Media-Agentur Schaefer - Dr. Frauke Schaefer - Inselstraße 20 -D-04103 Leipzig
Phone: +49 341/30 10 620 - Fax: +49 341/30 10 621 - info@media-schaefer.de

Where are they going...

Your target groups,
visitors,
customers,
business partners...?

...where are they off to?

We'll bring you together.

Media-Agentur Schaefer
worldwide advertising agent of K. G. Saur GmbH, a publisher of leading international reference works and specialist journals for art, music, literature, libraries and universities

www.media-schaefer.de

International Directory of Arts

INTERNATIONALES KUNST-ADRESSBUCH
ANNUAIRE INTERNATIONAL DES BEAUX-ARTS
ANNUARIO INTERNAZIONALE DELLE BELLE ARTI
ANUARIO INTERNACIONAL DE LAS ARTES

29th EDITION 2005

VOLUME III

INDEX OF PERSONS
Directors, curators, presidents
and scientific staff of museums
INDEX OF INSTITUTIONS AND COMPANIES

REGISTER DER PERSONEN
Direktoren, Kuratoren, Präsidenten und
wissenschaftliche Mitarbeiter der Museen
REGISTER DER INSTITUTIONEN UND FIRMEN

K·G·SAUR MÜNCHEN 2005

Redaktion:
K. G. Saur Verlag GmbH
Redaktion Art Address
Luppenstraße 1b
04177 Leipzig
Tel.: +49 (0)341/48699-12
Fax: +49 (0)341/48699-13
E-Mail: saur.artaddress@thomson.com

Bibliographic information published by Die Deutsche Bibliothek
Die Deutsche Bibliothek lists this publication in the Deutsche Nationalbibliografie;
detailed bibliographic data are available in the internet at http://dnb.ddb.de.

Advertising Representatives:

Worldwide:
Media-Agentur Schaefer
Inselstraße 20
D-04103 Leipzig
Tel.: +49 (0) 341 3010620
Fax: +49 (0) 341 3010621
E-Mail: marlen.kuenitz@media-schaefer.de
www.media-schaefer.de

France: MG Publicité, 22 Rue Drouot, F-75009 Paris,
Tel.: (01) 48 01 86 86, Fax: (01) 48 01 86 82, E-Mail: mgpub@magic.fr

Great Britain and Ireland: A.R.T. Publicity, 281 Cricklewood Lane, GB-NW2 2JJ London,
Tel.: (020) 8 455 7667, Fax.: (020) 8 455 1772, E-Mail: lornanoble@artpublicity.co.uk

Italy: Marlies Burget, Via della Treggia 1, I-06125 Ponte Rio,
Tel.: (075) 58 99 259, Fax: (075) 58 97 147, E-Mail: m.burget@tin.it

Printed on acid-free paper

© K. G. Saur Verlag, München 2005
Printed in the Federal Republic of Germany

All rights reserved. No part of this publication may be reproduced,
stored in a retrieval system, or transmitted in any form or by any means,
electronic, mechanical, photocopy, recording, or otherwise,
without permission in writing form from the publisher.

Cover marbling: Petra Weinmann, Ansbach
Typesetting: Da-TeX Gerd Blumenstein, Tanovski & Wündisch, Leipzig
and bsix information exchange GmbH, Braunschweig

Printed and bound by Strauss GmbH, Mörlenbach

ISBN 3-598-23104-0

Contents

page

Volume I

Source of Supply Listing ... 1
Museums and Public Galleries ... 11
Universities, Academies, Colleges ... 955
Associations ... 1009
List of Advertisers ... 1051

Volume II

Art and Antique Dealers, Numismatics ... 1
Art and Antiques Fairs ... 419
Galleries ... 437
Auctioneers ... 729
Restorers ... 775
Art Publishers ... 893
Art Periodicals ... 935
Antiquarians and Art Booksellers ... 959
List of Advertisers ... 1039

Volume III

Index of Persons (Directors, curators, presidents and scientific staff of museums) ... 3
Index of Institutions and Companies ... 119

Inhalt

Seite

Band I

Bezugsquellenverzeichnis ... 1
Museen und Öffentliche Galerien ... 11
Universitäten, Akademien, Schulen ... 955
Vereinigungen ... 1009
Verzeichnis der Inserenten ... 1051

Band II

Kunst- und Antiquitätenhandel, Numismatik ... 1
Kunst- und Antiquitätenmessen ... 419
Galerien ... 437
Auktionatoren ... 729
Restauratoren ... 775
Kunstverleger ... 893
Kunstzeitschriften ... 935
Antiquariate und Kunstbuchhandlungen ... 959
Verzeichnis der Inserenten ... 1039

Band III

Register der Personen (Direktoren, Kuratoren, Präsidenten und wissenschaftliche Mitarbeiter der Museen) ... 3
Register der Institutionen und Firmen ... 119

Aalund, Dorothy 045957
Aamodt, David 044727
Aaraas, Olav 031093, 031094
Aarhus, Aasne 030774
Aaronson, Diana 048652
Aarsen, John 043831
Aarsrud, Christian 036756
Aarstrand, Kjetil 030994
Aartomaa, Ulla 009785
Aarts, H.J. 030414
Aartsen, J. 029435
Aasberg, Dagny 030854
Aase, Jean 030952
Aaserud, Anne 031276
Aashagen, Kjersti Haugen 031137
Aasland, Odd 005306
Aasted, Elsebeth 008806
Aav, Marianne 009518
Abab, Khamib Hj. 027988
Abad, Dr. Andres 009197
Abad, María Jesús 036005
Abadesa, R.M. 035002
Abadese, M. 035484
Abadom, Monica 030689
Abadzic, Sabaheta 003941
Abadzieva, Sonia 027919
Abal de Russo, Prof. Clara 000433
Abaño, Isidro C. 031741
Abaraonye, Dr. Felicia Ihuoma 030677
Abbas, Muhammad 031386
Abbasi, Saeed 022609
Abbassi, Q. 022555
Abbate, Dr. Vincenzo 025081
Abbott, Dan 042413
Abbott, James 041969
Abbott, P. 039959
Abbott, Phyliss 042059
Abbott, Will 044569
Abcouwer, Dr. N.F. 029862
Abdo Mahgoub, Prof. Dr. Mohamed 009281
Abdol-Alipoor, M. 022630
Abdol-Alipour, Mohammad 022608
Abdolalipour, Mohammad 022605, 022612, 022614, 022615, 022618, 022622, 022627, 022642
Abdoolrahaman, S. 028065, 028068, 028069, 028072, 028073, 028074
Abdulla, K. 037861
Abdullah, Mohamed Yusuf 027984
Abdullin, Rif Mudarisovič 033989
Abdullina, Svetlana Aleksandrovna 034090
Abdunov, Georgi 004765
Abdurazakov, A. 038274
Abe, Hiroshi 026575
Abegg, Dr. Angelika 020038
Abejide, Ola 030704
Abel, Marianne 016605
Abel, Dr. Susanne 020885
Abel, Tiina 009398
Abelanet, Jean 014916
Abele, S. 020372
Abele, Susan 046477
Abeler, Jürgen 021022
Abell, Carl T. 045746
Abella, Carmencita T. 031739
Abella, Jordi 035185
Abels, Peggy 044943
Abensour, Dominique 013972
Abildgaard, Hanne 008957
Abitz, Gerald 044980
Ablak, Mehmet 038118
Abner, Steve 042959
Abraham, Debbie 000815
Abraham, Heidrun 016028
Abraham, Julian 038632
Abraham-Roelants, Josiane 003291
Abrahams, Katy 034616
Abrahams-Willis, Gabeba 034583
Abrahamson, Dana 044170
Abram, Ruth J. 046358
Abramek, Bogusław 032495
Abramović-Miletić, Ljiljana 034163
Abrams, Catherine 047581
Abrams, Linda C. 045396
Abrão, Flávio Jorge 004042
Abravanel, Claude 022971
Abrell, Dr. Herbert 001762
Abreu, Jorge M. de 032697
Abreu, Juana Ines 028474
Abreu Nunes, Dr. Maria Luisa 032639
Abric, Christian 011320
Abril, Joana Mari 036055
Abring, Hans-Dieter 017064
Abrojan, Ėlvira Vartanovna 033133
Absi, Nuha 027376
Absolon, Eric 041327
Abu Hadba, Abdul Aziz H. 031405
Abubakar, Ali Mohamed 027427
Abueg, Dr. Nelle F. 031766
Abungu, Lorna 053813
Aburai, Masakazu 027111
Acalija, Sanja 007733
Accardi, Dr. Giuseppina 023745
Acda, G.M.W. 029643, 029644
Acevedo Basurto, Sara 031567
Aceves Romero, David 028444
Achaah Ndumbi, Patrick 004973
Achatz, Erika 001908
Achenbach, Dr. Nora von 017715
Achenbach, Dr. Sigrid-Ute 016109
Achi, Y. 022986
Achuri, Julio César 007520, 007521
Ackerman, Andrew S. 046312
Ackerman, Mary Anne 044027
Ackermann, Dr. Marion 020356
Ackermann, Paul R. 049096
Ackerson, Rex D. 048577
Ackley, Clifford S. 042334
Ackroyd, Paul 040241
Acorn, Eleanor 006202
Acosta Guerrero, Elena 035624
Acosta Mohalem, José de Jesús .. 007563
Acton, David 049309
Adachi, Hogara 026641
Adachi, Takanori 027327
Ådahl, Dr. Karin 036642
Adair, Mary J. 045204
Adam, Thomas 016460
Adamczyk-Pogorzelska, Bożena .. 032125
Adami, Valerio 024660
Adamik, John 044265
Adamo, Giuseppe 025302
Adams, Anne 044645
Adams, Dr. Beverly 047011
Adams, Bill J. 047832
Adams, Celeste M. 044275
Adams, Cheryl 043318
Adams, Cindy 045098
Adams, David 039546
Adams, E. Charles 048630
Adams, Elizabeth 043116
Adams, Eloise 046117
Adams, F. 005240
Adams, G. Rollie 047485
Adams, Henry 042985
Adams, J. Marshall 044799
Adams, Jay 041906
Adams, Jean 039344
Adams, J.M. 038846
Adams, John D. 006742
Adams, Kate 041923
Adams, Kathy 047117
Adams, Kenneth 006115
Adams, Larry 042303
Adams, Lorraine Margaret 049584
Adams, Mazie M. 045131
Adams, Mel 047115
Adams, N.C. 038837
Adams, Roxana 045612
Adams, Stephen 038501
Adams, Steve 047300
Adams, Vivian 042140
Adams Muranaka, Dr. Therese ... 047841
Adamsom, Noel 001395
Adamson, Alberta 049138
Adamson, J. 039509, 039791
Adamson, Tony 038493
Adamsson, Anneli 036325
Adamyan, M.S. 000694
Adar, Yossi 022884
Addenbrooke, Rosie 039152
Adderley, D.E. 006733
Addison, K.A. 021099
Addoms, Andrew 044555
Adedayo, Oluremi F. 030696
Adediran, Nath Mayo 030692
Adelantar, Jonas O. 031790
Adelsberger, Paul 017004
Aderman, Ella 048047
Adesina, Bode 030685
Adey, Dr. Elizabeth 040357
Adiletta, Dawn C. 044458
Adisumarto, Dr. Soenartono 022436
Adkin, Tammy 005790
Adkins, Dean 048289
Adkins, Todd 045786
Adlbauer, Dr. Karl 001938
Adleman, Debra 046012
Adler, Helmut 002768
Adler, Peter 001302
Adler, Rosa 002276
Adler, Tracy L. 046347
Adlı, Nadir 038054
Adlung, Dr. Philipp 017682
Adolfsson, Stig 036310
Adolphs, Dr. Volker 016329
Adorno, Prof. Francesco 024192
Adriaens Pannier, Anne 003316
Adriaensens, Annemie 003196
Adriaenssens, Werner 003353
Adrian, Dolab Jorge 000164
Adriani, Prof. Dr. Götz 020498
Adriansen, Inge 009112
Adrimi-Sismani, Vassiliki 021521
Adsenius, Mikael 036645
Adsett, Virginia 039053
Adunka, Roland 001683
Adžemlerski, Svetoslav 004804
Aebersold, Marianne 037764
Aebi, Richard E. 037554
Aescht, Dr. Erna 002243
Afzal, Dr. Muhammad 031370
Agarwal, R.C. 022178
Agee, Sheila 048194
Ageeva, Marina Vladimirovna 033573
Agenjo, Xavier 035810
Ager, Kathleen 039545
Agliati Ruggia, Dr. Mariangela 037432
Agnelli, Marella 026082
Agnelli Caracciolo, Marella 026263
Agner, Raul Dumas 031794
Agnesi, Prof. V. 025093
Agostini, Giuseppe 025153
Agostini, Dr. Grazia 024116
Ågotnes, Dr. Anne 030763, 030765
Agrawal, Rajesh 022092
Agrech, F. 014693
Ågren, Gertie 036380
Agrenius, Helen 036361
Agresti, Giannicola 023204
Agten, Beate 019332
Agthe, Dr. Johanna 017168
Aguayo, José 043412
Agudo Cadarso, Christina 035995
Ague, Jay 046226
Aguero Moras, Alfonso 031480
Aguiar Branco, Dr. Fernando 032679
Aguilar Piedra, Raúl 007667
Aguillera, Kristin 046371
Aguiló, Anna 034816
Aguiló Ribas, Catalina 035603
Aguinaldo, Rosalinda 031681
Aguirre, David 048633
Aguirre, Joel O. 028142
Brandão Aguirre, Maria Beatriz ... 004513
Aguirre, Pierre 011379
Agúndez García, José Antonio 035459
Agusti, Jorge 035728
Ahern, Maureen 044947
Ahlberg, Leif 036407
Ahlbrecht, Helmut 020177
Ahlefeldt Laurvig Bille, Michael ... 009004
Ahlers, Silvia 004217
Ahlfort, Barbro 036296
Ahlqvist, Ingemar 036548
Ahlstrand, J.T. 036447
Ahmad, Awang Haji Adam bin Haji 004612
Ahmad, Mushtaq 031379
Ahmad, Dr. Razi 022293
Ahmady, B. 022640
Ahmaogak, George N. 041709
Ahmas, Kristina 009725
Ahmed, Amrani 029042
Ahmedzade, T.Z. 003082
Ahola, Tuija 010231
Ahonon, Léonard 003888
Ahrendt, Dorothee 020750
Ahrens, Claus 019473
Ahrens, Elke 016164
Ahrens, Regi 044919
Ahrndt, Dr. Wiebke 016426
Åhsberger, Douglas 036264
Ahtela, Eero 009834
Ahtola-Moorhouse, Leena 009515
Ahumada Valencia, Jacob 006948
þahýn, Seracettin 038102
Aichelburg, Dr. Wladimir Graf 001698
Aicher, Ernst 019009
Aichner, Dr. Ernst 018070
Aida, Susumu 026939
Aidara, Abdoul Hadir 034137
d'Aigneaux, Jean 014612
Aigner, Carl 002619
Aigner, Ottilie 002194
Aigremont, Robert d' 012462
Aiken, Dr. Edward A. 048456
Aikens, C. Melvin 043746
Ailonen, Riitta .. 009517, 009568, 009577, 009586
Aimé About, Assamoa 007688
Ainhirn, Karola 001708
Ainsley, Anne 038639
Airey, Laura 041628
Aistars, John 042661
Aitken, Catherine 036863
Aitken, Terry 049319
Aizpurua, Inaki 034787
Ajmetov, Ramis Kijamovič 033249
Ajzenberg, Prof. Dr. Elza 004529
Akabiamu, Martin 003895
Akam, Prof. Michael 038972
Akamati-Lilimbaki, Dr. Maria 021426
Akanbiemu, Martin Ogunayo 030690
Akasheh, Anahid 046370
Akazijeva, Tetjana Abaštajevna ... 038248
Akbar, Prof. Dr. Omar 016684
Akbulut, Nazım 038146
Åkerman, Charlotte 036332, 036333
Akers, Charlene 048209
Akers, John 048522
Akers, Lloyd 047113
Akersten, Dr. William A. 047107
Åkesson, Bernt-A. 036568, 036570
Akgül, Nebi 038079
Akgün, Ünal 038121
Akgulian, Mark 042880
Akimova, G. 027388
Akın, Gülşen 038063
Akin, Joseph 047625
Akinpelu, David Ano 030690
Akins, Ken 043302
Akins, Louise 044758
Akins, Rebecca 045791
Akioka, Yasuji 026570
Akira, Nagoya 027170
Akiyama, Yoshi 045622
Akkaya, Mustafa 038082, 038086
Akker, C. 030144
Akmamedova, Maja 038211
Aknazarov, N.A. 027402
Akomolafe, Tunde 030700
Akpan, Aniefiok Udo 030699

Akramov, N. . . . 049405
Aksajskij, Ivan Grigorjevič . . . 033948
Aksënova, Alisa Ivanovna . . . 034040
Aksoy, Sule . . . 038102
Al-Arifi, Dr. Nassir S. . . . 034123
Al-Bubu, Sana' . . . 027384
Al-Diban, Martina . . . 019182
Al-Esawi, Talaat . . . 009334
Al-Farsi, Said Ali Said . . . 031349
Al-Hameed, Hazim A. . . . 022668
Al-Khalifa, Nayla . . . 003094
Al-Maamari, Moussa . . . 027813
Al-Qaisy, Rabie . . . 022663
Al-Robaae, Dr. Khalaf . . . 022666
Al-Saud, Abdullah S. . . . 034125
Al-Shibli, Alae . . . 022661
Al-Sid, Siddig M. Gasm . . . 036152
Al-Wohaibi, Dr. Fahed . . . 027632
Alam, Dr. Shamsul . . . 003107, 003113, 003115, 003117
Alam, Syamsir . . . 022485
Alan, David . . . 048909
Aland, Prof. Dr. Barbara . . . 019140
Alaniz, Gilbert . . . 047441
Alaoui, Brahim . . . 013659
Alarcão, Adília . . . 032605
Alarcon, Anne . . . 048328
Alarcón, Enrique . . . 034925
Alarcón Lotero, José Félix . . . 007576
Alarcón Osorio, Gonzalo . . . 028442
Alario, Prof. Leonardo . . . 023697
Alasalmi, Jikka . . . 010253
Alaurin, Alice A. . . . 031667
Alausy, Abdalla . . . 027433
Alba, Dominique . . . 013736
Alba Alvarez, Dionisio . . . 036096
Albacete, M.J. . . . 042606
Alban, Marc . . . 012470
Albaneso, Virginia . . . 042873
Albani, Lino . . . 023936
Albarian, Kimberly . . . 045067
Albee, Suzanne . . . 049049
Albendea Solis, Juan Manuel . . . 035853
Alber, Merike . . . 009402
Alberdi, Juan B. . . . 000658
Alberg, Dr. Werner . . . 016846
Alberigi, Merry . . . 047921
Alberrán, Fernando . . . 028973
Albers, Birgit . . . 001762
Albers, Edward S. . . . 045037
Albers, Hannes . . . 015951
Albers, Dr. M. . . . 029691, 029692, 030164
Albers, Mary . . . 006235
Albert, Dr. J.S. . . . 044103
Albert, Karen T. . . . 044506
Albert, Peggy . . . 014363
Albert, Shea . . . 034584
Albertelli, Prof. Giancarlo . 024317, 024326
Alberti, Dr. Walter . . . 024710
Albertin, Anne-Marie . . . 011832
Albertini, L. . . . 036856
Albertis, Serge de . . . 013417
Alberto, Dr. Giordano . . . 024263
Albertsson, Kristinn J. . . . 021932
Albertus, Dana . . . 018594
Albertus, Jürgen . . . 018525
Alberty, Beth . . . 042457
Albiol Sampietro, Vicente F. . . . 035524
Albisetti, Guiseppe . . . 036819
Alborino, Dr. V. . . . 016887
Albrecht, Constanze . . . 016004
Albrecht, Marvin . . . 049132
Albrecht, Wolfgang . . . 049321
Albrecht-Weinberger, Dr. Karl . . . 002918, 002964
Albrechtsen, Bo . . . 021552
Albright, Dr. L. Barry . . . 043851
Albright, Liz . . . 046695
Albright, Shirley . . . 048605
Albright, Terrence . . . 046520
Albufera, E. d' . . . 013169
Alcock, Rodney . . . 041360
Alcolea Blanch, Santiago . . . 034915
Alcouffe, Daniel . . . 013685
Aldama, Dulce . . . 048520
Aldeguer Gordiola, Daniel . . . 034817
Aldema, Yehuda Levy . . . 022981
Alder, Barbara . . . 037267
Alder, M. . . . 039655
Alder, Ruedi . . . 037660
Alderdice, Dr. David . . . 001520
Alderfer, Joel D. . . . 044431
Alderfer, Kenny . . . 047582
Alderton, Michéle . . . 006243
Aldhizer, H.T. . . . 043964
Aldini, Tobia . . . 024234
Aldrich, William M. . . . 046572
Aldridge, Carolyn . . . 041154
Aldridge, G.E. . . . 038900
Aldunate del Solar, Carlos . . . 006928
Alebo, Lena . . . 036572
Alegria, Dr. Ricardo E. . . . 032738
Alegría Manegat, María . . . 034919
Aleksandrova, Marija . . . 004954
Aleksandrova, Nataša . . . 004809
Aleksandrović, Natalja Jurjevna . . 033293
Aleksandrovna, Marija . . . 004953, 004955
Alekseev, Nikolaj Makarovič . . . 033707
Alekseev, Vladimir Petrovič . . . 033049
Alekseeva, Aida Nikolaevna . . . 033188
Alekseeva, Galina Ivanovna . . . 033023
Aleksiuk, Galina A. . . . 034057
Aleksoska-Baceva, Zaharinka . . . 027919
Alemany, Uiso . . . 036062
Alemany, Véronique . . . 012847
Alencar, Vera de . . . 004330, 004337
Alessio, Pado . . . 026080
Alex, Erdmute . . . 016682
Alex, Dr. Reinhard . . . 016682
Alexander, Andrew . . . 042340
Alexander, Beatrix . . . 018322
Alexander, Brian . . . 041743
Alexander, Darsie . . . 041969
Alexander, Eric . . . 044278
Alexander, G. . . . 041398
Alexander, H.E. . . . 040144
Alexander, Irene O. . . . 043069, 043070
Alexander, Jane . . . 001172, 041018
Alexander, Jean . . . 048572
Alexander, Julia . . . 046227
Alexander, Karen . . . 040095
Alexander, Kimberly . . . 047741
Alexander, Kristi . . . 043026
Alexander, Margareta . . . 042882
Alexander, Nancy . . . 047369, 055004
Alexander, Prof. Richard D. . . . 041734
Alexander, Robert . . . 000966
Alexander, Ron J. . . . 045968
Alexandre, Claude . . . 012603
Alexie, Eric . . . 047469
Alexis, Gerald . . . 021602
Alfageme Sánchez, Vitaliano . . . 036095
Alfaro, Ana . . . 035978
Alfaro Castillo, Andrés José . . . 007431
Alfter, Dr. Dieter . . . 015770
Algar, Maria Angela . . . 036893
Algeri, Dr. Giuliana . . . 024606
Alhaainen, Kari M. . . . 009678
Alho, Anna-Liisa . . . 009574
Ali, H.-A. . . . 022662
Ali, Mazhar . . . 031404
Ali, Mohamed . . . 037850
Ali, Samirah Mohd . . . 027982
Ali, Sanaa . . . 009271
Alicante, Apolinario . . . 031743
Aliev, Kazi Magomet Ibragimovich . 033079
Alig, Joyce L. . . . 042682
Alilović, Ivica . . . 034192
Alimonti, Keith . . . 005674
Alin, Margareta . . . 036443
Alisch, Joachim . . . 016254
Aliyasak, Munasor . . . 027954
Alkema, J. . . . 029270
Allaire, Kay . . . 046319
Allan, David . . . 040755
Allan, John . . . 039465
Allan, Laurie . . . 041850
Allan, Randy . . . 042191
Allan, Shona . . . 040673
Allansson, Jón . . . 021929
Allard, Bob . . . 038617
Allard, Jeanine . . . 047635
Allard, Sarah . . . 039225
Allas, Anu . . . 009398
Allason-Jones, L. . . . 040552, 040553
Allderidge, Patricia . . . 038650
Allegrini, Prof. Piero . . . 024649
Allemand, Eolo . . . 023331
Allemand, Evelyne-Dorothée . . . 015007
Allemand, Jacqueline . . . 014649
Allemanlus, Elizabeth . . . 045102
Allemann, Martin . . . 037362
Allen, Anne . . . 041773
Allen, Armin . . . 046464
Allen, Babara . . . 048368
Allen, Brian . . . 049187
Allen, Bruce . . . 048160
Allen, Catherine . . . 043043
Allen, Dale . . . 043370
Allen, David . . . 038509, 038510
Allen, Dick . . . 048735
Allen, Graham . . . 038723
Allen, Jeff . . . 046835
Allen, Jill . . . 039993
Allen, Kay . . . 045420
Allen, Kim . . . 005885
Allen, Louise . . . 039589
Allen, Lucy . . . 044804
Allen, Marilyn . . . 042288
Allen, Nancy L. . . . 046539
Allen, Richard . . . 043276, 044657
Allen, Roger . . . 042075
Allen, Susan . . . 047996
Allen, Suzanne . . . 040519
Allen, Timothy S. . . . 048618
Allen, Trudy J. . . . 044224
Allen, Virginia S. . . . 042306
Allen, William M. . . . 047462
Allen Fleming, Kathy . . . 047612
Allender, Chris . . . 041480
Allie, Stephen J. . . . 043938
Allikvee, Anu . . . 009398
Allington, Peter . . . 040905
Allione, Patricia . . . 012211
Allison, C. . . . 041383
Allison, David . . . 030446
Allison, Glenn . . . 006771
Allison, Jim . . . 042817
Allison, N. . . . 030541
Allison, Tammy . . . 045394
Allison Rogers, Traude . . . 049589
Allman, Mary . . . 045348
Allman, William G. . . . 048960
Alloisi, Dr. Sivigliano . . . 025480
Allsop, Julie . . . 040944
Allwood, Rosamond . . . 039990
Alm, Björn . . . 036305
Alm, Göran . . . 036616
Almagro Gorbea, M.J. . . . 035417, 035428
Almarri, Ali . . . 038433
Almeda, Ermelo . . . 031749
Almeev, Robert V. . . . 049385
Almeida, Joel . . . 032638
Almeida Campos, Diogenes de . . . 004373
Almeida Dias, Manuel Mateus de . 000097
Almeras . . . 012644
Almirante, Julián . . . 035978
Almosara, Emelita V. . . . 031732
Almquist, Katarina . . . 036554
Almquist, Kathleen . . . 048694
Alms, Barbara . . . 016667
Alonso, Alejandro G. . . . 008009
Alonso, Alicia . . . 035377
Alonso, Jésus . . . 036083
Alòs Trepat, Carme . . . 034891
Alowan, Zoe . . . 046870
Alper, Mara . . . 046124
Alper, Richard . . . 048917
Alphons, Alois . . . 002047
Alpözen, T. Oǒuz . . . 038026
Alram, Dr. Michael . . . 002934
Alsaker, Sigmund . . . 031152
Alsobrook, Dr. David E. . . . 043044
Alsteens, S. . . . 013568
Alston, David . . . 039179
Alston, Joseph . . . 044259
Alsvik, Elling . . . 031287
Alswanis, Hope . . . 048140
Altamont, Earl of . . . 022874
Alteen, Glenn . . . 006698
Altenkirch, Gunter . . . 017389
Alter, Klaus . . . 021017
Alterio, Italo . . . 007643
Althaus, Marceline . . . 037380
Althoff, Bruno . . . 020908
Althoff, Ralf . . . 016855
Altmann, Ferdinand . . . 002316
Altmann, Katja . . . 019695
Altmeder, Prof. Susanne . . . 002955
Altner, Renate . . . 016181
Altstatt, Rosanne . . . 019467
Alvarado Gonzalo, Manuel de . . . 035015
Alvarez, Helena . . . 036641
Alvarez, José Carlos . . . 032652
Alvarez, Josefina . . . 000542
Alvarez, Juan . . . 043575
Alvarez, Sergio Antonio . . . 000137
Alvarez, Walter . . . 042163
Alvárez Arévalo, Miguel . . . 021583
Alvárez Masso, Montserrat . . . 034935
Alvárez Polo, Giesela . . . 008060
Alvarez Rojas, Antonio . . . 035021
Alvarez Valverde, Dr. José J. de . . 009156
Alves, C. Douglass . . . 048212
Alves, Hélio Osvaldo . . . 032619
Alves, Dr. Sónia . . . 032670
Alves Costa, Catarina . . . 032650
Alves de Sousa, Dr. Pio G. . . . 032585
Alves Gomes, José António . . . 004204
Alves Pinto, José F. . . . 032619
Alvina, Corazon S. . . . 031726
Alvina, Corazón S. . . . 031733
Alvud, Laura . . . 042908
Alymer, John . . . 038812
Amack, Rex . . . 046169
Amadei, Daniel . . . 006104
Amann, Bernd . . . 002057
Amann, Henry . . . 011208
Amarel Gourgel, Dr. Anicete do . . . 000095
Amaro das Neves, António . . . 032619
Amash, Carissa . . . 042146
Amat Amer, José Maria . . . 035171
Amato, Ann . . . 047180
Amato, Prof. Domenico . . . 024776
Amato, Pietro . . . 049422, 049428, 049434
Ambroise, Guillaume . . . 013750
Ambrose, David . . . 048859
Ambrose, Pamela E. . . . 047680
Ambrose, Richard . . . 042748
Ambrosetti, Dr. Giancarlo . . . 025411
Ambrosino, Guy . . . 047962
Ambrosio, Prof. Augusto C. . . . 025319
Ambrosio, Piero . . . 023492
Ambrosio, Thomas J. . . . 045977
Amdreoli, Prof. Annararie . . . 024275
Amelin, Olov . . . 036651
Amelingmeier, Dr. Eckard . . . 021001
Amell, Alexander . . . 043539
Amemiya, Tadashi . . . 027151
Amend, Brad . . . 043628
Amend, Debbie . . . 043628
Amendolagine, Dr. Beatrice . . . 024652
Ament, Sharon . . . 040245
Amer, Prof. Mordechai . . . 023047
Ames, Gerhard . . . 019960
Ames Sheret, Mary . . . 045743
Ametrano, Dr. Silvia . . . 000390
Amic, S. . . . 013210
Amidon, Catherine . . . 047102
Amidon, Eleanor . . . 044420
Amies, Sandra . . . 038652
Aminova, Svetlana Gašimovna . . . 033342

Amir, H. 028070
Amir, Mohammad 022404
Amiranišvili, S.J. 015406
Amiri, M. 022597
Amlow, Lothar 016194
Ammann, Christopher 037206
Ammann, Prof. Dr. Gert ... 002097, 002133
Ammann, Hugo 037820, 037822
Ammann, Katharina 037577
Ammann, Sandra 036863
Amnehäll, Jan 036306
Amo, Dr. Toshino 027141
Amo y de la Era, Mariano del 035595
Amon, Prof. Dr. Karl 001708
Amonson, John 048836
Amor, Kebbour 000071
Amoretti, Guido 026076
Amoriñ, Prof. Dr. José L. 000205
Amoroso, Dr. Domenico 023589
Amoroso, Richard L. 046713
Amory, Dita 046325
Amprimoz, M.F.X. 014972
Ampuero, Gonzalo 006918
Amrein, Dr. Heidi 037784
Amsallem, Christiane 014839
Amselgruber, Prof. Dr. 020375
Amsler, Cory 043506
Amstad, Hans 037792
An, Tran Huy 049536
Anand, Dr. Y.P. 022088
Anati, Prof. Emmanuel 023642
Anawalt, Patricia 045421
Ancheotti, Dr. Angelo 024104, 024111
Ančiporov, A.I. 033673
Anda, Tone 030719
Andami, Parisa 022631
Ander, Dr. Angelika 002971
Ander, Heike 019073, 053313
Andergassen, Dr. Leo 023527
Anderjack, George M. 047949
Anderl, Dick 049312
Anderle, Charlotte 002180
Anderle, Peter 002022
Anderlik, Heidemarie 016011
Anders, Brian 049370
Anders, Ines 017453, 017454
Anders, Win 006862
Andersen, Britta 008817
Andersen, Håkon 031283
Andersen, H.C. 008885
Andersen, Jeffrey W. 046664
Andersen, Jens 008890
Andersen, John 008870
Andersen, Kjell 030850
Andersen, Kurt 009014
Andersen, Lise 008888, 008889
Andersén, Peter 009897
Andersen, Randi 030995, 030996
Andersen, Thyge 009035
Andersen, Verginia 004261
Anderson, Annette 043009
Anderson, Ary 043352
Anderson, Betsy 045374
Anderson, Bonnie 047970
Anderson, Bruce 042356
Anderson, Carol 041439
Anderson, Christine 048189
Anderson, Claude 048110
Anderson, Claudia 048521
Anderson, Craig 042866
Anderson, D. 044272
Anderson, Dale W. 044465
Anderson, David 040307, 046656
Anderson, Donald B. 047551
Anderson, Douglas 042423
Anderson, Duane 044616, 047971
Anderson, Dr. Duane 047973
Anderson, Ellen 006595
Anderson, Eve 048547
Anderson, Fred 047427
Anderson, Garry 005307
Anderson, George 043968
Anderson, Hilary 045270
Anderson, J. 030275
Anderson, Jill 045168
Anderson, Joe 045215
Anderson, Judy 045658
Anderson, Kathi 045300
Anderson, Kathy . 049016, 049072, 049073
Anderson, Kris 045128
Anderson, Lynn 048471
Anderson, Margaret 000705
Anderson, Mark 043166
Anderson, Maxwell 046418
Anderson, Michael 044763, 044764
Anderson, Peter 048098
Anderson, Ray 048564
Anderson, Richard R. 048207
Anderson, Rolf 048980
Anderson, Steve 047379
Anderson, Susan K. 042022
Anderson, Susan M. 042268
Anderson, Tracy D. 044616
Anderson, W.M. 048146
Anderson-Densmore, Mari C. 045053
Andersson, Beritne 009481
Andersson, Göran 036300
Andersson, Henrik 036639
Andersson, Karin 036530
Andersson, Lars 036374, 036406
Andersson, Solveig 036312
Andersson, Ulla 036577
Andersson Flygare, Irene 036744
Andersson Møller, Vibeke 008999
Andjap, Gabriela Vasylivna 038409
Andjelković Dmitrijević, Branislava 034165
Ando, Barbara 042161
Andorfer, Gregory Paul 041996
Andrade, Rosemary 036163
Andral, Jean-Louis 010426, 010431
Andrási, Gábor 021680, 021681
André, Frédéric 003657
André, Dr. Georges 003383
André, Mervyn 001023
André-Schellner, Prof. Brigitte 002955
Andreadaki-Vlasaki, Maria 021225, 021447
Andreasen, Vagn 009017
Andreassen, Dag 031097
Andreassi, Dr. Giuseppe . 023336, 025622, 025988
Andreasson, Sven-Glov 036212
Andreeva, Antonina Borisovna ... 034029
Andrefsky, William 047282
Andrell, Pauline 030575
Andren, Martin 036443
Andres, Louis M. 045516
Andres, Morrie 043204
Andresen, Thomas Bjorkan 031200
Andreu, Dr. Jaime Sancho 035977
Andrew, K.J. 040505
Andrew, Marcia 048802
Andrews, Bernice 005212
Andrews, Janine 005412
Andrews, Kathy 041788
Andrews, Dr. Peter 038764
Andrews, Richard 048081
Andrews, Schuyler Gott 047659
Andrews, Shelly L. 041593
Andrews, Susan 044331
Andrews, Thomas F. 045445
Andrews Trechsel, Gail 042223
Andriamanantena, Ranaivoarivelo . 027932
Andrian-Werburg, Dr. Irmtraud Freifrau von 019352
Andrich, Dr. Uwe 017539, 017541
Andries, Pool 003161
Andrieu, Esther 000475
Andrishak, Steve 005422
Andrušaite, Dzintra 027746
Anelli, Dr. Giuseppe 025879
Anene, Francis 030673
Angarita Jiménez, Edgar 007556
Angel de Marco, Dr. Miguel 000142
Angelett, Prof. Luciana Rita 025536
Angelinetti de Elizalde, Sara 000329
Angelo, Therese 030457
Angeloni, Araldo 025700, 025701
Angelov, Anastas 004663
Angelov, Emil 004914
Angelova, Ilka 004900
Anger, Maksymilian 032101
Anger, Virginia 006178
Angerbauer, Dr. W. 019424
Angerer, Ferdl 002665
Angerer, Prof. Dr. Dr. Joachim 001890
Angerer, Dr. Martin 019752, 019754, 019757, 019759
Angert, Rina 023020
Anglin Burgard, Timothy .. 047857, 047871
Angst, H. 015678
Anguiano Lozano, Juan Manuel .. 028505
Angus, Barbara J. 043638
Angus, E. 041222
Anh, Tran Hong 049539
Anheuser, Kilian 037128
Anibas, Martin 003075
Anić, Hanja 007798
D'Aniello, Dr. Antonia 025715
Anılır, Burhanettin 038025
Aniol, Roland 020038
Anisi, Ali Reza 022635
Aniz Montes, Mercè 035180
Anken, Thomas 037079
Ankert, Kerstin 036265
Ankudinova, Elena Andreevna 033193
Anlagan, Çetin 038097
Anna, Dr. Susanne 016845, 016846
Annear, Judy 001505
Annemans, Jan 003210
Annett, John 040318
Annibaldi, Dr. Cesare 025448, 026263
Annicchiarico, Silvana 024698
Annison, F. 030532
Anosovskaja, Alla Vasiljevna 033195
Anraku, Yoshio 027040
Ansel, Dr. Valerie 014873
Ansell, Erynne 044659
Anselm, Gudrun 036511
Anselm, Paul S. 046616
Ansett, Tony 001050
Anthenaise, Claude d' 013633
Anthes, Hedi 018936
Anthes, Prof. Helmut 018936
Anthoine, Robert 046304
Anthony, Ginger 048686
Anthony, James S. 006599
Anthony, Jo 039559
Anthony, Lenard 005736
Anthony, Vincent 041851
Antihi, Adriana 032938
Antillano Armas, Sergio 049466
Antinori, Alessandra 025555
Antipas 021422
Antipenkov, Boris N. 033470
Antl, Prof. Gerhard 002711
Antognini, Marco 037286
Antoime, Janeen 047849
Antoine, Elisabeth 013719
Antoli Candela, Fernando 036062
Antonelli, Dr. Angelo 025393
Antonen, Rusty 045111
Antoniadou, Sofia 021211
Antonić, Dr. Dragomir 034147
Antonietti, Thomas 037211, 037565
Antonino, Dr. Biancastella . 023421, 023454
Antoniuk, Aleksander 031827
Antonoglou, Manolis 021453
Antonov, Anton 004673
Antonov, Teodosi 004752, 004755
Antonova, Irina A. 033458
Antonova, Ljubov Vladimirovna ... 034024
Antonsen, Lasse B. 046524
Antti-Poika, Jaakko 009578
Anttila, Eila 010010
Anttila, R. 005039
Anttila, Ritva 009629
Antweiler, Dr. Wolfgang 017920
Anyanwu, Dr. Starling E.N. 030676
Anzai, Ikuro 026743
Anzola, Sonia 049466
Anzuoni, Robert 043893
Aoki, Shigeru 026779
Aoki, Yoshiharu 026822
Apalkov, Jurij Aleksandrovič 033041
Apap Bologna, Daniela 028036
Aparin, Dr. Boris F. 033731
Apelbaum, Laura C. 048917
Apetrei, Maria 032910
Apfel, Prof. Kurt 002867
Apking, Barbara 045040
Aponte, Dr. Nilda E. 032718
Aponte Galvis, Alonso 007628
Apostolou, Eva 021207
Apostolov, Šanko 004923
Apostolova, Anna 004637
Apostolova, Lili 004691
Apothéloz, Gustave 037162
Apovnik, Dorothea 017192
Appel, G. 029909
Appel, H.H. 008991
Appel, Dr. Michaela 019122
Appelboom, Prof. Thiérry 003321
Appelhof, Ruth 043567
Appenzeller, Hans 020222
Appignanesi, Paolo 023881
Appleby, Roger 040120
Applegate, Matthew 040637
Appleton, Maggie 041095
Aprill, Gregg 042616
Aprison, Dr. Barry 042865
Apschnikat, Kenneth 044565
Apsega, Alejo 000493
Apsemetov, Azhibay 027400
Aquilera Cerni, Vicente 036062
Aquiloni, Laura 024869
Aquilué, Dr. Xavier 035175
Aquino, Amelia M. 031705
Ara, Judith 035429
Arab, Mona 000070
Arai, Toshizo 026590
Arakčeev, Boris Serafimovič 033750, 033823
Aralica, Miodrag 034281
Aramaki, Teiichi 026738
Aramova, Lidija Grigorjevna 034095, 034096, 034097
Aranburu, Xabier 034976
Aranda-Alvarado, Rocio 044860
Arango, Jaime 007551
Arango Trujillo, Ignacio 007473
Aranjo, Dr. Augusto C. de 000096
Aranne, Heikki 009652
Araño, Susana 034807
Arapoyanni, Xeni 021147
Araújo, Emmanoel 004560
Araujo, Marcelo 004555
Araujo, Samuel M. 004336
Aravantinos, Dr. Vassilis 021485
Arbart, Kazimierz 031901
Arbelo de Mazzaro, Prof. Aurora Catalina 000319
Arbeteta, Letizia 035420
Årbu, Grte 031070
Arbuckle, John B. 045246
Arbucó, Susana Maria 000234
Arbulla, Dr. Deborah 026139
Arbury, Steve 047307
Arcand, Jessica 047039
Arcangel, Norberto 031708
Arcangel, Norberto S. 031709
Arcangeli, Lino 023269
Arce Torres, Susana 031527
Arces, Prof. Antonio 024378
Arch, Nigel 040271
Archabal, Nina M. 047705
Archambault, Alan H. 043944
Archangelskij, Venjamin 033569
Archer, James Ronald 030975
Archer, Kent 006418
Archer, Prof. Michael 001507
Archibald, Allene 047458
Archibald, Dr. Joanna 039054

Archibald, Dr. Robert R. 047670
Archimanaritis, Alexios 021379
Archontidou-Argyri, Aglaia 021231, 021389, 021393
Archuleta, Margaret 047009
Arco-Zinneberg, Ulrich Graf 002535
Arcos, Hermana Ana Rosa 007572
Arcuri, Arthur 004174
Ardid, Jordi 034904
Ardila, Marsha T. 043086
Arduini, Dr. Franca 024138
Arefyeva, Galyna V. 038399
Arell, Berndt 009527
Arena, Albert A. 048849
Arena, Dr. Maria Stella 025515
Arenas Abello, Rosaema 007437
Arenas i Sampera, Josep A. 034929
Arenas Morales, Lía Esther 007519
Arends, Dr. T. 029837
Arens, A. 017398
Arenz, Deb 044265
Arenz, Deborah 045307
Arestizáhal, Irma 000184
Arfelli, Guido Arch 026014
Argente Oliver, José Luís . 034834, 035886
Argun, A.A. 015404
Argungu, Emir of 030674
Arhaldo, Liboni 024933
Ariano, Terry 048214
Arickx-George, M. 003663
Arih, Prof. Aleš 034514
Ariizumi, Haruhiro 026640
Arima, Shin-Ich 026775
Arisholm, Torstein 031095
Aristizábal Giraldo, Tulio 007479
Arizzoli-Clémentel, Pierre . 015187, 015189
Arkadjevna, A.A. 034013
Arkio-Laine, Leena 009523, 009529, 009540, 009545, 009549, 009563, 009566, 009567, 009584, 009585, 009589
Arkley, J. 040877
Arko-Pijevac, Milvana 007783
Arman, Kıvanç 038089
Armand-Delille, Lionel 012851
Armater, Raymond J. 047212, 047214
Armella Maza, Virginia 028485
Armenta Camacho, Juan 028673
Armin, Karlen 037636
Arminio, Roberta Y. 046743
Armirail, Sandrine 012651
Armiros, Konstantinos 042848
Armitage, Dr. Philip L. 038870
Armour, David A. 045551, 045552
Armour, Erica 043808
Armstrong, Alison C. 039835
Armstrong, Charlotte 046367
Armstrong, Elizabeth 046468
Armstrong, Fredrick 042749
Armstrong, James A. 042561
Armstrong, Jane C. 045550
Armstrong, Joan T. 045687
Armstrong, Lauraine 005472
Armstrong, Richard 047043
Armstrong, Steve 047520
Armstrong-Gillis, Kathy ... 047800, 047807
Armstrong Touchine, Maxine 042913
Arna, Angela 020310
Arna, Dr. Angela 020311
Arnaudo de Schanton, Veldis 000503
Arnaudova, Bojanka 004860
Arnault, Jean-Charles 011351
Arnăutu, Nicoleta 032780
Arndt, Gerda 016367
Arnemann, Heinrich 015730
Arneodo, Sergio 025738
Arnesson, Ingemar 036633
Arnesson, Kerstin 036263
Arnhold, Dr. Hermann 019156
Arning, Bill 042565
Arnold, Beate C. 020984
Arnold, Dr. Charles D. 006890
Arnold, Clara von 036586
Arnold, Dorothea 046364
Arnold, Erich 036986
Arnold, Francis 044968
Arnold, Gotthard 020220
Arnold, J. 040524
Arnold, Karl Heinz 017187
Arnold, Dr. Ken 040304
Arnold, Lothar 019019
Arnold, Mary Bea 044244
Arnold, Peter S. 043552
Arnold, Prof. Rainer 021030
Arnold, Sarah 045211
Arnold, Susan 038551
Arnold, Dr. Sven 016061
Arnold, Ute U. 021060
Arnold-Biucchi, Carmen F. 046287
Arnolli, G. 029837
Arnon, Carmella 022999
Arnot, Sally 043752
Arnott, Alastair 041060, 041061
Arnould, Marie-Agnès 011319
Arnoult, Hubert 013864
Arnoux, François 011235
Arnoux, Louis 013137
Arnst, Caris-Beatrice 015979
Arobba, Daniele 024134
Arocha Rovira, José A. 008170
Aron, Dr. Alfred 001938
Aron, Kathy 044928, 055036
Aronowitz-Mercer, Richard 040087
Arons, Dr. Kārlis-Ēriks 027761
Aronson, Julie 042919
Arpin, Odette 011008
Arpin, Pierre 006732
Arpin, Roland 006222, 006224
Arraras, Maria Teresa 032744
Arrasmith, Anne 042227
Arrate-Hernandez, Danilo M. 008122
Arriaga, Brenda 042772
Arrieta, Katrin 019901
Arriola, Juan Carlos Juárez 035336
Arroues, Heidi 044422
Arroyo, Marta 035976
Arroyo Martín, Dr. José Víctor 034988
Arsak, Mychajlo Mychajlovyč 038287
Arsenault, Linda 006184
Arseneau, Steve 043499
Arslan, Dr. Ermanno A. ... 024690, 024692
Arteaga, Agustín 000168, 028491
Artëmov, Evgenij 033751
Arterburn, Lesa 042072
Artero-Pamplona, Rafael 035561
Arthur, Catherine 041986
Arthur, Lloyd 005550
Articus, Dr. Rüdiger 017698
Artime, José 012577
Artman jr, Paul C. 044343
Artmann, Dr. 002178
Arts-Vehmeyer, M. 030289
Artykov, B.R. 049392
Aru, Krista 009414
Arunga Sumba, Owen 027423
Aruz, Joan 046364
Arvola, Silja 030938
Arzadeh, Kamal 022639
Arzur, Anna-Vari 013861
Asakura, Tetsuo 026681
Ašanin, Snezana 034180
Asano, Toru 026881
Asánsi Catalán, Maria Dolores ... 035442
Asbury, Michael J. 040712
Ascarelli Blayer Corcos, Dr. Anna . 025539
Ascencio, Michaelle 049464
Aščeulova, Tatjana Stanislavovna . 033581
Asch, Georges 013869
Aschauer, Manfred 002229, 002230
Asche, Dr. Susanne 018167, 019456
Aschengreen Piacenti, Dr. Kirsten . 024197
Aschim, Jan 047498
Aschkenes, Anna M. 047035
Aschwanden, Stefan 037542, 037784
Aselmeier, Marianne 018809
Asensio Llamas, Susana 035221
Ash, Carol 043939
Ash, Nancy 046975
Ash Ezersky, Lorinda 046327
Ashaye, Ibironke P. 030687
Ashcroft, Robert 042122
Ashdjian, Peter H. 008210
Ashe, James S. 045205
Ashe, Janet 042985
Asher, Dave 030588
Asher, Dorothy J. 043688
Ashley, Brian 040616, 040624
Ashley, Catherine 043509
Ashley, James 044818
Ashley, Raymond E. 047834
Ashman, Stuart A. 047974
Ashooh Lazos, Marylou 045620
Ashraf, Dr. Mohammad 031402
Ashton, Alan 040371
Ashton, Joanne G. 046193
Ashton, Kate 001235
Ashton, L. 040936
Ashton, Lynn 045489
Ashton, Dr. S. 038962
Ashton, Vicki 047128
Ashworth, A. Lawrence 041276
Ashworth, Ben 038562
Ashworth, Jim 001116
Ashworth, Meg 040944
Ashworth, S. 039922
Ashworth, Sue 039840
Ašimbaeva, N. 033760
Aširov, Jagšimurad 038206
Askali, Nurhusih 031675
Askew, J. 039432
Aslani, Q. 022577
Asmaramah, Rasanubari 027966
Asmundsson, Johann 021956
Asmus, Cathy 048350
Asmuss, Dr. Burkhard 016011
Aso, Keiko 027287
Asolati, Dr. Michele 025053
Asomaddin, Abdugayyumi 037840
Asparuchov, Milko 004783
Asparužov, Dr. Milko 004786
Aspe, Virginia Armella de 028543
Aspen, Peder 039382
Aspenwall, Jim 046066
Aspes, Dr. Alessandra 026287
Asprov, Ognian 004736, 004774
Assaàd, Khaled 037834
Assadulina, Maja 038209
Assaf, Amnon 023013
Assel, Dr. Marina von 015917
Assmann, Dr. Peter 002243, 002249, 002256
Assoghba, Romain-Philippe 003894
Assouline, Hadassah 022945
Assunção, Dr. Ana Paula .. 032659, 032660
Ast, Hiltraud 001996
Astaa, Mikko 009525
Astachova, Irina Valerjevna 034054
Aster, Robert 046194
Astika, Tjokorda Bagus 022529
Astini, Piero 024558
Astley Cooper, Patricia 040311
Astro, C. 013409
Åström, Kjell 036599
Åströmad, Kenneth 036255
Astrua, Dr. Paola 026051
Astrup, Yngve 030822
Astrup Bull, Knut 031283
Astui, Aingeru 034977
Asunción Mateo, María 035683
Asztalos, István 021617
Atac, Robert 048416
Atagarev, A. 038203
Atanasova Tsoneva, Neli 004767
Atanga, Peter S. 004972
Atasever, Gülümser 038177
Atasever, Yaşar 038141
Ateş, Sevim 038038
Athanasiadis, Tasos 021209
Athanasiadis, Yanni 000943
Athani, Shankar S. 022062
Athayde, Sylvia 004443
Athens, Joe 042913
Atherly, Mary 041685
Atherton, Lois 047100
Atiti, Abel 027424
Atiyeh, Walid 040195
Atkins, Michael 048682
Atkinson, Elmer F. 046947
Atkinson, J. 001521
Atkinson, Jennifer 042426
Atkinson, Jo 040241
Atkinson, Karen 045461
Atkinson, Lesley 040736
Atkinson, N.K. 038520
Atkinson, Scott 047838
Attack, Paul H. 005872
Attali, Zohara 022889
Atter, Kerri 043411
Attewell, Alex 040147
Attila, Dimény 032958
Attum, Elaine 043600
Attuquayefio, Dr. Dan K. 021111
Attwood, Maryon 049310
Atvur, Orhan 038171
Atwater, William F. 041561
Atwell, Cheryl 043329
Atwell, Michael 049085
Atwood, Carol Ann 043836
Atwood, John R. 045549
Atwood, Leland 043040
Atwood, Valdine C. 045549
Aubagnac, Gilles 011656
Aubele, Jayne 041621
Aubert, Ben 043625
Aubert, Glenda 005116
Aubert, L. 037130
Aubrecht, Dr. Gerhard 002243, 002243
Aubrun, Max 011331
Aubry, Françoise 003346
Aucella, Frank J. 048961
Auchterlonie, Fiona 039374
Audinet, Gérard 013630
Audisio, Aldo 026075
Audley, Paul 042407
Auel, Lisa B. 044104
Auer, Dr. Alfred 002094, 002934
Auer, Dr. Anita 020592
Auer, Helmut 001662
Auer, Wilfried 020051
Auerbach, Dr. Konrad 018448, 018449
Auffant, Luisa 009158
Auffret, M.J. 012490
Aufgebauer, Peter 016353
Augé, Jean-Louis 011151
Auger, Michele 045510
Augier, Jean-Pierre 012652
Augustat, Dr. Claudia 002961
Augusti, Dr. Adriana 026234
Augustin, Josef 001733
Aujard-Catot, Eliane 010596
Aulan, Comte d' 010542
Aulich, C. 020814
Ault, Lee 038875
Aumüller, Prof. 018827
Aunela, Jorma A. 009995
Aupetitallot, Yves 012017, 037246
Auping, Michael 044011
Aurandt, David 006330
Aurél, Szakál 021771
Aurell, Pirkko 010237
Auserve, Philippe 013305, 013306
Ausfeld, Margaret Lynne 045995
Ausiàs, Vera 011771
Auska, Adolf 001915
Austad, Dan 048407
Austigard, Bjørn 031030
Austin, George 045191
Austin, Kelly 043590
Austin, Pat 045041
Austin, Ramona 044415
Austin, Rowe 048445
Auth, Dr. Susan 046425
Autio, Tuula 036735, 036744

Auvergnat, Dr. Arielle 014989
Auwärter, Konrad 020344
Auwera, Joost Vande 003315
Auxerre, Alain 011653
Auzet, Didier 010598
Avalos Valenzuela, Ana 006947
Avant, Joanne 047790
Avdeeva, M.V. 033582
Avdeeva, Taisija Dmitrievna 033909
Avendaño, Clarissa L. 031741
Averjanova, Ėlvira Valentinovna 033275, 033660
Averoff-Ioannou, Tatiana 021161, 021380
Avery, Dr. D.M. 034586
Avery, Dr. G.A. 034586
Avery, Joseph T. 046336
Avery, Kim 005559
Avery, Laura 048001
Avery, Louise 005720
Avery-Gray, Adrienne 039973
Avesani, Ricciarda 025051
Avest, H.P. ter 029674
Avić, Mirsad 003941
Avila Bardají, José R. 035396
Avila de Monroy, María 007532
Avila Martínez, Jairo Hernando 007534
Avramenko, Mychajlo Pavlovyč 038392
Avrandt, David 006081
Avril, Ellen 044791
Avsom, Richard 044275
Awald, John C. 042450
Awouters, Maria 003333
Awouters, Mia 003353
Awwal, Dr. Iftikhar ul 003099, 003102
Ax, Goeran 036557
Ax, Michael 009095
Ayalon, E. 023083
Ayalon, Dr. E. 023084
Aydın, M. Sezai 038027
Ayerbe, Santiago 007585
Ayers, Betty 005232
Ayers, Marilyn L. 042137
Ayerve, José M. 009184
Ayesha, Abdulla 038423
Aykaş, Satı 038034
Aylesbury, Pat 001309
Ayling, Emma 041393
Aymon, Marie-F. 037310
Ayob, Dato Muslim 027980
Ayrault, Jacqueline 010365, 010366
Ayres, Dr. Anne 045457
Ayres, William 048377
Ayscue, Gene 049210
Aytar, Sefer 038195
Aytuğ, Şükriye 038014
Ayvaz, Melahat 038183
Azarcon, Romualdo A. 031752
Azarmehr, G. 022562
Azeim Mahmoud, Dr. Rifa'at Abdel 009309
Azevedo Abreu, Arienei 004301
Azevedo de Silva, Dr. Nearch 004368
Azimi, Esmail 022633
Aziz, Kapt Nazri 027980
Azizbekova, P.A. 003083
Aznar, Henry 000105
Aznar-Alfonso, Dr. Lydia 031661
Azuar, R. 034819
Azuma, Hisao 027330
Azzarelli, Vincent 044624
Baad Pedersen, Margit 008891
Baagøe, Jette 008935
Baalbergen, W. 029974
Baartman, H. 034618
Baartvedt, Randi 031302
Baas, F.K. 018058
Baatz, Henning 015490
Babajceva, Nadežda Borisovna 033939
Babanazarova, Marinika 049399
Babb, Ellen 045174
Babboni, Dr. Marina 023673
Babcock, Catherine 045162
Babcock, Sidney H. 046394
Babel, Jerzy 032083
Babelon, Jean-Pierre 011836
Babenko, Valerij Volodymyrovyč 038277
Baber, Charlotte 041058
Babić, Nikola 003930
Babic, Sherry 042780
Babin, Anikca 007733
Babini, Tino 025619
Babre, Dace 027736
Bacallado Aránega, Juan José 035795
Bacalles, Lorraine 046300
Baccetti, Dr. Nicola 025042
Baccheschi, Dr. Edi 024309
Bacchetta, Véronique 037117
Baccini, Dr. Stefano 024806
Baccolo, Maria Grazia 023749
Baccrabere, G. 014985
Bačeva, Irina 004850
Bach, Beverly 046774
Bach, Dana 019488
Bach, Kim 044075
Bach-Nielsen, Hanne 009106
Bach Østergaard, Bjarne 008988
Bachčevanov, Ivan 004880
Bachelder, Laura 047502
Bacher, Fabian 015508
Bachler-Rix, Margit 002635
Bachman, Dona R. 042619
Bachmann, Alois 037220
Bachmann, Gaby 036859
Bachmann-Tonelli, Karen 006494
Bachmisov, Ėduard Konstantinovič 033062, 033063
Bachniakon, Vaso 000034
Bachorz, Hanna 032536
Bachvarov, Ivan 004828, 004832
Bacigalupi, Dr. Don 047838
Bacin, Mark S. 046776
Bâciu, Dr. Florea 032846
Back, Lane 048630
Backer, Julie P. 042973
Backer, Kathleen L. 048873
Backhaus, Dr. 020725
Backhaus, Fritz 017178, 017190
Backhouse, Andrew 041153
Backhurst, Timothy D. 046054
Backlund, Connie 043857
Backström, Ragnar 009742
Bacon, Caroline 038656
Bacon, Weldon 005354
Bacourou, Emilia 021392
Bacquet, Emmanuel 013291
Bačvarov, Ivan 004690, 004831
Bączyk, Jarosław 032241
Badaró Nadal, Enrique 041502
Badas, Ubaldo 026336
Badault, Albert 011218
Badder, Susan 048891
Badders, Hurley E. 046868
Bade, Mary 045004
Badel, Doris 018277
Badenhorst, S. 034731
Bader, Joerg 037116
Badgley, Carole 006048
Badham, Mark 005703
Badoúin, Gerhard 019731
Badovinac, Zdenka 034481, 034485
Badre, Dr. Leila 027808
Badura-Triska, Dr. Eva 002965
Bächle, Anke 020365
Bäcker, Erich 016740
Bähr, Gustav-Adolf 019287
Baehr, Dr. M. 019132
Baehrend, John 042810
Baeke, Jan 029180
Bækkelund, Björn 030822
Baele, A. 003873
Baena Alcántara, María Dolores 035113
Baensch, Joachim 017482
Baensch, Norbert 017465
Baepler, Dr. Donald H. 045192
Bär, Dr. Frank P. 019352
Baer, Jan Hodges 044515
Baer, Dr. Rudolf 036851
Bärnighausen, Hendrik 019006
Baerwaldt, Wayne 006621
Baeten, Herman 003702
Baets, A. de 003640
Báez Plaza, Anastasio 034967
Baggenstos, Thomas 037693
Bagheri-Zenouz, Dr. E. 022565
Bagle, Eyvind 031097
Bagnell, Warren 005803
Bagnoli, Dr. Alessandro 025894
Bahadar Khan, Mohammad 031362
Baharin Bin Buyong, Dr. Kamarul 027975, 028005, 028017
Bahe, Michelle 041908
Bahena García, Jaime Arturo 028473
Bahm, Linda 041625
Bahn, Erich 003040
Bahn, Dr. Peter 016447
Bahnmaier, Paul M. 045227
Bahrami, M. 022638
Baier, Berthold 018023
Baier, Patrick 016454
Baik, Jo Gang 027444
Bail, Anne le 015380
Bailey, Ann S. 046436
Bailey, Billie K. 048983, 048984, 048985, 048986
Bailey, Chris H. 042417
Bailey, Colin B. 046333
Bailey, Courtney 047309
Bailey, David 044267
Bailey, Elizabeth 042614
Bailey, Erin 041860
Bailey, Fiona 039998
Bailey, Jack C. 048320
Bailey, Jann L.M. 005658
Bailey, Margaret 046517
Bailey, Michael 038560, 044371
Bailey, Patricia 005142
Bailey, Patricia E. 044289
Bailey, Prof. Reeve M. 041734
Bailey, Robert 040557
Bailey, Stephen F. 046784
Bailey, Steve 038618
Bailleux-Delbecq, Martine 011759
Bailly-Maitre, Marie-Christine 012390
Bain, Heather 045499
Bainbridge, Carol 046487
Bainbridge, David S. 048226, 048227, 048230
Baird, James 046912
Bairlein, Prof. Dr. Franz 020895
Baitchiba-Afalna, Kloumtouin 006905
Baiza, Lee 047538
Baj, Janina 032006
Bajada, John 028043
Bajanik, Dr. Stanislav 034326
Bajcurová, Dr. Katarína 034337
Bajević, Maja 003940
Bajic, Svetlana 003941
Bajko, Daria 046416
Bajpayee, Aparna 022032
Bajuk, Laura 045476, 045477
Bak, Aase 008799
Bak, Anna 032309
Bak, Jolán 021726
Bak, Dr. S.M. 029837
Bakajutova, Ljudmila M. 033732
Bakal, Jeniffer 046340
Bakalarz, Krystyna 032169
Bakalov, Michail 004879
Bakărdžieva, Cenka 004724
Bakărdžijev, Dimităr 004704
Bakarić, Lidija 007828
Bakay, Prof. Dr. Kornél 021777
Bakels, Dr. P. 029335
Baker, Alex 046972
Baker, Dr. Allan 006627
Baker, Alyson 045393
Baker, Amanda 001247
Baker, Barbara J. 041638
Baker, Billy P. 044204
Baker, Charlotte 041667
Baker, Chris 039209
Baker, Christopher 039406
Baker, Diane 001559
Baker, Gary E. 046496
Baker, James 046917, 047727, 047728, 048609
Baker, James W. 047098
Baker, Janet 041448
Baker, Dr. Janet 047011
Baker, Janet 047945
Baker, Jeanne 049042
Baker, John 040541, 041108, 041110
Baker, Joyce 047303
Baker, Kathryn 040893
Baker, Kendall 042547
Baker, Larry L. 042252
Baker, Peggy M. 047097
Baker, Rachel 042855
Baker, Dr. Robert 045513
Baker, Scott 048913
Baker, Sue 043214
Baker, Susan K. 049012
Baker, Warren L. 041638
Baker Driscoll, Dr. Jeanne 048882
Bakić, Ljiljana 034281
Bakker, C. 029775
Bakker, F. 029444
Bakker, G. 029172
Bakker, Henriette den 029449
Bakker, Dr. Lothar 015619
Bakker, W. 029300
Bakkevig, Sverre 031221
Bakouti, Moncef 037974
Bakr, Nemat 009269
Bakreeva, Ljubov Anatoljevna 033359
Bákula Budge, Cecilia 031546
Bal, Danielle 012021
Balabanov, Dimitar 004824
Balagtas, Alex 031706
Balagtas, Alex L. 031704
Balakina, Natalja Michajlovna 033796
Balan, Sandrine 013136
Balandraud, O. 012819
Balanza, Ferran 035476, 035477
Balao, Angel 035439
Balard, Prof. Michel 014883
Balas, Shawna 006856
Balaštíková, Eva 008675
Balatti, Ambrogio 023852
Balawejder, Edward 032136
Balázs, Dr. György 021678
Balbaugh, Joe 044902
Balciunas, Vytautas 027866
Bald, H. 018680
Baldaia, Peter J. 044693
Baldarrago Umpire, Prof. Miguel 031458
Baldellou, Vicente 035286
Baldemair, Vinzenz 002298
Balden, Friedesine 017550
Baldeón, Dr. Amelia 036081
Balderi, Felice 024545
Balderstone, Michael 001332
Baldeschi, Nino 026172
Baldewijns, Jeannine 003451
Baldini, Marino 007774
Baldit, Alain 013990
Baldoni, Lorenzo 024770
Baldwin, Deirdre 044170
Baldwin, Jane 041977
Baldwin, Susan 042847
Baldwin Rehbein, Valerie B. 047389
Balen, Dubravka 007828
Balen, Jacqueline 007828
Balestra, Nino 025591
Baley, Susan G. 046507
Balfet, Hélène 011805
Balic, Haris 002979
Balie, Dr. Isaac 034615
Baligand, Françoise 011641
Bálint, Magdolna 021697
Balist, Valerie 044662
Balistrieri, Bruce 046842
Balk, Dr. Claudia 019047

Balkanska, Veneta 004751
Ball, Baldev 047973
Ball, Dr. Daniela 037256, 037549
Ball, Elizabeth 005236
Ball, Glenys 001588
Ball, JoAnn 047074
Ball, Rex 047796
Ball, Sabine 017811
Balla, Wesley 041597
Ballak, Theo 020109
Ballantine, Dr. David 032718
Ballantine, Thomas 005563
Ballantyne, Dorothy 044561
Ballantyne, Weyman 030584
Ballard, Margot 047474
Ballard, Mark 046453
Ballbé, Xavier 035031
Ballerini, Rosangela 024545
Ballesta, J. 036033
Ballesta Gómiz, Pedro 035530
Ballesteros, Prof. Miguel 000529
Balletto, Prof. Emilio 026068
Ballinger, James K. 047011
Ballinger, J.C. 045686
Ballot, Prof. Dr. G.M. 034711
Ballweber, John 042636
Balmer, John 049325
Balogh, Mihály 021685
Balsama, Joseph 048446
Balsamo, Prof. Renato 023976
Balta, Zdravko 003948
Baltasar Coll Tomas, M.I.S.D. 035612
Baltensperger, Marianne 037597, 037598, 037599
Baltes, Peter 016615
Baltz, Gerald W. 047664
Balza, Raimundas 027851, 027852, 027854, 027858, 027859, 027867
Balzekas, R. 042823
Balzekas, Robert 042823
Balzekas, Stanley 042823
Bamala, Louis 007661
Bambara, Parfait Z. 004962
Bamberger, Gerald 016231
Bambery, Anneke 039225
Bamert, Markus 037544
Bamesa, Prof. Tshungu 007657
Bamforth, Janice 042129
Ban, Gheorghe 032935
Bana, Giovanni 023254
Banach, Wiesław 032308
Banach, Witold 032205
Banai, Merav 022926
Bańbura, Prof. Dr. Jerzy 032116
Banchieri, Daria 026211
Bancroft, William 043121
Bandaranaike, Sunethra 036129
Bandeira, Dr. Dione da Rocha 004166
Bandes, Dr. Susan J. 043574
Bandrowski, Margaret 048302
Bandt, J. 001277
Bandurraga, Peter L. 047372
Bandy, Mary Lea 045389
Bandyopadhyay, Dr. Banya 022011, 022371
Banfi, Enrico 024704
Banfield, Audray M. 000728
Bang, Mogens 008892
Bang Andersen, Sveinung 031221
Bang Larsen, Bent 009089
Bangcas, Salamon L. 031670
Bangcaya, Regino Z. 031778
Bange, Maja 031083
Banghard, Karl 019445
Banholzer, Dr. Max 037573
Banière, François 010350
Banker, Amy 043399
Banker, Maureen 047318
Bankert, John 042608
Bankes, Dr. G. 040406
Bánki, Esther 029891
Banks, Jaqueline 039229
Banks, R. 001105
Banks, Robert 048579
Bannicke, Elke 016120
Bannister, Jenny 001051
Bannister, R. 038769
Bannon, Anthony 047480
Banova, V. 004947
Banova, Vera 004946
Banović, Miroslav 034206
Bantivoglio, Barbar 046418
Bantle, Tom 044278
Banu Syed, Rehana 029116
Banz, Richard 049348, 049349
Banzato, Dr. Davide 023258, 025048, 025050, 025067
Baptista, Dr. Teresa 032606
Baptista Pereira, Fernando António 032688
Baquero, Dr. Angeles Ramos 031432
Baquero Velásquez, Ramón 007454
Bar-Gera, Dov 022890
Bar-Gera, Kenda 022890
Bar-Or, Galia 022906
Bar Semech, Vered 022901
Bar-Yosef, Dr. O. 022966
Barabaş, Dr. Neculai 032775
Barahona, Rolando 007674
Baral, Jody 045436
Barale, Joseph 012004
Baran, Iwona 032378
Barañano, Kosme de 035976
Barandun, Plasch 037674
Barangulova, Farida F. 033992
Baranova, M.N. 033844
Baranowska, Janina 040260
Baranowski, Dr. Jerzy 032163
Bárány, Anders 036651
Barattuci, Maurizio 047987
Barbagallo, Dr. Alfredo I. 000214
Barbalić, Željko 007782
Barbanera, Prof. Marcello 025516
Barbara, Sibille 013459, 013461
Barbeau, Bruce 006618
Barber, Dan 046082
Barber, Jacquey 042161
Barber, John 001645
Barber, R.G. 040960
Barberet-Girardin, E. 015093
Barberini, Maria Giulia 025550
Barbier, Jean 032764, 032766
Barbier, Jean-Paul 037127
Barbier, Nicole 011850
Barbier-Ludwig, Georges 011508
Barbier-Mueller, Monique 037127
Barbieri, Frances T. 048114
Barbieux, José 015005
Barbina, Prof. Alfredo 025468
Barbizet, Laure 013676
Barbosa, Artemio 031685
Barbosa Godefroid, Leonardo 004255
Barbour, Mark 042632
Barbour Strickland, C. 044344
Barbry jr, Earl J. 045689
Barbu, Cristian 032813
Barcel, Ellen 048258
Barcellos, Lauro 004424
Barcik, Jan 032032
Barclay, Craig 039887
Barclay, Don 043472
Barcus, Leisha 043425
Bardeau, Andreas Graf 001843
Bardelli, Alvaro 023239
Bardiaux, David 014833
Bardiová, Dr. Mariana 034301
Bardo, Antoine 012416
Bareinz, Reinhard 016535
Barendsen, J.E. 029681
Barens, H. 046632
Barents, Els 029189
Barés, Athos 000536
Baretow, Steven G. 045775
Barger, Judith M. 045124
Barghini, Sandra 046795
Bargholz, Christina 017709
Bargiel, Réjane 013645
Barillas, Nuria E. de 031426, 031433
Barilleaux, Rene Paul 044799
Barina, Miloslav 008528
Barisch, G. 016234
Barisch, M. 016234
Barišić, Josip 007810
Barison, Mara 023313
Baritault du Carpia, M. de 012990, 012991
Barjou, François 012646
Barkefeld, Anna 020250
Barkemeyer, Dr. Werner 017131
Barker, Alex 043270
Barker, Amy 038596
Barker, Betty 047323
Barker, Deborah 046751
Barker, G. 001516
Barker, G. Carl 045995
Barker, Garry 046022
Barker, Lisa M. 046105
Barker, Marie 048110
Barker, Dr. Nicolas 039161
Barker, Ray 041473
Barker, Rod 043536
Barker, Stuart 038890
Barker, Wendy 043730
Barker, William 046474
Barketov, Vladimir Aleksandrovič 033858
Barkhofen, Dr. Eva-Maria 015991
Barkley, Terry 042412
Barkoun, Gennady 003130
Barksdale, Daryl 045668
Barlek, Josip 007832
Barlow, Keith 040591
Barlow, Martin 040052
Barlow, Victoria 040158, 041317
Barmore, Jim 042635
Barndollar, Lue 043031
Barnea, Dr. Jackob 002320
Barnes, Althemese 048484
Barnes, James H. 043964
Barnes, Judy 045742
Barnes, Lolly 042211
Barnes, Lucinda 042166, 042288
Barnes, Marion 041470
Barnes, Ralp 048544
Barnes, Richard 044667
Barnes, William 040816
Barnet, Peter 046315, 046364
Barnett, Eric B. 043619
Barnett, George 039976
Barnett, James F. 046160
Barnett, James K. 041712
Barnett, Jim 048966
Barnett, June 048143
Barnett, Lawrence 048805
Barnett, Norman 048143
Barney, Edres 047022
Barnhart, Audrey 049192
Barnhill, Michael 042084
Barnhill, Pam 046113
Barnosky, Anthony 042163
Barnum, Lorie 047486
Barnwell, Andrea D. 041874
Barocelli, Prof. Francesco 025129
Baroff, Deborah 045215
Baroies-Fronty, Isabelle 013043
Baron, David 006263
Baron, Donna 049128
Baron, Dr. Jacques 013298
Barón, Javier 035429
Baron, Richard 043633
Baron, Robert 042717
Baroni, Fabio 023692
Baroni, Laura 024039
Baronne, Gerìool 046261
Barons, Richard I. 048255
Barr, Cheryl B. 042159
Barr, Edward 048582
Barr, Mike 039090
Barr, Norma 005344
Barr, Dr. Peter J. 041580
Barr, Tom 043947
Barr, Warren N. 046580
Barracane, Gaetano 023341
Barrachina, Jaime 035650
Barraclough, Bruc 046332
Barral Iglesias, Alejandro 035823
Barrand, Janine 001237, 001248
Barrera Bassols, Marco 028462
Barrett, Candace 045416
Barrett, Maurine 048275
Barrett, Michael 000733
Barrett, Wendy 047762
Barrett-Lennard, Amy 001449
Barrie, Brooke 044397
Barrientos, J. Oscar 021582
Barringer, George Martin 048909
Barrington, Robin 005852
Barro, Aminata 007690
Barron, G.D. 030492
Barron, Stephanie 045441
Barroso Panatieri, Angélica 004284
Barrow, Ira E. 006628
Barrowclough, Dr. George F. 046286
Barry, Alexis 048439
Barry Byrne, Brenda 005435
Barryte, Bernard 048319
Barsalou, Victoria 006122
Barsch, Dr. Barbara 016080
Barsch, Wolfgang 021068
Barson, Jerry 047962
Barsotti, Gianfranco 024511
Barstow, Norman 044381
Barsuglia, Dr. Bruno 024545
Barszcz, Janusz 032412
Barszczewska, Krystyna 032540
Bart, Barbara M. 044689
Barta, Andy 049192
Barta-Fliedl, Dr. Ilsebill 002919, 002921
Bartel, Janet 047824
Bartels, Dr. Christoph 016276
Bartels, Wolfgang 017752
Bartenev, Aleksandr Igorevič 033778
Barter, Judith A. 042820
Barth, Dr. Angelika 020426
Barth, Frank 017694
Bárth, Dr. János 021757, 021758, 021759, 021762
Barth, Linda J. 045468
Barth, Luiz Fernando 004289
Barth, Dr. Robert 037560
Barth, Dr. Robert L. 047187
Barthel, Günter 018369
Barthel, J. 019171
Barthelmess, Dr. Stephan N. 017954
Bartholow, Cheryl 042457
Bartík, Dr. Juraj 034317
Bartków-Domagala, Jadwiga 032524
Bartkowski, Gregor 016462
Bartl, Anna 036885
Bartl, Johanna 016676
Bartlett, Prof. Christopher 048595
Bartlett, Margaret 000924
Bartlett, R.W. 039672
Bartley, James A. 049244
Bartlinski, Jim 041998
Bartmuß, Prof. Dr. Hans-Joachim 017253
Bartolf, M. 006111
Bartolini Bussi, Prof. Maria Giuseppina 024750
Bartolomé Arraiza, Alberto 035425
Barton, Anita S. 045664
Barton, C. Michael 048520
Barton, Fayette Belle 045561
Barton, William R. 046808
Barton Billman, Hilary 044951
Barton Brown, Ann 049067
Barton Campbell, J.A. 047421
Barton Thurber, T. 044426
Bartoś, Magdalena 032151
Bartos, Paul I. 044234
Bartoš, Václav 008662
Bartosz, Adam 032384
Bartosz, Anna 032383
Bartram, Rita 044086
Bartsch, Monika 019086
Bartuś, Marta 031831

Bartz, Rolf-Peter 020681
Barufke, Regina 015755
Barwick, Kent 046368
Bary, Bertrand de 014142
Barzakova, Maria 004652
Barzen, Jeb 042018
Bas, Michael le 038764
Basamakov, Christo 004619
Basamakov, Ilko 004797
Basanieri, Giovanni 023980
Basante, Enar 007568
Basart 004531
Basbous, Alfred 027820
Bascom, Mansfield 045609
Başer, İsmail 038157
Basile, Kenneth A. 047760, 047761
Basir, Abdul 022539
Baškirova, Marija Michajlovna 033129
Bašnjak, Jurij Michajlovič 033029
Bass, Anneta Jakovlevna 033723
Bass, Carol 049263
Bass, Clayton 046618
Bass, Jacquelynn 042158
Basseches, Joshua 042559
Bassegoda Nonell, Juan 034921
Bassett, Christa 042621
Bassett, Fannie 042812
Bassett, Dr. M.G. 038990
Bassi, George 045199
Bassi, Dr. Roberto 026248
Bassi, Rosemarie 019790
Bassin, Aleksander 034483
Bassinger, Marilyn 046624
Bassler, Roseli Fischer 004080
Basso, Dr. Laura 024707
Bassús, María M. 000165
Bast, Douglas G. 042305
Bastard, Laurent 015017, 015018
Basterretxea-Moreno, Dr. Amaia 034984
Bastia, France 003309
Bastidas, Hugo Xavier 044859
Basu Ray Chaudhuri, S. 022284
Bata, Philippe 013868
Bata, Sonja 006582
Bataillard, Marianne 037055
Batchelor, Elisabeth 044924
Batchelor, Trevor 006114
Bateman, Jill 041836
Bateman, Dr. Richard 040245
Bateman, Suellen 044260
Bater, John 044030
Bates, Charles 045292
Bates, Craig D. 049357
Bates, F. 041021
Bates, Geoffrey 045361
Bates, Michael L. 046287
Bates, Sandy 046883
Bates, Tom 045874
Bateva, Mimi 004741
Bath, Marquess of 041301
Bathe, I. 006079
Batista, Alvaro 032570
Batkin, Jonathan 047980
Batkin, Norton 041738
Batori, Dr. Armicla 025521
Batova, Anna Nikolaevna 033639
Battaglini, Dr. Giuseppe 025339
Battcher, Reinhard 042421
Battel, Angelo 025734
Batten, Andrew C. 046332, 046780
Batterson, Lorna 045327
Battinou, Zanet 021171
Battins, Niccholas 046395
Battle, Dr. Thomas C. 048914
Batty, Tim 039255
Baty, Catherine 049116
Bauch, Herbert 018497
Bauch, Hermann 002650
Bauche, Dean 006032
Bauchhenß, Dr. Gerhard 016333
Baucum-Fields, Penny 046788
Baud, Arlette 036861
Baud, Georges 012114
Baud-Berthier, Gilles 010908
Bauder, Charles C. W. 044164
Baudet, Jean-Charles 015102
Baudet, Jean-Michel 013832
Baudisson, C. 012338
Bauduin, Jean-Loup 012325, 012326, 012330
Bauer, Arthur 002894
Bauer, Christoph 020219
Bauer, Douglas F. 043874
Bauer, Franz 002538
Bauer, Fritz 021092
Bauer, Georg 002956
Bauer, Gudrun 017869
Bauer, Hans 016203
Bauer, Heidrun 020393, 020394
Bauer, Dr. Helmut 019086
Bauer, Herbert 015517
Bauer, Prof. Dr. Ingolf 019039, 019403
Bauer, Lloyd 048172
Bauer, Dr. Markus 017455
Bauer, Peter 018659
Bauer, Richard 048522
Bauer, Sigrud 016203
Bauer, Stéphane 016106
Bauer, Susan 005865
Bauermeister, Janneke 019153
Bauernfeind, Günther 019246
Baulard, Hervé 011245
Baule, John A. 049327
Baum, Bruce 042349
Baum, Prof. Dr. E. 020940
Baum, Jo Ann 042306
Baum, Kristina 020667
Baum, Prof. Peter 002250
Baum, Rainer 036885
Baum, Wolfgang 020195
Bauman, Victor-Henrich 032962
Bauman Taylor, Paula 044025
Baumane, Inta 027696
Baumann, Anton 002418
Baumann, Daniel 036930
Baumann, Evelies 016592
Baumann, Dr. Kirsten 016684
Baumann, Klaus 017519
Baumann, Leonie 016151, 053518
Baumann, Dr. Maria 019745, 019746
Baumann-Eisenack, Dr. Barbara 020384
Baumann-Huber, Margrit 037720
Baumbach, Susan M. 040724
Baumberger, Moritz 037389
Baume, Nicholas 044463
Baumeier, Prof. Dr. Stefan 016691
Baumeister, Dr. Annette 016846
Baumeister, Dr. Ralf 015676
Baumgärtel, Dr. Bettina 016841
Baumgärtner, I. 019715
Baumgärtner, Iris 019717
Baumgardner, George 042635
Baumgardt, Manfred 016171
Baumgarten, Detlef 016381
Baumgarten, Dr. K. 015768
Baumgarten, Ute 018011
Baumgartner, Josef 001813
Baumgartner, Dr. Jutta 001946
Baumgartner, Dr. Michael 036930
Baumgartner, Dr. Sieglinde 002527
Baumstark, Prof. Dr. Reinhold 019030, 019038, 019095, 019110, 019123
Baur, Andreas 017083, 017087
Baur, Karl 037512
Bausart, Lucie 003182
Bause, George S. 046823
Bausier, Karine 003203
Bauske, Clay R. 044722
Baussan, Magali 015121
Baußmann, Dr. Edda 019153
Bavnshøj, Peter 008816
Bavoni, Dr. Umberto 026367
Bawden, Dr. Garth L. 041618
Bawinkel, Betty 044072
Bawinkel, Russel 044072
Baxter, Alan 038927
Baxter, Clare 038494, 038495
Baxter, Connie 006282
Baxter, Ellen 047043
Bayard, Jean 004976
Bayard, Pierre 004977
Bayarri, Carlos 035751
Bayden, Ian 048835
Bayer-Niemeier, Dr. Eva 018433
Bayet 003810
Bayles, Jennifer 042498
Baylis, Lisa 047472
Baylis, Timothy 041395
Bayliss, Joan 038592
Bayliss, Keith 041173
Bayliss, Dr. Paul 034638
Baymuradov, N. 037843
Bayona, Wilhelm A. 031804
Bayou, Charlie 013998
Bayram, Metin 038076
Baysal, H. Hüseyin 038047
Bayuelo Castellar, Soraya 007493
Bazanov, Valerij Anatoljevič 033102
Bazely, Sue 005699
Bazennerye, Dr. Jean 015234
Bazin, J. 013076
Bazley, Shirley 001256
Bazzoni, Maurizio 025397
Bazzotti, Prof. Ugo 024601
Beach, James 045205
Beach, Jane 042688
Beach, Dr. Milo C. 048884
Beady, Charles H. 047030
Beal, Bradley L. 046217
Beal, Graham W.J. 043444
Beal, Isabel C. 044365
Beal, Robert J. 047000
Beale, Arthur C. 042334
Beale, Carolyn 043221
Beale, Denise 039243
Beall, Brent 046645
Beall, Charlotte 048078
Beall, William 045035
Beam, Michael J. 046071
Beam, Michael N. 042797
Beamis, Frances D. 042494
Bean, Dr. Susan 047741
Beans, Daniel J. 048045
Bearcroft, Don 038460
Beard, David 046951
Beard, Dr. James S. 045715
Beard, Rick 041847
Beard-Simpkins, Doreen 048464
Beardsley, Theodore S. 046346
Beardsmore, R.J. 030562
Bearis, Lynn 005928
Beasley, James M. 048301
Beasley, Lorraine 041911
Beasley, Pam 048202
Beaton, Stuart 005118
Beattie, Natalie 001375
Beattie, Stuart 040854
Beatty, Brett 044702
Beatty, Steven 045003
Beatty, Thomas P. 048793
Beatyy, John T. 047515
Beaucamp, Dr. Barbara 018809
Beaud, Marie-Claude 027889
Beaudin Saeedpour, Dr. Vera 042461
Beaudry Dion, Jacqueline 006378
Beauffet, Jacques 014271
Beaufort, Dr. Christian 002912
Beaufort-Spontin, Dr. Christian 002934
Beaugrand, Prof. Dr. Andreas 016239
Beaumont, Helen 022761
Beaumont, Robert N. 048837
Beauregrand, Becky 043206
Beauvau, Princesse de 012070
Beavers, Randell A. 044653
Beavin, H.A. 039754
Beavis, Dr. Ian 041245
Beccari, Giuseppe 026361
Beccaria, Marcella 025448
Beccart, Christine 011984
Becchi, Casimiro 025188
Bećević, Azra 003941
Bech, Marianne 009078
Bechelet, Florence 040931
Becher, Inge 017369
Bechers, H.H 030211
Bechet, Georges 027895
Bechly, Dr. Günter 020364
Bechtel, Anna 042817
Bechtold, Dr. Ekkehard 001787
Bečić, Berina 003941
Beck, Alison 041923
Beck, Gerald 043813
Beck, Prof. Dr. Herbert 017195, 017196
Beck, Jane C. 045835
Beck, Jerry 042342
Beck, Mike 044684
Beck, Monica 048423
Beck, Noldi 027845
Beck, Rolf 020846, 020849
Beck, Stefan 037413
Beck, Tom 041962
Beck-Lipsi, Gabrielle 014114
Beck Silveria, Sheli 046456
Beckelman, Laurie 046404
Beckemeyer, Clemens 018924
Becken, Ellen 008825
Becker, Addie 048245
Becker, Dr. Annette 017156
Becker, Dr. Christoph 037777
Becker, Douglas L. 042002
Becker, Edwin 029239
Becker, Gail R. 045492
Becker, Dr. H. 017322, 017323
Becker, Horst R. 017171
Becker, Dr. Ingeborg 016002
Becker, Jürgen 017058
Becker, Lawrence 049309
Becker, Lisa 045511, 045537
Becker, Marjorie 045066
Becker, Dr. Michael 001969
Becker, Peter 017581
Becker, Dr. Peter-René 016426
Becker, Dr. Rayda 034649
Becker, Dr. Rolf 020343
Becker, Dr. Rudolf 019959
Becker, Sara 041648
Becker, Scott R. 048969
Becker, Ulrich 018665
Becker, Ulrike 002934
Becker, Ursula 020148
Beckers, Marion 016190
Beckett, D. 039435
Beckett, Michael D. 045213
Beckford, Chip 049063
Beckley, Frank J. 040851
Beckmann, Michael 001130, 001474
Beckmann, Dr. Ralf 017109
Beckmann, Werner J. 016851
Becks, Jürgen 020824, 020825
Becks, Dr. Leonie 018306
Beckstrøm, Alf 031227
Becucci, Dr. Sandra 023734, 025930
Bedal, Albrecht 020116
Bedal, Prof. Dr. Konrad 015837, 015838
Bedaux, Dr. R. 029854
Bedell, Lisa 046367
Bedenham, M.D. 039046
Bedenig, Dr. K. 037804
Bedford, Emma 034587
Bedia García, Juana 035285
Bedouin, Regan 043543
Bedoya de Rendón, Martha Elena 007578
Bedula, Jane 046035
Bee, Dr. Andreas 017188
Beebe, John 043724
Beebe, Mary L. 045069
Beech, Mike 039521
Beeck, Sonja 016684
Beeden, Keith 041000
Beeker, Angela 044550
Beeks, Bonny 044236
Beele, F. 003163

Beer, Dieter 037764
Beer, Dr. Günther 017468
Beer, Dr. Manuela 018336
Beerli, Klaus 037353
Beerts, Harry 003745
Beesch, Ruth 046352
Beeson, George 043356
Beets-Anthonissen, M. 003167
Beevers, David 038850
Begg, Ken 000888
Beggin, Suzy 044073
Begić, Veselko 007812
Bégin, Carmelle 005504
Begley, John P. 045494
Begouin, Bernard 011059, 011060, 011063, 011064
Begue, Christelle 014948
Béguin, Gilles 013622
Béguin, Pierre Henri 036967
Behler, Mark 049058
Behlmann, Cletus 047801
Behm, Stefan 001986
Behne, Dr. Axel 019537
Behnke, Jean 046896
Behnke, Martin 017572
Behr, Lothar 020555
Behr Richards, Anita 042295
Behrends, Carey F. 046625
Behrendt, Klaus 002979
Behrendt, Martina 016174
Behrens, Friedrich 020008
Behrens, Sarah 046819
Behrens, Todd 045124
Behrndt, Helle 008973, 052857
Behroozy, N. 023086
Behwke, Arlene 046896
Beier, Aasmund 031123, 031124
Beier, Dr. H.-J. 020803
Beier-de Haan, Prof. Dr. Rosmarie . 016011
Beiersdörfer, Dr. Kurt 019549
Beiersdorf, Maciej 032046
Beil, Judith 048505
Beil, Leslie 048242
Beilharz, Horst F. 020968
Beilmann-Schöner, Dr. Mechthild . 019822
Beimel, Alice 047688
Bein, Peter von 020821
Beiranvand, Asadollah 022571
Beirne, T. 039687
Beisel, P. 019192
Beisken, Angela 017795
Béistegui de Robles, Dolores 028436
Beitchman, Marsha 046282
Beitl, Dr. Klaus 002998
Beitl, Matthias 002132, 002976
Beitz, Dr. Uwe 016881
Bejenaru, Ionel 032857, 032931
Bekmuradov, I. 049395
Bekouan, Hortense Zagbayou 007685
Bela, Dr. Zbigniew 032043
Bélafi, Dr. B. 020434
Belai, George 021636
Bélair, Guy 005926
Belaja, Z.A. 033912
Belan, Judy 045959
Belbin, J. 001320
Belčeski, Rubinčo 027915
Belčeva, Tonja .. 004674, 004675, 004676
Belda Navarro, Dr. Cristóbal 035534
Beldeanu, Katharina 018379
Belder, Marie de 003773
Beldon, Stanford T. 041657
Belenis 021342
Belfield, John 001315
Belgado Camblor, Victoria 035046
Belgin, Dr. Tayfun 002172
Belie, Liesbeth de 003315
Belin, Jacques 011052
Belinskis, Andrejs 027766
Belisario, Alessandro 024199
Beljaev, A.A. 033920
Beljaeva, Nadešda V. 033652
Beljaeva, Svetlana A. 033926
Belk, Brad 044881, 044883
Belkowitz, Shirley S. 047411
Bell, Brendan 034701
Bell, Chee Chee 044712, 044713
Bell, Christine 038583
Bell, Doug 045739
Bell, Elizabeth 042639
Bell, Eunice 046615
Bell, Dr. Graham A.C. 005948
Bell, Greg 048467
Bell, Gregory 045013
Bell, Harold 044222
Bell, Julia 040461
Bell, Lynn 041923
Bell, Margaret 030552
Bell, Michael 006098
Bell, P.J. 009002
Bell, Robert 000888
Bell, Steve 042194
Bell, Valerie 043778, 045350
Bella, Miguel Angel di 000526
Bellah, Suzanne 046775
Bellaigue, Dominique de 010862
Bellais, Leslie 045595
Bellamore, Stan 030573
Bellamy, James 044516
Bellamy, Dr. Martin 040951
Bellamy-Jawor, Deborah 042876
Bellando, Francesco 023331
Bellanger, Françoise 013550
Bellani, Giancarlo 024390
Bellanová, S. 034452
Bellar, Gail 044435
Bellas, Gerald M. 042928
Bellaton, Jean-Louis 014301
Bellavia, Kim 045029
Bellazzi, Dr. Pietro 026324
Bellec, Henri 006332
Bellehumeur, Alain 005096
Beller, Janet 045503
Bellerby, Greg 006692
Bellettini, Dr. Pierangelo . 023416, 023424, 023427
Belli, Dr. Gabriella 025609, 025610, 026107
Bellier, C. 003815
Bellifemine, Graziano 023406
Bellin, Ines 015992
Bellinger, David 043926
Bellini, Lucette 011096
Bellini, R. 036854
Bellmore, Audra 048242
Bello Morales, Marinelly 049454
Belloni, Luigi Mario 025030
Bellucci, Alberto Guillermo 000225, 000227
Bellucci, Dr. Bruno 025716
Belluscio, Dr. Costantino 023180
Belluscio, Lynne J. 045217
Belluscio, Tara 045978
Bellwald, Tony 037211
Belmondo, Dr. Rosalba 025815
Belmonte, Patty 046672
Bělochová, Olga 008422
Belonovič, Ėleonora Nikolaevna .. 033855
Belonovich, Galina Ivanovna 033277
Belotti, Dr. Ione 023844
Beloubek-Hammer, Dr. Anita 016109
Belousova, Natalj Aleksandrovna . 033258
Belov, Vladimir Ivanovič 034064
Belova, N.H. 033813
Belser, Eduard J. 036892
Belsey, Hugh 041155
Belsham, J. W. 041076
Belsley, Kathryn 046881
Belt, Virginia 041902
Belter, Rüdiger 019073, 053313
Beltrán, Carlos 028292
Beltran, Josel 031752
Beltrán Figueredo, Martín 007546
Beltrán Lloris, Miguel ... 036104, 036105, 036106, 036107
Beltrani, Francesco 024634, 024635
Belušić, Andreja 007841
Belvin, Robert 046205
Bem, Marek 032507
Beman, Lynn S. 041697
Bemis, William 041693
Bemmes, Robert 047343
Bemporad, Dr. Dora Liscia 024191
Ben, Dr. Arie 023080
Ben-Barak, I. 023006
Ben-Chaôbane, Abderrazzak 029026
Ben-Gal, Dr. Ely 022996
Ben-Nuftali, Aya 023097
Ben-Shimon, Eytana 023102
Benachetti, Sandra 015106
Benavides Becquis, Maria del Carmen 007422, 007596
Benayahu, Dr. Y. 023094
Benbow, Colin 003897
Benbow, Julie 047873
Benda, Susanne 048581
Bender, Brynn 048646
Bender, Claudia 016846
Bender, Joseph 048308
Bender, Patricia L. 043683
Bender, Phil 043415
Bender Hadley, Joy 045695
Bender-Wittmann, Uschi .. 018952, 018953
Bendixen, Maren 017676
Bendixen, Uwe 017676
Bendyukova, Natalia Oleksandrivna 038386
Benedetti, Prof. Laudomia 024643
Benedetti, Sergio 022763
Benedict, Hope 047767
Benedict, Kay 042644
Benedik, Dr. A. Christian 002845
Benedik, Kristie 043530
Beneš, Dr. Luděk 008506
Benesch, Dr. Evelyn 002855
Benetti, Attilio 026223
Benezra, Neal 047885
Benford, Joseph 046980
Bengston, Rod 041590
Bengtson, Keith 044544
Bengtson, Prof. S.A. 036448
Bengtsson, Bengt 036608
Benington, Jon 038633
Benítez, Antonio Maria 007614
Benitez, Moya 031714
Benito, Fernando 035978
Benito Goerlich, Dr. Daniel 035981
Benjamin, Bart 047450
Benjamin, Brent 047676
Benjamin, Jeremy 046320
Benjamin, Dr. Tritobia H. 048913
Benke, Dr. Harald 020330
Benke, Uwe 015995
Benn, Carl 006611
Benner, Sue 000839
Bennerhag, Carina 036438
Benneth, Dr. Solbritt 036643, 036671
Bennett, Dr. Betsy 047315
Bennett, Charles 047973, 047975
Bennett, Christobel 001497
Bennett, Dorthy E. 042570
Bennett, Fernanda 047547
Bennett, Graham 041269
Bennett, Harold D. 042570
Bennett, Isabel 022687
Bennett, James 043819, 044198
Bennett, James A. 040661
Bennett, Judson E. 043946
Bennett, Kurt Updegraff Mary 042530
Bennett, Michael 042985
Bennett, Michael W. 045363
Bennett, Dr. Nicholas 040005
Bennett, Dr. Peter 042380
Bennett, Ruby 006176
Bennett, Sally B. 046040
Bennett, Sandra 041875
Bennett, Sharon 042728
Bennett, Shelley 047912
Bennett, Susan 039433
Bennett, Swannee 045344
Bennett, Tony 003088
Bennett, Valerie 041934
Bennett, William P. 044529
Bennington, Jeanette 044594
Bennington, Seddon 047045
Bennyworth, J.P. 038590
Benova, Katarina 034337
Beňovský, Jozef 034389
Benscheidt, Dr. Anja 016430, 016432
Bensen, Pat 048004
Benson, Barbara E. 049203
Benson, Benjamin Foley 047991
Benson, Claire 041834
Benson, Dave 005257, 005260
Benson, Patricia 043649
Bentabet, Mohamed 000043
Bente, Jodi 045057
Bente, Klaus 017685
Bente, Prof. Dr. Klaus 018578
Bentheim, Oskar Prinz zu 015656
Bentinck, Baron B.W. 029197
Bentley, Alan 039707
Bentley, Donna 046453
Bentz, Sylviane 014084
Benvie, R. 040496
Benvie, Rachel 040495
Benyovsky, Lucija 007841
Benz, Edward 042311
Benz, Paul 019986
Benz, Robert G. 049294
Benzel, S. 018260
Beran, Antonia 017364
Beran, Helmut 015921
Beran, Pavel 008691
Beránek, Petr 008551
Beránková, Dr. Helena 008286
Beránková, Dr. Jana 008369, 008469
Bérard-Azzouz, Odile 010269
Béraud, Isabelle 011889
Berberkić, Alija 034273
Berchoux, Pierre 011033
Berchtold, Marianne 036927
Berding, Dr. Hans-Henning 017732
Berdjajeva, Tatjana Jurjevna 033895
Bereczky, Dr. Lóránd 021671
Beresford, P. 041403
Bereska, Norbert 019181
Berežanskij, Aleksandr Samuilovič 033330
Berg, Hans-Jürgen 020274
Berg, Dr. Heinz 019659
Berg, Kaare 031077
Berg, Karin 031105
Berg, Kristian 036629, 036668
Berg, Manfred 015950
Berg, Peter 015781
Berg, Dr. Richard B. 042535
Berg, Roger 044932
Berg, Dr. Stephan 017761, 053375
Berg Lofnes, Solveig 031186, 031188
Bergamaschi, Cirillo 024395
Bergamini, Dr. Giuseppe . 026161, 026162, 026164
Bergdahl, Ewa 036504
Bergé, Pierre 029026
Bergen, Terry 041754, 044938
Bergendahl, Mathias 047718
Bergenthal, Dr. T. 018090
Bergeon, Annick 010882
Berger, Aaron 041595, 045665
Berger, Prof. Albert 001933
Berger, Andrea 001752
Berger, Dr. Andreas 018053
Berger, Claudio 037328
Berger, Elfriede 002754
Berger, Erwin 015711
Berger, Dr. Eva 019491, 019495
Berger, Eva-Marie 015537
Berger, Ewald 001933
Berger, Dr. Frank 017176
Berger, Georg 016911
Berger, Ingrid 031164
Berger, Jerry A. 048301
Berger, Karin 015711
Berger, Marianne 019943
Berger, Michael 020484, 020866

Berger, Moshe Tzvi 022967
Berger, Paul 036954
Berger, Shelly 049156
Berger, Teresa J. 045832
Berger, Theodor 018705
Berger, Tobias 030430
Berger, Dr. Ursel 016050
Bergeret, Anne-Marie . . . 012107, 012108, 012109
Bergeret, Jean 012703, 014305
Bergero, Susana 000313
Bergeron, André 005937, 005941
Bergeron, Arthur W. 046905
Bergeron, Myrna 046266
Bergès, Catherine 010269
Berges, Sylvie 010811
Berggård, Ingeborg 031299
Bergggruen, Oliver 017192
Berggten, Jan 036680
Bergheger, Brian F. 043687
Bergholm, Synnöve 009996
Berghout, Dr. P.-J. 029535
Bergin, Christer 036265
Bergler, Andrea 016607
Bergman, Bill 047300
Bergman, Ingela 036193
Bergman, Kaj 036285
Bergmann, Eva-Maria 019317
Bergmann, Jóhanna 021940
Bergmann, Prof. Marianne 017472
Bergmann, Sven 016835
Bergmann, Ulrike 016953
Bergra, Cliff 047229
Bergroth, Tom 010176
Bergs, Irene-Annette 018156
Bergs, Lilita 047514
Bergsten, Wayne 045904
Bergström, Anna-Lena 036511
Bergström, Anne 009949, 009950, 009951
Bergström, Carin 036584
Bergström, Eva-Lena 036648
Bergström, Lars 036276
Bergström, Matti 009597
Bergstrom, Prof. Stig M. 043110
Bergstrøm, Ture 008979
Bergundthal, Hermann 037182
Beringer, Emile 011807
Berinskat, Michael 017996
Berke, Debra 048951
Berkel, R.R. 030212
Berkemeier, Dr. Marie-Claire 036884, 036885
Berkes, Jill 043715
Berkes, Peter 036894
Berkey, Vernon 048217
Berkmen, Çetin 038031
Berkovitz, Sam 047061
Berkowitz, Dr. Roger M. 048569
Berktold, Dr. Werner 002051
Berkvens, Dirk 003161
Berlichingen, Hans Reinhard Freiherr von 018101
Berliet, Paul 012807
Berlin, K.W. 001476
Berliner, Nancy 047741
Bérlinš, Guntis 027698
Berman, Elizabeth Kessin 048888
Berman, Jerôme 042193
Berman, Tosh 048757
Berman-Miller, Cynthia 044579
Bernabo Brea, Dr. Luigi 025987
Bernabò Brea, Dr. Maria 025119
Bernard, A. 003329
Bernard, Charles 011822
Bernard, Christian 037124
Bernard, Fernand 003706
Bernard, Goetz 013140
Bernard, Loic 005771
Bernard, Marie-Thérèse 014602
Bernard, Mary Ann 045091
Bernard, Michel 003438
Bernard-Grit, Jeanne 014420
Bernardi, Dr. Vito 026005
Bernardini, Dr. Carla 023456
Bernardini, Paolo 025771
Bernardini, Toni 023277
Bernardinis, Domenico de 037159
Bernasconi, John G. 039889
Bernat, Chris 042298
Bernat, Clark 006023
Bernatzky, Eva 002680
Bernaudeau, Chloé 012702
Bernauer-Keller, Christine 016627
Bernay, Claude 013220
Berndes, Claske 048869
Berndt, Siegfried 020788
Berner, Dr. Hermann 018986
Berner, Dr. Klaus 053439
Bernesconi, César 041555
Berney, Adrienne 046259
Bernhard, Friedolin 017425
Bernhard-Walcher, Dr. Alfred 002934
Bernhardt, Harold O. 042649
Bernhardt, Josef 001858, 052532
Bernier, Ronald R. 049175
Bernier, Suzie 005291, 005292
Bernini, C. 037804
Bernklau, Maria 002971
Berns, Christiane 027894
Berns, Marla C. 045421, 047952
Berns, Peter 029625, 029626
Bernsmeier, Dr. Uta 016411
Bernstein, Bruce 046383
Berntsen, Gunnar 031171
Bero, Meg 041913
Beron, Prof. Petar 004870
Beroza, Barbara L. 049357
Berraute, Luis Bernardo 000565
Berrend, Nico 027904
Berreth, David S. 044055
Berridge, Peter 039117
Berrin, Kathleen 047857, 047871
Berrones-Molina, Patricia 046493
Berry, A. Joyce 047640
Berry, Barbara 049017
Berry, Diane 043599
Berry, James M. 044831
Berry, Jim 043862
Berry, Dr. P.F. 001377
Berry, Susan 048176
Berry, Violet 047100
Berry, Warren 039234
Berry, William B. 042163
Berryman, Jill 047375
Berryman, Val 043575
Bers, Miriam 016042
Bersirov, A.M. 033349
Berswordt-Wallrabe, Prof. Dr. Kornelia von 018711, 020147, 020150
Bert, James 048769
Bert, Putter 042115
Bertalan, Karin 019440
Bertani, Licia 024140
Bertaud, Henri 010351
Bertazzolo, Prof. Luigi 025593
Berthaud, Gérard 012994
Bertheaud, Michael 048975
Berthelsen, David 001048
Berthod, Dr. Bernard 012811
Berthold-Hilpert, Monika . . 017288, 020062
Bertholi, Jean 014540
Berti, Dr. Fausto 024850
Bertie, Dr. David M. 038586, 039534, 039810, 040479, 040703, 041125
Bertini, Dr. Pierluigi 024580
Bertl, Richard 002488
Bertling, Dr. Markus 019144
Bertola, Carinne 037384
Bertolini, Madalen 048327
Bertone, Aureliano 023867
Bertout, Ernest 012895
Bertram, Dr. Marion 016136
Bertram-Neunzig, Evelyn 018338
Bertrand, Claire 039859
Bertrand-Sabiani, Julie 013515
Bertsch, Patricia 046078
Bertschi, Victor 037144
Bertuleit, Dr. Sigrid 020141
Bertus, Jean-Paul 012900
Beruete Calleja, Francisco 035182
Berup, Christina 036382
Berwick, Hildegarde 040470
Beryt, Andrzej 032137
Besio, Remo 037731
Beširov, Ilija 004950
Beskrovnaja, Nina Sergeevna 033273
Besom, Bob 048280
Bessa Luis Baldaque, Laura Mónica 032680
Bessant, Louise 040367
Bessborough, Madeleine 039359
Besse, Nadine 014270
Besseiche, Daniel 015207
Bessignano, Timothy 046893
Bessire, Mark 047159
Besson, Christine 010394
Besson, Elisabeth 012021
Bessone, Dr. Silvana 032654
Bessor, Joyce M. 049375
Beštáková, Dr. Kamila 008539
Besten, G.J. den 029972
Besterman, Tristram 040406
Beštok, Chabas Korneevič 033540
Bestrom, Beth 047290
Betancourt, Julián 007427
Betancur, Víctor Raúl 007391
Betanio, Nemesio V. 031747
Bétemps, Alexis 025627
Bethell, Chris 040221
Bethell, Philip 041464
Bethge, Dr. Ulrich 018588
Bethmann-Hollweg, C. von 015504
Betrim 029082
Betschart, Madeleine 036952
Betscher, Hermann 018623, 018624
Betsky, Aaron 030096
Betsy, Dr. Bryan 041990
Bett, David 039525
Betta, Dr. Carlo 023776
Bettendorf, Josef 018955
Bettenhausen, Brad L. 048558
Bettens, Doug 001386
Bettison, Dr. Cynthia Ann 048177
Betton, Richard A. 044337
Betton, Thomas 026380
Betts, Jonathan 041219
Betts, Kathleen 048945
Betts, Shirley 006099
Betts, Wendy 005481
Betz, Eden 046632
Betz, Julia P. 046790
Betz, Martin 045603
Beu, Liliana Marinela 032921
Beuchel, Thomas 002555
Beuf, Jean-Claude 014481, 014482
Beugeling, Dr. Niels 029220
Beuker, J. 029279
Beukers, Prof. H. 029847
Beukes, Engela 034760
Beumer, A.C. 030386
Beumers, C.E.L. 030108
Beurskens, N. 029632
Beuster, Stephanie 019971
Beutelspacher, Prof. Dr. A. 017412
Beutelspacher, Martin 018952, 018953
Beuze, Lyne-Rose 028057
Bevan, Jennifer 000955
Beveridge, Albert J. 045279
Bevers, Dr. Holm 016109
Bevilacqua, Jean-Paul 011183
Bevilecqua, Emanuele 025580
Bex, Florent 003173
Beyeler, Ernst 037451
Beyer, Patrick 006062
Beyer, René 037807
Beyer, Dr. Roland 016761
Beynon, Jon 041197
Bezbach, Illja Vasil'ovyč 038414
Bezemek, Dr. Ernst 002060
Bezerra Rolim, Valéria Laena 004116
Bezin, C. 015089
Bezlaj Krevel, Ljudmila 034495
Bezold, Franz 019352
Bezzola, Dr. Tobia 037777
Bhagwati, Dr. Annette 016061
Bhan, Kuldeep K. 022367
Bhandari, Dr. J.S. 022077
Bhargava, P.C. 022043
Bhatt, Vikas 022034
Bhattacharya-Stettler, Therese . . . 036930
Bhaumik, P.K. 022093
Bhave, Dr. S.M. 022303
Bhering Cardoso, Marcio 004345
Bhikul, Tassanee 037897
Bhreathnach-Lynch, Dr. Sighle . . . 022763
Bhullar, Akbar Ali 031386
Bhuyan, G.N. 022119
Biagini, Lorena 025707
Bianchi, Loredana 036917
Bianchi, Matteo 036918
Bianchi Gilangon, Sergio 024166
Bianchini, Dr. Gregorio 026118
Bianchino, Dena 045823
Bianco, Prof. Vito Donato 025647
Biancolini, Daniela 023126, 026081
Bianconi, Teresa 025544
Biasini, Cathèrine 020263
Biasio, Elisabeth 037808
Biass-Fabiani, Sophie 012963
Biba, Prof. Dr. Otto 002903
Bibbins, M. Wyllis 042557
Bibby, Deirdre 044463
Biberin, Vladimir Nikolaevič 033986
Bibler, Helen Ann 044396
Bibra, G. von 001197
Bickel, John 038538
Bickell, Lara 047131
Bickford, Christpher P. 045017
Bickford, George P. 042985
Bickford-Berzock, Kathleen 042820
Bicklmeier, Lori 005328
Bicknell, Katharine 045772
Bicknell, Terry 030640
Bidar, A. 013411
Bidault, Alain 013039
Biddlecombe, Julie 039794
Biderman, Ellen 047977
Bidstrup, Wendy 045682
Bidwell, John 046394
Bidwell, Paul 041049
Bidwell, Richard 049013
Biec, Odile 013746
Biedenharn, Murray 045967
Biedermann, Dr. Gottfried 001925
Biefel, H. 016998
Biefel, I. 016998
Bieg, Werner 015430
Biegel, Dr. Gerd 016381, 020793
Biegel, Gerd 020954
Biegel, Susanne 015628
Biehl, Martin 031084
Bielamowicz, Zbigniew 032261
Bielański, Janusz 032052
Bielby, Jane 038837, 041037
Bielejec, Stephanie 041889
Bielinski, Regula 037574
Bielkin, Kenneth 046285
Biemans, Johan 029309
Biemans, Dr. Jos A.A.M. 029228
Bienedell, Arturo Alberto 000559
Biener, Herbert 001914
Bieńkowski, Joachim 032419
Bier, Carol 048948
Bier, F. 011692
Bierens de Haan, J.C. 029826, 030243
Bieri, Susanne 036936
Bieri Thomson, Helen 037143
Bierinckx, Cis 045922
Biermann, Prof. Dr. Günther 002284
Biersack, Werner 017506
Bierwisch, Heidi 017012
Biesboer, Dr. P. 029653

Biesenbach, Klaus 016110
Bieske, Dr. Dorothee 017130
Bievenour, Ginger 044741
Biezaitis, M. 000850
Biffiger, Steffan 037603
Bigay, Victorino 031621
Bigda, Daisy R. 042744
Bigelow, May 049124
Biggart, Norman 042518
Biggs, Kate 041044
Biggs-Craft, Katherine 006356
Bignasca, Dr. Andrea 036879
Bihan, Olivier le 010885
Bihler, A. 016915
Bijelić, Dubravka 034163
Bijleveld, W. 029216
Bijleveld van Lexmond, Caspar 037208
Biktaševa, Natalija Nikolaevna 033706
Bilanoha, Ewald 003009
Bilbey, Sue Ann 048766
Bilderback, Jeffrey 048029
Bilek, Alena 002852
Bilenduke, Florence 006125
Biles, Leanna S. 043983
Biles, LeAnna S. 043984
Bilgin, Mehmet 038164
Biličenko, Valentina Andreevna 033771
Bilich, Ivanka 007733
Billard, Marie Claude 010589
Billerbeck, Barb 046435
Billich, Dorie 005523
Billier, Philippe 014705
Billig, Pamela 042433
Billinge, Rachel 040241
Billings, Larry 042492
Billings, Loren 042864
Billings, Vernon N. 045158
Billingsley, Pam 047550
Billisics-Rosenits, G. 001823
Billops, Camille 046344
Billups, Di 040856, 040858
Biloparlović, Ivo 007783
Biloslav, Toni 034469, 034510
Bin Ismail, Halal 027974
Binaud, Daniel 010834
Binder, Caroline 040963
Binder, Christian 017257
Binder, Doug 039660
Binder, Gerhard 021043
Binder, Hanspeter 037408
Binder, Stefi 036871
Bindereif, Hugo 019475
Bindija, Mosar 034189
Bines, Dr. Joan P. 049121
Binette, Dennis 043804
Bing, Jens 008863
Bingham, David S. 043966
Binikowski 020694
Binkley, David 048925
Binnendijk, S. 030230
Bins, Coleen 043620
Bintz, Carol 048569
Biqijand, Colette 015038
Biran, Prof. Avraham 022982
Biraud, Guy 010389
Bircher, Prof. Dr. Martin 037026
Bircumshaw, John 047012
Bird, David M. 043662
Bird, P. 006196
Bird, Richard 042694
Bird, S. 038623
Birdick, Birdy 046689
Birdsall, Derrick 044695
Birdseye, William S. 048900
Birdsong, Sherri 042087
Bireley, Ellen K. 044747
Birk, Sherry C. 048938
Birk, Walter 019965
Birkebæk, Frank A. 009079, 009081
Birker, Susanne 017731
Birklid, Richard 043968
Birks, Mary 045766
Birley, Robin 039745
Birman de Bessudo, Raquel 028479
Birmanova, M. 027393
Birnbaum, Dr. Daniel 017191
Birney, Elmer C. 045914
Birnie, Ian 045441
Birnie Danzker, Jo-Anne 019093
Biro, Miriam 048474
Bırol, Çiğdem 038092
Birrer, Sibylle 036808
Birsak, Dr. Kurt 002567
Birthälmer, Dr. Antje 021021
Birtwhistle, Marjorie 049229
Bisanz-Prakken, Dr. Marian 002845
Bisbano, Beth 043074
Bischler, Gaston 019091
Bischof, Klaus 020362
Bischoff, Dr. Cäcilia 002934
Bischoff, Dieter 020252
Bischoff, Dr. Franz 016101
Bischoff, Dr. Harald 017010
Bischoff, Dr. Ulrich 016787
Bischoff, Walter 021049
Biscoito, M.J. 032618
Bishof, John 048104
Bishop, Adrian 039009
Bishop, Art 047831
Bishop, Barbara 044202
Bishop, Dr. C. 038591
Bishop, Eliza H. 043222
Bishop, Dr. Gale 048339
Bishop, Gale A. 047335
Bishop, Henry 005323
Bishop, Janet C. 047885
Bishop, Jean 045786
Bishop, Knox 043271
Bishop, Dr. Leslie 047399
Bishop, Dr. Michael 040566
Bishop, Michael 040567
Bishop, Dr. Mike 040568
Bishop, Ron 043957
Bishop, Russell J. 048151
Bishop, Tommy 048696
Bishopone, Iain R. 041241
Biskupić, Margareta 007818
Bisol, David 047949
Bissell, James 042986
Bisset, El 030474
Bissette, Carolyn B. 041947
Bissière, Caroline 013050
Bissonnette, Anne 044967
Bissonnette, Daniel 006722
Biström, Prof. Olof 009521
Biswas, Dr. T.K. 022372
Bither, Philip 045922
Bitner, Carol 047769
Bitomsky, Michael 016030
Bitsch, Dr. Helmut 019743
Bitschnau, Dr. Martin 002097
Bittel, Dr. Christoph 015750
Bitterli, Konrad 037493
Bittner, Regina 016684
Bivens, Peg 045030
Bivingou-Nzeingui 007665
Bixler, Ed 048040
Bizzarri, Laura 023331
Bjarnason, Páll V. 021958
Bjarnesen, Lynne 043299
Bjelić, Dobrila 034190
Bjerg, Ida 008854
Bjerkestrand, Steinar 030872, 030873
Bjerre, Henrik 008988
Bjerregaard, Jørgen O. 008818
Bjerregaard, Kirsten 008836
Bjerring Jensen, Knud 009090
Bjerrkjar, Anne 008934
Björk, Barbro 036692
Björklund, Anders 036623, 036663
Björkman, Sten 009472
Björn, Eva 036739
Björnemalm, Barbro 036744
Bjørgen, Asle B. 030991, 030992
Bjork, Alan 047558
Bjork, Tim 047019
Bjørklund, Prof. Kjell R. 031078
Blaas, Karl 037701
Blacharska, Wiktoria 031911
Black, Barbara 048217
Black, Bettye 045157
Black, Bill 001391
Black, Prof. C.M. 040235
Black, George B. 046131
Black, Jack 043827
Black, Jay 048819
Black, Joe 044265
Black, Kenneth N. 047505
Black, L. 001178
Black, William N. 043978
Black Petersen, S. 008895
Blackaby, Anita D. 044444
Blackburn, Dr. Bob 043537, 043713, 046652, 047766
Blackburn, M.A.S. 038962
Blackburn, Rachael 044921
Blackman, Barbara W. 047835
Blackman, Leona 043868
Blackmar, Charles B. 044847
Blackwelder, Martha 047804
Blackwood, Frank E. 005547
Bladen, Martha 048775
Blades, John M. 046795
Blades, Julian 041438
Blades, Kent 005217
Bladt, Inger K. 008798
Blæsild, Benno 008806
Blaettler, Roland 037125
Blagg, Margaret 041605
Blagg, Tim 044326
Blagov, Jurij Alekseevič 033253
Blair, Allan 006003
Blair, A.R. 045135
Blair, David 045421
Blair, Kay 049159
Blair, Robert 001336
Blair, William 038578
Blajan, Ion 032813
Blake, Dan 048713
Blake, Dr. Eugenia 045116
Blake, Janet 045095
Blake, Leo D. 042578
Blake, Paul 041465
Blake, Ruby 047573
Blake, Steven 039053
Blake Roberts, Gaye 041124
Blakey, Ellen Sue 048542
Blanc, Monique 013668
Blanchard, Cathérine 013532
Blanchard, Marian 030577
Blanchard, P.E. 006314
Blanchard, Raoul 037170
Blanchard-Gross, Diana 046472
Blanchebarbe, Prof. Dr. Ursula 020201
Blanchegorge, Eric 011448, 011449
Blanchette, Normand 005363
Blanchette, Odile 040937
Blanck, Denis 015362
Blanco, Bobby 031800
Blanco, Cristina 035405
Blanco, Hipólito S. del 000330
Blanco Sansa, Helena 034952
Bland, Bart 048338
Bland, Bruce F. 043556
Bland, Gaye K. 047523
Bland, Julia W. 046258
Blank, Maxine 045020
Blankenberg, Dr. H.M. 030233
Blankenship, Blanton 044371
Blankenship, Ken 042793
Blanquez, Juan 035771
Blas Pascual, Javier 035757
Blaschke, Shirley 046644
Blaser, Christophe 037249
Błaszczyk, Bożena 032282
Blatchford, Ian 040307
Blatter, Bernard 037679
Blauert, Elke 016101
Blaugrund, Dr. Annette 046380
Blavia, Francisco 049445
Blazevic, April 048193
Błazewicz, Sławomir 032446
Blazewiczea, Stanisław 031899
Blazwick, Iwona 040319
Blazy, Guy 012816, 012822, 014456
Blazy, Simone 012825
Bleakley, Bruce 047830
Bleathman, William 001114
Bled, Max 014831
Bleecker Blades, Margaret 043994
Bleiberg, Elizabeth W. 045560
Bleich, Gerhard 016509
Bleistein, Joachim 019364
Bleker, Klaus 016081
Bles, H. de 029463
Blessing, Jennifer 046404
Blethen, H. Tyler 043241
Bley, Karl 019319
Bley, Werner 019682
Bleymehl-Eiler, Dr. Martina 015795
Blicher-Moritz, Tine 008982
Blicke, Linda 042495
Blickle, K.H. 017816
Blickle, Ursula 018391
Bliemeister, Jeffrey 049034
Blinov, Viktor Filippovič 033018
Bliss Coleman, Amy 044393
Blitz, Amy 046278
Bljudova, Ljudmila Grigorjevna 033105
Bloch, Dorete 009449
Bloch Ravn, Thomas 008806
Block, Deborah 046320
Block, Diana 043396
Block, Isabel 045823
Block, Merle 044253
Block, Phillip 046348
Block, René 018190
Bloem, H. 029564
Bloem, M. 029230
Bloemen, H.A.C. 029566
Blohm Pultz, Janet 043358
Blok, R.S. 013568
Blok, Dr. W. 030302
Blom, J. 029336
Blomberg, M.G. 036267, 036268
Blomberg, Nancy 043404
Blome, Prof. Peter 036879
Blomen, Bärbel 020899
Blommaert, Georges 003156
Blommel, Henry H. 043129
Blomquist, Fredrik 036511
Blomquist, Shirley 042551
Blomstedt, Severi 009574
Blomster, Pontus 010138
Blondel, Madeleine 011603, 011605
Blondin, Linda 006672
Bloom, Alan 039242
Bloomer, Harlan 045643
Bloomfield, Sara J. 048952
Blosser, Jack 046711
Blouin, Mike 043431
Blount, Rob 048404
Blue, John 006520
Blübaum, Doris 017315
Blühm, Andreas 029239
Bluhm, Hans-Georg 018223
Blum, Dilys 046975
Blum, Jürgen 018021
Blum-Spicker, Helene 016750
Blumberg, Linda 047858
Blume, Dr. Eugen 016055
Blume, Sharon 048315
Blume, Torsten 016684
Blumenthal, Arthur R. 049261
Blumenthal, Prof. Dr. W. Michael 016084
Blumentritt, R. 020012
Blundell, Kathi 048279
Blustain, Malinda S. 041723
Blyth, Mary 041010
Blyth-Hill, Victoria 045441
Boa, Valerie N.S. 039640
Boal, Robert 046603

Boal Lee, Mathilde 042279
Boano, Giovanni 023664
Boarman, Don 044507
Boarowy, Innocenta 032408
Boas, Bob 040215
Boas, Heinz 019919
Boas, Natasha 047994
Boase, Colin 001591
Boast, Mair 040750
Boatman, Linda 042872
Boatright, Neva 043423
Bob, Murray L. 044827
Bobar, Maja 003940
Bober, Anna 031848
Bober, Jonathan 041927
Boberg, Scott 045170
Bobinger, Wanda L. 045355
Bobkina, Tatjana Gennadjevna ... 034023
Bobkov, Konstantin Vasilevič 033354
Bobnjarić, Venija 007712
Bočanová, Vanda 008609
Bočarov, Lev Nikolaevič 034050
Bocca, Massimo 023834
Boccanera, Prof. Giacomo 023605
Boccardo, Dr. Piero 024298
Bocchieri, Prof. Franco 026137
Bocci, Giampiero 023799
Boccolari, Prof. Giorgio 024766
Bochenek, Marceli 032385
Bochenek, Dr. Władysław 032299
Bochenski, Leslie 047468
Bochmann, Deb 041663
Bochnakov, Nikola 004800
Bock, Britta 017037
Bock, Dr. Robert 017153
Bockelman, James 048120
Bockius, Dr. Ronald 018792, 018794
Bockwoldt, Michael 043340
Bocquier 010924
Bocvarova-Plavevska, Marika 027919
Bod, Roy 042878
Bode-Hempton, Sharon 045177
Bodenstein, Anton 002818
Bodenstein, John Gilbert 019324
Bodilsen, Inge 008869
Bodine jr, William B. 047042
Bodine jr., William B. 047050
Bodine jr, William B. 047051
Bodingbauer, Prof. Adolf Karl 002704
Bodinger, John 043732
Bodini, Prof. Arturo 024701
Bodini, Prof. Floriano 023675
Bodini, Mauro 025917
Bodirsky, Peter 016580
Bodish, Glenn 042533
Bodnaryk, Randy 006427
Bodner, Connie 046082
Bodó, Dr. Sándor 021642
Bodoky, Dr. Tamás 021646
Bodorová, Olga 034418
Bodrova, Zoja Evgenjevna 033857
Bodsch, Dr. Ingrid 016322, 016334
Bøe, Kaare 030751
Böcher, Friederike 015737
Böcher, Hans-Georg 017826
Böck, Elfriede 017734
Boeck, Lorraine 048321
Boeckh, Dr. Hans 037138
Böckle, Karlheinz 020220
Bödewadt, Uwe 036633
Böge, Rainer 015483
Bögels, C. 030226
Boeglin, Yves 014923
Böhle, Hans-Theo 016688
Böhle, Rainer 015779
Böhler, Dr. Bernhard 002895
Böhm 019832
Böhm, Helmut 002980
Boehme, Dr. Sarah E. 043029
Böhme, Prof. Dr. Wolfgang 016337
Böhmer, Otmar 016834
Böhmer, Sylvia 015425
Böhnert, Marlies 017155
Böhnke, Bärbel 016948
Böhnlein, E. 019320
Böker, Wolfgang 036935
Boelen, Jan 003501
Boelens, Christ 030152
Bölke, Dr. Wilfried 015545
Böller, Susanne 019124
Bömer, Jana 008619
Bönig, Dr. Jürgen 017709
Böning, Heinrich 019681
Bönnen, Dr. Gerold 020980
Bönnighausen, Helmut 016771
Bönninghausen, D.E.J. von 029207
Bönsch, Dr. Peter 002338
Boer, A. den 029523
Boer, Dr. A.M. 029435
Boer, F.G. de 029997
Boer, P. den 029495
Börjesson, Klas 036371
Boers, T. 029203
Boers, Waling 016005
Boersma, W. 029995
Börste, Dr. Norbert 019547, 019550
Bösch, Dr. Gabriele 002157
Böse, Hans-Joachim 020927
Böser, Wolfgang 017416, 020309
Boesmans, Annick 003449
Boesner, Robert 002715
Böthig, Dr. Peter 019823
Boëthius, Lena 036296
Böttcher, Andreas 016391
Boettcher, Chris 047879
Böttcher, Dr. Ronald 020364
Boetzkes, Prof. Manfred 017925
Boffa, Prof. Giovanni 036819
Bogan, Alan 043955
Bogan, Dr. Michael A. 041619
Bogardus, Lorraine B. 046039
Bogatyrev, E. 033408, 033424
Bogdan, Gene 044875
Bogdanov, Pavel 033379
Bogdanova, Lidija Aleksandrovna . 033984
Bogdanova, Marija 004638
Bogdanović, Nikola 007797
Bogdanovna, Vera Ivanovna 033902
Bogdanowicz, Prof. Wiesław 032443
Bøge Henriksen, Kirsten 009071
Bogetti, Dr. Anita 023288
Boggio, Stefano 026206
Boggs, Mac 048262
Boggs, Rex 043898
Bogman, Suzanne 029239
Bognanni, Filippo 025217
Bogner, Peter 002927
Bogoljubskaja, A.V. 034085
Bogomolova, M.T. 033472
Bogurat, W. 032389
Bogusky, Alfred M. 005718
Boguszewicz, Ireneusz 031857
Boguwolski, Ryszard ... 031951, 031952, 031953
Bogyirka, Enil 021688
Boheme, Prof. Dr. Enrico 025575
Bohl, Samuel D. 042264
Bohlen, Dr. H. David 048284
Bohlin-Davis, Stephen 048026
Bohlmann, Dieter-Theodor 018127
Bohman, Stefan 036647
Bohnenkamp-Renken, Anne 017167
Bohnert, G. 018463, 018464
Bohórquez, Jorge Alfonso 007525
Bohr, G. Ted 046677
Boice, Linda S. 041894
Bois, Dr. M. de 029279
Boiseneau, Gerard 043702
Boissard, Jerome de 011930
Boisselle, Lynn 006133
Boissevain, C.F.C.G. 029474, 029475
Boissière, Yves 011897
Boitani, Dr. F. 025554
Boits, Paul 003183
Bojani, Prof. Gian Carlo ... 024070, 025178
Bojar, Hans-Peter 001938
Bojarczuk, Helena 031956
Bojarskij, Dr. Viktor I. 033827
Bojko, Elena Michajlovna 033905
Bojko, Nina Vladimirovna 033304
Bojkova, Irina Petrovna 034077
Bojkova, Margarita Alekseevna ... 033114
Bojović, Nevenka 034180
Bojović, Radivoje 034180
Bok, Franciszek 032358
Bok, Klaus 018005
Bokbot, Dr. Youssef 029028
Bokchun, Youngja 027544
Bol, Marsha C. 047970
Bol, Prof. Dr. Peter C. 017196
Boland, Angela 000846
Boland, Raymond 042586, 045597
Bolas, Gerald D. 042713
Bolderman, J.C.L. 029269
Bolduan, Anka 016426
Bolenz, Dr. Eckhard 019723
Boley, Shawn 042220
Bolge, George S. 042282
Bolger, Doreen 041969
Bolger, Dr. Francis 005248
Bolick, Dr. Margaret R. 045313
Bolin, Jerry 045558
Boling, Ron 047787
Bolipata, Alfonso Corpus 031781
Bolívar, Julián Gil 007401
Bolla, Dr. Margherita 026285, 026290, 026291
Bolle, Pierre 003371
Bolleville, Jean 012549
Bolling, Richard G. 044337
Bologna, Alberto 024490
Bolognani, Betty 047350
Bolotov, Valentin A. 033453
Bolotova, G.P. 033737
Bolsinger, Daniel 036887
Bolster, Jane 046281
Bolster, Molly 047192
Bolt, Ed L. 047015
Bolten, Harald 018403
Bolten Rempt, Dr. H. 029855
Boltesilverman, Diane 043789
Bolton, Bruce D. 005913, 005946
Bolton, David 039465
Bolz, Dr. Peter 016017
Bombard, LuAnn 049070
Bomberger, Bruce 045149
Bomford, David 040241
Bommerlyn, Loren 043213
Bommert, Rainer 016412
Bonaccorsi, R. 012338
Bonačić Mandinić, Maja 007798
Bonagura, Pasquale 026263
Bonamini, Eros 027838
Bonansinga, Kate 043639
Bond, Anthony 001505
Bond, Debra 046877
Bond, Emma 039763, 041234
Bond, Hallie 042275
Bond, Karen 044155
Bond, Kaye 046887
Bond, Wanda L. 044358
Bond-Fahlberg, Margareta 036651
Bondar, Dr. Vitalij Vjačeslavovič ... 033291
Bondareva, Valentina Nikolaevna . 033140
Bondaz, Gilles 014941
Bondil, Nathalie 013718
Bondjers, Rune 036265
Bone, Oliver 041207
Bonemaison, Michel 012808
Bonet Armengol, Jordi 034960
Bonet Correa, Antonio 035408
Bonet Planes, Juan Manuel 035422
Bonet Rosado, Helena 035980
Bonev, Ivan 004894
Boneva, Leonora 004863
Bongaarts, J. 029723
Bongaerts, Ursula 025467
Bongard, Rolf B. 016218
Bongers, H. 030088
Bonias, Zisis 021320
Bonifay, Suzanne 014247
Bonilla, Irene 035976
Bonilla, Mary Yamilet 049503
Bonin, Flavio 034511
Bonini, Julia 001204
Bonini, Laurie 001204
Bonn, Greg 045112
Bonnard, Jacques 013588
Bonnard Yersin, Pascale 037680
Bonnefille, J. Lovis 014221
Bonnefoi, Geneviève 011951
Bonnet, P. 029396
Bonnet Borel, Francoise 037665
Bonnett, Dr. Richard B. 044683
Bonnevialle, Gilles 014235
Bonnier, Bernadette 003668
Bonnin, Jean-Claude 012956
Bono, Sam 041620
Bonofiglio, Marta Maria 000520
Bonoli, Prof. Fabrizio 023433
Bonomi, Prof. Alfredo 025161
Bonomi, Dr. S. 023124
Bonsanti, Dr. Giorgio 024179
Bonvalet, Louis-Georges 012988
Bonzel, Helen 017301
Boo, Irene de 038726
Booknight, Alice 043082
Boomstra Van Raak, M.A.C. 029836
Boon, Loren 047443
Boone, Nathaniel A. 045623
Boonmark, Urith 037889
Boonstra, Dr. J.R. 029173
Booream, Rick 046482
Boorsch, Suzanne 046228
Boos, Dr. Andreas 019752
Boot, C. 030209
Boot, Kay 046739
Boot, M. 029230
Booth, Amanda 040571
Booth, Beverley 030466
Booth, C.M. 040850
Booth, Helen 005655
Booth, William H. 048567
Boothman, Colin 040325
Bootman, Karen 039409
Bora, Dr. D.K. 022176
Borbolla, Dr. Sol Rubin de la 028518
Borchardt, Dr. Albert 017825
Borchardt, Felicitas 015543
Borchardt, Susan A. 045723
Borchers, Karl-Hans 020560, 020561
Borchert, Till Holger 003262, 003269, 003270
Borčić, Goran 007802
Bordaz, Odile 015311
Bordeau, Annette 028995
Borden, Tamika 046272
Bordinskich, Gennadij Aleksandrovič 033891
Bore, Ove Magnus 031223, 031224, 031234
Boreham, Peter 040847
Borek, Henning 016394
Borel, François 037376
Borel, Dr. Gilles 037244
Borén, Ingjerd 036303
Borettaz, Omar 023218
Borg, Carles 028032
Borg, Prof. Dr. Vince 028025
Borgegård, Eva 036764
Borges, Prof. F. Sodré 032676
Borges, Grethe 030862
Borges, Richard 042146
Borges, Wolfgang 018493
Borges Rosales, Prof. J.C. 049501
Borgeson, Jaquelyn L. 042711
Borggrefe, Dr. Heiner 018607
Borghi, Gian Paolo 024106
Borić Brešković, Bojana 034173
Borisenko, Irina Gavrilovna 033509
Borisenko, Viktor Ivanovič 033975
Borisov, Boris 004807

Borisova, Diana . 004668, 004669, 004670
Borisova, Tanja . . . 004802
Borisova, Valentina Vladimirovna . 032987
Borja-Santiago, Monina Katherina . 031729
Borja-Villel, Manuel J. . . . 034922
Bork, Prof. Dr. Hans Rudolf . . . 019777
Borkopp-Restle, Dr. Birgitt . . . 019039
Borman, Dennes . . . 045991
Borman, R.Th.A. . . . 029270
Borms, Gwen . . . 003163
Born, J.G.M. . . . 029698
Born, Richard . . . 042838
Bornacelli Guerrero, Humberto . . . 007609
Bornecrantz, Mona . . . 036692
Bornemann, Daniel . . . 014852
Bornfriend, Carl . . . 044087
Bornman, A.R. . . . 034547
Borns, Harold . . . 046726
Borodavkin, Andrej Viktorovič . . . 033598
Borodina, Valentina Ivanovna . . . 033089
Borošak Marjanović, Jelena . . . 007841
Borovinskich, Nadežda Petrovna . . 033964
Borowski, Batya . . . 022942
Borowsky, Gwen . . . 046968
Borpuzari, D. . . . 022139
Borremans, Dr. R. . . . 003487
Borriello, Dr. Mariarosaria . . . 024894
Borromeo, Dr. Georgina . . . 047258
Borrowdale-Cox, Deborah . . . 045266
Borrup, Tom . . . 045913
Borsanyi, Jackie . . . 045751
Borsboom, Leo . . . 030343
Borščenko, Lidija Mychajlivna . . . 038331
Borsdorf, Prof. Dr. Ulrich . . 017076, 017078
Borselli, Lucilla . . . 025836
Borsig, Josef . . . 008261
Bortolan, Gino . . . 026256
Bortolotti, Dr. Marco . . . 023415, 023436
Borusiewicz, Mirosław . . . 032118, 032120
Borut, Križ . . . 034509
Bory, Jean-René . . . 037033
Borys, Stephen . . . 046607
Borysova, Galyna Stepanivna . . . 038418
Borzan, Maria . . . 032923
Bos, Agnès . . . 011680
Bos, Saskia . . . 029232
Bos, W. . . . 030159
Bosano Ansaldo, Dr. Carlos de . . . 000106
Bosch i Cornellà, Salvador . . . 035783
Boscher, Jean-Yves . . . 010882
Boschi, Prof. Enzo . . . 024052
Boschiero, Dr. Gemma . . 023287, 023289, 023291
Boser, Dr. Elisabeth . . . 016618, 016620
Boserup, Dr. Ivan . . . 008961
Boshoff, Jaco . . . 034583
Boshouwers, F. . . . 029634
Bosi, Erio . . . 024545
Bosinski, Prof. Dr. Gerhard . . . 018794
Bosioković, Sava . . . 034177
Boskamp, Ute . . . 017973
Boškova, Tatjana . . . 027920
Bošković, Dora . . . 007841
Bosma, M. . . . 030226
Bosman, K. . . . 003319, 003319
Bosmans, A. . . . 003163
Bošnakov, Nikola . . . 004781
Bosnar Salihagić, Željka . . . 007858
Bošniak, Jurij Michailovič . . . 033987
Bošnjak, Karlo . . . 007727
Boss, George . . . 039338
Boss, Dr. M. . . . 017028
Bossa Herazzo, Donaldo . . . 007478
Bossaert . . . 003609
Bossan, Marie-Josèphe . . . 014095
Bossart, Hans Peter . . . 037777
Bosse, David . . . 043369
Bossé, Laurence . . . 013630
Bosse, Maurice . . . 042537
Bosshard, Daniel . . . 037409
Bosshard, Reymond . . . 037347
Bosshard-Frischknecht, Hulda . . . 037658
Bosshard-Gorrite, Nuria . . . 037340
Bossine, Lesley . . . 039857
Bostanci, Gülten . . . 008254
Bostander, Nellie . . . 034771
Bostic, Connie . . . 041791
Boston, A. . . . 038938
Boston, David . . . 041346
Boston, J. Audrey . . . 038937
Boston, Katrina M. . . . 046471
Bostrem, Lidija Andreevna . . . 032996
Boswell, Mary Rose . . . 045084
Bosworth, John . . . 038750
Bot, Nadia . . . 037120
Bot Riera, Issa . . . 036056
Botero, Dr. Clara Isabel . . . 007436
Botha, R. . . . 034553
Bothe, Günter . . . 015712
Bothe, Heinrich . . . 016287
Bothe, Prof. Dr. Rolf . . . 020736, 020748, 020752, 020754
Bothmer, Dietrich von . . . 046364
Botineau, Pierre . . . 010878
Botirov, I.T. . . . 049414
Botsaris, Markos S. . . . 021158
Botsen, Jean-Pierre . . . 013807
Botte, Prof. Virgilio . . . 024913
Bottengård, Else . . . 031279
Bottero, Giuliana . . . 026077
Bottini, Dr. Angelo . . . 024168
Bottlaender, Michael . . . 017731
Bottrel Tostes, Vera Lúcia . . . 004401
Botwinick, Michael . . . 049338
Botzong, A. . . . 010817, 010818
Bouaïche, Claire-Lise . . . 037429, 037430
Bouchard, Guy . . . 006298
Bouchard, Marie . . . 013618
Bouchard, Yann . . . 014703
Bouché, R. . . . 020372
Boucher, George . . . 043571
Boucher, Michel . . . 010959, 010960
Boucher, Sid . . . 001387
Bouchet, Denis . . . 012622
Bouchet, J.-C. . . . 010348
Bouchon, Chantal . . . 013668
Bouchon, Juan Santiago . . . 000457
Bouck, Jill . . . 043603
Bouckaert, Odile-Marie . . . 003274
Boudia, Soraya . . . 013625
Boudier, Pierre . . . 011268
Boudou, Dominique . . . 013256
Boudreau, Luce Marie . . . 005264
Boudrot, Donna . . . 005026
Bouffault, Colette . . . 013493
Boughton, Peter . . . 039061
Bougia, Polyxeni . . . 021207
Bouglé, Frédéric . . . 014929
Boujamid, Azzouz . . . 029019
Boukli, Aïcha . . . 000046
Boulanger, Patrick . . . 012938
Boulanger, Sylvie . . . 011318
Boulbes, M. . . . 011736
Bould, Gillian . . . 040991
Boulet, Jean . . . 015108
Boulliard, Jean-Claude . . . 013566
Boulton Elliott, Helen . . . 006756
Boulton Stroud, Marion . . . 046940
Bounous, Jewell P. . . . 048727
Bouquet, B. . . . 013561
Bourassa, Marie . . . 006157
Bourbon, Prof. Giulio . . . 023681
Bourbon Busset, Jean-Louis de . . 010632
Bourbonnais, Alain . . . 005078
Bourbonnais, Caroline . . . 011584
Bourcier, Paul . . . 045595
Bourdais, Jany . . . 011533
Bourdin, Monika . . . 014554
Bourdon, Don . . . 005065
Bourdon, Kate . . . 006284
Bourdon, Michel . . . 011356
Boureima, Konfé . . . 004960
Bourel, Yves . . . 014454
Bouret, Brigitte . . . 014065
Bourgat, Robert . . . 013788
Bourgeois, Jean . . . 003843
Bourgeois, Valérie . . . 006659
Bourgoin, Colette . . . 005210
Bourgougnon, Eric . . . 010803, 013183
Bourgoz, Michel . . . 036860
Bourke, Marie . . . 022763
Bourlet, Michel . . . 011583
Bournazel, Comtesse de . . . 013947
Bourne, Susan . . . 038909
Bourque, Bruce . . . 041905
Bourriaud, Nicolas . . . 013734
Bouše, Petr . . . 008498
Bouska, Marianne . . . 042907
Bousmanne, Bernard . . . 003291
Bousquet, Nicolas . . . 010336
Boussard . . . 013493
Bousska, Prof. Dr. Vladimira . . . 002880
Boustany, Bernadette . . . 012350
Bouteiller, Hubert . . . 011554
Bouthat, Chantal . . . 006218
Boutry, Pierre . . . 034101
Bouttemy, Marie-Françoise . . . 012680
Bouvier, Prof. Dr. Beatrix . . . 020480
Bouvy, Michel . . . 011085
Bouvy, P. . . . 029890
Bouwman, J.W.M. . . . 029123
Bouxin, Marc . . . 014012
Bouzón Gallego, Avelino . . . 035959
Bovewizer, Austin . . . 022850
Bovey, Patricia E. . . . 006873
Bowden, Cindy . . . 041870
Bowden, Mitchell D. . . . 047007
Bowdery, J. . . . 039117
Bowdrey, Jeremy . . . 039122
Bowen, Allyson . . . 046326
Bowen, Duncan . . . 039619
Bowen, Graham . . . 038710
Bowen, John . . . 047252
Bowen, Linnell R. . . . 041739
Bower, Alan . . . 041185
Bower, Barbara A. . . . 043915
Bower, Corinna . . . 041316
Bower, Finn . . . 006456
Bower, Helen . . . 039961
Bower, Mary . . . 043767
Bowers, Prof. M. Deane . . . 042354
Bowes, Murray . . . 001600
Bowes, Peter . . . 041319
Bowes-Crick, C.P. . . . 040274
Bowie, Dr. Gavin . . . 038912
Bowle, Jean . . . 039471
Bowles, G. . . . 039046, 039047
Bowman . . . 039938
Bowman, Beth . . . 047954
Bowman, Dr. S. . . . 040097
Bowman, Travis . . . 042979
Bowman, Trina . . . 044463
Bownan, JoAnn . . . 046038
Bownan, Leslie Green . . . 049265
Bowron, Julian . . . 001261
Box, David . . . 001131
Boxall, Michael . . . 038699
Boxer, David . . . 026385
Boxer, Graham . . . 040035
Boxhall, Patricia . . . 000865
Boxley, Robert F. . . . 049232
Boyce, David Y. . . . 045232
Boychev, Petr . . . 004908, 004909
Boyd, Beatrice . . . 048773
Boyd, L. . . . 005639
Boyd, Peter . . . 041023
Boyd, Robert . . . 042140
Boyd, Susan . . . 048901
Boydell, Owen . . . 039360
Boyden, Dr. P. . . . 040240
Boyer, Cindy . . . 047478, 047484
Boyer, Jean-Marc . . . 014787
Boyer, John Vincent . . . 044459
Boyer, Sylvain . . . 010591
Boyette, Kathrin . . . 042574
Boyette, Todd . . . 041795
Boylan, Olive S. . . . 046089
Boyle, Catherine . . . 042624
Boyle, Chris . . . 044177
Boyle, Dorothy . . . 047757
Boyle, Gail . . . 038859
Boyle, William J.S. . . . 006647
Boym, Per Bj. . . . 031087
Boynton, Hugh . . . 039698
Boysen, Jesper . . . 008928
Boysen, Renate . . . 018509
Boysson, Bernadette de . . . 010884
Bozell, John R. . . . 045307
Božič, Bojan . . . 034471
Božko, Boris Stepanovyč . . . 038381
Bozkurt, Batuhan . . . 038142
Bozok, Erdoğan . . . 038065
Braack, Craig R. . . . 042127
Braam, Dr. P. . . . 029536
Braarud, Reni . . . 031062
Braat-Voorhuis, T.M.A. . . . 030387
Braaten, Alicia L. . . . 042943
Braaten, Ivar Gunnar . . . 030719
Braaten, Trond . . . 030752
Brabant, Diane . . . 006281
Brabec, Jiří . . . 008663
Brace, Denise . . . 039410, 041048
Brace, Jeffrey C. . . . 005036
Bracegirdle, H. . . . 040562
Bracegirdle, Robert . . . 040340
Brachaczek, Zofia . . . 032357
Bracher, Sylvia . . . 037745
Brachner, Dr. Alto . . . 019045
Brack, Dr. P. . . . 037767
Brack, Peter . . . 037781
Bracke, Norbert . . . 003577
Brackenreg, Philip . . . 000753
Brackenridge, Kirsty . . . 040659
Bracker de Hugo, M. . . . 014465
Bradbury, Christopher . . . 041401
Bradbury, David . . . 040165
Bradbury, J. Robert . . . 006000
Bradbury, Karen . . . 040028
Brademann, Margret . . . 016482
Braden, Gerald . . . 047362
Bradfield, Gerald . . . 045107
Bradford, Anna . . . 005591
Bradford, Dr. Bruce C. . . . 043334
Bradford, Colleen . . . 042414
Bradford, Jan . . . 046253, 046254
Bradford, Mary . . . 048341
Bradić, Mihajlo . . . 007709
Bradley, Allen . . . 046435
Bradley, Betsy . . . 044799
Bradley, Bob . . . 040424
Bradley, Dean . . . 006266
Bradley, Douglas E. . . . 046574
Bradley, Fiona . . . 039390
Bradley, Graeme . . . 030544
Bradley, J. . . . 040643
Bradley, J.M. . . . 039233
Bradley, Laurel . . . 046549
Bradley, Loris . . . 047892
Bradley, Richard . . . 046109
Bradley, Ron . . . 006746
Bradley, Dr. William Steven . . . 043304
Bradman, Susan . . . 039165
Bradshaw, Bill . . . 045343
Bradshaw, John P. . . . 047467
Bradshaw, Julia . . . 030517
Bradshaw, Paul . . . 049233
Bradt, Rachelle . . . 046419
Bradtke, Jerzy . . . 031921
Brady, Christine . . . 038690, 039885
Braekeleer, Catherine de . . . 003563
Brändle, Christian 037765, 037788, 037797
Brändle, Hans . . . 037369
Bräuer, Jörg . . . 015551
Bräunlein, Dr. Peter J. . . . 018828
Brafford, C.J. . . . 046011
Bragagnolo, Dr. Pietro . . . 024125
Bragg, Cheryl H. . . . 041745
Bragg, Gary O. . . . 046882
Bragotă, Gheorghe . . . 032861
Braham, George O. . . . 006657
Braham, Helen . . . 040126
Brahim, Natalia Majluf . . . 031550

Brahm-Lindberg, Lisa 049313
Brahma Chary, P. 022200
Braica, Silvio 007799
Braillard, Marie-Christine 014651
Brain, Danielle 044317
Bramah, Edward 040092
Bramberger, Alfred 001886
Bramlette, Teresa 041845
Branca, Luigi 025291
Brancaccio, Jim 045262
Brancaleoni, V. 003780
Brancati, Prof. Antonio 025174
Brancato, Prof. Francesco 025086
Brancel, Esther 049113
Brancelj, Andreja 034503
Brancucci, Dr. Michel 036899
Brand, Hermann 021012
Brand, Dr. Michael 047429
Brand, Dr. Ruth 036978
Brand, Ruth 037791
Brand-Claussen, Dr. Bettina 017835
Brânda, Nicolae 032781
Brandaeur, Aline 047970
Brandão, J. 032645
Brandaó, Maria Luiza 004131
Brandauer, Aline 047973
Brandenburg, Dr. Hajo 017680
Brandenburg, Dr. Winfried 019988
Brandenburger-Eisele, Dr. Gerlinde 019457
Brandenstein, Ameli von 020050
Brander, Prof. A. 009482, 009484
Brander, Alli 009625
Brandl, Andrea 020139
Brandl, Franz 001755
Brandler, Gotthard 017527, 017528
Brandoli, Susan 006728
Brandon, Cath 000917
Brandon, G. 005284
Brandon, Reiko 044598
Brandson, Lorraine 005270
Brandt, Dr. Joachim 016101
Brandt, Dr. Klaus 020038
Brandt, Dr. Klaus J. 020358
Brandt, Dr. Michael 017921
Brandt, Monique 005371
Brandt, Dr. Reinhard 020778
Brandt, Thomas 019273
Brandt, Tova 043358
Brandt, Wayne 043781
Brannon, Jim 048623
Branscome, Curtis 048374
Branscome, Kimberly 046810
Bransom, Jennifer 043274
Brantley, R. Brit. 042776
Braquilanges, Guy de 011171
Brascamp, M.H. 029811
Brasie, Jeff. 042918
Brasil do Amaral, Paulo Cesar 004294
Braslavsky, Noam 016028
Braß, Dr. M. 020372
Brassel, Dirk 016360
Braswell, Alvin L. 047315
Bratčenko, Tetjana Georgiïvna 038249
Bråthen, Magne 030945
Bratke, Dr. Elke 016329
Bratschi-Tschirren, Max 037070
Brattig, Dr. Patricia 018330
Bratton, Clara Ann 045161
Bratton, D. 040787
Bratton, Randall 049257
Bratuž, Ciril 034511
Brauen, Dr. Martin 037808
Brauer, Gerald J. 043374
Braufman, Sheila 042162
Braun, Dr. Andreas 002812
Braun, Annette 012191
Braun, Dr. Claudia 018809
Braun, Dr. Emanuel 016909
Braun, Hannes 002571
Braun, Dr. J.K. 046509
Braun, Joseph 012190
Braun, Karen 047306
Braun, Märta 036791
Braun, Mary E. 047695
Braun, Matthew 044789
Braun, Monika 018170
Braun, Peter 002557
Braun, Thomas 015817
Braun, Wilhelm 018994
Braunegger, Reinhold 002425
Braunlein, John 044143
Braunlein, John H. 046268
Braunová, Helena 008423
Brauns, Dmitri G. 047876
Braunstein, Susan L. 046352
Braunsteiner, Dr. Michael 001660
Braut, Else 030984
Bravo, John 048064
Braxton, Gail G. .. 044061, 044063, 044064
Bray, Alida 047897
Bray, Bill 043872
Bray, Rick 043288
Bray, Tamara 043457
Bray, Xavier 040241
Brayer, Hermione 012612
Brayner, Vânia 004318
Braz Teixeira, Dr. Madalena 032653
Brázdová, Marie 008775
Brearley, A. 039620
Brebeck, Wulff E. 016497
Brecciaroli, Dr. Luisa 026061
Brechbühl, Christof 037604
Brecht, Fatima 046369
Brechter, Steves 046759
Breckner, Thomas W. 045468
Bredenkamp, Dalene 034570
Bredereck, Wolfgang 000946
Bredow, Florentine C. 017958
Bredow, Sabine 015429
Bredsdorff, Eva B. 040066, 040581, 041331
Breede, Claus 005517
Breen, John D. 048024
Breese, Dr. Kathryn 044803
Breeze, Margaret 049167
Bregar, Marjeta 034509
Bregeaut, Pierre 011071
Bregovac Pisk, Marina 007841
Brehm, Georgia 045518
Brehm, Dr. Margrit 002560, 002565
Brehm, Dr. Thomas 019352
Brehme, Sylvia 015986
Breidbach, Prof. Dr. Dr. O. 018103
Breiler, Ronald 019918
Breinegaard, Jens 008896
Breiter, Michael 041598
Breitfuß, Dr. Anton 002569
Breithaupt, Brent H. 045167
Breithaupt, Julia 016834
Breitkreuz, Petra 017198
Breitmeier, Uwe 016635
Breitner, Suzy 045815
Breitwieser, Dr. Sabine 002902
Brejon, Barbara 012680
Brejon de Lavergnée, Arnauld 012680
Breker, Uwe H. 018332
Brekke, Borghild 031064
Brekke, Paul D. 048274
Brembeck, Josef 018960
Bremer, D. Neil 043686
Bremer, Stanley 030108
Bremner, R.W. 039286
Brendel-Pandich, Susanne 048505
Brendow, Dr. Volker 015824, 015828
Brendstrup, Dagmar 008839
Brengle, Anne B. 046190
Brennan, Anita 046038
Brennan, Anne G. 049216
Brennan, Edward 046397
Brennan, Kate 041038
Brennan, Nancy 047098
Brennan, Paul 042403
Brennan, Robert 022779
Brenneman, David 041862
Brenneman, Jan 044014
Brenner, Itzhak 023058
Brenner, Dr. Klaus-Peter 017470
Brenner, Theo E. 037773
Brennsteiner, Hans 002322
Brent, Brian 039167
Brent, Marty 006050
Bréon, Emmanuel 010909
Breščak, Mateja 034487
Breslauer, David 046035
Bresler, Zinaida Ivanovna 032984
Bresnahan, Bob 045787
Bresser, G.J. de 029740
Bressi, Dr. Nicola 026139
Bresticker, Stanley 047036
Breth, Renata 047993
Breton, Audrée 006334
Breton, Gérard 012510
Bretón, Prof. Raúl 028441
Bretscher, Peter 037091
Bretscher, Renzo 037145
Bretschneider, Jürgen 019774
Brettner, Friedrich 001901
Breu, Zita 003009
Breuer, Brad 047786
Breuer, Dieter 020869
Breuker, P. 029589
Breunesse, Caroline 029239
Breuze, Marc 010677
Brevik, Bernt 031218
Breville, Tristan 028071
Brewer, Billy 041679
Brewer, Constance 042948
Brewer, Dr. Douglas J. 048712, 048713
Brewer, Esther Vivian 043452
Brewer, R. 038990
Brewster, Carrie 046019
Brewster, Christine 038709
Brewster, Linda 039336, 039337
Brewster, Pete 005062
Brewster, Rae 001495
Brewster, Suzanne G. 041569
Brewster, William F. 045597
Brey, F.J. 017102
Brey, Karen 042587, 042588, 046786
Brez, Wendy 043877
Breza, Bogusław 032490
Breza, Michael 046737
Brian, J. Andrew 045809
Brichet, Michel 003320
Brichtová, Dobromila 008502
Brick, Elizabeth M. 046538
Bricka, Olena Mykolaïvna 038252
Brickman, Penny 048038
Bridenstine, James A. 044899
Bridge, Louise 006641
Bridger, Tozzy 039489
Bridges, Edwin C. 045993
Bridges, Dr. E.M. 039474
Bridges, Mary 041669
Bridges, Roger D. 044078
Bridges, Tim 041447
Bridgford, Todd C. 044417
Bridgman, Norma 034620
Briedenhann, M.M. 034559, 034560
Briedis, Agris 027733
Briel, Gerhard 017960
Briend, J. 013632
Brier, Ida 044662
Briere, Florence 012483
Briese, Jodie G. 049279
Briest, Francis 015195
Brigandi, Phil 047894
Briggs, Kate Halle 048259
Briggs, Michael 038629
Briggs, Dr. Peter S. 048644
Briggs-Jude, Wendy 006796
Briggs Murray, James 046399
Brigham, David 049309
Bright, Bill 044032
Bright, Robert 049173
Brighton, T. 039621
Brillonet, Jean-Marc 014530
Brind, R.A. 038655
Brindeau, Irène 012493
Brindle, Nicole 006215
Brindley, Lynne 040096
Bringager, Frithjof 031089
Brink, Siegfried 020832
Brink, Dr. Sonja 016841
Brinkley, Mike 044801
Brinklow, R. 039308
Brinkman, L.D. 044976
Brinkmann, Dr. Bodo 017195
Brinkmann, Dr. Jens-Uwe 017473
Brinkmann, Petra 018952, 018953
Brinkmann, Dr. Vinzenz 019117
Brinkmann, Dr. W. 037795
Brisch, Brigitte 017206
Brisebois, Marcel 005934
Brissard, Michel 015214
Brissette, Serge 011815
Brisson 013757
Brisson, Steven C. 045551, 045552, 045554, 045556
Brito Joao, Benedito 029055
Brito Moreira, Alvaro de 032685
Britschgi, Markus 037067
Britt, Nelson 043512
Britton, Marion 045367
Britz, Günther 015930, 015931
Brivio, Dr. Ernesto 024711
Brix, Thorsten 011537
Břízová, Zuzana 008361
Brkić, Staniša 034207
Broach, Barbara K. 043865, 043867
Broad, Sandy 006489
Broadbert, D. 042242
Broaderick, Tom 042025
Broadfoot, Jan 049214
Broady, Duncan 040399
Brobst, William A. 047208
Brocas, Jon 030533
Brock, Mary 047023
Brocke, Dr. Edna 017059
Brockhaus, Prof. Dr. Christoph 016861
Brockhoff, Joan 006524
Brockmeier, Royna L. 044518
Brocksch, Dr. Dieter 019394
Brodanec, Vlado 007832
Broderick, Janice K. 047654
Brodeur, Bill 006127
Brodie, Ian J. 030624
Brodie, Suzanne M. 043860
Brodl, Michaela 002971
Brodneva, Adelja Vladimirovna 033299
Broege, Wallace W. 047454
Broeker, Dr. Holger 020965
Broekgaarden, A. 029194
Brönner, Dr. Melitta 016136
Brogiolo, Prof. G. Pietro 025640
Broglie, Charles Edouard Prince de 011212
Broidl, Erich 002718
Brok, Dr. Barbara den 037267
Broker, David 001036
Brolsma, Allen 043224
Brom, Jodi 049249
Bromberg, Dr. Anne 043269
Brombierstäudl, Andreas 018081
Bromley, Fran 044439
Bromovsky, Fabia 041270
Broo, Dr. Hanno 016638
Broocks, Steven 048080
Brook, G.W.T. 001097
Brooke, Janet M. 005692
Brooke, Patrick 041225
Brooker, Melanie 038446
Brooking, Charles 039208
Brookman, Philip 048891, 048892
Brooks, Carol 049371
Brooks, Carolyn 045486
Brooks, Daniel F. 042221
Brooks, Dr. Earl 041725
Brooks, Eric 045256
Brooks, Leonard L. 046218
Brooks, Lindsay 040942
Brooks, Maggie 044292
Brooks, Peggy 044169

Brooks, Philip R.B. 041461
Brooks, Ruth 049102
Brooks jr., William F. 045836
Brooks Joyner, J. 046680
Brooks-Myers, Inez 046598
Brooksbank, Mike 039592
Brooslin, Michael 048295
Brophy, Dr. Gerald P. 041695
Broschinski, Dr. Annette 017765
Brose, Barbara H. 043260
Brose, David S. 044154
Brose, Lawrence F. 042504
Brosi, Dr. Sibylle 018162, 018169
Brosnahan, Seán 030489
Brosnan, Susan 046224
Brost, Leif 036341
Brothers, Michael M. 043330
Brotherton, Barbara 048091
Brouard, Michael 037481
Broucke, Remi 003376
Brougher, Kerry 048912
Broughton, H.E. 040427
Brouillet, Johanne 006460
Brouillette, Denis 006528
Brouillette, Penny 042645
Broun, Elizabeth 048941
Broun, Dr. Elizabeth 048943
Brousseau, Francine 005503, 005504
Brouwer, Dr. M. 029961
Brouwer, Norman 046406
Brouwer, T. de 029977
Brovčenkova, Valentina Ivanovna . 033065
Brovinsky, Boris 034495
Brow, Charlotte 044077
Brower, Ken 049090
Brower, Paul 042120
Browes, Judi 039152
Brown, Alastair 030804
Brown, Alex 041216
Brown, Anne 047384
Brown, Anthony 001114
Brown, Ashley 041832
Brown, Bern Will 006030
Brown, Bruce 047507
Brown, Carol 034598, 040084
Brown, Charles B. 044959
Brown, Charles T. 045867
Brown, Dr. Charlotte V. 047316
Brown, Dr. Christopher 040653
Brown, Dr. Claudia 047011
Brown, Curtis E. 046960
Brown, Dan 047761
Brown, Daniel 047431
Brown, Dr. Daniel T. 047621
Brown, Dr. Dann 047153
Brown, Darlene 044882
Brown, David 026385, 042648
Brown, David Alan 048924
Brown, Don 044286, 044598
Brown, Dona 045335
Brown, Dorothy 006687
Brown, Elizabeth A. 048081
Brown, Ellsworth H. 047045
Brown, Eric 038744
Brown, Forrest 046550, 046552
Brown, Geoffrey I. 049235
Brown, Georgina 005355
Brown, Gordon 040800, 040801
Brown, Hannah 048664
Brown, Harold 006192, 044563
Brown, Harold L. 044440
Brown, Helen 039053
Brown, Ian 039125, 039327, 039328, 039533, 039842, 040980, 040982, 040983
Brown, James A. 044473
Brown, Jane 042739
Brown, Janene 044911
Brown, Jean 039939
Brown, Jocelyn 030571
Brown, Johanna 049254
Brown, Julia 046404
Brown, Karon 048530
Brown, Kate 041316
Brown, Kevan 040452
Brown, Kevin 040074
Brown, Leanne 048820
Brown, Lee N. 013426
Brown, M. 005050
Brown, Margaret 038705, 038706, 038707
Brown, Marjorie 044402
Brown, Marlene 048718
Brown, Marlin 005467
Brown, Mary Anne 042897
Brown, Michael K. 044648
Brown, Nancy 049112
Brown, Nancy F. 045924
Brown, Neil 006543
Brown, Nicolas 047255
Brown, Patricia 042981
Brown, Peter B. 041476
Brown, Rich 047041
Brown, Richard D. 043795
Brown, Rick 045056, 045058, 045059
Brown, R.J. 047633
Brown, Robert 038648
Brown, Robert M. 045933
Brown, Rondalyn 006301
Brown, Dr. S. 038729
Brown, Scott 041485
Brown, Stephen 048093
Brown, T. Robins 044560
Brown, Terrence 046402
Brown, Vinita 043881
Brown, Vivian A. 031768
Brown, W. 040596
Brown, William 044395
Brown, Dr. William 044596
Brown Hirst, Kaye 047764
Brownawell, Christopher J. 043587
Browne, Charles C. 047638
Browne, J. 022675
Browne, Mary-Louise 030438
Browne, Patrick 043550
Brownell, Carlton C. 045337
Browning, Dawn C. 045730
Browning, Mark 045862
Brownlee, Reuben 048823
Browns, Doug 044308
Brownson, Ron 030431
Broy, Erich 018556
Brubaker, Bob 049031
Bruce, Donald 046272
Bruce, Dorene 042103
Bruce, E. 005079
Bruce, Elspeth 040699
Bruce, Jeffrey 044415
Bruce, Michael 044374, 044375
Bruch, Claudia 017093
Bruchhäuser, A. 016216
Bruck, Anton 002990
Brück, Martin 016684
Brueck, Siegfried 020243
Brückner, Heike 016684
Brückner, Sigrid 020399
Brüderlin, Dr. Markus 037451
Brüggerhoff, Dr. Stefan 016276
Brühlmann, Fritz 036868
Brülisauer, Annemarie 037417
Brüning, Henning 016684
Brüninghaus-Knubel, Cornelia 016861
Bruer, Dr. Stephanie-Gerrit 020314, 020316
Brugeman, Tim 043845
Brugge, Dr. J.P. ter 030276
Bruggeman, Jean 015267
Bruggen, Bill 044744
Brugger, Dr. Ingried 002855
Brugnoli, Renzo 025611
Brugnoli Bailoni, Francisco 006930
Brugo, Carlo 025589
Bruguière, Philippe 013640
Bruhin, Felix 037094
Bruhn, Thomas P. 048384
Bruijn, Dr. J. de 029186
Bruijn, J.A. 029471
Bruin, Joan 045442
Bruin, Dr. R.E. de 030226
Bruinjes, Wilhelm 016866
Bruintjes, Jaap C.N. 029508
Brulomié, Agnes 010882
Brumbauch, Mary 045526
Brumbaugh, Lee 047372
Brumberg, Esther 046373
Brumder, Robert B. 049018
Brumelis, Andrew 006609
Brumen, Patrizia 001943
Brumgardt, Dr. John R. 042728
Brummer, Guntram 020517
Brummer, Hans Henrik 036657
Brun, Dominique 012807
Brun, Laura 047867
Brunacci, Prof. Dr. Aldo ... 023278, 023283
Brunacci, Maurizio 023799
Brunckhorst, Dr. Friedl 015724
Brundin, Martha 043311
Brune, Thomas 017841, 020374
Brunecker, Frank 016219
Brunel, Georges 013623
Brunelle, Danielle 005925
Brunet, P. 013245
Brunette, T. 006707
Brunetti, Armando 023854
Brungard, Charlene K. 042106
Bruni, Dr. Gaetano 025484
Bruni, Giovanni 023771
Bruni, Stephen T. 049202
Brunin, Ph. 003811
Bruning, Angela 016237
Brunius, Staffan 036623
Brunn-Lundgren, Maria 036292
Brunnemann, Eric 021569
Brunner, Dr. 012815
Brunner, Alois 019569
Brunner, Dieter 017852, 017853
Brunner, Dorla 042208
Brunner, Heinz 002975
Brunner, Dr. Michael 020516
Brunner, Paul 015751
Bruno, Prof. Gianfranco 024309
Brunovský, Ferdinand 034443
Bruns, James H. 048934
Brunscheen, Scott 043428
Brunschwyler, Greta 046576
Brunson, Jeana 048483
Brunson, Neal E. 044858
Brunson, Theodore 044858
Brunson Frisch, Marianne 047092
Bruschetti, Dr. Paolo 023979
Bruse, Ralf 019219
Brusila, Johannes 010169
Brussa, Carlos A. 041542
Brussat, Tracey K. 047251
Brussee, G.J. 030017
Brust, Alexander 036893
Bruton, Prof. David L. 031078
Brutvan, Cheryl 042334
Bruun Beyer, Mette 008970
Brūvere, Solvita 027725
Bruwier, Marie-Cécile 003657
Bruy, Pauline 003599
Bruyn, Dr. Jean-Pierre de 003457
Bruyn, M.A. de 030129
Bruyninx, Prof. Dr. E. 003454
Brvar, C. 030230
Bryan, Dr. Betsy 041964
Bryan, Dr. Charles F. 047428
Bryan, Tim 041177, 041180
Bryan, Tracey 047428
Bryan Hood, Mary 046761
Bryant, James 047460
Bryant, Jim 047151
Bryant, Julius 041251
Bryant, Steve 040095
Bryck, Jack 041957
Bryde, John A. 031150
Bryer, Stephen 041369
Bryman, Donna 005343
Bryson, Mary 048614
Bryzensky, Nicole 001489
Brzeziński, Prof. Tadeusz 032367
Brzeziński, Dr. Wojciech 032480
Brzon, Narveen 047381
Brzozowski, Jerzy 032351
Brzozowski, Leszek 031946
Bsteh, Prof. Dr. Andreas 002325
Bubb, Shirley 045150
Buberl, Dr. Brigitte 016767
Buccellato, Prof. Laura 000170
Buccheri, Prof. G. 025093
Bucci, Jonathan 048959
Bucciferro, Rose 045360
Buccino Grimaldi, Marchese Luigi . 025927
Buccleuch, Duke of 040979, 040981
Buch, Carl E. 030882, 030883
Buchal, Dr. Sabine 019473
Buchan, Andrew 039996
Buchanan, David 044745
Buchanan, Dennis 038901
Buchanan, John 001088
Buchanan jr., John E. 047178
Buchanan, Karen 045529
Buchanan-Dunlop, R. 040155
Buchel, M. 029217
Bucher, Friedrich 002407
Bucher, Prof. Dr. H. 037795
Bucher, Hans 017259
Bucher, Regina 037331
Bucher-Häberli, E. 037171
Buchheim, Prof. Dr. Lothar-Günther 016209
Buchholtz, Annegret 018334
Buchholz, Sabine 018196
Buchholz-Todoroska, Małgorzata . 032329
Buchi, Danielle 010953
Buchner, Dr. Gabriele 019634
Buchner, U. Ernest 005438
Buchs, Denis 036989
Buchtmann, Hans-Georg 020559
Bučinskaja, Valentina Stanislavovna 027390
Buck, Dennis 041909
Buck, Prof. Dr. Elmar 018340
Buck, Kathleen 048654
Buck, Kurt 019560
Buckaloo, Terence 048351
Buckellew, Shari Spaniol 042258
Buckie, Valerie 005009
Buckingham, John 040669
Buckley, Annette 038640
Buckley, Juanita 047013
Buckley, Kerry W. 046544
Buckley, Laurene 043879, 046202
Buckley, Oliver 041286
Bucknill, Greg 040702
Buckridge, Martin 040734
Buckson, Deborah 046623
Bucur, Corneliu-Ioan 032934
Buczkowski, Hans 002452
Buczynski, Bodo 016173
Budarov, Viktor Viktorovič . 034078, 034080
Budde, Bernhard 016409
Budde, Dr. Rainer 018341
Buddle, Allan 044758
Buderer, Dr. Hans-Jürgen . 018806, 018809
Budiastra, Putu 022412
Budiati, Dr. Tinia 022422
Budimir, Dr. Ante 007805
Budka, Mikołaj 031832
Budko, Prof. Dr. Anatolij A. 033836
Budney, Jen 006100
Budrovich, Tony 045414
Budrys, Milda 042854
Budrys, Romualdas 027863
Budzynski, Lillian 043140
Büche, Wolfgang 017672
Büchler, Dr. Hans 037261
Büchler-Mattmann, Dr. Helene ... 036945
Bücken, Véronique 003315
Buecker, Thomas R. 043207
Bückling, Dr. Maraike 017196
Bügel, Christian 018324
Buehler, J. Marshall 049272
Bühler, R.E. 037740
Bühlmann, Isolde 037064

Bühner, Dr. Jan-A. 020345
Buell, Pamela 006199
Buendía García, Mercedes 036006
Buenrostro Alba, Manuel 028487
Bürger, Joachim de 016847
Bürger, Werner 015556
Bürgin, Christoph 037306
Bürgin, Dr. Toni 037497
Bürke, Dr. Bernhard 037047
Bürki, Prof. Hermann 036926
Buerlein, Robert A. 047408
Buermeyer, Chris 044377
Büscher, Marietta 019157
Buesing, Kay 045385
Büsser, Roger E. 037704
Bütikofer, Prof. Alfred 037719, 037730
Bützer, Michael 016842
Büyükçapar, Ahmet 038114
Bufano, Ralph A. 048085
Buford, Elizabeth F. 047314
Bugaeva, Galina Alekseevna 033917
Bugalho Semedo, C.M. 032631
Bugalová, Dr. Edita 034325
Bugarski, Astrida 003941
Bugg, Mathias 037510
Buggeland, Tord 030984
Buggle, Claudia 020762
Bugnon, Prof. Pierre-André 037677
Buhler, Leslie L. 048949
Buhlmann, Dr. Britta E. 018135
Buić, Evgenije 034163
Buijs, H.W.J. 030259
Buijs, J. 013568
Buisson, René 005944
Bujakowska, Beata 031957
Bujić, Marija 034163
Bujold, Michel 006161
Bukač, Václav M. 008380
Bukačová, Dr. Irena 008453, 008497
Bukowska, Halina Lubomiła 032160
Bulaty, Dr. Milan 016189
Bulei, Gheoghe 032947
Bulei, Gheorghe 032944, 032945, 032946
Bulgarelli, Grazia Maria 025555
Bulger, Ralph 006071
Bulgin, Lloyd 005378
Buljević, Zrinka 007798
Bull, Hege Sofie 030978
Bullard, E. John 046263
Buller, Osmo 010112
Bullinger, Dr. Thomas 009149
Bullock, Christopher 041402
Bullock, Margaret 047178
Bulova, Gretchen M. 041641
Bulthuis, P. 030372
Bumgardner, Tim 044792
Bumiller, Manfred 015876
Bumpass, Terry 047965, 047970
Bunbury, Theresa 005016
Bunce, Mark 038864
Bunch, Lonnie G. 042834
Bunch, Nancy B. 043079
Bunch, Rosemary 049299
Bund, Dr. Konrad 017520
Bung, Maria-Hildegard 015851
Bungert, Petra 003294
Bunke, Jim 048097
Bunker-Lohrenz, Jackie 047578
Bunkichi, Ito 027329
Bunyan, Vicki 001220
Buol-Wischenau, Karin 001943
Buonanno, Prof. Roberto 025495
Burak, Marek 032520
Buran, Dr. Dusan 034337
Buranelli, Dr. Francesco 049418, 049422
Burbank, Jane 047433
Burbano, Ignacio 007573
Burch, Danielle 044501
Burch, Ivan 005949
Burch, Prof. John B. 041734
Burch, Wanda 044870
Burchard, Helen 042096
Burchfield, Stanley G. 047738, 047743
Burckhardt, Dr. Daniel 036899
Burdak, Elisabeth 037815
Burdick, Funi 043773
Burdick, Richard L. 047539
Burdychová, Milena 008342
Burel, Bernard 013905
Burford, Beverley 040160
Burganov, Aleksandr 033461
Burge, Don 047230
Burge, Roisin 039737
Burge, Sarah 038806
Burger, Bernadette 037294
Burger, Dr. Hans 036827
Burger, Richard L. 046226
Burger, W. 018057
Burgère, André 011500
Burgess, Brian 001138
Burgess, Cynthia 048809
Burgess, Jerry G. 043941
Burgess, Jo 042267
Burgess, Ken 045855
Burgess, Norman 040295
Burgess, Robert 046276
Burgess, Susan M. 039437
Burghardt, Glenn 046588
Burghardt, Dr. Rainer 002327
Burgiss, Ken 030495
Burgos Cantor, Roberto 007417
Burgraff, Joseph 003472
Burik, Tatjana Borisovna 033907
Burkarth, Dr. Axel 020374
Burke, Adele 045464
Burke, Bonnie 005158
Burke, Bridget 043401
Burke, Daniel 046954
Burke, Gregory 030551
Burke, Jo 043375
Burke, Joan T. 042785
Burke, Marcus B. 046346
Burke, Maryellen 047186
Burke, Susan M. 005717
Burkel, Don 042038
Burkert, Richard A. 044872, 044873
Burkhalter, Françoise 037334
Burkhardt, Guido 015960
Burkhardt-Aebi, Rosmarie 037196
Burkhart, Linda 042791
Burki, Erika 036992
Burleson, D. 005580
Burleson, Rita 045171
Burlingham, Cynthia 045425
Burluaux-Blanchard, Odile 013630
Burman, Michael 041311
Burman, Peter 036568
Burman, Rickie 040188, 040189
Burmann, Peter 036570
Burmeister, Artur 018496
Burmeister, Prof. Dr. E.-G. 019132
Burmeister, Helmut 017962
Burmester, Dr. Andreas 019048
Burn, Dr. L. 038962
Burn-Murdoch, R.I. 040917
Burne, Colleen 043462
Burnett, Dr. A. 040097
Burnett, Kay Taylor 046159
Burnett, La Jean 044562
Burnett, Mark R. 042010
Burnett, Richard 039614
Burnett, Wayne 047634
Burnette, David 046068
Burnham, Laura 044853
Burns, Courtney 046712
Burns, Jane 043661
Burns, Kelly S. 044701
Burns, Laura 042003
Burns, Nancy 046870
Burns, Norman O. 046140
Burns, Pamela 005962
Burns, Richard 038919
Burns, Rick 043658
Burns McAndrew, F. 047649
Burnside, Madeleine H. 044989
Burny, Jeannine 003348
Burojević, Zoran 007795
Buron, Gildas 010667
Buron, René 014469, 014470
Burpee, Jane 005370
Burr, Dr. Brooks M. 042619
Burrell, J.E. 038839
Burresi, Dr. Mariagiulia 025270
Burri, Mario 037753
Burris, Erna 042571
Burroughs, Judy 047370
Burroughs, Stuart 038626
Burscheidt, Margret 017086
Bursell, Barbro 036639
Bursey, M.L. 034608
Bursić, Herman 007777
Burt, Ann 046724
Burtch, Michael 006430
Burton, John 043852, 045122
Burton, Margaret 044209
Burton, Val 000853
Burtschi, Mary 048751
Busack, Dr. Stephen 047315
Busceme, Greg 042080
Busch, Anna 036651
Busch, Fritz B. 020951
Busch, Dr. Ina 016638
Busch, Ingo 017763
Busch, Jean 048585
Busch, Wolf-Rüdiger 017335
Buschhoff, Dr. Anne 016418
Busching, Dr. Wolf-Dieter 018364
Buser, Pierre 037277
Busetto, Dr. Giorgio 026250
Bush, Dianne 005843
Bush, Walter 047021
Bush Tomio, Kimberley 048681
Bushby, Debra L. 038601
Busine, Laurent 003520
Busjan, Béatrice 020921
Busk Laursen, Bodil 008963
Buskirk, Dr. William H. 047399
Buskov, Poul 009151
Buss, Leo W. 046226
Bussac, Monique 010406
Busse, Dr. Klaus 016337
Busse, Valerie 045706
Bussees, Dr. Helena 003313
Bussers, Dr. Helena 003315
Bussers, Helena 003315
Bussinger, André 010969
Bußmann, Prof. Dr. Klaus 019156
Bustard, Wendy 046120
Bušueva, Margarita Viktorovna 033613
Busuladžić, Adnan 003941
Butala, Daniel 007732
Butler, Charles Thomas 043093
Butler, Connie 045451
Butler, David 040494, 049152
Butler, Gay 042772
Butler, Gerald 042040
Butler, John 038700
Butler, Joyce 047165
Butler, Maria V. 046876
Butler, Mary 042055
Butler, Maurice 006316
Butler, R. 034691
Butler, Samuel 046390
Butler, S.R. 039994
Butler, T. 039813
Butler, Tony 039158, 040567
Butnaru, Ioan 032902
Butt, Raymond 040749
Buttacavoli, Eva 041921
Buttar, Lyn 030651
Buttarazzi, Silvestro 023686
Buttel, Larry 044072
Butter, Jelena 016138
Butter, Mary 040966
Butterfield, DeAnne 042350
Butterfield, Tom 042246
Buttini, Eric 027895
Buttlar-Elberberg, Dr. Gertrud 003036
Button, Lawrence 044040
Butts, H. Daniel 045647
Butty, Dr. Pierre 037675
Butz, Dr. Herbert 016134
Buurma, Hilbrand 030163
Buurman, H. 029424
Buus, Henriette 008878
Buvelot, Q. 029434
Buyandelger, U. 029015
Buyko, Malgorzata 032023
Buys, C. 029854
Buyssens, Danielle 037113
Buzenschi, Florentina 032909
Buzzi, Alessandro 025320
Buzzoni, Dr. Andrea 024102, 024112, 024115
Byambasüren, P. 029003
Byčkova, Marina Nikolaevna 034007
Bye, Joellen 046187
Byers, Bill 042398
Byers, James B. 048882
Byh, Per-Olov 036386
Bykov, Dr. Aleksandr 034070
Bykova, Jekaterina Vladimirovna 033559
Bykovceva, L.P. 033443, 033466
Bylicki, Tomasz 032424
Byman, Bertyl 009859
Bynum, Marci 045343
Byong, Ha Min 027611
Byrd, Cathy 041859
Byrd, Eugene 048323
Byrn, Brian 043661
Byrne, Debra J. 048080
Byrne, Douglas 040975
Byrne, Lisa 000827, 001216
Byrne, Paddy 022782
Byrne, Roger 042163
Byrne, Sue 039589
Byrtusová, Jana 008326
Byström, Lars 036645
Bytkovskij, Oleg 033617
Byvanck, Dr. F.V. 029924
Byzewski, Leah 044260
Caballero Barnard, Prof. José M. 028869
Cabanes, Francisco 035987
Cabano-Dempsey, Annali 034545
Cabaret, Michel 014020
Cabel, Oswalda A. 031676
Cabell, Kathleen 044245
Cabello Carro, Dr. Paz 035397
Cabezas, Hervé 012249, 014501
Cable, Christopher B. 041714
Cabot, Ian 040930
Cabot, Lee A. 043758
Cabot, Paul 006635
Cabral, Dr. Elisabeth 032633, 032639
Cabrera, Asun 035443
Cabrera, E. 043802
Cabrera, Geles 028497
Cabrera Cachón, Teresa 028895
Caccia, Antonietta 025834
Cachola Schmal, Peter 017156
Cad, Gabriel 031666
Cadavid López, Susana 007617
Cadenne, Ivan 011260
Cadier, Gérard 013943
Caes, Ward 003157
Cagigós i Soró, Antonio 035850
Cagli, Prof. Bruno 025179
Çağman, Dr. Filiz 038100
Cahen, Daniel 003354
Cahen, Joël J. 029190
Cahen-Delhaye, Anne 003353, 003353, 003356
Cahill, Ann 040629
Cahill, John 022852
Cahill, Kevin M. 046284
Caho, Ismet 034214
Caiado, José Pedro 032650
Caianiello, Dr. Tiziana 018280
Caicedo, Iván 007490
Caicedo de Gómez, Hilda María 007466
Caicedo Lourido, María Isabel 007475
Caille, Georges 037637

Cain, Glena 047014
Cain, Prof. Dr. Hans-Ulrich 018559
Caines, M. 039331
Caivano, Felice 044464
Caji, Jaroslav 034141
Čajka, Vladimir Michailovič 034047, 034058, 034060
Čajkovskij, Bogdan M. 038345
Çakmak, Hacı 038017
Calame, Caroline 037275
Calandra, Eliana 025092
Calasan, Koviljka 034142
Calatayud Cases, José Vte 035700
Calbiac, Christoph de 012726
Calboutin, A. 034776
Caldeira, Ernesto 049298
Caldeira, Prof. Dr. Helena 032599
Caldeira, Vasco 004530
Calder, Jacqueline 046006
Calderan, Gianni 025569
Calderer Serra, Joaquín 035882
Caldwell, Brenda B. 048671, 048672
Caldwell, Carey 046598
Caldwell, Desiree 043117
Caldwell, Frank 041184
Caldwell, Joan G. 046267
Caldwell, Dr. J.P. 046509
Caldwell, Judy 045755
Caldwell, K. 039197
Caldwell, Roy 042163
Calhoun, Angela 044043
Calhoun, Ralph 045967
Calisi, Dr. Marinella 025495
Calkins, Christopher 046908
Calkins, Jack 005413
Call, Linda 049334
Callaghan, Madelein 006434
Callaghan, Richard 039363, 039364, 039365
Callahan, Christine 046463
Callahan, Colin J. 043123
Callahan, Colleen 047426
Callahan, Elizabeth 043578
Callahan, Martin L. 043973
Callahan, William 043088
Callan, Josi Irene 048468
Callanan, Mary 022796
Calland, Gary 041129
Callatÿ, François de 003291, 003293
Callaway, Judson 047780
Callebert, Fernand 003724
Calleen, Dr. Justinus Maria 020931
Callegher, Dr. Bruno 025053
Callen, Bonnie 005443
Callewaert, Ferdy 003720
Callies, Prof. Dr. H. 020272
Callis, Charles 030647
Callison, Brian 039310
Callison, Chris 048714
Calloway, Bertha 046679
Calomiris, Ellen 045384
Calonne, Sylvain 015268
Caltik, Heidi 002945
Calvarin, Margaret 011025, 011506
Calvert, Peter S. 047406
Calvesi, Prof. Maurizio 023893
Calvi di Bergolo, Ippolito 025778
Calvin, Prudence K. 048997
Calvo, B. 035419
Calvo, Ernesto 007674
Calvo, Luis María 000602
Calvocoressi, Richard 039384, 039424
Calzada, S. 034918
Camacho, Dr. João Carlos 032591
Camacho Cadaval, Fernando 035867
Camara, Dr. Abdoulaye 034136
Camara, Calvin 041751
Camara, Prof. Edeltrudes 004001
Camasse, Dr. Michele M. 024472
Camber, Diane W. 045824
Cameron, Dan 046386
Cameron, E. 030432
Cameron, Elizabeth 039303
Cameron, Fran 006104
Cameron, Gary L. 045707
Cameron, John 038761
Cameron, Joyce M. 048275
Cameron, Rosanna 001115
Cameron of Lochiel, Sir Donald 041078
Camfield, Paul 044054
Camin, Philippe 013110, 014656
Camm, Simon 040815
Cammarata, Paolo 025633
Cammarota, Dr. Giampiero 023444
Camnitzer, Luis 046325
Camós Alvarez, Pilar 036101
Camoys, Lord 039729
Camp, Janet G. 048433
Camp, Kimberly 045788
Campagna, Dr. Francesca 024681
Campagnolo, Matteo 037128
Campanalli, Dr. Adele 023864
Campbell, Bruce 040563
Campbell, C.A. 041101
Campbell, Catherine L. 044135
Campbell, Clayton 047986
Campbell, Colin 049180
Campbell, Connie 006021
Campbell, D. 039710
Campbell, Daniel T. 048216
Campbell, Deborah 041727
Campbell, Ellen F. 043980
Campbell, Francis D. 046287
Campbell, George 005677
Campbell, Ina 042251
Campbell, Jacklyn 041871
Campbell, Prof. J.D. 030485
Campbell, John 046230
Campbell, Kathleen 047367
Campbell, Kathryn 048073
Campbell, Kay 001479
Campbell, Lesa 043517
Campbell, Levin 042331
Campbell, Loraine 048616
Campbell, Lorne 040241
Campbell, Mabel 006124
Campbell, Mei 045513
Campbell, Mungo 039559
Campbell, Nancy 049033
Campbell, Neil 005811
Campbell, Richard 045918
Campbell, Roy G. 047315
Campbell, Sara 046833
Campbell, Shearon 042910
Campbell, Tacie N. 043514
Campbell, Tracey 045995
Campbell, Wallace 046852
Campbell-Ferguson, Gail 042396
Campbell McMurray, H. 040770
Campbell-Shoaf, Heidi 044049
Camphausen, Ute 018572
Campo, Marta 034911
Campodonico, Dr. Piero 024323
Campofiorito, Italo 004242
Campos, Alexander 044824
Campos, Prof. Antonio Celso de Arruda 004224
Campos, Maria Lucia Rocha 004537
Campredon, Elisabeth 011564
Campuzano Ruiz, Enrique 035832
Camus, Marie-France 012406
Canal, Dr. Guillermo C. de la 000172
Canales, Rocio Gonzalez de 028563
Cañamás, Marita 035976
Canbey, Maşuk 038193
Cândea, Ionel 032787
Candeloro, Ilaria 025613
Cândido, Maria João 032688
Candlin, Dierdre 040245
Candon, Anthony 040644
Candy, Ron 006726
Caneer, Ann 047119
Canini, Alberto 025518
Canizales Montoya, Luis Fernando 007579
Cankova, Tatjana 004682
Cannata, Dr. Roberto 025483
Cannatella, David C. 041936
Cannegieter, Dr. D.A.S. 029569
Canning-Lacroix, Johane 005950, 006380
Cannon, Annetta 046566
Cannon, Janet 005551
Cannon, P. 040542
Cannon-Brookes, Peter 039913
Cano, Luis Martín 028542
Cano, Rose Marie 045458
Cano de Martín, Marta 000293
Cano Rivero, Ignacio 035864
Cano Salas, Gilda 028480
Canogar, Rafael 036062
Canonne, Xavier 003366
Canovai, Dr. Roberto 024545
Canright, Steve 047883
Cantinho, Dr. Manuela 032644
Cantley, John 048451
Cantor, Helen 044040
Canulli, Richard G. 048785
Capa, José 035614
Capa Eiriz, Dr. José 035138
Capanna, Prof. Ernesto 025523
Capano, Dr. Antonio 026269
Capazza, Gérard 013317
Capdevila, Dr. Ricardo 000179, 000186
Capella Molas, Anna 035192
Capin, Djordje 034193, 034194
Capin, Jean 014969
Capion, Ole 008805
Capistrano Barker, Dr. Florina H. 031697
Capitani, Dr. François de 037422, 037784
Capitanio, Fabrizio 023379
Čapková, Dr. Jana 008383
Capomolla, Soccorso 024860
Capon, Barry 038882
Capon, Edmund 001505, 001506
Capon, S.H. 041345
Capot, Stéphane 012692
Capovilla, Prof. Sergio Carlos 000553
Cappelletti, Prof. Vincenzo 025262
Capper, Rosi 039832
Capponi, Dr. Carlo 024728
Capps, Jennifer 044754
Capps, Larry 044694
Capralos, Souli 021114, 021165
Caproni di Taliedo Guasti, Firmina 025492
Carabo, Lucille 042144, 042145
Caradec, Marie-Anne 011555
Caramazza, O.G. 024645
Caramelle, Dr. Franz 002078
Caramelli, Fernando 025240
Carazzetti, Prof. Riccardo 037272, 037273, 037278
Carbajal, Londi 047977
Carbajal, Sergio 028493
Carballo, José Rodriguez 035825
Carbert, R.W. 005874
Carbery, David 022786
Carbonell, Sílvia 035905
Carbonell i Esteller, Eduard 034955
Card, Nan 044078
Cardarelli, Andrea 024755, 024756
Cardelli, Patrice 012834
Carden, Martha 043331
Carden, Willie F. 042930
Cárdenas Marcaida, María Caridad 007911
Cárdenas Tovar, Jairo Simón 007638
Cardenas Troncoso, Gloria 006910
Carder, Julia 040027
Cardim Ribeiro, José 032692
Cardin, Deborah 041989
Cardinaels, Marie-Jeanne 003258
Cardinale, Vincenzo 016342
Cardini, Giuliano 025959
Cardon, Dorothy 047289
Cardon, Véronique 003316
Cardona, Hermana Martha 007612
Cardone, Veronique 012467
Cardoner, F. 034901
Cardoso, Prof. Dr. António 032576
Cardoso Botelho, Americo G. 032581
Cardot, A. 037668
Carduner, Michel 014393
Cardwell, E. 040643
Carevic Rivera, Alvaro 006916
Carey, Betsy 048499
Carey, Edith 037679
Carey, Hon Hug L. 046284
Carfano, M. Susan 049360
Cargeeg, G. 001609
Cariello, Dr. Rubina 025927
Carignani, Dr. Mario 024898
Cariou, André 013979
Carl, Christine S. 044131
Carl, Christy 044128
Carlano, Annie 047972
Carle, Michele 043905
Carlén, Staffan 036416
Carles, Gilbert 015013
Carlestam, Håkan 036317
Carleton, Dr. Don 041923, 048721
Carli, Dr. Laura 025970
Carlier, Sylvie 015258
Carlier, Yves 011850
Carlile, Janet 005029
Carlin, Scott 001582
Carlosama Mora, Rosa Cecilia 007522
Carlquist, Thomas 036577
Carlsen, Dr. Charles 046754
Carlsen, Margaret 047242
Carlson, Elizabeth 049246
Carlson, Jeffrey 046876
Carlson, Jim 048176
Carlson, Joseph 043660
Carlson, Linda 043903
Carlson, Norman P. 044829
Carlson, Robert 042298
Carlson, Dr. Shawn 048973
Carlsson, Ann-Britt 036725
Carlsson, Eva 036265
Carlström, Dr. Ann-Kristin 036498
Carlstrom, Terry 044437, 048129, 048906, 048919, 048939
Carmack, Brent 045307
Carman, Michael D. 047004, 047007
Carmen Lema Pensado, María del 041535
Carmer, Craig 045405
Carmichael, Dr. Ian 042161
Carmichael, J. 040182
Carmichael, Kristina 042755
Carmona Lancheros, Carlos Alberto 007463
Carmount, Laurie 005564
Carnahan, John W. 045972
Carnap-Bornheim, Prof. Dr. C. von 016526
Carnap-Bornheim, Prof. Dr. Claus von 020038
Carnazzi, Umberto 023396
Carner, Gil 045092
Carnerini, Carla 025129
Carnes, Griffiths 044975
Carnes, John 045292
Carnes, William H. 043925
Carney, Barbara 048535
Carney, Dr. Margaret 041651
Carney, Terry J. 039626
Carniello, Peter 005463
Carolan, Janet 039246
Carollo, Albert H. 048807
Carollo, Eugene R. 048807
Caron, Euclid 046736
Caron, Jacqueline 005654
Carpenter, Dean 042695, 043594
Carpenter, Ele 041160
Carpenter, Frank 039251
Carpenter, Dr. M.A. 038970
Carpenter, Matthew 041754
Carpenter, Dr. Richard 043346
Carpenter, T.F. 039042
Carpenter Correa, Laura 042443
Carpenter Troccoli, Joan 043404
Carpentier, Régine 003290
Carpio, Agustín 000467
Carr, Carolyn 048933
Carr, Eve 049212
Carr, Josh 046278

Carr, Layton 048115
Carr, Lucia C. 045569
Carr, N.J. 038815
Carr, Shelvie 043327
Carr-Griffin, Paul 040059
Carr-Whitworth, Caroline 039248
Carradice, Prof. Ian A. 040898
Carrara, Dr. Giancarlo 023859
Carraro, Dr. Francine 044809
Carré, Dr. Enrique González 031566
Carreau, Raphaële 011325, 011326
Carreck, Marjorie W. 039726
Carregha, Luz 028737
Carreira, Dr. Isabel 032606
Carrel, Michel 014507
Carreño, Irving 049451
Carreño Díaz, Prof. Esboardo 028225
Carrera Hontana, Enrique de 035410
Carretero Rebes, Salvador 035811
Carrier, Alan 046728
Carrier, Nicole M. 044792
Carrlee, Ellen 044890
Carrol, Brian 042481
Carroll, Daine L. 048603
Carroll, M. Lyda 044356
Carroll, Richard E. 049097
Carroll, Rowan 030581
Carroll, Scott 044888
Carroll, Sue 047266
Carroll, William B. 039765
Carron, Christian G. 044278
Carruthers, Karen 038767
Carruthers, Ray 006555
Carruzzo, S. 037676
Cars, Laurence des 013678
Carson, Heather 040232, 040316
Carson, John 047338
Carson, Michael 042881
Carstensen, Dr. Jan 016691
Carswell, A.L. 039408
Cart, Doran L. 044923
Cartacci, Marcello 025576
Carter, Bennett 044301
Carter, Curtis L. 045889
Carter, Dr. Curtis L. 045898
Carter, Hazel 045679
Carter, John S. 046951
Carter, Julia 044577, 044577
Carter, Kathy 045065
Carter, Martha C. 048276
Carter, Michael 046315
Carter, Mike 042380
Carter, Penelope 039406
Carter, R. 000848
Carter, Susan 048489
Carter, W.J. 039141
Cartwright, Colin M. 038689
Cartwright, Derrick R. 044426
Cartwright, Thomas 044044
Carty, Paul 022746
Caruana, Sebastian 028050
Carucci, Arturo 025638
Carus, Benno 016074
Carusi, Corina 042847
Caruso, Dr. Ida 023912
Caruso, Romy 049041
Carustrom, Terry 041779
Carvalho, Joseph 048293, 048294
Carvallo, Henri 015221
Carver, Dan 046789
Carver, Kate 039770
Carvey-Stewart, Elizabeth 047491
Cary, Farrin 043567
Cary, PeeWee 043529
Carzou, Jean-Marie 012877
Čas, Alenka 034462
Casadei, Dr. Sauro 024073
Casado Soto, José Luis 035812
Casagrande, Louis B. 042321
Casagrande, Rodrigo Fernando 004586
Casagrande, Tiziana 024087, 024088
Casal, Gabriel 031712
Casaldi, Silvano 024934
Casale, Tommaso 025982
Casalini, Dr. Antonio 025118
Casanelles, Eusebi 035907
Casanovas, María Antonia 034926
Casaro, Massimo 024727
Casarola, Albino 024870
Casartelli, Marisa Helena Cestari . 004470
Casas, Imma 034961
Cascales Ayala, Manuel 034842
Caselli Wijsbek, H.E.J. 030248
Casetti, Christoph 037020
Casey, Dawn 000829, 000889
Casey, Laura 048134
Casey, Lynn R. 044140
Casey, Prof. Michael T. 022835
Cash, Reva 043425
Cash, Sarah 048891, 048892
Cashatt, Dr. Everett D. 048284
Cashbaugh, Todd M. 041731
Cashman, William 042091
Casini, Dr. Stefania 023376
Casjens, Laurel 047778
Câşlaru, Constantin 032779
Casler, Jennifer R. 044009
Caso, Kristin 041595
Caspers, Martha 017176
Caspersen, Kim 039383
Cass, Michael 040307
Cass-Hassol, Nicholas 046385
Cassan, Dagmar de 002232
Cassan, Ferdinand de 002232
Cassanelli, Dr. Roberto . . . 024875, 024877
Cassell, Valerie 044637
Cassels, Patrick 038618
Casseminho Meira, Mariana 004301
Cassiano, Dr. Antonio 024484
Cassidy, Terry P. 048979
Castagnoli, Prof. Pier Giovanni . . . 026050
Căstăian, Mihai 032906
Castaño Cruz, Hermana Cecilia . . . 007468
Castañón Albo, Luis 035396
Castanyer Bachs, Narcis 036023
Castel, Marie-Chantal 013814
Castel-Branco Pereira, Dr. João . . 032634
Castele, Theodore J. 042993
Castellà Reial, Josep 035677
Castellana, Dr. Gruiseppe 023132
Castelletti, Dr. Lalfredo 023948
Castelletti, Dr. Lanfredo . 023943, 023946, 023947
Castelnuovo, Sheri 045591
Casteret, Norbert 011840
Castex, Jessica 013630
Castier, Annie 012680
Castilla, Francisca 035978
Castillo Tovar, Carlos Arturo 007505
Castle, Charles E. 045068
Castle, Lynn P. 042079
Castle, Myra 044355
Castleberry, May 046418
Castor, A. 013790
Castor González, Jesús . . . 028469, 028489
Castrillón Urrera, Carlos Alberto . . 007400
Castro, Milagos 032731
Castro Benítez, Daniel . . . 007403, 007405
Castro Mejía, María Eugenia 007399
Castro Meza, Raúl 028761
Castronovo, Simona 026052
Català Gorgues, Angel 035973
Cataldi, Dr. Maria 025990
Cataldi Gallo, Dr. Maria 024299
Catchpole, Julie 030569, 030570
Catchpole, Nancy 038619
Catchpole, Ron 039812
Cate, Phillip Dennis 046206
Cates, David L. 003089
Cates, Michael 040793
Catford, B.L. 001359
Cathcart, Rosemary 039450
Cathrin, Marcel 014437
Catleugh, Jon 040131
Catlin, Erica 042462
Catlin-Legutko, Cinnamon 046895
Cato, John S. 048425
Catolin, Eufemia B. 031811
Catron, Joanna D. 044055
Catroppa, Frank 041865
Catrysse, Bernard 026959
Catta, Javier 009224
Cattaneo, Claudia 037718
Cattaneo, Pascal 037327
Cattelain, P. 003815
Catton, Jonathan 039626
Cau, Ettore 026364, 026365
Caubet, Annie 013685
Caudoux, Michel 015140
Cauk, Françoise 010619
Cauldwell, Amanda 047396
Caulkins, Bethel I. 047394
Caumon, Annette 012793
Caurie, Philippa 041449
Čauševa, Dora 004706
Caussinus, Dany 010383
Cauvin, Sylvette 015113
Cauwe, Nicolas 003353
Cavaglion Bassani, Laura 023035
Cavagnis Sotgiu, Dr. Maria Carla . . 025502
Cavaillès, Maria 013744
de Paiva Cavalanti, Lauro Augusto 004415
Cavalcante, Raquel 004024
Cavalchini, Pieranna 042328
Cavalho-Roos, Dr. T. Rosa de 029256
Cavalier, Odile 010591
Cavalier, Sebastien 012829
Cavalli, Attilio 024714
Cavalli, Germano 026334
Cavalli-Björkman, Åsa 036619
Cavalli-Björkman, Görel 036648
Cavanaugh, Gwendolyn 043188
Cavanaugh, Joe 044053
Cavatrunci, Claudio 025555
Cavazzi Palladini, Dr. Lucia 025473
Cavelti, Dr. Urs J. 037155
Cavendish, Kim L. 043934
Cavenee, Dee 042496
Cavić, Aldo 007809
Cavnor, Julie Ann 041993
Cay Henry, Mary 043183
Cayer, Richard 041662
Çaylak, İsmail 038041
Cayphas, Jean-Paul 003538
Cazacu, Silvia 032813
Cazakoff, Ingrid 006448
Cazarez-Rueda, Luis 044242
Cazé, Sophie 012138
Cazes, Daniel 014998
Ceballos, Orlando Toro 007601
Ceballos Carrero, Rosa Maria 028316
Cebrián, Enriqueta 035978
Cebucoprea, Dr. Alexandru 032795
Ceccarelli, Giampiero 025941
Cecchetto, Dr. Giacinto 023716
Cecchi, Dr. Alessandro 024156
Ceccini de Dallo, Ana María 000609
Cech, Christine 003009
Cecil, William A.V. 041790
Čecov, Prof. Dr. V.P. 033507
Cederlund, Dr. Johan 036738
Cedersand, Kerstin 036623
Cederstrøm, Elisabeth 008988
Cedro, Dr. Bernard 032366
Ceesay, B.A. 015399
Ceesay, Hassoum 015399
Cega, Fani Celio 007813
Čekerinac, Bora 034266
Čeko, Franko 007792
Celant, Germano 046404
Celayır, İsmail Hakkı 038090, 038108
Celenko, Theodore 044748
Celestina, Susan 047005
Céleyran, Tapié de 013357
Celi, Maria 046320
Siqueira Celidonio, Helio Fernando 004017
Celio-Scheurer, Marie-Eve 037345
Celis, Augustin de 036062
Celli, Jeanann 048330
Celma, Cécile 028053
Celuzza, Dr. Mariagrazia 024373
Celuzza, Dr. M.G. 024376
Cembrano, Rita 031637, 031640
Cembrola, Robert 046462
Cendo, Nicolas 012934
Ceni, Giuseppe Riccardo 026289
Ceniceros Herreros, Javier 035538
Cenni, Mario 024545
Censky, Ellen J. 048382
Centore, Prof. Giuseppe 023655
Čepič, Taja 034496
Cepon, Miloska 034495
Čeran, Branko 007849
Cerar, Estera 034495
Čerba, Larisa Valerjanovna 033982
Čerče, Peter 034511
Ceriotti, Guido 023554
Cerişer, Nicolae 032873
Čerkalin, Sergej Dmitrievič 033708
Čerkasova, Olga Anatoljevna 033183
Černá, Margit 008507
Cernat, Ivona Elena 032875
Černavin, Lev Davidovyč 033794
Černín, Dr. Svatomír 008699
Černjak, Ėduard Isaakevič 033965
Černobai, Prof. Dr. Juri 038360
Černova, Vita Vasylivna 038280
Cerny, Dr. P. 006858
Cerny, Zbynek 008328
Ceron, Clodualdo N. 031750
Cerón, Pablo 028467
Cerón Mireles, Prof. José Luis . . . 028465
Ceroni, Nadia 025401
Cerovac, Branko 007779
Cerović, Dr. Ljubivoje 034228
Cerretelli, Claudio 025364, 025365
Certo, Michael 041625
Ceruti, Mary 045392
Cerutti, Dr. Antonio 025383
Cerutti, Lilia P. de 000673
Cervellino, Miguel 006915
Cervetti, Dr. Valerio 025111, 025117
Cervini, Dr. Fulvio 026046
Cesari, Gene 049238
Cesbron, Pierre 014374
Češková, Stanislava 008660
Česnova, Ljudmila Alekseevna . . . 033122
Cession Louppe, Jacqueline 003657
Cetinić, Ljiljana 034158
Ceulemans, Louisa 003509
Ceunynck, Christoph de . . 011535, 011536
Ceut 011948
Ceynowa-Barth, Tatjana 017434
Chabard, Dominique 010563
Chabert, Noëlle 013731
Chacala Nuñulo, Pedro 000092
Chačatrian, Šahen 000686
Chačikjan, Svetlana Melkonovna . . 033703
Chadbourne, Janice 042318
Chadima, John 043149
Chadli, Mohammed 029020
Chadwick, Adam 040218
Chadwick, Phyllis 046734
Chadwick, P.J. 034743
Chadwick-Case, Wendy 044829
Chadžiev, N. 004861
Chafe, Dr. K.S. 030691
Chaguaceda Toledano, Ana 035738
Chai, Paris K. 044601
Chaik, Pak In 027442
Chaimerez, M. G. 023024
Chainé, Françoise 006665
Chait, Karen 046278
Chakraborti, R.M. 022268
Chakravarti, Rasmohan 003098
Chakravarti, Dr. S.K. 022220
Chald, Elisabeth 040902
Chalfant, Rhonda 048102
Chalker, Mary 001536
Challen, John . . 039103, 039104, 039105, 039816
Challener, Elisbeth 048003

Challis, Liz . . . 000977
Challis, Paul . . . 000977
Chalmers, Kim . . . 042369
Chalmers, Sir Neil . . . 040245
Chalmers, Dr. Neil R. . . . 041241
Chalmers, Peggy . . . 040242
Chalupa, Josef . . . 008529
Chamay, Jaques . . . 037030
Chambareau, René . . . 010536
Chamberlain, Brewster . . . 048952
Chamberlain, Lori . . . 006396
Chamberlin, Edward M. . . . 044138
Chambers, Coleen B. . . . 044730
Chambers, Cullen . . . 048678
Chambers, Elizabeth . . . 047178
Chambers, Emma . . . 006019
Chambers, Keith . . . 000937
Chambers, Kristin . . . 042984
Chambers, Michael A. . . . 006093
Chambers, T.B. . . . 001268
Chambon, Cati . . . 012487
Chambon, Fabrice . . . 013230
Chambon, Marion S. . . . 046247
Chamil, Iskhakov . . . 008280
Chamonikola, Dr. Kaliopi . . 008290, 008291
Champanil, Vira . . . 037873
Chan, Elise . . . 048994
Chan, Peng Sam . . . 007187
Chanazarov, Kalbay . . . 049398
Chance, Delores . . . 042675
Chance, Dr. John . . . 048520
Chancel-Bardelot, Béatrice de . . . 010935, 010938, 010940
Chandès, Hervé . . . 013582
Chandler, Charles . . . 043377
Chandler, Christine . . . 043305
Chandler, Kenneth . . . 044745
Chandler, Pam . . . 044745
Chandon, Melissa . . . 043313
Chandran, P.R. . . . 022351
Chandžieva, Evelina . . . 004667
Chandžieva, Radka . . . 004650
Chanel, Pierre . . . 012793
Chankers, Natalie . . . 038584
Chanler, James . . . 046442
Channels, Noreen . . . 044464
Channer, L.J. . . . 040177
Channing, Susan R . . . 043000
Channon, Ann . . . 039042
Chanson, Robert . . . 037517
Chansou, Dr. Michel . . . 037476
Chapalain, Jean-Philippe . . . 012725
Chapin, Angela . . . 006295
Chapin, Jean . . . 048878
Chapin, Mona . . . 042919
Chaplin, Sylvia . . . 040376
Chapman, Alan . . . 038533
Chapman, Allison . . . 045602
Chapman, A.T. . . . 005139
Chapman, Gordon . . . 001592
Chapman, H. . . . 040556
Chapman, Dr. Jefferson . . . 045039
Chapman, J.R. . . . 040828
Chapman, Dr. S.T. . . . 040688
Chapman, Prof. Stanley . . . 040863
Chapman Banks, Barbara . . . 045304
Chapnick, Harold . . . 043877
Chapoose, Betsy . . . 043913
Chapp, Belena S. . . . 046421
Chappaz, Jean-Luc . . . 037128
Chappey, Frédéric . . . 012707
Chapron, Philippe . . . 010682
Chapuis, Julien . . . 046315
Charbonneau, Reine . . . 005901
Charette, Joanne . . . 006104
Charette, Luc A. . . . 005895
Chariot, C. . . . 003833
Charitatos, Katerina . . . 021386
Charitonov, Christo . . . 004936
Charles, Dorothée . . . 013668
Charles, Steve . . . 048090
Charlier, P. . . . 003672
Charlot, Colette . . . 013201
Charlton, Dr. Christopher . . 039183, 039184
Charlton, K. . . . 030614
Charlton-Jones, D. . . . 030555
Charmayne Young, J. . . . 047628
Charmelo, Julie . . . 042870
Charpentier, Corinne . . . 011569
Charrière, Edmond . . . 037012
Chartier, Catherine . . . 014384
Chartrain, Michèle . . . 011992
Charzynska, Jadwiga . . . 031905
Chase, Ed . . . 041802, 041803
Chase, Jim . . . 042683
Chaserant, Françoise . . . 012519, 012520, 012521
Chassaing, Jean-François . . . 012157
Chassé, Sonia . . . 005777
Chasseval, Geneviève de . . . 012210
Château, Georges . . . 014390
Chatelain, Prof. E. . . . 012898
Chatenet, Georges . . . 014993
Chatfield, Linda . . . 043489
Chatland, Gordon . . . 043843
Chatman, Patrina . . . 043437
Chatterjee, Dr. H.J. . . . 040159
Chatterjee, Dr. Sankar . . . 045513
Chatterjee, Sunil Kumar . . . 022152
Chaturvedi, Naresh . . . 022267
Chaudet, M.-H. . . . 037676
Chauffeteau, Claude . . . 010883
Chaumet, Danièle . . . 013834
Chauvel, Marie Claire . . . 012216
Chauvin, Dr. Robert S. . . . 043334
Chauvirviere, Comte de la . . . 014899
Chavanne, Blandine . . . 013324
Chavannes, Virgile Alexandre . . . 000567
Chavarria, Antonio . . . 047971
Chaves, Dr. Julio César . . . 031453
Chaves, Manuel Wenceslao . . . 031448
Chavez, Melinda N. . . . 048494
Chavez, Thomas . . . 047975
Chavez, Walter J. . . . 032751
Chayes, William . . . 042162
Chazal, Gilles . . . 013740
Cheatham, Jim . . . 043460
Chebanova, N. . . . 049411
Chebitwey, Jane . . . 027422
Checefsky, Bruce . . . 042997
Chedal, Jean-Claude . . . 013414
Cheetham, Elizabeth . . . 040866
Cheevers, James W. . . . 041744
Chefdebien, Anne de . . . 013712
Cheikh, Aboubakar . . . 007649
Chelbi, Fethi . . . 037950
Chelius, Margot . . . 019211
Chellah, Mwimanji Ndota . . . 049566
Chemera, Lyn . . . 043557
Chen, Jian Ming . . . 007030
Chen, Julie . . . 046412
Chen, Lucia . . . 046412
Chen, Shih-Bey . . . 007374
Chen, S.S.H. . . . 029430
Chen, Zu-E . . . 007274
Chen-Lee, Margaret . . . 007368
Chenault, Amanda . . . 043024
Cheney, Dotty . . . 044122
Cheney, Dr. John T. . . . 041695
Cheney, Rebecca . . . 039041
Cheng, Hon Seng . . . 047860
Cheng-Sheng, Tu . . . 007372
Chenoufi, Brahim . . . 000077
Chenoweth, Bob . . . 048260
Chenoweth, Richard . . . 047983
Chepp, Mark . . . 048304
Cherchi Usai, Paolo . . . 047480
Cherek, Dr. Janina . . . 031869, 031870
Cherif, Housine Med . . . 000076
Cherix, Dr. Daniel . . . 037245
Chermak, Glenda L. . . . 045087
Cherry, Stella . . . 022719
Chesbrough, Herbert A. . . . 048006
Chesebrough, David . . . 042502
Chesi, Prof. Gert . . . 002664
Chesneau-Dupin, Laurence . . . 011415, 011825
Chester, Timothy J. . . . 044278
Chesters, Dr. Robin . . . 040043
Cheval, François . . . 011195
Chevalier, Alain . . . 015327
Chevalier, Ann . . . 003587, 003588
Chevalies, Ségolène le . . . 011618
Chevallier, Bernard . . . 012123, 014154
Chevallier, Denis . . . 012945
Chew, Nigel . . . 040955
Chew, Ron . . . 048095
Chew Matsuda, Fay . . . 046372
Chez Checor, José . . . 009165
Chia, Khoo Boo . . . 028009
Chiacchierini, Prof. Ernesto . . . 025531
Chiappini, Dr. Marco . . . 023255
Chiappini, Dr. Rudy . . . 036969, 037002, 037287, 037288
Chiara Bettini, Dr. Maria . . . 023665
Chiaramonte, Dr. Giuseppe . . . 025092
Chiarchiaro, Charles . . . 046762
Chiarini, Dr. Marco . . . 024137, 024160
Chiarucci, Dr. Giuseppe . . 023146, 024456
Chiba, Mizuo . . . 027283
Chicharro Chamorro, José Luis . . . 035303
Chicoineau, Pierre . . . 012044
Chidavaenzi, R.P. . . . 049579
Chidsey, Dr. Jennifer L. . . . 042049
Chiego, William J. . . . 047798
Chiesa, Franco . . . 036999
Chiesi, Dr. Giuseppe . . . 036913, 036916
Chikhaoui-Trachene, Prof. Henia . . 029021
Chikkamare Gowda, B.M. . . . 022015
Chilcote, Doug . . . 047647, 047648
Chilcote, Gary . . . 047647, 047648
Child, M. . . . 041073
Childress, Ann . . . 043250
Childress, P.L. . . . 046782
Childrey, Brooke . . . 044785
Chilton, D.G. . . . 040948
Chilton, Meredith . . . 006600
Chimello, Sylvain . . . 014932
Chimier, Brigitte . . . 015081
Chiminelli, Baldassare . . . 023717
Chin, Song-gi . . . 027516
Chin Foo, Brenda . . . 015394
Chinea Brito, Carmen D. . . . 035317
Chinen, Satoru . . . 026533
Chinery, Derek . . . 040818
Chinwe Anyaegbuna, Felicia . . . 030679
Chiocchetti, Dr. Fabio . . . 025349
Chiong, Dr. Chew Tuan . . . 034299
Chiriac, Aurel . . . 032903, 032904, 032905
Chiritá, Lenuta . . . 032882
Chitaley, Dr. Shya . . . 042986
Chitoshi, Matsuo . . . 026606
Chivers, Jim . . . 030424
Chižnjak, Olga Romanivna . . . 038270
Chlebarova, Marija . . . 004643
Chlebecek, Friedrich . . . 002122
Chlobystin, Andrej . . . 033808
Chlopinska, Ljudmyla Dmytrivna . . 038364
Chmara, Gitta von . . . 018004
Chmelinova, Dr. Katarina . . . 034337
Chmelnickaja, Ljudmila . . . 003140
Chmielak, Jadwiga . . . 032130
Chmielewska, Wiesława . . . 032297
Chmielewski-Hagius, Dr. Anita . . . 018099
Chmurzyński, Wojciech . . . 032445
Cho, Byoung Soon . . . 027610
Choate, J.R. . . . 044490, 044490
Chocholáč, Ivo . . . 008527
Chodasiewicz, Jerzy . . . 032359
Choe, Sung Eun . . . 027552
Choetf, Betsy . . . 044729
Choi, Prof. Duck-Keun . . . 027602
Choi, Eric . . . 007182
Choi, Il Sung . . . 027472
Choi, Kim Sang . . . 027437
Choi, Man-Li . . . 027500
Choiselat, Roland . . . 006027
Choisne, Franck . . . 014700
Cholette, Yvon . . . 006552
Cholewa, Anita . . . 045914
Chołodowska, Małgorzata . . . 032563
Chomenko, Tamara Jevgenivna . . 038307
Chomič, Svetlana Viktorovna . . . 033279
Chong, Alan . . . 042328
Chongkol, Chira . . . 037885
Chopping, George C. . . . 006816
Choremi, Dr. Alkestis . . . 021181
Choremis, Alketis . . . 021208
Choriev, Kiem . . . 049381
Chorunženko, V.A. . . . 033142
Chou, Ju-Hsi . . . 042985
Choudhury, B. . . . 022118
Choudhury, Dr. R.D. . . . 022120
Chow, Kai-Wing . . . 048713
Chow, Kim-Fung . . . 007122
Chowdhuri, Dr. M.K. . . . 022217
Chowdhury, Prof. Dr. Saifuddin . . . 003116
Chrest, Gwen . . . 043011
Chrisanov, Petr Aleksandrovič . . . 033890
Chrisholm, Donna . . . 039869
Chrisman, D. Kent . . . 047467
Christ, Hans D. . . . 020373
Christ, Nelda M. . . . 042262
Christaffersen, Erna . . . 008908
Christen, Benoît . . . 010778
Christen, François . . . 037380
Christen, Thomas . . . 036986
Christensen, Henry . . . 030536
Christensen, J.O. . . . 008991
Christensen, Lisbeth . . . 008885
Christensen, Margaret . . . 005642
Christensen, Peter M. M. . . . 008928
Christensen, Ruth . . . 027838
Christensen, Svend . . . 008928
Christenson, Goran . . . 036459
Christian, J.A. . . . 047577
Christian, Jay . . . 043818
Christian, John . . . 048000
Christian, Joshua W. . . . 041991
Christiansen, Calvin . . . 048989
Christiansen, Jette . . . 008982
Christiansen, Prof. Dr. Jörn . . . 016411, 016420
Christiansen, Sherie . . . 048131
Christie, David . . . 046870
Christie, Gordon A. . . . 039507
Christie, Nancy . . . 046870
Christman, David C. . . . 044506
Christodoulakos, Yannis . . . 021225
Christoffel, Udo . . . 016093, 016195
Christoffer, Ed . . . 005468
Christoph, Susi . . . 002736
Christopher, Terry . . . 048172
Christophersen, Axel . . . 031290
Christou, Dr. Demos . . . 008235
Christov, Christo . . . 004677
Christov-Bakargiev, Carolyn . . . 025448
Christova, Emilia . . . 004709
Chrzan, Stanisław . . . 031841
Chrzanowski, Jerzy . . . 032557
Chu, Dr. Christina . . . 007115
Chu, Doris . . . 042346
Chubbuck Weinstein, Elizabeth . . . 042044
Chudjakova, Lidija Aleksandrovna . 033116
Chughtai, Arif Rahman . . . 031377
Chuma-Ibe, Gloria Chianu . . . 030693
Chunchu, Ai . . . 006972
Chung, Prof. Jing-Won . . . 027456
Chung, Yang-Ho . . . 027589
Chuoc, Cu Van . . . 049529
Chupin, Olivier . . . 011070
Church, B. A. . . . 043764
Church, Dorian . . . 040999
Church, Rena J. . . . 041910
Church, Susan . . . 044719
Churchill, Viscount . . . 039443
Churchill, Edwin . . . 041905
Churchill, Robin . . . 041969
Chushupal, E.N. . . . 027643
Chusnutdinova, Rušanija Salichovna . . . 033243

Chutiwongs, Dr. N. 029854
Chwałek, Roman 032303
Chwaliński, Andrzej 032178
Chwalisz, Zofia 032512
Chylak, Ana 038523
Chytilo, Prof. Lynne 041610
Ciamos, Christian 010342
Ciancio, Dr. Angela 024344
Cianciulli, John 044041
Ciapponi Landi, Bruno 024575
Ciaran, Dr. Fiona 030604
Ciardi, Dr. Roberto Paolo 025717
Ciarla, Dr. Roberto 025548
Ciavolino, Prof. Giuseppe 026087
Cibulová, Dr. Vlasta 008643
Cicala, Francesco 025102, 025104
Cicala Campagna, Dr. Francesca .. 025901
Cicali, Francesco 025103
Çiçeksız, İbrahim 038080
Ciceri, Angela 024051
Cichecka, Barbara 032486
Cichocki, Max 015989
Cicierski, Ernest 006856
Cicimov, Aleksandar 027925
Cicimurri, David 042974
Cicognani, Giorgio 023532
Cidenova, Rita Badmaevna 033999
Ciecholewski, Dr. Roman 032217
Ciecior, Gabriele 017758
Ciepiela, Elżbieta 032543
Cierna, Katarína 034337
Cierpka, Heinz 017551
Cieślak, Bogdan 032513
Cifelli, Dr. R.L. 046509
Cifuentes, Joaquín 028504
Ciganok, Nina 038255
Cigarroa, Melissa 045172
Cigliano, Flavia 042337
Cihan Özsayıner, Zübeyde 038101
Čikin, Vladimir Iljič 038384
Čilašvili, L.A. 015413
Cilona, Filippo Ferdinando 024086
Cimdiņa, Ruta 027735
Činč-Juhant, Dr. Breda 034491
Cinc-Mars, François 006562
Cindi, F. 034667
Cingolani, Lauro 025405
Cingolani, Lilias 045012
Cini, Amato 026175
Cini, Stephen 028039
Činovec, Igor 008683
Cinquepalmi, Angela 024084
Cintulova, Erika 034360, 034362
Cioce, Dr. Pasquale 023407
Cioci, Antonio 024166
Ciôfalo, Manfred 026008
Cioffari, Gerardo 023337
Cioppi, Dr. Elisabeth 024182
Cipolletti, Dr. Maria S. 016313
Cipollone, Dr. Rosa 025008
Ciprian, Dr. Pavel 008289, 008293, 008298, 008791, 008792, 008793, 008794
Cipriani, Curzio 024187
Cirani, Simona 025654
Cirill, T. 021808
Cirillo, Gail 046508
Cirjakovic, Ivana 034180
Čirkova, Larisa I. 033767
Ciro Galotta, Brás 004554
Cīrule, Astrīda 027713
Ciseri, Dr. Ilaria 024805
Cisle, Carrie 047332
Cisneros, Jose 044852
Cisneros, Mario Toledo 028711
Cist, O. 002239
Ciubotă, Dr. Viorel 032930
Ciugudean, Horia Ion 032771
Civai, Mauro 025888
Číž, Marian 034436
Claassen, Garth 042545
Claassen, Uwe 018534
Clabby, Paul 046223
Claes, Gabrielle 003337
Claessens Peré, Nanette 003196
Claesson, Anna Maria 036361
Clair, Cynthia 046210
Clam-Martinic, Dr. M.C.D. 002149
Clancey, Erin 045464
Clancy, John L. 048780
Clap, Sylvestre 010593
Clapham, Peter 041236
Clapperton, Raymond 030494
Clarck, Trinkett 041692
Clare, Roy 040243, 040279
Clarés, María Jesús 035978
Claret, Sawador 035875
Claret de Gouvêia, Antônio M. 004256
Clarin jr., Oligario L. 031688
Clark, Andrew 001474
Clark, Becky 046604
Clark, Charles T. 042968
Clark, Christa 047285
Clark, Donald 044257
Clark, Elaine R. 044320
Clark, Gayle 047436
Clark, Helen 039412
Clark, James 046932
Clark, Joann 045858
Clark, Kathy M. 046710
Clark, L.R. 001178
Clark, Mary K. 047315
Clark, Michael J. 048725, 048726
Clark, Neva 042527
Clark, Dr. Niki R. 047141, 047143
Clark, Patrick S. 048034
Clark, Peter 044067
Clark, Peter P. 043139
Clark, Phillip 045396
Clark, Richard H. 049096
Clark, Robert A. 038704
Clark, Roger 038810, 038859
Clark, Ronilee 047828
Clark, Scott 047646
Clark, Tom 048750
Clark, Vicky A. 047058
Clark, William 044955
Clark jr., William 046351
Clark, William H. 042099
Clark-Bedard, Sharon 006036
Clark-Langager, Sarah 042120
Clarke, A.H. 000858
Clarke, Alicia 047940
Clarke, B. 038962
Clarke, Cliff 005423
Clarke, David 030423
Clarke, Ignatius 022829
Clarke, Jane 047542
Clarke, Jay 042820
Clarke, Jeremy 040847
Clarke, Jerrie 048728
Clarke, Jo 040944
Clarke, Judith 040688
Clarke, Michael 039406
Clarke, Patrick 048346
Clarke, Robert 038467
Clarke, Ron 039152
Clarke, Sandi 000876
Clarke, T. Henry 049024
Clarke Di Vico, Carol 042026
Clary, Owen 041582
Clason, Anders 036297
Clatworthy, J.C. 038732
Claude, Ètienne 003287
Clausen, Charles 045869
Clausen, H. Erhardt 008815
Clausen, Jochen 018490
Clausen, Kim .. 008900, 009100, 009102, 009103, 009104
Clausen, Kirstin 005155
Clausen, Williy 037075
Clausnitzer, Regina 017564
Clauß, Dr. Gisela 018794
Clauß, Horst 018784
Claussen, Louise Keith 041901
Clavel, Sylvie 013634
Clavier, Michel 003645
Clavijo, Martha Isabel 007621
Clavijo Colom, Moraima 008006
Clawson, Rita 042072
Clay Chace, Helen 046333
Clayden, K. 040114
Clayden, Stephen 006354
Cleal, Rosamund 038550
Clear, Celia 040299, 040300
Clearwater, Bonnie 045817
Cleary, Chris 001372
Cleasby, I.W.J. 038518
Cleere, Sonny 047785
Clegg, R.E. 005598
Clegg, Dr. W.H. 041226
Clemens, George 042148
Clemens, Dr. Lukas 020483
Clemens, M. 012912
Clemens, William 043294
Clemens, William A. 042163
Clemenson, Gaye 044920
Clement, Christine 040284
Clement, Constance 046227
Clement, M. 013187
Clement, Rika 042289
Clement, T.A. 041431
Clement von Rehekampff, Uta 018505, 053236
Clemente, Milagros 031631
Clements, D.E. 040225
Clements, Gayle 048653
Clements, Louis 047385
Clements, Lynn B. 048799
Clemons, Veda 045697
Clendaniel, Dianne 042016
Clerc, Jacques 036968
Clergue, Yolande 010469
Clette, Michele 003332
Cleveland, David 040604
Cleveland, James C. 047384
Cleveland, Richard L. 048080
Cleven, E. 029346
Clevenger, A. Colin 044048
Clevenger, Martha 047670
Clevenger, Martha R. 045397
Clews, Stephen 038630
Cleyet-Merle, J.J. 012621
Cliffe, L. 041022
Clifford, B. 040268
Clifford, Timothy 039406, 039424
Clifton, Dan 043559
Clifton, James 044648
Clifton, Dr. James 044655
Clifton, Julia 047971
Clin, Marie-Véronique 013677
Cline, Garry 041703
Cline, Kim 044081
Cline, Raymond 046577
Clinger, Melinda 047470
Clinkingbeard, Brion 045490
Clinton, Tom 044279
Clitheroe, G. 040713
Clodfelter, Lee 042442
Clos Llombart, Jordi 034945
Close, Elisabeth 000974
Close, Freddy 003415
Close, Oliver 000857
Cloudman, Ruth 045498
Clouter, Carl 005494
Clow, John R. 049061
Clow, Jon 044856
Clow, Wayne 048412
Cluff, Raydene 047600
Cluver, Dr. M.A. 034592
Clyve, Lynda 042011
Coates, G. 005546
Coates, Ross 047283
Cobarg, Dr. Merete 019218
Cobb, Myrna 005235
Cobban, Janet 005607, 006833
Cobbe, Toy L. 045714
Cobble, Kelly 047301
Cobbold, A.G.B. 038926
Cobert, William 046284
Cobo, Maria 042462
Cobos Colmenares, Carlos Eduardo 007591
Cobos Wilkins, Juan 035499
Cobridges, Robert 046028
Coburn, Dr. Carol 044931
Coburn, Oakley H. 048264
Cocartă, Adrian 032862
Cocea, Sergio Eduardo 000676
Cochat, L. 014939
Cochener, Margaret M. 047466
Cochran, Barbara 042642
Cochran, Dorothy 046414
Cochrane, G. 039282
Cochrane, Tim 044271
Cockrill, Pauline 000732, 000737
Cocks, Dr. R. 040245
Cocordas, Eleni 046351
Cocuz, Prof. Ioan 032943
Coday, Jean C. 045646
Codding, Mitchell A. 046346
Codega, Antonio 025369
Codicé Pinelli, Dr. Ferruccio 023540
Codreanu, Elena 032895
Cody, George 046208
Coe, John G. 042816
Coekelbergs, Prof. R. 003856
Coelewij, L. 029230
Coelho, Conceição 032682
Coelho Bartholo, Dr. Maria de Lourdes 032586
Coellen, Claudia 037760
Coenen, Luc 003603, 003604
Coënen, Michel 015368
Coers, Frits 030227
Coetzee, F.P. 034720
Coffelt, Jon 042220
Coffen, Charles 006452
Coffey, Jeanne 044554
Coffey, John W. 047313
Coffrini, Ermes 023515
Cogan, Stanley 043876, 043878
Cogar, William 046116
Cogeval, Guy 005938, 013718
Cogswell, Arnold 044526
Cohalan, Mary Lou 043572
Cohen, A. 023053
Cohen, David A. 047169
Cohen, Evelyne 013639
Cohen, Françoise 013418, 013422
Cohen, Jack 046974
Cohen, Janie 042526
Cohen, Judith 023059
Cohen, Marvin H. 045843
Cohen, Nancy 048424
Cohen, Patricia 000229
Cohen, Richard S. 046836
Cohen, Sandor 041931
Cohen, Sylvia 043636
Cohen-Straytner, Barbara 046390
Cohn, Arthur B. 048761
Cohn, Marjorie B. 042560, 042560
Cohon, Dr. Robert 044924
Cohrs, Karin 018036
Cohrs, Peter 018036
Coibanu, Doina 032820
Coish, Theresa 046189
Coker, Gylbert 048550
Čolakov, Dimităr 004899
Colardelle, Michel 013717
Colardelle, Renée 012019
Colassi, David 046340
Colato, Juan 045472
Colazo, Susana 000509
Colbert, Brigitte de 013206
Colburn, Bolton 045095
Colby, James 044828, 044830
Coldren, James 043677
Cole, Burna 041674
Cole, Everett 042667
Cole, Felicity 040575
Cole, Garrett 042010
Cole, Geoffrey 038565
Cole, Ina 040918, 040922

Cole, Jane . . . 005980
Cole, K. . . . 034608
Cole, Paul B . . . 006788
Cole, Richard . . . 040238
Cole, Vicki . . . 047910
Cole, William H. . . . 041970
Cole-Will, Becky . . . 042013, 042014
Colegial Gupierrez, Juan Diego . . . 007460
Coleman, C. Allen . . . 047015
Coleman, Don . . . 043873
Coleman, Dorothy J . . . 046246
Coleman, Evelyn . . . 022815
Coleman, Jane . . . 042368
Coleman, Mary Ruth . . . 041637
Coleman, Rhonda . . . 047792
Coleman, Roddy . . . 040154
Coleman, Winifred E. . . . 049079
Coles, Alec . . . 040547, 040550, 041049, 041163
Coles, David . . . 040950
Coley, Dwaine C. . . . 044531
Colin, N. . . . 003439
Colina, Gay . . . 048978
Colitti, Raffaele . . . 023619
Coll, Tom . . . 049352
Coll Conesa, Dr. Jaume . . . 035985
Coll Gormley, Jean . . . 044497
Colla, Francis . . . 003434
Collado, Elisa . . . 035584
Collas, Josiane . . . 011629
Colle, Jean-Pierre . . . 011951
Colle, Marcella . . . 003512
Collens, David R. . . . 046079
Collett, Keith L. . . . 000851
Collett, Morine . . . 044773
Collett, V. . . . 040660
Collette, Dr. Alfred T. . . . 048456, 048460
Collette, Louis Jeffery . . . 045807
Collier, Caroline . . . 038855
Collier, Ric . . . 047775
Collier, Shirley . . . 040095
Collin, Dr. Gérard . . . 010789
Collin, Ludo . . . 003467
Colling, Guy . . . 027895
Collings, Donna . . . 005903
Collins, Anne . . . 041329
Collins, Belva . . . 042244
Collins, Craig . . . 042309
Collins, D. . . . 045627
Collins, D. Cheryl 045628, 045631, 045632, 045633
Collins, David . . . 046214
Collins, Dr. Des . . . 006627
Collins, George . . . 044322
Collins, James H. . . . 043473, 045958
Collins, John . . . 042275
Collins, Lin . . . 040539
Collins, Louanne . . . 040379
Collins, Lynn . . . 001582
Collins, Mary . . . 047282
Collins, Michael . . . 045519
Collins, Paul W. . . . 047951
Collins, Philip . . . 040451
Collins, Thom . . . 042922
Collins, Thomas F. . . . 042554
Collins, Toni I. . . . 043716
Collins, Vickie . . . 046967
Collins Blackmon, Mary . . . 041924
Collins Coleman, Clara . . . 047668
Collinson, Howard . . . 044768
Collu, Cristiana . . . 024978
Colman, Devin A. . . . 047702
Colombi Ferretti, Dr. Anna . . . 024071
Colombié, Ervé . . . 014452
Colombino, Carlos . . . 031439, 031446
Colombo, Dr. Tarcisio . . . 023752
Colombo Dougoud, R. . . . 037130
Colomer, Laia . . . 034809
Colon, Anibal . . . 047627
Colon, Constance B. . . . 048375
Colonna, Cécile . . . 014125
Colonna, Vittoria . . . 023609
Colonna Ceccaldi, Michel . . . 015186
Colossi, David . . . 046340
Colović, Milosav . . . 034259
Colpaert, Hilde . . . 003539, 003540
Colt, Elizabeth R. . . . 049059
Colton, Elizabeth . . . 047891
Colton, Fiona . . 039702, 039703, 039704, 039833
Columbano, Dr. Juan Carlos . . . 000429
Columbo, Colleen . . . 005518
Colvia, Dr. Anna . . . 025542
Colvin, Richard D. . . . 045601
Colwell, Bruce . . . 046551
Comanducci, Dr. Francesco . . . 025743
Comas Estatella, Dr. Antonio . . . 036042
Comba, Steve . . . 042938
Combe, Anette . . . 037404, 037405
Combe, Jean . . . 037669
Comber, Robert James . . . 005622
Combs, Dr. Dave . . . 045414
Combs, Robert K. . . . 043942
Comeau, Cy . . . 005077
Comeault, Maurice . . . 006385
Comer, Karen . . . 041853
Comer, Michael . . . 046243
Comingore, B.J. . . . 048107
Comish, James R. . . . 046585
Comlan Godonou, Alain . . . 003893
Commandeur, Beatrix . . . 015970
Commock, Tracy . . . 026385, 026392
Communeau, Matthieu . . . 011568
Compagno, Dr. L.J.V. . . . 034586
Compagno-Roeleveld, M.A. . . . 034586
Compaore, Benilde . . . 004962
Comparin, Guy . . . 012012
Complo, Jennifer . . . 044737
Compton, Richard . . . 040839
Comte, Philippe . . . 013748
Comtois, George S. . . . 045269
Cona, Dr. Cherubino . . . 025770
Conable, Mary . . . 048867
Conceição Correia, Maria da . . . 032609
Condeescu, Dan Alexandru . . . 032805
Conder, Marjorie D. . . . 047774
Condette, Jean-François . . . 015050
Condos, Lena . . . 000968, 000969
Condurache, Val . . . 032884
Cone, Ellen . . . 046778
Coneva, Tanja . . . 004845
Confessore, Lisa-Marie . . . 047997
Conforti, Michael . . . 049187
Cong, Pham Van . . . 049540
Conger, Ivan A. . . . 046763
Conihout, Isabelle de . . . 013555
Conijn, G.H. . . . 029520
Conijn, N.W. . . . 029256
Conisbee, Philip . . . 048924
Conkle Davis, Gloria . . . 041830
Conklin, David . . . 043435
Conklin, Jo-Ann . . . 047253
Conkright, Lance . . . 049069
Conley, Alston . . . 042811
Conley, Angela . . . 040416
Conley, Carolyn . . . 049165
Conley, Maria . . . 041576
Conlon, Beth . . . 042963
Conlon, Tim . . . 043512
Connaughton, Vincent . . . 022828
Conneau, Jean-Claude . . . 011459
Connell, Dr. D.P. . . . 039884
Connell, John . . . 005256
Connell, Louise . . . 040618
Connelly, Nancy . . . 043074
Connelly, Stephen . . . 038953
Connemann, Elfi . . . 016546
Connemann, Hans-Joachim . . . 016546
Conner, Dorisanna . . . 046787
Conner, Jill . . . 044207
Connolly, Thomas . . . 043746
Connolly, Tracy . . . 030480
Connor, Brian . . . 030487
Connor, Kathy . . . 047480
Connor, Lorraine . . . 045582
Connors, Dennis . . . 048459
Conocido, Domicilio . . . 028225
Conopask, Karen . . . 046849
Conover, Margaret . . . 048117
Conrad, Dr. Christofer . . . 020365
Conrad, Geoffrey . . . 042266
Conrad, Dr. J. . . . 017414
Conrads, Margaret . . . 044924
Consagre, Franesca . . . 047676
Consey, Kevin . . . 042166
Considine, Brian . . . 045433
Conso, Prof. Giovanni . . . 025588
Console, Dr. Ester Maria . . . 049422
Constable, S. . . . 040596
Constant Noanti, Mahoun . . . 003890
Constantino De La Penna, Carol . . 035881
Constantopoulos, Dr. Jim . . . 047152
Consuelo Dominguez Cuanalo, Delia del . . . 028675
Contarino, Dr. Giuseppe . . . 023114
Contassot, Cécile . . . 012013
Conte, Cynthia . . . 042765
Conte, Dr. Robert S. . . . 049145
Conte, Roxana Diaz . . . 000502
Contessa, Gregorio . . . 024594
Conti, Prof. Dr. Luigi Francesco . . . 024284
Conti, Richard C. . . . 046502
Conti, Roberto . . . 024876
Conticello, Prof. Dr. Baldassare . . . 023502, 025933
Conticello, Dr. Baldo . . . 024746
Contiguglia, Georgianna . 043401, 048610, 048611, 048613
Contini, Dr. Roberto . . . 016049
Contreras, Mamerto . . . 031765
Contreras, Pilar . . . 028471
Contreras Martínez, José Eduardo . 028889
Contro, Antonia . . . 042856
Conway, Allen C. . . . 046186
Conway, Cari . . . 046443
Conway, James . . . 043443
Conway, Steven . . . 003902
Conwell, Idella M. . . . 045650
Conyers, Wayne . . . 045571
Conzen, Dr. Fritz . . . 016825
Conzen, Dr. Ina . . . 020365
Coode, Linda . . . 039589
Coogan, Steve . . . 047500
Cook, Emma . . . 041320, 041336
Cook, Janel . . . 045535
Cook, Jenny . . . 047279
Cook, Joyce A. . . . 043878
cook, Judith H. . . . 047403
Cook, Lee . . . 048050
Cook, Mary Jo . . . 046087
Cook, Patrick . . . 041389
Cook, Robert . . . 046817
Cook, Silas B. . . . 047171
Cook, Steven . . . 005359
Cook, Thomas . . . 043075
Cook, Wendy . . . 041445
Cooke, Bill . . . 045260
Cooke, Glenn . . . 001474
Cooke, Krista . . . 006118
Cooke, Lynne . . . 042069, 046324
Cooke, Michael 026382, 026386, 026388, 026398
Cooke, Pat . . . 022757, 022768
Cooke, Patrick . . . 039254
Cooke, Pattie . . . 045480
Cooke, Susan . . . 040341
Cooke, Victoria . . . 046263
Cooke, Vina . . . 040538
Cookendorfer, Betty . . . 044448
Coolidge, Jennifer . . . 043332
Coolidge, John . . . 045150
Coombe, JoAnne . . . 043523
Coombs, Charles R. . . . 043548
Coombs, Gary B. . . . 044240
Coombs, Dr. Margery C. . . . 041695
Coombs, Robert . . . 049149
Coombs, Dr. Walter A. . . . 041695
Coomer, Robert . . . 043681, 048752
Cooney Frelinghuysen, Alice . . . 046364
Coopen, Barry . . . 041944
Cooper, Andrea . . . 043047
Cooper, Avis . . . 030493
Cooper, Bernard F. . . . 048187
Cooper, Grant . . . 030470
Cooper, Harry . . . 042560
Cooper, Helen . . . 046228
Cooper, Jo-Ann . . . 001238
Cooper, John . . . 040034
Cooper, Linda G. . . . 049356
Cooper, Linda L. . . . 049039
Cooper, Norman . . . 005817
Cooper, Rhonda . . . 048379
Cooper, Robert L.D. . . . 039393
Cooper, Ronna . . . 046922
Cooper, Rosemary . . . 040565
Cooper, S. . . . 039782
Cooper, Todd . . . 045752
Cooper, Virginia . . . 006589
Cooper Case, Carolyn . . . 047404
Coopmans, H. . . . 029265
Coote, Sylvia . . . 041144
Cop, Eddy . . . 003190
Cope, Michael W. . . . 039838
Copeland, Jackie . . . 042006
Copeland-Burns, Carla . . . 045274
Copeley, William N. . . . 043124
Copp, V.E. . . . 038794
Coppens, Marguerite . . . 003353
Coppernoll, Lee . . . 045898
Coppieters, Pierre . . . 003653
Coppola, Gianfranco . . . 025663
Coppola, Regina . . . 041696
Coppus, G.M. . . . 030182
Coquemelle, Lucie . . . 012718
Coral, Laurent de . . . 014346
Corazza, Dr. Carla . . . 024103
Corbat, Marc . . . 037416
Corbet, Glenn . . . 047437
Corbett, Agnes . . . 042580
Corbett, Gary . . . 001303
Corbett, Patricia . . . 012869
Corbett-Cyr, Susan . . . 006126
Corbier, René . . . 011095
Corbin, Dr. James E. . . . 046119
Corbin, Kendall W. . . . 045914
Corblet de Fallerans, J. . . . 015001
Corbould, Lola . . . 001031
Corbu, Emilia . . . 032942
Corcoran, M. . . . 022765
Corcos, Sidney . . . 022965
Corcuera, Catalina . . . 028423
Cordaro, Dr. Michele . . . 025474
Cordell, Prof. Linda S. . . . 042354
Corder, Russ . . . 047090
Cordero, Dr. Mario . . . 024012
Cordero Miranda, Prof. Gregorio . . 003918
Cordes, D. . . . 030453
Cordes, David . . . 043431
Cordonnier, Aude . . . 011667
Cordova-Gonzalez, Julia . . . 006909
Coreth, Peter . . . 002805
Corey, Mark . . . 044320
Coria, Rodolfo . . . 000477
Corio, Amedeo . . . 026275
Corkern, Wilton C. . . . 041574
Corkill, Nick . . . 040679, 040680
Corkum, Kate . . . 046191
Cormack, Anna E. . . . 041247, 041248
Cormack, Malcolm . . . 047429
Cormier, Angèle . . . 005897
Cormier, George Ann . . . 047136
Cormier, Lisette . . . 005263
Cornejo Gutiérrez, Miguel Angel . . 031504
Cornelis, J.P. . . . 003691
Cornelissen, Leo M. . . . 029233
Cornelissen, S. . . . 030085
Cornelius, Betty L. . . . 046825
Cornelius, Patsy . . . 049021
Cornelius, Dr. St. . . . 034687, 034688
Cornelius, Steffi . . . 016213
Corner, Rita . . . 006572
Cornet, Josep . . . 034924

Cornett, James 046798
Cornez, G. 003725
Corniani, Maurizio 024602
Cornick, N. 003705
Cornini, Dr. Guido 049422
Cornu, Bernard 012867
Cornwall, Bev 045028
Cornwell, John 001152
Coroiu, Dr. Ioan 032839
Corominas de Basso, Raquel 000397
Coronel, Maria Delia 031658
Corrado, Fabrizio 026052
Correa Sutil, Dr. Sofía 006935
Correia, Dr. Alberto 032702, 032703
Correia, Dr. Virgilio H. 032607
Corrigan, David J. 044461
Corrin, Lisa 048091
Corry, Corrine 006283
Corry, L. 040643
Corser, Elizabeth 005285
Corsini, Principessa 024154
Cort, Cynthia 044292
Cort, Louise 048884, 048908
Cortenova, Prof. Giorgio 026283
Cortes, Prof. Erlinda S. 031803
Cortés Gomez, Carlos 028428
Cortese, Prof. Gemma 025534
Corteville, Julie 013176
Cortez, Miguel 042875
Cortina, Leonor 028445
Cory, David H. 047601
Cory, Jeff 042827
Corzo, Miguel-Angel 046985
Corzo Sánchez, Jorge Ramón 035859
Cosandier, Juliane 037241
Coşereanu, Valentin 032885
Cosgrove, Patricia 041892
Coski, Dr. John M. 047421
Cosmetatos, Helen 021145
Cossa, Egidio 025555
Cossart, Graham 000863
Cossignani, Dr. Tiziano 024016
Cosson, Maurice 011275
Costa, Diane 047936
Costa, Elisabeth 032639
Costa, Dr. Gian Paolo 024067
Costa, Prof. Giovanni 023765
Costa, John 047386
Costa jr., Luís da 029052
Costamagna, Dr. Alba 025542
Costamagna, Liliana 025939
Costantini, Dr. Lorenzo 025548
Costar, John 030599
Costard, Matthew P. 040903
Costas Loyola, José E. 032721
Coste, Pierre 010650
Costello, Noel 001141
Costelloe, Jean 022848, 022849
Costely, Nigel 041228
Coster, Annie de 003860
Costersian, John 044202
Costescu, Cornelia 032927
Costie, Gord 005013
Costopoulos Weeks, Jeanne 042848
Costoulas, Costas 021278
Coté, Michel 012831
Cote, Richard 048896
Cotie, Donna 006391
Cott, Peter 039628
Cotter, Patrick 022721
Cotter, Suzanne 040659
Cotter, William 048999
Cotterill, F.D.P. 049579
Cottino, Prof. Alberto 026064
Cottino, Peter 023194
Cotton, Areca 049380
Cotton, Carol 044197
Cotton, Gordon A. 048778
Cottrell, Robert 048495
Cotty, Céline 012378
Couaille, C. le 013203
Couch, Charles Walter 041799
Coudrot, Jean-Louis 011317
Coudurier, Yvonne 013318
Coughlan, M. 001320
Coughlin, Richard J. 045022
Coulombe, Marie-Christine 006678
Coulombier, Jean-Luc 014356
Coulon, François 014023
Coulon, Gérard 012304, 014160
Coumans, Paul 029147
Coumans, P.M.W. 029156
Counot, Bernard 012668
Cour Dragsbo, Peter la 009112
Courson, Bruce A. 047934
Courtelarre, Henry 011081
Courter, Sally 042301
Courtial, M.C. 012788
Courtiour, Jon 041233
Courtney, Janice 047623
Courtney, Kathryn 044067
Courtney, Vernon 049171
Courtois, Jean-Pierre 003473
Couser, Carol 045343
Cousillas, Ana María 000192
Cousin, M. 010735
Cousino, Beate 010687
Cousinou, Olivier 012934
Coutagne, Denis 010296
Coutheillas, Didier 011748
Coutts, Herbert 039429
Coutts, Howard 038596
Couturas, Francis 013773
Couture, André 006229
Couture, Llyr E. 043493
Couture, Raoul F. 043493
Couty, Paul-Henry 010806
Coventry, Susan 040192
Covey, Dustin 005399
Cowan, Joan 005428
Cowart, Jack 048891
Cowburn, Ian 012427
Cowden, Chris 041940
Cowden, Dorothy C. 048491
Cowell, Lorraine 048827
Cowell, R. 040030
Cowell, Tom 006815
Cowley, Liz 038693
Cowley, Paul 039300
Cowling, A. 040596
Cowling, Dr. Mary 039431
Cowling, Sue 046702
Cox, Arrington 043080, 043083
Cox, Charlotte 046017
Cox, Dan 045666
Cox, Dr. Douglas C. 047273
Cox, Eileen 039322
Cox, Janet 042980
Cox, Janson L. 042235
Cox, Katherine 044684
Cox, Marilyn 046010
Cox, N.R. 039590
Cox, Richard 042459
Cox, Rosemary 042081
Cox, Steven 041905
Cox-Paul, Lori 044725
Coxe, Trudy 046464
Coxson, Michael 041467
Coyle, D.C. 006212
Coyne, Richard F. 042992
Cozza, Prof. Lucas 025488
Crabtree, Andrew 038791
Crabtree, John 048691
Cracket, Alan 041111
Craft, John J. 046931
Crago, Jody 049135
Craig, Gerry 047563
Craig, Joanna 042582
Craig, Len 001418
Craig, Martin 049085
Craig, Neil 041106
Craighead, Linda 046804
Crailsheim, Freiherr Ortholf von . . 015534
Crain, Sandra 044750
Cramer, Carole 047249
Cramer, Jeffrey S. 045300
Cramer, John 048977
Cramer, Patricia T. 049110
Cramer, Sue 001517
Cramer, Wendy 046232
Cramer-Petersen, Lars 008827
Crampton, Lewis S.W. 047497
Crampton, S. 034565
Crampton, Sharon 034562
Crandall, Daniel T. 047177
Crane, Karen R. 044888, 048197
Crane, Prof. Peter 039858
Crane, Susan 048060
Cranson, Diane 000727
Craughwell-Varda, Kathy 048038
Craven, Jane 044815
Craven, K. 040944
Craven, Tim 041058
Crawford, C. 006277
Crawford, Dr. Clifford 044105
Crawford, Henry B. 045513
Crawford, James 042591
Crawford, Louise J. 045955
Crawford, Nina 005327
Crawford, Dr. Richard 044263
Crawford, Robert 040402
Crawford, R.W.K. 040182
Crawford, Shirley 041629
Crawford, Vivian 026385
Crawford-Gore, Betsy 045176
Crawley, Tracey 041089
Creal, Carolyn 048263
Creamer, Winifred 043373
Crean, Kristen 047163
Creary, Marilou 046564
Creasey, Michael 047265
Creddes, Jean 005626
Credland, Arthur G. 039883, 039888, 039890
Creech, C.L. 045033
Creecy, Kerry 001083
Creedon, Denise 046014
Creemers, Guido 003798, 003799
Creemers, Harry 042760
Crégut, Dr. Evelyne 010597
Creighton, Martha 048843
Crelot, Stefan 003644
Cremer, Kurt 015426
Cremers, Filip 003818
Crenshaw, Louise 043052
Crenzien, Helle 008938
Crépin-Leblond, Thierry . 010843, 010845, 010848
Crésis, Eric 003568
Crespo, Michael 042052
Crespo-Burgos, Dr. Antonio 009252
Crespo Gulíérrez, Victoria 035433
Cressey, Dr. Pamela J. 041634
Creste, Chantal 013198
Creutzburg, Gerlinde 019517
Creutzburg, Ralf 018200
Creuz, Serge 003305
Crevecœur, Claude F. 003850
Crew, Keith 046998
Crews, Gerald 005528
Crick, Monique 037121
Crider, Gwendolyn 041919
Cripe, Roy 045332
Crippa, Flavio 024278
Crippen, Donna 043630
Crişan, Eva 032834
Crise jr., Robert 043442
Crispini, Prof. Giuseppe 025685
Cristofoli, Raoul 026057
Cristofoli, Vincent 012276, 013441, 013443
Cristofolini, Prof. Renato 023761
Critchlow, William H. 005856
Crites, Dr. Gary 045039
Crittin, Jean-François 037008
Crnković, Prof. Vladimir 007838
Crociata, Mariano 024623
Crocker, P.A. 038942
Crocker, Piers 031228
Croft, Brenda L. 000888
Croft, Evelyn 047604
Crofts, Nicholas 037128
Croke, Fionnuala 022763
Croker, R.C. 030447
Crokett, James 041981
Croll, Prof. Dr. Gerhard 002556
Croll, Helen 000885
Crombe, Polly 046696
Cromer, Lorelei 043871
Cromie, Cheryl-Anne 034639
Crompton, John 038783
Cronin, J.J. 039786
Cronin, Michael 046388
Cronin, Thomas E. 048835
Cronlund, Carl-Johan 036655
Crook, Rosemary 039658
Crook, Rosie 039663
Cropera, Dr. Carla 024118
Cropp, Aubrey 030456
Cros, Caroline 013630
Crosby, Bill 039638
Crosby Tasker, Sheila 047507
Crosman, Christopher B. 047506
Cross, Christine 042090
Cross, Dave 006886
Cross, Sharon 038954
Cross, Tony 038499, 038500
Crossland, Leonard B. 021110
Crossland, Maynard 045237
Crothers, George M. 045268
Croton, G. 030508
Crotti, Pierre 037243
Crouch, Ned 042954
Crouch, Philip 041448
Crous, Dr. D. 034585
Crouy-Chanel, Bernard de 012275
Crowdy, Hannah 039995
Crowe, Dr. D. 041833
Crowe, K.L. 041067
Crowell, Darryl 005191
Crowell, Stephen 047290
Crowell, Stewart A. 046268
Crowl, Bill 046451
Crowley, Noel 022784
Crowley, Terry 001067
Crowter, Philip 038821
Croy, David E. 043185
Crozemarie, Gilles 011372
Crozzolin, Umberto 026123
Crué, Emmanuel 011388
Cruège, Robert 014934
Crüzer, Cristina 037595
Cruise, Sandra 040805
Crum, Katherine 048254
Crum, Dr. Katherine B. 046596
Crum, Patricia 047277
Crum, Rebecca 048970
Crump, Caroline 034658
Crusan, Ronald L. 044023
Crusoe, Lewis D. 045553
Crutchfield, Sharon 041878
Cruvinel, Márcio Borges 004589
Cruz, Amparo Magdaleno de la . . . 035993
Cruz, Fe M. de la 031727
Cruz, Martin 036016
Cruz, Prudenciana C. 031716, 031738
Cruz, Sumra I. de la 031679
Csaplar, Dr. Ferenc 021659
Csar, Mary 042281
Cséfalvay, Pál 021723
Cserei, Dr. Ladislav 034420
Cseri, Dr. Miklós 021886
Cserményi, Vajk 021872
Cservenyák, László 021781
Csillag, Péter 021675
Csobádi, Jozef 034419
Csütörtöky, Jozef 034363
Čtvrtník, Dr. Pavel 008645, 008771
Cuadrado, Emeterio 035527
Čubareva, Roza Petrovna 033614
Cubrić, Ljiljana 034173
Cucchi, Franco 025881
Cuccuini, Dr. Piero 024181

Čučković, Lazo . . . 007732
Cuda, Dr. Maria Teresa . . . 023830
Cudahy, Michael J. . . . 045887
Cudbill, Carolyn . . . 038832
Čudnova, Lidija Aleksandrovna . . . 033899
Cudworth, Keith R. . . . 045334
Cuello, Juan Pablo . . . 041543
Cuervo de Jaramillo, Elvira . . . 007450
Cuevas, Elena . . . 031736
Cuevas y Lara, Mónica . . . 028524
Čuhelová, Blanka . . . 008703
Čuk, Prof. Dragan . . . 034286
Cukić, Milica . . . 034163
Ćuković, Petar . . . 034186
Cukrov, Tonćika . . . 007854
Culbertson, Gary . . . 049334
Čulig, Igor . . . 007732
Cullen, Deborah . . . 046369
Cullen, Maggie . . . 039225
Cullen, M.L. . . . 041264
Culligan, Jenine . . . 044684
Cullinan, Deborah . . . 047865
Cullingford, N.A. . . . 039369
Cullman, Lewis B. . . . 048254
Cullmann, Dorothy . . . 048254
Culot, Maurice . . . 003300, 003314
Culpepper, Marilyn . . . 045951
Culver, Michael . . . 046635
Cumbey, Susan G. . . . 041639
Cumming, Glen . . . 006830
Cummings, Dorothy A. . . . 034288
Cummings, Ernst E. . . . 043803
Cummings, Fern P. . . . 042517
Cummings, Mary Lou . . . 046224
Cummings, Ruth S. . . . 045736
Cummins, Alissandra . . . 003124
Cummins, Dr. D. Duane . . . 042176
Cummins, Heather . . . 041036
Cummins, Karen . . . 048605
Cummins McNitt, R. . . . 041672
Cunard, Gail C. . . . 044252
Cunia, Claudia . . . 003032
Cunliffe-Lister, E.S. . . . 038915
Cunning, Lois . . . 043616
Cunningham, Beth . . . 045395
Cunningham, Clark . . . 048713
Cunningham, Deirdre . . . 047480
Cunningham, Denyse M. . . . 043930, 043931
Cunningham, Eleanor W. . . . 044329
Cunningham, Jewel . . . 006361, 006373
Cunningham, Jo . . . 041163
Cunningham, Kim . . . 044822
Cunningham, Michael R. . . . 042985
Cunningham, Noreen . . . 040573, 040574
Cunningham, Patrick . . . 006861
Cunningham, Patrick J. . . . 042501
Cunningham, Scott . . . 044822
Cuno, Prof. James . . . 040126
Cunz, Dr. Rainer . . . 017765
Cunz, Dr. Reiner . . . 017766
Cupitt, John . . . 040241
Cupp, Franzas . . . 048450
Curbastro, Riccardo Ricci . . . 023653
Curda, Dr. Andreas . . . 002897
Curdy, Philippe . . . 037563
Curiger, Bice . . . 037777
Curling, Marianne J. . . . 044459
Curran, Donald . . . 044529
Curran, Emily . . . 042338
Currat, Joseph . . . 037669
Currell, M. . . . 000770
Currey, David . . . 046155
Currie, Gloria . . . 006406
Currier, Janice . . . 045502
Currin, Robert . . . 044123
Curry, Collette . . . 041110
Curry, Larrie Spier . . . 044454
Curry, Michael . . . 045372
Curry, Michael P. . . . 044414
Curtet, Jean-Christophe . . . 037112
Curtin, Donna D. . . . 047099
Curtis, Brian . . . 045793
Curtis, Dr. J. . . . 040097
Curtis, John . . . 041654
Curtis, Linda . . . 004992
Curtis, Neil . . . 038449
Curtis, Nellie K. . . . 046614
Curtis, Penelope . . . 039953
Curtis, Ron . . . 000825
Curtis, S. . . . 004998
Curtis, Sue . . . 039199
Curtis, Vaughn . . . 040827
Curtiss, Courtney P. . . . 042282
Curto, Argeo . . . 007785
Curto, Domenico . . . 023663
Curto i Homedes, Albert . . . 035949
Čus Rukonić, Jasminka . . . 007710, 007761
Čušenkov, Valerij Gennadjevič . . . 033537
Cushing, Dr. Paula E. . . . 043406
Cushing, Raymond L. . . . 042991
Cushing, Stanley . . . 042315
Cushman, Brad . . . 045346
Cusiac, Dragoş . . . 032919
Cusick, Bonnie A. . . . 043519
Cusming, J.R. . . . 039475
Čusova, Elena . . . 033393
Cussner, Alice . . . 049328
Cutler, Scott . . . 043634
Cutler, Walter L. . . . 048920
Cutright, Marjorie E. . . . 044674
Cuyper, Chris de . . . 003857
Cuyper, Meve jo de . . . 003143
Čvančara, Alois . . . 008475
Cvetaw, Dragica . . . 007730
Cvetkova, Natalija . . . 004679
Cvetković, Branislav . . . 034195
Cvetković, Marija . . . 034151
Cvitanović, Ivan . . . 007806
Čvorović, Božena . . . 003941
Cybulski, Antoni . . . 032509
Cygański, Janusz . . . 032192
Cyman, Patricia . . . 041618
Cyncar, Nadia . . . 005409
Cypress, Billy L. . . . 042196
Cyr, Jean-Claude . . . 005112
Cytacki, Joe . . . 043934
Cywin, Allison . . . 047264
Czajka, Jacek . . . 032334
Czajkowski, Józef . . . 032440
Czankus, Ruth . . . 042128
Czapiewska, Aleksandra . . . 040258
Czaplewski, Dr. N.J. . . . 046509
Czapska, Zofia . . . 032311
Czarny, Eugenunsz . . . 031962
Czchodzińska-Przybysławska, Anna . . . 032293
Czech, Tony . . . 042950
Czerannowski, Dr. Barbara . . . 016680
Czére, Dr. Andrea . . . 021694
Czerniak, Robert Michał . . . 032276
Czernin, Dr. Martin . . . 002962
Czerw, Ewa . . . 032498
Czerwinski, Bogdan . . . 032342
Czichos, Raymond L. . . . 049227
Czoma, László . . . 021765
Czopek, Sylwester . . . 032301
Czub, Zofia . . . 032306
Czubaczyński, Ryszard . . . 032111
Czuma, Stanislaw . . . 042985
Czymmek, Dr. Götz . . . 018341
Czyżyk, Władysław . . . 032537
Da Pra Galanti, Dr. Lorenzo . . . 025449
Daalder, Dr. R. . . . 029216
D'Abate, Richard . . . 047160, 047165
Dabell, Simon . . . 038754
Dabić, Ljubica . . . 034172
Dabižić, Miodrag . . . 034284
Dabney, Mary K. . . . 046945
Dąbrowska, Anna . . . 031873
Daby, Rebecca . . . 001646
Daccó, Dr. Gian Luigi . . . 024487, 024488, 024489
Dacey, Tim . . . 042005
Dachnenko, Lidija Oleksandrivna . . . 038420
Dackerman, Susan . . . 041969
Dadabaev, K. . . . 049397
Dae, Sung Kwon . . . 027584
Daele, Durandy van den . . . 012418
Daelemans, Danny . . . 003425
Daelemans, Frank . . . 003291
Daellenbach, Dennis . . . 044274
Daems, Gérard . . . 014798
Daenens, L. . . . 003452
Daenzer, Denise . . . 037791
D'Afflitto, Dr. Chiara . . . 025274
Dagan, Zvi . . . 022956
Dagdar, L. . . . 022613
Dage, Carol J. . . . 044721
Dagon, Yoav . . . 023088
Dagorne, Richard . . . 013125, 013127
Daguerre de Hureaux, Alain . . . 014992
Dahan, Arie . . . 023032, 023041, 023095
Dahesh, Dr. A.S.M. . . . 027807, 027810
Dahl, Erling . . . 031119
Dahl, Torveig . . . 030932
Dahlberg, Anne Marie . . . 036639
Dahlbring, Magnus . . . 036306
Dahle, Bernhard . . . 017487
Dahle, Sigrio . . . 006837
Dahlgren, Dorothy . . . 043030
Dahlie, Paul N. . . . 045356
Dahlitz, Ray . . . 000768
Dahlstrom, Harry . . . 044570
Dahm, Klaus . . . 019037
Dahmani, Dr. Saïd . . . 000050
Dahmke, Prof. Dr. A. . . . 018244
Dai, Linyan . . . 007305
Daijoji, Yoshifumi . . . 027349
Dailey, John R. . . . 048922
Dailledouze . . . 014541
Daily, Charles . . . 047967
Daily, Greg . . . 048459
Daily, Steven L. . . . 045893
Daim, Prof. Dr. Falko . . . 002327, 018794
Dajani, Virginia . . . 046281
Daker, Emma . . . 041430
Dakin Hastings, Lynne . . . 048594
Dalborg, Björn . . . 036666
Dalby, Åge . . . 030985
Dale, A.P. . . . 038458
Dale, Charles . . . 047614
Dale Zemlansky, Denise . . . 044400
Dalen, Mary G. . . . 005721
D'Alessandro, Laura . . . 042871
Daley, Jean . . . 043652
Dalhousie, Earl of . . . 039307
Dalichow, Dr. Bärbel . . . 019655
Dalla Vecchia, Fabio M. . . . 024792
Dallago, Antonio . . . 026311
Dallaj, Dr. Arnalda . . . 024692
Dallam, Fred . . . 043588
Dallas, John . . . 038566
Dalleo, Bruce . . . 046211
Dalli, Alberto . . . 025767, 025769
Dallman, Armin . . . 048808
Dallman, Dr. John E. . . . 045594
Dallmeier, Dr. Martin . . . 019748, 019750
Dalous, Pierre . . . 014999
Daloze, M. . . . 003251
Dalsgaard Larsen, Keld . . . 009090
Dalton, Bryan . . . 042523
Dalton, Carolyn . . . 039249
Dalton, Jake . . . 043704
Dalton, Ron . . . 045831
Dalton, Shirley B. . . . 047148
Daly, Beth . . . 048600
Daly, Dr. Eleanor . . . 044800
Daly, James . . . 046366
Daly, Tess . . . 030602
Daly, Thomas . . . 048737
Dalyell, Kathleen . . . 040016
Dám, Dr. László . . . 021802
Dam-den-Gnam, Pithaya . . . 037933
Dama, Prof. Salvatore Cirillo . . . 006925
Damamme, Jeanne . . . 013865, 013866
Daman, F.J. . . . 003164
Damaskinos . . . 021334
D'Amato, Dr. Alfonso . . . 023445
D'Amato, Aurelia . . . 025621
Dambaev, Munko Žartam . . . 032973
Dambergs, Guntis . . . 027799
D'Ambrosio, Anna T. . . . 048719
D'Ambrosio, Dr. Antonio . . . 025304
D'Ambrosio, Paul . . . 043137
D'Ambrosio, Paul . . . 043138
Damdinsuren, Tsedmaa . . . 029005
Damdoumi, Vasiliki . . . 021516
Dame, Susan . . . 043475, 047757
Damgaard, Ellen . . . 009009, 009010
Damgaard Sørensen, Tinna . . . 009084
Damian, Paul . . . 032810
Damianov, Nikola . . . 004843
D'Amico, Prof. Claudio . . . 023443
Damito, Dr. Ronaldo . . . 004402
Damjanova, Katerina . . . 004644
Damm, Dr. Inciser . . . 018339
Dammel, Werner . . . 019183
D'Amore, Dr. Paola . . . 025548
Dampman, Allan . . . 044698
Damsgaard, Nina . . . 009142
Damy, Ken . . . 023523
Dana, Rae . . . 049056
Dana, Richard . . . 042552
Danailov, Boris . . . 004849
Dance, Pat . . . 006868
Dancey, Jenny . . . 040445
Danchev, Dancho . . . 004717
Dăncuş, Mihai . . . 032937
Dandaura, M. . . . 030690
Dander, Dr. Marilena . . . 024435
Dandison, Basil . . . 049332
Dandwate, P.P. . . . 022302
Danelzik-Brüggemann, Dr. Christoph . . . 016841
Danesi, Claudio . . . 024024
Dangel, Gerhard . . . 017228
D'Angelo, Starlyn . . . 046662
Danh, Prof. Dr. Trinh . . . 049527
Daniel, Alain . . . 010538
Daniel, Andy . . . 044248
Daniel, Françoise . . . 010983
Daniel, Mary . . . 043378
Daniel, Rochette . . . 003312
Daniel McElroy, Susan . . . 040918, 040922
Daniels, Christopher . . . 044344
Daniels, John P. . . . 046873
Daniels, Marsha . . . 042705
Daniels, R. . . . 039686
Danielsson, Ing-Mari . . . 036692
Danielsson, Ralf . . . 036224
Danielsson, Rolf . . . 036226
Danielsson, Dr. Roy . . . 036448
Danini, Gianluca . . . 024414
Daniylopoulou, Olga . . . 021252
Danjo, Prof. Tatsuo . . . 026433
Dankbar, Johannes . . . 020471
Danker-Carstensen, Peter . . . 019903
Dankl, Dr. Günther . . . 002097
Danly, Dr. Laura . . . 043406
Dann, Alan O. . . . 045692
Dann, Gaston . . . 012666
Danna, Tracy . . . 042080
Danne, Rainer . . . 018088
Danneel, M. . . . 003319
Dannhus, H. . . . 018604
Dano, Dr. Ján . . . 034371
Dansako, Tetsuya . . . 027319
Dansberger, Dorthory . . . 043332
Danson, Stuart . . . 001610
Danšova, Olga Nikolajevna . . . 033597
Dante Coronel, Hugo . . . 000113
Dantinne, Claude . . . 012574
Danzer, Dr. Gudrun . . . 001943
Danzl, Barbara . . . 002663
Dapkyunas, Jeanne . . . 003134
Dapsens, J.-C. . . . 003628
Darakčieva, Uljana . . . 004756
Darakčijska, Uljana . . . 004754
Darby, Daniel . . . 006888
Darde, Dominique . . . 013421
Darga, Dr. Robert . . . 020204
Darke, Don F. . . . 044905

Darling, Denise L. 043323
Darling, L.A. 006651
Darling, Sharon 048041
Darling-Finan, N. 041007
Darmstädter, Dr. Beatrix 002934
Darr, Alan P. 043444
Darst, Lise 044132
Dart, John 038994
Dary 014637
Dary, Anne 010448, 011621, 012743
Das, Chandranath 022069
Das, Dilip A. 046209
Dasbach, Th. P. 029274
Dashiell, David A. 046995
Dassas, Frédéric 013640, 013718
Date, Tatumi 027205
Daubendiek, James 044842
Daubert, Debra 046737
Dauda, J.Y. 030695
Daudelin, Robert 005921
Dauge, Alexandra 012247
Daugelis, Osvaldas 027848
Daughdrill, Kay 043300
Daughhetee, Mark 044888
Daughterman-Maguire, Dr. Eunice 041990
Dauphin, Jean 003572
Daure, Regine 011133
Dauskardt, Dr. Michael 017628
Dautermann, Dr. Christoph 018400
Dautermann Ricciardi, Dana 044024
Dauth, Louise 000891
Dautović, Andrea 003941
Dauwe, Marc 003575
Dávalos de Camacho, Maya 028515
Davaras, Dr. C. 021120
Davatz, Dr. Jürg 037368
Davenport, Kimberly 044652
Davey, Arnold 040774
David, Dr. 042986
David, Dr. A.R. 040406
David, Catherine 030109
David, Johan 003479
David, Josiane 013047
David, Karen 043657
David, Mihai 032786
David, Norma Jean 044341
David, Paul 041386
David, Romeo G. 031643
David, Walfried 017309
David, Wendy 013369
David-Weill, Hélène 013638, 013645, 013668, 013724
Davidov, Dr. Dinko 034151
Davidović, Jasna 034266
Davidović, Jelena 034207
Davidow, Joan 043266
Davidse, I. 030010
Davidson, Anne 046806
Davidson, Prof. C.W. 038786
Davidson, Dan 043205
Davidson, Denny 047037
Davidson, Heather A. 006878
Davidson, John H. 040583
Davidson, Kate 001509
Davidson, Scott 005545
Davies, Alan 039272
Davies, Andrew 039917
Davies, Brian 040735
Davies, Deborah 038771
Davies, Eluned 040044
Davies, Erica 040150
Davies, Hugh M. 045068, 047825
Davies, Jane 005455, 006288
Davies, Jean S. 047072
Davies, Jenny 040364
Davies, Kate 043501
Davies, Kirsty 001587
Davies, Lucy 040073
Davies, M.P. 039304
Davies, Pascal 010539
Davies, Peggy 039587
Davies, R.H. 038758
Davies, Rick 045844
Davies, Rita 006594
Davies, S. 001516
Davies, Simon 040633, 040634
Davies, Steve 040364
Davies, Su 039854, 039856
Davies, Suzanne 001250
Davies, Dr. W.V. 040097
Davignon, Ètienne 003355
Dávila, Alejandro 000306
Davila, Julio V. 031564
Davis, Alice M. 043757
Davis, Dr. Ann 005196
Davis, Ann 041841
Davis, Audrey P. 041635
Davis, Beryl 006549
Davis, Beth 043062
Davis, Betty J. 046678
Davis, Carol A. 043796
Davis, Catherine 043821
Davis, Darwin R. 047642
Davis, David L. 046715
Davis, Dustin P. 044091
Davis, Ellen 046182
Davis, Elliot 042334
Davis, Gainor B. 046006
Davis, Gordon 041908, 041908
Davis, Helen 045677
Davis, Jacqueline B. 043973
Davis, Janet 006790
Davis, Jaqueline Z. 046390
Davis, Joanne 049026
Davis, John 043987
Davis, Karen Lee 045914
Davis, Kate 006258
Davis, Katherine 046395
Davis, Kay 043027
Davis, Kieth 030520
Davis, Dr. Leroy 046707
Davis, Lesia 005207
Davis, Dr. Leslie B. 042375
Davis, Lloyd 046602
Davis, M. 022929
Davis, Michael 048375, 048376
Davis, Nancy 042000
Davis, P.A.C. 030587
Davis, Phillip V. 048288
Davis, Priscilla 005373
Davis, Robert O. 047774
Davis, Ron 005724
Davis, Ruth 041628
Davis, Sarah 046285
Davis, Susan S. 045005
Davis, Tod 048599
Davis, Todd A. 006747
Davis, Walter R. 042609
Davis, William B. 042387
Davis, William J. 046497
Davis, Zina 049076, 049077
Davis Anderson, Brooke . . 046283, 046329
Davis Gardner, Katie 043055
Davison, Fiona 040168
Davison, Hazel 039852
Davison, Liane 006539
Davison, Dr. Patricia 034583
Davisson, Scott 048205
Davletov, B. 049387
Davson, Victor 046422
Davy, Geukens 003561
Davydova, Linaida Aleksandrovna . 033730
Davydova, Natalja Alekseevna . . . 033682
Dawans, Francine 003592
Dawe, Phillip 039535
Dawey, Dr. Chris 045930
Daws, Russell S. 048485
Dawson, Amy 047879
Dawson, Barbara 022749
Dawson, Chris 042989
Dawson, David 038833, 041190
Dawson, E.A. 039029
Dawson, J. 038962, 039134
Dawson, Dr. Mary R. 047044
Dawson, P. 022808
Dawson Penniman, H. 046955
Day, Brenda 041958
Day, Edward 047451
Day, Ginette 012105
Day, Jackie 048377
Day, John A. 048764
Day, Michael . . 039606, 040173, 040911, 040912, 040913, 040916
Day, Patricia 044337
Day, Richard 039051, 048789
Day, Sally 038475
Day, Theodorsa 046815
Dayan, Prof. T. 023094
Dayrit, Marina 031719
Dayson, Diane H. 046408
De Angelis, Prof. Giuseppe 025441
De Filippis, Dr. Elena 026209
De Floren, R. 041577
De Franceschi, Antonio Fernando . 004344
De Herdt, René 003464
De Kelver, Jan 003412
De Lorentiis, Decio 024578
De Luca, Dr. Bianca 023861
De Luca, Maurizio 049422
De Lucia Brolli, Maria Anna 023908
De Marchi, Dr. Andrea G. 025478
De Marco, Dr. Marco 024122
De Martin, Prof. Gian Candito 025235
De Martin, Prof. Giancandido 025231, 025232, 025234
De Mier Riaño, Elisa 007441
De Paepe, Pantxika 010263
De Palma, Prof. Luigi Michele 024776
De Palma, Dr. Maria Camilla 024310, 024311
De Paolis, Rosario 024482
De Pasquale, Vicenzo 024655
De Polo Saibanti, Claudio 024186
De Pompeis, Claudio 025185
De Reymaeker, Michel . . . 003650, 003652
De Rochambeau, M. 014943
De Santi, Claudio 024787, 024788, 024789
De Siena, Antonio 024684
De Simone, Dr. Emilio 023186
De Smet, Urbain 003848
De Strobel, Dr. Anna Maria 049422
De Vincentiis, Prof. Italo 025586
De Vito, Natalie 006613
De Waal, Dr. Lydia M. 034757, 034758
De Witte, Hubert 003263, 003264, 003265, 003266, 003268
Deagan, Dr. K.A. 044103
Deakin, G.T. 001193
Deal, Cliff 045091
Dealy, Anne F. 044164
Dean, Deborah 040615
Dean, Don 048674
Dean, Jeanne 048674
Dean, Jim 046026
Dean, Kevin 048001
Dean, M. 039239
Dean, Sharon 042986
Dean Krute, Carol 044463
Dean Stock, Michele 047731
Deaner, Beth J. 046235
Deans, Arthur 038439
Dear, Elizabeth 044299
Dearing, Vicki 042490
Dearinger, Dr. David 046380
Deaton, Linda 048485
Debain, Yvette 005048
Debal-Morche, Anne 010357, 010360
Debarge, René 012069
Deblanc Magnée, Marie-Paule . . . 003824, 003826
Debo, Thomas A. 047109
Debočički, Valentin 004720, 004721, 004722, 004723, 004725
Dębowska, Alina 031833
Debrabandère, Béatrice 013402
Debrah, Dr. Issac N. 021098
Debray, Cécile 013630
Debrincat, Saviour 028040
DeBruyn, David L. 044278
Debruyn, Raphaël 003578
Debry, Jaques 011304
Debryn, Johan 003763
Debus-Steinberg, Astrid 020369
DeBuse Potter, Gail 042697, 044904
Deca, Eugen 032921
Decames, Jean-Claude 012970
DeCamp, Alta J. 046174
Decán Gambús, Ivanova 049483
Decatur, Raylene 043406
Decavele, Dr. Johan 003460
Dechaux, Carine 003718
Decker, Carla 046437
Decker, E. 014684, 014685
Decker, Dr. K.P. 016489
Decker, Raymond 015185
Decker, Scott E. 044730
Deckers, Yolande 003163
Decoodt, Wim 003163
Decraene, A. 003163
Decroix, Philippe 014183
Decron, Benoît 012639
Decter, Avi Y. 041989
Dectot, Xavier 013719
Dedenroth-Schou, Poul 008997
Dedic, Bernard 007807
Dedíková, Soňa 008307
Deecke, Prof. Dr. Thomas 016421
Deedes, C.M.J. 039250
Deegan, Dr. Ann 042903, 047321, 047362, 049368, 049369
Deegan, Denise 042748
Deer, Naomi 044774
Deering, Stan 005223
Deernose, Kitty 043230
Deerpalsingh, Salni 028066
Deeva, Valentina Kirillovna 033175
Defauwes, Georges 003384
Defeo, Prof. Rúben D.F. 031773
Defferrard, Jacky 012595
Degel, Hermann 020365
Degel, Kirsten 008938
Degen, Dr. Ch. 037661
Degen, Jenna 046981
Degen, Kurt 019997
Deggelsegger, M. 002609
Degon, Pierre 014132
Degreif, Dr. Uwe 016219
DeGroft, Aaron 047999
Degueurce, C. 012857
Deguglielmo, M. 010635
Deguillaume, Marie-Pierre 014888
DeGuzman, Rene 047892
Deharde, Ewald 016527
Dehejia, Dr. Vidya 048884, 048908
Dehrkoop, Prestene 043642
Deiber-Kumm, Michele 042791
Deigendesch, Roland 019134
Deigendesch, Dr. Roland . . 019135, 019136
Deiker, Dr. Tom 042790
Deimel, Dr. Claus 018581
Deiser, Leopoldine 001829
Deisler-Seno, Jane 043163
Deitsch, Elka 046345
Deitz, Judith 048171
Deitz, M. Ph. 003596
Dejardin, Dr. Fiona M. 046692
Dekiert, Dr. Markus 019038
Dekker, H. 029679
Dekker, M. 029247
Deknop, A. 003292, 003304
Del Bagno, Rober 046389
Del Falco, Vittorio 025572
Del Frate, Dr. Gabriella 025100
Del-Prete, Sandro 037203
Del Testa, Luise 021063, 021064
Del Vivo, Tommaso 024047
Dela, Feliks 032158
Delacoste, Raymond 037332
Delacote, Goery 047861
Delaender, Georges 003838
Delage, Dominique 014826
Delahant, John M. 047996

Delahaye, Marie-Claude 010568
Delaine, Joël 013293, 013297
Delaney, Chris 039002
Delaney, C.J. 039002
Delangle, J.F. 010804
Delannoy, Agnès 014309
Delannoy, Jean 012686
Delany, Max 001028
Delaousie, Renée 013488
Delaquis, Christian 006840
Delarge, Alexandre 011895
Delattre, Jean-Luc 003678
DeLay, Matthew 041684
Delay, Matthew 041685
Delbaere, Stefaan 029268
Delbos, Andrée 014214
Delcourt, Dr. Marianne 003805
Delehanty, Suzanne 045814
Delépine, Francine 003310
Delgado, Alvaro 035369
Delgado, Avella 035302, 035304
Delgado, Eric 010535
Delgado, James P. 006715
Delgado, Jane 046278
Delgado, Lino Torres 028085
Delgado, Sally 041838
Delgado Restrepo, Gloria 007467
Delhaise, Christophe 003252, 003253
Delisle, André J. 005940
DeLisle, Godfray 005282
Delivorrias, Prof. Dr. Angelos 021188
Delker, Martin 016975
Dell, Roger 043848
Dell, Sharon 030627
Della Casa, Bettina 037285
Della Fina, Giuseppe M. 025023
Della Toffola, Leomberto 026251
Dellacroce, Raymond 043796
Dellamore, Hilona 010831
Dell'Antonia, Dario 015279
Dellantonio, Elio 025368
Dellbeck, Johan 036744
Dellin, Edward J. 045166
Dellinger, Mary H. 044057
Dell'Oca Fiordi, Dr. Angela 025919
Delmas, Jean 014085
Delmas, Luc 015239
DelMonico, Mary 046418
Delmont, Patrick 015334
Delobel, Jean 010630
Deloffre, Véronique 010676
Deloing, Evelyne 010477
Deloncle, Jacques-Gaspard 013785
DeLong, Dr. Marilyn 047697
DeLorme, Harry 048031
Delorme, Yves 014064
Delperdange, Roland 003213
Delporte, Luc 003817
Delroy, A. 001377
Deltedesco, Franco 024506
Deltour-Levie, Claudine 003353
Delye, Emmanuel 003589
Demaerschalk, Sylvain 003288
DeMaio, Bonnie 047557
Demard, Jean-Christophe 011230
Demaret, Nicole 003807
Demarez, Leonce 003206, 003207, 003235
DeMars, Louise L. 042418
Demarteau, J. 029379
Demazure, Michel 013733
Dembiniok, Marian 031881
Dembski, Prof. Dr. G. 001835
Dembski, Prof. Dr. Günther 002934, 002997
Dembski, Dr. Ulrike 002979
Demčenko, Ljubov Grigorjevna ... 033091
Demeester, Veerle 003163
Demel, Dr. Bernhard 002966
DeMenocal, Linda 042097
Demere, Dr. Thomas 047840
Demerling, Rod 006477
Demetis, Ioannis 021531
Demetriou, Maro 008212
Demetriou, Myra 001265
Demetz, Dr. Stefan 023469
Demeurie, Dirk 003405
Demidenko, Olga Moiseeva 033535
Demidovich, Peter 044681
Deminey, E. 034617, 034657
Deming, Diane 047373
Demirci, Süheyla 038179
Demke, Siegfried G. 045445
Demo, Dr. Željko 007828
Dempsey, Rey 022767
Dempsey, Terrence E. 047672
Demski, Tadeusz 032319
Demuth, Renate 019820
DeMuzio, David 046975
Denaro, Dolores 036949
Denelli, Gjergj 000031
Denenberg, Thomas 044463
Denford, Geoffrey 041401
Denford, Dr. G.T. 041408
Dengate, James 048713
Denis, Paul 006627
Denise, Danièle 011850
Denison, Ruth 039106
Denizli, Hikmet 038006
Denk, Dr. Roswitha 002934
Denker, Eric 048892
Denman, Ron 005268
Dennerly, Peter 030478
Denney, Alan 038959
Denning, Elizabeth 043804
Dennis, Mary 045046
Dennis, Sue M. 046414
Dennison, Foster K. 006794
Dennison, Lisa 046404
Dennler, William V.A. 048568
Denny, Tyra 044910
Dennys, Vincent 010395
Densapa, Tashi 022117
Densen, Paul M. 047927
Dent, G.J.H. 040711
Denton, Amy 043780
Denton, Joanna 041070
Dentraygues, D.J. 010451
Denys, Lama 010498
Denysenko, Jevgen Ivanovyč 038263
Denzel, H. 001684
Deon, Luca 037293
DeOrsay, Paul B. 043038, 046951
Deparpe, Patrice 012568
Depauw, Carl 003189
Depierre, Marie-Colette 012445
DePietro, Anne 044680
Depoid, Henry 011453
DeQueiroz, Prof. Alan 042354
Dequidt, Luk 003704
Deranian, Janet 043124
Derbic, Rupert 001776
Derbier, Josselin 014072
Derby, Newton 048393
Derbyshire, Janine 039225, 039227
D'Ercole, Dr. Vincenzo 023864
Dercon, Chris 019061
Dercon, C.P.E. 030088
Dercourt, J. 012088
Derda, Dr. Hans-Jürgen 016381
Derefaka, Dr. Abi Alabo 030706
Derenthal, Dr. Ludger 016101
Deriks, M. 030183
Dering, Dr. Florian 019086, 019105
Dering, Dr. Peter 015933
Derion, Brigitte 010882
Derjabin, Vladimir Ignatevič 033728
Derjužina, Alla Vasylivna 038250
Derksen, J. 029498
Derksen, J.J.V.M. 030225
Dermitzakis, Prof. Dr. M.D. 021210
DeRosa, Donald 048372
Derosier, Paul 046547
Deroux, Kenneth 044888
Derriks, Claire 003657
Dertazzo, Ludovico M. 025052
Desai, Vishakha N. 046297
Desaint, Jeanne 012989
DeSantis, Diana Ortega 047973
Desaulniers, Guy 005044
Desbarax, Dr. P.M. 003175
Desbenoit, Martine 010927
Desborough, Jeff 049167
Descamps, Patrick 012086
Desel, Jochen 015729
DeSeyter, Craig 044573
Desfossés Le Page, Carmen 006661
DeShon, Richard N. 047649
Deshpande, Dr. P.N. 022108
Désirat, Georges 014648
DesJardins, Edward 047559
Desjardins, Robert Y. 006449
Desjardins-Ménégalli, Marie-Hélène 011790, 011791
Desmarais, Charles 042922
Desmedt, An 003163
Desmet, Don 044899
Desmet, Viviane 003330
Desmules, Olivier 012899
Despotidis, Emmanouil 021129
DesRoches, C. 005844
Desse, Daniel 015200
Dessens, H.J.A. 029216
Desserud, Thore 030818
Dessornes, Maria E. 048551
Destefanis, Joseph 028993
DeStefano, Giacomo R. 046842
Desvigne, M. 014674
Desy, Dr. Elizabeth A. 045702
Desy, Margherita 042348
Detch, Rosalie S. 045245
Dethlefs, Dr. Gerd 019156, 053641
Detrani, Geoffrey 046417
Detrée, Jean-François 014561
Detrich, Kalman 046377
Detten, Jayne 047118
Dettmer, Dr. Frauke 019800
Dettmer, Hans-Georg 017487
Deuber-Ziegler, E. 037130
Deuchar, Stephen 040299
Deuchert, Dr. Norbert 016522
Deutmann, Karl Heinrich 016767
Deutsch, Franz 003060
Deutsch, Prof. Dr. H. 036919
Deutsch, Dr. J. 036919
Deutschbauer, Franz 002660
Dev, Anand 022095
Devaney, Richard 039194
Devanik, Dave 005956
Devaux, Bernard 013652
Devé, Jean 011950
Deveau, Bertha 047927
Deveau, Carole 005894
Devendorf, Meredith 045859
Devereux, Dr. B.J. 038960
Devereux, David . 039011, 039901, 039902
DeVille, Sue 046699
Devin, Pierre 011646,
Devine Nordstrom, Alison 043331
Devine-Reed, Pat 042825
Devlin, Dr. Felicity 022759
Devlin, Joseph T. 046989
Devonshire, Amana 041427
DeVonyar-Zansky, Jill 047092
Devos, Danny 003181
Devos, E. 003728, 003729, 003730
Devries, Fred 045829
DeVries, Karl 048032
Devroye-Stilz, Anne 013398
Devynck, Danièle 010321
Dewald, Ann 046793
DeWalt, Billie R. 047044
Dewan, L. Georg 006070
Deweerdt, Jean 011668
Dewey, Alice 039424
Dewey, S. 041280
Dewhurst, Dr. C. Kurt 043575
Dewhurst, Stephen 042069, 046324
Dewilde, Annick 003559
Dewilde, Jan .. 003531, 003532, 003533, 003534, 003535
Dewing, David 040152
DeWitt, Martin 043524
Dewitz, Dr. Bodo von 018302
DeWys-VanHecke, Amy 043443
Dexter, James 000898
Dexter, Susan 043847
Deyle, Betty 042143
DeYoung, Jeri 043855
Deyoung, Mildred 045078
Deysenroth, Paul 049119
Dezellus, Eric 014144
Dezutter, Willy P. 003280, 003283
Dhaene, Sylvie 003456
Dhaliwal, Theresa 040203
Dhaulakhandi, V.N. 022297
Dholakia, P.V. 022192
Dhombres, M. Jean 013601
Di Belgiojoso, Dr. Giuseppe B. 025768
Di Fabio, Clario .. 024297, 024307, 024315
Di Felice, Dr. Paola 026004
Di Flumeri, Dr. Gabriella 025548
Di Geronimo, I. 023764
Di Girolami, Dr. Paola ... 023753, 023951, 024379, 024810, 024854, 025443, 025606, 025649
Di Grazia Costa, Ivani 004530
Di Ianni, Angelo 025198
Di Lorenzo, Maria Teresa 025724
Di Malfetta, Dr. Felice 024776
Di Mario, Dr. Mario 026015
Di Martino, Maria 025248
Di Niro, Dr. Angela 023620
Di Paolo, Luciana 025240
Di Pascale, Paolo 023331
Di Pietrantonio, Dr. Giacinto 023375
Di Pietro, Gaetano 025186
Di Stefano, Dr. Carmela Angela ... 025082
Di Tommaso, Francis 046417
Diaconescu, Nicolae 032815
Diaconescu, Petru 032944
Diakite, Sinkoun 021594
Diallo, Ibrahima 047837
Diamantakis, Stavros 002411
Diamond, Dr. Judy 045313
Dianto, Herkus 022444
Dianzinga, Dias-Théodore 007665
Diaper, Dr. Hilary 039965
Diaper, Hilary 039965
Dias, Dr. Maduro 032578
Dias, Robério 004420
Dias Duarte, Luiz Fernando 004404
Diaw, Amadou Tahirou 034130
Díaz, Dr. Jimena Perera Diaz 041538
Díaz, Joaquín 035965
Díaz, Luis H. 007487
Díaz, Miguel 032749
Díaz de Mazzoldi, Olga 007567
Díaz Díaz, José Antonio 035330
Díaz García, José Luís 035541
Díaz Padrón, Matías 035429
Díaz Pardo, Isaac 034856
Díaz-Tusham, Rafael 046281
Díaz Ungría, Dr. Adelaida de 049503
Dibbets, W.A.G. 029284
Dičeva, Vera 004866
Dick, Hans-Gerd 021080
Dick, James 047555
Dicke, James F. 046199
Dickens, Denise 047310
Dickenson, Joanne 047150
Dickenson, Victoria 005930
Dickerman, Dr. Robert W. 041619
Dickermann, Dr. Fred 002141, 052569
Dickerson, Amy 044108
Dickerson, Patricia 046655, 055114
Dickerson, Robin 044088
Dickerson Lind, Anne 048019
Dickey, Michael 041785
Dickhaut, Monique F.A. 029896
Dickinson, Cindy 041691
Dickinson, Gary 046275

Dickinson, Pat 006632
Dickinson, Robert 041178, 041181
Dickinson, Roger 046213
Dickson, Carl A. 044442
DiCosimo, Joanne 006092
Didier, Alain 013971
Didier, Prof. Arturo 025997
Didier, Hebert 012688
Didrichsen, Maria 009519
Didrichsen, Peter 009519
Diebel, C. 030432
Dieck Jackson, Anke Tom 048254
Dieckhoff, Dr. Reiner 018322
Diederen, Roger 046320
Diederichs, Dr. Urs 019796
Diedrich, Dr. Stephan 018334
Diehes, Dr. Gerhard M. 001930
Diehl, Reinhard 018687
Diehl, Dr. Richard 048661, 048663
Diehl, Dr. Ruth 016329
Diekmann, Klemens 015653, 015654
Diekmann, Rolf 020377
Dieleman, Peter A. 029967
Diem, Peter 037215
Diemer, Dr. Kurt 015794
Diene, Baidy 034132
Dienes, Dr. Gerhard M. 001932, 001947
Dienst, Robert 002212
Dierking, Gary R. 043970
Dierks-Staiger, Regine 020365
Dießner, Dr. Petra 018592
Dietel, Volker 019234
Dieter, Raymond 042851
Diethorn, Karie 046950
Dietl, Dr. Gerhard 020364
Dietrich, Bev 005556, 005557
Dietrich, Dorothea 046206
Dietrich, Eva 037773
Dietrich, Dr. Gerhard 018330
Dietrich, Dr. Helmut 017522
Dietrich, Suzanne 043618
Dietrich, Tanja 037267
Dietschi, Jean-Pierre 037755
Dietz, Günter 020685
Dietz, Karl-Heinz 016859
Dietz, Paddy 049207
Dietz, Stefanie 020706
Dietz, Steffen 015448
Dietz, Thomas A. 044900
Dietz, Ulysses G. 046425
Díez, José Luis 035429
Diez Valdez, Oscar 031478
DiFerdinando, Charles A. 043535
Diffily, James P. 044007
Difuccia, Mike A. 045962
Digby, Linda 005381
Digel, Brigitte 020967
Digger, Jo 041286
Dignef, Leo 003222
Dijkstra, J.G. 029956
Dijkstra, Rob 029638
Dijols, Pierre 013214
Diklev, Torben 021546
Dikun, Z.M. 033281
Dilas, Milica 007779
Dilcher, Dr. D.L. 044103
Dill, Chris 044304, 044305
Dill, Cynthia 046269
Dillard Mitchell, Shannon 045346
Dillard Rech, Lori 046927
Diller, Douglas 047949
Diller, Dr. J. 019132
Dilley, Cherry 034748
Dilley, Mary Lou 045694
Dillon, Alice 048424
Dillon, Idelle 046871
Dillon, John 047879
Dillon, Mike 040700
Dilly, Georges 010754
Dilo, Lefter 000023
Dilts, Bonnie 046003
Dimaandal, Carmelita 031721
Dimaki, Sofia 021153
DiMaria, Tom 046593
DiMeo Carlozzi, Annette 041927
Dimitrić, Dragan 034255
Dimitrijević, Bora N. 034283
Dimitrov, Ass.Prof. Dr. Bojidar 004863
Dimitrov, Ivan 004808
Dimitrova, Stanka 004918
Dimmick, Walter 045205
Dimova, Ljubov Ivanovna 034074
Dimpelfeld, William 048043
Dimuchametova, Svetlana Aleksandrovna 033653
Dina, Diana le 037250
Dinard, N. Jean 012188
Diner, Mónica 028508
Dinger, Brigitte 017000
Dingertz, Stig 036637
Dinges, Christiane 018303
Dings, Mindie M. 042752
Dingwall, Fiona 039516
Dinkelspiel, Florence 045386
Dinkhauser, Lienhard 002826
Dinkins, Dr. Leon 047038
Dinsmoie, Elizabeth 005426
Diogo, Joanne 042576
Diogo Ribeiro, José 032607
Dion, Jean-Noël 006342
DiPaolo, Michael 045240
Dippel, Robert 048816
Dippold, Günter 015920
Dippold Vilar, Dalmo 004548
Dirican, Alan 041969
Dirnbacher, Karl 001900
Dirnbacher, Kurt 001700
Dirnbacher, Sonja 001699, 001701
Dirschel, Angelika 017829
Dirun, Moh Lativ 027981
Dishman, Jay 045798
Disney, Betty 043255
Disney, Jenny 047757
Distel, Anne 013678
Distel, Dr. Barbara 016619
Díte, Dr. Tibor 034447
Ditmanson, Dennis 049006
Dittberner, Stephen 047222
Dittertová, Dr. Eva 008327, 008328
Dittler, Ingeborg 016778
Dittmann, Britta 018718
Dittmar, Monika 020574
Dittmar, Volker 018849
Dittrich, Dr. Erika 017267, 017268, 017269
Divall, Colin 041480
Divelbiss, Maggie 047279
Dixey, Judy 040082
Dixon, Annette 041736
Dixon, Bonnie 044141
Dixon, Carol 045635
Dixon, David J. 042215
Dixon, Debbie 047998
Dixon, Elaine 047287
Dixon, Gerald 044247
Dixon, Hugh 040455
Dixon, Jill P. 043499
Dixon, Kate 045761
Dixon, Rick 041176
Dixon, Wendy M.C. 001171
Dixon, William 048562
Diz Ardid, Emilio 035566
Djabbar, Abd. 022527
Djačenko, N.D. 038395
Djadaibaev, Amir Jalinovich 027390
Djalal, Dr. Zaidir 022435
Djamba K. Shungu, Joseph 007657
Djanguenane, Nayondjoua 037942
Djepbarov, Redjep 038208
Djevori, Bozidar 034252
Djordjević, Nenad 034207
Djordjević, Zivadin 034260
Djurdjekanović, Sladjana 034177
Djurdjevič, Ivo 007814
Djuve, Kjetil 031180
Dlin, Elliott 043268
Dlugač, Vladimir Vladimirovič 032997
Długoszewska-Nadratowska, Hanna 031878
Dłużwska-Sobczak, Anna 032092
Dmitriev, Prof. I.S. 033776
Dmitrovic, Katarina 034180
Dmytrykiw, Danylo 044418
Doak, Elaine M. 045022
Doane, Erin 048008
Dobbelstein, H. 029556
Dobbie, Allison 030483
Dobbie, Dave 005964
Dobbratz, Alferna 044622
Dobke, Dr. Dirk 017686
Dobkowski, Mieczysław 031860
Dobney, Jayson 048763
Dobosi, Dr. Viola 021917
Dobras, Dr. Wolfgang 018791
Dobrea, George 042999
Dobrev, Marin 004884
Dobrianowa-Bauer, Dr. Snejanka D. 017177
Dobrik, Dr. Istváan 021792
Dobrik, Dr. István 021790, 021791
Dobrileit, Margitta 016847
Dobritzsch, Elisabeth 017489
Dobson, Stewart 038739
Docenko, Alina Vasylivna 038247
Dočev, Spas 004742
Dočeva, Penka 004726
Dočeva-Peeva, Elka 004863
Docog, Angelica 045793
Dodd, Dr. Donald B. 042226
Dodd, Jennifer 044533
Dodd, Nicholas 041429, 041432
Dodd, Nick 041001
Dodd, Philip 040184
Dodd, Roger 039126
Dodds, E. 039813
Dodds, Richard 048212
Dodge, Alan 001375
Dodge, Carol A. 048223
Dodge, Laura 043704
Dodier, Virginia 042626
Dodina, Tatjana Alekseevna 034066, 034068
Dodson, Gin 049014
Dodson, Howard 046399
Dodsworth, Roger C. 039290
Dodwell, A. 040205
Dodwell, P. 040205
Döllinger, Theodor 019565
Dörfer, Dr. Anja 019336
Dörhöfer, Friedrich 016484
Döring, Dr. Jürgen 017715
Döring, Martel 019380
Döring, Dr. Thomas 016385
Dörnenburg, Manuela 016248
Doerr, Marjorie A. 043694
Doersch, Lee 043616
Doetsch, Dr. Rainer 018297
Doezema, Marianne 048240
Doffey, Marie-Christine 036936
Dogan, Salih 038107
Dogariu, Octavian 032957
Doggatt, Henry 048443
Doherty, Ann 046348
Doherty, Laura 043549
Doherty, Peggy M. 043375, 043376
Doherty, Roisin 022838
Dohertyld, Erin 030454
Dohnal, Karel 008394
Dohrman, Stewart. 048023
Doht, Sabine 016921
Doiron, Sue 006338
Dojčev, Nejčo 004768
Dolan, Douglas C. 043503, 043506
Dolan, Joseph J. 043560
Dolata, Jan 032398
Dolby, Joe 034587
Dolby, Malcolm J. 040822, 041450
Dolce, Dr. Sergio 026127, 026139
Dolczewski, Zygmunt 032252
Dolenz, Dr. Heimo 002432
Doletsky-Rackham, Nina 043464
Doleva, John 048295
Dolgopolova, Zinaida Stepanovna 033897
Doll, Mary H. 045000
Doll, Nancy 044338
Dollinger, Hannes 037548
Dolor, Danny 031686
Doltenkov, V.V. 033022
Dolženko, Fëdor Nikolaevič 033104
Domagała, Roman 032390
Domaine, Elmo 024090
Domański, Edward 032460
Dombrowski, Dieter 020585
Domènech, Glòria 034907
Domenech de Celles, Yann 012024
Domenighim, Attilio 024166
Domingos, Tadeu 000088
Dominguez, Antonio Franco 034887
Domínguez, German 006934
Domínguez Cabrera, Gonzalo 008061
Domínguez Cadeño, Nelson 007949
Domínguez Salazar, José Antonio 035408
Dominjak, Aleksandr Vladimirovič 033647
Domitruk, Daryl 005959
Dommer, Olge 016771
Dompierre, Louise 005587
Dompnier, Pierre 014350
Domröse, Ulrich 015991
Don Angelo, Maria 024381
Donadio, Emmie 045834
Donadoni Roveri, Dr. Anna Maria 026069
Donahue, Gail 041650, 046073
Donahue, John J. 043051
Donahue, Susan F. 043766
Donaldson, E. 000779
Donaldson, John 038967
Donaldson, Susan 048277
Donat, Olivier 015297
Donath, David A. 049294
Donath, Wolfram 016161
Donati, Prof. Bruno 037004, 037147
Donati, Dario 037808
Donbaz, Veysel 038093
Donchez Mowers, Charlene 042181, 042182, 042183, 042185
Donders van den Aardweg, M.G. 029272
Dondo-Tardiff, Michelle 006088
Donegá, Dr. Giuseppe 026263
Donelli, Ivo 007798
Donelly, P. 039922
Donetzkoff, Alexis 012680
Donevski, Peti 004895, 004896, 004897, 004898
Donlon, Dr. D. 001513
Donnell, Courtney G. 042820
Donnellon, Maureen 000805
Donnelly, George J. 045077
Donnelly, John 048750
Donnelly, Peter 039868, 039921
Donner, Drs. E.M. 029196
Donner, Josef 002511, 003043
Donnermeyer, Reinhold 018925
Donoghue, Gail 048711
Donoghue, Michael 046226
Donohue, Deidre 046348
Donohue, Lorena 045348
Donoso Guerrero, Rosa 035434
Donzé, Frédéric 037477
Donzé, Roger 037427
Donzelli, Rodolfo 025588
Dooley, Bill 048666
Doove, Edith 003398
Dopffer, Anne 010838
Doppelfeld, Dr. Basilius 020130
Doppelstein, Jürgen 020695
Doppermann, Cäcilia 002641
Doppler, Prof. Dr. Alfred 002554
Doppler, Elke 003017
Doppler, Margarete 001761
Dor, Ehud 023007
Doračić, Damir 007828
Dorado Ortega, Oscar Javier 007471
Doran, J. 041043
Doran, Patricia A. 045053

Dordević, Radisav 034254
Dore, Dr. Anna 023425
Dore, Giovanni 025980
Dorée, Yves 014658
Doren, Jo-an' Van 043017
Dorgans 010644
Dorgerloh, Prof. Dr. Hartmut 019659
Dorhs, Michael 017962
Doring Van Buren, Denise 042070
Doriot, Sylvie 037255
Dorling, M. 038970
Dorman, Craig 048650
Dornan, Duncan 039353
Dornan, Vorin 046729
Dorner, Ernst 002182
Dornert, Nadine 010812
Dornieden, Horst 020416
Dornisch, Richard 047688
Doroshenko, Peter 003469, 045890
Dorosiev, J. 004731
Dorsaz, Pierre 037673
Dorsch, Dr. Klaus J. 019725, 019727
Dorsch, Roberta 045660
Dorsett, A.G. 039002, 040056
Dorst, A. 030128
Dortch, Steve 043713
Dose, Dr. Hanna 015765, 015766
Doseva, Iva 004863
Dosi, Ferdinando 025570
Dosik, Jeffrey 046408
Dossi, Dr. Barbara 002845
Dost, Dr. Wolfgang 020935
Doth, Diane 006851
Doubek, Franz 001835
Doublard du Vigneau, Simone 012046
Doucet, C. 015093
Doucet, Donna 005538
Doucet, Jean 010822
Doucet, M. 015092
Doudiet, Norman 042653
Dougherty, Erin 046036
Dougherty, Marijo 041603
Dougherty, Molly 046946, 046956
Dougherty, Thomas A. 046352
Doughty, P.S. 038669
Doughty, Richard 039643
Douglas, Dr. B. 001284
Douglas, Marietta 036426
Douglass, Amy A. 048522
Douglass, Ardith 045749
Douglass, Larry 042414
Douglass, Michael 047220
Douroux, Xavier 011598, 011600
Douvette, Herny d'Otreppe de 003829
Dow, George F. 046491
Doway, Stella 034287
Dowell, Michael B. 047280
Dowell, Wanda S. 041639
Dowie, Peggy 041068
Dowlan, Neil 039955
Dowling, J.R. 041268
Dowling, Valerie 022759
Down, Geoffrey 001369
Downend, A.V 040876
Downer, Dr. 022694
Downes, Elizabeth 001184
Downes, Marcia W. 046432
Downey, Dharmena 045657
Downey, Martha J. 042233
Downey, Dr. Robert H. 042384
Downie Banks, Dr. Margaret 048763
Downing, Clayta 048865
Downs, Alex 041573
Downs, Gerald 046722
Downs, John 044035
Downs, Stuart 044450
Doyle, John 046698
Doyle, Louise 000874
Doyle, Paul 022705
Doyon, Jean-Pierre 005912
Drabow, Kerstin 019668
Drachman, Lorraine 048632
Dräger, Ulf 017672
Draganić, Danica 007820
Draganov, Dr. Dimitar 004696, 004697
Dragićević, Mate 003932
Drăgoi, Dr. Livia 032837
Dragoni, Prof. G. 023442
Dragsbo, Peter 008826
Dragt, G.I.W. 029493, 029929
Draheim, Heidi 016828
Drahoňovský, Jan 008487
Drahošova, Viera 034425
Drake, Chip 046041
Drake, Ellen Mary 005741
Drake, Lisa 043812
Drake, Pia 017757
Drake, Tommi 044288
Dran, Jean-Luc 011963
Draper, Amanda 040778
Draper, Jill 038466
Draper, Jo 040365
Draper, Steven C. 043920
Drapkin, Adrienne 044765
Draps, M. Willem 003345
Drašković, Dragan 034208
Draughn, Raymond 047519
Drayman-Weisser, Terry 042006
Draževa, Conja G. 004647
Dražić, Jovanka 034266
Dražin Trbuljak, Lada 007854
Drda, Dr. Miloš 008689, 008690, 008705, 008751
Drechsler, Dr. Wolfgang 002965
Dreckow, T. 000928
Drees, Dr. Jan 020039
Dreezen, J. 003511
Dreher, Derick 046984
Dreher, Nancy 046043
Dreier, Bruno 018206
Dreier, Prof. Martin 036937
Dreier, Max 036870
Dreishpoon, Douglas 042498
Drejholt, Nils 036639
Drempetić-Hrcic, Nikola 007722
Drenker-Nagels, Dr. Klara 016317
Dresch, Dr. Jutta 018158
Drescher, Georg 020138
Dresco, Jean-Pierre 037406
Dressel, Barry 041893
Dressel, Ina-Maria 015567
Dressel, Jan 046584
Dressler, Iris 020373
Dreuzy, Jehan de 014287
Drew, Alejandrina 043644
Drew, Stephen E. 047587
Drewes, C. 034708
Drewnowski, Benedykt 037576
Drews, Ute 020038
Drexel, Hermann 002505
Drexler, Ray 044952
Drexler, Toni 020081
Dreycus, Dominique 012738
Dreydoppel, Susan M. 046168
Dreyer, Dr. Andreas 030874
Dreyer, Chris 046579
Dreyer, Dr. Elfriede 034732
Dreyer, K. 017331
Dreyer, Prof. L. 034724
Dreyer, Dr. Wolfgang 018253
Dreyfus, Renee 047857, 047871
Dreyfuss, James 044412
Drezgić, Olivera 034266
Drias, Lakhdar 000047
Driesbach, Janice 045311
Drieselmann, Jörg 016020
Driesens, F.J.J. 030057
Driessen, Hendrik 030210
Driessens, Mevrouw Colette 003429
Driewer, Ginny L. 049346
Drinjaković, Milica 034180
Drinkard, Joel F. 045488
Drioli, Anton 002553
Driscoll, David 045595
Driskell, Julia 042270
Driver, Rod 000983, 000984
Drlić, Predrag 007764
Drobney, Dr. Jeffrey A. 044957
Drocklehurst, E. 040251
Drögemöller, Inka 017192
Dröscher, Elke 017718
Drössler, Stefan 019054
Drößler, Stefan 019086
Droguet, Vincent 011850
Dromgoole, P.S.B.F. 039544
Dronkers, Ben 029184
Dronkers, S.L. 029137
Dror, Mira 022968
Drosinou, Paraskevi 021225
Droste-Vischering-Galen, Hubertus 001919
Drozd, Henryk 032310
Dru Burns, Mary 041652
Druček, A.A. 033473
Drucha-Graber, Barbara 002675
Druesedow, Jean 044967
Druick, Douglas 042820
Drummer, Karen A. 045592
Drummond, H. Maury 042045
Drutt, Matthew 044645
Družak, Antonija 007732
Dryfhout, John 043157
Dsuve, Kjetil 031243
du Fayet de la Tour, Alain 011830
Duarte, Carlos F. 049461
Duarte Ferreira, Selma 004579
Duarte Rodríguez, Rafael Enrique 007443
Dubarry, Dominique 052903
Dubb, Prof. Asher 034639
Dubé, Lisa 041657
Dubedat, Paul 014543
Dubick, David 043601
Dubler, Linda 041862
Dubois, Alan B. 045342
Dubois, Arlette 014129
Dubois, Danielle 005945
Dubois, Michel 037516
Dubois, Oliver 013994
Dubrisay, Pascal 012721
Dubrović, Ervin 007780
Dubrovin, Sergej Michajlovič 033587
Dubrovin, V.M. 032985
Dubuc, André 012658
Ducastelle, Jean-Pierre 003203, 003204, 003622
Ducey, Dr. Peter K. 043171
Duchamp, Luc 012920
Duchemin, Michael 045411
Duchesne, Prof. Jean-Patrick 003584
Duchesne, Jean-Patrick 003600
Duckers, Peter 041024
Duckworth, Elisabeth 005659
Duclos, Jean-Claude 012020, 012022
Duco, D.H. 029223
Ducor, J. 037130
Ducourau, Vincent 010684, 010686
Ducreux, Anne-Claire 012880
Duda, Eugeniusz 032040
Duda, Igor Mykytovyč 038402
Dudant, Didier 003149, 003150
Dudar, Dr. Wiesław 032219
Dudavt, Didier 003151
Dudeck, Dr. Volker 021072, 021073, 021074
Dudenhöffer, Franz 020264
Dudley, Andrew 001474
Dudley, Caroline 041243
Dudley, Clarissa 044613
Dudnik, I.E. 038320
Dudź, Jerzy 032371
Dudzik, Przemysław 031967
Dueck, Lois 005088
Dücker, Dr. Elisabeth von 017709
Düğer, Şaban 038175
Dühr, Dr. Elisabeth 020486
Duell, Charles H.P. 042741
Duell, Marshall 047946
Dümas, Dieter 018809
Dümmel, Karlheinz 019222
Duenkel, Bob 043932
Dünnebier, Dr. Michael 016821
Duensing, Darrell 047221
Duerr, Mark 045593
Dürrenmatt, Dieter 036905
Dürüce, Servet 038198
Düspohl, Martin 016094
Düsterwald, Dr. Brigitte 018565
Dütschler, H.R. 037631
Dufek, Mike 044159
Dufet-Bourdelle, Rhodia 013620
Duff, Ana 042443
Duff, Doris 049043
Duff, James H. 042692
Duffels, Dr. J.P. 029245
Duffy, Prof. A. 034735
Duffy, Henry J. 043157
Dufilho, Diane 048160
Dufour, Albertine 048369
Dufour, Christophe 037377
Dufour, Gary 001375
Dufour, Pierre 006679
Dufrasne, F. 003780
Dufrenne, Michèle 028997
Dugajeva, Tetjana Igorivna 038234
Dugall, Berndt 017194
Dugan, Walter 038692
Duggan, Ervin S. 046796
Duggen Below, Ina 019619
Dugmore, I.M. 034613
Dugot, Joël 013640
Dugué, Prof. J. 013710
Duguid, Meg 042879
Dugulin, Dr. Adriano 026126, 026128, 026129, 026130, 026131, 026132, 026134, 026135, 026140
Duhm, Burghard 016684
Duits, Th. te 029835, 030088
Duivesteijn, John 029456
Dujardin, Paul 003355
Dujmović-Kosovac, Ljubica 007779
Dukat, Zdenka 007828
Duke, Jacqueline 047972
Duke, Judy 043134
Dulaban, Alta 043015
Dulaney, H.G. 041923, 042297
Dulaney, W. Marvin 042725
Dulda, Mustafa 037991
Dulgheru, Lia Maria 032913, 032915, 032965, 032966
Dulibić, Ljerka 007856
Dulière, Cecile 003657
Dulin, Ètienne 015243
Dumalag, Filemon R. 031622
Dumančić, Ljubica 007822
Dumanoir, Thierry 012290, 014013
Dumaret, Isabelle 036998
Dumas, Cyril 012608, 012609, 012611, 012612
Dumitrescu, Horia 032863, 032864
Dumitrescu, Ilinca 032812
Dumitroaia, Gheorghe 032782, 032911, 032955
Dumitru, Ţeicu 032924
Dummer, S. 039813
Dumon, Noël 003271
DuMont, Bruce 042859
Dumont, Fabienne 003296
Dumont, Françoise 003592
Dumortier, Christian 014327
Dumortier, Claire 003353
Dumortier, Philippe 014327
Dumoulin, J. 003812
Dumville, John P. 043792, 044660, 047564, 048306, 048391
Dunand, Michele 012321
Dunbar, Elizabeth 049152
Dunbar, Lisa 046873
Duncan, Jenepher 000925
Dundass, Kay 030546
Dundon, Margo 044818
Dundore, Mary Margaret 047168
Dunfjeld, Sigbjørn 031202
Dunford, Fred 042399

Dungan, Erica Howe 042374
Dunham, Anne 047904
Dunham, Elizabeth L. 048492
Dunina, Elena Michajlovna 033313
Dunkelman, Arthur 045827
Dunkerton, Jill 040241
Dunkley, Diane L. 048894
Dunkley, Tina 041854
Dunlap, Melissa L. 045362
Dunlap, Susan 047521
Dunlop, J.M. 039449
Dunn, Alberta 044161
Dunn, Carol 047908
Dunn, Cathey 045397
Dunn, David W. 048394
Dunn, Deborah F. 044599, 044604
Dunn, Delores 046245
Dunn, Forrest 048159
Dunn, Hedy 045408
Dunn, Lawren 043822, 047110
Dunn, Lindsley A. 042945
Dunn, Madeline 043490
Dunn, Nancy 041786
Dunn, Richard 039041
Dunne, John 022832
Dunne, Maxine 005445
Dunning, Fred 039676
Dunning, Louise 039225
Dunton, Anna Mary 042590
Duparc, F.J. 029434, 029452
Duperray, Eve 010872, 011839, 011841
Dupeux, Cécile 014870
Duplančić, Arsen 007798
DuPont, Diana 047950
DuPont, George 045119
Dupont, Jean-Pierre 015169
Dupont, Joel 014536
Dupont, Paule 003522
Dupont, Roland 015308
Dupont-Bauverie, Caroline 010808
Dupont-Logié, Cécile 014731
Dupré, Hans Jörg 016628
Duprat, Andrés 000124, 000127
Duprat, Jean-Marie 014826
Dupraz, Cathérine 011293
Dupree, Sherry 043449
DuPree Richardson, Jane 048429
Dupret, Sandra 043439
Dupriez, Françoise 003846
Dupuis, Burno 013006
Dupuis-Sabron, Geneviève 010882
Dura, Ulrike 018594
Duraj, Paweł 032228
Durán Gómez, Eduardo 007457
Durán Nájera, Juan José 028412
Durán Solís, Leonel 028523
Durand, Agnes 012935, 012946
Durand, Alain 011738
Durand, André 011015
Durand, Micheline 010572, 010574
Durand, Régis 013564, 013599
Duranthon, Francis 014999
Durben, Silvan 046756
Durden, Chris J. 041936
Durdyeva, Tuvakbibi Kurbanovna 038204
Duret, Evelyne 014518
Duret, Michel 011786
Durham, A. Scott 046081
Durhône, Marise 010705
Durić, Vladimir 034146
Durkin, Birgid 043289
Durko, Prof. Janusz 032442
Durman, Prof. Mick 038722
Durmaz, Ş. Nihal 038160
Durnford, Louise 006257
Durnoff, M. 011875
Durr, Andy 038847
Durracq, Roger-Pierre 011957
Durrani, Prof. Farzaud 031391
Durrleman, Sophie 013638, 013645, 013668, 013724
Durschlag, Richard 049023
Dursi, Jen 046805
Durst, Duane R. 044424
Durst, John 048423
Dursum, Brian A. 043147
Durye, Joseph 015281
Dusar, Mark 003770
Duscher, Michael 002158
Dusheshe, Tanny 021569
Dussex, Armand 036844
Dutescu, Mihai 032850
Dutoit, Albert 037341
Dutra, James 049008
Dutschke, G.K. 001403, 001404
Duty, Michael W. 044977
Duval, Dennis 042941
Duval Reese, Becky 043637
Duvall, Tracy 048630
Duvernois, Bruno 012067
Duvivier, Christophe 013912, 013913
Duvoisin, Olivier 037348
Duvosquel, Jean-Marie 003843
Duyckaerts, E. 003617
Duysters, K. 029270
Duzenberry, Jeanelle 047109
Dvir, Orah 023009
Dvořáková, Dr. Hana 008286
Dwyer, Christine M. 041607
Dwyer, Tessa 001027
Dybbro, Inge 008948
Dybing, Leif 030810, 030811
Dyck, Angela 006782
Dyckmans, Heinrich 019170
Dye, Dr. Joseph M. 047429
Dyer, David 045936
Dyer, Deborah 042015
Dyer, John 001080
Dyer, John T. 048953
Dyer, Michael P. 048126
Dyer, Thomas 045191
Dyes, Brian 039814
Dykhuis, Peter 005565
Dyl, Stanley J. 044632
Dynak, Sharon 042970
Dysart, William 047834
Dzalilov, A. 049393
Džanaeva, Alla Akimovna 034034
Dzeko, Lebiba 003941
Dzeranov, Timur Efimovič 034038
Dzhalilov, I. 037841
Dziechciaruk-Maj, Bogna 032033
Dzięciołowski, Edwin 031932
Dziedzic, Bogusław 031822
Dziembowski, Bettina von 019233, 053449
Dziewior, Yilmaz 017705, 053388
Dziurzyński, Tadeusz 032030
Dzjadik, Jevgenija Mychajlivna 038356
Džuma, Galina Ivanivna 038339
Eade, Coila 044419
Eager, Barry W. 042168
Eakin, Eric 042065
Eames, Fred 001636
Earenfight, Philip 044673
Earenfight, Dr. Phillip 042622
Earl, L.M. 001209
Earl, Phillip I. 047372
Earle, Edward 046348
Earle, Susan 045206
Earls-Solari, Bonnie 047854
Early, Dr. Ann M. 041769
Early, J. W. 030432
Early, Judy 041783
Earnest, Ola May 047089
Earnst, Arlene E. 043486
Eastleigh, Lord 028990
Eastman, James 046744
Easton, Elizabeth 042458
Easton, Lois 044970
Easton-Moore, Barbara 043196
Eastty, Gary 043272
Eastwood, S.A. 038996
Eatman-Jackson, Rebecca 043833
Eaton, Alex 041260
Eaton, Jennifer 046332
Eaton, Kenneth M. 044588
Eaton, Mary Candace 046914
Eaton, Nellie 006112
Eaton, Virginia M. 047322
Eatts, M. 001154
Eayrs, Walter F. 042451
Ebbers, Klaus 018392
Èbedžans, Svetlana Georgievna 033575
Eberhardt, Dr. Hans-Joachim 019118
Eberl, Dr. Wolfgang 018298
Eberle, Josef 027840
Eberle, Lidia 032433
Eberle, Dr. Martin 016380, 016393
Eberle, Urs 037058, 037059
Eberli, Ulrich 037818
Ebert, Glenn 005080
Eberwein, Dr. Roland 002142
Ebie, Teresa H. 043637
Èbinger, Margarita Astemirovna 033097
Ebner, Dr. Lois 002235, 002384
Ebnet, David F. 047626
Ebtehaj, V. 022604
Echeverría Llanos, Clemente 007603
Ecjanov, A. 027397
Eckardt, Hans J. 037529
Eckenrode-Lewis, Emma 044691
Ecker, Dr. Berthold 002952
Ecker, Reingard 002832
Eckerbom, Jonas 036382
Eckerle, Dr. Klaus 018158
Eckerson, Rosemary 047290
Eckert, Lisa 048322
Eckert, Dr. Rainer 018596
Eckert-Schweizer, Angela 016841
Eckertn, Bob 045615
Eckhardt, Prof. Dr. Andreas 016318
Eckhardt, Cyndy 046518
Eckhardt, Mária 021665
Eckhardt, Susan 044899
Eckhel, Nerina 007832
Eckhoff, Audun 030756, 030757, 030758
Eckhout, Debbra 042151
Eckloff, Dr. Wolfram 018723
Eckmann, Sabine 047683
Eckstein, Beate 016326
Eckstrom, Carolyn 043704
Edblommery, Mats 036635
Eddie, I. 030566
Èdeleva, Inessa Aleksandrovna 033233
Edelmam, Asher B. 037428
Edelmann, Dr. Martina 020565
Eden, Dave 045973
Edenfield, W. Vernon 044058
Eder, Dr. Johanna 020364
Ederer, Walter 019301
Ederndorfer, Gerhard 002895
Edgar jr., Arthur C. 045857
Edge, Yvonne 040413
Edgert, Elizabeth 046127
Edgren, Bengt 036319
Edhofer, Elisabeth M. 002971
Edidin, Stephen R. 046320
Edina, Mèri 021812
Edinborough, Lisa 039097
Edinger, Dorothy 030660
Edison, Carol 047770
Edison, Robert D. 048629
Edland, Svein 045397
Edler, Dr. Doris 017357
Edler, Hans 002623
Edlinger, Matth. 002368
Edlund, D. 039088
Edmondson, J. 040030
Edmonson, Dr. James M. 042990
Edmunds, Allan L. 046929
Edo, Austin 031437
Edson, Gary 045513
Edson Way, Dr. J. 047965
Eduard, Ebner 001795
Edvardsen, Erik Henning 031080
Edward, Barbara 041396
Edwards, Ashley 048005
Edwards, Darwin 048855
Edwards, David 048471
Edwards, Denise 039064
Edwards, Geoffrey 001049
Edwards jr., Harford 043972
Edwards, Janet 000821
Edwards, Jim 045365
Edwards, John 038440
Edwards, Karen 006051
Edwards, Kathy 044768
Edwards, N. 038490
Edwards, Nancy E. 044009
Edwards, Nat 038489
Edwards, Pamela 046245
Edwards, Paul C. 046309
Edwards, Paula 044517
Edwards, Rita 044114
Edwards, Dr. Scott 048075
Edwards, Dr. S.R. 040406
Edwards, Susan H. 044936
Edwards, Wanda 044818
Edwards, William 040156
Eekhof, H.R. 030227
Eekhout, L.L.M. 029831
Eenhuis, Drs. M.C. 029430
Effenberger, Prof. Dr. Arne 016173
Efimovskij, A.F. 033294
Efrati, Y. 023105
Eftekhari, M. 022634
Egami, Namio 027186
Egan, Caroline 038818
Egan, Dominic 022689
Egawa, Tokusuke 026921
Egbaylar, Enis 038169
Egbert jr, Francis 044857
Egelseder, Berthold 002308
Egermann, Gerhard 002453, 002454
Egg, Prof. Dr. Markus 018794, 018794
Egge, Dr. Reimer 020520
Eggen, S. 003148
Egger, Dr. Franz 036885
Egger, Norbert 002140
Eggers, Bernardo 006920
Eggers, Dr. José Carlos 004491
Eggerstorfer, Alfred 002024
Eggl, Christine 002684
Eggleston Jamieson, Grace 042718
Egholm, Aage 008931
Egilsson, Kristjan 021985
Egipciaco, Wanda 046278
Egli, Markus 037317
Egloff, Prof. Dr. Michel 037181
Egloffstein, Dr. Albrecht Graf von und zu 019562
Egorova, Ljudmila Semenovna 034020
Egoryčev, Viktor Vasiljevič 033400
Egounlety, Micheline 003891
Egret, Daniel 013557
Eguía, Dr. José 036079, 036080, 036085
Ehls, Heiner 017962
Ehm, Rainer 019747
Ehn, Prof. Friedrich 001810
Ehrenberg, Johanna 037161
Ehrenberg, Rolf 018991
Ehrenfellner, Dr. Karl 002567
Ehrenheim, Jacob von 036250
Ehrenhuber, Franz 001721
Ehrenkranz, Joel S. 046418
Ehrentraud, Adolf 001980
Ehres, Maria 036764
Ehrhart, Bernhard 018531
Ehrle, Dr. Peter Michael 018156
Ehrlich, Dr. Richard 042041
Ehrlich, Richard L. 043004
Ehrmann-Schindlbeck, Anna-Maria 018104
Ehry, Carl A. 043664
Ehser, Claudia 019333
Eibl, Simon 018528
Eiblmayr, Dr. Silvia 002080
Eichelberger, Allison 045150
Eichenauer, Jürgen 019454
Eichenberger, Peter 036928
Eichhorn jun., Georg 002844
Eichhorn, Dr. Helmut 016963
Eichhorn, Herbert 016242

Eichler, Heidrun 018837
Eichmann, Erland 037713
Eichorn, Cornelia 041587
Eickhorst, Dr. William S. 044925
Eickmann, Margaret 047179
Eickmann, Theodore 043571
Eidam, Hardy 017016
Eidemüller, Gisela 016246
Eidlin, Nathan 023061
Eidsaune, Thor Helge 031017
Eielson, Kerry 041710
Eifrig, Jennifer S. 049128
Eigler, Gerd 017781
Eigner, Gerda 002972
Eikelmann, Dr. 018041
Eikelmann, Dr. Renate . . 018233, 018234, 019039, 019411, 019412, 019416, 019760
Eiken, Dr. Douglas 045083
Eikenoord, R.G. 030104
Eikermann, Silke 016475
Eiland, William U. 041832
Eilat, Galit 022935
Eilertsen, John 047452
Eilertson, Orie 047222
Eillott, John 001488
Eilschou Holm, Niels 008986
Eimbeck 029080
Eimer, Prof. Gerhard 018025
Eimert, Dr. Dorothea 016823, 016824
Einarsdóttir, Björg 021986
Einecke, Claudia 046680
Einhorn, Peggi 042457
Einreinhofer, Nancy 049029
Eins, Annaleen 029106
Einstein, Laura 046208
Eipper, Paul-Bernhard 037820
Eiraku, Toru 026999
Eirola, Martti 029092
Eis, Ruth 042162
Eiselt, Gerhard 018739
Eisenberg, Joseph 000752
Eisenburger, Dr. C.M.S. 029307
Eisenhofer, Dr. Stefan 019122
Eisenmann, Mark 046216
Eisl, Sigmund 002722
Eisler, Dr. János 021694
Eisley, Patricia 048830
Eisley, Susan 047067
Eisner, Michael 045099
Eissenhauer, Dr. Michael . 015826, 018179, 018180, 018183, 018186, 018187, 018191, 018196, 018198, 018200, 018203, 018204
Eitam, David 022923
Eiynck, Dr. A. 018661
Eizenberg, Arie 022898
Ek-Nilsson, Katarina 036675
Ekberg, Anna 036511
Ekblom, Bengt 036742
Ekelhart-Reinwetter, Dr. Christine . 002845
Ekinci, H. Ali 038030
Eklund, Dr. Sigrid 036652
Ekpo, Violeta I. 030708
Ekström, Börje 036438
Ekström, Kjell 009857, 009860
Ekström Söderlund, Birgitta 009504
El-Amrani, Dr. Ahmed 029043
El-Aziz, Fatma Abd 009310
El-Bahtimi, M. 009295
El-Bedawi, Mohammed Ahmed . . . 009293
El-Hajj, Amal Abu 022946
El-Hajraoui, Mohamed Abdelwahed 029030
El-Husseini, Dr. Mehrez 009282
El-Kasri, Houceine 029032
El-Moussli, Majed 037833
El-Nur, Prof. Osama A. . . . 036148, 036151
El-Ouafi, Prof. Boubker 029022
El-Younsi, Dr. Amin 029040
Elas-Necel, Karol 031867
Elayyan, Khaled 031406
Elba La Gioiosa, Rosa 000353
Eldamaty, Dr. Mamdouh 009297
Elder, E.J. 006821
Elder, Kym 048907
Elderfield, John 045389
Eldredge, Bruce B. 045315, 048275
Eldridge, Harold 038889
Eldridge, Karen 045232
Eldridge, Ruth 039076
Elen, A. 030088
Elerd, Udo 019473
Elfström, Gunnar 036424
Elgen, Fran 042202
Elger, Dr. Dietmar 017769
Elgstrand, Greg 005181
Elias, Prof. Giacomo 026105
Elias, Ramon Jan 044843
Elias Ortiz, Alejandrina 028783
Eliasen, Kirstin 009033
Eliason, Sara 036798
Eliasson, Ulla 036614
Eliëns, Prof. Dr. T.M. 029424
Eliezer-Brunner, Henrietta 023072
Eliot, D. 041192
Elis, Dr. Karlpeter 001929
Elk, Sara Jane 046935
Elkhadem, Hossam 003291
Elkin, Geoff 040466
Elkin, G.U. 033378
Elkington, Marian 038506
Elkington, Peter 038506
Elkjær, Trine 008806
Ellen, David M. 040508
Ellenbroek, Dr. F.J.M. 030208
Ellender, Dan 045100
Ellensint Kremer, M. 020547
Eller, E. 020114
Ellerman, Deborah L. 041788
Ellermann-Minda, Petra 001927
Ellermeier, Dr. Friedrich 017774
Ellermeyer, Dr. Jürgen 017709
Ellersdorfer, Heinz 002627, 002628, 002630
Ellin, Simone 041989
Ellingsen, Harry 030783, 030784
Ellington, Howard W. 049164
Elliott, Dana R. 043829
Elliott, Fiona 039963
Elliott, George 006872
Elliott, J.H. 041849
Elliott, Lucy 043516
Elliott, Mary Gene 041849
Elliott, Patrick 039424
Elliott, Rachael 001091
Ellis, Amy 044463
Ellis, Anita 042919
Ellis, Caroline . . . 040095, 040233, 041245
Ellis, David W. 042335
Ellis, Evelyn M. 045324
Ellis, George R. 044598
Ellis, Gillian 038737
Ellis, J. 022709
Ellis, J.C. 045187
Ellis, Joe 042647
Ellis, Lori 005065
Ellis, Pam 042662
Ellis, Robert E. 044898
Ellis, Steven 042640
Ellis-Peckham, Courtney 043734
Ellison, Dr. Curtis W. 046774
Ellison, Rosemary 041707
Elliston Weiner, Sarah 046365
Ellmers, Prof. Dr. Detlev 016429
Ellmeyer, Stephan 002518
Ellsworth, Lynn 046062
Ellwood, Tony 001246
Elmén Berg, Anna 036540
Elmore, Fletcher L. 045497
Elmore, George 045175
Elmqvist, Inga 036653
Elo, Maija 010093
Elorduy, Julieta Gil 028079
Elorza Guinea, Juan Carlos 035004
Eloy, Paul 003618
Eloy, Vicente 036034
Elsasser, Kilian 037305
Elsbree, Carl J. 042254
Elsbury, Kathy 042528
Elsen, 19.-21. Jh., Dr. Thomas . . . 015609
Elsen, Dr. Thomas 015617
Elsen-Schwedter, Dr. Beate 018432
Elšin, Sergej Veniamovič 033264
Elsner, Dr. Tobias von 018769
Elsom, Sarah 040002
Elsposch, Friedrich 016854
Elston, Tim 046870
Elsworth, Jo 038869
Elustondo, André 014347
Eluyemi, Dr. Omotoso 030669, 030672
Elvira Barba, Miguel Angel 035394
Ely, Bruno 010293, 010298
Elyasiv, Isaac 023057
Elzenga, Dr. E. 029256
Elzinga, Dr. C. 029837
Éma, Robert 012835
Emack Cambra, Jane 048507
Emanuel, Ludovít 008644
Emanuel, Nina 018554
Emanuelli, Dr. Giuseppe 025210
Ember, Dr. Ildikó 021694
Embertsén, Lena 036439
Emenegger, Ashley 049082
Emerick, Emily W. 045961
Emerson, David 041890
Emerson, Francis 049323, 049324
Emerson, Julie 048091
Emerson, Lucius J. 022854
Emerson, Myra 045139
Emerson, Pam 048591
Emerson, Philip G. 049182
Emerson, Robert L. 049358
Emery, Dominique 011894
Emery, Dr. K.F. 044103
Emigholz, Dr. Björn 020576
Emiliani, Prof. Andrea 023461
Eminger, Dr. Jürgen 020458
Emmanuel, Victoria 038734
Emmendörffer, Dr. Christoph 015614
Emonson, Janet 006447
Emont Scott, Deborah 044924
Encinas, Isabel 035405
Enciso Núñez, José Antonio 028171
End, Reinhard 017363
Ende, Arlyn 048118
Endenburg, Constanze 030100
Enders, Don 047630
Enders, Donald L. 047774
Endersbe, Susan U. 048057
Endert, D. van 015530
Endicott, John 039039
Endo, Koichi 027110
Endraß, Max 015560
Endzweig, Pamela 043746
Enei, Flavio 025756
Enei, Vicente 000469
Enevoldsen, V. 008991
Engberg, Siri 045922
Engdahl, Sarah 042965, 042966
Engel, Beate 036940
Engel, Birgit 015992
Engel, Donald J. 043571
Engel, Edmée 027895
Engel, Melissa 043555
Engel, Michael 045205
Engel, Robert 042430
Engel, Volker 016320
Engel, Dr. Walter 016830
Engelbach, Dr. Barbara 020200
Engelbosch, Christa 003768
Engelbrecht, Dr. C.M. . . . 034556, 034557, 034562
Engelbrecht, Dean Mark. 041686
Engelkemier, Catherine 041677
Engelmann, Christine 019278
Engelmann, Judith 017949
Engels, C.L.M. 029576
Engels, D. 030416
Engels, Kim 020865
Engels, Maria 015421
Engelsman, Dr. S.B. 029854
Engeman, Richard 047174
Engen, Jorunn 030816
Engen, Luc 003528
Engeseter, Aage 030934
Engesser, Dr. Burkart 036899
Engfors, Christina 036614
Enghoff, Dr. Henrik 008993
England, Ann 041859
Englebright, Steven E. 048378
Englert, Emil 020763
Englick, Gerd 015791
English, Catherine 006274
English, Charles L. 049236
English, Donise 047210
English, Louella F. 049236
English, Marie 046768
English, Patrick 046334
Engström, Johan 036615
Engström, Urban 036466
Enguita, Nuria 034907
Enkhtsetseg, Dashdavaa 029004
Enne, Eva 002312
Ennen, Dr. J. 020372
Enriqueta del Castillo y Mejía, María 028500
Enriquez, Felonilla D. 031664
Enseki, Carol 042457
Ensign, Garald 044665
Enslow, Ellen 049068
Ensslen, D. 005411
Enticott, Delyth 040543
Entin, Daniel 046392
Entwistle, R. 039813
Enz, Peter 037762
Enzler, Jerome A. 043513, 043514
Epp, Bear 005377
Eppensteiner, Heinz 002238
Eppich, Linda 047257, 047264
Epping, Nancy J. 043650
Eppinger, Virginia 042416
Epple, Sabine 018572
Eppler, Dr. Peter 003017
Eppler-Jehle, Ursula 015469, 015472
Epprecht, Dr. Katharina 037789
Epps, Renee 046358
Erancis, Dr. R.W. 041328
Erasmus, Prof. Theuns 034714
Erašova, Galina 033578
Erb, Christian 017169
Erbach-Erbach, Franz Graf zu 017001
Erbentraut, Dr. Regina 017601
Erbguth, Dr. Horst 019744, 019747
Erbschwendtner, Josef 002582
Ercolani, Fausto 026222
Erdem, Emin 038126
Erdem, Mehmet 038075
Erdenebat, P. 029011
Erdmann, Walter Johannes 017488
Erdoğan, Mustafa 038199
Eregina, Galina Nikolaevna 033759
Eremina, Natalija Aleksandrovna . . 033615
Erf, Lisa K. 042843
Erffa, Dr. Axel von 018176
Erftemeijer, A.F.W. 029653
Ergert, Bernd E. 019044
Ergin, Muhlis 038088
Ergino, Nathalie 012936
Erhart, Heinrich 002652
Erhart, Ingeborg 002096
Erhatic Širnik, Romana 034495
Erias Martinez, Alfredo 034980
Ericani, Dr. Giuliana 023352, 023355
Erice Lacabe, Romana . . . 036103, 036108
Erich, Frasl 002519
Erichsen, Dr. Johannes . . . 018442, 018443
Erichsen, John 008937
Erichson, Ulf 019826
Ericini, Carlo 023495
Erickson, Bruce R. 047709
Erickson, Florence 005840
Erickson, Marsha 044937
Erickson, Ruth 046896

Erickson, Willis D. 041961
Eriksson, Håkan 036744
Eriksson, Maud 036430
Eriksson, Nadja 036375
Eriksson, Susan C. 042245
Eringen, P. 047320
Eritsyan, Elena Sergeevna 033459
Erk, Werner 017426
Erkelens, Dr. A.M.L.E. 029256
Erkinova, Rimma Michajlovna 033152
Erlande-Brandenburg, Alain 011680
Erlandsen, Roger 031246
Erlindo, Vittorio 024748
Erlinger, Fritz 002573
Ermacora, Dr. Beate 018399
Ermeling, Andreas 019152
Ermert, Axel 016081
Ermischer, Dr. G. 015586
Ermolaeva, Ljudmila Nikolaevna 033361
Ernet, Dr. Detlef 001938
Ernst, Alfred 019000
Ernst, Gay 041952
Ernst, Hannelore 020246
Ernst, Joey 034569
Ernst, Jürgen 018577
Ernst, Mathias 020246
Ernst, Dr. Rainer 017123
Ernst-Adolf, Kloth 017864
Ernstell, Eva-Sofi 036639
Erochin, Viktor Ivanovič 033997
Erol, Dr. Erdogan 038057, 038130, 038132, 038133, 038136, 038137, 038138
Erramah, Mourad 037958
Erskine, David 038555
Eršova, Valentina Petrovna 033674
Ertel, Dr. Christine 002300
Ėrtjukova, Nadežda Semenovna 033185
Ertman, Willis 044556
Erts, Keith 042514
Erwin, Douglas H. 048930
Erwin, Renee 044007
Erwin, Sarah 048653
Eržen, Miro 034505
Erzsébet, Dr. Kovácsné Bircher 021845
Escalas, Román 034932
Escallon, Ana Maria 048883
Escandor, Beatriz 045421
Escat, Monique 014383, 014837
Esche, Charles 029550, 036462
Eschebach, Dr. Erika 016393
Eschenburg, Dr. Barbara 019124
Escobar, Ticio 031439
Escobar, Washington 041556
Escoffier, André 014695
Escriche, Carmen 035910
Escriche Jaime, Carmen 035860
Escrivà, J. Ramon 035976
Escudero, Juan Miguel 031783
Esera, T. 034108
Esguerra, Liwliwa 031638
Eshenroder, Glenda 044628
Eskildsen, Prof. Ute 017075
Eskritt, Jodi Ann 005036
Esman, J. 030209
Esparza, Richard R. 047460
Espeland, Else 031071
Espinagosa Marsà, Jaume 035898
Espinola, Vera 047715
Espinós, Adela 035978
Espinosa, Deborah 047276
Espinosa, Gina Agnes 031673
Espinosa Jiménez, Eleazar 008111
Espinosa Rodriguez, Antonio 028033, 028045
Espinosa Ruiz, Antonio 036065
Espinosa Yglesias, Angeles 028648
Espinoza, Carlos A. 006932
Espinoza, Felipe 028450
Espinoza Arrubarrena, Luis 028460
Espinoza Mella, Adelaida 007432
Espinoza Pérez, Egdar 030665
Espírito Santo Bustorff Silva, Dr. Maria João 032629
Espiritu Gaston, Lynell 031789
Espointour, Elizabeth 041818
Espuiagosa Marsa, Jaume 035897
Eßbach, Elke 021097
Esseiva, Renato 037591
Essen, Dr. Manfred von 019331
Esser, Dr. Werner 019378
Essers, Dr. Volkmar 016834
Essig, Timothy 045149
Estall i Poles, Vicent 035560, 035562
Esteban Darder, Vicente 035950
Estep, Connie 047393
Esterhuizen, Valerie 034734
Estes, Dr. James R. 045313
Estes, Judith 044678, 044679, 044681
Esteve, Y. 012101
Estévez González, Fernando 035316
Estham, Inger 036739
Estrada, Cesar P. 031649
Estrada Sánchez, Ramiro 028109
Estrela, Tiago 006896
Etches, Richard A. 044113
Etgar, Raphie 022970
Ethelberg, Per 008885
Etling, Russell 045816
Ettema, Michael J. 049168
Etter, Dr. Walter 036899
Ettrich, Berthold 016594
Eubanks, Ray 048265
Eugster, Willi 037508
Euler, Dr. Andrea 002256
Euler-Schmidt, Dr. Michael 018322
Eure, Linda Jordan 043602
Eutsler, Therese 045323
Eva, Jan 000852
Evan, Paul 039959
Evangelinos, Aris 021401
Evangelist, Andrea 045536
Evanich, Joan 049246
Evans, Bob 005982
Evans, Catherine 043106
Evans, Cathy 042737
Evans, D.W. 040707
Evans, Ed 005120
Evans, Eddie L. 042095
Evans, Edward 040656
Evans, Elaine A. 045039
Evans, G.H. 039002
Evans, Helen H. 044037
Evans, Jonathan 040276
Evans, Linda 048430
Evans, Margaret 043104, 044405
Evans, Megan E. 044394
Evans, Michael 042055
Evans, N. 030590
Evans, Paul 040268
Evans, Steven 042069, 046324
Evans, Sylvia B. 047430
Evans, Viola 005441
Evares, J. 041266
Evascovich, Mildred 041592
Evdokimov, Vladimir Aleksandrovič 033371
Evdokimov, Vladimir Nikolaevič 033134, 033135
Eveleigh, David J. 038858, 038859
Eveler, Kimberly 048227
Evelyn, Douglas E. 046383
Evensen, Anne Bjørg 030988
Everard, R.H.A.J. 029658
Everbrand, Lars-Åke 036209
Everett, Julienne 005089
Everett, Martin 038827
Everly, Nancy 043215
Evers, Prof. Dr. Bernd 016101
Evers, Bisse 036303
Evers, Cécile 003353
Evers, Richard 044529
Evers, Dr. Ulrika 019581
Eversberg, Dr. Gerd 018038
Eversmann, Pauline K. 049265
Evetts, Deborah 046394
Evgenidou, Despina 021207
Evgeniev, Todor 004648
Evstigneeva, Irina V. 033829, 033831
Evtimov, Dejan 004887
Ewald, Jill 046553
Ewell, Matson 043797
Ewen, Les 046024
Ewers, William 042872
Ewert, George H. 045946, 045950
Ewertowski, Zbigniew 032170
Ewigleben, Dr. Cornelia 020263
Ewing, Phyllis 044436
Ewing, Steve 046068
Ewing, William A. 037249
Ewington, Julie 001474
Ex, Dr. K.M.T. 030226, 030239
Exnarová, Alena 008341
Eyb, Alexander Freiherr von 020947
Eyb, Silvia Freifrau von 020947
Eychner, George 044757
Eyland, Cliff 006846
Eyler, Carolyn 044250
Ezell-Gilson, Carol 042730
Ezquerra, Beatriz 035910
Ezsöl, Adolf 002667
Fabbri, Fabio 025162
Fabbri, Dr. Francesco 023371
Fabbri, Dr. Franco 024224, 024225, 024226, 024227, 024230, 024233
Fabbri, Jennifer S. 034705
Fabela, Pamela K. 048583
Fabényi, Dr. Júlia 021676
Faber, Alain 027895
Faber, Dr. Elfriede 002874
Faber, Dr. Michael 018866
Faber, Dr. Monika 002845
Faber, O. 029297
Faber, Ole 008820, 008821, 008822, 009029, 009054, 009055, 009138, 009139, 009140
Faber, P. 029194
Faberman, Hilarie 048319
Fabian, Dr. Claudia 019037
Fabian, Rick 042685
Fabiani, Rossella 026147
Fabiankowitsch, Gabriele 002945
Fabich, Uwe 018529
Fabing, Suzannah 046545
Fabiny, Dr. Tibor 021648
Fabisiak, Wojciech 032325
Fabre, Eric 011998, 013641, 013642
Fabre, Jean-Louis 013919
Fabregues, M. de 012975
Fabrezi, Dr. Marissa 000538
Fabricius, Karen M. 008800, 008801, 008802, 009111
Fabris, Dr. Corrado 023275
Fabris, Jean 014665
Fabritius, Dr. Ruth 019821
Fabrizio, Fernando di 025155
Fabyan, Dr. E. Joseph 048791
Facchinetti, Claudio 023652
Facchini, Prof. Fiorenzo 023440
Faccinto, Victor 049251, 049259
Facciolongo, Sabino 023633
Fachrudin, H. 022441
Fadani, Dr. Andrea 020531
Fadden, John 046686
Fadeev, Igor 033379
Fae Kamm, Marie 043272
Fährig, Ute 017654
Faelmar-Abad, Mary 031651
Faenzi, Giovanna 024159
Færøy, Frode 031091
Fässler, Klaus 036848
Fagaly, William A. 046263
Fagbohunmi, Johnson 030684
Fage, André 013586
Fagerli, Karl A. 031054
Fagerstedt, Elisabeth 036721
Fagnant, Susan 045203
Faherty, William B. 044496
Fahey, John M. 048903
Fahey, Peggy 005604
Fahl, Dr. Andreas 017755
Fahl-Dreger, Axel 020563
Fahlund, Michael 046320
Fahrenbruch, Melanie 043176
Fahrer, Uwe 016401
Fahy, Everett 046364
Faietti, Dr. Marzia 023419
Failla, Dr. Donatella 024304
Faille d'Huysse, B. Baron della 003872
Faine, Susan 001448
Fair, Eileen 047936
Fair Sleeper, Sara 041627
Fairbank, Lynn 043360
Fairbanks, Theresa 046227
Fairclough, Oliver 038990
Fairfax, Anne 046363
Fairfax, James A. 048953
Fairfull, Thomas M. 043908
Fairman, Elisabeth 046227
Fairweather, Valerie A. 041102
Faißner, Waltraud 002249
Faivre, Bernard 012283
Fakundiny, Robert H. 041599
Falabrino, Ugo 026150
Falaschi, Prof. Pierluigi 023599, 023607
Falcão, Prof. José Antonio 032574
Falco, João 004047
Falco, Joseph 015229
Falconbridge, Liz 039877
Fales, Allen 044784
Falgayrettes, Christiane 013627
Falk, Dr. Birgitta 017063
Falk, Martin 001885
Falk, Rita 002096
Falke, Ulla 012177
Falkenberg, Edward 006588
Falkenberg, Dr. Regine 016011
Falkenberg, Dr. Uwe 016791
Falkenstien-Doyle, Cheri 047980
Falkner, Dr. Gerd 019630
Fallet, Estelle 037129
Falletti, Dr. Franca 024158
Fallon, Steve 048819
Falomir, Miguel 035429
Faltings, Dr. Dina 017834
Falvy, Dr. Zoltán 021703
Falz, A. 020156
Falz, Andreas 017836, 018810
Falz, Bernd 017889
Famà, Dr. Maria Luisa 026101
Famuyiwa, M.B. 030683
Fanciotto, Cristiana 025199
Fanelli, Doris 046937
Fang, Madeleine 042165
Fangarezzi, Dr. Riccardo 024952
Fankhauser, Heinz 036993
Fanni, Dr. Ignazio 026332
Fanning, Dale A. 047269
Fanony Fulgence 027937
Fansa, Prof. Dr. Mamoun 019471
Fanti, Mario 023447
Fanzun, Jon 037621
Farabee, Ann 042248
Farah, Ahmed 034541
Farahmanesh, Nazi 022571
Farar, Bill 043233
Farbaky, Dr. Péter 021661
Farber, Janet 046680
Faria, Dr. João Carlos Lázaro 032571
Farina, Dr. Ermes 026267
Fariña Busto, Francisco 035579, 035701
Faringdon, Lord 039485
Faris, Douglas D. 048130
Faris, M.P. 022723
Faris, Peter 041908
Farkas, Jesse 043728
Farley, G. 044490
Farley, Gayle 046642
Farley, Henry G. 048590
Farley, Dr. Linda E. 043400
Farley-Harger, Sara 044034
Farmer, Caroline 001366
Farmer, Dennis 042808
Farmer, Dorothy 005360

Farmer, Sid 040796
Farnden, Bob 001157
Farnell, C. 039687
Farnham, Priscilla 043800
Farnhill, Elizabeth 039048
Farnós y Bel, Alex 034838
Farnyk, Patricia Barnett Diane 046333
Farooqi, Dr. Anish 022087
Farr, Amanda 040582
Farr, Fonda 046606
Farr, Raye 048952
Farrajota Ataide Garcia, Dr. Maria Madalena 032639
Farrand, Dr. William R. 041733
Farrar, Ellyn M. 048553
Farrar, H.D. 046636
Farrar, Robert A. 044541
Farre, Pascal 037267
Farrell, Harold 038780, 038781
Farrell, Kathleen 047481
Farrell, Laurie 045388
Farrell, Lesley 041064
Farrell, Thomas L. 047219
Farrenkopf, Dr. Michael 016276
Farrington, Charles W. 046525
Farrington, Jane 038723
Farsan, Dr. N.M. 017831
Farver, Bonnie 042270
Farver, Jane 042565
Farwell, Richard S. 045818
Farwell-Gavin, Robin 047972, 047973
Fasching, Josef 001783
Fasciati, Luciano 037089
Fasel, André 037101
Fasold, Dr. Peter 017152
Fasold, Dr. Regina 017846
Fassati, Tomáš 008265
Fassbinder, Dr. S. 017524
Fasse, Dr. Norbert 016345
Fasser, Ernst 037503
Fast, Dr. Kirsten 017085, 017086
Fastlicht, Dr. Samuel 028477
Fateh, Suzanne 048878
Fatehi, F. 022561
Fatimah, T. 022397
Fatka, Jaroslav . 008594, 008600, 008601, 008606, 008607, 008652
Faton, Louis 013563
Fauchille, Bernard 013141
Faude, Wilson H. 044462
Faul, Beverly 047156
Faulds, W. Rod 042286
Faulkner, D. Lindsay 030608
Faulkner, John 042959
Faulkner, Peter 001550
Faulkner, Rebecca 046327
Faulkner, Tim 039848
Faull, Dr. Margaret 041274
Faure-Comte, Karen 015227
Fauria, Dr. Carmen 034947
Faust, Alexis 048635
Faust, Pierre-Paul 014134
Faust, Dr. Sabine 020483
Fautin, Daphne 045205
Fauver, Lynn N. 046064
Fava, Lourdes 028963
Favata, Alexa 048487
Favell, Gene H. 045028
Favell, Georg 044651
Favre, Lee M. 045364
Favre, Dr. Pascal 037267
Favre, Séverine 037681
Favro, Diane 042828
Fawaz, Salma 027817
Fawell, Anne 045068
Fawzi, Ibrahim 022975
Faxe, Birgitta 036371
Faxon, Susan 041721
Fay, David 043810
Fay, Joyce 042519
Fay, Martin 044471
Fayard, Armand 012026
Faydali, Erol 038159
Fayet, Dr. Roger 037524
Fayet, Roger 037786
Fazekas, Patricia L. 046207
Fazel, Asghar M. 022637
Fazia, Gloria 024208
Fazzi, Kim 047438
Fazzini, Richard 042458
Fazzone, Mary Ann 046214
Fearn, Peter 001176
Feaster, Richard 046320
Feather, Philip H. 045225
Fechter, E. 017635, 017636
Fedele, Prof. F.G. 024905
Federico, Jean 041640
Federle Orr, Dr. Lynn 047857, 047871
Fediw, Mary 046967
Fedorenko, Tamara Grigorjevna . . 033789
Fëdorova, Ljubov Nikolaevna 033593
Fëdorova, Ljudmila Ivanovna 033225
Fëdorova, Natalja Viktorovna 033170
Fedorowicz, Władysław 032074
Fedyna, Holger 019200
Fedynsky, Andrew 043003
Feeley, Betsey 046281
Feely, Dr. Martin 022790
Feeney, Lawrence 043100
Feeney, Warren 030461
Feest, Prof. Dr. Christian 002961
Feffee, Claudette 047207
Fefjuca, T.A. 038226
Fehér, Béla 021786
Fehér, Dr. György 021670
Fehérvári, Béla 021773
Fehle, Dr. Isabella 018790
Fehlemann, Dr. Sabine . . . 021019, 021021
Fehlhammer, Prof. Dr. Dr. Wolf Peter 019045
Fehlhammer, Prof. Dr. Wolf Peter . 019046
Fehlhammer, Prof. Dr. Dr. Wolf Peter 019413
Fehr, Horst 018675
Fehr, Dr. Michael 017624, 017625
Feichtlbauer, Brunhilde 001688
Feickert, Rudolf 020724
Feigel, Martine 013292
Feihler, Tim 042294
Feil, Fr. Carl 048573
Feinberg, Larry 042820
Feitknecht, Dr. Thomas 036936
Fejös, Dr. Zoltán 021678
Fekeza, Lidija 003941
Felbauer, Josef 002209
Felbauer, Maria 002209
Felber, René 037180
Felbermayer, Dietrich 002468
Feldbauer, Sara 044474
Feldberg, Michael 046285
Feldborg, Jan 030914
Feldes, Angelika 020257
Feldkamp, Dr. Jörg 016564
Feldkamp, Ursula 016429
Feldman, Kaywin 045764
Feldman, M.M 022955
Feldmane, Milda 027717
Feldmann, Dorothee 019648
Feldmer, Peter 017789
Felgenhauer-Schmiedt, Prof. Dr. Sabine 002742
Felhösné-Csiszár, Dr. Sarolta 021916
Felice, Silvio 028024
Felisati, Vittorio 024105
Fellay, André 037006
Felley, Jean-Paul 037110, 054173
Fellmeth, Dr. Ulrich 020360
Fellner, Fritz 001868
Fellner, Manuela 003009
Fellner, Marianne 007530
Felsher, Lynn 046370
Felshin, Nina 045840
Felz, Joseph 044094
Fenger, Lars 008938
Fennema, A.T. 029400
Fenner, Gloria J. 048646
Fenoglio, Norma 000496
Fenoglio, Norma C. 000497
Fensterstock, Lauren 047584
Fenton, David 048748
Fenton, Dr. Frank M. 049189
Fenton, John 000872
Fentress, Steven 047483
Ferarresi, Roberto 024132
Ferasin, Luigi 012661
Ferber, Linda 042458
Ferchland, Andrea 015992
Ferdi, Sabah 000079
Ferebee, Peggy V. 044337
Ferenczy, Dr. Mária 021655
Ferez Kuri, Maria del Carmen 028527
Fergola, Dr. Lorenzo 026085
Ferguson, Ian 030631
Ferguson, Moira 039875
Ferguson, Patricia 006600
Ferguson, Randy 047236
Ferguson, Ray 047512
Ferguson, Robert S. 039569
Fergusson, Ian L.C. 040273
Feria, Dr. Rafael 035405
Ferigo, Dr. Giorgio 026041
Ferino-Pagden, Dr. Sylvia 002934
Ferleger Brades, Susan 040172
Fermont, W.J.J. 029854
Fernan, Marissa N. 031660
Fernandes, Albano 032575
Fernandes, Isabel Maria 032620
Fernandes Gomes, João José 032573
Fernández, Dr. Antonio 006911
Fernández, Jorge H. 035160, 035162
Fernandez, Jorge Osvaldo 000190
Fernández, José Antonio 035953
Fernández, Kathleen M. 042293
Fernández, Luis Alfonso 003919
Fernandez, Luisito F. 031769
Fernández, Maria Angélica 000499
Fernandez, Nohema 044778
Fernández Bal, María Luisa 035701
Fernández Camargo, Gustavo 007623
Fernández Castañón Carrasco, José Antonio 035585
Fernández Cid, Miguel 035816
Fernández de Calderón, Cándida . . 028501
Fernández de Córdova Marquesa de Mirabel, Dr. Hilda 035658
Fernández de Henestrosa, Carlos . 035438
Fernández de Ulibarri, Rocío 007673
Fernández Gómez, Fernando 035858
Fernández Lóp, Olga 036005
Fernández Ugalde, Antonio 035158
Fernández Villaverde, Duque Alvaro 035439, 035761
Fernholm, Ragnhild 036426
Fernier, Jean-Jaques 013522
Ferolla Frizzi, Dr. Vanda 023691
Ferrandi, Dr. Giuseppe 026112
Ferrara, Giovanni 024922
Ferraresi, Roberto 024131
Ferrari, Alessio 024850
Ferrari, Amedeo 023995
Ferrari, Ciro 023750, 024607
Ferraris, Francesco 026276
Ferraris, Pietro 023141
Ferrazzini, Petra 037000
Ferré, Rosario 032722
Ferreau, Christine 019391
Ferreira, Bernardo 043290
Ferreira, Claudia Marcia 004375
Ferreira, Ivette Senise 004520
Ferreira, João Carlos A. 004381
Ferreira, José 000100
Ferreira Brandão, Dr. Carlos Roberto 004541
Ferreira Calado, Dr. Luis 032630
Ferreira da Costa, Paulo 032650
Ferreira da Cunha, Sergio Henrique 004278
Ferrell, John 042888
Ferren, Dick 048856
Ferrer jr., Dominador 031737
Ferrer Ciari, Agustín 034833
Ferrer Dalgà, María Rosa 035235
Ferrer-Joly, Fabien 010531
Ferrer Soria, José Luis 035213
Ferrero, Marcelo 000144
Ferres, Katleen 044275
Ferreyra, Prof. Carlos Alfredo 000380
Ferries, D. 040577
Ferrill, Winifred 045128
Ferriol 014904
Ferris, Alison 042487
Ferriso, Brian 045892
Fersen, Vera von 009555
Fertig-Möller, Heidelore 020810
Fesik, Kateryna Borysivna 038378
Festa, Mario 023111
Festanti, Dr. Maurizio 025413
Festini, Prof. Zvonko 007834
Fett, T. 030764
Fetter, Rosemary 041979
Feuß, Prof. Dr. Axel 017680
Fewkes, Nancy 042836, 042861
Fewster, Dr. Kevin 001525, 001575
Feyertag, Gertrude 002287
Feyler, Gabrielle . 014715, 014716, 014718
Fiala, Claudia 018055
Fiala Erlich, Chris 044188
Fiallo Hernández, Eduardo 009164
Fiaschetti, Maria Egizia 025544
Fibicher, Dr. Bernhard 036929
Fibiger, Susanne 008912
Fichner-Rathus, Prof. Dr. Lois 048601
Fick, Dr. Astrid . 018034, 018035, 018037, 020780, 020782
Fickert, Hildegard 016513
Fideucci, Elaine 044470
Fidler, Stephen David 040821
Fiechter, Hermann 037647
Fiedler, Dr. Elisabeth 001943
Fiedler, Marek 032275
Fiedler, Uwe 016565
Fiedler Streng, Evelyn 048106
Fiege, Kirsten 018432
Field, Caroline 001210
Field, Hannah 038544
Field, Monica . . . 005311, 005312, 006670
Field, Peter 040593, 040594, 040596
Field, Dr. Richard 044732
Fielden, Dr. Kate 038949
Fielding, Andrew 040599
Fielding, James 006865
Fields, Edward D. 042290
Fields, Hoyt 047923
Fields, Laura 042069
Fields, Vilma S. 042775
Fierro Gossman, Julieta N. 028544
Fierz, Gaby 036893
Fietsam, Robert 042107
Fiette, Alexandre 037128
Fietz, Dr. Rudolf 019469
Fifield, Donald 048545
Fifiiţă, Mariana 032870
Figari, G.B. Roberto 023610
Figlarowicz, Stefan 031908
Figueiredo, Alexandrine 011504
Figueres, Roger 012976
Figueroa, Elisa 006946
Figuerolar, Prof. I. 034931
Figuti, Midory Kimura 004512
Fike, Nancy J. 048689
Filieri, Dr. Maria Teresa . . . 024547, 024548
Filina, Larissa 033419
Filipčić-Maligec, Vlatka 007722
Filipetti, Dr. Giuseppe 024475
Filipova, F. 004944
Filipová, Maria 008578
Filipović, Marica 003941
Filipow, Dr. Krzystof 031829
Filipowicz, Zygmunt 032350
Filippi, Dr. Giorgio 049422
Filippo, Giuseppe 023296
Filippone, Christine 046981
Filippova, Ėleonora Anatoljevna . . . 033146

Fillman, Joseph B. 041658
Filtvedt, Per Kr. 031128
Fimpeler-Philippen, Annette 016845, 016846
Finaldi, Dr. Gabriele 035429, 040241
Finamore, Dr. Daniel 047741
Finamore, Prof. Nino 025796
Finat, Joelle 012532
Finch, Jon 040010, 040012
Finch, Patricia 041166
Finch, Rick 048715
Finch, Sarah 038946
Finch-Crisp, Sarah 041175
Finckh, Dr. Gerhard 018628
Finding, Gerhard 002137
Findley, Alvin 006488
Findley, David 047313
Fine, Ruth 048924
Fink, David G. 041587
Fink, Martin 019612, 019613, 019614
Fink, Dr. Verena 017715
Fink, Prof. William L. 041734
Finke, Karl 016980
Finkele, Diana 019966
Finkelstein, Christine 044397
Finkelstein, Jacqueline A. 004403
Finkelstein, Lori Beth 045585
Finks, Harvey 043483
Finlay, James 041479
Finlay, John 049091
Finlay, Nancy 044457
Finlayson, Prof. J.C. 021112
Finlayson, Jim 001064
Finley, James P. 043921
Finley, Janet 044235
Finley, Valerie 005810
Finneiser, Klaus 015979
Finnemore, Donnice 049000
Finnemore, Harry 049000
Finnerty, Sinéad 049082
Finney, Libby 039249, 039977
Finnigan, Stephen 044364
Finotti, Franco 025608
Finweg, Sabine 021070
Finžgar, Maja 034485
Finzi, Dr. Ranny 023065
Fionik, Doroteusz 031834
Fioning, Dr. Hubertuns 017062
Fiorentino, Alessandro 025926
Fiorenza, Joseph 044129
Fiori, Dennis A. 042000
Fiori, Dr. Pietro 024724
Fiorillo, Anthony 043270
Fiorio, Dr. Maria Teresa . . 024692, 024693, 024695, 024707
Fiouri, E. 008217
Firl, Wolfgang 017430
Firmenich, Andrea 015725
Firnges, Jörg 017933
Firstenberg, Jean 045410
Firszt, Stanisław 031971
Firth, Neil 041150
Fischbacher, Marianne 037198
Fischer, Dr. Alfred 018334
Fischer, Andrea 019988
Fischer, Angelika 017640
Fischer, Barbara 005889
Fischer, Christian 009090
Fischer, Dr. Eberhard 037789
Fischer, Dr. Eckhard 020962
Fischer, Felice 046975
Fischer, Dr. Fritz 015628, 020374
Fischer, Dr. Gert 020196
Fischer, Gertrud 002979
Fischer, Gottlieb 018848
Fischer, Hannelore 018319
Fischer, Dr. Hartwig 036890
Fischer, Helmut 016570, 016571
Fischer, Hermann von 037204
Fischer, Ilse 017696
Fischer, Ingrid 016875
Fischer, Karl-Günther 016379
Fischer, Klaus 016670
Fischer, Magdalena 002945
Fischer, Manfred W.K. 002387
Fischer, Dr. Manuela 016017
Fischer, Mark 044496
Fischer, Prof. Dr. Martin S. 018112
Fischer, Martina 018892
Fischer, Peter 002592, 037299
Fischer, Reinhold 019380
Fischer, Ron 042727
Fischer, Steffen 017439
Fischer, Susanne 017138
Fischer, Thomas 015946
Fischer, Prof. Dr. Volker 017183
Fischer, Dr. Werner 018921
Fischer-Elfert, Prof. Dr. Hans-W. . . 018557
Fischer-Huelin, Danièle 037128
Fischer Jonge, Ingrid 008977, 008980
Fischetti, Amy 043864
Fischhaber, Martin 018938
Fischlin, Jean-Mario 036862
Fisecker, August 002058
Fish, Paul 048630
Fish, Suzy 048630
Fishback, Pat 047424
Fisher, Alice 043201
Fisher, Claire 041217
Fisher, Clive 040741, 040742
Fisher, Debra 042425
Fisher, D.L. 030532
Fisher, Forest K. 045254
Fisher, Frederick J. 048911
Fisher, F.S. 042721
Fisher, Jay 041969
Fisher, John R. 048513
Fisher, Kathleen 046013
Fisher, Kathryn 006433
Fisher, Kevin M. 045285
Fisher, Larry 042017
Fisher, Lilian 048781
Fisher, M. 043556
Fisher, Susan 046376
Fisher, Ted 047455
Fisher, Dr. Wesley 046969
Fisher Sterling, Dr. Susan 048932
Fishman, Bernard P. 041659
Fisk, Jan 044954
Fiske, David A. 048347
Fiske, Nancy E. 048326
Fiske, Patricia 048925
Fisken, Judith A. 039478
Fiskesjö, Dr. Magnus 036654
Fisseha, Girma 019122
Fisson, Bruno 011808
Fitch, James A. 044177
Fite, Susan 043043
Fitschen, Dr. Jürgen 016413
Fitts, Catherine 048947
Fitz, Erwin 001764
Fitz, Prof. Jenoë 021868
Fitz, Péter 021649
Fitzgerald, Annamary 046670
Fitzgerald, E. 047303
Fitzgerald, Elizabeth 047669
Fitzgerald, Jane 045882
Fitzgerald, Mary Ann 045590
Fitzgerald, Maryann 048008
Fitzhugh, Robin 043793
Fitzpatrick, Gareth 039855
Fitzpatrick, M. 049579
Fitzpatrick, Mike 022824
Fitzpatrick, Pat 006880
Fitzpatrick, Robert 042860
Fitzpatrick, Tom 022973
Fitzsimmons, Rita 044903
Fitzsimons, Gray 045506
Fitzsimons, Dr. J. Michael 042049
Fiumi, Prof. Enrico 026368
Fix, Dr. Andrea 018698
Fjellhøi 030716
Fjermedal, Torkell 031323
Flacke, Dr. Monika 016011
Flacke, Robert 045107
Flagge, Prof. Dr. Ingeborg 017156
Flaherty, Mary A. 041715
Flaherty, Tom 047045
Flaksman, Sandy 045489
Flanagam, Michael 049147
Flanagan, Anne 001505
Flanagan, Brendan 039914
Flanagan, I.D. 039343
Flanagan, Shelia M. 045950
Flannery, Kent V. 041733
Flannery, Prof. Tim 000713
Flashar, Dr. M. 017227
Flask, David 045572
Flasza, Jan 031842
Flatau, Astrid . . 019049, 019050, 019051, 019113, 019131
Flaud, Jackie 015069
Flavin, Samantha 039948
Flechas Corredor, Jorge Arturo . . . 007636
Fleck, Robert 013332
Fleck, Dr. Robert 017683
Fleckenstein, Jutta 017288, 020062
Fleet, Dr. A. 040245
Fleet, Judy 044158
Flegel, Andreas 016916
Flegel-Wantier, Klaus 020177
Fleisch, Prof. Henri 027809
Fleischer, Alexander Franz 002989
Fleischer, Donna H. 048058
Fleischer, Dr. Martina 002901
Fleischman, Stephen 045591
Fleischmann-Heck, Dr. Isa 018396
Fleishman, Eve 044640
Fleissner, Alfred 002290
Fleming, Anne 040095
Fleming, Dr. David 040747
Fleming, Elizabeth A. 042733
Fleming, Elvis 047553
Fleming, Jeff 043424
Fleming, Jennifer 044083
Fleming, Leslie 046595
Fleming, Marty 048962
Fleming, Sam 038577
Flensburg, Birgitta 036296
Flensburg, Brigitta 036503
Flentje, Rachel 042268
Fletcher, Ann 030502
Fletcher, Carrol 045704
Fletcher, Charles 046110
Fletcher, Corinne 049219
Fletcher-Williams, Ann 039537
Fletling, Walter 017216
Flett, Dr. Alistair M. 038453
Flett, Harry 039674
Fleurov, Ellen 043729, 043731
Fleury, Nathalie 037042
Flick, André 013470
Fliegel, Brigitte 018594
Flieger, Erwin 018804
Flinn, Karen 048605
Flinsch, Stefanie 002567
Flinspach, Joan L. 044000
Flintoff, Paul 038751, 038753, 038755
Flodin, Göran 036613
Flögel, Dr. Evelyn 020643
Flögel-Kostić, Lela 034171
Flörl, Johann 002010
Flößer, Dr. Reinhard 015685
Flon, André 014372
Flon, Dominique 013322, 013326
Flood, Ellen 045790
Flood, Richard 045922
Flood, Rick 049336
Flood, Robert 045790
Flood, Timothy 042877
Florance, Robyn 001347
Florentino, M. Raquel 032636
Florenzano, Clorinda 024881
Florer, Michael R. 044183
Flores, Ana 032682
Flores, Antonio 031652
Flores, Crystal 045296
Flores, Juan C. 049502
Flores, Ricardo E. 031518
Flórez, Alberto 007625
Flórez, Helmer de Jesús 007618
Flórez de Grajales, Aura 007626
Florian, Carmen 032808
Floridi, Dr. Massimiliano 024327
Floris, Prof. Giovanni 023569
Floris, Lene 008920
Florizoone, Jan 003682
Flory, Maurice 012783
Floryan, Dr. Margrethe 008990
Flotow, Julia von 006622
Flour, Joke 003819
Flourentzos, Dr. Pavlos 008217
Flowers, Betty Sue 041931
Floyd, Alex 046479
Floyd, David 042051
Floyd, Roger 048103
Flucker, Turry 044805
Flude, Kevin 040249
Flückiger, Dr. Peter F. 037401
Flügge, Matthias 015981
Flühler, Dr. Dione 037784
Flug, Josef 002352
Fluke, Pam 041013
Fluke, Phil 041013
Fluksi, Josip 007828
Fluri, Annette 036904
Flury, Dorothea 036904
Flutsch, Laurent 037253
Flynn Johnson, Robert . . . 047857, 047871
Flynt, Suzanne 043369
Foa, Piers 000786
Foa, Robyn 000786
Foanaota, Lawrence 034540
Foard, Douglas 045230
Fobbs, Archie 048929
Focht, Brenda 047460
Focht, John 042071
Foe, Peter 048487
Föller, R. 017084
Foelsche, Gudrun 002327, 002330
Fölster, Dieter 020537
Först, Dr. Elke 017698
Foerster, Dr. Cornelia 016236
Förster, Karin 020374
Förster, Roswitha 019708
Föttinger, Franz 002696
Fogarasi, Zsuzsa 021756
Fogarty, Lori 048019
Fogliazza, Virginio 024521
Foissner, Elisabeth 002969, 002970
Foister, Dr. Susan 040241
Fojtík, Miroslav 008552, 008755
Fok, Oliver 018120
Folch, María Jesús 035976
Folch, Stella 034909
Foldøy, Oddveig 031221
Foley, Doris 046184
Foley, J.A. 030613
Foley, Jim 042807
Foley, Mim 047125
Foley, Suzanne 042770
Foley, W.M. 038837
Folga-Januszewska, Dorota 032456
Folger, Peter 044956
Folger, Willibald 001770
Folgić-Korjak, Angelina 034163
Folie, Dr. Sabine 002930
Folk, Luther 042385
Folkins, Alice 005356
Follbert, Léon 010483
Follett, Joanna 041042
Follin, Ann 036660
Follmann-Schulz, Dr. Anna-Barbara 016333
Folsach, Dr. Kjeld von 008964
Foltin, Viktorija Tyborivna 038406
Folwell Krueger, Hilary 043995
Fong, Lawrence 043742
Fonio, Prof. Ezio 026066
Fonseca Ferreira, Aurora da 000093
Fonsmark, Anne-Birgitte 008829
Font, Walter 043996
Font-Réaulx, Dominique de 013678

Font Sentias, Josep 035263
Fontaine, Axel 011342
Fontaine, Christian 014976
Fontaine, Patrick 013845
Fontaine, Dr. Thomas 020483
Fontana, Armon 037089
Fontana, Dr. Eszter 018585
Fontana, Lilia 045812
Fontaneda, Cristina 034839
Fontenioue, Henri du 011852
Fontenot, Michelle 046259
Fontenote-Jamerson, Belinda 045449
Fontenoy, Paul 042075
Fonts-Reaulx, Dominique de 013718
Foote, W.T. 001475
Fopp, Dr. Michael A. 040267
Foppa, Christian 037019
Forand, Ed 049080
Forand, Peggy 048251
Foray, J.-M. 010810
Foray, Jean-Michel 013407, 015107
Forbes, A.A. 038477
Forbes, Duncan 039425
Forbes, Jamie 006650
Forbes, Dr. John M. 041959
Ford, Chris 043364
Ford, Cynthia 043404
Ford, Dabney 046120
Ford, David 005525
Ford, H. 006412
Ford, Peggy A. 044304
Ford, Richard I. 041733
Ford, Dr. S.D. 047038
Ford jr., Thomas 031671
Førde, Anne-Marie 031337
Forder, Ron 040454
Fordham, Gerald J. 047730
Fordham, Michael 039657
Fordyce, Dr. R. Ewan 030485
Forellad, Dolors 035727
Foreman, Martin 039887
Forero, Dr. Enrique 007426
Foresman, Dr. Kerry 045936
Forest, Dominique 013668
Forest, Gilles 012094
Forest, Marie-Cécile 013700
Forgan, Dr. Sophie 041364
Forgang, David M. 049357
Forgeng, Jeffrey L. 049306
Forget, Patrice 015318, 015320, 015322
Forhaug, Helén 036418
Forkl, Dr. Hermann 020358
Forman, Bob 046913
Forman, Weldon 043136
Formanek, Verena 037451
Formanová, Markéta 008572
Forment, Francina 003353
Formery, Valerie 003564
Formicone, Luigi 024956
Fornals Villalonga, Francisco 035064
Fornara, Livio 037118, 037123
Fornari Schianchi, Dr. Lucia 025116
Fornasari, Giuseppe 024870
Forner Caballero, Ester 036075
Forney, Jack D. 043407
Forni, Prof. Gaetano 025768
Forrer, Dr. M. 029854
Forrest, Richard 005812
Forrester, Gillian 046227
Forrester, Hugh 038667
Forrester, Jim 040402
Forsberg, Anders 031221
Forsberg, Helena 036732
Forsberg, Dr. Peter K. 044474
Forsberg, Virpi 009498
Forschler, Dr. Anne 042223
Forssblad, Marianne 048087
Forster, Helen 005031
Forster, Michael 015512
Forster, Werner 019039
Forsythe, Dee 045203
Fort, Thomas A. 043609
Fortenberry, Kay 046162
Forti, Fabio 023487
Forti, Dr. Micol 049422
Fortin, James 006531
Fortin, Verna 045573
Fortino, Sally 015741
Fortunat Černilogar, Damjana 034528
Fortune, C.F. 034659, 034662, 034663, 034664
Fortune, Linda 034578
Foschi, Dr. Pier Luigi 025432, 025434
Fosdick, Pamela A. 045979
Fosen-Schlichtinger, Petra 001671
Fosmine, Francis G. 042124
Foss, Birgit 031133
Foss, Marybeth 048481
Fossati, Alessandro 037286
Fosse, Martine 011075
Fossum, Finn 030755
Foster, Alasdair 001362
Foster, Dr. Allan 006881
Foster, Carter 042985
Foster, Clarence 005253
Foster, David R. 046911
Foster, Dr. E.J. 039957
Foster, Kathleen 046975
Foster, Keith 045793
Foster, Laura 046634
Foster, Linda 048651
Foster, Marusia 006869
Foster, Preston 043136
Foster, R.A. 040030
Foster, Stephen 041057, 047766
Foster, Velma 006121
Foster Owen, J. 047765
Fotchi Chian, Mansoor 022599
Fotoghi, M. 022590
Fotter, Ludwig 001680
Foucart, Bruno 010906
Foucher, Jean-Pascal 014742
Fouhse, Sally 044081
Foulds, Kris 004984
Foulon, Pierre-Jean 003657
Fouray, Monique 014127
Fourie, Dr. H. 034731
Fournet, Claude 013405
Fournier, Johanne 005842
Fournier, Lydia 036844
Fournier, Dr. M. 029850
Fourny-Dargere, Sophie 012542, 015286
Foust, Dorothy 045574
Fouts, Chris 005059
Fouts, David 044963, 054833
Fowkes, Dudley 040837
Fowler, James 047922
Fowler, Jon 048632
Fowler, Martin 039026
Fowler, Sophie 039061
Fowler, Stephen 000873
Fowler, Victoria 049114
Fowler, William M. 042331
Fowler Shearer, Christine 045130
Fox, Andrew 038513
Fox, Catherine 039096
Fox, Charles 048217
Fox, Christopher D. 048553
Fox, Emily 048299
Fox, Eugene 044352
Fox, Dr. Georgia 042892
Fox, Howard 045441
Fox, Jill 041081
Fox, Julie 041236
Fox, Maureen 030522
Fox, Michael 045411
Fox, Mike 042817
Fox, Patric 043057
Fox, Richard 046800
Fox, Dr. Ronald 045803
Foyer, Marle 012485
Fraas, Susanne 017969
Fraaye, Dr. R.H.B. 029344
Fraboni, Anne 005281
Fraccaro, Prof. Marco 025145
Frady, Jackie L. 047371
Fraipont, J. de 003663
Fraisset, M.M. 010290
Frakes, Rita 045734
Framke, Dr. Gisela 016763, 016767
Framnes, Svein 031013
Franc, Karl 002739
França, Prof. Alexandre 004594
France, Glenda 043204
Francell, Larry 041669
Francès, Henry 011421
Franceschini, Luca 024631
Franceschini, Maria Anna 024163
Francesconi, Gino 046396
Francia, Ennio 049433
Franciolli, Marco 037285
Franciosi, Dr. Ario 023823
Francis, Dr. Carl A. 042564
Francis, Dermot 040331
Francis, Elaine 038917
Francis, Jerry 047070
Francis, Jesse 042807
Francis, John 041011
Francis, Kathy 042328
Francis, Dr. R. 039515
Francis, Tim 048311
Francis, Wayne 045696
Francisco, Emmanuel J. 045848
Francisco, Irving 048575
Francisco, Lisa 045753
Francisco, Silvestre António 000094
Franck, Dr. Frederick 048869
Franck, Marketta 010124
Franco, Alfredo 046206
Franco, Barbara 048910
Franco, Leoncio Verdera 035129
Franco, Patà 037581
François, Lionel 011749
Franconville 015165
Francou, Dr. Carlo 023723
Francová, Zuzana 034324
Frâncu, Simona 032784
Frandsen, Lene B. 008821, 008822, 009029, 009054, 009055, 009138, 009139, 009140
Frangos, Ioannis 021528
Frank, Claude 011431
Frank, Donald 044022
Frank, Dr. Günter 016446
Frank, Heinrich 004298
Frank, Larry 045220
Frank, Peggy 046128
Frank, Richard J. 042282
Frank, Richard W. 043938
Frank, Stuart M. 048126
Frank, Thomas 018068
Frank, Thomas H. 018434
Franke, Anselm 016110
Franke, Dr. Judith A. 045251, 048284
Frankel, Joan 046936
Frankel, Robert H. 047950
Frankel Nathanson, Marjorie 043016
Frankenberger, Anette 016209
Frankignoul, Daniel J. 003311
Frankl, Beatrice 019100
Franklin, Ailesia 043533
Franklin, Dr. David 006104
Franklin, Joyce 041708
Franklin, Karen S. 042438
Franko, Blanche 006499
Franková, Božena 008685, 008721
Franković, Dr. Bernard 007704
Franks, Carolyn J. 041766
Franks, Clara 045703
Franks, Curtis J. 042725
Franks, R.J. 005968
Fransen, Dr. H. 034580
Fransen, Linda 049234
Fransen, Martin 006275
Fransson, Elisabeth 036429
Frantz, James H. 046364
Frantz, Lewis 045021
Frantzen, Ole L. 008991
Frantzen-Heger, Gaby 027907
Franulic, Markita 007854
Franz, Dr. Erich 019156, 019156
Franz, Prof. Dr. G. 020485
Franz jr., L.R. 044103
Franze, Dr. Manfred 016868
Franzel, Frank E. 045731
Franzén, Ann 036649
Franzen, Darlyne S. 049294
Franzén, Eva-Lotta 036363
Franzke, Dr. Jürgen 019348
Franzolin Trevisan, Amélia 004554
Frapporti, Giovanni 022947
Fraser, David 039225
Fraser, Dr. Nicholas C. 045715
Fraser, Nonie 005244, 005425, 006534
Fratelli, Dr. Maria 024688, 024723
Fratzke, Dieter 018144
Frauendorfer, Dr. Bernd 017681
Traueneder, Dr. Hildegard 002550
Frawley, Sylvia 022761
Frayler, John 047744
Frayling, Prof. Christopher 040272
Frazer, John 005087
Frazer, Kay J. 045046
Frazer, Robert 046122
Frazier, Ronald F. 043359
Freaney, Linda 049293
Frèches, Claire 013678
Frechuret, Maurice 010876
Freddi, Dr. Loris 023779
Frederici, Joan 042400
Frederick, Frances 047041
Frederick, Karen 048038
Fredj, Jacques 013687
Free, Abigail 046537
Free, Adam 000703
Freece, David W. 044950
Freed, Douglass 048101
Freed, Howard 043824
Freed, Peter 043824
Freed, R. Mitchell 043701
Freed, Rita E. 042334
Freedman, Myron 047670
Freedman, Robert A. 042972
Freegman, David 040691
Freeland, Clara 042574
Freeland, George W. 045096
Freeling, Dr. Doris 043265
Freeman, A. 040847
Freeman, B.J. 041833
Freeman, Craig C. 045205
Freeman, D. Carl 043458
Freeman, Dottie 049114
Freeman, George 045109
Freeman, Lenette 046085
Freeman, Marina 045378
Freeman, Michael 038464
Freeman, Dr. Patricia W. 045313
Freeman, Rusty 046141
Freeman, Sue 044821
Freemantle, Andrew 040740
Freer, Elene J. 005127, 005128
Frehner, Dr. Matthias 036930
Frei, Beat 036960
Frei, Prof. Dr. Hans 019226
Frei, Hans-Peter 036980
Frei, Thomas 037549
Frei, Urs-Beat 037471, 037472
Freidberg, Dr. A. 023094
Freises, M. 014780
Freitag, Dr. Anne 037245
Freitag, Matthias 019754
Freitag, Winfried 016873
Freitag-Mair, Claudia 020100, 020101, 020102, 020103
Freitas, Dr. Henrique de 004127
Freixinet, Mercè 035344
Freland, Colin 030440
Frémaux, Thierry 012830
Frembgen, Dr. Jürgen 019122
Fremd, T. 045001
French, Ann 040416
French, B.G. 041566

French, Brenda . . . 039215
French, David . . . 040125
French, Dr. Frank . . . 048339
French, Mary . . . 043071
Frenkley, Helen . . . 023025
Frennet, Raymond . . . 003147
Frenssen, Dr. B. . . . 017524
Frenz, Achim . . . 017176
Frenz, Dr. Hans Gerhard . . . 018794
Frenza, James P. . . . 041728
Frenzel, Hans-Holger . . . 015581
Frerichs, Dr. Klaus . . . 016532
Frésard, Claude . . . 037363
Freschi Conti, Dr. Graziella . . . 023494
Frese, Dr. Annette . . . 017829
Fresk, Klas . . . 036595
Fresneda Padilla, Eduardo . . . 035258
Freudenberg, Dr. Mechtild . . . 020038
Freudenheim, Tom L. . . . 040153
Freuenschlag, Jörg . . . 002139
Freund, Franzika . . . 002819
Freus, Dan . . . 043846
Frey, Barbara . . . 043114
Frey, Dietrich . . . 020791
Frey, Dr. Eberhard . . . 018170
Frey, Dr. Georg . . . 020511
Frey, Dr. Jennifer K. . . . 047153
Freyberg, Wolfgang . . . 016937
Freyburger, J.-Claude . . . 013331
Freyer, Bryna . . . 048925
Freymann, Dr. Klaus . . . 019045
Friary, Donald R. . . . 043368
Frías Acosta, Alvaro Francisco . . . 007647
Friberg, Gösta . . . 036235
Friborg, Flemming . . . 008982
Frick, C. Kevin . . . 047422
Frick, William R. . . . 045893
Fricke, Inge . . . 018480, 018481
Fricke, Dr. Ronald . . . 020364
Frickman, Linda . . . 043904
Fridfinnsson, Jóhann . . . 021984
Frieb, M.T. . . . 015873
Friebel, V. . . . 018530
Fried, Grace . . . 043591
Fried, S. . . . 036624
Friedel, Prof. Dr. Helmut . . . 019124
Friederich, Dr. Christoph . . . 017036
Friederich, M. . . . 037237
Friedhofen, Barbara . . . 015943
Friedl, Gerlinde . . . 015709
Friedlander, Michal . . . 042162
Friedman, Dr. Alan J. . . . 043877
Friedman, Maxine . . . 048337
Friedman, Robert . . . 043069, 043070
Friedrich, Hanns . . . 015734
Friedrich, Heinz-Jürgen . . . 021055
Friedrich, Holger . . . 020221
Friedrich, Dr. Sven . . . 015910, 015913, 015923
Friedrich, Till . . . 016779
Friedrich-Sander, Harald . . . 017959
Friel, Dr. I. . . . 039068, 039071
Frieling, Robert . . . 044574
Frielinghaus, Volker . . . 016282
Friemark, Dan . . . 042169
Friemerding, Wolfgang . . . 016629
Friend, Charlotte . . . 046603
Friend, Glenda . . . 048877
Frierson, Amy H. . . . 042779
Fries, Dee . . . 042143
Friese, Dr. Elisabeth . . . 018229, 018230
Friesen, Steve . . . 044232, 044232
Friesenbichler, Gerhard . . . 002504
Friesenecker, Josef . . . 002608
Friesinger, Prof. Dr. Herwig . . . 001885
Friis, Birte . . . 008915, 009028
Friis-Hansen, Dana . . . 041921
Friis Møller, Søren . . . 009557
Frimodig, Heidemarie . . . 020073
Frinchillucci, Dr. Gianluca . 024095, 024097
Frinsko, Linda M. . . . 044249
Fripp, Gayle H. . . . 044332
Frisbee, John L. . . . 043124
Frisch, Patricia L. . . . 048210
Frisk Coffman, Mary . . . 046574
Frith, Caroline . . . 039756
Fritsch, Julia . . . 013719
Fritsch, Martin . . . 016088
Fritts, Teresa . . . 043529
Fritz, Anita . . . 045064
Fritz, Beatrice . . . 017830
Fritz, Dr. Ingomar . . . 001938
Fritz, Dr. U. . . . 016807
Frizzi, Dr. Vanda . . . 023690
Frlan, Damodar . . . 007832, 007832
de Froberville . . . 011473
Frodl, Dr. Gerbert 002006, 002853, 002969, 002970
Froehlich, Conrad G. . . . 042709, 042710, 042711, 042712
Fröhlich, Günter . . . 003017
Frohriep, Monika . . . 019980
Froitzheim, Dr. Eva-Marina . . . 016296
Frolcova, Dr. Milada . . . 008732
Frolec, Dr. Ivo . . . 008732
Frolova, Aleksandra Anatoljevna . . 033101
Frolova, T.V. . . . 034084
From-Brown, Kristy . . . 044690
Frommhage-Davat, Gudrun-Sophie 020854
Fromont, Chantal . . . 010704
Froning, Prof. Dr. H. . . . 018816
Froning, Dr. Hubertus . . . 017075
Frontalini, Costantino . . . 023882
Frorud, Harald . . . 031192, 031193
Frosdick, Fiona . . . 038684
Frost, Cheryl A. . . . 044714
Frost, Katarina . . . 036394
Frost, Natalie . . . 040550
Frost, R. . . . 039435
Frost-Pennington, Peter . . . 040797
Frotscher, Matthias . . . 018520
Froud, Alan . . . 000888
Fry, Judith . . . 001269
Fry, Stephen . . . 005585
Fryberger, Betsy . . . 048319
Frýda, Dr. František . . . 008571, 008576
Fryda, Hildegard . . . 019047
Fryer, Jonathan . . . 040992
Fryer, Molly . . . 043790
Fu, Dr. Tse Tak . . . 007126
Fuchs, Dr. Carl Ludwig . . . 017829, 017837
Fuchs, Dr. Detlef . . . 019825
Fuchs, E. . . . 032108
Fuchs, Elisabeth . . . 002344
Fuchs, Dr. Emanuel . . . 002893
Fuchs, Ernfried . . . 002935
Fuchs, Dr. Friedrich . . . 019745, 019746
Fuchs, Dr. Gerald . . . 002186
Fuchs, Matthias . . . 002622
Fuchs, Max . . . 037060
Fuchs, Monique . . . 014878
Fuchs, Dr. Rainer . . . 002965
Fuchs, Ronald . . . 002344
Fuchs, Sandra . . . 049072, 049073
Fuchssteiner, Ingrid . . . 002052
Füköh, Dr. Levente . . . 021728
Füllner, Dr. Karin . . . 016832
Fülöp, Dr. Eva Maria . . . 021903
Fülöp, Dr. Éva Maria . . . 021904
Fülöp, Dr. Gyula . . . 021807, 021872
Fünfgeld, F. . . . 017861
Fünfgelder, Konrad . . . 019583
Fünfschilling, Sylvia . . . 036863
Fürészné-Molnár, Anikó . . . 021906
Fürle, Gisela . . . 020575
Füvessy, Anikó . . . 021907
Fugami, Tracey . . . 046325
Fugaro, Anthony F. . . . 048762
Fugate, Charlotte . . . 046697
Fugate, Dody . . . 047971
Fugazza, Prof. Stefano . . . 025205
Fugazzola Delpino, Maria Antonietta . . . 025555
Fuge, Rex . . . 000914
Fugger-Babenhausen, Markus Graf 015635
Fuglie, Gordon L. . . . 045438
Fuglsang, Harald . . . 008870
Fuhrman, Loretta . . . 047111
Fuji, Hishizu . . . 026807
Fujii, Miyako . . . 026714
Fujii, Yoshitugu . . . 026714
Fujii, Zenzaburou . . . 026714
Fujisaki, Aya . . . 026533
Fujita, Chikako . . . 026960
Fujita, Kyoko . . . 026685
Fujita, Yukio . . . 026458
Fukagawa, Masafumi . . . 026645
Fukuda, Hiroko . . . 026533
Fukuda, Mamoru . . . 026591
Fukuhara, Yoshiharu . . . 027264
Fukuji, Eiji . . . 026502
Fukushima, Hiroyuki . . . 027286
Fulconis, Marie-Madeleine 014276, 014277
Fulda, Anna-Barbara . . . 037021
Fulfer, Glenn . . . 046077
Fulford, Prof. M.G. . . . 041029
Fulga, Ligia . . . 032791
Fulghum, Joyce . . . 044065
Fuller, Alfred W. . . . 042479
Fuller, Candy . . . 043928
Fuller, C.D. . . . 029577
Fuller, Craig . . . 047779
Fuller, Don Michael . . . 048487
Fuller, Elaine L. . . . 043240
Fuller, Elizabeth E. . . . 046984
Fuller, Ellen . . . 042515
Fuller, Janae . . . 045271
Fullerton, Jane . . . 006354
Fullhart, W.C. . . . 046653
Fulop, Lajos . . . 032851
Fulton, Jeff . . . 048030
Fulton, William . . . 041159
Fulton, William Duncan . . . 043507
Funck, Ludwig . . . 016448
Funk, Dr. Frank E. . . . 049217
Funk, Michael . . . 016771, 019594
Funk, Tamara . . . 045906
Funk, Uli . . . 016034
Funsho Adedayo, Oluremi . . . 030702
Furber, Rich . . . 047275
Furey, Linda . . . 046557
Furey, Patrick W. . . . 047651
Furger, Dr. Alex . . . 036863
Furger, Dr. Andres . . . 037107, 037784, 037785, 037798
Furgol, Dr. Edward . . . 048937
Furiesi, Dr. Alessandro . . . 026369
Furingsten, Agne . . . 036400
Furlan, Giuseppe . . . 023274
Furlong, James . . . 046357
Furlow, Elizabeth . . . 048086
Furman, Evelyn E. . . . 045221
Furnival, Gloria . . . 046528
Furrer, Dr. H. . . . 037795
Furry, Nancy . . . 048454
Fursdon, E.D. . . . 038936
Furshong, Peg . . . 043814
Fursova, Irina Alekseevna . . . 033592
Furtner, Alois . . . 015516, 015518
Furtwengler, Marusia . . . 015714
Furtwengler, U. . . . 015850
Furu, Helen . . . 031095
Furuta, Ryo . . . 027256
Fusi, Pietro . . . 023746
Fustig, Manuela . . . 017403
Futter, Christina . . . 044924
Futter, Ellen V. . . . 046286
Futzel, Charles . . . 048886, 054641
Fux, Franz . . . 001894
Fyfe, R. . . . 030460
Fyke, James . . . 046146
Fylypčuk, Dr. Olga Ivanivna . . . 038236
Gaaff, G. . . . 029396
Gaál, Dr. Attila . . . 021875, 021876
Gaasch, Cynnie . . . 044068
Gabarra, Josep Feliu . . . 034857
Gabat, Waltraud . . . 002827
Gabay, Oshra . . . 023033
Gabbard, Dennis . . . 044007
Gabbitas, Victoria . . . 039214
Gabet, Francis . . . 037252
Gabici, Dr. Franco . . . 025399
Gable, Edward . . . 042253
Gaborit, Jean-René . . . 013685
Gabra, Dr. Gwadat . . . 009294
Gabriel, Prof. Reinhold . . . 002154
Gabriel, Rosemary . . . 046283
Gabriel, Siegfried . . . 017200
Gabrielson, Bengt . . . 036376
Gabršek Prosenc, Meta . . . 034501, 034502
Gabyševa, Asja Lvovna . . . 033189
Gachet, Louis-Jean . . . 011211
Gačková, Dr. Lýdia . . . 034392
Gadd, Richard W. . . . 045984
Gaddis, Eugene R. . . . 044463
Gaddy, Kenneth . . . 048665
Gadebusch, Raffael D. . . . 016130
Gądor, Józef . . . 032273
Gädeke, Dr. Thomas . . . 020039
Gaedtke-Eckardt, Dr. Dagmar . . . 017765
Gähler, Walter . . . 037150
Gänsheimer, Dr. Susanne . . . 019124
Gänsicke, Christian . . . 016861
Gärtner, Monika . . . 002074
Gäßler, Prof. Dr. Ewald . . . 019468, 019473
Gafert, Alfred . . . 017875
Gaffino Rossi, Rodolfo . . . 026059
Gaffney, T.J. . . . 047133
Gafurov, G.G. . . . 049382
Gagarina, Dr. Elena . . . 033401, 033513
Gage, Mike . . . 044307
Gagge, Carl-Magnus . . . 036766
Gagnaison, Jean-Claude . . . 014719
Gagneur, Didier . . . 010447
Gagneux, Dominique . . . 013630
Gagneux, Yves . . . 013602
Gagnon, Rhéal . . . 005726
Gagosian, Robert . . . 049288
Gagro, Ivan . . . 007828
Gaida, Dr. Maria . . . 016017
Gaier, Dr. Claude . . . 003590
Gaigalat, Michael . . . 019391
Gaillard, Dr. Karin . . . 029843
Gain, Prof. D.B. . . . 034625
Gaines, Robert . . . 043692
Gair, Michael . . . 005061
Gais Muller, Deborah del . . . 047258
Gaisbauer, Ernst . . . 001708
Gaisberger, Karl . . . 001708
Gaissert Jackson, Mary . . . 041636
Gaitán de Santamaria, Magdalena 007492
Gaither, Edmund B. . . . 042336
Gajdukova, Nadežda Michajlovna . 033237
Gajewski, Dr. Pawel . . . 024647
Gajski, Zora . . . 007841
Gajuk, Volodymyr Vasil'ovyč . . . 038346
Galabuts'ka, Galina Michajlivna . . 038300
Galan, Brenda de . . . 003475
Galanti Papola, Mary . . . 046958
Galassi, Peter . . . 045389
Galassi, Susan Grace . . . 046333
Galasso, Prof. Elio . . . 023368
Galasso, Dr. Giovanna . . . 023363
Galati, Dr. Roberto . . . 023380
Galatis, Bill . . . 042345
Galbert, Antoine de . . . 013608
Galbraith, Marie . . . 048979
Galbreath, Desiree . . . 046155
Galčenko, Sergij A. . . . 038324
Gale, Marilyn . . . 049108
Galea, Victoria . . . 028048
Galeazzi, Dr. Claudio . . . 025318
Gałecki, Zdzisław . . . 032449
Galendo, Dr. Pedro G. . . . 031740
Galeotti, Prof. Piero . . . 023873
Gałęza, Jarosław . . . 032200
Galicer, Jorgelina . . . 000425
Galicki, Piotr . . . 031826
Galiègue, Josette . . . 010722
Galili, Avner . . . 023023
Galimberti, Dr. Paolo . . . 024735
Galindo, Luis . . . 049466

Galindo Rosales, Hortensia 028439
Galindo Steffens, Margarita 007398
Galkina, Inna Konstantinovna 033015
Galkina, Tatjana Ivanovna 033683
Gallacher, Daniel T. 005504
Gallagher, Marlys 042148
Gallagher, Marsha V. 046680
Gallagher, Patrick 022814
Gallagher, Susan 044265
Gallagher, Dr. Thomas H. 043667
Galland, Madelon 046347
Gallant, Aprile 046545
Gallant, Cécile 005884
Gallant, Greg 005251
Gallardo, Luis 028538
Gallasch, Harold E. 001092
Gallatin, Morgan Dean 048863
Galleano, Dr. Franco 024276
Gallego Londoño, María Elena 007594
Gallegos Franco, Francisco 028814, 028815
Gallen-Kallela-Sirén, Dr. Janne 010134
Galler, Peter 037453
Gallert, Andrea 020992
Galli, Dr. Cinzia 023997
Galli, Fiorenzo 024725
Galli, Mario 037318, 037319
Gallico, Prof. Claudio 024604
Gallifant, David W. 041341
Galliffet, P. de 012605
Galliker-Tönz, Robert 036945
Gallimore, Janet 049009
Galliot, Gérard 010772
Gallivan, Dr. P.A. 001106
Galljamova, Dolaris G. 033128, 033130
Gallo, Denis 047893
Gallo, Prof. Pietro 025524
Gallois, J.L. 010356
Galloway, Dr. Ian 001473
Galluzzi, Prof. Paolo 024164
Galočkina, Svetlana Jurjevna 034030
Galonska, Ann 048383
Galonska, Julie 043978
Galopim de Carvalho, Prof. A.M. 032651
Galscott, Joseph 001071
Galtier, Jacques 013420
Galvani, Bill 044993
Galvin, Frank 041110
Galvin, John E. 045578
Galvin, Maureen 042497
Galvis, Hermana Martha Lucía 007539
Gálviz Muñoz, Rosalba 007562
Galyckyj, Mikola Oleksandrovyč 038281
Gama Mota, Prof. Dr. Paulo 032596
Gamache 011452
Gamasin, Gleb 016684
Gamazo Barrveco, Mercedes 035410
Gambin, Kenneth 028044
Gamboa, Lyn 031789
Gamboa, Marilyn B. 031623
Gamet, Prosper 015063
Gamillscheg, Prof. Dr. Ernst 002971
Gammersvik, Aagot 030845
Gammersvik, Ågot 030984, 031307
Gamolin, Vladimir Danilovič 033623
Gamperer, Franz 002297
Gamsjäger, Rudolf 002016
Gamsjäger, Siegfried 002392
Gamwell, Lynn 042218
Gamzatova, Patimat Saidovna 033340, 033341
Gancarski, Jan 032077
Gančev, Rumjan 004821
Gandee, Cynthia 048489
Gandhi, K.M. 022331
Gandhi, M. 022261, 022375
Gandino, Guido 024301
Gandioso, Carmen Roman 004576
Gandolfi, Dr. Lia 024686
Gandon, Gérard 010330
Ganebnaja, Nina Evgenjevna 033109
Gangi, Sabine 015193
Gangkofner, M. 021091
Gangloff, Deborah 043338
Gangloff, Roland 043780
Gangwere, Stanley K. 043458
Ganiev, A. 049404
Ganijon, Alijonov 049396
Ganino, Luigi 023217
Gannett, Michael R. 043158
Gannon, Thomas 043522
Ganozova, Radoslava 004855
Ganpat, Ganesh 042679
Gansohr-Meinel, Dr. Heidi 016333
Gansz, Kevin 048193
Gantenberg, Anette 019391
Gantner, Bernard 012229
Gantner, Ellen 049151
Gantner, Dr. Hildegard 037267
Gantt, Judy M. 041861
Gantzert-Castrillo, Erich 019048, 019048
Ganz, James A. 049187
Ganzelewski, Dr. Michael 016276
Ganzer, Dr. Gilberto 025324
Ganzkow, Martin 017987
Ganzoni, Ursina 037546
Gappmayer, Helga 002301
Gappmayer, Sam 041845
Garami, Erika 021639
Garanne Modise, Rogoff 003955
Garaudy, Roger 035110
Garavaglia, Gianluigi 024009
Garavaglia, Dr. Giuseppe 024686
Garay, Nora Cecilia 007392
Garbarini Islas, Dr. Guillermo 000243
Garbe, Dr. Detlef 017707
Garbes, Pam 030528
Garbutt, Kirstie 038710
Garcia, Denis 015124
Garcia, Elizabeth F. 045565
Garcia, Françoise 010877
García, Joaquín Emilio 007602
Garcia, José 045814
Garcia, Julian 035013
García, Lola 035978
Garcia, Magdalena A. 046681
Garcia, Noah 047794
Garcia, Rene R. 031798
Garcia, Susana 036108
García Arévalo, Manuel Antonio 009166
García de Del Valle, Prof. Delia 049503
García de la Rosa, Ignacio 035318
García-Frias Checa, Carmen 036011
García Limón, Fernando 028668
García López, Dr. J.R. 035240
Garcia-Lorca de los Ríos, Laura 035249
García Martinez, Carlos 035828
García Menárguez, Antonio 035268
García Moreno, Beatriz 007416
García Mota, Francisco 035451
García Muriano, Felipe O. 034973
Garcia-Nakata, Lorraine 047870
Garcia Paz, Dr. Carlota 035822
García Pérez, Fernando 035814
García Rozas, Rosario 036097
García Ruíz, María Esther 028150
García Serrano, Rafael 035914, 035918, 035921, 035922
García Soto, Rubén 031581
García-Tuñon, Guillermo 035223
García Vanegas, Rubén Darío 007543
García Velasco, Francisco 035178
Garcías y Truyols, Joan 034864
Gard, Jean-Michel 037312
Gard, Jean-Noël 010986, 013408, 013713, 013921, 014076, 014079, 014560, 014979, 014980
Gardent, Bruno 012274
Gardi, Dr. Bernhard 036893
Gardi Dupré, Maria Grazia 024123
Gardiner, Mary N. 041810
Gardner, David 001385
Gardner, John 044804
Gardner, Nicki 041430
Gardner jr., William F. 045576
Gardner Begell, Ruth 048722
Gardner Broske, Janet 046421
Gardner Gates, Mimi 048091, 048092
Gardner-Stilwell, Jill 043902
Garduño Pulido, Blanca 028447, 028498
Garey, Rose 048452
Garfield, Leonard 048086
Garía, Susana 036103
Garibaldi, Dr. Patrizia 024301, 024316
Garibaldi, Dr. Vittoria 025165
Gariboldi, Leopoldo 024876
Garifdžanova, Roza G. 033092
Garimorth, Julia 013630
Garín Llombart, Felipe Vicente 035978
Garín Ortiz de Tarancón, Felipe 035978
Garland, Jeff 044361
Garland, Joan 045595
Garland, Kathleen 044924
Garland, Steve 038778
Garland, Wilma 041808
Garlinski, M. 037130
Garlits, Donald G. 046612
Garmer, Lars 036578
Garncarzová, Hana 008301
Garner, Les 046072
Garner, Sheila 001572
Garnham, Peter 006469, 006470
Garniche, Marie José 012231
Garnier 014370
Garnier, J.F. 015283
Garnier, Laurent 011376
Garnier, Maurice 013616
Garnier, Nicole 011236
Garrels, Gary 045389
Garret, Patty 042549
Garretson, Stacey 046045
Garrett, Anne 006492
Garrett, Franklin M. 041847
Garrett, Jim 045530
Garrett, Jural J. 045455
Garrido, Emilio M. 031724
Garriga, Francesc 035780
Garrigue, Philippe 014634
Garrison, Elizabeth 047178
Garrity, Lois 006567
Garrity, Marilyn 045153
Garrity jr, Marilyn 045154
Garrott, Martha 047436
Garrut, Dr. J.M. 034901
Garry, William 044889
Garside, Sioux 001526, 001528
Garstenauer, Karl 002514
Garton, Diane 006122
Garua, Marina Prieto 034800
Garuti, Alfonso 023669
Garweg, Udo 021021
Garwood, Pat 044704
Gary, Grace 041820
Garza, Michael A. 043945
Garza Camino, Dr. Mercedes de la 028514
Gasc, Michel 013068
Gasco, Yves 010696
Gascon, France 005653
Gąsior, Stanisław 032223
Gąska, Wiesław 032302
Gaskell, Ivan 042560
Gaskin, Vivienne 039549,
Gaspar, Burghard 001809
Gaspar, Filorena 032570
Gaspari, Prof. Gianmarco 024722
Gaspari, Kristin H. 049090
Gašparović, Miroslav 007853
Gasperment, Dr. Philippe 014604
Gass, Monika 017948
Gassen, Dr. Richard W. 018707
Gasser, Dr. Christoph 023868
Gasser, Ferdinand 023869
Gasset y Salafranca, Josep M. 035345
Gaßner, Prof. Hubertus 017075
Gast, Dr. Otto 019352
Gastal, Ney 004295
Gastaut, Amélie 013645
Gaston, Elizabeth 045897
Gastou, François-Régis 014988
Gateau, Fabienne 012660
Gateau, Laurence 013414
Gatellier, Michel 011855
Gately, Barbara 043057
Gatenbröcker, Dr. Silke 016385
Gates, Andrea 046898
Gates, Charles 041912
Gates, Daphnea 030525
Gates, Jay 048940
Gates, Jim 043139
Gates, Merryn 000698
Gates, Michael 041312
Gates, Pat 040990
Gates, Sue 041559
Gates, William 043109
Gatewood, Bill 045345
Gatti, Dr. Sandra 025097
Gattineau-Sterr, Dr. Susanne 019101
Gatzweiler, Wilfried 016328
Gau, Sönke 037799
Gaubert, Philippe 012310
Gaudencio de Germani, Marta 000216
Gaudet-Blavignac, Richard 037027
Gaudichon, Bruno 014121
Gaudio, Jennifer 045533
Gaudio, Linda 042085
Gaudlitz, Winfried 020031
Gaudnek, Prof. Dr. Walter 015520
Gaudzinski, Dr. Sabine 018794
Gaudzinski, Prof. Dr. Sabine 019299
Gauffin, Sten 036529
Gaugele, Roland 017449
Gaughran, Gerard 048257
Gauhar, Hasan 031398
Gaul, Roland 027876
Gauley, Sherrie 046680
Gaulke, Dr. Karsten 018180
Gault, Sam 039006
Gaulupeau, Yves 014133
Gaumé, Jean-Charles 013268
Gaurilius, K.K. 027865
Gausling, Helga 015450
Gauss, Dr. Ulrike 020365
Gaustad, Randi 031084
Gauthier, Jacques A. 046226
Gautier, Irène 013168
Gautier, Jean 003772
Gautier, Sandra K. 034600
Gautschi, Karl 037361
Gautschin, Hanspeter 036994
Gauvagan, Mary 039924
gavin, Glenda 048559
Gavin, John 042814
Gavín Moya, Julio 035733
Gaviria, Alba 007464
Gavish, Galia 022957
Gavran, Dr. Ignacije 003946
Gavranić, Cynthia 037763
Gavranic, Cynthia 037788
Gavrilaki, Eirini 021225
Gavrilova, Marija Jurjevna 033562
Gavrilović, Miladin 034274
Gay, Hebe Dina 000296
Gay, Millicent 047515
Gay, Pierre-Raymond 011417
Gayler, Billie Sue 048651
Gazda, Elaine K. 041732, 041732
Gazengel, Alcide 013063
Gazzaway, Ofiera 049300
Gealt, Adelheid M. 042263
Gear, Emily T. 048328
Gear, Dr. Gilian 040085
Gearan, Donald 044145
Gearinger, Robert E. 044051
Geary, Adam 039870
Gebhardt, Hans 015908
Gebhardt, Matt 047447, 047448
Gebhardt, Dr. Rainer 015548
Gebhardt, Dr. Ute 018170
Gebühr, Dr. Michael 020038
Geddes, Jim 030503
Geden, Dennis 006039
Gedeon, Lucinda H. 047285

Gee, Christina M. . . . 040191
Gee, Rosalyn . . . 041172
Gee, Rosalyn P. . . . 041174
Geeraerts, Liene . . . 003751
Geerdinck, J.J.M. . . . 029869
Geeroms, Luc . . . 003142
Geerts, Dr. T. . . . 029569
Geeslin, Phyllis . . . 044754
Gefahun, Dr. Abebe . . . 009443
Geft, Liebe . . . 045463
Gehlfuß, Gundula . . . 016831
Gehör, Dr. Seppo . . . 009936
Gehri, Emil . . . 037167, 037168
Gehrig, Bruno . . . 036955
Gehrig, Elisabeth . . . 015585
Gehrmann, Lucas . . . 002930
Gehrmann, Rudi . . . 016272
Gehrt, Gertrude . . . 041666
Geibig, Dr. Alfred . . . 016576
Geidner, Oskar . . . 020959
Geier, Bob . . . 046630, 046631
Geiger . . . 019409
Geiger, H. . . . 018414, 018415, 018416
Geiger, Hans . . . 020660
Geiger, Maurice . . . 013825
Geiger, Michael . . . 002169
Geiger, R. . . . 017317
Geiges, Michael . . . 037782
Geigle, R. . . . 015815
Geil, Bernd . . . 018461
Geir, Reinhard . . . 002918
Geiser, Alain . . . 037028, 037029
Geiser, Anne . . . 037251
Geisler, David A. . . . 046091
Geisler, John . . . 046091
Geißel, Helmut . . . 020904
Geisser, Hans . . . 036849
Geissl, Gerhard . . . 003033
Geißler, G. . . . 019729
Geissler, Josef . . . 002377
Geißler, Ramona . . . 019842
Geist, Dr. Joseph E. . . . 043828
Gelao, Clara . . . 023345
Gelburd, Dr. Gail . . . 045228
Geldenhuys, M. . . . 034561
Geldin, Sherri . . . 043112
Gelfer-Jørgensen, Mirjam . . . 008963
Gélinas, Cécile . . . 006461
Gelius, Dr. William . . . 008990
Gelszinnis, Hans Joachim . . . 019868
Gelzer, Bev . . . 046494
Gemmell, Michael . . . 006513
Gemmingen, Freiherr von . . . 017791
Gencer, Necdet . . . 038127
Gencsi, Zoltán . . . 021744
Gendre, Cathérine . . . 015188
Gendron, Christian . . . 013427, 013429, 013430
Generalli, Genevieve . . . 043008
Genev, Hristo . . . 004712
Genger, Angela . . . 016840
Genod, Jean-Claude . . . 037250
Genorio, Rado . . . 034497
Gens, María L. Alonso . . . 035526
Genschow, Cäcilia . . . 019665
Gentele, Glen P. . . . 047668
Gentet, M.A. . . . 037479
Gentile, Dr. Gerardo . . . 025183
Gentile, Mannie . . . 044278
Gentili, Lamberto . . . 025938, 025942
Gentilini, Dr. Anna Rosa . . . 024069
Gentis, Thierry . . . 042423
Gentle, Bill . . . 042815, 043485, 043895
Gentry, Dr. Johnnie L. . . . 043830
Gentry, Marsha . . . 045710
Gentry, Vicki . . . 045540
Geoffroy, Pierre . . . 014945, 014946
Geominy, Dr. Wilfred . . . 016312
Geoppa, Judith . . . 043301
Georg, Rolf . . . 020241
George, Dave . . . 047789
George, Hardy . . . 046649
George, Kerrianne . . . 001529
George, M.R. . . . 001178
George, Prof. Ron . . . 041273
George, Sarah B. . . . 047778
George, Tamsen E. . . . 042343
Georgel, Chantal . . . 013678
Georgel, Pierre . . . 013714
Georges, Joseph . . . 037178
Georges, Sonia . . . 037465
Georgescu, Valeriu . . . 032890
Georget, Luc . . . 012944
Georghiades, A. . . . 008217
Georghiou, G. . . . 008217
Georgia, Karamitrou . . . 021345
Georgia, Olivia . . . 048334
Georgieva, Elene . . . 004666
Georgieva, Taničkа . . . 004822
Georgieva, Teodora . . . 004945
Georgsson, Agust . . . 021948
Geppert, K. . . . 019927, 019928
Gerace, Gloria . . . 045426
Geraci, Ester . . . 023944
Gérard, Peter . . . 020761
Gérard, Raphaël . . . 011023
Gerasimčuk, Olga . . . 033812
Gerasimidi, Elena Ivanovna . . . 033009
Gerbauckas, Maryanne . . . 049089
Gerber, Bruno . . . 037039
Gerber, Daniel . . . 037141
Gerber, Jan . . . 043205
Gerber, Olive . . . 048138
Gerber, Dr. Peter R. . . . 037808
Gerber, Theodore . . . 042316
Gercke, Hans . . . 017827, 053230
Gerdur-Gunnardóttir, Gudny . . . 021958
Gereau, Rebecca . . . 044212
Gerena, Victor M. . . . 032748
Gergely, Dr. Katalin . . . 021653
Gergen, Rich . . . 047032
Gerhards, Dr. Eva . . . 017226
Gerhardt, Barbara . . . 036973
Gerhardt, E. Alvin . . . 044321
Gerhardt, Dr. Gunther . . . 020661
Gerharz, Michael . . . 019711
Gerhold-Knittel, Dr. Elke . . . 020374
Gerichhausen, Heinz . . . 020700
Gerini, Fiorenzo . . . 023149
Gerke, Lucien . . . 003845
Gerlach, Murney . . . 047264
Gerlach, Walter . . . 016651
Germain, P. . . . 011654
Germann, Joachim . . . 017684
Germann, Philip . . . 047298
Germann-Bauer, Dr. Peter 019752, 019754, 019757
Germano, Anna . . . 026221
Germanova, Galina . . . 004863
Germiny, Comte Gabriel de . . . 013907
Gerner, Dr. Cornelia . . . 016069
Gerner, Dr. Joachim . . . 020533
Gerold, Alfons . . . 037562
Gerrard, Jane . . . 040873
Gerrietts, Frank . . . 042082
Gershon, Stacey . . . 046310
Gertjejansen, Doyle . . . 046251
Gertsch, Fritz . . . 037254
Gertsch, Liliane . . . 037481
Gervais, Alex . . . 004994
Gervais, Louise . . . 043249
Gervaise, Pascale-Grémont . . . 014522
Gesemann, Dr. Björn . . . 018794
Gęsicki, Waldemar . . . 031851
Gesing, Dr. Martin . . . 015932
Gesquière, Dominique . . . 012525, 013007
Gessener, Andrew . . . 046322
Gesser, Susanne . . . 017176, 017179
Gessie, Dwight . . . 006564
Gessl, Paul . . . 002171
Gestin, Jean-Pierre . . . 014538
Gestsson, Magnús . . . 021938
Gestwicki, Theone . . . 043154
Getchell, Katherine . . . 042334
Gether, Christian . . . 008942
Getman, Z.D. . . . 033801
Getson, Ralph . . . 005808
Gettinger, Maria . . . 002170
Gettler, Peter . . . 019463
Geurts, Joe . . . 005504, 006096
Geus, Prof. Dr. Armin . . . 019223
Geuze, M.A. . . . 030148
Gevas, Sophia . . . 043784
Geyer, Prof. Dr. A. . . . 018102, 018114
Geyer, Jeannette . . . 034631
Geyer, Dr. Roderich . . . 002759, 002762
Gfeller, Claude . . . 037276
Gfeller, Irma E. . . . 045322
Ghaeni, Farzaneh . . . 022604
Ghandgar, J. . . . 022600
Gharrity, Mary Lou . . . 045866
Gherardi, Dr. Pierluigi . . . 025228
Ghesquières, L.-E. . . . 012683
Ghez, Prof. Claude . . . 037139
Ghez, Susanne . . . 042877
Ghiara, Prof. Maria Rosaria . . . 024924
Ghidini, Elena . . . 024972, 024973
Ghini, Dr. Giuseppina . . . 024930
Ghiorsi-Hart, Carol . . . 048204
Ghiron, Yves . . . 012867
Ghisalberti, Annie . . . 000892
Ghită, Ioana . . . 032821
Ghoniem, Atef . . . 009305
Ghorbani, M. . . . 022650
Ghoshroy, Kajal . . . 045178
Giacometti, Florence . . . 012263
Giacomini, Dr. Giovanni . . . 023728
Giacomini, Dr. Pietro . . . 023878
Giaimo, Catherine L. . . . 046959
Giaj, Ezio . . . 025247
Giamarchi, Paulette . . . 012334
Giambuti, Lia . . . 026334
Giampaolo, Francesca . . . 024508
Gianadda, Léonard . . . 037311, 037314, 037315
Gianaroli, Onofrio . . . 023457
Gianelli, Ida . . . 025448
Gianelli, Sarah . . . 046320
Gianfranco, Armando . . . 023506
Giannasi, Dr. D. . . . 041833
Giannetti, Prof. Antonio . . 025439, 025440, 025445
Giannetti, Elio . . . 025018
Gianni, Dr. Ginsberti . . . 023440
Gianora, Giulietta . . . 037552
Giarmoleo, Giuseppe . . . 025552
Gibavic, Annette . . . 045239
Gibb Roff, Samantha . . . 043728
Gibbon, Richard . . . 041480
Gibbon, Wilda V. . . . 006510
Gibbons, Cindy . . . 006239
Gibbons, Michael L. . . . 041966
Gibbs, Gail . . . 005723
Gibbs, Ivor . . . 040859
Gibbs, Judith . . . 041969
Gibbs, Margaret . . . 043655
Gibbs, Marie . . . 022853
Gibbs, Roger . . . 045084
Gibbs, Vivienne W. . . . 006617
Gibert-Balboni, Françoise . . . 015056
Gibson, Charlotte . . . 048615
Gibson, Hilda . . . 041363
Gibson, John . . . 040576
Gibson, Keith E. . . . 045283, 046244
Gibson, Ken . . . 045596
Gibson, Ralph . . . 049166
Gibson Garvey, Susan . . . 005570
Gică, Secţie-Bâeştean . . . 032929
Giebelhaus, L. . . . 006723
Gieben, Servus . . . 025541
Gielen, J.K. . . . 029698
Gier, Dr. Helmut . . . 015604, 015621
Gier, Dr. Klaus . . . 017680
Gieschen, Margarete . . . 017437
Giese, Dr. Dale F. . . . 048177
Giesen, Sebastian . . . 017689
Giesenschlag, Bill . . . 042548
Giesler, Dr. Jochen . . . 016333
Giesler, Dr. Ulrike . . . 018339
Giezendanner, Heini . . . 036839
Giffault, Michèle . . . 010527
Gifford, P. . . . 041115
Gigandet, Eric . . . 037438
Giglierano, Geoff . . . 046387
Giglio, Alessia . . . 037287
Giglio, Alessio . . . 037002
Gigou, Laure . . . 012628, 013806
Giguet, Aurore . . . 045192
Gil, Dr. Euzebiusz . . . 032085
Gil de los Reyes, Soledad . . . 035055
Gil de Prado, Eva . . . 035321
Gil Imaz, Maria Cristina . . . 036110
Gilardi Polar, Hernando . . . 007409
Gilbert, Abby . . . 046944
Gilbert, André . . . 006232
Gilbert, Barbara . . . 045464
Gilbert, Chris . . . 043424
Gilbert, David . . . 040857
Gilbert, Glen L. . . . 047183
Gilbert, Rendal B. . . . 048680
Gilbert, Sylvie . . . 005929
Gilbertson, Elsa . . . 041578
Gilbertson, Laurann . . . 043358
Gilchrist, Angela . . . 048942
Gilchrist, Dr. Ellen . . . 046611
Gilchrist, Rod . . . 047859
Gilder, T.J. . . . 039523
Giles, Laura . . . 047240
Giles, Mel . . . 005421
Giles, Nicole . . . 039424
Giles, Sue . . . 038859
Gilfillan, Richard M. . . . 049050
Gilg, Karen . . . 041904
Gilhaus, Dr. Ulrike . . . 016771
Gili, Dr. Antonio . . . 037290
Gill, B. . . . 030432
Gill, Cecil . . . 045822
Gill, John . . . 040116
Gill, Peter . . . 001304
Gill, Stephen J. . . . 027823
Gill, T. D. . . . 038598
Gillatt, V. . . . 001396
Gillcrest, Christopher H. . . . 045779
Gille, Martha . . . 029095
Gille, Prof. Dr. P. . . . 019090
Gillerist, Christopher . . . 048762
Gilles, Dr. Karl-Josef . . . 020483
Gilles, Matthieu . . . 011714
Gillespie, Gordon . . . 047244
Gillespie, Margaret . . . 042927
Gillespie, Maria . . . 038785
Gillespie, Marilyn . . . 045188
Gillespie, Rosemarie G. . . . 042159
Gillespie, Sarah . . . 022715
Gillespie, Shane . . . 022794
Gillett, Marnie . . . 047881
Gillette, Dr. David D. . . . 043851
Gilliam, Georgen . . . 046126
Gilliam-Beckett, Elizabeth . 044940, 045287
Gilliand, Michel . . . 036864
Gillies, A. . . . 041384
Gillies, Rachel . . . 030622
Gillioz, Jean-Maximin . . . 037200
Gillis, Jean . . . 047932
Gillis, Nancy S. . . . 042007
Gillis, Stuart . . . 039641
Gillman, Derek . . . 046972
Gillow, Norah . . . 040320
Gilman, Robert G. . . . 044504
Gilmore, Jerry . . . 042351
Gilmore-House, Gloria . . . 045405
Gilmour, J.A. . . . 040643
Gilmour, K. . . . 039907
Gilmour, Rosemary . . . 039068, 039071
Gilpin, Deborah J. . . . 041576
Gilpin, Melinda . . . 045684
Giltaij, J. . . . 030088
Gimborn, C.H. von . . . 016971
Gimenez, Carmen . . . 046404
Giménez Carrazana, Dr. Manuel . . 003921, 003922, 003923
Ginalski, Jerzy . . . 032307

Ginette, Eric 042540
Ginger, Greg 042114
Gingerich, Jim 048412
Gini, John 044877
Ginlund, Hans 009463
Ginnever, J. 038837
Ginter, Donald W. 046527
Ginton, Ellen 023092
Gioacchini, Delfo 025014
Giobbi, Maria Paola 023270
Giombini, Dr. L. 023897
Gion, Alois 047368
Gionio, Maria Teresa 024734
Giordano, Prof. Christian 037097
Giordano, Claudio 023650
Giorgetti, Pia 037286
Giorgi, Dr. Angelo 023513
Giorgi, Dr. Marisa 025548
Giorolano, Fabris 026124
Giovanna 025476
Giovanni, Ferrini 037581
Giovetti, Dr. Paola 023425
Giovine, Dr. Francesco Paolo 026219
Gips, Terry 043041
Giradeau, Ted 005198
Girard, Alain . . . 010626, 010627, 013896, 013897, 015276
Girard, Benoît 037418
Girard, Hélène 005044
Girard, Robert 006227
Girardin, Daniel 037249
Giraud, Milou 013770
Giraudy, Daniele 012928
Girgenti, Cecilia 000135
Girić, Milorad 034198
Giroir Luckett, Jeannie 047123
Gironde, Herberto 000264
Girouard, Terry 043061
Girousse, Laurent 010720
Giroux, Patrice 006163
Girsberger, Jürg 037057
Girst, Roswitha 017175
Girvan-Brown, Chris 001040
Gisbert, María Isabel 035429
Gisbert Santonja, Josep Antoni . . . 035146
Gisep, Claudio 037421
Gish, William 048716
Gisler, H. 037567
Gisler-Jauch, Dr. Rolf 036831
Gittelman, Steve 042686
Giubilei, Dr. Maria Flora . 024293, 024322, 024331
Giudice, Rosa Maria 025080
Giuliani, Prof. Dr. Luca 019088
Giuliano, Prof. Carlo 026049
Giuliano, Dr. Laura 025548
Giuntini, Trey 045767
Giurescu, Dinu C. 032813
Giuricco, Judith 046408
Giusti, Dr. Annamaria 024179
Givnish, Gerry 046971
Gizatulin, Marat R. 033643
Gjedsted, Kirsten 009005, 009006, 009007
Gjerdi, Trond 031101
Gjipali, Ilir 000037
Gjmacan 035902
Gjurašin, Hrvoje 007796
Gjurinovic Canevaro, Pedro 031549
Gladiß, Dr. Almut von 016131
Gladstone, Prof. M. 022059
Gladwin, Jim 043371
Gläser, Dr. Manfred 018728
Gläßel, Adolf 020649
Glaister, Jane 039835
Glaizot, Dr. Olivier 037245
Glanzer, Harvey W. 047394
Glanzer, Michelle 042450
Glaser, Prof. Dr. Franz . . . 001898, 002142, 002220
Glaser-Schnabel, Dr. Silvia 019352
Glasgow, Istiharoh 045412
Glaskova, Vera Evgenjevna 034043
Glass, Brent D. 043735, 048562
Glass, Dorothy F. 046315
Glass, Frank 006305
Glass, Jennifer 043995
Glass, Patrice 042776
Glassel, Jim 043882
Glasser, Susan 047416
Glasser, W. 001544, 001545
Glassman, Elizabeth 042884
Glassman, Susan 046995
Glassner, Prof. Dr. Gottfried 002307
Glasson, Michael 041287
Glaubinger, Jane 042985
Glauser, Daniel 037482
Glauser, Lori 006895, 052779
Glavočić, Daina 007779
Glaw, Dr. F. 019132
Glaz, Kazimir 006636
Glaze, George 042247
Gleason, Catherine 043731
Gleaton, Henry 046173
Gleaton, Sonja 046173
Gleeson, Elizabeth 000979, 001285
Gleffe, Waltraud 015546
Gleichenstein, Elisabeth von 018379
Gleirscher, Dr. Paul 002142
Gleissner, Stephen 049163
Gleixner, Johann 020612
Gleizer, Raquel 004557
Glenholme, Ian 039962
Glenn, Constance W. 045378
Glenn, Sherrain 045127
Glevenko, Elena Jurjevna 033763
Glick, Dr. Shmuel 022978
Glimme, Dr. Hans Peter 016961
Gliozheni, Lorenc 000027
Glistak, John 001432
Gliszczyńska, Elżbieta 031817
Glock, Walter 019839
Glocker, Dr. Jürgen 016338, 017503, 019984
Glöckner, Prof. Harry 002872
Gloor, Dr. Lukas 037802
Gloria, Dr. Heidi K. 031669
Gloria, Rogelia 031698
Gloßner, F.X. 019251
Glósz, Dr. József 021876
Glot, Claudine 011456
Gloudemans, M. 029983
Glover, Jack 048434
Glover, Lynn 047163
Glover, Mike 040781
Glover, Sarah Elizabeth 005084
Glover, Thomas 044399
Gluchova, Tatjana Vladimirovna . . 033181
Gluck, Daniel 046375
Gluck Steinberg, Judith 046283
Glüber, Dr. Wolfgang 016638
Glückert, Ewald 018527
Glueckert, Stephen 045931
Glüsing, Dr. Jutta 017129
Glušenkova, Ljudmila Nikolaevna . 033050
Gluškov, Viktor Ivanovyč 038372
Gluskova, Marina 033265
Glusstein, Bruno 037099
Glutting, Keith 046315
Glynn, Kathleen D. 047400
Gmelch, Christa 019811
Gnecco, Prof. María Julia 000572
Gnidovec, Dale 043110
Gnilšak, Ida 034515
Go, Sugil 027468
Gobbi, Elmar 024667, 024669
Gobel, Mary 044896
Goble, Rebecca 043354
Gockel-Böhner, Christoph 019552
Gockerell, Dr. Nina 019039, 020334
Gockov, Ilija 004640
Gócsáné-Móró, Csilla 021902
Gocz, Teodor 032403
Godart, Freddy 003382
Godbout, Dominique 005729
Goddard, Stephen 045206
Godefroy, Hubert 014394
Godelet, Andre 003529
Godfrey, Gerard 041293
Godfrey, Honor 040322
Godfrey, Judith 041567
Godfrey, Stephen J. 048212
Godkin, David 040241
Godlewska, Mirosława 032330
Godoli, Antonio 024156
Godoy, Arnaldo Augusto 004003
Godoy, Eliana 046294
Godoy, José 037128
Godoy Muñoz, Maria Antonieta . . . 021572
Godwin, Mary 040753
Godwin, Sharon 006568
Goebel, Susanne 015467, 015468, 015471
Göbel, Prof. Dr. Dr. Ulf 016161
Göçmen, Ali Bülent 038201
Goedicke, Dr. Christian 053548
Goegel, Ina 016684
Gökten, Serdar 038008
Göldner, Andrea 020770
Göller, Luitgar 015868
Görcke, Bärbel 019277
Gördüren, Petra 018247
Göres, Dr. Burkhardt 016082, 016167, 016168, 016169, 019480, 019659
Görgner, Ernst 016679
Goerke-Shrode, Sabine 048722
Görlich, Manfred 003019
Görner, Dr. Irina 018204
Görner, Klaus 017188
Görner, Veit 017756, 053256
Goertzen, Peggy 044542
Goertzen, Peter 005539
Goes, B.R. 029223
Goes, Dr. Georg 015892
Goess-Enzenberg, Ulrich Graf 002102
Goessen, J. 029903
Gößwald, Udo 016141
Göthberg, Elisabeth 036474
Goethert, Dr. Klaus-Peter 020482
Goethert-Polascheck, Dr. Karin . . . 020483
Götte, Dr. Gisela 016422, 019271
Götz, Matthias 036895
Götz, Dr. Norbert 019086
Götz, Rudolf 037688
Goetz, Scott 048248
Götz, Dr. Ulrike 017245
Götze, Barbara 016197
Götze, Dr. Bettina 019720
Götze, Dr. Jürgen 001661
Goetze, Lisel 043737
Götze, Robby Joachim 017428
Goetzman, Richard 044782
Goff, Alex P. 043584
Goff, Nick 041349
Goffe, Gwendolyn H. 044648
Goffman Cutler, Judy 046461
Goheen, Marion 047392
Golay, Laurent 037250
Golay, Muriel 037555
Golbin, Pamela 013638
Gold, Dr. Helmut 017186
Gold, Ruth C. 048215
Gold Levi, Vicki 041880
Goldbacher, Alexandra 002854
Goldberg, Beth 047920
Goldberg, Beverly 048700
Goldberg, Elizabeth 048116
Goldberg, Marsea 045456
Goldberg, Shalom 042285
Golden, Jacqueline 040709
Golden, Julia 044769
Golden, Rorey 046307
Golden, Thelma 046409
Goldenkova, Vera Anatoljevna 033850
Goldfinger, I. 022912
Goldfinger, Yaffa 023092
Goldfuhs, Ingeborg 001805
Goldin, Rafael 031082
Golding, Norman 030582
Goldman, Debra 046419
Goldman, Martin 048952
Goldman, Stephen M. 047714
Goldman, Steven 046720
Goldnagl, Friedrich 001782
Goldner, Cheri 046429
Goldner, George R. 046364
Goldovski, Dr. Boris 033446
Goldsmith, A. 041091
Goldsmith, Cynthia A. 046518
Goldsmith, Jeremy 041090
Goldsmith, John 039785
Goldsmith, Robert B. 046333
Goldstein, Ann 045451
Goldstein, Carolyn 045506
Goldstein, G. 048440
Goldstein, Gabriel M. 046419
Goldstein, Lisa 043704
Goldstein, Sid 047676
Goldwasser, Edwin 048928
Goley, Mary Anne 048904
Golf, Anamani 044838, 044839
Golikova, Ljudmyla Vasylivna 038390
Golinelli, Jean 015154
Golinski, Dr. Hans Günter 016281, 017794, 017796, 017797, 017799
Goll, Jürg 037007, 037360
Goll, Dr. Jürg 037666
Gollberg, Maralee 041795
Golloway, Zoe C. 047295
Gollwitzer, Horst 019352
Golofast, Larisa 038389
Gologranc Zakonjšek, Bronislava . 034462
Golonka, Jan 031889
Golovčenko, Ljudmila 038389
Golshan, J. 022621
Goltz, R. von der 016111
Gołubiew, Zofiasz 032056
Golz, Dr. Jochen 020741
Gomá Lanzón, Javier 035388
Gombert, Florence 012680
Gomel, Luc 013424
Gomendio Kindelán, Montserrat . . 035426
de Menezes Gomes, Geraldo 004538
Gomes, José Antonio Alves 004205
Gomes, Maryann 040412
Gomes de Pinho, António 032677
Gomes Leite, Gisélia Antonia 004449, 004450
Gómez, Arley 007528
Gomez, Carla 047963
Gómez, Carlo Humberto 007430
Gomez, Nadine 011594
Gómez, Roque Manuel . . 000445, 000540, 000541
Gomez, Victor 043632
Gómez Arnanz, Miguel 034877
Gómez Ayvilera, Fernando 035899
Gomez Hildawa, Isidro 031728
Gómez Hildawa, Sid 031754
Gómez Macías, Juan Antonio 035771
Gomig, Dr. Leo 001785
Gomozkova, Marina 033402
Mendes Gonçalves, Maria Arlete . . 004380
Gončar, Petro Ivanovyč 038309
Gončarenko, Larisa Fedorivna 038272
Gončarova, Elena Alekseevna 033169
Goncérut-Estèbe, Véronique 037111
Goncharov, Kathleen 042565
Gong, Stephen 042166
Gonos, Arthur 043988
Gonschior, Dr. Hannelore 019037
Gonseth, Marc-Olivier 037376
Gonyea, Ray 044737
Gonzaga Bastidas Ortíz, Rodrigo . . 007500
Gonzalas, Fabian 048883
Gonzales, Ben 031751
Gonzales, Gil 044078
Gonzales, Michael E. 046641
Gonzales Baldoui, Mariano 036087
Gonzales-Belleza, Erlinda 031684
Gonzalez, Arturo Gonzalez 028699
González, Aurelio 035324
Gonzalez, Christine 011870
González, Jaime 007620

González, Jorge 007402, 007410
Gonzalez, Dr. Juan G. 032718
González, Julieta 049464
Gonzalez, Manuel 046310
González, Milagros 049464
Gonzalez, Sylvie 014253
González Antón, Rafael 035794
González Aranda, Lucilia 007458
Gonzalez Azcoaga, Miguel Fernando 000320
González Cevallos, María A. 000165
Gonzalez-Cid, Malena 047793
González Cristóbal, Margarita 035439
González de Amezúa, Mercedes .. 035408
González de Aspuru Hidalgo, Sara . 036082
Gonzalez de Durana, Javier 036077
González de León, Antonio 028446
Gonzalez de Santiago, Ignacio María 035005
González Entidad, María Inocencia 007600
Gonzaléz Gonzàlez, Ignacio 028838
González Gozalo, Dr. Elvira 035176
González-Hontoria y Allendesalazar, Guadalupe 035398
González Lorente, Margarita 007942
González Padrón, Antonio María .. 035901
González Parra, Samuel 007395
González Penagos, Claudio 007384
Gonzalez Pons, Esteban 035290
González Rodríguez, Rosalía 035307
Gonzalo Andrade, Luis 007631
Good, Les 038859
Good, Liz 046264
Good, Patricia 045293
Goodale, Thomas 043761
Goodband, Lara 041483
Goodchild, Anne 040996
Goode, Barb 004990
Goode, Dr. David 006523
Goode, Mack 046348
Goode, Rita 039591
Goodell, Steve 048952
Goodend, Olivia 041417
Goodger, Margaret 038925
Goodin, Kitty 044887
Gooding, Brian 040019
Gooding, Janda 001375
Goodlett, Chris 045489
Goodman, A. 005133
Goodman, Barbara 044813
Goodman, Carl 041821
Goodman, Norman 041377
Goodman, Susan 046352
Goodman, Wallace 048549
Goodrich, Dr. James W. 043073
Goodridge, Janet 039744
Goodridge, W. 041170
Goodsell, Leo J. 042171
Goodwin, John 043709, 043711
Goodwin, Marsi 046898
Goodwin, Murray 030500
Goodwin, Robert 046234
Goodwin, Sue 048209
Goodwinl, Patricia 046114
Goody, Dick 047471
Goodyear jr., Frank H. 047009
Goodyear, Hal E. 049038
Goolsby, Elwin L. 048148
Goos, D. 016473
Goossens, Dr. E.J.H.P. 029197
Goossens, Gerda 003858
Gor-Arie, D. 023044
Gorbenko, Anatolij Aleksandrovič . 033011
Gorbey, Ken 030653
Gorbunova, Éleonora Grigorjevna . 033172
Gorczyca, Krzyštof 032154
Gorczynski, Bohdan 042874
Gordenker, Emilie 039406
Gordon, Alec 039288
Gordon, Alexander 038587
Gordon, B. 034591
Gordon, David 045892
Gordon, Dr. Dillian 040241
Gordon, Don 006440
Gordon, Donnarae 047378
Gordon, Lindsay 038450
Gordon, Nick 039973
Gordon, Stanley 048841
Gordon-Smith, Peter 039248
Gorduza, Victor 032777
Gordy, Christopher D. 043352
Gordy Edwards, Esther 043454
Goren, Dr. M. 023094
Goren, Nili 023092
Goreta, Aleksandra 007732
Goretti, Ndayarinze M. 004964
Gorewitz, Shalom 045599
Gorham, Linda 041960
Gorham, Marilyn R. 045305
Gori, Beatrice 023780, 023781
Gorini, Prof. Giovanni 025053
Gorini Esmeraldo, Eugênia 004530
Gorjão, Sérgio .. 032664, 032665, 032666
Gorka, Steffi 017013
Gorman, Jill 042116
Gorman, Dr. Martyn 038441
Gorman, N. 001368
Gormley, John 048625
Gormley, Nina Z. 048259
Gormsen, Gudrun 009099
Gorny, Dagmar 019552
Goroch, Tansija Vladimirovna 033967
Gorochov, Vladimir Aleksandrovič . 033311
Gorodnij, Aleksandr Ivanovič 034044
Gorove, Margaret 046769
Gorroño de Crespo, Maria del Carmen 000382
Gorschlüter, Peter 016837
Gorski, Michelle D. 048991
Górski, Mirosław 032008
Gorski, Stefan 032162
Gorsline, Marie 011035
Gosden, Dr. Chris 040665
Goshen, R. 023007
Goshow, Nancy 046366
Gosse, Rita 048122
Gosselin, Claude 005919
Gossy, Reinhard 002597
Gostick, Misha 005907
Gostisha, Don 041665
Gostwick, Martin 039180
Goswami, Raj Ratna 022300
Goswamy, Samares 022216
Ágota, Kasper 021928
Gotcher, Jack 041884
Gotgelf, Lev K. 032978
Goto, Hidehiko 027310
Gottfried, Claudia 019723
Gottfried, Heinz 002339
Gottfried, Dr. Michael 043575
Gotthardt, Ruth 002971
Gottlieb, Jaromir 008409
Gottlieb, Paul 046304
Gottschalk, Dr. Jack W. 041948
Gottskálksdóttir, Júlíana 021964
Gou Vernet, Assumpta 036051
Gouble, Philippe 011532
Goudry, Gail 005131
Goudy, David 046571
Gough, David 043449
Gough, Joan 000878
Gouinguenet, Hélène 010445
Goujat, Bérangère 010449
Goulaine, Marquis de 012078
Goulandris, Niki Angelos 021325
Gould, Alac 049355
Gould, Alec 044836
Gould, Claudia 046952
Gould, Jonathan H. 049052
Gould, Marilyn 049225
Gould, Richard 047381
Gould, William 044233
Goulden, M.R.R. 039711
Goulding, Kathleen 047261
Goumand, Bruno 012976
Gounarie, Dr. Emmanuela 021499
Gourcuff, Isabelle de 011217
Gourdin, Michel 003249
Gouriotis, G. 021354
Gouriotis, Lena 021352
Gourley, Hugh J. 048999
Gout, Jacques 011301
Goutayer, Virginie 011410
Goutorche, Christian 011560
Gouveia, Tiago Patricio 032588
Gouy-Gilbert, Cécile 012397
Govan, Michael 042069, 046324
Gove, Domingos Zefanias 029053
Gover, Isabel H. 041947
Gowdy, Marjorie E. 042213
Gowing, Laura 043773
Goycea, Ana Maria 000392
Gozani, Tal 045464
Gozdowski, Krzysztof 032352
Gozzi, Dr. Fausto 023788, 023790
Graaf, D.Th. de 029898
Graaf, F.M. de 030344
Graas, Lucette 003198
Grabar, Olga 038389
Grąbczewski, Wiktoryn 032462
Grabensberger, Dr. Peter 001949
Graber, Claudia 036932
Graber, Cleon 044070
Grabert, Walter 017597
Grabher, Gerhard 001763
Grabka, Dr. Marion 016637
Grabner, Adolf 001978
Grabner, Dr. Sabine 002969
Grabovec'kyj, Volodymyr Vasil'ovyč 038268
Grabow, Astrid 016689
Grabowska, Genowefa 032296
Grabowska-Chaiłka, Janina 032377
Grabowski, Dr. Jörn 016197
Graça, Filipe 032687
Grachos, Louis 047979
Gradin, Eva 036438
Gradova, Dina Aleksandrovna 033735
Gradwohl, Hans 001735
Graefe, Frank 020365
Graells, Eulàlia 034901
Grämiger, Hans 037488
Graen, Dr. Monika 019547, 019552, 019555
Graepler, Dr. Daniel 017472
Gräser, Dr. 020792
Grässlin, Karola 016386
Graeve-Ingelmann, Dr. Inka 019038
Graf, Andre 037305
Graf, Dr. Angela 017715
Graf, Prof. Dr. Bernhard 016081
Graf, Bernhard 037454
Graf, Brigitte 016183
Graf, Felix 037785
Graf, Dr. Rudolf 036829
Graf, Ulrich 017833
Graf, Werner 036996
Grafenauer, Michael 001710
Graff, Allison 043172, 043173
Graff, Elizabeth 044385
Graff, Nicholas 047613
Graff, Terry 006420
Graffagnino, J. Kevin 044031
Graffam, Olive 048894
Grafton, Duke of 041209
Graham, Lady 040515
Graham, Angela 041118
Graham, Barry 040141
Graham, Douglass J.M. 048002
Graham, Fiona 039977
Graham, J. 039435
Graham, Sir James 040515
Graham, John 001443
Graham, John R. 045564
Graham, Kenneth 022859
Graham, Michael S. 046218
Graham, Sir Peter 038446
Graham, Dr. Rusell W. 043406
Graham, Shelby 047956
Graham, Tom 042723
Graham LeBlanc 005218
Graham Lee, Jean 046222
Graham Wade, Karen 042934
Grahn, Göran 036669
Grahn, Martin 039152
Grai, K. 041405
Gralter, Margaret 040206
Gram, Dr. Magdelena 036652
Gramatikov, Georgi 004656
Gramatikov, Jančo 004798
Grambye, Lars 036458
Gramer, Kevin 043398, 043409
Gramm, Jean-Jacques 037457
Grammenos, Dr. D. 021489
Grams, Greg 048806
Grančarov, Michail 004782, 004784, 004785
Grančarova, Kamelia 004641
Grand, Stanley I. 042613
Grandchamp, Gilbert 037336
Grande, Prof. Dr. Nuno 032686
Grande, Prof. Nuno 032686
Grander, Johann 002105
Grandidier, Daniel 014260
Grandjean, Gilles 012555, 013577
Grandmont, Jean-François 005730
Grandrud, Dr. Reba 043483
Grange, Bill 039225
Grangé, Claire 010315
Grange, Sylvie 011163, 011165
Granger, Brenda 043612
Granier, Jean-Marie 013709
Granitto, Andrew 049327
Granitz, Gerhard 002334
Grannan, Jill 043443
Grannis, Sue Ellen 045730
Granomont, Josée 006663
Granqvist, Eirik 009994, 014143
Grant, A.E. 038516
Grant, Anne 001405
Grant, Bronwyn 030578
Grant, Elinah 003953
Grant, Elizabeth 038629
Grant, Frank F. 005774
Grant, Gillian 030421, 030422
Grant, Hugh 043421
Grant, J. 038573
Grant, Laurence . 005556, 005557, 038552
Grant, Rachel 039583
Grant, Richard 043091
Grant Morrisey, Marena 046719
Grantčarov, Michail 004692
Granville, Lee Z. 048200
Granville, Sharon 040592
Grape-Albers, Dr. Heide .. 017765, 017765
Grapin, Claude 010335
Grasberger-Lorenz, H. 020688
Graskoski, Debra 046565
Grasmann, Lambert 020598
Grasmug, Dr. Rudolf 001844
Grass, Yasmin 000708
Grasse, Carola 016966
Grasse, Marie-Christine . 011996, 012001, 012002
Grassegger, Karl 002697
Grasselli, Margaret Morgan 048924
Grassetti, Jessica 043187
Grassi, Dr. Renzo 025889
Graßmann, Dr. A. 018727
Grassmayr, Johannes 002081
Grasso, Giacomo 024314
Graswinkel, J. 029407
Gratacós Teixidor, Georgina 034896
Grate, Steve 045466
Grattan, Patricia 006360
Gratte, Stan 001590
Gratvol, Eran 023033
Gratz, Dr. Reinhard 002548
Gratzer, Heinz 002961
Grau, Prof. Dr. Jürke 019042
Grau, Salvador 036055
Grau Lobo, Luís A. 035328, 035329
Graudina, Anna 047514

Grauer, Michael R. 042609
Graumlich, Anne 048760
Grauwiller-Straub, Kathrin 037264
Grave, Marion 041261
Gravel, Mabel 005068
Graves, Tolley 045255
Graves-Brown, Carolyn 041170
Gray, Alan 030580
Gray, Dr. Anna 000888
Gray, Bonnie 005828
Gray, Campbell B. 047272
Gray, Ian 005193
Gray, John 030628
Gray, John L. 045411
Gray, Les 001156
Gray, Michael 039916
Gray, Muriel 001156
Gray, Peter 001454, 040590, 040782
Gray, Richard 039131
Gray, Sam 046663
Gray, Sarah 038555
Gray, Dr. Sharon R. 048310
Gray, Susan Inskeep 043782
Gray, Xanthi 047184
Graybill, Maribeth 041736
Grayburn, Patricia 039648
Graze, Sue 041928
Grąziewicz-Chludzińska, Barbara 032489
Graziola, Claudio 025216
Grazzini, Patricia J. 045918
Grbic, M. 030147
Greaves, Debbie 041201
Greaves, Kerry 048771
Grébert, Eliane 014589
Grečenko, Ljudmila Pavlovna 033302
Grech, Frances 028042
Gredler, Martin 002553
Grédy, Jean 037276
Greeff, I.B. 034576
Green, Cheryl 046381
Green, Chris 038682, 040883, 040887, 040891
Green, Dr. D. 040406
Green, E. 040002
Green, Erica 000716
Green, Eveleth 043671
Green, James 040778
Green, John F. 048266
Green, Jonathan 047455
Green, Linda 048300
Green, Lisa 000797
Green, Louise 048146
Green, Nancy 044791
Green, Richard 041483
Green, R.M. 001331
Green, Dr. William 042132
Green, William Davis 047576
Green, Dr. William E. 042609
Greenbaum, Elizabeth R. 042268
Greenberg, Joel 048022
Greenberg, Judy A. 048916
Greene, A. Wilson 046905
Greene, Joseph A. 042561
Greene, Lynda 047088
Greene, Marilyn 040170
Greene, Rose Mary 047379
Greene, Virginia 046993
Greener, Peter 038545
Greenfield, Mark S. 045470
Greenfield, Prof. Susan 040220
Greenhill, John 041196
Greenhow, Dr. Desna 038899
Greenlee, Hal 043179
Greenlee, Nina 045683
Greenlee, Sandy 043096
Greeno, Judy 006764
Greenough, Sarah 048924
Greensted, Mary 039053
Greenwald, LouAnne 049083
Greenway, Lord 040557
Greenwood, E.F. 040030
Greenwood, Gail 000707
Greenwood, Mike 041000
Greenwood, Tom 044981
Greer, Alberta 047479
Greer, Connie 045808
Greer, Judy 047330
Greer, Kim E. 047759
Greer, Rina 006640
Greer, William 006611
Greff, Ken 048076
Greff, Pierre 014859
Greffrath, Dr. Bettina 020961, 020963, 020966
Grefstad, Ola 031287, 031287
Gregersen, Bo 009088
Gregersen, Thomas 043383
Gregg, David 042423
Gregg, David W. 049123
Gregg, Rosalie 043356
Gregl, Dr. Zoran 007828
Gregoire, Jean 010440
Gregoor, Yves 029233
Gregori i Berenguer, Joan 035989
Gregors, Tommy 041596
Gregory, Gail 006630
Gregory, Joseph 042163
Gregory, Linda 032752
Gregory, Susan 042161
Gregory, Tabitha 048728
Gregson, Brian 001088
Greguski, Eva 048377
Greif, B. 016602
Greiff, Dr. Susanne 018794
Greig, John 039187
Greimel, Susanne 002560, 002565
Grein, Gerd J. 019545
Greinwald, Dr. Elisabeth 001715
Greisenegger, Dr. Vana 002979
Grelier, Joseph 014377
Grella, Consalvo 023305
Grellier, Gérard 012497
Gremillet, E. 014897
Grenda, Edward 005697
Grenis, Dr. Michael 042216
Grenon, Prof. Ernesto A. 000620
Grenter, Steve 041458
Grenville, John H. 005693
Grépier, Gabriel 011575
Greppi, Graciela B. 000523
Grepstad, Ottar 030913
Greschny, Nicolaï 012922
Greuter, Prof. W. 015997
Greve, Jürgen 017731
Grever, T.F. 029207
Grewenig, Dr. Meinrad Maria 020604
Grexa, Dr. Susanne 016101
Grezinger, August 018650
Gribble, Michael 030542
Gribbon, Deborah 045433
Grice, Jean 038817
Gricenko, Vladimir Petrovič 033972
Grider, George 043298
Griebel, Dr. Rolf 019037
Griebl, Monika 002949
Griebler, Reinhold 002523
Grieder, Susanne 036938
Griepink, Dr. B. 030031
Grieshofer, Prof. Dr. Franz 002132, 002976, 002998
Grießmair, Dr. Hans 023537, 023578
Griff, Hanna 046327
Griffeuille, Marie F. 014322
Griffeuille, Marie-Françoise 014320
Griffin, Dale 041884
Griffin, Dave 043403
Griffin, David J. 022750
Griffin, Elizabeth P. 044650
Griffin, Jennifer 043489
Griffin, Jonathan 039481
Griffin, Kjerstin 031221
Griffin, O.T. 040008
Griffis, Larry L. 045326
Griffith, Lee Ellen 044069
Griffith, William 046770
Griffiths, A. 040097
Griffiths, Bill 040474
Griffiths, Caitlin 041393
Griffiths, David 008332
Griffiths, D.F. 040057
Griffiths, Dr. G. 038861
Griffiths, Jayne 038830
Griffiths, Jean 039129
Griffiths, Mary 040416
Griffiths, Pauline 040513
Griffiths, Peter 040601
Griffiths, R. John 040776
Griffo, Dr. Alessandra 023238
Griffo, Dr. Pietro 024746
Griggs, David W. 042629
Griggs, K. 001229
Grignon, Prof. Georges 015122
Grigo, Dr. M. 018312
Grigorian, Anelka 000691
Grigorian, Prof. Dr. Gurgen G. 033519
Grigorjeva, Tamara Andriïvna 038285
Grigorova, Emiliya 004687
Grigsby, Roger 043154
Gril, Cajetán 002537
Grimaldi, Dr. David 046286
Grimaldi, Floriano 024532, 024533
Grimaldi, Gloria 021613
Grimaud, Patricia 013402
Grimes, John 047741
Grimm, Albert 037692
Grimm, Dr. Alfred 019121
Grimm, Dr. Eric 048284
Grimm, Prof. Dr. Günter 020482
Grimm, Monika 018975
Grimm, Tess C. 043767
Grimmer, Dietgard 002552
Grimod, Dr. Ivana 025628
Grimpe, Rusty 048654
Grimsrud, Halvard 031139
Grinage, Jeanine 041599
Grinbaum, Blanche 011352
Grinell, Sheila 047006
Grinenko, Lucy 038389
Griner, Robert F. 047439
Grinëv, Nikolaj N. 034028
Gringmuth-Dallmer, Prof. Dr. Eike 016136
Grinnell, Debbie 046128
Gripenberg, M. 009480
Grisebach, Dr. Lucius 019369
Grišina, Ekaterina Vasiljevna 033680
Grissom, Don 045546
Grissom, Joi 048135
Griswold, Sarah 049282
Gritt, Stephen 006104
Grjaznova, Ann 033683, 033800
Groat, John 046242
Grob, Dr. B.W.J. 029850
Grobler, I. 034749
Groce, Prof. Aldo A. 000606
Groce, Dr. W. Todd 048025
Grodskova, Tamara 033852
Grodwohl, Marc 015073
Grodzicki, Prof. Andrzej 032518
Gröbl, Dr. Lydia 002934
Gröger, Walter 002189
Groen, Ir.B. 029256
Groen, M.F. 030086
Grönbold, Dr. Günter 019037
Groenendijk, Drs. G.H. 029408
Groenendyk, Ed 046739
Groeneveld, A. 030108
Groeneveld, A.C. 030136
Groenewald, A. 034561
Groenewald, M. 034670
Groenewold, Rod 048804
Groenewoud, G.J.M.M. 029442
Grönholm, Kirsti 009537
Gróf, József 021767
Groff, John M. 046997
Groft, Tammis K. 041597
Groh, Dr. Klaus 016885
Groihofer, Brigitte 002934
Groiß, Dr. Albert 001678
Groleau, Michel 006341
Gromer, Kim 048522
Gromova, Ljudmila Ivanovna 033766
Grondman, Dr. A.C.M. 029473, 029711, 030412
Gronenborn, Dr. Detlev 018794
Gronert, Dr. Stefan 016329
Grøngaard Jeppesen, Torben 008811, 009043, 009044, 009047, 009048, 009049
Groninga, Janet 041565
Grønn Iversen, Trine 031063
Gronne, Claus 008982
Grønnegaard, Torben 009050
Gronning, Norman 048124
Grønvold, Ulf 031069
Groom, Gloria 042820
Groom, Simon 040039
Groos, Dr. Ulrike 016837
Grooss, Dr. K.S. 029850
Groot, E. de 030088
Groot, J.P. de 029647
Groot, Rolf de 019401
Grooth, Dr. M. de 029893
Grootveld, Cor 029234
Grootveld, Robert W. 047351
Grootveld-Parrée, C. 030077
Gros, C. 037130
Gros, Dr. Patrick 002561
Grosboll, Sue 042668
Groschner, Dr. Gabriele 002564
Grosfeld, Dr. J.F. 029349
Groß, Hans Kurt 002203
Groß, Helmut 016990
Gross, Jennifer 046228
Groß, Klaus M. 019843
Gross, Miriam 046308
Gross, Renee 046308
Groß, Thea 018869
Grosshans, Dr. Rainald 016049
Grossi, George 046898
Großkinsky, Dr. Manfred 017170
Grossman, Cissy 046318
Grossman, David J. 043048
Grossman, Grace Cohen 045464
Grossman, Richard 042341
Großmann, Prof. Dr. G. Ulrich 019352, 019353, 019371
Grossmann, Robert 014853
Grosspietsch, J. 020387
Grøtan, Geir A. 031043
Grote, Dr. Dietmar 019497
Grote, Dr. Hans-Henning 020957
Grote, Dr. Udo 019141, 019142, 021035
Grothe, Hans 016857
Grotkamp-Schepers, Dr. Barbara 020236
Grotz, Helmut 020582
Grove, David 047667
Grover, Ruth 042778
Groves, Bonnie Sue 043479
Grower, Steve 000881
Grozdanić, Nadežda 034257
Grozin, Vladimir 033403
Gruat, Philippe 012386, 013229, 014786
Grub, Adolf 016247
Grubb, Tom 043833
Grubbauer, Alfred 001687
Grube, Walter 019164
Gruber, Erich 002088
Gruber, F. 002188
Gruber, Franz 001954, 001977
Gruber, Dr. Gabriele 016638
Gruber, Dr. Gerlinde 002934
Gruber, Herbert 001759
Gruber, Dr. Herbert 016862
Gruber, Petra 019573
Gruber, Rosina 001976
Gruber, Thilo 018566
Gruber, Wolfgang 001769
Grubessi, Prof. Dr. Odino 025532
Grubler, Mitchell 043876
Grubola, Prof. James 045482
Grubola, James 045495
Grudzinska, M. 016829
Grüger, Dr. Andreas 020331

Grün, Maike 019048, 019048
Gründel, Dr. Winfried 016545
Gründig, Rita 017672
Grünwald, Karin 018769
Grünwald, Manfred 002472
Grünwald, Prof. Michael 001878
Grünzweil, K. 040596
Grütter, Daniel 037524
Gruetzmacher, Mark 048492
Gruetzner, Sara Jane 005186
Gruffydd, Alun 038647, 040060
Gruhs, Ernie 005625
Grujić, Dragana 034177
Grunaugh, Darlene 048138
Grunberg, Evelina 004311
Grund, Dr. Rainer 016803
Grundnig, Christine 002146
Grundschober, Dr. Franz 002957
Grunenberg, Christoph 040039
Grunewald, Curtis 048014
Grunz, Karin 016032, 016036
Grupe, Prof. Dr. Gisela 019032
Grusman, V.M. 033826
Gruzdeva, Tatjana Aleksandrovna . 033916
Gruzska, Larysa Petrivna 038421
Grygiel, Prof. Ryszard 032109
Grygorenko, Iryna Vasylivna 038244
Grynszpan, Anna 031966
Grynsztejn, Madeleine 047885
Grys, Dr. Iwona 032467
Gryspeert, Hans 003478
Grzechca-Mohr, Dr. Ursula 017195
Grzegorczyk, Dr. Detlef 019157
Grzesiak, Marion 044860
Grześkowiak, Andrzej 031948
Grzymkowski, Andrzej 032150
Gschwantler, Dr. Kurt 002892, 002934
Gschwendtner, Stefan 002256
Gsöllpointner, Peter 001660
Gstrein, Josef 002070
Guadarrama Guevara, Jorge 028463
Gualdoni, Flaminio 026211
Guardiola, Juan 034922
Guarino, Dr. Ariberto 025557
Guarnieri, M. Chiara 024066
Guati Rojo, Prof. Alfredo 028520
Guay, Serge 006162
Guayasamín, Pablo 009245
Gubb, A.A. 034609
Gubčevskaja, Ljudmila Aleksandrovna 033901
Gubel, Eric 003353
Guben, Eva-Maria 016847
Gubin, V.V. 033396
Gudde, Irene 046177
Gudina, Jurij Volodymyrovyč 038351
Gudmundsdottir, Anna Lísa 021958
Gudmundson, Per 036265
Gudnadòttir, Kristin 021963
Gudnason, Thorarinn 021946
Gue, Robin 048172
Gügel, Dominik 037483
Gül, Sebahat 038102
Guelbert de Rosenthal, Eva 000449
Güler, Ali 038007
Güler, M. Güven 038109
Güllüoğlu, F. Nevin 038168
Guenat, François 037420
Günaydın, Celal 038046
Gündogdu, Veysel 038043
Gündüz, Yaşar 038144
Guenette, Irene 006525
Guennec, Aude Le 011375
Günter, Werner 019430
Güntert, Prof. Dr. Marcel 036933
Günther, Albert J. 016912
Guenther, Bruce 047178
Günther, Clas 036623
Günther, Michael 018377, 053399
Günther, Rolf 017248
Günther, Dr. Sigrid 001819
Guenther, Todd 045152
Günzler, Lilo 017173
Guerbabi, Ali 000078
Guerber, Steve 042291
Guerci, Prof. Antonio 024312
Guerdy Lissade, Joseph 021606
Guerin, Charles A. 048644
Guerin, Kerry 001357
Guerlain, Daniel 012629
Guerlain, Florence 012629
Guermont, Mauricette 014524
Guerra, Jairo 007640
Guerra, Yolanda 007640
Guerra Pizòn, Olga 009214
Guerrero, Doris 007472
Guerrero, Javier 047839
Guerrero Alvarez, Guillermo 007574
Guerreschi, Prof. Antonio 025847
Guerri, Dr. Roberto 024713, 024716, 024718
Gürtler, Dr. Eleonore 002097
Gürtler, Dr. W. 001823
Guest, Fiona 038521, 039849
Guest, P. 038939
Guest, Raechel 048979
Gueury, Marie-Claire 003588, 003599
Guevara Hernández, Jorge 028846
Güzel, Selahattin 038067
Guffee, Eddie 047076
Guffee, Patti 047076
Gugelberger, Rachel 046417
Guggenberger, Hans 002168
Gugger, Beat 037542
Gugole, Jean 013216
Guhl, Klaus 037046
Guibal, Jean 010437
Guichard, Christiane 014427
Guichard, Marie-Claire 012135
Guichard, Vincent 013145
Guichaumon, Jean-Louis 012892
Guichon, Françoise 010300, 010301
Guidon, Suzanne 011490
Guidotti, Prof. Francesco 024666
Guidotti, Nives 023551
Guidry, Keith 046700
Guiducci, Dr. Anna Maria 025894
Guiffre, Florence 043883
Guigo, Elsa 013630
Guihaumé, Antoine 014430
Guilardian, D. 003324
Guilbaud, Laurence 015161
Guilbert, Manon 005504
Guilbot 012165
Guilbride, Kurt 005734
Guild, John 048329, 048337
Guilhot, Jean-Olivier 011726
Guillard, Alain 012719
Guillaut, Laurent 011067
Guillemin, Daniel 010466, 012055
Guillemin, Jean-Claude 010760
Guillemot, Hélène 012464
Guillén Jiménez, Marilú 028902
Guillerme, Lucienne 013283
Guillermo, Joseph 031619
Guilliem Arroyo, Salvador 028481
Guillot-Chene, G. 011763
Guimarães, Prof. Dr. Edi Mendes . . 004015
Guinid, Rosario 031682
Guinn, Kevin 044581
Guinness, Alison 043732
Guinness, Robert 022860
Guion, Jacques 014244
Guiotto, Prof. Dr. Mario 025955
Guisolan, Dr. M. 037608
Guiver, Pam 041298
Gulbina, Anna Alekseevna 034055
Gulbrandson, Alvhild 030987
Guldemond, J. 030088
Guljaev, Vladimir Andreevič 033529
Gullickson, Nancy 043516
Gullsvåg, Per Morten 031325
Gulyes, Andreas 002975
Gumă, Nicoleta 032831
Gumerman, George J. 048630
Gumpert, Lynn 046340
Gunarsa, Dr. Nyoman 022464
Gunby, Stephen G. 043094
Gundel, Dr. Marc 017852, 017853
Gunder, Jacques 012591, 012592
Gunderson, Catherine F. 006421
Gunderson, Dan 043333
Gunderson, Robert A. 044720
Gundlach, Prof. F.C. 017699
Gundler, Dr. Bettina 019046
Gundry, Beverly F. 044416
Gunér, Tullan . . . 036381, 036382, 036385
Gunjić, Ranko 007718
Gunn, Lorna 005670, 005674
Gunn, Robert 046783
Gunnarsson, Ann-Marie 036265
Gunnarsson, Torsten 036648
Gunning, Judy 001474
Gunnlaugsdóttir, Elin 021932
Gunter, Kristen C. 045124
Gunther, Minette 043037
Gunther, Paul 046389
Gunther, Uwe 034733
Guo, Xingjian 007049
Guohua, Gu 007207
Gupta, Chitta Ranjandas 022044
Gupta, Preeti 043877
Gupta, Dr. Vibha 022377
Gupta, V.N. 022203
Guralnik, Nehama 023092
Guratzsch, Prof. Dr. Herwig 016487, 017547, 020039, 020042
Gurba, Norma 045136, 045137
Gurevič, Dr. E. 033485
Gurgel, Felizardo Jesus 000090
Gurkina, Tatjana Aleksandrovna . . 033350
Gurley, Diana 005058
Gurney, Helen 039742
Gurney, Marilyn 005575
Gurney-Pringle, Chantal 000750
Guse, Ann 045733
Gusel, Erich 002201, 002203
Gusenleitner, Fritz 002243
Gusev, Vladimir 033753, 033754
Gushulak, Ruth 005449
Gust, Donald F. 042113
Gustafson, Donna 043016
Gustafson, Elaine D. 048493
Gustafson, James 045314
Gustafson, Sharon 045303
Gustafsson, Harry 005132
Gustafsson, Malin 036296
Gustafsson Ekberg, Kent 036198
Gustavson, Carrie 042231
Gustavson, Todd 047480
Gustavsson, Karin 036333
Gustavsson, Lars-Åke 036333
Gut, Andreas 016941
Gut, Ursula 037533
Gut, Werner 037642
Gutbrod, Dr. Helga 019214
Gutek, Dr. František 034310
Guth-Dreyfus, Dr. Katia 036886
Guthier, Mark 045596
Guthman, Howard 043800
Guthrie, Alyce N. 044181
Guthrie, C. Gay 006074
Guthrie, Giles 040389
Guthrie, Jeanne 042549
Guțică-Florescu, Laurențiu 032940, 032941
Gutiérez, Marisa 047592
Gutiérrez, Ana 035429
Gutiérrez, Guillermo Giraldo 007533
Gutiérrez, José A. 000188
Gutiérrez Alba, D. Julio 035867
Gutiérrez Campos, Yolanda Milagros 008195
Gutiérrez Carcia, Inés 008013
Gutiérrez Coto, Fernando 007669
Gutiérrez García, María Angeles . . 035531
Gutiérrez Jodar, Ricard 034910
Gutiérrez Salamanca, Carlos Julio . 007547
Gutierrez-Solana, Carlos 042465
Gutiérrez Velásquez, Amado 007461
Gutker de Geus, Sven E. 030021
Gutman, Kevel Jane 043502
Gutmann, Gabriela 002859
Guttormsen, Sissel 031285
Guy, Dr. A. 040240
Guy, Frances 039073
Guy, Grant 006837
Guy, Troger 013032
Guye, Francis 037480
Guyonneau, Olivier 012287
Guzman, Antonio 015098
Guzmán, Manuel Gil 028461
Guzzi, B. Anthony 044522
Guzzo, Enrico Maria 026286
Guzzo, Prof. Pietro Giovanni 023718, 024053, 025304, 026085
Gvišiani, G.M. 015407
Gwan, Pak Yong 027443
Gwara, Czesław 032327
Gwarda, Zofia 032346
Gweki Booi, Vuyani 034543
Gwiazda, Bronislaw 032226
Gwilim, Ian 038436
Gwyn, Brenda 045687
Gye, Peggy 040429
Gyger, Patrick 037743
Gyger, R. 037670
Gyllenberg Pernevi, Bodil 036303
Gyllenhaal, C. Edward 042493
Gyllkrans, Monika 036708
Györe, Pál 021615
Gysin, Jacques 037365, 037367
Gyula, Dr. Ernyey 021668, 053675
Haag, Olinde S. 046273
Haag, Dr. Sabine 002934
Haagen Pictet, Loa 037133
Haak, Dr. Bill 044220
Haakanson, Sven 045044
Haakestad, Jorunn 030771
Haaland, Anders 030770
Haamer, Kaia 009408
Haan, David de 039817
Haan, Maartje de 029441
Haan, Drs. Peter de 030240
Haapala, Anu 010243
Haar, Frauke von der 018982
Haar, Dr. Frauke von der 019046
Haas, Gordon 043780
Haas, Prof. Dr. Helmuth 002885
Haas, James R. . 043365, 043366, 043367
Haas, Josef 008354
Haas, Dr. Richard 016017
Haas, Ruth 049212
Haas, Sabine 018475
Haas, Dr. U. 018381
Haase, Prof. Dr. Claus-Peter 016131
Haase, Dr. Evelin 016393
Haase, Werner 021005
Haavaldsen, Per 031221
Habartova, Dr. Romana 008732
Habditch, Max 040365
Habecker, Dr. Eugene B. 046334
Habegger, Dr. Ueli 037303
Haberhauer, Günther 015831, 015832, 015835
Haberman, Patty 045792, 048521
Habermann, Dr. Sylvia 015911
Habermann, Yvonne 019956
Habersatter, Dr. Thomas 002564
Haberstroh, Sarah 045886, 045900
Habes, Scott 043042
Habibi, Mohammed 029031, 029038
Habrich, Prof. Dr. Dr. Christa 018071
Hachet, Michel 014970
Hachmer, Hendrik 030255
Hack, Angelica 016545
Hack, Dr. C. 029751
Hack, Janice 045106
Hack, Shery N. 042600
Hackenburg, Randy 042623
Hacker, Deannaopher 041915
Hackett, Brian 043322
Hackett, I. O. M. 040626

Hackett, Phoebe 047973
Hackford, Clive 039234
Hackhofer, Wilhelm 002575
Hackl, Prof. Dr. A. 002822
Hackler, Cornelia 020144
Hackman, John 010167
Hacksley, Malcolm 034594
Hacksley, M.M. 034623
Hackstein, Hermann 017623
Haddad, Regina Clélia 004592
Hadders, Rieks 029180
Haddington, Earl of 039605
Haddock, Brent 047229
Haddow, Carol 039109, 040500
Hadjicosti, Dr. M. 008217
Hadjisavvas, Dr. Sophocles 008209, 008220, 008227, 008229
Hadjistephanou, Prof. Costas E. . . 008213
Hadjusarnas, S. 008208
Hadland, Brian 006210
Hadley, Diana 048630
Hadley, V.J. 039156
Haduch, Henryka 031815
Haeck, Jules 003436
Häcki, Iren 037766
Haedo, Dr. José Antonio 000583
Häffner, Martin 020489
Häfliger, Pius 036827
Häfliger, Toni 037293
Hägele, U. 016694
Häggman, Gunvor 009924
Häggström, Stig 009503, 009666
Haenel, Johanna 001722
Haenel, Dr. Matthias 019037
Hänggi, Dr. Ambros 036899
Hänggi, Dr. Christoph 037550
Hänggi, René 036978
Hänsel, Dr. Alix 016136
Hänsel, Dr. Volker 002753
Häring, Dr. Friedhelm . . . 017407, 017408, 017410, 017413
Haese, Jürgen 017429
Häßler, Dr. Hans-Jürgen 017765
Häuser, Dr. Christoph 020364
Häußler, Theodor 015636
Hafenecker, Ingo 016869
Haffenden, Peter 001221
Haffner, Dr. Marianne 037793
Haffner, Z. 021732
Hafner, Dr. Mark S. 042049
Hafok, Barbara 003009
Hagan, Annemarie 005888, 005890
Hagan, Marylee 048532, 048535
Hagberg, Magnus 036189
Hagdorn, Dr. Hans 018063
Hagedorn Olsen, Claus 008933
Hagedorn-Saupe, Monika 016081
Hagemeier, Anna Mae 048350
Hagen, Dr. Bettina 002901
Hagen, Dr. Harold H. 048067
Hagen, Inga 016687
Hagen, John 044388
Hagen, Rien 029180
Hagen, Werner 002210
Hagendorfer, Dr. Johann 002050
Hager, Franz 002293
Hager, H. 034630
Hager, Joan DiChristina 042908
Hager, Joyce 046086
Hager, Dr. Michael W. 047840
Hagerup, Asbjørn 031044
Haggart, M.W. 005847
Hagler, James 043956
Hagloch, Jenny 047750
Hagnau, Dr. Carola 018336
Hagström, Lars 036422
Hagström, Torkel 036300
Hahling, Albert 036823
Hahn, Dr. Andreas 016314
Hahn, Prof. Dr. Dietbert 021006
Hahn, Gabriele 001835
Hahn, Dr. Klaus-Dieter 017095
Hahn, Dr. Sylvia 017244
Hahn Pedersen, Morten 008844
Hahnenberg, Tom 046064
Hahnl, Prof. Dr. Adolf 002298
Haider, Adolf 003079, 003080
Haider, Prof. Gertrude 002751
Haider, Johann 003051
Haigh, Brian 038636, 039237
Haigh, Louise 001290
Haight, Pete 049245
Haiko, Pertti 009815
Haile, Priscilla F. 048427
Hailey, Dabney 049046
Hain, Dr. Beatrix 003009
Hainard, Jacques 037376
Haindl, Dominik 001696
Haine, Heiko 016933
Haine, Prof. Dr. Malou 003333
Haine, Malou 003353
Haines, Jeniffer 041890
Hainfellner, Gerhard 002738
Haininger, Robert 001738
Hair, Denny G. 044644
Hair, Julia 044442
Haja, Simion 032968
Hajdamach, Charles 039753, 041128
Hajdamach, Charles R. 039290
Hajduk, Stjepan 007817
Hájek, A. 008638
Hájiček, Dr. Jaroslav 034345
Hakamata, Akihiro 026495
Hakasalo, Kalevi 009881, 009882
Hake, Helga 019615
Hakenjos, Dr. Bernd 016833, 016844
Hakes, Jay E. 041867
Hakobyan, Lilit 000678
Halamish, Uzi 023011
Halbgebauer, Peter 002901
Halbreich, Kathy 045922
Haldemann, Dr. Anita 036890
Haldemann, Dr. Matthias 037817
Halder, Dr. U. 036810
Haldimann, Marc-André 037128
Haldner, Bruno 036895
Haldo, Soeren 030993
Haldy, Lanny 041677
Hale, Donald G. 047008
Hale, J.K. 039720
Hale, Pat 043529
Hale, Dr. Stephen 048339
Halén, Widar 031084
Halevy, Maya 022943
Haley, Helen 006495
Haley, Jeanette 042708
Halfpenny, Geoff 049204
Halilagić, Rasim 034191
Hall, Alan 001594
Hall, Alma 049274
Hall, Anne M. 047890
Hall, Brian 038910
Hall, Charles W. 044655
Hall, D. 041428
Hall, Dale 046915
Hall, Doug 001474
Hall, Eli 031284
Hall, Gail 045272
Hall, Herbert 047195
Hall, Jenny 038637
Hall, Jim 043939
Hall, Mark 040697, 045719
Hall, Marlene 042575
Hall, Melissa 040532
Hall, Michael D. 043209
Hall, Mike 046092
Hall, M.J. 040534
Hall, Nancy 049231
Hall, Peter J. 034650
Hall, Philip 040676
Hall, Robert 039780
Hall, Robin 040435
Hall, Russell J. 042623
Hall, Tim 049237
Hall-Dodd, Jean 044812
Hall-Patton, Mark P. 044510
Hallam, Doug 006438
Hallan, Knut Christian 031092
Hallas-Murula, Karin 009397
Hallatt, Kim 047487
Hallberg, Sara 046607
Halldorsson, Gudni 021950, 021951
Hallé, Antoinette 014788
Hallen, Phillip 043772
Haller, Prof. Dr. Heinrich 037749
Haller, Dr. Kerstin 016427
Haller, Dr. Klaus 019037
Haller, P. 015458
Hallett, Bob 006094
Hallett, Vic 041212
Hallgrimsdóttir, Margrét 021972
Halliday, Tom 041680
Hallin, Jens 008928
Halling, Finn 031212
Halliwell, Richard 041295
Hallman, Charles V. 048703
Hallman, Christina 036650
Hallmanns, Dieter 018060
Hallmark, Dr. Donald P. 048283
Hallock, Robert 043203
Hallonová, K. 034452
Hallová, Dr. Markéta 008456, 008522, 008627
Halls, E.J. 038676
Hally, Dr. D.J. 041833
Halma, Sidney 046479
Halmágyi, Dr. Pál 021778, 021779
Halmová, Dr. Mária 034384, 034388
Halonen, Maija-Liisa 010111
Halota, Marianna 032062
Halouzková, Marcela 008769
Halsey Gardiner, Margaret 046363
Halstead, Graham 038731
Halter, Marc 012115
Halusa, Gerhard 002975
Ham, Jenny 046347
Ham, Mrs. Robert 043726
Hama, Atsushi 026443
Hamacher, Werner 017061
Hamada, Naotsugu 027052
Hamada, Dr. Takashi 026677
Hamann, Dr. Klaus 017746
Hamann, Dr. Matthias 019352
Hamano, Tokuei 027058
Hamans, Dr. P. 030201
Hamberger, Heike 018292
Hamblin, Edward L. 042195
Hambolu, Dr. M.O. 030698
Hambrecht, Dr. Rainer 015880
Hamed, Dr. Dawi Musa 036153
Hamed, Mohammed 036149
Hamel, W.A. 029457
Hamelin, Joël 012179
Hamelmann, Cordula 016721
Hamer, Diana 000516
Hamer, Fritz 043088
Hamer, Linnea 048938
Hamilton, Duke of 039652
Hamilton, Barbara 040697
Hamilton, Betsy 046188
Hamilton, Dan 043271
Hamilton, David 042732
Hamilton, Elaine 030595
Hamilton, Gaye 001251
Hamilton, James 038721
Hamilton, Dr. James 038729
Hamilton, James 038740
Hamilton, Jimmy V. 045758
Hamilton, John 000856
Hamilton, Laura 039551
Hamilton, Lynn 042407
Hamilton, Mary 042617
Hamilton, Mary Ellin 042021
Hamilton, Mort 041765
Hamilton, Olivia 040738
Hamilton, Roy 045421
Hamilton, R.V. 001178
Hamilton, S. 040936
Hamilton, W. 030505
Hamilton-Smith, Katherine 049009
Hamlin, Frank 046452
Hammar, Britta 036443
Hammell, Brian 048201
Hammell, Peter 048007
Hammer, Anders 036456
Hammer, Bettina 016637
Hammer, C. 039046
Hammer, Dr. Karen Elisabeth 019509, 019510, 020983, 020988
Hammer, William R. 047493
Hammerman, Toby 000971
Hammern, Dr. Karen-Elisabeth . . . 020986
Hammerschmidt, Elmar 018086
Hammerschmied, Gerhard 002761
Hammersla, Keith E. 045713
Hammond, Barbara M. 042920
Hammond, Eleanor A. 042358
Hammond, Gary R. 041957
Hammond, Georgina 039625
Hammond, Karen L. 044113
Hammond, Niall 038745
Hammond, Theresa N. 044333
Hammond-Tooke, Prof. W.D. 034647
Hammontree, Nina 046142
Hamoniaux, Jacky 011616
Hamooya, C. 049572
Hamp, Steven K. 043344
Hampshire, Camilla 039465
Hampson, Leslie 040357
Hampson, Louise 041484
Hampton, Jan 030468
Hamraeva, G. 049409
Hamran, Ulf 030734, 030736
Hamre, Harald 031233
Hamrin, Örjan 036265
Hamshere, John 040993, 040998
Hamzabegović, Amra 003941
Hamzaev, A. 049390
Han, Yong 006971
Han Keuk 027474
Hanak, Werner 002918
Hanau, E. 034721
Hanauer, Christine 044258
Hance, Ben 046601
Hanchant, Deanne 001547
Hancock, Robert 047421
Hand, John 048924
Handerson, Dr. Harold 041778
Handler, Jeremy 043002
Handley, Jerry 043097
Handley, Neil 040098
Handley, Pamela 006037
Handlon, Jerry 048042
Handlos, Donald 047389
Handlos, Helga 018655
Hando, Justin 037848
Handy, Ilke 020053
Hanebutt-Benz, Dr. Eva-Maria 018788
Hanejko, Eugeniusz 032388
Hanemann, Dr. Regina . . 015872, 015879, 015883
Hanemza, Jarett 047575
Hanes, Alice C. 047198, 047202
Hanfstengel, E. 016913
Hangl 020686
Hanhardt, John 046404
Hanhart, Karin 006511
Hanisak, Dr. Dennis 043962
Hank, Jack 042606
Hankel, Lillian 000920
Hankewych, Jaroslaw J. 042885
Hankins, Roger 043311, 049307
Hanley, James 049202
Hanley, Joanne 043822
Hanley, Robin 039878, 039880
Hanley, Theresa 046694
Hanlin, Dr. R. 041833
Hann-Ruff, Stacey 042371
Hanna, Annette Adrian 043422
Hanna, Dan 043693
Hanna, Martha 006091, 006104
Hanna, Rebecca 042909

Hanna, Richard . . . 046385
Hannah, Dr. Michael . . . 030633
Hannay, Rosemary . . . 040678
Hannecart, Jean . . . 011384
Hanner, Frank . . . 043888
Hannesen, Dr. Hans Gerhard . . . 015981
Hannibal, Dr. Joseph . . . 042986
Hannick, P. . . . 003198, 003199, 003201
Hanniffy, Constance . . . 022682
Hanniffy, Kieran . . . 022682
Hannula, Betsy . . . 043849
Hannus, L. Adrien . . . 048190
Hanor, Stephanie . . . 045068
Hanreich, Georg . . . 002459, 002461
Hanreich, Liselotte . . . 002459
Hansch, Dr. Wolfgang . . . 017850, 017853
Hansel, Anna-Elisabeth . . . 017566
Hanselman, David S. . . . 043915
Hansen, Arlette . . . 043339
Hansen, Arne . . . 005512
Hansen, Barbara . . . 047232
Hansen, D. . . . 001114
Hansen, David J. . . . 043249
Hansen, David K. . . . 048749
Hansen, Don . . . 046896
Hansen, Dr. Dorothee . . . 016418
Hansen, Emma . . . 043029
Hansen, E.P.H. . . . 003768
Hansen, Eva Maria . . . 047001
Hansen, Dr. Harriet M. . . . 009023
Hansen, Jean . . . 046896
Hansen, Jeff . . . 041773
Hansen, Jesper Vang . . . 008987
Hansen, Klaus Georg . . . 021550
Hansen, Larry . . . 044228
Hansen, Maiken . . . 009070, 009133
Hansen, Mogens 008810, 008879, 008880, 008880, 009152
Hansen, Moya . . . 043401
Hansen, Nicola . . . 040962
Hansen, Palle Birk . . . 009025
Hansen, Prof. Pearl . . . 049028
Hansen, Shannon . . . 047126
Hansen, Sidsel . . . 031168
Hansen, Dr. Stephen D. . . . 048186
Hansen, Thor Gunnar . . . 031009
Hansen, Prof. Dr. Dr. Volkmar . . . 016831
Hansen, Wayne . . . 042814
Hansford, Michele . . . 042643
Hansky, Sabine . . . 019045
Hanslok, Andreas . . . 016730
Hanson, Brent . . . 047631
Hanson, Chris . . . 045942
Hanson, Christopher . . . 044979
Hanson, Collen W. . . . 048116
Hanson, Dr. John . . . 044572
Hanson, Justin . . . 048050
Hanson, Lisa . . . 046015
Hanson, Luther D. . . . 043940
Hanson, Stephen . . . 042736
Hanson, Sue . . . 047405
Hanson, William R. . . . 042697, 044904
Hanssen, L.H. . . . 030108
Hanssen-Bauer, Françoise . . . 031089
Hanssens, Marjolaine . . . 003746
Hansson, Hans-Erik . . . 036259
Hanta, Dr. Rajoharison . . . 027935
Hantschmann, Dr. Katharina . . . 019039, 019416
Hanus-Möller, Christl . . . 020007
Hanz, Dr. Günter Martin . . . 019999
Hanzal, Andrea . . . 003017
Hapkemeyer, Andreas . . . 023467
Happe, Michael . . . 017970
Haque, Dr. Enamul . . . 003119
Hara, Toshio . . . 027059, 027171
Harada, Heisaku . . . 026798
Harada, Minoru . . . 026523
Harbert, Dave . . . 041716
Harbige, Sarah . . . 038553
Harbin, Melanie M. . . . 043022
Harboe, Jytte . . . 008999
Harck, Lorraine A. . . . 045086
Hard, John . . . 041599
Hardacre, John . . . 041409
Hardberger, Linda . . . 047798
Harden, Bob . . . 048568
Harden, R. . . . 038627
Harden, Victoria A. . . . 042179
Hardenbrook, Ruth . . . 048321
Harder, H. . . . 029798
Harder, Katie . . . 005349
Harder, Dr. Matthias . . . 017435
Harder, Dr. Ruth E. . . . 037529
Hardiati, Dr. Endang Sri . . . 022440
Hardiman, Thomás . . . 022789
Hardiman, Tom . . . 047189
Hardin, Jennifer . . . 047717
Hardin, Pam . . . 041637
Harding, J.C. . . . 041211
Harding, Keith . . . 040598
Harding, Maureen . . . 049066
Harding, Shelley . . . 006168
Harding-Davis, Elise . . . 005008
Hardingham, Dennis . . . 039334
Hardjonagoro, K.R.T. . . . 022521
Hardman, Dean . . . 049125
Hardman, Genee . . . 047552
Hardman, Robert . . . 042665
Hardmeier, Prof. Dr. Christof . . . 017523
Hardt, Nis . . . 016632
Hardwick, Tommy . . . 005309
Hardy, Anne . . . 041430
Hardy, Channing C. . . . 043654
Hardy, Dr. Florent . . . 042046
Hardy, G.A. . . . 041299
Hardy-Marais, Laurence . . . 012971
Hare, Sandra J.. . . . 044974
Harel, Joram . . . 002932
Harent, Sophie . . . 013324
Hargaden, Mary . . . 045871
Harger, Sara . . . 044036
Harima, Michihiro . . . 027260
Harinen, Dot . . . 006187
Harju, Jouni . . . 009751
Harker, Robert . . . 048137
Harkins, Michael J. . . . 042029
Harleman, Kathleen . . . 042114
Harlen, Willie . . . 047732
Harling, Nick . . . 038751, 038753
Harltow, Harvey . . . 006493
Harman, Elizabeth . . . 044580
Harman, Fred C. . . . 046791
Harman, Robert L.B. . . . 043808
Harmon, Darla . . . 044134
Harmon, Elaine . . . 043906
Harmon, Horace E. . . . 045276
Harmon, Leonard . . . 046542
Harmon, Mark S. . . . 043500
Harmsworth, Lord . . . 040136
Harn, Alan D. . . . 045251
Harnesk, Helena . . . 036744
Harnett, Margaret . . . 042231
Harnly, Marc . . . 045433
Harnoncourt, Anne d' . . . 046975, 046983
Haro, Jambo . . . 027431
Harold, Steve . . . 045634, 048597
Harp, Ann . . . 005190
Harper, Avis . . . 042034
Harper, Mary Kay . . . 047515
Harper, Robert W. . . . 047608
Harper Lee, Laura . . . 042366
Harrauer, Prof. Dr. Hermann . . . 002971, 002986
Harre Hérin, A. . . . 003641
Harreld Love, Josephine . . . 043450
Harrell, Deloris . . . 045649
Harrer, Anton . . . 002306
Harrer, Nicole . . . 002975
Harrewijn, H. . . . 029607
Harriett, Rebecca . . . 044430
Harrington, Beverly . . . 041753
Harrington, Bill . . . 001271
Harrington, Caren Anne . . . 042102
Harrington, Gary . . . 044775
Harrington, Judith A. . . . 048988
Harrington, Katie . . . 044500
Harrington, Lisa . . . 046766
Harrington, Sian . . . 040100
Harris, Adam Duncan . . . 044809
Harris, Amy . . . 041730
Harris, Dr. C. . . . 040665
Harris, Deborah . . . 006580
Harris, Dee . . . 047757
Harris, Dr. E.C. . . . 003901
Harris, Florence E. . . . 048321
Harris, Gene E. . . . 042692
Harris, Harper . . . 044957
Harris, Ivan . . . 006590
Harris, James T. . . . 042018
Harris, Jane . . . 046289
Harris, Jennifer . . . 040416
Harris, Joanna Ruth . . . 046195
Harris, Joe . . . 044541
Harris, Prof. Judith A. . . . 042354
Harris, Kaye . . . 001093
Harris, Mac R. . . . 045179
Harris, Miriam B. . . . 043900
Harris, Nathanial C. . . . 045978
Harris, Neville . . . 030637
Harris, Ottawa . . . 043397
Harris, René . . . 043638
Harris, Rhian . . . 040149
Harris, Richard . . . 041031
Harris, Rosemary . . . 040269
Harris, Sandra L. . . . 045189
Harris, Scott H. . . . 046244
Harris, Sharon . . . 038502
Harris, Tina B. . . . 044841
Harris-Fernandez, Al . . . 048185
Harrison, Betsy . . . 046082
Harrison, Camilla . . . 041480
Harrison, Christina . . . 040503
Harrison, Eunice . . . 040784
Harrison, Harrie . . . 046918
Harrison, Dr. J. . . . 034731
Harrison, Jefferson . . . 046496
Harrison, John . . . 038712, 041238
Harrison, Kathy . . . 044054
Harrison, M. . . . 040030
Harrison, Marie . . . 030612
Harrison, Michael . . . 038965
Harrison, Monica . . . 045595
Harrison, Myra . . . 042452, 042453
Harrison, Stephen . . . 039268, 041862
Harriss, Joan . . . 006547
Harrow, Edward D. . . . 048640
Harsch, René . . . 036855
Harstad, Peter T. . . . 044742
Hart, Brooks . . . 006041
Hart, Karen . . . 044633
Hart, Katherine . . . 044426
Hart, Macy B. . . . 044802
Hart, Myrna . . . 048967
Hart, Nancy . . . 044028
Hart, Peter R. . . . 039341
Hart, Robert L. . . . 045179
Hart, Ron . . . 048748
Hart, Susan E. . . . 049211
Hart, William . . . 047655
Hart Hennessey, Maureen . . . 048367
Harte, Jeremy . . . 039462
Harte, Miriam . . . 038645
Hartenhoff, Nancy . . . 042448
Hartfield, Libby . . . 044800
Harth, Marjorie L. . . . 042938
Harthorn, Sandy . . . 042288
Hartigan, Lynda R. . . . 048943
Hartkopf, Herbert . . . 016883
Hartl, Christa . . . 019572
Hartl, Georg L. . . . 016208
Hartlage, Ken . . . 044356
Hartland, Ian . . . 041218
Hartleb, Silvia Waltraud . . . 003069
Hartleben, Ralph Erik . . . 019112
Hartleib, Dr. Rudolf . . . 017189
Hartley, C. . . . 038962
Hartley, David B. . . . 047018
Hartley, Keith . . . 039424
Hartley, Kristin . . . 047595
Hartman, Bruce . . . 046754
Hartman, C. . . . 034674
Hartman, Janice . . . 041672
Hartman Becker, Heather . . . 045145
Hartmann, Andy . . . 037509
Hartmann, Bonnie . . . 048410
Hartmann, Felix . . . 037509
Hartmann, Joseph . . . 015637, 017118
Hartmann, K. . . . 019881
Hartnigk-Kümmel, Dr. Christa . . . 018159
Harto, Edward S. . . . 045875
Hartshorn, Willis . . . 046348
Hartung, Lee . . . 044216
Hartweger, Hans . . . 002975
Hartwell, Carroll T. . . . 045918
Hartwell, Jane . . . 040223
Hartwich, Bernd . . . 019592
Hartwick, Sue . . . 043887
Hartwig, Laurie . . . 047027
Hartwigsen, Peter Lorenz . . . 019306
Hartz, Jill . . . 042770
Hartz, Susanne . . . 008938
Hartzell, Matthew D. . . . 043388
Hartzold, Susan . . . 042261
Harvey, A.M. . . . 034685
Harvey, Conrad . . . 043209
Harvey, Deborah . . . 048339
Harvey, G.J. . . . 038837
Harvey, Iris . . . 040423
Harvey, Liz . . . 045378
Harvey, M. . . . 040936
Harvey, Paul . . . 043136
Harvey, Phyllis . . . 046402
Harville, Vickie . . . 045521
Harwon, Ipn . . . 000838
Haryu, Tsutomu . . . 026708
Haşdeu, N. Titus . . . 032790
Hasegawa, Koichi . . . 026614
Hasegawa, Mariko . . . 027172
Hasegawa, Sakae . . . 027227
Hasegawa, Takashi . . . 026801
Hasegawa, Tei . . . 027009
Hasegawa, Tokushichi . . . 026632
Hashagen, Joanna . . . 038596
Hashimoto, Akinobu . . . 026411
Hashimoto, Isao . . . 026505
Hashimoto, Kentarou . . . 027225, 053801
Hashimoto, Masao . . . 026708
Hashimoto, Takeshi . . . 026685
Hashimoto, Tsutomu . . . 026833
Hashimov, Bahodir Djuraevič . . . 049389
Hashitomi, Hiroki . . . 026705
Hashtroodi, A. . . . 022600
Hasitschka, Dr. Peter . . . 002957
Haskell, Barbara . . . 046418
Haskell, Dr. Eric T. . . . 042936
Haskell, Heather . . . 048293, 048294
Haskins, James . . . 043805
Håskoll Haugen, Liv . . . 030944, 030946, 030948
Haslauer, Dr. Elfriede . . . 002934
Haslehner, Hubert . . . 002426
Hasler, Norbert W. . . . 027839, 027843
Hasprunar, Jill . . . 044039
Haß, Heike . . . 017825
Hassan, Syed Jamal . . . 022078, 022084
Hassbecker, Egon . . . 017832
Hassdenteufel, Dr. Erwin . . . 018787
Hasse, Dr. Claus-Peter . . . 018769
Hasselbalch, Kurt . . . 042566
Hassen, Carol . . . 049326
Hassinen, Esa . . . 009783
Hassler, Donna . . . 048619
Hassler, Hermann . . . 027844
Hassmann, Dr. Elisabeth . . . 002934
Hassol, Milton D. . . . 046385
Hasson, Janet S. . . . 046140
Hasson, Rachel . . . 022963
Hastaba, Dr. Ellen . . . 002097
Hasted, Rachel . . . 039186
Hastedt, Catherine A. . . . 043045
Hastie, J. Drayton . . . 042740

Hastings, Lord 040974
Hastings, Bill 045348
Hasvold, Carol 043358
Haszprunar, Prof. Dr. Gerhard 019132
Hata, Nobuyuki 026512
Hataguchi, Minoru 026532
Hatchell, Steven J. 043060
Hatcher, Alexandra 006320
Hatcher, Alison 042260
Hatcher, Stephen 039174
Hatcher, V. 040622
Hatfield, P. 039459
Hathaway, Merle 001118
Hathaway, Michael 045088
Hathaway, Nadine 047981
Hathaway, Wesley 044007
Hatibu, Hadji 037858
Hatoum, Hassan 037835
Hatschek, Christoph 002910
Hatswell, D.A. 039349
Hattam, Edward 001182
Hattingh, J. 034566
Hattori, Gene 042635
Hattrick, Elspeth 040241
Hatzitaki-Kapsomenou, Prof. Ch. . . . 021492
Hau, Hal 045019
Haubold, Prof. Dr. H. 017659, 017660
Hauck, Richard 046633
Haudiquet, Annette 012509
Haudot, Charles 012295, 012296
Hauer, Armin 017206
Hauer, Karl 002876
Hauer, Ulrich 017651
Hauff, Rolf Bernhard 017995
Haufschild, Kurt 020180
Haug, Prof. Dr. Andreas 017034
Haug, Dr. Tilman 019089
Hauge, Tore 031022, 031160, 031210
Haugen, Charleen 047540
Hauger, Therese 030829
Haugg, Hans 016531
Hauglid, Anders Ole 030845, 030984
Hauk, Roman 032194
Haumesser, Giselher 018148
Haun, Elizabeth 043237
Haupenthal, Dr. Uwe 019307
Haupt, Eva 018211
Haupt, Dr. Herbert 002934
Hauptmann, Dr. Andreas 016276
Hauptner, Brigitte 002969
Hauregard, Léon J. 003146
Haurie, Michel 013524
Haus, Anny-Claire 014851
Haus, Mary 046418
Hausammann, Hans Peter 037601
Hauschild, Dr. Jan-Christoph 016832
Hausding, Michaela 016793
Hauser, Emil 037195
Hauser, Erin 048822
Hauser, Hans-Jörg 018156
Hauser, Larry 044513
Hauser, Monika 019887
Hauser, Peter 037774
Hauser, Reine 042507
Hauser, Robert 046190
Hauser, Urban 036971
Hauser-Schäublin, Prof. Dr. Brigitta 017474
Hausmann, Dr. A. 019132
Hausmann, Doris 046831
Hauss, M. 012149
Haußmann, Dr. Eberhard 016871
Haussonville, Comte d' 037032
Haussteiner, Franz 001759
Haustein-Bartsch, Dr. Eva 019739
Hauswald, Dr. Kenneth 041801
Haut, Sheryl 043304
Hautekeete, Stefaan 003315
Hauthaway, Elisabeth L. 047096
Havard, Carine 003692
Havas, Sandra H. 046628
Havassy, Péter 021734
Havel, Joseph 044648
Havelund, Jørgen 009069
Havens, Patricia 048183
Havens, Ron 044325
Haveri-Nieminen, Marja-Liisa 010070
Haverkamp, Frode 031089
Haverkamp-Begemann, Egbert . . . 046394
Havlíček, Jaroslav 008687
Havlíčková, Dr. Miloslava 008499
Havron, Rina 022896
Haw, Jane 046840
Hawadi, T. 049581
Hawelka, Dr. Walter 017378
Hawell, Dr. Steve 048075
Hawes, Denise 046864
Hawes, Irene 048691
Hawfield, Michael C. 044587
Hawhsford, Catherine 044664
Hawk, Alan 048929
Hawk, Bob 044764
Hawke, Jenny 034610
Hawke-Smith, Cameron 038958
Hawkes, Juliet 038865
Hawkey, Diane 048520
Hawkins, Del 043742
Hawkins, Lynda 043197
Hawkins, Marilyn 045543
Hawkins, Renee 045399
Hawkins, Dr. Ruth 044879
Hawkins, Dr. Seth C. 047701
Hawkins, Trystan 038793
Hawley, Anne 042328
Hawley, Greg 044929
Hawley, Henry 042985
Hawley, Ken 041220
Hawley, Pam 005457, 005458
Haworth, Brenda 044535
Hawvermale, Hettie G. 042167
Haxhiu, Prof. Dr. Idriz 000035
Haxton, Jason 045023
Hay, Irma 040083
Hay, Malcolm 040252
Hay, Mary 039824
Hay, Susan 047258
Hayashi, Hirotumi 027192
Hayashi, Kiichiro 026579
Hayashi, Masayoshi 027345
Hayashi, Misa 027166
Hayashibara, Ken 026940
Haycock, Dr. Lorna 039235
Hayes, C. Daniel 043777
Hayes, Chuck 046759
Hayes, David 039005
Hayes, Fiona 039568
Hayes, Neila C. 048173
Hayes, Randall 046676
Hayes, Virginia B. 048321
Hayhow, Simon 039504
Haylings, Peter 041440
Hayman, Judy 043505
Hayman, Louise 043606
Haynes, Bruce 005521
Haynes, Carol 044583
Haynes, Jackie 041724
Haynes, John H. 041077
Haynes, Peter 000886, 001546
Haynes, Tom 039468
Haynie, Ron 048959
Hayoz, Roger 037349
Hays, Bonnie 046801
Hays, George W.S. 047748
Haysom, David 041169
Hayter, Stephen 005140
Hayton, Brian 039885
Hayward, Alexander 039815
Hayward, Gardner 045269
Hayward, Merle 044705
Hayward, M.R. 039813
Hayward, Ron 030428
Hayward, Susan P. 041152
Haywood, Dr. C. 022772
Hayworth, P. 041434
Hazelrigg, Scott 041805
Hazelwood, Bevyn L. 043405
Head, Sandra 005141
Headland, R.K. 038969
Headley, Dr. David 047130
Headrick, Dennis 045371
Heady, Karen 046740
Healy, James 045452
Heaman, Ken 005596
Hearn, Brian 046649
Hearn, Redell 045413
Heath, Amie 047364
Heath, Betty 048349
Heath, Hether 006497
Heath, Pat 039912
Heathcote, Richard 001249
Heaton, Alice 042020
Heaume, R.L. 039513
Heaver, Stephen G. 045523
Heazlewood, Brenton 001611
Hebden, M.J. 039631
Heberling, Judith A. 044672
Hebestreit, Dr. Franz 019112
Hebler, Ingo 016470, 016471
Hebron, Victoria 041411
Hebsacker, Friedrich 020515
Hecher, Markus 020466
Hecht, Dr. Winfried 019931, 019932, 019933, 019934
Heck, Brigitte 018158
Heck, Suzanne 044536
Heckenbenner, Dominique 014683
Heckenberg, Dr. Norman 000840
Heckendorf, Kitty 044509
Heckert, Virginia 049091
Heckes, Jürgen 016276
Heckscher, Morrison H. 046364
Hectors, Jan 003426, 003427
Heddon, Gordon 040064
Hedegaard, Esben 009121, 009123, 009124, 009125
Hedel-Samson, Brigitte 010810
Hedelin, Jean-Louis 010543
Heder, Terence 045787
Hedger, Michael 000882
Hedges, Kenneth 047839
Hedin, Marika 036651
Hedin, Svante 036545
Hedinger, Dr. Bärbel 017680, 017700
Hedrick, Nancy 045253
Hee, Lee Hyun 027606
Heege, Dr. Elke 016919
Heen, E. de 030289
Heer, Ed de 029204
Heerebout, G.R. 029804
Heerink, B. 029649
Heermann, Dr. Ingrid 020358
Heey, H.F. 040533
Hefele, Bernhard 019037
Hefele, Dr. Gabriel 018651
Hefermehl, Norbert 016230
Hefferhan, Tom 001263
Heffern, Marion 006408
Heffley, Scott 044924
Heflin, Kirk 043955
Heflin, Tori 047839
Hefner, L. 019396
Hegan, M. 038579
Hege, Betsy 043283
Hegel, Andrea von 016011
Hegeman, Carol A. 044183
Heger, Gabriele 002700
Heggade, Dr. D. Veerendra 022104
Heggen, Bert 030247
Hegnar von Ubisch, Frederikke . . . 030917, 030918
Hegseth Garberg, Ann Siri 031287
Heguerte de Soria, María del Carmen 041520
Heibein, Debbie 047938
Heide, Dr. Birgit 018790
Heide, Diana 007832
Heidecke, Dr. D. 017674
Heidemann, Dr. Stefan 018111
Heiden, Karl-Josef zu 020232
Heidenkreis, Walfart 037600
Heidenreich, Barbara 031874
Heidenreich, Walter 002214
Heidrich, Dr. Hermann 018989
Heigl, J. 015442
Heij, Dr. J.J. 029279
Heijmans, Dr. H.G. 029406, 029416
Heil, Gerd 019896
Heil, Jean-François 010553
Heilbrun, Françoise 013678
Heilbrunn, Margaret 046389
Heiliger, Don 045004
Heiligmann, Dr. Jörg 018374
Heilman, Anna Bea 045545
Heilman, Patrick 042069
Heilmann, Dr. Angela 018654
Heiman, Mary-Ellen 005146
Heimann, Sybille 020670, 020671
Heimann-Jelinek, Dr. Felicitas . . . 002918
Heimberg, Dr. Ursula 016333
Heimrath, Dr. Ralf 019175
Heimühle, Bernd 015745
Hein, Carolyn 005840
Hein, Ivar-Kristjan 009398
Hein, Jørgen 008956
Hein, Lisbet 008936
Hein, Louise 044155
Heinämies, Kati 009532
Heinänen, Seija 009641, 009645
Heindl, Alex 045192
Heindrichs, Horst 016985
Heine, Sabine 016337
Heinemann, Dr. Christiane 018773
Heinemann, Ingo F. 018015
Heinerud, Jans 036732
Heines, Carolyn 044279
Heinicke, Dr. Janet 044755
Heinisch, Dr. Severin 002171
Heinlein, Roland 015675
Heinmiller, Lee D. 044388
Heinonen, Jouko 009781, 009782, 009783, 009784, 009785, 009786, 009788, 009790
Heinrich, Dr. Chirstoph 017694
Heinritz, Dr. Reinhard 015869
Heins, Dr. 030463
Heintzelman, Scott A. 048429
Heintzman, John 046879
Heinz, Dr. Marianne 018198
Heinz, Ulrich von 016078
Heinzelmann, P. 017842
Heinzer, Dr. F. 020372
Heinzerling, Werner 019045
Heinzl, Richard 003006
Heischmann, Dr. Günter 019127
Heise, Bernd 016799
Heise, Dr. Brigitte 018726
Heise, Dr. Karin 018915
Heiser, Jerry 042075
Heising, Cornelia 016834
Heiss, Herbert 037073
Heiß, Ulrich 018212
Heißig, Prof. Dr. Kurt 019099
Heitele, Thomas 018424
Heitmann, Dr. Bernhard 017715
Heitz, Henri 014716
Heizer, Lois 048172
Heizmann, Dr. Elmar 020364
Hejdová, Dagmar 008356
Heks, Silke 019207
Helavuori, Hanna-Leena 009581
Helbig, Gabriele 017101
Helbig, Heike 019945, 019946
Helbling, R. 037598, 037599
Helbling, Regine 037597
Held, Peter 044502
Helfenstein, Dr. Josef 042704
Helfenstein, Marie-Therese 037553
Helfrich, Kurt 047952
Helg, Lukas 037062
Helgesson, Michael 036382
Helke, Dr. Gabriele 002934
Hellberg, Kerstin 015660
Helleland, Allis 008988
Hellenkemper, Prof. Dr. Hansgerd . 018339

Heller, Barbara 043444
Heller, Dr. Erna 046334
Heller, Kurt 002977
Heller, Laura 047287
Heller, Margot 040292
Heller-Karneth, Dr. Eva 015528
Heller-Winter, Dr. Elisabeth 019086, 019101
Hellfaier, Detlev 016689
Hellmann, Birgitt 018117
Hellmund, Dr. M. 017659, 017660
Hellrung, Reinhard 017356, 017357
Hellstern, Dr. John R. 041630
Helm, Charles 043112
Helm, Cherie 048432
Helm, Erika 003062
Helm, Lorna 042943
Helm, Dr. Reinhardt 020731
Helm, Richard S. 044267
Helmberger, Dr. . 015580, 015582, 015583
Helmberger, Dr. Werner . . 015878, 018712
Helme, Andrew 040490
Helme, Mekis 009401
Helmecke, Gisela 016131
Helmerding, Willy 015767
Helmerson, Klas 036663, 036681
Helmig, Loeda 045375
Helminen, Hilkka 009612
Helminen, Liisa 009548
Helminen, Ritva 010091
Helms, Cheryl V. 046465
Helmus, L.M. 030226
Helmy, Kwathar 009275
Helsby, Kenneth M. 047035
Helsell, Charles P. 043910
Helstrom, Linnea 046274
Helton, Debra M. 048165
Helviö, Helena 009791
Helzel, Florence 042162
Helzer, Richard 042376
Héman, S. 029230
Hemby, Lisa 043267
Hemdal, Jay F. 048568
Hemdorff, Olle 031221
Hemetsberger, Matthias 002673
Hemm, Marsha 047245
Hemm, Michael 001759
Hemmendorff, Ove 036529
Hemmer, J. 029347
Hemmes, H.H. 030227
Hempel, Dr. Gudrun 002976
Hemsley, Jacqueline 000847
Henar, A.F. 029894
Henatsch, Dr. Martin 019139
Henchley, Gillian 040307
Hendel, Dr. Margarete 019227
Hendeles, Ydessa 006646
Hender, Diane 041722
Henderby, D. 039297
Henderson, Cherel 045037
Henderson, Diana 038534
Henderson, Donald C. 044332
Henderson, D.T. 039200
Henderson, E. Ray 042931
Henderson, G. 001377
Henderson, Graeme 001043
Henderson, Jai 045413
Henderson, Kevin 030572
Henderson, M. 001187
Henderson, Marie 006271
Henderson, Robbin L. 042157
Henderson, Sam R. 043854
Henderson, Stan 006468
Henderson Fahnestock, Andrea . . . 046378
Hendler, Karla 016154
Hendricks, Albert J. 048587
Hendricks, Dr. Alfred 019157
Hendricksh, M. 034682
Hendrickson, Dean A. 041936
Hendrickson, Riley 045908
Hendricx, Hilde 003765
Hendrikx, R. 030404, 030405
Hendrix, Lee 045433
Hendrix, Mittie B. 047722
Hendryx, Michael 049366
Heneberry, June L. 046268
Hengelhaupt, Regine 018641
Hengstenberg, Thomas 020186
Hengster, Sabine 017742, 017744
Hengstman, G. 029460
Henke, James 042998
Henke, Jerry D. 044018
Henkens-Lewis, Helen 039043
Henley, Michael 047177
Henmi, Yoshiharu 026917
Henn, Catherine E. C. 042338
Henn, Char 047355
Hennaut, Eric 003314
Henneman, Inge 003161
Hennessey, Dr. William . . 046496, 046501, 046505, 048792
Hennessy, Thomas F. 048536
Hennig, Eckhard 017579
Hennig, Lutz 019006
Henning, Darrell D. 043358
Henning, Dirk 019957
Henning, Ulrich 019795
Henning, William T. 047278
Hennuy, Claude 003793
Hennze, Dr. Joachim 017851, 017853
Henriksen, Kenneth Roy 008897
Henrikson, Steve 044888
Henrikssen, Tracey 006568
Henrion, Pierre 003600
Henriot, André 013217
Henriot, Elisabeth 011493
Henry, Barbara 046406, 046598
Henry, Cassandra L. 045514
Henry, Chris 039610
Henry, Christopher 039483
Henry, John B. 043861
Henry, Karen A. 005168
Henry, Lawrence 046102
Henry, Patricia 042895
Henry-Barnaudière, Elise 015377
Henrykowska, Anna 032274
Henrysson, Harald 036228
Henschke, Dr. Ekkehard 018599
Hensel, Diethardt 019276
Hensel, Dr. Karen 043564, 043565, 043566, 043569, 043570
Henseler, Petra 019253
Henseler, Rainer 019952
Henshall, Barbara E. 042711
Henshall, W.A. 041481
Henshaw Jones, Susan 048923
Hensley, Dr. Dannie 032718
Hensley, Trevor 041437
Henson, Harvey 042619
Henson, Leonora 042506
Henson, Trevis 041984
Hente, Joke 029208
Henton, Marty 045262
Hentschel, Barbara 018579
Hentschel, Dr. Martin 018399
Henwood, Peter C. 030526
Hepburn, Lorna 039578
Hepp, Dr. Frieder 017829, 017837
Héran, Emmanuelle 013678
Herb, Reinhard 020737
Herbage, M.-B. 014264
Herbata, Peter P. 003035
Herbaugh, Karen 045504
Herber, Bob 048698
Herberg, Mayde 047947
Herberger, Mark 048282
Herberstein, Andrea Gräfin 002037
Herbert, Jacky 014755
Herbert, Lynn M. 044637
Herbert, Sharon C. 041732
Herbert, Susan 000888
Herbst, Detlev 020552
Herbst, Dr. Helmut 020624, 020626
Herbst, John H. 043846
Herbuveaux, Arlette 014913
Herce, Ana I. 035910
Herda, Isabel 017234
Herdits, H. 001823
Heredia Cortés, Gabriel 028950
Herger, Madleine 037297
Herger, Dr. Peter 037301
Herger-Kaufmann, Josef . . 037586, 037653
Hergovich, Marianne 002934
Herholdt, Nancy 042749
Herkenhoff, Paulo 004405
Herlinger, Andreas 002975
Herlinger, Grete 002975
Hermalyn, Dr. Gary D. . . . 042431, 042435, 042440
Herman, Eileen 043256
Herman, Judy 044479
Herman, Monica 044014
Herman, Richard 043962
Hermand, Michel 013502
Hermand, Nathalie 003573
Hermann, Prof. A. 020720
Hermann, Adolf 020473
Hermann, Claudia 037297
Hermann, Dr. Oliver 020928
Hermann, Reyh 020023
Hermann, Dr. Siegfried W. 002444
Hermann-Szabó, Sara 009159
Hermans, Georges 003498
Hermansdorfer, Mariusz . 032523, 032527, 032530
Hermellin, G. 014758
Hernandez, Annie 014587
Hernández, Carlos Arturo 007414
Hernández, Jo Farb 047899
Hernandez, John 045215
Hernández, Rodolfo 028531
Hernandez, Sofia 046288
Hernández Carrión, Emiliano 035311
Hernández Gutiérrez, Jorge 007459
Hernández Hervás, Emilia 035735
Hernández Nieves, Román 034886
Herne, Shawn 041965
Herold, G. 019370
Herold, Dr. Inge 018806
Herold, Joyce L. 043406
Herold, Prof. Roland 002866
Herold, Prof. Roland-Peter 002118
Herr, Beth 043229
Herrán, Alfonso Carcero 007518
Herranen, Merja 009996
Herrbach-Schmidt, Dr. Brigitte . . . 018158
Herreman, Frank 045388
Herren, Hans 036962
Herren, Robert 037333
Herren, Walter 037185
Herrera Acosta, Elvira 028532
Herrera de la Muela, Ignacio 035723
Herrera Salazar, Germán 007499
Herrero, Prof. Eutimio 035275
Herreshoff, Halsey C. 042424
Herrick, Phyllis M. 044772
Herrick O'Hara, Virginia 042692
Herring, Madeline 042036
Herring, Sarah 040241
Herrman, Diana 041902
Herrmann, Ger-Ulrich 020170
Herrmann, John 042334
Herrmann, Jürgen 020654
Herrmann, Karen 047802
Herrmann, Dr. Klaus 020347
Herrmann, Matthias 003023
Herrmann, Samuel 037232
Herrmann, Uwe 018149
Herrmann, Dr. Volker 017926
Herrmann Fiore, Dr. Kristina 025542
Herron, James 046828
Herron, Mary 044710
Herselman, D.E. 034754
Hershfield, Shauna 045982, 045983
Herskowitz, Sylvia A. 046419
Herta, Ana 032769
Hertel, Prof. Dr. Hannes 019042
Hertford, Marquess of 038470
Hertiš, Iris 034462
Hertner, Max 037534
Hertzlieb, Gregg 048741
Hervey Bathurst, James & Sarah . . 039947
Herzer, Wolfgang 020707
Herzog, Dr. Georges 037204
Herzog, G.H. 017199
Herzog, John E. 046371
Herzog, Melinda 045612, 048817
Herzog, Rainer 016882
Herzogenrath, Prof. Dr. Wulf 016418
Heske, Immo 016381
Hesketh-Campbell, Lorraine 040453
Heslewood, Emma 040778
Hess, Carsten 008944
Hess, Dr. Daniel 019352
Hess, Roman 037803
Hessaby, Mohandes Iraj 022619
Hesse, Gisela 018092
Hesse, Dr. Sabine 020374
Hesse-Mohr, Dr. Petra 018809
Hesselund, Birgit 008799
Heston, Charlton 043783
Heston, Dana 045086
Heth, Charlotte 046383
Hett, Ulrike 016047
Hettingg, Mary Jane 049016
Heuberger, Georg 017178, 017190
Heuberger, Vera 037391
Heublein, Dr. Brigitte 017487
Heuckeroth, Erwin 018882
Heuer, Christoph 020177
Heufelder, Jochen 018327
Heufelder, Michael 019069
Heukemes, Dr. Berndmark 018458
Heulot, Laurent 010387
Heunemann 020284
Heusden, G. van 029665
Heuser 016802
Heuser, Prof. Dr. August 017159
Heuser, Frederick J. 046979
Heuser, Dr. Mechthild 036936
Heusinger, Prof. Dr. Lutz 018818
Heußner, Karen 020565
Heuwinkel, Christiane 016237
Heuwinkel, Dr. Hubert 016847
Hevers, Dr. J. 016392
Hevia, Agustin 035586
Hew Wing, Micheal 046372
Hewitt, H.D. 040641
Hewitt, Karen 042704
Hewitt, Susan 001584
Hewitt, Timothy M. 046625
Hewitt-Dower, Bill 000934
Hewson, Alan 038461
Hewson, Karen E. 006057
Hewson, Paul 000715
Hewson, Rose 030563
Hewson, Shirley O. 001629
Heyburn, Tim 039811, 039813
Heyd, Paul 019439
Heyden, Dr. Thomas 019369
Heyen, Lora 041950
Heyes, John 039400
Heyl, Cornelius A. von 020982
Heyler, Joanne 045467
Heym, Dr. Sabine 019107, 019108, 019111
Heymans, Dr. Hubert 003619
Heyneman, C. 003277
Heynen, Arnold 037706
Heynen, Dr. Julian 016835
Hibbitt, Karen 048894
Hickey, Leo J. 046226
Hickey, Michael 005200
Hicklin, Karen 042895
Hickman, Carole S. 042163
Hickman, Gerry 041883
Hickman, Warren 048859
Hickmann, Manfred 019627
Hickock, Paul 044629
Hicks, Anna Lee 046198
Hicks, Christine 013939
Hicks, Hilarie M. 046195
Hicks, Hugh Francis 041999

Hicks, Louis 041635
Hidasi, Prof. José 004126
Hidber, Alfred 037821
Hideo, Kurita 026424
Hideshima, Tatsumi 026419
Hidook, Tatjana 038264
Hiebel, Kaye 045695
Hiebler, Prof. Dr. Herbert 002793
Hieblinger, Faith 005716
Hiekisch-Picard, Sepp 016281, 017799
Hiéret, Jean-Pierre 010882
Hiesinger, Kathryn B. 046975
Hiesmayr, Herbert 002624
Higginbotham, Evangeline 047589
Higgs, Jane 039375
High, Laura 041768
High, Steven S. 047373
Hightower, John B. 046470
Higman, David 040048
Hignette, Michel 013716
Higuchi, Dr. Keiji 026886
Higuchi, Dr. Takayasu 026769
Higueras Rodríguez, Dolores 035430
Hiis Søftestad, Hanne 030725
Hijiwara, Takshi 026954
Hilaire, Michel 013204, 013210
Hilberg, Thomas D. 045747
Hilberg, Dr. Volker 020038
Hilbrand, Ingrid 001708
Hilbun, Dorinda 042048
Hildawa, Isidro 031757
Hildebran, Julia 043024
Hildebrand, Carla 049169
Hildebrand, Dr. Josephine 016104
Hildebrand, Walter 001883
Hildebrandt, Alexandra 016118
Hildebrandt, Sandra 046441
Hildenbrand, Manfred 017786
Hiles, Wayne 049007
Hilger, Charles 047957
Hilger, H. 020372
Hilger, Dr. Wolfgang 002952
Hilgers, Patrick 003217
Hilkenbach, Rainer 018241
Hilkhuijsen, J. 029408
Hill, Andrew 046226
Hill, Andrew F. 038588
Hill, Barbara A. 046132
Hill, Brian O. 048607
Hill, Carla 042037
Hill, Carolyn 046649
Hill, Charlie 006104
Hill, Christine C. 044449
Hill, Dr. Christopher L. 042375
Hill, Donald C. 045071
Hill, J. Bennett 049032
Hill, John 046652
Hill, June 039658
Hill, Katherine 043335
Hill, Lindsay 006175
Hill, Mary 047754
Hill, Michelle 042264
Hill, Pamela K. 044338
Hill, Peter 039778
Hill, Ray 045355
Hill, Robert D. 044443
Hill, Robin 039861
Hill, Sergej Ivanovič 032975
Hill, Shannen 043418
Hill, Steve 041798, 044745
Hill Carter, Charles 042720
Hill-Festa, Lisa 048087
Hill Perrell, Franklin 047547
Hillam, Penelope 000746
Hillard, Elbert R. 044797
Hillebrand, Dr. Melanie 034705
Hiller, Dr. Hilde 017236
Hiller, Dr. Hubertus 020086
Hiller, N. 030460
Hiller von Gaertringen, Dr. Julia 016689
Hiller von Gaertringen, Dr. Rudolf 018561, 018569, 018597
Hillerman, Barbara 003011
Hillesheim, Dr. Jürgen 015604
Hillhouse, David 038717
Hillhouse, Susan 047954
Hilliard, Elbert R. 044798
Hillier, Kenneth 038536
Hillis, Florence E. 045034
Hillsman, Matthew 047150
Hillstrom, Richard L. 045916
Hilpert Stuber, Susanne 037334
Hiltermann, Elisabeth 015772, 015958
Hilti, Joseph 037156
Hiltula, Leena 010225
Hilz, Dr. Helmut 019045
Hilzhood, Nancy 044936
Himanen, Hilke Liisa 009823
Himawan, Joice 041570
Himber, René 011153
Himmelbauer, Robert 002045
Himmelein, Prof. Dr. Volker 020374
Himmelstrand, Erik 036784
Hincapié, Alberto 007510
Hincapié Santa Maria, Jaime 007566
Hinchliffe, Robin 047918
Hind, Charles 040137, 040200
Hindelang, Eduard 018499
Hinderer, S. 017316
Hindman, James 045410
Hinds, Roger 042180
Hine, Marjorie 006668
Hine, N.A. 039059
Hinerman, Lenore 044197
Hines, Tommy 048252
Hingst, Eckhard 017946
Hinkley, Marilyn J. 049331
Hinman, Marjory 044439
Hinnant, Vandorn 044336
Hinrichsen, Dr. Torkild 017680, 017697
Hinsch, Werner 018524
Hinson, Tom E. 042985
Hintermaier, Dr. Ernst 002556
Hinton, Dr. Brian 039526
Hinton, Verdell 044700
Hinton, William 045481
Hinz, Günther 016232
Hinz, Dr. Hans-Martin 016011
Hiott, William D. 042975, 042976
Hippe, Margarethe 002532
Hipps, Will 041995
Hipschman, Dorrie 048370
Hipwell, John 006754
Hír, Dr. János 021813
Hirabayashi, Kunio 026949
Hirako, Akihiko 026473
Hiramatsu, Hideki 026445
Hirano, Irene 045434
Hirano, Itaru 027009
Hirano, Naoki 027191
Hirata, Shozo 027124
Hirayama, Miyako 027009
Hirci, Andrej 034487
Hird, Maureen 040349
Hirner, Dr. René 017840
Hiroshi, Doi 026524
Hiroshi, Ito 027272
Hiroya, Yukiatu 026995
Hirsch, Jan 048162
Hirsch, John 041929
Hirsch, Marjorie 048747
Hirschbiegel, Dieter 018394
Hirschel, Anthony G. 044748
Hirschler, Christa 020248
Hirst, M. 034667
Hirst, Marlys 042058
Hirth, Dr. Antoine 010799
Hirthe, Dr. Thomas 017765
Hirtle, Wade 005738
Hirvonen, Anna-Riikka 009702, 009703
Hiscock, Rosella 006190
Hislop, Kare 047352
Hiss, Elfi 037354
Hitchings, Sinclair 042318
Hitchmough, Dr. Wendy 039501
Hite, Andy 047034
Hite, Jessie Otto 041927
Hittaller, Hans Martin 001748
Hitzing, Jörg 019803
Hiukka, Toini 009930
Hjermind, Jesper 009150
Hjorth, Carl-Gustav 036698
Hladky, Sylvia 019046
Hlaváčková, Dr. Miroslava 008670
Hlôška, L. 034452
Hnateyko, Olha 046416
Ho, Keimei 026703
Ho, Lynn 041852
Ho Ho, Ying 034292, 054048,
Hoag, Everett H. 046191
Hoard, Constance G. 042485
Hoare, Adrian D. 041462
Hoare, Nell 041407
Hobaugh, J.H. 048015
Hobbs, Patricia A. 045280
Hobein, Beate 017626, 017627
Hoberg, Dr. Annegret 019124
Hobin, Ellen 005590
Hobolth, Nina 008799
Hobson, Marlena 048343
Hobson, Richard 038596
Hoch, Manfred 020009
Hochberg, Dr. F.G. 047951
Hochberger, Ernst 018161
Hochdörfer, Achim 002965
Hoche, Frank 017811, 019505
Hochleitner, Dr. Martin 002249
Hochscheid, Christian 016847
Hochstrasser, M. 037580
Hochuli, Dr. P. 037795
Hochuli-Gysel, Dr. Anne 036865
Hocking, Sheldon 048759
Hockman, Winnie 006294
Hodel, Daniel E. 037291
Hodel, R. 029837
Hodge, Anne 022763
Hodge, Dr. G. Jeannette 046248
Hodges, Rhoda 043629
Hodgins-Wollan, Sonya 005648
Hodgson, Beverly 044395
Hodgson, Clarence 005451
Hodgson, Kenneth O. 046490
Hodgson, Tom 039117, 039120
Hodkinson, Wendy 040406
Hodslavská, Lenka 008444, 008445
Hodson, Janice 042562
Höbler, Dr. Hans-Joachim 018578
Höck, Anton 002097
Höck, Dr. Christoph 018156
Höck, Georg 002184
Höfchen, Dr. Heinz 018135
Höfer, Dr. Hubert 018170
Höfer, Dr. Klaus 020513
Hoeffel, Joan 048058
Höfler, Franz 002482
Höfler, Werner Oskar 017861
Höfliger, Yvonne 037662
Höfling, Eckart Hermann 004369
Høeg, Asger 008893
Högberg, Lena 036672
Hoegen, Friedrich 018911
Hoegh Brand, Anne 031113
Högl, Dr. Günther 016765
Höglander, Agneta 036511
Höhl, Dr. Claudia 017921
Höhne, Annett 017537
Höibo, Roy 031163
Hoeker, Kristen 046106
Hoeksema, B.W. 029851
Hoekstra, Drs. Ridsert 030072
Hoekstra-van Vuurde, C.J. 029431
Hoel, Arild 031059
Hoel, Randall 048127
Höller, Silvia 002093
Hoelscher, Dr. Monika 015486
Hölscher, Dr. Petra 019096
Hölscher, Prof. Tonio 017823
Höltge, Dr. Kathrin 016385
Höltl, Georg 015705, 019574, 020445
Hoeltzel, Susan 042439
Hölz, Marjatta 020507
Hölzel, Josef 001736
Hoelzeman, Buddy 046030
Hölzer, Dr. Adam 018170
Hölzinger, Nora 016637
Hölzl, Dr. Christian 002934
Hölzl, Dr. Regina 002934
Höneisen, Markus 037524
Hoenig, Thomas M. 044926
Hönigmann, Alexandra 003017
Hönigmann, Andrea 003017
Höper, Dr. Corinna 020365
Hoepner, Leon 042190
Höppl, Birgit 018846
Hörker, Alois 002059
Hörmann, Barbara 017903
Hörmann, Fritz 002837
Hörner García, Gabriel 028684
Hoerschelmann, Dr. Antonia 002845
Hösch, Jürgen 017189
Höser, Dr. Norbert 015502
Hoesgen, Jennifer 005628
Hoesli, Hans Rudolf 036972
Hösli, Marc 037482
Hoeve, S. ten 030167
Höylä, Risto 009712
Hofbauer, Erwin 001861
Hofbauer, John D. 042193
Hofer, Manfred 002099
Hofer, Rudolf 002196, 002197
Hoff, Dr. Marlise 016096
Hoff, Svein Olav 030983
Hoff Jørgensen, Jan 030821
Hoffberger, Rebecca 041963
Hoffer, Andreas 002157
Hofferer, Robert 002273
Hoffert, Tonia 048554
Hoffman, Dan 005993
Hoffman, Hollace 046078
Hoffman, Dr. Kerstin 016856
Hoffman, Marilyn 048131
Hoffman, Max 043575
Hoffman, Michael E. 046304
Hoffman, Dr. Richard S. 045715
Hoffman, Thomas 047937
Hoffmann, Almut 016136
Hoffmann, Audrey 001602
Hoffmann, Christian 010177
Hoffmann, Dr. H. 016729
Hoffmann, Helmut W. 019285
Hoffmann, Jörn 016428
Hoffmann, John 042864
Hoffmann, Justin 019073, 053313
Hoffmann, Karen 016115
Hoffmann, Kim 048228
Hoffmann, Paul 002077
Hoffmann, Dr. Per 016429
Hoffmann, Dr. R.J. 019125
Hoffmann, Susanne 019566
Hoffmann, Tobias 018074
Hoffmann, Walter 019880
Hoffmann, Will 027902
Hoffpauer, Diane 043232
Hofinger, Franz 002084
Hofmacher, Anna 002479
Hofman, Andreas 017348
Hofman, Jack 045204
Hofman, O. 023044
Hofmann 019651
Hofmann, Dr. Alexander 016134
Hofmann, Dr. B. 036933
Hofmann, C. 029102
Hofmann, Christa 002971
Hofmann, Dr. Ernst 020249
Hofmann, Gertrud 018213
Hofmann, Helmut 002288
Hofmann, Irene 042255, 046468
Hofmann, Jürgen 018052
Hofmann, Lois 043301
Hofmann, Martina 019008
Hofmann, Rainer 019660
Hofmeister, Walter 017975

Hofschen, Dr. Heinz-Gerd 016411
Hofstad, Turid 031331
Hofstätter, Dr. Ulrike 001938
Hofstetter, Adolf 019573
Hofstetter, Willy 037747
Hofwolt, Gerald 044612
Hogan, Jacqueline 042218
Hogan, Tim 042354
Hogben, Barbara 001061
Hogben, Ian 001061
Hoge, Joan R. 043588
Hoge, Philip 049206
Høgestøl, Mari 031221
Hogg, C.G.O. 038683
Hogg, Gavin 041454
Hogsved, Åse 036612
Hogue, Kate 045019
Hoguet, Anne 013655
Hohbaum, R. 017376
Hoheisel, Tim 048996
Hoheisel-Huxmann, Reinhard 016429
Hohenberg, Anita Fürstin von 001698
Hohenlohe, Prinz Constantin von .. 020024
Hohenlohe-Bartenstein, Ferdinand Fürst zu 020104
Hohenlohe-Langenburg, Fürst zu . 018503, 018506
Hohenlohe-Oehringen, Katharina Fürstin zu 019235
Hohenlohe-Waldenburg, F.K. Fürst zu 020639
Hohensee, Falko 016747
Hohensinner, Harald 001836
Hohenzollern, Dr. Johann Georg Prinz von 019071
Hohl, Erhard 001748
Hohl, J. 015842
Hohmann, H.-J. 017886
Hohri, Sasha 046298
Hohut, Khrystyna 005408
Høibo, Roy 030893
Høie, Bjørn K. 031039
Højer Petersen, Anne 009020
Højgaard, Johnny 008858
Hokanson, Randi 046031
Hol Haugen, Bjørn Sverre 030819
Holben Ellis, Margaret 046394
Holbrook, Maureen 001262
Holc, Elwira 032199
Holcomb, Gary 043748
Holcomb, Grant 047487
Holcombe, David C. 042987
Holcombe, Holly 043001
Holden, Charles 039629
Holden, Florence 043125
Holden, Sally 038975
Holden, Steve 044119
Holden, Thomas 043521
Holder, Heidi 045388
Holderegger, Katharina 037721
Holderness, Christine 042389
Holdren, Greg 042189
Holdsworth, Jane A. 046467
Hole, Frank 046226
Holeman, Claude A. 043317
Holen, Dr. Stephen 043406
Holeva, Daniel 045854
Holländer, Tove 010177
Holland, J. 001516
Holland, Kim 046550
Holland, M. 034636
Holland, Rudolf 021081
Holland-Beickert, Dana 045764
Hollander, Stacy 046283, 046329
Hollander, Volker 016660
Hollein, Max 017192
Hollender, G. 037804
Holler, Christiane 001938
Holler, Dr. Wolfgang 016797
Holler-Schuster, Günther 001943
Hollerbach, Dr. R. 018312
Holleufer, Lars 008804
Holliday, Dr. John 039827
Holliger, C. 036977
Hollinetz, Alfred 002789
Hollinger, Gail 041713
Hollingworth, John 040101
Hollingworth, Mar 045413
Hollis, Phil 039940
Hollister, Jack 042061
Holloman, Jim 042808
Hollosy, Gyuri 045784
Holloway, Douglas 047855
Holloway, James 039425
Holloway, Leonard B. 046488
Hollstein, Dr. Wilhelm 016803
Hólm, Geir 021941
Holm, Torben 009119
Holm-Johnsen, Hanne 030909
Holm Sørensen, Bodil 008952
Holman, Clyde 049002
Holman, Graham 005999
Holman, Kurt 046889
Holman, Paul 042889
Holman, William M. 043481
Holmes, Carolyn C. 042763
Holmes, Erskine J. 038673
Holmes, Saira 038731
Holmes, Selean 042840
Holmes, Willard 046418
Holmes, Dr. William 045793
Holmes, William C. 043055
Holmes Helgren, Heidi 042597
Holmesland, Liv 031199
Holmgrain, Ardith 046281
Holmgren, Bengt 036538
Holmlund, Bertil 009924
Holmquist, Dr. Jeffrey G. 032718
Holmstrand-Krueger, Lena 036581
Holmström, Lars 010130
Holo, Dr. Selma 045420
Holodňáková, Dr. Radmila 008774
Holowacz, Eric V. 042077
Holozet, Andrée 015392
Holpainen, Anja 009689
Holsbeke, Mireille 003158
Holst, Prof. Dr. Christian von 020365
Holst, Gerd 020990
Holst, Lars 008899
Holstein, Lars 036732
Holsten, Christina 036323
Holsten, Dr. Siegmar 018169
Holt, Daniel D. 041563
Holt, Frank 046717, 046721
Holt, Joyce 045625
Holt, Phillip 000875
Holtby, J.M. 039621
Holte, Bettye 042956
Holten, Arnfinn J. 030744
Holten, Lars 009008
Holthof, Marc 003160
Holthuis, Dr. Gabriele ... 020110, 020111, 020112
Holtman, Marjorie 048234
Holton, Linda 044246
Holtz, Jerzy 036664
Holtz, Wolfgang 016073
Holtzapple, John C. 043089
Holtzhausen, A. 034692
Holubizky, Ihor 005672
Holverson, John H. 048096
Holvët, Brigitte 012240
Holz, Uwe 016258, 020953
Holzer, Dr. Elmar 020728
Holzer-Weber, Ruth 037813
Holzinger, Hans 019104
Homa-Rożek, Ewa 031890
Homann, Dr. Klaus 020542
Homberger, Lorenz 037789
Homburg, Cornelia 047676
Homen, Prof. Zoran 007749
Homering, Liselotte 018809
Hommell, Michel 012729
Homolova, Dr. Alexandra 034337
Homs-Chabbert, Arlette 013163
Honadel, Elroy 046581
Honcoopova, Dr. Helena 008603
Honda, Masami 026622
Honda, Masuo 027017
Honda, Shizuo 026803
Honermann, Josefine 016828
Honerød, Anne Grete 031153
Honeyman, Robert E. 043753
Hong, Kathleen 044592
Hong, Trinh Van 049536
Honkanen, Pekka 009575
Hood, Betty 042634
Hood, Michael 044733
Hood, Sadie Ann 049217
Hoogenboom, W. 029305
Hoogendonk, M.H. 029653
Hook, I.D. 039046, 039049
Hook, John 001474
Hook, Sam 046142
Hooker, Saralinda 042593
Hooks, Terri 043132
Hooper, C.L. 039672
Hooper, Dr. John 001473
Hoopes, John 045204
Hoopfer, Ann 048597
Hoops, Erik 016429
Hoorn Bakker, A. 030115
Hoover, Bessie 047349
Hoover, Charles 047602
Hoover, Rhonda J. 048862
Hooymayers, Dr. J.M.M. 029850
Hoozee, Dr. Robert 003465
Hope, Eve 005611
Hopfengart, Dr. Christine 036930
Hopfinger, Rebecca 042962
Hopfner, Dr. Rudolf 002934
Hopgood, Dr. James F. 044537
Hopkin, Dieter 041480
hopkin, Dr. Steve 040806
Hopkins, Anthea 039021
Hopkins, Dave 006315
Hopkins, Debra 048060
Hopkins, Linda 043612
Hopkins, S.K. 040954
Hopkins, Terri M. 045716
Hopkins Coughlin, Joan 049049
Hopkinson, Susan 040970, 040971, 040972
Hopmann, Gerd 016977
Hopp, Doris 017167
Hoppe, Barbara G. 045049
Hoppe, Günther 018362
Hoppe, Martin 017741
Hoppe, Michael 016770
Hoppe, Dr. Werner 015848
Hoppe-Oehl, Dr. Ulrike 018671
Hoppenworth, Bodo 017691
Hopper, Barbara 048850
Hopping, Robert 001397
Hoptman, Laura 047043
Horacio Aranguren, Juan José ... 000564
Horat, H. 037292
Horat, Dr. Heinz 037297
Horber, Dr. R. 014178
Hordyński, Piotr 032065
Horgen, Randi 030917
Hori, Robert 045423
Hori, Tomosaburo 026680
Horkheimer, Jack 045816
Horký, Milan 008314
Horman, Trevor 000718
Horn, Damian 040930
Horn, David 040163
Horn, Elizabeth 047241
Horn, Dr. Gabriele 019659
Horn, Henning 020346
Horn, Ken 045430
Horn, Dr. Luise 019073, 053313
Horn, Murray 047065
Horn, Dr. Reinhard 019037
Horn, Robert 042866
Horn, Sigrun 019898
Hornback, Kristina 044081
Hornbostel, Prof. Dr. Wilhelm 017715
Hornburg, Rainer 017925
Hornby, D. Mary 039099
Horndasch, Mickey 041782
Horne, Daphne 001090
Horne, Gene 030660
Horne, Graham 001044
Horne, Meade B. 048502
Horner, John R. 042375
Hornig, Dieter 020989
Hornik, Dr. Heidi 048813
Hornstrup, Nils 008893
Hornung, Herb 047810
Hornung, Prof. Dr. Maria 002978
Hornyak, Deanna 041787
Horowitz, Lawrence P. 048089
Horpeniak, Dr. Vladimír ... 008431, 008701
Horray, Henrietta 044251
Horrigan, William 043112
Horsley, Juliet 041157, 041163
Horsnall, P. 039470
Horst, Bill 047156
Horst, Dr. Katarina 018158
Horst, Prof. Dr. Kurt 018745
Horst, Randy 043471
Horsten, Frans 003519
Horsting, Archana 042160
Horstmann, Dr. G.G. 029279
Horton, Lon 042680
Hortz, Laura 048193
Horváth, Dr. Béla 021725
Horvath, Eugen 002262
Horváth, György 021671
Horváth, Dr. István 021721
Horváth, Dr. László 021797
Horvath, Dr. Michael J. 047137
Horvath, Ursula 002345
Horvatić, Franjo 007737
Horwath, Alexander 002973
Horwitz, Leon 042217
Horwood, Michelle 030627
Horžen, Vesna 034519
Hosack, George 042806
Hosaka, Kenjiro 027256
Hosar, Kåre 030984
Hose, Henry 048602
Hoskin, Rebecca 000807
Hoskins, Jeff 044545
Hoskins, Rebecca 046033
Hoskins, William J. 048193
Hoskinson, Susan 047080
Hoskisson, Don 045964
Hoško, Dr. Franjo Emanuel 007781
Hošková, Jitka .. 008587, 008708, 008723
Hosley, William 044456
Hosoe, Eikoh 027109
Hosokawa, Morisada 027159
Hosokawa, Toshiro 027199
Hossain, Shamsul 003096
Hossaka, Luiz 004530
Hosseloot, Eric 010987
Hosta Rebés, Assumpció 035227
Hostetter, David 045091
Hostyn, Norbert . 003685, 003687, 003688
Hotalling, Don 047332
Hotard, Patrick 042210
Hotchner, Holly 046282
Hoti, Prof. Afrim 000015
Hotvedt, Heidi 042529
Hotz, Benedict 037301
Hotz, Claus-Dieter 017512
Hotz, Dr. Gerhard 036899
Houby-Nielsen, Dr. Sanne 036642
Houdamer, Chloé 010934
Hough, Douglas R. 046809
Hough, Katherine 046798
Hough, Melissa E. 046930
Houghtling, Kim 006544
Houghton, J. 046107
Hougue, Veronique de la 013668
Houkjaer, Ulla 008963
Houlden, Penny 006368
Houliston, Laura 040192
Hoult, R. 030467
Hourant, Francis 003781, 003783

House, George M. 041591
House, Kirk 044407
Houseago, Avril 040608
Housego, Bill 000981
Housen, Jean 003600
Houssinot, Jean-Claude 014191
Houston, David 042977
Houston, Joe 047500
Houston, John 047441
Houston, L.S. 045806
Houston, Dr. Margaret 045202
Houston, Sandra J. 042810
Houts, Mary D. 044523
Houzet, Bernard 011546
Hovagimian, Vahan 002954
Hoveng, Dot 041784
Hovens, P. 029854
Hovi, Jouko 009459
Hovington, Raphael 005054
Hovish, Joseph J. 044738
Høvsgaard, Thomas 009116
Howard, Donna J. 045125
Howard, J. 034544, 040346
Howard, James 046098
Howard, Jan 047258
Howard, Jerome 006068
Howard, Jerry 045793
Howard, John 044050
Howard, John H. 044834
Howard, Louise 046128
Howard, Nora 041943
Howard, Paul 041487
Howard, Stephen R. 042810
Howard, Val 044393
Howe, Eileen 047334
Howe, Katherine S. 044648
Howe, Kathleen 041625
Howe, Philip 030605
Howe, Sherman M. 049295
Howell, A.C. 040936
Howell, Beverly 045176
Howell, Busser 048621
Howell, George L. 043691
Howell, Karen 040249
Howell, Kathy 048803
Howell, N. 040560
Howells, David 041142
Howese, Stephen 043245
Howett Smith, Catherine 041866
Howland, Robert 048237
Howoldt, Dr. Jenns E. 017694
Hoyd, Ed 043160
Hoyer, Dr. Eva Maria 018572
Hoyer, Klaus 015576
Hoyer, Lindy 046683
Hoyle, Gary 041905
Hoyle, Prof. R.W. 040807
Hoyle, Wayne 046870
Hoyos, Hans 002541
Hoyos Galarza, Melvin 009214
Hoyt, Marilyn 043877
Hoyt, Richard P. 049026
Hoyt, Robert 041655
Hoyum, Wanda 042138
Hrabánková, Dr. Světlana . 008462, 008463
Hrastović, Ivica 007750
Hrebíčková, Marta 034416
Hrisenková, Nataša 034391
Hristov, Dr. Ivan 004863
Hristov, Dr. Martin 004863
Hristova, Mariana 004865
Hristova-Radoeva, Vessela 004876
Hroch, David 008682
Hron, Vincent 042271
Hrtánková, Valéria 034337
Hruška, Václav 008446, 008661
Hsieh, Kun-Shan 027838
Huang, Kuang-Nan 007371
Huang, Yaohua 007225
Huard, Micheline 006442
Huart, Nicole d' 003335
Hubacher, Dr. Hans 037647
Hubbard, Bob 044279
Hubbard, Dr. Charles M. 044455
Hubbard, Dr. Jane 041421
Hubbard, Wendy L. 045658
Hubbs, Heather 042883
Hubbs, Jenice 005004
Huber, Alfred 037257
Huber, Arthur 036974
Huber, Dr. Bernhard 016337
Huber, Christoph Anselm 003302
Huber, Franz 002781
Huber, Markus 037523
Huber, Mary 042667
Huber, Dr. Waldemar 001887
Huber, Wolfgang 002156
Huber-Bitzer, Anne 020365
Hubert, François 014019, 014021
Hubinger, Horst 001703
Huchard, Viviane 013719
Huck, Thomas 017494
Huckaby, Barbara 044627
Hudák, Julianna 021729
Huddleston, David 006454, 006455
Hudeczek, Dr. E. 002217
Hudeczek, Dr. Erich 001945
Hudson, Fred 042109
Hudson, Giles 040661
Hudson, Dr. Julian D. 042957
Hudson, Louise 047326
Hudson, Mark S. 044049
Hudson, Dr. Neville 030437
Hue, Michel . . . 011462, 011675, 012585, 012708, 013070, 013073, 015097
Hueber, Prof. Dr. Friedmund 001708
Hueber, Régis 011430
Hübl, Prof. Dr. Richard 002762
Hübner, Dr. A. 019609
Hübner, Heinz 001658
Hübner, Dr. John 001953
Hübner, Dr. Ute 017314
Hübsch, Norbert 015905
Hückel, Angela 019086
Hückstädt, Antje 019531
Hüls, Johannes 016271
Hülsewig-Johnen, Dr. Jutta 016237
Hülsmann, Gaby 019822
Huemer, Dr. Peter 002097
Huenefeld, Wesley C. 041916
Hünninghaus-Böckmann, Ute 002707
Hürkey, Dr. Edgar J. 017150
Huerta, Benito 041774
Huerta, Enrike 035156
Hüsam, Gernot 016588
Huescar, Duque de 035390
Hüsers-Doehmen, Dr. Katharina . . 017517
Hüsken, Wim . . . 003635, 003636, 003637
Hüßner, Reinhard 018079
Huet, Dr. 012815
Hueter, Diana 043277
Hütt, Dr. Michael 020592
Hüttel, Dr. Richard 018579
Hüttner, Rudolf 002791
Huff, Richard E. 044779
Huffman, Bill 006527
Huffman, Joan 044453
Huffman, John 048387
Huffman, Vincent 005848
Hufnagl, Prof. Dr. Florian 019096
Hufschmid, Thomas 036863
Hufschmidt, Dr. Anke 016846
Hufschmied, Richard 002910
Hug, Guy 012653
Hug, Hannes 036900
Hug, Shamsul 003118
Hugel, André . . . 012192, 014058, 014060
Hugentobler, Hanspeter 037202
Huges, Bryn 039684
Huggert, Anders 036732
Hughbanks, Bette 047388
Hughes, Anne-Marie 038596
Hughes, Dr. David 049156
Hughes, Debra 049205
Hughes, Elaine M. 043555
Hughes, Eugene M. 043851
Hughes, Gareth 040878, 041030
Hughes, Gary 006354
Hughes, Ginny 048142
Hughes, Helga 039601
Hughes, James T. 048990
Hughes, Janet 000888
Hughes, John 040061
Hughes, Kathleen 048662
Hughes, K.C. 041415
Hughes, Marianne 046212
Hughes, Mark 040573
Hughes, P. 001114
Hughes, Philip 040873
Hughes, Richard Ll. 040051
Hughes, Susan 006634
Hughes, Thomas A. 046438
Hugo 034572
Hugonich, J. Yves 014620, 014621, 014622, 014623
Huguet, Jean-Pierre 037373
Huhtamäki, Tuula 010256
Huhtamäki, Ulla 009569
Hui, Hwang Sun 027440
Huijs Janssen, Dr. Paul 029736
Huijts, Stijn 030156
Huiskes, Bert 030283
Huizi, María Elena 049464
Hulbert, Dr. Richard C. 048339
Hull, Prof. Andrea 001481
Hull, Dale 046913
Hull, Howard 039133
Hull, Karen 040808, 040810
Hull, Priscilla 038898
Hullah, S. 039547
Hulló, István 034271
Hulse, E. 038822
Hulse, Sir Edward 038821
Hulse, Robert 040102
Hulser, Kathleen 046389
Hulshof, G. 029278
Hulston, Nancy 044912
Hultgren, Mary Lou 044415
Humbert, Jean-Baptiste 031416
Humbert, Vincent 012375
Hume, J. Wilbert 005229
Hume, Ted 005505
Humer, Diethard 002144
Humer, Franz . . . 001711, 002423, 002424
Humes, Alex B. 046945
Hummel, Alfred 018860
Hummer, Hermann 002976
Humphrey, J. Steven 043590
Humphrey, L. 038957
Humphrey, M. 001516
Humphrey, Rosanne 042354
Humphrey, Sylvia 040548
Humphreys, Mary 041298
Humphreys, Richard 040299
Humphries, Alan 039963
Humphries, Martin 040119
Humphries, Michael E. 043065
Humpl, Christine 002157
Hundt, Graf W.-D. von 015607
Hundt-Esswein, Hans U. 016467
Hùng, Nguyễn Quốc 049545
Hunger, Mattli 037473
Hunnewell, Elizabeth 049047
Hunold, Andrew 047615
Hunold, Dr. Angelika 018794
Hunt, Adrian P. 041621
Hunt, Alice 047365
Hunt, C. 041067
Hunt, Christopher J. 040403
Hunt, Clare 041063
Hunt, Dr. D.A. 039997
Hunt, David 046703
Hunt, Dr. Donald W. 041840
Hunt, Eugene A. 044942
Hunt, Michael 043585
Hunt, Phillip 042317
Hunt, Rhonda 001304
Hunt, Dr. Robert M. 045313
Hunt, Tony 030499
Hunt, Wilma 043181
Hunt Chamberlain, Carola 048028
Hunt Miller, Lee 047857, 047871
Hunter, Charles 049374
Hunter, Elizabeth 005004, 006147, 038524
Hunter, Fredericka 045662
Hunter, Jamie 005866
Hunter, Jessica 044301
Hunter, Jim 039087, 039511
Hunter, John 044851
Hunter, Judith 041418
Hunter, Julia 041905
Hunter, Ken 041082
Hunter, Lance 046758
Hunter, Liz 039706
Hunter, Paul 046328
Hunter, Richard 046703
Hunter, Terry 044475
Hunter, Thomas 048459
Hunter, Tom 044129
Hunter, Valerie 039406
Hunter-Stiebel, Penelope 047178
Huntington, Jeffrey L. 047654
Huntoon, Katherine 046504
Huntzinger, John 045865
Hunziker, Armando T. 000290
Hunziker, John 047474
Huo, Prof. Wei 007045
Huopainen, Raili 010043
Hupponen, Elina 010047
Huret, J. 014928
Hurezan Pascu, Geoghe 032886
Hurezan Pascu, George 032773
Hurkmans, Riek 029600
Hurley, Arthur L. 042750
Hurley, Richard 039138
Hurry, S.P. 039238
Hursey, Dick 045289
Hurtado Londoño, Gloria 007423
Hurum, Prof. Jørn H. 031078
Hurvitz, Uri 023096
Hurwitz, Avi 023026
Hušáková, Ivana 008685
Husband, John 030522
Husband, Timothy 046315
Husedžinović, Meliha 003940
Huskisson, Christine 044173
Husmann, Karin C.E. 029975
Huss, John 045616
Hussaini, Syed Mohammad 022581
Hussein, Dató Ibrahim 028008
Husseini, Frederic 027811
Husseini, Frédéric 027816
Hussey, Noelene 030531
Hussey-Arntson, Kathy 049199
Husslein-Arco, Dr. Agnes . 002560, 002565
Husso, Tuula 009967
Husted, Charlene 044155
Huston, Louise 048340
Husty, Peter 002567
Huszár, Zoltán . 021814, 021815, 021816, 021817, 021818, 021819, 021821, 021822, 021824, 021825, 021827, 021828, 021829
Hutchcrot, Sally 045030
Hutchings, Lamar 045233
Hutchins, Patricia 042653
Hutchins Bobyrk, Dawn 048184
Hutchinson, J. Dwight 045842
Hutchinson, John 022736
Hutchinson, Lawrence 042257
Hutchinson, Lydia C. 045842
Hutchinson, Susan 001470
Hutchison, John 043284
Huth, Nancy 046083
Huthwohl, Joël 013556
Hutin, Albert 042714
Hutt, Marilyn 048350
Hutter, Dr. Ernestine 002567, 002570
Hutterer, Dr. Karl 047951
Hutterer, Dr. Rainer 016337
Hutto, Dr. Richard 045936
Hutton, Susan 048178

Hutula, Betsy 042847
Hutz, Dr. Ferdinand 001768
Huuskola, Arto 010115
Huuskonen, Kari 009620
Huvenne, Dr. Paul 003163
Huwer, Elisabeth 017825
Huwyler, Dr. Edwin 036973
Hux, P. Meinrado 000410
Huxley, Geralyn H. 047039
Huyge, Dirk 003353
Huygens, Ch.E.C. 030108
Huysza, Hans 003047
Huzel, Karl 018551
Hwang, Pae Gang 027547
Hyams, Prof. Dr. Helge-Ulrike 018824
HyangAn, Kim 027615
Hyatt, John 041361
Hýbl, Dr. František 008655
Hyde, H. 040584
Hyde, J.R. 045768
Hyde, Lex 022805
Hyer, Warren W. 049316
Hygate, Nadine 039168
Hyland, Douglas 046202
Hylmarsová, Eva 008496
Hyman, Dr. P. 040357
Hyman, Ryan 046035
Hynes, Patricia 046282
Hynes, William Q. 048155
Hyross, Dr. Peter 034316, 034319, 034320, 034321, 034323, 034324, 034327, 034328, 034334, 034339
Hyšková, Veřa 008381
Hyson, Dr. John M. 041979
Hyss, Dr. Lothar 019158
Hytha, Prof. Dr. Robert K. 002394
Iaconoy, Nello 044208
Iacopi, Dr. Irene 025465, 025561
Iaing, Bonnie 005376
Iancu, Emilia 032916
Ianeva, Olga 004863
Iannelli, Dr. Maria Teresa 026303
Iannucci, Anna Maria 025398
Ibarra, Jorge A. 021578
Ibbertson, Prof. H.K. 030435
Ibbotson, Michael P.S. 030529
Ibing-Harth, Krista 015926
Ibragimov, T.S. 027410
Ibragimov, Ulykbek Šarachynovič . 027395
Ibrahim 027425
Ibrahim, Abbas 028018
Ice, Dr. Joyce 047972, 047973
Icershaw, Mary J. 039677
Ichijo, Akiko 027256
Ickowicz, Pierre 011586, 013134
Ide, Evan 042454
Ide, Richard 020090
Idemitsu, Shosuke 027175
Idiens, Dale 040523
Idleman, Paul 042703
Idris, Hassan Hussein 036152
Idrisov, G. 027413
Idshinnorov, S. 029009
Idzikowski, Waldemar 032236
Iemura, Katsuyuki 027310
Iercoşan, Neţa 032832
Ieronymidou, M. 008217
Ievleva, Nina Vasiljevna 033714
Ifland, Dorothee 015993
Ifsits, Marguerite 003017
Igel, Dr. Walter 017226
Iglesias Grande, Manuel 035079
Igna, Ion 032840
Igna, Mary Ann 041819
Ignatev, Viktor Jakovlevič 033287
Igrakova, Natalja Ivanovna 033665
Ihrenberger, Elisabeth 002565
Ikeda, Sakae 027131
Ikeda, Yushi 026522
Ikefuji, Kiyoshi 027232
Ikejima, Kazuo 027312
Ikitian, H. 000693
Iles, Chissie 046418
Ilg, Werner 037219
Ilg, Dr. Wolfgang 001847
Ilias, Sakalis 021150
Ilić, Dragica 034163
Ilich-Klančnik, Breda 034485
Iliescu, Prof. Constantin 032871
Iliev, Christo 004653
Iliev, Petăr 004764
Ilieva, Marija 004661
Ilisch, Dr. Peter 019156
Iljin, Vadim Jurjevič 033054
Iljina, Ljudmila Ivanovna 033001
Ilkjær, Marianne 008914
Ilkosz, Jerzy 032516
Illa i Vilà, Montserrat 036050
Ille-Kopp, Regina 016241
Illich, Dr. Inge 002561
Illuzzi, Dr. Michael C. 048063
Ilmonen, Anneli 010135
Ilon, Gabor 021811
Ilse-Neuman, Ursula 046282
Ilshöfer, B. 020556
Imai, Yoko 027256
Imami-Paydar, Niloo 044748
Imamura, Prof. Keiji 027266
Imanse, G. 029230
Imbeault, Nisk 005897
Imber, Sofia 049462
Imbernor, Laurence 014023
Imbert, Christiane 011124, 011126, 011127, 011128
Imhoff, Bert C. 006399
Imiela, Edward 032337
Immel, Dr. Wolfgang 016658
Immenkamp, Dr. Andreas 016771
Immerzeel, A.A.G. 029764
Immisch, T.O. 017672
Immonen, Kari 010180
Immonen, Olli . . 009801, 009802, 009804, 009805, 009807
Imori, Tsugio 026944
Imponente, Anna 024464
Impraim, Mary 021098
Imychelova, E.C. 034003
Inaba, Hisao 026919
Inaba, Yoshinori 027009
Inai, Keijirô 027167
Inama, Dr. Johannes 002056
Inauen, Roland 036846
Inazuka, Hiroko 027287
Inbar, Yehudit 022953, 022989
Inboden, Prof. Dr. Gudrun . 020365, 020365
Incardona, Dr. Angela 023136
İnce, R. Sefa 038180
Ince, Sterling 006395
Inch, John 030476
Incze, Dr. Kálmán 021656
Indahl, Trond M. 030771
Indāns, Juris 027742
Indeck, Dr. Jeff 042609
Indra, Dr. W.I. Pandji 022430
Ineba, Pilar 035978
Infante, Victor Manuel 000292
Ingber, Abie 042926
Ingebrigtsen, Dr. Kristian 031099
Ingelheim, gen. Echter von Mespelbrunn, Graf zu 018919
Ingilby, Sir Thomas C.W. 040838
Ingle, R. 039040
Inglis, Elspeth 044900
Inglis, Marion L. 005149
Inglis, R. 041229
Inglis, Robin 006045, 006046
Inglis, Stephen 005504
Ingmarsson, Niklas 036443
Ingram, Bill 043806
Ingram, Cathy 048907
Ingram, Daniel 044872, 044873
Ingram, Doris 042804
Ingram, J. 038613
Ingram, Jack 030598
Ingram, Jack E. 043949
Ingram, Lynn 042163
Ingvordsen, Jens 008806
Iniesta González, Montserrat 036043
Inkova, Mariela 004863
Inman, Edward 038964
Innes, J.F. 006079
Innes, Kathryn V. 047363
Innes, Moira 039956
Innocenti, Pierluigi 023205
Ino, Hironobu 026529
Ino, Koushin 027010
Inojatov, K.Ch. 049407
Inostroza Saavedra, Jorge E. 006945
Inoue, Kouki 026462
Inoue, Tadashi 026553
Inselmann, Andrea 044791
Inserra, Margaret 048528
Internoscia, David 045675
Intihar Ferjan, Jana 034485
Inui, Kazuo 026577
Io, Lau Si 007191
Ioanid, Radu 048952
Ion, Prof. Dr. I. 032877
Ionesco, G. 013581
Ionescu, Ruxandra 032824, 032914
Ionesov, Anatoly 049402
Ioniţă, Ionel 032794, 032796, 032797
Ioniţa, Ionel 032798
Ioniţă, Ionel 032802, 032804
Iotta, Ivana 023996
Iovinelli, Maria Teresa 025578
Iozzo, Mario 023871
Iprajian, Avedis 022977
Ireland, Lynne 045544
Ireland, Terese 043455
Irén, Kállai 021631
Iriarte, Prof. Elba Esther 000549
Iribarren Avilés, Rodrigo 006949
Irie, Yoshiro 027256
Irie, Yoshiyuki 026607
Irinina, Elena . . . 004628, 004629, 004630
Ironside, A. 041062
Irša, Dr. Rudolf 034380
Irvin, Mary A. 042189
Irvin, Stan 041925
Irving, Gillian 039152
Irving, James 040283
Irving, Mary L. 048523
Irwin, Charles W. 042300, 046627
Irwin, Ruth E. 045156
Irwin Meyer, Elaine 046510
Irwinnson, Charles W. 042302
Isaac, Preston 039081
Isajiw, Sophia 048660
Isakova, Ksenija Viktorivna 038261
Isaković, Aziz 003931
Isaksen, Knud Fink 008886
Isawumi, Prof. Dr. M.A. 030686
Isbell, Linda 047319
Iseki, Masaaki 027265
Iser, Wunibald 019180
Isert, Ingo Rüdiger 020354
Ishag, Ali 031397
Ishibashi, Kentaro 026533
Ishiga, Harue 026521
Ishihama, Beniko 026974
Ishii, I. 026485
Ishii, Mitsuru 026653
Ishii, Susumu 027022
Ishikawa, Chiyo 048091
Ishikawa, Koichi 026684
Ishikawa, M. 026488
Ishikawa, MitsuoSakari 027311
Ishikawa, Tetsuko 026533
Ishizuka, Kaname 026494
Ishtiaq Khan, Muhammad 031371
Isifidis, Kaplanis 021321
Iske, Gary 042111
Iskender, Prof. Kemal 038095
Islamova, Tatjana Michajlovna . . . 033958
Isler, Andreas 037808
Isler, Prof. Dr. H.P. 037759
Isler, Jacques 037738
Isler, Norman J. 048585
Ismai, Reza 022641
Isman, Eileen 006879
Isohauta, Teija 009634
Isomäki, Irmeli 009515
Ison, Susan P. 045502
Isoz, Nicolas 036821, 036822
Israel, Sue 045678
Israfilovglu, I.R. 003084
Issanjour, Guy 012036
Isshi, Kaihei 026548
Istas, Dr. Yvonne 020319
István, Dr. Berta 021663
Itai, Josef 023003
Itami, Kaneo 027347
Iten, André 037119
Ito, Masakazu 026939
Ito, Tomoyuki 026951
Itoa, Yukio 026646
Itoh, Hiroji 026909
Itoh, Ikutaro 026987
Itter, Wolfgang 018352
Ittmann, John 046975
Ivančević, Nataša 007779
Ivanenko, Pjotr Ivanovič 038279
Ivannikova, Ljudmila 033442
Ivanov, Aleksandr Aleksandrovič . . 033347
Ivanov, Ivan 004805, 004813, 004910
Ivanov, Stefan 004732
Ivanov, Vladimir Alexandrovič 033698
Ivanova, Galina Olegovna . 033259, 033990
Ivanova, Katja 004867
Ivanova, Maja I. 033699
Ivanova, Natalja Vasiljevna 033069
Ivanova, Silvia 042218
Ivanova, Tatjana Nikolaevna 034092
Ivanovski, Nikola 027911
Ivanuš, Rhea 007841
Ivask, Krista 009398
Ivaškina, Ljudmila 034008
Ivčević, Sanja 007798
Ivelic, Milan 006936
Ivens, R. 029880
Iversen, Mette 009150
Iverson, Dr. John B. 047399
Iverson, Stephen C. 045384
Ives, Alicia 041629
Iveson, Jon 039274
Ivetić, Marija 007773
Ivey, Donald J. 045174
Ivić, Prof. Vinko 007849
Ivica, Križ 034509
Ivkanec, Ivanka 007832
Ivory, Ken 030623
Ivory, Margaret 030564
Iwamoto, Mitsuo 026568
Iwasaki, Yohachiro 026551
Iwata, Tadao 026566
Iyoku, Hideaki 027202
Izaqirre, Manu 034788
Izdebska, Barbara 032426, 032472
Izsatovska, Dora 004635
Izui, Hidekazu 027009
Jaacks, Prof. Dr. Gisela 017713
Jaakkola, Markku 009500
Jaatinen, Aija 009762
Jaatinen, Carina 009472
Jaatinen, Toimi . 010117, 010118, 010123, 010132
Jaber Al-Jaber, Ibrahim 032759
Jablonská, Dr. Beáta 034337
Jablonska, Teresa 031868
Jabłońska, Teresa 032550
Jabłońska, Tereza 032546
Jablovska, Gaida 027763
Jabtonska, Teresa 032549
Jackley, Michael 043950
Jacklitch, Prof. Paul 042154
Jackowska, Anna 032392
Jackson, Bee 005505, 006436
Jackson, Bev 041608
Jackson, Bryan 005461
Jackson, G.B. 039025
Jackson, Henry 039492

Jackson, Jerry 047519
Jackson, Kenneth T. 046389
Jackson, Margaret 043147
Jackson, Paul 034103
Jackson, Robert L. 041575
Jackson, Sailor 042046
Jackson, Steven B. 042375
Jackson, Susan 040105
Jackson, Toby 040300
Jackson, Tony 038800, 041412
Jackson-Forsberg, Eric 046485
Jackson Quillen, Debra 045062
Jacob, Dr. Christina 017847, 017853
Jacob, Eric 012119
Jacob, François 037122
Jacob, John 040315
Jacob, Milner 030426
Jacob, Dr. Wenzel 016328
Jacob-Friesen, Dr. Holger 018169
Jacobacci, Emilia 025544
Jacobeit, Dr. Sigrid 017281
Jacobi, Dr. Fritz 016152
Jacobi, H.W. 029848
Jacobs, Charles 045727
Jacobs, Edwin 030013
Jacobs, F.J. 034566
Jacobs, Flora Gill 048957
Jacobs, John 044311
Jacobs, Joseph 046425
Jacobs, Karen 047939
Jacobs, Marty 046378
Jacobs, Ted Seth 012615
Jacobsen, Anne Marie 008885
Jacobsen, Bent Sonne 009026
Jacobsen, Gaute 030984
Jacobsen, Harald 031221
Jacobsen, Robert 045918
Jacobsen, Signe 009142
Jacobson, Alice 043708
Jacobson, Andrew 046518
Jacobson, Harold 044953
Jacobson, L. 034662
Jacobson, LouAnn 043478
Jacobson, Sally 043714
Jacobson, Thomas N. 046884
Jacobson, Thora E. 046988
Jacobson Zuckerman, Heidi 042166
Jacobsson, Ingela 036716
Jacobsson, Nils E. 036537
Jacobsson, Yvonne 036632
Jacoupy, Charles 014803
Jacquat, Jeannine 037419
Jacquat, Marcel S. 037014
Jacqué, B. 014063
Jacquemin, Hervé 014268
Jacquemyn, Erik 003638
Jacques, Annie 013575
Jacques, Gary E. 042521
Jacques, R.A. 014884
Jacquesson, Alain 037113
Jacquet, Alain 015015
Jacquot, Dominique 014875
Jadid Hashim Bin, Mohamed 004610, 004611
Jadoda, Rachel 045444
Jaeger, Anders 008823
Jäger, Dr. Hagen 016922
Jäger, Hans 002398
Jäger, Dr. Joachim 016055
Jäger, Leo 017440
Jäger, Dr. M. 016775
Jaeger, Dr. Monika 001936
Jaeger, Steven D. 045899
Jäger, Veronika 017962
Jaegere, Isabelle De 003557, 003558, 003560
Jaeggi, Dr. Annemarie 015988
Jäggi, Hans 037177
Jaehner, Inge 019493, 019495
Jämbäck, Juha 009996
Jäppinen, Jere 009529
Järliden, Barbro 036387
Järvinen, Marja-Liisa 010056
Järvinen, Vesa 009506
Jaffe, Steven 046389, 046406
Jagdfeld, Monika 017835
Jagenteufel, Hermann 003068
Jager, Dr. G.W.M. 030141
Jaggi, Konrad 037784
Jahan-Giry, Dr. Ali 022576
Jahn, Dr. Peter 016122
Jahn, Thomas 018209
Jahn, Dr. Wolfgang 016961
Jahnigen, Rick 042920
Jahnke-Lowis, Ilse 019207
Jaillet, G. 037667
Jain, Dr. Jyotindra 022081
Jaindl, Franz 002775
Jajčević, Zdenko 007844
Jakeman, Estelle 041326
Jakeuchi, Yoichi 026671
Jakeway, Robert 047502
Jaki, Barbara 034487
Jakibčuk, Mykola Mychajlovyč . . . 038266
Jaklin, Dr. Ingeborg 002874
Jakober, Yannick 034812
Jakobi, Paul 018950
Jakobsen, Björn M. 036342
Jakobsen, Egil Olav 030830
Jakobsen, S.E. 008906
Jakobson, Hans-Peter 017371
Jakobsons, Imants 027652
Jakomin, Dušan 026144
Jakoubĕová, Dr. Vladimíra 008727
Jakovleva, G.A. 033483
Jakovleva, Marina Dmitrievna 033828
Jakovleva, Nadežda Petrovna 034021
Jakovljević, Goran 007700
Jakubowski, Dr. Krzysztof 032478
Jakuševa, Valentina Maksimovna . 034091
Jalal, Masoody 022652
Jalandoni, Carlos L. 031673
Jalava, Mari . . . 009656, 010195, 010196, 010197
Jaletzke, Christian 016362
Jalilian, S.J. 022624
Jalon, Rita 003154, 003178
Jamal, Syed 027967
Jambon, Marcel 012202, 012203
James Jr., Alton 046381
James, Beth 043627
James, Betty 005436
James, Debbie 038634
James, Jon G. 049273
James, Louise 049301
James, Marion E. 043539
James, Sigrid 005452
James-Sarazin, Ariane 013656
Jamieson, Louise 001603
Jamieson, P.M. 005957
Jaminon, Martine 003586
Jamison, Wayne 043389
Jamkhedkar, Dr. A.P. 022325
Jammot, Dr. Dominique 013517
Jampen, Ulrich 037741
Jamro, Ron D. 046129
Jamščikova, Natalja Borisovna . . . 034032
Jan, Darja 034462
Janas, Stanisław 032216
Jančár, Dr. Ivan 034322
Jancekova, Vera 034445, 034446
Jančenko, Natalja Andreevna 034056
Janda, Martin 002663
Jandl, Ferdinand 001695
Janecek, James 047250
Janek, Eva 021679
Janes, Todd 005398
Janev, Georgi 004883
Jangoux, Prof. M. 003330
Janics, Dr. Hunert 001985
Janik, Michael 002142
Janjić, Gordan 034215
Jankavs, Peter 036577
Janke, Volker 020148
Jankov, Dr. Peter 020532
Jankova, Julia 004693
Jankova Kazakova, Rumjana 004662
Janković, Ljubica 034258
Jankovskyj, Anatolij Andrijovyč . . . 038243
Jankowski, Andrzej 032000
Janků, Miloslav 008336
Jankulovski, Plamen 004779
Janneau, O. 011036
Jannek, Norbert 018132, 018290
Jannet, Monique 013403
Jannke, William 048998
Janović, Ognjana 007765
Janovy, Karen 045311
Janovyč, Oleksandr Vasyljovyč . . . 038376
Jans, Mares 037103
Janscó, Istvan 004502
Janse, K.P.J. 029222
Jansen, Edward 048537
Jansen, F.W. 029759
Jansen, G. 030088
Jansen jr, John D. 043076
Jansen, Kristian 030841
Jansén, Maija 010165
Jansen, Siri 030759, 030767
Jansen, Dr. Steve 045208
Jansen Bramer, T. 030295
Janser, Andres 037788
Janssen, David 042673
Janssen, Dr. J.A.M.M. 030172
Janssen, Laura 049102
Janssen, Peter G. 018427
Janssen, S. 003163
Janssens, Dominique-Charles 010566
Janssens, Jan 003673
Jansson, Björn 036603
Jansson, Kyle R. 047752
Jansson, Tarja 009813
Jantsch, Karl 001996
Janu, Jan A. 002721
Janus, Jerzy 031871
Januszkiewicz, Bolesław 032251
Janzen, Thomas 018399
Janzweert, Jan 017634
Jaouen, Jean-Pierre 010765
Jaques, S.A. 040395
Jara, Dr. Holguer 009231
Jaramillo Agudelo, Darío 007425
Jaramillo Salazar, Juan Andrés . . . 007584, 007588
Jardim, Frank 043928
Jarh, Dr. Orest 034495
Jarmoljuk, Ol'ga Mikolaivna 038343
Jarocka-Bieniek, Jolanta 032363
Jaros, John R. 041909
Jaros, Susan 042985
Jaros, Urszula Maria 032213
Jarosch, Jessica 001716
Jaroševskaja, Valentina Michajlovna 033297
Jaroszewicz, Mieczysław 032321
Jarova, Galina Ivanivna 038306
Jarquín Pacheco, Ana María 028400
Jarratt, Ardell 047234
Jarrell, Gordon 043780
Jarrige, Jean-François 013715
Jarron, Matthew 039313
Jarvie, Robert 040697
Jarvis, Anthea 040398, 040404
Jarvis, Antony 040006
Jarvis, P.D. 039936
Jarzembowski, Prof. Dr. E. 040389
Jasbar, Dr. Gerald 020534
Jasim, Dr. Sabah 038430
Jasiuk, Jerzy 032312, 032470
Jaskanis, Paweł Olaf 032458
Jaskowiak, Jennifer 045420
Jaskulski, Janusz 032246
Jastram-Porsche, Sabine 019516
Jastrebova, Raisa 033580
Jastrzębski, Jerzy 032121
Jatti Bredekamp, Prof. Henry C. . . 034573, 034574, 034579
Jaukkuri, Maaretta 009542
Jaupaj, Arben 000011
Jauslin, Dr. J.-F. 036936
Jávor, Anna 021671
Jaworowicz, Hanna 031975
Jay, Hilary 046934
Jaynell, Chambers 045008
Jaysane, A. Patricia 045209
Jean, Louis 038473
Jeanbrau, Hélène 012610
Jeandron, Angela 044992
Jeanes, K.I. 034617
Jeanmart, Jacques 003666
Jeanneney, Jean-Noël 013559
Jeannot, Bernard 013651, 013735
Jeanselme, Brigitte 015020
Jeansson Kock, Brgitta 036664
Jebreil Zadeh, A. 022589
Jecha, James 045055
Jecht, Heidrun 018158
Jeck, Siegrun 018013
Jeckel, J. 030227
Jedda McNab, Barbara 047673
Jędrzejewski, Antoni 032372
Jefferies, Dr. Chris 043528
Jefferies, Richard 039130
Jefferies, Susan 006600
Jeffery, Gordon 006669
Jeffet, William 047719
Jeffrey, Susan 039903
Jeffries, Bill 006047
Jegorov, Boris Michajlovič 032990
Jehl, Dr. Rainer 018082
Jehle, Michael 046190
Jehle-Schulte Strathaus, Dr. Ulrike 036880
Jeitler, Johannes 002800
Jekov, Vasko 004864
Jelavić, Zeljka 007832
Jeletich, Dr. F. 029551
Jelfs, Ann 030586
Jeličić, Janko 007841
Jelinek, Dr. Zdeněk 008592
Jelinková, Jaroslava 008783, 008784
Jeliseeva, Tatjana 038329
Jelvakova, Irena A. 033420
Jemison, Gerald Peter 048780
Jenal, Christian 037487
Jenal, Ludwig 037487
Jenderko-Sichelschmidt, Dr. Ingrid 015575, 015579, 015584, 015586
Jenisch, R. Dietlinde 017448
Jenkins, Adrian 038596
Jenkins, Carol 046901
Jenkins, Charles 038771
Jenkins, Donald 047178
Jenkins, Frances Susong 044174
Jenkins, Sabra 048196
Jenkins, Sue 038604
Jenkner, Ingrid 005577
Jenko, Helena 034490
Jenko, Lilija Dmytrivna 038265
Jenko, Mojca 034487
Jenks, Tracey 041752
Jenne, Hans-Jörg 016967
Jenneman, Eugene A. 048598
Jenni, Rudi 000919
Jennings, Lucille 046605
Jennings, Peter 040902
Jennings, Sibley 041743
Jensch, Dr. Rainer 020673
Jensen, B. 030596
Jensen, Carol Ann 043708
Jensen, Ellen Elisabeth 009136
Jensen, Erik 008985
Jensen, Harold 041950
Jensen, Herbert 018046
Jensen, Dr. Inken 018809
Jensen, Dr. Jacob B. 008932
Jensen, James 044592, 044593
Jensen, Johan M. 008970
Jensen, Kathleen A. 048305
Jensen, Ken 045698
Jensen, Loring 048418
Jensen, M. Wayne 048556
Jensen, Mona 008805

Jensen, Niels Erik 009000
Jensen, Ole G. 021551
Jensen, Otto 009135
Jensen, Pam 043371
Jensen, Sterling 005994
Jensen, Tom 031072
Jensen, Vivi 008997
Jensner, Magnus 036332
Jenssen, Ragnar 030794
Jentsch, Dr. F. 017221
Jenvold, Birgit 008997
Jeppesen, Hans 008897
Jepson, D. 040627
Jerg, Alfred 018533
Jerković, Dragan 034172
Jerlich, Walter 001712
Jerner, Ingbritt 036536
Jerome, Jeff 041980
Jerris, Rand 043810
Jervois, W. 034622
Jésman, Prof. Czesław 032115
Jesretić, Miroslav 034266
Jessat, Mike 015502
Jesse, Bernd 042820
Jessewitsch, Dr. Rolf 020237
Jessop, L. 040548
Jessup, Scott 001338
Jeszenszky, Dr. Sándor 021666
Jette, Carol 041702
Jette, David 046415
Jetzer, Gianni 037492
Jeufroy, Pierre 011942
Jeutter, Dr. Ewald 016578
Jevdjević, Ivana 003940
Jevsejeva, Olga Jevgenivna 038246
Jevtović, Jevta 034149
Jevtović, Mila 034163
Jewell, Brian 039680
Jeziorowski, Tadeusz 032256
Jezler, Peter 036927, 037076, 037391
Jezmann, Meike 020423, 020424
Ježowitzová, Jiřina 008402
Ji, Gon Gil 027503
Ji, Qian 007205
Jian, Li 043320
Jibah, Matassim Bin Haji 004613
Jillis, Nellie 034631
Jiménez, Angel 035781
Jimenez, Mercedes 028558
Jiménez Chávez, Alma Rosa 028540
Jiménez Espejo, Francisco J. 035521
Jiménez Vásquez, Gustavo 007569
Jimeno Santoyo, Myriam 007449
Jiminez, Jill A. 045949
Jimison, Tom 046095
Jimmie, Charles 044388
Jin, Jon Moon 027438
Jing, Guo 007167
Jing Weng, Liao 007015
Jirmusová, Hana 008322
Joachim, Karin 015761
Joannette, Michelle 005644
Joans, Dr. Barbara 046595
Jobin, Pamela A. 049216
Jobke, Ryszard 032157
Jobst-Rieder, Marianne 002971
Joch, Peter 016642
Jochem, Marlene 018136
Jochims, Richard 017338, 017859
Jochum, Franz 002382
Jockel, Nils 017715
Jodice, Dorothy 045616
Jodłowski, Prof. Antoni 032494
Joel, Judy 040921
Joenniemi, Sirpa 010133
Jönsson, Bertil 036257
Jönsson, Tomas 036387, 036499
Jörg, Christiaan 029638
Jöris, Dr. Olaf 018794, 019299
Joffre, Roland 012554
Joger, Prof. Dr. Ulrich 016392
Johannessen, Arild 030839
Johannessen, Jeanette 048842
Johannessen, Kåre 009108
Johannessen, Preben L. 030904
Johannesson, Birgitte 008968
Johannewes, Alice 048477
Johannsen, Hermann 018508
Johannsen, Ilona 020916
Johannsen, Karin 017444
Johannsen, Ruby 044699
Johannson, Sigfus 005807
Johansen, Annette 009096
Johansen, Jens 008928
Johansen, Rikke 009150
Johansson, Börje 036166
Johansson, Conny 036443
Johansson, Hjördis 036692
Johansson, Jan 036432
Johansson, Karin 036505
Johansson, Kennet 036455, 036460, 036461, 036463, 036464
Johansson, Ketty 009031, 009032
Johansson, Kjell 036400, 036640
Johansson, Lars G. 036419
Johansson, Marie 036709, 036725
Johansson, Sonny 036719
Johansson, Tina 036692
Johansson, Ulf 009925
Johansson, Ulrica 036732
John, J. 008562
John-Willeke, Bettina 016636, 016645
Johncock, M. 001143
Johnes, John 041848
Johns, Dana 041976
Johns, Daniel 044675
Johns, Sharleen 043529
Johns, Valerie 044266
Johnsen, Aksel 031249
Johnsen, Berit Åse 030933
Johnsen, Duane 044072
Johnson, Alfred E. 045204
Johnson, Allen 044514
Johnson, Amy Jo 047108
Johnson, Andrew 039380
Johnson, Anne J. 046814
Johnson, Arden 044478
Johnson, Audrey 048261
Johnson, Barbara B. 044810
Johnson, Brooks 046496
Johnson, Byron 046098
Johnson, Byron A. 048818
Johnson, C. 040406
Johnson, C. Clayton 047194
Johnson, Carl 006292
Johnson, Christine 030648
Johnson, Colin 038993
Johnson, Craig 047694, 047700
Johnson, D. Thomas 042056
Johnson, Dale 038584
Johnson, David 047049
Johnson, David A. 048668
Johnson, David T. 042929
Johnson, Diana 046142
Johnson, Diane 043244
Johnson, Dorothy E. 042251
Johnson, Drew 046598
Johnson, Dwayne 044133
Johnson, Edward 048338
Johnson, Dr. Eileen 045513
Johnson, Elsie 005603
Johnson, Frank 034655
Johnson, Gerardo 021610
Johnson, Gina 048359
Johnson, Grace 047839
Johnson, Harold 048034
Johnson, Dr. Heide-Marie 045793
Johnson, James 042796
Johnson, James L. 043862
Johnson, Jean 042758
Johnson, Jeanne 047935
Johnson, Jennifer L. 043105
Johnson, Jeremy 000763, 000765
Johnson, Jerome Martin 045093
Johnson, Joan 041246
Johnson, Dr. John R. 047951
Johnson, Kathleen E. 048504
Johnson, Kaytie 044318
Johnson, Kenneth R. 044121
Johnson, Kevin 038714
Johnson, Dr. Kirk R. 043406, 043406
Johnson, Kurt 043555
Johnson, Laurel 000762
Johnson, LaVern M. 045534
Johnson, Lewis 049130
Johnson, Libba 043101
Johnson, Louis 046278
Johnson, Lydia 042663
Johnson, Mark M. 045995
Johnson, Marlo L. 044941
Johnson, Mary 049135
Johnson, Mary A. 047773
Johnson, Maurianna 045215
Johnson, Maxine 048765
Johnson, Melinda 046106
Johnson, Melissa 045472
Johnson, Nancy T. 045970
Johnson, Ned K. 042164
Johnson, Nichola 040612
Johnson, Nina 044304
Johnson, Patricia 001094
Johnson, Penny 040157
Johnson, Polly 045026
Johnson, Richard 042345
Johnson, Dr. Richard E. 047281
Johnson, Robert E. 048768
Johnson, Robert S. 043948
Johnson, Robin 039152
Johnson, Dr. Ron 006773
Johnson, Sandra L. 046875
Johnson, Sarah 044177
Johnson, Sharon 043257, 048512
Johnson, Sheila A. 006885
Johnson, Steven 043358
Johnson, Stuart 046097
Johnson, Suni 041992
Johnson, Terry 045800
Johnson, Thomas B. 049345
Johnson, Tom 049343
Johnson, Twig 045978
Johnson, Vanessa 048459
Johnson, William C. 044158
Johnson, William M. 043430
Johnson Bowles, Kay 043826
Johnsson, Anders 036243
Johnston, Alan 039368
Johnston, Catherine 006104
Johnston, Phillip 047258
Johnston, Renée 005597
Johnston, Richard 047715
Johnston, Sally 042004
Johnston, Sona 041969
Johnston, Stephen 040661
Johnston, Virginia 043468
Johnston, William R. 042006
Join-Diéterle, Catherine 013697
Jojo, Eva 045927
Jokulo Cooper, Jimmie 041987
Jolie, Renee 047972
Jolivel, D. 011129
Jolliff, Dawna 044509
Jolly, Dr. Anna 037455
Jolly, Guy 012139
Jomppanen, Tarmo 009610
Jonaitis, Aldona 043780
Jones, Alan 041059
Jones, Amanda C. 045659
Jones, Andy B. 049159
Jones, Anita 041969
Jones, Ann 039395
Jones, Anne 039491
Jones, Prof. B. 005401
Jones, Barbara L. 044340
Jones, Brenda 049154
Jones, Dr. Cheri A. 043406
Jones, Claire 038596
Jones, Clive 039072
Jones, C.R. 043137, 043138
Jones, Cynthia L. 044389
Jones, D. Keith 039157
Jones, D.L. 039813
Jones, Donna 006423
Jones, Donna P. 048211
Jones, Dr. Douglas S. 044103, 044103
Jones, Duffie 044866
Jones, E. Michael 003904
Jones, E.B. 030617
Jones, Edward 044093
Jones, Prof. E.L. 038728
Jones, Elisabeth 042921
Jones, Eric 039086
Jones, Erin 044348
Jones, Glenn 044295, 046183
Jones, Gwyneth 039137
Jones, Harvey 046598
Jones, Hugh R. 045524
Jones, Huw 039152
Jones, Jeanne 040339
Jones, Jeff 046760
Jones, Jill 048084
Jones, J.M. 039333
Jones, Joan 041120, 041122
Jones, Joanna 041069
Jones, Joy 005814
Jones, Julie 046364
Jones, Kathy 005211, 043598
Jones, Keith 000988, 039600
Jones, Larry A. 045478
Jones, Lester 039072
Jones, Lial A. 047588
Jones, Linda 042690, 043227, 048362
Jones, Lisa 000842
Jones, Lowell N. 042901
Jones, Margaret Ann 046705
Jones, Marilyn . . 044797, 047215, 048439
Jones, Mark 040307, 040523
Jones, Mike 048485
Jones, Nia 040484
Jones, R. 005955
Jones, Rhian 041616
Jones, Richard 038989
Jones, Dr. Robert 044800
Jones, Ronald D. 042541
Jones, Sian 041061
Jones, Stephen 047112
Jones, Sue 039510
Jones, Suzi 041711
Jones, Thomas 045854
Jones, Prof. Tom 038727
Jones, Trevor 039276
Jones, W.J. 030614
Jones Cox, Beverly 048933
Jones Harper, Suzanne 045566
Jong, C.C. de 029775
Jong, Dr. H. de 029245
Jong, Dr. Jutta de 020991
Jong, L. de 003163
Jong, Dr. M.A. de 029450
Jong, S. de 030088
Jonge, Eddy de 029638
Jonge, J.M. de 029687
Jonge, P. de 030015
Jongh, Marja de 030058
Jongh-Vermeulen, Dr. A. de 029151
Jonghe, Mieke de 003385
Jongs, Carel 005460
Jongstra, Jaap 029843
Jonin, Marie-Thérèse 011308
Jonker, Dr. A. 029465
Jonsson, Ingrid 036598
Jónsson, Petur 021937
Joo-Sik, Kim 027521
Joohee, Kim 027567
Joos, Cristian 037752
Joppien, Dr. Rüdiger 017715
Joppig, Dr. Gunther 019086, 019094
Jordaens, Lode 003426, 003427
Jordan, Brenda . . 045056, 045058, 045059
Jordan, Daniel P. 042769
Jordán, Dr. František 008767
Jordan, Kurt 017613
Jordan, Prof. Dr. Lothar 017204

Jordan, Manuel . . . 048319
Jordan, Mary Alice . . . 047925, 047926
Jordan, Peter . . . 037580
Jordan, Robert . . . 005322
Jordan, Thomas E. . . . 044189
Jordan Wass, Catherine H. 046496, 048792
Jordanov, Ivan . . . 004799
Jordanova, Zojca . . . 004624
Jordanović, Branislava . . . 034168
Jordon, G. . . . 000870
Jordon, J. Greg . . . 043704
Jørgensen, Anja . . . 009000
Jørgensen, Erik . . . 008885
Jørgensen, Mogens . . . 008982
Jorgensen, Roy . . . 043847
Jorikson, Håkan . . . 036311
Joris, J.L. . . . 003530
Joris, Yvònne G.J.M. . . . 029734
Jorquera Caro, Sonia Alexandra . . 028611
Jorrand, C. . . . 012421
Jorrín García, J.A. . . . 035535
Josanu, Vitalie . . . 032955
Joselu, Sergio . . . 023483
Joseph, Carolyn . . . 044482
Joseph, Jean-Louis . . . 010440
Joseph, Laurel . . . 039043
Joseph, Sarah . . . 044277
Joseph-Debaque, Sandrine . . . 011361
Josephson, Magnus . . . 036511
Josephsson, Eva . . . 036509
Joshi, Prof. B.D. . . . 022150
Joshi, Mallickarjun . . . 022373
Joshi, Vishwanath N. . . . 022288
Josias, Anthea . . . 034551
Josić, Zoran . . . 034140
Josifovich, Jorge A. . . . 000472
Joslin, Stewart . . . 048571
Joss, Laura . . . 041983
Jossifova, Maria . . . 004863
Jost, Gerda . . . 017352
Jost, Loren . . . 047463
Jost, Stephan . . . 046596
Jost-Prześlakowska, Maria . . . 032379
Josvai, Jason . . . 044838, 044839
Jósvai, Dr. Katalin Dankó . . . 021835
Jotov, Petko . . . 004872
Jotterand, Suzanne . . . 036820
Joubeaux, Hervé . . . 011266
Joubert, Alain . . 012278, 012279, 012958, 013451
Jouen, Jean-Pierre . . . 012235
Joüon des Longrais, F. . . . 014018
Jourdan, Aleth . . . 010331, 010332
Jourdan, Patrick . . . 013242
Jouzeau, Marie-Hélène . . . 013334
Jovanov, Dr. Jasna . . . 034226
Jovanović, Igor . . . 034177
Jovel Castro, Walter E. . . . 007680
Jovelić, Marijana . . . 034172
Jović, Vukašin . . . 034177
Joy, Catdlind . . . 035662
Joyaux, Alain . . . 046083
Joyce, Dan . . . 044961
Joyce, Martin J. . . . 022680
Joyce, Rosemary . . . 042165
Joyeux, Y. . . . 003251
Joyner, Elizabeth . . . 048776, 048779
Joyner, Roger D. . . . 044337
Ju, Calvin . . . 007369
Juárez, Marcelo O. . . . 000208
Juárez Nieto, M. Magdalena Sofía . 028667
Juaye, Comte Pierre du Manoir de 011221
Juchli, Cornelia M. . . . 037585
Juchniewich, Daniel . . . 045638
Judd, Martha . . . 044577
Judge, Joseph M. . . . 046498
Judge, Vancy . . . 049246
Judson, E. . . . 034722
Judson, Etta . . . 034738
Judson, Dr. Horace . . . 047085
Judson, Jack . . . 047797
Judson, William D. . . . 047043
Juelich, Clarence . . . 049139
Jülich, Dr. Theo . . . 016638
Jüllig, Carola . . . 016011
Jürries, Wolfgang . . . 018436
Jufa, Marija . . . 033659
Juffinger, Dr. Roswitha . . . 002564
Juhl, Kirsten . . . 031221
Jul, Ole . . . 009131
Jules Kouloufoua, Jean Gilbert . . . 007664
Julia, I. . . . 013721
Julia y Macias, Manuel . . . 035503
Juliusburger, Thomas . . . 042409
Julkunen, Pirjo . 009873, 009874, 009875, 009876
Jullian, Nathalie . . . 013570
Jullien, Pierre . . . 014982
Jumalla, Joesilo C. . . . 031639
Jumalon, Julian N. . . . 031634
Jumalon, Prof. Julian N. . . . 031657
Jumelet, J. . . . 029361
Jumping Bull, Calvin . . . 047026
Juncà Bonal, Mariona . . . 034896
Juncosa, Enrique . . . 022753
Juneau, Madeleine . . . 005943
Junek, David . . . 008583, 008584, 008585
Jung, H. . . . 029979
Jung, Heinrich . . . 017518
Jung, Ilse . . . 002934
Jung, Ludwig . . . 019837
Jung, Mark . . . 045896
Jung, Dr. Michael . . . 025548
Jungbluth, Carmen . . . 042302
Junge, Brigitte . . . 015631
Junge, Claudia . . . 018561
Junge, Dr. Michael . . . 017983
Junge, Dr. Peter . . . 016017
Junghans, Dr. Günther . . . 018825
Junginger, Ernst . . . 018500, 018501
Jungmann, Judith . . . 002945
Junhem, Inga . . . 036679
Junier, Caroline . . . 037375
Junker, Almut . . . 017176
Junker, Patricia . . . 044002
Junkins, Tom . . . 041770
Junno, Johanna . 010244, 010247, 010248
Junno-Pennanen, Johanna . . . 009942
Junod, Barbara . . . 037788
Juntikka, Ilse . . . 009939
Juntunen, Judy . . . 047002
Juranek, Christian . . . 020816
Jurčenko, Oleg Grygorovyč . . . 038284
Jurchuk, Dmitri . . . 016083
Jurdana, Ela . . . 007841
Jurdyga, Judy . . . 006426
Jurecka, Małgorzata . . . 032281
Jurevićius, J. . . . 027850
Jurgemeyer, Marne . . . 043954
Jurić, Radomir . . . 007762, 007823
Jurica, Varina . . . 007722
Jurkāne, Anna . . . 027778
Jurkiewicz, Jan Gustaw . . . 032542
Jurovics, Toby . . . 047240
Jurriaans-Helle, Dr. G. . . . 029163
Jusić, Enisa . . . 003928
Jussila, Neil . . . 042206
Just, Arthur . . . 002975
Just, Helmut . . . 002868
Just, Dr. Johannes . . . 016806, 016810
Just, Rüdiger . . . 017673
Justus, Dr. Antje . . . 018794, 019299
Justus, Dirk . . . 017687
Justus, Mary Beth . . . 041831
Jutkeit, A. . . . 019147
Juton, Alain . . . 013069
Jutras, Michel . . . 006658
Juul, Steffen . . . 009094
Juul Holm, Michael . . . 008938
Juva, Antti . . . 009978, 009979
Juvonen-Eskola, Annamari . . . 009472
Juzwenko, Dr. Adolf . . . 032534
Kaack, Dr. Joachim . . . 019038
Kaak, L. Joachim . . . 018298
Kaarto, Sari . . . 010025
Kaasen, Gunnar . . . 031023, 031025
Kaasen, Svanhild Alver . . . 030852
Kaba, Sory . . . 021589
Kabat, Nora . . . 047979
Kabayama, Koichi . . . 027189
Kabić, Dušan . . . 034177
Kábrtova, Jiřina . . . 008554
Kabrud, Jack . . . 045911
Kabus, Dr. Ronny . . . 018746
Kačalova, Alisa D. . . . 033044
Kačírek, Ľuboš . . . 034327
Kaczarová, Iveta . . . 034379
Kaczmarczyk, Witold . . . 032343
Kaczynski, Prof. Dr. R. . . . 019074
Kadake, Henrich . . . 044895
Kaden, Antje . . . 016498
Kadlec, Dr. František . . . 008598, 008614, 008615, 008618, 008622, 008641, 008647
Kadota, Keizo . . . 026802
Kadovitz, Sherri . . . 045474
Kadowaki, Akira . . . 027280
Kadurina, Elena . . . 004814
Kadurina, Emilija . . . 004815
Kadyrov, A.S. . . . 037838
Käär, Pekka . . . 010174
Käch, Robert . . . 037440
Kaehr, Roland . . . 037376
Kaelcke, Wolfgang . . . 019563, 019564
Kämpf, Michael . . . 018454
Kämpfner, Gabriele . . . 016350
Kaenel, Gilbert . . . 037243
Känsälä, Risto . . . 009684
Kärgling, Dr. Karlheinz . . . 018769, 018772
Kärki, Sirpa . . . 036497
Kärnefelt, Prof. Ingvar . . . 036440
Käs, Rudolf . . . 019358, 019375
Kaeser, Dr. Bert . . . 019117
Kaeser, Dr. Marc-Autoine . . . 037784
Kaeser, Olivier . . . 037110, 054173
Kaesler, Roger L. . . . 045205
Kästner, Dr. Klaus Peter . . . 016817
Kästner, Dr. Klaus-Peter . . . 017902
Kästner, Ursula . . . 015986
Kästner, Dr. Volker . . . 015986
Käyhkö, Unto . . . 009691
Kafetsi, Anna . . . 021204
Kager, Stephen J. . . . 049281
Kagioka, Masanori . . . 026672
Kahan, Mitchell . . . 041586
Kahari, Prof. George P. . . . 049583
Kahin, Dr. Sharon . . . 043511
Kahle, Patricia . . . 046236
Kahle, Sharon M. . . . 043446
Kahler, Caroline . . . 045328
Kahn, David M. . . . 044457
Kahn, Leo . . . 047978
Kahn, Tammie . . . 044636
Kahng, Eik . . . 042006
Kaijt, W.P.A.M. . . . 029243
Kailashnathan . . . 021989
Kaindl, Heimo . . . 001928
Kaiqu, Liu . . . 006976
Kaire, Inese . . . 027728
Kaiser, Dr. Barbara . . . 001950
Kaiser, Friederike . . . 019029
Kaiser, F.W. . . . 029424
Kaiser, H. . . . 018031
Kaiser, Dr. Hermann . . . 016572
Kaiser, Michael . . . 019351
Kaiser, Miriam . . . 028530
Kaiser, Peter . . . 037399
Kaiser, Philipp . . . 036890
Kaiser, Sara . . . 037039
Kaiser, Dr. Stephan . . . 018356
Kaiser-Reka, Berol . . . 016366
Kaißer, Paul . . . 020615
Kaizuka, Tsuyoshi . . . 027148
Kaján, Imre . . . 021724
Kajanus, Pirkko . . . 009598
Kajikawa, Yoshitomo . . . 026724
Kajitani, Nobuko . . . 046364
Kakko, Leena . . . 010122
Kakourou-Chrossi, Dr. Georgia . . . 021476
Kakuda, Arata . . . 026533
Kakui, Hiroshi . . . 027241
Kakusei, Miki . . . 026608
Kal, W.H. . . . 029194
Kalajainen, Jason . . . 044574
Kalanj, Marko . . . 034185
Kalantzes, Isabelle . . . 047777
Kalašnik, Tatjana Nikolajevna . . . 033178
Kalašnikov, Nikolaj Ivanovič . . . 033904
Kalčev, Kamen . . . 004685
Kalčev, Petar . . . 004885
Kalchthaler, Peter . . . 017228, 017235
Kaldewei, Dr. Gerhard . . . 016664, 016666
Kaldor, Cynthia . . . 045732
Kaldy, Robert . . . 002972
Kale, Matt . . . 045148
Kalela-Brundin, Maarit . . . 036449
Kalenberg, Angel . . . 041531
Kalenitchenko, Liliane . . . 014153
Kalicki, Jerzy . . . 032019
Kalina-Vidić, Ivana . . . 034163
Kalinová, Dr. Alena . . . 008286
Kalinsky, Nicola . . . 039425
Kalista, Dagmar . . . 002985
Kaljnyj, Dmytro Pavlovyč . . . 038382
Kalkhoff, Gabriele . . . 019472
Kalkmann, Hans-Werner . . 015784, 053323
Kallas, Nick . . . 048688
Kallberg, Ulla . . . 010162
Kallicas, Antonia . . . 008202, 008203
Kalligas, P. . . . 021154
Kallinich, Prof. Dr. Joachim . . . 016132, 016332
Kallio, Maija-Riitta . . . 009785
Kallista, Dr. Antonín . . . 008335
Kalmite, Lelde Alida . . . 045828
Kalmring, Sven . . . 020038
Kalnins, Indulis . . . 047596
Kalokerinos, Alexis . . . 021285
Kalpakova, Akgul . . . 038212
Kalpickaja, Elena Jakovlevna . . . 033755
Kalsan, Prof. Vladimir . . . 007706
Kaltenberger, Johann . . . 002599
Kaltenbrunner, Regina . . . 002566
Kalter, Prof. Dr. Johannes . . . 020358
Kaltsas, Dr. Nikolaos . . . 021183
Kaltved, David . . . 043739
Kalus, Dr. Jaromír 008545, 008547, 008549
Kamada, Masataka . . . 027017
Kamakura, Gizo . . . 026498
Kamal, Hassan . . . 037829
Kamansky, David . . . 046834
Kamarun, Prof. Ham Rabeah . . . 028014
Kamber, Ljubomir . . . 034207
Kamber, Pia . . . 036885
Kamber, Robert . . . 037234
Kamber, Urs . . . 036817
Kamburg, Petra . . . 017798
Kamenov, Dr. Petar . . . 004863
Kamer, S.J. . . . 029942
Kamerling, Leonard . . . 043780
Kamii, Monsho . . . 027307
Kamijo, Kazuo . . . 027073
Kamilia, Gharbi . . . 037961
Kamino, Yoshiharu . . . 026676
Kaminski, Jane . . . 015990
Kamiya, Yukio . . . 026499
Kamm, David . . . 043357
Kamm, James J. . . . 045757
Kammel, Dr. Frank Matthias . . . 019352
Kamp . . . 019947
Kamp, Dr. Diane D. . . . 048508
Kampe, Allen . . . 046274
Kamper, Gerard de . . . 034713
Kamphausen, Dr. Donat . . . 019660
Kamps, F. . . . 029698
Kamps, Toby . . . 045068
Kamuhangire, Dr. E . . . 038220
Kamyšova, Antonina Abramovna . . 033058
Kan, G. . . . 030351
Kan, Zhung . . . 007340
Kana Anderson, Gail . . . 046507
Kanabe, Albert . . . 005424
Kanaga, Marian . . . 045321

Kanaseki, Hiroshi 026923
Kanavrov, Darin 004626
Kanazawa, Tadao 026817
Kandeler-Fritsch, Martina 002945
Kandl, Veronica 044278
Kane, Debbie 043773
Kane, Debra 030600
Kane, Katherine 044458
Kane, Linda 005317
Kane, Patricia 046228
Kane, Randy 049192
Kane, Richard 046358
Kane, Robert E. 049185
Kaneichi, Ninomiya 026559
Kaneko, Kenji 027256
Kaneko, Yuriko 027009
Kanev, Ivajlo 004863
Kang, Prof. Joeng-Won 027602
Kania, Rolf 019391
Kania-Schütz, Monika 017584
Kankaala, Katri 009880
Kannan, Dr. R. 022057
Kanner, Debbie 043773
Kannu, T. 034294
Kano, Betty 046600
Kano, Kenji 026662
Kano, Takumi 027277
Kanowski, Dr. Claudia 020039
Kant Monteith, Joanita 045943
Kanter, Dr. Karin 018769
Kanter, Laurence B. 046364
Kantvilas, G. 001114
Kao, Deborah 042560
Kapches, Dr. Mima 006627
Kapelkova, Kristina 004863
Kapeller, Anne 037784
Kapfer, Otto 002378
Kapfer, Rudolf 002767
Kapinan, Catherine 048893
Kapinčeva, Dr. Iskra 004920
Kaplan, Dave 045339
Kaplan, David 045045
Kaplan, Ilee 045378
Kaplan, Luděk 008378
Kaplan, Nitzah 022909
Kaplan, Dr. Susan A. 042488
Kaplan, Wendy 045441
Kapler, Joseph 045595
Kapp de Thouzellier, Annemarie . . 017561
Kappeler, Richard 046779
Kappelmark, Ragnhild 036699
Kapronczay, Dr. Károly . . . 021635, 021693
Kaptain, H.J. 008835
Kaptein, Helen 001502
Kapusta, Jan 008518
Kapustina, Nadežda Ivanovna 038256, 038258, 038259, 038260
Karabaic, Milena 019391
Karačevcev, Vladimir F. 033147
Karadi, Gabriella 006611
Karadontis, Fleurette 021134
Karajotov, Dr. Ivan 004646
Karakas, Steve 047166
Karakuzov, Kumekbay 027405
Karamaliki, Nota 021225
Karaman, Antun 007707, 007721
Karamanou, Aglaia 021238
Karamanou, Dr. Aglaia 021242
Karamitrou-Mentesidi, Georgia . . . 021123
Karamzin, Alex 047876
Karanitsch, Peter 002327
Karantzali, Efthymia 021349
Kararadeva, Svetozara 004839
Karas, Lourdes 047058
Karasawa, Masahiro 027256
Karaseva, Alevtina Pavlovna 033003
Karaska, Dušan 034350
Karastamati, Dr. Helen 021182
Karbacher, Ursula 037499
Kardon, Nina 043992
Kardong, Don 048273
Kardosh, Judy 006701
Karegar, M. 022628
Karetsou, Al 021284
Kargar 022623, 022636
Karge, Dr. Wolf 020152
Karhoff, Brent 043608
Karhu, Jari 009561
Karhunen, Pentti 009474
Karibo, Lou 044033, 044037
Karijord Snørvik, Kjersti 031138
Karinen, Helge 036607
Karingi, Lina 027429
Karinja, Snježana 034511
Karis, Sirje 009425
Karjalainen, Tuula 009542
Kārkliņa, Rūta 027737
Karlinger, Friedrich 002771
Karlsdottir, Anna Stella . . . 031157, 031158
Karlsson, Anders 036732
Karlsson, Eva-Lena 036471
Karlsson, Henrik 009858
Karlsson, Lars Olov 036169
Karlsson, Stig 036206
Karlsson, Willy 036539
Karlstedt, Harry 009924
Karman Ohlberger, Christina 036507
Karmazin, N.I. . . . 033332, 033334, 033336
Karnath, Sonja 020253
Karnauchova, Galina Georgievna . . 033004
Karner, Dr. Regina 003017
Karnes, Andrea 044011
Karneth, Dr. Rainer 015528
Karojeva, Ljudmyla Rostislavivna . 038415
Károly, Simon 021657
Karon, Stephen A. 048457
Karosas, Gintaras 027862
Karov, Zdravko 004794
Karpf, Kurt 002542
Karpińska, Zofia 032391
Karpova, M.I. 033864
Karpowicz, Ewa 032349
Karppinen, Eira 009740, 009741
Karppinen, Hannu 009456, 009457
Karr, Ed F. 046850
Karrenbrock-Berger, Anneli 018296
Karsalainen, Tuula 009528
Karsch, Sylvia 018753
Karsmizki, Kenneth W. 042375
Karstadt, Bruce N. 045907
Karstens, E. 034740
Kartio, Kai 009512
Karttunen, Matti 009697
Karvonen-Kannas, Kerttu 009473
Karwatzki, Dr. Barbara 019810
Karwowski, Lech 032364, 032368, 032369, 032370
Kasal, Václav 008373, 008541
Kaschkat, Dr. Hannes 019414
Kasfir, Dr. Sidney 041866
Kashima, Noriyuki 026819
Kashima, Teishin 027350
Kasilag, Emma Y. 031769
Kaširin, Oleg Semënovič . 033971, 033977, 033981
Kasl, Ronda J. 044748
Kasperovič, K.K. 038225
Kasperska, Helena 032079
Kaspruk, Stepan Dmytrovyč 038269
Kass, Emily S. 048493
Kassal-Mikula, Dr. Renate 003017
Kaštelan, Jure 007850
Kastell, Christina 042677
Kastler, Daniel 010637
Kastler, Dr. Raimund 002567
Kastner, Carolyn 047875
Kastner, Erich 002972
Kasumov, Nazym Kasumovič 033099
Kasym, Sofija Vesiljevna 033772
Kaszak, Carole 040860
Kąsziołka, Stanisław 032562
Kaszubkiewicz, Andrzej 032093
Katagishi, Shoji 027287
Katakami, Syusaku 027008
Katalin, Dr. Keserü 021647
Katanekwa, K.V. 049568
Katanekwa, N.M. 049569, 049570
Kataoka, Chogoro 026997
Katayama, Takashi 027106
Katerinkino, Lidija P. 033329
Kates, Sam W. 043482
Katevenidou, Tassoula 021225
Kathane, M. Y. 022279
Katili, Dr. Ekki Husein 022424
Katiskoski, Kaarina 010180
Katkevich, Walter 042422
Katkova, Maria 033523
Kato, Bruce 044888, 048197
Kato, Jatsuo 027107
Kato, Sadao 026815, 027201
Katoh, Yuji 026645
Katona, Dr. András 021663, 021674, 021700
Katsalaki, Georgia 021285
Katsiff, Bruce 043505
Katsimpalis, Tom 045502
Katsura, Nobuo 027033
Kattanek, Prof. Dr. Siegfried 018774
Katz, Alain 011373, 011374, 011375
Katz, Jane 041982
Katz, Paul 041681
Katzenbach, Dr. Annette 016961
Katzensteiner, Peter 002842
Katzinger, Dr. Willibald . . . 002251, 002252
Kauder, Hans-Peter 002155
Kauder-Steiniger, Dr. Rita 019153
Kauders, Audrey S. 044944
Kauffmann, André 010442
Kaufmann, Bert Antonius 016841
Kaufmann, Carol 034587
Kaufmann, Dr. Christian 036893
Kaufmann, Christoph 018594
Kaufmann, Don 043126
Kaufmann, Heinz 037364
Kaufmann, Jürg 037041
Kaufmann, Sabine 020263
Kaukiainen, Hannu 009501
Kaukiainen, Heli . 009743, 009744, 009747
Kaulbach, Dr. Hans-Martin 020365
Kaumanns, Kurt 015942
Kaumeyer, Kenneth 048212
Kaupang, Brit 031084
Kaus, Dr. K. 001823, 002676
Kaus, Peter 015581
Kauschat, Gerda 016983
Kauth, K.O. 044699
Kauth, Robert R. 043930
Kava, Ritva 009505
Kavanagh, Dr. R. 005483
Kavanagh, Thomas 042266
Kavanash, Donald 047548
Kavanaugh, Martha 005213
Kavasch, E. Barrie 048976
Kavrečić, Ivan 007695
Kawabata, Hiroshi 027202
Kawaguchi, Kei 026882
Kawaguchi, Kimio 027189
Kawaguchi, Masako 027189
Kawai, Masaki 027290
Kawai, Suyako 026725
Kawaiaea, Daniel 044939, 044939
Kawakami, Kunihiko 026634
Kawanabe, Kusumi 027317
Kawasaki, Matsuju 026540
Kawasaki, Shoichiro 027154
Kawashima, Etsuko 026965
Kawiorski, Wacław 032081, 032175, 032176, 032229
Kay, Hannah 038749
Kay, Jeremy 047984
Kaya, Settar 038117
Kaye, Carole 045415
Kaye, Jennifer 006615
Kayombo, Dr. Norbert Andrew 037851
Kaysel, Dr. Roger 036873
Kayser, Christine 012785
Kayser, David 047744
Kayser, Gisela 016039
Kayser, Horst 019282
Kayser, Thomas A. 044528
Kaźmierczyk, Adam 031954
Kazus, Igor A. 033413
Kazutoschi, Kato 026450
Kazychanova, Marisa Grigorjevna . 034061
Kazyhanov, E.B. 027396
Keall, Dr. Edward 006627
Kean, John 048693
Kean, Roger 047233
Keane, Terry 046676
Kearney, Brian 042263
Kearney, John 042837
Kearney, Lynn 042837
Keasal, Debra L. 040468
Keasler, Suzy 045663
Keates, Eve 004995
Keating, Neal B. 044659
Keatinge, H.D.H. 041406
Keaveney, Raymond 022763
Keck, Gabriele 036927
Keck, John 044369, 048385
Keckeisen, Robert J. 048581
Kedde, M.C. 029465
Kędzierski, Sławomir 032473
Kędziora, Prof. Dr. Andrzej 032254
Keeble, Phyllis 039148
Keech, Brenda 044879
Keefe, John 046263
Keefer, Dr. Erwin 020374
Keegan, Daniel T. 047902
Keegan, Dr. W.F. 044103
Keenan, Edward 048901
Keene, John 034746
Keene, Rochelle 034639
Keene Fields, Catherine 045333
Keene Muhlert, Jan 048703
Keery, John 041148
Keesecker, Martin 045713
Kehrer, Helma 015525
Keil, Dirk 019664
Keil, Franka 018386
Keil, Matthias 002223
Keim, Cheryl 043208
Keim, Dr. Helmut 015532
Keinänen, Timo 009574
Keinan, Ofra 022882
Keiper, Elke 020646, 020647
Keiper, Dr. Joe 042986
Keisch, Dr. Christiane 016104
Keisuke, Iwamoto 026428
Keith, Barbara W. 043936
Keith, Dorothy 045608
Keith, Jack 041881
Keith, Larry 040241
Kejariwal, Dr. O. P. 022094
Kejzar, Josef 002631
Kekäle, Leena 010023
Kekeke, Daniel O. 030681
Kéler, Yves 014776
Kell, Dr. Klaus 018003
Kellams, Marty 043650
Kellar Mahaney, Edie 049377, 049378
Kellein, Dr. Thomas 016237
Keller, Dr. Christine 037784
Keller, Esther 036885
Keller, Dr. Eva 037764
Keller, Janet 048713
Keller, Jaroslav 008325
Keller, Linn 044432, 044433
Keller, Dr. Peter 002548
Keller, Peter C. 047945
Keller, Pierre 037240
Keller, Dr. Rolf 037819
Keller, Sylvia M. 047044
Keller, Tim 048351
Keller, Urs Oskar 036924
Kellerer, Anna 001994
Kellerhoff, Reinhard 020807
Kellett, Deborah 042294
Kellett, John 041968
Kelley, Barbara 042223
Kelley, Joyce J. 047340
Kelley, Timothy 046767

Kellgren, Ola 036732
Kelling, Paisley 046859
Kellner, Heike 002346
Kelly, Agnes R. 045659
Kelly, Amanda 048381
Kelly, Barbara 042354
Kelly, Bonny 047641
Kelly, Dr. Christopher 038966
Kelly, Cindy 041982, 041986
Kelly, D. 005337
Kelly, Eamonn 022759
Kelly, Elaine 042216
Kelly, Franklin 048924
Kelly, Gemey 006318
Kelly, Gillian 039323
Kelly, Jack 046034
Kelly, Jim 048082
Kelly, Karen 046324
Kelly, Linda 006453
Kelly, Michelle 038505
Kelly, Nancy 046684
Kelly, Rose 047396
Kelly, Sheila 006268
Kelly, Vonda 042269
Kelly, Wendy 042407
Kelm, Bonnie G. 047952, 049183
Kelm, Rüdiger 015465
Kelnberger, Raimund 019866
Kelner, Sara 044639
Kelsey Foley, Kathy 049015
Kelso, J. 040437
Kelthoum Kitouni, Daho 000058
Keltti, Pia 009462
Kemdal, Anne Louise 036676
Kemkes, Martin 015428
Kemkes, Dr. Martin 019409, 019931
Kemm, B. 036946
Kemmer, Kim 043815
Kemmerer, Allison 041721
Kemp, Alan 040862
Kemp, Blanch 045547
Kemp, Jane 043357
Kemp, Jo 040619
Kemp, N.R. 001114
Kemp, Dr. T.S. 040663
Kemp, W. Bradley M. 045205
Kemper, Heinrich 016856
Kemper, Julie 045279
Kemper Fields, Laura 044916
Kempf, Jürgen 010227
Kempf, Klaus 019037
Kempf, Peter 020207
Kempling, Steven 005361
Kempton, Peggy 044471
Kenagy, Dr. James 048075
Kendall, Andrew 041815
Kendall, Andy 043246
Kendall, Clifford P. 041672, 043825
Kendall, Harvey 038897
Kendrick, Marcia 042774
Kendrigan, Ernie 001168
Kenen, Susan 046204
Kenkel, Jens 019925
Kennedy, Arlene 005791
Kennedy, Dr. Brian 000888
Kennedy, Caroline 047123
Kennedy, Cheryl 045598
Kennedy, Chris 039225
Kennedy, Clay W. 042484
Kennedy, Elaine 039296
Kennedy, Elizabeth 042884
Kennedy, Dr. George L. 047819
Kennedy, Ian 044924
Kennedy, Mary C. 041913
Kennedy, R.H. 006624
Kennedy, Sally E. 047391
Kennedy, S.B. 038669
Kennedy, Tim 005180
Kennedy, William 043318
Kennedy, Prof. W.J. 040663
Kenney, Chris 042607
Kenney, Kimberley 042607
Kennis 029308
Kenny, Jessica 039124
Kenny, Kevin 043883
Kenny, Michael 022761
Kensler, Terry 032729
Kent, Dr. Jacquelyn S. 043958
Kent, Jerry 047669
Kent, Joan 047147
Kent, Liz 044714
Kent, Rachel 001517
Kenworthy, M. 038657, 038883
Kenwright, Carole 039036
Kenwright, Peter 041193
Kenyon, Colleen 049292
Kenyon, Sir George 039184
Kenyon, Kathleen 049292
Kenyon, Sarah 040880
Keo, Pich 004970
Keogh, Anthony J. 034705
Keough, Tracey 047259
Kepford, Kris S. 046933
Kephart, Betsy 046816
Keppert, Jozef 034354
Keracher, Susan 040897
Kerber Walrond, Frances 047661
Kerefov, Betal Muradinovič 033543
Kerekesh, Michael 047200
Kerelezova, Vera 004863
Keren, S. 022931
Kerimova, L.L. 049384
Kerkhoven, Dr. R. 029435
Kermode, Deborah 038731
Kern, Dr. Georg von 018070
Kern, James E. 048734
Kern, Robert 015775
Kern, Steven 047838
Kern, Ursula 017176
Kernaghan, Nan 006674
Kernan, Thomas J. 045340
Kerndler, Werner 001708
Kerner, Johann 018502
Kernhan, John 006013
Kerr, Andrea J. 040673
Kerr, Fred 001000
Kerr, John 039370
Kerr, Paul K. 042131
Kerr, Peter 001350
Kerr-Wilson, Ian 005592
Kerrin, Nancy 044829
Kerschbaum, Rupert 003017
Kershaw, Mary J. 039679
Kersing-Blok, Drs. I. 029404
Kersten, Michiel C.C. 029653
Kerstges, Andrea 016157
Kersting, Dr. Hannelore 018978
Kersting, Rita 016839
Kert, Christian 010291
Kervern, Jeannine 010807
Kervezee, Ruth 029239
Kerwood, Adrian 039058
Kesaeva, E.A. 034039
Keskküla, Prof. Ando 049922
Kesler, Jonathan G. 047296
Kesselman, Steve 047744, 048012
Kessler, Adolf 037388
Kessler, Earl 022097
Keßler, Matthias 020038
Kessler, Dr. Michael 036901
Kessler, Monika 016643
Kessler, Nava 022985
Kessler, Werner 037175
Kestel, Michael 020313
Kesteman, Emile 003309
Kestenbaum, Stuart J. 043363
Kester, Marilyn 042569
Ketchum, Clark 044323
Ketelsen, Dr. Thomas 016797
Ketner, Joseph D. 048847
Ketteler, Georg 016273
Kettemann, Dr. Otto 018421, 018422
Kettula, Suvi 009472
Keulen, W.J. 029221
Keunecke, Dr. Hans-Otto 017031
Keurs, P. ter 029854
Keuter, J.H.G. 029292
Keutgens, Eric 003227
Kevenhörster, Markus 001848
Keweloh, Hans-Walter 016429
Key, Eric 049157
Keyaerts, Geneniève 014444
Keyaerts, Magali 014444
Keyes, George S. 043444
Keyser, Ignace de 003333, 003353
Keyser, Ralph 042657
Keyworth, John 040081
Kezich, Giovanni 025713
Khabibullaev, Nozim 049410
Khachatrian, Shahen 000684
Khalid, Syed Ali 027972
Khan, Aurangzeb 031395
Khan, Gulzar Muhammad 031403
Khan, M. Ikramullah 031388
Khan, Muhammad Afzal 031381
Khan, Nazir Ahmad 031401
Khan Jatoi, Saeed 031390
Khasanov, S.R. 049408
Khasawneh, Alia 027380
Khazam, Sandra 001448
Kheel-Cox, Claudia 046259
Khevenhüller-Metsch, Maximilian . 002208
Khewhok, Carol D. 044598
Khewhok, Sanit 044597
Khodair Kassim, Kassim 027631
Khotko, P.S. 003133
Khulani-Mkhize, Leo 034635
Kibritova, Vanja 004769
Kida, Takuya 027256
Kidd, Benton 043072
Kidd, Jane 040673
Kidd, Pat 040867
Kidner, Laura 041451
Kidston, Jamie 006727
Kieberl, Wolff 001850
Kiebert, Susan 047928
Kiedel, Klaus-Peter 016429
Kiefer, Theresia 018707
Kieffer-Olsen, Jakob 009065, 009068
Kiehl, David 046418
Kiel, Dennis 042919
Kielak, Bernard 032204
Kielholz, Walter B. 037777
Kielland, Morten 031332
Kielwein, Dr. Matthias 016786
Kiely, Ann 041333
Kiely, David 041333
Kiemele, E. 017045
Kiendl, Anthony 005064
Kienholz, Kathleen 046281
Kienitz, Gerlinde 019296
Kientz, J.J. 011020
Kienzle, Karen 047953
Kiereś, Małgorzata 032497
Kiermeier-Debre, Prof. Dr. Joseph . 018905
Kiers, J. 029203
Kietlińska-Michalik, Dr. Barbara . . 032044
Kiewel, Ann 044571, 044575
Kift, Dr. Dagmar 016285, 016771
Kiger, Robert W. 047052
Kihiyo, Jackson M. 037852
Kihlberg, Eva 036726
Kiiski-Finel, Päivi 010180
Kilaghbian, Elia 026249
Kilani, Huda 027371, 027372
Kilby, Virginia 044869
Kilger, Dr. Gerhard 016762
Kilham, D.D. 044438
Kilian, Ewa 032141
Kilian, Dr. H. 020372
Kilian, Dr. Ruth 018780
Kilian Dirlmeier, Dr. Imma 018794
Kiliti, Zsuzsanna 021770
Killacky, John 047892
Killoran, Elizabeth 046851
Kilpatrick, Susie 041960
Kilroy, Frank 040372
Kilsdonk, Betty 043737
Kilvington, Ken 039673
Kim, Chi-Eun 027601
Kim, Christine Y. 046409
Kim, Hongnam 027554
Kim, Jin-Hyuck 027477
Kim, Jong Chull 027475
Kim, Dr. Ke Chung 048701
Kim, Kumja Paik 047853
Kim, Nam Kyun 027619
Kim, Sun-Jung 027504, 027543
Kim, Sung-Rae 027526
Kim, Sunggu 027522
Kim, Wook-Han 027504
Kim, Yun Soon 027626
Kimball, Cathy 047901
Kimball, Kathryn A. 046156
Kimfoko-Madoungou, Joseph 007666
Kimihiko, Hori 026447
Kimmig, Ingeborg 020357
Kimsey, Dr. Lynn S. 043314
Kimura, Hidenori 027138
Kimura, Shigenobu 026664
Kin, Wook-Han 027543
Kincaid, Jean E. 005045
Kincses, Károly 021761
Kindgren, Hans 036725
Kindler, Dr. Gabriele 018158
Kindrachuk, William 006760
Kindred, Peter 039522
Kindschy, Errol 049098, 049099
Kindt, Diane 045954
Kindt, Jean 003477
King, Alan 046570
King, Andy 038859, 038860
King, B.R. 041194
King, Brad 040176
King, Brian 005183
King, Carolyn 022699, 042819
King, Charles 042584
King, Dexter Scott 041864
King, D.F. 046449
King, Douglas R. 047679
King, Dr. Duane H. 045466
King, Edward . . . 038799, 039844, 039846
King, Elspeth 041107
King, Dr. F.W. 044103
King, George G. 047964
King, G.J. 001178
King, Graham 039143
King, Gwen G. 046793
King, Harry 045042
King, Hugh R. 043568
King, John 030490
King, Karma S. 045042
King, Lyndel 045910
King, Margaret H. 039514
King, Margery 047039
King, Michael D. 039281
King, Prof. Phillip 040266
King, Tamara 045933
King, William C. 045775
King Torrey, Ella 047889
Kingan, Beryl A. 041452
Kingdon, Charles 005879
Kingery, James 044210, 046428
Kingsbury, Bernard 030475
Kingsbury, Paul 046142
Kingsford Hale, James 039721
Kingsley, April 043574
Kingston, Jean T. 049220
Kinnear, J. 040696
Kinno, Seiichi 026830
Kinoshita, Kyuichiro 027170
Kinoshita, Masafumi 026792
Kinoshita, Yumi 044080
Kinsell, Tracey 045771
Kinsey, Danna 043063
Kinsman, Jane 000888
Kinsolving, Lucie 046380
Kinson, Alan 000756
Kintisch, Christine 002859
Kinzinger, Nancy 048415
Kioseva, Ass.Prof. Dr. Tsvatana . . . 004863
Kipiani, M.A. 015408

Kipkorir, Daniel 027419
Kipnis, Jeffrey 043112
Kippes, Dr. Wolfgang 002919, 003001
Kiprop, Nancy 027420
Kiràly, Elvira 021677
Kirby, Chris 041205
Kirby, Jo 040241
Kirby, John 005543
Kirby, Michael 049184
Kirch, Patrick V. 042165
Kirchhauser, Hannes 018170
Kirchmayer, Christian 002174
Kirchmeier Andersen, J.C. 008991
Kirchner, Dr. Ferdinand 002563
Kirchner, Gertrud 002052
Kirchweger, Dr. Franz 002934
Kiričenko, E.I. 033269
Kiričenko, Galina Vladimirovna . . . 033295
Kirigin, Branko 007798
Kirilova, Lena 004668, 004669
Kirk, Natalie 048853
Kirk, Ruth 043090
Kirk, Wendy 040133
Kirkbride, Cinoy 005429
Kirkby, Patrick 041404
Kirkeby Andersen, Dorte 009091
Kirker, Anne 001474
Kirkham, Thomas G. 038666
Kirklin, Deborah 047990
Kirkman, John 001022
Kirkpatrick, Andrea 006354
Kirkpatrick, David 039185
Kirkpatrick, Dr. Gail B. 019139
Kirkpatrick, May 038577
Kirkwood, Michael 043641
Kirmeß, Max 019417, 019418
Kirnbauer, Dr. Martin 036898
Kirov, Stefan 004919
Kirrane, Siobhan 040357
Kirsch, Eva 047812
Kirsch, Dr. Jeffrey W. 047829
Kirsch, Dr. John A.W. 045594
Kirsch, Dr. Steven 045150
Kirschberg-Grossman, Reva G. . . . 046318
Kirschensteiner, Brian 043575
Kirwan King, Martin 048441
Kirwin, Timothy B. 044642
Kischkewitz, Dr. Hannelore 015979
Kisdemaker, Drs. R.E. 029196
Kisëv, Ërdan 004829
Kishida, Tamiya 027328
Kishioka, Yukio 026420
Kisić, Anica 007719
Kisielowicz, Marcin 032455
Kisjova, Vera 004793
Kisler, Mary 030431
Kisler, Shuli 023092
Kisman, A.K. 029490, 029491
Kiss, K. 040129
Kisser, Gerhard 001891
Kissi, Flavio 025026
Kissiov, Kostadin 004789
Kissling, Bertrand 037410
Kißro, Reinhard 019487
Kistner, Hans-Jürgen 018143
Kitagawa, Kazuo 026760
Kitagawa, Seika 026918
Kitagawa, Shigeto 027166
Kitamura, Hitomi 027256
Kitamura, Sadao 026705
Kitauo, Tsuguto 026843
Kitazawa, Toshio 027093
Kitchen, Dr. M. 039332
Kitchin, Cameron 048795
Kitchin, Simon 039068, 039071
Kitching, Matthew 034645
Kite Powell, Rodney 048492
Kittelmann, Udo 017188
Kittleson, Darrell 041961
Kittner, Ed 044624
Kittredge, Cindy 044300
Kityo, Robert Martin 038216
Kitz, Hilary 048653
Kitzler, Gottfried 002374
Kitzmann, Andrew 048454
Kiuchi, Kazuhiro 026423
Kiupčupov, Georgi 004840
Kivi, Mirja 010134
Kivimäe, Juta 009398
Kivimäki, Kati 010024, 010027
Kiziltan, Sabri 038093
Kiziltan, Zeynep 038093
Kjær, Birgitte 008806
Kjeldbæk, Esben 008965
Kjeldgaard, Inge Merete 008842
Kjeldsberg, K. 030907
Kjeldsberg, Peter Andreas 031285
Kjeldsen, Kjeld 008938
Kjellberg, Anne 031084
Kjems, Folke 008925, 008927
Kjerström Sjölin, Eva 036443
Kjupčupov, Georgi 004838, 004841
Kjuptčupov, Georgi 004836
Klaasen, Lizet 003163
Kładna, Dr. Aleksandra 032367
Klages, Dr. Claudia 016333
Klameth, Wolfgang 017166
Klammt, Annerose 017453
Klang Eriksson, Eva 036443
Klanicová, Dr. Evženie 008277, 008278
Klapczyński, Stanisław 031865
Klapthor, Frances 041969
Klar, Annika 036381, 036382, 036385
Klar, Herma 019177
Klarić, Josip 007855
Klassen, John 045724
Klasson, Gunnar 036725
Klatt, David . . . 005953, 006034, 006413, 006429, 006893, 006894
Klatt, Dr. Ingaburgh 018721
Klauda, Manfred 018405, 018406, 018407, 018408, 018409, 018410
Klaus, Franz Josef 002238
Klaus, Judy 030543
Klaus, Dr. Sabine 048763
Klauser, K.D. 003741
Klaußecker, Fritz 020525
Klebe, Kurt E. 047164
Klee, Sonja 018432
Kleeberg, John M. 046287
Kleeblatt, Norman 046352
Kleefisch, Stephen J. 047081, 047082
Kleemann, Kurt 019792
Kleespies, Gavin 046069
Klei, Mary 045224
Klein, A. 029830
Klein, Adaire 045463
Klein, Dr. Angela 016381
Klein, Anton 002944
Klein, Beatrixe 020865
Klein, Carolyn 043678
Klein, Christhilde 029653
Klein, Christophe 013106
Klein, Dr. Emanuel 046137
Klein, Janice B. 043760, 043763
Klein, Jean-Claude 014212
Klein, Matthias 015568
Klein, Dr. Michael 018790
Klein, Peter 048428
Klein, Regine . . . 019612, 019613, 019614
Klein, Thomas 016722, 016723
Klein, Dr. Ulrich 020374
Klein, Valérie 013078
Klein-Langner, Wolfgang 021008
Kleindorfer-Marx, Dr. Bärbel 020640
Kleine, Dr. Joachim 021061
Kleiner, Gerald 045974
Kleiner, Michael 020571
Kleiner-Frick, Beat 037790
Kleiner-Frick, Dorothee 037790
Kleinert, Dr. Annette 018040
Kleinertz, Dr. Everhard 018316
Kleinhans, M. . . . 034764, 034765, 034766
Kleinhofer, Erna 003016
Kleinschmidt, Torsten 018102
Kleinschmidt-Altpeter, Dr. Irene . . . 016329
Kleipaß, Dr. Herbert 016973
Kleisner, Ted J. 049145
Kleist, Monika von 015668
Klejman, N.I. 033460
Klemenz, Wolfgang 018438
Klemińska, Izabella 032461
Klemm, Dr. Christian 037777
Klemm, Federico 000150
Klemm, Randy 044308
Klemm, Susanne 017115
Klemp, Dr. Klaus 017180
Klencke, Lippold von 016976
Klenner, Hans-Christian 019659
Klenow, Rosemary E. 043582
Klepač, Koraljka 007783
Klerk, Frank de 029615
Klerk, Prof. Dr. L.F.W. de 029733
Klesman, Kees 029198
Klettner, Emmi 001919
Kletz, Ursula 019124
Kley, Dr. Stefan 019365
Klicka, Dr. John 045192
Kliege, Dr. Melitta 019369
Klietmann, Wolfgang 002716
Klim, T.B. 033396
Klimaszewski, Cathy 044791
Klimek, Larry 045937
Klimenova, Tamara Aleksandrovna 033085
Klimesch, Dr. Gertraud 001821
Klimmer, Hans 002437
Klimov, Vladislav Petrovič 033070
Klimova, Anna Danilovna 033098, 034093, 034094
Klimova, Elena Michajlovna 033943
Kline, John 043136
Kline, Dr. John 043434
Kline, Katy 042487
Kling, Burkhard 020299
Kling, Gudrun 036932
Klingelhöfer, Claudia 020194
Klinger, Dr. H.C. 034586
Klinghardt, G. 034586
Klinghardt, Gerald 034583
Klingler, Michael 002097
Klingman, Catherine 043443
Klink, Alfonso Caballero 035096
Klink, R. 020492
Klinkow, Michaela 019469
Klis, Dr. Rita 018287
Kljajić, Damijan 034535
Kljueva, Valentina Ivanovna 033107
Klobe, Tom 044610
Kloch, Ove 009148
Klochko, Deborah 047862
Klöpfer, Anette 018487
Kloosterboer, A.E. 030064
Klootwijk, L.P. 030067
Kloppenborg, David N. 043475
Klos, Günther 017993
Klose, Dr. Dietrich 019119
Klose, Simon 000793
Kloster, Johan 031095
Klostermeier, David 047618
Klotzer, Dr. Georg 024668
Kloub, Ola 027385
Klucas, Kevin 043291
Kluchko, Halya 006643
Klučina, Petr 008620
Klüver, Heinrich 018644
Klug, Dr. C. 037795
Kluge, Dr. Arnd 017957
Kluge, Prof. Arnold G. 041734
Kluge, Prof. Dr. Bernd 016120
Kluge, Martin 036882
Kluge, W. 018838
Kluger, Reinhard 001771
Klukina, Anna I. 033379
Klumpe, Josef 016978
Klumpp, Sibylle 013299
Klupp, Krzysztof 032255
Kluska, Adam 032344
Kluss, Dr. Maciej 032268
Kluza, Radosław 032140
Klykova, Galina Ivanova 033618
Klytcheva, Bibi 038205
Kmieck, Anne T. 042987
Kmínek, Petr 008266, 008781
Knabe, Hans-Jürgen 019852
Knape, Gunilla 036293
Knapen, I.A.M. 030040
Knapp, D.R. 040062
Knapp, S. 040062
Knapp, Steve 046764
Knapp, Trevor 041291
Knappertsbusch, Dr. Michael 036899
Knauer, Wilfried 020955
Knauss, Carol 041728
Knauss, Dr. Florian 019117
Knauss, Jürgen 016606
Kneale, John Brian 040901
Knebelsberger, Caroline 042119
Knee, Arthur 001538
Knee, Lurline 001538
Kneubühl, Dr. Urs 036938
Kneuss, Martine 037583
Knibb, Dennis 006353
Knibiely, Philippe 014396, 014397
Knick, Dr. Stanley 046865
Kniefeld, Lothar 020421
Knieriem, Dr. Michael 021013, 021016
Knierriem, Peter 018602, 019854
Knigge, Horst 017751
Knigge, Prof. Dr. Volkhard 020739
Knight, Bob 049158
Knight, David J. 044538
Knight, Frank 049094
Knight, Gregory 042833
Knight, Irene 006060
Knight, Jean 039007, 040110
Knight, Jeremy 039773
Knight, Jim 043088
Knight, Katie 044502
Knight, Michael 047853
Knight, Robert 042209
Knight, V.M. 040165
Knight, Yvonne 044850
Knill, Phyllis 043679
Knipe, Peter 044559
Knipp, Otto 018027
Knippenberg, Dr. W.H.Th. 029983
Knipping, Mark 044316
Knipprath, Ute 016333
Knittel, Pierre 015366
Knittel, W. 019241
Knížák, Dr. Milan 008634
Knízák, Milan 008651
Knobloch, Stephan 017195
Knoch, Francis 027885
Knoch, Susan 043806
Knoche, Norma 043480
Knocke, Erich 017072
Knode, Marilu 045890
Knöchlein, Dr. Bernhard 020212
Knödel, Dr. Susanne 017716
Knödler-Kagoshima, Brigitte 018156
Knöpfel, Sylvia 017330
Knofler, Dr. Monika 002937
Knogler, Helmut 002494
Knoke, Christine 046833
Knol, Egge 029638
Knoll, Andrew H. 042556
Knoll, Annegret 018384
Knolle, Dr. P. 029569
Knoop, Ulrich 017905
Knop Kallenberger, Christine 048656
Knopp, Dr. Hans-Georg 016061
Knoppers, K. 029346
Knorowski, Mariusz 032202
Knorre, Dr. Alexander von 017891, 017892, 017893
Knott de Arechaga, Deborah 047407
Knowles, A.M. 039063, 039066
Knowles, Elizabeth 040692
Knowles, John 046142
Knowles, Prof. Lacey 041734
Knowles, P. 022703

Knowles, Peter 048203, 048794
Knox, J. 038668
Knox, Judy 042386
Knox, Lu 046543
Knox, R. 040097
Knuab, Donald E. 043390
Knubben, Dr. Thomas 019734
Knudsen, Ann Vibeke . . . 008883, 009075, 009076
Knudsen, Henning 008959
Knudsen, Herluf 009059
Knudsen, Jesper 008909
Knudsen, Karsten 009101
Knudsen, Svend Aage 008828
Knudsen, Trine-Lise 031078
Knuth, Dr. Michael 016051, 016173
Knutsen, Jim 048268
Kob, Karin 036863
Kobald, Peter 002111
Kobayashi, Akira 027079
Kobayashi, Fumio 027275
Kobayashi, Kiroku 027027
Kobayashi, Koichi 027136
Kobayashi, Moriaki 027316
Kobayashi, Naoji 026454
Kobayashi, Saburo 027203
Kobayashi, Shigeko 027236
Kobayashi, Tadashi 026436
Kobayashi, Dr. Tatsuo 026852
Kobayashi, Toshinobu 026629
Koblik, Steven S . . . .
Kobosil, Karel 008282
Kobusiewicz, Zofia 032149
Koç, Sema 038010
Koca, Osman 038150
Kočankov, Dr. Nikolaj 004863
Kočarženko, Jevgenija Ivanivna . . 038398
Koçςoban, Cahit 038111
Kocebenkova, Vera Ivanovna 033213
Kočevar, Sanda 007732
Koch, Dr. Alexander 037784
Koch, Christian 049093
Koch, Claudia 002901
Koch, Cynthia M. 044707
Koch, Friederike 018145
Koch, Heidemarie 021020
Koch, Ira 017600
Koch, Johannes Hugo 019294
Koch, Dr. Lars-Christian 016017
Koch, Dr. Michael 019039
Koch, Prof. Dr. Rainer 017176
Koch, Sven 017169
Koch, Werner 016291
Koch, Wilhelm 018913
Kochanova, Ljudmila Petrovna . . . 034022
Kochendörfer, Reinhard 018532
Kočík, Zdeněk . 008324, 008429, 008630, 008631
Kociolek, J. Patrick 047856
Kock, G.M. de 030202, 030204
Kock, Prof. Hans 018245
Kock, Peter 018954
Kock, R.D. de 034627
Kocsis, Dr. Gyula 021706
Koczur, Anton 001965
Koda, Harold 046364
Kodama, Ikuo 026827
Kodani, Susan 044600
Köb, Edelbert 002965
Köberl, Rudolf 002431
Koechlin, Bernard 037133
Köck, Dr. Michaela 002867
Köcke, Dr. Ulrike 017075
Koefoed, Lizette 009003
Köger-Kaufmann, Dr. Annette 018550
Kögl, Reinhard 020060
Kögler, Johannes 017262
Köhl, Gudrun 019128
Köhler, Birte 017715
Köhler, Eva 019939
Köhler, Georg 002825
Köhler, Dr. Juliana 017614
Köhler, N. 029653
Köhler, Otto 017971
Köhler, R. 017768
Köhler, Dr. Thomas 020965
Köhlmeier, Ernst 002017
Köhn, Regine 016668
Koehnline, Lyn 042713
Kölbl, S. 016266
Kölbl-Ebert, Dr. M. 019059
Kölbl-Ebert, Dr. Martina 016910
Köll, Helmut 002637
Köllhofer, Dr. Thomas 018806
Kölmel, Dr. Reinhard 015865
Könenkamp, Dr. Wolf 018894, 018895
König, G. 016256
König, Dr. Gabriele 017301
König, H. 015808
König, Heinz 017863
König, Helmut 017962
König, Josef 002877
König, Prof. Kasper 018334
König, Lotte 002972
König, Dr. Margarethe 020483
König, Reginald 020356
Koenig, Robert J. 048526
König, Prof. Dr. Viola 016017, 016087
Koenigsmarková, Dr. Helena 008650, 008726
Koeninger, Kay 043321
Könke, Dr. Jörn 015456
Köntös, László 021809
Köpf, Prof. Ernst Ulrich 017536
Köpke, Ingeborg 017273
Köpke, Prof. Dr. Wulf 017716
Köppen, Thomas 020856
Koerber, Susannah 047465
Koerhuis, E. 030400
Környei, Dr. Attila 021796, 021843, 021844, 021846, 021848, 021849
Koesoemowarni, Endang 022497
Köster, Dr. Barbara 019470
Köster, Hein 016165
Köster, Dr. Reinhard 018794
Koevend, Mary Helen de 046165
Kofler, Claudia 002945
Kofler, Gertraud 002063
Kofuku, Akira 027189
Koga, Kim 045453
Kogan, Lee 046283, 046329
Kogler, Leopold 002820
Kogure, Susumu 026554
Kohan, Carol E. 049065
Kohlbauer-Fritz, Dr. Gabriele 002918
Kohlberg, Ilona 017253
Kohler, Ruth 048136
Kohlschmidt, Ulrich 019240
Kohn, Klaus G. 016390
Kohn Loncarica, Prof. Dr. Alfredo G. 000178, 000219
Kohnke, Dr. Hans-Georg . . 016372, 016373
Kohout, K. 001835
Kohút, Dr. Teodor 034358
Koike, Tomio 026887
Koja, Dr. Stephan 002969
Kojaev, M. 027414
Kok, Harry de 003821
Kokki, Kari-Paavo 009510, 009511
Kokkotidis, Dr. Klaus Georg 020374
Kokošinek, Nataša 034465
Kokoska, Monika 017057
Kokot, Juliusz 031836
Kokroko, Grace Juliet 021103
Kolarić, Dr. Juraj 007831
Kolb, Jennifer 045595
Kolb, Nancy D. 046978
Kolb, Rainer 015576
Kolbach, B. 029708
Kolbasina, Larisa Aleksandrovna . . 033584
Kolbe, Joachim 018498
Kolber, Peggy 049011
Kolberg, Dr. Gerhard 018334
Kold, Anders 008938
Kolde, H. 018133
Kolenberg, Hendrik 001505
Koles, L.A. 001370
Kolesnikova, Ljudmila Arsenjevna . 033203
Kolesnikova, Ljudmila Petrovna . . . 033397
Kolesov, S.N. 033918
Koletsky, Susan 042067
Kolev, Cvetan 004902, 004905
Koll, Kersti 009394, 009398
Kolland, Dr. Dorothea 016097
Kollar, Mary 045324
Kollbaum, Marc 047663, 047666
Kollbaum-Weber, Jutta 021031
Koller, Dr. Johann 019048
Koller, Karl 002883, 003028
Koller, Margaret H. 043379
Koller-Jones, Kimberly B. 046214
Kollmann, Dr. Karl 017051
Kollmann-Caillet, Virginie 010463
Kolltveit, Bård 031095
Kolm, Herbert 002441
Kolmos, Dr. Alfred S. 049148
Kolner, Brian A. 042384
Kolodziejak, Adeline 005859
Kołodziejski, Dr. Adam 032354
Kolomceva, Raisa Michajlovna . . . 033439
Kolonas, L. 021423
Kolonas, Lazaros 021121, 021143
Kolonia, Rozina 021246
Kolonoas, Lazaros 021235
Koloski, Laura 043994
Koloskova, T.G. 033475
Kolosov, V. 049388
Kolosova, Ekaterina Matveevna . . . 033790
Kolsio, Hannele 009986
Kolsteren, Steven 029638
Kolt, Ingrid 006539
Kolt, Sheryl 006868
Kolter, Horst 017792
Koltz, Jean-Luc 027894
Koludrović, Ivana 007818
Kolveši, Željka 007849
Kolyesnik, Ljudmila Michajlovna . . 033158
Komanecky, Michael 043320, 047011
Komarek, Beverly 044298
Komarl, Debra 041618
Komarov, Ilja Iljič 033417, 033434
Komatu, Nario 027019
Kombu, Anatolij Stepanovič 033323, 033324
Komick, J. 006723
Komissarov, Eha 009398
Komnenović, Ilija 034223
Komor, Valerie 046389
Komzyuk, Vera 038286
Končakovs'kyj, Volodymyr Petrovyč 038304
Koncevaja, Tatjana Leonidovna . . . 033887, 033889
Kondakova, Nina Viktorovna 033974
Kondratenko, Tatjana Michailovna . 033290
Kondziela, Mariusz 032333
Konečná, Katarína 034401
Konecny, Dr. Andreas 001711
Konevskaja, Tatjana Ivanovna 033704
Konieczny, Marian 032189
Konieczny, Władysław 032381, 032539
Konkle, Scott 005012
Konnikov, Boris Aleksandrovič . . . 033602
Kono, Osamu 026691
Konomi, Thomas 000018
Kononov, Alexander 034671
Kononova, Natalia 034671
Konova, Ljubava 004863
Konrád, György 015981
Konst, Thomas 042631
Konstantinus, Lahurakis 021512
Konstantios, Dr. Dimitris 021163
Konsten, Marie-Thérèse 029628
Konukiewitz, Insa 016452
Konvalinka, Danilo 049270
Konz, Klaus 018619
Kooiman, R. 030249
Kooiskra, L. 029621
Kooistra-Manning, Kevin 042208
Koolkin, Kenneth 022898
Koolmees, Dr. P. 030231
Koontz, Darlene 043364
Koop, Kathy 046277
Koopmans, G. 029837, 029845
Koopmans, J.J.G. 030107
Koopmans, Y. 029270
Koopmans-Witt, C.E. 029319
Koos, Greg 042261
Kooten, C.V. 030015
Kopálová, Dr. Danka 034406
Kopbosinova, R.T. 027390
Kopco, Mary A. 043338, 043339
Kopczak, Dr. Chuck 045414
Kopec, Diane 042013, 042014
Kopecky, Carle J. 048045
Kopeinig, Josef 002725
Koperkiewicz, Adam 031912, 031917
Koperski, Kate 046485
Kopf, Sibylle 015928
Kopf, Vicki C. 049258
Koponen, Sanna 010030
Kopówka, Edward 032018
Kopp, Klaus 020863
Kopp, Dr. Marianne 015759
Kopp, Siegfried 002507
Kopp, Werner 016160
Koppel, Greta 009398
Koppel, John 008814
Koppel, Merike 009398, 009408
Koppel de Ramírez, Elsa 007447
Koppenhöfer, Dr. Johanna 017268
Koppensteiner, Dr. Erhard 002567
Koppensteiner, Norbert 003037
Kopplin, Dr. Monika 019150
Koppy, Ann 046514
Kopydłowski, Janusz 031861
Koralova, Ilina 018568
Korb, Uwe 018772
Korčagin, E.N. 033734
Korčevnikova, I.L. 033480
Kordina, Julia 002172
Kordiš, Ivan 034468
Kordowska, Barbara 032508
Koref, Barbara 015641
Koren, Elisabeth 030741
Koren, Johannes 001940
Korff, David 047132
Korhonen, Paavo 010120
Korhoven, Teppo 009535
Korir, David 027421
Korkmasova, Maimusat Arslan-Alievna 033343
Korkmaz, Abdurrahman 038135
Korman, Sandy 005234
Korn, Brigitte 015436
Korn, Dr. Werner 016577
Kornacki, Krzysztof 031979
Kornatek, Anna 032416
Kornejeva, Galina Viktorivna 038349
Kornetchuk, Elena 048121
Korobar, Klime 027917
Korotaeva, Ljudmila Dmitrievna . . 034072, 034073
Korotkij, Aleksandr Nikolaevič 033337
Korovina, Vera Vasiljevna 033670
Korppi, Svea 009990
Korres, Manolis 021176
Koršikov, Anatolij Semënovič 033619
Korsmeier-Humbert, Helga 019146
Kort, Pamela 017192
Kort, Drs. Toon 029148
Korte-Böger, Dr. Andrea 020197
Korten, Noel 045443
Korteweg, Drs. A. J. 029430
Kortländer, Dr. Bernd 016832
Kortlander, Christopher 044153
Kortschak, Dr. Werner 002841
Kortunova, M. 033782
Korzeniewska, Iwona 032041
Kos, Dr. Peter 034488
Kos, Stanisław 032304

Kos, Dr. Dr. Wolfgang . . . 002860, 002863, 002909, 002947, 002948, 002968, 002982, 002983, 002988, 002994, 002995, 003003, 003004, 003008, 003012, 003014, 003016, 003017
Košacký, Petr 008407
Košambekova, Rayan K. 027389
Kosanji, Kozo 027293
Kosasih, Dikdik 022388
Koschatko, Alois 002788
Koschnik, Dr. Leonore 016011
Kościńska, Halina 031854
Kościołko, Eugeniusz 032128
Koshalek, Richard 045451
Kosiba, Leokadia Ewa 031978
Kosicka, Anna 032395, 032396
Kosinski, Dr. Dorothy 043269
Kosinski, Joan 042874
Koski, Ann 045595
Koski, Elizabeth 041816
Koski, Janne 010026
Koskijoki, Maria 009476
Koskimies-Envall, Marianne 010203
Koskinen, Maija 010177
Koskinen, Pekka 010218
Kośko, Maria 032243
Kosler, Barbara 019066
Kosmadaki, Polina 021134
Kosok, Dr. Lisa 017709
Kosonen, Elina 010005
Kosonen, Juhani 009831
Kosorić, Despa 034238
Kosova, Parim 034250
Koss, Sarah 044950
Kossatz, Dr. Tilman 021000
Kost', Ljubov Vasylivna 038341
Kosta, Bernard 044460
Kostadinova, Snežana 004811
Kostecka, Edyta 002934
Kostede, Ulrich 018142
Kostelny, Elizabeth 047418, 048203, 048441, 048794, 048797
Koster, Dr. A. 029961
Koster, F. 029585
Koster, Dr. J. 029793
Koster, John 048763
Koster, Koos 029887
Koster, Richard de 049095
Kostet, Juhani . 009943, 010160, 010164, 010174, 010175, 010176
Kostina, N.V. 033922
Kostková, Magda 034435
Kostołowski, Andrzej 032558
Kostov, Georgi 004931
Kostova, Penka 004625
Kostrowicki, Andrzej 032231
Kostyál, Dr. László 021925
Kostynowicz, Roman 032365
Kosunen, Mirja . 009919, 010067, 010068, 010069
Kosvincev, Boris Jurjevič 033033
Kosvinceva, Tatjana Dmitrievna . . . 033032
Koszkul, Jan 032340
Kosznik, Danuta 031993
Koszutski, Oskar 032230
Kot, Malgorzata 042874
Kotai-Ewers, Trisha 001503
Kotasiak, Wojciech 032206
Kothe, O. 018549
Kothe, Robert J. 044191
Kotik, Charlotta 042458
Kotilainen, Eija-Maija 009546
Kotilainen, Kari 010054
Kotitonenko, Nadija Oleksiïvna . . . 038397
Kotkin, Lauren 041576
Kotljakova, N.V. 033352
Kotooka, Mitsushige 026689
Kotouč, Friederike 020139
Kotrba, Dr. M. 019132
Kotrošan, Dražen 003941
Kotsch, Natalie 044688
Kotschwar, Sandra 002249
Kotsiubynsky, Igor 038230
Kottcamp, Edward 043777
Kottenbrink, Magdalene 019702
Kotterer, Michael 019755
Kottmann, Ingeborg 020593, 020597
Kotula, Krystyna 032506
Kotzan, Peter 018640
Kotzur, Dr. H.J. 018786
Kouakou Thierry, Konan 007691
Kouchi, Osami 027288
Koukal, Petr 008546
Koukal, Dr. Vitezlaw 008674
Koumantakis, Prof. I. 021536
Kourinou, Eleni 021183
Kourouma, Moussa 021593
Koutsomallis, Kyriakos 021134
Kouvaras, Fotini 021479
Kouvoutsakis, Panagiotis 021326
Kouzin, E. 033221
Kouzmin, Alexander 033746
Kovačev, Dimitar 004620
Kovačević, Dr. Bojan3a 034157
Kovačić, Goranka 007722, 007747
Kovačić, Marcelo 007783
Kovačić, Vladimir 007774
Kovács, Irén 021690
Kovács, Péter . . 021865, 021866, 021867, 021871
Kovács, Dr. Tibor 021672
Kovácsné Ládi, Katalin 021784
Kovacsovics, Dr. Wilfried . . 002547, 002567
Kovalenko, Donna 048080
Kovalskij, Sergej Viktorovič 033726
Kovanen, Marja-Leena 009756
Kovarik, Jiri 008433
Kovrakis, Stavros 021409
Kovtun, Vladimir Vasiljevič 034099
Kowalczyk, Longin 032138
Kowalczyk, Wiktor 031991
Kowald, Dr. Margaret 001473
Kowalewska, Dr. Agnieszka 032504
Kowalewski, S. 041833
Kowalski, Beth 045595
Kowalski, Dr. James A. 046306
Kowalski, Michael 018071
Kowalski, Zygfryd 032152
Kowarik, Prof. Wilfried 002307
Kowark, Dr. Hannsjörg 020372
Kowski, Robert 044335
Kox, Jo 027886
Koyama, Dr. Hiroshi 027156
Koyama, Miturn 026455
Kozáková, K. 034452
Kozel, Jennifer 046312
Kozen, Hiroshi 026740
Kozerski, Paweł 031852
Kozhachev, M. 027399
Kozijn, W.I. 029363
Kožišková, Lenka 008503
Kozlova, T.D. 033738
Kozlova, Vera Danilovna 033046
Kozlovskaja, Nadežda Borisovna . . 033051
Kozlowski, Kazimiera 042599
Kozma, LuAnne 043575
Kozubek, Gwalbert 031894
Kožucharov, Dimitar 004757
Kozyra, Peter H. 005086
Kozyreff, Chantal 003353
Kraber, Rosa 048413
Kraciak, Aniela 032267
Kracke, Toni 045653
Kräftner, Dr. Johann 002942
Krähenbühl, Dr. Hans 037389
Krämer, Dirk 016860
Krämer, Gerd 015968
Kraemer, Jörg 016343
Krafczyk, Alois 017787
Kraft, Gro 021970
Kraft, Joe C. 046180
Kraft, Karl Ludwig 015733
Kraft, Dr. Perdita von 016593
Kraft, Dr. R. 019132
Kragelund, Patrick 008972
Kragh, Birgitte 008796
Kragh, Mogens 009137
Kraglund, Ivar 031091
Kragness, Kurt K. 042093
Krahn, Susan 005506
Krahn, Dr. Volker 016173
Krajasisch, Dr. P. 002692
Krajewski, Sara 045591
Krajneva, Anna Anatoljevna 033356
Krajniak, Paul J. 045887
Krakauer, Dr. Thomas H. 043547
Krakow, Peter 018575
Kralev, Krali 004881
Kralevska, Julijana 027919
Kraljević, Marija 007741
Kramarczyk, Andrea 016565
Kramatschek, Christopher 019035
Kramer, Dr. Dieter 002433, 017168, 017182
Kramer, Prof. Dr. Diether 001952
Kramer, Dr. E. 029837
Kramer, Finn Erik 008910
Kramer, Hermann 002758
Kramer, M. 019607
Kramer, Drs. M. 029430
Kramer, Dr. Mario 017188
Kramer, Trudy C. 048254
Kramme, Dr. Mike 046063
Kramp, Dr. Mario 018296
Krane, Susan 042351
Kranjc, Igor 034485
Kranjc, Katja 034485
Krankenhagen, Prof. Gernot 017709
Kranl, Christine 001744
Kranner, Romana 002029
Kranz, Betsy 044734
Kranz, Prof. Dr. P. 017028
Kranzelbinder, Norbert 001796
Krapež, Mateja 034487
Krapf, Eva 002861
Krapf, Dr. Michael 002969, 002970
Krapish, Anne 044224
Krasilnikov, Grigorij Vladimirovič . . 032971
Kraske, Bernd M. 019780, 019781
Kraskin, Sandra 046400
Krasnokutskaja, Lidiya Ivanovna . . 033667
Krasovskaja, Nonna 038389
Krasowska, Dorothy 046322
Kraspycki, Dr. Sylvia 017182
Krasteva, Dimitijka 004863
Krăsteva, Natasha 004708
Krátká, Drahomíra 008681
Kratochvíl, Jiří 008544
Kratochvílová, Alena 008664
Kratochvílová, Irena 008379
Kratochwil, Franz 002877
Kratsas, James R. 044274
Kratzert, Martin 018095, 018097
Kraupe, Thomas W. 017720
Kraus, E. 024798
Kraus, Gerhard 015477
Kraus, Jeannie W. 042075
Kraus, Dr. Jürgen 018070
Kraus, Dr. Michael 002540
Kraus, Peter 020535
Kraus, Dr. Stefan 018323
Kraus, Werner 019885
Krause, Bernd 016408
Krause, Ines 018700
Krause, Dr. Jürgen 019156
Krause, Manfred 020238
Krause, Dr. Markus 016985
Krause, Martin F. 044748
Krause, Ortrud 017487
Krause, Dr. Siegfried 019352
Krause, Walt 047387
Krause-Willenberg, Horst 017611
Krauß, M. 018125
Krauss, Dr. Rolf 016136
Kravcov, Igor Nikolaevič 033910
Kravcova, Ljudmila Petrovna 033256
Krazmien, Mindy 044826
Kreamer, Todd A. 045950
Krebernik, Prof. Dr. Manfred 018108
Krech, Shepard 042423
Krečič, Peter 034477
Kreem, Tiina-Mall 009398
Kregar, Tone 034462
Krehe, Lynette 042888
Kreibich, Matthias 016899
Kreim, Dr. Isabella 018073, 053389
Krein, Sandra 045533
Kreindl, Richard 002207
Kreiner, Dr. Michael 002938
Kreisel, Dr. Gerd 020358
Krejči, Irena 008743
Krejci, Jim 049346
Krekel, Dr. Michael 015726
Kremer, Elisabeth 016684
Kremer, Dr. Roberta 006714
Krempel, Prof. Dr. Ulrich 017769
Kremsreiter, Hans 019603
Kren, Thomas 045433
Krenn, Prof. Dr. Peter 001939
Krens, Thomas 046341, 046404
Krenzlin, Kathleen 016046
Kreps, Dr. Christina 043413
Kress, Brady 042573
Kreß, Hannelore 017574
Kress, Dr. Theo 018864
Krestin, Steffen 016598, 016599
Kret, Robert A. 042780, 046773
Kretschmer, Karl 019001
Kretzschmar, Dr. R. 020352
Kretzschmar, Ulrike 016011
Kreuger, S.C.P. 029935
Kreul, Dr. Andreas 016418
Kreutz, Ellen 016826
Kreutzer, Teresa 044475
Kreuzberger, Robert 047882
Kreuzer, Dr. Barbara K. 048242
Kreuzer, Hermine 002939
Krichman, Michael 047821
Krick, Robert K. 044056
Krieg, M. 010657
Krieger, Edino 004364
Krieger, Friedrich 001983
Kriegsman, L. 029851
Kriemler, Andrea 036893
Krier, Jean 027894
Krier, Patricia 043746
Krikken, J. 029851
Kriller, Beatrix 002934
Krings, Dr. Michael 019099
Krippner, Regina 020063
Krischel, Dr. Roland 018341
Krischka, Karl 002216
Krishnappa, Dr. M.V. 022015
Krishtalka, Dr. Leonard 045205
Kristament, Werner 002300
Kristan, Dr. Markus 002845
Kristensen, Hans H. 009112
Kristensen, Tenna 008885
Kristfinnsson, Örlygur 021980
Kristiansen, Peter 008956
Kristic, Dr. Danilo 021888
Kristinsdottir, Gudrun 021931
Kristinsson, Axel 021936
Kristjansdottir, Gudbjorg 021953
Krištof, Andreas 002945
Kristoffersen, Åge 030844
Kristy, Ben 044001
Kritsotakis, Dr. Konstantin 018794
Kritzas, Charalambos 021169
Kritzman, George 045466
Kriuacrk, Kathi 047298
Krivitz, James 045894
Krivokapič, Momičilo 034202
Krivoshejev, Vladimir 034279
Krivova, N.N. 033568
Krizanac, Milica 034163
Krizner, L.J. 046389
Krjakunova, Nadežda PProkofjevna 033112
Krjukov, Anatolij Charlampievič . . . 033148
Kroča, K. 008427
Kroča, Květoslav 008425, 008790
Krock, Andreas 018809
Kroczak, Czesław 031862
Kroczyński, Hieronim 032011

Kroeber-Wolf, Dr. Gerda .. 017168, 017182
Kröger, Dr. Jens 016131
Kröhnert, Gesine 020148
Kröhnert, Dr. Gesine 020151
Krönke, Rudolf 018354
Krönsjö, Marianne 036547
Kroeper, Dr. Karla 015979
Kröplin, Detlef 021040
Krösche, Klaus 016847
Krog, Paul 037810
Krogedal, David 043239
Krogh, Leila 008868
Krogh-Nielsen, Anna 008805
Krogstad, Bjørn R. 031016
Krohm, Prof. Dr. Hartmut 016173
Krohm-Steinberg, Sabine 016847
Krohn, Robin 042212
Król, Adam 032214
Królik, Janusz 032195
Kromann, Erik 009021
Kronbichler, Dr. Johann 002616
Kronenbers, Johannes 017079
Kronenfeld, Daniel 046278
Kronenwett, Heike 015854
Kronig, Karl 036932
Kronjäger, Dr. Jochen 018806
Kronquist, Bo 010192
Kroon, Rita 009398
Kropevec', Sergij Pavlovič 038318
Kropf, Dr. Christian 036933
Kropf, Joan 047719
Kropivka, Georgij Andrijovyč 038417
Kroqh, Finn E. 031229
Krotky, Gene 045330
Krouse, Dr. Susan 043575
Krouthen, Mats 031285
Kroy, Eadwierd 046682
Krpan, Sonja 007828
Krpata, Dr. Margit 002961
Krucký, Marian 008734
Kruczyński, Dr. Andrzej 032469
Krueger, Alice F. 045789
Krüger, Frank 017862
Krüger, Dr. Gundolf 017474
Krüger, Hans 015574
Krueger, Hilary 048975
Krueger, Dr. Ingeborg 016333
Krüger, Prof. Dr. Kersten 019895
Krüger, Dr. M. 034731
Krüger, Martin 018732
Krueger, Thomas 017282
Krüger, U. 018697
Krüger, Ulrich 018267
Krüper, Jochen 017080
Krug, Martina 017749
Krug, Wolfgang 002619
Kruger, Gert 029103
Kruk, Karol 032510
Krukowski, Wojciech 032421
Krull, Regine 016987
Krumova, Božura 004857
Krumpöck, Dr. Ilse 002910
Krupa, Alain-Gérard 003594
Krupa, Dr. Vladimír 034408
Krupp, Dr. Ingrid 020759
Kruppa, Gail 048588
Kruschen, Franziska 006877
Kruse, Anette 009080
Kruse, Hans 008954
Kruse, Dr. Hans-Joachim 019640
Kruse, James 043780
Kruse, Prof. Dr. Joseph A. 016832
Kruseman, Pauline W. 029164, 029210
Kruska, Peter 018251
Kruszynski, Dr. Anette 016834
Krutina, Dr. Ivan 008274
Krutisch, Dr. Petra 019352
Krutova, Marina Anatoljevna 032979
Kruus, Ülle 009394, 009398
Kruytz, Rick 044079
Krużel, Krzysztof 032027
Krylov, V.M. 033820, 033835
Krylova, Raisa Nikolaevna 033900
Kryza-Gersch, Dr. Claudia 002934
Krzemiński, Jerzy 032305
Krzemiński, Prof. Wiesław 032059
Krzesinska, Caroline 040999
Krzeszowiak, Aleksander 032345
Krzmarzick, Pam 046276
Krznarić, Stjepan 007697
Krzykowska, Zofia 032386
Krżyzaniak, Prof. Lech 032239
Kseniak, Dr. Mieczysław 032135
Kubadinow, Irina 002934, 002971
Kubassek, Dr. János 021720
Kube, Dr. Alfred 016430, 016432
Kube, Jan K. 015839, 020379
Kubiak, Anna 031824
Kubizek, Mathilde 001721
Kublanovskaja, Natalija Alekseevna 033577
Kubli, Dr. Renate 018526
Kuboschek, Andreas 017486
Kuboshima, Seiichiro 027301
Kubota, Gaylord 047288
Kubota, Dr. Tadashi 027084
Kubrak, Zygmunt 032124
Kucharski, Karen 043690
Kuchorenko, Konstantin Gavrilovič 033218
Kuchyňka, Zdeněk 008434
Kučinskij, Stanislav A. 033749
Kuck, Barbara 047252
Kuckertz, Josefine 015979
Kucra, Scott 042075
Kučuk, Julija Valerjevna 033335
Kuczek, Irena 032156
Kuczyńska, Urszula 032172
Kudo, Masahide 026525
Kudrjavcev, Aleksandr Abakarovič . 033913
Kudrjavceva, Olga 033736
Kübler, Christof 037784
Kübler, Dr. Gabriele 019814
Kübler, Sabine 015756
Küchler, Dr. Thomas 016240
Kuefstein, Elisabeth Gräfin 002533
Kühbacher, Andrea 002097
Kühebacher, Dr. Egon 025659
Kühhas, Margareta 002796
Kuehhas, Thomas A. 046779
Kuehl, Tracey K. 042187
Kühle, Sandra 019377
Kühling, Karin 018594
Kühn, Christine 016101
Kühnel, Dr. Anita 016101
Kuehnert, Leonard A. 041670
Kümmel, Dr. Birgit 015644, 015645
Künnapuu, Kalver 009432
Künnecke, Otto 016286
Kuenzel, Kurt 044148
Künzl, Dr. Ernst 018794
Künzl, Dr. Susanna 018794
Künzle, Fredy 037260
Künzler, Walter 037578
Kürten, Hans Peter 019791
Küster, Babette 018572
Küster, Dr. Bernd 019470
Küster-Heise, Katharina 018809
Küttner, Sybille 017698
Kufel, Tadeusz 032193
Kufeld, Klaus 018701
Kugel, Natalija Arkadjevna 033637
Kugina, Marija Borisovna 033020
Kugler, Andrea 019323
Kugler, Georg 002943
Kugler, Hans 016903
Kugler, Dr. Lieselotte 016012
Kugler, Dr. Walter 037050
Kuhfeld, Ellen 045908
Kuhl, Jane R. 045575
Kuhl, Dr. Uta 020039
Kuhlmann-Hodick, Dr. Petra 016797
Kuhn, Anja 016771, 017800
Kuhn, Prof. Dr. Axel 018618, 053194
Kuhn, Dieter 037738
Kuhn, Reinhilde 018156
Kuhn, Thomas G. 042900
Kuhn, Werner 019201
Kuhnke, Manfred 017104
Kuijers, Arie 034558
Kuiper, A. 029774
Kuiper, Dr. J. 029396
Kuiper, J. 029418
Kuitunen, Antero 009627
Kujukina, Tatjana Savvateevna 033986
Kujundžić, Zilka 003941
Kukk, Inge 009429
Kukko, Timo 010004
Kukla, Gabriele 016027
Kukla, Dr. Jon 042472
Kuklik, Mirosław 032270
Kuklová, Zdenka 008789
Kukovalska, Nelya M. 038326
Kukuruzova, Nina V. 033757
Kulakov, Viktor Evegenevič 033088
Kulczycka, Wanda 031849
Kuldna, Kersti 009398
Kulęgowski, Mieczyslaw 032224
Kulemeyer, Jorge Alberto 000596
Kulesa, Chester . 041812, 043601, 048066
Kulhanek, Karin 002934
Kulichikchin, Vladimir 038257
Kulik, Gary 049265
Kulik, Zbigniew 031981
Kulikowski, Jenny 047317
Kulinčenko, Galina Aleksandrovna 033338
Kulinič, V'jačeslav Jakovyč 038297
Kuljachtina, Ljubov Fëdorovna 033145
Kulkarni, B.S. 022106
Kulke, Willi 016771, 018459
Kullenberg, Ulrika 036549
Kulling, Catherine 037250
Kullnigg, Johann 002792
Kulmala, Matti 010186
Kulnytė, Birutė 027864
Kulygina, Svetlana Sergeevna 033599
Kumada, Tsukasa 026986
Kumar, Jitendra 022247
Kumar, Samarendra 022233
Kumar, Dr. Sarvash 022072
Kumasaka, Yoshihiro 026656
Kumazawa, Hiroshi 027169
Kume, Atsuko 027194
Kumela, Marjut 009513
Kumirai, Albert 049576, 049579
Kumler, Delorise M. 042958
Kumler, Phyllis 042117
Kummer, Edelbert 037450
Kummer, Prof. Dr. Stefan 021000
Kumpfmüller, Peter 002538
Kunac, Ana 007755
Kunar, Dr. Arun 022071
Kundar, Cynthia A. 046200
Kunde, Harald 015422
Kung-Haga, Vivian 045757
Kuniholm, Thor H. 029036
Kunow, Prof. Dr. Jürgen 020993
Kunst, Beate 015990
Kuntz, Edward 043136, 046753
Kunz, Hartmut 002525
Kunz, John 048995
Kunz, Jürgen 019037
Kunz, Mary Ellyn 046042
Kunz, Richard 036893
Kunz, Veronika 002525
Kunze, Prof. Dr. Max 020316
Kunze, Prof. Dr. Walter ... 002335, 002336
Kunzemann, Dr. Thomas 019670
Kuo, Shi Yu 007327
Kuononoka, Américo António 000098
Kuosmanen, Hannes 009599
Kupec, Dr. Tomas 008637
Kuper, A. 029250
Kupiec, Janina 032496
Kupka, Andreas 018129
Kuprijanov, Aleksandr Alekseevič . 033479
Kuragina, Ljudmila Anatoljevna 033268
Kuraishi, Dr. Mahmud 003101
Kurant, Dr. Bogdan 032448
Kuraya, Mika 027256
Kurban, Michael J. 042858
Kurčakova, Olga Mykolaïvna 038377
Kurdiovsky, Horst W. 001865
Kurella, Dr. Doris 020358
Kuri, Prof. Vilson 000036
Kuring, Alfons 019557
Kuring, Gertrud 019557
Kurosawa, Hiroshi 027203
Kuroyanagi, Tetsuko 027152
Kurpik, Maria 032459
Kurre 017910
Kurth, Joanna 010180
Kurtz, Dr. John K. 042495
Kurtz Schaefer, Guillermo S. 034884
Kurućev, Dragana 034281
Kurz, A. 019935
Kurz, Birgit 020356
Kurz, Elmar 002294
Kurz, Friedhelm 019010
Kurz, Helma 017117
Kurz, Dr. Herbert 016746
Kurz, Dr. Hugo 036878
Kurz, Jürgen 016989
Kurz, Manfred 020884
Kurze, Gisela 018598
Kurzel-Runtscheiner, Dr. Monica .. 002934, 003015
Kurzenberger, Jim 048219, 048220
Kusche, Dagmar 019055
Kushwaha, M.R.S. 022244
Kusnecova, Anna Grigorevna 032972
Kussé, Kristel 003418
Kussi, Kurt 021050
Kussmann-Hochhalter, Andreas .. 019398, 019399
Kuster, Emma Maria 015703
Kuster, Dr. P. 030093
Kusuma, Agung 022532
Kusumajaya, Dr. Made 022416
Kutluay, Sevgi 038102
Kutsioğlu, F. Suzan 038019
Kutter, Fritz 001715
Kutz, Artur 015875
Kuuioka, Yasuo 027282
Kuusk, Sven 001150
Kuuskemaa, Jüri 009398
Kuutsa, Tommi 009668
Kuvšinskaja, Ljudmila Anatoljevna 033204
Kuwahara, Keiichi 026463
Kuysters, Janneke 029867
Kuzeev, Rail Gumerovič 033993
Kuzel, Prof. Hans-Jürgen 017032
Kuzina, Marina Nikolaevna 033980
Kužma, Pavel 034344
Kuźma, Teresa 031997
Kuzmanić Pierotić, Ivo 006908
Kuzmić, Zdenko 007849
Kuzmin, Aleksej 033834
Kuzmin, Kirill Stanislavovič 033761
Kuzmits, Dr. Wolfgang 001825
Kuznecov, Nikolaj 033580
Kuznecova, Ljudmila Valentinovna 033724
Kuznecova, Natalija 033777
Kvaran, Gunnar B. 031070
Kvaran, Dr. Olafur 021966, 021975
Kvisle, Colleen 006819
Kvist, Kari 009498
Kwack, Dong Suk 027497
Kwakernaak, A.D. 030064
Kwang-ho, Dr. Hahn 027563
Kwasigroh, David 046749
Kwaśniewicz, Dr. Włodzimierz 032099
Kwasnik, Elizabeth I. 038560, 038561
Kwiadas-Wierzbicka, Ludwika 031980
Kwiatkowski, Prof. Marek 032450
Kwiatkowski, Phillip C. 045163
Kwiatkowski, Zygmunt 031943
Kwiecinski, William 043632
Kwok, Dr. Kenson 034290
Kwok, Kian Chow 034296
Kyas, Dr. Vojtěch 008294
Kyazim, K.M. 003085
Kyek, Martin 002561
Kyle, Peter 040287

Kyler, Duane 042941
Kyllönen, Elva 009472
Kyø Hermansen, Cathrine 008859
Kyparissi-Apostolika, Dr. Aikaterini 021153, 021349
Kyriazi, Nelli 021190
Kyriazopoulos, Prof. Basil 021388
Kyriazopoulou, Katerina 021225
Kytr, Hobe 044716
Kyupchupov, Georgi 004837
La Bianca, Domenico 024048
La Fayette, Aubert 015332
La Gamba, Prof. Filippo 023128
La Katos, Donald R. 045226
La Malfa, Francesca 024654
La Morgia, Dr. Jasmine 024545
La Porte, John Thomas 045140
La Regina, Prof. Adriano 025556
La Roche, A.J. 030567
La Rosa, Jean-Louis 011434
Laabs, Dr. Annegret 018770
Laajo, Eero 009605
Laaksonen, Tapio 009759, 009760
Laballe, Gérard 011279
Labanič, Eugen 034366
LaBar, Laurie 041905
Labarque, Ineke 003163
Labarre, Angélique de 011145
Labarthe, Olivier 037132
Labastar, Henri 005383
Labaste, Jacqueline 013555
Labat, Béatrice 015217
Labaune, Patrick 015094
L'Abbate, Vito 023957
Labbé 012443
Labbe, Armand 047945
Labbe, Daniel 015020
Laber, Philip 045718
Laberee, E.F. 005384
LaBier, Brenda 048795
Labonne, Michel 010708
Laborderie, Gérard 014896
LaBorwit, Melanie 045194
Labourdette, Anne 015184
Labovvić Marinković, Liljana 003925
Labrador, Ana Maria Theresa P. . . . 031776
Labrails, Marie-Dominique 014999
Labuda, Dr. Jozef 034308
Labuschagne, L. 034683
Lacabanne, Marie 005298
Lacabe, Jean-Marc 014983
Lacasse, Johanne 006459
Lacchi, G. 024383
Lăce, Mara 027771
Lace, Simon 040391, 040832
Lacena, Daniel L. 031665
Lacerna, Daniel L. 031677
Lacey, Eileen A. 042164
Lacey, Michael 001010
Lacey, Susan J. 042031
LaChance, Michelle 006729
Lachatenere, Diana 046399
Lacher, Gerhard 003002
Lachinger, Dr. Johann 002240
Lachish, Z. 023073
Lachmuth, Uwe 016888
Łaciuk, Adam 031850
Lackey, Doris 045151
Lackner, Franz 002990
Lackner, Dr. Helmut 003009
Lackner, Thomas 002280
LaComb, Gerald 046573
Lacovara, Dr. Peter 041866
Lăcrămioara, Marin 032776
Lacy, Kyleen 044756
Laczko, Valerie 043798
Ladd, Audrey 046442
Ladenburger, Dr. Michael 016318
Ladi, Adrian 043451
Ladier, E. 013129
Ladišić, Jure 007754
Ladleif, Dr. Christiane 015578
Ladlow, Nick 039970, 039977
LaDouceur, Philip Alan 049374
Laduceur, H. 006346
Laenen, Marc 003766
Läufer, Egbert 017717
Laevskaja, Galina Leonidovna 033590
Lafargue, Guy 010875
Lafer, Celso 004506
Laffon, GÈrard de 011961
Laffon, Juliette 013630, 013630
LaFollette, Diane 045343
LaFollette, Mary 044080
Lafon, Alain 012749
Lafond, Frédéric 012291
Lafont-Couturier, Hélène 010882
LaFontaine, Charles 047890
LaFontaine, Mary 048571
Lafontant Vallotton, Chantal 037374, 037375
Laforet, Andrea 005504
Lafragette, Florence 014578
LaFrance, Liselle 041598
Lagabrielle, Sophie 013719
Lagardere, Geneviève 014819
Lagaso, N. Trisha 047886
Lagercrantz, Jacob 036546
Lagercrantz, Kristian 036623
Lagerkrans, Jacob 036236, 036237, 036777
Lagerwaard, Drs. Cornelieke 019996
Łagiewski, Dr. Maciej 032519
Lagiglia, Dr. Humberto A. 000593
Lagnel, Cosette 037251
Lagoria, Georgiana 044592, 044593
Lagos, Marta 043435
Lagoutte, Claudine 010611
Lagree, Dr. Kevin 044755
Laguiche, Comte R. de 010468
Lagumdžija, Ermana 003941
Lagvik, Elisabeth 036253, 036254, 036256
Lahcéne, Zghidi Mohamed 000062
Laher, Herman 001679
Lahikainen, Dean 047733, 047741
Lahn, Tore 030821
Lahr, Jason 048228
Lahti, Markku 009634
Lahtinen, Maija 010078
Lahulla, F. 035416
Lai, Piero 024213
Lai, Selina 016028
Laier, Dr. Heinrich 016477
Lainesse, M. Sylvain 006681
Laing, D.W. 038932
Laing, Greg 044481
Laing, Henry 003903
Laing-Malcolmson, Bonnie 044301
Lainhoff, Thomas A. 045723
Lais, Bruno 020068
Laitinen, Suvi 009519
Laitman, Nanette 046282
Lajevs'kij, Sergij Lazarevič 038232
Lajoie, Léon 005656
Lajos, Asperjan 021748
Lajos, Dargay 021748
Lajoux, Jacques 011949
Lake, Susan 048912
Laken, L. 029698
Lakin, W.G. 040683
Lal Gaur, Banwari 022080
Lalaounis, Ioanna 021177
Lalev, Ivan 004699, 004743, 004744
Lalevic, Olga 003941
Lallemant, Marie-Françoise 011148
Lally, Michael H. 045510
Lalošević, Aleksander 034234
LaLouche, Judith 047356
Laloue, Christine 013640
Laluc 013495
Lam, Andrew 007127, 007128
Lam, Anita 045600
Lam, Prof. Peter Y.K. 007113
Lam, Tiffany 007119
Lama, Luís 031542
Lamaestre, Laurence de 011943
Lamard, Maria 018648
Lamasters, Raymond 044378
Lamb, Donna 041889
Lamb, Jennifer 001076
Lamb, Joseph 041735
Lamb, Nancy 048053
Lamb, Rebecca B. 041796
Lamb, Susan 040918, 040922
Lambacher, Lothar 016104
Lambaša, Gojko 007791
Lambel, T. de 011827
Lambers, Drs. P. 030240
Lambert, Al 045619
Lambert, Alice 046851
Lambert, Anne 045589
Lambert, Don 048202
Lambert, Françoise 037678
Lambert, Dr. Frederick A. 049140
Lambert, Helen 043858
Lambert, John 039330
Lambert, Kirby 044503
Lambert, Marianne 041876
Lambert, Marie-Jeanne . . 011225, 012741
Lambert, Ruth 040381
Lambert, Susan 040307
Lambert, Thierry 003623, 003624
Lambert, William E. 043164
Lambert, Yves 010588
Lambertson, John Mark 044727
Lambertye, Jean de 011470
Lambeth, Linda 005289
Lambilly, Comtesse Louis de 014613
Lambley, Alex 040922
Lambon, Corinne 014653
Lambousy, Greg 046259
Lambraki-Plaka, Prof. Dr. Marina . 021170
Lambrecht, Miriam 003353
Lambrechts, Lilian 042324
Lambrigger, Josef 037358
Lambropoulos, Iraklis 021441
Lamesch, Chantal 011396
Laminou, Souley 030668
Lammassaari, Taina 009492
Lammertse, F. 030088
Lamonaca, Marianne 045826
Lamontagne, Nicole 006337
Lamouret, Prof. Alfredo Daniel . . . 000147
Lamp, Frederick 041969
Lampard, D. 039813
Lampe, Dr. Karl-Heinz 016337
Lampens, Dieter 003163
Lampinen, Pekka 009496
Lampl, Brigitte 001943
Lampl, Johann 002793
Lampl, Dr. Sixtus 020557
Lamprecht, Anett 018572
Lamprecht, M.S. 034707, 034708
Lamschus, Dr. Christian 018741
Lamy, Laurence 015061
Lancaster, Robert 039989
Lancelot, Antoine 014182
Lancmanis, Imants 027693, 027721
Land, Mary 039102
Land, Winfried 001849
Landau, Dr. Sandra 019168
Landauer, Susan 047902
Lande Moe, Tore 031244
Landen, A. Wayne 006108
Landeraasen, Paul 048050
Landert, Markus 037697
Landes, Carolyn 045794
Landis, Prof. Dr. Anna Maria 024399
Landis, Ellen 041613
Landis, Jamye 047924
Landis, Judy 046915
Landis, Mary Ann 041682
Landman, Dr. Neil H. 046286
Landmann, Jörg 015600
Landmann, Jürgen 019238
Landois, Marie-Ange 010835
Landová, Blanka 034395
Landress, Helen T. 042036
Landrum-Bittle, Jenita 041839
Landry, Edmond 005527
Landry, Frédéric 005609, 005633
Landsbergen, Michael 001575
Landsmann, Hannah 002964
Lane, Dr. Andrew 039881
Lane, Dr. John R. 043269
Lane, Joshua W. 043368
Lane, Kathleen 048773
Lane, Kerstin 042882
Lane, Margaret Anne 042076
Lane, Maria 049230
Lane, Martin 006101
Lane, Nick 039445
Lane, Oliver 038585
Lane, Richard B. 047624
Lane, Steve 039152
Lane, William 049150
Lang, Alfred 016209
Lang, Anton 002869
Lang, Prof. Berthold 002972
Lang, Brian 043770
Lang, Brian J. 047056
Lang, Elisabeth 014881
Lang, Ewald 017576
Lang, Frank 020374
Lang, Gabriele 019623
Lang, Dr. Helmut 002971
Lang, Irma 034262
Lang, Manfred M. 002540
Lang, Merike 009405
Lang, Dr. Odo 037061
Lang, Paul 037128
Lang, Sabine 019137
Lang, Tom 047944
Lang, Ulrich 017188
Lang Walker, Barbra 005178
Langan, Lorie 047500
Langbein, Wolfram 019933
Langberg, Dr. Harald 008992
Lange, Dr. Albert de 019449
Lange, Allynne 045013
Lange, Andrzej 032317
Lange, Christian 018907
Lange, Cortina 036625
Lange, Dieter G. 019793
Lange, Dietmar 020682
Lange, Prof. Frederick W. 042354
Lange, Gerhard 020202
Lange, Jane 047920
Lange, Dr. John 040660
Lange, Dr. Justus 016393
Lange, Karl Wilhelm 017277
Lange, Monika 018809
Lange, Rich 048630
Lange Malinverni, Jonas R. 004178
Langel, Carmen 042678
Langelan, Mary 048942
Langelier, Jacques 014707
Langer, Dr. 018488, 019828
Langer, Agnes von 021850
Langer, Brian 001532
Langer, Dr. Brigitte 016511, 018221, 018482, 019224
Langer, Dr. Heiderose 020568
Langford, E. 041149
Langham, B. 001198
Langhammer, Peter 002166
Langhammerová, Dr. Jiřina 008639
Langhof, Jörgen 036271
Langhoff, Helmut 020823
Langhorne, Richard 038672, 041127
Langkafel, Sonja 017883
Langland, Leo 045793
Langley-Ware, Lyntia 043131
Langlois, Daniel 006390
Langman, David 030643
Langner, Inge 017485
Langner, Kerstin 018574
Langos, Barbara 015495
Langrell, Opal 006882
Langsbury, Hoani 030491
Langston, Linda 042677
Langton, B.R. 038835

Langton jr., Sara 047898
Långvik-Huomo, Marianne 009472
Lanham, Tracy 045868
Lanier, Lance 048743
Lanigan Wood, Helen 039447
Lankford, Éamon 022856
Lannerbro Norell, Maria 036265
Lanning, Bruce 048063
Lannon, John 042315
Lannoye, Henri 003243
Lansdown, Robert R. 042033
Lanser, Dr. Klaus Peter 019157
Lansky, Aaron 041694
Lanszweert, Willem 003683
Lanth, Lynn 043372
Lantos, Titus 002186, 002433
Lantz, Jerry A. 044124
Lantz, Marcel 014395
Lantz, William 043660
Lanyon, Scott M. 045914
Lanz, Dr. Hanspeter 037784, 037814
Lanzarini, Viviana 023435, 023441, 023453, 023458
Lanzinger, Dr. Michele . . . 024778, 026113
Lapa, Dr. Pedro 032642
Lapalus, Marie 012839, 012840
Lapetra, Damaso 034841
Lapeyre, Jean-François 014999
Lapi Ballerini, Dr. Isabella 024194
Łapiak, Dorota 031879, 031880
Laplana, Josep de C. 035509
Lapor, Ardin 048428
Laporte, Gerald 041778
Lapp, Holger 019041
Lappalainen, Ari 010038
LaPrelle, Robert 043262
Lapsley, Peter 003899, 052694
Laqua, Prof. Dr. Wolfgang 017411
Laquatra, Carolyn 042767
Laqueste, Marc 011556
Laquindanum, Felicidad 031764
Laranjeira de Schroeder, Prof. Viviana Nuñes 000361
Laray, Carolyn J. 044580
Larcher, Pedro Bruno 004175
Larco de Alvarez Calderon, Isabel . 031545
Lareida, Andrea 037051
Larey, Frank 039283
Large, Carol 046667
Large, Christine 038768
Large, Joan T. 046964
Large, Stephen 001392
Larguem, Salima 000073
Lark, Thomas C. 041613
Larkins, Catherine 049024
Larl, Rupert 002079
Larner, Bronwyn 001186
Laroche, Walter Ernesto 041517
Larocque, Peter 006354
LaRosa, Gail 042016
LaRose, Helen 005751
LaRowe, Annette 044341
Larque, Beverley 045222
Larquin, Olivier 013708
Larrañaga, Juan Ramón 035324
Larrañaga, Maria Isabel de 000171
Lars, Rogen 012399
Larsch, Georg 017126
Larsen, Carsten U. 008958, 008981
Larsen, Karen 049118
Larson, Dr. Andre P. 048763
Larson, Ara 048474
Larson, Barbara 048856
Larson, Bradley 046737
Larson, Donald 048278
Larson, Francine 043374
Larson, Harry 048152
Larson, John 044621
Larson, Dr. Judy L. 047465
Larson, Julie 047750
Larson, Neal L. 044541
Larson, Sidney 043073
Larson, Silvia 006800
Larson, Steve 048249
Larsson, Åke 036192
Larsson, Hans-Ove 036625
Larsson, Hugo 036511
Larsson, Lars-Erik 036618
Larsson, Peter 036426
Larsson, Thorbjörn 036622
Larsson, Ulf 036651
Larsson Modin, Anita 036705
LaRue, Dr. Hélèna 040654
LaRue, Dr. Hélène 040665
Lárusdóttir, Unnur 021958
Larvová, Hana 008606
Lary, Christian de 012979
Lasansky, Jeannette 045244
Lasansky, Leonardo 047698
Lasfargues, Jacques 012812, 014531
Lash, Michael 042867
Lasheras Corruchaga, José Antonio 035833
Lasić, Višnja 007732
Lasius, Dr. Angelika 018888
Laskey, Jane 040431
Lasley, Tom 047498
Lasmane, Daina 027776
Lasowa, Teresa 032488
Lassen, Thomas W. 009018, 009019
Lassere, Odile 013375
Lassnig, Johann 037201
Lasson, Dr. E. 019451
Lassotta, Dr. Arnold 016274, 016771
Lastic, Henri de 014187
Laštovková, Dr. Věra 008474
Lastra, Cristina 000180
Lastu, Didier 015023
László, Dr. Gabor 021869
László, Dr. Péter 021810
Laszlo, Želimir 007854
Latady, Bill 042355
Latanza, Dr. Antonio 025549
Lategan, L. 034561
Laterza Parodi, José 031450
Latham, Charles 048545
Latham, Stanley A. 048812
Latimer, Dr. Bruce 042986
Latondress, Paul 005283
Latour, Patrick 013555
Latourelle, Philippe 014513
Latsay, Brenda 005869
Latschar, Dr. John A. 044183, 044184
Lattanzi, Dr. Elena 024004, 024005, 026303
Lattanzi, Vito 025555
Latu, Jacques 013128
Latuconsina, Dr. Achmad 022449
Laturner, Sybille 020038
Latvala, Anja 010050
Lauand, Débora 004530
Laub, Dr. Peter 002567
Laub, Dr. Richard S. 042502
Laubach, Simone 018100
Laube, Kurt 019124
Laube, Robert 016771, 017800
Laubenberger, Dr. Manuela 002934
Laubie, M. 015132
Laubier, Lucien 013562
Laudat, František 008640
Laudenbacher, Konrad 019048
Lauder, Leonard A. 046418
Lauder, William T. 041699
Lauderdale, David 044811
Laue, Christoph 017883
Lauenborg, Michael 008841
Lauens, Joël 012408
Lauer, Dr. Bernhard 018181
Lauer, Keith G. 041846
Lauermann, Dr. Ernst 001702, 002748
Lauermann, Frank 045676
Laughlin, Patricia J. 048348
Laughlin, Phyllis 043626
Laughton, Barbara 042786
Laughton, Rodney 048037
Laugier, Pierre-Henri 010420
Laukkanen, Rauni 010213, 010214
Launchbury, Michael 040230
Laurencin, André 011196
Laurent, Dominique 005502
Laurent, Elizabeth M. 046989
Laurent, Isabelle 003369
Laurenza, Joseph 044254
Lauridsen, Henning Ringgaard . . . 009147
Lauridsen, Inger 008919, 009132
Lauridsen, Laurie 046241
Laurière, Claudine 013260, 013263
Lauring, Kåre 008897
Lauritzen, Ruth 044313
Lauro, Dr. Maria Giuseppina 025514
Laus, Harry 004107
Lausson, Mirja 036682
Lautanen-Raleigh, Marcia 043687
Lautenberg, W. 034589
Lauter, Prof. Dr. H. 018816
Lauter, Dr. Marlene 021003
Lauter, Dr. Rolf 018806
Lautz, Thomas 018311
Lauwers, J. 003180
Lauxerois, Roger 015210
Lauxmann, Dr. U. 020364
Lauzière, Yves 006462
LaValle, Nancy 043743
Lavalle Argudín, Mario 028507
Lavanchy, Jean-Claude 036932
Lavanchy, John 043483
Lavandera López, José 035625
Lavandeyra-Schöffer, Eléonore de . 013551
Lavarnway, Carrie 042450
Laveck, Jocelyn 006814
Lavédrine, Marc 011186
Lavelle, Phyllis 042382
Lavergne, Laurence 012036
LaVerne, Thomas 048172
Laverty, Bruce 046924
Lavery, Sally Ann 041689
Lavie, Pierre 012657
Lavigue, Emma 013640
Lavin, Lucienne 048976
Lavino, Jane 044809
Laviolette, Suzanna 047685, 047686
Lavis, Tom 005505
Lavoie, Suzanne 006350
Lavoy, Carl L. 005261
Lavoyer, Martin 011016
Lavrenjuk, Benedykt Antonovyč . . 038403
Law, Erica 040817
Lawes, Glen 039107, 039816
Lawitschka, Valérie 020495
Lawley, I. 041121
Lawrance, Sarah 039140
Lawrason, Helena 005320
Lawrence, Brad 006255
Lawrence, D.R. 001415
Lawrence, John 045062, 045559
Lawrence, John H. 046255
Lawrence, T.G.B. 040823
Lawrence, Wade 042731
Lawrimore, Katrina P. 044176
Lawson, Amanda 000774
Lawson, H. William 049359
Lawson, Julie 039425
Lawson, Karol 045528
Lawson, Pam 001122
Lawson, Paul 039795
Lawson, Paul W.G. 038804
Lawson, Scott J. 047294
Lawton, Ann L. 043027
Lawton, Peter 040772
Lawton, Rebecca 044002
Lawton, Simon R. 041203, 041204
Laxton, Ailisa 038628
Lay, Chan Kim 027989
Lay, Diana 038916
Layher, Hermann 020220, 020265
Layne, Janice 044127
Layton, Dwight 042197
Lazareva, Lilija Georgievna 033086
Lázaro López, Agustín . . . 035003, 035006
Lazárová, Eva 034313
Lazarus, Fred 041995
Lazenby, William C. 046905
Lazer, Laurie 047868
Lažetić, Predrag 034172
Lazov, Gavrail 004863
Lazzarini, Dr. Antonio 025267
Le, Ma Luong 049523
Le, Trung 049544
Le Bail, Jean-Marc 013840
Le Bailly de Tilleghem, Serge Baron 003809
Le Bihan, Olivier 013402
Le Blanc, Lisette 030332
Le Brun, Foni 027894
Le Cieux, Laurence 032762
Le Foll, Typhaine 013237
Le Gall, Régine 013335
Le Gendre, Bernard 012446
Le Grange, Judy 034632
Le Grelle, Daniël Graaf 003184
Le Harivel, Adrian 022763
Le Leyzour, Philippe 010610, 015016
Le Maître, Claude 010907
Le Nouëne, Patrick 010392, 010394, 010397, 010398
Le Rouzic-Giovanneli, Gisèle 012723
Le Saux, Marie-Françoise . 015126, 015127
Le Stum, Philippe 013978
Le Tissier, P. 040936
Le Van Ho, Mireille 013555
Le Vay, Jonathan 040485
Leach, John 041225
Leach, Mark 042761
Leach, Patricia 044522
Leader, Prof. Mary 022771
Leafdale, Norris 044440
League, Alice 043466
Leah, Mervyn 039983
Leahy, K.A. 040972
Leahy, Mary 046007
Leal, José H. 047943
Leal Spengler, Eusebio 007980
Leaman, David L. 048579
Leandry, Mario 005280
Lear, Paul 046746
Leatherman, Lawrence 048457
Leavesley, Dr. James 001498
Leavey, Jane 041877
Leavitt, Christie 044509
Leavitt, Tracey 005871
Lebas, Frédéric 017715
Lebeau, Monique 013303
Lebedeev, P.I. 033391
Lebedeva, Alla Markovna 033561
Lebegern, Robert 020448
Leberknight, Alan 042002
LeBlanc, Bernard 005900
LeBlanc, Denise 041576
LeBlanc, Guy R. 048250
Leblanc, Jacqueline 014523
LeBlanc, Karen M. 048845
Leblanc, Pascal 015054, 015055
LeBlanc, Suzanne 045190
LeBlond, Dan 047101
Lebouteiller, Claire 015336
LeBouthillier, Louis 005219
Lebrasseur, Marie-Josée 006119
Lebrero Stals, José 035854
Lebrun, Jacques 015182
Lebsack, Ren 006240
LeCato, J.M. 042726
Lečev, Dečko . . 004746, 004747, 004787, 004788, 004886, 004888, 004889, 004890, 004891, 004893
Lecher, Belvadine 042695
Lechien Durant, Françoise 003317
Lechner, Dr. Gregor Martin 001878
Lechner, Martin 002744
Lechowski, Andrzej 031830
Lechuga, Dr. Ruth 028448
Leclair, Alain 012393
Leclair, Tom 006078
Leclef, Louis 003172

LeCleire Taylor, Gay 045876
Leclerc, Claudette 006853
Leclerc, Marie-Andrée 005902
Leclerc, Patrick 010964
Leclerc, Paul 046390
Leclerc, Paul-André 005727
Leclercq, Jean-Paul 013638
Leclert, Hélène 014100
LeCompte, Sarah 041952
Leconte, Philippe 003607
Lecoq-Ramond, Sylvie . . . 011433, 011433
L'Ecotais, Emmanuelle de 013630
LeCount, Charles 047314
Lecouturier, Yves 011053
Lecuillier, Michel 010678
Lecuyer, Françoise 013435
Leder, Carolyn R. 040250
Lederer, Carrie 048839
Lederer, Irene 017908
Lederer, Nan 042354
Ledermair, Martin 002666
Ledet, Claudette 006221
Ledford, Thomas G. 045527
Ledoux, François 005825
Leduc, Dawn 005000
Lee, Bok Hyung 027525
Lee, Chris 040673
Lee, Christopher 042279
Lee, Colin 039999
Lee, Cynthia 046372
Lee, David L. 047777
Lee, David S. 047315
Lee, Ellen W. 044748
Lee, Eric M. 046507
Lee, Hee-Jae 027607
Lee, Hyun-Sook 027577
Lee, Jackie 048866
Lee, Janie C. 046418
Lee, Jean 046220
Lee, Prof. Jong-Sang 027602
Lee, Karen 006029
Lee, Lawrence 043059, 046676
Lee, Lila J. 048684
Lee, Linda 039999
Lee, Molly 043780
Lee, Ra Hee Hong 027627
Lee, Robert 046298
Lee, Roslyn 039748
Lee, Seung-Koo 027483
Lee, Steven 041974, 041985
Lee, William B. 047919
Lee, William D. 042450
Lee, Wuh-Kuen 007363
Lee Lindsey, Treva 042708
Lee Moss, Barbara 048740
Lee Pederson, Laura 046401
Lee Reid, Katharine 042985
Leebrick, Gilbert 044345
Leech, William J. 042280
Leeder, P.G. 041206
Leedy, Harriet 044156
Leedy, Sherry 044922
Leen, Frederik 003316
Leen, Mary 042566
Leenes, Tony 029864
Lees, Diane 040224
Leestma, Jeffrey K. 043341
Leeuw, G. de 029515
Leeuw, Prof. R. de 029226
Lefarth, Ute 020965
Lefébure, Amaury 011850
Lefebvre, Pascal 003585
Lefebvre-Canter, Michelle 042942
Lefever, Joel 044575
Lefevre, Gérard 013222
LeFevre, John 043062
Lefèvre, Prof. Patrick 003352
LeFevre-Stratton, Leslie 046268
Leff, Kathy 045826
Lefftz, M. 003617
Lefki, Michaelidou 008222, 008223
Lefort, Jacques 013197
Lefour, Pierre 014960
Lefrançois, Michèle 010909, 010910
Lefrançois, Thierry 012320, 012322, 012324
Lefrancq, Janette 003353
Legac, Mirjana 007783
Legarda, Eduardo 031700
Legarda, Rosalita R. 031700
LeGath, Judith B. 048503
Legault, Jocelyne 006772
Legendre, Françoise 014123
Legêne, Dr. S. 029194
Legg, Dr. G. 038846
Legget, J.A. 039974
Legleiter, Kim 045992
Legout, Gérard 010488
Legrand, Edith 012219
Legrand, Sybille 003249
Legros, Charles 003828
Leh, Dennis E. 042372
Lehan, Kathy 038820
Lehberger, Prof. Dr. Reiner 017695
Lehmann, Christine 019975, 019976
Lehmann, Gérard 012650
Lehmann, Dr. Hans-Ulrich 016797
Lehmann, Kai 020053
Lehmann, Dr. Karin 020164
Lehmann, Klaus 017934
Lehmann, Randall 044163
Lehmann, Dr. Ulrike 018707
Lehmann, Ursula 020809
Lehmann-Enders, Christel 018543, 018716
Lehnemann, Dr. Wingolf 018747
Lehner, Adam 046325
Lehnert, Marie Josée 027898
Lehnherr, Dr. Yvonne 037096, 037100
Lehodey, Colette 014014
Lehr, Dr. André 029283
Lehr, William 044445
Lehtinen, Dr. Martti 009543
Leiber, Christian 017588, 017589
Leibnitz, Dr. Thomas 002971
Leibrand, Sue 048050
Leich, Jeffrey R. 044026
Leicht, Walter 019884, 019888
Leichty, Erle 046993
Leidner, Udo 019288
Leidy, Susan 045618
Leif, Elizabeth 048386
Leighton, John . . 029239, 029441, 029451
Leijen, A.J.M. 029310
Leijerzapf, Dr. I.Th. 029852
Leijon, Anna-Greta 036625
Leijten, C.J.M. 029583
Leikauf, Barbara 001938
Leilund, Helle 008999
Leimu, Tuula 010220
Lein, Sharon 043387
Leinfelder, Prof. Dr. R. 019099
Leinicke, Kris G. 047494
Leinonen, Paula 010117
Leinweber, Dr. Ulf 018203
Leinz, Dr. Gottlieb 016861
Leipold-Schneider, Gerda 001763
Leiseth, Sylvia 049002
Leismann, Burkhard 015452
Leistner, Dr. Gerhard 019755
Leite, Ana Cristina 032632, 032636, 032657
Leite, Prof. Michael 042696
Leitgeb, Dr. Franz 001844, 001932
Leitgeb, Otto 002150
Leitmeyer, Wolfgang 020263
Leitnaker, Connie 045142
Leitner, Andreas 002757
Leitner, Dr. Friedrich W. 002142
Leitner, Norbert 002639
Leitner, Stefan 001675
Leitner-Böchzelt, Susanne 002224
Leitner-BÖchzelt, Susanne 002225
LeJambre, L.A. 042310
Lejeune, Louis 003201
Lejnieks, Dr. Janis 027740
Lekholm, Kerstin 036303
Lekson, Steve 042354
LeLacheur, Melinda 041690
Lelieur 013558
Leloup, Michel 011780
Lemaire, Michèle 010937
Lemaire, Philippe 014785
Lemal Mengeot, Chantal 003367
Lemańska, Stefania 031927
Lemaster, Leroy 045735
Lemasters, Howard 042023
Lemback, Jack 045751
Lembert, Dan 041958
Lembke, S. 016111
Lemcke, J. Peter 016554
Lemelle, François 013553
Lemercier, Christian 010900
Lemeunier, Albert 003593
LeMieux, Linda D. 043061
Leming, C.F. 041063
Lemire, Marie 005939
Lemky, Barbara 005314
Lemle, Robert 044141
Lemmon, Dr. Alfred 046255
LeMoine, Dr. Geneviève 042488
Lemoine, Serge 013678
Lemons, C.R. 043928
Lemos, Nikolas S. 021412
Lemothe, Peter Thomas 046225
Lempka, Wayne 046269
Lenaers, J.H. 029531
Lenaghan, Patrick 046346
Lenarczyk, Leszek 031935
Lenarduzzi, Nelson 000369, 000370
Lenarz, Michael 017178
Lencquesaing, May-Eliane de 013753
Lengerken, Prof. Dr. Dr. von 017667
Lenglet, Marie-Cornélie 012677
Lengyel-Kiss, Katalin 021682
Lenk, Elfriede 002455
Lenk, Dr. Sabine 016828
Lenkiewicz, Jolanta 032053, 032055
Lenković, Mario 007787
Lennard, John Barret 000956
Lennig, Dr. Petra 015990
Lenoir, Yves 003291
Lensen, Jean-Pierre 003835
Lenski, Jean-Pierre 014738
Lenssen, Dr. Jürgen 020609, 020994
Lent, Eric 042586
Lentini, Dr. Maria Constanza 024286
Lentino, Miguel 049451
Lentz, Lamar 047555
Lentz, Dr. Thomas 048884, 048908
Lenz, Berta 017423
Lenz, Gerhard 016344
Lenz, Helmut 017163
Lenz, Iris 020355
Lenz, Mary Jane 046383
Lenz-Weber, Dr. Diana 017731
Leo, Dana 046757
León, Imelda de 028171
Leon, Lamgen 046372
León Rivera, Jorge de 028440
León Rivera, Melba Rocío 007439
Leonard, Amy 041576
Leonard, Claude 013186
Leonard, Douglas 005065
Léonard, Georges 003437
Leonard, Glen M. 047774
Leonard, Jessie 045884
Leonard, Jim 006142
Leonard, Mark 045433
Leonard, R.A. 039258
Leonard, Robert 045609
Leonardo-Finger, Jascin 046125
Leoncini, Dr. Luca 024313
Leone, Carol 048853
Leonhardt, Günter 018453
Leonhardt, Rainer 018959
Leonori, Dr. Maria Chiara . 024093, 024098
Leontiev, Andrej 033701
Leontjeva, Sofija Jakovlevna 033595
Leopardi, Anna 025402
Leopold, Prof. Dr. Rudolf 002940
Léotoing, Comte de 015008
Lepage, Jean 013351, 013354
Lepdor, Catherine 037246
Lepe, Marcella 028681
Lepičić, Janko 034187
Lépine, André 003364
Lepine, Brigitte 010551
Lépine, Luc A. 006322
Lepley, John G. 043889, 043890
Leppala, Vesa 009507, 010063
Lepper, Beate 020735
Lepper, Dr. Katharina B. 016861
Leppiniemi-Järvinen, Anita 009675
Leproust, Evelyne 013980
Lepší, Miroslav 008424
Leray, Victor 012782
Lerch, Michaela 013615
Lerebours, Lionel 021603
Leresche, Anne 037250
Léri, Jean-Marc 013579, 013621
Leritt, Sarah 039968
Lernbaß, H. 018435
Lerner, Adam 041976
Lerner, Peter 042441
Lernout, Françoise 010369
Lerolle, Aggy 013685
Leron-Lesur, Pierre 014515
Lerouge-Benard, Jean-Pierre 012000
Leroux, Doug 006128
Leroux, Jean-François 015237
Lerov, Trifon 004695
Leroy, Gilbert 012737
Leroy, Jacques 010567
Leroy, Vincent 001910
Lerrick, Dr. Yacob 022465
Lervy, Annick 013065
Lesaffre, Jean-Marie 012681
Lesák, Dr. Barbara 002979
Leschhorn, Prof. Dr. Wolfgang 016385
Lescombes, Germain 011069
Lescroat-Cazenave, Elizabeth 013499
Lesdorf, Svitlana Pavlivna 038391
Leser, Rupert 015820
Lesher, Ronald E. 047692
Leshikar, Howard B. 048524
Leskien, Dr. Hermann 019037
Lesko, Diane B. 048028, 048031
Leskova, Marina 027919
Leskovar, Jutta 002256
Leskovar, Peter 034524
Leskovec, Ivana 034464
Leslie, James 038581
Leslie, Mike 046647
Lesniewicz, Paul 017824
Leśniewska, Józefa Ewa 032091
Lesser, Ann 048861
Lesser van Waveren, Hans-Georg . 015907
Lessmann, Dr. Johanna 017715
Leßmann, Dr. Sabina 016329
Lester, Colleen C. 048624
Lester, Ellen 045045
Lester, Mary P. 049322
Lestraden, M.P. 029311
Leszczyński, Wojciech 032532
Letenayova, Dr. Zdenka 034333
Letendre, Julie 043360
Letertre, J.B. 014893
Leth, Gwen I. 047393
Letourneur, Céline 011779
Letroye, Marcelle 003627
Letschert, Edmund 020726
Lettany, Lieve 003635
Lettner, Christoph 002638
Letts, A. 034612
Letz, Andrea 018290
Leu-Barthel, Angelika 017683
Leuba, Marion . . 010714, 010715, 010717
Leumann, Alexander 037091
Leuschner, Dr. Jörg 019971
Leušin, Viktor Vladimirovič 033031
Leutenegger, Dr. Marco . . . 036857, 037575
Leutenegger-Kröni, Tanja 037163

Leuzinger, Dr. Urs 037092
Lev-Ari, Y. 022998
Levá, Kimmo 009658
Levander, Karin 036764
Levčenko, Vitalij Vasiljevič 033319
Levens, Dwight R. 043438
Leventon, Melissa 047857, 047871
Leverton, Raymond 044782
Lévesque, André 006404
Levey, Georges 014716
Levi, A. 023001
Levi, Preston 043932
Levièvre, Francine 005947
Levin, Annika 013597
Levin, Dalia 022933
Levin, Mai 009398
Levin, Nikolaj Iljič 033898
Levin, Pamela 048061
Levine, Beverly 043992
Levine, Janet 046408
Levine, Kenneth 046401
Levine, Dr. Louis 046373
Levine, Phyllis 046348
Levinho, José Carlos 004385
Levinthal, Beth E. 044680
Levitt, S. 039971, 039974
Levkin, Jaroslav Borisovič 033664
Levy, David C. 048891, 048892
Levy, Harry A. 045810
Levy, Sue M. 046930
Lew, Dr. Irena 032182
Lewallen, Constance 042166
Lewandowski, Marian 032240
Lewandowski, Ryszard 032165
Lewars, James 049278
Lewenhaupt, Dr. Inga 036493
Lewerken, Dr. Heinz-Werner 016811
Lewicki, Ireneusz 032144
Lewin, Jackie 047650
Lewin, S.J. 039033
Lewis, Anne V. 047059
Lewis, Forrest 049215
Lewis, Frank C. 041755
Lewis, George 048324
Lewis, Greg 048707
Lewis, Larry 049292
Lewis, Lesley 006620
Lewis, Louise 046558
Lewis, Maisie 000781
Lewis, Merri 041620
Lewis, Michael 041618
Lewis, Oli 045185
Lewis, Richard 046905
Lewis, Robert 041905
Lewis, Robert K. 045256
Lewis, Steve 043775
Lewis, T. 038826
Lewis, Vel A. 037945
Lewis, William 049174
Lewis, William R. 047002
Lewis-Crosby, Meg 038541
Lewis Schaal, Cynthia 042753
Ley, Dr. Andreas 019082, 019086
Leyoudec, Maud 014737
Leypold, Denis 014877
Leys, K. 003289
Leys, Kathleen 003303
Leysen, Veerle 003613
Leyten, C.J.M. 030220
Leyva, Maria 048883
Lezarrdiere, A. de 012228
Lhagvasüren, I. 029007
L'Hostis, Denez 011642, 011643
Li, Lifu 007025
Li, Linna 007090
Li, Qianbin 007097
Liabeuf, Brigitte 014930
Liagouras, Angelos 021235
Liaño, Marta 049464
Liao, Kui-Yin 007365
Liapis, Kostas 021118
Liavas, L. 021187
Libbus Boon, Edna 005366
Libby, Reis 047611
Liberatore, Laurie 043690
Libert, Laura L. 046959
Libin, Laurence 046364
Liby, Håkan . . . 036735, 036744, 036744, 036748
Lică, Paul 032829, 032830
Lichenecker, Christian 002719
Lichovyj, Igor Dmytrovyč 038278
Lichte, Dr. Claudia 020999
Lichtin, Christoph 037299
Lichtlé, Francis 012192
Lichty, Robert C. 042605
Lickleder, Dr. Hermann 018222
Lickteig, Dorothy L. 044149
Licky, Maurice 006898
Liczkov, Sergej Nikolajevič 032972
Liddell, Lynne 039867
Liddle, Peter 039253
Liddle, Dr. Peter 039960
Lideń, Magnus 036740
Lidequist, Dr. Christina 036590
Lidman, Roger 047014
Lidtke, Thomas D. 049064
Līduma, Ilze 027716
Lieb, Hartmut 017616
Liebelt, Glenn T. 001189
Liebenberg, O.J. 034561
Lieber, Vincent 037385
Lieberman, Chrissy 048645
Lieberman, Richard K. 045387
Lieberman, William S. 046364
Liebgott, Dorion 006583
Liebgott, Niels-Knud 008956
Liebhart, Prof. Dr. Wilhelm 015521, 015522
Liebich, Haimo 019067
Liebscher, Sabine 018769
Liechtenstein, Friedrich 002530
Liechti, W. G. 037592
Liedekerke Beaufort, Comte Hadelin de 003363
Liekonen, Marita 009694
Lien, Mary 047106
Lienau, Jennifer 047960
Lienerth, J. 017082
Lienhard, Kurt 036906
Lienhard, Ulrich 037756
Liensdorf, Klaus 020437
Liepe, Heidrun 019659
Liepold-Moser, Bernd 001959
Lierville, Sylviane 011687
Liesbrock, Dr. Heinz 016352
Liesch, F. 018939
Liesens, Liliane 003314
Lieth, Elke-Luise von der 016195
Lif, Malka 023066
Lifshitz, S. 023016
Liggett, G. 044490
Light, Brad 049242
Light, Dr. Helen 001448
Light, Lyn 039540
Light, Natalie de 019345, 053008
Lightbourn, Brian 003896
Lightfoot, Ricky 043169
Lighthall, Penny L. 006668
Ligne, Michel Prince de 003225
Lignori, Prof. Laura 026058
Ligon, Doris H. 043067
Ligon, Dr. J. David 041619
Ligon, Samantha M. 042401
Ligthart, Elisabeth 002975
Ligúde, Ginsa 027694
Liikkanen, Hilkka 010046
Liknes, Fern 005440
Lilienthal, Dr. Georg 017615
Lillehammer, Grete 031221
Lilley, Clare 041334
Lilly, Bruce 047706
Lilly, Stephanie 042749
Lilly, Tina 045577
Lim-Yuson, Dr. Nina 031730
Lima, Alida de la 031424
Lima, Dr. Francisco 032578
Lima Greene, Alison de 044648
Limbach, Dr. Adelheid 020589
Limbacher, Dr. Gabor . . . 021620, 021833, 021857
Limburg-Stirum, Comtesse F. de . . 014947
Limme, Luc 003353
Limón Delgado, Antonio 035863
Limpo Pérez, Luis Alfonso 035554
Lin, Lee Chor 034297, 034298
Linaeque, Dr. P.M. 029089
Linasi, Marjan 034523
Linciano, Dr. Antonio 024264
Lincoln, Lee 043377
Lincoln, Louise 042839
Lind, Axel 009093
Lind, Dr. Christoph 018809
Lind, Ed 047272
Lind, Evgenij Alekseevič 033773
Lind-Sinanian, Gary 048992
Lind-Sinanian, Susan 048992
Lindahl, Per 036333
Lindauer, H. 030593
Lindberg, Annika 036732
Lindberg, David R. 042163, 042163
Lindberg, Janelle 046676
Lindberg, Kathy M. 043835
Lindbom, tina 036436
Lindemann, Prof. Dr. 020502
Lindemann, Prof. Dr. Bernd 036890
Lindemann, Prof. Dr. Bernd Wolfgang 016049
Linden, Grace 048186
Linden, Jaap ter 030094
Lindén, Lena M. 036352
Linden, Peppy G. 042771
Lindenhofer, Harald 002975
Linder, Brad 045743
Linder, Prof. H. P. 037762
Linder, Karin 036316
Linder, Maria 036387
Linder, Marja-Liisa 010134
Linderer, Steve 045175
Linderman, Mike 043765
Lindert, Reinhard 017467
Lindgren, Göran 035478
Lindh, Anders 036498
Lindh, Marianne 036781
Lindhartseni, Ole 031318
Lindhorst, André 019496
Lindley, Ralph 040841
Lindloff, Dr. Axel 020958
Lindmayr, Burgi 002556
Lindner, Gerd 015700
Lindner, Dr. Helmut 016819
Lindner, Mathias 016562
Lindner, Walter 017358
Lindquist, Carl 044767
Lindquist, Everett 048754
Lindquist, Sven-Olof 036796
Lindqvist, Catharina 036651
Lindqvist, Per-Inge 036383
Lindqvist, Svante 036651
Lindsay, Frances 001246
Lindsay, Judy 039256
Lindsay, Mike 041827
Lindsay, S.J. 040698
Lindsay, Tom 047896
Lindsay Baker, Dr. T. 044546
Lindsberger, Josef F. 001970
Lindseth, Knuth 031006
Lindsey, David 039829
Lindsey, Jack 046961, 046975
Lindsey, Jimmy 041596
Lindsey, Rob 045088
Lindström, Anneli 009580
Lindstrom, Janet 046208
Lindvall, Karin 036511
Lineberry, Heather S. 048517
Lineros, Ricardo 035056
Lines, S. 039221
Ling, Steven 041812, 048066
Lingier, Rafael 003397
Lingstadt, Kirsty 039352, 039669
Linhares, Philip 046598
Linhart, Dr. Eva 017183
Linke, Irmgard 002440
Linkov, Krasimir 004792
Linkowski, Zdzislaw 031947
Linley, Jim 039803
Linn, Joe Dale 047235
Linna, Markku 010148
Linnehan, Sharon 043467
Linnel, Eric 042273
Linnemann, Dr. Ulf 016805
Linnerr, Pip 001327
Linnertz, Rudolf 016377
Linnichenko, Antonina 038328
Linnie, Martyn J. 022778
Linnikova, Nina Jakovlevna 033807
Linou, Marie-Josée 014051, 014052
Lins, P. Andrew 046975
Linschinger, Josef 001911
Linsenmaier, Dr. Walter 037053
Linsky, Carol 047508
Linsmann, Dr. Maria 020487
Linthorne, Marguerite 005113
Linton, Dr. M. 001038
Linton, Meg 047948
Lintott, B. 030464
Linus, Frederick 044871
Linville, Tony 048361
Liot, David 014007
Liotta, Jorge 000588
Lipchinsky, Zelek L. 042152
Lipfert, Nathan 042039
Lipinski, Henry 039727
Lipka, Dieter 015713
Lipkens, Myriam 003499
Lipo, Frank 046584
Lipońska-Sajdak, Jadwiga 031987
Lipovanski, Georgi 004874
Lippe, Edward J. von der 044337
Lippens, Kathleen 003332
Lippert, Dr. Wolfgang 019042
Lippi, Angelo 024543
Lippi, Dr. Emilio 026120
Lippincott, Louise 047043
Lippman, Irvin M. 043106
Lippman, Judith 041997
Lipps, Jere 042163
Liptuga, Tatjana Ivanivna 038373
Lisai, Virginia 049118
Lisberg Jensen, Ole 008984
Liščáková, Daniela 008525
Lisenko, Mychajlo Lukyč . . 038379, 038380
Lisicyn, Viktor Borisovič 034069
Lisk, Susan J. 044382
Lisk-Hurst, Corrie 044331
Liška, Dr. Pavel 019755
Líška, Peteras 034441
L'Isle, Viscount de 040690
Lisnjak, Katerina Jevgenivna 038282
Lisowski, Silvia 020811
Liss, David 006054
Lissague, Bernard 010958
Lissens, Paul 003318
Listen, Simon 039345
Lister, Alison 040186
Listoe, Philip 006419
Listopad, John 048319
Lithén, Hans-Olof 010202
Litochleb, Dr. Jiří 008646
Little, Faye 039053
Little, John 042451
Little, L. 043692
Little, Tom 047497
Little, Tricia 044525
Littlefield, Jennifer 047018
Littleton, Kim 048555
Littlewood, Barry 039154
Litvak, Silvia 000315
Litwin, Dr. Jerzy 031904, 031920, 031922, 031923, 031931, 031955, 032387
Litz, Dr. Christine 018334
Litzenburg, Thomas V. 045281
Liu, Cary Y. 047240

Liu, Guang Rui 007050
Liu, Guang Tang 007057
Liu, Yuchuan 007051
Lium, Randi N. 031288
Lively, Carter C. 041742
Livengood, Donald L. 049158
Livengood, R. Mark 045234
Liverani, Dr. Paolo 049422, 049423, 049426, 049429
Livesay, Thomas A. 042121
Livezey, Dr. Bradley C. 047044
Livingston, Glenda A. 048821
Livingston, Jan 047401
Livingston, Judith 045333
Livingston, Dr. Valerie 048108
Livingstone, Judy A. 005339, 005340
Livland, Haakon 030947, 031270
Livneh, M. 022998
Livsey, Karen E. 044829
Liwei, Cheng 006985
Lixfeld, Gisela 020097
Lizarazo, Plata 007396
Lizon, Sylvian 013903
Lizzadro, John S. 043688
Ljiljak, Aleksandar 003938
Ljøkjell, J. 030931
Ljubaščenko, Anna Ivanovna 033940
Ljubić, Josip 007819
Ljubimov, Vladimir Alekseevič 032991
Ljubović, Prof. Blaženka 007789
Ljungberg, Louise 036563
Llabrés, Pere-Joan 035616
Llagostera Martínez, Dr. Agustín 006926
Llanas, Joan 036055
Llanes, Manuel 035915
Llanes-Myers, Susan 044641
Llazari, Vasil 000032
Llewellyn, David 039736
Llewellyn, Mike 039705
Llinas, Chr. 013205
Llobet, Guy 011421
Llongarriu, Marissa 035556
Llorens, Tomás 035438
Llorente, Sofía 035405
Llorente, Tina 044648
Lloveras, Fernando 032719
Lloyd, Alan 001505
LLoyd, Alison 040693
Lloyd, Deanna S. 045654
Lloyd, Kenita 045388
Lloyd, Kristin B. 041646
Lloyd, Stephen 039425
Lloyd Harvey, Peter 040731
Lmas, Jean de 011730
Lo Schiavo, Dr. Fulvia 025804
Loaring, A. 040542
Lobanova, Galina Pavlovna 033110, 033118
Lobaõ, Dr. Paulo 032578
Lobas, Aleksandr 027401
Lobb, Muriel 045319
Lobb, Sylvia 044829
Lobbig, Lois 041671
Lobjakas, Kai 009402
Lobkareva, Antonina Vasilevna 034005
Lobo, Dr. Wibke 016017
Lobos Lápera, Victor 006913
Lochman, Dr. Tomas 036879, 036908
Lochmann, Reinhart 015445
Lochrane, Dr. Charles G. 047825
Lock, Alan 039347
Lock, Victoria A. 045074
Lock-Weir, Tracey 000703
Locke, Dr. H. 005998
Locke, Michelle 043161
Lockett, Daniel 040354
Locklair, Paula 049254
Lockwood, Dave 043497
Lockwood, David 039296, 039298, 039299, 039300
Lockwood, D.C. 030611
Lockwood, Dr. Yvonne 043575
Loderer, Klaus J. 015640
Lodewijk, W. 029671
Lodge, Penny 047059
Lodowski, Dr. Jerzy 032514
Loeb, Gwen 047915
Löb, Heidrun 037791
Löbach, Prof. Bernd 016604
Loeben, Dr. Christian E. 017757
Löber, Eva 018759
Löbert, Dr. Horst W. 020376
Löbke, Dr. Matthia 017849, 053379
Löcken, Monika 015593
Loeffler, Robert J. 046016
Löffler, Ruth 016855
Löfström, Lena. A 036689
Löher, Jochen 016767, 016772
Löhr, Dr. Alfred 016411
Löhr, H. 017670
Löhr, Dr. Hartwig 020483
Loehr, Scott W. 041895
Löliger-Henggeler, Elisabeth 037423
Lönnebo, Lovisa 036645
Lönnström, Yvonne 010211
Loera Chávez y Peniche, Dr. Margarita 028519
Loers, Dr. Veit 018978
Lösch, Bernhard 025659
Lösche, Wolfgang 019058
Loest, Mark A. 047657
Lötsch, Prof. Dr. Bernhard 002967
Lövgren, Amanda 036591
Löwenkopf, A.Z. 022902
Lofgren, Donald 042939
Lofgren, John Z. 048771
Loft, Elaine P. 044620
Lofthus, Brian 044262
Loftin, Jack 041763
Loftin, Jim 044101
Loftus, John 020154
Loftus, Sydney L. 046687
Logan, Brad 045204
Logan, Burt 042348
Logan, Joyce 006167
Logan, Judy 044346
Loge, Øystein 030806, 030807
Logger, R. 029225
Logghe, Marc 003801, 003803, 003804
Lohberg, Gabriele 020481
Lohe, Michael 019073, 053313
Lohiniva, Leena 010046
Lohmann, Dr. Frank 037307
Lohmann, J.H.A. 029689
Lohmann, Uwe 020760
Lohmeier, Prof. Dr. Dieter 018248
Lohrenz, Mary 044798
Lohse, Dr. E.S. 047107
Loichemol, Hervé 011799
Loidl, Josef 001726
Loikkanen, Kirsi 009923
Loiko, Patricia 042334
Loisel, Dr. Ulrike 002448
Loitfellner, Tamara 002969
Loizeau, Sigolène 010882
Loizou Hadjigavriel, Loukia 008221
Lojdová, Ivona 008698, 008706
Løken, Trond 031221
Lokensgard, Dr. Lynne 042083
Lokin, Dr. D.H.A.C. 029411, 029412, 029413
Lokki, Juhani 009552
Lomaheftewa-Slock, Tatiana 047967
Lomakov, Dmitrij Aleksandrovič 033418
Loman, D.E. 029637
Lomatter, Odilor 037470
Lomax, James 039961
Lomax, Jenni 040107
Lombardi, Gloria R. 046473
Lombardi, Michele 012674
Lombardo, Dr. Giovanna 025548
Lombardo, Marta Alicia 000351
Lombardo, Romualda 031422
Lombino, Mary-Kay 045378
Łonak, Wojciech 032187
Londoño, Jaime Manzur 007429
Londos, Eva 036361
Londt, Dr. Jason 034700
Lonergan, Gillian 040845
Long, Avis 042512
Long, Betty 044237
Long, Charles 047799
Long, Greg 049304
Long, J. Grahame 042728
Long jr., Paul V. 047227
Long, Philip 039424
Long, Phillip C. 042929
Long, Sachia 043501
Long, Steve 046358
Longbourne, Dr. D. 040447
Longcore, Robert R. 046478
Longenecker, Martha W. 047823
Longenecker, Vickie 043941
Longevialle, Ghislain de 011962
Longhauser, Elsa 047988
Longhi, Alberto 025618
Longhi, Janice 038876
Longhi, L.A. 038873
Longley, Dione 045841
Longo, Prof. Giuseppe 026008
Longtin, Barbara C. 046103
Longuein, Paul 014565
Longwell, Alicia 048254
Lonnberg, Thomas R. 043766
Look, Johannes 015933
Looper, Gail S. 048205
Loose, Annegret 017646
Loose, Helmut 015642
Loosli, Jean-Pierre 037335
Lopas, Julie 044310
Lopata, Robert 042184
Łopatkiewicz, Zdzisław 031968
Lopatkin, Michail Vasiljevič 033894
Lopes, Manuel Teixeira 032700
López, Al Ignatius G. 031772
López, Ana María 035925
Lopez, Donald 048922
López, Edgar 007481
López, Jorge 028513
Lopez, Julie Anna 047963
López, Magdalena 035405
López, Manuel R. 009353
López, María Jose Muñoz 035115
López, Mónica Alejandra 000137
López Alvárez, Joaquín 035222
López de Arriba Reyes Durán, Mercedes 035405
López Fernández, Francisco Javier 035098
López Franco, Amparo 007526
López Hervás, Maria Victoria 035410
López Ortiz, Amparo 035813
López Pimentel, María del Carmen 007943
López Portillo Romano, Carmen 028478
López-Vidriero, Luisa 035439
López Wehrli, Silvia 036076
Loppa, Linda 003166
Lopreato, Paola 023904
Loquenz, Norbert 002522
Lorbeer, Marie 016115
Lorblanchet, Hélène 013200
Lorck, Bjorn 029099
Lord, Allyn 047523
Lord, Anne 001567
Lord, Gary T. 046555
Lord, Victoria 044979
Lord, Victoria A. 044978
Lorek, Amy E. 044534
Loren, Diane 042567
Lorenčak, Marja 034487
Lorenz, Dr. Angelika 019156
Lorenz, Barbara 001742
Lorenz, Dr. Harald 017478
Lorenz, Margaret 039882
Lorenz, Dr. Ulrike 017373, 017374, 019755
Lorenzen, Dr. Heidrun 019899
Lorenzi, Franco 024696
Lorenzi, Georges 014805
Lorenzo, Liliana Ema 000230
Lorenzo Rosales, Elaine 008045
Lorenzoni, Dr. Mario 025891
Loret, John 045626
Lorian, F. 015612
Loring Brace, C. 041733
Łos, Ewa 032132
Los, Dr. W. 029245
Losavio, Sam 042044
Losch, Michael 049115
Loshi, Ygal 023042
Loskott, Herbert 001666
Lossnitzer, Carin 016573
Lossnitzer, Dr. Hans 016573
Lotfullin, Galim F. 033594
Loth, Jan 045174
Lott-Büttiker, Dr. Elisabeth 037210
Lottermann, W. 015678
Lotz, Theo 049261
Lotze, Manfred 018636
Lotze, Ulrich 015964
Lotzwig, Hartmut 020189, 020190
Lou, Xia 007278
Louati, Ali 037984
Loud, Patricia C. 044009
Louderback, Paul 048654
Lõugas, Anne 009398
Loughton, Gregory 006626
Louis, Dr. Eleonora 002560
Louis, Hubert 010917, 010918
Louma, Mark 046088
Lounsbury, Kathryn 041564
Lourdes Barreto, Maria de 004102
Loureiro Saavedra Machado, João de 032663
Louring, Aage 008874
Loustau, Alain 012645
Louvencourt, Amaury de 011174
Louvi, Dr. Aspasia 021248, 021472, 021477, 021500
Louw, Prof. D.J. 034753
Louw, J.P. 034693
Louw, P. 034669
Louwagie-Neyens, Linda 006394
Louwman, E.V.N. 030051
Lovdžieva, Marija 004853
Love, Jackie 046519
Love, Mindi 043604
Loveland, Linda 048300
Lovell, Carol 045291, 048397
Lovell, Charles M. 048497
Lovell, Russell A. 047935
Lovell, Shirley 005637
Lovén, Lucie 031110
Lovenz, Marianne 045186
Loverin, Jan 042635
Lovett, Margaret 045291
Lovick, Emily 043978
Lovie, Robert 039529
Loving, Charles R. 046574
Lovis, Dr. William 043575
Lovrinović, Nikola 003942
Low, Dr. James 005705
Low, William 045248
Lowe, Carole 047114
Lowe, Dr. D. 040253
Lowe, Janet 005278
Lowe, John 043509
Lowe, Joseph 043108
Lowe, Susan 028047
Lowell, Kathleen 044579
Lowell, Molly W. 043506
Lowenfeld, David 042995
Lowly, Tim 042826
Lowrey, Annie 049162
Lowrey, Carol 046381
Lowrey, Timothy K. 041619
Lowry, Dale 005225
Lowry, Glenn D. 045389, 045390, 046374
Loxa, Juan de 035207
Loyau, Anne 010692, 010693
Loynes, G. 041435
Loyrette, Henri 013685
Lozada Arias, José 007386
Lozado de Solla, Noemi 000110

Lozano, Prof. Luis-Martín 028457
Lozano Forero, Martha Janet 007641
Lozano Peña, Carlos 007645
Lozanova, Dr. Ralitsa 004863
Lu, Wensheng 007155
Lu Allen, Dr. Marti 047274
Lubac, Marcel 011896
Lubbe, T.A. 034563, 034564, 034567, 034696, 034750, 034775, 034777
Lubic, James E. 044447
Lubimova, L.M. 033410, 033411
Lubina, Michail 032294
Lubitz, Dr. Telse 017821
Lubowsky Talbott, Susan 043424
Luboznski, Joe 044052
Luca, Claudia 032964
Lucas, Annemarie 019143
Lucas, Cynthia L. 044321, 044322
Lucas, Daniel 013043
Lucas, Enriqueta T. 031801
Lucas, Judith S. 042925
Lucas, Martyn 039980
Lucas, Mike 038896
Lucas, Palma B. 046974
Lucas, Ritchie 043145
Lucas, Robert 044550
Lucchese, Dr. Angiolo del 026272
Lucchesi Ragni, Dr. Elena 023517, 023525, 023526
Lucchini, Mario 037146
Luce, Donald T. 045914
Luce, H. Christopher 046314
Lučevnjak, Silvija 007760
Lucey, Denis 022809
Luchetti, Dr. Glauco 024129
Luchs, Alison 048924
Luchter-Krupińska, Lidia 031893
Lucidi, Augusto 023799
Luck, Barbara R. 049177
Lucke, Dr. Arne 017935
Luckeneder, Walter 002643
Luckhardt, Prof. Dr. Jochen 016385
Luckhardt, Dr. Ulrich 017694
Luckhurst, Ailene 042949
Luckow, Dr. Dirk 018247
Łuczkowski, Jan 032196
Luderowski, Barbara 047055
Ludewig, Dr. Thomas 019271
Ludington, Link 045580
Ludvigsen, Lucia 021553
Ludvigsen, Peter 008957
Ludwig, Andreas 016929
Ludwig, Dr. Jochen 017234
Ludwig, Jürgen 016717
Ludwig, Dr. Renate 017829
Ludwig, Rudolf 002127
Ludwig, Ursula 015799
Luebbers, Dr. Leslie 045753
Lübbers-Ukena, A. 016686
Lübeck, Elisabet 036378
Lübeck, Karla-Kristine 020148
Lüchinger, Paul 037659
Lüder-Zschiesche, Adelheid von .. 016783
Lüders, Dr. Klaus 019728
Lüderwaldt, Dr. Andreas 016426
Lüdi, Heidi 037268
Lüdke, Dr. Dietmar 018169
Lueg, Dr. Gabriele 018330
Lührs, Günter 017249
Lüll, M. 020372
Lüpkes, Dr. Vera 018607
Lüps, Dr. P. 036933
Lüps, Dr. Peter 037663
Lüscher, Hans 037812
Lüscher, Regula 037499
Lütgens, Dr. Annelie 020965
Lüth, Dr. Friedrich 017557, 019999
Lueth, Virgil W. 048210
Lüthi, Werner 036993
Lüthy, Dr. Hans A. 037001
Lütkemeyer, Ursula 019822
Lütken, Ilona 020361, 020365
Lüttichau, Dr. Mario-Andreas von . 017075
Lufkin, John C. 043430
Luft Dávalos, Rafaela 028638
Lugaski, Dr. Thomas P. 047377
Lugger, Leopold 002282
Luginbill, Troy 045531
Luginbühl-Wirz, Regula 036927
Lugosi, Dr. József 021652
Lugtenburg, Anneke 034717
Luh, Willi 016490
Luhs Agrilar, José María 035468
Luhta, Caroline 042994
Luijten, G. 029227
Luisi, Vincent 043532
Luisi-Potts, Billy 048113
Lukáč, Ján 034357
Lukacs, Maria 032868
Lukas, Clemens 015906
Lukasch, Dr. Bernd 015547
Lukasiewicz, Nancy 041834
Łukaszewski, Andrzej 032320
Lukaszuk-Ritter, Joanna 002950
Lukatis, Dr. Christiane 018187
Luke, Gregorio 045381
Luke, Suzanne 006776
Lukeš, Dr. Michal 008636
Lukesch, I. 002911
Lukeschitsch, H. 002772
Lukić, Ivan 034181
Lukičeva, Alla Stepanovna 033407
Lukina, Inna Nikolaevna 033678
Lukowczyk, Evelyn 017672
Lukšić, Hilar 007784
Lulav, S. 022902
Lum, Shawn 048722
Luma, Ramon E.S. 031771
Lumley, SimonWhite 040083
Lummel, Heinz 018175
Lummel, Dr. Peter 016022
Lumpkin, Libby 045182
Luna, Juan J. 035429
Luna Moreno, Luís 036003
Lunardi, Prof. Ernesto 024300
Lund, Arnstein 031287
Lund, Elaine H. 045699
Lund, Mikael 008946
Lund, Tora Jervell 030821
Lundberg, Åsa 036732
Lundberg, Carl-Anders 009750
Lundbergh, Hans 036753
Lunde, Oeivind 031281
Lundgreen, James 045641
Lundgren, Britta 036732
Lundgren Nielsen, Hanne 008902
Lundh, Göran 036582
Lundin, Sally 047255
Lundkvist, Anders 036267, 036268
Lundrigan, Dr. Barbara 043575
Lundström, Dr. Agneta .. 036601, 036606, 036627, 036646, 036658, 036661, 036664
Lundström, Agneta 036667
Lundström, Sven 036324, 036325
Lungarotti, Dr. Maria Grazia 026042
Lunger, Brian 005646
Lunger-Valentini, Eva 002195
Lunghi, Enrico 027886
Lungu, Alexandru 032935, 032936
Lunn, Will 046690
Lunning, Elizabeth 044645
Lunsford, P. Celina 017162
Lunsingh Scheurleer, Dr. R.A. 029163
Lunt, Amanda 041442
Lunt, Sara 039635, 040003, 041460
Luojus, Susanna 010177
Lupal, Kimberly A. 005167
Luperini, Prof. Ilario 025259
Luptáková, Eva 034349, 034396
Lupton, Ellen 046319
Lurie, Doron J. 023092
Lusa Monforte, Guillermo 034917
Lusardi, Richard A. 047383
Lusardy, Martine 013595
Lusby, D.A. 030591
Luse, Vel 044973
Lushear, Jen 046264
Lussi, Kurt 037081, 037297
Lussky, Richard 043330
Luštinec, Jan 008414
Lutaenko, Konstantin Anatoljevič . 034052
Luten Schuitema, E.A. 030256
Luterbach-Renggli, Hansjörg 037537
Luterbacher, Hannes 037164
Luther, Charles 043150
Luti, Claudio 024975
Lutnes, Kjell 030785
Lutnesky, Dr. Marvin 047153
Lutsic, Jennifer 047845
Luttinger, Ingrid 002096
Lutyens-Humfrey, A. 039046
Lutz, Dr. Albert .. 037770, 037789, 037796
Lutz, Gottlob 037179
Lutz, Marian 044648
Lutz, Nancy 048631
Lutz, Peter 020882
Lutz, Robert 042483
Lutz, Tina 048659
Lutz, Dr. Volker 002701
Lutz, William 043995
Lux, D. Ruth 046733
Lux, Simonetta 025544
Lux, Ulla 016838
Luxán, Elena 035415
Luxford, Bob 030568
Luyken, Dr. Gunda 015991
Luz, David W. 046872
Luz, Henrique 004530
Luz Paula Marques, Maria da 032674
Luz Ramirez Estrada, Maria de la . 007970
Luzin, Sergej Stepanovič 033272
Álvarez Lopera, José 035429
Lyall, Clare 041242
Lyall, Dr. D.C. 020372
Lybeck, Shirley 042800
Lydakis, Prof. Dr. Stelios 021200
Lydon, Andrea 022763
Lydon, Kate 047062
Lyell, D.I. 040437
Lyke, Linda 045471
Lyle, Charles T. 044152
Lyle, Janice 046798
Lyles, Pelham 049247
Lynam, Seamus 022761
Lynch, Cindy 043098
Lynch, Geraldino 022833
Lynch, Harry P. 041588
Lynch, Kevin 040003
Lynch, Thomas F. 042491
Lynch, Thomas J. 042373
Lyndaker, Vernon 043223
Lynesmith, P. 040489
Lyngby, Thomas 009112
Lynn, Bob 030427
Lynn, Judy G. 043194
Lynn, Ralph 005866
Lynx, David 049327
Lyon, David Peter 001353
Lyon, Katharine 045341
Lyons, Don 043498
Lyons, Jana 048946
Lyons, Joan 043498
Lyons, Dr. John D. 045594
Lyons, Michael 041375
Lyons, Michele 042179
Lyons, Rex 044029
Lyra, Fernando Soares 004318
Lysogórski, Krzysztof 031933
Lyssaris, Agelos 021469
Lytjen, Lokey 044808
Lytle Lipton, Susan 046352
Lytton Cobbold, Martha 039910
Lytwyn, Stephen 006876
Ma, Wei-du 006986
Maanit, G. 023007
Maarek, Lucien 014813
Maas, Klaus 016860
Maas, Wilhelm 019248
Maaß, Prof. Dr. Michael 018158
Maass, R. Andrew 043933
Maat, Erik 029608
Maaz, Dr. Bernhard 015984, 017573, 020738, 020742, 020743, 020746, 020751, 020753, 020755, 020758
Mabon, Richard 039433
Mabungule Chissano, Alberto 029054
Mac Phee, S.D. 005430, 049785
MacAdam, Barbara J. 044426
McAfee, Michael J. 049096
McAffee, Dionne 006648
MacAffer, John 041602
McAlister, Judith 042358, 043809
McAllister, Lowell 046634
McAlpine, Clark 044085
McAlpine, Dr. Donald 006354
McAnliffe, Dr. Chris 001242
McArthur, Meher 046834
MCarty, Kenneth W. 046959
MacAulay, Donald 005053
MacAulay, Margot 005053
McAuley, Joyce 041949
McAuley, Kathleen A. ... 042431, 042435, 042440
McAuley, Paul 039423
McBay, Ann 040716
Macbeth, James A. 047608
McBratney-Stapleton, Deborah ... 041716
MacBride, Frank 000837
McBride, Heather 041569
McBride, Joe 041706
McBride, Michael A. 044370
McBride, Peggy 047304
McCabe, C. Kevin 048688
McCafferty, Estelle 048305
McCaffrey, John 040307
McCall, Janet L. 047062
McCalla, Mary Bea 044126
McCallum, Cheryl 044636
MacCallum, Jack 005129
McCallum, Sue 046900
McCalman, Dr. Janet 001245
McCamphill, Debbie 038530
McCandless, Barbara 044002
McCann, Mac 042544
McCarroll, Stacey 042319
McCarte jr., John W. 042841
McCarter, John W. 042842
McCarthy, Christine 047268
McCarthy, Frances 042742
McCarthy, J. 001626
McCarthy, John J. 047973
McCarthy, Judith 022820
McCarthy, K. 030460
McCarthy, Robert 042308
McCarthy, Wayne 048848
McCartney, Dr. Nancy G. 043830
McCarty, Cara 047676
McCarty, Gayle 047341
McCarty, Kimberly 046042
McCarty, Laura 044023
McCarty, R. Paul 043914
McCaskey, Jane 046004
McCauley, John F. 042313
McCay, Bill 044845
Macchi, M. 014812
Macciotta, Prof. Giampaolo 023566, 023570
McClain, Ronald 044425
McCleave, John 006278
McClellan, Nancy 046506
McClelland, Jesse 042856
McClenny, Bart 041674
McCloskey, Anne M. 045358
McClung, Elizabeth 045845
McClure, Donna 046000
McClure, Kent 046000
McClure, Nancy 048149
McClure, Richard 048854
McCluskey, Holly H. 049140
McClusky, Pamela 048091
McCollough, Pam 045980
McCollum, Jay 043052

McComb, Joseph 046029
MacComb, Prof. Leonard 040266
McConachie, Jackie 041621
McCone, John 041688
MacConnel, Cal 043886
McConnell, Bridget 039548, 039563, 039571, 039574, 039575
McConnell, Glenn 046657
MacConnell, Raymond 042155
McCooey, Patrick 005530
McCord, Dr. Robert 045793
McCord-Rogers, Suzette 044536
McCormick, Donald 046390
McCormick, Edgar L. 044965
McCormick, Todd 042105
McCorquodale, Ross 001489
McCosh, John 030497
McCourt, Frank A. 046742
McCourt, Steve 000778
McCowan, Kurt 047539
McCoy, James P. 046920
McCoy, Jeff 047572, 047574
McCoy, Kathy 045975
McCoy, Nancy 045402
McCracken, Patrick 041678
McCracken, Ursula E. 048948
McCrary, Joel 043006
McCrary, Patrick C. 045506
McCray, Phil 048459
McCreary, Kathleen 044584
McCree, Timothy 041606
McCudden, Bruce 038816
McCue, Debbie 042195
McCue, Denise 048782
McCue, Donald 047360
McCue, Kaz 048534
McCuistion, Mary Ann 048767
McCullagh, Suzanne 042820
McCullick, Nancy 045728
MacCulloch, Alexandra 038555
McCulloch, Bruce 030557
McCulloch, Judith 044222
McCullough, Catherine 038526
McCullough, Hollis K. 048031
McCully, Robert 043909
McCurtis, Barbara S. 047818
McCusker, Alisa 045388
McCusker, Carol 047827
McDaid, Cecilia 039903
McDaniel, George W. 042731
McDaniel, Phyllis 044042
McDaniel, Robert 043535
McDaniels, Warren E. 046262
McDermott, Robin 041475
McDianmid, Gordon 005136
MacDonald, Catherine 039946
McDonald, Colin 040729
MacDonald, Colinn 039012, 041278
MacDonald, Craig 006458
McDonald, Donald M. 001287
McDonald, Doris 006084
McDonald, Douglass W. 042921
MacDonald, Elizabeth H. . . 046977, 054986
McDonald, Garry 005359
MacDonald, Dr. George 048075
MacDonald, Gerald J. 046346
Macdonald, I.H. 041097
MacDonald, Jessie 006391
McDonald, Jim 044801
McDonald, John 039800
McDonald, J.P. 045519
McDonald, Dr. L. 001435
McDonald, Marty 042516
MacDonald, Mary V. 043342
McDonald, Michael 043509
McDonald, Michele A. 045818
MacDonald, Ned 005643
McDonald, Paul 041890
MacDonald, Peter 039906
McDonald, Rebecca A. 044643
Macdonald, Robert R. 046378
MacDonald, Ruby 005295
MacDonald, S. 040255
McDonald, Susan 042471
McDonald, Sussanne 005454
McDonald, Tessa 044615
MacDonald-MacLeod, Beryl 006183
McDonnell, Jeanne 047891
McDonnell, Dr. Patricia 048469
McDonough, Stephen 041689
MacDougal, Bruce 047788, 047806, 047811
McDougall, Jamie 005119
McDougall, Kim 005504
McDowell, Anna 040989
MacDowell, Dr. Marsha 043575
McDowell, Susanne 016549
McDowell, Suzanne 043241
McEachern, Mark 048588
Macedonio, Prof. Giovanni 024052
Macek, Stanislav 008359
McElhone, William K. 042230
McElroy, L.J. 046133
McElroy, Prof. Michael B. 042564
McElroy, Sara 041927
McElwee, J.A.C. 039630
McEneaney, Eamonn 022872
McEnroe, Natasha 040136
McEntee, Holly 045594
MacEnulty, Bill 043053
Maceroni, Prof. Giovanni 025428
McEwen, Amy 046297
McEwen, Bob 044784
McEwen, Gloria 044784
MacFadden, Dr. B.J. 044103
McFadden, David 046282
McFadden, Lila 005288
McFadden, P. 034595
McFalls, W.J. 005601
McFarland, Seth 042915
MacFarlane, Aynsley 005051
MacFarlane, Nathalie 006480
MacFarlane, Sheena 040640
McFeely, Marie 022763
McFerrin, Jean 047783
McGahen, DeAnn 041653
McGarry, John H. 046105, 046106
McGary, Nancy 046352
McGaugh, Houston 048973
McGee, Maureen 045425
McGee, Prof. Mike 044095
McGee, Patrick 022744
McGehee, Thomas C. 048541
McGill, Forrest 047853
McGill, Shirley 043492
McGillivray, Allan 006677
McGillivray, Don 005986
McGillivray, Dr. W. Bruce 005404
McGinley, Edward 048872
McGinley, Dr. Jack 022752
McGinnis, Melissa S. 048464
McGirr, Margo 048345
McGivern, Andrew J. 049015
McGlumphy, D. 048655
McGlynn, Robert 046390
McGovern, Robert M. 042655
McGovern, Thomas 045443
McGowan, Jeanie L. 042620
McGrady, Dr. Patrick J. 048703
McGranahan, Doris 046649
McGrath, Joe 000904
McGrath, Steph 049135
McGraw, Linda 043133
McGraw, Steve 048078
McGreevy, Candace 048400, 048401, 048403
MacGregor, Neil 040097, 040241
McGrew, Rebecca 042938
McGuffie, Ian 006696
McGuinne, Niamh 022763
McGuinness, Ben 000978
McGuinness, Jim 049333
McGuire, Donna 006065
McGuire, Janice 044019
McGuire, Dr. Jim A. 042049
McGuire, Raymond J. 046409
MacGunnigle, Bruce C. . . . 043561, 043563
Mach, Jiří 008350
Machan, Dallas 039340
McHenry, Kathryn 049251
Macheret, Elisabeth 037026
Machhammer, Helmut 001816
Machinek, Hubert 020199
Machkovski, Petko 004758, 004935
Machneva, Margarita A. 033261
Macho, Erwin 002953
Machon, Abdurremane 029045
McHugh, Eileen 041888
McHugh, Dr. J. 041833
McHugh, Joseph 006713
McHughs, David 044021
MChuny, V.B. 034617, 034657
Macías Ramos, María Teresa 036018
Maciejewski, Andrzej 032444
Maciejunes, Nannette V. 043106
McIlhargey-Wigert, Dawn 044279
MacIlreith, Rob 005090
McInerney, Gay 042060
McInnes, Marilyn 039188
McIntosh, Jean 006168
McIntosh, Mildred 045729
McIntosh, Muriel 039584
McIntyre, Art 006299
McIntyre, Barbara 006386
McIntyre, Chris 039695, 040886
MacIntyre, Ronald 040636
Macintyre, Roy 039531
McIntyre, Stella 038766
Macintyre, Trish 040393
MacIsaac, Kim 046853
McIver, Duncan 044417
McIver, J.H. 042390
Mack, Angela 042733
Mack, J. 040097
Mack, Jeanne P. 044205
Mack, Joanne 046574
Mack, Joseph 044733
Mack, Vanessa 001516
McKague, Margot 005666
McKale, William 043971
MacKay, Allan 005718
Mackay, Andrew 041039
Mackay, Angus 039972
Mackay, Jim 041646
Mackay, John L. 042756, 042762
McKay, Kelly 005489
MacKay, Kevin 005117
MacKay, Dr. Lachlin 045024
McKay, Maria 048144
McKay, Mary Alice 046385
McKay, Patrick 047473
MacKay, Robert B. 043039
Mackay, Thomas 041221
Mackay, W.A.F. 006262
Mackechnie, John 039556
McKee, Barry 005595
McKee, Julia 046106
McKee, Kathleen 043790
McKee, Marshall 039766
McKee, Pamela 041742
McKee, Paul 039053
MacKellar, Dr. John 001280
McKellar, Stacey 005145
McKelvey, Anna 045043
McKenna, George L. 044924
McKenna, James 046660
McKenna, Sharon L. 046853
McKenrick, Fremont 043598
Mackensen, Dr. Götz 016426
Mackenzie, Althea 039731
McKenzie, Cameron 039287
McKenzie, Colin 046297
McKenzie, Graham 039549,
Mckenzie, Micahel 034571
McKenzie, Molly 042542
Mackenzie, Philippa 039662
MacKenzie, Stuart C. 042904
McKenzie, Wendy 005660
McKenzie Smith, An 039391
McKeown, Jack J. 044227
McKernan, Robert 042903, 047321, 049369
McKernan, Robert L. 047362
Mackey, Brian 040020
Mackey, David M. 044617
Mackey, Estel 048777
Mackey, Marjorie R. 041827
Mackey, Ted 048777
Mackie, Louise 042985
Mackie, Thomas 043181
McKillop, Joan 040642
Mackin, Richard E. 043953
Mackinlay, Betty 043993
McKinlay, Dawn 005854
McKinlay, Iain A. 039015
McKinley, Iain 039017, 039018
McKinley, Nancy R. 045853
McKinley, Robert 044676
McKinney, D. Frank 045914
McKinney, David 046364
McKinney, Frank B. 042717
McKinney, Jack 048811
McKinney, Janice 049161
McKinney-Tandy, Ruth 043720
McKinsey, Kristan H. 046880
McKitterick, Michael 048105
McKnight, Peg 042104
Mackowiak, Reinhild 018737
Maclagan, Dr. Helen 041307
Maclagan, Helen 041309, 041310
McLain, Charles 044994
McLain, Guy 048292
McLallen, Helen M. 045002
McLaren, Hazel 042024
McLaren, M. 001174
McLary, Kathleen 044744
McLaughlin, Belinda J. 042795
McLaughlin, Pat 046367
McLaughlin, Robert 048307
McLaughlin, Stacey B. 047541
McLaughlin, William F. 043453
McLaughlir, Dr. John 005478
McLaurin, Genette 046399
McLea 047769
McLean, Al 041011
McLean, Genetta 045248
McLean, Dr. Janice V. 041668
McLean, Kathleen 006049
McLean, Libby 039321
McLean, Linda E. 044662
Maclean, Marge 005548
MacLean, Roderick 005566
MacLean, Rusty 040869
McLean, Steve 040548
McLean Ward, Dr. Barbara 047188
McLellan, Darlene 043613
MacLellan, Heather 006155
MacLellan, Iain 045617
McLellan, Richard A. 042693
Maclennan, F. 039915
MacLeod, Cynthia 047423
MacLeod, Dr. Ian 001377
MacLeod, Kathleen 005351
MacLeod, Patricia 047745
McLeod, Roddy 039565
McLeod, Susan M. 043595
McLerran, Jennifer 041838
McLorys, Jan 042874
McLoughlin, Kevin 038845
MacLoy, David 000813
McMahon, Cynthia 042876
McMahon, James 044523
McMahon, James E. 044187
MacMahon, Rose 040065
McMahon, Stephen 048366
McMahon, Steve 048365
McManus, Carol 047933
McManus, Greg W. 030589
McManus, Marcia 043924
McManus Zurko, Kathleen 049302
McMaster, Shannon 044279
McMasters, Thomas O. 043974

McMeekin, Rebeeca B. 047328
McMenamin, Brendan 040329
McMichael, Sindy 043385
MacMillan, Bruce 043443
MacMillan, C.J. 039928
Macmillan, Prof. Duncan 039428
McMillan, Edward 043014
McMillan, Dr. R. Bruce 048284
McMorris, Sharon 043292
McMullen, Darlene 006069
McMurtie, I. 039378
McMurtrie, I. 039401
McNabb, Debra 006509
MacNabb, Vicky 047710
McNaboe, Tracey 039434
McNally, Ginger 049358
McNally, Margaret 001558
McNamara, C. J. 043863
McNamara, Carole 041736
McNamara, Mary E. 046414
McNaught, William 038615
McNeal, Joanne 043221
McNealy, Terry 046234
McNear, Sara 042861
McNeely, Don 048318
MacNeil, Malcolm 039822
McNeill, Anne E. 041477
McNeill, C. 001573
McNeilly, Kath 000929
McNelly, Dennis 046987
McNichol, Susan 006134, 006485
McNicol, Jean 006791
McNicol, Morag 040468
McNulty, E.C. 043755
McNulty, F.M. 044035
McNulty, J.L. 043755
McNutt, Jim 047809
Macon, Robert 046874
McOuat, Gordon 005875
McOwan, Daniel 001096
MacPhee, Dr. Ross D.E. 046286
McPherson, Beth Ann 046829
McPherson, Dan 043252
MacPherson, Kate 039240
McPherson, Loretta 001025
McPherson, Mark 044362
McPherson, Tommy 046829
McQuaid, Matilda 046319
Macquart, Bruno 013711
Macquart-Moulin, X. 013388
McQueen, Jack 047911, 047913
McQuillis Iscrupe, Shirley 045290
McReynolds, Anne 038664
McScowan, James 040923
McVay, Darice 048744
McWayne, Barry 043780
McWhorter, Nancy 045398
McWilliams, Edward R. 043490
McWilliams, Mary 042560
Macyszyn, Dr. Jacek 032474
Maczulis, Norbert 031984
Madanian, M. 022587
Madden, Jennifer 047932
Madden Leitner, Cynthia 043712
Maddox, Iva Jean 043963
Maddox, Margaret 045036
Madec 013849
Mader, Annita 002933
Mader, Dr. Gerald 002689
Maderek, Dorota 032292
Madersbacher, Dr. Ernst 002389
Madin, John 039465
Madjarov, Mitko 004657
Madkour, Christopher 045624
Madonia, Ann C. 049183
Madrid, Candy L. 047520
Madrid Rojas, Juan José 007599
Madsen, Inge 008884
Madsen, Jan Skamby 008916
Madsen, John 048630
Madsen, Lennart S. 008885
Madsen, Orla 008885
Madsen, Per Kristian 009143
Madshus, Eva 031069
Madurini, Dr. Giulio 024701
Madžarac, Nada 034485
Madzik, Józef 031820
Maeder, Edward F. 043368
Mädl, Else 015914
Mädl, Wilhelm 015914
Maeght, Adrien 013261
Mähl, Andrea 020953
Maek-Gérard, Dr. Michael 017195
Mäkelä, Asko 009576
Mäkelä, Sirkku 009850, 009851
Mäkeläinen, Reijo 009872
Mäki, Riitta 009800
Mäkinen, Antti 009651
Mäkinen, Marketta 009638
Mael, Stephen 039984
Mänd, Anu 009408
Maeng, Injae 027523
Männchen, Dr. Julia 017523
Mänttäri, Roy 009574
Märker, Dr. Peter 016638
Maerz, Jürgen 017203
Maes de Wit, Yvan 003639
Maesen, Mathieu 003711
Mäuser, Dr. Matthias 015877
Maeyama, Mikio 027285
Maeyama, Yuji 027009
Maffia, Prof. Cesare 024833
Maffioli, Dr. Monica 024186
Mafre, Christian 010322
Magacz, Joanna 016792
Magajne, Miljojka 034464
Magalhães, Carlos 004555
Ribeiro de Magalhães, Thales 004378
Magaña Cota, Gloria E. 028301
Magdich, Bob 048568
Magdolna, Simon 021760
Magee, Eileen M. 046924
Magee, Eugene 005803
Magee, Henry J. 046941
Magendans, J.R. 029853
Mager, Gerald Paul 019932, 019934
Mager, Dr. Karl 002075
Magersuppe, Karl 020300
Maggi, Ersilio 025375
Maggi, Gianfranco 023145
Maggi, Roberto 023846
Maggioli, Andrea 023446
Magglo-Serra, Dr. Rosanna 026047, 026074
Magidson, Phyllis 046378
Magielsen, A.F. 029809
Magill, Ronald E. 047747
Magill, Scott 046234
Magill, Tina M. 047122
Magilton, Jack 005702
Magiru, Maria 032843
Maglica, Nadja 007832
Magnago, José Carlos 000575
Magnaguagno, Guido 036897
Magnan, Oscar 044861
Magnetti, Daniela 026080
Magnin 010621
Magnin, B. 010620
Magnini, Prof. Marsilio 024026
Magnussen Svare, M. 008979
Magnusson, Inga-Lill 036404
Mago, Norma A. 031810
Magolfi, Dr. Miria 024215
Magomedova, Seir Seitovna 033945
Magras, M. 021560
Magré, Piet 029787
Magro, Antonio 023233
Magro, Pasquale 023284
Magsaysay, Dr. Eulogio Amang ... 031721
Maguin-Gonze, J. 037247
Maguindanao, Macmod 031742
Maguire, Cathy 048007
Maguire, Dr. Eunice 041964
Maguire, Nancy 042577
Magun', Marija Karpivna 038348
Magurany, J.D. 047663, 047666
Mahaffay, Suzanne 048840
Mahamadou, Kelessé 030667
Mahé, Lucien 012043
Mahecha Useche, Ernesto 007513, 007514
Mahéo, Noël 010369
Maher, Kathleen 042406
Maher, Kristie 047019
Maher, Michael 022698
Maher, Tina 038484
Maher-Kamprath, Audrey 047087
Mahida, Bhamini A. 022346
Mahilom, Mila M. 031663
Mahlknecht, Dr. Eduard 002138
Mahmoud, Assad 037831
Mahmudor, N. 049401
Mahnert, Volker 037137
Mahon, Rose 040825
Mahran, Younes 009291
Mai, Prof. Dr. Ekkehard 018341
Mai Hung, Prof. Dr. Pham 049532
Maia e Castro, Catarina 032680
Maiben, Dean 042029
Maier, Daniela .. 017090, 017091, 017092
Maier, Erhard 002600
Maier, Jakob 015533
Maier, Josef 002403
Maier, Marco 037609
Maier, Stefan 020335
Maier, Thomas 022972
Maier-Schöler, Barbara 020622
Maierhofer, Fritz 002160
Maikweki, James 027430
Mailer, Allison 006690
Mailhot, Philippe R. 006327
Maillard, Anne 012995
Maillé, Jacqueline 014252
Maillot, Suzanne 032760
Main, Sally 046265
Mainds, Paul E. 039728
Maine, Ian 038475
Mainella, Fran P. 041750
Mainieri Piedade, Leticia 004362
Mainland, Katrina 038743
Mainzer, Prof. Dr. Udo 018993
Mair, Walter 001909
Maire, Marcel 013501
Mairesse, François 003657
Mairinger, Jutta 002840
Mairot, Philippe 014638
Mairs, Kirsty 041265
Mais, Dr. Karl 002922
Maisak, Dr. Petra 017167
Maisel, Oscar 015918
Maislinger, Gerlinde 001833
Maison, Jack 046314
Maissen, Prof. Alfons 037198
Maistrello, Roberto 024588
Maitilasso, Mario 026154
Maitland, Richard 048445
Maitre-Allain, Olivier 013436
Maiwald, Dr. Christine 017715
Maiwald, Gabriele 018489
Majahad, Carol 046512
Majboroda, Ljudmyla Oleksiïvna .. 038233
Majburova, Irina Borisovna 033120
Majcen, Jože 034476
Majewska, Grażyna 032201
Majka, Mary 006296
Major, Jürgen 020326
Majorov, Aleksandr Gennadjevič .. 033154
Majstorovic, Prof. Božo 007800
Majstorović, Ljuba 034172
Majstorski, Georgi 004926
Majumdar, Prof. Swapan 022327
Makabe, Tadahiko 026698
Makarewicz, Anna 032406
Makarov, Nikolaj Michajlovič 033057
Makarova, N.B. 033396
Makeeva, I.F. 034014
Maketz-Anderle, Sabine 002180
Makholm, Kristin 045892
Maki, Linda 042954
Makkonen, Esko 010041
Maklansky, Steven 046263
Makoev, Feliks H. 033869
Makoni, P. 049579
Makovičková, Marie 008514
Makowiecki, Wojciech 032235
Makowska, Bożena 031900
Maksić, Nemanja 034266
Maksić, Slobodan 034266
Maksimova, L.D. 033697
Makwana, R.K. 022364
Mal, Olivia 006575
Malá, Olga 008606
Malagón Castro, Dimas 007412
Malak, Gregory 042942
Malakar, Diana 044162
Malao, N. 034722
Malaspina, Bartolomeo 026070
Malatare, Marilyn 048583
Malatesta, Giuseppe 023265
Malausssena, Paul-Louis 013396
Malawski, Wiesław 031990
Malceva, Ljudmila Dmitrievna 033702
Malcolm, Megan 030589
Malcom, Corey 044989
Maldent, Dominique 010904
Maldon Fitch, M. Derek 040392
Maldonado, Eduard M. 042835
Maldonado, Laural R. 047525
Maldonado, Nivia 042491
Malec, Dr. Franz 018197
Maleev, Dr. Michail 004868
Malek, Peter 002713
Maleković, Vladimir 007860
Malenfant, Robert 006291
Malenke, Patti 043180
Malet Ybern, Rosa María 034908
Malewicz, J. 029829
Malewicz, P.A. 029829
Malgeri, Dina G. 045604
Malgin, Andrej 038393, 038394
Malgorzewicz, Anna 000975, 001241
Malherbe, C. 034731, 034731
Malich, Adolf Mykolajovyč 038369
Malicky, Michael 002243
Maliet, Vincent 010779
Malik, Sajid Anwar 031384
Malikova, D. 034452
Malin, Regula 037764
Malinar, Branka 043586
Malinick, Cynthia B. 048895
Malinová, Miluše 008565
Malinverni, Pierluigi 024557
Mališeva, Valentina Pavlovna 033280
Maljković, Rada 034151
Malkočev, Angel 004632, 004633
Małkowski, Dr. Krzysztof 032435
Mallalieu, William P. 003121
Mallamo, J. Lance 042686
Mallery, W. David 043836
Mallinson, Justin 038838
Mallo Area, Alberto 035474
Malloy, Dean 006596
Malmberg, Brita 036792
Malme, Arnfinn 030974
Malme, Heikki 009515
Malmlöf, Maria 036372
Malmquist, Hilmar 021954
Malnati, Dr. Luigi 024626
Malniča, Andrej 034508
Malocha, Mary 047603
Malone, Gail 006371
Malone, Mary 022690
Malone, Pam 045171
Malone, Peter 042460
Malone, Terry 006490
Malonly, Rachelle 048676
Malov, Nikolaj Michajlovič 033859
Malsch, Dr. Friedemann 027841
Maltais, Marie E. 005487
Maltby, Janet .. 006545, 006546, 006547, 006548
Maltezou, Prof. Chryssa 026252
Malushi, Petrit 000021

Małuszyńska, Krystyna 031887
Maluţan, Cornelia 032853
Malý, Dr. František 008294
Malý, Karel 008412, 008707
Malyševa, Tatjana Vasiljevna 033260
Mamaev, Aleksandr A. 033005
Mambetova, D. 027638
Mamer, Helen 006801
Mampaso Boj, Loreto 035434
Mamuro, Yoshitake 027262
Man, Grigore 032778
Manabe, Masahiko 026781
Manakidou, Dr. Eleni 021499
Manakou, Paraskevi 021497
Manau, Ferran 035775
Mančal, Dr. Josef 015615
Mancaş, Ioan 032967
Manceau, Sophie 012539
Manchak, Barry 005410
Manchester, Dr. S.R. 044103
Mancinelli, Dr. Fabrizio 049418
Mancini, Prof. Franco 026030
Manconi, Dr. Dorica 025167
Manconi, Francesca 025332
Mancuso, Francesco 025083
Mandanas Esquito, Joven 031725
Mandel, David 041621
Mander, Gabriela 018141
Mandeville, Jeffrey 045275
Mandeville, Joyce 046005
Mandis, Alexander 021142, 021149, 021400
Mandiwana, T. 034731
Mandracchia, James 046846
Manera, Brigida 013783
Manera, Settimo 025344
Manes, John 043955
Maness, David C. 046473
Manfredini, Prof. Alessandra 025520
Manfrina, Mario 037199
Manfull, William 047193
Mangan, Dianne 001593
Mangan, Richard 040216
Mangani, Elisabetta 025555
Mangani, Dr. Elisabetta 025885
Mangels, W. Gilbert 047115
Mangia, Dr. Paola 025542
Mangiagalli, B. 034761
Mangiagalli, Tizzie 034761
Mangion, Eric 012930
Mangis, Julie 041777
Mangnus, G. 029964
Mango, Dr. E. 037759
Mangus, John 048862
Manguso, John M. 043973
Manhart, Marcia Y. 048656
Manhart, Patty 044076
Manheim, Drs. Ron 015933
Manhès, Bruno 012361
Manibusan, Rose 021569
Manicastri, Dr. Claudio 025500
Maniez, Erica S. 044788
Maniguet, Thierry 013640
Maninger, Peter 017327
Manini, Paula ... 048610, 048611, 048613
Maniurka, Dr. Piotr 032198
Manka, Riitta 009947
Manke, Elke 018447
Mankin Kornhauser, Elizabeth 044463
Mańkowska, Ewa 032078
Mankus, Edward 042823
Mann, Esther 040207
Mann, Harald J. 019703
Mann, Dr. James 045186
Mann, Judith 047676
Mann, LaDonna 049022
Mann, Dr. Stephan 017439
Mann, Theresa 048265
Mann, Vivian 046352
Mannberg Wretin, Karin 036744
Manne, Robert 048051
Manneby, Hans 036577
Manneby, Dr. Hans 036725
Mannering, Ken 038597
Manni, Dr. Riccardo 025533
Manning, Anne 041927
Manning, Carolyn 044354, 045395
Manning, Gladys E. 042086
Mannini, Maria Pia 025361, 025366
Manns, John 001630
Mano, Livio 024012
Manojlović, Miroljub 034246
Manrho, Jet 030083
Manring, Yvonne 049109
Mansell, Jefferson 042076, 042078
Manser, Jurg 037292
Mansfield, Dr. Bernard M. 044125
Mansfield, Lisa 046320
Mansfield, Nicholas 040411, 040414
Manske, Dr. Hans-Joachim 016424
Manson, Wayne 045027
Mansour Naguib, Sylvia 041867
Mansperger, Linda W. 046741
Manssen, W.J. 029294
Mantel, Ken 040239
Mantovani, Prof. Giuseppe 026090
Mantzke, Irmgard 018328, 053398
Manuel, R.S. 006130
Manuhutu, W. 030229
Manus, Dieter 018066
Manyon, Ellen 049137
Manzanares, Rick 043916
Manzanilla, Dr. Linda 028488
Manzato, Prof. Eugenio ... 026119, 026121
Manzini Gazzani, Giorgio Mario ... 007575
Mapfarakora, Jacques 004965
Maphet, L. Ernestine 044155
Maple, William T. 046124, 046125
Maples, Philip G. 047477
Maquet, Nadine 003594
Maquiso, Dr. Teresita R. 031746
Mara, Kanfela 021596
Marafioti, Dr. Sergio 025102, 025103, 025104, 025105
Marais, Caroline 040262
Marandel, J. Patrice 045441
Marangon, Maria 021449
Marapana, P.B. 036141, 036142
Maraval, P. 010729
Maravelaki, Noni 021225
Marazzi, Laura 026212
Marbach, Wilhelm 016569
Marble, Lori L. 046178
Marc, Denis 015086
Marcantel, Gregory 044854
Marcantonio, Donna 042558
Marcato, Paolo Stefano 025041
Marcel, Louis 012082, 012422
Marcet, Roger 034953
March, Dr. Eugene 045484
March and Kinrara, Earl of 039070
Marchado, Philippe 012373
Marchant, Dr. D.J. 038837
Marchant, Dr. R. 037244
Marchant Smith, Dick 041391
Marchante, Carlos M. 007989
Marchart, Bruno 002529
Marchenko, Leonid V. 038389
Marchesi, Dr. Marinella 023425
Marchetti, Prof. P.G. 023418
Marchetti, Roberto 023286
Marcheville, de 012435
Marchington, Andrea 038775
Marchini, Gian Paolo 026292
Marchione, Kenneth 048315
Marchois, Bernard 013693
Marcia, Graff 047655
Marció, Pietro 024867
Marco, Sixio 035166
Marcode Flores, Giancarlo 031559
Marcon, Gaby 013166
Marcos, Ludovic 013637
Marcos, Mariano 014909
Marcos V., Emilio 035585
Marcu, Aurora 032865
Marcum, Donald 043563
Marcum-Estes, Leah 046587
Marcus, Evelyn 044426
Marcus, Jed 046401
Marcus, Joyce 041733
Mård, Hans 036484
Mardles, Tracey 039893
Maréchal, Dominique 003316
Marechal, Ph. 003789
Marek, Danuta 031944
Marek, Stanisław 032177
Marenco, Jean-Jacques 014119
Mareneo, Simeone 026083
Mareno, Luisa López 035862
Marepo Eoe, Soroi 031435
Mares, Dr. Michael A. 046509
Marešić, Jagoda 007798
Maret, J.F. 029912
Marfà i Riera, C. 035480, 035482
Marghieri, Roland 013410
Margita, George 006487
Margkudilaga, Sufwandi 022450
Margles, Judy 047175
Margolis, Bernard 042318
Margrey, Peter 042617
Margulies, Stephen N. 042770
Mariani, Prof. Franco 024062
Mariani, Gabriel 013761
Mariani, Giuseppe Antonio 023863
Máriássy, Eva-Maria von 017528
Marić, Dušan 034143
Marichal, Rémy 013782
Maričić, Dušanka 034172
Maricki-Ostojić, Vesna 034266
Maries, John 038486
Marijan, Jassmina 034487
Marin, Dr. Emilio 007758
Marin, Prof. Emilio 007798
Marín, Fabio 007462
Marin, Jean-Yves 011054
Marin, Jeanne 014156
Marín Vázquez, Gilberto 028438
Marinac, Bogdana 034511
Marinazzo, Dr. Angela 023528
Marincig, Harald 003025
Marincola, Michele 046315
Marinelli, Dr. Giampiero Gabrio ... 024290
Marines, Sheila R. 045585
Maringer, Christine 003017
Marini, Gabriele 024460
Marini, Dr. Giorgio 026290
Marini, Mariagrazia 025821
Marini, Marinella 025821
Marini, Dr. Paola 026288, 026290
Marinis, Dr. Giuliano de 023197
Marinković, Ive 007701
Marino, Mari 004533
Marinoiu, Vasile 032948, 032949
Marinoiu, Prof. Vasile 032950
Marinov, Evstati 004943
Marinska, Dr. Rouja 004856, 004873
Marioni, Tom 047874
Mariono, Christy 042088
Marits, Ülle 009365
Mark, Guido 002785, 002810, 002811
Mark, Lory 046731
Markel, Stephen A. 045441
Markelova, Nina Konstantinovna .. 033536
Marken, Kevin 048720
Marker, Peggy 045927
Markert, Leo 017583
Markgraf, Monika 016684
Markham, Philip 030642
Markiewicz, Katarzyna 032265
Markina, Natalja Petrovna 033941
Markishtum, Merlee 048090
Markko, Helvi 009611
Markland, Eleanor 040357
Marko, Dr. Eva 001936
Markoe, Glenn 042919
Markon, Genya 048952
Markonish, Denise 042426
Markoulaki, Stavroula 021225
Markov, Dr. Nikolaj 004863
Markovčič, Albin 034513
Marković, Mirjana 034261
Marković, Prof. Slavica 007845
Markovič, Srdjan 034212
Markowicz, Kazimierz 032082
Markowitz, John 046877
Marks, Dede 041485
Marks, Edward 048354
Marks, Jacqueline 020840
Marks, Jacqueline S. 047325
Marks, John C. 044164, 044534
Marks, Katherine Duer 045329
Marks, Michael 020840
Marks, Michael J. 044552
Marks, Sherry 045192
Markus, Russell P. 043328
Marler, Brooke 043759
Marley, Rita 026381
Marlow, Martha 043515
Marlowe, Dean 048245
Marloyannis, Georgi 021431
Marmier, Maurice 014263
Marmolejo, Martha Lucía 007496
Marnetté-Kühl, Dr. Beatrice 016393
Maroević, Prof. Igor 007818
Maroević, Igor 007829
Marović, Metodija 007828
Marøy Hansen, Arild 030761
Marquardt, Claudia 019369
Marquardt, Regine 020145
Marquardt, Dr. W.H. 044103
Marquart, Dr. M. 015586
Marques, Luiz 004530
Marques, Willy 037444
Marquet, Helmut 003145
Marquet, Jean-Claude ... 012499, 012964
Marquet, Sybil 014267
Marquete, Ronaldo 004351
Márquez Martínez, Teresa 028525
Márquez Rojas, Margoth 007531
Marquis, Jean M. 036998
Marren, James 048739
Marri, Dr. Franca 024357
Marriott, Wayne P. 030548
Marsac, Michel 014319
Marsan, Geneviève 012780
Marsch, Peter 030655
Marschall, Jolanta 032287
Marsden, Dale 045548
Marsden, Melinda 044385
Marsden, Peter 039694
Marsden, Susan 006208, 006209
Marseille, Barbara 047141
Marseille, Jeremias 023098
Marsh, Geoff 040302
Marsh, Joanna 044463
Marsh, John S. 046894
Marsh, Tracy 005287
Marsh, Warwick 000732
Marsh-Matthews, Dr. F. 046509
Marshall, Alan 012814
Marshall, Dr. Cora 046201
Marshall, Danny 047636
Marshall, Francis 040778
Marshall, Jerry 046111
Marshall, Karen 045053
Marshall, Dr. Larry 045793
Marshall, Robert A. 044379
Marshall, Steven 040366
Mársico de Larribité, Viviana 000128
Marsland, Joanna Ruth 048072
Marson, Luigi 026356
Marstein, Nils 031104
Marszalec, Roman 032073
Marszałek, Zygmunt 032438
Marszewski, Tadeusz 032289
Marte, Philomena 006198
Marteljanova, Elisaveta Vladimirovna 033629
Martens, Caspar 029638
Martens, H.E.D. 029270
Martens, Jean 003236
Martens, Prof. Dr. K.R.I.M. 029245

Martens, Melissa 041989
Martens, Warburg 019517
Martensen, Robert L. 044912
Marth, Dr. Regine 016385
Martí Aixalà, Joseph 035891
Martí Armengol, Teresa 034908
Martí Bonet, José María 034944
Martí i Llambrich, Miquel 035592
Martig, Dr. Peter 037204
Martin, Alvia D. 046661
Martin, Amanda 040927
Martín, Andrés Peláez 034824
Martin, Anthea 034596
Martín, Aurora 035232, 035963
Martin, Bob 046259
Martin, Carol 006584
Martin, Collen 044983
Martin, Corlene 042909
Martin, Danny 040528
Martin, Erin L. 046215
Martin, Eva 019369
Martin, François 011273, 011274, 011492, 012285, 014175, 015136
Martin, Frank 046707
Martin, Jacques 005415
Martin, James E. 047335
Martin, Jay C. 045639
Martin, Jean-Claude 010329
Martin, Jean-Hubert 016841
Martin, Jennifer 046036
Martin, Jerry 049283
Martin, J.G. 039973
Martin, JoAnne 005024
Martin, Dr. Joanne M. 041984
Martin, John 043740
Martin, L.A. 039089
Martin, Larry 045205
Martin, Loretta 048612
Martin, Loris 005333
Martin, Dr. Lutz 016193
Martin, M. 039975
Martín, Macarena Alés 035335
Martin, Marietta 042023
Martin, Marilyn 034587
Martin, Mary C. 043525
Martin, Dr. Michael 018476
Martin, Michael 046687
Martin, Otto-Walter 016217
Martin, Pascal 013234
Martin, Paul 043899
Martin, Dr. Paula 039027
Martin, Dr. Peter-Hugo 018158
Martin, Pierre de 014849
Martin, Rebecca J. 048581
Martin, Richard 043386
Martin, Rick 043707
Martin, Robert 040961
Martin, Roger 005100
Martin, Sandra 040404
Martin, Dr. Shéonagh 039392
Martin, Terry 044098
Martin, Ètienne 014874
Martin, Tracy N. 042479
Martin, William 049122
Martin, William J. 047426
Martin, Wilson 047779
Martín Flores, Alfonso 035410
Martin-Vignes, Nicole 010295
Martindale, Bruce 006559
Martindale, Wendy 006242
Martínek, Jaroslav 008405, 008512, 008720
Martinelli, Massimo 024436
Martinelli, Patricia A. 044409
Martinelli, Dr. Roberta 025337, 025338
Martinet, Jean-Louis 012376
Martínez, Dr. Armando Luis 028482
Martinez, Connie 047896
Martinez, Daniel 044611
Martinez, Edward 047374
Martínez, Gonzalo 007506
Martínez, José Luis 028492
Martínez, Maite 035976
Martínez, Margarita 049451
Martínez, Ramiro 028534
Martinez, Ray 041572
Martínez, Ricardo Ariel 007581
Martínez Alvárez, Dr. José María 035492
Martínez Arvizu, Jesus 028608
Martínez Cortés, Ariel 007607
Martínez Fuentes, Dr. Antonio J.F. 007954
Martínez Mestre, Miguel 028499
Martínez Rodríguez, Andrés 035362
Martinez Saravia, Carlos A. 000202
Martínez Sarria, Victoria 007587
Martínez Vargas, Enrique 028400
Martini, Prof. Dr. Erlend 019649
Martini, Dr. Luciana 025398
Martiniani-Reber, Marielle 037128
Martiniz-Lemke, Tania 045439
Martínková, Jana 008511
Martino, Giuseppe 024032
Martino, Mike 047518
Martino, Dr. Ronald L. 044683
Martinović, Jovan 034201
Martinović, Niko 034217
Martins, Josephine 044944
Martins, Michael 043804
Martins Carneiro, José Manuel 032693
Martins Catharino, Henriqueta 004453
Martins e Silva, José 032640
Martins Fernandes, Francisco R. 032619
Martinson, Gordon 042393
Martis, Ela Helgi 009427
Martis, Val 042823
Martoana, Alan 045738
Martonová, T. 008375
Martorell, Jaume 035609
Marty, Michel 014317
Martykánová, Marie 008732
Martynova, Nina Petrovna 033263
Martynova, Raisa Fëdorovna 033180
Marugg, Richard 037545
Maruschke, Thomas 016364
Marusic, Irena 034495
Maruszeczka, Dave 005621
Maruyama, Mariko 026469
Maruyama, Masatake 027254
Maruyama, Tamiko 027287
Marvin, Anne 048133
Marvin, Anne M. 048581
Marwell, Dr. David G. 046373
Marwick, Fiona C. 039520
Marwick, Guy 046613
Marx, Dr. Erich 002547, 002549, 002567, 002568, 002570
Marx, Prof. Dr. Harald 016789
Marx, Mary 046597
Marx, Prof. R. 034669
Maryon, Mike 038916
Marzahn, Dr. Joachim 016193
Marzatico, Dr. Franco 023386, 026106
Marzio, Frances 044648
Marzio, Peter C. 044648
Marzolf, John G. 041907
Marzoli, Dr. Dirce 020374
Más Vilaplana, Antonio 035338
Masahide, Maekawa 027023
Masana, Megan 045995
Masanori, Ichikawa 026878
Mašanović, Pavle 034276
Masaracı, Yasemin 038023
Mašátová, Ivana 008269
Masau Dan, Dr. Maria 026133
Masayuki, Ogata 026823
Mascarenhas, Dr. Aubrey A. 022264
Mascherbauer, Michael 001693
Mascheroni, Achille 025766
Mascia, Sara 048506
Maseberg, G. 017649
Maselli Scotti, Dr. Franca 023223, 023224
Masemore, Dr. Ira 045359
Masen, Larz 045917
Masing, Maia 009408
Masino, H. 020631
Masjoan, Prof. Estela 000242
Maske, Andrew 047741
Maslarova, Iljana 004942
Maslov, V.I. 033508
Mason, Barbara 048288
Mason, Bonnie N. 046773
Mason, Carl 041751
Mason, Charles 046607
Mason, D.A. 006452
Mason, Darielle 046975
Mason, Erik 045397
Mason, G. 040548
Mason, Julia 038828
Mason, Dr. Kevin 038771
Mason, Laurie 005952
Mason, Michael E. 043619
Mason, Ngahirika 030431
Mason, Rainer Michael 037114
Mason, Richard 041342
Mason, R.P. 039419
Mason, Wally 046727
Mason, William J. 044380
Mason-Chaney, Lisa 043676
Maspoli, Guido 037286
Masriera, Alicia 034928
Massada, Satê 027379
Massalsky, Joachim 016434
Massari, Dr. Stefania 025551
Massaro, Marilyn 047251, 047259
Massart, Claire 003353
Massenbach, Elisabeth von 019085
Massengill, Myers 047029
Massey, Lewis 041872
Massey, S.L. 006260
Massey, William P. 042755
Massicotte, Jean 005823
Massie Lane, Rebecca 048448
Massimbe, Julieta 029051
Massobrio, Dr. Giulio 023165
Masson, Colette 005733
Masson Rusinowski, Fabienne 003512
Massy, Jean-Baptiste 037684
Mastemaker, Lorie 044410
Master-Karnik, Paul 045297
Masterson, Judy 043771
Mastorgio, Carlo 023259
Mastoris, Steph N. 039108
Mastorito, Susana 000336
Mastrogiuseppe, Joy 047282
Mastrovic, Mikica 007837
Masuda, Hideaki 026503
Masuda, Rei 027256
Mašulovic, Branimir 034263
Masuo, Tano 026673
Masuyer, François 011565
Mata, Rene Luis S. 031718, 031737
Mata González, Juan C. de la 035439
Matajis, Andrijana 034163
Matakieva, Ass.Prof. Dr. Teofana 004863
Matamoros, Joséphine 011178, 011423
Matasci, Mario 037623
Matat, Leonid Nykonorovyč 038294
Matauschek, Katja 020365
Mataušić, Nataša 007841
Mátéffy, Dr. Balázs 021643
Matei, Rodica 032809
Matejić, Slavoljub 034139
Matenga, Edward 049588
Maternati-Baldouy, Danielle 012951
Materón Salcedo, Edgar 007474
Maters, Drs. Petra 030255
Mateu y Miró, Josep 035065
Mateva, Borjana 004694
Matharan, Paul 010882
Matheis, Adam 018783
Matheny, Paul 043088
Mathes, Wayne 046591
Matheson, Susan 046228
Matheson, Trueman 005794
Mathew, Helen 047353
Mathewes, Charles P. 046195
Mathews, George K. 046473
Mathews, Mary 043319
Mathews, Nancy 044961
Mathews, Susan 039443
Mathez, Dr. Edmond A. 046286
Mathias, Gérard 011792
Mathiassen, Tove E. 008806
Mathieson, Julia 006359
Mathieu, Caroline 013678
Mathieu, Dr. Kai R. 016538, 017351, 020183, 020727
Mathis, Bernhard 037066
Mathis, Walti 037297
Mathison, Judy 048802
Mathusa, Parker D. 048109
Matias, Bienvenida 045909
Matijaca, Ivo 007742
Matijevič, Jožef 034509
Matile, Michael 037768
Matilla, José Manuel 035429
Matilsky, Barbara 042713
Matino, Dr. Lucia 024731
Matiskainen, Dr. Heikki 010035, 010037
Matkin, Dan 044781
Matland, Susan 030982
Mato, Nancy 046796
Matochik, Dr. John A. 043914
Matos, Dr. Lúcia de 032680
Matos Moctezuma, María Fernanda 028277
Matos Reis, Dr. António 032698
Matoušek, Dr. Branislav 034338
Matoušková, Martina 008654
Matschiner, Dieter 002625
Matskási, Dr. István 021673
Matson, Dr. Timothy 042986
Matsubayashi, Hosai 027306
Matsuda, Hiroshi 026533
Matsuda, Motoi 026945
Matsuhashi, Hiroto 026479
Matsumoto, Takeshi 026842
Matsumoto, Tohru 027256
Matsuo, Yasumasa 026805
Matsuoka, Masao 026872
Matsuoka, Mieko 027198
Matsura, Akira 026516
Matsushita, Kensuke 026405
Matsuura, Kunio 027079
Matsuzaki, Yukiko 027169
Matsuzawa, Shigefumi 027337
Matt, Edvin 045214
Matt, Dr. Gerald 002930, 002931
Mattausch-Schirmbeck, Dr. Roswitha 015721
Matteotti, Mario 025447
Matter, Kuno 037531
Matter, Victor 037259
Mattern, Dr. T. 018816
Mattes, Glenda 043492
Matteson, Judith M. 043923
Mattet, Laurence 037127
Matthäi, Bernhard 018323
Matthaes, Goffried 024706
Matthes, Lilian 008885
Matthes, Olaf 017712
Matthew, A.T. 034613
Matthew, Malcom 047805
Matthewman, Su 041480
Matthews, Anita 022839
Matthews, B. 046143
Matthews, Dr. B. 046509
Matthews, Dr. B.E. 039389
Matthews, Christy 043437
Matthews, Daniel Paul 046415
Matthews, John 000771
Matthews, Julia 006627
Matthews, Keith 041474
Matthews, Marsha 047174
Matthews, Martin 039722
Matthews, Nancy 048920
Matthews, Zara 039441
Matthews Hoffmann, Catherine 045273
Matthey, Prof. François 037344
Matthias, Diana 046574
Matthias, Kevin 039223
Matthiesen, Kjell Marius 030984
Matthiessen, Joy A. 043432

Matti, Arnold 037823
Matticks, Rebecca 043628
Mattila, Karen 005967
Mattioni, Fernando 025240
Mattl-Wurm, Dr. Sylvia 003017
Mattlin, Håkan 009467
Matton, A. 003493, 003494
Matton, Ann 003492
Mattox, Boyd 048513
Mattson, James 043659
Mattsson, Christina 036652
Matukova, Marija Bajramovna 033205
Matuschka, Dagmar Gräfin von 020000
Matuska, Mike von 036630
Matuss, Dr. Márta 021716
Matuszczyk, Andrzej 032066
Matveeva, Tatjana Sergeevna 032994
Matvenov, Evgenij Rostitovič 033138
Matyniak, Margaret 048868
Matz, Darrell 048470
Matzke, Klaus 020030
Matzon, Ea 009114
Maubano, M. 012506
Maubant, Jean-Louis 015297
Maudet, Serge 027838
Maué, Dr. Hermann 019352
Mauerhan, Joëlle 010773
Mauersberger, Dr. Klaus 016812
Maugain, Gregory 013253
Mauldin, Barbara 047972, 047973
Mauler, Norbert 001956
Maulhardt, Dr. Heinrich 020592
Maulsby, Richard 041781
Maumont, A. 014999
Maung, U Min Khin 029062
Mauoloux, Herman 003782
Maur, Dr. Karin von 020361
Maurer, C.F. William 045691
Maurer, Eberhard 020371
Maurer, Eleonore 002044
Maurer, Ellen 045860
Maurer, Prof. Dr. Friedemann 017806
Maurer, Dr. Rudolf 001746
Maurer, Sherry C. 047490
Maurer, Simon 037772
Maurer-Zilioli, Dr. Ellen 019096
Maurice-Chabard, Brigitte 010561
Maurin, Ange 013962
Maurin, Bernard 014664
Maurin, Ray 044775
Maurirere, Naomi 030501
Maurizio, Dr. R. 037593
Maurizio, Dr. Remo 037594
Mauron, Christophe 036989
Mausel, Olivia 044585
Mautner-Markhof, Dr. Marietta 002845
Mauws, Eveline 006193, 052769
Mavric, Kaye 000940
Mavrodiev, Zdravko 004875
Mavrotas, Takis 021273
Mavuso, Makana R. 036162
Maw, Dr. Martin 040664
Mawdsley, Simon 030807
Mawe, Theodore 031436
Mawleke, M. 034657
Maxey, Michael 047754
Maxfield, Dorothy 049221
Maxfield, Mike 040408
Maxham, Marjorie P. 042384
Maxham, R.S. 043972
Maxheimer, Greta 043371
Maxholmes, Thomas 001651
Maxim, Dr. Elena 032799
Maximilien, Diana 037641
Maxwell, Gregory 049368
Maxwell, Jennifer 041146
Maxwell, Lowell 046893
Maxwell, Robert N. 044711
Maxwell, Robyn 000888
Maxwell, Dr. Thomas 046441
Maxwell Stuart, Catherine 039799
May, Eve 038777
May, Guy 027903
May, J. Alan 044154
May, James 041679, 044744
May, Jane 039977
May, John M. 043058
May, Pauline 041053
May, Philip 046617
May, Thérèse 027903
Mayberg, Magnus 036628
Mayberry, Matthew 043055
Mayer, August 002653
Mayer, Gregory C. 045594
Mayer, Günter 002826
Mayer, Günther 002851
Mayer, H. 020368
Mayer, Hedwig 001792
Mayer, Herbert 002916, 002971
Mayer, Jannie 013680
Mayer, John 047191
Mayer, M. 018904
Mayer, Olafa 018858
Mayer, Ronald 048237
Mayer, Walter 042500
Mayer-Thurman, Christa C. 042820
Mayers, Lise 047216
Mayes, Catherine 043549
Mayes, James 047511
Mayfield, Signe 046804
Mayhew, Kim 046434
Mayle, A.H. 040151
Maynard, Helen B. 044175
Maynard, Marie-Noëlle 011113
Maynard, Rex 042134
Mayo, Dr. Margaret Ellen 047429
Mayo, Martha 045508
Mayo, Marti 044637
Mayor, N. 010931
Mayorga Sanchón, D. Juan 035923
Mayou, Roger 037133
Mayr, Dr. Helmut 019099
Mayr, Herbert 018803
Mayr, Josef 001860
Mayr, Jürgen 017604
Mayr, Karin 017391
Mayr, Manfred 016703
Mayr, Peter 002837
Mayr, Walter 002493
Mayr-Oehring, Dr. Erika 002564
Mayrhofer, Martin 002674
Mayrhofer, Meinrad 002460
Mayrhofer, Monika E. 003065
Mayrhuber, Petra & Gerti 002804
Mays, N. 000754
Maysonnaue, J. 015379
Maytk, Paul 049036
Maywald-Pitellos, Dr. Claus 018788
Maza, Roberto Ramos 028901
Mazeika, Dr. Rasa 005892
Mazepov, Jurij Ivanovyč 038387
Maziarka, Włodzimierz 031960
Mazitova, Svetlana Vladimirovna 033289
Mazlish, Anne 048221
Mazlumoğlu, Hasan 038060
Maznev, Kostadin 004718
Mazonowicz, Douglas 046335
Mazor, Robin 044933
Mazourek, Paul 001614
Mazow, Dr. Leo 048703
Mazur, Leonid Viktorovič 034087
Mazurkiewicz, Janina 032394
Mazza, Germana 023680
Mazza, Thomas C. 046316
Mazzari, Roberto 023409
Mazzei, Dr. Lapo 024177
Mazzei, Marina 024597
Mazzeo, Dr. Donatella 025548
Mazzerioli, Paolo 025169
Mazziotti Gillan, Maria 046840
Mazzocchi, G. 025617
Mazzolti, Prof. Mario 025396
Mazzoni, Anne-Hélène 014102
Mazzoni, Prof. Francesco 023802
Mazzoni de Bravo, Helga 000255
Mazzotta, Gabriele 024700
Mazzotti, Dr. Stefano 024103
Mazzullo, Thomas 043018
Mbe, John C. Jacques 040988
Mbodji, Abdoulaye 034138
Mbokashanga, Nyimi Kuete 007662
McGarry, James R. 044991
Mead, Barry 038539
Meade, C. Wade 047577
Meade, Diane 043557
Meade, John 045219
Meador-Woodruff, Robin 041732
Meadors, William 045373
Meadows, Larry G. 042959
Meagher, George E. 042724
Meagher, Kathy 005485
Meagher, Tom 005802
Mealey, Brian 045816
Mealing, David 030521, 030644
Mearwah, Reena 022143
Mecham, Denny H. 047765
Mechan, Dallas 038911
Mechell, Barbara 048815
Mechler, Sabine 017835
Meck, Gerhard 019657
Mecklin, Kai 010148
Mecredy, Stephen D. 005695
Medaković, Anica 034281
Medeiros, Francisco 032623
Medek, Prof. Robert 002882
Medernach, Marcel 027891
Mederski, Mark 047016
Medica, Dr. Massimo 023428
Medicus, Christine 002561
Medina, Dennis H.J. 041563
Medina i Montes, Susana 035908
Medley, Mark 046142
Medlin, Tina 044640
Medlock, Leon 047120
Medlycott, Sir Mervyn 040953
Medri, Prof. Gianluca 024072
Medri, Dr. Litta 024162, 025293
Medurić, Jovan 034144
Medvedev, Nikolaj Jurjevič 033726
Medvedow, Jill 042327
Medzihradská, Dr. Elena 034376
Meehan, Brian 005783, 005792
Meehan, Joseph M. 043850
Meek, Kenneth 042033
Meek, Noel 030496
Meeke, Dr. Noel 039739
Meeker, David 040095
Meekers, Christa 003501
Meena, K.L. 022187
Mees, Dr. Allard 018792, 018794
Meester de Heyndonck, B. de 003205
Meeusen, M. 003800
Meewis, Menno 003182
Meffre, Pierre 015088
Meglio, Luciano di 024417
Mehaska, Dr. Walter 044444
Mehl, Dr. Heinrich 020039
Mehler, Sarah 037799
Mehring, Albert G. 044444
Mehring, Karen 043880
Mehta, A.P. 022007
Meiborg, E. 029926
Meidell, Bjarne A. 030769
Meidenbauer, Roy 046192
Meidinger, Ronald J. 041814
Meier, Andreas 037411
Meier, Anton C. 037742
Meier, Helmut 037153
Meier, Jürgen 017487
Meier, Michelle 046417
Meier, Rupert 036911
Meier, Stefan 036882
Meier, Dr. Werner 037614
Meier, Wolfgang 017137
Meighörner, Dr. Wolfgang 017272
Meijer, M. 029270
Meillat, Eric 010344
Meillat, Joël 013167
Meillon, Anne 012036
Meinderts, Drs. A.J.M. 029425
Meinderts, Drs. A.J.M 029438
Meindre, Colette 012753, 014157
Meinelschmidt, C. 017965
Meiners, Dr. Jochen 016545
Meiners, Prof. Dr. Uwe 016572
Meinig, U. 015625, 015626
Meinrad-Meier, Dr. Anton 037165
Meir, Cecilia 023081
Bastos Gambogi Meireles, Alexa 004044
Meiring, Barbara 043969
Meiringer, Susanne 001790
Meirose, Jan-Dirk 016886
Meirovics, Prof. Imauts 027745
Meisch, Jim 027895
Meisser, Dr. N. 037244
Meissimilly-Rosin, Martine 015194
Meissner, Roman 032238
Meißner, Uwe 017673
Meissonnier, J. 011696
Meister, Arthur 036981
Meister, Mark 043318, 043325
Meister, Nicolette 042132
Meiszies, Dr. Winrich 016848
Meixner, J. Alfred 015807
Mejdahl, Ulla 008843
Mejer, Robert Lee 047297
Mejia, Javier 007606, 007610
Mejía Maya, Rafael 007639
Méla, Prof. Dr. Charles 037026
Melamed, Nuril 023082
Melander, Dr. Torben 008990
Melcher, Horst 018993
Melcher, Dr. Ralph 019963
Melchionne, Kevin 046991
Meldgård, Bjarne 008903
Melencio, Jet 031696
Melgarejo Cabrera, Elizabet 008130
Meli, Pietro 024501
Melichar, Dr. Herbert 002327, 002327
Melisi, Prof. Francesco 024899
Melke, Gunta 027675
Melki, Dr. Loutfalla 027812
Melkonyan, Hasmik 000681
Mella, Joseph S. 046157
Mellander, Barbo 036171
Mellander, Barbro 036402
Mellbye, Maren-Otte 031274
Mellemsether, Hanna 031287
Meller, Dr. Harald 017666
Mellinger, A. Clair 044449
Mello, Luiz Carlos 004376
Mellon, Lori A. 043417
Mellor, Stephen 048925
Mellott, Tina 042419
Mellow, Ralph 005288
Melničuk, Andrej Fëdorovič 033650
Melnik, Alison G. 046157
Melnikova, I.F. 027409
Melnikova, Natalija Ivanovna 033164
Melnikova, Tamara Michajlovna 033325
Melnyk, Anatolij Ivanovič 038317
Melo, B. de 032579
Melo, Jorge Orlando 007407, 007408
Melo Miranda, Selma 004432
Melody, Paul 030534
Melomina, Olga Alekseevna 033006
Melone, Dr. Francesco 024974
Meloni, Alberto C. 047650, 048976
Melrose, A. 001114
Melson, Claudia 043490
Melton, Babs 048395
Meltzer, J.L. 034588
Meltzer, Lalou 034583
Melville, Terry 030620
Melzer, Ellen 017526
Melzer, Gustav 002438
Melzer, Dr. Miloš 008510
Melzer, Miloš 008700
Melzer, Dr. Miloš 008736
Melzer, Miloš 008772
Melzer, Dr. R. 019132
Memoire, Natalie 010895

Mena, Manuela . . . 035429
Mena Segarra, Prof. Enrique . . . 041500
Menaker Rothschild, Deborah . . . 049188
Ménard, Jean . . . 014422
Menard, Jean-Daniel . . . 014954, 014955
Menard, Joan . . . 041649
Menardi, Dr. Herlinde . . . 002098
Menato, Prof. Giuliano . . . 026186
Menconeri, Kate . . . 049292
Mencucci, Angelo . . . 025853
Mendel, Shlomoh . . . 023054
Mendell, Seth F. . . . 045726
Mendelssohn, Dr. Gabriele . . . 018065
Mendelssohn, Prof. H. . . . 023094
Mendenhall, Winnifred . . . 043027
Mendes, Albano . . . 021599
Mendes Bürgi, Dr. Bernhard . . . 036890, 036894
Mendes Marques, Dr. Maria da Concerção . . . 032621
Méndez, Dr. Marion . . . 017545
Méndez Lecanda, Dr. Elia Josefina 028535
Méndez López, Nohra Isabel . . . 007491
Mendoza Garriga, Cristina . . . 034923
Mendoza Ramírez, Patricia . . . 028449
Menefee, Antonio . . . 047561
Menegazzi, Dr. Alessandra . . . 025059
Meneguzzo, Giobatta . . . 024587
Meneses, Adriana . . . 049475
Meng, Jim . . . 041693
Meng, Qingjin . . . 007055
Meng, Ung Vai . . . 007184
Menga, Prof. Angelo . . . 024794
Mengden, Dr. Lida von . . . 018707
Menge, Heide . . . 016426
Mengele, Mark . . . 048422
Menghin, Prof. Dr. Wilfried . . . 016136
Mengis, Tim . . . 045538
Menhes, Prof. Dr. S.B.J. . . . 029245
Menig, Irene . . . 015841
Menis, Gian Carlo . . . 026165
Menk, S. . . . 019585
Menke, Dr. Annette . . . 020611
Menke, Hubertus . . . 018128
Menke, Wilhelm . . . 017776
Menke, William V. . . . 048788, 048790
Menn, Richard J. . . . 042627
Menna, Edith . . . 047773
Menne, Gilbert . . . 003446
Mennel, Suzanne . . . 036927
Mennicke, Christiane . . . 016796
Mennicken, R. . . . 003708
Mennucci, Dr. Antonello . . 025679, 025684
Mens, Drs. I.J.A. . . . 030383
Mensch, Bernhard . . . 019390
Mentzelopoulos, Constantine . . . 021506
Menu, Daniel . . . 015265
Menu, Louis . . . 003643
Menz, Dr. Cäsar 037111, 037114, 037118, 037123, 037125, 037128, 037129, 037131, 037136
Menz, Martin . . . 020177
Menzel, Joachim . . . 020271
Menzies, Donald . . . 049280
Menzies, G.M. . . . 038455
Menzies, Jackie . . . 001505
Meoard-Blondel, Anne . . . 012953
Merabet, Née . . . 000046
Meral, A. Seda . . . 038009
Merali, Shaheen . . . 016061
Mercadal i Fernández, Oriol . . . 035686
Mercado Lopez, Eugenio . . . 028584
Mercandino Jucker, Gabriella . . . 024697
Mercede, Nevin . . . 049337
Mercer, Anna . . . 040928
Mercer, Bill . . . 047178, 047433
Mercer, L.H.S. . . . 039136
Mercer, Régis . . . 015302
Mercier, Poppi . . . 042283
Mercuri, Joan B. . . . 042844, 046582
Mercuri, Mariano . . . 025202
Merdjanov, Plamen . . . 004698, 004733, 004734
Merdžanov, Plamen . . . 004748
Meredith, Jill . . . 041692, 041692
Meredith, Mary Ellen . . . 048472
Merene-Wiesbauer, Dr. Elisabeth . 002923
Merhiou, Olivier de . . . 013017
Merino Acosta, Dr. Luz . . . 008006
Merino Santisteban, José . . . 035460
Mèriot, Christian . . . 010888
Merk, Dr. Anton . . . 017742
Merk, Jan . . . 019025
Merk, Zsuzsa . . . 021619
Merkel, Dr. Michael . . . 017698
Merkert, Prof. Jörn . . . 015991
Merlin, Georges . . . 010609
Merlin-Anglade, Véronique . . . 013773
Merling, David . . . 042172
Merling, Mitchell . . . 047999
Mermet, Christian . . . 013283
Merrell, Ed . . . 043653
Merrell Domingo, Merle . . . 031687
Merriam, Robert W. . . . 043562
Merrill, Kimberly . . . 041591
Merrill, Dr. Linda . . . 048908
Merrill, Michael . . . 048179
Merrill, Robert . . . 040516
Merrill, Ross . . . 048924
Merrill-Mirsky, Dr. Carol . . . 045427
Merrill Roenke, H. . . . 044165
Merriman, Larry . . . 044466
Merrin, Keith . . . 039831
Merrit, Carrie . . . 044218
Merritt, Jody A. . . . 041879
Merritt, Roxanne M. . . . 043894
Mersseman, Denise . . . 003827
Merta, Klaus-Peter . . . 016011
Merten, Jürgen . . . 020483
Merten, Dr. Klaus . . . 020712
Mertens, Carlos Frederico . . . 000424
Mertens, Dr. Sabine . . . 018790
Mertens, Dr. Veronika . . . 015466
Mertes, Lorie . . . 045814
Merveldt, Catherine Gräfin von . . . 016759
Mery, Estelle . . . 015347
Merzenich, Hildegard . . . 019052
Mes, Dr. U. H. M. . . . 030268
Mesa, José de . 003909, 003911, 003912, 003913
Mesbahi, Sh. . . . 022613
Meščerina, Nadežda Alekseevna . . 033622
Meschede, Dr. Friedrich . . . 016007
Mesejo Maestre, Eduardo . . . 007945
Mešerjakov, Vladimir . . . 033780
Meserve, Edward N. . . . 048386
Meshke, R. . . . 005305
Meskin, Maria . . . 004778
Meslin-Perrier, Chantal . . . 012698
Mesnil du Buisson, Laurent du . . . 015240
Mesquida García, Dr. Mercedes . . 035640
Mesquita, Ivo . . . 004532
Messel, Nils . . . 031089
Messenger, Jane . . . 000703
Messenger, Janet M. . . . 046814
Messenger, Margaret . . . 005217
Messer, David J. . . . 044376
Messer, Jennifer . . . 047495
Messer, Renate . . . 019426
Messerli, Jakob . . . 036932
Messerli, N. . . . 037266
Messerli, Ursula . . . 037540
Messiaen, Marcel . . . 003542
Messika, Natalie . . . 023055
Messimer, Susan . . . 045149
Messinger, Carla . . . 041661
Messmer, Alois . . . 020425
Messmer, Dorothee . . . 037697
Messner, John . . . 040910
Messner, Kathrin . . . 002963
Messner, Reinhold . . . 023708, 023875
Meštan, Prof. Pavol . . . 034335
Mészáros, Dr. Ferenc . . . 021673
Métais, Michel . . . 013126
Metcalf, Charles D. . . . 049319
Metcalf, Craig . . . 006075
Metcalf, Elizabeth . . . 046325
Metcalf, Mike . . . 048175
Metcalf, Susan E . . . 043264
Metcalf, William E. . . . 046287
Metcalfe, Duncan . . . 047778
Metcalfe, Edward C. . . . 045693
Meteku Zekeke, Endalew . . . 009445
Metham, Penny . . . 001326
Methven, John . . . 001457
Metropolis, William C. . . . 042564
Mets, Esta . . . 009433
Mettala, Teri . . . 046638
Mette, Dr. Bettina . . . 016468
Metternich, Wolfgang . . . 017184
Mettjes, Dr. Gerd 020275, 020276, 020277, 020279
Metz, Edward . . . 041796
Metz, Lance . . . 043590
Metz, Thomas . . . 016884, 018294
Metz, Wolfgang . . . 018593
Metzger, Amy . . . 044386
Metzger, Frederick W. . . . 006685
Metzger, Dr. Wolfram . . . 018158
Metzler, Jeannot . . . 027894
Metzler, Dr. Sally . . . 042855
Metzner, Dietrich . . . 019765, 019766
Meulemeester, Jean Luc . . . 003697
Meulenbeld, B.C. . . . 029194
Meurant, Anne . . . 003333, 003353
Meurer, Dr. Heribert . . . 019931
Meûter, Ingrid de . . . 003353
Mevludin, Ekmečić . . . 003944
Mewborn, Frankie . . . 048852
Mewes, Claus . . . 017703
Mewton-Hynds, Sally . . . 041283
Meybohm, Amy E. . . . 041898
Meyer, Alain . . . 013246
Meyer, Alberto . . . 036932
Meÿer, Bob . . . 029192
Meyer, Charles G. . . . 041954
Meyer, Dr. Christian . . . 002329, 002850
Meyer, Dr. Christian A. . . . 036899
Meyer, Ellen L. . . . 041844
Meyer, Fifi . . . 034590
Meyer, Franz . . . 015787
Meyer, G. . . . 020127
Meyer, Helen . . . 045218
Meyer, Hélène . . . 037128
Meyer, Hubert . . . 014749
Meyer, Irin von . . . 017715
Meyer, Jackie-Ruth . . . 010317,
Meyer, J.B. . . . 029690
Meyer, Jochanan . . . 022894
Meyer, Dr. Jochen . . . 018813
Meyer, Karl . . . 019205
Meyer, Kurt . . . 019520, 019524, 019525, 019527
Meyer, Lioba . . . 019473
Meyer, M. . . . 029264
Meyer, Marc . . . 027895
Meyer, Marie-Emmanuelle . . . 015174
Meyer, Niels . . . 008806
Meyer, Peter S. . . . 008998
Meyer, Rachel . . . 046805
Meyer, Stefan . . . 019851
Meyer, Steve . . . 044658
Meyer, Dr. Susanne . . . 016361
Meyer, Thomas . . . 037761
Meyer, Werner . . . 017447, 020528
Meyer-Büser, Dr. Susanne 019073, 053313
Meyer-Friese, Dr. Boye . . . 017680
Meyer-Kröger, Hagen . . . 019070
Meyer Utne, Janneke . . . 030983
Meyer zu Schwabedissen, Doris . . 019193
Meyerdierks, Judith . . . 042650
Meyere, J.A.L de . . . 030236
Meyers, Amy . . . 046227, 047912
Meyers, Joel . . . 045228
Meyerson, Barbara . . . 045791
Meyerson, Randy . . . 048568
Meyrick, Robert . . . 038465
Meysner . . . 020401
Meza, Ruben . . . 044754
Mezan Barrera, Jesús Manuel . . . 028421
Mezhlumyan, G.B. . . . 000680
Mežinski, Jelena . . . 034151
Mezvinski-Smithgall, Elsa . . . 048940
Mezzatesta, Dr. Michael P. . . . 043542
Mhute, Josiah Rungano . . . 049586
Miano, Ederick C. . . . 031656
Michael, Dean . . . 001165
Michael, Dr. Eckhard . . . 018744
Michael, Dr. Elisabeth . . . 019037
Michael, Helene . . . 037752
Michael, Janet . . . 038947
Michael, Linda . . . 000925
Michael, William H. . . . 044717
Michaelidon, Maria . . . 021452
Michaelis, Bonni-Dara . . . 046419
Michaelis, Dr. Rainer . . . 016049
Michaelsen, Miah . . . 046556
Michailov, Christo . . . 004636
Michailov, Igor . . . 033785
Michajlov, A.B. . . . 033968
Michajlova, Ljudmila Vasiljevna . . 033788
Michajlova, Zdravka . . . 004740, 004892
Michajlovna, Jelena . . . 033402
Michalka, Matthias . . . 002965
Michalka, Prof. Dr. Wolfgang . . . 019713
Michaud, Bruce P. . . . 047745
Michaud, François . . . 013630
Michaud, Jean-Marc . . . 012494, 014081, 014688
Michaud, Raynald . . . 005942
Michavila, Joaquín . . . 036062
Michel, D. . . . 013209
Michel, Ernest W. . . . 046328
Michel, Gundega . . . 027747
Michel, Helmut . . . 020703
Michel, Jean-François . . 011314, 011315, 011316
Michel, Samuel . . . 037166
Michel, Prof. Dr. Thomas . . . 020358
Michelet, Annick . . . 013956
Michelotti, Dr. Francesca 034110, 034112, 034116, 034120
Michels, Dr. Anette . . . 020494
Michels, Dr. Hubertus . . . 016691
Michels, Dr. Norbert . . . 016675
Michélsen, Pia . . . 036446
Michie, Thomas . . . 047258
Michieli, Catalina Teresa . . . 000108
Michoutouchkine, N. . . . 049415
Mickelson-Lukach, Joan . . . 044024
Mickenberg, David . . . 043762, 049046
Micklich, Judy . . . 047755
Micklich, Dr. Norbert . . . 016638
Micklim, Lynne . . . 043432
Micko, Ingeborg . . . 002830
Mickschat, Klaus-Dieter . . . 019523
Miclescu, Constanţa . . . 032966
Micol, P.M. . . . 011837
Mičurová, M. . . . 034452
Micynska, Tamara Petrivna . . . 038253
Middag, B.M. . . . 029828
Middelbasch, Max . . . 030049
Middlemost, Thomas A. . . . 001585
Middleton, J. . . . 001114
Middleton, J.W. . . . 038974
Middleton, S.I. . . . 038974
Midleton, Viscount . . . 038924
Miedema, B. . . . 029323
Mielke, Dr. Heinz-Peter . . . 017517
Mielsch, Prof. Dr. Harald . . . 016312
Mierkiewicz, Edward . . . 032463
Mierzwiński, Mariusz . . . 032139
Miesbeck, Peter . . . 019883
Miesenberger, Martin . . . 002366
Miessgang, Dr. Thomas . . . 002930
Mießl, Peter . . . 002141, 052569
Mieth, Katja Margarethe . . . 020339
Miethe, Susann . . . 019517
Mietke, Dr. Gabriele . . . 016173
Miggitsch, Jörg . . . 002324
Miglbauer, Dr. Renate . . . 002828, 002829, 002830, 002831

Miglinas, Skirmante 042854
Migliori, Gabriele 024850
Mignot, D. 029230
Migritone Gondwe, Michael 027941
Miguet, Daniéle 011253, 011254
Mihai, Raul 032788
Mihail, Benoît 003359
Mihailović, Milica 034154
Mihalić, Jana 007732
Mihelić, Sanjin 007828
Mihevc, Bibijana 034497
Miho, Terao 026606
Mihovilić, Kristina 007776
Mihut, Elena 032816
Mijić, Suzanalav 034177
Mijin, Vesna 034269
Mijnlieff, E.M. 029625, 029626
Mikaelsen, Laila 021548
Mikelson, Mary 006809
Mikes, Johannes H. 001890
Mikeskova, Irina 004863
Mikeson, Mary 048321
Mikhalevsky, A.V. 027417
Mikkelsen, Dr. Egil 031074, 031079, 031088, 031112, 031114
Mikkelsen, Falk 008873
Mikkola, Ari 009886
Mikkola Huk, Eira 009834
Miklas, Lois 044523
Mikołajska, Ewa 032348
Mikonranta, Kaarina 009634
Mikoszewski, Jerzy 032485
Mikulaštík, Dr. Tomáš 008766
Mikus, Joan 043935
Mikuž, Marjeta 034486
Milani, Arch 046554
Milani, Dr. Domenico 025122, 025127
Milanich, Dr. J.T. 044103
Milano, Dean 043689
Milano, Prof. Ernesto 024752
Milbank, Bill 030626
Milbrath, Dr. S. 044103
Milchram, Gerhard 002918, 002964
Mildner, Dr. Paul 002142
Mildner, Dr. U. 019721
Miles, Bernice 044697
Miles, Blanche 047774
Miles, Bradley R. 042629
Miles, Carolyn P. 047652
Miles, Carolyn W. 041582
Miles, Christine M. 041597
Miles, David A. 049294
Miles, Ed 042214
Miles, Ellen 048933
Miles, Gwyn 040307
Miletić, Jelena 034177
Mileusnić, Slobodan 034166
Mileusnić, Snježana Radovanlija . . 007854
Milev, Svetoslav 004842
Milhazes, Dr. Maria Claúdia C. . . . 032582
Miliadzidou-Ioannou, Dr. E. 021491
Milian, Mihai 032961
Milius, James 044215
Milivojević, Radmila 034204
Milkofsky, Brenda 049129
Mill, Dennis J. 046709
Millan, William I. 038635
Millar, Jim 006187
Millar, Joyce 006164
Millard, Ellen 006555
Millard, Jamie 045259
Millard, Rhoda 005345
Millas, Dr. Rolando 045816
Millaud, Hiriata 015395
Millberg, Per-Olof 036360, 036361
Mille, Dr. Diana Dimodica 043787
Millen, A.J. 005030
Miller, Alan 000849
Miller, Dr. Albrecht 016938, 019361
Miller, Alison 038602
Miller, Andree . . . 041659, 042655, 043623
Miller, Angus 039622
Miller, Archie W. 006004
Miller, Bob 047457
Miller, Charles 046729
Miller, C.J. 044372
Miller, Corinne 039950
Miller, David 048009
Miller, David M. 045783
Miller, Denise 042836
Miller, Don 043976
Miller, Douglas 046042
Miller, E.M.J. 038606, 040370
Miller, Prof. George 044492
Miller, George 047086
Miller, Gerald J. 047906
Miller, Gordon 042862
Miller, Prof. Dr. H. 019059
Miller, Harriet 046433
Miller, Howard L. 044461
Miller, Jacky 038686
Miller, Dr. James 045265
Miller, Janelle 047590
Miller, John 041198, 044363
Miller, Dr. J.Y. 044103
Miller, Dr. Kathy Ann 048466
Miller, Kevin R. 043331
Miller, Kristin 041645
Miller, Dr. L.D. 044103
Miller, Lenore D. 048897
Miller, Linda L. 043665
Miller, Lisa 041657
Miller, Lois 044647
Miller, Margaret A. 048487
Miller, Marguerite 041655
Miller, Dr. Markus 016907
Miller, Mary 045490
Miller, Michael 047168, 048253
Miller, Nan L. 047412, 047412
Miller, Nancy Lee 042352
Miller, Pamela 047230
Miller, Paul F. 046464
Miller, R. Craig 043404
Miller, Randy 006354
Miller, Roger 049209
Miller, Rosemary 001112
Miller, Ruby 041577
Miller, Sammy 040526
Miller, Sandy 048392
Miller, Stephen 045108, 045149
Miller, Steve 046036
Miller, Steven 040871
Miller, Susan 047878
Miller, Tammy 043657
Miller, Terry J. 044117
Miller, Tom 005510
Miller, Tracy 042155
Miller, Walter 048458
Miller, William 039487, 040281
Miller, William K. 043520
Miller Batty, Nancy 049202
Miller-Betts, Christine 041899
Miller Zohn, Kristen 041595
Millereau, Marie-Pierre 010858
Millet, Florence 012436
Millet, Teresa 035976
Millett, Prof. Martin 038967
Milli, Konrad 018124
Milligan, Frank D. 046126
Milligan Ryan, Barbara 049332
Millin, Laura J. 045931
Milliner, Marcus 006105
Millman, David 045191
Millroth, Thomas 036806
Mills, Brendon 045113
Mills, Cynthia K. 042229
Mills, Dan 045241
Mills, David 046227
Mills, Dinah 048782, 048783
Mills, Ellsworth 044539
Mills, Gina 044849
Mills, J. 041399
Mills, John 039430
Mills, John K. 047243
Mills, Nigel 041321
Mills, R.G. 041306
Mills, Susan 038488
Milne, Julie 040550
Milne, Lee 001095
Milne, V. 000721
Milne, William K. 040479
Milne, W.K. 039787
Milner, Renate 048729
Milnor, Nancy 044132
Milojković, Jelica 034244
Milonjić, Miroslav 007786
Milosavljević, Branka 034172
Milošević, Prof. Ante 007793, 007803
Milosevich, Joe B. 044876
Milosis, Themis 021266
Miloux, Yannick 012690
Milovanović, Dušan 034163
Milson, Andrew 039453
Milstren, Dr. Gerhard 036704
Milton-Elmore, Kara 046541
Milton-Tee, Ann 030501
Milyov, Simeon 004863
Min, Choi Hyong 027436
Mina, Dr. Gianna A. 037269
Minahan, Nancy M. 048436
Minar, Rena 048482
Minard, Barbara 044716
Minarini, Dr. Laura 023425
Minassian, Levon 022560
Minchinton, J. 040596
Mindell, Prof. David P. 041734, 041734
Minder, Nicole 037679
Mine, William K. 038588
Mineau, Marc 006491
Mineeva, Valentina Alekseevna . . . 033064
Minegishi, Sumio 027115
Miner, Curt 044444
Miner, Donald J. 047605
Minerva, Michael 046373
Minetti, Dr. Alessandra 025797
Minish, Marveen 045774
Minke, Prof. Dr. Alfred 003430
Minkenberg, Dr. Georg 015419
Minkkinen, Aimo 010122
Minmeister, J.C. 011644
Minney, Michael J 045146
Minns, Dr. Jonathan E. 039776
Mino, Dr. Yutaka 026985
Minse, C. 029662
Minter, Sue 040115
Minto, Don 044835
Minto, Heather 044835
Minton, Dwayne 021569
Mints, Carolyn 042760
Mintz, Ann 047068
Mintz, Deborah Martin 043832
Minx, Jim 046650
Mion-Jones, Esta 041058
Miotkandal, Oddvar 031058
Mir, Dr. Ronen 041914
Mir-khalaf, A. 022561
Mira, Vegar 007699
Mira Bonomi, Angelo Vittorio 024269, 025871
Mirabdolbaghi, Zia 015157
Mirabella Roberti, Prof. Mario 026215
Miranda, Gaudenzio 024991
Mirelez, Cathy 044195
Mirmoghtadaie, S. 022562
Mirnik, Dr. Ivan 007828
Mirolo, Diana 036855
Miron, Dr. Andrei 019961
Miron, Dr. O. 023007
Mironneau, Paul 013752
Mironowicz-Panek, Maria 032161
Mirzejewska, Maria 032429
Misago, Dr. Kanimba 034100
Miscault, René de 012423
Mischke, Petra 017856
Mischkewitz, Franz 019219
Mišečkina, Marija V. 033155
Mishima, Tadao 026926
Mishima, Yashuhisa 026954
Mishima, Yoshinori 026954
Mishne, Merle H. 045748
Mishra, H. P 022037
Mišina, Ljudmila Aleksandrovna . . 033692
Misjuga, Bogdan Vasil'ovič 038358
Miskovic, Svetlana 006831
Miskowski, Anthony 048605
Mislej, Irene 034456
Misner, Mary 005205
Misočnik, Svetlana Michajlovna . . 033892
Misof, Dr. Bernhard 016337
Miss, Dr. Stig 008990
Mitanov, Petăr 004877
Mitchel, Gary 043227
Mitchell, Archie 048691
Mitchell, Barbara 044631
Mitchell, D.I. 041067
Mitchell, Freda 042394
Mitchell, Harold 000899
Mitchell, James 042749
Mitchell, Jena 047541
Mitchell, Joan 001006
Mitchell, Joanne 041647
Mitchell, Kay 046094
Mitchell, Leah 044833, 046426
Mitchell, Marjorie 047460
Mitchell, Paul 005304
Mitchell, Dr. Peter 040665
Mitchell, Renee 045006, 045007
Mitchell, Sandra 045606
Mitchell, Sue 001537
Mitev, P. 004816
Miteva, Kremena 004671
Mitheis, Christine 001706
Mitkevič, V.M. 032992, 032993
Mitkovs'ka, Tetjana Sergiïvna 038362
Mitne, Debra 044756
Mitre, Dr. Jorge Carlos 000223
Mitrev, Dimităr . . 004770, 004772, 004833
Mitrović, Miodrag 034280
Mitsuoka, Tadanari 026427
Mittas, Nicole 017232
Mittelberg, Antje 017680
Mitten, David 042560
Mittendorfer, Gabriele 002606
Mitterhöfer, Dr. Jakob 002325
Mitterwenger, Dr. Christine 002414, 002415, 002416, 002417
Mittmann, Dr. Hans-Walter 018170
Mittwoch, Wolfgang 017113
Mitzel, Horst 020789
Mitzel, June 005439
Mitzevich, Nick 001326
Mitzscherlich, Dr. Birgit 015899
Miwa, Kenjin 027256
Miyagawa, Ellen 046803
Miyaji, Nobuo 026942
Miyake, Akiko 026659
Miyake, Tetsuhisa 027338
Miyamoto, Akio 026602
Miyaoka, Kiyomi 027086
Miyatani, Masayuki 027104
Miyazaki, Katsumi 027148
Miyazaki, Takashi 026896
Miyazawa, Akimichi 026884
Miyazima, Hisao 027088
Mizerová, Hana 008590
Mizerski, Dr. Włodzimierz 032439
Mizina, Ljudmila V. 033923
Mizinga, Flexon Moono 049574
Mizukami, Iwao 026547
Mizukami, Takeo 027030
Mizukami, Takeshi 027140
Mizuno, Keizaburo 026851
Mizuno, Takashi 027009
Mizuno Elliott, Nancy 047397
Mizuta, Dr. Akira 026894
Mizutani, Takeshi 027256
Mjasiščeva, Olena Georgiïvna 038405
Mjøs, Lise 031113
Mlecz, Stella C. 047391
Mleczko, Radoslaw 032465
Mlynarčík, Dr. Jozef 034386
Mlynarski, Ryszard 032531

Mo, Charles . . . 042760
Moacir Maia, Prof. Pedro . . . 004445
Moberg, Jack . . . 045672
Mobley, Ree . . . 047972
Moc, Joan S. . . . 045734
Mochi Onori, Dr. Lorenza . 025479, 026173
Mochola, Tatiana . . . 031973
Mochoruk, Mike . . . 006026
Mochova, Jelena Fillipovna . . . 032972
Mock, Rayonna . . . 041666
Moctezuma, Allessandra . . . 047835
Modegi, Masaaki . . . 027248
Modelsee, Susanne . . . 017192
Modersohn, Christian . . . 019541
Modest, Wayne . . . 026385
Modi, Amrutbhai . . . 021990
Modonesi, Dr. Denise . . . 026291
Modotti, Luigi . . . 023905
Modrzejewska, Dr. Irena . . . 031823
Moe, Barbara . . . 044299, 044993
Moe, Helene . . . 031055, 031056
Moe, Richard . . . 048936
Möbius, Ingrid . . . 018997
Moed, G.J. . . . 029963
Moeferdt, Dr. Horst . . . 016725
Möhlenkamp, Dr. Klaus . . . 018979
Möhlmeyer, Erich . . . 019507
Möhring, Barbara . . . 017748
Möhring, Dr. Helmut . . . 019917
Moehring, Markus . . . 018670
Möller, Axel . . . 016051
Möller, Hilke Gesine . . . 018736
Möller, Kristina . . . 036594
Moeller, Prof. Magdalena . . . 016003
Möller, Marie von 030756, 030757, 030758
Möller, Peter . . . 036725
Möller, Dr. Reimer 020230, 020231, 020233
Möller, Dr. Werner . . . 016684
Möller-Arnsberg, Birgit . . . 019070
Moen, Eivind . . . 031268
Moench, Esther . . . 010594
Mönig, Dr. Roland . . . 018280
Mönkkönen, Mikko . . . 009935
Moens, Dominique . . . 003684, 003762, 003863
Moens, Karel . . . 003193
Mörgeli, Markus . . . 037351
Mörike, Dr. Doris . . . 020364
Moering, Dr. Renate . . . 017167
Moers, Rainer . . . 017653
Mörtinger, Franz . . . 001757
Mörzer Bruyns, W.F.J. . . . 029216
Moes, K. . . . 029249
Moeske, Ulrich . . . 016769
Mössinger, Ingrid . . . 016558
Mössner, Dr. Wolfgang . . . 018440, 018441
Moetlo, Nancy . . . 034730
Moffat, Jill . . . 044082
Mofford, Juliet . . . 041722
Moga, Jack . . . 044308
Moga, John . . . 044311
Mogensen, Ove . . . 009131
Moget, Layla . . . 014799
Mohamadi, Naghme . . . 022593
Mohammadrezaie, P. . . . 022570
Mohan, S. . . . 036159
Mohl, Dr. Max . . . 015885
Mohr, John . . . 048605
Mohr, Julie . . . 040409
Mohr, Peter . . . 040409
Mohr, Vibeke . . . 031191
Mohring, Marilyn . . . 047512
Moigne, Roland de . . . 010942
Moilanen, Arja . . . 010130
Moisala, Prof. Pirkko . . . 010169
Moisen Lechuga, Patricia . . . 028511
Moises, Loly Keith . . . 031683
Mojica, Brenda . . . 031680
Mojseeva, T.M. . . . 033803
Mojzer, Miklós . . . 021694
Mojžíšová, Dr. Olga . . . 008398, 008626
Mokarram Hossain, Mahmud . . . 003112
Mokhtar Bin Abu Bakar, Dato Mohamed . . . 028007
Mokre, Jan . . . 002905, 002971
Mol . . . 003808
Mol, I. . . . 029396
Mol, W. . . . 029351
Moland, Arnfinn . . . 031091
Moldenhauer, Susan . . . 045170
Molen, Dr. J.R. ter . . . 029256
Molenda, Remigiusz . . . 032045
Molesworth-Saint Aubyn, Lady Iona . . . 038776
Molin, Dr. Paulette . . . 044415
Molina, Prof. Mario . . . 031418
Molina Cabal, Alvaro José . . . 007495
Molina Pico, Horacio . . . 000633
Molinare, Rod . . . 040095
Molinari, Arno . . . 003018
Molinari, Danielle . . . 013605, 040937
Molinari, Giovanni . . . 025848
Molinaro, Ettore . . . 023509
Molinaro, Marcene J. . . . 044954
Molins, Javier . . . 035976
Molist, Miguel . . . 034920
Molitor, Anne . . . 003305
Mollano, Prof. Olga . . . 000466
Mollay, Catherine . . . 005836
Møller, Dan E. . . . 009150
Møller, Lars Kærulf . . . 008882
Møller, Stig B. . . . 008798
Møller-Hansen, Keld . . . 009153
Moller-Pedersen, Kurt . . . 008809
Moller-Racke, Heidi . . . 018789
Molles, Dr. Manuel C. . . . 041619
Mollett, Fran . . . 048605
Mollfulleda i Borrell, Joaquin . . . 034855
Mollo, B. . . . 039377
Molloy, Dr. Peter M. . . . 047008
Molnar, August J. . . . 046207
Molnár, Dr. Erzsébet . . . 021768, 021769
Molnár, Sándor . . . 021914
Mols, P. . . . 030263
Molsbergen, B. . . . 029435
Molteni, A. . . . 012620
Moltesen, Mette . . . 008982
Moltke-Hansen, David . . . 046949
Molvær, Edvard . . . 030719
Momas, Jacques . . . 010968
Mombrun, C. . . . 021555
Momčilov, Dimčo . . . 004707
Monachon, Danuta . . . 013583
Monaco, Dr. Giuseppe . . . 025495
Monaghan, A. . . . 040944
Monaghan, Bryan . . . 005396
Monaghan, Ciaran . . . 038438
Monaghan, Nigel . . . 022762
Monahan, Gloria . . . 005818
Monbron, Comte de . . . 012281
Moncrief, Dr. Nancy D. . . . 045715
Moncur, Shannon . . . 005110
Mond, Ulrike . . . 016323
Mondini, Massimo . . . 023510
Mondragón, Lourdes . . . 028427
Mondragón, Martín Antonio . . . 028806
Monds, Kathy . . . 047124
Monedoñedo Espinoza, Juan . . . 031569
Monery, Jean-Paul . . . 014558
Mones, Prof. Alvaro . . . 041532
Money, Eric . . . 040875
Monfort, Catherine . . . 003710
Mongan, Barbara . . . 043121
Monge, Janet . . . 046993
Monge, Maria de Jesus . . . 032701
Mongellaz, Jacqueline . . . 014701, 014704
Mongon, Alain . . . 010481
Moniak, Eugeniusz . . . 032566
Monigan, Michael F. . . . 048953
Moniot, François . . . 010882
Monk, Suny . . . 048447
Monkhouse, Christopher . . . 045918
Monmousseau, Patrice . . . 014698
Monnani, Walter . . . 001715
Monnet, C. . . . 012679
Monney, Paul . . . 037475
Monnier, Georges . . . 037555
Monnier, Jean-Laurent . . . 013767
Monod, Frédéric . . . 013086
Monot, Michel . . . 015304
Monrad, Kasper . . . 008988
Monroe, Dan L. . 047734, 047736, 047737, 047739, 047740, 047741
Monroe, Dr. Sam . . . 047126
Monschaw, Elline von . . . 022763
Montag, Dr. Ulrich . . . 019037
Montagne, Dr. C. . . . 029435
Montagu of Beaulieu, Lord 038878, 038879
Montaner, Jaume . . . 034933
Montani, Miro . . . 007836
Montanini, Deborah . . . 047029
Montaut . . . 014426
Montebello, Philippe de . . . 046364
Montefiore, Don . . . 001140
Monteil, Esclarmonde . . . 010988
Montenegro, Dr. Raffaele . . . 023348
Montenegro Carneiro, Maria Margarida V. . . . 032661
Montérémal, R. . . . 012565
Montero, Alberto E. . . . 006906
Montero, Prof. Paula . . . 004527
Montero Agüerz, Ildefonso . . . 035117
Montesano, Frank . . . 043165
Montesdeoca García-Sáenz, Antonio Daniel . . . 035627
Montet-White, Anta . . . 045204
Monteyne, Nathalie . . . 003163
Montfort, Helen G. . . . 044378
Montgomery, A. . . . 039802
Montgomery, Alexander . . . 006600
Montgomery, Alexandra . . . 040859
Montgomery, Cathie . . . 041133
Montgomery, D. Bruce . . . 042685
Montgomery, Erick D. . . . 041896
Montgomery, Florence . . . 042320
Montgomery, Dr. John . . . 047150
Montgomery, Küllike . . . 036734
Montgomery, N. . . . 034561
Montgomery, Dr. Sally . . . 038670
Montgomery, S.E. . . . 041308
Montgomery, Prof. W.I. . . . 038663
Montgomery Tyler, Kay . . . 042719
Monti, Canco Pietro . . . 024925
Monticelli, Dr. Paolo . . . 024965
Montileaux, Paulette . . . 047336
Montin, Kim . . . 010162, 010170
Montjalin, Olaf de . . . 014713
Montmany, Marta . . . 034934
Montñés García, Carmen . . . 036101
Montoya Soto, Sonia . . . 007485
Montserrat Martí, Dr. J.M. . . . 034938
Monzó, Josep Vicent . . . 035976
Moodie, Laura . . . 005171
Moodie, Sandra . . . 026389
Moody, Dr. Barry . . . 005017
Moody, Eric N. . . . 047372
Moody, Tammy . . . 043475
Mooij, Dr. Charles de . . . 029736
Moombolah-Goagoses, Esther U. . 029107, 029108
Moombolah-Joagoses, Esther U. . . 029104
Moon, Diane . . . 040214
Moon, John P.C. . . . 047414
Moons, L.J.M. . . . 029661
Moore, Anne . . . 040499
Moore, Barbara . . . 046765
Moore, Bennett . . . 044411
Moore, Carleton B. . . . 048519
Moore, Dr. Carlton . . . 045793
Moore, Dan . . . 041842
Moore jr., Dan . . . 041842
Moore, David . . . 038825
Moore, Dona . . . 005672
Moore, Duane . . . 048648
Moore, Dr. Dwight . . . 043706
Moore, Dr. Elizabeth A. . . . 045715
Moore, Fran . . . 005336
Moore, Gary F. . . . 048653
Moore, George . . . 043938
Moore, Harold D. . . . 048195
Moore, J. Roderick . . . 043839
Moore, James C. . . . 041613
Moore, Jennifer . . . 044330
Moore, Juanita . . . 044914
Moore, Kevin . . . 040780
Moore, Linda . . . 046112
Moore, Margaret . . . 046123
Moore, Margaret Jane . . . 042011
Moore, Michael R. . . . 047405
Moore, Nick . . . 039217, 039472, 039607, 040648, 040751, 040959
Moore, Richard . . . 001177
Moore, Richard H. . . . 044203
Moore, Rod . . . 039112
Moore, S. . . . 005384
Moore, Susan J. . . . 044623
Moore, Terry . . . 044524
Moore, Prof. Thomas E. . . . 041734
Moore, Dr. Viola . . . 046811
Moore, William J. . . . 044332
Moore, William S. . . . 043458
Moore Cole, Alisha . . . 044927
Moore Stucker, Kathryn . . . 047025
Moorefield, Amy G. . . . 047409
Moorer, Bill . . . 005504
Moores-Franklin, Lolisa . . . 047077
Moos, Dr. David . . . 042223
Moppett, Ronald . . . 005189
Moqimi-zadeh, Hamid . . . 022568
Mor, Judith . . . 023103
Mora, Alejandra . . . 028606
Mora, Dr. Rafael A. . . . 000187
Mora García, Carlos . . . 028928
Morabito, Dr. Leo . . . 024306
Moraes Branco, Pércio de . . . 004297
Moraes Sophia, Eunice . . . 004530
Moragas, Cora Romy . . . 006917
Moraitou-Apostolopoulou, Dr. Maria . . . 021537
Moral, Mary del . . . 046694
Morales, April . . . 045067
Morales, Dr. Michael . . . 043703
Morales-Coll, Eduardo . . . 032728
Morales Gómez, Antonio . . . 028593
Morales Gómez, David . . . 028594
Morales Pérez, Eduardo . . . 028898
Morales Ramón, José María . . . 035468
Moran, Liz . . . 041104
Moran, Maryann . . . 048062
Moran, Paula G. . . . 041589
Moran, Vivienne . . . 001562
Moran-Zerda, Leticia . . . 031735, 031744
Moraña, Prof. Oscar . . . 049457
Morand, J. . . . 005379
Morand, Lynn L. 045551, 045552, 045554, 045556
Morand, Marie-Claude . . 037478, 037563, 037564, 037565, 037566
Morandini, Dr. Carlo . . . 026166
Morante López, Dr. Rubén Bernardo . . . 028941
Morash, Terrence . . . 042341
Morath-Vogel, Dr. Wolfram 017006, 017008
Moravčík, J. . . . 034452
Moravec, Tomaš . . . 008553
Morawietz, Doris . . . 018230
Morawinska, Agnieszka . . . 032483
Mórawski, Karol . . . 032476
Morawski, Mike . . . 044984
Morbach, Philippe . . . 013707
Morbán Laucer, Dr. Fernando . . . 009163
Morbis, Daniela . . . 023351
Morcom, G. . . . 034608
Morcos Gayyed, Mervat . . . 009331
Mordasini, Andrea . . . 036992
Mordi, Pietro . . . 024443
More-Molyneux, Michael . . . 039649
Moreau, Susie K. . . . 005641
Morehouse, Dorothy V. . . . 045321
Morel, Michel . . . 005364
Morel, Pascal . . . 014258

Morel, Sylvie 005504
Morel-Deledalle, Myriame 012947
Morelli, Gianni 025401
Morello, Dr. Giovanni 049431, 049432
Morelock, Dr. Jerry 044099
Moreno, Amanda 038529
Moreno, Anne Marie 031791
Moreno, Barry 046408
Moreno, Enrique 035405
Moreno, María Cristina 007527
Moreño de Medellín, Patricia 028913
Moreno Garrido, Maria Jesús 035113
Moreno Ulloa, Graciela 007672
Moret, J.-L. 037247
Moretti, Dr. A. Maria 025554
Moretti, Dr. Giovanni 024064
Moretti, Dr. Mario 023807
Moretti, Prof. Mario 025729, 025731
Moretti, Dr. Mario 026349
Morey, Mark 041678
Morgan, B.V. 006005
Morgan, Chris 038934, 040529, 043917
Morgan, Dahlia 045805
Morgan, Dave 045950
Morgan, David 044804
Morgan, Gary 001041
Morgan, Dr. Gary 001377
Morgan, Dr. J.D. 047114
Morgan, Jeremy 006264
Morgan, Jessica 042327
Morgan, K. 030431
Morgan, Kerry 042704
Morgan, Martin 041761
Morgan, Peter J. 041033
Morgan, Peter M. 046144
Morgan, Ron 039150
Morgan, Zane 043642
Morgan-Welch, Beverly 042333
Morgenegg, Hans 037041
Morgenroth, Heiner 018286
Morhun, Sue 005462
Mori, Masatoshi 026550
Moriarty, M.J. 039067
Moriarty, Steve 046574
Morier-Genoud, Gabriel 037010, 037011
Morigi Govi, Dr. Cristiana 023425
Morillo León, Anabel 035856
Morin, Cathy J. 046104
Morin, Robert G. 046104
Morinelli, Dom Leone 023774
Morishigue, Akifumi 026957
Morison, J. 039666
Moritsch, Dr. Otmar 003009
Moritz, Craig 042164
Moritz, Franz 018346
Moritz, Heidi 016880
Moritz, Dr. Marina 017018
Moritz, Per 036438
Moriyama, Mayumi 027218
Moriyama, Ryoichi 026450
Mork, Eileen 044478
Morkowski, J. 037435
Morl, Dr. Claudia 024215
Morletta, Martine 040071
Morley, Stephen H. 042493
Morlok, Dr. Wolfgang 020093
Morman, C. 029364
Morna, Dr. Teresa 032641
Morneburg, Otto 015903
Moro, Alberto E. 000378
Moro, Luigi 023120
Moroder, Robert 025015
Moroyama, Masanori 027256
Morozov, Ivan Ivanovič 033303
Morozov, Vladimir Vasilevič 033477
Morozova, Ludmila Ivanovna 033666
Morozova, T.V. 033222
Morral, Eulàlia 035905
Morrall, Dr. Andrew 046300
Morran, Gerald 005542
Morretta, Rosemary 047435
Morrill, Andreu 042613
Morrin, Peter 045498
Morris, Charles 042749
Morris, C.I. 039590
Morris, Clive 038991
Morris, D. 039079
Morris, David 040416, 047385
Morris, Derek 040270, 054473
Morris, Jack 005667
Morris, Jeffory 047267
Morris, Joan 039934
Morris, John 003881
Morris, Johnathan 001016
Morris, Lynda 040609
Morris, Mark 047713
Morris, Martha 048927
Morris, Nell 045104
Morris, Pamela 047178
Morris, Patricia A. 047725
Morris, Susan 042162
Morris Hambourg, Maria 046364
Morrison, Andrew 038681, 039160, 039764, 040836, 041188, 041367
Morrison, Angela 040893
Morrison, Charlotte K. 043385
Morrison, Cindi 045148
Morrison, D. 001467
Morrison, David A. 005504
Morrison, Garth 039651
Morrison, James F. 044871
Morrison, Kim 044557
Morrison, Lynn 040880
Morrison, Lynne 045143
Morrison, Mark T. 047712
Morrison, Philip R. 046499
Morrison, Renee 041745
Morrison, Sandra 046820
Morrisroe, Julia 046065
Morrissey, Dr. Kris 043575
Morrissey, Tom 045318
Morsch, Prof. Dr. Günter 019478
Morsch, Nathalie 005105
Morsch, Sigrid 019425
Morscheck, Charles 046963
Morscher, Lukas 002082
Morscher, Dr. Lukas 002083
Morse, Carla 006604
Morse, F.E. 042914
Morsiani, Paola 044637
Mort, Mark 045205
Mortensen, Ingrid 009145
Mortenson, Marianne 045408
Morteveille, Gérard 014619
Morteyrol, Amélie 014936
Mortimer, Kristen 044231
Morton, Craddock 000890
Morton, Doug 042959
Morton, E. 006671, 040548
Morton, Geneva 046813
Morton, Lisa 043544, 054743
Morton, Susan 041272
Morucci, Alberto 025641
Moś, Ignacy 032247
Mosby, Dewey F. 044401
Moschig, Günther 002133
Mosco, Dr. Marilena 024170, 024176
Mosconi, Prof. Andrea 023994, 023999
Moscoso Möller, M.A. Fernando 021581
Mosdal, Brita 008877
Mosel, Günter 017750
Moseley, Bruce M. 046688
Mosena, David R. 042865
Mosenfelder, Mrs. Robert 043727
Mosenstine, Ken 042585
Moser, Audrey 043509
Moser, Dr. Bernd 001938
Moser, Christopher L. 047460
Moser, Dr. Juliane 017097
Moser, Rene 043223
Moser-Gautrand, Claire 011012
Moses, H. Vincent 047460
Moses, Stephen A. 046253, 046254
Moses Nesmith, Cynthia 043084
Mosharraf Hossain, M. 003097
Moshenson, Edna 023092
Moshier, Wendy 047756
Mosica, Phillippe 014469
Moskovaja, Ljudmila Ivanovna 033620, 033621
Mosneagu, Marian 032845
Moss, Ed 042490
Moss, Gillian 046319
Moss, Kay K. 044154
Moss, Kenneth 046366
Moss, Michael E. 049096
Moss, Rick 046589
Moss, Dr. Roger W. 046924
Mossman, Kate 005489
Moster-Hoos, Dr. Jutta 019468
Mostert, Antoinette 029083
Mothe, Florence 013926
Mothe, Hubert 012448
Motlotle, Ntikwe Pene 003953
Motornaja, Larisa Ivanovna 033555
Motoyama, Yoshiao 027185
Mott, Joyce 045246
Mottart, Eugène 003692
Motte, Vic 003790
Motte Saint-Pierre, Marquise de la 013177
Mottram, Graham 039792, 041471
Motyka, Jerzy 031877
Motyka, Maria 032076
Moudry, Mary Lou 042383
Mouely-Koumba, Marie-Agnès 015397
Mougel, René 012195
Moughdad, S. 037825
Mougin, Denis 012504
Mouillaud, Jean 011906
Mould, Laurel 005610
Moulias, Christos 021425
Moulin, Hélène 015096
Moulin, Pierre 010547
Moult, Lynne 039986
Mounier, Bernard 014895
Mount, Steven 046479
Mountbatten of Burma, Countess 038537
Mountfort, Dick 042204
Moura, Fernando 032638
Moura Delphim, Angelo Alberto de 004186
Mouralová, Blanca 016185
Mourão, R. 004252
Mourlet, Gérard 014610
Mousley, Patricia K. 044626
Moussa Nene, Djamil 006903
Mousseigne, Alain 014986
Moussellard, Renaud Pascal 011123
Mousset, Jean-Luc 027894
Moutashar, Michèle 010472
Mouton, Romona 045090
Mouw, Christine 049066
Movan, Lisa 040461
Movillon, Mario M. 031690
Mowat, Dr. P. 040643
Mowll Mathews, Nancy 049188
Mowrey, Debbie 041792
Mowry, Robert 042560
Moxeme, Oscar O. 047161
Moxley, Richard W. 047407
Moy, Henry 044710
Moya Pons, Frank 009162
Moya-Valgañón, José Gabriel 035439
Moyce, Greg 047960
Moye, L.M. 045522
Moye, Matthew M. 045522
Moyes, Nick 039225
Moyle, N. 040722
Moyle, Nicola 040721
Moynes, Debbie 005005
Moynihan, George P. 048089
Moyroud, Raymond 010977
Mozales, José 035247
Mpouna Coline, Samuel 021595
Mrabet, Ridha 037970
Mrachacz, Maria 018317
Mravlincić, Ivan 007811
Mraz, Dr. Gottfried 002907
Mroczkowski, Dennis P. 043953
Mršić, Vjekoslav 007858
Mrugalska-Banaszak, Magdalena 032245
Mrva, Dr. Marián 034452
Mrvová, J. 034452
Msemwa, Dr. Paul J. 037851
Msimanga, A. 049579
Msonge, Andreas 037857
Mtshiza, Zola 034587
Muceus, Cheryl 041571, 041573
Muchametčina, Lejla Munirovna 033285
Muchanov, Gennadij Stepanovič 033251
Muchitsch, Dr. Wolfgang 001938
Mucnjak, Prof. Alois 002873
Mudd, Margaret 045934, 045935
Mudd, Michael 044687
Muddiman, Susi 001078
Mühlbacher, Anton 002435
Mühlbacher, Peter 019761
Mühlbauer, Heinrich 018542
Mühlberger, Dr. Kurt 002849
Mühldorfer-Vogt, Christian 019683, 019685, 019687, 019689
Mühlegger-Heuhapel, Dr. Christiane 002979
Mühlemann, Yves 037021
Mühlhäußer, Werner 017607, 017608
Muehlig, Linda 046545
Mühne, Dr. Christian 019626
Mülhaupt, Freya 015991
Müllauer, Gerhard 003077
Müllejans-Dickmann, Dr. Rita 017338, 017859
Müller, A. 019938
Müller, Dr. Adelheid 019352
Müller, Andreas 017239
Müller, Anette 021088
Müller, Astrid B. 016081
Müller, Berit 020987
Müller, Bruno 001794
Mueller, Carlyn 045388
Müller, Dr. Christian 036890, 036891
Müller, Dr. Claudius 019122
Müller, Conrad 017275
Müller, Erwin 018934
Müller, Eugen 002239
Müller, Prof. Dr. Felix 036927
Müller, Gerda 017606
Müller, Dr. Gino 037247
Müller, Gisela 017211
Mueller, Dr. Gordon H. 046260
Müller, H. 016346
Müller, Dr. H. P. 037490
Müller, Hans 002838
Müller, Dr. Hans-Peter 018559
Müller, Heike 019464, 019465, 019466
Müller, Heinz-Willi 015648
Müller, Hermann 036959
Müller, Dr. Ingeborg 015979
Müller, Prof. Dr. Irmgard 016280
Mueller, Jane 042496
Müller, Johann 037459
Müller, Johann Paul M. 002086
Mueller, John 045539
Mueller, Judith 046342
Müller, Dr. Jürg P. 037018
Müller, Dr. Karsten 020356
Müller, Klaus 016359
Müller, Dr. Klaus-Peter 019469
Müller, Dr. Maria 016834
Müller, Dr. Markus 019145
Müller, Markus 036882
Mueller, Prof. Marlene 049028
Müller, Dr. Martin 016972, 017370, 017375, 021032
Müller, Matthias 017967
Müller, Dr. Maya 036893
Müller, Michael 018376
Müller, Peter 020391, 020392
Müller, Dr. Peter 021686
Müller, Dr. R. 020353
Müller, Dr. Róbert 021764
Müller, Dr. Roland 020366, 020367
Müller, Roland 037068
Müller, Rolf 037647

Müller, Rudolf 037702
Müller, Sabine 017214, 053470
Mueller, Shirley 049351
Müller, Dr. Siegfried 016276
Müller, Stefan 018999, 019002
Müller, Prof. Telmo Lauro 004491
Müller, Thomas 018589
Müller, Dr. Thomas 020381
Müller, Thomas 037757
Müller, Urs 036863
Müller, Dr. Volker 020588
Müller, Walter 015441
Müller, Werner 016834
Müller, Prof. Dr. Werner 019895
Müller, Wolfgang 016758, 016760
Müller, Zsuzsanna 036623
Müller-Bahlke, Dr. Thomas 017655
Müller-Gaebele, Erich H. 017271
Müller-Karpe, Dr. Michael 018794
Müller-Krumbach, Dr. Renate 015895
Müller-Merz, Dr. Edith 037578
Müller-Serre, Helga 019797
Müller-Späth, Esther 017962
Müller-Tamm, Dr. Pia 016834
Müller-Westermann, Dr. Iris 036645
Müller-Wirth, Sabine 018158, 018169
Münch, Eugen 020506
Muench Navarro, Pablo 028895, 028898, 028902
Münch-Severin, Kornelia 016029
Muenkel, Harold 045548
Münzel, Prof. Dr. Mark 018829
Mürner, Rolf 037301
Muertegui, Charles 031652
Müsch, Dr. Imgard 020374
Mugavero, C.J. 041656
Muggeridge, Rosalind 046367
Muhlena, David 042678
Muir, Eleanor 041105
Muirhead, Frank H. 039182
Mujta, Dr. Józef Stanisław 032009
Mukai, Tetsuya 027121
Mukai, Tomoko 027169
Mukanova, N. 027392
Mukasa, Josephine 038219
Mukela, Manyando 049567
Mukulu 029091
Mulcahy, Fran 043933
Mulcahy, Michael 022816
Mulder, Dr. E.W.A. 029469
Mulder, Jenny 029398
Muldoon, Patrick L. 046460
Mulford, Hansen 046719
Mulholland, Hugh 038665
Mulk, Dr. Inga-Maria 036366
Mulka, Denise 040440
Mulkey, Terry 046047, 046048
Mull, Astrid 014056
Mullally, Matt 047565
Mullen, Beverly J. 042899
Mullen, Cindy 046605
Mullen, Kathy 047147
Muller, Dena 046279
Muller, Donald 042417
Muller, Jean-Paul 013296
Muller, Joe 044630
Muller, John 043939
Muller, Judith 046336
Muller, M. Gilles 052915
Muller, Norman 047240
Muller, Pam 047641
Mullers Bast, G.J. 029670
Mulligan, Dermot 022700
Mulligan, Therese 047480
Mullin, Amanda 046934
Mullin, D. 038677
Mullin, Marsha A. 044522
Mullins, Colleen 047696, 052085
Mullins, James 022801
Mullins, Margaret 022787
Mullins, Monica 038507
Mullins, Rose 038782
Mullins, Roy 046848
Mullins, Sam 040213
Mullio, Cara 049083
Mullis, Connie 045999
Mulqueen, Grace 022819
Mulvaney, Rebecca 041560
Mulvany, Dr. John 042836
Mummery, Brian 039797
Mun, Kyong Hyun 027476
Munakata, Pariji 026613
Munch, Jytte 009126
Munck, Jacqueline 013630
Munday, Graham K. 038814
Mundel, Ernst 015785
Munder, Heike 037780
Mundorff, Angelika 017284
Mundus, Doris 018594
Mundwiller, Mollye C. 044521
Mundy, James 047211
Muney Moore, Julia 044746
Munk, Dr. Jan 008713
Munk Pedersen, Hans 008864, 008865, 008867
Munksgaard, Jan Henrik 030959
Munktell, Ing-Marie 036741
Munnerlyn, Ron J. 042145
Munns, Judith 048199
Muno, Ed 046647
Muno Jordan, Iris 043612
Munoz, Carol 043640
Muñoz, Concha Carmona 035472
Munrde, Pamela E. 045079
Munro, Dr. David M. 039897
Munro, Gale 048954
Munro, J.A. 038962
Munro, Lewis 039779
Munroe, Alexandra 046351
Munroe, Dan L. 047735
Munroe, Pam 048842
Munroe Hjerstedt, E. 046736
Munshi, Prof. Supriya 022022
Munsick, Lee R. 046807
Munson, Julie 044624
Munson, Larry 048141
Munson, Robin 044131
Munstermann, Leonard 046226
Munt, Martin 040956
Munteanu, Simona 032835
Munteanu, Vasile 032878
Munthe, Adam 040293, 040504
Muntildeoz Rivera, Lorena 007440
Munyer-Branyan, Cheryl 046161
Munyikwa, D. 049579
Muolo, Vicenzo 024795
Mur, Pilar 034989
Mura-Smith, Collin 046417
Mura Sommella, Dr. Anna 025464, 025490, 025558, 025583
Muradjan, Rima Gevkorovna 033534
Muradov, Oraz 038210
Murakami, Isamu 026533
Murakami, Toshimasa 027108
Muramatsu, Masafumi 027213
Muramatsu, Teijiro 026565
Murariu, Dr. Dumitru 032811
Murase, Masao 026459
Murat, Francine 021601
Murat de Chasseloup-Laubat, Prince 012902
Murata, Seiko 026894
Murati, Sulejman 034267
Muratore, P. Umberto 025958
Murauchi, Michimasa 026481
Murch, Cliff 005743
Murdin, Alexander 038797
Murdoch, Angus 047366
Murdoch, John 047912
Murdock, Gordon R. 045914
Murdock, Helen 001595
Murenina, G.P. 033856
Murerwa Kirigia, George 027426
Murgueítio de Montoya, Lucy 007480
Murillo Toro, Edificio 007453
Murken, Prof. Dr. Jan 019544
Murko, Matthias 019367
Murphey, F. Warren 044851
Murphy, Anne 047142, 047677
Murphy, Beth 045908
Murphy, D. 039419
Murphy, Dennis J. 046498
Murphy, J. 039258
Murphy, Dr. Jack A. 043406
Murphy, Joe 022826
Murphy, John 045881, 046970
Murphy, Kenny 041981
Murphy, Madge 044838
Murphy, Patricia 046608
Murphy, Patrick 043122
Murphy, Patrick T. 022730
Murphy, Paula 041673
Murphy, Randy 049362
Murphy, Rosalinde 022761
Murphy, Tricha J. 022722
Murphy, Valary 038653, 040202
Murra-Regner, Georg 016755
Murray, Alisdair 041357
Murray, Ann H. 046561
Murray, Holly 048298
Murray, Janice 041480
Murray, Jeffrey 044316
Murray, Johanne 005020
Murray, Karin G. 048730
Murray, Kay 022775
Murray, M. 005576
Murray, Mary 045984, 048719
Murray, Dr. Peter 000735, 000736
Murray, Peter 022720, 041334
Murray, Roddy 041126
Murrey, Grace 039863
Murzabekas, N. 027391
Musa, George 005160
Musango, Simon Peter 038220
Muscă, Luciana 032945
Muscat, Stefanie J. 044771
Muschg, Prof. Dr. Adolf 015980
Muschwitz, Tanja 015974
Mușețeanu, Dr. Crișan 032810
Musgrave, Lee 044237
Musil-Jantjes, Angela 031084
Muširovski, Volodymyr Makarovyč 038383
Muškalov, Sergej Michajlovič 033314
Musketa, Dr. Konstanze 017661
Musonda, Dr. Francis B. 049571
Musser, Bernice 043384
Musset, Daniele 012871
Mustaine, Beverly 045118
Musto, David F. 046226
Musty, Tony 039210, 039482, 039486, 039654, 040671, 040756
Muswasi, P. 036162
Musy-Ramseyer, Sylviane 037013
Muszała-Ciałowicz, Joanna 032278
Muto, Tetsu 027220
Muya Wa Bitanko, Dr. Kamuanga 007660
Muzii, Dr. Rossana 024917
Mveng, Engelbert 004981
Mya, U San 029071
Mychajlunow, Lorraine 005388
Myerow, Cathy 049214
Myers, Dr. Arnold 039388
Myers, Bob 041622
Myers, Dr. Charles W. 046286
Myers, Jane 044002
Myers, Jeff 044744
Myers, Laura H. 049305
Myers, Maryann 043556
Myers, Mickey 048390
Myers, M.R. 039682
Myers, Pam 045132, 045133
Myers, Pamela L. 041789
Myers, Prof. Philip 041734
Myers, Dr. Thomas P. 045313
Myers Breeze, Camille 048357
Mygh, Liselotte 009034
Myhrén, Sture 036300
Myhrvold, Sissel 031084
Myland, Conny 039367
Myland, Mel 039367
Myllyharju, Taina 009934
Myllylä, Pälvi 010212
Myllymaa, Marju 009469
Myllymäki, Viljo 009767
Myltygaševa, Ljudmila Petrovna 032970
Mylyadi, Dr. Wulan Rujiati 022423
Myon, Kim Ik 027435
Mytton-Famié, Elisabeth 011650
Myzgina, Valentina Vasylivna 038242
Myzina, Larisa Ivanovna 033257
Naab, Michael 044978, 044979
Naar, Harry I. 045212
Nabačikov, Dr. V.A. 033452
Nabaura, Trudy 022948
Nabika, Hideyuki 026745
Nachtigäller, Roland 019338
Nacimento Brito, M.F. do 004370
Nacke, Josef 017405
Nad-Jerkovic, Erika 007706
Nadan, José 012495
Nadel, D. 022929
Nader, Georges S. 021605
Nadkarni, Dnyaneshwar 022265
Nadler, Dr. Rajaa 019258
Nadler Thomas, Genny 042050
Nadzeika, Bonnie-Lynn 046032
Naef, W. 045433
Naegel, Marie-Luise 037501
Nägele, Dr. R. 020372
Näse, Li 009710
Näslund, Erik 036621
Naess, Jenny-Rita 031221
Naeßl-Doms, Vinzenz 018870
Nätscher, Dr. Wolfgang 019566
Nævestad, Dag 031095
Nafziger, Helen 041768
Nagai, Akio 026533
Nagai, Dr. Akira 027064
Nagai, Taizan 026490
Nagai, Yoshitaka 026511
Nagasaki, Motohiro 026939
Nagashima, Gyozen 026638
Nagashima, Kosuke 026605
Nagel, Prof. Günter 019077, 019092
Nager, Hans-Werner 036842
Naghawy, Aida 027370
Nagiełło, Zbigniew 032104
Nagl, Michaela 002852
Nagorskij, Nikolaj Viktorovič 033756, 033810
Nagueira, Dr. Lenita W. Mendes 004037
Nagy, Dr. Aniko S. 021669
Nagy, Dr. Árpád 021694
Nagy, Imre 021738, 021739
Nagy, Dr. István 021694
Nagy, László 021804
Nagy, Rebecca 044106, 047313
Nagy-Molnár, Dr. Miklós 021755
Nahabedian, Mildred 048992
Nahon, Pierre 015158
Nahser, Dr. Siegmar 016017
Naidoo, Peter 034640
Nail, Nancy 042944
Nairne, Andrew 040659
Naish, Carolyn 040196
Naito, Makio 027094
Naivne, Sandy 040244
Najafi, M. 022598
Najera, Lionel 048883
Naji Sari, Ahmed 049562
Nakabayashi, Kazuo 027256
Nakagawa, Hajime 027057
Nakagawa, Misao 027287
Nakajima, Atsushi 026423
Nakajima, Prof. Jimi Naoki 004590
Nakajima, Tokuhiro 026664
Nakamura, Hiroshi 026976, 027012
Nakamura, Junsuke 026898
Nakamura, Makoto 027009
Nakamura, Minoru 027221
Nakamura, Nobuo 026659
Nakamura, Reiko 027256

Nakamura, Saihachi 026434
Nakamura, Satoru 026438
Nakano, Masaki 026468
Nakano, Seijiro 027137
Nakano, Yuzo 042160
Nakashima, Kunio 026415
Nakashima, Michiko 026883
Nakayama, Prof. Kimio 027114
Nakazawa, Ryuhei 027351
Nakrem, Prof. Hans Arne 031078
Nally, Flaget 042021
Namiki, Masashi 026887
Nance, Paul J. 045376
Nanfeldt, Mikael 036303
Nanfeldt, Philippa 036296
Nannen, Eske 016958
Nanni, Romano 026342
Nanu, Dan Basarab 032866
Nanzer, Angel Omar 000574
Naoki, Togawa 027170
Naomichi, Ishige 027089
Napier, John H. 045994
Náplavová, Dr. Marie 008732
Nápoli, Prof. Dr. José 000193
Naramore, Bruce E. 042979
Narbutaite, Gražina 027856
Nardelli, Lucia 023472
Nardi, Christopher J. 043803
Nardin, A. 013654
Narinskaja, Natalija Efimovna 033710
Narr, Claudia 020053
Narzt, Karl 002607
Nasalski, Zygmunt 032133
Nasarov, N. 037844
Nasby, Judith M. 005558
Nascimento, Leo 004152
Nash, Alyce 046130
Nash, Carol 044540, 044540
Nash, Lesley 045117
Nash, Dr. Steven A. 047857, 047871
Nasi, Stefano 024831
Nasir, Pervin T. 031373
Naski-Multanen, Marke 010185
Naski-Multanen, Marki 010187
Nasko, Siegfried 002617
Nasky, Cindy 044231
Nason, Dr. James 048075
Nason Davis, Robert 047505
Nasset, Yvette 043812
Nassi, Talma 022910
Nasu, Takayoshi 026983
Nasybullin, Émir Salimovič 033248
Natali, Dr. Antonio 024156
Nathan, Jaqueline S 042370
Nathans, David 043018
Natier, Michel 012786
Natter, Dr. Tobias G. 002969
Natterer, Sylvia 002779
Naturel, Michèle 011302
Natuschke, Peter 015523
Naudascher, Josef 018779
Nauderer, Ursula Katharina 016617
Nauert, Prof. Dr. Dr. Claudia 017525
Nauhaus, Dr. Gerd 021088
Naukkarinen, Tiina 009547
Nault, Gilles 006401
Naumann, Prof. Dr. Clas M. 016337
Naumann, Dr. Friedrich 019089
Naumann, Gerd 019634
Naumann, Heike 016064
Naumann, Peter 019345, 053008
Naumann, Rolf 018119
Naumann, Thomas 020656
Naumann-Steckner, Dr. Friederike 018339
Naumer, Sabine 018200
Naumova, Nadija Grygorivna 038305
Naupp, Thomas 002787
Nause, Jean Pierre 011083
Nauta, Dr. J.F 029823
Nauta, Patience 043443
Naval Mas, Antonio 035287
Navarro, Daisy A. 031727
Navarro, Elías Terés 036036
Navarro, Dr. Fausta 024172
Navarro, Mariana Varela 007421
Navarro Guitart, Jesús 035350
Navarro Linares, Antonio 035245
Navas Gutiérrez, Mariano 007592
Navascués, Pedro 035424
Navascués Benlloch, Pilar 034999
Navascués Benlloch, Pilar de 035395
Nave, Dr. Francine de 003169, 003191
Naveau, Jaques 012178
Naveaux, Ralph 045971
Navia, Olga Lucía 007469
Naville, Marc F. 037755
Nawafleh, Sami 027383
Nawka, Tomasz 015900
Nawrocki, Czesław 031812
Naylor, Dr. Bruce G. 005362
Naylor, Eleanor 048353
Nazarov, Roman Grygorovyč 038254
Naziebło, Dr. Jerzy 032568
Nazionale, Nina 046389
Ndacyayisenga, Albert 034102
Ndege, Conchita F. 044336
Neaf, Oscar Angel 000385
Neagu, Marian 032822
Neal, George 044451
Neal, Dr. John R. 042896
Neale, Susan 006142, 006188
Nealis, Sharon 043242
Néar, Marie-José 015032
Neault, Caroline 043099
Neave, Ruth 039305
Nebel, Dr. Martin 020364
Nebes, Prof. Dr. Norbert 018111
Nebl, Rudolf 002648
Nebuloni, Dr. Gabriela 024492
Nečajeva, Paraskovija Mychajlivna 038241
Nečasová, Eva 008270
Necker, Hans 015742
Necker, L. 037031
Necker, Louis 014940
Nedelčeva, Cvetanka 004878
Nedeljković, Dragana 034266
Nedelkovska-Dimitrovska, Liljana 027919
Nedeva, Galja 004952
Nedoma, Petr 008610
Neeb, Vanessa 048568
Needham, Dr. Claude 046870
Needham, Melanie 006812
Needle, John 038724
Neef, Almut 020263
Neel, David 044293
Neely, Alastair 005785
Neergaard, Mogens de 008996
Nees Holcomb, Sara 045261
Neff, Emily 044648
Neff, Jean W. 041697
Neff, John 049256
Nefzi, Tarak 037948
Negro Cobo, Marta 035004
Nehrer, Manfred 002927
Neich, R. 030432
Neichl, Brigitte 002949
Neidert, David 041717
Neidhart, Herbert 002443
Neighbours, Dr. K.F. 046444
Neil, Erik 046265
Neill, Teda W. 043907
Neilsen, Henry L. 048870
Neilsen, Kathrine 049176
Nejdl, Josef 008353
Neka, Suteja 022418
Nekrasov, Aleksandr Michailovič 033685
Nekrasov, Sergej Michailovič 033837
Nel, M. 034561
Nelgares Raye, José 035301
Nelišerová, Dr. Eva 034336
Nelje, Kerstin 036438
Nelley, Betty 030539
Nelly, Catherin 013886
Nelsen, Rick 048514
Nelson, Amanda 044771
Nelson, Arthur 048845
Nelson, Bob 047496
Nelson, Bryan 005549
Nelson, Carolyn 045168
Nelson, Cindy J. 044960
Nelson, Cortland 042355
Nelson, Daniel A. 045168
Nelson, Darrel 043339
Nelson, Doug 043617
Nelson, Ellie 005122
Nelson, Eric 049362
Nelson, Geoff 041576
Nelson, Gwen 043475
Nelson, Harold B. 045380
Nelson, Helen 047893
Nelson, Henry 039128
Nelson, Howard 044577
Nelson, James R. 043167
Nelson, John 039850, 044384, 044385
Nelson, Julie D. 047299
Nelson, Dr. Larry 046888
Nelson, Lee Ann 044325
Nelson, Lori 005676
Nelson, Mike 047989
Nelson, Mindy Honey 046431
Nelson, Morris 042234
Nelson, Nancy 043118
Nelson, Philip 039850
Nelson, Sarah E. 041659
Nelson, Stephen R. 047917
Nelson-Balcer, Mona 049195
Nelson-Mayson, Lin 047706
Nelsson, Cecilia 036444
Nelsson, Sigvard 036481
Němeček, Jaroslav 008348
Nemes, András 021847
Nemeth, Alice 006832
Nemeth, Elaine 006566
Németh, Pál 021645
Németh, Dr. Péter 021803
Nemeth Ehrlich, Dorica 007828
Nemetz, Johann 003031
Nemetz, Norbert 020976
Nemiroff, Diana 006104
Nenno, Dr. Rosita 019453
Nenonen, Yrjo 010172
Nenov, Dr. Nikolai 004819, 004820, 004823
Nenquin, Prof. Dr. J. 003450
Nentwig, Dr. Franziska 016920
Nenz, Cornelia 019805
Nenzioni, Gabriele 025694
Nepi, Dr. Chiara 024181
Nepočatych, Viktor Alekseevič 033090
Nepomuceno, Susan 042092
Nepputh, Fritz 016918
Néray, Katalin 021664
Nerchesseau, Daniel 013650
Nerdinger, Prof. Dr. W. 015602
Nerdinger, Prof. Dr. Winfried 019034
Neretniece, Anastasija 027703
Nerheim, Gunnar 031097
Neri, Joanne 041458
Nero, Don 048854
Nesbilt, Bill 005591
Nesbitt, Bill 005589
Nesbitt, Dr. Elizabeth 048075
Nesbitt, Melissa 048538
Neset, Karsten T. 031264
Nesheim, Jan 045801
Neshushtan, M. 022995
Nesin, Jeffrey D. 045765
Nesje Bjørlo, Aslaug 031164
Nesme, H. 012348
Nesmith, Michael 047968
Nespoli, T. 029245
Ness, Arlin E. 041611
Ness, Gary C. 043109, 045669, 045673
Ness, Dr. Gary C. 046270
Ness, Kim G. 005594
Nessell Colglazier, Gail 045620
Nesselrath, Dr. Arnold 049419, 049422, 049435
Nestler, Dr. Iris 018663
Nestler-Zapp, Dr. Angela 015738, 015739
Nestorova, Ani 004654
Neszmelyi, Adrienne 043505
Netel, Lies 029934
Stille Neto, Bernardo 004382
Neto, Luis 032688
Nette, Mary 045674
Netten, Dr. John 006372
Netter, Esther 045474
Netterlund, Karin 036600
Netuschil, C.K. 016641
Netzer, Dr. Nancy 042811
Neu, Noreen 006251
Neu, Dr. Stefan 018339
Neu-Kock, Dr. Roswitha 018338
Neubauer, Alexandra 017177
Neubert, André 017978
Neubert, George W. 047804, 047804
Neubert, Hermann 018943
Neuburger, Dr. Susanne 002965
Neuer, D. 017828
Neufeld, Alice 006802
Neufeld, Carol E. 048465
Neuffer, Dr. Fr. O. 018793
Neugebauer, Rud. 015555
Neugebauer, Prof. Dr. Wolfgang 002889
Neugebauer-Maresch, Dr. J.-W. 002750
Neugent, Susan E. 041855
Neuhaus, A.F. 029818
Neuhaus, Dorothy E. 048765
Neuhaus, Johann Diederich 020923
Neuhoff, Stephan 018315
Neuhuber, Prof. Dr. W.L. 017027
Neuland-Kitzerow, Dr. Dagmar 016128
Neulinger, Adolf 001866
Neulinger, P. Maximilian 002193
Neumann, B. 001207
Neumann, Christoph 018969
Neumann, Dr. Dieter 002774
Neumann, Herbert 001865
Neumann, Timothy C. 043369
Neumann, Dr. U. 020499
Neumann-Eisele, Petra 018220
Neumayer, Dr. Heino 016136
Neumayer, W. 001684
Neumüllers, Marie 016684
Neuner, Ernst 003070
Neuner, Meinhard 002089, 002097
Neuner, Wolfgang 002097
Neunzert, Hartfrid 018477, 018479
Neuwirth, Karin 002979
Neuwirth, Karl 002710
Nevermann, Ulrike 017764
Neves, Julio 004530
Neves, Maria da Soledade S. 032619
Neveux, Yannick 013233
Nevill, Armanda 038808
Neville Blakey, W.H. 038841
Nevin, Michael E. 048801
Nevins, Christopher B. 043785
Nevitt, Elizabeth 041752
Nevraumont, Marcel 003474
Nevskaja, Galina N. 033044
Nevskij, Aleksej 033402
Newbery, C. 040769
Newbery, David 040766
Newbery, G. 040668
Newbery, Maria 040977
Newbury, Barbara 038792, 038913
Newcomb, Nancy 046389
Newhard-Farrar, Nancy 043009
Newhouse, Larry 049363
Newkirk, Sally 046185
Newland, Judy 042133
Newlands, David 005579
Newman, Ed 005595
Newman, Joanne K. 046115
Newman, Lilly 047402
Newnham, Kate 038859
Newsome, Mary 043533
Newsome, Steven C. 048881
Newton, Bette 043258, 044669
Newton, Christina 047410
Newton, Gael 000888

Newton, Paula H. 043668
Newton Gibson, Yasabel 046709
Neyer, Dr. Hans Joachim 017772
Neylon, Christina 022702
Neylon, Nicholas 046844
Neyses, Mechthild 020483
Neysters, Dr. Silvia 016841
Nezu, Kohichi 027216
N'Gele, Edward O. 027825
Nghien, Nguyen Thi 049533
Ngoubeli, Joseph 007664
Ngozi, Niobe 044636
Nguyên, T.P. 037109
Nhlane, Dr. Med 027939, 027942
Nias, Peter 038809
Niaufre, M. 014049
Niazi, Dr. Liaquat Ali Khan 031382
Nicandri, David L. 048471
Nicholas, Darcy 030579
Nicholas, Jeremy 041285
Nicholl, Boyd 042231
Nicholls, David 041711
Nicholls, Jane 046516
Nicholls, Stephen 039057
Nichols, Charlotte 048247
Nichols, John 047989
Nichols, Lawrence W. 048569
Nichols, Madeleine 046390
Nichols, Sarah 047043
Nichols, William O. 048779
Nicholsen, Charles 044564
Nicholson, Joseph 046996
Nicholson, Marilyn L. 044487
Nicholson, Robert 022756, 022777
Nicholson, Rosemary 040227
Nichterlein, Peter 020812
Nick, Lloyd 041868
Nickel, Douglas R. 047885
Nickell, Jeff 041955
Nickels, Sarah 046307
Nickens, Harry 047468
Nickerson, Cindy 043186
Nickerson, Dr. M.A. 044103
Nickl, Dr. B.E. 016198
Nicklaus, Jörg 015549
Nickles, Karen 043611
Nicod, Annelise 037128
Nicod, Bernard 037338
Nicod, Caroline 037246
Nicodemus, Dr. Victoria 029087
Nicola, A. 030277
Nicolai, Dr. B. 017647
Nicolai, David 046599
Nicolaisen, C. 009107
Nicolaisen, Dr. Jan 018579
Nicolas, Alain 012942
Nicolas, Jean 010414
Nicolau, Antoni 034943
Nicolau, Irina 032813
Nicolau, Sanda Gabriela 032965
Nicolaysen, Katja 030924
Nicolescu, Costion 032813
Nicoletta, Catherine 011433
Nicolini, Renato 025580
Nicoll, Jessica 047162
Nicolls, Andrea 048925
Nicolosi, Anthony S. 046462
Nicols, Marian 040357, 040358
Nicosia, Angelo 023226
Nicosia, Prof. Umberto 025533
Nicu, Mircea 032956
Niederalt, Michael 020135
Niederer, Robert 037186
Niederhöfer, Hans-Jörg 020364
Niederl, Dr. Reinhold 001938
Niedzielenko, Andrzej 032095, 032096
Niedźwiecki, Jan 032220
Niehaus, Dr. Andrea 016321
Niehoff, Dr. Franz 018483, 018484, 018487
Nield, M.J. 041262
Nield, Thenetta 048192
Niell-LLabrés, Francisca 035604
Nielsen, Anna Kathrine 008834
Nielsen, Anne-Marie 008982
Nielsen, Christin 036412, 036413
Nielsen, Debbie 006324
Nielsen, Erik 009120
Nielsen, Ervin 009046
Nielsen, Hans 009092
Nielsen, Jan 046626
Nielsen, Jennifer 044013
Nielsen, Jens N. 008798
Nielsen, Johannes 009072
Nielsen, Jytte 008940, 009129
Nielsen, Keld 008819
Nielsen, Kim 048937
Nielsen, Kori L. 043191
Nielsen, Niels Jul 008970
Nielsen, Ole 008885
Nielsen, Poul Bryde 009109
Nielsen, Teresa 009141
Nielsen, Wendy 006286
Nielson, Jay 043912
Niemann, Dr. Carsten 017770
Niemann, Willi 019149
Niemeyer, Kirk 046643
Niemi, Marja 010025
Niemitz, Prof. Dr. Hans-Ulrich 018562
Nienur, Jennifer 044275
Nier, Eberhard 015866
Nieraad, Karla 020533
Niermann, Katrin 016351
Niero, Antonio 026265
Niesel, Bernd 017303
Niesner, Dr. Tomáš 008301, 008458
Nieszczerzewska, Elżbieta 032184
Nieuwdorp, Hans 003168
Nieuwstraten, Frits 029652
Nievera, Dr. Eduardo 031734
Nievergelt, Frank 037709
Nieves, Marysol 042432
Nieweg, J. 029772
Niewęgłowski, Stanisław 032336
Niewerth, Herbert 016771, 020666
Niggemann, Dr. Stefan 018086
Nigratschka, Kurt 018024
Nigro, Dr. Lorenzo 049422
Niinistö-Alanne, Arja 009962
Niizeki, Kimiko 027169
Nijsten, J. 029556
Nikbakhsh, M. 022589
Nikiforov, Valerij Ivanovič 033510
Nikiforov, Viktor S. 038374
Nikita, Eleni S. 008225
Nikitine, Serge 012518
Nikitović, Lidija 034180
Niklasch, Wilfried 016650
Nikolaev, V.A.. 033727
Nikolaeva, Irina Alekseevna 033490
Nikolaeva, Lidija Dmitrievna 033548
Nikolajenko, Galina 038389
Nikolaou, Yorka 021207
Nikolasch, Dr. Franz 002314
Nikoleišvili, M.V. 015403
Nikolić, Dragan 034172
Nikolić, Dušica 034177
Nikolić, Jadranka 007714
Nikolov, Prof. Dr. Vasil 004844
Nikolova, Asja 004701
Nikolova, Ass.Prof. Dr. Diana 004863
Nikolova, Erika 004773
Nikolova, Petja 004863
Nikolova, Radka 004753
Nikoltsios, Vasilios 021504
Nikonov, Aleksandr K. 033373
Nikulin, Valerij S. 033845
Nill, Annegreth T. 043106
Nilsen, Laurel 049047
Nilsen, Rolf Erik 030863
Nilsen, Tore L. 030761
Nilson, Göran 036300
Nilson, Ylva 036577
Nilsson, Bo 036638
Nilsson, Christer 030822
Nilsson, Christin 036382
Nilsson, Håkan 036803, 036805
Nilsson, Harald 036747, 036747
Nilsson, Karin 036382, 036385
Nilsson, Marianne 036688
Nilsson, Rune 036340
Nilsson, Torsten 036498
Nimmich, Dr. Gunter 016044
Nimri, Mohamed 037988
Nimz, Tim 042298
Niniou-Kindeli, Vanna 021225
Nirša, Alla Mychajlivna 038366
Nisbet, A. 041466
Nisbet, Peter 042560
Nishi, Yukitaka 026708
Nishida, Dr. Hiroko 027216
Nishidera, Masaya 027102
Nishikawa, Kyotaro 027333
Nishimura, Atsushi 027325
Nishitakaesuji, Nobuyoshi 026448
Nishitani, Noboru 027229
Nishizawa, Jun-ichi 027050
Nishizawa, Keiichi 026937
Niskz, Siiri 010031
Nissen, Dan 008962
Nissen, M.A.J.M. 029547
Nit, A. 029680
Niţă, Gabriela 032947
Nitsch, Hubert 002245
Nitsch, Dr. Ulla M. 016423
Nitta, Hideo 026799
Nitter, Marianne 031221
Nittmann, Karl 001838
Nittve, Lars 036645
Nitzschke, Katrin 016782
Niven, Catharine 039808
Nivière, Marie-Dominique 010271
Niwa, Masatoshi 026564
Nix, Dr. J.C. 030105
Nix, M. 039682
Nix, Nicole 019261
Nixon, Chris 043494
Nixon, Isabelle 005747
Nixon, James D. 043494
Nixon, Nigel 039090, 040505
Nixon, Roderick A. 049112
Nixon, Taryn 040230
Nixon, W.A. 001164
Niyama, Sadamasa 027173
Nizamiev, Muzip Tazievič 033240
Nižegorodova, Elena Vladimirovna . 033028
Nko'o, Hulio 004982
Nlemchuku Anyanwu, Dr. Starling E. 030703
N.N. ... 016813, 016818, 017288, 017765, 017765, 018326, 018330, 019608, 020374, 020374, 020491, 022336, 034708, 045389
Noack, Wita 016119
Noah, Randy 048055
Nobis, Dr. Norbert 017769
Noble, Alexandra 040143
Noble, Douglas R. 044744
Noble, Dr. Douglas R. 045766
Noble, Rhonda 001244
Nóbrega, Enrique 049464
Noda, Renate 002961
Noda Gómez, Onaysi 007951
Nodine, Jane 048267
Nodzyńska, Marta 032545
Noe, Adrianne 048929
Noe, Per 009036, 009037, 009038, 009058
Noe, Pierre 003777
Noeding, Faye S. 048496
Nöhammer, Josef 001887
Noel, Albert 003378
Noël, Jacques 013336
Noël, Ètienne 014017
Noel, William 042006
Noelmans, L. 003797
Nörenberg, Bernd 015476
Noever, Prof. Peter 002904
Noever, Peter 002945
Noggler-Gürtler, Lisa 003009
Noguchi, Mitsunari 026482
Noguchi, Reiichi 027169
Nogueira, Abrelino 030434
Nogueira, Sandy 030434
Nogueira da Costa, Maria Inês ... 029050
Noh, Joon Eui 027623
Nohsoh, Toshio 026466
Noirot, André 010921
Noko, Oarabilke J. 003952
Nolan, Amy 047718
Nolan, Edward V. 048471
Nolan, Gail 040095
Nolan, Julia 039142
Nolan, Linda P. 046876
Nolan, Patrick B. 044695
Nolan, Peg 045661
Nolan Jones, Nancy 042982
Noland, Martin R. 047657
Nold, Carl R. ... 045551, 045552, 045554, 045556
Nolen, John 044348
Noli, Gino 029084
Noll, Linda M. 044485
Noll, Dr. Petra 016892
Nollar, Philip 048722
Nolle, Karl 016800
Nolley, Lance 045343
Nolte-Fischer, Dr. Hans-Georg 016637
Nombluez, Pieter 003507
Nomura, Harukata 026759
Nonesteid, Mark 043558
Nonestied, Mark 047035
Nonnenmacher, Eugen ... 016297, 016298
Noon, Patrick 045918
Noon, Rosemary 049120
Noordermeer, Aly 029239
Nooter Roberts, Mary 045421
Noppe, Catherine 003657
Nørager Pedersen, Erik 008805
Nørbach, Lars Chr. 009030
Nørbach, Lars Christian 008798
Nørballe, Inge 008862
Norbart, Rianne 029239
Norberg, Deborah 047902
Norbut Suits, Linda 048285
Norby, Lory 045587
Nordahl, Per 036775
Nordal, Bera 036575
Nordberg, Henri 010157
Nordbrock, Carol 041911
Norden, Linda 042560
Nordgren, Sune 031089
Nordheim, Lutz von 021054
Nordin, Maxine 005614
Nordine, Dr. Malki 000068
Nordlinder, Gunnar 036656
Nordlund, Ivar 009466, 010084
Nordmo, Per E. 030875
Nordmo, Sverre 030861
Nordon, Deborah 046370
Nordqvist, Jørgen 008824
Nordström, Lena 036527
Nordstrom, Ralf 010201
Norell, Dr. Mark A. 046286
Norgren, Philip E. 048314
Norheim, Kari 030868
Norheim, Svein 030868
Noriega, Natividad 031779
Norland, Lissie 030857
Norlund, Yvonne 036602
Norman, Dr. D.B. 038970
Norman, Heather L. 044120
Norman, Jan 044366
Norman, Margaret Jane 049130
Norman, W.H. 041315
Normanby, Lady 041368
Normand, P. 041047
Normand, Rick 046266
Normann, Mark 040653
Normann, Øystein 030879
Noro, Masahiko 018318
Norovtseren, Oyuntegsh 029016
Norrington, S. 001516
Norris, Adrian 039951

Norris, Andrea S. 045206
Norris, B. 030460
Norris, Baden N. 030465
Norris, Johnny 042385
Norris, Dr. Patrick 044900
Northam, J. 006237
Northcote, P.S. 030609
Northrop Adamo, Amy 046367
Northwood, John 001266
Norting, Jack 044283
Nortmann, Dr. Hans 020483
Norton, Elaine 042579
Norton, Fran 048420
Norton, George 049123
Norton, I.S. 001178
Norton, Jessica A. 041697
Norton, Lyle 045136
Norton, Mary Lynn 047488
Norton jr., Richard W. 048163
Norton, Scott L. 043943
Norton, Susan E.S. 048903
Norton Moffatt, Laurie 048367
Norvell, Edward 047764
Norwood, Nancy 047487
Nory, Jean-Marc 014168
Noryńska, Barbara 032318
Nose, Dr. Martin 019099
Nosek, Elizabeth 045128
Noske, Dr. H. 017108
Noskova, Alla Anatoljevna 033263
Nosovic, Milorad 034176
Nota, Dr. Maria Teresa 025496
Nothnagl, Hannes 002343
Nothnagl, Reinhold 002687
Notin, Véronique 012691, 012697
Nottage, James H. 044737, 045411
Notteghem, Patrice 012488
Notter, Annick 013516, 013519
Nougarède, Martine 013425
Nougué, Cendrine 013155
Nouvel, Odile 013668
Nouyrit, H. 011043
Novák, Dr. László 021798
Novák, Dr. Pavel 008418, 008464
Novak, Stanislav 007715
Novak, Timothy 043046
Nováková, Dr. Lenka 008286
Novakovska, Nada 027914
Novellis, Mark de 041254
Novgorodova, Prof. M.I. 033429
Novikov, Timur 033809
Novoselova, Rimma Vjačeslavovna 033648
Novotná, Dr. Mária 034373
Novotná, Mariana 034369
Novotny, Deborah 041631
Nowack, Meg 048961
Nowacki, Dr. Henryk 032012
Nowacki, Janusz 032236
Nowacki, Marek 032356
Nowak, Holger 016590, 018109, 018117
Nowak, Joanna 032288, 032353
Nowak, Romuald 032533
Nowak, Włodzimierz 032266
Nowakyniak, Dr. Edmund 032197
Nowers, John 039542
Nowobilski, Dr. Józef Andrej 032036
Nowojski, Paweł 031985
Noyes, Julia 045310
Nozaka, Motoyoshi 026500
Nozet, Hervé 015071
Ntsema Khitsane, Julia 027822
Nuber, Dr. W. 019163
Nuculov, Georgi 004803
Nudds, Dr. J.R. 040406
Nudelman, Robert 045429
Nüesch, Ernst 036875
Nüesch, Rosmarie 037625
Nugent, Charles 040416
Nugent, M. 005474
Nugent, Randolph 046414
Nuki, Tatuto 026610
Nummelin, Esko 009986
Nummelin, Maria 009465
Nummelin, Rauni 010113
Numonova, Gulchehra Tojitinovna 037839
Nunes, Dave 047129
Nunes de Vasconcelos junior, Walter 004395
Núñez, César Marku 036043
Nuñez, Ramon 035121
Núñez Centella, Ramón 035123
Nunley, John 047676
Nunley, Larry 048654
Nunn, Chris 041164
Nunn, Dr. Tey Marianna 047972, 047973
Nunziati, Anna 023666
Nupen, Nikki 029093
Nurfeisova, Nurshamal Bekvossunovna 027390
Nurger, Heli 009372
Nuri, Kedir 009447
Nurkkala, Yrjö 010155
Nurmi, Virpi 010025
Nurmi-Nielsen, Anna 010025
Nusbaum, Pat 043700
Nussbaum, Felix 019493
Nussbaum, Patricia 037350, 037400
Nussbaum, Prof. R.A. 041734
Nussbaumer, Christiana 002741
Nussbaumer, Paul 037000
Nußbaummüller, Winfried 001762
Nusupova, D.N. 027635
Nutkins, Geoff 041014
Nuttall, Rick 034565
Nuyttens, M. 003281
Nyakas, Dr. Miklós 021736
Nyamabondo, Constantinus M. 037845
Nyamenya, Peter 027423
Nybak, Arne 047908
Nye, Steve 040847
Nye, Tom 042434
Nyegaard, Georg 021547
Nyein, U Kyaw 029061, 029065
Nyerges, Alexander Lee 043320
Nyffenegger, Kathrin 036930
Nygaard, Knut M. 030833
Nygårds, Eva 036296
Nygren, Bitte 036614
Nygren, Kris 005471
Nykänen, Veijo 009999
Nykolyshyn, Z. 006848
Nylander, Jane 042326, 045299
Nylen, Bob 042635
Nylén, Lars 036754
Nyman, Ola 036636
Nyman, Sven-Eric 036758
Nynoen, Paal 031095
Nys, Wim 003196
Nystad, Marianne 031265
Nyström, Hazze 008956
Nysveen, Aagot 044543
Nyujtó, Zsuzsa 021640
Nyunt, Kyaw 029078
Oaklander, Christine I. 041657
Oakley, Lisa 045037
Oakley, Stephen 048483
Oaks, Martha 044225
Oandasan, Crescencion 031678
Oanh, Phan 049541
Oates, Sarah 041820
Oatman, Michelle 046198
Obal, Franc 034506
O'Bannion, Tami 045850
O'Baoill, Eilis 040585
Obedat, Nassim 027358
O'Beirne, M.J. 040183
Ober, Jerry 042300
Oberchristl, Monika 002249
Oberfrank, Wilhelm 002272
Oberg, Paul Chancy 030711
Oberhänsli, Silvia 037076
Oberhänsli, Dr. This 037305
Oberhaus, Betty 043218
Oberländer, Rolf 015801
Oberlin Steel, Virginia 042577
Obermaier, Dr. Walter 003024
Obermair, Sigrid 002945
Obermeier, Christoph 019262
Obermeyer Simmons, Helen 043849
Obernosterer, Beatrix 002136, 002148
Obhof, Dr. Ute 018156
O'Bomsawin, Nicole 006061
Obradović, Slobodan 034175
Obrascova, Maja Aleksandrovna 033716
Obrecht, Elsa 037578
O'Brian, John 043898
O'Brien, David 022840
O'Brien, Eileen 045620
O'Brien, Freda 030661
O'Brien, Dr. G.G. 039421
O'Brien, Judith 044580
O'Brien, Kevin 045089
O'Brien, Kevin J. 044983, 044987
O'Brien, Maureen 047258
O'Brien, Michael J. 043071
O'Brien, Pam 046257
O'Brien, Patrick J. 048758
O'Brien, Ruairí 016781, 016785
O'Brien, Suzanne 043734
Obrist, Hans-Ulrich 013630
O'Bryen, Antoinette 022724
Obud, Renate 002773
Ocampo, Juan Carlos 000452
Ocaña, Maria Teresa 034956
O'Carroll, Helen 022864
O'Casaide, Peadar 022701
Ocello, Claudia 046424
Ochi, Catherine Megumi 027157
Ochi, Yujiro 026664
Ochoa, Cristina 045460
Ochoa, Maria 044494
Ochonko, Nikolaj Anatoljevič 033911
Ochsenmeier, Peter 017304
Ockershausen, Cindy Lou 048933
O'Connell, Bernard 046999
O'Connell, Daniel M. 047066
O'Connell, Michael 022713
O'Connor, Andrew 022763
Oconnor, Prof. Barry M. 041734
O`Connor, David 000703
O'Connor, Karen 043887
O'Connor, M. 030575
O'Connor, Thomas P. 022739
O'Connor, Tony 041290
O'Conor Nash, Marguerite 022707
Odawara, Kaname 026707
Odden, Tor 031140
Ode, Robert 011136
Odegaard, Nancy 048630
Odehnal, Petr 008740
O'Dell, Kathryn 045891
Odendaal, E.A. 034755
Odenhoven, Dr. S.L. 030193
Odenthal, Dr. Johannes 016061
Oder, Karla 034517, 034517, 034518
Odess, Daniel 043780
Odin, Samy 013644
Odoj, Romuald 032341
O'Donnell, Janice 047261
O'Donnell, Molly 044849
O'Donnell, P. 040643
O'Donovan, Hugh J. 045961
Odrowąż-Pieniążek, Janusz 032451
Odum, R. Andrew 048568
Oechslin, Dr. Ludwig 037015
Oegema, D. 034725
Öhlinger, Walter 003017
Öhlknecht, Rupert 002679
Öhman, Nina 036678
Öhman, Volga 036433
Oehme, Ursula 018594
Oehms, Günter 019207
Öjesjö, Mona Lisa 036425
Ökten, Haydar 038154
Oellers, Dr. Adam C. 015424, 015425
Oelschlägel, Dr. Petra 015972
Oelschlaeger-Garvey, Barbara 045598
Oerichbauer, Edgar S. 044760
Örsi, Dr. Julianna 021911
Oertlin, Jean-Paul 013475
Oeschger, Dr. Bernhard 018158
Östberg, Maths 036793
Östberg, Wilhelm 036623
Österholm-Granqvist, Sonja 010202
Oesterlein, Arnulf 015687
Österlund, Petter 036690
Oesterreicher, Claudia 003017
Oesterwind, Dr. Bernd C. 018865
Oetterli, Christoph 037700
Oettingen-Wallenstein, Fürst zu 016341
Oettingen-Wallerstein, Fürst zu 017773, 020658
Oettinger, Dr. Marion 047804
Öttl, Josef 015904, 015922, 018437
Oexle, Dr. Judith 016798
Özbey, Şahin 038061
Özcan, Hilmi 038125
Özçelik, Serpil 038103, 038105
Özdemir, Abdulhalik 038021
Özek, Halil 038093
Özerdem, Hürrem 038003
Özeren, Öcal 038152
Özgen, Emine 038024
Özgerey, Mehmet 038098
Özkütük, Zafer 038029
Özsağır, Ahmet 038112
Öztürk, Erdal 038104
Offers, Donald 036863
Offringa, D.C. 034725
Offroy, Martine 014984
Offutt, Cathy 044728
O'Floinn, Raghnall 022761
O'Foighil, Prof. Diarmaid 041734
Ogata, Hisanobu 026487
Ogawa, Toshiro 027142
Ogden, Dale 044744
Ogden, Sharon 030459
Oggenfuss, Daniel 019124
Ogilive, Peter 040944
Ogle, Brian 038870
Ogle, Nigel 030515
Ogle, Susan F. 049201
Ogliari, Prof. Francesco 025388
Ogny, Jean d' 012223
O'Gorman, Dr. Jodie 043575
O'Gorman, Therese 041866
O'Gorman, Tim 043940
O'Grady, John 038921
Ogrodniczak, Tomasz 032242
O'Halloran, Jim 030601
O'Hanlon, Dr. Michael 040665
O'Hara, Bruce 048589
O'Hara, Michael 041297
Ohba, Masatoshi 027256
Ohe, Dr. Werner von der 016548
O'Hear, John 045929
O'Hern, John D. 043690
Ohl, Thomas 020823
Ohlsen, Dr. Nils 016958
Ohlsson, Birger 036215
Ohm, Ruth 042156
Ohmann, Agathe 009062
Ohmura, Etumasa 026832
Ohnemus, Dr. Sylvia 016426
Ohngemach, Dr. Ludwig 016896
Ohno, Akira 027334
Ohno, Masaji 026903
Ohrt, Hans Dieter 005675
Ohrt, Karsten 009052
Ohrt, Nils 009027
Ohsaki, Kuninori 026805
Ohta, Yoshinori 026472
Ohtsubo, Kenji 027287
Øien, Elisabeth Adelheide 030825
Oiler, Gary 048402
Oiler, Sue 048402
Oilliamson, Comtesse d' 011845
Oinas, Tapani 010044
Ojalvo Prieto, Roberto 007545
Ojeda Sato, Alonso 007549
Ojha, M.B. 022143
Okabe, Nobuyuki 027320

Okachi, Yukio 026879
Okada, Akiko 026555
Okada, Hidenori 027256
Okajima, Hasashi 027256
Okamoto, Takenobu 026699
Okániková, M. 034452
Okano, Kiheita 027080
Okawa, Eiji 026652
Okaya, Michiko 043589
Okazaki, Kyoichi 027320
Okazawa, Kunro 026924
O'Keefe, Barbara K. 043148
O'Keeffe, Cheryl W. 041898
O'Keeffe, Tony 038486
Oker-Blom, Teodora 009533
Okimoto, Hiroshi 026530
Okkenhaug, Eli . . 030756, 030757, 030758
Okoshi, Hisako 027009
Okubo, Tokiko 027327
Okumiya, Kaku 026708
Okumura, Yoshitsugu 026829
Okura, Haruhiko 026717
Olachea, Elena 028432
Olaczola, Juanjo 034882
Olano Trujillo, Manuel José 007586
Ólason, Vésteinn 021978
Olausson, Magnus 036471, 036648
Olbrantz, John 047751
Olde Dubbelink, R.A. 029986
Oldeman, Dr. L.R. 030305
Olden, Sam 049335
Oldenburg, Rie 021543
Oldenburger, Julie 041737
Oldham, Terry 047644
O'Leary, Daniel E. 047162
Olejniczak, Józef 032221
Olerud, Becky 043459
Oleščins'ka, Alla Pavlivna 038228
Olfra, Michelle 045966
Olijnyk, Michael 047055
Oliva, Francisco Miguel González de la 035244
Olivarelli, Sebastiano . . . 025102, 025103, 025104
Olivas, Art 047973
Olivas, Arthur 047975
Olive Garrard, Jacqueline 000639
Olivé Serret, Prof. Enric . . 035893, 035894
Nunes de Oliveira, Adilson 004099
Oliveira, Dr. José Carlos 032583
Oliveira, Nicolas de 040228
Oliveira Caetano, Dr. Joaquim 032610
Oliveira Mesquita Spränger, Paulo Roberto 004406
Oliveira Rodrigues, Adélia E. de . . 003994
Oliver, André 011224
Oliver, Dr. Graham 038990
Oliver, Graham 040342
Oliver, Katherine C. 045569
Oliver, Keith 006866
Oliver, Robyn 001124
Oliver Joliffe, Ruth 042315
Oliveri del Castillo, Patrizia 026346
Olivié, Jean-Luc 013668
Olivier, Prof. J. 034690
Olivier, Louis 014378
Olivo, Sandra 045834
Ollenburger, Jeff 044703
Ollikainen, Anja 010228
Ollingen, Elisabeth 002156
Ollman, Arthur 047827
Olmedo, Freddy 009205
Olmedo Patiño, Dolores 028495
Olmo Fernández, Jesús del 035009
Olmos Muñoz, Pedro 006919
Olmstead, Dr. Richard 048075
Oloffson, Jan 036234
Olsberg, Nicholas 005914
Olsen, Dr. Arnold 044503
Olsen, Betsy 043870
Olsen, Claus 009067
Olsen, Johanne 021549
Olsen, John 030980
Olsen, Dr. Knapp 046485
Olsen, Maude 049269
Olsen, Phyllis J. 044240
Olsen, Sandra H. 042507
Olsnes, Aanund 030915
Olson, Alice 042660
Olson, David 046477
Olson, Don 048462
Olson, Dona A. 047071, 047580
Olson, Dorothy 041858
Olson, Janis 042121
Olson, Joan 048172
Olson, Kathleen 045278
Olson, Kathryne 046755
Olson, Kathy 046760
Olson, Kristina 046027, 046028
Olson, Nicky L. 043259
Olson, Oliver 048321
Olson, Paula 043064
Olson, Roberta 048013
Olson, Ruth Ann 045203
Olson, Susanne 048846
Olson, Suzanne 047157
Olson, Thomas H. 047580
Olson, William 006159
Olson Peters, Ruth 045176
Olsson, Daniel Sven 036265
Olsson, Daniels Sven 036266
Olsson, Mari-Louise 036480
Olszak, Eliane 011899
Olszanowski, Zdzisław 032528
Oltean, Dr. Vasile 032793
Olthoff, Gabriele 020808
Oltjenbruns, Dr. Kevin 043903
Oltmans, Kay 042352
Olucha Montins, F. 035068
O'Malley, Dennis M. 047254
O'Malley, Jeanette 046836
O'Malley, Kathleen 043032, 043033, 043034
Oman, Dr. Hiltrud 002583
Oman, Richard G. 047630
Omar, Hadmar 037864
Omar, Hamad H. 037850, 037861, 037862, 037863
Omar, R.H. 034601, 034602, 034603, 034604
O'Mara, John F. 006362
O'Meara, John 041817
Omedes, Dr. Anna 034927
Omer, Gil 022938
Omer, Prof. Mordechai . . . 023074, 023092
Ometto, Giulio 026064
Omieczyński, Witold 032098
Ommen, Dr. Eilert 019315
Onaga, Stephen 047288
Ondevilla, Alex 031632
Ondish, Andrea 048699
Ondrejčeková, Zora 034337
Ondrušeková, Dr. Anna 034412
O'Neil, Paul 041967
O'Neill, Anthony 039689
O'Neill, Caroline 000725
O'Neill, Colleen 005294
O'Neill, Heidi 046325
O'Neill, John 046346
O'Neill, John J. 041972
O'Neill, Mark 039548, 039555
O'Neill, Peter 001627
O'Neill, Sheila C. 049126
O'Neill, Vicki 001355
Onodera, Hiroshi 026927
Onodera, Reiko 027169
Onorevoli, Dr. Giuseppe 026014
Onyejekwe, Dr. Umebe N. 030707
Oomen, Dr. Th. 003163
Oost, T. 003759, 003760, 003761
Oost, Tony 003757
Oostdijk, Dr. Alexandra E. 030290
Oosterbaan, A. 029396
Oosterhof, H. 030209
Oosthoek-Bogaard, A.W. 029875
Oostra, Dr. R.J. 029209
Ootukasa, Mitukuni 026954
Ooyama, Masaaki 026809
Op de Beeck, Bart 003291
Op de Beeck, Jozef 003633
Op de Beek, R. 029360
Opdenberg, Laurence 003299
Operta, Mevlida 003941
Opie, Robert 041385
Opinel, Annick 014369
Opolă, Valentina 027729
Opp, Edmund 043754
Oppenheim, Roy 037235
Oppenhimer, Ann 047415
Opperman, G. 034736
Oppermann, Prof. M. 017670
Oppitz, Prof. Dr. Michael 037808
Opstad, Jan-L. 031283
Oquendo, Dante 031782
Orač-Stipperger, Dr. Roswitha 001946, 002690
Oratowska, Barbara 032134
O'Rawe, A.C. 040643
Oražem, Prof. Dr. Vito 017077
Orbons, Dr. A. 029759
Orchard, Dr. Karin 017769
Ordine, Mauriziano 025961
Ordoš, Dr. Ján 034414
Ore, Phyllis 006300
Orear, Tammy S. 045532
Orebäck-Krantz, Elisabeth 036577
Oredsson, Prof. Lars-Göran 036442
Orefici, Giuseppe 031576
Oreglia, Luciano 023367
Orehovec, Martina 034495
O'Reilly, Margaret 048605
O'Reilly-Lawrence, Priscilla 046255
Oremus, Frederick L. 046176
Oren, Dan 022893
Orfali, Dalila 000048
Orgeix, Charles-Louis d' 012754
Orgonikidze, I. 015412
Oriol, Calvo 034858
O'Riordan, E. 022831
O'Riordan, Ian 039381
Orlandi, Giuseppe 026360
Orlando, Fran 046480
Orlando González, Jorge 007411
Orlić, Alfons 007827
Orloski, Julie 048063
Orlov, Evgenij Michajlovič 033808
Orlov, Viktor 033030
Orłowski, Jarosław 031963
Orlson Agbo, Raymond 021101
Ormerod, Robin 005714
Ormhaug, Knut . . 030756, 030757, 030758
Ormiston, O. 040579
Ormond, Dr. Rupert 040469
Ormonde, Dr. Helena 032578
Ornauer, Elisabeth 002979
Ornsby, Philip 039691
Oroianu, Silvia 032954
Orona, Blanca 043640
Oropeza Segura, Manuel 028686
Orosz, Helma 020787
Orozco, Prof. Margarita V. de 028273
Orozco, Sylvia 041932
Orozco Móron, Edna Maria 028522
Orr, Brenda P. 005899
Orr, Charlene 045796
Orr, Dr. Patrick J. 022790
Orr-Cahall, Christina 049091
Orrick, Mary Norton 046862
Orro, Leena 009632
Orsi, Dr. Oriana 024409
Orsini, Ph. 014974
Orskou, Gitte 008805
Ortal, Dr. R. 022954
Ortega, Enric 036055
Ortega, Luis Angel 035771
Ortega DeSantis, Diana 047975
Ortega Rivera, Enric 036055
Ortel, Gustav-A. 016489
Ortenzi, Prof. Alfio 023271
Ortiz, Emilio I. 047978
Ortiz, Gustavo A. 007418
Ortiz, Rosa 034942
Ortiz Crespo, Alfonso 009238
Ortíz Lan, José E. 028132
Ortíz Muñoz, Idania 007502
Ortiz Volio, Melania 007681
Ortmeier, Dr. Martin 018861, 018863
Ortner, Josef 002963
Ortner, M. Christian 002910
Orton, Anna 041330
Orton, Donald 048309
Oruch, Sam 046650
Orzsi, Zoltán 021626
Osamu, Dr. Izumi 027049
Osborn, Rachel 041657
Osborne, Bernard 049236
Osborne, Duncan 038485
Osborne, Lois I. 043005
Osborne, Peter 047135
Osborne, S. 040037
Osborne, Victoria 041483
Oscarsson, Ulla 036529
Oselies, David 004991
Oset, Hans Petter 030908
O'Shaughnessy, Margaret . 022788, 046332
O'Shea, Deborah H. 047535
O'Shea, John 041733
O'Shea, Patrick B. 022818
O'Shea, William A. 005802
O'Shea Schmieg, Shannon 041840
Oshel, Laurie 044139
Oshima, Seiji 027235
Oslen, John C. 005387
Oslund, Christopher 005561
Osman, Prof. Ali Mohamed 036146
Osmond, Lynn 042830
Ospina Cubillos, Carlos Enrique . . . 007448
Ospina de Muñoz, Esperanza 007561
Ospina Navia, Francisco 007608
Ospino de la Rosa, José 007497
Osrin, Myra 034575
Osses, Dietmar 016285, 016771
Ostapova, Svitlana Ivanivna 038368
Østergård, Niels Jøan 009105
Ostarhild, Dr. H. 018929
Ostaszewska, Stanisława 032373
Osten, Dr. Till 020364
Ostendorf, Dr. Thomas . . . 020417, 020418
Ostenrieder, Dr. Petra 019450
Østerås, Bodil 031238
Osterhus, Cynthia B. 047763
Ostermann, Françoise 037011
Ostermiller, Jerry 041823
Østervig, Torsten 009012
Osticresi, Dr. Patrizio 024178
Ostlund, Ralph 046274
Ostojić, Milan 034281
Ostrenko, Wit 048490
Ostritz, Dr. S. 019869, 020747
Ostrosky, Amelia 049092
Ostrouchova, Marina Georgievna . 033326
Ostrow, Mindy 046749
Ostrow, Victor 048059
Ostrowski, Prof. Jan 032070
Ostrum, Meg 045835
O'Suilleabhain, Sean 022683
O'Sullivan, Dr. A.M. 022875
O'Sullivan, Keith M.C. 038978
O'Sullivan, Mary 022813
Oswald, Dr. Niklaus 037784
Osyra, Tadeusz 032020
Ōta, Motoji 027230
Otani, Kazuhiko 027215
Otani, Shogo 027256
Otaola, Pablo 035976
Otavová, Marie 008773
Otero, Álvaro 007482
Otke, Natalja Pavlovna 032981
Otkovyč, Dr. Vasyl 038355
Otomo, Akira 027343
Otomo, Tsutomu 026877
O'Toole, Judith H. 044340

Otsuka, Ronald 043404
Otsuka, Yoshio 027296
Ott, Irene 017219
Ott, John H. 045270
Ott, Lili R. 046662
Ott, Wendell 048515
Ott, Wolfgang 020785
Otte, Prof. 003589
Otte, Andreas 016759
Otte, Stacey A. 041941
Otte, Wulf 016381
Ottenbacher, V. . . 016220, 016221, 016222
Otterspeer, Prof. Dr. W. 029846
Ottillinger, Dr. Eva 002921
Ottinger, Bénédicte 014760, 014761, 014762
Otto, John 042597
Otto, Kristin 021047
Otto, Martha 043109
Otto, Dr. Sigrid 015992
Otto, Veronika 019980
Otto-Hörbrand, Martin 020358
Ottomeyer, Prof. Dr. Hans 016011
Otton, Dr. William G. 043161
Ottosson, Jon Gunnar 021969
Ottou Onana, Irène 004974, 004978
Ottrubay, Dr. Stefan 001859
Otttaviani, Jean-Claude 010328
Otwell, Maureen 047705
Otzen, Dr. Peter 017433
Ouarzazi, Abdul Wahed 035021
Ouellet, Nicole 006217, 006230
Ouellet, Raynald 005905
Ouellette, Lenore 045509
Ourecky, Irma 049170
Ourmieres, Jean-Guy 014556
Outerbridge, Amanda 003905, 003906
Ovalle Neira, Pedro Ubert 007604
Ovečkinaova, Olga 033781
Overbeck, Prof. Dr. Bernhard 019119
Overbeck, Gertrud 016425
Overdiep, Dr. G. 029484
Overlie, Jill 045397
Overmyer, Lorraine 043534
Overstreet, Laura 041647
Overton, Jonathan 038632
Oviedo de Coria, Beatriz 000568
Ovsjankina, Ljudmila Vladimirovna 033959
Owczarski, Marian 046708
Owczuk, Tadeusz 032326
Oweis, Iman 027382
Owen, Ann 040063
Owen, Gwilym 040063
Owen, Paula 047800, 047807
Owen, Richard 039981
Owen, Thomas S. 048591
Owen Walker, Elizabeth 043411
Owens, Heather 046071
Owens, Joseph J. 048796
Owens, Marshall 044611
Owens, Sue Ellen 043349
Owens-Celli, Morgyn 045377
Owers, Lorna 039316
Owyoung, Steven D. 047676
Oxley, Nicola 040228
Oya, Mina 027189
Oyama, Prof. K. 026736
Oygur, Dr. Sule 046425
Oyuela, Raul M. 043146, 045813
Ozaki, Masaaki 027256
Ozanam, M. Yves 013679
Ozay, Alev 038102
Ožegova, Ljudmila Ivanovnă 033270
Ozola, Agrita 027789
Ozola, Ārija 027685
Ozolina, Vita 027729
Paajanen, Kyllikki 009700
Paap, Hans-Uwe 018513
Paarlberg, Bill 048244
Paarlberg, S. 029502
Paas, Dr. 016884
Paas, Dr. Sigrun 018790
Paaverud, Merl 042237, 049191
Paaverud, Merlan E. 042238, 042239, 046863
Pabian, Roger K. 045313
Pabst, Fieke 029239
Pabst, Stewart J. 043132
Pacciarelli, Dr. Marco 024409
Paccioretti, Cecilia 049031
Pace, Dr. Lorenzo 048708
Pace, Richard 041066
Pace-DeBruin, Margaret 042344
Pacere, Tifinga Frédéric 004959
Pačev, Nikolaj 004737
Pache, Pierre 037744
Pacheco, Anelise 004367
Pacheco, Diane 042427
Pacheco, Gustavo 004315
Pachiyanni, Phani 021338
Pachner, Joan 046079
Pachnicke, Prof. Peter 019390
Pacholik, Kazmimierz 032492
Pachomova, Nadežda Petrovna . . . 033119
Pachter, Marc 048927, 048933
Pacini, Marina 045756
Pacjukov, Vladimir V. 033339
Packard, Vance 043136
Packauskas, R. 044490
Packer, Dr. Claude 026387
Packer, Nancy 046934
Packheiser, Michael 018971, 018972
Paczkowski, Dr. Jörg 020819
Paczkowski, Dr. Renate 018248
Paczos, Andrzej 031972
Padalkina, Olga Viktorovna 033014
Paddock, D. 041323
Paddock, Eric 043401
Paddock, Dr. J.M 039093
Paddock, Dr. John 040597
Paderni, Loretta 025555
Padgett, Michael 047240, 047449
Padhy, Dr. K. P. 022230
Padhy, Dr. K.P. 022196, 022311
Padian, Kevin 042163
Padurariu, Nicolae 032813
Pärdi, Heiki 009424
Paesano, Dr. Ciro 024904
Pätzold, Winfried 017985
Pagac, Gerald J. 045940
Pagano, Dr. Denise Maria 024915
Pagano, Sergio 049417
Page, Casey 047689
Page, Chris 039172
Page, Eric 044913
Page, Gregory A. 048249
Page, John 038631
Page, Dr. Jutta Annette 043155
Page, Kathryn 046259
Pagé, Suzanne 013630
Pagella, Dr. Enrica 026052
Pagès, Solange 012537
Pagliardi, M. Nicoletta 025556
Pagnotta, Philippe 014660
Pagot, Serge 013350
Pagulayan, Teresita L. 031717, 031723
Pahlke, Dr. Rosemarie E. 016766
Pahlow, Martina 020461
Paige Linn, Nancy 047235
Paillard, Ph. 012818
Pailler, Henri 011744, 013143
Paillet, Antoine 014845
Paillet, Patrick 014412
Pain, Ron 040851
Paine, Susan W. 042334
Paine, Dr. Timothy D. 047456
Paine, Tony 030458
Paine, Wesley M. 046150
Painter, Bill 044898
Painter-De Monte, Y.Z. 048626
Païpetú, Andreas 021343
Pais de Brito, Joaquim 032650
Pais Pinto, Joaquim 000087
Paisley Cato, Dr. 047840
Paiva, Ricardo Luís 032689
Paizis-Paradelis, Constantin 021434
Pajović, Maja 034200
Pajskrová, Dr. Jana 008370
Pak, Valentin V. 027394
Pakesch, Peter 001937, 001938
Pakkala, Taru 009452
Pakoma, Katariina 009634
Pakuningrat, Maulana 022411
Pakzad, Dr. Amir 017767
Pal, Raj 041320, 041336
Pal, S.N. 022218
Pala, Valter 025677, 025680
Palacios i Manuel, Josep 035029, 035030, 035032
Palacpac, Remedios 031694
Palacz, Tomasz 032202
Palágyi, Dr. Sylvia 021919
Palamarz, Elisabeth 010102
Palavonov, D. 037837
Palella, Dr. Graciela Elizabeth 000309
Palermo, Jeanne 043319
Palisse, A. 014951
Páll, Dr. István 021851
Pall, Martina 001933
Palladino-Craig, Allys 048478
Pallan, Norbert 002471
Pallanca, Dr. Claude 028996
Pallavicini, Maria Camilla 025470
Pallestrang, Kathrin 002976
Pallmert, Sigrid 037784
Pallottino, Paola 024107
Pallozola, Christina 043049
Pálmason, Ólafur 021968
Palmberg Eriksson, Stina 036511
Palmeiri, John 042424
Palmenaer, Els de 003158
Palmer, Lord 039326
Palmer, A.B. 041887
Palmer, Cheryl 042760
Palmer, Dr. C.J. 039697
Palmer, Mike 038555
Palmer, Oonagh 039484, 039608
Palmer, Peregrine 041413
Palmer, Ros 041231
Palmer, Sharon S. 045002
Palmgren, Kaj 009468
Palmgren, Ola 036382, 036385
Palmquist, Dr. Lena 036652
Palmquist, Linda 043126
Palo-oja, Ritva 010128
Paloheimo, George B. 047963
Palokangas, Markku 009554, 009564, 009570, 009571
Palombo, Aldo 046540
Palombo, Ionah 022946
Palomero, Santiago 035925
Palomo, Antonio 021565
Palop, José Alcántara 034862
Palou Sampol, Joana M. 035615
Palov, Dr. József 021855
Palsa, Raija 009828, 009829
Palsa, Raja 009830
Pálsson, Lýdur 021942, 021943
Paltenghi, Barbara 037288
Paltrinieri, Roberto 023414
Paluck, Jayne 006426
Palzerová, Hana 008365, 008367
Pamart, Jean-Luc 013453
Pambrun, Sam 046866
Pamlényi, Klara 021754
Pamperin, David L. 045074
Pamuk, Ömer 038167
Pan, Giuseppe 025009
Pan, Junxiang 007240
Pan, Zheng 007244
Pan, Zhenzhou 007000
Panabière, Louis 028431
Panafieu, Bruno de 014360
Panagiotopoulou, Anastasia 021183
Panajotov, Vladimir 004738
Panamaroff, Emilia 006426
Pañares, Tonette 031659
Panaskin, Vladimir Vasiljevič 033053
Panawatta, Senarath 036140
Panayotova, Dr. S. 038962
Panazza, Dr. Gaetano 024524
Pančeva, Petrana 004623
Pančeva, Radka 004933
Pančuk, Fedir Vasil'ovyč 038412
Panczenko, Dr. Russell 045589
Panda, Prof. C. 022229
Pandey, A.K. 022281
Pandey, Dr. S.N. 022041, 022103
Pandilovski, Melentie 000706
Pandolfi, Sylvia 028537
Pandžić, Ankica 007841
Panek, Kornelia 016985
Paner, Henryk 031909
Panese, Prof. Dr. Francesco 037248
Pang, Toni 044776
Pangburn, D.A. 047437
Pange, Roland de 013542
Panhorst, Michael W. 048363
Panić, Djordje 034265
Paniccia, Antonio 026281
Panizza, Marco 025979
Panjević, Nikola 003945
Panjuškin, A.D. 033394
Pankok, Eva 018026
Pannabecker, Rachel K. 046529
Panne, Dr. Kathrin 016545
Panneton, Jean 006665
Pannewitz, Otto 020215
Panni, Frédéric 012056
Panoski, Naum 027923
Pansi, Dr. Heinz 002038
Pant, Kurt 003000
Pant, Dr. Madhu 022086
Panteghini, Ivo 023522
Pantellini, Claudia 037267
Panter, Dr. Armin 020113
Panter, John 047833
Pantoja, Dianne 042581
Pantoja, Hernán Gil 007541
Panțuru, Prof. N. Ioan 032806
Panvini, Dr. Rosalba 023590
Pany, Franz Norbert 019217
Panzanaro, Mauro 024461
Paola de Picot, Mercedes di 000166
Paoletta, Dr. Donald 045301
Paoli, Arturo 023596
Paoli, Feliciano 026169
Paolillo, Dr. Antonio 024002
Paolillo, Giuseppe 023347
Paolozzi Strozzi, Dr. Beatrice 024195
Paolucci, Dr. Antonio 024153
Papa, Prof. Cristina 023799, 026199
Papachristodoulou, Dr. Joannis . . . 021451
Papadakis, N. 021120
Papadakis, Dr. Nikos 021468
Papademetriou, Dr. Eleni 008214
Papadopoulos, A. 008217
Papadopoulos, Prof. N. 021192
Papadopoulou, Eleni 021225
Papadopoulou-Pangou, K. 021328
Papaefthymiou, Eleni 021207
Papageorgiou, Ioannis 021358
Papagno, Dr. Francesco Saverio . . 025172
Papait, Jean 011242
Papakonstantinou, Maria-Photini . 021349
Papaldo, Dr. Serenita 025466
Papangeli, Kalliopi 021254
Papantoniou, Ioanna 021402
Papararo, Jenifer 006613
Paparella Treccia, Raffaelle 025187
Paparone, Guiseppe 025981
Papazian, Aline 046840
Papazoglou, Lena 021183
Papco, Ján 034315
Papendieck, Dr. Christine 020668
Papendorf, Dorothee C. 020089
Papet, Edouard 013678
Papike, Dr. James J. 041616
Papillard, Marie Laure 015137
Papin-Drastik, Y. 011519
Papone, Elisabetta 024308
Papounaud, Benoît-Henry 014290

Papović, Stanko . . . 034179
Pappas, Elizabeth . . . 043773
Pappi, Evangelia . . . 021400
Papuc, Gheorghe . . . 032767, 032844
Paradis, Michèle . . . 006025, 006666
Paradowski, Dr. Stefan . . . 037690
Páramo, Amanda Lucía . . . 007387
Paramonov, Vladimir Aleksandrovič 033979
Paraskevas-Gizis, Evaggelos . . . 021507, 021509, 021510
Parberg, Dee . . . 047239
Pardee, Jean . . . 043573
Pardilla, Helena . . . 007629
Pardini, Prof. Edoardo . . . 024180
Pardo, Alfredo . . . 007415
Pardo, Rengifo . . . 007406
Pardue, Diana . . . 047009
Pardue, Diana R. . . . 046408
Pare, Glenn . . . 047932
Paredes Giraldo, Maria Camino . . . 035632
Parent, Béatrice . . . 013630
Parent, Geraldine . . . 006129
Parent, Dr. Thomas . . . 016771
Paret, John J. . . . 041907
Pargner, Dr. Birgit . . . 019047
Parham, Herbert S. . . . 044423
Parikka, Anne . . . 009489
Parillo, James D. . . . 048008
Parisch, Manfred . . . 002457
Parise, Dr. Roberta . . . 025053
Pariset, Jean-Daniel . . . 013680
Parish, Suzanne D. . . . 044898
Parisi, Prof. Vittorio . . . 025126
Park, Janette A. . . . 039905
Park, You Chul . . . 027465
Park Curry, Dr. David . . . 047429
Parke, David L. . . . 044523
Parke, Julie . . . 045491
Parke, Susan . . . 045052
Parker, Cheryl Ann . . . 049064
Parker, David . . . 043911
Parker, Donna . . . 042366
Parker, Eris . . . 030455
Parker, Harry S. . . . 047857, 047871
Parker, Herschell . . . 046149
Parker, John . . . 000893
Parker, Prof. John S. . . . 038963
Parker, Julia . . . 040122
Parker, Madeline . . . 041797
Parker, Margaret . . . 047116
Parker, P. . . . 040350
Parker, Robert . . . 044151
Parker, Sandi . . . 042094
Parker, Steve . . . 045257
Parker, Teresa . . . 043686
Parker, Tim . . . 006018
Parkes, Susan . . . 022769
Parkhurst, Jo . . . 043866
Parkin, Peg . . . 000791
Parkinson, C.D. . . . 038478
Parkinson, Glenn . . . 044026
Parks, Dennis . . . 048085
Parks, Gary W. . . . 045243
Parks, Dr. Raymond . . . 039388
Parks, Robert E. . . . 046394
Parks, Ron . . . 043192
Parks, Shirley . . . 049228
Parks McClain, Patti . . . 045086
Parlic-Barisic, Slobodanka . . . 027919
Parma, Raphaël . . . 013830
Parma, Dr. Rita . . . 025466
Parmalee, Dr. Paul . . . 045039
Parman, Susan . . . 044097
Parmentier, Damien . . . 013301
Parmentier, J.-P. . . . 012678
Parnell, Dr. G. . . . 040268
Parnes, Stuart . . . 043732
Parola, Publio . . . 000495
Parpagiola, Dr. Giuseppe . . . 024981
Parr, Jesse . . . 045729
Parr, Melissa . . . 046673
Parra, Raúl . . . 028536
Parra Casamun, Gerardo . . . 028509
Parra Santos, Alirio . . . 007489
Parratt, D.M. . . . 041087
Parreiras Horta, Maria de Lourdes . 004279
Parreño, Prof. Manuel . . . 027838
Parrilla de Alvarez, Estela . . . 028246
Parrinello, Prof. Nicolo . . . 025090
Parris, David . . . 048605
Parrish, M. . . . 039843
Parrott, Robert W. . . . 045717
Parrott, Shirley . . . 047557
Parry, Linda . . . 040321
Parry, Wendy . . . 040868
Parshall, Peter . . . 048924
Paršina, Lidija Semënovna . . . 033042
Paršina, Ljudmila Vladimirovna . . . 034026
Parson, Helen . . . 038855
Parsons, Brian . . . 000950
Parsons, Clare . . . 039891
Parsons, Jeffrey R. . . . 041733
Parsons, Julien . . . 039053
Parsons, K. . . . 001514
Parsons, Louise . . . 046640
Parsons, Ralph . . . 041085
Parsy, Paul-Hervé . . . 013480
Partin, Marc . . . 049320
Parton, Neville . . . 001113
Partyka, Józef . . . 032185
Parusel, Janina . . . 032555
Parušev, Todor . . . 004917, 004922
Pârvan, Lucia . . . 032785
Pârvan, Lucica . . . 032856, 032857
Pârvan, Lucicia . . . 032931
Parviainen, Helena . . . 009781
Paša, Natko . . . 007832
Pascal, Huston . . . 047313
Pascale, Mark . . . 042820
Pasch, Anne . . . 043555
Paschke, Ilona . . . 018731
Pascual, José . . . 035290
Pascucci, Marisa . . . 045995
Pashley, Bill . . . 038955, 040918, 040922
Pasiciel, Stanisław . . . 031941
Paskova, Spaska . . . 004689
Pasler, Hermann . . . 018784
Pasquali, Prof. Flavia . . . 025879
Pasquier, Alain . . . 013685
Pasquini-Barisi, Isabella . . . 026028
Passaglia, Elio . . . 024761
Passarin, Dr. Mauro . . . 026310
Passe, Eugene . . . 047349
Passi, Leena . . . 009454
Paßlick, Tonio . . . 020718
Pasté de Rochefort, Aymeri . . . 011458
Pastellas, Dominiue . . . 013703
Paster, Carol . . . 047120
Pasternak, Natalija Anisimovna . . . 033642
Pastor, Paloma . . . 035756
Pastor Vázquez, Prof. J.F. . . . 035996
Pastore, Heather . . . 043686
Pastore, Prof. Michele . . . 025989
Pastorek, Ivan . . . 034355
Pastoriza, Juan A. . . . 032716
Pasture, B. . . . 003651
Paszowski, Cindy . . . 005403
Patané, Dr. Rosario . . . 023791
Patchen, Dr. Jeffrey . . . 044735
Paten, Richard . . . 040701
Patenaude, Val . . . 005833
Pater, Dr. Józef . . . 032515
Paterson, Anne . . . 040487
Paterson, Blair . . . 006250
Paterson, John . . . 029088
Pathak, Dr. Bindeshwar . . . 022097
Pathak, G.M. . . . 022364
Patier, Xavier . . . 011216
Patin, Sylvie . . . 013678
Patka, Dr. Erika . . . 002996
Patka, Dr. Marcus G. . . . 002918
Patnode, J. Scott . . . 048274
Patocchi, Luca . . . 037284
Paton, W.J. . . . 030471, 030472
Patorska, Joanna . . . 032143
Patrich, Pat . . . 048609
Patrick, Brian . . . 030488
Patrick, J.A. . . . 038735
Patrick, R.E . . . 046075
Patrick, Ruth . . . 046917
Patrick, Stephen E. . . . 042360, 042361, 042362, 042363, 042364
Patros, Charlotte . . . 049190
Patry, J. Michael . . . 045249
Patten, Dan W. . . . 044268
Patterschal, Donald . . . 048236
Patterson jr., Aubrey B. . . . 048657
Patterson, James . . . 040095
Patterson, Ken . . . 005109
Patterson, Lillian . . . 041635
Patterson, Dr. Mark A. . . . 042509
Patterson, Richard . . . 048606
Patterson, Robert B. . . . 047716
Patterson, Ruth . . . 000888
Patterson-O'Regan, J.J. . . . 038711
Patteson, Rita . . . 048809
Pattie, M. . . . 030587
Pattinson, G. . . . 040957
Pattison, Alison . . . 039597
Patton, Jody . . . 048079
Patton, LuAnn W. . . . 041633
Patton, Robert . . . 048621
Patton, Dr. Sharon F. . . . 046607
Patton, S.M. . . . 041793, 041794
Patwa, Elizabeth . . . 010770
Patzak, Dr. B. . . . 002987
Patzer, George . . . 005601
Patzig, Eberhard . . . 018572
Paugh, James J. . . . 049311
Pauka, T.R. . . . 029255
Paukšte, Regīna . . . 027655
Paul, April . . . 046308
Paul, C.D. . . . 040623
Paul, Frédéric . . . 010805
Paul, Gayle . . . 047197
Paul, Renee . . . 030589
Paul, Ryan . . . 042664
Paul, Shimrath . . . 030488
Paul-Zinserling, Dr. V. . . . 018114
Paula, Alberto de . . . 000218
Paulay, Dr. G. . . . 044103
Păuleanu, Dr. Doina . . . 032842
Păuleanu, Doina . . . 032891, 032959
Pauletić, Mirjana . . . 007705
Pauley, Ed . . . 046826
Paulicka-Nowak, Dr. Lucja . . . 032013
Paulo, Dālia . . . 032614
Paulocik, Linda . . . 006806
Paulsen, Nils . . . 030835
Paulson, Christopher . . . 047306
Paulson, Dr. Dennis R. . . . 048466
Paulson, Warren . . . 005037
Paulsrud, Geir . . . 030827
Paulus, Norma . . . 047174
Pauly, Dorothy . . . 042698
Pausch, Gottfried . . . 001801
Pausch, Dr. Oskar . . . 002993
Pause, Dr. Carl . . . 019271
Paust, Dr. Bettina . . . 015933
Pautet, C. . . . 012985
Pautrizel, Françoise . . . 010795
Pavaloi, Dr. Margareta . . . 017838
Pavelčík, Dr. Jiří . . . 008732
Pavelcikova, Monika . . . 034346, 034433, 034434
Pavelec, Karen . . . 043745
Pavelka, Dr. Karel . . . 008741, 008766
Pavia, Prof. Giulio . . . 026065
Pavic, Stjepan . . . 003946
Pavić, Vladimira . . . 007854
Pavičić, Snježana . . . 007841
Pavlát, Dr. Leo . . . 008653
Pavletić, Mira . . . 007703
Pavlides, Paul . . . 011210
Pavliňák, Dr. Petr . . . 008555
Pavljuk, Vasil Mykolajovyč . . . 038239
Pavlov, Aleksandr Anatoljevič . . . 033047
Pavlova, Irina Vasiljevna . . . 034011
Pavlović, Ivo . . . 007711
Pavlu, Viktor . . . 002926
Pavlunina, Ljudmila Fëdorovna . . . 034086
Pavoni, Rosanna . . . 053752
Pavúková, Olga . . . 034393
Pavuljak, Jaraoslav Ivanovyč . . . 038401
Pawchuak, Linda . . . 047327
Pawłowska, Krystyna Iwona . . . 032502
Pawłowski, Dr. Antoni J. . . . 032087
Payet, Hugues . . . 032761
Payling, Catherine . . . 025486
Payne, Elizabeth . . . 005302
Payne, James . . . 048834
Payne, Mary . . . 045224
Payne, R.G. . . . 041067
Payne, Prof. Robert B. . . . 041734
Payne, Susan . . . 040697
Payrich, Wolfgang . . . 002042
Payton, Charles . . . 040767
Payton, Sidney . . . 043414
Paz, Boaz . . . 053548
Paz, Diego Alonso . . . 007583
Paz, Olivier . . . 013036
Paz Morales Osorio, Maria de la . . 028459
Pazmandy Horvath, Margaret . . . 047137
Pazoutova, Katerina . . . 008413
Pčelinceva, Nelli Sergeevna . . . 033282
Peabody, Ann F. . . . 044962
Peabody Turnbaugh, Sarah . . . 046852
Peace, Barb . . . 006758
Peach Lynch, Ann . . . 047535
Peacock, Pat . . . 048412
Peak, Marianne . . . 047301
Peake, Jane . . . 049128
Pealer, Dr. Casius . . . 046610
Pearce, Alan . . . 041012
Pearce, Andrew . . . 040844
Pearce, Barry . . . 001505
Pearce, John N. . . . 044059
Pearce, Michael . . . 039396
Pearce, Pelham G. . . . 042689
Pearce, Robert J. . . . 005789
Pearlstein, Elinor L. . . . 042820
Pearsall, Barbara . . . 046528
Pearson, A. Faye . . . 005600
Pearson, Dave . . . 041823
Pearson, Fiona . . . 039424
Pearson, Marion . . . 048663
Pearson, N. . . . 001232
Pearson, Paul . . . 042457
Pearsons, Don . . . 006838
Peaucelle, Denis . . . 010407
Peavy, John M. . . . 044814
Peces Rata, Felipe Gil . . . 035873, 035874
Pech, Edwin . . . 031983
Pecháček, Ivo . . . 008452
Pechal, Dorothy . . . 048524
Pecharromán, Ricardo . . . 035638
Pechlamer, Helmut . . . 001832
Pechová, Dr. Jarmila . . . 008286
Pecht, Ulrike . . . 017829
Peci, Innocenzo . . . 025444
Peck, Donald J. . . . 046892
Peck, Elsie . . . 043444
Peck, James F. . . . 048656
Peck, Scott . . . 043264
Peck, William H. . . . 043444
Peck Bracy, Tralice . . . 045960
Peckham, Cynthia A. . . . 047509
Pecoraro, Joseph P. . . . 042818
Peczelt, Ursula . . . 001851
Pedder, John . . . 040368
Pede, Miriam . . . 042150
Peden, Harold R. . . . 048705
Pedersen, Birgit . . . 008805
Pedersen, Hans . . . 031035
Pedersen, Jørgen . . . 008806, 008838
Pedersen, Kenno 008847, 008898, 009130
Pedersen, Knud . . . 008969
Pedersen, K.S. . . . 008991
Pedersen, Lisbeth . . . 008947
Pedersen, Lykke . . . 008999
Pedersen, Naja . . . 008938
Pedersen, T. . . . 008991

Pederson, Curt 045907
Pederson, Jennifer 042898
Pedevillano, Diane 047213
Pedlar, Arthur 045891
Pedneault, Richard 006751
Pedretti, Cornelia 037506
Pedretti, Robert 042587, 042588
Pedrini, Dr. Claudia 024400, 024404, 024407, 024408, 024409
Peduzzi, Francis 011073
Peebles, Cheryl 006785
Peebles, Virginia T. 043094
Peek, Andre 048164
Peek, Thomas 019660
Peel, Prof. John S. 036736, 036737, 036749
Peele, Anna M. 043989
Peeperkorn-van Donselaar, Dr. L.A. 030076
Peers, Dr. Laura 040665
Peers-Gloyer, Axel 019662
Peery, Richard 048605
Peeters, Herman 003399
Peeters, L. 003195
Peeters, Ludo 003401
Peeters Saenen, E. 003403
Pehlivaner, Metin 038016
Peić Čaldarović, Dubravka 007841
Peičinova, Chaterina 004631
Peiffer, Jacques 012095
Peik, Karl-Heinz 017709
Pein, Max Gerrit von 020350, 020359
Peine, Arnold 015874
Peiry, Lucienne 037238
Peitler, Karl 001941
Pejković, Božidar 007734
Pejnović, Nikola 007770
Peković, Mirko 034172
Pela, Premysl 046420
Peláez Arbeláez, Leopoldo 007446
Peláez Tremols, Dr. Lucía 035224, 035225
Pelagalli, Prof. G.V. 024904
Pelanne, Marja 009573
Pélatan, Martial 010277
Pełczyk, Antoni 032094
Pelegrini, Dr. Béatrice 037131
Péligry, Christian 013555
Pelikánová, Jaroslava 008530
Pelkey, Ann 047072
Pella, Nicholas W. 046674
Pellard, Sandra-Diana 011286
Pellegrinetti, Jerri 006577
Pellegrino, Ronald J. 044377
Pellen, Robin 039190, 039192
Pellengahr, Dr. Astrid 018215
Pellmann, Dr. Hans 018773
Pellow, Robin 039788
Pelon-Ribeiro, Laurence 011551
Pelosio, Prof. Giuseppe 025128
Pelrine, Diane 042263
Pelser, R. 034769
Pelsers, Dr. L. 029569
Peltier, Cynthia 045241
Pelz, H. 016458
Pelzl, Prof. Dr. Leopoldine 001687
Pemberton, David 001114
Peña, José María 000185
Peña Castillo, Agustín 028416
Peña Javier, Estrellita 031775
Peña Reigosa, Maria Cristina 007932
Peñalver Gómez, Henriqueta 049503
Penard, Michel 015307
Penati, Fabio 024880
Pence, Debra 044484
Pence, Noel 044666
Penčev, Ass.Prof. Dr. Vladimir 004863
Pender, Branko 007798
Pendleton, Chris 043956, 043959
Penent, Jean 014996, 014997
Penicaud, Pierre 011400
Penick, George 044440
Penick, Steven 047626
Penka, Bradley 045054
Penkina, Elena Ivanovna 033214
Penkov, Petio 004927, 004928, 004929, 004930, 004938, 004939, 004940
Penkova, Elka 004863
Penn, Joyce 043156
Penn, Michael 041077
Penn, Simon 038884
Penna, Liisa 041825
Pennanen, Tapani 010134
Pennant 003808
Pennas, Dr. Vasso 021164
Penndorf, Jutta 015501
Penner, E. Paul 006770
Penner, Lisa 041822, 041826
Pennestri, Dr. Serafina 026053
Penney, David 043444
Penney, S.F.J. 005983
Penney, Stephen 040600
Penning, Dr. Mark 034605
Pennington, Claudia 046470
Pennington, Claudia L. 044983, 044988
Pennington, Tom C. 044753
Pennino, Gaetano 025076
Penno-Burmeister, Karin 018456
Penny, Cheryl 006308
Penny, Dr. Nicholas 040241
Pensabene, Dr. Giovanni 024545
Pensom, Carole 005701
Pentrella, Dr. Ruggero 025553
Penvose, Jane 048576
Penz, Marta 026187
Penzin, Viktor 033484
Pèon, Marie-Thérèse 012837
Peoples, Jo 000712
Peora, Prof. Oscar Carlos 000229
Pepić, Eva 027837
Pepich, Bruce W. 047305
Pepion, Loretta 042477
Peppler, Tina 005161
Perac, Jelena 034163
Perales Piqueres, Rosa 035015
Peralta, Juan 031542
Peralta, Prof. Tole 006914
Peralta Juárez, Juan 034793
Peralta Vidal, Gabriel 006921
Perchinske, Marlene 043072
Percival, Arthur 039493
Perco, Daniela 023828
Percy, Ann B. 046975
Percy, David O. 042744
Perego, Graziella 024363
Pereira, Maria Isabel de Sousa 032580
Gomes Pereira, Prof. Sonia 004393
Pereira Cabral, Augusto J. 029048
Pereira de Araujo, J. Hermes 004400
Pereira Herrera, David M. 003908
Pereira Neto, Prof. João 032644
Pereira Viana, Dr. Maria Teresa 032680
Pereireira Reis, Brasiliano 004150
Perelló, Antonia M. 034922
Perepelkina, Aleksandra Fëdorovna 033893
Peretti, Pierre de 013202, 013208
Peretto, Prof. Raffaele 025614
Pereyra Salva de Impini, Prof. Nydia 000607
Perez, Anthony 047585
Pérez, Fernando Alberto 007580
Perez, Gabriel 046288
Pérez, Juan Fernando 009253
Perez, Patricia 031654
Pérez, Rosa María 021584
Pérez Aviles, José Javier 035967
Pérez Avilés, José Javier 035969
Pérez Basurto, Alejandro 028464
Pérez Camps, Josep 035462
Pérez Casas, Angel 034827
Pérez Espinosa, Juan Fidel 028654
Perez Gollan, Dr. José Antonio 000204
Pérez Gónzález, Melba 008124
Pérez Gutiérrez, Arturo 028483
Pérez Maldonado, Raúl 021574
Pérez Mesuro, Dolores 035937
Pérez Moreno, Rafael 035393
Pérez Navarro, Amalia 035410
Pérez Ornes, Nora 009157
Pérez Outeiriño, Bieito 035819
Pérez Quintana, José Andrés 007950, 007981
Pérez Recio, Manuel 035327
Pérez Ruán, Liliana 007642
Pérez Villarreal, Pedro 007615
Pergament, Allen 048215
Perger, Dr. Richard 002874
Pergola, Prof. Philippe 026271
Pería, Alejandra 028491
Pericoli, Prof. Cecilia 025491
Périer-d'Ieteren, C. 003297
Perillat, Shirley 005367
Perin, Giovanni 025870
Périn, Dr. Patrick 014310
Périnet, Francine 006058, 006059
Perini, Mino 025419
Perisho, Sally L. 043399
Perišin, Stane 007708
Périssère, Michèle 010893
Perkins, Allison 041969
Perkins, Bob 048076
Perkins, Bruce C. 049265
Perkins, Deborah 048111
Perkins, Larry David 044106
Perkins, Martin 043552
Perkins, Sophie 040130
Perkins, Stephen 044309
Perkins, Viola 044390
Perkko, Mariliina 009472, 009475
Perkone, Inga 027765
Perl, Alexander 016483
Perlee, A. 029001, 029006, 029014
Perlein, Gilbert 013397
Perlman, Patsy 041977
Perlon, Dr. Diane 045414
Perlstein, Barbara 046637
Perman, David 041296
Pernas Ojeda, Maria Emma 028458
Pernot, M.M. 048608
Pernu, Esko 010045
Peron, Claude 013827
Perot, Jacques 010838, 011450, 011451
Perraudin, Marguerite 037280
Perrault, Lise 006680
Perrefort, Dr. Maria 017731
Perren, Stephan 037748
Perrenoud, Raymond 037024
Perret, Gilles 037375
Perret, Pascale 037248
Perrier, Dr. Danièle 015692
Perron, Jean L. 006374
Perron, Michelle M. 043436
Perrons, Margot 040743
Perrot, Annick 013725
Perrot, C. 013270
Perrot, Mollie 046750
Perrottet, Marie-C. 037023
Perroud, Paul 012239
Perry, Andy 045485
Perry, Bob 042008
Perry, Ed 048772
Perry, Gregory P. 046206
Perry, Hadley 041116
Perry, John 049051
Perry, Michael L. 043282
Perry, Nancy 044915, 047197
Perry, Peter 000902
Perry, Rachel 046222
Perry, Shannon 045758
Perry, Sheila 045722
Persak, Erica 000888
Persan, Marquis de 011964
Perse, Marcell 018129, 018130, 018131
Persengieva, Marina 004760
Peršin, Vladimir 007732
Person, Tage 036281
Persson, Ann-Charlotte 036498
Persson, Bertil 036437
Persson, Curt 036438
Persson, Dr. Per-Edvin 010222
Persson, Thomas 036382
Pertin, B. 022176
Pertola, Esko 009720, 009721
Péru, Dr. Laurent 013328
Perucchi, Dr. Ursula 037733
Peruga, Iris 049464
Pesarini, Dr. Fausto 024103
Pescaru-Rusu, Adriana 032854
Pesch, Dr. Dieter 018866
Peschel, Tina 016128
Pescia, Sergio 037590
Pese, Dr. Claus 019352
Pešek, Dr. Ladislav 008476
Pesenecker, Marita 017538
Pesi, Dr. Rossana 024545
Pešková, K. 034452
Peso, Jean-Michel del 014399
Pesqueira de Esesarte, Prof. Alicia 028605
Pesqueur, Jean-Yves 011078, 011079
Pessa, Joanna 046366
Pessa, Loredana 024322
Pessemier 's Gravendries, Paul de 003565
Pessey-Lux, Aude 010326
Pessoa, Miguel 032607
Pestalozzi, Prof. Karl 037561
Pestalozzi, Dr. Martin 036812
Pestel, Michael 047047
Pestiaux, Pierre 003625
Petchey, Tim 041397
Peter, Carolyn 045425
Peter, Christopher 034744, 034745
Peter, Elmar 002125
Peter, Frank-Manuel 018305
Peter, Horst 016404
Peter, Jack 047615
Peter, Dr. Markus 036863
Petercsák, Dr. Tivadar 021717
Petermann, Jörg 016928
Petermann, Ralf 015596
Peterposten, Carlo 036825
Peters, Dr. Dirk J. 016429
Peters, Dr. Gustav 016337
Peters, Heinrich 016387
Peters, Dr. Hermann 016952
Peters, Irmtrude 016847
Peters, Karen 040125
Peters, Larry D. 048579
Peters, M. 029502, 043910
Peters, Michael 016771, 016771, 020926
Peters, Sandra 015620
Peters, Ted H. 047077
Peters, Dr. Ursula 019352
Peters, W. 005185
Peters-Barenbrock, Sabine 019515
Peters Bowron, Edgar 044648
Peterseim, Dr. Siegfried 019157
Petersen, Christopher 041235
Petersen, Flemming 008819
Petersen, Jan 043667
Petersen, Jerome 044508
Petersen, Jim 042169
Petersen, John 047843, 049111
Petersen, Viggo 008798
Peterson, Alan 048609
Peterson, Allan 046878
Peterson, Allan E. 047846
Peterson, Barbara 042991
Peterson, Brian 043505
Peterson, Dr. Cheryl D. 044846
Peterson, Dennis 048272
Peterson, Glenn 046370
Peterson, James L. 047709
Peterson, Karin 044964
Peterson, Karin E. 044456
Peterson, Mark F. 049248, 049249
Peterson, Merlin 044219
Peterson, Mildred 042130
Peterson, Paula 046526
Peterson, Rebecca 045635
Peterson, R.J. 043484
Peterson, Roger 047931
Peterson, Thomas 042253
Peterson, Tom 048628
Peterson, Townsend 045205

Peterson, William . . . 046116
Peterson-Moussaid, Kathleen . . . 041933
Petersson, Håkan . . . 036645
Petey-Hache, Philippe . . . 014942
Peti, Viktorija . . . 027913
Petit, Jean-Paul . . . 010840
Petit, René . . . 011160
Petit, Prof. Th. . . . 014872
Petke, Debra . . . 044459
Petkov, Dimităr . . . 004858
Petkov, Pavel . . . 004702, 004703
Petkov, Vladimir . . . 004825
Petout, Philippe . . . 014409, 014410
Petr-Marcec, Prof. Smiljana . . . 007706
Petranov, Borislav . . . 002908
Petre, John L. . . . 030576
Petre, Prof. Vasile . . . 032819
Petrelli, Dr. Flavia . . . 024916
Petrenko, Vladimir Grigorjevič . . . 033346
Petresu, Nicolae . . . 032810
Petri, Gerda . . . 008956
Petri, Susanne . . . 018579
Petrie, Hugh . . . 040118
Petrinski, Ivan . . . 004863
Petrioli, Annamaria . . . 024156
Petrioli Tofani, Dr. Annamaria . . . 024152, 024156
Petrone, P. Paolo . . . 024905
Petrov, Angel . . . 004639
Petrov, Evgenij . . . 038227
Petrov, Najden . . . 004827
Petrova, Lidija . . . 004912
Petrova, Nadežda . . . 033192
Petrova, Velička . . . 004710
Petrovic, Dejan . . . 034180
Petrović, Dragutin . . . 034281
Petrović, Marijana . . . 034163
Petrović-Raić, Marijana . . . 034163
Petrovnina, Galina Michajlovna . . . 033644
Petrovski, Zoran . . . 027919
Petrovszky, Dr. Richard . . . 020263
Petrucci, Stefano . . . 025193
Petruchno, Alla Sergeevna . . . 032976
Petrus, Jerzy T. . . . 032070
Petrus, Magdolna . . . 021923
Petrussen, Thomas . . . 021541
Petruța, Bliderişanu . . . 032926
Petry, Michael . . . 040228
Petryshyn, M. . . . 005657
Petschar, Dr. Hans . . . 002971
Petschek-Sommer, Birgitta . . . 016656, 016657
Pett, Joachim . . . 015591
Pettengill, Shirley . . . 048473
Pettersson, Jan . . . 036369
Pettersson, Kerstin . . . 036684
Pettersson, Lennart . . . 036296
Pettibone, Jody . . . 048882
Pettibone, John W. . . . 044223
Petty-Johnson, Gayle . . . 049347, 049349
Pétursdóttir, Brynhildur . . . 021933
Pétursson, Björn . . . 021944
Pétursson, Halldór . . . 021932
Petz, Emmerich . . . 001667
Petzal, Monica . . . 040148
Petznek, Dr. Beatrix . . . 001711
Petznek, Friedrich . . . 001769
Petzold, A. . . . 016731
Petzold, Lorraine . . . 005776
Peuckert, Valérie . . . 003199, 003200
Peukert, Jörg . . . 017254
Peuzin, Jean . . . 013989
Pevahouse, Jerry . . . 043206
Pevereit, S. . . . 040596
Peverelli, Maria de . . . 037001
Pevernagie . . . 003358
Pewitt, Dr. J. Dudley . . . 042226
Peyer, Ricard de . . . 040378
Peyer, Richard de . . . 040377
Peylhard, Anne-Marie . . . 010590
Peyre, P. . . . 013009
Peyton-Jones, Julia . . . 040286
Pezarro, D. . . . 029145
Pfaff, Patricia . . . 018809
Pfaffenberger, Dr. Gary . . . 047153
Pfaffenbichler, Dr. Matthias . . . 002934
Pfaffenhuemer, Dr. Johannes . . . 002309
Pfanner, Dario . . . 024549
Pfanner, Ute . . . 001763
Pfanz, Donald C. . . . 044056
Pfau, F.D. . . . 020045
Pfau, Gisela . . . 004193
Pfeifer, Anton . . . 001806
Pfeifer, Nezka . . . 047934
Pfeiffenberger, Deborah . . . 046203
Pfeiffer, Dr. Andreas . . . 017851
Pfeiffer, Brian . . . 042343
Pfeiffer, Gordon A. . . . 049203
Pfeiffer, Günter . . . 003744
Pfeiffer, Dr. Ingrid . . . 017192
Pfeiffer, Rainer . . . 020176
Pfeiffer, Wolfgang . . . 001692
Pfeifhofer, Elisabeth . . . 001906
Pfeifhofer, Helmut . . . 001906
Pfeil, Elke . . . 016001
Pfennings, Edgar . . . 006941
Pferdehirt, Dr. Barbara . . . 018792, 018794
Pfister, Emil . . . 037022
Pfister, Paul . . . 037777
Pfleger, Dr. Susanne . . . 020967
Pflüger, Helmut . . . 020913
Pflumm, Manfred . . . 020595
Pfnorr, Reinhard . . . 019302
Pfnuer, Linda . . . 015955
Pfosser, Dr. Martina . . . 002243
Pfotenhauer, Louise . . . 044311
Pfretzschmer, Prof. Dr. Hans-Ulrich . . . 020496
Phagan, Patria . . . 047211
Phaneuy, Jim . . . 042102
Phares, Jane . . . 045855
Pharo, R.G. . . . 039284
Phelan, Beverly . . . 042141
Phelan, Wynne . . . 044648
Phéline, Jean-Michel . . . 014654
Phelps, Kathleen D. . . . 049451
Pheney, Kathleen . . . 042042
Pheysey, Dawn . . . 047272
Phil, D. . . . 022229
Philbin, Ann . . . 045426
Philbin, Gail . . . 044279
Philbrick, Harry . . . 047434
Philbrick, Nathaniel . . . 046123
Philbrick, Ruth T. . . . 048924
Philbrook, Wyman . . . 048786
Philipon, Peter . . . 006530
Philipp, Dr. Claudia Gabriele . . . 017715
Philipp, Werner . . . 016053
Philippe, Pierre . . . 037042
Philippon, Annie . . . 014087
Philippot . . . 013131
Philipson, Jean . . . 001307
Philipson, Peter . . . 040214
Phillip, D.M. . . . 030473
Phillips, Amanda . . . 039950
Phillips, Ann . . . 039244
Phillips, Christopher . . . 046348
Phillips, Colin . . . 001239
Phillips, Dale . . . 048787
Phillips, Gene . . . 043426
Phillips, George . . . 006206
Phillips, G.R. . . . 034676
Phillips, James . . . 042613
Phillips, John . . . 038770
Phillips, Joseph R. . . . 041905
Phillips, Dr. Kenneth E. . . . 045414
Phillips, Lisa . . . 046386
Phillips, Melissa . . . 046418
Phillips, Robert F. . . . 048569
Phillips, Prof. Ruth B. . . . 006703
Phillips, Dr. Sandra S. . . . 047885
Phillips, Stephen . . . 048940
Phillips, Steven . . . 044041
Phillips, Wayne . . . 046259
Phillips Olmedo, Carlos . . . 028496, 028503
Phillipson, Prof. David W. . . . 038971
Phillp, John . . . 038779
Philo, P. . . . 040812
Philo, Phil . . . 040458
Philotheou, G. . . . 008217
Philp, B.J. . . . 039278
Philp, Brian . . . 040646
Philp, S. . . . 039907
Philpatt, Vandan . . . 047848
Philpot, Chris . . . 038708
Philpott, Vandean . . . 047880
Philson, William C. . . . 045783
Phinney, Chad . . . 048522
Phinney Kelley, Sarah . . . 045242
Phippin, Susan . . . 048048
Phipps, Rebecca J. . . . 042299
Phleps, Dr. Roland . . . 017238
Phuong, Pham Xuân . . . 049554
Phuong, Tran Thi Thuy . . . 049543
Piacentini, Dr. Paola . . . 025548
Pianca, Dr. Vittorino . . . 026355
Pianea, Dr. Elena . . . 025643
Piasecka, Grażyna . . . 032401
Piaskowski, Tadeusz . . . 031913
Piastrella, Dr. Carlo . . . 023992
Piatek, Bruce J. . . . 046797
Piątek, Jacek . . . 032257
Piatrowski, Kenn . . . 044579
Piatt, Margaret . . . 049086
Piatti, Verena . . . 002268
Piaty, Karl . . . 002802
Picard, Dr. Bertold . . . 016997
Picard, Dennis . . . 049101
Picard, Michel . . . 013824
Picard, Thomas . . . 046397
Picazo Verdejo, Elisa . . . 035203
Piccardi, Dr. Marco . . . 024180
Picciano, Eric . . . 042900
Piccioli, Prof. Rossana . . . 024441
Piccirilli, Guido . . . 025966
Piccirillo, M. . . . 022969
Piccoli, Prof. Adalberto . . . 023779
Piccottini, Prof. Dr. Gernot . . . 002432
Picelj, Zdenko . . . 034509
Picha, Krzysztof Vincenc . . . 031891
Piché, Thomas . . . 006753, 048455
Picher, Claude . . . 005241
Pichler, Gerd . . . 002437
Pichler, Dr. Isfried H. . . . 001669
Pichler, Jutta M. . . . 002171
Pichorner, Dr. Franz . . . 002934
Pickard, Carey . . . 045570
Pickard, Kelli L. . . . 044010
Pickering, Jane . . . 042563, 042566
Pickering, Mona . . . 045652
Pickin, John . . . 041134, 041135
Pickles, Verna . . . 005237
Pico, Dr. Teresa . . . 032704
Picollet, Auguste . . . 010315
Picon, Carlos . . . 046364
Picpican, Isikias T. . . . 031628
Pidault, Monique . . . 013812
Pidcock, James . . . 040269
Pido, Asuncion Q. . . . 031711
Pidpala, Nila Andriïvna . . . 038299
Piek, W. . . . 030347
Pieke, Hannelore . . . 015618
Pienimaa, Vilho . . . 009618
Pieplow, Jane . . . 043807
Pierard, Christiane . . . 003655
Pierce, Dr. Charles E. . . . 046394
Pierce, Donna . . . 043404
Pierce, Dr. Donna . . . 047963
Pierce, Gene . . . 041700
Pierce, Sally . . . 042315
Piergollini, Alberto . . . 024986
Pierides, Demetrios Z. . . . 008211
Pierini, Dr. Paolo . . . 025403
Pierrangeli, Prof. Carlo . . . 025477
Pierrot-Bults, Dr. A.C. . . . 029245
Piersantini, Dr. Michele . . . 026177
Piersol, Daniel . . . 046263
Pierson, Charles . . . 041589
Pierson, Stacey . . . 040254
Pieschacón González, Gabriel . . . 007633
Pieschel, Janet . . . 005184
Piet . . . 003723, 049728
Pieters, Dr. Georges . . . 003459
Pietri de Caldera, Alicia . . . 049471
Pietropaolo, Dr. Lisa . . . 024550
Pietrzak, Stanisław . . . 032397
Pietrzak, Ted . . . 042503
Pietrzyk, Prof. Zdisław . . . 032065
Pietsch, Dr. Ted . . . 048075
Pietsch, Dr. Ulrich . . . 016809
Pietscher, Charles . . . 044972
Pietschmann, Wolfgang . . . 017989, 017990
Piette, Jacques . . . 013437
Pigeat, Jean-Paul . . . 011328
Pihema, Joseph . . . 030501
Pihlak, Jaak . . . 009436
Pihlgren, Kjell . . . 036315
Piirainen, Sari . . . 009472
Piiroinen, Päivikki . . . 009749
Pijaudier-Cabot, Joëlle . . . 015264
Pijbes, W. . . . 030085
Pijeaux, Dr. Lawrence . . . 042222
Pijl, B.H. . . . 029826
Pika-Biolzi, Dr. M. . . . 037767
Pikal, Dr. Jaroslav . . . 008416
Pike, Alan . . . 034549
Pike, J.P. . . . 005707
Pike, Stephen J. . . . 045715
Pil, E. . . . 003163
Pilar, Jacquelin . . . 044080
Pilar Muñoz Jiménez, María del . . . 007434
Pilati von Thassul-Filo della Torre, Francesca Gräfin . . . 002018, 002528
Pilato, Dominique . . . 014600
Pilchowski, Władysław . . . 032147
Pilides, Dr. D. . . . 008217
Pilioko, A. . . . 049415
Pilkilton, Sue . . . 048669
Pilkinton, Hunter M. . . . 049019
Pillaert, E. Elizabeth . . . 045594
Pillay, Ruven . . . 040241
Piller, Ferdinand . . . 036939
Piller, Gudrun . . . 036885
Piller, Dr. Gudrun . . . 036885
Piller, Josienne N. . . . 047064
Pillet, Gaby . . . 037520
Pillichshammer, Johann . . . 002361
Pillsbury, Dr. Edmund P. . . . 043273
Pilotti, Bianca Maria . . . 023909, 023974
Pils, Walter . . . 002258
Pilven, Denis . . . 010941
Pilz, Anette . . . 020974
Pilz, Bernd . . . 017593
Pilz, Winfried . . . 015423
Pim, James . . . 047452
Pimentel, Cristina . . . 032678
Pimmins, Rose . . . 047319
Pinat, Bruno Augusto . . . 024356
Pincemin, Cecilia . . . 005690
Pindinelli, Prof. Elio . . . 024271
Pine, Lynda . . . 039768
Piñeiro, Alberto Gabriel . . . 000209
Pinelli, Prof. Antonio . . . 025261, 025264
Pinette, Matthieu . . . 014753
Pinette, Matthiew . . . 010368, 010369
Pingel, Carol . . . 044327
Pingeot, Anne . . . 013678
Pinheiro, Maria Joao . . . 032638
Pinheiro-Fankhauser, Marie-Anne . . . 037620
Pini, Lucia . . . 024703
Pinigina, Taisija Viktorovna . . . 033862
Pinilla, José . . . 007509
Pinnix, Cleve . . . 046839, 049243
Pino Morán, Mónica . . . 006951
Pinson, Dr. Patricia . . . 046618
Pintarić, Adam . . . 007811
Pintarić, Snježana . . . 007852
Pintarić, Tanja . . . 007818
Pintea, June . . . 043723
Pintea, Rodica . . . 032869
Pinto, Dr. Bianca Alessandra . . . 025481
Pinto, Dr. Ettore . . . 023762
Pinto de Matos, Maria Antonia . . . 032626

Pinto Simon, Elena 046300
Pinzl, Christoph 020975
Pinzón, Carlos 007646
Pinzón, Rito 007622
Pioch, Klaus 015992
Pionk, Richard 046397
Piot, Marc-Etienne 037055
Piotrovski, Michail 033743
Piotrowski, Jerzy 031837
Pipek, K. 008364
Piper, Catharina 036761
Piper, William 047661
Pipino, Dr. Giuseppe 025898
Pipkin, Roy 048425
Piquera, F. 012517
Piquereddu, Dr. Paolo 024979, 024980
Piquero López, Blanca 035408
Pirenne, R. 003816
Pires Martins, Prof. Calebe 004607
Pirie, Victoria 038795
Pirker, Hans 002521
Pirker, Rudolf 002778
Pirkkalainen, Heli 010177
Pirkmajer, Darja 034463
Pirkonen, Pekka 009770
Pirlot, Anne-Marie 003314
Pirnat, Miha 034487
Pirnie, M. 040719
Pisa, Regina M. 048218
Pisani, Ètienne du 034619
Pisano, Dr. Jane 046451
Pisano, Dr. Jane G. 045455
Pisarev, S.V. 033241
Pischl, Rupert 002736
Pişiren, Tuncay 038153
Piskal, Irina Leonidovna 033906
Piskur, Bojana 034485
Piso, Prof. Dr. Ioan 032838
Pistono Grand, Mario 025779
Pištora, Jiří 008316
Pistorius, Dr. Agnes 002979
Pitard, Wayne 048713
Piterskaja, Larisa Karlovna 033739
Piteša, Ante 007798
Pithie, Helen 000729
Pitkänen, Erkki 009501
Pitkänen, Maritta 009852
Pitman, Bonni 043269
Pitot 003806
Pitre, Marc 005732
Pitt, James 021554
Pitt Jones, Priscilla 043491
Pittaway, Louise D. 048376
Pittner, K. Heinz 020280
Pittock, Tina 038474
Pitts, Priscilla 030482, 030489
Pitts, Terence 042674
Pittz, Franeis 043053
Pitxot, Antoni 035194
Pitzen, Marianne 016323
Piuma, Dr. Fabio 026271
Pixley, Patricia 046678
Pixner, Albin 025698
Pizitz, Jackie 046441
Pizzigoni, Prof. Gianni 025099, 026274
Pizzinini, Dr. Meinrad 002089, 002097
Pizziolo, Marina 024720
Pizzo, Tony 048032
Pizzollo, Sissy 046962
Pjankova, Svetlana Anatoljevna . . 033071
Pla, Josefina 031442
Plaat, Jaanus 009416
Plaine, Jean 014022
Planas, Marta 000085
Planas, Ramón 034940
Planchard, Ch. 014177
Planchon, Jacques 011585
Planck, Prof. Dr. Dieter 018374
Planes Torregassa, Ramón 035883
Planisek, Dr. Sandra 045555
Plank, Benedikt 002595
Plánka, Dr. Ivan 008787
Plankensteiner, Dr. Barbara 002961
Plant, C.D. 039790
Plantalamor, Luis 035447
Plante, Stella 005797
Plasser, Dr. Gerhard 002567
Plaßmann, Dr. Otmar 020055
Plaßmeyer, Dr. Peter 016801
Plastow, N. 040324
Plata Vega, Edith 007635
Platen, Dr. Michael 017654, 018107, 018115
Platero, Ramon 035586
Plath, Dr. Carina 019155, 053649
Plath, Margie J. 048723
Platonova, T.V. 033139
Platt jr., Geoffrey 047420
Platt, Nicholas 046297
Platt, Ron 049258
Platt, Ronald 044338
Platteter, Janet 045085
Plattner, Fritz 002693
Platz, Daniela 020987
Platz, Dr. Gertrud 015986
Platzgummer, Hanno 001789
Plavan, Tamara 038389
Plavec-Butkovic, Lidija 007706
Player, Elizabeth 022763
Plaza, Ben 046697
Plazotta, Carol 040241
Plenković, Ivo 007702
Plenter, Dr. H.A. 030278, 030279
Plesher, Dan 043143
Pleská, Leona 008680
Plessis, H. 034725
Plessis, M. du 034737
Pletnjov, Valentinr 004925
Plevin, Leon M. 045130
Pleyn, Dieter 016426
Plitek, Dr. Karl-Heinz 021011
Plöchinger, Prof. Dr. Benno 002327
Plöckinger, Veronika 002132
Plötz, Dr. Robert 018240
Płotkowiak, Wiesław 031961
Plotoagă, Gabriela 032841
Plotzek, Dr. Joachim M. 018323
Ploug, Mariann . 008821, 008822, 009029, 009054, 009055, 009138, 009139, 009140
Plouin, Suzanne 010800
Plourde, Nelie 041939
Plowright, Georgina 039082, 039140, 039746, 039784
Pluciński, Dr. Józef 032360
Pluhařová, Jana 008756
Plukavec, Lina 007855
Plume, Thierry 011728
Plumier, J. 003662
Plumley, Nicholas 039771
Plummer, Bill 046648
Plummer, Marguerite R. 048161
Plummer, Mary Ann 044039
Plummer, Sue J. 041903
Plummer, Val 041430
Plunkett, Stephanie 048367
Pluntke, Margitta 015502
Pochman, Kathryn K. 046124, 046125
Pochwała, Stanisław 032050
Pocius, D. 001345
Pocius, Edward 042823
Počivalova, Elena Ivanovna 033177
Počivavšek, Marija 034462
Počivavšek, Prof. Marija 034462
Pocsainé Eperjesi, Eszter 021837
Podany, Evelyn D. 042951
Podany, Jerry 045433
Podedworny, Carol 006777
Podestá, Horacio 000244
Podlesnik, Mateja 034483
Podmaniczky, Christine B. 042692
Podnar, Franc 034521
Podos, Lisa Beth 046300
Podzorski, Patricia 045753
Pögelt, Erika 017654
Poel, Dr. Peter te 029893
Pölcher, Bertold 016927
Pöllmann, Rotraud 019834
Poelman, Shannon 006814
Pöppelbaum, H. 019818
Pöppelmann, Dr. Heike 018769
Pörnbacher, Prof. Dr. Hans 020305
Pöss, Ondrej 034329
Poessiger, Peter M. 043891
Pöstinger, Eberhard 002678
Poethe, Lothar 018564
Poethke, Prof. Dr. Günther 015979
Poette, Simonne 015141
Pöttler, E. 002723
Pöttler, Prof. DDr. V.H. 002723
Pötzsch, Herbert 018814
Pogačnik Grobelšek, Helena 034485
Poggendorf, Renate 019048
Poggi, Patrizia 025401
Poggi, Dr. Roberto 024302
Poggiani-Keller, Raffaella 023644
Pogliani, Dr. Marisa 026181, 026182
Pogonec', Olena Dmytrivna 038293
Pogorzelska, Renata 031882
Pogt, Dr. Herbert 021021
Pohanka, Dr. Reinhard 003017
Pohjakallio, Lauri 009483
Pohl, Burkhart 048543
Pohl, G. 016392
Pohl, Gerhard 018904
Pohl, Dr. Klaus-Dieter 016638
Pohl-Schneider, Nadine 018806
Pohlman, Lynette 041684, 041685
Pohlmann, Dr. Ulrich 019056, 019086
Pohowsky, Carolyn 045989
Pointal, Jean-Louis 010849
Poirel, Evelyne 014125
Poiret, Jean-Marie 013333
Poirier, Daphne 006431
Poirier, Diane 005264
Poirier, Ulric 006784
Poissant, Margaret 044634
Poitevin, B. 012731
Poivet, Clémence 015011
Poivet, Cllémence 015010
Pokorná, Blanka 008465
Pokorná, Libuše 008516
Pokorný, Jaroslav 008742
Pokorny, Klaus 002969
Pokorný, Zdeněk 008368
Pokorny-Nagel, Kathrin 002945
Pol, A. 029848
Poláčková, Dr. Dagmar 034337
Polacsek, John 043443
Polacsek, John F. 043447
Polak, Dr. Jerzy 031835
Polak, Dr. J.J.H. 030265
Polak, Sarah 041916
Polanco de Laverde, Cecilia 007516
Polanía Ramírez, Tiberio 007484
Polanich, Judith K. 042405, 048476, 048622
Polanská, Zuzana 008591
Polat, Cemal 038058
Pole, Len 039465
Pole, Merle 001360
Polenov, Juri A. 033126
Poleske, Lee E. 048119
Poletti, Catherine 011219
Poli, Cristina Tessari 023356
Polich, Debra 041729
Polichetti, Maria Luisa 025852
Polichetti, Dr. Massimilano A. 025548
Polifka, Marcus 044591
Polikarpova, Marina Alekseevna . . 033207
Polioudovarda, Anna M. 021219
Polis, Crystal A. 046921
Poliščuk, Natalja 038370
Poliščuk, Svetlana Alekseevna . . . 033037
Politopoulos, Catherine 045476
Poljakova, Valentina Alekseevna . . 034065
Polk, Vickie 049262
Poll, Lothar C. 016107
Poll, Walter 019220
Poll-Frommel, Veronika 019048
Pollák, Dr. Róbert 034368
Pollan, Carolyn 043981
Pollard, Brent 040667
Pollard, David 039146
Pollard, Ian 041006
Pollard, S. 030460
Polley, Amy E. 041775
Polli, Kadi 009398
Polli, Dr. Vittorio 026374
Pollini, Lucia 037286
Pollock, Mallory 042947
Polnick, Bill 006432
Polo, Laura W. 045736
Polonovski, Max 013674
Polott, E. Leslie 044663
Poloznev, Dmitrij F. 033227
Polozova, Natalja Ivanovna 034059
Pols, Dr. Ivor 034702
Polverari, Dr. Michele 023201
Polvi, Arvo 009598
Polyarnaya, Janna 033742
Polychronopoulos, Mari Elleneca . . 021408
Polymerou-Kamilakis, Dr. Aik. 021175
Polzine, Roxann L. 049315
Poma Swank, Anna-Maria 046315
Pomar, Maria Teresa 028171
Pomarede, Vincent 013685
Pomeroy, Dan E. 046154
Pomeroy, Marilyn 049291
Pomeroy Draper, Stacy 048619
Pommeranz, Dr. Johannes 019352
Pommies, Marie-Anne 010880
Pompa, Vince 041971
Pomponi, Luigi 025932
Ponce de León, Carolina 047863
Ponciş, Gheorghe 032907
Pond-Anderson, Marcia 046843
Ponder, Gary 047109
Pongracz, Dr. Patricia 046334
Ponomareva, Galina B. 033468
Ponomareva, Tatjana 033830
Pons, Marc 036055
Pons-Pons, Fermí 035729
Ponsonnard, Christian 012524
Ponsoy, Teresita 031807
Pont, Jeanne 037128
Ponte, Emily 044642
Ponte, Dr. Susanne de 019047
Ponton d'Amecourt, Jean de 012186
Pontual, Sylvia 004317
Pontvianne, Jean-Paul 012373
Poodt, J.G.M. 029734
Poolaw, Linda 041705
Poole, Helen 039656
Poole, Helen E. 041015
Poole, J.E. 038962
Poonsil, Banteng 037902
Poorter, Nora de 003188
Poot, J.A. 029230
Pop, Valer 032951, 032952, 032953, 032954
Popa, Gabriela 032939
Popal, Najibulla 000004
Pope, Clare 041424
Pope, Linda 047955, 049013
Popelier, Betty 006145
Popelka, Dr. Pavel 008733
Popescu, Dr. A. 038962
Popescu, Ioana 032813
Popivoda, Mileva 034207
Poplack, Robert 042126
Popolla, Don Gianluca 025972
Popov, Aleksandr Nikolaevič 034051
Popov, Gennadij Viktorovič 033369
Popova, Inna Sergiïvna 038388
Popova, L.B. 033616
Popova, Nina Ivanovna 033745
Popovčak, Borivoj 007856
Popović, Bojana 034163
Popovic, Miroslav 027919
Popović, Pavle 034266
Popovici, Dragomir 032810
Poppa, Dr. Rudolf 016714

Poppi, Dr. Cesare 025349
Popski, Dragoljub 034170
Por, Prof. F.D. 022951
Porada, Jerzy 032171
Poras, E. Linda 045505
Porenta, Tita 034533
Porfírio, José Luís 032649
Porignaux, Jonathan 003502
Pornin, Claudie 015054
Poroszlai, Dr. Ildikó 021856
Porra-Kuteni, Valérie 010734
Porras, César Augusto 007552
Porrelli, D.M. 040540
Porsmose, Erland 008950, 008951
Port, Jane L. 047097
Portanje, B.K. 029366
Portatius, Botho von 017233
Porte, Patrick 013720
Portele, Helmut 003027
Portell, Rosa 048315
Porteous, Ken 006863
Porter, Ann 042526
Porter, Barbara A. 046693
Porter, Barry 048554
Porter, Dr. C.M. 044103
Porter, Emily 042296
Porter, Frances J. 045695
Porter, Herman 006179
Porter, John R. 006228
Porter, Julian 038695
Porter, Marty 044911
Porter, Marye 039723
Porter, Paul 047750
Porter, Phil 045551, 045552, 045554, 045556
Porter, Phillip 005348
Porter, Richard T. 046693
Porter, Russ 001550
Porter, Suzanne 030553, 043545
Portet, Angel 035663
Portiabohn, Ivece 046393
Portiglia, Hélène 010485
Portigliatti Barbos, Prof. Mario ... 026062
Porttier, W. 003174
Portugal Ortiz, Max 003915
Portús, Javier 035429
Portz, Willi 019995
Porzenheim, Maria 016698
Posada, Teresa 035429
Posch, Eva 016567
Poser, Steffen 018594, 018600
Posinjak, Jurij Michajlovič 033967
Pospisilova, Dr. Alena 008447
Possehl, Gregory L. 046993
Posselt, Dr. Martin 018209
Possémé, Evelyne 013668
Possèmé, Gilles 014413
Possenti, Dr. Elisa 024982
Post, Alfred 016808, 053527
Post, Dr. K. 030338
Post, Dr. William 042728
Postek, Roman 032105
Postel, Mitchell P. 046786, 047364, 049289
Postema-George, Deborah 046106
Poster, Amy 042458
Postier, Wilfried 016099
Postl, Dr. Walter 001938
Postles, Suella 040616
Poston, Jonathan 042736
Poston, Roger D. 043084
Potapov, Roald Leonidovič 033843
Poteau, Gérard 011876
Poteete, Timothy 045215
Potempa, Dr. Harald 016114
Potet, Jean-Pierre 015294
Potgieter, M.J. 034763, 034763
Pothan, Scott 030658
Potirakis, Georges 040861
Potochick, Andrea 042288
Potocka, Maria Anna 032164
Pototschnig, Alfred 002604
Potsch 001751
Pott, Karin 016059
Pott, Dr. Ute 017646
Potter, Byrn 045466
Potter, Edmund 048346
Potter, J.E. 041256
Potter, Linda 044279
Potter, Ron 044728
Potter, Ted 047409
Pottier, Marie Hélène 011812, 011813
Potts, Albert 047395
Potts, Prof. Daniel T. 001521
Potts, Timothy 044009
Potucek, Delvin 048858
Potužáková, Dr. Jana 008575
Potvin, Ronald 046459
Poueymirou, Frank 046340
Pouget, Daniel 011810, 014373
Poulain, Ivan 012038
Poulis, Helen 005691
Poullain, Christine 012021
Poulliot, Elizabeth A. 046498
Poulos, Ann 048522
Poulsen, Hanne 008897
Poulter, Gill 039312, 039315
Pounis Guntavid, Joseph 027959
Pourtalès, Laure de 010345
Pourtalet, P. 011979
Pourtaud, François 012189
Povedano, Balbino 035110
Poviliúnas, Virgilijus 027861
Povšič, Sabina 034485
Powar, N.V. 022329
Powders, Dr. Vernon 041676
Powell, Bob 039896
Powell, Bobbie 047459
Powell, Bruce 042415
Powell, Earl A. 048924
Powell, Gwendolen 039955
Powell, JoAnne 042075
Powell, John T. 042402
Powell, Maurice F. 018193
Powell, Michael 040397
Powell, Nancy S. 046936
Powell, Shana 044112
Powell, William V. 045032
Powell-Cotton, C. 038712
Powell Harold, Fran 048026
Power, Cathy 040117
Power, Christopher 001323
Power, Deirdre 022705
Power, Dennis M. 046598
Power, Nicola 040944
Powers, Catherine 041804
Powers, Claire 006038
Powers, Heather 044045
Powers, James L. 044691
Powers, Leland 044489
Powers, Linda 045072
Powers, Dr. Ramon 046732
Poyner, Noelle 001161
Pozsonyi, József 021625
Pozzi, Dr. Raffaella 024078
Pozzuoli, Prof. María Cristina 000389
Ppili, Leleala E. 000081
Prace, David 046271
Prackwieser, Walter 024119
Prada Pérez, Isaac 007504
Pradat, Marc-Marie 011973
Prader, Angela 037040
Prado, César O. 031510
Präger, Dr. Christmut 018806
Prätzel, Maritta 019842
Prag, Dr. A.J.N.W. 040406
Prágay, Dr. István 021639
Prahase, Mircea . 032783, 032848, 032897
Prakapcov, Vladimir I. 003138
Prall, Steve 041805
Pralong-Salamin, Rachel 037557
Pralormo, Marcella 026082
Prammer, Dr. Johannes 020335
Pranza, Denise M. 047597
Prasch, Dr. Hartmut 002521, 002686
Prasolova, Elena Ivanovna 033799
Prasser, Gabriele 019368
Prasser, Karen L. 042983
Praßl, Johann 001844, 001845
Praszelik-Kocjan, Grażyna 032188
Prat, Jean-Louis 014468
Prather, Marla 046418
Prati, Dr. Luciana 024224, 024225, 024226, 024227, 024230, 024233
Pratt, Gordon 045114
Pratt, Dr. William 045192
Prause, W. 016625
Pray, Jim 043555
Prayitno, Dr. R. Joko 022472
Praz, Jean-Claude 037566
Praženilová, Dr. Viera 034413
Pražic, Rastko 007752
Préaux, Alain 014130
Prebushewsky Danylink, Janet ... 006427
Preece, Geoff 039249
Preininger, Kristina 034487
Preising, Dr. Dagmar 015425
Preiss, Prof. Heinz 002177
Preiss, Slawomir 032338
Preissler, Leonilda Maria 004143
Preiswerk-Lösel, Dr. Eva-Maria ... 036872
Prem, Prof. Dr. Hanns J. 016313
Premack, Ellen 043410
Premerl, Nada 007849
Premoli Silva, Adolfo 025215
Premoli Silva, Dr. Isabella 024717
Premović-Aleksić, Dragica 034221
Prendergast, Dr. D.V. 040831
Prendergast, Mary B. 022704
Přenosilová, Dr. Vera 008612
Prentice Burkett, Hazel 042173
Prentiss, Margo 047086
Prescott, Janice 048246
Presgrave, A.D. 001069
Presley, Priscilla 045760
Presnell-Weidner, Denise 047103
Pressl, Hannes 001708
Presson, Virginia 049027
Prest, Véronique 013630
Prestegard, Tom 048405
Preston, Carol 047879
Preston, Dr. Charles R. 043029
Preston, John 042894
Preston, Jules 041158
Preston, P. Anthony 030462
Preston, Dr. P.M. 039389
Preszler, Robert E. 047334
Pretola, John P. 048289
Pretorius, A.F. 034666
Pretsch, Dr. Peter 018171
Pretty, Carol Anne 005203
Preuß, Helmut 018374
Preuß, Jürgen 016931
Prévost, Jean-Marc 014073
Prévost-Bouré, Pascal 013415
Prevosti, Marta 035678
Prevratil, Joseph F. 045382
Prew, R. 039034
Prewer, Steven 038608
Prewett, Vickie 042911
Preyer, Josef 002456
Pría, Melba 028517
Přibáňová, Dr. Svatava 008294
Pribbernow, Marcus 018773
Přibil, Vladimír 008557
Přibyla, Radomír 008390
Prica, Stanko 034248
Price, Anita 005325, 005326
Price, Brenda 046890
Price, John 045622
Price, Dr. Marla J. 044011
Price, Marti 042825
Price, Renée 046384
Price, Robert 041745
Price, Sally Irwin 042063
Price, Stephen 038859
Price, Thomas E. 043089
Price Shanis, Carole 046973
Prickett, Marcus 029081
Prickett, N.J. 030432
Priddle, Th. 041489
Priddy, Dr. Bennie 020613
Prie, Jean-Yves 013838
Priego Fernández del Campo, Carmen 035387, 035421
Prière, Marc 010607
Prieto, Gabriel 007451
Prieto Vicioso, Esteban 009160
Prieur, Abel 015299
Prieur, P. 037160
Prigge, Dr. Walter 016684
Prikolota, Olga Vasylivna 038335
Přikrylová, Ludmila 008514
Priljeva, Srdjan 034285
Prillinger, Judith 002340
Prima, Dana D. 046312
Primack, Ilene 045815
Primozic, Melanija 034531, 034533
Prince, David 048456, 048460
Prince, J.R. 040394
Prince, Nigel 038731
Prince, Shannon 006040
Prince, Todd 042664
Pringle, Harry 047157
Pringle, Roger . 041137, 041138, 041139, 041140, 041141, 041143
Prinz, Gerhard 020374
Prinz, Ina 016315
Prinz, Peter 042227
Prinz, Dr. Ursula 015991
Prinzler, Hans Helmut 016018
Prior, Annette 036303
Prior, Claudine 005164
Prior, Terrence M. 046747
Pripačkin, I.A. 033318
Prister, Boris 007841
Prister, Lada 007841
Pritchard, Frances 040416
Pritchard, Leonard 043092
Pritchard, Philip 006605
Pritikin, Renny 047892
Prittwitz und Gaffron, Dr. Hans-Hoyer von 016333
Privette, David 045330
Prix, Jörg 001799
Prjamikova, Vera Pavlovna 033288
Probst, Heinz 019199
Probst, Peter 037572
Probst, Dr. Volker 017599
Procacci, Ugo 024174
Procelli, Dr. Enrico 025387
Prochaska, James J. 042690
Prochazka, Denise 043626
Prochina, Irina Evgenjevna 033493
Procopé Ilmonen, Susanne 009856
Procopiou, E. 008217
Proctor, Karen E. 046864
Proctor, R. 038962
Proctor, Rebecca 038958
Proctor, Vicki 043646
Próder, István 021915
Prod'Hom, Chantal 037242
Proebst, Walter 015447
Prösch, Dr. Christoph 021038
Prohaska, Prof. Dr. Wolfgang 002934
Prokisch, Dr. Bernhard ... 002256, 002258
Prokop, J. 008535
Prol, Elbertus 047440
Pronti, Dr. Stefano 025207
Propri, Mary Ann 048860
Prøsch Danielsen, Lisbeth 031221
Proschwitz, Ted von 036300
Proskynitopoulou, Rosa 021183
Pross, Ann 043428
Proß, Christian 019221
Prosser, M. 030587
Prota, Prof. Romolo 025800
Prothero-Brooks, C.C. 006465
Proto Pisani, Dr. Rosanna Caterina 024145, 024147, 024150, 024173
Protz, Edward L. 044135
Proud, Hayden 034587
Proust, Georges 013636

Prouty, Elisha 044256
Provick, A.M. 005433
Providi, Dr. Ioanna 021202
Provoyeur, M. Pierre 010591
Prpa Stojanac, Ika 007798
Prudhomme, James 046163
Prudhomme, Mary Louise 042046
Prudhomme, Suzanne M. 045969
Prugh, Burton 042513
Pruitt, John E. 048276
Prum, Richard O. 045205
Prunet, Pierre 014357
Prusinovsky, Rupert 019542
Pruska, Mariola 032090
Pryor, Eric 048424
Prys-Jones, Dr. R. 041240
Przeczewski, P. Marek 024248
Przekazinski, Andrzej 032430
Przigoda, Dr. Stefan 016276
Przybilla, Carrie 041862
Przybył, Grazyna 031934
Przybylska, Grażyna 032295
Przybysz, Jane 047903
Przygoda, Udo 017164
Przypkowski, Piotr Maciej 031969
Psarapoulou, Betty 021164
Psenner, Dr. Barbara 002079
Psota, Dr. Thomas 036927
Puccinelli, Lydia 048925
Puccini, Simonetta 026088
Puchner, Manfred 002253
Puckett, Jakobus 018043
Puckett, James 015633
Puckett, Margaret 042009
Puckett, Robert A. 049165
Puckett, Tom 043697
Puddy, Audrey 041298
Pudelska, Aleksandra 032240
Pudney-Schmidt, Birgid 016834
Puech, Laurent 012578
Pühle, Dr. Matthias 018777
Puentes de Valderrama, Ana Rosa 007613
Pürro, Gertrud 036979
Puerta, Prof. J. 035375
Puertas Tricas, Rafael 035453, 035454
Puerto, Dr. F. Javier 035406
Pütz, Ursula 019548
Püüa, Endel 009373, 009375, 009376
Puga, Rosa D. 006929
Pugačevskaja, Alla Aleksandrovna 033495
Puget, Catherine 013883
Puggaard, Ole 008930
Pugh, Connie 006166
Pugi, Guido 025362
Puharich, Nick 030477
Puhle, Dr. Matthias 018769, 018772
Puhlmann, Dr. Helga 019039
Puig, Felipe 041518
Pujol, Albert 034949
Pujol, Gloria 000083
Puklowski, Tracy 030535
Pule, Tickey 003950
Pulinka, Steven M. 046623
Pulle, Thomas 002621
Pullen, Bernice 046725
Pullen, Reg 046514
Pullen, Sue 039793
Pullin, Robert 039376
Pulnar, Janusz 032279
Pultz, John 045206
Pulvenis de Séligny, Marie-Thérèse 013406
Pumbaya, Ismael 031742
Pumphrey, Jim 042628
Pungerčar, Majda 034509
Puntman, Paul 030342
Pupo de Mogallón, Yolanda 007477
Purba, Suruhen 022474
Purdy, Dorothea 042528
Pure Via, Luis 036042
Purin, Bernhard 019065, 020062
Purin, Sergio 003353
Purke, Terry 048621
Purkis, Harriet 040327, 040328, 040330
Purrington-Hild, Sally 042557
Purslow, Martin 040089
Purves, W.M. 039402
Puscher 018370
Puschnig, Dr. André 036899
Pusineri, Prof. Adelina 031447
Pusineri Scala, Prof. Carlos Alberto 031445
Puste, Jennifer 042673
Pusterla-Cambin, Patrizia 037279
Pusztai, László 021667
Putman, Christy 046418
Putnam, Erna 041784
Putnam, Michael 042018
Putsch, Dr. Jochem 020238
Putyńska, Elżbieta 031853
Putz, Karl 020383
Putze, Alfred 018054
Puyplat, Lisa 017037
Puzanova, N.A. 027390
Puzo, Joseph 043170
Puzrina, Oksana Jurjevna 033363
Py, Cyille 014141
Py, Jacques 014898
Pyatt, John 030516
Pycke, J. 003812
Pyhrr, Stuart 046364
Pyka, Henryk 031986
Pykäläinen, Mari 010151
Pylkkänen, Heikki 009699
Pym-Hember, Peter 006087
Pynn, Jo Ann 006602
Pyrrou-Drivalou, Ourania 021168
Pysher, Ray 045740
Qëndro, Gëzim 000033
Qin, Xinghan 006997
Qiu, Fang 006968
Quaas, Achim 017709
Quaas, Dr. Gerhard 016011
Quackenbush, Bill 006786
Quackenbush, Laura J. 045234
Quackenbush, Molly 042506
Quackenbush, W.G. 005066
Quaghebeur, Marc 003286
Quail, Sarah 040760, 040761, 040762, 040763, 040768, 040771
Quairiaux, Yves 003657
Qualizza, Dr. Marino 026163
Qualmann, Kenneth 041410
Quam, Jeffery 045707
Quann, Byron 044446
Quarcooporne, Nii 046425
Quarles Van Ufford, Dr. C.C.G. 029157, 030243
Quartero, Dr. Luigi 026325
Quaß, Alois 003049
Quast, Dr. Dieter 018794
Quasthoff, Michael 017769
Quatember, Dr. Wolfgang 001798
Quattrocchi, A. 006134
Quattrociocchi, Maria Pia 025196
Quayle, Frederick M. 048442
Quéau, Jean-François 011080
Quellenberg, Björn 037777
Queree, Jennifer 030460
Querejazu Calvo, Dr. Jorge 003920
Quero Castro, Salvador 035410
Quetard, Patrice 010559
Quevedo, Emilio 007424
Quevedo, Jacinto 035626
Quibell, Batty J. 047598
Quick, Estelle 041183
Quien, Prof. Guido 007801
Quijano, Marcela 020530
Quilitzsch, Uwe 016682
Quilter, Jeffrey 048901
Quinata, Tom 021568
Quinet, Wladyslaw 003814
Quinlan, Karen 000794
Quinlan, M. 038674
Quinn, Betty 022729
Quinn, James F. 045952
Quinn, Thomas 022799
Quinn, Vivienne 038931
Quinquis, Pierre 015230
Quinsonas, M. de 012569
Quint, Eduard 029781
Quintanilla, Faustino 042066
Quintart, A. 003239
Quintelier, Johan 003475
Quintens, Patricia 003285
Quintens, Roger 003580
Quintern, Dr. Henry 002011
Quintero Durán, Miguel 007558
Quinto, Christine 039735
Quinton, Cathy 047776
Quirce, Sylvie 012125
Quirke, S. 040255
Quist, Kris N. 045985, 047905
Quoc Binh, Prof. Dr. Truong 049531
Quoc Quan, Phạm 049530
Raabe, Dr. Eva Ch. 017168, 017182
Raaber, Achim 002975
Raacke, Norbert 046263
Raade, Prof. Gunnar 031078
Raahauge, Kristine 021542
Raassen Kruimel, E.J.C. 029828
Raath, A. 034715
Rabal Merola, Victoria 035049
Rabano, Isabel 035418
Rabben, Anne Lise 031089
Rabbidge, Ted 030662
Rabeder, Dr. G. 001708
Rabeling, C.M. 029488
Raber, Christie 048710
Rabie, L.N. 034614
Rabino Massa, Prof. Emma 026063
Rabinovitch, Victor 005504
Rabinowitz, Rivka 023052
Rabner, Mario 028529
Rabner Cymerman, Mauricio 028280
Rabold, Dr. Joachim Martin 015925
Raboud, Isabelle 037675
Raby, Dr. Julian 048908
Race, Anne Katrin 015706
Racey, Nicholas 048396
Rachewiltz, Dr. Siegfried de 026024, 026025
Rachinger, Dr. Johanna 002971
Rachman Zeth, H.R.A. 022486
Rachmankulov, Ilgiz Šamiljevič 033242
Racine, Bruno 013711
Racine, Ellen 046547
Racine, Yolande 005267
Rack, Theo 017387
Racker, Barbara 047616
Rackham, J.E. 040000
Rackow, Marcia 046411
Racky, Kurt 019485
Raczka, Laurel 046971
Raczka, Robert 045737
Rada, Judith K. 048563
Radam, B. 041071
Radawetz, Natalia 006864
Radčenko, Olga Ivanovna 033722
Raddatz, Dr. Corinna 017716
Radday, Helmut 016569
Radecki, Ronald 048229
Rademacher, Henning 017722
Radford, Ron 000703
Radić, Danka 007813
Radić, Ljubica 007735
Radić, Mladen 007769
Radić, Nikola 007861
Radicke, Rüdiger 020074
Radigois, Bertrand 012682, 012684
Radigonda, Ron 046648
Radins, A. 027755
Radivojević, Milan 034174
Radley, Seán 022836
Radloff, Rodney 049172
Radman-Livaja, Ivan 007828
Radojčić, Milica 003926
Radovanović, Dragan 034240
Radović, Anđelija 034172
Radovič, Roman Bogdanovyč 038352
Radović, Slobodan 003939
Radschinski, Margitta 021072
Radtke, Christian 020038
Radtke, Edward 032102
Radulescu, Speranta 032813
Radulović, Ema 034210
Radulović, Ksenija 034162
Radwan, Krzysztof 032054
Radycki, Dr. Diane 042186
Radzak, Lee 048677
Radziewicz, Mary Ellen 042028
Radzilowicz, John 047045
Radzina, K. 027768
Raemdonck, André 003341
Rafey, Souhad 046281
Raffaelli, Prof. Mauro 024181
Raffel, Suhanya 001474
Raffelt, L. 019048
Rafferty, Pauline 006749
Raffi, Prof. S. 023452
Rafuse, Linda 005779, 005780
Ragan, Charlotte 042602
Ragionieri, Dr. Pina 024141
Ragni, Dr. Elena 023517
Rago, Kara 045343
Ragon, Jacques 014389
Ragsdale, Tammie 045558
Raguindin, Ethelinda A. 031625
Rahaman, F. 022341
Rahe, Dr. 018676
Rahe, Gebhard 019983
Rahlff, Reiner 016502, 020831
Rahman Chuchu, Abdul 004617
Rahman-Steinert, Uta 016134
Rahmani, Dr. A.R. 022267
Rahmatulaev, I. 049394
Rai, Archana 022032
Raidl, Dieter 001876
Raihle, Jan 036265
Raimond, Jean-Bernard 010738
Raimondi, Dr. Ludovico 024348
Rainbird, Stephen 001148
Rainbow, Prof. P. 040245
Rainer, Gerhard Florian 002961
Raineri, Maguerite 045060
Raines, James L. 047774
Raines, K. 005835
Rainsbury, Anne 039055
Raiola, Jonathan 046339
Rais, Dagmar 005970
Raisor, Jerry 047402
Raiss, Gerhard 017046
Rait, Eleanor 044506
Raith, Robert 016739
Raithel, Andreas 019172
Raja, Dr. Mohamad J. 022301
Rajaram, K. 022299
Rajčeva, Vasilka 004810
Rajchevska, Tsvetana 004863
Rajić, Delfina 034180
Rajkinski, Dr. Ivan 004948
Rajkinski, Ivan 004949
Rajkumar, Kimcha 006697
Rakke, Jim 044304
Rakonjac, Srdjan 034163
Rakotoarisoa, Jean-Aimé 027928
Raku XV, Kichizaemon 026762
Rakusanová, Marie 008606
Ral'čenko, Iryna Grygorivna 038229
Ralčev, Prof. Georgi 004871
Ralli, Efterpi 021207
Ralls, Nick 040865
Ralston, B. 030432
Ramachandran, V.S. 022231
Ramade, P. 015099
Ramaekers, M.T. 003778, 003779
Ramage, Alastair 039558
Raman, Anna 038092
Rambelli, Faustolo 024619
Rambert, Francis 013596
Rambo, Dr. Deborah 048115
Rambourg, Bernard 014002
Rambow, Charles 043950
Ramesh, J. 021991

Ramet, Nathan . . . 003632
Ramezan-nia, T. . . . 022584
Ramharter, Dr. Johannes . . . 002762
Ramírez, Angel Antonio . . . 007512
Ramirez, Jan . . . 046389
Ramirez, Joe . . . 042647
Ramírez, José Juan . . . 035899
Ramírez, Marcela E. . . . 028445
Ramirez, Mari Carmen . . . 044648
Ramírez, Suny . . . 028283
Ramirez Casali, María Eliana . . . 006937
Ramírez de Lara, Ligia . . . 007488
Ramírez Hernández, Jose Luis . . . 028803
Rammer, Gottfried . . . 002162
Ramón Vilarasau, Sandra . . . 049457
Ramond, Serge . . . 015183
Ramond, Sylvie . . . 012817
Ramoneda, Josep . . . 034903
Ramoneda, Prof. Luis Alberto . . . 000362
Ramos, Margarida . . . 032655
Ramos, Salome D. . . . 031797
Ramos Fernández, Dr. Rafael . . . 035165
Ramos Horta, Dr. José . . . 009168
Ramos Pérez, Froilán . . . 028400
Ramos Ruíz, Martha . . . 007550
Rampazzi, Filippo . . . 037286
Rampl, Dr. Franziska . . . 001745
Ramsauer, Dr. Gabriele . . . 002558, 002559
Ramsay, Gael . . . 000761
Ramsay, Peter . . . 001291
Ramsay, Susan . . . 006512
Ramsden, Alan R. . . . 005990
Ramsden, S. . . . 038837
Ramsden, William . . . 048400, 048403
Ramsden-Binks, T. . . . 039178
Ramseuer, Dr. Gabriele . . . 002586
Ramsey, Peter . . . 046671
Ramsey, Ron . . . 000888
Ramsey, Steve . . . 046517
Ramseyer, Dr. Denis . . . 037181
Ramskjaer, Liv . . . 031097
Ramušćak, Prof. Ljubica . . . 007706
Ramuschi, Maria Cristina . . . 026102
Ramut, Eliza . . . 031814
Rana, A.K. . . . 022073
Ranade, Dr. Hari Govind . . . 022310
Ranaldi, Prof. Franco . . . 025345
Rand, Michael . . . 049003
Rand, Patrick . . . 043023
Rand, Richard . . . 049187
Randall, R. Dennis . . . 044661
Randall, Ross . . . 041650
Randall, Ross G. . . . 046073
Randazzo, Giuseppe . . . 025091
Randić Barlek, Mirjana . . . 007832
Randow, Renate von . . . 020857
Raney, Floyd . . . 045349
Raney, Nancy . . . 042200
Ranftl, Helmut . . . 002257
Range, Dorothy . . . 049284
Rangström, Lena . . . 036639
Raninen-Siiskonen, Tarja . 009621, 009622
Ranjbaran, Sa'eid . . . 022607
Rank, Karin . . . 017220
Rank-Beauchamp, Elizabeth . . . 048127
Ranker, Prof. Thomas A. . . . 042354
Rankin, John L. . . . 005599
Rankin jr, P.R. . . . 043675
Rankin, Ray . . . 040121
Rankin, Shan . . . 043609
Ransom Lehman, Karen . . . 046597
Ransome Wallis, Rosemary . . . 040155
Ranšová, Eva . . . 008534
Rantanen, Reijo . . . 010241
Rao, D.V. . . . 022316
Rapetti, Rodolphe . . . 013723
Rapisarda, Alfredo Pablo . . . 000667
Rapkin, Grace . . . 046352
Rapmund, J. . . . 030088
Raposo, Luís . . . 032648
Rapp, Karen . . . 047461
Rappe-Weber, Dr. Susanne . . . 020937
Raptou, E. . . . 008217
Raptou, Dr. Eustathios . . . 008234
Rardin Johnson, Sara . . . 047194
Rarhein, Ingar . . . 030828
Rasajski, Javor . . . 034281
Rasario, Dr. Giovanna . . . 024185
Rasbury, Patricia . . . 046154
Rasch, Elisabeth . . . 036732
Rasch, Tone . . . 031097
Rasche, Dr. Adelheid . . . 016101
Raselli, Lilian . . . 036925
Rash, Roswitha M. . . . 046902, 046903, 046904, 046907, 046910
Rašidov, G.R. . . . 049412
Rasjid, A. . . . 022469
Rask, Sven . . . 008875
Rasmusen, Milo . . . 043021
Rasmussen, Alan H. . . . 008945
Rasmussen, Frank Allan . . . 008976
Rasmussen, Keith . . . 045061
Rasmussen, Dr. Pamela . . . 043575
Rasmussen, Robert . . . 046874
Rasmussen, William . . . 047428
Rasmusson, Allan . . . 036804
Raspail, Thierry . . . 012810
Rassweiler, Janet . . . 046424
Rastas, Perttu . . . 009542
Rašticová, Dr. Blanka . . . 008732
Rataiczyk, Matthias . . . 017665, 053451
Ratcliffe, Dr. Brett C. . . . 045313
Ratcliffe, Shirley . . . 039116
Rath, H. . . . 020025
Rath, Harald . . . 003020
Rath, Herbert . . . 001918
Rath, I. . . . 020025
Rath, L. . . . 017965
Rathbone, Eliza . . . 048940
Rathbun, Merrilyn . . . 043935
Rathburn, Robert R. . . . 042225
Rathfelder, Johannes . . . 002813
Rathgeber, Paul . . . 016540, 016542
Rathke, Dr. Christian . . . 019453
Rathman, Deane . . . 048732
Ratier, Hugo . . . 000459
Ratner, Phillip . . . 023104
Ratnikova, Marina Semënovna . . . 034088
Rattemeyer, Dr. Volker . . . 020877
Rattenborg, Cena . . . 046602
Rattenbury, Richard . . . 046647
Ratti, Dr. Enrico . . . 026242
Ratti, Dr. Marzia . . . 024440
Ratti, Pietro . . . 024436
Rattigan, John . . . 022783
Ratzeburg, Wiebke . . . 016390
Ratzenböck, Hans-Jörg . . . 002244
Ratzky, Dr. Rita . . . 021689
Ratzloff, Betty Lou . . . 046075
Rau, Lorraine . . . 043840, 043840
Rau, Dr. Patrick . . . 018374
Rau, Prof. Dr. Peter . . . 017724
Rauch, L. . . . 037545
Rauch, Margot . . . 002094, 002934
Rauch, Werner . . . 013523
Rauchbauer, Judith von . . . 015529
Rauchensteiner, Dr. Manfried . . . 002910
Rauchenwald, Alexandra . . . 001711
Raud, Anu . . . 009362
Raudsepa, Ingrida . . . 027729
Raudsepp, Renita . . . 009398
Rauf, Barb . . . 043217
Raulff, Dr. Ulrich . . . 018813
Raunio, Erkki . . . 009460
Rauø, Kåre William . . . 030834
Raus, Edmund . . . 045613
Rausch, Amalia . . . 003072
Rausch, Guy . . . 027890
Rausch, Jürgen . . . 019582
Rauschenberg, Chris . . . 047167
Rauscher, August . . . 002463
Rauscher, Hannelore . . . 020768
Raussmüller, Urs . . . 037522
Raussmüller-Sauer, Christel . . . 037522
Rauzi, Prof. Estebar . . . 000462
Ravagnan, Dr. Giovanna Luisa . . . 026239
Ravanelli Guidotti, Dr. Carmen . . . 024070
Ravaonatoandro, Aldine . . . 027931
Ravasi, Prof. Gianfranco . . . 024733
Ravasi, Gianfranco . . . 026213
Ravasio, Dr. Tiziana . . . 023359
Ravaux, J.-P. . . . 011199, 011201
Rave, Dr. August B. . . . 020365
Raved, Noga . . . 022897
Raveendran, K. . . . 022358
Raveh, Kurt . . . 023036
Ravel, Christian . . . 012883
Ravelo Virgen, Margarita . . . 028902
Ravenal, John . . . 047429
Ravenscraft, Pauline . . . 048732
Raverty, Norm . . . 001007
Ravid, Zami . . . 023029
Raviv, Efraim . . . 023049
Ravnik Toman, Barbara . . 034459, 034460, 034472, 034473, 034474, 034527
Ravoire, Olivier . . . 013513
Ravonatoandro, Aldine . . . 027930
Rawdon, David D. . . . 034678
Rawle, Caroline . . . 041332
Rawluk-Raus, Bożena . . . 032286
Rawstern, Sherri . . . 041559
Rawsthorn, Alice . . . 040134
Ray, Dulce Ivette . . . 044010
Ray, Dr. Ella Maria . . . 043406
Ray, Jeffrey . . . 046925
Ray, Justice A.N. . . . 022219
Ray, Randy W. . . . 044649
Ray, Romita . . . 041832
Ray, Shirley . . . 044969
Rayburn, Ella S. . . . 048067
Rayburn, Nicholas . . . 047579
Rayment, John . . . 039920
Raymond, David . . . 044911
Raymond, Nancy . . . 006724
Raymond, Richard . . . 049355
Raymond, Yvette . . . 005662
Rayne, Angela . . . 044231
Raynolds, Robert . . . 045648
Rayworth, Shelagh F. . . . 006502
Razafindratsima, Clarisse . . . 027934
Razzaq Moaz, Dr. Abdal . . . 037828
Read, Albert J. . . . 046691
Read, B. . . . 038483
Read, Bob . . . 045195
Read, Liz . . . 022761
Read, Peter . . . 030489
Read, Robert F. . . . 043251
Read, Rolly . . . 022761
Real, Nelson A. . . . 000346
Reale, Giuseppe . . . 024891
Reale, Dr. Isabella . . . 026162
Reale, Sara W. . . . 044829
Reap, Mary . . . 048065
Reason, Robert . . . 000703
Reber, Dr. Alfred . . . 037282
Reber, Eugene . . . 043029
Reber, Dr. Markus . . . 037571
Reber, Paul . . . 049255
Rebman, Dr. Jon . . . 047840
Rebmann, Dr. Martina . . . 018156
Réboli, Eliana Moro . . . 004094
Rębosz, Ireneusz . . . 032181
Rebuschat, Karlheinz . . . 017353
Recalt, Gustavo . . . 000259
Recanati, Harry . . . 006939
Recanatini, Cesare . . . 023199
Reček, Antonín . . . 008589, 008715
Rečev, Vasil . . . 004835
Rech, Prof. Dr. Manfred . . . 016411
Rechberger, Erwin . . . 002023
Recht, Roland . . . 014865
Rechter, Jerril . . . 001032
Recio Crespo, Miguel Angel . . . 035439, 035761
Recio Crespoz, Miguel Angel . . . 035932
Reck, Pat . . . 041615
Reckitt, Helena . . . 041845
Recouvrot, M. . . . 014519
Rector, P. . . . 034879
Recupero, Jacopo . . . 023211
Reczek, Krzysztof . . . 032021
Reddeker, Lioba . . . 002857, 002858
Reddell, James R. . . . 041936
Redding, Mary Anne . . . 042759
Redenbach, Marj . . . 005858
Redlaczyk, Janelle . . . 049167
Redlich, Daniela . . . 017177
Redlin, Jane . . . 016128
Redmann, Sheila K. . . . 047603
Redmond, Dr. Brian . . . 042986
Redmond-Cooper, Helen . . . 039405
Redolfi, Silke . . . 037486
Redpath, Donna . . . 005470
Redvale, Jolene . . . 049368
Reed, Andy . . . 001024
Reed, C. . . . 041067
Reed, Caroline M. . . . 040236
Reed, Dorothy . . . 045745
Reed, Gerard . . . 000701
Reed, Ian . . . 039440
Reed, J. . . . 040351
Reed, Leon B. . . . 043189
Reed, Mark . . . 047183
Reed, Mary . . . 046046, 046167
Reed, Michael . . . 044637
Reed, Patrick H. . . . 043960
Reed, Philip . . . 040106, 040182
Reed, Robin Edward . . . 047421
Reed, Sharon . . . 049295
Reed, Ursula . . . 046957
Reeder, Deborah . . . 047225
Reeder, Warwick . . . 001240
Reedie, K.G.H. . . . 038979, 038980
Reedy, Joan M. . . . 049359
Reekie, Clara . . . 046109
Reel, David M. . . . 049096
Reel, Paula . . . 041719
Reel, Robert . . . 045277
Reenberg, Holger . . . 008904
Rees, Diane . . . 044484
Rees, Elfan . . . 041348
Rees, James C. . . . 046074
Rees, Monica . . . 038693
Rees-Jones, Elizabeth . . . 039998
Reese, Dr. Beate . . . 021003
Reese, David L. . . . 046339
Reese, Frances S. . . . 047214
Reese, Gary . . . 048470
Reese, Julie . . . 046866
Reeskamp, E. . . . 030226
Reeve, Anthony . . . 040241
Reeve, William F. . . . 006182
Reevees, D.W. . . . 041444
Reeves, Dr. Deborah . . . 048763
Reeves, Dennis . . . 040031
Reeves, Don . . . 046647
Reeves, Kate A. . . . 046101
Reeves, Lee . . . 041704
Reeves, Dr. Nicholas . . . 039460
Refsum, Siri . . . 031113
Regan, Brian . . . 046394
Regan, Mary . . . 044139
Regan, Michael . . . 040108
Regêncio Macedo, Carlos António . 032603
Regenvanu, Ralph . . . 049416
Reggiori, Albino . . . 024481
Regibus, Raymond de . . . 037520
Regier, Charles . . . 046529
Regli, Kurt . . . 037176
Regnauer, Dr. A. . . . 020165
Regnier, Gérard . . . 013726
Regoli, Dr. Edina . . . 025601
Regull, Enrique . . . 036042
Řeháková, Dr. Hana . . . 008559, 008560
Rehberg, Dr. Rolf . . . 019676
Rehberg, Vivian . . . 013630
Rehberger, Prof. Dr. Dr. Karl . . . 002579
Rehde, Anders . . . 008850, 008852
Reher, Charles A. . . . 045169
Reher, Dr. Uwe . . . 018201
Rehm, Dr. Heinrich . . . 019482
Rehor, Ophelia . . . 015901

Rei, M. 034699
Reiblich, Luisa 018809
Reich, Dr. Annette 018135
Reich, Christopher J. 043305
Reich, Dindy 043610
Reich, Jacqueline 014566
Reichard, Tim 048568
Reichel, Antje 017811
Reichel, Maik 018749, 018750
Reichel, Reinhard 017424
Reichen, Quirinus 036927
Reichenbach, Dr. María Cecilia von 000388
Reichenbach, Svenja Gräfin von . . 016009
Reichert, Klara 018857
Reichholf, Prof. Prof. Dr. J. 019132
Reichl, Leo 002116
Reichmann, Dr. Christoph 018400
Reichmann, Hans-Peter 017157
Reichmann, Kurt 019485
Reichmuth, Bernhard 037197
Reickart, Harry 042969
Reid, Alan 039201
Reid, Alison 039496
Reid, David 039295
Reid, Dennis 006581
Reid, Gare B. 048126
Reid, Grace 042223
Reid, Graeme 045088
Reid, Dr. John S. 038442
Reid, Kevin 039241
Reid, Kim 006142
Reid, Marie-Claude 006333
Reid, Megan 049371
Reid, Michelle 044300
Reid, Richard 005534
Reid, Scott 040449, 040450
Reid, Prof. Seona 039557
Reid-Bavis, Glenda 005302
Reid Hardman, Mimi 045117
Reid-Wallace, Dr. Carolyn 046145
Reid Williamson, J. 042573, 044751
Reidel, Dr. Hermann 019745, 019746
Reidy, Susan 048706
Reifenscheid-Ronnisch, Dr. Beate . 018295
Reijmers, M. 029194
Reijnders, Dr. W. 029312
Reiles, Paul 027894
Reilly, Ann-Marie 046283
Reilly, Gerry 049141
Reilly, John W. 043552
Reilly, Margaret T. 039561
Reilly, Robin 005038
Reilly, Valerie A. 040673
Reimann, Rella 046838
Reimann, Urs 036894
Reimer, Wayne 006160
Reimonenq, H. 021563
Rein, Dr. Anette 017182
Rein, Elfriede 015750
Reinbacher, Adolf 001870
Reinbold, Dr. Michael 019470
Reinckens, Sharon 048881
Reinders, Dr. Carin E.M. 029252
Reinders, C.E.M. 030209
Reinders, P.J. 029507
Reinecke, Klaus 018147
Reinert, Frank 027894
Reinert, Hans-Walter 019389
Reines Josephy, Marcia 045444
Reinhard, Adelheid 019838
Reinhard, Erika 018382
Reinhard, Rolf 018382
Reinhard-Felice, Dr. Mariantonia . . 037606, 037729
Reinhardt, Dr. Brigitte 020530, 020534
Reinhardt, Dr. Georg 018628
Reinhardt, Hannelore 020519
Reinholdt, Bruce 048878
Reinholdt, Helle 009097
Reinig, Margot 017701
Reininghaus, Ruth 046397
Reinisch, Christine 002581
Reinisch, Dr. Tobias 002984
Reinius, Doris 017143
Reinke, Doris M. 043666
Reinsch, Prof. Dietmar 016388
Reis, Heitor 004444
Reis, Jennifer 046021
Reis, Dr. José 032606
Reisacher, Anton 036973
Reisch, Prof. Dr. Ludwig 017038
Reisetbauer, Hans 002578
Reising, Dr. Gert 018169
Reisner, Peter 019876
Reiss, Johannes 001827
Reisse, Hans Peter 018189
Reissenweber, E. 016466
Reißer, Gudrun . 016740, 016741, 016742, 016743, 016744, 016746
Reisz, Frederick S. 045440
Reiter, Alois 002634
Reiter, Carmen 001758
Reiter, Günther 002212
Reiter, Klaus Giselher 019112
Reiterer, Bruno 002567
Reithinger, Gilles 013572
Reitner, Prof. Dr. J. 017469
Reitz, Dr. E. 041833
Reitz, Thomas A. 005715
Reitzler, Anne 043551
Rejimbal, Tamara 046057
Rejn, J. Surya Narayara 022130
Rejune Adams, Gloria 043382
Rekker, L. 030260
Rell, Zofia 032233
Rem, Dr. P.H. 029256
Remaud 012636
Remen, Geir 031014
Remillon, Michel 012923
Remington, Charlotte 045375
Rémon, Régine 003583
Remsen, Dr. J.V. 042049
Remy 003811
Renaux, Jean-Pierre 014848
Renda, Dr. Gerhard 016236
Render, Lorne E. 045630
Rendić-Miočević, Prof. Ante 007828
Renfrew, Katherine A. 046497
Renfro, Francis 043487
Renfro, Gladys 044667
Renger, Dr. Konrad 019038, 019038
Rengnath, Rudi 016705
Renken, Dr. Lisa 045370
Renn, Wendelin 020596
Rennicke, Stefan 019391
Rennie, Heather 005058
Rennie, Ian 039298
Rennie, Jennifer A. 038468
Rennie, Mairi C. 048809
Renning, Kenneth 046242
Rennox, Munuma 029085
Renouf, Nicholas 046229
Renouf, Phil 001413
Rensberger, Dr. John M. 048075
Rent, Dr. Clyda S. 043102
Renting, Dr. A.D. 029256
Renton, Alan 040694
Renton, John 040602
Rentoul, A. 000998
Rentzhog, Sten 036529, 036530
Renvall, Dr. Pertti 009761
Renz, Joachim 019209
Renz, Ruth 048014
Renzl, Ludwig 002422
Renzo, Luigi 025605
Reo, Danielle 047821
Repetto, Arnaldo 024370
Rephann, Richard 046229
Reppe, C. 019678
Requejo, Angel 036064
Reris, L.S.D. 036135
Reser, Dr. Ladislaus 037301
Rességuier, Bernadette de 013279
Ressel, Dr. Stephen 042016
Ressiter, Jeremy 041316
Ressmeyer, Richard 042749
Restall, Robin 049451
Restif, Claire le 012144
Restle, Prof. Dr. Conny 016147
Resurreccion jr., Teodoro R. 031692
Retallick, Leslie 041232
Rethly, Akos 021695
Retière, Ch. 011617
Retière, Marie-Noëlle 013463
Retno, Dr. Sulistianingsih S. 022433
Rettenbeck, Georg 016716
Rettenmund, Jürg 037196
Rettig, Wolfram 017710
Retzlaff, Detlef 019219
Reublin, Patricia 044303
Reuland, G. 027881
Reumer, Dr. J.W.F. 030095
Reus, B. de 029995
Reuß, Carsten 018954
Reuße, Dr. Felix 017228
Reustle, M. Charles 043165
Reustle, Dr. S. 020914
Reuter, Cecelia 043927
Reuter, Horst 018535
Reuter, Laurel J. 044262
Reuter, Pat 043646
Reuter, Scott . . . 041822, 041825, 041826
Reuter, Simone 015803
Reuter, Dr. Wolfgang 017346
Reuther, Dr. Manfred 019245
Reutimann, Daniel 037657
Revelard, Michel 003233
Revilla Uceda, Mateo 035254, 035259
Rew, Christine 038451
Rex Svansson, Karin 036755, 036757
Rex Svensson, Karin 036756
Rexwinkel, Nancy 042449
Rey, Marie-Catherine 011680
Rey-Delqué, Monique 014994
Rey-Vodoz, Véronique 037386
Reyer, Manfred 015927
Reyer-Völlenklee, Silvia 002090
Reyes, Manuel 021573
Reyes, Patricia 046394
Reyes Flórez, Graciela 007483
Reyes Mota, Dr. Alicia 028443
Reymann, Patrick H. 043004
Reymond, Catherine 037340
Reynaldo, Pia 048723
Reynies, Béatrice de 013699
Reynolds, Craig 044682
Reynolds, David 045282
Reynolds, Earl 046063
Reynolds, Edmond 047632
Reynolds, Elsie 006287
Reynolds, Frank 006453
Reynolds, Janelle 006859
Reynolds, Jerry 049223
Reynolds, Jock 046228
Reynolds, Nancy 006633
Reynolds, R.G. 039003
Reynolds, Stanley G. 006799
Reynolds, Dr. Terry 045181
Reynolds, Valrae 046425
Reynolds Brown, C. 049213, 049216
Reys, M. 029911
Rezai, N. 022650
Rezeanu, Prof. Paul 032849
Rezler, Aleš 008461
Rezník, Branislav 034303
Rhamie, Barb 042679
Rhees, David J. 045908
Rhein, Dr. Stefan 018755, 018756, 018757, 018761, 018762
Rhi, Prof. Ju-Hyung 027602
Rhie, Dr. Jong-chul 027578
Rho, Jean 046320
Rhoades, John S. 045407
Rhoback, Kristine 041697
Rhode, Michael 048929
Rhodes, Carleen 047704
Rhodes, John 039542
Rhodes, Dr. Michael 041232
Rhodes, Ulysses S. 042474
Rhodes, William 046288
Rhomberg, Kathrin 018321
Rhymer, Clarence 005472
Rhys-Michael, Cellan 038856
Riaño Bernal, Wolfram Armando . . 007445
Riaño Lozano, Fernando . . 035430, 036076
Ribas San Emeterio, Neus 034854
Ribbert, Dr. Margret 036884, 036885
Ribbrock, Dr. Gerhard 019022
Ribé Monge, Genis 035730
Ribeiro, Agostinho 032624
Ribeiro, Francisca 032688
Ribeiro de Faria, Manuel José Marques 032647
Ribeiro Martins, António 032619
Ribero, Michel 015105
Ribes, Sonia 032763
Ribeton, Olivier 010685
Ribey, Barbara 006496
Riboreau, Brigitte 010943
Ricart, Dolors 034908
Ricci, Massimo 025741
Ricci, Pat 046249
Ricciardi, Prof. Mario 026073
Riccòmini, Prof. Eugenio . 023426, 023428, 023456
Rice, Annette 043704
Rice, Calvin 042572
Rice, Christopher 038718
Rice, David 039589
Rice, Donald 042191
Rice, Jane 047380
Rice, Nancy N. 047671
Rice, Sean 046226
Rice Irwin, John 046510
Rich, Andrea L. 045441
Rich, Beverly 048181, 048182
Rich, Hans 017231
Rich, Margaret 000761
Rich, Mark S. 047420
Rich, Merle 041786
Rich, Nancy 046545
Rich, Pat 047656
Richard, Alison F. 046226
Richard, Christopher 046598
Richard, Francis 013685
Richard, Jack 043254
Richard, Judy Morrissey 006571
Richard, Michel 012798
Richard, M.L. 006076
Richard, Nancy 042339
Richards, Beth 046938
Richards, Dolores 042292
Richards, Jane 041958
Richards, Janet 041732
Richards, John 039637
Richards, L. Jane 045933
Richards, Nancy 044612
Richards, Nancy E. 046195
Richards, Pat 048011
Richards, Paul 041001
Richards, Ron 044744
Richards, W.R. 038698
Richardson, Catherine 039813
Richardson, Darlene 047469
Richardson, Don H. 048352
Richardson, E. 039813
Richardson, Edgar 048050
Richardson, Gary 039286
Richardson, Dr. James B. 047044
Richardson, Jeanette 030619
Richardson, Katherine 048426
Richardson, Larry D. 042064
Richardson, Lindsey 046118
Richardson, Margaret 040289
Richardson, Mary 048050
Richardson, Meredith J. 046883
Richardson, Michael 043979
Richardson, Roy 030504
Richardson, R.T. 039959
Richardson, Sarah 040550
Richardson, Vivian 048864
Richardt, Ursula 018158

Richart, Brigitte 011615
Richart, Christian 041792
Richartz, Christoffer 015992
Richaud, Maurice 015262
Riche, Nicole 010788
Riche-Descamps, Jeannine 003710
Richelson, Paul W. 045949
Richerson, Jim 046880
Richey, Susan 043090
Richmond, Alan 041693
Richmond, Art 045230
Richmond, Patricia 042377
Richmond-Rex, Phyllis E. 030709
Richner, Trudi 037652
Richon, Marco 036951
Richoux, Sylvie 012939
Richter, Bob 005757
Richter, Dr. Burkhard 017731
Richter, Donald 043296
Richter, Dr. Erhard 017529
Richter, Gert 017661
Richter, Gunnar 017611
Richter, Dr. Helmut 017290
Richter, Helmut 020775, 020777
Richter, Hiltrud 019485
Richter, Jenett 006852
Richter, Jörg 017644
Richter, Paul 001812
Richter, Paula 047741
Richter, Dr. S. 017221
Richter, Susie 045075
Richter, Tanya 044523
Richter, Dr. Thomas 036927
Richter, Ursula 019889
Richthofen, Dr. Jasper von 017453, 017454
Richtsfeld, Dr. Bruno 019122
Richwagen, Sue 042490
Rick, Jane 040294
Rickards, Dr. R.B. 038970
Rickart, Eric 047778
Ricke, Dr. Helmut 016841
Rickenbach, Bertha von 037000
Rickenbach, Judith 037789
Ricker, Maria 006884
Ricker, Stephen A. 042101
Ricketts, Paul W. 048821
Rićko, Oka 007723
Rico Perrat, Gabriela 028136
Riddell, Dr. Richard 039262
Riddle, Janet 030660
Riddle, Lola 047470
Ridgely, Barbara S. 044172
Riding, Gillian 039756
Riding, Jacqueline 040171
Ridley, David J. 039094
Ridley, Jackie D. 039255, 039257
Ridley, Jacqeline 039260
Ridley, Dr. Michael 039261
Ridpath, Marjorie 042569
Rieche, Dr. Anita 016333
Rieche, Christiane 017661, 017668
Riechert, Claudia 020136, 020137
Riechert, Karl-Ludwig 017754, 019576
Rieck, Silvana 015679, 015680
Ried, Martha 018418
Riedel, Andrea 019441
Riedel, Angela 022761
Riedel, Gerd-Rainer 017020
Riedel, Heinz 003018
Riedel, Dr. Matthias 018339
Riedel, Uwe 018978
Riedel, Walter G. 046703, 046704
Rieder, Alfred 037671
Riederer, Prof. Dr. Josef 053548
Riedesel, Rikarde 015664
Riedl, Monika 015774
Riedmiller, Thomas 017291, 017293
Rieger, Sigrun 019039
Rieger-Jähner, Prof. Dr. Brigitte . . 017206
Riegler, Frank 002898
Riegler, Wolfgang 001674
Riego González, Angel 035041
Riehl, Ken 005163
Riek, Peter 016995, 016996
Riek, Rolf 018467
Rieken, Duane 044770
Riemann, Angelika 016750
Riemersma, Tiny 029462
Riepe, Ulrike 017779
Riepl, Heiner 020123
Riepniece, Ineta 027683
Riepula, Anne 009757
Ries, Christian 027895
Rieser, Gabriele 002803
Riesgo, Juan M. 035396
Riess, Gerhard 002953
Riestra de Cuevas, Bertha 028510
Riether, Dr. Achim 019118
Riethmüller, Dr. Marianne 017299
Riethmuller, Bruce 001535
Rietschel, Dr. Gerhard 018809
Rietvelt, Carol 044804
Rietzke, I. 015949
Rifaux, Yves 012884
Rife, Sandra B. 049185
Riffel, Carola 016954
Rifkin, Ned 048912
Riganti, Riccardo 026117
Rigby, Carol 039696, 041332
Rigby, S. 038751, 038753
Rigdon, Lois 042513
Rigdon, Marge 043529
Rigeade, Pascal 010733
Rigert, Markus 037718
Rigg, Frank 042329
Riggall, R.A. 001440
Riggins-Ezzell, Lois S. 046154
Riggio, Leonard 046324
Riggs, Carol 045520
Riggs, Gerry 043056
Riggs, Richard 045247
Riggs, Timothy A. 042713
Righetti, Olimpia L. 000617
Righolt, Niels 036332
Rigoli, Adriano 026183
Rigon, Lidia 025612
Řihová, Dr. Ivana 008695
Riibak, Renate 009407
Riker, Janet 042467
Rikkoert, A. 030143
Rikkonen, Mikko 010215
Riley, Angelika 017715
Riley, Barbara 044960
Riley, Cathy 048824
Riley, Cygred 043573
Riley, Grace 040288
Riley, Joseph P. 042730
Riley, Michael J. 047554
Riley, Norman 041891
Riley, Pat 044013
Riley, Peter 040945, 040946
Riley, Terence 045389
Rimer, G.J. 039959
Rimmö, Christina 036764
Rimoldi, Luciano 025046
Rimon, Ofra 022928
Rinaldi, Paolo 026013
Rinaldini, Dr. Francesco 023772
Rinck, Aksel 019322
Rinder, Lawrence R. 046418
Rindfleisch, Jan 043248
Rindlisbacher, Rolf 037354
Rindom Madsen, Finn 009013
Rindsfüsser, Annemarie 015753
Rinetti, Dr. Luigi 026299
Ring, Prof. Francis 038634
Ring, Klaus 016262
Ringelheim, Joan 048952
Ringgaard Lauridsen, Henning . . . 009150
Ringler, Sarah 049062
Ringstad, Jan Erik 031166, 031167
Rink, Christine 018567
Rinker, Dr. Dagmar 020530
Rintala, Liisa 010119
Rintoul, Dr. Gordon 039394, 039403, 039407, 039418, 040994, 040996, 040999
Rinuy, Anne 037128
Riolini-Unger, Dr. Adelheid 017260
Rionda, Patricia Elena 000624
Riopelle, Christopher 040241
Riordan, Mary Ann 044997
Riordon, Bernard 005477, 005567
Ríos de Molina, Martha 028470
Rios de Saluso, María Luisa Adriana 000463
Ríos Montero, Sylvia 006931
Rios Rigau, Adlin 032705
Rios-Samaniego, Milita 047589
Riottot El-Habib, Béatrice 013737
Rioux, Alfred 005755
Ripatti, Marja-Liisa 009490, 009495
Ripley, John W. 048918
Ripoll, Rafael Romá 034810
Ripperová, Dr. Marie 008748
Rippstein, Laurence 037679
Rippy, C. 048654
Rippy, Linda 047094
Risani Dossi, Dr. Carola 023961
Risch, Laurie 043198
Riseman, Henry 042456
Riser, Cherie 045700
Rish, Sarah 045292
Rishel, Joseph 046953
Rishel, Joseph J. 046975, 046983
Risskov Sørensen, Kurt 008949
Rister, Faye 005620
Risthein, Helena 009398
Ristola, Ruth 046698
Ritch, Irene 006393
Ritchey, Robert L. 047130
Ritchie, Christina 006694
Ritschard, Claude-Janine 037128
Ritter, Martin 019424
Ritter, Michael 019226
Ritter, Mildred 041700
Ritter, Dr. Nicole 016469
Ritter, Wolfgang 017053
Rittmann, Josef 002534
Rittwage, Roy 005154
Ritzmann, Dietrich-Wilhelm 020064
Riva, Davide 023636
Riva, Maurizio 023636
Rivard, Céline 006311
Rivas, Francisco 035622
Rivas, Helen 047158
Rivas Octavio, José A. 035413
Rivatton, Bernard 014273
Rivé, Isabelle 012806
Riveil, Gilbert 015071
Rivera, Dianna 042391
Rivera, George 047954
Rivera, Gigi 031784
Rivera, Mario 044710
Rivera, Prof. Osmin 021607
Rivera, Paula 048498
Rivero Borrell, Héctor 028502
Rivers, Gabrielle 040777
Rivers, Mildred B. 044412
Rivière, Danielle 012829
Rivière, Dr. Dominique . . . 013811, 015176
Rivoira, Prof. Giuseppe 025801
Rivolta, Barbara 048574
Riwar, Monique 037335
Rix, Peggy 042670
Rixhon, Maryse 003434
Rizzo, Antonio A. 000500
Rizzuto, Timothy C. 042045
Rjabcev, Igor Mykolajovyč 038283
Rjabov, Gennadij Evgenjevič 033929
Rjazanov, Aleksandr Michajlovič . . 033039
Rjazanova, Lilija Aleksandrovna . . 033106
Rjuken, Kjetil 030822
Roach, Ed 005759
Roaldset, Prof. Dr. Elen . . 031078, 031090, 031115
Robb, Doug 040610
Robb, Douglas 044407
Robb, Lisa 046859
Robbins, Anna 000783
Robbins, Carol 043269
Robbins, Carolyn 048060
Robbins, Daniel 040197
Robbins, Neil 039759
Robe, Sofia 032920
Robel, Sigrid 016596
Robelen, William G. 043381
Roberson, Jeanette W. 045109
Roberson, W. Allen 043085
Robert, Henri 011527
Robert, K.L. 005867
Roberts, Bette 045726
Roberts, Brady 047011
Roberts, Carty 046096
Roberts, Catsou 038855
Roberts, Coles 046518
Roberts, Dr. Dafydd 040044, 040046
Roberts, David 041000
Roberts, Day 005334
Roberts, Elaine 045210
Roberts, Gary 042803
Roberts, Sir Hugh 040264
Roberts, Hugh 040277
Roberts, James D. 048296
Roberts, Jan 042906
Roberts, Jill 046082
Roberts, John 038895
Roberts, Martin 039152
Roberts, Mary A. 048704
Roberts, Paige W. 042188
Roberts, Peg 042149
Roberts, Perri L. 043147
Roberts, Randy 048044
Roberts, Sir Samuel 039115
Roberts, Teresa 043170
Roberts-Douglass, Kathy 047511
Roberts-Walker, Gayle 042110
Róbertsdóttir, Gerdur 021958
Robertson, A. 038824
Robertson, Alexander 039950
Robertson, Beatrice L. 046873
Robertson, Beverly 045768
Robertson, Bruce 045441
Robertson, Byron 044167
Robertson, Charles J. 048943
Robertson, David 042838
Robertson, Dongwol Kim 043162
Robertson, Dr. H.G. 034586
Robertson, I. 040240
Robertson, I.G. 040954
Robertson, Lynn 043082
Robertson, Pamela B. 039559
Robertson, Pat 044691
Robertson, Preston 005971
Robertson, Rosalyn 047499
Robertson, Susan 048846
Robidoux, R.R. 046992
Robie, Kathlyn 048139
Robins, Dr. Gay 041866
Robinson, Alicia 040077
Robinson, Beulah 042890
Robinson, Bonnell 042314
Robinson, Bruce 001081
Robinson, Charles 039203
Robinson, Christine 048359
Robinson, Cliff 000877
Robinson, Dan 039061
Robinson, David 048761
Robinson, Deborah 041286, 041286
Robinson, D.N. 040346
Robinson, Don 041710
Robinson, Duncan 038962
Robinson, Franklin W. 044791
Robinson, Dr. George W. 044632
Robinson, Graham 030594
Robinson, Herb 005651
Robinson, Dr. James J. 044748
Robinson, John 043736
Robinson, John A. 001255
Robinson, Dr. Joyce 048703
Robinson, Julie 000703
Robinson, Katharine S. 042736, 042743
Robinson, Laurie 043149

Robinson, Louise 044015
Robinson, Malcolm J. 048625
Robinson, Michael 005187
Robinson, Michelle 043304
Robinson, Dr. Paul 039235
Robinson, Prof. Peter 042354
Robinson, Phaedra 043441
Robinson, Dr. Roger W. 044255
Robinson, Ruth 049193
Robinson, Thomas A. 043648
Robinson, Travis 045258
Robinson, William 042560
Robinson, William H. 042985
Robinson-Dowland, Martin 041249
Robison, Andrew C. 048924
Robles, José Angel 028730
Roblin, Laurent 011464
Robson, Judy 041816
Robson, Keith 041244
Roca, Teresa 035353
Rocca, Robert 011770
Rocchi, Dr. Silvano 025714
Roch, Dr. Heidi 017481
Roch, Neal 041623
Roch-Stübler, Dr. Heidi . . 017480, 017483, 017484
Rocha, Dr. Olivio 032578
Rocha Moreno, Leonor 007452
Rocha Virmond, Eduardo da 004086
Rochard, Dr. Patricia 018064
Rochat, Pierre 036910
Roche, Fr.S. 022353
Roche, James 042601
Rochefort, Hervé de 011528
Rochette, Christelle 012311
Rochette, Edward C. 043059
Rochmad, Edi 022381
Rockefeller, David 046288
Rockhill, King 046045
Rockhold, Jean 047553
Roda, Dr. Burkard von . . . 036884, 036885, 036892, 036898
Roda, Dr. Hortensia von 037524
Roďák, Dr. Jozef 034438
Rodazie, M. 012805
Rodd, H.C. 041394
Roddick, J.H. 006752
Roddis, William H. 045497
Rodee, Marian 041618
Rodekamp, Dr. Volker . . . 018558, 018584, 018590, 018593, 018594, 018595, 018600
Rodenburg, Teun 030364
Roder, Dr. Hartmut 016426
Roderick, Myron 048361
Rodes, David 045425
Rodeschini Galati, Dr. Maria Cristina 023375
Rodger, David 041187
Rodger, Robin 040697
Rodgers, James 045075
Rodgers, Jeff 042611
Rodgers, Kenneth G. 043546
Rodgers, Maureen 005138
Rodgers, Michael W. 043918
Rodgers, Michele 042638
Rodgers, Rachel A. 042615
Rodgers, Tommie 045199
Rodgers, Warren D. 044265
Rodgers, Z. 022776
Rodiek, Dr. Thorsten 018717, 018720, 018722, 018725, 018726, 018729
Rodimceva, I.A. 033377
Rodina, Lucia-Letiţia 032768
Rodini, Elizabeth 042838
Rodman, Vickie 047780
Rodney, Clayton 021600
Rodolfi, Rosanna 024221
Rodon, Francesc 036057
Rodrigo, Carmen 035978
Rodrigues, Dr. Paulo 004373
Rodrigues Meyer, Fernando 004290
Rodriguez, Carlos Armando 007465
Rodriguez, Carmen 043145
Rodriguez, Geno 046280
Rodriguez, John 043181
Rodríguez, José Alfonso 007470
Rodriguez, Roberto M. 042751
Rodríguez, Rosa 035978
Rodriguez, Teresa 048708
Rodríguez, Tomás 049464
Rodríguez Angarita, María Esther . 007404
Rodriguez-Boette, Taryn 047609
Rodríguez-Boette, Taryn 047611
Rodríguez Culebras, Dr. Ramón . . . 035838
Rodríguez de Montes, María Luisa 007385
Rodríguez del Camino, Marco 049464
Rodríguez Delucchi, Jorge 041524
Rodríguez Martín, Aurora 035378
Rodriguez-Mendoza, Amalia 041920
Rodríguez Ruza, Concepciòn 035139
Rodriquez, Jennie 047872
Rodríquez Culebras, Ramón 036062
Rodway, Em 043097
Röber, Dr. Ralph 018374
Röber, Wolf-Dieter 017428
Röck, Erwin 002477
Rödel, Klaus 008866
Roeder, Corinna 019469
Röder, Heinz 020934
Roeder, Paul 043216
Röder, Dr. Sabine 018399
Rödger, Ralf 015699
Rödiger-Diruf, Prof. Dr. Erika 018172
Röding, Lutz 016267
Roegiers, Prof. Dr. Jan 003579
Röhl, Johannes 015665
Roehmer, Dr. Marion 019326
Röhr, Angelika 003017
Röhrer-Ertl, Dr. Dr. O. 019032
Röhrig, Prof. Dr. Dr. Floridus 002156
Röhring, Micha 017962
Roelfsema-Hummel, Chris 047032
Roelink, Géke 029180
Röllig, Robert 019098
Roeloffs, Abigail 042284
Roelofs, Dr. P. 029961
Römer, Kurt 001727
Römer, Neria 037286
Römer, Stefan 019073, 053313
Römhild, Michael 017917
Roensch, Fred 045408
Röper, Dr. Martin 020244
Rösch, Dr. Mathias 019043
Röscher, Angela 017015
Roese, Ronnie L. 043264
Roesink, Macha 029141
Röske, Dr. Thomas 017835
Roesler, Henry E. 045976
Rösner, Dr. Corinna 019096
Rössl, Dr. Joachim 002515, 002819
Rößler, Dr. Hans 019230
Rössler, Heiner 018896
Rössler, Prof. Leopold 002906
Rössler, Dr. R. 016560
Roest-den Hartogh, G.C. 029744
Röver-Kann, Dr. Anne 016418
Roffia, Dr. Elisabetta 024029, 025904
Rogalski, Dr. Andrzej 037289
Rogdeberg, Guttorm A. 031040
Rogé, Monique 015033
Roger, Will 047855
Rogers, Dianne 049275
Rogers, Floretta 041800
Rogers, James 043655
Rogers, James A. 049110
Rogers, James R. 043891
Rogers, June 046266
Rogers, Malcolm 042334
Rogers, Patricia 043155
Rogers, Peggy 043657
Rogers, Philippa 001640
Rogers, Rachael 038457
Rogers, Richard 046281
Rogers, Robert 043684
Rogers, Roy 048784
Rogers jr, Roy Dusty 042388
Rogers, Ted 048270
Rogers, Dr. T.L. 005582
Rogers-Barnett, Cheryl 048784
Rogerson, J.-C. 039277
Rogerson, L. 040668
Rogge, Marc 003823, 003874
Rogger, Prof. Iginio 026110
Roggero, Prof. Mario Federico 023795
Roggero, Sue 039647
Roggmann, Bettina 015449
Roggow, B. 020970, 020971
Rogić, Milena 007788
Rogiest, Peter 003163
Rogin, Ned 043733
Rogina, Bojana 034485
Rogl, Rudolf 001872
Roglán-Kelly, Dr. Mark 043273
Rogne, Odd 031253
Rogozińska, Ewa 031819
Roh, Michael 043077
Roháček, Dr. Jindřich 008548
Rohan, Antoinette Duchesse de . . 012168
Rohde-Hehr, Patricia 017715
Rohdt, Erwin 015798
Rohlfs, Stefan 017025
Rohner, John R. 042354
Rohner, Rudolf 037183, 037184
Rohr, Dr. Gerlinde 018593, 018594
Rohrbach, John 044002
Rohrer, Norbert 037596
Rohrer, Susan 046673
Rohsmann, Dr. Arnulf 002146
Rohwer, Dr. Sievert 048075
Roig Toqués, Francisco 036049
Roige, Annabella 046990
Roiß, Dr. Hubert . . . 003050, 003051, 003052, 003055
Roitman, Dr. Adolfo D. 022979
Rojanova, Galina Iljinična 033223
Rojas de Moreno, María Eugenia . . 007632
Rojas Iragorri, Ximena 007428
Rojas Toro, Elizabeth 003923
Rojas y Cruzat, Oscar M. de 007900
Rojo Dominguez, Ana Cristina 035015
Rola, Stefan 032203
Roland, Dr. Berthold 015657
Roland, Debbie U. 047691
Roland, Greg 044324
Roland, Heather 043101
Roley, Scott 044722
Roll, Jarrod 042489
Roll, Kempton 041792
Rolla, Maureen 047043
Rolland, C. 011154
Rollenitz, Maria 002131
Roller, Dr. Hans-Ulrich 020636
Roller, Scott 045595
Roller, Dr. Stefan 020534
Rolley, Jean-Pierre 010333
Rollings, James R. 049093
Rollins, Avon W. 045032
Rollins, Fred H. 048994
Rollins, Ken 045173
Rolo Fajardo jr., Gaudioso 031785
Roloff, Prof. Dr. A. 020433
Romagnoli, Dr. Emilio 024867
Romagnoli, Martha Beatriz 000665
Romagnoli, Prof. Myriam Ruth . . . 000508
Romagnolo, Dr. Antonio 025615
Roman, Cynthia 044463
Román, Enrique 000315
Román Berrelleza, Juan Alberto . . 028494
Roman de Zurek, Teresita 007476
Romanelli, Prof. Giandomenico . . . 026228, 026229, 026230, 026232, 026238, 026243, 026245, 026246, 026254, 026262
Romanenko, Maja Petrovna 033541
Romanenko, Vera Vladimirovna . . . 033019
Romaniuc, Elvira 032872
Romanko, Jennifer 006798
Romano, Simona 024975
Romano, Socorro 035155
Romanova, Margarita Nikolevna . . 034001
Romanova, Raisa Michajlovna . . . 033059
Romanowska, Marta 032060
Romard, Judith 005802
Romdhane, Khaled Ben 037946
Romeo, Paolo 024683
Rømer Sandberg, Ole 030868
Romero, Dr. Edgardo J. 000157
Romero, Mark 047154
Romero Ardila, Dídimo Ernesto . . . 007523
Romero de Tejada, Pilar 035423
Romero de Torres, Rafael 035116
Roming, Lorenz 020095
Romińska, Elina 032180
Romito, Dr. Matilde 024944, 025070, 025634, 025636, 026321
Rommé, Dr. Barbara 019153
Rommel, Dr. Ludwig 017911
Romney, George 044726
Romney, George G. 044724
Romportlová, Simona 008294
Romsics, Imre 021749
Romualdi, Antonella 024156
Rona, Zeynep 038073
Ronaghan, Allen 005649
Ronald, William 001364
Ronchi, Dr. Benedetto 026099
Roncière, Florence de la 012859
Rončkevičová, Antónia 034428
Róncoli, Mónica 000106
Rondeau, James 042820, 042820
Rondot, Bertrand 013668
Ronfort, J.N. 013563
Ronig, Prof. Dr. Dr. Franz 020478
Ronning, Peggy 045688
Ronowicz, Małgorzata 032122
Ronte, Prof. Dr. Dieter 016329
Roode, I. de 029230
Roodt, Frans 034704
Roohfar, Z. 022628
Rooke, Daru 039955
Rooney, Dr. Brendan 022763
Rooney, Jan 046280
Rooney, Mary 030517
Roos, Dr. Klaus-Dieter 019196
Roosa, Jan 048774
Roose, B. 003281
Roosen, Jean-Paul 011031
Roosevelt, Christopher 045515
Roosing, Jan Jaap 021063, 021064
Root, Deane L. 047046
Root, Margaret 041732
Roots, Gerrard 040118
Roper, Donna K. 046868
Roper, Mark 039032
Ropp, Ann 044865
Ropp, Harry 043509
Roppelt, Dr. Tanja 016528
Ropponen, Liisa 009472
Roque Gameiro, Maria Alzira 032662
Roques, Thierry 011134
Roquette-Gept, Marie-Christine . . 014652
Rorem, Ned 046281
Rorschach, Kimerly 042838
Rosa, Jocelyn R. de la 031647
Rosa, Joseph 047043, 047885
Conceição Duarte Rosa, Maria da . 004250
Rosa, Mercedes 004438
Rosales, Felipe 031630
Rosales Huatuco, Dr. Odón 031455
Rosales Vergas, Manuel 028476
Rosanbo, Richard de 012419
Rosas de Silva Rebelo, Dr. Margarida 032680
Rosasco, Betsy 047240
Rosberg, Ingemar 036221
Rose, Ben 048980
Rose, Gilles 011338
Rose, Mary 045928
Rose, Dr. Murray 038643
Rose, Rebecca 047421
Rose, Sally 039372, 039373
Rose, Susan 006148
Rose, Wilhelm 015938

Roselli, Bart A. 048044
Roselli, David L. 043542
Roselló, Núria 036055
Rosemann, Günther 018673
Rosemann, Thomas 037777
Rosen, Steven W. 042047
Rosenbaum, Joan 046352
Rosenbeck, Dr. Hans 015954
Rosenberg, Dr. H.I. 005201
Rosenberger, Pat 042953
Rosenblattl, Christina 001783
Rosenbleeth, Herb 048928
Rosenblum, Amy 045814
Rosenblum, Robert 046404
Rosenbluth, Betsy 042524
Rosendahl, Paul 008845
Roseneck, Prof. Dr. Reinhard 017487
Rosenfeld, Alla 046206
Rosenfield, Jamie 046373
Rosenfield Lafo, Rachel 045297
Rosengren, Kerstin 036287
Rosenkranc, Milan 008347
Rosenkrantz, Baron Erik Christian 008929
Rosenmeier, Edith Marie 009117
Rosenquist, Perry E. 043226
Rosenstock, F. 015427
Rosensweig, Larry 043383
Rosenthal, Deborah 048410
Rosenthal, Dina R. 048335
Rosenthal, Ellen 043410
Rosenthal, Mark 046404
Rosentrater, Jil 044302
Rosero Solarte, Luciano 007570
Rosetti, Evelyn 046313
Rosewitz, Mindy 043952
Rosher, Fiona 039701
Rosiak, Andrzej 032491, 032565
Rosiek, Barbara 032569
Rosing, Emil 021544
Rosing, M. 008966
Rosini, Prof. Dr. Corrado 023237
Rosinski, Dr. Rosa 016233
Rosiny, Dr. Claudia 036928
Rosito, Massimiliano G. 024165
Rosjat, Dr. Erika 015902
Rośkiewicz, Wiesław 032355
Rosljakov, Sergij Mykolajovič 038363
Rosoff, Susan 046719
Ross, Dr. Cathy 040230
Ross, David A. 043892
Ross, Donald A. 001533
Ross, Dugald Alexander 039826, 041080
Ross, Ian D. 005165
Ross, Jan 006736
Ross, Jay 048654
Ross, Jerry 043747
Ross, Dr. J.P. 044103
Ross, Judy 044701
Ross, Mari B. 041971
Ross, Marian 048584
Ross, Martin J.E. 005473
Ross, Phill 044563
Ross, Richard 046824
Ross, Sandria B. 041740
Ross, Stewart 000951
Ross, Wendy 044935
Ross Noble, R. 040580
Rossacher, Walter 001943
Rossellini, Laurence 012952
Rosser, Merlin 006533
Rosset-Magnat, Chantal 014094
Rossetti, Evelyn 046378
Rossetti de Scander, Dr. Antonio 026143
Rossi, Dr. Francesco 023381
Rossi, Guido 024301
Rossi, John S. 043825
Rossi, Rochelle 042592
Rossiter, Shannon 045008
Rossolimo, Dr. Olga L. 033532
Rostami 022629
Rostek, Charlotte 039716
Rostek, L. 001561
Rostholm, Hans 008905
Rostworowska, Dr. Magdalena 032517
Rosu, Georgeta 032813
Roszko, Grzegorz 031942
Rota, Anna Francesca 023851
Rota, Dr. Laura 023638
Rotaru, Georgeta Monica 032888
Roten, Hortensia von 037784
Roth, André 011714
Roth, Dan 041837
Roth, Eric 046268
Roth, Flemming 008876
Roth, Gary G. 047312
Roth, John 000971, 042456
Roth, Jules 013368
Roth, Linda H. 044463
Roth, Prof. Dr. Martin 016816
Roth, Dr. Michael 016109
Roth, Dr. Peter 034411
Roth, Ronald C. 047347
Roth, Dr. Ursula 016832
Roth-Oberth, Dr. Erna 017112
Rothe-Wörner, Heidrun 017379
Rothen, Heidi 037302
Rothenberger, Manfred 019360
Rotheneder, Martin 002307
Rothermel, Barbara 045525
Rothfuss, Joan 045922
Rothkopf, Katherine 041969
Rothove, Billi R.S. 044157
Roths, Jaylene 046055, 046056, 048221
Rothschild, Eric de 013687
Rothschild, Baroness Philippine de 013755
Rotkale, Rita 027732
Rotonda-McCord, Lisa 046263
Rotovnik, Mitja 034480
Rotsart, John A. 047836
Rott, Dr. Herbert W. 019038
Rottermund, Prof. Andrzej 032484
Røtting, Dorrit 009016
Rottmann, Lee 047674
Rouchaud, Alain 014009
Roughley, Dr. R.E. 006849
Rouijel, Souad 029035
Roullot, Cédric 014551
Roulston, Peggy 045607
Roumm, David L. 044990
Rountree, Robin K. 048414
Rouquereol, N. 010550
Rouquet, Chantal 015047, 015052, 015053, 015054
Roura Güibas, Gabriel 035238
Roure, Patrick 012695
Rourke, Ralph 042437
Rouse, Virginia 043096
Rousseau, Marshall 047719
Roussel, Dominique 014814, 015289
Roussel, Louis 012861, 014783
Rousselot, Dr. Jean-Loup 019122
Rousset-Rouard, Yves 013010
Roussia, Pierre 012230
Roussier, François 015331
Routhier, Nathalie 005121
Routledge, M.A. 041163
Roux, Bertrand 011442, 014528
Roux, Jean-Pierre 011773, 011999
Roux, Nathalie 011397
Rovati, Clementina 025143
Rovine, Victoria 044768
Rowan, Edward 045619
Rowe, Alan L. 030560
Rowe, Ann 005209
Rowe, Ann P. 048948
Rowe, Barbara 049212
Rowe, C. 034703
Rowe, Donald 046668
Rowe, Dorothy 048172
Rowe, M. Jessica 043424
Rowe, Matthew 039366
Rowe, Michael 041355
Rowe, Timothy 041936
Rowe-Shields, Michele 048003
Rowinski, Dr. Stanislaw 017715
Rowland, Rodney 047191
Rowland Jones, Mark 038710, 041112
Rowles, H.E. 040614
Rowley, Dean 041865
Rowley, Matthew 046978
Rowley, Roger H.D. 047283
Rowold, Kathleen L. 042262
Rowsell, Wayde 006382
Rox-Schulz, Heinz 019958
Roxas Lim, Prof. Aurora 031770
Roxburghe, Duke of 039841
Roy, Dr. Archana 022215
Roy, Dr. Ashok 040241
Roy, Carolyn 047191
Roy, David T. 038559
Roy, Jan-Bernard 013363
Roy, Kenneth J. 046162
Roy, Nathalie 014125
Roy, Noëlle 013730
Royce, Bill 045096
Royce, Ralph 044134
Royer, Claude 012253
Royle, Ted 039045
Rozanov, Aleksej Jurjevič 033515
Rozenberg, Dr. Silvia 022974
Rozendaal, Prof. A. 034752
Rozenfeld, Boris Matveevič 033274
Rozewicz, Beverly L. 044504
Rozko, Laurie 047362
Rozłowski, Tadeusz 031992
Roznoy, Cynthia 048316
Rózsa, Gyula 021691
Rozsošyns'ka, Nina Leonidivna 038295
Rozzo, Dr. Ugo 026095
Rúa, Rosa Edith 007590
Ruas dos Santos, Dr. Margarida 032635
Rub, Timothy 042919
Ruban, Nikolaj Ivanovič 033080
Rubel, William 047958
Ruben, Bärbel 016065
Ruben Cuñeo, Dr. Nestor 000638
Rubidge, Prof. Bruce 034643
Rubin, Jane 046352
Rubin, Jean-François 037384
Rubin, Robert S. 042458
Rubinstein, Adam 047324
Rubinstein, Ernest 046414
Rubio, J. David 007511
Rubio Pediata, Luis 036120
Rubio Sánchez, Pedro 028235
Rucellai, Oliva 025873
Ruch, Pam 047238
Rucka, Barbara 032155
Ruckel, Jay G. 046337
Rucker, Dr. Henrike 020781
Rucker, Ken 048180
Ruckstuhl, Dieter 037108
Ruczynski, F.C.K. 029350
Ruda, M. 003951
Rudaz, Patrick 037009
Rudd, Karen 040947
Rudd, Robert 043710
Rudd, Shirley J. 046861
Ruddlesden, C. 039211
Ruddock, Joanna 039028
Rudi, Dr. Thomas 018572
Rudigier, Dr. Andreas 001888, 002657
Rudin, Vladimir Vasiljevič 033896
Rudisill, Horace F. 044468
Rudisill, Dr. Richard 047973, 047975
Rudkin, David J. 039069
Rudman, Karen 029094
Rudnik, Galina Anatolevna 033871
Rudolp, Dr. Andrea 019589
Rudolph, Beth 041626
Rudolph, Jeffrey N. 045414
Rudolph, Johanna 019691
Rudolph, Ulrich 017311
Rudzińska, Wanda M. 032425
Rübesam, Manfred 018587
Rücker, Dr. Thomas 002561
Rückert, Dr. Birgit 019969
Rückert, Hans 015446
Rueda, Horacio 009254
Rüdel, Dr. Holger 020040, 020041
Rüdiger, Bernd J. 017450
Ruedin, Pascal 037564
Rüede, Erich 037615
Rüger, Axel 040241
Ruegg, Dr. François 037097
Rühl, Karin 017209
Rühlig, Cornelia 018980, 018981
Rühmer, Erich 017977
Rührl, Helmut 016403
Rührnschopf, Elfriede 002862
Ruell, David 041808
Rünger, Dr. Gabriele 017094
Rürup, Prof. Dr. Reinhard 016184
Ruesch, Carol 049376
Rüschoff-Thale, Dr. Barbara 017894
Ruess, Andreas 015788, 015789
Rueß, Dr. Karl-Heinz 017445, 017446, 017451, 017452
Rüth, Dr. Uwe 018852
Rütsche, Dr. Claudia 037775
Ruette, Monique de 003353
Rütti, Beat 036863
Ruf, A. 018160
Ruf, Beatrix 037776
Ruf, Peter 018702, 018706
Ruf, Susanne 020365
Rufe, Laurie J. 047554
Ruff, Eric J. 006889
Ruff, Joshua 048377
Ruff, T.J. 041365
Ruffo, Joseph M. 045302
Ruggeri, Prof. Alessandro 023434
Ruggeri Augusti, Dr. Adriana 026244
Ruggiero, Dr. Laurence J. 049260
Rugoff, Ralph 046592, 047850
Rugsveen, Magne 030822
Rugunanau, S. 034629
Rugus, Dot 047420
Ruhe, Rikke 009000
Ruhl, Erwin 017881
Ruhl, Hans-Eberhard 016648
Ruhl, Horst 020708
Ruhlig-Lühnen, Dagmar 018058
Ruhnke, Steven 043971
Ruhstaller, Tod 048371
Ruivo, José 032607
Ruiz, Aureli 035698
Ruíz, Dimas Fernández-Galiano 035264
Ruiz, Jauier Luna 028711
Ruíz, Leticia 035429
Ruiz de Azua Murua, Asun 036094
Ruiz-Martinez, José D. 021538
Ruiz Sastre, Elena 035163
Ruiz-Torres, Maricarmen 046694
Rukavina, Vjeročka 007849
Ruley, Dennis 047541
Rulíšek, Dr. Hynek 008372
Rulle, Amy 048631
Rum, Piera 025391
Rumbach, Erseline 049125
Rumbaugh, Catherine 047637
Rumbaugh, Darlene 047001
Rumi, Satoh 027170
Rumjanceva, Valentina Pavlovna 033672
Rumly, Katrina 001326
Rummel, Dr. Michael 015616
Rummel, Dr. Ralf 016382
Rump, Elisabeth 042691
Rump, Elizabeth 047247
Rump, Dr. Oliver 017714
Rumpca, Ronette 047018
Rumrill, Alan F. 044945
Rumsby, J.H. 039782
Runde, Dr. Sabine 017183
Rundhovde, Eric 030762
Rundle, Stella 003949
Rundqvist, Dmitry V. 033398
Runey, Dennis I. 049277
Runia, E. 029434
Runte, Markus 019552
Runton, Bourke A. 048636
Runyon, Carol 045196

Ruossr, Dr. Mylène 037784
Rupert, Dr. Manfred 002133
Rupert Enriquez, Carola 041955
Rupf, Hans-Jürgen 020132
Rupley, Kathleen 047398
Rupp, Jane E. 045685
Ruppe, Dr. Harry O. 017112
Rupprecht, Dr. Klaus 015880
Rupprechter, Hanns-Michael 020370, 053568
Ruprechtsberger, Prof. Dr. Erwin M. 002252
Ruseckaitė, Aldona 027847
Rusev, Rusi 004627, 004847
Rush, Martin 040174
Rush, Dr. Michael 045120
Rushton, Ray 040211
Rusibaev, D.S. 049406
Rusina, Prof. Ivan 034337
Rusinová, Dr. Zora 034337
Ruske, Wolfgang 015804
Ruskule, Skaidrite 027741
Rusnell, Wesley A. 047554
Russe, Christel 017372
Russel, Jack 000795
Russell, Barry 005076
Russell, Brenda 005448
Russell, Brian J. 039609
Russell, Prof. Bruce 039894
Russell, Douglas 043175
Russell, J. Fiona 046546
Russell, John I. 042445
Russell, Kentdur 049306
Russell, Laurence J. 045861
Russell, Marilyn M. 047043
Russell, Nancy J. 045071
Russell, Pamela 043848
Russell, Paul 042890
Russell, Willie 048083
Russell Howe, Dr. Stanley 042178
Russi, Graciela 000341
Russo, Prof. Antonio 024753, 024762
Russo, Dr. Carmelo 023763
Russo, Dick 049290
Russo, Pam 049290
Russo, Ralph 045596
Russo de Fontela, Adriana 000554
Rust, Sandra 002934
Rust, Wilfried W. H. 043942
Rustichelli, Arlette 036860
Rustige, Rona 005092
Ruszczyc, Ferdynand B. 032456
Ruszel, Dr. Krzysztof 032300
Ruta Serafini, Dr. Angela 024059
Rutberg, Carl 048326
Ruthensteiner, Dr. B. 019132
Rutherford, Jessica 038848, 038852
Rutherford Conrad, Marth 005123
Rutherford Conrad, Martha 006077
Rutishauser, Werner 037524
Rutkowski, Czesław 032314
Rutledge, Ann 043026
Rutsch, Franz 019597
Rutte, Helgard 020053
Rutter, A. 039688
Rutter, Michael 005668
Rutter, Mike 039062
Ruttinger, Jacquelyn 044897
Ruttner, Nancy 047053
Ruus, Tina 042910
Ruuska, Aulis 010190
Ruy Van Beest Holle, C.J. du 030110
Ruyssinck, Micheline 003353
Ružić, Ivan 007849
Ruzo, Victor 037337
Rvijn, Benoît 003282
Ryan, Dana 044821
Ryan, Dr. E. 043911
Ryan, Graham 001344
Ryan, Hilary 040778
Ryan, Jack Dingo 046148
Ryan, Kay 048399
Ryan, Lynne 042097
Ryan, Michael 022734
Ryan, Paul 048343
Ryan, Robert 042307
Ryan, Steven P. 047354
Ryan, Thomas 045432
Ryan, Thomas R. 045147
Ryazonova, T.P. 027641
Ryba, Kurt 025109
Rybakov, Ivan Alekseevič 032972
Rybakova, Tamara Viktorovna 033427
Rybka, Walter P. 043724
Rybnikova, Larisa 033414
Rychener, Dr. Jürg 036863
Rychlik, Dr. Otmar 002380
Rychliková, Marie 008730
Rychtarik, John 042449
Ryckman, Heather 006055
Rycquart, Walter 003262, 003263, 003264, 003265, 003266, 003267, 003268, 003269, 003270, 003273, 003276, 003280, 003283
Rydel, Maria 032068
Ryder, Michael J. 040238
Rydergård, Evy 036511
Rydzewski, Dr. Jacek 032034, 032035
Rylance, Mark 040287
Ryland, James 045971
Rylands, Philip 026264
Rymkuß, Silke 016847
Rynd, Chase 046147
Rynierse, H. 029558
Ryol, Thae Pyong 027441
Ryšánková, Dr. Milada 008725
Rysin, Oleksandr Mykolajovyč 038367
Ryska, Norbert 019549
Rystedt, Prof. Eva 036445
Ryusawa, Aya 026887
Ryzdynski, Mark 044509
Ryžov, Stanislav 038389
Ryžova, Tamara Alaksandrovna 033561
Ryžova, Tamara Aleksandrovna 033553
Rzepecka, Mirosława 032207
Rzepiela, Urzula 032258
Rzeszotarski, Jan 032316
Sá Marques, Ana Rita 032650
Saabye, Marianne 008968
Saadé, William 010411, 010413
Saage, Wallace 044640
Saager-Bourret, Stephanie 047081, 047082
Saal, Agnès 013559
Saal, Dr. Wolfgang 018790
Saalmann, Ute 016858
Saar, A. 009403
Saaret, Tarmo 009398, 009408
Saarimaa, Hanna-Maija 009887
Saarinen, Jarmo 010162
Saarist, Tiiu 009385
Saarnio, Robert 047742
Saathoff, Joachim 019578
Saatsi, Niko 009915
Šabalin, Rostislav Viktorovič 033646
Sabaté, Antonio 036042
Sabaté i Piqué, Gemma 036022
Sabatini, L. 003595
Sabin, Carleen 045846
Sabin, Owen 045846
Sabina, Choclán 035334
Sabloff, Dr. Jeremy 046993
Sabogal, Bernardo 007498
Sabolic, Prof. Dubravka 007820
Sabotinova, Donka 004830
Sabran-Ponteves, E. Comte de 013946
Sabroe, Charlotte 009115
Šabunts, Natalja 038202
Sacarés Mas, Antoni 035881
Sacco, Louise R. 043361
Saccocci, Prof. Andrea 025053
Šachalova, Natalja Vladimirovna 033402
Sachanbiński, Prof. Michał 032521
Sachs, Charles L. 042465
Sachs, Samuel 046333
Sachs, Sid 046985
Sachse, Jutta 018609
Sack, Dr. Birgit 016788
Sack, Georg 020867
Sackett, Margot Magee 006323
Sackl, Dr. Peter 001938
Sackstetter, Susanna 016600
Sada, Ricardo J. 035306
Sadinsky, Rachael 045266
Sadion, Martine 011713
Sadjukov, Nikolaj I. 033061
Sadler, Bill 047914
Sadler, Dr. Donna 043348
Sadler, Patsy 046860
Sádlo, Dr. Václav 008519
Sadok, Nedjah 000063
Sadowski, Władysław 032039
Al-Saeed, Susan 031346
Saeed, Tahir 031376
Säkkinen, Senja 009948
Sæland, Frode 030946
Sälejoki-Hiekkanen, Leena 009583
Sänger, Dr. Reinhard 018158
Sæther, Per 030719
Sæthre, Ellen 031231
Sættem, Nils 008943
Saeverud, Dag H. 031198
Safarnia, P. 022577
Saffiotti Dale, Maria 045589
Safford, Pete 043336
Safin, Françoise 003592
Safina, Zulfira Midechatovna 033538
Šafr, Pavel 008319
Safronova, V.V. 033608
Safsafi, Nourddine 029035
Saft, Marcia 046352
Saganic, Livio 045583
Sagar, Scott 043074, 049185
Sagdalen, Betty Jo 044995
Sagebiel, Chris 047362
Sagel, Dietmar 019207
Sager, Judy 044003
Saghaar-Bessiére, Francoise 014459
Saghi, Mohamed 029034
Sagmeister, Dr. Rudolf 001762
Sagov, Magomet Zakrievič 033549
Sagrera, Enric 035237
Sagristà, Ferran 036055
Saheki, Ryoken 026556
Sahlstrand, James 043673
Sahm, Helena 000860
Said, Sanib 027986
Sailard, Olivier 013638
Sailer, Andreas 002636
Sain, Annette J. 047109
Saines, Chris 030431
Sainio, Tuulu 010160
Sainsbury, Derek 039458
Saint-Affrique, Olga de 012329
Saint-Bris, Jean 010359
Saint Hippolyte, Mary 048208
Saint-Maur, P. de 013692
Saint-Pierre, Adrienne 043786
Saint-Pierre, François 012583
Saint-Pol, Pierre P. 011656
Saint Romain, P.W. 047075
Sainte-Fare-Garnot, Nicolas 013703
Sáinz González, Elena 028442
Saire, Marcel 011877
Saisí, Enrique 000460
Saissac, Prof. Rosa A. 000512
Saito, Osamu 026911
Saji, Nobutada 027246
Sakaeva, Guzel Rinatovna 033246
Sakai, Tadayasu 026501
Sakai, Tetsuo 026465, 027294
Sakai, Dr. Toshihiro 027005
Sakai, Yasuo 027031
Sakamoto, Bishop 027113
Sakari, Marja 009542
Sakata, Toshitaka 026866
Sakazume, Hideichi 027237
Sakli, Dr. Mourad 037975
Sakmirda, Marta 020070
Šakova, Marjana Kušbievna 033542
Sakrausky, Oskar 001869
Sakwerda, Jan 032544
Sala, Susan M. 031659
Salabert, Patricia 016426
Salachova, P.Ch. 034010
Sălăjean, Ioan 032818
Salajić, Prof. Silvija 007820
Salameh, Khader 022958
Salamon, Nándor 021900
Salas, Jaime de 035955
Salas Vázquez, Eduardo 035410
Salatino, Kevin 045441
Salaverria, Ana 035149
Salazar, Ernesto 009249
Salazar, Evangeline 048721
Salazar, Lucila A. 031753
Salazar Soto, José Aníbal 007389, 007390
Salcedo Zambrano, Alonso 007571
Salcher, Hubert 003046
Salcher, Johann 002282
Salchli, Jacqueline 037457
Saldan, Kathryn 046941
Salden, Hubert 002008
Saldo, Josip Ante 007794
Šale, Majda 007696
Salé, Marie-Pierre 013678
Saleh, Ali Ibrahim 009298
Salehi, M. 022638
Salerno, Osvaldo 031439
Sales Marques, José Luís de 007182
Saletić, Momčilo 034188
Saletti, Prof. Cesare 025140
Salgo, Nicolos 047146
Salib, Dr. Mahar 009294
Saliga, Pauline 042828
Saliger, Dr. Arthur 002969, 002970
Saliklis, Ruta 041657, 043591
Salin, Anne-Maj 010200, 010204
Salina, Xavier 037342
Salisbury, Joyce 046064
Salisbury, R.D.N. 041028
Salisbury, Ruth 040942
Salje, Prof. Dr. Beate 016193
Salkin, Asen 004711
Salkoranta, Marja 009895, 010176
Sall, Joan C. 046976
Salleh, Dr. Badriyah B.H. 027993, 027998, 027999, 028000, 028002, 028003
Salleh, Dr. Badriyat B.H. 028001
Sallen, Sheila 043947
Sallinen, Kari 010217
Salmen, Brigitte 019168
Salmen, Nora 043092
Salmi, Lyle 043351
Salmon, Béatrice 013638, 013645, 013668, 013724
Salmon, Irit 022983
Salmon, Patricia 048338
Salmona, Paul 013685
Salmona, Riccardo 046283, 046329
Salmons-Perez, Carl 048012
Salo, B.M. 033389
Salo, Prof. J. 010163
Salomatin, A.V. 033502
Salome, Elizabeth 044731
Salomé, Laurent 014124, 014126, 014131
Salomeia, Paul 032874
Salomon, Joel 047503
Salomón Zuebi, Alex Faruk 031572
Salomone, Mario R. 000148
Salonen, Jouni 009975
Saloniemi, Marjo-Riita 010118
Salsi, Dr. Claudio 024689, 024691, 024694
Saltamanikas, P. 021417
Salter, Ann C. 047482
Saltiel, Solita 021494
Salton, Jenny 039782
Saltonstall, Patrick 045044
Salu, Luc 003161
Salus, Ernst R. 022997
Saluz, Prof. Eduard 017308
Salvador, Fred 005243
Salvador, Josep 035976
Salvador, Mari Lyn 041618

Salvador Zazurca, Alejandro 036099, 036100, 036113, 036114
Salvatierra, Julio 036062
Salvator, Markus 001723
Salvatore, Ferraro 023122
Salvatori, Prof. Franco 025513
Salven, Irmeli 009516
Salvesen, Ole Bjørn 031132
Salveson, Doug 043844
Salvi, Donato 037489
Salvig, Jakob 009127
Salvioni, Mario Casanova 036915
Salwiński, Jacek 032049
Salzgeber, Christoph 037436
Salzman, Alexej 008508
Salzmann, Prof. Dr. Dieter 019138
Samac, Dr. Šime 007821
Samaniego, Lydia 031756, 031761
Samarati, Dr. Luigi 024518
Samardžić, Nadežda 034172
Samek, Tomasz 019153
Sameli-Erne, Doris 037190
Sameshima, Satoru 026669
Sami-Azar, Dr. A.R. 022620
Samietz, Rainer 017492
Saminger, Herbert 002817
Sammallahti, Leena 009989
Sammer, Dr. Alfred 002966
Samochvalova, Ljudmila Nikolaevna 033262
Samodurov, Jurij Vadimovič 033449
Samon, Josep 036055
Samoy, Antenor R. 031624
Sampaio, Heli de Almeida 004452
Sampaolo, Prof. Valeria 024894
Sampil, Mamadou 021592
Sampson, Michael 043690
Samson, Dr. Bill 039309
Samson, Ditas R. 031697
Samson, Fr. Antonio S. 031644
Samson, James 030618
Samson, Louise 043929
Samson, Rémy 011309
Samsonova, Ėlvira Aleksandrovna . 033317
Samuels, Clifford 047682
Samuels, Philip 047682
Samuelson, Laura 046494
Samyn, John 003851
San Agustin, Leonora P. 031626
San Carlos, Duque de 035440
San Diego, Rodolfo 031749
San Martín, Luis Marín de 036031
San Quirce, Sylvie 012124
Sana, Costantino 023176
Sanborn, Colin J. 042940
Sanborn, Michael 049200
Sanchez, Artero 004535
Sanchez, Basilio 004534
Sanchez, Maria José 035808
Sánchez, Osvaldo 028455
Sanchez, Roger 047337
Sánchez, Tomás 035405
Sánchez Aguilera, Marco 006912
Sánchez de Velandia, Myriam 007381
Sánchez Fuertes, Caayetano 034853
Sanchez Garcia, Javier 028570
Sánchez Hernández, Américo 028512
Sánchez Mastranzo, Nazario A. . . . 028761
Sánchez Murguía, Socorro 028171
Sánchez Peña, José Miguel 035021
Sánchez Pérez, Luz María 028483
Sánchez Ramírez, Angeles 036117
Sánchez Recio, Miguel Angel 035391, 035392
Sánchez Rodríguez, Marciano 035745
Sánchez Ruiz, José Fernando 034805
Sánchez Trujillano, Teresa 035361
Sanchidrián, Rafael Ruiz 035414
Sanchis, Frank Emile 046368
Sanclemente Girón, Américo Alfonso 007507, 007508
Sand, Christiane 012232
Sand, Gabriele 017769
Sand, Karl 002450
Sand, Viki 046925
Sandahl, Jette 036306
Sandberg, Anja 010178
Sandberg, Fredrik 036265
Sandbichler, Veronika 002094
Sandbichler, Dr. Veronika 002934
Sandell, Stephen 045912
Sanden, Jarle 031028, 031030
Sander, Dr. Antje 018121, 018122
Sander, Dr. Birgit 017170
Sander, Dr. Dietulf 018579
Sander, E. 017385
Sander, Helmut 017715
Sander, Dr. Jochen 017195
Sanders, Dr. Albert E. 042728
Sanders, Boyd 048679
Sanders, G. 029256
Sanders, James 044721
Sanders, Jennifer 001575
Sanders, Mildred 049005
Sanders, William A. 043695
Sanderson, Cecil 043895
Sanderson, Dr. Dewey D. 044683
Sanderson, Eleonore P. 047189
Sanderson, R. 006465
Sanderson, Sue 049338
Sandheinrich, Bernard 047675
Sandkühler, Prof. Dr. St. 019249
Sandlofer, Michael 042442
Sandmann, Oskar 017899
Sandmeyer, Marilyn 046046
Sandmo, Sigurd S. 030768
Šandová, Dr. Miroslava . . . 008349, 008668
Sandoval, Josefina de 049447
Sandoval, Raquel 007397
Sandoval, Sonia 009246
Sandrini, Dr. Francesca 025115
Sandrock, Dr. Oliver 016638
Sandström, Birgitta 036486
Sandström, Paul 009924
Sandstrom, Ake 036345
Sandu, Ion 032767
Sandvoß, Hans-Rainer 016047
Sandweiss, Eric 047670
Saner, Gerhard 037612
Sanfelice di Bagnoli, Fabio 025475
Sanford, Dr. Beverly S. 049257
Sanftner, Phyllis 046038
Sangalang, Debbie 031744
Sangl, Dr. Sigrid 019039
Sangmanee, Kitti Cha 013689
Sangster, Gary 041976
Sanguinetti, María Isabel 000487
Sangvichien, Dr. Sanjai 037874
Sangvichien, Prof. Sood M.D. 037891
Sangwill, Richard 036252
Sani, Michele 024869
Sanita, Dennis 044715
Sankowski, Janusz 032447
Sanna, Maria Antonia 025999
Sannibale, Dr. Maurizio . . . 049422, 049425
Sano, Dr. Emily J. 047853
Sans, Bartolomé 034852
Sans, Jérôme 013734
Sansano Costa, Lina 035799
Sansom, Andrew 043642, 044242, 044794, 047228, 049071
Santa Ana Alvárez Ossorio, Florencio de 035436
Santa Elena, Barrio 007517
Santaca, Dr. Susanna 009530
Santamaria, Prof. Ulderico 049422
Santamarina, Guillermo 028435
Santana Quintana, Luis Carlos . . . 028437
Santandreu, Edmundo 000198
Santaniello, Giovanni 024947
Santiago, Isabel 032638
Santiago, Mark 041591
Santiago, Mildred 043958
Santiago, Rubio 035968
Santinacci-Boitelle, Françoise 012340
Santini, Roberto Mario 004471
Santis, Jorge 043933
Santomauro, Angelica M. 044391
Santoni, Dr. Vincenzo 023568
Santonja, Josep A. Gisbert 035147
Santonja, Dr. Manuel 035742
Santoro, Geraldine 046408
Santoro, Dr. Paola 024577
Santos, Prof. Eliane Aparecida . . . 004591
Teles Dos Santos, Prof. Dr. Jocelio 004437
Santos, Maria Soares dos . 014843, 014844
Santos, Osmar 041550, 041551
Santos, Turibio 004413
Santos Correia Victor, Ana Paula dos 000099
Santos González, José María 035840
Santos Ramírez, Marco Antonio . . 028949
Santos Sátz Gomes, Ilmo 035137
Santos Simões, Joaquim A. 032619
Santrot, Jacques 013341
Santzevlariz, David 035555
Santzevlàriz, David 035556
Sanucci, Dennis 045010
Sanz, Eduardo 036062
Sanz, Joaquim 035465
Sanz Gamo, Rubí 034792
Sanz Sánchez, Erundino 034895
Sanzi, Dr. Maria Rita 023860
Šapošnikova, Ljudmila Vasiljevna . 033428
Sapouna-Sakellaraki, Dr. Efi 021365
Sarabhai, Gira 021988
Saragoza, Florence 013719
Saraiva da Costa Pecorelli, Carlos . 032611
Saran, P.K. 022141
Saraver, Ida 005627
Sarda, Marie-Anne 010926
Sardella, Filomena 024910
Sardo, Delfin 032628
Sarelius, Seppo 010162
Sargeant, Erich 040095
Sargent, William 047741
Sargsyan, Zaven 000687
Sarholz, Dr. Hans-Jürgen 015693
Sari, Dr. Alireza 022646
Sarie, Pierre 012770
Sariego, Manuel Lucío Julio 007553
Sarioglu, M. Adnan 038022
Sariola, Helmiriitta 009515
Sarkisjan, David A. 033413
Sarl, P.M. 040934, 040935, 040936, 040938, 040939
Sarna, Micheal 042829
Sarosácz, György 021793
Saroyan, Ione 046389
Sarpong, Kwame 021102
Sarrail, Cécile 011121
Sarrazin, Dr. J. 016244
Sarrazin, Dr. Jenny 018737
Sarret, Françoise 012700
Sarsfield, Stanley 039202
Sarteanesi, Prof. Nemo . . . 023893, 023894
Sartes, Minna 010159, 010161
Sarti, Fabiola 025869
Sarto, Pietro 037340
Sartori, Dean 043421
Sartori, Dr. Michel 037245
Sartorio, Matteo 024729
Sartorio Pisani, Dr. Giuseppina . . . 025512
Sartorius, K. 016300
Sartorius, Tara 045995
Saruchanian, Saro 000689
Sarvis, Will 041703
Sas, Adrian 046293
Sasagawa, Takami 026782
Sasaki, Hideaki 026685
Sasaki, Hideya 026831
Sasaki, Masamine 027188
Sasaki, Yoneyuki 026721
Sasano, Takaaki 027032
Sasayama, Kazutoshi 026667
Saskiweicz, Sharon 047553
Şaşmaz, Abdülkadir 037995
Sassen, J.H. 029230
Sasso, Rosalie 043509
Sastri, C.L.N. 022006
Sastry, Dr. V.V. Krishna . . . 022155, 022317
Sasymanov, Y.A. 027640
Sata, Gorī 000020
Sather, Stanley 006763
Sato, Keichi 026694
Sato, Mitsuo 026628
Sato, Naoki 027189
Sato, Takeshi 026422
Sato, Toyozo 026887
Sato, Yoshio 026704
Sato, Yumika 027031
Satoko, Maemura 026606
Satsuma, Masato 027169
Sattelmair, Hartwig 017003
Satterfield, Foad 047922
Satterthwaitt, Dr. Leann 000836
Sattlecker, Dr. Franz 002919, 003001
Sattmann, Dietrich 003017
Satut, Jorge 041520
Satvé Oliván, Enrique 035732
Satyan, M.S. 022128
Satzer, Wolfgang 002189
Saubel, Katherine 042012
Sauceman, Jill 044880
Sauder, Carolyn 041762
Sauer, Dr. Albrecht 016429
Sauer, Daniel 004346
Sauer, Marc 010269
Sauer, Dr. Marina 015466
Sauer, Wilfrid 018012
Sauerborn, Ulrich 015428, 015433
Sauermann, Bernhard 018439
Sauers, Dr. Richard A. 048437
Sauerwein, Herbert 002215
Sauge, Birgitte 031069
Sauge, Brigitte 031069
Saul, Dainiel 005661
Saulieu, Pascal de 011562
Saulnier, Lydwine 014764
Saulsbery, Jeff 042259
Saumade, Jeanine 012117
Saunders, Dr. David 040241
Saunders, Dr. Gail 003089, 003092
Saunders, Kristin 041237
Saunders, P.R. 040949
Saunders, Dr. Rebecca A. 042049
Saunders, Richard 045711
Saunders, Richard H. 045834
Saunders, Stuart 000803
Saunders, Dr. Timothy 019328
Saunier, Bernard 015238
Saurage, Hank 042050
Saury-Serres, Claudine 012659
Sautai, Daniel 011034
Sauter, Pierre 036821
Sauter, Wolfgang 018215
Sautov, Ivan Petrovič 033679, 033681
Sautter, Dr. Heribert 017107
Sauvebeuf, B. de 011681
Savage, Harland 049226
Savage, Pamela 049226
Savage, Paula 030634
Savage, Ronald 041628
Savage, Terry 042317
Savard, Denise 006834
Savary, Lee 041625
Savčenko, Andrej Grigorjevič 033068
Savčenko, Nikolaj Jakovlevič 033944
Savcheva, Dr. Elizabeth 004863
Savel, Irena 034507
Savelja, Oleg 038389
Savelsberg, Dr. Wolfgang 016682
Savery, Suzanne T. 046902, 046903, 046904, 046907, 046909, 046910
Savi, Dr. Dario 026187
Savi, Dario 026188
Savickaja, Ljudmila Aleksandrovna 033316
Savidge, Amanda 041445
Savidis, Prof. G. 021388
Savigny, Marie-Anne 011680
Savill, Rosalind J. 040310
Saville, Ansley 047531

Saville, Jennifer 044598
Saville, R.J. 039930
Saville, Sue 039264
Saving, Barbara 045115
Savini, Thomas M. 046309
Savinič, Irina Borisovna 033841
Savko, Iraida Lvovna 033973
Savolainen, Kari 009782
Sawa, Ryuken 026710
Sawadogo, Alimata 004963
Sawauchi, Takashi 027204
Sawchuk, Barry 005638
Sawchuk, Sherry 046066
Sawdey, Michael P. 041913
Sawicka-Oleksy, Daniela 031875
Sawkins, Annemarie 045898
Sawyer, Carol 047429
Sawyer, Doug 047005
Sawyer, Ed 047599
Sawyer, Kenneth C. 000961
Sawyer, Laura 042277
Sawyer, Sean 042466
Sawyer, Tom 043820
Saxinger, Karl 020644
Saxsburg, Sheila 048641
Sayle, Kristina 038736
Sayler, John G. 045207
Sayunain, Selamat 027974
Sazdova, Katerina 027927
Sazonov, Valerij Petrovič . . 033638, 033640
Sazonova, T.V. 033357
Sbardellati, Max 003044
Sbarge, Robert 041885
Scafetta, Stefano 048943
Scaggs, Tom 048971
Scaglia, Orlando 000426
Scalera, Michelle 047999
Scalera Liaci, Prof. Lidia 023339
Scalia, Dr. Fiorenza 024161
Scalini, Mario 023800
Scalora, Salvatore 048384
Scandola, Dr. Pietro 036950
Scanlon, Scott B. 046748
Scannapieco, Carlos A. . . 000411, 000413, 000414
Scaramella, Julie 049088
Scaramellini, Guido 023852
Scărlătescu, Fl. 032852
Scarpetti, Ivo 024634
Scarpi, Prof. Paolo 025059
Scarratt, David 039399
Scarso Japaze, Eduardo 000238
Scenna, Prof. Desiderato 023865
Ščerbakova, I.T. 033231
Ščerban, Aleksandr Nikolaevič . . . 033035
Schaack, Judy 048242
Schaaf, Ania 003733
Schaaf, Petra 018820
Schaaff, Dr. Holger 018794
Schaafsma, Curtis F. 047973
Schaal, Agnes 042272
Schaar, Dana 042646
Schaar, Elke 018594
Schaatsenberg, W.J.M. 029510
Schachtner, Dr. Sabine 015970
Schachtschneider, Perdita 015503
Schachtsiek, Richard 045294, 046070
Schack von Wittenau, Dr. Clementine Gräfin 019862, 016576
Schächter, Willid 017802
Schädel, Gisela 017690
Schädle, Bernarda 015840
Schädler, Ulrich 037638
Schäfer, Andreas 037578
Schaefer, Barbara 018341
Schäfer, Bernd 017495
Schaefer, Dr. Claudia 016850
Schaefer, D.E. 034661
Schäfer, Dr. Dorit 018169
Schaefer, Elizabeth Meg 043075
Schäfer, Gerd . . . 018085, 018087, 018089
Schäfer, Prof. Dr. H.-P. 017360
Schaefer, Dr. Hartmut 019037
Schäfer, Prof. Dr. Hermann 016335
Schäfer, Julia 018568
Schäfer, Dr. Klaus 015539
Schäfer, Klaus 019017
Schäfer, Leane 017357
Schaefer, Scott 045433
Schaefer, Dr. Stacy 042892
Schäfer, Dr. Wolfgang 020553
Schäffel, Brigitte 002516
Schäffel, Karl 002516
Schaeffer, Astrida 043538
Schäffer, Prof. Dr. Dr. Johann 017771
Schäffer, Rudolf 017737
Schäfke, Dr. Werner 018322
Schael, Alfredo 049474
Schaeps, J. 029852
Schärer, Dr. Martin R. 037675
Schärli, Beatrice 036885
Schaetzel, Désiré 010853
Schafer, Colin 039871
Schaffer, Dale 043253
Schaffer, Dr. Herbert 002399
Schaffer, Dr. Nikolaus 002567
Schaffer-Hartmann, Richard 017742, 017743
Schaffers Bodenhausen, Dr. K. . . . 029427
Schaffgotsch, Marie-Elise Gräfin . . 002375
Schaffner, Arndt R. 020448
Schaffner, Ingrid 046952
Schafhausen, Nicolaus 017165
Schafmeister, Prof. Dr. Maria-Theresia 017522
Schafroth, Colleen 044237
Schagen, C. 029762
Schaible, Larry 048557
Schaible, Silvia 019018
Schaiek, Zvi 023099
Schakel, F. 029135
Schalhorn, Dr. Andreas 016109
Schalke, Prof. Dr. Thomas 015990
Schall, Jan 044924
Schall Agnew, Ellen 045528
Schallenkamp, Kay 043705
Schaller, Anne K. 048246
Schaller, Hydee 041741
Schaller, Irene 037610
Schallert, Dr. Elmar 001758
Schalles, Dr. Hans-Joachim 021034
Schallmayer, Prof. Dr. Egon 015722
Schaltenbrand, Therese 037267
Schaluschke, Anja 018200
Schamberger, Rolf 017295
Schampers, K.J.J. 029653, 029654
Schanche, Kjersti 031317
Schantl, Alexandra 002619
Schantz, Michael W. 046996
Schanz, K.H. 019380
Schaper, Henning 020965
Schapp, Rebecca M. 047953
Schardin, Anne 001303
Scharf, Tamara 039020
Scharfenberg, Bernd 017266
Scharff, Prof. Wolfram 019778
Scharioth, Dr. Babara 019063
Scharioth, Dr. Barbara . . . 019064, 019081
Scharloo, Dr. M. 029660
Scharnowski, Joachim 016074
Scharnweber, Karl 016732
Schaschl, Sabine 037093
Schaschl-Cooper, Sabine 037366
Schatorje, Dr. Jos 030267
Schatteman, Alice 045979
Schatten, Gereon 015830
Schatz, Duane 043651
Schatz, Günther 002319
Schatz, Dr. W. 037795
Schatzmann, Prof. Urs 036934
Schauber, Dr. Gregor 002513
Schauer, Karl 002291
Schauerte, Alfred 018847
Schauerte, Dr. Günter 016175
Schaufel, Shirley 046575
Schaufelberger-Breguet, Simone . 037496
Schaukal, Dr. Barbara 001927
Schaumann, Prof. Walther 002164, 002165
Schaumburg-Lippe, Wolfgang Prinz zu 002242
Schaunaman, Lora 041559
Schaus, Dick 044898
Schawaller, Dr. W. 020364
Schawe, Dr. Martin 019038
Schebesta, Dr. Kurt 002856
Scheck, Klaus Peter 020128
Scheckle, Marian 029084
Scheda, Nicole 019391
Schedin, Pernilla 036387
Schedler, Christian 018944, 018945, 018946, 018947, 018948, 018949
Scheef, Vera 016690
Scheele, Edward 041564
Scheele, Dr. F. 016961
Scheele-Schmidt, Gisela 029086
Scheelen, J. 003504
Scheen, Rolf 031076
Schefcik, Jerry A. 045182
Schefers, Dr. Hermann 018686
Scheffers, Albert A.J. 030234
Scheffler, Ina 016518
Scheffler, Jürgen 018605, 018606
Scheffner, Charles A. 047127
Schegg, Jakob 036941
Scheiber, Johann 002184
Scheiblechner, Margit 036863
Scheicher, Harald 002784
Scheid, Dr. Eva 017963
Scheifer, Joanne 048935
Scheifinger, Otto 002101
Schein, Valentin 034512
Schelde-Jensen, Bodil 008861
Schelfhaut, Andrée 003488
Schellack, Dr. Fritz 020213
Schellenberger, Simona 018368
Schelshorn, E. 020894
Schemm, Jürgen von 018806
Schemmel, Prof. Dr. Bernhard 015881
Schenck, Jean-Luc 014199
Schenck, Marvin 048683
Schenk, Joseph B. 045949
Schenk, L.J.B. 029194
Schenk, P. 029758
Schenk, Ueli 036932
Schenk Freiherr von Stauffenberg, Franz 018507
Schenker, Prof. Christoph 037778
Schepers, Heiner 018662
Schepers, Dr. Wolfgang 017757
Scheppink, Baukje 030349
Scher, Anne 046352
Scherbel, Dr. G. 019362
Scherer, Ernst 037538
Scherer, Jim 047104
Scherer, Dr. Kristine 017837
Scherer, Kurt 036867
Scherer, Manfred 037538
Scherer, Rodney 001288
Scherf, Angeline 013630
Scherf, Avner 022993
Scherney, Dr. Ingrid 001885
Scherrer, August 037607
Scherrer, M. 010970
Scherting, Bruce A. 044769
Scherzer, Beatrice 018017
Scheu, David R. 049209
Scheuerecker, Franz X. 019570
Scheuermann, Gernot 019643
Scheuers, Vera 019207
Scheuren, Elmar 018358
Scheurer, Bruno 037045
Schiborra, Ute 017646
Schick, Dr. Karin 020356
Schick, Martin 015638
Schick, Dr. Ulrike 019538
Schicklberger, August 002575
Schicklgruber, Dr. Christian 002961
Schidlowsky, V. 011200
Schieber, Matthias 019225
Schieber, Dr. Michael 019321
Schiebout, Dr. Judith A. 042049
Schieck, Dr. Martin 017206
Schiefelbein, Don 044548
Schiemann, Larry 041809
Schierle, Dr. Sonja 020358
Schiers, Jörge 015778
Schierz, Dr. Kai Uwe 017017
Schiess, Robert 036881
Schießl, Werner 016890
Schiestl, Dr. Michael 002107
Schietere de Lophem, A. de 003279
Schietinger, James 043351
Schietz, Ottar 031214
Schiff, Michael 043268
Schiffer, Tim 048760
Schiffino, Prospero 023611
Schiffmann, Dr. René 037091, 037696
Schilbach, Michael 019443
Schild, Hans 037616
Schild, Margit 016828
Schilder, A.M.Th. 029238
Schildkrout, Dr. Enid 046286
Schill, Jörg 020169
Schillemans, R. 029203
Schiller, J. 001198
Schilli, K. 017361
Schilling, Christiane 017765
Schilling, Wolfgang 020181
Schiltz, Kelly 044307
Schimek, Dr. Michael 017443
Schimmel, Dan 046939
Schimmel, Paul 045451
Schimmelpenninck Van der Oije, C.O.A. 030087
Schimpf-Reinhardt, Dr. Hans 015861, 015863
Schindlbeck, Dr. Ingrid 016017
Schindlbeck, Dr. Markus 016017
Schindler, Dr. Helmut 019122
Schindler, Dr. Margot 002976
Schindler-Kaudelka, Dr. Eleny 002432
Schinkel, Dr. Eckhard 016771, 020666
Schinnerl, Heimo 002143
Schinnerl, Dr. Heimo 002283, 002284
Schinnerling, Mechthild 021059
Schinović, Nataša 003947
Schiøtz, Ottar 031213
Schipper, P. 030372
Schipper, Drs. Peter W. . . 029392, 030202, 030204
Schirmbeck, Dr. Peter 019944
Schirmböck, Thomas 018805
Schisler jr, Lee C. 042420
Schitinger, Jim 043353
Schiwek, Thomas 020981
Schladebach, Tilman 015935
Schlag, Dr. Gerald 002218, 002390, 002676, 002692
Schlagkamp, Dieter 020191
Schlass, Gerhard 002962
Schlatter, Alexander 036896
Schlatter, Dr. Rudolf 018586
Schlegel, Adolf 020709
Schlegel, Dr. Konrad 002934
Schleher, Linda 042964
Schleich, Prof. Dr. H. Hermann . . . 021014
Schleicher, John 045307
Schleicher, Dr. Lennart 017551
Schleider, Holger 016416
Schlemmer, C. Raman 024990
Schlenk, Christoph 002092
Schleper, Dr. Thomas 019391
Schleushner, Evelyn 045200
Schleyerbach-Breu, Christiane . . . 018942
Schlicher, Fred J. 045738
Schlicht, Esther 017192
Schlicht, Udo 016236
Schlichting, Art 047139
Schlichting, Heike 015561, 015563
Schlicting, Eunice 043305
Schlieben, Katharina 037799
Schliebs, Des 001198

Schliefsteiner, Herbert 002356
Schliekau, Jürgen 015669
Schliemann, Ulrich 016436, 016438, 016443
Schlieper, Hans 020245
Schlimmgen-Ehmke, Katharina . . . 016691
Schlögl, Franz 002331, 002746
Schlombs, Dr. Adele 018331
Schloßbauer, Kurt 019712
Schlosser, Christa 019174
Schlosser, Christoph 037088
Schlosser, Prof. Katesa 018250
Schloßer, Rosemarie 016650
Schloter, John E. 047717
Schluchter, Dr. André 037084
Schluep, Charlotte 037193
Schlüter, Dr. Andreas 020364
Schlüter, D. 029469
Schlüter, Dr. J. 017708
Schlueter, Sue 045883
Schlüter, Dr. Wolfgang 019495
Schlup, Michel 037372
Schmälzle, Reinhard 020160
Schmalbrock, R.F. 018110
Schmalfuß, Dr. Helmut 020364
Schmaltz, Prof. Bernhard 018243
Schmalz, Lydia H. 046257
Schmandt, Dr. Matthias 016245
Schmauder, Dr. Michael 016333
Schmeh, Thomas J. 045031
Schmeja, Michael 001747
Schmelz, Dr. Bernd 017716
Schmid, A. 015793
Schmid, Dr. Anna 017765
Schmid, Debora 036863
Schmid, Elisabeth 037794
Schmid, Dr. Elmar D. 019097
Schmid, G. 019911
Schmid, Gerhard 037630
Schmid, Dr. Hanns 002492
Schmid, Hanspeter 037499
Schmid, Jakob 037671
Schmid, Dr. Margit 001786
Schmid, Dr. Peter 037787
Schmid, Reinhard 020580
Schmid, S. 019733
Schmid, U. 020364
Schmid, Dr. Ulla K. 020091
Schmid, Ute 046334
Schmid-Birri, Ingrid 037074
Schmid-Nafz, Gerlinde 018872
Schmidberger, Dr. Ekkehard 015826
Schmidberger, Prof. Dr. Ekkehard . 018191
Schmidl, Dr. H. 001835
Schmidl, Karin 015992
Schmidl, Matthias 002031
Schmidt, Aiko 016961
Schmidt, Dr. Alfons 019659
Schmidt, Andreas 021065
Schmidt, B. 020550
Schmidt, Dwight 044229
Schmidt, Erwin 018460
Schmidt, Dr. Eva 016414
Schmidt, Franz Xaver 020364
Schmidt, Franziska 017762
Schmidt, Gavin 042212
Schmidt, Georg 017421
Schmidt, Gudrun 015982
Schmidt, Dr. Hans-Günter 020997
Schmidt, Dr. Hans-Werner 018579
Schmidt, Harro 017759
Schmidt, Hartmut 020844, 020847, 020848, 020850
Schmidt, Jan 019048
Schmidt, Karl 016591
Schmidt, Kirsten 008928
Schmidt, Klaus 021010
Schmidt, Lawrence R. 046621
Schmidt, Martin 017765
Schmidt, Dr. Peter 019268
Schmidt, Philipp 001739
Schmidt, Rolf 016200, 016201
Schmidt, Roman 018690
Schmidt, Dr. Rüdiger 018156
Schmidt, Dr. S. 019132
Schmidt, Dr. Sabine Maria 016861
Schmidt, Sebastian 017942
Schmidt, Siegfried 020853
Schmidt, Teresa 048742
Schmidt, Dr. Theun-M. 016173
Schmidt, Thomas 016712, 016713
Schmidt, Volker 016415
Schmidt, Wayne W. 048855
Schmidt, Willi 020048
Schmidt-Bergmann, Prof. Dr. Hansgeorg 018164
Schmidt-Dengler, Prof. Dr. Wendelin 002971
Schmidt-Esters, Gudrun 017215
Schmidt-Glintzer, Prof. Dr. Helwig . 020956
Schmidt-Herwig, Dr. Angelika 017152
Schmidt-Lawrenz, Dr. Stefan 017817
Schmidt-Rutsch, Dr. Olaf . 016771, 020926
Schmidt-Surdez, Maryse 037372
Schmied, Peter 037647
Schmiegel, Karol A. 043488
Schmieglitz-Otten, Juliane 016545
Schmigalle, Dr. Günther 018156
Schmink, Donna 044745
Schmith, Andreas 015589
Schmitt, Horst 020479
Schmitt, Prof. Dr. Michael 016337
Schmitt, Robert 014751
Schmitt-Riegraf, Dr. Cornelia 019148
Schmitz, Dr. Bettina 017924
Schmitz, Brigitte 015984
Schmitz, Dr. Britta 016055
Schmitz, Doris 042665
Schmitz, Hans-Hermann 015965
Schmitz, Dr. Michael 017765
Schmitz, Silvia 017764
Schmitz, Uwe 016682
Schmitz von Ledebur, Dr. Katja . . . 002934
Schmocker, Susan 001505
Schmöhl, Thomas 015941
Schmölzer, Othmar 002488
Schmolka, Gerhard 003017
Schmollgruber, Friedrich 002698
Schmook, Dr. R. 015701
Schmucker, Kristine 044229
Schmuttermeier, Elisabeth 002945
Schmutz, Daniel 036927
Schmutz, Dr. Hans Konrad 037728, 037734
Schmutzler, Ruth 017195
Schnackenburg, Dr. M.-L. 019490
Schnall, Dr. Uwe 016429
Schneede, Prof. Dr. Uwe M. 017694
Schneeweis, Dr. Felix 002132
Schneider, Dr. Alfred 015535
Schneider, Prof. Dr. Angela 015984, 016055, 016152
Schneider, Dr. Carola 017068
Schneider, Claire 042498
Schneider, Dr. Cornelia 018788
Schneider, Don 046765
Schneider, E. Lina 016105
Schneider, Eckhard 001762
Schneider, Dr. Erich 020139, 020140, 020142, 020143
Schneider, Ester 018926
Schneider, Dr. G.C. 029105
Schneider, H. 018173
Schneider, Dr. Hans 037263
Schneider, Hansjörg 018374
Schneider, Hélène 013879
Schneider, Dr. Herbert 019752
Schneider, Joanne 045833
Schneider, John 049067
Schneider, Josef 016514
Schneider, Dr. K. 017674
Schneider, Karl-Heinz 019915
Schneider, Dr. Katja 017672
Schneider, Kerry 047049
Schneider, Klaus 016870
Schneider, Dr. Klaus 018337
Schneider, M. 019372
Schneider, Malou 014863
Schneider, Dr. Manfred 002097
Schneider, Michael 016639, 036893
Schneider, Nadja 037149
Schneider, Paul 045417
Schneider, Reisa Sniley 006709
Schneider, René 011032
Schneider, Dr. Thomas 019492
Schneider, Prof. Dr. Ulrich . 015426, 017183
Schneider, Dr. Ulrich 020039
Schneider, Ursula 017709
Schneider, Dr. Wolfgang . . 016638, 017420
Schneider-Kempf, Barbara 016176, 016177
Schneider-Mohamed, Rosemarie . 016828
Schneidler, Dr. Herbert 019759
Schneidmiller, Kenneth A. 044337
Schnell, Frank 043093
Schnell, Gertrude H. 044046
Schnell, M. 010817
Schnell, Ronald 048589
Schnellhammer-Ocist, Norbert . . . 002691
Schnepp, Patrick 012328
Schnepper, Mary S. 043766
Schneyer, Rosemary 048368
Schniek, Dr. Rüdiger 020038
Schnitzer, Dr. Claudia 016797
Schnitzler, Bernadette 014864
Schnitzler, Dr. Ludwig 015780
Schnurr, Marie 043557
Schober, Manfred 020159
Schober, Otto 001913
Schoberwalter, Anton 002153
Schobinger, Dr. Juan 000432
Schoch, Lois H. 041917
Schoch, Dr. R. 020364
Schoch, Dr. Rainer 019352
Schöb, Kathrin 037445
Schöbe, Lutz 016684
Schöbel, Dr. G. 020529
Schöbl, Ernst 002439
Schöck, Dr. Gustav 020374
Schoeller, Danielle 015274
Schöllmann, Dr. Lothar 019157
Schömann, Rainer 019048
Schoen, Kenneth 048822
Schön, Matthias D. 015650, 017621
Schönberger, Dr. Angela . . 016104, 016126
Schöne, Dr. Anja 020417, 020418
Schoene, Lynn 020099
Schoeneck, Edith 019404
Schönefeld, Dr. Bärbel 016159
Schönewald, Dr. Beatrix . 018069, 018075, 018076
Schönfelder, Kathleen 018558
Schönfellner, Dr. Franz . . . 002173, 002175
Schönhagen, Dr. Benigna 015611
Schönitzer, Prof. Dr. N. 019132
Schoenke, Marilyn 044605
Schönweger, Astrid 024670
Schoewe, Sherry 045121
Schofield, Roger 030657
Schokkenbroek, J. 029216
Scholl, Dr. Andreas 015986
Scholl, Ben 048572
Scholl, Dr. Lars U. 016429
Schollenberger, Werner 019380
Scholler, Dr. Markus 018170
Schollian, Gerd 017818
Schollmeier, Dr. Axel 019153
Scholtemeijer, G. 034725
Scholten, Lisa 042449
Scholz, Dr. Antony 001951
Scholz, C. 020372
Scholz, Carl 048409
Scholz, Dr. Dieter 016121, 016152
Scholz, Dr. G. . . . 016292, 016293, 016294
Scholz, Dr. Günter 016295
Scholz, Margitta 016371
Scholz-Bauer, U. 019831
Scholz-Strasser, Inge 003005
Scholze, Frank 015992
Schomers, Dr. Florian 002095
Schommers, Dr. Annette . . 019039, 019416
Schonewille, Dr. P. 029279
Schonlau, Ree 046675
Schoofs, M. 003548
Schooler, Jim 049370
Schoon, P.J. 029502
Schoonhoven Okken, W. 029388
Schoonover, Karen 006261
Schoonover, Larry 048275
Schoonover, Mary Ellen 041908
Schoppe, Karla 021085
Schopping, H. 030226
Schorta, Dr. Regula 037455
Schoske, Dr. Sylvia 019121, 020166
Schotsman, Liesbeth 003163
Schøtt, Vibehe 008856
Schott-Smith, Christine 021566
Schotte, Petra 018718
Schotten, Christoph 020569
Schou-Christensen, Jørgen 008963
Schoulepnikoff, Chantal de 037422, 037784
Schoutens, P. 029203
Schrade, Ewald 016895
Schrader, Kathleen 047429
Schrader, Wolfgang 019634
Schram, Prof. Dr. F.R. 029245
Schramer-Lorang, Fernande 027883
Schramm, Dr. Ágnes 034337
Schramm, Jeanne 049087
Schramm, Robert W. 049087
Schrank, Gustav 017940
Schratter, Rudolf 002064, 002065, 002066, 002067
Schreck, Anne-Katrin 019352
Schreiber, Dr. K. 020372
Schreiber, Mildred 042672
Schreier, Dr. Christoph 016329
Schreilechner, Waltraud 002085
Schrein, Catherine 042035
Schreiner, A. 020065
Schreiner, Josy 027872
Schreiner, Manuela 018374
Schrem, Wilfried 019216
Schrenk, Prof. Dr. Klaus 018169
Schrenk, Dr. Sabine 037455
Schrettl, Reinhold 002780
Schrick, Annette 015970
Schrijvers, N. 003163
Schriver, Stephanie 047959
Schroder, Dr. Anne 043542
Schrøder, Lise Lotte 008911
Schrøder Vesterkjær, Siri 031240
Schroeder, Allen 042650, 045906
Schroeder, Bob 043998
Schröder, Christoph 015498, 015499
Schroeder, Chuck 046647
Schroeder, Dorothy 042820
Schröder, Dr. Heike 015816, 020374
Schröder, Dr. Klaus Albrecht 002845
Schroeder, N.H. 038532
Schroeder, P. 041833
Schroeder, Patricia 043841
Schroeder, Sharon 047355
Schroeder, Stephan 035429
Schröder, Till 017709
Schröder, Dr. U. 017524
Schrödl, Dr. M. 019132
Schröter, Jürgen 020441
Schröter, Dr. P. 019032
Schröter, Wolfgang 020181
Schroll, Ludwig 016982
Schroth, Dr. Adella 047362
Schroth, Dr. Sarah W. 043542
Schrub, Antoine 013809
Schten, Abigail 043355
Schube, Inka 017769
Schubert, Armin 016369
Schubert, Jason 042915
Schubert, Dr. Kristina 015990
Schubert, Susan 016834
Schubert, Werner 002869
Schubert, Wolfgang 018576, 053483
Schuch, Herbert 018152

Schuchardt, Günter 016926
Schuchmann, Dr. Karl-Ludwig 016337
Schüle, Bernard A. 037784
Schuelke, Chris 043835
Schüllenbach, Konrad 029110
Schüly, Dr. Maria 017228
Schünemann, Dr. Gustav 015891
Schünemann, Karl 015474
Schünemann, Ulla 017359
Schüpbach, Beat 036930
Schüpbach, Ulrich 036954
Schürer 016902
Schürer, Ralf 019352
Schuerholz, Peter 048501
Schürmann, Dr. Kay U. 018826
Schütt, Charlotte 037783
Schütt, Dr. Jutta 017195
Schütt-Hohenstein, Dr. A. 020372
Schuette, Bobbie 044306
Schütte, Dr. Margret 020039
Schütz, Dr. Christian 020602
Schütz, Ilse 034781
Schütz, Jan 008338
Schütz, Dr. Karl 002934, 002934
Schütz, Volker 016252
Schütz, Wolfgang 020721
Schuh, Kurt 002958
Schuh, Walter 002370
Schuhmacher, Walter 017380
Schuhwerk, Dr. Franz 019042
Schulenburg, Gräfin Sonnhild von der 017099
Schulenburg, Stephan Graf von der 017183
Schuler, Romana 002940
Schuler, Shirley 047079
Schuler, Dr. Thomas 016565
Schulkin, Jerrold L. 045288
Schuller, Kurt 001844
Schuller, Tom 044980
Schuller tot Peursum-Meyer, Drs. J. 030240
Schullerus, M. 015506
Schulman, Daniel 042820
Schulman Jesse, Daniel 042820
Schulson, Henry H. 042777
Schulte, Dr. Birgit 017624, 017625
Schulte, Wolfgang 003508
Schulte-Hobein, Dr. Jürgen 015566
Schulte-Kemper, Hubert 018853
Schulte-Wülwer, Prof. Dr. Ulrich .. 017130
Schulten, Ton 030005
Schulters, Johannes 015870
Schultes, Alfred 002100
Schultes, Dr. Lothar 002249, 002256
Schultes, Peter 015521, 015522
Schultz, Brian 044470
Schultz, Douglas G. 042498
Schultz, Dr. Franz Joachim 015916
Schultz, Prof. Dr. Hartwig 017167
Schultz, J. Bernard 046028
Schultz, Jeffrey 044316
Schultz, Peter 036645
Schultze, Prof. Dr. H.-P. 016133
Schultze, Joachim 020038
Schulz, Dr. Ch. 037453
Schulz, Günther 015486
Schulz, Dr. Isabel 017769
Schulz, Marion 019776
Schulz, Max 045420
Schulz, Ralph J. 046143
Schulz, Rebekah 001123
Schulz, Regine 042006
Schulz, Volker 020826
Schulz-Hoffmann, Prof. Dr. Carla .. 019038
Schulz-Weddigen, Dr. Ingo 018375
Schulze, Dietmar 018590
Schulze, Dr. Sabine 017195
Schulze Altcappenberg, Prof. Dr. Hein-Th. 016109
Schulze-Dörrlamm, Dr. Mechthild . 018794
Schulze-Neuhoff, Eckart 016841
Schumacher, Caroline 019390
Schumacher, Dr. Doris 017646
Schumacher, Hans-Joachim 018276
Schumacher, Rainald 019109
Schumacher, Dr. Renate 016331
Schumacher-Gebler, Eckehart 018580
Schumann, Maurice 012133
Schumann, Peter 044226
Schumann, Romzin 027887
Schumard, Ann 048933
Schummel, Helle 009118
Schupbach, Marianne 036932
Schuppli, Madeleine 037629, 037633
Schur, Chantel 006328
Schure, Edeltraut 020943
Schurig, Dr. Roland 015429, 015430
Schurkamp, Trish 042299
Schusser, Dr. Adalbert 003017
Schuster, Anna 001852
Schuster, Dr. Erika 001904
Schuster, Erwin 002701
Schuster, Eva 020865
Schuster, Franz 001966
Schuster, Prof. Dr. Gerhard 018056, 020749
Schuster, Kenneth L. 042197
Schuster, Prof. Dr. Peter-Klaus ... 015984, 016055, 016121, 016148, 016152, 016175
Schuster, Robin 045545
Schuth, Anton 018983
Schutte, Maria Christina 000111
Schutz, Carine 013808
Schutz, David 046007
Schutz, John 047909
Schutz, Kenneth J. 047468
Schutzbier, Heribert 002277
Schwab, K. 015852
Schwab, Maria 017332
Schwab, Rosl 001705
Schwab, S. 038458
Schwab, Sibylle 018809
Schwab, Sigrid 016647
Schwab-Dorfman, Debbie 046352
Schwabach, Dr. Thomas . 020764, 020765, 020766, 020767
Schwabe, Uwe 018560
Schwager, Michael 047527
Schwaiger, Dr. Axel 017366
Schwaiger, Wilhelm 001889
Schwalenberg, Gregory 041966
Schwaller, M. 013432
Schwalm, Dr. Bodo 017532
Schwalm, Dr. Hans-Jürgen 019741
Schwalm, Helmut 020121
Schwank, Prof. Dr. Benedikt 016214
Schwanzar, Dr. Christine 002256
Schwar, Scott 046583
Schwark, Dr. Thomas 017755
Schwarm, Larry W. 043705
Schwarts, Eleanore 048432
Schwartz, Constance 047547
Schwartz, David 041821
Schwartz, Elizabeth 044911
Schwartz, Gary 048552
Schwartz, Janet 006610
Schwartz, Judith 006601, 006607
Schwartz, Michael 042988
Schwartz, Stephen H. 044071
Schwartzbaum, Paul 046404
Schwarz 019987
Schwarz, Dr. Dieter 037721
Schwarz, Ernst 002055
Schwarz, Dr. Helmut 019374
Schwarz, Prof. Dr. Karl 002896
Schwarz, Klaus 018113
Schwarz, Peter 019521, 019522
Schwarz, Walter A. 002910
Schwarzenberg, Karl Johann von . 002936
Schwarzjirg, Dr. Helmuth 002201
Schwarzkopf, C.G. 048389
Schwarzkopf, Craig 042093
Schweiger, Andrea 036904
Schweigert, Dr. Günter 020364
Schweiggl, Wolfgang 023975
Schwein, Florence 043634
Schweiss, Christoph 037225
Schweizer, Dr. Hans Ulrich 037769
Schweizer, Nicole 036930
Schweizer, Dr. Paul D. 048719
Schweizer, Dr. Rolf 019169
Schwelle, Dr. Franz 002315
Schwemer, Florian 019048
Schwenker, Polly 041579
Schwering, Dr. Burkhard 018240
Schwertner, Dr. Johann .. 002142, 002283, 002284
Schwind, Stefan 016795
Schwinden, Lothar 020483, 020483
Schwinn, Wolfgang 019770
Schwintek, Monika 020054
Schwinzer, Dr. Ellen 017731
Schwitter, Josef 037148
Schwoeffermann, Catherine 042217
Schwolger, David 045160
Schymalla, Joachim 019559
Sci, LaVerne 043324
Sciallano, Martine 012142
Scichilone, Dr. Giovanni 023864
Scirè Nepi, Dr. Giovanna 026236
Scoates, Christopher 047952
Scobey, Pati 041610
Scoccimarro, Fabio 026136
Scofield, P. 030460
Sconci, Maria Selene 025550
Scoon, Fergus 040363
Scotes, Helen 030474
Scott, Adrienne 042892
Scott, Andrew 041480
Scott, B. 001494
Scott, Barbara 046446
Scott, Bob 040410
Scott, Carol E. 046832
Scott, Dan 046893
Scott, Donna A. 046383
Scott, E. 034731
Scott, Elva 043553
Scott, Eric 047362
Scott, F.E. 039900
Scott, Dr. Gerry 047804
Scott, Jane 001613
Scott, John 001615, 044147
Scott, Julie 047900
Scott, Kitty 006104
Scott, Michael 041168, 045048
Scott, Preston 005105
Scott, Ron 006118
Scott, Rose 044287
Scott, Terri 043629
Scott, Vane S. 046447
Scott, Vanya 049160
Scott, Virginia 042354
Scott, William W. 048509
Scott Bouth, Karen 005718
Scott-Childress, Katie 044315
Scott Garrity, Noreen 042577
Scottez-de Wambrechies, Annie .. 012680
Scotti, Dr. Roland 037039
Scrase, D.E. 038962
Scribner, John C.L. 041937
Scriven, Brian 042652
Scriver, Lorraine 042478
Scriver, Dr. Robert M. 042478
Scrobotă, Paul 032770
Scudder, G.G.E. 006710
Scuderi, Helena 047145
Scudero, Domenico 025544
Scudieri, Dr. Magnolia 024185
Ščukina, Irina Anatolivna 038311
Sculley, John 041109
Scully, Cammie V. 048987
Scully, Robert J. 049173
Seabold, Thomas 044971
Seage Person, Robin 044354
Seager, Pamela 045383
Seal, Ray 040219
Seald-Chudzinski, Romi 047207
Seale, Sir David 003125
Searl, Majorie 047487
Searle, Ross 000844
Sears, Ann 043809
Sears, Dennis 044100
Seaver, Tom 022830
Šeba, Vasyl Stanislavovyč 038408
Sebastián, Dr. Amparo 035427
Sebastian, Padmini 001243
Sebastiani, Prof. Antonio 025585
Sebayang, Nas 022473
Šebek, Dr. F. 008561
Šebesta, Dr. Pavel 008328
Sebire, H. 040936
Sebolt George, Alberta 048406
Secher Jensen, Dr. Thomas 008808
Seck, Dr. Amadou Abdoulaye 034135
Sedano, Pilar 035429
Sedberry, Rosemary 042043
Seddon, Jane 039068, 039071
Seddon, Jeffrey 040263
Seddon, Joan 005758
Sedge, Jane 040986
Sedikova, Larisa 038389
Sedilek, F. 034452
Sedinko, Svetlana Alekseevna ... 033579
Sedioli, Giovanni 023430
Sedláček, Zbyněk 008320, 008449
Sedler, Irmgard 018385
Sedlmeier, Martin 019599
Sedlmeir, Wolfgang 016427
Sedman, Ken 040460
Sedova, Galina Michajlovna 033800
Sedova, Irina V. 033413
Seear, Lynne 001474
Seebeck, Eibe 016773
Seeber, Dr. Ekkehard 020558
Seeberg, Peter 001996
Seefried, Dr. Monique 041866
Seel, Dr. Peter C. 016061
Seele, Ralf-Michael 018885
Seeley, Daniel 045553
Seelig, Dr. Lorenz 019039, 019760
Seeliger, G. 020294
Seeliger, Dr. Matthias 017998
Seelinger, Evelyn 047779
Seemann, Esther 019799
Seemann, Hellmut 020744
Seemann, Hellmut Th. 020757
Seemann, R. 020677
Seewaldt, Dr. Peter 020483
Seewöster, H. 019236
Şefănescu, Radu 032789
Šefčík, Dr. Erich 008455
Sefcik, James F. 046259
Segal, Dror 023040
Segal, Merav 023056
Segalstad, Prof. Tom V. 031078
Segarra, Guido Barletta 032727
Segarra, Ninfa 046388
Seger, Joe 045929
Segerer, Dr. A. 019132
Segessenmann, Vreni 037404, 037405
Segger, Martin 006744
Seghatoleslami, Parvine Sadre ... 022617
Seghers, George D. 041643
Segieth, Dr. Clelia 016209
Seglie, Prof. Dario 025243, 025245, 025250
Segni Pulvirenti, Francesca 023571
Segovia Barrientos, Francisco 034954
Séguin, Louise 006379
Segura, Angela 036027
Segura, Avelino 043270
Segura Martí, J.M. 034808
Seib, Dr. Gerhard 019011, 019012, 019013, 019014, 019016
Seibel, Prof. Dr. Wilfried 016866
Seibert, Dr. Elke 020716, 020717
Seibert, Georg 020463
Seibert, Peter S. 045144
Seidel, Doris 019065
Seidel, W.A. 018457
Seidenberg, Ulrich 018931
Seider, Diana L. 045352
Seidl, Alfred 002002

Seidl, Dr. Katharina 002934
Seidl, Manfred 001822
Seif, Denise 042705
Seifermann, Ellen 019363
Seifert, Jörg 015550
Seiffert, Claudia 018158
Seifried, Doriann 005447
Seifriedsberger, Anna 002462
Seifriedsberger, Georg 002462
Seigo, Jinbo 027111
Seiji, Kamei 027055
Seilacher, Adolf 046226
Seiler, Prof. Dr. Michael 019659
Seiler, R. 037209
Sein, Joni L. 043614
Seip, Ivar 030901
Seipel, Prof. Dr. Wilfried . . 002933, 002934
Seisbøll, Lise 009022
Seissl, Maria 003013
Seitter, John R. 042576
Seitz, Anna 002731, 002733
Seitz, Becca 041969
Seitz, Erich 020690
Seitz, Oliver 015603
Seitz-Weinzierl, Beate 020881
Sejček, Zdeněk 008669
Šejleva, Gergana 004686
Sekera, Dr. Jan 008596
Sekerák, Jiří 008288
Sekete, A. 034566
Sekgwele, David 034639
Sekulian, Augustin 002954
Selbach, Josee 029638
Selbe, Nance 047570
Seleli, Prof. Y. 034597
Selenitza, Enin 000025
Self, Dana 044921
Selfridge, Anna B. 045292
Selfridge, Nancy 045986
Selig, Gary D. 005150, 005151
Seligman, Thomas K. 048319
Seligmann, Susan M. 048898
Seline, Janice 046649
Selirand, Urmas 009368
Selke, Gordon 046735
Sell, Manfred 020932
Sella, Lodovico 023393
Sellers, Kate M. 044463
Sellers, Mary B. 043429
Sellers, P. 001340
Sellers, P.E. 029154
Selles, Didier 013685
Sellés, José Pascual 034810
Selliere-Charon 003218
Sellinger, Dr. Günter 002714
Sellink, Manfred 003262, 003263, 003264, 003265, 003266, 003267, 003268, 003269, 003270, 003273, 003276, 003280, 003283
Sello, Thomas 017694
Selmayr, Prof. Dr. Gerhard 018807, 018808
Selmeczi, Dr. László 021709
Selmer, Jørgen 008970
Selmer Olsen, Knud 030732
Selmić, Leposava 034222
Selph, Judy 043394
Selsing, Lotte 031221
Selvorious, Clement 024291
Selway, Robert 047946
Selwyn, Sve 039476
Selzer, Erika 001708
Selzer, Helmut 003017
Semakova, Tatjana Gennadjevna . . 033264
Semënov, Ivan Grigorjevič 033574
Semenova, Galina 033489
Semënova, Tatjana Andreevna . . . 033174
Semff, Dr. Michael 019036, 019118
Semočkin, Aleksandr Aleksandrovič 033705
Sen Gupta, Pradip Kumar 003105
Senadheera, S. 036137
Senanster, Hvon de 013847
Sender, Becky 047240
Sendl, Thomas 019588
Sendra, Gemma 034922
Senén López Gómez, Felipe 035124
Senf, Erika 019502
Senften, Penny 045629
Seng, Dr. Joachim 017167
Senge, Takatoshi 027099
Sengele, J.-M. 013289
Senior, Caroline 022870
Senior, David 040434
Seniuk, Jake 047125
Sen'ko, Rostislav Oleksandrovyč . . 038312
Senn, Carol J. 043298
Senn, Dr. Matthias 037107, 037784
Sennequier, Geneviève 014125
Sens, Dr. Angelie 029220
Sensabaugh, David 046228
Sensen, Stephan 015493, 015494
Seo, Chiaki 027110
Seoighe, Mainchín 022696
Seokgi, Kim 027482
Sepioł, Afred 031964
Seppänen, Anne 036265
Sequeira, Dora 007676, 007682
Sequeira, Dora María 007677
Serafini, Flavio 024412
Serafińska-Domańska, Maria 032179
Serageldin, Dr. Ismail 009285
Seraja, Marina Leonidovna 034098
Serani Elliott, Daniela 006922
Šeravić, Ivana 007815
Şerban, Violeta 032908
Şerbănescu, Done 032901
Šerbec, Jože 034467
Šerbelj, Dr. Ferdinand 034487
Serdar, Elizabeta 007843
Serena, Dominique 010473
Serge, Pascal 015049
Sergeenko, Valentin Ivanovič 033657
Sergeeva, Elena Nikolaevna 034015
Sergeeva, I.N. 033132
Sergent Nemeth, Dana 041821
Serghini, Mohamed 029041
Seright, Susan 040853
Séris, Anne-Jean 012323
Serkownek, Edith 045778
Sermeno, Rhodora J. 031777
Serna, Marco A. 007537
Serna Muñoz, Martha Judith 007494
Serota, Sir Nicholas 040299, 040300
Serpe, Louis 014678, 014679
Serra, Florenci 036055
Serra, Sophie 012409
Serra de Manresa, Valentí 034946
Serra Ferreira, Dr. Ana Margarida . 032592
Serra Rexach, Eduardo 035429
Serradj-Remili, Nedjma 000044
Serrano, Delmy 046327
Serré-Van Wijk, Brenda 029198
Sersha, Tom 043769
Serson, Christine 003249
Sérullaz, Arlette 013722
Servais Lebrun, Françoise 003644
Service, Pam 043751
Servis, Nancy M. 043312
Servitje de Lerdo de Tejada, Marinela 028490
Sesić, Maria 034161
Šestakova, Tamara Nikolaevna . . . 033938
Sestan, Ivan 007832
Sethuraman, K. 022090
Setinský, Jiří 008302
Šetrakova, Svetlana N. 033432
Settle Cooney, Mary 048670
Settler, Faye 006870
Seuffert, Dr. Ottmar 016745
Seugwoo, Nam 027567
Sevastjanova, Lidija Ivanovna 033228
Ševčenko, Ol'ga Ivanivna 038298
Sevda, Dadasheva 003086
Ševeček, Dr. Ludvík 008786
Sevellec, Jacques 010982
Sever, Nancy 000697, 000699
Severance, Christopher C. 005250
Severens, Martha R. 044349
Ševereva, Tamara Anatoljevna . . . 033576
Severini, Pavel 034203
Sévery, Sébastien 014015, 014016
Sevi, Uriel J. 000220
Sevier, James 043380
Sevigney, Nichola 048871
Sevilla, Guillermo A. 000252
Sevınç, Nurten 038039
Ševkomud, Igor Dmitrievič 033081
Ševyrin, Sergej Andreevič 033651
Seward Hannam, Kim 005719
Sewell, Cynthia 042288
Sewell, Dennita 047011
Sewell, Jack 000957
Sewell, Jane S. 049117
Sexton, Nick 039169
Sexton, Robert 043299
Seybold, Russell G. 046521
Seybold, Silke 016426
Seyfried, Dr. Friederike 018557
Seyl, Susan 047174
Seymour, C. 001446
Seymour, Dr. Claire 040265
Seyrl, Harald . . . 002642, 002644, 003021
Seytkazieva, N.M. 027636
Sezen, Nuri 038015
Sezer, Tahsin 038093
Sezgin, Mustafa 038188
Seznec, A. 013977
Sforzi, Dr. Andrea 024375
Sfrappini, Dr. Alessandra 024564, 024566, 024568
Sgromo, V. Joseph 047585
Sgubin, Dr. Raffaella 024351, 024352, 024353
Sgubini Moretti, Dr. Anna Maria . . 023629
Shaak, Dr. Graig D. 044103
Shaath, Shawqi M. 037824
Shacham, Tzvi 023062
Shackelford, George T. M. 042334
Shady Solís, Dr. Ruth 031548
Shaffer, Marcy 041600
Shaffer, Randy 041749
Shaffer, Dr. Susan 045793
Shaffer, Terry 043575
Shaffer, Vivienne 048281
Shafi El-Sheikh, Hassan Abdel . . . 009283
Shagonaby, Joyce 044428
Shah, Hiralal P. 022007, 022008
Shahi, M. 022555
Shahzad, Tasneem 031396
Shaiboub, Dr. Abdullah . . 027828, 027829, 027830, 027831, 027832, 027833, 027834, 027835, 027836
Shaiman, Jason 043082
Shaker, H. 022551
Shalev, Avner 022953, 022989
Shalgosky, Sarah 039153
Shamis, Bob 046378
Shamsbod, Mahmoud 022616
Shanahan, Carl 044160
Shanahan, J.P. 001037
Shane, Dr. Orrin 047709
Shank, Nicholas 045915
Shankle, Kent 048987
Shanley, Ellen 046370
Shanmugam, Dr. P. 022054
Shannon, Dr. Helen 048605
Shannon, Steve 039334
Shapiro, Denise 045183
Shapiro, Lynda 043141
Shapiro, Michael 041862
Shapiro, Dr. Michael E. 041857
Shapiro, Selma 046586
Sharan, Michael 022920
Sharer, Robert 046993
Sharma, Dr. O. P. 022019
Sharma, R.D. 021997
Sharman, Glen 040212
Sharon, Dr. Douglas 047839
Sharp, Corwin 049295
Sharp, Ellen 043444
Sharp, James 045479
Sharp, Jane 046206
Sharp, Kevin 049091
Sharp, Lewis I. 043404
Sharp, Lindsay 041459
Sharp, Paige 045088
Sharp, Randall 043669
Sharp, R.W.D. 041263
Sharpe, D. 040794
Sharpe, Dr. Lindsay 040285
Sharpe, Yvonne 006745
Sharrock, D.J. 039851
Sharygin, G.V. 033518
Shastri, Nandan 022369
Shastri, N.H. 022370
Shattuck, Jennifer B. 045961
Shattuck, John 042329
Shaudys, Vincent 048231
Shaughnessy, Beth 005709
Shaul, Nissim 023045
Shaver, Steve 048137
Shaw, Cindy 040943
Shaw, D. 001433
Shaw, David 039152
Shaw, Deirdre 049075
Shaw, Elizabeth 041333
Shaw, Harry 039943
Shaw, J. 038778
Shaw, Karen 043572
Shaw, Lana 006086
Shaw, Lytle 046325
Shaw, Margaret 000888
Shaw, R. Douglas 049100
Shaw, R.W. 040022
Shaw, W. 039573
Shawe-Taylor, Desmond 040138
Shawhan, Jeff 045780
Shawn, Gene 046916
Shawn Barber, Barbara 046916
Shaylor, Ellen 041796
Shea, Carol 043286
Shea, John C. 044949
Sheads, Scott 041983
Sheaffer, Ed 048156
Shearer, I.M. 039362
Shearer, Linda 049188
Shearer, Thelma 001015
Shedd, Linda 042070
Shedd, Nancy S. 044672
Sheedy, Gilles 005085
Sheedy, Tom 022697
Sheehan, Ron 044863
Sheets, Arian 048763
Sheets, H.L. 045694
Sheets, Jeff 041562
Sheets, John W. 048864
Sheffer, Ann E. 049126
Sheffield, Sir Reginald 041165
Shefsiek, Kenneth 046268
Sheku, Nail 000038
Sheldon, Dr. Andrew 045936
Sheldon, Dr. Frederick H. 042049
Sheldon, Sara 042353
Sheley, David 044477
Shelhouse, Marvin 045864
Shellabarger, Harold L. 048348
Shelley, Majorie 046364
Shelley, Roger 039224
Shelley, Dr. Rowland 047315
Shelly, Roger 039225
Shelswell White, E.R.G. 022692
Shelton, L.T. 044849
Shelton, Ronald G. 043088
Shen, Dr. Lindsay 047697
Shendar, Yehudit 022989
Sheng, Yi Jia 007197
Shepard, Betty J. 045431
Shepard, Bruce 006416
Shepard, Charles A. 046238
Shepard, Joel 047892
Shephard, Diane 045533
Shepherd, Dr. Brian 000921

Shepp, James G. 045601
Sheppard, Jude 042904
Sheppard, Veronica 040259
Sheppy, Richard 038811
Sherck, Robin 041565
Sherer, Aaron 046738
Sherhofer, Ronald F. 048968
Sheridan, Barry 038843, 039665
Sheridan, Joan 048848
Sheridan, Tom 048630
Sheriff, Alice 046239
Sherin, Pamela V. 047237
Sherman, Alan 023039
Sherman, Cathy R. 043151
Sherman, Jacob 006008
Sherman, Mimi 046363
Sherman, Nancy 047353
Sherman, Seán 040167
Sherman, Sean 040246
Sherman, William 041743
Sherrer, John 043081
Sherrill, Sarah B. 046300
Sherry, Thomas 049111
Sherwood, Frederick 043571
Sherwood, Penelope 048783
Shestack, Alan 048924
Shetler, John 048596
Shetty, Prof. N.R. 022085
Shexnayder, Charlotte 043525
Shick, Andrew F. 046841
Shickles, Tim 043862
Shieh, Suewhei 048593
Shields, Ann 048702
Shields, Charlotte. 044539
Shields, Dorothy 045320
Shields, R. Michael 006708
Shields, Scott 047588
Shiels, Margaret M. 043508, 049267
Shiffman, Carol 047140
Shifman, Barry L. 044748
Shigaki, Betty 047475
Shih, Chia-Chun 044009
Shih, Minfa 007380
Shikada, Norimitsu 026925
Shikata, Miho 027306
Shilliday, Charles 006843
Shilo-Cohen, Nurit 022976
Shimada, Kazutaka 027203
Shimada, Kunio 027083
Shimazu, Misato 027169
Shimizu, Minoru 027079
Shimp, Dr. Robert E. 043029
Shin, Chul-Won 027477
Shin, Prof. Kwang Cho 027518
Shin, Tak Keun 027450
Shin, Young Koog 027604, 027622
Shin-tsu Tai, Susan 047950
Shinn, Deborah 046319
Shinoda, Aishin 026648
Shipley, Sandra 042921
Shipp, Kim 005784
Shippee Lambert, Lisa 042609
Shirahra, Yukiko 048092
Shirbacheh, Tahereh 022608
Shireman, Joyce A. 046166
Shirley, Pippa 041270
Shirley, Rosie 041058
Shirley, Shirley 048662
Shives, Jenny 045503
Shivvers, Mel 043426
Shlomo, Eli Ben 023031
Shlomo, Eliyahu-Ben 022908
Sho, Masaki 026970
Shoaff, Jeanne 043905
Shock, Helen 044676
Shockley, Richard 005765
Shoemaker, Innis H. 046975
Shoemaker, John 045103
Shoemaker, Rene D. 041835
Shokoofi, M.R. 022645
Sholl, Rachel 040049
Shonk, Scott L. 043716
Shôno, Prof. Susumu 027096
Shook, Rays 043323
Shopland, A. 005301
Shoreman, Mark 006765
Shorey, Prof. C.D. 001514
Short, John D. 044752
Short, William 047916
Shorter, Daniel A. 041675
Shoshani, Jesheskel 043458
Shostak, Anthony 045248
Shozo, Tamura 026606
Shrago, Esther 043309
Shrago, Mindy 043309
Shrake, Peter 042019
Shrestha, Dr. Keshab 029117
Shrigley, Ruth 040400, 040404
Shriver, James M. 049117
Shriver, Karen K. 044618
Shriver, Thomas L. 041747
Shrum, L. Vance 044812
Shubert, Gabrielle 042465
Shugart, Dr. Gary 048466
Shugart, Dr. Sanford 046716
Shulman, Steven E. 048880
Shultz, Cathee 045452
Shuman, Greg 041680, 048811
Shuman, Lynne 045670
Shupeck, Fern 045885
Shust, Maria 046416
Shuttleworth, Alec 038488
Shuttleworth, John 044677
Shydlovskyy, Ihor 038337
Siachoono, Stanford Mudenda 049575
Siano, Mary Ann 042439
Siber, Hans Jakob 036814
Sibeth, Achim 017168
Sibeth, Dr. Achim 017182
Sibille, Marie-Hélène 010470
Sibiril, Marceline 013003
Sibley, S.F. 041415
Sibley, Shelia M. 046477
Siboroski, Paul 043934
Sibson, Tracy 030600
Sibutha, Addelis 049578
Sicard, D. 014448
Sicilia, Fiorella 025420
Sidebottom, D.J. 039616
Siders, Phyllis 043449
Sidibé, Samuel 028019
Sidiropoulos, Kleanthis 021285
Sidner, Rob 047823
Sidorov, Konstantin Nikolaevič 033067
Sidorova, Elena Iljinična 033184
Siebenmorgen, Prof. Dr. Harald 016455, 016541, 018158, 018163, 018166, 019506, 020293
Sieber, W. 015624
Sieber Kirk, Ellen 042266
Sieberer, Dr. Wido 002133
Siebert, Andreas 015744
Siebert, Dr. Anne Viola 017757
Sieblist, Kerstin 018594
Siebol, Michael 049327
Siebrecht, Silke 019738
Siede, Dr. Irmgard 018809
Siedell, Daniel 045311
Siefert, Chris 047059
Siefert, Dr. Helge 019038, 019543
Siegal, Robert L. 032754
Siegel, Bernard 048154
Siegel, Bob 045781
Siegel, Eric 043877
Siegel, Gerlinde 017580
Siegel, Nancy 044673
Siegenthaler, Gustavo Bernardo 000612
Siegfried, Clifford A. 041599
Siegman, Joe 023039
Siegmann, William 042458
Siegrist, Urs 037756
Sielewonowski, Zenon 032313
Siembor, Natalie 046747
Siemen, Palle 008843
Siemen, Wilhelm 015571, 017969, 020181
Siener, William 042500
Sienkiewicz, Joanna 032285
Sierpowski, Prof. Dr. Stanisław 032014
Sierra Bello, Prof. Luz 028456
Sierra de la Calle, Blas 036004
Sierra Jones, Alvaro 007542
Siersma, Betsy 041696
Sietz, Phillip 046933
Sievernich, Gereon 016117
Sievers-Flägel, Dr. Gudrun 019344
Sievert, Annette 017683
Sifkovits, Dr. Adam 001724, 001725
Sigal, Bronia 028506
Sigal, Laurence 013628
Sigaud, Anne 012787
Sigg, Thierry 012144
Siggins, Michael 042280
Sigl, Bärbel 015956
Sigmond, Prof. P. 029226
Signore, Joseph A. 043390
Signorell, Victor 037518
Signorini, Prof. Rodolfo 024605
Sigo, Charles 048439
Sigurdardottir, Aldis 021982
Sigurdardóttir, Elin S. 021935
Sigurdardóttir, Maria Karen 021967
Sigurdardòttir, Sigridur 021983
Sigurdarson, Erlingur 021934
Sigurdson, Annchristine 036393
Sigurdsson, Helgi 021958
Sigurjonsdottir, Iris Olöf 021939
Sigurjónsson Jonsdottir, Sigrun Asta 021957
Sigurpålsson, Jón 021952
Sigwing, Marty 049153
Sihm, Marcel Agang-Ang 031636
Sijarić, Mirsad 003941
Šikić, Vojko 007717
Sikorska, Janina 031958
Sikorski, Marek 031859
Sila, Dr. Ante 007851
Silas, Anna 048100
Silber, Dr. Evelyn 039951
Silber, H. 020497
Silber, Karl-Heinz 017733
Silcox, David 006644
Silek, Suzanne 044090
Siler, Charles 046259
Šilina, Ljudmila Semënovna 033882
Silla, Dr. Chiara 024151
Silla, Dr. Chiaretta 024169, 024184, 024190, 024198, 024201
Sillaks, A. 038880
Sillanpää, Pirkko 009472
Silliman, Thomas 045990
Sillner, Helmut 001737
Šilnikova, Inna Evgenjevna 033988
Šilov, Lev Alekseevič 033641
Šilov, Viktor Valentinovič 033870
Šilova, Tatjana Ėduardovna 032980
Silva, Cyro Advincula da 004366
Silva, Dr. Heliodoro 032578
Silva, Isabel 032584
Silva, Ivan Mariano 004227
Silva, John 031648
Silva, Dr. Leonardo D. 004319
Silva, Mark 047267
Silva, Dr. P.H.D.H. de 036139, 036143
Silva, Pilar 035429
Silva de Oliveira, António Manuel 032669
Silva Montauntildea, Margarita 007616
Silva Silva, Párroco Isaac 007548
Silveira, Prof. Maria Auxiliadora 004241
Silveira Godinho, Isabel 032656
Silver, Jessica 046415
Silver, Joshua M. 046959
Silverio, Prof. Franco di 025221
Silverio, Dr. Loca di 025221
Silverman, David 046993
Silverman, Judd 046278
Silverman, Lanny 042833
Silvester, Suzanne 046646
Silvestre, Ines K. 031758
Silze, Peter 017687
Sim, Angela 034295
Sim, Lee 027574
Sim, Robin 046639
Simak, Ellen 042780
Simanjuntak, Pareli 022383
Simard, Guylaine 005725
Simard, Julie 006402
Simavi, Çigdem 038092
Simcock, Dr. J.P. 030435
Simeonova, Maria 004863
Simerly, E. 045720
Simić, Prof. Jasna 034266
Simina, Nicolae-Marcel 032932
Simister, Kirsten 039885
Simkins, Barbara 005739
Simková, Dr. Anežka 008694
Simmons, Amy 045466
Simmons, Arlene 045227
Simmons, Denise P. 048844
Simmons, Ian 040606
Simmons, Jamie 048538
Simmons, Julie M. 006535
Simmons, Mark 040697
Simmons, Susan 043572
Simo, Colleen M. 045228
Simon, C.M. 047026
Simon, Gerlinde 015613
Simon, Hal 043274
Simon, Helen 043794
Simon, Dr. László 021878, 021879, 021880, 021881, 021882, 021883, 021884, 021885, 021887, 021889
Simon, Nancy 049215
Simon, Robert 043427
Simon, Rolf 015673
Simon, Ronald 046376
Simon, Susanne 016867
Simona, Dr. Rafanelli 026298
Simončič, Alenka 034487
Simone, Suzanne 028991
Simoneau, Christiane 006660
Simonelli, Lynn 043318
Simonett, Dr. Jürg 037021
Simonetti, Dr. Farida 024299
Simoni, Kate 007828
Simoni, Rino 024280
Simonnet, Philippe 014005
Simons, Ulrich 019512
Simonson, George 045252
Simpel, Francis de 003843
Simpson, Ann 039424
Simpson, Colin M. 038716
Simpson, Helen J. 039342
Simpson, J.L. 041182
Simpson, John W. 005798
Simpson, Ken 038562
Simpson, Laurence 046332
Simpson, M.A. 005080
Simpson, Paula 040778
Simpson, Shannon 049021
Simpson, Shona 030559
Simpson, Prof. S.J. 040663
Simpson, Tracy 041457
Simpson, Wendell 048658
Sims, Judith 041921
Sims, Patterson 045978
Sims, Richard 047226
Sims-Burch, Wylene 043068
Simui, Muyoyeta 049573
Simundson, Peter 006623
Simunec, Josip 007862
Šimunić, Ljerka 007816
Sin, Jang Jong 027439
Sinaga, T. Moesa 022493
Sinanovitch, Laura 036903
Sinčić, Branko 007863
Sinclair, Dr. Bradley 016337
Sinclair, H.M. 041163
Sinclair, James J. 043292
Sinclair, Mark E. 044525
Sindermann, Sabine 019906
Sinding Steinsvik, Tone 030726
Singer, Ilana 022930

Singer, June . . . 041558
Singer, Karl . . . 018610
Singer, Dr. Marijane . . . 046701
Singh, Dr. Bhanu Pratap . . . 022201
Singh, Himmat . . . 022179
Singh, Prof. I.B. . . . 022241
Singh, S. . . . 022045
Singh, S. Amolak . . . 022009
Singh, Spoony . . . 045428
Singh, Vidya Nand . . . 022051
Singhvi, Dr. L.M. . . . 022085
Singleton, Ed . . . 043053
Singleton, G. David . . . 048656
Singley, Eric . . . 045418
Sinha, Prof. Anshu Kumar . . . 022237
Sinick, Chris . . . 047802
Sinisalo, Soili . . . 009515
Šinjaev, Nikolaj Ulanovič . . . 033136
Sinn, Margaret . . . 048874
Sinn, Prof. Dr. Ulrich . . . 021000
Sinnig-Haas, Christiane . . . 011282
Sinnott, George . . . 006153
Sinopoli, C. . . . 041733
Sinopoli, P.A. . . . 000528
Sinsheimer, Karen . . . 047950
Sintes, Claude . . . 010471
Sinyard, Elizabeth . . . 006007
Siokalo, Zoriana . . . 043505
Sipes, Robert L. . . . 047650
Šípková, Želmíra . . . 034454
Sirech, Alexander . . . 007985
Siri, Marta . . . 025129
Širin, Jurij . . . 033580
Širkanova, Maja Konstantinovna . . . 033603
Sirot Smith, Martin . . . 041156
Siry, Renaud . . . 013439
Sisdal, Odelbjørn . . . 031251
Sisi, Dr. Carlo . . . 024155
Sisi, Carlo . . . 024156
Sisi, Dr. Carlo . . . 024157, 024193
Šišigin, Egor Spiridonovič . . . 033187
Siska, József . . . 021891
Šiškin, Anatolij Aleksandrovič . . . 033747
Šiškova, Živka . . . 004664
Sisley, Alan . . . 001358
Sitar, Dr. Gerfried . . . 002613
Sitarski, Steve . . . 046937
Sithole, R. . . . 049579
Sitjar, Corazon . . . 031703
Sitkowska, Maryla . . . 032428
Sitt, Dr. Martina . . . 017694
Siudziński, Kazimierz . . . 031928
Siváček, Dr. Vladimír . . . 034394
Šivačev, Stefan . . . 004795, 004796
Sivan, Pnina . . . 022916
Sivcova, Natalja Viktorovna . . . 033547
Sivertson, Al . . . 004989
Sivkov, Dr. Janaki . . . 004924
Sivkova, Svetlana G. . . . 033217
Sivonen, Esa . . . 009810
Sivrić, Marijan . . . 034275
Sivrikaya, İsmet . . . 038163
Sivula, Leena . . . 009904
Sivusaari, Tiina . . . 009891
Sivyer, M.J. . . . 001206
Siwecki, Barbara . . . 043326
Siwek, Alberyk . . . 032407
Siwek, Jan . . . 031813
Sixbey, Peter . . . 043430
Siximons, Les . . . 001045
Sizemore, Bernice . . . 042100
Sjöberg, Ursula . . . 036664
Sjöberg-Pietarinen, Solveig . . . 010166
Sjöblom, Seth . . . 036780
Sjöö, Robert . . . 036284
Sjöskog, Per . . . 009827
Sjöström, Mats . . . 010176
Sjösvärd, Lars . . . 036283
Skaarup, Bi . . . 008970
Skaarup, J.C. . . . 009077
Skaarup, Jørgen . . . 009086
Skamby Madsen, Jan . . . 008917
Skandera, Franz . . . 020118
Skanis, M. . . . 027662
Skar, Anne Kari . . . 031221
Škarić, Mila . . . 007828
Skarpia-Heupel, Prof. Dr. Xanthippi . . . 021496
Skarsbø, Einar . . . 031120
Skarstein, Sigrid . . . 031310
Skarstøl, Gunnar . . . 030808
Skartsounis Schwab, Diane . . . 037016
Skatov, Nikolaj Nikolaevič . . . 033762
Skavhaug, Kjersti . . . 030905
Skeide, Cecilie . . . 030983
Skelly, David . . . 046226
Skenbuch, Urban . . . 036652
Škiljan, Maja . . . 007841
Skinner, J.F. . . . 041065, 041067
Skip, R. . . . 043402
Skippings, Lin . . . 040109
Skirtz Althea Warren, Stefan A. . . . 042916
Skjølberg, Erik . . . 030831
Sklar, E. . . . 005511
Sklenářová, Vilma . . . 008750
Skobeleva, T.P. . . . 033864
Škoberne, Želimir . . . 007849
Skoda, Joan . . . 047641
Skodak, Maria . . . 002005
Skog, Fredik . . . 036651
Skoghäll, Lars . . . 036522
Skoglund, Eric Y.W. . . . 036353
Skoglund, Ivar . . . 030754
Skoglund, Urban . . . 036580
Skonecki, Leonard . . . 044017
Skopec, Dr. Manfred . . . 002946
Skorikova, Svetlana Nikolaevna . . . 033084
Skoruls'ka, Oksana Mykytivna . . . 038313
Skory, Gary F. . . . 045848
Skotheim, Hege . . . 030941
Skott, Inga . . . 010199
Skov, Torben . . . 008923, 008926
Skov Kristensen, Henrik . . . 009061
Skowranet, Heide . . . 020356
Skriebeleit, Jörg . . . 017135
Škrinjarić, Srećko . . . 007828
Skrobov, Sergej . . . 033124
Skudal, Tina M. . . . 030788
Skuja, Andrejs . . . 027752
Škulj, Božica . . . 007857
Škurko, Dr. A.I. . . . 033399, 033522
Skutecki, Andreas . . . 020784
Škvařilová, Božena . . . 008613
Skvarla, Diane K. . . . 048955
Škvarnová, M. . . . 034452
Skwarlová, Alena . . . 008779
Skwirowski, Krzysztof . . . 032323
Skye, Stephen . . . 043236
Slabá, Jaroslava . . . 008399
Slabakova, Ganka . . . 004659, 004660
Slade, Norman . . . 045205
Sladen, S. . . . 041074
Slader, John . . . 043896
Sladky, Vaclav . . . 002991
Slamenová, Dr. Zuzanah . . . 034332
Slaney, Deb . . . 041613
Slanina, Súsanne . . . 020283
Slapinski, Tim . . . 042543
Slastunin, A.A. . . . 033252
Slater, Elizabeth A. . . . 040033
Slattery, Fiona . . . 040697
Slavick, Allison D. . . . 042539
Slavik, Jan . . . 036306
Sławski, Marek . . . 032290
Slear, Gary . . . 045244
Śledź, Edward . . . 031907
Sledzik, Paul . . . 048929
Slehofer, Vera . . . 036879
Slej, Dr. Karen . . . 036642
Slenczka, Dr. Eberhard . . . 019352
Slettjord, Lars . . . 031048
Sleurs, Jean-Pierre . . . 003490
Slichter, Jennifer . . . 045502
Slim, Soumaya . . . 028533
Slimon, Gary . . . 006097
Slinger, Frederico . . . 041544
Slivac, Barbara . . . 045191
Śliwiński, Eugeniusz . . . 032015
Sliwinski, Jennifer . . . 043503
Sloan, Brent . . . 047771
Sloan, Catherine . . . 040347
Sloan, Mark . . . 042734
Sloan, Sarah . . . 028209
Slobodzian, John . . . 005330
Slocum, Kay . . . 042630
Sloof Vermeij, P. . . . 029459
Sloss, Tencha . . . 042482
Slotta, Prof. Dr. Rainer . . . 016276
Slover, Louise . . . 044512
Slovin, Rochelle . . . 041821
Slowe, V.A.J. . . . 039134
Složenikina, Valentina Ivanovna . . . 033671
Sluis, R. ter . . . 029645
Slyngborg, Mette . . . 008843
Smadar, Harpazi . . . 023093
Smailes, Helen . . . 039406
Smal, M. . . . 034728
Small, Jim . . . 044320
Small, Lawrence M. . . . 048944
Small, Lisa . . . 046320
Small, Luke . . . 006839
Small, Nicole G. . . . 043270
Smalley, Patricia . . . 046369
Smallman, Anne . . . 043043
Smart, Pansy . . . 044773
Šmatov, Victor . . . 003137
Smedt, Raphaël de . . . 003291, 003342
Smeets, H. . . . 030229
Smerdel, Inja . . . 034492
Smidt, D.A.M. . . . 029854
Smidt, Erzsébet . . . 021899
Smidt-Jensen, Jörgen . . . 009063
Smietana, Evelyn . . . 045172
Smiley, Kristine . . . 045801, 045802
Smiljković, Koviljka . . . 034272
Smilova, Dimitrina . . . 004651
Smirnova, Natalja Petrovna . . . 033867
Smirnova, N.V. . . . 033096
Smit, K. . . . 029529
Smit, Sandra . . . 034550
Smit, Toril . . . 031113
Smith, A. . . . 039583
Smith, Adam . . . 046735
Smith, Agnes L. . . . 043897
Smith, Alan . . . 001005, 001484
Smith, Alistair . . . 040416
Smith, Allan . . . 030431
Smith, Amanda . . . 048531
Smith, Dr. Amy C. . . . 040811
Smith, Ann . . . 039095, 041006, 048979
Smith, Anne . . . 047435
Smith, Antony . . . 041338
Smith, Art . . . 006272
Smith, Becky . . . 044163
Smith, Bertyne . . . 042028
Smith, Betsy . . . 043506
Smith, Bill . . . 041827
Smith, Dr. B.J. . . . 001178
Smith, Bradley . . . 048394
Smith, Brian . . . 045215
Smith, Bruce . . . 043095
Smith, Byron C. . . . 044976
Smith, Calvin B. . . . 048814, 048817
Smith, Carol . . . 043552
Smith, Carole . . . 045838
Smith, Caron . . . 047838
Smith, Chris . . . 039346
Smith, Chuck . . . 047048
Smith, Clive . . . 030527
Smith, Colin . . . 041373
Smith, D. Ryan . . . 042089
Smith, Daniel J. . . . 049063
Smith, Darryl . . . 047868
Smith, David . . . 005824, 045614
Smith, Dr. David A.S. . . . 039458
Smith, Deborah A. . . . 042489
Smith, Diane . . . 048222
Smith, Dr. Donald . . . 039398
Smith, Donna . . . 005431, 005432
Smith, Donna M. . . . 005074
Smith, Dottie . . . 047358
Smith, Doug . . . 041693
Smith, Duane . . . 044671
Smith, Dwight . . . 043448
Smith, Earl . . . 049025
Smith, Elizabeth . . . 042860, 048269
Smith, Elizabeth A. . . . 046012
Smith, Francis . . . 005108
Smith, Francis X. . . . 042021
Smith, Fred T. . . . 044966
Smith, Frederick G. . . . 042785
Smith, Gary . . . 044366
Smith, Gary D. . . . 044443
Smith, Gary N. . . . 043274
Smith, Gary T. . . . 047758
Smith, Gloria A. . . . 042644
Smith, Guy . . . 047941
Smith, Dr. H. Duane . . . 047273
Smith, Heather . . . 005954
Smith, Howard . . . 040404
Smith, Ian . . . 040803
Smith, J. . . . 030460, 041252
Smith, Dr. James N.M. . . . 006695
Smith, Jan . . . 045638, 046171
Smith, Jane . . . 042483
Smith, JaNeen M. . . . 044051
Smith, Janet . . . 005775
Smith, Janice . . . 005588
Smith, Jay . . . 044704
Smith, J.B. . . . 046845
Smith, Jean . . . 005985
Smith, Jerry . . . 048956
Smith, Joel . . . 047211
Smith, John T. . . . 044850
Smith, Judy . . . 047973
Smith, Kelleen . . . 045192
Smith, Kent . . . 042850, 048284
Smith, Kevin . . . 042502, 045165
Smith, Kevin P. . . . 042423
Smith, Kory . . . 045459
Smith, Kristine . . . 044398
Smith, Kym . . . 000796
Smith, Lisa Deanne . . . 006648
Smith, M. . . . 006387
Smith, Mariann . . . 042498
Smith, Marilyn . . . 005768, 006116, 043161
Smith, Mark . . . 040476
Smith, Mary . . . 006107, 006109
Smith, Maureen M. . . . 047239
Smith, Maurice . . . 005706
Smith, Michael . . . 046086
Smith, Michael J. . . . 045504
Smith, Michael O. . . . 043430
Smith, Michele L. . . . 048746
Smith, Dr. M.P. . . . 038732
Smith, Nancy . . . 022861
Smith, Norman . . . 045878
Smith, Owen . . . 041907
Smith, Pamela . . . 047975
Smith, Pat A. . . . 043019
Smith, Patricia F. . . . 045292, 049276
Smith, Pauline M. . . . 041846
Smith, Peggy . . . 045141
Smith, R. . . . 005188
Smith, R.D. . . . 039959
Smith, Rebecca . . . 044163
Smith, Rebecca A. . . . 045809
Smith, R.E.G. . . . 006204
Smith, Richard . . . 048339
Smith, Dr. R.M.H. . . . 034586
Smith, Robert A. . . . 048546
Smith, Robert H. . . . 048924
Smith, Robert J. . . . 045204
Smith, Ron . . . 006201
Smith, Ronald . . . 045382
Smith, Sam . . . 043210
Smith, Scott . . . 048027
Smith, Shana . . . 047129
Smith, Sharon . . . 041259
Smith, Shauna . . . 048300
Smith, Sheila . . . 038785
Smith, Shirley . . . 044089
Smith, Stan . . . 043470

Smith, Stephanie 042838
Smith, Steve 048238
Smith, Sue 001436
Smith, Susan 048147
Smith, Terri 046141
Smith, Thomas 047068
Smith, Tim 044669
Smith, Tobi 047985
Smith, Todd 043815
Smith, Trevor 001375
Smith, Vivian DuRant 046426
Smith, Warwick 030556
Smith, Wayne C. 045134
Smith, W.D. 039004
Smith-Christmas, Kenneth L. 047291
Smith de Tarnowsky, Andrea 046139
Smith-Ferri, Sherrie 048683
Smith-Speelman, Dr. Khristina ... 043013
Smith Woods, Karen 042030
Smitherman, Joy 048068
Smithline, Howard 023019
Smitten, Al 005546
Smoak, Janet 047779
Smogór, Anna 031821
Smola, Dr. Franz 002853, 002969
Smolders, R. 029470
Smole Gavrilovic, Margita 003941
Smolek, Michael A. 047651
Smolík, Luboš 008436
Smoljaninova, Iryna Mykolaïvna .. 038302
Smolkin, Robert 042192
Smorenburg, D. 030249
Smorodinsky, Marina 045418
Smrcka, Mariann 045741
Smrekar, Dr. Andrej 034487
Smucker, Linda 049373
Smurthwaite, D. 040240
Smutná, Silva 008744
Smylski, Brian 006015
Smyth, Deirdre 039806
Smyth, R. 005793
Smyth, Victor 046399
Snars, Frank 001218
Sneddon, Russell C. 043622
Šneiter, G.G. 033388
Snell, Dr. Gesa 017730
Snell, Dr. Howard L. 041619
Snell, Prof. Ted 000798
Snetselaar, Rebecca 049194
Snibbe, Robert M. 042971
Snichelotto, Paolo 025737
Snider, Gary 006508
Snider, James B. 044078
Snider, Katherine 046358
Snider, Phyllis 041776
Śniegocki, Michał 032464
Snoddy, Stephen 040473
Snoddy, Suzie 048417
Snodgrass, Dianna H. 044379
Snoeys, Johan 003183
Snørteland, Dr. Målfrid 031041
Snørteland, Målfrid 031042
Snørtzland, Dr. Målfrid 031046
Snow, David H. 047975
Snowden, Gilda 043445
Snowden, Karen 040967, 040969
Snowdon, Sam T. 043834
Snydacker, Daniel 046459
Snydal, Dave 005143
Snyder, Barbara C. 045740
Snyder, Craig 041642
Snyder, Howard 005226
Snyder, James 022960, 047331
Snyder, James S. 022974
Snyder, Jill 042984
Snyder, Jim 049357
Snyder, Marion 049013
Snyder, Michael B. 044819
Snyder, Rob 047283
So, Gretchen 046372
So, Dr. Jenny 048884, 048908
So, Nguyen 049538
Soane, Sir John 040257
Soans, Hanno 009398
Soares, Dr. Marie-Christine 037784
Soares de Souza, Prof. Jonas 004156
Sobczyk, Pawel 032503
Sobel, Dean 041819
Sobezyk, Stéphanie 011660
Sobieraj, Edward 032225
Sobieraj, Janusz Szczepan 031950
Sobieszek, Robert 045441
Sobiesznak-Marcimak, Margaret . 032454
Sobita Devi, Dr. K. 022170
Soboleva, L.L. 033286
Sobolik, Bonnie 044262
Søborg, Hans Christian 030722
Sobótek, Czesław 032554
Socarrás, Carlos 007605
Soccoro R. Samson, Marlene 031662
Sochovolsky, Z. 023087
Socias, Luis G. 035603
Socorro Mallorca, Maria 031674
Sodagar, L. 022640
Soden, Jack 045760
Soden, Joanna 039420
Soechting, Dr. Dirk 020235
Söderlind, Lars 036525
Söderlind, Prof. Solfrid 036648
Söderlund, Göran 036657
Söderström, Marita 010176
Soeharto, Ki 022535
Soejanto, B.U.W. 022393
Soekiman, Dr. Djoko 022543
Sölder, Wolfgang 002097
Söllner, Jürgen 020106
Soemaatmadja, Atang 022438
Sömmer, Hermann 015681
Sönmez, Dr. Necmi 017074, 017075
Söptei, István 021838
Sörensen, Steinar 030821
Sörries, Prof. Dr. Reiner 018195
Soesilo Hadi, Dr. Hidayat 022534
Soetjipto, Dr. 022516
Soffiantino, Paola 026052
Softić, Dr. Aiša 003941
Softic, Ajsa 003941
Soganci, Dr. Marion 019178
Soggin, Gian Piero 025000
Sogoba, Djaié 028021
Sohal, Neena 041052
Sohinki, Arnie 047513
Sohl, Katrin 018594
Sohlern, Gilbert von 017461
Sohnle, Dr. W. 020372
Søholt, Petter ... 031015, 031287, 031287
Soika, Dr. Aya 038968
Soileau, Malbae 048965
Soja, Henryk 032007
Sojková, Dr. Jana 008761
Šoka, Milan 034304
Sokač-Štimac, Prof. Dubravka ... 007775
Soklove, Deborah 048893
Sokol, Vladimir 007790
Sokól-Augustyńska, Maria 032277
Sokolov, Dr. Aleksej 033729
Sokolov, Dr. Nikolaj N. 033387
Sokołowska, Beata 032538
Sokołowska, Renata 032375
Sokolowski, Thomas 047039
Sol i Bachs, Josep M. 034952
Solà Turell, Ramón 035661
Solander, Terry J. 044150
Solańska, Krystyna 032061
Solberg, Chet 048050
Solberg, Per 030763
Šolc, Dr. Josef 008501
Soldaini, Julio E. 000165
Soldatova, Nina Ivanovna 033866
Soldatova, Tamara Mikolaïvna ... 038303
Soldini, Dr. Simone 037325
Sole, Allen 029090
Sole, Laura M. 039831
Solé, Maties 035513, 035514
Soler García, José María 036069
Soles, Mary Ellen 047313
Solheim Pedersen, Einar 031221
Solias i Aris, Josep 035283
Šolić, Dr. Marija-Edita 007756
Solimon, Ron 041615
Solis, Claudia 044634
Solis, Isabel 006950
Solivar, Sonia 031641
Solms, Fürst zu 016376
Šolochov, Aleksandr Michajlovič .. 034031
Solomatenko, Marg 006200
Solomko, Juri 033423
Solomon, Elizabeth 046997
Solomon Kiefer, Carol 041692
Solórzano Pérez, Diana 028285
Solovev, Aleksandr Borisovič 033748
Solovëva, E.A. 003128
Solovjeva, Ljubov Pavlovna 033176
Soloyeni, Joanna 021396
Soltek, Dr. Stefan 019455
Soltis, Dr. P.S. 044103
Solymosi, Rosalia 021641
Some, Porosper 004957
Somers, David 005132, 005134
Somers, Stephen G. 043159
Somerville, Ann 030589
Somerville, Robert 005208
Somma, Dr. Thomas P. ... 044060, 044062
Sommani, Dr. Donatella 026091
Sommer, Dr. Achim 016958
Sommer, B.A. 006538
Sommer, Lawrence J. 045307
Sommer, Mogens 008846
Sommer, Dr. Roswitha 016485
Sommer, Susan 046390
Sommer, Dr. Susanne 016855
Sommer Ribeiro, José A. 032627
Sommerfeld, Renate 020071
Sommerfeldt Gikas, Carol 042044
Sommerhuber, Christian 002705
Sommers, Joyce A. 044746
Sommers, Larry 045312
Somoza, Maria E. 032735
Sonder, Lucien 046327
Søndergaard, Sidsel 008982
Sonderman, Jacque 046838
Song, Prof. Ki-Ho 027602
Sonke, Denton 042232
Sonnabend, Dr. Martin 017195
Sonnabend, Regina 016684
Sonnberger, Gerwald 046384
Sonnenberger, Dr. Franz . 019346, 019347, 019357, 019358, 019367, 019373, 019374, 019375, 019377
Sonnenburg, Hubert von 046364
Sonno, Dr. Viviana 023279, 023285
Sonntag, Dr. Dina 020374
Sonntag, Gabrielle 012796
Sonntag, Dr. Hans 018890
Sonntag, Johannes 016960
Sonntag, Dr. Johannes-Hendrik ... 017394, 017395, 017396, 017397
Sonoyama, Hiroshi 027180
Soohey, Shirron 048742
Soosloff, Philip 047501
Sopóliga, Dr. Miróslav 034439
Sorber, Frieda 003166
Soregaroli, Dr. Art 005155
Sorell, M.E. 045777
Soren, Joshua 048070
Sørensen, Anne Birgitte 008885
Sørensen, Anny 008855
Sørensen, Einar 030807
Sørensen, Jens 009056, 009057
Sørensen, Jens Erik 008805
Sørensen, Marianne 009142
Sørensen, Ove 009042
Sørheim, Helge 031221
Soriano, Alain 010381
Soriano, Dr. Corazon 031745
Soriano, Dolores 034947
Sormsen, Ellen C. 047443
Sorokin, Igor Vladimirovič 033853
Sorokina, N.I. 033445
Sorsak, Maks 034485
Sosič, Sarival 034483
Sošin, Aleksandr Pavlovič 033201
Šošmin, Aleksandr Aleksandrovič . 033824
Sosnovs'ka, Tatjana Viktorivna ... 038301
Sosnovskaja, Marina Jurjevna ... 033113
Sossenheimer, Doris 020859
Sotheran, Cheryll 030653
Soto, Jules M.R. 004145
Soto Bastida, Nicolás 028486
Součková, Dr. Jana 008473, 008632
Souichi, Takahata 026992
Souka Séko, Cisse Nèe 003892
Soule, Robert M. 042783
Soult 016026
Souplet, Michel 012392
Sourakli, Judy 048081
Sousa, Maria José Rego 032590
Souster, L. 040427
Souter, Jill 047806
Souter, Teri 005630
South, Allison 047775
Southall, A. 040682
Southall, Tom 041862
Southard, Edna Carter 046773
Southern, John 039245
Southern, Kathy Dwyer 048890
Southwell, Carey 044232
Southworth, Edmund ... 038908, 039719, 039919, 039920, 039921, 039922, 039923, 039925, 040030, 040779
Soutif, Prof. Daniel 025359
Souza, Amandio 032616
Sovaudjieva, Natalia 004672
Sovluk, Viktor Ivanovič 033300
Sowada, Dr. Karin 001521
Sowder, Marvin 043285
Sowers, Russ 044608
Sowinski, Larry 046224
Soyhan, Cihat 038102
Soylu, Nilüfer 038134
Sozio, Janet L. 046059
Space, Fred 048444
Space, Parker 048444
Špaček, Jaroslav 008311
Spackman, A.J. 040217
Spadavecchia, Fiorella 026244
Spadea, Dr. Roberto 024004, 024005
Späth, Annette .. 015670, 015672, 015732
Spagnola, Gina 044136
Spahr, Elisabeth 037087
Spahr, P. Andrew 045618
Spaid, Sue 042922
Spalding, Jeffrey 005769
Spalding, Jeffrey J. 046609
Spalek, Dr. Ladislav 034381, 034432
Spancer, Donald B. 045564
Spang, Mathias 016225
Spang, Veronika 020365
Spangenberg, Kristin 042919
Spangenberg, L. 034669
Spanke, Dr. Daniel 020897
Spanos Nordan, Antoinette 042228
Spargo, Janet 038956
Sparks, Brian 045353
Sparks, Kevin S. 049218
Sparre, Comte de 015002
Sparrow, John 040704
Sparrow, Judy 040704
Spas'ka, Larisa Ivanivna 038350
Spassibenko, A.V. 027415
Spathari, Elizabeth 021131, 021141, 021289
Špatný, Jan 008688
Spaulding, Daniel 041745
Spautz, Andrea 017765
Spear, June 005456
Spear, Robert N. 044682
Speare, Jed 042332
Spearman, Grant 041709
Spears, Carolyn 046119
Spears, Dolores 044854
Spears, Kimberly 041718

Spears, Susan . . . 045705
Specht Corsi, Martha . . . 025949
Speciale, Giovanni . . . 023592
Speciale, Michael P. . . . 049240
Speckels, Gabriele . . . 019546
Specter, David . . . 046385
Spector, Nancy . . . 046404
Spedding, J.H.F. . . . 039853
Spedding, Michael . . . 030501
Spedini, Prof. Gabriella . . . 025526
Speierl, Dr. Charles . . . 043017
Spelak, Lucyna . . . 032168
Speler, Dr. Ralf-Torsten . . . 017664
Spellazza, William Salvador . . . 043765
Speller, Margaret . . . 039279
Spen, Cathryn . . . 038622
Spence, Millie . . . 006171
Spence, Talbert B. . . . 042257
Spencer, Elizabeth . . . 039225, 039227
Spencer, Georgia . . . 044800
Spencer, Jeff . . . 046870
Spencer, Jim . . . 042959
Spencer, Leonard H. . . . 042540
Spencer, Ted . . . 043139
Spencer, Wendy . . . 047684, 048480
Spencer-Davies, Jenni . . . 041171
Spencer-Longhurst, Dr. P. . . . 038720
Spendel, Dr. Cölestin . . . 002612, 003058
Spender, Michael . . . 039355
Sperath, Albert . . . 046100
Sperber, Dr. G. . . . 005392
Sperber, Dr. Lothar . . . 020263
Sperebet, Yilmaz . . . 008257
Sperl, Karl Eberhard . . . 018867
Sperling, F.A.H. . . . 042159
Sperling, Marion . . . 043618
Speth, John D. . . . 041733
Spicer, Joaneath . . . 042006
Spicer, Margaret E. . . . 044426
Spichtig, Klara . . . 037514
Špička, Dr. Dušan . . . 008460, 008710
Spiegel, Elisabeth . . . 018339
Spiegel, Lisa J. . . . 042354
Spiegel, Marty . . . 048088
Spiegelberg, Dr. U. . . . 017931
Spiegelman, Deborah . . . 045815
Spieler, Dr. Reinhard . . . 036991
Spielmann, Prof. Heinz . . . 017682
Spies, Heike . . . 016831
Spies, Uta . . . 019571
Spieß, Dieter . . . 020845
Spiessens, Frans . . . 003244
Spigo, Dr. Umberto . . . 024504
Spilka, Abby R. . . . 046373
Spilker, Rolf . . . 019498
Spillemaecker, Chantal . . . 012243
Spiller, Harriet . . . 042499
Spiller, Mortimer . . . 042499
Spiller, Steven T. . . . 047359
Spillman, Jane S. . . . 043155
Spillman, W.B. . . . 045135
Spindle, Carol . . . 047205
Spindler, Gabriele . . . 002249
Spindler, Jean-Charles . . . 010854
Spinelli-Flesch, Marie . . . 010768
Spinner, Helmut . . . 017804
Spinola, Dr. Giandomenico 049422, 049430
Spires, Ruth . . . 041045
Spiridonov, Jurij Ivanovič . . . 033310
Spiro, Stephen B. . . . 046574
Spitler, Bing G. . . . 048128
Spitzack, Maynard A. . . . 043816
Spitzbart, Ingrid . . . 001912
Spivak, Lisa . . . 043416
Spivey, Towana . . . 043977
Splaine, Shirley . . . 041807
Šplíchalová, Vladimíra . . . 008768
Spliethoff, Dr. M. . . . 029256
Splitt, Jerzy Aleksander . . . 031976
Splitter, Dr. Rüdiger . . . 018179
Spooner, Zoe . . . 045925
Sporea, Radoje . . . 034145
Sporer-Heis, Dr. Claudia . . 002089, 002097
Sportiello, Anne . . . 012950
Spotts, George . . . 044312
Spowart, Cliff . . . 001412
Spoz, Andrzej . . . 032417
Sprain, Donald . . . 049113
Sprankling, Miriam . . . 046441
Spratt, Andrew . . . 040884
Sprayue, John . . . 047454
Sprecher, Dr. Eva . . . 036899
Sprecher, Dr. Dr. Thomas . . . 037804
Spree, Tommy . . . 015985
Spreer, Elmar . . . 017054
Sprem Lovrić, Branka . . . 007751
Spriggs, Lynne . . . 041862
Spring, Marika . . . 040241
Springer, Bill . . . 042404
Springer, Donald C. . . . 048836
Springer, Ernst . . . 002054
Springer, Fred . . . 048523
Springer, Jonathan . . . 047348
Springer, Kathleen . . . 047362
Springer, Dr. Tobias . . . 019352
Springhorn, Prof. Dr. Rainer . . . 016690
Sprink, Claus-Dieter . . . 016066
Sproat, Dr. John G. . . . 043080, 043083
Spruill, Sarah C. . . . 042789
Spruill Redford, Dorothy . . . 043219
Spruit, R.J. . . . 029775
Sprung, Sigrid . . . 002969
Sprung, Y. . . . 022902
Spuler, Dr. Christof . . . 015420
Spur, Birgitta . . . 021965
Spurgeon, Lucy . . . 049303
Spurney, Dr. Robert . . . 048125
Spychała, Jerzy . . . 032110
Spyropoulos, Prof. Dr. Theodoros . 021151, 021276, 021371, 021474, 021482, 021514
Squier, P.H.M. . . . 039074
Squiers, Carol . . . 046348
Squire, Richard J. . . . 042098
Squires, Ann . . . 044855
Sretenovic, Vesela . . . 047253
Srimal, Swdip . . . 022223
Srinivasan, Shanta . . . 022096
Srivastava, Dr. G.P. . . . 022237
Sroka, Steven . . . 048766
Sroka, Teresa . . . 031949
Srp, Karel . . . 008606
St. Onge, Dave . . . 005694
Staarman, A. . . . 029408
Staat, D.W. . . . 029269
Staber, Deborah . . . 044553
Stableton, Mike . . . 048050
Stachel, G. . . . 018504
Stachel, M. . . . 018504
Stack, Joan . . . 043072
Stack, Lotus . . . 045918
Stack, R. . . . 001516
Stackpole, Matthew . . . 043603
Stackpole, Renny A. . . . 048073
Stacy, Kaye . . . 001469
Stade, Anette . . . 037056
Stadelmann, Kurt . . . 036932
Stader, Anette . . . 037355
Stadler, Eva Maria . . . 001931, 052539
Stadler, Herbert . . . 019357
Stadler, Hilar . . . 037224
Stadler, Dr. Peter . . . 002327
Stadler, Wilhelm . . . 002544
Stadtman, Kenneth L. . . . 047271
Staebell, Sandra . . . 042366
Städtler, Leopold . . . 001928
Stäheli, Charles E. . . . 037201
Stähli, Alois . . . 037502
Stämpfli, Markus . . . 036963
Stäuble, Dr. Nicole . . . 037675
Staffen, Dr. Zdeňek . . . 008333
Stager, Prof. Lawrence . . . 042561
Stagg, Barbara . . . 047566
Stagleder, Linda . . . 043817
Stagno, Dr. Laura . . . 024327
Stahel, Urs . . . 037717
Stahl, Alan M. . . . 046287
Ståhl, Elizabet . . . 036265
Stahl, Dr. Johannes . . . 016316
Stahl, Judith R. . . . 042053
Stahl, Kathleen P. . . . 042583
Stahl, Konrad . . . 018995
Stahl, Mongerité . . . 012664
Stahl, Patricia . . . 017176, 017181
Stahl, Prof. Paul H. . . . 032807
Ståhlberg, Ninaka . . . 010048
Stahlecker, Robert C.G.A. . . . 029443
Stahn, Frank . . . 017065
Staikova, Evdokia . . . 004863
Stainback, Charles . . . 048010
Stajčić, Milorad . . . 034209
Staker, Mark L. . . . 047774
Staker, Ron . . . 043799
Stalder, Dieter . . . 037265
Stalf, Oscar . . . 020655
Stalling, Dr. Gesine . . . 019352
Stallings, Diane G. . . . 044836
Stallings, Tyler . . . 045095
Stallwitz, Kurt . . . 043526
Stalskaja, Lidija Mirzejusofovna . . 033000
Stalvey, Dorrance . . . 045441
Stalvey, Rip . . . 048488
Stambach, Dr. Rudi . . . 037463
Stambaugh, James D. . . . 049134
Stambrau, Doris I. . . . 017182
Štambuk, Slobodan . . . 007725
Stamhuis, I.M. . . . 030217
Stamm, Hannelore . . . 015951
Stamm, Jörg . . . 037627
Stamm, Dr. Rainer . . . 016419
Stamm, Wolfgang . . . 020172
Stammers, Michael . . . 040032
Stammers, Mike . . . 040035
Stancati, Antonella . . . 025542
Stanciu, Ştefan . . . 032867
Stancu, Dr. Radu . . . 032912
Standen, J. . . . 040949
Standen, Roger . . . 039660
Standenat, Peter . . . 002326
Standley, Janet . . . 041422
Standring, Timothy . . . 043404
Stanek, Barbara . . . 032190
Stanek, Dr. Christian . . . 002959
Stângă, Ion . . . 032858, 032859
Stange, Lorraine . . . 047726
Stangel, John . . . 045637
Stangier, Thomas . . . 018487
Stangl, Bernhard . . . 002161
Stangl, Denise . . . 042184
Stangl, Reinhard . . . 018691
Stangler, Prof. Dr. Ferdinand . . . 002327
Staniczek, Dr. Arnold . . . 020364
Stanimitović, Angelina . . . 034278
Stanislav, Dr. Ján . . . 034302
Stanislavska, Ljudmyla Pavlivna . . 038275
Štankina, Irina Valeriïvna . . . 038231
Stankiritz, Gina . . . 041888
Stankov, Vesna . . . 034281
Stanland, Richard C. . . . 043081
Stanley, Allein . . . 044154
Stanley, B. . . . 048899
Stanley, Diane . . . 043699
Stanley, Eric . . . 047994
Stanley, Michael . . . 038731
Stanley, Tom . . . 047489
Stansberry, Lucy . . . 043656
Stanshev, Stansho . . . 004684
Stanton, Dr. J.E. . . . 001319
Stanton, Meridith Z. . . . 042477
Stanulis, Roxanne M. . . . 043488
Stapel, R. . . . 020949
Stapf, Arnulf . . . 019316
Stappaerts, Greet . . . 003182
Starbuck, robin . . . 042124
Starcky, Emmanuel . . . 011608, 011612
Starham, J.T. . . . 040436
Stark, Dr. Barbara . . . 018379, 018380
Stark, Dr. Frank . . . 042896
Stark, Julie . . . 049367
Stark, Linda . . . 006424
Stark, Ole . . . 020695
Stark, Peter . . . 046622
Stark, William . . . 044490
Stark, William G. . . . 045164
Starke, Jörg . . . 016182
Starkey, Marsha B. . . . 044437
Starkey, Patsy . . . 045948
Starlin, Mildred . . . 041585
Starling, Kate . . . 040230
Starling, P.H. . . . 038476
Starnes, Wayne . . . 047315
Starodubcev, Gennadij Jurjevič . . . 033320
Starr Hart, Leslie . . . 044869
Stasch, Dr. Gregor . . . 017298, 017302
Stasinopoulou, Elisavet . . . 021183
Stasiuk, Savelia . . . 006712
Staski, Edward . . . 045181
Stastna, Dr. Eva . . . 034337
Staton, James D. . . . 048419
Stattler, Rick . . . 047264
Staub, Bettina . . . 037619
Staub, Edith . . . 036866
Štauber, Dr. Bedřich . . . 008490, 008492
Stauber, Reinhard . . . 017947
Stauber, Richard . . . 037351
Staubermann, Dr. K. . . . 030240
Staubli, Gallus . . . 036932
Stauder, Heiner . . . 018653
Staudinger, Wilhelm . . . 017154
Staudt, Benno . . . 017242
Stauffacher, Ueli . . . 037227
Stauffer, Nancy . . . 047568
Staunton, Bob . . . 040333
Stauß, Christian . . . 019037
Stave, Pari . . . 046299
Stavem Arrowsmith, Valorie . . . 042568
Stavitsky, Gail . . . 045978
Stavropoulos, Savvas . . . 021407
Stavrou, Dr. Patroclos . . . 021286
Stawarczyk, Prof. Tadeusz . . . 032525
Stawarz, Dr. Andrzej . . . 032457
Stawowy, Grzegorz . . . 032347
Stayton, Kevin . . . 042458, 042458
Stažić, Andjelko . . . 007846
Steacy, Archie M. . . . 006689
Stead, Miriam . . . 041131
Steadman, Dr. D.W. . . . 044103
Stearns, Emily . . . 049059
Stebbins, Theodore . . . 042560
Steblecki, Edith . . . 042340
Stecher, Anton . . . 002071
Stecher, Dr. Hans Peter . . . 002246
Stecker, Heidi . . . 018568
Stecker, Prof. Dr. Raimund . . . 019789
Steckley, John . . . 044159
Stedall, Tony . . . 041191
Steed, Martha J. . . . 042216
Steehler, Dr. Kirk W. . . . 043721
Steel, David H. . . . 047313
Steel, Martin . . . 046349
Steel, Philip . . . 030513
Steele, Curtis . . . 044878
Steele, Jeffrey . . . 044519
Steele, Joe . . . 006028
Steele, Robert . . . 046805
Steele, Steven . . . 043416
Steele, Dr. Valerie . . . 046370
Steen, Johan . . . 029587
Steen, Dr. Jürgen . . . 017176
Steen, Laura . . . 043047
Steen Jacobsen, Jan . . . 008918
Steen Jensen, Jørgen . . . 008971
Steen-Zuniga, Britt . . . 042687
Steenbeek, Dr. T.G.D. . . . 030291
Steenbruggen, Han . . . 029638
Steensma, Jennifer . . . 044279
Ştefan-Nicolin, Mihail . . . 032803
Štefančíková, Dr. Alica . . . 008491
Stefanelli, Claudio . . . 025192, 025194
Stefanescu, Dan . . . 032813
Ştefănescu, Radu . . . 032792
Stefani, Claude . . . 011266
Stefani, L. . . . 021518

Stefanidou-Tiveriou, Prof. Dr. Th. . 021499
Stefanko, V.M. 038289
Stefanov, Georgi 004678
Stefanova, Morena 004863
Stefánsdóttir, Ragnheidur 021930
Steffan, Anton 001779
Steffan, Ferdinand 020687
Steffan, Günther 001779
Steffan, Roland 037500
Steffan, Dr. Wallace A. 047497
Steffan, Wallen A. 048440
Steffen, Carlos 004293
Steffen, Geneviève 043556
Steffen, Paul 037531
Steffian, Amy 045044
Steffl, John 043518
Stege, Frank 018940
Stege, Dr. Heike 019048
Stegeman, E. 029346
Steger, Adrian 037716
Stegmann, Dr. Markus 037524
Steguweit, Dr. Wolfgang 016120
Stehlin, Vera 036896
Stehphan, H. J. 016780
Steidl, Erwin 002134
Steidl, Dr. Thomas 002297
Steiger, Ivan 008623, 019116
Steiger, Ricabeth 037784
Steigert, Roger 048303
Steigerwald, Steve 044846
Steigman, Kenneth 045560
Stein, Christin L. 044829
Stein, Hanspeter 002408
Stein, Jutta 016684
Stein, Longest F. 016040
Stein, Peter 047869
Stein, Simcha 023026
Stein, Susan R. 042766
Stein, Dr. Wolfgang 019122
Steinau, Marlies 020134
Steinau, Norbert 016545
Steinberg, Dr. David 042476
Steinborn, Vera 016771
Steinbrenner, Theophil 020247
Steinbring, Wally 005068
Steinbrügge, Bettina 018742, 053227
Steinegger, Karl 002009
Steiner, Barbara 018568
Steiner, Charles 027827
Steiner, Charles K. 049163
Steiner, Chris 041613
Steiner, Dietmar 002848
Steiner, Dr. Erich 002619, 002619
Steiner, Dr. Peter B. 017244
Steiner, Ralph 040882
Steinhauer, Dr. George . . . 021113, 021430
Steinhauser, H. J 020167
Steinhauser, Prof. Dr. Monika 016279, 016284
Steinhauser, Norbert 017271
Steinhof, Dr. Monika 016426
Steininger, Prof. Erich 002618
Steininger, Florian 002855
Steininger, Prof. Dr. Fritz F. 017193
Steinkeller, Prof. Piotr 042561
Steinlage, Forrest F. 044850
Steinle, Dr. Christa 001943
Steinle, E. 020119
Steinle, Karl-Heinz 016171
Steinmann, Dr. Axel 002961
Steinmetz, Robert 010780
Steinmetz, Dr. Walter 002518
Steinmetz, Wolf-Dieter 016381
Steinmetz, Wolf Dieter 020954
Steinwendtner, Hans 001998, 001999
Stejskal, Václav 008731
Stejskalová, Eliška 008558
Štekar-Vidic, Verena 034457, 034475, 034515, 034516
Stelfox, Evearad 043744
Stella, Dr. Clara 023526
Steller, Tom 046598
Stellmacher, Bernhard 020206
Stellwes, Carla 047791
Stelzhamer, Ernst 002833
Štem, Galina Michajlovna 033045
Stemmer, Dr. Klaus 015978
Stemmrich, Dr. Daniel 019391
Stenberg, Gunilla 036349
Stender, D. 017093
Steneberg, Suzanne 036732
Steneker, J. 029334
Stengel, Karin 018184
Stengel, Tom 045944
Stengert, Monika 049285
Stenhouse, Roderick 040488
Stenkamp, Dr. Hermann-Josef . . . 016274, 016771
Stenkula, Anna 036651
Stenman, Paul 009724, 009726
Stenning, Howard 038504
Stensholt, Morten Chr. 031254
Stenstrop, Georg 008871
Stepančič, Lilijana 034482
Stepanova, Anna Alekseevna 033947
Stepanova, Ljudmila Vasiljevna . . . 033087
Stepanova, Maria 033143
Stephan 018768
Stephan, Eric 018117
Stephan, Peter 019694
Stephan, Ralph 020218
Stephen, Charla 042284
Stephen, Virginia 005393
Stephen Weppner, Mary Dessoie . . 042203
Stephens, Dawn 042450
Stephens, John R. 044255
Stephens, Matt 039887, 039891
Stephens, Retha 044958
Stephens, Ruby A. 047728
Stephens, Spencer 048166
Stephens, Xavier 045615
Stephens Kruize, Pricilla G. 045806
Stephenson, Holly 044897
Stephenson, Tim 039171
Stepic, Barbara 042470
Stepken, Angelika 018157
Šter, Janez 034533
Stergar, Branka 007772
Šterk, Slavko 007849
Sterly, Marita 017866, 017868
Stermer, Jenifer 045260
Stern, Barry 042476
Stern, Gail F. 047239
Stern, Günter 002992
Stern, Hans 004396
Stern, Jean 044777
Stern, V. 029719
Sternath-Schuppanz, Dr. Marie-Luise 002845
Sternback, Mike 043190
Sternberg, Dr. Carsten 018979
Sternecker, Dieter 015675
Sternschulte, Agnes 016691
Sternweiler, Dr. A. 016171
Stertz, Dr. Stephen 042431
Stets, Mary Anne 046116
Stetson, Daniel E. 045124
Steuer, Matthias 016946
Steuert, Patricia 045509
Steurbaut, W.W.G. 029254
Stevan Bathoorn, H. 030315
Steven, H. 001398
Steven, Jackie 043310
Stevens, Andrew 045589
Stevens, Dr. Crosby 039248
Stevens, F. Scott 049345
Stevens, George 042399
Stevens, H. 029408
Stevens, Jane 042850
Stevens, Jean 044900
Stevens, Jon 042110, 049196
Stevens, Lawrence 040728
Stevens, N. Lee 044444
Stevens, Norman S. 044908
Stevens, Scott . 049340, 049341, 049342, 049343, 049344
Stevens, Timothy 040175
Stevens Hardeman, Dr. H.J.M. . . . 029242
Stevensen, Sara 039425
Stevenson, Candace 005969
Stevenson, Colin 030607
Stevenson, Esma 030607
Stevenson, Fenners W. 042301
Stevenson, Judy 039731
Stevenson, Moira 040404
Stevenson, Victor 006684
Števko, Anton 034399
Steward, James 041736
Steward, Maureen 005562
Steward, Travis 046389
Stewardson, Joanne 039963
Stewart, Ann 022763
Stewart, Barbara 039818
Stewart, Beth A. 047101
Stewart, Brian 039480
Stewart, Doug 006102
Stewart, Fiona 000833
Stewart, Heather 040095
Stewart, Dr. I. 038443
Stewart, Lorelei 042846
Stewart, Mary 043762
Stewart, Pamela 048378
Stewart, Rick 044002
Stewart, Sarah 041215
Stewart, W. Lyn 005047
Stewart, Wilma 005819
Stewart-Leach, Sheila . . . 045567, 045751
Stewart-Young, J. 039308
Steyer, Dr. Bernd 020567
Steyer, Rosemarie 021021
Steyn, Andrew 034742
Steyskal, Josef 002876
Stiassny, Dr. Melanie L.J. 046286
Stiawa, Wolfgang 002816
Štíbr, Dr. Jan 008479, 008481
Štíbrová, Eva 008480
Stichel, Dr. Rudolf 016637
Stidolph, Diana 030537
Stieb, Ernst 006021
Stief, Gerhard 016719
Stiefelmayer, Ulrike 017157
Stiefmiller, Helen 044374, 044375
Stiegel, Dr. Achim 016104
Stiegemann, Prof. Dr. Christoph . . 019548
Stieglitz, Leo von 020374
Stiehler, Ursula 015721
Stieneker, Uwe 018613
Stiepani, Ute 016047
Stieper, Jürgen 016504
Stier, Dr. Christine 020364
Stier, David 048297
Stierhof, Dr. Horst 017944
Stieve, Mary Farrell 042019
Stiewe, Dr. Heinrich 016691
Stiffler, David L. 041575
Stiggens, D.C. 029660
Stijns, H.J.M.R. 030043
Štika, Dr. Jaroslav 008674
Stilje, Emma Kristina 036802
Stilling, Niels Peter 008928
Stillström, Gunilla 036692
Stimson, Judy 040681
Stinchcomb, Donna 047279
Stinzendörfer, Heidi 018135
Stipperger, Prof. Walter 002025
Stippich, Wolfram 018238
Stirratt, Betsy 042265
Stiso Mullins, Kathleen 046008
Stitely, David 045744
Stiver, Louise 047973
Stiverson, Gregory 043606
Stiwich, Undine 016631
Stob, Susan E. 049135
Stobbs, Neil T. 038659
Stochr, Bernard 011432
Stock, S. 001276
Stockar, Rudolf 037286
Stockebrand, Marianne 045662
Stocker, Gerfried 002241
Stockhammer, Prof. Dr. Helmut . . . 002145
Stockhaus, Heike 020695
Stockhoff, Val 048694
Stockinger, Dr. Ursula 001938
Stockman, Edgard 003238
Stockman, Dr. René 003461
Stockmann, Robert 018039
Stockwell, Denis 038651
Stoddard, Leah 042768
Stoddard, Sheena 038859
Stoddart, Simeon 043029
Stöckl, Gottfried 001756
Stöckler, Elisabeth 002049
Stöckli, Edi 036899
Stöckli, Werner 037347
Stöckmann, Birgit 016055
Stögner, Stefan 001677
Stöllner, Dr. Thoms 016276
Stölting, Dr. Siegfried 016429
Stölzel, Eckhard 021095, 021096
Stössel, Dr. Iwan 037524
Stoessinger, Caroline 046278
Stößl, Dr. Marianne 019411, 019412
Stofferan, Jan 048169
Stoga, Alan 046288
Stoga, Dr. Andrzej 032427, 032450
Stohler, Peter 037786
Stoianov, Georgi 004817
Stoica, Georgeta 032807
Stojanov, Georgi 004749, 004750
Stojanov, Stojan . 004668, 004669, 004762
Stojanovic, Jelena 044790
Stojič, Jelena 034281
Stojneva, Nadežda 004665
Stokes, Mike 041023
Stokes Sims, Lowery 046409
Stokesbury, Bria 005681
Stolberg-Wernigerode, Alexander Graf zu 019484
Stolk, Ton 030274
Stoll, Dr. Wilhelm 016637
Stolle, Dr. Walter 016638
Stoller, Blanche 046001
Stollman, S. 030460
Stolwerk, Rick 030616
Stolwijk, Chris 029239
Stolyarov, Gwen 046340
Stolzenburg, Dr. Andreas 017694
Stomberg, John R. 042319
Stone, Donna K. 044619
Stone, Gaynell 043113
Stone, Karen 041811
Stone, Linda 042033
Stone, Margaret 038844
Stone, Mike 039077
Stone, Nancy E. 044138
Stone, Nathan 047308
Stone, Pat 044357
Stone, Paul 006057
Stone, Robert E. 046536
Stone, Thelma 044008
Stone, Walker S. 043541
Stone, Walter 047262
Stone-Gordon, Tammy 043575
Stone-Miller, Dr. Rebecca 041866
Stoner, Sheila 048412
Stooss, Toni 036845, 036847
Stoppelaar, Dr. J.D. de 030240
Stoppioni, Maria Luisa 023773
Stopps, R.A. 038853
Storch, Nancy 045868
Storch, Dr. Ursula 003017
Storch, Prof. Dr. Volker 017839
Storck, Dr. Ekkehard 020414
Storer, Prof. Robert W. 041734
Storer, Russell 001517
Stork, Dr. Simone 016864
Storm, Alex 005801
Storms, Dale C. 046568
Storto, Fred 016709
Storvik, Jehans 031311
Storz, Dr. Dieter 018070
Stoscheck, Dr. Jeannette 018579

Stoter, Dr. M. 029837
Stothoff, Richard H. 043859
Stottrop, Ulrike 017073, 017078
Stoughton, Kathleen 045070
Stoullig, Claire 010771
Stoumann, Ingrid 008843
Stout, Patricia 038523
Stovall, Linda Joy 049132
Støvern, Håvard 031126
Stowell, Elwood A. 044368
Stoyas, Yannis 021207
Stoye, Wilfried 021086
Stoyell, Sue 046020
Strachova, Alevtina Gennadjevna . 033626, 033627
Strackerjan, Wilfried 020584
Straczek, Dr. Tomasz 032471
Stradeski, Leigh-Anne 039661
Stradiotti, Dr. Renata ... 023517, 023519, 023525, 023526
Straehly, Christiane 010343
Straka, Barbara 016060
Stramm, Günter 019991
Strandberg, Hindrik 009534
Strandberg Aieta, Janelle 042954
Strandberg Olofsson, Prof. Margareta 036292
Strander, Esa 010025
Strandgaard, Kirsten 009040, 021539
Strang, Craig 042161
Strang, T.H. 049081
Strang, Tim 048168
Strange, Georgia 042265
Strange, Shirley 043010
Stránsky, Jiří 008340
Strassen, Hermann zur 018419
Straßer, Dr. Josef 019096
Straßer, Wilfried 019227
Strassner, Andrea 048233
Strate, Kenneth 042136
Strate, Ursula 017715
Stratfold, Graham 041480
Strathy, Mark 046201
Stratmann, Dr. Wilhelm 018979
Stratton, Ceilia M. 043919
Stratton, David C. 047748
Stratton, Frances R. 044783
Straukamp, Werner 019337
Straus, Gail 047411
Strauss, Dorothea 053357
Strauss, Dr. Frank B. 048053
Strauß, Josef 002019
Strauss, Dr. Karl W. 016568
Strauss, Linda 045411
Strauß, Michael . 016494, 016495, 016496
Strazar, Dr. Marie D. 044551
Streatfield, George C. 039594
Street, Dr. Martin 018794, 019299
Street Settleman, Henry 046278
Streetman, John W. 043766
Streets, Kim 041001
Strehl, Dieter 003007
Streicher, Dr. Gebhard 015515
Streiff, Elsie 037433
Streiff, Dr. Hans Jakob 037044
Streihammer, Dr. Rudolf 003071
Streisselberger, Josef 002358
Streit, Ruth 048767
Streitberger, Christine 002270
Streitt, Ute 002256
Strekalova, Valentina Michajlovna . 033927
Strelnitski, Vladimir 046124, 046125
Stremel, Ted 005423
Strémoouhoff, Catherine 014912
Strempfl, Dr. Heimo 002147
Stremsterfer, Joanne 047677
Strenge, Bernhard von 019247
Strick, Jeremy 045451
Strickland, Alice 044238
Strickland, Dan 006818
Strickland, D.H. 042397
Strickland, Katherine F. 047469
Strickland jr., William 047054
Strickler, Susan E. 045618
Strid, Prof. Dr. Karl-Gustav 036302
Strieder, Dr. Barbara 015933
Strigl, Alfred 002651
Striker, Don 041824
Strinati, Dr. Claudio 025550
Strine, Linda T. 047346
Stringer, Clare 040768
Strittmatter, Gabi 037236
Stritzinger, Wolfgang 003009
Stritzler-Levine, Nina 046300
Strižnikova, Svetlana S. 033405
Strnadová, Z. 008628
Strobbe, Johan 003721
Strobel, Barbara 015973
Strobel, Margaret 042852
Strobel, Sigruth 019514
Strobl, Dr. Andreas 019118
Strocka, Prof. Dr. V.M. 017227
Strode, Molly 044848
Strode, Wendell 042367
Stroebel, G. 034561
Ströbele, Dr. Werner 019807, 019809
Ströle-Jegge, Dr. Ingeborg 019718
Strömbäck, Stig 036370
Strömberg, Karin 036691
Strömberg, Ulla 008989
Strömfors, Göran 009855
Strömsdörfer, Thomas 020133
Strohfeldt, Guido 017286
Strohhammer, Andreas 002252
Strohmaier, Franz 002266, 002267
Strom, George 043698
Strom, Peter 043726, 043727
Stromberger, Franz 002821
Strombo, Cathryn J. 048435
Strondl, Ruth 002934
Strong, Charles 042126
Strong, Dan 044359
Strong, Michael 000871
Stroobants, Dr. A. 003392, 003393, 003394, 003395
Stroobants, Bart . 003635, 003636, 003637
Stroppel, Alice 048099
Stroud, Michael 028034
Strubel, Howell 047376
Struhs, David B. 042671
Štrumej, Lara 034485
Strumia, Prof. Franco 023576
Stryker, Richard R. 043163
Stryker Lewis, Evelyn 046179
Stuani, Guido 023749
Stuart, Ann 043393
Stuart, Bruce F. 045366
Stuart, Jacqueline 005041
Stuart, Jan 048884, 048908
Stuart Elliott, David 027209
Stubbe, Els 029233
Stubbe Østergaard, Jan 008982
Stubbendieck, James 045303
Stubbs, Fred 043443
Stubbs, Ruth 006236
Stubing, Paul 043362
Štubova, Elena Valentinovna 033117
Stuchlík, Ladislav 008467, 008468
Stuckenbruck, Corky 043395
Stucker, Noah Lon 047025
Stucker, Richard 046571
Stuckey, Robert 048744
Stuckless, Allyson 006364
Stucky, Anton 037511
Studencka, Jolanta 032004
Studencki, Zbigniew 032332
Studenroth, Zachary 046562
Studer, Dr. Daniel 037491
Studer, Winfried 019228
Studinka, Felix 037788, 037797
Studley, David 047781
Stüben, Jürgen 017715
Stüber, Dr. E. 002322
Stüber, Prof. DDr. Eberhard 002561
Stüning, Dr. Dieter 016337
Stütz, Michael 018343, 018344
Stüwe, Hartmut 018218
Stuhlman, Theresa 046982
Stuhr, Joanne 048642
Stulić, Anselmo 007778
Stults, Jeannine 046476
Stumpe, L. 040030
Stumpf, Dr. Gerd 019119
Stumpf, Magdalena 003072
Stuppner, Dr. Alois 002915
Šturc, Libor 008649
Sturdy, Tom C. 005840
Sturgell, Ron 044296, 046183
Sturgeon, Ava 005536
Sturgeon, Keni 045965
Sturgis jr, Ewell G. 043087
Sturm, Kirk 047923
Sturm, Martin 002255,
Sturm, Ulli 002141, 052569
Sturtevant, Naomi 042805
Sturtz, Rodney 048057
Stussi, Edmond 015347
Stutzer, Dr. Beat 037017, 037506
Stutzinger, Dr. Dagmar 017152
Stuvøy, Ingunn 031188
Štvánová, Jana 008524
Štýbrová, Miroslava 008788
Styles, Bertha 048547
Stylianou, Petros 008215
Štyrkalo, Jaroslav Jevgenovyč ... 038267
Styron, Thomas W. 044349
Suanda, Wayan 022500
Suárez, José 007595
Suárez, Margarita 007975
Suárez Baldrís, Jordi 035697
Suárez Zuloaga, María Rosa 036122
Subler, Craig A. 044918
Šubová, Dana 034377
Suchan, Laura 006080
Suchanov, M.K. 033512
Suchinina, Svetlana Jurjevna 033849, 033851
Suchocki, Wojciech 032250
Suchy, Ladislao 024820
Suchy, Theodore D. 045331
Šuckaja, Galina Konstantinovna .. 033522
Sudarmadji, Dr. 022448
Suddaby, R.W.A. 040182
Sudduth, William M. 041856
Sudnischnikowa, Jaqueline 002985
Sudwidja, Ketut 022508
Südekum, Dr. Karl 020997
Süel, Mustafa 038011
Sünkel, Werner 019871
Sünwoldt, Sabine 020107
Sütterlin, Hans 036863
Sützl, Werner 001657
Suezo, Uwano 026478
Suffolk, Randall 044213
Sugawara, Eikai 026920
Sugden, K. 040406
Suggett, Martin 040030
Suggitt, Mark 038803, 038805
Suggs, Patricia 042074
Sugimoto, Lisa Ann 044931
Sugimoto, Yukio 026810
Sugino, Hideki 027287
Sugonjako, Mykola Mykolajovič .. 038365
Suhr, Dr. Norbert 018790
Suhrbier, Dr. Birgit 017168, 017182
Suhre, Terry 047662
Sui, Dr. Claude 018809
Suk, Joo-sun 027609
Sukpramool, Patcharin 037900
Sukumaran, Dr. C. 022040
Sulaiman, Dr. Nasruddin 022384
Sulayman, Dr. Tawfiq 037836
Šulce, Baiba 027661
Suldina, Elena Nikolaevna 034006
Şulea, Ioan 032952
Sulebust, Jarle 030719
Šuleř, Dr. Petr 008283, 008292
Suliga, Dr. Jan Witold 032481
Sullivan, B. 001178
Sullivan, Carole 041777
Sullivan, Christine M. 045879
Sullivan, Cyndi 047496
Sullivan, Irene 042442
Sullivan, Joanne 044480
Sullivan, John 045352
Sullivan, Kathryn D. 043107
Sullivan, Dr. Lynne 045039
Sullivan, Martin E. 047690
Sullivan, Michael 045945, 045947
Sullivan, P.O. 022800
Sullivan, Dr. Robert M. 044444
Sullivan, Tracy L. 041644
Sullivan Sturgeon, Catherine 042891
Sullivanons, Mary Louise 046920
Sully, Georges 012414
Sultan, Samir M. 009330
Sultan, Terrie ... 044656, 048891, 048892
Sumalde, Dr. Augusto 031689
Sumalvico, Ulrike 020796
Sumawilaga, H. Djamhir 022512
Sumberg, Dr. Barbara 047972
Sumbulova, Nadežda Georgievna . 033546
Sumers, Anne R. 046812
Summerfield, Jan 038983, 041223, 041283
Summers, Carl 045357
Summers, Jacquie 039267
Summers, John 006611, 042962
Summers, Marcia J. 046121, 047968
Summers, Ruth 041797
Summersgill, Robert H. 042339
Šumnaja, Dr. T.G. 033395, 033494
Sumner, Kent 043178
Sumoza, Rosa María 007486
Sumrall, Robert F. 041744
Šumskaja, Ljubov Vladimirovna .. 033360
Sun, Dr. Dennis 007129
Sun, Jixin 007038
Sunday Oyegbile, Olayinka 030670
Sundblad, Stefan 036593, 036596
Sundborg, Peter 036692
Sundelin, Åsa 036651
Sundell, Eva 036282
Sundell, Karin 036692
Sundin, Sven-Olov 036535
Sundström, Susanne 036732
Sundvoll, Bjorn 031078
Suné, Prof. J.M. 034931
Sunier, Sandra 036932
Suominen, Tapio 010134
Supamena, M.S. 009167
Supanz, Ewald 001872
Superchi, Toni 044154
Superior, P. 034677
Supriyatno, Y. 022537
Surace, Dr. Angela 023742
Šurdić, Borislav 034160
Sureau, Jean-Louis 011366, 014782
Surma, Henryk 032183
Surmann, Dr. Ulrike 018323
Surrett, Janet 048123
Surroca i Sens, Joan 035233, 035236
Surup, Axel 020938, 020939, 020941
Suryana, Otong 022389
Surzyńska-Błaszak, A. 032247
Suščenko, Evgenija Michajlovna .. 033583
Sušić, Željka 007858
Šušková, Helena 034308
Suslova, Natalija Oleksandrivna .. 038276
Susoj, Elena Grigorjevna 033711
Šuštar, Branko 034494
Susumu, Shimasaki 026623
Sutakovič, Nataša 034249
Šutalo, Kata 007839
Suter, Daniel 036863, 037305
Suter, Dick 000820
Suter, Josef Ignaz 036944
Suter, Mary 043830
Sutherland, Cara 041780
Sutherland, Gordon 005782
Sutherland, Maire-Claire 003732
Sutherland, Maureen 005759
Sutherland, Norma 041482

Sutherland, Rene 000994
Sutherland, Dr. Stuart 006704
Suthers, Terence 039670
Sutloff, Catherine 042260
Sutoyo, R. 022517
Sutphin, Derik 048608
Sutschek, Felix 016340
Sutton, Cynthia 044906
Sutton, J.M. 038497
Suvitie, Osmo 010006
Suvorova, Tatjana 033216
Suwanasai, Avudh 037935
Suwentra, I. Ketut 022414
Suzuki, Katsuo 027256
Suzuki, Keizo 026615
Suzuki, Koji 026429
Suzuki, Makoto 027021
Suzuki, Naomitsu 027178
Suzuki, Prof. Norihiko 026813
Suzuki, Takatoshi 026490, 027269
Suzuki, Yoshikazu 026569
Suzuki, Yusai 026950
Švachová, Jarmila 008439
Svae, Karin 036511
Svanascini, Prof. Osvaldo 000226
Svartgrund, Anita 009736
Svedberg, Berit 036673
Svedfeldt, Bjorn 036589
Svedlow, Andrew Jay 045621
Švedova, Inga 038389
Svendsen, Sverre J. 030961
Svens, John-Erik 010250
Svenshon, Dr. Helga 016637
Svensson, Else Marie 036201
Sverrir Árnason, Gísli 021949
Svetina, Ivo 034493
Sviblova, Olga 033431
Svirčević, Rosa 034233
Sviridova, Tetjana Mykolaïvna 038333
Svitkova, Ani 004848
Svoboda, Dr. Christa 002567
Svoboda, Kurt 002004
Swaan, Trudy 006207
Swadley, Ben H. 048055
Swagemakers, Walter 029180
Swager, Karen 043082
Swaile, B.D. 005124
Swain, Adrian 046022
Swain, Hedley 040230
Swain, Kristin 043156
Swainston, M. .. 000722, 000723, 000724
Swallow, Debby 040307
Swan, Daniel C. 048653
Swan, Delores 044285
Swanagan, Don Jo 043206
Swanee, Lois 044578
Swaner, Ivan 044387
Swank, Scott T. 042600
Swanson, Alan 049314, 049315
Swanson, Ann 047536
Swanson, Brook 049012
Swanson, Erik 043220
Swanson, Robert 005162, 045729
Swanson, Dr. Vern G. 048310
Swantek, John E. 049001
Swart, Donna 043256
Swartout, Dennis W. 044264
Swartzlander, Martha 047537
Swasey, Gilvano 003881
Swatosch-Dore, Michael 002972
Swatschina, Wilhelm 002054
Sweasy, Lisa 043951
Sweeney, Alan 048062, 048985
Sweeney, Bill 044745
Sweeney, Colin 041351
Sweeney, Dennis F. 046333
Sweeney, John 042454
Sweeney, Karen 047382
Sweeney, Margie 047537
Sweeney Price, Mary Sue 046425
Sweets, Henry 044423
Sweets, Judy 045208
Sweha, Dr. Fawzi 009308
Sweitzer, Rick 044263
Swensson, Lisa C. 046472
Swettenham, Christine 041353
Świda, Piotr 032452
Swiderski, Christine 006619
Swift, Carolyn 042618
Swift, John 047354
Swift, Juli 046196
Swift, M. 039813
Swift, R.G. 041253
Swigart, Arthur L. Stewart 048738
Swigart, Patricia B. 044674
Swigart, Stacey A. 048737
Swim, Ann 042598
Swinford, Mervyn 039500
Swingle, Mark 048799
Swinkels, Dr. L.J.F. 029961
Śwircz, Kazimierz 032075
Świst, Lucyna 032005
Switlik, Matthew C. 045971
Swozilek, Dr. Helmut 001763
Sy, Joaquin 031713
Syahali, Teuku Sahir 022451
Sydow-Blumberg, Karen von 019467
Sykes, Diana A. 040894
Syljuk, Anatolij Michajlovyč 038330
Sylla, Aline 013685
Sylvester, Judith 042266
Sylvester, Morten 009134
Syme, John 030445
Symes, Dr. Robert F. 041027
Symmes, Edwin C. 041869
Symmes, Marilyn 046319
Symons, Gwendolyn 045203
Symons, Prof. T.H.B. 006141
Synder, Judith 042576
Syndram, Prof. Dr. Dirk 016790
Syre, Dr. Cornelia 019038
Syré, Dr. Ludger 018156
Syring, Marie Luise 016841
Syrjänen, Anneli 009940
Syrjänen, Inkeri 010141
Šyškina, Raïsa Petrivna 038271
Systad, Gunnhild 030846
Sytek, Wioletta 032237
Šytikov, Viktor Mychajlovyč 038262
Syverson, Duane 043718
Syvertsen, Per Ole 031017, 031018
Szabo, Dr. Agneza 007849
Szabo, Andras 032893
Szabó, Dr. Botond Gáborjáni 021711
Szabo, Ernst 002770
Szabó, Dr. J. József 021890
Szabó, Lajos 021696
Szabó, Lilla 021701
Szabolcs-Király, Dr. István 021752, 021753
Szakacs, Dennis 046386
Szakmary, Joanna 046134
Szalay, Prof. Dr. Mikloš 037808
Szameit, Prof. Dr. Erik 001885
Szaniawska, Wanda 032434
Szaraniec, Dr. Lech 031989
Szathmáry, László 021737
Szatmári, Dr. Imre 021628, 021629
Szczebak, Dr. Władysław 032382
Szczech, Bernard 032541
Szczepański, Marek 032361
Szczesiak, Rainer 019219
Szczygieł, Andrzej 032048
Szczypiorski, Krzysztof 032148
Szeemann, Dr. H. 036856
Szekely, Linda 048367
Szekeres, Viv 000709
Szentkuti, Károly 021795
Szevera, Dr. Walter 003009
Szewczuk, Mieczysław 032280
Szewczyk, Kazimierz 032413
Szewczyk-Smith, Diane 046106
Szinai, Stephan 002962
Szinvavölgyi, Oszkár 021788
Szkop, Henryk 031902
Szmolicza, József 021745
Szöke, Dr. Mátyás 021922
Szoényi, Dr. Eszter 021733
Szpakiewicz, Alina 031910
Szpakowska, Ewa 032272
Szram, Dr. Antoni 032112, 032117
Szuber, Robert 031970
Szücs, Dr. Judit 021708
Szücs-Irén, B. 021627
Szura, Andrzej 032001
Szuromi, Béla 021830
Szvircsek, Dr. Ferenc 021834
Szygenda, Lynn 039355
Szymańska, Dobrochna 032415
Szymańska, Ewa 031906
Szymczyk, Adam 036889
Szymusiak, Dominique 012478
Szyndzielorz, Albert 031937
Taaffe, Renee 045931
Taawo, Kjell 036511
Tabacu, Jenica 032823
Tabah, Béatrice 015054
Tabaka, M. 006012
Tabakoff, Sheil 046385
Tabakoff, Sheila 046567
Tabakov, Michail Ivanovič 034062
Tabaraud, Georges 011472
Tabata, Chihiro 027316
Tabb, Kathy 045263
Tabbernor, Christine 006855
Tabbert, Mark 045270
Tabeaud, Marcel 011769
Tabel-Gerster, Margit 017715
Taber, David 045547
Tac An, Dr. Nguyen 049549
Tackett, William 044847
Tadahisa, Sakai 027297
Tadaya, Imamura 027182
Tadiello, Dr. Roberto 026231
Taeckens, Michel 012681
Täube, Dr. Dagmar 018336
Täubrich, Hans-Christian . 019347, 019373
Taft Andrews, Nathalie 045496
Taga, Yoshiya 026633
Tagaev, Muchtar 027639
Tagage, L.M. 029901
Tagesen, Fran 042967
Taggart, Travis 044490
Taghiyeva, Roya 003087
Taglang, Barbara-Ulrike 018743
Tagliasacchi, Dr. Paolo 023965
Taguchi, Yasuo 026587
Taha, Dr. Haji Adi bin Haji 028005
Taher, Salah E. 009311
Tahon, Eva 003273, 003276
Tait, Dr. Edward 040457
Tait, Leslie Bussis 046382
Tait, L.P. 034692
Tait, Ronald 038685
Tajedin-Noureldaim, Yousif 009355
Takács, Dr. Imre 021694
Takács, Mária 021841
Takahara, Mayako 026444
Takahashi, Akiya 027189
Takahashi, Prof. Susumu 027271
Takahide, Hidenobu 027335
Takakusa, Shigeru 026856
Takanashi, Mitsumasa 027189
Takano, Masahiro 026444
Takano Yoshizawa, Hirohisa 026444
Takase, Tamotsu 027289
Takashi, Prof. Sutoh 027053
Takashina, Shuji 026701, 026702
Takata, Yoshikazu 026658
Takebe, Toshio 026899
Takeda, Sharon 045441
Takehana, Rintaro 026410
Takemoto, Hiroshi 027348
Takenaka, Yasuhiko 027315
Takeuchi, Jun-ichi 027169
Takeuchi, Makoto 026679, 027158
Takeuchi, Tadashi 026885
Taki, Shigeko 026938
Takita, Minoru 026678
Taksami, Prof. Čuner 033774
Taktak, Fehmi 038078
Tal, Felix 029241
Tal, Ilan 022994
Tal, Dr. Nissim .. 022913, 022922, 022926
Talaga, Sally 044590
Talajić, Mirko 007713, 007720
Talalay, Lauren 041732
Talamo, Prof. Giuseppe 025499
Talamo-Kemiläinen, Maarit 010176
Tálas, Dr. László 021896
Talazov, Veselin 004735
Talbert, Candy 048682
Talbot, Dennis 040407
Talbot-Stanaway, Susan .. 046107, 046787
Talerman, Margaretha 046921
Talero Pinzón, Claudia 007648
Tales, Sofia 025060
Tall, J.J. 039611
Talla, Primitiva C. 031802
Talland, Valentine 042328
Talley, Dan R. 045051
Talley, Roy 042062
Talsky de Ronchi, Prof. Alicia 000604
Talvio, Tuukka 009562
Talzrow, Michael 044311
Tamari, Dr. Dov 023070
Tamba, Dumitru Gheorghe 032969
Tambini, Michael 038796
Tamblin, J. 040721
Tamburini, Pietro 023464
Tamindarova, Miljauša Amirovna .. 033236
Tamir, Peleg 023079
Tamis, Catherine M. 047548
Tamla, Toomas 009396
Tammen, Mike 045586
Tammenoksa, Paavo 009812
Tammiksaar, Erki 009419
Tamminen, Jukka A. 009832
Tamminen, Marketta 009992, 009993, 009996, 009997
Tamminen, Osmo 009458
Tamplin, Illi-Maria 006136
Tanabe, Emi 026926
Tanabe, Mikinosuke 027189
Tanaka, Iwao 026793
Tanaka, Masayuki 027189
Tanaka, Takeyoshi 026418
Tanaka, Toshiya 026489
Tanaka, Yoshiaki 026786
Tănăsescu, Gabriela 032917
Tanata, Charles 044832
Tandefelt, Petra 009579
Tandy, Virginia .. 040400, 040404, 040417
Taneva, Radosveta 004863
Taneva, Valentina 004826
Tangco, Manny 031701
Tange, Ellen 008995
Tangen, Eigil 031127
Tangen, Kirsten 030795
Tani, Gohei 026660
Taniguchi, Dennis 047866
Taniguchi, Harumichi 027098
Tanino, Dr. Akira 027330
Tanke, Dr. Walter 016768
Tanko, Majda 034509
Tankoano, Ounteni Ernest 004957
Tannehill, Suzette 042048
Tannen, Jason 042893
Tannenbaum, Barbara 041586
Tannenbaum, Judith 047258
Tannenbaum, Myles 046969
Tanner, Julia 039690
Tanner, Matthew 038868
Tanner, Paul 037768
Tannert, Christoph 016095,
Tanninen-Mattila, Maija 009530
Tannous, Youssef 027819
Tantaquidgeon, Gladys 048687
Ţanţăreanu, Ecaterina 032772
Tantoco, José P. 031705
Tapias Moreno, Rito Antonio 007634
Tapié, Alain 011056
Tàpies, Miquel 034907

Tapken, Dr. Kai Uwe 019133, 019719
Tapliss, Sue 038614
Tappan, Amanda 043538
Tappe-Pollmann, Dr. Imke 016690
Tapsell, P. 030432
Taracchini, Alfredo 024402
Taragin, Davira 048569
Tarasek, Władysław 031895
Tarasenko, Tatjana Ivanovna 034018
Tarasova, Nadežda Petrovna 033115
Tarawneh, Khaled 027359
Tarbell, Mike 044659
Tarcalova, Dr. Ludmila 008732
Tardiem, Robert 012803
Targan, Alfons 016442
Taricco, Dr. Bruno 023836
Tarjeson, Jane 045641
Tarmann, Dr. Gerhard 002097
Tarnawesky, Prof. M. 006871
Tarnovskaja, Tatjana Nikolaevna .. 033586
Tarnow, Rosmarie 019330
Tarnowski, A. 039228
Taron, Dr. Douglas 042829
Tarplee, Peter 039945
Tarr, Blair D. 048581
Tarr, Dr. Edward H. 015782
Tarrant, Josh 000933
Tarrats Bou, Francesc ... 035550, 035895, 035896
Tarrús Galter, Josep 034895
Tarshish, Noa 022925
Tartaglio, Michael 042410
Tartarini, Jorge D. 000201
Tarus, Käpy 010066
Taruvinska, Pascall 049582
Tarver, Paul 046263
Tasaka, Sharon 044610
Tasanen, Terni 010153
Taschenmacher, Peter 015728
Tasić, Nikola 034167
Tasick, Julian 045644
Tasker, Diana 043669
Tašlaj, Ljudmyla Borysivna 038361
Taşlialan, Dr. Mehmet ... 038110, 038196, 038197
Tasma, G.L. 029591
Tassell, C.B. 001178
Tassi, Prof. Franco 023404, 023913, 026339
Tassianari, Duilio 023275
Tassignon, Jean-Marie 003362
Tassini, Francesco 023891
Tatangelo, Mireille 015163
Tataru, Marius J. 017605
Tate, Barbara L. 046360
Tate, Belinda 049252
Tate, Pat G. 048110
Tatewaki, M. 026400
Tatlıcan, Zerefşan 038174
Tátrai, Dr. Vilmos 021694
Tatro, Ron 043625
Tatsch, Madeleine 016589
Tatter, Paul 041614
Tatum, Dana Lee 044692
Taub, Liba 038973
Taube, Dr. Angelika 018355
Tauerová, Dr. Jarmila 008625
Taufi 029101
Taupe, Christina 035291
Taupe, Georg & Ingrid 002777
Taut, Dr. Konrad 018571, 018767
Tautorat, Ina 016087
Tavares Garcia, Sonia Maria 004271
Tavassoli 022644
Tavčar, Dr. Lidija 034487
Tavel, Dr. Hans Christoph von 036931
Taveneaux, Benoît 014453
Tavernier, Bertrand 012830
Tavernier, Marc 014098
Taviani, Prof. Emilio Paolo 025571
Tavlakis, Ioannis 021116
Tawalba, Dia 027380
Tayler, Jayne 039892
Taylor, Alison 040357
Taylor, Barbara 038923
Taylor, Barbara E. 044534
Taylor, Chris 039660, 041829
Taylor, Darrell 042666
Taylor, David 038444
Taylor, David G. 006411
Taylor, Deborah 044693
Taylor, Denise M. 045110
Taylor, Donald B. 044020
Taylor, Edith 045205
Taylor, Gloria 005877
Taylor, Howard 047782, 047785
Taylor, J. Lawrence 044806
Taylor, J. William 042789
Taylor, Jeanette 005206
Taylor, Jeff 043862
Taylor, Jennifer 039299
Taylor, Jenny Lou 042894
Taylor, Jill E. 041258
Taylor, June 043647
Taylor, Kathryn T. 049105
Taylor, Kathy 040247
Taylor, Lillian 044408
Taylor, Linda 041704
Taylor, Lloyd 039836
Taylor, Dr. Louise 040127
Taylor, M. 040537
Taylor, M.A. 040697
Taylor, Marilyn S. 047650
Taylor, Mary Rose 041863
Taylor, Michael 040696
Taylor, Mike 030575
Taylor, Dr. Peter 034599
Taylor, Richard 042001
Taylor, Robertine 046390
Taylor, Ron 006574
Taylor, Saddler 043082
Taylor, Simon 043567
Taylor, S.K. 001226
Taylor, Sue Ellen 043036
Taylor, Susan H. 046233
Taylor, Susan M. 047240
Taylor, Thomas C. 048398
Taylor, Tom 045205
Taylor, Tracey 040459
Taylor, Dr. Trevor 040357
Taylor Bennett, Cheryl 048227
Tazlari, Marianne 020818
Tazzoli, Vittorio 025141, 025142
Tchen, Dr. John K. W. 046372
Tckcli, Gonul 038102
Teachout, Gerald E. 047017
Teagle, Rachel 045068
Teague, John 001100
Teague, Lynn 048630
Tear, Paul 040310
Teatero, Barbara E. 005167
Tebani, Shahzor Ali 031365
Tebbutt, J. Bernard 039675
Tebbutt, Michael L. 040439
Tecce, Dr. Angela 024888, 024901
Teckman, Jon 040095
Tederick, Lydia 048960
Tedeschi, Dr. Carlo 025974, 025976
Tedeschi, Martha 042820
Tedesco, Joseph 028038
Tedesco, Paul H. 043491, 043492
Tedesko, Frank W. 043868
Tedford, Catherine L. 042603
Tedrow, Allen 047107
Teehan, Virginia 022822
Teerimäki, Matti 009452
Teeson, Douglas H. 046116
Teeter, Stephen 046259
Teeter, Wendy 045421
Teets, James W. 048529
Teets, Robert G. 048529
Teets, Ruth E. 048529
Teeuwisse, Dr. J.B.J. 029436
Tegin, Taylan 038013
Tegou, Eva 021225
Teig, Catherine 046637
Teinilä, Soile 010255
Teinonen, Markku 009593
Teisen, Michael 008994
Teitelbaum, Jesse 049174
Teitelbaum, Matthew 006581
Teixeira, Joaquina B. 047262
Tejada, Susana 042498, 045424
Tejada Jiménez, Natalia 007536
Tekampe, Dr. Ludger 020263
Tekatlian, Dominique 011033
Tektaş, Mehmet 038004
Telford, D.B. 030452
Telford, Helen 030549
Tellechea, Helena C. 000208
Tellenbach, Dr. Michael 018809
Telleria de Gallardo, Prof. María E. 000371
Tellier, Arnaud 037138
Tellier, Dr. Cassandra 043111
Tellini, Dr. Alberto 026210
Tello Figueroa, Jimmer Jesús 007456
Telltingsrude, Rebecca 044303
Telsemeyer, Ingrid 016771, 020926
Tělupilová, Marielav 008477
Temkin, Ann 046975
Temmer, James D. 045886, 045900
Temming, Dr. S.N. 030036
Tempal, Denison 044982
Tempel, B. 030085
Tempel, Norbert 016771
Tempelaars, P.A. 029583
Temperli, R. 037806
Tempesti, Giorgio 023309
Tempestini, Luciano 025275, 025277
Temple, Ann 022728
Temple, Prof. J. 039404
Temple, Patty 040535
Templeman, Jack 006874
Templer, Peggy 045773
Templin, Brigitte 018729
Tempone, Mario C. 041525
Tena, Asunción 035978
Tenabe, Gabriel S. 041988
Tenbergen, Dr. Bernd 019157
Tenenbaum, Ann 046324
Teneva, Dr. Nadežda 004862
Tengblad, Stefan 030659
Tengku, Abdul Hamid 027979
Tennent, Elaine 044609
Tennent, Mike 047723
Tennyson, Daniel 038511
Tenorio Vera, Ricardo 035252
Tent, J. 029526
Tentoni, Dr. Damiana 025285
Teofilov, Teofil 004937
Tëplyj, Nikolaj Ivanovič 033740
Ter Assatouroff, C. 003339
Tera, Mitsuhiko 027292
Teramoto, John 044748
Teran, Reba Jo 043990
Terasima, Yoko 027189
Terblanche, E. 034561
Tercan, Şenel 038070
Terčon, Nadja 034511
Terechov, Anatolij Vladimirovič ... 033656
Terechov, Vladimir Michajlovič ... 033552
Terentev, I.S. 033957
Terentjev, Vladyslav Sergijovyč ... 038400
Terezhchuk, Volodymyr 038404
Tergun, Dr. Alimuddin 022434
Terlouw, Dr. Willem 029843
Terlutter, Dr. Heiner 019157
Terman Frederiksen, Finn 009064
Teropšić, Tomaž 034461
Terpening, Virginia L. 044743
Terra, Prof. Pedro 004212
Terrail, Claude 013738
Terrell, Walter D. 048039
Terrettaz, Roger 037313
Terrier, Claude-Cathérine 011130
Terrier, France 037744
Terry, A. 039435
Terry, Blanche S. 048778
Terry, Christopher J. 006089, 006090
Terry, Joe 045996
Terry, Ray 047539
Tersew, Sylvie 021558
Teruzzi, Dr. Giorgio 023385
Tervahauta-Kauppala, Liisa 009682
Terziev, Penjo 004713
Terzo, Dr. Fatima 026308
Tesch, Ilse 020302
Tesch, Sten 036565, 036566
Teschner, Adelheid 019007
Tesfatsion, Costentinos 009441
Teshigara, Akane 027242
Teske, Christe 016396
Teske, Robert T. 045893, 049018
Tesseraux, Hartmut 017939
Tessman, Norm 047226
Testoni, Marcus 000903
Testoni, Theresa 000903
Tétaz, Marie Noëlle 011394
Tête, Michel 011589
Tetlow, David 040399
Tetterode Ravestein, Elke 029575
Tetzlaff, Reinhild 016820
Teufel, Tina 002560
Teunissen, J. 030226
Tew, Julie 039538
Tewes, Max 018487
Texel, Mark 046033
Teysen, Kenneth 045557
Thacker, Murray 030558
Thackeray, Dr. F. 034731
Thakkar, V.M. 022364
Thal, Denise 043344
Thaler, Dr. Herfried 002252
Thaler, Janice M. 044126
Thalheimer, Patricia 043330
Thaller, Toni 037751
Thalmann, Jacqueline 040657
Thalmann, Rolf 036904
Thames, Charles 047693
Thangwa, Josephine 027428
Thaxton, Kate 040611
Thaxton Soule, Debora 047495
Thaxton-Ward, Vanessa 044415
Thayer, Candace 045988
Thayer, Dorothy 045830
Thayer, Patricia 047617
Théberge, Pierre 006104
Thein, U Soe 029060
Thein, Udo 017872
Theis, Heinz-Joachim 016089
Theis, Wolfgang 016171
Theissen, A. 016178
Theißen, Dr. Peter 016721
Thellung, Caterina 026052
Theodorescu, Roxana ... 032795, 032800, 032801, 032809, 032817
Theol, Christopher R.M. 038902
Thériault, Serge 006104
Theriot, Edward C. 041936
Therre, Marie-Line 015204
Therrien, Richard 005416
Thestrup, Poul 009045
Thestrup Truelsen, Susanne 008849
Theune-Großkopf, Dr. Barbara ... 018374
Theunis, Karin 003353
Thévenin, M. Claude 014233
Thevenon, Luc F. 013396, 013412
Theyhsen, Annette 015933
Theys, Guido 003555
Thi, Nguyen Toan 049537
Thi Nu, Ha 049551
Thiagarajan, Dr. Deborah 022272
Thibault, Barbara 042325
Thibault, Pascale 013957
Thibodeau, Tony 047971
Thiébaut, Philippe 013678
Thiel, Dr. Ulrich 017222, 017224
Thiels-Mertens, Lydia 003402
Thieme, Thomas 036304, 036778
Thieme, Wulf 017698
Thiemler, Dagmar 020238
Thier, Dr. Bernd 019153

Thier, Wolfgang 002046
Thierbach, Melanie 015606
Thierer, Prof. Dr. Manfred 018627
Thierry, Olivier 011135
Thiery, Robert 013190
Thiesen, Barbara A. 046530
Thiesen, Bill 045639
Thiesen, John D. 046530
Thiessen-Schneider, Gudrun 019232, 053372
Thijsse, L. 029414
Thill, Edmond 027894
Thimme, Danae 042263
Thingvold, Terje 031028
Thipodeau, Richard G. 043451
Thir, Karl 001665
Thir, Dr. Mike 020364
Thiroy, Richard 003756
Thistle, Paul C. 005331
Thoben, Peter 029544
Thobois, Elisabeth 002845
Thöner, Wolfgang 016684
Thöny, Christof 001774
Thörn, Eva 036706
Thörnberg, Magnus 036431
Thörne, Michael 036604
Thøgersen, Mogens 008913
Thogersen, T. 030848
Thole, Dr. Bernward 018820
Thoma, Ludwig 002353
Thoman-Oberhofer, Elisabeth 002087,
Thomanek, Kurt 002014
Thomann, Marcel 012913
Thomas, Abigail 039777
Thomas, Angela 038778
Thomas, Anne 006104
Thomas, Dr. Beth 040907
Thomas, Beth A. 044373
Thomas, Brad 043308
Thomas, Celestine 026385
Thomas, Charles 042254
Thomas, Charles C. 044976
Thomas, David 040241
Thomas, Dean V. 039132
Thomas, Don 049264
Thomas, Eleanor 040360
Thomas, Dr. Floyd R. 049171
Thomas, Harold Pratt 042743
Thomas, Heidi 048833
Thomas, Joe 042946
Thomas, Kathryn 047667
Thomas, Linda L. 041695
Thomas, M. Simon 030088
Thomas, Marcel 021015
Thomas, Marge 046581
Thomas, Mark 039699
Thomas, Maureen 047753
Thomas, Nancy K. 045441
Thomas, Nicholas 041084
Thomas, Raymond 010496
Thomas, Prof. Dr. Renate 018339
Thomas, Robert G. 040359, 040361
Thomas, Rosalyn 041181
Thomas, S. 003795
Thomas, Sarah 000703
Thomas, Steve 047455
Thomas, Susan 044301
Thomas, Thelma 041732
Thomas, Valerie 013323
Thomas, Valérie 013329
Thomas, William G. 047883
Thomas, William T. 043050
Thomas, Y. 012234
Thomas-Ziegler, Sabine 018866
Thomason, Henry 048056
Thomasson, J.R. 044490
Thome, Teresa L. 044276
Thomenius, Kristina 009763
Thommen, Lynn 046352
Thommesen, Nils H. 030733
Thompson, Anna 036651
Thompson, Anna M. 047643
Thompson, Barb 005006
Thompson, Barbara 044426
Thompson, Bernard J. 006892
Thompson, Bernell 048071
Thompson, Brian 041093
Thompson, Brian C. 046371
Thompson, Carol 041862
Thompson, Claudia 045298
Thompson, Deborah 036745, 048018
Thompson, Dixie 042699
Thompson, Dr. F.G. 044103
Thompson, Ida 044646
Thompson, Isobel 041181
Thompson, J. 042617
Thompson, Jim 041780
Thompson, Jo 049206
Thompson, Joe H. 048033
Thompson, John 042534, 048018
Thompson, Joseph 046511
Thompson, Karen 044598
Thompson, Kathy 043234
Thompson, Kelly 045047
Thompson, Livia 046354
Thompson, Marc 043645
Thompson, Margaret 039732
Thompson, Mervyn 039242
Thompson, Murray 001400
Thompson, Dr. P. 039752
Thompson, P. 039922
Thompson, Paul 030641, 039152
Thompson, Pauline 006716
Thompson, Peter 041214
Thompson, Ronda 049054
Thompson, Roy 005713
Thompson, S. 040972
Thompson, Scott 043510
Thompson, Susan 046229
Thompson, Wilma 043242
Thomsen, Douglas 043559
Thomsen, Sanciea 043559
Thomson, Beth 040795
Thomson, Bruce 005492
Thomson, C. 038759
Thomson, David 039820
Thomson, Frances 001564
Thomson, Frank E. 041789
Thomson, Prof. K.S. 040663
Thomson, Dr. Philip 001109
Thømt, Torill 031050
Thonet, Anke 017144
Thongthew, Suvaporn 037927
Thorarinsson, Einar 021955
Thorbjornsdottir, Sonny 021971
Thorburn, Ken 038881
Thorkildsen, Åsmund 030807
Thorlacius, Ethel 048858
Thorláksson, Eiríkur 021959
Thorláksson, Eiríkur 021960, 021962
Thormann, Dr. Olaf 018572
Thorn, Brett 038555
Thorndahl, Jytte 008819
Thorndike, Ellen 048390
Thorne, Lynne 003901
Thorne, Martha 042820
Thornton, Leigh 040507
Thornton, Pam 046771, 046772
Thorp, Barbara 044793
Thorpe, Christine 039014
Thorpe, Linda 039135
Thorpe, Timothy 039878
Thorsager, Carl F. 031330
Thorsell, William 006627
Thorsen, Sue 048198
Thorsteinsson, Arne 009448
Thoulouze, Daniel 013669
Thouret, Nicole 010512, 010513
Thowsen, Atle 030761
Thrailkill, Helen 048323
Thrane, Finn 009053
Thresher, Leon 044429
Throckmorton, C. 038469
Throl, Dr. Hans-Joachim . . 020964, 053249
Thron, Rudolf 002534
Thümmler, Dr. Sabine 018183
Thuesen, Søren T. 021545
Thum, Marvin 048054
Thurley, Dr. Simon 040230
Thurlow, Irja 045995
Thurmann, Dr. Peter 018247
Thurmer, Robert 042988
Thurner, Ludwig 002351
Thúroczy, Dr. Csaba 021776, 021898
Thurow, Dr. Beate 019812, 019813
Thurow, Chuck 042849
Thuy, X. de 013219
Thwaites, Dr. Peter 038952
Thygesen, Anker 008885
Thykier, Claus 009128
Thyrring, Ulla . . . 008901, 008905, 008907
Thys, Joseph 003331, 003852
Tiacci, Giovanni Battista 025168
Tibbits, Michaela 045615
Tibbs Thurlow jr., E. 048902
Tiberi, Prof. Romolo 025022
Tiberio, Dr. Artioli 025238
Tichenor, Daryl L. 048800
Tichobajeva, Galina Vasylivna 038354
Tichonov, Dr. Igor L. 033791
Tichonov, Vladimir Viktorovič 033156
Tiderman, Conny 036280
Tidow, Klaus 019254
Tiedemann, Klaus 019726
Tiedemann, Nicole 017680
Tiefenbach, Dr. J. 001823
Tiefenbach, Oskar 001844
Tielman, Prof. R.A.P. 030271
Tiendrebeogo, Prosper . . . 004956, 004961
Tierney, J. 038837, 039603
Tierney, Janet 041037
Tiescen, Doug 043707
Tiesing, F. 029346
Tietjen, Hinrich 018643
Tietken, Antje 019468
Tietmeyer, Dr. Elisabeth 016128
Tietz, R.M. 034609
Tietzel, Prof. Dr. Brigitte 018396
Tiffany, Harold 044495
Tiffany, Sharon 048356
Tigchelaar, I. 030167
Tigert, Jennifer 005238
Tiitsar, Ketli 009402
Tijdink, W. 029327
Til, Barbara 016841
Tilarinos, George 046906
Tilbrook, Val 000918
Tildesley, J.M. . . 039293, 039550, 039820
Tiley, Sian L. 034718
Till, Dr. Wolfgang 019086
Tillequin, Prof. François 013662
Tiller, Helmut 002951
Tilley, Nicola 040921
Tilley, Peter 040139
Tilliabaev, R.A. 049383
Tillmann, Dr. Doris 018246
Tillmann, Michael 016930, 016932
Tillmann, Ulrich 018334
Tillmann, Walter 019207
Tilmant, France 003626
Timbrook, Mark 045926
Timlin, Aaron 043440
Timm, Kristal 043869
Timm, Robert 045205
Timmelmayer, Andreas 002975
Timmerman, B.W. 030232
Timmermann, Dietrich 008978
Timmermans, L. 029892
Timmins, John 030489
Timmons, P.J. 041305
Timms, Peter 043848
Timofeeva, Nina Vasiljevna 033903
Timothy, John 046108
Timotijevic, Milos 034180
Timpano, Anne 042923
Tinčev, Valentin 004680
Tindale, Bruce 001282
Tindel, Raymond D. 042871
Tindell, Daniel F. 044116
Ting, Dr. Joseph 007125
Ting, Dr. Joseph S. P. 007124
Ting, Joseph S.P. 007118
Tingley, Charles A. 047611
Tinguy de la Giroulière, Dominique de 012407
Tinius, Joanna 048021
Tinjum, Larry 047218
Tinnell, Jack L. 046658
Tinney, Donal 022858
Tinney, Harle H. 046457, 046466
Tinte, Francisco 000636
Tintori, Dr. Andrea 024414
Tio, Dr. Teresa 032705
Tió, Teresa. 032715
Tip, J.C. 030007
Tippmann, Rainer 016565
Tira, Masa Morioka 044606
Tirado, Vincent 045819
Tirelli, Dr. Margherita 025376
Tirion Beijerinck, I.H. 030088
Tironi, Ivan 007766
Tischer, Achim 016417
Tisdale, Brenda 043643
Tisdale, Shelby J. 048498
Tisken, Jörg 020488
Tisserand, Gérard 011398
Tissier, Gève 011437
Tissier de Mallerais, Martine 012886
Titova, Larisa Michajlovna 033278
Titova, Valentina Vasiljevna 033612
Tittoni, Dr. Maria Elisa . . . 025534, 025535
Tittoni Monti, Dr. Elisa 025547, 025581
Tivadar, Petercsák 021719
Tixier, Guy 012893
Tixier, J.M. 013880
Tiziani, Andrea 037726
Tjäder, Jan-Börge 031095
Tjan, R. 029365, 030226
Tjardes, Tamara 047972
Tjentland, L. 049234
Tjomlid, Steinar 031266
Tjupina, Lidija Afanasjevna 033038
Tjutčeva, Valentina Sergeevna . . . 033744
Tkačeva, Irina Vladimirovna 033854
Tkach, Steven 048967
Tkačuk, Jaroslava Juriïvna 038288
Tkešelašvili, A.V. 015415
T'Kint de Roodenbeke, Juan Graaf 003390
Toase, Charles 040323
Tobe, Carol B. 045483
Tober, Barbara 046282
Tobias, Todd 047832
Tobin, Shelley 038872
Tobler, Beatrice 036932
Tobler, Dr. M. 037819
Tobón Arbeláez, Elvira 007598
Tocev, Petăr 004683
Tocheva, Natalia 004771
Tochigi, Akira 027256
Toczewski, Dr. Andrzej 032561
Tod, Chris 041098
Toda, Masayasu 026954
Todd, Carol 045981
Todd de Iramain, Margarita Tula . . 000585
Todolí, Vicent 035976
Todorov, Todor 004812
Todorova, Ani 004658
Todorova, Pepa 004705
Todorova-Stojanova, Kresa 004775
Todts, Herwig 003163
Toedtemeier, Terry 047178
Toejner, Poul Erik 008938
Toelle, Wolfgang 017514
Toepfer, Lutz 015736
Törmälä, Satu 009472
Törnblom, Görel 036381, 036382
Törnig-Struck, Jutta 018906
Tövsayhan, G. 029008
Toftegaard, Kirsten 008963
Toftgaard Poulsen, Søren 008905
Tohjoh, Kohkoh 026706
Toit, Elizabeth du 034634

Toivanen, Pekka 009614
Toivanen, Yrjö 010224
Toka, Arnita 027748
Tokarczyk, William 044166
Tokarski, Longin 031864
Tokuda, Toshiaki 026626
Tokugawa, Narimasa 026821
Tokugawa, Yoshinobu 026887
Toledo, Eva 031702
Tolentino, Onofre R. 031760
Tolhurst, Robert 038874
Tollefson, Roy 005966
Tollet, André 011228
Tolmačeva, Valentina Michajlovna 033201, 033202
Tolmoff, Mati 009417
Tolnay, Dr. Alexander 016153, 053521
Tolnick, Judith E. 045018
Tolonen, Tatiana 010180
Tolson, Peter 048568
Tolstoj, Vladimir I. 033200
Tolstrup, Dr. Inger 009000
Tolton, Ray 005043
Tolu, Giuseppe 023366
Toluse, Joe 042291
Toma, Shiichi 026888
Tomaka, Janice 042506
Tomamichel, Leonhard 036964
Tomana, Makoto 027031
Tomar, Y.P.S. 022305
Tomaschett, Dr. Pius 037645
Tomasi, Marie-Cécile 010565
Tomašik, Gennadij Aleksandrovič 033034
Tomasović, Nives 007724, 007726
Tomassetti, Larissa 001903
Tomassini, Gabriella 026012
Tomasson, Thordur 021981
Tomaszewski, Robert 032159
Tomaz do Couto, Dr. Matilde 032587
Tombs, Sebastian 039417
Tomczak, Bogdan 032535
Tomea Gavazzoli, Dr. Maria Laura 024961, 024962, 024963, 024966
Tomey, J.K. 039101
Tomiyama, Hideo 027148
Tomiyasu, Reiko 026444
Tomkins, John 047083
Tomkins, Rachel 040659
Tomlin, Julian 040416
Tomlinson, Dr. Janis A. 048887
Tomlinson, Lori 047284
Tomljenović, Zvjezdana 007828
Tommassen, W. 029926
Tomobe, Naoshi 026649
Tomot, Dr. Michael 045404
Tomov, Lazar 004863
Tomova, Krasimira 004921
Tompkins, Jack D. 047360
Tomplak, Darinka 034530
Toms, Art 044281
Toms, Donald D. 045219
Toms, Dr. R. 034731
Tondre, Mary L. 047091
Toner, Dominga N. 042175
Toner, Eden R. 047363
Toney, Brian E. 041202
Tonezzer, Lucia 037007
Tonge, V. 040389
Toniolo, Elia 026284
Tonković, Snježana 007728
Tonneau-Ryckelynck, Dominique 012009
Tønneberg, Ingrid 031219
Tonnier, Nicole 020356
Tonon, Dr. Marco 023521, 025325
Tooby, Michael 038990
Tooker, Chad 047616
Toom, Maire 009398
Toomet, Tiia 009426
Toomey, Dr. Richard 048284
Toone, Keith 005179
Tooze, M. 038773
Toplovich, Ann 046153
Topoleanu, Florian 032963
Topoleanu, Florin 032860, 032960, 032961, 032962
Topolinsky, Verna 005014
Toraason, Mary C. 048716
Torataro, Yoneyama 027144
Torchia, Richard 044214
Torchia, Robert W. 045757
Torchio, Maurizio 026045
Torfs, Freya 003182
Torgersen, Ulf E. 031047
Torki, Nasser 022557
Torm, Helge 009001
Tornborg, Kay 045429
Torno, Janet E. 042229
Torp, Lisbet 008979
Torra, Eduardo 036098, 036102
Torra, Emilio 024428
Torralba, Casiana C. 031642
Torrance, Joshua C. 043685
Torre, Antonio 025566
Torre, Prof. Danilo 024182
Torre, Fuensanta García de la 035114
Torre, Graciela de la 028516
Torre, José Ramón de la 032734
Torre, Dr. Paola 025548
Torre Bonachera, José Luis la 034965
Torre González, Norberto de la 028736
Torre Prados, Francisco de la 035455
Torremocha Silva, Antonio 034818
Torrence, Gaylord 044924
Torrent í Bagudà, Enric 035946
Torrente, Virginia 036005
Torrents, Carme 035195
Torrenzieri, Claudio 026014
Torres, Prof. Emmanuel 031771
Torres, John 047971
Torres, Julio 035405
Torres, Pedro Pablo Alberto 007577
Torres Correa de Migliorini, Beatriz 000586
Torres Orell, Francisca 035461
Torres Valderrama, Hernando 007442
Torres Varela, Hilda 000503
Torruella Leval, Susanna 046369
Tortolero, Carlos 042857
Tortosa, Guy 010710
Torunsky, Dr. Vera 016333
Tosatto, Guy 012021, 013339
Tosdevin, M. 040721
Tošev, Miroslav 004761
Toševa, Svetla 004846
Tosi, Dr. Maria Teresa 025278
Tosini Pizzetti, Simona 024590
Tosswill, Richard 006730
Tostado, Dr. Conrado 028468
Tostevin, Patrick 040826
Toteva, Teodora 004642
Totevski, Totjo 004907
Toth, Elizabeth 043318
Tóth, Hajnalka 021910
Tóth, János 021746, 021926
Toti, Dr. Odoardo 023175
Tottis, Jim 043444
Touche, Hugues de la 013019, 013020, 013021, 013022, 013023
Touhey, Paula 044961
Toulmond, Dr. André 014111
Toumazis, Yannis A. 008210
Toumit, François 011057
Touret, Lydie 013663
Tourneux, Alain 011251
Tourta, A. 021498
Tourtillotte, William 048228
Tous, Rafael 034916
Toussaint, Christophe 014668
Toussaint, Jacques 003665
Toussaint, Yolaine 005908
Towe, Andrew C. 043365, 043366, 043367
Towe, Ruth 042205
Towell, Debbie 006737
Towell, Gerry 040510
Tower, Joan B. 041583
Towl, Betsy 042714
Town, Geri 049334
Townley, Kim 030635
Townsend, Clifford 043605
Townsend, Richard F. 042820
Townsend, Richard P. 042032
Townsend, Simon 038584
Townsend, Wayne 006304
Townsend, Wilma T. 042594
Toyama, Tohru 027204
Toyoda, Takao 026695
Trabert, Ilona 015986
Trabitsch, Dr. Thomas 002979
Tracey, D. 038679
Tracy, Duane 046135
Tracy, Susan 006584
Träger, Anne 016592
Träger, Béatrice 020059
Trafford, Lynne 030545
Tragent, Henry 045838
Trager, Neil C. 046269
Tragner, Dr. Manfred 003009
Trahan, Eric 042591
Traikasem, Saengchan 037906
Trainor, Eugene N. 048049
Trakospoulou, Helen 021327
Traljić, Seid 007826
Trâmbaciu, Şefan 032826
Trămbaciu, Stefan 032825
Tramer, Nancy 043477
Tramonte, Pietro 025374
Tramp, Lana 048350
Tramposch, Dr. Bill 030653
Transier, Dr. Werner 020263
Tranter, Rachel 041254
Trapani, Prof. Salvatore 025095
Trapnell, Simon H. 039593
Trapness, Thor 030916
Trapp, Gaudenz Graf 002786
Trapp, Graf Johannes 025905
Trapp, Dr. Oswald Graf 002786
Trappeniers, Maureen 029736
Trask, David 049262
Trask, Richard B. 043294
Tratebas, Ed 046138
Trauffer, Walter 036973
Traugott, Joseph 047970, 047973
Traunecker, Claude 014857
Trautmann, Charles H. 044793
Trautwein, Dr. Wolfgang 015981, 015982
Trauzettel, Ludwig 016682
Travella, Eugenio A. 000527
Travelyan, Vanessa 040603
Travers, John 040468
Travis, Betsy L. 047206
Travis, David 042820
Travis, P. 030615
Traxler, Dr. Herbert 002632
Trazegnies, Marquis de 003377
Trček Pečak, Tamara 034487
Trebbi, Marco 030766
Trebilcock, Evelyn 044662
Trebilcock, Joanie 043468
Trebilcozk, Samantha 038859
Trebitsch, Dr. Thomas 002900
Tréboit, Marcel 012973
Treen, Robin 047903
Treff, Dr. Hans-Albert 019089
Trefný, Martin 008671
Tregaskis, Kate 039427
Tréguier, Frank 011593
Trehin, E. 013585
Tremain, Robert 005529
Trembath, Lynne 040208
Tremblay, Diane 006312
Tremblay, Ermenegildo 025327
Tremblay, M. Joland 005936
Tremble, Steve 048077
Treml, Robert 020649
Tremp, Prof. Ernst 037494
Tremper Hanover, Lisa 043047
Trendler, Meg 043749, 043750
Trenkmann, Heidemarie 017007
Trentin-Meyer, Maike 015750
Trepesch, Dr. Christof 015605, 015609, 019963
Treskow, Dr. Sieglinde von 016368
Tresnak, Lenka 023536
Tresseras, Miquel 036030
Trethewey, Graham 001373
Tretjakov, Nicolaj S. 033630
Tretjakova, Vera Dmitrievna 033103
Trett, Robert 040563
Treude, Dr. Elke 016690
Treuherz, Julian 040038, 040041
Trevelyan, Vanessa 039181, 040614
Treves, Dr. Samuel B. 045313
Trevisani, Dr. Enrico 024103
Trevisani, Dr. Filippo 024751, 024765
Trezzi, Daniela 026057
Triandaphyllos, Diamandis 021333
Triantafyllidis, Jutta 017033
Triantis, Alice 021235
Triapitsyn, Serguei V. 047456
Tribouillois, Serge 014505
Trice, Robbert 046870
Trickett, Jessica D. 049359
Trickett, Peter 041025
Tridente, Tommaso 024774
Triebel, Dr. Dagmar 019042
Trier, Dr. Markus 018339
Triesch, Dr. Carl 017716
Triet, Dr. Max 036907
Triffaux, J.M. 003198, 003201
Trifonova, Mariana 004951
Trifut, Viorica 032774
Trillos Lozano, Ariel 007503
Trimbacher, Hans-Peter 002740
Trimpe, Pam 044768
Tringali, Mario 026201
Trinidad, Miguel Angel 028574
Tripanier, Romain 006326
Trischler, Prof. Dr. Helmuth 019045
Trivelli, Mari Frances 047919
Trividic, Claude 013885
Trnek, Dr. Helmut 002934
Trnek, Dr. Renate 002901
Troché, Bruno 012233
Tröger, Dr. Beate 019154
Tröster, Dr. G. 017475
Trofast, Jan 036617
Trofimova, Nadežda Nikolaevna 033873
Troha, Nevenka 034529
Troiani, Dr. Stefano 025809, 025810, 025811, 025813
Troll, Tim 043469
Trollerudoy, Elin 031237
Trollope, John 045009
Troman, Louise 041284, 041289, 041388
Trommer, Markus 019126
Tromp, C.P. 030122
Tromp, Dr. G.H.M. 030052
Tron, Prof. Federico 024847
Tronchetti, Dr. Carlo 023561
Trone, Peter 047094
Tronem, Donatella 024736
Troniou, Marie-France 012846
Tronrud, Thorold 006569
Trop, Sandra 048455
Tropeano, Placido 024677
Trosper, Robert 041757
Trost, Maxine 042322
Trost, Dr. V. 020372
Trotnow, Dr. Helmut 015983
Trotter, Mark A. 043791
Trotter, Ruth 040550
Trotti-Bertoni, Prof. Anna 024072
Trottmann, Dr. Kajo 016846
Troubat, Catherine 011823
Troughton, Betty 048828
Trouplin, Vladimir 013661
Trout, Amy L. 046225
Trouw, Bernward 017923
Trowles, Peter 039557
Trox, Dr. Eckhard 018735
Troy, Gloria 046368
Troyer, Herbert 002680

Trtheway, Linda 043592
Trubicyna, Tatjana 033564
Truc, Sylvie 012018, 012025
Truchina, Galina Vasiljevna 034076
Trucksis, Jane 049317
Trudel, Marianne 005010
Trudgeon, Roger 000763
Trudzinski, Dr. Meinolf 017765
True, Marion 045433
Trueb, Linda 045205
Trücher, Karl 001780
Trueman, Debbie 005978, 005981
Trümper, H.-J. 016162
Trümpler, Dr. Charlotte 017060
Trümpler, Rico 036874
Trümpler, Dr. Stefan 037460
Trufanov, E.I. 034089
Trufini, Antonio 024819
Trullén i Thomàs, Josep María . . . 036052
Trulock, Sue 047024
Trulock, Trent 042604
Trulssen, Torbjorn 031277
Truman, Nell 042086
Trumble, Edward P. 042353
Trumbower, Sarah P. 042174, 045877
Trummer, Manfred 002945
Trummer, Thomas 002853, 002969
Trumpie, Dr. Ank 029843
Trumps, Patricia 043112
Trumpy, Sigrid 041744
Trupp, Adam 048580
Truque, Angeles Penas 035126
Trusch, Dr. Robert 018170
Truškin, Michail Danilovič 033308
Tsafrir, Prof. Yoram 022941
Tsai, Eugenie 046418
Tsakos, Konstantinos 021444
Tsaneva, Svetla 004863
Tsang, Gerard C.C. 007117
Tsang, Kathleen 006810
Tsaoussis, Vassilis 021462
Tsatsos, Irene 045440
Tschach, Dr. M. 001823
Tschachotin, Peter 020365
Tschamber, Théo 013491
Tscherter, Erwin 015112
Tschirner, Manfred 016152
Tschoeke, Dr. Jutta 019346, 019354
Tscholl, Erich 037360, 037666
Tschopp, Walter 037375
Tschorsnig, Dr. Hans-Peter 020364
Tschudi, Gabriele 017835
Tse Bartholomew, Terese 047853
Tselekas, Panayotis 021207
Tselos, George 046408
Tsenoglou, Dr. Eleni 021285
Tsenor, Carey 005585
Tsipopoulou, Dr. M. 021120
Tsomondo, Tarisai 049580
Tsoukalas, P. 021502
Tsourti, Eos 021207
Tsoutas, Nicholas 001634
Tsugaru, Yoshisaburo 027048
Tsuji, Shigebumi 026922
Tsujii, Dr. Tadashi 026402
Tsujimoto, Isamu 026414
Tsujimoto, Karen 046598
Tsujimura, Tetsuo 027256, 027258
Tsukada, Masahiko 027189
Tsukitani, Atsufumi 026787
Tsuneishi, Fumiko 027256
Tsutsumi, Seiji 026630
Tsuzuki, Chieko 027256
Tua, Jean 037135
Tubaja, Roman 032393
Tucci, Franco 024367
Tuček, Helga 018689
Tuch, Gabriele 016061
Tuchel, Dr. Johannes 016047, 016048
Tucher, Bernhard Freiherr von 018138
Tucker, Andrew 039235
Tucker, Anne W. 044648
Tucker, Bob 044737
Tucker, Kevin W. 043077
Tucker, Mark S. 046975
Tucker, Michael S. 047586, 047594
Tucker, Paul L.C. 044799
Tucker, Prof. Priscilla K. 041734
Tucker, Sara 046324
Tucker, Suasan A. 045998
Tucker, Sue 043845
Tucker, Susan A. 045997
Tuckett, Noreen 000826
Tuckhorn, Nancy 048894
Tucoo-Chala, Jean 013278
Tudeer, E. 010099
Tudor, Kim 041083
Tuffs, Peter 041038
Tufrow, Kate 047887
Tugarina, Polina Innokentjevna . . . 033163
Ţuglui, Traian 032889
Tuhumwire, Joshua 038214
Tuitjer, Regine 017765
Tulaeva, Marina Aleksandrovna . . . 033976
Tulekova, Margarita Vasiljevna . . . 033048
Tuleškov, Vencislav 004739
Tulku, Doboom 022098
Tulku, Mynak R. 003907
Tull, Earl B. 048069
Tullos, Mark A. 048810
Tumanova, Anna Andreevna 033847
Tumanyan, Tamar 000692
Tumidei, Stefano 023426
Tuminaro, Craig 041650
Tung, Wu 042334
Tungarova, Saran-Tèrèl Sultimovna 034002
Tunheim, Arne 030858
Tunis, Dr. Angelika 016017
Tunnell, Bill 045953
Tunnicliff, Iris 041362
Tunsch, Dr. Thomas 016131
Tuomi, Marja-Liisa 009551
Tuomi, Timo 009574
Tuomi, Tuulia 009479
Tuominen, Laura 009472
Tuomola, Satu-Miia 010025
Tupper, Christine 005873
Tupper, J. 040786
Tupper, J.A. 005808
Tupper, Jon 005245
Tura, Jordi 034849
Turán, Róbert B. 021687
Turbanisch, Gérard 013275
Turcanu, Dr. Senica 032876
Turci, Dr. Mario 025773
Turdo, Mark A. 046168
Turek, Stanisław 031866
Turekanov, E.T. 027637
Turekian, Karl K. 046226
Turgeon, Christine 006226
Turicyna, T.K. 034012
Turk, James F. 047747
Turkov, Shura 022895
Turkova, Helga 008779
Turley, G. Pasha 042912
Turley, James 042057
Turnbow, Chris 047971
Turnbull, A. 000927
Turner, A.K. 030523
Turner, Annette 001191
Turner, David 043054
Turner, Edward E. 049096
Turner, Dr. Elaine 018794, 019299
Turner, Elizabeth 001114
Turner, Elizabeth Hutton 048940
Turner, Grady T. 046375
Turner, J. Rigbie 046394
Turner, Kathy 044762
Turner, Dr. Kenneth R. 044247
Turner, Laura 039885
Turner, Linda 048540
Turner, Nathan 044374, 044375
Turner, N.S. 040623
Turner, Sheridan 049198
Turner, Dr. Thomas F. 041619
Turnham, Stephanie 042135
Turnquist, Jan 043120
Turnquist, Dr. Jean E. 032729
Turovski, Jevgenij 038389
Turpin, Susan . . . 047521, 048263, 049287
Turton, Alan 038610
Turunen, Eija 010014
Tusa, Prof. Vincenzo 025746
Tuschell, Peter 002999
Tustin, S. 034773
Tut, Dr. Ye 029077
Tutorov, Jasmina 034286
Tuttle, Barbara 043921
Tuttle, Lyle 047888
Tuttle Miller, Elisabeth 042917
Tutty, Lauren 005778
Tuve, Richard L. 045658
Tuyttens, Deborah 006795
Tuzar, Dr. Johannes M. 001808
Tvers'ka, Ljudmila Volodymyrivna . 038291
Tvrtković, Dr. Nikola 007840, 007842, 007847
Twalba, Dia'a 027387
Tweneboa-Kodua, Maxwell Ohene 021105
Twist, William 005740
Twitchell, Linda 005872
Twohill, Nicholas 030603
Tworek, Dr. Elisabeth 019083
Twyford, Mark 043577, 046067
Txabarri, Myriam Gonzalez de 036116
Ty, Agustin 031650
Tyack, Gerry V. 040497
Tyagi, Prof. K.N. 022257
Tyamzarne, G.W.T. 049590
Tybring, Tina 036489
Tych, Felix 032479
Tychenko, Volodymyr Oleksandrovyč 038310
Tydesley, Carole 041386
Tyler, Dr. Alan 040647
Tyler, Fielding L. 048798
Tyler, Frances P.B. 042719
Tyler, Grant 006847, 006857
Tyler, Jayne 039886
Tyler, Jean 044254
Tyler, John C.P. 049237
Tyler, Kim 000772
Tyrefelt, Ronny 036274
Tyrell, Dr. Albrecht 019722
Tysdal, Bobbie Jo 046445
Tyson, Rose 047839
Tytgat, Christiane 003353
Tzekova, Katia 004863
Tziafalias, Athanasios 021261, 021351
Úbeda, Andrés 035429
Ubl, Prof. Dr. Hansjörg 002759
Uburğe, Baiba 027729
Uccello, Vincenza 049079
Uchida, Akihiko 027200
Uchida, Toshio 026785
Uchiyama, Takeo 026741
Uchtmann, Daniel 002934
Ucik, Dr. Friedrich 002142
Uda, Makoto 026528
Uddin, Belen Y. 031676
Udø, Ovin G. 030954
Uduwara, J.S.A. 036126
Ueda, Ichiro 027024
Ueda, Shinya 027130
Uehira, Mitsugi 026746
Uehling, Russel 044076
Ueland, Hanne Beate 031070
Uelsberg, Dr. Gabriele . . . 019020, 019021, 019022
Ueltschi, Hans-Peter 037602
Ueno, Katami 027247
Ueno, Takaaki 027322
Ueno, Tetsukazu 026426
Ürgová, Dana 007630
Uerscheln, Gabriele 016847
Uetz, Kitty 042932
Uffmann, Rüdiger 016236
Ufimcev, Valeri K. 033125
Ugarte-Peña, Alfredo 006927
Ugat, Pedro R. 031622
Ugawa, Masahiro 027018
Ugent, Dr. Donald 042619
Ugo, Prof. Gianni 000417
Ugren, Dragomir 034225
Uhernik, Boris 007746
Uhlemann, Dr. Silvia 016637
Uhlig, Dietmar 020380
Uhlig, Rainer 016660
Uhlmann, Klaus 016031
Uhrmacher, Erwin 015727
Ujiie, Seiichiro 027263
Ujváry, Dr. Péter 021694
Ukdah, Radi 037832
Ukena, H. 016686
Ul-Haq, Saleem 031381
Ulak, Dr. James 048884, 048908
Ulbrich, Marorie 041612
Ulbrich, Thomas 027563
Ulbricht, Dr. Ingrid 020038
Ulčar, Mirko 034458
Ulenberg, Dr. S.A. 029245
Uliančić-Vekić, Prof. Dr. Elena 007774
Ulinskyte, Vilija 027855
Ulitin, Valerij G. 033836
Ullmann, Silke 018830
Ulloa, Gina 028567
Ulloa Rojos, Sergio 006942
Ullock, Jack 005882
Ullrich, Prof. Dr. Ferdinand 019739, 019740, 019741
Ullrich, Tyrena 019951
Ulm, Dagmar 002256
Ulm zu Erbach, Franz Freiherr von 016999, 020683
Ulmann, Dr. Arnulf von 019352
Ulmer, Dr. Renate 016644, 016646
Ulmer, Sean 041736
Ulmis, Janis 027708
Ulrich, Alan 047342
Ulrich, Matthias 017192
Ulrich-Hicks, Barbara 044704
Ultan, Prof. Lloyd 042431
Umari, Suna 044654
Umberger, Eugene 044311
Umberger, Leslie 048136
Umemoto, Michio 026539
Umeñaca, Juan 035630
Umezu, Gen 027009
Uminowicz, Glenn 043293
Umney, Nick 040307
Umorbeckov, Baytursun Esjanovič . 027390
Unbehaun, Dr. Lutz 019936, 019937, 020131
Underwood, Katie 045822
Undesser, Gottfried 002920
Unge-Sörling, Suzanne 036642
Unger, Dr. Achim 053548
Unger, P. Karl 002603
Ungerfeld, M. 023067
Uno, Tomohisa 027233
Unraw, Peter 005963
Unruh, Dr. Frank 020483
Unsain, José María 035155
Untch, Katharine 047429
Unterdörfer, Dr. Michaela 037498
Unterreiner, Katrin 002919
Unterschultz, Judy 006514
Untersteiner, Eva 003076
Unverfehrt, Dr. Gerd 017466
Unzueta Reyes, Prof. Ana Geraldina 028452
Uoti, Maunu 009955
Uotila, Dr. Pertti 009539
Upeniece, Daiga 027729
Upp, Janeanne A. 048469
Upshaw, Lisa 047757
Upton, Alastair 039501
Upton, Graham 039361
Upton, Jan 039361
Uracz, Andrzej 032186
Urakova, Ljudmila Evgenjevna . . . 033179
Uranić, Igor 007828
Uranija, Valentin 007825

Urban, Dr. Andreas . . . 017755
Urban, Bettina . . . 002969, 002970
Urban, Elke . . . 018591
Urban, Erin . . . 048331, 048332
Urban, Heinz . . . 018877
Urban, Robin . . . 042207, 042536
Urban, Wolfgang . . . 019926
Urbaneck, Rotraud . . . 020813
Urbanek, Erich . . . 001920
Urbanek, Dr. Wilhelm . . . 002865
Urbanelli, Lora . . . 047258
Urbani, Vittorio . . . 026261
Urbanová, V. . . . 034452
Urbański, Andrzej . . . 032552, 032553
Urbanski, Prof. Dr. Krysztof . . . 031999
Urbas, Herbert . . . 001853
Urbons, Klaus . . . 019023
Urey-Weeks, Burdie . . . 027826
Urgesi, Prof. Domenico . . . 024679
Uribe, Gloria Zea de . . . 007419, 007420
Uribe Ramón, Jorge . . . 007624
Urio, Leonarda . . . 036998
Urioste Avana, Jaime . . . 003923
Urmas, Olli . . . 009739
Urquina Llanos, Henry . . . 007501
Urquiola, Beatriz S.A. . . . 031722
Urrea, Ana Isabel . . . 007644
Urrutia, Larry . . . 047838
Urrutibehety, Clément . . . 014463
Ursachi, Vasile . . . 032925
Urschel, Joe . . . 041780
Urschitz, Charlotte . . . 001935
d'Ursel, Robert . . . 003417
Ursić, Desanka . . . 006924
Ursu, Mihai . . . 028985
Urumov, Vanko . . . 004911
Urumova, Rumjana . . . 004649
Ušakov, Prof. S.A. . . . 033505
Ušakova, Tamara Ivanovna . . . 033296
Usanov, Evgenij Nikolaevič . . . 032977
Usaquén Ramos, Martha Lucía . . . 007393
Usberghi, Dr. Gianni . . . 026138
Uschner, Ralf . . . 015749
Ushakoff, Doreen . . . 042188
Ushkov, Konstantin . . . 027408
Usik, Boris Grigorjevič . . . 034063
Uslaner, Diane . . . 006608
Usler, Dr. Alexander . . . 017404
Usquhart, Donald R. . . . 038517
Ussenko, Valentina . . . 027404
Ussing Olsen, Peter . . . 009015
Ustaeva, Anna . . . 038207
Ustinov, Vladimir Jurjevič . . . 034083
Ustvedt, Østein . . . 031108
Ustvedt, Øytein . . . 031089
Utech, Dr. Frederick H. . . . 047044
Uthardt, Lorenz . . . 009854
Uthemann, Ernest W. . . . 019964
Utili, Dr. Mariella . . . 024906
Utriainen, Onerva . . . 010125
Utry, Dr. Attila . . . 021789
Utsunomiya, Akiko . . . 026533
Utter, Dr. Brad L. . . . 048981
Utz, Karen . . . 042225
Utz, Laura Lee . . . 046535
Uure, Sarah . . . 046468
Uvarova, Elena Anatolevna . . . 033986
Uyttenhove, Prof. Dr. J. . . . 003462
Uzubalieva, K.N. . . . 027634
Uzunov, Nikolai . . . 004681
Vaccaro, Dr. Luis Fernandez . . . 000151
Vaccaro, Prof. Mario . . . 023588
Vache, Bernd . . . 017588, 017589
Vačiullin, Gali Fajzrachmanovič . . . 033995
Väisänen, Raija . . . 009637
Väkeväinen, Lea . . . 009582
Välicki, Antti . . . 009623
Vaelske, Urd . . . 002567
Värtinen, Lea . . 009455, 009461, 009602, 009603, 009774, 009845, 009914, 009973, 010062, 010189
Vaessen, J.A.M.F . . . 029271
Väterlein, Dr. Christian . . . 015628
Vahey, John . . . 042316
Vahl, Heidemarie . . . 016832
Vaida, Lucian . . . 032896
Vaillancourt, Sandra . . . 047961
Vaillant, L. le . . . 030432
Vaimbois, Laurent . . . 013325
Vainorius, Julius . . . 027860
Vaireaux, Bernard . . . 014082
Vairo, Carlos Pedro . . . 000649
Vaitkute, Karile . . . 042823
Vajnerman, Viktor Solomonovič . . . 033601
Vajšnorajte, I.A. . . . 033983
Valadés Sierra, Juan M. . . . 035015
Valaison, Marie-Claude . . . 013789
Valat, Georges . . . 011480
Vălčev, Aleksandăr . . . 004869
Valcke, Ludo . . . 003221
Valdeny da Rocha, Manoel . . . 004567
Valderas, Elena Ruiz . . . 035059
Valderrama de Díaz, Maritza . . . 007554
Valdes, Nieves . . . 031635
Valdes Gonzalez Salas, Ana Luisa . 028424
Valdez, Ana Luisa . . . 028466
Valdez, E.A. . . . 045082
Valdez, Juan Carlos . . . 028624
Vale, Jessica . . . 038832
Vale, Prof. Dr. Maria da Graça Pratas do . . . 032600, 032606
Valemtová, Dr. Jarmila . . . 008448
Valencia, Alvaro Pío . . . 007589
Valencia, Maria L. . . . 032704
Valencia, Dr. Niels . . . 031555
Valencia de Redondo, María Eugenia . . . 007582
Valencia Ospina, José Aníbal . . . 007382, 007383
Valenteijn, R. . . . 030070
Valentin, J.C.P. . . . 029582
Valentin, Jocelyne . . . 014842
Valentin, Noel . . . 046369
Valentine, Eunice E. . . . 048840
Valentine, James W. . . . 042163
Valentine, Kathryn . . . 040468
Valentine, P. . . . 034568
Valentiner, Gitte . . . 008812
Valentini, Paolo . . . 026037
Valentová, Dr. Jarmila . . . 008441
Valerio, Michele . . . 023342
Valette, Jean . . . 011904
Valeza, Luisa S. . . . 031645
Valk, Marika . . . 009394, 009398, 009407, 009408
Vall Petitpierre, Carmina . . . 034925
Vallat, Pierre . . . 010971
Valle, Dr. Marco . . . 023377
Valle, Martha . . . 047278
Valle Pérez, Dr. José Carlos . . . 035667
Vallee, Dianne . . . 005615
Vallejo Laso, Manuel . . . 035688
Vallejo Triano, Antonio . . . 035111
Vallery, Tullio . . . 026266
Valles, Dave Anthony . . . 031663
Valles-Bled, M. . . . 012727
Vallette, Philippe . . . 010913
Valley, Derek R. . . . 046673
Valley, Mohawk . . . 041701
Vallianos, Dr. Christopher . . . 021525
Valliant, John R. . . . 047692
Vallvieille, Michel de . . . 014606
Valor, E. . . . 000629
Valowitz, Rhoda . . . 048552
Valter, Dr. Claudia . . . 020141
Valtere, Māra . . . 027690
Valtere, Mara . . . 027781
Valuska, Dr. David . . . 045050
Valz, Jean-Paul . . . 010299
Vametova, Farida H. . . . 033131
Vámos, Dr. Éva . . . 021684
Van Adrichem, J. . . . 029230
Van Allen, Victor . . . 005277
Van Alphen, Jan . . . 003158
Van Amerongen, R.A.M. . . . 029406
Van Arsdel, Sara . . . 046718
Van Autzen, Henning . . . 020365
Van Baren, J.H.V. . . . 030305
Van Beek, Dr. R. . . . 029163
Van Beekhofff, D. . . . 029146
Van Beers, H. . . . 029230
Van Beheemen, P. . . . 029475
Van Berge-Gerbaud, M. . . . 013568
Van Berge Henegouwen, Dr. A.L. . . . 029435
Van Bergen, W.J. . . . 029734
Van Blyenburgh, Dr. Ninian Hubert 037130
Van Boheemen, P. . . . 029474
Van Boorne, Geert . . . 003470
Van Bossche, André . . . 003489
Van Boven, Dr. M.W. . . . 029446
Van Boxtel, E. . . . 030088
Van Brakel, J.H. . . . 029194
Van Brakel, J.W. . . . 030304
Van Broeckhoven, Greet . . . 003163
Van Broekhoven, L. . . . 029854
Van Bussel, Gerard W. . . . 002961
Van Campen, Dr. Jan . . . 029843
Van Campenhout, Nico . . . 003611
Van Cauteren, J. . . . 030316, 030317
Van Clardt, V. . . . 034778
Van Cleve, David . . . 042312
Van Daele, Dr. Rik . . . 003611
Van Damme . . . 003553
Van Damme, I. . . . 003319
Van de Beuque, Guy . . . 004354
Van de Guchte, Dr. Maarten . . . 044812
Van de Kerkhof, Véronique . . . 003189
Van de Maele, Maurice . . . 006923
Van de Perre, M. . . . 003141
Van de Schoor, Dr. F.C.M. . . . 029961
Van de Velde, Hildegard . . . 003187
Van de Voorde, Veronique . . . 003658
Van de Voort, Dr. J.P. . . . 030276
Van de Wiele, Johan . . . 003458
Van Delen, Wieke . . . 034583
Van den Abeele, Jean-Pol . . . 003773
Van den Akker, Ad . . . 044576
Van den Berg, R. . . . 029557
Van den Berg, S. . . . 030046
Van den Bosch, Paula . . . 029893
Van den Branden, Walter . . . 003839
Van den Brink, Dr. Peter . . . 029893
Van den Broeke, J. . . . 030261
Van den Bussche, Willy . . . 003543, 003686
Van den Donk, Drs. H.P.S.M. . . . 029924
Van den Driessche, B. . . . 003617
Van den Eijnde, Jerden . . . 030299
Van den Elzen, Dr. Renate . . . 016337
Van den Hout, A.H.P.J. . . . 030230
Van den Meiracker, C. . . . 030108
Van den Steen de Jehay, Comte Guy . . . 003545
Van den Valentyn, Heike . . . 016841
Van den Veen, J. . . . 029978
Van der Auwera, M. . . . 003505
Van der Beele, P. . . . 029777
Van der Burgh, Dr. J. . . . 030237
Van der Donckt, Marie-Claire . . . 003694
Van der Elst, Els . . . 003353
Van der Goes, Drs. André W.A. . . . 016794
Van der Haegen, Erik . . . 003853
Van der Heever, Chast . . . 034739
Van Der Heijden, Merijn . . . 044291
Van der Holst, A.P.J. . . . 030137
Van der Kemp, Gerald . . . 011955
Van der Laan, Anke . . . 029653
Van der Laar, P. . . . 030081
Van der Lelie, H. . . . 029849
Van der Lugt, Dr. P. . . . 029697
van der Meiden, Kees . . . 029642
Van der Meijden, Dr. Hellebora . . . 036879
Van der Merwe, Jake . . . 005066
Van der Merwe, T. . . . 034592
Van der Merwe, Thijs . . . 034583
Van der Meulen, G.P. . . . 029580
Van der Ploeg, J. . . . 030392
Van der Ploeg, P. . . . 029434
Van der Spek, Dr. T.M. . . . 029850
Van der Veer, Hugh G. . . . 048398
Van Der Vin, J.P.A. . . . 029848
Van der Wall, Dr. Frauke . . . 020999
Van der Werdt, E.F.L.M. . . . 029803
Van der Westhuizen, V. . . . 034708
Van der Zalm, Leo . . . 029611
Van der Zijpp, Sue-An . . . 029638
Van der Zwaag, M. . . . 029197
Van Deun, Charles . . . 003754
Van Deurs, Lone . . . 008830
Van Deventer, Anriët . . . 034704
Van Dijck, Leen . . . 003152
Van Dijk, E.A. . . . 030414
Van Dijk, J. . . . 029194
Van Dongen, A.G.A. . . . 030088
Van Dongen, P.L.F. . . . 029854
Van Dooren, Rita . . . 003168
Van Doorne, Geert . . . 003468
Van Doorne, Veerle . . . 003391
Van Dorst, Drs. M.H.J. . . . 030269
Van Duuren, D.A.P. . . . 029194
Van Dyck, Ann . . . 003161
Van Dyk, Pieter . . . 001389
Van Dyk, Stephen H. . . . 046319
Van Dyke, Dore . . . 041883
Van Dyke, Jonathon . . . 044445
Van Egmond, C. . . . 029720
Van Endert, Dr. Dorothea . . . 018948
Van Faasen, Drs. S.A.J. . . . 029430
Van Frank, M. . . . 044545
Van Geluwe, Johan . . . 003842
Van Gennip, J. . . . 029659
Van Genuchten, S. . . . 030306
Van Gerwen, Dr. Ch. . . . 030252
Van Gijseghem, A.M. . . . 003466
Van Ginneken, Lily . . . 029455
Van Gompel, F. . . . 003646
Van Grevenstein, Alexander . . . 029893
Van Grootheest, J. . . . 029435
Van Haaften, Joel . . . 045368, 045369
Van Haaren, Joke . . . 029653
Van Haaren, S. . . . 030230
Van Haarlem, Dr. W.M. . . . 029163
Van Hablem, M. . . . 029934
Van Haecke, Bert . . . 003387
Van Harinxma, Barones K.L. . . . 030260
Van Harten Boers, H. . . . 030161
Van Hattem, M. . . . 029408
Van Heerden, H. . . . 034669
Van Heerden, Martie . . . 029103
Van Hees, Eva . . . 045814
Van Heesch, Dr. A. . . . 029961
van Helmond, Mary . . . 038976
Van Hengstum, R. . . . 029851
Van Heugten, Sjraar . . . 029239
Van Heuven-Van Nes, Dr. E. . . . 029256
Van Hoof, Werner . . . 003194
Van Hoofstat, Jan . . . 003743
Van Hoonacker, Albin . . . 003574
Van Hoonacker, Marie-Henriette . . 003574
Van Hoorn, Dr. M.A.M. . . . 029660
Van Horn, Walter . . . 041711
Van Hout, I.C. . . . 029194
Van Hout, N. . . . 003163
Van Huis, Edwin . . . 029749
Van Huy, Prof. Dr. Hguyen . . . 049522
Van Kampen, Dr. Iefke Johanna . . 024235
Van Kerkhouen, Laurence . . . 003262
Van Kerkhoven, Geertrin . . . 003695
Van Klinken, M.F. . . . 029260
Van Koughnett, W.J. . . . 005106
Van Krimpen, W. . . . 029424
Van Krugten, Dr. D. . . . 018098
Van Kruistum, G. . . . 029806
Van Laar, Barb . . . 048191
Van Laarhoven, H. . . . 029313
Van Laarhoven, Dr. Jan . . . 029704, 029736
Van Laer, M. . . . 003435
Van Leeuwen, P.C. . . . 029294
Van Leeuwen, P.P.H. . . . 030363
Van Lennep, Jacques . . . 003316
Van Leverink, J. . . . 029914
Van Liebergen, Dr. L.C.B.M. . . . 030213
Van Lier, F.J. . . . 029373

Van Lingen, C. 030085
Van Loo, R. 003505
Van Loon, V. 029244
Van Looy, Walter 003715
Van Marion, A.J.H. 030235
Van Meerbeeck, Patrick 003562
Van Meerten, M.M. 030388, 030390
Van Melsen, Frances 034606
Van Mensch, Dr. 029748
Van Mol, Bruno 003649
Van Mullekom, Elisabeth 001119
Van Ness, Sally D. 044027
Van Nieuwenhuijzen, M. 029230
Van Noort, Dr. S. 034586
Van Noten, Francis 003301, 003338, 003357
Van Nüss, Berndt 020898
Van Oijen, M.J.P. 029851
Van Olst, C. 029767
Van Orman, John 046076
Van Pelt, Peter 043554
Van Peteghem, Dr. Sylvia 003471
Van Pottelberghe, Michel 003843
Van Praët, Michel 013592
Van Proyen, Mark 047855
Van Putten, J.H.J. 036161
Van Raalte, Christopher 047864
Van Raalte, Ronald C. 047543
Van Raay, Stefan 039073
Van Raemdonck, Mieke 003353
Van Ravensteyn, Fr. 003444
Van Regteren, R. 029966
Van Remoortel, P. 003251
Van Rensburg, F.S. 034729
Van Rijnswall, M. 029891
Van Rijswick, Dr. A. 030192
Van Rosmeilen 029096
Van Schalkwyk, Frieda 034723
Van Schalkwyk, Thea 034723
Van Schie, A. 030227
Van Seters, A.G.J. 029240
Van Shields 045542
Van Shields, W. 047488
Van Soest, Dr. R.W.M. 029245
Van Sprang, Sabine 003315
Van Straaten, Dr. E.J. 030015
Van Stuivenberg, F. 029567
Van Suchtelen, A. 029434
Van 't Veen, Cees 029843
Van Tilborgh, Louis 029239
Van Tilburg, B. 030030
Van Tilburg, C. 029696
Van Tol, J. 029851
Van Tooren, M.M. 029410
Van Tuyl, Prof. Gijs 020965
Van Tuyll Van Serooskerken, Dr. C. Baron 029660
Van Twist, Kees 029638
Van Veen, J.W. 029643
Van Vierzen, Barb 006142
Van Vilsteren, Dr. V.T. 029279
Van Vleet, Sue 047612
Van Vlijmen, Dr. P.M.L. 030235
Van Vollenharen, A.C. 034747
Van Volsem, Cindy 006168
Van Voorhis, Joan 042068
Van Voorst Van Beest, R. 029660
Van Wagner, Alison G. 041724
Van Waterschoot, J. 029202
Van Weelden, J.F. 029504
Van Wegen, Dr. Rik 029893
Van Wesemael, Willy 003791
Van Westerop, W.C.J. 030137
Van Wetten, Katja 020365
Van Wezel, H. 029860
Van Willigen, Samuel 037784
Van Zante, Gary 042566
Van Zijl, J.J.R. 034559
Van Zijl, M.I.E. 030226, 030226
Van Zyl, S. 034706
Van Zÿverden, J. 030086
Váňa, R. 008273
Vanadziņs, A. 027671
Vanater, Holli M. 043334
Vanausdall, John 044737
Vanautgaerden, Alexandre 003289, 003303
Vance, Alex D. 046171
Vance, Ann 049106
Vance, Tom 045237, 045238
Vanco, John L. 043721
Vančugov, V.P. 038375
Vandamme, Dr. E. 003163
Vandamme, Heidi 029239
Vandecan, Suzanne 003669
Vandekerchove, Veronique 003582
Vandelannoote, Jean-André 014336
Vanden Berghe, E. 003275
Vandenbroek, Dr. Paul 003163
Vandenbulcke, Anne 003292, 003304, 003339
Vandenheuvel, William 046559
Vandenven, Marc 003188
Vandepitte, Dr. Francisca . 003313, 003316
Vandeput, Ann 003500
Vander, Joan 044326
Vanderbeck, LeeAnne 047323
Vanderhenst, Clara 003171
Vanderhust, Guido 003308
VanderLeest, Merlyn 046860
Vanderlip, Dianne 043404
Vandermaesen, M. 003281
Vanderpijpen, Willy 003291
Vanderpool, Guy C. 048538, 048539
Vanderschooten, Alain 014616
Vandervellen, Pascale 003333, 003353
Vanderwerff, Laverne 041784
Vandever, William 043987
Vandevivere, I. 003617
Vándor, Dr. László 021924, 021925
Vandormael, Dr. H. 003441
Vandulek, Márta 021662
Vandura, Djuro 007856
Vane-Wright, R. 040245
Vanegas López, Walberto 007515
Vanek, Helga 003017
Vanerck, Patricia 003370
Vanhaelen, M. 003334
Vanhalewijn, Rudy 003552
Vanheusden, Margot 003181
Vanja, Dr. Christina 017638
Vanja, Prof. Dr. Konrad 016128
Vanlatum, Anne 014686
Vannini, Prof. Marco 024188
Vannoni, Filippo 024171
Vanns, Michael 038887, 039830
Vannson, Françoise 010348
Váňová, Kristina 008692
Vanreuerm-Rossetto, Roxane 011669
Vanrie, André 003664
Van't Veen, Dr. Cees 029837, 029842
Vantrimpont, Jean-Denis 003566
Varadinis, Mirjam 037777
Varaksina, Tamara Ivanovna 033016
Varaldo, Prof. Carlo 023147, 023148, 023150, 023480
Vardanjan, Irina Valerjevna 033607
Vare, Talis 009358
Varela, Katia 008005
Varela, Matias 042125, 055024
Varenius, Linnéa 036361
Varga, Vincent J. 005722
Vargas, Heriberto 007524
Vargas, Maria Cristina 007413
Vargas, Mercedes L. 031762
Vargas Cuervo, Roberto 007555
Vargas de Martínez, Evelia 007559
Vargas Guadarrama, Dr. Luis Alberto 028539
Vargoz, Sylvine 013643
Vargyas, Herbert 002543
Varignana, Dr. Franca 023417
Varjonen, Risto 009516
Varnado, R. Brien 042728
Vârnav, Prof. Remus 032898, 032899
Varno, Edward 042594
Varrak, Maruta 009412
Vartiainen, Ulla 009878
Váry, Dr. László 021698
Vasconcelos, Maria João . 032672, 032674
Vaseva Dimeska, Viktorija 027921
Vasher-Dean, April 046221
Vasić, Dr. Voislav 034169
Vasicek, Werner 001808
Vasileva, Dineta 004901
Vasileva, Rumjana 004859
Vasilevič, Georgij N. 033689
Vasiliu, Lucian 032879
Vasilui, Lucian . 032880, 032881, 032883, 032894
Vassallo, Dr. Adriana 025531
Vassallo de Cettour, Crsitina 000286
Vasseur, Bernard 014190
Vasseur, Dominique 048304
Vasseur, Marie-Madeleine 012402
Vassiliadis, Dimitrios 021334
Vassilika, Dr. Eleni 017924
Vassilyeva, Valentina 027403
Vasudeva Bhatta, K. 022017
Vašut, Karel 008746
Vatksy, Sharon 043879
Vatutin, Konstantin Ivanovič 033589
Vaucher, Laurence 037346
Vaughan, Ellen 042764
Vaughan, Dr. Gerard 001246
Vaughan, Dr. Jefferson 044263
Vaughan, Roger 038563, 039152
Vauth, Henry 016834
Vavilova, Anna Pavlovna 033668
Vavilova, N.I. 033663
Vavra, Jan 049159
Vázquez Agraz, Joaquín 028171
Vázquez Ramírez, Nelson 028109
Vazquez Zuleta, Sixto 000363
Vazzana, Dr. Angelo 025409
Vdovin, Dr. Gennadij Viktorovič . . . 033435
Vecarić, Nenad 007708
Vecchio, Marji 042821
Večerková, Dr. Eva 008286
Vedeznikova, Galina I. 033454
Vedjaeva, Natalja Anatoljevna 033636
Védrine, Laurent 014291
Védrine, Mireille 011209
Vedsted, Jakob 008837
Veeneman, Dr. G.A.C. 029850
Veenvliet, J. 029469
Veerabhadra Rao, K. 022129
Veerman, Hein 030286
Vees, L. 017816
Vega, Carmen L. 032742
Vegelin Van Claerbergen, Ernst . . . 040126
Vegesack, Alexander von 020719
Vegesack, Baron Henrik von 036659
Vehma-Çiftçi, M. 019479
Vehniä, Harri 009765, 009766
Vehns, Johannes 017735
Veil, Dr. Stephan 017765
Veisz, Ottó 021780
Veit, Johann 001668
Veit, Prof. Dr. Willibald 016134
Veitch Alexander, Mary 045795
Vejle, Jan 008831, 008832, 008833
Vejlstrup, Tove 008938
Vela de la Torre, Antonio 035793
Velado Craña, Bernardo 034870
Velani, Dr. Livia 023231
Velaochaga Rey, Irene 031552
Velasquez, Dr. Geraldine 045129
Vélasquez, Dr. M. Manuel 032578
Velázquez, Agustín 035492
Velazquez, Efrain 042172
Velázquez Martínez del Campo, Roxana 028526
Velde-Conyers, Ellayne 045701
Velder, Linda 046448
Velers, J.B.A. 029988
Vélez, Jesús Hernán 007529
Velez, Pedro 042883
Vélez, Pilar 034936, 034948
Velfl, Dr. Josef 008657
Velghe, Brita 003306, 003316
Velikanova, Olga Alekseevna 033806
Velikova, Elena 004818
Velikova-Kesheleva, Violeta 004863
Velilla Moreno, Pilar 007535
Vella, Antonino 041277
Vella, John J. 028026
Vellacott, Robert B. 000980
Vellekoop, Marije 029239
Veller, Prof. M. 034646
Velluto, Giovanna 026153
Veloccia Rinaldi, Dr. Maria Luisa . . 024236, 026026, 026027
Veloso, Abraã9 032699
Veltheim, M. von 017865
Veltzke, Dr. Veit 018954, 020823
Venborg Pedersen, Dr. Mikkel 009000
Vences, Dr. M. 029245
Vendeuvre, Elyane de 015160, 015159
Veneman, Katherine 048829
Venizelos, Eleftherios 021201
Venkataraman, R. 022249
Venkatesh Jois, Dr. K.G. 022202
Vento, Minna 009472
Ventre, Dr. Riccardo 023655
Ventrudo, Meg 046371
Ventsch, Warren 048736
Venturo Rubino, Donata 023177
Vera, Gina C. de 031633
Vera, Teresa N. de 031691
Verardo, Bonnie 041625
Verbanck Piérard, Annie 003657
Verbeeck, Luc 003241
Verbrugghen, Johanna M. 046822
Vercler, Dr. 043130
Verderame, Dr. Lori 041660
Verdi, Prof. Richard 038720
Verdugo Santos, Javier 035834
Veremeeva, Irina Lukivna 038316
Veres, Dr. László 021787
Vereščagina, Tatjana Fëdorovna . . 034016
Verey, A.P. 041416
Vergara, Alejandro 035429
Vergara Rodríguez, Ancízar 007388
Vergara Torres, David 006938
Verge, Laurie 043012
Verger, Sylvestre 013686
Vergho, Dr. Helge 015939, 018255
Vergne, Philippe 045922
Vergnetta, Angela 025809
Vergun, Neonila Rodionivna 038357
Verhaagh, Manfred 018170
Verhaard, A.J.G. 029989
Verhaeghe, Y.-C. 003814
Verhoeff, R.N.S. 029663
Verhoeven, Carolina 029258
Verkest, Idesbalo 003144
Vermeesch, Gerald 042219
Vermeulen, S. 034561
Verna, Gaëtane 005762
Verner Hamilton, Elizabeth 042732
Verneulen, W. 030015
Verney, Antoine 010679
Vernon, C.J. 034608
Vernon, G.N. 034608, 034609
Verone, Amy 046781
Verrando, Joyce 044472
Verrill, John H. 046685
Verroen, Dr. Th.L.J. 029496
Verschelden, G. 003788
Verschoor, M. Lynn 042449
Verschuur, P. 029533
Versluis, John 044178
Versluis, P. 029270
Verster, J.L. 030074
Vertenten, A. 003419
Verthamon, Henri de 010374
Verwey, Drs. A.D.M. 029183
Verwiebe, Dr. Birgit 015984
Verwimp, Gunter 003163
Verževikina, Marina 033937
Verzosa, Fe Angela 031720
Verzuh, Valerie 047971

Vesio-Steinkamp, Susan 042917
Veskovic, Esad 003941
Vest, Ladonna 042716
Vest, Windsor 048206
Vestergaard, Ole Schou 008880
Vestermanis, Margers 027731
Vettel, Greg 044262
Vetter, J.W.M. 029547
Vetter, Manfred 019286
Vetter, Maureen 045309
Vetter, Remo 037624
Veyradier, Henri 012541
Vezzosi, Alessandro 026341
Via, Marie 047487
Vial, Marie-Paule 012944
Vialla, Andre 012167
Vialla, Gérard 013970
Vianin, Georges 037754
Viar, Javier 034982
Viatgé, Karine 010425
Viatte, Françoise 013685
Vibe, Ellen S. de 031072
Vice, Lola 042483
Vice, Mary L. 047721
Vice, Michael L. 044184
Vicente, Jaime D. 035910
Vicini, Dr. Donata 025139, 025144, 025146
Vicini, Maria Lucrezia 025483
Vicino, Giuseppe 024134
Vickers, Irene 040027
Vickery, Michael 045228
Vicq Carvalho, Beatriz de 004397
Victor, S. 034667
Vida, Štefan 034404
Vidal, Nélida 028454
Vidal, Pierre 013660
Vidal, Silvia M. 049499
Vidal de Alba, Beatriz 028521
Vidal Huguet, Carme 035352
Vidal Inglès, Anton 035187
Vidali, Dr. Gloria 026255
Vidarte, Juan Ignacio 034985
Vidovic, Prof. Josip 007706
Vidulich, Tullio 026111
Viehmeier, Klaus 020890
Vienet, Bernard 012014
Vienonen, Inga 009925
Viens, Katheryn P. 048507
Viera, Ricardo 042184
Vierhauser, Emil 001868
Vierk, Viola 017723
Vierny, Dina 013708
Vierock, Ronald 016129
Vietti, Paola 025426
Vietze, Arwed 021072, 021074
Vieux, Jacky 011959
Vigarani, Guido 024764
Vigié-Chevalier, Béatrice 012947
Vigna Taglianti, Prof. Augusto 025537
Vignau-Wilberg, Dr. Thea 019118
Vigorelli, Prof. Giancarlo 024722
Vigreux, Jean 014209
Viguier, Florence 013130
Vihovde, Anne Brit 030763
Viinikainen, Kari 009821
Viita, Jorma 009731
Vikan, Dr. Gary 042006
Vikström, Lena 036479
Viktorova, Jelena 027729
Vikulova, V.P. 033384
Vila, Dominique 011306, 011307
Vila, Emma R. 000126
Vilà Noguera, Francesc 035464
Vilà Planas, Xavier 036055
Vilademunt, Josep 036055
Vilain, André 003576
Vilain, Jacques 013045, 013614
Vilaplana, Susana 035978
Vilas, Felipe Arias 035073
Vilchez Vilchez, Carlos 035251
Viler, Darko 034464
Viletová, Dagmar 008776, 008777
Vilhu, Raimo 009488
Viljanskyj, Oleksandr Oleksijovyč 038238
Viljoen, H. 034719
Viljoen, L. 034561
Vilks, Dr. Ilgonis 027734
Vilkuna, Janne 009639, 009640
Villa, Azucena ... 031786, 031787, 031799
Villadier, Francis 013044
Villagran Valdespino, Manuel Angel 028627
Villamayor Coto, José 028484
Villamizar Duarte, Eduardo Adolfo 007564
Villamizar Lamus, Eduardo 007565
Villanueva, Gustavo M. 030663
Villarroya i Font, Joan 034888
Ville, Roy de 041631
Ville, Roy V. de 041632
Villegas de Aneiva, Teresa 003916
Villela, Milu 004532
Villeneove, Daniel 006216
Villeneuve, Pat 045206
Villeon, H. de la 012624
Villiers, Jaline de 034694
Villiger, Dr. Verena 037100
Villoutreix, Pascal 012631
Vilman, Vladimir 034495
Vilsmeier, Cäcilie 019297
Vilus, Ljiljana 007832
Vimpari, Maritta 009885
Vimpère, Jean 012218
Viñayo, Antonio 035331
Vincent, Ariel 014590
Vincent, François 005799
Vincent, Dr. Gilbert T. 043137, 043138
Vincent, Glenda 048421
Vincent, Hélène 012021
Vincent, Jean-Claude 013769
Vincent, Victor 045816
Vincentelli, Moira 038463
Vincenti, Dr. Patrick 044484
Vincenzi, Marco 024044
Vine, Pat 047835
Viner, David 039091
Vingtain, Dominique 010598
Vinje, Tor 031036
Vinke, Albert 019819
Vinogradov, Z. 022902
Vinogradova, Vira Illivna 038314
Vinsen, Bob 030550
Vinyet Estebanell, Josep 035356
Vinzens, Brigitte 037732
Vio, Ettore 026247, 026258
Virasoro, Carlos Alberto 000608
Virgin, Louise 049309
Virieu, A. de 011836
Virole, Agnès 014308
Virtanen, Prof. Ismo 009534
Virtanen, Risto 009937
Vis-Best, A. 029928
Visbach, Alida 006211
Vischer, Dr. Theodora 037356
Visentin, Prof. Dr. Mario 023934
Visini, Patrick 015078
Viskari, Leena 009824
Višnevskaja, Julija 033500
Vispi, Maria 024392
Visser, Dr. Anna Maria 024099
Visser, H. 029230
Visser, Johann 019329
Visser, Mattijs 016841
Visser, Dr. S. H. 029288
Visser, Susan R. 048228
Visser, Tina 005427
Viswanadham, M. 022339
Vitáček, Zdeněk 008313, 008351
Vitagliano, Carol Edith 000213
Vital, Christophe 012616, 014841
Vital, M. 011853, 013119
Vitali, Christoph 037451
Vitali, Samuel 036930
Vitali, Tiziana 024869
Viti, Paolo 026263
Vitie, Heikki 009558
Vitković Zikić, Milena 034163
Vitmayer, Janet 040179
Vitous, Frantisek 008517
Vitt, Dr. L.J. 046509
Vivanco Vega, Manuel 007444
Viver, F. Xavier 035934
Vivies, Bertrand de 011912, 011914
Vizi, Dr. József Kriston 021763
Vizi, Ondrej 034243
Vizirito, Jackie 042662
Vjalikov, P.F. 033368
Vjalych, Ljudmila Makarovna 033321
Vješnic, Borko 007798
Vlachou, Elia 021207
Vlack, Donald J. 046390
Vladimirova, Galina A. 033817
Vlaemynck, Joris 003406
Vlasáková, Beata 034437
Vlašić, Andrija 007767
Vlasova, Tetjana Mykolaïvna 038336
Vlatković, Radmila 034237
Vlcek, Dr. Tomas 008599
Vliegenthart, Dr. A.W. 029254
Vlieghe, Prof. Dr. Hans 003155
Vlk, Antonin 008426
Vlnas, Dr. Vit 008616, 008617
Vlnas, Dr. Vít 008648
Vlok, Rochelle 034771
Voce, Yolanda 047813
Vodret, Dr. Rossella 025479
Vögele, Dr. Christoph 037577
Völcker-Janssen, Dr. Wilhelm 018383
Voélin-Dubey, Monique 037385
Voelkel, David B. 044059
Völker, Angela 002945
Voelker, Gary 045192
Völker, Heike 015992
Völker, Reinhard 020526
Völkl, Rosemarie 019744
Voelkle, William M. 046394
Vörös, Dr. Gabriella 021858, 021862
Voet, Albert 003186
Vötter-Dankl, Susanna 002360
Vogeding, Dr. Ralf 020390
Vogel, Christian 019352
Vogel, Klaus 016784
Vogel, Dr. Michael 015957
Vogel, Robert 048358
Vogel, Wilhelm Dieter 017197
Vogelaar, Dr. C.J.J. 029855
Vogelbacher, Martin 020444
Vogeler, Dr. Hildegard 018726
Vogels, J.J. 029625, 029626
Vogelsang, Harald 016278
Vogelsang, W.J. 029854
Vogelstein, John L. 046352
Vogl, Elisabeth 020385
Vogler, Franz 002867
Vogler-Zimmerli, Brigitta 036930
Vogt, Barbara 027842
Vogt, George L. 049205
Vogt, Dr. Renate 016336
Vogt, Sharon L. 046018
Vogt, Wolfgang 018947
Vogtenhuber, Peter 002243
Vogue, Louis de 011444
Vogüé, Comte B. de 013484
Vogüé, Patrice de 012854
Vogüé, T. Comtesse de 015025
Voicu, Mariana 032913
Voigt, Dr. Kirsten 018169
Voigt, Sigrun 017972
Voigt, Dr. Wolfgang 017156
Voigt Andersen, Mogens 021540
Voisin, Bernard 011346
Voisin-Thiberge, Claire 013343
Voithofer, Waltraud 001760
Vojtenko, Vladimir Georgievič 033571
Vokotopoulou, Dr. Julia ... 021249, 021440
Volbers, Dr. Wilfried 015898
Volkert, James 046383
Volkmann, Jürgen 017553
Volkov, Sergej Pavlinovič 033566
Volkova, Valentina Borisovna 033226
Volkwein, Peter 018077
Vollert, Adalbert 017172
Vollgraaff, Helene 034583
Vollmer, David 048533
Vollmer, Erich 044934
Vollmer, Janis 044158
Vollmer, Jennifer 043592
Vollnhals, Rudolf 021084
Volmar, Michael 044471
Voločkova, Olga Kuzminična 033677
Volosenkova, Nadežda 033884
Volosova, Galina Pavlovna 033838
Vološyna, Ljubov Vasylivna 038340
Volovenskaja, Ljudmila Vladimirovna 033173
Volpe, Jorge 000154
Volskij, Svjatoslav O. 033585
Volz, Günther 015658
Volz, Jochen 017191
Volz, Robert L. 049186
Vomm, Dr. Wolfgang 015967, 015972
Vomsattel, Gerold 037683
Von der Mieden, O.J.E. 030292
Vondras, Barbara 045272
Vonhof, M.J. 030015
Vonier, Franz 001788
Vonk-Hennig, Davien 029128
Voogt, Leo 029440
Vookles, Laura L. 049338
Voordendaf, A.G. 030187
Voorhies, Dr. Michael 045313
Vorachek, Pamela 047749
Vorano, Tullio 007753
Vorel, Otakar 008415
Vorländer, Dr. Hermann 019229
Vormaier, Andreas 003009
Vorobjova, Solomija Oleksandrivna 038353
Voropanov, Vladimir Valentinovič 034071
Vorre, Birgit 008999
Vorres, George 021414
Vorres, Ian 021414
Vorsteher, Dr. Dieter 016011
Vort-Ronald, Michael P. 001136
Vorwig, Dr. Carsten 018866
Vos, H.N. 034755
Vos, K. 029854
Voss, Dr. J. 003597
Voss, Kurt 044136
Voß, Dr. Rolf 019219
Voss, William J. 044007
Vostrikov, Vladimir Ivanovič 033694
Votaw, John F. 049136
Votroubková, Dr. Iva 008328
Voute, Dr. A.M. 030240
Vovk Čepič, Taja 034484
Voyadzis, G. 021200
Voyame, Christian 036932
Voyles, Robert 043912
Voza, Dr. Giuseppe 025745, 025902
Voznickyj, Boris Grygorovyč 038344
Voznjuk, Dr. Volodymyr Oksentijovyč 038237
Vrabec, Vesna 007849
Vraesos, Alexis 010707
Vrat, Prof. Prem 022322
Vrba, Elisabeth 046226
Vrčic, Vjeko 007729
Vrebos, M. 003292, 003304
Vrellis, Paul P. 021281
Vriarte, Miriam de 047875
Vriend, Anita 029239
Vries, D.P. de 029844
Vries, J. de 029492
Vries, Dr. M.E.A. de 029134
Vrieze, John 029158
Vroede, Erik de 003517
Vrousos, Alexis 014338
Vrtiska, Floyd 048461
Vuadens, G. 037669
Vuigner, J.L. 037323
Vuille, Roger 037474
Vuilloud, R. 037332
Vujčić, Davorin 007734
Vujičić, Jasminka 007832

Vujnović, Andrej 034153
Vuk, Vili 034500
Vukadin, Hela 007849
Vukašinović, Dragomir 034220
Vukotić, Biljana 034163
Vuković, Prof. Radovan 007859
Vukovich, Franz 002292
Vulf, Galina Gerasimovna 033305, 033306, 033307
Vuorikoski, Timo 010126
Vuorinen, Pirjo 009635
Vusoniwailala, Kate 009450, 030511
Vuyk, Dr. K. 029236
Vydrina, Ljudmila Sergeevna 033795
Vykoukal, Dr. Jiří 008329
Vykydal, Vlastimil 008296
Vyntu-Terycanu, Dr. Olena Dmytrivna 038240
Vyskocil, Hubert 002999
Vysockij, Nikita Vladimirovič 033416
Vysockyj, Viktor Ivanovyč 038332
Vyvyan-Robinson, Richard 038774
Waage, Einy 031057
Waal, M. de 034561
Wachna, Pamela 006612
Wachs, Diane C. 045258
Wachsmund, Ulrike 016979
Wachten, Dr. Johannes 017178
Wachter, Dr. Markus 002423, 002424
Wacker, Ursel 021057
Wackerfuß, Winfried 017125
Wacs, Darin 046805
Wada, Kunibo 027105
Wade, Blake 044499, 044589
Wade, Dennis 000901
Wade, Don 048431
Wade, Dr. Edwin L. 043851
Wade, Hilary 038998, 038999
Wade, J. Blake 042031
Wade Thomas, Randall 044074
Wadensten, Hillevi 036732
Wadsley, Amanda 039588
Wadsworth, David H. . . . 043032, 043033, 043034
Wächter, Gabriele 018219
Waechter, James 047401
Wäldchen, Günter 020240
Wälder, Manfred 018635
Wærdahl, Tove 030920
Wäre, Dr. Ritva 009572
Waern, Karl Erik 036176
Wäspe, Roland 037493
Wagemakers, C. 029178
Wageman, Patty 029638
Wagener, Danièle 027888, 027892, 027897
Wagensberg, Jorge 034930
Wagesreiter, Viktoria 003017
Waggener, Lynda 045870
Waghorne, N. 040847
Wagini, Dr. Susanne 019118
Wagner, Connie 047571
Wagner, Dieter 016822
Wagner, Eckard 020226
Wagner, Florence 045545
Wagner, Gerhard A. 016375
Wagner, Günther 019624
Wagner, Herbert 001867
Wagner, Hermann 001850
Wagner, Dr. Jens-Christian 019334
Wagner, Kay 047817
Wagner, Lynn 044953
Wagner, Maria 001730
Wagner, Patrice 042157
Wagner, René 019696
Wagner, Rita 018322
Wagner, Ruth 048138
Wagner, Dr. Siegfried 019186, 019187
Wagner, Thomas K. 043596
Wagner, Dr. Velten 016986
Wagner, Vivian 042930
Wagner-Gnan, Angela 019379
Wagoner, Ian 041618
Wagrodzki, Jerzy 032477
Wagstaff, Sheena 040299, 040300
Wahdan, Tracey 039273, 040959
Wahl, Hans-Rudolf 037750
Wahl, Johann 002807
Wahl, Sonja 042963
Wahle, Michael 016225
Wahlöö, Claes 036443
Wahlquist, Håkan 036623
Wahnsiedler, Angel 046222
Wain, Lisa 000960
Waintraub, Aron 022904
Waisbrot, Ann 045708
Waite, Dawn D. 042659
Wajima, Kunio 026578
Wakamatsu, Motoi 027287
Wake, David B. 042164
Wake, William 039329
Wakeling, Melissa 005083
Waker, William 047743
Wakitani, Masami 027120
Wakiyama, Yoshitaka 026491
Wal, Eva 016327
Walaszczyk, Anna 032559
Walaszczyk, Antoni 031959
Walberczyk, Jerzy 031892
Walburg, Dr. Reinhold 017169
Walch, Heribert 001830
Walch, Nicole 003291
Walch, Peter 041625
Walch, Timoth 049066
Wald, Albrecht 017128
Walde, Prof. Dr. Elisabeth 001785, 002090, 002234
Walden, Ian N. 039289
Waldherr, Johann 002420
Waldherr, Kaspar 018615
Waldkirch, Bernhard von 037777
Waldman, Glenys A. 046959
Waldmann, Fritz 037635
Waldmann-Glaser, Dr. Erich 002724
Waldmeier, Kurt 037051
Waldon, Arnold 046999
Waldren, Dr. William 035143
Waldron, Richard 046921
Walentowicz, T. 039046
Walgamott, Libby 047363
Walgenbach, H. 030081
Walgrave, René 003580
Waligurski, Carolyn M. 044696
Waligurski, Stephen S. 044696
Walk, Deborah 047999
Walk, Stephen G.W. 046465
Walkensteiner, Wolfgang . . 002141, 052569
Walker, Alexandra 040778
Walker, Anita 043430
Walker, Anne Noel 048511
Walker, Barry 044648
Walker, Bill 040889
Walker, Carol 040587
Walker, Catherine 039769
Walker, Celia 046141
Walker, Christopher 038903
Walker, Daniel 046364
Walker, David A. 039581
Walker, Dean 046975
Walker, Edwin G. 043350
Walker, Eleanor 006067
Walker, Gavin 040864
Walker, Gerald 047566
Walker, I. 041428
Walker, John 041478
Walker, June 045009
Walker, Kate 001578
Walker, Dr. K.J. 044103
Walker, Lauren 006775
Walker, Lulen 048909
Walker, Neil 040617
Walker, Nicola 040416
Walker, Pam 049272
Walker, Peter 038759
Walker, Rob 005060
Walker, Roslyn A. 048925
Walker, Sam 040090
Walker, Scott 046427, 046430
Walker, Sonia 041949
Walker, Stephen 041040, 048654
Walker, Tim 030518
Walker, William 045616
Walker Mecky, Debra 044351
Wall, Dora 005820
Wall, Gordon 043597
Wall, Kathleen 005556, 005557
Wallace, A. 006803
Wallace, Amanda 040404
Wallace, Anaret 034560
Wallace, Brian 046956
Wallace, Dr. C. 001563
Wallace, George 046557
Wallace, Hilt 006767
Wallace, I. 040030
Wallace, J. Don 045852
Wallace, James A. 045769
Wallace, James E. 044031
Wallace, Joseph 044377
Wallace, Judy 045769
Wallace, Lynda 030420
Wallace, Meghan 041698
Wallace, Mike 045902, 046886
Wallace, Pat 039145
Wallace, Dr. Patrick F. . . . 022705, 022759, 022761, 022762
Wallace, Stephen R. 047583
Wallace, Teresa 043118
Wallace, Dr. Terry 048643
Wallace, William D. 049308, 049311
Wallach, Nancy 044936
Wallbrecht, Dr. Andreas 016451
Wallcraft, Wilma K. 005728
Waller, Bret 044736
Waller, Richard 047425
Waller, Susan R. 047763
Wallers-Bulot, Danielle 011385
Wallet, Marie 011097, 011098
Walley, G.P. 040623
Walling, Mary 046352
Wallis, Brian 046348
Wallis, Deborah L. 045308
Wallis, Jonathan 039225
Wallis, W.-C.K.H. 039506
Wallmann, Dr. Margarete 002132
Wallner, Sabine 002875
Wallner, Dr. Thomas 037576
Wallner-Bărbulescu, Luminiţa 032887
Walloschek, Arnold 019993
Wallwork, John 044044
Wallwork-Wright, Jan 039456
Walmsley, Frances 005977
Walser, Stefan 037660
Walseth, J. 008991
Walsh, Alice 047256
Walsh, Brian 022780
Walsh, David 046716
Walsh, Debbie 022717
Walsh, H. Ben 044239
Walsh, John 001499
Walsh, Larry 022825
Walsh, Mary 046044
Walsh, Nigel 039950
Walsh, Noa Martin 022711
Walsh, Pat 047376
Walsh, Paul 045920
Walsh-Piper, Kathleen 045266
Walsted, Anne-Lise 008957
Walt, Barbara 037517
Waltenberg, Horst 016867
Waltenspül, Walter 036834
Walter, A. 019386
Walter, Alfred 016724
Walter, Andreas 016261
Walter, Bernadette 037768
Walter, H. 020287
Walter, Katharina 002097
Walter, Max 002490
Walter, Michael 020220
Walter, Patricia 042108
Walter, Philippe 013231
Walter, Susanne 019284
Waltereit, Manfred 016956
Waltermire, Joan 046571
Walters, Cheryl 048548
Walters, Cliff 038766
Walters, John A. 048344
Walters, Margaret 049172
Walters, N. 034727
Walther, Alois 016803
Walther, Gerd 017289
Walther, Hubert 015370
Walther, Jim 041620
Walther Cuevas, Georgina 028422
Walton, Ann 043988
Walton, John 001008
Walton, Karin . . . 038859, 038863, 038867
Walton, Les 040783
Waltoś, Prof. Dr. Stanisław 032063
Walty, J. 037151
Waltz, James 042615
Walujo, Dr. Ekoparoto 022403
Walz, Dr. Alfred 016385
Walz, Carol 046060
Walz, Glenn 006505
Walz, Jack 046060
Walzer, Herwig 002341
Wam, H. ten 029478, 053897
Wamers, Prof. Dr. Egon 017152
Wamser, G. 020405
Wamser, Prof. Dr. Ludwig 017591, 019033, 019213, 019575, 020776
Wamulungwe, Patrick Lisina 049569
Wan, Jamaluddin 027972
Wan, Norhiyati Ibrahim 027973
Wan, Robert 015393
Wan, Yusoff 027972
Wan Ahmad, Wan Ali Bin 027958
Wanachiwanawin, Prof. Darawan . 037886
Wand-Seyer, Dr. Gabriele . 017891, 017892
Wander, Evelyne 014242
Wandrei, Ellen A. 042100
Wandrooij, O.D. 029568
Wandschneider, Dr. Andrea 019547, 019552, 019555, 019556
Wang, Prof. Lianmao 007227
Wang, Mian Hou 007256
Wang, Ragnhild 031110
Wang, Xi Rong 007241
Wånge, Cecilia 036333
Waning, Alexander 029863
Wankel, James 005419
Wanner, Prof. Dr. E. 018434
Wanostrocht, C.A. 040958
Wappenschmidt, Dr. Kathrin 019877
Wappis, Erich 002142
Warburton, Stuart 039967, 039968
Warchałowski, Walerian 032123
Ward, Alberta 041873
Ward, Andrew 039170
Ward, Barry J. 045076
Ward, Barry K. 043527
Ward, David D. 039242
Ward, Esmé 040416
Ward, Joan 041257
Ward, Kathy 042056
Ward, Kimberley D. 043527
Ward, Dr. Lauck W. 045715
Ward, Mark 041963
Ward, Michael 040382
Ward, Mike 038482
Ward, Nancy 044874
Ward, Prof. Paul 037811
Ward, Ralph E. 044454
Ward, Robert W. 049042
Ward, Roger B. 049091
Ward, Scott 047325
Ward Grubb, Barbara 046926
Ward Povse, Sandra 048065
Ward Shannon, Dr. George 042075
Ward Shannon jr., George 047131
Warda, Rebecca M. 042802
Warden, Donald 048174
Warden, P. 037847

Wardius, Janine . 030756, 030757, 030758
Wardlaw, Alivia 044648
Wardle, Michelle 044965
Wardropper, Ian 042820, 046364
Ware, Katherine 046975
Ware, Mark 048217
Ware, Robert 041617
Warfel, Stephen G. 044444
Warger, Julia M. 048380
Wargo, Richard 042295
Warigai, Tsutomu 026540
Waring, Brian 040483
Waring, H.B.H. 040390
Waring, Jeff 046948
Warinsie Kankpeyeng, Benjamin . . 021100
Warkiewicz Laine, Christian K. . . . 042831
Warming, Dagmar 009011
Warne, Pam 034587
Warner, Henry 039656
Warner, Jan 045338
Warner, Joanne 046319
Warner, John D. 048089
Warner, Judith 048046
Warner, Malcolm 044009, 046227
Warner, R. 038669
Warnes, Dr. Carl E. 046084
Warp, Harold G. 045903
Warren, David B. 044635, 044648
Warren, Eleanor 042948
Warren, Elizabeth 046283, 046329
Warren, Emma 039895
Warren, Harry 049146
Warren, Katherine V. 047461
Warren, Maggie 040700
Warren, Rebecca 042787
Warren, Sally 006142
Warrilow, Walt 038988
Warstler, Pasqua 043728
Wartenberg, Ute 046287
Warth, Werner 037710
Warther, David R. 043495
Wartke, Dr. Ralf-Bernhard 016193
Warton, Sue 041021
Warwick Thompson, Paul 046319
Warzecha, Newton M. 044243
Warzecha, Zygmunt 032362
Washbrook, Harry 005385
Washington jr, W. Curtis 042745
Washington Goyaud, Rolando 000367
Washizuka, Hiromitsu 026897
Waskowic, Lorraine 006197
Wass, Ann 047451
Wass, Janice 048284
Wasser, Larry 047714
Wasserman, Nadine 046269
Wassermann, Fred 046352
Wassing, A. 030108
Wassmann, Harry 042141
Wassmer, Edouard 037102
Wassnig, Gerhard 002236
Wat, Kathryn 041586
Watanabe, Hisashi 026848
Watanabe, Junko 026528
Watanabe, Kiriko 027287
Watanabe, Kousho 027020
Watanabe, Makoto 026506
Watanabe, Osamu 027133
Watanabe, Seiichiro 026412
Watanabe, Shinsuke 027189
Watanabe, Taeko 026812
Watanabe, Takao 026761
Watanabe, Yasuhiro 027210
Watanate, Akiyoshi 027196
Watari, Shizuko 027273
Watelet, Pierre 013340
Waterlow Oam, Nick 001363
Waterman, Amy E. 046327
Waters, Davis 043540
Waters, Deborah D. 046378
Waters, F. 040578
Waters, Martha 043037
Watkin, Alan 041453
Watkin, Jeffrey 039944
Watkin, Mel 047658
Watkins, Dr. David K. 045313
Watkins, Jonathan 038731
Watkins, Kathleen 040919
Watkins, Rod 045888
Watkinson, Patricia 043998
Watne, Eva 031320
Watson, Andy 043019
Watson, Bob 039604
Watson, Claudia 043322
Watson, Daryl 044115
Watson, Sir David 038854
Watson, Doreen 038658
Watson, Edwin W. 044057
Watson, Helen 040968
Watson, Iain 040548
Watson, Dr. Ian 040657
Watson, John 001501
Watson, Julian 040161
Watson, Julie 040550
Watson, Lisa 040778
Watson, Mark 039199
Watson, Maureen 041378
Watson, Maxine 046222
Watson, Philip 038723
Watson, Ronald 044012
Watson, Dr. Rubie 042567
Watson, Sara C. 044353
Watson, Scott 006702
Watson, Sheena 040795
Watson, Dr. Sheila 039632, 039633, 039634, 039636
Watson, Wendy 048241
Watson, Wendy M. 048240
Watson, William S. 039426
Watson-Armstrong, Francis 038582
Watt, David 039385
Watt, James C.Y. 046364
Watt, Michael 048525
Watt, Robert 005007
Watt, T. 039325, 039987, 039988
Watteck, Arno 002322
Wattenberg García, Eloisa 035998
Wattenmaker, Dr. Richard J. 048882
Watters, Frank X. 047057
Watters, Jane 001522
Watterson, Norma 043593
Watteyne, Damien 003736, 003737, 003739, 003740
Watton, Graham C. 030565
Watton, Janet 047328
Watts, Kelly 044582
Watts, L. 001410
Watts, Martin 039789
Watts, Michael 042722
Watts, Pete 049334
Watts, Peter . . . 001014, 001346, 001438, 001442, 001510, 001512, 001519, 001524, 001582, 001589
Watts, Steve 039992
Watts McKinney, Sylvia . . . 042455, 046973
Waugh, Carmen 006933
Waurick, Dr. Götz 018794
Wawrzyk, Henryk 032173
Wawrzyniak, Andrzej 032431
Wawzonek, Donna 006319
Way, Angela 042200
Way, Catherine A. 044827
Way, Paul 039371
Way-Jones, M.F. 034622
Wayne, Cynthia 041962
Wayne, Kenneth 042498
Wcześny, Marek 032174
Weadick, Nathalie 022804
Weaner, Arthur 044182
Wear, Lisa 047763
Wearne, Richard B. 046170
Weatherby, Ken 005881
Weathers, Allen 045785
Weaver, Henry 005624
Weaver, John 041746
Weaver, Luella 045754
Weaver, Nigel 040879
Weaver, Pat 047724
Weaver, R. 039813
Weaver, Randall 041787
Weaver, Sarah 044998
Weaver, Susan 044511
Weaver, Suzanne 043269
Weaver, Vey O. 041564
Webb, Alan 038829
Webb, Belinda 001527
Webb, Eddie 047203
Webb, Heather 006137
Webb, Hugh 047173
Webb, Judy 047516
Webb, Keith 041302
Webb, Dr. S.D. 044103
Webb, Vaughan 043839
Webber, Barry 046495
Webber, Chris 040336
Webber, Eddie 000818
Webber, Maurie 040638
Webel, Sophie 013584, 013772
Weber 020301
Weber, Dr. Annette 017178
Weber, Brigitta 021076
Weber, C. Sylvia 018432, 020117
Weber, Cornelia 036930
Weber, C.S. 018431
Weber, Dr. Erich 020504
Weber, Francis J. 045928
Weber, Dr. Gerhard 018235
Weber, Dr. Gregor J.M. 018186
Weber, Hans Ruedi 037777
Weber, Heidi 037771
Weber, Heiko 018963
Weber, Jean 027910
Weber, Johanne 020378
Weber, John S. 047885
Weber, Karl 015724
Weber, Dr. Klaus 015988
Weber, K.R. 047982
Weber, Dr. Marion 007544
Weber, Michael 029099
Weber, Olaf 017123
Weber, Otto 019380
Weber, Dr. Peter 032892
Weber, Robin 006209
Weber, Stephan W. 001669
Weber, Ute 019435
Weber, Vera 041709
Weber, Warren 047913
Weber, Drs. W.I.M. 030284
Weber, Dr. Winfried 020477
Weber, Yvette 012885
Weber-Brosamer, Dr. Bernhard . . . 016853
Weber-Lehmann, Dr. Cornelia 016279
Weber Soros, Dr. Susan 046300
Weberg, William 047244
Webersberger, Josef 002297
Webley, Dr. L. 034621
Webley, Dr. W. 034622
Webster, Barbara 042532
Webster, Harvey 042986
Webster, Robert 048568
Webster, Roger J. 038772
Webster, Susan 044332
Webster, Prof. William 001513
Wechner, Wilma 002097
Wechs, Thomas 015717
Wechsler, Jeffrey 046206
Weckbacher, Vernon 045539
Weckerle, Prof. Hans 017725
Weckström, Gunnar 010221
Weddegjerde, Per 030719
Weddle, Sam 045401
Weeda, K.A. 029563
Weedmark, Lillian 006482
Weekley, Carolyn 049177, 049178, 049179
Weekly, Nancy 042503
Weeks, Ross 048511
Weems, Marcia 048668
Weenink, G.J. 029870
Weerdt, G.A. de 030197
Wefers, Dr. Sabine 018118
Wegener-Welte, Kathrin 015652
Wegge, Aslak 031329
Wegmann, Dr. Peter 037723, 037727
Wegner, Gene 031646
Wegner, Hartmut 016260
Wegner, Karl-Hermann 018202
Wehgartner, Dr. Irma 021000
Wehling, Arno 004386
Wehmeyer, Egon 015651
Wehmeyer, Pete 041926
Wehrberger, Gerhard 002301
Wehrberger, Kurt 020534
Wehrle, Karl 019772
Weibel, Prof. Peter 001943, 018165, 018174
Weibezahn, Dr. Ingrid 016410
Weibull, Nina 036674
Weichselbaum, Dr. Hans 002554
Weichselbaum, Karl 002388
Weichselberger, Ingrid 002685
Weick, Wolfgang E. 016763, 016766, 016767
Weick-Krohn, Dr. Helga 017178
Weidel, Geraldine 044662
Weidemann, Dr. Friedegund 016055
Weidinger, Alfred 002845
Weidisch, Peter 015731
Weidl, Beverly 044617
Weidner, Dr. Thomas 019086
Weidner, Timothy 044212
Weidner, William 047103
Weiermair, Prof. Peter 023420
Weigel, Jay 046250
Weigelt, Jürgen 016205
Weight, A. 040182
Weigl, Stephan 002243
Weigle, Petra 019364
Weiglin, Peter 042125, 055024
Weigt, Karin 016680
Weil, Benjamin E. 047885
Weil, Gilbert 010954
Weil, Dr. Mark S. 047683
Weil-Seigeot, Claude 011386
Weiland, Linde 017300
Weilepp, Bruce 048231
Weiler, Gerhard 020995, 021004
Weiler-Streichsbier, Dr. Doris 019470
Weilter, Theresia 002391
Weimert, Dr. Helmut 017843
Weinberg, Adam D. 041721
Weinberg, H. Barbara 046364
Weinberger, Prof. Gabriel 003048
Weinelt, Hannes 001963
Weinelt, Wendeline 017294
Weinert, Renate 015698
Weingärtner, Rudi 002210
Weingartner, Heinrich 002960
Weinhart, Dr. Martina 017192
Weinheber-Janota, Brigitte 002130
Weinheimer, Corinna 031285
Weinig, Prof. Dr. 020348
Weinke, Jane 049015
Weinland, Dr. Martina 016139
Weinmayr, Stefanje 018486
Weinmeister, Konstanze 017550
Weinshrott, William J. 043882
Weinstein, Michael 046327
Weintraub, Aviva 046352
Weinzapfel, Connie 046220
Weir, Margaret 040468
Weir, Margaret S. 048408
Weirauch, Annette 019626
Weisbach, Rainer 016684
Weisberg, Frank F. 045494
Weise, Sigrid 015992
Weiserová, Dr. Jana 008392, 008624
Weiskircher, Arrand 014834
Weisman, Billie Milam 045422
Weisman, Bruce 044996
Weiss, Alfred 002327
Weiß, Bernd 019600
Weiß, Berthold 001880
Weiss, Brigitte 016553

Weiss, Christian 018257
Weiß, E. 020035
Weiß, Ferdinand 001839
Weiß, Frank 019634
Weiss, Dr. Gabriele 002961
Weiss, Ján 034341
Weiss, Jeffrey 048924
Weiß, Johannes 001763
Weiss, Lois 048039
Weiss, Martin 043877
Weiss, Olga 042880
Weiss, Prof. Dr. Rainer-Maria 017698
Weiss, Sabine 020696
Weiss, Dr. Thomas 016681, 016682, 016683, 019477, 020944, 020945
Weiß, Dr. Ulrike 017755
Weissenbach, Peter 036859
Weißenböck, Jarmila 002979
Weissend, Patrick 042038
Weissengruber, Dr. Thekla 002256
Weisser, Amy S. 042069
Weisser, Dr. Bernhard 016120
Weisser, Dr. Jürgen 017610
Weit, Janina 016333
Weitzendorfer, Dr. Alfred 002222
Weium, Frode 031097
Welander-Berggren, Elsebeth 036303
Welborn, Ann 048623
Welborn, Patricia 049318
Welch, Richard 043821
Welch, Robert M. 044100
Weldon, Eleanor 005898
Wellens, Luc 003196, 003196
Weller, Dennis P. 047313
Weller, Susan J. 045914
Wellicome, Lavinia 041426
Wellington, John P. 048015
Wellington, Judith 042746
Wellman, Lesley 044426
Wells, Edna 043433
Wells, Elizabeth 040229
Wells, Gerald 040309
Wells, Keith 047283
Wells, Kenneth D. 042372
Wells, Licia A. 047877
Wells, Nicole 046389
Wells, Penny 005531, 005532
Wells, Peter 044382
Wells, Stephen D. 043942
Wells, Trevor C. 027838
Wells-Cole, Anthony 039961
Wells Zaia, Kay 046569
Wellspeak, Charles 043286
Wellwood, Bridget 030574
Welsh, Caroline 042275
Welsh, Jane 043043
Welsh, Melissa 046106
Welsh, Susan 039053
Welter, Barbara 036869
Welter, Matt 044311
Welty, Claude 013295
Welu, James A. 049309, 049309
Welzig, Ingrid 019341
Wemhoff, Prof. Dr. Matthias 019553
Wemmlinger, Raymond 046343
Wemyss, Dallas 039899
Wendel, Candice 044756
Wendel, Michael G. 042234
Wendel, Siegfried 019940
Wendel, Vickie 041746
Wendl, Dr. Tobias 015912
Wendling, Britt 036532
Wendling, Pia 012063, 012064
Wendling, Urs 037268
Wendorf, Richard 042315
Wendt, Birgitta 036622
Wenger, Rhona 005552
Wenham, Julia 041393
Weniger, Prof. Dr. Gerd-C. 018928
Weninger, Gehard 002420
Wenn, Diane 006783
Wenn, Norbert 016474
Wennerholm jr., Roy 047630
Wentworth, Peggy 042011
Wenzel, Gundula 020773
Weon-Kettenhofen, Hae-Yon 016337
Wepfer, Dr. Hans-Ulrich 037223
Wepler, Bill 044744
Weppelmann, Dr. Stefan 016049
Werd, Drs. Guido de 018280, 018281
Werf, Hans van der 014882
Werkmäster, Daniel 036506
Werkmäster, Lisskulla 036265
Wern, Christine 017178
Werneburg, Dr. Ralf 020044
Wernecke, Dr. Ingrid 019688
Werner, Dr. Anne-Marie 019963
Werner, Bernd 017669, 017671
Werner, Constanze 019381
Werner, Dietrich 047545
Werner, Dr. Edwin 017661, 017668
Werner, Harald 001694
Werner, Heinz 017904
Werner, Jane 047059
Werner, Dr. Sigrid 020163
Werner, Dr. Winfried 019099
Wernevik, Lena 036511
Wernicke, Prof. Dr. Joachim 019526, 019528, 019530
Wernz-Kaiser, Heike 015760
Werring, Ole A. 031075
Wert, Nancy L. 045873
Werth, Linda 048998
Wertkin, Gerard C. 046283, 046329
Wertz, Dinyelle 046930
Wéry, Benoît 003830
Weschenfelder, Dr. Klaus . 016576, 019862
Wescoat, Dr. Bonna D. 041866
Wesenberg, Dr. Angelika 015984
Wesler, Kit W. 049169
Wesney, Russell 030561
Wessel, Marilyn F. 042375
Wessel, Dr. Ruth 016847
Wesseler, Jürgen 016431
Wessels, E.M. 034566
Wessels, Reinhard 017777
West, Andrew 030519
West, Barbara 044761
West, Chris 038860
West, Gerald C. 042902
West, J. Martin 045290
West, J. Thomas 005197
West, Janis 045608
West, Jeff 043275
West, Jenny 030510
West, Pat 038590
West, Dr. Patricia 045003
West, Penelope A. 045290
West, Richard 047583
West, Richard V. 048080
West, Thomas 044381
West, W. Richard 046383
Westbrook, Nicholas 048553
Westbrook, T.G. 039291, 041445
Westby, Alan 046735
Westenhuber, Karl-Heinz 019752
Wester la Torre, Carlos 031540
Westerbeck, Colin 042820
Westerkamp, P.W. 029413
Westerlund, Jens 009110
Westermann-Angerhausen, Prof. Dr. Hiltrud 018336
Westers, Drs. Abraham 029947
Westfall, Deborah 042250
Westfehling, Dr. Uwe 018341
Westheider, Dr. Rolf 017603
Westhoff, Julia 016407
Westholm, Gun 036796
Westling, Stefan 036403
Westlund, Frances 005855
Westmacott, Jean 044110
Westman, Anne 036203
Westmoreland, Debra 046032
Westmorland, Lamont 045419
Westoby, Carolyn 005375
Weston, Catherine 038555
Weston, D.W.V. 038997
Weston, E. 040418
Weston, Gill 040442
Weston-Lewis, Aidan 039406
Westphal, Jean 012294
Westphal, Dr. Martin 019801
Westphal, Ursula 016674
Westra, J.F. 029166
Westrop, Dr. S. 046509
Westwood, Ros. 038935
Wetenhall, Dr. John 046141
Wetenhall, John 047999
Wetherell, Virginia 043837
Wetherington, Mark V. 045487
Wetmore, Shirley 048643
Wettengl, Dr. Kurt 017176
Wetter, Ellen de 006194
Wetterau, G. 043965
Wetton, Allan 000747
Wettre, Håkan 036296
Wetzel, Brigitte 017547
Wetzel, Dietrich 019633
Wetzel, Elaine 042294
Wetzel, James K. 043384
Wetzel, Walter 036983
Wetzstein, Jim 046090
Weydemann, Ingrid 002365
Weyerhaeuser, Charles A. 043549
Weyers, E. 034708
Weygandt, Virginia 048303
Whaley, Martha 044867
Whallon, Robert 041733
Whang, Prof. Won-Koo 027617
Whatmoor, D.J. 040652
Wheary, Dale C. 047420
Wheatcroft, F.B. 039010
Wheaton, R. 001426
Wheeldon, Jenny 042483
Wheeler, Karla 042132
Wheeler, Lawrence J. 047313
Wheeler, Mary 044932
Wheeler, Matthew 038678
Wheeler, Robert K.L. 045861
Wheelock, Arthur 048924
Whelan, Mary C. 046620
Wheldon, G.H. 039839
Wheltle, Bruce 041772
Whetstone, Lucy 040549
Whisman, Evelyn 047294
Whissell, Raymond 006321
Whistance, John 041387
White, A.C. 041255
White, Adam 038456, 039961
White, Babs 043301
White, Barbara 048162
White, Betsy K. 041569
White, Blair H. 044864
White, Courtney 046405
White, C.S. 040770
White, David 006656, 040303, 045323
White, Diane 043901
White, Donald 046993
White, Donna 005540
White, Donny 005851
White, Elisa 046280
White, Gail W. 048570
White, Sir George 040123, 040199
White, James J. 047052
White, Joe L. 044999
White, Julia 044598, 049228
White, Kathryn 038636
White, Kristy 043153
White, Marcelle 043285
White, Mark 048360
White, Mary 041023
White, Matthew 046522, 046523
White, Maylon 048799
White, Metthew 042087
White, Richard S. 048639
White, Dr. Sally 041451
White, Tim 042163
White, Timothy J. 042815
White, Turner 044920
White, Warren O. 043624
Whitehead, F. 038940
Whitehead, J.K. 040840
Whitehouse, Adrienne 039714
Whitehouse, C.M. 038725
Whitehouse, David B. 043155
Whiteley, Jim 045215
Whiteman, Rowland 044217
Whiter, Robert 001009
Whitey, Matthew 039950
Whitfield, Carol 005802
Whiting, Dr. Cliff 030653
Whitley, Ann Marshall 048449
Whitlock, Pamela 001060
Whitlow, Paula 006063
Whitmal, Angela M. 041594
Whitman-Grice, Lisa 047395
Whitmore, Damien 040307
Whitmore, Dennis 041992
Whitney, Richard 043463
Whitt, Teresa C. 048235
Whittaker, Dr. J. 039024
Whittall, Dafydd 040069
Whitten, Norman 048713
Whittington, Michael 042760
Whitworth, Kent 045037
Whitworth, Peggy 042673
Whorlow, David 039681
Whyel, Rosalie 042116
Whyte, Alan 006769
Whyte, Robert A. 047873
Wiatr, Al 042707
Wiberg, Ewa 036677
Wible, Carole 044580
Wiblé, François 037315
Wible, Dr. John R. 047044
Wichert-Meissner, Dr. Susanne . . . 016328
Wichrowski, Zbigniew 032071, 032072
Wick, Peter 037295
Wick, Susan B. 048685
Wick Reaves, Wendy 048933
Wickenden, N.P. 039046
Wickers, Tine 008988
Wickham, Ann 039645
Wickham, W.C. 044427
Wicklund, Doug 043783
Wickman, Viktor 028049
Wickramasinghe, Dr. Nanda 036130, 036134
Wicks, Alice 048402
Wicks, Dr. Fred 006627
Wicks, Phyllis 049269
Wicks, Stephen C. 045040
Widbom, Mats 036660
Widdowson, Prof. J.D.A. 041003
Widemann, Norbert 017226
Widén, Britt-Marie 036296
Widener, George D. 046983
Widenheim, Cecilia 036645
Widjeskog, Susanna 009996
Widmann, Dr. Marion 016333
Widschwendter, Martin 001772
Widulin, Navena 015990
Wiebe, Charles M. 048121
Wiebe, Dave 044542
Wiebel, Dr. Christiane 016576
Wiechert, Ralph D. 047681
Wiechmann, Dr. A.H.C.A. 029850
Wieczorek, Prof. Dr. Alfried 018809
Wieczorek, Jan 032253
Wied, Fürst zu 019955
Wied, Dr. Alexander 002934
Wied, M. Prinz zu 019955
Wiedemann, Dr. Konrad 018188
Wiedemann, Wilfried 018676
Wiedenhofer, Dr. Josef 002296
Wieg, Cornelia 017672
Wiegand, Dawn Michelle 043663
Wiegand, Gesine 017487
Wiegand, Otto 018901
Wiegand, Tanya 005147
Wiegand, Winfried 018883, 018884, 018886

Wiegmann, Dr. Karlheinz 018304
Wiehager, Dr. Renate 016008
Wiehart, Michael 002962
Wiehl, Wolfgang 018535
Wieklander, Dan 048875
Wielek, Jan 032103
Wiell, Stine 008885
Wiemann, Dr. Elsbeth 020365
Wiemer, Regine 018668
Wienand, Paul 020723
Wiene, Inger 008970
Wienecke, Joachim 017878
Wieninger, Johannes 002945
Wiens, Dr. John J. 047044
Wier, Nan 046700
Wier, Tom 047703
Wierecky, Norbert 017721
Wiermann, Susanne 015676
Wierzbicka, Alina 032153
Wierzbowska, Ilona 031856
Wiese, Dr. André 036879
Wiese, Joyce 048565
Wiese, Kerstin 018563
Wiese, Larry 045794
Wiese, Prof. Dr. Rolf 018988, 019882
Wiese, Dr. Rüdiger 020745
Wiese, Sharon A. 041784
Wiese, Dr. Stephan von 016841
Wiese, Dr. W. 019716
Wieseman, Betsy 042919
Wiesen, Richard A. 042500
Wiesenhofer, Franz 002478, 002480
Wiesenmüller, H. 020372
Wieser, Gertrud 003017
Wiesmann-Emmerling, Adelheid 016638
Wiesner, Tomáš 008737
Wietholt, Charlotte 029653
Wiethorn, Hans 020266
Wieting, Margaret 044766
Wiewelhove, Dr. Hildegard 016238
Wiget, Dr. Josef 037541, 037543
Wiggins, Denise 045595
Wigh, Leif 036645
Wight, Anthony 042845
Wight, David 044695
Wigmore, John R. 006735
Wijesooriya, Bandusena 036125
Wijn, Drs. J.J.A. 030158
Wikström, Anne-Maj 010145
Wikström-Haugen, Inger 036299
Wilcox, Bill 049065
Wilcox, Dr. David R. 043851
Wilcox, John 043136
Wilcox, Mike 043614
Wilcox, Richard 045690
Wilcox, Scott 046227
Wilcox, Susan 043850
Wilcox, Thomas R. 042039
Wilcox, Tim 040404
Wilczak, Susan 047642
Wilczek jun., Alexander Graf 002727
Wild, Jane 006142
Wild, Maxine F. 001018
Wild, Norbert 037765, 037788
Wildberger, Anne-Käthi 036879
Wilde, Cathleen 047115
Wilde, Dr. Eliane de 003316
Wilde, Kevan A. 030621
Wilde, Dr. Manfred 016661, 016662
Wildeman, G.J.D. 029216
Wilder, Cecile 047327
Wilder, Jacalin W. 042446, 042447
Wilder, Sofie 003181
Wildes, Deborah 045883
Wildgans, Ilse 002323
Wildgust, D. 040733
Wildgust, Patrick 039161
Wildhagen, Harald 017811
Wildman, Janet 039612
Wildman, S.G. 039926
Wildung, Prof. Dr. Dietrich 015979
Wilekans, Martine 030175
Wiles, Stephanie 045839
Wiley, E.O. 045205
Wiley, Florence 043479
Wiley, John 005874, 041441
Wilezek, Alexander 002302
Wilfong, Terry 041732
Wilhelm, Ada 043092
Wilhelm, Angelika 021024, 021026
Wilhelm, Elliot 043444
Wilhelm, Franz 016897
Wilhelm, Martin 001863
Wilhelm, Robert 044488
Wilhelmer, Erika 015836
Wilhelmer, Hans-Sieghart 001691
Wilhelmson, Pia 009841
Wilhelmy, Dr. W. 018786
Wilhite, Janet 043263
Wilk, Zbigniew 031925
Wilke, Erich 020902
Wilkens, Dr. Barbara 024545
Wilkens, Prof. Dr. Horst 017728
Wilker, Klaus-J. 020462
Wilkes, Regi 047194
Wilkes, Woody 043934
Wilkie, Jo-Anne 046052
Wilkins, Prof. David G. 047064
Wilkins, Margaret 039499
Wilkinson, D.J. 040076
Wilkinson, MaryAnn 043444
Wilkinson, Patty 042276
Wilks, John 039206
Will, Heinz 017617
Willander, Dr. Alfred 002536
Willard, David 044157
Willburger, Dr. Nina 020374
Willeboordse, A. 030165
Willeboordse, A.C.J. 029125
Willeboordse, Arco 030166
Willems, Alfons 003854
Willems, Carmen 003798
Willems, Jean 003631
Willemsen, M. 029408
Willenbrink, Brunhilde 016749
Willer, Thérèse 014854
Willers, Prof. Dietrich 036925
Willers, Dr. Johannes 019352
Willesme, Jean-Pierre 013560
Williams, Alice 044176, 045282
Williams, Barb 047363
Williams, Bill 045493
Williams, Bob 044526
Williams, Clay 044804
Williams, Dr. D. 040097
Williams, David 040036
Williams, Debby 048135
Williams, Don 046278
Williams, Dorothy 043981
Williams, Ed 041965, 043676
Williams, Edna 045633
Williams, Eric K. 046489
Williams, Fred 043142
Williams, Gareth H. 038941
Williams, Dr. George 049104
Williams, Gloria 046833
Williams, Greg 047822, 047833, 047845
Williams, Henry G. 041601
Williams, Hilary 040477, 041453
Williams, I.B. 038570, 041463
Williams, Janice C. 047314
Williams, Jay 043082
Williams, Jenny 039733
Williams, Jimmy 047203
Williams, Judy 030645
Williams, Karen 005376, 030597
Williams, Kathy 043979
Williams, Kay P. 046195
Williams, Dr. Keith 049058
Williams, Kevin 045914
Williams, Laura 040168
Williams, Linda 040874
Williams, Lisa 045536
Williams, Dr. Lorraine 048605
Williams, Lyle 047798
Williams, M. 041833
Williams, Mary-Louise 001508
Williams, Michael 040616, 040620, 040624
Williams, Dr. Michael 042986
Williams, Morag 039294
Williams, Dr. N.H. 044103
Williams, Pamela 042363
Williams, Paul 047776
Williams, Peter J. 001617
Williams, Richard 039724
Williams, Robert J. 048124
Williams, Stacy 047772
Williams, Stephen 040193
Williams, Stephen R. 047133
Williams, Teri 041843, 041870
Williams, Thomas 045655
Williams, Tommy 045388
Williams, Victoria 039692, 039693
Williams-Davies, John 040907
Williamson, Armand J. 042464
Williamson, Eleanor 048312
Williamson, J. Reid 044740
Williamson, Jan 047986
Williamson, Jane 043838
Williamson, Mary 042654
Williamson, Paul 040307
Williamson, Roberta 043856
Willis, Carol 046401
Willis, James 042091
Willis, Dr. Jeff 049287
Willis, Kelly B. 045256
Willis, Leanne 001466
Willis, Michael 047121
Willis, Pamela 040234
Willis, Patricia 040091
Willis, Robert 043262
Willis, William 047224
Willisch, Susanne 019048
Willits, Mary Lou 044290
Willmann, Prof. Dr. R. 017475
Willmer, Prof. P.G. 040892
Willmitch, Thomas R. 042276
Willmont, Joanne 045250
Willms, Dr. Christoph 017152
Willms, Karl 016435
Willomitzer, Gerry 006813
Willoughby, Alan 046014
Willoughby, Brenda 043297
Willoughby, Sue 047225
Willour, Clint 044130
Willow, Hai Chang 046314
Wills, Carol 047650
Willscheid, Bernd 019298
Wilmes, Dr. Ulrich 018334
Wilmot, Patricia J. 044467
Wilmot, Robert 039396
Wilms, Kurt 015659
Wilner Stack, Trudy 048631
Wilpert, Dr. Clara B. 036893
Wilsdon, D.E. 001482
Wilsey, Bart 043821
Wilson, A. 040544
Wilson, Dr. A. 041086
Wilson, Alan 001474
Wilson, Dr. Alan 038542, 038543
Wilson, Amy 043691
Wilson, Arnold 038620
Wilson, Audrey 005814
Wilson, B. 041151
Wilson, Beth 042538
Wilson, Carol 044580
Wilson, Chris 022710, 038437, 040047, 049222
Wilson, Christine 039190, 039192
Wilson, Clifford 041804
Wilson, Courtney B. 041965
Wilson, Dale 043628
Wilson, Dan 044289
Wilson, Diane 042109
Wilson, Dorothy 038733
Wilson, Eric 041000
Wilson, Floyd S. 042754
Wilson, Gill 041322
Wilson, Gillian 040814, 045433
Wilson, Gordon 047607
Wilson, Gordon J. 047606
Wilson, H. 038794
Wilson, I.A. 038589
Wilson, Inge 005623
Wilson, J. Keith 045441
Wilson, Jane 046761
Wilson, Jay 049351
Wilson, Jerry 043316
Wilson, Jim 044413
Wilson, John 038669, 045126
Wilson, Karen L. 042871
Wilson, Kay 044360
Wilson, Keri 039582
Wilson, Kevin 001543
Wilson, Dr. L. 046692
Wilson, Lamar 048142
Wilson, Lesley 039060
Wilson, Marc F. 044917, 044924
Wilson, Mark 029638
Wilson, Michael 040241
Wilson, Nancy 045519
Wilson, Peter 040299, 040300
Wilson, Prof. R.J.A. 040625
Wilson, Rob 047357
Wilson, Robert C. 048385
Wilson, Robin 040708
Wilson, Dr. Rodney 030432
Wilson, Roger N. 046476
Wilson, Roy 040717
Wilson, Sophia 039053
Wilson, Steven 044455
Wilson, Tom 049257
Wilson, Wayne 005670, 005673
Wilson, William 040369
Wilson Davine, Blossom 047246
Wilson Jenkins, Kay 044359
Wilson-McKee, Marie 042817
Wilsony, Thomas A. 047973
Wilsterman, James 043625
Wiltfang, Helga 019325
Wiltzius, Ruth 046896
Wiluś, Bogusława 032212
Wilusz, Mike 048373
Wilz, Mick 042475
Wimberger, Dr. Peter 048466
Wimmer, Franz 002438
Wimpress, Kate 038514
Wimsett, Brian 039271
Win, U Kyaw 029077
Winans, Cathie 048125
Winbladh, Marie-Louise 036642
Winch, Barbara 048243
Winchell, Jane 047741
Winchester, Dr. Judi A. 043029
Wincke, Claus-Jürgen 015629
Wind, D.A. 030133
Winders, Dr. Bruce 047786
Windham, Michael 047778
Winding, Dr. Norbert 002561
Windl, Dr. Helmut 001702, 002748
Windle, Ann S. 045581
Windrum, Robert 006519
Windsor, Deirdre 045504
Windsor, Noel 000800
Wine, Dr. Humphrey 040241
Winegrad, Dr. Dilys V. 046923
Wines, Claudia 043667
Winey, Michael J. 042623
Wingate, Lloyd R. 034667, 034668
Wingfield, Carolyn 040880
Wingo, Calvin 043740
Winkelmeyer, Iris 019124
Winklbauer, Andrea 002964
Winkler, Anke 017428
Winkler, Axel 020356
Winkler, Dr. G. 001823
Winkler, Gerhard 001714
Winkler, Dr. Gerhard 001826
Winkler, Howard 041771
Winkler, J. 045854

Winkler, Dr. Kurt 016056, 016116, 016127, 016137, 016140, 016142, 016143, 016145, 016146, 016149, 016181
Winkler, Paul 044638
Winkler, Dr. Raffael 036899
Winkler, Reinhard 020657
Winkler, Steffen 017428
Winkler, Susanne 003017
Winkler, Ursula 018231
Winkler-Hermaden, Burkhardt 002112
Winkler Prins, Dr. C.F. 029851
Winkworth, David R. 039113
Winn, Allan 041354
Winnekes, Dr. Katharina 018323
Winnicki, Tomasz 032404
Winnicott, Caroline 040659
Winning, Fiona 001425
Winnink, Dr. G.J.G. 029387
Winrerborham, Nick 039964
Winslow, Bruce B. 045847
Wint, Dennis M. 046943
Winteler, Florence 036822
Winter, Amy 043875
Winter, Dr. B. 005170
Winter, C. 030484
Winter, Emil 017914
Winter, Gerhard 017802
Winter, Dr. Heike 017169
Winter, Dr. Heinz 002934
Winter, Hilda 040345
Winter, Joan G. 000861
Winter, Kevin 043780
Winter, Małgorzata 031855
Winter, Petra 016197
Winter-Berger, Robert 046343
Winterbotham, N. 039948
Winterbotham, Nick 038456, 039950, 039955, 039961
Winterhalter, Greg 042147
Winterick, Douglas E. 042520
Winters, Laurie 045892
Wintersteen Parmenter, Marian ... 047852
Wintgens, Dr. D. 029855
Wintz, Klaudius 002176
Winzeler, Marius 017453, 017454
Winzen, Dr. Matthias 015853
Winzingerode, Margit Freifrau von . 019661
Wiotte-Franz, Claudia 019965
Wippermann, Hartmut 018897
Wippert, Bernd 018411
Wipplinger, Hans-Peter 019571
Wirenfeldt Asmussen, Marianne .. 009087
Wirnsberger, Karlheinz 001948
Wirsperger, Dr. Peter 002301
Wirtanen, Lyle 043183
Wirth, Dr. Klaus 018809
Wirth, Peter 047977
Wirth, Prof. Dr. Volkmar 018170
Wirthgen, G. 018573
Wirz, Arno 015884
Wirz, Charles 037134
Wise, Ann 041451
Wise, Carol 044902
Wise, Philip 039117
Wise, Raymond 040241
Wise, Dr. Stephen R. 046827
Wise, Tess 045600
Wise, Theodore F. 043918
Wiséhn, Ian 036634
Wiseman, Christopher ... 044881, 044883
Wiseman, William 049121
Wishart, E. 001114
Wismar, Franz Werner von 019798
Wismeijer, P.J. 029503
Wismer, Beat 036807
Wisowaty, Elaine 045351
Wißkirchen, Dr. Hans 018718, 018719
Wissler, Richard 043105
Wissler-Thomas, Carrie 044441
Wistar, Caroline 046954
Wistoft, Birgitte 008985
Wisuri, Marlene 043021
Wit, B.H. de 029328
Wit, Prof. Dr. G.W. de 030097
Witcherly, Zak 049142
Witcox, David E. 046492
Witenstein, Michael 045379
Withnell, J.H. 005386
Withycombe, C. 038962
Witkofsky, Adrien 044350
Witmer, Linda F. 042621
Witschey, Walter R.T. 047424, 047432
Witschi, Heinz 037204
Witschi, Dr. Peter 037187
Witt, David 048497
Witt-Dörring, Dr. Christian 002904
Witt-Dörring, Christian 002945
Witte, Amy 042491
Witte, David 048188
Witte, Hubert De 003267
Witte de Haelen, Didier de 003483
Wittenbauer, Christine 018633
Wittendorfer, Dr. Frank 019112
Witter, Thomas 018289
Wittig, Peer 015547
Wittington, Dr. Stephen 049253
Wittke, Norbert 017854
Wittkopp, Gregory M. 042255
Wittmann, Dr. Helmut 002561
Wittmer, Heike 019621
Wittmer, Marcilene 043147
Wittstock, Dr. Jürgen 018825
Witty, Anne 042039
Witty, Robert M. 047822, 047833, 047841, 047845
Witzbauer, Dr. Harald 002565
Witzleben, Alexander von 018104
Witzmann, Nora 002976
Witzmann, Dr. Reingard 003017
Wlattnig, Robert . 001800, 002142, 002784
Włodarczyk, Tadeusz 032526
Wodiunig, Tina 037791
Woehl, Betty 048054
Wöhrer, Hannes 001713
Wöhrer, Josef 002292
Woelfl-Graff, Elisabeth 003017
Woelk, Dr. Moritz 016815
Wörlen, Hanns Egon 019571
Woertman, Rick 029169, 053878
Wörtz, Walter ... 018224, 019203, 019874
Wörz, Dr. Arno 020364
Wöß, Gerhard 002766
Woestenburg, K. 030041
Wognum, Nick 043523
Wohlgemuth, Werner 017243
Wojciechowski, Jerzy 031995
Wojciechowski, Zbigniew 031926
Wójcik, Adam 032380
Wojewoda, Maciej 032328
Wojtowicz, Wit Karol 032089
Wojtusiak, Prof. Janusz 032064
Wojtysiak, Władysława 032127
Wolanin, Dr. Barbara A. 048950
Wolbert, Dr. Klaus 016644, 016646
Wolde, H.B. ten 029795
Wolden, Arnold 048016
Wolenitz, Dorit 023050
Wolf, Alexandra 002751
Wolf, Dr. Barbara 015602
Wolf, Dr. Beate 020365
Wolf, Connie 047869
Wolf, Dieter 016530
Wolf, Dr. Helmut 015597, 018430
Wolf, Prof. Dr. Jörn Henning 018249
Wolf, Martha Leigh 047238
Wolf, Maurice de 003690
Wolf, Patricia B. 041711
Wolf, Reinmar 002327
Wolf, René 029180
Wolf, Sabine de 003163
Wolf, Sara 042760
Wolf, Sarah 047498
Wolf, Sylvia 042820, 046418
Wolf, Vicki 047842
Wolf, Werner 001942
Wolfe, Adam 001054
Wolfe, Dr. Cheri L. 044005
Wolfe, Douglas 045793
Wolfe, L. 006001
Wolfe, Sara 046304
Wolfe, Susan 044211
Wolfe, Townsend 045342
Wolfensberger, Dr. Rolf 036932
Wolfer, Johannes 001783
Wolfer, Dr. Martin 001783
Wolff, Martha 042820
Wolff, Dr. Tobias 016427
Wolff, W. 018541
Wolford, Craig 042960
Wolfová, Dr. Eva 008642
Wolfs, R. 030088
Wolfschlag, Robert 045579
Wolfson, R.D. 029923
Woliung, Dorothy 042117
Wolkow, Gary 043337
Woll, Gunda 020508, 020509, 020510
Wollan, Alexa 005648
Wollert, Christian 015987
Wolleswinkel, E.J. 030056
Wollkopf, Peter 018379
Wollmann, Dr. Klaus 019554
Wollner, Dr. Bernd 018930
Wołodko, Wiesław 031915
Wolpers, Emily G. 047122
Wolsdorff, Dr. Christian 015988
Wolsk, Nancy 045264
Wolter, Bernd 019767
Wolters, R. 029358
Wolters, Prof. Dr. Reinhard 020501
Wolters, Susan 047492
Wolterstorff, Robert 047164
Wolthoorn, Dr. R. 029855
Woltman, Bob 041613
Wolz, Robert J. 044986
Wolzogen, Wolf von 017176
Womack, Gayle 047914
Wombell, Paul 040256
Wong, Allison 044592, 044593
Wong, Carly 040416
Wong, Michele 046340
Wong, S.J. 005867
Wong-Uparaj, Acharn Damrong ... 037872
Wonisch-Langenfelder, Dr. Renate 002567, 002568
Wood, Brian 005144
Wood, Bryen 038929
Wood, Carolyn 042713
Wood, Charles A. 047291
Wood, David 043117
Wood, Dr. Donald A. 042223
Wood, Edward 044190
Wood, Elaine 042757
Wood, H. 041119
Wood, James N. 042820
Wood, Jeff 045850
Wood, Jeremy 040228
Wood, Katherine 039119
Wood, Kaye 000808
Wood, Lydia 043065
Wood, Mara-Helen 040555
Wood, Margaret 046896
Wood, Margaret K. 044251
Wood, Marion 039196
Wood, Nancy 001401
Wood, P. 039031
Wood, Ronald M. 045517
Wood, Vicki 039749
Wood, Virginia 048774
Wood, Willis 049037
Wood, Wilma 005767
Woodage, Claire 039220
Woodcock, Vivi 046913
Woodings, David J. 030524
Woodrey, Mark 044800
Woodrow, James 038649
Woods, Christine 040416
Woods, Claude N. 044498
Woods, Dana V. 047509
Woods, James C. 048673
Woods, Jean 044386
Woods, John S. 046500
Woods, Margaret M. 042375
Woods, Mark H. 045837
Woods, Pearley 043867
Woods, Trudy 045400
Woods, William 043761
Woodson, Shirley 043452
Woodson, Yoko 047853
Woodward, Charles J. 039195
Woodward, Christopher 038624
Woodward, Geoff 041282
Woodward, Hiram 042006
Woodward, John 038798
Woodward, Mac 044695
Woodward, Martin 038671
Woodward, Peter 039256
Woodward, Richard 047429
Woodward, Robert F. 047427
Woodward, Roland H. 049068
Woody Cywink, Linda 047967
Woof, Dr. Robert 039623
Woog, Dr. Friederike 020364
Woolcott, Isabelle S. 043182
Woolf, Derrick 040522
Woolfall, Steve 039061
Woolliscroft, Pam 041123
Woolmore, J.D. 039075
Woolrich, Gill 041001
Woolsey, Sam 043281
Woosley, Anne 048516
Woosley, Dr. Anne I. 043507
Wooten, Jerry 048252
Wootton, James E. 042763
Worcester, Mike 043035
Word, Levi 042368
Worden, Gretchen 046965
Worden, John 047458
Worden, Pamela 042347
Workington, Dawn 040778
Workman, David A. 048828
Workman, Robert 044002
Workmann, Tom 044901
Worm, Dr. Heinz-Lothar 018656
Wormald, M. 001198
Worn, Ethel 043247
Worschech, Kathrin 015502
Worschech, Thomas 017157
Worsdale, Godfrey 040460
Worswick, Clark 047741
Worth, Claudia R. 049133
Worth, Cyril 044577
Worth, Tim 006842, 006860
Worthen, Amy N. 043424
Worthen jr., William B. 045344
Worthington, Gary 047084
Worton, Graham 039290
Worton, James 047674
Worts, Martin 030881
Wotovic, Audrey 011797
Woycicki, Dr. Kazimierz 018570
Woyda, Stefan 032259
Woytowicz, Barbara 046348
Wpadhyays, Dr. Chandrakant B. .. 021994
Wradzidlo, Dr. Isolde 016240
Wragg, Gary 038611
Wray, JaLayne 049160
Wrębiak, Celestyn 031825
Wretemark, Mia 036577
Wrey, Dr. James D. 046870
Wright, Amina 038624
Wright, Anthony 030460
Wright, Belinda 000864
Wright, Carolyn 043280
Wright, David M. 049277
Wright, Ethan 044745
Wright, George 039508
Wright, Henry T. 041733
Wright, Joanne 040617
Wright, John 044543
Wright, Kevin 047448
Wright, Lesley 044359
Wright, Lynne 004984

Wright, M. 040949
Wright, Margot 038449
Wright, Mavis 049074
Wright, Michael 044804
Wright, Nigel 039083
Wright, Raymond 049030
Wright, Rita 030425
Wright, Dr. Robin K. 048075
Wright, Dr. S. 040623
Wright, Simon 000841
Wright, Steven J. 046931
Wright, Vicki C. 043538
Wright Millard, Elizabeth 047658
Wright-Parsons, Ann 043373
Wrigley, John 000880
Wrobel, Horst 017415
Wróbel, Leszek 032248
Wróblewska-Straus, Hanna 032437, 032482
Wróblewski, Jerzy 032208
Wroczyńska, Ewa Maria 032402
Wroz, Winfried 018216
Wu, Cheng-Shang 007370
Wu, Chu Pang 007186
Wu, Dang Wei 007252
Wu, Hongzhou 007238
Wu, Hung Yuen 007063
Wu, Ke Shun 007265
Wu, Prof. Shi-Kuei 042354
Wu, Dr. Shun-Chi 016017
Wudel, Tom 045941
Wünsche, Prof. Dr. Raimund 019117
Würgler, Andreas 037321
Würmli, Dr. M. 020511
Würsch, Paul 037536
Würthner, Robert 002103
Würzelberger, Jörg 002760
Wüst, Léonard 037617
Wüthrich, Dr. Lucas 037439
Wulf, Karin 016310
Wulf, Rüdiger 016767
Wulkan, Reba 046419, 046419
Wunderer, Dr. Hansjörg 019756
Wunderlin, Dominik 036893
Wunsch, G. 017136
Wurda, Andreas 018763, 018764
Wurfel, Max 001381, 001382, 001383
Wurmfeld, Sanford 046347
Wurster, F. 019610
Wurzer, Günther 002142
Wurzinger, Erika 001996
Wustrack, Dr. Michael K. 017151
Wuthenau von Pietsch, Carlota von 028787
Wyatt, Frederica 044886
Wyatt, Mary Pat 044890
Wyatt, Shannon 047420
Wyatt, Steve 046454
Wyckoff, Dr. D. 046509
Wyczółkowski, Mariusz 031996
Wydler, Henry 037305
Wye, Deborah 045389
Wykersloot, Baron E. de 003254
Wyld, Lesley 040432
Wyldster, Martin 040241
Wylie, Charles 043269
Wyman, Devik 042123
Wyman, James 041838, 044109
Wymbs, Norm 043474
Wÿnandts, Dr. H. 029838
Wynn, Rachel 047148
Wynne, M.V 039080
Wynnemer, Donald 048874
Wyrsch, Dr. Jürg 037686
Wyse Jackson, Dr. Patrick N. 022745
Wysk, Susan C. 048388
Wyss, Matthias von 037640
Xamena, Miguel A. 000254
Xanke, Uwe 016711
Xavier, Andrew 040135
Xerri, Alda 028046
Xiae, Guo Cui 007209
Xiao, Runjun 007352
Xiejun, Chen 007242
Xin, Xue Jian 042456
Xinmiao, Zheng 007003
Xiong, Qiu Shi 007253
Xu, Jay 042820, 048092
Xun, Gao You 007168
Xylander, Prof. Dr. Willi 017457
Y, Dr. Rainer 020374
Yaacobi, Effi 023039
Yabacıoğlu, Ömer 038044
Yabe, Yoshiaki 026688
Yager, Bob 045636
Yaghobi 022643
Yagid, Meira 023092
Yahn Kramer, Bettie 048170
Yajima, Loretta 044595
Yakar, Saffet 038077
Yalakki, C.S. 022349
Yaldız, Fethiye 038074
Yaldiz, Prof. Dr. Marianne 016130
Yamada, Rikuzou 027007
Yamada, Yasuhisa 027323
Yamaga, Motoko 026515
Yamagishi, Youichi 026953
Yamaguchi, Kakutaro 026427
Yamaguchi, Matsuzo 027287
Yamakawa, Kazutoshi 027056
Yamamoto, Akira 026413, 027250
Yamamoto, Atsuo 026841
Yamamoto, Chikyo 026690
Yamamoto, Kazumaro 026826
Yamamoto, Dr. Masao 026844
Yamamoto, Shuji 027315
Yamamoto, Yasukazu 026887
Yamamoto, Yoshiko 047847
Yamanaka, Osamu 026662
Yamanaka, Sadanori 027253
Yamazaki, Midori 026685
Yamazaki, Tomiji 027276
Yambo, Francisco Xavier 000091
Yanagi, Munemichi 027090
Yanagi, Sori 027223
Yanagihara, Masaki 027287
Yanamoto, Akira 027143
Yanari, Sachi 043998
Yancey, Shirley S. 049020
Yande, R. 003198, 003201
Yandle, Ashley 042744
Yaneff, Greg 005177
Yanega, Doug A. 047456
Yáñez Anllo, Lucila 035367
Yang, Xiaoneng 044924
Yanik, Kadir 038182
Yaniv, Shosh 022984
Yank, Paul 042680
Yanko, Dick 042367
Yankov, Dr. Angel 004791
Yano Bretón, Dr. Sabino 028862
Yantorno, Suzanne 046320
Yap, Priscilla M. 031766
Yap, Virgilio 031653
Yapelli, Tina 047844
Yard, Dr. Sally 047820
Yarlow, Loretta 042468, 046395
Yaroshchuk, Mariya 038290
Yarsinske, Amy Waters 046503
Yasin, Dr. Walid 038422
Yassin, Robert A. 048642
Yasuda, Haruki 027216
Yasui, Teruo 026700
Yasuo, Hasimoto 026943
Yates, Jane M. 042729
Yates, R. 034586
Yates, Royden 034583
Yates, Sam 045038
Yates, Dr. Steve 047973
Yates, Dr. Steven A. 047970
Yates, Dr. Terry L. 041619
Yatim, Prof. Dr. Othman 027976
Yatras-Dehove, Elena 021160
Yazbeck, Janine 027818
Yeager, Shelley 046531
Yeager, William 006476
Yeatts, David L. 049294
Yébenes, M. Sierra 035110
Yee, Lydia 042432
Yeffeth, Laura 046417
Yelavich, Susan 046319
Yeler, Nihat 038005
Yellis, Ken 046458
Yellow Horn, Jo-Ann 005157
Yener, Emin 038018
Yerdon, Lawrence J. 047069
Yerhot, Judith 042268
Yerkovich, Dr. Sally 046424
Yeroulanos, Marinos 021188
Yersin, Jean-Marc 037680
Yetkin, Mehmet 037994
Yeudall, Robert 005395
Yeung, C.T. 007135
Yi, Shu 007001
Yi, Zhu 006983
Yıldız, Adem 038050
Yıldız, Hacı Ahmet 037993
Yılmaz, Ayla 038094
Yip, Chee-Kuen 007121
Ylioja, Merja 010054
Ylvisåker, Anne Britt 030771
Yochim, Jordan 045205
Yoder, Harold E. 047345
Yoder, Robert Lee 045063
Yoder, Sandy 048715
Yoki, Aharon 048486
Yokomizo, Hiroko 027169
Yoneya, Tetsuo 027035
Yoneyama, Torataro 027234
Yoon, Prof. Se-Young 027576
York, Beverly 049190
York, Brian 041805
Yorty, Faith A. 048301
Yosef, A. 023083
Yoshida, Kazuo 027028
Yoshida, Mitsuo 026818
Yoshida, Shoji 027281
Yoshihisa, Suto 026425
Yoshikata, Ishihara 027139
Yoshikawa, Miho 026887
Yoshinaka, Yasumaro 026534
Yoshioka, Akemi 027216
Yoshioka, Kenjiro 027082
Yoshioka, Yoji 026431, 026492
Yotsutsuji, Hideki 026887
You, Mee Chung 027584
Youck, Ingrid 006517
Young, Amber M. 044344
Young, Bobbie 043168
Young, Brian 045342
Young, C. 039308
Young, Charles 044273
Young, Cynthia 043443
Young, Dan 005573
Young, Dede 047285
Young, Dr. D.J. 039452
Young, Ernest 044939
Young, Frank 049103
Young, Gary 006417
Young, Holly 047014
Young, Jocelyn 041711
Young, John J. 006570
Young, Joyce 046679
Young, Judi 006588
Young, Karen S. 048500
Young, Kyle 046142
Young, Dr. Marcia 042259
Young, Marvin R. 048161
Young, Mary Jane 042142
Young, Michael 001452
Young, Sir Nicholas 040099
Young, Patrice 048319
Young, Richard L. 042646
Young, Steve 043786
Young Lee, Nan 027505
Young-Sanchez, Margaret 043404
Young-Vignola, Eilee 046942
Youngken, M. Joan 046459
Youngs, Christopher 047344
Younker, Randall W. 042172
Younkin, Elva 047433
Yount, Frank 045284
Yount, Sylvia 041862
Youssoufian, Jerry 006024
Yozak, Roman 038342
Ysel, H.J.D. 034712
Ysenburg und Bündingen, Casimir Erbprinz zu 019878
Yu, Louis 007129
Yu, Sun 006994
Yu, Teng Kuei 007375
Yüksek, Mustafa 038120
Yuergniaux, Danièle 013929
Yuichi, Tatsuno 026533
Yuki, Ryogo 026857
Yuko, Isazawa 027170
Yun, Jang Sub 027562
Yunus bin Zakaria, Dr. Mohd 028010
Yut, Joyce 042607
Yzereef, Dr. Gerard 029150, 029152
Zabarovskij, Vladimir Ivanovič 033372
Zabehlicky-Scheffenegger, Dr. Susanne 002432
Zabel, Barbara 032010
Zabel, Igor 034485
Zabel, Jürgen 021094
Zabusch, Prof. Stephanie 002871
Zaccaguini, Dr. Marisa 025479
Zaccome, Dr. Gian Maria 026058
Zacepina, Olga Vasiljevna 033860
Zachariou, E. 008217
Zacharkiw, Irene 048857
Zacharuk, Dr. Richard 017177
Zache, D. 019577
Zacher, J. 000759
Zachorowska, Maria 032042
Zachos, Dr. K. 021277
Zachou, Eleni 021153, 021349
Zack, Wendy 005286
Zadgorska, Valentina 004863
Zadka, Ruth 022940
Zadorožna, Nadija Fedorivna 038385
Zäch, Benedikt 037722
Zaffarano, Antonio 026314
Zaffino, Antonio 025860
Zafran, Eric 044463
Žagar, Zora 034511
Zagnoli, Roberto 049422, 049427
Zagrina, Natalja Aleksandrovna . . . 033696
Zahaniciuc, Marcel 032827
Žahirović, Prof. Šaban 003933
Zahler, Robert 001718
Zahn, Donald 042933
Zahn-Biemüller, Dr. Eva 020999
Zahner, Anton 037371
Zahrádka, Jiří 008294
Zahradník, Dr. Zdeněk . . . 008389, 008765
Zaitsev, Nikolai Alekseevič 027418
Zaitsu, Nagatsugi 027068
Zając, Zdzisława 032547
Zajączkowski, Wiesław . . . 031903, 031938
Zajceva, Natalija Leonidovna 033266
Zajic, Václav 008435
Zak, Thomas 042986
Zakatova, Anastasija Vasiljevna . . 033052
Zakian, Michael 045605
Zakrevskaja, G.P. 033733
Zakrzewski, R.J. 044490
Zakythinos, Prof. D. 021388
Zalba, Pat E. 042698
Zaldivar, Brenda Projas 028791
Zaleski, Pierre 013610, 013617
Zamanillo, Jorge 045809
Zamarchi Grassi, Dr. P. 023236
Zambrano de Gentile, Flor 049458
Zamora Canellada, Alonso 035845, 035848
Zanche, Prof. Vittorio de 025057
Zander, Charlotte 016299
Zander, Dr. Gisela 018771
Zander-Seidel, Dr. Jutta 019352
Zandler, Richard 045197
Zanella, Prof. S. 024266
Zanella Manara, Dr. Emma 024267

Zanelli, Dr. Gianluca 024299
Zanetta, Michèle 037030
Zang, Dr. Joachim 018044
Zangenfeind, Hermann 002577
Zangs, Dr. Christiane 019271, 019272
Zankman, Pat 044270
Zannas, D.K. 021504
Zanni, Dr. Annalisa 024726
Zannieri, Nina 042340
Zanola, Oscar Pablo 000648
Zansitis, Peter Paul 042854
Zant, Herbert 002199
Zantfrisco, Liana 003508
Žantudieva, Elizaveta Magamedovna 033539
Zapałowa, Jadwiga 032234
Zapałowa, Kazimiera 031998
Zapata, Marian 021608
Zapolis, Frank 042823
Zaporožskaja, Valentina Aleksandrovna 033082
Zappa, Armanda 037489
Zappa, Giancarlo 037036
Zaracki, Kathleen 045979, 045979
Zaragüeta, Vicente 035154
Zarb, Michael 006748
Zaremba, Ewa 032264
Zaremba, Tadeusz 032227
Zarev, Dr. Kosio 004715, 004716, 004719
Zarimi, Dominique 014720
Zarina, Elena Gennadjevna 033661
Zarling, Ronald 046231
Zarri, Dr. Enrico 024545
Zarrilli, Dr. Carla 025890
Zarubin, V.I. 033444
Zarzuelo Villaverde, Manuel 035637
Zarzycka, Joanna 032418
Zarzycka, Dr. Zyta 032097
Zasur, Dahas 004360
Zatloukal, Dr. Pavel 008542
Zatulovska, Olena Petrivna 038235
Zau, Daw Nu Mya 029069
Zausch, Bärbel 017672
Zavada, Jeanne L. 046849
Závala, Ignacio M. 034880
Zavattaro, Dr. M. 024180
Zavjalova, Irina Vasiljevna 033239
Zavodnick, George A. 049353
Zawisza, Norbert 032106
Zawol, Zofia 032411
Zawrel, Dr. Peter 002886
Zayani, Abdelhak 029027
Zbarnea, Tudor 028984
Żbikowska, Janina 032260
Zbikowski, Dr. Dörte 018247
Zborowski, Janusz 032145, 032146
Zdesenko, Vjačeslav Iosifovič 033151
Zdravkovski, Dr. Dragiša 027918
Zea, Philip 043368, 044835, 046439, 046440, 047190, 048364, 049333
Zealand, A. 039308
Zeberg, Rolf 036373
Zecca, Walter 026167
Zecha, Horst 020217
Zeder, O. 013210
Zegadłowicz-Rudel, Atessa 032409
Zegher, Catherine de 046325
Zeh, Manfred 002026
Zehavi, Zvi 023016
Zehentmeier, Dr. Sabine 020181
Zehnder, Angela 034587
Zehnder, Prof. Dr. Frank Günter 016333
Zehnder, W. 037668
Zehnter, Dr. Annette 016684
Zeidler, Ingrid 019697
Zeigerer, Wolfgang 018251
Zeik, Travis 049140
Zeileis, Georg 001882
Zeillinger, Josef 002463
Zeiner, Ulrich 017657
Zeipel, Agneta von 036725
Zeitler, Dr. Kurt 019118
Zeitlin, Marilyn 048517
Zekaria, Ahmed 009439
Zekorn, Beate 017174
Zeković, Marina 034172
Zeldenrust, I. 029435
Zelenović, Radoslav 034159
Želev, Ivan 004759
Železnik, Adela 034485
Zelfel, Prof. Dr. Hans Peter 001824
Zelfel, Dr. Hans Peter 002327
Zelie, M. 034762
Zella, Robbin 042408
Zelleke, G. 042820
Zeller, Anselm 002787
Zeller, Kurt W. 002013, 002015
Zeller, Regine 016831
Zemanová, Jana 008684
Zemanova, Zita 008717
Zembala, Dr. Dennis 043443
Zembik, Andrzej 031886
Zemer, Avshalom 022926
Zemovičs, Elmārs 027759
Zemp, Dr. Heinrich 037305
Zemter, Dr. Wolfgang 020925
Zenegas-Millan, Dorenda 046856
Zenks, Ralph 020637
Zentz d'Alnois, Philippe 010947
Zenz, Gerhard 002474
Zepeczaner, Eugen 032900
Zeppenfeld, Dr. Burkhard 019391
Zerah, Dov 013639
Zerdina, V. 027749
Zerrudo, Eric 031755
Žertogova, Izabella Jakovlevna 033078
Zeschick, Dr. Johannes 019875
Zeskinskaja, Nelly 038371
Zettel, Ernest 001916
Zetterström, Margareta 036633
Zettl, Charleen 042395
Zettler, Richard 046993
Zeuli, Prof. Errico 025528
Zeuli, Maria Francesca 025544
Zevallos Quinones, Dr. Jorge 031605
Zevi, Dr. Anna Gallina 025031, 025032, 025033
Zevi, Anna Gallina 025559
Ževrnja, Prof. Nediljko 007804
Zgaga, Višnja 007854
Zhang, Cheng Zhi 007237
Zhang, Jing 007086
Zhang, John 042153
Zhang, Lizhi 007321
Zhang, Wei 007025
Zhang, Wen Long 007294
Zhang, Xiao Jun 007215
Zhi, Yunting 007257
Zhitao, Huang 007210
Zhou, Zhao 007041
Zhu, Jiping 007243
Zhuber-Okrog, Karoline 002934
Ziąbka, Leszek 031977
Ziauddin, Muhammad 003103
Zibelius-Chen, Prof. Dr. K. 020491
Zibelo, Fisseha 009444
Zibler, Barbara 016072
Zichner, Prof. Dr. L. 017158
Zidić, Igor 007848
Zidlick, Pauline 042027
Zieglar, Ken 047000
Ziéglé, Anne 010882
Ziegler, Christiane 013685
Ziegler, Dr. Reinhard 020364
Ziegler, Dr. Susanne 016017
Ziehe, Dr. Irene 016128
Zielinski, Melissa L. 041760
Zielke, Bridgett 045597
Zielonka, Mariusz 032322
Ziemann-Heitkämper, Sonja 017883
Zierden, Martha 042728
Zierke, Franciszek 032556
Zieselman, Ellen 047970
Ziessow, Dr. Karl-Heinz 016572
Zięzio, Ryszard 032002
Ziffer, Dr. Irit 023069
Zifferero, Dr. Andrea 026040
Žigalov, Valerij Alekseevič 033875
Žiganova, Nina Iljinična 033245
Zigler Becker, Janis 042079
Zigmunde, Alida 027767
Zijp, R.P. 029563
Zika, Paul 001111
Zilianti, Dr. Romualdo 023448
Žiljanina, Tatjana Vladimirovna 033209
Zillenbiller, Prof. Dr. Erwin 020577, 020578
Zimina, I.D. 033985
Zimmer, Jim L. 045361
Zimmer, Patricia 005046
Zimmerer, Kathy 042633
Zimmerman, Anne 042672
Zimmerman, Daniel W. 043909
Zimmerman, Diane 047517
Zimmerman, Ryan 043079
Zimmerman, Sara C. 046436
Zimmerman, Vickie 043529
Zimmermann, Grety 036948
Zimmermann, Dr. Karl 036927
Zimmermann, Prof. Dr. Konrad 019902
Zimmermann, Dr. Margret 017228
Zimmermann, Oliver L. 018293
Zimmermann, Paul 017966
Zimmermann, Pedro 036965
Zimmermann, Peter 015982
Zimmermann, Pius 037324
Zimmermann, Tina 020365
Zimmern, Emily F. 042758
Zindler, Debra 045776
Zingarelli, Thomas V. 043787
Zingg, Ernst 037402
Zink, Bob 045914
Zinke, Dr. Detlef 017228
Zinn, Nancy 042006
Zinnkann, Dr. Heidrun 017183
Zintel, Diana 046222
Zintz, Daniel 014798
Ziolkowski, Anne 043212
Zippelius, Dr. K. 018168
Zipursky, Gerry 006709
Zirnitis, P. 027762
Zischka, Dr. Ulrike 019086
Ziswiler, Prof. V. 037787
Žitko, Duška 034511
Zitko, Salvator 034470
Zižić, Olivera 034239
Zjablicki, A.J. 027411
Zjumčenko, Ljudmila Petrovna 033888
Zlatar, Milena 034522
Zlattinger, Klaus 002685
Zlobina, Nina Nikolaevna 033267
Żmuda, Anna 032126
Żmuda, Maurycy 032086
Znamenov, V.V. 033752
Žnidarič, Dr. Marjan 034499
Znojek, Jerzy 032222
Zoe, Vivian F. 049078
Zöhrer, Georg 001972
Zöller, Achim 020184, 020185
Zöller, Dr. Helge 020999
Zöller-Stock, Dr. Bettina 018726
Zoer, J.A. 029501
Zoete, Johan de 029656
Žogina, Viktorija Stepanovna 033779
Zoli, Renato Giancarlo 026014
Zolli, Barbara T. 047093
Zolotareva, Tatjana Nikolaevna 033669
Zolotina, I.A. 033764
Zolotinkina, Dr. Larissa Igorevna 033768
Zoltán, Kató 032933
Zombork, Márta 021912
Zomborka Szűcsné, Márta 021913
Zomlefer, W. 041833
Zommer, Raya 022907
Zona, Louis A. 049360
Zonneveld-Kouters, M.C. 030027
Zopes, Elaine 043774, 046237, 047185, 048017, 048232
Zopf, August 001874, 002337
Zopf, Johann 002694
Zorbo, Lorrie 042054
Zorić, Ivanka 034163
Zoridis, Pandeli 021372
Zorn, Dr. Olivia 015979
Zorzi, Dr. Marino 026237
Zoubek, Ernst 002763
Zrebiec, Alice 043404
Zrelov, Vladimir Andreevič 033713
Zsidi, Dr. Paula 021634
Zsuzsa, Dr. Fodor 021919
Zuback, Lynne 044892
Zubčie, Pavao 007763
Zuber, Michaela 017141
Zuberer, Peter 020715
Zubiaurre, Pablo 000122
Zubov, Aleksandr Nikolaevič 034004
Zubrij, Elena Stanislavovna 033157
Zuccali, Jean-Pierre 012740
Zuckerman, B. Michael 042614
Zuckriegel, Dr. Margit 002560
Zuckriegl, Dr. Margit 002565
Züchner, Dr. Christian 017038
Zünd, Peter 037393
Züst, Ernst 037739
Zueva, Ljubov Vasiljevna 033933
Zufferey, Anne-D. 037484, 037559
Žugan, Vitalij Ivanovič 033946
Zugay, Gabriele 002934
Zugaza Miranda, Miguel 035429
Zugni Tauro, Anna Paola 024089
Zuidervaart, Dr. Huib J. 030002
Žuk, Oksana Jaroslavivna 038338
Żuk, Stanisław 031844
Žukauskienė, Genovaite 027853, 027857
Zukauskienė, Genovaite 027859
Zukiwski, Wilson 006826
Zukowsky, John 042820
Zukulis, Ivars 027756
Zuleta, Pilar 007433
Zumaeta Zúñiga, Hector 006943
Zumbini, Vincenzo 023981
Zumpfe, Dr. Dieter 002327
Zuna-Kratky, Dr. Gabriele 003009
Zunk, Bodo 019782
Zupančič, Mirina 034466
Žuravlev, M.N. 003127
Žuravleva, Tatjana Jurjevna 033544
Zurawski, Jarosław 032560
Zurbuchen, Max 037257
Zurcher, Sarah 037098
Zurfluh, Dr. Anselm 037425
Zurfluh, M. 011311
Zuris, Donald P. 043163
Zuris, Kay A. 044278
Zuskinová, Dr. Iveta 034374
Zutautas, Sofia 042833
Žutikov, Aleksandr Ivanovič 033609
Zutter, Dr. Jorg 000888
Zuver, W. Marc 048905
Zvelebil, Miloš 008673
Zviguilsky, Dr. Alexandre 010905
Zvirin, Prof. Yoram 022927
Zwaenepoel, Dr. J. 003515
Zwaka, Petra 016086
Zwanger, Meryl 046325
Zwart, A. 029788
Zweifel, Gwen 005490
Zweifel, Regula 037784
Zweite, Prof. Dr. Armin 016834, 016835
Zwez, Annelise 037646
Zwez, John 048851
Zwicker, Jörg 001924, 002518
Zwickl, Alfred 037735, 037736
Zwicky, P. 036947
Zwiener, Walter 016243
Zwierzyna, John 044444
Zwink, Dr. E. 020372
Zwolak, Adam 031816
Zydlik, Stanisław 032414
Zygmun, Kathy 047822
Zykaner, Michaela 002946
Zykov, Andrej Viktorovič 033255
Zyman, Daniela 045446

Index of Institutions and Companies

Register der Institutionen und Firmen

008 Antiquités, Paris 065340
1 2 3... Art Now, Bruxelles 096122
1 Over 1a Gallery, Denver 115957
100% Natural, Cancún 128496
100 et 1 Collections, Montluçon . . 064705
De 1001 Dingenhal, Alkmaar 077707
100th Bomb Group Memorial Museum, Dickleburgh 039238
The 100th Meridian Museum, Cozad 043204
103rd Ohio Volunteer Infantry Memorial, Sheffield Lake 048138
104 Antiques & Collectables, Regina 059080
107 Workshop Gallery, Shaw 114410
1078 Gallery, Chico 042888
108 Fine Art, Harrogate 113187
10th Avenue Antiques, Calgary 058776
11 Duke Street, London 113419
111 Place Gift Antiques, Tulsa 093276
11th Avenue Grafic Visuals, Regina 097169
12 Below Arts Counsel, New York . . 117533
12 Sedie, Torino 076753
12 Vancouver Service Battalion Museum, Richmond 006279
121 Photography Gallery, San Antonio 119384
1220 Productions, Los Angeles . . . 116689
123 Watts Gallery, New York 117534
1301 PE, Los Angeles 135377
1301 Projects & Editions, Los Angeles 116690
13th Street Gallery, Omaha 118681
14-1 Galerie, Stuttgart 104961
14 Sculptors Gallery, New York 117535
1405 Art Gallery, New York 117536
150 ans de Couture, Aix-les-Bains . 010299
15th Field Artillery Regiment Museum, Vancouver 006684
15th Street Gallery, Salt Lake City . 119323
16th Street Gallery, Salt Lake City . 119324
17 Reasons, San Francisco 119574
1708 Gallery, Richmond 047406
1708 Gallery, Richmond 119092
1719 Galerie, Alkmaar 107611
1796 Bantry French Armada Exhibition Centre, Bantry 022691
The 1811 Old Lincoln County Jail and 1839 Jailer's House Museum, Wiscasset 049267
1822-Forum Frankfurter Sparkasse, Frankfurt am Main 102739
1859 Jail-Marshal's Home and Museum, Independence 044719
1874 House Antiques, Portland . . . 091879
1890 House-Museum and Center for Victorian Arts, Cortland 043170
19. Sajandi Tartu Linnakodaniku Muuseum, Tartu 009413
19 Vek, Sankt-Peterburg 080288
1900-1970, Bruxelles 057793
1900 Monceau Antiquités, Paris . . . 065341
1904 Antiques, Portland 091880
1908 Cash Register, Tampa 093095
1910 Boomtown, Western Development Museum, Saskatoon 006413
1914 Plant City High School Community Exhibition, Plant City 047078
198 Gallery, London 040073
19th Century Shop, Baltimore 142217
2 Ravens, Kirkby Stephen 141698
20/20, Dublin 135851
20 North Gallery, Toledo 120073
2000 Art Galleries, Sydney 095264
2000 Cadres & Idées, Paris 124537
2000 Ciutat Vella, Barcelona 129310
2004 L, J. de, Amsterdam 140275
20.21 Galerie Edition Kunsthandel, Essen 102666, 133912, 139052
2023 Antiques, Louisville 089950
2040 Gallery, Austin 114947
20first Century Art, Godalming 113137
20th Century Antiques, Vancouver . 059324
20th Century Antiques, Wellington . 079310
20th Century Consortium, Kansas City 089480, 122933
20th Century Gallery, Baltimore . . . 087628
20th Street Art Gallery, Sacramento 119131
21 Grand Gallery, Oakland 118621
21 Notre Dame O, Montréal 058890
217 Art Contemporain, La Croix-de-Rozon 111376
21st Centuary Gallery, Bungay 112752
21st Century Antics, Salisbury 086487
21st Century Bob, San Diego 092596
222 Westlake Antique Mall, Seattle 092942
23rd Street Antique Mall, Oklahoma City 091448
24 Carat, Damascus 083049
24 Hour Museum, The National Virtual Museum, Brighton 136145
24HR Art, Northern Territory Centre for Contemporary Art, Parap 001366
26 Martyrs Museum, Nagasaki 026857
26th Field Artillery Regiment Museum, Brandon 005135
274 Gallery, Northbridge 094986
275 Antiques, London 085044
280 Modern, New York 117537
Le 29, L'Isle-sur-la-Sorgue 063914
29 Palms, Fresno 088894
291 Antiques, London 085045
2AH, Grenoble 063041
2bis Editions, Paris 133507
2X de Afstand, Zaltbommel 108269
3 Arts Studio, Honolulu 088925
3 Day Gallery, Dallas 115813
3 Day Gallery, Dallas 115814
3-Dimentions Art and Architecture, Wien 133173
3 Falk Gallery, Tucson 120096
3 Monkeys, Portland 091881
3 Ten Haustudio, Atlanta 114841
303 Gallery, New York 117538
313 Antiques, London 085046
33rd Street Galleria, New York 117539
33rd Street Galleria, New York 117540
34., Beograd 080385
364 Hayes Street Gallery, San Francisco 119575
390th Bomb Group Memorial Air Museum and British Resistance Organisation Museum, Framlingham 039522
3A Antiques, Norwich 086106
3AR, Versailles 125016
3D Galerie, Dänischenhagen 102334
3d Gallery, Bristol 112711
3F, Versailles 068788
Le 3L, Toulon (Var) 124958
3M Art Collection, Saint Paul 047693
4 Art, Chicago 115317
4 Cats Gallery, Abbotsford 094111
4-F Gallery, Los Angeles 116691
4-H Schoolhouse Museum, Clarion . 042944
4 Ladies Art Gallery, Chicago 115318
4 Star Gallery, Indianapolis 116435
40 George Street Contemporary Art, Mount Eden 079161
404, Braunschweig 133836, 135734
41 Artecontemporanea, Torino 106654
A la 42ème Ligne, Paris 138271
43rd Street Gallery, Richmond 119093
448th Bomb Group Memorial Museum, Seething 040976
450 Broadway Gallery, New York . . 117541
4599 Antiques, Miami 090112
45th Infantry Division Museum, Oklahoma City 046641
4711-Museum, Köln 018301
4731 Gallery, Detroit 116075
The 4th Floor Gallery, Surry Hills . . 095246
4th Infantry Division Museum, Fort Hood 043919
5 Art, Tampa 120016
5 Clock Gallery, Lausanne 111608
Le 5 Elément, Paris 138272
5 Green Boxes, Denver 115958
5-Star Collectibles, Honolulu 088926
50 Penn Place Art Gallery, Oklahoma City 118651
500 X Gallery, Dallas 115815
50er Jahre Erlebniswelt, Zusmarshausen 021081
50er-Jahre-Museum, Büdingen . . . 016488
511 Gallery, New York 117542
51st Avenue Art, Calgary 096783
539 Gallery, New Orleans 117381
54 the Gallery, London 113420
55 Antiques, Kingston-upon-Hull . . 130847
56 Group Wales, Cardiff 054264
57th Street Antique Mall, Sacramento 092123
5BE Gallery, New York 117543
5th and J Antiques, San Diego 092597
5th Avenue Books, San Diego 142895
6 Pence, Fukuoka 077039
63 Gallery, Seoul 107203
64 Steps, Toronto 097204
66 Cuadros, Valencia 110793
68elf Förderverein junger Kunst e.V, Köln 053006
7. Antykwariat, Warszawa 140770
7 Galerie, Athinai 105379
El 7 Peus, Barcelona 080778
77 Gallery, New York 117544
779, Paris 099899
799 Art Gallery, New York 117545
7ciris, Tarrega 081626, 129748
7th Avenue Antique Mall, Saint Paul 092336
82 Picture Gallery, Hong Kong 097745
824 Gallery, Jacksonville 116503
825 Art, Denver 115959
82nd Airborne Division War Memorial Museum, Fort Bragg 043893
82nd Street Beanies, Indianapolis . 089257
871 Fine Arts, San Francisco 119576, 142920
901 Gallery, Fort Worth 116126
918 Antique Gallery, Los Angeles . . 089668
A-1 Antiques and Auction House, Houston 088985
A-1 Furniture, San Jose 132919
A-1 Furniture Refinishing, Los Angeles 132228
A-1 Furniture Refinishing, Los Angeles 132229
A-1 Galerie, Maastricht 108111
A-1 Galerie, Maastricht 108112
A-1 Jewelry and Coin, Chicago . . . 087996
A 1 Upholstery, San Antonio 132799
A-3, Moskva 109477
A 5, Saint-Pierre 121959
A & A, Osnabrück 073227
A & A, Praha 060085
A & A Antique Restoration, Long Beach 132221
A A Antiques, Christchurch 079002
A & A Antiques, Milwaukee 090264, 122966
A & A Antiques, Pittsburgh 091780
A & A Art, Denver 115960
A & A Art and Frame, Washington . . 120235
A & A Galeria, Poznań 109039
A & A Upholstery Company, San Antonio 132800
A & A Upholstry, New Orleans 132407
A à Z Antiquités, Lannion 063529
A Ages Ago, Denver 088633
A Althée, Marseille 138189
A-Antikvariaatti, Pori 137983
A-Antique, Long Beach 132222
A Antiques, New Orleans 090497
A Antiques Consigned, New Orleans 090498
A Arte, Milano 106143
A-Auction by Jer, Cincinnati 122849
A & B Antique Furniture, Albuquerque 087357
A & B Antique Furniture, San Antonio 132801
A & B Antiques, Hampton 055945
A & B Art Gallery, New York 117546
A & B Subastadores, Madrid 122029
A Barn Full of Brass Beds, Conisholme 084074
A Better Antique Buyer, Baltimore . . 087629
A Big Difference, Eagle Heights . . . 094500
A Bit of the Past, Austin 087544
A Book A Brac Shop, Miami 142545
A Booksearch, Nelson 140642
A & C Black, Huntingdon 135160
A & C Gallery, London 113421
A & C Upholstery, San Francisco . . . 132862
A Cappella Book, Atlanta 142194
A Child's Heart, Pittsburgh 091781
A Coin Gallery, Jacksonville 089360
A Collector's Bookshop, Saint Louis 142851
A Contrario, Limoges 099501
A Country Place Antiques, Saint Louis 092193
A Creative Eye, Goulburn 094600
A D Antiquités, Labastide-d'Armagnac 063470
A & D Antiquity, Birmingham 087727
A & D Gallery, London 113422
A Damn Fine Artist, Austin 114948
A Different Angle, Oakland 118622
A Doll Affaire, Sacramento 092124
A Dong Gallery, Ha Noi 120440
A Dong Gallery, Ha Noi 120441
A & E Downtown Antiques, San Antonio 092471
A&E Graphics Complex, Houston . . 116257
A & F Galleries, Tweed Heads South 095355
A Field of Dreams, Oklahoma City . 091449
A & G Gallery, New York 090647
A Galerie, Amsterdam 107646
A Gallery, Göteborg 110901
A Gallery, London 113423
A Gallery, New York 117547
A Gallery, Salt Lake City 119325
A Gallery for Fine Photography, New Orleans 117382
A Gathering of the Tribes, New York 117548
A Gift for All Seasons, Honolulu . . . 116192
A Gift of Art, Tampa 120017
A Glas of Beauty, Amsterdam 077767
A Glory to Behold, Tucson 093188
A Good Buy, Los Angeles 089669
A & H Antiques, Milwaukee 090265
A Hotcakes Gallery, Milwaukee . . . 117159
A&I Stripping & Refinishing, Albuquerque 131733
A J Antiques, Bath 083409
A & J Glas-Porslinslagning, Stockholm 129854
A Joy Forever Antiques, Brighton, Victoria 055545
A L Fine Arts, Paris 099900
A la Belle Epoque, Caen 061856
A la Belle Epoque, Giromagny 063002
A la Belle Epoque, Provins 066988
A la Belle Epoque, Sallanches 068095, 124922
A la Belle Epoque, Sarreguemines . 068132
A la Bonne Brocante, Paris 065342
A la Bourse d'Or, Paris 065343
A la Brocante de l'Eglise, Douai . . . 062722
A la Brocante du Musoir, Le Tréport 063722
A La Capucine, Québec 059053
A la Carte Antik, Stockholm 081904
A la Corne de Jouvence, Paris 065344
A la Cour de France, Montreuil-sur-Mer 064770
A la Grange, Sains-en-Amienois . . . 067341
A la Maison, Sammeron 068106
A la Manière, Rouen 101105
A la Mûrisserie, Le Mans 063651
A la Porte de Sologne, Argent-sur-Sauldre 060957
A la Porte Notre Dame, Cambrai . . . 061917
A la Poussière d'Or, Marin 064286
A la Recherche du Temps Perdu, Cabourg 061847
A la Recherche du Temps Perdu, Le Puy-en-Velay 063695
A la Reine Margot, Paris 065345
A la Vieille France, Metz . . 064515, 124444
A la Vieille Russie, New York 090648

A l'Age de Bronze, Murat (Cantal) . . 064843
A l'Ancien Temps, Ajaccio 060732
A l'Ancien Temps, Ajaccio 060733
A l'Art Antique, Marly-le-Roi 064289
A l'Art Notre, Périgueux 100988
A l'Enseigne du Commissaire Maigret, Liège 137514
A l'Espace des Arts, Saint-Rémy-de-Provence 101225
A l'Espace des Particuliers, Clamart 062313
A l'Estampille, Metz 064516
A Likely Story, Alexandria 142192
A l'Imagerie, Paris 065346, 099901
A Literary Saloon, Seattle 142974
A Little Bit of Kiwi, Roxburgh 108555
A & M Antique, Albuquerque 087358
A&M Galerie, Ostseebad Binz 104555
A & M Table Pads, Windsor, Ontario 123860
A Marie Stuart, Paris 065347
A Muse Gallery, Columbus 115754
A New Doll in Town, Miami 090113
A Niche in Time, Chicago 087997
A Nitch in Tyme, Norfolk 091362
A & P, Palermo 076120
A. Paul Weber-Museum, Ratzeburg 019725
A Piece of History, Launceston 056086
A Place in Time, Jacksonville 089361
A Pleasant Cove, Jacksonville 089362
A Plus Furniture, Houston 088986
A Quaint Little Shoppe, Atlanta 087438
A Refinishing Touch, Jacksonville . . 132167
A Renaissance Book Shop, Milwaukee 142564
A Restoration Centre, Dun Laoghaire 074959, 127102
A Room With a Vieux, Boston 087789
A Room With A View, Kortrijk 058257
A Rug Importer, Tucson 093189
A Ruth Creation, Cincinnati 115596
A Saint-Benoît-des-Prés, Paris 138273
A Samarcande, Montrichard 099769
A. Schiiwesch Musée Rural, A. Schiiwesch Museum für ländliche Kultur, Binsfeld 027871
A Second Look Books, Calgary 137615
A Second Look Books, Kitchener . . 137645
A Secret Closet, Chicago 087998
A Select Few, New York . . 090649, 132427
A Simpler Time, Minneapolis 117231
A. Sohos Museum, Tinos 021507
A Soldier's Life, Regimental Museum of the 15th/19th The King's Royal Hussars and Northumberland Hussars and Light Dragoons, Newcastle-upon-Tyne . 040544
A Space, Toronto 006578
A Space, Toronto 097205
A Super Head Shot, New York 117549
A & T, Dahlewitz 070172
A & T Kunsthandel, Plaidt 073337
A-Top Art Gallery, New York 117550
A Touch of Asia, San Francisco 092703
A Touch of France, Boston 115134
A Touch of Mystery, Norfolk 091363
A Touch of Nostalgia, Edmonton . . . 058814
A Touch of the Past, Maryborough, Queensland 056164
A Unique Antique, Chicago 087999
A Unique Blend, Salt Lake City 092408
A Upholstering Company, Nashville 132394
A Vintage Boutique, Saint Louis 092194
A Votre Servies, 's-Hertogenbosch . 078510
A1 Antiques, Baltimore 087630
A1 Furniture Restoration, Wellington 128969
A1 Jukebox and Nostalgia, Baltimore 087631
A1A Antiques, Ulverston . . 086980, 131627
A.A. Antik, Göteborg 081788
AA Antik-Schatzkammer, München . 072625
A.A. Gallery, Ho Chi Minh City 120495
AAA Art, Los Angeles 116692
AAA Auction, Cincinnati 122850
A.A.A. Gallery, Bruxelles 057794
A.A.A. Invest, Gent 058166
A.A.A.Aabenraa, Berlin 069547
Aaaz Scris, Liège 058279
AAB Antiquités, Bruxelles 057795
Aabenhus Århus Antikvariat, Århus . 137861
Aabenraa Museum, Aabenraa 008796
AABP, Bruxelles 057796
Aachen, A., Miami 090114
Aachener Kunst- und Antiquitätenhändlerverband 1976 e.V., Aachen 053007
Aachener Kunstblätter, Köln 135735
A.A.D.A. News, Corte Madera 136284
AAF Contemporary Art Fair, New York 093958
AAF Museum, Washington 048879
Aagaard, Kongens Lyngby 060391
Aagaard & Co, Robert, Knaresborough 084880
Aakar Art Gallery, Mumbai 105750
Aal-Jays, Las Vegas 089532
Aalbers & Israëls, Enschede 078366
Aalborg Historiske Museum, Aalborg 008798
Aalborggaarden, Kragerø 079395
Aalderink, Amsterdam 077768
Aalholm Automobil Museum, Nysted 009041
Aaltense Oorlogs- en Verzetscollectie 1940-1945, Aalten 029122
AAM, Tübingen 074108
Aamiri, Berlin 069548
Aan de Oude Delft, Delft 078138
Aanblick Galerie, Groningen 108029
Aandacht, Utrecht 128853
Aankoop Alle Antiek, Antwerpen . . . 057666
Aankoop en Verkoop Antiek, Antwerpen 057667
De Aanschouw, Rotterdam 108172
De Aanschouw, Rotterdam 108173
Aanzet, Rossum 128817
Aaor, Denver 088634
Aar-te Galerie, Hameln 103235
Aaragon Museum, Ilupeju 030688
Aarde, Almere 077735
Aardewerk, A., Den Haag 078156
Aardewerk & Zoon, Betty, Den Haag 078157
Aardewerkvermuseum Petrus Pegout, Noordbroek 029969
Aardogi, Paris 099902
Aardvark, Chicago 115319
Aardvark, Fyshwick 055847
Aardvark, Milwaukee 142565
Aardvark, Moorak 056253
Aardvark, San Francisco 142921
Aardvarks, Christchurch 079003
Aardvarks, Christchurch 079004
Aareena, Castle Hill 055643
Aarehüsi, Thun 111943
Aargauer Kunsthaus, Aarau 036807
Aargus, Frankfurt am Main 070723
Aaron, Calgary 137616
Aaron, Chicago 115320
Aaron Bros., Fort Worth 116127
Aaron, Fort Worth 116128
Aaron, Fort Worth 116129
Aaron Bros., Houston 116258
Aaron Bros., Houston 116259
Aaron, London 085047
Aaron, New Orleans 090499
Aaron, Tunbridge Wells . . 086930, 142123
Aaron, A., Singapore 109753
Aaron, Anton, New York 090650
Aaron, David, London 113424, 122577, 130912
Aaron, Didier, London 085048, 113425
Aaron, Didier, New York 117551
Aaron, Didier, Washington 120236
Aaron, John, Denver 115961
Aaron's Art, Indianapolis 116436
Aaron's Galerie, Hamburg 103082
Aaronson House, Zichron Yaakov . . 023105
Aarquebus Antiques, Saint Leonards-on-Sea 086462
Aars, Buenos Aires 136690
A'Arte, Saint-Ouen 067694
Aart's Masters, Saint-Emilion 101143
Aarwun, Ngunnawal 094961
Aasiaat Katersugaasiviat Museum, Aasiaat Museum, Aasiaat 021538
Aasland Museum Taxidermy, Cranbrook 005306
A.A.T.A. Newsletter, Mundelin 136285
Aatma, Helsinki 137926
Aauld Antiques, Tauranga 079257
Aavikute Majamuuseum, Saaremaa Muuseum, Kuressaare 009375
Aavishkar, Kolkata 105732
AB Antik, Praha 060086
AB Antik, Praha 060087
A.B. Antiquités, Bruxelles 057797
AB Antiquités, Toulon (Var) 068436
AB Antiquités, Versailles 068789
AB Antykwariat, Kraków 079613
AB Artefacts, Marcoola 056159
AB Books, Croydon 136871
AB Furniture, Caulfield South 055655
AB-Grass, Wien 137282
AB Killsberg Bokhandel, Helsingborg 141113
A.B. Works, Pittsburgh . . . 091782, 132660
A.B.A. Bookhouse, Saint Kilda, Victoria 137080
ABA International Olympia Book Fair, London 093903
Aba la Esquina, Buenos Aires 055144
ABA Militaria, Saint-Fargeau-Ponthierry 067471
Abaad Antigüedades Boedo, Buenos Aires 055145
Ababord Antiquités, Marseille 064301
Abac, Bruxelles 137421
Abaca, Bordeaux 061568
Abaca, L'Aigle 063490
Abaca, Libourne 063813
Abaca, Marseille 064302
Abaca, Nice 065015
Abaca, Nice 065016
Abaca Conservation-Restauration, Paris 124538
Abacadabra, Nice 065017
Abacadabra, Nîmes 065165
Abacanthe, Pornic 066949
Abacar Antics, Valencia 081635
Abaco, Valencia 081636
Abaco-Borgobello, Julio M., Florida Oeste 055270
Abacule, Aix-en-Provence 060691
Abacus, Roma 127901
Abacus, Roma 127902
Abacus, Michel, Montréal 058891
Abacus Antiques, Louisville 089951
Abacus Art, Ashwood 123187
Abacusgomberi, Milano . . 075570, 140038
Abad Duato, Antonio, Zaragoza . . . 129798
Abada, Felix, New York 117552
Abadan Museum, Abadan 022545
Abadi, Berlin 101769
Abadía Compra, Buenos Aires 055146
Abadie, Alain, Artix 061001
Abafe, Saint-Thibéry 068012
Abakus, Gdańsk 129006
Abalache, Oklahoma City . 091450, 142714
Abandoned Planet Bookstore, San Francisco 142922
Abanico del Arte, Bogotá 098091
Abanicos Publicitarios Neder, Barcelona 080779
Abante, Portland 118962
Abante, Stockholm 110995
Abantos Restauracion, Madrid 129547
Abaris, Norwalk 135470
Abaris, Stuttgart 139748
Abarzua, Victor, Montréal 123779
Abascal, Ana & Patricia Medina, Sevilla 081565
Abashiri Kyodo Bijutsukan, Abashiri 026399
Abashiri Kyodo Hakubutsukan, Abashiri 026400
Abásolo, Bilbao 129419
Abatemps, Lyon 138128
Abaúj Antikvárium, Budapest 074656, 121634
Abaziou, Hélène, Marseille 064303
Abbacus, Den Haag 078158
Abbadie, Marie-Claude, Bordeaux . 061569
Abbakuse, Malmö 081858
Al-Abbar, Al-Kamara 112444
Al-Abbar, Dubai 112446
Al-Abbar, Dubai 112447
Abbas Antiques, Sherborne 086574
The Abbasid Palace Museum, Baghdad 022658
A Abbatia, Lisboa 079841, 140814
Abbaye Antiquité, Romainville 067199, 138584
Abbaye Antiquités, Montivilliers . . . 064699
Abbaye de Cluny, Cluny 011410
Abbaye de Flaran, Valence-sur-Baise 015097
Abbaye de Saint-Amand de Coly, Saint-Amand-de-Coly 014174
Abbaye des Moines, Bruxelles 057798
Abbaye des Moines, Bruxelles 057799
Abbaye du Val Richer, Saint-Ouen-le-Pin 014460
Abbaye Saint-André, Villeneuve-lès-Avignon 015275
Abbé, Christophe, Seynod 068239
Abbe Museum at Downtown, Bar Harbor 042013
Abbe Museum at Sieur de Monts Spring, Bar Harbor 042014
Abbeville, New York 135404
Abbeville, Paris 133508
Abbey, Ron, Bowral 136811
Abbey and Stones Museum, Margam 040421
Abbey Antiquarium, Knaresborough 141700
Abbey Antiques, Dublin 074888
Abbey Antiques, Hemel Hempstead 084648, 130780
Abbey Antiques, Norwood 056384
Abbey Antiques, Ramsey, Cambridgeshire 086325
Abbey Antiques, Romford 131425
Abbey Antiques, Stirling . . 086708, 131536
Abbey Antiques, Winnipeg 059445
Abbey Antiques & Art, Auckland . . . 078903
Abbey Artifacts, Duns 112970
Abbey Bookshop, Paris 138274
Abbey Cane and Rush Seaters, Loughborough 131238
Abbey Clock Clinic, Austin 131790
Abbey Clock Clinic, Austin 131791
Abbey Galleries, Bath 083410, 130345
Abbey Green, Utrecht 078787
Abbey House, Derby 084158, 130632
Abbey House Museum, Leeds Museums and Galleries, Leeds 039948
Abbey Museum of Art and Archaeology, Caboolture 000871
Abbey Pumping Station Museum, Leicester 039967
Abbey Road Gallery, London 113426
Abbey Visitor Centre, Bury Saint Edmunds 038922
Abbeydale Industrial Hamlet, Sheffield 040993
Abbeygate Gallery and Antiques, Grimsby 084535
Abbeys Auctions, Box Hill 120568
Abbona, Alessandro, Genova 075428
Abbot Hall Art Gallery, Kendal 039844
Abbot's, Kansas City 132202
Abbot's House, Arbroath 038519
Abbotsford House, Melrose 040443
Abbott, London 085049
Abbott, Woodbridge 122758
Abbott, A., Ipswich 084797
Abbott, Dick, Burwell 112770
Abbott, Nicholas, Hartley Wintney . . 084596
Abbott & Holder, London . 085050, 113427
Abby Aldrich Rockefeller Folk Art Museum, Williamsburg 049177

ABC, Amsterdam 140276
ABC Antiquariat, Bonn 138889
ABC-Antiquariat, Hamburg 139164
ABC Antiquariat, Zürich 141316
ABC Antiques, Knokke-Heist 058236
ABC Antiques, Books and Collectables, Port Macquarie 056474, 137050
A.B.C. Antiquités, Marseille 064304
ABC Architectuurcentrum Haarlem, Haarlem 029650
ABC Book Store, Toronto 137688
ABC Books and Posters, Denver . . . 115962, 142376
ABC Chalonnaises, Chalon-sur-Saône 062077
ABC Coin Company, Cincinnati 088204
ABC Coin Company, Indianapolis . . 089258
ABC Coinarama, San Francisco . . . 092704
ABC Collectibles, Tucson 093190
ABC Collections, Tonnay-Charente . 068427
ABC de la Carte Postale Ancienne, Lyon 064045
ABC del Marco, Santiago de Chile . 059482
ABC Depôt, Tinqueux 068422
ABC Dépôt Vente, La Valette-du-Var 063458
ABC-Galerie, Ansfelden 001692
ABC Galerie, Bruxelles 096123
ABC Gallery, Poznań 109040
ABC-Kirja, Turku 137994
ABC Librairie, Nancy 064855
Abc Pascal, Clamart 062314
ABC Pascal, Paris 065348
ABC & Viccari, Hove 130808
A.B.C.D, Châteauneuf 062198
A.B.C.D., Louviers 064016
Abcdaire, Angers 060840
ABCL, Liège 137515
ABCollectables, Lobethal 056108
Abd El-Fatah El-Sayed Soliman, Alexandria 060415
ABD Group, Chicago 115321
Abdeen Palace Museum, Cairo 009289
Abderhalden, Emil, Forch 135012
Abdij Museum, Sint-Truiden 003764
Abdis, Maulette 064427
Abdis, Sorel-Moussel 068262
Abdou, Casablanca 077629, 128510
A.B.D.S., Anglet 060867
A.B.D.S., Pau 066695
Abdül Antik, İstanbul 083112
Al-Abdul Wahab, Riyadh 080370
Abe, Calgary 058777
Abé, A., Aalst 057656
ABEAM Antique Restoration, Northolt 131325
Abecassis, Maxime, Mitry-Mory . . . 064571
Abecassis, Paul, Saint-Ouen 067695
ABECEDA Antiquariat, München . . . 139492
l'Abécédaire, Nice 138248
Abegg-Stiftung, Riggisberg 037455
Abeille, Argenteuil 060961
Abeille Antiquité, Saint-Ouen 067696
Abeille Débarras, Auzits 061112
Abel, Los Angeles 132230
Abel, Oslo 079407
Abel, Saint-Ouen 067697
Abel, A., Paris 099903
Abel, Esther, Paris 124539
Abel & Armand, Bruxelles 057800
Abel Tasman Kabinet, Lutjegast . . . 029882
Abelard, Bruxelles 137422
Abelard, Toronto 137689
Abelein-Windsheimer & Windsheimer, Blaufelden 069866
Abell, A.N., Los Angeles 122942
Abella, Antibes-Juan-les-Pins 060910
Abella, Barcelona 080780
Abella, Monaco 077593
Abels, Enschede 140419
Abencerage, Paris 065349, 138275
Abend, Denver 115963
Abendstern, Heuchelheim, Kreis Gießen 071507
Abeni Guerra, Brescia 127201
Mario Abeni & Stefano Querciagrossa, Modena 127714
Abeno Ueda Bijutsu-ten, Osaka . . . 077171
Abenteuermuseum Saarbrücken - Sammlung Heinz Rox-Schulz, Saarbrücken 019958
Aberbach, New York 117553
Aberbach, Susan, New York 117554
Abercauph, Carole, Philadelphia . . . 132603
Aberconwy House, Conwy 039135
Abercron, von, München 104133
Aberdeen Art Gallery, Aberdeen . . . 038438
Aberdeen Arts Centre, Aberdeen . . 038439
Aberdeen House Antiques, London . 085051
Aberdeen Maritime Museum, Aberdeen 038440
Aberdeen University Natural History Museum, Aberdeen 038441
Aberdeen University Natural Philosophy Museum, Aberdeen 038442
Aberdeenshire Farming Museum, Mintlaw 040479
Aberdona Gallery, Alloa 038487
Aberfeldy Gallery, Aberfeldy 112483
Aberford Antiques, Aberford 083245
Abergavenny Art Gallery, Toodyay . . 095340
Abergavenny Museum, Abergavenny 038457
Aberle, Bruxelles 120716
Abernethy Museum, Abernethy 038459
Abernethy Nature Heritage Museum, Abernethy 004985
Aberseer Heimathaus, Lipphaus-Museum, Strobl 002722
Abertillery Museum, Abertillery . . . 038460
Aberystwyth Arts Centre, Aberystwyth 038461
Aberystwyth Yesterday, Aberystwyth 038462
Abe's Antique Attic, Indianapolis . . 089259
Abe's Antiques, Atlanta 087439
ABGG's Gallery, Makati 108818
Abgineh Va Sofalineh, Teheran 022604
Abguss Sammlung antiker Plastik, Berlin 015978
Abgußsammlung antiker Skulpturen, Institut für Altertumswissenschaften der Friedrich-Schiller-Universität Jena, Jena 018102
Abhai Smarak Panchal Sangrahalaya, Bareilly 022019
Abhey Arts, Bromley 112742
Abid, Ezzedine, Saint-Nazaire (Loire-Atlantique) 067682
Abigael's Antiques, Annerley 055347
Abigail Adams Smith Museum, New York 046367
Abim-Pljus, Sankt-Peterburg 080289
Abingdon, New York 117555
Abingdon House Antiques, Ilminster 084789
Abingdon Museum, Abingdon 038466
Abinger Bazaar, Abinger Hammer . . 083250
Abington, Finningham . . . 084407, 141614
Abington, Philadelphia 091595
Abington Art Center, Jenkintown . . 044853
Abington Museum, Northampton . . 040593
Abis, Bonaria Giuseppa, Cagliari . . . 075196
Abitat, Ascona 111133
Abiuso, Benito, Roma 127903
Abkar Museum, Sa'd-Abad Museum, Teheran 022605
A.B.L, Chassy 062177
Able, Houston 088987
Able, Saint Paul 092337
Able Art, Rotorua 108550
A.B.L.E. Tyson China Repairs, South Yarra 123306
Ableart, Houston 116260
ABM, Saint-Ouen 138602
ABM-Utvikling, Oslo 053938
ABN Numismatique, Colmar 062399
ABN Numismatique, Saint-Louis . . . 067590
Abner, Tampa 093096
A.B.O, Plouénan 066867
Aboa Vetus - Arkeologis-historiallinen Museo, Turku 010159
Abode, Providence 119067
Aboitiz Badiola, Oscar, Santiago de Chile 059483
ABOL, Paris 065350
Abon, Louis, Dijon 062637
Abony Lajos Falumúzeum, Abony . . 021615
Aboriginal and Pacific Art, Ivanhoe . 094663
Aboriginal and Pacific Art, Sydney . 095265
Aboriginal and Tribal Art Centre, Sydney 095266
Aboriginal Art, Echuca 055787
Aboriginal Art and Artifacts, Perth . . 056451
Aboriginal Art and Culture Centre, Alice Springs 094132
Aboriginal Art Centres, Paddington . 095012
Aboriginal Art Centres, Sydney 095267
Aboriginal Art Galerie, Speyer 104931
Aboriginal Art Galleries of Australia, Melbourne 094802
Aboriginal Art Gallery Concept Store, Sydney 056663, 095268
Aboriginal Art Museum, Utrecht . . . 030222
Aboriginal Art Online, West End . . . 056814
Aboriginal Art Prints, Darlinghurst . . 094450
Aboriginal Artists of Australia, Newcastle 056329
Aboriginal Arts, Vancouver 097406
Aboriginal Arts Adelaide, Adelaide . 055309
Aboriginal Desert Art Gallery, Alice Springs 094133
Aboriginal Dreamings Gallery Ginninderra, Nicholls 094962
Aboriginal Fine Arts Gallery, Darwin 094456
Aboriginal Gallery of Dreamings, Melbourne 056180, 094803
Aboriginalartworks.com, Perth 056452
Aboriginart, Toronto 097206
Abos, Nérac 064972
Abott's, Turramurra 056744
Abou & Mireille Benibre, Thérèse, Toulouse 068473
Abou Dabou, Berlin 138729
Abou Jurab, Isa, Damascus 083050
Aboucaya, Georges, Paris 065351
Aboudaram, Christian, La Roquebrussanne 063443
Abousleiman, Farid, Beirut 140219
About Antiques, Westbourne Park . . 056817
About Studio Gallery, Bangkok 112224
About Time for Clocks, Greenwich . 055916
Abovecloud, Los Angeles . 089670, 142485
ABP, Vincennes 125036
ABPi, Lausanne 111609
Abracadabra, Bordeaux 061570
Abracadabra Bookshop, Rockfort . . 142834
Abracadabroc, Vernon 068785
Abraham, Eleanor, New York 090651
Abraham & Co., Jackie, Miami 090115
Abraham Gallery, Southsea 114468
Abraham Krinizi Museum, Ramat Gan 023048
Abraham Lincoln Birthplace, Hodgenville 044565
Abraham Lincoln Book Shop, Chicago 142270
Abraham Lincoln Museum, Lincoln Memorial University, Harrogate . . 044455
Abraham Ojanperän Museo, Liminka 009828
Abrahams, Hamburg 103083
Abrahams, Christine, Richmond, Victoria 095135
Abrahams, Mike, Lichfield 141730
Abraham's Mosterdmakerij, Eenrum 029529
Abral Artproduct, Bucureşti 129213
Abrams, Harry N., Benteld 134798
Abrams, Harry N., New York 135405
Al-Abrar, Sharjah 083208
Abrash, Dubai 112448
Abravanel, Maren, Cully 141239
Abraxas Studio, San Diego 132837
Abreu, Belo Horizonte 058401
Abreu, Sacramento 119132
Abreu, Francisco F. Plácido, Porto . 109362
Abreu, Iara, Belo Horizonte 096451
Abreu, M., Fritzlar 070901
Abri du Passé, Castres . . . 062025, 138068
Abri du Passé, Marseille 064305
Abri Pataud, Gisement Préhistorique et Musée, Les Eyzies-de-Tayac-Sireuil 012619
Abri Préhistorique de Laugerie Basse, Gisement Préhistorique, Les Eyzies-de-Tayac-Sireuil 012620
Abrocadabra-Passé par Ici, Neuilly-sur-Seine 064983
Abrocantique Antiquités Brocantes, Chalon-sur-Saône 062078
Abrons Arts Center, Gallery of Henry Street Settlement, New York 046278
Abs, Hans-Joachim, Essen 102667
ABSA Group Museum, Johannesburg 034638
Absalom's Gallery, Broken Hill 094299
Absenta, León 110393
Abside Restauraciones, Madrid . . . 129548
Absidial, Plaudren 101010
Absinthe, Angers 060841
Absinthe Antiquité, Angers 060842
Absolu, Notre-Dame-des-Landes . . 065235
Absolute Antiques, Cincinnati 088205, 122851
Absolute Art, Nottingham 114170
Absolute Art Company, Mermaid Beach 094838
Absolute Art Gallery, Knokke-Heist . 096315
Absolute Art Gallery, New Orleans . 117383
Absolutely, Toronto 059111
Absolutely North, Toronto 059112
Abstein, Atlanta 114842
Abstract Books, Indianapolis 142448
Abstractie Versus Realisme, Amsterdam 107647
Abstrait, Toulouse 101326
Abstrakt Creations, Chicago 115322
Absynthe Antiquité, Angers 060843
ABTart, Stuttgart 104962
Abteilung Handwerk und dörfliches Leben des Heimatmuseums Neu-Ulm, Neu-Ulm 019212
Abteilung Kunsterziehung, Universität Mozarteum Salzburg, Salzburg . . 049644
Abteilung Kunstgeschichte, Südasien Institut, Ruprecht-Karls-Universität Heidelberg, Heidelberg 050125
Abu Ahmed, Dubai 083181
Abu Ahmed, Ibraham, Manama . . . 057615
Abu Al-Mudhyaf, Ruwi 079519
Abu Qais, Madinat Al-Sultan Qaboos 108766
El Abuelito Arturo, Bogotá 059800
Abuelo, Valparaíso 059561
Abuk Staraja Kniga, Sankt-Peterburg 140923
Aburaya, Sendai 077207
Aburto V., Juan Carlos, Concepción 059477
ABV Antik-Servis, Velikij Novgorod . 080341
ABV Services, Paris 065352
Abyss Marine, Liège 058280
Abysse, Morges 111750
Abysses, Donville-les-Bains 062714
A.C., Roma 076261
A.C. Gilbert's Discovery Village, Salem 047749
AC Vent, La Roche-sur-Yon 063413
A.C. White Gallery, Bloemfontein . . 034554
ACA Galleries, München 104134
ACA Galleries, New York 117556
Acacia, Madrid 129549
Acacia Antiques, Berwick 055499
Acacia Out Of Print, Adelaide 136765
Acacia Tree, Singapore 080412
Academia, Freiburg im Breisgau . . . 139103
Academia Anticuario Euroartes, Bogotá 059801, 123889
Academia Art, Salzburg 095714
Academia Brasileira, Rio de Janeiro 049753
Academia Brasileira de Arte, São Paulo 004496
Academia Brasileira de Arte, São Paulo 049757

Academia Brasileira de Letras, Rio de Janeiro 004329
Academia Chilena de Bellas Artes, Santiago de Chile 049838
Academia de Arte George Enescu, Iaşi 050624
Academia de Arte Vizuale Ioan Andreescu, Cluj-Napoca 050622
Academia de Artes Plásticas San Alejandro, Marianao 049883
Academia de Bellas Artes, Universidad Autónoma Tomás Frías, Potosí 049744
Academia de Bellas Artes Remigio Crespo Toral, Universidad de Cuenca, Cuenca 049915
Academia de Dibujo y Pintura Mirart Mirasierras, Madrid 050720
Academia de España ó Storia, Archeologia e Belle Arti, Roma 050414
Academia de Letras e Artes do Planalto, Luzmiânia 049749
Academia de San Carlos, Universidad Nacional Autónoma de México, México 050533
Academia do Saber, Rio de Janeiro 137567
Academia Gallery of Heffers Virgin Academy, Erevan 094107
Academia Music, Tokyo 140181
Academia Nacional de Belas-Artes, Lisboa 050612
Academia Nacional de Bellas Artes, Buenos Aires 049593
Academia Nacional de Bellas Artes Hernando Siles, La Paz 049742
Academia Polona Artium, Roma 050415
Academia Polona Artium, Polish University London, München 050184
Academia Provincial de Bellas Artes, Cádiz 050715
Academic File International News and Photo Syndication, London 136146
Academie Beeldende Kunsten, Oudenaarde 049726
Academie Beeldende Kunsten Maastricht, Hogeschool Zuyd, Maastricht 050563
Academie Brasschaat, Brasschaat 049679
Académie d'Auguste, Le Puy-en-Velay 099453
Académie des Antiquaires de France, Maubourguet 052885
Academie des Arts de Woluwe-Saint-Pierre, Bruxelles 049681, 133254
Academie des Arts et Métiers Constantin Meunier, Bruxelles 049682
Académie des Beaux-Arts, Kinshasa 049872
Académie des Beaux-Arts, Paris 049968
Académie des Beaux-Arts, Verviers 049737
Académie des Beaux-Arts Alphonse Darville, Charleroi 049693
Académie des Beaux-Arts de la Ville de Tournai, Tournai 049735
Academie des Beaux-Arts de Namur, Namur 049723
Académie des Beaux-Arts de Saint-Josse-ten-Noode, Bruxelles 049683
Académie des Beaux-Arts et Arts Décoratifs de la Ville de Binche, Binche 049678
Académie des Beaux-Arts Saint-Gilles, Bruxelles 049684
Académie des Inscriptions et des Belles-Lettres, Paris 049969
Académie des Sciences, Arts et Belles-Lettres de Dijon, Dijon 049946, 052886
Académie des Sciences, Belles Lettres et Arts, Lyon 049953
Academie en Vaktekenschool, Temse 049733
Académie Internationale de la Céramique, Genève 054164
Académie Libanaise des Beaux-Arts, Beirut 050518
Académie R. Defossez, Spa 049731
Académie Royale des Beaux-Arts, Liège 049715
Académie Royale des Beaux-Arts de Bruxelles, Bruxelles 049685
Académie Royale des Sciences, des Lettres et des Beaux-Arts de Belgique, Bruxelles 049686
Academie van Bouwkunst, Groningen 050558
Academie voor beeldende Kunst en Vormgeving Arnhem, Arnhem 050554
Academie voor Beeldende Kunsten, Sint-Truiden 049730
Academie voor Beeldende Kunsten Mol, Mol 049721
Academie voor Schone Kunsten, Brugge 049680
Academie voor Schone Kunsten, Turnhout 049736
Academisch Historisch Museum van de Universiteit Leiden, Leiden 029846
Academy Art Museum, Easton 043587
Academy Billiard Company, West Byfleet 087084
Academy Books, Portsmouth 131392, 142007
Academy Fine Books, Las Vegas 142481
Academy Galleries, Wellington 030632
The Academy Gallery, Beverly Hills 042192
Academy Gallery, New Orleans Academy of Fine Arts, New Orleans 046246
Academy Hall Museum of the Rocky Hill Historical Society, Rocky Hill 047518
Academy of Art College, San Francisco 052119
Academy of Arts, Cairo 049918
Academy of Arts, Pepperdine University, Los Angeles 051629
Academy of Arts of the Ukraine, Kyïv 050795
Academy of Arts of Uzbekistan, Taškent 052416
Academy of Design and Decoratives Art, Brisbane 049610
Academy of Fine Arts, Berhampur 050293
Academy of Fine Arts, Kolkata 050309, 105733
Academy of Fine Arts and Literature, Delhi 105644
Academy of Fine Arts Museum, Kolkata 022211
Academy of Natural Sciences of Philadelphia Museum, Philadelphia 046917
Academy of Pencraft, Stone Carving, Calligraphy and Painting, Shanghai 049855
Academy of Spherical Arts, Toronto 006579
Academy of the Fine Arts, Hong Kong 049850
Academy of Wall Artistry, Alexandria 050883, 114839
Academy Picture Restorations, Sydney 123313
Academy Upholstery, Kingston-upon-Hull 130848
Acadia Art & Rare Books, Toronto 137690
Acadia University Art Gallery, Wolfville 006877
L'Acajou, Beirut 077379
Acajou, Liège 123644
Acajou Bambou, Paris 065353
Acala Gallery, Bangkok 112225
Acanthe, Ambert 060790
Acanthe, Auch 061047
Acanthe, La Varenne-Saint-Hilaire 063463
Acanthe, Le Vésinet 063729
Acanthe, Marseille 064306
Acanthe, Nice 065018
Acanthe, Saint-Raphaël 067982
Acanthe, Vannes (Morbihan) 068711
Acanthe, Versailles 068790
Acanthe Antiquités, Grenoble 063042
Acanthus, Cincinnati 088206
Acanthus, New York 117557
Acanthus, Nottingham 086128, 131335
Acanthus, Oslo 134847
Acanthus, Twello 128848
Acanthus, Utrecht 140541
Acanthus, Versmold 074198
Acanthus Books, New York 142625
Acanthus Leaf Antiques, Houston 088988
Acanthus Miniature, Firenze 106026
Acanto, Donostia-San Sebastián 129495
Acanto, Roma 076262
Acanto Cuadros, Almeria 110091
Acapulco Arte Galería, Bogotá 098092
ACC Galerie Weimar, Weimar, Thüringen 105184
Accademia Albertina di Belle Arti, Torino 050438
Accademia Cignaroli di Pittura e Scultura, Affresco ed Incisione, Verona 050449
Accademia dei Concordi, Rovigo 050433
Accademia dei Virtuosi, Roma 140094
Accademia del Libro Usato S. Gallo, Firenze 134577
Accademia di Architettura, Università della Svizzera Italiana, Mendrisio 050771
Accademia di Belle Arti, Bari 050352
Accademia di Belle Arti, Bologna 050355
Accademia di Belle Arti, Carrara 050357
Accademia di Belle Arti, Catania 050359
Accademia di Belle Arti, Catanzaro 050361
Accademia di Belle Arti, Foggia 050372
Accademia di Belle Arti, Frosinone 050374
Accademia di Belle Arti, L'Aquila 050380
Accademia di Belle Arti, Lecce 050382
Accademia di Belle Arti, Macerata 050386
Accademia di Belle Arti, Napoli 050397
Accademia di Belle Arti, Palermo 050402
Accademia di Belle Arti, Reggio Calabria 050413
Accademia di Belle Arti, Sassari 050434
Accademia di Belle Arti, Urbino 050441
Accademia di Belle Arti, Venezia 050444
Accademia di Belle Arti A. Galli, Como 050362
Accademia di Belle Arti di Brera, Milano 050387
Accademia di Belle Arti di Ravenna, Ravenna 050412
Accademia di Belle Arti di Roma, Roma 050416
Accademia di Belle Arti e Liceo Artistico, Firenze 050365
Accademia Giacinto Gigante, Napoli 106356
Accademia Italiana di Restauro, Milano 050388
Accademia Leonardo da Vinci: Journal of Studies and Bibliography of Vinciana, Florence 135858
Accademia Ligustica di Belle Arti, Genova 050377
Accademia Nazionale dei Lincei, Roma 050417
Accademia Nazionale di Belle Arti, Parma 050404
Accademia Nazionale di San Luca, Roma 050418
Accademia Petrarca di Lettere, Arte e Scienze, Arezzo 050351
Accademia Tedesca, Roma 050419
Accart, Paris 099904
Accent Antiques, Austin 087545
Accent Arts, Minneapolis 117232
Accent Fine Art, Phoenix 118857
Accent Fine Gifts, Phoenix 118858
Accent Gallery, Wembley 095384
Accent Office Art, Dallas 115816
Accent on, Portland 091882
Accent on Antiques, Pittsburgh 091783
Accent on Books, Wellington 140668
Accent on Design, Philadelphia 091596
Accent Your Home, Jacksonville 089363
Accents and Beyond Consignment, Minneapolis 090333
Accents Antiques, Miami 090116
Accents Toniques, Marseille 138190
Accès Bijoux, Montréal 058892
Access Art, Auckland 108294
Access Art, West Perth 123327
Access Artisans, New York 117558
The Accokeek Foundation, Accokeek 041574
Accord Galéria, Budapest 105485
Accordeon en Harmonica Museum, Malden 029905
Accou, Pascal, Seichamps 068196
Accra, Ille-sur-Têt 063203
l'Accroche-Coeur-Ducloy, Mons 058336
L'Accrosonge, Paris 099905
Accumulations, Birmingham 087728
Accurate Antiques, Columbus 088372
Ace Art, Winnipeg 006837
Ace Art, Winnipeg 097569
Ace Auctions, Ferntree Gully 120583
Ace Coin Shop, Salt Lake City 092409
ACE Contemporary Exhibitions, Los Angeles 116693
Ace Furniture Refinishers, San Antonio 132802
Ace Gallery, New York 117559
Ace International, Boronia 055523
Ace of Clubs House, Texarkana 048538
Ace Traders, Palmerston North 079212
Ace Upholstery, Albuquerque 131734
Aceña Bonilla, Margarita, Madrid 129550
Acero, Giuseppe, Roma 127904
Acervo Antiguidade, Belo Horizonte 123686
Acervo Artístico Cultural dos Palácios do Governo, São Paulo 004497
Acervo Didático de Invertebrados I e II, Instituto de Biociências, São Paulo 004498
Aces High Aviation Gallery, Wendover 114661
Acetres, Sevilla 081566
Acevedo, Alicante 080754
Acevedo, William, Cali 059870, 123914
ACF, Montpellier 064727
ACF Art Collector's Fund, Zürich 112023
ACF les Sculptures, Yverdon-les-Bains 112011
Achallé, Marc, Fontenay-le-Comte 062902
Achard, Dominique, Bligny-sur-Ouche 098975
Acharya Jogesh Chandra Purakirti Bhavan, Bangiya Sahitya Parisat Bishnupur Branch, Bishnupur 022044
Achat 22, Šumen 137608
Achat Antiquité Brocante, Athis-Mons 061017
Achat Antiquités, Nice 065019
Achenbach & Costa, Düsseldorf 133885
Achermann, Jeannette, Luzern 130097
Achète Tout, Bruxelles 057801
Achète Tout Antiques, Bruxelles 057802
Achille, Nice 065020
Achilles, H. & E., Eschershausen 070611
Achkal, Jounieh 077430
Achleitner, Karl, Steyr 137266
Achnamian, Pierre, Le Rouret 063706
Achour, Paris 065354
Acht-Eins, Stuttgart 073950
Acht P!, Bonn 102175
Achtelik, Peter-Michael, Gelsenkirchen 070955
Achter de dikke Deur, Hoogeveen 140463
Achter de Zuilen, Overveen 030037
Achter 't Hoes, Emmen 108013
Achterhoeks Museum 1940-1945, Hengelo, Gelderland 029726
Achternkamp, Petra, Darmstadt 125442
Achternkamp, Stefan, Obernzenn 126579
Achtiani, Mehdi, Tours 068575
ACI-Antique Chine Import, Concarneau 062441
Acker, Rolf, Freiburg im Breisgau 070818
Acker, Rolf, Freiburg im Breisgau 070819
Ackerbürgermuseum, Gartz 017329
Ackerbürgermuseum, Reichenbach, Oberlausitz 019775
Ackerbürgermuseum Haus Leck, Grebenstein 017514
Ackerl, Walter, Graz 123357
Ackerman, Waitara 056792
Ackermann, München 134212
Ackermann, Wilhelm, Wuppertal 074519
Ackermann & Johnson, London 085052, 113428

Ackersgott, A., Duisburg 070472
Ackland Art Museum, Chapel Hill . . 042713
Acland Coal Mine Museum, Acland . 000696
Acme, Boston 131841
Acme, San Francisco 119577
ACME Art Gallery, Columbus 043104
ACME Books, Houston 142420
ACME Fine Art, Boston 115135
ACME Gallery, Los Angeles 116694
Acme Gallery, New Orleans 117384
ACME Studios, London 054265
A.C.O. Art de Chine & d'Orient, Paris 065355
Acoma, Firenze 135859
Aconerre Arte Conservazione Restauri, Milano 127508
Acorn, Armadale, Victoria 055354
Acorn, Chicago 088000
Acorn, Sheffield 086551
Acorn Antiques, Deganwy 084155
Acorn Antiques, Dulverton 084225
Acorn Antiques, London 085053
Acorn Antiques, Worthing 087263
Acorn Auctions, Salford 122683
Acorn Books, San Francisco 142923
Acorn Bookshop, Columbus 142348
Acorn Furniture, Atlanta 131757
Acorn Galleries, Billingshurst 112641
Acorn Hall House Museum, Morristown 046032
Acorn Lane Antiques, Seattle 092943
Acquario, Roma 106479
Acquario Associazione Culturale, Roma 053724
Acquavella Galleries, New York . . . 117560
Acquilino, Silvio, Milano 127509
Acquire, Arnhem 107845
Acquisitions, Atlanta 087440
Acquisitions, Charlotte 087922
Acquisitions, London 085054
Acquisitions, Los Angeles 089671
Acquisitions, Prahran 056486
A.C.R., Paris 124540
ACR Antiquités, Rouen 067235
ACR Edition Internationale, Courbevoie 133464
ACR Gallery, Yoxford 114757
Acri Ciro, Napoli 075932
Acropolis, Nice 065021
Acrostiche, Saint-Étienne 067434
ACS Editions, Milano 134601
Act Conservation Services, Baltimore 131811
ACT Galerie, Champigny-sur-Marne 099111
Acta Historiae Artium/Academiae Scientiarium Hungaricae, Budapest 135838
Acta International, Roma 106480
Actana, Paris 065356
Act'Art, Marmande 124387
Acte 2, Paris 099906
Actée, Charenton-le-Pont 099118
Actes Sud, Arles 133450
Acti dei Convegni di Studi Sulla Magna Grecia, Roma 135860
Action, Columbus 131974
Action, Indianapolis 132146
Action &CO, Indianapolis 132147
Action Auction Bendigo, Bendigo . . 120564
Action Auction Bendigo, Bendigo East 120566
Action Auktioner i Östjämtland, Hammarstrand 122151
Action Images, Lincolnwood 122940
Action Sports Cards, Cleveland 142327
Actions Timbres Monnaies Minéraux, Angers 060844, 120894
Active Imagination, Albuquerque . . 087359
Activité Bois, Marseille 124388
Acton Scott Historic Working Farm, Church Stretton 039090
Actor, Tokyo 077229
Actua, L'Isle-sur-la-Sorgue 063915
Actualité des Arts Plastiques, Paris . 135681
Actuel Art, Paris 099907
Actuell & Antiques, Flensburg 070696
Acuarela, Badajoz 110096
Açude Museum, Museus Castro Maya, Rio de Janeiro 004330
Acuña, José Antonio, Bogotá 098093
Acuna & Hansen, Los Angeles 116695
Acuñaciones, Barcelona 080781
Acworth, Semaphore 056583
Acxelle Antique, Hyères 063185
AD, Athinai 105380
A.D., Milano 075571
AD Antiques, Johannesburg 080698
AD Antiques, Woodseaves 087234
Ad-Art Decor, İstanbul 136134
Ad Art Decoration, Firenze 127283
A.D. Buck Museum of Natural History and Science, Nothern Oklahoma College, Tonkawa 048577
Ad-Dukkan, Sharjah 141375
A.D. German Warehouse, Richland Center 047394
Ad Infinitum Galleries, San Juan . . . 108859
Ad Invest, Napoli 106357
Ad Lib, Hong Kong 059584
Ad Plus, Praha 137812
Ad Sumos Antiguidades, Rio de Janeiro 058532
ADAC, Paris 099908
Adac Grafica, Modena 106344
Adachi Institute of Woodcut Prints, Tokyo 107007
Adachi Museum of Art, Yasugi 027327
Adalbert-Stifter-Haus, Oberösterreichisches Literaturmuseum und Adalbert-Stifter-Gedenkraum, Linz 002240
Adam, Bath 130346
Adam, Luxembourg 077468
Adam, Melbourne 056181, 094804
Adam, Neckargemünd 072950
Adam, Paris 065357
Adam, Alice, Chicago 115323
Adam, Costas, Athinai 134482
Adam, David, Lindfield 085003
Adam, F., Halle, Saale 103060
Adam, Günter, Lauenburg 072164
Adam, Henry, Tarbes 121264
Adam, Jacques, Vannes (Morbihan) 101426
Adam, James, Dublin 121659
Adam, Pasquale, Köln 103576
Adam, Philippe, Paris 065358
Adam, Philippe, Pompièrre 066901
Adam Art, Wellington 108607
Adam Auctions, Burnham-on-Sea . 122441
Adam & Dave's Group, Buffalo 087855
Adam E. Treganza Anthropology Museum, San Francisco State University, San Francisco 047847
Adam East Museum Art Center, Moses Lake 046047
Adam & Eve, London 141743
Adam & Eve Antiques, Dallas 088449
Adam Gallery, Bath 112567
Adam Gallery, London . . . 085055, 113429
Adam Gallery, Penarth 114222
Adam-Ries-Museum, Annaberg-Buchholz 015548
Adam & Sheridan, London 130913
Adam Thoroughgood House, Virginia Beach 048792
Adam & Ziege, Kleinmachnow 103563
Ādama Alkšņa Memoriālais Muzejs, Rūjiena 027773
Adamar, Miami 117012
Adamczyk, Michał, Warszawa 134858
Adamec, Eugen, Rožňava 080635
Adami, Paolo, Torino 076754
Adami Casaravilla, H., Montevideo . 122769
Adami & Pagano, Milano 127510
Adamiak, Unna 074159
Adamiak, Werl 074338
Adamiec & Schmidt, Hannover 071374, 125861
Adamo, Las Vegas 116597
Adam's, Brescia 075136
Adams, Chester 083947, 130555
Adams, Milwaukee 090266
Adams, München 072626, 126342
Adam's, Pittsburgh 132661
Adams, Richmond 092053
Adam's, San Antonio 132803
Adams, Ansel, Fresno 116169
Adams, B.J., Washington 120237
Adams, George, New York 117561
Adams & Co., G.H., London 130914
Adams, Henry, Chichester 122464
Adams, Jacqueline, Atlanta 087441
Adams, John, London 113430
Adams, John, New York 117562
Adams, Mary, Birmingham 087729
Adams, Maurice, Miami 117013
Adams, Norine, New York 132428
Adams, Norman, London 085056
Adams, Pamela, Birchgrove 055503
Adams, Robert Henry, Chicago 115324
Adams, Rodney, Pwllheli 086319
Adams, Tony, Ipswich 084798
Adams, V., Frome 141620
Adams Antiques, Nantwich 086032
Adam's Aukcja Antyków, Poznań . . 121896
Adams Avenue Bookstore, San Diego 142896
Adams County Historical Museum, Decatur 043354
Adams County Historical Society Museum, Gettysburg 044182
Adams County Historical Society Museum, Lind 045322
Adams County Museum, Brighton . . 042416
Adams Davidson, Washington 093374, 120238
Adams House, Deadwood 043338
Adams Igloo Wildlife Museum, Smithers 006481
Adams Mark, London 113431
Adams Museum, Deadwood 043339
Adams National Historical Park, Quincy 047301
Adams Old Stone Grist Mill, Bellows Falls 042122
Adams Room Antiques, Dorking . . . 084183
Adams State College Luther Bean Museum, Alamosa 041593
Adamski, Konstanz 072045, 121483
Adamski, Frehrking & Wiesehöfer, Köln 103577
Adamson, David, Washington 120239, 135521
Adamson, M., Toronto 097207
Adamson, Nigel, Harrogate 084567, 130759
Adamson Armoury, Skipton 086622
Adamson-Duvannes, Los Angeles . 116696
Adamson-Eric Museum, Eesti Kunstimuuseum, Tallinn 009394
Adamstuen, Oslo 140695
Adana Arkeoloji Müzesi, Adana Müzeleri, Adana 037990
Adana Devlet Güzel Sanatlar Galerisi, Adana 037991
Adana Etnografya Müzesi, Adana Müzeleri, Adana 037992
Adare Antiques, Adare 074853
Adare Trinity Museum, Adare 022675
Ada's Place, Millthorpe 094851
Aday, Pazo de, Alicante 080755
ADC, Firenze 075265
Adda, Robert, Saint-Ouen 067698
Addams, Amanda, Bulleen 120571
Addenda Art Expressions, Lyon . . . 064046
Addenda Espace Image, Lyon 064047
Addenda Galerie d'Art, Lyon 099533
Addi, Las Vegas 116598
Addington - Ryde House of Heritage, Ryde 001444
Addison, Oakland 091403
Addison & Assoc., San Francisco . . 119578
Addison, Toronto 059113
Addison Fine Art, London . 085057, 130915
Addison Gallery of American Art, Andover 041721
Addison & Ripley, Washington 120240
Addison Ross, London 113432
Addisow, Ronald, Krefeld 072063
Adducci, Massimo, Roma 127905
ADEC, London 085058
Adega, Houston 088989
Adel, Tomas, Berlin 101770
Adelaide Antiquarian Books, Adelaide 136766
Adelaide Artistic Glass, Glenelg . . . 094588
Adelaide Arts Society, North Adelaide 052449, 094970
Adelaide Booksellers, Adelaide 136767
Adelaide Central Gallery, Norwood . 001344
Adelaide Central School of Art, Norwood 049616, 094991
Adelaide City Council Civic Collection, Adelaide 000701
Adelaide Exchange, Adelaide 055310
Adelaide Gaol, Thebarton 001547
Adelaide House Museum, Alice Springs 000732
Adelaide Hunter Hoodless Homestead, Saint George 006338
Adelaide Junction Antiques, Wellington 079311
Adélaïde le Grenier, Pontlevoy 066942
Adelaide Lithuanian Museum and Archives, Norwood 001345
Adelaide Masonic Centre Museum, Adelaide 000702
Adelaide Old Books, Kent Town . . . 136960
Adelaide River Railway Heritage Precinct, Adelaide River 000718
Adelaide's Antiques and Gallery, Wentworth Falls 056813
Adelantado, Luis, Valencia 110794
Adelca, Pointe-à-Pitre 134494
Adele's Gallery of Fine Arts, Canterbury 094367
Adelhausermuseum, Natur- und Völkerkunde, Freiburg im Breisgau 017226
Adelin, Antwerpen 057668
Adelman, J., San Antonio . 092472, 119385
Adelmann von Adelmannsfelden, Jörg Graf, Abtsgmünd 121291
Adelphi, Milano 134602
Adelphi, Montevideo 087301
Adelphi, Punta del Este 087353
Adelphi, Redlynch Salisbury 114301
Adelson, New York 117563
Adelson, Paul, Dallas 115817
Aden Society of Arts, Aden 055124
Adena State Memorial, Home of Thomas Worthington, Chillicothe 042897
Ader, Françoise, Arcachon 060949
Ader, Geoffroy, Paris 065359
Ader, Rémi, Paris 121106
Aderton, Stockholm 141137
Adès, Ginette, Saint-Ouen 067699
Adet, Jean-Louis, Longnes 063982
Adfontes, Verein für Grafische Gestaltung am Platz Wien, Wien 052501
Adhoc, Vigo 110859
Adi-Art, Łódź 108999
ADI Art Gallery, Kathmandu 107572
Adia-M, Sankt-Peterburg 134881
Adiex, Paris 065360
Adin, Antwerpen 057669
Adina, Oberwil 111794
Adirondack Center Museum, Elizabethtown 043655
Adirondack Museum, Blue Mountain Lake 042275
Adıyaman Müzesi, Adıyaman 037994
Adjinsoff, Roger, Saint-Ouen 067700
Adjutant General's Corps Museum, Winchester 041399
ADK - Actuele Kunst, Amsterdam . . 107648
Adkins, Houston 088990
Adkins, Gary, Minneapolis 090334
Adkins, Keith, Launceston 136969
Adler, Frankfurt am Main 102740
Adler, Genève 082387

Adler, Gstaad 111537
Adler, Paris 099909
Adler & Co., San Francisco 119579
Adler, Arno, Lübeck 139424
Adler, Carl, Dresden 138985
Adler, Julian, Cape Town 080673
Adler, Kurt S., Tampa 093097
Adler, Rachel, New York 117564
Adler & Conkright, New York 117565
Adler Kit, Los Angeles 089672
Adler Museum of Medicine, Johannesburg 034639
Adlerberg, Sankt Gallen 111863
Adlerskij Kraevedčeskij Muzej - Muzej Istorii Adlerskogo Rajona, Soči 033887
Adlitzer, Traiskirchen 137271
ADM Art Gallery, Philadelphia 118728
Admella, Mount Gambier 137012
Admiral Digby Museum, Digby 005350
Admiral Nimitz National Museum of the Pacific War, Fredericksburg 044053
Admiral Upholstery, Tulsa 132992
Admiral Vernon Antiques Market, London 085059
Admiralty Antiques, Crows Nest, New South Wales 055725
Admiralty House Antiques, Seattle . 092944
Admirer, Sofia 096714
ADN, Luxembourg 077469
Ado, Gdańsk 108868
Adobe, San Francisco 142924
Adolf, Monika, Regensburg 126686
Adolf, Stephanie, Wiesbaden 127006
Adolf-Bender-Zentrum, Sankt Wendel 019995
Adolf-Dietrich-Haus, Berlingen 036924
Ādolfa Alunāna Memoriālais Muzejs, Jelgava 027691
Adolfs, M., Münster 072893
Adolfsson, Huddinge 110945
A.D.O.M., Paris 065361
Adonis Antiquités, Saint-Parres-aux-Tertres 067936
Adopt-A-Chair, Ulverstone 056762
Ador, Toulouse 124969
Ador'B, Saint-Paul-de-Vence 101194
Adornments, Paddington, Queensland 056425
Adornments Contemporain, Albuquerque 131735
Adornos Arañas Antiguas, Buenos Aires 055147
Adornos Art et Deco, Rosario 055291
Adornos Villaflor, Santiago de Chile 123871
Adracare, Busselton 136834
Adrénaline Antiquités, Marseille . . . 064307
Adri-Art-16, Barcelona 110100
Adriaan, Den Haag 078159
Adriaan's Antiques, New Orleans . . 090500
Adrian, David, Knokke-Heist 096316
Adriani, Henrich, Pulheim 126664
Adrianno's Fine Art Gallery, Forrestfield 094554
Adrian's Ashgrove Antiques, Ashgrove 055411
Adriatica, Bari 139981
Adrien Numismatic, Dijon 062638
Adro de Santos, Lisboa 079842
A.D.S., Léguevin 063738
A.D.S., Paris 065362
ADS Antiques, Miami 090117
Adscriptio Iberica Librariae Antiquariorum, Palma de Mallorca 054073
Adsera Carvajal, Maria Teresa, Barcelona 080782
Adsmore Museum, Princeton 047234
Advanced Coatings, San Diego 132838
Advanced Graphics London, London 113433
Advanced Plating, Nashville 132395
Advanced Refinishing, Nashville . . . 132396
Advanced Wood Finishing, San Diego 132839
Advances in Art, Kansas City 116552
Advenia-Art'E, Madrid 110418
Advertising and Graphic Design Department, Southwestern Community College, Sylva 052233
Advertising Art Department, Chattanooga State Technical Community College, Chattanooga 051101
Advertising Art Design Department, State University of New York at Farmingdale, Farmingdale 051324
Advocate, London 113434
Ady Endre Emlékmúzeum, Endre Ady Memorial Museum, Budapest . . . 021632
Adyar, Sydney 137100
Adyar Art Club, Chennai . . 053685, 105617
Adygejskij Respublikanskij Kraevedčeskij Muzej, Majkop 033348
Adze Gallery, York 114746
A.E. Seaman Mineral Museum, Michigan Technological University, Houghton 044632
Äänekosken Kaupunginmuseo, Äänekoski 009451
Æbelholt Museum, Hillerød 008908
Aebischer, Elisabeth, Schwarzenburg 111898
Aebischer, Erwin, Basel 082112
Aebischer, Erwin, Frenkendorf 082375
Aebischer, Johann, Fribourg 111410
Aebli, Marlyse, Bern 111240
Aeby, François, Fribourg 111411
Ädelfors Gruvmuseum, Holsbybrunn 036347
Die Ägayrischen Gewölbe, Viechtach 020580
Aegean Maritime Museum, Mykonos 021386
Aëgerter, Bernard, Marseille 064308
Aegerter, Bernard, Nice 065022
Aegerter, Claude, Chêne-Bourg . . . 082307
Aegidius, Bad Honnef 101660
Aegis, Ulm 139806
Ägyptische Sammlung der Universität/ Museum Schloß Hohentübingen, Tübingen 020491
Ägyptischer Kulturladen, Berlin . . . 101771
Ägyptisches Museum der Universität Leipzig - Interim, Leipzig 018557
Ägyptisches Museum und Papyrussammlung, Staatliche Museen zu Berlin - Stiftung Preußischer Kulturbesitz, Berlin 015979
Aegyptus - Rivista Italiana di Egittologia e Papirologia, Milano 135861
Ähtärin Kotiseutumuseo, Ähtäri . . . 009452
AEKO Veilingen, Hasselt 120763
AEL Ethnic Gallery, Lesneven 099476
Aelbrecht Galerie, Rotterdam 108174
Äldre Ting, Aakersberga 081771
Aele, Madrid 110419
Älvsborgs Länsmuseum, Vänersborg 036756
Ämmäkosken Kanava, Kajaani 009653
Ängelholms Auktionskammare, Ängelholm 122093
Aenigma, Amsterdam 140277
Aequitas, Lyon 064048
A.E.R Archeologia e Restauro, Bologna 127127
AER Verlag, Bolzano 134555
Aera Memorial Museum, San Pablo 031783
Aerial Arte, Valencia 129749
Aerial House Antiques, Long Melford 085830
Aernouts, Régis, Paris 065363
Aero, Helsinki 060495
Aero Limited, New York 117566
Aéro-Musée de l'Aviation, Mèze . . . 013053
Ærø Museum, Ærøskøbing 008800
Aero Space Museum of Calgary, Calgary 005179
Aeronauticum - Deutsches Luftschiff- und Marinefliegermuseum Nordholz, Nordholz 019336
Aeroplastics Contemporary, Bruxelles 096124
Aérospatiale, Toulouse 014981
Aerts, S., Bruxelles 057803
AES, Chicago 115325
Aeschbach, Max, Derendingen 082339
Aesthetic Art Services, Los Angeles 116697
A.F. Antic, Constanța 140888
A.F. Antiquités, Bruxelles 057804
AFA-Antiquité Franco Anglaise, Paris 065364
A.F.C., Barcelona 080783, 140978
AFC Edition, Wiesbaden . . 105240, 134457
Afdeling Nuttige en Fraaie Handwerken, Openluchtmuseum Het Hoogeland, Uithuizermeeden 030218
Affabile, Salvatore, Roma 106481
Affair Art Gallery, Mumbai 105751
Affaire d'Antique, Eindhoven 078326
Affaire d'Eau, Amsterdam 077769
Affairs Art Gallery, Mumbai 105752
Affairs of the Art, Toronto 097208
Affaitati, Antonio, Napoli 075933
Affaitati, Giuseppe, Napoli 075934
Affari d'Epoca, Firenze 075266
L'Affiche, Milano 106144
L'Affiche, Milano 106145
L'Affiche, Milano 134603
L'Affiche, Nantes 099799
Affiche, Palermo 106411
Affiche Museum Hoorn, Hoorn 029770
Affiches, Genève 111418
Affiches Anciennes, Paris 065365
The Affinity Art Gallery, Midsomer Norton 114082
Affinity's Antiques, Regina 059081
Afford-a-Bulls, Bulls 078999
Affordable Aboriginal Arts, Indooroopilly 056011
Affordable Antiques, Ashby-de-la-Zouch 083340
Affordable Antiques, Hale . 084551, 130754
Affordable Art, Dallas 115818
Affordable Art, London 113435
Affordable Art, Oklahoma City 118652
Affordable Art, Virginia Beach 120211
Affordable Art Fair Bristol, Bristol . . 093904
Affordable Art Fair London, London 093905
Affordable Art Gallery, Chicago 115326
Affordable Black Art, Jacksonville . 116504
Affordable Books and Collectables, Phoenix 091706, 142756
Affordable Modern Art, New York . . 117567
Affordable Posh, Mittagong 056236
Affresco di Piero della Francesca, Monterchi 024857
Affrica-African Art, Washington . . . 120241
Afif Abad Military Museum, Shiraz . 022596
Afinsa, Granada 122027
Afinsa, Madrid 122030
Åfjord Bygdetun, Åfjord 030713
Afkari, Richard, New York 090652
Afnan, Cairo 098604
Afnan, Cairo 098605
Afnan, Cairo 098606
Afnan, Cairo 098607
Africa, Cairo 060424
Africa Calls, Dublin 105855
Africa Cultural Gallery, Nairobi 107157
Africa Curio, Milano 075572
Africa Dreaming, Gawler Belt 055862
Africa Exclusive, Delft 078139
Africa Exklusiv - Galerie für Afrikanische Kunst, Wien 095785
Africa Just, Armadale, Victoria 094158
Africa Museum, Seoul 027542
Africa-Museum, Tervuren 003789
Africa Visions Two Thousand One, Las Vegas 116599
Africa Within, Cincinnati 115597
African Accents, San Diego 119468
African Accents Hawaii, Honolulu . . 088927
African American Art, Charlotte . . . 115271
African American Art Gallery, New York 117568
African-American Historical and Cultural Society Collection, San Francisco 047848
African American Movie Posters, Los Angeles 089673
African American Museum, Cleveland 042982
African American Museum, Dallas . 043261
African-American Museum at Oakland, Oakland 046589
The African American Museum in Philadelphia, Philadelphia 046918
African American Museums Association, Chicago 054554
African and Tribial Art Gallery, Berlin 101772
African Art, Elzach 070551
African Art, Saint-Denis 109408
African Art and Designs, Miami . . . 117014
African Art Center, Houston 116261
African Art Centre, Durban 034596
African Art Gallery, San Francisco . .092705, 119580, 123101
African Art Gallery, Tampa 120018
African Art Museum of Maryland, Columbia 043067
African Art Museum of the S.M.A. Fathers, Tenafly 048526
African Art Production, New York . . 117569
African Art Room, Houston 116262
African Art-Shop, Düren 070345
African Arts, Los Angeles 136286
African Arts, Tucson 120097
African Arts Center, New York 117570
African Attractions, Virginia Beach . 120212
African Connection, Saint Ives, Cornwall 114357
African Crafts Corp, Rosebank 134899
African Cultural Art Forum, Philadelphia 046919
African Gallery, Bramsche 069973
African Gems, Denver 115964
African Hands, Washington 120242
African Herbalist Shops, Museum for Man and Science, Johannesburg 034640
African Heritage, Amsterdam 077770
African Heritage, Nairobi 107158
African Heritage Gallery, Dallas . . . 115819
African Imports, Dallas 115820
African Imports, Fort Worth 116130
African Legacy Gallery, Kirup 094707
African Muse Gallery, Paris 099910
African Mystical Arts, Balwyn 094207
African Mystical Arts, Forest Hill . . . 094552
African Odyssey, San Antonio 119386
African Palace, Indianapolis 116437
African Safari, Chicago 115327
African Safari and Veteran Car Museum, Dvůr Králové nad Labem 008357
African Tribal Art, Haarlem 108052
African Village, Detroit 116076
Africana, Zürich 112024
Africana Museum, Mariannhill 034677
Africana Museum, Monrovia 027825
Afric'Art, Château-Thierry 062188
Africoin, Bruxelles 057805
Afrika Centrum, Cadier en Keer . . . 029379
Afrika Museum, Berg en Dal 029307
Afrika-Museum, Bergen, Kreis Celle 015964
Afrika-Museum, Zug 037815
Afrikaans Music Museum, Bloemfontein 034555
Afrikaanse Taalmuseum, Paarl 034693
Afrikahaus Museum und Nold-Namibia-Bibliothek, Sebnitz 020158
Afrikana Gallery, South Melbourne . 095204
Afrique Congo, Liège 058281
Afrique Congo Sculptures, Liège . . . 058282
Afro-American Cultural Center, Charlotte 042753
Afro-American Historical Society Museum, Jersey City 044858
Afrocrafts, Manama 095986
Afrodisiyas Müzesi, Geyre Köyü Karasu Aydın 038072
Afrodite Antik, Stockholm 081905
After Noah, London 085060
After Noah, London 085061, 130916
After the Paint, Saint Louis 092195
After-Words, Chicago 142271

Afterimage, Rochester 136287
Afterimage Gallery, Dallas 115821
Afton, Totland Bay 114588
Afton, Totland Bay 135308
Afval-Museum, Zwolle 030410
Afyon Devlet Güzel Sanatlar Galerisi, Afyon 037995
Afyon Etnografya Müzesi, Afyon . . . 037996
Afyon Müzesi, Bolvadin Müzesi, Zafer Müzesi ve Dumlupınar Müzesi, Afyon 037997
A.G. Ar., Roma 076263
Aga Khan Museum of Islamic Arts, Marawi 031742
Agabio, Cagliari 075197
Agaméde, Paris 099911
Agape, Albuquerque 087360
Agape, Cleveland 115679
Agapi, Bordeaux 098983
Agar, Rosie, Saintfield 086480
AgArt, Warszawa 134859
Agartha, Paris 099912
Agartha, Rio de Janeiro . . 058533, 137568
Agassiz-Harrison Historical Museum, Agassiz 004987
Agatha Antikvariat, Täby 141181
Agathe, Saint-Ouen 067701
Agathon Oudheden, Antwerpen . . . 057670
Agathonos Monastery Collection, Ypati 021530
Agatunet, Nå 031040
Agave, Valencia 129750
Agawa Bay Exhibition Centre, Wawa 006778
Agder Naturmuseum, Kristiansand . 030954
L'Age d'Or, Bad Breisig 069270
l'Age d'Or, Bonn 069908
L'Age d'Or, Charleroi 137487
L'Age d'Or, Paris 138276
L'Age d'Or, Parma 076191
Age of art, Pinneberg 073329
Age of Elegance, Whitchurch, Shropshire 087132
Age Of Grace Antiques, Christchurch 079005
Age of Jazz, Whitby 087126
The Age of Steam Railroad Museum, Dallas 043262
Agecroft Hall, Richmond 047407
The Aged Art Jia Association, Guangzhou 052786
The Aged Art Society, Anshan 097636
The Aged Art Society, Fuxin 097715
The Aged Art Society, Taiyuan 098004
The Aged Art Society Jinzhou, Dalian 097708
Aged on High, Mount Waverley 056299
Agei Saranda Monastery, Spárti . . . 021473
Ageing Fancies, Seattle 092945
Ageless Treasures, Saskatoon 059095
Agem Produtora Cultural, São Paulo 096658
Agen Philatélie, Agen 060663
Agence Alsacienne de l'Or et des Méraux précieux, Strasbourg . . . 068284, 121263
Agence Alsacienne Or et des Méraux Précieux, Nancy 064856
Agence Art Process, Paris 099913
Agence C.B.S., Boulogne-Billancourt 099016
Agência Arte, Porto Alegre 096542
Agencia Cultural Oboe Financeira, Fortaleza 096510
Agência de Leilões Xira, Lisboa . . . 121923
Agensteinhaus und Simmentaler Hausweg, Erlenbach im Simmental 037070
Ageo Bustillo, Milagrosa, Sanlúcar de Barrameda 129719
Ages, Roma 134666
Ages Ago, Vancouver 059325
Agesilas, Claude, Fontaine-Lavaganne 062891
Agesilas, Corinne, Paris 065366
Agfa Photo-Historama, Museum Ludwig, Köln 018302
Agharkar Museum, Botany Department Museum, Allahabad 022000
Agharta, Żurawski & Walas, Warszawa 109085
Agia Lovra Monastery, Kalavryta . . 021297
Aginskij Okružnoj Kraevedčeskij Muzej im. G. Cybikova, Aginskoe 032973
Agion Panton Church Museum, Metéora 021377
Agios Andreas Monastery Museum, Agios Andreas 021117
Agios Stephanos Monastery, Metéora 021378
Agios Vissarion Monastery, Trikala . 021511
Agir Editora, Rio de Janeiro 133301
Agis-Verlag, Baden-Baden 133738
A Aglaia, Porto 080062
Agliozzo, Manlio, Firenze 075267
AGM, Zagreb 133400
Agneray, Josette, Paris 124541
Agnes Etherington Art Centre, Kingston 005692
Agnes Gallery, Birmingham 042220
Agnes Jamieson Gallery, Minden . . 005876
Agnes-Miegel-Haus, Bad Nenndorf . 015759
Agnes Photography and Book Arts, Birmingham 115093, 142233
Agnew's, London 085062, 113436
Agniel, Aigues-Vives 060680
Agnini, Elena, München 126343
Agora, Honfleur 063162
Agora, Lyon 064049, 138129
Agora, New Orleans 090501
Agora, New York 117571
Agora, New York 117572
Agorá, Prato 076248, 127884
Agora Antiguedades, Salamanca . . 081536
Agora Museum, Athinai 021154
Agora Restauraciones de Arte, Madrid 129551
Agora Verlag, Berlin 133745
Agoraï Mozzanico Leckie, Manuela, Carouge 082286
Agostinelli, Berardo, Roma 106482, 121717
Agostinelli, Roland, Marseille 124389
Agostinho, Orlanda, Paris 124542
Agostini, Roma 127906
Agostini, Giuseppe, Roma 076264
Agostini, Nino, Roma 127907
Agostinucci, Andrée, Nice 124495
Agouridis, Nik., Thessaloniki 074630
Agouridou, Chrisoula, Thessaloniki . 074631
Agra, María Teresa & Vicente, Valladolid 081684, 141084
Agra-Art, Warszawa 121899
Agrar- und Forstmuseum, Wittenburg 020929
Agrar- und Freilichtmuseum, Crimmitschau 016606
Agrarhistorisches Aktionsmuseum, Trendelburg 020467
Agrarhistorisches Museum, Alt Damerow 015488
Agrarhistorisches Museum, Schlepzig 020037
Agrarisch en Wagenmuseum, De Waal 029401
Agrarisch Museum Westerhem, Middenbeemster 029927
Agrarmuseum, Greußen 017530
Agrarmuseum Wandlitz, Wandlitz . . 020668
Agre, Michel, Toulouse 124970
Agricultural Heritage Museum, Hamilton 030509
Agricultural Museum, Coate 039110
Agricultural Museum, Faisalabad . . 031361
Agricultural Museum, Giza 009330
Agricultural Museum, Jasin 027951
Agricultural Museum, Miyazaki, Miyazaki-ken 026825
Agricultural Museum, Yangon 029072
Agricultural Museum at Stone Mills, La Fargeville 045060
Agricultural Museum Brook, Dover . 039271
Agricultural Museum of Entre Douro e Mino, Vila do Conde 032699
Agricultural Museum of Jeollanam-do, Samho 027539
Agricultural Museum of New Brunswick, Sussex 006541
L'Agriculture au Fil du Temps, Maniquerville 012872
L'Agriculture Bressane Musée, Ecomusée de la Bresse Bourguignonne, Saint-Germain-du-Bois 014307
Agriculture Museum, Imphal 022165
Agropolis Muséum, Montpellier . . . 013197
Agrotechnorama, Ettenhausen 037079
Agrupación de Acuarelistas de Cataluña, Barcelona 054074
Agtsch, K., Creglingen 070162
Água Forte, Lisboa 109259
Aguado, Logroño 110409
Agüera-Madrid, Juan, Bourges 061718
Aguéli, Stockholm 110996
Aguélimuseet, Sala 036554
Aguer, Hélène, Saint-Jean-de-Luz . 067533
Aguiar, Henri de, Beaune 061267
Aguilar, Granada 129523
Aguilar, Madrid 134933
Aguilar, Leo, Houston 088991
Aguilera, Madrid 129552
Aguilera Puntas, Córdoba 081045
Aguilera Silva, Carmen, Santiago de Chile 059484
Aguilera y Restauracion, Madrid . . . 129553
Aguinaleo Narvaez, Fernando, Málaga 081412
Agung Rai Museum of Art, Ubud . . . 022528
Agurcho Iruretagoiena, Pamplona . . 081505
Aguttes, Issoudun 063222, 121016
Aguttes, Vierzon 068868, 121285
Aguttes, Claude, Neuilly-sur-Seine . 064984
Aguttes, Claude, Neuilly-sur-Seine . 121091
Aguttes, Claude, Paris 065367
Ah, Theo von, Sachseln 082763
AH Antique Mall, Las Vegas 089533
Ah Sam, San Francisco 132863
Ah-Tah-Thi-Ki Museum, Big Cypress Seminole Indian Reservation 042196
AHA Courses, London 054266
Ahlat Müzesi, Ahlat 037998
Ahlberg, Lund 081848
Kurt Ahlbrecht & Dr. Gerhard Röper, Hamburg 103084
Ahler Kråm - Volkskundliche Sammlung, Partenstein 019566
Ahlers, Göttingen 102975
Ahlers, Fred, München 072627
Ahlgrim, Harald, Gaienhofen 070923
Ahlheim, Ulrich, Dortmund 070281
Ahlner, Stockholm 110997
Ahlström, B., Stockholm . . 081906, 122246
Ahmadi, Manama 095987
Ahn, Byongchan, Seoul 128453
Ahnert, Knut, Berlin 138730
Ahnert-Krutzke, H., Gleichen 139140
Aholan Talomuseo, Keitele 009687
Helga Ahrend & Anna-Maria Wager, München 072628
Ahrens, Varel 074180
Ahrens & Hamacher, Düsseldorf . . . 139004
Ahsan Manzil Museum, Bangladesh National Museum, Dhaka 003099
Ahtausmuseo, Kotka 009740
Åhus Museum, Åhus 036171
Ai, Nara 106938
Ai Baffi, Oberwil-Lieli 111796
Aibido, Tokyo 077230
AIC News, Washington 136288
AICA Internationale Gesellschaft der Kunstkritiker, Sektion Österreich, Wien 052502
Aichberger, Helga, Neunkirchen, Niederösterreich 057190
Aichelbaum, Léon, Paris 138277
Aichele, Frieder, Stuttgart 073951
Aichelmann & Hawelka, Oberursel . 073161
Aichholzer, Manfred, Pörtschach am Wörther See 095705
Aichi-ken Bijutsukan, Nagoya 026878
Aichi-ken Toji Siryokan, Seto 027055
Aichi-kenritsu Geijutsu Daigaku, Nagakute 050466
Aichinger & Comp., Wien 137283
Aichmaier, Johann, Salzburg 057233
Aidan Gallery, Moskva 109478
L'Aidjolate, Saint-Ouen 067702
Aiello, Denver 115965
Aiello, Roberto, Roma 127908
Aifacs Gallery, Delhi 105645
Aigantighe Art Museum, Timaru . . . 030604
Aigenbauer-Schindler, Maria, Krems 057121
L'Aigle Impériale, Marseille 064309
L'Aigle Impériale, Paris 065368
L'Aiglon, Polliat 066897
Aiglonnes du Moulin de Mérouvel, Alençon 060762
Aigner, Christoph Wilhelm, Salzburg 133133
Aigner, Johannes, Deutschlandsberg 056956
Aiguier, Jean-Louis, Le Pradet 063691
Aiguière de Cuivre, Montlhéry 064702
Aikawa Folk Museum and Exhibition Hall of Folk Crafts, Aikawa 026403
Aikawa Kokokan, Isesaki 026573
Aiken County Historical Museum, Aiken 041582
Aiken Thoroughbred Racing Hall of Fame and Museum, Aiken 041583
Aileen's Antiques, Vancouver 059326
Ailene's Antiques and Collectibles, Albuquerque 087361
Ailes d'Anges, Genech 062981
Les Ailes du Temps, Béziers 061426
D'Ailleurs, Beirut 077380
Ailsa Gallery, Twickenham 086962
AIM Enterprises, Cleveland 115680
Al-Ain Gallery, Cairo 098608
Ain Mondial Chapiteaux, Balan 098910
Aina̧žu Jūrskolas Memoriālais Muzejs, Ainaži 027653
Aineen Taidemuseo, Tornio 010155
Aineh va Roshananal Museum, Yazd 022651
Ainger, E.J., Richmond, Victoria . . . 120631
Ainhoa Ziganda Apaolaza, Donostia-San Sebastián 129496
Ainola, Järvenpää 009612
Ainscough Contemporary Art, London 113437
Ainsley, Sandra, Toronto 097209
Ainsley, Sandra, Toronto 097210
Ainsley House, Campbell 042587
Ainslie, Perth 086222
Ainslie, Alan, Pretoria 110069
Aintzinatekarien Azoka, Bilbao 093860
Ainu Museum, Hokkaido Daigaku Shokubutsuen Hakubutsukan, Sapporo 027024
Aion Antiquities, Chicago 088001
Air Classic Museum of Aviation, Sugar Grove 048416
Air Command Headquarters Museum and Air Park, Winnipeg 006838
Air de Chasse, Paris 065369
Air de Paris, Paris 099914
L'Air du Temps, Bordeaux 061571
L'Air du Temps, Brie-Comte-Robert 061793
Air du Temps, Gironville-sur-Essonne 063004
Air du Temps, La Ferté-Alais 063367
Air du Temps, Nantes 064889
L'Air du Temps, Paris 065370
Air du Temps, Schoelcher 077555
Air du Temps, Varces-Allieres-et-Risset 068724
Air Force Armament Museum, Eglin Air Force Base 043622
Air Force Flight Test Center Museum, Edwards Air Force Base 043617
Air Force Heritage Museum and Air Park, Winnipeg 006838
Air Force Museum, Christchurch . . 030457
Air Force Museum, Delhi 022075
Air Force Museum, Ha Noi 049520
Air Force Museum, Teheran 022606

Air Galleries, New York 117573
Air Galleries, New York 117574
Air Gallery, London 113438
Air Gallery, New York 046279
Air Heritage Museum of Santa Barbara/Goleta, Goleta 044239
Air Museum, Carrara San Giorgio 023676
Air of Art Museum, Bologna 023414
Air Power Park and Museum, Hampton 044413
Air Victory Museum, Medford 045740
Airault, Jean-Marc, Brigueuil 061801
Airborne and Special Operations Museum, Fayetteville 043831
Airborne Forces Museum, Aldershot 038474
Airborne Museum Hartenstein, Oosterbeek 029995
Airbrush Action, Lakewood 136289
Airbrush Art School, Werribee 095387
Aird, John B., Toronto 097211
Aireloom, Honolulu 132088
Airmen Memorial Museum, Suitland 048419
Airoldi, Isabella, Breganzona 129985
L'Airone, Messina 106133
Airport Gallery 1 & 2, Frankfurt am Main 017151
Airport Museum, Cairo 009290
Airpower Museum, Ottumwa 046752
Airvault, Philippe, Châtelaillon-Plage 062213
Aisle 7 Antiques, Chicago 088002, 131877
Aisne Collections, Bucy-le-Long 061833
Aisthesis, Jérôme Cordie, Paris 124543
Aithousa Skoufa, Athinai 105381
Aitihasic Puratatva Sangrahalaya, Delhi 022076
Aitonevan Turvemuseo, Kihniö 009704
Aître Saint-Saturnin, Blois 010843
Aittouarès, Paris 099915
Aiwen e Rifat Museum and Art Gallery, Karachi 031371
Aix Antiquités, Saint-Cannat 067388
Aix-en-Provence Antiquités, Aix-en-Provence 060692
Aixia, Las Rozas de Madrid 129712
Aizenman, Buenos Aires 136691
Aizkraukles Vēstures un Mākslas Muzejs, Aizkraukle 027655
Aizpuru, Juana de, Madrid 110420
Aizpuru, Juana de, Sevilla 110759
A.J. Antiquités, Paris 065371
AJ Net, Montigny-les-Cormeilles 064694
A.J. Snyder Estate, Rosendale 047545
Ajak-Nostalgie, Emersleben 070554
Ajanpatina, Helsinki 060496
Ajassa, Torino 076755
Ajasse, Lyon 138130
Ajax Museum, Amsterdam 029162
Ajdan, Moskva 109479
Ajisai, Kobe 106875
AJNA, Amiens 060803
A.J.'s Antiques, El Paso 088782
A.J.'s Auction and Antiques, Oklahoma City 091451
A.J.'s Posters and Prints, Chicago 115328
A.J.'s Toys, El Paso 088783
Ajtte Museum, Jokkmokk 036365
Ájtte - Svenskt Fjäll- och Samemuseum, Jokkmokk 036366
Ajucla, Salamanca 110731
AK Artist Run Centre, Saskatoon 097186
AK-Express, Essen 135736
A.K.A. Gallery, Saskatoon 006414
Aka Salon Antykow, Kraków 079614
Aka-you, Verviers 123675
Akademia e Arteve, Tiranë 049591
Akademia Sztuk Pięknych, Gdańsk 050599
Akademia Sztuk Pięknych, Łódź 050603
Akademia Sztuk Pięknych, Poznań 050604
Akademia Sztuk Pięknych, Warszawa 050607
Akademia Sztuk Pięknych, Wrocław 050610
Akademia Sztuk Pięknych im. Jana Matejki, Kraków 050600
Akademiai Kiadó, Budapest 134498
Akademie der Bildenden Künste, München 050185
Akademie der Bildenden Künste in Nürnberg, Nürnberg 050205
Akademie der bildenden Künste Wien, Wien 049648
Akademie der Künste, Berlin 015980
Akademie der Künste, Berlin 015981
Akademie der Künste, Kunstsammlung der Stiftung Archiv, Berlin 015982
Akademie Franz-Hitze-Haus, Münster 050199
Akademie für Bildende Kunst Vulkaneifel, Steffeln 050239
Akademie für Eurythmische Kunst, Dornach 050761
Akademie für Kunst und Kunsttheorie Hessen, Groß-Umstadt 050095
Akademie Sankelmark, Sankelmark 050230
Akademie Schloss Solitude, Stuttgart 050240
Akademie Verlag, Berlin 133746
Akademie voor Architectuur en Stedebouw, Tilburg 050568
Akademie voor Beeldende Kunsten en Vormgeving, Akademie Minerva, Groningen 050559
Akademie voor Kunst en Vormgeving, 's-Hertogenbosch 050560
Akademie Výtvarných Umění, Praha 049891
Akademija, Vilnius 107357
Akademija Likovnih Umetnosti Sarajevo, Sarajevo 049746
Akademija za Primenjene Umetnosti, Beograd 050674
Akademische Druck- und Verlagsanstalt, Graz 133073
Akademisches Kunstmuseum der Universität, Antikensammlung, Bonn 016312
Akademisches Münzkabinett, Institut für Altertumswissenschaften der Friedrich-Schiller-Universität Jena, Jena 018102
Akademkniga, Moskva 140893
Akademkniga, Moskva 140894
Akademkniga, Moskva 140895
Akademkniga, Moskva 140896
Akademkniga Magazin N1, Sankt-Peterburg 140924
Akademkniga Magazin N3, Sankt-Peterburg 140925
Akademkniga Magazin N4, Sankt-Peterburg 140926
Akademkniga Magazin N5, Sankt-Peterburg 140927
Akademski Slikar, Koper 109939
Akadimia Athinon, Athinai 050269
Akadomari-mura Folk Museum, Akadomari 026407
Akai, Nanmeido, Nara 077158
Akainyah, Chicago 115329
Akalo, Bordeaux 061572
Akalo, Bordeaux 061573
Akama-jingu Treasure House, Shimonoseki 027065
Akane, Nagoya 106913
Akant, Praha 060088
Akant, Praha 060089, 098411
Akant, Praha 123969
Akant, Wrocław 079795
Akant, Wrocław 129124
Akanthos, Antwerpen 057671
akanthus, Berlin 125159
Akar Prakar, Jaipur, Rajasthan 105719
Akariya, Tokyo 077231
Åkarps Antikvariat, Lund 141119
Akasaka Green Gallery, Tokyo 107008
Akashi-shiritsu Tenmon Kagakukan, Akashi 026408
Akateeminen Kirjakauppa, Helsinki 137927
Akbank Bahariye Sanat Galerisi, İstanbul 112265
Akbank Bebek Sanat Galerisi, İstanbul 112266
Akbank Beylerbeyi Sanat Galerisi, İstanbul 112267
Akbarzadeh-Glatthard, A., Oberdiessbach 111786
Akbarzadeh-Glatthard, Antoinette, Bern 111241
Akcent, Kwidzyn 108996
Akcent, Warszawa 109086
Akcija, Moskva 080214
Akcija, Moskva 080215
Akcija, Moskva 109480, 121961, 140897
akd-forum, Basel 082113
Akemi, Singapore 080413
Aken-Antik, Aken 069125
Akers, Timothy, Beckenham 130362
Åkers Hembygdsmuseum, Strängnäs 036683
Akershus Fylkesmuseum, Strømmen 031246
Akhenaton, Troyes 101388
Akhtary, M., Berlin 069549
AKI-Akademie voor Beeldende Kunst en Vormgeving, Enschede 050557
Akiba, Miami 090118
Akimoto, Nagoya 077145
Akin, Boston 087790
Akin, A.R., Birmingham 087730
Akinci, Amsterdam 107649
Akir, Oslo 079408
Akita Daigaku Kozangakubu Fuzok u Kogyo Hakubutsukan, Akita 026409
Akita-kenritsu Hakubutsukan, Akita 026410
Akita-kenritsu Kindai Bijutsukan, Yokote 027346
Akita Prefectural Art Gallery, Akita 026411
Akita Senshu Museum of Art, Akita 026412
Akiyama, Tokyo 107009
Akiyoshidai Kagaku Hakubutsukan, Shuuhou 027085
Akka, Paris 099916
Akka Arte del Mañana, Valencia 110795
Akko Gallery, Bangkok 112226
Akko Municipal Museum, Akko 022884
Akkolades, Den Haag 078160
Akomena, San Zaccaria 128245
Akon, Warszawa 079719
Akpol Museum, Semarang 022502
Akránum, Budapest 074657
Akriti, Delhi 105646
Akron Art Museum, Akron 041586
Akropolis, Brescia 075137
Akros Gallery, Bilbao 110267
AKS Holographie-Galerie, Essen 102668
Aksanat Resim Galerisi, İstanbul 112268
Aksent 167, Leuven 096370
Akshaya Kumar Maitreya Museum, Siliguri 022341
Aksoy, Akin, Tübingen 126918
Aksum Archaeology Museum, Aksum 009444
Akta, Gabrovo 096702
Akta Lakota Museum, Chamberlain 042699
Aktaion, Zaandam 140574
Die Aktgalerie, Berlin 101773
Aktien-Galerie, Überlingen 074132
Aktien-Galerie, Wien 095786
Aktion Museum M, Mistelbach an der Zaya 002315
Aktionsforum Praterinsel, München 019028
Aktionsgalerie Bern, Wohlen bei Bern 112005
Aktives Museum Spiegelgasse für Deutsch-Jüdische Geschichte in Wiesbaden, Wiesbaden 020861
Aktives Museum Südwestfalen, Siegen 020198
Aktuaryus, Strasbourg 101279, 124937
Akumulatory 2, Poznań 109041
Akvamarín, Znojmo 098517
Akvarel', Kyïv 112388
Akvarius, Chimki 109465
Akvarius, Moskva 109481
Akwarel Parcenier, Toulouse 101327
Akwesasne Museum, Hogansburg 044566
Akzente, Bremen 138933
Akzente, Burgwedel 102294
Akzente, Mettmann 072534
Akzente, Nettetal 072961
Akzente, Telgte 105038
Al-Ain Museum, Al-Ain 038422
Al Bassir, Hiba, Damascus 130276
Ål Bygdemuseum, Ål 030715
A.L. Fetterman Educational Museum, Fort Valley 043988
Al Gallery, Podgorica 109740
Al-Harithy, İzmir 112372
Al Ibriz Orcadre, Rabat 077687, 107559
Al-Karak Museum for Archaeology and Folklore, Al-Karak 027359
Al Kassaba Museum Thafer al Masri Foundation, Nablus 031417
Al-Khor Museum, Al-Khor 032755
Al Mada'in Museum, Baghdad 022659
Al-Mahatah - Sharjah Aviation Museum, Sharjah 038428
Al-Mansora Museum Dar-ibn-Luqman, Daqahlia 009327
Al Mawsil Museum, Nineveh 022672
Al Montepío Antigüedades, Buenos Aires 055148
Al-Mukalla Museum, Al-Mukalla 049560
Al-Muntaza Palace Museum, Alexandria 009272
Al Portico di Grazioli, Verona 076985, 128411
Al Pozzo, Venezia 076914
Al-Rawi, Idris, Paris 099917
Al Shaheed Monument and Museum, Baghdad 022660
Al Sulaimaniya Museum, Sulaimaniya 022674
Al Tempio Antico, Lugano 082588
Al-Toyan Tower Trading, Ruwi 079520
Al-Wakra Museum, Al-Wakra 032756
Al Zubara Fort, Doha 032757
Ala, Salvatore, Milano 106146
Ala Moana, Honolulu 088928
Alabama Art Agency, Klagenfurt 095610
Alabama Arts Magazine, Montgomery 136290
Alabama Auction Room, Birmingham 122820
Alabama-Coushatta Indian Museum, Livingston 045354
Alabama Furniture, Houston 088992
Alabama History Museum, Montgomery 045993
Alabama Mining Museum, Dora 043479
Alabama Museum of Natural History, Tuscaloosa 048661
Alabama Museums Association, Tuscaloosa 054555
Alabama Music Hall of Fame, Tuscumbia 048668
Alabama Pastel Society, Birmingham 054556
Alabarces Jimenez, Jose, Palma de Mallorca 081463
Alabaster Bookshop, New York 142626
Alabastri, Anne, Paris 124544
Alabau, Valencia 129751
Alacahöyük Müzesi, Alaca 038001
La Alacena, Málaga 081413
Aladdin, Leiden 140474
Aladdin Antiques, Montmorency 056244, 123268
Aladdin Antiques, Wellington 079312
Aladdin Book Shoppe, Oklahoma City 142715
Aladdin Finishers, Portland 132681
Aladdin Gallery, Houston 088993
Aladdin's Antique Alley, Saint Paul 092338
Aladdin's Cave, Freshwater 084439, 141619
Aladdin's Cave, Leeds 084924
Aladdin's Cave, Swansea 086809
Aladdins Cave Antiques, Berry 055491
Aladin, Bruxelles 137423
Aladin, Dijon 062639
Aladin, Grenoble 063043
Aladin, Guérande 063094
Aladin, Lille 063827
Aladin, Versailles 135682
Aladin Antik, Praha 060090

Aladin Antik, Zürich 082932, 130227
Aladine, Paris 065372
Aladjem, Sabitaï, Aubervilliers 098871
Alaerts, J.P., Bruxelles ... 057806, 096125
Alagarda Irriberri, Maria, Barcelona 080784
Alaimo, Providence 119068
Alaimo, Michele, Milano 075573
Alain, Bernard, Fontenay-sous-Bois 062906, 138092
Alain, Levent, Athies-sous-Laon ... 061014
Alain, Michel, Bruxelles 057807
Alain Encadreur, La Rochelle 099402
Alal, Paris 124545
El-Alam El-Arabi, Cairo 060425
Alamance Battleground, Burlington 042523
Alamanda, Saint-François 105469
Alamannenmuseum, Weingarten, Württemberg 020760
Alamannenmuseum Ellwangen, Ellwangen 016941
Alambee Auto and Folk Museum, Echuca 001004
Alamo, Montpellier 064728
The Alamo, San Antonio 047786
Alamo Antique Mall, San Antonio .. 092473
Alamo City Galleries, San Antonio .. 119387
Alamo City Galleries, San Antonio .. 119388
Alamo City Galleries, San Antonio .. 119389
Alamo City Galleries, San Antonio .. 119390
Alamo Military Collectables, Saint Louis 092196
Alamo-Mo Book Shop, San Diego .. 142897
Alamo Township Museum-John E. Gray Memorial, Kalamazoo 044896
Alampo Orazio, Catania .. 075232, 127256
Alan, Adrian, London 085063
Alan Jones Scout Memorabilia Museum, West Perth 001609
Alan Macpherson House, Napanee . 005983
Alana, Seattle 092946
Ålands Jakt och Fiskemuseum, Eckerö 009465
Ålands Konstmuseum, Mariehamn . 009856
Ålands Museum, Mariehamn 009857
Ålands Sjöfartsmuseum, Mariehamn 009858
Alaniesse, Jacques, Lyons-la-Forêt 064196
Alankrita Antiques, Bangalore 074762
Alankritha Arts Gallery, Hyderabad . 105691
Alan's Antique, Woking 131705
Alan's Antiques, Leatherhead 084916, 130865
Alan's Antiques, Omaha 091546
Alan's Collectables, Gosford 055901
Alanteaks, Jacksonville 089364
Alantic, Lyon 064050
Alapítvány Érc és Ásványbányászati Múzeum, Rudabánya 021830
Alarannan Antikvariaatti, Tampere . 137990
Alarce, Madrid 129554
Alarcon, Pedro Lopez, Madrid 081197
Alaska Aviation Heritage Museum, Anchorage 041710
Alaska Centennial Center for the Arts, Fairbanks Arts Association, Fairbanks 043779
Alaska Indian Arts, Haines 044388
Alaska Museum of Natural History, Eagle River 043555
Alaska Northwest Books, Portland . 135479
Alaska Shop of Chicago, Chicago .. 115330
Alaska Shop of New York, New York 117575
Alaska State Council on the Arts Communique, Anchorage 136291
Alaska State Museum, Juneau 044888
Alaska Watercolor Society, Anchorage 054557
Alatornion Pitäjämuseo, Tornio 010156
Alaux, Jean, Paris 065373
Alauzet, Yvon, Millau 064555
Alauzet, Yvon, Millau 064556
Alauzet, Yvon, Millau 138209
Alauzet, Yvon, Millau 138210
Alazarine, Pierre, Gordes 063017
Alazraki, Daphne, New York 090653
ALB Antiquités, Paris 065374
Alba, Madrid 081198
Alba, Iulia, Palma de Mallorca 081464
Alba Burguillos, Antonio, Bilbao ... 129420
Alba Cabrera, Valencia 110796
Alba Editorial, Barcelona 134901
Alba Longa, Madrid 081199
Albadia Museum, Arab Bedouin Heritage Center, Osafia 023043
Hijos de Albaladejo García, San Pedro del Pinatar 122082
Alban, Cristin, Noce 065205
Alban, Eduard, Seligenstadt 073797
Albano, Jean, Chicago 115331
Albany Antiques, Hindhead 084688
Albany Antiques, Malvern, Victoria . 056141
Albany Civil Rights Movement Museum, Albany 041594
Albany Gallery, Cardiff 112804
Albany Gallery, London ... 085064, 113439
Albany Hill, Albany 078901, 128893
Albany Historical Museum, Sabetha 047582
Albany Institute of History and Art, Albany 041597
Albany Museum, Grahamstown ... 034621
Albany Museum of Art, Albany 041595
Albany Regional Museum, Albany .. 041604
Albany Residency Museum, Albany 000721
Albarium, Zaragoza 129799
Albarium, Zaragoza 129800
Albarran, Margarita & Rodriguez Armijo, Sevilla 110760
Albatros, Milano 106147
Albatros, Moskva 109482
Albatros, Moskva 109483
Al.ba.tro's, Toulouse 068474
Albatros de Pitcairn, Etables-sur-Mer 062810
Albatrossmuseet, Romakloster 036545
Albayalde, Donostia-San Sebastián 129497
Albemarle Gallery, London 113440
Alber, Herbert, Bregenz 095484
Alber, Martin, Haidershofen 057051
Alberdi, Buenos Aires 055149
Albergo-Museo Atelier sul Mare, Castel di Tusa 023705
Alberni Valley Museum, Port Alberni 006168
Albers, Memphis 116973
Albers, Manning, San Francisco ... 119581
Albert, Atlanta 087442
Albert, Daniel, Sedan 068183
Albert, Dr. Rainer, Speyer 073875
Albert, Susan Carol, São Paulo 058668
Albert Cuijp Antiquiteiten, Amsterdam 077771
Albert Edelfeltin Ateljeemuseo, Porvoo 009991
Albert Engström-Museerna, Grisslehamn 036315
Albert & Herbert Antikbod, Stockholm 081907
Albert Kersten GeoCentre, Broken Hill 000846
Albert-König-Museum, Unterlüß ... 020542
Albert Lane Antiques, Berry 055492
Albert Park Gallery, Albert Park ... 094127
Albert & Partner, Palma de Mallorca 081465
Albert-Schweitzer-Gedenk- und Begegnungsstätte, Weimar, Thüringen 020735
Alberta Art Foundation Collection, Edmonton 005387
Alberta Association of Registered Nurses Museum, Edmonton 005388
Alberta Aviation Museum, Edmonton 005389
Alberta Beach and District Museum, Archives Society, Alberta Beach .. 004990
Alberta Central Railway Museum, Wetaskiwin 006797
Alberta College of Art & Design, Calgary 049777
Alberta Forestry Service Museum, Hinton 005619
Alberta Hospital Museum, Ponoka . 006165
Alberta Museums Association, Edmonton 052719
Alberta Print Makers Society, Calgary 052720, 096784
Alberta Railway Museum, Edmonton 005390
Alberta Society of Artists, Edmonton 052721
Alberta Sports Hall of Fame and Museum, Red Deer 006240
Alberta Wheat Pool Grain Museum, Calgary 005180
Albertella, R., Genova 127431
Albertfalvai Helytörténeti Gyûjtemény és Iskolamúzeum, Budapest 021633
Alberth, Marina, Bad Mergentheim . 069325
Alberti, Bilbao 129421
Alberti, Nice 065023
Alberti, Bianca Maria, Milano 127511
Alberti Gallery, London 113441
Albertiina, Helsinki 060497
Albertina, Wien 002845
Albertine, Becherel 098944, 138029
Albertis, Hanau . 103249, 121442, 125859, 139227
Albertland and Districts Museum, Wellsford 030655
Alberto Galerija, Vilnius 107358
Alberto Jose, Salamanca . 081537, 129714
Alberto Savio, Milano 075574
Alberton, Auckland 030429
Alberton Museum, Alberton 004992
Alberts, Almelo 077720
Alberts, Jacksonville 089365, 132168
Albert's Antiquariat, Detmold 138978
Albert's Bookshop, Guyra 136925
Alberts-Langdon, Boston 115136
Alberts-Van Smirren, Amsterdam .. 077772
Albgaumuseum, Museum der Stadt Ettlingen, Ettlingen 017090
Albi, Vincent, Bordeaux .. 061574, 124110
Albigeois Antiquités, Albi 060745
The Albin O. Kuhn Gallery, University of Maryland-Baltimore County, Baltimore 041962
Albino Books, Birmingham 141415
Albino Tableaux, Paris 099918
Albinson-Kurz, Eutin 070670
Albion, London 130917
Albion Academy Historical Museum, Edgerton 043605
Albion Antique Auction Centre, Albion 120559
Albion Books, Vancouver 137722
Albion Gallery, Saint David's 114353
Albisetti, Alain, Cuzac 062588
Albo Antiques, Hamilton 058846
Albonetti, Domestici Mara, Roma .. 106483
Albrecht, Berlin 069550
Albrecht, A., Zinnowitz 074570
Albrecht, C.P., Nürnberg 073093
Albrecht, Donata, Burgdorf, Kreis Hannover 125414
Albrecht, E., Augsburg 069214
Albrecht, Frank, Schriesheim 134387, 139716
Albrecht, H., Buchen 070075
Albrecht, Mario, Aue, Sachsen 069212
Albrecht, Martina, Isernhagen 103441
Albrecht, Susanne, München 104135
Albrecht-Daniel-Thaer-Gedenkstätte-Landesausstellung, Reichenow .. 019777
Albrecht-Dürer-Antiquariat, Nürnberg 139599
Albrecht-Dürer-Gesellschaft, Kunstverein Nürnberg, Nürnberg 019345, 053008
Albrecht-Dürer-Haus, Museen der Stadt Nürnberg, Nürnberg 019346
Albrecht-Kemper Museum of Art, Saint Joseph 047644
Albrechtsburg, Meißen 018888
Albrici, Antonio, Brescia 075138
Albrici & Paderni, Firenze 075268
Albright-Knox, Buffalo 115246
Albright-Knox Art Gallery, Buffalo .. 042498
Albrow & Sons, Norwich 086107
Albry, Berrima 055487
Album, Paris 138278
Album, Letras & Artes, Madrid 136068
Album Verlag, Berlin 133747
Album-Verlag für Photographie, Wien 133174
Albums Books, New York 142627
Albuquerque, Celma, Belo Horizonte 096452
Albuquerque, Michael & Jane de, Wallingford 087003, 131639
Albuquerque Art Business Association, Albuquerque 054558
Albuquerque Coins, Albuquerque .. 087362
Albuquerque Furniture, Albuquerque 131736
The Albuquerque Museum of Art and History, Albuquerque 041613
Albuquerque & Sousa, Lisboa 079843
Alburda, Lyon 138131
Albury Antiques, Albury 055328
Albury Regional Art Gallery, Albury . 000728
Albury Regional Museum, Albury .. 000729
Alby, Cagliari 127238
Alby Auktionsfirma, Alby 122096
Alcade, Lyon 138132
Alcal, Houston 132094
Alcalá, Madrid 122031
Alcan Aluminium Corporate Art Collection, Montréal 005906
Alcarria, Sevilla 129726
Alcaston Gallery, Fitzroy 094527
Alcázar, Sevilla 035851
Alcázar de los Reyes Cristianos, Córdoba 035109
Alcázar de Segovia, Segovia 035840
Alchemist Gallery, Yarmouth 114743
Alchemy: The Group for Collections Management in Yorkshire and Humberside, Halifax 054267
Alcheringa, Bodegraven 140364
Alchimia, Roma 076265, 127909
Alchimie, Saint-Étienne 101145
Alcobas Fernandez, Juan Miguel, Cartagena 110293
Alcoforado, Washington 093375
Alcolado, Marcos Diez, Madrid 110421
Alcolea, Barcelona 080785, 110101
Alcolea, Madrid 081200, 110422
Alcolea, Jorge, Madrid 110423
Alcon, Houston 132095
Alcónii, Fernando Vicente, Castellón de la Plana 129476
Alcott, Houston 142421
Alcott, Los Angeles 116698
Alcuin, Phoenix 142757
Alcuvilla, Jérôme, Rivieres 067160
La Aldaba, A Coruña 081052
El Aldabon, Bogotá 059802
Aldag, Eva, Buxtehude 121365
Aldborough Roman Town Museum, Boroughbridge 038789
Aldea del Tiempo, Bucaramanga .. 059865
Aldea Galery, Buenos Aires 094054
Aldebert, Alain, Neuville-de-Poitou . 064996
Aldebert, Comdor, Castres 062026
Aldeburgh Museum, Aldeburgh ... 038471
Alden, Denver 088635, 132028
Alden, Michael, New Orleans 117385
Alden B. Dow Creativity Center, Northwood University, Midland 051709
Alden Hamilton, Richmond 092054
Alden Historical Society Museum, Alden 041628
Alden House Museum, Duxbury ... 043548
Alder, Ha Noi 120442
Alder Cocinas, Alicante 129300
Aldermaston Antiques, Aldermaston 083262
Alderney Railway - Braye Road Station, Alderney 038472
Alderney Society Museum, Alderney 038473
Aldersey Hall, Chester 083948
Aldershot Military Museum and Rushmoor Local History Gallery, Aldershot .. 038475
Aldessan Gallery, Glasgow 113098

Aldfaers Erf Route, Museumdorp Allingawier, Allingawier 029135
Aldheidskeamer Uldrik Bottema, Aldeboarn 029129
Aldidea, León 081167
Aldidea, León 081168
Aldine, Los Angeles 142486
Aldo Castillo Gallery, Chicago 115332
Aldonga Auctions, Wodonga 120656
Aldous-Cook, David, Sutton 135306
Aldredge, Dallas 142359
Aldrich Museum of Contemporary Art, Ridgefield 047434
Aldridge, Bath 122399
Aldridge, F.W., Takeley 131572
Aldus, Braşov 140872
Aldus, Frederiksberg 137866
Ale-Kirja, Oulu 137980
Alefeld, A.W., Bonn 069909
Alegria, Mandaluyong 108830
Alegria, San Antonio 092474, 132804
Alegria, Luis, Porto 109363
Alejndra's Upholstery, Chicago 131878
Aleksandra Rusteiķa Memoriālais Muzejs, Jūrmala 027695
Aleksandrovskaja Sloboda - Gosudarstvennyj Istoriko- architekturnyj i Chudožestvennyj Muzej-zapovednik, Aleksandrov 032976
Aleksandrovskij Chudožestvennyj Muzej, Aleksandrov 032977
Aleksandrovskij Dvorec - Gosudarstvennyj Muzej Carskoje Selo, Puškin 033679
Aleksandrovskij Literaturno-chudožestvennyj Muzej Mariny i Anastasii Cvetaevych, Aleksandrov 032978
Aleksandrovskij Narodnyj Muzej M.E. Pjatnickogo, Aleksandrovka 032979
Aleksiev, Rajko, Sofia 096715
Aleksis Kiven Syntymäkoti, Palojoki 009947
Ålen Bygdetun, Ålen 030717
Alencastro, Porto Alegre 096543
Aleph, Bruxelles 096126
Aleph Art Books, Utrecht 140542
Aleppo National Museum, Aleppo . . 037824
Aléry, Annecy 060882
Ales, Saint Paul 132758
Alésina, Eric, Clairvaux-les-Lacs . . 062312
Alésina, Eric, Saint-Étienne 067435, 124894
Alessandri, Roma 127910
Alessandri, Alessandra, Roma 127911
Alessandri, Roberto, Roma 106484
Alessandrino, Carmelo, Milano 127512
Alessandro, Danny, New York 090654
Alessi, Warszawa 079720
Ålesunds Museum, Ålesund 030718
Aleteja Publishing House, Sankt-Peterburg 134882
Alex, Susanne, Geseke 070981
Alex Brown Cycle History Museum, Thornhill, Dumfriesshire 041216
Alex Gallery, Washington 120243
Alex Mylonas Museum, Athinai 021155
Alex Robertson Museum, Alonsa . . 005002
Alex Youck School Museum, Regina 006246
Alexander, Haarlem 128685
Alexander, Henfield 084656
Alexander, Houston 088994
Alexander, New York 090655
Alexander, New York 090656
Alexander, San Francisco 092706
Alexander, Sofia 096716
Alexander, David, London 085065
Alexander, Julian, London 085066
Alexander, Keith, Vancouver 097407
Alexander and Baldwin Sugar Museum, Puunene 047288
Alexander Antiques, Portrush 086296
Alexander & Bonin, New York 117576
Alexander Brest Museum, Jacksonville 044811
Alexander & David Fax, Kristen, Canberra 136845
Alexander Fleming Laboratory Museum, London 040074
Alexander Gallery, Bristol 083724
Alexander Gallery, Bristol 112712
Alexander Graham Bell National Historic Site, Baddeck 005051
Alexander Keiller Museum, Avebury 038550
Alexander-Mack-Museum, Bad Berleburg 015662
Alexander McKay Geological Museum, Wellington 030633
Alexander Ramsey House, Saint Paul 047694
Alexander Verlag Berlin, Berlin 133748
Alexander & Victor, New Orleans . . 117386
Alexander's, Oklahoma City 091452
Alexander's, San Francisco 092707
Alexanders, Titchfield 086887, 131594
Alexander's Antiques, Richmond . .092055, 123069
Alexander's Antiques, Saint Louis . . 092197
Alexander's Galerie, Telgte 105039
Alexander's Gallery, Saint Louis . . . 119171
Alexander's Sculptural Service, New York 117577
Alexandra Antiquité, Groslay 063086
Alexandra Galleries, Beckenham . . 112597
Alexandra Galleries, London 113442
Alexandra Museum, Alexandra 030421
Alexandra Timber Tramway and Museum, Alexandra 000730
Alexandre, Fort-de-France 140241
Alexandre, Namur 058349
Alexandre, New York 117578
Alexandre, Toronto 137691
Alexandre, Charles, Montréal 096964
Alexandre, Jean-Christophe, Bavilliers 061226
Alexandre d'Or, Paris 065375
Alexandria Antiques, Brighton 083681
Alexandria Antiques, Brighton 083682
Alexandria Archaeology Museum, Alexandria 041634
Alexandria Black History Resource Center, Alexandria 041635
Alexandria Livros, Lisboa 140815
Alexandria Museum of Art, Alexandria 041631
Alexandria Press, London 135171
Alexandris, Konst., Patrai 074625
Alexandroff, Arnaud, Bénodet 061348
Alexandros Papanastassiou Museum, Levidion 021356
Alexandrovics, Ivanhoe 094664
Alexa's Treasures, Ballarat 055426
Alexej von Jawlensky-Archiv, Locarno 037271
Alexejew, Wien 133175
Alexeline, Chalon-sur-Saône 062079
Alexia Gallery, Washington 120244
Alex's Antique Clocks and Watches, Toronto 123823
Alex's Art Galerie, Klosters 111587
Aleyne, Noelle, Paris 099919
Alf Lechner Museum, Ingolstadt . . . 018067
Alfa, Bologna 134547
Alfa, Brno 137767
Alfa 2, Gdynia 079592
Alfa Antikvariat, Stockholm 141138
Alfa Antikvariat Väst, Stockholm . . . 141139
Alfa-Art, Moskva 080216, 121962
Alfa Art, Sankt-Peterburg 121967
Alfa Böcker, Malmö 141126
Alfa - Galerie Díla, Praha 098412
Alfa Haganum, Den Haag 140386
Alfa-Omega, Karlovy Vary 098369
Alfa Restauri, Roma 127912
Alfabeta, Stockholm 134963
Alfano, Simone, Palermo 127816
Alfarrábios, Lisboa 140816
Alfarrabista Candelabro, Porto 140861
O Alfarrabista Livraria, São Paulo . . 137579
Alfarrabista Livro Aberto, Porto 140862
Alfazema, Porto Alegre 058481
Alfea, Milano 075575, 140039
Alfea sa Libreria, Lugano 141267
Alfia, Cluj-Napoca 140884
Alfican, Bruxelles 096127
Alfie's Antique Market, London 085067
Alföldi Galéria, Hódmezővásárhely . 105561
Alfoëldi Galéria, Tornyai János Múzeum, Hódmezővásárhely 021738
The Alfoldy Gallery, Canyon 005215
Alfombras Ghali, Alicante 129301
Alfombras Miguel, Zaragoza 129801
Alfombras y Kilims, Madrid 081201, 129555
Alfons Graber-Museum, Steinach . . 002693
Alfonsin, Marinete Rejane Zanetti, Porto Alegre 058482
Alford Heritage Centre, Alford, Aberdeenshire 038481
Alford House-Anderson Fine Arts Center, Anderson 041716
Alford Manor House Museum, Alford, Lincolnshire 038483
Alford Studio and Gallery, Jacksonville 116505
Alfort, J.M., Stockholm 081908
Alfred East Art Gallery, Kettering . . 039854
Alfred Ost Museum, Zwijndrecht . . 003876
Alfred-Vogel-Museum, Teufen 037624
Alfred-Wegener-Gedenkstätte, Zechlinerhütte 021040
Alfrēda Kalniņa Memoriālais Muzejs, Cēsis 027669
Alfreds Antik, Sandnes 079489
Alfred's Antiques, Burpengary 055586
Alfreton Antiques Centre, Alfreton . 083266
Alfriston Antiques, Alfriston 083268
Alf's Antiques, Toronto 059114
Alger, Minneapolis 090335
Alger County Heritage Center, Munising 046087
Alghalaf, Saleh, Manama 095988
Algonquin College Museum, Nepean 005991
Algonquin Culture and Heritage Centre, Golden Lake 005519
Algonquin Park Logging Museum, Whitney 006818
L'Alguer, La Bisbal d'Empordá 081001, 129452
L'Algver, La Bisbal d'Empordà 129453
Alhambra, Maracaibo 093548
Alhambra Antigüedades, Buenos Aires 055150
Alhambra Books, Edmonton 137630
Alhamra Art Gallery, Lahore 108777
Alhena, Fontainebleau 062895
Ali, Rahma, Köln 103578
Ali Baba, Le Havre 063623
Ali-Baba, München 072629
A Aliança Livros, Lisboa 140817
Alianza, Boston 115137
Alianza Artística, Barranquilla 098085
Alianza Editorial, Madrid 134934
Alianza Gallery, Louisville 116924
Alias, Paris 065376, 133509, 138279
Alibek, Hamburg 071186
Alibert, Daniel, Albi 124064
Alibert, Lisette, Paris 099920
Alibrandi, Firenze 106027
Alica, Angelo, Milano 127513
Alice Austen House Museum, Staten Island 048326
Alice C. Sabatini Gallery, Topeka and Shawnee County Public Library, Topeka 048579
Alice in The Wonderland, Venezia . . 106721
Alice Springs RSL War Museum, Alice Springs 000733
Alice T. Miner Colonial Collection, Chazy 042785
Alice's, London 085068
Alice's Bookshop, Belconnen 136796
Alice's Bookshop, Carlton North . . . 136850
Alice's Old Furniture, Vancouver . . . 059327
Alicke, Paul, Mörfelden-Walldorf . . 139483
Alien Libros, Buenos Aires 136692
Alienor, Albi 060746
Aliénor 2000, Duras 062753, 099245
Alig, K., Schwenda 104866
Alikartano, Numminen 009914
Alimentarium, Musée de l'Alimentation-Une Fondation Nestlé, Vevey 037675
Fratelli Alinari, Firenze . . . 106028, 134578
Aline, Fryde, Saint-Ouen 067703
Alinea, Knokke-Heist 058237
Aline's Antiques, Louisville 089952
Alingsås Museum, Alingsås 036172
Aliprandi, Gianantonio, Milano 075576
Alis, Bucureşti 121960
Alisan Fine Arts, Hong Kong 097746
Alisgården, Lapinkylä 009799
Alison, Chennai 074786
Alison, Chennai 074787
Alisson RP 42, Saint-Étienne 067436
Alivertti, René, Vésenaz 082875
Aliwal North Museum and Church Plein Museum, Aliwal North 034544
Alix, Jean-Bernard, Paris 124546
Alix, Pierre, Chinon 120977
Aliya, Atlanta 114843
Alizarin, San Francisco 119582
Alizarine, Albi 060747, 098806
Alizarine, Auvers-sur-Oise 098882
Alizés, Ronnet 067214
El Aljibe, Don Torcuato 055257
Aljira Center for Contemporary Art, Newark 046422
Alkader, Antwerpen 096054
Alkader, Antwerpen 096055, 123545
Alkader, Mechelen 096382
Alkame, Milano 075577
Alkent Actuel Art, İstanbul 112269
Alkgård, Peter, Gnesta 122140
Alkgårds Auktionskammare, Södertälje 122241
Alkmaar Galeries voor Hedendaagse Kunst, Alkmaar 107612
Alkonost, Sankt-Peterburg 140928
Alkoven, Basel 082114
All Aboard, Wallington 056797
All About Antiques, Oklahoma City . 091453
All About Antiques, Wagga Wagga . 056787
All About Art, Albuquerque 114764
All About Coins, Salt Lake City 092410
All About Pictures, Cincinnati 115598
All American Vogue, Denver 088636
All-Antik, Stockholm 081909
All Antique Glass, Norfolk 091364
All Art 1900, Bruxelles 057808
All Art & Antique Restorer, Kardinya 123247
All Art Gallery, Houston 116263
All Art is Quite Useless, Antwerpen . 096056
All Arts Bookshop, Woollahra 137142
All Booked Up, Jacksonville 142459
All Booked Up and More, Louisville 142523
All Books Used and Rare, Houston . 142422
All-Brite, Philadelphia 132604
All-China Association of Fine Arts Workers, Beijing 052787
All Hallows Undercroft Museum, London 040075
All in Good Time Antiques, Strathalbyn 056635
All in Luck, Baltimore 087632
All-India Fine Arts and Crafts Society, Delhi 053686
All Most Antiques, Toronto 059115
All My Relations, Indianapolis 089260
All Our Yesterday, Sandwich 086517
All Our Yesterdays, Glasgow 084459
All-Ram, Limhamn 110951
All Star Collectibles, Cleveland 088299
All the Best Antiques, Buffalo 087856
All the Right Angles, Seattle 119870
All The Way Militaria, Rotterdam . . 078693
All Things Considered, Columbus . . 088373
All Things Old and Interesting, Yackandandah 056890
All Uppköpet, Stockholm 081910
Alla Corte del Re, Cagliari 075198
Alla Corte Interiors, Padova 076066
Alla Prima Arts, Portland 118963
Alla Prima Gallery, Towcester 114594

Alla Prima Studios, Dallas 115822
Alla Stazione, Genova 106078
Allahabad Museum, Allahabad 022001
Allain, Françoise, Plurien 066880
Allaire-Aigret, Paris 099921
Allam, Newbridge-on-Wye 086058, 131302
Allan, C.A., Adelaide 136768
Allan, N.S., New York 090657
Allan Shivers Museum, Woodville . . 049299
All'Angolo, Torino 076756
All'Angolo, Torino 128250
Allanix, Carouge 111330
Allan's Antiques and Reproductions, Cheadle Hulme 083912
Allard, Saint Ignatius 123083
Allard, Isabelle, Annecy 124077
Allard, Serge, Montbenoit 064652
Allard Pierson Museum Amsterdam, Archeologisch Museum der Universiteit van Amsterdam, Amsterdam 029163
Allardi, Jean-Philippe, Paris 121107
Allary, Irène, Pradelles 066974
Allbooks, Leidschendam 140485
Allcroft, Michael, Disley 084165
Allcroft, Michael, Hayfield 084634
Allcroft, Michael, Newmills 086073
Alldecor, Kirchberg (Sankt Gallen) . 111582
Allecto, Tallinn 137912
Allée du Roy, Willgottheim 069052
Allegan County Historical and Old Jail Museum, Allegan 041655
Allegany County Historical Museum, Cumberland 043242
Allegany County Museum, Belmont 042127
Alleghany Highlands Arts and Crafts Center, Clifton Forge 043009
Allegreto, Lisboa 109260
Allegri, Claude, Flendruz 082371
Allegrini, Wiesbaden 074393
Allegro, Barcelona 129311
Allegro - Galerie Díla, Praha 098413
Allemand, Philippe, Issoire 124264
Allemandi, Umberto, Torino 134688
Allemandi & Beltrametti, Brescia . . 075139
Allemann, Jean-Pierre, Valdoie . . . 125005
Allemann, Pierre, Evette-Salbert . . . 124237
Allen, Baltimore 142218
Allen, Pittsburgh 091784
Allen, Anthony, New Mills 131299
Allen, J., San Francisco 092708
Allen, John, Norwich 114159
Allen, M., Four Oaks 084430, 130716
Allen, Martin, Prahran 056487
Allen, Michael, East Brisbane 055780
Allen, Robert, San Francisco 119583
Allen, Tricia, Nungurner 094999
Allen, William H., Philadelphia 142732
Allen County-Fort Wayne Historical Society Museum, Fort Wayne 043996
Allen County Historical Museum, Iola 044763
Allen County Museum, Lima 045292
Allen Gallery, Alton 038499
Allen Memorial Art Museum, Oberlin College, Oberlin 046607
Allen R. Hite Art Institute, University of Louisville, Louisville 045482
Allen Sapp Gallery, North Battleford 006032
Allen & Townsend, Dublin 121660
Allena, Costanzo Giovenale, Torino . 128251
Alleno, Janine, Amboise 060796
Allen's, Branksome 083643
Allen's Antiques, North Shore 079186
Allenspach, Kurt, Azmoos 082102
Allentown Art Festival, Buffalo 115247
Allentown Art Museum, Allentown . 041657
Allentuck, Gary, Washington 120245
AllerArt, Bludenz 095480
Allerhand, Ansbach 101586
Allerhande, Hippolytushoef 029753
Allerton, Mornington 094882
Allerton, New York 117579
Allerton Books, Leeds 141711
Allerts, A., København 060262
Allery, Toronto 059116, 097212
Alles, I., Baden-Baden 069408
Alles Antik, Bremen 070005
Alles-Kitsch Curiosa, Den Haag . . . 078161
Alletru, Frédéric, Noyant 065241
Alley Cat, Saint Louis 092198
Allez Art, Bad Homburg v.d.Höhe . . 069288
Allgäu-Museum, Kempten 018231
Allgäuer, Robert, Vaduz 140223
Allgäuer Auktionshaus, Kempten . . 121463
Allgäuer Burgenmuseum, Kempten 018232
Allhallows Museum of Lace and Antiquities, Honiton 039767
L'Alliance, Toulon (Var) 138625
Alliance and District Museum, Alliance 004997
Alliance Biblique des Antilles Françoises, Baie Mahault 139905
Alliance Européenne des Experts, La Guéroulde 052887
Alliance Française Galerie, Ha Noi . 120443
Alliance of Artists' Communities, Providence 054559
Allianz deutscher Designer e.V., Braunschweig 053009
Allie Griffin Art Gallery, Weyburn . . . 006801
Allied Air Force Museum, Allentown 041658
Allied Artists of America, New York . 054560
Allied Arts Association, Richland . . 054561
Allied Arts Center and Gallery, Richland 047392
Allied Arts Council of Lethbridge, Bowman Arts Center, Lethbridge 052722
Allied Arts of Seattle, Seattle 054562
Allier Antiquités, Vichy 068852
Les Alliés, Paris 099922
Les Alliés, Paris 099923
Alligri, Dominique, Bischheim 061497
Alliierten-Museum Berlin, Berlin . . . 015983
Alling Coverlet Museum, Palmyra . . 046799
All'Insegna del Sole, Genova 075429
Allison, Miami 090119
Allison, Marie, Nashville 090410
Allison-Antrim Museum, Greencastle 044319
Allisonville Road Antique Mall, Indianapolis 089261
Allix, Brix 061817
Allmendinger, Rolf, Vaihingen 126940
Allmer, Helmut, Graz 056997
Allo, Robert, Menton 064488
Allobroc, Savigny-sur-Orge 068168
Allongue, Michel, Fayence 062847
Allongue, Michel, Tourrettes 068572
Allora Historical Museum, Allora . . . 000740
Allora Treasures, Allora 055341
Alloy, Los Angeles 132231
Allpine, London 130918
Allpress Antiques, Malvern, Victoria 056142, 123257
Allroggen, Sabine, Brühl, Rheinland 125403
Allroggen, Silke, München 126344
Allschwiler Kunst-Zentrum, Allschwil 036828
Allschwiler Kunstverein, Allschwil . 054165
Allsop, Duncan M., Warwick 142140
Allsop, Jonathan, Mouilleron-en-Pareds 064808
Alltime Antiques, Bairnsdale 055420
Alluard, Régis, Andéchy 124072
Alluchon, Bernard, Paris 065377
Allure, Brugge 057757
Allure Antiques, Perth 056453
Alluto, Annalisa, Torino 128252
Allwardt, Amorbach 069164
Allwardt, R., Amberg, Oberpfalz . . . 069160
Allwood Antiques, Nowra North . . . 056394
Allwood Furniture Repair, Calgary . . 123737
Allwood House, Hurstbridge 001122
Ally, Saint Paul 142863
ALM Déco, Le Pré-Saint-Gervais . . 124307
Alma, Montpellier 099749
Alma, Praha 060091
Alma, Saint-Jean-de-Luz 101160
Alma Firehouse and Mining Museum, Alma 041665
El Almacen, Fuengirola 081103
Almacén a la Bina, Bogotá 059803
Almacén Anticuario Antigüedades Bazaar, Bogotá 059804
Almacén Bazar la Subasta, Bogotá . 059805
Almacén Galeria de Arte, Rio de Janeiro 096584
Almacén Jalan Dahlan, Bogotá 059806
Almacén Jalan Dhalan, Cartagena . 059889
Almacenes el Hogar, Santa Cruz de Tenerife 110737
Almaden, San Jose 132920
Almaden-Espacio Arte, Madrid 110424
Alman Arkeoloji Enstitüsü, İstanbul . 050792
Almanar, Casablanca 107546
Almandine, Paris 065378
Almar, Conilhac-Corbières 062463
Almar, C. & A., Bucureşti 080137
Almarza, Santiago de Chile 059485, 123872
Almaz-Lombard, Balakovo 080204
Almaznyj Fond, Gosudarstvennyj muzej-zapovednik Moskovskij Kreml, Moskva 033364
Almazova, Moskva 109484
Almazovo, Moskva 109485
Almecap-Arte-Creacion, Bogotá . . . 098094
Almeda Antique Mall, Houston 088995
Almeda Antique Mall, Houston 088996
Almediheem, Khalid, Riyadh 080371
Almehagen, Anita, Firenze 106029
Almeida, Arlette de, Ville-sur-Jarnioux 068886
Almeida, Monica Filgueiras de, São Paulo 096659
Almeida, Vitória Silva, Lisboa 079844
Almeida Franco, Lisboa 079845
Almeida Fuentes, Alejandra, Zaragoza 129802
Almeida & Sousa, Lisboa 079846
Almelek, İstanbul 112270
Almenningen Galleri, Bergen 108674
Alméras, Jacky, Anduze 060836
Almira Restauradores, Madrid 129556
Almirah Antiques, Bangalore 074763
Almoina, Palma de Mallorca 081466
Almond Valley Heritage Centre, Livingston 040043
Almoneda, Madrid 081202, 129557
Almoneda, Valencia 081637
Almoneda Abando, Bilbao 080964
Almoneda Altamira, Vigo . 081696, 122091
Almoneda Angelo, Málaga 081414
Almoneda Arienza, Madrid 081203
Almoneda Bastero, Madrid 081204, 122032, 141022
Almoneda el 23, Madrid . . 081205, 122033
Almoneda la Catedral, Pamplona . .081506, 122080
Almoneda la Fuentecilla, Madrid . . 081206
Almoneda Trastienda, Pontevedra . 081528
Almoneda Verona, Madrid 081207
Almonedas Muñecas, Madrid 081208
Almonry Heritage Centre, Evesham 039461
Almorial, Paris 099924
Almost All New Zealand Books, Oamaru 140649
Almost Heaven, Tucson 093191
Almshouses Arcade, Chichester . . . 083969
Almusbah, Shuaa, Jeddah 080355
Almviks Tegelbruksmuseum, Västervik 036769
Alne Bank, Gerringong 001055
Alnot, Colette, Saint-Ouen 067704
Alnwick Antiques, Alexandra 055336
Aloha, Brugheas 061822
Aloha Antiques, Honolulu 088929
Aloha Images, Honolulu 116193
Aloha Wood Art, Honolulu 116194
Along the Way, Baltimore 087633
Alonso, Jean-Claude, Aillant-sur-Tholon 060682
Alonso, Jose, Miami 117015
Alonso, Ricardo, Córdoba 055250
Alonso Castrillo, Isabel y Jose Ramon, Madrid 081209
Alonso-Defrocourt, Paris 065379
Alonso Novoa, Málaga 110630
Alonzo's, Salt Lake City 132778
Alopaşalı, Kütahya 083168
Alosery, Almere 107627
Alostum, Mathias, Aalst 057657
't Aloude, Utrecht 078788
Alouette, San Diego 092598
Alp' Antiquités, Moutiers-Tarentaise 064823
Alp-Museum Fasons, Seewis-Dorf . 037551
Alp'Antic, Goncelin 063010
Alpen-Adria-Galerie im Stadthaus, Klagenfurt 002136
Alpenländische Galerie, Zweigmuseum des Bayerischen Nationalmuseums, Kempten 018233
Alpenrail Swiss Model Village and Railway, Claremont, Tasmania 000919
Alpenrose, Moskva 109486
Alpenverein-Museum, Innsbruck . . 002074
Alper, Maurice, Terrasson-Lavilledieu 068373
Alper, Sherri, Nashville 090411
Alpermann, Sabine, Erlangen 102651
Alpha Antiques, Baltimore 087634
Alpha Antiquites, Saint-Ouen 067705
Alpha Arts Enchères, Lyon 121041
Alpha Collection, Paris 065380
Alpha Fine Art, Cape Town 110014
Alpha Gallery, Boston 115138
Alpha House Gallery, Sherborne . . . 114427
Alpha Museum, Bangalore 022013
alpha nova, Berlin 101774
Alpha Numis, Lagor 063488
Alpha-Presse, Frankfurt am Main . . 133935
Alpha Space, Sapporo 106980
Alphagraphics, Chicago 115333
Alpha's Dolls, Dallas 088450
Alphaville, New York 117580
Alphaville, Rio de Janeiro . 096585, 120794
Alphecca, Chard 124187
Alphecca, Paris 099925
Alpin- und Heimatmuseum, Hohe Wand-Stollhof 002053
Alpine, London 135172
Alpine Antiques, Astley Bridge 083345
Alpine Art, Salt Lake City 119326
Alpine Coin Company, Portland 091883
Alpine Design, New York 090658
Alpines Ballonsport-Museum, Mürren 037359
Alpines Museum, Zermatt 037747
Alpines Museum des Deutschen Alpenvereins, München 019029
Alpineum, 3D-Alpenpanorama/ Diorama, Luzern 037291
Alpinmuseum, Zweigmuseum des Bayerischen Nationalmuseums, Kempten 018234
Alpinmuseum Dachstein, Ramsau am Dachstein 002496
Alpmuseum Riederalp, Riederalp . . 037450
Alp'Ours, Annecy 060883
Alps, Atlanta 114844
Alpsennereimuseum, Hittisau 002048
Alresford Gallery, Alresford 112498
Alro's Antiques, Woody Point 056850
Al's Collectables and Antiques, Denver 088637
Al's Fine Art, Nashville 117330
Al's Gallery, Nashville 117331
Als Hjemstavnsmuseum, Hadsund . 008888
Alsace, Strasbourg 068285
Alsacienne-de-l'Or et des Métaux Précieux, Metz 064517
Alsaticarta, Mulhouse . . . 064825, 138226
Alsatroc, Strasbourg 068286
Alschweig, Frank, Schwabach 126781
Alsina Antigüedades, Buenos Aires . 055151
Alsleben, Berlin 069551, 125160
Alsmeier, Esther, Nordhorn 126556
Alšova Jihočeská Galerie, Hluboká nad Vltavou 008372

Alster Philatelie, Hamburg 071187
Alsters Herrgård, Karlstad 036386
Alstertalmuseum, Hamburg 017679
Alstin's Antique Gallery, Hamilton, Victoria 055940, 120590, 123235
Alston Antiques, Alston 083282
Alt, Hamilton 123768
Alt, Konrad, Schillingsfürst 073689
Alt, Manfred, Saarbrücken 073621
Alt & Antik, Buxtehude 070116
Alt-Arnstorf-Haus, Arnstorf 015569
Alt-Freden-Sammlung, Freden 017216
Alt-Gut, Bad Nauheim 138699
ALT Production, Paris 099926, 133510
Alt-Refrath, Bergisch Gladbach . . . 101759
Alt-Rothenburger Handwerkerhaus, Rothenburg ob der Tauber 019912
Alt & Schön, Mayen 072475
Alt-Segeberger Bürgerhaus, Bad Segeberg 015798
Alt-Stade im Baumhaus, Stade 020274
Alt Wien Kunst, Wien 057360, 120677
Alta, R., Tilburg 078765
L'Alta Epoca, Brescia 075140
Alta Mira, Eivissa 110345
Alta Museum, Alta 030722
Altadena Antiques, Birmingham . . . 087731
Altai, Milano 106148
Altair, Palma de Mallorca 110669
Altajskij Gosudarstvennyj Institut Iskusstv i Kultury, Barnaul 050625
Altajskij Gosudarstvennyj Kraevedčeskij Muzej, Barnaul 033014
Altajskij Respublikanskij Kraevedčeskij Muzej im. A.V. Anochina, Gorno-Altajsk 033152
Altamira, Caracas 120422
Altamira, Warszawa 079721
Altamiradeco, Bournemouth 083591
Altamont Press, Asheville 135319
Altamura, Altamura 135862
Altbuchdienst Luegerplatz, Wien . . 137284
Altdenzlinger Heimethüs mit Otto-Raupp-Stube, Denzlingen 016672
Altdorfer Universitäts-Museum, Altdorf bei Nürnberg 015491
Alte Anton Bruckner-Schule, Windhaag bei Freistadt 003049
Alte Börse, Stadtgeschichtliches Museum Leipzig, Leipzig 018558
Das Alte Bureau, Berlin 069552
Alte Cuesterey, Essen 017058
Alte Fabrik, Bonn 069910, 125347
Alte Feste, National Museum of Namibia, Windhoek 029104
Alte Feuerwache Loschwitz e.V., Kunst- und Kulturverein, Dresden . . 053010, 102420
Alte Försterei, Ilmenau 103425
Alte Galerie, Landesmuseum Joanneum, Graz 001925
Alte Galerie Enge, Zürich 082933
Alte Huf- und Wagenschmiede, Dietmanns 001781
Alte Kachelofenfabrik, Neustrelitz . . 104436
Alte Kirche Friedensdorf, Dautphetal 016651
Alte Kunst, Wien 057361
Alte Kunst & Militaria, Wien 057362
Alte Marktschmiede, Lasberg 002205
Alte Möbel, Berlin 069553
Alte Mühle Schrattenberg, Schrattenberg 002655
Alte Nationalgalerie, Staatliche Museen zu Berlin - Stiftung Preußischer Kulturbesitz, Berlin 015984
Alte Oberamtei, Gerabronn 017376
Alte Pinakothek, Bayerische Staatsgemäldesammlungen, München 019030
Alte Saline Bad Reichenhall, Bad Reichenhall 015772
Alte Schatztruhe, Wien 057363
Alte Schmiede, Mühlbeck 139486
Alte Schule mit Clara-Zetkin-Gedächtnisstätte, Königshain-Wiederau 018351
Alte Seifenfabrik, Lauterach 002210
Der Alte Stil, Kippenheim 071851
Alte Synagoge, Hechingen 017816
Alte Synagoge, Museen der Stadt Essen, Essen 017059
Alte und Neue Kunst, Paderborn . . . 135737
Alte Universitäts-Galerie, Wien 095787
Alte Wache, Groitzsch bei Pegau . . 017548
Alte Wassermühlen und Museum Des Bauern Sach und Zeug, Maria Luggau 002282
Das Alte Zollhaus Heimatmuseum, Hitzacker 017934
Altea, Madrid 110425
Altea Maps & Books, London 130919, 141744
Altenau, G., Diekhusen-Fahrstedt . . 070244
Altenburg, Berlin 121317
Altendorf, Irmeli & Wolfgang, Freudenstadt 102878, 133960
Alter, New York 090659
Alter, Anneliese, Hamburg 071188
Alter, Hélène, Malakoff 064230
Alter Dinge Hof, Wels 057350
Alter Ego, Parma 076192
Alter Spielzeug Trödelladen, Innsbruck 057072
Alterio, Pasquale, Roma 127913
Altermann, Santa Fe 119868, 123110
Alterna, Warszawa 129075
L'Alternance, Arras 098862
Alternariato, Torino 076757
L'Alternative, Paris 065381
Alternative Antiques, Warrnambool . 056804
Alternative Ink, San Antonio 119391
Alternative Museum, New York 046280
Alternatives, Tucson 120098
Altero, Nicole, Paris 065382
Alterosa Arte Comtemporanea e Antiga, São Paulo 096660
Altertumssammlung der Benediktinerabtei, Engelberg 037066
Altertumstresor, München 072630
Altes am Graben, Graz 056998
Altes Amtshaus, Karl-Pollender-Stadtmuseum, Werne 020810
Altes en vogue, Basel 082115
Altes Hafenamt, Ständige Ausstellung für Hafen und Schiffahrt, Dortmund . 016761
Altes Haus, Greifenstein 017518
Altes Rathaus, Lüneburg 018739
Altes Rathaus-Potsdam Forum, Potsdam 019652
Altes Rathaus Wilster, Wilster 020906
Altes Residenztheater, München . . . 019031
Altes Schloß Schleißheim, Oekumenische Sammlung Gertrud Weinhold Das Gottesjahr und seine Feste, Bayerisches Nationalmuseum, Oberschleißheim 019411
Altes Schloß Schleißheim, Sammlung zur Landeskunde Ost- und Westpreußens, Bayerisches Nationalmuseum, Oberschleißheim 019412
Altes & Schönes, Barsinghausen . . 069473
Altes Schoß, Abteilung Gemäldegalerie und Kunsthandwerk, Oberhessisches Museum und Gail'sche Sammlungen, Gießen 017407
Altes und Besonderes, Wien 057364
Altes und Neues Schloß Eremitage, Bayreuth 015904
Altes Zeughaus Landenberg, Sarnen 037513
Altesse, Nendeln . 077444, 107333, 134739
Altesse, Wien 137285
Altfield, Hong Kong 059585
Altfriesisches Haus, Sylt-Ost 020391
Althorp Museum, Althorp 038498
Altia Oyj, Rajamäen Tehdasmuseo, Rajamäki 010017
Altiero, Thierry, Le Thor 063711
El Altillo, Montevideo 087302
El Altillo, Zaragoza 081730
Altius, Warszawa . 079722, 109087, 121900
Altkirch Antiquités, Mulhouse 064826
Altkunst Josefstadt, Wien 057365
Altländer, Jork 103455
Altmärkische Antiquariats & Kunsthandlung, Gardelegen 070933, 139130
Altmärkisches Museum, Stendal . . 020314
Altman, Robert, New York 090660
Altmann, Aspremont 061013
Altmann, Gerhard, Tulln 095773
Altmeyer, R., Paderborn 073279
Altmühltaler Mühlenmuseum, Dietfurt 016705
Altnöder, Ferdinand, Salzburg 095715
Altomani & Sons, Milano 075578
Altomani & Sons, Milano 075579
Alton Museum of History and Art, Alton 041671
Altona Antikviteter, Malmö 081859
Altonaer Antiquariat, Hamburg 139165
Altonaer Antiquitätenhof, Hamburg .071189, 125798
Altonaer Museum in Hamburg, Norddeutsches Landesmuseum, Hamburg 017680
Alträucher, Köln 071900
Altrama, Madrid 129558
Altri Tempi, Taranto 076742
Altstadt Antiquariat, Erfurt 139043
Altstadt Antiquariat, Freiburg im Breisgau 139104
Altstadt-Antiquariat, Zürich 141317
Altstadt-Galerie, Bern 111242
Altstadt-Galerie, Mainz 103994
Altstadt Galerie, Remscheid 104712
Altstadt Galerie Hall, Hall in Tirol . . 095556
Altstadtantiquariat, Innsbruck 137194
Altstadtgalerie, Greiz 102999
Altstadtgalerie, Rheda-Wiedenbrück 104738
Altstadtrathaus, Städtisches Museum Braunschweig, Braunschweig . . . 016380
Altube Barandiaran, Fernando, Donostia-San Sebastián 110330
Altun Ha Archaeological Site, Altun Ha 003877
Altunizade Kültür Merkezi, İstanbul 112271
Alturath, Manama 057616
Altus, Berlin 069554, 121318
Altus, San Isidro 055298
Altxerri, Donostia-San Sebastián . . 110331
Altza, Donostia-San Sebastián 129498
Alūksnes Novadpētniecības un Mākslas Muzejs, Alūksne 027657
Alumni Museum, Catonsville 042658
Alumny Creek School Museum, Grafton 001077
Alun, Pierre d', Bruxelles 133255
Aluna Gallery, Washington 120246
Alupka State Palace and Park Preserve, Alupka 038225
Aluštinskij Literaturno-Memorialnyj Muzej S.N. Sergeeva-Censkogo, Alušta . 038226
Alutiiq Museum and Archaeological Repository, Kodiak 045044
Alva DeMars Megan Chapel Art Center, Saint Anselm College, Manchester 045617
Alvar Aalto Museum, Jyväskylä . . . 009634
Alvarenga, Eliana, Rio de Janeiro . . 058534
Alvárez e Hijos, Buenos Aires 055152
Alvarez, New York 132429
Alvarez, Orléans 065290
Alvarez, Porto 109364
Alvárez, Ernesto, Buenos Aires 055153
Alvarez, John Jairo, Medellín 098247
Alvárez, Julietta, Medellín 098248
Alvarez, Robert, Bayonville-sur-Mad 098934
Alvárez Reyes, Carlos, Santiago de Chile 059486, 123873
Alvarez Rodrigo, Maria Pilar, Zaragoza 129803
Alvarez Soleil, Levroux 063805
Alvarez White, María Cecilia, Bogotá 098095, 123890
Alvargonzalez, Madrid . . . 081210, 122034
Alvaro Chirveches, Carlos Javier, Madrid 129559
Alvaro Galeria, Sevilla 110761
Alvdal Museum, Alvdal 030723
Alvear, Don Torcuato 055258
Alvear, Washington 120247
Alvear, Helga de, Madrid 110426
Alvear Antiques, Buenos Aires 055154
Alvear Art Galerie, Buenos Aires . . . 055155
Alvensleben, München 104136
Karen Alvermann & Heiko Geier, Bensheim 069522
Alverton, Northallerton 131322
Alves, Carlos, Miami 117016
Alves, Leonardo Donizete, São Paulo 058669
Alves, Maria Fernanda, Coimbra . . . 140811
Alves, Maria Fernanda, Coimbra . . . 140812
Alves-Albich, Helenice, Friedberg, Hessen 102882
Alves Beato, Manuel, Lisboa 079847
Alves & Marques, Lisboa 079848
Alves & Rodrigues, Coimbra 079816
Alvillos, San Miguel de Tucumán . . 055301
Alwane, Casablanca 107547
Alwane, Sarba Kaslik 077439
Always Buying Antiques, Jacksonville 089366
Always Collectible, Austin 087546, 142213
Alwin, Goult 063021
Alwun, Phoenix 118859
Alyea's Jewellers, Ottawa 059025
Alyed, Marrakech 077679
Alys Antiques 1906, Waikato 079280
Alyskewycz, Jorge, Paris 099927
Alyth Museum, Perth Museum and Art Gallery, Alyth 038503
Alzgalerie, Truchtlaching 105071
Alzon, Yves, Hirsingue 063158
A.M. de Jonghuis, Nieuw Vossemeer 029944
Am Dragos, Madrid 110427
Am Ellinger Tor, Weißenburg in Bayern 074325
AM Galeria de Artes, Belo Horizonte 096453
Am Quadros, São Paulo 058670
A.M Real French Polishing, London 130920
AM Trading, Aldgate 055334
AM Visual Arts Management, Elizabeth Bay 055791
AMA Galerie, Braunschweig 102214
Amabile Kunst & Mode, München . . 072631
Amacla, Toulouse 101328
Amadei, Maria Luigia, Bologna 075038
Amadeus, Wien 057366
Amadeus Antikues, Bucureşti 080138
Amadeus Antiques, Tunbridge Wells 086931
Amadeus Antiquités, Paris 065383
Amadeus Maroc, Casablanca 077630
Amado, Gonçalo, Lisboa 109261
Amador de los Rios, Madrid 110428
Amador-Livermore Valley Museum, Pleasanton 047088
Amagasaki Bunka Art Gallery, Amagasaki 026413
Amager, København 133422
Amagerbro Antik, København 060263, 137877
Amagermuseet, Dragør 008831
Amakusa Kirishitankan, Hondo 026546
L'Amalgame, Alès 060769
Amalienborg, Danske Kongers Kronologiske Samling, København 008956
Åmåls Hembygdsmuseum, Åmål . . 036176
Åmåls Järnvägsmuseum, Åmål . . . 036177
Åmåls Konsthall, Åmål 036178
Amalthea Verlag, Wien 133176
Amana, Aix-en-Provence 098779
Amanda's Collectibles, Houston . . . 088997
Amanda's of Mogo, Mogo 094865
Amanda's Secondhand Hypermarket, Newport, Shropshire 086079
Amandi, Oestrich-Winkel 104523
L'Amandier Artémis, Auxerre 061094
Amandine, Bouguenais 061678
Amann, Johannes, Weißenhorn . . . 126990
Amann, Sandra, New York 132430

Amano, Kazuo, Osaka 106950
Amanosan Kongo-ji Treasure House, Kawachi-Nagano 026637
Amapola Gallery, Albuquerque 114765
Amar Nadège, Lioux 063906
Amaral, Adriano, Porto 129186
Amarante, Grenoble 063044
Amarante, La Rochelle 063422
Amarante, Lyon 064051
Amarante, Marcq-en-Barœul 064270, 124386
Amarante, Montrouge 064776
Amarante & Zebrano, Paris 124547
Amararte, Lugo 081190, 110412
Amarica, Paul, Paris 099928
Amarilli, Torino 076758
Amarillo Art Association, Amarillo . . 054563
Amarillo Museum of Art, Amarillo . . 041678
Amarna, Maastricht 108113
Amarna, Maastricht 108114
Amartiste, Courseulles-sur-Mer . . . 099182
Amaryl, Groningen 140429
Amaryllis, Bruxelles 096128
Amaryllis, Bruxelles 096129
Amasra Müzesi ve Tarihçesi, Amasra 038002
Amaste Comunicacion, Bilbao 110268
Amasya Devlet Güzel Sanatlar Galerisi, Amasya 038003
Amasya Müzesi, Kral Mezarları, Hazeranlar Konaği ve Alpaslan Müzesi, Amasya 038004
Amate, Moreno & Garcia, Paris 099929
L'Amateur, Beirut 107325
L'Amateur, Buenos Aires 136693
L'Amateur d'Art, Beirut 107326
L'Amateur de Musique, Paris 065384
Amateurs d'Art, Perros-Guirec 066763
Amathole Museum, King William's Town 034667
Amato, Nice 065024
Amatto, Hasparren 099325
Amaury Goyet Galerie, Aix-en-Provence 060693
Amayoube, Paris 099930
Amazeum, München 019055
Amazing Adventures Collectibles, San Francisco 092709
Amazing Grates, London . 085069, 130921
Amazonite, Casablanca 077631
't Ambacht, Enschede 128666
Ambalama, Amstelveen 077757
Ambalangoda Mask Museum, Ambalangoda 036125
Ambassador Antiques, Albion 055324
Ambena, Paris 099931
Amber, Nijmegen 078649
Amber, B., Seattle 092947
Amber Antiques, Auckland 078904
Amber Antiques, Southampton 086647, 131516
Amber Arts, Edinburgh 112981
Amberes, Antwerpen 120702
Amberg, Tönisvorst 074066
Amberg, Hardy, Schleusingen 126771
Amberg, Michael, Würzburg 127038
Ambergate, A.A., Ripley, Derbyshire 086370
Ambergris Museum and Cultural Centre, Ambergis Caye 003878
Amberia, Gdańsk 079576
Amberina, Siraya, Antwerpen 057672
Amberley Working Museum, Amberley 038504
Ambiance Antiques, San Francisco . 092710
Ambiance Antiquités, Montréal 058893, 123780
Ambiance Art and Antiques, Los Angeles 089674, 132232
Ambiance Deco, La Rochelle 063423
Ambiance et Discernement Antiquités, Montréal 058894
Ambience, Kolkata 105734
Ambience Antiques, New Orleans . . 090502
Ambient Art, Amsterdam 107650
Ambiente, Bad Sachsa 069361
Ambiente, Cuxhaven 070165
Ambiente, Grindelwald 082485
Ambiente, Norderstedt 073070
Ambiente, Plön 073346, 126634
Ambiente, Rotterdam 078694
Ambiente, Seebad Heringsdorf 104876
Ambiente, Zwartsluis 128889
Ambiente 51, Heidelberg 071443
Ambiente Antik, Aschaffenburg . . . 069188
Ambiente Antik, Bad Münstereifel . 069331
Ambiente de Antaño, Medellín 059893
Ambienti, Casablanca 077632
Ambijenta, Beograd 080386, 109680
Ambika, Lisboa 079849
Ambika, Paris 138280
Ambit Find, New Orleans 090503
Ambit Galeria, Barcelona 110102
l'Amboine, Bruxelles 057809
Ambra, Milano 127514
Ambre, Besançon 061375
Ambre, Cenon 062049
Ambre, Compiègne 062436
Ambre Antiquités, Casablanca 077633
Ambre Congo, Bruxelles 057810
Ambre de Chaldée, Strasbourg 068287
Ambre Jaune, Gentinnes 123636
Ambridge Ferazzutti, Toronto 059117
Ambrogi, Walter, Roma 127914
Ambrosanio, Nello, Roma 127915
Ambrose, Cleveland 088300
Ambrose & Assoc., Columbus 088374
Ambrose, Loughton 122606
Ambrosia, Los Angeles 142487
Ambrosia Books, Balmain 136792
L'Ambrosiana, Milano 106149
Ambrosini & Marinari, Livorno 075521
Ambrossino, Miami 117017
Ambrozik, Henryk, Warszawa 079723
Ambühl, H.-R., Thalwil 111942
Ambühl & Wackerle, Luzern 111677
A.M.C., Mulhouse 099784, 133501
Ame, Paris 099932, 124548
Ame du Bois, Béziers 061427
Amedeo, Zürich 082934
Amelang, Hamburg 103085
Amelang, J., Berlin 125161
Amelia Douglas Gallery, New Westminster 006002
Amelia Earhart Birthplace Museum, Atchison 041828
Amelia Island Museum of History, Fernandina Beach 043836
Amelia's, Ashburton 078902
Amelia's Antique, Wagga Wagga . . 056788
Amelia's Retro-Vogue and Relics, Austin 087547
Ameliasburgh Historical Museum, Ameliasburgh 005004
Amélie Antiquités, Paris 065385
Ameline, Paule, Paris 124549
Åmell, Verner, London . . . 085070, 113443
Åmell, Verner, Stockholm 081911
Åmell's Konsthandel, Stockholm . . 110998
Ameln, Eilika, Koblenz 071888
Amend & Assoc., E.M., Dallas 115823
Amend, E.M., Dallas 131992
Amendola, Adriano, Roma 127916
Amendolara, Robert, Providence . . 092030
Amenity, Machida 077140
América Antigüedades, Buenos Aires 123147
América Móvel, Lisboa 079850
America West Primitive and Modern Art Gallery, Tucson 120099
Americabilia, Las Vegas 089534
American Abstract Artists, New York 054564
American Academy in Rome, New York 136292
American Academy in Rome, Roma 050420
American Academy in Rome. Memoirs, Roma 135863
American Academy of Appraisers of Art, Antiques and Rug, Bridgeville . . . 122828
American Academy of Art, Cambridge 051061
American Academy of Arts and Letters, New York 051808
American Academy of Arts and Letters Art Museum, New York 046281
American Advertising Museum, Portland 047166
American Airlines C.R. Smith Museum, Fort Worth 044001
American Airpower Heritage Museum, Midland 045850
American Antiquarian Society, Worcester 054565
American Antique Mall, Tucson . . . 093192
American Antiques, Cleveland 088301
American Art, Baltimore 115028
American Art, Washington 136293
American Art and Antiques, Chicago 122840
American Art Antiques, Chicago . . . 088003
American Art Gallery, München . . . 104137
American Art Journal, New York . . . 136294
American Art Publishing, San Francisco 135486
American Art Resources, Houston . 116264
American Art Review, Kansas City . 136295
American Artisan, Nashville 117332
American Artist, New York 136296
American Artists Professional League, New York 054566
American Arts Alliance, Washington 054567
American Arts Antiques, Chicago . . 088004
American Association for Museum Volunteers, Denver 054568
American Association for State and Local History, Nashville 054569
American Association of Dealers in Ancient, Oriental and Primitive Art, New York 054570
American Association of Museums, Washington 054571
American Baptist Museum, Rochester 047476
American Bicycle and Cycling Museum, Santa Fe 047961
American Bronzes, Las Vegas 116600
American Catholic Historical Society Museum, Philadelphia 046920
American Center, Sofia 096717
American Ceramic Society, Westerville 054572
American Classical II, Nashville . . . 090412
American Classical Music Hall of Fame and Museum, Cincinnati 042916
American Classics, Minneapolis . . . 090336
American Clock and Watch Museum, Bristol 042417
American Coin and Currency, Omaha 091547
American Coin and Jewelry, Oklahoma City 091454
American Coin Collectibles, Columbus 088375
American Coin Company, Cleveland 088302
American Coin Exchange, Fort Worth 088828
American Coin Exchange, Miami . . 090120
American Coins, Portland 091884
American Collectibles, Las Vegas . . 089535
American Collectibles, Norfolk 091365
American Color Print Society, Princeton 054573
American Cotton Museum, Greenville 044350
American Council for the Arts, New York 054574
American Cowboy and Indian Art, Chicago 088005
American Craft, New York 136297
American Craft Museum, New York 046282
American Craftsmen, Portland 132682
American Craftsmen, Portland 132683
American Estates, Milwaukee 090267
American Estates and Antiques, Portland 091885
American European Art, New York . 054575
American-European Art, New York . 117581
American Federal Rare Coins, Phoenix 091707
American Federation of Arts, New York 054576
The American Film Institute, Los Angeles 045410
American Fine Art and Frame, Dallas 115824
American Fine Arts Gallery, New York 117582
American Fine Arts Society, New York 054577
American Folk Art Museum, New York 046283
American Garage, Los Angeles 089675
American Handweaving Museum, Clayton 042963
American Helicopter Museum & Education Center, West Chester 049067
American Heritage Big Red Fire Museum, Louisville 045501
The American Historical Foundation Museum, Richmond 047408
American Historical Print Collectors Society. Newsletter, Fairfield 136298
American History Unlimited, Chicago 142272
American Illustration, New York . . . 136299
American Illustrators Gallery, New York 117583
American Independence Museum, Exeter 043773
American Indian Art Magazine, Scottsdale 136300
American Indian Contemporary Arts, San Francisco 047849
American Institut of Conservation of Historic and Artistic Works. Journal, Washington 136301
American Institute for Conservation of Historic and Artistic Works, Washington 054578
American Institute of Architects, Washington 054579
American Institute of Graphic Arts, New York 054580
American Interiors, Norfolk 132553
American Irish Historical Society Museum, New York 046284
American Jazz Museum, Kansas City 044914
American Jewelers and Coin Company, Chicago 088006
American Jewish Art Club, Chicago 054581
American Jewish Congress, New York 054582
American Jewish Historical Museum, New York 046285
American Journal of Archaeology, Boston 136302
American Labor Museum, Haledon . 044391
American Legacy Gallery, Kansas City 116553
American Legation Museum, Tanger 029036
American Living Press, Allston 136303
American Maple Museum, Croghan 043223
American Memorabilia, Las Vegas . 089536
American Merchant Marine Museum, Kings Point 045010
American Military Museum, Charleston 042724
American Motorcycle Museum, Raalte 030049
American Museum in Britain, Bath . 038615
American Museum of Asmat Art, Saint Paul 047695
American Museum of Cartoon Art, Santa Monica 047984
American Museum of Fire Fighting, Hudson 044661
The American Museum of Fly Fishing, Manchester 045622
American Museum of Magic, Marshall 045699
American Museum of Natural History, New York 046286
American Museum of Radio, Bellingham 042118

American Museum of Science and Energy, Oak Ridge . . . 046585
American Museum of Straw Art, Long Beach . . . 045377
American Museum of the Miniature Arts, Dallas . . . 043263
American Museum of the Moving Image, Astoria . . . 041821
American Numismatic Association, Colorado Springs . . . 054583
American Numismatic Society, New York . . . 054584
American Numismatic Society Museum, New York . . . 046287
American Plating, Phoenix . . . 132642
American Police Center and Museum, Chicago . . . 042818
American Precious Metals, San Jose . . . 092911
American Precision Museum, Windsor . . . 049238
American Primitive, Columbus . . . 088376
American Primitive Gallery, New York . . . 090661, 132431
American Printing House for the Blind, Callahan Museum, Louisville . . . 045483
American Quarter Horse Heritage Center and Museum, Amarillo . . . 041679
American Rare Coin and Collectibles, Minneapolis . . . 090337
American Rare Coin and Jewelry, Kansas City . . . 089481
American Rare Coins, Charlotte . . . 087923
American Red Cross Museum, Washington . . . 048880
American Refinishing, Jacksonville 132169
American Renaissance for the 21st Century, New York . . . 054585
American Review, Cranford . . . 136304
American Romanian Academy of Arts and Science. Journal, Sunland . . . 136305
American Royal Museum, Kansas City . . . 044915
American Saddlebred Horse Museum, Mexico . . . 045801
American Saddlebred Museum, Lexington . . . 045255
American School of Classical Studies at Athens, Athinai . . . 050270
American School of Classical Studies at Athens, Princeton . . . 051989
American Showcase, New York . . . 135406
American Society of Apparaisers, Portland . . . 054586
American Society of Appraisers, Houston . . . 054588
American Society of Appraisers, Kansas City . . . 054587
American Society of Classical Realists, Minneapolis . . . 054589
American Society of Contemporary Artists, New York . . . 054590
American Society of Portrait Artists, Montgomery . . . 054591
American Space, New York . . . 117584
American Sport Art Museum and Archives, Daphne . . . 043300
American Studio Plus, Washington . 120248
American Swedish Historical Museum, Philadelphia . . . 046921
American Swedish Institute, Minneapolis . . . 045907
American Table Design, Tampa . . . 093098
American Textile History Museum, Lowell . . . 045504
American Trading Company, Cincinnati . . . 088207
American University Studies. Series 20. Fine Arts, New York . . . 136306
American Visionary Art Museum, Baltimore . . . 041963
American Visions, Saint Louis . . . 119172
American Watchmakers-Clockmakers Institute, Harrison . . . 044447
American Watercolor Society, New York . . . 054592
American Watercolor Society Newsletter, New York . . . 136307
American West Heritage Center, Wellsville . . . 049054
American Work Horse Museum, Lexington . . . 045277
Americana Antiques, Miami . . . 090121
Americana House, Chicago 088007, 142273
Americana Manse, Whitney-Halsey Home, Belmont . . . 042128
Americana Museum, El Paso . . . 043632
Americana Museum, Terra Alta . . . 048529
Americans for the Arts, Washington 136308
America's Black Holocaust Museum, Milwaukee . . . 045884
America's Ice Cream and Dairy Museum, Medina . . . 045746
America's National Music Museum, Vermillion . . . 048763
Americas Society Art Gallery, New York . . . 046288
America's Stonehenge, North Salem . . . 046536
Amerigo Tot Múzeum, Pécs . . . 021814
Amerika Museum Nederland, Cuijk . 029388
The Amerind Foundation, Dragoon . 043507
Ameringer, Will, Howard & Yohe, New York . . . 117585
Amerongs Historisch Museum/ Tabaksmuseum, Amerongen . . . 029145
Amersham Auction Rooms, Amersham . . . 122386
Amersham Museum, Amersham . . . 038507
Ames, Jacksonville . . . 116506
Ames, Los Angeles . . . 122943
Ames y Ropke, Madrid . . . 110429
Ameublement Comme Neuf Antiquités, Montréal . . . 058895
Amev Verzekeringsmuseum, Utrecht . . . 030223
Ameye, Croix . . . 099190
Amfora, Constanța . . . 109453
Amfora, Oostende . . . 058355
Amgad, Elnily, Fgura . . . 077511
Amherst County Museum, Amherst 041698
Amherst History Museum, Amherst 041690
Amherst Museum, Amherst . . . 041697
l'Ami de Musée, Paris . . . 135683
L'Ami des Lettres, Bordeaux . . . 098984
Ami Voyage, Avignon . . . 138018
Amiano, Juan, Pamplona . . . 110714
Amiaux, Christiane, Sainte-Ruffine . 068077
Amicale des Brocanteurs du Poitou Charentes, Niort . . . 052888
Amici, Francesco, Venezia . . . 106722
Amici Antiques, Nashville . . . 090413
Amicis, Alberto de, Rio de Janeiro . 058535
De Amicis Point, Milano . . . 075580
Amico dell'Arte Cristiana, Milano . . 135864
Amics de les Arts i Joventus Musicals, Terrassa . . . 054075, 110787
Amics de los Museos de Cataluña, Barcelona . . . 054076
Amida-ji Treasure Storehouse, Hofu 026542
Amiel, Lucia, Paris . . . 099933
Amiens & Asta-Richard, Lyon . . . 124333
Amieva Mexico, Madrid . . . 081211
Amieva Mexico, Madrid . . 081212, 141023
Amighini, Enzo, Verona . . . 076986
Amigos de los Museos, Barcelona . 054077
Amigos del Arte, Asunción . . . 053968
Los Amigos del Libro, Cochabamba 133300
Amilien Attic, San Diego . . . 092599
Aminta, Skopje . . . 077495
Amiralai, Mannheim . . . 134186
Amire and Co, Ménerbes . . . 064479
Amirouche, Réda, El Mouradi . . . 055135
Amirouche, Réda, Staoueli . . . 055139
Amiry, Los Angeles . . . 116699
Amis des Arts, Aix-en-Provence . . . 098780
Amis des Arts, Neuchâtel . . . 111765
Amis du Château de Pau. Bulletin, Pau . . . 135684
Les Amis du Dessin, Bruxelles . . . 052640
Amis du Vieux Marche le Brol, Bruxelles . . . 057811
Amis Galerie d'Art Bagatelle, Aix-les-Bains . . . 098799
Amistad, San Antonio . . . 119392
Amities, Minneapolis . . . 117233
Amitin, Saint Louis . . . 142852
Amity and Woodbridge Historical Society Museum, Woodbridge . . . 049280
Amity Gallery, Albany . . . 094124
Amivi, Castello de la Plana . . . 110299
A.M.J.P. Antiquités, Montlouis-sur-Loire . . . 064704
AMK, Grafing bei München . . . 071081
AMK Kunsthandel, München . . . 072632
AMM Newsletter, Winnipeg . . . 135620
Amma, Antwerpen . . . 096057
Ammann, Zürich . . . 135079, 141318
Ammann, Arnold, Bern . . . 082194
Ammann, Helmut, Pöcking . . . 104617
Ammann, Thomas, Zürich . . . 112025
Ammann Arte Moderne, Locarno . . 111648
Ammen, T., Delmenhorst . . . 070212
Ammendolea, Luigi Fortunato, Messina . . . 075551
Ammering, Ernst, Ried im Innkreis . 095710
Ammirata, Alessandro, Palermo . . . 106412
Ammitzbøll, Anne, København . . . 060264
Ammoniet, Hasselt . . . 096307
Amodio, Antonio, Verona . . . 128412
Amon Carter Museum, Fort Worth . 044002
Amor, Albert, London . . . 085071
Amorati, Mauro, Bologna . . . 075039
Amorgos, Aglantzia . . . 098294
Amorim, Pedro, São Paulo . . . 058671
Amorotti, Bernard, Nice . . . 065025
Amorotti, Bernard, Nice . . . 124496
Amors of Evenly Antiques, Barley Mow . . . 083381
Amory Regional Museum, Amory . . 041700
Amos, Diana & Eric, Saint George's 096432
Amos, Eno, New York . . . 117586
Amos Andersonin taidemuseo, Helsinki . . . 009512
Ámos-Anna Gyűjtemény, Ferenczy Múzeum, Szentendre . . . 021878
Amos Eno Gallery, New York . . . 046289
Amos Herr House, Landisville . . . 045155
Amourette, Daniel, Rouen . . . 101106
Amourette, Gérard, Ivry-la-Bataille . 063227
Amouyal, Zouzou, Lyon . . . 064052
Amparo, Madrid . . . 129560
Amparo Barbero Ferrandiz, Alicante 110084
Amparo Cabrera, Guadalajara . . . 107469
Amparo Caro Gancedo, Maria, Madrid . . . 129561
Amparo Gamir, Madrid . . . 110430
Ampersand, San Francisco . . . 119584
Amphora Galleries, Balfron . . . 083372
Ampir, Beograd . . . 080387
Ampir, Sankt-Peterburg . . . 129243
Ampir limited, Moskva . . . 080217
AM.PM Gallery, Hong Kong . . . 097747
Ampollini, Piero, Milano . . . 127515
Ampthill Antiques, Ampthill . . . 083293
Ampthill Emporium, Ampthill . . . 083294
Amrein, Werner J., Luzern . . . 082616
Amreli Archaeological and Art Museum, Amreli . . . 022007
Amrit Art Gallery, Kanpur . . . 105731
Amro, Abdou-Ibrahim, Paris . . . 065386
Amrumer Museum und Windmühle, Nebel . . . 019189
Amsler & Ruthardt, Berlin . . . 069555
Amstein, Philippe, Basel . . 082116, 129907
Amstel Antiques en Curiosa, Amsterdam . . . 077773
Amsteltuin, Amstelveen . . . 107643
Amsterdam Antiques, Denver . . . 088638
Amsterdam Art Gallery, Amsterdam 077774
Amsterdam Avenue Antiques, Atlanta . . . 087443
Amsterdam University Press, Amsterdam . . . 134767
Het Amsterdams Automuseum, Zwanenburg . . . 030407
Amsterdams Beeldhouwers Kollektief, Amsterdam . . . 053876, 107651
Amsterdams Historisch Museum, Amsterdam . . . 029164
Amsterdams Openbaar Vervoer Museum, Amsterdam . . . 029165
Amsterdamsch Venduhuis, Amsterdam . . . 121776
Amsterdamse Hogeschool voor de Kunsten, Academie van Bouwkunst, Amsterdam . . . 050551
Amstutz, Edi, Wil . . . 130216
AMT, Rouen . . . 067236
Amtshofmuseum, Gernsbach . . . 017382
Amtsrichterhaus, Schwarzenbek . . 020132
Amtsturm-Museum, Wendländischer Altertumsverein, Lüchow, Wendland . . . 018732
L'Amuleto, Perugia . . . 140091
Amuri Historical Museum, Waiau . . 030609
Amurin Työläismuseokortteli, Tampereen Museot, Tampere . . . 010117
Amurskij Gorodskoj Kraevedčeskij Muzej, Amursk . . . 032980
Amurskij Oblastnoj Kraevedčeskij Muzej im. G.S. Novikova-Daurskogo, Blagoveščensk . . . 033034
L'Amusette, Musée Interactif pour Enfants, Mesvin . . . 003644
AMV Marcos y Cuadros, Santiago de Chile . . . 059487
AMVC-Letterenhuis, Antwerpen . . . 003152
A.M.Y. Japan, Yokohama . . . 077331
Amyot, Paris . . . 099934
Amyot, Elisabeth, Paris . . . 099935
Amyris, Bruxelles . . . 133256, 135587
Amy's Antiques, Portland . . . 091886
Amy's Attic, Oklahoma City . . . 091455
Amz Artz, Okato . . . 108530
An, Thanh, Ha Noi . . . 120444
An Amazong Gallery, New York . . . 117587
An Antique Affaire, Los Angeles . . . 089676
An Antique Store, Chicago . . . 088008
An Dun Transport and Heritage Museum, Ballinahown . . . 022682
AN - Galeria, Łódź . . . 109000
An Iodnlann, Isle-of-Tiree . . . 039827
An Lanntair, Stornoway . . . 041126
AN Magazine, Newcastle-upon-Tyne . . . 136147
An Odd Volume, Seattle . . . 142975
An Tairbeart Museum, Tarbert . . . 041186
Ana Chiclana, Madrid . . . 081213
Ana Ros, Barcelona . . . 080786
ANA World's Fair of Money, Baltimore . . . 093959
Anabas-Verlag, Frankfurt am Main . 133936
Anabel's Galerie, Barbizon . . . 098915
Anacleto, Joaquim, Lisboa . . . 079851
Anacortes Museum, Anacortes . . . 041703
Anacostia Museum, Washington . . . 048881
Anadarko Philomathic Museum, Anadarko . . . 041704
Anadolu Medeniyetleri Müzesi, Ankara . . . 038006
Anaesthetic Museum, London . . . 040076
Anaf, Saint-Priest (Rhône) . . . 121251
Anaf, Jean-Claude, Lyon . . . 121042
Anagnostaras, Marie-Béatrice, Pully 082731
Anagramme, Montpellier . . . 064729
Anaheim Museum, Anaheim . . . 041708
Anahy Alta Joyeria, Cancún . . . 077556
Anais, München . . . 104138
Anakita Oriente, Burgos . . . 081010
Analecta, Versailles . . . 138651
Analepse, Paris . . . 065387
Anales de Historia del Arte, Madrid 136069
Analogon, Hannover . . . 139228
Anamnese, Jarnac . . . 063233
Anamnesis, Balaclava . . . 055422
Anamorfose, Kortrijk . . . 096366
Anamorfosis, Barcelona . . . 080787
Anamur Kültür Merkezi, Anamur . . . 038005
Ananda, Baltimore . . . 115029
Ananda, Nice . . . 099827

Ananda, Paris 065388
Ananda Niketan Kirtishala, Bagnan . 022011
Anandhaa Nilayam, Chennai 139946
Ananse, Houston 116265
Ananse, Houston 116266
Anapskij Archeologičeskij Muzej-zapovednik, Anapa 032982
Anares, Bremen 138934
Anars, Ljubljana 109947
Ana's Attic, Omaha 091548
ANA's National Money Show, Portland 093960
Anasazi, Phoenix 142758
Anasazi, Saint-Tropez 101233
Anasazi Heritage Center, Dolores . . 043478
Anasazi State Park, Boulder 042355
Anastacia's Antiques, Philadelphia . 091597
Anastasio, Adriana, Roma 076266, 127917
Anastasis, Gent 058167
Anatoli's Restoration, New York . . . 132432
Anatomisch Museum, Groningen . . 029635
Anatomisch Museum, Utrecht 030224
Anatomisch Museum Nijmegen, Nijmegen 029958
Anatomisch Museum van de Rijksuniversiteit Leiden, Leiden . . 029847
Anatomische Sammlung, Friedrich-Alexander-Universität Erlangen-Nürnberg, Erlangen 017027
Anatomische Sammlungen des Institut für Anatomie und Zellbiologie, Martin-Luther-Universität Halle-Wittenberg, Halle, Saale 017652
Anatomisches Museum, Greifswald 017521
Anatomisches Museum, Institut für Anatomie der Universität Innsbruck, Innsbruck 002075
Anatomisches Museum Basel, Basel 036878
Anatomy and Pathology Museum, Alexandria 009273
Anatomy Museum, Aberdeen 038443
Anatomy Museum, Chennai 022053
Anatomy Museum, Dunedin 030480
Anatomy Museum, Medical College, Mumbai 022260
AnBau 35 - Galerie und Edition, Bonn 102176, 133827
Anbriosa, Antwerpen 057673
Ancelo, Helsinki 124039
Ancely, Jacques, Paris 099936
Ancestor House Antiques, Toledo . . 093161
Ancestors Alive, Philadelphia 142733
Ancestral, Lisboa 129145
Ancestrale, Saint-Lô 067588
Ancestry, Mumbai 074818
Ancestry Antiques, Rozelle 056555
Anchor, London 085072
Anchor Art Gallery, Saint-Barthélemy 105467
Anchor Fine Arts, Christchurch 108376
Anchor House Antiques, Honolulu . . 088930
Anchorage Gallery, Port Chalmers . 108546
Anchorage Museum of History and Art, Anchorage 041711
L'Ancien Carmel, Tarbes 014908
Ancien Couvent de Vagnas, Vagnas 068673
Ancien Merv Historical Site, Mary . . 038208
l'Ancien Palais de Justice, Dakar . . 034128
Ancienne Abbaye de Fontcaude, Musée de Site, Cazedarnes 011167
Ancienne Douane, Strasbourg 014850
Ancienne École de Médecine Navale, Rochefort (Charente-Maritime) . . 014076
Ancienne Mairie-Musée Annexe, Lillebonne 012687
Ancienne-Mans, Le Mans 063652
Ancienne Salle de Ventes, Le Neubourg 063672
Anciennement Vôtre, Gondreville . . 063014
Anciennement Vôtre, Nancy 064857
Ancient and Honorable Artillery Company Museum, Boston 042313
Ancient and Modern, Blackburn, Lancashire 083547, 130402
Ancient and Modern Bookshop, Blandford Forum 141420
Ancient and Oriental, Grimston 084537
Ancient Antique Furniture, Singapore 080414
Ancient Antiques, Indianapolis 089262
Ancient Architecture Museum, Beijing 006960
Ancient Art and Coins, London 085073
Ancient Art of the New World, New York 090662
Ancient Artefacts and Egyptian Antiquities, Saint Kilda, Victoria 056562
Ancient Arts, Long Beach 089618
Ancient Arts, Long Beach 089619
Ancient Asia Gallery, Tulsa 093277
Ancient Basics, Los Angeles 089677
Ancient City, Samut Prakan 037927
Ancient & Classic, New York 090663
Ancient Coins Museum, Beijing . . . 006961
Ancient Craft, Singapore 080415
Ancient Earth Indigenous Art Gallery, Cairns 055595
Ancient Gallery, Ha Noi 093556
Ancient Gallery, Ho Chi Minh City . . 093559
Ancient Greek and Roman Coins, Portland 091887
Ancient Grounds, Seattle 092948
Ancient High House, Stafford 041081
Ancient House Museum, Thetford . . 041207
Ancient Mariner Art Effects, Singapore 080416
Ancient & Modern Art Gallery, New York 090664, 117588
Ancient Monuments Society, London 054268
Ancient of Days, Oklahoma City . . . 091456
Ancient Order of Foresters, Southampton 041054
Ancient Pearl, Las Vegas 089537
Ancient Spanish Monastery of Saint Bernard de Clairvaux Cloisters, Miami . . . 045803
Ancient Traditions Gallery, Albuquerque 087363
Ancient Treasure, Sacramento 092125
Ancient Valley, Singapore 080417
Ancora Ancora, San Jose 092912
Ancre Aldine, Lyon 138133
Ancre de Miséricorde, Saint-Malo (Ille-et-Vilaine) 067604
Anczok, Maximilian, Stuttgart 073952
Anczykowski, Caspar, Wuppertal . . 127047
A.N.D., Paris 065389
And Antiques, Calgary 058778
AND Gallery, Saint Paul 119269
AND Gallery, Trnava 109924
And So To Bed, London . . 085074, 130922
Andalusien Art, Worpswede 074485
Andancas, Rio de Janeiro 096586
Andanti, Schwäbisch Gmünd 139718
Andarte, Renens 111827
Andelos, Amsterdam 128527
Andena, Buenos Aires 055156
Andenken, Denver 115966
Andera, Maastricht 078591
Anderberg, Christin, Lund 129844
Die Andere Galerie, Zürich 112026
Andere Welten, Hamburg 103086
Anders Svors Museet, Hornindal . . . 030906
Andersch, Nürnberg 073094
Andersen, Eskilstrup 124013
Andersen, Annamarie M., Zürich . . 112027
Andersen, Bent, København 060265
Andersen, Mikael, København 098533
Andersgalerie, Düsseldorf 102468, 133886
Anderson, Burford 112754
Anderson, Cremorne 136869
Anderson, Markranstädt 104034
Anderson, Oakland 091404
Anderson, Saint Paul 092339, 132759
Anderson, San Francisco 092711
Anderson, A., Minneapolis 090338
Anderson, Alistair, Glasgow 130727
Anderson, Evelyn, Nashville 090414
Anderson & Son, F.E., Welshpool . . 087073
Anderson, H. & A., Stanwell Park . . 056629
Anderson, Judith, Auckland 108295
Anderson, Ruth, London 096937
Anderson, Vivien, Caulfield North . . 094385
Anderson Alistair, Glasgow 113099
Anderson County Arts Center, Anderson 041718
Anderson County Arts Council, Anderson 054593
Anderson County Historical Museum, Garnett 044149
Anderson County Museum, Anderson 041719
Anderson Gallery, Richmond 047409
Anderson & Garland, Newcastle-upon-Tyne 122627
Anderson & Garland, Ryton 122674
Anderson Hill, Kingston-upon-Thames 113329
Anderson Museum, Cairo 009291
Anderson Museum of Contemporary Art, Roswell 047551
Anderson O'Brien, Omaha 118682
Anderson O'Day, London . 113444, 135173
Anderson Park Art Gallery, Invercargill 030522
Anderson Park Art Gallery, Invercargill 108475
Anderson & Paul, Dunedin 079078, 128931
Anderson Slater, Settle . . . 086536, 131463
Andersons, A., Clayfield 055680
Andersonville Prison, Andersonville 041720
Andersson, Staffanstorp 122245
Andersson, F., Vevey 082877
Andersson, Herman, Tollarp 129884
Andersson & Söner, Richard, Eskilstuna 122123
Andersson, Thomas, Uppsala 141183
Anderssonhall, London 113445
Anderwereld, Groningen 108030
Andhra Academy of Arts, Vijayawada 050334
Andhra Pradesh State Museum, Hyderabad 022155
Andhra Sahitya Parishat Government Museum, Kakinada 022194
Andia Blanco, Javier, Murcia 081438
Andiamo, Milwaukee 117160
Andina, Miami 117018
Andino, Pretoria 080727
Andino, J.P. de, Washington 120249
Andipa Gallery, London . . 085075, 113446, 130923
Andi's Gallery, Jakarta 105834
Andižanskij Kraevedčeskij Muzej, Andižan 049382
Andjić, Beograd 109681
Andler & Co., A.R., Saint Paul 119270
Ando, Sendai 077208
Ando, Tokyo 107010
Andó, Fabio, Roma 076267
Andoe, Tulsa 120180
Andong Folk Museum, Andong 027446
Andover, New York 117589
Andover Historical Society Museum, Andover 041722
Andover Museum, Andover 038509
Andøymuseet, Risøyhamn 031137
Andra, Antwerpen 057674
Andrade, Gecy C., Belo Horizonte . . 058402
Andrade, José, Lisboa 079852
Andrä, Ernest Leopold, Krems 057122
Andraeas, Hamburg 103087
Andraz Antique, Bucureşti 080139
André, Paris 124550
André, Roma 106485
André, Anthony, Saint-Pierre-des-Corps 067953
André, Jacques, Etampes 062811
André, Michel, Coutevroult 062537
André Antiquités, Belfort-du-Quercy 061329
Andre Emile, Vancouver 097408
Andre Garitte Foundation, Berchem 003226
Andrea, Dallas 131993
Andrea Robbi-Stiftung, Sils in Engadin 037560
Andréani, Jean-Claude, L'Isle-sur-la-Sorgue 063916
Andreani, Luciano, Bern 082195
Andreas, S.C., Timişoara 080187
Andrea's Antiques, San Francisco .092712, 132864
Andrea's Antiques, Tauranga 079258
Andreassons, Järpås 141116
Andréemuseet, Stiftelsen Grännamuseerna, Gränna 036311
Andreescu-Bernhardt, Despina, Saarbrücken 073622
Andreevskij spusk 3, Kyïv 112389
Andréewitch, Stephan, Wien 057367
Andréhn-Schiptjenko, Stockholm . . 110999
Andreini, Milano 075581
Andreini, Elsa, Milano 121694
Andreja Pumpura Muzejs Lielvārdē, Lielvārde 027703
Andreja Upīša Memoriālmāja, Skrīveri 027779
Andreja Upītša Memoriālais Muzejs, Rīga 027728
Andrejcak, Bent K, København 060266
Andreotti, Angelo, Bologna 127128
Andres, Marie-Christine, Mutzig . . . 064850
Andre's Art Gallery, San Diego 119469
Andres Gonzalez, Jose Angel, Zaragoza 110877
Andrés Mayoral, Madrid 129562
Andresen, Elke, Geesthacht 070943
Andretta, Bonnie, New York 117590
Andreu, Tomás, Santiago de Chile . 097617
Andrew, Chicago 131879
Andrew, Zurrieq 077551, 128486
Andrew, Brian, Chicago 088009
Andrew, William, New York 135407
Andrew and District Local History Museum, Andrew 005014
Andrew Carnegie Birthplace Museum, Dunfermline 039316
Andrew County Museum, Savannah 048034
Andrew, Hilditch & Son, Sandbach . 122687
Andrew J. Blackbird Museum, Harbor Springs 044428
Andrew Johnson National Historic Site, Greeneville 044320
Andrew Logan Museum of Sculpture, Welshpool 041329
Andrew Ross Museum, Kangaroo Ground 001142
Andrew-Safford House, Peabody Essex Museum, Salem 047733
Andrews, L., München 072633
Andrews, Marilyn, Nelson 108507
Andrews, Meg, Harpenden 084565
Andrews, Michael, Milford, Surrey . 085991
Andrews, Stephen, Saint Peter Port 086471
Andrew's Collectibles, Buffalo 087857
Andrew's Pueblo Pottery and Art Gallery, Albuquerque 114766
Andrew's Refinishing, Dallas 131994
Andrien Antiquités, Dampmart 062594
Andriesse, Paul, Amsterdam 107652
Andrieu-Bourelly, Edmonde, Fumel . 062950
Andrighetti, Vancouver 097409
Andrin, Joël, Antibes-Juan-les-Pins 060911
Andriola, Thom, Houston 116267
Andriot, Bernard, München 072634
Andriotto, Fabio, Roma 127918
Andrischewski, Heinz Joachim, Düsseldorf 070353
Andrle, V., Praha 060092
Andrlová, Marie, Praha 060093
Android's Dungeon, Oklahoma City 091457
Androna degli Orti, Trieste 076885
Androscoggin Historical Society Museum, Auburn 041887
Androt, Pierre, Beaulieu-sur-Mer . . 061255
Androutsopoulou, Evangelia, Chalkida 105418
Androx, Vigo 110860
Andrøymuseet, Polar- og Fiskerimuseet, Andenes 030730

Andruchowicz, Dietlinde, Bodenheim 102164
Andwells, Hartley Wintney 084597
Andy Warhol Art Authentication Board, Andy Warhol Foundation, New York . . . 054594
The Andy Warhol Museum, Pittsburgh 047039
Andy's Antiquitäten, Karlsruhe 071706
Andy's Corner, Norwood 056385
Andy's Curio Shoppe, Gisborne . . . 079099
Ané, Patrick, Foix 099266, 124239
Aneks, Kraków 108924
Anelim, Lisboa 079853
Anet Antiquités, Anet 060839
Anew Fine Consignment, Columbus 088377
Anfield Museum, Liverpool 040025
Anfiteatro, Milano 106150
Angarskij Gorodskoj Vystavočnyj Zal, Angarsk 032983
Angarskij Muzej Časov, Angarsk . . . 032984
Angarskij Muzej Mineralov, Angarsk 032985
Angaston Abbey Trading, Angaston . 055345
Angate, New York 090665
l'Ange Bleu, Lausanne 082528
Ange du Bizarre, Carouge 082287
Ånge Zoologiska Museum, Ånge . . . 036185
Angel, David, Miami 090122
Angel Añor, Tarragona 110782
Angel Antiques, Petworth 086235
Angel Antiques, Redditch 086340
Angel Antiquités, Marseille 064310
Angel Arcade, London 085076
The Angel Bookshop, North Walsham 141959
L'Angel d'Or, Palma de Mallorca . . . 081467
Angel Gento, Valencia 081638
Angel Mounds Historic Site, Evansville 043765
Angel Orensanz Foundation Center for the Arts, New York 046290
Angel Row Gallery, Nottingham . . . 040615
Angel Town, Albuquerque 087364
Angela, Neue Wiener Werkstätte, Wien 095788
Angela & J's Gallery, New York 090666
Angela & J.'s Gallery, New York . . . 090667
Angelburger Kunst- und Kulturhaus, Angelburg 015540
Angele, Montendre 064674
Angelfall Studios, Baltimore 115030
Angelfish, Denver 115967
Angélic'Art, Genève 082388
Angelini, Alessandra, Roma 076268
Angelique's Cottage, El Paso 088784
Angeliter, Quern 073398
Angell Gallery, Toronto 097213
Angell Street Curiosities, Providence 092031
Angelos and Angeliki Giallina Gallery, Corfu 021237
Angelou, Michel, Saint-Étienne . . . 067437
Angelou, Michel, Saint-Genest-Malifaux 067483
Angelov, J., Sofia 123731
Angel's Antiques, Toronto 059118
Angels Divine, Louisville 089953
Angels Eagles Dolls, Sacramento . . 092126
Angel's on the Walk, Mount Tamborine 056295
Angelus, Buenos Aires 094055
Angenard, Pierre, Beaucé 061250
Angerer, Vomperbach 095778
Angerer, D., Gerbstedt 070972
Angermuseum, Erfurt 017006
Angers Hof, Wernigerode . 105216, 139839
Angevaren, W.J.L.M., Den Haag . . . 078162
Angie, Singapore 109754
The Angkor Conservation, Siem Reap 004971
Angkorwat Art of Cambodia, Long Beach 089620
Anglade-Barthelemy, New Orleans . 117387
Angle, Saint-Paul-Trois-Châteaux . . 101222
Angler, Denver 115968
Angles of Art, Theale 114567
Anglesea Antiques, Dun Laoghaire . 074960
Anglian Art, King's Lynn 113324
Anglican Cathedral Museum, Saint John's 006359
Anglicana Aste, Roma . . . 076269, 121718
Anglim, Paule, San Francisco 119585
Anglo American Antiques, Albuquerque 087365, 131737
Anglo Antiques, Invercargill 079122
Anglo-Persian Carpet, London 085077, 130924
L'Angolo dé Buttieri, Bologna 075040
L'Angolo del Lume, Roma 076270
L'Angolo del Passato, Venezia 076915
L'Angolo dell'Antico, Torino 076759
Angono National Museum, Angono . 031619
Angost, Paris 065390
Angourie Road Antiques, Yamba . . . 056894
Angrenskij Kraevedčeskij Muzej, Angren 049384
Angsana, Bangkok 083090
Angstmann, Weiden, Oberpfalz 074297
Angstrom, Dallas 115825
Anguera Maura, Salvador, Palma de Mallorca 081468
Angulo, Oviedo 110659
Angus Antique Furniture, Richmond, Victoria 056525, 120632
Angus Antiques, Dundee 084228
Angus & Co, Toronto 059119
Angus Fine Art, Kirriemuir 113338
Angus Folk Museum, Glamis 039545
Angustin, Miguel de, Helsingborg . . 110939
Anguz, Saint-Aygulf 067369
Anhaltische Gemäldegalerie, Schloß Georgium, Dessau, Anhalt 016675
Anhaltische Verlagsgesellschaft, Dessau, Anhalt 133861
Anhaltischer Kunstverein Dessau e.V., Dessau, Anhalt 053011
Anhui Fine Arts Publishing House, Hefei 133357
Anhui Sheng Bo Wu Guan, Hefei . . . 007111
Anica Art, Leura 094735
Anicroche, Eze 099256
Aniela, Kangaroo Valley 094679
Aniha, Delhi 105647
Anila Arts and Crafts, Chennai 074788
Anima, Bergamo 135865
Animal and Fish Museum, Evros . . . 021259
Animal Arts, Canterbury 112799
Animal Museum, Amman 027361
Animal World, Las Vegas 089538
Animal World, Las Vegas 089539
Animas Museum, Durango 043535
Animation Art, Amsterdam 107653
Animation Art, Edmonton 096859
Animation Art Gallery, Honolulu . . . 116195
Animation Art Gallery, London 113447
Animation Connection, Toronto 097214
Animation USA, Seattle 119871
Animazing Gallery, New York 117591
Aninat, Isabel, Santiago de Chile . . 097618
Anita Déco, Marseille 064311
Anita Gallery, San Antonio 031781
Anita's Corner Mall, Oklahoma City 091458
Anıtkabir-Atatürk ve Kurtuluş Müzesi, Ankara 038007
Anitlar Müzeler, Ankara 054247
Anixis, Baden 111150
Anjalan Kartanomuseo, Anjalankoski 009455
Anjali, Sangeeta, Hyderabad 105692
Anjavie, d', Heerlen 078498
Anjely, Austin 087548
Anjou, Bernard d', Rouen 121236
Anjou Antiquités, Avrillé 061149
Anjou Antiquités, Craon 062544
Ank-Tiek, Amsterdam 077775
Anka Tomy, Paris 121108
Ankara Atatürk Kültür Merkezi, Cumhuriyet Devri Müzesi, Ankara 038008
Ankara Devlet Güzel Sanatlar Galerisi, Ankara 038009
Ankara Sanat ve El Sanatları Fuarı, Ankara 093899
Anker, Arnhem 128567
Het Anker, Dordrecht 107972
Het Anker, Zele 120792
de Ankerburg Wagner, Wacław, Kraków 129026
Anker's House Museum, Chester-le-Street 039062
Ankh Antiquarian Books, Chadstone 136857
Ankkapurhan Teollisuusmuseo, Anjalankoski 009456
Ankner, Dietrich, Kiedrich 126039
Anmoder, Madrid 081214
Ann, Nagoya 077146
Ann Arbor Art Association, Ann Arbor 054595
Ann Arbor Art Center, Ann Arbor . . . 041727
Ann Arbor Hands-On Museum, Ann Arbor 041728
Ann Bryant Art Gallery, East London 034607
Ann & Ed's Antiques, Oklahoma City 091459
Ann & Neil Antiques, Phoenix 091708, 123051
Ann-Teeks, Toronto 059120
Ann-Tiques, Townsville 056728
Ann-Tiques and More, Jacksonville 089367
Anna, Den Haag 078163
Anna, Sankt-Peterburg 109614
Anna Antiek, Leeuwarden 078548
Anna Antikvitás, Budapest 074658, 139909
Anna Art Studio and Gallery, Bellevue Hill 094235, 123189
Anna Bahr-Mildenburg-Gedenkraum & Hermann Bahr-Gedenkraum, Wien 002846
Anna Bemis Palmer Museum, York . 049346
Anna Eaton Stout Memorial Art Gallery, Owensboro 046758
Anna Fresko, İstanbul 083113
Anna Leonowens Gallery, Halifax . . 005565
Anna Miller Museum, Newcastle . . 046445
Anna, Ollia & Maude, Omaha 091549
Annabelle, Seattle 092949
Annabelle Antiques, Los Angeles . . 089678
Annabelle's Antiques, Subiaco 056642
Annabelle's Attic, Cincinnati 088208
Annabellinski, Orange 056404
Annabell's Attic, Tucson 093193
Annaberger Kunst- und Kulturverein e.V., Annaberg-Buchholz 053012, 133722
Annaka, Annaka 077034
Annales d'Ethiopie, Addis Ababa . . 135674
Annali dell'Istituto Italiano di Numismatica, Roma 135866
Annalina, Briançon 099032
Annals Antique, Singapore 080418
Annam Héritage, Paris 065391
Annan Gallery, Glasgow 113100
Annandale Galleries, Annandale . . . 094155
Annandale National Historic Site, Tillsonburg 006572
Annapolis Valley Macdonald Museum, Middelton 005864
Annas Brigaderes Memoriālais Muzejs, Tērvete 027784
Anna's Old Wares, Morwell 056263
Anne, Paris 065392
Anne, Jean-François, Paris 065393
Anne, Vincent, Paris 065394
Anne Antiquités, La Baule-Escoublac 063284
Anne Antiquités, Le Mans 063653
Anne Frank Center USA, New York . 046291
Anne Frank Huis, Amsterdam 029166
Anne Grimdalens Minne, Dalen i Telemark 030802
Anne Hathaway's Cottage, Shakespeare Birthplace Trust, Stratford-upon-Avon 041137
Anne Hvides Gård, Svendborg 009121
Anne Murray Centre, Springhill 006501
Anne of Cleves House Museum, Lewes 039992
Anne of Green Gables Museum, Kensington 005677
Anne & Pénélopé, Paris 065395
The Anne Spencer Memorial Foundation, Lynchburg 045524
Anne & Thierry Antiquités, Lyon . . . 064053
Anneberg-Samlingerne, Nykøbing Sjælland 009039
Année Galerie, Haarlem 108053
Années 1900, Bétaille 061409
Les Annees 50, Bruxelles 057812
Les Années de l'Or, Nîmes 065166
Années Folles, Bordeaux 061575
Années Folles, Villenave-d'Ornon . . 068909
Anne's Antiques, Cape Town 080674
Anne's Attic, Tampa 093099
Anne's Books, Annerley 136784
Annett Antique, Vanløse 060411
Annette Antiques & Collectables, Lincoln 084995, 130895
Annette's Antiques, San Jose 092913
Annette's of Rue Royal, New Orleans 090504
Annetts, Horsham 113276
Annex, Los Angeles 116700
Annex, Portland 091888
Annex Antique, New York 090668
Annex Art Centre Gallery, Toronto . . 006580
Annex Books, Toronto 137692
Annex Gallery, New York 117592
Annex Gallery, San Diego 119470
L'Annexe, Clermont-Ferrand 099139
Annia, Salamanca 110732
Annicchiarico, Ciro, Roma 127919
Annick Vidal, Versailles 068791
Annick's Antiques, Sorell 056599
Annie E. Woodman Institute, Dover . 043493
Annie Herold et Philippe, Sens 068213
Annie Riggs Memorial Museum, Fort Stockton 043983
Annie's, Cleveland 088303
Annie's Affordable Art, Seattle 119872
Annie's Antiques, Cooden 084079
Annie's Antiques, Farnham 084385
Annie's Antiques, Jacksonville 089368
Annie's Antiques and Collectibles, Jacksonville 089369
Annies Art Gallery, Malmö 110958
Annie's Attic, Louisville . . 089954, 142524
Annie's Book Stop, Portland 142784
Annie's Bppk Company, Calgary . . . 137617
Annie's Gallery, Norbreck 114146
Annie's Old Things, Camp Hill 055610
Annie's Petroleum, Columbus 088378
Annie's Sales, Milwaukee 090268
Annima, Helsinki 060498
Anniston Museum of Natural History, Anniston 041745
Annly, Shanghai 059728
Annmary Brown Memorial, Providence 047249
Anno, Feusisberg 082366
Anno 1666, Zwolle 078885
Anno 1850, Groningen 078396
Anno 1850, Groningen 078397
Anno 1881, Altenberg, Erzgebirge . 069147
Anno 1900 - 1930, Hamburg 071190
Anno 85, Breda 078077
Anno Aktuell, Rheda-Wiedenbrück . 073507
Anno - Antikes aller Art, Berlin 069556
Anno Antikvitás, Sopron 074751
Anno Antiquitas, Budakeszi 074655
Anno Dazumal, Wolfenbüttel 074467
Anno Domini, Meißen 072504
Anno Domini, Osnabrück 073228
Anno Domini, Völklingen 139819
Anno Domini Antiques, London 085078
Anno Tubak, Luxembourg 077470
L'Annonciade, Musée de Saint-Tropez, Saint-Tropez 014558
Ann's Antiques, Houston 088998
Ann's Antiques, Stoke-on-Trent . . . 086731
Ann's Art, Groningen 108031
Ann's Caning Service, Baltimore . . 131812
Annterior Antiques, Plymouth 086274
Anntiques, Dallas 088451

Annuaire General des Beaux-Arts, Bruxelles . . . 135588
Annual Antique Ethnographic Art Show, Santa Fe . . . 093961
Annual Antique Indian Art Show, Santa Fe . . . 093962
Annual August Antiques Show, Nantucket . . . 093963
Annual Journal of the Ruskin Society, Oxford . . . 136148
Anodyne Contemporary, Vancouver 097410
Anoka County Historical and Genealogical Museum, Anoka . . . 041746
Anola and District Museum, Anola . 005019
Anomaly, Portland . . . 091889
Anon, Paris . . . 133511
Anonimo e d'Autore, Roma . . . 076271
Another Age Antiques, Austin . . . 087549
Another Antique Shop, Louisville . . 089955
Another Chance, Philadelphia . . . 091598
Another Man's Treasure, El Paso . . 088785
Another Period in Time, Baltimore . 087635
Another Time, San Francisco . . . 092713
Another Time, Seattle . . . 092950
Another Time Antiques, Christchurch . . . 079006
Another Time Antiques, Detroit . . . 088755
Anouk Miga, Maastricht . . . 078592
Anoyanakis Collection, Athinai . . . 021156
Anqing Municipal Museum, Anqing . 006953
Anquez, Etaples . . . 062813
Ans, Levanger . . . 121855
An's Rommelzoo, Haarlem . . . 078440
Ansaldi, Adriano, Brescia . . . 127202
L'Anse aux Medows National Historic Site, Saint-Lunaire-Griquet . . . 006384
Ansel, Jochen, Stuttgart . . . 126840
Anselme, Philippe, Saint-Bonnet-du-Gard . . . 067378
Anselmi, Andrea, Firenze . . . 127284
Ansermet, Pierre-Jean, Fribourg . . . 082376
Anshan City Museum, Anshan . . . 006954
Ansichtssache, Dresden . . . 102421
Ansichtssache, Lübeck . . . 103959
Ansley, Ruby, Birmingham . . . 087732
Anson, Tampa . . . 120019
Anson-Cartwright, Hugh, Toronto . . 137693
Anson County Historical Society Museum, Wadesboro . . . 048821
Ansorena, Madrid . . . 081215
Ansorena, Madrid . . . 110431
Ansorena, Madrid . . . 110432
Ansorena, Madrid . . . 122035
Ansorena, Madrid . . . 122036
Anstead, Mary, San Diego . . . 123097
Anstensen, Kim, Göteborg . . . 110902
Anstey Galleries, Harrogate . . . 113188
Ant Hill Gallery, Broken Hill . . . 094300
Ant Hill Gallery, Wynnum . . . 095435
Antal & Társa, Budapest . . . 074659
Antalya Devlet Güzel Sanatlar Galerisi, Antalya . . . 038015
Antalya Müzesi, Antalya . . . 038016
Antami Libros, Buenos Aires . . . 136694
Antan, Luxembourg . . . 077471
Antano, Buenos Aires . . . 055157
Antaño, Buenos Aires . . . 136695
Antaño, Estepona . . . 081097
Antar, Latifeh, Zghorta . . . 077440
Antea Antiques, Basel . . . 082117
Antéart, Dijon . . . 062640
Antebellum, Blois . . . 061517
Antebellum Antiques, New Orleans . 090505
Antelope County Historical Museum, Neligh . . . 046174
Anten-Gräfsnäs Järnväg, Alingsås . 036173
L'Antenato, Milano . . . 075582
Antenne de l'Imprimerie de la Presse, Louhans . . . 012758
Anterieur, Leiden . . . 078559
Antes, Den Haag . . . 078164
Anthea, Quimper . . . 067012
Anthea's, Mitchelton . . . 056235
Anthea's Antiques, Auckland . . . 078905
Antheaume, Christiane, Rouen . . . 067237
Anthéaume, Fabrice, Foussemagne 062934
Anthemion, Bruxelles . . . 057813
Anthemion, Cartmel . . . 083889
Anthemion Gallery, Toronto . . . 059121
Anthéos, Bordeaux . . . 061576
Anthèse, Arcueil . . . 133449
Anthia, Charleville-Mézières . . . 062153
Anthill, Richmond . . . 092056
Anthinéa Brocante, Saint-Quentin (Aisne) . . . 067970
Anthony, Dublin . . . 074889
Anthony, Hong Kong . . . 097748
Anthony, Dorette, Hamburg . . . 071191
Anthony, Ivan, Auckland . . . 078906
Anthony, John, Bletchingley . . . 083561
Anthony, John, Kitchener . . . 058868
Anthony Antigüedades, Fuengirola . 081104
Anthony Henday Museum, Delburne 005338
Anthony's, Minneapolis . . . 132375
Anthony's Antiques and Fine Arts, Salt Lake City . . . 092411
Anthropological-Ethnological Museum, Athinai . . . 021157
Anthropological Museum, Beijing . . 006962
Anthropological Museum, Gauhati . 022118
Anthropological Museum, Department of Anthropology, Guwahati University, Guwahati . . . 022131
Anthropological Museum, Manipur University, Canchipur . . . 022048
Anthropological Museum of Xiamen University, Xiamen . . . 007310
The Anthropological National Folklore Museum, Amman . . . 027362
Anthropologische Sammlung der Universität Göttingen, Göttingen . . . 017464
Anthropologische Staatssammlung, München . . . 019032
Anthropology at Creswick, Creswick 055723
Anthropology Museum, Brisbane . . 000836
Anthropology Museum, DeKalb . . . 043373
Anthropology Museum, Delhi . . . 022077
Anthropology Museum, Ranchi . . . 022319
Anthropology Museum, Sri Jai Narain Degree College, Lucknow . . . 022234
Anthropology Museum and Resource Centre, Johannesburg . . . 034641
Anthropos, Fribourg . . . 136118
Anti-Aircraft Museum, Ha Noi . . . 049521
Anti-Keer, Hengelo, Overijssel . . . 140456
Anti-Kriegs-Museum, Berlin . . . 015985
Anti-Saloon League Museum, Westerville . . . 049107
Antiauariat FBV, Köln . . . 139331
Antic, Arras . . . 060985
Antic, Restinclières . . . 101090
Antic 190, Barcelona . . . 080788
Antic 1900, Villeurbanne . . . 068936
Antic 2000, François, Roquebrune-Cap-Martin . . . 067218
Antic 80, Abbeville . . . 060650
Antic Art, Toulon (Var) . . . 068437
Antic Art Connexion, Bezons . . . 061446
Antic Art et Déco, Lege-Cap-Ferret . 063735
Antic . Arte, Roma . . . 076272
Antic Arts and Crafts, Atlanta . . . 087444
Antic Atelier Cresta, Brienz, Graubünden . . . 082271
Antic Bisbal, La Bisbal d'Empordá . 081002
Antic Bisbal, La Bisbal d'Empordá . 081003
Antic Brocante, Barcelona . . . 121993
Antic Center Informatique, Nice . . . 065026
Antic Comimpex, Bucureşti . . . 080140
Antic Daro, La Bisbal d'Empordá . .081004, 129454
Antic Deco, Grenoble . . . 063045
Antic Déco International, Loupian . . 064012
Antic Décor, Montcaret . . . 064660
Antic Design, Saint-Étienne . . . 067438
Antic Dolls, Nice . . . 065027
Antic Dolls-Toys, Lyon . . . 064054, 124334
Antic Ex Libris, Bucureşti . . . 140873
Antic Julie & Renato, Toulon (Var) . . 068438
Antic-Kaufhaus Falkenried, Hamburg . . . 071192, 125799
Antic-Land, Saint-Étienne . . . 067439
Antic-Line, Perpignan . . . 066733
Antic Restauro, Barcelona . . . 129312
Antic Saint-Maclou, Rouen . . . 067238
Antic Shop, Neuilly-sur-Seine . . . 064985
Antic - Starožitnosti, Ústí nad Labem . . . 060198
Antic Sud Loire, Saint-Melaine-sur-Aubance . . . 067671
Antic-Tac, Paris . . . 065396, 124551
Antica, Angers . . . 060845
Antica, Braunschweig . . . 069976
Antica, Gex . . . 062991
Antica, Madrid . . . 129563
Antica, Marines . . . 064287
Antica, Olomouc . . . 060058
Antica, Paris . . . 065397
l'Antica, Sion . . . 082810, 111905
Antica, Tarbes . . . 068361
Antica, Vitry-aux-Loges . . . 069011
Antica Antiques, Claremont . . . 055671
Antica GS, Sarreguemines . . . 068133
Antica Libreria Cappelli, Bologna . . 139983
Antica Opera Romana, Bari . . . 105927
Antica Persia, Napoli . . . 075935
Anticaja, Roma . . . 076273, 127920
Anticaja & Petrella, Roma . 076274, 127921
Anticamente, Roma . . . 076275
Antic'Ange, Saint-Cassien . . . 067392
Anticariat, Craiova . . . 140889
Anticariat Curtea Veche, Bucureşti . 140874
Anticariat Galeria Halelor, Bucureşti . . . 109415, 140875
Anticariat Nr. 2, Bucureşti . . . 140876
Anticariat Nr. 4, Bucureşti . . . 140877
Anticariat Nr. 9, Bucureşti . . . 140878
Antic'Art, Ajaccio . . . 060734
Antic'art, Bouere . . . 061669
Antic'Arts, L'Absie . . . 063477
Antic'Arts, Parthenay . . . 066689
Antic'Brocante, Bayonne . . . 061229
Antic'Diffusion, Clermont-Ferrand . 062324
Antiche Armi, Milano . . . 075583
Antiche Belle Cose, Bologna . . . 075041
Antiche Fantasie, Roma . . . 076276
Antichi Maestri Pittori, Torino . . . 106655
Antichitá, Firenze . . . 075269
Antichita, Glebe . . . 055880
Antichitá, Roma . . . 076277
Antichitá, Roma . . . 076278
Antichitá Al Collegio, Bologna . . . 075042
Antichità al Faro, Biasca . . . 082254
Antichitá al Teatro di Duse, Bologna 075043
Antichitá Alla Porta, Bologna . . . 075044
Antichitá As, Messina . . . 075552
Antichitá Barberia, Bologna . . . 075045
Antichitá Belsito, Roma . . . 076279
Antichitá Biedermeier, Milano . . . 075584
Antichitá Carlo III, Napoli . . . 075936
Antichitá Casartelli, Torino . . . 076760
Antichitá & Curiositá, Roma . . . 076280
Antichitá dal Luzzo, Bologna . . . 075046
Antichitá Dante, Palermo . . . 076121
Antichitá del Corso, Bologna . . . 075047
Antichitá della Moscova, Milano . . . 075585
Antichitá due Torri, Bologna . . . 075048
Antichitá Due Torri, Verona . . . 076987
Antichitá e Arte, Milano . . . 075586
Antichitá Federico II, Bari . . . 075005
Antichita Gattamelata, Padova . . . 076067
Antichità Giardini, Modena . . . 127715
Antichitá Giulia, Roma . . . 076281
Antichita Grand Tour, Roma . . . 076282
Antichità Il Cherubino, Cagliari . . . 127239
Antichitá il Leone, Bologna . . . 075049
Antichitá Isabella, Milano . . . 075587
Antichita M.M., Napoli . . . 075937
Antichità Mona Lisa, Ascona . . . 082095
Antichitá Nirone 5678, Milano . . . 075588
Antichitá Nova, Milano . . . 075589
Antichitá Piantarose, Perugia . . . 076228
Antichitá Porta Venezia, Milano . . . 075590
Antichitá Rialto, Bologna . . . 075050
Antichitá Rinascimento, Roma . . . 076283
Antichitá Ripetta, Roma . . . 076284
Antichitá San Basso, Venezia . . . 076916
Antichitá San Maurizio, Venezia . . . 076917
Antichitá San Salvatore, Bologna . . 075051
Antichitá San Samuele, Venezia . . . 076918
Antichitá San Vitale, Bologna . . . 075052
Antichitá Santa Giulia di Borelli, Brescia . . . 075141
Antichità Sturni, Roma . . . 076285
Antichitá Vecci, Firenze . . . 075270
Antichitá Venezia, Milano . . . 075591
Antichitá Volta, Milano . . . 075592, 140040
Antichitati Lu & Ad, Cluj-Napoca . . 080174
Antic'Inn, Beauvoisin . . . 061316
Antická Gerulata v Rusovciach, Mestské Múzeum v Bratislave, Bratislava . 034316
Anticmag, Clermont . . . 062323
Antico, Marlene, Paddington . . . 095013
Antico e Antico, Roma . . . 076286
L'Antico Forziere, Torino . . . 076761
Antico Frantoio, Massa Marittima . . 024636
Antico Mania, Modena . . . 127716
Antico Mondo, Köln . . . 071901
Antico per Antico, Milano . . . 075593
Antico Splendore, Modena . . . 127717
L'Antico Viaggiointorno Ad Un Oggetto, Roma . . . 076287
Antic'Oro, Brescia . . . 075142
Antics, Paris . . . 065398
Antics, Saint-Martin-d'Heres . . . 067642
Antics Lleida, Lleida . . . 081176
Anticthermal, Nancy . . . 121082
Anticua, Barranquilla . . . 098086
Anticuaria, Oviedo . . . 081455
Anticuaria de la Casa Verde, Guatemala . . . 074647
Anticuaria del Retiro, Buenos Aires . 136696
Anticuaria el Callejon, Madrid . . . 081216
Anticuaria en Muebles, Medellín . . 059894
El Anticuario, Arequipa . . . 079533
El Anticuario, Medellín . . . 059895
El Anticuario, La Palmas de Gran Canaria . . . 081498
El Anticuario, Vigo . . . 081697
Anticuario Cotanda, Madrid . . . 081217
Anticuario El Arcón, Cartagena . . . 059890
Anticuario el Fin del Afán, Medellín 059896
Anticuario El Museo de Santa Severa, Bogotá . . . 059807
El Anticuario Francés, Cali . . . 059871
Anticuario Frances, Cochabamba . .058395, 123684
Anticuario H & S, Bogotá . . . 059808
Anticuario La Candelaria, Bogotá . . 059809
Anticuario Las Palmas, Medellín . . . 059897
Anticuario Pallarols, Buenos Aires .055158, 123148
Anticuario San Antonio, Cartagena . 059891
Anticuarios Agrupacion Profesional de Anticuarios de las Rea, Barcelona 054078
Anticuarios Arte Decorativo, Medellín . . . 059898
Anticums, Les Anglès . . . 063753
Anticus, Hannover . . . 071375, 125862
Anticus, Russell . . . 079232
Anticus, Warszawa . . . 079724
Anticus-BDC, Stratford-upon-Avon . 142092
Anticuus, Roma . . . 076288
Anticuus, Roma . . . 076289
Antiek, Gouda . . . 078383
Antiek Brocante, Antwerpen . . . 057675
Antiek Brocante Royal, Brugge . . . 057758
Antiek Care, Boxtel . . . 128600
Antiek Care, 's-Graveland . . . 128678
Antiek & Curiosa, Amsterdam . . . 077776
Antiek & Design Centre, Eindhoven 078327
Antiek en Wijn, Breda . . . 078078
De Antiek-Express, Hoogeveen . . . 128729
Antiek Franky, Hasselt . . . 058222
Antiek Garden en Pine, Mechelen . . 058333
Antiek Oud Aelst, Aalst . . . 057658, 123542

Antiek Paris Provence, Brugge 057759
Antiek Roosendaal, Roosendaal . . . 078684
Antiek Show Case, Antwerpen 057676
Antiek Stockhouse, Gent 058168
Antiekbeurs, Schoorl 093823
Antiekbeurs A'dam 700, Amsterdam 077777
Antiekcenter, Kortrijk 058258
De Antieke Schuit, Dordrecht 078295
De Antiekhoek, Almelo 077721
De Antiekhoek, Leiden 078560
't Antiekhuis, Breda 078079
Antiekimport Oss, Oss 078664
Antiekmarkt Leiden, Leiden 078561
Antietam National Battlefield, Sharpsburg 048129
Antifaschistische Mahn- und Gedenkstätte, Lieberose 018640
L'Antiga, Denia 081067, 129492
Antiga Libros, Palma de Mallorca . .081469, 141066
Antigamente, Porto 080063
Antigo, A Coruña 081053, 129485
Antigo Lavradio, Rio de Janeiro . . . 058536
Antigona, Ciutadella de Menorca . . 081042
Antigonish Heritage Museum, Antigonish 005022
Antigua, Cheptainville 062273
Antigua Cárcel de Jaruco, Jaruco . . 008032
Antigua Casa de los Marqueses de Campo Florido, San Antonio de los Baños 008116
Antigua Casa Histórica, Buenos Aires 055159
Antigua de Mexico, Tucson 093194
Antigua Librería, Buenos Aires 136697
Antigua Upholstery, San Diego 132840
Antigualla, Santa Cruz de Tenerife . 081549
Antigue Bookshop, Buenos Aires . . 136698
Antiguedades, Madrid 081218
Antiguedades, Valencia 081639
Antiguedades Abraham, Palma de Mallorca 081470
Antiguedades Antaño, Jerez de la Frontera 081162
Antiguedades Antiqua, Donostia-San Sebastián 081071
Antiguedades Arcangel, Sevilla . . . 081567
Antiguedades Atenas, Granada 081140
Antiguedades Atrio, Valencia 081640
Antiguedades Barros, Valladolid . . . 081685
Antiguedades Capileida, Santa Cruz de Tenerife 081550, 129721
Antiguedades Carlota, Barcelona . . 080789
Antiguedades Castellarnau, Tarragona 081621
Antiguedades Claudio, Madrid 081219
Antiguedades Consuelo Roman, Madrid 081220
Antiguedades Dato 12, Zaragoza . . 081731
Antiguedades del Sureste, Cancún . 077557
Antiguedades el Hallago, Monterrey 077583
Antiguedades el Sol, Guadalajara . . 077559
Antiguedades Emilio, Madrid 081221
Antiguedades Esperanza, Oviedo . . 081456
Antiguedades Juan Antonio, Madrid 081222
Antiguedades la Flora, Burgos 081011
Antiguedades la Peregrina, La Palmas de Gran Canaria 081499
Antiguedades la Salamandra, Monterrey 077584
Antiguedades Linares, Toledo 081630
Antiguedades Luna, Sevilla 081568
Antiguedades Macor, Madrid 081223
Antiguedades Maite, Santa Cruz de Tenerife 081551
Antiguedades Martin, Madrid 081224
Antiguedades Miguel Angel, Madrid 081225
Antiguedades Montelongo, Sevilla . 081569
Antiguedades Montenegro, Vigo . . . 081698
Antiguedades Palacios, Madrid 081226
Antiguedades Paris, Palma de Mallorca 081471
Antiguedades Perojo, La Palmas de Gran Canaria 081500
Antiguedades Querol, Valencia 081641
Antiguedades Raiz, Donostia-San Sebastián 081072
Antiguedades Rey Don Pedro, Burgos 081012
Antiguedades Romero, Madrid 081227
Antiguedades Santa Teresa, Sevilla 081570
Antiguedades Santiago Marti, Barcelona 080790
Antiguedades Segundo, Sevilla . . . 081571
Antiguedades Siloe, Valencia 081642
Antiguedades Talavera, Valencia . . 081643
Antiguedades Tandem, Barcelona . . 080791
Antiguedades Union, Guadalajara . . 077560
Antiguedades Viera, La Palmas de Gran Canaria 081501
Antigüedades, Bogotá 059810
Antigüedades, Montevideo 087303
Antigüedades, Santiago de Chile . . 059488
Antigüedades, Santiago de Chile . . 059489
Antigüedades Alabastro, Cali 059872
Antigüedades Alfonso XII, Jaén . . . 081160
Antigüedades Antiques, Bogotá . . . 059811
Antigüedades Arlequín, Santiago de Chile 059490
Antigüedades Atelier Inroma, Lima . 079535
Antigüedades Barón, Madrid 081228, 141024
Antigüedades Bío Bío, Santiago de Chile 059491
Antigüedades Bohemia, Buenos Aires 055160
Antigüedades Bohemia, Viña del Mar 059566
Antigüedades Britania, La Palmas de Gran Canaria 081502
Antigüedades Cambalache, Badajoz 080773
Antigüedades Caoba, Almeria 080769
Antigüedades Carlos III, Pamplona . 081507
Antigüedades Challer Palace, Barranquilla 059799
Antigüedades Claudio, Madrid 081229
Antigüedades Cuca Romero, Madrid 081230
Antigüedades de la Fuente, Bilbao .080965, 129422
Antigüedades de los Abuelos, Medellín 059899
Antigüedades El Andamio, Santiago de Chile 059492
Antigüedades el Arcón, Lima 079536
Antigüedades El Coleccionista, Viña del Mar 059567
Antigüedades el Museo, Sevilla . . . 081572
Antigüedades el Nene, Buenos Aires 123149
Antigüedades el Patio, Sevilla 081573
Antigüedades el Polo, Lima 079537
Antigüedades el Rastro de San Telmo, Buenos Aires 055161
Antigüedades Esmeralda, Buenos Aires 055162
Antigüedades Gorer, Buenos Aires . 055163
Antigüedades Guemes, Buenos Aires 055164
Antigüedades Karlos, Madrid 081231, 141025
Antigüedades la Calesa, Castello de la Plana 081034
Antigüedades la Caverna, Murcia . .081439, 141064
Antigüedades La Dehesa, Santiago de Chile 059493
Antigüedades la Ocasión, Barcelona 080792
Antigüedades la Portada de Prado Centro, Medellín 059900
Antigüedades La Rueda, Buenos Aires 055165
Antigüedades la Telaraña, Medellín 059901
Antigüedades la Telaraña, Medellín 059902
Antigüedades la Verja, Oviedo 081457
Antigüedades La Yapa, Buenos Aires 055166
Antigüedades Laura, Medellín 059903
Antigüedades Los Reyes, Cali 059873
Antigüedades Macor, Madrid 081232
Antigüedades Maria Teresa, Medellín 059904
Antigüedades Marta Rosa, Santiago de Chile 059494
Antigüedades Matusalén, Castello de la Plana 081035
Antigüedades Milagros, Lima 079538
Antigüedades Nuria, Murcia 081440
Antigüedades Ondarbide, Donostia-San Sebastián 081073
Antigüedades Pantim, Buenos Aires 055167
Antigüedades PM, Buenos Aires . . . 055168
Antigüedades Rodas, Vigo 081699
Antigüedades San Expedito, Medellín 059905, 123929
Antigüedades San Lorenzo, Medellín 059906
Antigüedades Santa Clara, Cáceres 081022
Antigüedades Santander, Bogotá . . 059812
Antigüedades Siglo XVII, Lima 079539
Antigüedades Sisi, Santiago de Chile 059495
Antigüedades Sonia, Cali 059874
Antigüedades Tres Morillas, Jaén . . 081161
Antigüedades Trueque, Pamplona . . 081508
Antigüedades Valladolid 2000, Valladolid 081686
Antigüedades Veintiseis, Santiago de Chile 059496
Antigüedades Venus, Valencia 093554
Antigüedades Vieja Estación, Don Torcuato 055259, 123163
Antigüedades y Arte San Antonio, Bogotá 059813
Antigüedades y Artesanias La 5a, Cali 059875
Antigüedades y Avaluos, Medellín . 059907
Antigüedades y Decoración San Telmo, Bogotá 059814
Antigüedades y Segundas, Medellín 059908
Antigüedades y Subastas de Sevilla, Sevilla 081574, 122084
Antigüedades Z.S., Pamplona 081509
Antiguidades Doll's, Lisboa 079854
Antiguidades Doll's, Lisboa 079855
Antiguidades e Velharias Fim do Século, Funchal 079832
Antiguidades Escritorio de Artes, Rio de Janeiro 058537
Antiguidades Estima, São Paulo . . . 058672
Antiguidades Fortaleza, Lisboa 079856, 140818
Antiguidades Francisco, São Paulo . 058673
Antiguidades Galera São Pedro, Funchal 079833
Antiguidades la Gemme, Rio de Janeiro 058538
Antiguidades Laura, São Paulo 058674
Antiguidades Mayflower, Coimbra . 079817
Antiguidades Minha Avo Tinha, São Paulo 058675
Antiguidades Mobel, Funchal 079834
Antiguidades Opera, São Paulo 058676
Antiguidades Ouro Velho, Belo Horizonte 058403
Antiguidades Sampaio Rocha, São Paulo 058677
Antiguidades São Sebastião, Rio de Janeiro 058539
Antiguidades Serralves, Porto 080064, 129187
Antiguitats Capri, Tarragona 081622
Antiguitats Duch, Barcelona 080793
Antiguo, Alicante 080756
Antiguo, Alicante 080757
Antiguo Ayuntamiento y Cárcel de Bejucal, Bejucal 007882
Antiguo Recinto del Congreso Nacional, Buenos Aires 000142
Antiik, Tallinn 060480
Antiik, Tallinn 060481
Antiik & Käsitöö, Tallinn 060482
Antiikin ja Keräilyesineiden Osto-, Myynti- ja Vaitotapahtuma, Tampere 093645
Antiikki Erik, Helsinki 060499
Antiikki ja Entisöinti, Jokela 060600
Antiikki- ja Keräilymessut, Vaasa . . 093646
Antiikki Jokela, Pori 060619
Antiikki & Nykyaika, Helsinki 060500
Antiikki PP, Turku 060635
Antiikki Trianon, Helsinki 060501
Antiikkihalli, Helsinki 060502
Antiikkiliike Kaappi & Kello, Helsinki 060503
Antiikkiliike Vanha Rouva, Pori 060620
Antiikkilinja, Helsinki 060504
Antik, Beuzeville 061417
Antik, Burgwedel 070108
Antik, Castres 062027
Antik, České Budějovice 059996
Antik, Glücksburg, Ostsee 071009
Antik, Hamm, Westfalen 071360
Antik, Helsingborg 093882
Antik, Holice v Čechách 060018
Antik, İstanbul . . . 122379, 135110, 141373
Antik, København 060267
Antik, Koblenz 071889
Antik, La Garenne-Colombes 063391
Antik, Milano 075594
Antik, Moskva 080218
Antik, Náchod 060054
Antik, New York 090669
Antik, Pardubice 060071
Antik, Pécs 139940
Antik, Plzeň 060079
Antik, Praha 060094
Antik, Přerov 060183
Antik, Samara 080284
Antik, Schopfheim 073719
Antik, Schwieberdingen 073779
Antik, Wolfsburg 074479
Antik, Znojmo 060204
Antik 141, Frederiksberg 060222
Antik 1800, Malmö 081860
Antik 19, Frederiksberg 060223
Antik 2000, Sankt Leon-Rot 073670
Antik 2000, Strasbourg 068288
Antik 22, Karlsruhe 071707
Antik 7, Oslo 079409
Antik 77, København 060268
Antik & Acente, Köln 071902
Antik A+J, Mariánské Lázně 137795
Antik am Deutschhof, Heilbronn . . . 071469
Antik am Hafen, Husum, Nordsee . . 071597
Antik am Marstall, Delingsdorf 070210
Antik am Meer, Bremen 070006
Antik am Zoo, Leipzig 072191
Antik am Zoo, Wuppertal 074520
Antik and More, Immenhausen 071616
Antik-Antikvariat, Praha . . 060095, 137813
Antik & Antikvariat MH, Ústí nad Labem 060199, 137857
Antik & Art, Hannover 071376
Antik & Art, Karlsruhe 071708
Antik Art, Moskva 080219
Antik - Art Antonio, Genova 075430
Antik Art Centrum, Trnava 080642
Antik-Art Deco, Bremen 070007
Antik Art Lüneburg, Lüneburg 072353
Antik-Atelier, Balje 069440
Antik Atrium, Göttingen . . 071040, 139143
Antik & Auksjon, Sandnes 121875
Antik Bansin, Seebad Bansin 073781
Antik-Basar, Waghäusel 074237
Antik Bazaar, Toronto 059122
Antik-Bazar, Brünig 082273
Antik Bazar, Košice 080616
Antik Bazar, Leissigen 082573
Antik Bazar, Nancy 064858
Antik Bazar, Svitavy 060193
Antik-Blaes, Bruxelles 057814
Antik-Blankenburg, Blankenburg, Harz 069864
Antik Böngészde, Budapest 139910
Antik Bútor - Régiség, Pécs 074744
Antik Center, Köln 071903
Antik-Center-Wiesenburg, Wildenfels 074436
Antik-Centr, Sankt-Peterburg 080290
Antik Centrum, Bratislava 080597
Antik Centrum, Dvůr Králové nad Labem 060014

Antik & Chic, Halstenbek 071182
Antik Daniel, Fürth, Bayern 070910
Antik D+D, Znojmo 060205
Antik & Dekor, İstanbul 136135
Antik & Dekoration, Sundbyberg . . . 082045
Antik Depó, Enese 074735
Antik & Design, Aalborg 093638
Antik & Design, Eckernförde 070501
Antik & Design, Konstanz 072046
Antik & Design, Ludwigsburg, Württemberg 072304
Antik & Design, Anne, Mainz 072386, 126255
Antik-Diele, Burweg 070112
Antik-Diele, Heede 071439
Antik e Nuovo, Horw 082501
Antik-Eck, Hannover 071377
Antik-Eck, Lemgo 072221
Antik-Ecke im Sand, Bamberg 069442
Antik-Eggli, Luzern 082617
Antik-Eppi, Jena 071653
Antik Exclusiv, Karlstein am Main . . 071739
Antik Extra, Hochstetten-Dhaun . . . 071537
Antik Fascination, Timişoara 080188
Antik-Forum, Zürich 082935
Antik France, Marseille 064312
Antik-Frühling, Gaggenau 093695
Antik Galéria, Zalaegerszeg 074759
Antik-Galerie, Broderstorf 070061
Antik-Galerie, Vaduz 077450
Antik Galerie Braunschweig, Braunschweig 069977
Antik-Galerie im Lichtental, Wien . . 057368
Antik-Galerie Vaduz, Vaduz 077451
Antik-Galerie zum Storchen, Diessenhofen 082341
Antik & Genbrug, Frederiksberg . . . 060224
Antik-Hall, Haguenau 063111
Antik Halle, Kassel 071742
Antik-Haus, Butzbach 070115
Antik Haus, Herne 071491
Antik Haus, Reinbek 073478
Antik-Haus, Verl 074196
Antik-Haus, Westoverledingen 074376
Antik Haus Sankt Leon-Rot, Sankt Leon-Rot 073671
Antik Hillerød, Hillerød 093639
Antik Hof, Delmenhorst 070213
Antik-Hof, Kümmersbruck 072103
Antik-Hof, Wokuhl-Dabelow 074466
Antik im Hinterhof, Waiblingen 074238
Antik im Hof, Osnabrück 073229
Antik im Odeon, Darmstadt 070178
Antik JN, København 060269
Antik JZ, København 060270
Antik Kaltenkirchen, Kaltenkirchen . 071688
Antik-Karussell, Metelen 072531
Antik-Kate, Frederiksberg 060225
Antik KF, Oberursel 073162
Antik-Klasik, Praha 060096
Antik & Kunst, København 060271
Antik & Kunst, Remagen 073484
Antik & Kunst, Wien 137286
Antik & Kunst Heilbronn, Heilbronn . 093696
Antik & Kuriosa, Malmö 081861
Antik Lager, Schwanenstadt 057307
Antik Lageret, København 060272
Antik & Lamper, København 060273
Antik Landemærket, København . . . 060274
Antik Lar, Moskva 080220
Antik Luma, Praha 060097
Antik Mignon, Karlovy Vary 060032
Antik & Militaria, Stockholm 081912
Antik & Modern, Bensheim 069523
Antik & Modern, Budapest 074660
Antik-Möbel-Restaurierung, Bad Homburg v.d.Höhe 125098
Antik & Möbelformedlingen, Stockholm 081913
Antik-Möbelhaus, Kapellen-Drusweiler 071702
Antik-Mühle, Bruchsal 070064
Antik Mûhely - Antikvitás, Pécs . . .074745, 127082
Antik Nordwest, Frankfurt am Main 102741
Antik Nostalgie, Lingen 072276
Antik of the Future, Stockholm 081914
Antik og Gammelt, Stavanger 079496
Antik og Lopper, København 060275
Antik Oriental, Tampa 093100
Antik Original, Nettetal 072962
Antik Oskar, Helsinki 060505
Antik Øst, Oslo 079410
Antik-Palette, Freising . . . 070873, 139125
Antik-Régiségbolt, Pécs 074746
Antik Restaurator., Budapest 127074
Antik Russo, Nürnberg 126559
Antik-Sammelsurium, Limburg an der Lahn 072255
Antik Sanat Galerisi, İstanbul 083114
Antik Sankt Rupert, Salzburg 057234
Antik-Scheune, Unna 074160
Antik Schlößchen, Schwetzingen . . 073776
Antik Sofie-Amalie, København . . . 060276
Antik & Souvenir, Quedlinburg 073393
Antik Stadel Wifling, Wörth, Kreis Erding 074464
Antik-Stadl, Bad Leonfelden 056936
Antik-Stadl, Donzdorf 070272
Antik Starožitnosti, Mladá Boleslav . 060052
Antik-Stube, Hinzert-Pölert 071529
Antik-Stube, Hirzenhain 071534
Antik-Stübchen, Erfurt 125595
Antik-Stübchen, Friedrichstadt 070898
Antik-Stübchen, Konz 072052
Antik Style, Mainz 072387
Antik Svítidla, Praha 060098
Antik-Tage Landau, Landau in der Pfalz 093697
Antik-Tage Rosenheim, Rosenheim 093698
Antik Tanulmanyok, Budapest 135839
Antik Treff, Radlberg 057217
Antik Treff, Rheda-Wiedenbrück . . . 073508
Antik & Trends, Wangen im Allgäu . 074273
Antik & Trödel, Estedt 070663
Antik & Trödel, Grünhainichen 071130
Antik & Trödel, Hannover 071378
Antik Trödel, Leipzig 072192
Antik & Trödel in der List, Hannover 071379
Antik Troja, Mersch 077485
Antik-Truhe, Hilchenbach 071512
Antik u. Sammlerstube, Dresden . . 138986
Antik und Art, Hannover 071380
Antik und Deko, Mantel 072442
Antik- und Geschenkestube, Geeste 070942
Antik und Kunst, Cottbus 070156
Antik und Kunst im Turm, Neuleiningen 073001
Antik und Kunsthandel, Idar-Oberstein 071605
Antik und Kunsthandel, Tangermünde 074039
Antik- und Kunstkabinett, Bonn . . . 069911
Antik und Raritäten Cabinet, Magdeburg 072368
Antik und Trödel, Sohland 073849
Antik und Trödelcenter, Magdeburg 072369
Die Antik-Werkstatt, Münchberg . . . 072622
Antik West, Göteborg 081789
Antik West, London 085079
Antik Winkeltje, Aurich 069243
Antik Z, Malmö 081862
Antik Zentrum Bochum, Bochum . . 069880
Antik Žiro, Trjavna 058774, 137611
Antika, Graz 056999
Antika, Mainz 139442
Antika, Seattle 092951
Antika 1, Lyon 064055
Antika Kranj, Kranj 080646
Antika Lyon Terreaux, Lyon 138134
Antika Tizian, Ljubljana 080647
Antika Vedspisar och Kaminer, Sigtuna 081894
Antikaffären PHM, Stockholm 081915
Antikarat, Luxembourg 077472
Antikarnas, İstanbul 083115
Antik'Art et Déco, Sète 068233
Antikas, Kaslik 077436, 128456
Antikavriata Veikals, Rīga 140216
Antikayes, Le Touquet-Paris-Plage . 063714
Antikboden, Oslo 079411
Antikboden, Sävedalen 081890
Antikboden i Västertorp, Hägersten 081828
Antikdoktor, Köln 126061
Antike Fundgrube, Bayreuth 069486
Antike-Fundgrube, Gronau, Westfalen 071107
Antike Kunst, Basel 136119
Antike Puppen, Nürnberg 073095
Antike Welt, Mainz 135738
Antikea, Törökbálint 074757
Antiken-Kabinett, Frankfurt am Main 070724
Antiken- und Abgußsammlung des Archäologischen Seminars, Marburg 018816
Antikenmuseum Basel und Sammlung Ludwig, Basel 036879
Antikenmuseum der Universität Leipzig, Leipzig 018559
Antikenmuseum und Abgußsammlung des Archäologischen Instituts der Universität Heidelberg, Heidelberg 017823
Antikensammlung, Bern 036925
Antikensammlung, Kunsthalle zu Kiel, Kiel 018243
Antikensammlung, Staatliche Museen Kassel, Kassel 018179
Antikensammlung, Staatliche Museen zu Berlin - Stiftung Preußischer Kulturbesitz, Berlin 015986
Antikensammlung der Friedrich-Alexander-Universität Erlangen-Nürnberg, Erlangen 017028
Antikerie, Hollen 071563
Antikes, Freiburg im Breisgau 070820
Antikes, Goslar 071062
Antikes am Deich, Hamburg 071193
Antikes & Modernes, Wesel 074351
Antikes & Schönes, Murnau 072936
Antikes vom Land, Graz 057000
Antikes Wohnen, Klagenfurt 057102
Antikes Wohnmuseum, Weinheim, Bergstraße 020761
Antikgalleriet, Oslo 079412
Antikgården, Mariefred 081881
Antikhallarna, Göteborg 081790
Antikhalle, Verden 074190
Antikhalle Hanau, Johann-Georg, Hanau 071369
Antikhalle-Torgau, Torgau 074070
Antikhandel Anna Luisenhof, Anna Luisenhof 069170
Antikhandel Bonn, Königswinter . . . 072036
Antikhandl, Náchod 060055
Antikhandlung Gohlis, Leipzig 072193
Antikhane, İstanbul 083116
Antikhaus, Dötlingen 070267
Antikhaus, Hilden 071514
Antikhaus, Velbert 074185
Antikhaus Jever, Jever 071666
Antikhof, Aspenstedt 069211
Antikhof, Lingen 072277
Antikhof, Michelhausen 057181
Antikhof, Ottweiler 073272
Antikhof Dreieich, Dreieich 070303
Antikhof Kloschwitz, Wettin 074379
Antikhof Kropp, Kropp 072096
Antiki Aro, Sofia 058759, 137599
Antikimport, Montréal 058896
Antikk & Brukt, Oslo 140696
Antikkeller, Saarbrücken 073623
Antikkhuset Hamar, Furnes 121851
Der Antikladen, Frankfurt am Main . 070725
Antiklädchen, Rauschenberg 073437
Das Antiklager, Warmsen 074279
Antikmagasinet- Lampverkstad, Stockholm 081916
Antikmarknad Antikviteum, Gustavsberg 081827
Antikmarkt, Bickenbach, Bergstraße 069815
Antikmarkt, Darmstadt 070179
Antikmarkt am Alex, Berlin 069557
Antikmarkt Basel, Basel . . 082118, 129908
Antikmarkt R.O.S.A., Bamberg 069443
Antikmarkt Süd, Wien 057369
Antikmöbel, Berlin 069558, 125162
Antikmöbel, Schefflenz 073679
Antikmöbelmarkt, Landau in der Pfalz 072127
Antikmuseet, Göteborg 036292
Antik'n, Oslo 079413
Antikname, İstanbul 083117
Antikören Mynthandel, Göteborg . . 081791
Antikoteca, Montevideo 122770
Antikparadies, Bad Ischl 056928
Antikriegshaus Sievershausen, Lehrte 018545
Antiks, Sankt-Peterburg 080291
Antik's, Thomery 068401
Antiks Design, Lisboa 079857
Antikscheune Elmschenhagen, Kiel 071819
Antikschopf, Rheinmünster 073527
Die Antikstube, Wiefelstede 074386
Antikstübli, Sankt Gallen 082770
Antikt, Surry Hills 056651
Antikt, Gammalt och Nytt, Stockholm 081917
Antikt och Modernt, Stockholm . . . 081918
Antikum, Mainz 103995
Antikurmakaren, Malmö 081863
Antikva, Frýdek-Místek 060015
Antikva-Art, Brno 059971
Antikva Mikos, Třebíč 060196
Antikva Nova Kodl, Praha . 060099, 120851, 137814
Antikva Nova Praga, Praha 120852
Antikva Radio Praha, Praha 060100
Antikva René, Praha 060101
Antikva - Starozitnosti, Bratislava . . 080598
Antikvaar, Tallinn 060483
Antikvaar, Tallinn 060484
Antikvaar, Tallinn 137913
Antikvaarinen Kirjakauppa, Helsinki 137928
Antikvar, Irkutsk 080206
Antikvár, Miskolc 139938
Antikvar, Nižnij Novgorod . 080280, 140921
Antikvar, Sankt-Peterburg 080292
Antikvar-Metropol, Moskva 080221
Antikvar na Mjasnickoj, Moskva . . . 080222
Antikvaria Bökkeri, Helsinki 137929
Antikvaria Poopa Joe, Espoo 137921
Antikvariaat, Tallinn 137914
Antikvariaatit, Helsinki 137930
Antikvariaatit, Helsinki 137931
Antikvariaatti Anno Domini, Vantaa . 138004
Antikvariaatti Brigitta, Helsinki 137932
Antikvariaatti Grafika, Tuusula 138001
Antikvariaatti Lumikannas, Helsinki 137933
Antikvariaatti Syvä uni, Helsinki . . .060506, 137934
Antikvariaatti Tyrwää, Vammala . . . 138003
Antikvariaatti Vistan Divari, Paimo . 137982
Antikvariát, Frýdek-Místek 137781
Antikvariat, Kaliningrad 140892
Antikvariát, Kroměříž 137789
Antikvariat, Murska Sobota 080666, 140970
Antikvariát, Olomouc 137799
Antikvariát, Olomouc 137800
Antikvariát, Praha 137815
Antikvariát, Praha 137816
Antikvariát, Praha 137817
Antikvariát, Praha 137818
Antikvariát, Prešov 140962
Antikvariat, Rīga 140217
Antikvariat, Rostov-na-Donu 080283, 140922
Antikvariat, Samara 080285
Antikvariat, Sankt-Peterburg 080293
Antikvariat, Sofia 137600
Antikvariát, Třebíč 137855
Antikvariát, Zlín 137859
Antikvariat 2B, København 137878
Antikvariat Antiqua, Stockholm . . . 141140
Antikvariát Arcanum, Třebíč 137856

Antikvariat Åsnan, Uppsala 141184
Antikvariat Athenaeum, Stockholm . 141141
Antikvariat August, Stockholm 141142
Antikvariát Bělehradská, Praha . . . 137819
Antikvariat Bibliomanen, Uppsala . . 141185
Antikvariat Böcker & Kuriosa, Lund 141120
Antikvariat Boken, Stockholm 141143
Antikvariat Bokstödet, Stockholm . . 141144
Antikvariát Dali, Bratislava 140956
Antikvariat Erato, Stockholm 141145
Antikvariat Felix Jenewein, Kutná Hora 137790
Antikvariát Globus, Liberec 137791
Antikvariát-Kuriozity, Praha 137820
Antikvariat Läslustan, Lund 141121
Antikvariat Můstek, Praha 137821
Antikvariat na Bronnoj, Moskva . . . 080223
Antikvariat na Manežnoj, Moskva . . 080224
Antikvariát Nazca, Žilina 140965
Antikvariat Pan, Göteborg 141095
Antikvariát Pařížská, Praha 137822
Antikvariát Pegasus, Bratislava . . . 140957
Antikvariát Ptolomaeus, Praha 137823
Antikvariat Röde Orm, Göteborg . . . 141096
Antikvariát Runa, Jablonec nad Nisou 137786
Antikvariát Š, Chrudim 137778
Antikvariat Sør, Kristiansand 140694
Antikvariat - Starožitnosti, Domažlice 060011, 137780
Antikvariát Steiner, Bratislava 140958
Antikvariát v Suterénu, Ostrava . . . 137803
Antikvariát Valentinská, Praha 137824
Antikvariát Votobia, Olomouc 137801
Antikvariát Votobia, Přerov 137851
Antikvariát za Věží, České Budějovice 137773
Antikvariatet, København 137879
Antikvariatet, København 137880
Antikvariatet, Valby 137909
Antikvariatet Bokmalen, Göteborg . 141097
Antikvariatet PUK, København 137881
Antikvariít Čajka, Trenčín 140964
Antikvarijat Danica, Beograd 080388
Antikvarijat i knjižara Matice srpske, Beograd 140946
Antikvarijat Jesenski i Turk, Zagreb 137762
Antikvarijat Jesenski i Turk, Zagreb 137763
Antikvarijat Knjiga Mali Neboder, Rijeka 059946, 137761
Antikvarijat Matice srpske, Novi Sad 140950
Antikvarijat Tin Ujević, Zagreb 137764
Antikvariska Bokhandeln, Helsingborg 141114
Den Antikvariske Samling, Ribe . . . 009065
Antikvárium, Makó 139936
Antikvárium, Szeged 139941
Antikvárium - EX-Libris, Budapest . 139911
Antikvárium - Font, Budapest 139912
Antikvarnaja Galereja, Moskva 080225
Antikvarnaja Galereja, Sankt-Peterburg 080294
Antikvarnaja Galereja Archipova, Sankt-Peterburg 080295
Antikvarnaja lavka, Moskva 080226
Antikvarnaja Mebel, Moskva 080227
Antikvarnica Galerija Mirjana, Beograd 080389, 109682
Antikvarnica i Galerija, Sombor . . .080411, 109748
Antikvarnica Konzul, Beograd 080390
Antikvarno-Bukinističeskij Salon, Sankt-Peterburg 080296, 140929
Antikvarno-Numizmatičeskij Magazin, Sankt-Peterburg 080297
Antikvarno-restavracionnaja Masterskaja, Jaroslavl 080207
Antikvarnyj Aukcion, Sankt-Peterburg 121968
Antikvarnyj Centr, Sankt-Peterburg . 080298
Antikvarnyj Juvelirnyj Magazin, Moskva 080228
Antikvarnyj Magazin, Moskva 080229
Antikvita, Nymburk 060057
Antikvita-Starožitnosti, Praha 060102
Antikvitás, Budapest 074661
Antikvitás, Budapest 074662
Antikvitás Régiségbolt, Miskolc . . . 074741
Antikvitete MK, Maribor 080659
Antikviteten, Skodsborg 060400
Antikviteter i Forum og Internationale Møntbørs, Frederiksberg 093640
Antikviteter på Børsen, København . 093641
Antikvity, České Budějovice 059997
Antikvity Art Aukce, Brno . 059972, 120846
Antikwest, Helsinki 060507
Antillaise, Fort-de-France 140242
Antillaise, Le Lamentin 140247
Antillaise, Rivière-Salée 140251
l'Antillaise Art Gallery, Austin 114949
Antille, Fernand, Sierre 082808
Antilles Médailles, Chevilly-Larue . . 062283
Antilope, Casablanca 077634
L'Antilope, Lyon 099534
Antim, Bruxelles 057815
Antin, Brenda, Los Angeles 089679
Antin, Jean-Pierre, Lavérune 063560
Antinori, Giovanni Luca, Torino 076762
Antipodean Gallery, Nedlands 137021
Antipodean Map and Print Gallery, Subiaco 137094
Antipodes, Paris 099937
Antiq' Art, Saint-Raphaël 067983
Antiq Déco, Quiberon 067007
Antiq Photo Gallery, Toulouse 068475
Antiq'Ardenne, Libramont 093592
Antiqart, Košice 080617, 140961
Antiq'Arts, Courthiezy 062526
Antiqe och Qriosa, Stockholm 081919
Antiqitäten und Wohnen, Essen . . . 070617
Antiqlädeli, Frauenfeld 082373
Antiqua, Amsterdam 140278
Antiqua, Athinai 074585
Antiqua, Firenze 075271
Antiqua, Göteborg 081792
Antiqua, Heidenau 125903
Antiqua, Hradec Králové 060019
Antiqua, Jihlava 060027
Antiqua, Qormi 073390, 126668
Antiqua, Santiago de Chile 059497
Antiqua, Verona 076988
Antiqua, Warszawa 140771
Antiqua Domus, Palermo 076122
Antiqua-Nova, Köln 071904
Antiqua Novis, Funchal 079835
Antiqua Res, Roma 076290
Antiqua Russos, Setúbal 080123
Antiqua - Starožitník, Jihlava 060028
Antiquae, Burgos 129456
L'Antiquaire, Albi 060748
L'Antiquaire, Benfeld 061343
L'Antiquaire, Montréal 058897
Antiquaire, Provins 066989
L'Antiquaire, Sainte-Clotilde 080132
Antiquaire, San Francisco 092714
Den Antiquaire, Tuntange 077493
Antiquaire de Quinsac, Quinsac . . . 067029
Antiquaire des Gâtines Rouges, La Chaussée-d'Ivry 063329
L'Antiquaire du Fourneau, Balbigny 061179
Antiquaire du Village, Saint-Leu-la-Forêt 067586
Antiquaire d'Yerres, Yerres 069059
l'Antiquaire Galerie, Lefkosia 059952
L'Antiquaire Joyal, Montréal 058898
Antiquaire Suisse, Bruxelles 057816
Antiquaires de la Geôle, Versailles . 068792
Antiquaires de la Pauline, La Garde 063386
Antiquaires de Lignane, Puyricard . 067003
Antiquaires de Sant-Vincens, Perpignan 066734
Les Antiquaires de Stockel, Bruxelles 057817
Antiquaires Drouot, Paris 065399
Les Antiquaires du Château, Plougoumelen 066870
Antiquaires du Château d'Allaman, Allaman 082079
Antiquaires du Rhin, Strasbourg . . . 068289
Antiqualha, Porto 080065, 129188
Antiqualhas Brasileiras Livraria, Rio de Janeiro 137569
Antiquália, Lisboa 079858
Antiqualia Salinha de Arte, São Paulo 058678
AntiquaNova, Wiesbaden 139846
Der Antiquar, Norderstedt 139597
Antiquaren Boekenbeurs Utrecht, Utrecht 093824
Antiquária, Lisboa 121924
Antiquaria, Sliema 077530, 140240
Antiquaria, Tours 068576
Antiquaria Bok- & Bildantikvariat, Göteborg 141098
Antiquaria di La Rosa & C., Catania 075233
Antiquaria-English Antiques, Tours . 068577
Antiquaria Padova, Padova 093756
Antiquaria Sant'Angelo, Roma 076291
Antiquariaat De Koppelpoort, Amersfoort 140272
Antiquariaat De Oude Wereld, Antwerpen 137393
Antiquariaat Friesland, Leeuwarden 140471
Antiquariaat Sint Joris Maritiem, Amsterdam 077778, 128528, 140279
Antiquariaat Smedeman, Nieuw Vennep 140502
Antiquarian, Plattsburgh 136309
Antiquarian, San Diego 092600
Antiquarian and Fine Books, Belfast 141402
Antiquarian and Landmarks Society Museum, Hartford 044456
Antiquarian and Pre-Owned Books, Miami 142546
Antiquarian Antiques, London 058875
Antiquarian Book Mart, San Antonio 142879
Antiquarian Book Shop, Washington 143036
Antiquarian Bookcrafts, Dublin 127089, 139959
Antiquarian Booksellers, Glebe 136916
Antiquarian Booksellers Association, London 054269
Antiquarian Booksellers Association of America, New York 054596
Antiquarian Booksellers Association of Canada, Victoria 052723
Antiquarian Bookseller's Association of Japan, Tokyo 053774
Antiquarian Booksellers Association of Korea, Seoul 053816
Antiquarian Building, Chicago 088010, 142274
Antiquarian Horological Society, Ticehurst 054270
Antiquarian Horologist, New York . . 132433
Antiquarian Horologists, New York .090670, 132434
Antiquarian Maps and Prints, Potts Point 137053
Antiquarian of Dallas, Dallas 142360
Antiquarian on Tedder, Main Beach 136988
Antiquarian Print Gallery, Unley . . .123323, 137122
Antiquarian Restorers, New York . . 132435
Antiquarian & Trading, Kingston . . .077029, 140155
Antiquarian's Delight, Philadelphia .091599, 142734
Antiquariat, Bowral 136812
Antiquariat Academica, Gießen 139137
Antiquariat Ad Forum, Goslar 139149
Antiquariat Aix-La-Chapelle, Aachen 138666
Antiquariat Alt-Breisach, Breisach am Rhein 138932
Antiquariat Althoheneck, Ludwigsburg, Württemberg 139421
Antiquariat am Bachhaus, Eisenach 139034
Antiquariat am Bäckerbrunnen, Wiesbaden 139847
Antiquariat Am Ballplatz, Mainz . . . 139443
Antiquariat am Bayerischen Platz, Berlin 138731
Antiquariat am Dom, Trier 139787
Antiquariat am Domshof, Bremen . . 138935
Antiquariat am Fischtor, Mainz 139444
Antiquariat am Gendarmenmarkt, Berlin 138732
Antiquariat am Hermannplatz, Berlin 138733
Antiquariat am Kräherwald, Stuttgart 139749
Antiquariat am Marktplatz, Solothurn 141301
Antiquariat Am Neutor, Michelstadt 139477
Antiquariat am Prater, Berlin 138734
Antiquariat am Stadtbach, Memmingen 139475
Antiquariat an der Herderkirche, Weimar, Thüringen 139830
Antiquariat an der Moritzburg, Halle, Saale 139159
Antiquariat an der Nikolaikirche, Leipzig 139387
Antiquariat Athenaeum, Stockholm . 141146
Antiquariat B, Wernigerode 139840
Antiquariat Beim Steinernen Kreuz, Bremen 138936
Antiquariat Bibermühle, Ramsen . . 141289
Antiquariat Blechtrommel, Jena . . . 139286
Antiquariat Buchstabei, Oldenburg, Oldenburg 139626
Antiquariat Bücher consum, Mühlbeck 139487
Antiquariat Bücherkiste, Wuppertal 139881
Antiquariat Bücherwelt, Pfullendorf 139658
Antiquariat carpe diem, Koblenz . . . 139329
Antiquariat Claraplatz, Basel 141195
Antiquariat der Braunschen Universitätsbuchhandlung, Karlsruhe 139292
Antiquariat der Literatur, Zürich . . . 141319
Antiquariat der Schwalm, Schwalmstadt 139721
Antiquariat FBV, Köln 139332
Antiquariat für Bücher, Rostock . . . 139697
Antiquariat Goethe & Co., Heidelberg 139246
Antiquariat Grimbart, Burgdorf, Kreis Hannover 138956
Antiquariat Hagenbrücke, Braunschweig 138915
Antiquariat Heinrich Heine, Freiburg im Breisgau 139105
Antiquariat Hierana, Erfurt 139044
Antiquariat Hoheluft, Hamburg 139166
Antiquariat im Baldreit, Baden-Baden 138708
Antiquariat Im Hof, Grenzach-Wyhlen 139153
Antiquariat im Hopfengarten, Braunschweig 138916
Antiquariat-im-Internet, Dresden . . 138987
Antiquariat im Lenninger Tal, Lenningen 139409
Antiquariat im Schnoor, Bremen . . . 138937
Antiquariat Im Seefeld, Zürich 141320
Antiquariat im Willy-Brandt-Haus, Berlin 138735
Antiquariat Karla, Lüneburg 139432
Antiquariat Les-Art, Gerlingen 139134
Antiquariat Leseband, Freiburg im Breisgau 139106
Antiquariat Libresso, Buxtehude . . . 138958
Antiquariat Libretto, Soest 139733
Antiquariat Lipresso, Bacharach . . . 138692
Antiquariat Magister Tinius, Falkensee 139067
Antiquariat Maxvorstadt, München . 139493
Antiquariat Mercurius, Köln 139333
Antiquariat Mitte, Berlin 138736
Antiquariat Mittlere Mühle, Baden . 141194
Antiquariat Numero 45, München . . 139494
Antiquariat-Papierier, Sint Jansteen 140532
Antiquariat Querido, Düsseldorf . . . 139005
Antiquariat Roter Stern, Marburg . . 139457
Antiquariat Sankt Georg, Eisenach . 139035
Antiquariat Silvanus, Bonn 138890
Antiquariat Tagedieb, Leipzig 139388
Antiquariat-Teetz, Teetz 139778

Antiquariat und Antik, Langen in Hessen 139377
Antiquariat und Galerie im Rathausdurchgang, Winterthur . .111995, 141312
Antiquariat und Kunst, Husum, Nordsee 139282
Antiquariat Unter der Muren, Velbert 139814
Antiquariat Walkmühle, Frankfurt am Main 139074
Antiquariat Zeitzeichen, Neukirchen-Vluyn 139587
Antiquariat zum Rathaus, Bern 141223
Antiquariat Zwiebelfisch, Weimar, Thüringen 139831
Antiquariate Nr. 1, Nr. 2, Nr. 3, Feldberg, Mecklenburg 139070
ANTIQUARIATO, Chiesuol del Fosso 093757
Antiquariato, Milano 135867
Antiquariato, Parma 076193
Antiquariato, Pisa 076238
Antiquariato 800, Roma 076292
Antiquariato del Novecento, Genova 075431
Antiquariato del Novecento, Genova 075432, 140029
Antiquariato Europeo, Roma 076293
Antiquariato Florida, Napoli 075938, 140075
Antiquariato Indie, Firenze 075272
Antiquariato Librario Bado e Mart, Padova 076068, 140082
Antiquariato Librario Bisello, Milano 075595, 140041
Antiquariato Navale, Milano 075596
Antiquariats, Rīga 140218
Antiquariats-Messe Zürich, Zürich . 093887
Antiquariatsgesellschaft, Berlin . . . 138737
Antiquariatsmesse Köln, Köln 093699
Antiquaries Journal, London 136149
Antiquario, San Francisco 092715
Antiquario, Wellington . . . 079313, 128970
Antiquario da Atlantica, Rio de Janeiro 058540
Antiquário do Chiado, Lisboa 140819
Antiquario DPL Numismatica, Rio de Janeiro 058541
Antiquario Epocas, São Paulo 058679
L'Antiquario Gemmologo, Padova . . 076069
Antiquario Genesi, Rio de Janeiro . . 058542
Antiquário HR, Fortaleza 058468
Antiquario Retalhos do Tempo, Rio de Janeiro 058543
Antiquário Sé, Faro 079828
Antiquario Soho, Rio de Janeiro . . . 058544
Antiquarios, San Francisco 092716
Antiquarische Fundgrube bei der Volksoper, Wien 137287
Antiquarische Gesellschaft in Zürich, Zürich 054166
Antiquarium, Agropoli 023135
Antiquarium, Ariano Irpino 023244
Antiquarium, Avella 023304
Antiquarium, Borgia 023484
Antiquarium, Brescello 023515
Antiquarium, Buccino 023539
Antiquarium, Caldarola 023579
Antiquarium, Castelseprio 023742
Antiquarium, Cesenatico 023825
Antiquarium, Cimitile 023880
Antiquarium, Filadelfia 024128
Antiquarium, Golasecca 024349
Antiquarium, Houston 142423
Antiquarium, Loreto Aprutino 024534
Antiquarium, Lugnano in Teverina . 024554
Antiquarium, Manduria 024594
Antiquarium, Massarosa 024646
Antiquarium, Mergozzo 024678
Antiquarium, Minturno 024746
Antiquarium, Monasterace 024783
Antiquarium, New York 090671
Antiquarium, Nonantola 024951
Antiquarium, Numana 024976
Antiquarium, Palazzolo Acreide . . . 025075
Antiquarium, Partinico 025130
Antiquarium, Patti 025133
Antiquarium, Porto Torres 025332
Antiquarium, Prato 025356
Antiquarium, San Marzano sul Sarno 025709
Antiquarium, Santa Flavia 025746
Antiquarium, Serravalle Scrivia . . . 025866
Antiquarium, Tindari 026021
Antiquarium, Trieste 026125
Antiquarium, Anfiteatro Romano, Santa Maria Capua Vetere 025750
Antiquarium, Chiostro di San Francesco, Fondi 024219
Antiquarium, Museo Archeologico, Sant'Antioco 025771
Antiquarium, Museo Statale di Crotone, Crotone 024004
Antiquarium, Uomo e Ambiente nel Territorio Vesuviano, Boscoreale . 023502
Antiquarium, Villa Rufolo, Ravello . . 025393
Antiquarium Cantianense, San Canzian d'Isonzo 025661
Antiquarium Civico, Bagnolo San Vito 023323
Antiquarium Civico, Vazzano 026220
Antiquarium Civico, Vico del Gargano 026314
Antiquarium Comunale, Nettuno . . . 024933
Antiquarium Comunale, Colleferro . 023929
Antiquarium Comunale, Contessa Entellina 023955
Antiquarium Comunale, Milena . . . 024740
Antiquarium Comunale, Monte Romano 024815
Antiquarium Comunale, Roma 025464
Antiquarium Comunale, Sezze 025879
Antiquarium Comunale, Sutri 025974
Antiquarium Comunale, Tiriolo 026023
Antiquarium Comunale N. Pansoni, Cossignano 023987
Antiquarium del Castello Eurialo, Siracusa 025900
Antiquarium del Parco della Forza, Ispica 024424
Antiquarium del Seminario Vescovile, Nola 024947
Antiquarium del Serapeo, Villa Adriana, Tivoli 026026
Antiquarium del Teatro Greco-Romano, Taormina 025987
Antiquarium del Varignano, Portovenere 025342
Antiquarium delle Grotte di Catullo, Sirmione 025904
Antiquarium di Agrigento Paleocristiana Casa Pace, Valle dei Templi, Agrigento 023130
Antiquarium di Canne, Barletta 023346
Antiquarium di Himera, Termini Imerese 026007
Antiquarium di Megara Hyblaea, Augusta 023301
Antiquarium di Monte Cronio, Sciacca 025843
Antiquarium di Nervia, Ventimiglia . 026270
Antiquarium di Poggio Civitate, Murlo 024887
Antiquarium Di Sant'Appiano, Barberino Val d'Elsa 023329
Antiquarium di Tesis, Vivaro 026358
Antiquarium di Villa Romana, Patti . 025134
Antiquarium e Archeologica Museo, Cuglieri 024010
Antiquarium e Mosaico Romano, Bevagna 023388
Antiquarium e Zona Archeologica, Lugagnano Val d'Arda 024553
Antiquarium Forense, Roma 025465
Antiquarium Hungaricum, Budapest 121635, 139913
Antiquarium Ipogeo dei Volumni, Perugia 025163
Antiquarium Jetino, San Cipirello . . 025665
Antiquarium Lucio Salvio Quintiano, Ossuccio 025030
Antiquarium Sestinale, Sestino 025869
Antiquarium Tellinum, Palazzo Besta, Teglio 025998
Antiquarium Torre Cimalonga, Scalea 025830
Antiquarium - Villa Maritima, Minori 024745
Antiquarius, London 085080, 141745
Antiquarius, North Shore 140644
Antiquarius, Roma 076294
Antiquarius, Roma 140095
Antiquarius, San Francisco 092717
Antiquarius, Vancouver 137723
Antiquarius, Zürich 082936
Antiquarius Center, Los Angeles . . . 089680
Antiquarius of Ampthill, Ampthill . .083295, 130300
Antiqu'art, Berck-sur-Mer 061353, 098949
Antiquart, Mouscron 120781
Antiquary, Nelson 079172
Antiquary, Tulsa 093278
L'Antiquasi, Torino 076763, 128253
Antiquated, Petworth 086236
Antiquax, Madrid 081233
Antiquax-Victoria, Auckland 128894
Antique, Levoča 080626
Antique, Lisboa 079859
Antique, Nová Baňa 080630
Antique, Plzeň 060080
Antique, Spišská Nová Ves 080639
Antique, Wolfenbüttel 074468
Antique 2000, Los Angeles 089681
Antique 2000, Paris 065400
Antique 21, Reims 067051
Antique 24, Düsseldorf 070354
Antique Accents, New York 090672
Antique Accents, Salt Lake City . . . 092412
Antique Accents, Tulsa 093279
Antique Acquisitions, New Orleans . 090506
Antique Addict, Oklahoma City 091460
Antique Adoption, Long Beach 089621
Antique Affaire, Kings Park 056054
Antique Affaire, Wanganui 079302
Antique Age, Los Angeles 132233
Antique Alcove, Denver 088639
Antique Alley, Auckland 078907
Antique Alley, Honolulu 088931
Antique Alley, Phoenix 091709
Antique Alley, Portland 091890
Antique Alley, Seattle 092952
Antique & Ancient Coins, Beijing . . 059571
Antique and Art Around Florida, Fort Lauderdale 136310
Antique and Art Exchange, San Francisco 092718
Antique and Collectable Restoration, Omaha 132585
Antique and Collectible Dolls of Seattle, Seattle 092953
Antique and Collectibles Dealer Association, Huntersville 054597
Antique and Collectibles Marketplace, Sacramento 092127
Antique and Collector's Books, Southport 137088
Antique and Collector's Gallery, Las Vegas 089540
Antique and Concept Gallery, Miami 090123
Antique and Country Pine, Crewe . . 084109
Antique and Country Pine, Crewkerne 084110
Antique and Decorative Lighting Dealers Association, Littleton, Somerset . 054271
Antique and Design, Canterbury . . .083855, 130501
Antique and Doll Affaire Shoppe, Sacramento 092128
The Antique and Hobby Shop, Hong Kong 059586
Antique and Modern Caners, Morden 131283
Antique and Resale Shop, Chicago . 088011
Antique and Thrift Store, Chicago . . 088012
Antique Angle, Dallas 088452
Antique Antiques, New York 090673
Antique Antiques, Singapore 080419
Antique Appraisers Association of America, Garden Grove 054598
Antique Arcade, Cleveland 088304
Antique Architectural Decor, Saint Louis 092199
Antique Arms and Armour, Nowergup 056393
Antique Art, Bucureşti 129214
L'Antique-Art, Montréal 058899
Antique-Art, Saint-Jean-de-Luz . . . 067534
Antique Art, Salon-de-Provence . . . 068101
Antique & Art, Warszawa 079725
Antique Art and Arms, Minneapolis . 090339
Antique Art Gallery, Oklahoma City . 091461
Antique Arts Gallery, Hong Kong . . . 059587
Antique Asylum, Toronto 059123
Antique Auto and Race Car Museum, Bedford 042095
Antique Auvergne, Ambert 060791
Antique Bad Company, Emsworth . . 084331
Antique Barn, Toledo 093162
The Antique Barometer Company, London 085081, 130925
Antique Bed Shop, Halstead 084561
Antique Bed Specialists, Tyabb 056749
Antique Beds, Hove 084744, 130809
Antique Bidaikan, Sendai 077209
Antique Bishamon, Hiroshima 077050
Antique Boat Museum, Clayton . . . 042962
Antique Bookshop, London 141746
Antique Bottle and Glass Collector, East Greenville 136311
Antique Boutique, Edmonton 058815
Antique Boutique, New York 090674
Antique Boutique, Richmond 092057
Antique Broadway Broker, Denver . 088640
Antique Buildings, Dunsfold 084234
Antique Buyers of Melbourne, Yarraville 056902
Antique Buying, Columbus 088379
Antique Cache, New York 090675
Antique Caméras, Paris 065401
Antique Castings, San Diego 092601
Antique Cellar, Regina 059082
Antique Center, Néa Kifissia 074624
Antique Center, San Antonio 092475, 132805
Antique Center Antiquarios, Rio de Janeiro 137570
Antique Center at Federal Hill, Baltimore 087636
Antique Center-Milwaukee, Milwaukee 090269
Antique Center of Texas, Houston . . 088999
Antique Center of Tucson, Tucson . . 093195
Antique Center on Broadway, Denver 088641
Antique Center-Walker'S Point, Milwaukee 090270
Antique Centre, Cleobury Mortimer . 084030
The Antique Centre, Kidderminster .084835, 130842
Antique Centre, Oakland 091405
Antique Centre, Oklahoma City 091462
Antique Centre, Oklahoma City 091463
Antique Centre, Preston 086308
Antique Centre of Devonport, North Shore 079187
Antique Centre of Hawthorn, Hawthorn, Victoria 055959
Antique Centre of Stonnington, Armadale, Victoria 055355
The Antique Centre on the Quay, Exeter 084354, 141604
Antique Chairs and Museum, Launceston 084907
Antique Chapelle, La Chapelle-d'Armentières 063311
Antique Church Furnishings, Walton-on-Thames 087013
Antique Circus, Baltimore 087637
The Antique Circus, Baltimore 087638
Antique City, Atlanta 087445
Antique-City, Knokke-Heist 058238
Antique City, Rozelle 056556
Antique Clock Gallery, Long Beach .089622, 132223
Antique Clock Repair, Dallas 131995

Antique Clock Repair and Antiques, Bowral 055527, 123193
Antique Clock Restoration, Columbus 131975
Antique Clock Shop, Saint Paul . . .092340, 132760
Antique Clock Shop, Shanghai 059729
Antique Clocks, Harston 084594
Antique Clocks by Mike, Oklahoma City 091464
Antique Coins, Saint Paul 092341
Antique Collecting, Woodbridge . . . 136150
The Antique Collector, London 058876
Antique Collector, Zürich 082937
Antique Collector's Club, Wappingers' Falls 135520
Antique Collectors' Club, Woodbridge 135315, 142166
Antique Company, Houston 089000
The Antique Company, Sacramento 092129
The Antique Company, Sacramento 092130
Antique Connection, San Antonio . . 092476
Antique Connections, Fort Worth . . 088829
Antique Conservation, New York . . . 132436
Antique Consignment, Los Angeles . 089682
Antique & Contemporary Leasing, Washington 093376
Antique Cooperative, Albuquerque . 087366
Antique Cooperative, Oklahoma City 091465
Antique Corner, Bristol . . . 083725, 130451
Antique Corner, Fort Worth 088830
Antique Corner, Narrandera 056319
Antique Corner, Oxenford . 056413, 120623
Antique Cottage, Albuquerque 087367
Antique Cottage, San Antonio 092477
Antique Cottage, San Diego 092602
Antique Cottage at Estes Park, Omaha 091550
Antique Country Furniture and Interiors, Sandgate 086503
Antique de la Radio, Madrid 081234
Antique Dealer and Collectors' Guide, London 136151
Antique Dealers, Shepparton 056589
Antique Dealers Association of California, San Francisco 054599
Antique Dealers Association of New South Wales, Paddington 052450
Antique Dealers' Association of Poland, Kraków 053976
Antique Decor, Armadale, Victoria . 055356
Antique Decoration, Cluj-Napoca . .080175, 129228
Antique Decoration Art Noveau, Braşov 080133
Antique Department Store, Glebe . . 055881
Antique Depot, Richmond 092058
Antique Design, Philadelphia 091600
Antique Design Center, Norfolk 091366
Antique Detours, Sacramento 092131
Antique Doctor, Tucson . . 093196, 132979
Antique Doll Restorers, Auckland . . 128895
Antique Dolls and Bears, Torbay . . . 079274
Antique Dream, Chicago 088013
Antique Drive, Hong Kong 059588
Antique East, Singapore 080420
Antique Effects, Ballarat 055427
Antique Elements, Leichhardt 056094
Antique Emporium, Albuquerque . . 087368
Antique Emporium, Dallas 088453
Antique Emporium, Healesville 055971
Antique Emporium, Nashville 090415
Antique en Stock, Rouen 067239
Antique English Windsor Chairs, Chipping Norton 083987
Antique Engravings, Camperdown . 055615
Antique Estate Jewelry Gallery, New Orleans 090507
Antique Europa, Houston 089001
Antique Exchange, Baltimore 087639
Antique Exchange, Denver 088642, 122880
Antique Exchange, Winnipeg 059446
Antique Eyes, Stockbridge 086710
Antique Firearms, Dommershausen 070269
Antique Fireplace Centre, Hartlepool 084595
Antique Fireplace Restoration, Dublin 074890, 127090
Antique Fireplaces, Liverpool 085020
Antique Fireplaces, Manchester . . . 085908
Antique Forum, Newcastle-under-Lyme 086062
Antique Four, Bower Ashton 083617
Antique Furniture, Baltimore 087640
Antique Furniture, Los Angeles 132234
Antique Furniture, Sherwood 123303
Antique Furniture, Toledo 132967
Antique Furniture Restoration, London 130926
Antique Furniture Services, Miami .090124, 132333
Antique Furniture Warehouse, Houston 089002, 132096
Antique Furniture Warehouse, Stockport 086719
Antique Furniture Workroom, New York 090676, 132437
Antique Galerie, Düsseldorf 070355
Antique Gallery, Atlanta 087446
Antique Gallery, Cleveland 088305
Antique Gallery, Los Angeles 089683
Antique Gallery, Memphis 090048
Antique Gallery, Nairobi 077347
Antique Gallery, New York 090677
Antique Gallery, Philadelphia 091601
Antique Gallery, Phoenix 091710
The Antique Gallery, Sutton 114525
Antique Gallery Meguro, Tokyo 077232
Antique Garage, Yokohama 077332
Antique Garden, Saint Paul 092342
Antique Gas and Steam Engine Museum, Vista 048804
Antique Gatherings, Phoenix 091711
Antique General Store, Narrabeen . 056317
Antique Guild, Denver 088643
Antique Guild, Kyoto 077087
Antique Guild, Los Angeles 089684, 132235
Antique Guild Japan, Tokyo 053775
Antique Guild United Kingdom, Burnley 054272
Antique Hardware Store, Oklahoma City 091466
Antique Heaven, Miami 090125
Antique Heritage, Chipping Campden 083982
Antique Home Improvement, Los Angeles 089685
Antique House, Cairo 060426
Antique House, Chicago 088014
Antique House, Göteborg 081793
Antique House, Honolulu 088932
Antique House, Jacksonville 089370, 132170
Antique House, Oklahoma City 091467
Antique House, Waikato 079281
Antique Importers, Seattle 092954
Antique Importers of Western Australia, Mount Lawley 056288
Antique Imports, Hutt City 079118
Antique Inspirations, Houston 089003
Antique Interiors, Charlotte 087924
Antique Interiors, Twickenham 086963
Antique Iron Market, Nashville 090416
Antique Jewelry, Saint Paul 092343
Antique Junction, Columbus 088380
Antique Junque Shoppe, Walcha . . 056794
Antique Kaprova, Praha 060103
Antique Kingdom, Charlotte 087925
The Antique Lamp Shop, London . . 085082
Antique Lamp Shop, Maylands, Western Australia 056175
Antique Legacy, Sacramento 092132
Antique Light, Abbotsford 055308
Antique Lighthouse, Philadelphia . .091602, 132605
Antique Lighting, Ottawa 059026
Antique Lighting Company, Seattle . 092955
Antique Lighting Remains, New York 090678
Antique Liquidators, Seattle 092956
The Antique Look, New York 090679
Antique Mall, Edmonton 058816
The Antique Mall, Las Vegas 089541
Antique Mall, Regina 059083
Antique Mall, San Diego 092603
The Antique Mall, Tucson 093197
Antique Mall of Austin, Austin 087550
Antique Mall of Creve Coeur, Saint Louis 092200
Antique Mall of Green Hills, Nashville 090417
Antique Mall of Irvington, Indianapolis 089263
Antique Mall of Midtown, Memphis 090049
Antique Mall of Palma Ceia, Tampa 093101
Antique Mall of West Seattle, Seattle 092957
Antique Mall on Clark, Chicago . . . 088015
Antique Mall on Montgomery Street, Fort Worth 088831
Antique Mall Village, Houston 089004
The Antique Man, Baltimore 087641
Antique Man, Buffalo 087858
Antique Man, Chicago 088016
Antique Manor, La Richardais 063406
Antique Manor, Tréméreuc 068624
Antique Map & Book Shop, Dorchester 141554
Antique Map & Print Gallery, Hallow 141640
Antique Maps, Belmont 136798
Antique Maps and Fine Prints, Dallas 142361
Antique Maps and Fine Prints, Dallas 142362
Antique Maps and Prints, Miami . . . 142547
Antique Maps Room, Toronto 059124, 137694
Antique Market, Adelaide 055311
Antique Market, Denver 088644
Antique Market, Hay-on-Wye 084631
Antique Market, Phoenix 091712
Antique Market, Sacramento 092133
Antique Market, Vancouver 059328
Antique Market, Vancouver 059329
Antique Market of Warrnambool, Warrnambool 056805
Antique Marketplace, Austin 087551
Antique Mart, Richmond, Surrey . . . 086351
Antique Mart, Saint Paul 092344
Antique Master, Nairobi 077348
Antique Mattress, Houston 089005
Antique Max, Praha 060104
Antique Memories, San Jose 092914
Antique Menagerie, Saint Louis . . . 092201
Antique Merchants Mall, Nashville . 090418
Antique Mini-Mall, Tucson 093198
Antique & Modern Jewellery Xchange, Auckland 078908
Antique Moderne, København 060277
Antique Möbel, Brno 059973
Antique Niche, New York 090680
Antique Odyssey, Seattle 092958
Antique Oise, Saint-Samson-la-Poterie 067998
Antique Oriental Rug Buyers, Miami 090126
Antique Oriental Rugs, Pittsburgh . .091785, 132662
Antique Oriental Rugs Center, Las Vegas 089542
Antique Outdoor Market, Long Beach 089623
Antique Outpost, Phoenix 091713
Antique Panache, Houston 089006
Antique Park, Bordeaux 061577
Antique Parlor, San Diego 092604
Antique Passion, Aulnay-sous-Bois 061064
Antique Pavilion, Houston 089007
Antique Pendulum, Washington . . . 133019
Antique Pine, Harrogate 130760
Antique Pine & Country Furniture Shop, Driffield 084218, 130656
Antique Place That, Houston 089008
Antique Plus, Las Vegas 089543
Antique Plus, Los Angeles 089686
Antique Pohořelec, Praha 060105
Antique Presidio, Tucson 093199
Antique Print, Main Beach 056123
Antique Print Gallery, Christchurch .079007, 140609
Antique Print Room, Sydney 056664, 137101
Antique Print Shop, East Grinstead .084246, 130660, 141564
Antique Print Shop, Redbourn 086336
Antique Prints, Dublin 139960
Antique Prints, Hawthorn; Victoria . 055960
Antique Prints, Pittsburgh 142770
Antique Properties, Nairobi 077349
Antique Radio and Audio Repair, San Diego 132841
Antique Radio Store, San Diego . . . 092605
Antique Refinishers, San Diego . . . 132842
Antique Refinishing, Virginia Beach 133008
Antique Repair, Cincinnati 131923
Antique Repair, Tucson 132980
Antique Repair Madeira Junction, Cincinnati 131924
Antique Resources, Chicago 088017
Antique Resources, Tulsa 093280
Antique Restoration, El Paso 132060
Antique Restoration, New York 090681, 132438
Antique Restoration, Providence . . . 132708
Antique Restoration 45 Rose, San Francisco 092719, 132865
Antique Restoration Atelier, Washington 133020
The Antique Restoration Centre, Cheltenham 130530
Antique Restoration Service, Nashville 132397
Antique Restoration Services, Box Hill 123194
Antique Restoration Services, East Norriton 132059
Antique Restoration Studio, Denver 132029
Antique Restoration Studio, Stafford 131522
Antique Restorations, Christchurch . 079008
Antique Restorations, Christchurch . 128916
Antique Restorations, Christchurch . 128917
Antique Restorations, Hawkes Bay . 128937
Antique Restorations, Salt Lake City 132779
Antique Restorations, Tulsa 132993
Antique Restorations of Unley, Unley 123324
Antique Restoring, Nairobi 077350
Antique Riviera, Helsinki 060508
Antique Rooms, Maldon 085897
Antique Row, Dallas 088454
Antique Row on South Broadway, Denver 088645
Antique Salad, Vancouver 059330
Antique Salvage, Dundrum 074970
Antique Sampler Shoppes, Kansas City 089482
Antique Sampler Shoppes, Las Vegas 089544
Antique Services of Texas, San Antonio 092478
Antique Shop, Acassuso 055140
Antique Shop, Blaenau Ffestiniog . . 083556
Antique Shop, Bruton 083773
The Antique Shop, Chester 083949, 130556
Antique Shop, Donegal 074886
Antique Shop, Ferbane 074973
Antique Shop, Godalming 084479
Antique Shop, Hamilton, New South Wales 055934
The Antique Shop, Kirkcudbright . . 084876
Antique Shop, Kjustendil 058754
The Antique Shop, Langholm 084903
Antique Shop, Lille 063828
Antique Shop, Martínez 055277
The Antique Shop, Newtonmore . . . 086084
Antique Shop, Omaha 091551
The Antique Shop, Saint-Nom-la-Breteche 067689
Antique Shop, Sutton Bridge 086797
Antique Shop Saborna, Plovdiv 058758

Antique Shoppe, Ottawa 059027
Antique Shoppe, Salt Lake City . . . 092413
Antique Shoppe, Tauranga 079259
Antique Show, Dallas 088455
Antique Showcase, Philadelphia . . . 091603
The Antique Silver Company, Balaclava 055423, 123188
Antique Specialty Mall, Albuquerque 087369
The Antique Square, Hong Kong . . . 059589
Antique Station, Tulsa 093281
Antique Stove Heaven, Los Angeles 089687, 132236
Antique Studio, El Paso 132061
Antique Styles, Loganholme 056111
The Antique Superstore, Hamilton . 058847
Antique Swan, Austin 087552
Antique Textiles & Lighting, Bath . . 083411
Antique Thrift Shop, San Diego 092606
Antique Timepiece, Hong Kong 059590
Antique Touch, Seattle 092959
Antique Toy and Board Collector, Salt Lake City 092414
Antique Toy World, Chicago 136312
Antique Toy World Magazine, Chicago 088018
Antique Toys & Dolls, Milwaukee . .090271, 132360
Antique Toys et Collectible, Dunkerque 062747
Antique Trade Center, Dallas 088456
Antique Trader, Denver 088646
Antique Trader, Iola 136313
The Antique Trader, London 085083
Antique Trader Weekly, Iola 136314
Antique Traders, Bourne 083586
Antique Traders, San Francisco . . . 092720
Antique Trading, Dublin 074891
Antique Trading Company, Wellington 079314
The Antique Travelshop, Bussum . . 078124
Antique Treasure Traders, Toronto . 059125
Antique Treasurers, Phoenix 091714
Antique & Unique Treasures, Indianapolis 089264
Antique Village, Manchester 085909, 131253
Antique Village, Toronto 059126
Antique Warehaus, Houston 089009
Antique Warehouse, Baltimore 087642
Antique Warehouse, Claremont . . . 055672
Antique Warehouse, Fort Worth . . . 088832
Antique Warehouse, London 085084
Antique Warehouse, Memphis 090050
The Antique Warehouse, Vancouver 059331
Antique Warehouse, Winnipeg 059447
Antique Warehouse, Worcester 087249
Antique Watch and Clock Repair, Minneapolis 132376
Antique Watch Gallery, Hong Kong . 059591
Antique Way, Los Angeles 089688, 132237
Antique Week, Knightstown 136315
Antique Wholesalers, Miami 090127
Antique Wholesalers, Salt Lake City 092415
Antique Within, Leek 084932, 130874
Antique Wooden Horse, Jacksonville 089371, 132171
Antique Workshop, Cincinnati 131925
Antique Workshop, Detroit 132048
Antique World, Calgary 058779
Antique World, Surrey . . . 059109, 123822
Antique World, Winnipeg 059448
Antique Zoo, Denver 088647
Antiquéa, Genève 082389
Antiqueland USA, Austin 087553
Antiqueland USA, Dallas 088457
Antiqueland USA, Fort Worth 088833
Antiqueland USA, San Antonio 092479
Antiqueline, New York 090682
Antiqueria, New York 090683
Antiquerie Médoc-Antiquités-de-Lescapon, Queyrac 067006
Antiquers, Toronto 059127
Antiques, Bucureşti 080141
Les Antiques, Dallas 088458
Antiques, Edinburgh 084273
Antiques, Fochabers 084416
Antiques, Kiel 071820
Antiques, Kingston 077030
Antiques, London 130927
Antiques, Marazion 085926
Antiques, Menston 085975
Antiques, Minsk 057651
Antiques, Minsk 057652
Antiques, Minsk 057653
Antiques, New York 090684
Antiques, Saint-Florent-sur-Cher . . 067476
Antiques, Toronto 059128
Antiques, Vancouver 059332
Antiques 1071, Napier 079162
Antiques 4 USA, San Diego 092607
Antiques AAA, Indianapolis 089265
Antiques & Accessoires, Stuttgart . . 073953
Antiques across the World, Nottingham 086129
Antiques ACT, Fyshwick 055848
Antiques Ad Hoc, Ashburton 083334
Antiques Adventure, Coventry 084089
Antiques Allentown, Buffalo 087859
Antiques am Heuberg, Basel 082119
Antiques Amended, Memphis 090051, 132314
Antiques and Angels, North Shore . 079188
Antiques and Art, Hobart 055986
Antiques and Art, Miami . . 090128, 132334
Antiques and Art, Seattle 092960
Antiques and Art in Queensland, Bondi Junction 135534
Antiques and Art in Victoria, Bondi Junction 135535
Antiques and Art Independent, Edinburgh 136152
Antiques and Arts, Dubai . 083182, 112449
Antiques and Auction News, Mount Joy 136316
Antiques and Beyond, Atlanta 087447
Antiques and Bricabrac, Miami 090129
Antiques and Bygones, Chichester . 083970
Antiques and Bygones, Durban 080694
Antiques and Bygones, Rochdale . . 086384
Antiques and Classical Interiors Fair, Naxxar 093814
Antiques and Collectables, Coolangatta 055711
Antiques and Collectables, Geelong 055863
Antiques and Collectables, Honolulu 088933
Antiques and Collectables, North Fremantle 056357
Antiques and Collectables, Scunthorpe 086526, 131461
Antiques and Collectables Centre, Ballarat 055428
Antiques and Collectables Fair, London 093906
Antiques and Collectibles Newsletter, New York 136317
Antiques and Collectors Centre, Diss 084167
Antiques and Country Living, Frome 084445
Antiques and Crafts Centre, Chorley 084002
Antiques and Curios, Peterborough .086229, 131373
Antiques and Curios, Worcester . . .087250, 131713
Antiques and Decorative, Tampa . . 093102
Antiques and Decorative Art, Tampa 093103
Antiques and Everything, Triabunna 056737
Antiques and Fine Art, Omaha 091552
Antiques and Fine Art, Penzance . .086209, 131368
Antiques and Fine Art, Watertown . 136318
Antiques and Furnishings, Bournemouth 083592
Antiques and Gifts, Aberdour 083243, 130281
Antiques and Gifts, Downham Market 084216
Antiques and Interiors, Nashville . . 090419
Antiques and Interiors, Norwich . . . 086108
Antiques and Interiors, Philadelphia 091604
Antiques and Interiors on Selwyn, Charlotte 087926
Antiques and Meubles, North Fremantle 056358
Antiques and Modern Arms Fair, Canterbury 093566
Antiques and Modern Arms Fair, Maitland 093567
Antiques and Modern Arms Fair, Wayville 093568
Antiques and More, Indianapolis . . . 089266
Antiques and More, Las Vegas 089545
Antiques and More, Long Beach . . . 089624
Antiques and More, Miami 090130
Antiques and More, Tulsa 093282
Antiques and Oddities, Portland . . . 091891
Antiques and Pearl, Austin 087554
Antiques and Piano Restoration, London 130928
Antiques and Restoration by Irina, San Francisco 092721, 132866
Antiques and Stuff, Denver 088648
Antiques and Stuff, San Diego 092608
Antiques and Stuff by Ruth, San Diego 092609
Antiques and Things, London 085085
Antiques and Things, New Orleans . 090508
Antiques and Treats, Albuquerque . 087370
Antiques Anonymous, Washington . 093377
Antiques - Antigüedades, La Paz . . 058396
Antiques Antiques, San Francisco . . 092722
Antiques Anywhere, Baltimore 087643
Antiques Art, Rotterdam 078695
Antiques, Art and Investment Fair, Seinäjoki 093647
Antiques & Art Australia, Armadale, Victoria 133043
Antiques & Arts, Toronto . . 059129, 097215
Antiques As Well, Heidelberg 055974
Antiques at 115 Broadway, San Antonio 092480
Antiques at 80 Charles, Boston . . . 087791
Antiques at 99 Charles, Boston . . . 087792
Antiques at Budleigh House, East Budleigh 084245
Antiques at Dunlavy, Houston 089010
Antiques at Forge Cottage, Gargrave 084451
Antiques at Glen Harrow, Belgrave . 055468
Antiques at Heritage, Woodstock . . 087235
Antiques at Hyde Park, London 058877
Antiques at India Point, Providence . 092032
Antiques at Pike Place, Seattle 092961
Antiques at Redbank, Redbank 056521
Antiques at Rummel Creek, Houston 089011
Antiques at Saint Lawrence Market, Toronto 059130
Antiques at Spruce Meadows, Calgary 093618
Antiques at the Beach, San Diego . 092610
Antiques at the Market, Las Vegas . 089546
Antiques at Weldwood, London . . . 058878
Antiques Avignon, Hackney 055929
Antiques Avignon, Moret-sur-Loing 064787
Antiques Barometers, Ramsey, Cambridgeshire 086326, 131404
Antiques Books, Woolloongabba . . . 137144
Antiques, Books, Ephemera and Collectibles, Atlanta . . . 087448, 142195
Antiques Brass Lantern, Hiroshima . 077051
Antiques by Billy, Toronto 059131
Antiques by George, Tucson 132981
Antiques by Lillian, Miami 090131
Antiques by Loraine, Milwaukee . . . 090272
Antiques by Ralph, Miami 090132
Antiques by Rebecca, Miami 090133
Antiques by Rudy, Virginia Beach . . 093343
Antiques by Sandy, Miami 090134
Antiques by the Wishing Corner, Portland 091892
Antiques by Three Lions, Jacksonville 089372
Antiques Bye Wells, Toronto 059132
Antiques Canada, Toronto 093619
L'Antiques Center, Cherbourg 062275
The Antiques Centre, Trowbridge . . 086924
Antiques Centre at Olney, Olney . . . 086161
Antiques Centre of Wellington, Wellington 079315
Antiques Centre York, York 087284
Antiques Chicago, Chicago 093964
Antiques & Co, Nantes . . . 064890, 124472
Antiques & Collectables, Auckland . 078909
Antiques & Collectibles Magazine, Westbury 136319
Antiques & Collecting Magazine, Chicago 136320
Antiques Collections, New York . . . 090685
Antiques Colony, San Jose 092915
Antiques Consortium, Albuquerque . 087371
The Antiques Council, Warren 054600
Antiques & Curiosities, Auckland . . 078910
Antiques de France, Montréal 058900
Antiques de Provence, New Orleans 090509
Antiques Decor and More, Saint Paul 092345
Antiques Diary, Twyford 136153
Antiques Down Under, Coffs Harbour 055700
Antiques & Dreams, Birmingham . . 087733
Antique's du Monde, Los Angeles . . 089689
Antiques & Eccentricities, Columbus 088381
Antiques & Elegant Junk, Wanganui 079303
Antiques Emporium, Tetbury 086846
Antiques et cetera, Brighton 083683, 130441
Antiques Etc., Atlanta 087449
Antiques Etc, Auckland 078911
Antiques Etc., Boston 087793
Antique's Etc., Denver 088649
Antiques Etc., Sacramento 092134
Antiques Etc., Stretton 086780
Antiques Etcetera, El Paso 088786
Antiques Exchange, Bournemouth .083593, 130414
Antiques Fair, Naxxar 093815
Antiques Fair Chester, Chester 093907
Antiques & Fine Art Dealers and Auctioneers: Business Ratio Plus, Hampton 136154
Antiques & Fine Furniture, Sevenoaks 086540, 131464
Antiques Fleamarket, San Diego . . . 092611
Antiques for All, Miami 090135
Antiques for Everyone, Birmingham 093908
Antiques Forever, Phoenix 091715, 132643
Antiques & Funk, Winnipeg 059449
Antiques Gallery, Lyndhurst 131247
Antiques & Gallery, Praha 060106
Antiques Garage, New York 090686
Antiques & Gardens, Birmingham . . 087734
Antiques Hall, Fyshwick 055849
Antique's House, Thessaloniki 074632
Antiques Houston, Houston 089012
Antiques Idées, Chelles 062268
Antiques Imp-Exp, Midwoud 128778
Antiques Import Export, Stockport .086720, 131541
Antiques in Indy, Indianapolis 089267
Antiques in NSW, Bondi Junction . . 135536
Antiques in Sassafras, Sassafras . . 056575
Antiques in the Bank, Cleveland . . . 088306
Antiques in the Rough, San Francisco 092723
Antiques in Time, Cleveland 088307, 131950
Antiques in Wales, Kidwelly 084837
Antiques & Interiors, Genova 075433
Antiques International, Houston . . . 089013
Antiques International, Miami 090136
Antiques International, West Hollywood 093447
Antiques & Knick Knacks, Nairobi . . 077351
Antiques Magazine, Birmingham . . 136155
Antiques Magazine, New Orleans . . 090510
Antiques Marie-Claire, Bussum . . . 078125
Antiques Market, Hobart 055987

Antiques Market, Knokke-Heist . . . 058239
Antiques Memories, Qormi 077523
Antiques & Militaria, Toronto 059133
Antiques Minnesota Midway, Saint Paul 092346
Antiques 'n Stuff, Oklahoma City . . 091468
Antiques 'n Stuff, Tampa 093104
The Antiques Network, Cincinnati . . 088209
Antiques News, Edinburgh 136156
Antiques Notre Dame, Montréal . . . 058901
Antiques of Brentwood, Nashville . . 090420
Antiques of Cool Springs, Nashville 090421
Antiques of Denver, Denver 088650
Antiques Of Epsom, Auckland 078912
Antiques of Georgetown, Washington 093378
Antiques of Penrith, Penrith 086201
Antiques of Shadyside, Pittsburgh . 091786
Antiques of Sherborne, Sherborne .086575, 131482
Antiques of Southside, Birmingham 087735
Antiques of the Orient, Singapore . . 080421
Antiques of the Orient, Singapore . . 080422
Antiques of the Orient, Singapore . . 140951
Antiques of Tomorrow, Pretoria . . . 080728
Antiques of Western NY, Buffalo . . .087860, 131851
Antiques of Woodstock, Woodstock 087236, 131712
Antiques on Broadway, Vancouver . 059333
Antiques on Ellsworth, Pittsburgh . . 091787
Antiques on High, Armadale, Victoria 055357
Antiques on High, Oxford . 086176, 131352
Antiques on Hildebrand, San Antonio 092481
Antiques on Lloyd, Moe 056240
Antiques on Macquarie, Hobart . . . 055988
Antiques On Manukau, Auckland . . 078913
Antiques on Memorial, Houston . . . 089014
Antiques on Michigan, Chicago . . . 088019
Antiques On Mount Pleasant, Toronto 059134
Antiques on Nineteenth, Houston . . 089015
Antiques On Queen, Toronto 059135
Antiques on Railway, Boonah 055521
Antiques on the River, Detroit 088756
Antiques on the Square, Indianapolis 089268
Antiques on View, Bendigo 055475
Antiques Plus, Los Angeles 089690
Antiques-Point Chev Plaza, Auckland 078914
Antiques Productions, Houston 089016
Antiques Provencal, New York 090687, 132439
Antiques Puces Libres, Montréal . .058902, 123781
Antiques Restoration, Dublin 127091
Antiques Restoration, New York . . . 132440
Antiques Rich Man Poor Man, Montréal 058903
Antiques Riverwalk, Minneapolis . . 090340
Antiques Services, Bruxelles 057818
The Antiques Shop, Pittenweem . . . 086271
Antiques Splinters, Forster 055834
Antiques Starozitnosti, Bratislava . . 080599
Antiques & Stuff, Houston 089017
Antiques Super Mall, Houston 089018
Antiques @ The George, Burford . .083783, 141461
Antiques, Tiques & Toys, Pittsburgh 091788
Antiques @ Tirau, Waikato 079282
Antiques To Go, Winnipeg 059450
Antiques Tour, Auckland 078915
Antiques Trade Gazette, London . . .135174, 136157
Antiques Trade Space, Newark-on-Trent 086049
Antiques Unique, Dallas 088459
Antiques Warehouse, Bath 083412
The Antiques Warehouse, Bristol . .083726, 130452
Antiques Warehouse, Buxton 083828, 130494
The Antiques Warehouse, Farnham 084386, 130703
The Antiques Warehouse, Glasgow . 084460
Antiques Warehouse, Marlesford . . 085953
Antiques Warehouse, San Antonio . 092482
Antiques Warehouse, Tucson 093200
Antiques Warehouse, Uxbridge 086992
Antiques Warehouse, Whangarei . .079362, 128982
Antiques White Bear, Saint Paul . . . 092347
Antiques Within, Memphis 090052
Antiques Workshop, San Antonio . . 132806
Antiques World, Brugge 057760
Antiques World Belgium, Bruxelles . 057819
Antiques'Atelier, Camblain-l'Abbé . 061915
Antiques@Chicago, Chicago 088020
Antiquest-Verity, Toronto 059136
Antiquetrade, Roma 076295
Antiqueweek-Central, Knightstown . 136321
Antiqueweek-Eastern Edition, Knightstown 136322
Antiquitäten 1900, Klagenfurt 057103
Antiquitäten am Danteplatz, Heidelberg 071444
Antiquitäten am Franziskanerplatz, Würzburg 074490, 139868
Antiquitäten am Hafenplatz, Bad Karlshafen 069306
Antiquitäten am Kosttor, München . 072635
Antiquitäten am Kurpark, Bad Ems . 069277
Antiquitäten am Marktplatz, Heidelberg 071445
Antiquitäten am Schauspielhaus, Leipzig 072194
Antiquitäten am Schloß, Bedburg-Hau 069508
Antiquitäten am Schloß, Kiel 071821, 121464
Antiquitäten am Schloßpark, Bad Homburg v.d.Höhe 069289
Antiquitäten am Schwabentor, Freiburg im Breisgau 070821
Antiquitäten am See, Rottach-Egern 073598
Antiquitäten Am Steinweg, Marburg 072443
Antiquitäten am Thielenplatz, Hannover 071381
Antiquitäten am Zielemp, Olten . . . 082716
Antiquitäten am Zielemp, Rickenbach (Solothurn) 130148
Antiquitäten An der Alten Wache, Potsdam 073357
Antiquitäten an der Heiliggeistkirche, Landshut 072141
Antiquitäten an der Königstraße, Elmshorn 070546
Antiquitäten an der Paulskirche, Frankfurt am Main 070726
Antiquitäten Anno-Domini, Wissen . 074452
Antiquitäten auf der Breite, Schaffhausen 082796
Antiquitäten Colonnaden 70, Hamburg 071194
Antiquitäten Diele, Wiefelstede 074387
Antiquitäten Eck, Bayreuth 069487
Antiquitäten Freund, Stadtprozelten 073892
Antiquitäten-Galerie, Abtwil 082075, 129892
Antiquitäten Gengenbach, Gengenbach 070964
Antiquitäten Heiligkreuz, Sankt Gallen 082771
Antiquitäten Hofgut, Mannheim . . . 072412
Antiquitäten im alten Zollhaus, Wallerfangen 074265
Antiquitäten im Bachgau, Großostheim 071123
Antiquitäten im Bennohaus, Meißen 072505
Antiquitäten im Holländerviertel, Potsdam 073358
Antiquitäten im Kolerschloß, Lauf an der Pegnitz 072167
Antiquitäten im Landhausstil, München 072636
Antiquitäten im Mühlenhof, Kalkar . 071687
Antiquitäten im Neuwerk, Rendsburg 073497
Antiquitäten im Taunus, Wehrheim . 074295
Antiquitäten im Tetzelhaus, Pirna . . 073336
Antiquitäten im Wolfgang-Borchert-Haus, Hamburg 071195
Antiquitäten in Altdorf, Altdorf bei Nürnberg 069144
Antiquitäten in der Königshauspassage, Leipzig 072195
Antiquitäten in Herrenhausen, Hannover 071382
Antiquitäten Kaufhaus, Leipzig 072196
Antiquitäten Kaufhaus, Leipzig 072197
Antiquitäten-, Kunst- und Sammlermarkt, Ulm 093700
Antiquitäten - Münzen, Quedlinburg 073394
Antiquitäten Pavillon, Andrea, Stuttgart 073954
Antiquitäten-Salon Augsburg, Augsburg 093701
Antiquitäten-Salon Ludwigsburg, Ludwigsburg, Württemberg 093702
Antiquitäten-Salon Rosenheim, Rosenheim 093703
Antiquitäten-Salon Stuttgart, Stuttgart 093704
Antiquitäten Scheune, Schöneck, Hessen 073713
Antiquitäten-Sommer, Heiligenhafen 093705
Antiquitäten Spatenmühle, Wöllstein 074460
Antiquitäten-Tage Münster, Münster 093706
Antiquitäten & Teppiche, Bad Pyrmont 069353
Antiquitäten und Holz, Heidelberg . . 071446
Antiquitäten- und Kunsttage Wolfratshausen, Wolfratshausen . 093707
Antiquitäten- und Münzengalerie, Leipzig 072198
Antiquitäten-Zeitung, München . . . 135739
Antiquitäten zum Hochrad, Ermatingen 082357
Antiquitätengalerie, Potsdam 073359
Antiquitätengalerie Oben, Halle, Saale 071173
Antiquitätenhalle Schüttorf, Schüttorf 073734
Antiquitätenhandel, Unterach am Attersee 057335
Antiquitätenmarkt, Köthen, Anhalt . 072042
Antiquitätenstübchen, Riedbach . . . 073530
Antiquitätenzentrum, München 072637, 126345
Antiquitás, Budapest 074663
Antiquitás, Budapest 074664
Antiquitás, Győr 074736
Antiquitat, Balatonfüred 074653
Antiquité, Cahors 061894
Antiquite, Dallas 088460
Antiquité, Québec 059054
Antiquite 56, Saint-Ouen 067706
Antiquité AJR, Saint-Maur-des-Fossés 067656
Antiquité Art Ancien, Pérouges 066729
Antiquité Art Ancien, Vaujours 068733
Antiquité Art Contemporain, Nice . . 065028
Antiquité au Chiabout, Luppy 064034
Antiquité au Temps Jadis, Carcassonne 061969
Antiquité Au Temps Qui Passe, Paris 065402
Antiquité Bonheur D'Autrefois, Montréal 058904
Antiquité Brancion, Paris 065403
Antiquité Brocante, Coux 062540
Antiquité Brocante A, Reims 067052
Antiquité Brocante du Lac, L'Isle-Jourdain 063911
Antiquité Brocante du Laonnois, Mons-en-Laonnois 064609
Antiquité Brocante Guibert, Narbonne 064958
L'Antiquité Classique, Louvain-la-Neuve 135589
L'Antiquité Curiosité, Montréal 058905
Antiquité de Geneston, Pont-Saint-Martin 066933
Antiquité de la Chapelle, Plouigneau 066876
Antiquité de la Couronne, Québec . 059055
Antiquité de la Place, Codognan . . . 062375
Antiquité de la Prefecture, Orléans . 065291
Antiquité de la Reine, Bourg-la-Reine 061711
Antiquité de l'Abbaye, Hambye 063120
Antiquité de l'Almanarre, Hyères . . 063186
Antiquité de l'Eglise, Sainte-Geneviève 068059
Antiquité Décor, Dieppe 062622
Antiquité Décoration, Montville 064784
Antiquité des Marais, Guérande . . . 063095
Antiquité des Seigneurs, Strasbourg 068290
Antiquité des Templiers, La Baule-Escoublac 063285, 121019
Antiquité du Chalet, Caluire-et-Cuire 061910
Antiquité du Château, Nantes 064891
Antiquité du Château, Rambouillet . 067038
Antiquité du Hanau, Philippsbourg . 066819
Antiquité du Lac, Saulxures-sur-Moselotte 068146
Antiquité du Musée, Troyes 068641
Antiquité du Rest, Pleuven 066856
Antiquité du Village Fleuri, Rémérangles 067087
Antiquité Ehrmann, Metz 064518
Antiquité et Decoration, Hyères . . . 063187
Antiquité Fontaine aux Bretons, Pornic 066950
Antiquité Franco Anglaise, Villiers-le-Bel 068989
Antiquité la Barbotine, Alençon . . . 060763
Antiquité La Méridienne, Le Pellerin 063678
Antiquité la Vigie, Quiberon 067008
Antiquité le Grenier de Saint-Lié, Charleville-Mézières 062154
Antiquité le Grenier de Saint-Lié, Charleville-Mézières 062155
Antiquité les Deux Chênes, Coutiches 062538
Antiquité Marie Rue Subes, Dax . . . 062603
Antiquité Saint-Maur, Martel 064408
Antiquité Saint-Prix, Saint-Prix 067967
Antiquité TDC, Castres 062028
Antiquiteas, Brockenhurst 083763
Antiquites, Aubigny 061041
Antiquités, Bougival 061670
Antiquites, Kraków 079615
Antiquités 165 vh, Paris 065404
Antiquités 1900-1950, Cannes 061931
Antiquités 2000, Chalon-sur-Saône 062080
Antiquités 2000, Juvisy-sur-Orge . . 063270
Antiquités 29, Brest 061761
Antiquités 34, Nancy 064859
Antiquités 44, Vertou 068825
Antiquités 56, Marolles-en-Brie . . . 064299
Antiquités 80, Saint-Ouen 067707
Antiquités 87, Limoges 063877
Antiquités 88, Paris 065405
Antiquités 89, Essey-lès-Nancy . . . 062807
Antiquités 95, Deuil-la-Barre 062617
Antiquités A&G, Montréal 058906
Antiquités A la Clef d'Or, Genève . .082390, 130030
Antiquités ABC, Genève 082391
Antiquités Ada, Montréal 058907
Antiquités Allais, Honfleur 063163
Antiquités and Co, Guérande 063096
Antiquités Antonio, Boisseuilh 061545, 124106
La Antiquités Art, Strasbourg 068291
Antiquités Art et Grenier, Nevers . . . 065001
Antiquités Arts Artisanats, Lons-Montmorot 063996
Antiquités Arts et Antiques, Beaulieu 061253
Antiquités au Cadran Solaire, Mathieu 064423
Antiquités au Palais, Rennes (Ille-et-Vilaine) 067094
Antiquités au Palais du Grand Yaka, Bouillac 061679
Antiquités au Saint-Hubert, Rieulay 067141

Antiquités au Sourire du Passé, Marboué 064259, 124385
Antiquités Auberchicourt, Auberchicourt 061035
Antiquités aux Tonneaux, Méounes-lès-Montrieux 064497
Antiquités B comme Brocante, Biscarrosse 061494
Antiquités Bagatelle, Thonon-les-Bains 068403
Antiquités B.G., Rennes (Ille-et-Vilaine) 067095
Antiquités Blancoises, Le Blanc 063568
Antiquités Broc Troc, Narbonne 064959
Antiquités Brocante au Fond du Chemin, Notre-Dame-de-Sanilhac 065234
Antiquités Brocante Barbéris, Nice 065029
Antiquités-Brocante des Vertus, Saint-Aubin-sur-Scie 067365
Antiquités Brocante du Murier, Angoulême 060874
Antiquités Brocante & Lustincone, Aléria 060768
Antiquites Brocantes, Valbonne 068677
Antiquités Brocantes du Faubourg, Troyes 068642
Antiquités Brocantes le Phare, Sète 068234
Antiquités Brocant'Stock, Bergerac 061355
Antiquités Broquantes, Puttelange-aux-Lacs 067000
Antiquités Caroline, Montréal 058908
Antiquités Claude, Puteaux 066999
Antiquités Colombette, Toulouse 068476
Antiquités Contemporain, Binic 061488
Antiquités Croix Rousse, Lyon 064056
Antiquités Croix Rousse, Lyon 064057
Antiquités d'Alet, Alet-les-Bains 060776
Antiquités d'Assise, Québec 059056
Antiquités de Bailly, Bailly 061174
Antiquités de Beure, Beure 061414
Antiquités de France, Hommarting 063161
Antiquites de Grand-Papa, Vetheuil 068830
Antiquités de la Baie, Perros-Guirec 066764
Antiquités de la Bonne Etoile, Confolens 062459
Antiquités de la Carderie, Saint-Martin-Labouval 067649
Antiquités de la Cathédrale, Auxerre 061095
Antiquités de la Cave au Grenier, Moings 064574
Antiquités de la Choisille, Saint-Cyr-sur-Loire 067414
Antiquités de la Cité, Troyes 068643
Antiquités de la Dronne, Aubeterre-sur-Dronne 061038
Antiquités de la Garde, La Garde 063387
Antiquités de la Gare, Beaurepaire 061310
Antiquités de la Landriais, Dinard 062684
Antiquités de la Madeleine, Verneuil-sur-Avre 068778
Antiquités de la Maison Carrée, Nîmes 065167
Antiquités de la Pêcherie, Lyon 064058
Antiquités de la Place, Épinal 062785
Antiquités de la Poste, Cavaillon 062039
Antiquités de la Rabine, Landaul 063510
Antiquités de la Renaissance, Hem 063142
Antiquités de la Sucrerie, Chavenay 062260
Antiquités de l'Ancienne Poste, Sainte-Geneviève-des-Bois 068062
Antiquités de l'Angoumois, Gond-Pontouvre 063011
Antiquités de l'Assomption, Sainte-Maxime 068067
Antiquités-de-l'Autie, Saint-Ouen 067708
Antiquités de l'Eglise, Etréchy 062819
Antiquites de l'Estel, Avignon 061124
Antiquités de l'Ile Saint-Louis-ISL, Paris 065406
Antiquités de l'Ill, Strasbourg 068292
Antiquités de l'Océane, Carnac 061989
Antiquités de Locquemeau, Tredrez-Lacquemeau 068618
Antiquités de Mauperthuis, Mauperthuis 064435
Antiquités de Meaux, Meaux 064456
Antiquités de Saint-Michel en Grève, Saint-Michel-en-Grève 067676
Antiquités de Sainte-Agathe, Longuyon 063990
Antiquités de Thueyts, Thueyts 068416
Antiquités de Vaux, Cesson-Sévigné 062060
Antiquités de Verneuil, Verneuil-sur-Seine 068784
Antiquités Déco, Binic 061489
Antiquités Décor et Confort de France, Montréal 058909
Antiquités Décoration, Sausset-les-Pins 068155
Antiquités des Bateliers, Les Rosiers-sur-Loire 063778
Antiquités des Bateliers, Saumur 068147
Antiquités des Bords du Cher, Saint-Aignan (Loir-et-Cher) 067343
Antiquités des Carmes, Avignon 061125
Antiquités des Cordeliers, Dinan 062679
Antiquités des Corps Saints, Avignon 061126
Antiquités des Emmurées, Rouen 067240
Antiquités des Escoulettes, Rocbaron 067171
Antiquités des Halles, Airvault 060690
Antiquités des Mercoeurs, Murat (Cantal) 064844
Antiquités des Mesnuls, Les Mesnuls 063772
Antiquités des Meulières, La Ferté-sous-Jouarre 063374
Antiquités des Plantades, La Garde 063388
Antiquités des Provinces de France, Pézenas 066790
Antiquités des Quatre Fontaines, Narbonne 064960
Antiquités des Rochettes, Nantes 064892
Antiquités des Souvenets, Le Lude 063650
Antiquités des Ternes, Paris 065407
Antiquités du 12, Paris 065408
Antiquités du Barry, Vaujours 068734
Antiquités du Beffroi, Rivière 067159
Antiquités du Bourg, Martigny 082648
Antiquités du Canal, Troyes 068644
Antiquités du Château, Aubenas 061028
Les Antiquités du Château, Cagnes-sur-Mer 061890
Antiquités du Château, Le Château-d'Oleron 063598
Antiquités du Cloître, Jonzac 063249
Antiquités du Grand Bras, Saint-Georges-sur-Loire 067494
Antiquités du Lavoir, Labosse 063476
Antiquités du Manoir de Bellanton, Thouare-sur-Loire 068412
Antiquités du Marais, Challans 062073
Antiquités du Marché, Levallois-Perret 063799
Antiquités du Mas Chatelan, Mallemort 064240
Antiquités du Matelot, Québec 059057
Antiquités du Meneyer, Bénodet 061349
Antiquités du Moulin, Clamart 062315
Antiquités du Moulin, Saint-Gelais 067482, 124901
Antiquités du Palais, Albi 060749
Antiquités du Palais, Niort 065192
Antiquités du Parc, Lyon 064059
Antiquités du Parc de l'Europe, Saint-Étienne 067440
Antiquités du Parc de l'Europe, Villeurbanne 068937
Antiquités du Pont, Bruxelles 057820
Antiquités du Pont, Monnières 064604
Antiquités du Pont des Arches, Liège 058283
Antiquités du Pont Neuf, Paris 065409
Antiquités du Port, Antibes-Juan-les-Pins 060912
Antiquités du Port Royal, Paris 065410
Antiquités du Poulbenn, Crach 062543
Antiquités du Roy, Pacé 065320
Antiquités du Théatre, Noyon 065244
Antiquités du Théatre, Valence (Drôme) 068683
Antiquités du Val de Loir, Bazouges-sur-le-Loir 061248
Antiquités du Vieux Bourg, Villersexel 068934
Antiquités du XXe Siècle, Genève 082392
Antiquités En Top, Montréal 058910
Antiquités et Brocante Glainoise, La Chapelle-Glain 063315
Antiquités et Curiosités, Monaco 077594
Antiquités et Puces, Annecy 060884
Antiquités Félibien, Nantes 064893
Antiquités Ferme Sainte-Marie, Doncourt-lès-Conflans 062713
Antiquités Finkwiller, Strasbourg 068293
Antiquités Galerie d'Art, Guerlesquin 063101
Antiquités Gisèle, Lyon 064060
Antiquités Guy, Montréal 058911, 096965
Antiquités Hors Château, Liège 058284
Antiquités Jasper, Aubenas 061029
Antiquités Jean Boyvin, Dole 062696
Antiquités Jean-Claude, Montréal 058912
Antiquités Jean Macé, Nantes 064894
Antiquités JPS, Montréal 058913
Antiquités la Bigarderie, Blaye 061510
Antiquités la Chine du Port, Capbreton 061962
Antiquités la Comtoise, Montauroux 064643
Antiquités la Comtoise Fleurie, Narbonne 064961
Antiquités la Farandole, Allauch 060779
Antiquités la Grange, Châteauneuf-Val-Saint-Donat 062209
Antiquités la Grange, Chinon 062291
Antiquités la Grange, Gourdon 063023
Antiquités la Grange, La Vallée-au-Blé 063462
Antiquités La Maladière, Bourg-de-Péage 061704
Antiquités La Musardière, Saintes 068084
Antiquités la Pinsonnière, Chaville 062261
Antiquités la Vieuserie, Le Quesnel 063703
Antiquités Le Cerisiers, Quillan 067010
Antiquités le Damiette, Rouen 067241
Antiquites le Grenier Olarguais, Olargues 065261
Antiquités le Guillou, Brest 061762
Antiquités le Louis XV, Magagnosc 064210
Antiquités le Marchand d'Oublis, Bondues 061551
Antiquités le Padoue, Molesmes 064584
Antiquités Le Plessis, Saint-Urbain 068029
Antiquités le Presbytère, Limoges 063878
Antiquités le Presbytère, Rilhac-Lastours 067145
Antiquités le Prieuré, Varades 068723
Antiquités le Roi Soleil, Sanary-sur-Mer 068110
Antiquités le Vertugadin, Villefranche-sur-Mer 068899
Antiquités le Village, Wambrechies 069041
Antiquites le Voltaire, Narbonne 064962
Antiquités les 3 Fontaines, Lancon-Provence 063507
Antiquités les Cinq, Thonon-les-Bains 068404
Antiquités les Puces Angevines, Angers 060846
Antiquités les Remparts, Vannes (Morbihan) 068712
Antiquités les Vieilleries, Vannes (Morbihan) 068713
Antiquités Longchamp, Paris 065411
Antiquités Lormaye, Lormaye 064008
Antiquités Lyonnaises, Vaulx-en-Velin 068735
Antiquités Magasin, Montréal 058914
Antiquités Marilyn, Lyon 064061
Antiquités Martine, Pons 066903
Antiquités Milord, Montréal 058915
Antiquites & Modern Design, Roma 127922
Antiquités Montréal, Montréal 058916
Antiquités Montréal Universels, Montréal 058917
Antiquités Nazareth, Toulouse 068477
Antiquités Nicolas, Aubenas 061030
Antiquités Parcheminerie, Nevers 065002
Antiquités Passion, Cognac 062376
Antiquités Passion, Javrezac 063241
Antiquités Pierrejean Patrick, Châlons-en-Champagne 062094
Antiquités Plestin, Plestin-les-Grèves 066850
Antiquités pour la Table, Montréal 058918
Antiquités Privilège, Québec 059058
Antiquités Renaissance, Montréal 058919
Antiquités Restauration, Montréal 123782
Antiquités Rhône Alpes, Villeurbanne 068938
Antiquités Rocaille, Paris 065412
Antiquités Rond Point Elysées 7, Paris 065413
Antiquités Saint-Antoine, Lucciana 064021
Antiquités Saint-Christophe, Le Merlerault 063667
Antiquités Saint-Eloi, Clermont-Ferrand 062325
Antiquités Saint-Honoré, Arnay-le-Duc 060977
Antiquités Saint-Louis, Versailles 068793
Antiquités Saint-Maclou, Pontoise 066943
Antiquités Saint-Nicolas, Lunéville 064033
Antiquités Saint-Spire, Corbeil-Essonnes 062467
Antiquités Sainte-Anne, Paris 065414
Antiquités Salon de Thé, Bordeaux 061578
Antiquités Scientifiques, Genève 082393
Antiquités Seconde Chance, Montréal 058920
Antiquités sous Lu Barri, Saint-Paul-de-Vence 067938
Antiquités Transformation Ebénisterie, Baudreville 061224
Antiquites Trésor d'Ivoire, Montréal 058921
Antiquités Vence, Vence 068749
Antiquités Viaud, Château-Arnoux-Saint-Auban 062178
Antiquités Voltaire, Nantes 064895
Antiquities, Arundel 083309
Antiquities, Auckland 078916
Antiquities, Wolverhampton 087207
Antiquities Dealers' Association, London 054273
Antiquities International, Las Vegas 089547
Antiquities Kerikeri, Kerikeri 079134
Antiquities Museum, Bibliotheca Alexandria, Alexandria 009274
Antiquities Museum of Tel Aviv-Yafo, Eretz Israel Museum, Tel Aviv 023062
Antiquities of Nevada, Las Vegas 089548
The Antiquities Shoppe, London 058879
Antiquitum, Québec 059059
Antiquity, Cambridge 136158
Antiquity and European Work of Art, New York 090688
Antiquity Furniture, Indianapolis 132148
Antiquity Hands of the Hills, Singapore 080423
Antiquity Shop, Nairobi 077352
Antiquity Workshop, Austin 131792
Antiquorum, Genève 082394, 122319
Antiquorum, New York 122985
Antiquorum, Paris 065415
Antiquorum, Roma 076296
Antiquorum Italia, Milano 121695
Antiquus, Christchurch 079009
Antiquus, London 085086
Antiquus, Vauhallan 068732
Antiquus, Venezia 076919
Antiquus, Venezia 076920
Antiquus, Venezia 076921
Antiquus, Wrocław 079796, 140802
Anti's, Milano 075597
Antis Jonáš, Chrast u Chrudimě 060008
Antix Brocante, Clermont-Ferrand 062326
Antix e Artes, Rio de Janeiro 058545
Antix-Stadl, Dornbirn 056959
Antler River Historical Society Museum, Melita 005856
Antoine, Claude, Liège 096374
Antoine, Michel, Bruxelles 057821

Antoinette, San Diego 092612
Antoinette's, Salt Lake City 092416
Antologia di Belle Arti, Torino 135868
Antom, Stockinish 131540
Anton, Henri, Montreuil-sur-Mer . . . 121080
Anton Bruckner-Museum, Ansfelden 001693
Anton Galerie, Berlin 101775
Anton Galerie, Paris 065416
Anton Hanak-Museum, Langenzersdorf 002201
Anton-Museum, Zwettl, Niederösterreich 003074
Anton Pieck Museum, Hattem 029680
Anton Van Wouw House, University of Pretoria, Brooklyn 034569
Anton Wildgans-Haus, Mödling 002323
Antona Austriņa Memoriālais Muzejs, Vecpiebalga 027794
Antonacci, Paolo, Roma 076297
Antonelle, Patrick, New York 117593
Antonelli, Felice, Genova 075434
Antonelli, Massimo, Roma 076298
Antonelli Institute of Art and Photography, Cincinnati 051136
Antoni, Gerhard, Buborn 125406
Antoni, Philippe, Mézy-sur-Seine . . 064554
Antoni, Philippe, Paris 065417
Antonia's Antiques, Washington . . . 093379
Antonietti, François, Nantes 121085
Antonini, Antoinette, Monaco 077595
Antonini, Maria Maddalena, Milano 075598
Antônio Antiguidades, São Paulo . . 058680
Antonio Rinaldini & Figlie, Napoli . . 106358
Antonio's Antiques, San Francisco .092724, 132867
Antonitsch, Alma & Josef, Mannheim 134187
Antonopouleion Archeological Museum, Pylos 021444
Antonopoulou, Ang., Athinai 105382
Antonow, Dr. Alexander, Frankfurt am Main 133937
Antons & Co, Kim, København 060278
Anton's Antikk, Oslo 079414
Antonucci, Cosima, Milano 075599
Antony, Daniel, Fleurance 062875
Antony, Henrietta, Montréal 058922
Antony & Woodgate, Brighton, Victoria 055546
Antony's, Oberstaufen . . . 073151, 121569
Antqiues and Bric-a-Brac Market, Wellingborough 087065
Antunes, Lisboa 140820
Antunes, Angela, Belo Horizonte . . . 058404
Antunes, Manuel, Lisboa 079860
Antwerp Antiques Markt, Antwerpen 057677
Antwerps Tram- en Autobusmuseum, Berchem 003227
Anty-Raj, Warszawa 079726
Antyk, Gdańsk 079577, 129007
Antyk, Gdańsk 140716
Antyk, Kraków 079616
Antyk & Art, Kraków 079617
Antyk Salon Sztuki Dawnej, Lublin . 079677
Antyki, Dąbrowa Górnicza 079575
Antyki, Katowice 079607
Antyki, Kęty 079608, 129021
Antyki, Kobyłka 129022
Antyki, Kraków 079618
Antyki, Kraków 129027
Antyki, Poznań 079685
Antyki, Warszawa 079727
Antyki, Warszawa 079728
Antyki Ars Silesiae, Wrocław 079797, 140803
Antyki Biżuteria Salon Sztuki, Kraków 079619
Antyki i Dzieła Sztuki, Przemyśl . . .079702, 140766
Antykwariat, Jelenia Góra 079605, 140728
Antykwariat, Łomianki 140757
Antykwariat, Sopot 140767
Antykwariat, Warszawa 079729
Antykwariat, Warszawa 140772
Antykwariat, Warszawa 140773
Antykwariat Akademicki, Kraków . . 140730
Antykwariat bibliofilski, Warszawa . 140774
Antykwariat DAES, Wrocław 079798
Antykwariat Gdański Salon Sztuki Dawnej, Gdańsk 079578, 140717
Antykwariat i Galeria Sztuki Współczesnej, Szczecin 109081, 140769
Antykwariat i Salon Plastyki Współczesnej, Szczecin 079717
Antykwariat Naukowy, Kielce 140729
Antykwariat Naukowy, Kraków 140731
Antykwariat Naukowy, Łódź 140752
Antykwariat Naukowy, Wrocław . . . 140804
Antykwariat Rara Avis, Kraków 140732
Antykwariat Staromiejski, Warszawa 140775
Antykwariat Szkolny, Warszawa . . . 140776
Antykwariat Sztuka Dawna i Przedmioty Kolekcjonierskie, Słupsk 079706
Antykwarnia Księgarnia Niezależna, Częstochowa 140715
ANU Antiques and More, Albuquerque 087372
Anubis Ancient Art, Rotterdam 078696
l'Anverre-Atelier, Antwerpen 096058
Anvil Antiques, Leek 084933
Anvil Gallery, Saintfield 086481
Anvill Antiques, Hartley Wintney . . . 084598
Any Amount of Books, London 141747
Anyang Yin Xu Bo Wu Yuan, Anyang 006955
Anything Goes, London 085087
Anything Goes, Tucson 093201
Anything Goes On Bay, Toronto 059137
Anýž, Komárov 060038
ANZ Banking Museum, Melbourne . 001230
A.N.Z. Gallery Fine Art, Brunswick . 094319
Anza-Borrego Desert Museum, Borrego Springs 042312
Anzac Cottage Museum, Mount Hawthorn 001291
ANZAC Memorial, Sydney 001504
Anzali Military Museum, Bandar-Anzali 022548
Anzidei, Roberto, Roma 127923
Anzilotti, Benedetta, Firenze 127285
Anzilotti, David & Stefano, Roma . .076299, 127924
Anzoátegui, Hugo M., Buenos Aires 055169
AOC, Lyon 064062
Aoiya, Kyoto 077088
Aoki, Fukuoka 077040
Aomori-kenritsu Kyodokan, Aomori 026415
Aouizerats, Alain, Job 063242
Aoyama, Tokyo 077233
Aoyama, Tokyo 077234
Aoyama Yanagawa, Tokyo 077235
AP-Art, Knokke-Heist 096317
A.P Art, Lille 099481
APA, Amsterdam 134768
Apa, Nagoya 106914
Apa Tani, Paris 065418, 124552
APAA Newsletter, San Pedro 136323
Apache Coin, Minneapolis 090341
Aparatus Som e Imagem, Rio de Janeiro 096587
Apart, London 113448
Aparté, Pézenas 138571
Apartheid Museum, Ormonde 034689
the apartment, Athinai 105383
APC Galerie, Köln 103579
APC-Ringmaurer, Murten 111761
APD Singapore, Singapore 134889
Apeiron, Amsterdam 140280
Apeiron, Palermo 106413, 127817
Apeldoorns Museum, Apeldoorn . . . 029252
Apellaniz, Vitoria-Gasteiz . 081712, 110869
Apellaniz Saez de Ibarra, Juan Antonio, Vitoria-Gasteiz 081713
Apelle, Paris 124553
Apelstein, Katherine, Saint-Ouen . . 067709
Aperture, New York 136324
Aperture Foundation, New York . . . 135408
Aperture Photo Gallery and EMU Art Gallery, Eugene 043741
Apestaart, de, Enschede 078367
Apesteguy, Anne, Deauville 099197
Apex, Los Angeles 116701
Apex Art, New York 046292
APEX Gallery, Washington 120250
Apex Museum, Atlanta 041842
Apexim '93, Bucureşti 109416
Aphaia Verlag, Berlin 133749, 138738
Aphold, Roland, Allschwil 111114
Aphold, Roland, Weil am Rhein 105175
Apiary, Denver 088651
Apice Art, São Paulo 058681
Apicella-Bergner, Gabriela, Köln . . . 103580
Apis, Pézenas 066791
Apitz, Joachim, Babenhausen, Schwaben 069250
Apitz, Manfred, Hamburg 071196
Aplicaciones Vane, Barcelona 129313
Apocalypse Boutique, Denver 115969
Apogee, New York 117594
Apogee, Seattle 092962
Apolinario Mabini Birthplace Museum, Tanauan 031799
Apolinario Mabini Shrine and Museum, Manila 031711
Apollo, Bucureşti 109417
Apollo, Helsinki 120880
Apollo, Indianapolis 116438
Apollo, Zeist 078861
Apollo, The International Magazine of Art and Antiques, London . . 135175, 136159
Apollo Antik och Konsthandel, Stockholm 081920
Apollo Antiques, Warwick 087034
Apollo Apparao Galleries, Mumbai . 105753
Apollo Art Books, Den Haag 140387
Apollo Galleries, Westerham 087095
Apollo Gallery, Dublin 105856
Apollo Gallery, Dublin 105857
Apollo Gallery, Taipei 098059
Apollo Raamatuaja, Tallinn 137915
Apollo Southerns, Tonypandy 131599
Apollon Galerie, Frei-Laubersheim . 102850
Apolloni, Maria Pia, Roma 076300
Apolloni, W., Roma 076301
Apollo's Art, Doetinchem 078287
Apolonia, Denver 088652
APOM Informações, Actas dos colóquios, Lisboa 136041
Apostolos, Lemesos 098309
Apostroph Verlag, Stuttgart 134405
L'Apostrophe, Montréal 058923
Apothécairerie de l'Hôtel Dieu-le-Comte, Troyes 015047
Apothecary, Chicago 115334
Apotheken-Museum, Schiltach 020025
Apothekenmuseum, Hofgeismar . . . 017959
Apothekenmuseum Bad Schwalbach, Stadtmuseum, Bad Schwalbach . 015795
Apothicairerie, Centre Hospitalier de Gonesse, Gonesse 011966
Appalachian Center for Crafts, Smithville 048205
Appalachian Spring, Washington . . 120251
Appaloosa Horse Club of Canada Senior Citizens Museum, Claresholm . . . 005274
The Appaloosa Museum and Heritage Center, Moscow 046045
Appap, Paris 065419
Apparcel, Yannick, Lyon 124335
Apparences, Villeneuve-les-Avignon 101475
Appartamenti Monumentali, Firenze 024137
Appay, Gairoard & Besch, Cannes . 120961
Appel, Dr., Berlin 138739
Appel, Eric, New York 090689
Appel, Hélène, Paris 099938
Appel, Vera-M. & Anton, Weßling . . 139844
Appel d'Air, L'Isle-sur-la-Sorgue . . . 063917
Appel & Troschke, Frankfurt am Main 102742
Appelfeld, New York 142628
Appenzeller Brauchtumsmuseum, Urnäsch 037660
Appenzeller Schaukäserei, Stein, Appenzell-Ausserrhoden 037609
Appenzeller Volkskunde-Museum, Stein, Appenzell-Ausserrhoden 037610
Appia, Grenoble 099299
Appin Wildlife Museum, Appin 038515
Apple, Annie, Tampa 093105
Apple Barrel, Honolulu 116196
Apple Barrel Antique Mall, Oklahoma City 091469
Apple Blossom Antique Mall, Oklahoma City 091470
Apple Card Studios, Kingston-upon-Hull 135164
Apple Gallery, Godalming 113138
Apple Market Stalls, London 085088
Apple Orchard Antique Mall, Oklahoma City 091471
Apple Press, London 135176
Apple Tree Gallery, Saundersfoot . . 114398
The Apple Trees Museum, Burlington 042512
The Appledore Gallery, Appledore, Devon 112512
AppleGum Antiques, Bega 055467
Apples & Pears Gallery, Tarleton . . . 114549
Appleton Art Center, Appleton 041752
Appleton Galleries, Vancouver 097411, 120825
Appleton Museum of Art, Ocala . . . 046609
Appletree Press, Belfast 135119
Applewood, Charlotte 115272
Applewood Studio Gallery, Bega . . . 094230
Appleyard, Roger, Rotherham 086406
Appliance Plus, Tucson 093202
Applicat, Paris 099939
Applied Art College, Rīga 050514
Applied Arts Magazine, North York . 135621
Applin, Jess, Cambridge 083840
Appolo Subastas, Bilbao 122016
Appomattox Court House, Appomattox 041756
Appraisal Services, New York 090690
Appraisers Association of America, San Francisco 054601
Appraising Association, Nashville . . 054602
Appreciating Antiques, New York . . 090691
Apricot Gallery, Ha Noi 120445
Apricot Gallery, Ho Chi Minh City . . 120496
Apriķu Novada Muzejs, Apriķi 027659
Aprilborn, Saint Paul 092348
April's Gallery, New York 117595
Apriori Antiques, San Francisco 092725
Apropos Antiques, Richmond 092059
Apropos Galleries, Saint Paul 119271
Apsara, Long Beach 116662
Apsara, Singapore 080424
Apsley, Den Haag 078165
Apsley, Miami 090137
Apsley House, London 040077
APT Galerie d'Art, Houston 116268
Apta, Paris 065420
Apteekkimuseo, Kouvola 009743
Apteekkimuseo ja Qwensel, Turku . 010160
Apter-Fredericks, London 085089
Aptos Cruz, Stirling 095225
Aptucxet Trading Post Museum, Bourne 042358
Adnan Al-Aqel & Khaled Al-Mallah, Damascus 083051
Aqua, Koshigaya 077086
Aqua 20th Century Modern, Austin . 087555
Aqua Blues, Le Lavandou 099444
Aqua-Blues, Les Sables-d'Olonne . 063781
Aqua-Design, Aichach 138674
Aquafortis, Firenze 075273
Aqualeon Parc de la Natura, Albinyana 034795
L'Aquamanile, Lyon 064063
Aquamarin Verlag, Grafing bei München 133986
Aquamarina, Madrid 110433
Aquarell Verlag, Lauda-Königshofen 134142
Aquarella, Les Trois-Ilets 107460
Aquarelle, Kortrijk 058259

Aquarelle Gallery, London 113449
Aquarelles de Loire, Angers 098829
Aquarellisten Förlag, Göteborg 134957
Aquaria Vattenmuseum, Stockholm 036613
The Aquarium, London 113450
Aquarium-Musée de la Mer, Laboratoire Maritime de Dinard, Dinard 011617
Aquarium-Musée-Institut Paul Ricard, Le Brusc 012473
Aquarius, Dubai 112450
Aquarius Antik, Drammen 079383
Aquarius Antiques, Leeds 084925
Aquarius, Loudon & Thys, Würzburg 074491
Aquarius Rare Coins, Miami 090138
Aquarius Wassermuseum, Mülheim an der Ruhr 019019
The Aquary Museum, Tucson 048626
Aquatic Hall of Fame, Museum of Canada, Winnipeg 006839
Aquatics Museum - Institute of Oceanography and Fisheries, Suez 009346
Aquila Books, Calgary 137618
Aquilanti, Buenos Aires 136699
Aquiles Adler, Richmond 119094
Aquincumi Múzeum, Budapesti Történeti Múzeum, Budapest 021634
Aquitaine, Bordeaux 061579
A.R. Bowman Memorial Museum, Prineville 047244
A.R. Mitchell Memorial Museum of Western Art, Trinidad 048609
Ar Stal, Brest 061763
Ar Stal, Concarneau 062442
Ar Stal, Pontivy 066941
Ar Stal, Quimper 067013
Ara, Lisboa 109262
ARA, Rekken 128809
Arab International Services, Cairo . 060427
Araba Fenice, Cagliari 075199
Arabesque, Beirut 077381
Arabesque, Cairo 098609
Arabesque, Paris 065421
Al-Arabesque Gallery, Manama . . .057617, 095989
Arabesques, Castres 062029
Arabia, Pascual, San Francisco . . . 132868
Arabia Museum-Gallery, Helsinki . . 009513
Arabian Trade House, Riyadh 080372
Arabic Museum, Cairo 009309
Arabic Typewriters, New York 090692
Arad Museum, Arad 022888
Arader, W. Graham, Houston 089019
Arader, W. Graham, Houston 089020
Arader, W. Graham, Houston 142424
Arader, W. Graham, New York 090693, 142629
Arader, W. Graham, Philadelphia . . .091605, 142735
Arader, W. Graham, San Francisco .092726, 142925
Arader Graham, W., New York 117596
Arader Graham, W., Philadelphia . . 118729
Aragão, Antónia, Lisboa 079861
Araghi, Genova 106079
Aragon, Paris 065422
Aragon, Modeste, La Coucourde . . . 063348
Aragon, Modeste, Savasse 068162
Aragon Diaz, Lopez de, Madrid 081235
Arai Memorial Museum of Art, Iwanai 026590
Arai-shiritsu Hakubutsukan, Arai . . 026417
Al-Araimi Gallery, Al-Qurum 108764
Āraišu Muzejparks, Ezerpils, Drabeši 027677
Aral, A Coruña 129486
Araldi, Albin, Chaumont (Haute-Marne) 062245
Araluen Centre, Alice Springs 094134
Aram, Den Haag 078166
ARAM Kunstmagazin, Wien 135543
Arama, Maurice, Paris 065423
Arami Galería, Bucaramanga 098201, 123913
Arana, Getxo 081110
Aranaz Darras, Donostia-San Sebastián 081074
Arango, Guillermo, Medellín 059909
Arango, Maria, Las Vegas 116601
Aranha, Silvia de Souza, São Paulo 058682
Arany János Múzeum, Nagykőrös . . 021798
Arany Sas Patika, Pharmacy Museum, Budapest 021635
Arar, Florian, Bordeaux 061580
Ararat Gallery, Ararat 000746
Ararat Trading Post, Ararat 055350
Arario Gallery, Cheonan 107179
Araripe, Nilda, Rio de Janeiro 096588
Aras, Ravensburg 104667, 134357
Aras, Patrick, Lamorlaye 063499
Arash, New York 117597
Arasi, Chennai 105618
Arati, Kathmandu 107573
Aratoi Wairarapa Museum of Art and History, Masterton 030535
Arauco, Nürnberg 104471
Araujo, Evly da Rosa, Porto Alegre . 058483
Araujo, Oliva, Madrid 110434
Araujo, Oliva, Madrid 110435
Arax Orientmattor, Stockholm 081921
Araya, María Esther, Santiago de Chile 059498
Araya Vera, Sergio, Santiago de Chile 123874
Arbæjarsafn, Reykjavík Museum, Reykjavík 021958
Arbalet, Minsk 057654
Arbatskaja Iverija, Moskva 109487
Arbatskaja Nachodka, Moskva 080230, 140898
Arbaud, Aix-en-Provence 060694
Arbeia Roman Fort and Museum, South Shields 041049
Arbeidsgenot, Oudtshoorn 034690
Arbeiterfotografie Galerie, Köln . . . 103581
Arbeitsgemeinschaft bildender Künstler am Mittelrhein e.V., Koblenz 053013
Arbeitsgemeinschaft der Künstler- und Kulturfreunde Steiermark, Mürzzuschlag 052503
Arbeitsgemeinschaft der Kunstbibliotheken, München 053014
Arbeitsgemeinschaft der Restauratoren-Museen-Denkmalpflege-Grabungstechnik; Berufsverband staatlich geprüfter RestauratorInnen; Bundesverband Deutscher Diplom-RestauratorInnen; Deutscher Restauratoren Verband; Deutscher Verband Freiberuflicher Restauratoren; Restauratoren Fachverband; Restauratorenverband Sachsen, Bonn 053589
Arbeitsgemeinschaft des Kunsthandwerks Nordrhein- Westfalen, Düsseldorf 053015
Arbeitsgemeinschaft Deutscher Kunstvereine - Projektbüro, Hannover 053016
Arbeitsgemeinschaft Diessener Kunst, Dießen am Ammersee 053017
Arbeitsgemeinschaft kirchlicher Museen und Schatzkammern, Würzburg . . 053018
Arbeitsgemeinschaft Kunsthandwerk Bremen, Bremen 053019
Arbeitsgemeinschaft Malen und Zeichnen, Chemnitz 053020
Arbeitsgemeinschaft Mittelfränkischer Münzensammler e.V., Dinkelsbühl 053021
Arbeitsgemeinschaft Schweizer Keramiker, Sursee 054167
Arbeitsgemeinschaft Selbstständige Industrie-Designer, Beendorf 053022
Arbeitsgruppe für Theoretische und Angewandte Museologie, Wien . . 133177
Arbeitskreis 68, Künstlergemeinschaft Wasserburg am Inn, Wasserburg am Inn 053023
Arbeitskreis Bild- und Kunstbuchverlage im Börsenverein des Deutschen Buchhandels e.V., Frankfurt am Main 053024
Arbeitskreis deutscher Kunsthandelsverbände, Köln 053025
Arbeitskreis für Grafikforschung, München 053026
Arbeitskreis Moderne Graphik, Frankenthal, Pfalz 053027
Arbeitskreis Stadtzeichner, Alsfeld .053028, 133720
Arbejder-, Håndværker- og Industrimuseet, Horsens 008930
Arbejdermuseet, København 008957
Arbeo, Barcelona 080794
The Arbery Centre, Wantage 087017
Arbetets Museum, Norrköping 036498
Arbil Museum, Arbil 022656
Arbin, Lars, Stockholm 081922
Arbiter, Wallasey 087000
Arboga Bryggerimuseum, Arboga . . 036188
Arboga Museum, Arboga 036189
D'Arbois, Bruxelles 123571
El Arbol de Dios, San Salvador 098684
Årbols Skolmuseum, Åmål 036179
Arbor, Jacksonville 089373
Arbor, Jacksonville 089374
Arbor Antiques, Jacksonville 089375, 132172
Arbor Lodge, Nebraska City 046169
Arboré, Jean-François, Paley 065332
Arboreus, Chur 111354
Arbour Antiques, Stratford-upon-Avon 086772
Arbousse Bastide, Patrice, Avallon . 061114
Arbousse-Bastide, Patrice, Thory . . 068411
Arbras, London 085090
L'Arbre à Collections, Bazoche-Gouet 061246
Arbre à Pain, Grenoble 063046
L'Arbre aux Papiers, Le Mans 133478
Arbre Bleu, Gillonnay 062999
Arbre de Jessé, La Carité-sur-Loire 138110
Arbroath Art Gallery, Arbroath 038520
Arbroath Museum, Arbroath 038521
Arbur, Milano 106151
Arbuthnot Museum, Peterhead 040703
Arc, Edinburgh 112982
Arc Abatement, Austin 087556
Arc Antique, Nantes 124473
Arc Communicatio, Subotica 109749
The Arc Contemporary Crafts, Chester 112850
L'Arc en Seine, Paris 065424
A.R.C. Gallery, Chicago 042819
Arc Linea, Milano 075600
Arc One Gallery, Melbourne 094805
Arc Prints, Saint Louis 119173
ARC Yinnar, Yinnar 095455
L'Arca, Brescia 075143
L'Arca, Genova 075435
L'Arca, Milano 140042
L'Arca, Modena 127718
L'Arca, Modena 127719
Arca da Tia Lecas, Porto 080066
Arca das Velharias, Lisboa 079862
Arca de L'Àvia, Barcelona 080795
Arca do Tempo, Lisboa 079863
Arcache, Beirut 077382
Arcache, Lucien, Paris 065425
Arcad, Annecy 098835
Arcad'art, Grenoble 063047
Arcadas São José, Lisboa 079864
Arcade, Apeldoorn 078029
Arcade 127, Paris 065426
Arcade Art, New Orleans 117388
Arcade Books, Belfast 141403
Arcade Books, Toronto 137112
Arcade Chausse-Coqs, Genève 111419
Arcade Colette, Paris 099940
Arcade Historical Museum, Arcade . 041758
Arcades, Rennes (Ille-et-Vilaine) . . 067096
L'Arcadia, Brescia 075144
Arcadia, Firenze 127286
Arcadia, Madrid 110436
Arcadia, Milano 075601
Arcadia, Montréal 058924
L'Arcadia, Napoli 075939
Arcadia, New York 117598
Arcadia, Oswestry 086169
Arcadia, Phoenix 091716
Arcadia Antichità, Bologna 075053, 105939
Arcadia Antiques, Bristol 083727
Arcadia Antiques, Toronto 059138
Arcadia Books, Ballarat 136788
Arcadia Books, Mylor 137020
Arcadia Booksellers, Oxford 141979
Arcadia Galerie, Lyon 064064
Arcadia Press, New York 135409
Arcadia Township Historical Museum and Furniture Museum, Arcadia 041759
Arcadia University Art Gallery, Glenside 044214
Arcadian Antiques, Auckland 078917
Arcadian Books and Art Prints, New Orleans 142604
Arcadian Clock &CO, New York 132441
Arcadiane, Paris 099941
Arcadie, Jouars-Pontchartrain 063254
ARCAM Galerie, Amsterdam 029167
A.R.CA.M.S., Autun 124085
Arcana, Colmar 062400
Arcana, Roquefort-les-Pins 067220
Arcana Artis, Warszawa 140777
Arcane, Versailles 068794
L'Arcantica, Torino 076764
Arcaz, Madrid 129564
ARCE, Madrid 134935
ARCE Subastas, Barcelona 080796, 121994
Arceneaux, Birmingham 115094
Arch Angel Antiques, Hong Kong . . 059592
Arch Angel Art, Amsterdam 107654
Arch Angel Contemporary Art, Hong Kong 097749
Arch Gallery, London 113451
Archaeological and Historical Museum, Ramat Hashofet 023054
Archaeological Collection, Baltimore 041964
Archaeological Collection, Kibbutz Ruhama 023018
Archaeological Collection, Yehi'am . 023100
Archaeological Collection of Youth Village Nitzanim, Doar-Na Evtach 022904
Archaeological Museum, Amaravati 022006
Archaeological Museum, Amman . . 027363
Archaeological Museum, Anuradhapura 036126
Archaeological Museum, Anyang . . 006956
Archaeological Museum, Bedung . . 027947
Archaeological Museum, Bijapur . . 022042
Archaeological Museum, Bodhghaya 022045
Archaeological Museum, Colombo . 036128
Archaeological Museum, Dedigama 036136
Archaeological Museum, Delhi 022078
Archaeological Museum, Gorakhpur 022124
Archaeological Museum, Guntur . . . 022129
Archaeological Museum, Gwalior . . 022141
Archaeological Museum, Halebidu . 022145
Archaeological Museum, Hampi . . . 022146
Archaeological Museum, Hardwar . 022148
Archaeological Museum, Jaunpur . . 022183
Archaeological Museum, Kamalapur 022196
Archaeological Museum, Karachi . . 031372
Archaeological Museum, Khajuraho 022203
Archaeological Museum, Kibbutz Ein Dor 022999
Archaeological Museum, Kibbutz Gat 023003
Archaeological Museum, Konarak . 022230
Archaeological Museum, Lemesos . 008226
Archaeological Museum, Mahastangarh 003113
Archaeological Museum, Mainamati 003114
Archaeological Museum, Myohaung 029064
Archaeological Museum, Nalanda . 022281
Archaeological Museum, Neishaboor 022588
Archaeological Museum, Old Goa . . 022285
Archaeological Museum, Pagan . . . 029065
Archaeological Museum, Paharpur . 003115
Archaeological Museum, Pune 022302
Archaeological Museum, Sanchi . . . 022323
Archaeological Museum, Sarnath . . 022328

Archaeological Museum, Spanish Town . . . 026397
Archaeological Museum, Swat . . . 031402
Archaeological Museum, Taxila . . . 031403
Archaeological Museum, Udaipur . . 022359
Archaeological Museum, Vaisali . . . 022368
Archaeological Museum, Varanasi . 022371
Archaeological Museum, Zadar . . . 007823
Archaeological Museum, Department of Antiquities, Tripoli . . . 027831
Archaeological Museum, Louisville Presbyterian Theological Seminary, Louisville . . . 045484
Archaeological Museum Blitar, Blitar . . . 022402
Archaeological Museum Harappa, Harappa . . . 031362
Archaeological Museum Kediri, Kediri . . . 022460
Archaeological Museum Konarak, Puri . . . 022311
Archaeological Museum Moen-Jo-Daro, Moen-Jo-Daro . . . 031390
Archaeological Museum of Ancient Corinth, Ancient Corinth . . . 021131
Archaeological Museum of Argos, Argos . . . 021142
Archaeological Museum of Baluchistan Quetta, Quetta . . . 031397
Archaeological Museum of Epidaurus, Asklepieion Lygourio . . . 021149
Archaeological Museum of Isthmia, Isthmia . . . 021289
The Archaeological Museum of Kfar Saba, Kfar Saba . . . 022992
Archaeological Museum of Nemea, Archaia Nemea . . . 021141
Archaeological Museum of Patiala, Patiala . . . 022291
Archaeological Museum of Piraeus, Piraeus . . . 021430
Archaeological Museum of Siteia, Siteia . . . 021468
Archaeological Museum of Thebes, Thebes . . . 021485
Archaeological Museum Peshawar, Peshawar . . . 031391
Archaeological Museum Red Fort Delhi, Delhi . . . 022079
Archaeological Museum Saidu Sharif, Saidu Sharif . . . 031401
Archaeological Museum Taj Mahal, Agra . . . 021987
Archaeological Museum Umarkot, Umarkot . . . 031404
Archaeological Museums of Chania and Rethymnon, Chania . . . 021225
Archaeological Preserve Nicopolis ad Istrum, Veliko Tărnovo . . . 004927
Archaeological Receipts Fund, Athinai . . . 053661
Archaeological Resource Centre, York . . . 041472
Archaeological Site Museum, Alampur . . . 021998
Archaeological Site Nimrud (Calah), Nimrud . . . 022671
Archäologie-Museum, Städtische Museen Heilbronn, Heilbronn . . . 017847
Archäologiemuseum, Künzing . . . 018433
Archäologiemuseum im Fränkischen Freilandmuseum, Archäologische Staatssammlung München, Bad Windsheim . . . 015837
Archäologisch-Ethnographische Lehr- und Studiensammlung des Instituts für Altamerikanistik und Ethnologie der Universität Bonn, Bonn . . . 016313
Archäologisch-Ökologisches Museum, Albersdorf . . . 015465
Archäologische Ausgrabung Borg, Perl . . . 019590
Archäologische Ausstellung in der Schule, Nassenfels . . . 019180
Archäologische Gedenkstätte, Klosterneuburg . . . 002154
Archäologische Sammlung, Ruhrlandmuseum, Essen . . . 017060
Archäologische Sammlung der Universität, Freiburg im Breisgau . . . 017227
Archäologische Sammlung der Universität Zürich, Zürich . . . 037759
Archäologische Sammlung des Historischen Museums, Luzern . . . 037292
Archäologische Sammlung Keltenhaus, Historisches Rathaus, Taufkirchen, Kreis München . . . 020407
Archäologische Sammlung mit Heimatvertriebenenstube und Kruk-Sammlung, Königsbrunn . . . 018345
Archäologische Sammlung Warmbad-Villach, Villach . . . 002772
Archäologische Staatssammlung München, Museum für Vor- und Frühgeschichte, München . . . 019033
Archaeologische Verzameling der Rijksuniversiteit, Utrecht . . . 030225
Archäologischer Park Cambodunum - APC, Kempten . . . 018235
Archäologischer Park Carnuntum, Petronell . . . 002423
Archäologischer Park Magdalensberg, Landesmuseum Kärnten, Pischeldorf, Kärnten . . . 002432
Archäologischer Park mit Museums-Turm, Kellmünz . . . 018224
Archäologischer Park Xanten, Xanten . . . 021032
Archäologisches Freilichtmuseum, Groß Radern . . . 017559
Archäologisches Freilichtmuseum Oerlinghausen, Oerlinghausen . . . 019445
Archäologisches Landesmuseum, Wünsdorf . . . 020993
Archäologisches Landesmuseum, Stiftung Schleswig-Holsteinische Landesmuseen Schloß Gottorf, Schleswig . . . 020038
Archäologisches Landesmuseum Baden-Württemberg, Konstanz . . . 018374
Archäologisches Landesmuseum Mecklenburg-Vorpommern, Freilichtmuseum Groß Raden, Groß Raden . . . 017557
Archäologisches Museum, Burgheim . . . 016517
Archäologisches Museum, Donauwörth . . . 016740
Archäologisches Museum, Frankfurt am Main . . . 017152
Archäologisches Museum, Rimpar . 019846
Archäologisches Museum Carnuntinum, Archäologischer Park Carnuntum, Bad Deutsch-Altenburg . . . 001711
Archäologisches Museum der Stadt Kelheim, Kelheim . . . 018220
Archäologisches Museum der Stadt Weißenhorn, Weißenhorn . . . 020784
Archäologisches Museum der Universität Münster, Münster . . . 019138
Archäologisches Museum des Historischen Vereins für Oberfranken, Bayreuth 015905
Archäologisches Museum Essenbach, Essenbach . . . 017081
Archäologisches Museum Gablingen, Gablingen . . . 017310
Archäologisches Museum im Rathaus, Weichering . . . 020704
Archäologisches Museum in der Feldmühle, Rennertshofen . . . 019802
Archäologisches Museum Lavant, Lienz . . . 002234
Archäologisches Museum Neu-Ulm, Archäologische Staatssammlung München, Neu-Ulm . . . 019213
Archäologisches Pilgermuseum Hemmaberg-Juenna, Globasnitz . 001898
Archäologisches Zentrum Hitzacker, Hitzacker . . . 017935
Archaeology, New York . . . 136325
Archaeology Centre, Bagshot . . . 038565
Archaeology Museum, Allahabad . . 022002
Archaeology Museum, Chennai . . . 022054
Archaeology Museum, Nsukka . . . 030697
Archaeology Museum, Victoria . . . 028039
Archaeology Unit and Transport Museum, Gloucester . . . 039588
Archaeos, Fitzroy . . . 055820
Archäothek Schlag Keg, Salzburg . . 095716
Archaïa, Lyon . . . 064065
Archambault, Guy, Vitry-le-François 121288
l'Archange, Paris . . . 099942
Archangelos Mihail İkon Müzesi, Girne . . . 008241
Archangelskij Gosudarstvennyj Muzej Zodčestva i Narodnogo Ikusstva - Malye Karely, Archangelsk . . . 032989
Archangelskij Literaturnyj Muzej, Archangelsk . . . 032990
Archangelskij Oblastnoj Kraevedčeskij Muzej, Archangelsk . . . 032991
Archangelskij Oblastnoj Muzej Izobrazitelnych Iskusstv, Archangelsk . . . 032992
Archangelskij Sobor, Gosudarstvennyj muzej-zapovednik Moskovskij Kreml, Moskva . . . 033365
Archdiocesan Museum of Manila, Manila . . . 031712
Arché, Milano . . . 075602
L'Arche, Paris . . . 133512
Arche de Noé, Orléans . . . 065292
Archea, Amsterdam . . . 077779
Archelaus Smith Museum, Cape Sable Island . . . 005217
Archéo-Musée du Kronos, Espace Patrimoine, Albens . . . 010313
Archeo Plan, Delft . . . 128619
L'Archéodrome de Bourgogne, Meursault . . . 013047
Archeologia Classica, Roma . . . 135869
Archeologica di Sovana, Sorano . . . 025924
Archeological and Land Study Collection, Alumot . . . 022887
Archeological and Natural History Museum, Nacionalni Park Brijuni, Brijuni . . 007703
Archeological Collection, Agios Kirikos . . . 021119
Archeological Collection, Anafi . . . 021130
Archeological Collection, Apeirathos 021139
Archeological Collection, Astypalaia 021152
Archeological Collection, Dimitsana 021247
Archeological Collection, Drama . . . 021250
Archeological Collection, Edessa . . 021251
Archeological Collection, Ermoupolis . . . 021257
Archeological Collection, Farsala . . 021261
Archeological Collection, Feneos . . 021262
Archeological Collection, Feres . . . 021263
Archeological Collection, Filiatra . . 021264
Archeological Collection, Folegandros . . . 021269
Archeological Collection, Galaxidi . . 021270
Archeological Collection, Geraki . . . 021272
Archeological Collection, Grevena . 021274
Archeological Collection, Grevena . 021275
Archeological Collection, Gythion . . 021276
Archeological Collection, Ios . . . 021282
Archeological Collection, Istiaia . . . 021290
Archeological Collection, Kardamyli 021304
Archeological Collection, Kastro . . . 021318
Archeological Collection, Kea . . . 021323
Archeological Collection, Kimolos . . 021329
Archeological Collection, Kos . . . 021339
Archeological Collection, Kozani . . . 021344
Archeological Collection, Liknades . 021357
Archeological Collection, Lindos . . . 021359
Archeological Collection, Lixouri . . . 021364
Archeological Collection, Loutra Aidipsou . . . 021365
Archeological Collection, Maroneia . 021367
Archeological Collection, Mégara . . 021372
Archeological Collection, Messinia . 021376
Archeological Collection, Mithymna 021382
Archeological Collection, Molyvos . 021383
Archeological Collection, Navpaktos 021404
Archeological Collection, Néa Anchialos . . . 021406
Archeological Collection, Neos Skopos . . . 021410
Archeological Collection, Paramythia . . . 021418
Archeological Collection, Platanos . 021438
Archeological Collection, Preveza . . 021443
Archeological Collection, Pythagoreion . . . 021446
Archeological Collection, Serrai . . . 021461
Archeological Collection, Siatista . . 021463
Archeological Collection, Sifnos . . . 021466
Archeological Collection, Symi . . . 021480
Archeological Collection, Tanagra . . 021481
Archeological Collection, Tsotili . . . 021515
Archeological Museum, Andros . . . 021132
Archeological Museum, Argostolion 021143
Archeological Museum, Arhaia Olympia . . . 021147
Archeological Museum, Atalanti . . . 021153
Archeological Museum, Chaironeia 021222
Archeological Museum, Chalkida . . 021223
Archeological Museum, Chios . . . 021231
Archeological Museum, Chora . . . 021235
Archeological Museum, Corfu . . . 021238
Archeological Museum, Delos . . . 021245
Archeological Museum, Dion . . . 021249
Archeological Museum, Elefsis . . . 021254
Archeological Museum, Eresos . . . 021255
Archeological Museum, Eretria . . . 021256
Archeological Museum, Florina . . . 021265
Archeological Museum, Iráklion . . . 021284
Archeological Museum, Kabos . . . 021291
Archeological Museum, Kalamata . 021292
Archeological Museum, Kalamos . . 021296
Archeological Museum, Kalymnos . 021302
Archeological Museum, Kastelli Kisamou . . . 021315
Archeological Museum, Kavala . . . 021320
Archeological Museum, Kiato . . . 021324
Archeological Museum, Kilkis . . . 021327
Archeological Museum, Kórinthos . 021338
Archeological Museum, Kos . . . 021340
Archeological Museum, Lamia . . . 021349
Archeological Museum, Lárissa . . . 021351
Archeological Museum, Mykonos . . 021387
Archeological Museum, Myrina . . . 021389
Archeological Museum, Mytilini . . . 021393
Archeological Museum, Naxos . . . 021405
Archeological Museum, Paros . . . 021420
Archeological Museum, Patrai . . . 021423
Archeological Museum, Plaka . . . 021437
Archeological Museum, Polygyros . 021440
Archeological Museum, Rethymnon 021447
Archeological Museum, Rhodos . . . 021451
Archeological Museum, Salamina . . 021455
Archeological Museum, Samos . . . 021456
Archeological Museum, Samothráki 021460
Archeological Museum, Sicyon . . . 021465
Archeological Museum, Spárti . . . 021474
Archeological Museum, Tegea . . . 021482
Archeological Museum, Thassos . . 021483
Archeological Museum, Thera . . . 021486
Archeological Museum, Thermo . . . 021488
Archeological Museum, Tinos . . . 021508
Archeological Museum, Trichur . . . 022357
Archeological Museum, Vathy . . . 021517
Archeological Museum, Vravrón . . . 021526
Archeological Museum, Yiokaleion Foundation, Karystos . . . 021313
Archeological Museum of Agrinion, Agrinion . . . 021121
Archeological Museum of Aiani, Aiani . . . 021123
Archeological Museum of Aigina, Aegina . . . 021113
Archeological Museum of Astros, Astros . . . 021150
Archeological Museum of Delphi, Delphi . . . 021246
Archeological Museum of Durrës, Durrës . . . 000015
Archeological Museum of Ioannina, Ioannina . . . 021277
Archeological Museum of Komotini, Komotini . . . 021333
Archeological Museum of Nafplion, Nafplion . . . 021400
Archeological Museum of Pella, Pella . . . 021426
Archeological Museum of Somothraki, Palaiochora . . . 021415

Archeological Museum of Stavros, Stavros Ithakis 021479
Archeological Museum of Veroia, Veria 021518
Archeological Open Air Museum in Březno u Loun, Okresni Muzeum, Louny . . . 008490
Archeological Site Avedat, Avedat . 022892
Archeologičeska Ekspozicija Kreposta, Silistra 004828
Archeologičeska Ekspozicija v Džamia Achmed Bej, Istoričeski Muzej, Kjustendil 004720
Archeologičeski Institut s Muzej, Bălgarska Akademija na Naukite, Sofia 004844
Archeologičeski Muzej, Burgas 004646
Archeologičeski Muzej, Plovdiv . . . 004789
Archeologičeski Muzej, Radnevo . . 004807
Archeologičeski Muzej, Septemvri . 004826
Archeologičeski Muzej, Sozopol . . . 004879
Archeologičeski Muzej, Varna 004910
Archeologičeski Muzej, Veliko Tărnovo 004928
Archeologičeski Rezervat Starijat Grad Šumen i Šumenska Krepost, Šumen 004886
Archeologičeskij Muzej, Čerepovec 033072
Archeologičeskij Muzej, Rostovskij Oblastnoj Muzej Kraevedenija, Azov 033010
Archeologičeskij Muzej Kazanskogo Universiteta, Kazanskij gosudarstvennyj universitet, Kazan 033229
Archeologické Muzeum, Břeclav . . . 008277
Archeologické Múzeum, Slovenské Národné Múzeum, Bratislava 034317
Archeologické Pracoviště, Slezské zemské muzeum, Opava 008545
Archeologické Sbírky, Západočeské muzeum, Plzeň 008569
Archéologie Monnaies, Montpellier . 064730
Archéologie Monnaies Médailles, Montpellier 064731
Archeologiemuseum, Stein 030183
Archeologisch Centrum C.W. Bruinvis, Alkmaar 029130
Archeologisch en Paleontologisch Museum Hertogsgemaal, 's-Hertogenbosch 029731
Archeologisch Museum, Oudenaarde 003694
Archeologisch Museum, Harelbeke 003492
Archeologisch Museum, Mechelen . 003631
Archeologisch Museum Abdij, Affligem 003144
Archeologisch Museum Haarlem, Haarlem 029651
Archeologisch Museum Van Bogaert-Wauters, Hamme 003489
Archeologisch Museum van de Universiteit, Gent 003450
Archeologisch Openluchtmuseum Eerste Wereldoorlog, Zillebeke 003866
Archeology Museum, Shamir 023060
Archeology Museum of Kozani, Kozani 021345
Archeonet, Bruxelles 057822
Archéoscope, Le Mont-Saint-Michel 012533
Archéosite, Aubechies 003206
Archéosite de la Chapelle Saint-Julien, Martigues 012961
Archéosite de la Vallée des Merveilles, Tende 014918
Archéosite de l'Hospice des Pèlerins de Saint-Jacques-de-Compostelle, Pons 013877
Archéosite de l'Oppidum Celto-Ligure d'Entremont, Aix-en-Provence . . . 010289
Archéosite du Château et Village Médiéval, Montségur 013230
Archéosite et Exposition de la Cité Militaire Romain de la VIII Légion, Mirebeau-sur-Bèze 013075
Archéosite Gallo-Romain des Flaviers, Mouzon 013284
Archéosite Gallo-Romain Ruscino, Perpignan 013782
ArchéoSite Gaulois de Saint-Julien, Saint-Julien 014364
Archeosite Militaire, Groupe Fortifié l'Aisne, Verny 015185
Archéosite Préhistorique de Cambous, Saint-Martin-de-Londre 014419
Archéosites Gallo-Romains, Fontvieille 011861
Archer, London 130929
Archer, Sorell 056600
Archer, Barbara, Atlanta 114845
Archer, R.G., Lavenham 141708
Archer, R.G., Sudbury, Suffolk 142099
Archer County Museum, Archer City 041763
Archer Gallery, Clark College, Vancouver 048747
Archer Street Antiques and Gallery, Longford 056113
Archer's Antique, Olney 086162
Les Arches, Paris 099943
Arches Museum of Pioneer Life, Winona 049248
Archetto, Salvatore, Napoli 075940
Archétype, Bruxelles 096130
Archétype, Paris 065427, 099944
Archetypes, Hyères 099361
Archeus Fine Art, London 113452
Archevêché, Rouen 067242
Archi-Noire, Paris 065428
ArchiArt, Port Douglas 095082
Archibald, New York 117599
Archibald Graham McIlwaine House, The Petersburg Museums, Petersburg 046902
Archibald Historical Museum, La Rivière 005728
Archibalds, Wellington 108608
Archibook Verlag, Berlin 133750
Archicendolo, Napoli 075941
Archief en Museum van het Vlaams Leven te Brussel, Bruxelles 003285
Archie's, Chicago 088021
L'Archimede, Roma 106486
Archimede Staffolini, Lefkosia 098297
Archimedes, Leipzig 139389
Archipel, Paris 065429, 124554
Archipel Antiek, Den Haag 078167
Archipelago, Sheffield 114411
Archipelago Art, Griffith 094605
Archipelago Press, Singapore 134890
Archipelagos, Skiathos . . . 074629, 105444
Archipelagos Cultural Center, Athinai 021158
Architects' Journal, London 136160
Architectura, München 135740
Architectura et Natura, Amsterdam 134769
Architectural Antiques, Albuquerque 087373
Architectural Antiques, Atlanta 087450, 131758
Architectural Antiques, Bedford . . . 083471
Architectural Antiques, Denver 088653
Architectural Antiques, Dublin 074892
Architectural Antiques, Kendal 084824
Architectural Antiques, London 085091, 130930
Architectural Antiques, Miami 090139
Architectural Antiques, Minneapolis 090342
Architectural Antiques, Oklahoma City 091472
Architectural Antiques, Ottawa 059028
Architectural Antiques, San Antonio 092483
Architectural Antiques, Vancouver . 059334
Architectural Antiques Exchange, Philadelphia 091606
Architectural Art Glass Studio, Cincinnati 131926
Architectural Artifacts, Chicago . . . 088022
Architectural Artifacts, Denver 088654
Architectural Artifacts, New York . . 090694
Architectural Artifacts, Toledo 093163, 123126, 132968
Architectural Association, London .054274, 113453
Architectural Association Publications, London 135177
Architectural Colonial Antiques of Indianapolis, Indianapolis 089269
Architectural Decor, Austin 087557
Architectural Design, Chichester . . 136161
Architectural Digest, Los Angeles . . 136326
Architectural Heritage, Birmingham 087736
Architectural Heritage, Taddington . 086820
Architectural Imports, Edmonton . . 058817
Architectural Recovery, Portland . . . 091893
Architectural Relics, Phoenix 091717
Architectural Review, London 136162
Architectural Salvage, Denver 088655
Architectural Salvage, Kansas City . 089483
Architectural Salvage, Louisville . . . 089956
Architectural Salvage of San Diego, San Diego 092613
Architectural Warehouse, Auckland 078918
Architectural Warehouse Antiques, San Antonio 092484
Architecturals, Philadelphia 091607
Architecture and Art School, Architect Union of Armenia, Erevan 049605
Architecture Foundation, London . . 040078
Architecture in Greece, Athinai 135833
Architecture Museum, Bérat 000010
Architektur Forum Zürich, Zürich . . 037760
Architektur Galerie Berlin, Berlin . . 101776
Architektur im Ringturm, Wien 002847
Architektur- und Kunstgeschichte 20./21. Jahrhundert, Universität Hannover, Institut für Geschichte und Theorie, Hannover 050119
Architekturforum Aedes East, Berlin 101777
Architekturforum Aedes West, Berlin 101778
Architekturgalerie e.V, München . . .053029, 104139
Architekturgalerie Luzern, Ausstellungsraum Partikel, Luzern 037293
Architekturmuseum, Basel 036880
Architekturmuseum der Technischen Universität München, Pinakothek der Moderne, München 019034
Architekturmuseum Schwaben, Augsburg 015602
Architekturnaja Galereja, Moskva . . 109488
Architekturno-chudožestvennyj Ansambl byvšego Spaso-Jakovleskogo Monastyrja, Gosudarstvennyj muzej-zapovednik Rostovskij Kreml, Rostov (Jaroslavskaja obl.) 033700
Architekturno-ėtnografičeskij Muzej Angarskaja Derevnja, Bratskij gorodskoj objedinennyj muzej istorii osvoenija Angary, Bratsk 033045
Architekturno-ėtnografičeskij Muzej Derevjannogo Zodčestva Chochlovka, Perm 033645
Architekturno-etnografski Muzej Etăr, Gabrovo 004680
Architekturno-istoričski Muzej-rezervat, Boženci 004643
Architekturno-muzeen Rezervat Arbanassi, Architectural Museum Preserve Arbanassi, Veliko Tărnovo 004929
Architekturno-muzeen Rezervat Carevec, Veliko Tărnovo 004930
Architekturno-parkov Kompleks Dvorceva, Balčik 004624
Architekturzentrum Wien, Wien . . . 002848
Architektuur Centrum Amsterdam, Amsterdam 029168
Architus Antiques, Kirkby Lonsdale . 084872
Archiv Bürgerbewegung Leipzig e.V., Leipzig 018560
Archiv der deutschen Jugendbewegung, Witzenhausen 020937
Archiv der Universität Wien, Schausammlung, Wien 002849
Archiv für die Waldviertler Urgeschichtsforschung, Horn 002062
Archiv für Dorfgeschichte, Badeborn 015847
Archiv für Philatelie der Museumsstiftung Post und Telekommunikation, Bonn 016314
Archiv und Kollektion Paul Kaiser-Reka, Brandenburg an der Havel 016366
Archiv und Museum des Heimatkreises Leitmeritz, Fulda 017294
Archiv Verlag, Wien 133178
Archival Conservation Center, Cincinnati 131927
Archive, Caen 061857
Archive, Toronto 097216
Archive Books and Music, London . 141748
Archive of Experimental and Marginal Art, Lund 134961
Archives, Paris 138281
Archives Antiques, Belfast 083478
Archives et Musée de la Littérature, Bruxelles 003286
Archives Fine Books, Brisbane 136819
Archives Museum - Temple Mickve Israel, Savannah 048022
Archives of American Art, Smithsonian Institution, Washington 048882
Archives of American Art Journal, New York 136327
Archives of Asian Art, New York . . . 136328
Archivia Decorative Arts Book Shop, New York 142630
Archivio Delle Arti, Milano 127516
Archivio Segreto Vaticano, Città del Vaticano 049417
Archivio Storico Fiat, Torino 026045
Archivio Storico-Museo dello Studio-Biblioteca, Bologna 023415
Archivo Español de Arte, Madrid . . . 136070
Archivo-Museo Don Alvaro de Bazán, Viso del Marqués 036076
Archivo Museo Histórico Municipal, La Línea de la Concepción 035336
Archivo-Museo San Juan de Dios-Casa de los Pisas, Granada 035242
L'Archivolto, Genova 075436
Archway Books, Falmouth 141606
Archway Gallery, Aberdeen 112473
Archway Gallery, Houston 116269
Arcila Castaño, Alvaro, Medellín . . . 059910
Arcimboldo, Torino 140121
Arckx, Argenteuil 060962
El Arco, Gijón 081121
Arco, Oslo 079415
Arco, Praha 137825
L'Arco del Tempo, Milano 075603
Arco & Haenle, München . 104140, 134213
Arcofi, Paris 099945
Arcola Museum, Arcola 005024
Arcor Restauració, Barcelona 129314
Arcorest, Valencia 129752
Arcos Verlag, Ergolding 133911
The Arctic Bear, Toronto 097217
Arctic Corsair, Kingston-upon-Hull . 039883
Arctic Experience Gallery, Hamilton 096909
d'Arcy, Montréal 058925
Arcy, Philippe d', Lyon 064066
Ardalan, Behzad, Saint-Ouen 067710
Ardavin, Anthony, Atlanta 114846
Ardéco, Avignon 098886
Ardeco, Delft 078140
Ardeco, Fremantle 055839
Ardeco, Versailles 101452
Ardell Burchard, Saint Louis 119174
Ardelt, Frank, Dessau, Anhalt 125454
Ardelt, Herbert, Schlangenbad 104825
Arden, Boston 115139
Arden, West Hollywood 093448
Arden, Woollahra 095415
Arden, C., Hereford 141661
Arden Gallery, Buntingford 112753
Arden Gallery, Henley-in-Arden . . . 084658
Arden Gallery, Henley-in-Arden . . . 113226
Ardengo, Roma 140096
Ardeta, Paris 065430
Ardeta, Paris 124555
Ardies, Jacques Paul Andre, São Paulo 096661
Ardingly International Antiques and Collectors Fair, Ardingly 093909
Arditi, Amsterdam 077780
Arditti, J.L., Christchurch . 084005, 130578
Ardor, Auckland 108296
Ardos, Hoffelt 107389
Ardress House and Farmyard Museum, Annaghmore 038511

Ardrossan Historical Museum, Ardrossan . . . 000749
Ards Art Centre, Newtownards . . . 040585
Ardshiel Gallery, Whiting Bay . . . 114684
Ardustyl, Paris . . . 065431, 124556
Ardy, Bernardino, Genova . . . 140030
Aré, Roma . . . 106487
Area, Houston . . . 089021
Area de Anitua, Madrid . . 081236, 129565
Aremark Historielag, Aremark . . . 030732
Arena, Gent . . . 058169, 137492
Arena, Sofia . . . 096718
Arena, Sofia . . . 096719
Arena Artists Studio, Arena Art and Design Association, Liverpool . . . 054275
Arena International, Taunton . . . 114552
d'Arenberg, Bruxelles . . . 057823
Arend Dieperink Museum, Potgietersrus . . . 034712
Arendal Bymuseum, Arendal . . . 030733
Arendall, Memphis . . . 090053
Het Arendonks Heemmuseum, Arendonk . . . 003197
Arends, Ijmuiden . . . 128731
Arends, Tynaarlo . . . 128849
Arends, Venlo . . . 078830
Arends, Uwe, Witzenhausen . . . 074458
Arends-Kossack, Uwe, Berkatal . . . 069545
Arends & Tammes, Amsterdam . . . 107655
Arendt, München . . . 072638
Arendt, Gerhard, Bielefeld . . . 069816
Arenhövel, Dr. Willmuth, Berlin . . . 133751
Arens, Meppen . . . 104063
Arens, A., Freiburg im Breisgau . . . 070822
Arens, Luis Fernando, München . . . 072639
Arens, Renate, Berlin . . . 069559
Arent, Petra, Lübeck . . . 126238
Arenthon, Paris . . . 099946, 138282
Arentshuis, Stedelijke Musea, Brugge . . . 003262
Arenz, Jürgen & Petra, Bermel . . . 069797
Ares Esmoriz, Luis, A Coruña . . . 129487
Ares Sanat Evi, İstanbul . . . 112272
Ares Vapen & Antikt, Göteborg . . . 081794
Aresco, Breda . . . 128601
Areta, Varna . . . 096761
Areté, Milano . . . 106152
Aretè, Roma . . . 127925
Arete, Zürich . . . 112028
Arethusa, Roma . . . 127926
Arets, Bruxelles . . . 096131
Årets Kunstmesse i Forum, Frederiksberg . . . 093642
Arévalo, Maresa, México . . . 107474
Arfa, Knokke-Heist . . . 058240
Arfaoui, Habib, Paris . . . 138283
ARG Antique, Dubai . . . 083183
Argar, Barcelona . . . 080797
Argar Galería, Almeria . . . 110092
Argauisch Kantonales Weinbaumuseum, Tegerfelden . . . 037622
Arge, Griffith . . . 055919
Argence-Lecaillé, Aurore, Carcassonne . . . 061970
Argenor Numismatique, Paris . . . 065432
Argenson, Paule, Saint-Didier-au-Mont-d'Or . . . 067425
Argent, Bronze & Cuivre, Bordeaux . 124111
Argenterie Abadie, Nice . . . 065030
Argenterie de Turenne, Paris . . . 065433
Argentium, Broughton . . . 112747
Argentum, Double Bay . . . 055754
Argentum Antiques, Coggeshall . . . 084049
Argenville, Louis d', La Rochelle . . . 099403
Argeu, Ananias, Belo Horizonte . . . 123687
Argile Gallery, London . . . 113454
Argiles, Paris . . . 065434
Argo, Athinai . . . 105384
Argo, Knokke-Heist . . . 096318
Argo, Lefkosia . . . 098298
Argo, Warszawa . . . 109088
Argo Gold Mine and Mill Museum, Idaho Springs . . . 044711
Argonaut Book Shop, San Francisco . . . 092727, 142926
L'Argonaute, Cité des Sciences et de l'Industrie, Paris . . . 013550
Les Argonautes, Paris . . . 065435, 138284
Argor, Valenciennes . . . 068687
The Argory, Dungannon . . . 039319
Argos, İstanbul . . . 112273
Argosy, New York . . . 142631
Argosy, Ottawa . . . 137669
Argoud, Jean-Claude, Paris . . . 124557
Argraphie, Montreuil-sous-Bois . . . 133499
Argus, Brugge . . . 096110
Argus, Bruxelles . . . 057824
Argus Livres Anciens, Québec . . . 137679
ARGVS Vereniging van Kunstexperts, Bruxelles . . . 052642
ARGVS Vereniging van Kunstexperts, Knokke-Heist . . . 052641
ARGVS Vereniging van Kunstexperts, Mechelen . . . 052643
Argyle, Goulburn . . . 136922
Argyle Street Galleries, Moss Vale . 056272
Argyll and Sutherland Highlanders Regimental Museum, Stirling . . . 041101
Arhaiologiko Mouseio Thassaloniki, Thessaloniki . . . 021489
Arheološka Zbirka, Budva . . . 034178
Arheološka Zbirka, Metković . . . 007758
Arheološka Zbirka, Nin . . . 007762
Arheološka Zbirka Crne Gore, Podgorica . . . 034239
Arheološka Zbirka i Lapidarij Dr. Grga Novak, Hvar . . . 007724
Arheološka Zbirka Osor, Nerezine . . 007761
Arheološki Muzej, Prizren . . . 034249
Arheološki Muzej Istre, Pula . . . 007776
Arheološki Muzej u Splitu, Split . . . 007798
Arheološki Muzej Zagreb, Zagreb . . 007828
ARHIS, Paris . . . 133513
Arhitekturni Muzej Ljubljana, Ljubljana . . . 034477
Arhitext Design, Bucureşti . . . 136045
Århus Bymuseum, Århus . . . 008804
Aria, Saint-Ouen . . . 067711
Aria Antiques, San Francisco . . . 092728
L'Aria del Tempo, Milano . . . 075604
Ariadne, New York . . . 117600
Ariadne, Stockholm . . . 081923
Ariana, Delft . . . 107886
Arians, Remels . . . 073486
Arians, Horst, Leer . . . 072178
Arians, Horst, Uplengen . . . 126937
Aribaud, C., Cornebarrieu . . . 062484
Arical, Barcelona . . . 110103
Aricchi, Akie, Paris . . . 099947
Ariel, Kraków . . . 108925
Ariel, Paris . . . 099948
Arielle, Paris . . . 065436, 124558
Ariëns Kappers, E.H., Amsterdam . . 140281
Ariental, Bruxelles . . . 057825
Ariental, Gent . . . 058170
Arienti, Franco, Milano . . . 075605
Aries, Dubai . . . 083184
Aries, Grabenstätt . . . 133982
Arieta, Valerie, London . . . 085092
L'Ariete, Bologna . . . 105940
L'Ariete, Padova . . . 106391
Arigoni, Catherine, Paris . . . 065437
Arild's Antikk, Oslo . . . 079416
Arimani, E., Tarragona . . . 110783
Arimon, Järvenpää . . . 137966
Arin, Moskva . . . 080231
Arin, Moskva . . . 080232
Ariodante, New Orleans . . . 117389
Arion Press, San Francisco . . . 135487
Arioso, Stockholm . . . 111000
ARIS, Lund . . . 136108
Arise-Gallery, Washington . . . 093380
Arise-Window to the East, Washington . . . 093381
Aristeuros, Barcelona . . . 140979
Aristocrat Gallery, San Diego . . . 119471
Aristocratz, Bristol . . . 083728
Aristoloches, Grenoble . . . 063048, 099300
Aristos, Getxo . . . 081111
Aristos, Getxo . . . 081112
Aristos, New York . . . 136329
Aristos Broc's, Vannes (Morbihan) . 068714
Aristote, Paris . . . 065438
Arita Toji Bijutsukan, Arita . . . 026418
Arithmeum, Rechnen einst und jetzt, Bonn . . . 016315
Aritza, Bilbao . . . 110269
Ariz, Tucson . . . 120100
Ariz, Coree, Tucson . . . 093203
Arizona Antiques, Tucson . . . 093204
Arizona Artist Guild, Phoenix . . . 054603
Arizona Artists Guild News, Phoenix 136330
Arizona Coins, Phoenix . . . 091718
Arizona Commission on the Arts, Phoenix . . . 054604
Arizona Gallery, Tucson . . . 048627
Arizona Hall of Fame Museum, Phoenix . . . 047004
Arizona Historical Cache, Phoenix . 091719
Arizona Historical Society Museum, Central Arizona Division, Tempe . . . 048516
Arizona Historical Society Museum, Headquarters and Southern Arizona Division, Tucson . . . 048628
Arizona Historical Society Pioneer Museum, Flagstaff . . . 043850
Arizona Mining and Mineral Museum, Phoenix . . . 047005
Arizona Museum For Youth, Mesa . . 045791
Arizona Pastel Artists Association, Glendale . . . 054605
Arizona Science Center, Phoenix . . 047006
Arizona-Sonora Desert Museum, Tucson . . . 048629
Arizona State Capitol Museum, Phoenix . . . 047007
Arizona State Museum, Tucson . . . 048630
Arizona State University Art Museum, Tempe . . . 048517
Arizona Watercolor Association, Phoenix . . . 054606
Arizzi, Giovanni, Parma . . . 076194
Ark Antiques, Bishop's Castle . . . 083540, 130400
Ark Kyoto, Kyoto . . . 077089
Ark-La-Tex Antique and Classic Vehicle Museum, Shreveport . . . 048158
ARK Restoration and Design, New York . . . 132442
Arka, Amsterdam . . . 107656
Arka, Paris . . . 065439
Arka, Vilnius . . . 107359
Arka, Warszawa . . . 079730, 109089
ARKA Kulturwerkstatt, Essen . . . 053030, 102669
Arkada, Gdańsk . . . 108869
Arkada, Wrocław . . . 109211
Arkade, Linz . . . 095649
ARKADE, Münster . . . 139560
Arkade, Zemun . . . 109750
Arkadi Monastery Collection, Rethymnon . . . 021448
Arkadia, Gdańsk . . . 108870
Arkadia, Palermo . . . 106414
Arkadyan, San Francisco . 119586, 142927
Arkaeologisk Museum, Korsør . . . 009001
Arkahna, Nantes . . . 099800
Arkane, Ajaccio . . . 060735, 098802
The Arkansas Arts Center, Little Rock . . . 045342
Arkansas Museum of Natural Resources, Smackover . . . 048202
Arkansas Museum of Science and History - Museum of Discovery, Little Rock 045343
Arkansas Museums Association, Little Rock . . . 054607
Arkansas Post Museum, Gillett . . . 044189
Arkansas Post National Memorial, Gillett . . . 044190
Arkansas State University Art Gallery, Jonesboro . . . 044878
Arkansas State University Museum, Jonesboro . . . 044879
Arkaringa Gallery, Black Rock . . . 094255
Arke Galerie, Dortmund . . . 102392
Arkea, Nice . . . 065031
Arkea Antiques, Bath . . . 083413, 130347
Arkell & Monk, Dorking . . . 084184
Arken Museum of Modern Art, Ishøj 008942
Arkeologisk Museum i Stavanger, Museum of Archaeology Stavanger, Stavanger . . . 031221
Arkeologiskt Museum Vuollerim 6000 år, Vuollerim . . . 036802
Arkeoloji Müzesi, Konya . . . 038129
Arkeoloji Müzesi, Kütahya . . . 038139
Arkeoloji ve Arkeologlar Derneği Istanbul Şubesi, İstanbul . . . 054248
Arkeoloji ve Etnografya Müzesi, Elazıg . . . 038056
Arkeos Arte Precolombino, Bogotá . 098096
Arkesteijn, P.J.M., Delft . . . 078141
Arkhan, Paris . . . 065440
Arkitektur Förlag, Stockholm . . . 134964
Arkitekturmuseet, Stockholm . . . 036614
Arkitekturmuseet, Nasjonalmuseet for Kunst, Oslo . . . 031069
Arklow Maritime Museum, Arklow . 022678
Arkoloji ve Etnografya Müzesi, Edirne . . . 038053
Arkona Lion's Museum, Arkona . . . 005027
Arkos, Clermont-Ferrand . . . 099140
Arkos, Clermont-Ferrand . . . 099141
Arktisk Museum Nanoq, Jakobstad 009613
Arkway, Richard B., New York . . . 142632
The Arkwright Society, Cromford . . 039183
Arkwright Traders, Dunedin . . . 079079
L'Arlecchino, L'Isle-sur-la-Sorgue . 063918
Arlequín, Buenos Aires . . . 136700
Arlequin, Grand-Lancy . . . 111529
Arlequin, Madrid . . . 081237
Arlequin, Paris . . . 065441
Arlequín Antigüedades, Don Torcuato . . . 055260, 123164
Arleston, Flinders . . . 055830
Arli International, New York . . . 117601
Arlinghaus, H., Boxberg, Baden . . . 069968
Arlington, Columbus . . . 088382
Arlington Arts Center, Arlington . . . 041777
Arlington Books, Ottawa . . . 137670
Arlington Court, Arlington . . . 038523
Arlington Heights Historical Museum, Arlington Heights . . . 041782
Arlington Historical Museum, Arlington . . . 041778
Arlington Historical Society, Arlington . . . 041771
Arlington House - The Robert E. Lee Memorial, Arlington . . . 041779
Arlington Mill Museum, Bibury . . . 038697
Arlington Museum, Birmingham . . . 042221
Arlington Museum of Art, Arlington . 041773
Arlington Upholstery and Design, Columbus . . . 131976
ARLIS News-sheet, Bromsgrove . . . 136163
Arlo, Warszawa . . . 079731
Arlogos, Paris . . . 099949
Arlotta, G., Winterthur . . . 082909
Arlt, Maria, Dresden . . . 070307, 125484
Arlt, P., Holdenstedt . . . 103399
Arlt, Peter, Jena . . . 071654
Armada Gallery, Plymouth . . . 114254
Armadale Antique Centre, Armadale, Victoria . . . 055358
Armadale Community Museum, Armadale . . . 038524
Armadale Watch Gallery, Armadale, Victoria . . . 055359
Armadillo, Chicago . . . 142275
Armádní Muzeum Žižkov, Praha . . . 008592
Armagh County Museum, Armagh . 038526
Armand, Nice . . . 065032
Armand, Pittsburgh . . . 118897
Armand, Philippe, Enghien-les-Bains . . . 062775
Ármándia Katonai & Hadtörténeti Régiségek Boltja, Budapest . . . 074665
Armando Museum, Amersfoort . . . 029147

Armando Vitrales, Bogotá 123891
Armandos, Sacramento 132728
Armando's Antiques, Miami 090140
Armanet, Andrée & Marc, Bourgoin-Jallieu 061731
Armarius, Koudum 140469
Armchair Books, Edinburgh 141569
Armchair Bookstore, Portland 142790
Armed Forces Museum, Taipei 007364
Armed Forces of the Philippines Museum, Quezon City 031769
Armed Forces Survey Department Museum, Bangkok 037867
Armeemuseum 'Friedrich der Große', Kulmbach 018437
Armel, Pleudaniel 066852
Armémuseum, Stockholm 036615
Armen, Toronto 097218
Armengau, Patrick, Avignon 120915
Armengaud, Josy, Paris 065442
Armenia Editions, Nyon 135054
Armenian Artistic Union, Cairo 052865
Armenian Cathedral and Museum, Isfahan 022560
Armenian Center for Contemporary Experimental Art, Erevan 094108
Armenian Museum, Jerusalem 031413
Armenian Museum of America, Watertown 048992
Armenjon, Michel, Appenai-sous-Bellême 060936
Armentani, Gaetano, Taranto 128246
Armeria, Mondavio 024787
Armeria Reale, Torino 026046
Les Armes Anciennes, Nice 065033
Armes du Chevalier, Chevry-Cossigny 062288
Les Armes du Chevalier, Paris 065443
Armes & Traditions, Strasbourg . . . 068294
Armetal, Paris 065444
Armfelt Museo, Helsinki 009514
Armi e Bagagli, Torino 076765
Armidale and District Folk Museum, Armidale 000751
Armin Hott, Kandel 103483
Armit, Jenny, Los Angeles 116702
Armit, Jenny, West Hollywood 120372
Armitage Antique Gallery, Chicago .088023, 131880
Armitage Auctions, Launceston . . . 120600
Armitano, Caracas 135528
Armoire Amoureuse, Bollène 061548
Armoire Charolaise, Baron 061212
Armoires and More, Dallas 088461
Armondi, Brescia 075145
Armoni, İstanbul 112274
Armonie, Palermo 076123
Armonie, Paris 099950
Armonie, Roma 076302
Armor, Garsington 130724
Armor Antiquités, Nantes 064896
Armory Art Gallery, Blacksburg 042243
Armory Center for the Arts, Pasadena 046831
Armour Antiques, Indianapolis 089270
Armour-Winston, London . 085093, 130931
The Armoury of Saint James' Military Antiquarians, London 085094
Arms and Armor, Minneapolis 090343
The Arms and Armour Society, London 054276
Arms and Armour Society Journal, London 136164
Arms Collecting, Alexandria Bay . . . 136331
Arms Family Museum of Local History, Youngstown 049359
Arms Gallery Hunters House, Frederiksberg 060226
Armson, Michael, Wilstone 087156
Armstark, Bad Griesbach im Rottal . 069285
Armstark, Richard, Schärding 057300, 123467
Armstrong, Coventry 141540
Armstrong, Fort Worth 088834
Armstrong, Harrogate 084568
Armstrong, Las Vegas 089549
Armstrong, Sandringham 056571
Armstrong, Anthony, Glasgow 113101
Armstrong, Richard Reed, Chicago . 115335
Armstrong Browning Library, Waco . 048809
Armstrong Collection, Olivet College, Art Department, Olivet 046668
Armstrong Gallery, Cornell College, Mount Vernon 046072
Armstrong-Prior, Phoenix 118860
Armstrong-Spallumcheen Museum and Art Gallery, Armstrong 005028
Armurerie Caderot, Berre-l'Etang . . 061372
Armu's Antiques, Montevideo 087304
Army Medical Corps Centre Museum, Lucknow 022235
Army Medical Services Museum, Aldershot 038476
Army Museum, Halifax 005566
Army Museum, Paddington 001361
Army Museum and Fort Copacabana, Rio de Janeiro 004331
Army Museum of Infantry Center, Phachuab Khiri Khan 037918
Army Museum of South Australia, Keswick 001150
Army Museum of Western Australia, Perth 001374
Army Physical Training Corps Museum, Aldershot 038477
Arn, Willy, Lyss 130113
Arnaboldi, Roma 076303
Arnak, Buffalo 115248
Arnau, Barcelona 110104
Arnau, Miami 117019
Arnaud, Florence, Paris . . 065445, 099951, 138285
Arnaud, François, Boulogne-Billancourt 099017
Arnaud-Vannier, Langres 121027
Arnaudin, Laurent, Paris 065446
Arnault, Jean Claude, Stockholm . . 111001
Arnaune-Prim, Beauzelle 120921
Arnaune & Prim, Toulouse 121268
Arndean, London 113455
Arndean, London 113456
Arndt & Partner, Berlin 101779
Arndt Gebr., Elmshorn 102615
Arndt, Dr., Unterleinleiter 074163
Arndt, D., Graal-Müritz 071070
Arndt, Doris, Biberach an der Riß . . 102104
Arndt, Doris, Witten 127026
Arndt, Elisabeth, Bayreuth 101743, 121314
Arndt, Volker, Hamburg 071197
Arndt, Volker, Hamburg 071198
Arne, Rolf, Froland 128988
Arnemann, Gaby, Kamen 103475
Arnheim, Brighton, Victoria 094281
Arnhems Oorlogsmuseum 1940-45, Arnhem 029263
Arnim, Christoph Graf von, Gerabronn 070969, 125720
Arno, Paris 124559
Arno, Raquel, São Paulo 058683
Arnol Blackhouse Museum, Arnol . . 038531
Arnold, Christchurch 140610
Arnold, Frankfurt am Main 121401
Arnold, Rochy-Condé 067188
Arnold, Peter, Prahran 137056
Arnold, Phyllis, Donaghadee 084172, 130638, 141553
Arnold, Roy, Needham Market 086042, 141950
Arnold, Sean, London 085095
Arnold & Co., Susan, Tulsa 093283
Arnold, Willi, Uznach 082870
Arnold Schönberg Center, Wien . . . 002850
Arnold Theiler Museum for African Diseases, Onderstepoort 034687
Arnoldi, Bruxelles 096132, 137424
Arnoldi-Livie, Angelika & Bruce, München 072640, 104141
Arnoldsche Verlagsanstalt, Stuttgart 134406
Arnolfini, Bristol 038855
Arnon, Monique, San Francisco . . . 092729
Arnot, Herbert, New York 117602
Arnot Art Museum, Elmira 043690
Arnoud, Liliane, Bourmont 061733
Arnoux, Paris 099952
Arnoux, Christian, Paris 065447
Arnoux, Jean-Paul, Dun-sur-Auron . 062746
Arnprior and District Museum, Arnprior 005029
Arnus, Evaristo, Barcelona 080798
Aroca Verlag & Galerie, Landsberg am Lech 103822, 134139
Arohonka, Anssi, Helsinki 137935
Arohonka, Mika, Hämeenlinna 137924
Aroma D.D, Ha Noi 120446
Aromda, Paris 099953
Aronow, Louis, San Francisco 119587
Aronowitsch, Stockholm 111002
Arons, J., Brugge 123566
Aronson, Amsterdam 077781
Aronson, Chatswood 055663
Aronson, Frances, Atlanta 114847
Aros Aarhus Kunstmuseum, Århus . 008805
Arossita, Sofia 096720
Around the Clock, Brixham 083753, 130462
Around the Clock, Chicago 131881
Around the Corner, Albuquerque . . . 114767
Around the World Books, San Francisco 142928
Arovell-Galerie, Gosau 095516
Arovell-Kunstzeitschrift, Gosau 135544
Arovell-Verlag für Kunst, Gosau . . . 133072
Aroya, Zaragoza 110878
ARP Museum Bahnhof Rolandseck, Remagen 019789
Arpad Johan, Vezelay 068834
Arpe, Cannes 099059
Arquebus Krigshistorisk Museum, Haugesund 030880
Arqueologia Clasica, Barcelona . . . 080799
Arquivo Histórico e Museu de Canonas Dr. Sezefredo Azambuja Vieira, Canoas 004054
Arrademento Dekorasyon, İstanbul . 136136
Arrademento Mimarlık Tasarım Kültürü Dergisi, İstanbul 136137
Arran Heritage Museum, Brodick . . 038880
The Arrangement, San Antonio 092485
Arrangerie, Antwerpen 123546
Arrantzaleen Museoa, Bermeo 034977
Arranz Gozalo, Loreto, Madrid 081238, 129566
Array, Singapore 080425
Arreda, Simona Marletta, Catania . . 075234
Arrêt sur Image, Bordeaux 098985
Arretini, Giuliano, Firenze 127287
Arretini, Marco, Firenze 075274
Arreton Manor, Arreton 038532
Arribas Parra, Santiago, Valladolid .081687, 129788
Arrighi, Bastelicaccia 061215, 124092
Arrigo, Alice, Zürich 112029
Arrigucci, Daniela, Firenze 140008
Arrivabene, Gilberto, Milano 075606
Arrizabalaga Garcia, Manuel, Córdoba 110312
Arrojo Alfredo, Monica, A Coruña . . 081054
Arrow, Chicago 088024
Arrow, Vijfhuizen 128868
Arrow Rock State Historic Site, Arrow Rock 041785
Arrowmont School of Arts and Crafts, Gatlinburg 051378
Arrowmont School of Arts and Crafts Collection, Gatlinburg 044157
Arroyave, Fernando, Medellín 123930
Arruda, Miguel, Lisboa 079865
Arruda, Virgínia, Brasília 058457
ARS, Bratislava 136063
Ars, Český Krumlov 098347
Ars, Madrid 110437
Ars, Malbork 109029
Ars, Skopje 107421
Ars, Verona 076989
Ars, Wrocław 129125
Ars 2000 - Galerija Krvina, Gorenja Vas 109936, 134894
ARS 6000 Alter Militärring 5, Köln . 071905
Ars Antica, Baden 082106
Ars Antiqua, Bad Abbach 069254
Ars Antiqua, Bruxelles 057826
Ars Antiqua, Genève 082395
Ars Antiqua, Genk 058157
Ars Antiqua, Madrid 129567
Ars Antiqua 2000, Milano 075607
Ars Antiquités, Ars-sur-Formans . . . 060998
Ars Artis, Köttmannsdorf 095627
Ars Artis, Oxford 141980
Ars Boutique, Tallinn 098692
Ars Ceramica, Glen Head 136332
Ars Contemplativa, Basel 111160
Ars Contempora, Bremerhaven 070051
Ars Domus, Düsseldorf 070356
Ars Domus, Krefeld 072064
ars Edition, München 134214
Ars Electronica Center, Linz 002241
Ars Erotica Nova, Verein zur Förderung zeitgenössischer erotischer Kunst, Wien 052504
Ars Felix, Binningen 054168, 135000
Ars-Forum, Jaroslavl 109469
Ars Futura, Zürich 112030
Ars Graphica, Schermbeck 104822
Ars in Fine, Paris 099954
Ars (Iskusstvo Petrograda), Sankt-Peterburg 136052
Ars Islamica, Bruxelles 057827
Ars Italica, Milano 106153
Ars Labor, Lugano 082589, 130091
Ars Labor Restauro, Roma 127927
Ars Libraria, Milano 127517
Ars Libri, Boston 142242
Ars Libri, Madrid 134936, 141026
Ars Ligni, Münchwald . . . 072892, 126491
Ars Liturgica, Maria Laach 072455, 134194, 139464
Ars Longa, Kraków 129028
Ars Longa, Kraków 129029
Ars Longa, Milanówek 109030
Ars Longa, Paris 124560
Ars Longa, Rīga 107316
Ars Millennia, Roma 076304
Ars Mundi, Hannover 134034
Ars Mundi, Timişoara 080189
Ars Nova, Breda 107874
Ars Nova, Innsbruck 057073
Ars nova, Petersberg, Kreis Fulda . . 104600
Ars Nova - Nykytaiteen Museo, Turku 010161
Ars Pictórica, Lisboa 109263
Ars Polona, Warszawa . . . 109090, 134860
Ars Publicita - Galerija Gasspar, Piran 109998
ARS Recup', Nancy 064860
Ars Restaurandi, Roma 127928
Ars Restauro, Sevilla 129727
Ars Temporis, Reifnitz 095708
Ars Temporis, Reims 067053
Ars Vivendi, Grünwald 071134
Ars Vivesco, Québec 097122
Arsa Kunstakademie, Schönenwerd . . 050774, 111894, 135066
d'Arschot & Cie, Bruxelles 057828
Arsenal, Kraków 079620, 140733
Arsenal Antiques, Pittsburgh 091789
Arsenal Gallery, Bialystok 108861
Arsenal Gallery, New York 046293
Arsenal Museum, London 040079
Arsenal/Surrealist Subversion, Evanston 136333
Arsenale Editrice, San Giovanni Lupatoto 134685
Arsenic and Old Lace, Salt Lake City 092417
Arsenik-Schauhütte des Bezirksheimatmuseums Spittal im Pöllatal, Rennweg 002521
Arser, Cellatica 134566
Arsinopia, Saint-Ouen 067712

Arslan, Bilge, Berlin 125163
Arslibri Verlag, Luzern 135041
Arstudio B, Knokke-Heist 096319
Årsunda Viking Museum, Årsunda . 036195
Art, Burgas 096695
Art, Chrudim 098354
Art, Eivissa 110346
Art, Genova 075437
Art, Leeds 113362
Art, Ljubljana 080648
Art, Ljubljana 080649
Art, Ljubljana 109948
Art, Ljubljana 109949
Art, Ljubljana 129285
Art, Ljubljana 129286
Art, London 113457
Art, Lublin 109025
Art, Maribor 080660, 109983
Art, Mińsk Mazowiecki 109031
Art, Silsden 114436
Art È, Torino 128254
Art, Venezia 106723
Art, Venezia 106724
Art, Warszawa 109091
Art, Das Kunstmagazin, Hamburg . . 135741
Art 11, Paris 099955
Art 123, New York 117603
Art-1900, Berlin 069560
Art 1930 Déco, Menton 064489
Art-2, Singapore 109755
Art 2001, Lauenburg 072165
Art 2001, Lauenburg 103841
Art 204, Paris 099956, 133514
ART 21, Alfortville 098817
Art 3, Paris 124561
Art 3, Valence (Drôme) 101408
Art 36, Sofia 096721
art 4 art, halle für kunst, Küsnacht . 111597
Art 4 Association, Caen 099045
Art 4 Business, London 113458
Art 4 Business, Philadelphia 118730
Art 4 d, Bangkok 136133
Art 4 Less, Tampa 120020
Art 4 U, Banbury 112550
Art 4 Uz, York 114747
Art 45, Montréal 096966
Art 47 Diffusion, Nogentel 065214
Art 6, Richmond 119095
Art 75, Paris 099957
Art 77, Auxerre 061096
Art 77, Paris 099958
Art 80, Houston 132097
Art 800, Miami 117020
Art 86, Poitiers 101013
L'Art a la Page, Paris 099959
Art à l'Affiche, Pessac 101002
Art a Motive, Minneapolis 117234
Art A2Z, Woollahra 095416
Art ab dä Gass, Haus zum Heidenkreis 333, Steckborn 037600
Art Ability, Dallas 115826
Art Academy of Cincinnati, Cincinnati 051137
Art Academy of Los Angeles, Sherman Oaks 052178
Art Access, Columbus 115755
Art Action (Art Galleries & Dealers), Singapore 109756
Art Actualité, Megève 064460
Art Actuel, Nogent-sur-Marne 099876
Art Actuel, Paris 099960
Art Advice Corporate, New York . . . 117604
Art Advisory Group, New York 117605
Art Advisory Services, New York . . . 117606
Art Affair, Las Vegas 116602
Art Affair, Torquay 114582
Art Affaire, Sorrento 095196
Art Affairs, Amsterdam 107657
Art Africa, Montréal 096967
Art Africa, New York 117607
Art Agencies International, Den Haag 107900
Art Agents Gallery, Hamburg 103088
Art Agentur Köln, Köln 103582
Art-Akademija, Moskva . . 080233, 109489, 129234
Art Alcove, Farmington 116122
Art & All That Jazz, Saskatoon 097187
Art Allée Antiquités, Vence 068750, 125012
Art Alley, Birmingham 115095
Art Alley, Houston 116270
Art Alliance, New York 117608
Art Alliance Bulletin, Philadelphia . . 136334
Art Alliance Philadelphia, Philadelphia 054608
Art Almanac, Sydney 095269
Art Almanac, Sydney 135537
Art Alp Décor, Chambéry 099105
Art Alt Praunheim, Frankfurt am Main 133938
Art Alternatives, Hoboken 136335
Art Ancien, Basel 082120
L'Art Ancien, Bordeaux 061581
Art Ancien, Orléans 099888
L'Art Ancien, Québec 097123
l'Art Ancien, Rabat 077688
Art Ancien, Roma 076305
Art and Antique Centre, Bangkok . .083091, 112227, 122375
Art and Antique Dealers League of America, New York 054609
Art and Antique Furniture, San Francisco 092730
Art and Antique Planet, Los Angeles 089691
Art and Antique Restorations, Oklahoma City 132576
Art and Antique World, Los Angeles 089692
Art and Applied Design Department, Lane Community College, Eugene 051308
Art and Architecture, Forest Row . . 054277
Art and Architecture, London 136165
Art and Architecture Department, Daley College, Chicago 051111
Art and Architecture Department, Oakton Community College, Des Plaines . 051256
Art and Architecture Exhibition Space, San Francisco 047850
Art and Art, Dallas 115827
Art and Art Education Department, Alabama A & M University, Normal 051851
Art and Art History Department, College of Saint Catherine, Saint Paul 052083
Art and Art History Department, Drury University, Springfield 052208
Art and Art History Department, Gustavus Adolphus College, Saint Peter . . . 052091
Art and Art History Department, Hamilton College, Clinton 051164
Art and Art History Department, Kalamazoo College, Kalamazoo 051539
Art and Art History Department, Loyola Marymount University, Los Angeles 051630
Art and Art History Department, New England College, Henniker 051457
Art and Art History Department, Providence College, Providence 047250
Art and Art History Department, Providence College, Providence 051992
Art and Art History Department, Saint Mary's College of Maryland, Saint Mary's City 052082
Art and Art History Department, University of California Davis, Davis 051229
Art and Art History Department, University of Richmond, Richmond 052022
Art and Art History Department, Virginia Polytechnic Institute and State University, Blacksburg 050991
Art and Arts, Torino 106656
Art and Arts Editeur, Bordeaux 133454, 138034
Art and Auction Magazine, New York 136336
Art and Charity, San Antonio 119393
Art and Clay Designs, Tucson 120101
Art and Creation, Jaipur, Rajasthan 105720
Art and Culture, Dubai 083185
Art and Culture Center of Hollywood, Hollywood 044579
Art and Design, Chicago 115336
Art and Design Department, Adrian College, Adrian 050869
Art and Design Department, Brenau University, Gainesville 051371
Art and Design Department, Columbia College Chicago, Chicago 051112
Art and Design Department, Lynn University, Boca Raton 051002
Art and Design Gallery, Hatfield . . . 039695
Art and Frame, İstanbul 112275
Art and Frame Direct, Dallas 115828
Art and Frame Direct, Los Angeles . 116703
Art and Frame Exhibition, Jeddah . . 080356
Art and Frame Expo, Dallas 115829
Art and Frame Gallery, Kansas City . 116554
Art and Frame Gallery, Saint Louis . 119175
Art and Frame Gallery, Saint Louis . 119176
Art and Frame Gallery @ Creve Coeur, Saint Louis 119177
Art and Frame Gallery @ Manchester, Saint Louis 119178
Art and Frame Workes, Cincinnati . 115599
Art and Frame World, Fort Worth . . 116131
Art and Framing Express, Washington 120252
Art and Framing Gallery, El Paso . . . 116100
Art and Framing Solutions, San Diego 119472
Art and Fun, Cleveland 115681
Art and Gold, Haifa 105904
Art and Humanities Department, Abraham Baldwin Agricultural College, Tifton 052262
Art and Humanities Department, Kennedy-King College, Chicago 051113
Art and Humanities Department, Malcolm X College, Chicago 051114
Art and Humanities Department, Olive-Harvey College, Chicago 051115
Art and Humanities Department, Truman College, Chicago 051116
Art and Humanities Department, Wright College, Chicago 051117
Art and Industrie, Armadale, Victoria 094159
Art and Industry Antiques, Auckland 078919
Art and Interior Design Program, Lasell College, Auburndale 050929
Art and Languages Department, College of the Redwoods, Eureka 051311
Art and Local History Collections, Mackay 001200
Art and Market, Chengdu 135644
Art and More, Columbus 115756
Art and Photography Department, Hartnell College, Salinas 052098
Art and Picture Works Gallery, Bowral 094272
Art and Print, Los Angeles 116704
Art and Sciences Division, Huron College, Huron 051492
Art and Soul, Saint Louis 119179
Art and Soul Furniture, Gerringong . 055875
Art and Soul Gallery, Milwaukee . . . 117161
Art and Technology Department, University of Maryland Eastern Shore, Princess Anne 051988
Art and the Artist, Fresno 116170
Art and Wine Birmingham, Birmingham 115096
Art Angels, Amsterdam 107658
Art Angle, Johannesburg 080699
Art Antiguidades, Belo Horizonte . . 058405
Art & Antik, Saarbrücken 073624
Art-Antik Galerie Black Box, Dresden 070308
Art Antique, Hamburg 071199
Art Antique, Košice 080618
Art Antique, Lindlar 072272
Art & Antique Essen, Essen 093708
Art & Antique Wiesbaden, Wiesbaden 093709
Art & Antiques, Atlanta 136337
Art & Antiques and Bridge Miniatures, Eton 084339, 130689
Art, Antiques and World Imports, Cincinnati 088210
Art-Antiquite, Bruxelles 057829
Art Antiquités Artisanat, Jugon-lès-Lacs 063264
Art Antyk, Warszawa 129076
Art Appeal, München 072641
Art Appraisal Company, Tulsa 120181
Art Approach, Kangaroo Ground . . . 056030
Art Aqua, Wien 057370, 095789
Art & Archival, Queanbeyan 123296
Art Arena Gallery, Wollongong 095404
Art Around Gallery, Philadelphia . . . 118731
Art asap, New York 117609
Art Asiatique, Marseille 064313
Art Aspects Gallery, Lismore 094740
Art Assets, New York 117610
Art Associates, Hawthorn, Victoria . 094620
Art Associates, New York 117611
Art Association of Harrisburg, Harrisburg 044441
Art Association of Harrisburg, Harrisburg 051442, 054610
Art Association of Jacksonville, Jacksonville 054611
Art Association of Richmond, Richmond 054612
Art at Buck Fizz, Suffolk Park 095236
Art at Eight, London 096938
Art at Home, Washington 120253
Art at Linden Gate, Yarra Glen 095446
Art at Work, Greenford 113155
Art Atelier Aquatinta, Lenzburg 111639
Art Atelier Galleries, Hawthorn, Victoria 094621, 123237
Art Athina, Athinai 093750
Art Attack, Cleveland 115682
The Art Attack, Jacksonville 116507
Art Attack, Manawatu 108489
Art Attack, Paraparaumu 108538
Art Attacks Too, New Orleans 117390
Art Attract, O'Connor 095001
Art Auction, Milano 121696
Art & Australia, Saint Leonards 135538
Art Authentique Asiatique, Lausanne 082529
Art Authority, Chicago 115337
Art Authority, Chicago 115338
Art Avenue, Toulouse 101329
Art Avenue Magazine, Vancouver . . 135622
Art Avenues, New York 117612
Art Bank, London 096939
Art Bank, Philadelphia 118732
Art Bank, Rosebery 056550
Art Bar, Albuquerque 114768
Art Baraka, Pamplona 110715
Art Barn, Washington 120254
Art Base, Singapore 109757
Art Base Book Research, Kitzingen . 139326
Art Basel Miami Beach, Miami Beach 093965
Art Beat Gallery, Louisville 116925
Art Beat International, Boston 115140
Art Beatus, Hong Kong 097750
Art Beatus, Vancouver 097412
Art Best, Saint-Ouen 067713
Art Bodensee, Dornbirn 093576
Art & Book, Hamburg 103089
The Art Book, Oxford 136166
Art Book Company, Taipei 133393
Art & Book Edition, Hamburg 133996
Art Book Services, Woodbridge . . . 142167
The Art Book Studio, Delhi 134511
Art Book Survey, London 135178
Art Books International, London . . . 135179
Art Books of London, London 141749
Art Boutique, Braintree 112692
Art Brokering, Los Angeles 116705
Art Brush, Saint George's 096433
Art Bubamara, Beograd 109683
The Art Bug, Norwich 114160
Art-Buks, Moskva 140899
Art Bulletin, New York 136338
Art Bureau NZ, Auckland 078920

Art Bureau & Werkstatt, Lamspringe 103817, 134137
Art Business News, Cleveland 136339
Art Business Today, London 135180, 136167
Art by Design, Farmington 116123
Art by Design, Houston 116271
Art by God, Dallas 115830
Art by God, Miami 117021
Art by Nature, Tulsa 093284
Art by the Sea, Auckland 108297
Art by Will, Philadelphia 118733
Art Byte, New York 136340
Art Caballero, Barcelona 080800
Art Cadre, Paris 099961
Art Cadre Dauphine, Paris 099962
Art Calendar, Upper Fairmount 136341
Art Cannon Gallery, Montréal 005907
Art Capital Group Gallery, New York 117613
Art Care, Singapore 129257
Art Care and Conservation, Dunedin 108424, 128932
Art Care Professional, Ellwangen . . 070540
Art Carnival, Toronto 059139
Art Casino 6000 Römer Str 85, Köln 071906
Art Cellar Exchange, San Diego . . . 119473
The Art Center, Bangkok 037868
The Art Center, Jeddah 080357
The Art Center, Mount Clemens . . . 046052
d'Art Center, Norfolk 118606
Art Center, Porto Alegre 058484
Art Center at Fuller Lodge, Los Alamos 045405
Art Center College of Design, Pasadena 051917
Art Center Gallery, Central Missouri State University, Warrensburg 048863
Art Center In Hargate, Saint Paul's School, Concord 043123
Art Center, Instituto Centro de Arte, Lima 053971
Art Center Lavradio, Rio de Janeiro 058546
Art Center of Battle Creek, Battle Creek 042054
Art Center of South Florida, Miami Beach 045823
The Art Center of Waco, Waco 048810
Art Center Sarasota, Sarasota 047997
Art Centr Puškinskaja 10, Sankt-Peterburg 033726
Art Centre, Barcelona 110105
Art Centre, Barcelona 110106
Art Centre, East London 110041
Art Centre, Haifa 022913
Art Centre, Kathmandu 107574
Art Centre, Stellenbosch 080748
Art Cetera Gallery of Memphis, Memphis 116974
Art Channel, Sendai 106990
L'Art Chez Soi, Baerenthal 061161
Art Chi, Düsseldorf 070357
Art Chicago, Chicago 093966
Art China, Shanghai 135645
Art Circle, Amsterdam . . . 077782, 107659
Art-Cite, La Chaux-de-Fonds 111344
Art Classics in Oil, New York 117614
Art-Clinique, Bruxelles 123572
Art Clipper, Helsinki 060509, 098713
Art Club, Roma 053725
Art Clubs of Omaha and Bellevue, Omaha 054613
Art & Co, Warszawa 079732
Art Co-Ordinates, Subiaco 056643
Art Coko, New York 117615
Art Collage, Khorram-Abaad University, Khorram-Abaad 050336
Art Collection, Acton 000697
Art Collection, Rotterdam 078697
Art Collection, San Francisco 119588
Art Collection, Stirling 041102
Art Collection Canada, Toronto 097219
Art Collection International, Amsterdam 077783
Art Collections, Tulsa 120182
Art Collections Outlet, Miami 117022
Art Collective, Minneapolis 117235
Art Collective Gallery, San Francisco 119589
Art Collector, Pisa 076239
Art Collector, San Diego 119474
Art Collector, Taupo 079254
Art Cologne, Internationaler Kunstmarkt, Köln 093710
Art & Com, Bruxelles 096133
Art Com, Paris 133515
Art Com, San Francisco 136342
Art Comes to Life, Milwaukee 117162
Art & Communication, Paris 099963, 121109, 133516, 138286
Art & Company, Amsterdam 077784
Art Company, Cincinnati 115600
Art Company, Eindhoven 107993
Art Company, Gütersloh 103031
Art Company, Pretoria 080729
Art Company, Tucson 120102
Art Company, Virginia Beach 120213
Art Company the Art Gallery, Edmonton 096860
Art Compass, Wellington 108609
Art Complex Museum, Duxbury . . . 043549
Art Concept, Amsterdam 077785
Art Concept, Enghien-les-Bains . . . 062776
Art & Concept, Frankfurt am Main . 102743
Art Concept, Nantes 064897, 099801
Art Concept, Paris 099964
Art Concepts, Berlin 069561
Art Concorde, Paris 099965, 133517
Art Conexion, Sabadell 110726
The Art Connection Eton, Eton 113031
Art Conseil, Paris 099966
Art Conseil & Expertise, Paris 065448
Art Conservation, Küsnacht 130057
Art Conservation, Vlaardingen 128869
Art Conservation Alliance, Chicago .054614, 131882
Art Conservation and Restoration, Cleveland 131951
Art Conservation Associates, New York 132443
Art Conservation Framers, Melbourne 123264
Art Conservation Research Foundation, New York 132444
Art Conservation Resource Center, Boston 131842
Art Conservation Service, Boston . . 131843
Art Consultant, Los Angeles 116706
Art Consulting, Praha 098414
Art Contact, London 113459
Art Contact, Marlborough 114060
Art Contacts, Maitland 110066
Art Corporation, London 113460
Art Cottage, Louisville 116926
Art Criticism, Stony Brook 136343
Art Critics' Association, Moskva . . . 054017
Art Cru Muséum, Bordeaux 010875
Art & Cuadros, Lima 079540
The Art Cube, Düsseldorf 070358
Art Cult Center - Tabakmuseum, Wien 002851
Art & Cultural Alliance, Johannesburg 110045
Art d'Aimer, Castillon-la-Bataille . . 062022
Art Dais, Hyderabad 105693
Art Dallas, Dallas 115831
Art d'Antan, Grenoble 063049
Art Data, London 135181
Art de Asia, San Francisco 092731
Art de Basse Normandie, Caen 135685
Art de Chine, Nice 065034
Art de la Chine et du Japon, Paris . 065449
Art de l'Enfance, Marcellaz-Albanais 012884
Art de Vivre, Carcassonne 061971
Art de Vivre, Carcassonne 061972
L'Art de Vivre, Hautefort 099326
Art de Vivre, L'Isle-sur-la-Sorgue . . 063919
l'Art de Vivre, New York 090695
L'Art de Vivre, Vevey 082878
Art Dealers Association of America, New York 054615
Art Dealers Association of California, Los Angeles 054616
Art Dealers Association of Canada, Association des Marchands d'Art du Canada, Toronto 052724
Art Dec, Bourg-Saint-Bernard 061714, 124155
Art Deco, Berlin 069562
Art Deco, Bruxelles 057830
Art-Deco, Disentis 082342, 111384
Art Decò, Genova 127432
Art Dèco, Kraków 079621
Art Dèco, Kraków . 079622, 108926, 129030
Art Deco, Mainz 103996
Art Deco, München 072642
Art Deco, München 072643
Art Deco, Oława 079681
Art Deco, Poznań 109042
Art Deco, Santiago de Chile 059499
Art & Deco, Warszawa 109092
Art-Deco, Warszawa 129077
Art-Deco, Zürich 082938
Art Déco 1930-1950, Nice 065035
Art Deco-Art Nouveau, Bruxelles . . 057831
Art Deco Collections, Oakland 091406
Art Deco en zo, Apeldoorn 078030
Art Deco en Zo, Hilversum 078532
Art Deco Etc, Brighton 083684
Art Deco Français, San Francisco . . 092732
Art Deco - Galerie Mili Vávrové, Praha 060107, 098415
Art Deco Gallery, Roma 076306
Art-Deco-House, Breda 078080
Art Deco Metropolis, Stuttgart 073955
Art Deco Society New York, New York 054617
Art Deco - Starožitnosti, Praha 060108
Art & Decor, Travemünde 074080
Art & Decoration, Breda 078081
Art & Decoration, Praha 093635
Art & Decoration, Venlo 078831
Art Decoy Gallery, Holt, Norfolk . . . 113256
Art d'elite, Ortenberg, Baden 073223
d'Art Demain, Broken Hill 094301
Art Department, Kwa Dlangezwa . . 050703
Art Department, San Diego 119475
Art Department, Abilene Christian University, Abilene 050864
Art Department, Acadia University, Wolfville 049835
Art Department, Agnes Scott College, Decatur 051238
Art Department, Alabama Southern Community College, Monroeville . 051738
Art Department, Alabama State University, Montgomery 051744
Art Department, Albertus Magnus College, New Haven 051790
Art Department, Alice Lloyd College, Pippa Passes 051952
Art Department, Allegany Community College, Cumberland 051214
Art Department, Allen County Community College, Iola 051504
Art Department, Alverno College, Milwaukee 051716
Art Department, Alvin Community College, Alvin 050891
Art Department, Amarillo College, Amarillo 050892
Art Department, Ancilla College, Donaldson 051264
Art Department, Anderson University, Anderson 050900
Art Department, Angelo State University, San Angelo 052103
Art Department, Anoka Ramsey Community College, Coon Rapids 051199
Art Department, Aquinas College, Grand Rapids 051402
Art Department, Ashland College, Ashland 050913
Art Department, Augsburg College, Minneapolis 051722
Art Department, Augustana College, Sioux Falls 052186
Art Department, Aurora University, Aurora 050932
Art Department, Averett College, Danville 051226
Art Department, Baker University, Baldwin City 050941
Art Department, Bakersfield College, Bakersfield 050939
Art Department, Baldwin-Wallace College, Berea 050972
Art Department, Barton College, Wilson 052389
Art Department, Bay de Noc Community College, Escanaba 051306
Art Department, Belhaven College, Jackson 051513
Art Department, Belleville Area College, Belleville 050961
Art Department, Bellevue College, Bellevue 050962
Art Department, Bellevue Community College, Bellevue 050963
Art Department, Benedictine College, Atchison 050915
Art Department, Berea College, Berea 050971
Art Department, Berry College, Mount Berry 051757
Art Department, Bethany Lutheran College, Mankato 051673
Art Department, Big Bend Community College, Moses Lake 051756
Art Department, Birmingham-Southern College, Birmingham 050987
Art Department, Black Hawk College, Moline 051734
Art Department, Black Hills State University, Spearfish 052200
Art Department, Bluefield State College, Bluefield 051001
Art Department, Boise State University, Boise 051003
Art Department, Bowling Green State University, Huron 051491
Art Department, Brazosport College, Lake Jackson 051575
Art Department, Briar Cliff University, Sioux City 052184
Art Department, Bridgewater College, Bridgewater 051029
Art Department, Bridgewater State College, Bridgewater 051028
Art Department, Bronx Community College, Bronx 051033
Art Department, Brookdale Community College, Lincroft 051611
Art Department, Brooklyn College, Brooklyn 051038
Art Department, Butler County Community College, El Dorado 051290
Art Department, Caldwell College, Caldwell 051059
Art Department, California Baptist College, Riverside 052030
Art Department, California Lutheran University, Thousand Oaks 052260
Art Department, California Polytechnic State University Pomona, Pomona 051969
Art Department, California State University, Carson 051080
Art Department, California State University,Chico, Chico 051133
Art Department, California State University Hayward, Hayward 051454
Art Department, California State University Long Beach, Long Beach 051622
Art Department, California State University Los Angeles, Los Angeles 051631
Art Department, Calvin College, Grand Rapids 051403
Art Department, Cameron University, Lawton 051596
Art Department, Cape Cod Community College, West Barnstable 052349
Art Department, Capitol Community Technical College, Hartford 051446

Art Department, Cardinal Stritch College, Milwaukee . . . 051717
Art Department, Carlow College, Pittsburgh . . . 051954
Art Department, Carroll College, Waukesha . . . 052339
Art Department, Carson-Newman College, Jefferson City . . . 051529
Art Department, Carthage College, Kenosha . . . 051546
Art Department, Castleton State College, Castleton . . . 051082
Art Department, Catonsville Community College, Catonsville . . . 051083
Art Department, Cedar Crest College, Allentown . . . 050885
Art Department, Central Missouri State University, Warrensburg . . . 052325
Art Department, Central Piedmont Community College, Charlotte . . . 051097
Art Department, Central University of Iowa, Pella . . . 051922
Art Department, Central Wyoming College, Riverton . . . 052034
Art Department, Cerritos College, Norwalk . . . 051863
Art Department, Chaffey Community College, Rancho Cucamonga . . . 052011
Art Department, Chapman University, Orange . . . 051890
Art Department, Citrus College, Glendora . . . 051388
Art Department, City College of New York, New York . . . 051809
Art Department, Clackamas Community College, Oregon City . . . 051895
Art Department, Clarion University of Pennsylvania, Clarion . . . 051147
Art Department, Cleveland State University, Cleveland . . . 051155
Art Department, Clinton Community College, Plattsburgh . . . 051963
Art Department, Cochise College, Douglas . . . 051265
Art Department, Coffeyville Community College, Coffeyville . . . 051169
Art Department, Coker College, Hartsville . . . 051448
Art Department, Colby College, Waterville . . . 052338
Art Department, Colby-Sawyer College, New London . . . 051797
Art Department, College of Lake County, Grayslake . . . 051407
Art Department, College of Mount Saint Joseph, Cincinnati . . . 051138
Art Department, College of Notre Dame of Maryland, Baltimore . . . 050942
Art Department, College of Saint Benedict, Saint Joseph . . . 052071
Art Department, College of Saint Elizabeth, Morristown . . . 051754
Art Department, College of Saint Mary, Omaha . . . 051884
Art Department, College of Southern Idaho, Twin Falls . . . 052285
Art Department, College of the Canyons, Valencia . . . 052302
Art Department, College of the Desert, Palm Desert . . . 051911
Art Department, College of the Siskiyous, Weed . . . 052346
Art Department, Colorado State University, Fort Collins . . . 051344
Art Department, Columbia Basin College, Pasco . . . 051919
Art Department, Columbia College, Columbia . . . 051179
Art Department, Community College of Allegheny County, Monroeville . . . 051739
Art Department, Compton Community College, Compton . . . 051197
Art Department, Concordia College, Bronxville . . . 051036
Art Department, Concordia College, Moorhead . . . 051749
Art Department, Concordia College, Seward . . . 052172
Art Department, Connecticut College, New London . . . 051796
Art Department, Cornell College, Mount Vernon . . . 051762
Art Department, County College of Morris, Randolph Township . . . 052012
Art Department, Cuesta College, San Luis Obispo . . . 052128
Art Department, Culver-Stockton College, Canton . . . 051070
Art Department, Daemen College, Amherst . . . 050898
Art Department, Dana College, Blair 050993
Art Department, Davidson College, Davidson . . . 051228
Art Department, DePauw University, Greencastle . . . 051411
Art Department, Des Moines Area Community College, Boone . . . 051005
Art Department, Doane College, Crete . . . 051212
Art Department, Dominican College of Blauvelt, Orangeburg . . . 051892
Art Department, Dominican University of California, San Rafael . . . 052134
Art Department, Drake University, Des Moines . . . 051254
Art Department, Earlham College, Richmond . . . 052020
Art Department, East Central College, Union . . . 052289
Art Department, East Central University, Ada . . . 050868
Art Department, East Los Angeles College, Monterey Park . . . 051742
Art Department, East Tennessee State University, Johnson City . . . 051533
Art Department, Eastern Arizona College, Thatcher . . . 052258
Art Department, Eastern Connecticut State University, Willimantic . . . 052382
Art Department, Eastern Iowa Community College, Clinton . . . 051161
Art Department, Eastern Kentucky University, Richmond . . . 052021
Art Department, Eastern Michigan University, Ypsilanti . . . 052415
Art Department, Eastern Wyoming College, Torrington . . . 052266
Art Department, Eastfield College, Mesquite . . . 051697
Art Department, Eckerd College, Saint Petersburg . . . 052092
Art Department, Edinboro University of Pennsylvania, Edinboro . . . 051284
Art Department, Elmhurst College, Elmhurst . . . 051298
Art Department, Everett Community College, Everett . . . 051316
Art Department, Feather River Community College, Quincy . . . 052002
Art Department, Florida Community College at Jacksonville, Jacksonville . . . 051519
Art Department, Fontbonne University, Saint Louis . . . 052073
Art Department, Fort Lewis College, Durango . . . 051274
Art Department, Franklin and Marshall College, Lancaster . . . 051582
Art Department, Franklin College, Franklin . . . 051355
Art Department, Franklin Pierce College, Rindge . . . 052025
Art Department, Fresno City College, Fresno . . . 051361
Art Department, Friends University, Wichita . . . 052370
Art Department, Garden City Community College, Garden City . . . 051375
Art Department, Gaston College, Dallas . . . 051220
Art Department, Gavilan College, Gilroy . . . 051385
Art Department, Georgetown College, Georgetown . . . 051382
Art Department, Georgia College, Milledgeville . . . 051714
Art Department, Goshen College, Goshen . . . 051397
Art Department, Goucher College, Baltimore . . . 050943
Art Department, Graceland University, Lamoni . . . 051580
Art Department, Grambling State University, Grambling . . . 051398
Art Department, Grand Canyon University, Phoenix . . . 051946
Art Department, Grand Rapids Community College, Grand Rapids . . . 051404
Art Department, Grand View College, Des Moines . . . 051255
Art Department, Grayson County College, Denison . . . 051245
Art Department, Green River Community College, Auburn . . . 050928
Art Department, Greenfield Community College, Greenfield . . . 051413
Art Department, Guilford College, Greensboro . . . 051414
Art Department, Hagerstown Junior College, Hagerstown . . . 051430
Art Department, Hannibal La Grange College, Hannibal . . . 051439
Art Department, Harold Washington College, Chicago . . . 051118
Art Department, Hartwick College, Oneonta . . . 051887
Art Department, Haskell Indian Nations University, Lawrence . . . 051591
Art Department, Hastings College, Hastings . . . 051449
Art Department, Henry Ford Community College, Dearborn . . . 051236
Art Department, Herbert H. Lehman College CUNY, Bronx . . . 051034
Art Department, Hesston College, Hesston . . . 051459
Art Department, Hibbing Community College, Hibbing . . . 051460
Art Department, Highland Community College, Freeport . . . 051360
Art Department, Hiram College, Hiram . . . 051466
Art Department, Holy Names College, Oakland . . . 051867
Art Department, Houghton College, Houghton . . . 051476
Art Department, Housatonic Community and Technical College, Bridgeport . . . 051027
Art Department, Hunter College, New York . . . 051810
Art Department, Huntington College, Huntington . . . 051486
Art Department, Imperial Valley College, Imperial . . . 051496
Art Department, Indiana Wesleyan University, Marion . . . 051680
Art Department, Iowa Wesleyan College, Mount Pleasant . . . 051759
Art Department, Iowa Western Community College, Council Bluffs . . . 051208
Art Department, Jacksonville State University, Jacksonville . . . 051518
Art Department, James H. Faulkner Community College, Bay Minette . 050957
Art Department, Jamestown College, Jamestown . . . 051527
Art Department, Jefferson Community College, Watertown . . . 052337
Art Department, Jefferson Davis Community College, Brewton . . . 051026
Art Department, Jersey City State College, Jersey City . . . 051530
Art Department, John Brown University, Siloam Springs . . . 052181
Art Department, Jones County Junior College, Ellisville . . . 051297
Art Department, Kansas State University, Manhattan . . . 051670
Art Department, Kansas Wesleyan University, Salina . . . 052097
Art Department, Kentucky Wesleyan College, Owensboro . . . 051906
Art Department, Kenyon College, Gambier . . . 051374
Art Department, Kingsborough Community College, Brooklyn . . . 051039
Art Department, Knox College, Galesburg . . . 051373
Art Department, La Grange College, La Grange . . . 051563
Art Department, La Sierra University, Riverside . . . 052031
Art Department, Lackawanna Junior College, Scranton . . . 052156
Art Department, Lake City Community College, Lake City . . . 051572
Art Department, Lake Erie College, Painesville . . . 051909
Art Department, Lake Tahoe Community College, South Lake Tahoe . . . 052193
Art Department, Lamar University, Beaumont . . . 050959
Art Department, Laney College, Oakland . . . 051868
Art Department, Le Moyne College, Syracuse . . . 052235
Art Department, Lenoir Community College, Kinston . . . 051554
Art Department, Lewis and Clark College, Portland . . . 051975
Art Department, Lewis and Clark Community College, Godfrey . . . 051391
Art Department, Lewis-Clark State College, Lewiston . . . 051600
Art Department, Lincoln College, Lincoln . . . 051608
Art Department, Lindenwood University, Saint Charles . . . 052068
Art Department, Linfield College, McMinnville . . . 051650
Art Department, Linn Benton Community College, Albany . . . 050877
Art Department, Long Island University - Brooklyn Campus, Brooklyn . . . 051040
Art Department, Longwood College, Farmville . . . 051329
Art Department, Lorain County Community College, Elyria . . . 051301
Art Department, Loras College, Dubuque . . . 051270
Art Department, Los Angeles City College, Los Angeles . . . 051632
Art Department, Los Angeles Harbor College, Wilmington . . . 052385
Art Department, Los Angeles Valley College, Valley Glen . . . 052306
Art Department, Lourdes College, Sylvania . . . 052234
Art Department, Lower Columbia College, Longview . . . 051625
Art Department, Luther College, Decorah . . . 051240
Art Department, Lutheran Brethren Schools, Fergus Falls . . . 051333
Art Department, Lynchburg College, Lynchburg . . . 051647
Art Department, McLean Arts Center, McLean . . . 051649
Art Department, MacMurray College, Jacksonville . . . 051522
Art Department, McMurry College, Abilene . . . 050865
Art Department, Macomb Community College, Warren . . . 052324
Art Department, McPherson College, McPherson . . . 051654
Art Department, Madonna College, Livonia . . . 051617
Art Department, Manchester College, North Manchester . . . 051855
Art Department, Mansfield University, Mansfield . . . 051675
Art Department, Marian College, Fond Du Lac . . . 051341
Art Department, Marietta College, Marietta . . . 051677
Art Department, Mars Hill College, Mars Hill . . . 051682
Art Department, Marylhurst University, Marylhurst . . . 051684
Art Department, Marywood University, Scranton . . . 052157
Art Department, Mercer University, Macon . . . 051652

Art Department, Meredith College, Raleigh 052007
Art Department, Merritt College, Oakland 051869
Art Department, Mesa State College, Grand Junction 051400
Art Department, Methodist College, Fayetteville 051331
Art Department, Metropolitan State College, Denver 051248
Art Department, Miami University, Oxford 051908
Art Department, Midland College, Midland 051711
Art Department, Midway College, Midway 051712
Art Department, Millersville State College, Millersville 051715
Art Department, Millikin University, Decatur 051239
Art Department, Minnesota State University, Mankato, Mankato 051674
Art Department, Miracosta College, Oceanside 051873
Art Department, Mississippi Gulf Coast Community College, Gautier 051379
Art Department, Mississippi State University, Mississippi State 051729
Art Department, Missouri Western State College, Saint Joseph 052072
Art Department, Monmouth College, Monmouth 051735
Art Department, Monroe Community College, Rochester 052039
Art Department, Montana State University Billings, Billings 050984
Art Department, Montgomery County Community College, Blue Bell . . . 050999
Art Department, Morehead State University, Morehead 051752
Art Department, Morningside College, Sioux City 052185
Art Department, Mount Marty College, Yankton 052409
Art Department, Mount Mary College, Milwaukee 051718
Art Department, Mount Mercy College, Cedar Rapids 051087
Art Department, Mount Saint Clare College, Clinton 051162
Art Department, Mount Saint Mary's College, Los Angeles 051633
Art Department, Mount San Antonio College, Walnut 052321
Art Department, Mount San Jacinto College, San Jacinto 052125
Art Department, Mount Vernon Nazarene College, Mount Vernon 051763
Art Department, Muskingum College, New Concord 051789
Art Department, Napa Valley College, Napa 051773
Art Department, Nassau Community College, Garden City 051376
Art Department, Navarro College, Corsicana 051204
Art Department, Nazareth College of Rochester, Rochester 052040
Art Department, Nebraska Wesleyan University, Lincoln 051609
Art Department, New Mexico State University, Las Cruces 051587
Art Department, Normandale Community College, Bloomington 050997
Art Department, North Arkansas Community College, Harrison 051444
Art Department, North Carolina Agricultural and Technical State University, Greensboro 051415
Art Department, North Central Michigan College, Petoskey 051933
Art Department, North Hennepin Community College, Brooklyn Park 051045
Art Department, North Idaho College, Coeur d'Alene 051168
Art Department, North Park University, Chicago 051119
Art Department, North Seattle Community College, Seattle 052161
Art Department, Northampton County Community College, Bethlehem . . 050977
Art Department, Northeastern Illinois University, Chicago 051120
Art Department, Northeastern Oklahoma A & M College, Miami 051704
Art Department, Northeastern State University, Tahlequah 052244
Art Department, Northern Kentucky University, Highland Heights 051463
Art Department, Northern State University, Aberdeen 050863
Art Department, Northern Virginia Community College, Annandale . . 050904
Art Department, Northland Pioneer College, Holbrook 051468
Art Department, Northwest College, Powell 051985
Art Department, Northwest Nazarene College, Nampa 051771
Art Department, Northwestern College, Orange City 051891
Art Department, Northwestern Michigan College, Traverse City 052269
Art Department, Notre Dame College, Manchester 051667
Art Department, Oklahoma State University, Stillwater 052220
Art Department, Olivet College, Olivet 051883
Art Department, Olympic College, Bremerton 051024
Art Department, Orange County Community College, Middletown 051708
Art Department, Palomar Community College, San Marcos 052130
Art Department, Paris Junior College, Paris 051914
Art Department, Peace College, Raleigh 052008
Art Department, Penn Valley Community College, Kansas City 051541
Art Department, Peru State Colllege, Peru 051930
Art Department, Piedmont College, Demorset 051244
Art Department, Pierce College, Woodland Hills 052402
Art Department, Pittsburg State University, Pittsburg 051953
Art Department, Plattsburgh State University College, Plattsburgh 051964
Art Department, Plymouth State College, Plymouth 051966
Art Department, Prairie State College, Chicago Heights 051131
Art Department, Pratt Community College, Pratt 051986
Art Department, Prince George's Community College, Largo 051586
Art Department, Queens College, Flushing 051340
Art Department, Radford University, Radford 052005
Art Department, Rhode Island College, Providence 051993
Art Department, Richard Bland College, Petersburg 051931
Art Department, Ripon College, Ripon 052026
Art Department, Rivier College, Nashua 051775
Art Department, Roanoke College, Salem 052095
Art Department, Roberts Wesleyan College, Rochester 052041
Art Department, Rochester Community College, Rochester 052038
Art Department, Rockland Community College, Suffern 052226
Art Department, Rocky Mountain College, Billings 050985
Art Department, Roger Williams College, Bristol 051030
Art Department, Rogers State College, Claremore 051146
Art Department, Rowan University, Glassboro 051386
Art Department, Rutgers University, Camden 051066
Art Department, Sacramento City College, Sacramento 052064
Art Department, Saint Ambrose University, Davenport 051227
Art Department, Saint John's University, Collegeville 051176
Art Department, Saint Louis Community College at Meramec, Saint Louis . 052074
Art Department, Saint Mary-of-the-Woods College, Saint Mary-of-the-Woods 052081
Art Department, Saint Mary's College, Raleigh 052009
Art Department, Saint Mary's University of Minnesota, Winona 052392
Art Department, Saint Olaf College, Northfield 051859
Art Department, Saint Thomas Aquinas College, Sparkhill 052197
Art Department, Salem College, Winston-Salem 052396
Art Department, Salem State College, Salem 052093
Art Department, Salisbury State University, Salisbury 052099
Art Department, Salve Regina University, Newport 051841
Art Department, Sam Houston State University, Huntsville 051490
Art Department, Samford University, Birmingham 050988
Art Department, San Bernardino Valley College, San Bernardino 052112
Art Department, San Diego Mesa College, San Diego 052114
Art Department, San Francisco State University, San Francisco 052120
Art Department, San Jacinto College North, Houston 051477
Art Department, San Juan College, Farmington 051327
Art Department, Santa Ana College, Santa Ana 052136
Art Department, Santa Clara University, Santa Clara 052139
Art Department, Santa Rosa Junior College, Santa Rosa 052145
Art Department, Seattle Pacific College, Seattle 052162
Art Department, Shepherd College, Shepherdstown 052176
Art Department, Sheridan College, Sheridan 052177
Art Department, Shippensburg University, Shippensburg 052179
Art Department, Shorter College, Rome 052058
Art Department, Siena Heights College, Adrian 050870
Art Department, Sierra Community College, Rocklin 052052
Art Department, Silver Lake College, Manitowoc 051672
Art Department, Simpson College, Indianola 051501
Art Department, Snow College, Ephraim 051303
Art Department, South Carolina State University, Orangeburg 051893
Art Department, South Dakota State University, Brookings 051037
Art Department, South Suburban College, South Holland 052192
Art Department, Southeastern State College, Durant 051275
Art Department, Southern Nazarene University, Bethany 050975
Art Department, Southern Oregon State College, Ashland 050914
Art Department, Southern University in New Orleans, New Orleans 051798
Art Department, Southern Utah State College, Cedar City 051085
Art Department, Southern Virginia College, Buena Vista 051053
Art Department, Southwest Baptist University, Bolivar 051004
Art Department, Southwestern College, Winfield 052390
Art Department, Southwestern Community College, Creston 051210
Art Department, Southwestern Oklahoma State University, Weatherford . . . 052344
Art Department, Southwestern University, Georgetown 051383
Art Department, Spoon River College, Canton 051069
Art Department, Spring Arbor College, Spring Arbor 052204
Art Department, State University of New York at Albany, Albany 050874
Art Department, State University of New York at Stony Brook, Stony Brook 052224
Art Department, State University of New York College at Cortland, Cortland 051205
Art Department, State University of New York College at Oswego, Oswego . 051902
Art Department, State University of West Georgia, Carrollton 051079
Art Department, Stephen F. Austin University, Nacogdoches 051770
Art Department, Stephens College, Columbia 051180
Art Department, Sterling College, Sterling 052218
Art Department, Stetson University, De Land 051234
Art Department, Suffolk County Community College, Selden 052170
Art Department, Surry Community College, Dobson 051263
Art Department, Tacoma Community College, Tacoma 052239
Art Department, Taft College, Taft . . 052243
Art Department, Tallahassee Community College, Tallahassee 052245
Art Department, Tarrant County Junior College, Hurst 051493
Art Department, Taylor University, Upland 052296
Art Department, Temple College, Temple 052253
Art Department, Texarkana College, Texarkana 052257
Art Department, Texas A & M University, Kingsville 051553
Art Department, Thomas More College, Crestview Hills 051211
Art Department, Tougaloo College, Tougaloo 052267
Art Department, Treasure Valley Community College, Ontario 051889
Art Department, Tulsa Junior College, Tulsa 052279
Art Department, Umpqua Community College, Roseburg 052059
Art Department, Union College, Barbourville 050952
Art Department, University of Alabama, Tuscaloosa 052283
Art Department, University of Arkansas, Fayetteville 051330
Art Department, University of Arkansas at Pine Bluff, Pine Bluff 051950
Art Department, University of Central Arkansas, Conway 051198
Art Department, University of Central Florida, Orlando 051896
Art Department, University of Evansville, Evansville 051314
Art Department, University of Findlay, Findlay 051335
Art Department, University of Indianapolis, Indianapolis 051498
Art Department, University of Massachusetts Boston, Boston . . 051008
Art Department, University of Memphis, Memphis 051689
Art Department, University of Missouri, Columbia 051181
Art Department, University of Nevada Reno, Reno 052017
Art Department, University of North Carolina at Chapel Hill, Chapel Hill 051092
Art Department, University of North Dakota, Grand Forks 051399

Art Department, University of Puget Sound, Tacoma 052240
Art Department, University of Redlands, Redlands 052016
Art Department, University of Saint Francis, Fort Wayne 051349
Art Department, University of Saint Thomas, Houston 051478
Art Department, University of South Carolina at Aiken, Aiken 050871
Art Department, University of Southern Indiana, Evansville 051315
Art Department, University of Southern Maine, Gorham 051396
Art Department, University of Texas at Arlington, Arlington 050910
Art Department, University of Texas at Brownsville and Southmost College, Brownsville 051047
Art Department, University of Texas Pan American, Edinburg 051285
Art Department, University of the District of Columbia, Washington 052327
Art Department, University of Vermont, Burlington 051058
Art Department, University of Wisconsin-Green Bay, Green Bay 051410
Art Department, University of Wisconsin, Marinette, Marinette 051678
Art Department, University of Wisconsin Parkside, Kenosha 051547
Art Department, University of Wisconsin River Falls, River Falls 052027
Art Department, Valencia Community College, Orlando 051897
Art Department, Valley City State College, Valley City 052305
Art Department, Vassar College, Poughkeepsie 051982
Art Department, Vermilion Community College, Ely 051300
Art Department, Victor Valley College, Victorville 052310
Art Department, Villa Maria College of Buffalo, Buffalo 051054
Art Department, Vincennes University Junior College, Vincennes 052313
Art Department, Virginia Wesleyan College, Norfolk 051849
Art Department, Viterbo College, La Crosse 051559
Art Department, Wabash College, Crawfordsville 051209
Art Department, Waldorf College, Forest City 051342
Art Department, Walla Walla Community College, Walla Walla 052319
Art Department, Washington and Jefferson College, Washington 052336
Art Department, Wayne State College, Wayne 052341
Art Department, Webster University, Saint Louis 052075
Art Department, Wenatchee Valley College, Wenatchee 052348
Art Department, Wesleyan College, Macon 051653
Art Department, West Liberty State College, West Liberty 052354
Art Department, West Valley College, Saratoga 052148
Art Department, West Virginia State College, Institute 051502
Art Department, West Virginia University at Parkersburg, Parkersburg 051915
Art Department, Western Connecticut State University, Danbury 051224
Art Department, Western Illinois University, Macomb 051651
Art Department, Western Kentucky University, Bowling Green 051018
Art Department, Western Montana College, Dillon 051262
Art Department, Western Oklahoma State College, Altus 050890
Art Department, Western Washington University, Bellingham 050964
Art Department, Western Wyoming College, Rock Springs 052049
Art Department, Westfield State College, Westfield 052359
Art Department, Westminster College, New Wilmington 051807
Art Department, Wharton County Junior College, Wharton 052363
Art Department, Wheaton College, Norton 051862
Art Department, Whitman College, Walla Walla 052320
Art Department, Whitworth College, Spokane 052201
Art Department, Wilberforce University, Wilberforce 052374
Art Department, William Jewell College, Liberty 051606
Art Department, William Paterson College, Wayne 052342
Art Department, William Penn College, Oskaloosa 051901
Art Department, William Woods University, Fulton 051367
Art Department, Williams College, Williamstown 052381
Art Department, Willmar Community College, Willmar 052383
Art Department, Wilmington College, Wilmington 052387
Art Department, Winston-Salem State University, Winston-Salem 052397
Art Department, Wittenberg University, Springfield 052210
Art Department, Worcester State College, Worcester 052405
Art Department, York College, York . 052411
Art Department, Agricultural and Technical College, State University of New York, Cobleskill 051166
Art Department, Art Division, Pacific University in Oregon, Forest Grove 051343
Art Department, Bernard M. Baruch College, City University of New York, New York 051811
Art Department, College of Arts and Sciences, Governors State University, University Park 052294
Art Department, Division of Communications and Fine Arts, Grossmont College, El Cajon 051289
Art Department, Division of Creative Arts, Monterey Peninsula College, Monterey 051741
Art Department, Division of Fine Arts, Antelope Valley College, Lancaster 051581
Art Department, Division of Fine Arts, Howard College, Big Spring 050983
Art Department, Division of Fine Arts, Limestone College, Gaffney 051368
Art Department, Division of Humanities and Fine Arts, College of Saint Francis, Joliet 051535
Art Department, Fine Arts Division, College of the Sequoias, Visalia 052314
Art Department, Fine Arts Division, Concordia College, Saint Paul . . . 052084
Art Department, Fine Arts Division, Shasta College, Redding 052015
Art Department Gallery, Community College of Rhode Island, Warwick 048871
Art Department, Humanities Division, Delta College, University Center 052292
Art Department of the Mary Baldwin College, Staunton 052216
Art Depot, Aggsbach Markt 095462
Art Depot, London 113461
Art Depot, Minneapolis 117236
Art Dépôt, Paris 065450
Art Depot, Wien 095790
Art & Design, Montabaur 104118
Art Design, Paimpol 065327
Art Design ans Multimedia Program, Lansing Community College, Lansing 051584
Art & Design Gallery, Kaikoura 108481
Art Design Service, Salt Lake City . 119327
Art Designs, Detroit 116077
Art Development, Detroit 116078
Art Développement ADT, Genève . . 135014
Art d'Gott, La Paz 096438
Art Diagonal, Internationaler Club bildender Künstler, Wien 052505
Art Dialogue Gallery, Buffalo 115249
Art Dictionaries, Edition Münster, Münster 134291
Art didacta, Igls 049628
Art Dimensions, Saint Louis 119180
Art Direct, Oakland 118623
Art Direct, Sevenoaks 114405
Art Direct of Saint Paul, Saint Paul . 119272
Art Directions Book Company, Stamford 135508
Art Directors Club, New York 054618
Art Directors Club für Deutschland e.V, Berlin 053031
Art Division, Maryville University of Saint Louis, Saint Louis 052076
Art Division, Washington and Lee University, Lexington 051604
Art Division, Department of Humanities, Avila College, Kansas City 051542
Art Domaru, Plzeň 098407
Art d'Orient, La Courneuve 063356
Art du Nord, Groningen 108032
L'Art du Table, Paris 065451
Art du Temps, Cassis 062006
Art du Temps, Cassis 062007
Art du Temps, Cogolin 062380
Art du Temps, Mouriès 064817
L'Art du Temps, Paris 065452
L'Art du Temps, Toulon (Var) 068439
Art e Dossier, Firenze 134579
Art-e-Fax, Holt, Norfolk 113257
Art e Mobili, Winterthur . . 082910, 130219
Art-East, Kyïv 112390
Art Education, Reston 136344
Art Education Department, Coahoma Community College, Clarksdale . . 051148
Art Education Program, State University of New York College at New Paltz, New Paltz 051805
The Art Effect, Otley 114195
Art Egypte Centre, Casablanca 077635
Art Eko, Košice 080619
Art Elements Gallery, Milwaukee . . 117163
Art Emporium, Louisville 116927
Art Emporium, Vancouver 097413
Art-en-Direct, Boulogne-Billancourt 099018
Art-en-Liberté, Bandol 098912
Art en Maguscule, Montréal 096968
Art en Marge, Bruxelles 096134
L'Art en Mouvement, Paris 099967
Art en Noir, Wien 057371
Art en Nostalgie, Groningen 078398
Art en Stalles, Pouzac 013933
Art Enables, Washington 120255
Art Encounter, Dallas 115832
Art Encounter, Las Vegas 116603
Art Enterprise, Toronto 123824
Art Equity, Sydney 056665
Art-Erhaltung, Contemporary Art Open Space, Berlin 101780
Art Eritorija, Kaunas 107345
Art Espace Galerie, Blagnac 098974
Art Estampe, Gentilly 099288, 133471, 138094
Art et Affiche, Nice 138249
Art et Antiques, Loches (Indre-et-Loire) 063972
Art et Architecture, Paris 099968
Art et Art, Marsa 112250
Art et Bois, La Possession 129208
Art et Cadre, Versoix 111962
Art et Cadres, Fribourg 111412
Art et Cadres, Troyes 101389
Art et Collections, Montélimar 064671
Art et Comédie, Paris 133518
Art et Conservation, Toulouse 124971
Art et Cristal, Saint-Ouen 067714
Art et Decoration, Firenze 127288
Art et Décoration, Fougères (Ille-et-Vilaine) 099271
Art et Découvertes, Saint-Vaast-la-Hougue 101236
Art Et Facts, Edinburgh 112983
Art et Innovation, Vic-Fezensac . . . 068841
L'Art et la Manière, Reims 067054, 124855
L'Art et la Mer, Paris 135686
Art et les Grandes Civilisations, Paris 133519
Art et Lithographies, Pontarlier 101042
Art et Lumière, Digne-les-Bains . . . 062632
Art et Passion, Hautmont 063135
Art et Passions, Mortagne-au-Perche 099773
Art et Patrimoine, Bourbon-l'Archambault 061702
Art et Patrimoine, Challuy 062076
Art et Poésie, Pagny-sur-Meuse . . . 135687
Art et Société, Rennes (Ille-et-Vilaine) 135688
Art et Style d'Aquitaine, Bordeaux . 061582
Art et Tendances, Rouen 101107
Art et Troc, Sarrebourg 068130
Art et Veline, Dinard 099224
Art Etc, Cape Town 110015
Art Etc., Portland 118964
Art Etcetera, Singapore 109758
Art-Etche, La Rochelle . . . 063424, 099404
Art Evasion, Hoenheim 063160
Art Exchange, Columbus 115757
Art Exchange, London 096940
Art Exchange, San Francisco 119590
Art Exclusive, Wetzlar 105235
Art Exhibition House, Ha Noi 120447
Art-Expo, Hattingen 103309
Art Expo, Parow 110068
Art Expo-Galerie Deprez-Bellorget, Paris 099969
Art Export, Pézenas 066792
Art Exposure Gallery, Glasgow 113102
Art Express, Miami 117023
Art Expressions, Calgary 096785
Art Expressions, Windsor, Ontario . . 097550
Art Expressions Gallery, San Diego . 119476
Art Expressions/Publications, Loenen aan de Vecht 135992
Art Factors, Portland 118965
Art Factory No. 1, Amersfoort 077744
Art Factory Outlet, Las Vegas 116604
Art Fair.International Fair Poster Competition, Plovdiv 093617
Art First, London 113462
Art First, New York 117616
Art Focus, Singapore 109759
The Art Folio, Highgate, Western Australia 123242
Art Folio, Kuala Lumpur 107434
Art for All, Chichester 112856
Art for All, Little Hallingbury 113403
Art for All, Los Angeles 116707
Art for Animals, Tucson 120103
Art for Art's Sake, Christchurch . . .079010, 108377
Art For Arts Sake, Wellington 108610
Art For Arts Sake, Wellington 108611
Art For Arts Sake, Wellington 108612
Art for Change, New York 046294
Art for Colour, Byron Bay 094335
Art for Eyes, Glasgow 113103
Art for Interiors, London 113463
Art for Life, Nottingham 114171
Art for Offices, London 113464
Art for Sale!, Wien 095791
Art for the Soul, New Orleans 117391
Art for You, Minneapolis 117237
Art for Your Office, London 113465
art + form, Dresden 102422
Art Formel, Paris 065453
Art Forum, Antwerpen 096059
Art Forum, Bangkok 112228
Art Forum, México 107475
Art Forum, Milngavie 114083
Art Forum, Singapore 109760
Art Forum Berlin, Internationale Messe für Gegenwartskunst, Berlin 093711
Art Forum - Kunstverein, Graz 052506
Art Forum Riehen, Riehen 111835

Art Foundry Gallery, Sacramento . . 119133
Art Foyer Décor, Toulouse 101330
Art & Frame, Apeldoorn 093825
Art & Frame, Christchurch 108378
Art Frame, Jeddah 080358
Art & Frame, Malvern, South Australia 094775
Art + Frame, Wien 095792
Art Frame Gallery, Hong Kong 097751
Art & Framing, Greenside 110043
Art from Art, Gent 096282
Art From Russia, Dallas 115833
Art From the Heart, Portland 118966
Art Front Gallery, Tokyo 107011
art fundus, München 072644
Art Furniture, London 085096, 130932
Art-FX, Cootamundra 094434
Art-Galereja Dača, Moskva 109490
Art-Galereja Dača, Žukovka 109666
Art Galéria, Liptovský Mikuláš 109918
Art Galerie, Detmold 102358
Art Galerie, Garmisch-Partenkirchen 102918
Die Art Galerie, Hildesheim 103378
Art Galerie, Künzelsau 103806
Art Galerie, La Baule-Escoublac . . . 099372
Art Galerie, Ludwigsburg, Württemberg 103942
Art Galerie, Möhnesee 104082
Art Galerie, Saarbrücken 104787
Art Galerie, Wolfenbüttel 105318
Art Galerie 94, Nijmegen 078650
Art-Galerie an der Stadtkirche, Bayreuth 101744
Art Galerie No, Baden-Baden 101719
Art-Galerie-Rudenz, Meiringen 111729
Art-Galerie zur alten Post, Appenzell 111122
Art Galerija, Čačak 109728
Art Galery, Medellín 098249
Art Galleries, California State University Northridge, Northridge 046558
Art Galleries and Ceramics, New York 117617
Art Galleries Association Singapore, Singapore 054047
Art Galleries at UAH, Huntsville 044690
Art Galleries of Ramapo College, Mahwah 045599
Art Gallery, Amsterdam 107660
Art Gallery, Atlanta 041843
Art Gallery, Avignon 098887
Art Gallery, Bangalore . . . 074764, 105600
Art Gallery, College Park 043041
Art Gallery, Edmonton 096861
The Art Gallery, Edmonton 096862
Art Gallery, Etobicoke 005437
Art Gallery, Ha Noi 120448
Art Gallery, Haifa 022914
The Art Gallery, Hillsborough 039751
Art Gallery, Ho Chi Minh City 120497
The Art Gallery, Hong Kong 097752
Art Gallery, Houston 116272
Art Gallery, Hyderabad 105694
Art Gallery, İstanbul 112276
The Art Gallery, Kuala Lumpur 027965
Art Gallery, Los Angeles 116708
Art Gallery, Miami 117024
Art Gallery, Portland 118967
Art Gallery, Roma 106488
Art Gallery, Ruislip 114330
Art Gallery, Santiago de Chile 059500
Art Gallery, Wiesbaden 105241
Art Gallery, Zürich 112031
Art Gallery, James Prendergast Library, Jamestown 044827
The Art Gallery, John C. Calhoun State Community College, Decatur 043346
Art Gallery, North Hennepin Community College, Brooklyn Park 042471
Art Gallery, Pierce College, Woodland Hills 049286
The Art Gallery, University of Meryland, College Park 043042
The Art Gallery, University of New Hampshire, Durham 043538
Art Gallery, University of Texas at San Antonio, San Antonio 047787
Art Gallery 2, Trieste 106714
Art Gallery 3, Singapore 109761
Art Gallery 78, Gdynia 108904
Art Gallery Amedeo, Torino 106657
Art Gallery and Framing, New York . 117618
Art Gallery and Framing, Tulsa 120183
Art Gallery and Museum, Bootle . . . 038788
Art Gallery at the Westin Copley, Boston 115141
Art Gallery Collections, Surfers Paradise 095238
Art Gallery de la Rivoire, Bourgoin-Jallieu 099023
Art Gallery Groeninge, Brugge 096111
Art Gallery Hillsborough, Hillsborough 113242
Art Gallery Irena, Ljubljana 109950
Art Gallery Kendall, Miami 045804
Art Gallery Lai, Lenzerheide 111640
Art Gallery Lichtstrahl, Widen 111991
Art Gallery Marist College, Poughkeepsie 047210
Art Gallery Natascha, Knokke-Heist 096320
Art Gallery Newcastle Region, Newcastle 094937
Art Gallery of Algoma, Sault Sainte Marie 006430
Art Gallery of Bancroft, Bancroft . . . 005058
Art Gallery of Bishop's University, Lennoxville 005762
Art Gallery of Calgary, Calgary 005181
Art Gallery of Fells Point, Baltimore 115031
Art Gallery of Greater Victoria, Victoria 006732
Art Gallery of Hamilton, Hamilton . . 005587
Art Gallery of Hamilton, Hamilton . . 096910
Art Gallery of Mississauga, Mississauga 005887
Art Gallery of New South Wales, Sydney 001505
Art Gallery of Newfoundland and Labrador, Saint John's 006360
Art Gallery of Northumberland, Cobourg 005282
Art Gallery of Nova Scotia, Halifax . 005567
Art Gallery of Ontario, Toronto 006581
Art Gallery of Peel, Brampton 005132
Art Gallery of Peterborough, Peterborough 006136
Art Gallery of Seikado Library, Tokyo 027144
Art Gallery of South Australia, Adelaide 000703
Art Gallery of Southwestern Manitoba, Brandon 005136
Art Gallery of Sudbury, Sudbury . . . 006527
Art Gallery of Swift Current National Exhibition Centre, Swift Current . . 006544
Art Gallery of the College of Fine and Applied Arts, Sudan University of Science and Technology, Khartoum 036146
Art Gallery of the Faculty of Painting, Sculpture and Graphic Art, Bangkok 037869
Art Gallery of the Municipality and Town of Mesolongion, Mesolongion 021374
Art Gallery of the South Okanagan, Penticton 006129
Art Gallery of Western Australia, Perth 001375
Art Gallery of Windsor, Windsor, Ontario 006830
Art Gallery of Windsor, Windsor, Ontario 097551
Art Gallery of York University, North York 006049
Art Gallery One, Zürich 112032
Art Gallery Sint-Raphaël, Hasselt . . 096308
Art Gallery Sultan, Honfleur 099331
Art Gallery Tours, New York 117619
Art Gallery Wholesales, Indianapolis 116439
Art Gallia, Paris 065454
Art-Garage, Zug 112207
Art Garaža, Beograd 109684
Art Garden, San Francisco 119591
Art Garden Kawasaki, Kawasaki . . . 106872
Art Gate, Manama 057618, 095990
Art Gilding, Rosebery 123299
Art Glass Repair and Restoration, Jacksonville 132173
Art Glass Show, Portland 093967
Art Global, Hoisbüttel 071562
Art Gluchowe, Glauchau 017427
Art Grafic, Wolfsburg 105322
The Art Group, Las Vegas 116605
Art Guild, Farmington 054619
Art Guild of Burlington, Burlington . 054620
Art Guild of Burlington Gallery, Burlington 042513
The Art Gym, Marylhurst University, Marylhurst 045716
Art Haus, Bramsche 102213
Art Haus, Wien 095793
Art-Helsinki, Helsinki 098714
Art Heritage, Delhi 105648
Art History, Oxford 136168
Art History and Archaeology Department, University of Missouri, Columbia . 051182
Art History Department, Emory University, Atlanta 050919
Art History Department, Sweet Briar College, Sweet Briar 052232
Art History Department, University of California Riverside, Riverside . . . 052032
Art History Department, Faculty of Arts and Science, McGill University, Montréal 049798
Art History Program, University of Massachusetts Amherst, Amherst 050895
Art Holdings, Minneapolis 117238
Art & Home, Holywood 113262
Art-Home, Singapore 109762
Art Horizon, Chicago 115339
Art House, Camborne 112784
Art-House, Dornbirn 056960, 095494
Art House, Hasselt 096309
Art House, Houston 116273
The Art House, Middlesbrough 114081
Art House Gallery, Paget 096430
Art-House Gallery, Peterborough . . 114241
Art House Gallery, Rushcutters Bay 095164
Art House of Collectors, Hong Kong 097753
Art House Reproductions, Newstead 094947
Art House Studio, Oklahoma City . . 118653
Art & Image, Amsterdam 077786
Art Image, Atlanta 114848
Art Image Gallery, Vancouver 097414
Art Images, Dallas 115834
Art Images Gallery, Norwood 094992
Art Immédiat, Paris 099970
Art Impressions, Columbus 115758
Art in America, New York 136345
Art in Architecture, Los Angeles . . . 051634
Art in Asia, Hong Kong 097754
Art in Bark Display, Toowoomba . . . 095344
Art in Bulgaria, Sofia 135613
Art in Fiber, Washington 120256
Art in Florence, Firenze 106030
Art in General, New York 117620
Art in Progress, Genova 106080
Art in Wisconsin, Sturgeon Bay . . . 136346
Art in Your Home, Great Coxwell . . . 113151
Art Incorporate, Surry Hills 095247
Art Incorporated, San Antonio 119394
Art Incorporated, Southport 114463
Art Index, Amsterdam 107661
Art Index, Mie 140166
Art Index, Milano 135870
Art Index, A Guide to Asian Art on the Internet, New York 136347
Art Indus, Delhi 105649
Art & Industry, Berlin 069563
Art Information Centre, Middelburg . 134823
Art Initiative, Atlanta 114849
Art Inspiration, Lemgo 103901
Art Institute of Atlanta, Atlanta 050920
Art Institute of Boston at Lesley University, Boston 051009
The Art Institute of Boston Main Gallery, Boston 042314
The Art Institute of Chicago, Chicago 042820
Art Institute of Chicago, Publications Department, Chicago 135344
Art Institute of Dallas, Dallas 051221
Art Institute of Fort Lauderdale, Fort Lauderdale 051346
Art Institute of Houston, Houston . . 051479
Art Institute of Philidelphia, Philadelphia 051934
Art Institute of Pittsburgh, Pittsburgh 047040
Art Institute of Seattle, Seattle 052163
Art Institute of Southern California, Laguna Beach 051569
Art Instruction Schools, Minneapolis 051723
Art & Interiors, New York 117621
Art Interiors, Toronto 097220
Les Art International, Johannesburg 110046
Art International Publishers, Paris . . 133520
Art Internationale, Québec 097124
Art & Investissement, Paris 099971
Art Investment, San Francisco 132869
Art Ireland Exhibition, Dublin 093753
Art Ireland Summer Exhibition, Dublin 093754
Art-is, Sofia 096722
Art Is Heaven, Nashville 117333
Art Is In, Miami 117025
The Art is In, Salt Lake City 119328
Art is Life, Verein zur Förderung unabhängiger Kunst, Wien 052507
Art is OK Gallery, Albuquerque 114769
Art Is Vital Gallery, Calgary 096786
Art Isanat, Eching 125565
Art Issues, West Hollywood 136348
Art Journal, New York 136349
Art-Junives, Lviv 112426
Art K, Paris 099972
art kaleidoscope für Frankfurt und Rhein-Main, Frankfurt am Main 135742
Art Kandyna, Warszawa 129078
Art-Kapella, Schkeuditz 104824
Art Kids, Amsterdam 053877
Art Kids, Amsterdam 077787
Art Kiosk, Bruxelles 096135
Art Kitchen, Amsterdam 107662
Art Kite Museum für Kunst & Flugobjekte, Detmold 016687
Art-Kollegija, Sankt-Peterburg 109615
Art-Komitet, Moskva 080234
Art Konstant, Lisboa 109264
Art Konsult, Delhi 105650
Art Kontakt, Český Krumlov 123955
Art Korner, Den Haag 107901
Art Lab, Makati 108819
Art Land Indooroopilly, Indooroopilly 094658
Art Las Vegas, Las Vegas 093968
Art League, Indianapolis . . 054621, 116440
Art League of Houston, Houston . . . 044634
Art League of Houston, Houston . . . 054622
Art League of Manatee County, Bradenton 042377
Art League of Manatee County, Bradenton 054623
Art League of Rhode Island, Newport 054624
Art Legacy, Odiham 114184
Art Lending of Ottawa, Ottawa 097093
Art Libraries Journal, Bromsgrove . 136169
Art Libraries Society of North America, Kanata 052725
The Art Libraries Society of the UK & Ireland, Bromsgrove 054278
Art Library, Leeds 039949
Art Libre Edition, Wien 133179
Art Life, Clyst Saint George 112882
Art Life, Tokyo 134718
Art Life Design, Ottawa 097094
Art Limited, Houston 116274
Art-Line, Augsburg 101610

Art Line, London 136170
Art-Line, Mannheim 072413
Art Line, Singapore 109763
Art Line Gallery, Riyadh 109674
Art Link, Oslo 079417
Art Lithographies, Paris 099973
Art Littoral Galerie, Dinard 099225
Art Location, Hildesheim 103379
Art Loft, Port 111815
Art Loft Gallery, New York 117622
Art Loft Studio, Birmingham 115097
Art Loss Register, Köln 134096
The Art Loss Register, London 135182
Art Loss Register, New York 135410
Art Loss Register, Sankt-Peterburg . 134883
The Art Lounge, Birmingham 112643
Art Lounge, Coogee 094423
Art Lover's Art and Craft Fair Bulletin, Palatine 136350
Art Lovers Gallery, New York 117623
Art Lovers League, Baltimore 054625, 115032
Art-M, Kraków 108927
Art M, Trjavna 096759
The Art Magazine, Néa Psychico . . 135834
Art-Mah, Genève 111420
Art Makers Studio Gallery, Heidelberg 094631
Art Man Gallery, Cairo 098610
Art Market, Milwaukee 117164
Art-Market, Piaseczno . . . 079682, 129058
Art Market, Tulsa 120184
Art Market, Warszawa . . . 079733, 129079
Art Mart, Omaha 118683
Art Mart, Tampa 120021
Art Mart, Tampa 120022
Art-Mart.Co.Uk, Chelmsford 112840
Art Masters, Auckland 128896
Art Masters, El Paso 116101
Art Masters, New York 117624
Art Masters, Oklahoma City 118654
Art Masters Association, Boston . . . 054626
Art Matters, Makati 108820
Art Media Resources, Chicago 115340
Art Media Resources, Chicago 142276
Art, Media, Theatre Department, Vanier College, Saint Laurent 049813
Art Melange, Buenos Aires 094056
L'Art Meme, Bruxelles 135590
Art Memories, Villeurbanne 068939
Art Mexicano, Columbus 115759
Art Miami, Contemporary and Modern Art, Miami Beach 093969
A.R.T Mimo, Marseille 124390
Art (Minneapolis), Minneapolis 136351
Art Miya, Tokyo 107012
Art MLS, Miami 117026
Art Mob, Battery Point 094219
Art Mode Gallery, Calgary 096787
Art Mode Gallery, Ottawa 097095
Art Monaco, Monaco 121771
Art Montage, Stockholm 111003
Art Montfalcon, Barcelona 110107
Art Monthly, London 136171
Art Monthly, Nanjing 135646
Art-Most, Moskva 109491
Art Motif, Delhi 105651
Art Motors, Milano 106154
Art Móveis, Belo Horizonte 058406, 123688
The Art Movement, London 113466
Art Multi, Paris 133521
Art Multiple Décoration, Meyzieu . . 064551
Art Multiple Décoration, Meyzieu . . 064552
Art Multiples, Amsterdam . 107663, 134770
Art Mûr, Montréal 096969
Art Museum, Thiruvananthapuram . 022349
The Art Museum at Florida International University, Miami 045805
Art Museum of Dazu Rock Carvings in Chongqing, Chongqing 007049
Art Museum of Greater Lafayette, Lafayette 045088
The Art Museum of Los Gatos and the Nature Museum of Los Gatos, Los Gatos 045476
Art Museum of Missoula, Missoula . 045931
Art Museum of South Texas, Corpus Christi 043161
Art Museum of Southeast Texas, Beaumont 042079
Art Museum of the Americas, Washington 048883
Art Museum of the Chinese Univertity of Hong Kong, Hong Kong 007113
Art Museum of the University of Memphis, Memphis 045753
Art Museum of Western Virginia, Roanoke 047465
Art Music Antic, Nice 065036
Art, Music & Theatre Department, Armstrong Atlantic State University, Savannah 052150
Art Musings, Mumbai 105754
Art Mystique, Tucson 120104
Art 'n Frame Warehouse, Dallas . . . 115835
ART-n-more, Uelzen 074135
Art 'n' Such, Bundaberg 094326
Art N'Co, Nantes 064898
Art Nest, Dubai 083186
Art New England, Brighton 136352
Art New Media, Warszawa 109093
Art New Zealand, Auckland 136010
Art Newc Project, Kyïv 112391
The Art Newspaper, London 135183, 136172
Art Next - Saga, Vigo 110861
Art Nexus, Bogotá 135661
Art Nocturne Knokke, Knokke 093593
Art Noir, Philadelphia 118734
Art North Gallery, Gordon 094597
Art Not Terminal Gallery, Seattle . . . 119873
Art Nova, El Paso 116102
Art-Nova, Katowice 108919
Art Noveaux, Cairo 098611
Art Novell, Barcelona 110108
Art Novum, Warszawa 109094
Art Now Gallery, Göteborg 110903
Art Now Gallery Guide: Boston-New England, Clinton 136353
Art Now Gallery Guide: Chicago-Midwest Edition, Clinton 136354
Art Now Gallery Guide: International Edition, Clinton 136355
Art Now Gallery Guide: New York Edition, Clinton 136356
Art Now Gallery Guide: Philadelphia Edition, Clinton 136357
Art Now Gallery Guide: Southeast Edition, Clinton 136358
Art Now Gallery Guide: Southwest Edition, Clinton 136359
Art Now Gallery Guide: West Coast Edition, Clinton 136360
Art Now International, Johannesburg 110047
Art Nuvo, Buderim 094322
Art of Animation, Adelaide 094113
Art of Deco Galerie, Alkmaar 077708
Art of Eastern Europe, Denver 115970
Art of Facts, Houston 116275
Art of Georgia, Berlin 101781
Art of Hands, Long Beach 116663
Art of History, Cincinnati 115601
Art of Living, Zollikon 082931
The Art of Michael Lees, Ellingham 113016
Art of Money, Portland 091894
Art of Persepolis, New York 090696
Art of Sieglar, Troisdorf 074103
Art of the 20th Century, New York . . 093970
Art of the Past, New York 090697
Art of the West, Minnetonka 136361
Art of This Century, New York 117625
Art of Time, New York 090698
Art of Velvet Gallery De Stierenstal, Montfoort 029931
Art-Office, Mouvaux 099783
Art On 5th, Austin 114950
Art on Aplin, Cairns 094341
Art on Argyle, Picton 095071
Art on Cairncross, Maleny 094767
Art on Canvas, Saint Louis 119181
Art On Line Sociéty, Tours 052889
Art on Paper, New York 136362
Art on Paper, Praha 137826
Art on Paper Fair, London 093910
Art on the Avenue, Detroit 116079
Art on the Edge, Philadelphia 118735
Art on the Edge, West Hollywood . . 120373
Art on the Wall, Paisley 114217
Art on Wheels, Göteborg 110904
Art One, Toronto 097221
Art One Gallery, Los Angeles 116709
Art One Studio, Hong Kong 097755
Art Option, London 096941
Art Options, San Francisco 119592
Art Options - Latin American Fine Art, London 113467
Art or Not, Bath 112568, 135117
Art Original, Bristol 112713
Art Outlet, Minneapolis 117239
Art Pack, Makati 108821
Art Palm Beach, West Palm Beach . 093971
Art-Pap, Gdańsk 108871
Art Papers, Atlanta 136363
Art Paris, Paris 093649
The Art Partnership, London 113468
Art-Passepartout, Berlin 069564
Art Passion, Mulhouse 064827
Art Peinture, Toulon (Var) 068440
Art & Photographs, London 113469
Art' Place, Lille 099482
The Art Place, Rotorua 108551
Art Place Gallery, Dorrigo 094483
Art Placement, Saskatoon 097188
Art Placement International, New York 117626
Art Plakat, Braunschweig 102215
Art-Plakat, Oldenburg, Oldenburg . . 104535
Art-Plakat Museumsshop, Oldenburg, Oldenburg 104536
Art Plaza, Osaka 106951
Art Pluralis, Paris 099974
Art Police, Minneapolis 136364
Art Poster Gallery, Zürich 112033
l'Art pour Art, Tucson 120105
Art Praha, Praha 098416
Art Premier, Bruxelles 096136
Art Présent, Cannes 099060
Art Présent, Paris 099975
Art Preserve, Saint Paul 119273
Art Preserve, Saskatoon 097189
Art-Press, Hajdúszoboszló 135840
Art Press, Lübeck 134170
Art Press, Paris 135689
Art-Presse, Kraków 134855
Art & Presse Diffusion, Les Brenets 136120, 141236
Art Print Gallery, Madrid 110438
Art Print Japan, Tokyo 107013
Art Print Japan, Tokyo 107014
Art Print Verlag, Saalbach 133132
Art Prints, Mayland 114068
Art Program, Maui Community College, Kahului 051538
Art Program, Pfeiffer College, Misenheimer 051728
Art Program, Saint Mary College, Leavenworth 051597
Art Program, Trinity College, Washington 052328
Art Program, Tyler Junior College, Tyler 052287
Art Project A16, Zürich 112034
Art Projects, London 113470
Art Projects International, New York 117627
Art-Projekt, Süstedt 074025
Art Prom PS 88, Alkmaar 107613
Art Promotion Gallery, Bruxelles . . . 096137
Art Proofing Gallery, Paris 133522
Art Provenance, Chicago 115341
Art & Public, Genève 111421
Art Public, Paris 099976
Art Publicity, Köln 103583
Art Publishing International, London 135184
Art Quarterly, London 136173
Art-Ray, München 126346
Art Reach, Jacksonville 116508
Art Reference Collection, Westport . 136365
Art Reference Services Quarterly, Binghamton 136366
Art Reflex, Den Haag 078168
Art Reflexx, Lübeck 072319
Art Rental & Sales, Winnipeg 097570
Art & Repro, Westerkappeln 074364
Art Resource Gallery, Columbus . . . 115760
Art Resources, Tulsa 120185
Art Resources, West Hollywood . . . 093449
Art Resources Gallery, Minneapolis 117240
Art Resources Gallery, Saint Paul . . 119274
Art Resources International, Washington 054627
Art Restauration Technique, Marseille 124391
Art-Restauro, Valencia 129753
Art Restoration, Quakers Hill 123295
Art Restoration and Conservation, San Antonio 132807
Art Restoration Services, London . . 130933
Art Restoration Studio, Toronto 123825
The Art Restoration Studios, Chichester 130561
The Art Restoration Studios, Haslemere 130771
Art Restorations, Dallas 131996
Art Retreat, A Private Museum, Singapore 034289
Art Review, London 136174
Art Revue Magazine, Loveland 136367
Art & Ride, Tholey 105047
Art Room, Lengnau (Aargau) 111637
Art Room, Malmö 110959
The Art Room, Nottingham 114172
The Art Room, Taunton 114553
Art Room Gallery & Print Bin, Hyde Park 094657
The Art Room in Beatties, Wolverhampton 114723
Art Route Studio, Camps Bay 080672
D'Art Royale, Québec 097125
Art Sacré, Eze 011772
Art Saint Louis, Saint Louis 119182
Art Sales Index, Egham 135145
Art Salon, Bangsar Baru 107433
Art Salon, Chiba 106835
Art Salon, Kaliningrad 109470
Art Salon, Long Beach 116664
Art Sans Frontieres, Carlton, Victoria 055634
Art Sans Frontieres, Kew 056044
Art Sauf, Lyon 064067
Art Savvy International, Fort Worth . 116132
Art Scene China, Hong Kong 097756
Art Scene Sacramento, Sacramento 119134
Art-Scenic, Le Faou 063617
Art School, Education Alliance, New York 051812
Art School Maa, Helsinki 049923
Art School of the Hong Kong Art Centre, Hong Kong 049851
Art Search, London 113471
Art Seek, Appledore, Devon 112513
Art Seen, New York 136368
Art Seiller, Saint-Paul-de-Vence . . . 101195
Art Seoul, Seoul 107204
Art Service, Paris 099977
Art Service, Internationale Kunstbücher, Karlsruhe 139293
Art Services International, Alexandria 054628
Art-Servis, Moskva 109492
The Art Shed Gallery, Red Hill 095116
The Art Shop, Abergavenny 112486
Art Show, Atlanta 114850
Art Signum, Žilina 109926
Art Singel 100, Amsterdam 107664
Art Sintez, Kyïv 112392
Art Society Gallery, Queanbeyan . . . 095107

Art Society of India, Mumbai 053687
Art Solutions, Tulsa 120186
Art & Soul Gallery, Singapore 109764
Art Source, Denver 115971
The Art Source, Los Angeles 116710
Art Source, Phoenix 118861
Art Source, San Francisco 119593
Art Source, Tulsa 120187
Art Source and Design, Charlotte . . 115273
Art Source and Design, Oklahoma City 118655
Art Sources, Miami 117027
Art Space, Saint Ives, Cornwall 114358
Art Space 111, Fort Worth 116133
Art Space Gallery, London 113472
Art Space Seoul, Seoul 107205
Art-Spektor, Sankt-Peterburg 080299
Art Stall Gallery, Seattle 119874
Art Stock, Stuttgart 134407, 139750
Art Stop, Denver 115972
Art-Store, Arnhem 078042
Art Store, Dublin 105858
Art Store, Indianapolis 116441
The Art Store, Le Raincy 099456
Art Store, Paris 099978
Art Store Gallery, Pittsburgh 118898
Art Stuc, Barcelona 129315
Art Student Showcase, New York . . 117628
Art Students League News, New York 136369
The Art Studio, Beaumont 042080
Art Studio, Berlin 101782
ART Studio, Köln 103584
Art-Studio, München 104142
The Art Studio, Newcastle, Staffordshire 114118
Art Studio, Podgorica 109741
Art Studio, Tauranga 108573
Art Studio, Vaduz 107340
Art Studio 1, Deinste 102353
Art Studio 56, Winnipeg 097571
ART Studio 6000 Fürst-Pückler-Str 70, Köln 071907
Art Studio Department, State University of New York College at New Paltz, New Paltz 051806
Art Studios International, Hawthorn, Victoria 094622
Art-Styl, Warszawa 079734
Art & Style, Höxter 103387
Art & Style, Néris-les-Bains 064976
Art Sud, Toulouse 101331
Art Sun, Ha Noi 120449
Art Symbol, Paris 099979
Art Tableaux, Collonges-au-Mont-d'Or 062398
Art Tageblatt, Esch-sur-Alzette 107385
Art-Talk, Scottsdale 136370
Art Taller la Glicina, Barcelona 129316
Art & Tapis, Beirut 077383
Art-Tech, Silicon Valley Institute of Art Technology, San Jose 047895
Art & Tech Art, Travemünde 074081
Art Tecnica, Valencia 129754
Art Temple, San Francisco 092733
Art-Tendence, Kehl am Rhein 071773
Art Territory, West Hollywood 120374
Art + Text, Paddington 135539
Art-Thé, Antibes-Juan-les-Pins . . . 098847
Art Thema Galerie, Bruxelles 096138
Art Therapy, Mundelein 136371
Art Times, Saugerties 136372
Art To Treasure, Willingham 114697
Art Today, Delhi 105652
Art Total, Köln 071908
Art Tours of Manhattan, New York . 117629
Art Trade Center, Bucureşti 109418
Art Trading, Zaandam 078848
Art Trading France, Paris 065455
Art Trak, Dallas 115836
Art Transfer, München 072645
Art Treasures Gallery, Hong Kong . . 059593
Art-Treff, Gifhorn 102958
Art Trend, Graz 057001
Art Trend Gallery, Singapore 080426
Art Tribal, Paris 135690
Art Tribal Himalaya, Nevers 065003
The Art Trust, South Melbourne . . . 056608
The Art Trust, Woollahra 056851
Art & Unart, Köln 103585
Art und Bijou, Köln 103586, 134097
Art und Business, Katsdorf 133097
Art-und Design-Studio-Galerie, Werl 105205
Art und Weisss, Morbach 104122
Art & Understanding, Albany 136373
Art-Uni, Lučenec 080629
Art Unique, Lichfield 113390
Art Unlimited, Amsterdam 134771
Art Unlimited, Neustadt an der Weinstraße 104425
Art Unlimited, New Orleans 117392
Art Unlimited Postcard Gallery, Amsterdam 107665, 134772
Art Up Déco, Lyon 099535
Art Up Deco, Paris 099980
Art Up Déco, Paris 099981
Art USA, Dallas 115837
Art USA Gallery, Austin 114951
Art USA Gallery, Austin 114952
Art Vegas, Las Vegas 116606
Art Ventures, Charlotte 115274
Art Verneuil, Paris 099982
Art Verre, Eindhoven 107994
Art-Via Investment, Den Haag 107902
Art-Vie, Paris 099983
Art Viet Nam Gallery, Ha Noi 120450
Art Village Gallery, Memphis 116975
Art + Vision, Bern 111243, 134990
Art Vision Enterprise, Singapore . . . 109765
Art Visions, Las Vegas 116607
Art Vitam, Miami 117028
Art Vue, New York 117630
Art Walk, Mumbai 105755
Art Warehouse, Miami 117029
Art + Wave, Hamburg 103090
Art Werk Gallery, Chicago 115342
Art Werks, Portland 118968
Art Wise, New York 117631
Art Wood, Reims 067055, 124856
Art Work, Düsseldorf 102469
Art Work, Nindorf 073061
Art Work, Zürich 112035
Art Work Australia, Hawthorn East . 055956
Art Work Galerie, Duisburg 102576
Art Workers Guild, London 054279
Art Workers Guild Annual Report, London 136175
Art Works, Amsterdam 107666
Art Works, Christchurch 108379
Art Works, Minneapolis 117241
Art Works, Newcastle-upon-Tyne . . 114120
Art Works, Vancouver 097415
Art Works Gallery, Norfolk 118607
Art Works Paris, Paris 065456
Art Workshop, Lemesos 098310
Art World, Chennai 105619
Art World, Christchurch 108380
Art World, Edmonton 096863
Art World, Edmonton 096864
Art World, Osborne Park 095009
Art World, San Diego 119477
Art X Art, Milano 106155
Art-X Galéria, Budapest 105486
Art Zone, Dunedin 079080
Art Zone, New Orleans 117393
Artă, Bucureşti 136046
Arta Gallery, Jerusalem 105906
Arta-Mangon, Bruxelles 057832
Artacasa, Amsterdam 107667
Artache, Milano 106156
Artacraft, Minneapolis 117242
Artact Art, Artarmon 055402
Artadentro, Faro 109249
Artaffect, Groningen 078399
D'Artagnan, Buenos Aires 136701
d'Artagnan, Eindhoven 107995
Artagor, Caen 099046
Artagra, Grimaud 063081
Artakut Kunstprojekte, Paderborn . . 104565, 134341
Artal, Allaman 122301
Artal, Strasbourg 101280
Artal Borruel, Jose, Zaragoza 129804
Artalia, Palermo 106415
Artamation, Milwaukee 117165
Art'an, Aix-en-Provence 060695
Artani, Stuttgart 073956
Artanne, Sittard 108225
Artantic, Montpellier 064732
Artantique, Brasília 058458
Artareal, Timişoara 080190
Artaria, München 072646
Artaria & Co., Wien 057372, 133180
Artarmon Galleries, Artarmon 000753
Artas, Cochem 102320
Artas Folklore Museum, Bethlehem 031407
Artasia, Milwaukee 090273, 117166
Artasia, San Francisco 092734
Artasia Gallery, Newtown, New South Wales 094954
Artatelier, Bucureşti 136047
Artaud, Jean-Pierre, Marseille 064314
Artaut, Myriam, Albi 060750
Artavia Gallery, Caerleon 112776
Ar'Tawoo, Guérande 099318
Artax Kunsthandel, Düsseldorf 102470
Artazart, Paris 099984
Artbank, London 113473
Artbank, Rosebery 095159
Artbank Gallery, London 113474
Artbeat, Paraparaumu 108539
Artbibliographies Modern, Oxford . . 135289
Artbox, Mattersburg 002296
Artbox Galerie der Editionen, Frankfurt am Main 102744
Artbox Studio, Adelaide 094114
The Artbunker, Auckland 108298
Artburn, Birmingham 112644
Artcade, Murten 111762
Artcade Gallery, Bruxelles 057833
Artcadre-Berès, Paris 065457
Artcanal, Paris 099985
Artcentr+, Moskva 109493
Artchet, Paris 124562
Artchivum, Budapest 021636
Artcite Hot, Windsor, Ontario 097552
Artclass, Kraków 129031
Artclub, Lyon 064068
Artclub Gallery, Paris 099986
Artco, Leeds 113363
Artco France, Saint-Ouen-l'Aumône 101193
Artcol, Montrouge 064777
Artcom Puces de Reims & Nancy, Reims 067056
Artcor Barcelona, Barcelona 129317
Artcore, Toronto 097222
l'Artcothèque, Granville 099295
Artcour, Paris 065458
Artcube, Paris 065459
Artcurial, Paris 121110
Artcurial, Paris 121111
Artdata Verlag, Ascheberg, Westfalen 133725
Artdekko.ch, Bern 111244
Artdomain, Glenside 094594
D'Arte, Barcelona 129318
Arte, Budapest 105487, 121636
L'Arte, Catania 106015
Arte, Coimbra 109242
Arte, Milano 135871
De Arte, Nantes 099802
Arté, Roma 076307
Arté, Roma 076308
Arte, San Marino 129252
Arte, Tokyo 077236
De Arte, Valladolid 110848
Art'e', Villanova di Castenaso 134711, 135872
Arte, Witten 074453
Arte 10, Madrid 110439, 134937
Arte 43, Madrid 110440
Arte 63, Bogotá 098097
Arte '800, Roma 076309
Arte 92, Milano 106157
Arte Afrocaribeña, Amsterdam 077788
Arte Al Borgo, Palermo 106416
Arte Americas, Fresno 116171
Arte Andino, Bogotá 098098
Arte Andino, Bogotá 098099
Arte Antica, Buenos Aires . 055170, 123150
L'Arte Antica, Livorno 075522
L'Arte Antica, Livorno 127492
Arte Antica, Messina 075553
Arte Antica, Napoli 075942
Arte Antica, Roma 127929
L'Arte Antica, Torino 076766
Arte Antica, Torino 076767
L'Arte Antica, Torino 140122
Arte Antica Rufini, Roma 076310
Arte Antica Rufini, Roma 076311
Arte Antiga, Belo Horizonte 058407
Arte Antiga, Lisboa 079866
Arte & Antiguidades, Porto Alegre . . 058485
Arte Arredo, Roma 076312
Arte & Arte, Palermo 106417
Arte Bello, Cali 098227
Arte Cafe, Medellín 098250
Arte Canarias, La Palmas de Gran Canaria 110704
Arte Canarias, La Palmas de Gran Canaria 110705
Arte Capital, Brescia 075146
Arte Centro Due, Milano 106158
Arte Club, Genova 075438
Arte Colonial, Arequipa 079534
Arte Colonial, Bogotá 059815
Arte Colosseo, Roma 106489
Arte Contemporanea Italiana, Milano 106159
Arte Contemporanea Maiocchi, Milano 106160
Arte Contemporaneo, Bucaramanga 098202
Arte & Cornice, Milano 135873
Arte Creativo, Bogotá 098100
Arte Creativo, Bogotá 098101
Arte Cristiana, Rivista Internazionale di Storia dell'Arte e di Arti Liturgiche, Milano 135874
Arte Cuadro, Néa Erythraia 105435
Arte de Coleccíon, Bogotá 098102
Arte de Relojes, Madrid 081239
Arte de Vivir, Madrid 136071
Arte del Restauro, Messina 127498
Arte del Siglo XX, Madrid 110441
Arte do Objeto, Brasília 123693
arte domo, Stuttgart 073957
Arte Domus, Kortrijk 096367
Arte DOS Gráfico, Bogotá 133397
Arte Due, Milano 106161
Arte e Antichitá, Verona 076990
Arte e Antiguidade, Rio de Janeiro . 058547
Arte e Antiquariato, Bologna 075054
Arte e Archeologia. Studi e documenti, Firenze 135875
Arte e Arte, Bologna 105941
Arte e Dossier, Firenze 135876
Arte e Estúdio, Lisboa 109265
Arte e Estúdio, Lisboa 109266
Arte e Naturalezza, Palermo 106418
Arte e Personae, Firenze 075275
Arte em Dobro, Rio de Janeiro 096589
Arte En Tela, México 107476
Arte Esposito, Torino 106658
Arte et Opera, Ajaccio . . . 060736, 138008
Arte Extremeña, Badajoz 110097
Arte Factum, Reinharz 134365
Arte Fato Galeria, Porto Alegre 096544
Arte Fino, Zürich 112036
Arte Fino Barroco, Guadalajara 107470
Arte Florentia, Palermo 106419
Arte Galeria, Fortaleza 096511
Arte Galeria, Santa Cruz de Tenerife 110738
Arte Galería Visbal, Bogotá 098103

Arte Galicia, Revista de Información de las Artes Plásticas Gallegas, Ferrol . . 136072
Arte Gallery, Cleveland 115683
Arte Garduño, Sevilla 110762
Arte Gráfico en Madrid, Madrid . . . 136073
Arte Heraldica, Rio de Janeiro 058548
Arte Heraldica, Rio de Janeiro 058549
El Arte Hispano, Panamá City 108782
Arte Ignorante, Palma de Mallorca . 110670
Arte Imagen, A Coruña 110315
Arte in, Venezia Mestre 135877
Arte in Movimento, Roma 106490
Arte Incontro in Libreria, Milano . . . 135878
Arte, Individuo y Sociedad, Madrid . 136074
Arte Información y Gestión, Madrid 122037
Arte Inversión, Guatemala 105473
Arte Italiana, Buenos Aires 055171
Arte Italiano, Bucaramanga 098203
Arte La Quimera, Caracas 093520
Arte Lancia, León 110394
Arte Lancia, León 110395
Arte Las Americas, Houston 116276
Arte Lombarda, Cesano Maderno . . 135879
Arte Lugano Galleria, Lugano 111658
Arte Madrid, Madrid 129568
Arte Maya Tz'utuhil, San Francisco . 047851
Arte Medievale, Cinisello Balsamo . 135880
Arte Mia, Erftstadt 102637
Arte Moderna, Erlangen 102652
Arte & Molduras, Fortaleza 096512
Arte Mundi France, Paris . 099987, 133523
Arte nel Tempo, Bologna 105942
Arte Novo, Madrid 110442
Arte Núcleo, México 107477
Arte Padova, Padova 093758
Arte Periférica, Lisboa 109267
Arte Pictoris, Medellín 098251
Arte Piú, Catania 106016
Arte Primitivo, New York 117632
Arte Publico Press, Houston 135366
Arte Redenta Produzioni, Genova . . 053726
Arte Religioso Venecia, Bogotá . . . 059816
Arte Religioso y Comtemporaneo, Medellín 098252
Arte + Restauro, Heidelberg 125896
Arte Reyes, Granada 081141
Arte Sacra Antiguidades, Belo Horizonte 058408
Arte Salutari, Lisboa 079867
Arte Santana, La Palmas de Gran Canaria 110706
Arte Santana, La Palmas de Gran Canaria 110707
Arte Santerasmo, Milano 106162
Arte Serrano 207, Madrid 110443
Arte Sol, Solothurn 111917
Arte Stampa, Savona 135881
Arte Struktura, Centro Internazionale d'Arte Contemporanea, Milano 053727, 134604
Arte Til, Fortaleza 096513
Arte Tiless, Zaragoza 110879
Arte Topaz, Barcelona 110109
Arte & Tradizione, Catania 075235, 106017, 127257
Arte Unico, Los Angeles 089693
Arte Universale, São Paulo 058684
Arte Vária, Coimbra 109243
Arte Veneta, Milano 135882
Arte Veneta, Venezia 106725
Arte Vinci, Bucaramanga 098204
Arte Vita Stil', Moskva 109494
Arte Viva, Frankfurt am Main 102745
Arte Viva, Levallois-Perret 099478
Arté Wallhof Galerie, Basel 111161
Arte X Arte, Buenos Aires 094057
Arte Xerea, Valencia 110797
Arte XXI, Madrid 110444
Arte y Collecciones, Madrid 122038
Arte y Color, Bogotá 098104
Arte y Diseño, Málaga 110631
Arte y Folklore, Guatemala 105474
Arte y Formas, Bucaramanga 098205
Arte y Marquetería la 35, Medellín . 098253
Arte y Naturaleza, Madrid 110445
Arte y Parte, Santander 136075
Arte y R, Málaga 110632
Arte y Reliquia, México 128502
Arte y Representaciones, Málaga . . 110633
Arte y Restauración, Barcelona . . . 129319
Arte y Restauracion de Antigüedades, Bogotá 059817, 123892
Arte y Ritual, Bogotá 059818
Arte y Ritual, Madrid 110446
Artea Centr, Varna 096762
Artealcontrario, Modena 106345
Arte'Alp, Leysin 111641
Artearredo, Roma 076313
Arteasel, Winnipeg 097572
Arteaspoon, Bruxelles 096139
Arteatelier, São Paulo 096662
Arteauction, Miami 122959
Arteba, Zürich 112037
Arteba Galleria, Lugano 111659
Artebene, Lüdinghausen 134173
Artec, Denia 081068
Artec, Denia 129493
A.R.T.E.C, Toulouse 124972
Artec Consulting, Bondi Junction . . 123190
Artecasa, Ciudad Real 081041
Artecc, Genova 075439
Arteclio, Pamplona 081510
Arteclio, Pamplona 081511
Artecum, Dardilly 099196
Arteder, Madrid 134938
Arteemu, Helsinki 098715
Artefact, Den Haag 107903
Artefact, Oosterbeek 128796
Artefact, Strasbourg 068295
Artefact Gallery, Saint Kilda, Victoria 095170
Artefacts, Bangalore 074765
Artefacts, Hobart 094637
Artefacts Conservation, Auckland . . 128897
Artefakt, Basel 111162
Artefakt, Gdańsk 108872
Artefakt, Karlsruhe 071709
Artefakt, Kassel 071743
Artefakt, Linz 057151
Artefakt, Lyon 064069
Artefakt, Tuttlingen 105078
Artefino, Cleveland 115684
Artefiz - Kunsthalle Zeitgenössischer KüntlerInnen, Zürich 112038
Arteforum, Bologna 105943
Artegma, Panamá City 108783
Artegrafica, Helsinki 098716, 124040, 133440
Artegrafica Silva, Collecchio 134573
Artegrafica Sociale, Cittadella 134571
Artegres, Cali 059876
Arteguia, Madrid 136076
Arteide, Palermo 076124, 127818
Arteincornice, Torino 106659
Arteinvest, Roma 106491
Artekon, Helsinki 124041
Artel Galéria, Budapest 105488
Arteleku, Donostia-San Sebastián . 050717
Artelier, Berlin 125164
Das Artelier, Bremen 102229
Artelier Tatort Spittelberg, Wien . . . 095794
Artelite, Milano 106163
Artem, Paris 138287
Artem, Quimper 101058
Artem Galleria, Palermo 106420
Artemar, Nice 065037
Artemarco, Viña del Mar 059568
Artemare, Roma 076314
Artemartell, Bogotá 059819, 123893
Artemedia, Altmünster 133058
Artemedia Pronto, Birsfelden 111295
Artemercato, Palermo 106421
Artemesia, Aix-en-Provence 098781
Artemesia, Alresford 083275
Artemida, Moschheim 072600
Artemis, Atlanta 087451
Artemis, Donostia-San Sebastián . . 129499
Artemis, Hong Kong 059594
Artemis, Hong Kong 059595
Artemis, İstanbul 112277
Artemis, Liverpool 113405
Artemis, Miami 117030
Artemis, München 072647
Artemis, New York 117633
Artemis, Paris 065460
Artemis, Strasbourg 068296
Artemis Archery Collection, Oldland 040641
Artemis Collection, Athinai 021159
Artemis Fine Arts, London 113475
Artemis Fine Arts, Paris 099988
Artemis Gallery, New York 117634
Artemis Gallery, Richmond 119096
Artemis Gallery, Seattle 119875
Artemisa - Arte Antica, Madrid 081240
Artémise, Dinard 099226
Artemise, Napoli 075943
Artemisia, Madrid 110447
Artemisia Gallery, Chicago 042821
Artemision, Palermo 127819
Artemision e.V., Görlitz 053032
Artemon, Zeuthen 074568, 134477
Artempório, Lisboa 109268
Artemus, New York 090699
Artemus, Portland 091895
Artemusa, Bogotá 098105
Artemusa, Bogotá 098106
Arten, Paris 099989
Arten Galéria, Budapest 105489
ArteNa, Waltenschwil 111983
Artenciel, Paris 065461
Artengo, Tholey 074057
Artenostrum, Dieulefit 099205
Artenova, New York 117635
Artense, Amersfoort 077745
Artenvielfalt, München 134215
Artenz, Waikato 108587
Arteoggi, Livorno 106114
L'Arteologo, Roma 076315
Arteology, Colne 112896
Artepe, İstanbul 112278
Arteranzoni, Milano 127518
Arterestauro, Firenze 127289
Arteria, Groningen 108033
Artéria Galéria, Szentendre 105580
Arterial Gallery, Parkside 095057
Arteries, Glasgow 113104
artery berlin, Berlin 133752, 135743
Artery Gallery of Photography, Kaslo 005665
Artery Melbourne, Fitzroy 094528
Artes, Annecy 060885
Artes, Bamberg 069444, 125129
Artes, Knokke-Heist 096321
Las Artes, Montevideo 087305
Las Artes, Montevideo 087306
Artès, Paris 065462
Artes, Rheda-Wiedenbrück 134366
Les Artes, San Diego 119478
Artes & Artes, Lisboa 109269
Artes Beatriz, Cali 123915
Artes Cova, Murcia 110646
Artes de México, México . 134756, 135990
Artes Design, Uppsala 082056
Artes-Galerie, Merlischachen 111731
Artes Goya, Santiago de Chile 059501
Artes Gráficas y Venereo, México . . 134757
Artes Monet, Santiago de Chile . . . 059502
Artes Platicas Vital, Brasília 096488
Artes Renoir, Santiago de Chile . . . 059503
Artes y Antigüedades, Bogotá 123894
Artes y Oficios, Monóvar 035510
La Artesa, Valencia 129755
Artesan, Barcelona 080801, 129320
Artésania, La Chaux-de-Fonds 082298, 129995
Artesanía Marquet, Mendoza 094101
Artesania Puerto, Valencia 129756
Artesania y Antiguedades, Madrid . 129569
Artesanias Bueno, Zaragoza 129805
Artesano Lugo, Madrid 081241
Artesanos ex Casa Maple, Buenos Aires 123151
Artesia, Catania 106018
Artesia Historical Museum and Art Center, Artesia 041786
Artespacio, Bogotá 098107
Artestile, Roma 076316
Artestudio, Milano 106164
Artetecnica Cornici, Bologna 105944
Arteum, Ljubljana 109951
Arteum, Ljubljana 109952
Artevalori, San Marino 129253
Artevera, Pohlheim 073351
ArteVino, Uetendorf 111951
Artevinum, Hamburg 071200
Artex, Chicago 115343
Artexpo, Bruxelles 135591
Artexpo, Cluj-Napoca 093846
Artexpo Atlanta, Atlanta 093972
Artexport, La Paz 096439
Artexte, Centre d'Information en Art Contemporain, Montréal 133316
art.fair, Enjoy Contemporary Art, Köln 093712
Artfinder, Bruxelles 096140
Artfirm, New York 117636
Artfit, Phoenix 118862
Artfix, Chicago 131883
ArtFocus, Toronto 135623
Artfocus Gallery, Brookvale 094310
Artfolio, Singapore 109766
Artforms Gallery Manuyunk, Philadelphia 046922
Artforum, Hannover 103257
Artforum, Ostrava 137804
Artfour, Elchingen 121391
ArtFrame Gallery, Tavistock 114558
Artframed, Ormskirk 114191
Artfrance, Paris 099990
Artful Arts, Harrogate 113189
Artful Deposit Galleries, Allentown . 041656
Artful Dodger, Charlotte 115275
Artful Dodger, Los Angeles 089694
Artful Dog, Nashville 117334
Artful Hand Gallery, Boston 115142
Artful Posters, New York 117637
Artfull Enterprises Mobile Gallery, Christchurch 112869
Artfully, Auckland 078921
Artfully Yours, Angaston 094152
Art'G, Béziers 098956
Artgalerie am Schloss, Bad Bergzabern 101628
Artgarbs Gallery, Saint Paul 119275
Artgarden, Grassington 113148
ARTgerecht, Eberbach, Baden 102588
Artginal, Paris 099991
Artgo Studio, Vancouver 097416
Artgold, Montréal 096970
Artgrafic, Barcelona 110110
Artgrafic, Barcelona 110111
Artgument, Esure-sur-Indre 099251
Arth Art and Crafts, Ahmedabad . . . 105593
Artha, Alkmaar 128521
Arthaud, Paris 133524
Arthaud, Damien, Lyon 064070
Arthaus, Wien 057373
Arthaus, Zwickau 105373
Arthe, Musée de la Veilleuse-Théière, Dinan 011614
Arthea Galerie, Wiesloch 105289
Ar'them Gallery, Paris 065463
Arthèmes, Cormeray 062480
Arthemis, Mulhouse 064828
Arthémuse, Bordeaux 098986
Arthena, Herzogenbuchsee 111555
Arthès, Bruxelles 120717
Artho, Edwin, Chez-le-Bart 129998
Arthobler, Porto 109365
The Arthonse, Christchurch 079011, 108381
Arthotel Billie Strauss, Kirchheim unter Teck 103554
Arthouse, Ahrensburg 101546
Arthouse, Bergheim, Erft 069533
ArtHouse, Fischerhütte 070692
Arthouse, Frederiksberg 060227

Arthouse, San Francisco ... 119594
Arthouse, Twistringen ... 105083
ArtHouse Gallery, Sittingbourne ... 114437
Arthouse Oakland, Oakland ... 118624
Arthouse Studios and Gallery, Farmington ... 116124
Arthur, Elizabeth, Hamilton, Victoria 055941
Arthur, John, Dorking ... 112952
Arthur A. Houghton Jr. Gallery and the Great Hall Gallery, New York ... 046295
Arthur Antiquités, Le Vicel ... 063731
Arthur Cottage, Ballymena ... 038577
Arthur Griffin Center for Photographic Art, Winchester ... 049230
The Arthur J. Moore Methodist Museum, Saint Simons Island ... 047721
Arthur M. Sackler Gallery, Washington ... 048884
Arthur M. Sackler Museum, Cambridge ... 042555
Arthur Manley Society, Tampa ... 054629
Arthur Rackham Society. Journal, Grosse Pointe ... 136374
Arthur Ross Gallery, University of Pennsylvania, Philadelphia ... 046923
Arthurdale Heritage Museum, Arthurdale ... 041787
Arthus-Bertrand, Paris ... 065464
Arthus-Bertrand, Paris ... 065465
Arthus Galéria, Pécs ... 105569
Arti, Alkmaar ... 134764
Arti, Roma ... 127930
Arti Capelli II, 's-Hertogenbosch ... 108070
Le Arti Decorative, Parma ... 076195
Arti Doria Pamphily, Roma ... 106492
Arti e Restauro Associazione Culturale di Volontariato, Bologna ... 127129
Arti et Amicitiae, Amsterdam ... 029169, 053878
Arti et Industriae, Den Haag ... 107904
Arti Grafiche, San Francisco ... 135488
Arti Grafiche Friulane, Tavagnacco . 134687
Arti Tessili, Genova ... 075440
arti-unique.com, Gilfach Goch ... 113092
Artia, Knokke-Heist ... 096322
Artia, Oslo ... 079418, 108701, 140697
Artia Russian Art, Toronto . 059140, 097223
Artiaco Alfonso, Napoli ... 106359
Artiarticle, Mablethorpe ... 114022
Artibus Asiae, Zürich ... 135080, 136121
Artice, Koondoola ... 056063
Artichoke, Vancouver ... 135624
Article, Charlotte ... 115276
ARTicle, Köln ... 103587
Articles Fine Arts Gallery, Stanwell Park ... 095222
Artico, Münster ... 104353
Articulate Gallery, WVSA Arts Connection, Washington ... 048885
Articule, Montréal ... 096971
Artiek, Groningen ... 078400
Artifact Book & Art Conservation, Kyneton ... 123252
Artifacts, Accrington ... 112489
Artifacts, Bruxelles ... 057834
Artifacts, Nashville ... 090422
Artifacts (Columbia), Columbia ... 136375
Artifacts Gallery, Indianapolis ... 116442
Artifakt Gallery, Deloraine ... 094471
Artifex, Brugge ... 096112
Artifex, Sutton Coldfield ... 114526
Artifexgallery, Wellington ... 108613
Artificial Design und Objekte, Nürnberg ... 073096
Artificio, Firenze ... 134580
L'Artificio, Torino . 076768, 106660, 128255
Artificium, Berlin ... 101783, 138740
Artificium, Witten ... 105310
Artifoni, Emanuele, Torino ... 128256
Artig Galerie, Frankfurt am Main .. 102746
Artiges & Fils, C., Bruxelles 096141, 123573
L'Artigiana, Milano ... 127519
Artigiana, Perugia ... 127868
Artigiana Cornici, Roma ... 106493
Artigiano Gallery, Auckland ... 108299
Artigo, Leigh-on-Sea ... 113377
Artika, Zürich ... 082939
Artikviteten, Oslo ... 079419
Artilleriemuseum Solothurn, Solothurn ... 037571
Artillery Company of Newport Military Museum, Newport ... 046455
Artillery Museum of Finland, Hämeenlinna ... 009488
Art'im, Paris ... 099992
art.image, Graz ... 133074
Art'Image Galerie, Aix-les-Bains ... 098800
Artimanha, Lisboa ... 079868
Artimer, Turku ... 060636
Artimex, Bruxelles ... 096142
Artimo, Rotterdam ... 108175
Artin, Varna ... 096763
Artin Evolution, Phoenix ... 118863
Artina, Paris ... 099993
Artina, Zug ... 112208
Artinf, Buenos Aires ... 135530
Artinfo, Moskva ... 134876
Artinform, Kyïv ... 112393
Artinoe, Huelva ... 129539
ArtInque, Buderim ... 055576
Artinside, Basel ... 136122
Artinteriors, Watford ... 114653
Artinvest, Thalwil ... 082845
Artio, Athinai ... 105385
Artion Gallery, Hong Kong ... 097757
Artiquaria, Burgos ... 081013, 129457
Artique, Guatemala ... 074648
Artique, Houston ... 132098
Artique, New York ... 117638
Artique, New York ... 117639
Artique, Tetbury ... 086847
Artique, Watford ... 114654
Artique Fine Art Gallery, Cremorne . 094438
Artique Galleria, Minneapolis ... 090344
Artique Galleries, Leicester ... 113369
Artique Gallery, San Antonio ... 119395
Artiquity of Orient, Armadale, Victoria ... 055360
Artirex, Bucureşti ... 129215
Artis, 's-Hertogenbosch ... 108071
Artis, Lyon ... 099536
Artis, Milano ... 106165
Artis, Paris ... 099994
Artis, Pont-Aven ... 101018
Artis, Salamanca ... 110733
Artis, Venezia ... 106726
Artis, Warszawa ... 109095
A.R.T.I.S. Anticariat, Bucureşti ... 140879
Artis Gallery, Auckland ... 108300
Artis Geologisch Museum, Amsterdam ... 029170
Artis-Historia, Mechelen ... 133293
ARTISA, Grenoble ... 093650
Artisaani, Helsinki ... 098717
Artisan, Berlin ... 101784
Artisan, Botany ... 123191
Artisan, Den Haag ... 128623
Artisan, Epping ... 113027
Artisan, New York ... 135411
Artisan, Roosendaal ... 128814
Artisan Antiques, Cleveland ... 088308
Artisan Antiques, Miami ... 090141
Artisan Books, Fitzroy ... 136897
L'Artisan Ebéniste, Prunay ... 124854
L'Artisan Encadreur, Paris ... 124563
Artisan Furniture Refinishing, Vancouver ... 123845
Artisan Galleries, Woodford Green . 114728
Artisan Gallery, Greenhithe ... 113158
Artisan Gallery, Robigana ... 095150
Artisan House, Los Angeles ... 116711
Artisan House, Phoenix ... 132644
Artisan Net, San Antonio ... 119396
Artisan Picture Gallery, Subiaco ... 095229
l'Artisan Pratique, Lausanne ... 130062
Artisan Sanat Galerisi, İstanbul ... 112279
Artisanat Réalité, Paris ... 099995
l'Artisane, Villars-sur-Ollon ... 082889
Artisania, Sale ... 107566
Artisans, Chennai ... 105620
Artisans 21 Gallery, Chicago ... 115344
Artisan's Alley, London ... 096942
Artisans Antiques Emporium, Jacksonville ... 089376
Artisans Art, Washington ... 120257
Artisans d'Art, Honfleur ... 099332
Artisans du Bois, San Diego ... 132843
Artisans Gallery, Akaroa ... 108290
Artisans Gallery, Cardiff ... 112805
Artisan's Gallery, San Antonio ... 119397
Artisan's Studio Gallery, Dallas ... 115838
Artisart, Maastricht ... 108115
Artischocke, Lörrach ... 072288
Artiscope, Bruxelles ... 096143
Artisforma, Stuttgart ... 104963
Artishock, Bischofszell ... 111296
Artisin, Enschede ... 078368
Artisjok, Rotterdam ... 078698
Artisjoke Maastricht, Maastricht ... 108116
Artison, Budapest ... 074666
Artissum, Den Haag ... 107905
Artist, Amsterdam ... 077789
Artist, Taipei ... 135655
The Artist, Tenterden ... 136176
Artist Alley Gallery, Las Vegas ... 116608
Artist Association, Mumbai ... 053688
Artist Atelier of Atlanta, Atlanta ... 114851
Artist Cooperative, Detroit ... 116080
Artist Cooperative Gallery, Omaha . 118684
Artist-Craftsmen of New York, New York ... 054630
Artist Design Group, New Orleans . 054631, 117394
Artist Doorway, Lilydale ... 136976
d'Artist Framery, Singapore ... 109767
d'Artist Gallery, Singapore ... 109768
Artist Gallery, San Francisco Museum of Modern Art, San Francisco ... 047852
artist Kunstmagazin, Bremen ... 135744
The Artist Market, New Orleans ... 117395
Artist Paintbrush, Sacramento ... 119135
Artist Product Gallery, New York ... 117640
Artist Publishing, Taipei ... 133394
Artist Quarters, Chicago ... 115345
Artist Run, Amsterdam ... 107668
Artist Showcase, Denver ... 115973
Artist Studio, Hyderabad ... 105695
Artist Studio, Hyderabad ... 105696
Artist Studio, Hyderabad ... 105697
Artist Studio Gallery, Delhi ... 105653
Artist Trade, Ljubljana ... 109953
artist window, Bremen ... 135745
Artista, Firenze ... 135883
Artistea, Pretoria ... 080730
Artistenmuseum, Marburg ... 018817
Artistes & Artisan du Quartier, Saint-Étienne ... 101146
Artistes de France - Comité European des Beaux Arts, Saint-Étienne ... 052890
Artistes-de-Notre Temps, Rauville-la-Bigot ... 067044
Artistes sans Frontières, Paris ... 099996
Artistic, Atlanta ... 131759
Artistic, San Antonio ... 132808
Artistic Accents, Regina ... 097170
Artistic Antiques, Miami ... 090142
Artistic Collections, Seattle ... 119876
Artistic Endeavors, San Antonio ... 119398
Artistic Frame Works, Silverton ... 080745
Artistic Galleries, Cincinnati ... 115602
Artistic Ideas, Toronto ... 097224
Artistic Imports, Atlanta ... 087452
Artistic Impressions, Miami ... 117031
Artistic License Gallery, North Adelaide ... 094971
Artistic Metal, Cincinnati ... 131928
Artistic Services Unlimited, Washington ... 120258
Artística Colorama, Córdoba ... 055251
Artistically Bent, Columbus ... 115761
Artistically Speaking Gallery & School of Fine Art, Edmonton ... 096865
Artistik, Indianapolis ... 116443
Artistix, London ... 096943
Artistixx, New Orleans ... 117396
Artistry Galleries, Hawthorn, Victoria ... 094623
Artists Abode, Semaphore ... 095189
Artists Alliance of California, Nevada City ... 054632
Artists and Framers, Baltimore ... 115033
Artist's and Graphic Designer's Market, Cincinnati ... 136376
Artists and Illustrators, London ... 136177
Artists and Illustrators Exhibition, London ... 093911
Artists' and Photographers' Press, London ... 135185
Artists Army Studios, San Francisco 119595
Artists Association of Nantucket, Nantucket ... 054633
Artists Association of Nantucket Museum, Nantucket ... 046122
Artists Association of New Mexico, Las Cruces ... 054634
Artists Bookworks, Forest Row ... 135150
Artists' Camp Antiques, Cremorne . 055722
Artists Center and Foundation, Makati ... 031695
Artists' Collaborative Gallery, Sacramento ... 119136
Artists Consultant, Philadelphia ... 118736
Artists' Cooperative Gallery, Omaha 046674
Artists Creations, Las Vegas ... 116609
Artists Eye, Dee Why ... 094470
Artists' Fellowship, New York ... 054635
Artists' Forum, San Diego ... 119479
Artists' Gallery, Austin ... 114953
Artists Gallery, Parañaque ... 108847
Artists Gallery, Virginia Beach ... 120214
Artist's Gallery of Seattle, Seattle .. 119877
Artists Garden, Fitzroy ... 094529
Artists' General Benvolent Institution, London ... 054280
Artist's Handicrafts Association, Chennai ... 053689, 105621, 134510
Artists Historical Society, London .. 054281
Artists House Tel Aviv, Israel Painters and Sculptors Association, Tel Aviv .. 023063
The Artist's Magazine, Cincinnati .. 136377
Artists on Santa Fe, Denver ... 115974
Artists Own Gallery, Brisbane ... 094284
Artists Realm, Gisborne ... 094584
Artists See Boston, Boston ... 115143
Artist's Space, New York ... 046296
Artists Space, New York ... 117641
The Artists Studio, Pwllheli ... 114291
Artists to Watch, Saint Paul ... 119276
Artists' Union of Armenia, Erevan .. 052448
Artists' Union of Azerbaijan, Baku .. 052629
Artists' Union of Georgia, Tbilisi ... 053005
Artists' Union of Kazakhstan, Almaty ... 053809
Artists' Union of Latvia, Rīga ... 053832
Artists' Union of the Moldova Republic, Chişinău ... 053866
Artists' Union of Turkmenistan, Ašgabat ... 054259
Artists Unlimited, Bielefeld ... 102109
Artists Unlimited, Tampa ... 120023
Artists's Union of Tajikistan, Dušanbe ... 054240
Artistuff, Swindon ... 114538
Artitude, Paris ... 099997
Artitudes, Memphis ... 116976
Artitudine, Genova ... 106081
Artium, Essen, Oldenburg ... 133921
Artium Art Gallery, Luxembourg ... 107390, 134749
Artium Art Magazine, Luxembourg . 135986
Artium - Centro Museo Vasco de Arte Contemporáneo, Vitoria-Gasteiz . 036077
Artium Kristall, Göteborg ... 110905
Artizen Gallery, Bendigo ... 094239
Artjärven Kotiseutumuseo, Artjärvi . 009459
ArtJaz Gallery, Philadelphia ... 118737
Artkids, Pretoria ... 080731, 129296

Artkraft Diffusion, Paris 099998
Artlab, Wien 095795
Artlab Australia, Adelaide 123173
Artland, Indooroopilly 123244
Artland, Mumbai 105756
Artland Gallery, Hong Kong 059596
Artlands, Hillington 113241
Artlantis Kunst und Design, Stuttgart 104964
Artlibris, Paris 138288
Artlife Gallery, New York 117642
Artline, Amsterdam 107669
Artline, Heilbronn 103330
Artline, Heilbronn 103331
Artline, Münster 104354
Artline Gallery, Zürich 112039
ArtLink, Virginia Beach 120215
Artloan, Bristol 112714
Artlonga, Berlin 101785
Artlounge-Hamburg, Hamburg 103091
Artlovers, Artarmon 055403
Artlynk Gallery, Beverley 112626
Art.M., Warszawa 109096
Artmakers Trust, Hamilton 108457
Artmann, Dr. Wolfgang Adolf, Krenglbach 095635
Artmaori, Taranaki 108564
Artmaori, Taranaki 108565
Artmark Galerie, Spital am Pyhrn . . 095763
Artmedia Art Gallery, Beograd 034146
Artmetro, Cleveland 115685
Art.Metz, Exposition d'Art Contemporain, Metz 093651
Artmill, Plymouth 114255
Artmobile, Newtown 046480
Art'monie, Nice 065038
Artmosphere, Graz 095518
Artmosphère, Vence 101431
Artmosphere Gallery, Seattle 119878
Artmost, Moskva 109495
Art'n Card, Bremen 102230, 133839
Artnau Espai d'Art, Girona 110364
Artner, Gertrud, Krenglbach 057132
ArtNet, Genève 111422
Artnet, İstanbul 112280
artnet.com, New York 136378
ArtNetwork, Nevada City 054636
Artnews, New York 136379
Artnex, San Diego 119480
Arto, Bruxelles 133257
Arto, Gent 120754
Arto Kunsthandel, Enschede 108016
Arto Nivo, Brugge 096113
Artobjekt, Öhringen 104521
Artocratia, Zürich 112040
Artofficial, Den Haag 107906
Artom, Domat/Ems 111386
Artonef, Aix-en-Provence 098782
Artonnet, München 104143
Artonomy, Cincinnati 115603
Artop, Lille 099483
Artop, Roubaix 101103
Artop-Atelier Restauration Tableaux et Objets Polychromes, Héry 124259
Artos, Sofia 096723
Artoteek Oost, Amsterdam 107670
Artoteket, Oslo 108702
Artothek, Köln 018303
Artothek der Stadt und Regionalbibliothek Erfurt, Erfurt 017007
Artothek der Zentral- und Landesbibliothek Berlin, Berlin 015987
Artothek Frankfurt (Oder), Frankfurt/ Oder 102841
Artothek-Galerie, Wien 002852
Artothek im Bonner Kunstverein, Bonn 016316
Artothek Worpswede, Worpswede . 020983
Artothèque, Angers 010386
Artothèque Antonin Artaud, Marseille 012926
Artothèque de Montréal, Montréal . 096972
Artothèque-Sud, Nîmes 013417
L'Artothèque Sud, Nîmes 099863
Artourage, 's-Hertogenbosch 078511
Artous, Paul & Fils, Montauban 064625
Artower Art, London 113476
Art+Photo Theiler, Matten 111721
Artplace, Perth 095065
Artpleasure, Paris 099999
Artplus, Prades 066975, 101049
Artport, Auckland 108301
Artpreciation, Hong Kong 097758
Artpresents 6000 Simrock Str 74, Köln 071909
Artprice.com, Saint-Romain-au-Mont-d'Or 133700
Artprice.com, Saint-Romain-au-Mont-d'Or 133701
Artprint, Kaiapoi 108480
Artprint on Canvas, Miami 117032
ArtProfil, Mannheim 135746
Artprojects, Vettweiß 074201
Artquest, Saint Louis 119183
Artra, Genova 106082
Artrad Art et Traditions, Maisons-Laffitte 099627
Artrade, Heerlen 108068
Artrade, Maastricht 078593
Artradex, L'Union 099530
Artrageous, San Diego 119481
Artrageous, San Diego 119482
Artrageous La Jolla, San Diego . . . 119483
Artrain, Ann Arbor 041729
Artraktion, Bern 111245
Artreasury, New York 090700
Artreich, Kalletal 103474
Artrent, Berlin 101786
Artrent, Frankfurt am Main 102747
Artrepco Galerie, Zürich 112041
Artrepreneur, New York 117643
Art'Restauré, Bordeaux 124112
Artréyu, Düsseldorf 102471
Artribú, Roma 106494
Artrium, Reutlingen 104722
Artrium Galerie, Ibbenbüren 103417
Artrium Kunstgalerie, Stäfa 082830, 111930
Artrock, San Francisco 119596
Artropica Innisfail Studio Gallery, Innisfail 094659
Artrujillo, Minneapolis 117243
ARTS, La Mézière 124278
A.R.T.S, Saint-Cyr-en-Val 067412
Art's, Sumy 112435
Les Arts, Vancouver 097417
Les Arts, Versailles 101453
Art's, Wellington 108614
Arts Affaires, Boulogne-Billancourt . 099019
Arts Alive Gallery, Oamaru 108529
Arts Alliance Center at Clear Lake, Nassau Bay 046159
Arts Anciens, Grasse 063036
Arts and Artisans, Chicago 115346
Arts and Artisans, Chicago 115347
Arts and Associates Gallery, Pasay . 108849
Arts and Carpets, Manama 057619
Arts and Communications Department, Christopher Newport College, Newport News 051843
Arts and Crafts Association of Meriden, Meriden 054637
The Arts and Crafts Furniture Company, London 085097, 130934
Arts and Crafts Museum, Bhavnagar 022027
Arts and Crafts School, Tripoli 050521
Arts and Hobby Centrum, Warszawa 079735
Arts and Humanities Department, Red Rocks Community College, Lakewood 051578
Arts and Humanities Division, Jamestown Community College, Jamestown . 051525
Arts and Humanities Division, Leeward Community College, Pearl City . . . 051921
Arts and Letters Club of Toronto, Toronto 052726
Arts and Media Division, Southampton College of Long Island University, Southampton 052195
Arts and Papers, Stuttgart 139751
Arts and Science Center for Southeast Arkansas, Pine Bluff 047023
Arts and Science Council, Charlotte 054638
Arts and Sciences Cluster, Central Community College, Columbus Campus, Columbus 051189
Arts and Sciences Division, New Mexico Junior College, Hobbs 051467
Arts and The Islamic World, London 136178
Arts Antiques, Buttevant 074868
Arts, Antiques & Auctions, Gent . . . 135592
Arts Antiquités, Bordeaux 061583
Arts Antiquités, Castres 062030
Arts Asiatiques, Paris 135691
Arts Association of Harare, Harare . 055126
Arts & Autographes, Paris 133525, 138289
Arts Bibliographic, London 141750
Arts Bridge, Chicago 054639
Arts Bridge, Chicago 115348
Arts Broc, Talence 068350
Arts & Business, London 054282
Lez Arts-Cachés, Bruxelles 096144
The Arts Center of the Capital Region, Troy 048617
Arts Center of the Ozarks, Springdale 048279
Arts Centre, Singapore 080427
Arts Centre, Washington 041313
The Arts Centre, South Essex Arts Association, Leamington 005759
Arts Centre (Far East), Singapore . . 080428
Arts Centre of Christchurch, Christchurch 030458
Arts Club, Montréal 096973
Arts Club of Chicago, Chicago 054640
Arts Club of Washington, Washington 048886, 054641
Arts Collector Gallery, Singapore . . 109769
Arts Company Nashville, Nashville . 117335
Arts & Concept, Singapore 109770
Arts Council England, London 054283
Arts Council England, East Midlands, Nottingham 054284
Arts Council England, South East, Brighton 054285
Arts Council England, South West, Exeter 054286
Arts Council Nelson, Nelson 053912, 108508
Arts Council of Fayetteville, Fayetteville 043832
Arts Council of Fayetteville-Cumberland County, Fayetteville 054642
Arts Council of New Orleans, New Orleans 054643
Arts Council of Northern Ireland, Belfast 054287
Arts Council of Pakistan, Karachi . . 053963
Arts Council of Richmond, Richmond 052727
Arts Council of Southwestern Indiana, Evansville 054644
Arts Council of the Blue Ridge, Roanoke 054645
Arts Council of the Mid-Columbia Region, Richland 054646
The Arts Council of Wales, Cardiff . 054288
Arts Council of Wales, Mid and West Wales Office, Carmarthen 054289
Arts Council of Wales, North Wales Office, Colwyn Bay 054290
Arts Council of Wayne County, Goldsboro 044238
Arts & Crafts Depot, Berlin 069565, 101787
Arts d'Afrique, København 060279
Arts d'Afrique Noire, Arnouville-les-Gonesse 098861, 133451, 135692
Art's Déco Gallery, La Seyne-sur-Mer 099409
Les Arts Décoratifs, Bruxelles 057835
Arts Décoratifs, Düsseldorf 070359
Arts Decoratifs, West Hollywood . . . 093450
Arts Décoration Extrême-Orient, Valence (Drôme) 068684
Arts Department, Framingham State College, Framingham 051354
Arts Department, Kellogg Community College, Battle Creek 050956
Arts Department, Saint Clair County Community College, Port Huron . . 051971
Arts Department, University of Science and Arts of Oklahoma, Chickasha 051132
Arts Design, Tampa 120024
Arts Desire, Auckland 078922, 108302
Arts d'Extrême Orient, Lyon 099537
Arts Division, Emma Willard School, Troy 052273
Arts Division, Fordham University, New York 051813
Arts Division, Merced College, Merced 051695
Arts Division, Portland Community College, Portland 051976
Arts Division, Rosemont College, Rosemont 052060
Arts Division, Wilkes Community College, Wilkesboro 052377
Arts du Marbre, Palaiseau 124534
Arts du Monde, New York 117644
Arts du XXème Siécle, L'Isle-sur-la-Sorgue 063920
Arts Education Policy Review, Washington 136380
Arts et Antiquités d'Alisson, Montmorency 064717
Arts et Bijoux, Melun 099702
Arts et Boiseries, Paris 065466
Arts et Civilizations, Quimper 067014
Arts et Collections, La Charité-sur-Loire 063323
Arts et Création, Limoges 063879
Arts et Décors, Zürich 082940
Arts et Métiers Graphiques, Paris . . 133526
Arts et Passions-Espace Collections, Blois 061518
Arts et Techniques, Paris 124564
Arts et Vestiges, Bouloc . . 061684, 099015, 124153
Arts Extended Gallery, Detroit 116081
Arts Extension Service, Amherst . . . 054647
The Arts Factory, Las Vegas 116610
Art's Factory, Paris 100000
Arts Faculty, Department of Fine and Applied Arts, Pretoria 050706
Arts for Health, Manchester 054291
Arts Forum, Courchevel 099176
Arts & Frames Millenium, Ottawa . . 097096
The Arts Gallery, Hong Kong 097759
Arts Gambetta, Montigny-lès-Metz . 099746
Arts Graphiques, Maisons-Alfort . . . 133490
Arts Graphiques d'Aquitaine, Libourne 133482
Arts Guild, Swindon 142107
Art's Haggle, Nantes 099803
Arts Hawaii, Honolulu 088934
Arts, Humanities and Communications Division, Modesto Junior College, Modesto 051733
Arts in Harmony, Indianapolis 116444
Arts in Progress, Boston 054648
Arts in the Academy, Washington . . 048887
Arts Indiana Magazine, Indianapolis 136381
Arts Infinite, Hong Kong 097760
Arts Institute at Bournemouth, Poole 050854
Arts League of Michigan, Detroit . . 054649
Arts Limited, Richmond 119097
Arts Litho, Paris 100001
Arts & Livres, Luxembourg 077473, 140239
Arts Magazine (New York), Forest Hills 136382
Arts Magna, Miami 117033
Aux Arts Majeurs, Paris 138290
Arts Management Weekly, London . 136179
Arts Massilia, Marseille 099639
Arts Midland Galleries, Midland . . . 045847
Arts Midwest, Minneapolis 054650
Arts & Mirrors, Toronto 097225
Arts NDG, Montréal 096974
Arts Nouveaux, Verona 076991
Arts of Africa, New Brunswick 136383

Arts of Asia, Armadale, Victoria . . .055361, 094160
Arts of Asia, Ho Chi Minh City 120498
Arts of Asia, Hong Kong 135647
Arts of Asia Publications, Hong Kong 133358
Arts of Iran, San Francisco 119597
Arts of Paradise, Honolulu 116197
Arts on the Green, Omaha 118685
Arts Options, Mendlesham Green . . 114077
Arts Palace, Cairo 098612
Arts Partnership of Greater Spartanburg, Spartanburg 054651
Arts Pluriels, Fort-de-France 107458
Arts Primitifs, Arnay-le-Duc 060978
Les Arts Production, Bruxelles 096145
Arts Project Australia, Northcote . . .001342, 052451
Arts Quarterly, New Orleans 136384
Arts-Recherche Photographiques, Bruxelles 096146
Arts Resource, San Francisco 119598
Arts Tamborine, Mount Tamborine . 094911
Arts & Tradition, Beirut 077384
ArtsAtlantic, Halifax 135625
Artscan, Houston 116277
Artscape, New York 136385
Artscape Gallery, Palmerston North 108534
Artscape West International, San Francisco 119599
Artsconnexion, Mons 052644
Artsconnexion, Mons 096389
ArtScope, Chicago 136386
Artscope, New York 117645
Artseal Gallery, San Francisco 119600
Artsearch Databank, Cincinnati . . . 115604
Artset, Limoges 063880
Artsfocus, Colorado Springs 136387
Artsgora, Barcelona 110112
Artshaus.Co.Uk, Caister-on-Sea . . . 112779
Artshouse Gallery, Northbridge 094987
Artshow, Milano 135884
Artside Gallery, Seoul 107206
Artsiphartsi, Tampa 120025
Artsland, Birmingham 115098
Artslink, Hong Kong 135648
Artsmart, Christchurch 108382
Artsonje Center, Seoul 027543
Artsonje Museum, Gyeongju 027504
Artsoum, Nice 099828
Artsource, Denver 115975
Artsource, London 113477
Artsource International, New York . . 117646
ArtSource Quarterly, Nevada City . . 136388
ArtSouth Gallery, Gore Invercargill . 108454
Artspace, Auckland 030430
Artspace, Ha Noi 120451
Artspace, Hong Kong 097761
Artspace, Peterborough 006137
Artspace, Raleigh 047309
Artspace, Richmond 047410
Artspace, Richmond 119098
Artspace, Woolloomooloo 001634
Artspace-Lima, Lima 045293
Artspeak, Vancouver 097418
Artspeak Studio Gallery, Warrandyte 095370
ArtsPost, Hamilton 108458
ArtSquare, London 113478
Artstil, Moskva 140900
Artstudio, München 072648
Artstyl, Warszawa 129080
Artsud, Conques 099171
Artsud, Villeneuve-d'Aveyron 101474
Artsud Beyrouth, Beirut 093809
Artsud Dubai, Dubai 093901
Artsud Moscou, Moskva 093847
Artsville, Nashville 117336
Artswatch, Louisville 045485
Artswatch, Louisville 116928
Artswest, Seattle 119879
Artsyndication, Düsseldorf 070360
Arttalk, Beacon 136389
Arttech, West Thurrock 114669
Arttemple, Hyderabad 105698
Artterra, Praha 098417
Artterra Int, Groningen 108034
Arttig, Milwaukee 117167
art.tm, Inverness 113296
art.tm, Inverness 113297
art.tm, Inverness 135162
Arttown, London 113479
Artuel, Paris 100002
Artur, Ramon, Barcelona 080802
Artur Media, Bucureşti 080142
Artus & Associés, Paris 121112
Artveler, Paris 100003
Art'Vigne, La Chaux-de-Fonds 111345
Artvillage, Hausmannstätten 052508
Artvision, La Tranche-sur-Mer 099410
Artvue, Atlanta 114852
Artware, München 134216
Artware, San Diego 119484
Artware, Stuttgart 073958
Artware Consulting, Wien 095796
Artware Fine Art, London 113480
Artwaves, Saint Just 114378
Artways, Toulouse 101332
Artweek, San Jose 136390
Artword Artist Forum, Toronto 135626
Artwork Mexican, Phoenix 118864
Artwork Publishing, San Francisco .119601, 135489
Artworks, Austin 114954
Artworks, Bradford 112688
Artworks, Calgary 096788
Artworks, Cincinnati 115605
Artworks, Paris 065467
Artworks, Trenton 048600
Artworks 21, Sacramento 119137
Artworks Company, Tianjin 098007
Artworks Cornwall, Saint Austell . . 114349
Artworks Gallery, Dubai 112451
Artworks Gallery, Dunedin 108425
Artworks Gallery, Southport 095215
Artworks of Kansas City, Kansas City 116555
Artworks on Q, Mermaid Waters . . . 094839
ArtWorkz, Lowestoft 114002
Artworld Europe, Largo 136391
ArtWorld Hotline, Nevada City 136392
ArtXchange, Seattle 119880
Arty Bee's Books, Wellington 140669
Artyard Sculpture Gallery, Denver . . 115976
Artyfacts, Brighton 136180
Artyfacts, Bromsgrove 112745
Artyfacts, Padstow 114208
Artyfacts, Wadebridge 114634
Artyp, Bruxelles 096147
Artz, Petersfield 114245
Artz, Martina, Wetzlar 074380
ArtZ FartZ, Milwaukee 117168
ArtZ FartZ, Milwaukee 117169
Artz Plus, Edmonton 096866
Artz y Gifts, Chicago 115349
Artzan Canada, Toronto 097226
Artzco, Vancouver 097419
Artzone, Glasbury 113097, 135152
Artzonia, Vancouver 097420
Artzu Gallery, Manchester 114038
Aru, Maria Pia, Cagliari 127240
Aruid-Panajotovi, Ruse 096708
Arun, Lalitpur 107601
Arundel, Los Angeles 142488
Arundel Bookshop, Arundel 141387
Arundel Clocks, Arundel . . 083310, 130304
Arundel Museum and Heritage Centre, Arundel 038533
Arundel Toy Museum Dolls House, Arundel 038534
Arusha Declaration Museum, Arusha 037845
Arvada Center for the Arts and Humanities, Arvada 041788
Arval, Cali 123916
Arv'Art, Chamonix-Mont-Blanc 099107
Arvel, Dainville 062589
Arvidsjaurs Hembygdsmuseum, Arvidsjaur 036196
Arvika Fordonmuseum, Arvika 036198
Arvika Museum, Arvika 036201
Arvim, Roma 076317
Arvis, Gabrielle, Paris 065468
Arvore, Porto 109366
Arxiu del Monestir, Sant Joan de les Abadesses 035784
Ary, Patricia F., Fortaleza 096514
Ary Jan, Mathias, Paris 065469
Aryan, Delhi 134512
Aryana, Lyon 064071
Arzamasskij Gosudarstvennyj Literaturno-Memorialnyj Muzej A.P. Gajdara, Arzamas 032998
Arzamasskij Istoriko-chudožestvennyj Muzej, Arzamas 032999
Arzat, Paris 065470, 124565
Arzemju Mákslas Muzejs, Rīga 027729
Arzenal, Praha 098418
Arzenál Galéria, Budapest 105490
Arzile, Jean-Claude, Bordeaux 124113
AS 220 Studio, Providence 119069
A.S. Antique Galleries, Manchester .085910, 131254
AS Art, Köln 071910
Les As de la Renovation, Les Abymes 127072
A.S. Starožitnosti, Pardubice 060072
A.S. Starožitnosti, Praha 060109
As Time Goes By, Edmonton 058818
As Time Goes By, Hamilton, New South Wales 055935
As Time Goes By, Louisville 089957
AS Verlag, Zürich 135081
ASA Artisan, Palatine 136393
Asa Packer Mansion, Jim Thorpe . . 044863
Asagaya Bijutsu Senmon Gakko, Tokyo 050476
Asagaya Some Kenkyujo, Tokyo . . . 050477
Asahi, Sendai 106991
Asahi, Tokyo 077237, 107015
Asahi Bijutsukan, Tokyo 135971
Asahi-yaki Pottery Museum, Uji, Kyoto 027306
Asahikawa Youth Science Museum, Asahikawa 026421
Asaka, San Francisco 119602
Asakichi, San Francisco 092735
Asakura Sculpture Gallery, Tokyo . . 027145
As'Art, Paris 100004
Asashi Seimei Gallery, Tokyo 107016
Åsavallen, Postmuseum, Skolmuseum och Bruksmuseum, Edsbro 036240
Asbæk, København 098534
Asboth, Wien 095797
Asbury, Peter, Birmingham 083525, 130386
ASC Deco, Dallas 088462
ASC-Kunstobjekte, Aachen 101499
Les Ascenceurs du Calal Historique du Centre, Houdeng-Aimeries 003521
Ascencio, Alain, Toulon (Var) 068441
Ascencio, Robert, Maureilhan 064438
Ascent Auction Galleries, Saint Leonards-on-Sea 122680
Aschanska Gården, Eksjö 036241
Aschauer, Franz, Wieselburg an der Erlauf 057599
Asche, Johann, Berlin 138741
Aschehoug & Co., H., Oslo 134848
Aschenbrenner, Ernst, Hohenwarth . 071560
Aschendorffsche Verlagsbuchhandlung, Münster 134292
Andreas Aschoff & Anna Petri, Jena 139287
Ascot, Saint Marys 137082
Ascot Antik, Monchy-Saint-Eloi . . . 064592
Ascot Antique, Wellington 079316
Ascot Antiques, Blackpool 083551
Ascot Antiques, Invercargill 079123
Ascott House, Leighton Buzzard . . . 039982
Asele Institute Nimo, Nimo 050577
Asenbaum, London 085098
Asenbaum, Renate, Wien 137288
Asesepän Paja, Naarva 009896
Asfhan, Sharjah 083209
Ash, London 085099, 141751
Ash, New York 117647
Ash, Westcliff-on-Sea 114672
Ash, Edward, Orpington 114192
Ash, Jim & Pat, Llandeilo 085030
Ash, Norma, Memphis 132315
Ash Hill Towers, Kilmallock 074984
Ash Lawn-Highland, College of William and Mary, Charlottesville 042763
Ashanti, Atlanta 114853
Ashanti, Jacksonville 089377
Ashbey's Galleries, Cape Town 121979
Ashbourne Antiques, Ashbourne . . . 083324
Ashbourne Gallery, Ashbourne 112523
Ashbrook, Ottawa 059029
Ashburton Art Gallery, Ashburton . . 108292
Ashburton Aviation Museum, Ashburton 030424
Ashburton Books, Ashburton 141388
Ashburton Marbles, Ashburton 083335
Ashburton Museum, Ashburton . . . 030425
Ashburton Museum, Ashburton . . . 038535
Ashburton Vintage Car Club Museum, Ashburton 030426
Ashby, Queenscliff 056511
Ashby, San Diego 119485
Ashby, Vanessa, Armadale, Victoria 055362
Ashby-de-la-Zouch Museum, Ashby-de-la-Zouch 038536
Ashby-Hodge Gallery of American Art, Fayette 043828
Ashby Moody, M., Tampa . 093106, 143019
Ashcombe Coach House, Henfield . 084657
Ashcroft Museum, Ashcroft 005031
Ashe Antiques Warehouse, Wickham Market 087145, 131685
Asher, Portland 091896
Asher & Co., A., IJmuiden 140465
Ashern Pioneer Museum, Ashern . . . 005032
Asher's Bazar, Caracas 093521
Asheville Art Museum, Asheville . . . 041789
Ashford Gallery, Dublin 022730
Ashford Museum, Ashford 038537
Ashgate Publishing, Aldershot 135115
Ashgrove Clocks, Brighton, Victoria 055547, 123195
Ashione, New York 117648
Ashish Balram Nagpal, Mumbai . . . 105757
Ashitaba, Sendai 077210
Ashiyana Enterprises, Jaipur 074814
Ashkenazy, Los Angeles 116712
Ashland, Cincinnati 088211
Ashland - Henry Clay Estate, Lexington 045256
Ashland Historical Museum, Ashland 041804
Ashland Historical Society Museum, Ashland 041813
Ashland Logging Museum, Ashland 041802
Ashland Logging Museum, Ashland 041803
Ashland Railroad Station Museum, Ashland 041806
Ashley, Cleveland 088309
Ashley, Houston 089022
Ashley, Houston 089023
Ashley, Houston 089024
Ashley, Houston 089025
Ashley, Houston 089026
Ashley, Houston 089027
Ashley, Jacksonville 089378, 122924
Ashley, Louisville 116929
Ashley, Miami 117034
Ashley, Omaha 091553
Ashley, Portland 091897
Ashley, Diane, Philadelphia 118738
Ashley Jackson, Holmfirth 113251
Ashley Park Antiques, Waitotara . . . 079300
Ashley Pine, Saintfield . . . 086482, 131447
Ashman, Jacksonville 089379
Ashmolean Museum of Art and Archaeology, Oxford University, Oxford 040653
Ashmolean Museum Publications, Oxford 135290

Ashok, Amsterdam 107671
The Ashridge Decorative and Fine Arts Society, Berkhamsted 054292
Ashtabula Arts Center, Ashtabula . . 041816
Ashtabula County Historical Society Museum, Geneva-on-the-Lake . . 044168
Ashtabula Plantation, Pendleton . . . 046867
Ashtead Park Lane Fine Arts, Ashtead 112529
Ashton, Chicago 115350
Ashton, Saint Paul 092349
Ashton, K., Gants Hill 084450, 130722
Ashton Court Visitor Centre, Bristol . 038856
Ashton-Drake Galleries, Baar 111147
Ashton Drake Galleries, Wolfurt . . . 095976
Ashton Gallery, Winnipeg 097573
Ashton & Gower, Stow-on-the-Wold 086738
Ashton Villa, Galveston 044128
Ashton's Antiques, Brighton 083685
Ashtree, Fresno 088895
Ashtree Arts, Northallerton 114149
Ashvita Art Object, Chennai 105622
Ashwell Gallery, Ashwell 112531
Ashwell Village Museum, Ashwell . 038545
Ashworths Treasures of the Earth, Home Hill 001116
A.S.I. Posten, Minneapolis 136394
Asia 2000, Hong Kong 133359
Asia-Africa Museum, Genève 037109
Asia America, Portland 091898
Asia Art Archive, Hong Kong 007114, 133360
Asia Art Gallery, Mandaluyong 108831
Asia Arts, Bangkok 083092
Asia Arts and Crafts Syndikat, Kuala Lumpur 077497
Asia-Australia Arts Centre, Sydney . 095270
Asia Bookroom, Belconnen 136797
Asia Contemporary Art, London . . . 113481
Asia Crate, Oklahoma City 091473
Asia Gallery, Bangkok 112229
Asia-Pacific Culture & Arts, Singapore 109771
Asia Rustic, New York 090701
Asia Society and Museum, New York 046297
Asia Tide, Armadale, Victoria 055363
Asian-African Conference Museum, Bandung 022387
Asian-American Arts Centre, New York 046298
Asian American Arts Centre, New York 117649
Asian and Primitive Art Gallery, Paddington 095014
Asian Antique Gallery, Denver 088656
Asian Antiques, Bangkok 083093
Asian Antiques and Furniture, Los Angeles 089695
Asian Antiques Center, Houston . . . 089028
Asian Art Center, Washington 133021
Asian Art Gallery, London 113482
Asian Art Gallery, New York 117650
Asian Art Gallery, Woollahra 095417
Asian Art in London, London 113483
Asian Art Museum of San Francisco, San Francisco 047853
Asian Art News, Hong Kong 133361, 135649
The Asian Art Newspaper, London . 136181
Asian Art Options, Singapore 109772
Asian Arts, New York 090702
Asian Arts and Culture Center, Towson 048593
Asian Center Museum, Quezon City 031770
Asian Civilisations Museum, National Museums of Singapore, Singapore 034290
Asian Connection Galleries, Noosa Heads 056350
Asian Cultures Museum, Corpus Christi 043162
Asian Design, New York 090703
Asian Essence, Chicago 088025
Asian Feeling, Bruxelles 057836
Asian Galleries, Art Gallery of New South Wales, Sydney 001506
Asian Home Decor, Chicago 088026
Asian House of Chicago, Chicago . . 088027
Asian Resource Gallery, Oakland . . 046590
Asian Style, Bolzano 075124
Asian Style, Seattle 092963
Asian Watercolors by Suzanna, San Francisco 119603
Asianart, North Newton 086091
Asiart Corner, Hong Kong . 059597, 137747
Asiatic, Singapore 080429
Asiatic Arte, Buenos Aires 094058
Asiatic Society, Kolkata 053690
Asiatic Society Museum, Kolkata . . 022212
Asiatica-Buchhandlung, Zürich 141321
Asiatika, Stuttgart 073959
Asiattitude, Senlis 068209
Asibelle, Couesmes 062500
A.S.I.E., Marseille 064315
Asie Antique, Paris 065471
Asien Antik, Berlin 069566
Asikkalan Kotiseutumuseo, Asikkala 009460
Asil, Damascus 083052
Asil, Manama 057620, 095991
Asila, Cairo 098613
El Asilo del Libro, Valencia 141075
Asilva, Ariane-Essor, Paris 100005
Asín Remírez de Esparza, F., Zaragoza 141088
L'Asino, Livorno 075523
Aşiyan Müzesi, İstanbul 038079
Aska Antik, Sorunda 081899
Askanders, Indianapolis 132149
Askeladden Antikk, Stavanger 079497
Askéo, Paris 100006
Asker Museum, Hvalstad 030917
Askeri Müze ve Kültür Sitesi Komtuanlıği^BE, İstanbul 038080
Askersunds Auktionskammare, Askersund 122103
Askim Museum, Askim 030746
Askon Museo, Lahti 009780
Aslı Tunca, İstanbul 083118
Åsmundarsafn, Listasafn Reykjavíkur, Reykjavík 021959
Asociace Starožitníků, Praha 052834
Asociación Amigos del Museo Nacional de Bellas Artes, Buenos Aires 052442
Asociación Colombiana de Museos, ACOM, Bogotá 052808
Asociacion de Amigos de los Museos Militares, Madrid 054079
Asociación de Anticuarios de Aragón, Zaragoza 054080
Asociación de Artistas Plásticos de Madrid, Madrid 054081
Asociación de Artistas Visuales de Euskal Herria, CreaZ, Donostia-San Sebastián 054082
Asociación de Artistas Visuales de Euskal Herria Mediaz, Bilbao 054083
Asociación de Empresarios de Almonedas y Antigüedades de Madrid, Madrid . 054084
Asociación de Escritores y Artistas, Madrid 054085
Asociación de Museos de Guatemala, AMG, Guatemala 053671
Asociacion de Profesionales en Arte Antiguo y Moderno, Madrid 054086
Asociación del Amigos de Museo Nacional de Arte Decorativo, Buenos Aires . 052443
Asociación Española de Archiveros, Bibliotecarios, Museólogos y Documentalistas, ANABAD, Madrid 054087
Asociación Española de Museólogos, Madrid 054088
Asociación Española de Pintores y Escultores, Madrid 054089
Asociación Española de Profesionales del Diseño, Madrid 054090
Asociación Fotográfica Cordobesa, Córdoba 054091
Asociación Galega de Artistas Visuais, Vigo 054092
Asociación Internacional Mujeres en las Artes, Madrid 054093
Asociación Madrileña de Artistas Visuales Independientes, Madrid 054094
Asociacion Madrileña de Galerias de Arte, Madrid 054095
Asociacion Nacional Profesional de Galerias de Arte, Madrid 054096
Asociación Numismática Española, Barcelona 054097
Asociación Plástica Latina Internacional de Chile, Santiago de Chile 052783
Asociación Venezolana Amigos del Arte Colonial, Caracas 055118
Asociatia Nationalá a Muzeelor in aer Liber - România, Bucureşti 054012
Aspect Design, Hobart 094638
d'Aspect Jacques, Marseille 138191
Aspects Gallery, Blairgowrie 094260
Aspects Gallery in Appleby, Nelson . 108509
Aspects of Art, Leyburn 113389
Aspekt Galerie, Brno 098325
Aspen, Denver 088657
Aspen Art Museum, Aspen 041819
Aspen Historical Society Museum, Aspen 041820
Asperger, Berlin 101788
Aspidistra Antiques, Finedon 084402, 130709
Aspidistra Antiques, Woking 087204
Aspinall, Walter, Sabden 086428
Aspingtons, Stockholm 141147
Aspire, Cleveland 122863
Aspö-Tosterö Hembygdsmuseum, Strängnäs 036684
Aspöck, Dr. Hubert, Ried im Innkreis 137242
Asppan, Rivas-Vaciamadrid 134952
Asprey, Jacques, London 113484
Asquier, Marie-Pierre, Veigné 125010
ASR, Hamburg 125800
Asri Environmental Education Center, Bristol 042420
Assadi, D., Nyon 111782
Assam, Ingeborg, Villach 095775
Assam Forest Museum, Gauhati . . . 022119
Assam Forest Museum, Guwahati . 022132
Assam State Museum, Gauhati 022120
Assam State Museum, Guwahati . . 022133
Åssamuséet, ÅSSA-Industri- och Bilmuseum och ÅSSA Spårväxlar och Signalfabriks, Åtvidaberg 036206
Assay, Caroline d', Paris 124566
Asseff, Henry, Cali 059877
Assembly Antiques Centre, Bath . . . 083414
Assembly Rooms Market, Lancaster 084896
Assets Antiques, Buffalo 087861
Assfalg, Siegfried, Biberach an der Riß 102105
Assiginack Historical Museum and Norisle Heritage Park, Manitowaning 005824
Assila, Giza 098683
Assinck, Ruud, Lochem 128753
Assiniboia, Regina 006247
Assiniboia and District Historical Society Museum, Assiniboia 005034
Assiniboia Gallery, Regina 097171
Assiniboine Historical Society Museum, Brandon 005137
Assioma, Prato 106472
Assmann, Franz Josef, Graz 057002
Assoc Numismatique du Centre, Orléans 065293
Associação Brasileira de Conservadores-Restauradores de Bens Culturais, Rio de Janeiro 052702
Associação Brasileira de Livreiros Antiquarios, Petrópolis 052703
Associacão Portugesa Antiquários, Lisboa 054001
Associacão Portugesa de Museologia, Lisboa 054002
Associacija Muzeev Rossii, Tula . . . 054018
Associacija Muzej, Varna 052706
Associació Art Bacelona, Barcelona 054098
Associacio Arts, Palma de Mallorca 054099
Associació Cultural i Artística Els Esquirol, La Massana 052438
Associacio d'Amics de les Antiguitats, Barcelona 054100
Associació d'Artistas Visuals de Catalunya, Barcelona 054101
Associació d'Artistas Visuals de la Comunitat Valenciana, Valencia . . 054102
Associació d'Artistas Visuals de les Illes Baleares, Palma de Mallorca 054103
Associació del Museo de la Ciència i de la Tècnica i d'Arqueologia Industrial de Catalunya, Terrassa 054104
Associaciò Difusora d'Obra Gràfica Internacional-ADOGI, Barcelona . .054105, 134902
Associated Artists of Pittsburgh, Pittsburgh 054652
Associated Artists of Pittsburgh Gallery, Pittsburgh 047041
Associated Artists of Winston-Salem, Winston-Salem 054653, 120421
Associated International, Los Angeles 116713
Association Alberto et Annette Giacometti, Paris 052891
Association Art Promotion, Liège . . 052645
Association Artistique Général Gérard, Ligny 052646
Association Culturelle des Peintres Sculpteurs, Marseille 099640
Association Culturelle Terre des Arts, Galerie Mistral, La Bégude-de-Mazenc 099384
Association des Amis de Cholaïc, Ayer 054169
Association des Amis des Arts et de la Culture, Monaco 053867
Association des Amis du Musée Asia-Africa, AMA, Genève 054170
Association des Antiquaires Brocanteurs et Negociants en Oeuvres d'Art du Poitou, Poitiers 052892
Association des Antiquaires de la Province de Liège, Liège 052647
Association des Antiquaires du Golfe, Saint-Tropez 052893
Association des Antiquaires du Haut-Rhin, Hirsingue 052894
Association des Antiquaires et Brocanteurs de la Charente, Angoulême 052895
Association des Antiquaires et Brocanteurs de la Creuse, Peyrat-la-Nonière . . 052896
Association des Antiquaires et Brocanteurs de la Place du Foirail, Pau 052897
Association des Antiquaires et Brocanteurs de la Vendée, Les Sables-d'Olonne 052898
Association des Antiquaires et Brocanteurs des Deux-Sèvres, Chauray 052899
Association des Brocanteurs et Antiquaires de Loire-Atlantique, Nantes 052900
Association des Conservateurs d'Antiquités, Athinai 053662
Association des Conservateurs et du Personnel Scientifique des Musées de la Ville de Paris, Paris 052901
Association des Galeries d'Art Actuel de Belgique, Bruxelles 052648
Association des Galeries d'Art Contemporain, Montréal 052728
Association des Galeries d'Art Contemporain de Montréal, Montréal 052729
Association des Galeries d'Art Parisiennes, Paris 052902
Association des Musées Automobiles de France, Paris 052903
Association des Musées et Centres pour le Développement de la Culture Scientifique, Technique et Industrielle, AMCSTI, Dijon 052904
Association du Patrimoine Artistique, Bruxelles 052649
Association Européenne des Musées d'Histoire des Sciences Médicales (AEMHSM), Paris 052905
Association for British Transport and Engineering Museums, London . . 054293

Association for Cultural Advancement through Visual Art, London 054294
Association for Cultural Enterprises, Worcester 054295
Association for Living History, Farm and Agricultural Museums, North Bloomfield 054654
Association for Studies in the Conservation of Historic Buildings, London 054296
Association for Visual Arts, Cape Town 054063, 110016
Association Française des Amateurs d'Horlogerie Ancienne, Besançon 052906
Association Française des Conservateurs-Restaurateurs, Paris 052942
Association Française des Directeurs de Centres d'Art, Pougues-les-Eaux . 052907
Association Française des Musées d'Agriculture et du Patrimoine Rural, AFMA, Paris 052908
Association Française des Régisseurs d'Œuvres d'Art, AFROA, Paris . . . 052909
L' Association Francophone des Musées de Belgique, Liège 052650
Association Générale des Conservateurs des Collections Publiques de France, Paris 052910
Association Genevoise des Galeries d'Art Moderne, Genève 054171
Association Internationale de Management des Arts et de la Culture, Montréal 052730
Association Internationale des Amis de Nicolas Schöffer, Paris 052911
Association Internationale des Arts Plastiques, Paris 052912
Association Internationale des Critiques d'Art, Paris 052913
Association Internationale des Musées d'Armes et d'Histoire Militaire, Liège 052651
Association Internationale des Musées d'Histoire, Paris 052914
Association Internationale des Numismates Professionels, Bruxelles 052652
Association Museum and Industries, Paris 052915
Association Museums New Brunswick, Fredericton 052731
Association Nationale des Artistes Professionnels des Arts Plastiques, Ouagadougou 052713
Association Nationale des Conseillers aux Arts Plastiques, Orléans 052916
Association Nationale des Directeurs d'Ecole d'Art, Cergy 052917
Association Nayart, Nay 099822
Association Numismatique de Monaco, Monaco 053868
Association of American Editorial Cartoonists, Raleigh 054655
The Association of Art and Antique Dealers - LAPADA, London 054297
Association of Art and Antique Dealers of Saint Peterburg, Sankt-Peterburg 054019
Association of Art Historians, London 054298
Association of Art Historians Bulletin, London 136182
Association of Art Museum Directors, New York 054656
Association of Art/Object Handlers and Allied Professionals, London 054299
Association of Artists in Ireland, Dublin 053710
Association of British Picture Restorers, Hayling Island 054317
Association of British Transport and Engineering Museums, Rugby . . . 054300
Association of Children's Museums, Washington 054657
Association of College and University Museums and Galleries, Norman . 054658
Association of Community Arts Agencies of Kansas, Salina 054659
Association of Czech Moravian and Silesian Museums, Praha 052835
Association of European Open Air Museums, Hagen, Westfalen 053033
Association of Greek Antiquarians and Art Dealers, Athinai 053663
Association of Hawaii Artists, Honolulu 054660
Association of Hispanic Arts, New York 054661
Association of Icelandic Curators, Reykjavík 053679
Association of Icelandic Visual Artists, Reykjavík 053680
Association of Illustrators, London . 054301
Association of Independent Colleges of Art & Design, San Francisco 054662
Association of Independent Museums, Bristol 054302
Association of Independent Museums Bulletin, Cocking 136183
Association of Indian Museums, Delhi 053691
Association of Indiana Museums, Indianapolis 054663
Association of International Photography Art Dealers, Washington 054664
Association of Islandic Painters, Reykjavík 053681
Association of Manitoba Museums, Winnipeg 052732
Association of Master Upholsterers, Newport, Gwent 054303
Association of Midwest Museums, Saint Louis 054665
Association of Museum Professionals of the Republic of Macedonia, Skopje . . 053848
Association of Museums and Galleries of Czech Republic, Praha 052836
Association of Museums in Seoul, Seoul 053817
Association of Museums of the Indian Ocean, Victoria 054045
Association of Northern, Kimberley and Arnhem Aboriginal Artists, Darwin 052452
Association of Painters and Sculptors, Tiranë 052435
Association of Railway Museums, Washington 054666
Association of Railway Preservation Societies, Watford 054304
Association of Science-Museum Directors, San Diego 054667
Association of Science-Technology Centers, Washington 054668
Association of South Dakota Museums, Sioux Falls 054669
Association of Systematics Collections, Washington 054670
Association of the State Literary Museums of the Republic of Belarus, Minsk 052637
Association pour la Recherche Scientifique sur les Arts Graphiques, ARSAG, Paris 052918
Association pour le Respect de l'Intégrité du Patrimoine Artistique, ARIPA, Issy-les-Moulineaux 052919
Association pour les Musées de Marseille, Marseille 052920
Association Prof. Marcel Hoc pour l'Encouragement des Recherches en Numismatique, Louvain-la-Neuve 052653
Association Professionnelle de Restaurateurs d'Œvres d'Art, Beroepsvereniging voor Restaurateurs van Kunstvoorwerpen, Wezembeck Oppem 052654
Association Professionnelle des Galeries d'Art du Luxembourg, Luxembourg 053846
Association Suisse des Experts et de Conseils, ASEXCO, Genève 054172
Associazione Amici del Museo Bagatti Valsecchi, Milano 053728
Associazione Amici di Brera e dei Musei Milanesi, Milano 053729
Associazione Antiquari d'Italia, Firenze 053730
Associazione Artisti Bresciani, Brescia 053731
Associazione Artisti Martino Dolci, Brescia 053732
Associazione Artisti Martino Dolci, Brescia 105990
Associazione Culturale, Trieste 053733
Associazione Culturale Arte e Ricambi, Verona 053734, 106788
Associazione Culturale d'Arte Contemporanea, Perugia 053735
Associazione Internazionale Mosaicisti Contemporanei, Ravenna 053736
Associazione Italiana Gallerie d'Arte Contemporanea, Milano 053737
Associazione Librai Antiquari d'Italia, Firenze 053738
Associazione Napoletana Antiquari, Napoli 053739
Associazione Nazionale dei Musei dei Enti Locali ed Istituzionali, ANMLI, Brescia 053740
Associazione Nazionale dei Musei Italiani, Roma 053741
Associazione Nazionale Musei Scientifici, ANMS, Firenze 053742
Associazione Piemontese Antiquari, Torino 053743
Assouline, Paris 133527
Den Ast, Buggenhout 003360
Asta Ambrosiana, Milano 121697
Astamangala, Amsterdam 077790
Astan-e-Qods-e Razavi Museums, Mashad 022581
Astano, Nice 065039
Astarté, Genève 082396
Astarte, Lugano 082590, 122333
Astarte, Madrid 110448
Astarte Antichitá, Palermo 076125
Aste - Ifir Piemonte, Torino 121730
Aste Mecenate, Milano 121698
Asteggiano, Frédéric, Malemort-sur-Corrèze 124383
Astelle, Lyon 124336
Astier, Françis-Sébasti, Saint-Chaffrey 067397
Astley-Cheetham Art Gallery, Stalybridge 041086
Astley Hall Museum and Art Gallery, Chorley 039083
Astley House, Moreton-in-Marsh . . 086009
Astley House, Moreton-in-Marsh . . 086010
Astley House, Moreton-in-Marsh . .114090, 131284
Astley House, Moreton-in-Marsh . . 131285
Astley Street Gallery, Wynnum 095436
Aston, Charters Towers 055662
Aston Hall, Birmingham Museums, Birmingham 038718
Aston Manor Transport Museum, Birmingham 038719
Aston Pine Antiques, Faringdon . . . 084382
Astor, Memphis 090054
Astor, New York 090704
Astor House Hotel Museum, Golden 044231
Astori, Carlo, Milano 127520
Astoria Coins, Astoria 087437
Astorre, Bologna 105945
Astors' Beechwood-Victorian Living History Museum, Newport 046456
Astra House Antiques Centre, Hemswell Cliff 084652
Astrachanskaja Gosudarstvennaja Kartinnaja Galereja im. B.M. Kustodieva, Astrachan 033001
Astrachanskij Gosudarstvennyj Obedinennyj Istoriko- architekturnyj Muzej-zapovednik, Astrachan 033002
Astrachanskij Kraevedčeskij Muzej, Astrachanskij muzej-zapovednik, Astrachan 033003
Astrachanskij Kreml, Astrachanskij muzej-zapovednik, Astrachan 033004
Astraea, Leuth 140487
Astrapas, Niš 109732
Astree, Rouen 067243
Astro-Zombies, Albuquerque 087374
Astrof, David, Montréal 096975
Astrolabe, Le Touquet-Paris-Plage . 063715
Astrolabe, Peymeinade 066786
Astrolabe Booksellers, Hobart 136941
Astrolabe Gallery, Ottawa . 059030, 097097
Astrolavos Artlife, Athinai . 105386, 134483
Astrolavos Dexameni, Athinai 105387, 134484
Astrolavos Piraeus, Piraeus 105439, 134491
Astrologo Eugenio, Roma 076318
Astronautics Museum, Beijing 006963
Astronomisch Compensatieuurwerk Kamiel Festraets, Sint-Truiden 003765
Astronomisch-Physikalisches Kabinett, Staatliche Museen Kassel, Kassel 018180
Astruc, Stéphane & François-Xavier, Bordeaux 061584
Astruc-Plijnaar, J.M.Th., Rotterdam 078699
Astrup Fearnley Museet for Moderne Kunst, Oslo 031070
Astruptunet, Skei i Jølster 031186
Asturiol Estany, Andres, Barcelona .080803, 129321
Asuka, Tokyo 107017
Asuka Shiryokan, Nara-Kokuritsu Bunkazai Kenkyujo, Asuka 026428
Asutosh Museum of Indian Art, Kolkata 022213
Asuurkeraamika, Tallinn 098693
Asyl der Kunst, Häuslingen 017619
Asylum House Antiques, Bradford-on-Avon 083628
At-Bristol, Bristol 038857
AT-Fachverlag, Fellbach 133928
At First Sight, Soisy-sous-Montmorency 068254
At Home Antiques, Toronto 059141
At Home Antiques, Vancouver 059335
At Home Galerie, Salins-les-Bains . 101246
At the Sign of the Chest of Draws, London 085100
ATA Arts Centre, Singapore 109773
ATA - Český Antikvariat, Praha 137827
Atala, Marseille 064316
Atala & Chactas, Valencia 081644
Atalante, Madrid 081242, 110449
Atalante, Saint-Aygulf 067370
Ataloa Lodge Museum, Muskogee . 046108
Atascadero Historical Society Museum, Atascadero 041827
Atatürk Kitaplığı Sanat Galerisi, İstanbul 112281
Atatürk Köşkü, Diyarbakır 038048
Atatürk Kongre ve Etnografya Müzesi, Sivas 038179
Atatürk Kültür Evi, İstanbul 112282
Atatürk Kültür Merkezi Sanat Galerisi, İstanbul 112283
Atatürk Müzesi, Bursa 038032
Atatürk Müzesi, İzmir 038109
Atatürk Müzesi, Konya 038130
Atatürk ve Etnografya Müzesi, Akşehir 037999
Ataürk Müzesi, Şişli 038177
Ataz, Minneapolis 117244
ATC Gallery, Ho Chi Minh City 120499
Atchinson, Topeka and Santa Fe Depot, Alden 041627
Atchison, Birmingham 115099
Atchison County Historical Society Museum, Atchison 041829
L'Atelier, Angers 060847, 098830
Atelier, Barcelona 129322
Atelier, Brive-la-Gaillarde 099037
Atelier, Cairo 098614
Het Atelier, Deventer 107966
Atelier, Épinal 124231
O Atelier, Faro 129143
L'Atelier, Firenze 127290
Atelier, Köln 135747
L'Atelier, La Clayette 063335
Atelier, Lannion 063530
Das Atelier, Lippstadt 103928
L'Atelier, Madrid 110450
Atelier, Nîmes 065168
l'Atelier, Pignans 101009
Atelier, Portland 118969
L'Atelier, Toronto 059142
Atelier, Vélizy-Villacoublay 068746

l'Atelier, Washington 093382
Atelier 13, Ellwangen 016942
Atelier 142, San Francisco 119604
Atelier 2000, Recklinghausen 104680
Atelier 25, Chinon 099133
Atelier 31 2500 First Av, Seattle . . . 119881
Atelier 340 Muzeum, Bruxelles 096148, 133258
Atelier 35, Bucureşti 109419
Atelier 3a, Wien 095798, 133181
Atelier 4, Courpière 062518
Atelier 4, Honolulu 116198
Atelier 43, Sankt Veit an der Glan . .095747, 137255
Atelier 49, Vallauris 101414
Atelier 5+1, Unterseen 111953
Atelier 52, Saint-Maur-des-Fossés . 067657
Atelier 67, Nantes 099804
Atelier 68 - Kreativzentrum Floridsdorf, Wien 095799
Atelier 71, Fareham 113055
Atelier 82, Bern 129945
Atelier 91, Paris 124567
Atelier 98 - Galerie auf der Uhlenhorst, Hamburg 103092
Atelier A, Basel 129909
Atelier A-E, New York 117651
Atelier A2, Saint-Paul-de-Vence . . . 067939
Atelier A3, Eferding 095499
Atelier Adam, Bruxelles 123574
Atelier Alexander, Winterthur 111996
Atelier Alpha Bleue, Paris 133528
Atelier am Chelebüel, Muri (Aargau) 111760
Atelier am Glanzhügel, Neumarkt am Wallersee 095694
Atelier Am Tönniesberg, Hannover . 103258
Atelier am Weidendamm, Hannover 103259
Atelier Anna, Sankt Johann in Tirol . 057292
L'Atelier Anne-Marie Frere, Contern 077462, 128466
Atelier Aquitain de Restauration, Etude Patrimoine Archéologique, Villeneuve-sur-Lot 125029
Atelier Art ad Absurdum, Hamburg . 103093
Atelier Arte Meditativa, Ascona . . . 111134
Atelier Artes, Plzeň 123967
Atelier Arts, Regina 097172
Atelier Augarten - Zentrum für zeitgenössische Kunst der Österreichischen Galerie Belvedere, Gustinus Ambrosi-Museum, Wien 002853
Atelier B, Aarau 111098
Atelier B, Knokke-Heist 096323
Atelier B, Vence 101432
Atelier Block 16, Hannover 103260
Atelier Boab, Saint-Malo (Ille-et-Vilaine) 101169
Atelier Bois et Décoration, Bischwiller 061499
Atelier Bonaparte, Nice 124497
Atelier Bonaparte, Paris . . 065472, 100007
Atelier Brera, Milano 127521
Atelier Cantoisel, Joigny (Yonne) . . . 099370
Atelier Casa Antica, Stuttgart 073960, 139752
Atelier Cezanne, Marseille 099641
Atelier Charlemagne, Paris 124568
Atelier Conseil, Nice 124498
L'Atelier Conseils, Lille 063829
Atelier Coperta, Bruxelles . 057837, 123575
L'Atelier Création d'Art, Nice 099829
Atelier Damrémont, Paris 124569
Atelier d'Art Damrémont 25, Paris . 065473
Atelier d'Art Drussant, Clermont-Créans 099138
Atelier d'Artistes Réunis, Paris 065474
Atelier de Conservation, Nantes . . . 124474
Atelier de la Courtine, Saint-Paul-de-Vence 101196
L'Atelier de la Ramejane, La Pomarède 124282
L'Atelier de la Reinière, Nice 065040
L'Atelier de la Reinière, Nice 065041
Atelier de la Renaissance, Reims . . 124857
Atelier de la Renaissance, Toulouse 124973
Atelier de la Tour Saint-Nicolas, Dijon 062641
Atelier de l'Argenteur, Nantes 124475
Atelier de l'Ebéniste, La Baule-Escoublac 124274
L'Atelier de Maîtré Poupée, Paris . . 124570
L'Atelier de Nicolas Schöffer á la Villa des Arts, Paris 013551
Atelier de Pan, Tournes 068561
Atelier de Recherche et de Création des Arts et Métiers (ARCAM), Paris 133529
Atelier de Restauration de Tableaux, Gévezé 124249
Atelier de Restauration de Tableaux, Saint-Germain-en-Laye 124903
Atelier de Restauro, Belo Horizonte 123689
Atelier de Tristan, Paris 100008
Atelier Décor, København 060280
Atelier Dedieu, Villeurbanne 125031
Atelier degli Artisti, Brescia 105991
Atelier del Restauro, Roma 076319, 127931
Atelier d'Endoume, Bretagne G. Point, Roudouallec 133695
Atelier des 3 Visages, Arras 098863
Atelier des Artistes, Knokke-Heist . 096324
Atelier des Arts et Techniques, Paris 124571
Atelier des Bastides, Monpazier . . . 013102
Atelier des Grames, Gigondas 133472
Atelier des Guillemites, Paris 065475
Atelier des Marches, Paris 124572
Atelier des Ombres, Lyon 099538
Atelier des Peintres du Marais, Paris 100009
Atelier des Petits Champs, Paris . . . 124573
Atelier des Produits Résineux Vidal, Ecomusée de la Grande Lande Marquèze, Luxey 012799
l'Atelier des Tableaux Carina, Nice .099830, 124499
Atelier d'Estampe Imago, Moncton . 005894
Atelier d'Estienne, Pont-Scorff 101041
L'Atelier d'Eugène, Ollainville 065264
Atelier d'Hermance, Hermance 111551
Atelier di Restauro, Parma 127843
Atelier Diverso, Betzdorf 102100
Atelier DL, L'Isle-sur-la-Sorgue . . . 063921
Atelier do Papel, Porto Alegre 058486
Atelier d'Onze Heures, Tours 068578, 101376
Atelier d'Or, Brighton, Victoria 123196
Atelier d'Ornano, Bordeaux 124114
Atelier du 18ème, Nevers . 065004, 124493
Atelier du Bois, Lodève 063975
Atelier du Bois Doré, Paris 124574
L'Atelier du Bronze, Pantin 124536
Atelier du Caire, Cairo 098615
Atelier du Change, Tours 101377
Atelier du Châpitre, Roquemaure . . 067222
Atelier du Cuir, Tréguier . . 068621, 125001
L' Atelier du Décorateur, Marseille . 124392
Atelier du Doreur, Rennes (Ille-et-Vilaine) 067097, 124871
Atelier du Meuble, Cogolin 062381, 124206
Atelier du Meuble, Le Chambon Feugerolles 124293
l'Atelier du Meuble, Nice 124500
Atelier du Mobilier, Strasbourg 068297
'Atelier du Peintre, Bastia 098926
Atelier du Peintre, Gap 099279
l'Atelier du Peintre, Lyon 099539
Atelier du Poële-en-Faïence, Strasbourg 068298
L'Atelier du Temps Passé, Paris . . . 124575
Atelier du Val de Grace, Paris 124576
Atelier-Editions Fanal, Basel 111163
Atelier Engramme, Québec 097126
Atelier Ernst Hecker, Aue, Sachsen . 015595
Ateliér Fiala, Praha 060110, 123970
Atelier Freies Glas, Haibach 095554
Atelier Freiraum, Regensburg 104689
Atelier für Architektur und Kunst, Kassel 103507
Atelier für Intarsien, Wil 111992
Atelier für Kunst und Handwerk, München 104144
Atelier für Kunst und Rahmen, Stuttgart 126841
Atelier für Maler, Bildhauer & Restauratoren, Innsbruck 057074, 123388
Atelier für Möbel- & Gemälderestaurierung, Innsbruck 123389
Atelier für Restaurierung, Regensburg 126687
Atelier G, Amiens 124067
Atelier-Galerie, Andelfingen 111121
Atelier Galerie, Toulon (Var) 101316, 124959
Atelier-Galerie, Wabern 111975
Atelier Galerie du Richard Rak, Coutures 011521
Atelier-Galleriet, Herlev 098530
Atelier Gallery, Vancouver 097421
Atelier GF, Toronto 097227
Atelier Guidoux, Nantes 064899
Atelier Herenplaats, Rotterdam 108176
Atelier Histoire de Tours, Tours 015014
Atelier HL, Den Haag 128624
Atelier III, Matthias, Barmstedt 101738
Atelier im Bärenhof, Zürich 082941
Atelier im Hof, Bassum 101741
Atelier im Hof, Berlin 101789
Atelier Intarsia, Verona 128413
Atelier Intarsio, Paris 124577
Atelier Ivan Meštrović, Ivan Meštrović Foundation, Zagreb 007829
Atelier Kea Homan, Assen 029277
Atelier Klex, Rheine 104747
Atelier Königshof, Dresden 102423
Atelier-Kreativ, Bad Mergentheim . . 101670
Atelier la Giradière, Charentay 124188
Atelier La Patine, Nouan-le-Fuzelier 065238
Atelier Ladywood Museum, Ladywood 005736
Atelier Limited, Münster . . 104355, 134293
Atelier Livre & Pinturas Especiais, Fortaleza 058469
Atelier M, Chicago 115351
Atelier Manoli-Musée et Jardin de Sculpture, La Richardais 012302
Atelier Matisse, São Paulo 049758
L'Atelier Metal, Martigues 099692
Atelier Mind Art, Neupölla 095696
Atelier Mistral, Hyères 099362
Atelier Municipal de Passementerie, Assoiation Soierie Vivante, Lyon . 012805
Atelier-Musée de la Soie, Taulignan 014914
Atelier-Musée des Tisserands et de la Charentaise, Varaignes 015130
Atelier-Musée du Bâton Basque, Larressore 012432
Atelier-Musée du Chapeau, Chazelles-sur-Lyon 011338
Atelier-Musée du Sabotier, Lautrec . 012441
Atelier Musée du Verre, Ancienne Verrerie Parant, Trélon 015040
Atelier-Musée du Vitrail et des Métiers d'Art du Verre, Gréoux-les-Bains 012027
Atelier-Musée Livre et Typographie, Grignan 012035
Atelier Na-iem, Gees 029596
Atelier Nordfelder Reihe 13, Hannover 103261
Atelier Ocre d'Art, Châteauroux . . . 099123
Atelier Opus, Saumur 124929
Atelier Oriental Rugs, Louisville . . . 089958
Atelier Otto Niemeyer-Holstein, Die Neue Galerie, Koserow 018386
Atelier Outlet, Berlin 069567, 101790
Atelier Paul Cézanne, Aix-en-Provence 010290
Atelier Produzioni d'Arte, Milano . . 106166
Atelier Régional de Restauration, Bignan 124100
Atelier Renaissance, Nantes 124476
Atelier Repinto, São Paulo 058685
L'Atelier Restauracion de Muebles, Madrid 129570
Atelier Robert, Barcelona 129323
Atelier Römerberg, Wiesbaden 105242
Atelier Saint Antoine, Reims 067057, 124858
Atelier Saint-Honoré, Paris 100010
Atelier Saint-Luc, Fribourg 130016
Atelier Saint-Michel, Le Havre 063624, 099435, 124298
Atelier Saint-Romain, Rouen 101108
Atelier Sala d'Art, Barcelona 110113
Atelier Salem, Salem bei Ratzeburg 073653
Atelier-Sankt-Georg, Innsbruck . . . 123390
Atelier-Sankt-Georg, Meiningen . . . 123418
Atelier Schinkelstraße, Düsseldorf . 070361
Atelier Sebastian, Wien 057374
Atelier Segantini, Maloja 037307
Atelier SpessArt, Aschaffenburg . . . 133723
Atelier Steendam, Gent 058171
Atelier Stéphane, Cadaujac 124166
Atelier T, Wien 095800
Atelier Tiama'o, Papara 101492
Ateliér Triton, Praha 060111, 123971
Atelier Verlag, Köln 134098
Atelier Viktoria, Bocholt 102144
Atelier XVIIIème, Montbrison 064655
Atelier zum Eck, Speicherschwendi 082824
l'Ateliere, Liège 058285
Ateliergalerie In den Gerbgruben, Neusiedl am See 095698
Atelierhaus, Akademie der bildenden Künste Wien, Wien 049649
Atelierhaus Aachen, Aachen 101500
Atelierhaus F34, Stuttgart 104965
Atelierhaus Philipp Harth, Bayrischzell 015926
Ateliers Couleurs Sud, Toulouse . . . 068478
Ateliers d'Art, Paris 124578
Ateliers d'Artistes de la Ville de Marseille, Marseille 133491
Les Ateliers de la Mabilais, Noyal-sur-Vilaine 124528
Ateliers de l'Abeille, Chavignon . . . 011335
Les Ateliers de Vence, Vence 101433
Ateliers du Parc, Champigny-sur-Marne 099112
Les Ateliers du Prisme, Paris 065476
Les Ateliers du Roy, Le Haillan 124297
Ateliers Gai, Lille 063830
Ateliers im Alten Schlachthof e.V., Sigmaringen 104903
Ateliersammlung Herbert Hiesmayr, Sankt Thomas am Blasenstein 002624
Atelierul de Restaurari, Bucureşti . . 129216
Ateliéry Praha, Praha 123972
Ateljé Ebéniste, Stockholm 129855
Atelje Firul, Negotin 109731
Atelje-galerija Rebeka, Ljubljana . . 109954
Ateljé Nygammalt, Stockholm 081924
Ateljé Treklövern, Jönköping 110946
Atelje za Umetnost in Obrt, Metlika 080665, 109994, 129291
Atena, Warszawa . 079736, 109097, 121901
Atena Gallery, Ha Noi 093557
Ateneo Art Gallery, Ateneo de Manila University, Quezon City 031771
Ateneo de Madrid, Madrid 054106
Ateneo de Valencia, Valencia 049515
Ateneo Puertorriqueno Gallery, San Juan 032728
Ateneumin Taidemuseo, Valtion Taidemuseo, Helsinki 009515
Atezart, Avignon 098888
Atha Cliath, Dublin 127092
Athabasca, Edmonton 137631
Athanassakeion Archeological Museum, Volos 021521
Athanassiadou, Zina, Thessaloniki . 105445
Athanor, Parma 127844
Athar, Casablanca 077636, 107548
Athelhampton House, Dorchester . . 039254
Athelstan Museum, Malmesbury . . 040394
Athena, Compiègne 099163
Athena, Livorno 106115
Athena, Palermo 076126
Athena, Palermo 076127
Athena, Southampton 114454
Athena Antiquités, Casablanca 077637
Athena Art Gallery, Kortrijk 096368
Athena Fine Art, Blackrock 074861
Athena Impresa di Restauro, Bari . . 127106

Athena Münzen der Antike, München 072649, 121518
The Athenaeum, Alexandria 041636
Athenaeum, Pavia 135885
Athenaeum of Philadelphia, Philadelphia 046924
Athenars, Roma 076320
Athena's Antiques, Portland 091899
Athena's Upholstery, San Diego . . . 132844
Athene, Miami 142548
Athenoux, Robert, Arles 060968
Athens University Museum, Athinai 021160
Atherton Antiques, Atherton 055415
Athesia, Bolzano 134556, 139999
Athey, G.M., Alnwick 083271, 130290
Athlone, Calgary 123738
Athlone Castle Museum, Athlone . . 022679
Athol Murray College of Notre Dame Museum, Wilcox 006819
Atholl Antiques, Aberdeen 083233
Atholl Country Life Museum, Blair Atholl 038761
The Atholl Gallery, Dunkeld 112966
ATI Auction Gallery, Pittsburgh 123055
Atica, Buenos Aires 094059
Atica, Echandens 082348
El Atico de Los Angeles, Maracaibo 093549
Atienza, Granada 129524
Atikokan Centennial Museum, Atikokan 005037
Atimo-Personnel, Fribourg 111413
Atkins, Christopher J.G., Bruxelles .057838, 123576
Atkins, Garry, London 085101
Atkins, T. J., Taunton 086827
Atkinson Art Gallery, Southport 041069
Atlan, Alain, Paris 065477
Atlanta Antiques and Auction, Atlanta 087453, 122797
Atlanta Art Gallery, Atlanta 114854
Atlanta Art Services, Atlanta 114855
Atlanta Book Exchange, Atlanta . . . 142196
The Atlanta College of Art, Atlanta . 041844
Atlanta College of Art, Atlanta 050921
Atlanta Contemporary Art Center and Nexus Press, Atlanta 041845
The Atlanta Cyclorama, Atlanta . . . 041846
Atlanta Furniture, Atlanta 131760
Atlanta Furniture, Atlanta 131761
Atlanta Galleries, Atlanta 114856
Atlanta History Museum, Atlanta . . 041847
Atlanta International Museum of Art and Design, Atlanta 041848
Atlanta Museum, Atlanta 041849
Atlanta Panorama, Atlanta 114857
Atlanta Restauracion, Barcelona . . . 129324
Atlantic 1 Museum, Swampscott . . 048445
Atlantic Art Gallery, Cape Town 110017
Atlantic Bay Gallery, London 085102, 130935
Atlantic Canada Aviation Museum, Bedfords 005090
Atlantic City Historical Museum, Atlantic City 041880
Atlantic County Historical Society Museum, Somers Point 048215
Atlantic Gallery, New York 117652
Atlantic Gallery of Georgetown, Washington 120259
Atlantic Provinces Art Gallery Association, Wolfville 052733
Atlantic Salmon Museum on the Miramichi River, Doaktown 005353
Atlantic Statiquarium Marine Museum, Louisbourg 005801
Atlantic Wildfowl Heritage Museum, Virginia Beach 048793
Atlántica Internacional, Las Palmas de Gran Canaria 136077
Atlantik Verlags- und Mediengesellschaft, Bremen 133840
Atlantiquasie, Le Bono 063574
Atl'Antique, Rochefort (Charente-Maritime) 067174
Atlantique City Fall Festival, Atlantic City 093973
Atlantique City Spring Festival, Atlantic City 093974
Atlantique Restores and Conservationists, Devonshire 123681
Atlantiques, Long Beach 089625
Atlantis, Houston 132099
Atlantis, Stockholm 134965
Atlantis Antichità, Milano 127522
Atlantis Antiques, Louisville 089959, 132286
Atlantis Bookshop, London 141752
Atlantis Discovered, San Antonio . . 092486
Atlantisia, Toronto 097228
Atlas, Chicago 131884
Atlas, London 136184
Atlas Antiquariaat, Rotterdam 140516
Atlas Antiquités, Montréal 058926
Atlas Galleries, Chicago 115352
Atlas Galleries, Chicago 115353
Atlas Galleries, Chicago 115354
Atlas Gallery, London 113485
Atlatl- National Native Arts Network, Phoenix 054671
Atlin Historical Museum, Atlin 005039
Atmosfera, Helsinki 060510
Atmosphere, Bruxelles 057839
Atmosphère, Dijon 062642
Atmosphere Antique and Unique, Göteborg 081795
Atmosphère Antiquités, Creteil 062563
Atmosphère d'Ailleurs, Lorient 063998
Atmosphère d'Antan, Ménilles 064484
Atmosphères, Paris 065478
Atnabrufossen Vannbruksmuseum, Atna 030747
Atom Antiques, Chicago 088028
Atom Museum, Haigerloch 017635
Atomic Passion, New York 090705
Atomik Pop 2, Oklahoma City 091474
Atomium, Bruxelles 003287
Atout Coeur, Calais 099052
Atrandom, Gifu 106849
Atrax, Přerov 098495
Atre, Lipsheim 063907
Atrema, Orléans 065294
Atreo, Zaragoza 081732
Atribut, Moskva 080235
Atrio, Santiago de Chile 059504
Atrion, Thessaloniki 105446
Atrium, Oberhausen, Rheinland . . . 073142
Atrium, Plzeň 098408
Atrium, Waibstadt 074241
Atrium 1, İstanbul 083119
Atrium 2, İstanbul 083120
Atrium an der Schleuse, Brunsbüttel 016473
Atrium du Casino, Monaco 107522
Atrium Galerija, Beograd 109685
Atrium Gallery, Bath 112569
Atrium Gallery, Clifton Beach 094406
Atrium Gallery, Fort Worth 044003
Atrium Gallery, Saint Louis 047652
Atrium Gallery, Saint Louis 119184
Atrium Gallery, Salt Lake City 047768
Atrium na Žižkově, Praha 098419
Atrium Showcase Gallery, San Antonio 119399
Atrozos, Madrid 129571
Atsuta-Jingu Museum, Nagoya 026879
Attal, Jeffrey C., Austin . . 087558, 142214
Attali, Ange, Le Perreux-sur-Marne 063680
Attali, Jean-Hubert, Paris 100011
Attendi, London 113486
Attenson, Mitchell, Cleveland 088310, 142328
Attention to Detail, Columbus 115762
Attias, Annemarie, Zürich 082942
Attias, Fortunato Jose, Rio de Janeiro 058550
Attic, Baldock 083368
The Attic, Delhi 074801
The Attic, Newton Abbot 086080
The Attic, San Francisco 092736
Attic Antiques, Blackburn South . . . 055507
Attic Antiques, Indianapolis 089271, 132150
Attic Antiques, Saintfield 086483
Attic Books, Cheltenham 141498
Attic Finds, Tucson 093205
The Attic Gallery, Leven 113386
Attic Gallery, Portland 118970
Attic Gallery, Swansea 114532
Attic Treasures, Louisville 089960
Attic Treasures, New Orleans 090511
Attic Treasures, Norfolk 091367
Attic Treasures, Vancouver 059336
Attica, Edmonton 058819, 123756
Attica Furniture Restoration, Edmonton 123757
El Attico, Guatemala 074649, 105475
Atticus, Warszawa 140778
Atticus Books, Grays 141632
Atticus Books, Toronto 137695
Atticus Bookshop, Lancaster 141703
Attienaj, Toronto 059143
Attik 18, København 060281
Attila József Memorial Room, Budapest 021637
Åttingen Hantverk och Lantbruksmuseum, Aneby 036182
Attinger, Victor, Neuchâtel 135050
Attingham Park, Shrewsbury 041018
Attique, Tulsa 093285
Attitude Art Publishers, Salt Lake City 135485
Attitude Exact, Washington 120260
l'Attitude Gallery, Boston 115144
attitudes, Espace d'Arts Contemporains, Genève 037110, 054173
Attleboro Area Industrial Museum, Attleboro 041882
Attleboro Museum, Attleboro 041883
Attmore-Oliver House, New Bern . . 046193
Atualidades Panoramica e Galeria de Arte, Rio de Janeiro 058551, 096590
Åtvidabergs Bruks- och Facitmuseum, Åtvidaberg 036207
Atw Antiques, Hamilton 058848
Atwater Kent Museum - The History Museum of Philadelphia, Philadelphia 046925
Atwell House Gallery, Alfred Cove . . 000731
Atwell-Wilson Motor Museum, Calne 038948
Atwood Memorial Center, Saint Cloud State University, Saint Cloud 047623
Atypique, Brignais 061796
Atzig, Peter, Pforzheim 126626
Au Bleu de Longwy, Herserange . . . 063151
Au Bois Dore, Saint Peters 123301
Au Bon Diable, Le Conquet 063605
Au Bon Maitre d'Armes, Le Castellet 063585
Au Bon Usage, Paris 065479
Au Bon Vieux Temps, Belvès 061341
Au Bon Vieux Temps, Chalon-sur-Saône 062081
Au Bon Vieux Temps, Luxembourg . 077474
Au Bon Vieux Temps, Royan 067306
Au Bonheur d'Antan, Duclair 062744
Au Bonheur d'Ombeline, Toulouse . 068479
Au Bonheur du Jour, Genève 082397
Au Bonheur du Jour, Lausanne 082530
Au Bonheur du Jour, Neuchâtel . . .082687, 130123
Au Bonheur du Jour, Paris 100012
Au Bonheur du Jour, Valence-d'Agen 068682
Au Bonheur du Meuble, Mées 064459, 124442
Au Bonheur du Tour, Douai 062723
Au Bouffon du Roy, Les Rosiers-sur-Loire 063779
Au Bouquiniste, Le Havre 138114
Au Bout de la Cour, Maulette 064428
Au Bric à Brac, Metz 064519
Au Capharnaum, Perpignan 066735
Au Carré de Jouy, Provins 066990
Au Charme d'Antan, Cerizay 062057
Au Charme d'Antan, Saint-Omer . . 067690
Au Charme d'Autrefois, Luxembourg 077475
Au Charme d'Autrefois, Pont-de-Briques-Saint-Etienne 066916
Au Charme du Logis, Bruxelles 057840
Au Charme du Passé, Saint-Cloud . 067402
Au Charme du Passé, Tel Aviv 075001
Au Charme du Temps, Pont-Audemer 066911
Au Chat Botté, Basel 082121
Au Cherche-Midi, Bruxelles 057841
Au Chevalier Bayard, Grenoble 063050
Au Chevalier Noir, Lausanne 082531
Au Chiabout, Metz 064520, 124445
Au Chien Vert, Pézenas 066793
Au Chineur, Gardonne 062968
Au Chineur Vaudois, Lausanne 082532
Au Chin'Eure, Saint-André-de-l'Eure 067353
Au Clair de la Lune, Dozule 062735
Au Clair Obscur, Dinan 062680
Au Coeur du Temps, Sarzeau 068138
Au Coin des Ombres, Pau 066696
Au Coin du Meuble, Québec 059060
Au Coin Littèraire, Strasbourg 068299
Au Col Bleu, Brest 061764
Au Collectionneur, Paris 065480
Au Collectionneur, Tournai 058378
Au Comptoir des Hallettes, Montivilliers 064700
Au Debotté, Paris 065481
Au Décor d'Autrefois, Strasbourg . . 068300
Au Dénicheur, Lomme 063978
Au Dénicheur, Saint-Ouen-du-Breuil 067932
Au Duc de Chartres, Paris 065482
Au Facteur Cheval, Paris 065483
Au Faubourg, Reims 067058, 124859
Au Feuillet Jauni, Waterloo 137541
Au Fil des Ans, Bois-Colombes 061535
Au Fil des Siècles, Fauverney 062840
Au Fil des Temps, Saint-Ouen 067715
Au fil du temps, Beirut 077385
Au Fil du Temps, Bruxelles 057842
Au Fil du Temps, Bruz 061828
Au Fil du Temps, Caen 061858
Au Fil du Temps, Cortaillod 082329
Au Fil du Temps, Douai 062724
Au Fil du Temps, La Coucourde . . . 063349
Au Fil du Temps, Montauban 064626
Au Fil du Temps, Paris 065484
Au Fil du Temps, Pézenas 066794
Au Fil du Temps, Vigeois 068871
Au Fond de la Cour, Paris 065485
Au Foyer d'Autrefois, Lausanne . . . 082533
Au France, New York 090706
Au Furet, Bois-Guillaume 061538
Au Garage, Tour-de-Trême 082858
Au Glaize Village, Defiance 043372
Au Grand Bazar, Paris 065486
Au Gré du Temps, Albi 060751
Au Grenier, Champenoux 062121
Au Grenier, Vouvry 082894
Au Grenier d'Ango, Dieppe 062623
Au Grenier de Beauvallon, Sainte-Maxime 068068
Au Grenier de l'Azergues, Lyon 064072
Au Grenier de Lucie, Saint-Ouen . . 067716
Au Grenier de Lucie, Saint-Ouen . . 067717
Au Grenier de Monette, Gannat . . . 062959
Au Grenier d'Elise, Bar-le-Duc 061192
Au Grenier des Soyeux, Lyon 064073
Au Grenier du Louvre, Maulette . . . 064429
Au Grenier Normand, Le Tréport . . . 063723
Au Jardin Antique, Casablanca 077638
Au Jeton d'Argent, Rennes (Ille-et-Vilaine) 067098
Au Jeu de Paume, Montpellier 064733
Au Jouet d'Autrefois, Lyon 064074
Au Lac Art Gallery, Ho Chi Minh City 120500
Au Lion d'Argent, Gisors 063005
Au Lion des Neiges, Woollahra 056852
Au Louis d'Or, Caen 061859
Au Mee Co, Doetinchem 078288

Au Mobilier Vendéen, Les Essards (Vendée) . . . 063763, 124312
Au Mobilier Vendéen, Saint-Jean-de-Monts . . . 067543
Au Nom de la Rose, Aubagne . . . 061021
Au Palais du Meuble, Changy . . . 062135
Au Papier Monnaie, Nantes . . . 064900
Au Paradis, Bordeaux . . . 061585
Au Passage Gambetta, Biarritz . . . 061448
Au Passé Entreposé, Lyon . . . 064075
Au Passé Présent, Maureillas-las-Illas . . . 064440, 138202
Au Passé Simple, Aix-les-Bains . . . 060719
Au Passé Simple, Amiens . . . 060804
Au Passé Simple, Ardenay-sur-Mérize . . . 060955
Au Passé Simple, Nogent-le-Roi . . . 065208
Au Passé Simple, Paris . . . 065487
Au Passé Simple, Poitiers . 066887, 124846
Au Pays d'Ardenne - Original Museum, Bastogne . . . 003213
Au Petit Bonheur, Beaumont (Vienne) . . . 061265
Au Petit Bonheur, Den Haag . . . 078169
Au Petit Grenier, Cluses . . . 062370
Au Petit Grenier, Nice . . . 065042
Au Petit Paris on the Corner, Los Angeles . . . 089696
Au petit Trésor, Basel . . . 082122
Au Pin de Campagne, Liège . . . 058286
Au Point du Jour, Troyes . . . 125003
Au Reflets d'Antan, Aubigny-au-Bac 061042
Au Regard des Anges, Forgès . . . 062919
Au Réveil du Temps, Saint-Nabord . 067681
Au Roi de Rome, Nice . . . 065043
Au Roy Soleil, Antibes-Juan-les-Pins . . . 060913
Au Semainier Antiquités, Lausanne 082534
Au Siècle Passé, Bois-Colombes . . 061536
Au Singe Violet Antiquités, Paris . . . 065488
Au Sol d'Aix, Aix-en-Provence . . . 060696
Au Soli, Megève . . . 064461
Au Sou d'Or, Béziers . . . 061428
Au Sourire d'Ariane, Saint-Ouen . . . 067718
Au Temps Conte, Cely-en-Biere . . . 062048
Au Temps Jadis, Buironfosse . . . 061835
Au Temps Jadis, Challans 062074, 124177
Au Temps Jadis, Den Haag . . . 078170
Au Temps Jadis, Fontenay-sous-Bois . . . 062907
Au Temps Jadis, Huisseau-sur-Cosson . . . 063184
Au Temps Jadis, Montagnac . . . 064616
Au Temps Jadis, Rumegies . . . 067327
Au Temps Jadis, Sailly-lez-Lannoy . 067337
Au Temps Jadis, Saint-Quentin (Aisne) . . . 067971
Au Temps Jadis, Vétraz-Monthoux . 068832
Au Temps Passé, Amiens . . . 060805
Au Temps Passé, Mamers . . . 064241
Au Temps Perdu, Lausanne . . . 082535
Au Temps qui Passe, Courville-sur-Eure . . . 062527
Au Trésor de Paris-ATP, Paris . . . 065489
Au Troc Cevenol, Florac . . . 062880
Au Troc Malouin, Saint-Malo (Ille-et-Vilaine) . . . 067605
Au Vase de Delft, Paris . . . 065490
Au Verre à Pied, Le Mans . . . 063654
Au Verre Luisant, Voiron . . . 069023
Au Vieil Artisan Bressan, Confrançon . . . 062461
Au Vieu Parchet, Flumet . . . 062883
Au Vieux Bibelot, Charleroi . . . 058137
Au Vieux Bougeoir, Marseille . . . 064317
Au Vieux Canon, Genève . . . 082398
Au Vieux Chaudron, Lannebert . . . 063528
Au Vieux Chêne, Metz . . . 064521
Au Vieux Chevreuse, Chevreuse . . . 062285
Au Vieux Chinois Antiquités, Paris . 065491
Au Vieux Colombier, Aubencheul-au-Bac . . . 061034
Au Vieux Dijon, Dijon . . . 062643
Au Vieux Document, Paris . . . 138291
Au Vieux Fiacre, Mont-Saint-Martin 064614
Au Vieux-Gothard, Chêne-Bourg . . . 082308
Au Vieux Grenier, Bergerac . . . 061356
Au Vieux Grenier, Fléac . . . 062870
Au Vieux Logis, Ploisy . . . 066860
Au Vieux Magasin, Bruxelles . . . 057843
Au Vieux Manoir, Bapaume . . . 061190
Au Vieux Marché, Chinon . . . 062292
Au Vieux Minervois, Rieux-Minervois . . . 067143
Au Vieux Paris, Paris . . . 065492
Au Vieux Paris, Tournai . . . 058379
Au Vieux Quartier, Colmar . . . 062401
Au Vieux Quartier, Namur . . . 137534
Au Vieux Rodez, Rodez . . . 067190
Au Vieux Saint-Georges, Pérouges . 066730
Au Vieux Saint-Pierre, Calais . . . 061904
Au Vieux Saussaies, Paris . . . 065493
Au Vieux Souvenir, Versailles . . . 068795
Au Vieux Tournay, Tournai . . . 058380
Au Vieux Tours, Tours . . . 068579
Au Violon d'Ingres, Casablanca . . . 077639
Au Violon d'Ingres, L'Isle . . . 082508
Au Voltaire, Châtillon-d'Azergues . . 062228
Au XXème Siècle, Paris . . . 065494
l'Aubaine, Liège . . . 058287
L'Aubaine, Paris . . . 065495
L'Auberge du Hussard, Brantome . . 061748
Auberlehaus, Trossinger Heimatmuseum, Trossingen . . . 020488
Aubert, Fabrègues . . . 062834
Aubert, Jacques, Gerbéviller . . . 062987
l'Aubier, Neuchâtel . . . 082688, 141282
Auböck, Carl, Wien . . . 095801
Auböck, Max, Hallwang . . . 123377
Aubonnière, Chaille-sous-les-Ormeaux . . . 011191
Aubour, Michel, Limoges . . . 063881
Aubrey Brocklehurst, London . . . 130936
Aubri, Christophe, Einvaux . . . 062769
Aubri, Michèle, Xeuilley . . . 069057
Aubry, Alain, Ménil . . . 064482
Aubry, Eric, Paris . . . 065496
Aubry, Geneviève, Rosières-aux-Salines . . . 067226
Aubry, Jacques, Pont-l'Abbé . . . 066923
Aubry, Jean, Paris . . . 065497
Aubry, Roger, Morges . . . 082671, 111751
Auburn Antiques, Auckland . . . 078923
Auburn-Cord-Duesenberg Museum, Auburn . . . 041885
Auburn Gallery, Auburn . . . 094181
Aubusson, Chrystian, New York . . . 090707
Auchère-Merle, Marie-Hélène, Brantôme . . . 099025, 124160
Auchinachie & Son, G.L., Woollahra 056853
Auchincloss, Pamela, New York . . . 117653
Auchindrain Museum of Country Life, Inveraray . . . 039800
Auckland Antique Shop, Auckland . 078924
Auckland Art Gallery - Toi o Tāmaki, Auckland . . . 030431
Auckland Collectors Centre, Auckland . . . 078925
Auckland Museum and Auckland War Memorial Museum, Auckland . . . 030432
Auckland Photo Restorers, South Auckland . . . 128954
Auckland Society of Arts, Ponsonby 053913
Auction Broker, Oakland . . . 123027
Auction Center of Oldham County, La Grange . . . 122935
The Auction Centre, Cambridge . . . 120574
Auction Gallery, Richmond . . . 123070
The Auction Guild, Fayette . . . 136395
Auction Partners, Königswinter . . . 121482
Auction Place, Welshpool . . . 120652
Auction Rooms, Falkirk . . . 122508
Auction Trader, Cheltenham, Victoria . . . 120578
Auctioneer, Bruxelles . . . 120718
Auctioneer Associates, Miami . . . 122960
Auctioneers, Cantallops . . . 122020
Auctioneers, Cantallops . . . 122021
Auctioneers Association, New York . 054672
Auctioneers Association Canada, Edmonton . . . 052734
Audap, Pierre Emmanuel, Paris . . . 121113
Auden, Bad Homburg v.d.Höhe . . . 101650
Audeoud, Georges, Genève . . . 082399
Audi Museum Mobile, Ingolstadt . . 018068
Audibert, Paray-Vieille-Poste . . . 099898
Audibert, François, Toulon (Var) . . . 124960
Audibert, Jean-Marie, Nîmes . . . 065169
Audiello, New York . . . 117654
Audiger, Christian, Breteuil-sur-Iton 061784
Audley End House, Saffron Walden . 040878
Audorfer Museum im Burgtor, Oberaudorf . . . 019382
Audouard Franck, Pordic . . . 066948
Audouze, Jean-François, Pau . . . 066697
Audrain Historical Museum, Graceland Museum, Mexico . . . 045802
Audrey, New York . . . 117655
Audrey, C., New York . . . 117656
Audreys Antiques, Auckland . . . 078926
Audrey's Place, Indianapolis . . . 089272, 132151
Audubon Antiques, New Orleans . . . 090512
Audubon Artists, New York . . . 054673
Audubon House, Key West . . . 044981
Audubon State Historic Site, Saint Francisville . . . 047629
Aue Verlag, Möckmühl . . . 134204
Auer, Saint Louis . . . 092202
Auer, Walsrode . . . 074268
Auer von Welsbach Museum, Althofen . . . 001683
Aufbau Antiquariat, Zürich . . . 141322
Aufbau-Verlag, Berlin . . . 133753
Auffenbauer, Dieter, Perleberg . . . 126619
Auffret, Catherine, L'Isle-sur-la-Sorgue . . . 063922
Auffret, François, Olonzac . . . 065266
Aufgemöbelt, Bielefeld . . . 069817
Auge, Jens, Krainhagen . . . 126141
Augen, Portland . . . 118971
Augenladen, Mannheim . . . 104019
Auger, Françoise, Nançay . . . 064852
Auger, Roger, Québec . . . 137680
Auger, Roger, Québec . . . 137681
Augestad Magne, Sandnes . . . 108747
AuGIAS, Juziers . . . 063273
Augier, Albert, Carpentras . . . 061996
Auglaize County Historical Society Museum, Saint Marys . . . 047687
Augsburger, Jean-Jacques, Concise 111366
Augsburger Kunstauktionshaus Petzold, Augsburg . . . 121296
Augsburger Puppentheatermuseum Die Kiste, Augsburg . . . 015603
August Antiques, Houston . . . 089029
August Antiques, Moreton-in-Marsh 086011
August Deusser-Museum, Zurzach . 037820
August-Gottschalk-Haus, Gedenkstätte und Ausstellung zur neueren Geschichte der ostfriesischen Juden - Jüdisches Museum, Esens . . . 017053
August-Holländer-Museum, Emsdetten . . . 016978
August Horch Museum Zwickau, Zwickau . . . 021084
August House Studio, Chicago . . . 115355
August Kitzbergi Tubamuuseum, Karksi . . . 009370
August Macke Haus, Bonn . . . 016317
August-Suter-Museum, Eptingen . . 037069
Augusta, Indianapolis . . . 089273
Augusta Historical Museum, Augusta . . . 000756
Augusta Historical Museum, Augusta . . . 041902
Augusta Museum of History, Augusta . . . 041895
Augusta Richmond County Museum, Augusta . . . 041895
Augustana College Art Gallery, Rock Island . . . 047490
Auguste, Alençon . . . 060764
Auguste, François, Saint-Nicolas-lez-Arras . . . 067688
Auguste, François, Saint-Ouen . . . 067719
Auguste Gallery, Houston . . . 116278
Augustin, Lübeck . . . 072320
Augustin, Claude, Les Chères . . . 063761
Augustin, N., Middelburg . . . 078635
Augustin, Peter, Innsbruck 057075, 095576
Augustinermuseum, Freiburg im Breisgau . . . 017228
Augustinermuseum, Rattenberg, Inn 002505
Aujourd'hui Jadis, Le Luc . . . 063647
Aukčná Spoločnost SOGA, Bratislava . . . 080600, 121976
Aukční Síň Nuselská, Praha . . . 120853
Aukrug, Innien . . . 071629
Auksjonshuset, Ramme og Bruktgalleriet, Oslo . . . 079420, 121861
Auktion Haus Mallorca, Palma de Mallorca . . . 122077
Auktioner Sållarps, Tranås . . . 122279
Auktionerverket, Eskilstuna . . . 122124
Auktions-Magasinet, Grums . . . 122146
Auktions- und Kunsthaus, Wiesbaden . . . 121623
Auktionsbyrån, Trollhättan . . . 122281
Auktionsgalerie am Baldeneysee, Essen . . . 121398
Auktionsgården, Mönsterås . . . 122216
Auktionsgården, Sankt Olof . . . 122237
Auktionsgodsaffären Billinge, Billinge . . . 122105
Auktionshallen, Gävle . . . 122138
Auktionshallen, Helsingborg . . . 122157
Auktionshallen, Järbo . . . 122166
Auktionshallen, Karlskoga . . . 122176
Auktionshallen Ekeby, Ekeby . . . 122119
Auktionshallen i Alingsås, Alingsås . 122097
Auktionshallen-Överskottslagret, Solna . . . 122243
Auktionshaus am Brandenburger Tor, Berlin . . . 121319
Auktionshaus am Dom, Köln . . . 121468
Auktionshaus Baden-Baden, Baden-Baden . . . 121309
Auktionshaus Dorotheum, Düsseldorf . . . 121378
Auktionshaus für Historica, Spiesen-Elversberg . . . 121603
Auktionshaus Hansa, Bremen . . . 121358
Auktionshaus Höchst, Frankfurt am Main . . . 121402
Auktionshaus im Schloß Potzneusiedl, Potzneusiedl . . . 120672
Auktionshaus Königsallee, Düsseldorf . . . 121379
Auktionshaus Markus, Leipzig . . . 121493
Auktionshaus Nitschareuth, Jena . . 121459
Auktionshaus Nymphenburg, München . . . 072650, 121519
Auktionshaus Rheinsberg, Rheinsberg . . . 121588
Auktionshaus Sankt-Peter-Ording, Sankt Peter-Ording . . . 121595
Auktionshaus Satow, Satow . . . 073676
Auktionshaus Viktualienmarkt, München . . . 121520
Auktionshaus Walldorf, Walldorf, Baden . . . 121620
Auktionshaus Zofingen, Zofingen . . 122359
Auktionshuset, Hørsholm . . . 120864
Auktionshuset Anders Antik, Eslöv . 122125
Auktionshuset Anders Antik, Landskrona . . . 122188
Auktionshuset i Sundbyberg, Sundbyberg . . . 122268
Auktionshuset Kåremo, Kalmar . . . 122172
Auktionshuset Metropol, Stockholm 122247
Auktionskammaren, Rättvik . . . 122229
Auktionskammaren Hallsberg, Hallsberg . . . 122149
Auktionskammaren i Åmål, Åmål . . 122098
Auktionskammaren i Varberg, Kungsbacka . . . 122185
Auktionskammaren i Varberg, Varberg . . . 122292
Auktionskompaniet, Göteborg . . . 122141
Auktionskompaniet AB, Stockholm . 122248

Auktionsregister Gemälde, Münster 135748
Auktionstjänst i Fagersta, Västerfärnebo 122287
Auktionsverket Eda Gamla Skola, Charlottenberg 122115
Auktionsverket Gamla Tiden, Uddevalla 122283
Auktionsverket Gefle, Gävle 122139
Auktionsverket i Karlskrona, Karlskrona 122177
Auktionsverket Kronprinsen, Malmö 122206
Aula Didáctica de Prehistoria de Tito Bustillo, Ribadesella 035703
Aula Didáctica del Castro de Coaña, Coaña 035102
Aulagnon, Soillès Pont 124936
Aulanier, Marc, Langeac . . 063514, 124290
Aularge-Danigo, Quimper 138575
AULD Alliance Art Gallery, Nashville 117337
The Auld Kirk Gallery, Aberdeen . . . 112474
Auld Kirk Museum, Auld Kirk and Barony Chambers, Kirkintilloch 039903
Auld Sköll, Fair Isle 039473
Auldearn Antiques, Auldearn 083354
Aulestad, Karoline og Bjørnstjerne Bjørnsons Hjem, Follebu 030845
Aulet, Barcelona 129325
Auletta, Giovanni, Bologna 105946
Auli Mølle, Årnes 030737
Aulich, Thomas, Berlin 101791
Aulnette, Saint-Nazaire (Loire-Atlantique) 067683, 121248
Aulock, Andrea von, Münster 072894, 126493
Aulos Musica, Genève . . . 111423, 141244
AUM Gallery, Denver 115977
Aumann, Thomas, Hildesheim 071524, 125927
Aumont Bernard, Paris 065498
Aunan, Ingvild, Oslo 079421
Aunkan Galeria, Barcelona 110114
Aunt Betty's Antiques, Dallas 088463
Aunt Edna's Treasures, Moonee Ponds 056247
Aunt Hattie's Attic, Miami 090143
Aunt Margaret's Museum of Childhood, Dufresne 005369
Aunt Ruth's Antiques, Salt Lake City 092418
Aunt Shelly's Treasures, Fresno . . . 088896
Auntie's Affic, Whyalla 056820
Aunties Attic, Portland 091900
Auprete Delagenest, Guy, Nice 065044
Aura, Bromma 081775
Aura Antiques, Masham 085960
L'Aura des Arts, Mallemort 099630
Aura Galerías, México 107478
Aurantica, Roma 076321
Aurantique, Nice 065045
Aurea Charta, Parma 127845
Aurélie, Paris 065499
Aurelio Sevilla Alvero Library and Museum, Pasay 031753
Aurelio's Refinishing, Houston 132100
Aurelius Ink, Nashville 090423
Áureo, Barcelona 121995
Aureola, Bucureşti 080143
Aurévane, Aixe-sur-Vienne 060730, 124062
Auriel, Toulouse 101333
Auriga, Barcelona 134903
L'Auriga, Firenze 075276
Aurland Bygdetun og Lensmannsstova, Aurland 030748
Aurnhammer-Sammlung, Treuchtlingen 020469
Aurobindo Gallery, Delhi 105654
Aurobora, San Francisco 135490
Aurora, Vancouver 097422
Aurora Antiques, Columbus 088383
Aurora Fine Books, New York 142633
Aurora Galerie, Knokke-Heist 096325
Aurora Historical Museum, Aurora . 041909
Aurora Historical Society Museum, Aurora 041917
Aurora History Museum, Aurora . . . 041908
Aurora-Kunstverlag, Sankt-Peterburg 134884
Aurora Museum, Aurora 005041
Aurora Public Art Commission, Aurora 041910
Aurskog-Høland Bygdetun, Hemnes i Høland 030886
Aurum Press, London 135186
Aurygem, Madrid 129572
Aus-Art, Wien 052509
Aus dem Antiquariat, Frankfurt am Main 135749
Aus Forschung und Kunst, Klagenfurt 135545
Aus-Tex Coins, Austin 087559
Ausada Duran, León 110396
Ausart International, Cheltenham, New South Wales 055666
Ausems, Hilversum 128718
Ausgrabungen Wüstung Hard, Thaya 002742
Ausgrabungsdokumentation 6000 Jahre Wohnberg Oberleis, Ernstbrunn . . 001838
Ausgrabungsmuseum Esslinger Stadtkirche, Esslingen 017082
Ausgrabungsstätte Schanzberg, Gars am Kamp 001885
AuSi Gallery, Tucson 120106
Auskjonshuset, Oslo 121862
Ausmeyer & Gerling, Bremen 070008
Aušros Avenue Mansion, Šiauliai Aušros Museum, Šiauliai 027852
Aussandon, Yves, Aubagne 061022
Aussen, Rob, Amsterdam 077791
Aussie Art Store, Sydney 095271
Aussie Books, Coopers Plains 136866
Aussiedlermuseum im Schüttkasten, Allentsteig 001672
Ausstellung der Kantonalen Schnitzerschule, Brienz, Bern . . . 036971
Ausstellung der Schweizerischen Geigenbauschule, Brienz, Bern . . 036972
Ausstellung Faszination und Gewalt - Dokumentationszentrum Reichsparteitagsgelände, Museen der Stadt Nürnberg, Nürnberg 019347
Ausstellung Fontane und Hankels Ablage, Zeuthen 021061
Ausstellung Haus Wysburg und Ruine Wysburg, Remptendorf 019794
Ausstellung Heinrich Federer, Sachseln 037471
Ausstellung Hittisauer Lebensbilder aus dem 19. Jahrhundert, Hittisau . . . 002049
Ausstellung Juden in Buttenhausen, Münsingen 019134
Ausstellung Kirche Zillis, Zillis 037751
Ausstellung Max-Kommerell, Münsingen 019135
Ausstellung zur Erd- und Vorgeschichte, Breitscheid, Hessen 016406
Ausstellungen im Bosch-Archiv, Stuttgart 020343
Ausstellungsforum FOE 156, München 019035
Ausstellungsfoyer der Bundesdruckerei, Berlin 101792
AusstellungsHalle, Frankfurt am Main 017153
Ausstellungshalle für Zeitgenössische Kunst Münster, Münster 019139
Ausstellungsräume der Staatlichen Graphischen Sammlung, München 019036
Ausstellungsraum 25, Zürich 112042
Ausstellungsraum Klingental, Basel 036881
Ausstellungsraum Sankt Anna-Kapelle, Passau 019570
Ausstellungsraum Schloß Büchsenhausen, Innsbruck 002076
Ausstellungssaal Katharinen, Sankt Gallen 037490
Ausstellungszentrum Heft, Hüttenberg 002064
Ausstellungszentrum Heiligenkreuzer Hof, Universität für Angewandte Kunst Wien, Wien 002854
Ausstellungszentrum im Schloss, Schlettau 020043
Ausstellungszentrum Kloster Cismar, Stiftung Schleswig-Holsteinische Landesmuseen Schloß Gottorf, Grömitz 017547
Ausstellungszentrum Kroch-Haus, Leipzig 018561
Ausstellungszentrum Lokschuppen, Rosenheim 019883
Aust-Agder Museet, Arendal 030734
Aust & Köckritz, Ortrand 126597
Austefjord Museum, Austefjorden . . 030749
Austin, Paris 065500
Austin & Co, San Jose 092916
Austin, John, Colchester 135136
Austin, Peter & Helen, Dorking 084185, 130645
Austin Antiques, Austin 087560
Austin Artworks, Austin 114955
Austin Auction Company, Austin . . .087561, 122805
Austin Children's Museum, Austin . 041919
Austin-Desmond, London . 085103, 113487
Austin Galleries, Austin . . 087562, 114956
Austin History Center, Austin 041920
Austin Museum of Art, Austin 041921
Austin Nature and Science Center, Austin 041922
Austin Pastel Society, Austin 054674
Austin Presence, Austin 114957
Austin Rare Coins, Austin 087563
Austin Spirit Gallery, Austin 114958
Austis Prodejní, Znojmo 098518
Australia Council for the Arts, Surry Hills 052453
Australian Aboriginal Art, Zollikerberg 112019
Australian Aboriginal Dreamtime Gallery, Alice Springs 094135
The Australian Aboriginal Fine Art Gallery of New York, New York 117657
Australian Abstracts, Coburg 094411
Australian and New Zealand Arms Company, Box Hill 055532
Australian and New Zealand Association of Antiquarian Booksellers, Frankston 053914
Australian and New Zealand Association of Antiquarian Booksellers, West Leederville 052454
Australian Antarctic Division Display, Kingston 001158
Australian Antique Arms Auctions, Doncaster East 120580
The Australian Antique Dealers Association, Malvern 052455
Australian Antiques, Fyshwick 055850
Australian Antiques and Fine Art Fair, Moore Park 093569
Australian Art Auctions, Kareela . . . 120595
Australian Art Connection, Sydney . 095272
Australian Art Informs, Sydney 095273
Australian Art Link, Greenwich 055917
Australian Art Resources, South Melbourne 056609
Australian Art Resources, Woollahra 056854
Australian Art Resources, Woollahra 095418
Australian Art Sales, Kareela 133050
Australian Book Auctions, Prahran . 120627
Australian Branch of China Relics, Ferny Creek 123223
Australian Centre for Contemporary Art, Southbank 001479
Australian Centre for Photography, Paddington 001362
Australian Children's Folklore Collection, Museum Victoria, Melbourne 001231
Australian Commercial Galleries Association, Saint Kilda, Victoria . 052456
Australian Council of University Art and Design Schools, Perth 052457
Australian Electric Transport Museum, Saint Kilda, South Australia 001446
Australian Exhibition Center, Chicago 042822
Australian Federation of Friends of Museums, Sydney 052458
Australian Flying Museum, Archerfield 000748
Australian Freethought Heritage Library, Balwyn 000768
Australian Galleries, Collingwood . . 094417
Australian Galleries, Collingwood . . 094418
Australian Galleries, Paddington . . . 095015
Australian Galleries, Paddington . . . 095016
Australian Galleries, Paddington . . . 095017
Australian Galleries, Paddington . . . 133052
Australian Gallery of Sport and Olympic Museum, Jolimont 001134
Australian Gold Exchange, Melbourne 056182
Australian Guild of Realist Artists, Camberwell 052459, 094357
Australian Heritage Print Company, Randwick 056518
Australian Institute of Genealogical Studies, Blackburn 000809
Australian Mallee Art, Cheltenham, Victoria 055667
Australian Mallee Art, Cheltenham, Victoria 055668
Australian Museum, Sydney 001507
Australian Naive Art, Paddington . . 095018
Australian National Maritime Museum, Sydney 001508
Australian Originals, Portland 118972
Australian Pearling Exhibition, Darwin 000973
Australian Print Workshop, Fitzroy . 094530
Australian Prints & Paintings, Blackwoode 055515
Australian Racing Museum, Caulfield South 000904
Australian Railway Museum, Melbourne 001232
The Australian Shop, Gent 096283
Australian Stockman's Hall of Fame and Outback Heritage Centre, Longreach 001192
Australian Toy Museum, Collingwood 000941
Australian War Memorial, Campbell 000881
Australian Wildlife Art Gallery, Munro 094922
Australiana-Africana, Caloundra . . . 055604
The Australiana Aspect, Warrandyte 056800
Australis Old Wares, Caringbah . . . 055631
Austråt Slott, Opphaug 031060
Austrått Fort, Brekstad 030794
Austråttborgen, Trondheim 031280
Austruy, Jean-Claude, Niort 065193
Aut. Pressaut., Königsdorf 133106
Autant, en Emporte le Temps, Paris 065501
Autantiquité, Lille 063831
Autegarden, Bruxelles 057844
Auterbe, Jean-Louis, Menton 064490
Auth, G., Duisburg 070473
Authentic Aboriginal, Gembrook . . . 055872
Authentic Aboriginal Art Centre, Sydney 095274
Authentic Africa, New York 117658
Authentic Africa, Philadelphia 118739
Authentic African Arts, Houston . . . 116279
Authentic City, Singapore 080430
Authentic French Antiques, Lievin . 063819
Authentic Lighting, Red Hill 056520
Authentic Namur, Namur 093594
Authentiek, Gent 058172
l'Authentique, Bruxelles 057845
L'Authentique, Lyon 064076
Authier, Thierry, Périgueux 066720
Author Bookstore, Calgary 137619
Autiero, Antonio, Napoli 075944
Autistic Specialists, Baltimore 115034
Auto Museum Dr. Carl Benz, Ladenburg 018457
Auto-Museum Fritz B. Busch, Wolfegg 020951
Auto Museum Moncopulli, Osorno . 006920
Auto Pinto, Lisboa 079869
Auto-Sammlung Gut-Hand, Aachen 015416

Auto & Technik Museum, Sinsheim 020220
Auto- und Motorrad-Museum, Öhringen 019439
Auto- und Motorradmuseum, Erlebnispark Ziegenhagen, Witzenhausen 020938
Auto- und Spielzeugmuseum Boxenstop, Tübingen 020492
Autoart - Edition Automobile, Rangendingen-Höfendorf 104655, 134352, 139674
Autobook World, Sydney 137102
Autochrome, Lyon 064077
Les Autodidactes, Paris 138292
L'Autographe, Genève 141245
Les Autographes, Paris 138293
Autographs and More, Louisville . . 142525
Autographs of Sports Legends Gallery, Indianapolis 142449
Autographs Plus, Saint Louis 142853
Automates Avenue, Falaise 011779
Automatik-Museum, Leipzig 018562
Automative Fine Art - A Journal by the Automative Fine Arts Society, Lake Orion 136396
Automative Fine Arts Society, Lake Orion 054675
Automne, Bruxelles 096149
Automobil-Museum, Asendorf bei Bruchhausen-Vilsen 015591
Automobil Museum Alte Garage, Rorschach 037462
Automobil-Museum Siegfried Marcus, Stockerau 002713
Automobil- und Motorradmuseum Austria, Mitterndorf an der Fischa 002320
Automobil-Veteranen-Salon, Gundelfingen an der Donau 017604
Automobilhistorisches Museum, Linz 002242
Automobilia, Hebden Bridge 039712
Automobilmuseum, Aspang 001699
Automobilmuseum Dresden, Dresden 016780
Automobilmuseum Stainz, Graz 001926
Automoción Costa, Valencia 129757
Automotive Hall of Fame, Dearborn 043341
Automusa, Bergeijk 029308
Automuseum Deventer, Deventer . . 029471
Automuseum Engstingen, Engstingen 016988
Automuseum E.R. Prihoda, Praha . . 008593
Automuseum Histo-Mobil, Giethoorn 029608
Automuseum Old Timer, Lo-Reninge 003609
Automuseum Schagen, Schagen . . 030123
Automuseum Störy, Bockenem 016286
Autoren Galerie 1, München 104145
Autorska Galeria, Gdańsk 108873
Autotron, Rosmalen 030075
Autour de Bois, Aléas, Le Robert . . 128493
Autour de l'Art, Antibes-Juan-les-Pins 098848
Autoworld, Bruxelles 003288
Autre Chose, Paris 065502
l'Autre Galerie, Bruxelles . 057846, 096150
Autre Reg'art, Bruxelles 096151
Autre Temps, Bordeaux 061586
Autrefois, Annecy 060886
Autrefois, Chartronges 062173
Autrefois, Fayence 062848
Autrefois, Genève 082400
Autrêfois, Jounieh 077431
Autrefois, Martigues 064414
Autrefois, Paris 065503
Autrefois, Paris 138294
Autrefois, Poussan 066973
Autrefois, Saint-Étienne 138595
Autrefois, Tours 068580
Autrefois, Vendôme 068756
Autrefois Antiques, Boston 087794
Autrefois en Gascogne, Vic-Fezensac 068842
Autrement Qu'Ainsi, Marcq-en-Barœul 099636
Autres Choses, Lyon 064078
Autrum-Mulzer, Swantje, München . 126347
Autry Museum of Western Heritage, Los Angeles 045411
Autumn Gallery Jewellery, Brighton, Victoria 055548
Autumn London Park Lane Arms Fair, London 093912
Auvergne Médailles, Vichy 068853
Auvermann, Detlef, Glashütten, Taunus 139138
Auvermann, Dirk, Königstein im Taunus 139357
Auversoise de Décoration, Auvers Saint-Georges 061092
Auwärter-Museum, Stuttgart 020344
Aux 3 Aches, Lyon 099540
Aux Affaires Anciennes, Massy 064422
Aux Armes d'Antan, Paris 065504
Aux Armes de Lorraine, Lerrain . . . 063748
Aux Armes de Lorraine, Mirecourt . 064563
Aux Arts et Caetera, Saint-Brieuc . .067381, 101134
Aux Arts Etc, Clermont-Ferrand . . . 062327
Aux Arts Etc, Tours 068581
Aux Arts...Etc, Oingt 099886
Aux Beaux Arts, Mantes-La Jolie . . 064251
Aux belles Antiquités, Basel 082123
Aux Bons Livres, Nice 138250
Aux Cases à Bulles, Paris 138295
Aux Charmes d'Antan, Mulhouse . . 064829
Aux Collectionneurs, Caen 138059
Aux Compagnons d'Hastings, Merville-Franceville-Plage 064507
Aux Couleurs de Provence, Montréal 096976
Aux Coups de Coeur, Nevers 065005
Aux Déménageurs Héraultais, Montpellier 064734
Aux Deux Anges, Labastide-d'Armagnac 063471
Aux deux Arts, Saulieu 068142
Aux Drapeaux Dimu, Saint-Étienne . 067441
Aux Fils du Temps, Paris 065505
Aux Fruits des Arts, Meudon 099721
Aux Merveilles d'Asie, Paris 065506
Aux Merveilles de l'Asie, Paris 065507
Aux Merveilles de l'Asie, Paris 065508
Aux Merveilles de l'Asie, Paris 065509
Aux Merveilles de l'Asie, Paris 124579
Aux Merveilles de l'Asie, Paris 124580
Aux Meubles Anciens, Besançon . . 061376
Aux Monnaies de la Bourse, Paris . 065510
Aux Mystères de l'Art, Marrakech . . 077680
Aux Naufrages du Temps, Saint-Malo (Ille-et-Vilaine) 101170
Aux Neiges d'Antan, Font-Romeu-Odeillo-Via 062887
Aux Occasions, Dijon 062644
Aux Plaisirs du Collectionneur, Paris 065511
Aux Portes du Temps Passé, Bézu-Saint-Eloi 061447
Aux Puces, Marseille 064318
Aux Puces de Plainfaing, Plainfaing 066838
Aux Puces Lavalloises, Laval (Mayenne) 063549
Aux Quartiers de France, Saint-Ouen 067720
Aux Reflets du Passé, Asnières-sur-Seine 061008
Aux Reflets du Passé, Paris 065512
Aux Remparts, Belfort 061324
Aux Rêves d'Antan, Le Mans 063655
Aux Siécles Passés, Bordeaux 061587
Aux Siècles Passés, Le Lardin-Saint-Lazare 063643
Aux Sièges d'Autrefois, Clermont-Ferrand 062328
Aux Soldats d'Antan, Paris 065513
Aux Soldats d'Antan, Paris 065514
Aux Temps Anciens, Grenoble 063051
Aux Tortues, Paris 065515
Aux Tresors Perdus, Saint-Ouen . . . 067721
Aux Trois Clés, Villeurbanne 068940
Aux Trois Marchés, Auxerre 061097
Aux Trois Marchés, Auxerre 061098
Aux Trois Marchés, Auxerre 124086
Aux Trois Marches, Paris 065516
Aux Trois Siècles, Sallanches 068096, 138611
Aux Trouvailles de Pasteur, Coudekerque-Branche 062498
Aux Trouvailles Galerie, L'Isle-sur-la-Sorgue 063923
Aux Vestiges Habis, Jounieh 077432
Aux Vieilles Portes, Cogolin 062382
Aux Vieiseries, Halloy 063117
AV Gallery, Limerick 022821
Av Goldteam, Paris 065517
A.V. Recycle Center, Tokyo 077238
Ava Gallery, Bangor 112556
Avallone Immacolata, Napoli 075945
Avalon, Christies Beach 136859
Avalon, Houston 132101
Avalon, Las Vegas 116611
Avalon, Portland 091901
Avalon, Saint Paul 119277
Avalon Postcard and Stamp Shop, Chester 083950
Avalook Antiques, Berrigan 055486
Avalun, München 139495
Avanersuup Katersugaasivia, Thule Museum, Qaanaaq 021546
Avanidis, Filip A., Athinai 074586
Avanlache NCG, Obertshausen 134324
Avant Art, Lüdinghausen 072350
Avant Art, Lüdinghausen 134174
Avant Garde, Padstow 114209
Avant Garden Bookshop, Daylesford 136876
Avante Galleries, Nashville 117338
Avantgarde Gallery, London 113488
Avantgarde Gallery, Möhnesee 104083
Avantgart, Heimbach, Eifel 071479
La Avanzada, Valencia 081645
Avdelnigen för Konstvetenskap, Lunds Universitet, Lund 050748
Ave-Art, Šumperk 098501
Ave Galeria, Kraków 108928
Avedis-Bahadourian, Paris 065518
Aveline, Paris 065519, 100013
Avelingh, in de, Maastricht 078594
Avelino, Pedro, Rio de Janeiro 096591
Avenida Art Gallery, Calgary 096789
Avent Designs, London 113489
Aventinum, Praha 133413
Aventinus, Abensberg 121290
Aventinus-Museum, Abensberg . . . 015437
Aventura, Miami 090144
Aventurine, Bruxelles 057847
Avenue, Oostende 058356
Avenue 30, Cairo 060428
Avenue A Cards, New York 117659
Avenue Antiques, Boston 087795
Avenue Antiques, Scarborough 056578
Avenue Antiques, Tauranga 079260
The Avenue Art Gallery, Calgary . . . 096790
Avenue Gallery, Austin 114959
Avenue Gallery, Baltimore 115035
Avenue Victor Hugo Bookshop, Boston 142243
Averoff Gallery, Athinai 021161
Averoff Gallery, Metsovon 021380
Averøy Skolemuseum, Averøy 030750
Averty, Clair, Nantes 124477
Avery, Ashley, Denver 088658
Avery, Ashley, Sacramento 092135
Avery County Museum, Newland . . 046452
Avery Fine Art, Atlanta 114858
Avery Historical Museum, Smethwick 041043
Avery Research Center for African American History and Culture, Charleston . . 042725
Avesta Auktionstjänst, Avesta 122104
Avetisians Museum, Erevan 000677
Aviamy, Dallas 131997
Aviation Art Gallery, Bankstown . . . 094212
Aviation Art Gallery, Orange 136397
Aviation Art Studio, Lincoln 113395
Aviation Gallery, Sacramento 119138
Aviation Heritage Museum of Western Australia, RAAF Association, Bull Creek 000858
Aviation Museum of Kentucky, Lexington 045257
AVICOM International Committee for Autovisual and New Technologies Museums, Liverpool 054305
Avid, New York 117660
AVID, Wellington 079317
Avier, Philippe, Bar-sur-Seine 061199
Avignon House Antiques, New Orleans 090513
Avignone Rossa, Giorgio, Torino . . . 140123
Avila Gómez & Cia., Ricardo, Bogotá 059820
Aviso, Washington 136398
Avison, Wellington 079318
Avivson, London 135187
Avlea, Lyon 064079
A.V.M., Paris 100014
Avner, Saint-Ouen 067722
AVOA, Paris 065520
Avoca Beach Antiques, Avoca Beach 055417
Avogadro & Doneda, Milano 127523
Avog's Crash Museum, Lievelde . . . 029869
Avoid the Middle Man, San Diego . . 092614
Avon-Anglia Publications, Weston-super-Mare 135312
Avon Antiques, Bradford-on-Avon . . 083629
Avon Books, Bristol 141446
Avon Historical Society Museum, Avon 041943
Avon House Antiques, Kingsbridge . 084853
Avon River Heritage Museum, Hants County 005602
Avon Valley Art Society, Northam . .052460, 094985
The Avonbridge Antiques and Collectors Market, Salisbury 086488
Avoncroft Museum of Historic Buildings, Bromsgrove 038884
Avondale Discovery Farm, Beverley 000801
Avondale Galleries, Oklahoma City . 118656
Avondale House, Rathdrum 022848
Avonds, Ludo, Antwerpen 057678
Avonds, Pierre, Turnhout 123674
Avonlea, Jacksonville 089380
Avonlea, Young 137147
Avonlea and District Museum, Avonlea 005045
Avonturen, Den Haag 078171
Avos, Los Angeles 132238
Avshalom, Eitan, New York 117661
Avtorskaja Galereja, Moskva 109496
Avusturya Kültür Ofisi, İstanbul 112284
A.W. Campbell House Museum, Strathroy 006522
Awa, Warszawa . .079737, 134861, 140779
Awa Camara, Bruxelles . . 057848, 123577
A.W.A. Electronic-Communication Museum, Bloomfield 042253
Awangarda, Wrocław 109212
Award Antik, Stockholm 081925
Awarji, Joseph, Damascus 083053
Awashi, Sato, Kamakura 106863
Aweart, Bournemouth 112678
AX Galeria, Bensheim 101754
The AXA Gallery, New York 046299
The AXA Gallery, New York 117662
Axana, Saint-Ouen 067723
Axbridge Museum, Axbridge 038553
Axe, Richard, Harrogate 141643
Axe Néo-7 Art Contemporain, Gatineau 005500
Axel, West Hollywood 093451
Axel Ebbes Konsthall, Trelleborg . . . 036715
Axel Stenross Maritime Museum, Port Lincoln 001397
Axelle, New Orleans 117397
Axels Bücherstube, Chemnitz 138961
Axia Art Consultants, London 085104
Axia Modern Art, Armadale, Victoria 094161
Axial, Lyon 099541

Axiom, Liverpool 136979
Axiom Centre for Arts, Cheltenham . 039050
Axis Fine Art, Brno 098326
Axis Gallery, Tokyo 107018
Axis - Visual Arts Information Service, Leeds 054306
Axitoys, Paris 100015
Axminster Museum, Axminster 038554
Axpe-Chaplain, Eric, Château-l'Eveque 062186
Axpe & Saillard, Périgueux 066721
Aya İrini Kilisesi Müzesi, Ayasofya Müzesi, İstanbul 038081
Ayac's, Amsterdam 107672
Ayala Museum, Vigan 031805
Ayala Museum - Gallery III, Makati . 031696
Ayala Museum of Philippine History, Makati 031697
Ayala Rodriguez, G., Madrid 081243, 141027
Ayasofya Müzesi, İstanbul 038082
Ayasofya Müzesi, Trabzon 038187
Aycliffe and District Bus Preservation Society, Newton Aycliffe 040576
Aydin, H., Berlin 069568
Aydın Devlet Güzel Sanatlar Galerisi, Aydın 038017
Aydın Müzesi, Aydın 038018
Ayer & Co., Bogotá 059821
Ayer & Hoy, Caracas 093522
Ayera, Zaragoza 081733
Ayerego, Toronto 137696
Ayesse, Odette, Rennes (Ille-et-Vilaine) 067099
Ayios Dimitrios Crypt Museum, Thessaloniki 021490
Aylmer and District Museum, Aylmer 005046
Aylmer Military Collection, Brading . 038812
Aylward, Wooroloo 095433
Aymara, Metzingen 104067
Ayme, Bernard, Marseille 124393
Aynalıkavak Kasrı, İstanbul 038083
Aynsley & Martel, Louisville 089961
Les Ayres, Bordeaux 138035
Ayres, Fort Worth 132070
Ayres, Donald, Thornhill 114570
Ayrshire Yeomanry Museum, Ayr . . 038558
Ayscoughfee Hall Museum, Spalding 041074
Ayşe ve Ercümend Kalmık Vakfı-Müzesi, Gümüşsuyu 038073
Ayubi, Thomas, Hochstadt, Pfalz . . 125946
Ayuka, Stevenage 086700
Ayuntamiento de Almeria, Almeria . 110093
Ayutthaya, Atlanta 114859
Az Arts Espace, Aigues-Mortes 098771
AZ Location, Aubière 098872
AZ Project, Sapporo 077192
Azabache, México 134758
Azabu Kasumicho Gallery, Tokyo . . 107019
Azadi Museum, Teheran 022607
Azaïs, Jean, Mougins 064803
Azalea House Antiques, Norfolk . . . 091368
Azaleen-Museum, Bremen 016407
Azani, Chicago 115356
Azar, Carl A., Atlanta 131762
Azarbayezan Museum, Tabriz 022600
Azcarate, Juan F.F. de, Buenos Aires 094060
Azeglio, Bologna 105947
Azemar, Christophe, Nice 065046
Azen, Louis, Damascus 083054
Azerbaijan State Museum of Fine Arts, Baku 003081
Azerbaijan State University of Arts, Baku 049669
Azeredo, José Mota, Porto 129189
Azevedo, António Manuel Guimarães, Lisboa 079870
Azevedo, António Manuel Guimarães, Lisboa 079871
Azimio la Arusha Museum, Arusha . 037846
Azimont, Jean-Pierre, Baillargues . 061172
Azimuth, Rousson 067305
Ažio, Kyïv 112394
Aziz, Teheran 074839
Aziz, Abdat, Amsterdam 077792
Aziz, Antoun, Cairo 060429
Azoulay, Daniel, Miami 117035
Azovskij Kraevedčeskij Muzej, Azov 033011
Azpitarte, Florence, Paris 065521
Aztalan Museum, Jefferson 044846
Aztec Graphics, San Diego 119486
Aztec Museum and Pioneer Village, Aztec 041944
Aztec Ruins, Aztec 041945
Azuchi, Osaka 106952
Azuchi-do, Tokyo 140182
Azul, Padova 076070
Azul Cobalto, São Paulo 058686
Azum, Sylvane, Bagnères-de-Luchon 061164
Azuma, New York 117663
Azuma, Sapporo 077193
Azuma, Seattle 119882
Azumino Mountain Art Museum, Hotaka 026547
Azur, Fréjus 062936
Azur Démolition, Cannes 061932
Azusa, Tokyo 107020
Azzlo, Tokyo 107021
Azzola, Max, Toulouse 068480
Azzopardi, Marseille 064319
Azzopardi, C., San Giljan 077525
Azzopardi & Sons, Valletta 077536
B-4 It Was Cool, New York 090708
B 42, Frankfurt am Main 102748
B & A, Tauranga 128962
B & B, Den Haag 078172
B & B Antiques, Stickney 086703
B B Antiques, Zabbar 077548, 128484
B. & B. Art, Venezia 106727
B. & B. Art, Venezia 106728
B & B Art Gallery, New York 117664
B & B International Gallery, New York 090709
B. Bissoondoyal Memorial Centre, Tyack 028074
B & C Art, Omaha 118686
B & C Carpet Company, New York . . 090710
B C Graphics, Baltimore 131813
B Contemporary, London 113490
B & D, Milano 106167
B & D Furniture Repair, Saint Louis . 132741
B-Gallery, Richmond 119099
B H, Raon-l'Etape 067042
B & H Antiques, Miami 090145
B & H Clock, San Jose 132921
B J Antiquités, Marseille 064320
B & J Booksellers, Coopers Plains . 136867
B & J Refinishing and Upholstery, Memphis 132316
B-Lumen, Schiltigheim 068177
B M Birla Science and Technological Museum, Hyderabad 022156
B & M Clock Repair, Houston 132102
B & M Gallery, Meito 106910
B & N Verlag und Edition, Bad Homburg v.d.Höhe 133730
The B & O Railroad Museum, Smithsonian Institution, Baltimore 041965
B & O Railroad Station Museum, Ellicott City 043676
B & O Starožitnosti, Praha 060112
B & Q Art Gallery, Long Beach 116665
B & R Fittings, Jolimont 056021
B & S Upholstery, El Paso 132062
B-semi Schooling System, Yokohama 050505
B. & T. Antiques, London 085105
B & W Antiques, Seattle 092964
B & W Collector Books, Salt Lake City 142871
BA 47 Antikviteter, Oslo 079422
Ba Bi, Song, Shanghai 097903
BA-CA Kunstforum, Wien 002855
Baader, Joachim, München 104146
De Baaien Rok, Bussum 078126
Baal, Bielefeld 102110
Baarle's Museum, Baarle-Hertog . . 029287
Baas, Seattle 119883
Baba & Társa, Budapest 074667
Baba Antiques, Mumbai 074819
Baba Nyonya Heritage Museum, Melaka 027989
Babaada, Batheaston 083452
Babault, Alain, Gondrecourt-le-Château 063012
Babcok, New York 117665
Babe Didrikson Zaharias Museum, Beaumont 042081
Babe Ruth Birthplace & Museum, Baltimore 041966
Babel, Murcia 110647
Babel Galeria, Gdańsk 108874
Babendererde, Peter, Lübeck 139425
Babendererde, Rosemarie, Stockelsdorf 073923
Babilla, Milano 075608
Babilônia Antiguidades, Porto Alegre 058487
Babinot, Francine, Aigues-Mortes . . 060678
Babits Mihály Emlékház, Szekszárd 021875
Bablon, Béatrice, Paris 138296
Babls Uhrensammlung, Waffenbrunn 020616
Babol Museum, Babol 022547
Babon, Frédéric, Pézenas 066795
Bab's Collectibles, Jacksonville . . . 089381
Babuino Novecento, Roma 106495
Babushka Antiques, Auckland 078927
Babylon Museum, Babylon 022657
Babylon Oriental Rug, Los Angeles . 089697
Babylone, Nice 065047
Babylonian Jewry Museum, Or Yehuda 023042
Bac, Georges, Paris 065522
Bac Saint-Germain-Editions Callithos, Paris 100016, 133530
Baca House, Trinidad History Museum, Trinidad 048610
Bacarelli, Riccardo, Firenze 075277
Les Bacchanales, Neuilly-sur-Seine 064986
Bacchi, Antonio, Roma 076322
Bacchin, Paolo, Verona 128414
Bacchus Antik, Stockholm 081926
Bacci, Gregorio, Venezia 106729
Bacciocchi, Ilde, Milano 127524
Baccjo, Warszawa 109098, 121902
Baccus Marsh Antiques, Bacchus Marsh 055419
Bace, Bill, New York 117666
Bacelos, Vigo 110862
Bach, Los Angeles 132239
Bach, Detlef, Winterbach, Kreis Bad Kreuznach 127023
Bach, G., Carouge 082288
Bach, G., Genève 082401
Bach, Hans Jürgen, Düsseldorf . . . 121380
Bach, M., Roetgen 073563
Bach-Gedenkstätte im Schloß Köthen, Köthen, Anhalt 018362
Bach-Museum, Bach-Archiv Leipzig, Leipzig 018563
Bachčisaraj State Historical and Cultural Preserve, Bachčisaraj 038227
La Bacheca, Cagliari 106009
La Bacheca, Catania 075236
Bachelier, Saint-Ouen 067724
Bachelier, Chantal, Nice 124501
Bachelier Foucauld, Nantes 064901, 138234
Bachelier-Glotin, Gaëlle, Nantes . . . 064902, 138235
Bachellier, Monique, Revigny 067126
Bachelor's Club, Tarbolton 041187
Bacher, Adam, Portland 118973
Bacher, Franz, Raubling 073435
Bacher, Véronique, Belp 129944
Bacher-Museum, Zellerndorf 003068
Bachet, Vouvray-sur-Loir 069035
Bachet, Pierrette, Château-du-Loir . 062181
Bachfischer, Regensburg 104690
Bachgau-Museum, Großostheim . . 017576
Bachhaus Eisenach, Eisenach 016920
Bachkovski Manastir muzej, Bachkovo 004622
Bachmann, Luzern 111678
Bachmann, D., Zürich 082943
Bachmann, Erika, Puchheim 073379
Bachmann, Irène, Luzern 111679
Bachmann, Josef, Grüt 082487
Bachmann, Nora, Marquartstein . . . 072468
Bachmann, Petra, Bornheim, Rheinland 125369
Bachmann & Berthold, Crimmitschau 070163
Bachmann & Eckenstein, Basel . . . 082124, 111164
Bachmann-Museum Bremervörde, Ehemalige Erzbischöfliche Kanzlei, Bremervörde 016436
Bachofer, C., Frickenhausen, Württemberg 125677
Bachrach, Richmond 092060
Bachschmid, Stephan, Kaufbeuren . 126021
Bacht, Richard, Essen 133913
Bachus, Warszawa 079738
Bacin de Plata, La Paz 058397
Back, Michael, Memmelsdorf 126304
Back Alley Antiques, San Antonio . . 092487
Back Alley Books, Chicago 142277
Back Copies, Melbourne 136995
Back of Beyond, Gisborne 079100
Back Pages Books, Stirling 137092
Back Porch, San Diego 119487
Back Roads Art, Austin 114960
Back to Africa, New York 117667
Back to Back Galleries, Cooks Hill . 094424
Back to the Picture, San Francisco . 119605
The Backdoors Warehouse, Washington 093383
Backert, Hilmar, Andernach 101581
Backerworks Skilled Welding, Albuquerque 131738
Backhausen, Bernd, Mönchengladbach 072564
Backker, L. de, Bruxelles 057849
Backlot, Los Angeles 116714
Back'N'Time Antiques, Waihi 079277
Backspace, Portland 118974
Backstreet Antiques, Calgary 058780
Backstreet Galleries, Los Angeles . 116715
Backstreet Gallery, Dallas 115839
Backus Heritage Village, Port Rowan 006189
Backwoods Tin, Milwaukee 090274
Baclayon Church Museum, Baclayon 031622
Bacon, Philip, Fortitude Valley 094556
Bacon & Cie, Saujon 068141
Baconnais, Jean, La Baule-Escoublac 099373
Bacon's Castle, Surry 048441
Bacot, Jacques, Paris 065523
Bacot, Odette, Chalon-sur-Saône . . 062082
Bacqueville, Paris 065524
Bacqueville, Paris 065525
Bacstreet, Paris 065526
Baculo, Madrid 110451
Bączek, Beata, Poznań 109043
Bad Boys Gallery, Baltimore 087644
Bad Gasteiner Museum, Bad Gastein 001715
Bad Reichenhaller Salzmuseum, Bad Reichenhall 015772
Bad Salzufler Kunst & Antiquitätenhaus, Bad Salzuflen 069363, 121306
Bad Schwalbacher Kur-Stadt-Apotheken-Museum, Bad Schwalbach 015795
Badaling Art Cooperative, Beijing . . 097640
Badarelli, Albertville 060743
Badawang, Cleveland 115686
Badcocks Gallery, Newlyn 114131
Baddack, J., Hildburghausen 071513
Baddow Antique Centre, Chelmsford 130527

Baddow Antique Centre, Great Baddow . . . 084503, 130743
Badè Institute of Biblical Archaeology and Howell Bible Collection, Berkeley . 042156
Badeeb & Sons, Mohammed Ahmed, Sanaa . . . 093562
Bademuseum, Bad Elster . . . 015691
Baden Antik, Karlsruhe . . . 071710
Baden-Powell House, London . . . 040080
Badener Puppen- und Spielzeugmuseum, Baden bei Wien . . . 001742
Bader, Eilenburg . . . 102607
Bader, Tübingen . . . 139792
Bader, Ulm . . . 139807
Bader, A., Neu-Isenburg . . . 072966
Bader, Alexander, Berlin . . . 069569
Bader, Alfred, Milwaukee . . . 117170
Bader, Patick, Eloie . . . 062774
Bader, Peter, Luzern . . . 082618, 111680
Bader-Koller, Edith E., Lugano . . . 082591, 111660
Badest, Milwaukee . . . 117171
Badger, Worthing . . . 142174
Badger Creek Museum, Cartwright . 005233
Badger Mine and Museum, Shullsburg . . . 048168
Badgers Books, Buderim . . . 136829
Badgerys Attic, Lawson . . . 056092
Badhaus Museum und Galerie, Kulmbach . . . 018438
Badiali, Maria Grazia Marisa, Modena . . . 075895, 106346
Badin, Paris . . . 065527
Badin, Giraud, Paris . . . 065528
Badin, Giraud, Paris . . . 138297
Badin de Montjoye, Dominique, Sucy-en-Brie . . . 068336
Badische Antiquitäten- und Kunsttage, Donaueschingen . . . 093713
Badische Gesellschaft für Münzkunde, Karlsruhe . . . 053034
Badische Landesbibliothek, Karlsruhe . . . 018156
Badischer Kunstverein, Karlsruhe . . 018157
Badischer Kunstverein, Karlsruhe . . 053035
Badisches Bäckereimuseum und Erstes Deutsches Zuckerbäckermuseum, Kraichtal . . . 018389
Badisches Landesmuseum Karlsruhe, Karlsruhe . . . 018158
Bado & Mart, Padova . . . 140083
Badorfer, Brühl, Rheinland . . . 138951
Badorrek, Manfred, Bad Kissingen . 138696
Badum, Georg, Bamberg . . . 121311
Bae, Andrew, Chicago . . . 115357
Bächler, Hubert, Zürich . . . 112043
Baechtold, Brigitte, Lausanne . . . 130063
Baecker, Inge, Köln . . . 103588
Bäckerei- und Dorfgeschichtliches Museum, Bremervörde . . . 016437
Bäckereimuseum, Krummhörn . . . 018426
Bäckereimuseum, Rimpar . . . 019847
Bäckermuseum, Wien . . . 002856
Bähler, Hermann, Vordemwald . . . 082893
Bäkmann, Hans-Joachim, Rinteln . 073540
Bänder, Klaus, Düsseldorf . . . 102472
Bänninger, Erica, Basel . . . 082125
Bär, Arnold, Altnau . . . 082088
Baer, Barbara, Jacksonville . . . 089382
Bär, Manfred, Berlin . . . 125165
Bärbeline, Lübeck . . . 072321
Bärchen, Heidi, Stuttgart . . . 073961
Baere, de, Beaufort . . . 055459
Bären Galerie, Birr . . . 111293
Bärenmaler, Leipzig . . . 103855
Bärner Heimatstube, Langgöns . . . 018515
Bärnstensmuseet, Höllviken . . . 036341
Bärtschi, Guy, Genève . . . 111424
Bärtschi, Tobias, Luzern . . . 130098
Baerveldt, Joure . . . 121795
Bärwaldt, Maastricht . . . 078595
Bärwinkel, Eike, Langenbach, Kreis Freising . . . 139379
Bästkustens Auktionstjänst, Svenshögen . . . 122275
Baeten, Antwerpen . . . 057679
Baetica, Málaga . . . 136078
Baets, I. de, Gent . . . 096284
Bättig, Armin W, Luzern . . . 111681
Baetzner, Herilt, Hamburg . . . 071201
Baeuerle, Jochen, Stuttgart . . . 139753
Baeuerle, Klaus, Konstanz . . . 103753
Bäuerliche Gerätesammlung, Buch bei Jenbach . . . 001772
Bäuerliche Sammlung, Obertilliach . 002391
Bäuerliches Gerätemuseum und Venezianer-Gatter, Innervillgraten 002073
Bäuerliches Heimatmuseum der Landtechnik, Geiselhöring . . . 017340
Bäuerliches Museum im Achentaler Heimathaus, Rohrdorf . . . 019876
Bäumler, Peter, Regensburg . . . 104691, 134359
Baez, Ricardo B., Buenos Aires . . . 136702
Baez-Yankovic, Dinko V., Luxembourg . . . 128469
Bafkham, Limburg an der Lahn . . . 072256
The BAG, Baguio . . . 136019
Bag and Art, Wien . . . 095802
Bag One Arts, New York . . . 117668
Bagamoyo Historical Museum, Bagamoyo . . . 037849
Bagatela, Belo Horizonte . . . 058409
La Bagatelle, La Seyne-sur-Mer . . . 063447
Bagatelle Antiques, Barton, Cambridgeshire . . . 083406, 130343
Bagatelle Brocante, Bègles . . . 061321
Bagatti, Arturo, Milano . . . 075609, 140043
Bagchee, Delhi . . . 139947
Bagdad Gallery, Portland . 091902, 123063
Bagdaschwili, Remscheid . . . 073489
Baggins, Rochester . . . 142021
Baggins, B., Saint Louis . . . 092203
Baggot Framing, Dublin . . . 105859
Baggott, Stow-on-the-Wold . . . 086739
Baggott, Duncan J., Stow-on-the-Wold . . . 086740
Baghai Sain Shapoor, Torino . . . 076769
Baghcheh-Jaq Palace, Urmieh . . . 022647
Baghdad Museum, Baghdad . . . 022661
Bagherys, Genève . . . 082402, 111425
Baghgheh Chogh Palace, Maku . . . 022578
Baghino, Annalisa, Roma . . . 076323
Bagiau, Asnières-sur-Vègre . . . 061012
Baginski, M., Großefehn . . . 071118
Bagira, Moskva . . . 109497
Bagland, Mauricette, Conches-en-Ouche . . . 062446
Bagn Bygdesamling, Bagn . . . 030752
Bagnai Alessandro, Firenze . . . 106031
Bagnai Alessandro, Siena . . . 106649
Bagno di Nerone, Pisa . . . 106464
Bagnolati, Giancarlo, Bologna . . . 075055
Bagnoréa, Annecy . . . 098836
Bagnoud & Roppa, Crans-sur-Sierre 082333
Bagpipe Music Museum, Ellicott City . . . 043677
Bagshaw, Uttoxeter . . . 122732
Bagshaw, G., Siddington . 086616, 131500
Bagshaw Museum, Batley . . . 038636
Bagué, M.A., Girona . . . 110365
Bagué, Santiago, Barcelona . . . 129326
Baguio-Mountain Provinces Museum, Baguio . . . 031626
Bahamas Historical Society Museum, Nassau . . . 003089
Bahamas Museum, Nassau . . . 003090
Bahawalpur Museum, Bhawalpur . . 031357
Bahawalpur State Museum, Bhawalpur . . . 031358
Bahay Laguna Museum, Liliw . . . 031685
Bahay Nakpil-Bautista, Manila . . . 108840
Bahay Tsinoy Museum, Manila . . . 031713
Bahlburg, Hamburg . . . 071202
Bahnwärterhaus, Galerien der Stadt Esslingen, Esslingen . . . 017083
Bahr & Kemper, Bremen . . . 138938
Bahrain Art Center, Manama . . . 095992
Bahrain Arts Society, Manama . . . 052631
Bahrain Arts Society Gallery, Manama . . . 003093
Bahrain Contemporary Art Association, Manama . . . 052632
Bahrain Fine Arts School, Manama . 049671
Bahrain National Museum, Manama 003094
Bai, Beijing . . . 097641
Bai, New York . . . 117669
La Baia delle Favole, Milano . . . 127525
Baibo Hua Yuan, Qingdao . . . 097884
Baicao, Urumchi . . . 137754
Baie Verte Peninsula Miners' Museum, Baie Verte . . . 005057
Baier, Fred, Tucson . . . 120107
Baier, Sibylle, Wiesbaden . . . 105243
Baier, Zilly, Oberstdorf . . . 104508
Baierweinmuseum, Bach an der Donau . . . 015636
Baihan Al Qasab Museum, Wadi Baihan . . . 049565
Baihua Literature and Art Publishing House, Tianjin . . . 133385
Baihuazhou Literature and Art Publishing House, Nanchang . . . 133373
Baik, Honolulu . . . 088935
Baik-Song, Seoul . . . 107207
Baikal, Paris . . . 065529
Baiken, Kyoto . . . 106889
Le Bail Weissert, Paris . . . 138298
The Baildon Furniture, Baildon . . . 083361
Baile de Laperrière, Charles, Calne 135127
Bailen la Trastienda, Ourense . . . 081447
Bailer Donat, München . . . 072651
Bailey, Austin . . . 087564, 131793
Bailey, Honolulu . . . 088936
Bailey, Murwillumbah . . . 137019
Bailey & Co., Oklahoma City . . . 091475
Bailey, Thirlmere . . . 095329
Bailey, Andrew, Haverfordwest . . . 113205
Bailey, Beezy, Cape Town . . . 110018
Bailey, E., Milford, Surrey . . . 085992
Bailey, F.O. & Co, Portland . . . 123061
Bailey House Museum, Mauri Historical Society, Wailuku . . . 048824
Bailey-Matthews Shell Museum, Sanibel . . . 047943
Bailey & Nelson, Seattle . . . 119884
Baileys, Ross-on-Wye . . . 086399
Bailiffgate Antique Pine, Alnwick . . 083272
Baillet-Lefrére, René, Tourcoing . . . 068557
Bailleul, Didier, Le Mans . . . 063656
Bailleul, Patrick, Saint-Hilaire-du-Harcouët . . . 101159
Bailleul & Nentas, Bayeux . . . 120916
Baillif, Roland, Genève . . . 122320
Bailly, Charles & André, Paris . . . 100017
Bailly, Jacques, Paris . . . 100018
Bailly, Jacques, Paris . . . 100019
Bailly, Jean-Jacques & Francois, Paris . . . 124581
Bailly, Thierry, La Chapelle-Montlinard . . . 063318
Bailly Gutenberg, Paris . . . 133531
Baimasi Han Wei Gucheng Display Center, Luoyang . . . 007177
Baimbridge Antiques, Hamilton, Victoria . . . 055942
Bainbridge & Co, A., Ruislip . . . 122672
Baines, Henry, Southborough . . . 086652
Baines, James, Malanda . . . 094765
Bains, Christchurch . . . 079012
Les Bains d'Aphrodite, L'Isle-sur-la-Sorgue . . . 063924
Baiocco, Fabiola, Roma . . . 076324
Bair, Salt Lake City . . . 119329
Baird, Robert M., Salt Lake City . . . 132780
Baird Institute Museum, Cumnock . 039195
Bairnsdale Antiques, Bairnsdale . . . 055421
Bairnsdale Museum, Bairnsdale . . . 000758
Bairro Alto, Lisboa . . . 129146
Bairstow Eves Fine Art, Whitby . . . 122744
Baisden, Tampa . . . 120026
Baishing, Singapore . . . 080431, 109774
Bait Al Zubair, Muscat . . . 031345
Bait Muzna Gallery, Muscat . . . 031346
Baitson, Gilbert, Kingston-upon-Hull 122554
Baituna al Talhami Museum, Bethlehem . . . 031408
Bajahr, Rainer, Bendorf, Rhein . . . 069519
Bajaj Art Gallery, Mumbai . . . 105758
Bajardi, Marion, Graz . . . 123358
Bajcsy-Zsilinszky Emlékmúzeum, Veszprém . . . 021918
Bajer, André, Oslo . . . 140698
Bajocchi, Pietro, Cairo . . . 060430
Bajolet, Léon, Montigny-lès-Metz . . 064695
Bajor Gizi Emlékmúzeum, Szinháztörténeti Múzeum, Budapest . . . 021638
Bajt Dan, Charkiv . . . 112378
Bajuwarenmuseum Waging am See, Waging . . . 020619
BAK, Almelo . . . 107621
Bak Negara Muzium Matawang, Kuala Lumpur . . . 027966
Bakar Local History Museum, Bakar 007695
Bakara, Biarritz . . . 061449
Bakarat, Kraków . . . 108929
Bakari, Wilkinsburg . . . 135524
Bakehouse, Ohaupo . . . 079203
Bakehouse Gallery, Patonga . . . 095060
Bakehouse Museum, Crystal Brook 000961
Bakelants, Ivo, Deurne . . . 058156, 133283
Bakélite, Clermont-Ferrand . . . 062329
Bakelite Museum, Williton . . . 041389
Het Baken, Almelo . . . 107622
Baker, Denver . . . 122881
Baker, Paddington . . . 095019
Baker, A.P. & R., Wigtown . . . 142157
Baker, Edith, Dallas . . . 115840
Baker, Frederick, Chicago . . . 115358
Baker, G., Horncastle . . . 084734, 130805
Baker, Gordon F, London . . . 058880
Baker, Gregg, London . . . 085106
Baker, J. & J., Lavenham . . . 084909
Baker, Jeffrey, Coffs Harbour . . . 094413
Baker, Keith, Woking . . . 087205
Baker, Norma, Fort Worth . . . 088835
Baker, R.J., Canterbury . . 083856, 130502
Baker, T., Langford, Nottinghamshire . . . 084901
Baker, T.R., Stockbridge . . . 086711
Baker-Cederberg Museum, Rochester . . . 047477
Baker Truesdale, Fortitude Valley . . 055837
Bakers Auction, Paramount . . . 123041
Bakers Dozen Antiques, Vancouver 059337
Bakersfield Museum of Art, Bakersfield . . . 041954
Bakfickan, Stockholm . . . 141148
Bakhtari, Mehdi, Paris . . . 065530
Bakhtiyar, Stockbridge . . . 086712
Bakirzoglu, Erika, Wien . . . 057375
Bakkemuseet, Frederiksberg . . . 008862
The Bakken, Library and Museum of Electricity in Life, Minneapolis . . . 045908
Bakker, Ad, Dordrecht . . . 078296
Bakker, Aletta, Sarlat-la-Canéda . . 101256, 124926
Bakker, Bartje, Amsterdam . . . 077793
Bakker, James R., Cambridge . . . 122834
Bakker, Wim, Rotterdam . . . 078700
Bakker - Leeskamer van Maastricht, Tjerk, Maastricht . . . 140492
Bakkerij Museum, Oosterhout . . . 029998
Bakkerijmuseum, Geel . . . 003442
Bakkerijmuseum, Groot-Bijgaarden 003482
Bakkerijmuseum, Huizen . . . 029783
Bakkerijmuseum, Veurne . . . 003827
Bakkerijmuseum De Grenswachter, Luijksgestel . . . 029880
Bakkerijmuseum de Meelzolder, Almelo . . . 029136
Bakony Múzeum, Veszprém . . . 021919
Bakonyi Természettudományi Múzeum, Zirc . . . 021928
Bakri Gazzaz, Hussein, Riyadh . . . 080373
Baks, E., Den Haag . . . 107907
Baksa, Prof. Dr. Jean Pierre von, Wien . . . 095803
Baku, Fukuoka . . . 106840

Baku Art Gallery, Bucureşti 109420
Baku Museum of Education, Baku . 003082
Bal Gandharva Rang Mandir, Pune . 105823
Bal Sangrahalaya, Lucknow 022236
Bala Like Railway Museum, Bala . . 038569
Balaam, Barcelona 129327, 140980
Balachninskij Kraevedčeskij Muzej, Balachna 033012
Baladna, Amman 107154
Balai Seni Lukis Negara, Kuala Lumpur 027967
Balalaika Arts, New York 117670
Baland, Torsten, Berlin 138742
Balandier, Michel, Saint-Étienne . . . 124895
Balanghai Archeological Site Museum, Butuan 031637
Balao-Balao Gallery, Angono 108813
Balasch, Hermann, Sattledt 057299, 123466
Balassa Bálint Múzeum, Esztergom 021721
Balassi, Kiadó, Budapest 134499
Balastre, Jacqueline, Varzy 068729
Balatoni Múzeum, Keszthely 021764
Balaÿ, Charles, Lyon 064080
Balay Negrense Museum, Silay . . . 031789
Balboa 13, Madrid 110452
Balboa Art Conservation Center, San Diego 132845
Balboa Park Gallery, San Diego Art Institute, San Diego 047814
Balbon, Denise, Saint-Ouen 067725
Balboni, Strasbourg 124938
Balcaen, Ets Claude, Paris 065531, 124582
The Balch Institute for Ethnic Studies, Philadelphia 046926
Balcli's, Barcelona 080804, 121996
Balcombe Fine Art, Croydon 123218
Balconi Ricciardi, Angela, Milano . . 075610
Baldacchino, Los Angeles 089698
Baldaia, Laurindo Pinto, Porto 129190
Baldaia, Laurindo Pinto, Porto 129191
Baldaia, Laurindo Pinto, São Mamede de Infesta 129205
Baldari, Antonio, Roma 127932
Baldari, Benito, Roma 127933
Baldem, İstanbul 112285
Baldes, Carsten, Göppingen 071026
Baldfaced Stag, Ashurst, Kent 083344
Baldi, Padova 076071
Baldi, Lella, Verona 076992
Baldi, Rino, Vénissieux 101445
Baldin, Torino 076770
Baldinger, Artuur, Amsterdam 107673
Baldo, Antonio Juan, Alicante 129302
Baldo, Veronese, Verona 076993
Baldomero Aguinaldo House, Kawit 031680
Baldoni, Nicole, Pignans 066831
Baldus, Siegbert, Karlsruhe 071711
Baldwin, Vineyard Haven 143035
Baldwin & Sons, A.H., London 085107, 122578
Baldwin, M. & M., Cleobury Mortimer 141524
Baldwin, M. & M., Kidderminster . . 141693
Baldwin, Peter, Mullumbimby 137016
Baldwin County Heritage Museum, Elberta 043647
Baldwin Historical Society Museum, Baldwin 041957
Baldwin Photographic Gallery, Middle Tennessee State University, Murfreesboro 046095
Baldwin-Reynolds House Museum, Meadville 045736
Balestra, Marseille 064321
Balestra, Louis, Marseille 064322
Balestra, Louis, Marseille 064323
Balfe, Dublin 121661
Balfet, Christian, Le Pradet 063692
Balfet, Olivier, Mazamet 064443
Balfour, Toronto 137697
Balfour Museum of Hampshire Red Cross History, Winchester 041400
Bălgarka, Burgas 096696
Bălgarski Chudožnik, Sofia 133308
Balgoma, Madrid 081244
Bali-Africa, Bruxelles 057850
Bali Bay Trading, Tampa 093107
Balian, Paris 065532
Balias, D., Serans 068226, 101273
Balikcioglu, S., Köln 071911
Balıkesir Devlet Güzel Sanatlar Galerisi, Balıkesir 038019
Baliki, Saint-Paul 080131
Balke, Evelyn, Berlin 125166
Balke, H., Alpirsbach 069138
Balkema, A.A., Rotterdam 134828
Balkhausen, Weilerswist 074303
Balkhausen, I., Köln 071912
Balkwill, Ray, Exmouth 113046
Ball, David, Leighton Buzzard 084963, 130882
Ball, O., Hüffenhardt 071585
Ball & Claw Antiques, Tetbury 086848
Ball State University Museum of Art, Muncie 046083
Balla-Wein, Portarlington 056481
Ballack, F.H.H., München 072652
Ballan Shire Historical Museum, Ballan 000760
Ballance House, Glenavy 039582
Ballangen Bygdemuseet, Ballangen 030754
Ballantine Books, New York 135412
Ballarat Clayfire Gallery, Magpie . . . 094759
Ballarat Fine Art Gallery, Ballarat . . 000761
Ballard, Seattle 132928
Ballard & Fetherston, Seattle 119885
Ballarin Marin, Enrique, Zaragoza . . 081734
Ballario, Georges, Le Cannet 063583
La Balle de Plomb, Eguilles 062766
Ballerup Egnsmuseet, Ballerup 008818
Ballestrem, C. Gräfin von, Münster . 072895
Ballet, Eddy, Thorey-Lyautey 124957
Ballinamore Local Museum, Ballinamore 022683
Ballis, Ian, North Geelong 056366
Ballon- en Luctvaartmuseum Zep/Allon, Lelystad 029858
Balloni, Andrea, Milano 075611
Ballonmuseum Gersthofen, Gersthofen 017391
Ballot, Saint-Étienne 121244
Ballot, Michel & Dany, Romenay . . . 067205
Ballpark Gallery, San Francisco . . . 119606
Ball's Falls Historical Park, Allanburg 004996
Ballufin, Charles, Grenoble 063052
Bally, Miami 132335
Bally, Miami 132336
Bally, Maurice & Gisèla, Colmar . . . 062402
Bally Schuhmuseum, Schönenwerd 037533
Ballybunion Heritage Museum, Ballybunion 022685
Ballycastle Museum, Ballycastle . . 038574
Ballyheigue Maritime Centre, Ballyheigue 022688
Ballymena Museum, Ballymena . . . 038578
Ballymoney Museum, Ballymoney . 038580
Balmain Framers and Gallery, Balmain 094203
Balmer, H.R., Zug 141366
Balmes Richelieu, Pierre, Paris 065533
Balmoral, Toronto 059144
Balmoral Art Galleries, Hamlyn Heights 094614
Balmoral Grist Mill, Tatamagouche . 006554
Balnarring Gallery, Balnarring 094206
Balneologické Múzeum, Piešťany . . 034408
Balocco Arte, Torino 106661
Il Balon 2, Roma 076325
Al-Baloushi, Khalid Rasool Buksh Osman, Muttrah 079514
Balsalobre Oliva, Fernando, Cartagena 081030
Balsan, Paris 100020
Balsano, Rosario, Torino 076771
Balser, Helmuth, Gernsbach 070976, 125725
Balser, Shirley, Baltimore 142219
Balsiger, Otto, Delémont 111379
Balsiger, Walter, Bad Ragaz 082105, 129904
Baltazar, Bruxelles 096152
Baltazar, Ostrava 060065
Balteau, Alain, Liège 058288
Balter, Steven F., Seattle 132929
Baltes, Bernd, Holzwickede 134066
Baltes, I., Holzwickede 103402
Baltic Crossroads, Los Angeles . . . 116716
Baltic Imports, Minneapolis 117245
Baltimore Book Company, Baltimore 122808, 142220
Baltimore Civil War Museum, Baltimore 041967
Baltimore Clayworks, Baltimore . . . 115036
Baltimore County Historical Museum, Cockeysville 043026
Baltimore Gallery, Baltimore 115037
Baltimore Gold & Silver Center, Baltimore 087645
Baltimore Maritime Museum, Baltimore 041968
The Baltimore Museum of Art, Baltimore 041969
Baltimore Museum of Industry, Baltimore 041970
Baltimore Paint Removing Company, Baltimore 131814
Baltimore Public Works Museum, Baltimore 041971
Baltimore Streetcar Museum, Baltimore 041972
Baltimore's Black American Museum, Baltimore 041973
Balvu Vēstures un Mākslas Muzejs, Balvi 027660
Balzac, Toronto 097229
Balzaretti, Daniela, Milano 075612
Balzeau, Liliane, Tours 068582
Balzekas Museum of Lithuanian Culture, Chicago 042823
Balzo, Roland del, Grenoble 063053
Bama Ngappi Ngappi Aboriginal Corporation, Yarrabah 056900
Bambach, Klaus, Wiesbaden 074394
Bamberger, Alan, San Francisco . . . 142929
Bamberger, Peter, Nürnberg 121563
Bamble Museum, Langesund 030969
Bamboo, Jacksonville 116509
Bamboo, Kathmandu 107575
Bamburgh Castle, Bamburgh 038582
Bame, Chris, Dallas 131998
Bamian Museum, Bamian 000001
Bammert, Urs, Luzern . . . 082619, 130099
Bammler, Thomas, Traunstein 074075
Bamps, Véronique, Bruxelles 057851
Bampton Gallery, Bampton, Devon .083376, 130327
Bamses Auktioner, Svedala 122274
Bamyan, Paris 065534
Ban Kao Prehistoric Museum, Kanchanaburi 037901
Banaemah, Jeddah 080359
Bananenmuseum, Sierksdorf 020206
Banas, Alessandro Pietro, Milano . . 127526
The Banbury and District Art Society, Banbury 054307
Banbury Cross Antiques, Sacramento 092136
Banbury Cross Fine Arts and Antiques, Ascot 055406
Banbury Fayre, London 085108
Banbury Museum, Banbury 038584
Banc Public, Sainte-Cecile-d'Andorge 101239
Banch, Davide, Firenze 075278
Banchory Museum, Banchory 038586
Banco 22, Firenze 075279
Banco Libri, Bologna 139984
Banco-Münzcabinett, Münster 072896
Bancroft, Cleveland 115687
Bancroft Mill Engine Trust, Barnoldswick 038598
Bancroft Mineral Museum, Bancroft 005059
Bancroft's Decorative and Fine Arts Society, Loughton 054308
Bandamora, Katoomba 094681
Bandaranaike Museum, Colombo . . 036129
La Bande des Six Nez, Bruxelles . . 096153
La Bande des Six Nez, Bruxelles . . 137425
Bandeira, Rosário, Setúbal 109404
Bandekow, Fred, Vollerwiek 105131
Bandele, Phoenix 142759
Bandelier Site, Los Alamos 045406
Bandello, Rocco, Genk 058158
Bandigan, Sydney 095275
Bandinelli, Benito, Firenze 127291
Bandkowski, Andrzej, Wrocław . . . 109213
Bandol Antiquités, Bandol 061184
Bandol Antiquités, Bandol 061185, 124090
Banes, Richmond 132709
The Banff Centre, Banff 049774
Banff Museum, Banff 038588
Banff Park Museum, Banff 005061
Bang, Cape Town 110019
Bang, D.C., Frederiksberg 060228
Bangabandhu Shek Mujibur Rahman Museum, Dhaka 003100
Bangally, New York 117671
Bangalow Antiques, Bangalow 055447
Bangalow House Antiques, Lismore 056103
Bangbu City Museum, Bangbu 006957
Bangen, Wolfram, Havixbeck 125888
Bangert, Dr. Albrecht, München . . . 134217
Bangerter, Bern 082196, 129946
Bangiya Sahitya Parisad Museum, Kolkata 022214
Bangkok Capital Antique, Hong Kong 059598
Bangkok University City Gallery, Bangkok 037870
Bangla Academy Folklore Museum, Dhaka 003101
Bangladesh National Museum, Dhaka 003102
Bangladesh Shamorik Jadughar, Dhaka 003103
Bangor Historical Society Museum, Bangor 042009
Bangor Museum and Art Gallery, Bangor, Gwynedd 038590
Bangs, Christopher, London 085109
Bangsbo Museum, Frederikshavn . . 008864
Bangunan Alat Kebesaran Diraja, Bandar Seri Begawan 004610
Banicke Múzeum, Rožňava 034419
Baniel, Irit, New York 117672
Bank, München 072653
Bank Gallery, Darlinghurst 094451
Bank Gallery, Los Angeles 116717
The Bank House Gallery, Norwich . . 086109
Bank House Gallery, Norwich 114161
The Bank House Gallery, Norwich . . . 131326
Bank Leumi Museum, Tel Aviv 023064
Bank Museum of Kansallis-Osake-Pankki, Helsinki 009516
Bank of America Galleries, San Francisco 047854
Bank of England Museum, London . 040081
Bank of Ireland Arts Centre, Dublin . 022731
Bank of Ireland Gallery, Thurles . . . 105903
Bank of Mississippi Art Collection, Tupelo 048657
Bank of Montreal Museum, Montréal 005908
Bank of Valletta Museum, Sliema . . 028029
Bank of Victoria Museum, Yackandandah 001638
Bank One Fort Worth Collection, Fort Worth 044004
Bank Street Antiques, Ottawa 059031
Bank Street Gallery, Newquay 114138
Banker's Furniture, Phoenix 091720
Bankert, Schildow 126766
Bankfield Museum, Halifax 039658
Banking and Currency Museum, Kadina 001136
Bankmuseet, Stavanger 031222
Banknote and Coin Collection of the National Bank of Hungary, Budapest 021639

Banks, M.G., Christchurch 079013, 108383
Banks, Robert H ., Dallas 115841
Banks, Simon, Finedon 084403
Banks, Yvonne, Seattle 119886
Banks Peninsula Antiques, Akaroa . 078898
Banksia Grove Gallery, Lake Cathie 094721
Bankside Gallery, London 040082
Banmuseet, Ängelholm 036169
Bannach, Jürgen, Siegsdorf 073814
Bannehr, Pamela-Britt, Lüchow, Wendland 126245
Banner County Historical Museum, Harrisburg 044440
Bannier, Yves, Saint-Brandan 067380
Banning, J., New York 117673
Banning Residence Museum, Wilmington 049200
Bannister, David, Cheltenham 130531, 141499
Bannister, Penny, Fremantle 136907
Bannock County Historical Museum, Pocatello 047106
Bannockburn Heritage Centre, Stirling 041103
Bannow, Günther, Lübeck 072322
Banovsky, Chomutov 060007
Banovsky, Michel, Bagneux 061166
Banpo, Paris 065535
Banq, Eric, Castres 062031
Banque du Livre, Saint-Étienne . . . 138596
Banquels, J., Courville-sur-Eure . . . 062528
Banqueting House, London 040083
Banské Múzeum v Prírode, Banská Štiavnica 034305
Bantock House, Wolverhampton . . . 041429
Bantry House, Bantry 022692
Banyan Tree, Hong Kong 059599
Bányászati Múzeum, Salgótarján . . 021832
Banys Arabs, Palma de Mallorca . . 035600
Banzhaf, Tübingen 139793
Banzon Antiques, Manila 079562
Bao, Ly, Hoi An 120542
Bao Tàng Dân Tôc Hoc Viêt Nam, Ha Noi 049522
Bao Tàng Hai Phong, Hai Phong . . . 049534
Bao Tàng Quan Doi, Ha Noi 049523
Bao Tàng Văn Hóa Các Dân Tôc Viêt Nam, Thai Nguyen 049551
Baobab, Amsterdam 077794
Baptist Amandus, Bergen op Zoom . 107869
Baptista, A.M. Salgueiro, Lisboa . . . 079872
Bar Bookstore, Scarborough 142050
Bar David Museum, Kibbutz Bar Am 022996
Bar Harbor Historical Society Museum, Bar Harbor 042015
Bara Art, Lalitpuru 107609
Baraban, Lyon 064081
Barabas, Ladislav, Bratislava 080601
Barabe, Nicolas, Rennes (Ille-et-Vilaine) 067100
Barabinskij Kraevedčeskij Muzej, Novosibirskij oblastnoj kraevedčeskij muzej, Barabinsk 033013
Baracchi, Paolo, Firenze 075280
De Baracquen Museum voor Bourtanger Bodemvondsten, Bourtange 029338
Barahona, Victor, Santiago de Chile 059505
Barailler, Jean-Pierre, Nice 065048
Baraka, San Diego 119488
Barakat, Beit Lahm 079523
Barakat, Samir, Cairo 098616
Barakat Gallery, London 113491
Barake, Herbert, São Paulo 058687
Barale, Patrick, Ezanville 062833
Barale, Paula, Moulins (Allier) 064811
Baramasa, Manila 108841
Baran de Bordeaux, Auckland 078928
Barandela Blancoq, Jaime, Saint-Maurice 067663
Baranès, Martine, Paris 133532
Barangay Museum, Mandaluyong . . 031707
Baranov Museum, Kodiak 045045
La Baraque, Lichtenvoorde 128751
Barasoain Church Museum, Malolos 031703
Barat, Jean-Luc, Le Dorat 063614
Baratta, Maria Celeste, Messina . . . 075554
La Baratte, Megève 064462
Baratte, Frédérique, Chauny 062255
Baratti, Giorgio, Milano 075613
Baraz, İstanbul 112286
Barazer, Guillaume, Roscoff 101101
Barb, Tucson 120108
Barba, Javier, Lima 079541
Barbacana, Montevideo 087307
Barbáchano & Beny, Cercedilla . . . 129482
Barbáchano & Beny, Madrid 129573
Barbados Museum, Saint Michael . 003124
Barbagallo, Sebastiano, London . . . 085110
Barbagallo, Sebastiano, London . . . 085111
Barbakan, Warszawa 109099
Barbanel, Claude, Paris 065536
Barbanel, Claude, Saint-Ouen 067726
Barbara F., Bremen 070009
Barbara Fritchie House, Frederick . 044047
Barbara Galeria, Warszawa 109100
Barbara Hepworth Museum and Sculpture Garden, Saint Ives, Cornwall 040918
Barbara's Books, South Auckland . . 140651
Barbara's Dolls, Fort Worth 088836
Barbara's kleine Welt, Schorndorf, Württemberg 073723
Barbareschi, Valentina, Torino 128257
Barbarian Book Shop, Wheaton . . . 143053
Barbarians, Saint Paul 119278
Barbarisi, Elisabetta, Roma 076326
Barbarlık Müzesi, Lefkoşa 008253
Barbarot, Claude, Jaulny 063237
Barbaroux, Suzanne, Marseille 064324
Barbatelli, Nicola, Napoli 075946
Barbaud, Nantes 064903
Barbaud, Jean-Pierre, Soisy-sous-Montmorency 068255
Barbaud, Jean-Yves, Nantes 064904
Barbazán, Manuel J., Buenos Aires 055172
Barbe, Christophe, Caen 061860
Barbe, Ludovic, Toulouse 068481
Barbe, Ludovic, Vicdessos 068851
Barbe, Patrice, Paris 065537
Barbe-Lafarge, Francis, La Calmette 063301
Barber, Alison, West Haddon 087085, 131665
Barber, D., Würzburg 139869
Barber, John M., Richmond 119100
Barber, Ron, Wellington 108615
Barber Institute of Fine Arts, Birmingham 038720
Barber Kennedy, Mat, Chicago 115359
Barbera, Evelyne, Saint-Ouen 067727
Barbera, Olivia, Saint-Ouen 067728
Barbero, A., Madrid 129574
Barberousse, Jeanlin, Gruissan . . . 063088
Barberousse, Michel, Paris 065538, 100021
Barbers, Market Drayton 122612
Barbers, Woking 122755
Barbers, Ashley, Redfern 056522
Barber's Book Stores, Fort Worth . . 142408
The Barber's Clock, Worcester 087251, 131714
Barberton Museum, Barberton 034547
Barbéry, Paris . . . 065539, 100022, 138299
Barbery, Lia, Montevideo 087308
Barbesol, Christian, Ladon 063480
Barbetti, Roberto, Genova 106083
Barbian, Martin, Saarbrücken 139702
Barbican, Manama 095993
Barbican Antiques Centre, Plymouth 086275
Barbican Art, London 040084
Barbican Art Gallery, London 113492
Barbican Bookshop, York 142176
Barbican Gallery, Plymouth 114256
Barbican Gallery Comes to Town, Plymouth 114257
Barbie, Manuel, Barcelona 110115
Barbier, Antoine, Blumeray 061533
Barbier, Gérard, Dordives 062717
Barbier, Gérard, Sermaise 068228
Barbier, Hélène, Marseille 124394
Barbier, Martine, Metz 064522
Barbier, Michel, Le Bizot 063567
Barbière, Brigitte, Mazan 064447
Barbieri, Adriano, Firenze 127292
Barbieri, Carlo, Modena 127720
Barbisch, Sankt Gallenkirch 057289
Barbizon, Arnhem 078043
Barbizon, Paris 100023
Barbj Lavorazione, Firenze 075281
Barboni, Magda, Milano 075614
Barboni, Piero, Genova . . . 075441, 134593, 140031
Barbosa, António J. Rodrigues, Braga 129138
Barbotin, Frédéric, Le Pouliguen . . . 063690
Barbotine, Mont-Louis 064613
Barbotine, Saint-Martin-de-Ré 067630
Barbour's General Store Museum, Saint John 006351
Barbuino, Roma 121719
Barby Antiques, Tucson 093206
Barcala Diaz, Juan Ramon, Jerez de la Frontera 081163
Barcaldine and District Historical Museum, Barcaldine 000769
Barcellino, Nino R., Pittsburgh 091790
Barcellona, Federica, Genova 106084
Barcellos, Livia de Alencar Chaucs, Porto Alegre 096545
Barcelo, Ignacio, Córdoba 110313
Barcelona, Bad Reichenhall 101689
Pereira Barcínio & Araújo, Porto . . . 109367
Barcino, Barcelona 080805
Barclay, Headington 084640
Barclay, M.J. & D., Friockheim 084444
Barclay-Samson, Richard, London . 085112
El Barco, Madrid 129575
Barco, Praha 060113
Del Barco Arte, Sevilla 110763
Barcsay Gyüjtemény, Ferenczy Múzeum, Szentendre 021879
The Bard Graduate Center for Studies in the Decorative Arts, Design, and Culture, New York 046300
Bardas, Galaţi 140890
Bardawil, Eddy, London . . 085113, 130937
Bardean, Albuquerque 114770
Bardeau'sches Kultur- und Ausstellungszentrum, Feldbach . . 001843
Bardelaere Museum, Lembeke 003575
Barden House Antiques, Tonbridge . 086893
Bardet, Jacques, Plougoumelen . . . 066871
Bardez, Jean-François, Paris 124583
Bardhaman Science Centre, Bardhaman 022018
Bardini, Genova 140032
Bardith, New York 090711
Bardon, Brooklyn 135337
Bardón Mesa, Luis, Madrid 141028
Bardoux, Patrick, Grimaud 063082
Bardu Bygdetun, Salangsdalen 031160
Bārdu Dzimtas Muzejs Rumbiņi, Pociems 027723
Barducci, Alberto, Bologna 127130
Bardwell, S., Dronfield 084223
Bare Cove Fire Museum, Hingham . 044555
Bare-Delhaise, Liège 058289
Bare Hands Gallery, Birmingham . . 115100
Bare Wood, Birmingham 131830
Barebones Art Space, Bangalow . . . 094209
Barefoot, Colombo 081757
Barefoot Gallery, Christchurch 108384
Barekat, Torino 128258
Baren Woodcut, Aloha 054676
Bareo, Singapore 109775
Barès, Paris 100024
Bares, Nello, Milano 075615
Barewood, London 130938
Bareyre, Martine & Gérard, Agen . .060664, 124058
Barfield, Donna J., Jacksonville . . .089383, 142460
Barfino, Barcelona 080806
Barfoot, Craig, East Hagbourne . . .084247, 130662
Barfüßerkirche, Angermuseum, Erfurt 017008
Barfuß, Matto H., Herrieden 103361
Bargac, Philadelphia 091608
Bargain Barn, Elliot 055792
Bargain Box, Luton 085871
Bargain Corner, Chicago 088029
Bargain Upholstery, Saint Paul 132761
Barganhata Comercio de Usados, Rio de Janeiro 058552
Bargaro Beach Gallery, Bargara . . . 094216
Barge, Annie, Ambierle 060793
Bargera, Kenda, Köln 103589
Barghini, Isa, Milano 075616
Barham, London 085114
Baria, Tristan, Sees 068186
Baria, Tristan, Sees 068187
Barilleau, Bruno, Le Chesnay 063600
Barillet, Marie José, Milano 075617
Barin Carpets Restoration, London . 130939
Barioz, Christian, Lyon 064082
Baripada Museum, Baripada 022020
Barist, Joan, New York 090712
Barjavel, Françoise, Arry 060992
Barjol, Michel, Malaucene 099628
Bark House Gallery, Newquay 114139
Barkenhoff Stiftung Worpswede, Worpswede 020984
Barker, Buffalo 087862, 131852
Barker, Alyce, Los Angeles 116718
Barker & Son, F.J., Bayview 055458
Barkerville Historic Town, Barkerville 005066
Barkham, Julian, Wellington 128971
Barkham Antique Centre, Barkham 083380, 130332
Barking Box, New York 090713
Barkley East Museum, Barkley East 034548
Barkowski, Rolf, Recklinghausen . . 073442
Barkwell, Kansas City 089484
Barletta & Morcos, Paris 065540
Barletti, Geom. Giulio, Torino 128259
Barley, Robert, London 085115
Barley Twist, Charlotte 087927
Barleylands Farm Museum, Billericay 038708
Barlier, Francis, Paris 065541, 100025
Barling Fine Porcelain, Wickham Bishops 087144
Barlow, New Orleans 117398
Barlow, Tulsa 132994
Barlow, Isiaha, Wanganui 108602
Barlow, PM & MA, Malanda 056127
Barlow Collection of Chinese Ceramics, Bronzes and Jades, Brighton 038845
Barmbecker Antiquariat, Hamburg . 139167
Barmet, Edy, Wauwil 082901
Barmorr, San Diego 092615
Barmouth Sailors' Institute Collection, Barmouth 038593
The Barn, Nairobi 077353
The Barn, Petersfield 086233
Barn Antiques, Barnstaple 083395
Barn Antiques, Nantwich 086033
Barn Antiques Centre, Long Marston 085828
The Barn at Bislington, Bisington . . 083546
Barn Book Supply, Salisbury 142043
Barn Court Antiques, Templeton . . . 086840
Barn Galleries, Henley-on-Thames . 113229
Barn Museum and Rail Depot Museum, Troutdale 048614
Barna, J., Hamilton 123769
Barnacle Historic State Park, Coconut Grove 043028
Barnadas, Jordi, Barcelona 110116
Barnard & Nedin, Lund 081849
Barnard's Mill Art Museum, Glen Rose 044203
Barnegat Bay Decoy and Baymen's Museum, Tuckerton 048625
Barnes, Andrew, Prahran 137057
Barnes, Daisy, Hutton-le-Hole 113283
Barnes, Jane, Honiton 084713
Barnes, R.A., Bicester 083508

Barnes Candace, San Francisco ... 092737
Barnes County Historical Museum, Valley City ... 048736
Barnes Foundation, Merion ... 045788
Barnes & Noble, Cleveland ... 142329
Barnet, Bertrand, Gournay-en-Bray 063024
Barnet Cattanach, Anne-Marie, Borehamwood ... 083575, 130410
Barnet Historical Society Museum, Barnet ... 042024
Barnet Museum, London ... 040085
Barnett, Jacksonville ... 116510
Barnett, David, Milwaukee ... 117172
Barnett, Roger, Eton ... 084340
Barney, Daniel, New York ... 090714
Barnicott, Linda, Pittsburgh ... 118899
Barnizados & Lacados, Hontoria ... 129536
Barnizados J. & M. Martínez, L'Hospitalet de Llobregat ... 129537
Barnizados Mayoral, Madrid ... 129576
Barnizados y Lacados, Segovia ... 081562, 129725
Barnola, Antonio de, Barcelona ... 110117
Barnoud, Dijon ... 099209
Barnowicz, Sue Ellen, Main Beach . 056124
Barnsdale Gallery, Yoxford ... 114758
Barnsdall Art Center, Los Angeles .. 116719
Barnsdall Junior Arts Center, Los Angeles ... 045412
Barnt Green Antiques, Barnt Green .083401, 130340
Barntiques, Colchester ... 084053
Barnum House Museum, Grafton .. 005526
Barnum Museum, Bridgeport ... 042406
Barnwell County Museum, Barnwell 042027
Barnyard International, Atlanta ... 087454
Barockberichte, Informationsblätter des Salzburger Barockmuseums, Salzburg ... 135546
Barockjagdschloß Eckartsau, Eckartsau ... 001801
Barockmuseum, Reidling ... 002515
Barockschloß Riegersburg, Riegersburg, Niederösterreich ... 002528
Baroco, Neuilly-sur-Seine ... 064987
Baroda Museum and Picture Gallery, Vadodara ... 022364
Barois, Philippe, Aire-sur-la-Lys ... 060685
Barok, Prigorje Brdověko ... 123945
Barokh, R.M., West Hollywood ... 093452
Baroko, Louny ... 123962
De Barometer, Rotterdam ... 078701
Barometer Shop, Leominster ... 084968, 130884
Barometer World, Merton . 085981, 131275
Barometer World Museum, Merton . 040451
Le Baron, Casablanca ... 077640
Baron, Chester ... 083951, 130557
Baron, Miami ... 090146
Baron, Bertrand, Melle ... 064473
Baron, H., London ... 141753
Baron Art, Holt, Norfolk ... 084701
Baron & Boisanté, New York ... 117674
Baron & Boisanté, New York ... 117675
Baron & Boisanté, New York ... 135413
Baron Fine Art, Chester ... 112851
Baron Hermanos, Barcelona ... 080807
Baron & Ribeyre, Paris ... 121114
Barone, Hamilton ... 137637
Barone, Marseille ... 124395
Barong, Padies ... 065324
Baroni, Milano ... 075618
Baroni, Jean-François, Paris ... 100026
Baroni, Loris, Venezia ... 076922
Baroni, Maurizio, Parma ... 076196
Baroni, Silvia, Bologna ... 127131
Baroni & Segre, Milano ... 127527
Baronian-Francey, Bruxelles ... 096154
Baroniet Rosendal, Rosendal ... 031153
La Baroquante, Saint-Maime ... 067600
Baroque, Copponex ... 062466
Baros Books, Trowbridge ... 142120
Barossa, Angaston ... 136781
Barossa Valley Historical Museum, Tanunda ... 001533
Baroti, Klaipėda ... 107350
Barovier, Marino, Venezia ... 106730
Barozzino, Giovanna, Lisboa ... 079873
Barquet, Ramis, New York ... 117676
Barquet, Ramis, New York ... 117677
Barr, Houston ... 116280
Barr, B., Denver ... 122888
Barr & Barr, New York ... 117678
Barr Colony Heritage Cultural Centre, Lloydminster ... 005781
Barr & Ochsner, Zürich ... 082944
Barra González, Sergio, Santiago de Chile ... 059506
Barrachina-Ramoneda, Barcelona . 129328
Barrack Cottage, Hobart ... 055989
Barragan, Madrid ... 129577
Barral, Angel, Buenos Aires ... 055173
Barran, Julian, Castle Cary ... 112823
Barranco, Madrid ... 081245
Barrand, Grace, Nutfield ... 114181
Barrandov, Praha ... 137828
Barras, David, Bulle ... 082280
Barrat, Vichy ... 068854
Barraud, Jean-Marie, Castelnau-le-Lez ... 062014
Barraud, Patrick, Saint Prex ... 082766
Barraud & Bonnet, Le Crès ... 063608
Barrault, Alain, Puisserguier ... 066996
Barrault, Anne, Paris ... 100027
Barre, Claire, Bordeaux .. 061588, 124115
Barré, Gérard, Saint-Malo (Ille-et-Vilaine) ... 067606
Barre, Laurent-Claude, Dampierre-en-Yvelines ... 062592
Barré, Nicolas, Orléans ... 065295
Barre Historical Museum, Barre ... 042028
Barreau, Rennes (Ille-et-Vilaine) ... 067101
Barreau, Thorigné-Fouillard ... 068409
Barreau, Jean-Louis, Chinon ... 138075
Barreau, Patrick, Tours ... 068583
Barreau Le Maistre Art Gallery, Jersey Museum, Saint Helier ... 040911
Barrel, Genova ... 106085
Barrere, Charles, Saint-Ouen ... 067729
Barrère, Jacques, Paris ... 065542
Barrett House, Forest Hall, New Ipswich ... 046237
Barrett Street Antique Center, Virginia Beach ... 093344, 123133
Barrette, Kelly, Boston ... 115145
Barrhead and District Centennial Museum, Barrhead ... 005068
Barridoff, Portland ... 123062
Barrié, P., Paris ... 065543
Barrie H Coleman, Great Somerford 113153
Barrientos, Guatemala ... 074650
Barrie's Birthplace, Kirriemuir ... 039907
Barrington, Christchurch ... 140611
Barrington, London ... 135188
Barrington, David, Brasted ... 083646
Barrington, Michael, Dorchester ... 130639
Barrington Area Historical Museum, Barrington ... 042029
Barrington-Doulby, Edward, Barnard Castle ... 083386, 130334
Barrington Galley of London, New York ... 117679
Barrington Living History Farm, Washington ... 048971
Barrington Woolen Mill Museum, Barrington ... 005071
Barrios, Montevideo ... 122771
Barrister, New Orleans ... 117399
Barrister, San Antonio ... 142880
Barro, Maos de, Belo Horizonte ... 058410
Barro, Sacramento ... 092137
Barrocco, Montfort-l'Amaury ... 099743
Barrocos Galería, Bucaramanga ... 098206
Barron Arts Center and Museum, Woodbridge ... 049281
Barron County Historical Society's Pioneer Village Museum, Cameron ... 042585
Barros, Antonio M. Ferreira, Lisboa 079874
Barros, Dario, São Paulo ... 096663
Barros, Maria Beatriz, Porto ... 080067
Barrow, Loughborough ... 113997
Barrows, Martinborough ... 108497
Barry, Kevin, Los Angeles ... 116720
Barry & Rare, Minehead ... 141946
Barrymore, Albuquerque ... 087375
Barry's Antiques, Berrima ... 055488
Barry's Antiques, Great Yarmouth .. 084526
Barry's Auction, Albuquerque ... 122792
Le Bars, Montauban ... 064627
Barsa Mûtárgykaptár, Budapest ... 105491
Barsacq Schaefli, Sylvie, Biarritz .. 061450
Barsanti, G. & Figli, Pisa ... 106465
Barse, Gilles, Saint-Cannat ... 067389
Barsley, Belmont ... 055471
Bart, Betty & Jane, New York ... 090715
Barta, Manfred, Salzburg ... 057235
Barta & Marquardt, Berlin 069570, 125167
Bartel, Irmgard, Konstanze & Christian, Bonn ... 069912
Bartels, Gudrun, Friedland, Kreis Göttingen ... 133964
Bartels, Heinz, Libbesdorf ... 126218
Bartels, Karla, Bernau bei Berlin ... 138867
Bartelt, Giedre, Berlin ... 101793
Bartens, Helga, Hannover ... 071383
Barter, Alnwick ... 141384
Barter, Johannesburg ... 080700
Bartfield, J.N., New York . 090716, 132445, 142634
Barth, Frankfurt am Main ... 070727
Barth, H., Köln ... 103590
Barth, Klaus, Heidelberg ... 125897
Barth, Dr. Ute, Zürich ... 112044
Barth Erben, Walter, Zug . 083043, 141367
Bartha, Miklos von & Margareta von, Basel ... 111165
Bartha, N. von, London ... 113493
Barthel, Claudia, Graz ... 057003
Barthel & Tetzner, Berlin .. 101794, 133754
Barthelmess & Wischnewski, Berlin ... 069571, 101795
Barthelmy, Roberto L., Buenos Aires ... 055174
Bartholomäus-Schmucker-Heimatmuseum, Ruhpolding ... 019950
Bartholomew County Historical Museum, Columbus ... 043096
Bartın Kültür Evi, Bartın ... 038020
Bartke, Hans, Möhnesee ... 072558
Bartko-Reher, Berlin ... 138743
Bartleby & Co., Bruxelles ... 133259
Bartleby, Washington ... 143037
Bartlesville Area History Museum, Bartlesville ... 042030
Bartlett, Michael, Saint-Ouen ... 067730
Bartlett, Nigel A., London ... 085116
Bartlett, Philipp, Nantes ... 064905
The Bartlett Museum, Amesbury .. 041688
Bartlow, Peter, Chicago ... 115360
Bartók 32 Galéria, Budapest ... 105492
Bartók Béla Emlékház, Budapest .. 021640
Bartoli, Cincinnati ... 088212
Bartoli, Herminé & Saliceti, Ajaccio 060737
Bartoli, Rodolfo, Firenze ... 075282
Bartolomé, Jordi, Barcelona ... 080808
Bartolomei-Roussel, Yvon, Corbières ... 062469
Bartolomeo, Roberto, Milano ... 075619, 127528
Bartolomeu Dias Museum Complex, Mossel Bay ... 034683
Bartolotta, Giuseppe, Firenze ... 127293
Bartolozzi, Guido, Firenze ... 075283
Barton, Sacramento ... 119139
Barton, Saint Louis ... 119185
Barton County Historical Society Village and Museum, Great Bend ... 044298
Barton Museum, Bhavnagar ... 022028
Barton Museum, Wilson ... 049222
Barton-Sharpe, New York ... 090717
Bartow History Center, Cartersville . 042638
Bartow-Pell Mansion Museum, Bronx ... 042430
Bartrick, Steven D., Gloucester ... 141628
Bart's Coins, Chicago ... 088030
Barts Wonderwinkel, Gent ... 123618
Bartsch, C., Meckenheim, Rheinland ... 072482
Bartsch, Heine Robert, Charlottenlund ... 060216
Bartsch, Helge, Rettenberg ... 126715
Bartsch, Monika, München ... 126348
Bartsch & Chariau, München ... 104147
Bartscht, K. & G., Leipzig ... 072199
Baruc, São Paulo ... 058688
Baruch, Anne & Jacques, Chicago . 115361
Baruffaldi, E.-M., Göttingen ... 071041
Barwinski, Lothar, Meschede ... 126310
Barwon, Queenscliff ... 137065
Barwon Booksellers, Geelong ... 136914
Barzel, Berlin ... 069572
B.a.S., Venezia ... 106731
B.a.S., Venezia ... 106732
B.a.S., Venezia ... 106733
Bas Art, Buenos Aires ... 055175
Basaglia, Gianpietro, Livorno ... 075524
Basai International, Shanghai ... 059730
Basak, İstanbul ... 112287
Basalt, Amsterdam ... 107674
Basantapur, Kathmandu ... 107576
Baschek, Jörg, Hadamar . 071160, 125779
Bascourt, Antwerpen ... 057680
Base Art Gallery, Cincinnati ... 115606
Base Ball Cards, Columbus ... 088384
Base Borden Military Museum, Borden ... 005118
Base Gallery, Tokyo ... 107022
Base Space, Brookvale ... 094311
Baseball Card Corner, Cincinnati .. 142305
Basecraft, Yorklea ... 095456
Basedau, Hamburg ... 071203
Baseline, Providence ... 119070
Basement Art, København ... 098535
Basement Gallery, Enniskillen ... 113022
Basement Gallery, Los Angeles ... 116721
Bases, Saint Paul ... 092350
Bases Loaded, Buffalo ... 087863
Bashar, Manama ... 095994
Bashert, Albuquerque ... 114771
Bashford, Auckland ... 078929
Bashford, Dobson, Christchurch ... 108385
Basho Memorial Museum, Ueno ... 027303
Basho Museum, Tokyo ... 027146
Basic, Luka, Wien ... 057376, 133182
Basic Antic, La Fouillouse ... 063381
Basile, Melbourne ... 056183
Basilian Fathers Museum, Mundare 005970
Basilica Collegiata di Santa Maria Assunta, San Gimignano ... 025677
Basílica de Nuestra Señora del Pilar, Zaragoza ... 036098
Basilica del Santo Niño Museum, Cebu ... 031650
Basilica Museum, Schatkamer van de Onze-Lieve-Vrouwbasiliek, Tongeren .. 003797
Basilique Notre-Dame de Montréal, Montréal ... 005909
Basilique Royale Saint-Denis, Saint-Denis (Seine-Saint-Denis) ... 014252
Basilisk, Basel ... 141196
Basilisk, Morges ... 111752
Basilisk Bookshop, Fitzroy ... 136898
Basilisken-Presse, Marburg ... 134191
Basin Head Fisheries Museum, Prince Edward Island Museum and Heritage Foundation, Souris ... 006492
Basin Müzesi Sanat Galerisi, İstanbul ... 038084
Basing House, Basing ... 038610
Basingstoke Canal Exhibition, Mytchett ... 040507
Basis Actuele Kunst, Utrecht ... 108239
Basis Antiquariat, München ... 139496
Basis Wien, Wien ... 002857
Basis Wien, Wien ... 002858
Basix, Singapore ... 080432
Baskerville, Petworth ... 086237
Baskerville, Lee, Richmond ... 119101
Baskerville Bindings, Holt, Norfolk . 141673

Baskerville Books, Wadhurst 142137
Baskett, Mary, Cincinnati 115607
Baskin Visual Arts, University of California Santa Cruz, Santa Cruz 052140
Baškirskij Respublikanskij Chudožestvennyj Muzej im. M.V. Nesterova, Ufa . . . 033989
Baskom, Moskva 121963
Basler Kunstverein, Basel 054174
Basler Papiermühle, Schweizerisches Museum für Papier, Schrift und Druck, Basel 036882
Baslerhof, Luzern 111682
Basmadjian, Garig, Paris 100028
Basnet Art, Kathmandu 107577
Basnier, François, Caen 061861
Basquin, Christine, Sains-du-Nord . 067339
Basrah Museum, Basrah 022665
Bass Museum of Art, Miami Beach . 045824
Bass Museum of Brewing, Burton-upon-Trent 038916
Bassali, Paris 065544
Bassam, Arès 060956
Bassamat, Casablanca 107549
Bassani, Rossella, Verona 128415
La Basse Fontaine, Vence 101434, 138645
Bassenge, Gerda, Berlin . . 069573, 121320, 138744
Bassereau, Nicole, Paris . 100029, 133533
Bassery, François, Lille 063832
Bassery, François, Lille 063833
Bassery, François, Lille 124314
Basset, Jean-Claude, Auray 061067
Bassetlaw Museum and Percy Laws Memorial Gallery, Retford 040822
Bassett Hall, Williamsburg 049178
Bassett House Museum, Okanagan Falls 006067
Bassi, N., Memphis 090055
Bassler, Freiburg im Breisgau 070823, 102854
Bassof, Lawrence, Beverly Hills . . . 135328
Bassoi, São Paulo 123712
Bassola, Ettore, Firenze 127294
Bastejs, Rīga 107317
Baster, Halina, Kraków 129032
Bastian, Jean, Strasbourg 068301
Bastianacci, Vittorio, Firenze 127295
Bastide, Catherine, Bruxelles 096155
Bastide, Gil, Orléans 065296
Bastide Gallery, Tournon-d'Agenais 068562
La Bastidiole, Paris 138300
Bastien, J., Bruxelles 096156
Bastier, Patrick, Coligny 062393
Bastilippo, Sevilla 081575
Bastings, Charles, Oss 078665
Bastings, Frans & Geryon, Oss 078666
Bastings & Van Tuyl, Oss 078667
Bastion, Nanaimo 005978
Al Bastione, Palermo 076128
Il Bastione Antichità, Cagliari 075200
Bastogne Historical Center, Bastogne 003214
Teixeira Bastos, Lisboa 079875
Basualto López, Romilio Segundo, Santiago de Chile 059507
Bata Shoe Museum, Toronto 006582
Batagianni, Vaso, Athinai 105388
Batalla, Valentín, Cáceres 081023
Batanero, Stephane, Marseille 124396
Batavia Art, Singapore 109776
Batavia Depot Museum, Batavia . . . 042037
Batavia-Werf, Lelystad 029859
Batchworth Lock Canal Centre, Rickmansworth 040834
Bate Collection of Historical Instruments, Oxford 040654
Le Bateau Lavoir, Grenoble 099301
Le Bateau-Lavoir, Paris . . 100030, 133534
Le Bâteau Livre, Montpellier 138217
Batel, Bruno, Fanjeaux 062838
Bateman, J. & R., Chalford 083907, 130523
Bateman, June, New York 117680
Bateman Historical Museum, Bateman 005075
Bateman's, Etchingham 039456
Bateman's Kipling's House, Burwash 038917
bateria - Zeitschrift für Kunst und Literatur, Fürth, Bayern 135750
Bates College Art Department, Lewiston 051601
Bates College Museum of Art, Lewiston 045248
Bates-Scofield Homestead, Darien . 043301
Bath Abbey Heritage Vaults, Bath . . 038616
Bath and Bradford on Avon Antique Dealers Association, Batheaston 054309
Bath Galleries, Bath 083415
Bath Industrial Heritage Centre, Bath 038626
Bath Old Books, Bath 141392
Bath Police Museum, Bath 038617
Bath Postal Museum, Bath 038618
Bath Royal Literary and Scientific Institution, Bath 038619
Bath Saturday Antiques Market, Bath 083416
Bath Stamp and Coin Shop, Bath . . 083417
Bath Street Gallery, Auckland 108303
Batheaston, Corsham 130606
Bathke, Axel, Hamburg 103094
Báthory István Múzeum, Nyírbátor . 021802
Bathurst, Georgina, Paddington, New South Wales 056415
Bathurst Agricultural Museum, Bathurst 034549
Bathurst and District Historical Museum, Bathurst 000773
Bathurst Books, Hobart 136942
Bathurst Regional Art Gallery, Bathurst 000774
Bathurst Street Antiques Centre, Hobart 055990
Bathurst Teddy Bear Shop, Bathurst 055452
Batik, Barcelona 136079
Batik Gemi Müzesi, Girne 008242
Batik International Art, Barcelona . . 134904
Batillat, La Ferriere-aux-Etangs . . . 063365
Batiran, Kamil, Berlin 069574
Batisse, Michel, Colombes 062423
Batista, Antônio S., Fortaleza 096515
Batley Art Gallery, Batley 038637
Batlle, Barcelona 140981
Batman Kültür Merkezi, Batman . . . 038021
Batoche National Historic Site, Batoche 005079
Batoche National Historic Site, Rosthern 006308
Baton Rouge Gallery, Baton Rouge . 042042
Batra Art Gallery, Mumbai 105759
Båtsamlingarna på Bassholmen, Uddevalla 036724
Batsford, B.T., London 135189
Båtsmanskasernen, Karlskrona . . . 036381
Batsto Village, Hammonton 044409
Batstone, Hilary, London 085117
Batta, Gio, Brescia 105992
Battaglia, Cristina, Torino 140124
Battaglia, Francesco, Troissereux . . 068633
Battaglia, Riccardo, Roma 127934
Battaglia Antonio, Milano 106168
Battaglia-Merkle, Maria, Ettlingen . 070667
Battaglino, Bruno, Genova 127433
Battais, Fougères (Ille-et-Vilaine) . . 062923
Battais, Francis, Fougères (Ille-et-Vilaine) 062924
Battais, Francis, Rennes (Ille-et-Vilaine) 067102
Battais, Gilles, Fougères (Ille-et-Vilaine) 062925
Battarbee, L., Dallas 142363
Batteau, Yves, Tourcoing 068558
Battei, Luigi, Parma 134653
Battenberg, München 134218
Batten's Jewellers, Bridport 083676, 130439
Batters Cage, Indianapolis 089274
Battifoglio, Giacomo, Monaco 107523
Battistella, Aldo, Luneray 064031
Battistoni, Giorgio, Verona 076994
Battle, David, Umberleigh 131628
Battle Abbey, Battle 038638
Battle and Farm Museum, Naseby . 040514
Battle Museum, Kibbutz Gesher . . . 023004
Battle Museum of Local History, Battle 038639
Battle of Lexington State Historic Site, Lexington 045271
Battle Shop, Oostende 058357
Battlefield, Minneapolis . . 090345, 142575
Battlefield House Museum, Stoney Creek 006512
Battlefield Military Antiques, Minneapolis 090346
Battleford National Historic Site, Battleford 005080
Battles Museums of Rural Life, Girard 044196
Battlesbridge Antique Centre, Battlesbridge 083454
Battlesbridge Motorcycle Museum, Battlesbridge 038641
Battleship Cove - Maritime Heritage Museums, Fall River 043803
Battleship North Carolina, Wilmington 049209
Battleship South Dakota Memorial, Sioux Falls 048188
Battleship Texas, La Porte 045076
Battolo, Luigi, Genève 082403
Battou, Remiremont 067089
Baturins'kyj Deržavnyj Istoričnyj Zapovidnyk Get'mans'ka Stolicja, Baturin . . . 038228
Bau-Bau, Amsterdam 107675
Bau de Antiguidades, Rio de Janeiro 058553
Bau-Xi Gallery, Toronto 097230
Bau-Xi Gallery, Vancouver 097423
Baublis, Warszawa 079739
Bauch, Hannover 139229
Bauch, H., Oberried 139619
Bauché, Dominique, Le Pont-Chrétien-Chabenet 063687
Bauchet, Christian, Clermont-Ferrand 062330
Baudelaire, Antwerpen 096060
Baudenkmal Hopfenhaus - Landwirtschaftliche Gerätesammlung - Alt-Seilerei - Ostdeutsche Heimatstube, Aidlingen 015461
Baudet, Eric, Le Havre 099436
Baudet, Laure, Toulouse 068482
Baudiere, Max, Combaillaux 062431
Baudin, Jean-Paul, Gimeux 063000
Baudini, Andrea Angelo & Daniele Oreste, Milano 075620
Baudouin, René, Chauconin-Neufmontiers 062242
Baudoux-Boitel, Francis, Compiègne 062437
Baudouy, Toulouse 124974
Baudry, Villeurbanne 068941
Bauer, Charleville-Mézières 120970
Bauer, Hamburg 103095
Bauer, Kevelaer 071811
Bauer, Portland 118975
Bauer, Sedan 121258
Bauer, Agnes, Warngau 126969
Bauer, Arthur, Berlin 138745
Bauer, B., Frickenhausen, Württemberg 125678
Bauer, Christophe, Paris 124584
Bauer, Doris, Mainz 072388
Bauer, E., Kleinostheim 071871
Bauer, Erich, Rosenheim 126736
Bauer, Erich Alois, Hart bei Graz . . . 057055
Bauer, Frank, Mannheim 104020
Bauer, Gregor, Leipzig 126181
Bauer, Gretel, München 139497
Bauer, Harald, Leipzig 103856
Bauer, Horst, München 104148
Bauer, I., Kühlungsborn 072101
Bauer, Inge & Aloys, Landkern 103821
Bauer, Jens-H., Hannover 071384, 103262, 134035, 139230
Bauer, Klaus, Satow 121596
Bauer, Marie-Luise & Harald, Beltheim 069516
Bauer, Max, Sankt Gallen 111864
Bauer, Dr. Michael, Kronberg im Taunus 139370
Bauer, Michael, Wien 137289
Bauer, Peter, Gmund 071012
Bauer, R.M., Itzstedt 071649
Bauer, Robyn, Paddington, Queensland 095046
Bauer, Dr. Wilhelm, Wien 123488
Bauer, Wolfgang, Bad Aussee 056923
Bauer & Abraham, Béziers 120930
Bauer-Bornemann, Bamberg 125130
Bauer-Empl, Regina, Freising 125675
Bauer & Leible, Trödelmarkt, Renchen 073495
Bauerfeind, Hartmund, Berg, Kreis Ahrweiler 069527
Bauerle, Jimmy, København 060282
Bauermeister, Olivier, Neuchâtel . . . 082689
Bauern-Technik-Museum, Steyr-Gleink 002706
Bauern- und Handwerker-Museum, Malgersdorf 018801
Bauern- und Heimatmuseum Haigermoos, Sankt Pantaleon 002610
Bauern- und Waldmuseum, Haidmühle 017630
Bauerngerätemuseum des Stadtmuseums, Ingolstadt 018069
Bauernhaus 1809 vor der Industrialisierung, Simonsfeld 002681
Bauernhaus-Museum, Bielefeld . . . 016233
Bauernhaus-Museum, Lindberg . . . 018655
Bauernhaus-Museum, Muttenz . . . 037365
Bauernhaus-Museum, Ruhmannsfelden 019949
Bauernhaus-Museum, Wolfegg . . . 020952
Bauernhausmuseum, Bad Füssing . 015702
Bauernhausmuseum, Grafenau, Niederbayern 017499
Bauernhausmuseum Altburg, Calw . 016539
Bauernhausmuseum Amerang des Bezirks Oberbayern, Amerang 015532
Bauernhausmuseum des Landkreises Erding, Erding 017003
Bauernhausmuseum Hattingen, Hattingen 017794
Bauernhausmuseum Hof Haina, Biebertal 016228
Bauernhausmuseum Hohenstein, Württemberg, Hohenstein, Württemberg 017981
Bauernhausmuseum Knechtenhofen, Oberstaufen 019420
Bauernhausmuseum Schniderlihof, Oberried 019408
Bauernhofmuseum, Buchhofen . . . 016479
Bauernhofmuseum Hof, Kirchanschöring 018258
Bauernhofmuseum Jexhof, Schöngeising 020081
Bauernkriegsmuseum, Weinstadt . . 020764
Bauernkriegsmuseum Kornmarktkirche, Mühlhäuser Museen, Mühlhausen, Thüringen 019011
Bauernkriegsstube Baltringen, Mietingen 018939
Bauernmöbelmuseum Propstkeusche, Malta 002274
Bauernmühle-Dorfmuseum, Finkenstein 001855
Bauernmuseum, Schmannewitz . . . 020056
Bauernmuseum, Zahna 021037
Bauernmuseum Althuus, Gurbü . . . 037171
Bauernmuseum Blankensee, Trebbin 020461
Bauernmuseum Großklein, Großklein 001971
Bauernmuseum Guntersdorf, Guntersdorf 001988
Bauernmuseum im Grottenhof, Kaindorf an der Sulm 002109
Bauernmuseum im Holz, Bützberg . 036988
Bauernmuseum Inzigkofen, Inzigkofen 018078

Bauernmuseum Landkreis Bamberg, Frensdorf 017250
Bauernmuseum Lanzenkirchen, Lanzenkirchen 002204
Bauernmuseum Liebenau, Liebenau bei Dippoldiswalde 018636
Bauernmuseum mit Kräutergarten, Nitschareuth 019318
Bauernmuseum Mühlhausen, Villingen-Schwenningen 020591
Bauernmuseum Ostdorf, Balingen . 015860
Bauernmuseum Osternach, Ort im Innkreis 002400
Bauernmuseum Pfarrscheuer, Bösingen 016304
Bauernmuseum Rothenburg, Rothenburg, Oberlausitz 019920
Bauernmuseum Sollinger-Bauer, Maria Schmolln 002285
Bauernmuseum Spannberg, Spannberg 002683
Bauernmuseum Wittstock, Wittstock bei Prenzlau 020934
Bauernmuseum Zabeltitz, Zabeltitz . 021036
Bauernstube, Ellwangen 016943
Baugeschichte der ehemaligen Fürstbischöflichen Residenz Schloß Neuhaus, Ausstellung im Remter des Schlosses, Paderborn 019547
Baugeschichtliches Archiv der Stadt Zürich, Haus am Rech, Zürich 037761
Baugh, J.Earl, Louisville 132287
Bauhaus-Archiv, Museum für Gestaltung, Berlin 015988
Bauhaus Art Gallery, Brisbane 094285
Bauhaus Books, Seattle 142976
Bauhaus Design, Oklahoma City . . . 091476
Bauhaus-Museum, Stiftung Weimarer Klassik und Kunstsammlungen, Weimar, Thüringen 020736
Bauhofer, Monika, Prien 104639
Baukunst Galerie, Köln 103591
Baukus & Kühr, Jagsthausen 103446
El Baul, Logroño 081179
El Baúl de La Abuela, Maracaibo . . 093550
El Baúl de Las Pulgas, Bogotá 059822
El Baúl de los Recuerdos, A Coruña 141013
El Baul de los Recuerdos, Sevilla . . 081576
Il Baule Blu, Venezia 076923
Baum, Leipzig 072200, 126182
Baum, Frank, Meiningen 072500
Baum, Jan, Los Angeles 116722
Baum, P., Kirchzarten 071863
Baum, Sabine, Ludwigsburg, Württemberg 126228
Bauman, New York 142635
Bauman, D., Philadelphia 142736
Baumann, C., Carouge 082289
Baumann, Frank, Naumburg, Saale 072942
Baumann Nachf., H., Varel 074181
Baumann, Hansjörg, Baar 082103, 129903
Baumann, Harald, Bad Ischl 056929
Baumann, Helmut, Trendelburg . . . 074086
Baumann, Irmtrud, Monschau 104114
Baumann, Joachim, Schwäbisch Hall 073743
Baumann, Lasse, København 060283
Baumann, Dr. Wolfgang, Regensburg 073450
Baumann & Städeli, Zürich 082945
Baume, Poitiers 066888
Baume, Hervé, Avignon 061127
Baumeister, Nürnberg 073097
Baumeister, Nürnberg 073098
Baumeister, L., Abenberg 069106
Baumgärtel, Mike, Schönheide, Erzgebirge 139714
Baumgaertner, François & Nicole, Innenheim 063209
Baumgart, F., Paderborn 104566
Baumgart, Torsten, Ratingen 073426
Baumgarte, Samuelis, Bielefeld . . . 102111
Baumgarten, Albert, Freiburg im Breisgau 102855
Baumgartl, Andreas, München 104149
Baumgartner, Chicago 131885
Baumgartner, Gerhard, Gordola . . .082480, 130039
Baumgartner, Herbert, Klagenfurt . . 057104
Baumgartner, Katharina, Salzburg . 057236
Baumhauer, Josef, Aachen 069075
Baumkotter, London 085118, 113494
Baur, Erich, Nidau 082700
Baur, M. Johannes, München 126349
Baury, Raymond, Saint-Hilaire-Saint-Florent 067522
Bausback, Franz, Mannheim 072414
Bausch, Wiesbaden 105244
Bauscher, Traudl, Potsdam 104621
Bause, S., Usedom 074168
Bauskas Novadpētniecības un Mākslas Muzejs, Bauska 027661
Bauskas Pils Muzejs, Bauska 027662
Bausmann, Eric, Mainz 103997
Bautahaugen Samlinger, Hedalen . . 030885
Baute, Daniel, Jurancon 063266
Baute, Daniel, Pau 066698
Bautista, Alba, Bogotá 098108
Bautzner Münzhandlung, Bautzen . 069485
Bauve, Coulommiers 120983
Bavaria Airways-Museum, Kirchdorf an der Amper 018261
Bavastro, Eugenio, Montevideo . . . 122772
Baveux Le Pennec, Claire & Didier, Perriers-sur-Andelle 066762
Baviera, Silvio R., Zürich 112045
BAWAG Foundation, Wien 002859
Bawden, Keith, Cheltenham 130532
BAX Antykwariat, Lubin 079676
Baxeras, Magdalena, Barcelona . . . 110118
Baxter, Archerfield 055351
Baxter, Paris 100031
Baxter, B., Indianapolis 122917
Baxter & Sons, H.C., London 085119
Baxter, Chang & Patri, San Francisco 119607
Baxter House Museum, Gorham . . . 044249
Baxter & Mansfield, Auckland 140585
Baxter Springs Heritage Center and Museum, Baxter Springs 042059
Baxter Warner, Philadelphia 091609
Bay, Elliott, Seattle 092965
Bay Area Discovery Museum, Sausalito 048019
Bay Area Museum, Seabrook 048068
Bay Auctions, Tauranga 121833
Bay Books, Cleveland 142330
Bay Bookshop, Colwyn Bay 141534
Bay Bookshop, Colwyn Bay 141535
Bay City Books, Los Angeles 142489
Bay Furniture Restoration, Oakland 132565
Bay of Islands Gallery, Paihia 108533
Bay of Spirits Gallery, Toronto 097231
Bay Sala, Bilbao 110270
Bay Tree Antiques, Wilton, Salisbury 087157
Bay Tree Gallery, Bradford-on-Avon 112689
Bay Tree Gallery, Holywood 113263
Bay & Vidal, Montevideo 087309
Bay View Historical Museum, Bay View 042062
Bayanihan Folk Arts Museum, Manila 031714
Bayard Antique Village, Jacksonville 089384
Bayarré, Fabrice, Paris . . . 100032, 138301
Bayat, Paris 065545, 124585
Bayat Inuit Gallery, Winnipeg 097574
Baycrafters, Bay Village 042063
Bayer, Bietigheim-Bissingen 102133
Bayer, Alois, Schwandorf 073752
Bayer, Gerhard, Baden-Baden 069409
Bayer, Konrad, Andrechs am Ammersee 101583
Bayer & Bayer, Praha 098420
Bayerische Akademie der Schönen Künste, München 050186
Bayerische Münztage, Internationale Münzen-, Banknoten- und Wertpapierbörse, München 093714
Bayerische Numismatische Gesellschaft, München 053036
Bayerische Staatsbibliothek, München 019037
Bayerische Staatsgemäldesammlungen, Direktion, München 019038
Bayerisches Armeemuseum, Ingolstadt 018070
Bayerisches Brauereimuseum Kulmbach, Kulmbach 018439
Bayerisches Eisenbahnmuseum, Nördlingen 019320
Bayerisches Moor- und Torfmuseum, Torfbahnhof Rottau, Grassau, Chiemgau 017512
Bayerisches Nationalmuseum, München 019039
Bayerisches Schulmuseum, Ichenhausen 018041
Bayerisches Strafvollzugsmuseum, Kaisheim 018137
Bayet, Max, Villeurbanne 068942
Bayet Aisha Fahmi (Mogamaa el-Fonoon), Cairo 009292
Bayin Guoleng Zhou Museum, Kuerle 007166
Bayle Museum, Bridlington 038835
Bayles, Buntingford 122440
Baylis, Chris, Woodstock 087237
Bayliss, D.W. & A.B., Ludlow 085861
Bayly Art Museum of the University of Virginia, Charlottesville 042770
Baynton-Williams, Arundel 083311
Bayntun, George, Bath . . . 130348, 141393
Bayo, Vitoria-Gasteiz 081714
Bayo Studios, New York 117681
Bayou Bend Collection, Houston . . . 044635
Bayreuther Münzhandlung, Bayreuth 069488
de Bayser, Bruno, Paris 100033
Baysgarth House Museum, Barton-upon-Humber 038607
Bayside Antiques, Oakland 091407
Bayside Antiques Centre, Hampton . 055946
Bayside Books, Wynnum 137145
Bayside Galleries, Fukuoka 106841
Bayside Galleries, Yokohama 107139
Bayside Treasures, Toledo 120074
Bayview Galleries, Mona Vale 094869, 123267
Bayview Gallery, San Francisco . . . 092738
Baz, Antoine Rovi, Paris 065546
Bazaar, Cairo 060431
Bazaar, Prato 076249
Bazaar, Whitby 087127
Bazaar 17, Viganello 082887
Bazalar, Lima 079542, 129000
Bazan, Dordrecht 107973
Bazar Antik, Praha 060114
Bazar Bizar, Groningen 078401
Bazar de Antiguedades Cuauhtemoc, Monterrey 077585
Bazar de Belen, Guadalajara 077561
Bazar de las Oportunidades, Cali . . 059878
Il Bazar di Milú, Cagliari 075201
Bazar el Escarabajo, México 077569
Bazar King David, Rio de Janeiro . . 058554
Bazar Kny, Praha 060115
Bazar na Dvoře, Brno 059974
Bazar Odessa, Monterrey 077586
Bazar San Javier, Monterrey 077587
Bazar - Starožitnosti, Pardubice . . . 060073
Bazar Traslapuerta, Valparaíso 059562
Bazaren, Mariehamn 060612
Bazarez, Hiroshima 106853
Bazarka Antik, Brno 059975
Bazille, Anne-Marie, Bagnoles-de-l'Orne 061167
Bazin, Nîmes 065170
Bazin, Paris 065547
Bazin, Jean-Marie, Jouy (Eure-et-Loir) 063262
Bazin, Pascal, Brécey 061754
Bazza, Anthony, New York 132446
Bazzani, Verona 140151
Bazzanti & Marinelli, Firenze 106032
Bazzi de Alvez, Mirta, Montevideo . 087310
Bazzicalupo, Claudia, Parma 127846
Bazzolo, Stefania, Torino 076772
B.B., Paris 065548
BB International Fine Arts, Pfäffikon (Schwyz) 111807, 135056, 141288
BB Selections, Bussum 078127
BBC Books, London 135190
BBC Experience, London 040086
BBC Homes and Antiques, Bristol . . 136185
BBD Galerie, Amersfoort 107634
BBK-Galerie, Oldenburg, Oldenburg 104537
B.B.M. Jewellery & Antiques, Kidderminster 084836, 130843
BBR Auctions, Barnsley, South Yorkshire 122398
BC Antiques, Singapore 080433
B.C. Fine Art Gallery, Sanctuary Cove 095178
B.C. Galleries, Armadale, Victoria . . 055364
B.C. Galleries, Woollahra 056855
BC Kunstverlag, Wuppertal 134473
B.C. Metalcrafts, London . 085120, 130940
BCI Fine Art, Johannesburg 080701
BCN Art Directe, Barcelona 110119
B.D.E., Paris 065549
B.D.V, Saint-Ouen 067731
Be-Bop, Chicago 115362
Be-Bops, San Antonio 092488
Be Precedento, Vilnius . . . 077455, 140229
Béacco, Toni, Nazelles-Négron 124492
Beach Antique, Toronto . . 059145, 137698
Beach Antiques, Clevedon 084031
Beach Art, Thirroul 095330
Beach Books, Jacksonville 142461
The Beach Gallery, Toronto 097232
Beach Gallery, Virginia Beach 120216
Beach Street Gallery, San Francisco 119608
Beaches Antique Gallery, Jacksonville 089385
Beaches Art and Frame Gallery, Jacksonville 116511
Beaches Arts Center, Jacksonville . 116512
Beachhead Gallery of Contemporary Art, Warrnambool 095374
Beachville District Museum, Beachville 005083
Beacon Hill Antiques, Frankfurt am Main 070728
Beacon Historical Society Museum, Beacon 042068
Beacon Street Gallery, Chicago . . . 115363
The Beacon Whitehaven, Whitehaven 041370
Beaconsfield Historic House, Prince Edward Island Museum and Heritage Foundation, Charlottetown 005244
Bead Art, Amsterdam 107676
The Bead Goes On, Toronto 059146
Bead Harbor, Boston 087796
Beag Kunstverlag, Emmenbrücke . . 135009
Beagle Books, Sway 142106
Beajaim, Pontevedra 081529
Beajaim, Pontevedra 081530
Beaker, Tampa 120027
Beakys, Tuggeranong 137115
Beale, G.S., Thorpe-le-Soken 131592
Bealey, Christchurch 108386
Beall, Miami 090147
Bealu, Jean-Jacques, Blanzay 061507
Béalu & Fils, J.M., Paris 065550
Beam, Nijmegen 108147
Beam Ends Galleria, Hartley Wintney 113195
Beaman, Atlanta 087455
Beaminster Museum, Beaminster . . 038643
Beamish, the North of England Open Air Museum, Beamish 038645
Bean, S.A., San Antonio 092489
Bean Row Gallery, Hathersage 113204
Beaners, Houston 089030
Beanie Babies Collector's Shop, Las Vegas 089550
Beanie Planet, El Paso 088787
Bear Butte State Park Visitors Center, Sturgis 048411

Bear Creek Glass, Birmingham 115101
Bear Island Bokks, Cardiff 141485
Bear Mountain Trailside Museums Wildlife Center, Bear Mountain 042071
Bear Museum, Petersfield 040704
Bear Paths, Cleveland 115688
The Bear Press, Bayreuth 133741
Bear Steps Antiques, Shrewsbury . . 086597
Bearclaw Gallery, Calgary 096791
Bearclaw Gallery, Edmonton 096867
Beard Outlet, Portland 118976
Beardall, Clive, Maldon . . 085898, 131249
Beare, John & Arthur, London 085121, 130941
Bearks, Paris 065551
Bearly, Portland 142791
Bearly Collectibles, Milwaukee 090275
Bearly Trading of London, London . 085122
Béarn, Pau 066699
Bearne, Exeter 122504
Bears, A., Yackandandah 056891
Bear's Collection, Indianapolis 089275
Bea's Silver Hummingbird, Albuquerque 114772
Beasle, Chicago 142278
Beasley, P.T., Farningham 084392
Beast Creations, Flinders 094548
Beat, Sacramento 119140
Beatles Museum, Halle, Saale 017653
Béatrice B le Passage des Créateurs, Bourg-en-Bresse 061705, 099022
Beatrix Potter Gallery, The National Trust, Hawkshead 039706
Beatriz Antiguedades, Getxo 081113
Beatties Historic Photograph Museum, Dodges Ferry 000985
Beatty, Darlinghurst 094452
Beatty, Seattle 142977
Beatty Museum, Newport Pagnell . . 040569
Beau, Didier, Sceau-Saint-Angel . . 068173
Beau Fort Plantation Home, Bermuda 042170
Beau-Gest, L'Hôtellerie 063812
Beau Matthews, Philadelphia 091610
Beau Nash Antiques, Tunbridge Wells 086932
Beau Village Museum, Saint Victor . 006397
Beauarts Studios, Chicago 115364
Beaubourg, Paris 100034
Beaubourg, Vence 101435
Beaubourg, Gana, Paris 100035
Beaubourg, R. & L., Paris 100036
Beaubreuil, Guy, Feytiat 062860
Beauchamp & Beauchamp, Québec 097127
Beauchamp Newman Museum, Elizabeth 043652
Beaucourt, Eric, Maulette 064430
Beaucousin, Catherine, Louviers . . 064017
Beaudesert Museum, Beaudesert . . 000781
Beaudet, Royan 067307
Beaudoin, Philippe, Romorantin-Lanthenay 067208
Beaudran, Pierre, Mirande 121074
Beaufield Mews Antiques, Stillorgan 074996
Beaufils, Serge, Thorigné-Fouillard 068410
Beaufort, Robert, Chauray 062257, 124195
Beaufort County Arts Council, Washington 054677
Beaufort Historic Site, Beaufort . . . 042074
Beaufort Museum, Beaufort 042076
Beaufort West Museum, Beaufort West 034550
Beaufour, Pierre-Louis, Dieppe 062624
Beauger, Jacques, Moulins (Allier) . 064812
Beaugrand, Prof. Dr. Andreas, Bielefeld 102112
Beaujean, Jean-Pierre, Chaumont-en-Vexin 062244
Beaujeu, Anne de, Bruxelles 057852
Beaulé, Montréal 058927
Beaulieu Abbey Exhibition of Monastic Life, Brockenhurst 038878
Beaulieu Collection, Montréal 005910
Beaulieu Fine Arts, Brockenhurst . . 112740
Beaumarie, Jean, Ville-d'Avray . . . 068879
Beaumaris Castle, Beaumaris 038646
Beaumaris Gaol and Courthouse, Beaumaris 038647
Beaumé, J.J., Paris 100037
Beaumel, Gérard, Cajarc 061903
Beaumont, Dordrecht 078297
Beaumont, Montréal 058928
Beaumont, Jean, Die 062621
Beaumont, Jean, Saumur 068148
Beaumont, Odile, Mussey-sur-Marne 064849
Beaumont, Robin de, London 141754
Beaumont Antique Furniture, Hamilton, New South Wales 055936
Beaumont Art League, Beaumont . . 042082
Beaumont Art League, Beaumont . . 054678
Beaumont Hall, Saint Albans 114342
Beaumontpublic & Königbloc, Luxembourg 107391
Beauport-Sleeper-McCann House, Gloucester 044221
Beaupuis, Hubert de, Saint-Victor-l'Abbaye 068033
Beauquis, Philippe, Annecy 060887
Beauregard-Keyes House, New Orleans 046247
Beaussant & Lefèvre, Paris 121115
Les Beautés, Québec 059061
Beautiful Memories, Ocho Rios . . .077033, 106831
Beautiful Plains Museum, Neepawa 005986
Beautiful Tibet, New York 090718
Beauty and the Beach, Mornington . 094883
Beauty Antique, Singapore 080434
Beauty Galleria, Los Angeles 116723
Beauvais, Philippe, Paris 065552
Beauvais, Séverine, Montmorency . 064718
Beauvais Heritage Center, Clark . . . 042949
Beauvoir, Moustiers-Sainte-Marie . 064819
Beauvoir, Nice 065049
Beauvoir, Jefferson Davis Home and Presidential Library, Biloxi 042210
Beaux Arts, Bath 112570
Beaux-Arts, Dallas 135356
Les Beaux Arts, Hilden 103373
Beaux Arts, London 113495
Beaux Arts Gallery, Miami 117036
Beaux Arts Magazine, Paris 135693
Les Beaux Jours, Rouen 067244
Beaux'Arts Ecole Superieure Le Mans, Le Mans 049951
Beaver, Atlanta 142197
Beaver, Deakin 094467
Beaver Bros., San Francisco 092739
Beaver Coin Room, London 085123
Beaver College Art Gallery, Glenside 044214
Beaver Corner, Gent 058173
Beaver Island Historical Museum, Beaver Island 042091
Beaver River Museum, Beaverton . . 005089
Beaverbrook Art Gallery, Fredericton 005477
Beaverhead County Museum, Dillon 043470
Beazor & Sons, John, Cambridge . . 083841
Bebb, Ludlow 114004, 131242
Bebensee, Hamburg 103096
Beber, Bad Münder 101671
Bébert, Rotterdam 134829
Bebes & Jouets, Edinburgh 084274, 130673
Bebob, Amsterdam 107677
Bebop, Göteborg 081796
Beca Fine Arts, Wellington 079319
Bécassine, Arnhem 078044
Beccaletto, Cristiano, Milano 127529
Beccia, Fernanda, Milano 075621
Becciolini, Paolo, Firenze . 075284, 127296
Beccles and District Museum, Beccles 038649
Beccles Gallery, Beccles . 112596, 130359
Beceren, Zürich 082946
Bech, København 060284, 098536
Bechauf, Bielefeld 102113
Bechelsdorfer Schulzenhaus, Schönberg, Mecklenburg 020072
Becher, Renate, Hof, Saale 071545
Bechman, København 098537
Bechter, Jutta, Landsberg am Lech 072134
Bechtermünz, München 134219
Bechtle, Esslingen 133922
Bechtloff, R., Aalen 101533
Bechtold, Jeroen, Amsterdam 107678
Bechtold, U., Pforzheim 139654
Béchu, Jean-Baptiste, Nantes 124478
Bechu, Johan, Blois 061519
Beciani, A., Charleroi 096273
Beck, Nürtingen 073130
Beck, Shepparton 137085
Beck, Tampa 120028
Beck jr., Arthello, Dallas 115842
Beck, Astrid & Manfred, Überherrn . 074131
Beck, B., Chicago 142279
Beck, B., Freiburg im Breisgau 070824
Beck, C.H., München 134220
Beck, Gerhard, Lörrach 072289
Beck, Heinz, Meilen 082652
Beck, James, Fakenham 122507
Beck, K., Sontheim an der Brenz . . 104928
Beck, Markus, Kirchheim unter Teck 071859
Beck, Monika, Homburg . . 103403, 134067
Beck, Roland M., Nürnberg 073099
Beck, Thomas L., Jacksonville 132174
Beck Cultural Exchange Center, Knoxville 045032
Beck & Eggeling, Düsseldorf 102473
Beck Head Books and Gallery, Kirkby Lonsdale 141697
Beck Isle Museum of Rural Life, Pickering 040713
Beck & Nalley, Sacramento 092138, 142836
Beckel-Odille-Boïcos, Paris 100038
Beckenham Antique Market, Beckenham 083468
Becker, Bad Kreuznach . . 069314, 101666
Becker, Bremen 070010
Becker, Cannes 061933
Becker, Lüchow, Wendland 072343
Becker, Vanves 068721
Gebr. Becker, Zeist 078862
Becker, Albert Z., Saint Louis 119186
Becker, Anne, Borken, Hessen 125367
Becker, Arleen G., New York 117682
Becker, C., Waake 074232
Becker, D., Houston 142425
Becker, Dieter, Immenstadt 125968
Becker, Dirk, Hamburg 071204
Becker, Emanuelle, Luxembourg . . 077476
Becker, Enno, Berlin 101796
Becker, Eugène, Paris 065553
Becker, Fred, Luxembourg 107392
Becker, H., Haarlem 140439
Becker, Hans Robert, Westergellersen 074362
Becker, Ingeborg, Hannover 139231
Becker, J., Amsterdam 077795
Becker, J.H., Zeist 078863
Becker, Jürgen, Hamburg 103097
Becker, Karl-Ernst, Duisburg 070474
Becker, Larry, Philadelphia 118740
Becker, Michael, Fröndenberg 070902
Becker, Michael, München 126350
Becker, Rita & Dagmar, Münster . . . 072897
Becker, Robert, Badem 069406
Becker, Susan, Walton-on-Thames . 087014
Becker, Thomas, Siek 073816
Becker, Ulrich, Würzburg 139870
Becker, Wolfgang, Pritzwalk 126662
Becker County Historical Museum, Detroit Lakes 043459
Becker-Kater, Vechta 105106
Becker-Kater, Angelika, Diepholz . . 102364
Beckers, Darmstadt 133852
Beckers, Eindhoven 078328
Beckers, Anita, Frankfurt am Main . 102749
Beckers, E. & L., Burscheid, Rheinland 070111
Beckers, Harald, Jüchen 125984
Beckert, Wolfgang, Aschheim 069209
Beckett, Toronto 097233
Beckford's Tower and Museum, Bath 038620
Beckham, New Orleans 142605
Beckholmen, Renée, Stockholm . . .111004, 134966
Beckie's Antiques, Dallas 088464
Beckmann, Edemissen . . . 070502, 125569
Beckmann, Toledo 120075
Beckmann, Erich, Hannover 071385
Beckmann, Marlies, Rheine 104748
Beckoning Hills Museum, Boissevain 005109
Beckschäfer, H., Arnsberg 069180
Beckstones, Greystoke 113164
Beckwith & Son, Hertford . 084671, 130790
Becky's Old Wares, Rivett 056534
Becq, Pierre, Metz 064523
Becq, Pierre, Senon 068212
Becquer-Rastrillo, Madrid 081246
Becuadro, Madrid 110453
Bed Bazaar, Framlingham 084431, 130717
Al-Bedaa, Dubai 083187
Bedale, David, Mobberley 085996
Bedale Museum, Bedale 038651
Le Bedane, Bruxelles 123578
Bede Art BGallery, Mount Marty College, Yankton 049329
Bedel, Pleurtuit 066853
Bedel de Buzareingues, Bertrand, Paris 124586
Bede's World, Jarrow 039831
Bedford, Bilbao 080966
Bedford, P.E.L., Bridport 083677
Bedford Central Library Gallery, Bedford 038654
Bedford City/County Museum, Bedford 042100
Bedford Gallery, Johannesburg 110048
Bedford Gallery at the Dean Lesher Regional Center for the Arts, Walnut Creek 048839
Bedford Historical Society Museum, Bedford 042098
Bedford Museum, Bedford 038655
Bedfordshire and Hertfordshire Regiment Association Museum Collection, Luton 040355
Bedi, Margaret, Billingham 083514
Bédier, Claude, Carqueiranne 062002
Bedingfield Inn Museum, Lumpkin . 045521
Bednarczyk, C., Wien 057377
Bedos, Raphaël, Paris 065554
Bedot, André, Tarascon (Bouches-du-Rhône) 068357
Bedouin Market, Cairo 098617
Bedrijfsmuseum NUON-ENW Amsterdam, Amsterdam 029171
Bedriye Kazancıgil, İstanbul 083121
Bedsteads, Bath 083418, 130349
Bedwell, Peter, Prahran 056488
Bee, New Orleans 117400
Bee, Kay, Boston 087797
Bee & Bear, Nagoya 140168
Beech, J.M. & A.J., Sheffield 086552
Beeches & Rale, Hawthorn, Victoria 055961
Beechey, Neville, Colac 055706
Beechmountain Art Gallery, Beechmont 094224
Beechwold, Columbus 142349
Beechwood Gallery, Newport, Gwent 114134
Beechworth Antiques, Beechworth . 055460
Beechworth Curiosity Shop, Beechworth 055461
Beechworth Gallery, Beechworth . . 094225
Beechworth Historic Court House, Beechworth 000782
Beechworth Past and Present, Beechworth 055462
Beecroft Antiques, Beecroft 055465
Beecroft Art Gallery, Southend-on-Sea 041063
Beecroft Treasure House, Beecroft . 055466
Beedham Antiques, Hungerford . . . 084751
Beehive, Salt Lake City 092419

Beehive Art Space, Albury 094130
Beehive House, Salt Lake City 047769
Beehive Old Wares, Maldon 056129
Beek, Johan, Barneveld 140359
Beekhuizen, Jan, Amsterdam 077796
Beekmans en Waning, Haarlem . . .078441, 128686, 140440
Beeld en Aambeeld Galerie, Enschede 108017
Beeld in Beeld, Nijmegen 108148
Beeldentuin Belling Garde, Bellingwolde 029301
De Beeldenwinkel, Amsterdam 107679
Beeldlijn, Amersfoort 107635
Beenleigh and District Museum, Beenleigh 000787
Beer, Franz X., Auerbach, Niederbayern 125069
Beer, Franz X., München . 072654, 126351
Beer, Hans-Peter, Québec 059062, 123804
Beer, Mike, Düsseldorf 125521
Beer, Mike, Köln 071913, 126062
Beer & Co., Monika, Wien 057378
Beer Collectables, Beer 083475
De Beer Studios, London 130942
Beerents, Anouk, Amsterdam 077797, 128529
Beerhost, Ursula, Karlsruhe 125995
Be'eri Archaeological Collection, Be'eri 022896
Beermann, York-Werner, Garmisch-Partenkirchen 070934
Beers, Sacramento 142837
Bees Antiques, Woodstock 087238
Beese, Martina, Großräschen 125768
Beese-Koch, Siglinde, Limburg an der Lahn 103912
Beesley & Pace, Salt Lake City 132781
Beesley's, Paignton 122647
Beeston Castle, Tarporley 041188
Beethoven Emlékmúzeum, Martonvásár 021780
Beethoven Eroicahaus, Wien Museum, Wien 002860
Beethoven-Gedenkstätte in Floridsdorf, Wien 002861
Beethoven-Haus, Bonn 016318
Beethoven Heiligenstädter Testament, Wien Museum, Wien 002862
Beethoven Pasqualatihaus, Wien Museum, Wien 002863
Beethovenhalle, Bonn 016319
Beethovenhaus, Krems 002170
Beethovenhaus Haus der Neunten, Baden bei Wien 001743
Beetles, Chris, London . . . 085124, 113496
The Beetroot Tree, Draycott 112957
Beetz, Alwin, Lübeck 126239
Before My Time, Toronto 059147
Befreiungshalle Kelheim, Kelheim . 018221
Le Befroi et le Musée des Frères Caudron, Rue 014151
Bega Valley Regional Art Gallery, Bega 000789
Began, São Paulo 058689
Begas, G., Heerlen 108069
Bege, Aigues-Mortes 098772
Begg, Jan, Stanmore 123309
Begijnhofkerk, Provinciaal Centrum voor Cultureel Erfgoed, Sint-Truiden . . 003766
Begijnhofmuseum, Dendermonde . . 003392
Begijnhofmuseum, Herentals 003509
Begijnhofmuseum, Kortrijk 003556
Bégin, Québec 097128
Bégin, Québec 097129
Begleiter, Baltimore 131815
Bégné, Jean-Luc, Bordeaux 061589
Begoña Alcorta Egaña, Donostia-San Sebastián 081075
Begoña Alcorta Egaña, Donostia-San Sebastián 081076
Begsteiger, Günther, Linz 057152
Begüm, İstanbul 083122
Begüm, İstanbul 083123
Beguiling, Toronto 137699
Béguinage d'Anderlecht, Bruxelles . 003289
Bégulin, Vérena, Saint-Imier 082765
Begunk, J., Stendal 073914
Běhal, Ilja, Olomouc 123963
Běhal, Jiří, Olomouc 123964
Behar, Renée, São Paulo 058690
Behavka, Karl, Wien 057379
Behind the Boxes - Art Deco, London 085125
Behm & Brock, Toronto 059148
Behmann, Fritz & Gabriele, Hannover 071386
Behncke-Brahmer, D., Hamburg . . . 103098
Behnhaus/ Drägerhaus, Museum für Kunst und Kulturgeschichte der Hansestadt Lübeck, Lübeck 018717
Behnke, Frank, Ahrensburg 138673
Behold the Antique, New York 090719
Het Behouden Blik, Uithuizermeeden 030219
Behr, A.A., Kaiserslautern 103464
Behr, H.W., Augsburg 125071
Behr, Winfried, Zellingen 074561
Behr Thyssen, New York 117683
Behrend, U., Konz 072053
Behrendt, Petra, Amrum 101579
Behrendt, Petra, Wittdün 105309
Behrendt, R., Bad Mergentheim . . . 069326
Behrendt, Thomas, Erfurt 070583
Behrendt & Markus, Berlin 125168
Behrens, Hannover 125863
Behrens, Leck 072175
Behrens, Ludwigsburg, Württemberg 103943
Behrens, B. & T., Leck 072176
Behrens, Heinz Alb., Timmenrode . . 126903
Behrens, Thomas, Rastede 073421
Behringer, Werner, Fürth, Bayern . . 121414
Behringer-Crawford Museum, Covington 043198
Behrmann, Johann, Bremen 102231
Behrmann, Kurt von, Phoenix 118865
Behrmann, Patrick, Bremen 102232
Behruz, Prahran 056489, 123288
Behzad Museum, Sa'd-Abad Cultural-Historic Complex, Teheran 022608
Bei, Ningbo 097878
Beiarn Bygdetun, Moldfjord 031032
Beier, Belgershain 069512
Beier, Hartmut, Hameln 071359
Beier, Hartmut, Leipzig . . . 072201, 139390
Beier, Klaus, Augsburg 069215
Beier, R., Erfde 070582
Beier, Ulrich & Monika, Berlin 121321
Beier, Viola, Köln 126063
Beifang Literature and Art Press, Harbin 133355
Beijers, J.L., Utrecht 121806, 140543
Beijing Animation Art Museum, Beijing 006964
Beijing Antique City, Los Angeles . . 089699
Beijing Art Gallery, Beijing 097642
Beijing Art Gallery, Beijing 097643
Beijing Art Museum, Beijing 006965
Beijing Arts and Crafts Publishing House, Beijing 133332
Beijing Changcheng Hua Ren Huai, Beijing 006966
Beijing Classic Art, Beijing 059572
Beijing Cloisonne, San Francisco . . 092740
Beijing Cultural Relic Protection Foundation, Beijing 006967
Beijing Dabaotai Western Han Tomb Museum, Beijing 006968
Beijing Drawing House, Beijing 097644
Beijing Fine Arts and Photography Publishing House, Beijing 133333
Beijing Folklorish Museum, Beijing . 006969
Beijing Gu Guanxiang Station, Beijing 006970
Beijing Imperial Art Academy, Beijing 049841
Beijing Museum, Beijing 006971
Beijing Natural History Museum, Beijing 006972
Beijing Opera Museum, Beijing . . . 006973
Beijing Telephone History Museum, Donghuang 007065
Beijing Wen Shi Art Galley, Beijing . 097645
Beik Thano, Yangon 077699
Beilun Art Cooperative, Ningbo 097879
Beim Antiquaire, Machtum 077482
Beiner-Büth, Silke, Hamburg 125801
Beirut Antiques Fair, Beirut 093810
Beisac, Wiesbaden 074395
Beisac, Hermien de, Wiesbaden . . . 074396
Beisler, Weilheim, Oberbayern 139829
Beisler, W., Aschaffenburg 069189
Beissel, R., Bad Honnef 069300
Beissert, H.-W. & V., Wildeshausen . 105295
Al-Beit, Dunia, Riyadh 080374
Beit al-Ajaib Museum with House of Wonders Museum, Zanzibar 037861
Beit-Alfa Ancient Synagogue, Kibbutz Chefzi-bah 022997
Beit Hagdudim, Avihail 022893
Beit-Hagefen Art Gallery, Haifa 022915
Beit Hameiri, Zefat 023103
Beit Hankin, Kfar Yehoshua 022994
Beit Ha'Omanim, Jerusalem 022940
Beit Hatefutsoth, Tel Aviv 023065
Beit Lohamei Haghetaot, Yad Layeled, Lohamei-Hageta'ot 023026
Beit Miriam-Museum, Kibbutz Palmachim 023016
Beit-Shean Museum, Beit Shean . . 022898
Beit Shturman Museum, Kibbutz Ein Harod 023001
Beiteddine Museum, Shouf 027821
Beiträge zur Kunst des Christlichen Ostens, Recklinghausen 135751
Beitzel, David, New York 117684
Bejannin, Saint-Ouen 067732
Bejannin, Saint-Ouen 067733
Bejšovec, Jan, Praha 123973
Bekaert, Bruxelles 123579
Beker, Buenos Aires 136703
Békési Galéria, Békés 105484
Bekking & Blitz, Amersfoort 134765
Bekko Museum, Nagasaki 026858
Bekler, Klaus, Duisburg 070475
Bekman, Amsterdam 077798
De Bekoring, Gent 058174
Bel Age, Las Vegas 089551
Bel Air Gallery, Bournemouth 112679
Bel Air Gallery, London 113497
Bel Air Gallery, London 113498
Bel Air Gallery, Sheffield 114412
Bel-Aire Coin, Saint Paul 092351
Bel Art, Novi Sad 109737
Bel Art, Québec 097130
Bel Art Gallery, Vancouver 097424
Bel Art Gallery, Vancouver 097425
Bel-Arte, Lengnau (Bern) 111638
Bel-Canto Antiek, Hilversum 078533
Le Bel Ecrin, Nice 065050
Bel Etage, Wien 057380
Bel Etage, Zürich 082947
Bel Mondo, Karlsruhe 103486
Belair, Villeurbanne 068943
Belair Mansion, Bowie 042360
Belair Stable Museum, Bowie 042361
Belaja Galereja, Ekaterinburg 109467
Belaja Luna, Odesa 112429
Béland, D.M., Montréal 096977
Belanger, Michael, Los Angeles . . . 089700
Belarussian State Academy of Arts, Minsk 049673
Belarussian University of Culture, Minsk 049674
Belasting en Douane Museum, Rotterdam 030076
Belaych, Christian, Paris 065555
Belaž, Sankt-Peterburg 109616
Belbezier, Lille 063834
Belcarra Eviction Cottage, Castlebar 022704
Belcher, Robert, Droitwich 084222
Belcher Studios, San Francisco . . . 119609
Belcourt Castle, Newport 046457
Belda, Praha 098421
Belen de los Santos, Dominga, Madrid 129578
Belenky Bros., New York 117685
Belerion Gallery, Penzance 114230
Beleva, Kristina, Sofia 123732
Belfast Book, Belfast 141404
Belfast International Antique and Fine Art Fair, Belfast 093913
Belfast Museum, Kapuatohe Historic Reserve, Christchurch 030459
Belfast Traders, Christchurch 079014
Belforte, Livorno 134596, 140036
Belga Traders, Sint-Niklaas 058370
Belgazou, Rouen 067245
Belger, Frank, Annaberg-Buchholz . 069171
Belgorodskij Gosudarstvennyj Chudožestvennyj Muzej, Belgorod Art Museum, Belgorod 033018
Belgorodskij Gosudarstvennyj Institut Iskusstv i Kultury, Belgorod 050627
Belgorodskij Gosudarstvennyj Istoriko-Kraevedčeskij Muzej, Belgorod . . 033019
Belgrave Antique Centre, Darwen . . 084138
Belgrave Carpet Gallery, London . . . 085126
Belgrave Gallery, London 113499
Belgrave Gallery, Saint Ives, Cornwall 114359
Belgrave Hall and Gardens, Leicester 039968
Belgravia, San Giljan 121761
Belgravia Books and Treasures, Edmonton 137632
Belgravia Gallery, London 113500
Belhaven Memorial Museum, Belhaven 042104
Les Béliers, Cellule 062047
Believers, Phoenix 091721
Belija Kvadrat, Sofia 096724
Belin, D ., Detroit 116082
Belin, Étienne, Périgueux 066722
Belinki & DuPrey, Portland 118977
Belinskij Rajonnyj Kraevedčeskij Muzej, Penzenskij gosudarstvennyj obedinennyj kraevedčeskij muzej, Belinskij . . . 033021
Belisle, Maurice E., Denver 088659, 132030
Belize Audubon Society, Belize City 003879
Belize Maritime Terminal and Museum, Belize City 003880
Belk, Andrea & Gerd, Petersberg, Kreis Fulda 126620
Belkhandi Museum, Belkhandi 022023
Belkhayat, Casablanca 077641
Belkin, Ronald A., Long Beach 089626
The Belknap Mill Museum, Laconia 045084
Belk's Refinishing, Charlotte 131868
Bell, Berrima 094245
Bell, Chicago 115365
Bell, Latrobe 056081
Bell, Nashville 117339
Bell, Winchester 131694
Bell, Woodbridge 142168
Bell, Anne, Kingston Southeast 056059
Bell, Darrell, Saskatoon 097190
Bell, J. & H., Castletown 083892
Bell, Mary, Chicago 115366
Bell, Paul-J., Falkensee 125628
Bell, Peter, Edinburgh 141570
Bell & Co., Robert, Horncastle 122546
Bell, Zillah, Thirsk 114569
Bell Antiques, Fresno 088897
Bell Antiques, Grimsby 084536
Bell Antiques, Romsey 086397
Bell Antiques, Twyford, Berkshire . . 086970
Bell Canada Telephone Historical Collection, Montréal 005911
Bell County Museum, Belton 042135
Bell Court Auction Rooms, Bidford-on-Avon 122412
The Bell Gallery, Belfast 083479
The Bell Gallery, Belfast 112606
The Bell Gallery, Belfast 130366
Bell Gallery, Storrington 114498
Bell Homestead, Brantford 005144

Bell House Antiques, Cambridge, Gloucestershire 083852
Bell Passage Antiques, Wickwar . . .087147, 131686
Bell Pettigrew Museum, Saint Andrews 040892
Bell Rock Mill Museum, Verona . . . 006730
Bell & Wyatt, Invercargill 079124
Bella, Virginia Beach 120217
Bella Antique, New York 090720
Bella Arte Internacional, Medellín . . 098254
Di Bella Concetta, Catania 106019
Bella Coola Museum, Bella Coola . . 005091
La Bella Epoca, Panamá City 079524, 128997
Bella G, Los Angeles 089701
Bella Luna Gallery, Tucson 120109
Bella Valeria, Milano 075622, 106169
Bella Vista Gallery, Chicago 115367
Bella Vita, Düsseldorf 102474
Bella Vita, Oakland 091408
Bellachioma, Roma 076327, 106496
Bellacorium, Houston 116281
Belladonna - Pro Na, Senden, Westfalen 134397
Bellaghy Bawn, Magherafelt 040383
Bellagio Gallery of Fine Art, Las Vegas 116612
Bellamy, Dunedin 108426
Bellamy, Fremantle 094568
Bellamy, Wellington 140670
Bellamy Mansion Museum of History and Design Arts, Wilmington 049210
Bellange, Stockholm 111005
Bellanger, Nantes 138236
Bellanger, Patrice, Paris . . 065556, 100039
Bellapais Manastiri, Girne 008243
Bellarine Historical Museum, Drysdale 000991
Bell'Art Gallery, Bellville 110012
Bellarte, Bielefeld 102114
Bell'Arte, Maastricht 108117
Bellas Artes, Gijón 110356
Bellas Gallery, Fortitude Valley 094557
Bella's Market, Saint Louis 092204
Bellavista Gallery, South Auckland . 108559
Bellcourt Books, Hamilton, Victoria . 136930
Belle, H.F., Dieren 128645
Belle, Kay, Chicago 088031
Belle Arte, Kraków 079623
Belle Arte, West Hollywood 120375
Belle & Belle, Paris 100040
Belle Cheminée, Dublin 074893
La Belle Chimaera, Rio de Janeiro . 058555
Belle Chose, Calvi 061912
Belle Cose, Napoli 075947
Belle Epoque, Alès 060770, 124065
Belle Epoque, Belo Horizonte 058411
A la Belle Epoque, Biarritz 061451
Belle Epoque, Bougival 061671
Belle Epoque, Bourges 061719
Belle Epoque, Brest 061765
La Belle Epoque, Jarmenil 063231
A la Belle Epoque, Le Havre 063625
Belle Epoque, Morlaix 064792
La Belle Epoque, München 072655
La Belle Epoque, München 072656
Belle Epoque, Münster 072898
La Belle Epoque, Néris-les-Bains . . 064977
La Belle Epoque, Ronchin 067212
La Belle Epoque, Santiago de Chile 059508
La Belle Epoque, Strasbourg 068302
Belle Epoque, Toronto 059149
Belle Epoque, Traunstein 074076
Belle Epoque, Vatan 068730
La Belle Epoque Gallery, New York . 090721
Belle Framing and Gallery, Woollahra 095419
Belle Grove Plantation, Middletown 045845
Belle Ile-en-Mer, Béziers 061429
La Belle Maison, New York 090722
Belle Maison, Porto Alegre 058488
Belle Meade Gallery, Nashville 117340
Belle Meade Interiors, Nashville . . . 090424
Belle Meade Plantation, Nashville . . 046140
La Belle Nouvelle Orleans, New Orleans 090514
Belle Starr Antiques, Saint Louis . . 123084
Bellearti, Madrid 129579
Belleau, Christopher R., Providence 119071
Bellecour, San Francisco 092741
Bellemare, Roger, Montréal 096978
Bellemin, Patrick, Chambéry 062101
Bellenger, Gérard, Elbeuf-sur-Seine 062770
Beller, Dettingen unter Teck 070234
Bellerio, Locarno 082580, 130085
Belles Années, Saint-Erme-Outre-et-Ramecourt 067433
Belles Choses, Strasbourg 068303
Belles et Bonnes, Trans-en-Provence 068615
Belles Marchandises, Bruxelles . . . 057853
Belletti, Piero & Chiara, Torino 076773
Belleville Area Museum, Belleville . 042109
Bellevue Antique Mall, Nashville . . . 090425
Bellevue Art Museum, Bellevue . . . 042114
Bellevue Gallery, Edinburgh 112984
Bellevue House, Kingston 005693
Bellflower Genealogical and Historical Society Museum, Bellflower 042117
Bellfoundry Museum, Loughborough 040340
Belli, Armando, Bologna 139985
Belliard, F., Rouen 067246
Bellier, André, Nantes 124479
Bellier, Jean-Claude, Paris 100041
Bellier, Luc, Paris 100042
Bellin, Angela, Ueken 082865
Bellinger, Rommerskirchen 073567
Bellinger, Carl, Barnet 083393
Bellinger, Katharina, Unteralba 126933
Bellinger, Katrin, München 072657
Bellingrath Home, Theodore 048541
Bellini, Luigi, Firenze 106033
Bellini, Philip, New York 090723
Bellini, Philip, New York 132447
Bellini, Tino, Milano 075623
Bellino, Rodolphe, Nice 124502
Bellint-Lamarque, Hélène, Paris . . . 100043
Bellinzona, Oreste, Milano 106170
Bellissimo, Knutsford 113340
Bellman, C.M., Stockholm 111006
Bellman, John, Billingshurst 122413
Bello, Andrés, Santiago de Chile . . . 133331
Bello, Claudio, Roma 127935
Bello, Stefano, Bologna 127132
Il Bello Ritrovato, Roma 076328
Il Bello Ritrovato, Roma 076329
Belloc, Preignac 066980
Belloc Lowndes, Chicago 115368
Bellon, Orlando, Trieste 128370
Bellon, Renaud, Luzillé 064043
Bellos, Gelson Carlos, Porto Alegre . 058489
Bellotti, Magda, Madrid 110454
Bellou, Guy, Paris 065557
Bellou, Guy, Paris 124587
Bellport-Brookhaven Historical Society Museum, Bellport 042124
Bell's, Christchurch 121816
Bell's, Christchurch 121817
Bells Antiques, Christchurch 079015
Bellu, Emmanuel, La Châtre 063327
Bellucci, Marius, Roche-lez-Beaupré 067172
Bellucci, Paolo, Firenze 127297
Bellucci, Ugo, Roma 127936
Belluco, Maurizio, Padova 076072
Belly Art, Brighton, Victoria 123197
Belmer Antiquitätenhof, Belm 069514
Belmont and District Museum, Belmont 005093
Belmont Antiques, Chicago 088032
Belmont Antiques, Nashville 090426
Belmont Antiques, Norfolk 091369
Belmont Booksellers, Portland 142792
Belmont Collection, Throwley 041219
Belmont, Gari Melchers Estate and Memorial Gallery, Fredericksburg 044055
Belmont & Landon, Richmond 092061
Belmundo, Buchs, Sankt Gallen . . . 111312
Belmundo, Zürich 112046
Belmundo, Zug 112209
Belo Belo, Braga 109237
Beloit Historical Society Museum, Beloit 042131
Belokranjski Muzej, Metlika 034503
Bel'or, Paris 065558
Belorusskij Gosudarstvennyj Muzej Istorii Velikoj Otečestvennoj Vojny, Minsk 003130
Belos Tempos Moveis de Decoracoes, Rio de Janeiro 058556
Belot, Judin, Zürich 112047
Belotti, Francesco, Milano 075624
Beloveżskaja Pušča Muzej, Beloveżskaja Pušča 003127
Below Stairs, Hungerford 084752
Belozerskij Istoriko-chudožestvennyj Muzej, Belozersk 033023
Belozerskij Muzej Narodnogo Dekorativno-prikladnogo Iskusstva, Belozersk . 033024
Belriguardo, Ferrara 134575
Belser, Stuttgart 134408
Belser Kunst Quartal, Ostfildern . . . 135752
B'Eltaller, Getxo 081114
Beltane, Taden 068348
Belter, Rüdiger, München 104150
Belton House, Grantham 039619
Beltramelli, Angeline, Lyon 064083
Beltrami County Historical Museum, Bemidji 042138
Beltramini, Giuliano, Cagliari 127241
Beltz, Tina, Essen 070618
Belussi, Gianangelo, Milano 075625
Beluxurious, Los Angeles 116724
Belvárosi Aukciósház, Budapest . . .105493, 121637
Belvárosi Galéria, Szekszárd 105579
Belvárosi Régiségbolt, Budapest . . 074668
Belvedere, Chicago 131886
Belvèdere, 's-Hertogenbosch 078512
Belvedere, München 121521
Belvedere, Unna 074161
Belvedere Antiques, New York 090724
Belvedere Reproductions, Ipswich . 130826
Belvedere - Zeitschrift für bildende Kunst, Wien 135547
Belvidere Gallery, Aberdeen 112475
Belvoir Gallery, Grantham 113143
Belye Palaty, Moskva 109498
Bélyegmúzeum, Budapest 021641
Belz, Rainer, Kassel 071744
Belz, T., Brühl, Rheinland 070072
Be.Ma., Milano 075626
Bemark Galeria, Raszyn 109069
Bembridge Maritime Museum and Shipwreck Centre, Bembridge . . . 038671
Bembridge Windmill Museum, Mottistone 040501
Bement-Billings Farmstead, Newark Valley 046433
Bemis Center for Contemporary Arts, Omaha 046675
Bémon, Gerald, Nice 065051
Ben, Thanh, Ho Chi Minh City 120501
Ben-Ami, Ramat Aviv 121673
Ben-Gurion House, Tel Aviv 023066
Ben-Hur Museum, Crawfordsville . . 043208
Ben & Johnny's Attic, Los Angeles . 089702
Ben Shahn Galleries, Wayne 049029
Ben Uri Gallery, London Jewish Museum of Art, London 040087
Benador, Jacques, Genève 111426
Benalcazar, R. de, Paris 065559
Bénalcazar, Robert de, Issy-les-Moulineaux 063226
Benalla Costume and Pioneer Museum, Benalla 000792
Benalla Market, Benalla 055472
Benalla Regional Art Gallery, Benalla 000793
Benamou, Albert, Paris 100044
Benappi, Vittorio, Torino 076774
Benardout, Raymond, Los Angeles . 089703
Benards Gallery, Llandudno 085032, 113415, 130907
Benares Historic House, Mississauga 005888
Benato, Flavia Maria, Verona 128416
Benavente, Madrid 081247
Benavides, Madrid 081248
Benchaïb, Paris 100045
Benchamabophit National Museum, Bangkok 037871
Benchmark Antiques, Bridport 083678, 130440
Benchmark Books, Salt Lake City . . 142872
Bencich, Buenos Aires 136704
Bencik, Pforzheim 073315
Bencteux MM, Falaise 062836
Benczúr, Budapest 105494
Bend in the River, Gainsborough . . . 113084
Bendel, Gregor, Bad Neuenahr-Ahrweiler 101679
Bendel, J., Edesheim 070504
Bendel, Judit, Szada 127084
Benden & Klimczak, Köln 103592
Bender, El Paso 088788
Bender, A., Mannheim 139451
Bender, M., Völklingen 139820
Bender, Renate, Maisach 104012
Bender, Renate, München 104151
Bender, Udo, Bremen 070011
Bendig, Hanfried, Bremen 070012
Bendigo Antique Centre, Bendigo . . 055476
Bendigo Art Gallery, Bendigo 000794
Bendin, Müssen 072933
Bendrat, Julia, Jesteburg 125983
Bendschneider, K., Demmin 070216
Bendt, Marilen, Freigericht 070869
Béné, Paris 124588
Benecke, Lars, Buchholz in der Nordheide 138953
Benedektinerabtei und Abteimuseum, Seckau 002669
Bénedet, Alain, Saint-Cybardeaux . 067408
Bénedet, Alain, Saint-Jean-d'Angély 067528
Benedetti, Cristina, Roma 076330
Benedetti-Fahrenkrug, Lüneburg . . 072354
Benedetto, Saint Petersburg 123094
Bénédétto, Alain, Grimaud 063083
Benedick, Alain, Postroff 066963
Benedicta Arts Center, College of Saint Benedict, Saint Joseph 047643
Benedictine Monastery - Church of the Multiplication of Loaves and Fish Tabgha, Tiberias 023098
Benedictis, Henri de, Montpellier . . 064735
Benedikt, Mödling 057184
Benedikt-Nimser-Haus, Wilhelmsdorf, Württemberg 020893
Benediktinerstift und Stiftssammlungen, Altenburg 001678
The Benedykt Dybowsky Zoological Museum, Lviv 038337
Benefit Street Antiques, Providence 092033
Beneforti, Simone, Firenze 127298
Bénelli, Jacques, Paris 138302
Benelux Art and Framing Trade Show, Professionele Beurs voor de Inlijster en Kaderfabrikant, Haasrode 093595
Beneš, Václav, Plzeň 137810
Benesch, Leipzig 103857
Benesch, Sankt Andrä-Wörden 057284
Benesch, H., Ebringen, Breisgau . . 070498
Beneton, Guy, Paris 065560
Benetti, Antonella, Roma 076331
Beneun, Neuss 104420
Benezet, Dublin 074894
Bénézit, Henri, Paris 100046
Benézit, M., Paris 100047
Benga Oral Historic Centre, Dandenong 000968
Bengal Gallery of Fine Arts, Dhaka . 096035
Bengal Natural History Museum, Darjeeling 022068
A Bengala, Porto 080068

Bengelsträter, Jutta, Iserlohn 103438
Bengler, Michael, Dingolfing 125468
Bengoechea Carriedo, Elena, Valencia 110798
Benguet Museum, La Trinidad 031683
Benhabbou, Mohamed, Casablanca 077642
Benham, Seattle 119887
Benhamidi, Mohamed, Zürich 082948
Benheim, Naomi, Camberwell 094358
I Beni Culturali, Roma 135886
Benichou, Edmond, Marseille 064325
Bénichoux, Nancy 064861
Benicia Historical Museum, Benicia 042141
Benik-Kaiser, Birgit, Neckarsulm . . 072954
Beningbrough Hall, York 041473
Benitez, Bien, Los Angeles 116725
Benitez Gonzalez, Elba, Madrid . . . 110455
Benjaman's Art Gallery, Buffalo . . . 115250
Benjamin, Ottawa 137671
Benjamin, A.A., Houston 089031
Benjamin, Marcus, Columbus 115763
Benjamin and Dr. Edgar R. Cofeld Judaic Museum of Temple Beth Zion, Buffalo 042499
The Benjamin Banneker Museum, Baltimore 041974
Benjamin Franklin House, London . 040088
Benjamin Patterson Inn Museum Complex, Corning 043154
Benjamins, John, Amsterdam 134773, 140282
Benjamin's Books, Queanbeyan . . . 137064
Benkert, Ralf, Garmisch-Partenkirchen 139132
Benli, Paris 065561
Bennati, Michel, Beynac et Cazenac 061423
Bennati, Michel, Sarlat-la-Canéda . 068124
Bennazar, Paul, Saint-Ouen 067734
Bennazar, Pierre, Boulogne-Billancourt 061685
Bennemann, Markus, Köln 126064
Benner, Gloria, Baden-Baden 125124
Bennett, Bedale 083470, 130363
Bennett, Louisville 132288
Bennett, Nashville 117341
Bennett, Vancouver 059338
Bennett, Alan, Truro 086925
Bennett, John, London 113501
Bennett, Paul, London 085127
Bennett Mitten, New York . 090725, 132448
Bennett Place State Historic Site, Durham 043540
Bennett Street Gallery, Atlanta 114860
Bennie Museum, Bathgate 038635
Benninger, Horst, Köln 103593
Bennington Battle Monument, Old Bennington 046659
Bennington Battlefield Exhibition, Walloomsac 048838
The Bennington Museum, Bennington 042146
Benny Chia, Hong Kong 097762
Benny's, Attard 077505, 128471
Benoit, Buenos Aires 055176
Benoit, Adolf, Bindernheim 061487
Benoît, Anne, Paris 065562
Benoit, Jacky, Fontvieille 062913
Benoit, Jean-Loup, Beaumont (Vienne) 061266
Benoît, Pierre, Paris 065563
Benoit, Raymond, Saint-Jean-du-Corail 067547
Benoît-Latour, Dominique, Nevers . 065006
Benoldi, Luca, Parma 076197
Benot, Cádiz 110291
Benrido, Kyoto 134712
Benriya, Settsu 077223
Benrubi, Bonni, New York 117686
Ben's Rocking Horses, Sacramento 092139
Bensi Santini, Antonella, Milano . . . 075627
Bensmann, Hagen am Teutoburger Wald 103042
Benso, Alessandro, Firenze 075285
Benson, Paris 065564
Benson, Singapore 109777
Benson Veteran Cycle Museum, Benson 038675
Bensusan Museum of Photography, MuseuMAfricA, Johannesburg . . . 034642
Bensussan, Gérard, Montgiscard . . 064688
Bent, Michael J, Mulgrave 120617
Bent Cover, Phoenix 142760
Bent Tree Gallery, Dallas 115843
Bentancour, César, Montevideo . . . 122773
Benteli, Wabern 135074
Bentleg, South Grafton 095203
Bentler, Bernd, Bonn 125348
Bentley, Albuquerque 087376, 122793
Bentley, Calgary 058781, 123739
Bentley, Cape Town 080675
Bentley, Pretoria 110070
Bentley, William, Hungerford 084753, 130816
Bentley for Books, Huonville 136950
Bentley & Skinner, London 085128
Bentley's, Blackburn 112662
Benton County Historical Museum, Philomath 047002
Benton County Historical Museum, Prosser 047248
Benton Fine Art, Moreton-in-Marsh 086012, 114091
The Benton Homestead, Tolland . . . 048570
Bentonville Battleground State Historic Site, Four Oaks 044020
Bent's Old Fort, La Junta 045071
Bentz, Peter, Milwaukee 090276
Bentz, Werner, Ettlingen 133924
Benucci, Ponte San Giovanni 134659
Benucci, Roma 076332, 106497
Benucci, Roma 106498
Benxi City Museum, Benxi 007019
Benz, G., Freiburg im Breisgau 070825
Benz, Gertrud & Marcus, Meilen . . . 141277
Benz, Gertrud & Marcus, Zürich . . . 141323
Benz, N., Damp 070174
Benz, Philmon, Basel 111166
Benz, Willy, Zürich 141324
Benzacar, Ruth, Buenos Aires 094061
Benzakein, Cape Town 080676
Benzenberg, A., Seeshaupt 073789
Benzenberg, Annemarie, Tutzing . . 074123
Benzi & Vagnone, Torino 128260
Benzie Area Historical Museum, Benzonia 042151
Benziger, Düsseldorf 133887
Beobide Lantoki Museoa, Zumaia . . 036121
Beolibel, Beograd 080391
Beothuck Village, Grand Falls-Windsor 005531
Beothuk Interpretation Centre, Boyd's Cove 005126
Beowulf Galleries, Woollahra 056856, 095420
Beppu Daigaku Fuzoku Hakubutsukan, Beppu 026433
Bep's Antiques, New Orleans 090515
Ber, Claude le, Camaret-sur-Mer . . 099055
Beranoaguirre, Rosa, Donostia-San Sebastián 081077
Berardo, Silvia, Roma 076333
Beraud, Marc, Marclopt 064269
Berauer, Strasbourg 068304
Berbé, M., Bruxelles 057854
Berbé, M., Bruxelles 057855
Berbere, Los Angeles 089704
Berbey, Janine, Seurre 068236
Berceo Librería, Madrid 141029
La Berceuse, Fort-de-France 128488
Berceuses Dugal & Cie, Québec . . . 097131
Berche, Maguy, Capdenac-Gare . . . 099082
Berche & Pagis, Paris 138303
Berchem, Essen 125609
Berchi, J. Fernandez, Madrid 081249
Berchtold, M., Allschwil 082084
Bercker, Lucien, Aix-en-Provence . 060697
Berden, Roermond 078678
Berdery, Jean-Pierre, Aire-sur-l'Adour 060687
Berdini, Andrea, Bologna 075056
Berea College Burroughs Geological Museum, Berea 042152
Berea College Doris Ulmann Galleries, Berea 042153
Beredskapsmuseet, Viken 036790
Beregi Múzeum, Vásárosnamény . . 021916
Berenberg, Boston 115146
Berend Lehmann Museum, Halberstadt 017643
Berendes, Lüder, München 072658, 126352
Berengo, Amsterdam 107680
Bérenguer, Joseph, Auch . 061048, 124084
Bérenguer-Topacio, Makati 108822
Berenkamp, Innsbruck 133089
Berensen, Montréal 096979
Berensmann, Barbara, Stuttgart . . . 073962
Berès, Paris 065565, 100048
Berès, Pierre, Paris 133535, 138304
L'Béret Vert, Toulon (Var) 068442
Beretta, Egidio, Milano 127530
Beretti, Sandro, Milano 127531
Béreyziat, Pierre, Tournus 068565
Bereznikovskij Istoriko-kraevedčeskij Muzej, Berezniki 033028
Berg, Carlingford 094373
Berg Bros., Cincinnati 088213
Berg, Paris 133536
Berg, Paris 133537
Berg, A., Toronto 123826
Berg, Annette, Hannover 125864
Berg, B., Friedersdorf, Niederlausitz 070892
Berg, B., Waldshut-Tiengen 074259
Berg, Christine, Kempen 103529
Berg, Gary, Seattle 119888
Berg, J., Homberg, Efze 071573
Berg, M., Barntrup 138718
Berg, Otto, København 060285
Berg, Reinhard, Wiesbaden 105245
Berg, Reinhold, Regensburg 073451, 139682
Berg, Ulrike, Stühlingen 073945
Berg, Werner, Bleiburg 095477
Berg & Berg, Hamburg 071205
Berg-Isel-Museum der Tiroler Kaiserjäger mit Andreas Hofer-Galerie, Innsbruck 002077
Berg-Klönhammer, Ottobrunn 126606
Berg-Kragerø Museum, Kragerø . . . 030952
Berg- und Stadtmuseum, Obernkirchen 019401
Bergama Arkeoloji Müzesi, Bergama 038022
Bergamini, Andrea, Modena 127721
Bergartsmuséet, Sandviken 036559
Bergauer, Peter, Thun 082850
Bergbau- und Greifenstein-Museum, Ehrenfriedersdorf 016898
Bergbau- und Heimatmuseum, Gloggnitz 001899
Bergbau- und Heimatmuseum, Goldkronach 017477
Bergbau- und Heimatmuseum, Jochberg 002104
Bergbau- und Heimatmuseum Paulushof, Essen 017061
Bergbau- und Industriemuseum Ostbayern, Kümmersbruck 018430
Bergbau- und Mineralienmuseum, Oberwolfach 019430
Bergbau- und Stadtmuseum Weilburg, Weilburg 020723
Bergbaudokumentation Hansa Empelde, Ronnenberg 019880
Bergbauernmusem mit Galerie, Frankenfels 001862
Bergbauernmuseum, Alpbach 001673
Bergbauernmuseum, Telfs 002734
Bergbauernmuseum, Wildschönau . 003045
Bergbaumuseum, Altenberg, Erzgebirge 015498
Bergbaumuseum, Deuben 016696
Bergbaumuseum, Grünbach am Schneeberg 001981
Bergbaumuseum, Hall in Tirol 002007
Bergbaumuseum, Hausham 017808
Bergbaumuseum, Horgen 037193
Bergbaumuseum, Mühlbach am Hochkönig 002339
Bergbaumuseum, Oelsnitz, Erzgebirge 019441
Bergbaumuseum Achthal, Teisendorf 020415
Bergbaumuseum Graubünden mit Schaubergwerk, Davos Platz 037038
Bergbaumuseum Heilige Barbara, Mürzzuschlag 002342
Bergbaumuseum im Besucherbergwerk Tiefer Stollen, Aalen 015427
Bergbaumuseum Klagenfurt, Klagenfurt 002137
Bergbaumuseum Leogang, Leogang 002227
Bergbaumuseum mit Mineralienschau und Schaubergwerk, Hüttenberg 002065
Bergbaumuseum Peißenberg, Peißenberg 019583
Bergbaumuseum Pöllau, Neumarkt in Steiermark 002367
Bergbaumuseum Schachtanlage Knesebeck, Bad Grund 015710
Bergbaumuseum und Schaubergwerk Röhrigschacht, Wettelrode 020834
Bergbaumuseum und Schaustollen, Fohnsdorf 001857
Bergbauschaustollen, Pölfing-Brunn 002444
Bergdon, Toronto 059150
Bergemann, Berlin 069575, 125169
Bergemann, Margot, Düsseldorf . . . 070362
Bergen, de, Eindhoven 078329
Bergen County Historical Society Museum, River Edge 047447
Bergen Kunst- og Antikvitetsformidling, Minde 079401
Bergen Kunsthandel, Bergen 079371
Bergen Kunstmuseum, Bergen 030756
Bergen Kunstmuseum - Rasmus Meyers Samlinger, Bergen 030757
Bergen Kunstmuseum - Stenersens Samling, Bergen 030758
Bergen Marsjandise, Bergen 079372
Bergen Museum, Bergen 030759
Bergen Museum of Art and Science, Hackensack 044376
Bergen Museum of Art and Science, Ho-Ho-Kus 044559
Bergen Museum of Local History, Bergen 042155
Bergen & Putman, New Orleans . . . 117401
Bergen Skolemuseum, Bergen 030760
Bergens Kunstforening, Bergen . . . 053939
Bergens Sjøfartsmuseum, Bergen . 030761
Bergens Tekniske Museum, Bergen 030762
Berger, Mulhouse 064830
Berger, Nieder-Olm 104443
Berger, Schwerin 104867
Berger, Stuttgart 126842
Berger, Alain, Beaune 061268
Berger, André, Saint-Denis-en-Bugey 067420
Berger, Andreas S., Warstein 074281
Berger, Betty, Augsburg 069216
Berger, Ferdinand, Wien 057381
Berger, François, Paris 065566
Berger, Jimmy, København 060286
Berger, Max, Paris 065567
Berger, Michael, Benshausen 069521
Berger, Michael, Pittsburgh 118900
Berger, Michael, Pittsburgh 118901
Berger, Peter, Stuttgart 126843
Berger, Reinhold, Vellberg 126943
Berger, Rudolf, Bern 082197, 129947
Berger, Simon, Wabern 130208
Berger-Levrault, Nancy 133502
Berger & Marletta, Roma 076334
Bergères et Marquises, Paris 065568
Bergerhaus, Gumpoldskirchen 001987
Bergerie, Persac 066773
Bergerie, Ury 068661
Bergeron, Christian, Québec 097132
Bergeron, D.L., Windsor, Ontario . . 097553
Bergeron, Jean-Claude, Ottawa . . . 097098
Bergeron, J.F., New Orleans 117402
Bergeron-Guerpillon, Quimper 121228

Berges, Jean-Louis, Saint-Pe-d'Ardet . . . 067948
Berggren, Anders, Saltsjöbaden . . . 110988
Berggruen, Paris . 100049, 133538, 138305
Berggruen, John, San Francisco . . . 119610
Berghammer, Peter, Hohenbrunn . . 139275
Berghen, Bergen op Zoom . . . 140360
Berghoff, Tampa . . . 120029
Berghuis, Jan, Voorschoten . . . 128873
Bergische Bücherstube, Overath . . 139645
Bergisches Freilichtmuseum für Ökologie und bäuerlich-handwerkliche Kultur, Lindlar . . . 018660
Bergisches Museum für Bergbau, Handwerk und Gewerbe, Bergisch Gladbach 015967
Bergisches Museum Schloß Burg, Solingen . . . 020235
Bergkerk Deventer, Deventer . . . 029472
Bergkerk Museum, Hannema-de Stuers Fundatie, Deventer . . . 029473
Bergkristallmuseum, Saalbach . . . 002545
Bergler & Nitsche-Bergler, Schwarzenbach an der Saale . . . 073757
Berglöf, Malmö . . . 081864
Berglöf, M., Stockholm . . . 081927
Bergmännisches Traditionskabinett mit Besucherbergwerk, Breitenbrunn, Erzgebirge . . . 016404
Bergman, Las Vegas . . . 089552
Bergman, Stockholm . . . 111007
Bergman, Harry, Stockholm . . . 111008
Bergmann, Celle . . . 102303
Bergmann, Hamburg . . . 071206
Bergmann, Christine, Au, Breisgau . 101609
Bergmann, Franz, Schwarzenbach an der Saale . . . 073758
Bergmann, S., Köln . . . 126065
Bergmann, Thomas, Erlangen . . . 121396
Bergmans & Brouwer, Gorinchem . . 140426
Bergner, Falk, München . . . 126353
Bergner & Job, Wiesbaden . . . 105246
Bergoglio, Torino . . . 140125
Bergoglio, Danile, Torino . . . 128261
Bergoglio, Gian Marco, Torino . . . 128262
Bergoglio, Marco, Torino . 076775, 128263
Bergsjö Konsthall, Bergsjö . . . 036214
Bergslagens Motor Museum, Grängesberg . . . 036309
Bergsma, Wiego, Utrecht . . . 128854
Bergstens Konstförlag, Tyresö . . . 134973
Bergström, Siwert, Malmö . . . 110960
Bergstrom, Kalle, Paris . . . 100050
Bergstrom-Mahler Museum, Neenah . . . 046171
Bergsturz-Museum Goldau, Goldau 037153
Bergtheil Museum, Westville . . . 034776
Le Bergueleven, Saint-Martin-des-Près . . . 067641
Bergwerkmuseum Grube Glasebach, Straßberg . . . 020333
Bergwerksmuseum, Penzberg . . . 019587
Bergwerksmuseum Schacht Mehren, Mehren . . . 018880
Bergwinkelmuseum, Schlüchtern . . 020049
Berinson, Hendrik A., Berlin . . . 101797
Berk, Harlan J., Chicago . 088033, 142280
Berke, Peter, Weinbach . . . 126983
Berkei, Ilona, Zeuthen . . . 127063
Berkeley, Saint Louis . . . 092205
Berkeley Antiques, Tewkesbury . . .086874, 131586
Berkeley Antiques Market, Berkeley 083491
Berkeley Art Center, Berkeley . . . 042157
Berkeley Art Museum, Berkeley . . . 042158
Berkeley Castle, Berkeley . . . 038676
Berkeley Civic Arts Program, Berkeley . . . 054679
The Berkeley Costume and Toy Museum, New Ross . . . 022845
Berkeley Editions, Darling Point . . .094449, 133047
Berkeley Plantation, Charles City . . 042718
Berkelouw, Berrima . . . 136802
Berkelouw, Paddington, New South Wales . . . 137038
Berkelouw, H., Los Angeles . . . 142490
Berkelouw, Leo, Leichhardt . . . 136973
Berkenkopf, Peter, Köln . . . 126066
Berkes, Peter, Basel . . . 129910
Berkhout, P.Y.M., Den Haag . . . 128625
Berkman, Philadelphia . . . 091611
Berko, Knokke-Heist . . . 096326
Berko, Paris . . . 100051
Berko, Patrick, Bruxelles . 096157, 133260
Berks Art Alliance, Reading . . . 054680
Berkshire Antiques, Windsor . . . 087180
Berkshire Antiques Centre, Midgham . . . 085985
Berkshire Artisans, Pittsfield . . . 047066
Berkshire County Historical Society Museum at Arrowhead, Pittsfield . . . 047067
Berkshire Metal Finishers, Sandhurst, Berkshire . . . 086515, 131456
Berkshire Mill Museum, Moora . . . 001278
The Berkshire Museum, Pittsfield . . 047068
Berkshire Scenic Railway Museum, Lenox . . . 045236
Berkswell Village Museum, Berkswell . . . 038679
Berl, Ulrich, Lauda-Königshofen . . . 072162
Berland, Edinburgh . . . 084275
Berland, Didier, Paris . . . 065569
Berleux, Gilles, Boutenac-Touvent . 061736
Berlevåg Havnemuseum, Berlevåg . 030773
Berlijn, Ger, Amsterdam . . . 077799
Berlijn, Paul, Haarlem . . . 078442
Berlin-Antiquariat, Berlin . . . 138746
Berlin Art and Historical Collections, Berlin . . . 042168
Berlin Connection Association, Luzern . . . 111683, 135042
Berlin Design, Achim . . . 133714
Berlin Historical Society Museum of Local History, Berlin . . . 042169
Berlin Projects, Berlin . . . 101798
Berlina, Los Angeles . . . 116726
Berline, Grenoble . . . 063054
Berliner Antiquariatsmarkt, Berlin . . 138747
Berliner Auktionshaus für Geschichte, Berlin . . . 121322
Berliner Bilder Galerie, Berlin . . . 069576
Berliner Bilder Galerie, Berlin 101799, 125170
Berliner Bilderzauber, Berlin . . . 125171
Berliner Hundemuseum, Ostseebad Binz . . . 019519
Berliner Impressionisten Galerie, Potsdam . . . 104622
Berliner Kinomuseum, Berlin . . . 015989
Berliner Medizinhistorisches Museum der Charité, Berlin . . . 015990
Berliner Münzauktion, Berlin . . . 121323
Berliner S-Bahn-Museum, Potsdam 019653
Berlinghof, Heidelberg . . . 121448
Berlinghof, Leimen, Baden . . . 121492
Berlinische Galerie, Landesmuseum für Moderne Kunst Fotografie und Architektur, Berlin . . . 015991
Berlins Gem and Historical Museum, South Nanango . . . 001476
Berlioz, Annonay . . . 060904
Berlioz, Guy, Maraussan . . . 064257
Berman, Torino . . . 106662
Berman, Bob, Philadelphia . . . 091612
Berman, D., Austin . . . 114961
Berman &Co., Ted, Sacramento . . . 132729
Berman Hall, Jerusalem . . . 022941
Bermann, Gisèle, Bruxelles . . . 057856
Bermanne, Marsillargues . . . 064403
Bermans, Dover . . . 122891
Bermondsey, Madrid . . . 081250
Bermondsey Antiques Market, London . . . 085129
Bermuda Arts Centre, Dockyard . . . 096416
Bermuda Editions Contemporary Art, Saint George's . . . 096434
Bermuda Historical Society Museum, Hamilton . . . 003897
Bermuda Maritime Museum, Mangrove Bay . . . 003901
Bermuda Memories, Saint George's 096435
Bermuda National Gallery, Hamilton 003898
Bermuda National Trust Museum, Saint George's . . . 003902
Bermuda Natural History Museum, Flatts . . . 003896
Bermuda Society of Arts, Hamilton .003899, 052694
Bermúdez Antiques Art's, Maracaibo . . . 093551
Berna, Patrick, Le Mas . . . 063665
Bernabei, Firenze . . . 127299
Bernack, Worpswede . . . 105327
Bernadac, Saint-Paul-de-Vence . . . 101197
Bernadette's Galleries, North Vancouver . . . 006043
Bernadette's Galleries, Vancouver . 097426
Bernadis, Leonardo, Balerna . . . 082111
Bernadottebiblioteket, Stockholm . . 036616
Bernaerts, Antwerpen . . . 120703
Bernal, Marie, Strasbourg . . . 124939
Bernal S., José, Santiago de Chile . 059509
Bernal Troncoso, Pedro, Santiago de Chile . . . 097619
Bernam, Bogotá . . . 098109
Bernandino Jalandoni Ancestral House, Silay . . . 031790
Bernard, Macclesfield . . . 114023
Bernard, Montréal . . . 096980
Bernard, Alain, Meyzieu . . . 064553
Bernard, Antoinette, Paris . . . 065570
Bernard, Christian, Paris . . . 065571
Bernard, Christine, Cheminot . . . 062270
Bernard, Claude, New York . . . 117687
Bernard, Claude, Paris . . . 100052, 133539
Bernard, Henri, Bordeaux . . . 061590
Bernard, Jean-Claude, Montélimar . 064672
Bernard, Marion, Champlitte . . . 099113
Bernard, Michel, Bougnon . . . 124152
Bernard, Michel, Lyon . . . 064084
Bernard, Michel, Nolay . . . 065225
Bernard, Theo, Erlenbach am Main . 070603
Bernard Historical Museum, Delton 043386
Bernard Price Institute Paleontology Museum, Johannesburg . . . 034643
Bernardi, San Marino . . . 109668
Bernardi, Toronto . . . 059151, 097234
Bernardi, A. de, Aachen . . 101501, 133710
Bernardi & Sons, Bea Tullio, Pretoria . . . 121987
Bernardi, Franco, Torino . . . 128264
Bernardi, Lorenzo, Firenze . . . 127300
Bernardi, Marino, San Marino . . . 080343
Bernardi, Riccardo, Roma . . . 127937
Bernardini, Cecilia, Roma . . . 127938
Bernardino & Soares, Lisboa . . . 079876
Bernardis, Massimiliano, Chiasso . . 082311
Bernardis, Sergio, Torino . . . 140126
Bernardoff, Braidwood . . . 055536
Bernarducci & Meisel, New York . . . 117688
Bernardus Verlag, Grevenbroich . . . 133988
Bernareggi, Federico Ferdinando, Milano . . . 075628
Bernasconi, Enrica, Milano . . . 127532
Bernasconi, Roger, Marseille 064326, 124397
Bernat Galeria, Barcelona . . . 110120
Bernau, K., Weimar, Thüringen . . . 139832
Bernaudat, Guy, Sainte-Savine . . . 068078
Bernaudo & Sicuro, Torino . . . 128265
Bernauer, Robert, Frankfurt am Main . . . 102750
Bernays, Dallas . . . 115844
Bernberg Fashion Museum, Museum Africa, Johannesburg . . . 034644
Berndt, Köln . . . 103594
Berndt, Brigitta, Solothurn . . . 130181
Berndt, Pierre, Genève . . . 082404
Berndt, Rudolfo, Buenos Aires 055177, 123152
Berndt Museum of Anthropology, University of Western Australia, Nedlands . . 001319
Berné, Mulhouse . . . 099785
Bernecker, J., Bötzingen . . . 138888
Berner Kunst- und Antiquitätenmesse, Bern . . . 093888
Berner Kunstmitteilungen, Bern . . . 136123
Berners, Richard, Köln . . . 103595
Bernesga, León . . . 110397
Bernet-Neumann, Ulrike, Erlenbach (Zürich) . . . 130010
Bernett, F.A., Boston . . . 142244
Bernhammer, Horst & Frank, Bischoffen . . . 069853
Bernhard & Vögeli-Müller, Winterthur . . . 082911, 130220
Bernhardt, Rainer, Lübeck . . . 126240
Bernhardt, Torsten, Hamburg . . . 139168
Bernheim, Panamá City . . 079525, 108784
Bernheim-Jeune, Paris . . . 100053
Bernheim-Jeune, Paris . . . 100054
Bernheim-Jeune, Paris . . . 138306
Bernheim-Jeune, Paris . . . 138307
Bernheimer, Fine Old Masters, München . . . 072659
Berni, Carla, Firenze . . . 075286
Bernicat, G., Roanne . . . 067162
Bernice Pauahi Bishop Museum, Honolulu . . . 044591
Bernier / Eliades, Athinai . 105389, 134485
Bernigaud, Fabrice, Saint-Martin-du-Mont . . . 067644
Bernini, Andrea, Livorno . . . 075525
Bernini, Dario, Parma . . . 127847
Bernini, Manola, Firenze . . . 127301
Bernou, Robert, Asunción . . . 079530
Berns, Christiane & Günter, Neuwied . . . 073044
Berns, Perry, Dallas . . . 115845
Bernstein, New York . . . 117689
Bernstein, M., Los Angeles . . . 142491
Bernstein & Co., S., San Francisco .092742, 142930
Bernstein Museum, Bad Füssing . . 015703
Bernsteinmuseum, Ostseebad Sellin . . . 019533
Berntsen, Kaare, Oslo . . . 079423, 108703
Bernwieser, Christian, Wien . . . 137290
Beronnet, Marcel, Villeurbanne . . . 068944
Berquat, Pascal, Marseille . . . 121060
Berquat, Pascal, Marseille . . . 121061
Berr, Ernst & Susanna, München . . 104152
Berr, Karl, Tirschenreuth . . . 074064
Berra, Clementina, Milano . . . 075629
Berra, Clementina, Milano . . . 075630
Berra, Paola, Milano . . . 075631
Berre, Alain le, Kerlaz . . . 063279
Berretta Lemoine, Veronique, Toulon (Var) . . . 068443
Berrima District Art Gallery, Bowral 000822
Berrima District Museum, Berrima . 000799
Berrima Galleries, Berrima . . . 094246
Berrino, Monaco . . . 107524
Berrios Valenzuela, Orlando, Santiago de Chile . . . 059510
Berry, Saint-Maur . . . 067654
Berry, J.J., Windsor, Ontario . . . 059438
Berry, Lesley, Flamborough . . . 084410
Berry, Ray, Maylands, Western Australia . . . 056176
Berry, Sandra, New Orleans . . . 117403
Berry Antiques, Moreton-in-Marsh . 086013
Berry Art Gallery, Berry . . . 094247
Berry & Growther, Huddersfield . . . 130812
Berry-Hill, New York . . . 117690
Berry Museum, Berry . . . 000800
Berry Street Bookshop, Wolverhampton . . . 142163
Berryware, Tucson . . . 120110
Berselli, Milano . . . 127533
Berset, Marika, La Conversion . . . 082324
Bersham Heritage Centre and Ironworks, Wrexham . . . 041453
Bersia, Milano . . . 075632
Berson, Toronto . . . 059152
Bert, Providence . . . 119072
Bert, Dominique, Paris . . . 100055
Das Berta-Hummel-Museum im Hummelhaus, Massing . . . 018860

Bertacchi, Orfeo, Modena 075896
Bertacchini, Gabriella, Modena 127722
Bertana, Isabel S. de, Buenos Aires 055178
Bertarini, Aldo, Modena 075897
Bertaux, Baltimore 115038
Berte Museum, Slöinge 036587
Bertha V.B. Lederer Fine Arts Gallery, Geneseo 044160
Berthas Kunsthandel, Buchholz in der Nordheide 070078
Berthelin, Manuel, Cognac 062377
Berthelot, Paris 124589
Berthelot, Saint-Denis-de-l'Hôtel . . 067417
Berthelot, Bertrand, Remouillé 067092
Berthelot, Jean-Louis, Bourg-Beaudouin 061703, 124154
Berthelot-Vinchon, Paris 065572
Berthet, Anne-Sophie, Saint-Pourcain-sur-Sioule 067965
Berthet-Aittouarès, Paris 100056
Berthet André, Lyon 064085
Berthier, Renée, Limoges 063882
Berthiller, Claude, Villeurbanne 125032
Berthold, Gelsenkirchen 102927
Berthold-Auerbach-Museum, Horb . 018005
Bertholier, Joël, Le Pont-de-Beauvoisin 063688, 124306
Berthommier & Dominique Langlet, Geneviève, Rivarennes 067156
Berthoud, Le Vésinet 063730
Berti, Firenze 075287
Berti, Adriana, Firenze 075288
Berti, Luciano, Bern 082198
Berti, Marusca, Prato 127885
Bertin, Paris 065573
Bertin Poirée, Paris 100057
Bertocchi, Bologna 139986
Bertogalli, Parma 076198
Bertola, Carlo, Torino 128266
Bertola, Lauro, Torino 128267
Bertold Gallery, London 113502
Bertoli, Matteo, Milano 127534
Bertolin, Livano, München 126354
Bertolin, Silvano, Haimhausen 125784
Bertolotti, Luciano, Brescia 127203
Bertoncelj, Danilo, Ljubljana 080650, 129287
Bertoncelli, Maurizio, Bologna 075057, 139987
Bertone, Flavio, Torino 128268
Bertoni, Andrea, Bologna 127133
Bertoni, Félix, Magagnosc 064211
Bertouy, Didier, Lyon 064086
Bertram, W., Bremen 070013
Bertram House Museum, Iziko Museums of Cape Town, Cape Town 034573
Bertran, Jean-Pierre, Villeneuve-sur-Lot 068915
Bertran, Michel, Rouen 067247
Bertran, Michel, Rouen 101109
Bertran, Michèle & Etienne, Rouen .067248, 138585
Bertrand, Lisboa 134867
Bertrand, Ribaute-les-Tavernes . . . 067128
Bertrand, Tassin-la-Demi-Lune . . . 138624
Bertrand, Alex, Vendôme 068757
Bertrand, Arthus, Palaiseau 065331
Bertrand, Dominique, Cambrai 120960
Bertrand, Michel, Noron-l'Abbaye . . 065229
Bertrandy, Philippe, Le Puy-en-Velay 138117
Bert's Antiques, San Diego 092616
Bertsch, Karlsruhe 103487
Bertulli, Mario, Roma 127939
Bertus, Rotterdam 078702
Berufsgruppe des Salzburger Kunst- und Antiquitätenhandels, Salzburg . . . 052510
Berufsverband Bildender Künstler, Bezirksverband Bergisch-Land, Wuppertal 053037
Berufsverband Bildender Künstler, Bezirksverband Ostwestfalen-Lippe, Herford 053038
Berufsverband Bildender Künstler Aachen/ Euregio, Aachen 053039
Berufsverband Bildender Künstler Berlins e.V., Berlin 053040
Berufsverband Bildender Künstler Frankfurt/ Main, Frankfurt am Main 053041, 102751
Berufsverband bildender Künstler Hamburgs e.V, Hamburg 053042
Berufsverband Bildender Künstler Landesverband Bayern e.V., München 053043
Berufsverband Bildender Künstler München und Oberbayern, München 053044
Berufsverband Bildender Künstler Niederbayern e.V., Fürstenzell . . . 053045
Berufsverband Bildender Künstler Nürnberg e.V., Hilpoltstein 053046
Berufsverband Bildender Künstler Oberbayern-Nord und Ingolstadt, Ingolstadt 053047
Berufsverband Bildender Künstler Schwaben-Nord und Augsburg e.V., Augsburg 053048
Berufsverband Bildender Künstler Schwaben-Süd, Kempten 053049
Berufsverband Bildender Künstler Unterfranken, Würzburg 053050
Berufsverband Bildender Künstler Westfalen e.V., Dortmund 053051
Berufsverband Bildender Künstlerinnen und Künstler, Regionalverband Wiesbaden, Wiesbaden 053052
Berufsverband Bildender Künstlerinnen und Künstler Braunschweig e.V., Braunschweig 053053
Berufsverband Bildender Künstlerinnen und Künstler Oberfranken e.V., Bamberg 053054
Berufsverband Bildender Künstlerinnen und Künstler Südhessen, Groß-Umstadt 053055
Berufsverband Handwerk Kunst Design e.V., Bundesverband Kunsthandwerk, Frankfurt am Main 053056
Berufsverband österreichischer Kunst- und Werkerzieher, Wien 052511
Berufsverband österreichischer Kunst- und Werkerzieher, Landesgruppe Niederösterreich, Baden bei Wien 052512
Arbeitsgemeinschaft der Restauratoren-Museen-Denkmalpflege-Grabungstechnik; Berufsverband staatlich geprüfter RestauratorInnen; Bundesverband Deutscher Diplom-RestauratorInnen; Deutscher Restauratoren Verband; Deutscher Verband Freiberuflicher Restauratoren; Restauratoren Fachverband; Restauratorenverband Sachsen, Bonn 053589
Berufsvereinigung Bildender Künstler Oberösterreichs, Landesverband Oberösterreich, Linz 052513
Berufsvereinigung bildender Künstler Salzburg, Salzburg 052514
Berufsvereinigung der bildenden Künstler Österreichs, Bundesverband und Landesverband für Wien, Niederösterreich und Burgenland, Wien 052515
Berufsvereinigung der bildenden Künstler Österreichs, Landesverband für Steiermark, Fürstenfeld 052516
Berufsvereinigung der bildenden Künstler Österreichs, Landesverband Kärnten, Klagenfurt 052517
Berufsvereinigung der bildenden Künstler Österreichs, Landesverband Vorarlberg, Bregenz 052518, 133062
Berwald, London 085130
Berwick, Officer 056400
Berwick Barracks, Berwick-upon-Tweed 038681
Berwick Borough Museum and Art Gallery, Berwick-upon-Tweed 038682
Berwick Pakenham Historical Museum, Pakenham 001364
Beryl's Boutique Gallery, Bundoora . 094327
Beryl's Old Charm Antiques, Chatswood 055664
Berzel, Speyer 073876
Berzeliusmuseet, Stockholm 036617
Berżera, Warszawa 109101
Bērzgales Pagasta Vēstures Muzejs, Bērzgale 027666
Berzolari, Andrea, Milano 127535
Besættelsessamlingen 1940-45, Grindsted 008879
Besançon, Jacques & Dominique, Bordeaux 061591, 138036
Besançon, Philiberte, Aix-en-Provence 060698
Besch, Constant, Mâcon 064201
Besch, Gérard, Juziers 063274
Beschek, Helmut, Linz 095650
Besenmuseum & Galerie, Ehingen, Donau 016895
Besenval, Jean-Pierre, Paris 124590
Besichtigungsstätte der Mumie des Ritter Kahlbutz, Neustadt, Dosse 019289
Beside the Wave, Falmouth 113050, 135147
Besiktas Kultur Merkezi, İstanbul . . 112288
Besim, Adil, Wien 057382
Besler, Frankfurt am Main 102752
Besley, Beccles 130360, 141401
Besnard, Alain, Orléans 065297
Besnard, Christian, Nançay 064853, 099790, 124467
Besnard, Michel, Mortagne-au-Perche 064797
Beso Ur och Antik, Göteborg 081797
Besold & Tauche, Sankt Veit an der Glan 137256
Bespeckled Trout, New York 090726
Besrest, Jean-Jacques, Paris 065574
Bessard, Ghislaine, Velines 068745
Besseiche, Daniel, Courchevel 099177
Besseiche, Daniel, Dinard 099227
Besseiche, Daniel, Paris 100058
Besseiche, Daniel, Paris 100059
Besseiche, Daniel, Pont-Aven 101019
Besselaar, Utrecht 108240
Besselaar, Utrecht 108241
Bessels, Hendrik-W., Oslo 079424
The Bessemer Gallery, Sheffield . . . 114413
Bessemer Hall of History, Bessemer 042175
Besser, Erika, Bad Orb 069351
Besser, Manfred, Hamburg 103099
Bessi, Andrea, Firenze 127302
Bessie Surtees House, Newcastle-upon-Tyne 040545
Bessière, Georges, Ambérieu-en-Bugey 060788
Bessire, Jythe, Maisoncelle-Saint-Pierre 064223
Bessler, Frank, Stuttgart 104966
Bessler, Wilhelm, Augsburg 069217
Besson, London 113503
Besson, Jean-Louis, Aurillac 061071
Best, Bad Oeynhausen 101682
Best, Chaskovo 096699
Best, Detmold 102359
Best, Ray, Newton Tony 086083
Best, Wolfgang, Stellichte 073912
Best Art Restoration, Dallas 131999
Best Finishing Company, Houston . . 132103
Best Friend of Charleston Museum, Charleston 042726
Best Friends Antiques, Tampa 093108
Best Little Wordhouse in the World, Calgary 137620
Best Loved Books, Emerald 136890
Best of Brass, Hereford 113236
Best of the West Antique Expo, Abbotsford 093620
Bester, Béatrice & Alain, Vincennes 068992
Bestman, Delft 078142
Besucher-Bergwerk Hüttenstollen, Orts- und Bergwerksmuseum Osterwald, Salzhemmendorf 019973
Besucher-Dienste, Staatliche Museen zu Berlin - Stiftung Preußischer Kulturbesitz, Berlin 015992
Besucherbergwerk Bad Friedrichshall-Kochendorf, Heilbronn 017848
Besucherbergwerk Drei Kronen und Ehrt, Elbingerode, Harz 016934
Besucherbergwerk Finstertal, Asbach bei Schmalkalden 015573
Besucherbergwerk Grube Fortuna, Solms 020240
Besucherbergwerk Grube Gustav, Meißner 018893
Besucherbergwerk Schiefergrube Christine, Willingen, Upland 020900
Besucherbergwerk Vereinigt Zwitterfeld zu Zinnwald, Tiefer-Bünau-Stollen, Zinnwald-Georgenfeld 021068
Bet Gordon, Deganya Aleph 022902
Bet Hashomer Museum, Kibbutz Kfar Giladi 023008
Bet Pinhas Museum of Nature, Haifa 022916
Beta Railway Station Historic Museum, Alpha 000741
Beta Verlag, Rastatt 134353
Bétabois, La Charité-sur-Loire 063324
Betbeder, Catherine, Anglet 060868
Betbeder, Catherine, Biarritz 061452
Betbeder Espacio de Arte, Tandil . . 094106
Betesaraki, Donostia-San Sebastián 129500
Beth Ahabah Museum and Archives, Richmond 047411
Beth-Nell Antiques, Greystones . . . 074977
Beth Tzedec Reuben and Helene Dennis Museum, Toronto 006583
Bethany, Bendigo 094240
Bethany College Art Department, Mingenback Art Center, Lindsborg 051612
Bethel Historical Society's Regional History Center, Bethel 042178
Bethenod, C, Paris 065575
Bethesdas, København 137882
Bethge, Wolfgang, Erfurt 102643
Bethlehem Art Gallery, New York . . 117691
Bethlehem Historical Association Museum, Selkirk 048109
Bethlehem Museum, Bethlehem . . . 034552
Bethlem Royal Hospital Archives and Museum, Beckenham 038650
Bethmann, Jean de, Bordeaux 061592
Bethmann-Hollweg, Asta von, Berlin 069577, 101800
Béthon, Patrick, Paris 065576
Beth's Antiques, Meeniyan 056179
Bethune Memorial House, National Historic Site of Canada, Gravenhurst 005545
Bethunes, Wellington 121841
Betis, Jean-François, Versailles . . . 138652
Betonzeitschiene, Plattenbaumicromuseum, Dresden 016781
Betsey Williams Cottage, Providence 047251
Betsy Ross House, Philadelphia . . . 046927
Bett, North Hobart 094974
Bettcher, Miami 117037
Bettenbühl, Irmgard, Kronberg im Taunus 126155
Bettencourt Frères, Bagnolet 124089
Better Buy Books, Nerang 137023
Better Coins, Houston 089032
Better Days, Menai Bridge 085972
Better Days Antiques, Mornington . 056257
Better Homes, San Antonio 092490
Better Times Antiques, New York . . 090727
Betti, Roger, Toulouse 101334
Bettina und Achim von Arnim Museum, Wiepersdorf bei Jüterbog 020859
Bettinardi, Giorgio, Milano 127536
Bettinger, Marc T., Portland 091903
Bettini, Firenze 127303
Bettini, A. & F., Karlsruhe 071712
Bettles, Ringwood 114315
Bettoni, Arturo, Brescia 075147
Betts House Research Center, Cincinnati 042917
Betty Brinn Children's Museum, Milwaukee 045885
Bettyann & Jimbo, Dallas 088465
Betty's Antiques, Long Beach 089627
Betty's Bookstore, San Diego 142898
Betuws Fruitteelt Museum, Erichem 029578
Between Cultures, Seattle 119889
Betws-y-coed Motor Museum, Betws-y-coed 038688

Betz, Houston 116282
Betzel, Aurel, Berlin 125172
Betzwieser, Christopher, Miltenberg 126318
Beuche, Bernard, Mazan 064448
Roger Beuchert & Hermina Szabo-Beuchert, Marloffstein 104037
Beugnot, Claire & Xavier, Versailles 125017
Beulah, Amsterdam 077800
Beulecke, Rebecca, Hilpoltstein . . . 125938
Beumers, Manfred, Aachen 069076, 101502
Beuneker, Leeuwarden 078549
Beuroner Kunstverlag, Beuron 133821
Beurret, Nicolas, Herrliberg 111554
Beurrier, Dominique, Déville-lès-Rouen 062620
Beurs van Berlage Museum, Amsterdam 029172
Beurskens, Roermond 078679
Beurville, Claudine, Méry-sur-Oise . 064508
Beuse, C., Amersfoort 128523
Elka Beutel & Susan Gülzow, Potsdam 126644
Beuthner, Manfred, La Roche-Bernard 099401
Beutler, E., Bremen 138939
Beutler, Felix, Berlin 125173
Beutler, Gerhard, Calw 070119
Bev & Dale, Oklahoma City 091477
Bevan, Rupert, London 130943
Beveled Edge, Baltimore 115039
The Beveled Edge, Richmond 119102
Beveled Edge, Tampa 120030
Beverage Containers Museum, Millersville 045874
Beverley, London 085131
Beverley Art Gallery, Beverley 038690
Beverley Decorative and Fine Arts Society, Newbegin 054310
Beverly Antiques, Chicago 088034
Beverly Art Center, Chicago 042824
Beverly Hills Antiquarian, Los Angeles 089705, 142492
Beverly Hills Gallery, Chicago 115369
Beverly Historical Museum, Beverly 042188
Bévilacqua, Raphaël, Burlats 061838
Bevo, Saint Louis 092206
Bewdley Antiques, Bewdley 083505, 130379
Bewdley Museum, Bewdley 038693
Bewer, Petra, Stuttgart 139754
Bewitched, Chicago 131887
Bewley's Café Museum, Dublin . . . 022732
Bexelius & Co, Uppsala 111088
Bexfield, Daniel, London 085132
Bexhill, Saint Leonards-on-Sea . . . 086463
Bexhill Museum, Bexhill-on-Sea . . . 038695
Bexhill Museum of Costume and Social History, Bexhill-on-Sea 038696
Bexley, Columbus 088385
Bexley Historical Society Museum, Bexley 042195
Bexley Museum, London 040089
Bey, Patrick, Cavaillon 062040
Beyeler, Ernst, Basel 111167, 134980, 141197
Beyer, Claudia, Vellberg 126944
Beyer, Dagmar, Seeg 073785
Beyer, Dagmar, Stötten 073924
Beyer, Harry, München 072660
Beyer, Thomas, Wernigerode 074343
De Beyerd, Centrum voor Beeldende Kunst, Breda 029346
Beyoğlu Belediyesi Sanat Galerisi, İstanbul 112289
Beyoglu Sanat Merkezi, İstanbul . . 038085
Beyond Baroque Art Gallery, Venice 048757
Beyond Futons, Charlotte 087928
Beyond the Fridge Door Childrens Art, London 096944
Beyond The Mount Fine Art Conservation, Castlemaine 123206
Beyond the Wall, Chicago 115370
Beyond the Wall, New York 117692
Beyond the Wall, Saint Louis 119187
Beyond the Wall, Seattle 119890
Beyreuther, Jürgen, Neuengönna . . 072981
Beyrie, New York 117693
Beyul, New York 090728
Bezalel Academy of Arts and Design Jerusalem, Jerusalem 050349
Bézard, Xavier, Maintenon 064220
Bezert, Jean-Pierre, Cosne-d'Allier 062490
Bézert, Jean-Pierre, Marseille 124398
Ter Beziens, Kolhorn 029815
Béziers, Dominique, Le Havre 124299
Bežigrajska Galerija, Mestna Galerija Ljubljana, Ljubljana 034478
Bežigrajska Galerija 2, Mestna Galerija Ljubljana, Ljubljana 034479
Bezirksgalerie Alsergrund, Wien . . . 002864
Bezirksheimatmuseum, Völkermarkt 002784
Bezirksheimatmuseum mit Zdarsky-Skimuseum, Lilienfeld 002238
Bezirksmuseum, Buchen 016477
Bezirksmuseum Alsergrund, Wien . 002865
Bezirksmuseum Brigittenau, Wien . 002866
Bezirksmuseum Dachau, Dachau . . 016617
Bezirksmuseum Döbling, Wien 002867
Bezirksmuseum Donaustadt, Wien . 002868
Bezirksmuseum Favoriten, Wien . . 002869
Bezirksmuseum Floridsdorf, Wien . 002870
Bezirksmuseum Hernals, Wien 002871
Bezirksmuseum Hietzing, Wien . . . 002872
Bezirksmuseum Höfli, Zurzach 037821
Bezirksmuseum Innere Stadt, Wien 002873
Bezirksmuseum Josefstadt, Wien . . 002874
Bezirksmuseum Josefstadt, Außenstelle Alte Backstube mit Museum, Wien 002875
Bezirksmuseum Landstraße, Wien . 002876
Bezirksmuseum Leopoldstadt, Wien 002877
Bezirksmuseum Margareten, Wien . 002878
Bezirksmuseum Mariahilf, Wien . . . 002879
Bezirksmuseum Marzahn-Hellersdorf, Berlin 015993
Bezirksmuseum Meidling mit Galerie, Wien 002880
Bezirksmuseum Neubau, Wien 002881
Bezirksmuseum Ottakring, Wien . . . 002882
Bezirksmuseum Penzing, Wien 002883
Bezirksmuseum Simmering, Wien . 002884
Bezirksmuseum Stockerau, Stockerau 002714
Bezirksmuseum Währing, Wien . . . 002885
Bezirksmuseum Wieden, Wien 002886
Bezirksverband Bildender Künstlerinnen und Künstler Karlsruhe e.V., Karlsruhe 053057
Bezirksverband Bildender Künstlerinnen und Künstler, Regional Mannheim e.V., Mannheim 053058
Bezoekerscentrum Binnenhof, Den Haag 029419
Bezoekerscentrum de Meinweg, Herkenbosch 029729
Bezoekerscentrum Mijl Op Zeven, Ospel 030010
Bezoekerscentrum Oortjespad, Kamerik 029797
Beztchi, Josef, Frankfurt am Main . 070729
B.F. Larsen Gallery, Provo 047270
BFAS-Blondeau Fine Art Service, Genève 111427
BGC, Paris 065577
B.H.A., Bibliography of the History of Art, Vandœuvre-lès-Nancy 135694
Bhagalpur Museum, Bhagalpur . . . 022024
Bhagavan Mahavir Government Museum, Cuddapah 022065
Bhakta Bahadur Sreshtha, Kathmandu 077703
Bharany's Curio House, Delhi 074802
Bharat Bhawan Museum, Bhopal . . 022031
Bharat Itihas Samshodhak Mandal Museum, Pune 022303
Bharat Kala Bhavan, Varanasi 022372
Bharatiya Adim Jati Sevak Sangh Museum, Delhi 022080
Bharatiya Kala Prasarini Sabha, Pune 050321
Bhartiya Vidya Bhavan, Hyderabad . 105699
Bhavan's Art Gallery, Bangalore . . . 105601
Bhavya Art Gallery, Bangalore 074766
Bhirasri Museum of Modern Art, Bangkok 037872
BHL, Soustons 068278
BHNY Fine Art, New York 117694
Bhuri Singh Museum, Chamba 022050
Bi Gakko, Tokyo 050478
Bi-Hand, Bristol 112715
Bia, Marta, Verona 076995
Biaggi, Alexandre, Paris 065578
Biaggi, Anne-Marie, Menton 121072
Biagiarelli, Roma 076335
Biagiotti, Caterina Diana, Firenze . . 075289
Biagiotti, Roberta, Firenze 075290
Biagiotti & Sarti, Firenze 127304
Bialik-Museum, Tel Aviv 023067
Białostockie Muzeum WSI, Państwowe Muzeum w Białymstoku, Wasilków 032487
Bianca, Buenos Aires 123153
Biancarelli, François, Paris 065579
Bianchera, Mario, Zürich 130228
Bianchetti, Carla & Mario, Brescia . 075148
Bianchi, Beat, Aarau 111099
Bianchi, Donatella, Milano 127537
Bianchi, Lucia, Milano 127538
Bianchin, Luisa Maria Laura, Milano 075633
Bianchini, Roma 076336
Bianchini, Emilia Maria, Milano . . . 127539
Bianco, Piergiorgio, Milano 075634
Bianconi, Renata, Milano 106171
Biapo Artes, São Paulo 058691
Biarom Design, Bucureşti 080144
Biartea, Asociación Artesana de Bizkaia-Bizkaiko Artisau Elkartea, Bilbao . 054107
Biasio Antichitá, Padova 076073
Biasio Mobili, Padova 076074
Biasoli, Monique, Bazas 098935
Biasutti, Giampiero, Torino 106663
Biasutti & Biasutti, Torino 106664
Biau, Jean-Francois, Montpellier . . 064736
Biazzi, Tina Cecilia & Leonarda Vercelli, Torino 076776
Bibak Museum, Benguet, Ifugao Bontoc, Apayao and Kalinga Museum of Culture, Baguio 031627
Biban, Daniele, Venezia 076924
Bibbo, Canio, Roma 076337
Bibby, Anna, Auckland 108304
Bibelgalerie Meersburg, Meersburg 018869
Bibelmuseum, Rutzenmoos 002544
Bibelmuseum, Beuron 016214
Bibelmuseum, Münster 019140
Bibelmuseum Stuttgart, Stuttgart . . 020345
Bibelocik, Kraków 079624
Bibelocik, Kraków 079625
Bibelot, 's-Hertogenbosch 078513
Bibelot, Honolulu 116199
Bibelot, Warszawa 140780
Bibelot, Warszawa 140781
Bibelot Snuisterij, Heerlen 078499
Bibelots and Books, Seattle 142978
Biber, Jeffery L., Philadelphia 091613
Biberger, Peter, Salzburg 057237
Biblarte, Lisboa 079877, 140821
Bible Lands Museum Jerusalem, Jerusalem 022942
Bible Museum, Trilofo 021513
Bible Museum, Dizengof House, Tel Aviv 023068
Biblia Rara, Würzburg 134467
Biblical Arts Center, Dallas 043264
Biblical Heritage Collection, London 141755
Biblical Museum of Canada, Vancouver 006685
Biblical World Gallery, Budapest . . . 074669
Biblio-Globus Torgovyj Dom, Moskva 140901
Bibliographicum, Heidelberg 139247
Biblioludothèque, Maison de la Nature, Paris 013552
Bibliomania, Oakland 142706
Biblionia Books, Sendai 140177
Bibliophile, Paddington, New South Wales 137039
Bibliophile Bookshop, Norfolk 142704
Bibliophilen-Gesellschaft Köln, Köln 053059
The Bibliopole, Surry Hills 137096
Bibliosfera, Moskva 109499
La Biblioteca, Milano 140044
Biblioteca Antônio Perdigão, Museu e Arquivo da Cidade, Conseilheiro Lafaiete 004068
Biblioteca d'Arte, Milano 024686
Biblioteca Fundaziun Planta Samedan, Samedan 037485
Biblioteca Luis-Angel Arango, Bogotá 007402
Biblioteca Medicea Laurenziana, Firenze 024138
Biblioteca y Museo Histórico Médicos de Valencia, Valencia 035971
Bibliotéka Antikvárium, Budapest . . 139914
Biblioteka, Muzeum i Archiwum Warszawskiego Towarzystwa Muzycznego im. Stanisława Moniuszki, Warszawa 032417
Biblioteka Narodowa, Warszawa . . 032418
Biblioteka Sejmowa, Wydzial Muzealiów, Warszawa 032419
Biblioteksmuseet, Borås 036221
Bibliotheca Gastronomica, Zürich . . 141325
Bibliotheca Mystica, Luzern 141270
Bibliotheca Rara, Münster 134294
Bibliotheca Wittockiana-Musée de la Reliure et du Hochet, Woluwe-Saint-Pierre 003860
Bibliothek Otto Schäfer, Museum für Buchdruck, Graphik, Kunsthandwerk, Schweinfurt 020138
Bibliothème, Reims 138577
Bibliothèque d'Art ENSAV de la Cambre, Fondation Isabelle Errera de l'Ecole nationale des Arts Visuels, Bruxelles 003290
Bibliothèque d'Art et d'Archéologie des Musées d'Art et d'Histoire de la Ville de Genève, Genève 037111
Bibliothèque d'Art et d'Archéologie Jacques Doucet, Paris 013553
Bibliothèque de l'Arsenal, Paris . . . 013554
Bibliothèque des Arts, Lausanne . . 135031
Bibliothèque d'Histoire de l'Art, Genève 037112
Bibliothèque d'Histoire de l'Art Emile-Bertaux, Université Lyon II, Lyon . 049954
Bibliothèque Marmottan, Boulogne-Billancourt 010906
Bibliothèque Mazarine, Paris 013555
Bibliothèque-Musée, Toulouse 014982
Bibliothèque-Musée de la Comédie-Française, Paris 013556
Bibliothèque-Musée de l'Observatoire, Paris 013557
Bibliothèque-Musée Forney, Paris . 013558
Bibliothèque-Musée Valéry Larbaud, Vichy 015203
Bibliothèque Publique et Universitaire, Salle Ami Lullin, Genève 037113
Bibliothèque Publique et Universitaire, Salle Rousseau, Neuchâtel 037372
Bibliothèque Royale Albert Ier, Bruxelles 003291
Bibliothèque Royale de Belgique, Bruxelles 003291
Bibra, V. Freifrau von, Köln 071914
Bical, Lydia, Neuilly-sur-Seine 064988
Bican, İstanbul 083124
Bicentennial Art Center and Museum, Paris 046814
Bicentennial Historical Museum, Cunnamulla 000964
Bich, Cau, Ho Chi Minh City 120502
Bichlmeier, Annemarie, Holzkirchen, Oberbayern 071571
Bichon, Vendargues 068754
Bichon, Claude, Pornic 101043
Bickel, Minnette D., Pittsburgh 118902
Bickleigh Castle, Bickleigh 038699
Bicoca Antic, La Bisbal d'Empordá . 081005

Bicycle Culture Center, Tokyo 027147
Bicycle Museum, Šiauliai Aušros Museum, Šiauliai 027853
Bicycle Museum of America, New Bremen 046199
Bida Loca, Albuquerque 114773
Bidasoa, Hondarribia 081154
Bidder-Up Auctioneers, Oklahoma City 123029
Biddington, New York 117695, 122986
Biddle & Webb, Birmingham 122415
Biddulph, Peter, London 085133
Bideford Pottery, Bideford 112635
Bidges, Birmingham 087737
Bidjara C.D.E.P., Charleville 055661
Bidner, Franziska, Passau 073294
Bidonlivre, Montréal 137647
Bidorini, Serena, Venezia 128378
Bidwell House, Monterey 045988
Bidwell Mansion, Chico 042889
Biebergrund-Museum, Biebergemünd 016226
Bieberle, Andreas, Magdeburg 121507
Bieberle, Matthias, Glindenberg . . . 139141
Biebl, Jürgen, Bremen 121359
Biedenharn Museum and Gardens, Emy-Lou Biedenharn Foundation, Monroe . 045967
Bieder, Hans, Liestal 082578
Biederberg, Suzanne, Amsterdam . 107681
Biedermann, Jean-Paul, Colmar . . . 062403
Biedermann, Manfred, Heeselicht . . 125895
Biedermann, Margit, Igls 057069
Biedermann, Dr. Margret, München 104153
Biedermann, Peter, Gera 070967
Biedermann, R., Billigheim 069848
Biedermeier, Nijmegen 078651
Biedermeier, Roosendaal 078685
Biegas, Detroit 116083
Bieker & El Sayed, Vettweiß 074202
Bielański, Warszawa 140782
Bielefelder Kunstverein e.V., Bielefeld 053060
Bielen-Säge Museum, Unterschächen 037653
Bielitz, Volker, Leipzig 126183
Bieman de Haas, Elisabeth den, Amsterdam 107682
Biemann, R., Bad Bevensen 069265
Bien, Thaddäus, Hamburg 139169
Bien Phong Museum, Ha Noi 049524
Bienaimé, Bruxelles 057857
Bienaimé, Eric, Hazebrouck 063139
Bienaimé, Pierre, Commercy 062435
Bienal de Arte de Pontevedra, Pontevedra 093861
Bienefeld, Martin, Lüdenscheid . . . 103971
Bienefeld, Mirabel, Kempen 071784
Bienen- und Wagnereimuseum, Grieskirchen 001958
Bienenkundemuseum, Felsberg . . . 017110
Bienenkundemuseum, Münstertal . 019159
Bienenmuseum, Alberswil 036826
Bienenmuseum, Quetzin 019692
Bienenmuseum, Stadtmuseum Berlin, Berlin 015994
Bienenstein, Ingeborg, Wien 057383
Bienfait, Fréderic, Octeville-sur-Mer 065260
Bieniek, Campbell Town 094365
Bieniek, Wuppertal 127048
Biennale d'Art Contemporain, Lyon . 093652
Biennale des Antiquaires de Monaco, Monaco 093820
Biennale des Antiquaires Paris, Paris 093653
Bienvenu, Christian, Beaumont-sur-Sarthe 061263
Bienvenue, Arnhem 078045
Bienville Gallery, New Orleans 090516
Bier, Elmira, Washington 120261
Bierbaum, R., Vlotho 074222
Bierbrauer, Josepha von, Braunschweig 125373
Bierhaus, Hans-Jürgen, München . 072661
Bierhinkel, H., Rheinau 073512
Bierhuizen, Tilburg 128842
Biermaier, B., Minneapolis 142576
Biermann, Dirk Benedikt, Dortmund 070282
Biermann, Karl H., München 072662
Biermuseum, Laa an der Thaya . . . 002187
Bierreclamemuseum, Breda 029347
Bies, J.H.P., Eindhoven 128661
Bies, Marie-José, Eindhoven 078330
Biesalski, Marion Eva, München . . . 126355
Biesbosch Museum, Werkendam . . 030321
Biesenbruch, Wolfgang, Mettmann . 072535
Biesenkamp, Hürth 071593
Bietz, Egon & Irene, Nieder-Olm . . . 104444
Bietz-Hoth, Berlin 101801, 125174
Biffarino, Brescia 075149
Big Apple Antiques, New York 090729
Big Apple Art Gallery, New York . . . 117696
Big Apple Art Gallery, New York . . . 117697
Big Apple Country Auction, New York 122987
Big Apple Visual Group, New York . . 117698
Big Bear Antiques, Omaha 132586
Big Bear Trails Museum, Loon Lake 005798
Big Beaver Nature Centre and Museum, Big Beaver 005097
Big Bell Gu Zhon Museum, Beijing . 006974
Big Ben, Bergisch Gladbach 069538
Big Ben, Buenos Aires 055179
Big Ben Antique Clocks, London . . . 085134
Big Bone Lick State Park Museum, Union 048690
The Big Book, Glen Innes 136921
Big Book Store, Detroit 142400
Big Canvas, Freshwater 113081
Big Cat Gallery, New York 117699
Big Cat Press, Chicago 135345
Big Dipper, Portland 091904, 132684
Big Don's Sport Card Shop, Columbus 088386
Big Hole National Battlefield, Wisdom 049273
Big Jar, Philadelphia 142737
Big Orbit Gallery, Buffalo 115251
Big People Toys, Seattle 092966
Big People Toys, Seattle 092967
Big Picture, Huddersfield 113278
The Big Picture, London 113504
Big Pig Gig, Cincinnati . . . 115608, 122852
Big Pit National Mining Museum of Wales, Blaenavon 038759
Big Red Barn Gallery, Clearmont . . 042970
Big River Art Gallery, Dargaville . . . 108422
Big River Memorial Museum, Big River 005098
Big Shed Antiques, Shepparton . . . 056590
Big Shell Museum, Tewantin 001541
Big Shot, Oakland 118625
Big Sky in Mind, Quezon City 108853
Big Springs Museum, Caledonia . . . 042549
Big Thunder Gold Mine, Keystone . . 044994
Big Well, Greensburg 044339
BigArt, Grantham 113144
Bigden, Edward, Debenham 084148
Bigelow House Museum, Olympia . 046670
Biger, Yves-Marie, Pont-l'Abbé 066924, 124850
Biggar Gasworks Museum, Biggar . 038702
Biggar Museum and Gallery, Biggar 005099
Biggenden Museum, Biggenden . . . 000802
Biggio, Giuseppina, Torino 076777, 140127
Biggör, Paul, Goppertsweiler 125745
Biggs, Richmond 092062
Biggs Museum of American Art, Dover 043488
Biggs Powell, Memphis 090056
Bigler, Marc, Bern 129948
Bigler, Dr. Robert, Rüschlikon 111853
Bignell, Graham, London 130944
Bigorneau Langoureux, La Flotte . . 063379
Biguet, Paule, Antibes-Juan-les-Pins 060914
Bigwood, Brasted 083647
Bigwood Auctioneers, Stratford-upon-Avon 122715
Bihan Antiquités, Saint-Lunaire . . . 067594
Bihar Tribal Welfare Research Institute Museum, Ranchi 022320
Bihari Múzeum, Berettyóújfalu 021631
Bihler, Maria-Ana, Magstatt-le-Bas 064217
Bijan, Bolzano 075125
Bijan Royal, New York 090730
Bijbels Museum, Amsterdam 029173
Bijbels Openluchtmuseum, Heilig Landstichting 029704
De Bijenkorf, Nijmegen 078652
Bijenmuseum Hengelhoef, Houthalen 003524
Bijenteeltmuseum De Bankorf, Amen 029144
Bijenteeltmuseum Kalmthout, Kalmthout 003548
Bijkerk, Willem Fredrik, Enschede . 108018
Bijl, A., Dordrecht 078298
Bijlokemuseum, Gent 003451
Le Bijou Art Glass, San Diego 119489
Bijoux-Bijar, Charleroi 058138
Bijskij Kraevedčeskij Muzej V.V. Bianki, Bijsk 033030
Bijutsu Kenkyu, Tokyo 135972
Bijutsu Shi, Tokyo 135973
Bijutsu-shi Gakkai, Tokyo 053776
Bijutsu Shuppan-sha, Tokyo 134719, 135974
Bijutsu Techo, Tokyo 135975
Bijutsushi Kenkyushitsu, Tohoku Daigaku Bungaku-bu, Sendai 050474
Bijzonder Goed, Deventer 078272
BIL-DAX, Düsseldorf 125522
Bilall, Myri, Berlin 069578, 121324
Bilall, Myri, Berlin 121325
Bilanzuoli, Lucio & Buccio, Pasqualino, Modena 075898
Bilbao Antigue, Bilbao 080967
Bilbao XXI Subastas, Bilbao 122017
Bilboko Arte Eder Museoa / Museo de Bellas Artes de Bilbao, Bilbao . . . 034982
Bilby, Port Douglas 095083
Bild & Rahmen-Fachhandel, Oberhausen, Rheinland 104496
Bild Schön, Georgsmarienhütte . . . 102936
Bild und Rahmen, Bremen 102233
Bild und Rahmen, Norderstedt 104459
Bild- und Tonarchiv, Landesmuseum Joanneum, Graz 001927
Bildarchiv Foto Marburg, Marburg . 018818
Bildbuch Verlag, Wien 133183
Bildegalleriet, Oslo 108704
Bildens Hus, Sundsvall 036690
Bilder-Galerie & all-in-one Museum, KulturKunststatt Prora, Ostseebad Binz 019520
Bilder Galerie Minden, Minden, Westfalen 104076
Bilder im Hof, Flensburg 070697
Bilder till salu, Stockholm 111009
Bilder und Rahmen, Kassel 103508
Bilder und Rahmen Galerie, Mönchengladbach 104090
Bilder und Zeichen der Frömmigkeit - Sammlung Rudolf Kriss, Zweigmuseum des Bayerischen Nationalmuseums, Straubing 020334
Bilderbogen, Bayreuth 101745
Bilderbogen-Galerie, Neuruppin . . . 019266
Bilderbuero, Calw 070120
Bilderdijkmuseum, Vrije Universteit, Amsterdam 029174
Bildergalerie, Düsseldorf 102475
Bildergalerie, Solingen 104914
Bildergalerie Venlo, Venlo 108264
Das Bilderhaus, Frankfurt am Main 102753
Das Bilderhaus, Höchstadt an der Aisch 103385
Bilderhaus, Mörlenbach 104106
Bilderhaus Fürth, Fürth, Odenwald . 102905
Bilderhaus Krämerbrücke, Erfurt . . 102644
BilderLaden Köpenick, Berlin 101802
Bilderrahmen & Postershop, Salzburg 095717
Bilderstube Leuebrüggli, Obersteckholz 111793
Bildhauerfoyer Bahnhof Westend, Berlin 101803
Bildhauergalerie für Kleinplastik, Berlin 101804
Bildhauermuseum, Plau am See . . . 019631
Bildkunst-Akademie Hamburg, Hamburg 050109
Bildmuseet, Umeå 036730
Bildt, Klaus, Krefeld 072065
Bilecik Devlet Güzel Sanatlar Galerisi, Bilecik 038024
Bilger, Ricco, Zürich 135082, 141326
Bilhaud, Alain, Paris 100060
Bilhenry, Milwaukee 117173
Bilinelli, L., Bruxelles 096158
Bilio-Noack, Karin, Eulgem 102716
Biljarskij Gosudarstvennyj Istoriko-Architekturnyj i Prirodnyj Muzej-Zapovednik, Biljarsk 033031
Bilkin Arte Garaikidea, Bilbao 110271
Bílkova Vila, Galerie Hlavního Města Prahy, Praha 008594
Bílkův Dům v Chýnově, Galerie Hlavního Města Prahy, Chýnov u Tábora . . . 008344
Billabong, Coolangatta 136864
Billamoz, Emmanuel, Chambéry . . . 062102
Billantique, Yverdon-les-Bains 082922
Billard, Alain, Roquefort-les-Pins . . 067221
Billardmuseum, Wien 002960
Billardmuseum, München 019040
Billcliffe, Roger, Glasgow 084461
Billcliffe, Roger, Glasgow 113105
Billebaude, Avallon 061115
Billebaude, Chalon-sur-Saône 062083
Billedhuggerskolen Charlottenborg, Kongelige Danske Kunstakademi, København 049897
Billedhuggerskolen Frederiksholms Kanal, Kongelige Danske Kunstakademi, København 049898
Billedkunstnernes Forbund, København 052843
Billedkunstskoler, Kongelige Danske Kunstakademi, København 049899
Biller, Georg, Grabenstätt 071073
Billesberger, Siegfried, Moosinning 104121
Billett, Allan, Kanahooka 056028
Billett, Darren, Kanahooka 056029
Billiard Room Antiques, Chilcompton 083979
Billich, Sydney 095276
Billich at the Rocks, Sydney 056666
Billig, Heike, Koblenz 071890
Billing, Gaby & Gert, Baar 111148
Billingham Art Gallery, Billingham . . 038710
Billings Estate Museum, Ottawa . . . 006085
Billings Farm and Museum, Woodstock 049294
Billis, George, New York 117700
Billmair, Peter, München 126356
Billmann, Bert, Aachen 069077
Billnäsin Kirvesmuseo, Pohja 009980
Billon, Montmarault 064714, 124453
Bill's Antiques, Miami 090148
Bill's Beanie Babies, Omaha 091554
Bill's Sports Collectibles, Denver . . 088660
Bill's Tobacco Antiques, Cincinnati . 088214
Bill's Upholstery, Tampa 132948
Bill's Used Furniture, Pittsburgh . . . 091791
Billy, André, Montpellier 121077
Billy, Dominique, Les Ulmes 063792
Billy, Gérard, Soudat 068267
Billy, Jean-Charles, Le Touquet-Paris-Plage 099457
Billy-Andrieu, Montpellier 121078
Billy Bishop Heritage Museum, Owen Sound 006107
Billy Graham Center Museum, Wheaton 049134
Billycan Emporium, Coolgardie 055714
Bilø, Jens, København 060287
Biloxi Art Association, Gulfport 054681
Bils, Christophe, Lyon 064087
Bilsak, İstanbul 112290

Bilston Craft Gallery, Wolverhampton 041430
Biltmore Estate, Asheville 041790
Bilton, Vancouver 097427
Bily Clock Museum and Antonin Dvorak Exhibition, Spillville 048271
Bilyara Gallery, Bournda 094269
Bim-Köhler, Schornsheim 104844
Bimba-The Art Hut, Chennai 074789, 105623
Bimbo-Martinez, Madrid 129580
Bimbo-Martinez, Sevilla 129728
Bimbo-Martinez, Zaragoza 129806
Bimier, Michel, Villemomble 068906
Bimmerle, Louisville 116930
Binaghi, A.-P., Fiez 082367
Binalong Motor Museum, Binalong . 000803
Binapfl, Alfred, Friedberg, Bayern . . 125679
Binard, Éric, Verneuil-en-Halatte . . 068777
Binc, Oklahoma City 142716
Binchester Roman Fort, Bishop Auckland 038745
Binchi, Silvia, Firenze 075291
Binck, Hooge Zwaluwe 128727
Binder, Alfred, Frankfurt am Main . . 102754
Binder, Alfred, Wien 057384
Binder, Andreas, München 104154
Binder, Andreas, Pregarten 057215
Binder, D. & A., London 085135
Bindereimuseum Hofbräu Kaltenhausen, Hallein 002012
Binders, Charlotte 115277
Bindi, Newcastle 056330
Bindi, Alessandro, Firenze 106034
Binet, Patrick Roger, Paris 100061
Bineth Gallery, Tel Aviv 105916
Bing, Seoul 107208
Bingara Museum, Bingara 000804
Binger, København 060288
Binger, Heike, Flensburg 125638
Bingham, Salt Lake City 119330
Bingham, Tony, London 085136
Bingham Library Trust Art Collection, Cirencester 039091
Bingham & Vance, Cleveland 088311, 115689
Bingley, Robert, Wing 087184
Bingley Antiques, Haworth 084630
Bingold, Hans, Nürnberg 104472
Bini, Singapore 080435
Bini, Angelo, Cagliari 127242
Bini, Dr. Leo, Roma 127940
Bink, Portland 118978
Binnenhuis 1900, Den Haag 078173
't Binnenhuys, Antwerpen 057681
Binnenschifffahrts-Museum Oderberg, Oderberg, Mark 019435
Binnenskamers, Gent 058175
De Binnentuin, Almelo 107623
Binner, Barbara, Wuppertal 105346
Binnington, Peter, Wareham 131646
Binoche, Jean-Claude, Paris 121116
Binoche & De Maredsous, Orléans . 121101
Binor, Balakovo 080205
Binos Collection, Mytilini 021394
Binrest, Barcelona 129329
Binscarth and District Gordon Orr Memorial Museum, Binscarth 005101
Binsch, Harald, Reutlingen 073499
Binsfeld, Ursula, Ras-Al-Khaimah . . 130277
Binst, Jean, Pont-l'Abbé 066925
Bintz, Offenbach am Main 134325
Binz & Andrey, Sankt Antoni 082769, 130157
Binz & Krämer, Köln 103596
Biodiversity Museum, Dehradun . . . 022071
Biodôme de Montréal, Montréal . . . 005912
Biohistoricum, Museum und Forschungsarchiv für die Geschichte der Biologie, Neuburg an der Donau . 019223
Biola University Art Gallery, La Mirada 045073
Biolchini, Stefano, Milano 075635
Biological Museum, Imphal 022166
Biological Sciences Collection, Birmingham 038721
Biologiezentrum des Oberösterreichischen Landesmuseums, Linz 002243
Biologiska Museet, Örebro 036516
Biologiska Museet, Södertälje 036593
Biologiska Museet, Uppsala 036733
Biologiska Museet, Stiftelsen Skansen, Stockholm 036618
Biology Department Teaching Museum, Muncie 046084
Biology Museum, Amman 027364
Biology Museum, Saskatoon 006415
Biomedical Museum, Institute of Medical Research, Kuala Lumpur 027968
Biondi, Massimo, Zürich . . 082949, 130229
Biong, Oslo 079425
Biosca Galería, Madrid 110456
Bipasha Ghosh, London 113505
Bira Gallery, Balaclava 094195
Biraben, Aurèle, Bergerac 120924
Biraben, Aurèle, Bordeaux 120934
Biraben, Aurèle, Sarlat-la-Canéda . 121256
Birbal Sahni Institute of Palaeobotany Museum, Lucknow 022237
Dr. Birbaumer & Eberhardt, Timmendorfer Strand 074059
Birch, Robert, Toronto 097235
Birchall, J., Cleversulzbach 070142
Birchall, John, Neuenstadt 072983
Bircham Contemporary Arts, Holt, Norfolk 113258
Birchills Canal Museum, Walsall . . . 041284
Birchington Antiques, Birchington . . 083519
Birchip Local History Museum, Birchip 000805
Birchmann, Friedrich, Wien 057385
Birchwood Art Gallery, Winnipeg . . . 097575
Bird, Joanna, London 113506
Bird, John, Petworth 086238
Bird in Hand, Washington . 120262, 143038
Birdie, Klaaswaal 121796
Birds Birds Birds, Faversham 113060
Bird's Nest Miniatures, El Paso 088789
Birds of Paradise Lampshades, Toronto 123827
Birds of Vermont Museum, Huntington 044682
Birdsey, Paget 096431
Birdsville Working Museum, Birdsville 000806
Birdtail Country Museum, Birtle . . . 005102
Birger Sandzén Memorial Gallery, Lindsborg 045326
Biri Auksjonsforretning Ans, Biristrand 121846
Biribisso, Milano 127540
Birimbao, Sevilla 110764
Birjand Museum, Birjand 022550
Birka Vikingastaden, Adelsö 036164
Birkdale Antiques, Southport 086656, 131518
Birkenes Bygdemuseum, Birkeland 030775
Birkenhagen, D., Quedlinburg 073395
Birkenhead Antique Centre, Rozelle 056557
Birkenhead Priory and Saint Mary's Tower, Birkenhead 038713
Birkenhead Tramways and Taylor Street Large Object Collections, Birkenhead 038714
Birkhäuser Verlag, Neu-Isenburg . . 134303
Birkholz, Siegfried, Leukersdorf . . . 126216
Birks, Edmonton 096868
Birks Museum, Decatur 043350
Birla Academy of Art and Culture, Kolkata 050310
Birla Academy of Art and Culture Museum, Kolkata 022215
Birla Century Art Gallery,, Mumbai . 105760
Birla Industrial and Technological Museum, Kolkata 022216
Birla Museum, Bhopal 022032
Birla Museum, Pilani 022297
The Birman Gallery, Haywards Heath 113215
Birmingham Antique Centre, Birmingham 083526
Birmingham Antique Mall, Birmingham 087738
Birmingham Art Association, Birmingham 054682
Birmingham Bloomfield Art Center, Birmingham 042229
Birmingham Civil Rights Institute Museum, Birmingham 042222
Birmingham Coin and Jewelry, Birmingham 087739
Birmingham Historical Museum, Birmingham 042230
Birmingham Institute of Art and Design, Birmingham 038722
Birmingham Institute of Art and Design, University of Central England, Birmingham 050803
Birmingham Museum and Art Gallery, Birmingham 038723
Birmingham Museum of Art, Birmingham 042223
Birmingham Museums and Art Gallery, Publications Department, Birmingham 135121
Birmingham Nature Centre, Birmingham 038724
Birmingham Railway Museum, Birmingham 038725
Birnam, New York 117701
Birnbaumer, Josef Gerhard, Attnang-Puchheim 056922
Biro & Sons, San Francisco 132870
Biron 75ter, Saint-Ouen 067735
Bírósági, Budapest 074670
Birsfelder Museum, Birsfelden 036958
Birth & Gramm, Lamone-Cadempino 082521
Birthplace of John Wayne, Winterset 049262
Birties of Worcester, Worcester . . . 114735
Birtwhistle, David, Worcester 114736
Bis, Paris 124591
Bis, Aurelio, Paris 065580
Bis-Art, København 060289
Bisanzio, Roma 106499
Bisarri, Helsinki 060511
La Bisbal, La Bisbal d'Empordá . . . 129455
Bisbee Mining and Historical Museum, Bisbee 042231
La Biscaglina, Milano 075636
Bischöfliches Diözesanmuseum für christliche Kunst, Münster 019141
Bischöfliches Diözesanmuseum Klagenfurt, Klagenfurt 002138
Bischöfliches Dom- und Diözesanmuseum, Trier 020477
Bischöfliches Dom- und Diözesanmuseum Mainz, Mainz 018786
Bischof, Cäsar, Bettlach 129977
Bischof, Helena, Sydney 095277
Bischof, Petra, Oberhausen, Rheinland 073143
Bischofberger & Co., Bruno, Sankt Moritz 111881
Bischofberger, Bruno, Zürich 112048, 135083
Bischoff, Bernhard, Thun 111944
Bischoff, W., Zell am Harmersbach . 074559
Bischoff, Walter, Berlin 101805
Bischoff, Walter, Stuttgart 104967
Il Biscione, Milano 075637
Il Biscione, Milano 106172
Biscuit Tin Museum, Duns 039326
Bisel, Marcos y Molduras, Cartagena 110294
Bishnu Museum, Assam Regimental Centre, Shillong 022332
Bishop Asbury Cottage, West Bromwich 041335
Bishop Bonner's Cottage Museum, East Dereham 039348
Bishop Hill Colony, Bishop Hill 042233
Bishop Hill Heritage Museum, Bishop Hill 042234
Bishop Martin Museum, Natchitoches 046162
Bishop of Winchester's Palace Site, Witney 041423
Bishop Philpotts Gallery, Truro 114600
Bishop Suter Art Gallery, Nelson . . . 030549
Bishop's Gallery, Bishop's Castle . . 112660
Bishops' House Museum, Sheffield 040994
Bishop's Lodge Museum, Hay 001101
The Bishop's Palace, Galveston . . . 044129
Bishop's Stortford Local History Museum, Bishop's Stortford 038748
Bishops Waltham Gallery, Bishop's Waltham 112661
Bishops Waltham Museum, Bishop's Waltham 038750
Bishopsgate Antiques, York 087285
Bishopsgate Gallery, London 113507
Bishopston Books, Bristol 141447
Biskupska Pinakoteka, Dubrovnik . . 007713
Biskupský Dvůr, Moravské Zemské Museum, Brno 008281
Bisman, Jean-Jacques, Rouen 121237
Bismarck Antichitá, Bologna 075058
Bismarck-Museum, Bad Kissingen . 015731
Bismarck-Museum, Schönhausen, Elbe 020082
Bismarck-Museum, Fürstlich von Bismarck'sche Kulturstiftung, Friedrichsruh bei Hamburg 017273
Bisogno, Denis, Sanary-sur-Mer . . . 068111
Il Bisonte, Firenze 050366, 106035
Het Bisschopshof, Utrecht 140544
Bisselink, G.J.M., 's-Heerenberg . . 140455
Bissell, Sara H., Charlotte 087929
Bissingen und Nippenburg, A. Gräfin von, München 126357
Bissinger, George C., München 072663, 126358
Bissogianni, Diana, Athinai 105390
Bissonnet, André, Paris 065581
Bistarelli, Eric, Nice 124503
Bistrot, Washington 093384
Bistrots d'Autrefois, Paris 065582
Bitar, Mohammed & Ahmad, Damascus 083055
Bitforms, New York 117702
Bitouzet, Annie, Moulins (Allier) . . . 064813
Bits and Pieces, Amsterdam 077801
Bits and Pieces, Broken Hill 055566
Bits and Pieces, Egkomi 059948
Bits & Pieces, Kitchener 058869
Bits & Pieces, Pretoria 080732
Bits & Pieces, Ta' Xbiex 077534
Bitschnau, Walter, Kufstein 057136
Bitté Franck, Marckolsheim 064266
Bitter, Alain, Marckolsheim 064267
Bitterli, Ruth Rahel, Basel 082126
Bitterli, Ruth Rahel, Basel 082127
Bitterlich, Christine, Frauenberg . . . 102846
Bitterne Local History Centre, Southampton 041055
Bittersweet Antiques, Atlanta 087456
Bittners, Louisville 089962, 132289
Biuletyn Historii Sztuki, Warszawa . 136020
Biunno, Joseph, New York 090731
Biunno, Joseph, New York 090732
Biunno, Joseph, New York 132449
Biuro Wystaw Artystycznych, Zakopane 109235
Biv, Roy G., Columbus 115764
Biville, Laurent, Rouen 067249
Biwa-ko Bunkakan, Otsu 026997
Bix, Austin 131794
Bix, Kansas City 132203
Bix, Louisville 132290
Bix, Milwaukee 132361
Bix, Tucson 132982
Bix, Tulsa 093286, 132995
Biyun Xuan, Hangzhou 097734
Bizancio, Bogotá 098110, 123895
Bizarr, München 134221
Bizarre, London 085137
Bizarre Antiques, Bristol 083729
Bizarre Bazaar, New York 090733

Bizarre Decorative Arts North West, Altrincham 083284, 130296
Biz'Art, Paris 065583
Bize, Hervé, Nancy 099791, 138230
Bizen Pottery Traditional and Contemporary Art Museum, Bizen 026434
Bizet, Raymond, Beaulieu-sur-Mer . 098936
Bizeul, Michel, Taverny 068369
Bizományi Mûtárgybolt, Szeged . . . 074752
Bizy Bee's Books, Wellington 140671
Bizzarro, Catania 075237
Bizzy Lizzy, Bournemouth 141421
BJ Antiques, Chicago 088035
BJ Antiques, Toronto 059153
B.J. Hales Museum of Natural History, Brandon 005138
BJ Oldies, Houston 089033
BJ Run, Le Tampon 121958
Bjärnums Museum, Bjärnum 036215
Bjästa Auktioner & Loppmarknad, Bjästa 122107
Bjarkøy Museum, Bjarkøy 030776
Bjarne, Edmonton 137633
Bjarne Ness Gallery, Fort Ransom . 043967
Bjerget, København 060290
Bjerggaard, Bo, København 098538
Bjerre, Henrik, København 124027
B.J.F., Paris 065584
Björnberg, Stockholm 081928
Björnsson, Lund 122200
Björverud, Karin H., Lund 129845
Bjørgan Prestegård, Kvikne 030965
Bjorling & Grant, Minneapolis 090347
Bjørn West-Museet, Matredal 031012
Bjørnlund, Sussie, København 098539
Bjørns Antikvariat, København 137883
B.J.'s Antiques, Fort Worth 088837
B.J.'s Antiques, Jacksonville 089386
B.J.'s Antiques, Virginia Beach 093345
B.J.'s Auctions, Edwardstown 120582
BJ's Curiosity Shop, Toledo 093164
Bjugn Bygdatun, Bjugn 030780
BK Art Antiques, Gloucester 122520
B.K.I. Galerie, Darmstadt 102337
BKW-Museum, Mühleberg 037351
Blå Pakhus, København 060291
Blå Stolen, Stockholm 111010
Blaabjerg Egnsmuseum, Varde Museum, Nørre Nebel 009029
Blaase, Rieseby 073535
Blaase, Rieseby 126722
Blaavandshuk Egnsmuseum, Varde Museum, Oksbøl 009054
Blache, Pierre, Grenoble 121011
Black, Winnipeg 059451, 137734
Black, A. & C., London 135191
Black, David, London 085138, 130945
Black, Pétrita, Lausanne 111610
Black Ace Books, Los Angeles 142493
Black American West Museum and Heritage Center, Denver 043397
Black and White Gallery, San Francisco 119611
Black Art by Erni, Houston 116283
Black Art Collection, New Orleans . 117404
Black Art Gallery, New York 117703
Black Art Plus, Columbus 115765
Black Art Production, Oakland 118626
Black Arts, Houston 089034
Black Arts National Diaspora, New Orleans 046248
Black Artwork, Baltimore 115040
The Black Cat Bookshop, Leicester 141715
Black Chat Bookshop, Wendouree . 137136
Black Cherry Blues, Paris 138308
Black Country Living Museum, Dudley 039289
Black Creek Pioneer Village, North York 006050
Black Cultural Archives, London . . . 040090
Black Cultural Centre for Nova Scotia, Dartmouth 005323
Black Diamond Antiques, Bulli 055580
Black Dog Antiques, Bungay 083779
Black Dog Gallery, Virginia Beach . . 093346
Black Dot Gallery, Cremorne 094439
Black Dragon Society, Los Angeles .054683, 116727
Black Dragon Society, Salzburg . . . 052519
Black Fashion Museum, New York . 046301
Black Gull, London 141756
Black Hawk State Historic Site, Hauberg Indian Museum, Rock Island 047491
Black Heritage Gallery, Houston . . . 116284
Black Heritage Museum, Miami . . . 045806
Black Hill, Hamburg 103100
Black Hills Mining Museum, Lead . . 045219
Black Hills Museum of Natural History, Hill City 044541
Black Horse Antiques Centre, Norwich 086110, 131327
Black Images, Dallas 142364
Black Ink, Stow-on-the-Wold 114501
Black & Kausel, Paris 100062
Black Kettle, Mosgiel Dunedin 079158
Black Kettle Museum, Cheyenne . . 042813
Black Laboratory, Seattle 119891
Black Legends of Professional Basketball Museum, Detroit 043434
Black Letter Books, Winnipeg 137735
Black Masks, Bronx 136399
Black Mountain Circle, Abergavenny 112487
Black Mountain College Museum and Arts Center, Asheville 041791
Black Nugget Museum, Ladysmith . 005734
The Black Palette Gallery of Modern Art, Mandaluyong 108832
Black Peppers Gallery, Brisbane . . . 094286
Black Phoenix Galleries, Atlanta . . . 114861
Black & Pretty, Baltimore 115041
Black River Academy Museum, Ludlow 045518
Black River Historical Society of Lorain Museum, Lorain 045403
Black Rock Arts Foundation, San Francisco 047855
The Black Sheep, Tetbury 086849
Black Sheep Books, Jacksonville . . 142462
Black Sheep Gallery, Hawarden . . . 113207
Black Stump Books, Croydon 136872
Black Sun Books, New York 142636
Black Swamp Creek Antiques, Tiaro 056711
Black Swan, Oakland 142707
Black Swan Books, Richmond 142823
Black Swan Gallery, Congleton 112898
Black Tulip Antiques, Denver 088661
Black Watch of Canada Regimental Memorial Museum, Montréal 005913
Black & White Art, Halmstad 110935
Blackamoor Antiques, New Orleans 090517
Blackberry Farm-Pioneer Village, Aurora 041911
Blackberry Patch, Columbus 088387
Blackbird, San Francisco 119612
Blackbird Antiques, Naracoorte . . . 056313
Blackbird Pottery, Dunedin 108427
Blackbrook Antiques Village, Weeford 087063
Blackburn, Charles H., Neuilly-sur-Seine 064989, 138246
Blackburn, Norman, Stamford 086683
Blackburn Museum and Art Gallery, Blackburn, Lancashire 038751
Blacket Book's, Edinburgh 141571
Blackfish Gallery, Portland 118979
Blackflash, Saskatoon 135627
Blackfriars Bookshop, Victor Harbor 137125
Blackgang Sawmill and Saint Catherine's Quay, Blackgang 038754
Blackheath, London 141757
Blackheath Antiques, Mount Victoria 056296, 137014
Blackheath Gallery, London 113508
Blackley, Manchester 131255
Blacklock, Egham 141593
Blackman Museum, Snohomish . . . 048206
Blackmon, James, San Francisco . . 092743
Blackmore, Cassandria, Seattle . . . 119892
Blackpool Mill, Narberth 040512
Blackridge Community Museum, Blackridge 038756
Blackrock Upholstery, Blackrock . . 074862
Blacksburg Regional Art Association, Blacksburg 054684
Blacksmith Shop Museum, Dover-Foxcroft 043497
Blacksmiths Antiques, Blacksmiths 055514
Blacksmith's Cottage, Bacchus Marsh 000757
Blackstone, Honolulu 088937
Blackstone, Linda, Pinner 114249
Blackstone Valley Historical Society Museum, Lincoln 045317
Blackthorn Gallery, Riverton 095148
Blackville Historical Museum, Blackville 005103
Blackwater Draw Museum, Eastern New Mexico University, Portales 047150
Blackwater Pine Antiques, Truro . . .086926, 131611
Blackwater Valley Museum, Benburb 038673
Blackwell, London 141758
Blackwell, Oxford 135291
Blackwell Street Center for the Arts, Denville 043422
Blackwell - The Arts and Crafts House, Bowness-on-Windermere 038799
Blackwell's Rare Books, Oxford . . . 141981
Blackwood, Pittsburgh 118903
Blackwood, Simon, Hawick 130776
Blackwood Gallery, University of Toronto at Missisanga, Mississauga 005889
Blades, Katrina L., Birmingham . . . 087740
Bladud House Antiques, Bath 083419
Bläser, Markus, Leipzig 103858
Blaeser, Norbert, Steffeln . 104947, 134404
Blaess, Thomas, Bern 111246
Blätter für Grafik und Literatur, Trier 135753
De Blaeue Acolye, Vlissingen 140563
Blågårds Plads Antikvariat, København 137884
Blagbrough, Saint Louis 119188
Blagg, Daniel, Fort Worth 116134
Blagoveščenskij Sobor, Gosudarstvennyj muzej-zapovednik Moskovskij Kreml, Moskva 033366
Blaim, Adolf, Messern 095680
Blain, Claude, Montréal 058929
Blaine County Historical Museum, Hailey 044387
Blaine County Museum, Chinook . . 042904
Blaine House, Augusta 041903
Blaine Lake Museum, Blaine Lake . 005104
Blair, Brad, Los Angeles 089706
Blair, Robert, Richmond 092063
Blair Antiques, Blair Atholl 083557
Blair Castle, Blair Atholl 038762
Blair House Antiques, Washington . 093385
Blair House Museum, Kentville 005680
Blair Museum of Lithophanes, Toledo 048566
Blairman & Sons, H., London 085139
The Blairs Museum, Aberdeen 038444
Blais, Michel, Vancouver 097428
Blais, Michel, Vancouver 097429
Blais, Simon, Montréal 096981
Blaise, Benoît, Paris 124592
Blaise Castle House Museum, Bristol 038858
Blaizot, Claude, Paris 138309
Blake, Woodbridge 142169
The Blake Gallery, Crewkerne 112920
The Blake Gallery, York 114748
Blake & Hawkins, London 085140
Blake Museum, Bridgwater 038832
Blake's Lock Museum, Reading . . . 040810
Blakesley Hall, Birmingham 038726
Blakey, Colin, Nelson 086045, 131295
Blakey & Sons, J.H., Brierfield 083679
Blakstad Sykehus Museum, Asker . 030744
Blana, Matthias, Ketterschwang . . . 126033
Blanc, München 134222
Blanc, New York 090734
Blanc, Alain, Castres 062032
Blanc, Alain, Paris 100063
Blanc, André, Toulouse 068483
Blanc, Annie, Lyon 099542
Blanc, Anselme, Paris 065585
Blanc, Fernand, Riaz 082740
Blanc, Philippe, La Canourgue 063302
Blanc, Robert, Gaillac 099278
Blanc Bertrand, Marssac-sur-Tarn . 064405
Blanc et Bleu, Jouy-en-Josas 063261
Blanchaert, Milano 075638
Blanchard, Froxfield 084446
Blanchard, London 085141, 130946
Blanchard & Co., New Orleans 090518
Blanchard, Nîmes 065171
Blanchard, Tourtour 101383
Blanchard, Albert, Paris 138310
Blanchart & Cie., Gerard, Bruxelles . 133261
Blanche & Co., Los Angeles 089707
Blanche, Ariane, Nantes 124480
Blanchet, Deni, Montréal 058930
Blanchet, Monique, Ribérac 067130
Blanchet-Joron-Derem, Paris 121117
Blanchetière, Yves, L'Aigle 121026
Blanchetti, Jean-François de, Paris 065586
Blanchon, J.P., Lisboa 079878
Blanchy & Lacombe, Bordeaux 120935
Blanckaert, Alain, Reims 067059
Blanco, Marcelo, Buenos Aires 055180
Blanco, Mercedes, Pamplona 081512
Blanco Family Museum, Angono . . . 031620
Blanco Seco, Iván, Gijón 081122
Blanco y Negro, Valencia . 081646, 129758
Blancon, Gilles, Hannover 071387
Blancpain & Stepczynski, Genève . . 111428
Le Bland, West Wyalong 095394
Bland, Gerald, New York 090735
Bland District Historical Museum, West Wyalong 001610
Blanden Memorial Art Museum, Fort Dodge 043910
Blandford Art Society, Wimborne Minster 054311
Blandford Forum Museum, Blandford Forum 038764
Blank, Herbert, Stuttgart 139755
Blank, Hubert, Angelburg 101584
Blank, Peter, Wilburgstetten 074435
Blank, Reinhard, Bad Vilbel 121308
Blank, Thomas, Basel 129911
Blank Art, Kyïv 112395
Blank Canvass Art Gallery, Houston 116285
Blanke, Bernhard, Berlin . 101806, 138748
Blankenburger, Ingrid, Berlin 138749
Blankschmiede Neimke, Dassel . . . 016649
Blaquière, Geneviève, Sorèze 068263
Blas Bruni Celli, Caracas 143056
Blas Garcia, Jose Maria, Barcelona 129330
Blås & Knåda, Stockholm 111011
Blas Vega, Jose, Madrid 081251
Blasberg, Doris & Hartmut, Basberg 069479
Blasco, Monterrey 107516
Blasco, Francesco, Milano 075639
Blasco Querol, Maria Antonia, Sabadell 110727
Blaser, R., Lahnstein 072115
Blaser & Herrmann, Bern . 082199, 129949
Blasi, Angelo, Bologna 075059
Blasichc, Lima 079543, 129001
Blasingame, Fort Worth 088838
Blasinstrumenten-Sammlung, Zimmerwald 037753
Blaskovich Múzeum, Pest Megyei Múzeumok Igazgatósága, Tápiószele 021902
Blasmusik-Museum, Ratten 002504
Blason, A Coruña 081055
Blassiaux, Richard, Paris 124593
Blast From the Past, Kansas City . .089485, 132204
Blast From the Past, Milwaukee . . . 090277
Blasthaus, San Francisco 119613
Blasum, Gertrude, Hamburg 125802

Blaszczyk, Michael, Bad Homburg v.d.Höhe . . . 101651
Blatchfords, San Diego . . . 132846
Blatt, New York . . . 090736
Blatter, Hans-D., Münster . . . 139561
Blattner, Eggenfelden . . . 070511
Blatz, Almut, Konstanz . . . 072047
Blau, Daniel, München . . . 104155
Blau, Doris & Leslie, New York . . . 090737
Blau, Dorothy, Saint Louis . . . 119189
Blau, Siegfried, Düsseldorf . . . 102476
Blau-gelbe Viertelsgalerie, Industrieviertel, Bad Fischau . . . 001713
Blau-gelbe Viertelsgalerie, Mostviertel, Weistrach . . . 002820
Blau-gelbe Viertelsgalerie, Waldviertel, Zwettl, Niederösterreich . . . 003075
Blau-gelbe Viertelsgalerie, Weinviertel Weinviertel, Mistelbach an der Zaya . . . 002316
Blau & Scheibl, Wien . . . 057386
Die Blaue Eule, Essen . . . 102670, 133914
Blaue Galerie, Dreieich . . . 102418
Der Blaue Laden, Oberhausen, Rheinland . . . 104497
Blaues Schloß, Obernzenn . . . 019404
Het Blauwe Huys, Melick . . . 128770
De Blauwe Olifant, Maastricht . . . 078596
De Blauwe Tulp, Groningen . . . 078402
De Blauwe Vlinder, Haarlem . . . 108054
Blåvand Museum, Varde Museum, Blåvand . . . 008820
Blåvand Redningsbådsmuseum, Varde Museum, Blåvand . . . 008821
Blawnox Antiques, Pittsburgh . . . 091792
Blay, G.D., Dorking . . . 084186
Blayney Barnett, Olaf, London . . . 130947
Blaze, Bristol . . . 112716
Błażej, Piotr, Poznań . . . 129060
Blazing Sun, Cincinnati . . . 115609
Blazquez, Miguel, Madrid . . . 141030
Blazquez Barbero, Carmelo, Madrid 081252
Blázquez Barbero, Guillermo, Madrid . . . 141031
Bleachers, Cincinnati . . . 088215
Bleak House, Broadstairs . . . 038873
Bleakhouse Museum, Fogo Island . 005450
Blech, Wolfgang, Heilbronn 071470, 125905
Der Blecheimer, Düsseldorf . . . 070363
Blechschmidt, Gotthard, Frankfurt am Main . . . 070730
Blecks, Prof. G. H., Düsseldorf . . . 125523
Le Bled, Sophie, Requeil . . . 067123
Bledel, Marcos F., Buenos Aires . . . 094062
Bleeker Street, Chicago . . . 088036
Blehle, Karl, Seligenstadt . . . 104882
Blei, Karl, Reiskirchen . . . 073481, 126710
Bleibtreu, Clara, La Garenne-Colombes . . . 099398
Bleibtreu-Antik, Berlin . . . 069579
Bleibtreu Galerie, Berlin . . . 101807
Bleich-Rossi, Graz . . . 095519
Bleichhäuschen, Rheda-Wiedenbrück . . . 104739
Bleier Milton, A., New York . . . 117704
Bleijenberg, Amsterdam . . . 107683
Bleikeller, Sankt Petri Domgemeinde, Bremen . . . 016408
Bleisch, Adrian, Arbon . . . 111129
Blekinge Auktionsverk, Ronneby . . 122232
Blekinge Museum, Karlskrona . . . 036382
Bleloch Museum, Johannesburg . . . 034645
Blem, København . . . 060292
Blench & Son, John, Saint Helier . . 142036
Blend, Barry, Collioure . . . 099159
Blender, Paddington . . . 095020
BlendeVier, Oldenburg, Oldenburg . 104538
Blenheim, Fairford . . . 084370
Blenheim Palace, Woodstock . . . 041438
Blenko Museum of Seattle, Seattle . 048074
Blens & Hartmayer, Ofterdingen . . . 073192
Blenwell, San Francisco . . . 132871
Blésoise, Blois . . . 061520, 124104
Bleß, Hartmut, Großefehn . . . 103019
Bletchley Park Exhibition, Bletchley 038768
Bleu 214, Toulon (Var) . . . 068444
Bleu de Paris, Paris . . . 065587
Le Bleu du Ciel, Lyon . . . 064088
Bleu Galerie, Genève . . . 111429
Bleu Line, Lisboa . . . 129147
Bleu Passé Antiquités, Paris . . . 065588
Bleu Passion, Fréjus . . . 099274
Bleu Sonatine, Dinan . . . 062681, 099220
Bleu Vert, Fort-de-France . . . 107459
Bleu-Vert Antiquités, Paris . . . 065589
Bleue Comme Une Orange, Ajaccio 060738, 098803
Bleue Forêt, Salers . . . 101243
Blewbury Antiques, Blewbury . . . 083564
Blewett, E.K., Austin . . . 087565
Blewitt-Harrison-Lee Museum, Columbus . . . 043099
Bleymaier, E.A., Egling . . . 070514, 102603, 125572
B.L.G., Padova . . . 076075
Blicheregnens Museum, Kjellerup . 008954
Blichermuseet på Herningsholm, Herning . . . 008901
Blickensdorff, Berlin . . . 101808
Blickfang, Weilheim, Oberbayern . . 105181
Blickling Hall, Norwich . . . 040601
Blickpunkt, Düsseldorf . . . 070364
Blickpunkt, Erftstadt . . . 102638
Blickpunkt, Hamburg . . . 103101
Bligh Museum of Pacific Exploration, Bruny Island . . . 000856
Blikmuseum De Blikvanger, Renesse . . . 030055
Blind Tiger Gallery, Quezon City . . . 108854
Blindaž gde podpisan akt o kapituljacii, Oblastnoj istoriko-chudožestvennyj Muzej, Kaliningrad . . . 033211
Blindehistorisk Museum, Hellerup . 008892
Blinden-Museum, Berlin . . . 015995
Blindenmuseum, Landesbildungszentrum für Blinde, Hannover . . . 017750
Blindenmuseum, Staatliche Museen zu Berlin - Stiftung Preußischer Kulturbesitz, Berlin . . . 015996
Blinds & Shutters, Memphis . . . 132317
Blink Gallery, London . . . 113509
Blinky, Denver . . . 088662
Blissett, Gary, Long Preston . . . 113991
Blists Hill Victorian Town Open Air Museum, Madeley . . . 040382
Blitz, Amsterdam . . . 077802
BLM Bauernhaus-Museum Bortfeld, Braunschweigisches Landesmuseum, Wendeburg . . . 020793
Blob Art, Livorno . . . 106116
Bloc Acier, Rouen . . . 067250
Bloch, Berlin . . . 125175
Bloch, Oberhausen, Rheinland . . . 073144
Bloch, Peter Adolf, Innsbruck . . . 095577
Blochererschule, Berufsfachschule für Kommunikationsdesign & Innenarchitektur, München . . . 050187
Blochwitz, J., Hamburg . . . 071207
Block, René, Berlin . . . 101809, 133755
Block, Rolf, Berlin . . . 101810
Blocker, Peggy, San Antonio . . . 092491
Blockheads and Granary Antiques, Flore . . . 084414
Blockhouse Museum, Merrickville . 005861
Blocquel-Chapart, Françoise, Pau . .066700, 100981
Blodveimuseet, Bygdetunet, Saltnes, Rognan, Saltdal, Rognan . . . 031142
Blöcher, Heidi, Karlsruhe . . . 125996
Blöchle, Peter, Basel . . . 082128, 129912
Blödorn & Ewert, Krummwisch . . . 134134
Blohm, Reiner, Freiburg im Breisgau . . . 070826
Blois Antiquités, La Chaussée-Saint-Victor . . . 063330
Blokesch, Hildegard & Otto, Bamberg . . . 069445
Blokesch, Otto, Frensdorf . . . 070875
Blokken, Rotterdam . . . 140517
Blokkodden Villmarksmuseet, Engerdal . . . 030824
De Blokschaaf, Bussum . . . 078128
Blokwachterswoning Waterhuizen, Waterhuizen . . . 030314
Blom, Dordrecht . . . 107974
Blome, Dietmar, Worpswede . . . 134466
Blome, Lars, Hannover . . . 103263
Blome-Balogh, O., Buinen . . . 128614
Blomqvist, Minde . . . 079402
Blomqvist, Oslo . . 079426, 108705, 121863
Blomqvist & Co, Sollentuna . . . 122242
Blomskogs Bildemont & Auktioner, Årjäng . . . 122100
Blond Fine Art, St James . . . 056626
Blondeau & Associés, Paris . . . 065590
Blondel, Alain, Paris . . . 100064
Blondel, Jean-Michel, Talmontiers . 068354
Blondie's Antiques, Louisville . . . 089963
Bloom, San Diego . . . 092617
Bloom & Son, N., London . . . 085142
Bloom Mansion, Trinidad History Museum, Trinidad . . . 048611
Bloomfield, Bungendore . . . 094329
Bloomfield, London . . . 130948
Bloomfield, Pittsburgh . . . 091793
Bloomfield Academy Museum, Bloomfield . . . 042254
Bloomfield Science Museum Jerusalem, Jerusalem . . . 022943
Blooming Art Gallery, Los Angeles . 116728
Bloomington Art Center, Bloomington . . . 042268
Bloomington Historical Museum, Bloomington . . . 042269
Bloomsbury Antiques, Jolimont . . . 056022
Bloomsbury Book Auctions, London 122579
Bloomsbury & Co, Ottawa . . . 059032
Blore, Nottingham . . . 141969
Blosfield, Tampa . . . 132949
Bloss, Merzhausen . . . 121514
Blossom Street Gallery, Houston . . 116286
Blouet, Pascal, Mayenne . . . 121068
Bloume, Christian, Sainte-Marie . . . 129212
Blount-Bridgers House/ Hobson Pittman Memorial Gallery, Tarboro . . . 048502
Blount Mansion, Knoxville . . . 045033
Blowfly Art & Design, Brunswick . . 123198
Blowing Rock, Charlotte . . . 087930
Bloxham, London . . . 085143, 130949
Bloxham, John, London . . . 113510
Bloxham Village Museum, Bloxham 038770
Blu Old Sheffield, Roma . . . 076338
Bluart, Padova . . . 106392
Blue Antiques, Dallas . . . 088466
Blue Antiques, Toronto . . . 059154
Blue Beyond, Isle-of-Tiree . . . 113306
Blue Butterfly, Nice . . . 065052
Blue Dolphin Gallery, Mooloolaba . . 094875
Blue Dot Gallery, Bristol . . . 112717
The Blue Dot Gallery, Toronto . . . 097236
Blue Earth County Historical Museum, Mankato . . . 045641
Blue Elephant, Maastricht . . . 078597
Blue Flyer Auctions, Bendigo . . . 120565
Blue Fonz, Antwerpen . . . 057682
Blue Galerie, Mönchengladbach . . . 104091
Blue Gallery, Kansas City . . . 116556
The Blue Gallery, London . . . 113511
Blue Gallery, Richmond, New South Wales . . . 095129
Blue Gallery, Wolverhampton . . . 114724
The Blue Heron, Vancouver . . . 059339
Blue Hills, Grose Vale . . . 055922
Blue Hills Trailside Museum, Milton 045878
Blue House Antique, West Hollywood . . . 093453
Blue Lake Fine Arts Camp, Twin Lake . . . 052286
Blue Lias, Lyme Regis . . . 114010
Blue Licks Battlefield Museum, Mount Olivet . . . 046061
Blue Moon Antiques, Taranaki . . . 079249
Blue Moon Books, Waikato . . . 140661
Blue Moon Contemporary Art, Haslemere . . . 113196
Blue Moon Contemporary Art, Henley-on-Thames . . . 113230
Blue Moon Trading, Tampa . . . 093109
Blue Mountain Gallery, New York . . 117705
Blue Mountains Antiques, Woodford 056845
Blue Nile Papyrus, Cairo . . . 098618
Blue Oyster Gallery, Dunedin . . . 108428
Blue Pegasus, Albuquerque . . . 087377
Blue Penguin, Russell . . . 079233
Blue Pomegranate Studios, Omaha 118687
Blue Pony Gallery, Charlotte . . . 115278
Blue Pump Antiques, Toronto . . . 059155
Blue Ridge Institute and Museum, Ferrum . . . 043839
Blue Ruin, Pittsburgh . . . 118904
Blue Shore Gallery, Taurikura . . . 108581
Blue Sky, Oregon Center for the Photographic Arts, Portland . . . 047167
Blue Sky Books, San Francisco . . . 142931
Blue Space Gallery, Ho Chi Minh City . . . 120503
Blue Star Red Cloud, New York . . . 117706
Blue Steel Art, Bern . . . 082200
Blue Sun Gallery, Ha Noi . . . 120452
Blue Tulip Gallery, Windsor . . . 114708
Blue & White, Jerusalem . . . 105907
Blue Words, Lyon . . . 138135
Bluebell Railway, Uckfield . . . 041256
Blueberry Hill in Old Town, Sacramento . . . 092140
Bluebird Art Gallery, Louisville . . . 116931
Bluebird Studio, Indianapolis . . . 116445
Bluebottle Art Gallery 415 E Pine St, Seattle . . . 119893
Blüchermuseum, Kaub . . . 018206
Blüm, Bad Dürkheim . . . 069275
Bluemingdeal, Indianapolis . . . 089276
Blümmel, C. & N., Hasselberg . . . 071426
Bluemoon Gallery, Tunbridge Wells . 114608
Blueprint Galerie, Dinslaken . . . 102374
The Blueroom Gallery, San Francisco . . . 119614
Bluestocking Books, Boston . . . 142245
Bluestone Art, Lincoln . . . 113396
Bluestone Cottage and Museum, Coburg . . . 000935
Bluestone Gallery, Devizes . . . 112946
Bluestone Museum, Hinton . . . 044558
Bluestone Stables Gallery, Axedale . 094186
Bluette, Christian, Bordeaux . . . 061593
Bluewood Gallery, Redfern . . . 095124
Bluff Maritime Museum, Bluff . . . 030454
Bluff Park Antiques, Birmingham . . 087741
Bluff Park Rare Books, Long Beach 142483
Bluff Road Upholstery, Indianapolis 132152
Blum, New York . . . 090738
Blum, Charly, Antibes-Juan-les-Pins . . . 060915
Blum, Egon, Staad . . . 082827
Blum, Karlheinz, Spechbach 073873, 126817
Blum, Norbert, Marambat . . . 064252
Blum, Peter, New York . . . 117707
Blum & Magener, Uetikon am See . 130199
Blum & Poe, Los Angeles . . . 116729
Blum-Tuor, Ellen, Zürich . . . 082950
Bluma, Jed, Baltimore . . . 087646
Blumberger Mühle, NABU Erlebniszentrum, Angermünde . . . 015542
Blume, Birgitt, Hamburg . . . 071208
Blume, Claudia, Holzkirchen, Oberbayern . . . 103401
Blumenhof Galerie, Kehrsatz . . . 111578
Blumer, Rolf-Dieter, Schwäbisch Gmünd . . . 126782
Blumes antikvariat, Frederiksberg . 137867
Blumgarten & Co., Chicago . . . 115371
Blumka, Anthony, New York . . . 117708
Blunck, Uwe, Neumünster . . . 104415
Blunden, Vanessa, Wimborne . . . 114700
Blunderbuss, London . . . 085144
Bly, John, London . . . 085145
Bly, John, Tring . . . 086918
Blyburgate Antiques, Beccles 083465, 130361

Blyth, Manchester 114039
B.M, Bordeaux 124116
BM Çağdaş Sanat Merkezi, İstanbul 112291
B.M. Magazine, London 136186
BM Traders, Singapore 109778
BMB Galerie, Amsterdam 107684
BML Fine Arts, New York 117709
BMV Books, Toronto 137700
BMW Museum, München 019041
B'nai B'rith Klutznick National Jewish Museum, Washington 048888
B.N.C., Paris 065591
Bô, Aubagne 061023
BO!, Stockholm 081929
Bo Fang Shopping Arcade, Shenzhen 097971
B.O. Furniture Refinishing, El Paso . 132063
Bo-Jo's Antique Mall, Memphis . . . 090057
Bo-Kaap Museum, Iziko Museums of Cape Town, Cape Town 034574
Bø Museum, Bø i Telemark 030782
Bo Plastic, Paris 065592
Boa, Gianni, Padova 127799
BOA2000, Wil 141311
Boada Saquero, Agustin, Barcelona 080809
Boaden, Sandra, Richard & Chris, Hexham 084676
Boal Mansion Museum, Boalsburg . 042279
Boam, Clare, Horncastle 084735
Boandik Cultural Museum, Beachport 000778
Boardman, Haverhill 122539
Boardwalkart, Merimbula 094834
Boarman Arts Center, Martinsburg . 045712
Boase Antiques, Exmouth 084365
Boat Museum, Ellesmere Port 039434
Boat'art, Saint Paul 119279
Boatmen's National Bank Art Collection, Saint Louis 047653
Boats 'n Pieces, Paradise Point . . . 056438
Bob Burns Museum, Van Buren . . . 048743
Bob Campbell Geology Museum, Clemson University, Clemson 042974
Bob Jones University Museum and Gallery, Greenville 044348
Bob Marley Museum, Kingston 026381
Bobbins, Whitby 087128, 131680
Bobbitt Visual Arts Center, Albion . . 041610
Bobcat, Chicago 088037
Bobcat, Chicago 131888
Bober, Vitoria-Gasteiz 081715
Boberg & Kring, Jork 071669
Bobet, Rennes (Ille-et-Vilaine) 067103
Bobet, Rennes (Ille-et-Vilaine) 067104
Bobik, Peter Hans, Graz 057004
Bobik, Dr. W. & M., Graz 057005
Bobo-Gruppe, Bergisch Gladbach . . 053061
Bob's Attic Antiques, Saint Louis . . 092207
Bob's Coin Store, Milwaukee 090278
Bob's Coins, Milwaukee 090279
Bob's Comics, Birmingham 087742
Bob's Custom Woodworking, Columbus 131977
Bob's Used Furniture, Providence . . 092034
Bobsien, Winfried, Hamburg 071209
BOC Museum, The Charles King Collection, London 040091
Boca Raton Historical Society Museum, Boca Raton 042281
Boca Raton Museum of Art, Boca Raton 042282
Bocarra, Dario, Paris 065593
Bocca, Milano 134605
Bocca, Milano 140045
Bocca Tigris, Stockholm 081930
Boccador, Jacqueline, Paris 065594
Boccard, Olivier, Villemoyenne 068908
Boccarossa, Padova 076076
Bocchia, Ettore, Parma 076199
Bocchini, Ulderico, Perugia 127869
Boch, Eva, Kürnach 072106
Boche, H.F.A., Berlin 101811, 125176
Bochmann, K., Limburg an der Lahn 072257
Bocholter Brouwerij Museum, Bocholt 003236
Bochon, Pascal, Vincennes 068993
Bochumer Antiquariat, Bochum . . . 138882
Bochumer Künstlerbund e.V., Bochum 053062
Bock, Augsburg 069218
Bock, François de, Lille 124315
Bock, Friedel P., Wien 123489
Bock, Günter, Saarbrücken 073625
Bock, H.-P., Nörten-Hardenberg . . . 073063
Bock & Herchen, Bad Honnef 133732
Bock von Wülfingen, Regina, Lankau 126171
Bockrath, Cleveland 115690
Bockwindmühle Brehna, Brehna . . 016399
Bockwindmühlenmuseum, Trebbus 020462
Bocquet, Emmanuel, Frevent 062947
Bocquier, Gérard, Nantes 138237
Bocquillon, André, Honfleur 063164
Bodacious Books, Nashville 142594
Bodanrück-Bauernmuseum, Allensbach 015481
Bodart & Valter, Sipplingen 104911
Bodaskogs Affärs- och Postmuseum, Aneby 036183
Boddington, Pat, Mount Glorious . . 094905
Bode, K., Dissen am Teutoburger Wald 070259
Bode, Klaus, Borgholzhausen 069954
Bode, Klaus D., Nürnberg . 104473, 134317
Bode, Ralf, Bonn 069913
Bode, Stefan, Braunschweig 138917
Bode, Wolfgang, Meckenheim, Rheinland 072483
La Bodeguita del Medio Obrero, Medellín 098255
Bodek, Hannover 103264, 134036
Bodelwyddan Castle Museum, Bodelwyddan 038771
Bodenbinder, Anne-Louise, Menden 126306
Bodenheimer, Heinz, Frankfurt am Main 070731
Bodenheimer Heimatmuseum, Bodenheim 016289
Bodenschatz, Jeanine, Basel 111168
Bodensee-Galerie, Singen, Hohentwiel 104907
Bodensee-Naturmuseum, Konstanz 018375
Bodes & Bode, Den Haag 078174
Bodhi, Bergen op Zoom 078068
Bodhi, Portland 091905
Bodhi Tree Bookstore, Los Angeles . 142494
Bodhouse Antiques, Birkenhead . . . 083523
Bodiam Castle, Robertsbridge 040842
Bodie State Historic Park, Bridgeport 042405
Bodijn, Jan, Leiderdorp 128747
Bodin, Strasbourg 068305
Bodin, François, Tours 068584
Bodin, Sophie, Soussans 068277
Bodin, Thierry, Paris 138311
Bodin-Lemaire, Brigitte, Olonne-sur-Mer 065265
Bodis, Frank, Wiesbaden 127007
Bodmin and Wenford Railway, Bodmin 038772
Bodmin Antiques Centre, Bodmin . . 083567
Bodmin Town Museum, Bodmin . . . 038773
Bodnar, Joseph, New Brunswick . . 122977
Bodoque, J., Madrid 129581
Bodrum Sualtı Arkeolojisi Müzesi, Bodrum 038026
Body, Martin, London 130950
Body Focus, Providence 092035
Bodybuilder & Sportsman Gallery, Chicago 115372
Boe, Patrick, Marennes 064280
Böblinger Kunstverein, Böblingen . . 053063
Boeck, de, Antwerpen 133247
Böck, Anton, Wien 057387, 123490
Boeck, Paule de, Gent 096285
Boeck, Roswitha, Berlin 069580
Böck, Wilhelm & Sophie, Langenbach, Kreis Freising 126166
Boeckel, Heidi, Aschaffenburg 069190
Böckelmann, Uwe, Bretnig-Hauswalde 125395
Böcking, Heinrich, Ralingen 126677
Böckli, August, Aathal-Seegräben .082074, 129891
Böcksteiner Montanmuseum Hohe Tauern, Böckstein 001759
Böd of Gremista Museum, Lerwick . 039987
Böddeker & Schlichting, Jürgen, Paderborn 126609
Bödeker, Erich, Hannover 103265
Böer, Claudia, Hannover 134037
Bögge, Alfred, Hamm, Westfalen . . 071361
Böggemeyer, W., Hasbergen 071424
Boegler, Peter, Augsburg 121297
Boegly, Serge, Rupt-sur-Moselle . . 067332
Boehl & Oppermann, Bremerhaven . 070052
Böhlau, Wien 133184
Böhlau Verlag, Köln 134099
Böhlen, Hans, Belp 082191
Böhler, Julius, München 072664
Böhler, Lothar, Oppenweiler 073222
Böhler, Wolfgang, Bensheim 101755, 133742, 138725
Böhm, Potsdam 121577
Böhm, Bernhard, Freilassing 125674
Böhm, Harald, Berlin 069581, 138750
Böhm, J., Bielefeld 069818
Böhm, M., Karlsruhe 071713
Boehm Gallery, San Marcos 047910
Böhme, Husum, Nordsee 139283
Böhme, Cornelia, Gutenberg 071153, 103039
Böhme, Jürgen, Kassel 126013
Böhme, Sibylle, Berlin 138751
Böhme, Thomas, Dresden 125485
Böhringer, Georg, Düsseldorf 070365, 125524
Böhringer, Heinrich, Wunsiedel 139878
Boeijink, Nico, Haarlem 128687
Boek & Glas, Amsterdam 140283
Het Boekdorado, Den Haag 140388
Böke, Christiane, Neulingen, Enzkreis 126535
Boekelder, Südlohn 074020
Böken, Haitger, Reinheim 104706
De Boekenbeurs, Middelburg 140498
De Boekenboet, Alkmaar 140267
De Boekenboot, Hallum 140448
Boekendaal, Gouda 140427
De Boekenhof Emmen, Emmen . . . 140418
De Boekenkelder, Groningen 140430
't Boekenschuurtje, Warffum 140568
De Boekenvondst, De Bilt 140382
De Boekenvriend, Albergen 140266
De Boekerij, Baarn 140358
Boekhout, Phoenix 091722
Boekie Woekie, Amsterdam 107685
Boekie Woekie, Amsterdam 134774, 140284
Boe(k)tiekske, Mechelen 137527
't Boekwerk Antiquariaat, Nijmegen 140505
Boelens, Marian, Zwolle 078886
Bölicke, F., Schortens 073726
Böll, Klaus, Würzburg 074492
Böll, R., Flintbek 070711
Böllner, Herbert, Lauter 126177
Boema, Praha 098422
Boemboem, Utrecht 108242
Boer, H. de, Groningen 078403
Boer, M.L. de, Amsterdam 077803
Boer, Peter de, Amsterdam 077804
Boer, Theo de, Zandpol 140576
Boer, Wim de, Alkmaar 077709
Boer Tala Zhou Museum and Gallery, Bole 007020
Börde-Heimatmuseum, Lamstedt . . 018472
Börde-Museum Burg Ummendorf, Ummendorf 020536
Bördenheimatmuseum Heeslingen, Heeslingen 017819
Boerderij Klein Hulze, Almen 029139
Boerderij Museum Duurswold, Slochteren 030160
Boerderijmuseum De Bovenstreek, Oldebroek 029985
Boerderijmuseum De Lebbenbrugge, Borculo 029326
Boerderijmuseum Zelhem, Zelhem . 030381
Boeree, Philip, Haarlem 128688
Boerenantiek, Eindhoven 078331
Boerenbondsmuseum, Gemert 029600
Boerenkrijgmuseum, Overmere . . . 003701
Boerenwagenmuseum, Buren, Gelderland 029371
Börjeson, Malmö 110961
Börjesson, D., Göteborg 110906
Boerner, C.G., Düsseldorf . 102477, 139006
Boerner, C.G., New York 117710
Börner, Helmut, Dresden . 070309, 121375
Börnert, Armin, Eichenau 125575
Boerth, Richard, Seattle . . 092968, 132930
Bösch, W., Bayreuth 138720
Böschenstein, Thomas, Zürich 082951
Boesen, Hans, Mindelheim 104075
Boesendorfer, New York 090739
Böser, D., Weingarten, Baden 074313, 105193
Boesky, Marianne, New York 117711
Boesmans, M., Köln 071915
Bössmann, Osnabrück 139636
Bösterling, H. B., Köln . . . 071916, 126067
Böttcher, Melsdorf 104058
Boettcher, G., Hannover 071388
Böttcher, Gerhard, Fürstenfeldbruck 102894
Böttcher, H., Königswinter 072037
Böttcher, Ruth, Grafing bei München 125750
Böttger, Gunter, Leipzig 103859
Boetto, Genova 075442
Boetto, Genova 121688
Bœuf, Frederic, Toulon (Var) 124961
Boeuf, Robert, Toulon (Var) 101317
Bofors Industrimuseum, Karlskoga . 036377
Bog-Børsen, København 137885
Bogan House Antiques, Totnes 086904
Bogapott, Tallinn 098694
Bogart, Groningen 078404
Bogart, Bremmer & Bradley, Seattle 092969, 132931
Bogat, Baltimore 087647, 131816
Bogati, Québec 097133
Bogdanoff, New Orleans 117405
Bøger & Kuriosa, København 137886
Boggiano, H.Y.H., Buenos Aires . . . 094063
Boglio, Jean-Louis & Janet, Currumbin 136874
Bogner, Dorothe, Frankfurt am Main 070732
Bogner, E., Landshut 072142
Bogner, Willi, München 126359
Bognor Regis Museum, Bognor Regis 038777
Bogormen, København 137887
Bogorodickij Dvorec-muzej i Park, Bogorodick 033037
Bogstad Gård, Oslo 031071
Bogstadveien Antikk, Oslo 079427
Bogtrykmuseet, Esbjerg 008841
Bogwood Sculpture Artists, Newtowncashel 022846
Bogyoke Aung San Museum, Yangon 029073
Bohan, Ned, New York 090740
Bohard, Marie, Auch 061049
Bohec, Alain, Nantes 064906
La Boheme, Gisborne 140627
Bohemia, Bromsgrove 112746
Bohemia Antiques, Vancouver 059340
Bohemia Art, Ústí nad Labem 098509
Bohemia Galleries, Beverley 112627
Bohemia Paper, Praha . . . 098423, 123974
Bohen, D., Marcinelle 120779
The Bohen Foundation, New York . . 046302
Bohle, Ingrid, Kaarst 103462
Bohlenständerhaus, Amriswil 036839
Bohlken, Westerland 074365

Bohlmann, Dr. Carolin, Berlin 125177
Bohm, Siegfried, Göttingen 071042
Bohman, Lars, Stockholm 111012
Bohn, Carl, København 060293
Bohn, Henry, Liverpool 141737
Bohn & Schmidt, Köln 071917
Bohnhoff & Pluntke, München 072665
Bohnsack, Strausberg 073943
Bohnsack, Hans-Jörg, Strausberg . 073944
Bohol Museum, Balay Hipusanan sa Mgs Bilihong Butang sa Bohol, Tagbilaran 031797
Bohr, Meldorf 072508
Bohr, Ingrid, Graz 057006
Bohun Gallery, Henley-on-Thames . 113231
Bohusläns Museum, Uddevalla 036725
Boi, Tran, Hue 120544
Boiché, Isabelle, Bourgoin-Jallieu . 124158
Boidet, Philippe, Chambéry 099106
Boie, Ingeborg, Bremen 070014
Boige, Annie, Villennes-sur-Seine . . 101478
Boiler House Steam and Engine Museum, Kurwongbah 001163
Boille, Béatrice, Grasse 063037
Boillon-Tajan, Marie-Thérèse, Paris 100065
Boillot Maison, Rouen 067251
Boira & Barclay, Sant Cugat del Vallès 129720
Boireau, Benoît, Tours 138640
Bois, Robin des, Levallois-Perret . . 063800
Bois d'Acanthe, Liège 058290
Bois d'Acanthe-Bois d'Antan, Liège 123645
Bois d'Antan, Liège 123646
Le Bois Debout, Lyon 064089, 099543, 138136
Bois Doré, Paris 100066
Bois l'Epicier, Maulette 064431
Bois Rose, Toulouse 068484
Bois Sacré, Genève 111430
Bois Secula, Saint-Paul 129211
Boisard, Pierre, Barfleur 061206
Boisard, Pierre, Barfleur 061207
Bois'Arts, Villeurbanne . . . 068945, 125033
du Boisbaudry, Loïc, Paris 065595
Boise Art Museum, Boise 042288
Boisgirard, Claude, Paris 121118
Boisguérin, Annick, Guérande 063097
Boisnard, Jean Luc, Rouen 067252
Boisserée, Köln 103597, 139334
Boisseron Antiquités, Boisseron . . . 061542
Boisseuil, Marc, Paris 065596
Boissière, Nicole, Gazeran 062975
Boissieu, Frédéric de, Rouen 067253
Boisson, Thierry, Sarcey 068123
Boissonnas, Pierre, Lucien & Valentin, Zürich 130230
Boîte à Jouets, La Rochelle 063425
La Boîte à Musique, Paris 065597
Boîte à Onglets, Lyon 064090, 099544
La Boite à Sons, Villeurbanne 101481
Boix, Barcelona 080810
Boix, Christian, Paris 065598
Bojara & Kellinghaus, Osnabrück . . 139637
Bôk, Leeuwarden 140472
Bok, Dr. Vladimir, Praha 123975
Bokcheon Municipal Museum, Busan 027453
Boke, Nagoya 077147
Bokflorian, Stockholm 141149
Bokhoven, Josine, Amsterdam 107686
Bokhuset, Göteborg 141099
Bokkistan, Göteborg 141100
Bokmalen, Uppsala 141186
Bokn Bygdemuseet, Bokn 030786
Bokslussen Antikvariat, Sorunda . . 141136
La Bola, Barcelona 080811
Bolander, Lars, New York 090741
Bolaño, Lamas, Barcelona 080812
Bolaño, Lamas, Barcelona 080813
Bolaño, Lamas, Barcelona 121997
Bolaños, Madrid 081253
Bold, B., Carlton, Victoria 055635
Bold in Gold, Maleny 094768
Bolders, J.G., Roosendaal 128815
Boldon Auction Galleries, East Boldon 122494
Boldrini, São Paulo 058692
Bolduc, Louis, Québec 059063
Bolduc, Marcel, Québec 059064
Bolduc House Museum, Sainte Genevieve 047726
Boldyreff, Natalie, Paris . . 100067, 133540
Bolens, R., Bruxelles 057858
Bolerium, San Francisco 142932
Boletin de la ANABAD, Madrid 136080
Boletin del Seminario de Estudios de Arte y Arqueologia, Universidad, Valladolid 136081
El Boliche del Restaurador, Buenos Aires 055181
Bolin, Stockholm 122249
Bolin Wildlife Exhibit and Antique Collection, McKinney 045558
Bolinao National Museum, Bolinao . 031633
Bolinas Museum, Bolinas 042292
Bolivar, Arellano, New York 117712
Bolivar Gallery, Kingston . 106806, 140156
Bolivar Hall, San Antonio 047788
Bolkart, Josef, Augsburg 069219
Bolkart, Stefan, Augsburg 069220
Bollag, Arlette, Zürich . . . 112049, 122361
Bollag, Claudia, Unterstammheim . 111955
Bolland, Ton, Amsterdam 140285
Bolland & Marotz, Bremen 070015, 121360, 138940
Bolle, Pierre-Alain, Genève 082405
Bollen, Genk 058159
Boller, Kassel 139302
Bollerhey, Karl, Kassel . . . 071745, 139303
Bollian, C., Sinzheim 073837
Bollig, J., Schliengen 073700
Bolliger, Marlies, Lausanne 111611
Bolliger, Peter, Bremgarten (Aargau) 111305
Bolling Hall Museum, Bradford 038803
Bollinger Mill State Historic Site, Burfordville 042510
Bollmohr, Nienstädt 073059
Bollnäs Konsthallen, Bollnäs 036220
Bolognini, Françoise, Thionville . . . 101311
Boloqui Larraya, Mirian, Zaragoza . 081735
Bolot, Saint-Jean-de-Losne 067532
Bolour, Y. & B., Los Angeles 089708
Bolsa, Madrid 081254
Bolsa de Arte, Rio de Janeiro 096592
Bolsa de Arte Porto Alegre, Porto Alegre 096546
Bolšemuraškinskij Gosudarstvennyj Istoriko-chudožestvennyj Muzej, Bolšoe Muraškino 033040
Bolšoj Dvorec, Muzej-zapovednik Oranienbaum, Lomonosov 033331
Bolson, Harry N., New York 090742
Bolsoni, Bern 082201
Bolt, Lochem 128754
Bolt, Brian R., Portballintrae 086291
Bolt, Elsebeth, København 060294
Bolte, Nienstädt 073060
Bolte, H., Drensteinfurt 102419
Boltens, Berne 069801
Bolton, Martin, Paris 065599
Bolton, Richard, Mangerton 131259
Bolton Antique Centre, Bolton 083569
Bolton Historical Museum, Bolton . . 042294
Bolton Library, Cashel 022703
Bolton Museum and Art Gallery, Bolton 038778
Bolton Steam Museum, Bolton 038779
Boltons, Peter, Carnforth 112818
Boltz, Waltraud, Bayreuth 121315
Bolu Devlet Güzel Sanatlar Galerisi, Bolu 038027
Bolu Müzesi, Bolu 038028
Bolwerk, Bredevoort 140368
Bolzani, Milano 106173
Bolzau, J., Sankt Augustin 073663
Bomaderry Antiques, Bomaderry . . 055517
Bomani, San Francisco 119615
Bomann-Museum Celle, Celle 016545
Bomarsundmuseet i Prästö Lotsstuga, Sund 010101
Bomb, New York 136400
Bombara, Carl, New York 090743
Bombay &CO, Los Angeles 132240
Bombay Art Society, Mumbai 053692
Bombay Company, Tampa 093110
Bombe Chest Antiques, Washington 093386
Bombini, Leonardo, Milano 127541
La Bomboniera, Chicago 115373
Bommels, Amsterdam 077805
De Bommelzolder, Zoeterwoude . . . 030393
Bommen Elvemuseum, Vennesla . . 031328
Bommer, Rolf, Basel 129913
Bommer, Werner, Zürich . . 112050, 122362
Bompiani, R.C.S., Milano 134606
Bomsholmen Museum, Røed, Øyestad, Arendal, Arendal 030735
Bomsucesso, São Paulo . . 058693, 123713
Bomuldsfabriken, Arendal 108672
Bon, Kyoto 077090
Bon, Seoul 107209
Bon, Ellen, Tucson 093207
Bon, François-Xavier, Lyon 064091
Bon Accord, Edinburgh 141572
Bon-Accord Books, Aberdeen 141376
Bon Gloor, Henriette, Zürich 130231
Le Bon Petit Diable, Paris 100068
Au Bon Vieux Temps, Agen 060665
Bona, Cincinnati 131929
Bona-Wight, Vancouver 059341
Bonaccorso, Paolo, Palermo 076129
Bonacina, Alessia Erminia Ales, Milano 075640
Bonack, Berlin 125178
Bonade, Alexandre, Dinard 099228
Bonaffini, Marinella, Modena 127723
Bonafous-Murat, Arsène, Paris 100069, 138312
Bonakdar, Tanya, New York 117713
Bonali & Fasser, Brescia 127204
Bonamici, Maurizio, Roma 127941
Bonanni, Chantal, Gournay-sur-Aronde 063025
Bonanni, Chantal, Saint-Ouen 067736
Bonanno, Gloria, Messina 127499
Bonanova, Barcelona 080814, 121998
Bonaparte Galleria d'Arte, Milano . . 106174
Bonard, Pierre, La Sarraz 130172
Bonardi, Fabrizio, Brescia 075150
Bonatelli, Milano 075641
Bonavera & Cambiaso, Genova . . . 127434
Bonavista Museum, Bonavista 005113
Bonavista North Regional Museum, Wesleyville 006790
Bonazzoli, Giuseppe, Brescia 127205
Bonciani, Maurizio, Roma 127942
Boncopagni, Nicola, Roma 076339
Bond, San Francisco 119616
Bond, A.P., Unley Park 056773
Bond, J.V., San Diego 092618
Bond, Kent, Tampa 120031
Bond & Son, S., Colchester 084054, 130598
Bond County Museum, Greenville . . 044342
Bond Gallery, London 113512
Bond Store Port of Maryborough Heritage Museum, Maryborough, Queensland 001223
Bond Street Antique Centre, London 085146
Bond Street Antiques, Cromer 084118, 130618
Bond Street Silver Galleries, London 085147
Bond van Handelaren in Oude Boeken, Rotterdam 053879
Bondgate Gallery, Alnwick 038492
Bondu, Dominique, Paris 121119
Bondu, Jean-Philippe, Paris 121120
Bonduelle & Lancry, Corbeil-Essonnes 120981
Bondzio, Ulrich, Berlin 125179
The Bone Dude's, Christchurch . . . 108387
Bonechi, Firenze 134581
Bonello, Pierre, Reims 067060
Bo'ness and Kinneil Railway, Bo'ness 038783
Bo'ness Heritage Area, Bo'ness . . . 038784
Bonetsmüller, Adolf, Tuntenhausen . 126922
Bonfanti, Giuliano, Milano 140046
Bonfils, Olivier de, Bergerac 061357
Bonfini, Gabriel, Paris 124594
Bonfoey, Cleveland 115691
Bonfreschi, Stefano, Modena 127724
Bong Bong Books, Bowral 136813
Bong Sung, Daegu 107181
Bongartz, Aachen 069078, 121289
Bongartz & Partner, Hannover 103266
Bongers, Aurel, Recklinghausen . . . 134358
Bongers, Doris, Wesel 074352
Bongiorno, Paolo, Modena 140070
Bongiovanni, Paola, Bologna 105948
Bonhage jr., Joseph B., New Orleans 117406
Bonhagen, Anke, Oldenburg, Oldenburg 104539
Bonham, Waikato 079283
Bonhams, Banbury 122396
Bonhams, Bath 122400
Bonhams, Bedale 122404
Bonhams, Cambridge 122444
Bonhams, Cape Town 121980
Bonhams, Cardiff 122447
Bonhams, Carlisle 122448
Bonhams, Carmarthen 122451
Bonhams, Carouge 122315
Bonhams, Chester 122461
Bonhams, Edinburgh 122497
Bonhams, Edinburgh 122498
Bonhams, Exeter 122505
Bonhams, Glasgow 122515
Bonhams, Guildford 122529
Bonhams, Hale 122532
Bonhams, Henley-on-Thames 122541
Bonhams, Honiton 122544
Bonhams, Hove 122547
Bonhams, Ipswich 122551
Bonhams, Johannesburg 121984
Bonhams, Leeds 122560
Bonhams, London 122580
Bonhams, London 122581
Bonhams, London 122582
Bonhams, Market Harborough 122613
Bonhams, Monaco 121772
Bonhams, Nantwich 122623
Bonhams, Newcastle-upon-Tyne . . 122628
Bonhams, Norwich 122637
Bonhams, Nottingham 122640
Bonhams, Nueva Andalucía 122075
Bonhams, Oxford 122645
Bonhams, Par 122648
Bonhams, Plymouth 122657
Bonhams, Poole 122660
Bonhams, Reepham 122665
Bonhams, Retford 122666
Bonhams, Ringwood 122668
Bonhams, Sevenoaks 122691
Bonhams, Sevenoaks 122692
Bonhams, Sherborne 122697
Bonhams, Solihull 122701
Bonhams, Southport 122705
Bonhams, Tetbury 122725
Bonhams, Toronto 097237, 120815
Bonhams, Whitstable 122747
Bonhams, Winchester 122749
Bonhams & Brooks, London 122583
Bonhams & Butterfields, Los Angeles 122944
Bonhams & Butterfields, San Francisco 123102
Bonhams & Langlois, Saint Helier . . 122678
Bonheur, Saint Louis 119190
Bonheur des Jours, Perros-Guirec . 066765
Le Bonheur du Jour, Amiens 060806, 124068
Bonheur du Jour, Les Sables-d'Olonne 063782
Bonheur du Jour, Montauban 064628

Le Bonheur du Jour, Sainte-Fortunade . . . 068055
Bonhof, Apeldoorn . . . 078031
Bonhomme-Raynaud, Agnès, Cheveuges . . . 124198
Boni, Ilaria, Firenze . . . 075292
Bonifatius-Verlag, Paderborn . . . 134342
Bonillo, Albora F., Valencia 081647, 129759
Bonillo, Anselme, Rochegude . . . 067185
Bonino, Patrizia, Genova . . . 075443
Bonke, Andy, Reuver . . . 128810
Bonn, Lutz, Neuwied . . . 073045
Bonnadier, Régis, Limoges . . . 063883
Bonnafoux, Dolorès, Poitiers . . . 101014
Bonnafoux, Louis, Nice . . . 065053
Bonnal, Mende . . . 064475
Bonnal, Mende . . . 064476
Bonnal, Mende . . . 064477
Bonnar, Joseph, Edinburgh . . . 084276
Bonnard, Christian, Saint-Lubin-des-Joncherets . . . 067593
Bonnat, Marie, Chennevières-sur-Marne . . . 062272
Bonne Occase, Annemasse . . . 060901
A la Bonne Occaz, Lausanne . . . 082536
Bonnefantenmuseum, Maastricht . . 029893
Bonnefoi, Henri, Paris . . . 138313
Bonnefont, N., Villefranche-de-Rouergue . . . 068892
Bonnefous, Lyon . . . 124337
Bonnefoy, La Coucourde . . . 063350
Bonnefoy, Jean-Charles, La Coucourde . . . 063351
Bonnefoy, Pascale, Saint-Étienne . . 067442
Bonnefoy, Richard, Chécy . . . 062264
Bønnelycke, Holeby . . . 124022
Bonnemoy, Elisabeth, Thiers . . . 068388
Bonnemoy, Jean-Luc, Escoutoux . . 062800
Bonner Antiquitäten Centrum, Bonn 069914
Bonner County Historical Museum, Sandpoint . . . 047928
Bonner Kunstverein, Bonn . . . 053064
Bonnes Choses Antiquarios, Rio de Janeiro . . . 058557
Bonnet, Christian, Faverolles (Cantal) . . . 062844
Bonnet, Jean-Pierre, Nîmes . . . 065172
Bonnet, Marie-Claude, Toulouse . . . 068485
Bonnet House, Fort Lauderdale . . . 043930
Bonnetain, Paulette, Azé . . . 061153
Bonneton, Eric, Brignais . . . 061797
Bonneton 5060 Eric, Villeurbanne . . 068946
Bonnier, Genève . . . 111431
Bonnier, Peder, New York . . . 117714
Bonnimond, F., Paris . . . 124595
Bonnin, Bernard, Béziers . . . 061430
Bonnin, Bernard, Béziers . . . 061431
Bonnin, Christian, Béziers . . . 061432
Bonnin Serra, Jose, Barcelona . . . 080815
Bonnington Arts Centre, Nakusp . . . 005976
Bonno, Michel, Plougoumelen . . . 066872
Bonn'occase, Bonne . . . 061558
Bonnot, Thierry, Nice . . . 065054
Bonomo, Marilena, Bari . . . 105928
Bonomo, Marilena, Bari . . . 105929
Bons Tempos, Porto . . . 080069
Bonsai-Museum, Seeboden . . . 002672
Bonsai Museum Heidelberg, Heidelberg . . . 017824
Bonsignori, Roma . . . 134667
Bonson, S., Greenbank . . . 094602
Bonte-Sioen, Brugge . . . 120712
De Bonte Sonoy, Alkmaar . . . 077710
Bontoc Museum, Bontoc, Ifugao . . . 031635
Bontoc Museum, Bontoc, Mountain Province . . . 031636
Bonum, Kraków . . . 079626
Bonum, Solna . . . 110993
Bonvin, Crans-sur-Sierre . . . 082334
Bonvin, René, Sion . . . 082811
Bonvini, Bruno, Milano . . . 075642, 106175
Bonzi, Maurice, La Clusaz . . . 063337
Boobala, Norfolk . . . 091370
Boodja Aboriginal Art and Craft, Fremantle . . . 055840
Boodle & Dunthorne, Liverpool . . . 085021
Boodle & Dunthorne, Sydney . . . 056667
Boody, Saint Louis . . . 119191
Boogaard, Amsterdam . . . 077806
Book Adventure, Memphis . . . 142535
Book Affair, Carlton, Victoria . . . 136851
Book and Comic Exchange, London 141759
Book Ark, New York . . . 142637
Book Art & Architecture & Volume Gallery, London . . . 130951
Book Art Cooperative, Shanghai . . . 137752
Book & Art Shop, Sheffield 114414, 142058
The Book Bag, Fitzroy . . . 136899
Book Bank, Memphis . . . 142536
Book Bank, Toowong . . . 137109
Book Barn, Miami . . . 142549
Book Barn, Mullumbimby . . . 137017
Book Barn, Surry Hills . . . 137097
Book Basket, Memphis . . . 142537
Book Bay, San Francisco . . . 142933
Book Bazaar, Ottawa . . . 137672
Book Bazaar Ballarat, Ballarat . . . 136789
Book Bin, Detroit . . . 142401
Book Broker, San Diego . . . 142899
Book Browser, Houston . . . 142426
The Book Buff, Broadmeadow . . . 136825
The Book Bug, Hitchin . . . 141667
Book Buyers Shop, Houston . . . 142427
Book-Bytes, Hawthorn, South Australia . . . 136935
Book Case, Memphis . . . 142538
Book Cellar, San Antonio . . . 142881
Book-Chek, Sacramento . . . 142838
Book City Collectables, Los Angeles 142495
Book City Paradise, Portland . . . 142793
Book Collector, Houston . . . 142428
Book Collector, Parramatta . . . 137044
Book Collector, Sacramento . . . 142839
Book Connection, Dubbo . . . 136885
Book Connection, Invermay . . . 136952
Book Cultural Museum, Shaoguan . 007250
Book Den, Cessnock . . . 136856
Book Den, Hamilton . . . 137638
Book Den, San Antonio . . . 142882
The Book Depot, London . . . 141760
Book Discoveries, Nashville . . . 142595
Book Discoveries, Seattle . . . 142979
Book Emporium, Scarborough . . . 142051
The Book End, Hastings . . . 136933
Book Ends, Winnipeg . . . 137736
Book Exchange, Amsterdam . . . 140286
Book Exchange, Bussum . . . 140375
Book Exchange, Calgary . . . 137621
Book Exchange, Colchester . . . 141527
Book Exchange, Denver . . . 142377
Book Exchange Plus, Phoenix . . . 142761
Book Finding Services, Saint Andrews . . . 142033
Book Forum, Denver . . . 142378
Book Gallery, El Paso . . . 142404
Book Gallery, Jerusalem . . . 139978
Book Gallery, Moss Vale . . . 137010
Book Gallery, Phoenix . . . 142762
Book Garden, San Diego . . . 142900
Book Haven, Cleveland . . . 142331
Book Horizons, Miami . . . 142550
Book House, Dallas . . . 142365
Book House, Kirkby Stephen . . . 141699
The Book House, Ravenstonedale . 142014
Book House, Saint Paul . . . 142864
Book House in Dinkytown, Minneapolis . . . 142577
Book Hunter, Saskatoon . . . 137684
Book Inn, Whangarei . . . 140687
The Book Loft, Masterton . . . 140639
Book Lore, Lyneham . . . 136983
Book Mark, Dallas . . . 142366
Book Mark, Philadelphia . . . 142738
Book Mark It, Washington . . . 143039
Book Market, Bruxelles . . . 137426
Book Market, Ottawa . . . 137673
Book Museum, Bath . . . 038621
Book Nook, Atlanta . . . 142198
Book Now, Bendigo . . . 136800
Book Off, Kaida . . . 140158
Book Off, Kanie . . . 140159
Book Outlet, Miami . . . 142551
The Book Palace, London . . . 141761
Book Peddler, San Antonio . . . 142883
Book People, Richmond . . . 142824
Book Place, Memphis . . . 142539
Book Rack, Birmingham . . . 142234
Book Rack, Cincinnati . . . 142306
Book Rack, Cincinnati . . . 142307
Book Rack, Cincinnati . . . 142308
Book Rack, Cleveland . . . 142332
Book Rack, Columbus . . . 142350
Book Rack, Denver . . . 142379
Book Rack, Denver . . . 142380
Book Rack, Denver . . . 142381
Book Rack, Indianapolis . . . 142450
Book Rack, Jacksonville . . . 142463
Book Rack, Oklahoma City . . . 142717
Book Rack, Oklahoma City . . . 142718
Book Rack, Oklahoma City . . . 142719
Book Rack, Oklahoma City . . . 142720
Book Rack, Phoenix . . . 142763
Book Rack, Pittsburgh . . . 142771
Book Rack, Richmond . . . 142825
Book Rack, San Antonio . . . 142884
Book Re-View, Portland . . . 142794
Book Realm, Enoggera . . . 136892
Book Rendezvous, Baltimore . . . 142221
Book Restorer, Christchurch . . . 128918
Book Return, Birmingham . . . 142235
Book Returns, Auckland . . . 140586
Book Scene, Houston . . . 142429
Book Shelf, Oklahoma City . . . 142721
The Book Shop, Castle Donington . . 141497
Book Shop, Fort Worth . . . 142409
Book Shop, Hay-on-Wye . . . 141647
Book Shop at the Art Gallery of Ontario, Toronto . . . 137701
Book, Stamp and Picture Gallery, Hampton . . . 136931
Book Station, Caringbah . . . 136848
Book Store, Cincinnati . . . 142309
Book Swap, Fort Worth . . . 142410
Book Swap of Carrollwood, Tampa . 143020
The Book-Swop, Edinburgh . . . 141573
Book Trader, Minneapolis . . . 142578
Book Trader, Oklahoma City . . . 142722
Book Trader, Philadelphia . . . 142739
Book Traders, Memphis . . . 142540
Book Traffic, Amsterdam . . . 140287
Book Turn, Sendai . . . 140178
Book Warren, Brixham . . . 141459
Book World, Benoni . . . 080671
Book World, Indianapolis . . . 142451
Book World, Indianapolis . . . 142452
Book Worm of Noe, New Orleans . . 142606
Book Wormz, South Auckland . . . 140652
Bookarts Canberra, Griffith . . . 123232
Bookbarn, Bristol . . . 141448
Bookbeat Byron, Byron Bay . . . 136835
Bookbox, Cheltenham . . . 141500
Bookcase, Carlisle . . . 141490
Bookcase, South Brisbane . . . 137086
Bookcase, Winnipeg . . . 137737
Booked Out, Randwick . . . 137068
Booked Up, Washington . . . 143040
Bookends, Emsworth . . . 141598
Bookends, Fowey . . . 141617
Bookends, Greystones . . . 139974
Bookends, Louisville . . . 142526
Booker Lowe, Houston . . . 116287
Booker T. Washington National Monument, Hardy . . . 044430
Bookery, El Paso . . . 142405
Bookery, Fyshwick . . . 136909
Booketab, Ringwood . . . 137073
Bookfinders, Belfast . . . 141405
Bookfinders, Philadelphia . . . 142740
Bookfound, Edge Hill . . . 136889
Bookhaven, Philadelphia . . . 142741
Bookings Taken, Rozelle . . . 137075
Bookish, Waikato . . . 140662
Bookking International, Paris . . . 133541
Booklady, Miami . . . 142552
Bookleaves, New York . . . 142638
BookLovers, Bath . . . 141394
Bookmaker, Groningen . . . 140431
Bookman, Nashville . . . 142596
The Bookman, Norwich . . . 141961
Bookmans Halt, Saint Leonards-on-Sea . . . 142039
The Bookmark, Brighton . . . 141434
Bookmark, Falmouth . . . 141607
Bookmark, Oakland . . . 142708
Bookmart Editions, Leicester . . . 135165
Bookmine, Sacramento . . . 142840
Bookmonger, San Francisco . . . 142934
The Bookologist, Nowra . . . 137036
Bookplate, Hornsby . . . 136947
Bookrack, Louisville . . . 142527
The Book's, Cheltenham . . . 141501
Books, Cromer . . . 141548
Books, Nashville . . . 142597
Books Abound, Houston . . . 142430
Books Afloat, Weymouth . 087115, 142149
Books and Art on Beaumont, Hamilton, New South Wales . . . 136927
Books and Beyond, Chicago . . . 142281
Books and Boxes Plus, Houston . . . 142431
Books and Collectables, Underwood 137121
Books and Pages, Maroubra . . . 136992
Books and Pieces, Nottingham . . . 141970
Books Around, Geelong . . . 136915
Books by George, Birmingham . . . 142236
Books & Bygones, Weymouth . . . 087116, 142150
Books, Cases and Prints, Atlanta . . 142199
Books et Cetera, North Perth . . . 137034
Books Etc., Denver . . . 142382
Books Etc., Oklahoma City . . . 142723
Books for Collectors, Toddington . . 142115
Books for Cooks, Fitzroy . . . 136900
Books for Thought, Tampa . . . 143021
Books & More, Wettingen . . . 141309
Books 'n Bitz, Nerang . . . 137024
Books 'n Tees, Oklahoma City . . . 142724
Books 'n Things, Albany . . . 136777
Books 'n Things, Louisville . . . 142528
Books of Fifth Avenue, Palm Beach 137042
Books Of Oceania, Whangarei . . . 140688
Books of Paige's, Miami . . . 142553
Books of Wonder, New York . . . 142639
Books on Bronte, Waverley . . . 137135
Books on Dean, Albury . . . 136778
Books on High, Columbus . . . 142351
Books Rare and New Zealand, Dunedin . . . 140623
Books & Things, London . . . 141762
Books Unlimited, Denver . . . 142383
Books Unlimited, Edmonton . . . 137634
Books Unlimited, Indianapolis . . . 142453
Bookscene, Nottingham . . . 141971
Books@Devonport Wharf, North Shore . . . 140645
Booksearch, Chichester . . . 141513
Booksearch, Colchester . . . 141528
Booksearch, Launceston . . . 141706
Booksearch, Leicester . . . 141716
Booksearch, Saint Paul . . . 142865
Booksellers Row, Chicago . . . 142282
The Bookshelf, Cairns . . . 136837
Bookshelf, Winnipeg . . . 137738
The Bookshop, Bournemouth . . . 141422
Bookshop, Cambridge . . . 141467
Bookshop, Conwy . . . 141539
Booksmart, Miami . . . 142554
The Booksmith, Clayfield . . . 136861
Booksmith, Jersey City . . . 135371
Books'n'Print, Invercargill . . . 140634
Bookstacks, Wellington . . . 140672
Bookstall, San Francisco . . . 142935
Bookstein, Lori, New York . . . 117715

Bookstein, Lori, New York 117716
Bookstop, New Town 137026
Bookstop Gallery, Taranaki 108566, 140655
Bookstop Plus, Memphis 142541
The Bookstore, National Gallery of Canada, Ottawa 137674
Bookstore on West Twenty Fifth, Cleveland 142333
Booktalk, Richmond, Victoria 137071
Booktrader, København 137888
Bookwise, Wellington 140673
Bookworks, Chicago 142283
Bookworld, Oswestry 141978
Bookworm, Cincinnati 142310
The Bookworm, Edinburgh 141574
Bookworm, Evesham 141602
Bookworm, Holland-on-Sea 141671
Bookworm Book Store, Kansas City 142474
Bookworm & Bugjuice, Cleveland . . 142334
Bookworms Bookshop, Ferny Hills . 136895
Boolarra Historical Museum, Boolarra 000812
Booleroo Steam and Traction Museum, Booleroo Centre 000813
Boom, Cleveland 088312, 115692
Boomalli Aboriginal Artists, Leichhardt 056095
Boomerang, Kansas City 089486
Boomerang, San Diego 092619
Boomerang Art, Glenelg 094589
Boomerang Books, Seattle 142980
Boomerang's, San Diego 092620
Boomkwekerijmuseum, Boskoop . . 029336
Boon, Bruxelles 096159
Boon, Knokke-Heist 096327
Boone, Mary, New York 117717
Boone, Mary, New York 117718
Boone County Historical Center, Boone 042300
Boone County Historical Society Museum, Belvidere 042136
Boone's Lick Site, Boonesboro 042304
Boongar Arts & Crafts, Kuranda . . . 056068
Boonsborough Museum of History, Boonsboro 042305
Boonshoft Museum of Discovery, Dayton 043318
The Boorman House, Mauston 045728
Boos, Frank H., Bloomfield Hills . . . 122822
Boos, T. & G., Landau in der Pfalz . . 072128
Boos Antic Sud Est, L'Isle-sur-la-Sorgue 063925
Boos Antic Sud-Ouest, Condom . . . 062451
Booser, Luc de, Knokke-Heist 096328
Boot Hill Gallery, Beaumaris 094223
Boot Hill Museum, Dodge City 043475
Booth & Son, A.E., Ewell . 084353, 130694
Booth & Son, A.E., Torquay 131601
Booth, Fara, New York 090744
Booth, Joanna, London 085148
Booth, Richard, Hay-on-Wye 141648
Booth, Richard, Hay-on-Wye 141649
Booth 13 Vintage, Oklahoma City . . 091478
Booth-Clibborn, London 135192
Booth Museum of Natural History, Brighton 038846
Boothbay Railway Village, Boothbay 042307
Boothbay Region Art Foundation, Boothbay Harbor 042308
Boppard, Daniel, Cossonay-Ville . . . 082331
Boquet, Damien, Paris 100070
Boqui, Montevideo 114759
Bor - Art, Roma 106500
Boralevi, Alberto, Firenze 075293
Boralevi, Daniele, Firenze 075294
Boranup Galleries, Margaret River . 094787
Borås Galleri Antik, Borås 081774
Borås Idrottsmuseum, Borås 036222
Borås Konstmuseum, Borås 036223
Borås Museum, Borås 036224
Borboën, Marcel, Lausanne 130064
Borchardt, Peter, Hamburg 103102
Borcherdt, K., Braunschweig 102216
Borchert, Olaf, Willisau 082907
Borchi & Camiciottoli, Firenze 127305
Borck, Andrea, Hamburg 125803
Bord, Jacques, Saint-Étienne 067443
Bord, Jacques, Saint-Étienne 067444
Bord, M., London 085149
Bordas, Paris 100071, 133542
Borde, Thierry, Cosne-Cours-sur-Loire 062488, 124211
Bordeaux Centre, Hôtel de Vassal, Bordeaux 061594
Borden, Janet, New York 117719
Bordenave, Jean, Anglet 060869
Bordentown Historical Society Museum, Bordentown 042310
Border History Museum, Hexham . . 039744
Border Regiment and King's Own Royal Border Regiment Museum, Carlisle 038996
Borderland Antiques, El Paso 088790
Bordes, Alexis, Paris 065600, 124596
Bordes, Michel, Villeneuve-sur-Lot . 068916
Bordes, Patrick, Marnes-la-Coquette 064295
Bordes-Barrera, Jose R., New York . 117720
Bordet-Secrettand, Elisabeth, Vitteaux 069017
Bordier, Colmar 062404
Bordihn, München 072666
Bordin, Padova 076077
Bordin, Giuseppe, Torino 128269
Bords d'Eaux, Mers-les-Bains 064506
Borduas, Montréal 096982, 133317
Boréal Express, Paris 065601
Borej Art, Sankt-Peterburg 109617
Borelli, Colombes 099162
Borelli-Edwards, Pittsburgh 118905
Bores, Emile, Montauban 064629
Borg, Bernard, Bagneaux-sur-Loing 061162
Borg, Christina, New York 090745
Borg, Michel, Villeveyrac 068987
Borg, Paul, B'Kara 077506, 107443
Borg, Richard ter, Groningen 078405
Borg Verhildersum, Leens 029832
Borgarsyssel Museum, Sarpsborg . 031173
Borgeaud, Claude, Basel 082129
Borgen, Valby 133433
Borges Reis & Almeida, Lisboa 079879
Børgesen, Bent, København 060295
Borgheresi, Leonardo, Firenze 127306
Borghese, Rio de Janeiro 096593
Borghesi, Roberto, Trieste 076886
Il Borghetto, Milano 075643
Borgmann, T., Köln 103598
Nina Borgmann & Caroline Nathusius, Köln 103599
Borgmeier, Hagen, Westfalen 125780
Borgmuseum, Spøttrup 009116
Le Borgne, Daniel, Villeneuve-le-Guyard 068913
Borgo e Castello Medioevale, Torino 026047
Borgobello, Parma 076200
La Borgognona, Roma 106501
Borgsjö Hembygdsgård, Erikslund . 036251
Borinquen Art, Tampa 120032
Boris Antiquaire, Béziers 061433
Boriscothi Antiques, Chiang Mai . . . 083106
Borisoglebskij Kraevedčeskij Muzej, Borisoglebsk 033041
Borja, R., Valencia 081648, 110799
Bork, København 060296, 098540
Bork, Moshe, El Paso 088791
Bork, Dr. U., Freiburg im Breisgau . 070827
Borkener Galerie, Borken, Hessen . 102203
Borkowska, Monika, Nové Zámky . . 129278
Borkowski, Hannover 103267
Borla, Silvano, San Vittore 082768, 130156
Borlach-Museum, Bad Dürrenberg . 015686
Borlänge Auktionsbyrå, Borlänge . . 122111
Bormacher, Chicago 131889
Bormann, Herbert, Rodenbach 073549
Bormann, Thomas, Hamburg 139170
Bormshuis, Antwerpen 003153
Born, Barcelona 080816, 121999
Born Again, Baltimore . . . 087648, 131817
Born in the USSR, Houston 089035
Born-Néo, Montréal 096983
Bornemann, Dr. Bernd, Lübeck 103960
Børnenens Museum, Nationalmuseet, København 008958
Borner, Andreas, Rickenbach (Solothurn) 130149
Borner, Pia Anna, Luzern 111684
Bornhöft, Wolfgang, Seedorf bei Bad Segeberg 073783
Bornholms Kunstmuseum, Gudhjem 008882
Bornholms Museum, Hjorths Fabrik und Bornholmsk Keramikmuseum, Rønne 009075
Bornholt, Detlef, Kiel 071822
Borniger, U., Bacharach 069251
Bornkast, A., Siegburg 073803
Bornmann, M., Kassel 071746
Borno Museum Society, University of Maiduguri, Maiduguri 053934
Borno State Museum, Maiduguri . . 030694
Bornschein, Mike, Wismar 074450
Boros, R., Rietheim-Weilheim 073536
Borosch, Dortmund 125477
Borough Galleries, Eaglehawk 055776, 094501, 123221
Borough Museum and Art Gallery, Newcastle-under-Lyme 040543
Borow, Meckelfeld 072478
Borras Mari, Fermin, Barcelona . . . 080817
Borrazzi, Roberto, Roma 076340
Borri, Luciano, Roma 127943
Borroco N Roll, São Paulo 058694
Borromini, Torino 076778
Borsod Miskolci Múzeum, Miskolc . 021786
Borsotti, Mauro, Milano 127542
Bortolotti, Pierre, Albi 060752
Bortolussi, Victor, Toronto 123828
Bortorello, São Paulo 058695
Bortz, Philip, Cincinnati 088216
Borups Antik, Frederiksberg 060229
Boryeong Coal Museum, Boryeong . 027451
Borzo, 's-Hertogenbosch 078514
Bos, Marten, Leeuwarden 128741
Bos-de Groote, C.J.M.S., Baarn . . . 128573
Bos-Otten, Amsterdam 077807
Bosák, Luboš, Česká Lípa 059995
Bosc, Alain, Cannes 061934
Bosch, Barcelona 134905
Bosch, Barcelona 140982
Bosch, Mathias, Düsseldorf 070366
Bosch, Rudolf, Erlenbach (Zürich) . .082355, 130011
Boschan, W., Königs Wusterhausen 072030
Boschbach, M., Kerpen, Rheinland . 103532
Boscheck, Reinhard, Mülheim an der Ruhr 104129
Boscher, Daniel, Paris 121121
Boscher, Samuel, Cherbourg-Octeville 120976
Boscher Belleissue, Jacqueline, Saint-Brieuc 067382
Boscher & Oriot, Morlaix 121081
Boscher, Studer & Fromentin, Paris 121122
Boschert, Eberhard, Landau in der Pfalz 072129
Boschert, Eberhard, Neustadt an der Weinstraße 126543
Boschert, Hermann, Kaiserslautern 103465
Boschert, Hermann, Neustadt an der Weinstraße 104426
Boschetti, Enrica, Milano 127543
Boschi, Alessio, Bologna 105949
Boschi, Andrea, Parma 127848
Boschi, Rudolf, Innsbruck 057076
Boscia, S., Hausach 071436
El Bosco, Godoy Cruz 055271, 123168
Bosco, Luciano, Roma 076341
Bosco, Paul J., New York 090746
Boscobel House, Shropshire 041025
Boscobel Restoration, Garrison . . . 044152
Boscombe Militaria, Bournemouth . 083594
Boscombe Models & Collectors Shop, Bournemouth 083595
Bosdure Marzocchi, Bastia 061216, 098927
Bose, Anne-Dorothee, Wittlich 105313, 134462
Bose Pacia, New York 117721
Bosetti, Henri & Michèle, Rueil-Malmaison 067318
Bosi Artes, Roma 076342
Bosica, Ernani, Torino 128270
Bosinski, Monica, Mainz-Kastel . . . 126267
Bosio, Yves, Menton 064491
Boškov, P., Kjustendil 058755
Boskovitch, Bruxelles 057859
Bosmuseum, Amsterdam 029175
Bosmuseum, Hechtel 003503
Bosmuseum, Tessenderlo 003791
Bosmuseum Jan van Ruusbroec, Hoeilaart 003515
Bosmuseum Wildert, Essen 003425
Bosoni, Milano 106176
Bosque de Ciência, Manaus 004203
Bosque Galería Artdicré, México . . . 107479
Bosquet, Paris 100072, 133543
Boss & Co, Schönbühl-Urtenen . . . 135065
Boss, J., Ludwigsburg, Württemberg 072305
Boss, Thomas G., Boston . 115147, 142246
Bossaert, Brugge 057761
Bossanova, Seattle 119894
Bosse, Kitzbühel 095606
Bosse, P., Osnabrück 073230
Bosse, Sigrid, Cottbus 070157
Bosser, Fiederic, Paris . . . 100073, 133544
Bossmann, L., Siegen 126799
Bostelmann & Siebenhaar, Berlin . . 133756
Bosten, Aachen 069079
Bostock, J., London 113513
Boston, Derek, Salisbury 086489
Boston, Julia, London 085150
Boston Antique Cooperative, Boston 087798
Boston Antiques and Fine Arts Show, Boston 093975
Boston Art, Boston 115148
Boston Art, Boston 115149
Boston Art, Boston 115150
Boston Art Dealers, Boston 115151
Boston Artists Gallery, Tulsa 120188
Boston Athenaeum, Boston 042315
Boston Book Annex, Boston 142247
Boston Book Company, Boston 142248
Boston Center for the Arts, Boston . 115152
Boston Corporate Art Collection, Boston 115153
Boston Directors' Lab, Boston 115154
Boston Fire Museum, Boston 042316
Boston Gallery, Quezon City 108855
Boston Guildhall Museum, Boston . 038791
Boston House, Toronto 059156
Boston National Historical Park, Boston 042317
Boston Printmakers, Emmanuel College, Boston 054685
Boston Public Library Art Collections, Boston 042318
Boston Rare Maps, Boston 142249
Boston Sculptors, West Newton . . . 054686
Boston Sculptors Gallery, Boston . . 115155
Boston Towne Coin Exchange, Boston 087799
Boston University Art Gallery, Boston 042319
Boston Visual Arts Union, Newton . . 054687
Boswell, Ashgrove 136786
Boswell, Peter, London 130952
Boswell-Crowe, Los Angeles 116730
Boswell & Davis, London 130953
Boswell Museum and Mausoleum, Auchinleck 038547
Boswell Museum of Music, East Springfield 043580
Bosworth Antiques, Market Bosworth 085929
Bosworth Battlefield Visitor Centre and Country Park, Market Bosworth . . 040426
Bősze, Budapest 105495
Bot, Christiane de, Antwerpen 057683
Bot, G.P.L., Vlaardingen 128870

Botanic Gardens Museum, Southport . . . 041070
Botanical Museum, Rawalpindi . . . 031399
Botanical Museum of Harvard University, Cambridge . . . 042556
Botanical Museum of the National Gardens, Athinai . . . 021162
Botanical Survey Museum of India, Pune . . . 022304
Botanical Survey of India, Dehradun 022072
Botaničeskij Muzej, Sankt-Peterburg . . . 033727
Botanické Oddělení Národního Muzea, Průhonice . . . 008663
Botaniksektionen Utställingar, Uppsala Universitet, Uppsala . . . 036736
Botanische Staatssammlung München, München . . . 019042
Botanisches Museum, Hamburg . . . 017681
Botanisches Museum Berlin-Dahlem, Berlin . . . 015997
Botanisches Museum der Universität Zürich, Zürich . . . 037762
Botanisk Museum, København . . . 008959
Botaniska Museet, Lund . . . 036440
Botany Bay Prints, Turner . . . 056743
Botany Museum, Faizabad . . . 022113
Botany Museum, Gorakhpur . . . 022125
Botany Museum, Jaunpur . . . 022184
Botany Museum, Kanpur . . . 022197
Botany Museum, Lucknow . . . 022238
Botelho, Antonio Pedro Martinho, Lisboa . . . 079880
Botelho, Francisco Silva, Lisboa . . . 079881
Botelho, José Silva, Lisboa . . . 079882
Boterf, La Chapelle-Basse-Mer . . . 063309
De Botermolen, Keerbergen . . . 003550
Botero, Barranquilla . . . 098087
Botha, Cornelia, Hamburg . . . 125804
Bothorel, Marie, Pleyber-Christ . . . 066858
Bothorel, Yves, Berrien . . . 061373
Botkyrka Konsthall och Xet-Museet, Tumba . . . 036721
Bøtø Nor Gl. Pumpestation, Væggerløse . . . 009135
Botswana National Museum and Art Gallery, Gaborone . . . 003950
Bottarel & Foi, Brescia . . . 075151
Bottari, Torino . . . 106665
Bottaz, Bousson, Lyon . . . 124338
Botte Dorée, Vitré . . . 069008
La Bottega, Modena . . . 127725
La Bottega Antica, Genova 075444, 127435
Bottega Artigiana, Milano . . . 127544
Bottega d'Altri Tempi, Prato . . . 127886
Bottega d'Arte, Casablanca . . . 077643
Bottega d'Arte, Firenze . . . 106036
Bottega d'Arte, Firenze . . . 127307
Bottega d'Arte, Livorno . . . 106117
Bottega d'Arte, Roma . . . 076343
La Bottega d'Arte Antica, Napoli . . . 127752
La Bottega del Borgo Nuovo, Torino 076779
Bottega del Giano, Milano . . . 127545
La Bottega del Restauratore, Messina . . . 127500
Bottega del Restauro, Bari . . . 127107
Bottega del Restauro, Brescia . . . 127206
Bottega del Restauro, Milano . . . 127546
Bottega del Restauro, Modena . . . 075899, 127726
Bottega del Restauro, Torino . . . 076780
Bottega del Restauro, Verona . . . 128417
La Bottega del Vecchio Ceppo, Milano . . . 127547
La Bottega dell'Artigiano, Modena . 127727
Bottega Delle Arti, Padova . . . 140084
Bottega delle Occasioni, Palermo . . 076130
Bottega delle Stampe, Firenze . . . 106037
Bottega delle Stampe, Milano . . . 075644, 127548
Bottega di Restauro Bramante, Milano . . . 127549
La Bottega di San Luca, Torino . . . 076781
Bottega Farnese, Palermo 076131, 127820
La Bottega Margutta, Roma . . . 076344
Bottega Restauro Mobili Antichi e Cornici su Misura, Bologna . . . 127134
Bottega San Carlo, Locarno . . . 082581
Bottega San Felice, Firenze . . . 075295
La Bottega Solferino, Milano . . . 075645
Bottegantica, Bologna . . . 105950
La Bottegantica, Cagliari . . . 075202
El Botteghin, Milano . . . 075646
Bottéro, Maryse & Gérard, Nice . . . 065055
Botticcelli, Santiago de Chile . . . 059511
Botticelli, Firenze . . . 075296
Botticelli, Lima . . . 079544
Bottin, Peter, Vachendorf . . . 074177
Bottländer, Michael, Hamm, Westfalen . . . 125857
Bottland Gallery of Modern Art, Surry Hills . . . 095248
The Bottle Kiln, West Hallam Ilkeston . . . 114666
Botto, Maria, Roma . . . 076345
Bottom Drawer Antique Centre, Mooroduc . . . 056254, 137004
Bottom Feeders Studio Gallery, New York . . . 117722
Bottom of the Harbour Nautical Antiques, Sydney . . . 056668
Bottom of the Ninth, Cleveland . . . 088313
Botton, Isidoro, Milano . . . 075647
Botwood Heritage Centre, Botwood 005120
Botzenhardt, Walburga, Kempten . . 071787
Bou, Marie-Hélène, Decazeville . . . 062612
Boucard, Michelle, Paris . . . 124597
Boucaud, Paris . . . 065602
Boucaud, Charles et Philippe, Maraussan . . . 064258
Boucaud, Philippe, Béziers . . . 061434
Bouchardon, Odile, Langeais . . . 063515
Bouchart, Françoise, Granville . . . 063031, 138095
Bouchart, Philippe, Aire-sur-la-Lys . 060686
Bouché, Paris . . . 065603
Bouche, Bernard, Paris . . . 100074
Bouché, Lucette, Villeréal . . . 068927
Bouché, Olivier, Monpazier . . . 064605
Bouchelier Antiquité Brocante 71, Montceau-les-Mines . . . 064663
Bouchene, Nasreddine, Bouzaréah . 055132
Boucher, Amiens . . . 060807
Boucher, Gérard, Le Havre . . . 063626
Boucher, Kevin, Mount Evelyn . . . 094903
La Boucherie, Orvilliers . . . 065313
La Boucherie Antiquités, Maulette . 064432
Bouchetard, Catherine, Saint-Ouen 067737
Bouchiba, Strasbourg . . . 124940
Bouchoucha, Slim, Paris . . . 065604
Boučková, Vladimíra, Salorno . . . 128244
Le Bouclart, Maussane-les-Alpilles 064441
Boucle d'Or, Tours . . . 068585
Bouclet, Christian, Bessé-sur-Braye 061403
Boucq, Aubervilliers . . . 061037
Boucq, Paris . . . 065605
Bouda, Petr, Brno . . . 137768
Boudewijn, Ton, Nijmegen . . . 108149
Boudin, Arthur, Honfleur . . . 099333
Boudin, Gérard, Rouen . . . 101110
Il Boudoir della Nonna, Palermo . . . 076132
Boudon, Gilles, Ferrières-Saint-Mary . . . 062858
Boudoux, Bernard, Nointel . . . 065217
Boudreau, Montréal . . . 058931
Boudreaux, Houston . . . 132104
La Bouee de Noe, Ceton . . . 062063
Bouet, Jean-Loïc, Vaubadon . . . 068731
Boughton House, Kettering . . . 039855
Bougival Antiquités, Bougival . . . 061672
Bougo, Loyc, Saint-Congard . . . 067405
Bouguen, Bernard, Avignon . . . 138019
Bouhams, Palma de Mallorca . . . 081472, 122078
Bouhin, Jean-Michel, Montbard . . . 064648
Bouhours, Thierry, Château-du-Loir 062182, 124191
Bouhours, William, Châteaudun . . . 062191
Bouillet, Beaune . . . 061269
Bouillon, Christoph, Köln . . . 071918
Bouillon, Dominique, Paris . . . 124598
Bouillon, Michel, Autun . . . 061085
Bouillotte, Sainte-Anne-d'Auray . . . 068048
Bouillotte, Sannois . . . 068120
Bouin & Gardon, Paris . . . 124599
Boulade, Isabelle, Villeurbanne . . . 068947
Boulakia, Fabien, Paris . . . 100075
Boulan, Vigneux-sur-Seine . . . 133706
Boulandier, Bilbao . . . 141009
Boulanger & Fils, Paris . . . 124600
Boulanger, Patrice, Paris . . . 065606
Boularand, Jacques, Pézenas . . . 066796
Boulard, Stockholm . . . 141150
Boulard, Laurent, Ailly-le-Haut-Clocher . . . 060683
Boulard, Laurent, Saint-Riquier . . . 067995
Boulder City-Hoover Dam Museum, Boulder City . . . 042356
Boulder History Museum, Boulder . 042350
Boulder Pastel Painters Association, Boulder . . . 054688
Boul'Dingue Occasions, Lyon . . . 138137
Boul'Dingue Occasions, Lyon . . . 138138
Boule, Monaco . . . 064588
Boulenger, Bernard, Berck-sur-Mer 061354
Boulenger, Daniel, Hardelot-Plage . 063125
Boules, Betton . . . 061413
Boules de Canton, Paris . . . 065607
Boulestin, Patrick, Saivres . . . 068089
Boulet, Tulle . . . 068657
Boulet, Jean-Claude, Sébécourt . . . 068180
Boulet, Michelle, Paris . . . 100076
Boulevard Antique, Leicester . . . 084945
Boulevard Antiques, Whitstable . . . 087139
Boulevard Arts Center, Chicago . . . 042825
Boulevard de l'Art, Paris . . . 100077
Boulevard d'Unica, Utrecht . . . 108243
Boulevard Emporium, Dallas . . . 088467
Bouley, Alain, Villeurbanne . . . 068948
Bouley, Josiane, Villeurbanne . . . 068949
Bouley, Roger, Villeurbanne . . . 068950
Boulia Stone House Museum, Boulia . . . 000820
El Boulle, Milano . . . 106177
Boulle, Saint-Grégoire . . . 067510
Boullé, Claude, Paris . . . 100078
Boullé, Yvon, Moutiers . . . 064822
Boulogne, Pont-de-Briques-Saint-Etienne . . . 066917
Boulonnais, Anne, Vandières . . . 068707
Boulouk, Georges, Paris . . . 065608
Bouloux, Sylvie, Angers . . . 124073
Boulton, John, Broseley . . . 083770
Boulton & Cooper, Malton . . . 122610
Bouma, Groningen . . . 140432
Bouman-Buwalda, Amsterdam . . . 077808
Bound for Pleasure, Sacramento . . 142841
Bound To Be Found, Indianapolis . . 089277
Bound Words, Hampton . . . 136932
Boundary Gallery, London . . . 113514
Boundary Museum, Grand Forks . . 005533
Bounica, Genève . . . 082406
Bouniol, Denise, Issoudun . . . 099368
Bountiful Books, San Diego . . . 142901
Bountiful of Berry, Berry . . . 055493
Bounty Antiques, Topsham . . . 086897
Bouquet-Jacoillot, Colette, Condé-sur-Vesgre . . . 062450
Bouquinerie, La Chaux-de-Fonds . . 082299
Bouquinerie, Valence (Drôme) . . . 138644
Bouquinerie Comtoise, Besançon . . 061377, 138030
Bouquinerie de l'Institut, Paris . . . 100079, 138314
Bouquinerie des Carmes, Liège . . . 137516
Bouquinerie des Quais, Rennes (Ille-et-Vilaine) . . . 138578
Bouquinerie du Palais, Ajaccio . . . 138009
Bouquinerie le Fouineur, Lausanne . 141263
Bouquinerie Le Meridien, Bruxelles 137427
Bouquiniste, Bayonne . . . 138024
Bouquiniste, La Rochelle . . . 138112
Bouquiniste, Saint Andrews . . . 142034
Bouquiniste, Saint-Étienne . . . 138597
Bourassin-Rancon, Christian, Airaines . . . 060684
Bourbaki-Panorama Luzern, Luzern 037294
Bourbon-Hanby, London . . . 085151
Bourbon Street Gallery, New Orleans . . . 117407
Bourbonnais, Jean-Louis, Saint-Rémy-lès-Chevreuse . . . 067994
Bourcy & Paulusch, Wien . . . 137291
Bourdareau, Marcel, Chasseneuil-sur-Bonnieure . . . 062175
Bourdariat, Albert, Paris . . . 124601
Bourdely & Roig Diffusion, Grenoble 063055
Bourdette, Danielle, Honfleur . . . 099334
Bourdon, Daniel, Viriat . . . 069004
Bourdon, Louis, Guingamp . . . 063108
Bourdon, M., Mons . . . 058337
Bourdon-Smith, J.H., London . . . 085152, 130954
Bourdonnais Antiquités, Paris . . . 065609
Bourel, Jean-Paul, Annonay . . . 060905
Bourel, Jean-Paul, Annonay . . . 060906
Bouretz, Béthune . . . 061411
Bourey Caldarera, Marie-Christine, Avallon . . . 061116
Bourgaux, Anne, Bruxelles 057860, 096160
Bourgeneuf 1900, Saint-Julien-Chapteuil . . . 014365
Bourgeois, Besançon . . . 061378
Bourgeois, Daniel, Châtillon-sur-Seine . . . 062236
Bourgeois, Marie, Vaupillon . . . 068737
Bourgeois, Pierre, Lyon . . . 064092
Bourgeois Boheme, Los Angeles . . 089709
Le Bourget, Montréal . . . 096984
Bourgey, Sabine, Paris . . . 065610
Bourgogne Antiquités, Dunkerque . 062748
Bourgogne Antiquités, Mâcon . . . 064202
Bourgues, Christian, Cavaillon . . . 062041
Bourguet, Gérard, Québec 059065, 097134
Bourke, Limerick . . . 074986
Bourkel, Christian, Breteuil-sur-Iton 061785
Bourkel, Christian, Les Baix-de-Breteuil . . . 063757
Bourlet, Catherine, Genève 111432, 130031
Bourlot, Torino . . . 140128
Bourn, Hugh, Burnham-on-Crouch . 112764
Bourne, Edinburgh . . . 112985
Bourne, Michael, Columbus . . . 131978
Bourne, P., Edinburgh . . . 084277
Bourne & Co., Richard A., Hyannis Port . . . 122916
Bourne Antiques and Arts, Bourne . 083587
Bourne End Antiques Centre, Bourne End . . . 083588
Bourne End Auction Rooms, Bourne End . . . 083589, 122423
Bourne End Pictures Plus, Bourne End . . . 112677
Bourne Gallery, Reigate . . 114302, 131409
Bourne Hall Museum, Ewell . . . 039462
Bourne Mill Antiques, Farnham . . . 084387
Bournemouth Fine Books, Bournemouth . . . 141423
Bournemouth Natural Science Society Museum, Bournemouth . . . 038794
Bournemouth Transport Museum, Christchurch . . . 039084
Bournville Centre for Visual Arts, Birmingham . . . 038727
Bourquard-Furster, Pierre, Semur-en-Auxois . . . 068203
Bourquin, Claire, Miglieglia . . . 082659
Bourquin, René, Bessoncourt . . . 124099
Bourquin, Yveline, Dijon . . . 062645
Bourrasset, Daniel, Le Muy . . . 063671
Bourreau, Ravier, Noirmoutier-en-l'Ile . . . 099878
Bourret, Bernard, Avignon . . . 061128
La Bourrine à Rosalie, Sallertaine . . 014643
Bourrut, Lucienne, Vic-en-Bigorre . 068839
The Bourse Antiquarian Print Gallery, Brighton, Victoria . . . 055549
Bourse aux Affaires, Les Sables-d'Olonne . . . 063783

La Bourse aux Collections, Melun . . 064474
Bourse aux Livres, Tournai 137539
Bourse aux Timbres, Lyon 064093
Bourse Collectionneur, Paris 065611
Bourse d'Antiquités Militaires, Orléans 093654
Bourse du Jouet Ancien, Bordeaux . 093655
Bourse du Mobilier, Roanne 067163
Bourse et Collections, Toulon (Var) . 068445
Bourse Numismatique et Cartophile, Bourges 093656
Boury, Jean-Yves, Janzé 063230
Bouscary, Monique, Dijon 062646
Bouscasse, Alain, Carpentras 061997
Bouscayrol, Biarritz 098961
Bouscayrol, Bordeaux 098987
Bouscayrol, Pau 100982
Bousquet, Richard, Arcachon 060950
Bousquet, Richard, Paris 065612
Boussaroque, Claudine, Bordeaux . 061595
Boussat, Philippe, Felletin 062852
Boustead-Bland, Chester 083952
Bout-Croizé, Sandrine, Lieuran lès Béziers 124313
Bout d'Bois, La Baule-Escoublac . . 063286
Bout d'Bois, La Baule-Escoublac . . 063287
Bouteloup, Huguette, Saint-Ouen . . 067738
Boutemy, Paris 065613, 124602
Boutersky, Jacques, Paris 100080
Boutet, Lionel, Lumio 064025, 099529, 138126
Boutet Brousmiche, Poitiers 066889
Boutin, Josiane, Chamoux 062112
The Boutique, Hamilton 096911
Boutique, Opio 065273
Boutique Antiquités, Beaune 061270
Boutique d'Antan, Montcenis 064667
Boutique de Francine, L'Isle-sur-la-Sorgue 063926
Boutique de la Demolición, Coronel Dorrego 055256
Boutique de l'Antiquaire, Lourmarin 064014
Boutique de l'Histoire, Paris 138315
Boutique-de-l'Or, Rennes (Ille-et-Vilaine) 067105
Boutique dell'Arredamento, Modena 075900
Boutique du Collectionneur, Saint-Louis 067591
Boutique du Fou, Loix-en-Ré 063977
La Boutique du Marais, Paris 065614
Boutique Dunia, Montréal 096985
Boutique Folies, Québec 059066
Boutique Paris-Musées, Paris 138316
Boutique Paris-Musées, Paris 138317
Boutique Rosa, Casablanca 077644
Boutique Virgilio, Panamá City 108785
't Boutje, Breda 078082
Boutle & King, London 141763
Bouton, München 104156
Bouton, Heidi, Bernburg 102098
Boutreux, Patrick, Chouzé-sur-Loire 062304
Boutros, Zaki, Cairo 060432
Boutwell, Langenfeld 103832
Boutwell Draper, Redfern 095125
Bouveret, Luc, Paris 065615
Bouvet Ladubay, Saumur 101263
Bouvier, Bonn 138891
Bouvier, Jacques, Paris 065616
Bouvier, Jean-Louis, Saint-Quentin-Fallavier 067977
Bouvier, Michel, Paris 138318
Bouvrot, Koppingen 111590
Bouwen, Rina, Madrid 110457
Bouwhuis, G., Diever 128646
Bouwman, Arnhem 078046
Bouwman, Ivo, Den Haag 078175
Bov Museum, Padborg 009060
Bovani, Sabrina, Firenze 127308
Bovenschutte, Gelselaar 128671
Bovien, Ursula, Moghegno-Aurigeno 111737
Bovill, Miles, Malvern, Victoria 056143
Bow House, Hungerford 084754
Bow-well Antiques, Edinburgh 084278
Bow Windows Book Shop, Lewes . . 141721
Bowback Chair Company, Atlanta . . 087457
Bowden, Bryan, Harrogate 084569, 130761
Bowden, David, London 113515
Bowden, Jonathan, Riverside 095147
Bowden Pioneer Museum, Bowden 005122
Bowdery, M.J., Hindhead 084689
Bowdoin College Museum of Art, Brunswick 042487
Bowdoin College. Museum of Art. Occasional Papers, Brunswick . . . 136401
Bowdon, Clitheroe 141525
Bowen, Tianjin 098008
Bowen, Wellington 108616
Bowen, Annabel, Baltinglass 127088
Bowen House/ Roseland Cottage, Woodstock 049290
Bower, Mount Molly 056293
Bower, Peakhurst 056447
Bower House Gallery, Milton 094853
Bowerbank Mill, Deloraine 094472
Bowers, Francis, Peterborough 086230
Bowers Mansion, Carson City 042634
Bowers & Merena, Wolfeboro 123140
The Bowers Museum of Cultural Art, Santa Ana 047945
Bowers Science Museum, Cortland 043171
Bowery, Baltimore 087649
Bowery Gallery, New York 046303
The Bowes Museum, Barnard Castle 038596
Bowes Railway Heritage Museum, Gateshead 039535
Bowhaus, Los Angeles 116731
Bowhill Collection, Selkirk 040979
Bowie & Hulbert, Hay-on-Wye 113208
Bowie on Bowie Art, Fort Worth . . . 116135
Bowie Railroad Station and Huntington Museum, Bowie 042362
Bowinkel, Uberto, Napoli 075948
Bowitz, Frankenthal, Pfalz 070722
Bowkett, Knaresborough . 084881, 130856
Bowlby, Nicholas, Poundgate 114286
Bowlby, Nicholas, Tunbridge Wells .114609, 131614
Bowles, Franklin, New York 117723
Bowling Green State University Fine Arts Center Galleries, Bowling Green . 042370
Bowls New Zealand Museum, New Plymouth 030550
Bowman, Robert, London 085153
Bowman, Robert, London 113516
Bowman, Robert, London . 113517, 130955
Bowman, Russell, Chicago 115374
Bowman, Megahan and Penelec Galleries, Allegheny College, Meadville 045737
Bowmanville Museum, Bowmanville 005123
Bowmoore, Marlborough 085945
Bowne House, Flushing 043874
Bowood Antiques, Wendover 087075
Bowood House and Gardens, Calne 038949
Bowral Antiques, Bowral 055528
Bowraville Folk Museum, Bowraville 000823
La Box, Bourges 010934
Box Heart Expressions, Pittsburgh . 118906
Box of Delights, Skipton 142072
Box of Porcelain, Dorchester 084174
Boxart, Verona 106789
Boxenstopmuseum Auto-Zweirad-Spielzeug, Tübingen 020492
Boxer, Martínez 055278
Boxer, Henry, Richmond, Surrey . . . 114307
Boxes and Musical Instruments, London 085154, 130956
Boxfield Gallery, Stevenage 041094
Boxholms Auktionstjänst, Boxholm . 122112
Boxoyo, Cáceres 141012
Boxster, Nashville 090427
Boxy, P. & L., Knokke-Heist 058241
Boya, Shenzhen 097972
Boyce, Victoria, Tucson 120111
Boycott, Bruxelles 096161
Boyd, Annie, Stanmore 056627
Boyd, John, Castle Cary 130519
Boyd, Roy, Chicago 115375
Boyd, Vance, Memphis 090058
The Boydell Galleries, Liverpool . . .085022, 113406
Boyer, Argenton-sur-Creuse 060965
Boyer, Dorien, Saint-Hilaire-de-Brethmas 067514
Boyer, Serge, Paris 065617
Boyer Museum and National Marbles Hall of Fame, Wildwood 049173
Boyertown Museum of Historic Vehicles, Boyertown 042372
Boyes, Judy, Ambleside 112505
The Boyle House - Hot Spring County Museum, Malvern 045608
Boyles-Snyder &CO, Los Angeles . . 132241
Boyne Valley Historical Cottage, Ubobo 001574
Boys From the Bush Antiques, Woodside 056848
Boys Town Hall of History & Father Flanagan House, Boys Town 042373
Boz, Hay-on-Wye 141650
Bozar Shop, Bruxelles 137428
Bozart, Lisboa 109270
Bozart, Philadelphia 135475
Bozatlı, İstanbul 112292
Bozhou City Museum, Bozhou 007021
Bozsik, Budapest 074671
Bozzeto, Bilbao 110272
Bozzetto, Pedro, Porto Alegre 058490
Bozzi, Ivan, Bolzano 127192
Bozzi, Ugo, Roma 134668
Bozzini, Sonia, Milano 127550
BPA Collectables, Los Angeles 089710
BQ, Köln 103600
Braak, ter, Zwolle 108279
Braak, Peter ter, Groningen 078406
Braak, Peter ter, Groningen 078407
Braak, Peter ter, Groningen 128679
Braakhuis, P., Maastricht 078598
Braam, J.P.B., Bruxelles 123580
Braat & de Pater, Leiden 078562
Braatz, Rüdiger, Langwedel 139381
Brabant Antiquariaat, 's-Hertogenbosch 140459
Brabante, Madrid 129582
Brabants Etsenkabinet, Geldrop . . . 140424
Brabants Museum Oud Oosterhout, Oosterhout 029999
Brac, Jean, Mouleydier 064809
Brac de la Perrière, Lyon 124339
Bracaglia, Silverio, Roma 127944
Bracci, Angelino, Roma 076346
Bracci, Angelino, Roma 076347
Bracci, Claudio, Roma 076348
Bracciali, Carlo, München 072667
Bracher, Kathrin, Bern 129950
Brachert, Dr. Eva, Mainz 126256
Brachert, Dr. Thomas, Nürnberg . . . 126560
Brachot, Bruxelles 096162
Brachot, Bruxelles 096163
Bracht, Christa, Kassel 071747
Bracias Peñafiel, Sergio, Zaragoza . 081736
Bracken Community Museum, Bracken 005130
Bracken Hall Countryside Centre, Baildon 038566
Bracket, Toronto 097238
Bracket Clock, Córdoba 081046
Brackets, Tunbridge Wells 122729
Bracki Muzej, Škrip 007796
Brackley Antique Cellar, Brackley . . 083620
Brackley Antiques, Brackley 083621, 130422
Brackmann, C., Bruxelles 123581
Bracko, Calgary 123740
Bracksmayer, R., Bad Nauheim . . . 069336
Bradatsch-Wendler, Andrea, Leonberg, Württemberg 126213
Bradbury & Son, Edward, Cheltenham 083916, 141502
Bradbury, Roger, Coltishall 084065
Bradbury, Stuart, Paulton 131363
Bradbury Science Museum, Los Alamos 045407
Bradford, Baar 134978
Bradford, Cairns 055596
Bradford, Nashville 090428
Bradford Brinton Memorial, Big Horn 042197
Bradford Campbell, San Francisco . 119617
Bradford County Historical Society Museum, Towanda 048590
Bradford Creek Antiques, Bendigo . 055477
Bradford Historical Society Museum, Bradford 042382
Bradford Industrial Museum and Horses at work, Bradford 038804
The Bradford Museum of Collector's Plates, Niles 046486
Bradford-on-Avon Museum, Bradford-on-Avon 038810
Bradley, Houston 132105
Bradley, Portland 091906
Bradley, Richmond 092064
Bradley, A. & M., Petworth 086239
Bradley, Robert, Salisbury 086490
Bradley Brent, Portland 118980
Bradley Gallery of Art, Plymouth . . . 047103
Bradley Museum, Mississauga 005890
Bradran, Manama 095995
Brad's Custom Woodworking, Windsor, Ontario 123861
Bradshaw, Birmingham 087743
Bradshaw, Portland 118981
Bradshaw, W.F., Woollahra 056857
Bradstreet's Books, Hawthorn, Victoria 136936
Bradwell Antiques Centre, Bradwell 083634, 130427
Bradwin, Elizabeth, London 085155
Brady, Philadelphia 132606
Brady & Co., W.M., New York 117724
Brady & Turner, London 130957
Brae, Clarence, Paterson 056446
Brae-Mar Antiques, Woonona 056889
Braecklein, Wolfgang, Berlin 138752
Braem & Minetti, Toronto . 059157, 097239
Braemar, London 085156
Braemar, Springwood 095219
Braemar Castle, Braemar 038816
Brändl, Werner, Würzburg 074493
Brändström, Andreas, Stockholm . . 111013
Bräunlein, Dieter, Spalt 073869
Bräustüberlmuseum, Raab 002483
Braga, Martel 064409
Bragardo, Liège 058291, 123647
Bragegården, Vaasa 010199
Bragg, Jean, New Orleans 090519
Bragg, John, Lostwithiel 085851
Bragg, Kimberly, San Francisco . . . 092744
Bragg-Mitchell Mansion, Mobile . . . 045945
Bragge & Sons, Rye 086422, 131433
Braggiotti, Amsterdam 107687
Brahetrolleborg Skolemuseum, Faaborg 008848
Brahma, Pierre, Paris 065618
Brahms-Netski, New York 090747
Brahmshaus, Baden-Baden 015848
Brahmshaus, Heide, Holstein 017820
Brahuer Joyeros, Barcelona 080818
Braidwood and Rushbrook Museum, Edinburgh 039378
Braidwood Museum, Braidwood . . . 000830
Braig, Albrecht, Memmingen 072512
Brail-Millet, Alzonne 060786
Brailly, Amiens 060808
Brain, Marilyn, Constantia 080692
Brain Trust, Tokyo 107023
Brain-Watkins House, Tauranga . . . 030598
Brainard, C.R., Cleveland 115693
Braintree District Museum, Braintree 038817
Braintree Historical Society Museum, Braintree 042384
Braith-Mali-Museum, Biberach an der Riß 016219

Braithwaite Fine Arts Gallery, Cedar City . . . 042663
The Braithwaite Gallery, York . . . 114749
Braitman, Charlotte . . . 115279
Brajkovic, Berlin . . . 069582, 125180
Bralorne Pioneer Museum, Bralorne 005131
Brāļu Amtmaņu Muzejs, Valle . . . 027792
Brāļu Jurjānu Memoriālais Muzejs Meņģeļi, Ērgļi . . . 027681
Brāļu Kaudzīšu Memoriālais Muzejs, Vecpiebalga . . . 027795
Braly, Jean, New Orleans . . . 117408
Brama, Breda . . . 107875
Brama, Warszawa . . . 109102
Bramah Tea and Coffee Museum, London . . . 040092
Bramall Hall, Bramhall . . . 038818
Brambilla, Marco, Milano . . . 127551
Brambridge Antiques, Brambridge .083635, 130428
Brambuk Living Cultural Centre, Halls Gap . . . 001093
Brame & Lorenceau, Paris 065619, 100081
Bramley Antiques, Eye . . . 084367, 130697
Brammertz, Frank, Langenfeld . . . 103833
Brammertz, H., Stolberg, Rheinland 073925
Brampton Picture Gallery, Brampton, Cambridgeshire . . . 112693
Bramsnæs Museum og Arkiv, Kirke Hyllinge . . . 008953
Branca, Chicago . . . 115376
Brancaccio, Simonetta, Roma . . . 076349
Brancatelli, Calogero, Roma . . . 076350
Branchon, Lilia, Lyon . . . 124340
Branchvereniging Art & Frame, Utrecht . . . 053880
Branchville Railroad Shrine and Museum, Branchville . . . 042385
Branco, Catarina Faria, Lisboa . . . 079883
Branco, Catarina Faria, Lisboa . . . 079884
Branco, Maria Rosário, Porto . . . 080070
Branco, Pedro Aguiar, Porto . . . 080071
Brand, Den Haag . . . 078176
Brand, Roches-lès-Blamont . . . 067187
Brand, Joachim, Bern . . . 082202
Brand, Marianne, Carouge . . . 111331
Brand, W., Punthorst . . . 128805
Brand Library and Art Galleries, Glendale . . . 044207
Brand & Rauch, Bonn . . . 069915
Brand X Antiques, San Francisco . . 092745
Brandão, São Paulo . . . 137580
Brande, Halstenbek . . . 103081
Brande Museum, Brande . . . 008825
Brandeis, Miami . . . 142555
Brandel, Katrin, Berlin . . . 138753
Brandenburg-Preußen Museum, Wustrau . . . 021028
Brandenburgische Kunstsammlungen Cottbus, Museum für zeitgenössische Kunst, Fotografie und Plakat, Cottbus . . . 016593
Brandenburgischer Kunstverein Potsdam e.V., Potsdam . . . 019654, 053065
Brandenburgischer Verband Bildender Künstler e.V, Potsdam . . . 053066
Brandenburgisches Forstmuseum Fürstenberg/Havel, Fürstenberg, Havel . . . 017280
Brandenburgisches Freilichtmuseum Altranft, Altranft . . . 015523
Brandenburgisches Museum für Klein- und Privatbahnen, Gramzow . . . 017509
Brandenburgisches Textilmuseum Forst, Forst, Lausitz . . . 017141
Brander Museum, Huntly . . . 039787
Brander-Rodriguez, Luis, Nice . . . 124504
Brandes, W., Braunschweig . . .121353, 138918
Brandes 5060 L., Duisburg 070476, 125559
Brandi, Maurizio, Napoli . . . 075949
Brandicourt, Colette, Paris . . . 065620
Brandis, Agnes von, Hamburg . . . 125805
Brandis, Alexandra, Salzburg . . . 123438
Brandl, Eduard, Wien . . . 057388
Brandler, Brentwood . . . 130433
Brandler Galleries, Brentwood . . . 112698
Brandner, R., Berchtesgaden . . . 069526
Brandner, Reinhard, Klagenfurt-Wölfnitz . . . 095625, 133103
Brandon, Tulsa . . . 123128
Brandon, Elizabeth, Nashville . . . 117342
Brandon Heritage Museum, Brandon . . . 038819
Brandsdörfer, Thomas, Düsseldorf . 070367
Het Brandspuithuisje, Ijsselstein . . . 140466
Brandstätter, Dr. Christian, Wien . . . 133185
Brandstätter, Günther, Bergheim . . . 123342
Brandstorps Auktionsfirma, Brandstorp . . . 122113
Brandstrup Galleri, Stavanger . . . 079498
Brandt, London . . . 085157
Brandt, C., Itzstedt . . . 071650
Brandt, Christophe, Neuchâtel . . . 130124
Brandt, Tilman, Görlitz . . . 125735
Brandt, Walfried, Hövikodden . . . 128990
Brandtmayer, Horst, Seefeld in Tirol 057312
Brandval Museum, Brandval . . . 030793
Brandweermuseum, Wouwse Plantage . . . 030356
Brandweermuseum en Stormrampmuseum, Borculo . . . 029327
Brandweermuseum Wassenaar, Wassenaar . . . 030310
Brandy, Michel, Saint-Martin-de-Ré 067631
Brandywine Battlefield, Chadds Ford . . . 042691
Brandywine River Museum, Chadds Ford . . . 042692
Brandywine River Museum Antiques Show, Chadds Ford . . . 093976
La Branère, Labenne . . . 063475
Branger, François, Angers . . . 120895
Branigan Cultural Center, Las Cruces . . . 045177
Branko Deškovič Art Gallery, Bol . . 007701
Branksome, Martínez . . . 055279
Branksome Antiques, Branksome . . 083644
Brans, Clive & John, Mosman Park . 056269
Brans, Sylvaine, Paris . . . 124603
Branscheid, U., Lüdenscheid . . . 072345
Bransky, Weimar, Thüringen . . . 105185
Bransten, Rena, San Francisco . . . 119618
Brant, New York . . . 135414
Brant, Laird, Dallas . . . 088468
Brant Museum, Brantford . . . 005145
Brantes Wattebled, Paris . . . 065621
Brantwood, Coniston . . . 039133
Brantwood, Warwick . . . 087035
Brase, Bad Endorf . . . 101641
Brasher-Rucker, Memphis . . . 116977
Brasiello, Pasquale, Perugia . . . 127870
Brasil 40, Madrid . . . 129583
Brasil Europa Moveis e Antiguidades, Rio de Janeiro . . . 058558
Brasilianische Botschaft, Berlin . . . 015998
Brasilianisches Kulturinstitut, Berlin 015999
Brasilienmuseum im Kloster Bardel, Bad Bentheim . . . 015653
Brass, Lawrence, Bath . . . 083420, 130350
Brass & Son, Lawrence, Bristol . . . 130453
Brass, Lawrence, London . . . 130958
Brass Armadillo, Omaha . . . 091555
Brass Armadillo, Phoenix . . . 091723
Brass Bed Factory, Philadelphia . . . 132607
Brass Buff, Tulsa . . . 093287, 132996
Brass Eagle, Portland . . . 091907
Brass Eagle Antiques, Cincinnati . . 088217
Brass Foundry Castings, Brasted . . 130430
Brass Key Antiques, Salt Lake City . 092420
The Brass Knob, Washington . . . 093387
Brass Light Gallery, Milwaukee . . .090280, 132362
Brass Menagerie, New Orleans . . . 090520
Brass Monkey, New Orleans . . . 090521
Brass Monkey 407, New Orleans . . 090522
Brass & Nickel Plating, Portland . . . 132685
Brass Rubbing Centre, Edinburgh . . 039379
Brass Towne, Baltimore . . . 131818
Brass Works, Chicago . . . 088038, 131890
Brass Works, Chicago . . . 131891
Brassac, J.L., Villefranche-de-Rouergue . . . 068893
Brassel, Vera, Altstätten . . . 111118
Brasseur, Martine, Reims . 067061, 101069
Brassworks, Portland . . . 132686
Brassworks Company, Baltimore . .087650, 131819
Braswell, New York . . . 090748, 122988
Braswell Chase, New York . . . 122989
Bratří Špillarů, Domažlice . . . 098356
Bratskij Chudožestvennyj Vystavočnyj Zal, Bratskij gorodskoj objedinennyj muzej istorii osvoenija Angary, Bratsk . . 033046
Bratskij Gorodskoj Objedinennyj Muzej Istorii Osvoenija Angary, Bratsk . . 033047
Brattle, Boston . . . 142250
Brattle Farm Museum, Staplehurst . 041093
Brattleboro Museum and Art Center, Brattleboro . . . 042389
Bratz, Jörg P., Berlin . . . 069583
Brauckmann, Beatrice, Germering . 125722
Brauer, Elfriede, Hörbranz . . . 057062
Brauer, Gustav, Bremen . . . 133841
Brauer, Jörg, Rudolstadt . . . 073612
Brauer & Brauer, Rio de Janeiro . . . 096594
Brauer Museum of Art, Valparaiso . 048741
Brauerei-Kontor, Kleines Museum der Privatbrauerei Moritz Fliege, Bochum . . . 016275
Brauerei-Museum, Haßfurt . . . 017790
Brauerei-Museum, Nesselwang . . . 019205
Brauerei Museum Bürger-Bräu Hof, Hof, Saale . . . 017955
Brauereichäller Kulturforum, Laufen 037233
Brauereikulturmuseum Gut Riedelsbach, Neureichenau . . . 019263
Brauereimuseum, Aldersbach . . . 015473
Brauereimuseum, Altomünster . . . 015519
Brauereimuseum Bräu im Moos, Tüßling . . . 020506
Brauereimuseum im historischen Kronen-Brauhaus zu Lüneburg, Lüneburg 018740
Brauereimuseum im Stift Göß, Leoben . . . 002222
Brauereimuseum in der Brauerei Franz Xaver Glossner, Neumarkt, Oberpfalz . . . 019251
Brauereimuseum Schöneck, Schöneck, Vogtland . . . 020076
Brauhaus-Galerie, Freistadt, Oberösterreich . . . 001867
Brauhausmuseum, Stadtlauringen . 020285
Brauhinia Shire Bicentennial Art Gallery, Springsure . . . 001485
Braulio 2, Castello de la Plana . . . 110300
Braumuseum, Wieselburg an der Erlauf . . . 003040
Braumuseum-Wolff Giersings's Brauerbe, Stadt- und Kulturgeschichtliches Museum, Torgau . . . 020449
Braun, Saint Louis . . . 092208
Braun, Stockholm . . . 081931
Braun, Bernd, Stuttgart . . . 139756
Braun, Franz Josef & Fr. Werner, Memmelsdorf . . . 126305
Braun, Gabriele, Mühlacker . . . 126336
Braun, Hans-Gert, Wuppertal . . . 074521
Braun, Hans-Gert, Wuppertal . . . 074522
Braun, Hans-Gert, Wuppertal . . .105347, 139882
Braun, Hans-Gert, Wuppertal . . . 139883
Braun, Helmut, Hauenstein . . . 071434
Braun, Helmut, Rinnthal . . . 073539
Braun, Horst, Spalt . . . 073870
Braun, I., Detmold . . . 138979
Braun, Klaus, Stuttgart . . . 104968
Braun, Markus & Hans, Pirmasens . 126632
Braun, Martin, Rastede . . . 073422
Braun, R., Freiburg im Breisgau . . . 070828
Braun, Rheinhold, Regensburg . . . 073452
Braun, Werner, Lörrach . . . 072290
Braun, Wolfgang, Blieskastel . . . 069869
Braunauer Heimatmuseum, Forchheim, Oberfranken . . . 017137
Braunbehrens, von, München . . . 104157
Braunbehrens Nachf., von, Wolfratshausen . . . 105321
Braune, Brad, San Antonio . . . 119400
Braune, Irmgard, Edling . . . 070509
Braunmiller, Wilfried, München . . . 126360
Brauns, Thomas & Curt, Frechen . . 139102
Braunschweigisches Landesmuseum, Braunschweig . . . 016381
Braunschweigisches Landesmuseum, Abteilung Ur- und Frühgeschichte, Wolfenbüttel . . . 020954
Braunstein, Alain, Nice . . . 065056
Braunstein & Quay, San Francisco . 119619
Braunton and District Museum, Braunton . . . 038820
Braus, Heidelberg . . . 134047
Brausen, Hans, Dormagen . . . 102385
Brautsch, H. & M., Greding . . . 125753
Bravard, Frédéric, Monaco . . . 077596
Brave Old World, Portland . . . 132687
Braverman, Pittsburgh . . . 091794
Bravin, Tamara, Torino . . . 076782
Bravo, Quezon City . . . 079569
Bravo Carrion, Paulino, Madrid . . . 081255
Bravo Heredia, Francisco, Málaga . 081415
Bravo of Old Town, San Diego . . . 119490
Bravo Panadero, Oscar, Madrid . . . 081256
Bray Heritage Centre and Museum, Bray . . . 022695
Brayer, Nancy . . . 064862
Brayer, André, Damblain . . . 062590
Brayshaw Museum Park, Blenheim 030453
Brazen, Burnham Market . 083802, 141462
Brazier, Richmond . . . 119103
Brazil Galeria, Sydenham . . . 095263
Braziller, George, New York . . . 135415
Brazoria County Historical Museum, Angleton . . . 041724
Brazos Valley Antiques, Fort Worth . 088839
Brazos Valley Museum of Natural History, Bryan . . . 042491
Brazosport Museum of Natural Science, Brazosport . . . 042390
Brazosport Museum of Natural Science, Clute . . . 043025
Brazzini, Dario, Firenze . . . 127309
Bread & Puppet Museum, Glover . . 044226
Bread Street Gallery, Penzance . . . 114231
Breadalbane Folklore Centre, Killin . 039867
Breakspeare, Tetbury . . . 086850
Breamore Countryside Museum, Breamore . . . 038821
Breamore House Museum, Breamore . . . 038822
Breard, Hermann, Rouen . . . 101111
Breault & Sons, Dallas . . . 132000
Brebner Surgical Museum, Johannesburg . . . 034646
Brebsom & Co, Gerard-Michel, Luxembourg . . . 077477, 107393
Breche, Sevilla . . . 081577
Breche, Sevilla . . . 081578
Brechin Museum, Brechin . . . 038823
Brechmann, Hedwig, Bielefeld . . . 102115
Brechó, Elio & Clair, São Paulo . . . 123714
Brecht-Haus Weißensee, Kommunale Galerie Weißensee, Berlin . . . 016000
Brecht-Weigel-Gedenkstätte, Berlin 016001
Brechthaus, Augsburg . . . 015604
Brecknock Museum and Art Gallery, Brecon . . . 038825
Brecon Mountain Railway, Merthyr Tydfil . . . 040448
Breda Aude, Chantal de, Lyon . . . 064094
Breda's Begijnhof Museum, Breda . 029348
Breda's Museum, Breda . . . 029349
Bredase, Breda . . . 078083, 128602
De Brede, Maasbree . . . 029889
Brede, Horst, Zierenberg . . . 134478
Brede Værk, Kongens Lyngby . . . 008999
Bredgade Antikvariat, København . . 137889
Bredgade Kunsthandel, København 060297, 098541
Bredy Farm Old Farming Collection, Bridport . . . 038838

Breebaart, I.L., Amsterdam 128530
Breede, B. & J., Bremen 138941
Breede, Ulf, Berlin 069584
Breen, Kevin, West Melbourne 120653
Breendonk Fort National Memorial, Willebroek 003856
Breewood, Richmond, New South Wales 095130
Breeze, Geoffrey, Bath 083421
Bregenzer Kunstverein, Bregenz . . . 052520
Brégeot, Eric, Aire-sur-l'Adour 060688
Bregt Zijlmans, Vlijmen 128871
Bréhal'Antiques, Brehal 061757
Bréhélin, Jean, Rennes (Ille-et-Vilaine) 138579
Bréhéret, Paris . . . 065622, 100082, 133545
Bréhéret, Michèle, Angers 060848
Brehm, Krefeld 103773
Brehm, Gerda, Krefeld 072066
Brehm, Werner, Uettingen 074138
Brehm-Gedenkstätte, Renthendorf . 019803
Brehmer, Renate, München 104158, 139498
Breidablikk, Stavanger 031223
Breidenstein, Petra, Berlin 125181
Breier, Marianne, Dettingen unter Teck 070235
Breier, V., San Francisco 119620
Breier & Breier, Dettingen unter Teck 070236
Breil Jacques, Lyon 064095
Breitbach, Norbert, Boppard 121351
Breitenbach, Christa, Aschaffenburg 069191
Breitenbach, Christa, Laudenbach, Unterfranken 072163
Breitengraser, Berlin 101812
Breitfeld, Annaberg-Buchholz 069172
Breithaupt, Bettina, Gomaringen . . 125743
Breitmann, Hugo, Buenos Aires . . . 055182
Breitschchäuer, Bern 111247
Breitschuh, Klaus, Quedlinburg . . .073396, 121580
Breiz, Carnac 061990
Brem, Brigitte M., Stuttgart 073963
De Bremberg, Waalre 140566
Brembs, B., Schweinfurt 073765
Bremecke, Ratingen 104660
Bremens, Jean-Marc, Lyon 121043
Bremer, Berlin 101813
Bremer, Ijmuiden 128732
Bremer, Beverly, Atlanta 087458
Bremer, M., Essen 070619
Bremer, R., Heidelberg 071447
Bremer Numismatische Gesellschaft, Bremen 053067
Bremer-Röhner, Dr. Uta, Plön 104615
Bremer Rundfunkmuseum, Bremen 016409
Bremer Verband Bildender Künstlerinnen und Künstler, Bremen 053068
Bremerhavener Versorgungs- und Verkehrsmuseum, Bremerhaven . 016428
Bremermann, New Orleans 090523
Bremermann, Gerrie, New Orleans . 090524
Bremerton Naval Museum, Bremerton 042395
Bremilts, Jean-Louis, Lille 063835
Bremmer, Tilburg 108228
Bremmer, Barbara, Windhaag bei Perg 057603
Bremmers, Maastricht . . . 128758, 140493
Bren Art, Toronto 097240
Brenau University Galleries, Gainesville 044110
Brendlein, Heidelberg 139248
Brendow & Sohn, Joh., Moers 134208
Brennan, Patricia, Roma 076351
Brennan, Robyn, Annerley 055348
Brennan and Geraghty's Store Museum, Maryborough, Queensland 001224
Brennecke, Klaus-D., Berlin 101814
Brenner, Leo, Aachen 101503
Brenner, Michel, Vesoul 068828
Brenner, S., Gieboldehausen 070987
Brenner, Stefan, Stuttgart 073964
Brenner, Sylvia, Zwinge 074583
Brennereimuseum am Hitzlhammer, Sankt Oswald bei Freistadt 002606
Brennereimuseum Haselünne, Haselünne 017784
BrennGlas Verlag, Niddatal 134313
Brennig, Heribert, Bonn 138892
Brennpunkt, Schüpfen 111896
Brensbach Museum und Galerie im alten Rathaus, Brensbach 016444
Brenske, Helmut, Hannover 071389, 121443, 125865, 134038
Brenske, Dr. Stefan, München 072668
Brent, Keighley 113311
Brent, Saint Louis 092209
Brentwood, Nashville 117343
Brentwood Antik Auctions, Brentwood 122432
Brentwood Art Center, Los Angeles . 051635
The Brentwood Gallery, Warrington 114649
Brentwood Museum, Warley Hill . . . 041298
Brenzel, Steffen, Murnau 104383
Brenzett Aeronautical Museum, Romney Marsh 040851
Brenzett Museum, Romney Marsh . 040851
Breon, Gagny 062953
Brepols Publishers, Turnhout 133298
Brereton, Lorcan, Dublin 074895
Brès, de, Amsterdam 107688
Brès, Martin, Marseille . . . 064327, 099642, 138192
Bresaylor Heritage Museum, Paynton 006121
Bresinsky, H., Vilgertshofen 139817
Bresler Eitel, Milwaukee 117174
Bressan, Renzo, Venezia 128379
Bressem, J., Pasewalk 073293
Bresset & Fils, Paris 065623
Bressingham Steam Museum, Diss 039242
Bressoise Transactions, Le Crès . . . 063609
Bressol, Barcelona 080819
Brest, Christophe, Épernay 062780
Brest Philatélie, Brest 061766
Bret, André, Faverges-de-la-Tour . . 062843
Bret, Michel, Lyon 124341
Bretagne Ancienne, Guérande 063098
Bretagne Antik, Brest 061767
Bretaudiere, Hervé, Chalon-sur-Saône 120967
Bretin, Sophie, Lyon 124342
Bretón, Logroño 081180, 110410
Breton, Benoît, Bulgnéville 061836
Breton, Gérard, Saint-Léonard-de-Noblat 067583
Breton, Sylvie, Dijon 062647
Bretschneider, Giorgio, Roma 140097
Brett & Co, A.J., London 130959
Brett & Sons, Arthur, Norwich 086111
Brett Whiteley Studio Museum, Surry Hills 001500
Bretts, Christchurch 140612
Bretz, Simone, München 126361
Breu, Bernadette, Portland 091908
Breu, Toni J., Bonstetten 111301
Breu, Zita, Wien 123491
Breuberg-Museum, Breuberg 016448
Breuel, Ernst, Hamburg 133997
Breuer, Düsseldorf 102478
Breuer, A., Drochtersen 070337
Breuer, Eva, Woollahra 095421
Breughel, Pieter, Amsterdam 077809
Breughel, Pieter, Oss 078668
Breughel, Pieter, Venlo 078832
Breuil, Bellerive-sur-Allier 061336
Breunesse, Zeist 078864, 108273
Breunig, Eugen, Stuttgart 126844
Breuza & Larizza, Torino 076783
Brevan Art Gallery, Cape Town 080677
Brevard Museum, Cocoa 043027
Brevard Museum of Art and Science, Melbourne 045751
Brevik Bymuseum, Brevik 030795
Brew & Sterling, Broadbeach 055563
Brewarrina Aboriginal Cultural Museum, Brewarrina 000831
Brewer, Henry, West Bridgford 114664
Brewery Chapel Museum, Halstead 039667
The Brewhouse Gallery, Grantham . 113145
Brewhouse Yard Museum, Nottingham 040616
Brewster & Co., I., Philadelphia . . . 091614
Brewster & Co., I., Philadelphia . . . 091615
Brewster & Co., I., Philadelphia . . . 118741
Brewster & Brown, New York 090749
Breyne & Co., de, Bruxelles 057861
Brezina, Birmingham 131831
BRG Associés, Paris 124604
Brhel, B., Heidelberg 071448
Brhel, Sabine, Schwerin 104868
Brian, Buffalo 115252
Brian, Robert, San Francisco 092746
Brian & Anna's Collectibles, Houston 089036
Briance, Jean, Paris 100083, 138319
Briançon, Philippe, Marseille 064328
Briand, Daniel, Drémil-Lafage 133468
Briand, Josiane, Notre-Dame-de-Monts 065232
Brianes, Daniel, Gages 062952
Briani & Miotto, Cincinnati 115610
Brian's, Kaiapoi 079129
Brian's Books, Doubleview 136883
Brian's Books, Katoomba 136956
Brianza, Bruno, Kempten 071788
Briar Herb Factory Museum, Clyde . 030471
Briar Patch, Salt Lake City 092421
Briard, Alain, Marseille 124399
Briard, Claude, Marseille 124400
Briard, Thierry, Caen 061862
Briarpatch, Cincinnati 088218
Briarwood, San Jose 092917
Briata, Georges, Marseille 099643
Briatte, Williams, Jussy 063268
Briatte, Williams, Saint-Quentin (Aisne) 067972
Briau, Jacques, Blois 061521
Briau, Jacques, Paris 065624
Bribie Island Community Arts Centre, Bribie Island 000833
Bric a Brac, Buenos Aires 055183
Bric à Brac, Orléans 065298
Bric-a-Brac, Padova 076078
Bric à Brac, Saint-Ouen 067739
Bric-a-Brac, Truro 086927
Bric à Brac, Vercheny 068765
Bric à Brac d'Armelle, Ris-Orangis . 067153
Bric à Broc, Cluny 062365
Bricabraque Mobrel, Lisboa 079885
Brice, Memphis 090059
Brice, Bruce, New Orleans 117409
Brick House, Montgomery 045997
The Brick Row, Baltimore . 087651, 131820
Brick Row Book Shop, San Francisco 142936
Brick Store Museum, Kennebunk . . 044954
Brick Window Gallery, Naphill 114110
Brickell Village Gallery, Miami 117038
Bricolage Móveis Antigos, Porto Alegre 058491
Bricoles, Göttingen 071043
Bricout, Patrice, Marcq-en-Barœul . 064271
Bricus, Beirut 077386
Bride, Patrick, La Cluse-et-Mijoux . 063339
Bridenne, Franck, Boulogne-sur-Mer 061692
Bridewell Museum, Norwich 040602
Bridge, Christine, London . 085158, 130960
Bridge & Art, Braunschweig 102217
Bridge Books, Murray Bridge 137018
Bridge Books, Richmond, Tasmania 137070
Bridge Center for Contemporary Art, El Paso 043633
The Bridge Gallery, Northbridge . . . 094988
The Bridge Gallery, Southampton . . 114455
Bridge House Antiques, Hungerford 084755
Bridge House Gallery, Saint George's 096436
Bridgehampton Historical Society Museum, Bridgehampton 042403
Bridgeman, Taranaki 108567
The Bridgeman Art Library, London 135193
Bridgeman Art Library, New York . . 135416
Bridgepoint Books, Mosman 137008
Bridgeport Antiques, Chicago 088039
BridgeSpotters Collective, Pittsburgh 054689
BridgeSpotters Gallery, Pittsburgh . 118907
Bridgestone Bijutsukan, Ishibashi Zaidan, Tokyo 027148
Bridgetown Old Gaol Museum, Bridgetown 000834
Bridgewater Books, Lewes 135166
Bridgford Antiques, West Bridgford . 087079
Bridging Arts, San Francisco 119621
Bridgnorth Antiques Centre, Bridgnorth 083667, 130436
Bridgnorth Northgate Museum, Bridgnorth 038829
Bridgton Historical Museum, Bridgton 042413
Bridgwater, David, Bath 083422
Bridlington Harbour Museum, Bridlington 038836
Bridport Museum, Bridport 038839
Bridport Old Books, Bridport 141433
Brié, Alain, Saint-Alban 067345
Briefmarken Münzen Historika, Hamburg 071210
Briefmarkenmuseum im Kloster Bardel, Bad Bentheim 015654
Briels, Breda 107876
Briem, Anna, Sankt Johann in Tirol 095743
Briercrest and District Museum, Briercrest 005152
Brière, Michel, Sablé-sur-Sarthe . . 067334
Brierley Hill Glass Museum, Brierley Hill 038842
Brierly Jigsaw Gallery, Bridgetown . 000835
Brieux, Alain, Paris 065625, 138320
Brigand Trading, Schaan 107334
Brigandi, Donald E., New York 090750
Brigantini, C., Miami 117039
Briged Pasukan Polis Hutan, Kuching 027985
Brigg Verlag, Augsburg 133726
Briggs, F.E.A., Brook 083769
Brigham City Museum-Gallery, Brigham City 042414
Brigham Young University Earth Science Museum, Provo 047271
Brigham Young University Museum of Art, Provo 047272
Brigham Young's Winter Home, Saint George 047630
Brighenti, Andrea, Modena 075901
Bright, Albuquerque 087378
Bright, Saint Kilda, Victoria 095171
Bright Antiques, Bright 055542
Bright Art Gallery, Bright 094280
Bright Henderson, J., San Diego . . . 119491
Bright Metals of the Heights, Houston 132106
Brighthouse, Wickham 114693
Brightlingsea Museum, Brightlingsea 038844
Brighton, Dallas 088469
Brighton, Fort Worth 088840
Brighton, Houston 089037
Brighton, Kansas City 089487
Brighton, Murcia 081441
Brighton, Saint Louis 092210
Brighton, San Antonio 092492
Brighton, Tucson 093208
Brighton, Tulsa 093288
Brighton Antique Prints and Maps, Brighton, Victoria 136816
Brighton Antiques, Brighton, Victoria 055550
Brighton Architectural Salvage, Brighton 083686
Brighton Books, Brighton 141435
Brighton Fishing Museum, Brighton 038847
Brighton Flea Market, Brighton 083687
Brighton Galleries, Mortdale 094889

Brighton Lanes Antique Centre, Brighton 083688
Brighton Museum and Art Gallery, Brighton 038848
Brightwells, Leominster 122563
Brigl, G., Landsberg am Lech 072135, 126163
Brigl, G., München 072669, 126362
Brignell, Cambridge 130495
Brikettfabrik Hermannschacht Zeitz, Zeitz, Elster 021045
Brilhante, Manuel, Porto 080072
Brilke, Görlitz 102972
Brill, Leiden 134821
Brill, Gary, Milton 056226
Brill, Normelio, Porto Alegre 058492
Brillantes Ancestral House, Tayum . 031801
Brilleman, Fabienne, Lyon 124343
Brilliant Antiques, Saint Louis 092211
Brilliant Facets, Brisbane 094287
Il Brillocco, Roma 076352
Brim-Brim Gallery, Newtown, Victoria 094960
Brimaud, Carole, Paris 100084
Brimo de Laroussilhe, Paris 065626
Brimstone Museum, Sulphur 048421
Brimstones, Lewes 141722
Brin de Mer, Honfleur 099335
Brindle, T., Whalley 087121
Brindley Bank Pumping Station and Museum, Rugeley 040870
Brings, Mülheim an der Ruhr 126339
Brini, Andrea, Bologna 075060
Brink 7 Galerij, Yde 030357
Brink & Van Dijk, Deventer 078273
Brinkens Museum, Malax 009854
Brinkhus, Heike, Bremen 138942
Brinkman, Enschede 108019
Brinkman, A.P., Amsterdam 077810
Brinkman, H., Amsterdam 140288
Brinkman Russell, Nelson 079173
Brinkmann, Wuppertal 105348
Brinkmann, Karin, Köln 071919
Brinkmann, Volker, Mannheim 072415
Brinkmann & Verbeek, Köln 126068
Brinks & Partner, Köln 103601
Brinquin, André, Tours 068586
Brinsley Art Gallery, Dunedin 108429
Briolet-Lecaudey, Véronique, Saint-Vigor-le-Grand 068034
Brion, Jean-Bernard, Rochefort-en-Terre 067181
Brioni, Ernesto Antonio, Milano . . . 127552
Brioult, Lydie, Vernon 121277
Bris, Anja, Schwetzingen 073777
Brisbane and Provincial Antique Dealers Association, Tarragindi 052461
Brisbane Antique Market, Clayfield . 055681
Brisbane Auction Galleries, Bowen Hills 120567
Brisbane City Gallery, Brisbane 000837
Brisbane Galleries, Thornlands 095333
Brisbane Tramway Museum, Ferny Grove 001026
Brisbois, Marie-José, Paris 065627
Briscadieu, Alain, Bordeaux 120936
Brischen, Simone, Gleizé 063008
Briscoe, Woolloongabba 056881
Au Brise Bise, Saint-Maur-des-Fossés 124909
Brisigotti, London 085159
Brissaud, Poitiers 138573
Brissoni Marcellin, Audincourt 098875
Bristol, Oslo 079428
The Bristol Arts Library, Bristol 112718
Bristol Auction Rooms, Bristol 122439
Bristol Blue, Barcelona 129331
Bristol Books, Bristol 141449
Bristol Brocante, Bristol 083730
Bristol City Museum and Art Gallery, Bristol 038859
The Bristol Decorative and Fine Arts Society, Bristol 054312
Bristol Guild of Applied Art, Bristol . 083731
Bristol Historical and Preservation Society Museum, Bristol 042421
Bristol Industrial Museum, Bristol . . 038860
Bristol Trade Antiques, Bristol 083732
Bristow, Daniel, Tetbury 131581
Britain's Heritage, Leicester 084946, 130878
Britannia, Petiville 066783
Britannia Antigüedades, Lima 079545
Britannia Antiques, Cagliari 075203
Britannia Antiques, Hahndorf 055930
Britannia Antiques, Houston 089038
Britannia Antiques, Stepney 056631
Britannia Antiques and Fine Art Gallery, Nelson 079174, 108510
Britannia Art Publications, London . 135194
Britannia Gallery, Mellor Brook 114072
Britannia Gallery, Ottawa 097099
Britannia Heritage Shipyard, Richmond 006280
British Academy, London 050825
British Academy Publications, London 135195
British-American Arts Association, London 054334
British Antique Dealers' Association, London 054313
British Antique Dealers' Association Antiques and Fine Art Fair, London 093914
British Antique Furniture Restorers' Association, Dorchester 054314
British Antique Replicas, Burgess Hill 083798
British Antiques, New Orleans 090525
The British Antiques Connection Group, Santiago de Chile 059512
British Art and Design Association, Arena Art and Design Association, Liverpool 054275
British Arts Festivals Association, London 054315
British Association of Friends of Museums, Launceston 054316
British Association of Paintings Conservator-Restorers, Hayling Island 054317
British Association of Paper Historians, London 054318
British Aviation Preservation Council, Coventry 054319
British Balloon Museum, Newbury . 040541
British Brick Society, High Wycombe 054320
British Button Society, Tonbridge . . 054321
British Columbia Aviation Museum, Sidney 006468
British Columbia Congenital Heart Museum, Vancouver 006686
British Columbia Farm Machinery and Agricultural Museum, Fort Langley 005460
British Columbia Forest Discovery Centre, Duncan 005372
British Columbia Forest Service Museum, Victoria 006733
British Columbia Golf House Museum, Vancouver 006687
British Columbia Medical Association Museum, Vancouver 006688
British Columbia Mineral Museum, Victoria 006734
British Columbia Museum of Mining, Britannia Beach 005155
British Columbia Museums Association, Victoria 052735
British Columbia Orchard Industry Museum, Kelowna 005670
British Columbia Regiment Museum, Vancouver 006689
British Columbia Sports Hall of Fame and Museum, Vancouver 006690
British Columbia Sugar Museum, Vancouver 006691
British Commercial Vehicle Museum, Leyland 039996
British Council, Visual Arts, London 040093, 054322, 135196
British Cycling Museum, Camelford 038974
British Dental Association Museum, London 040094
British Empire and Commonwealth Museum, Bristol 038861
British Engineerium, Hove 039776
British Film Institute Collections, London 040095
British Gallery, Paris 065628
British Golf Museum, Saint Andrews 040893
British Horological Institute, Newark-on-Trent 054323
British Import, Neuilly-sur-Seine . . 064990
British Import Antiques, Paris 065629
British in India Museum, Colne 039128
The British Journal of Aesthetics, Oxford 136187
British Lawnmower Museum, Southport 041071
British Leisure Publications, East Grinstead 135138
British Library, London 040096
The British Library, London 135197
British Library Bookshop, London . . 141764
The British Museum, London 040097
British Museum Friends, London . . 054324
British Museum Press, London 135198
British Numismatic Trade Association, Hayling Island 054325
British Optical Association Museum, College of Optometrists, London 040098
British Oriental Rug Dealers' Association, Eton 054326
British Painting for Sale, Sheffield . 114415
British Photographic Museum, Totnes 041235
British Red Cross Museum and Archives, London 040099
British Society of Aesthetics, Eastbourne 054327
British Society of Master Glass Painters, London 054328
British Society of Painters in Oil, Pastels and Acrylics, Ilkley 054329
British Telecom Museum, Oxford . . 040655
British Trading Company, Dallas . . . 088470
Brito, Antonio Carlos, São Paulo . . . 058696
Brito, Jeannine de, Paris 065630
Britsch, Georg, Bad Schussenried . 069376
Britsch jun., Georg, Bad Schussenried 069377
Britschgi, Melchior, Zürich 141327
Brittany Upholstering, Ottawa 123795
Britten, Andrew, Malmesbury 085900
Britti, Maria Gabriella, Milano 106178
Britto, Miami 117040
Brittons, Clitheroe 084034
Britz, Sheila, New York 090751
Brive Numismatique, Brive-la-Gaillarde 061807
Briwax, Taranaki 128960
Brix Gallery, Makati 108823
Brixham Museum, Brixham 038870
Brixia, Brescia 075152
Brjanskij Gosudarstvennyj Obedinennyj Kraevedčeskij Muzej, Brjansk . . . 033049
Brjanskij Literaturnyj Muzej, Brjansk gosudarstvennyj obedinennyj kraevedčeskij muzej, Brjansk . . . 033050
Brjanskij Oblastnoj Chudožestvennyj Muzej, Brjansk 033051
B.R.M. Coins, Knutsford 084888
Brněnská Antikva, Brno 059976
Broad Bay China, Dunedin 079081
Broad Ripple, Indianapolis 132153
Broad Ripple Bookshop, Indianapolis 142454
Broad Ripple Vintage, Indianapolis . 089278
Broad Street Book Center, Hereford 141662
Broadbent, London 113518
Broadfield House Glass Museum, Kingswinford 039895
Broadfoot, Tony, Brighton 083689
Broadhurst & Co, C.K., Southport . . 142083
Broadstairs Antiques and Collectables, Broadstairs 083755
Broadview Museum, Broadview . . . 005156
Broadway, Andrew, Richmond, Victoria 095136
Broadway and Ninth Antiques, San Antonio 092493
Broadway Antique Market, Chicago 088040
Broadway Antiques, Denver 088663
Broadway Ceramics, London 113519
Broadway Clock Shop, Seattle 092970, 132932
Broadway Dolls and Bears, Broadway 130463
Broadway Gallery, Houston 116288
Broadway Gallery, Tucson 120112
Broadway Gallery, Vancouver 097430
Broadway Magic Experience, Broadway 038876
Broadway Modern, Broadway 112732
Broan, Cynthia, Brooklyn 115244
Broberg, Lars, Stockholm 081932
Broby Hembygdspark, Broby 036230
Broc 3000, Elbeuf-sur-Seine 062771
Broc Amélie, Saint-Dizant-du-Bois . 067427
Broc Ant Art, Bruxelles 057862
Broc-Antique, Paris 065631
Broc Antique, Thouars 068413
Broc Art, Basel 082130
Broc Bazar, Saint-Ambroix 067349
Broc de Brenaz Sud, Sault-Brenaz . 068144
Broc en Stock, Lille 063836
Broc en Tout, Paris 065632
Broc et Puces, Lambesc 063496
Broc et Puces, Le Havre 063627
Broc et Style, Beaune 061271
Broc et Troc, Arbus 060946
Broc & Kitch, Saint-Étienne 067445
Broc Line Lainet, Sampigny 068109
Broc Rennes, Rennes (Ille-et-Vilaine) 067106
Broc Shop, Bernay 061365
Broc Style, Claye Souilly 062321
Broc'a Boc', Voglans 069022
Broc'Adour, Biarritz 061453
La Brocalou, Les Alleuds 063749
Brocantaires, Megève 064463
Brocant'Art, Epone 062792
Brocante, Amsterdam 077811
Brocante, Basel 082131
La Brocante, Bruxelles 057863
La Brocante, Don Torcuato 055261
Brocante, Helsinki 060512
Brocante, Hondarribia 081155
Brocante, Nantes 064907, 138238
La Brocante, Oost-Cappel 065272
Brocante, Torino 076784
Brocante, Weybridge 087107
Brocante 51, Marseille . . . 064329, 124401
Brocante à la Campagne, Coulomby 062504
Brocante à la Ferme, Cambrai 061918
Brocante Abescat, Chaumont-sur-Tharonne 062252
Brocante Aixoise, Aix-les-Bains . . . 060720
Brocante Almere, Almere 077736
El Brocante Andaluz, Málaga 081416
Brocante Antiek, Den Haag 078177
Brocante Antiques Centre, Marlborough 085946, 131267
Brocante & Antiquitäten, Zäziwil . . . 082925
Brocante Antiquités, Neufchâteau . 064980
Brocante au Bonheur du Jour, Châteauneuf-du-Faou 062203
Brocante Automobile KR, Giriviller . 063001
Brocante Aux 4 Sous, Meysse 064550
La Brocante Baconnaise, Baconnes 061157
Brocante Barbotin, Marcilly-sur-Vienne 064264
Brocante Cadeaux du Donjon, Sainte-Geneviève-des-Bois 068063
Brocante Christophe, Oostende . . . 058358
Brocante d'Allonville, Nantes 064908
Brocante d'Augan, Augan 061060
Brocante de Bâlines, Balines 061180
Brocante de Bicêtre, Saint-Genest-Malifaux 067484
Brocante de Bischwiller, Bischwiller 061500

Brocante de Bourgneuf, Saint-Eloy-de-Gy . . . 067432
Brocante de Bransles, Bransles . . . 061747
Brocante de Callac, Callac . . . 061908
Brocante de Château, Château-Salins . . . 062187
Brocante de Félicie, Chemaudin . . . 062269
Brocante de la Bruyére, Le Meux . . 063670
Brocante de la Cathédrale, Soissons . . . 068249
Brocante de la Chasse, Bruxelles . . 057864
Brocante de la Gare, Mouy . . . 064824
Brocante de la Ratière, Sainte-Geneviève . . . 068060
Brocante de la Ronde, La Chaux-de-Fonds . . . 082300
Brocante de la Vallée de l'Arré, Airion . . . 060689
Brocante de la Valsainte, Cerniat . . 082295
Brocante de l'Aubreçay, Saint-Xandre . . . 068042
Brocante de l'Eglise, Arpajon . . . 060981
Brocante de l'Eglise, Courseulles-sur-Mer . . . 062521
Brocante de l'Epinay, Roncherolles-en-Bray . . . 067211
Brocante de Linthout, Bruxelles . . . 057865
La Brocante de Marie-Jeanne, Dijon . . . 062648
Brocante de Provence, Saint-Paulet-de-Caisson . . . 067945
Brocante de Retournac, Retournac . 067124
Brocante de Serris, Serris . . . 068230
Brocante de Sévrier, Sévrier . . . 068237
La Brocante-de-Tamié, Tamié . . . 068355
Brocante de Thoiry, Thoiry . . . 068399
Brocante d'Elisa, Montrond-les-Bains . . . 064774
Brocante des Chapelles, Archiac . . 060953
Brocante des Coteaux, Saint-Cloud 067403
Brocante des Emmurées, Rouen . . . 067254
Brocante des Fargues, Aurillac . . . 061072
Brocante des Isles, Pointe-à-Pitre . 074645
Brocante des Quatre Moulins, Cluny 062366
Brocante des Quatre Vents, Bourges . . . 061720
Brocante des Souvenets, Longué-Jumelles . . . 063986
Brocante des Valois, Angoulême . . 060875
La Brocante du Batiment, Azerailles 061154
Brocante du Bâtiment, Geispolsheim-Illkirch . . . 062976
Brocante du Bois, Merinchal . . . 064505
Brocante du Bourget la Barbotine, Le Bourget-du-Lac . . . 063576
Brocante du Château, Apremont . . . 060941
Brocante du Château, La Clayette . 063336
Brocante du Donjon, Domfront . . . 062703
Brocante du Faubourg, Sully-sur-Loire . . . 068341
Brocante du Florival, Guebwiller . . . 063089
Brocante du Forum, Villefranche-sur-Saône . . . 068901
Brocante du Kronthal, Marlenheim . 064288
Brocante du Lavoir, Saint-Pol-de-Léon . . . 067963
Brocante du Lude, Albi . . . 060753
La Brocante du Mas, Pierrelatte . . . 066827
Brocante du Moutet, Saint-Nicolas-de-la-Grave . . . 067686
Brocante du Noyer, Bruxelles . . . 057866
Brocante du Parc, Dijon . . . 062649
Brocante du Plot Art Populaire Savoyard, Groisy . . . 063084
Brocante du Point du Jour, Corné . . 062482
Brocante du Pont de Coise, Coise . . 062392
Brocante du Pont de Paris, Laval (Mayenne) . . . 063550
La Brocante du Port, Antibes-Juan-les-Pins . . . 060916
Brocante du Pressoir, Montgesty . . 064687
Brocante du Rempart, Eguisheim . . 062768
Brocante du Rohu, Saint-Pierre-Quiberon . . . 067961, 124917
Brocante du Taillan-Médoc, Le Taillan-Médoc . . . 063708
Brocante du Trieves, Mens . . . 064487
Brocante du Trieves, Saint-Baudille-et-Pipet . . . 067371, 124888
Brocante et Monnaie, Fréjus . . . 062937
Brocante et Vieilles Dentelles, Genève . . . 082407
Brocante la Petite Chine, Meillonnas . . . 064470
Brocante le Grenier des Iles, Surzur 068347
Brocante les Remparts, Sauzet . . . 068161
Brocante Merle, Pons . . . 066904
Brocante Minaret, Rabat . . . 077689
Brocante Normande, La Ferté-Macé 063370
Brocante Normande, Saint-André-de-l'Eure . . . 067354
Brocante Réalmontaise, Réalmont . 067045
Brocante Richard, Lentilly . . . 063743
Brocante Saint-Antoine, Lyon . . . 064096
Brocante Saint-Eloi, Arbonne-la-Forêt . . . 060945
Brocante Saint-Nicolas, Moisdon-la-Rivière . . . 064577
Brocante Sainte-Cécile, Albi . . . 060754
Brocante Service, Bellegarde-en-Marche . . . 061333
Brocante Vallée aux Loups, Le Plessis-Robinson . . . 063685
Brocante ZF, Alger . . . 055130
Brocante Zola, Sens . . . 068214
Brocant'Elle, Lyon . . . 064097
De Brocanterie, Arnhem . . . 078047
Brocanterie, Carcassonne . . . 061973
Brocanterie, Honfleur . . . 063165
La Brocanterie, Le Petit Quevilly . . . 063682
Brocanterie, Palermo . . . 127821
Brocanterie Annette, Haarlem . . . 078443
Le Brocanteur, Cape Town . . . 080678
Brocanteur Koloniaal Teak, Venlo . . 078833
Brocanteurs, Amsterdam . . . 077812
Brocanthèque, Chanceaux-sur-Choisille . . . 062131
Brocanthèque, Thionville . . . 068392
Brocanthosaurus, Épinal . . . 062786
La Broc'Antic, Bonnelles . . . 061559
Brocantic, Bouchain . . . 061667
Brocantic, Le Havre . . . 063628
Broc'antic, Lille . . . 063837
Brocantic, Milano . . . 106179
Brocantic, Nice . . . 065057
Broc'Antic, Novalaise . . . 065240
Brocantic, Oostende . . . 058359
Brocantic, Saint-Quentin (Aisne) . . . 067973
Broc'Antic'Collection, Courlaoux . . . 062515
Broc'Antics, Etampes . . . 062812
Brocantics, Torcy-le-Grand . . . 068429
Brocantik, La Coucourde . . . 063352
Brocantine, Corbigny . . . 062470
Brocantine, Ecully . . . 062762
Brocantine, Les Sables-d'Olonne . . 063784
Brocantine, Veneux-les-Sablons . . . 068761
La Brocantine d'Autrecourt, Mesnières-en-Bray . . . 064511
Brocantique, Carcassonne . . . 061974
Brocantique, Genève . . . 082408
Brocantique, Saint-Céré . . . 067393
Brocantix, Sarrians . . . 068134
Brocant'oc, Laloubière . . . 063495
Brocaphil Keller, Colmar . . . 062405
Brocapuce, Bern . . . 082203
Broc'Armony, Langon . . . 063518
Broc'Art, Genève . . . 082409
Brocart, Girona . . . 081131
Broc'Art, Lay . . . 063561
Broc'Art des Remparts, Calvi . . . 061913, 138063
Brocastel, Vivier-Danger . . . 069020
Broc'Avenue, Nice . . . 065058
Broccoletti, Remo, Roma . . . 106502
Broceliande, Le Mans . . . 138116
Brochart, Jean-Paul, Burlats . . . 061839
Brochart, Jean-Paul et Brigitte, Mazamet . . . 064444
Brochu, Jean, Tour-en-Sologne . . . 068556
Brock, Dülmen . . . 070342
Brock, Martin, Dülmen . . . 070343
Brock, Nick, Dallas . . . 088471
Brock, P. de, Knokke-Heist . . . 096329
Brock & Art, Liebefeld . . . 082575, 111643, 122332
Brockenstube, Brig . . . 082272
Brockhaus Antiquarium, Kornwestheim . . . 139366
Brockmann, Daniela, Lugano . . . 130092
Brockmann, Georg, Mering . . . 121513
Brockmann, H., Gescher . . . 070979
Brockow, Petra, Bad Tölz . . . 125116
Brocksden County School Museum, Stratford . . . 006518
Brockshus, Bremen . . . 125383
Brocksieper, Brigitte, Calw . . . 070121
Brockstedt, Hans, Berlin . . . 101815
Brockstedt, Hans, Hamburg . . . 103103
Brockville Museum, Brockville . . . 005158
Broc's-en-Stock, Massillargues Attuech . . . 064421
Broc'Shop, Auxon . . . 061111
Broc'Trente, Auxerre . . . 061099
Brocza, Rudolf, Melk . . . 057177
Brocza, Rudolf, Melk . . . 057178
Brocza, Rudolf, Melk . . . 123419
Brodar, Wien . . . 095804
Brodergave, København . . . 060298
Broderick, Portland . . . 118982
Brodersen, Peter, København . . . 060299
Brodhag & Wörn, Berlin . . . 101816
Brodick Castle, Brodick . . . 038881
Brodie Castle, Forres . . . 039516
Brodkorb, Martina, Eisenach . . . 102609
Brodney, Boston . . . 087800
Brodnig, Dr., Graz . . . 057007
Brodoux, Germaine, Agen . 060666, 098768
Brodsworth Hall & Gardens, Doncaster . . . 039248
Brody, Chicago . . . 088041
Brody, Dalton, Washington . . . 093388
Brödlin, J., Efringen-Kirchen . . . 070510
Brödlin, Johannes, Weil am Rhein . 074300
Bröhan, Torsten, Düsseldorf . . . 070368
Bröhan-Museum, Landesmuseum für Jugendstil, Art Deco und Funktionalismus (1889-1939), Berlin . . . 016002
Broeke, Henk, Den Haag . . . 078178
Bröker, B., Bassum . . . 069481
Broekhoff, Nijmegen . . . 078653
Bröll, Hans jun., Gessertshausen . . 070982
Broelmuseum, Stedelijke Musea Kortrijk, Kortrijk . . . 003557
Brönner, Mainz . . . 134178
Broes, K., Brugge . . . 096114
Broess, 's-Hertogenbosch . . . 078515
Bröstler, Horst, Marktheidenfeld . . . 134196
Brötje, G., Oldenburg, Oldenburg . . 073199
Brötzinger Antiquariat, Pforzheim . . 139655
Broeze, Edam . . . 128655
Broggiato, Daniele, Padova . . . 076079
Broglin, Colmar . . . 099160
Brohammer, Jürgen & Claudia, Wörth am Rhein . . . 127028
Brok, Barcelona . . . 080820, 122000
Brokbals, Wilhelm, Recklinghausen 073443, 126682
Broken Art, Chicago . . . 131892
Broken Hill Regional Art Gallery, Broken Hill . . . 000847
Brokensha, Anne, Unley . . . 056765
Brokidée, Marcq-en-Barœul . . . 064272
Brokx, Anna, Langenzersdorf . . . 137211
Brol, Jacques, Bruxelles . . . 057867
Brolga, Gundaroo . . . 136924
Brolly, Jean, Paris . . . 100085
Broman, Kalustamo, Helsinki . . . 124042
Brome County Historical Society Museum, Knowlton . . . 005723
Bromer, Boston . . . 142251
Bromfield, Boston . . . 115156
Bromfield Art Gallery, Boston . . . 042320
Bromfietsmuseum De Peel, Ospel . 030011
Bromham Mill and Art Gallery, Bromham . . . 038883
Bromley Galleries, Bromley . . . 112743
Bromm, Hal, New York . . . 117725
Broms, Helsinki . . . 098718
Bromsen, Maury A., Boston . . . 142252
Bromsgrove Museum, Bromsgrove . 038885
Bromsten, Spånga . . . 081900
Bromwell, Cincinnati . . . 115611
Broncería Mateu, Las Heras . . . 123169
Bronck Museum, Coxsackie . . . 043203
Bronda, Helsinki . . . 098719
Brøndum Antikvariat, Skørping . . . 137907
Bronet, Bruxelles . . . 057868
Bronidève, Viroflay . . . 069006
Bronikowska, Ewa, Warszawa . . . 109103
Bronne, Henri, Monaco . . . 107525
Bronner, L'Isle-sur-la-Sorgue . . . 063927
Bronner, Astrid, Teningen . . . 126898
Bronner, Christian, Coustellet . . . 062531
Bronold, Michael, Lauda-Königshofen . . . 126175
Brons, L., Amsterdam . . . 077813
Brønshøj Museum, Brønshøj . . . 008827
Bronsin, Bruxelles . . . 057869
Bronte Gallery, Mapua . . . 108495
Brontë Parsonage Museum, Haworth . . . 039707
Bronx Council on the Arts, Bronx . . 054690
Bronx County Historical Society Museum, Bronx . . . 042431
Bronx Museum of the Arts, Bronx . . 042432
Bronzart, Calgary . . . 096792
Bronze & Brass Museum, Bhaktapur . . . 029111
Bronze d'Art et Vitrinier, Paris . . . 124605
Bronzeplus, Birmingham . . . 112645
Bronzes et Sculptures, Metz . . . 064524
El Bronzino, Bogotá . . . 059823
Broocks, Gettorf . . . 070983
De Broodgalerie, Amsterdam . . . 107689
Broodthaers, M.-P., Bruxelles . . . 096164
Brook, Bad Homburg v.d.Höhe . . . 069290
Brook, Heidelberg . . . 071449
Brook, Michael, London . . . 130961
Brook, Minetta, New York . . . 117726
The Brook Gallery, Budleigh Salterton . . . 112750
Brook Street Collectables, Providence . . . 092036
Brookart, San Jose . . . 135496
Brooke, Alexander, New York . . . 117727, 135417
Brooke Gifford, Christchurch . . . 079016
Brookes, Los Angeles . . . 132242
Brookes, Diane, Tetney . . . 114565
Brookes-Smith, Forest Row . . . 084424
Brookfield, Healesville . . . 055972
Brookfield Craft Center, Brookfield . 042445
Brookfield Museum, Brookfield . . . 042446
Brookgreen Gardens, Murrells Inlet 046102
Brooking Collection, Dartford . . . 039208
Brookings, J.J., San Francisco . . . 119622
Brookings & Co., J.J., San Jose . . . 119848
Brookings Arts Council, Brookings . 042448
Brookings County Museum, Volga . 048805
Brookland, Washington . . . 120263
Brooklands Museum, Weybridge . . 041354
Brookline Auction Gallery, Brookline 122829
Brookline Historical Society Museum, Brookline . . . 042451
Brookline Village Antiques, Boston . 087801
Brooklyn Art Gallery, Cardiff . . . 112806
Brooklyn Arts Center, Jacksonville . 116513
Brooklyn Arts Council Gallery, Bronx 042433
Brooklyn Arts Council News, Brooklyn . . . 136402
Brooklyn Children's Museum, Brooklyn . . . 042457
Brooklyn Historical Society Museum, Brooklyn . . . 042470
Brooklyn Journal of Arts & Urban Affairs, Brooklyn . . . 136403
Brooklyn Museum of Art, Brooklyn . 042458

The Brooklyn Museum Report, Brooklyn . . . 136404
Brooklyn Sports Cards and Collectibles, Cleveland . . . 088314, 142335
Brooks, Den Haag . . . 078179
Brooks, Dublin . . . 074896
Brooks, Monaco . . . 077597, 121773
The Brooks, Overton Park . . . 136405
Brooks, Sacramento . . . 092141
Brooks, Washington . . . 133022
Brooks Academy Museum, Harwich 044473
Brooks and District Museum, Brooks . . . 005159
Brooksby, Angie Elizabeth, Firenze . 106038
Brookside Antiques, Kansas City . .089488, 132205
Brookside Art Gallery, Kansas City . 116557
Brookside Saratoga County Historical Society, Ballston Spa . . . 041960
Broome County Historical Society Museum, Binghamton . . . 042215
Broome Historical Society Museum, Broome . . . 000853
Broome Street Gallery, New York . . 117728
Broomehill Museum, Broomehill . . . 000854
Broomer, A.R., New York . . . 090752
Broomhead Junker & Cie., Paris . . . 065633
Broqua, Christophe, Aire-sur-l'Adour . . . 124060
Bror Hjorths Hus, Uppsala . . . 036734
Bros, Francoise, Bordeaux . . . 124117
Brosa, Berthe, Tettnang . . . 105044
Brosch, Loßburg . . . 103941
Broschek, Hamburg . . . 133998
Brose, Oliver, Hamburg . . . 071211
Brose, Oliver, Kayhude . . . 071772
Broßhauser Mühle, Solingen . . . 073850
Brossy, Robert, Rolle . . . 082745
Brot- und Mühlen-Lehrmuseum, Gloggnitz . . . 001900
Brother, Philadelphia . . . 091616
Brother Antique, Hong Kong . . . 059600
Brother Rice Museum, Waterford . . 022869
Brotherton, Naomi, Dallas . . . 115846
Brotonne, Frédéric, Feron . . . 062856
Brouard, Gilles, Gemages . . . 062977
Brouard, Gilles, Saint-Germain-de-la-Coudre . . . 067497
Les Broucants, Verona . . . 128418
Broughton, Berry . . . 055494
Broughton, Bob, Taroona . . . 137108
Broughton Books, Edinburgh . . . 141575
Broughton Gallery, Broughton . . . 112748
Broughton House and Garden, Kirkcudbright . . . 039900
Broughton House Gallery, Cambridge . . . 112786
Broughty Castle Museum, Dundee . 039305
Broughty Ferry Art Society, Dundee 054330
Brouillard, Patrick, Neuchâtel . . . 130125
Brouns, Konrad, Maastricht . . . 078599
Brous, Nancy, New York . . . 090753
Brousse, Didier, Lourmarin . . . 099525
Broutée, William, Paris . . . 065634
Broutta, Michèle, Paris . . . 100086, 133546
Brouwershuis, Antwerpen . . . 003154
Brouws Museum, Brouwershaven . 029360
Broward County Historical Museum, Fort Lauderdale . . . 043931
Brower, David, London . . . 085160
Brower, Robert, Cleveland . . . 115694
Browgate Antiques, Baildon . . . 083362
Brown, Glasgow . . . 084462
Brown, Kansas City . . . 089489
Brown, Newton Stewart . . . 131318
Brown, Oklahoma City . . . 091479
Brown, Seattle . . . 092971
Brown, Tain . . . 114546
Brown, Alasdair, London . 085161, 130962
Brown, Alexander, Cincinnati . . . 088219
Brown, B., Seattle . . . 142981
Brown, Cam, Eagle Farm . . . 120581
Brown, David, Memphis . . . 142542
Brown, David, Montréal . . . 058932
Brown, David, Saint Andrews 086443, 131439
Brown, Gavin, New York . . . 117729
Brown, Graeme, Toorak . . 056712, 123319
Brown, I. & J.L., Hereford . . . 084667
Brown, I. & J.L., London . . 085162, 130963
Brown, Iris, New York . . . 090754
Brown, James A., Charlotte . . . 087931
Brown, John & Val, Barnard Castle . 083387
Brown, Joseph, Prahran . . . 095104
Brown, Juanita C., Oklahoma City . 091480
Brown, Karen, Darwin . . . 094457
Brown, Linda L., San Antonio . . . 119401
Brown, Lou, Houston . . . 089039, 132107
Brown, Malcolm, Cleveland . . . 115695
Brown, Martina, Berlin . . . 069585
Brown, Murray, Pevensey . . . 086266
Brown, Paula, Toledo . . . 120076
Brown, P.J., Haslingden . . . 084611
Brown, Reinhold, New York . . . 117730
Brown, Robert, Washington 093389, 120264
Brown, Sally, Stockport . . . 114488
Brown, Sidney, San Francisco . . . 119623
Brown, S.J., Jacksonville . . . 132175
Brown, William C., Dubuque . . . 135359
Brown County Art Gallery and Museum, Nashville . . . 046137
Brown County Historical Society Museum, New Ulm . . . 046276
Brown County Historical Society Pioneer Museum, Nashville . . . 046138
Brown & Dewenter, Kassel . . . 071748
Brown House Museum, Sandersville 047925
Brown Ink Gallery, New York . . . 117731
Brown Lines, Hugo . . . 136406
Brown Mountain Restoration, Dallas 132001
Browne, Gayle, Austin . . . 087566
Browne, Martin, Potts Point . . . 095100
Browne & Assoc. Chuck, Tulsa . . . 093289
Browne & Co, Benny, Stoke-on-Trent . . . 114491
Brownella Cottage, Galion . . . 044124
Browning, G.R., Washington . . . 120265
Browning's of Wyoming, Cincinnati 115612
Brownlow, Faldingworth . . . 084376
Brownrigg, Petworth . . . 086240
Browns, High Wycombe . . 084681, 130794
Brownsbank Cottage, Biggar . . . 038703
Brownsboro Book Center, Louisville 142529
Brownstone, Chicago . . . 088042
Brownstone, Chicago . . . 088043
Brownstone, Houston . . . 089040
Brownstone & Cie., Gilbert, Paris . . 100087
Brownsville Museum of Fine Art, Brownsville . . . 042482
Browntown Museum, Lake City . . . 045104
Brownvale North Peace Agricultural Museum, Brownvale . . . 005160
Brownville Historical Society Museum, Brownville . . . 042483
Browse Antiques, Stafford 086678, 131523
Browse & Darby, London . . . 113520
Browse Inn, Virginia . . . 056784
Browser, Falmouth . . . 141608
Browsers Bookshop, Epping . . . 141599
Browsers Delight, Fremantle . . . 055841
Browsers Nook, San Francisco . . . 092747
Browsers Secondhands Books, Hamilton . . . 140628
Browsers Secondhands Books, Tauranga . . . 140659
Browzers, Broken Hill . . . 136826
Browzers, Manchester . . . 141934
Broyles, Kansas City . . . 089490
Brozzetti, Torino . . . 076785, 128271
Bru, Patrick, Septfonds . . . 068224
Brubacher House Museum, Waterloo . . . 006770
Bruc Antic, Barcelona . . . 129332
Bruce Castle Museum, London . . . 040100
Bruce County Museum, Southampton . . . 006496
Bruce Mines Museum, Bruce Mines 005161
Brucemore, Cedar Rapids . . . 042673
Bruce's, El Paso . . . 088792
Bruce's Antiques, San Jose . . . 092918
Bruce's Auctions, Adelaide . . . 120556
Bruchet-Méry, Jean-Luc, Rennes (Ille-et-Vilaine) . . . 067107
Bruchhausen, Heike, München . . . 072670
Bruckbacher Hoarstubn, Weyregg am Attersee . . . 002843
Brucke, Tokyo . . . 107024
Bruckhoff, Friedhelm, Berlin . . . 101817
Bruckmann, H., Horn-Bad Meinberg 071581
Brucknerzimmer, Kronstorf . . . 002181
Brucoli, Mauro, Milano . . . 075648
Brudavollen Bygdetun, Ørsta . . . 031064
Bruder, H., Bergheim, Erft . . . 069534
Bruder-Konrad-Museum, Altötting . 015513
Bruderer, Otto, Waldstatt . . . 111981
Die Brücke, Braunschweig . . . 016382
Die Brücke - Kärnten.Kunst.Kultur, Klagenfurt . . . 135548
Brücke Museum, Berlin . . . 016003
Brücke-Museum, Berlin . . . 135754
Brückenhausmuseum, Erfurt . . . 017009
Brückner, Christine, München . . . 104159
Brückner, Thomas, Geldern . . . 070949
Brueckner Museum, Albion . . . 041611
Brückner-Zündorff, Jutta, Bad Füssing . . . 101644
Brückturm-Museum über der 'Steinernen Brücke', Arbeitskreis Schiffahrtsmuseum Regensburg e.V, Regensburg . . . 019744
Brüder Grimm-Haus Steinau, Steinau an der Straße . . . 020299
Brüder Grimm-Museum Kassel, Kassel . . . 018181
Brüder-Grimm-Stube, Marburg . . . 018819
Brüggemann, Ernst, Mömbris . . . 072562
Brüggemann-Riemer, Simone, Lübbenau . . . 103956
Brüggen, Falk von der, Bremen . . . 125384
Brügger, Christine, Bern . . . 111248
Brügger Antiquitäten, Brügge, Holstein . . . 070067
Brühler Kunstverein e.V, Brühl, Rheinland . . . 053069
Brüll, Hans, Dorsten . . . 070278, 125475
Brüning, J. & M., Südlohn . . . 074021
Brüning, Thomas, Ratingen . . . 126680
Brünner Heimatmuseum, Schwäbisch Gmünd . . . 020109
Brüns, A., Lüneburg . . . 121505
Brünz & Rosowsky, Las Vegas . . . 116613
Bruet, Nicolas, Paris . . . 065635
Brüxer und Komotauer Heimatstuben, Palais Stutterheim, Erlangen . . . 017029
Bruford, W., Eastbourne . . 084257, 130666
Bruggemuseum - Archeologie, Stedelijke Musea Brugge, Brugge . . . 003263
Bruggemuseum - Belfort, Stedelijke Musea Brugge, Brugge . . . 003264
Bruggemuseum - Brugse Vrije, Stedelijke Musea Brugge, Brugge . . . 003265
Bruggemuseum - Gruuthuse, Stedelijke Musea Brugge, Brugge . . . 003266
Bruggemuseum - Onthaalkerk van Onze-Lieve-Vrouw, Stedelijke Musea Brugge, Brugge . . . 003267
Bruggemuseum - Stadhuis, Stedelijke Musea Brugge, Brugge . . . 003268
Brugger, Martin Robert, Klaus . . . 057117
Brugidou, Philippe, Paris . . . 065636
Brugier, Paris . . . 065637, 124606
Brugmann Antiquités, Bruxelles . . . 057870
Brugs Antiekhuis, Brugge . . . 057762
Brugwachterhuis, Dilsen-Stokkem . 003407
Bruhais, André, Le Loroux Bottereau . . . 124304
Bruhm, Wolfgang, Jena . . . 125982
Bruhns, Denver . . . 088664, 122882
Bruijn, de, Maastricht . . . 078600
Bruijn, Dick de, Amsterdam . . . 107690
Bruijn, W.M. de, Groningen . . . 078408
Bruijn & de Vaan, Nijmegen . . . 140506
Bruijne, Ellen de, Amsterdam . . . 107691
Bruijnzeels, Haarlem . . . 078444
Bruinen, Isabelle, Lille . . . 099484
Bruini, Renzo e Stefano, Modena . . 075902
Bruk, Kevin, Miami . . . 117041
Bruksmuseet i Robertsfors, Robertsfors . . . 036544
Bruksmuseet Smedsgården, Sandviken . . . 036560
Bruksmuseum, Eksjö . . . 036242
Brukt og Antikkhuset, Kristiansand . 079396
Bruktbu, Løvas, Stavanger . . . 140709
Brulain, Paris . . . 065638
Brullé, Pierre, Paris . . . 100088
Brumado, Rio de Janeiro . . . 058559
Brumaire, André, Pont-l'Évêque . . . 066929
Brument, Patrick, Rouen . . . 067255
Brumme, Frankfurt am Main 102755, 139075
Brumme, Siegfried, Mainz 072389, 139445
Brun, Jean-Claude, Grenoble . . . 063056
Brun, Jeanette G., Zürich . . . 082952
Brun Lea Antiques, Burnley . . . 083810
Brun Lea Antiques, Burnley . . . 083811
Brun-Leglise, Dominique, Paris . . . 100089
Brune, H.-J., Wolfhagen . . . 074475
Bruneau, Jean-Charles, Dinard . . . 062685
Bruneau, Philippe, Tours . . . 068587
Bruneaux Graveurs, Caen . . . 061863
Brunei Forestry Museum, Sungai Liang . . . 004617
Brunei Gallery, London . . . 040101
Brunel, Cannes . . . 061935
Brunel, Saint-Sever . . . 068007
Brunel, Shepton Mallet . . . 114424
Brunel, Didier, Digoin . . . 062634
Brunel Antiques and Collectors Fair, Uxbridge . . . 093915
Brunel Engine House, London . . . 040102
Brunelleschi, Remo, Genova . . . 127436
Brunelli, Fabio Marco, Bologna . . . 127135
Brunelli, Harold, Auxerre . . . 061100
Brunello, Paolo, Bologna . . . 127136
Brunet, Rio de Janeiro . . . 058560
Brunet, Elisabeth, Rouen . . . 138586
Brunet, Noemi, Gaillac . . . 062954
Brunet, Patrick, Lyon . . . 064098, 124344
Brunetti, Silvia, Paris . . . 124607
Brunia, Mascha, Breda . . . 078084
Bruniková, Květa, Liberec . . . 060042
Brunk & Sons, John, Phoenix . . . 123052
Brunke, Berthold, Bochum . . . 125340
Brunkeberg, Stockholm . . . 129856
Brunnarius, Karl, Bad Gandersheim 069283
Brunnen-Antiquariat, Düsseldorf . . 139007
Brunnen-Verlag, Basel . . . 134981
Brunnengräber, Christiane, Bonn . . 125349
Brunnenmuseum, Bad Vilbel . . . 015818
Brunnenmuseum, Goslar . . . 017479
Brunnenturm-Presse, Regensberg . 135059
Brunner, Höchst . . . 137191
Brunner, Andreas Christian, Schwanberg . . . 057306
Brunner, Elisabeth, Pfäffikon (Zürich) . . . 082725
Brunner, Fritz, Embrach . . . 130009
Brunner, G., Regensburg . . . 073453
Brunner, Gernot, Maria Wörth . . . 123417
Brunner, Giovanni, Roma . . . 127945
Brunner, Katia, Honfleur . . . 099336
Brunner, Klaus, Lörrach . . . 072291
Brunner Heimathaus mit Rudolf-Steiner-Gedenkstätte, Brunn am Gebirge . 001771
Brunner Mine Site, Dobson . . . 030479
Brunner-Wendel, Lieselotte, Steißlingen . . . 104950
Brunnier Art Museum, Iowa State University, Ames . . . 041684
Bruno & Fils, André, Paris . . . 124608
Bruno, Andrea, Torino . . . 128272
Bruns, Helga, München . . . 104160
Bruns, J.C.C., Minden, Westfalen . . 134203
Bruns, Thomas, Winsen, Luhe 074449, 105306
Brunsch, Josephine, München . . . 072671
Brunskogs Hembygdsgård, Brunskog . . . 036231

Brunswick Antiques, Penrith 086202
Brunswick Railroad Museum, Brunswick 042490
Brunswick Street Antiques, Fitzroy . 055821
Brunswick Town State Historic Site, Winnabow 049244
Brunswick Valley Museum, Mullumbimby 001297
Brusasca, Torino 076786
Brusato, Tebaldo, Brescia 140001
Brusberg, Dieter, Berlin 101818
Bruschelli, Perugia 076229
Bruschi, Paolo, Firenze 127310
Bruschi & Merry, Pittsburgh 118908
Bruschweiler, F.G., Rayleigh 086332
Brush Art Gallery and Studios, Lowell 045505
Brush Country Museum, Cotulla . . . 043188
Brush Gallery, Wingham 095402
Brushstokes, Middlebury 136407
Brushstrokes Art School, Dublin . . . 050342
Brushworks, San Diego 119492
Brushworks, Tulsa 120189
Brushworks Gallery, Salt Lake City . 119331
Brusquet, Thierry, Sene 068208
Brussels Ancient Art Fair, Bruxelles 093596
Brussels Non European Art Fair, Bruxelles 093597
Brussels Oriental Art Fair, Bruxelles 093598
Brutarian, Accokeek 136408
Bruton, Holmfirth 113252
Bruton, New York 117732
Bruton Classic Furniture Company, Bruton 130470
Brutschan, Katharina, Schaffhausen 082797
Brutscher, St., Oberstdorf 073154
Bruun, København 060300
Bruun, Lisse, København 098542
Bruun Rasmussen, København 060301
Bruun Rasmussen, København 060302
Bruun Rasmussen, København 120866
Bruun Rasmussen, København 120867
Bruun Rasmussen, Vejle . 060413, 120878
Bruunshåb Gamle Papfabrik, Viborg 009145
Bruxella 1238, Musée de la Ville de Bruxelles, Bruxelles 003292
Bruyer, Paris 100090
Bruyere, Alain, Toulouse 068486
Bruyere, Jean, L'Etrat 099477
Bruyères, Serge, Marssac-sur-Tarn 064406
Bruyn, Ch. de, Bruxelles 057871
Bry, François, Mortagne-au-Perche 064798
Bry Gallery, Monroe 045968
Bryan, Douglas, Cranbrook 084100
Bryan-Peach, N., Wymeswold 087274
Bryanston Graphics, Johannesburg 110049
Bryant, Houston 116289
Bryant, Kansas City 132206
Bryant, New Orleans 117410
Bryant, New Orleans 117411
Bryant, Jan, Gladesville 055877
Bryant Cottage, Bement 042137
Bryant-Russ, Los Angeles 132243
Brydone Jack Observatory Museum, Fredericton 005478
Bryggen, Bergen 079373, 108675
Bryggens Museum, Bergen 030763
Bryggeriet, Nyköping 081887, 129853
Brzezinski, Ewa, Rennes (Ille-et-Vilaine) 124872
BS Antique Trading, Singapore 080436
BSAT Gallery, British Sporting Art Trust, Newmarket 040561
BSMD, Paris 100091
BT Museum, London 040103
Bu Museum, Utne 031306
Bu Yue Zhai, Handan 097731
Buade, Québec 097135
Bub, Brigitte, Berlin 125182
Bubba's Baseball Bullpen, Albuquerque 087379
Bubbly, Singapore 080437
Bubbly Hills Vintage, Long Beach . . 089628
Buby, Trenčín 080641
Bucaro, León 081169
Bucat, Pierre, Paris 124609
Buccaneer, 's-Hertogenbosch 078516
Buccaneer Heaven, Tampa 093111
Bucceri, Padova 076080
Bucchi, Federica, Roma 076353
Bucci, Enrico, Santiago de Chile . . . 097620
Bucciarelli, Giovanni, Firenze 127311
Buccleuch Mansion, New Brunswick 046204
Buccony, Buco, Bratislava 080602
Bucerius Kunst Forum, Hamburg . . 017682
Buceti, D & S, Roma 076354
Buceti, Domenico, Messina 075555
Buch, Claudia, Oberhausen, Rheinland 073145
Buch, N.O, Brøndby 124011
Buch & Kunst, Braunschweig 102218, 138919
Buch-Kunstverlag Ettal, Ettal 133923
Buch & Schudrowitz, Berlin 125183
Buch- und Kunsthandlung der Benediktinerabtei St. Michael, Siegburg 139726
Buchal, P., Groß-Umstadt . 071114, 121419
Buchan, K.S., Leigh-on-Sea 084954
Buchanan, Duncan, Auckland 078930
Buchanan Center for the Arts, Monmouth 045962
Das Buchantiquariat, Ittigen 141260
Buchantiquariat am Rhein, Basel . . 141198
Bucharskij Gosudarstvennyj Muzej, Buchara 049385
Buchart, Antibes-Juan-les-Pins . . . 060917
Buchdreher, Freiburg im Breisgau . 139107
Buchdruckmuseum, Rohrbach in Oberösterreich 002538
Bucheit, Rita, Chicago 115377
Buchele, B.& H., Maselheim 072471
Bucheli, R.E., Bath 112571
Bucheon, San Francisco 119624
Bucher, Alois, Innsbruck 057077
Bucher, C.J., München 134223
Bucher, Herbert, Absam 056908
Bucher, Jeanne, Paris . . . 100092, 133547
Bucher, Stefan, Luzern 130100
Bucher, Viktor, Wien 095805
Buchfänger am Pferdemarkt, Oldenburg, Oldenburg 139627
Der Buchfreund, Wien 137292
Der Buchfreund, Wien 137293
Buchgeher, Christoph, Linz 057153
Buchhandlung beim Lederhaus, Ravensburg 139677
Buchhandlung Franz-Mehring-Haus, Leipzig 139391
Buchhandlung Johannesstift, Berlin 138754
Buchheim, Prof. Dr. Lothar-Günther, Feldafing 133926
Buchhold, Petra, Schrecksbach . . . 073731
Buchholz, Hannover 103268
Buchholz, Lisboa 140822
Buchholz, Daniel, Köln . . . 103602, 139335
Buchholz, Godula, Denklingen 102356
Buchholz, Karsten, Hamburg 071212
Buchholz, Ralf, Hildesheim 125928
Buchholz, Susanne, Kassel 126014
Buchholz & Pyroth, Hamburg 071213
s'Buchholze Hisli, Schuttertal 020105
Buchholzer Heimatmuseum, Buchholz in der Nordheide 016480
Buchinger, Josef, Spittal an der Drau 057318
Buchinger, Otto, Linz 057154, 095651
Der Buchladen, Saarbrücken 139703
Buchloh, Helmut, Schnaitsee 073708
Buchmann, Agra 111111
Buchmann, Köln 103603
Buchmann, Yvonne, Basel 129914
Buchmüller, J., Mülheim an der Ruhr 072609
Buchmuseum, Solothurn 037572
Buchmuseum der Sächsischen Landesbibliothek - Staats- und Universitätsbibliothek Dresden, Dresden 016782
Buchner, Christine, Pitten 133127
Buchner, Rudolf, Fürstenfeld 137170
Buchoul, Jean-Marc, Nantes 064909
Buchrestaurierung Leipzig, Leipzig . 126184
Buchs, André, Genève 082410
Buchs, Oskar, Gstaad 111538
Buchtip, Wien 137294
buchWeger, Frankfurt am Main . . . 139076
Buchwerkstatt, Bremen 125385
Buci, Paris 100093
Buck, Christopher, Sandgate 086504, 131453
Buck, J. de, Bruxelles 057872
Buck, Nicole, Strasbourg 101281
Buck, S. & H. de, Gent . . . 096286, 133285, 137493
Buck House Antique Centre, Beaconsfield 083458
Buck Mountain Treasures, Oklahoma City 091481
Buckboard Antiques, Oklahoma City 091482
Buckenham Galleries, Southwold . . 114470
Buckenmaier, Ulrich, Überlingen . . .105084, 126926
Buckfast Abbey, Buckfastleigh 038888
Buckham Fine Arts Project Gallery, Flint 043860
Buckhaven Museum, Buckhaven . . 038891
Buckhead, Atlanta 131763
Buckhead, Atlanta 142200
Buckhorn Museum, San Antonio . . 047789
Buckhorn School of Fine Arts, Buckhorn 049775
Buckie Drifter Maritime Museum, Buckie 038892
Buckies, Cambridge 083842, 130496
Buckingham, C.W., Cadnam 083833
Buckingham Antiques, Buckingham 083776, 130472
Buckingham Movie Museum, Buckingham 038894
Buckingham Palace, Royal Collections, London 040104
Buckinghamshire County Museum, Aylesbury 038555
Buckinghamshire Railway Centre, Quainton 040787
Buckland Abbey, Yelverton 041467
Buckland Gallery, Beechworth . . . 094226
Buckland Heritage Museum, Spruce Home 006503
Buckland Southerst, Vancouver . . . 097431
Buckler's Hard Village Maritime Museum, Buckler's Hard 038896
Buckley, Memphis 090060
Buckley, Penrith 056450
Buckley, Dave, Nottingham 086130
Buckley, W., Congleton 084072
Buckley Center Gallery, Portland . . 047168
Buckley Galleries, Dun Laoghaire . .074961, 105891, 121670
Buckley-Kohler, Columbus 088388
Buckleys Museum of Shops, Battle 038640
Buckleys Yesterday's World, Battle . 038640
Bucknall, Moya, Solihull 114444
Buck's Stove Palace, Portland 091909
Bucksport Historical Museum, Bucksport 042494
Buckwitz, Sybille, Kronberg im Taunus 103792
Bucx, Ben, 's-Hertogenbosch 128713
Bucyrus Historical Society Museum, Bucyrus 042495
Bud & Bettys, Winnipeg 059452
Budai Antik, Budapest 074672
Budai Krónika, Budapest 139915
Óbudai Társaskör Galéria, Budapest 105496
Budapest Galéria Kiallitohaza, Budapest 105497
Budapest Kiallitoterem, Budapest . . 105498
Budapesti Történeti Múzeum, Vármúzeum, Budapest 021642
Budatétényi Galéria, Budapest 105499
Budau, Norbert, Nordenham 073066
Budavári Mátyás Templom Egyházművészeti Gyüjteménye, Budapest 021643
Budawang Antiques, Milton 056227
Budde, Hermann, Lemgo 072222
Budde, Klaus, Warendorf 074277
Buddelschiff-Museum, Neuharlingersiel 019238
Buddelschiff-Museum, Tangerhütte 020396
Buddelschiff-Museum, Wedel 020694
Buddenbrookhaus, Heinrich-und-Thomas-Mann-Zentrum, Lübeck 018718
Buddenbrooks, Boston 142253
The Buddhist Art Museum, Yangon . 029074
Buddle Arts Centre, Wallsend 041281
Budd's Beach Gallery, Surfers Paradise 095239
Buddy Holly Center, Lubbock 045512
Bude-Stratton Museum, Bude 038897
Budeia, Oslo 079429
Budenz-Ház, István Király Múzeum, Székesfehérvár 021865
Buderim Pioneer Cottage, Buderim . 000857
Buderim Rare Books, Buderim 136830
Budget Antiques, Edmonton 058820
Budgino, K., Klaipėda 140227
BudiArt, Bussum 078129
Budil, S., Amsterdam 077814
Budinok-muzej A. Čechova, Sums'kyj oblasnyj krajeznavčyj muzej, Sumy 038397
Budinok-muzej Sevastopol's'ke Komunistične Pidpillja 1942-1944, Muzei geroïčnoï oborony i vyzvolennja Sevastopolja, Sevastopol 038385
Budrich & Schmidt, Friedeburg, Ostfriesland 070888
Budrus, Renate, Stadtallendorf 073889
Buechel, Louisville 089964
Buechel Memorial Lakota Museum, Saint Francis 047628
Bücher-Brockenhaus, Bern 141224
Bücher-Brocky, Basel 141199
Bücher-Brocky, Luzern 141271
Bücher-Brocky, Zürich 141328
Bücher-Ernst, Wien 137295
Bücherantiquariat Irchel, Zürich . . . 141329
Bücheratelier, Velbert 139815
Bücherbogen am Savignyplatz, Berlin 138755
Bücherbogen im Stülerbau, Berlin . 138756
Bücherbogen in der Knesebeckstraße, Film-Bühne-Tanz-Kostüm-Textil, Berlin 138757
Bücherbogen in der Knesebeckstraße, Internationales Modernes Antiquariat, Berlin 138758
Bücherbogen in der Kochstraße, Berlin 138759
Bücherbogen in der Nationalgalerie, Berlin 138760
Der Bücherdoktor, Hofheim am Taunus 139274
Büchergalerie Westend, München . 139499
Büchergilde Art Club, Frankfurt am Main 133939, 139077
Bücherhalle, Berlin 138761
Das Bücherhaus, Eldingen 133908, 139036
Bücherinsel, Leipzig 139392
Bücherladen Aussersihl, Zürich . . . 141330
Büchers Best, Dresden 138988
Bücherstube am See, Konstanz . . . 139361
Bücherstube Weinhaus, Wien 137296
Bücherwurm, Basel 141200
Der Bücherwurm, Heidelberg 139249
Bücherwurm, Kiel 139318
Bücherwurm, Kiel 139319
Bücherwurm, Schaffhausen 141298
Büchi, Monaco 107526
Büchi, Max, Bern 082204, 129951
Büchler, Josef, Pfaffenhofen an der Ilm 104601
Büchner, Coburg 070144
Büchner, H., Sinsheim 073833
Büchner, Thomas, Berlin 125184
Büchnerhaus, Riedstadt 019834

Büchsenmacher- und Jagdmuseum, Ferlach . . . 001853
Büchter, E., Rheine . . . 073519
Bücken, Walter, Herzogenrath . . . 103366, 125924
Bückmann, Monika, Krefeld . . . 072067
Büdenhölzer, Brigitte, Emmendingen . . . 070558
Büdke, C., Waren . . . 139826
Büecheler-Hus, Kloten . . . 037213
Büel, Otto, Luzern . . . 082620
Bühler, Aschaffenburg . . . 069192
Bühler, Stuttgart . . . 073965, 104969
Bühler, Edy, Wolfhausen . . . 122358
Bühler, Hans Peter, Nürtingen . . . 126572
Bühler, Irmtraud, Bremen . . . 070016
Bühler, Martin, Basel . . . 129915
Bühlmann, Astrid, Bern . . . 129952
Bühlmann, Dr. X., Luzern . . . 111685
Bühlmayer, C., Wien . . . 057389, 123492
Bühn, Josef, München . . . 134224
Bühnemann, Michael, Berlin . . . 069586
Bühnemann, Rainer L., Hannover . . 071390
Bühning, Bohmte . . . 069906
Bührer, Barbara, Neuhausen am Rheinfall . . . 130130
Buekenhout, Jean, Bruxelles . . . 057873
Büker, Eberhard, Hamburg . . . 071214
Bülow, Holger, Berlin . . . 125185
Bülow, J., Lübeck . . . 103961
Bülow, Rose-Marie, København . . . 060303
El Buen Orden, Buenos Aires . . . 055184
En Buen Uso, Logroño . . . 081181
Buena Park Historical Society Museum, Buena Park . . . 042496
Buena Vista, Dordrecht . . . 107975
Bündner Kunstmuseum, Chur . . . 037017
Bündner Natur-Museum, Chur . . . 037018
Bünger, Düsseldorf . . . 125525
Bünger, Th., Puchow . . . 073382
Bürck, Berlin . . . 138762
Büren, Fredy von, Savognin . . . 082795, 130173
Büren, Fritz von, Mettmenstetten . . 130118
Bürgel, Ludwig, Seekirchen am Wallersee . . . 095760, 133162
Bürger- und Bauernmuseum, Hilzingen . . . 017928
Bürgerhaus-Galerie, Castrop-Rauxel . . . 102299
Bürgerhaus Grünau, Kommunale Galerie Treptow-Köpenick, Berlin . . . 016004
Bürgerhausen, R., Aachen . . . 069080
Bürgerkorpsmuseum im Kanzlerturm, Eggenburg . . . 001807
Bürgermeister-Müller-Museum, Solnhofen . . . 020244
Bürgermeister-Ringenhain-Haus, Stadt- und Kulturgeschichtliches Museum, Torgau . . . 020450
Bürgerstiftung Kunst für Güglingen, Güglingen . . . 017594
Bürgi, Robert, Lyss . . . 082642
Bürgli, Gossau (Sankt Gallen) . . . 111525
Bürki, Bernhard, Sigriswil . . . 082809
Bürki, Hans, Ostermundigen . . . 111804, 130137
Bürkle, Raimund, Luzern . . . 082621
Büro Friedrich, Berlin . . . 016005
Büro für Kunst, Dresden . . . 102424
Büro Otto Koch, Dessau, Anhalt . . . 016676
Büromaschinen-Museum, Aspang . 001700
Büromuseum, Mülheim an der Ruhr 019020
Bürsten- und Heimatmuseum, Schönheide, Erzgebirge . . . 020083
Bürth, Karin, Greifswald . . . 071089
Büsch, Berlin . . . 101819
Bütow, Georg, Bad Oeynhausen . . . 069345, 101683
Büttiker, Katharina, Zürich 082953, 112051
Büttner, Anke, Geisenhausen . . . 125705
Büttner, W. & J., Hohenroth . . . 071559
Bützer, Judith, Düsseldorf . . . 125526
Büyük Saray Mozaik Müzesi, İstanbul . . . 038086
Buffa, Francesca, Palermo . . . 076133
Buffalo and Erie County Historical Society Museum, Buffalo . . . 042500
Buffalo and Erie County Naval and Military Park, Buffalo . . . 042501
Buffalo Bean Museum, Tompkins . . 006576
Buffalo Bill Cody Homestead, Princeton . . . 047233
Buffalo Bill Historical Center, Cody . 043029
Buffalo Bill Memorial Museum, Golden . . . 044232
Buffalo Bill Museum of Le Claire, Iowa, Le Claire . . . 045216
Buffalo Bill Ranch, North Platte . . . 046533
Buffalo Candle and Craft, Buffalo . . 087864
Buffalo Museum of Science, Buffalo 042502
Buffalo Nations Luxton Museum, Banff . . . 005062
Buffalo Society of Artists, Williamsville . . . 054691
Buffalo Stew Antiques, Tulsa . . . 093290
Buffalo Trails Company, Fort Worth . 116136
Buffalo Trails Museum, Epping . . . 043718
Buffalo Wholesale Antiques, Buffalo 087865
Buffet, Claude, Paris . . . 138321
Buffet Rouge, Lyon . . . 064099
Buffs Museum, National Army Museum, Canterbury . . . 038977
Bugatti Trust, Cheltenham . . . 039051
Bugdahn & Kaimer, Düsseldorf . . . 102479
Bugden, Potts Point . . . 137054
Bugeja, Victoria . . . 077542
Bugera & Kmet, Edmonton . . . 096869
Il Bugigattolo, Genova . . . 075445
Bugmann, Sabine, Nunningen . . . 130132
BuGok Railroad Exhibition Hall, Railroad Museum, Uiwang . . . 027622
Bugs & Benz, Houston . . . 132108
Buguruslanskij Istoriko-kraevedčeskij Muzej, Buguruslan . . . 033055
Buhard, Jean-Yves, Saint-André-sur-Vieux-Jonc . . . 067358
Buhard, Jean-Yves, Villeurbanne . . 068951
La Buhardilla, Monterrey . . . 077588
La Buhardilla, Pamplona . . . 081513
Buhl, Johannes, Regensburg . . . 104692
Buhler, Elfriede, Milano . . . 127553
Buhlinger, Petra, Walzbachtal . . . 126966
El Búho, Buenos Aires . . . 094064
El Búho, Cali . . . 098228
Buhr, Carl, Hamburg . . . 071215
Buhr, M. de, Dorum . . . 070298
Buhre, Unna . . . 105098
Buhs, D., Salzhemmendorf . . . 073655
Build Gallery, San Francisco . . . 119625
Building Arts, Pittsburgh . . . 091795
Building of Bath Museum, Bath . . . 038622
Buisine, Patrick, Lille . . . 063838
Buisson, Claude, Seloncourt . . . 068202
Buisson, Luc du, Cluny . . . 062367
Buisson, Monique, Dijon . . . 062650
Buisson, Roger, Paris . . . 124610
Het Buitenhuis, Amstelveen . . . 077758
Buitrago, Carlos Armando, Cali . . . 059879
Bujack, Karin, Kiel . . . 126040
Bujnakskij Istoriko-kraevedčeskij Muzej, Dagestanskij gosudarstvennyj objedinennyj istoriko-architekturnyj muzej, Bujnaksk . . . 033056
Bukara, Valencia . . . 081649
Bukhara, Sharjah . . . 083210
Bukinist, Moskva . . . 140902
Bukinist 7, Moskva . . . 140903
Bukinist na Litejnom, Sankt-Peterburg . . . 140930
Bukovac Art Gallery, Cavtat . . . 007707
Bukowski, Göteborg . . . 122142
Bukowski, Helsinki . . . 120881
Bukowski, Malmö . . . 122207
Bukowski, Lilla, Stockholm 081933, 122250
Bukowski, Rafał, Kraków . . . 129033
Bukyoung University Museum, Busan . . . 027454
Bulabula Arts, Winnellie . . . 056835
Bulang & Zorn, Marburg . . . 139458
BulArt, Varna . . . 096764
Buldrini, Roberto, Roma . . . 127946
El Bulevard dels Antiquaris, Barcelona . . . 080821
Bulfinch, Boston . . . 122823
Bulgarelli, Renato, Torino . . . 128273
Bulgarian Museum Chamber, Sofia . 052707
Bulger, Stephen, Toronto . . . 097241
Bulimba Gallery, Bulimba . . . 094323
Il Bulino, Milano . . . 075649
Buljanskaja, Alla, Moskva . . . 109500
Bulkens, Gustaaf, Antwerpen . . . 057684
Bulkley Valley Museum, Smithers . . 006482
Bull, Audrey, Carmarthen . . . 083881
Bull, Audrey, Tenby . . . 086841
Bull, John, London . . . 085163
Bull & Son, Walter, Cirencester . . . 084014, 130579
Bullet, Saint Paul . . . 092352
Bulletin de l'Antiquaire et du Brocanteur, Paris . . . 135695
Bulletin de l'Institut Royal du Patrimoine Artistique, Bruxelles . . . 135593
Bulletin du Musée National de Varsovie, Warszawa . . . 136021
Bulletin of Detroit Institute of Arts, Detroit . . . 136409
Bulletin van het Rijksmuseum, Amsterdam . . . 135993
Bulling, Rolf & Helma, Backnang . . 101621
Bullivant, Robert, Saint Louis . . . 119192
Bulloch Hall, Roswell . . . 047550
Bullock, Leslie, Haarlem . . . 078445
Bullpen, Fresno . . . 088898
Bullpen, Toledo . . . 093165
Bullrich Gaona Wernicke, Buenos Aires . . . 055185
Bulls, Bulls . . . 079000
Bulls in a China Chop, Burra . . . 055587
Bullseye Connection Gallery, Portland . . . 118983
Bully's Fifties, Rotterdam . . . 078703
Bulurru Australia, Marrickville . . . 056163
Bulwagang Helena Benitez Gallery, Manila . . . 031715
Bulzoni, Roma . . . 134669
Bum Steer, Fort Worth . . . 088841
Bumb, H.-Jürgen, Contwig . . . 070155
Bumble Hill Studio, Kulnura . . . 094710
Bumbles, Ashtead . . . 083342, 130314
Bumcke, Gerd, Idar-Oberstein . . . 103419
Bumper, Villenave-d'Ornon . . . 068910
Bumpers Antique, Sandgate . . . 056570
Bumpkin, Littlehampton . . . 056107
Bumps, Los Angeles . . . 089711
Bunbury Regional Art Galleries, Bunbury . . . 000860
Bunbury Watermill, Bunbury . . . 038901
Bunch, Kongens Lyngby . . 060392, 098592
Bund Bildender Künstler Leipzig e.V., Leipzig . . . 053070
Bund Bildender Künstler Lüneburg, Strachau . . . 053071
Bund Bildender Künstler Niedersachsen, Hannover . . . 053072
Bund Bildender Künstler Niedersachsen, Gruppe Hannover, Hannover . . . 053073
Bund Bildender Künstlerinnen Württemberg e. V., Stuttgart . . . 053074
Bund Deutscher Buchkünstler, München . . . 053075
Bund Deutscher Grafik-Designer e.V., Hamburg . . . 053076
Bund Deutscher Kunsterzieher e.V., Hannover . . . 053077
Bund Freischaffender Foto-Designer e.V., Stuttgart . . . 053078
Bunda, Veronica, Springwood . . . 056624
Bunda, Veronica, Sydney . . . 056669
Bundaberg Arts Centre, Bundaberg 000861
Bundaberg Historical Museum, Bundaberg . . . 000862
Bundaberg Railway Museum, Bundaberg . . . 000863
Bundanon Art, Cambewarra . . . 094361
Bundava, Sydney . . . 056670
Bundelkhand Chhatrasal Museum, Banda . . . 022012
Bundesberufsgremium Handel Briefmarken und Numismatika, Wien . . . 052521
Bundesbriefmuseum, Schwyz . . . 037541
Bundesverband Bild & Rahmen, Rheinbach . . . 053079
Bundesverband Bildender Künstler e.V., Landesverband Bonn/ Rhein-Sieg, Bonn . . . 053080
Bundesverband Bildender Künstler Landesverband Hessen e.V., Taunusstein . . . 053081
Bundesverband Bildender Künstler Niederbayern/Oberpfalz e.V, Regensburg . . . 053082
Bundesverband Bildender Künstler Rheinland-Pfalz e.V., Mainz . . . 053083
Bundesverband Bildender Künstler Saarland e.V., Saarbrücken . . . 053084
Bundesverband Bildender Künstlerinnen und Künstler, Bonn . . . 053085
Bundesverband Bildender Künstlerinnen und Künstler, Bezirksgruppe Stade-Cuxhaven, Buxtehude . . . 053086
Bundesverband Bildender Künstlerinnen und Künstler, Bezirksverband Aachen/ Euregio, Aachen . . . 053087
Bundesverband Bildender Künstlerinnen und Künstler, Bezirksverband Darmstadt, Darmstadt . . . 053088
Bundesverband Bildender Künstlerinnen und Künstler, Bezirksverband Mittelhessen e.V, Herborn, Hessen . . . 053089
Bundesverband Bildender Künstlerinnen und Künstler, Bezirksverband Münsterland, Münster . . . 053090
Bundesverband Bildender Künstlerinnen und Künstler, Bezirksverband Unterfranken e.V, Kempten . . . 053091
Bundesverband Bildender Künstlerinnen und Künstler, Landesgruppe Oldenburg, Oldenburg, Oldenburg . . . 053092
Bundesverband Bildender Künstlerinnen und Künstler, Landesverband Schleswig-Holstein, Kiel . . . 053093
Bundesverband Bildender Künstlerinnen und Künstler, Region Bergisch-Land, Wuppertal . . . 053094
Bundesverband Bildender Künstlerinnen und Künstler, Regionalverband Kassel-Nordhessen, Kassel . . . 053095
Bundesverband Bildender Künstlerinnen und Künstler, Bezirksgruppe Hildesheim, Hildesheim . . . 053096
Bundesverband Bildender Künstlerinnen und Künstler, Bezirksgruppe Ostfriesland im Landesverband Niedersachsen, Hannover . . . 053097
Bundesverband Bildender Künstlerinnen und Künstler, Bezirksverband Düsseldorf, Düsseldorf . . . 053098
Bundesverband Bildender Künstlerinnen und Künstler, Bezirksverband Heidelberg, Heidelberg . . . 053099
Bundesverband Bildender Künstlerinnen und Künstler, Bezirksverband Köln e.V., Köln . . . 053100, 103604
Bundesverband Bildender Künstlerinnen und Künstler, Bezirksverband Westfalen Süd/ Nord e.V., Dortmund . . . 053101
Bundesverband Bildender Künstlerinnen und Künstler Landesverband NRW e.V., Köln . . . 053102
Bundesverband Bildender Künstlerinnen und Künstler Niedersachsen, Hannover . . . 053103
Bundesverband Bildender Künstlerinnen und Künstler, Regionalverband Celle, Celle . . . 053104
Bundesverband Bildender Künstlerinnen und Künstler, Regionalverband Göttingen, Göttingen . . . 053105
Bundesverband Bildender Künstlerinnen und Künstler, Regionalverband Harz e.V., Goslar . . . 053106
Bundesverband Bildender Künstlerinnen und Künstler Südbaden, Freiburg im Breisgau . . . 053107

Bundesverband der Bibliotheken und Museen für Darstellende Künste e.V., Köln 053108
Bundesverband der Jugendkunstschulen und Kulturpädagogischen Einrichtungen e.V., Unna 053109
Bundesverband des Deutschen Kunst- & Antiquitätenhandels e.V., Drestadt 053110
Bundesverband Deutscher Auktionatoren, Delmenhorst 053111
Arbeitsgemeinschaft der Restauratoren-Museen-Denkmalpflege-Grabungstechnik; Berufsverband staatlich geprüfter RestauratorInnen; Bundesverband Deutscher Diplom-RestauratorInnen; Deutscher Restauratoren Verband; Deutscher Verband Freiberuflicher Restauratoren; Restauratoren Fachverband; Restauratorenverband Sachsen, Bonn 053589
Bundesverband Deutscher Galerien, Köln 053112
Bundesverband Deutscher Kunstverleger e.V., Frankfurt am Main 053113
Bundesverband Deutscher Kunstversteigerer e.V., Berlin 053114
Bundesverband Museumspädagogik e.V., München 053115
Bunel, Patrick, L'Isle-sur-la-Sorgue 063928
Bungalow Antiques, Oakland 091409
Bungalow Gallery, Indianapolis 116446
Bungalow Porslin, Stockholm 081934
Bungalow Upholstery, Auckland . . . 128898
Bungay Museum, Bungay 038902
Bungert & Wirtz, Trier 126907
Bunglemarr Trading, Bundaberg . . . 055582
Buninyong Antiques, Buninyong . . . 055585
Bunka Gakuen Fukushoku Hakabutsukan, Tokyo 027149
Bunkamura Museum of Art, Tokyo . 027150
Bunker d'Hitler, Musée de la Resistance, Brûly-de-Pesche 003284
Bunker Hill Museum, Charlestown . 042750
Bunker Museet, Frederikshavn 008865
Bunker Stalina, Samara 033712
Das Bunkermuseum, Emden 016957
Bunkier Sztuki, Kraków 108930
Bunnell Street Gallery, Homer 044586
Bunratty Castle and Folkpark, Bunratty 022697
Bunryu, Tokyo 140183
Bunt Stein BogenHaus, Obernburg . 104502
Buntin, Robyn, Honolulu . . 088938, 116200
Bunting, Peter, Bakewell 083363
Buonamici, Firenze 075297
Buonarroti, Michelangelo, Brugge . 057763
Buonasorte, Ugo, Milano 075650
Buono, Francesco, Roma 127947
Buonocore, Gennaro, Napoli 127753
Buonocore, Mario, Napoli . 075950, 127754
Buqaish, Sharjah 112464
Buqara, Rio de Janeiro 058561
Buque Museo Ex BAP América, Iquitos 031529
Buque-Museo Fragata Presidente Sarmiento, Buenos Aires 000143
Buque Museo Yaraví, Puerto de Puno 031587
Bur, Marie-France, La Celle-Saint-Cloud 063305
Buraczyński, Tomasz, Warszawa . . 129081
Burapha Museum of Art, Chon Buri 037899
Burbage-Atter, Leeds 141712
Burbank, San Jose 092919
La Burbuja-Museo del Niño, Hermosillo 028315
Burca, Eamon de, Blackrock 139954
Burcea, Ion, București . . . 080145, 129217
Burchard, Friedrich, Wuppertal 139884
Burchfield-Penney Art Center, Buffalo 042503
Burckardt, Helga, Bielefeld 069819
Burden, Clive A., Rickmansworth . . 142018
Burden Gallery, Aperture Foundation, New York 046304
Burden & Izett, New York 090755
Burdett, Melrose Park 056207
Burdett & Rawling, Kingston-upon-Hull 130849
Burdick, Washington 120266
Burdur Devlet Güzel Sanatlar Galerisi, Burdur 038029
Burdur Müzesi, Burdur 038030
Bureau, Anne, Gaure 099285
Bureau County Historical Society Museum, Princeton 047232
Burebank Book's, Norwich 141962
Burek, Michaela, Markdorf 126290
Burel, Thierry, Paris 065639
Burel, Y., Luneray 064032
Bures Antiques, Bures 130475
Buret, Roland, Paris 138322
Burford Antique Centre, Burford . . .083784, 130476
The Burford Gallery, Burford 083785, 112755
Burg-Antik, Nürnberg 073100
Burg Beeskow, Beeskow 015935
Burg Falkenberg, Falkenberg, Oberpfalz 017099
Burg Forchtenstein, Eisenstadt 001820
Burg-Galerie, Brüggen, Niederrhein 070069, 102273
Burg Galerie, Burg auf Fehmarn . . . 102288
Burg Giebichenstein, Hochschule für Kunst und Design Halle, Halle, Saale . . . 050096
Burg Gleichen, Wandersleben 020667
Burg Gnandstein, Staatliche Schlösser, Burgen und Gärten Sachsen, Kohren-Sahlis 018368
Burg Gößweinstein, Gößweinstein . 017461
Burg Greifenstein, Greifenstein 001953
Burg Hagen, Hagen bei Bremerhaven 017621
Burg Herzberg, Breitenbach am Herzberg 016402
Burg Hohenzollern, Bisingen 016254
Burg Kreuzen, Bad Kreuzen 001728
Burg Kreuzenstein, Leobendorf . . . 002226
Burg Kronberg, Kronberg im Taunus 018418
Burg Lauenstein, Ludwigsstadt . . . 018712
Burg Meersburg, Meersburg 018870
Burg Mildenstein, Leisnig 018602
Burg-Museum, Parsberg 019565
Burg Neuhaus, Wolfsburg 020961
Burg Neustadt-Glewe, Neustadt-Glewe 019292
Burg Pappenheim mit Naturmuseum und Historischem Museum, Pappenheim 019562
Burg Prunn, Riedenburg 019828
Burg Rabenstein, Frohnleiten 001873
Burg Schlaining mit Museum, Stadtschlaining 002689
Burg Sonnenberg, Wiesbaden 020862
Burg Stolpen, Stolpen 020326
Burg Trausnitz, Landshut 018482
Burg Trifels, Annweiler 015553
Burg- und Klosteranlage Oybin, Kurort Oybin 018447
Burg- und Mühlenmuseum Pewsum, Ostfriesisches Freilichtmuseum, Krummhörn 018427
Burg und Park Wilhelmsbad, Hanau 017736
Burg- und Schloßmuseum Allstedt, Allstedt 015483
Burg- und Stadtmuseum Königstein, Königstein im Taunus 018354
Burg Vischering, Münsterlandmuseum, Lüdinghausen 018737
Burg Wernstein, Wernstein am Inn . 002839
Burg zu Burghausen, Burghausen, Salzach 016511
Burg Zwernitz, Wonsees 020977
Burgan, Claude, Paris 065640
Burgart-Presse, Rudolstadt 134375
Burgaski Muzej, Burgas 004647
Burgassi, Lucia, Firenze 106039
Burgate Antique Centre, Canterbury 083857
Burgauer Galerie, Burgau, Schwaben 102289
Burgen und Schlösser, Braubach . . 135755
Burgenkundliche Sammlung im Burgenmuseum, Gossau (Sankt Gallen) 037155
Burgenkundliches Museum des Steirischen Burgenvereins, Bärnbach 001747
Burgenländische Landesgalerie, Eisenstadt 001821
Burgenländisches Brotmuseum, Bad Tatzmannsdorf 001735
Burgenländisches Feuerwehrmuseum, Eisenstadt 001822
Burgenländisches Landesmuseum, Eisenstadt 001823
Burgenländisches Schulmuseum, Lockenhaus 002261
Burgenländisches Steinmuseum, Landsee 002196
Burgenmuseum Eisenberg, Eisenberg, Allgäu 016927
Burger, Andreas, Heiligenkreuz im Lafnitztal 057057
Burger, Christa, München 104161
Burger, Robert, Los Angeles 132244
Burger Weeshuis, Zierikzee 030387
Burgersdijk & Niermans, Leiden . . . 140475
Burgersdorp Cultural Historical Museum, Burgersdorp 034570
Burgert, Strasbourg 068306, 124941
Burgert, Prof. Hans-Joachim, Berlin 133757
Burgess, Derek J., Parkstone 086191, 131362
Burgess, J & J, Cambridge 141468
Burgess Farm Antiques, Morestead 086008
Burgess Farm Antiques, Winchester 087171
Burgevin, Denis, Gien 062994
Burggalerie, Magdeburg 103985
Burggalerie Laa, Laa an der Thaya . 002188
Burghard, Rastatt 073419
Burghead Museum, Burghead 038904
Burghley House, Stamford 041087
Burghofmuseum, Stadtgeschichtliches Museum, Soest 020230
Burghold & Grazyna, Soest 126810
Burgi, Camille, Paris 065641
Burgin, Christine, New York 117733
Burgio, Emanuele, Palermo 076134
Burgio, Giuseppe, Palermo 076135
Burgmuseum, Güssing 001985
Burgmuseum, Höhr-Grenzhausen . . 017947
Burgmuseum, Kirschau 018273
Burgmuseum, Lenzen, Elbe 018617
Burgmuseum, Lisberg 018666
Burgmuseum, Ortenberg, Hessen . . 019484
Burgmuseum, Seebenstein 002671
Burgmuseum, Sulzberg 020386
Burgmuseum, Wolfsegg 020969
Burgmuseum Altnußberg, Geiersthal 017337
Burgmuseum Bad Bodenteich, Bad Bodenteich 015673
Burgmuseum Burg Guttenberg, Haßmersheim 017791
Burgmuseum Clam, Klam 002149
Burgmuseum der Wasserburg Kapellendorf, Kapellendorf 018149
Burgmuseum für Vor- und Frühgeschichte, Deutschlandsberg 001779
Burgmuseum Greifenstein, Greifenstein 017519
Burgmuseum Grünwald, Archäologische Staatssammlung München, Grünwald 017591
Burgmuseum Marksburg, Braubach 016375
Burgmuseum mit Folterkammer, Natur- und Jagdmuseum, Pappenheim 019562
Burgmuseum Reichenstein, Pregarten 002465
Burgmuseum Ruine Dürnstein, Wildbad-Einöd 003044
Burgmuseum Schlossfreiheit, Tangermünde 020397
Burgmuseum Schönfels, Schönfels 020080
Burgmuseum Waldeck, Waldeck, Hessen 020634
Burgruine Münzenberg, Münzenberg 019162
Burgruine Teufelsberg, Überherrn . . 020514
Burgturm Davert, Ascheberg, Westfalen 015588
Burgues, Catherine, Gentilly 124248
Burguet, Monique, Montrouge 064778
Burgverlag, Wien 133186, 137297
Burgwin-Wright Museum, Wilmington 049211
Buried Treasures, Denver 088665
Burijn, de, Nieuw en Sint Joosland . 128783
Buril, Madrid 081257
Buril, Sevilla 081579
Burin Heritage House, Burin 005164
Burjatskij Gosudarstvennyj Objedinennyj Istoričeskij i Architekturno-chudožestvennyj Muzej, Ulan-Udė 033998
Burjatskij Respublikanskij Chudožestvennyj Muzej im. C.S. Sampilova, Ulan-Udė 033999
Burkard, Gerhard & Viktoria, Buttenwiesen 070114
Burkard, Peter, Luzern . . . 111686, 122338
Burkart, Nürnberg 073101
Burkart, Rolf A., Bad Kreuznach . . . 133733
Burke, Los Angeles 089712
Burke, Memphis 142543
Burke, New York 090756
Burke & Sons, John F., Cahir 074869
Burke County Historical Powers Lake Complex, Powers Lake 047218
Burke Museum, Beechworth 000783
Burke Museum of Natural History and Culture, Seattle 048075
Burke News, Seattle 136410
Burkert, George, San Francisco . . . 132872
Burkhard, Essen 133915
Burkhardt, Vaihingen 105100
Burkhardt, Bianca, Steinbach, Taunus 126831
Burkhardt, Janet, Waramanga 137128
Burkhardt, Klaus-Joachim, Stuttgart 073966
Burkhardt-Spann, Gabriele, München 126363
Burlando, Mauro Silvio, Genova . . . 075446
Burle, Rio de Janeiro 096595
Burleson County Historical Museum, Caldwell 042548
Burlington, Denver 088666
Burlington, New York 090757
Burlington Art Centre, Burlington . . 005165
Burlington Bertie's, Auckland 078931
Burlington County Historical Society Museum, Burlington 042520
Burlington Historical Museum, Burlington 042518
Burlington Historical Museum, Burlington 042519
Burlington Magazine, London 136188
Burlington Magazine Publications, London 135199
Burlington Paintings, London 085164, 113521, 130964
Burlington-Rock Island Railroad and Historical Museum, Teague 048512
Burlövs Gamla Prästgård, Arlöv . . . 036194
Burman, Stratford-upon-Avon 086773, 131553
Burman, C. & L., London . 085165, 130965
Burmeister, Brigitte, Kiel 071823
Burmeister, J., Kerpen, Rheinland . 071802
Burmeister & Wain's Museum, København 008960
Burmese Fine Art, Singapore 080438
Burmester, James, Bristol 141450
Burnaby Art Gallery, Burnaby 005168
Burnaby Village Museum, Burnaby . 005169
Burnay, Luís P., Lisboa 140823
Burne, W.G.T., London . . . 085166, 130966
Burner, M., Isernhagen 071637
Burness, Victor, London 085167
Burnet, Amsterdam 140289
Burnet, Ross, Uralla 137123
Burnett, Richmond, Surrey 114308
Burnett House and Myilly Point Heritage Precinct, Darwin 000974

Burnham Deepdale Exhibitions, Burnham Deepdale . . . 112761
Burnham Model and Collectors Shop, Burnham-on-Sea . . . 083806
Burnham Museum, Burnham-on-Crouch . . . 038905
Burnham Tavern, Hannah Weston Chapter, National Society Daughters of the American Revolution, Machias . . . 045549
Burnie Regional Art Gallery, Burnie . 000864
Burning Embers, Aberdeen . . . 083234
Burning Issues Gallery, Whangarei . 108658
Burning Mountain Antiques, Wingen 056834
The Burning Question Studio, Vancouver . . . 097432
Burns, Catherine, Oakland . . . 118627
Burns, Greg, Oklahoma City . . . 118657
Burns, Stephanie, Deakin . . . 094468
Burns Cottage Museum, Alloway . . 038489
Burns & Graham, Winchester . . . 087172
Burns House Museum, Mauchline . 040437
Burns Visual Arts Society of Calgary, Calgary . . . 052736, 096793
The Burnside, Brodick . . . 112741
Burnside Plantation, Bethlehem . . . 042181
Burnstein, Carl, New York . 090758, 142640
Burnt House Museum, Jerusalem . . 022944
Burntisland Museum, Burntisland . . 038911
Buro Art, Edinburgh . . . 112986
BuroK, Leeuwarden . . . 108090, 134819
BuroK, Leeuwarden . . . 134820
Burøsund Bygdemuseum, Vannareid . . . 031315
Burot, Y., Châtillon-sur-Seine . . . 062237
Burpee Museum of Natural History, Rockford . . . 047497
Burr & Muir, Cape Town . . . 080679
Burra Mine Open Air Museum, Burra . . . 000866
Burralga, Brisbane . . . 094288
Burrangong Gallery, Young . . . 095457
Burrell, Marceline, San Francisco . . 092748
Burrell Collection, Glasgow . . . 039548
Burren Centre, Kilfenora . . . 022802
Burren College of Art, Ballyvaughan 050341
Burridge, John, Swanbourne . . . 056662
Burritt on the Mountain, A Living Museum, Huntsville . . . 044691
Burrowes Mansion Museum, Matawan . . . 045725
Burrows, David E., Osgathorpe . . . 086168
Burrus, Claire, Paris . . . 100094
Bursa Arkeoloji Müzesi, Bursa . . . 038033
Bursa Devlet Güzel Sanatlar Galerisi, Bursa . . . 038034
Bursa Türk-İslâm Eserleri Müzesi, Bursa . . . 038035
Bursledon Windmill, Bursledon . . . 038912
Burslem Antiques, Stoke-on-Trent . 086732
Burston Gallery, Toronto . . . 097242
Burston Strike School, Burston, Diss . . . 038914
Burstow & Hewett, Battle . . . 122401
Bursztyn Galeria, Gdynia . . . 108905
Burt County Museum, Tekamah . . . 048514
Burté, Bernadette, Nancy . . . 064863
Burth, K., Ettenheim . . . 070664
Burtnieku Pagasta Briedes Krogs, Burtnieki . . . 027667
Burton, Invercargill . . . 079125
Burton, Saint Paul . . . 119280
Burton, Ian, Auchterarder . . . 083350
Burton, John, Ebrington . . . 084269
Burton & Co., K.J., Balmain . . . 055444
Burton Agnes Hall, Burton Agnes . . 038915
Burton Antiques, Burton-upon-Trent 083814
The Burton Art Gallery and Museum, Bideford . . . 038700
Burton Ching, San Francisco . . . 092749
Burton Constable Hall, Kingston-upon-Hull . . . 039884
Burton Court, Eardisland . . . 039342
Burton-Garbett, A., Morden . . . 141947
Burton Lysecki, Winnipeg . . . 137739
Burton Marinkovich, Washington . . 120267
Burtons' Colossal Collectables Fair, Canterbury . . . 093570
Burt's Antiques, Salt Lake City . . . 092422, 132782
Burwell-Morgan Mill, Millwood . . . 045877
Burwell Museum, Burwell . . . 038918
Bury Art Gallery and Museum, Bury, Lancashire . . . 038919
Bury Saint Edmunds Art Gallery, Bury Saint Edmunds . . . 038923
Bury Transport Museum, Bury, Lancashire . . . 038920
Burzio, Vincenzo, Torino . . . 128274
Busacchi, Daniela, Verona . . . 128419
Busan Museum, Busan . . . 027455
Busan University Museum, Busan . 027456
Busan Woman's College Tea-ceremony Museum, Busan . . . 027457
Buscaroli, Francesca, Bologna . . . 127137
Busch, Bielefeld . . . 069820
Busch, Benno, Sondershausen . . . 126816
Busch, Bettina, Berlin . . . 125186
Busch, H., Detmold . . . 070225
Busch, Jürgen, München . 104162, 126364
Busch, Klaus, Stakendorf . . . 073893
Busche, Dr. Ernst A., Berlin . . . 101820
Busche, H., Detmold . . . 102360, 125456
Buschlen-Mowatt, Vancouver . . . 097433
Buschlinger, Ulrike, Wiesbaden . . . 105247
Buschmann, Heinz & Peter, Mönchengladbach . . . 126325
Buschulte, Heinz, Oberlahr . . . 139618
Busck, Arnold, København . . . 137890
Buscot House, Buscot . . . 038928
Buscot Park House, Faringdon . . . 039485
Buse, Adelheid, Erfurt . . . 125596
Buse, Peter-Jesko, Mainz 072390, 126257
Busetto, Fabio, Venezia . . . 128380
Bush, New Orleans . . . 090526
Bush & Partners, A.E., Attleborough 083348, 130315
Bush, Robert, London . . . 085168
Bush and Beach Artwork, Barwon Heads . . . 094217
Bush Antiques, Saffron Walden . . . 086430
Bush House Museum and Bush Barn Art Center, Salem . . . 047750
Bush 'n Beach Gallery, Collaroy . . . 094415
Bush 'n Beyond Studio Gallery, Broken Hill . . . 094302
Bushehri, Manama . . . 095996
Bushell, Seattle . . . 123111
Busher, Raad, Saarbrücken . . . 073626
Bushey Antique Centre, Bushey . . . 083825, 130492
Bushey Museum and Art Gallery, Bushey . . . 038929
Bushi d'Eau, Hitomi, Paris . . . 100095
Bushido Antiques, Honolulu . . . 088939
Bushman Site Museum, Estcourt . . 034611
Bushuven, Düren . . . 139001
Bushwhacker Museum, Nevada . . . 046180
Bushwood, Redbourn . . . 086337
Bushwood Books, Kew . . . 135163
Bushwood Studios, Windsor, Ontario . . . 097554
Bushy Park Ironworks, Dublin . . . 127093
Bushy Run Battlefield Museum, Jeannette . . . 044840
Busiello, Pasquale, Napoli . . . 127755
Busignani, Patricia, San Marino . . . 080344, 140944
Business and Creative Arts Division, College of San Mateo, San Mateo . . . 052132
Business Committee for the Arts, New York . . . 054692
Business Matters in the Visual Arts, San Francisco . . . 119626
Business Men's Art Institute, Montrose . . . 054693
Busnel, Jacques-Henry, Saint-Malo (Ille-et-Vilaine) . . . 067607
Busnel, Jacques-Henry, Saint-Malo (Ille-et-Vilaine) . . . 067608
Busnel, Jean-François, Saint-Malo (Ille-et-Vilaine) . . . 067609
Busse, Erfurt . . . 070584
Busse, Schleswig . . . 104826
Busse, Worpswede . . . 105328
Busse, Holger, Hamburg . . . 071216
Bussemakerhuis, Borne . . . 029335
Bussien, Pierre, Martigny . . . 082649
Bussière, Henry, Paris . . . 100096
Bussière Jannel, Paris . . . 100097
Bußmann, H., Ahlen . . . 101543
Bussolino, Roberto, Torino . . . 128275
Busson, Bernard, Saint-Ouen . . . 067740
Bussoni, Giuseppe, Milano . . . 075651
Bussotti, München . . . 126365
Bussy, J.H. de, Amsterdam . . . 134775
Al-Bustan, Manama . . . 057621
Busters, Atlanta . . . 087459, 131764
Busy Beaver Coins, Buffalo . . . 087866
Busy Bee Books, Mawson . . . 136993
But Is It Art, London . . . 096945
But is it Art, Reading . . . 114298
Butchart & O'Hara, Long Beach . . . 089629
Butchoff, Ian, London . . . 085169
Bute Museum, Rothesay . . . 040859
Buteau, Gérard, Clermont-Ferrand . 062331
Buten & Binnen, Wilhelmshaven . . . 074441
Buter, Paris . . . 065642, 100098
Butera School of Art, Boston . . . 051010
Butik Antik, København . . . 060304
Butik Antik, Küblis . . . 082519
Butler, Fort Worth . . . 088842
Butler, Brian D., Los Angeles . . . 116732
Butler, Edward, Dublin . . . 074897
Butler, Laurence, Glasgow . . . 084463
Butler, Peter, Teralba . . . 095325
Butler, Rita, Pangbourne . . . 086190
Butler, Robin, Clare . . . 084025
Butler, Roderick, Honiton . 084714, 130800
Butler County Historical Museum, Allison . . . 041663
Butler County Museum, Hamilton . . 044402
Butler County Museum and Kansas Oil Museum, El Dorado . . . 043628
Butler Gallery, Kilkenny . . . 022804
Butler Institute of American Art, Youngstown . . . 049360
Butler Street Gallery, Pittsburgh . . . 091796
The Butler & the Chef, San Francisco . . . 092750
Butler & Wilson, London . . . 085170
Butler's Corner, Baltimore . . . 087652
Butman, Alexander, Paris . 100099, 133548
Butnaru, Damian, Volxheim . . . 126954
Bútorbizományi, Budapest . . . 074673
Butrinti Museum, Butrint . . . 000014
Butt, Anthony, Baldock . . . 083369
Butte Montmartre, Paris . . . 100100
Butte Silver Bow Arts Chateau, Butte . . . 042533
The Butter Factory, Mannum . . . 056154
Butter Pat Museum, Bigfork . . . 042203
Butterfass, Julie, Villegly . . . 125024
Butterfield Trail Historical Museum, Russell Springs . . . 047575
Butterfields, Chicago . . . 122841
Butterflies Gallery, Pokolbin . . . 095074
Butterfly Alphabet, Washington . . . 120268
Butternut and Blue, Baltimore . . . 142222
Butters, Portland . . . 118984
Butterworth, Sarah, Aboyne . . . 112488
Buttet, Pierre de, Poisy . . . 124845
Buttin, Jean-Charles, Rumilly . . . 067328
Buttin, Philippe, Annecy . . . 060888
Buttmi, Mannheim . . . 072416
The Button Queen, London . . . 085171
Buttons Buttons Buttons, Sydney . . 056671
Butuan City Museum, Butuan . . . 031638
Butuan Diocesan Museum, Butuan . 031639
Butuan National Museum, Butuan . 031640
Butz, L., Steinhagen . . . 073908
Butzon & Bercker, Kevelaer 103534, 134087
Buvat, Madeleine, Pionsat . . . 066833
Buvens, Aarschot . . . 137392
Bux, Gelsenkirchen . . . 139133
Bux, Peter, Leipzig . . . 126185
Buxtehude Museum für Regionalgeschichte und Kunst, Buxtehude . . . 016532
Buxton Antiques Fair, Buxton . . . 093916
Buxton Autumn Antiques and Fine Art Fair, Buxton . . . 093917
Buxton Museum, North Buxton . . . 006040
Buxton Museum and Art Gallery, Buxton . . . 038935
Buy and Sell Olde Wares, Annandale . . . 055346
Buy Design, Ancrum . . . 112509
Buyenlarge, Philadelphia . . . 118742
Buyeo National Museum, Buyeo . . . 027464
Buyers, Toronto . . . 059158
Buysscher, C. de, Ladeuze . . . 120765
De Buytensael, Arnhem . . . 107846
Buz White Screenprint, Portland . . . 118985
Buzare, Hélène, Paris . . . 065643
Buzeczki, M., Bruchsal . . . 070065
Buzeczki, M., Ubstadt-Weiher . . . 074127
Buzelim, Belo Horizonte . . . 096454
Buzulukskij Gorodskoj Istoriko-kraevedčeskij Muzej, Buzuluk . . . 033057
BV-Galerie, Klagenfurt . . . 095611
BV Métaux Précieux, Paris . . . 065644
Bwlch Farm Stable Museum, Llanelli . . . 040055
By Antiqua, Roma . . . 076355
By George, Johannesburg . . . 080702
By George Antiques Centre, Saint Albans . . . 086435, 131436
By-Gone Days Antiques, Charlotte . 087932
By Many Hands, Minneapolis . . . 117246
By the Bay Museum, Lewisporte . . 005772
By the Book, Albury . . . 136779
By the Book, Phoenix . . . 142764
Bya Barros, São Paulo . . . 058697
Byam Shaw School of Fine Art, London . . . 050826
Byard Art, Cambridge . . . 112787
Byblos Bookshop, Mareeba . . . 136991
Bydee, Austin . . . 114962
Bydgoski Antykwariat Naukowy, Bydgoszcz . . . 121884, 140713
Byegones, Zebbug . . . 077549
Byers-Evans House Museum, Denver . . . 043398
Byethorpe, Barlow . . . 083382, 130333
Byfield and District Museum, Byfield . . . 000869
Bygdetunet Jutulheimen, Vågå Historielag, Vågåmo . . . 031311
Byggðasafn, Vestmannaeyjar . . . 021984
Byggðasafn Akraness og Nærsveita, Akranes . . . 021929
Byggðasafn Austur-Skaftafellssýslu, Höfn . . . 021949
Byggðasafn Borgarfjardar, Borgarnes . . . 021936
Byggðasafn Dalamanna, Búdardalur 021938
Byggdasafn Dalvíkur, Dalvík . . . 021939
Byggðasafn Dalvíkurbyggdar, Dalvík 021939
Byggðasafn Hafnarfjarðar, Hafnarfjörður . . . 021944
Byggðasafn Húnvetninga og Strandarmanna, Brú . . . 021937
Byggðasafn Rangæinga, Skogar . . . 021981
Byggðasafn Reykjanesbaejar, Reykjanesbaer . . . 021957
Byggðasafn Árnesinga, Eyrarbakki . 021942
Byggðasafn Skagfirdinga, Varmahlid . . . 021983
Byggðasafn Snæfellinga og Hnappdæla, Stykkishólmur . . . 021982
Byggðasafn Sudurnesja Vatnsnes, Reykjanesbaer . . . 021957
Byggðasafn Vestfjarda, Isafjörður . . 021952
Byggðasafnid Grenjadarstad, Húsavík . . . 021950
Byggförlaget, Stockholm . . . 134967
Bygland Museum, Bygland . . . 030799
Bygone, Richmond . . . 092065
Bygone Beautys, Leura . . . 056098
Bygone Days, Ottawa . . . 059033
Bygones, Angmering . . . 083305

Bygones, Burford 083786, 130477
Bygones, Huntly 084772, 130820
Bygones, Limerick 074987
Bygones, Worcester 087252
Bygones Antiques, Constantia 080693
Bygones at Holkham, Wells-next-the-Sea 041327
Bygones by the Cathedral, Worcester 087253
Bygones Museum, Claydon 039096
Bygones of Ireland, Westport 074997
Bygones Reclamation, Canterbury . 083858
Byham, P.J. & J.F., Barooga 055450
Byland Abbey, Coxwold 039160
Byles, Patrick K., Kingston 106807
Byles, Robert, Bampton, Devon . . .083377, 130328
Bymodellen, Oslo 031072
Bymuseet, Skjern 009100
Bymuseet Møntergården, Odense . . 009043
Byrd, Edward, Los Angeles 116733
Byrdie's, Jacksonville 089387
Byre Gallery, Stoneykirk 114497
Byrkley Books, Burton-upon-Trent . 141463
Byrne, Bendigo 055478
Byrne, Chester 122462
Byrne, Christopher C., Dallas 115847
Byrnes, James B., Los Angeles . . . 116734
Byron, Taranto 076743
Byron, Sandra, Woollahra 095422
Byron Fine Art Gallery, Byron Bay . . 094336
Byron Historical Museum, Byron . . 042538
Byron & Roche, Chicago 115378
Byrt, Gavin, Red Hill South 095121
By's Antigüedades, Caracas 093523
Byte Gallery, Northbridge 094989
Bytown Historical Museum, Ottawa 006086
Byzance Artes e Interiores, Rio de Janeiro 058562
Byzant, Prešov 080633
Byzantine and Christian Museum, Athinai 021163
Byzantine Collection, Chalkida 021224
Byzantine Museum, Paphos 008232
Byzantine Museum, Tinos 021509
Byzantine Museum and Art Galleries, Lefkosia 008213
Byzantine Museum of Antivouniotissa, Corfu 021239
Byzantine Museum of Katapoliani, Paros 021421
Byzantine Museum of the Metropolis of Samos and Ikaria, Samos 021457
Byzantium, Columbus 115766
C 2, Montsoult 064781
C & C Arts Gallery, Singapore 109779
C & C Auction Gallery, Larchmont . . 122937
C & C Coin, Phoenix 091724
C d M, Milano 075652
C & D Sports, Columbus 088389
C Fine Art, Wath-upon-Dearne 114655
C & G Auctions, Rivett 120633
C & G Furniture, Houston 132109
C-Galéria, Komárno 109916
C. Grier Beam Truck Museum, Cherryville 042797
C International Contemporary Art, Toronto 135628
C & M Arts, New York 117734
C Magazine, Toronto 133322, 135629
C/O Berlin, Berlin 101821
C-Plus, Strasbourg 101282
C & R Gallery, Milwaukee 117175
C & S Antiques, Honiton 084715
C & T Antiques, Houston 089041
C V B, Santiago de Chile 123875
C2 Gallery, Soulbury 114449
The C21 Shop, Mundesley 114101
Cá d'Oro, Bologna 075061
Ca' d'Oro-Galleria Giorgio Franchetti, Venezia 026234
Cá Venier dei Leoni, Venezia 106734
CAA Newsletter (New York), New York 136411
Caamano, Philippe, Saint-Martin . . 127073
Cabaia, Lisboa 079886
Cabalgata XVIII, Palma de Mallorca 081473
Caballero, Inocencio Lopez, L'Hospitalet de Llobregat 081158
Caballero Vela Arturo, Acapulco . . . 128494
Caballin Muñiz, David Armando, Gijón 081123
Cabalus, Vézelay 101462
Caban, Mirosław, Grodzisk Mazowiecki 129019
Cabane Identification, Paris 065645
Cabanel, Victoria, Paris 065646
Cabanis & Troschke, Esslingen 125620
Cabanne & Maisonneuf, Lurcy-Levis 064035
Cabanon de Le Corbusier, Roquebrune-Cap-Martin 014102
Cabaret Mechanical Theatre, London 040105
Cabarga Restauraciones, Bahía Blanca 123145
Cabat, Tucson 120113
Cabello Coderque, Jose Antonio, Sevilla 081580
Cabeza de Vaca, Mercedes, Madrid 081258
Cabib, P.F., Genova 075447
Cabinet, Berlin 125187
Cabinet d'Art Asiatique, Labarde . . 012356
Cabinet d'Art Contemporain, Bruxelles 096165
Le Cabinet de Curiosité, Bruxelles . 137429
Cabinet de l'Amateur, Paris 065647
Le Cabinet des Curieux, Paris 065648
Cabinet des Dessins, Genève 111433
Cabinet des Estampes du Musée d'Art et d'Histoire, Genève 037114
Cabinet des Estampes et des Dessins, Liège 003583
Cabinet des Estampes et des Dessins, Strasbourg 014851
Cabinet des Médailles, Bruxelles . . 003293
Cabinet des Médailles Cantonal, Lausanne 037251
Cabinet des Medailles et Antiques, Paris 013559
Cabinet des Monnaies et Médailles, Marseille 012927
Cabinet des Monnais et Médailles du Revest-les-Eaux, Le Revest-les-Eaux 012559
Cabinet d'Expertise Tastet Souchon, Amiens 060809
Cabinet d'Expertises Origine, Paris . 100101
Le Cabinet du Curiosité, Paris 065649
Cabinet Numismatique, Nantes . . . 064910
Cabinet Numismatique de Bretagne, Lorient 063999
Cabinet Numismatique de la Bibliothèque Nationale et Universitaire de Strasbourg, Strasbourg 014852
Cabinet of Discoveries, Campbell . . 055611
Cabinet Quercy, Toulouse 068487
Cabinet War Rooms, London 040106
Cabinets by Order, Louisville 132291
Cable Natural History Museum, Cable 042539
Cabo, Pascual de, Palma de Mallorca 110671
Cabon, Frédéric, Bordeaux 061596
Cabon, Frédèric, Libourne 063814
Caboodle, Edinburgh 084279
Cabot Historical Society Museum, Cabot 042540
Cabot Ma()cMullen, New York 117735
Cabot's Old Indian Pueblo Museum, Desert Hot Springs 043433
Cabotse, Michel, Paris 065650
Cabotse, Michel, Paris 100102
Cabourdin, Annie, Lille 063839
Cabral, Rio de Janeiro 137571
Cabral, Alice, Rio de Janeiro 096596
Cabral, Gilberto E.M., Rio de Janeiro 096597
Cabral, Jorge, Montevideo 087311, 142183
Cabral Moncada, Lisboa 121925
Cabrejas, Mariano, Zaragoza 081737, 129807
Cabrera Delfa, Montevideo 122774
Cabrera Moran, M.I., Madrid 110458
Cabri and District Museum, Cabri . . 005174
Cabrillo National Monument, San Diego 047815
Cabrol, Pierre, Toulouse 068488
Caburn Books, Lewes 141723
Cabuzel, Frédéric, Saint-Riquier . . . 067996
Caccamo, Bertrand, Brignais 061798
Cacchioni, Antonio, Roma 127948
Cacciabue-Drac, Delio, Château-Chinon 062180
Cacciatore, John, Albuquerque 114774
Cacciola, J., New York 117736
Cache, Málaga 081417
Cache Antiques, Atlanta 087460
Cache Antiques, Atlanta 087461
Cache Antiques, Atlanta 122798
Cache Antiques, West Hollywood . . 093454
Cachemire, Bessèges 061405
Cachet Seckinger, Hansueli, Basel .082132, 141201
Cachot, Den Haag 078180
Cachoux, Michel, Paris 100103
Cacialli, Giuseppe, Firenze 127312
Caco Velho, Porto 080073
Caco Velho, Rio de Janeiro 123700
Cad, Cincinnati 115613
C.A.D., Firenze 127313
Caddo-Pine Island Oil and Historical Society Museum, Oil City 046636
Caddoan Mounds, Cherokee County 042794
Caddy's Diner, Purmerend 030045
Cade, Denise, New York 117737
Cade, Denise, New York 117738
Cadeby Experience, Boston Collection and Brass Rubbing Centre, Cadeby . . 038937
Cadeby Light Railway, Cadeby 038938
Cadeiral, Coimbra 079818
Cadena de Moteles, Madrid 110459
Cadenet, Martine, Perpignan 066736
Cades Cove Open-Air Museum, Townsend 048592
Cadet, Rousselle, Arles 060969
Cadet, Rousselle, L'Isle-sur-la-Sorgue 063929
Cadet, Rousselle, Saint-Germain-en-Laye 067498
Cadi, Barcelona 080822
Cadia Vintage, Boston 087802
Cadiac, Béziers 061435
Cadillac Museum, Cadillac 005176
Cadimage, Lyon 064100
Cadogan, London 113522
Cadot, Farideh, Paris 100104
Cadot, Farideh, Paris 100105
Cadre, Épinal 062787, 124232
Cadre à Part, Paris 124611
Cadre de Vie, Paris 100106
Cadre Deco 47, Paris 100107
Au Cadre Doré, Genève 130032
Le Cadre Noir, Aulnay-sous-Bois . . 098877
Le Cadre Noir, Livry-Gargan 099516
Le Cadre Noir, Saint-Denis 109409
Cadrerie, Le Puy-en-Velay 099454
Cadrerie, Marseille 099644, 124402
Cadres Décors, Aurillac 098880
Cadrissimo, Clermont-Ferrand 099142
Cadrix, Montpellier 124455
Il Caduceo, Torino 076787
Cady, Robin, Portland 132688
Caedmon House, Whitby . 087129, 131681
Caelt, London 085172, 113523
Caelum Gallery, New York 117739
Caen Numisma, Caen 061864
Caernarfon Maritime Museum, Caernarfon 038940
Caerphilly Castle, Caerphilly 038944
Caesar, Benedict, Hamburg 103104
Caesarea Museum, Kibbutz Sedot Yam 023020
Café Aroma Photogalerie, Berlin . . . 101822
Café Art Gallery, Hue 120545
Cafe de Matisse, San Jose 119849
Café des Arts, Ha Noi 120453
Cafe Galeria, Brasília 096489
Café-Museum Zum Puppenhaus, Immenstaad 018059
Café Sting, Stavanger 108754
El Cafetal, Vitoria-Gasteiz 081716
Caffard, Guy, Colmar 062406
Il Caffè, Milano 140047
Caffé del Baraccano, Bologna 075062
Caffi, Franco, Brescia 075153
Cafiso, Milano 106180
Cafmeyer, Knokke-Heist 096330
Cagayan Museum, Tuguegarao . . . 031802
Cage, Robin, Richmond 119104
La Cage Aux Folles, Milano 075653, 106181, 121699, 127554, 140048
Caglia, Ugo, Torino 128276
Cagliani, Luigi, Milano 127555
Cagnard, T, Charenton-le-Pont 062146
Cagne, Edith, Lons-le-Saunier 063994
Cagny, Yves de, Paris 121123
Cagny-Perier, Hélène, Paris 124612
Caguana Indian Ceremonial Park and Museum, Utuado 032752
Cahaba Cottage Antiques, Birmingham 087744
Cahaya, Singapore 080439
Les Cahiers de la Peinture, Paris . . 135696
Cahill, David, Dun Laoghaire 074962
Cahit Sıtkı Tarancı Müze-Evi, Diyarbakır 038049
Cahn, Jean-David, Basel . 082133, 122302
Cahokia Courthouse State Historic Site, Cahokia 042542
Cahokia Mounds State Historic Site, Collinsville 043049
Cahoon Museum of American Art, Cotuit 043186
Caiati, Milano 075654
Caiati, Lino, Milano 127556
Caidian District Museum, Wuhan . . 007300
Caignard, Nantes 064911
Caignard, Nantes 064912
Cailac, Paule, Paris 100108
Caillaud, Alain, Sainte-Reine-de-Bretagne 068076
Caillaud, Florence, Bologna 127138
Cailler, Nane, Pully 111818
Caillet, Gérard, Payerne 082721
Cailleux, Pierre, Paris 065651
Cailliau, B., Bruxelles 057874
Cailly, Geneviève, Hanches 063122
Cain, Corinne, Phoenix 118866
Caio, São Paulo 096664
Caird, Jane, Raglan 108548
Cairdean nan Taighean Tugha, Innerleithen 054331
Cairncross & Sons, Filey 084400
Cairns Museum, Cairns 000873
Cairns Regional Gallery, Cairns 000874
Cairo Berlin Art Gallery, Cairo 098619
Cairo Geological Museum, Cairo . . . 009293
Cairo Museum, Vicksburg 048776
Cais, Seoul 107210
Caistor Antiques, Caistor 083836
Caithness District Museum, Wick . . 041381
Caitlyn, Saint Louis 119193
Caja de Castellon, Castello de la Plana 110301
Caja de Castellon, Castello de la Plana 110302
Caja Madrid, Zaragoza 110880
La Caja Negra, Madrid 110460
Čajkovskaja Kartinnaja Galereja, Permskaja gosudarstvennaja chudožestvennaja galereja, Čajkovskij 033058
Čajkovskij Kraevedčeskij Muzej, Permskij oblastnoj kraevedčeskij muzej, Čajkovskij 033059
Calabria, Gilles, Metz 064525
Calabria Nobilissima, Cosenza 135887
Calabrò Antichità 1968, Roma 076356
Calades, Avignon 098889

Calado, Humberto M. Sousa, Lisboa 079887
Calado, José Cândido, Lisboa 079888
Calahorra, Juan, Barcelona 110121
Calala Cottage, Tamworth 001531
Calamassi, Simone, Firenze 075298
Calame, Marlyse, Vence 101436
Calame Lelievre, Michèle, Argilliers 060966
Il Calamo, Torino 140129
Calanca, Jean-Pierre, Paris 065652
Calard, François, Jouvencon 063260
Calard, Jacques, Chénérailles 062271, 124197
Calart Actual, Genève 111434
Calaveras County Museum, San Andreas 047781
Calbourne Water Mill and Rural Museum, Calbourne 038945
Calçada da Estrela, Lisboa 079889
Calcografia, Istituto Nazionale per la Grafica, Roma 025466
Calcografia Nacional, Real Academia de Bellas Artes de San Fernando, Madrid 035369
Calcutta Painters, Kolkata 053693
Caldarella, Jack M., El Paso 088793
Caldas, Madrid 081259
Calderan, Torino 076788
Calderdale Industrial Museum, Halifax 039659
Calderglen County Park, East Kilbride 039351
Calderón G., Elsa V., Santiago de Chile 059513
Caldicot Castle, Caldicot 038946
Caldon Gallery, Cheddleton 112839
Caldwell, Ian, Walton-on-the-Hill . . 087015
Caldwell, J., Charlotte 087933
Caldwell, TOM, Belfast 112607
Caldwell & Snyder, San Francisco . 119627
Caldwell Snyder Gallery, New York . 117740
Caldwells, Elsternwick 055794
Caleb Lothrop House, Cohasset . . . 043032
Caleb Pusey House, Upland 048705
La Calebasse, Cabasse 061844
La Calebasse, Cabasse 061845
Caleca, Messina 075556
Calèche, Barneville-Carteret 061211
Calèche, Le Luc 063648
La Caleche, Pézenas 066797
Caledon Museum, Caledon 034571
Caledonia, Bilbao 080968, 110273
Caledonia Antiguedades, Madrid . . 081260
Caledonia Books, Glasgow 141621
Caledonian Antiques, Bristol 083733, 130454
Caledonian Gallery of Fine Antiques, Chicago 088044
Caledonian Images, Banff 112552
Calegari, Ezio & Dario, Milano 127557
Caleidos, Padova 106393
Caleidoscopio Arte, La Paz 096440
Calendas, Rio de Janeiro 058563
Calepinus, Paris 138323
Caler, John W., Sun Valley 135511
La Calesa, Castello de la Plana . . . 081036
Calestani, Alessio, Milano 106182, 121700
Caley, Auckland 108305
The Calgach Centre, Derry 039231
Calgary and Edmonton Railway Museum, Edmonton 005391
Calgary Book Exchange, Calgary . . 137622
Calgary Chinese Cultural Centre, Calgary 005182
Calgary Coin & Antique Gallery, Calgary 058782
Calgary Contemporary Arts Society, Calgary 052737, 096794
Calgary Highlanders Museum, Calgary 005183
Calgary Police Service Interpretive Centre, Calgary 005184
Calgary Science Centre, Calgary . . 005185
Calgary Summer Antique Show, Calgary 093621
Calgary Winter Antique Show, Calgary 093622
Calheiros, António M. Fernandes, Lisboa 079890
Calhoun County Museum, Port Lavaca 047136
Calhoun County Museum, Rockwell City 047516
Calhoun County Museum, Saint Matthews 047691
Caliban, Pittsburgh 142772
Calicchio, Lee, New York 117741
Calico, Essen 070620
Calico, X & F, Barcelona 080823
Calico Cat, Chicago 088045
Calico Cat, Milwaukee 090281
The Calico Cat, Tampa 093112
Calico Museum of Textiles, Sarabhai Foundation, Ahmedabad 021988
Califia, San Francisco 142937
California Academy of Sciences Museum, San Francisco 047856
California African-American Museum, Los Angeles 045413
California Art Gallery, San Marino . . 047911
California Art Institute, Westlake Village 052360
California Art Investment, Kansas City 116558
California Association of Museums, Santa Ana 054694
California Center for the Arts, Escondido 043729
California Child, Los Angeles 116735
California College of Arts and Crafts, San Francisco 052121
California Confederation of the Arts, Sacramento 054695
California Heritage Museum, Santa Monica 047985
California Institute of Arts, Valencia 052303
California Museum of Ancient Art, Beverly Hills 042193
California Museum of Photography, Riverside 047455
California Oil Museum, Santa Paula 047989
California Palace of the Legion of Honor, Fine Arts Museum of San Francisco, San Francisco 047857
California Science Center, Los Angeles 045414
California State Capitol Museum, Sacramento 047585
California State Indian Museum, Sacramento 047586
California State Mining and Mineral Museum, Mariposa 045688
California State Railroad Museum, Sacramento 047587
California State University-Long Beach Art Museum, Long Beach 045378
California Studies in the History of Art, Berkeley 136412
California Upholstering Company, Sacramento 132730
California Watercolor Association, Walnut Creek 054696
Calik, Krystyna, Kraków 108931
Calil, São Paulo 137581
Calil, São Paulo 137582
Calimala, Vessy 111964
La Calinière, Paris 065653
Call of the Wild Museum, Gaylord . . 044158
Calla, Lily, Salt Lake City 119332
Callahan County Pioneer Museum, Baird 041949
Callan, New Orleans 090527, 117412
Callan, New Orleans 135403
Callan, Thomas R., Ayr 122394
Callander Bay Heritage Museum, Callander 005203
Callant, Roland, Montay 064647
Callanwolde Fine Arts Center, Atlanta 041850
Callat & Cie., Paris 065654
Calle, Gerardo de la, Santiago de Chile 059514
Calle Sanchez, Carmen de la, Jerez de la Frontera 110390
Calle Sanchez, Carmen de la, Madrid 110461
Callegari, Roberto, Padova 076081
Calleja, Antwerpen 057685
Callejón Antiguo, Medellín 059911
Callejón Sanchez, José, Barcelona . 129333
Callendar House, Falkirk 039476
Calleva Museum, Silchester 041029
Callewaert, Henri, Jaux 063239
Calli Antik, København 060305
Callies, Bettina, Regensburg 104693
Callies, Gerhard, Dornhan 070275, 121374
Calligrammes, Ottawa . . . 097100, 123796
Callingham, Northchapel 086099
Callis, São Paulo 133303
Callkins Field Museum, Iowa Falls . 044770
Calloway, Susan, Washington 093390, 120269
Callsen, Gunter & Maximilian, Straßlach-Dingharting 073936
Callu-Mérite, Paris 100109
Callwey, Georg D.W., München 134225
Calmels, Simone, Toulouse 068489
CalmelsCohen, Paris 121124
Calmieri, Alessandro, Siegen 104893
Calne Antiques, Calne 083838
Caloundra Fine Art Gallery, Caloundra 094355
Caloundra Regional Art Gallery, Caloundra 000876
Calton Gallery, Edinburgh 084280
Calton Gallery, Edinburgh 112987
Calton Gallery, Edinburgh 130674
Calumet County Historical Society Museum, New Holstein 046231
Calumet-Nuzinger, Ch., Heidelberg . 103318
Calvari, Angelo, Roma 076357
Calvente, Madrid 081261
Calverley Antiques, Tunbridge Wells 086933, 131615
Calvert, Nashville 090429
Calvert, Washington 093391, 120270
Calvert, Karen, San Antonio 119402
Calvert Marine Museum, Solomons 048212
Calverton Folk Museum, Calverton . 038950
Calvet, Gérard, Paris 065655
Calvin Coolidge Memorial Room of the Forbes Library, Northampton 046543
Calvin Coolidge State Historic Site, Plymouth Notch 047105
Calvin West Upholstery, Dallas 132002
Calvinia Regional Museum, Calvinia 034572
Calvo, Valencia 129760
Calvo Gonzalez, Pablo, Segovia . . . 081563
Calypso, Xaghra 077546
Calzada, Marc, Barcelona 080824
Calzada Salavedra, Arcadi, Barcelona 110122
Calzavara, Luca, Venezia 128381
Camafeo, Alicante 080758
Le Camaïeu, Tournai 058381
Camara, Jose A., Madrid 081262
Cámara Santa de la Catedral de Oviedo, Oviedo 035583
Camard, Jean-Pierre, Paris 065656
Camarev, Norton Summit 056383
Camargo, Ricardo Pagotto, São Paulo 096665
Camargue, Spit Junction 056621
Camargue Gallery, Stoke-on-Trent . 114492
Camarote-Pizarro, Valencia 110800
Cambalache, Segovia 081564
Camberwell Antique Centre, Camberwell 055605
Camberwell Architectural Salvage & Antique, London 085173
Camberwell Auctions, Hawthorn East 120592
Camberwell Books and Collectibles, Hawthorn East 055957, 136934
Camberwell Bookshop, London . . . 141765
Camberwell College of Art, London . 050827
Cambi, Genova 075448
Cambieri, Marco, Milano 127558
Cambium, Madrid 129584
Cambon, Alain, Paris 138324
Camborne Museum, Camborne . . . 038956
Camborne School of Mines Geological Museum and Art Gallery, Pool . . . 040736
Cambria Books, Blackheath 136804
Cambria County Historical Society Museum, Ebensburg 043598
Cambria Historical Society Museum, New Providence 046272
Cambridge and County Folk Museum, Cambridge 038958
Cambridge Antiques, Waikato 079284
Cambridge Art Association, Cambridge 054697
Cambridge Auctioneering, Waikato . 121836
Cambridge Contemporary Art, Cambridge 112788
Cambridge Cottage, Bolwarra 055516
Cambridge Fine Art, Cambridge . . .083843, 112789, 130497
Cambridge Fine Art, Little Shelford . 113404
Cambridge Galleries, Cambridge . . 005205
Cambridge Glass Museum, Cambridge 042570
Cambridge Historical Museum, Cambridge 042557
Cambridge Museum, Cambridge . . 030455
Cambridge Museum, Cambridge . . 042569
Cambridge Museum of Technology, Cambridge 038959
Cambridge Pine, Bottisham 083584
Cambridge University Collection of Air Photographs, Cambridge 038960
Cambridge University Press, Cambridge 135130
Cambridge University Press, New York 135418
Cambronne, Paris 121125
Camden, Pontevedra 081531
Camden Archives and Museum, Camden 042580
Camden Arts Centre, London 040107
Camden Arts Trust, London 050828
Camden Bokks, Bath 141395
Camden County Historical Society Museum, Camden 042576
Camden Fine Art Gallery, Camden . 094362
Camden Haven Historical Museum, Laurieton 001179
Camden Historical Museum, Camden 000880
Camden Passage Antiques Market, London 085174
Camden Press, London 135200
Camden Society of Artists, Camden 052462, 094363
Camden Valley Antiques, Narellan . 056316
The Cameleon, Rotterdam 078704
The Camelford Gallery, Camelford . 112797
Camellia Grove Antiques, Eagle Heights 055773
Camelot, Boston 115157
Camelot, San Francisco 119628
Camelot Antiques, Toronto 059159
Camelú, Roma 106503
Cameo, Columbus 115767
Cameo, Vancouver 097434
Cameo Antiques, Chester 083953
Cameo Gallery, London 113524
Camera Austria International, Graz .095520, 133075, 135549
Camera Magenta, Wien 052522
Camera Obscura, Edinburgh 039380
Camera Obscura, Hainichen, Sachsen 017639
Camera Obscura, Paris 100110
Camera Obscura Gallery, Denver . . 115978
Camera Work, Berlin 101823
Camerawork, London 113525
Camerawork Books, San Francisco 142938
Camerer, Cuss & Co, London 085175, 130967
Camerino, Umberto, Roma 127949
Cameron, Portland 142795

Cameron, Donald, Kew 094693
Cameron, Patricia, Seattle 119895
Cameron Highlanders of Ottawa Regimental Museum, Ottawa 006087
Cameron & Hollis, Moffat 135284
Cameroon Maritime Museum, Douala 004973
Camet, Huguette, Saint-Ouen 067741
Camhi, Rebecca, Athinai 105391
Camiciotti, Ugo, Firenze 075299
Camilla's Bookshop, Eastbourne . . 141566
Camille, N., Bruxelles 057875
Camilleri, Paul, Balzan 128472
Camille's, Tucson 093209
Camin, Roberto, Bolzano 127193
Caminade, Corinne, Paris 100111
Caminade, Jean-Alain, Colmar 062407, 138078
Caminetti, Leonardo, Berlin 101824
Caminetti, Leonardo, München 104163
Caminetto, Bologna 105951
Caminha, Francisco B., Rio de Janeiro 058564
El Camino Gallery, Phoenix 118867
Càminul Artei, Bucureşti 109421
Çamlıca Sanat Evi, İstanbul 112293
Cammarata, Sebastiano, Catania . . 127258
Cammarella, Loretta, Milano 106183
Cammies Country Living, Paringa . . 056439
Camões, Lisboa 140824
Camoin-Damachy, Paris 065657
Camouflage Brussels, Bruxelles . . . 096166
Camp 6 Logging Museum, Tacoma . 048462
Camp Five Museum, Laona 045166
Camp Floyd, Fairfield 043791
Camp Gallery, Sweet Briar 048447
Camp Hancock, Bismarck 042236
Campabadal Torres, Barcelona 122001
Campagne, København 060306
Campagne, Brigitte, Paris 065658
Campagne, Yves, Sainte-Cathérine-lès-Arras 068049
La Campagne du Nord,, Rotterdam . 108177
Campagnola, Daniela, Verona 076996, 128420
Campaign for Museums, London . . 054332
Campalans, A., Barcelona 129334
Campana, Cannes 099061
Campana, Guérin, Corte 062486
Campaña, Luis, Köln 103605
Campana, Mario, Brescia . 105993, 127207
Campana, Pierre, Paris 065659
Campanella, Michele, Genova 106086
Campbell, Baltimore 087653
Campbell, Cleveland 088315
Campbell, Edmonton 096870
Campbell, London 085176
Campbell, Milton Keynes 131279
Campbell, Stirling 131537
Campbell, Andrew, Jesmond 084812
Campbell, Charles, San Francisco . 119629
Campbell, Duncan, London 113526
Campbell, Iain, Widnes . . 087148, 142155
Campbell & Assoc., J., Cincinnati . . 115614
Campbell, John, Nashville 117344
Campbell, J.T., Dallas 088472
Campbell, Lucy B., London 085177, 113527
Campbell, Mack, Toowoomba 137110
Campbell, Marcus, London 141766
Campbell, Meg, Southampton 086648
Campbell, Peter, Atworth 083349
Campbell, William, Fort Worth 116137
Campbell Collections, Mashu Museum of Ethnology and William Campbell Furniture and Picture Collection, Durban . . 034597
Campbell County Rockpile Museum, Gillette 044191
Campbell Grant, Christchurch 079017
Campbell Hall Gallery, Monmouth . . 045964
Campbell Historical Museum, Campbell 042588
Campbell House, Toronto 006584
Campbell House Museum, Saint Louis 047654
Campbell River and District Public Art Gallery, Campbell River 005206
Campbell River Museum, Campbell River 005207
Campbell River Optical Maritime Museum, Campbell River 005208
Campbell Town Croft Antiques, Campbell Town 055612
Campbell Whittlesey House, Rochester 047478
Campbell Wilson, Brighton 083690
Campbellford-Seymour Heritage Centre, Campbellford 005209
Campbelltown City Bicentennial Art Gallery, Campbelltown 000882
Campbelltown Print Gallery, Leumeah 094733
Campbeltown Museum, Campbeltown 038976
Campe, Nürnberg 104474, 139600
Camperdown and District Museum, Camperdown 000883
Camperdown Cemetery, Newtown, New South Wales 001330
Camperos, San Francisco 132873
Camphor-Hill, Baltimore 115042
Campi, Adriana, Milano 075655
Campidell, Walter, Feistritz an der Drau 123351
Il Campiello, Milano 075656
Campillo Monforte, Carlos, Barcelona 080825
Campion, Peter, Cheltenham 130533
Campion Gallery, Rye 114335
Campione, New York 117742
Campione, Santo, Milano 127559
Campisi, Gabriele & Rodolfo, Catania 075238
Campman, Zeist 078865
Campo, Antwerpen 120704
Campo, Carine, Antwerpen 096061
Campo, Carmen del, Córdoba 110314
Campo Antolin, Fernando del, Zaragoza 129808
Campo & Campo, Berchem 096108, 120710
Campo do Pozzi, Venezia 076925
Campobasso, Roberto, Napoli 075951
Campobello Island Museum, Welshpool 006787
Campogiani, Luca, Milano 075657
Campolmi, Alessandro, Firenze . . . 075300
Camponi, Enrico, Roma 076358
Camposanto e Museo dell'Opera, Pisa 025266
Campregher, J. & R., Steyr 057322
Campsie Antiques, Lennoxtown . . . 084967
Campus Art Gallery, Santa Rosa Junior College, Santa Rosa 047990
Campus Martius Museum, Marietta 045669
CampusGalerie, der British American Tobacco, Bayreuth 015906
Camron-Stanford House, Oakland . 046591
Camstra, Eleonore, Lochem 128755
Camu, Th., Charleroi 058139
Camugli, Lyon 138139
Camus, Saint-Ouen 067742
Camus, Saint-Ouen 067743
Camus, Jean, Bordeaux 061597
Camus Ares, Ricardo, Santander . . 081552
Can Art Handworks, Detroit 132049
Canaan Historical Society Museum, Canaan 042590
Canada 2000 Antiques, Vancouver . 059342
Canada Agriculture Museum, Ottawa 006088
Canada Aviation Museum, Ottawa . 006089
Cañada Cordero, Antonio, Madrid . . 081263
Canada House Gallery, London 040108
Canada Science and Technology Museum, Ottawa 006090
Canada West Antique Company, Vancouver 059343
Canada's Aviation Hall of Fame, Wetaskiwin 006798
Canada's Penitentiary Museum, Kingston 005694
Canada's Sports Hall of Fame, Toronto 006585
Canadeau, Québec 097136
Canadian Airborne Forces Museum, Petawawa 006135
Canadian Antique Dealers' Association, Toronto 052738
Canadian Arctic Gallery, Basel 111169
Canadian Art, Toronto 135630
Canadian Art Foundation, Toronto . . 052739
Canadian Art Museum Directors Organization, Ottawa 052740
Canadian Automotive Museum, Oshawa 006079
Canadian Baseball Hall of Fame, Toronto 006586
Canadian Centre for Architecture, Montréal 005914
Canadian Clay and Glass Gallery, Waterloo 006771
Canadian County Historical Museum, El Reno 043646
Canadian Embassy Art Gallery, Washington 048889
Canadian Federation of Friends of Museums, Toronto 052741
Canadian Fine Arts, Toronto 097243
Canadian Football Hall of Fame and Museum, Hamilton 005588
Canadian Force Base Gagetown Military Museum, Oromocto 006076
Canadian Golf Hall of Fame, Oakville 006057
Canadian Golf Museum, Aylmer . . . 005047
Canadian Lacrosse Hall of Fame, New Westminster 006003
Canadian Military Studies Museum, Limehouse 005774
Canadian Museum of Animal Art, Bolton 005111
Canadian Museum of Contemporary Photography, National Gallery of Canada, Ottawa 006091
Canadian Museum of Flight, Langley 005745
Canadian Museum of Health and Medicine, Toronto 006587
Canadian Museum of Nature, Ottawa 006092
Canadian Museum of Rail Travel, Cranbrook 005307
Canadian Museums Association, Ottawa 052742
Canadian Olympic Hall of Fame, Temple de la Renommée Olympique du Canada, Ottawa 006093
Canadian Plains Gallery, Winnipeg . 097576
Canadian Railway Museum, Saint Constant 006333
Canadian Scottish Regiment Museum, Victoria 006735
Canadian Scouting Museum, Ottawa 006094
Canadian Sculpture Centre, Toronto 006588
Canadian Ski Museum, Ottawa 006095
Canadian Society for Education through Art, Regina 052743
Canadian Society of Painters in Water Colour, Toronto 052744
Canadian War Museum, Ottawa . . . 006096
Canadian Warplane Heritage Museum, Mount Hope 005968
Canadian Wildlife and Wilderness Art Museum, Ottawa 006097
Canadiana Gallery, Toronto 006627
Canajoharie Library and Art Gallery, Canajoharie 042591
Çanakkale Anıtlari ve Savaş Müzesi, Çanakkale 038037
Çanakkale Devlet Güzel Sanatlar Galerisi, Çanakkale 038038
Çanakkale Müzesi, Çanakkale 038039
Çanakkale Seramik Sanat Galerisi, İstanbul 112294
Canal Fulton Heritage Society Museum, Canal Fulton 042592
Canal Furniture, New York 090759
Canal Museum, Linlithgow 040015
Canal Museum, Llangollen 040062
Canal Museum, Stoke Bruerne 041114
Canal Society of New York State Museum, Syracuse 048453
Canale, Paris 065660
Canaletto, Warszawa 109104
Canapé, Lisboa 079891
Canapé Claque, Sindelfingen 073824
Can'Art, Toulouse 101335
Cañas, Barcelona 080826
Canavese, Paris 065661
Canavese, Paris 124613
Canavez Filho, Nuno, Porto 140863
Canazza, Giuseppe, Padova 076082
Canbaz, Faruk, Hannover 125866
Canberra Antiques Centre, Fyshwick 055851
Canberra Bicycle Museum, Dickson 000983
Canberra Contemporary Art Space, Braddon 000827
Canberra Contemporary Art Space, Braddon 133045
Canberra Contemporary Art Space Manuka, Manuka 001216
Canberra Museum and Gallery, Canberra 000886
Canberra School of Art Gallery, Acton 000698
Canbulat Türbe ve Müzesi, Gazimağusa 008236
Canby Depot Museum, Canby 042595
Cancelliere Candida, Messina 075557
Il Cancello, Firenze 075301
La Cancha de la Mamita, Santa Cruz 058400
Cancino, María, Bogotá 059824
Cancino Chapinero, Bogotá 059825
Candace, Chicago 088046
Candale, J., Madrid 081264
Candeias, Vítor, Lisboa 079892
De Candelaer, Rotterdam 078705
Candelaria Rug Galleries, Albuquerque 087380
Candeloro, Carmela, Napoli 127756
Candide, Berlin 138763
Candido, Bilbao 080969
Candillier, André, Paris 100112
Candl, Virginia Beach 093347
Candle Lane Books, Shrewsbury . . 142070
Candlenut Gallery, Port Douglas . . 095084
Candlestick Books, Masterton 140640
Candover Gallery, Alresford 112499
Candyjacks Antique Store, Louisville 089965
Cane & Able, Bury Saint Edmunds .083820, 130489
Canelli, Milano 075658
Canepa, Sergio, Genova 075449
Canessa Gallery, San Francisco . . . 119630
Canesso, Paris 065662
Canestrelli, Claudia, Venezia 076926
Canevelli, Bernard, Genova 075450
Caney Valley Historical Society Museum, Caney 042596
Cangemi, Giuseppe, Roma 127950
Cango Caves Interpretive Centre, Oudtshoorn 034691
Cangxian Fenghua Calligraphy and Painting Gallery, Cangzhou 097691
Canillo, Christian, Toulouse 068490, 124975
Canillo, Philippe, Toulouse 068491, 124976
Caninenberg, Horst, München 072672
Canivet, Jehan, Bruxelles 057876
Canivet, Stéphane, Le Mans 063657
Cankarjev Dom, Ljubljana 034480
Cankarjeva Založba, Ljubljana 134895, 140966
Çankırı Devlet Güzel Sanatlar Galerisi, Çankırı 038041
Çankırı Müzesi, Çankırı 038042
Cannaviello, Enzo, Milano 106184
Cannell, M.D., Raveningham 086330
Cannella, Catania 075239
Canners & Upholders, Poole 131383
Cannery Antiques, Nashville 090430

Cannery Art Centre, Esperance 094512
Cannes Brocante, Cannes 061936
Canneva, Elio, Genova 127437
Canning, Jo, Fairfield 094520
Canning A.R.T.S., Yarrawonga 095452
Cannington Centennial Museum, Cannington 005212
Cannington Manor, Regina 006248
Cannon, Elizabeth, Colchester 084055
Cannon Falls Area Historical Museum, Cannon Falls 042597
Cannon Hall Museum, Barnsley, South Yorkshire 038599
Cannon Village Visitor Center, Kannapolis 044909
Cannonbury, Southwold 086668
Cannone, Domenico Antonio, Bari . 127108
Cano Granados, Manuel, Granada . 110371
Cano Puy, Miriam, Donostia-San Sebastián 129501
Canolfan Y Plase, Bala 038570
Canolfan Y Plase, Y Bala 041463
Canon City Municipal Museum, Canon City 042598
Canon España, Barcelona 110123
The Canon Gallery, Petworth 086241, 114246, 131376
Canon Gate Bookshop, Chichester . 141514
Canopia, Madrid 110462
Canova, Treviso 134702
Canowindra Trading Post, Canowindra 055625
Canso Museum, Canso 005213
Canta Attilio, Bari 075006
Cantaert, M., Brugge 057764
Cantalapiedra, Valencia 129761
Cantata Studio, Kuranda 094714
Cantelli, Prof. Patrizia, Bologna . . . 127139
Il Canterano di Romanazzi, Torino . . 076789
Canterbury, Christchurch 108388
Canterbury, Los Angeles 116736
Canterbury Antiques, Canterbury . . 055626
Canterbury Antiques, Canterbury . . 083859
Canterbury Antiques, Dallas 088473
The Canterbury Auction Galleries, Canterbury 122446
Canterbury Bookshop, Canterbury . 141480
Canterbury Cathedral Archives and Library, Canterbury 038978
Canterbury Fine Art Gallery, Canterbury 094368
Canterbury Heritage Museum, Canterbury 038979
Canterbury House Antiques, Jacksonville 089388, 122925
Canterbury Museum, Christchurch . 030460
Canterbury Roman Museum, Canterbury 038980
Canterbury Shaker Village, Canterbury 042600
Canto, Umberto, Roma 076359
Canto do Livro, Fortaleza 137556
Canton Antiques, Baltimore 087654
Canton Classic Car Museum, Canton 042605
Canton Gallery, Baltimore 115043
Canton Historical Museum, Canton . 042601
Canton Museum of Art, Canton 042606
Cantor, Lawrence J., West Hollywood 120376
Cantor Arts Center Journal, Stanford 136413
Cantor-Roughton, Dallas 115848
Cantore Antichitá, Modena 075903
Canty's Bookshop, Fyshwick 136910
Canuit, Eindhoven 107996
Canus, Evelyne, Basel 111170
Canus, Evelyne, Paris 100113
Canvas, Manchester 114040
The Canvas Collection, Lincoln 113397
Canvas Gallery, San Francisco 119631
Canwood Museum, Canwood 005214
Canyon State Collectables, Tucson . 093210
Canzanella, Napoli 127757
Canzi, Busan 107167
Cao Xue Qin Gallery, Liaoyang 097869
Caoba, Almeria 080770
Caoba, Santiago de Chile 059515
Caoba de Cuba, Valencia 129762
CAP Art Center and Don Sergio Osmeña Memorabilia, Cebu 031651
CAP Art Center and Price Mansion, Tacloban 031793
Cap-de-Bon-Désir, Bergonnes 005095
Cap-Sud, New York 090760
Capa Esculpuras, Bruxelles 096167
Capanema, José, Belo Horizonte . . 058412
Caparra Ruins Historical Museum, Guaynabo 032715
Caparrini & Corzani, Firenze 127314
CAPC Musée d'Art Contemporain, Bordeaux 010876
Cape, Jonathan, London 135201
Cape Ann Historical Museum, Gloucester 044222
Cape Bonavista Lighthouse, Bonavista 005114
Cape Breton Centre for Heritage and Science, Sydney 006545
Cape Breton Miners' Museum, Glace Bay 005510
Cape Clear Heritage Centre, Skibbereen 022856
Cape Coast Castle Museum, Cape Coast 021101
Cape Cod Clutter, San Diego 142902
Cape Cod Museum of Natural History, Brewster 042399
Cape Cod National Seashore Museum, Wellfleet 049048
Cape Cod School of Art, Provincetown 051996
Cape Fear Museum, Wilmington . . . 049212
Cape Gallery, Byron Bay 094337
The Cape Gallery, Cape Town 110020
Cape Henry Lighthouse, Virginia Beach 048794
Cape May County Historical Museum, Cape May Court House 042615
Cape Museum of Fine Arts, Dennis . 043390
Cape of Good Hope Art Gallery, Singapore 109780
Cape Spear National Historic Site, Saint John's 006361
Cape Town Holocaust Centre, Cape Town 034575
Cape Vincent Historical Museum, Cape Vincent 042617
Čapek, Třebíč 098504
Čapek, Petr, Brno 123950
Capel Mawr Collectors Centre, Criccieth 141547
A Capela, São Paulo 058698
Capella Brancacci, Firenze 024139
Capelle, Nano, Cahors 061895
Capelle Medicee, Firenze 024140
Capelle Nano, Cahors 061896
Capeluto, New York 117743
Capeluto, New York 117744
Ca'Pesaro Galleria Internazionale d'Arte Moderna, Venezia 026228
Capet, Patrick, Royan 067308
Capet, Paul, Le Gosier 127071
Capharnaum, Saint-Gilles-du-Gard . 067505
Capharnaum Ancient Synagogue, Kfar Nahum 022991
Capia, Robert, Paris 065663, 124614
Capitain, Gisela, Köln 103606
Capital Antiques, San Antonio 092494
Capital Antiques, Washington 093392
Capital Art Corporation, Taipei 098060
Capital Bookshop, Cardiff 141486
Capital Children's Museum, Washington 048890
Capital Corner, Bruxelles 096168
Capital Pawn & Gun, Regina 059084
Capital Restoration, Saint Louis . . . 132742
La Capitale Galerie, Paris 100114
Capitani Roberto, Milano 106185
Il Capitello, Torino 076790
Capitol Coin Company, Washington 093393
Capitol Furnishings, New York 090761
Capitol Hill Art League, Washington 054698
Capitol Hill Books, Denver 142384
Capitol Hill Books, Washington 143041
Capitol Reef National Park Visitor Center, Torrey 048587
Capitola Historical Museum, Capitola Village 042618
Capitole Echange Estimation, Toulouse 068492
Capitolino, Roma 127951
Capitolium, Brescia 121680
Capitolium, Roma 127952
Capítulo Uno, Buenos Aires 136705
Caplain-Matignon, Paris 100115
Caplow, Minneapolis 132377
Capo, Philadelphia 091617
Capo D'Arte, São Paulo 123715
Capodistria Museum, Koukouritsa, Evropouli 021343
Capolavori, I., Seattle 119896
Capomondo, Helsinki 060513
Capon, Patric, Bromley . . . 083766, 130469
Capone, Pietro, Palermo 076136
Capone, Silvia, Torino 076791
Capozzi, Alberto, Genova 075451
Capozzi, Marco, Genova 075452
Capp Street Project, San Francisco . 047858
Cappelen, J.W., Oslo 134849, 140699
Cappelens, Oslo 121864
Cappelens, J.W., Oslo . . . 121865, 140700
Cappella degli Scrovegni, Padova . . 025048
Cappelle Sistina, Sala e Gallerie Affrescate, Musei Vaticani, Città del Vaticano 049418
Cappelletti, Gabriele, Milano 106186
Cappelli, Bologna 134548
Cappellini, Firenze 140009
Cappellone, Olivier, Paris . 065664, 124615
Cappon House Museum, Holland . . 044571
Capponi, Ettore & C., Brescia 075154
Cappuzzo, Giuliano, Firenze 075302
Capra, Cleveland 088316, 122864
Caprara, Marisa, Bologna 127140
Capraro, Belisario, Milano 127560
Caprice, Bischwiller 061501
Caprice, Limburg an der Lahn 103913
Caprice d'Antan, Saint-Ouen 067744
Caprices, Levallois-Perret 063801
Caprices Antiquités, Paris 065665
Caprices du Temps, Angers 060849
Caprichoso, Graça & Miguel, Lisboa 079893
Capricia, Le Blanc 063569
Capricorn, Smethwick 114443
Capricorn Antiques, Toronto 059160
Capricorn West, Kojonup 056062
Il Capricorno, Venezia 106735
Capricorno, Washington 120271
Capro, Montréal 123783
Capstick-Dale, Simon, London 113528
Capsule Gallery, Cardiff 112807
CAPT Comics, Birmingham 087745
Capt Voyages et Galerie, Genève . . 111435
Captain Books, Innsbruck 137195
Captain Charles H. Hurley Library Museum, Buzzards Bay 042537
Captain Cook Birthplace Museum, Middlesbrough 040458
Captain Cook Memorial Museum, Whitby 041364
Captain Cook Schoolroom Museum, Great Ayton 039627
Captain Forbes House Museum, Milton 045879
Captain George Flavel House Museum, Astoria 041822
Captain Nathaniel B. Palmer House, Stonington 048375
Captain Phillips' Rangers Memorial, Saxton 048035
Captain Salem Avery House Museum, Shady Side 048123
Captain's Cottage Museum, Murray Bridge 001299
Captain's Courtyard Antiques, New Orleans 090528
Captain's House, Scarborough 114399
Captain's Saloon, München 072673
Captier, Bernard, Paris 065666
Captier-Barnes, Paris 065667
Captive Inspirations Photographic Gallery, Brisbane 094289
Captured on Canvas Paintings of Australia, Wembley Downs 095385
Captured Visions, Saint Paul 119281
Capuano, Emanuele, Napoli 075952
Capucine, Rochefort (Charente-Maritime) 067175
La Capucine, Saint-Joseph 140252
Capus, Jean, Senningen 077490
Caputo, Lorenzo, Bari 075007
Caputo, Luciano, Padova 127800
Car, Jean-Pierre, Gardanne 062967
Car and Carriage Museum, Pittsburgh 047042
Car Life Museum, Bonshaw 005117
Cara, Wiesbaden 105248
Cara y Cruz, Madrid 081265
Carabaux, New Orleans 117413
Carabe, Luis, Sevilla 081581
Carabinier, Montigny-lès-Metz 064696
El Carabo, Valencia 141076
Caracciolo, Antonio & Italo, Genova 127438
Caracol Archaeological Site, Mayan Ruins, Caracol 003882
Caractère, Paris 100116
Caractères, La Rochelle 063426
Caractères, La Foire du Livre d'Artiste, Bruxelles 093599
Caraffi, Maleny 094769
Carafizi, São Paulo 096666
Caral de Montety & Cornut, Aix-en-Provence 060699
Caram, F., São Paulo 058699
Caramanna, Stefania, Palermo 127822
Carambol, Basel 082134
El Carambolo, Sevilla 081582
Caramoor Center for Music and the Arts, Katonah 044934
Carápan, Monterrey 077589
Carare, Strasbourg 124942
Carat, Bordeaux 098988
Carat, Gdańsk 108875
Caratsch, de Pury & Luxembourg, Zürich 112052
Caravan, Teheran 074840
Caravan, Fil, New York 090762
Caravan Antiquités, Paris . 065668, 124616
Caravan Book Store, Los Angeles . . 142496
Caravanserai, Manama 095997
Caravanserail, Jounieh 077433
Caravansérail, Reims 067062
Caravati, Richmond 092066
Caravello, Beatrice, Palermo 106422
Caravello, Massimo & Giacomo, Palermo 106423, 127823
Carayol, Bayonne 120917
Carayol, Biarritz 061454, 120931
Carbajosa, Valentin Fernandez, León 081170
Carballo & Carballo, Montevideo . . 122775
Carberry, Valerie, Chicago 115379
Carberry Plains Museum, Carberry . 005220
Carbethon Folk Museum and Pioneer Village, Crows Nest, Queensland . 000959
Carbon Based Studios, Brisbane . . . 094290
Carbon County Museum, Rawlins . . 047340
Carbonari, Giuseppe, Verona 076997
Carbonaro, Davide, Roma 076360
Carbone, Torino 106666
Carbone Rieger, Toronto 097244
Carbonear Railway Station, Carbonear 005222
Carboolture Historical Village and Museum, Caboolture 000872
Carburantes Tarazona, Albacete . . . 110083
The Carby Art Gallery, Aberdeen . . . 112476
Carcamo, Iván, Santiago de Chile . . 059516
Carcanagues, Jacques, New York . . 117745
Carcoar Historic Village, Carcoar . . 000895
Card Traders of Austin, Austin 142215

Cardamom Antiques, Acassuso . . . 055141
Cardamom Antiques, Buenos Aires . 055186
Cardana, Amersfoort 077746
Cardani, Daniel, Madrid . . 081266, 110463
Cardellini, Otello, Roma 127953
Cardellini, Roberto, Roma 127954
Cardellino, Emanuele, Torino 076792, 134689
Cardenas Olaya, Enrique, Bogotá . . 059826
Cardi, Milano 106187
Cardi, Milano 106188
Cardi, Francis, L'Ile-Rousse 063825
Cardiff Antique Centre, Cardiff 083870
Cardiff Arts Center, Cardiff 038986
Cardiff Castle, Cardiff 038987
Cardiff Reclamation, Cardiff 083871
Cardiff School of Art and Design, University of Wales Institute, Cardiff, Cardiff 050806
Cardigan Heritage Centre, Cardigan 038995
Cardigan Street Gallery, Carlton, Victoria 094376
Cardilès, Jean, Onet-le-Château . . 065270
Cardin, Pierre, Paris 100117
Cardinal, Paris 065669
Cardinal, Suzanne, Voiron 069024
Cardinal Gallery, Annapolis 041739
Cardinal Ó Fiaich Heritage Centre, Áras an Chairdiméil Ó Fiaich, Cullyhanna . 039189
Cardingmill Antiques, Church Stretton 084010
Cardini, Andrea, Genova 075453
Cardini, Leon F., Los Angeles 132245
Cardona, Genova 075454
Cardona, Samwel, Zebbug 128485
Cardone, Roberta, Bari 075008
Cardoso, Amadeu, São Paulo 096667
Cardoso, Paulo Barreiros, Lisboa . . 129148
Cardwell Shire Museum, Tully 001569
Care of Collections Forum, Grangemouth 054333
Carel, Miami 117042
Carel, Jean-Lou, Le Castellet 099426
Carello Frères, Nice 065059
Carena, Adalberto, Torino 128277
Carette, Hervé, Linselles 063904
Caretto, Luigi, Torino 076793
Caretto, Patrizia, Torino . . 076794, 106667
Carew Manor and Dovecote, Beddington 038653
Carey, Mervyn, Cranbrook 122481
Carey Museum, Hooghly 022152
Ca'Rezzonico Museo del Settecento Veneziano, San Barnaba, Venezia 026229
Carfagna, Andrea, Roma 127955
Cargo, Hyères 063188
Cariano, Victoria 077543
Caribart, Amsterdam 107692
Caribbean Art Gallery, Montego Bay 106823
Caribbean Creations, Chicago 115380
Caribbean Gallery, Tampa 120033
Caribbean Primate Research Center Museum, San Juan 032729
Caricatura Galerie, Kassel 018182
Carillon Antigüedades, Olivos 055288
Carillon Antiques, Perth 056454
Carillon di Archita Calcante, Taranto 076744
Carillon Historical Park, Dayton . . . 043319
Carina Prints, London 113529
Carincotte, Delphine, Marseille 099645
Carinthia Verlag, Klagenfurt 133098
Cariou, Bernard, Grenoble 138096
Cariou, Jean-Loup, Pont-Aven 101020
Caris, Gordon, Alnwick . . . 083273, 130291
Caris, Gordon, Hexham . . 084677, 130792
Carisbrooke Castle Museum, Newport, Isle of Wight 040565
Carissa's Armoires and Antiques, Nashville 090431
Caristi, Dominic F., Boston 131844
Caritas Fotogalerie, Konstanz 103754
Carivari, Leipzig 134143
Carl, Hans, Nürnberg 134318, 139601
Carl, Victor, New York 090763
Carl Eldhs Ateljémuseum, Stockholm 036619
Carl G. Fenner Nature Center, Lansing 045161
Carl-Henning Pedersen og Else Alfelts Museum, Herning 008902
Carl-Hirnbein-Museum, Missen-Wilhams 018955
Carl Jularbo Museum, Avesta 036209
Carl Larsson-Gården, Sundborn . . . 036688
Carl-Lohse-Galerie - Stadtmuseum Bischofswerda, Bischofswerda . . 016253
Carl-Maria-von-Weber-Museum, Dresden 016783
Carl Michael Ziehrer-Gedenkraum, Wien 002887
Carl Nielsen Museet, Odense 009044
Carl Nielsens Barndomshjem, Årslev 008811
Carl Orff Museum, Dießen am Ammersee 016701
Carl Sandburg Home, Flat Rock . . . 043857
Carl Sandburg State Historic Site, Galesburg 044119
Carl-Schweizer-Museum, Murrhardt 019169
Carlborg, Hans & Jennifer, Woollahra 056858
Carle, Gerhard, Abstatt 125047
Carlen, Ottawa 097101
Carlén, Stockholm 081935
Carlen House, Mobile 045946
Carleo, San Diego 132847
Carles, Bruno, Lunel 064027
Carleton College Art Gallery, Northfield 046549
Carleton Gallery, Birmingham 141416
Carleton University Art Gallery, Ottawa 006098
Carletti, Maurizio, Roma 127956
Carli, L'Isle-sur-la-Sorgue 063930
Carli-Livre-Brocante, Marseille 064330, 138193
Carlier, Amiens 060810
Carlier, Hélène, Condom 062452
Carlier, Jean-Edouard, Paris 065670, 138325
Carlier Gebauer, Berlin 101825
Carlier & Imbert, Saint-Étienne 121245
Carlimpex Reproduction, Paris 100118, 133549
Carlin, Paris 100119
Carlina, Torino 106668
Carling Nichols, Washington 093394
Carlini, Alfonso, Roma 127957
Carlini, Alfredo, Lyon 124345
Carlini, Gesuino, Cagliari 127243
Carlini, Marcel, Saint-Raphaël 067984
Carlino, Las Vegas 089553
Carlino, Las Vegas 089554
Carlisle Antique and Craft Centre, Carlisle 083878
Carlisle Collection of Miniature Rooms, Nunnington 040631
Carlisle & Finch, Cincinnati 088220, 131930
Carlitos, Roma 076361
Carlo, Anita de, New York 090764
Carlos, Antonio, Fortaleza 096516
Carlos Alejandro, Santiago de Chile 123876
Carlos Gomes Museum, Centro de Ciências, Letras and Artes, Campinas 004037
Carlos P. Garcia Memorabilia, Manila 031716
Carlos P. Romulo Collection, Manila 031717
Carlotta, Roma 076362
Carlotti, Michel, Marseille 124403
Carlow County Museum, Carlow . . . 022700
Carl's, Bruxelles 057877
Carlsbad Caverns National Park, Carlsbad 042625
Carlsbad Children's Museum, Carlsbad 042624
Carlsbad Museum and Art Center, Carlsbad 042626
Carlsberg Museum Valby, Valby . . . 009137
Carlsen, Lymington 085876, 114013
Carlsen, H., Oslo 079430
Carlson Tower Gallery, Chicago . . . 042826
Carlson-Turner, Portland 142785
Carlsro Museum, Kristiinankaupunki 009749
Carlsson, C.J., Uppsala 122284
Carlton Antiques, Great Malvern . . . 084511
Carlton Clocks, Amersham 083289, 130299
Carlton Clocks, Little Chalfont 085010
Carlton County Historical Museum and Heritage Center, Cloquet 043021
Carlton-Davidson, London 085178
Carlton Hobbs, London 085179
Carlton Hollis, Harrogate 084570
Carlton House Antiques, Wingham . 087185
Carlton Rochell, New York 117746
Carlton-Smith, John, London 085180
Carlton Smith, M.D., London 113530
Carlucci, Roma 076363
Carlyle House, Alexandria 041637
Carlyle's House, London 040109
Carlyn, Dallas 115849
Carman House Museum, Iroquois . . 005647
Carmarthen Heritage Centre, Carmarthen 039001
Carmarthen Museum, Carmarthen . 039002
Carmarthen Museum. Publication, Carmarthen 136189
Carmarthenshire County Museum, Carmarthen 039002
Carmel, Claremont 110036
Carmel, Constantia 110038
Carmel, Sacramento 132731
Carmel Art Gallery, Ottawa 097102
Carmeline, Paris 065671
Carmen, Montevideo 087312
Carmen, Luis Martin del, Madrid . . 129585
Carmen Books, Granada 141019
Carmen Boreantiques, Vancouver . . 059344
Carmicheal-Stewart House, New Glasgow 005997
Carmignani, Thierry, Marseille 064331
Carmo, Marya, Porto Alegre 096547
Carnaby Collection of Beetles and Butterflies, Boyup Brook 000826
Carnazzi, Jean, Lyon 064101
Carnegie, Chris, Yealmpton 087282, 131722
Carnegie, D., San Francisco 092751
Carnegie Art Center, Walla Walla . . 048833
Carnegie Art Center, Rotunda and Fireplace Galleries, Mankato 045642
Carnegie Art Museum, Oxnard 046775
Carnegie Center for Art & History, New Albany 046185
Carnegie Hill Antiques, New York . . 090765
Carnegie Historical Museum, Fairfield 043788
Carnegie Magazine, Pittsburgh 136414
Carnegie Museum, Inverurie 039810
Carnegie Museum of Art, Pittsburgh 047043
Carnegie Museum of Natural History, Pittsburgh 047044
Carnegie Science Center, Pittsburgh 047045
El Carnero, Bogotá 059827, 137756
Carnet, J.P.H., Villedieu-sur-Indre . . 068890
Carnevali, Carlo, Firenze 075303
Carney, K.M. & W.A., Eaglehawk . . . 055777
Carney Gallery, Weston 049120
La Carnichette, Saint-Cyprien 067410
Carnifex Ferry Battlefield State Park and Museum, Summersville 048422
The Carningli Centre, Newport, Dyfed 086074, 131309
Carniola Antiqua, Ljubljana 080651
Carnot, Lorient 064000
Carnovale, Aurelio, Roma 076364
Carnton Plantation, Franklin 044043
Caro, Yvan, Chézy-sur-Marne 062289
Caro de Prielle, Bertrand, Bordeaux 124118
Caroje, Rennes (Ille-et-Vilaine) 101073
The Carole and Barry Kaye Museum of Miniatures, Los Angeles 045415
Carolee, Saint Louis 092212
Carolina Art Association, Charleston 054699
Carolina Augusta Art, São Paulo . . . 058700
Carolinas Aviation Museum, Charlotte 042754
Carol's, Edmonton 058821
Carol's Antiques, Adare 074854
Carolus Magnus, Düren 070346
Carolus Rex & Smulan, Göteborg . . 081798
Caron, Vancouver 097435
Caron, Daniel, Montreuil-sous-Bois 064766
Caron-Lestringant, Paris 065672
Carosi, Aldo, Roma 127958
Carosio, Gianmatteo, Genova 127439
Carosso, New York 117747
Carousel Auction, Sacramento 123078
Carowind Gallery, Portland 118986
Carp, Susanne, Köln 126069
Carpanely, Badajoz 080774
Carpe Artem, Paris 100120
Carpe Diem, Léon 063745
Carpe Diem, Monaco 077598
Carpe Diem Antiques, New York . . . 090766
Carpe Diem Antiques, Philadelphia . 091618
Carpe Diem Galleries, Bangkok . . . 112230
Carpe Diem Gallery, Wellington . . . 108617
Carpenter, John, Llanelli 085036
Carpenter, Rosemary, Truro 142121
Carpenter, Steve, Wisbech 087188, 131699
Carpenter Home Museum, Cle Elum 042965
Carpenter Museum of Antique Outboard Motors, Gilmanton 044193
Carpentier, Paris 100121
Carpentier, Jean, Danze 062598
Carpentier, Jean, Paris 065673
Carpentier, Jean, Saint-Ouen 067745
Carpetbagger Aviation Museum, Harrington 039675
Carpinteria 43, Madrid 129586
Carpinteria Valley Museum of History, Carpinteria 042629
Carpinus, Bussum 140376
Carr, Adam, New Orleans 090529
Carr, Harold J., Washington 087050
Carr, John B., Saint Albans 131437
Carr, Michael, Woollahra 056859
Carr, Ronald, Salisbury 086491
Carr, Virginia, Chicago 115381
Carr House, Victoria 006736
Carra, Charlotte, Saint-Lattier 067573
Carrabba, Austin 131795
Carracci, I., Bologna 075063
Carracedo Carracedo, Benjamin, Barcelona 110124
Carraig, Blackrock 139955
Carraig Books, Dublin 139961
Carrandi, New York 117748
Carranza, Madrid 081267
Carrara, Las Vegas 116614
Carrau, Gilbert, Cauneille . 062038, 124173
Carray Carron, Raymonde, Martigny 111719
Carré, Louis, Paris 100122
Carré Blanc, Sion 111906
Carré d'Art, Musée d'Art Contemporain, Nîmes 013418
Carré d'Artistes, Aix-en-Provence . 098783
Carré d'Artistes, Lyon 099545
Le Carre D'Or Antiguidades, Rio de Janeiro 058565
Carré noir, Landerneau 099420
Carré Rouge, Biarritz 061455
Carré Sainte-Anne, Montpellier . . . 099750
Le Carré-Scéne Nationale, Château-Gontier 011275
Carré Verre, Obernai 099885
Carrefour de la Création, Touvre . . .068614, 101384
Carrefour du Meuble, Saint-Jean-d'Angély 067529
Carrefour du Vitrail, Lavaudieu 012449
Carreiras, Carmen, Barcelona 080827
Carreño, Dunhe, Chicago 115382
Carreno Valenzuela, Iván Ricardo, Santiago de Chile 059517
Carrera, Bernard, Saint-Mariens . . . 067623
Carrera, Federico, New York 090767
Carrère, Xavier, Soustons . 068279, 101278

Carretero Garrido, Valencia 129763
Carri, Silvano, Firenze 127315
Carriage and Harness Museum, Beechworth 000784
Carriage Antiques, Jimboomba 056020
Carriage House Antique, Jacksonville 089389
Carriage House Antiques, Houston . 089042
Carriage House Antiques, Norfolk . . 091371
Carriage House Museum, Camden . 042579
Carriage House Museum, Colorado Springs 043053
Carriage Museum, Saint George's . 003903
Carriageway Gallery, New Orleans . 117414
Carrick, G., Gainsborough 084447
Carrick Hill, Springfield 095218
Carrick Hill Museum, Springfield . . 001484
Carrico, Memphis 132318
Carrie M. McLain Memorial Museum, Nome 046494
Carrie Secrist, Chicago 115383
Carrie Weedon Natural Science Museum, Galesville 044122
Carrière-Lenglet, Philippe, Ganges . 062958
Carrière Souterraine d'Aubigny, Taingy 014893
Carrigar, Houston 089043
Carrilhão, Belo Horizonte 058413
Carrillo Sanz, Julian, A Coruña 110316
Carrington & Co., London 085181
Carrington-Gallagher, San Antonio . 119403
Carrington House, Llanrwst 085042
Carrion Bolivar, Carmen, Santander 110745
Carro de la Luz, Madrid 110464
Carrobbio, Quarto Inferiore 135888
Carroll, San Francisco 142939
Carroll, Windsor, Ontario 097555
Carroll, A., Saint Paul 132762
Carroll County Farm Museum, Westminster 049114
Carroll Reece Museum, East Tennessee State University, Johnson City . . . 044864
Carroll's Clocks, Saint Paul 092353, 132763
Carrollton Junque and Antiques, New Orleans 090530
Carromato del Max, Mijas 035493
Le Carrousel, Tournai 058382
Carroza, Jorge, Santiago de Chile . . 097621
Carrozzo, Alfredo, Roma 127959
Carry A. Nation Home Memorial, Medicine Lodge 045745
C.A.R.S., Brighton 083691
Cars of the Stars Motor Museum, Keswick 039850
Carscadden's Museum, Plenty 006159
Carshalton Antique Galleries, Carshalton 083886
Carshalton Water Tower, Carshalton 039007
Carshalton Water Tower, London . . 040110
Carsley, Whetstone & Assoc, Montréal 058933
Carson, Dallas 115850
Carson, Vancouver 137724
Carson, Sandy, Denver 115979
Carson, Thomas J., Denver 115980
Carson Clark, Edinburgh 141576
Carson County Square House Museum, Panhandle 046811
Carson Pirie, Scott, Chicago 088047
Carss Cottage Museum, Blakehurst 000811
Carswell, Rush & Berlin, New York . 090768
c.art, Dornbirn 095495, 133066
Cart-Tanneur, Didier, Migé 138208
La Carta Bianca Studio Bibliografico, Genova 140033
Carta Turchina, Prato 127887
Carte d'Arte, Bologna 135889
Cartel Fine Art, Granada 110372
Cartel Fine Arts, Málaga 110634
Carten & Assoc., Austin 114963
Carter, Atlanta 114862
Carter, Edward, New York 117749
Carter, Katharine T., New York 117750
Carter, Mark, Fairford 084371
Carter, Roger & Angela, Lincoln . . . 130896
Carter, Stewart, Christchurch 108389
Carter Bowden, Fort Worth 088843
Carter-Coile Country Doctors Museum, Winterville 049266
Carter County Museum, Ekalaka . . 043624
The Carter House, Franklin 044044
Carter House Natural Science Museum, Redding 047356
Carter & Ormsby, Richmond, Victoria 056526, 137072
Carteret County Museum of History and Art, Morehead City 046023
Carters, Hampton East 120591
Carter's Grove Visitor Center, Williamsburg 049179
Cartes Anciennes Ptolémée Plus, Montréal 137648
Cartesius, Trieste 106715
Cartexpo, Vulaines-sur-Seine 133709
Cartier, Paul, Erlenbach (Zürich) . . . 111397
Cartier, Paul, Richterswil 111830
Cartier Co., Cairo 060433
Cartiere Vannucci, Milano 106189
Il Cartiglio, Firenze 075304
Il Cartiglio, Torino 076795, 140130
Cartmill & Parish, Tauranga 079261, 128963
Carton, Karin, Versailles 068796
Carton House, Maynooth 022834
Carton, Taquin, Delroisse, Bruxelles 123582
Cartonumis, Orléans 065299
Cartoon Art Gallery, Houston 116290
Cartoon Art Museum, San Francisco 047859
Cartoon City, San Antonio 092495
Cartoon City, San Antonio 092496
Cartoon Connection Studio, Brookvale 094312
Cartoon Factory, Salt Lake City . . . 119333
Cartoon Gallery, Sydney 095278
Cartoon Gallery, Sydney 095279
Cartoonfabrik, Berlin 101826
Cartophilie, Nantes 138239
Cartoplus 21, Dijon 138081
Cartouche, Montrouge 064779
Cartref Taid, Trevelin 000642
Cartrefle Antiques, Mathry 085963
Cartuja de la Asunción, Granada . . 035243
Cartwells of Tirau, Tirau 079273
Cartwheel, Mosta 077515
Cartwheel Antiques, Corrimal 055718
Cartwright, Michael, Denmark 094474
Cartwright Hall Art Gallery, Bradford 038805
Caruso, San Francisco 092752
Caruso, Antonio, Allaman 082080
Caruso, Antonio, Lausanne 082537
Caruso, Antonio, Lausanne 082538
Caruso, Concetto, Catania 127259
Caruso, Orazio, Catania 127260
Carvajal, Luis, Madrid 081268
Carvajal Cabello, Luis, Madrid 110465
Carvalho, António Tavares, Lisboa . 140825
Carvalho, Antonio Tavares, Lisboa . 140826
Carvalho, António Lima, Porto 080074
Carvalho, José, Belo Horizonte 058414
Carvalho, Julio C., Belo Horizonte . . 058415
Carvalho, Nilson Guimaraes, Rio de Janeiro 058566
Carvalho & Gil, Lisboa 079894
Carver County Historical Society Museum, Waconia 048820
Carverne, Tampa 093113
Carvers & Gilders, London 130968
Carvings International, San Jose . . 119850
Carwick, Koroit 056065
Cary Cottage, Cincinnati 042918
Caryl House, Dover 043491
Carzaniga & Ueker, Basel 111171
Casa, Bucureşti 080146
Casa, Essen 070621
Casa Adobe de San Rafael, Glendale 044208
Casa Amesti, Monterey 045980
Casa Antano, Córdoba 055252
Casa Antica di Caruso, Catania . . . 075240
Casa Antik, Kelkheim 071779
Casa Arte Sacra, Braga 129139
Casa Belchior, Porto Alegre 058493
Casa Bella, Cairo 098620
Casa Bella Collection, Valencia 081650
Casa Blanca, Firenze 075305
La Cas'à Bulles Martinique, Saint-Joseph 140253
Casa Buonarroti, Firenze 024141
Casa Cărţii, Iaşi 109458
Casa Ceramo, Belo Horizonte 058416
Casa Contadina, Forenza 024222
Casa Cuba, Miami 090149
Casa da Cultura, Machado 004201
Casa da Memória Arnaldo Estevão de Figueiredo, Campo Grande 004045
Casa da Noal, Treviso 026119
Casa d'Arte, Fortaleza 096517
Casa d'Arte Ascona, Ascona 111135
Casa das Artes, Brasília 096490
Casa das Artes-Galeria, São Paulo . 096668
Casa d'Asta della Rocca, Torino . . . 076796
Casa d'Aste Bottega dell'Arte, Lugano 082592, 122334
Casa d'Aste Capitolium, Brescia . . . 075155
Casa d'Aste della Rocca, Torino . . . 121731
Casa de America, Madrid 110466
Casa de Andrés Eloy Blanco, Cumaná 049486
Casa de Antigüedades, Lima 079546
Casa de Antigüedades Los Bosquesillos, Caracas 093524
Casa de Antigüedades y Hierro Forjado, Medellín 059912
Casa de Colón, San Sebastián de La Gomera 035772
Casa de Cora Coralina, Goiás 004129
Casa de Cultura Afrónio Peixoto, Lençóis 004188
Casa de Cultura João Ribeiro, Laranjeiras 004184
Casa de Deodoro, Rio de Janeiro . . 004332
La Casa de Don Angel, Santa Fé . . . 055303
Casa de Dulce María Loynaz, La Habana 007939
Casa de Hidalgo, Dolores Hidalgo . . 028222
Casa de José Bonifácio, Rio de Janeiro 004333
Casa de José Jacinto Milanés, Matanzas 008054
Casa de la Constitución de 1814, Apatzingán 028105
Casa de la Cultura, Enguera 035173
Casa de la Cultura, Museo Arqueológico, Museos Histórico y de la Ciudad, Curuzú Cuatiá 000324
Casa de la Cultura Augusto Rivera Garces, Museo Simón Bolívar, Bolívar . . . 007456
Casa de la Cultura Benjamín Carríon, Cuenca 009185
Casa de la Libertad, Sucre 003920
Casa de las Américas, La Habana . 052827
Casa de las Ciencias, A Coruña . . . 035121
Casa de las Dueñas, Sevilla 035852
La Casa de Las Lomas, México . . . 107480
Casa de Lavalleja, Museo Histórico Nacional, Montevideo 041498
Casa de les Roques, Valencia 035972
Casa de los Abuelos, Museo Folclórico, Sonsón 007617
Casa de los Arabes, La Habana . . . 007940
Casa de los Morlanes, Ayuntamiento de Zaragoza, Zaragoza 036099
Casa de los Tiros, Granada 035244
La Casa de los Tratados, Girón 009202
Casa de Madera, Mar del Plata . . . 094100
Casa de Manuel Mujica Láinez, La Cumbre 000375
Casa de Marinos, Aranjuez 034845
Casa de Miguel Failde Pérez, Matanzas 008055
Casa de Oliveira Vianna, Niterói . . . 004240
Casa de Osório, Rio de Janeiro 004334
La Casa de Palermo, Buenos Aires . 094065
Casa de Pilatos, Sevilla 035853
Casa de Rancho Cucamonga, Rancho Cucamonga 047321
Casa de Remate Esquina del Remate, Punta Arenas 059480, 120834
Casa de Subastas, México 121764
Casa de Subastas de Madrid, Madrid 122039
Casa de Subastes, Barcelona 122002
Casa de Unidad, Detroit 043435
Casa de Usados, Medellín 059913
Casa de Vacas, Madrid 110467
Casa de Velásquez, Madrid. Melanges/ Miscellanies, Paris 135697
Casa de Vitorino Ribeiro, Porto 032671
Casa del Arte, Aschaffenburg 069193
Casa del Arte de la Universidad de Concepción, Concepción 006911
La Casa del Balcón, Martínez 055280
Casa del Boccaccio, Certaldo 023802
La Casa del Coleccionista, Buenos Aires 055187
La Casa del Coleccionista, Vitoria-Gasteiz 081717
La Casa del Collezionista, Roma . . . 076365
Casa del Cordón, Vitoria-Gasteiz . . 036078
La Casa del Cuadro, Lima 079547, 129002
Casa del Escribano Real Don Juan de Vargas, Tunja 007628
Casa del Gatto, Brione 111308
Casa del General José Garibaldi, Museo Histórico Nacional, Montevideo . . 041499
Casa del Águila y la Parra, Museo Regional, Santillana del Mar 035830
La Casa del Mobile Vecchio, Roma . 076366
La Casa del Mobile Vecchio, Roma . 076367
Casa del Rey IV, Vitoria-Gasteiz . . . 081718
Casa dell'Ariosto, Ferrara 024099
Casa delle Aste, Chiavari 121684
Casa delle Aste Nuova Ifir, Milano . 121701
Casa Delmonte, Palma de Mallorca 081474
Casa Depa Antigüedades, Lima . . . 079548
Casa d'Esper, Miami 090150
Casa di Carlo Goldoni, Museo Correr, Venezia 026230
Casa di Giorgione, Castelfranco Veneto 023716
Casa di Goethe, Roma 025467
Casa di Lazzaro Spallanzani, Scandiano 025832
Casa di Petrarca, Arquà Petrarca . . 023258
Casa di Pirandello, Agrigento 023131
Casa di Pirandello, Roma 025468
Casa di Xilogravura, Campos de Jordão 004050
Casa do Brazão, Faro 079829
Casa do Escultor Ervin Curt Teichmann, Pomerode 004288
Casa do Livro Azul, São Paulo 137583
Casa do Livro Usado, Fortaleza . . . 137557
Casa dos Livros Usados, Fortaleza . 137558
Casa dos Presentes, Lisboa 079895
Casa dos Sete Candeeiros, Salvador 004435
Casa Editrice Francescana, Assisi . 134541
Casa Elizalde, Barcelona 110125
Casa España, Makati 108824
Casa Española, Buenos Aires 055188
Casa-Fuerte de Ponce de León, Santo Domingo 009154
Casa Gorordo Museum, Cebu 031652
Casa Grande History Museum, Casa Grande 042644
Casa Grande Ruins, Coolidge 043135
Casa H.A., Buenos Aires 055189
Casa Henas, Buenos Aires 055190
Casa Hidalgo, Segovia 035841
Casa International, Osaka 077172
Casa Jesús T. Piñero, Canóvanas . . 032711
Casa João Turin, Curitiba 004078
Casa Leopardi, Recanati 025402
Casa Linda Galleries, New York . . . 117751
Casa Lines, Buenos Aires 055191
Casa Loma, Toronto 006589
Casa Luis Barragán, México 028423
Casa Malanca, Brisighella 023530
Casa Manana, Waikato 079285
Casa Manila Museum, Manila 031718

Casa Manuel F. Zárate, Guarraré . . 031419
Casa Maria Esclasans, Barcelona . . 080828
Casa Memorială Gheorghe Dima, Braşov 032789
Casa Memorială Vasile Alecsandri, Mireşti 032894
Casa Mexicana, Dallas 115851
Casa Milchstrasse, Livorno 075526
Casa Municipal de Cultura. Sala de Exposiciones, Alcázar de San Juan 034803
Casa Munoa, Donostia-San Sebastián 081078
Casa Museo 20 de Julio de 1810, Bogotá 007403
Casa Museo A. Gramsci, Ghilarza . . 024337
Casa Museo A. Uccello, Palazzolo Acreide 025076
Casa Museo Alegre de Sagrera, Terrassa 035903
Casa Museo Almirante Miguel Grau, Piura 031582
Casa Museo Amado Nervo, Tepic . . 028823
Casa-Museo Antonio Machado, Segovia 035842
Casa Museo Antonio Nariñtildeo y Álvarez, Villa de Leyva 007636
Casa-Museo Azorín, Monóvar 035511
Casa Museo Bonsor, Mairena del Alcor 035449
Casa Museo Bruzzone, Mar del Plata 000422
Casa Museo Cadete Juan Escutia, Tepic 028824
Casa Museo Carlos Pellicer Cámara, Villahermosa 028930
Casa Museo Coronel Gregorio Méndez Magaña, Jalpa de Méndez 028355
Casa Museo Curros Enríquez, Celanova 035078
Casa Museo de Arrese, Corella 035119
Casa Museo de Cervantes, Valladolid 035993
Casa-Museo de Colón, Valladolid . . 035994
Casa-Museo de Lope de Vega, Madrid 035370
Casa Museo de Rafael Alberti, El Puerto de Santa María 035683
Casa-Museo de Unamuno, Salamanca 035738
Casa Museo de Zorrilla, Valladolid . 035995
Casa-Museo de Zúrbaran, Fuente de Cantos 035205
Casa Museo dei Puccini, Pescaglia . 025181
Casa Museo del Cima, Conegliano . 023953
Casa Museo dell'Alta Valle del Cervo, Rosazza 025596
Casa Museo di A. Oriani, Casola Valsenio 023693
Casa Museo di Dante, Firenze 024142
Casa Museo di Monticello Amiata, Cinigiano 023885
Casa Museo Emilia Pardo Bazán, Real Academia Galega, A Coruña 035122
Casa Museo F. Scaglione, Sciacca . 025844
Casa Museo Fantoni, Rovetta 025612
Casa Museo Federico García Lorca, Fuente Vaqueros 035207
Casa Museo Fernando Fader, Ischilín 000365
Casa Museo Francesco Baracca, Lugo 024555
Casa Museo G. de Chirico, Roma . . 025469
Casa Museo G. Mazzarino, Pescina 025196
Casa Museo Gene Byron, Guanajuato 028298
Casa Museo Giovanni Verga, Catania 023760
Casa Museo Ignacio Zuloaga, Zumaia 036122
Casa Museo Ivan Bruschi, Arezzo . . 023234
Casa Museo Joaquin Torrents Llado, Palma de Mallorca 035601
Casa-Museo Jorge Eliécer Gaitán, Bogotá 007404
Casa-Museo José Benlliure, Valencia 035973
Casa Museo José Clemente Orozco, Guadalajara 028273
Casa Museo José María de Cossío, Casona de Tudanca, Tudanca 035956
Casa Museo Julián Gayarre, Roncal 035718
Casa Museo La Moreña, La Barca . 028372
Casa-Museo La Sebastiana, Fundación Pablo Neruda, Valparaíso 006946
Casa-Museo León y Castillo, Telde . 035901
Casa Museo Leonardo Valdez Esquer, Etchojoa 028253
Casa Museo López Portillo, Guadalajara 028274
Casa Museo M. Moretti, Cesenatico 023826
Casa Museo Maestro Manuel Altamirano, Tixtla de Guerrero 028844
Casa-Museo Manuel de Falla, Granada 035245
Casa Museo Mario Urteaga, Cajamarca 031470
Casa-Museo Menéndez Pelayo, Santander 035810
Casa Museo Miguel Hernández, Orihuela 035565
Casa Museo Modernista, Novelda . 035544
Casa Museo Páez, Valencia 049516
Casa Museo Pavesiano, Santo Stefano Belbo 025780
Casa Museo Pérez Galdós, Las Palmas de Gran Canaria 035621
Casa Museo Piccione d'Avola, Geraci Siculo 024333
Casa Museo Pinazo, Godella 035239
Casa Museo Posada del Moro, Torrecampo 035940
Casa Museo Quinta de Bolívar, Bogotá 007405
Casa Museo R. Bendandi, Faenza . . 024065
Casa Museo R. Siviero, Firenze . . . 024143
Casa Museo Ricardo Gomez Campuzano, Bogotá 007406
Casa Museo Rosalía de Castro, Padrón 035589
Casa Museo Sa Domu Antiga, Santadi 025760
Casa Museo Signorini-Corsi, L'Aquila 024459
Casa Museo Silvestre Rodríguez, Nacozari de García 028591
Casa Museo Tito, Ûbeda 034964
Casa Museo Tiu Virgiliu, Suni 025968
Casa-Museo Tomás Morales, Moya 035526
Casa Museo V. Cermignani, Giulianova 024346
Casa Museo Valle Inclán, La Pobra do Caramiñal 035660
Casa Museo Vladimir Cora, Acaponeta 028077
Casa Museo Zenobia y Juan Ramón Jiménez, Moguer 035499
Casa Museu Abel Salazar da Universidade do Porto, São Mamede de Infesta 032686
Casa Museu Bissaya Barreto, Coimbra 032594
Casa-Museu Castell Gala Dalí, La Pera 035649
Casa-Museu de Almeida Moreira, Viseu 032702
Casa-Museu de Salvador Dalí de Cadaqués, Cadaqués 035017
Casa-Museu del Poeta Verdaguer, Folgueroles 035195
Casa-Museu dos Patudos, Alpiarça 032574
Casa-Museu Dr. Anastácio Gonçalves, Lisboa 032626
Casa-Museu Egas Moniz, Avanca . . 032579
Casa-Museu Gaudí, Barcelona 034901
Casa Museu Guerra Junqueiro, Porto 032672
Casa-Museu Pare Manyanet, Tremp 035952
Casa-Museu Prat de la Riba, Castellterçol 035071
Casa-Museu Teixeira Lopes, Vila Nova de Gaia 032700
Casa-Museu Teixeira Lopes e Galerias Diego de Macedo, Porto 032673
Casa-Museu Torres Amat, Sallent . 035748
Casa Natal de Aquileo Parra, Barichara 007394
Casa Natal de Cervantes, Alcalá de Henares 034800
Casa Natal de Jesús Montané Oropesa, Nueva Gerona 008073
Casa Natal de José Antonio Ramos Sucre, Cumaná 049487
Casa Natal de José María España, La Guaira 049498
Casa Natal de Legazpi, Zumárraga . 036123
Casa Natal de Regino Boti, Guantánamo 007934
Casa Natal de San Ignacio, Azpeitia 034879
Casa Natal de Sant Antoni María Claret, Sallent 035749
Casa Natal de Santa Teresa de Jesús, Avila 034875
Casa Natal de Sarmiento, San Juan 000568
Casa Natal del Libertador Simón Bolívar, Caracas 049447
Casa Natal del Pintor Wifredo Lam, Santa Clara 008136
Casa natale de Santiago Ramón y Cajal, Petilla de Aragón 035651
Casa Natale di A. Rosmini, Rovereto 025607
Casa Natale di Giosuè Carducci, Pietrasanta 025228
Casa Natale di Giuseppe Verdi, Busseto 023550
Casa Natale di Pascoli, San Mauro Pascoli 025712
Casa Natale di Pio V, Bosco Marengo 023500
Casa Natale di Raffaello, Urbino . . . 026172
Casa Natale di Toscanini, Parma . . 025111
Casa Natale di V. Monti, Alfonsine . 023168
Casa Natale Gaetano Donizetti, Bergamo 023374
Casa Natale Leonardo da Vinci, Vinci 026340
Casa National de Goya, Museo del Grabado, Fuendetodos 035203
Casa Navarro, San Antonio 047790
Casa Ofhir, Santiago de Chile 123877
Casa-Oficina de António Carneiro, Porto 032674
Casa Pedro Domingo Murillo, La Paz 003909
Casa Piú, Caracas 093525
Casa Postal, Madrid 081269
Casa Real, São Paulo 058701
Casa Real Shrine, Malolos 031704
Casa Rivera, Museo Histórico Nacional, Montevideo 041500
Casa Roche Pombo, Morretes 004230
Casa Romei, Ferrara 024100
Casa Ros, Ourense 081448
Casa Ros, Ourense 081449
Casa Rosada Abelardo Díaz Alfaro, Caguas 032708
Casa Salazar, San Antonio 119404
Casa Salsa, Cancún 128497
Casa San Isidro, Ciudad Bolívar . . . 049482
Casa Santuario de San Pedro Claver, Verdú 036024
Casa Schlatter, Firenze 075306
Casa Sheik, Porto Alegre 058494
Casa Siglo XIX, Fundación Sebastián, Chihuahua 028152
Casa Taller, Panamá City 050587
Casa Taller de Arte, Medellín 098256
Casa Velha Antiguidades, Belo Horizonte 058417
Casa Velha Antiguidades, Brasília . . 123694
La Casa Verde, Cancún 077558
Casa Vicente, Donostia-San Sebastián 081079
Casa Victoria, Los Angeles 089713
Casa Wolf, Firenze 075307
Casa y Museo de El Greco, Toledo . 035915
Casablanca Antique Lamps, New York 090769, 132450
Casablanca Bookshop, Kitchener . . 137646
Casablanca Verlag, Berlin 133758
Casadella, Ensie, Solliès-Pont 068258
Casadio, Diletta, Roma 076368
Casadio, Romeo, Brescia 105994
Casado, José, Collioure 062395
Casagrande, Adriano, Roma 127960
Casagrande, Giampiero, Lugano . . . 135037
Casagrande, Luciano, Roma 076369
Casagrande, Mario, Braunschweig . 069978
Casagwa National Museum, Daraga 031667
Casaj, Oakland 091410
Casal Balaguer, Palma de Mallorca 035602
Casal Balaguer, Palma de Mallorca 110672
Casal Solleric, Centre d'Exposicions i Documentació de l'Art Contemporai, Palma de Mallorca 035603
Casale, Serenella, Roma 106504
Il Casale dell'Antico, Roma 076370
Il Casale dell'Arte, Catania 075241
Il Casale dell'Arte, Catania 127261
La Casamaures, Saint-Martin-le-Vinoux 014427
CasaMia, Stein, Mittelfranken 073901
Casamit, Barcelona 122003
Casamonti, Roberto, Crans-sur-Sierre 111373
Casanelly, Lima 079549
Casanova, Alcino F.M., Porto 129192
Casanova, Alcino F.M., Vila Nova de Gaia 129207
Casanova Coleccio, Barcelona 080829, 122004
Casanovas Infiesta, Antonio, Madrid 110468
Casar Herrero, Santiago, Santander 110746
Casarão Azul Antiguidades, Porto Alegre 058495
Casares, Alberto, Buenos Aires . . . 136706
Casari, Stefano, Brescia 127208
Casariego, Madrid 081270
Casaril, Giacomo, Roma 127961
Casas Adobe's Collectibles, Tucson 093211
Casas Estrade, Barcelona 110126
Casatelier Restauração e Arte, Rio de Janeiro 123701
Casati, Alessandro, Milano 075659
Casati, Giorgio, Milano 075660
Casay, Anthony, San Diego 119493
Casbah, Amsterdam 107693
Cascade, Arnhem 078048
Cascade, Casablanca 077645
Cascade Auctions, Seattle 123112
Cascade Blue Antiques, Blackheath 055508
El Cascajero, New York 142641
Cascar Art, Bremen 102234
Cascianelli, Roma 140098
Casciello, Domenico, Paris 065674
Casciello, Domenico, Saint-Pryvé-Saint-Mesmin 067968, 124918
Cascina Museo della Civiltà Contadina, Cremona 023993
Cascione, Olimpia, Bologna 075064
Casco, Utrecht 108244
Casè, Fabio, Milano 127561
Case d'Art, Paris 100123
Casebow, Peter G., Worthing 131718
Casell, New Orleans 117415
Casella, Valencia 129764
Casella, West Hollywood 093455
Casella, Gianmaria, Brescia 127209
Caselli, Elio, Napoli 075953
Caselli, Lucia, Firenze 075308
Casemate Museum, Fort Monroe . . 043953
Casements, Swinton 131570
Caseneuve, Christiane, Aurillac . . . 098881
Caserío de Errecarte, Casa Natal del Hermano Francisco Gárate, Azpeitia 034880
Caseta de Balma, Castello de la Plana 081037
Caseta de la Musica, Madrid 081271
Casetti, Hélène, Cannes 061937
Casey, Jacksonville 089390
Casey, Las Vegas 089555
Casey, Narre Warren 120619
Casey & Assoc., San Francisco . . . 119632
Casey, Toledo 093166, 132969

Casey, William J., Warwick 087036
Casey Farm, Saunderstown 048017
Casey Jones Home and Railroad Museum, Jackson 044806
Casey Jones Museum, Vaughan . . . 048756
Casey Kaplan, M., New York 117752
Cash America, Portland 091910
Cash Paid, El Paso 088794
Cashan, Sharjah 083211
Cashi, Denver 088667
Casho, Cairo 098621
Casillas 1 Art-Studio, El Paso 116103
Casimir, Tournai 058383
Casimir, Jack, London 085182
Casini, Philippe, Paris 100124
Casino, Saint-Céré 101137
Casino dell'Aurora Pallavicini, Roma 025470
Casino Luxembourg - Forum d'Art Contemporain, Luxembourg 027886
Casino Restorations, Saint Paul . . . 132764
Casita del Príncipe, El Pardo 035635
Casnica, Cluj-Napoca 080176
Caso, Osaka 106953
Caso, Christiania, København 060307
Casoli, Sergio, Milano 106190
Cason del Buen Retiro, Madrid 035371
Caspar-David-Friedrich-Institut für Kunstwissenschaften, Ernst-Moritz-Arndt-Universität Greifswald, Greifswald 050094
Caspar Neher-Gedenkraum, Wien . 002888
Casperle, Bilbao 080970
Caspian Gallery, Paddington 095021
Caspian Oriental Rugs, Chicago . . . 088048
Casque, Tokyo 107025
Casque and Gauntlet Militaria, Farnham 084388, 130704
Cass, Maria, Nayland 086040, 131293
Cass County Historical Society Museum, Logansport 045366
Cass County Historical Society Museum, Plattsmouth 047086
Cass County Historical Society Museum, West Fargo 049072
Cass-Garr, New Orleans 090531
Cassagnaud, Joël, Auch 061050
Cassagne, Corinne, Romans-sur-Isère 121235
Cassagne, Joël, Langon 063519
Cassagnes, Bernard, Brousses-et-Villaret 061820
Cassandra Antiquités, Marseille . . . 064332
Cassandra's Art, Atlanta 114863
Cassandre, Saint-Raphaël 067985, 138608
Cassani, München 072674
Cassaro, Giovanni, Torino 128278
Cassé, Carmen, Paris 100125
Cassel & Lampe, Bonn 138893
Il Cassetto, Taranto 076745
Il Cassetto della Nonna, Torino 076797, 128279
Il Cassettone, Bologna 127141
Cassi, Marco, Firenze 075309
Cassia County Museum, Burley . . . 042511
Cassian de Vere Cole, London 113531
Cassidy, London 141767
Cassidy, Warminster 087025, 131651
Cassidy, Barry, Sacramento 142842
Cassidy, P.J., Holbeach 141670
Cassimus, Angelo, New Orleans . . . 090532
Cassina, Diego, Lugano 111661
Cassini, Giocondo, Venezia 140149
Cassiopée, Paris 065675
Cassiopeia Fine Arts, Chicago 115384
Cassissium, Nuits-Saint-Georges . . 013462
Cassius Forum Bonn, Forum für religiöse Kunst und Begegnung, Bonn 016320
Cassius Forum Bonn, Forum für religiöse Kunst und Begegnung, Bonn 053116
Casson, Guillaume de, Paris 100126
Castagner, Agathe, La Garenne-Colombes 063392
Castaing, Frédéric, Paris 065676
Castaing, Frédéric, Paris 138326
Castaing, Hugues, La Rochelle 063427
Castaing, Hugues, Le Bois-Plage-en-Ré 063573
Castaldi, Luigi, Napoli 127758
Castan, Echternach 107384
Castan, Nellie, Melbourne 056184
Castaño Cortes, Angel, Madrid 129587
Casteel-Linn House and Museum, Princeton 047235
Castel, Jeanne, Paris 100127
Castel Beseno, Besenello 023386
Castel Coira, Sluderno 025905
Castel Maraldo d 406, Modena 106347
Castel Prösels, Fié 024119
Castel Sant'Elmo, Napoli 024888
Castel Taufers, Campo Tures 023617
Castelar, Maria José de M., São Paulo 049759
Castel'Art, Le Castellet 099427
Castelin & Lhote, Dunkerque 062749
Castell Cartoixa Vallparadis, Museu de Terrassa, Terrassa 035904
Castell y Waun, Chirk 039080
Castella-Ayral, Toulouse 068493
La Castellana, Palermo 076137
Castellana 150, Madrid 122040
Castellana la Habana, Madrid 122041
Castellana Muebles, Madrid 122042
Castellana Serrano, Madrid 122043
Castellana Subasta d Joyas, Madrid 122044
Castellana Subastas Barcelona, Barcelona 122005
Castellani, Jean-Marie, Aix-en-Provence 098784
Castellani Art Museum, Niagara University 046485
Castellano Olmedo, Millan, Santander 081553
Castelli, Leo, New York 117753
Castellini, Brescia 075156
Castellino, Genève 082411
Il Castello, Milano 106191
Castelló 120, Madrid 110469
Castello dei Burattini - Museo Giordano Ferrari, Musei Civici di san Paolo, Parma 025112
Castello dei Visconti di San Vito, Somma Lombardo 025913
Castello del Buonconsiglio, Monumenti e Collezioni Provinciali, Trento 026106
Castello della Manta, Manta 024599
Castello di Donnafugata, Ragusa . . 025384
Castello di Giulio II, Ostia Antica . . . 025031
Castello di Masnago, Musei Civici, Varese 026211
Castello di Montebello, Archaeological Museum, Bellinzona 036913
Castello di Rivoli Museo d'Arte Contemporanea, Rivoli 025448
Castello di Sasso Corbaro, Bellinzona 036914
Castello di Stenico, Stenico 025948
Castello d'Issogne, Issogne 024425
Castello Ducale, Agliè 023126
Castello e Museo Civico F. Baldinucci, Lari 024468
Castello e Museo della Rocca, Roma 025471
Castello e Raccolta Archeologica, Montechiarugolo 024831
Castello Fénis, Fénis 024090
Castello Malaspina, Bobbio 023408
Castello Malaspina, Massa 024630
Castello Pallotta, Caldarola 023580
Castello Principesco, Merano 024667
Castello Reale, Moncalieri 024784
Castello Reale, Racconigi 025379
Castello Reale, Venaria 026226
Castello Reggia di Venaria Reale, Torino 026048
Castellon, Adora, Tresses 101386
Castellon, Alfredo, Bordeaux 061598
Castells & Castells, Montevideo . . . 122776
Castellum, Bovenden 069967
Castellvi, Maria Jose, Barcelona . . 110127
Castelnuovo, Tedesco Giovanni, Firenze 075310
Castera, Bordeaux 138037
Casteran, Eric, Toulouse 101336
Casterbridge Books, Chicago 142284
Casterman, Bruxelles 133262
Castiaux, France, Mairieux 064222
Castiglione, Paris 065677
Castilho, Manuel, Lisboa 079896
Castillo de Javier, Javier 035306
Castillo de Loarre, Loarre 035360
Castillo de los Tres Reyes del Morro, La Habana 007941
Castillo de San Felipe del Morro, San Juan 032730
Castillo de San Marcos Museum, Saint Augustine 047606
Castillo de Sobroso, Villasobroso . . 036068
Castillon, Toulon (Var) 101318
Le Castillon, Toulon (Var) 124962
Castillos de Guayana la Vieja, Guayana 049495
Castine Scientific Society Museum, Castine 042653
The Castle, Marietta 045670
Castle, Ian, Eppstein 125592
Castle Air Museum, Atwater 041884
Castle and Regimental Museum, Monmouth 040489
Castle Antiques, Burnham-on-Sea . 083807
Castle Antiques, Deddington 084153
Castle Antiques, Deganwy 084156
Castle Antiques, Downham Market . 084217
Castle Antiques, Gent 058176
Castle Antiques, Nottingham 086131
Castle Antiques, Orford 086165
Castle Antiques, Vancouver 059345
Castle Antiques, Waitara 056793
Castle Antiques, Warwick 087037
Castle Antiques Centre, Middleham 085983
Castle Antiques Centre, Westerham 087096, 131669
Castle Arte e Antiguidades, Rio de Janeiro 058567
Castle Arts, Canterbury 112800
Castle Ashby Gallery, Castle Ashby . 083891
Castle Ashby Gallery, Castle Ashby . 112822
Castle Ashby Gallery, Castle Ashby . 130518
Castle Book's, Edinburgh 141577
Castle Bookshop, Colchester 141529
Castle Brand Visitor Centre, Nenagh 022843
Castle Cary and District Museum, Castle Cary 039008
Castle Clinton, New York 046305
Castle Close Antiques, Dornoch . . . 084210
Castle Combe Museum, Castle Combe 039009
Castle Coole, Enniskillen 039446
Castle Cornet Military and Maritime Museums, Saint Peter Port 040934
Castle Douglas Art Gallery, Castle Douglas 039011
Castle Fine Art, Bridge-of-Weir 130435
Castle Frames, Caerphilly 112778
Castle Fraser, Sauchen 040962
Castle Galleries, Cape Town 080680
Castle Galleries, Cardiff 112808
Castle Galleries, Nottingham 114173
Castle Galleries, Salisbury 086492
Castle Galleries, Southampton 114456
Castle Galleries, York 114750
Castle Gallery, Inverness 113298
Castle Gate Antiques Centre, Newark-on-Trent 086050
Castle Gate Gallery, Dunster 112971
Castle Hill Books, Kington 141696
Castle Hill Gallery, Reading 114299
Castle Hill Museum, Pembroke 040681
Castle Hill National Historic Park, Placentia 006155
Castle Keep Museum, Newcastle-upon-Tyne 040546
Castle Menzies, Aberfeldy 038455
Castle Military Museum, Cape Town 034576
Castle Museum, Clitheroe 039099
Castle Museum, Colchester 039117
Castle Museum, Gonder 009445
Castle Museum, Norwich 040603
Castle Museum, York 041474
Castle Museum of Saginaw County History, Saginaw 047602
Castle of Antiquities, Hong Kong . . . 059601
Castle of Saint John, Stranraer 041134
Castle Park Arts Centre, Frodsham . 039527
Castle Point Transport Museum, Canvey Island 038985
Castle Reclamation, Martock 085959, 131271
Castle Restoration, Auchtertool . . . 130317
Castle Rushen, Manx National Heritage, Castletown 039015
Castle Story, Newark-on-Trent 040530
Castle Tucker, Wiscasset 049268
Castle Upholstery, Dublin 127094
Castle Ward, Downpatrick 039280
Castleford Museum Room, Castleford 039012
Castlegate House Gallery, Cockermouth 112884
Castlemaine Antiques, Castlemaine 055644
Castlemaine Art Gallery and Historical Museum, Castlemaine 000902
Castlemaine Collectors Centre, Castlemaine 055645
Castlemart, Geraldton 055873
Castleton, Indianapolis 089279
Castleton, Indianapolis 116447
Castleton Historical Society Museum, Castleton 042654
Castleton Village Museum, Castleton 039014
Castletown, Teach Chaisleán an Bhaile, Celbridge 022708
Castletown Museum, Gerston 039539
Častnyj Muzej Grammofonov i Fonografov, Sankt-Peterburg 033728
Casto, Gent 120755
Castor, Göteborg 081799, 110907
Castor, Zug 083044
Castor and District Museum, Castor 005237
Castorano, Luigi, Roma 127962
Castreau, Jean, Vernon 068786
Castrillo Libreria, Madrid 141032
Castro, Barcelona 080830
Castro, Amanda, Sacramento 092142
Castro, Antonio, Sevilla 141071
Castro, Juan Manuel de, Buenos Aires 136707
Castro, Meira, Rio de Janeiro 058568
Castro, Ricardo, Barcelona 080831, 129335
Castro e Rosa, Lizaura Marques de, Porto Alegre 123695
Castro & Silva, Lisboa 140827
Castropola, Pula 137760
Castrum, Eger 074731
Castrum Peregrini, Amsterdam 135994
Castrum Peregrini Presse, Amsterdam 134776, 135995
Casubolo, Mariangela, Roma 106505
Cat, Marianne, Marseille 099646
Cat, Tuong, Ha Noi 120454
Cat Alley, San Diego 119494
Cat & Fiddle Gallery, Upper Coomera 095358
Cat in the Window, Keswick 084831
The Cat & the Fiddle, Regina 059085
Catacombes, Paris 013560
Catala, Marie-Christine, Genève . . . 082412
Catala, Pierre-Yves, Moulins (Allier) 064814
Catala-Roca, Francesco, Barcelona 110128
Catalane, Céret 124174
Cataldi, Giorgio, Marseille 064333
Catalina, Tucson 093212
Catalina Island Museum, Avalon . . . 041941
Catalonia Grafic, Barcelona 110129
Catalpa, Nykøbing Falster 060395, 098596
Catalyst, Science Discovery Centre, Widnes 041383
Catanach, Armadale, Victoria 055365, 123179
Catanach, Amanda, Broome 055569
Catarsis, Madrid 110470

Catawba County Museum of History, Newton . . . 046479
Catawba Science Center, Hickory . . 044525
Catawissa Railroad Museum, Catawissa . . . 042656
Catch-All, Salt Lake City . . . 092423
Catch All Five, Los Angeles . . . 089714
Cátedra Ediciones, Madrid . . . 134939
Catedral Antiguidades, Rio de Janeiro . . . 058569
Catelin, Gilles, Montluçon . . . 064706
Catellani, Anna, Stockholm . . . 129857
Catenazzi, Luigi, Locarno . . . 082582
Cater Museum, Billericay . . . 038709
Catera, Carlo, Roma . . . 127963
Caters, Jacques-Emmanuel de, Bruxelles . . . 057878
Caters, Jacques-Emmanuel de, Bruxelles . . . 057879
Cates & Co., Mary, Dallas . . . 088474
Cathach, Dublin . . . 139962
Catharina, Groningen . . . 078409
Cathay, Paris . . . 065678
Cathay, Singapore . . . 080440
Cathcartston Visitor Centre, Dalmellington . . . 039202
Cathedral Gallery, Lichfield . . . 113391
Cathedral Jewellers, Manchester . . 085911
Cathedral Museum, Mdina . . . 028025
Cathedral of Saint John the Divine Museum, New York . . . 046306
Cathedral Treasury, Chichester . . . 039067
Cathedral Treasury Museum, Carlisle . . . 038997
Cathédrale d'Images, Les Baux-de-Provence . . . 012604
Cather & Brown, Birmingham . . . 142237
Cathers & Dembrosky, New York . . 090770
Cather's Furniture, Richmond . . . 132710
Cathey Antiques, Nottingham . . . 086132
Catholic Historical Society of the Roanoke Valley Museum, Roanoke . . . 047466
Cathrinesminde Teglværksmuseum, Broager . . . 008826
Cathy's Antiques, Dallas . . . 088475
Catley, Brendon, Tauranga 079262, 128964
The Catlin House Museum, Scranton . . . 048062
Catlins Historical Museum, Owaka . 030563
Cato, Jans 6000 Klosterwall 19-2 1, Hamburg . . . 103105
Cato, Lennox, Edenbridge 084270, 130672
Cato Crane & Co., Liverpool . . . 122574
Caton, Hyères . . . 063189
Caton, Peter, Brighton, Victoria . . . 094282
Catot, Olivier, Marseille . . . 124404
Catrice, Wasquehal . . . 069044
Catrina, Jeannette, Oetwil am See . 111798
Cats, Bernard, Bruxelles . . . 096169
Cats, Bernard, Knokke-Heist . . . 096331
Cats Eye, Chicago . . . 088049
Cats Paw, Cleveland . . . 088317
Catskill Fly Fishing Center and Museum, Livingston Manor . . . 045356
Cattai, Michela, Milano . . . 075661
Cattaneo & C., Natalina, Genova . . . 075455
Cattaraugus Area Historical Center, Cattaraugus . . . 042659
Cattedra di Archeologia e Storia dell'Arte Greca e Romana, Facolta di Lettera e Filosfia, Libera Universita Maria SS Assunta, Roma . . . 050421
Cattelani, Marco, Basel . . . 082135
Cattet, Alexandre, Paris . . . 065679
Cattiaux, Chantal, Douchy-les-Mines . . . 062728
Cattiaux, Didier, Josselin . . . 063252
Cattle, Barbara, York . . . 087286
Cattle Raisers Museum, Fort Worth 044005
Catto, Wien . . . 137298
Catto Gallery, London . . . 113532
Catucci, Elio, Genova . . . 127440
Catullus, Stockholm . . . 081936
Catus, Bologna . . . 105952
Caudine, Laurent, Moncayolle-Larrory-Mendibi . . . 124447
Caudron, Christian, Montreuil-sous-Bois . . . 124463
Caudwell's Mill & Craft Centre, Matlock . . . 040432
Cauet, Christian, Longueau . . . 063988
Caula, Jacqueline, Pertuis . . . 066777
Caulfeild Gallery, Vancouver . . . 097436
Caulfield Antique Warehouse, Caulfield South . . . 055656, 123210
Caulfield Auction Centre, Caulfield South . . . 120576
La Causa, Milwaukee . . . 117176
Causans, Etienne de, Paris 065680, 100128
Causeway School Museum, Bushmills . . . 038931
Causey Antique Shop, Gosforth, Tyne and Wear . . . 084485
Causse, Georges, Saint-Sulpice-de-Favières . . . 068010
Causse, Henri, Sainte-Enimie . . . 068054
Caussignac, Jean-Claude, Lavaur . 063557
Van Cauter, Johan, Sint-Niklaas . . . 123671
Cauthorn Memorial Depot and Sutton County Jail, Sonora . . . 048224
CAV Antiques, Providence . . . 092037
Cavalcade of Costume, Blandford Forum . . . 038765
Uchoa Cavalcanti, Rio de Janeiro . . 096598
Cavaleri, Carlo, Mendrisio . . . 082655
Cavaleri, Gianfranco, Genova . . . 075456
Cavalier, Chicago . . . 088050
Cavalier Antiques, Glenelg 055887, 123230
Cavalier Block, Halifax . . . 005568
Cavaliere, Giancarlo, Milano . . . 127562
Cavalière, Henri, Toulon (Var) . . . 068446
Cavalieri, Luciano, Roma . . . 127964
Cavaliero, New York . . . 117754
Il Cavalletto, Locarno . . . 111649
Cavallino Edizioni, Venezia 106736, 134704
Cavallo, Carlo, Torino . . . 076798, 128280
Cavallo, S., New York . . . 090771
Cavan County Museum, Ballyjamesduff . . . 022689
Cavanagh, Carrol, New York . . . 117755
Cavani Antichitá, Modena . . . 075904
The Cave, Washington . . . 120272
Cave, F. & C.H., Northampton . . . 086096
Cave & Sons, R.G., Ludlow . . . 085862
Cave and Basin National Historic Site, Parks Canada, Banff . . . 005063
Cave au Grenier, Montréal . . . 123784
Cave au Grenier, Paris . . . 065681
Cave au Grenier, Ségny . . . 068191
La Cave aux Curiosités, Lyon . . . 064102
La Cave aux Sculptures, Dénezé-sous-Doué . . . 011578
La Cave D'Arts, Louviers . . . 099528
Cave des Chartreux, Voiron . . . 015330
Caveau, Bologna . . . 075065
Caveau des Récollets, Château-du-Loir . . . 062183, 099121
Caveau Muséalisé, Cave Coopérative, Cabrières . . . 011044
Caveau-Musée des Jacobines, Santenay . . . 014666
Caveau-Musée Les Vignerons de Roueïre, Quarante . . . 013968
Cavecanem, Sevilla . . . 110765
Cavehill Gallery, Belfast . . . 112608
Cavellini, Piero, Brescia . . . 105995
Cavelti-Giuliani, Andreas, Gossau . . 141257
Cavenaghi, Gianfranco, Milano . . . 106192
Cavendish, Fremantle . . . 055842
Cavendish, Rupert, London . . . 085183
Cavendish Antiques, York . . . 087287
Cavendish Fine Arts, Sonning-on-Thames . . . 086639
Cavendish Laboratory, Cambridge . 038961
Cavendish Rose Antiques, Cavendish . . . 083893
Caveri & Caveri, Milano . . . 075662
La Caverne, Nangis . . . 064885
Caverne, Tampa . . . 093114
La Caverne d'Ali Baba, Cercles . . . 062053
La Caverne d'Ali Baba, Perpignan . . 066737
Caverne d'Antan, Hangest-en-Santerre . . . 063124
Caverne des Arts, Chantilly . . . 099116
La Caverne des Particuliers, Alfortville . . . 060778
Caverne des Particuliers, Créteil . . . 062564
Caverne des Particuliers Alma, Creil 062555
Cavernes de l'Abîme à Couvin, Couvin . . . 003379
Les Caves des Minimes, Bruxelles . 057880
Caves Muséalisées Byrrh, Thuir . . . 014951
Les Caves Rupestres, Rochecorbon 014074
Cavestany, Madrid . . . 081272
Caviart, Rouen . . . 101112
Cavicchi Vannoni, Prato . . . 076250
Cavicchioli, Rossella, Modena . . . 075905
Caviezel, Claudio, Bern . . . 129953
Caviglia, Enrico, Maroggia . . . 082647
Cavite City Library Museum, Cavite 031647
Cawdor Castle, Cawdor . . . 039023
Cawi, Elisabeth, Hamburg . . . 071217
Cawood Antiques, Cawood . . . 083895
Caxton, Dublin . . . 074898
Cayfosa, Mogoda . . . 134950
Caylar, Guy, Bédarieux . . . 061319
Caylus Anticuario, Madrid . . . 081273
Cayman Arts, Miami . . . 117043
Cayón, Madrid . . . 122045
Cayon, Troyes . . . 101390
Cayuga Museum, Auburn . . . 041888
Cayuga-Owasco Lakes Historical Society Museum, Moravia . . . 046020
Cazaban, Jean-Louis, Paris . . . 065682
Cazac, Abel, Perpignan . . . 066738
Cazal, Patrick, Biarritz . . . 061456
Cazals de Fabel, Paris . . . 065683
Cazanove, Michelle, Le Gosier . . . 105466
Cazaux, Christian, Bordeaux . . . 120937
Cazeau-Beraudière, Paris . . . 100129
Cazenave, Edwina, Biarritz . . . 061457
Cazenovia College Chapman Art Center Gallery, Cazenovia . . . 042661
Cazzulani, Massimiliano, Milano . . . 127563
C.B. Restauración, Burgos . . . 129458
CBA Gallery, Tokyo . . . 107026
CBC, Perugia . . . 127871
CBC Museum, Toronto . . . 006590
CBC Radio Museum, Saint John's . 006362
CBO Antiquités, Roanne . . . 067164
C.B.O-Comptoir Belfortain de l'Or, Belfort . . . 061325
Cc-22, Madrid . . . 110471
CC Arts Gallery, Vancouver . . . 097437
CC Kunst, Stuttgart . . . 104970
C.C. Silver and Gold, Phoenix . . . 091725
CCA-Centre for Contemporary Arts, Glasgow . . . 039549, 135153
CCA Galleries, Farnham . . . 039488
CCA Galleries, Farnham . . . 113056
CCA Galleries, Farnham . . . 135149
CCA Galleries, London . . . 113533, 135202
CCAA Glasgalerie Köln, Köln . . . 103607
CCAC Institute, California College of Arts and Crafts, Oakland . . . 046592
CCC-Cartoon-Caricature-Contor, München . . . 104164, 134226
CCC Weeks Gallery, Jamestown . . . 044828
CCNOA, Bruxelles . . . 003294
c.d.n. Galeria, Warszawa . . . 109105
CDS Gallery, New York . . . 117756
C.E. Smith Museum of Anthropology, California State University, Hayward . . . 044492
Čebelarski Muzej, Muzeji Radovljiške Občine, Radovljica . . . 034515
Čeboksarskij Vystavočnyj Zal, Čeboksary . . . 033060
Cebriá Saez, Vicente, Valencia . . . 129765
Cebrian, Miguel, Zaragoza . . . 081738
Cebu Archdiodesan Museum, Cebu 031653
Cebu City Museum, Cebu . . . 031654
Cebu City State College Museum, Cebu . . . 031655
CECA International Committee for Education and Cultural Action of Museums, Mumbai . . . 053694
Ceccarelli, Evelino, Perugia . . . 127872
Ceccarelli, Glauco, Basel . . . 129916
Ceccarelli, Luciano, Roma . . . 127965
Ceccatelli Piacenti, Sandra, Prato . . 127888
Ceccherelli, Renato, Genova . . . 075457
Cecchini, Perugia . . . 106458
Cecchini, Aldo, Roma . . . 127966
Cecchini, Rolando, Roma . . . 127967
Cecconi, Andrea, Wien . . . 057390
Ceccotti, Carlo, Roma . . . 127968
Cecelia Coker Bell Gallery, Coker College, Art Dept., Hartsville . . . 044466
Čech a Syn, Blansko . . . 059970
Cecil Clark Davis Gallery, Marion . . 045682
Cecil Higgins Art Gallery, Bedford . . 038656
Cecilie Antikk, Bergen . . . 079374
Cecille R. Hunt Gallery, Webster University, Sankt Louis . . . 047944
Cedar Antique Centre, Hartley Wintney . . . 084599, 130768
Cedar Cliff Collectibles, Saint Paul . 092354
Cedar Falls Historical Museum, Cedar Falls . . . 042665
Cedar Grove Galleries, Morpeth . . . 056260
Cedar Grove Historical Society Museum, Cedar Grove . . . 042669
Cedar Grove Mansion, Philadelphia Museum of Art, Philadelphia . . . 046928
Cedar Grove Mansion Inn, Vicksburg . . . 048777
Cedar House Antiques, Mullumbimby . . . 056302
Cedar House Gallery, Ripley, Surrey 114318
Cedar Key Historical Society Museum, Cedar Key . . . 042670
Cedar Key State Park Museum, Cedar Key . . . 042671
Cedar Lodge Antiques, Newtown, Victoria . . . 056341
Cedar Rapids Museum of Art, Cedar Rapids . . . 042674
Cedar Root Gallery, Vancouver . . . 097438
Cedar Street Galleries, Honolulu . . . 116201
Cedar Street Galleries, Honolulu . . . 116202
Cedar Valley Memories, Osage . . . 046730
CEDCO Publishing Company, San Rafael . . . 135498
Cederbergs, Sävedalen . . . 081891
Cederwall, San Francisco . . . 119633
CEDIAS Musée Social, Paris . . . 013561
Cédille, Paris . . . 100130
Los Cedros, Madrid . . . 081274, 129588
Cee-Jay, Richmond . . . 092067, 132711
Cefn Coed Colliery Museum, Neath 040516
Ceh, Gabriela, Buchen . . . 070076
Cein, Julio y Fernando, Córdoba . . . 055253
Ceiriog Memorial Institute, Glyn Ceiriog . . . 039595
Cejnar, Peter, Wien . . . 057391
Cejudo Perez, Rafael, Córdoba . . . 081047
Cel-Art, Hong Kong . . . 097763
Celadon, Rio de Janeiro . . . 058570
Celamuse - Porcelain Museum, Seoul . . . 027544
Celant, Geneviève, Clermont-Ferrand . . . 062332
Celantique, Paray-Vieille-Poste . . . 065337
Celbridge Motor Museum, Celbridge 022709
Celebration Antiques, Philadelphia . 091619
A Celebration of Immigration, London . . . 040111
Celebration of Irish Museum, Carrickmacross . . . 022701
Celebrity Art Galery, Paris . . . 100131
Celebrity Coin, Milwaukee . . . 090282
Celebrity Sports Gallery, Houston . . 142432
Čelekenskij Muzej, Čeleken . . . 038205
Celest, Varna . . . 096765
Celeste & Co., Las Vegas . . . 089556
Celeste & Eliot, Zürich . . . 112053
Celestial, Lynn, Chicago . . . 115385
Celestial Galleries, Fortitude Valley . 094558

Celi, Maria Liliana, Taranto 076746
Célia, B. Guedj, Lyon 099546
Celinda's Doll Shoppe, Minneapolis 132378
Céline Antiquaire, Montréal 058934
Celinogradskij Istoriko-Kraevedčeskij Muzej, Astana 027395
Čeljabinskaja Oblastnaja Kartinnaja Galerija, Čeljabinsk 033067
Čeljabinskij Oblastnoj Kraevedčeskij Muzej, Čeljabinsk 033068
Cellar Antiques, Hawes 084628
Cellar Antiques, Orroroo 056411
Cellar Coin, San Diego 092621
Cellar Gallery, Chippenham 112863
Cellar Stories, Providence 142815
Cellensia, Celle 138959
Cellier, Châtellerault 062216
Cellier, Jean-Pierre, Belfort 061326
Cellini, Berlin 101827
Cellini, Bridgnorth 112700
Cellini, Leiden 108099
Cellini, Portland 118987
Celma, Firenze 106040
Celma Albuquerque Galeria de Arte, Belo Horizonte 096455
Celma Delgado, Maria Carmen, Barcelona 080832
Celotti, Vincent, Vevey 082879
Cels, Hamburg 103106
Celsius, Amsterdam 077815
Celsius Artes e Antiguidades, Brasília 058459
Celtic Antique, Firenze 075311
Celtic Headquarters, Amsterdam . . 077816
Cemal Reşit Rey Galerisi, İstanbul . 112295
Cementmuseet Slemmestad, Slemmestad 031199
Cemerin, Lindau, Bodensee 103918
Cenacolo del Ghirlandaio, Firenze . 024144
Cenacolo di Sant'Apollonia, Firenze 024145
Cenacolo Vinciano, Milano 024687
Cenarius, Luanda 094049
Cénatus, Pont-Pean 066930
El Cencerro, Rosario 055292, 123172
Cencor, Lima 129003
Cendre, Jean-Luc, Prey 066983
Cenedella, Robert, New York 117757
Cennosti, Sofia 135614
Cent 8, Paris 100132
Cent 8, Paris 100133
Le Cent Garde, Nice 065060
Cent Noranta, Barcelona 080833
Centar Savremene Umjetnosti Crne Gore, Podgorica 034240
Centar za Fotografiju, Film i Televiziju, Muzej Suvremene Umjetnosti, Zagreb 007830
Centar za Grafiku i Vizuelna Istraživanja, Beograd 109686
Centar za Sovremeni Umetnosti Skopje, Skopje 027916
Centaur Boekhandel, Den Haag . . . 140389
Centaur Bookshop, Maylands, Western Australia 136994
Centaur Galleries, Las Vegas 116615
Centaurica, Amsterdam 107694
Il Centauro, Pisa 076240
Centelli, Franco, Firenze 127316
Le Centenaire, Hydra 055136
Centenary Antique Centre, Newcastle 056331
Centennial Art Gallery, Calgary 096795
The Centennial Museum at the University of Texas at El Paso, El Paso 043634
Centennial Museum of Canmore, Canmore 005211
Centennial Museum of Sheguiandah, Sheguiandah 006453
Centennial Museum of the Nanaimo Regional General Hospital, Nanaimo 005979
Centennial Park 1910 Logging Museum, Thunder Bay 006564
Centennial Village Museum, Greeley 044302
Center Art Gallery, Grand Rapids . . 044273
Center Art Studio, New York 132451
Center for Advanced Visual Studies, Massachusetts Institute of Technology, Cambridge 051062
Center for Agricultural Science and Heritage, Indianapolis 044734
Center for American Archeology, Kampsville 044906
Center for American History, Austin 041923
Center for American Music, Stephen Foster Memorial, Pittsburgh 047046
Center for Art and Design Studies, Cazenovia College, Cazenovia . . . 051084
Center for Arts Administration, Graduate School of Business, University of Wisconsin Madison, Madison 051659
Center for Arts Criticism, Minneapolis 045909
Center for Book Arts, New York . . . 046307
Center for Contemporary Art, Kyïv . 038292
Center for Contemporary Art, Sacramento 119141
Center for Contemporary Art Kitakyushu, Kitakyushu 026659
Center for Contemporary Arts of Santa Fe, Santa Fe 047962
Center for Contemporary Graphic Art and Tyler Graphics Archive Collection, Sukagawa 027091
Center for Creative Photography, University of Arizona, Tucson 048631
Center for Cultural Arts, Gadsden . . 044100
Center for Curatorial Studies, Annandale-on-Hudson 041738
Center for Emerging Art, Miami . . . 117044
Center for Exploratory and Perceptual Art, Buffalo 042504
Center for Intuitive and Outsider Art, Chicago 042827
Center for Jewish Art, Hebrew University of Jerusalem, Jerusalem . . 050350, 134535
Center for Maine Contemporary Art, Rockport 047507
Center for Photography at Woodstock, Woodstock 049292
Center for Puppetry Arts, Atlanta . . 041851
Center for the Arts, Tucson 120114
Center for the Arts, Vero Beach . . . 048771
Center for the Arts, University of Wisconsin La Crosse, La Crosse 051560
Center for the Arts, Wesleyan University, Middletown 051706
Center for the Arts at Yerba Buena Gardens, San Francisco 047892
Center for the Visual Arts, Denver . . 043399
Center for the Visual Arts, Brandywine Workshop, Philadelphia 046929
Center for Wooden Boats, Seattle . . 048076
Center Galleries, Detroit 043436
Center Galleries, Detroit 116084
Center Garo, Yokohama 107140
Center of Arts, Cairo 098622
Center of Attention, Carrboro 136415
Center of Attention, Virginia Beach . 120218
Center of Nautical and Regional Archaeology, Nahshonim 023036
Center of the Earth Gallery, Charlotte 115280
Center on Contemporary Art, Seattle 048077
CenterCity Contemporary Arts, Providence 119073
Centerville Historical Museum, Centerville 042687
Cento Anni, Bruxelles 057881
Cento Anni, Paris 065684
Centoira, Buenos Aires 094066
Centonze, Claudio, Firenze 075312
Centorb, Rossella, Catania 075242
Centr Iskusstv 2000, Moskva 080236
Centr Istorii Aviacionnych Dvigatelej im. N.D. Kuznecova, Samarskij gosudarstvennyj aėrokosmičeskij universitet, Samara 033713
Centr Sovremennogo Iskusstva, Moskva 054020, 109501
Centraal Museum, Utrecht 030226
Central Academy of Arts and Design, Beijing 049842
Central Antiques, Mount Lawley . . . 056289
Central Antiques, Phoenix 091726
Central Archives for the History of the Jewish People, Jerusalem 022945
Central Art Gallery, Ashton-under-Lyne 038541
Central Auctions, Fyshwick 120586
Central Australian Aviation Museum, Alice Springs 000734
Central Australian Museum, Alice Springs 000735
Central Avenue Strip Shop, Toledo . 132970
Central Book Exchange, Salt Lake City 142873
Central Butte District Museum, Central Butte 005239
Central Christian Supply, Phoenix . . 142765
Central City Coins and Antiquities, Brisbane 055555
Central City Opera House Museum, Central City 042689
Central Coin and Jewlery, Denver . . 088668
Central College Museum, Bangalore 022014
Central Furniture Refinishing, Winnipeg 123864
Central Gallery, London 085184
Central Goldfields Art Gallery, Maryborough, Victoria 094793
Central Hall Artists Newsletter, Great Neck 136416
Central Hawke's Bay Settlers Museum, Waipawa 030615
Central Institute of Fine Arts, Beijing 049843
Central Iowa Art Association, Marshalltown 054700
Central Iowa Art Museum, Marshalltown 045706
Central Luzon State University Museum, Muñoz 031746
Central Markets, Hutt City 121826
Central Mart, Colac 055707
Central Missouri State University Archives and Museum, Warrensburg 048864
Central Montana Historical Association Museum, Lewistown 045252
Central Museum, Bhopal 022033
Central Museum, Indore 022175
Central Museum, Nagpur 022279
Central Nation University Museum, Beijing 006975
Central National Herbarium, Botanical Survey of India, Haora 022147
Central Nevada Museum, Tonopah . 048578
Central New Brunswick Woodmen's Museum, Boiestown 005108
Central Park Gallery, Kansas City . . 116559
Central Park Gallery, Malvern East . 094773
Central Piedmont Community College Art Gallery, Charlotte 115281
Central Saint Martin's College of Art and Design, London 050829
Central Saint Martin's College of Art and Design, London 050830
Central Sikh Museum, Amritsar . . . 022009
Central Texas Area Museum, Salado 047729
Central Texas Museum of Automotive History, Rosanky 047539
Central Texas Pastel Society, Temple 054701
Central Washington Agricultural Museum, Union Gap 048698
Centralantikvariatet, Stockholm . . . 141151
La Centrale, Montréal 096986
La Centrale dell'Arte, Roma 106506
Centralivros, Lisboa 134868
Centralne Muzeum Jeńców Wojennych w Łambinowicach -Opolu, Opole . . . 032197
Centralne Muzeum Morskie, Gdańsk 031904
Centralne Muzeum Pożarnictwa, Mysłowice 032158
Centralne Muzeum Włókiennictwa, Łódź 032106
Centralnyj Dom Chudožnikov, Moskva 033367
Centralnyj Geologorazvedočnyj Muzej im. Akademika F.N. Černyševa, Sankt-Peterburg 033729
Centralnyj Gosudarstvennyj Muzej Kazachstana, Almaty 027389
Centralnyj Muzej Aviacii i Kosmonavtiki, Moskva 033368
Centralnyj Muzej Drevnerusskoj Kultury i Isskustva im. Andreja Rubleva, Moskva 033369
Centralnyj Muzej Federalnoj Pograničnoj Služby RF, Moskva 033370
Centralnyj Muzej MVD Rossii, Moskva 033371
Centralnyj Muzej Oktjabrskoj Železnoj Dorogi, Sankt-Peterburg 033730
Centralnyj Muzej Pochvovedenija im. V.V. Dokučaeva, Sankt-Peterburg 033731
Centralnyj Muzej Svjazi im. A.S. Popova, Sankt-Peterburg 033732
Centralnyj Muzej Velikoj Otečestvennoj Vojny, Moskva 033372
Centralnyj Muzej Vooružennych Sil, Moskva 033373
Centralnyj Muzej Vserossijskogo Obščestva Slepych, Moskva 033374
Centralnyj Muzej Železnodorožnogo Transporta, Sankt-Peterburg 033733
Centralnyj Voenno-morskoj Muzej, Sankt-Peterburg 033734
Centralnyj Vystavočnyj Zal g. Perm, Perm 033646
Centralnyj Vystavočnyj Zal Manež, Moskva 033375
Centralnyj Vystavočnyj Zal Manež g. Sankt-Peterburga, Sankt-Peterburg 033735
Centre Aeri, Vilanova i la Geltrú . . . 036048
Centre Archéologique Charles-Morel, La Canourgue 012212
Centre Artistic de Sant Lluc, Barcelona 110130
Centre Artistique de la Vallée de la Creuse, Fresselines 099276
Centre Artistique de la Vallée de la Creuse, Fresselines 099277
Centre Artistique et Médiéval, Richerenches 014042
Centre Artistique Jean Baffier, Sancoins 014663
Centre Belge de la Bande Dessinée, Bruxelles 003295
Centre Bonastruç ça Porta, Girona . 035227
Centre Commémoratif de l'Holocauste à Montréal, Montréal 005915
Centre County Historical Society Museum, State College 048325
Centre County Library Historical Museum, Bellefonte 042106
Centre Cultural de la Fundació La Caixa, Vic 036027
Centre Culturel Canadien, Paris . . . 100134
Centre Culturel Coréen, Paris 100135
Centre Culturel de Verdun, Verdun . 006724
Centre Culturel des Roches, Rochefort 003718
Centre Culturel du Mexique, Paris . 100136
Centre Culturel et Patrimonial la Poudrière de Windsor, Windsor, Québec . . . 006834
Centre Culturel-Exposition d'Artistes et d'Artisans, Collombey 037025
Centre Culturel Franco-Manitobain, Winnipeg 006840
Centre Culturel Marguerite Bourgeois, Troyes 015048
Centre Culturel Suédois, Paris 100137
Centre Culturel Suisse, Paris 100138
Centre d'Archéologique et Historique, Neuville-aux-Bois 013380
Centre d'Art, Baie-Saint-Paul 005055
Centre d'Art, Port-au-Prince 021601
Centre d'Art Contemporain, Avallon 010581
Centre d'Art Contemporain, Bignan 010805
Centre d'Art Contemporain, Bruxelles 003296
Centre d'Art Contemporain, Dijon . . 011598
Centre d'Art Contemporain, Genève 037115

Centre d'Art Contemporain, Ginals . 011951
Centre d'Art Contemporain, Istres . . 012141
Centre d'Art Contemporain, Lacoux-Hauteville-Lompnes 012373
Centre d'Art Contemporain, Meymac 013050
Centre d'Art Contemporain, Mont-de-Marsan 013109
Centre d'Art Contemporain, Pau . . . 013746
Centre d'Art Contemporain, Pougues-les-Eaux 013929
Centre d'Art Contemporain, Revin . 014039
Centre d'Art Contemporain, Tanlay . 014898
Centre d'Art Contemporain, École d'Art du Rueil-Malmaison, Rueil-Malmaison 014152
Centre d'Art Contemporain, Ferme du Buisson, Noisiel 013445
Centre d'Art Contemporain Bouvet-Ladubay, Saumur 014698
Centre d'Art Contemporain de Basse-Normandie, Hérouville-Saint-Clair 012094
Centre d'Art Contemporain de Brétigny, Brétigny-sur-Orge 010989
Centre d'Art Contemporain de Castres, Castres 011148
Centre d'Art Contemporain du Creux de l'Enfer, Thiers 101310
Centre d'Art Contemporain Georges Pompidou, Cajarc 011070
Centre d'Art Contemporain la Synagogue de Delme, Delme 011569
Centre d'Art Contemporain le Quartier, Quimper 013972
Centre d'Art Contemporain Théo Argence, Saint-Priest (Rhône) 014496
Centre d'Art de Cowansville, Cowansville 005303
Centre d'Art de Lévis, Lévis 005770
Centre d'Art de Saint-Georges, Saint-Georges, Quebec 006340
Centre d'Art du Crestet, Crestet . . . 011533
Centre d'Art du Mont-Royal, Montréal 005916
Centre d'Art en l'Ile, Genève 111436
Centre d'Art et de Culture, Soignies 003772
Centre d'Art et de Plaisanterie, Scène Nationale, Montbéliard 013138
Centre d'Art et d'Exposition Jacques-Henri Lartigue, L'Isle-Adam 012706
Centre d'Art et d'Histoire André Auclair, Cruas 011541
Centre d'Art Graphique, Hameau Petit Arran, Parly 013742
Centre d'Art International, Maison de la Céramique, Mulhouse 013290
Centre d'Art le Quai de la Batterie, Arras 098864
Centre d'Art Neuchâtel, Neuchâtel . 037373
Centre d'Art Nicolas de Staël, Braine-l'Alleud 003251
Centre d'Art Passerelle, Brest 099027
Centre d'Art Présence Van Gogh, Saint-Rémy-de-Provence 014513
Centre d'Art Sacré, Patrimoine Oeuvres d'Art Romain et Baroque, Ille-sur-Têt 012131
Centre d'Art Santa Mònica, Barcelona 034902
Centre d'Art Sébastien, Saint-Cyr-sur-Mer 014246
Centre d'Artistes Vaste et Vague, Carleton 005227
Centre d'Arts Plastiques, Voûtes du Port, Royan 101127
Centre Darts Visuels de L'Alberta, Edmonton 096871
Centre de Cultura Contemporània de Barcelona, Barcelona 034903
Centre de Cultura Sa Nostra, Palma de Mallorca 035604
Centre de Culture Catalane, C.D.A.C.C., Perpignan 013783
Centre de Culture Scientifique la Rotonde Ecole des Mines, Saint-Étienne . . 014268
Centre de Découvert du Marais Breton, Le Barre-de-Monts 012461
Centre de Découverte Martime, Penmarch 013766
Centre de Documentació i Museu Tèxtil, Terrassa 035905
Centre de Documentation Arabe, Timbuktu 028022
Centre de Documentation Archéologique du Roussillon, Perpignan 013784
Centre de Documentation du Patrimoine, D.R.A.C., Montpellier 013198
Centre de la Gravure et de l'Image Imprimée de la Communauté Française de Belgique, La Louvière 003563
Centre de la Mémoire d'Oradour, Oradour-sur-Glane 013494
Centre de la Mer, Institut Océanographique, Paris 013562
Centre de la Photographie Genéve, Genève 037116
Centre de la Vieille Charité, Marseille 012928
Centre de les Arts i de les Lletres, Escaldes-Engordany 052439
Centre de Paléontologie et Archéologie, Valréas 015120
Centre de Photographie de Lectoure, Lectoure 012583
Centre de Recherches et de Documentation du Sénégal, Saint-Louis 034137
Centre de Recherches et d'Etudes Technologiques des Arts Plastiques, Bruxelles 003297
Centre de Recherches Historiques sur les Maîtres Ebénistes, Paris 013563
Centre de Scriptophilie, Deinze . . . 137489
Centre de Secours Principal, Tourcoing 015004
Centre de Vente entre Particuliers, Angers 060850
Centre d'Edition Contemporaine, Genève 037117
Centre Départmental d'Art Contemporain Cimaise et Portique, Albi 010317, 133445
Centre des Antiquaires, Attin 061018
Centre des Antiquaires, Moirans . . . 064575
Centre des Arts Contemporains du Québec à Montréal, Montréal 005917
Centre des Arts de Shawinigan, Shawinigan 006449
Centre d'Etudes Archéologiques, Eyguières 011767
Centre d'Études Historiques et Archéologiques, Le Barroux 012462
Centre d'Exposition Archéologique de l'Orangerie, Étiolles 011753
Centre d'Exposition Art-Image, Gatineau 005501
Centre d'Exposition d'Amos, Amos . 005010
Centre d'Exposition de Rouyon-Noranda, Rouyn-Noranda 006311
Centre d'Exposition de Saint-Hyacinthe, Saint-Hyacinthe 006341
Centre d'Exposition de Val d'Or, Val d'Or 006678
Centre d'Exposition du Costume, Avallon 010582
Centre d'Exposition Langevin, Grande-Synthe 011986
Centre d'Exposition l'Imagier, Aylmer 005048
Centre d'Exposition Mont-Laurier, Mont-Laurier 005901
Centre d'Exposition Plein Sud, Longueuil 005795
Centre d'Exposition Raymond-Lasnier, Maison de la Culture de Trois-Rivières, Trois-Rivières 006658
Centre d'Exposition sur l'Industrie des Pâtes et Papiers, Trois-Rivières 006659
Centre d'Hébergement, d'Étude sur la Nature et l'Environnement, Allouville-Bellefosse 010340
Centre d'Histoire de la Résistance et de la Déportation, Lyon 012806
Centre d'Histoire de Montréal, Montréal 005918
Centre d'Histoire Locale, Tourcoing 015005
Centre d'Histoire Locale du Canton de Pompey, Pompey 013875
Centre d'Iconographie Genevoise, Genève 037118
Centre d'Interpretació p.n. d'Aigüestortes i Estany de Sant Maurici, Espot . . . 035180
Centre d'Interpretation de la Métabetchouane, Desbiens 005347
Centre d'Interpretation de l'Ardoise, Richmond 006281
Centre d'Interpretation de l'Histoire de Sherbrooke, Sherbrooke, Québec 006459
Centre d'Interprétation des Luys, Brassempouy 010967
Centre d'Interpretation du Parc de l'île-Bonaventure-et-du Rocher-Percé, Percé 006131
Centre d'Interprétation du Patrimoine de Sorel, Sorel-Tracy 006491
Centre du Livre d'Artiste Contemporain, Verderonne 015171, 052921, 138650
Centre du Visiteur, Braine-l'Alleud . 003252
Centre Européen d'Actions Artistiques Contemporaines, Strasbourg 014853
Centre Européen de la Paix, Souchez 014832
Centre Européen de l'Orgue, Marmoutier 012913
Centre Européen des Métiers d'Art, Givet 011957
Centre Expo du Meuble, Marseille . 064334
Centre for African Studies Collection, University of Cape Town, Rondebosch 034742
Centre for Art Tapes, Halifax 005569
Centre for Black and African Art and Civilization, Lagos 030693
Centre for Contemporary Photography, Fitzroy 001027
Centre for Contemporary Photography, Fitzroy 094531
Centre for Creative Communities, London 054334
Centre for Creative Photography, Stepney 095223
Centre for Exhibition and Art Exchange, Ha Noi 120455
Centre for Experimental Art and Communication, Toronto 006591
Centre for Fine Art, Bruxelles 052655
Centre for the Magic Arts, London . 040112
Centre for the Study of Greek Traditional Pottery, Athinai 021164
Centre for Visual Art, University of Natal, Scottsville 050708
Centre France Estimation, Cognat-Lyonne 062379
Centre Franco-Ontarien de Folklore, Sudbury 006528
The Centre Gallery, Calgary 096796
Centre Gallery, Miami 117045
Centre Gallery, Sunderland 114519
Centre Hill Mansion, The Petersburg Museums, Petersburg 046903
Centre Historique de la Mine, de la Machine à Vapeur et du Chemin de Fer, Oignies 013478
Centre Historique de la Résistance en Drôme et de la Déportation, Romans-sur-Isère 014094
Centre Historique Minier, Lewarde . 012658
Centre International d'Art Contemporain de Montréal, Montréal 005919
Centre International d'Art-Raymond du Puy, Le Poët-Laval 012548
Centre International des Artisans d'Art, Bordeaux 052922, 124119
Centre Jean Giono, Manosque 012875
Centre Jeanne d'Arc, Orléans 013511
Centre Minier de Faymoreau, Faymoreau-les-Mines 011789
Centre Missionnaire Sainte-Therèse, Montréal 005920
Centre Muséographique, Québec . . 006215
Centre National d'Artisanat d'Art, Ouagadougou 004961
Centre National de la Photographie, Paris 013564
Centre National de la Photographie, Paris 052923, 133550
Centre National des Arts Plastiques (CNAP), Paris 133551
Centre National d'Exposition, Jonquière 005654
Centre National Musée Jean Jaurès, Castres 011149
Centre of Contemporary Art, Christchurch 030461
Centre Permanent d'Exposition de Poupées Anciennes, Lyons-la-Forêt 012836
Centre Philatélique de Polynésie Française, Papeete 015392
Centre Photographique d'Ile-de-France, Pontault-Combault 013903
Centre pour l'Image Contemporaine Saint-Gervais, Genève 037119
Centre Provincial d'Hébergement Le Caillou, Maison Emile Verhaeren, Roisin . . 003725
Centre Régional d'Art Contemporain, Fontenoy-en-Puisaye 011856
Centre Régional d'Art Contemporain, Montbéliard 013139
Centre Régional d'Art Contemporain, Sète 014778
Centre Régional de la Photographie, Douchy-les-Mines 099241
Centre Régional de la Photographie Nord-Pas-de-Calais, Douchy-les-Mines 011646, 133466
Centre Régional de Restauration et Conservation d'Œuvres d'Art, Vesoul 125020
Centre Rhenan d'Art Contemporain, Altkirch 098818
Centre Social i Cultural de la Fundació La Caixa, Lleida 035344
Centre Tomi Ungerer, Musées de Strasbourg, Strasbourg 014854
Centricity, New York 090772
Centro Agost, Museo de Alfarería, Agost 034781
Centro Ambientale Archeologico, Archeologico Museo Civico, Legnano 024491
Centro Andaluz de Arte Contemporáneo, Sevilla 035854
Centro Andino de Tecnología Tradicional y Cultura de la Comunidades, Ollantaytambo 031578
Centro Arte Contemporanea, Napoli 024889
Centro Arte Contemporanea, Napoli 106360
Centro Arte La Tesoriera, Torino . . . 106669
Centro Arte Moderna, Pisa 106466
Centro Atlántico de Arte Moderno, Las Palmas de Gran Canaria 035622
Centro Camuno di Studi Preistorici, Capo di Ponte 023642
Centro Ceremonial de Caguana, San Juan 032731
Centro Comercio e Moveis Usados, Rio de Janeiro 058571
Centro Cultural Banco do Brasil, Rio de Janeiro 004335
Centro Cultural Conde Duque, Madrid 035372
Centro Cultural Contemporaneo Pelaires, Palma de Mallorca 110673
Centro Cultural Corp Group, Caracas 049448
Centro Cultural de la Fundació la Caixa, Barcelona 034904
Centro Cultural de la Raza, San Diego 047816
Centro Cultural España Córdoba, Córdoba 000288
Centro Cultural Isidro Fabela, México 028424
Centro Cultural Paraguayo-Americano, Asunción 031438
Centro Cultural Paraguayo-Argentino, Concepción 031451
Centro Cultural Torre de la Calahorra, Fundación Roger Garaudy, Córdoba 035110
Centro Culturale Polivalente, Bagnacavallo 023317
Centro d'Arte, Firenze 106041
Centro d'Arte Contemporanea Ticino, Bellinzona 036915

Centro d'Arte La Maddalena, Genova 106087
Centro d'Arte Puccini, Firenze 106042
Centro d'Arte Verrocchio, Casole d'Elsa 023694
Centro de Arqueologia Annete Laminge Emperaire, Lagoa Santa 004179
Centro de Arte Caja de Burgos, Burgos 035001
Centro de Arte Contemporaneo, Málaga 110635
Centro de Arte Contemporáneo la Fábrica, Abarca de Campos 034780
Centro de Arte Jaime Trigo, Pontevedra 081532
Centro de Arte Joven, Madrid 110472
Centro de Arte La Cañuela, Caracas 049449
Centro de Arte La Estancia, Caracas 049450
Centro de Arte Moderna da Fundação Calouste Gulbenkian, Lisboa 032627
Centro de Arte Moderno y Contemporáneo Daniel Vázquez Díaz, Nerva 035542
Centro de Arte Visuales, Lima 031542
Centro de Arte y Antiguedades, Guadalajara 077562
Centro de Artes e Comunicação, Universidade Federal de Pernambuco, Recife 049752
Centro de Artes Visuales, Museo del Barro, Asunción 031439
Centro de Artistas Plásticos, Montevideo 041501
Centro de Bellas Artes, Maracaibo . 052422
Centro de Biologia Marinha, São Sebastião 004561
Centro de Ciencia y Tecnología, Guadalajara 028275
Centro de Desarrollo de las Artes Visuales, La Habana 007942
Centro de Diseño Ambiental, La Habana 007943
Centro de Documentación Musical, Casa Museo Andrés Segovia, Linares . . 035333
Centro de Educação Ambiental Gralha Azul e Museu de História Natural, Cascavel 004059
Centro de Estudios Conservacionistas, Guatemala 021576
Centro de Estudios de Restauración de Obras de Arte, Madrid 129589
Centro de Estudios Folklóricos, Guatemala 021577
Centro de Estudios Árabes y Arqueológicos Ibn Arabi, Murcia 035528
Centro de Estudos Murilo Mendes, Juiz de Fora 004171
Centro de Exposiciónes de Geologia y Mineria, Buenos Aires 000144
Centro de Exposiciones La Casona de los Olivera, Buenos Aires 000145
Centro de Exposiciones Ses Voltes Parc de la Mar, Palma de Mallorca 035605
Centro de Fotografía, Santa Cruz de Tenerife 035793
Centro de Información e Interpretación del Parque de Pagoeta, Aia 034787
Centro de Interpretación del P.N. de las Hoces del Río Duratón, Sepúlveda 035849
Centro de Interpretación del P.N. del Cañon del Río Lobos, Ucero 035962
Centro de Interpretación del P.N. del Lago de Sanabria, San Martín de Castañeda 035762
Centro de Investigatión de las Artes Escénicas, Miramar 049884
Centro de Mesonero Romanos, Casa de la Panadería, Madrid 035373
Centro de Pesquisas Folclóricas, Rio de Janeiro 004336
Centro de Pesquisas Paleontológicas da Bacia do Araripe, Crato 004073
Centro de Restauración Irene, Madrid 129590
Centro de Restauración Los Leones, Santiago de Chile 123878
Centro del Bel Libro, Ascona 129900
Centro del Diseño, Bilbao 034983
Centro della Cornice, Milano 075663, 127564
Centro della Stampa Azed, Lugano . 135038
Centro Di, Firenze 140010
Centro di Arte Contemporanea, Roma 106507
Centro Di della Edifimi, Firenze . . . 134582
Centro di Documentazione Messapica, Oria 025002
Centro di Informazione e Documentazione Arti Visive, Archivio Biblioteca Arte Comtempoanea, Prato 025357
Centro di Palazzo Doria, Genova . . . 127441
Centro di Porta Altinate, Padova . . . 076083
Centro di Restauro, Firenze 127317
Centro di Restauro, Milano 127565
Centro di Restauro Artistico e Monumentale, Genova 127442
Centro di Scienze Naturali e Raccolta Natura ed Arte, Prato 025358
Centro di Scultura Contemporanea, Cagli 023557
Centro di Studi per la Storia dell'Architettura, Roma 050422
Centro di Studi Salentini, Lecce . . . 134595
Centro Escolar University Museum and Archives, Manila 031719
Centro Etnográfico Joaquín Díaz, Urueña 035965
Centro Ferroviário de Cultura, Volta Grande 004609
Centro Fotográfico Álvarez Bravo, Oaxaca 028602
Centro Galego de Arte Contemporáneo, Santiago de Compostela 035816
Centro Histórico-Cultural de Enfermagem Ibero- americana, Escola de Enfermagem / EE, São Paulo 004499
Centro Internazionale di Brera, Milano 134607
Centro Internazionale di Ceramica, Roma 050423
Centro Maggiori, Collezione di Disegni di Antichi Maestri, Monte San Giusto 024816
Centro Mundo Aborigen, Córdoba . . 000289
Centro Municipal de Exposiciones, Elche 035164
Centro Municipal de Exposiciones Subste, Montevideo 041502
Centro Museo Universitario di Storia Naturale e della Strumentazione Scientifica, Modena 024750
Centro Nacional de Conservación, Restauración y Museología, La Habana 123949, 133410
Centro Nacional de Documentação e Investigação Histórica, Luanda . . 000093
Centro Nazionale di Studi Alfieriani, Asti 023286
Centro Numismatico, Ascona 082096
Centro Opere d'Arte, Taranto 076747, 106650, 121729
Centro Parque Nacional Picos de Europa - Casa Dago, Cangas de Onis 035046
Centro per l'Arte Contemporanea Luigi Pecci, Prato 025359
Centro Pró-Memória do Club Athlético Paulistano, São Paulo 004500
Centro Pró-Memória Hans Nobiling do Esporte Clube Pinheiros, São Paulo 004501
Centro Regional de Arqueologia Ambiental, Piraju 004281
Centro Regional de Pesquisas Archeológicas Mário Neme, Piraju 004282
Centro Restauro Meranese, Merano 127497
Centro Restauro Mobili Antichi, Torino 076799, 128281
Centro Storico Fiat, Torino 026045
Centro Studi di Arte Comparata e Ricerche Interdisciplinari, Bari 053744
Centro Studi I. Silone, Pescina 025197
Centro Studi L. A. Muratori, Modena 053745
Centro Studi Naturalistici del Pollino Il Nibbio, Morano Calabro 024878
Centro Universitario Europeo per i beni Culturali, Ravello 050411
Centrum Arts and Creative Education, Port Townsend 047140
Centrum Beeldende Kunst, Groningen 029636
Centrum Beeldende Kunst, Nijmegen 108150
Centrum Beeldende Kunst Dordrecht, Dordrecht 107976
Centrum Beeldende Kunst Emmen, Emmen 029558
Centrum Beeldende Kunst Utrecht, Amersfoort 029148
Centrum Fornikling, Oslo 079431
Centrum Kultury i Sztuki Afrykańskiej, Kraków 032022
Centrum Kunsthistorische Documentatie, Katholieke Universiteit, Nijmegen 050565
Centrum Kunstlicht in de Kunst, Eindhoven 029537
Centrum Młodzieży, Kraków 108932
Centrum Muzeologiczne przy Muzeum Sztuki, Łódź 053977
Centrum Pamięci Gen. Józefa Hallera, Władysławowo 032499
Centrum Rysunku i Grafiki im. Tadeuza Kulisiewicza, Muzeum Okręgowego Ziemi Kaliskiej w Kaliszu, Kalisz 031975
Centrum Rzeźby Polskiej, Oronsko . 032202
Centrum Sztuki Studio im S.I. Witkiewicza, Warszawa 032420
Centrum Sztuki Współczesnej, Warszawa 032421
Centrum Sztuki Współczesnej Łaźnia, Gdańsk 031905
Centrum voor de Vlaamse Kunst van de 16de en de 17de Eeuw, Antwerpen 003155
Centrum voor Heiligenbeelden, Kranenburg 029822
Centrum voor Natuur en Landschap, Terschelling-West 030196
La Centuria, Buenos Aires 055192
Centuries, Birmingham 087746
Centuries, Minneapolis 090348
Centuries 46, Brno 059977
Centuries Old Maps and Prints, New Orleans 142607
Centurion Galleries, Chicago 115386
Century, Charlotte 087934
Century Antique Watch, Singapore . 080441
Century Antiques, Cleveland 088318
Century Arts and Antiques, New York 090773
Century Box, München 072675
Century Coins, Pittsburgh 091797
Century Fine Arts, Lymington 085877
Century Furniture Restoration, Hamilton 123770
Century Galleries, Henley-on-Thames 113232
Century Gallery, Slough 114441
Century Gallery, Sylmar 048451
Century Modern, Dallas 088476
Century of Stone Gallery, Louisville 116932
Century Pine, Loughrea 074991
Century Schoolhouse, Toronto 006592
Century Shop, Louisville 089966
Century Village Museum, Burton . . 042530
Ceol - Irish Traditional Music Centre, Dublin 022733
CEP Sanat Galerisi, İstanbul 112296
CEPA Photographic Galleries, Buffalo 115253
CEPACI, Promotion de l'Artisanat de Côte d'Ivoire, Bordeaux 098989
Cepade, Paris 100139
Cepade Centro Paulista de Arte e Design, São Paulo 049760
Cepcolor, Mâcon 099624
Cepheus, Stockholm 111014
Cera, Pedro Araújo, Lisboa 109271
C'era Una Volta, Genova 075458
Ceralacca, Brescia 075157, 140002
Ceram Antiek, Tilburg 078766
Cerami, Charleroi 058140
The Ceramic Collection, Aberystwyth 038463
Ceramic Collectors Society, North Sydney 052463
Ceramic Restoration, New York . . . 132452
Ceramic Review, London 136190
Cerámica, Madrid 136082
Ceramica Arte 4, Cartagena 123928
Ceramica Gallery, New York 090774
Ceramics Collector, Strasbourg . . . 068307
Ceramics Monthly, Westerville 136417
Ceramics Museum, Tel Aviv 023069
La Céramique Moderne, Paris 135698
Cerclaje, Madrid 110473
Cercle Bleu, Metz 099704
Cercle d'Art, Laval 005752
Cercle des Beaux-Arts de Liège, Liège 052656, 096375
Cercle des Beaux-Arts de Verviers, Verviers 052657, 096415
Cercle Royal Artistique de Schaerbeck, Bruxelles 052658
Čerdynskij Kraevedčeskij Muzej A.S. Puškina, Tcherdyn Regional Pushkin Museum, Čerdyn 033071
Cereal Prairie Pioneer Museum, Cereal 005240
Ceredigion Museum, Aberystwyth . 038464
Ceres, New York 117758
Ceres Antiques, Ceres 083896
Ceresa, Ferdinando, Maglio di Colla 111715
Ceri, M., Firenze 075313
Ceri, M., Firenze 075314
Cerino Canova, Laura, Torino 076800
Cerio, Silvia, Roma 127969
Cerisola Martinez, José, Montevideo 087313
Čerkechskij Muzej Jakutskaja Političeskaja Ssylka, Jakutskij gosudarstvennyj muzej istorii i kultury narodov severa im. Jaroslavskogo, Čerkech 033078
Cerkov Ionna Predteči, Jaroslavskij gosudarstvennyj istoriko-architekturnyj i chudožestvennyj muzej-zapovednik, Jaroslavl 033190
Cerkov Pokrova v Filjach, Moskva . 033376
Cerkov Položenija riz Presvjatoj Bogorodicy, Gosudarstvennyj muzej-zapovednik Moskovskij Kreml, Moskva 033377
Cerkov Roždestva Christova, Jaroslavskij gosudarstvennyj istoriko-architekturnyj muzej-zapovednik, Jaroslavl 033191
Cerkov Troicy v Nikitnikach, Gosudarstvennyj istoričeskij muzej, Moskva 033378
Cermamic Studio, New York 117759
Cernan Earth and Space Center, River Grove 047450
Cernara 6 Galeri, Jakarta 105835
Cerne Antiques, Cerne Abbas 083898
Černigivs'kyj Oblasnyj Chudožnij Muzej, Černigiv 038229
Černigivs'kyjy Literaturno-memorial'nyj Muzej-zapovidnik Mychajlo Kocjubynskogo, Černigiv 038230
Černivec'kyj Chudožnij Muzej, Černivci 038234
Černivec'kyj Krajeznavčyj Muzej, Černivci 038235
Černivec'kyj Literaturno-Memorial'nyj Muzej im. Ju.A. Fedkoviča, Černivec'kyj krajeznavčyj muzej, Černivci 038236
Černivec'kyj Literaturno-Memorial'nyj Muzej O. Kobyljans'koï, Černivec'kyj krajeznavčyj muzej, Černivci 038237
Černivec'kyj Muzej Bukovins'koï Diaspory, Černivci 038238
Černivec'kyj Muzej Narodnoï Architektury ta Pobutu, Černivci 038239
Cernuschi, Alberto, New York 117760
Cernuschi, Ursula, Paris 100140
Cerny, P., Erlangen 070596
Černý Pavouk, Ostrava 137805
Ceroa, Madrid 129591
Ceros, Paris 138327
Cerruti, Massimo, Milano 127566
Certainly Wood, Christchurch 128919
Certijn, Bussum 078130
Cerutti & Miller, New York 117761
Cervantes Antiquités, Saint-Ouen . . 067746
Cervera, Jose, Valencia 081651

Cervera, Marta, Madrid 110474
Cervini, Diana, Roma 076371
El Cesar, Bogotá 098111
Cesar & Daughter, Edith, Atlanta . . . 131765
César, Pape, Paris 100141
Cesaretti, Leonilde, Roma 140099
Cesaris Aroldi, Luisa, Milano 127567
Cesaro, Giorgio, Padova 076084
Cesaroni, Braşov 080134
Cesati, Alessandro, Milano 075664
Il Cesello, Firenze 106043
Česká Koruna, Praha 060116
České Centrum Fotografie, Praha . . 008595
České Muzeum Výtvarných Umění, Praha 008596
České Zdravotnické Muzeum, Praha 008597
Cessane, Bogotá 098112
C'est Chouette, L'Isle-sur-la-Sorgue 063931
C'est la Vie Antiques, San Diego . . . 092622
Cesteria Al Mare, Brescia 075158
Cēsu Izstāžu Nams, Cēsis 027670
Cēsu Vēstures muzejs, Cēsis 027671
Cettour, Bernard, Trouville-sur-Mer 068635
Četyre Iskusstva, Moskva 121964
Ceuleers, Jan, Antwerpen 137394
Ceuleneer, Reiner de, Antwerpen . . 057686
Cevenol, Saint-Martin-de-Valgalgues 067638
Cévenols, Le Vigan (Gard) 063732
Ceviz, İstanbul 083125
CEWEs Auktioner, Boden 122108
Ceylon, Dallas 088477
Ceylon Society of Arts, Colombo . . . 054125
Cèzanne, Bardowick 069468
Cézanne, Bardowick 101737
Cezanne, Bardowick 121313
Cezart.com, Lyon 064103
CFB Esquimalt Naval Museum and Military Museum, Victoria 006737
C.F.C., Milano 075665
CFCC Webber Center, Ocala 046610
CFM Gallery, New York 117762
CG Park, Saint-Paul-de-Vence 067940
C.G.B., Paris 065685
C.G.B. Galerie, Honfleur 099337
C.G.F., Paris 065686
CG's Curiosity Shop, Cockermouth . 084043
CH Art, Miami 117046
Ch. Frenkelis Mansion, Šiauliai Aušros Museum, Šiauliai 027854
C.H. Moore Homestead, Clinton . . . 043010
C.H. Nash Museum-Chucalissa Archaeological Museum, Memphis 045754
Chaa Creek Natural History Centre, San Ignacio 003886
Chabanian, Annecy 098837
Chabanian-le Baron, Annecy 098838
Chabanian-le Baron, Courchevel . . 099178
Chabanian-le Baron, Honfleur 099338
Chabanian-le Baron, Megève 099696
Chabanian-le Baron, Saint-Paul-de-Vence 101198
Chabanian-le Baron, Saint-Paul-de-Vence 101199
Chabanis, Roselyne, Bourg-Saint-Andeol 061713
Chabanne, Michel, Pranles 066978
Chabannes, Cavaillon 062042
Chabarovskij Gosudarstvennyj Institut Iskusstv i Kultury, Chabarovsk . . . 050629
Chabarovskij Kraevoj Kraevedčeskij Muzej im. N.I. Grodekova, Chabarovsk . . 033080
Chabarovskij Muzej Archeologii im. A.P. Okladnikova, Chabarovsk 033081
Chabolle, Jean-François, Paris 065687
Chabot Museum, Rotterdam 030077
Chac & Mool, West Hollywood 120377
Chácara do Céu Museum, Museus Castro Maya, Rio de Janeiro 004337
Chacártegui Cirerol, Jorge, Palma de Mallorca 110674
Chacewater Antiques, Chacewater . 083899
Chaco, Bielefeld 069821
Chaco Culture National Historical Park, Nageezi 046120
Chacon, Miguel, Vic-le-Comte 068844
Chacon, Rodriguez, Madrid 129592
Chacun, Christian, Paris 065688
Chacur, New York 117763
Chadde, Patricia, Neustadt am Rübenberge 134310
Chadelaud, Limoges 063884
Chadelaud, Paris 065689
Chadron State College Main Gallery, Chadron 042694
Chadupi, François, Wien 137299
Chadwell, Audrey & Jesse, Buffalo . 087867
Chadwick, Richmond 092068
Chadwick, Dolby, San Francisco . . . 119634
Chadwick, Howard, Boston 087803
Chadwyck-Healey, Cambridge 135131
Chadz Antiques, Taranaki 079250
Chaffal, Roger, Morance 064785
Chaffee Center for Visual Arts, Rutland 047579
Chaffey, Pat, Tamworth 095313
Chagall Gallery, Barcelona 110131
Chagall House, Haifa 022917
Chagall Museum, Vitebsk 003140
Chagas, Funchal 121921
Chagas, Funchal 121922
Chagas, Onedina L., Belo Horizonte 058418
Chagford Galleries, Chagford 112830
Chagot, Francis, Tulle 068658
Chagrin Falls Historical Society Museum, Chagrin Falls 042698
Chai Ma, Bangkok 083094
Chai Ma, Bangkok 112231
Chaieb, Daniel, Porto Alegre 058496
Chailloux, Maria, Amsterdam 107695
The Chaim Gross Studio Museum, New York 046308
The Chain, Amsterdam 077817
Chaineau, Jean-Marc, La Roche-Clermault 063408
Chaintreuil, Georges, Ferney-Voltaire 062853
Chair Doctor, Nashville 132398
Chair Re-Glue and Furniture Repair, Saint Paul 132765
The Chair Set Antiques, Woodstock 087239
La Chaise Antique, Stow-on-the-Wold 086741, 131547
Chaise de Bois, Angers 060851
Chait, Ralph M., New York 090775, 117764
Chaix, Corine, Toulon (Var) 068447
Chaix, Corinne, Camps-la-Source . . 061930
Chaiya National Museum, Surat Thani 037936
Chakasskij Respublikanskij Kraevedčeskij Muzej, Abakan 032970
Chakdara Museum, Chakdara 031359
Chak's, Hong Kong 059602
Chalabi Antik, İstanbul 083126
Chalais Brocante, Chalais 062072, 124176
Chalancon, Saint-Étienne 067446
Chalermnit, Bangkok 141369
Le Chalet, Allouis 060782
Le Chalet, Villefranche-sur-Cher . . . 068898
Châlet de l'Etambeau, Château-d'Oex 037010
Chalet of the Golden Fleece, New Glarus 046216
Chalifour, Gérald, Bessé-sur-Braye . 061404
Chalk House, Saint Ives, Cornwall . 114360
Chalkwell Auctions, Southend-on-Sea 122704
Challiss, San Francisco 092753
Chalmeton, Chappes 062144
Chalmont, Christophe, Durtal 062756
Chalmont, Richard, Paris 065690
Chalon, Nick, Chard 083909
Chalon Collections, Chalon-sur-Saône 062084
Chalvet, Mado, Houston 116291
Chalvignac Isabelle, Versailles 068797
Chalvin, Yves, Lyon 099547
Chamarajendra Academy of Visual Arts, Mysore 050318
Chamarande, Bruxelles 057882
Chamarilero, Madrid 081275
Chamberlain, Denver 132031
Chamberlain, Dennis, Los Angeles . 116737
Chamberlain Museum of Pathology, Birmingham 038728
Chamberlayne School of Design, Mount Ida College, Newton 051844
Chambers, New York 117765
Chambers, Utrecht 078789
Chambers, Graham H., Lancaster . . 084897
Chambers, Ronald G., Petworth . . . 086242
Chambers & Crosthwaite, Hamilton, Queensland 055939
Chambers Gallery, Ipswich 113301
Chambet, Jean-Paul, Saint-Germain 067496
Chamblin, R., Jacksonville 142464
El Chambo, Vigo 081700
Chambon, C., Nogent-sur-Seine . . . 065213
Chambon, Claude, Favars 062841
Chambon, Claudie, Saint-Aubin . . . 067363
Chambon, Philippe, La Chapelle-la-Reine 063317
Chambord, Virginia Beach 093348
Chamboux, Jean-François, Tours . . 068588
La Chambre, Rotterdam 078706
Chambre, Claire, Annecy 098839
Chambre Belge des Experts en Œuvres d'Art, Bruxelles 052659
La Chambre Blanche, Québec 097137
Chambre d'Amis, Amsterdam 077818
Chambre Européenne des Experts-Conseils en Oeuvres d'Art, Paris 052924
Chambre Nationale des Commissaires-Priseurs Judiciaires, Paris 052925, 121126
Chambre Nationale des Experts Spécialisés, Paris 052926
Chambre Professionnelle Belge de la Libraire Ancienne et Moderne, Liège 052660
Chambre Royale Belgo-Luxembourgeoise des Salle des Ventes aux Encheres, Bruxelles 052661
Chambre Royale des Antiquaires de Belgique, Koninklijke Kamer van de Antiquairs van Belgie, Bruxelles . . 052662
Chambre Syndicale de l'Estampe, du Dessin et du Tableau, Paris 052927
Chambre Syndicale des Salles de Ventes de Belgique, Bruxelles 052663
Chambrelin, Joëlle, Attin 061019
Chambrion, Martine, Lyon 064104
Chambure, Marie de, Paris 100142
Chameleon, Seattle 142982
Chameleon Antique Lighting, New York 090776
Chameleon Antiques, New York . . . 090777
Chameleon Gallery, Masterton 108499
Chaminade, Jacques, Lyon 138140
Chamizal National Memorial, El Paso 043635
Chammard, Monique de, Paris 100143
Chamonal, Rodolphe, Paris 138328
Chamoroff, Bianca C., Beirut 077387
Chamouleau, Armand, Limoges . . . 063885
Chamouleau, Armand, Paris 065691
Chamouleau, Jean-Claude, Fouquebrune 062930
Champ de Mars, San Francisco . . . 092754
Champ des Possibles, Noirmoutier-en-l'Ile 099879
Champ Libre, Montréal 096987
Champagne dit Lambert, Ottawa . . 059034
Champaign County Historical Museum, Champaign 042703
Champaign County Historical Museum, Urbana 048714
Champaloux, Emile, Limoges 099502
Champavert, Toulouse 138631
Champeaux, Dominique, Thil 068391
Champetier, Michelle, Cannes 099062
Champignonnière-Musée du Saut aux Loups, Montsoreau 013233
Champion, Alain, Nantes 064913
Champion, Alain, Nuille-le-Jalais . . 065248
Champion, Gondrand, Bourgoin-Jallieu 120951
Champion, Josy, La Sauvetat 063445
Champion, René-Paul, Cognac 120979
Pierre Champion & Françoise Kusel, Nîmes 121097
Champion Mill, Champion 042706
Champions Lighting, Houston 089044
Champion's Refinishing, Houston . . 132110
Champkins, Paul, London . 085185, 130969
Champlain Trail Museum, Pembroke 006126
Champod, Michel, Genève 082413
Champs Chapel Museum, East Hendred 039350
Champvallins, Jacqueline de, Paris 100144, 133552
Chamsori Gramophone and Audio Science Museum, Gangneung 027486
Chan, San Francisco 092755
Chan, Liu, Taipei 098061
Chan, Peter, Toronto 059161
Chan, P.F., Singapore 080442
Chan, Pui Kee, Singapore . 080443, 129258
Chan & Co., Tony, Hong Kong 097764
Chan & Co., Tony, Hong Kong 097765
Chan Ngee, Singapore 080444
Chan Pui Hoe, Howard, Hong Kong . 097766
Chan Shing Kee, Hong Kong 059603
Chance Operations Gallery, Denver . 115981
Chancellor Robert R. Livingston Masonic Library and Museum, New York . . 046309
Chancenotte, Jacques, Dijon 124218
Chancery Lane Antiques, Nashville . 090432
Chandan Bulchand, La Palmas de Gran Canaria 081503
Chandelier, Maurice, Atlanta 087462
Chandeliers, Clancy, Dublin 074899
Chandjian, W., München 072676
Chandler, R.A., Tiverton 131595
Chandler Gallery, Randolph 047328
Chandler Museum, Chandler 042707
Chandos Books, Bristol 141451
Chandradhari Museum, Darbhanga 022067
Chang, Bobby, Singapore 109781
Chang, Theo, Caracas 093526
Chang, W.C., Taipei 059793, 137755
Chang Foundation Museum, Taipei . 007365
Chang Jiang, Hong Kong 097767
Chang Wei Hwa, Taipei 059794
Changan Art Cooperative, Xian 098051
Changcheng, Baoding 097638
Changcheng, Wuxi 098028
Change des Saints Pères, Paris . . . 065692
Change du Port, Marseille 064335
Change Plus, Biarritz 061458
Changement de Décor, Châlons-en-Champagne 062095, 099104
Changement de Décor, Épernay . . . 062781
Changi Village Antiques, Singapore 080445
Changji Mulei County Museum, Changji 007026
Changjizhou Museum, Changji 007027
Changning District Revolutionary Display Center, Shanghai 007229
Changping Yanjing Art Cooperative, Beijing 097646
Changqing County Museum, Jinan . 007150
Changsha City Museum, Changsha 007029
Changshu Calligraphy and Painting Gallery, Changshu 097693
Changshu City Museum, Changshu 007032
Changshu Engraved Stone Museum, Changshu 007033
Changshu Mausoleum of Fallen Heroes, Changshu 007034
Changy, D. de, Bruxelles 057883
Changyanbao Prefecture Art Association, Xian 052788, 098052
Chania Byzantine and Postbyzantine Collection, Chania 021226

Chankit, Glenda, Toronto 059162
Le Channel, Galerie de l'Ancienne Poste, Calais 011073
Channel Folk Museum, Lower Snug 001197
Channel Islands Galleries, Saint Peter Port 086472, 142040
Channel Islands Military Museum, Saint Ouen 040930
Channel-Port-aux-Basques Museum, Channel-Port-aux-Basques 005242
Chanoit, Fréderic, Paris 065693
Chan's Ancient Jade and Art, Hong Kong 059604
Chan's Art Gallery, Vancouver 097439
Chantal, Francesca, Roma 127970
Chantal, Karli, Lausanne 130065
Chantal Muñoz, Rognac 124880
Chantebois, Chantilly 062140, 124185
Chantek, Rumah, Singapore 109782
Chanteloup, Marie de, Paris 065694
Chantérac-Geiss, Alois, Völklingen 126952
Chanticleer, London 130970
Chantilly, Kelvin Grove 056038
Chantrel, Estelle, Rennes (Ille-et-Vilaine) 124873
Chantry, Léon-Noël, Tours 068589
Chantry Bagpipe Museum, Morpeth 040499
Chantry Bookshop & Gallery, Dartmouth 084137, 141550
Chantry House Gallery, Ripley, North Yorkshire 114317
Chanty-Mansijskij Okružnoj Kraevedčeskij Muzej, Chanty-Mansijsk 033087
Chanu, Cedric, Narbonne 064963
Chanut, François, Paris 138329
Chao Hua Art Cooperative, Beijing 097647
Chao Phraya Gallery, Washington 093395
Chaos Art Gallery, Budapest 105500
Chaos Collectables, Christchurch 079018
Chaoyang City Museum, Chaoyang 007036
Chap Hin, Hong Kong 097768
Chapé, København 060308, 098543
Chapeau, Antwerpen 096062
Chapeau Clacque, Berkel-Enschot 140362
La Chapeauthèque, Anduze 010383
Chapel, Pittsburgh 132663
Chapel Antiques, Barmouth 083384
Chapel Antiques, Nantwich 086034, 131290
Chapel Antiques Centre, Sheffield 086553
Chapel Art Center, Saint Anselm College, Manchester 045617
Chapel Art Gallery, Riseley 114319
Chapel Books, Chepstow 141505
The Chapel Brae Gallery, Braemar 112690
Chapel Emporium Antique Centre, Long Sutton, Lincolnshire 085846
Chapel Gallery, Bracebridge 005127
Chapel Gallery, North Battleford 006033
Chapel Gallery, West Newton 049088
Chapel Hill Museum, Shag Harbour 006445
Chapel House Fireplaces, Holmfirth 084699
The Chapel of Art, Criccieth 112922
Chapel off Chapel, Prahran 095105
Chapel Place Antiques, Tunbridge Wells 086934
Chapel Street Antiques Arcade, Penzance 086210
Chapel Street Bazaar, Prahran 056490
Chapel Walk Antique Centre, Leominster 084969
Chapelaine Antiquitités, La Chapelle-sur-Erdre 063321
Chapelle de Bailly, Saint-Bris-le-Vineux 014208
Chapelle des Indiens, Tadoussac 006552
Chapelle Matisse, Vence 015156
Chapelle-Musée Saint-Nicolas, Vitré 015318
Chapelle Sainte-Radegonde, Musée du Vieux Chinon, Chinon 011362
Chapellerie des Arcades, Brest 061768
Chapellerie Houssin, Le Havre 063629
Chapelotte, Jean-Claude, Luxembourg 107394
Chaphariz, Brasília 058460
Chapin, Bill, Toledo 093167, 132971
Chapin Library of Rare Books, Williamstown 049186
Chapitre Un, Montréal 137649
Chapleau Centennial Museum, Chapleau 005243
Chaplier, Ghyslaine, Paris 065695
Chaplin-Archiv, Frankfurt am Main 017154
Chapman, Milwaukee 117177
Chapman, Chas, London 096946
Chapman, Hilary, London 113534
Chapman, Lee, Keswick 113316
Chapman, Manuka, Griffith 094606
Chapman, Michael, Cley 112877
Chapman, Peter, London 085186, 130971
Chapman & Friedman, Louisville 116933
Chapman Gallery, Salford 040941
Chapman Historical Museum, Glens Falls 044212
Chapman Museum, Brandon 005139
Chapotot, Claude & Sonia, Nanterre 064886
Chapoulie, Agen 060667
Chappell, Bakewell 083364
Chappell, New York 117766
Chappell, Alice, Boston 115158
Chappell, Jordan, Houston 089045
Chappell Art Gallery, Chappell 042715
Chappell Hill Historical Society Museum, Chappell Hill 042716
Chappell & McCullar, San Francisco 092756
Chappuis, Jean-Marc, Neuchâtel 111766
Chapron, Hubert, Saint-Marcel 067622
Chaptard, Jeannine, Le Coteau 063607
Chapter and Verse, Pune 139952
Chapter House, London 040113
Chapter House Books, Mornington 137006
Chapter House Books, Sherborne 131483, 142067
Chapter One, London 085187, 141768
Chapter & Verse, Rye 142025
Chapters, Dublin 139963
Chapu, Marie-Françoise, Paris 065696
Chapuis, Nice 138251
Chapuis, Frédéric, Saint-Ouen 067747
Chapuis, Geneviève, Gacé 062951
Chapusot, Jean-Claude, Langres 063522
Chaput, Nicole, Tournus 068566
Le Charabia, Bruxelles 137430
Characters Art Gallery, Bolton 112670
Charaire, Jean, Agen 060668
Charaire, Jean, Aubiac 061040
Charbit, Adolphe, Draguignan 120993
Charbo, Amsterdam 140290
Charbonneau, Boris, Cahors 061897, 138061
Charbonneaux, Catherine, Paris 121127
Charbonnel, Alain, Loches (Indre-et-Loire) 063973
Charbonnet & Charbonnet, New Orleans 090533
Charbonnier, Georges L., Genève 082414
Charbonnier, Michel, Marseille 064336
Charbonnier, Noël, Paris 124617
Chard and District Museum, Chard 039031
Chard Antique Centre, Chard 083910
Chard Coins, Blackpool 083552
Chardon, Yves, Hauterives 063134
Charef, Guy, Douvres-la-Delivrande 062734
Charèl, Amsterdam 077819
Charel, New York 090778
Charents Literary Memorial Museum, Erevan 000678
Charfa, Skopje 107422
Charil, Grégory, Nemours 064970
Charim, Miryam, Wien 095806
Charing Cross Books, Annerley 136785
Chariot, Earlwood 055779
Le Chariot d'Or, Lyon 064105
Charitonenko i Syn, Sumy 112436
Charivari, Knokke-Heist 096332
Charkivs'kij Chudožnij Muzej, Charkiv 038242
Charkivs'kij Istoryčnyj Muzej, Charkiv 038243
Charkivs'kij Literaturnyj Muzej, Charkiv 038244
Charlbury Museum, Charlbury 039034
Charlemagne, Paris 124618
Charles, Rouen 067256
Charles, Salt Lake City 132783
Charles, Whitwick 087142
Charles, Bernard, Pont-de-Briques-Saint-Etienne 066918
Charles, Daniel, Ashbourne 083325, 130312
Charles, Jean, Valenciennes 068688
Charles, Mary, Neuville-de-Poitou 064997
Charles, Oliver, Petworth 086243
Charles, Sylvain, Saint-Julien-les-Morey 067562
Charles A. Grignon Mansion, Kaukauna 044938
Charles A. Weyerhaeuser Memorial Museum, Little Falls 045338
Charles A. Wustum Museum of Fine Arts, Racine 047305
Charles Allis Art Museum, Milwaukee 045886
Charles Antiques, Leamington Spa 130864
Charles B. Aycock Birthplace, Fremont 044077
Charles B. Goddard Center for Visual and Performing Arts, Ardmore 041765
Charles Carroll House of Annapolis, Annapolis 041740
Charles & Charles, Los Angeles 089715
Charles Dickens Birthplace Museum, Portsmouth 040760
Charles Dickens Centre, Rochester 040846
Charles Ferguson Museum, Mentone 001253
Charles Gates Dawes House, Evanston Historical Society Museum, Evanston 043758
Charles H. MacNider Museum, Mason City 045722
Charles H. Scott Gallery, Vancouver 006692
Charles H. Taylor Arts Center, Hampton 044414
Charles H. Wright Museum of African American History, Detroit 043437
Charles-Harold Collection, Tampa 120034
The Charles Hosmer Morse Museum of American Art, Winter Park 049260
Charles International Antiques, Wrotham 087272
Charles M. Auampato Discovery Museum, Charleston 042746
Charles R. Conner Museum, Pullman 047281
Charles Rennie Mackintosh Society, Glasgow 054335
Charles River Museum of Industry, Waltham 048845
Charles River Street Antiques, Boston 087804
Charles Surt University Art Collection, Wagga Wagga 001585
Charles Towne Landing 1670, Charleston 042727
Charlesfort Antiques, Manakau 079140
The Charleston Museum, Charleston 042728
Charleston Trust, Firle 039501
Charlestown Shipwreck and Heritage Centre, Saint Austell 040901
Charlesworth, Benny, Great Harwood, Lancashire 084508
Charleville Historic House Museum, Charlesville 000907
Charlie Finds Great Old Stuff, Seattle 092972
Charlier, Guy, Trier 126908
Charlier, Wilhelm, Erding 125594
Charlier & Michiels, Bruxelles 057884
Charlie's Art Studio and Gallery, Jacksonville 116514
Charlie's Restoration, Columbus 131979
Charlie's Used Furniture, Pittsburgh 091798
Charlot, Jack, Bessey-lès-Cîteaux 061406
Charlotte and Philip Hanes Art Gallery, Wake Forest University, Winston-Salem 049251
Charlotte Antiques and Collectibles Show, Charlotte 093977
Charlotte Berlins Museum, Ystad 036803
Charlotte County Museum, Saint Stephen 006393
Charlotte Museum of History and Hezekiah Alexander Homesite, Charlotte 042755
Charlotte Some Times, Lyon 064106
Charlotte Street Gallery, London 113535
Charlottenlund Antik, Skodsborg 060401
Charlotte's Web, Seattle 092973
Charlott's Antik, Stockholm 081937, 129858
Charlott's Antiques, San Antonio 092497
Charlton Hall Galleries, Columbia 122869
Charlton House Antiques, London 085188
Charm of Yesteryear, Houston 089046
Charmasson, Danielle, Uzès 068666
Le Charme, Milano 075666
Charme Antique, Québec 059067
Charme d' Antan, Ribecourt-Dreslincourt 067129
Charme d'Antan, Beirut 077388
Charme d'Antan, Fresnes-sur-Escaut 062944
Charme du Passé, Le Havre 063630
Charmerie, Bourges 061721
La Charmerie, Saint-Denis 109410
Charming You, Jacksonville 089391
Charmoy, Xavier, Blois 138033
Charney Basset Mill, Wantage 041294
Charney Bassett Mill, Charney Basset 039035
Charnley-Persky House Museum, Chicago 042828
Charnwood Antiques, Sawbridgeworth 086519, 131458
Charnwood Museum, Loughborough 040341
Charo Alfaro, Madrid 081276
Charo y Pat, Ciutadella de Menorca 081043
Charpentier, Denis, Metz 064526
Charpentier, Fabrice, Verdun (Meuse) 068767
Charpentier, Françoise, Paris 100145
Charpentier, Marc, Châtelaillon-Plage 062214
Charpentier, Marc, La Rochelle 063428
Charpentier, Marc, Metz 064527
Charpentier, Patrice, Evreux 062827
Charpille, Jean-Pierre, Saint-Étienne 067447
Charra Franck, Saint-Péray 067949
Charrette, Bernay 061366
Charrier, Fabrice, Bonneval 061561
Charrier-Villepreux, Brigitte, La Châtre 063328
CHArt Computers and the History of Art, School of History of Art, Film and Visual Media, London 054336
Chart House, Shenfield 086570
Charta, Milano 134608
Chartered Insurance Institute's Museum, London 040114
Chartered Society of Designers, London 054337
Charterhouse School Museum, Godalming 039596
Charton, Hubert, Salins-les-Bains 068093
Charton, Roland, Avignon 098890
Charton, Roland, Avignon 098891
Chartouni & Sehnaoui, Beirut 077389, 121752
Chartrain, Flers 062871
Chartres, Neuilly-sur-Seine 064991
Chartres, Stéphane, Ribérac 067131
Chartres Antiquités, Chartres 062169
Chartreuse International, Seattle 092974
Les Chartreux, Toulouse 138632
Chartwell House, Chartwell 039036
Charveriat, Jean, Lyon 099548
Charvet Arnaud, Paris 100146
Charytonowicz, Zbigniew, Warszawa 079740
Chasamp, Cincinnati 115615
Chase, Dolores, Salt Lake City 119334

Chase and District Museum, Chase 005254
Chase Art Centre, Wadebridge 114635
Chase Art Gallery, Wadebridge 114636
Chase County Museum, Cottonwood Falls 043184
Chase Fine Art, Stafford 114473
Chase Gallery, Boston 115159
Chase Home Museum of Utah Folk Art, Salt Lake City 047770
The Chase Manhattan Bank Art Collections, New York 046310
Chasen, Richmond 119105
Chass, Pittsburgh 091799, 132664
Chassagne, Annie & Jean-Pierre, Toulouse 068494
Chassaigne, Yvette de la, Pont-Aven 101021
Chassaing, Hervé, Toulouse 101337
Chassaniol-Bénard, Elisabeth, Vire .069001, 138664
Chassany, Georges, Le Broc 063580
Chassany, Raphaël, Le Broc 063581
Chassay, Christiane, Montréal 096988
La Chasse aux Trésors Antiques, Montréal 058935
Châsse Sainte-Bernadette et Musée, Nevers 013386
Chasset, Patrick, Rouen 067257
Chasseurs d'Horizons, Chamonix-Mont-Blanc 062108
Chassin, Joëlle, Saint-Ouen-d'Attez 067928
Chastagner, André, Lyon 064107
Chastagnier, Bernard, Bandol 061186
Chaste, Durban 080695
Chastel, Aline, Paris 065697
Chastenay, Florence de, Paris 138330
Chat Nam, Leung, Hong Kong 097769
Chatarras Luque, Alicante 080759
Château, Aigle 036820
Château, Arlay 010468
Château, Assier 010504
Château, Belvoir 010749
Château, Castries 011152
Château, Duilhac-sous-Peyrepertuse 011663
Château, Gruyères 037170
Château, Lacave 012371
Château, Larra 012430
Château, Larroque-Toirac 012433
Château, Les Ternes 012642
Château, Moncley-Recologne 013092
Château, Prudhomat 013957
Château, Rousson 014142
Château, Saint-Ouen 067748
Château, Saint-Quintin-sur-Soule . . 014506
Château, La Sarraz 037516
Château, Vogue 015328
Château, Bernard, Augnax 061061
Chateau Ancient Arte, Tampa 093115
Château Beaufief, Mazeray 012988
Château Bisso, Voiron 069025
Château Chic, Phoenix 091727
Chateau d' Arts, Singapore 109783
Château d'Aigremont, Seraing 003747
Château d'Angers, Angers 010387
Château d'Antoine d'Abbadie, Hendaye 012088
Château d'Arcelot, Arceau 010452
Château d'Auvers, Voyage au Temps des Impressionnistes, Auvers-sur-Oise 010565
Château d'Auzers, Auzers 010579
Château d'Avignon, Saintes-Maries-de-la-Mer 014624
Château d'Azay-le-Ferron, Azay-le-Ferron 010610
Château de Beaumanoir, Quintin . . 013983
Château de Beloeil, Beloeil 003225
Château de Biron, Monpazier 013103
Château de Bonaguil, Saint-Front-sur-Lemance 014294
Château de Bonneval, Coussac-Bonneval 011518
Le Château de Bouchons, Saint-Loubès 101168
Château de Bouges, Bouges-le-Château 010904
Château de Bourbilly, Vic-de-Chassenay 015201
Château de Boury-en-Vexin, Boury-en-Vexin 010947
Château de Busca-Naniban, Mansencôme 012879
Château de Buzay, La Jarne 012281
Château de Castelnou, Castelnou . . 011147
Château de Cazeneuve, Préchac . . 013946
Château de Cénévières, Cénévières 011171
Château de Champchevrier, Cléré-les-Pins 011392
Château de Châteaudun, Châteaudun 011285
Château de Chevannes-Saint Racho, La Clayette 012236
Château de Chillon, Montreux 037333
Château de Coppet, Coppet 037032
Le Château de Craon, Craon 011526
Château de Crazannes, Crazannes . 011528
Château de Deulin, Fronville 003440
Château de Dufau, Coarraze 011412
Château de Fénelon, Sainte-Mondane 014614
Château de Fernelmont, Fernelmont 003433
Château de Fleurac, Rouffignac-Saint-Cernin 014135
Château de Fleurigny, Thorigny-sur-Oreuse 014947
Château de Fougères-sur-Bièvre, Fougères-sur-Bièvre 011876
Château de Fourquevaux, Fourquevaux 011883
Château de Frolois, Frolois 011902
Château de Galard, Terraube 014921
Château de Gandels, Garrevaques . 062970
Château de Germolles, Mellecey . . 013004
Château de Grandson, Grandson . . 037161
Château de Gratot, Exposition Permanente Historique Huit Siècles de Vie, Gratot 012005
Château de Hautefort, Hautefort . . . 012080
Château de Jannée, Pessoux 003703
Château de Kergrist, Ploubezre . . . 013847
Château de la Bastie d'Urfé, Saint-Étienne-le-Mollard 014280
Château de la Baume, Prinsuéjols-Marvejols 013952
Château de la Brède, La Brède 012209
Chateau de la Compagne, Los Angeles 089716
Château de la Guerche, La Guerche 012275
Château de la Motte-Tilly, Centre des Monuments Nationaux, La Motte-Tilly 012290
Château de la Renaissance et Donjon de 1320, Fléville-devant-Nancy 011827
Château de la Roche-Guyon, La Roche-Guyon 012307
Château de Labrède, Labrède 012366
Château de Lacypierre, Saint-Crépin-Carlucet 014238
Château de Langeais, Langeais . . . 012406
Château de l'Angotière, Domjean . . 011626
Château de Lastours, Baziège 061245
Château de Léhélec, Béganne 010731
Château de l'Ermitage, Cercle Historique et Archéologique de Wavre et de la Region, Wavre 003847
Château de l'Hermitage, Condé-sur-l'Escaut 011459
Château de Lichtenberg, Lichtenberg 012666
Château de Losse, Thonac 014936
Château de Lourmarin, Lourmarin . 012783
Château de Louvignies, Notre-Dame-de-Louvignies 003679
Château de Luynes, Luynes 012800
Château de Maisons-Laffitte, Centre des Monuments Nationaux, Maisons-Laffitte 012859
Château de Meillant, Meillant 013000
Château de Messilhac, Raulhac . . . 013994
Château de Meux, Jonzac 012165
Château de Mogère, Montpellier . . 013199
Château de Monbazillac, Monbazillac 013090
Château de Montaigut, Camares . . 011077
Château de Montaner, Montaner . . 013122
Château de Montignies-sur-Roc, Montignies-sur-Roc 003656
Château de Montméry et son Parc, Ambazac 010345
Château de Montmuran, Les Iffs . . . 012624
Château de Pongamp, Plouguenast 013854
Château de Prades, Lafox 012377
Château de Puymartin, Marquay . . . 012916
Château de Ratilly, Treigny 015037
Château de Reinhardstein, Robertville 003717
Château de Rixensart, Rixensart . . . 003716
Château de Rochambeau, Thoré-la-Rochette 014943
Château de Rochefort-en-Terre, Rochefort-en-Terre 014081
Château de Roquedols, Meyrueis . . 013052
Château de Rosanbo, Lanvellec . . . 012419
Château de Saint-Aubin-sur-Loire, Saint-Aubin-sur-Loire 014192
Château de Saint-Jean-de-Beauregard, Saint-Jean-de-Beauregard 014341
Château de Sauvan, Mane 064247
Château de Solre-sur-Sambre, Solre-sur-Sambre 003774
Château de Sombreffe, Sombreffe . 003775
Château de Sourdis, Gaujacq 011925
Château de Spontin, Yvoir 003865
Château de Sully-sur-Loire, Sully-sur-Loire 014886
Château de Talcy, Marchenoir 012886
Château de Tarascon, Musée du Château du Roy René, Tarascon (Bouches-du-Rhône) 014901
Château de Temniac, Sarlat-la-Canéda 014674
Château de Thoury, Saint-Pourçain-sur-Besbre 014492
Château de Trazegnies, Trazegnies . 003813
Château de Vascœuil, Centre d'Art Musée Michelet, Vascœuil 015137
Château de Vaurenard, Gleize 011962
Château de Véves, Celles 003363
Château de Villegongis, Villegongis 015259
Château de Villeneuve, Saint-Germain-Lembron 014314
Château de Villeneuve, Vence 015157
Château de Voltaire/Centre des Monuments Nationaux, Ferney-Voltaire 011799
Le Château d'Eau, Toulouse 014983
Le Château des Allymes, Ambérieu-en-Bugey 010346
Château des Baux, Les Baux-de-Provence 012605
Château des Ducs d'Epernon, Cadillac 011049
Château des Pêcheurs, La Bussière 012210
Château des Rois Ducs, Sauveterre-la-Lémance 014711
Château des XIVe-XVIIe s, Époisses 011716
Château d'Ételan, Saint-Maurice-d'Ételan 014432
Château d'If, Musée Carcéral, Marseille 012929
Château d'Oiron, Oiron 013480
Château d'Oron, Oron-le-Châtel . . . 037406
Château du Chassan, Faverolles (Cantal) 011787
Château du Clos de Vougeot, Vougeot 015339
Château du Fosteau, Leers-et-Fosteau 003574
Château du Haut-Koenigsbourg, Orschwiller 013523
Château du Lude, Le Lude 012516
Château du Rivau, Lemere 012594
Château du Vert-Bois, Bondues . . . 010864
Château du XVIe s, Ancy-le-Franc . 010378
Château d'Ussé, Rigny-Ussé 014047
Château et Musée de Filain-Fort, Filain 011814
Château et Musée de Valangin, Valangin 037665
Le Chateau Export, Tampa 093116
Le Chateau Export, Tampa 093117
Château Feodal, Corroy-le-Château 003377
Château Féodal de Beynac, Beynac et Cazenac 010784
Château Ferme, Falaën 003431
Château Fort, Bouillon 003248
Château-Fort de Robert-le-Diable, Moulineaux 013266
Château Franc-Waret, Franc-Waret 003439
Château Frontenac, Québec 097138
Château la Garenne, Bruxelles 057885
Château Le Temple, Valeyrac 015101
Château Les Bories, Antonne-et-Trigonant 010434
Château Logue, Maniwaki 005825
Château Malromé, Saint-André-du-Bois 014183
Château Médiéval de Tancarville, Tancarville 014897
Château Médiéval et Musée Delporte, Thy-le-Château 003794
Château Montauban, Fontvieille . . . 011862
Château Morin Antiquités, Sablonnières 067335
Château-Musée, Aulan 010542
Château-Musée, Boën-sur-Lignon . 010850
Château-Musée, Brissac-Quincé . . 011010
Château-Musée, Carrouges 011130
Château-Musée, Collonges-lès-Bévy 011427
Château-Musée, Cons-la-Grandville 011470
Château-Musée, Cormatin 011484
Château-Musée, Davayat 011562
Château-Musée, Ferrières-en-Brie . 011803
Château-Musée, Haroué 012070
Château-Musée, Heudicourt 012101
Château-Musée, La Barben 012198
Château-Musée, Lavardens 012448
Château-Musée, Lavoûte-sur-Loire 012458
Château-Musée, Le Bourg-Saint-Léonard 012468
Château-Musée, Le Plessis-Brion . . 012545
Château-Musée, Lenoncourt 012595
Château-Musée, Maillebois 012851
Château-Musée, Menthon-Saint-Bernard 013017
Château-Musée, Meung-sur-Loire . 013046
Château-Musée, Montmirail 013189
Château-Musée, Pange 013542
Château-Musée, Pirou 013823
Château-Musée, Poudenas 013928
Château-Musée, Roche-la-Molière . 014070
Château-Musée, Saint-Vidal 014571
Château-Musée, Tourrette-Levens . 015013
Château-Musée, Valprivas 015119
Château-Musée, Vendeuvre 015159
Château-Musée, Villandry 015221
Château-Musée, Virieu-sur-Bourbre 015316
Château-Musée, Musée des Beaux-Arts, Boulogne-sur-Mer 010911
Château-Musée Anjony, Tournemire 015008
Château-Musée d'Andurain, Mauléon-Licharre 012975
Château-Musée d'Anet, Anet 010385
Château-Musée d'Art Populaire et Religieux, Clermont-en-Genevois 011394
Château-Musée d'Aulteribe, Sermentizon 014770
Château-Musée de Bois-Chevalier, Legé 012588
Château-Musée de Bonneville, Chamblac 011212
Château-Musée de Brie, Champagnac-la-Rivière 011221
Château-Musée de Bussy-Rabutin, Bussy-le-Grand 011034
Château-Musée de Cany, Cany-Barville 011101
Château-Musée de Château Dauphin, Pontgibaud 013907
Château-Musée de Chémery, Chémery 011342
Château-Musée de Chenonceau, Chenonceaux 011345

Château-Musée de Combourg, Combourg 011440
Château-Musée de Condé, Condé-en-Brie 011458
Château-Musée de Courson, Courson-Monteloup 011514
Château Musée de Cugney, Cugney 011546
Château-Musée de Culan, Culan 011548
Château-Musée de Dampierre-sur-Boutonne, Aulnay (Charente-Maritime) 010543
Château-Musée de Dieppe, Dieppe 011586
Château-Musée de Filières, Gommerville 011964
Château-Musée de Jussy, Jussy-Champagne 012186
Château-Musée de la Batisse, Chanonat 011235
Château-Musée de la Gataudière, Marennes 012902
Château-Musée de la Grange, Manom 012874
Château-Musée de la Nature, Bonnefamille 010867
Château-Musée de la Possonnière, Couture-sur-Loir 011520
Château-Musée de la Roche, Chaptuzat 011241
Château-Musée de la Roche-Racan, Saint-Paterne-Racan 014465
Château-Musée de la Rochelambert, Saint-Paulien 014474
Château-Musée de la Trémolière, Anglards-de-Salers 010399
Château-Musée de Lacassagne, Saint-Avit-Frandat 014193
Château-Musée de Lamartine, Saint-Point 014488
Château-Musée de Lantheuil, Lantheuil 012418
Château-Musée de Maupas, Morogues 013248
Château-Musée de Miromesnil, Tourville-sur-Arques 015025
Château-Musée de Montaigu, Laneuveville-devant-Nancy 012403
Château-Musée de Montal, Saint-Jean-Lespinasse 014360
Château-Musée de Montfleury, Avressieux 010607
Château-Musée de Montgeoffroy, Mazé 012987
Château-Musée de Panloy, Port-d'Envaux 013917
Château-Musée de Pont-Chevron, Ouzouer-sur-Trézée 013530
Château-Musée de Préhistoire, Belesta-de-la-Frontière 010734
Château-Musée de Puyguilhem, Villars (Dordogne) 015230
Château-Musée de Ravignan, Perquie 013791
Château-Musée de Ripaille, Thonon-les-Bains 014940
Château-Musée de Selles, Cambrai 011082
Château-Musée de Serrant, Saint-Georges-sur-Loire 014303
Château-Musée de Teillan, Aimargues 010283
Château-Musée de Terre-Neuve, Fontenay-le-Comte 011852
Château-Musée de Vaulaville, Tour-en-Bessin 015001
Château-Musée de Veauce, Ébreuil 011676
Château-Musée de Villeprévost, Tillay-le-Péneux 014958
Château-Musée de Villersexel, Villersexel 015294
Château-Musée de Villesavin, Tour-en-Sologne 015002
Château-Musée de Vollore, Vollore-Ville 015332
Château-Musée d'Effiat, Aigueperse 010275
Château-Musée des Ducs, Duras 011669
Château-Musée des Martinanches, Saint-Dier-d'Auvergne 014261
Château-Musée des Rochers-Sévigné, Vitré 015319
Château-Musée des XVIe-XVIIe s, Tanlay 014899
Château-Musée du Fort La Latte, Rennes (Ille-et-Vilaine) 014018
Château-Musée du Grand-Saussay, Ballancourt-sur-Essonne 010632
Château-Musée du Maréchal Lyautey, Thorey-Lyautey 014945
Château-Musée du Moulin, Lassay-sur-Croisne 012435
Château-Musée du Plessis-Bouré, Ecuillé 011681
Château-Musée du Plessis-lès-Tours, La Riche 012303
Château-Musée du Rhône, Tournon-sur-Rhône 015009
Château-Musée du Suscinio, Sarzeau 014688
Château-Musée du Touvet, Le Touvet 012569
Château-Musée du Val, Lanobre 012414
Château-Musée du XVe et XVIIIe Siècle, Commarin 011444
Château-Musée du XVIIe Siècle, Fontaine-Française 011843
Château-Musée d'Urtubie, Saint-Jean-de-Luz 014346
Château-Musée et Ecuries de Chaumont-sur-Loire, Chaumont-sur-Loire 011328
Château Musée Grimaldi, Cagnes-sur-Mer 011059
Château-Musée la Fayette, Chavaniac-Lafayette 011333
Château-Musée le Denacre, Wimille 015363
Château-Musée Listran, Jau-Dignac-et-Loirac 012152
Château-Musée Mansart, Sagonne 014162
Château-Musée Marguerite de Burgogne, Couches 011494
Château-Musée Municipal, Nemours 013362
Château-Musée Renaissance, Azay-le-Rideau 010611
Château-Musée Turcan, Ansouis 010419
Château-Musée Verdus, Saint-Seurin-de-Cadourne 014541
Chateau Napoleon, Los Angeles 089717
Le Chateau of Antiques, Dallas 088478
Château Petit Versailles, Parentignat 013548
Château-Promenade des Parfums, Chilleurs-aux-Bois 011361
Château Royal, Musée de la Côte Catalane, Collioure 011420
Château Royal d'Amboise, Amboise 010355
Château Suffren, Saint-Tropez 068013
Chateaubriand Antiques Centre, Burwash 083817
Chateauminois, Cyrille, Dardilly 124216
Chateauminois, Marc, Toulon (Var) 124963
Chatelet Chaume, Didier, Roanne 067165
Chatelherault, Ferniegair 039495
Chatelus, Alain, Lyon 124346
Chatham College Art Gallery, Pittsburgh 047047
Chatham Islands Museum, Waitangi, Christchurch 030620
Chatham-Kent Museum, Chatham, Ontario 005257
Chatham Railroad Museum, Chatham, Ontario 005258
Chatilez, Guy, Tourcoing 101374
Chatillon-DeMenil Mansion, Saint Louis 047655
Chatre, Martine & Thibault de la, Paris 100147
De Chats en Chats, Toulouse 068495
Chatsworth, Mamaroneck 122955
Chatsworth House, Bakewell 038567
Chattahoochee Valley Art Museum, La Grange 045061
Chattanooga African-American Museum, Chattanooga 042775
Chattanooga Regional History Museum, Chattanooga 042776
Chattel, Dallas 132003
Chattel Changers, Milwaukee 090283
Chattels, Lija 077512
Chattels Antiques, Warrandyte 056801
Chattels Antiques, Wonga Park 056843
Chatterley Whitfield Mining Museum, Stoke-on-Trent 041115
Chattishgarh Mudra Sangrahalaya, Katora Talab 022201
Chatto & Windus, London 135203
The Chatton Gallery, Chatton 112837
Chau, K.H., Hong Kong 059605
Chaubard, Dominique & Claude, Fontanes 062899
Chaucer, London 085189
Chaucer Bookshop, Canterbury 130503, 141481
Chaucer-Head Bookshop and Art Gallery, Stratford-upon-Avon 142093
Chaudesaigues, Stéphane, Vaison-la-Romaine 101398
Chaudoir, M.-C., Bruxelles 057886
Le Chaudron Magique, Brugnac 011016
Chaufour, Chatellerault 062217
Chaume Gonzalez, Miguel Pablo, Valencia 129766
Chaumeil Expo, Clermont-Ferrand 099143
Chaumet, İstanbul 083127
La Chaumière, Paris 124619
Chaumière d'Antan, Mérignac (Gironde) 064503
Chaumière Rustique, Saint-Jean-de-Monts 067544
Chaussat, Dominique, Thairé 068378, 124953
Chaussavoine-Delecroix, Paule, Rennes (Ille-et-Vilaine) 067108
Chaussin, Jacques, Lyon 121044
Chaussin, Bremens & Guillaumot, Villefranche-sur-Saône 121286
Chaussinand, Yves, Villeurbanne 068952, 125034
Chauveau, Pierre, Hyères 063190
Chauvin, Didier, Chambéria 124180
Chauvin, J M, Rouen 067258
Chauvin Egaze Ghislaine, Longny-au-Perche 063983
Chauzy, François, Tournus 068567
Chavanne, Henriette, Cormatin 099174
Chave, Alphonse, Vence 101437
Chaves Ferreira, Lisboa 134869
Chavey, Felix, New York 132453
Chavez, George, San Antonio 132809
Chawkandi Art, Karachi 108771
Chawner, John, Birchington 083520, 130385
Chaya-machi Gallery, Osaka 106954
Chaye, Honfleur 099339
Chayette & Cheval, Paris 121128
Cheap Antiques, Kansas City 089491
Cheap Art, Athinai 105392
Cheatle, Zelda, London 113536
Chebellas, Trina, Sacramento 092143
Chebský Hrad, Krajské Muzeum Cheb, Cheb 008327
Cheddar Man and the Cannibals, Cheddar 039044
Cheddleton Flint Mill, Cheddleton 039045
Chedworth Roman Villa, Yanworth 041464
Chedworth Roman Villa Museum, Cheltenham 039052
Cheekwood Museum of Art, Nashville 046141
Cheekwood Nashville's Home of Art and Gardens, Nashville 051776
Cheese Factory Studio Gallery, Meadows 094799
Cheever, San Antonio 142885
Cheffertons, Antwerpen 057687
Cheffins, Cambridge 122445
Chegai, Pietro, Firenze 106044, 134583
Chégaray, Sylvie, Honfleur 063166
Chehel-Sotoon Museum, Qazvin 022589
Chehel-Sotoon Palace Museum, Isfahan 022561
Chehel-Stoun Museum, Ghazvin 022552
Cheim & Read, New York 117767
Cheiro de Mofo, Belo Horizonte 058419
Chelan County Historical Museum, Cashmere 042645
Chelan County Public Utility District, Wenatchee 049055
Chelesa Art, Hong Kong 097770
Chelines, Hondarribia 081156
Chelini, A. & C., Firenze 075315
Chelini, Fabio, Livorno 075527
Chelley's Antiques, Dunedin 079082
Chellini & C., Silvano, Firenze 075316, 127318
Chelmer, Chelmsford 112841
Chelminski, London 113537
Chelminski, Hilary, London 085190
Chelmsford Historical Museum, Chelmsford 042787
Chelmsford Historical Society Museum, South Chelmsford 048236
Chelmsford Museum, Chelmsford 039046
Cheloudiakoff, Belfort 098947
Chelsea, Laufen 111606
Chelsea, Philadelphia 132608
Chelsea Antichitá, Firenze 075317
Chelsea Antique Mirrors, London 085191, 130972
Chelsea Antiques, Los Angeles 089718
Chelsea Antiques, Strandon Taranaki 079246
Chelsea Antiques and Decorative Art Centre, Albion 055325
Chelsea Antiques Fair, London 093918
Chelsea Art Fair, London 093919
Chelsea Art Museum, Miotte Foundation, New York 046311
Chelsea Book Shop, San Francisco 142940
Chelsea Books, London 141769
Chelsea Ceramic Guild, New York 054702, 117768
Chelsea Clocks and Antiques, London 085192
Chelsea College of Art and Design, London 050831
Chelsea Court House Museum, Chelsea 000909
Chelsea Galleria, Miami 117047
Chelsea Galleries, Kingston 106808
Chelsea Gallery, London 141770
Chelsea Gallery, Tulsa 120190
Chelsea Gallery, Wynberg 110082
Chelsea House Publishers, Broomall 135340
Chelsea Physic Garden, London 040115
Chelsey, Metford 056216
Chelston Gallery, Torquay 114583
Cheltenham Antique Market, Cheltenham 083917
Cheltenham Art Gallery and Museum, Cheltenham 039053
Cheltenham Center for the Arts, Cheltenham 051104
Chelwood, Cheltenham 112844, 135135
Chem, M.A., Rotterdam 078707
Chemin Christian, Rivedoux-Plage 067158
Chemin de Fer-Musée Blonay-Chamby, Lausanne 037237
Chemin de la Soie, Molière-Cavaillac 013087
Le Chemin de Table, Paris 065698
Chemin des Arts, Paris 138331
Le Chemin du Fauvisme, Réseau Culturel Terre Catalane, Collioure 011421
La Cheminée Antiquitées, Paris 065699
Chemini, Claudie, Darnieulles 062602
Chemins Privés, Hyères 063191
Chemnitzer Künstlerbund e.V., Chemnitz 053117
Chemnitzer Verlag, Chemnitz 133849
Chemould, Kolkata 105735
Chemould, Mumbai 105761
Chemstrip, Regina 059086, 123809
Chemung Valley History Museum, Elmira 043691
Chen, J.F., Los Angeles 089719
Chen, J.F., West Hollywood 093456
Chen Peiqiang, Perugia 076230
Chen & Wiedemann, München 072677

Chen Xin Tang, Nanjing 097872
Chenal, Jacques, Grenoble 063057
Chenal, Jacques, Seyssinet-Pariset 068240
Chenango County Historical Society Museum, Norwich 046568
Le Chêne dans la Maison, Tournai . 058384
Le Chêne d'Or, Rouen 067259
Chenel, Alain-Pierre, Nice 065061
Cheneviere, Antoine, London 085193
Chenevière, Pierre, Antibes-Juan-les-Pins 060918
Cheney, Sacramento 092144
Cheney, Robert, Finedon 084404
Cheney Cowles Museum, Spokane . 048275
Cheney Homestead, Manchester . . 045614
Cheng Ka Yung, Hong Kong 097771
Cheng Shuang Kuei, Hong Kong . . . 059606
Chengdu City Museum, Chengdu . . 007040
Chengdu Painting Gallery, Chengdu 097697
Chenkier, Strasbourg 068308, 101283
Chenkier, M., Scharrachbergheim . 068176
Chenoir, Lidie, Thouars 068414
Chenonceau, Washington 093396
Chenu, Jean, Lyon 121045
Chenu, Scrive & Bérard, Lyon 121046
Chenue à la Croix de Lorraine, Clichy 062360
Cheo, Oakland 118628
Cheongdam Gallery, Seoul 107211
Cheongju Early Printing Museum, Cheongju 027467
Cheongju National Museum, Cheongju 027468
Cheongju University Museum, Cheongju 027469
Chepstow Museum, Chepstow 039055
Cheraw Lyceum Museum, Cheraw . 042789
Chercheur d'Art, Metz 099705
Chereau, Jacques, Sannerville 101255, 124925
Cherif, Sidi Bou Saïd 112255
Cherishables, Washington 093397
Cheriton, Narberth 131292
Cherner, Bruce, Boston 087805
Cherokee Coins and Jewelry, Louisville 089967
Cherokee County Historical Museum, Murphy 046099
Cherokee Heritage Centre, Tahlequah 048472
Cherokee Moon, Houston . 089047, 122904
Cherokee Strip Land Rush Museum, Arkansas City 041770
Cherokee Strip Museum, Alva 041675
Cherokee Strip Museum and Henry S. Johnston Library, Perry 046887
Chéron, Henry, Bernay 061367
Cheroutre, J., Oostende 123667
Cherrier, Francis, Agnac 060671
Cherrington, T.A., Teddington 142109
Cherruault, Isabelle, Verneuil-sur-Avre 068779
Cherry, Washington 093398
Cherry, Peter, Hahndorf 055931
Cherry Antiques, Hemel Hempstead 084649
Cherry Art Studio, San Francisco . . 119635
Cherry County Historical Society Museum, Valentine 048732
Cherry Creek Art Association, Denver 054703
Cherry Holt Studio, Sutterton 114524
Cherry Lane, Toronto 059163
Cherry Orchard Antiques, Wellington 079320
Cherry Pelavin Fine Arts, New York . 135419
Cherry Ripe Antiques, Concord 055709
Cherry Street Antiques, Columbus . 088390
Cherry Street Interiors, Kansas City 089492
Cherry Valley Museum, Cherry Valley 042796
Cherrys' Art Center, Columbus 115768
Chertsey Antiques, Chertsey 083939
Chertsey Museum, Chertsey 039057
Cherub, Carshalton 083887
Cherub, Washington 093399
Cherub Antiques, Skipton 086623
Cherwell Framing Gallery, Kidlington 113321
Cheryl & Pete's, Yackandandah . . . 056892
Chesapeake and Ohio Canal Tavern Museum, Sharpsburg 048130
Chesapeake Bay Maritime Museum, Saint Michaels 047692
Chesapeake Beach Railway Museum, Chesapeake Beach 042798
Chesham, Singapore 109784
Chesham Graphics Gallery, Chesham 112847
Chesham Town Museum, Chesham 039058
Cheshire Antiques and Fine Art Fair, Knutsford 093920
Cheshire Brick & Slate, Tarvin 086824, 131573
Cheshire County Museum, Keene . . 044945
Cheshire Military Museum, Chester 039059
Chesney, New York 090779
Chesney's Antique Fireplace Warehouse, London 085194
Chess Antiques, Chesham 083941, 130551
Chess Expo, 's-Hertogenbosch 108072
Chessler, Baltimore 115044
Chest of Drawers, London 085195
The Chest of Drawers, Tetbury 086851
Chester, Peter & Catherine, San Diego 092623, 132848
Chester Art Guild, Chester 042804
The Chester Beatty Library, Dublin . 022734
Chester County Historical Society Museum, West Chester 049068
Chester County Museum, Chester . 042803
Chesterfield, Fresno 088899
Chesterfield Antiques, Birmingham . 083527
Chesterfield County Museum, Chesterfield 042808
Chesterfield Historical Society of Verginia Museum, Chesterfield 042808
Chesterfield Museum and Art Gallery, Chesterfield 039063
Chesterholm Museum Roman Vindolanda, Hexham 039745
Chester's Closet, Denver 115982
Chesterton, Margaret, Saint Austell 086446
Chesterwood Museum, Stockbridge 048363
Chestico Museum, Port Hood 006185
Chestnut Hill Antiques, Philadelphia 091620
Chestnut Hill Resale, Philadelphia . 091621
Chet Krupski, Tampa 093118
Chethams's Hospital and Library, Manchester 040397
Chetopa Historical Museum, Chetopa 042812
Chetwynd Stapylton, Portland 118988
Cheugn, Alberto Manuel, New York . 117769
Cheung, Sacramento 092145
Cheung King, Hong Kong 059607
Chevailler & Pache, Valentin S., Yverdon-les-Bains 082923
Chevalerias, Stéphane, Dirac 062691
Chevalet d'Eon, Salon-de-Provence 101247
Chevalier, Paris 065700
Chevalier, Bernard, A Saint-Eterne, Soings-en-Sologne 068248
Chevalier, S.A., Courbevoie 062510, 124212
Chevalier-Bourdiol, Marie-Joëlle, Saint-Cannat 067390
Chevalley, Annie, Montreux 111741
Chevallier, Stéphane, Guillestre . . . 063107
Les Chevau-Légers, Lorient 064001
Les Chevaux du Vent, Paris 065701
Le Cheverny, Bruxelles 057887
Chevertons of Edenbridge, Edenbridge 084271
Chevillon, Gilles, Corcelles-en-Beaujolais 062472
Cheviot, Cincinnati 088221
Cheviot, Los Angeles 132246
Cheviot Museum, Cheviot 030456
Chevrier, Guy, Montréal 058936
Chevrier Franck, Chaumont (Haute-Marne) 062246
Chevy Chase Antiques, Washington 093400
Chevy Chase Antiques Show, Bethesda 093978
Chevy Chase Gallery, Washington . . 120273
Chew, Betek, Singapore 109785
Cheyenne Frontier Days Old West Museum, Cheyenne 042814
Cheyne, Patrick, Altrincham 122385
Cheyne House Antiques, Rye 086423
Chez, Carl, Pézenas 066798
Chez, Françoise, Annesse-et-Beaulieu 060902
Chez, Jean, Bruxelles 057888
Chez, Jean, Bruxelles 120719
Chez, Joanne, Piaseczno 109038
Chez Annamarie, Praha 098424
Chez Antique, Sacramento 092146
Chez Arsène, Batz-sur-Mer 061220
Chez Betty, Charleroi 058141
Chez Chalon, Chard 083911, 130525
Chez Colombine, Auvers-sur-Oise . 061093
Chez Daniel, Les Fourgs 063765
Chez Dany, Saint-Ouen 067749
Chez Desserey, Le Pailly 063675
Chez François, Grenoble 099302
Chez Grand'Mère, Cabestany 061846
Chez Maxine, Montréal 058937
Chez nos Anciens, Boulogne-sur-Mer 061693
Chez Pierrot, Notre-Dame-de-Riez . 065233
Chez Will, Paris 065702
Chi, Los Angeles 116738
Chi Fang, Dandong 097713
Chi Hong, Taipei 059795
Il Chiacchierino, Bari 075009
Chiais, Valentina, Venezia 076927
Chianelli, Rosario, Roma 127971
Chiang Mai Contemporary Art Museum, Chiang Mai 037895
Chiang Saen National Museum, Chiang Rai 037898
Chiappetta, Claude, Aix-en-Provence 060700
Chiara, Warszawa 109106
Chiara Antichitá, Modena 075906
Chiari, Firenze 140011
Chiari, Dorothea, Fulda 125693
Chiaroscuro, Richmond 119106
Chiarugi, Simone, Firenze 127319
Chiavarini, Paola, Parma 076201
Chiazzese, Domenico, Palermo . . . 127824
Chiba City Museum of Art, Chiba . . 026436
Chiba-kenritsu Awa Hakubutsukan, Tateyama 027135
Chiba-kenritsu Bijutsukan, Chiba . . 026437
Chiba-kenritsu Boso Fudoki-No-Oka, Sakae 027010
Chiba-kenritsu Chuo Hakubutsukan, Chiba 026438
Chiba-kenritsu Kazusa Hakubutsukan, Kisarazu 026654
Chiba-kenritsu Sonan Hakubutsukan, Isumi 026576
Chiba-shi Kasori Kaizuka Hakubutsukan, Chiba 026439
Chiba Sogo Museum of Art, Chiba . 026440
Chic & Antique, Solingen 073851
The Chicago Academy of Sciences Peggy Notebaert Nature Museum, Chicago 042829
Chicago Antique Centre, Chicago . . 088051
Chicago Antique Mall, Chicago 088052
Chicago Antiques Fair, Chicago . . . 093979
Chicago Architectural Arts, Chicago 131893
Chicago Architecture Foundation, Chicago 042830
Chicago Art Dealers Association, Chicago 054704
Chicago Art Group, Chicago 115387
Chicago Art Source, Chicago 115388
Chicago Artists' Coalition, Chicago . 054705
Chicago Artists' News, Chicago . . . 136418
The Chicago Athenaeum - Museum of Architecture and Design, Chicago 042831
Chicago Center for the Print, Chicago 115389
Chicago Children's Museum, Chicago 042832
Chicago Coin Company, Chicago . . 088053
Chicago Coin Company, Chicago . . 088054
Chicago Connection, San Antonio . . 092498
Chicago Conservation Center, Chicago 131894
Chicago Cultural Center, Chicago . . 042833
Chicago Design Show, Annual Contemporary Furnishings Forum, Chicago 093980
Chicago Gallery News, Chicago . . . 136419
Chicago Gold, Chicago 088055
Chicago Gold Gallery, Chicago 088056
Chicago Historical Society, Chicago 042834
Chicago International New Art Forms Exposition, Lakeside 136420
Chicago Printmakers Collaborative 4642 N Western Av, Chicago 054706
Chicago Watch Brokers, Chicago . . 088057
Chicagoland Polish Books, Chicago 142285
Le Chicchere Cose Cosi, Roma 076372
Chiché, Bertrand, Bouin 061680
Chichester Antiques Centre, Chichester 083971, 130562, 141515
Chichester Bookshop, Chichester . . 141516
Chichester Decorative and Fine Arts Society, London 054338
Chichester District Museum, Chichester 039068
Chichester Gallery, Chichester 083972
Chichester Gallery, Chichester 112857
Chichester Gallery, Chichester 130563
Chichester Gallery, Chichester 141517
Chichi Antiquités, Montréal 058938
Chichibunomiya Kinen Supohtsu Hakubutsukan, Tokyo 027151
Chicho Campanera, Barcelona 080834
Chickamauga-Chattanooga National Military Park, Fort Oglethorpe 043960
Chickasaw Council House Museum, Tishomingo 048559
Chickasaw County Historical Society Museum, Bradford Village, Nashua 046135
Chicken Street, Leiden 078563
Chickies, Edmonton 058822
Chico Museum, Chico 042890
Chicochai, Vancouver 059346
Chicory Gallery, Alkmaar 107614
Chiddingstone Castle, Chiddingstone 039076
Chide, François, Dinard 062686
Chido Museum, Tsuruoka 027297
Chidori, Seattle 092975
Chief John Ross House, Rossville . . 047549
Chief Oshkosh Native American Arts, Egg Harbor 043620
Chief Plenty Coups Museum, Pryor . 047275
Chiefs & Spirits, Den Haag 107908
Chiefswood Museum, Ohsweken . . 006063
Chieftain Auctions, Saint Albans . . . 122676
Chieftains Museum, Rome 047531
Chiellini, Livorno 106118
Le Chien d'Or, Québec 097139
Chieng Huat Antique, Bangkok 083095
Chiesa, Carlo Alberto, Milano 140049
Chiesa, Mario, Torino 128282
Chiesa di Santa Maria Maddalena de Pazzi, Sala Capitolare Crocifissione del Perugino, Firenze 024146
Chiffonnier, Jarmenil 063232
Chiffonnier d'Art, Beuzeville 061418
Les Chiffonniers, Meschers-sur-Gironde 064509
Chifley Home, Bathurst 000775
Chignoli, Patrizia, Milano 075667
Chihiro Art Museum Azumino, Nagano 026842
Chihiro Art Museum Tokyo, Tokyo . . 027152
Chihuly, Seattle 119897
Chikatetsu Hakubutsukan, Tokyo . . 027153
Chikkyo Art Museum Kasaoka, Kasaoka 026633
Chikubushima Treasure House, Shiga 027062

Chikueido, Kyoto 077091
Chikuho-do, Yokohama 077333
Chikurin-ji Treasure House, Kochi . . 026670
Chikusendo, Hiroshima 077052
Childers Pharmaceutical Museum, Childers 000911
Childhood and Costume Museum, Bridgnorth 038830
Children Art Palace, Islamabad 031366
Children's Art Museum, San Angelo 047782
Childrens Art Museum, Tako 027131
Children's Discovery Museum of Central Illinois, Bloomington 042258
Children's Discovery Museum of North San Diego, Carlsbad 042624
Children's Discovery Museum of San Jose, San Jose 047896
Children's Discovery Museum of the Desert, Rancho Mirage 047323
The Children's Discovery Museum of Vermont, Burlington 042524
Children's Hands-On Museum, Tuscaloosa 048662
Children's Health Museum, Charlottesville 042764
Children's Heritage and Science Museum, Amman 027365
Children's Library Museum, Marondera 049587
The Children's Metamorphosis, Londonderry 045374
Children's Museum, Bhavnagar . . . 022029
Children's Museum, Detroit 043438
Children's Museum, Holyoke 044584
Childrens Museum, Imphal 022167
Children's Museum, Quezon City . . 031772
Children's Museum, Qurm 031352
The Children's Museum, Seattle . . . 048078
Children's Museum, Shanghai 007230
Children's Museum, Museo de Los Niños, San Diego 047817
The Children's Museum, Museum Wharf, Boston 042321
Children's Museum at La Habra, La Habra 045067
The Children's Museum at Saratoga, Saratoga Springs 048005
Children's Museum at Yunker Farm, Fargo 043812
Children's Museum Big Bang, Sakai 027011
Children's Museum in Dartmouth, South Dartmouth 048237
The Children's Museum in Easton, North Easton 046526
Children's Museum in New Braunfels, New Braunfels 046196
Children's Museum of Boca Raton, Boca Raton 042283
The Children's Museum of Cleveland, Cleveland 042983
Children's Museum of Denver, Denver 043400
The Children's Museum of Green Bay, Green Bay 044306
Children's Museum of History, Natural History and Science at Utica, New York, Utica 048718
The Children's Museum of Houston, Houston 044636
The Children's Museum of Indianapolis, Indianapolis 044735
The Children's Museum of Kansas City, Kansas City 044911
Children's Museum of Lake Charles, Lake Charles 045100
Children's Museum of Los Angeles, Los Angeles 045416
Children's Museum of Maine, Portland 047157
Children's Museum of Manhattan, New York 046312
The Children's Museum of Memphis, Memphis 045755
Children's Museum of Oak Ridge, Oak Ridge 046586
Children's Museum of Portsmouth, Portsmouth 047184
Children's Museum of Richmond, Richmond 047412
The Children's Museum of Rose Hill Manor Park, Frederick 044048
Children's Museum of South Carolina, Myrtle Beach 046113
Children's Museum of Spokane, Spokane 048273
Children's Museum of Stockton, Stockton 048370
Children's Museum of Tampa - Kid City, Tampa 048486
Children's Museum of the Arts, New York 046313
The Children's Museum of Utah, Salt Lake City 047771
Children's Museum of Virginia, Portsmouth Museums, Portsmouth 047196
Children's Own Museum, Toronto . . 006593
Children's Planet, Louisville 089968
The Children's Science Center, Cape Coral 042611
Childress County Heritage Museum, Childress 042894
Childs, Boston 115160
Childs, Graham, Newbury 131303
Childventure Museum, Fort Washington 043992
Chile & Tomate, Houston 116292
Chillagoe Historical Centre, Chillagoe 000913
Chillariz, Dnipropetrovs'k 112384
Chillida Leku, Hernani 035279
Chilliwack Museum, Chilliwack . . . 005268
Chiltern Athenaeum, Chiltern 000914
Chiltern Motor Museum, Chiltern . . 000915
Chiltern Open Air Museum, Chalfont Saint Giles 039028
Chilton, Miranda 056232
Chilton, Juliet, Shrewsbury 086598
Chimène, Meylan 064545
La Chimera, Roma 076373
Chimera Foundation, Mumbai 105762
Chimera Oriental Art Books, Hurstpierpoint 141685
La Chimère, Cannes 061938
Chimère Antiquités, Paris 065703
Chimes Textbook Exchange, New Orleans 142608
Chimmey Point Tavern, Addison . . . 041578
Chimney Mill Galleries, Bury Saint Edmunds 083821
Chimney Mill Galleries, Bury Saint Edmunds 112771
Chimneyville Crafts Gallery, Jackson 044796
Chin, Geraldton 055874
Chin Fung Tong Gallery, San Francisco 119636
China 2000, New York 117770
China Academy of Art, Hangzhou . . 049849
The China Antique, Breda 078085
China Antique Furniture, New York . 090780
China Antique Link, Shanghai 059731
China Antiques, Shanghai 059732
China Antiques, Shanghai 059733
China Art Exposition, Beijing 093630
China Art Gallery, Beijing 006976
China Art Gallery, Bruxelles 057889
China Art Objects, Los Angeles 116739
China Arts, Kuala Lumpur 077498
China Arts, Paris 065704
China Arts Far East Trading, Beijing 059573
China Arts Hangzhou, Hangzhou . . . 059581
China Arts Trade and Development, Beijing 059574
China Attic, Bruxelles 057890
China Avant-Garde, New York 117771
China Aviation Museum, Beijing . . . 006977
China Bazaar, Honolulu 088940
China Book Centre, Auckland 140587
China Calligraphy Art Museum, Xian 007314
China Cat Antiques, Jacksonville . . 089392
China China, Toronto 059164
China Chine, Chatou 062240
China City, Al-Qurum 079511
China Contemporary Literature Museum, Beijing 007001
China Cultural Relic Newspaper, Beijing 135650
China Curio Centre, Hong Kong . . . 059608
China Federation of Literary and Art Circles, Chinese Artists' Association, Beijing 052789
China Fine Art Institute, Hangzhou . 097735
China First History Archive Museum, Beijing 006978
China from China, Amstelveen 077759
China Great Wall Museum, Beijing . 006979
China Handicraft Company, Penang 077501
China Institute Gallery, New York . . 046314
China International Book Trading Corporation, Beijing 133334
China Jia Long, Singapore 080446
China Jia Wu Zhan Zhen Museum, Weihai 007299
The China Locker, Lamberhurst . . . 084895
China Museum of Buddhist Literature and Heritage, Beijing 006980
China National Association of Literature and Arts, Taipei 052805
China National Museum, Beijing . . . 006981
China Nationalities Museum of Inner Mongolia, Tongliao 007293
China Nationalities Photo-Arts Publishing House, Beijing 133335
China Original, Heidelberg 134048
China Painter, Oklahoma City 136421
China Photographic Publishing House, Beijing 133336
The China Repairers, Doughton . . . 130654
China Repairers, London 130973
China Silk Museum, Hangzhou 007100
China Society for the Study of Folk Literature and Art, Beijing 052790
China Sports Museum, Beijing 006982
China Stamp Museum, Beijing 006983
China Standard Cao Book Society, Nanjing 137751
China Town Coin Center, New York . 090781
China Trade Center Art Gallery, San Francisco 119637
China Tradition Medicine Museum, Chongqing 007050
China Treasures, Hong Kong 059609
China Works, Auckland 078932
China Xiamen Huaqiao Museum, Xiamen 007311
De la China y del Viento Sudan, Madrid 110475
China Yin Xue Museum, Hangzhou . 007101
Chinard, Blacourt 061504
Chinati Foundation, Marfa 045662
Chinatown Art, New York 117772
Chinchilla and District Historical Society Museum, Chinchilla 000917
Chinderah Bay Antiques, Chinderah 055669
La Chine, Amsterdam 077820
Chine Antique, Dijon 062651
Chine et Japon, Marseille 064337
Chine Gallery, Hong Kong 059610
Chine Gallery, Hong Kong 059611
La Chine Populaire, Uzès 068667
Chinerie, Riom 067147
Chines Antiques, Nantes 064914
Chinese-American Fine Art Society, Boston 054707
Chinese Antique Repair, Oakland . . 132566
Chinese Antiques, Limoges 063886
Chinese Art Association of America, San Francisco 054708
Chinese Art Gallery, Dallas 115852
Chinese Arts and Crafts, Hong Kong 059612
Chinese Arts and Crafts, Hong Kong 059613
Chinese Association of Museums, Taipei 052806
Chinese Association of Natural Science Museums, Beijing 052791
Chinese Carpets, Sharjah 083212
Chinese Contemporary, London . . . 113538
Chinese Country Antiques, New York 090782
Chinese Culture Center of San Francisco, San Francisco 047860
Chinese Decorative Art Studio, Singapore 080447
Chinese Dynasty Furnishings, Honolulu 088941
Chinese Export Antique Furniture and Traditional Artworks Fair, Shanghai 093631
Chinese Fine Art, Manama 095998
Chinese Heritage, Singapore 080448
Chinese House Museum, Echo 043599
De Chinese Kunsthandel, Rotterdam 078708
Chinese Medicine Museum, Hangzhou 007102
Chinese Museum, Melbourne 001233
Chinese Museum of Military Weaponary, Tongzhou 007294
Chinese Painting Academy, Beijing . 049844
Chinese Painting and Calligraphy Institute, Wuhan 098026
Chinese Painting Gallery, Shanghai 097904
Chinese Painting Gallery, Wuxi 098029
Chinese People's Political Confutative Conference Calligraphy and Painting Gallery, Ningbo 097880
Chinese Photographers Association, Beijing 052792
The Chinese Porcelain Company, New York 090783
Chinese Society of Museums, Beijing 052793
Le Chineur du Marais, Paris 065705
Chineurs, Dieppe 062625
Ching, C.P., Hong Kong 059614
Ching Ting Chen, Hong Kong 059615
Chinikhaneh Museum, Sheikh Sati Mausoleum, Ardebil 022546
Chink in the Wall, Barton-upon-Humber 112564
Chino, Vancouver 097440
Chino-shi Togariishi Jomon Kokokan, Chino 026443
Chinoh, New York 117773
Chinqua-Penn Plantation, North Carolyna State University, Reidsville 047370
Chiocchini, Franca, Perugia 127873
Chios Museum of Byzantine and Postbyzantine Art, Chios 021232
Chiostro dello Scalzo, Firenze 024147
Il Chiostro di Manfredi, Genova . . .075459, 140034
Chiotakis, Ioannis, Athinai 139896
Chip n' Dale's Antique Mall I, Memphis 090061
Chip n' Dale's Antique Mall II, Memphis 090062
Chiparus, Parthenay 066690
Chiparus, Parthenay 066691
Chippendale Eastlake, Houston . . . 089048
Chippendale Society, Leeds 054339
Chippenham Museum and Heritage Centre, Chippenham 039077
Chippewa County Historical Society Museum, Montevideo 045991
Chippewa Valley Museum, Eau Claire 043595
Chipping Norton Antique Centre, Chipping Norton 083988
Chipping Norton Museum of Local History, Chipping Norton 039079
Chippokes Farm and Forestry Museum, Surry 048442
Chirac, Chantal, Aubusson 061045
Chirco, Toulon (Var) 124964
Chiricahua Museum, Willcox 049176
Chiron, Marie-Christine, Nantes . . . 064915
Chirone L'Arte, Verona 076998
Chisenhale Gallery, London 040116
Chishaku-in Temple Storehouse, Kyoto 026709
Chishoken, Imai, Kyoto 077092
Chisholm & Larsson, New York 117774
Chisholm Trail Heritage Center Museum, Duncan 043528
Chisholm Trail Historical Museum, Waurika 049014

Chisholm Trail Museum, Kingfisher . 045006
Chisholm Trail Museum, Wellington 049050
Chislehurst Antiques, Chislehurst . . 083997
Chisolm, New York 117775
Chisseaux Rive Gauche, Paris 100148
Chista, New York 090784
Chistina's Cupboard, Toronto 059165
The Chiswick Fireplace Company, London 085196, 130974
Chiswick House, London 040117
Chita-shi Rekishi Minzoku Hakubutsukan, Chita 026445
Chitari Academy Of Fine Arts,, Pune 105824
Sri Chitra Art Gallery, Gallery of Asian Paintings, Thiruvananthapuram . . 022350
Chitrakoot, Kolkata 105736
Chitram, Rekha, Kolkata 105737
Chittagong University Museum, Chittagong 003096
Chittenango Landing Canal Boat Museum, Chittenango 042908
Chiucchiù, Alessandro, Roma 127972
Chivers, Los Angeles 089720
Chiverton House Museum, Northampton 001340
Chivré, Claire de, Dieulefit 099206
Chiyoda Designer Gakuin, Tokyo . . 050479
Chiz, Pittsburgh 118909
Chizky, Jean, L'Isle-sur-la-Sorgue . 063932
Chladecká, Žilina 080643
Chlebovec, Ondřej, Olomouc 060059
Chloe Antiques, Worthing 087264
Chloupek, Zagreb 123946
Chmelik, Dietmar, Leipzig 103860
Chmel'nyc'kyj Chudožnij Muzej, Chmel'nyc'kyj 038251
Chmel'nyc'kyj Oblasnyj Krajeznavčyj Muzej, Chmel'nyc'kyj 038252
Cho, Seoul 107212
Chobot, Wien 095807
Chochon, Chochon, Barré & Allardi, Paris 121129
Chochou, Maria, Rhodos 105442
Chock, Déborah, Paris 100149
Chocol Art Gallery, Ashburton 108293
Choctaw Museum, Hugo 044666
Chodoff, Chirstopher, New York . . . 090785
Chodorowski, Wiesław, Starogard Gdański 129073
Chodová, Alena, Přibram 060184
Chofu Museum, Shimonoseki 027066
Chofu-shiritsu Hakabutsukan, Chofu 026446
Chohung Museum of Finance, Seoul 027545
Choice, Bergen op Zoom 078069
Choice, Delhi 105655
Choice Antiques, Warminster 087026
Choice Art Gallery, Dallas 115853
Choice Galeria de Arte, São Paulo . 096669
Choice Gallery, Birmingham 112646
Choices Recovery Centers, New York 090786
Choisy Antiquités, Choisy-le-Roi . . .062297, 124199
Chojagahara Kokokan, Itoigawa . . . 026581
Chojin Lama Museum, Ulaanbaatar 029001
Choko, Tokyo 107027
Chokoku no Mori Bijutsukan, Hakone 026490
Cholet, Nicole, Busseol 099040
Chollet, Stéphane, Paris 124620
Chollet Vuaillat, Paris 065706
Cholmondeley, Peter, Stuart Park . . 056641
Choma Museum and Crafts Centre, Choma 049566
Chomarat, Gérard, Lyon 099549
Chomarat, Michel, Lyon 133486
Chome Fine Art, Bath 112572
Chomette, Michèle, Paris 100150
Chomienne, Véronique, Nice 099831
Chomsioglou, Maria, Thessaloniki . 074633
Chomsioglou, Maria, Thessaloniki . 074634
Chonbuk University Museum, Jeonju 027518
Chongjak, Seoul 107213
Chongming County Museum, Shanghai 007231
Chongqing Chinese Painting Gallery, Chongqing 097704
Chongqing History Calligraphy and Painting Gallery, Chongqing 097705
Chongqing Museum, Chongqing . . . 007051
Chongqing Natural Museum, Chongqing 007052
Chongro, Seoul 107214
Chongwen Zhai Art Cooperative, Jinan 097856
Chonigbaum, Antony 060932
Chonnam University Museum, Gwangju 027501
Choo Seng & Co., Yangon 077700
ChooChoo Train Depot, Houston . . . 089049
Chopin, Bruxelles 057891
Choquet, Caroline, Paris 065707
Choraku Homotsukan, Kamo, Izu . . 026616
Chorfi, Casablanca 107550
Chorfi, Casablanca 107551
Chorley-Burdett, Bournemouth 083596
Chornspycher, Inkwil 111569
Chorosinski, K., Köln 071920, 126070
Chorožskij Istoriko-Kraevedčeskij Muzej, Chorog 037837
Chorus, Firenze 127320
Chorus-Verlag für Kunst und Wissenschaft, München 134227
Ch'ose, Genolier 111511
La Chose, Saint-Dizier 067428
Chosun, Pymble 056507
Chosun, Seoul 077363
Chosun, Seoul 107215
Chosun-Ilbo, Seoul 107216
Chouakri & Brahms, Berlin 101828
Chouchou, Magny-Lormes 064216
Choucroun, Richard, Houston 089050
Chouet-Darbois, Claude, Beaune . . 061272
La Chouette, Montolieu 138214
Chouinard, Hong Kong 097772
Chourlet, Vence 101438
Chourlet, Céline, Paris 100151
Chow, Carin, San Francisco 092757
Chow, Raymond, Vancouver 097441
Choyce, Ware 114644
Choyce Gallery, Saint Albans 114343
Chrämai, Anduze 098827
Chrétien, Jean, Paris 138332
Chrétien, René, Paris 065708
Chrétienne, Le Lorrain 140248
Chrétienne La Foi, Fort-de-France . 140243
Chris, R., Paris 065709
Chris' Antiques, Healesville 055973
Chris Art & Antique, Bucureşti 080147
Chris'Ary, Villeneuve-d'Ascq 068911, 125028
Chrisday, Paris 065710
Chrismas, Douglas, Los Angeles . . 116740
Chriss Antix, Roanne 067166
Chris's Crackers, Carhampton 083877
Chrissy, Auckland 078933
Christ, Hans, Krefeld 121485
Christ, Sabine, Kirchheim unter Teck 126048
Christ Boelens Jukeboxen Museum, Sint Oedenrode 030152
Christ Child Opportunity Shop, Washington 093401
Christ Church Cathedral Treasury, Oxford 040656
Christ Church Community Museum, Lakefield 005740
Christ Church Picture Gallery, Oxford 040657
Christ the King College Museum, Calbayog 031646
Christa's Limited, Chicago 088058
Christchurch Art Gallery Te Puna o Waiwhetu, Christchurch 030462
Christchurch Auctions, Christchurch 121818
Christchurch Carpets, Christchurch 084006
Christchurch Mansion, Ipswich 039811
Christchurch Tricycle Museum, Christchurch 039085
Christelijke Hogeschool voor de Kunsten Constantijn Huygens, Kampen . . . 050561
Christel's Antiek, Utrecht 078790
Christen, Mario, Luzern 130101
Christen, Richard K., Louisville 089969
Christen-Fankhauser, Jetta, Reinach (Basel-Land) 082737
Christensen, Bent, Ahrensburg 069119
Christensen, Janni & Steen, Hellerup 060251
Christensen, Reinhold, Frederiksberg 060230
Christensen, Reinhold, Frederiksberg 098525, 124014
Christi, Neuss 073013
Christian, Peter & Ann, Blackpool . . 083553
Christian Art Distributors, Vereeniging 134900
Christian Arts, London 054340
Christian C. Sanderson Museum, Chadds Ford 042693
Christian Daniel Rauch-Museum, Museum Bad Arolsen, Bad Arolsen 015644
Christian Gallery, Merano 106131
Christian-Wolff-Haus, Stadtmuseum Halle, Halle, Saale 017654
Christiania Auktionsforretning, Oslo 121866
Christianity and the Arts, Chicago . . 136422
Christian's, Guatemala 105476
Christians, Hamburg 133999
Christianssands Billedgalleri, Kristiansand 030955
Christiansted National Historic Site, Saint Croix 047627
Christie, Cairo 060434
Christie, Midland 137000
Christie, Ottawa 059035
Christie, Robert, Carrickfergus 083885
Christie Antique Show, Dundas 093623
Christie Galerie, Mougins 099775
Christie's, Adelaide 120557
Christie's, Aix-en-Provence 120890
Christie's, Amsterdam 121777
Christie's, Andover 122387
Christie's, Ardmore 122796
Christie's, Ashbourne 122390
Christie's, Athinai 121632
Christie's, Atlanta 122799
Christie's, Bangkok 122376
Christie's, Barcelona 122006
Christie's, Beijing 120838
Christie's, Beirut 121753
Christie's, Berlin 121326
Christie's, Beverly Hills 122817
Christie's, Bologna 121678
Christie's, Bordeaux 120938
Christie's, Boston 122824
Christie's, Bruxelles 120720
Christie's, Buenos Aires 120551
Christie's, Cape Town 121981
Christie's, Cheltenham 122457
Christie's, Chicago 122842
Christie's, Dallas 122871
Christie's, Dublin 121662
Christie's, Düsseldorf 121381
Christie's, Edinburgh 122499
Christie's, Frankfurt am Main 121403
Christie's, Genève 122321
Christie's, Genova 121689
Christie's, Glin 121671
Christie's, Greenville 122899
Christie's, Hamburg 121424
Christie's, Harrogate 122535
Christie's, Helsinki 120882
Christie's, Hong Kong 120839
Christie's, Jakarta 121651
Christie's, Johannesburg 121985
Christie's, Kuala Lumpur 121758
Christie's, Lisboa 121926
Christie's, London 122584
Christie's, London 122585, 135204
Christie's, Lugano 122335
Christie's, Luxembourg 121756
Christie's, Madrid 122046
Christie's, Melbourne 120608
Christie's, México 121765
Christie's, Milano 121702
Christie's, Monaco 121774
Christie's, Montevideo 122777
Christie's, München 121522
Christie's, Mumbai 121650
Christie's, New Orleans 122978
Christie's, New York 122990
Christie's, New York 122991
Christie's, Newport 123023
Christie's, Oklahoma City 123030
Christie's, Palm Beach 123039
Christie's, Paris 121130
Christie's, Penrith 122649
Christie's, Petworth 122656
Christie's, Plymouth 122658
Christie's, Ponsacco 121716
Christie's, Praha 120854
Christie's, Ramsey, Isle of Man . . . 122662
Christie's, Rio de Janeiro 120795
Christie's, Roma 121720
Christie's, Rotterdam 121801
Christie's, Saint-Denis (Seine-Saint-Denis) 067422
Christie's, San Francisco 123103
Christie's, San Pedro Garza Garcia . 121770
Christie's, Santiago de Chile 120835
Christie's, São Paulo 120797
Christie's, Shanghai 120841
Christie's, Singapore 121973
Christie's, Souance-au-Perche 121262
Christie's, Stockholm 122251
Christie's, Stuttgart 121604
Christie's, Subiaco 120641
Christie's, Taipei 120844
Christie's, Tel Aviv 121675
Christie's, Templecombe 122723
Christie's, Tokyo 121743
Christie's, Torino 121732
Christie's, Toronto 120816
Christie's, Venezia 121737
Christie's, Washington 123136
Christie's, Wien 120678
Christie's, Woollahra 120659
Christie's, Zürich 122363
Christie's Gallery, Dallas 115854
Christie's International Magazine, London 136191
Christie's Publications, London . . . 135205
Christie's Publications, New York . . 135420
Christin, Jean, Genève 122322
Christin Gallery, Toronto 097245
Christinaz, Alain, Biel 082256
Christine Antiquité, Noisy-le-Grand 065223
Christine's Adapon Fine Arts, Makati 108825
Christine's Art Gallery, Baguio 108816
Christine's Curiosity Shop, Tucson . 093213
Christine's Time, Helsinki 060514
Christine's Vintage Specialty Shop, Cleveland 088319
Christmann, Wiesbaden 139848
Christmas Closet, Jacksonville 089393
Christmas Morning, Dallas 088479
Christmas Museum Gallery, Horsley Park 001119
Christodoulou, D.E., Amsterdam . . . 140291
Christof, Franz, Schleusingen 073698
Christof, Franz, Weimar, Thüringen . 074307
Christofski, Motueka 079159
Christoph &Co., Holger, Bonn 138894
Christophe, Clément, Embrun 099247
Christophe Raymond, Auterive 061084
Christopher, Birmingham . 087747, 131832
Christopher, Alexander, Duncraig . . 123219
Christopher, Radko, Pittsburgh 091800
Christopher, Virginia, Calgary 096797
Christopher's, Farnham . . 084389, 130705
Christopher's Collectibles, El Paso . 088795

Christopher's Discoveries, New Orleans 090534
Christophs Friseur-Museum, Leipheim 018555
Christos Capralos Museum, Aegina 021114
Christos Capralos Museum, Agrinion 021122
Christos Capralos Museum, Athinai 021165
Christ's Hospital Museum, Horsham 039771
Christusbruderschaft Selbitz Buch- und Kunstverlag, Selbitz 134395
Christy's Antiques, Virginia Beach . 093349
Chroma, Salt Lake City 119335
Chroma, San Francisco 119638
Chromatic Arts, Swindon 114539
Chromos, Belo Horizonte 096456
Chromos, Belo Horizonte 096457
Chromosome, Berlin 101829
Chronicle Books, San Francisco . . . 135491
Chronique d'Egypte, Bruxelles 135594
Chronis, Nikol., Iráklion 074622
Chronos, Brugge 057765
Chrysalis, East Melbourne 094502, 133049
Chrysalis, Manchester 114041
The Chrysler Museum of Art, Norfolk 046496
Chrysochoidis, Dimitrios, Athinai . . 074587
La Chrysolite, Auxerre 061101
Chrysolite, Paris 065711
Chryssikou, Angeliki G., Kifissia . . . 105429
Chrystals Auctions, Ramsey, Isle of Man 122663
Chrzan, Mieczysław, Poznań 079686, 140759
CHTJ Southard House Museum, Richmond 047404
Chu, Lauran, Paris 100152, 133553
Chu, Sammy, Los Angeles 116741
Chu, Shing, New York 090787
Chuan Cheng Art Center, Taipei . . . 007366
Chuangxin Antique Store, Shanghai 059734
Chubu, Nagoya 106915
Chuck, San Francisco 092758
Chuck and Barb's Baseball Cards, Columbus 088391
Chudalla, Albert, München 126366
Chudarek, Rudolf, Wien 057392
Chudleigh Park of Sassafras, Sassafras 095184
Chudožestvena Galerija, Balčik . . . 004625
Chudožestvena Galerija, Blagoevgrad 004640
Chudožestvena Galerija, Burgas . . . 004648
Chudožestvena Galerija, Chaskovo . 004654
Chudožestvena Galerija, Čirpan . . . 004659
Chudožestvena Galerija, Drjanovo . 004673
Chudožestvena Galerija, Gabrovo . . 004681
Chudožestvena Galerija, Gălăbovo . 004686
Chudožestvena Galerija, Karlovo . . 004704
Chudožestvena Galerija, Kavarna . . 004709
Chudožestvena Galerija, Kazanlăk . 004712
Chudožestvena Galerija, Levski . . . 004739
Chudožestvena Galerija, Loveč . . . 004742
Chudožestvena Galerija, Mezdra . . 004751
Chudožestvena Galerija, Michajlovgrad 004752
Chudožestvena Galerija, Pernik . . . 004773
Chudožestvena Galerija, Plovdiv . . . 004790
Chudožestvena Galerija, Provadia . . 004803
Chudožestvena Galerija, Provadija . 004806
Chudožestvena Galerija, Radnevo . . 004808
Chudožestvena Galerija, Silistra . . . 004829
Chudožestvena Galerija, Smoljan . . 096713
Chudožestvena Galerija, Sozopol . . 004880
Chudožestvena Galerija, Velingrad . 004941
Chudožestvena Galerija, Vidin 004943
Chudožestvena Galerija, Žeravna . . 004952
Chudožestvena Galerija Boris Denev, Veliko Tărnovo 004931
Chudožestvena Galerija Darenie Kollekcia Svetlin Russev, Pleven 004778
Chudožestvena Galerija Dobrič, Dobrič 004667
Chudožestvena Galerija Elena Karamichajlova, Šumen 004887
Chudožestvena Galerija Georgi Papazov, Jambol 004695
Chudožestvena Galerija Ilija Beškov, Pleven 004779
Chudožestvena Galerija Kiril Petrov, Montana 004755
Chudožestvena Galerija Nikola Marinov, Targovište 004899
Chudožestvena Galerija Nikolaj Pavlovič, Svištov 004894
Chudožestvena Galerija Petar Persengiev, Novi Pazar 004760
Chudožestvena Galerija Prof. Ilija Petrov, Razgrad 004812
Chudožestvena Galerija Ruse, Ruse 004818
Chudožestvena Galerija Stanislav Dospevski, Pazardžik 004768
Chudožestvena Galerija Varna, Varna 004911
Chudožestvennaja Galereja - Dom Kukly Tatjany Kalininoj, Petrozavodsk . . 033658
Chudožestvenno-grafičeskij Fakultet, Kubanskij Gosudarstvennyj Universitet, Krasnodar 050640
Chudožestvenno-memorialnyj Muzej K.S. Petrova-Vodkina, Chvalynsk 033089
Chudožestvenno-pedagogičeskij Muzej Igruški - Kulturno-delovoj Centr, Sergiev Posad 033867
Chudožestvenno-vystavočnyj Kompleks, Muzej Istorii i Kultury Srednego Prikamja, Sarapul 033849
Chudožestvennyj Moskovskij Gusudarstvennyj Akademičeskij Institut im. V.I. Surikova, Moskva 050643
Chudožestvennyj Muzej, Staryj Oskol 033905
Chudožestvennyj Muzej, Valujki . . . 034022
Chudožestvennyj Muzej im. A.N. Radiščeva, Saratov 033852
Chudožestvennyj Muzej im. M.S. Tuganova, Vladikavkaz 034034
Chudožnij Muzei, Sevastopol 038386
Chudožnij Muzej, Žytomyr 038420
Chudožno-memorial'nyj Muzej Ivana Truša, Nacionalnij Muzej u Lvovi, Lviv . . 038338
Chudožno-memorial'nyj Muzej Leopol'da Levyc'kogo, Nacionalnij Muzej u Lvovi, Lviv 038339
Chudožno-memorial'nyj Muzej Oleksi Novakivs'kogo, Nacionalnij Muzej u Lvovi, Lviv 038340
Chudožno-memorial'nyj Muzej Oleni Kul'čic'koï, Nacionalnij Muzej u Lvovi, Lviv 038341
Chudožnyj Muzej im. O. Šovkunenka, Cherson 038247
Chudžandskij Istoriko-Kraevedčeskij Muzej, Chudžand 037838
Chuey, Los Angeles 116742
Chugeisha, Takaoka 077225
Chugg, Keith, Swansea 086810
Chughtai Museum Trust, Lahore . . . 031377
Chugoku, Kyoto 077093
Chugoku, Sapporo 106981
Chumacero, Lourdes, México 107481
Chumbhot-Punthip Museum, Bangkok 037873
Chun & Co., Peggy, Honolulu 116203
Chun Chan, Beijing 097648
Chun Tian, Tianjin 098009
Chunfeng Literature and Art Publishing House, Shenyang 133381
Chung, Hong Kong 059616
Chung, Seoul 107217
Chung, Marguerite, Fontanil-Cornillon 062900
Chung-Cheng Art Gallery, Saint John's University, Jamaica 044823
Chung-Cheng Aviation Museum, Taipei 007367
Chungju Museum, Chungju 027471
Chungnam Telecommunication Museum, Daejeon 027478
Chungnam University Museum, Daejeon 027479
Chuo Bijutsu Gakuen, Tokyo 050480
Chuo Gallery, Nagoya 106916
Church Corner Antiques, Christchurch 079019
Church Farm Museum, Skegness . . 041036
Church Farmhouse Museum, London 040118
Church Gallery, Chagford 112831
Church Gallery, Claremont 094399
Church Hall Farm Antique, Broxted . 083772
Church Hill Antiques, Los Angeles . 089721
Church Hill Antiques Centre, Lewes 084978
The Church Hill Gallery, Knutsford . 113341
Church House Antiques, Weybridge 087108
Church House Design, Congresbury 112900
Church Lane Antiques, Claremont . 055673
Church Lane Antiques, Cranebrook 055721
Church of Scotland Committee on Artistic Matters, Edinburgh 054341
Church of the Holy Apostles Collection, Parga 021419
Church on the Lane Antiques, Columbus 088392
Church Street Antiques, Altrincham 083285, 130297
Church Street Antiques, London . . .085197, 130975
Church Street Antiques, Stow-on-the-Wold 086742
Church Street Antiques, Wells-next-the-Sea 087071
Church Street Centre, Woodbridge . 087216
Church-Waddel-Brumby House Museum, Athens 041831
Churchgate Antiques, Empingham . 084330
Churchhill Clocks, Midhurst 085986, 131278
Churchill, London 135206
Churchill, North Fremantle 056359
Churchill County Museum and Archives, Fallon 043807
Churchill House Museum and Hatton Gallery, Hereford 039731
Churchill Island Agricultural Museum, Newhaven 001329
Churchill & White, Boston 087806
Churchilliana, Sacramento 142843
Churchills Gallery, Nazeing 114111
Churrinche, Buenos Aires 055193
Churt Curiosity Shop, Churt 084012
Churzee Gallery, London 113539
Chusonji Sankozo, Hiraizumi 026518
Chvalynskij Kraevedčeskij Muzej, Chvalynsk 033090
Chybulski, Schaanwald 107337
Ci-Gong, Daegu 107182
CIA Museum, McLean 045562
Cia Rosa Art, São Paulo 058702
CIAC, Pertuis 101000
Ciăsa Granda, Stampa 037593
Ciambrelli, Carlo Filippo, Roma . . . 106508
Cian Conservando el Arte, Madrid . 129593
Cianci, Tullio, Davos Platz 082336
Ciancimino, London 085198
Cianella, Pietro, Roma 076374
Cianferoni, Piero, Firenze 127321
Ciani, Andrea, Genova 106088
Ciaralli, Mario, Roma 127973
Ciaravino, Carlo, Torino 128283
Ciarlo Brothers, San Francisco 132874
Cibeles, Madrid 122047
Ciccarelli, Lyon 064108
Ciccarelli, Dino, Roma . . . 076375, 127974
Ciccarelli, Nelly, Vaulx-en-Velin . . . 068736
Cicco, de, Lyon 064109
Cicconi, Alberto, Roma 127975
Cicerano, Alessandra, Napoli 075954
Cicerano, Carlo Giuseppe, Napoli . . 140076
Cicero, Krummhörn 072097
Cicero, Jan, Chicago 115390
Cicero Presse, Sylt-Ost . . 134426, 139777
Cicerone, Giuseppe, Roma 127976
Cicogna, Michele, Venezia 128382
Cicogna Casanova, Rolando, Torino 076801
Le Cid Antiquités, Marseille 064338
Cider House Galleries, Bletchingley 083562
Cider House Galleries, Bletchingley 112667
Cider Museum, Hereford 039732
Cider Press Antiques Centre, Taunton 086828, 131575
CIDOC International Committee for Documentation, København 052844
Cielo, Portland 091911
Cieluch, Zbigniew, Poznań 109044
Ciências Educação e Artes Luiz de Queiráz, Escola Superior de Agricultura Luiz de Queiroz / ESALQ, Piracibaba 004280
Ciencias Naturales P. Ignacio Sala, Valencia 035974
Ciervo, Francesco, Napoli 075955
Cieslik, Marianne, Jülich 134074
Ciferri, Armando, Brescia 105996
Cifola, Stefano, Roma 127977
Çifte Medrese Müzesi, Kayseri 038123
Cigarini Fin'art, Genève 082415
Cigarpe, Cartagena 110295
Cigarpe, Cartagena 110296
Cigit, Buenos Aires 136708
Cigliutti, Carole, Colombes 062424
Cigna, Antonino, Roma 076376
Cigna Museum and Art Collection, Philadelphia 046930
Il Cigno, Milano 075668
Cigüe, Saint-Étienne 138598
Cihan Antika, İstanbul 083128
Cilena, Maria, Milano 106193
Cilfynydd Art Society, Mountain Ash 054342
Ciliento, Franco, Richwiller 067137
Cilindri, Alessio, Prato 076251
Cilla, Serge, Lyon 064110
CIMA Art Gallery, Kolkata 105738
Cimabue, Mendoza 094102, 123171
La Cimaise, Besançon 061379
Cimaise, Besançon 098950
Cimaise, Cordes-sur-Ciel 099172
Cimaise d'Or, Metz 099706
Cimal, Valencia 136083
Cimarron Valley Railroad Museum, Cushing 043251
Cimetière, Jean, Bourbon-Lancy . . 061701
Cimino, Luca, Genova 127443
Čimkentskij Istoriko-Kraevedčeskij Muzej, Čimkent 027396
CIMUSET International Committee for Science and Technology Museums, Delhi 053695
Cinà, Marcella, Palermo 127825
Cinabre, Paris 065712
Cincinnati Academy of Design, Cincinnati 051139
Cincinnati Antiques Festival, Sharonville 093981
Cincinnati Art Club, Cincinnati 054709
Cincinnati Art Galleries, Cincinnati .115616, 122853
Cincinnati Art Museum, Cincinnati . 042919
Cincinnati Fire Museum, Cincinnati 042920
Cincinnati Gallery, Cincinnati 115617
Cincinnati Gallery, Cincinnati 115618
Cincinnati Museum Center, Cincinnati 042921
Cincinnati Plating and Repair Company, Cincinnati 131931
Cindy's Dolls, Las Vegas 089557
Cine Art Gallery, London 113540
Ciné-Images, Paris 100153
Cine-Qua-Non, Amsterdam 140292
Cinédoc, Paris 100154, 138333
Cinelli, Marzio, Firenze 075318
Cinema Books, Seattle 142983
Cinema Bookshop, London 141771
Cinema Collectors, Las Vegas 089558
Cinema Collectors, Los Angeles . . .089722, 142497
Cinema Graphics, Denver 115983
Cinema Museum, London 040119
La Cinémathèque de Toulouse, Toulouse 014984
Cinémathèque Historique, Toulouse 014984
Cinémathèque Québécoise - Musée du Cinéma, Montréal 005921
Cinemonde, Nashville 090433

Cinemonde, Nashville 090434
Cineteca Nazionale, Roma 025472
Ciney Antiquites, Ciney 093600
Cini, Giovanni Battista, Genova 075460
Çini Müzesi, Kütahya 038140
Çinili Köşk Müzesi, İstanbul 038087
Cinissimo, München 139500
Cinnamon Hill Antiques, Nashville . 090435
Cinolter, Martin, Praha 060117
Cinque Gallery, New York 117776
Cinquemani, Rosario, Palermo 076138
Cinquième Galerie, Paris 100155
Ciocca Arte Contemporanea, Milano 106194
Cioffi, Amelia, Verona 128421
La Ciotola, Verona 076999
Ciparis Lennox, Toronto 097246
Cipolat, Manduel 064246
Circa, Arles 060970
Circa, Fort Worth 088844
Circa, Indianapolis 089280
circa 1900, Liverpool 085023
Circa 1904 Antiques, Portland 091912
Circa 1910, Los Angeles 089723
Circa 610, New York 090788
Circa Ad, Portland 091913
Circa Antiques, Birmingham 087748
Circa Antiques, Jacksonville 089394
Circa Antiques, Los Angeles 089724
Circa Antiques, San Antonio 092499
Circa Antiques, Unley 056766
Circa Art Magazine, Dublin 135852
Circa Design Center, Dallas 088480
Circa Gallery, Minneapolis 117247
Circa Interiors and Antiques, Charlotte 087935
Circa Vintage, Glasgow 084464
Cirçé, Strasbourg 068309
Circhirello, Carole, Montpellier 124456
Circle Art and Antiques, Miami 090151
Circle Books, Bristol 141452
Circle Centre Gallery, Indianapolis . 116448
Circle Craft, Vancouver 097442
Circle Craft Gallery, Vancouver 006693
Circle Press Publications, London . . 135207
Circolo Artistico di Arezzo, Arezzo . 053746
Circolo degli Artisti, Torino 053747
Circolo degli Artisti, Casa di Dante, Firenze 053748
Circolo dei Librai Antiquari, Torino . 053749
Circuit Association d'Art Contemporain, Lausanne 054175
Circuit Géologique des Boves, Arras 010484
Circular Word, Buffalo 142261
Circulo Cinco, Belo Horizonte 058420
Círculo de Bellas Artes, La Paz 052695
Círculo de Bellas Artes, Madrid . . . 054108
Círculo de Bellas Artes de Valencia, Valencia 054109
Circus City Festival Museum, Peru . 046893
Circus Museum, Rapperswil, Sankt Gallen 037433
Circus World Museum, Baraboo . . . 042017
Cirencester Arcade, Cirencester . . . 084015
Cirencester Lock-Up, Cirencester . . 039092
Cirieco, Georges, Grenoble 063058
Ciriello, New Orleans 132408
Cirilla, Kraków 140734
Ciriza Vega, Jesus Carlos, Pamplona 110716
Cirkel Galerie, Almere 107628
Cirklaff, Dieter, Rodgau 104756
Cirkon, Sankt-Peterburg 080300
Cirone, Pierfrancesco, Roma 076377
Cirrus Gallery, Los Angeles 116743
Cirrus Gallery, Winnipeg 097577
Ciruito Museale Urbano, Palazzo Santi, Cascia 023689
Ciry, Micheline, Paris 065713
Cisar-Holt, Tulsa 093291
Císařová, Praha 123976
Císařská Konírna, Prague Castle Gallery, Praha 008598
Čišinski-Gedenkstätte, Panschwitz-Kuckau 019557
Cislaghi, Carlo, Milano 075669
Cissy, George, Memphis 116978
Cistercian Museum, Hailes 039654
The Citadel Archives and Museum, The Military College of South Carolina, Charleston 042729
Citadel Trading, Dubai 083188
Citadelles & Mazenod, Paris 133554
Citadel's Artspace, Saint Helens . . . 040908
Cité d'Art, Genève 111437
Cité de la Mer ESTRAN, Dieppe . . . 011587
Cité de l'Énergie, Shawinigan 006450
Cité Deco, Montréal 058939
La Cité des Antiquaires, Villeurbanne 068953
Cité des Métiers de Tradition, Saint-Laurent-de-la-Plaine 014377
Cité des Sciences et de l'Industrie, Paris 013565
Citigold, Brisbane 055556
Čitinskij Oblastnoj Chudožestvennyj Muzej, Čita 033093
Citiscapes, Seattle 119898
City and County Museum, Lincoln . 040005
City and Guilds of London Art School, London 050832
City Antik, Gävle 081785
City Antik, København 060309
City-Antik, Wien 057393
City Antiques, Los Angeles 089725
City Antiques, Portland 091914
City Antiques, Rochester 086385
City Art, Birmingham 112647
City Art, Christchurch 108390
City Art, San Francisco 119639
City-Art, Tampere 060623
City Art Centre, Edinburgh 039381
City Art Gallery, Saint Paul 119282
City Art Gallery, Sevilla 110766
City Art Gallery, Vancouver 097443
City Art Gallery, Wagga Wagga 001586
City Art Gallery, Leeds Museums and Galleries, Leeds 039950
City Art Works, Atlanta 114864
City Art Works, Pratt Fine Arts Center, Seattle 052164
City Auction Rooms, Dunedin 121821
City Auksjon, Oslo 121867
City Auktion, Bern 122311
City Barn Antiques, New York 090789
City Basement Books, Melbourne . . 136996
City Books, Pittsburgh 142773
City Clocks, London 085199, 130976
City County Pioneer Museum, Sweetwater 048450
City Exhibition Space, Sydney 001509
City Galerie, Hamburg 103107
City-Galerie, Linz 095652
City Galerie, Regensburg 104694
City-Galerie, Wien 057394, 095808
City Galerie, Zürich 112054
City Gallery, Leicester 039969
The City Gallery, London 113541
City Gallery, Nottingham 114174
City Gallery at Chastain, Atlanta . . . 041852
City Gallery East, Atlanta 041853
City Gallery Wellington, Wellington . 030634
City Hall Council Chamber Gallery, Charleston 042730
City Island Nautical Museum, Bronx 042434
City Kunsthandel, København 060310
City Museum, Ahmedabad 021989
City Museum, Makale 009446
City Museum, Saint Louis 047656
City Museum, Yirgalem 009447
City Museum, Leeds Museums and Galleries, Leeds 039951
City Museum and Art Gallery, Gloucester 039589
City Museum and Art Gallery, Plymouth 040721
City Museum and Records Office, Portsmouth 040761
City of Belmont Museum, Belmont . 000791
City of Bowie Museums, Bowie . . . 042363
City of Brea Gallery, Brea 042391
City of Gosnells Museum, Gosnells . 001075
City of Ketchikan Museum, Ketchikan 044978
City of Las Vegas and Rough Riders Memorial Museum, Las Vegas . . . 045194
City of London Police Museum, London 040120
City of Melbourne Collection, Melbourne 001234
City of Norwich Aviation Museum, Horsham Saint Faith 039774
City of Richmond and Burnley Historical Museum, Richmond, Victoria 001430
City of Saint John Gallery, Saint John 006352
City of Unley Museum, Unley 001578
City of Wayne Historical Museum, Wayne 049027
City of York Museum, York 006892
City Park Radio Museum, Launceston 001175
City Pride, Canterbury 083860
City Salvage, Minneapolis 090349
City Streets Gallery, Toronto 097247
City Strippers Restoration, Wellington 128972
City Traders, Rockhampton 056542
City View Antique Mall, Dallas 088481
City Wide Antiques, Detroit 088757
City Wide Antiques, Detroit 088758
City Wide Antiques, Detroit 132050
City Wide Antiques, Detroit 132051
Cityn kirja ja pap, Rovaniemi 137985
La Civetta, Pisa 135890
Le Civette, Trieste 076887
Civic Bookshop, Newcastle 137028
Civica Galleria d'Arte Contemporanea, Lissone 024505
Civica Galleria d'Arte Contemporanea F. Scroppo, Torre Pellice 026090
Civica Galleria d'Arte G. Sciortino, Monreale 024796
Civica Galleria d'Arte Moderna, Milano 024688
Civica Galleria d'Arte Moderna, Palazzo Pubblici Uffici, Gallarate 024266
Civica Galleria d'Arte Moderna, Villa Serra, Genova 024293
Civica Galleria d'Arte Moderna E. Restivo, Palermo 025080
Civica Galleria di Palazzo Rocca, Chiavari 023845
Civica Pinacoteca V. Crivelli, Convento dei Filippini, Sant'Elpidio a Mare 025776
Civica Raccolta d'Arte, Medole 024659
Civica Raccolta d'Arte, Roseto degli Abruzzi 025599
Civica Raccolta d'Arte B. Biancolini, Potenza Picena 025346
Civica Raccolta delle Stampe Achille Bertarelli, Milano 024689
Civica Raccolta di Terraglia, Museo Internazionale Design Cermico, Laveno Mombello 024481
Civica Raccolta e Ceramiche Rinascimentali, Camporgiano . . . 023627
Civiche Raccolte Archeologiche e Numismatiche, Castello Sforzesco, Milano 024690
Civiche Raccolte d'Arte, Palazzo Cicogna, Busto Arsizio 023553
Civiche Raccolte d'Arte Applicata, Milano 024691
Civici Musei di Villa Paolina, Pinacoteca L. Viani, Viareggio 026300
Civici Musei e Gallerie di Storia ed Arte, Udine 026161
Civico Gabinetto dei Disgeni, Civiche Raccolte d'Arte, Milano 024692
Civico Museo, Cairo Montenotte . . . 023573
Civico Museo Antropologico, Balestrate 023326
Civico Museo Archeologico, Acqui Terme 023120
Civico Museo Archeologico, Arsago Seprio 023259
Civico Museo Archeologico, Camogli 023610
Civico Museo Archeologico, Ozieri . 025040
Civico Museo Archeologico e di Scienze Naturali Federico Eusebio, Alba . . 023145
Civico Museo Archeologico L. Barni e Pinacoteca C. Ottone, Vigevano . . 026322
Civico Museo Bibliografico Musicale, Bologna 023416
Civico Museo Biblioteca dell'Attore del Teatro, Genova 024294
Civico Museo d'Arte Contemporanea, Palazzo Reale, Milano 024693
Civico Museo d'Arte Moderne, Anticoli Corrado 023211
Civico Museo d'Arte Orientale, Trieste 026126
Civico Museo degli Strumenti Musicali, Milano 024694
Civico Museo del Finale, Finale Ligure 024134
Civico Museo del Mare, Trieste 026127
Civico Museo del Merletto al Tombolo, Rapallo 025391
Civico Museo del Risorgimento e Sacrario Oberdan, Trieste 026128
Civico Museo della Risiera di San Sabba, Trieste 026129
Civico Museo di Guerra per la Pace Diego de Henriquez, Trieste 026130
Civico Museo di Scienze Naturali, Domodossola 024034
Civico Museo di Storia ed Arte e Orto Lapidario, Trieste 026131
Civico Museo di Storia Naturale della Lombardia, Jerago con Orago . . . 024429
Civico Museo Dianese, Diano Marina 024031
Civico Museo e Antiquarium Comunale, Lanuvio 024456
Civico Museo Flaminio Massetano, Massa Martana 024645
Civico Museo Frignanese, Pavullo nel Frignano 025147
Civico Museo G. Galletti, Domodossola 024035
Civico Museo G.V. Parisi-Valle, Maccagno 024563
Civico Museo Ingauno, Palazzo Vecchio del Comune, Albenga 023147
Civico Museo Insubrico di Storia Naturale, Induno Olona 024414
Civico Museo Morpurgo, Trieste . . . 026132
Civico Museo Naturalistico, Ovada . 025039
Civico Museo Naturalistico Ferruccio Lombardi, Stradella 025956
Civico Museo Revoltella e Galleria d'Arte Moderna, Trieste 026133
Civico Museo Sartorio, Trieste 026134
Civico Museo Setificio Monti, Abbadia Lariana 023108
Civico Museo Storico, Palmanova . . 025100
Civico Museo Storico Archeologico, Savona 025823
Civico Museo Teatrale di Fondazione Carlo Schmidl, Trieste 026135
Civico Studio Museo Francesco Messina, Milano 024695
Civil Engineer Corps and Seabee Museum, Port Hueneme 047131
Civil War Museum, Philadelphia . . . 046931
Civil War Museum, McCook House, Carrollton 042631
Civil War Museum of Lone Jack, Jackson County, Lone Jack 045375
Civil War Store, New Orleans 090535
Civile, Andrea, Roma 076378
Civilian Conservation Corps Museum, Highlands Hammock State Park, Sebring 048098
Civilization Art Gallery, Columbus . . 115769
La Civita Pietro, Bologna 075066
Civitat, Zwolle 078887
Civran, Fiorenza, Venezia 128383
Cizeron, Marie-Claude, Le Crozet . . 063613
Cizeron, Marie-Noël, Romans-sur-Isère 067201
Çizgi, İstanbul 112297

Čížková, Jitka, Česká Lípa 137772
C.J. Pictures, Hornchurch 113272
C.J.'s Upholstery, Albuquerque 131739
CK Collection, Singapore 080449
C.L. Alexander Museum, Tumby Bay 001570
Claassen-Schmal, Barbara, Bremen 102235
The Clachan Gallery, Glasgow 113106
Clackmannshire Council Museum, Alloa 038488
Claër, Eric, Brignais 061799
Claes, Sävedalen 081892
Claes, Jules, Genk 096278
Claeshallen, Malmö 081865, 122208
Claffey, Patricia, München 104165
Clagahé, Lyon 138141
Clair de Lune, Port-Louis 101045
Clair Obscur, Montréal 058940
Le Claire, Thomas, Hamburg 071218, 139171
Claire Lane Antiques, Jacksonville . 089395
Clairemont, San Diego 092624
Clairgeonette, Paris 065714
Clairon-Labarthe, Paris 124621
Clampart, New York 117777
Clan Armstrong Museum, Langholm 039929
Clan Cameron Museum, Spean Bridge 041078
Clan Donnachaidh Museum, Pitlochry 040716
Clan Grant Museum, Alness 038491
Clan Gunn Museum, Latheron 039935
Clan Macpherson House and Museum, Newtonmore 040579
Clanart Gallery, Enniskillen 113023
Clancy, Bray 074866
Clandestine Immigration and Naval Museum, Haifa 022918
Clapham Art Gallery, London 113542
Clapham Art Gallery, London 113543
Claphams, Lane Cove 056079
Claphams Clock Museum, Whangarei 030657
Clapson, Jenny, Kingscote 094703
Clara Barton Birthplace, North Oxford 046531
Clara Barton Home, Glen Echo 044200
Clara Charle's, Lyon 064111
Clara-Zetkin-Museum, Birkenwerder 016248
Clara-Ziegler-Stiftung, München . . 019047
Claradon, Saint Michael 057650
Clara's Attic, Seattle 092976
Clare Ancient House Museum, Clare 039094
Clare Antique Warehouse, Clare . . .084026, 130586
Clare Hall Company, Sudbury, Suffolk 086784, 131557
Clare Heritage Centre, Corofin 022724
Clare Museum, Ennis 022783
Clare National Trust Museum, Clare 000918
Claremont Antiques, Tunbridge Wells 086935
Claremont Museum, Claremont . . . 042940
Claremont Museum, Claremont, Western Australia 000920
Claren, Latrobe 056082
Clarence House Antiques, Watchet .087052, 142142
Clarencetown and District Historical Museum, Clarencetown 000923
Clarendon Books, Leicester 130879, 141717
Clarendon House, Nile 001331
Claresholm Museum, Claresholm . . 005275
Clarfeld, Sabine, Seevetal 073791
Clarges Gallery, London 113544
Claridge's Fine Art and Antiques Fair, London 093921
Clarin Ancestral House, Loay 031688
Clarinbridge Antiques, Marton 079145
Clarine's Hang-Ups, Jacksonville . . 132176
Claringbold, Berry 055495
Clark, Montréal 096989
Clark, Towcester 086910, 131603
Clark, Annarella, Stow-on-the-Wold 086743
Clark, Catharine, San Francisco . . . 119640
Clark, Christopher, San Francisco . . 119641
Clark, Edward, Armadale, Victoria . 055366
Clark, Garth, Long Island City 116687
Clark, Garth, New York 117778
Clark & Co., Jonathan, London 085200, 113545
Clark, Mark, San Francisco 092759
Clark, Penelope, San Francisco . . . 092760
Clark, Peter, Birmingham . 083528, 130387
Clark, Stephen L., Austin 114964
Clark Art, Northwich 114156
Clark Atlanta University Art Galleries, Atlanta 041854
Clark County Historical Museum, Vancouver 048748
Clark County Historical Society Museum, Springfield 048303
Clark County Museum, Henderson . 044509
Clark County Museum, Marshall . . . 045698
Clark Galleries, Towcester 114595
Clark House Museum Complex, Wolfeboro 049275
Clark Humanities Museum, Claremont 042936
Clark & Smith, Bordeaux 061599
Clarke, Cape Town 140972
Clarke, Westbury 056818
Clarke, Christopher, Stow-on-the-Wold 086744
Clarke, Graham, Maidstone 114030, 135279
Clarke, Janet, Bath 141396
Clarke, Janet, Freshford 141618
Clarke County Historical Museum, Berryville 042174
Clarke Hall, Wakefield 041272
Clarke Hall, J., Deal 141551
Clarke House Museum, Chicago . . . 042835
Clarke Memorial Museum, Eureka . 043751
Clarke Museum, Orono 006077
Clark's Antiques, Charlotte 087936
Clarkson Historical Museum, Clarkson 042951
Clarksville, Austin 114965
Clarksville, Austin 114966
Clarksville-Montgomery County Museum-Customs House Museum, Clarksville 042954
Claro, Tucson 120115
Clary & Co., New York 090790
Clasic Stylle, Praha 060118
Clasic V & G, Bucureşti 109422
Clásica, Buenos Aires 136709
Clasicas Adriano, Sevilla 081583
Clasing, Münster 104356, 126494
Clasing & Langer, Osnabrück 073231
Class, Bakel 128576
Classen Street Potters, Oklahoma City 118658
Classensgade Antikvariat, København 137891
Classic, Akaroa 078899
Classic, Cairo 060435
Classic, Freiburg im Breisgau 070829
Classic, Taranaki 128961
Classic, Wiesbaden 074397
Classic Age, West Hollywood 093457
Classic Antik, Göteborg 081800
Classic & Antique, Qormi 077524
Classic Antique Iron Beds, New York 090791
Classic Antique Wood, Charlotte . . .087937, 131869
Classic Antiques, Edmonton 058823, 096872
Classic Antiques, Jacksonville 089396, 132177
Classic Antiques, Philadelphia 091622, 132609
Classic Art, Albuquerque 087381
Classic Art, Attard 107442
Classic Art, Bromley 112744
Classic Art Gallery, Groningen 078410
Classic Artforms, West Hollywood . 120378
Classic Attic, Charlotte 087938
Classic Bindings, London . 130977, 141772
Classic Book Shop, Haymarket 136938
Classic Cars Museum, Salt Lake City 047772
Classic Century Square, Albuquerque 087382
Classic Chapters, Broken Hill 136827
Classic Coins Hawaii, Honolulu 088942
Classic Collectibles, Phoenix 091728
Classic Collection, Birmingham . . . 087749
Classic Collections, San Antonio . . . 092500
Classic Consignment Center, Albuquerque 087383
Classic Custom Upholstery, San Antonio 132810
Classic Desks, Wellington 079321, 128973
Classic Dreams 1960, Atlanta 087463
Classic Fine Arts, Mansfield 114053
Classic Finish Art, San Jose 132922
Classic Furniture, Milwaukee 090284
Classic Furniture Service, Salt Lake City 132784
Classic Hall, Hellerup 060252
Classic Home, Budapest 074674
Classic Image, London 113546
Classic Jewellery, Christchurch . . . 079020
Classic Lighting Emporium, Philadelphia 091623
Classic Picture Company, Dallas . . . 115855
Classic Reproductions, Leicester . . 113370
Classic Reproductions, Pewsey . . . 131379
Classic Restoration Company, Cleveland 131952
Classic Rocking Horses, Thirsk . . . 086881
The Classic Source, Mumbai 105763
Classic Toy, Lyon 064112
Classic Toys, New York 090792
Classic Traders, Auckland 078934
Classic Troc Cannes, Cannes 061939
Classic Upholstery, Philadelphia . . . 132610
Classic Woods, Portland 132689
Classic World Imports, Dallas 088482
Clássica, Lisboa 079897
Classica, Sofia 096725
The Classical Quarterly, Oxford 136192
Classical Realism Journal, Minneapolis 136423
Classical Restorations and Design, New York 132454
The Classical Review, Oxford 136193
Classical Strings, Milwaukee 090285
Classico, Binningen 082263
Classics Antiques, Miami 090152
Classics Bookshop, Oxford 141982
Classics Kunstatelier, Brugge 057766
Classique, Lyon 138142
Classy, Houston 116293
Clastres, Jacques, Villeblevin 125023
Clatteringshaws Forest Wildlife Centre, Clatteringshaws 039095
Clau, Rio de Janeiro 058572
Claude, Daniel, Gampelen 082385
Claude Bernard Galerie, Villedomer 068891, 101469
Claude Crayston Museum, Glenora . 005513
Claude & Lima, Paris 065715
Claude & Martine, Saint-Ouen 124913
Claudel, Jean-Jacques, Saussines . 068157
Claudelands, Waikato 079286
Claudia's Antik, Bärnsdorf 069433
Clausen, Dormagen 102386
Clausen, København 060311, 098544
Clausen & Sons, Arthur, Edmonton . 120801
Clausen, Grethe, København 124028
Clausen Memorial Museum, Petersburg 046900
Clauss, André, Strasbourg 124943
Claustro, Segovia 110756
Claux, Paris 100156
Clavel, Bonnaz & Lecomté, Marseille 121062
Clavell & Morgades, Barcelona 080835
Claveria, Emmanuel, Artigues-près-Bordeaux 061000
Clavreuil, Bouchemaine 061668
Clavreuil, Jean, Paris 138334
Clawson Historical Museum, Clawson 042958
Clay, Memphis 132319
Clay, D.K., New Orleans 117416
Clay, John, London 085201, 130978
Clay County Historical Museum, Liberty 045285
Clay County Museum, Moorhead . . 046015
Clay Pan Gallery, Dubbo 094492
Clay Products Interpretive Centre, Medicine Hat 005850
Clay Studio, Philadelphia 046932
Clay Tobacco Pipe Museum, Broseley 038887
Clayart Gallery, Manwatu 108494
Claydon House, Middle Claydon . . . 040456
Clayfield Antique Market, Clayfield . 055682
Claypool, Esther, Seattle 119899
Claypool-Young Art Gallery, Morehead 046021
Clayton, Saint Louis 092213
Clayton, Tampa 120035
Clayton, Tim, King's Lynn . 084848, 130846
Clayton Collection Museum, Chollerford 039082
Clayton Collection Museum, Humshaugh 039784
Clayton McLain Memorial Museum, Cutknife 005319
Clayton-Payne, Andrew, London . . . 085202
Clayton-Payne Andrew, London . . . 113547
Clayways, Austin 114967
Cle Elum Telephone Museum, Cle Elum 042966
Clean is Wood, Bruxelles 123583
Clear Creek Gallery, Tenterfield . . . 095324
Clear Lake Area Historical Museum, Clear Lake 042968
Clear View Art Gallery, Hamilton Parish 096429
Clearfield County Historical Society Museum, Clearfield 042969
Clearing House, Charlotte 087939
Clearing House, Jacksonville 089397
Clearwater County Historical Museum, Shevlin 048152
Clearwater Historical Museum, Orofino 046725
Cleary, John, Houston 116294
Clédic, Bar-sur-Aube 061198
Cleeve, Bristol 083734
Cleeve Picture Framing, Bishop's Cleeve 083542, 130401
La Clef, Uzès 068668
Clef du Passé, Reims 067063
The Cleft Art Gallery, Donaghadee . 112948
Clegg, Benedict, Tunbridge Wells . . 131616
Clegg & Sons, G.D., Poole 131384
Clegg, John, Ludlow 085863
Clegg's Museum of Horse-Drawn Vehicles, Hamiota 005598
Clematis Press, London 135208
Clemenceau, Pau 138568
Clémençon Meillat, Martine, Bosmoreau-les-Mines 061666
Clémençon Meillat, Martine, Bourganeuf 061716
Clemens, Solingen 104915
Clemens-Sels-Museum, Neuss . . . 019271
Clement, Bonn 138895
Clément, Culan 062583
Clément, Montluçon 064707
Clement, Guy, Roubaix 067229
Clément, Louis, Cohade 062389
Clement, Piet, Amsterdam 107696, 134777
Clemente, Nice 065062
Clemente, Antonio, Torino 128284
Clementine, New York 117779
Clements, Forney 122896
Clemont & Co., Hong Kong 097773
Clendening History of Medicine Library and Museum, University of Kansas Medical Center, Kansas City 044912
Clent Books, Bewdley 141410

Cléo Antiquités, Saint-Dyé-sur-Loire . . . 067431
Cleo Redd Fisher Museum, Loudonville . . . 045479
Cléon, Michel, Rouen . . . 067260
Cleopatra Bazar, Alexandria . . . 060416
Cleo's Black Cat, San Francisco . . . 092761
Clepsidra, Bogotá . . . 098113
Clepsidra, Lisboa . . . 079898
Cléquin, Daniel, Villevallier . . . 068986
Cler Relojeros, Fernando, Madrid . . 081277
Clerc, Alain, Cour-Cheverny . . . 062508
Clerc, Catherine F., Lausanne . . . 111612
Clerc, Pierre, Montpellier . . . 138218
Clerck, F. de, Brugge . . . 057767
Clergiot, Georges, Sainte-Menehould . . . 068071
Clergiot, Michel, Sainte-Menehould 068072
Clergy House, Alfriston . . . 038484
Clérigo Galeria, Lugo . . . 110413
Clermont, Pézenas . . . 066799
Clermont, Pézenas . . . 066800
Clermont Collections, Clermont-Ferrand . . . 062333
Clermont State Historic Site, Clermont . . . 042979
Clerval, Xavier De, Colombes . . . 062425
Clés de Saint-Pierre, Dax . . . 062604
Clés de Saint-Pierre, Hossegor . . . 063174
La Clessidra, Messina . . . 106134
La Clessidra, Trieste . . . 076888
Cletienne, Olivia, Paris . . . 124622
Cleve, Anna von, Kleve . . . 103564
Cleve-Artline, Kevelaer . . . 103535
Cleve National Trust Museum, Cleve 000927
Clevedon Court, Clevedon . . . 039098
Clevedon Salerooms, Clevedon . . . 122472
Cleveland Art Association, Cleveland . . . 054710
Cleveland Artists Foundation at Beck Center for the Arts, Lakewood . . . 045130
Cleveland Center for Contemporary Art, Cleveland . . . 042984
Cleveland County Historical Museum, Shelby . . . 048142
Cleveland Crafts Centre, Middlesbrough . . . 040459
Cleveland Institute of Art, Cleveland 051156
Cleveland Ironstone Mining Museum, Skinningrove . . . 041038
Cleveland Living Arts Centre, Dunedin . . . 030481
Cleveland Museum of Art, Cleveland . . . 042985
Cleveland Museum of Natural History, Cleveland . . . 042986
Cleveland Police Museum, Cleveland . . . 042987
Cleveland Public Art, Cleveland . . . 115696
Cleveland State University Art Gallery, Cleveland . . . 042988
Cleveland Studies in the History of Art, Cleveland . . . 136424
Cleverdon, Douglas, London . . . 135209
Cleversulzbach, Neuenstadt . . . 072984
Clewiston Museum, Clewiston . . . 043006
Clichés du Passé, Marseille . . . 064339
Cliffe Antiques Centre, Lewes . . . 084979
Cliffe Castle Museum, Keighley . . . 039835
Clifford, Dublin . . . 074900
Clifford Gallery, Olney . . . 114187
Clifford-Smith, Boston . . . 115161
Clifton, T. Joseph, Memphis . . . 116979
Clifton and District Historical Museum, Clifton . . . 000930
Clifton Art Gallery, Karachi . . . 108772
Clifton Community Historical Society, Clifton . . . 043007
Clifton Gallery, Aberdeen . . . 112477
The Clifton Gallery, Bristol . . . 112719
Clifton Park Museum, Rotherham . . 040856
Climat, Les Sables-d'Olonne . . . 099470
Climax Community Museum, Climax . . . 005277
Clin d'Oeil, Clermont-Ferrand . . . 062334
Clin d'Oeil, Paris . . . 065716
Clinco, Carlo, Torino . . . 128285
Clínica de Arte, Cali . . . 059880, 123917
Clínica de Muñecos Casas Reyes, Bogotá . . . 123896
Clínica de Porcelanas, Bogotá . . . 123897
La Clínica del Mueble, Valencia . . . 129767
Clinique de l'Ours, Paris . . . 124623
Clinique de Poupées, Nice . . . 124505
Clinique des Poupées, Lyon . . . 124347
Clinique des Poupées, Nancy . . . 064864, 124468
Clinique du Meuble Ancien, Abrest . 060656, 124056
Clink Prison Museum, London . . . 040121
Clinton, Jacksonville . . . 122931
Clinton Academy Museum, East Hampton . . . 043564
Clinton Art Association, Clinton . . . 054711
Clinton County Historical Museum, Plattsburgh . . . 047083
Clinton County Historical Society Museum, Saint Johns . . . 047637
Clinton County Museum, Frankfort . 044028
Clinton Street Antique Centre, Milwaukee . . . 090286
Clinton Street Antiques, Portland . . 091915
Clintonville Antiques, Columbus . . . 088393
Clio, Paris . . . 138335
Clio Antic, Bucureşti . . . 080148
Clio Calvi, Milano . . . 075670
Clipper, Vannes (Morbihan) . . . 068715
Clipper Ship Cutty Sark, London . . . 040122
Clisby, Bryan, Hartley Wintney . . . 084600, 130769
Clist, Gerry, London . . . 130979
Clive House Museum, Shrewsbury . 041019
Cliveden House, Philadelphia . . . 046933
Cloarec, Didier, Pornichet . . . 066951
Cloche d'Or, Foix . . . 062884
Cloches de Corneville, Pont-Audemer . . . 013880
Clock and Watch Service Centre, Coffs Harbour . . . 055701
Clock Clinic, London . . . 085203, 130980
Clock Doctor, Atlanta . . . 087464, 131766
Clock Gallery, London . . . 130981
The Clock Gallery, North Killingholme . . . 131320
Clock-House, Aalst . . . 057659
Clock House, Leavenheath 084917, 130866
Clock House Antiques, Keighley . . . 084818
Clock Manor, Kansas City . . . 132207
Clock Shop, Hurstpierpoint 084778, 130821
Clock Shop, Saint Albans . 086436, 131438
The Clock Shop, Winchcombe . . . 087166, 131693
Clock Shop of Richmond, Richmond . . . 092069, 132712
Clock Shop Weybridge, Weybridge . 087109, 131674
Clock Tower, Saint Albans . . . 040881
Clock Tower, Sapporo . . . 027025
Clock Tower Antiques, Philadelphia 091624
Clock Tower Archive Centre, Youghal . . . 022878
The Clock-Work-Shop, Winchester . 087173, 131695
Clock Workshop, Caversham . . . 083894, 130520
Clockmaster, Saint Louis . . . 132743
Clocks and Collectables, Eltham . . . 055796
Clocks and Collectibles, Jacksonville . . . 089398, 132178
Clocks and More, Albuquerque . . . 087384, 131740
Clocks Unique Antique Mart, Tampa . . . 093119, 132950
Clocktower Museum, Elsham . . . 039438
Clockwise, Emsworth . . . 084332, 130685
Clockwise, Henfield . . . 130783
Clockwise, Launceston . . . 056087
Cloisonne, Ando, Tokyo . . . 077239
The Cloisters, North Sydney . . . 056374
The Cloisters, Metropolitan Museum of Art, New York . . . 046315
Cloisters Antiques, Ely . . . 084325, 141594
Cloisters Antiques Fair, Norwich . . . 086112
Cloître de Cadouin, Le Buisson-de-Cadouin . . . 012476
Clola Antiques Centre, Clola by Mintlaw . . . 084038
Clonalis House, Castlerea . . . 022707
Cloncurry and District Museum, Cloncurry . . . 000931
Clonfert Diocesan Museum, Loughrea . . . 022829
Clonfert Museum, Clonfert . . . 022714
Clonmel Potters Gallery, Kingston . . 106809
Cloots, Christiane, Bruxelles . . . 096170
Clos Arqueologic Torre Llauder, Mataró . . . 035480
Clos Arsene Lupin, Maison Maurice Leblanc, Etretat . . . 011756
Clos de la Fontaine, Nîmes . . . 065173
Le Clos des Cimaises, Saint-Georges-du-Bois . . . 067491
Le Clos Saint-Roch, Betoncourt-Saint-Pancras . . . 061412
Close, David, Collyweston . . . 112895
Close, Henry H., Abergavenny . . . 083246
Closet, Sacramento . . . 092147, 142844
Closset, Jean-Jacques, Paris . . . 124624
Closson, Cincinnati . . . 115619
Closson, Cincinnati . . . 115620
Clot Bramsen et Georges, Paris . . . 100157
Clothing and Textiles Museum, University of Manitoba, Winnipeg . . . 006841
Clotworthy Arts Centre, Antrim . . . 038514
Le Clou, Zürich . . . 112055
Cloud County Historical Museum, Concordia . . . 043126
Clough, Sallie, Auckland . . . 108306
Clough-Hanson Gallery, Rhodes College, Memphis . . . 045756
Clovelly Collectables, Clovelly . . . 055696
Cloverdale Antique Mall, Surrey . . . 059110, 120814
Clowes Fund Collection, Indianapolis . . . 044736
Clowes Nash, Norwich . . . 122638
Cloyne Pioneer Museum, Cloyne . . 005279
Club degli Artisti, Foggia . . . 053750
Il Club dell'Arte e della Cultura, Roma . . . 106509
Club of American Collectors of Fine Arts, New York . . . 054712
Club Paradoxe, Strasbourg . . . 101284
Clüver, Hanna, Loxstedt . . . 072302
Clun Local History Museum, Clun . . 039101
Clune Galleries, Potts Point . . . 095101
Clunes, Francis, Paris . . . 065717
Clunes Museum, Clunes . . . 000932
The Clunky Mantel, Edmonton . . . 058824
Cluny, Edinburgh . . . 141578
Cluny Auteur, Cluny . . . 099157
Clusella Piñana, Carmen, Barcelona 110132
Cluthé, Marie, Toronto . . . 059166
Clutter House Antiques, Dallas . . . 088483
Clutterboxe Antiques, Cleveland . . . 088320, 131953
Cluttered Cupboard, Chicago . . . 088059
Clutters, Toronto . . . 059167
Cluva, Venezia . . . 134705
Cluzel, Patrick, Cannes . . . 124168
Cluzel, René, Paris . . . 065718, 138336
Clwyd Auction Centre, Deeside . . . 122487
Clydach Antiques, Swansea . . . 086811
Clyde Antiques, Patrington . . . 086195
Clyde Historical Museum, Clyde . . . 030472
Clydebank Museum, Clydebank . . . 039102
Clydebuilt, Scottish Maritime Museum, Glasgow . . . 039550
Clyde's Antiques, Oklahoma City . . 091483
Clymer Museum of Art, Ellensburg . 043669
CM Antik, Uttenreuth . . . 074173
C.M. Bellman Museum, Stockholm . 036620
C.M. Bookshop in Silverlake, Los Angeles . . . 142498
C.M. Booth Collection of Historic Vehicles, Rolvenden . . . 040850
C.M. Russell Museum, Great Falls . 044299
CMA Gallery, Saint Louis . . . 119194
C.M.B. Marseille Numismatique, Marseille . . . 064340
C.M.C., Paris . . . 100158
C.M.P, Paris . . . 065719
Cmuk, Wiesbaden . . . 105249
CMZ-Verlag, Rheinbach . . . 134367
CN Galeria, Bogotá . . . 098114
CN Galería, Bogotá . . . 098115
CNAP, Lisboa . . . 109272
CNCE, Aix-les-Bains . . . 060721
Cnock, Knokke . . . 120764
CNRS Editions, Paris . . . 133555
Co, Xhan, Ha Noi . . . 120456
Co. Art, Genova . . . 127444
C.O. Card Home, Cardston . . . 005225
CO-Libri, Bremen . . . 138943
C.O. Müller-Galerie, Eichstätt . . . 016908
Co. Re. Ar., Roma . . . 127978
Coaccioli, Romina, Roma . . . 127979
The Coach House, London . . . 085204
Coach House Antiques, Canterbury . 083861
Coach House Antiques, Gomshall . . 084482, 130734
Coach House Antiques, Hastings . . 084616, 130774
Coach House Antiques, Moss Vale . 056273
Coach House Antiques, Stanley . . . 086693, 131528
Coach House Antiques, Whitby . . . 087130
Coach House Books, Toronto . . . 133323
The Coach House Gallery, Eastwood 112979
Coach House Museum, Langton Matravers . . . 039930
Coachman, San Jose . . . 092920
Coad, Jim, Albuquerque . . . 087385
Coad & McCure, Margate . . . 056161
Coal Creek Heritage Village, Korumburra . . . 001161
Coal Miners' Museum, Van Lear . . . 048745
Coalfields Antiques, Greymouth . . . 079104
Coalfields Museum, Collie . . . 000940
Coalition of Women's Art Organizations, Port Washington . . . 054713
Coalport China Museum, Coalport . 039106
Coarte, A Coruña . . . 110317
Coast, Fresno . . . 088900
Coast & Country Browns Bay, Auckland . . . 108307
Coast Gallery, Long Beach . . . 116666
Coast Gallery, Mombasa . . . 107156
Coast Salish Arts, Vancouver . . . 097444
Coast to Coast, Tampa . . . 120036
Coastal and Maritime Art, Narrabeen . . . 094928
Coastal Center for the Arts, Saint Simons Island . . . 047722
Coastal Curiosities, Opunake . . . 079206
Coastal Discovery Museum, Hilton Head Island . . . 044552
Coastal Heritage Museum, Crystal River . . . 043234
Coastal Painting Gallery, Qingdao . . 097885
Coastal Peoples, Vancouver . . . 097445
Coatalem, Eric, Paris . . . 100159
Coats, A., London . . . 085205
Cobalt's Northern Ontario Mining Museum, Cobalt . . . 005281
Cobb & Co., Box Hill . . . 055533
Cobb, Clive & Lesley, Hove . . . 130810
Cobb, Timothy, Milwaukee . . . 117178
Cobb and Co Museum, Toowoomba 001556
Cobb County Youth Museum, Marietta . . . 045664
Cobb Institute of Archaeology Museum, Mississippi State . . . 045929
Cobb Lane Art Gallery, Birmingham 115102
Cobb Museum of Art, Marietta . . . 045665
Cobbaton Combat Collection, Chittlehampton . . . 039081
Cobbitty Arts, Crafts & Antiques, Cobbitty . . . 055698
The Cobbled Yard, London . . . 085206
Cobblers Garden Gallery, Millthorpe 094852

Cobblestone, Houston 089051
Cobblestone, Seattle 092977
Cobblestones, Portland 091916
Cobblestones Museum, Greytown . 030508
Cobdogla Irrigation and Steam Museum, Cobdogla 000934
Cobh Museum, Cobh 022716
Cobham Bus Museum, Cobham . . . 039111
Cobham Galleries, Cobham 084041
Cobisi, Giuseppe, Roma 127980
Cobisi, Vincenzo, Roma 127981
Cobland, Depden 084157, 130631
Cobo, Pepe, Sevilla 110767
Cobo, Pepe, Sevilla 110768
Cobra & Bellamy, London 085207
Cobra Cafe Galleri, København 098545
Cobra Museum voor Moderne Kunst, Amstelveen 029158
Coburg, Jacksonville 089399
Coburger Münzhandlung, Coburg . . 070145
Coburger Puppen-Museum, Coburg 016573
Coburn, Annandale 123176
The Coburn Gallery, Ashland College Arts & Humanities Gallery, Ashland 041809
Cobweb, Miami 132337
Cobweb, New York 090793
Cobweb Antiques, Cullompton 084128, 130622
Cobweb Corners, Omaha 091556
Cobwebs, London 085208
Cobwebs, Salt Lake City 092424
Cobwebs, Southampton . . 086649, 142077
Cobwebs Collectables, Wanganui . . 079304
Coca-Cola Memorabilia Museum of Elizabethtown, Elizabethtown . . . 043654
The Coca-Cola Pavillion, Santa Cruz 031784
Coca-Nuts & Co., Oklahoma City . . 091484
Cocalico Valley Museum, Ephrata . . 043715
Cocardasse, Den Haag 078181
Cocchi, Nicola, Firenze 127322
Le Cocguen, Jean-Claude, Plouaret 066864
La Cochera de Pepe, Jerez de la Frontera 081164
Cochet, Dourdain 062732
Cochet, Paulette, Genève 082416
Cochise, Firenze 075319
Fergus Cochrane & Warren Leigh, London 085209
Cochrane-Nelson House, Westfield . 049113
Cochrane Railway and Pioneer Museum, Cochrane 005283
Cocinas Montañez, Málaga 081418
Cock-A-Too, Calgary 058783
Cockaigne, George, Lismore 056104
Cockatoo Art Gallery, Cairns 094342
Cockatoo Gallery, Broome 094314
Cockburn Museum, Edinburgh 039382
Cockermouth Antiques, Cockermouth 084044
Cockermouth Antiques Market, Cockermouth 084045, 130595
Cockrell Antiques, Surbiton 086791
Coco, Kyoto 106890
Coco, Melissa, Catania 075243
Coco-De-Mer, Singapore 080450
Cocoa, Cheltenham 083918, 130534
Coconut Grove Gallery, Miami 117048
Coco's Galleria, Kansas City 116560
Cocozza, Antonio, Roma 127982
Cocusse, Claudine, Reims 067064
Cocusse, Claudine, Reims 067065
Coda Gallery, New York 117780
Codaccioni Gallo, Rose-Marie, Marseille 064341
Code Red Art Gallery, Claremont . . 094400
Codex, Stockholm 141152
Codington County Heritage Museum, Watertown 048996
Codman House - The Grange, Lincoln 045296
Côdô, Ha Noi 120457
Codosero, Luis, Madrid 081278
Codt, de, Bruxelles 123584
Cody Country Art League, Cody . . . 054714
Coe Hall, Oyster Bay 046778
Coed Hills Rural Artspace, Cowbridge 112904
Coelho, José António, Porto 080075
Toca Coelhos, Lisboa 079899
Coemans, Bruxelles 057892
Coen, Roma 076379, 134670
Coenen, Heide, Essen 070622
Coenen, Heide, Essen 070623
Coens, Grevenbroich 103003
Coerten, Jacques, Le Paradou 099450
Cöster, Offenbach am Main 104528
Coeur, Jacques, Bourges 061722
Coeur d Capitol Gallery, Washington 120274
Coeur d'Art, Brioude 061806, 099036
Coffee Cat, Los Angeles 142499
Coffee House Press, Minneapolis . . 135396
Coffin House, Newbury 046439
The Coffin School Museum, Nantucket 046123
Coffineau, Béatrice & Guy, La Roche-sur-Yon 063414
Coffman & Co., Boston 087807
Cofides, Saint-Ouen 067750
Cofion Books & Postcards, Tenby . . 142111
Cogges Manor Farm Museum, Witney 041424
Coggeshall Farm Museum, Bristol . 042422
Coggeshall Heritage Centre and Museum, Coggeshall 039116
Coggins, Anthony, Bristol 130455
Coggins, Ray, Westbury 087092
Cogito, Setúbal 080124, 109405
Cognard, Christian, Pont Audemer . 124849
Cognitive Arts, Boston 115162
Cohan, James, New York 117781
Cohan, Leslie & Browne, New York . 117782
Cohen, New York 090794
Cohen, New York 117783
Cohen, Saint Louis 092214, 132744
Cohen, Byron C., Kansas City 116561
Cohen, Ethan, New York 117784
Cohen, James, New York 117785
Cohen & Sons, James H. & Jerald L., New Orleans 090536
Cohen, Michel, Paris 065720
Cohen, Philip, London 085210
Cohen, R., San Francisco 119642
Cohen, Rick, Ringwood 123298
Cohen, Stephen, Los Angeles 116744
Cohen, Valerie, Paddington 095022
Cohen-Aloro, Claude, Paris 133556
Cohen & Cohen, London 085211
Cohendy, Jean-Charles, Moissat . . 064583
Cohet & Feraud, Montauban 121075
Cohn, E., Berlin 069587
Cohn, George & Peter, London 085212, 130982
Cohn Edelstein, Rio de Janeiro 096599
Cohnen, H.D., Bonn 069916
Cohnen, Karl, Mönchengladbach . .072565, 104092
Cohrs-Zirus, Ingrid, Worpswede . . . 105329
Cohu, Stephen, Saint Ouen 086470, 131443
Cohuna Historical Museum, Cohuna 000936
Coimbra, Rosa Martins, Lisboa 129149
Le Coin, Pampigny 082719
Coin and Jewellery Shop, Accrington 083253
Coin and Stamp Gallery, Phoenix . . 091729
Coin and Stamp USA, Miami 090153
Coin de Montcalm, Paris 065721
Coin Dealer, New York 090795
Le Coin des Arts, Paris 065722
Coin du Miroir, Dijon 011599
Coin Exchange, Pittsburgh 091801
Coin Galleries of Seattle, Seattle . . 092978
Coin, Gold and Silver Report, Las Vegas 089559
Coin Invest Trust, Balzers 077441
Coin Mart, Kansas City 089493
Le Coin Perdu, Utrecht 078791
Coin Shop, Chicago 088060
Coin Shop, Cleveland 088321
Coin Shop, Houston 089052
Coin Shop, Indianapolis 089281
Coin Star, Chicago 088061
Coin Vault, New Orleans 090537
The Coinage Hall Antiques Centre, Truro 086928, 131612
Coinex II, Los Angeles 089726
Coins, Tel Aviv 075002
Coins, Michael, London 085213
Coins and Curios Centre, Mumbai . 074820
Coins and Currency, Miami 090154
Coins for Tomorrow, Dallas 088484
Coins Museum, Amman 027366
Coins & Notes Museum, Kingston . . 026389
Coins Plus, Cincinnati 088222
Coins Plus, Cincinnati 088223
Coins Plus Gems, Milwaukee 090287
Coisas & Coisas, Rio de Janeiro . . . 058573
Coisas de Família, Lisboa 079900
Cojan, Anne-Marie, Vitry-sur-Seine 069015
Cokato Museum and Akerlund Photography Studio, Cokato 043035
Cokkie Snoei, Rotterdam 108178
Le Col Rouge, Aix-en-Provence . . . 060701
Cola Collection, Houston 089053
Colac Otway Shire Hammerton Bottle Collection, Colac 000937
Colacicco, Giovanni, Roma 127983
Colacicco, Michele, Torino 128286
Colaert, P., Antwerpen 057688
Colangelo, Philippe, Saint-Ouen . . . 067751
Colantonio, Luciano, Brescia 075159
Colanzi, Domenico, Milano 106195
Colas, Alain, Lyon 124348
Colas, Christine, Paris 100160
Colasanti & Colasanti, Roma 076380
Colbert, Paris 100161
Colboc, Laurent, Meylan 064546
Colborne Lodge, Toronto 006594
Colburn Gem and Mineral Museum, Asheville 041792
Colby & Son, Ralph, Portland 132690
Colby College Museum of Art, Waterville 048999
Colchester Historical Museum, Truro 006668
Colcţia Muzeală a Mănăstirii Lainici, Bumbeşti-Jiu 032818
Cold Spring Harbor Whaling Museum, Cold Spring Harbor 043038
Coldharbour Mill, Working Wool Museum, Uffculme 041258
Coldstream Antiques, Coldstream . . 084059
Coldstream Gallery, Ulmarra 095356
Coldstream Museum, Coldstream . . 039125
Coldwater Canadiana Heritage Museum, Coldwater 005284
Cole, A.E., London 130983
Cole, E.J., Houston 089054
Cole, John, Devonport 136880
Cole, S.J., Birmingham 130388
Cole, Sylvan, New York 117786
Cole County Historical Museum, Jefferson City 044847
Cole Harbour Heritage Farm Museum, Cole Harbour 005285
Cole Land Transportation Museum, Bangor 042010
Cole Museum of Zoology, Reading . 040806
Cole Pratt, New Orleans 117417
Coleção Assis Pegado - Museu da Moto, Fortaleza 004113
Coleção de Artes Visuais, São Paulo 004502
Coleção do Palácio do Governo de Campos do Jordão, Campos de Jordão . . . 004051
Coleção Entomológica de Referência, Faculdade de Saúde Pública / FSP, São Paulo 004503
Colecção Maritima do Comandante Ramalho Ortigão, Faro 032611
Coleccion 21, Guatemala City 074652
Colección Amazónica, Madrid 035374
Colección Anatomía, Madrid 035375
Colección Arqueológica, Génova . . 007505
Colección Arqueológica, Pijao 007580
Colección Arqueológica Municipal, Besalú 034978
Colección Benedito, Madrid 035376
Colección Carlos Alberto Pusineri Scala, Asunción 031440
Colección de Anestesioloxía e Reanimación, Santiago de Compostela 035817
Colección de Arqueología, Ciudad Real 035093
Colección de Arqueología y Etnografía Americana, Madrid 035377
Colección de Arte Carmen Rodríguez Acosta, Granada 035246
Colección de Arte y Museo Botero, Banco de la República, Bogotá 007407
Colección de Geología, Vilajüiga . . . 036044
Colección de la Biblioteca Musical, Madrid 035378
Colección de la Caja de Ahorros, Valencia 035975
Colección de la Casa de Alba, Epila 035174
Colección de la Casa de Alba, Madrid 035379
Colección de la Facultad de Filosofía y Letras, Madrid 035380
Colección de la Real Academia de la Historia, Madrid 035381
Colección de los Iconos, Torrejón de Ardoz 035942
Colección de los Padres Escolapios, Madrid 035382
Colección de Minerales y Arqueología, Villanueva 007644
Colección de Mineralogía, Madrid . 035383
Colección de Numismática, Vitoria-Gasteiz 036079
Colección de Pintura y Recuerdos Históricos del Castell de Balsareny, Balsareny 034893
Colección de Roberto Montenegro, Instituto de las Artesanías Jaliscienses, Guadalajara 028276
Colección del Banco de España, Madrid 035384
Colección del Observatorio de Cartuja, Granada 035247
Colección del Poeta Baudilio Montoya, Clarcá 007485
Colección Etnográfica, Colexió Público Mosteiro de Caaveiro, Capela . . . 035048
Colección Instrumentos Musicales Folklóricos y Cerámica Española, Rupit-Pruit 035726
Colección Municipal, Granada 035248
Colección Municipal de Arte Contemporáneo, Madrid 035385
Colección Museística de San Mateo, San Mateo 035765
Colección Museográfica Parroquial, Lucena del Cid 035365
Colección Museográfica Permanente de Municipal, Moncada 035504
Colección Numismática, Banco de la República, Bogotá 007408
Colección Ornitológica W.H. Phelps, Caracas 049451
Colección Osuna, Sevilla 035855
Colección Parroquial, Colmenar Viejo 035105
Colección Parroquial, Gascueña . . . 035216
Colección Parroquial, Nuevo Baztán 035546
Colección Parroquial, San Mateo . . 035766
Colección Parroquial, Traiguera . . . 035951
Colección Parroquial, Iglesia Santiago Apóstol, Liétor 035332
Colección Veri, Marratxinet 035475
Colección Vivot, Palma de Mallorca 035606
Colecciones Biológicas de Referencia, Barcelona 034905
El Coleccionista, Buenos Aires 055194
El Coleccionista, Cuenca 081065
El Coleccionista, México 077570
Colecţia de Artă Plastică Fr. Storck şi Cecilia Cecilia Cuţescu Stock, Bucureşti . 032794
Colecţia de Istorie a Farmaciei Cluj-Napoca, Cluj-Napoca 032834
Colecţia Etnografică, Poiana Sibiului 032918
Colecţia Etnografică, Răşinari 032922

Colecţia Muzeală de Istorie, Săcueni . . . 032928
Colectivo Multimédia Perve, Lisboa 109273
Sibyl Colefax & John Fowler, London . . . 085214
Colegiata de Santa María la Mayor, Toro . . . 035936
Colegio de Artes Plásticas, Universidad Autónoma de Centro América, San José . . . 049875
Colegio de Santa Isabel Museum, Naga . . . 031748
Colegio del Rey, Alcalá de Henares . 034798
Colegio Dominicano de Artes Plásticas, Santo Domingo . . . 049911
Coleham Pumping Station, Shrewsbury . . . 041020
Coleman, Chicago . . . 115391
Coleman, Garrick D., London . . . 085215
Coleman, Garrick D., London . . . 085216
Coleman, J., Cincinnati . . . 142311
Coleman, Kathleen, Houston . . . 116295
Coleman, Lynda, Austin . . . 114968
Coleman, Mary L., Pittsburgh . . . 118910
Coleman, Simon, London . . . 085217
Coleman, Spencer, Beverley . . . 112628
Coleman, Spencer, Lincoln . . . 113398
Coleman, Spencer, Stamford . . . 114479
Coleman House Museum, Ainsworth . . . 041584
Colemore, Jolimont . . . 056023
Colemore-Williams, Patricia, Russell . . . 079234
Coleraine Bookshop, Coleraine . . . 141533
Coleraine Local History Museum, Coleraine . . . 000939
Coleridge Cottage, Nether Stowey . 040522
Coles, Ronald, Kenthurst . . . 094690
Coles, Sadie, London . . . 113548
Colesberg/Kemper Museum, Colesberg . . . 034591
Coleshill Antiques, Coleshill . . . 084064
Colesville and Windsor Museum at Saint Luke's Church, Harpursville . . . 044439
Colette, Den Haag . . . 140390
Coleurs d'îles, Fort-de-France . . . 134755
Coley Homestead and Barn Museum, Weston . . . 049119
Coliboeuf, Caroline, Pau . . . 066701
Colibri Edition, Coupvray . . . 133463
Colicchio, Carlo, Napoli . . . 075956
Colin, Cardiff . . . 141487
Colin, Jean-Pierre, Saint-Benigne .067374, 124889
Colin-Maillard, A., Paris . . 065723, 100162
Coliseum, Lugo . . . 081191
Coliseum Antiquariato, Belo Horizonte . . . 058421, 137543
Coliseum Antiques, Mayfield . . . 056170
Coll-Rotger, Paris . . . 065724
Colla, Joseph, Montpellier . . . 124457
Collado Aucejo, Carmen, Valencia . 110801
Collage 20th Century Classic, Dallas . . . 088485
Collage Gallery, San Francisco . . . 119643
Collalti, Filippo, Roma . . . 127984
Collalti, Sergio, Roma . . . 076381
Collard, Pontrieux . . . 066946
Collard, Totnes . . . 142117
Collay, Jean-Louis, Lyon . . . 064113
Collcción Museográfica Permanente, Siete Aguas . . . 035872
Collecció de la Unió Excursionista de Catalunya, Olesa de Montserrat . . 035551
Collecció la Magrana, Vilajüiga . . . 036045
Collecció la Porciuncula, L'Arenal . . 034852
Collecció Marroig, Deià . . . 035142
Collecció Museogràfica d'Arqueologia Local, Riba-Roja de Turia . . . 035700
Collecció Parroquial, Naut Aran . . . 035539
Collecció Parroquial, La Salzadella . 035752
Collección Carlos Ferreyros Díaz, Bogotá . . . 007409
Colleccíon de Instrumentos Musicales Monsenór José Ignacio Perdomo Escobar, Bogotá . . . 007410
Collección del Santo Rosario, Aroche . . . 034860
Colleció d'Autòbils de Salvador Claret Sargatal, Sils . . . 035875
Colleció de la Tossa de Montbui, Santa Margarida de Montbui . . . 035802
Colleció de Sant Andreu de la Barca, Sant Andreu de la Barca . . . 035774
Collecio Thyssen-Bornemisza, Barcelona . . . 034906
Collecíon de Antigüedades, San Andrés de Sotavento . . . 007603
Colleción de Arte y Ciencias Naturales, Ciudad Real . . . 035094
Collecion du Louvre, Belo Horizonte 058422
Colleción Eugenio Fontaneda, Ampudia . . . 034839
Colleción Parroquial, Albocácer . . . 034796
Collecions Municipals del Foment Arqueològic Excursionista Sallentí, Sallent . . . 035750
Colleck, Philip, New York . . . 090796
Collect-Art, Amersfoort . . . 107636
Collectabears, Portland . . . 091917
Collectabel Trader, Bondi Junction . 135540
Collectable Books, London . . . 141773
Collectable Creations, Toowoomba . 056717
Collectables, Cowes . . . 055720
Collectables, Honiton . . . 084716
Collectables, Kingston-on-Spey . . . 084857
Collectables and Antiques, Willunga 056824
Collectables From Yesteryear, Greerton Tauranga . . . 079103
Collectamania, Waikato . . . 079287
Collectible Antiques, New Orleans . 090538
Collectible Art Gallery, Philadelphia 118743
Collectible Caboose, Austin . . . 087567
Collectible Toys Unlimited, Sacramento . . . 092148
Collectible Trains and Toys, Dallas . 088486
Collectibles, Dubai . . . 083189
Collectibles, El Paso . . . 088796
Collectibles, El Paso . . . 088797
Collectibles Etc., Oklahoma City . . . 091485
Collectie A. Veltman, Bussum . . . 029377
Collectie Anderson, Losser . . . 029878
Collectie D.H.G. Bolten, Den Haag . 029420
Collectie H.H.F. Salomon, Den Haag 029421
Collectie in het Gemmeentehuis, Brummen . . . 029363
Collectif d'Expression Artistique-C.E.A, Bayonne . . . 098930
Collecting Doulton, London . . . 136194
Collectio Navalis, Berlin . . . 138764
The Collection, Columbus . . . 088394
Collection, Denver . . . 088669
The Collection, Los Angeles . . . 089727
The Collection, Manama . . . 057622
The Collection, Padstow . . . 114210
Collection, Taipei . . . 135656
The Collection, West Hollywood . . . 093458
Collection 2000, Saint-Étienne . . . 067448
Collection A, Spreitenbach . . . 111927
Collection A, Zürich . . . 112056
Collection Archéologique, Bram-le-Lauragais . . . 010961
Collection Archéologique, Garin . . . 011923
Collection Archéologique, Laure-Minervois . . . 012438
Collection Archéologique, Marmoutier . . . 012914
Collection Archéologique, Tramont-Emy . . . 015030
Collection Archéologique, Villarzel-Cabardes . . . 015233
Collection Archéologique de la Maison des Fouilles et Maison du Memontois, Malain . . . 012861
Collectión Banco de la República, Bogotá . . . 007411
Collection Capital, Toulouse . . . 068496
Collection Cérès Franco, Lagrasse . 099415
Collection Charles de l'Escalopier, Amiens . . . 010365
Collection d'Affiches de la Période Révolutionnaire, Château Saint-Hugues, Semur-en-Brionnais . . . 014754
Collection d'Archéologie, Belmont-Luthézieu . . . 010746
Collection d'Archéologie Biblique USH, Strasbourg . . . 014855
Collection d'Art, Amsterdam . . . 107697
Collection d'Art, La Côte-Saint-André . . . 012241
Collection d'Art, Pauillac . . . 013753
Collection d'Art Céramique, Longfosse . . . 012733
Collection d'Art et d'Histoire Religieuse, La Lucerne-d'Outremer . . . 012284
Collection d'Art Religieux Ancien, Prunay-en-Yvelines . . . 013958
Collection d'Arts Décoratifs, Cazaux-Saves . . . 011166
Collection d'Arts Décoratifs, Salers 014633
Collection d'Arts Décoratifs, Villevielle . . . 015301
Collection d'Arts Populaires, Coren-les-Eaux . . . 011482
Collection d'Arts Populaires, Oberdorff . . . 013466
Collection d'Automates, Gilley . . . 011947
Collection de 2000 ex-voto, Monthermé . . . 013172
Collection de Cloches, Morteau . . . 013252
Collection de Costumes Alsaciens J. Bossert, Strasbourg . . . 014856
Collection de Faïences, Nevers . . . 013387
Collection de la Chapelle Royale Saint-Louis, Dreux . . . 011659
Collection de la Fondation in Memoriam Comtesse Tatiana Zoubov, Genève 037120
Collection de la Guerre de 1870, Le Bourget (Seine-Saint-Denis) . . . 012469
Collection de l'Abbaye de l'Ile Chauvet, Bois-de-Céné . . . 010860
Collection de l'Art Brut, Lausanne . 037238
Collection de l'Art Brut Publications, Lausanne . . . 135032
Collection de l'Aventure Automobile, Poissy . . . 013864
Collection de l'Hôtel de Ville, La Rochelle . . . 012315
Collection de l'Institut d'Égyptologie, Strasbourg . . . 014857
Collection de Locomotives à Vapeur, Obermodern . . . 013467
Collection de l'Outillage de Tonnellerie, Pauillac . . . 013754
Collection de Matériel Ancien de Cuvier, Margaux . . . 012905
Collection de Matériel Ferroviaire, Burnhaupt-le-Haut . . . 011032
Collection de Minéraux de l'Université Pierre et Marie Curie, Paris . . . 013566
Collection de Peintures, Cavaillon . . 011162
Collection de Peintures, Issac . . . 012136
Collection de Peintures, Lanildut . . 012413
Collection de Peintures, Exposition Ven Hard, Saint-Siffret . . . 014544
Collection de Peintures Héraldiques, Sainte-Julie . . . 014599
Collection de Sculptures, Peillon . . 013761
Collection de Sculptures, Viry-Noureuil . . . 015317
Collection de Tapisseries d'Aubusson et des Flandres, Saint-Chamant . . . 014216
Collection de Téléphones Anciens, Saint-Jean-du-Gard . . . 014358
Collection de Tire-Bouchons, Saint-Christophe-des-Bardes . . . 014222
Collection de Tonnellerie, Boersch . 010853
Collection de Tonnellerie, Dambach-la-Ville . . . 011559
Collection de Vieilles Étiquettes de Grands Crus, Cussac-Fort-Médoc . . . 011550
Collection de Vieux Avions, Habsheim . . . 012061
Collection de Vieux Coffres, Le Quiou-Évran . . . 012557
Collection de Vieux Pressoirs, Paulx 013757
Collection de Voitures Anciennes de S.A.S. Le Prince de Monaco, Monaco . . . 028989
Collection de Voitures Hippomobiles, Rosières-aux-Salines . . . 014116
Collection des Pressoirs des Ducs de Bourgogne, Chenôve . . . 011347
Collection des Serrures Fontaine, Paris . . . 013567
Collection d'Etains, Sierre . . . 037557
Collection d'Étendards, Beynac et Cazenac . . . 010785
Collection Deyrolle, Paris . . . 133557
Collection d'Histoire Naturelle, Le Locle . . . 037274
Collection Discographique et Bibliographique du Jazz, Villefranche-de-Rouergue . . . 015250
Collection d'Orgues Mécaniques, Palais des Orgues Mortier, Herzeele . . . 012096
Collection d'Outillage Ancien de Tonnellerie, Cussac-Fort-Médoc . . . 011551
Collection d'Outillage Vini-Viticole, Bégadan . . . 010730
Collection d'Outillage Viticole dans la Cave, Saint-Estèphe . . . 014267
Collection du Château d'Attre, Attre 003205
Collection du Château des Princes, Chimay . . . 003374
Collection du Moulin du Cros, Montagnac-sur-Lède . . . 013117
Collection du Musée Archéologique, Guise . . . 012055
Collection Entomologique, Chaveyriat . . . 011334
Collection Eugène Pesch, Oberkorn 027899
Collection Ferroviaire, Sospel . . . 014827
Collection Forum, Washington . . . 136425
Collection Frits Lugt, Paris . . . 013568
Collection Gallo-Romaine, La Roquebrussanne . . . 012334
Collection Guido Van Deth, Amsterdam . . . 029176
Collection Historial Cognacq-Jay, Paris . . . 013569
Collection Historique, Saint-Barthélemy . . . 021561
Collection Historique, Assas . . . 010503
Collection Historique, Auch . . . 010528
Collection Historique, Pennautier . . 013768
Collection Historique, Ossuaire Tour, La Wavrille, Douaumont . . . 011644
Collection Historique de Fouets, Les Micocouliers, Sorède . . . 014823
Collection Historique de la Marqueterie d'Art Spindler, Boersch . . . 010854
Collection Historique Maritime, Brest . . . 010979
Collection Internationale d'Épinettes, Sapois-Menaurupt . . . 014668
Collection J.M., Amiens . . . 060811
Collection Jules Romains, Falicon . 011781
Collection Jules Verne, Amiens . . . 010366
Collection Lambert, Musée d'Art, Avignon . . . 010588
Collection Lapidaire, Gimont . . . 011948
Collection Lapidaire et Historique sur l'Histoire de l'Abbaye de la Grasse, Lagrasse . . . 012379
Collection Minéralogique, Mizerieux 013080
Collection of Archaeology and Land Study, Nahshonim . . . 023037
Collection of Byzantine and Postbyzantine Art, Kythira . . . 021348
Collection of Icons and Curch Heiröooms at Pyrgos, Thera . . . 021487
Collection of Martinware Pottery, Southall . . . 041052
Collection of the Church of Koimissis tis Theotokou, Panagitsa Pellis . . . 021416
Collection of the Church of the Evangelistria, Kastron Agiou Georgiou . . . 021319
Collection of the Church of the Pangia, Agiassos . . . 021115
Collection of the Dominican Priory, Stari Grad . . . 007807
Collection of the Evangelismos tis Theotokou, Skiathos . . . 021469
Collection of the Koroni Monastery, Karditsa . . . 021305

Collection of the Mega Spileon Monastery, Kalavryta . . . 021298
Collection of the Metropolis of Kefallinia, Argostolion . . . 021144
Collection of the Metropolis of Monemvassia and Spárti, Spárti . 021475
Collection of the Metropolis of Xanthi, Xanthi . . . 021527
Collection of the Monastery of Agios Andreas, Peratata . . . 021428
Collection of the Monastery of Agios Nikolaos, Apoaika . . . 021140
Collection of the Monastery of Odigitria, Kolymvari . . . 021331
Collection of the Monastery of Saint Ignatios, Kalloni . . . 021301
Collection of the Monastery of Saint John the Divine, Antissa . . . 021138
Collection of the Panagia Tourliani, Ano Mera . . . 021137
Collection of the Proussou Monastery, Karpenission . . . 021311
Collection of the Rendina Monastery, Karditsa . . . 021306
Collection of the Saint John the Divine Monastery, Patmos . . . 021422
Collection of the Tatarna Monastery, Karpenission . . . 021312
Collection of the Worshipful Company of Clockmakers, London . . . 040123
Collection Pierre Bouton, Berneuil . 010763
Collection Préhistorique Pagès, Le Moustier . . . 012537
Collection Prevee, Miami . . . 117049
Collection Rare de Tracteurs Viticoles, Savigny-les-Beaune . . . 014722
Collection Républicaine, Urimenil . . 015075
Collection Schlumpf, Musée National de l'Automobile, Mulhouse . . . 013291
The Collection Shop, Miami . . . 090155
Collection Singulière d'Art Contemporain Insolite, Sénas . . . 014757
Collection Ski-Montagne, Briançon . 010990
Collection sur le Vin et la Gastronomie, Université du Goût, Grezels . . . 012032
Collection Vini-Viticole et de Tonnellerie, Caveau J. Becker, Zellenberg . . . 015386
Collection Viti-Vinicole, Coopérative de l'Étoile, Banyuls-sur-Mer . . . 010642
Collection Viticole, Mardeuil . . . 012900
Collectionantes, Nantes . . . 064916
Collectionneur, Clermont-Ferrand . . 062335
Le Collectionneur, Middelburg . . . 078636
Collectionneur, Nevers . . . 065007
Collectionneur, Roanne . . . 067167
Le Collectionneur Cevenol, Alès . . . 060771
Collectionneur Impuni, Paris . . . 138337
Le Collectionnisme, Wattignies . . . 069048
Collections, Christchurch . . . 079021
Collection's, Saint-Ouen . . . 067752
Collections 71, Autun . . . 061086
Collections Antiques, Indianapolis . 089282
Collections Archéologiques, Parmain . . . 013743
Collections Artistiques de l'Université de Liège, Liège . . . 003584
Collections Baur-Musée des Arts d'Extrême-Orient, Fondation Alfred et Eugénie Baur-Duret, Genève . . . 037121
Collections Brassicoles, Brasserie Kronenbourg, Strasbourg . . . 014858
Collections Claeyssens, Wambrechies . . . 015348
Collections d'Anciens Outils de Tonnellerie, Listrac-Médoc . . . 012713
Collections d'Art et d'Histoire, Clermont (Oise) . . . 011402
Collections d'Arts Décoratifs du Château de Longpra, Saint-Géoire-en-Valdaine . . . 014299
Collections d'Arts Populaires, Eschau . . . 011724
Collections de la Bibliothèque, La Bernerie-en-Retz . . . 012205
Collections de la Bibliothèque Municipale, Auxerre . . . 010570
Collections de la Bibliothèque Sainte-Geneviève, Paris . . . 013570
Collections de la Commanderie, Neuilly-sous-Clermont . . . 013373
Collections de la Fondation de Coubertin, Saint-Rémy-lès-Chevreuse . . . 014522
Collections de la Fondation Marius Vazelles, Meymac . . . 013051
Collections de la Fondation Roger-van-Rogger, Bandol . . . 010637
Collections de la Maison de la R.A.T.P., Paris . . . 013571
Collections de la Maison Henri IV, Saint-Valery-en-Caux . . . 014564
Collections de la Mine Saint-Louis, Sainte-Marie-aux-Mines . . . 014603
Collections de la Salle des Martyrs-Chapelle-Crypte, Paris . . . 013572
Collections de la Serrurerie Dantin, Paris . . . 013573
Collections de la Tour Eiffel, Paris . . 013574
Collections de l'Abbaye Bénédictine de Saint-Louis-du-Temple, Vauhallan 015143
Collections de l'Auberge du Cygne, Tôtes . . . 014967
Collections de l'Ecole Nationale Supérieure des Beaux-Arts, Paris . . . 013575
Collections de Papier Peint, Saint-Pandelon . . . 014464
Collections d'Histoire Locale, Bourganeuf . . . 010933
Collections d'Histoire Naturelle, Asson . . . 010505
Collections d'Objets de Chais et Tonnellerie, Listrac-Médoc . . . 012714
Collections d'Outils de Tonnellerie et d'Appareils Viticoles Anciens, Listrac-Médoc . . . 012715
Collections du Centre d'Instruction Navale de Brest, Brest . . . 010980
Collections du Château, Châteaubriant . . . 011283
Collections du Château, Loches (Indre-et-Loire) . . . 012720
Collections du Château, Xaintrailles 015374
Collections du Château de Born, Saint-Europe-de-Born . . . 014281
Collections du Château de Courances, Courances . . . 011507
Collections du Château de Gizeux, Gizeux . . . 011961
Collections du Château de la Thibaudière, Juigné-Béné . . . 012180
Collections du Château de Lantilly, Cervon . . . 011188
Collections du Château de Sury-le-Comtal, Sury-le-Comtal . . . 014891
Collections du Château d'Epernon, Angoulême . . . 010401
Collections du Château des Rohan, Pontivy . . . 013909
Collections du Château du Bouchet, Rosnay . . . 014117
Collections du Château du Breil de Foin, Genneteil . . . 011930
Collections du Château Médiéval des Cars, Les Cars . . . 012614
Collections du Conseil Général, Angers . . . 010388
Collections du Donjon, Bazoges-en-Pareds . . . 010692
Collections du Groupe de Conservation de Vehicules Militaires, MVCG Paris Ile de France, Issy-les-Moulineaux . . . 012139
Collections du Haras, La Roche-sur-Yon . . . 012310
Collections du Passé, Saint-Germain-en-Laye . . . 138601
Collections du Relais Louis XIII, Paris . . . 013576
Collections du Restaurant Procope, Paris . . . 013577
Collections du Service Historique de l'Armée de l'Air, SHAA, Armées . . 010475
Collections et Découvertes, Montauban . . . 064630
Collections Galerie, Paris . 065725, 100163
Collections Historiques, Menou . . . 013015
Collections Historiques du Château Fort des XIe-XVe s, Montcornet-en-Ardenne . . . 013149
Collections II, New Orleans . . . 090539
Collections in Situ de l'Unesco, Paris . . . 013578
Collections Internationales, Verdun (Meuse) . . . 068768
Collections Internationales de Marionnettes, Charleville-Mézières . . . 011248
Collections Littéraires, Kolbsheim . 012195
Collections Livres, Bruxelles . . . 133263
Collections Municipales d'Art et d'Histoire, Condé-sur-l'Escaut . . . 011460
Collections of Cypriot Painting, Sculpture and Graphics, Kolonaki . . . 021330
Collections of Harpenden, Harpenden . . . 113185
Collectique, Fresno . . . 088901
Collective Antiques, San Francisco . 092762
Collective Art Gallery, Indianapolis . 116449
Collectophile Librairie, Montréal . . . 137650
The Collector, Barnard Castle . . . 083388, 130335
The Collector, Cape Town . . . 110021
The Collector, Clevedon . . . 084032
The Collector, Haarlem . . . 078446
The Collector, London . . . 085218
The Collector, London . . . 136195
The Collector, Murrumbeena . . . 120618
Collector Book and Print Gallery, Cincinnati . . . 115621, 142312
Collector Book & Print Gallery, Newport . . . 118605, 142703
Collector Heaven, Atlanta . . . 087465
Collector Items, Seattle . . . 092979
Collector Magazine and Price Guide, Dubuque . . . 136426
The Collector Newsmagazine, Roswell . . . 136427
Collectormaniac, Mount Gambier . . 056281
Collector's, Parma . . . 076202
Collectors Art, San Diego . . . 119495
Collectors Art Gallery, New York . . . 090797
Collectors Attic, Denver . . 088670, 122883
Collectors Authority, San Antonio . . 092501
Collectors Books and Cards, Calgary . . . 137623
Collectors Books and Records, Vancouver . . . 137725
Collectors Cabinet, Aachen . . . 138667
The Collectors Centre, Saint Peter Port . . . 086473, 142041
Collectors Centre - Antique City, London . . . 085219
Collector's Choice, Denver . . . 088671
Collectors Choice, Modbury . . . 085998
Collectors Choice, Omaha . . . 091557
Collector's Choice, Saskatoon . . . 097191
The Collectors Club, New York . . . 046316
Collectors Coin Exchange, Phoenix . 091730
Collectors Connection, Cincinnati . . 088224
Collector's Corner, Burnie . . . 136832
Collectors Corner, Calgary . . . 058784
Collectors Corner, Carshalton . . . 083888, 141494
Collectors Corner, Columbus . . . 088395
Collectors Corner, Columbus . . . 088396
Collectors' Corner, Faversham . . . 084394
Collectors Corner, Greenslopes . . . 055914
Collector's Corner, Greenslopes . . . 055915
Collectors Corner, Marieholm . . . 081883
Collectors Corner, Napier . . . 079163
Collectors Corner, Northallerton . . . 086095
Collectors Corner, Oakland . . . 091411
The Collectors Corner, Oklahoma City . . . 091486
Collector's Corner, Omaha . . . 091558
Collector's Corner, Toledo . . . 093168
Collector's Corner, Truro . . . 086929
Collector's Corner, Zürich . . . 082954
Collector's Covey, Dallas . . . 115856
Collectors Covey, Dallas . . . 115857
The Collector's Den, Dublin . . . 074901
Collectors Den, Indianapolis . . . 089283
Collectors Den, Pittsburgh . . . 091802
Collector's Den, Valletta . . . 077537
Collectors Dream, Sacramento . . . 092149
Collectors Emporium, Buffalo . . . 087868
Collector's Emporium, Los Angeles 089728
Collectors Fine Art, Honolulu . . . 116204
Collectors Firearms, Houston . . . 089055
Collectors Gallery, Bannesdorf . . . 101735
The Collectors Gallery, Calgary . . . 096798
Collector's Gallery, Kalamaria . . . 105424
Collectors Gallery, Kooyong . . . 094708
Collectors' Gallery, Shrewsbury . . . 086599
Collector's Gazette, Kirkby-in-Ashfield . . . 136196
Collector's Heaven, Dallas . . . 088487
Collectors International, Oakland . . 091412
Collectors News & the Antique Report, Grundy Center . . . 136428
Collectors Old Book Shop, Richmond . . . 142826
Collectors Old Toy Shop and Antiques, Halifax . . . 084557
Collectors Paradise, Albuquerque . . 087386
Collectors' Paradise, Leigh-on-Sea 084955
Collector's Paradise Watches, Chennai . . . 074790
Collectors Path, Honolulu . . . 088943
Collectors Pieces, Mount Eliza . . . 056280
Collector's Place, Shrewsbury . . . 086600
The Collectors Shop, Edinburgh . . . 084281
Collector's Showcase, Jacksonville 089400
Collectors Showcase, Winnipeg . . . 059453
Collector's Sports Books, Earlwood 136886
The Collector's Store, Hamilton . . . 058849
Collectors Superstore, Virginia Beach . . . 093350
Collector's Toystop, Milwaukee . . . 090288
Collector's Warehouse, Cleveland . 088322
Collectors World, Cromer . . . 084119
Collectors World, Nottingham . . . 086133
Collectors World, Pittsburgh . . . 091803
Colleen's Art, New Orleans . . . 117418
Colleen's Books, Houston . . . 142433
Colleen's Collectables, Columbus . . 088397
Colleen's Station Gallery, Miami . . . 117050
College Art Association, New York .054715, 136429
College Art Collections, London . . . 040124
College Art Gallery, New Paltz . . . 046269
The College Art Gallery, College of New Jersey, Ewing . . . 043771
College Book Rack, Jacksonville . . 142465
College Bookstore, Houston . . . 142434
Collège de France, Paris . . . 049970
College Football Hall of Fame, South Bend . . . 048225
College Museum, Epsom . . . 039452
College Museum, Lancing . . . 039927
College Museum, Maynooth . . . 022835
College of Architecture, Clemson University, Clemson . . . 051152
College of Architecture, Georgia Institute of Technology, Atlanta . . . 050922
College of Architecture, Illinois Institute of Technology, Chicago . . . 051121
College of Architecture, Texas A & M University, College Station . . . 051174
College of Architecture, University of Illinois at Chicago, Chicago . . . 051122
College of Architecture and Design, Kansas State University, Manhattan . . . 051671
College of Architecture and Design, Lawrence Technological University, Southfield . . . 052196
College of Architecture and Environmental Design, Arizona State University, Tempe . . . 052251
College of Architecture and Fine Arts, University of Santo Tomas, Manila 050594
College of Art, Delhi . . . 050298
College of Art, Kwame Nkrumah University of Science and Technology, Kumasi . . . 050268
College of Art, Maryland Institute, Baltimore . . . 050944
College of Art and Architecture, University of Idaho, Moscow . . . 051755
College of Art and Design, Philadelphia . . . 051935

College of Art and Design, Center for Creative Studies, Detroit 051257
College of Art and Design, Watkins Institute, Nashville 051777
College of Art and Humanities, Humboldt State University, Arcata 050908
College of Art Gallery, Kwame Nkrumah University of Science and Technology, Kumasi 021104
College of Arts, Hue University, Hue 052433
College of Arts, Nihon University, Tokyo 050481
College of Arts, University of Baghdad, Baghdad 050340
College of Arts and Crafts, Patna University, Patna 050319
College of Arts and Crafts, Faculty of Fine Arts, Lucknow University, Lucknow 050314
College of Arts and Crafts Museum, Lucknow 022243
College of Arts and Humanities, University of Maine at Augusta, Augusta ... 050931
College of Arts and Sciences, Seton Hall University, South Orange 052194
College of Arts and Sciences, University of Massachusetts Amherst, Amherst 050896
College of Creative Arts, West Virginia University, Morgantown 051753
College of Eastern Utah Art Gallery, Price 047229
College of Eastern Utah Prehistoric Museum, Price 047230
College of Fine and Applied Arts, Sudan University of Science and Technology, Khartoum 050743
College of Fine Arts, Carnegie-Mellon University, Pittsburgh 051955
College of Fine Arts, Sookmyung Women's University, Seoul 050510
College of Fine Arts, University of Montevallo, Montevallo 051743
College of Fine Arts, University of New Mexico, Albuquerque 050879
College of Fine Arts, University of New South Wales, Paddington 049617
College of Fine Arts, University of the Philippines, Quezon City 050597
College of Fine Arts, Wichita State University, Wichita 052371
College of Fine Arts and Architecture, Jawaharlal Nehru Technological University, Hyderabad 050305
College of Fine Arts of Seoul National University, Seoul 050511
College of Fine Arts - School of Visual Arts, Boston University, Boston 051011
College of Imaging Arts and Sciences, Rochester Institute of Technology, Rochester 052042
College of Liberal Arts, Azusa Pacific University, Azusa 050938
College of Liberal Arts, Dakota State University, Madison 051658
College of Liberal Arts and Education, Tuskegee University, Tuskegee .. 052284
College of Liberal Arts and Sciences, University of Florida, Gainesville . 051369
College of Marin Art Gallery, Kentfield 044968
College of Media Arts & Design, Drexel University, Philadelphia 051936
College of New Jersey Art Gallery, Trenton 048601
College of Photographic Art and Sciences, Rochester Institute of Technology, Rochester 052043
College of Textile Technology Museum, Hooghly 022153
College of the Arts, Ohio State University, Columbus 051190
College of the Arts, University of Southwestern Louisiana, Lafayette 051568
College of Visual and Performing Arts, Kutztown University, Kutztown ... 051558
College of Visual and Performing Arts, University of Massachusetts Dartmouth, North Dartmouth 051854
College of Visual Arts, Saint Paul .. 052085
College of Visual Arts Gallery, Saint Paul 047696
The College of Wooster Art Museum, Wooster 049302
College Park Aviation Museum, College Park 043043
Collegi d'Arquitectes de Catalunya, Barcelona 050710
Collegio del Cambio - Museo d'Arte, Perugia 025164
Collegium Hungaricum, Berlin 101830
Collem, V., Bruxelles 057893, 120721
Collet, Catherine, Saint-Mihiel 067679
Collet, Henri, Saint-Denis-d'Anjou . 067416
Colleton Museum, Walterboro 048843
Collett Art Gallery, Belfast 112609
Colletti, Chicago 088062
Collezionando di Palazzo Giampiero, Firenze 075320, 140012
Collezione A. Checchi, Fucecchio .. 024256
Collezione Berenson, Firenze 024148
Collezione Borsari, Parma 025113
Collezione Calderara, Fondazinone Calderara, Ameno 023193
Collezione Civica d'Arte, Palazzo Vittone, Pinerolo 025243
Collezione Contini-Bonacossi, Firenze 024149
Collezione d'Arte della Banca Carige, Genova 024295
Collezione d'Arte di Santa Maria di Piazza, Ostra 025035
Collezione d'Arte Religiosa Moderna, Musei Vaticani, Città del Vaticano 049419
Collezione d'Arte Sacra, Saludecio . 025642
Collezione di Carrozze, Villa Barbaro, Maser 024627
Collezione di Ceramiche Mostra Permanente, Fiorano Modenese . 024135
Collezione di Farfalle, Guardia Sanframondi 024386
Collezione di Marionette Ferrari, Istituto San Paolo, Parma 025114
Collezione di Minerali e Fossili, Semione 037552
Collezione di Violini, Cremona 023994
Collezione Ducati Fratelli Saltarelli, Senigallia 025850
Collezione Entomologica, Sassari .. 025800
Collezione Etnografica, Forni Avoltri 024237
Collezione Fisica e Medicina, Pavia 025138
Collezione G. Lorenzi, Milano 024696
Collezione Jucker, Milano 024697
Collezione Martini Carissimo, Oria . 025003
Collezione Memorie della Comunità, Romano di Lombardia 025592
Collezione Meo-Evoli, Monopoli ... 024793
Collezione Minici Zotti, Un Museo di Magiche Visioni, Padova 025049
Collezione P. Mariani, Desio 024030
Collezione Permanente del Design Italiano '45-'90, Milano 024698
Collezione Preistorica, Castaneda .. 037003
Collezione Privata di Attrezzi ed Utensili Contadini, Camerota 023608
Collezione Scaglione, Locri 024515
Collezione Straka-Coppa, Villa Fidelia, Spello 025931
Collezione Tessile de Tela Umbra, Città di Castello 023892
Collezione Titta Ruffo, Pisa 025259
Collezione Wolfson, Genova 024296
Collezioni d'Armi e Ceramiche della Rocca Sforzesca, Imola 024400
Collezioni d'Arte della Cassa di Risparmio, Savona 025824
Collezioni d'Arte e di Storia della Cassa di Risparmio, Bologna 023417
Collezioni degli Istituti di Geologia e di Paleontologia, Milano 024699
Collezioni del Dipartimento di Entomologia e Zoologia Agraria, Portici 025327
Collezioni dell'Istituto Universitario Orientale, Napoli 024890
Collezioni di Presepi del Convento Muri-Gries, Bolzano 023466
Collezioni Egittologiche dell'Università di Pisa, Dipartimento di Scienze Storiche, Pisa 025260
Collezioni Naturalistiche del Museo Comunale, Imola 024401
Collezionoe Sarda L. Piloni, Cagliari 023559
Collier, Mark, Fordingbridge 084422
Collier County Museum, Naples ... 046129
Collier Memorial State Park and Logging Museum, Chiloquin 042901
Colliers, Newcastle-upon-Tyne 114121
Colliette, Marie-Agnès, Semur-en-Auxois 121259
Colligan, Dennis, Houston 089056
Collignon, Audun-le-Roman 061058
Collignon, Daniel, Mont-Bonvillers . 064610
Collignon, Daniel, Nancy 064865
Collignon, Gildas, Troyes . 101391, 138643
Collignon, Sylvie, Paris 065726
Collignon & Laurent, Soissons 121261
Collin, Jean-François, Paris 065727
Collin County Farm Museum, McKinney 045559
Collinge Antiques, Llandudno 085033, 130908
Collinge & Clark, London 141774
Collingwood Antiques, Johannesburg 080703
Collingwood Gallery, Collingwood .. 094419
Collingwood Museum, Collingwood 005287
Collingwood Museum on Americanism, Alexandria 041638
Collins, Houston 089057
Collins, München 126367
Collins, San Diego 092625
Collins, Bernadette, Minneapolis .. 117248
Collins, C.P., Leichhardt 136974
Collins, F.G. & C., Wheathampstead 087123, 131679
Collins, Frank, Mendlesham Green . 085974
Collins & Son, J., Bideford 083509, 130382
Collins, Jim, Vancouver 097446
Collins, Louis, Seattle 142984
Collins, M.E., New York 090798
Collins, Tricia, New York 117787
Collins & Chandler, Toronto 059168, 097248
Collins Gallery, Glasgow 039551
Collins Gallery, London 113549
Collins & Hastie, London . 113550, 130984
Collins & McCullough, Miami 090156
Collins Street Gallery, Melbourne .. 094806
Collinsville Depot Museum, Collinsville 043050
Colliton Antique Centre, Dorchester 084175, 130640
Collomb, Agnès, Le Grand-Saconnex 082482
Collot, Longué-Jumelles 063987
Collu, Giovanni, Cagliari .. 075204, 127244
Collyer, Jean, Boughton 083585
Collyer, R., Birmingham .. 083529, 130389
Colman, Michael, Malvern, Victoria 056144, 123258
Colmar, Marcel, La Garde 063389
Colnaghi & Co., P. & D., London ... 085220
Colnard, Marc, Pringy 066984
Colne Valley Museum, Golcar 039598
Colobert & Letresor, Etampes 121001
Colomb, Alain, Chanac 062130
Colomb, Olivier, Saint-Estève 124893
Colombani, Dominique, Marseille ..064342, 124405
Colombano, Gianbeppe, Torino 106670
La Colombe d'Or Art Gallery, Houston 116296
Colombelle, Paris 065728
Colombi, Elda, Milano 075671
Colombi, Giuliana, Milano 127568
Colombine, Amsterdam 140293
Colombine, Montcaret 064661
Colombo, Alberto, Milano 127569
Colombo, Angelo, Zürich 082955
Colombo, Maria Grazia, Bologna .. 075067
Colombo, Nicoletta, Milano 106196
Colombo National Museum, Colombo 036130
Colomé, Raoul, Toulouse 124977
Colomo, Lorenzo, Valladolid 110849
Colon XVI, Bilbao 110274
Colonel Ashley House, Ashley Falls . 041815
Colonel Davenport Historical Foundation, Rock Island 047492
Colonel Stephens Railway Museum, Tenterden 041198
Colonel William Jones House, Gentryville 044169
Colonels' Choice, Milwaukee 090289
Coloneum, Regensburg 073454
La Colonia, Medellín 059914
Colonial Antiguidades, Rio de Janeiro 058574
Colonial Antiques, Tulsa 093292
Colonial Art Gallery, Oklahoma City 091487
Colonial Art Gallery, Oklahoma City 118659
Colonial Art Gallery, Oklahoma City 123031
Colonial Art Gallery, Russell 108556
Colonial Arts, San Francisco 092763
Colonial Attic Antiques, Spotswood 056623
Colonial Auctions, Philadelphia 123043
Colonial Brass, Houston 132111
Colonial Burlington Foundation, Burlington 042521
Colonial Classics, Ascot Vale 123185
Colonial Concept, Saint-Ouen 067753
Colonial Cottage Antiques, Rockhampton 056543
Colonial Cottage Antiques, Virginia Beach 093351
Colonial Cottage Museum, Wellington 030635
Colonial Desks, Christchurch 079022
Colonial Discount Jewelers, Cleveland 088323
Colonial Estate Buyers, Minneapolis 090350
Colonial Fair Antiques, Dannevirke . 079076
Colonial Frontiers, Tucson 093214
Colonial Industrial Quarter, Bethlehem 042182
Colonial Michilimackinac, Mackinaw City 045554
Colonial Pemaquid Historical Site, New Harbor 046219
Colonial Pennsylvania Plantation, Media 045744
Colonial Restorations, Auckland ...078935, 128899
Colonial Times, Cross-in-Hand 084122
Colonial Trading Company, Boston . 087808
Colonial Williamsburg, Williamsburg 049180
Colonies Market, Oklahoma City ... 091488
Colonna, București 109423
La Colonna, Roma 076382
Le Colonne, Firenze 075321
Les Colonnes, Paris 065729
Colonnese, Napoli 140077
Colony Furniture Shops, Charlotte . 087940
Color, München 072678
Color Art, Saint Louis 119195
Color Association of the US, New York 054716
Color Connection Gallery, Tulsa ... 120191
Color-Fast, Los Angeles 116745
Color Genesis, Atlanta 114865
Color Impressions, Charlotte 115282
Color y Forma, Medellín 098257
Colorado Gallery of the Arts, Araphoe Community College, Littleton 045347
Colorado Historical Society Museum, Denver 043401
Colorado Institute of Art, Denver ... 051249
Colorado Photographic Arts Center, Denver 043402
Colorado Railroad Museum, Golden 044233
Colorado River Indian Tribes Museum, Parker 046825
Colorado School of Mines Geology Museum, Golden 044234
Colorado Ski Museum and Ski Hall of Fame, Vail 048723

Colorado Springs Fine Arts Center, Taylor Museum, Colorado Springs 043054
Colorado Springs Museum, Colorado Springs 043055
Colorado University Art Galleries, Boulder 042351
Colorado University Heritage Center, Boulder 042352
Colorado Watercolor Society, Westminster 054717
Colorado-Wyoming Association of Museums, Sheridan 054718
Il Colore, Cagliari 106010
Colore Luna, Essen 102671
De Colores, Albuquerque 114775
Colorfield Art Space, Taipei 098062
Coloris-Art, Villeneuve (Vaud) 111974
Colorworks Studio, New York 117788
Colory, Berlin 101831
Colosseum Art Gallery, Haifa 022919
Colour Museum, Bradford 038806
Colourbox, Otley 114196
Colours, Cairo 098623
Colours, Edinburgh 112988, 130675
Colours, Masterton 108500
Colportages, Rouen 138587
Colter Bay Indian Arts Museum, Colter Bay Village 043063
Coltishall Antiques Centre, Coltishall 084066, 130604
Colton, Gary, Kelvedon . . . 084821, 130839
Colton Area Museum, Colton 043064
Colton Hall Museum, Monterey . . . 045981
Coltsfoot, Leominster 084970, 130885
Coluccia, Lucrezia, Bari 075010
Coluccia, Pietro, Bari 075011, 127109
Coluccini, Franco, Roma 127985
Columbia City Gallery, Seattle 119900
Columbia Coins, Portland 091918
Columbia College Art Gallery, Chicago 042836
Columbia County Historical Museum, Lake City 045103
Columbia County Historical Society Museum, Kinderhook 045002
Columbia County Historical Society Museum, Saint Helens 047633
Columbia County Museum, Bloomsburg 042270
Columbia Fire Department Museum, Columbia 043076
Columbia George Interpretive Center, Stevenson 048356
Columbia Journal of Law & the Arts, New York 136430
Columbia Museum of Art, Columbia 043077
Columbia Rarities Group, El Paso . . 088798
Columbia River Exhibition of History, Science and Technology, Richland 047393
Columbia River Maritime Museum, Astoria 041823
Columbia State Historic Park, Columbia 043066
The Columbian Museum and Art Center, Wamego 048850
Columbiana-Fairfield Township Museum, Columbiana 043092
Columbus, Groningen 078411
Columbus Antique Broker, Columbus 088398, 122870
Columbus Art Gallery, New York . . . 117789
Columbus-Belmont Civil War Museum, Columbus 043098
Columbus Circle Gallery, New York . 117790
Columbus College of Art and Design, Columbus 051191
Columbus Cultural Arts Center, Columbus 043105
The Columbus Museum, Columbus 043093
Columbus Museum of Art, Columbus 043106
Columbus Park Museum, Discovery Bay 026379
Columbus Sportscards, Columbus . 088399
Column, Elmira 136431
Columna 32, Zaragoza 081739
Las Columnas, San Salvador 098685
Colussi, Franco, Seven Hills 123302
Colville Lake Museum, Norman Wells 006030
Colvin, Richard, Denver 132032
Colwyn Books, Colwyn Bay 141536
Colystock Antiques, Stockland 086718
Colzium Museum, Kilsyth 039873
Com Arca, Bucureşti 080149
Com Art Graz, Verein zur Förderung von Computerkunst, Graz 052523
Com Arte Projetos Culturais, Belo Horizonte 096458
Comali, Den Haag 107909
Comanche Crossing Museum, Strasburg 048392
Comarca, Cartagena 059892
Il Comaro, Iaşi 080184
Comart, Madrid 129594
Comatra, Colombes 062426
Comatra, Paris 065730
Comba, Marcus, Sankt Gallen 130158
Combalbert, Françoise, Saint-Magne-de-Castillon 067599
Combalbert, Jean-Louis, Quinsac . . 067030
Combalia Dexeus, Maria Victoria, Barcelona 110133
Combasteix, Hervé & Robert, Le Grand-Lucé 063622
Combat Air Museum, Topeka 048580
Combe, Michel, Batz-sur-Mer 061221
Combe Martin Museum, Combe Martin 039129
Combe Mill Beam Engine and Working Museum, Long Hanborough 040333
Comber and District Historical Society Museum, Comber 005288
Comber Pioneer Village, Holland Centre 005622
Comberton Antiques, Comberton . . 084071
Combes, Dominique, Toulouse 101338
Combes, Michèle, Pouilly-sous-Charlieu 066970
Combi, Gian Luigi, Torino 076802
Combined Auctions, Ultimo 120649
Combret, Didier, Villefranche-de-Rouergue 068894
Combs, Gary, New York 142642
Combs, Sharon, Tulsa 093293
Come in, Aalen 069105
Comeau, André, Montréal 058941
Comed, Milano 135891
Comenius-Antiquariat, Hilterfingen . 141259
Comenius Museum, Naarden 029934
Comenos, George L., Boston 087809
Comeprima, Toulouse 101339
Comer Museum, Morgantown 046026
Comércio de Arte Oriental Macau Antigo, Lisboa 079901
Comerlati, Didier, Paris 065731
Comes, Giovanna, Catania 127262
Comet Slices Gallery, Louisville . . . 116934
Cometa Arte Comercio, Belo Horizonte 058423
Cometalledo, Barcelona 080836
Comic Book World, Cincinnati 142313
Comic-Forum, Wien 133187, 135550
Comic Galerie, Wien 095809
Comic-Galerie Grober Unfug, Berlin 101832
Comic-Galerie Grober Unfug, Berlin 101833
Das Comic-Museum, Wiener Neustadt 003030
Comic Point, Reutlingen 139690
Comic Warehouse, Albuquerque . . . 142190
Comicladen-Kollektiv, Hamburg . . . 139172
Comicopia, Boston 087810
Comics Bazar, Roma 076383
Comics Bazar, Roma 140100
Comics-Galerie, Pulheim 104643
Coming of Age Antiques, Withcott . 056837
Comisión Nacional de Arqueología y Monumentos Historicos, Panamá City 053966
Comisión Nacional de Museos y de Monumentos, Buenos Aires 052444
Comitê Brasileiro do ICOM, Porto Alegre 052704
Comité Nacional del Consejo Internacional de Museos, ICOM, Bogotá 052809
Comité National Français de l'ICOM, Paris 052928
Comité National Monégasque de l'Association Internationale des Arts Plastique, Monaco 053869
Comité Peruano del Consejo Internacional de Museos, ICOM Peru, Lima 053972
Comité Professionnel des Galeries d'Art, Paris 052929
Comitée National de ICOM Centralafrique, Bangui 052781
Comitée National de ICOM de Algérie, Alger 052436
Comma 5, Milano 075672
Command Museum, San Diego . . . 047818
Commanda General Store Museum, Commanda 005290
La Commanderie d'Arville, Arville . . 010499
Commandery Museum, Worcester . 041442
Comme Art, Paris 100164
Comme Autrefois, Montauban 064631
Comme Avant, Ars-en-Ré 060993
Commedia, Münster 139562
Commedia Dell'Arte, Montpellier . . 099751
Commencement Art Gallery, Tacoma 048463
Commerce Bancshares Fine Art Collection, Kansas City 044916
Commercial and Industrial Museum, Kanpur 022198
Commercial and Technical Art Department, South Central Technical College, North Mankato 051856
Commercial Art, Salt Lake City 119336
Commercial Art Department, Guilford Technical Institute, Jamestown . . 051526
Commercial Art Department, Honolulu Community College, Honolulu . . . 051472
Commercial Art Department, Luzerne County Community College, Nanticoke 051772
Commercial Arts Services, Dallas . . 115858
Commercial Museum, Gauhati 022121
Commercial Museum, Gauhati University, Guwahati 022134
The Commercial Press, Hong Kong . 133362
Commeter, Persiehl & Co., Hamburg 103108
Commissaires-Priseurs de Chartrons, Bordeaux 120939
Commissaires Priseurs de Montpellier, Montpellier 121079
Commissariat House, Saint John's . 006363
Commissariat Store Museum, Brisbane 000838
Commission a Portrait.Com, London 113551
Common Ground, New York 117791
Common Ground Gallery, Windsor, Ontario 097556
Common Market, Memphis 090063
Common Space Center for Creativity, Toledo 120077
Common to Key Coin, Sacramento . 092150
Commonwealth Air Training Plan Museum, Brandon 005140
Commonwealth Antiques, Boston . . 087811
Commonwealth Association of Museums, Calgary 052745
Commonwealth Books, Boston 142254
Commonwealth Fine Art, Boston . . 115163
Commonwealth Institute, London . . 040125
Commonwealth Museum, Boston . . 042322
Commonwealth of the Northern Mariana Islands Museum of History and Culture, Saipan 030711
Commune du Pouancé, Pouancé . . 101047
Communication Arts, Menlo Park . .135390, 136432
Communication Arts Department, Madison Area Technical College, Madison . 051660
Communications and History Museum of Sutton, Washington 048891
Communications Monument, Seoul 027546
Community Artists' Collective, Houston 054719
Community Arts Centre, Wanganui . 030625
Community Arts Council Museum, Goldsboro 044238
Community Arts Gallery, Detroit . . . 043439
Community Arts Project, Cape Town 054064
Community College Art Gallery, Baltimore 041975
Community Council for the Arts, Kinston 054720
Community Fine Arts Center, Rock Springs 047495
Community Historical Museum, Maxwell 045729
Community Historical Museum of Mount Holly, Belmont 042129
Community Memorial Museum of Sutter County, Yuba City 049367
Community Museums Association of Prince Edward Island, Charlottetown . . . 052746
Community of Christ Musuem, Independence 044720
Comocer, Castellón de la Plana . . . 129477
La Cómoda, Madrid 129595
Comode, Simone, Autun 061087
Comoglio, Georges, Paris 065732
Comox Air Force Museum, Lazo . . . 005757
Compagnia della Pietra, Verona . . . 128422
Compagnia delle Indie, Firenze 075322
Compagnia di Belle Arti, Milano . . . 106197
Compagnie Avignonnaise de Change, Avignon 061129
Compagnie d'Artistes, Lorient 099520
Compagnie de la Bourse, Paris 065733
Compagnie de la Chine et des Indes, Paris 065734
Compagnie de l'Or et des Métaux Précieux, Thionville 068393
La Compagnie des Antiquaires, Paris 052930
Compagnie des Arts, Strasbourg . .068310, 138616
Compagnie des Commissaires-Priseurs, Aubervilliers 120908
Compagnie des Commissaires Priseurs de la Région Parisienne, Paris 052931
Compagnie des Commissaires Priseurs de Paris, Paris 121131
Compagnie des Experts en Ameublement, Objets d'Art et de Collection près la Cour d'Appel et le Tribunal de Grande Instance de Paris, Paris 052932
Compagnie des Libraires Experts de France, Paris 138338
Compagnie d'Expertise en Antiquités et Objets d'Art, Paris 052933
Compagnie d'Experts Français en Antiquités, Paris 052934
Compagnie Française des Arts Graphiques, Neuilly-sur-Seine 133503
Compagnie Française des Experts en Objets d'Art et Antiquités, Paris 052935
Compagnie Générale de l'Or, Paris . 065735
Compagnie Nationale des Experts, Paris 052936
Compagnie XIX, Paris 065736
Compagnon, Emilie, Sains-du-Nord 067340
Compagnon Franck, Rouen 067261
Compagnons Ebénistes Associés, Paris 124625
Compañia Literaria Granadina, Granada 141020
Compas, Les Mars 063770
Compas Antiquités, Les Mars 063771
Compass Gallery, Glasgow 113107
Compendium Gallery, Auckland . . . 108308
Complejo Histórico Chivilcoy, Chivilcoy 000274
Complejo Museológico La Estación, Cruz Alta 000323
Complejo Museos Históricos Militares, La Habana 007944
Complément d'Objet, Paris 065737
Complément d'Objet, Paris 065738
Complément d'Objets, Brantome . . 061749
Complementz', Dallas 088488

Complesso Museale di Santa Chiara, Napoli . . . 024891
Complete Pictures, Houston . . . 116297
Complete Post, Los Angeles . . . 089729
Complete Traveller Bookstore, New York . . . 142643
Complex Muzeal de Ştiinţele Naturii, Galaţi . . . 032865
Complexe Muséographique Arche de Noé, Saint-Clément-des-Baleines . . . 014233
Complexul Monumental Curtea Domnească, Târgovişte . . . 032944
Complexul Muzeal Arad, Arad . . . 032773
Complexul Muzeal Bucovina, Suceava . . . 032943
Complexul Muzeal de Stiinţe ale Naturii Constanţa, Constanţa . . . 032841
Complexul Muzeal de Stiintele Naturii Ion Borcea, Bacău . . . 032775
Complexul Muzeal Goleşti, Goleşti . 032871
Complexul Muzeal Măldăreşti, Măldăreşti . . . 032889
Complexul Naţional Muzeal Astra, Sibiu . . . 032934
Compliments, Buffalo . . . 087869
Componere, Saint Louis . . . 119196
Compositions Gallery, San Francisco . . . 119644
Compostella, Mario, Napoli . . . 127759
Compra - Venta, Málaga . . . 081419
Compra y Venta de Antigüedades Belle Epoque, Bogotá . . . 059828
Compra y Venta de Oro y Plata, Madrid . . . 081279
Compraventa Libros & Muebles, Bogotá . . . 059829, 137757
Compta Martinez, Antoni, Barcelona 129336
Le Comptoir, Sète . . . 101274
Comptoir aux Occasions, Nantes . . 064917
Comptoir Bordelais de Monnaies et Change, Bordeaux . . . 061600
Comptoir d'Achat Or et Argent, Blois . . . 061522
Comptoir d'Achat Or et Argent, Tours . . . 068590
Comptoir de Change, Toulon (Var) . . 068448
Comptoir de la Chine, Mulhouse . . . 064831
Comptoir de la Chine, Strasbourg . . 068311
Comptoir de la Main d'Or, Paris . . . 065739
Le Comptoir de l'Aviation, Paris . . . 065740
Comptoir de l'Occasion du Centre, Aurillac . . . 061073
Comptoir de Zélie, Chamalières . . . 062099
Comptoir des Métaux Précieux, Auxerre . . . 061102
Comptoir des Monnaies Ancienne, Lille . . . 063840
Comptoir des Monnaies Anciennes, Épernay . . . 062782
Comptoir des Monnaies Anciennes, Reims . . . 067066
Comptoir des Tuileries, Paris . . . 065741
Comptoir des Tuileries, Paris . . . 065742
Le Comptoir du Collectionneur, Thionville . . . 068394
Comptoir du Meuble Ancien, Bruxelles . . . 057894
Comptoir du Troc, Saint-Melaine-sur-Aubance . . . 067672
Comptoir Français de l'Or, Paris . . . 065743
Comptoir Marseillais de Bourse, Marseille . . . 064343
Comptoir Numismatique, Nevers . . 065008
Comptoir Numismatique, Orléans . . 065300
Comptoir Numismatique, Villeneuve-sur-Lot . . . 068917
Comptoir Numismatique du Roannais, Roanne . . . 067168
Comptoir Numismatique et Philatélique, Bergerac . . . 061358
Comptoir Numismatique la Semeuse, Creutzwald . . . 062566
Comptoir Numismatique Troyen, Troyes . . . 068645
Comptoir Parisien de l'Or, Le Mans . 063658
Comptoir Savoyard de Change, Annecy . . . 060889
Comptoirs du Chineur, Paris . . . 065744
Compton, Lucinda, Ripon . . . 131418
Compton Cassey Gallery, Withington . . . 114715
Compton Castle, Paignton . . . 040670
Compton County Historical Museum, Eaton Corner . . . 005384
Compton & Schuster, London . . . 130985
Compton Verney Collections, Compton Verney . . . 039131
Compulsive Collector, New York . . . 142644
Computer Assisted Arts Association, Zwijnaarde . . . 052664
Computermuseum Aachen, Aachen 015417
Comstock Historic House, Moorhead . . . 046016
Comte, Lausanne . . . 082539
Comte, Olivier, Genève . . . 082417
Comte, Roland, Genève . . . 111438
Comteroux, Perpignan . . . 066739
Comtoise, Cannes . . . 061940
Con Edison Energy Museum, New York . . . 046317
Con Foster Museum, Traverse City . 048597
Cona, Nairobi . . . 077354
Conan, Lyon . . . 121047
Conart, Bucureşti . . . 129218
Conca d'Oro, Messina . . . 106135
Concept Art, Granville . . . 099296
Concept Art Gallery, Pittsburgh . . . 118911
Conception Bay Museum, Harbour Grace . . . 005604
Conceptions Art, Calgary . . . 096799
Conceptions Southwest, Albuquerque . . . 136433
Concetta D-Gallery, Albuquerque . . 114776
Concord, Hong Kong . . . 097774
Concord, New York . . . 132455
Concord Art Association, Concord . . 054721
Concord Art Association Museum, Concord . . . 043116
Concord Heritage Museum, Concord . . . 000942
Concord Museum, Concord . . . 043117
Concordia Historical Institute Museum, Saint Louis . . . 047657
Concordia University-Wisconsin Art Gallery, Mequon . . . 045780
Concourse Aboriginal Gallery, Winnipeg . . . 097578
Condamin, Jacques, Nantes . . . 099805
Condamin, Jean-Paul, Saint-Laurent-d'Agny . . . 067575
Condé, Monica de, Vichy . . . 138657
Conde, Susan, New York . . . 117792
Conde Gonzalez, Cesar, Madrid . . . 081280
Condemine, Annie, Sens . . . 068215
Condettan, Boulogne-sur-Mer . . . 061694
Condettan, Le Touquet-Paris-Plage 063716
Condor Ap Contract, Bucureşti . . . 080150
Condotti Fine Arts, Roma . . . 076384
Condotti Fine Arts, Roma . . . 076385
Condrau, Alexa, Disentis . . . 111385
Conduit Gallery, Dallas . . . 115859
Conejo Valley Art Museum, Thousand Oaks . . . 048551
Confederate Memorial Hall-Bleak House, Knoxville . . . 045034
Confederate Memorial State Historic Site, Higginsville . . . 044532
Confederate Museum, Crawfordville 043211
Confederate Museum, New Orleans 046249
Confederation Centre Art Gallery and Museum, Confederation Centre of the Arts, Charlottetown . . . 005245
Confédération Internationale des Négociants en Oeuvres d'Art (C.I.N.O.A.), Bruxelles . . . 052665
Conference House, Staten Island . . 048327
Confluences, Paris . . . 052937
Conforti, Firenze . . . 140013
Confucian Shrine and Chinese Museum, Nagasaki . . . 026859
Confucianist Society of Japan, Tokyo . . . 053777
Congdom Anatomical Museum, Bangkok . . . 037874
Congdon-Clelford, Paul, Chandler's Ford . . . 130524
Congé, Michèle, Paris . . . 124626
Congedo, Galatina . . . 134592
Congo Arts, Bruxelles . . . 096171
La Congrega, Brescia . . . 075160
Congregation Emanu-el Museum, New York . . . 046318
Congressional Arts Caucus, Washington . . . 054722
Conifer Grove Antiques, South Auckland . . . 079237
Conil, Monique, Paris . . . 065745
Coningsby Gallery, London . . . 113552
Coninx Museum, Zürich . . . 037763
Conjunt Monumental de la Esglésias de Sant Pere, Museu de Terrassa, Terrassa . . . 035906
Conjunto Arqueológico de Baelo Claudia, Tarifa . . . 035890
Conjunto Arqueológico de Carmona, Necrópolis y Anfiteatro Romano de Carmona, Carmona . . . 035055
Conjunto Arqueológico de Itálica, Santiponce . . . 035834
Conjunto Arqueológico de Madinat Al Zahra, Córdoba . . . 035111
Conjunto Cultural de Caixa, São Paulo . . . 004504
Conjunto de la Ferrería y Molinos de Agorregi, Aia . . . 034788
Conklin Reed Organ and History Museum, Hanover . . . 044425
Conkright, Charles, New York . . . 117793
Conley, Buffalo . . . 087870
Conlibro Buch und Kunst Verlagsgesellschaft, Darmstadt . . 133853
Conlon, Dublin . . . 074902
Conlon, James M., Chicago . . . 088063
Conn, Jack M., Dallas . . . 088489
Connaissance de la Suisse, Genève 054176
Connaissance de l'Art, Lausanne . . 054177
Connaisseur, Kraków . . . 079627
Connaisseur, Warszawa . . . 079741
Connaisseur, Warszawa . . . 079742
Connally, Oklahoma City . . . 091489
Connan, Reynald, Paris . . . 065746
Connaught Brown, London 085221, 113553, 130986
Connaught Galleries, London . . . 085222
Connaught Gallery, Frinton-on-Sea . 113082
Conneaut Railroad Museum, Conneaut . . . 043128
Connecticut Audubon Birdcraft Museum, Fairfield . . . 043785
Connecticut Avenue Collection, Washington . . . 093402
Connecticut Historical Society Museum, Hartford . . . 044457
Connecticut Institute of Art, Greenwich . . . 051425
Connecticut Museum Association, Roxbury . . . 054723
Connecticut Pastel Society, Newtown . . . 054724
Connecticut River Museum, Essex . 043732
Connecticut State Museum of Natural History, Storrs . . . 048382
Connecticut Trolley Museum, East Windsor . . . 043584
Connecticut Valley Historical Museum, Springfield . . . 048292
Connecticut Watercolor Society, Farmington . . . 054725
Connell, Atlanta . . . 114866
Connell, John, Wargrave . 087022, 131649
Connell, Michael, Dublin . . . 074903
Connelly, John, New York . . . 117794
Connemara History and Heritage Centre, Clifden . . . 022711
Conner, Washington . . . 120275
Conner & Daniels, Memphis . . . 132320
Conner Prairie Living History Museum, Fishers . . . 043846
Connex Caribe Mexico, Cancún . . . 128498
Connoiseur Antiques, Toronto . . . 059169
The Connoisseur, Governor's Harbour . . . 057613
Connoisseur, Toronto . . . 059170
Connoisseur, Valletta . . . 077538
Connoisseur Antiques, West Hollywood . . . 093459
Connoisseur's Antiques Fair, Show of the Art and Antique Dealers League of America, New York . . . 093982
Connoisseur's Collection, Chicago . 115392
Connoisseur's Connection, Baltimore . . . 087655
Connoisseurs Fine Antiques, Birmingham . . . 087750
Connoisseurs Gallery, Paris . . . 100165
Connoisseurs' Store, Toorak . . . 056713
Connor, Barry, Moss Vale . . . 056274
Connor, L., Blackburn, Lancashire . 130403
Connors Museum, Connors . . . 005291
Conor Fennessy, San Francisco . . . 092764
Conquaret, Evelyne, San Francisco . 092765
Conquaret, Evelyne, San Francisco . 092766
Conquest House Antiques, Canterbury . . . 083862
Conquet, Perpignan . . . 066740
Conrad, Basel . . . 111172
Conrad, Fresno . . . 116172
Conrad, Arnold, Tübingen . . . 074109
Conrad, Ch., Berlin . . . 069588
Conrad, H., Alfter . 069131, 101557, 133718
Conrad, Michel, La Colle-sur-Loup . 063341
Conrad, René, Woippy . . . 069055
Conrad, Ulrich, Göttingen . . . 125739
Conrad, Wolfgang, Lutherstadt Eisleben . . . 126249
Conrad Mansion Museum, Kalispell 044903
Conrad Weiser Homestead, Womelsdorf . . . 049278
Conrads, Düsseldorf . . . 102480
Conrads, Gerhard, Aachen . . . 069081
Conrads, Mathias, Wuppertal . . . 127049
Conrads, Walter, Düsseldorf . . . 102481, 133888
Conradt, Margrit, Grömitz . . . 071106
Conrest2, München . . . 126368
Conroy, T.W., Baldwinsville . . . 122807
Cons Art, Craiova . . . 129229
Consadori, Annamaria, Milano . . . 075673
Consart, Helsinki . . . 124043
Conseil, Philippe, Antibes-Juan-les-Pins . . . 120901
Conseil Bruxellois de Musées, Bruxelles . . . 052666
Conseil Québécois de l'Estampe, Montréal . . . 052747
Consejo de Arte, Barcelona 110134, 122007
Consejo Nacional de Conservación y Restauración de Monumentos Históricos y Artísticos, Lima . . . 053973
Consejo Provincial de las Artes Plasticas, Santiago de Cuba . . . 052828
Conservacion 3-a, Madrid . . . 129596
Conservacion y Gestion de Patrimonio, Madrid . . . 129597
Conservación y Restauración del Patrimonio Artístico, Valencia . . . 129768
Conservación y Restauración del Patrimonio Artistico, Valencia . . . 129769
Conservación y Restauración Siglo XXI, Madrid . . . 129598
Conservation Center for Art and Historic Artifacts, Philadelphia . . . 132611
Conservation Centre Presentation, Liverpool . . . 040026
Conservation Départementale Musées des Pays de l'Ain, Bourg-en-Bresse . . 010925
Conservation News, London . . . 136197
Conservation of Art, Los Angeles . . 132247
Conservation Resource Centre, Glebe . . . 001062
Conservation Studio, London . . . 130987
Conservation Studio, Thame . . . 131588
Conservation Studio for Art, Philadelphia . . . 132612

Conservatoire Air et Espace, Mérignac (Gironde) . . . 013030
Conservatoire Botanique National de Brest, Brest . . . 010981
Conservatoire de la Faune Sauvage de Sologne, Ménestreau-en-Villette . 013012
Conservatoire de l'Estuaire de la Gironde, Blaye . . . 010834
Conservatoire de l'Outil Maison de Pays des Crètes, Évigny . . . 011761
Conservatoire des Machines de Guerre Médiévales, Tiffauges . . . 014954
Conservatoire du Machinisme et de Pratiques Agricoles, Vouillé . . . 015340
Conservatoire du Patrimoine Religieux, Liessies . . . 012667
Conservatoire Maritime Basque, Ciboure . . . 011379
Conservatoire National des Arts et Métiers, Paris . . . 049971
Conservatoire Vinicole, Plassac . . . 013832
Conservatoni du Musée, Gravelines 012007
Conservatorio di Santa Chiara, San Miniato . . . 025714
Conservatory of Fine Arts, Ha Noi . . 052425
Conservazione Beni Culturali, Roma 127986
Consigli, Igino, Parma . . . 076203
Consiglieri, Sergio, Livorno . . . 075528
Consign Design, Chicago . . . 088064
Consignment 1st, Charlotte . . . 087941
Consignment Cellar, Louisville . . . 089970
Consignment Collection, Houston . . 089058
Consignment Collections, West Hollywood . . . 093460
Consignment Company, Salt Lake City . . . 092425
Consignment Connection, Richmond . . . 092070
Consignment Connection, Tulsa . . .093294, 123129
Consignment Cottage, Los Angeles 089730
Consignment Galleries, Dallas . . . 088490
Consignment Galleries, Washington 093403
Consignment Gallery, Portland . . . 091919
Consignment Interiors, Albuquerque 087387
Consignment Shop, Indianapolis . . . 089284
Consignment Store, Dallas . . . 088491
Consignment Treasures, Tulsa . . . 093295
Consignments, Memphis . . . 090064
Consignments 'n More, Houston . . . 089059
Consignpointe, Memphis . . . 090065
Consolini, Enrica, Roma . . . 076386
La Consolle, Palermo . . . 076139
Consolo, Giuseppe, Genova . . . 127445
Consorti, Augusto, Roma . . . 106510
Consortium, Chicago . . . 088065
Le Consortium, Dijon . . . 011600
Consortium for Pacific Arts and Cultures, Honolulu . . . 054726
Constable & Co, London . . . 135210
Constables Studio, Fowey . . . 113076
Constant Reader Books, Toronto . . . 137702
Constant Reader Bookshop, Milwaukee . . . 142566
Constantino Fioratti, Helen, New York . . . 090799
Constitution Chronicle, Boston . . . 136434
Constitution Convention Museum, Port Saint Joe . . . 047138
Constitution Island Association Museum, West Point . . . 049095
Constitution Museum, Tabriz . . . 022601
Constitution Square, Danville . . . 043297
Constitutional History Gallery, Bandar Seri Begawan . . . 004611
Consuelo, Modena . . . 075907
Consuelo Sierra Arranz, Madrid . . . 081281
Consulart, Milano . . . 106198
Consultant Press, Rhinebeck . . . 135482
contact:c4, Forum internationaler Kunst aus Berlin, Berlin . . . 016006
Contact Editions, Toronto . . . 137703
Contact Gallery, Warszawa . . . 109107
Contafili, Firenze . . . 127323
Container Warehouse, Honolulu . . . 088944
Containers for Collectibles, Houston 089060
Contardo, A., Bruxelles . . . 057895
Contavalli, Nino, Lima . . . 079550
Fratelli Conte, Bari . . . 075012
Conte, Las Vegas . . . 089560
Conte, Paris . . . 065747
Conte, Gérard, Paris . . . 065748
Conte, Guglielmo, Roma . . . 127987
Contempary Temporary Art Space, Cardiff . . . 112809
Contempo, Eindhoven . . . 107997
Contempo, Rotterdam . . . 108179
Contemporary, London . . . 136198
Contemporary African Art, New York 117795
Contemporary Art Australia, South Yarra . . . 095208
Contemporary Art Center of Fort Worth, Fort Worth . . . 044006
Contemporary Art Center of Virginia, Virginia Beach . . . 048795
Contemporary Art Centre, Kingston 106810
Contemporary Art Centre of South Australia, Parkside . . . 001367
Contemporary Art & Craft Artisanat, Perth . . . 114237
Contemporary Art for San Antonio Blue Star Art Space, San Antonio . . . 047791
Contemporary Art Gallery, Oklahoma City . . . 118660
Contemporary Art Gallery, Vancouver . . . 006694
Contemporary Art Gallery, Vancouver . . . 097447
Contemporary Art Gallery, Zürich . . 112057
Contemporary Art Gallery, Greenaway Gallery, South Yarra . . . 001478
Contemporary Art Holdings, Cirencester . . . 112872
Contemporary Art Institute - CAI School of Art, Sapporo . . . 050472
Contemporary Art Museum, Raleigh 047310
Contemporary Art Museum, University of South Florida, Tampa . . . 048487
Contemporary Art Museum of Saint Louis, Forum for Contemporary Art, Saint Louis . . . 047658
Contemporary Art Museum of Yerevan, Erevan . . . 000679
Contemporary Art Review, Stamford 136435
Contemporary Art Services Tasmania, Hobart . . . 094639
Contemporary Art Shares, New York 117796
Contemporary Art Society, London . 054343
The Contemporary Art Society for Wales, Cardiff . . . 054344
Contemporary Art Society of Australia, Greenaway Gallery, South Yarra . . 052464
Contemporary Art Workshop, Chicago . . . 042837
Contemporary Art Workshop, Chicago . . . 115393
Contemporary Arts and Crafts, Pune 074831
Contemporary Arts Center, Cincinnati . . . 042922
Contemporary Arts Center, New Orleans . . . 046250
Contemporary Arts Collective, Las Vegas . . . 116616
Contemporary Arts Museum, Houston . . . 044637
Contemporary Asian Art Fair, Singapore . . . 093858
Contemporary Ceramics, London . . 141775
Contemporary Christian Art Gallery, New York . . . 117797
Contemporary Crafts Association Museum, Portland . . . 047169
Contemporary Crafts Museum and Gallery, Portland . . . 047169
Contemporary Fine Art Gallery, Eton 113032
Contemporary Fine Arts Center, Ha Noi . . . 120458
Contemporary Fine Arts Galerie, Berlin . . . 101834
Contemporary Gallery, Dallas . . . 115860
Contemporary Gallery, Taipei . . . 098063
Contemporary Graphic Art Dealer's Association of Japan, Tokyo . . . 053778
Contemporary History Museum, Teheran . . . 022609
Contemporary Impressions, Peachtree City . . . 136436
Contemporary Museum, Baltimore . 041976
The Contemporary Museum, Honolulu . . . 044592
The Contemporary Museum at First Hawaiian Center, Honolulu . . . 044593
Contemporary Posters, New York . . 117798
Contemporary Print Portfolio, Shawnee Mission . . . 136437
Contemporary Studio Pottery, Chagford Newton Abbot . . . 112833
Contes d'Orient, Hong Kong . . . 059617
Contessa, Arnhem . . . 107847
Contessa, Michel, Miami . . . 090157
Contessa Art Gallery, Austin . . . 114969
Contessa Gallery, Cleveland . . . 115697
Conti, Adriana & C., Catania . . . 106020
Conti, Alessandro, Firenze . . . 127324
Conti, Andrea, Firenze . . . 140014
Conti, Giovanni, Firenze . . . 075323
Conti, Nadia, Roma . . . 127988
Conti, Pietro, Brescia . . . 127210
Continental, Praha . . . 098425
Continental Precious Metals, San Jose . . . 092921
Contini, Camillo, Parma . . . 127849
Contorno, Rio de Janeiro . . . 096600
Contour Contemporary Art, Newlyn . 114132
Contrada Scura, Trieste . . . 076889
Contrada Scura, Trieste . . . 076890
A Contrario, Paris . . . 138339
Contrast, Barcelona . . . 110135
Contrast Gallery, Bruxelles . . . 096172
Contrastarte, Lisboa . . . 109274
Contraste e Antiguidades, Belo Horizonte . . . 058424
Contraste Rustico e Antigo, Belo Horizonte . . . 058425
Contrasten, Rotterdam . . . 078709
Contrastes, Paris . . . 065749
Contreras, San Diego . . . 132849
Contreras, Tala, Mandaluyong . . . 108833
Contretype, Bruxelles . . . 096173
Contrisciani, Mara, Bari . . . 075013
Control Magazine, London . . . 136199
Controversial Bookstore, San Diego 142903
Convent dels Minims, Santa María del Cami . . . 035805
Convent Gallery, Daylesford . . . 094464
Convento de San Antonio el Real, Segovia . . . 035843
Convento de San Plácido, Madrid . . 035386
Convento de Santo Domingo el Antiguo, Toledo . . . 035916
Convento dell'ex-Convento di Sant'Onofrio detto di Fuligno, Firenze . . . 024150
Convergence, Nantes . . . 099806
Conversation Piece, Clayton South . 055693
Conway, Catherine, New York . . . 117799
Conway, Susan, Washington . . . 120276
Conway Fire Museum Aka Vintage Fire Engines, New Albany . . . 046186
Conway Scenic Railroad, North Conway . . . 046521
Conwy Valley Railway Museum, Betws-y-coed . . . 038689
Cony, Singapore . . . 080451
Conzada, Milano . . . 075674
Conzen, F. G., Frankfurt am Main . . 102756
Conzen, F.G., Düsseldorf . . . 102482
Conzen-Sammlung, Düsseldorf . . . 016825
Coo-ee Aboriginal Art, Bondi Beach 094263
Coo Lyon, Maximiliano, Santiago de Chile . . . 059518
Cooch & Son, Fred, Houston . . . 132112
Coogan, Hobart . . . 055991
Cooinda Gallery, Sawtell . . . 095186
Cook, Boston . . . 087812
Cook, New York . . . 117800
Cook, David, Denver . . . 115984
Cook, Geoff C., Gloucester . . . 113136
Cook, I.C., Exeter . . . 113037
Cook, J., San Francisco . . . 092767
Cook, L.J., Camberwell . . 055606, 123202
Cook, Martyn, Woollahra . . . 056860
Cook, Randal, Fort Worth . . . 088845
Cook, Richard, Béziers . . . 098957
Cook, R.L., Sheringham . . . 142068
Cook, Sheila, London . . . 085223
Cook, Stephen, Broadway 083756, 130464
Cook, William, London . . . 130988
Cook, William, Marlborough 085947, 131268
Cook County Historical Museum, Grand Marais . . . 044270
Cook Hope, Beate, Oslo . . . 140701
Cook Inlet Historical Society Museum, Anchorage . . . 041712
Cooke, New York . . . 132456
Cooke, Mary, London . . . 085224, 130989
Cooke, Sandy, Long Melford 085831, 131228
Cooke, Sue, Wanganui . . . 108603
Cooke's Antique, New York . . . 132457
Cookeville Art Gallery, Cookeville . . 043133
Cookeville Depot Museum, Cookeville . . . 043134
Cookham Antiques, Cookham . . . 084080
Cookhouse Gallery, Ambleside . . . 112506
Cookhouse Gallery, Keswick . . . 113317
Cook's Creek Heritage Museum, Dugald . . . 005370
Cooks Hill Galleries, Cooks Hill . . . 094425
Cookstown Antiques, Cookstown . . 084081
Cooktown School of Art Gallery, Cooktown . . . 000944
Cookworthy Museum of Rural Life in South Devon, Kingsbridge . . . 039882
Cool-Art Gallery, Coolum Beach . . . 094428
Cool Saigon Company, Ho Chi Minh City . . . 120504
Cooljunk, Waimate . . . 079299
Coolspring Power Museum, Coolspring . . . 043136
Coolstore Gallery, Mapua . . . 108496
Coolyah, Shanghai . . . 059735
Cooma Cottage, National Trust of Australia (NSW), Yass . . . 001646
Coomalie Culture Centre, Batchelor 055451
Coombe Street Gallery, Lyme Regis 114011
Coombes, J. & M., Dorking . . . 084187
Cooner, Joel, Dallas . . . 115861
Cooper, Brasted . . . 083648
Cooper, Cardiff . . . 141488
Cooper, Phoenix . . . 091731
Cooper, Brad, Tampa . . . 120037
Cooper, Ian, Looe . . . 113994
Cooper, John, Saint Helier . . . 086447
Cooper, Jonathan, London 113554, 130990
Cooper, Melanee, Chicago . . . 115394
Cooper, Paula, New York . . . 117801
Cooper, Sonia, Aberfeldy . . . 083244
Cooper, Suzanne, Kansas City . . . 089494
Cooper Gallery, Barnsley, South Yorkshire . . . 038600
The Cooper Gallery, Bideford . . . 083510
The Cooper Gallery, Bideford . . . 112636
Cooper Hay Rare Books, Glasgow . . 141622
Cooper-Hewitt National Design Museum, New York . . . 046319
Cooper Hirst, Chelmsford . . . 122455
Cooper Regional History Museum, Upland . . . 048704
Cooper & Tanner, Frome . . . 122514
The Cooper Union - School of Art, New York . . . 051814
Cooper Young Gallery, Memphis . . . 116980
Cooperation Arts and Crafts Unlimited, Wien . . . 052524
Cooperativa Archeologia, Firenze . . 127325
Cooperativa di Solidarietà Sociale Elios, Bolzano . . . 127194
Cooperativa per Il Restauro, Milano 075675, 127570
Cooperative Store Museum, Albany 000722
Coopernook Antiques, Coopernook . 055715
Coopers, Epping . . . 055802

Coopers of Ilkley, Ilkley . . 084787, 130823
Coopersmith, Ellen, Washington . . . 093404
Cooperstown Art Association, Cooperstown 054727
The Coopersville Area Historical Society Museum, Coopersville 043140
Coopmans, L., Venlo 140560
Coop'ren Duikhelm, Giethoorn 029609
Cooran Art Gallery, Cooran 094431
Coorevits, A., Gent 058177
Coos Art Museum, Coos Bay 043141
Coos Art Museum School, Coos Bay 051200
Coos County Historical Society Museum, North Bend 046514
Coosemans, P., Bruxelles 120722
Copacetic Comics, Pittsburgh 118912
Cope Livros e Revistas, Brasília . . . 137551
Copeland, Albert, Dallas 088492
Copeland Fine Art, Columbus 115770
Copeland & de Soos, Woollahra . . . 056861
Copelia Artes, São Paulo 096670
Copello, Alessandro, Milano 127571
Copello & Rizzo, Milano 121703
Copenhagen Art Gallery, København 098546
Copercini & Giuseppin, Padova 076085
Coperta, Bruxelles 057896
Copet, Christian, Bruxelles 123585
Copin, Michel, Paris 065750
Copley, Boston 115164
Copley, Keith, New York 117802
Copley Society of Boston, Boston . . 054728
Coploff, Jeffrey, New York 117803
Coplu, Nevşehir 112374
Copnal, Crewe 141545
Coppelia Antiques, Plumley 086273
Coppens, Helene, Bruxelles 096174
Coppens, Josephine, Saint Arnaud . 095168
Copper Art Gallery, Woodburn 095409
Copper Cliff Museum, Sudbury 006529
Copper Country Antique Mall, Tucson 093215
Copper Kettle Antiques, Vancouver . 059347
Copper King Mansion, Butte 042534
Copper Village Museum and Arts Center, Anaconda 041702
Copperbelt Museum, Ndola 049575
Copperfields, Hawkes Bay 079110
Coppergate Gallery, York 114751
Coppertown U.S.A., Calumet 042552
Coppin, Jean-Patrick, Sougy-sur-Loire 068271
Coppini Academy of Fine Arts, San Antonio 052104
Coppini Academy of Fine Arts Gallery and Museum, San Antonio 047792
Coppola, Alessandro, Roma 127989
Copshaholm House Museum and Historic Oliver Gardens, South Bend 048226
Coptic Museum, Cairo 009294
Copyright, Antwerpen 137395
Copyright, Paris 133558
Copyright Artbookshop, Gent 137494
Coquelet, Sophie, Bourges 061723
Coquery, Jean-Jacques, Paris 124627
Coquet, Nicole, Saint-Maurice-sur-Eygues 067666
Coquet-Pourvis, Nyons 065250
La Coquille, Haarlem 078447
Coquille River Museum, Brandon . . 042386
Coquille Valley Art Association, Coquille 054729
Cor e Forma, Rio de Janeiro 096601
Cor Fontein, Zutphen 078872
Côr On Line, Lisboa 109275
Coraddi, Greensboro 136438
Corak Rinesi, Karmen, Roma 127990
Coral Gables, Miami 090158
Coral Gables Gallery, Miami 117051
Coral Gables Merrick House, Coral Gables 043144
Coral Garden, Pittsburgh 118913
Coral Springs Museum of Art, Coral Springs 043148
Corau, Alain, Bordeaux 120940
Coray, Pieter, Montagnola 111739
Corazon, Houston 116298
Corbally Stourton, Mascot 056168
Corban Estate Arts Centre, Auckland 030433
Le Corbeau, Bern 082205
Le Corbellier, Paris 124628
Corbet, Auguste, Monthuchon 064690
Corbett, Cynthia, London 113555
Corbetta, Glória, Porto Alegre 096548
Corbin, Tampa 093120
Corbin, D.A., Poole 131385
Corbin, Marc, Miami 090159
Corbo, Montevideo 122778
Corbridge Roman Site Museum, Corbridge 039140
Corcelle, Thierry, Paris . . . 065751, 138340
Corcione, Rosaria, Napoli 106361
Corcoral, Guy, Pibrac 066822
Corcoran, Cleveland 115698
Corcoran College of Art and Design, Washington 052329
Corcoran Gallery of Art, Washington 048892
Cordé, Amsterdam 077821
Cordeiros, Porto 109368
Cordelia & Perdy's, Lichfield 084988
Cordelia Street Antique and Art Centre, Brisbane 055557
Les Cordeliers, Montpellier 064737
Les Cordeliers, Montpellier 064738
Cordero Garcia, Monica, Madrid . . . 129599
Cordes, Kiel 139320
Cordier, Heilbad Heiligenstadt 134055
Cordier, Joël, Irancy 063212
Cordier, Patrice, Pontarlier 066938
Cordier-Dornat, Maurice, Appoigny . 060937
Cordoba, Bucaramanga 098207
Cordoba, Francisco, Roma 106511
El Córdobes, Buenos Aires 055195
Cordouan, La Palmyre 099400
Cordova Historical Museum, Cordova 043151
Cordy, John, Auckland 121810
Core, Denver 043403
Core New Art Space, Denver 115985
Co.Re.Ca., Brescia 127211
Corenger, Den Haag 078182
Coresal, Madrid 129600
Corfe Castle Museum, Corfe Castle 039141
Corfield Potashnick, London 085225
Corfu Byzantine Collection, Corfu . . 021240
Corfu Museum of Shells, Kastellanoi Mesis 021314
Corge, Colette, Monflanquin 064601
The Corgi Heritage Centre, Heywood 039747
Corgialenios Historical and Cultural Museum, Argostolion 021145
Cori, Anna, Roma 127991
Corianne, Paris 100166
Corin Maman Ashdod Museum, Ashdod 022889
Corinium Galleries, Cirencester . . . 122467
Corinium Museum, Cirencester . . . 039093
Corinna, Giuseppe, Bari 127110
Corinto, Buenos Aires 055196, 123154
Corinto, Medellín 059915
Coriolan, Lyon 124349
Cork Brick Antiques, Bungay 083780
Cork Butter Museum, Cork 022718
Cork Public Museum, Cork 022719
Cork University Press, Cork 134525
Corkin, Jane, Toronto 097249
Corlett, Oliver, Los Angeles 089731
Corley, David, Dallas 088493
Corlouer, Gilbert, Paris 124629
Corman, Thomas, London 113556
Cormano, Wauwil 111986
Corn Maiden Gallery, Gordon Park . 094598
Corn Mill Antiques, Skipton 086624
Cornacchia, Madrid 129601
Cornall, Graham, Armadale, Victoria 055367
La Corne d'Abondance, Fontaine-les-Gres 062893
Corneillan, Arnaud de, Meaux 121069
Corneli, Garmisch-Partenkirchen . . 102919
Cornelis, Rotterdam 078710
Cornelissen, Wiesbaden 105250
Corneliu, Florin, Iaşi 080185
Cornelius, L.A.U., Rotterdam 078711
Cornelius, Peter, Halle, Saale 071174
Cornelius Low House/Middlesex County Museum, Piscataway 047035
Cornell, Volker, Obertshausen 104511
Cornell Museum, Delray Beach . . . 043382
Cornell University Press, Ithaca . . . 135369
Corner Antiques, Las Vegas 089561
Corner Antiques, Windsor, Ontario . 059439
Corner Antiques, Worthing 087265
Corner Collectables, Oamaru 079200
Corner Cupboard, Albuquerque 087388
Corner Cupboard Curios, Cirencester 084016
Corner Farm Antiques, Shifnal 086592
Corner of Arts, Singapore 109786
The Corner Portobello Antiques Supermarket, London . . 085226, 130991
Corner Shop, Bradford 083625
Corner Shop, Helsingborg 141115
Corner Shop, Oxford 086177
Corner Shop Antiques, Camelford . . 083853
Corner Store, Dallas 088494
Cornerhouse Publications, Manchester 135280
Corners, Charlotte 115283
Cornerstone, Portland 091920
Cornerstone Antiques, Toronto 059171
Cornerstone Gallery, Saint Ives, Cornwall 114361
Cornet à Dés, Quimper 067015
Cornette de Saint-Cyr, Pierre, Paris 121132
La Cornice, Catania 106021, 121683
La Cornice, Padova 076086
La Cornice, Padova 076087
La Cornice, Roma 076387
Cornice Museum of Ornamental Plasterwork, Peebles 040677
Cornier, Patrick, L'Isle-sur-la-Sorgue 063933
Corning Museum of Glass, Corning . 043155
Cornish Antiques, Fort Worth 088846
Cornish College of the Arts, Seattle 052165
Cornish Mines, Engines and Cornwall Industrial Discovery Centre, Pool . 040737
Cornkammer, Kuddewörde 103802
Corno, Montréal 058942
Cornstalk, Glebe 136917
Cornstalk, Newtown, New South Wales 137030
Cornu, Jean-Pierre, Balacet 061177
Cornucopia, London 085227
Cornucopia, Roma 076388
Cornucopia, Roma 076389
La Cornucopia, Torino 076803
Cornucopia Antiques, Hebden Bridge 084643
Cornucopia Magazine, İstanbul 135111, 136138
Cornucopia: Turkey for Connoisseurs, Hawick 136200
Cornwall, Heidi, Flensburg 070698
Cornwall Aero Park, Helston 039720
Cornwall Galleries, Newquay 114140
The Cornwall Gallery, Kingston 106811
Cornwall Geological Museum, Penzance 040691
Cornwall Historical Museum, Cornwall 043158
Cornwall Iron Furnace, Cornwall . . . 043159
Cornwall Regional Art Gallery, Cornwall 005296
Cornwall Traders, Auckland 078936
Cornwater Fine Art, Ravenshead . . 114297
Cornwell, Earl E., Indianapolis 122918
CO.R.O.Art, Clermont-Ferrand 124201
Coroforte, Roberto, Roma 127992
Coroller & Gilbon, Paris 124630
Coromandel, Riec-sur-Belon 067138
Coromandel School of Mines Museum, Coromandel 030473
La Corona, Ascona 082097, 129901
Corona, Spišská Nová Ves 140963
Corona Antiques, Montréal 058943
Corona Boned, Eivissa 081095
Coronach District Museum, Coronach 005299
Coronado National Memorial, Hereford 044516
Coronado-Quivira Museum, Lyons . 045535
Coronado Studio, Austin 114970
Corpel, Jean-Guy, Nice 065063
Corporate Art, Atlanta 114867
Corporate Art, London 113557
Corporate Art, New York 117804
Corporate Art, Norwood 056386
Corporate Art, West Burleigh 095389
Corporate Art Association, New York 054730
Corporate Art Services, Kansas City 116562
Corporate Art Source, Chicago 115395
Corporate Art West, Phoenix 118868
Corporate Fine Art International, London 113558
Corporate Image, Long Beach 116667
Corporate Images, Chicago 115396
Corpsmuseum van het Utrechtsch Studenten Corps, Utrecht 030227
Corpus Christi Museum of Science and History, Corpus Christi 043163
Corpus der Mittelalterlichen Glasmalerei Österreichs, Wien 135551
Corpus Vasorum Antiquorum. Italia, Roma 135892
Corpus Vitrearum, Paris 135699
Corradi, Daniele, Roma 140101
Corradi, Paola, Genova 075461
Corrado, Mario, Roma 076390
Corraini, Maurizio, Mantova 134599
Corrales Miura, Angelina, Cáceres . 081024
Corran, Carmarthen 141492
Corrarello, Rosa, Roma 127993
Corre, François, Rennes (Ille-et-Vilaine) 138580
Le Corre Guy, Mougins 099776
Correa, Ruta, Freiburg im Breisgau . 102856
Correct Dental Arts, Tampa 120038
Corredor, Luis Fernando, Bogotá . . 059830
Corredor, Luis Fernando, Bogotá . . 059831
Corredor de Arte Antiguo, Bogotá . . 059832
Corredor, Gallery of the College of Fine Arts, University of the Philippines Diliman, Quezon City 031773
Correia, Hagen, Westfalen 103043
Correia, Domingos da Silva, Porto . 129193
Correia, G., Hagen, Westfalen 103044
Correia, Maria C. Pereira, Braga . . . 079806
Correia, Renato Silva, Lisboa 079902
Corrèze, Den Haag 078183
Il Corricolo, Napoli 075957
Corridor Gallery, Glenrothes 039586
Corridors of Colour, Bangalore 105602
Corrie ten Boomhuis, Haarlem 029652
Corrigan, Paisley 086189
Corrigan, Singleton 056597
Corrigin Museum, Corrigin 000950
Corrin, John, Douglas, Isle of Man .084213, 130655
Corris Railway Museum, Machynlleth 040380
Corroyer-Signature, Lyon . 099550, 124350
Corry Area Historical Society Museum, Corry 043167
Corry's, Leicester 084947, 130880
Cors, Inga-Birgit, Bonn 125350
Corsale, Maria Pia, Napoli 127760
Corsaren Antikvariat, København . . 137892
Corsesca, Martínez 055281
Corsham Court, Corsham 039145
Corsi, Clara, Roma 076391
Corsi, Mario, Altendorf 082085
Corsi Arte Antiquaria, Milano 075676

Corsi Internazionali di Cultura Sull'Arte Ravennate e Bizantina. Atti, Ravenna 135893
Corsini, Piero, New York 117805
Corski, Bucureşti 129219
Corson, Yves, Plestin-les-Grèves . . 066851
Corssmit, Breda 128603
Cortada, Xavier, Miami 117052
Cortade, Jean Claude, Montauban . 064632
La Corte Arte Contemporanea, Firenze 106045
La Corte Restauro Mobili Incisioni, Brescia 127212
Cortemilia, Milano 127572
Cortes, Armando Maria, Lisboa . . . 079903
Cortes, Carlos, San Antonio 119405
Cortés, Filip, Český Krumlov 060003
Cortes Casaña, Francisco Javier, Castellón de la Plana 129478
Cortese, Porto Alegre 058497
Cortese, Raffaella, Milano 106199
Cortijo Bacardi, Málaga 035450
Le Cortil, Falaên 003432
Cortile Bisignano, Napoli 075958
Cortina, Roma 106512
Cortina, R., Milano 106200
Cortland County Historical Society Museum, Cortland 043172
Cortland-Leyten, Chicago 115397
Cortona, Enrico, Milano 075677
CortonAntiquaria, Cortona 093759
Corum, Angle, Montpellier 099752
Çorum Devlet Güzel Sanatlar Galerisi, Çorum 038044
Çorum Müzesi, Çorum 038045
Coruzzi, Alessandra, Milano 127573
Corvaglia, Gianluigi, Torino 128287
Corvallis Art Center, Oregon State University, Corvallis 043174
Corve Street Antiques, Ludlow 085864
Corven Art, Howey 113277
Corvi, Alessandra, Roma 076392
Corvina Books, Budapest 134500
Corvinos, Pascal, Billom 061484
Corvol, Marie-France, Paris 100167
Cory, San Antonio 092502
Corzine & Co., Nashville 090436
Cosa, London 113559
Cosac & Naify, São Paulo 133304
Cosar, Michael, Düsseldorf 102483
Cosas, Groningen 078412
Cosas de Entonces, Madrid 081282
Cosas de l'Avia, Girona 081132
Cose Antiche, Milano 135894
Le Cose del 900, Milano 075678
Le Cose del 900, Milano 075679
Cose del Passato, Firenze 075324
Cose del Passato, Firenze 075325
Cose del Passato, Lugano 082593
Cose del Passato, Torino 076804
Cose d'Epoca, Milano 075680
Cose d'Epoca, Roma 076393
Le Cose di Ieri, Perugia . . 076231, 127874
Cose di Vecchie Case, Padova 076088
Cose nel Passato, Milano 075681
Cosediunaltromondo, Milano 127574
Cosentino, Los Angeles 089732
Cosevecchie Riviera di Chiaia, Napoli 075959
Cosgrove, Omaha 123033
Cosgrove, Leila M ., Omaha 091559, 123034
COSI Columbus, Columbus 043107
Cosi Toledo, Toledo 048567
Coskun, London 113560
Cosma Elite, Médis 064458
Cosmic Art, Fukuoka 106842
Cosmic Galerie, Paris 100168
Cosmo, Tokyo 077240
Cosmocaixa, Alcobendas 034807
Cosmodôme, Laval 005753
Cosmopolis, Vancouver 097448
Cosmopolitan Book Shop, Los Angeles 142500
Cosmopolitan Gallery, New York . . . 117806
Cosmos Gallery, Incheon 107199
Cossa, Gabor, Cambridge 083844
Cossit House Museum, Cape Breton Centre for Heritage and Science, Sydney 006546
Cosson, Robert, Luxeuil-les-Bains . 064039
Costa, Nice 065064
Moreira da Costa, Porto 140864
Costa, Alberto, Buenos Aires 136710
Costa, Alexander, Furth im Wald . . . 102912
Costa, Andrea, Padova 127801
Costa, António, Lisboa 079904
Costa, Benito, Roma 076394
Costa & Cia, C.A., Brasília 058461
Costa, Elisabeth, Pontresina 111811
Costa, Eugenio, Genova 106089
Costa, Giancarlo, Milano 127575
Costa, Maria Pereira, Lisboa 079905
Costa, Pedro Felner, Lisboa 079906
Costa, Rodrigo Vieira, Porto 109369
Da Costa, Rosane Aguiar Fernandes, Porto Alegre 096549
Costa Azul, Don Torcuato 055262
Costa Brocante, Riscle 067155
Costa de Diego, Oviedo 110660
Costa-Dupuy, Marie-Louise, Toulouse 068497
Costa Guido, Torino 106671
Costa Martinez, Jorge, Barcelona . . 110136
Costa & Rodrigues, Sesimbra 080122
Costalunga Antique Restorations, Malvern East 123256
Costantini, Paolo, Venezia 076928, 106737, 128384
Costanzo, Alfio, Catania . . 075244, 127263
Costas, Milano 106201
Costela, Bucureşti 109424
Costella, Cincinnati 131932
Costentin, Michel, Brionne 061803
Coster, Laurens Jansz, Haarlem . . . 140441
Costermans, Bruxelles 057897
Costes, Pierre & Sylvie, Plouha 066874
Costey, Jean-Paul, Paris 065752
Costil, Jean-Jacques, Rouen 067262
Costin, Iuliu-Ventin, Gernsbach . . . 125726
Costta, Juçara, Belo Horizonte 096459
Costume Museum of Canada, Dugald 005371
Cosy Corner, Antwerpen 137396
Cosy Corner, Toulouse 068498
Cosy Home, Eguilles 062767
Cota, West Hollywood 093461
Cotabato National Museum, Cotabato 031665
Cotanda Anticuario, Madrid 081283
Côté, Paris 065753
Cote, Villeurbanne 068954
Coté, François, Montréal 137651
Côte Basque, Bayonne 061230
Côté Cave, Rueil-Malmaison 067319
Coté Cour, Chauny 062256
Côte d'Azur Antiques, Los Angeles . 089733
La Côte des Arts, Marseille 135700
Côte Jardin Antiques, Washington . 093405
Côté Nord Antiek, Eindhoven 078332
Côte Ouest, Arcachon 060951
Côté Provence, Ascot Vale 055407
Côte Sud, Bruxelles 057898
Côté Versailles, Saint-Denis (Seine-Saint-Denis) 067423
Cotehele House, Saint Dominick, Cornwall 040904
Cotham Antiques, Bristol 083735
Cotham Galleries, Bristol 083736
Cotham Gallery 101, Kew 094694
Cothey Bottom Heritage Centre, Newport, Isle of Wight 040566
Cotinaud, Marie-Claire, Paris 065754
Cotiso, Bucureşti 080151
Coto, Rosy, Riom 067148
Cotswold, Cirencester 112873
Cotswold, New York 090800
Cotswold Antique Dealers Association, Stow-on-the-Wold 054345
Cotswold Antiques, Winchcombe . . 087167
The Cotswold Auction Company, Cheltenham 122458
The Cotswold Auction Company, Gloucester 122521
Cotswold Galleries, Stow-on-the-Wold 086745, 131548
Cotswold Heritage Centre, Northleach 040597
Cotswold Motoring Museum and Toy Collection, Bourton-on-the-Water 038796
Cotswold Pine and Associates, Middle Aston 085982, 131276
The Cottage, Johannesburg 080704
The Cottage, Kanturk 074979
Cottage, San Antonio 092503
Cottage, Tulsa 093296
Cottage and Garden Antiques, Portland 091921
Cottage Antiques, Houston 089061
Cottage Antiques, Los Angeles 089734
Cottage Antiques, Margate 085927, 131261
Cottage Antiques, Nashville 090437
Cottage Antiques, Oklahoma City . . 091490
Cottage Antiques, Pontefract 086285, 131382
Cottage Antiques, Ringway 086365
Cottage Antiques, Sanson 079235
Cottage Antiques, Stepney 056632
The Cottage Antiques, Tucson 093216
Cottage Antiques, Walsden 087012
Cottage Antiques, Zürich 082956
Cottage Blundell's, Canberra 000887
Cottage Bookshop, Queenstown 137066
Cottage-Buchhandlung, Wien 137300
Cottage Collectables, Holt, Norfolk . 084702
Cottage Craft Gifts & Fine Arts, Calgary 096800
Cottage Curios, Allonby 083270
Cottage Door, Omaha 091560
Cottage Farm Antiques, Chipping Campden 083983
Cottage Gallery, Huntingdon 113282
Cottage Gallery, San Diego 119496
The Cottage Gallery, Skipton 114438
Cottage Grove Museum, Cottage Grove 043182
Cottage Holdings, North Fremantle . 056360
Cottage House Mall, Memphis 090066
Cottage Lawn, Oneida 046687
Cottage Museum, Lancaster 039919
Cottage Rose, South Auckland 079238, 128955
Cottage Style Antiques, Rochester . 086386
Cotte, Sabine, Paris 124631
Cotte de Mailles, Avallon 061117
Cottees, Wareham 122736
Cotten, Martine, Pont-Aven 101022
Cottet, Jean-Claude, Lausanne . . .082540, 130066
Cotthem, Bruxelles 096175
Cotthem Gallery, Barcelona 110137
Cottier, Sarah, Redfern 095126
Cottin, Frechen 070808, 121411
Cottin, Irene, Köln 071921, 121469
Cotting-Smith-Assembly-House, Peabody Essex Museum, Salem 047734
Cottingley Antiques, Bradford 083626, 130425
Cotton, Joan, West Bridgford 087080
Cotton, Lynda, Watchet 114651
Cotton, Mary, Houston 116299
Cotton, Nick, Watchet . . . 087053, 131654
Cotton, Yvonne, Vandoeuvres 130202
Cotton Country Antiques, Phoenix . . 091732
Cotton Museum, Cairo 009295
Cottone, Alessandra, Verona 128423
Cottonlandia Museum, Greenwood . 044354
Cotton's Attic, Los Angeles 089735
Cottonwood County Historical Society Museum, Windom 049234
Cottreau, Thierry, Saint-Ouen 067754
Cottrell, Catherine, New Orleans . . 090540
Coudert, Michel, Meyrals 064549
Coué, Nantes 064918
Coué, Jean-Yves, Nantes 064919
Coué, Philippe, Véretz 068772
Coueffé, Dominique, Lyon 138143
Couet, Martin de, Aachen 069082
Couffon de Trévros, Charles, Rennes (Ille-et-Vilaine) 067109
Cougart, Paris 100169
Cougart Gallery, Paris 065755
Coughton Court, Alcester 038469
Coughton Galleries, Arthingworth . . 112520
Cougoule-Devergne, Sophie, Saint-Ouen 067755
Coulborn & Sons, Thomas, Sutton Coldfield 086800, 131563
Coulet, Jean-François, Valence (Drôme) 068685, 101409
Coulet, Laurent, Paris 138341
Coulet & Faure, Paris 138342
Couleur du Sud, Paris 065756
Couleur du Temps, Saint-Ouen 067756
Couleur-en-Musique, Cherrueix . . . 099132
Couleur Konsthandel, Stockholm . . 111015
Couleur Sud, Le Thor 063712
Couleur Syracuse, Paris 065757
Les Couleurs, Bornheim, Pfalz 102205
Couleurs d'Asie, Auray 061068
Couleurs du Siam, Marans 064253
Couleurs du Sud, Nîmes 099864
Couleurs du Temps, Genève 111439
Couleurs et Bois, Saint-Denis 080126
Couleurs Primaires, Lyon 099551
Coulibaly, Yousfouph, Montréal 058944
Les Couloirs du Temps, Champigny-la-Futelaye 062123
Les Couloirs du Temps, Pacy-sur-Eure 065321
Coulon, Le Havre 063631
Coulon, Dominique, Paris 100170
Coulon, Jean, Paris 100171
Coulter, Robert, York 087288
Coulter Robert, York 114752
Coultershaw Beam Pump, Petworth 040708
Coumantaros Art Gallery of Sparta, National Gallery, Spárti 021476
Council, Michael, Columbus 088400
Council for Museum Anthropology, Tucson 054731
Council for Museums, Archives and Libraries, London 054346
Council for the Prevention of Art Theft, Warminster 054347
Council of American Jewish Museums, New York 054732
Council of American Maritime Museums, Bath 054733
Council of Australian Art Museum Directors, Canberra 052465
Council of Australian Museum Directors, Canberra 052466
Council of Museums in Wales, Cardiff 054348
Counter Culture, London 136201
Countermedia, Portland 142796
Counterpoint, El Paso 116104
Counterpoint Records and Books, Los Angeles 142501
Country and Eastern, Norwich 086113
Country and Garden, Esslingen 070658
Country Antique Showroom, San Francisco 092768
The Country Antiques, Antrim 083306, 130303
Country Antiques, Auckland 078937
Country Antiques, Bagshot 083360
Country Antiques, Kidwelly 084838
Country Antiques, Killearn 084842
Country Antiques, Long Melford . . . 085832
Country Bear, Sacramento 092151
The Country Bedroom, Keswick . . . 084832
Country Chaircraft, Halesowen 130755
Country Charm, Masterton 079146
Country Charm Antiques, Tulsa 093297
Country Chattels, North Tamborine . 056376
Country City, New York 090801
Country Clocks, Tring 086919, 131608

Country Club Antiques, Denver 088672
Country Clutter, Fresno 088902
Country Clutter, Phoenix 091733
Country Collector, Pickering 086268
Country Cottage, Dallas 088495
Country Cottage Antiques, Deniliquin 055748
Country Cottage Interiors, Kingsley . 084854
Country Cousins, San Diego 092626
Country Cupboard Antiques, Tanunda 056695
Country Depot, Fresno 088903
The Country Doctor Museum, Bailey 041947
Country Eclectic Antiques, Willoughby 056823
Country Emporium Antiques, Tucson 093217
Country Fine Arts, Llanddeusant . . . 113414
Country Friends, Indianapolis 089285
The Country Gallery, Ballyclare 112543
Country Gallery, Dereham 112945
Country Garden Antiques, Dallas . . 088496
Country Gentleman, Houston 089062
Country Home, Salt Lake City 092426
Country Home, Tucson 093218
Country Home, Tucson 093219
Country House, Saint Mary 086468
Country House, Wien 057395
Country House and Antiques, São Paulo 058703
Country House Antiques, Manuka . . 056156
Country House Antiques, Seething . 086534
Country in Time, San Antonio 092504
Country Life Antiques, Bushey 083826
Country Life Antiques, Glen Iris . . .055885, 123229
Country Life Antiques, Meadows . . 056178
Country Life Museum, Yeovil 041469
Country Line Antiques, Denver 088673
Country Living Antiques, Callington 083837
Country Looks, Healesville 094627
Country Manor, Cincinnati 088225
Country Markets Antiques, Chilton .083980, 130567, 141520
Country Music Hall of Fame and Museum, Nashville 046142
Country Oak Antiques, Harrogate . . 084571
Country Peddlers, Miami 090160
Country Peddlers of America, Jacksonville 089401
Country Pine, Newport, Gwent 131311
Country Pine Antiques, Market Bosworth 085930
Country Pine Shop, West Haddon . . 087086
Country Roads, Ottawa 059036
Country Sailor, Torino 076805
Country Scene Art Gallery, Molong . 094868
The Country Seat, Huntercombe . . . 084770
The Country Seat, Llandudno 085034, 130909
Country Seat Antiques, Newby East 086061
Country Shoppe, Pittsburgh 091804
Country Shops Antiques, Omaha . .091561, 132587
Country Times, Rockhampton 056544
The Country Trader, Waterloo 056806
Country Treasures, Galston 055858
Country Treasures, Kerikeri 079135
Country Village, Palmerston North .079213, 128951
The Countrymans Gallery, Leicester 113371
Countryside Museum, East Budleigh 039345
Countrystyle, London 130992
County Antiques, Ashford 083341
County Antiques, Ilminster 084790
County Antiques, Linlithgow 085006
County Donegal Railway Heritage Centre, Donegal 022728
County Hall Gallery, London 113561
County Museum, Fufeng 007072
County Museum, Sligo 022858
County Museum Dundalk, Dundalk . 022780
County Museum Technical Centre, Halton 039668
County of Grey-Owen Sound Museum, Owen Sound 006108
County of Los Angeles Fire Museum, Los Angeles 045417
Coup de Cour de Vesna, Sucy-en-Brie 068337
Coup de Foudre, Vence 068751
Coup de Gras, Chicago 115398
Coupé, Michel, Cuvilly 062587
Coupes Languedoc Provençe, Avignon 061130
Coupure Galerie, Gent 096287
Couque, Janine, Saint-Ouen 067757
Couque, Philippe, Paris 065758
Cour Beaudeval, Faverolles (Eure-et-Loir) 062845
Cour Carrée, Paris 065759
Cour d'Albane, Rouen 101113
La Cour d'Antan, Acquigny 060658, 124057
Cour de Rouen, Rouen 067263
A la Cour des Adieux, Fontainebleau 062896
La Cour des Arts, Arles 098859
Cour des Miracles, Figeac 062861, 138087
La Cour des Miracles, Reignier 067050
Cour des Miracles, Vannes (Morbihan) 068716
Cour des Mirascles en Bourgogne, Marcigny 064262
La Cour Freville, Anduze 098828
Cour Renaissance, Strasbourg 068312
Courage Shire Horse Centre, Maidenhead 040385
Courant d'Art, Clermont-Ferrand . . 062336
Courant d'Art, Mulhouse 099786
Courant d'Art, Paris 100172
Courant d'Art, Paris 138343
Courants d'Ere, Paris 065760
Courault, Noël, Gueugnon 063103
Courbet, Francis, Carpentras 061998
Courbis, Michel, Nice 065065
Courbois, Emile, Abbeville 060651
Courbois, R.M., Haarlem 078448
Courbois, R.M., Haarlem 078449
Courbon, Saint-Étienne 067449
Courbon, Armand, Saint-Étienne . . 067450
Courchet, Thierry, Cagnes-sur-Mer . 120957
Courchet, Palloc & Fede, Nice 121093
Courchinoux, Marie-Rose, Paris . . . 100173
Courcoux & Courcoux, Stockbridge 114486
Court Gallery, Calne 112781
Court Gallery, Nether Stowey 086046, 131297
Court Hall Museum, Sittingbourne . 041032
Court House and Museum, Pevensey 040711
Court House Antique Centre, Sheffield 086554, 142059
Court House Arts Centre, Busselton 094332
Court House Museum, Stroud 001496
Court'Art, Paris 065761
Courtauld Institute Gallery, London . 040126
Courtauld Institute of Art, University of London, London 050833
Courteaux-Enault, Paris 065762
Courtenay and District Museum and Paleontology Centre, Courtenay . . 005301
Courtenay's, Bournemouth 112680
Courthouse Gallery, Portsmouth Museums, Portsmouth 047197
Courthouse Museum, Berrien Springs 042171
Courthouse Museum, Exira 043776
Courthouse Museum, Newport 046453
Courthouse Square Museum, Charlotte 042752
Courtiade, Bernard, Toulouse 124978
Courtial, Maria & Jörg, Darmstadt . 102338
Courtier, Laurent, Pacy-sur-Eure . . 065322
Courtieux, Suresnes 101305
Courtin, Grégoire, Baugé 061225
Courtney, Richard, London 085228
Courtney and Lemmerman Galleries, New Jersey City University, Jersey City 044859
Courtois, Georges, Massangis 064420
Courtois & Chauviré, Angers 120896
Courtois de Viçose, Germaine, Toulouse 068499
Courtoy, R., Bruxelles 057899
The Courtroom Gallery, Lampeter . . 113345
Courts Miscellany, Leominster 084971
Courtville Antiques, Dublin 074904
Courtyard, Brackley 083622, 130423
Courtyard Antiques, Brasted 083649, 130431
Courtyard Antiques, Coxley 084098
Courtyard Antiques, Williton 087152
Courtyard Antiques Market, Seaford 086527
Courtyard Art Gallery, Austin 114971
Courtyard Collectables, Saint Ives, Cornwall 086457
Courtyard Gallery, Appleby-In-Westmorland 112511
The Courtyard Gallery, South Crail . 114451
The Courtyard Gallery, Wokingham . 114719
Courtyard Gallery, Washington Studio School, Washington 048972
Courtyard Living Gallery, Portland . . 118989
Cousas de Antanho, Lisboa 079907
Cousens, Peter, Newtown, New South Wales 123279
Cousin, Jacqueline, Les Andelys . . 121034
Cousins & Son, E.W., Ixworth 084809, 130834
Cousland Smiddy, Cousland 039149
Coustal, Catherine, Villeseque-des-Corbieres 101480
Coutant, Claude, Paris 065763
Coutard, Eve, Paris 100174
Coutau-Bégarie, Olivier, Paris 121133
Coutinho, Bussum 134803
Coutinho, Francisco Pereira, Lisboa 109276
Coutinho, Salvador Ferreira, Porto . 080076
Coutinho, Sebastião L., Rio de Janeiro 058575
Couton, Bertrand, Nantes 121086
Coutoula, Martine, Beynac et Cazenac 061424
Coutoula, Martine, Sarlat-la-Canéda 068125
Coutts, London 130993
Coutts Memorial Museum of Art, El Dorado 043629
Couturier, Los Angeles 116746
Couturier, Eric, Paris 121134
Couturier-Nicolay, Paris 121135
Couven Museum, Aachen 015418
Couvent des Cordeliers, Forcalquier 011865
Couvent des Cordeliers, Fribourg . . 130017
Couvent des Ursulines, Liège 058292, 123648
Couvrat Desvergnes, Paris 065764
Gebr. Couvreur, Breda 078086
Couvreur, Breda 078087
Couvreur, Breda 140365
Couvreur, R., Oosterhout 128799
La Cova, Barcelona 080837
Cova, Cartagena 081031
Covatti, Assunta, Roma 076395
Cove Curios, Cove 084088
Cove Landing, New York 090802
Covent Garden Flea Market, London 085229
Coventry Toy Museum, Coventry . . 039150
Coventry Watch Museum, Coventry 039151
Cover to Cover Bookshop, Winnipeg 137740
Covered Bridge Antique Mall, Cincinnati 088226
Coves Quay Gallery, Salcombe 114384
Covet Design Store & Gallery, Kerikeri 108485
Covington, Tucson 120116
Covington Antique Market, Oklahoma City 091491
Cow Hollow Woodworks, San Francisco 132875
Cowall, Bernd, Den Haag . 107910, 128626
Cowan Vertebrate Museum, Vancouver 006695
Cowboy Artists of America Museum, Kerrville 044977
Cowboy Museum, Sunset 048434
Cowboy-Museum Fatsy, Linz 002244
Cowboys and Indian Antiques, Albuquerque 087389
Cowbridge and District Museum, Cowbridge 039157
Cowbridge Antique Centre, Cowbridge 084091, 130611
Cowderoy, John, Eastbourne 084258, 130667
Cowdery, Richard, New York 117807
Cowdy Gallery, Newent 114129
Cowes Maritime Museum, Cowes . 039158
Cowichan Bay Maritime Centre, Cowichan Bay 005304
Cowichan Valley Museum, Duncan . 005373
Cowleigh Gallery, Malvern 114035
Cowles, Minnetonka 135399
Cowles, Charles, New York 117808
The Cowley County Historical Museum, Winfield 049242
Cowlitz County Historical Museum, Kelso 044950
Coworth Gallery, Sunningdale 086790
Cowpens National Battlefield, Chesnee 042799
Cowper and Newton Museum, Olney 040642
Cowra Museums, Cowra 000953
Cowri, Seattle 092980
Cowtown Antique Mall, Fort Worth . 088847
Cowwarr Art Space, Cowwarr 094436
Cox, Bruxelles 137431
Cox & Co., London 113562
Cox, Claude, Ipswich 130827, 141690
Cox, Edd, Seattle 119901
Cox, Jon, Louisville 132292
Cox, Robert, London 130994
Cox, Udo, Gerolzhofen 125727
Cox's Architectural Reclamation Yard, Moreton-in-Marsh 086014
Coyaba Gardens and Awarak Museum, Ocho Rios 026395
Coyote Gallery, Oroville 046728
Coyote Point Museum for Environmental Education, San Mateo 047915
Cozze, Houston 089063
Cozzetto, Maxine, Portland 091922
Cozzolino, Floriana, Livorno 075529
C.P. Art Centre, Chennai 105624
C+P Galerie, Groß-Gerau 103015
C.P. Nel Museum, Oudtshoorn 034692
CPH Restoration, Salt Lake City . . . 132785
C.P.R. Antiques and Services, Barrhead 083403
Crabbe, Peter Ian, Cambridge 083845
Crabble Corn Mill, Dover 039272
Crabnet, New Orleans 117419
Crabtree, Evelyn, New York 117809
C.R.A.C, Paris 100175
Cracker Country Museum, Tampa . . 048488
Cracker Factory Antique Center, San Diego 092627
Cracker Trail Museum, Zolfo Springs 049380
Crackerbox Palace, Cairns 094343
Crackerjack, Seattle 119902
Crackers, Portland 091923
Craddock, Kay, Melbourne 136997
Cradle of the Sun, San Francisco . . 119645
Cradlewell Antiques, Jesmond 084813
Crafoord, Eslöv 141093
Crafoord, Göteborg 122143
Crafoord, Lund 122201
Crafoord, Stockholm 122252
Crafoord-Nellemann & Thomsen, København 120868
Craft Alliance Gallery, Saint Louis . . 047659
Craft Art, Hong Kong 097775
The Craft Factor, Saskatoon 135631
Craft in the Bay, Cardiff 112810
Craft Museum, Kuala Lumpur 027969
Craft Potters Association, London . . 054349
Craftart & Gallery, Cape Town 110022
Crafted Toys International, Salt Lake City 092427

Crafthouse, Vancouver 097449
Craftiques, San Antonio 092505
Craftivist, New Orleans 117420
Crafts Council, London 136202
Crafts Council Collection, London .. 040127
Crafts Council of the Northern Territory, Darwin 052467, 094458
Crafts Council Shop, London 113563
Crafts Museum, Delhi 022081
Crafts Museum, Mequon 045781
Crafts Nouveau, London .. 085230, 130995
Craftselijke Zadelmakerij Museum, Bellingwolde 029302
Craftsman Antiques, Cleveland 131954
Craftsman Antiques, Oakland 091413
Craftsman Farms Foundation, Parsippany 046829
Craftsman Furniture Service, Sacramento 132732
Craftsman Gallery, Swansea 114533
The Craftsman Magazine, Driffield . 136203
Craftsmens Gallery, Woodstock ... 114730
Craftspace Gallery, Winnipeg 097579
Crafty Olde Things, Rangiora 079228
Craggsdan, Altona 094151
Cragside House, Rothbury 040855
Craig, Tucson 120117
Craig, York 131725
Craig, Edmund, Fort Worth 116138
Craig Heritage Park Museum, Parksville 006114
Craigavon Museum, Craigavon 039164
Craigdarroch Castle Historical Museum, Victoria 006738
Craighead-Green, Dallas 115862
Craiglea, Edinburgh 084282, 130676
Craig's, Buffalo 087871
Craik, Brian & Caroline, Bath 083423
Crail Museum, Crail 039165
Crailo State Historic Site, Rensselaer 047378
Crake, Johannesburg 110050
Crakehall Water Mill, Crakehall ... 039166
Crals, Liège 096376
Cralyn, Manawatu 079141
Cramalot Inn Antiques, Stroud 056640
Cramer, Den Haag 078184, 107911
Cramer, Barbara, Bonn 102177
Cramer, Hans, Zuoz 083046
Cramer, Patrick, Genève .. 111440, 135015, 141246
Crameri, Arnold, Chur 111355
Crames, W., Bergheim, Erft 069535
Crampton Tower Museum, Broadstairs 038874
Cranage Lane, Phoenix 091734
Cranbrook Academy of Art, Bloomfield Hills 050994
Cranbrook Antique Centre, Cranbrook 084101
Cranbrook Art Museum, Bloomfield Hills 042255
Cranbrook Gallery, Cranbrook 112914, 141544
Cranbrook House and Gardens Auxiliary, Bloomfield Hills 042256
Cranbrook Institute of Science, Bloomfield Hills 042257
Cranbrook Museum, Cranbrook ... 039167
Cranbury Historical and Preservation Society Museum, Cranbury 043206
Crane & Assoc., Stefan, Dallas 115863
Crane Bag, Dublin 135853
Crane Collection Gallery, Wellesley . 049045
Crane Gallery, Seattle ... 092981, 119903
Crane Hill Publishers, Birmingham . 135330
Crane Museum, Dalton 043286
Crane Point Hammock Museum, Marathon 045654
Cranford, Knutsford 084889
Cranglegate Antiques, Swaffham .. 086806
Crankos, Invercargill 079126
Cranston, Toller, Toronto 097250
Crantock Forge Gallery, Crantock .. 112915
Crantock Gallery, Crantock 112916
Crapie, Péronnas 066727
Crapper & Co., Thomas, Stratford-upon-Avon 086774
Craque Allure, Haarlem 108055
Crary Art Gallery, Warren 048861
Crater of Diamonds State Park Museum, Murfreesboro 046092
Craters of the Moon, Arco 041764
Crathes Castle, Banchory 038587
Craven, Freiburg im Breisgau 070830
Craven Gallery, London 085231
Craven Museum, Skipton 041039
Cravens House, Lookout Mountain . 045401
Cravinho, Vitorino P. Silva, Lisboa .. 079908
Craviolatti, Pier Carlo, Torino 128288
Crawford, Memphis 132321
Crawford, J., Sacramento 142845
Crawford, Matthew, London 130996
Crawford, R.E., Richmond 092071
Crawford Arts Centre, Saint Andrews 040894
Crawford Auto-Aviation Museum, Cleveland 042989
Crawford County Historical Museum, Pittsburg 047037
Crawford Doyle, New York 142645
Crawford Municipal Art Gallery, Cork 022720
Crawford, Owen & Zachery, Louisville 116935
Crawford W. Long Museum, Jefferson 044841
Crawfordjohn Heritage Venture, Biggar 038704
Crawley, Marie Louise, London 130997
Crawley & Asquith, London 085232, 141776
Crawley Museum Centre, Crawley . 039168
Le Crayon Gris, Sisteron 101277
Les Crayons Bleus, Marseille 099647
Crazy Collecting, Miami 090161
Crazy Mountain Museum, Big Timber 042202
Crazymport, Milano 075682
Cre-Art-Ive Flair, Nelson 108511
Creaciones M.S., Bogotá 098116
Créahm, Region Wallonne, Liège .. 052667
Creamery Museum, Eriksdale 005431
Creange, Colette, Avignon 061131
Créartdis, Saint-Martin-Boulogne .. 067625
Crearte, Bogotá 098117
Creatabilitoys! - Museum of Advertising Icons, Coral Gables 043145
Creation, Christchurch 108391
Création d'Ambiance, Gstaad 082488
Creationists Konsortium, Denver .. 115986
Créations, Mouans-Sartoux 135701
Creations by Elaine, Indianapolis .. 116450
Créations RB, Marseille .. 064344, 099648
Créations Tesoro, Paris 065765
Creatistic Fine Art, Calgary 096801
Creativ Art, Lüneburg 072355
Creative Art, London 096947
Creative Art, New York 117810
Creative Art, Philadelphia 118744
Creative Art Centre, Dubai 083190
Creative Art Concepts, Cincinnati .. 115622
Creative Art Conservation, Burwood 123200
Creative Art Galleries International, Miami 117053
Creative Art Gallery, Dallas 115864
Creative Art Gallery, Saint Louis ... 119197
Creative Arts, Cairo 098624
Creative Arts, Stuttgart 073967
Creative Arts, Vancouver 097450
Creative Arts Center, Kansas City .. 044917
Creative Arts Center, Pontiac 047120
Creative Arts Department, West Virginia Institute of Technology, Montgomery 051747
Creative Arts Division, Bradford College, Bradford 051023
Creative Arts Division, DeAnza College, Cupertino 051215
Creative Arts Division, Western Oregon University, Monmouth 051736
Creative Arts Guild, Dalton 043284
Creative Arts Guild, Dalton 054734
Creative Arts Maker, Los Angeles .. 132248
Creative Arts Program, Charles River School, Dover 051267
Creative Arts Unlimited, Durbanville 121983
Creative Burnings, Saint Louis 092215
Creative Camera, London 136204
Creative Closets, Columbus 131980
Creative Connections, Albuquerque 114777
Creative Discovery Museum, Chattanooga 042777
Creative Eye, Denver 115987
Creative Finishing Specialists, Vancouver 123846
Creative Furniture, Los Angeles ... 089736
Creative Galleries, Los Angeles ... 116747
Creative Galleries, Nashville 117345
Creative Growth Art Center, Oakland 046593
Creative Imagery, Columbus 115771
Creative Impressions Gallery, Sacramento 119142
Creative Insprations Gallery, Belmont 094237
Creative Memories, Chicago 088066
Creative Napier, Hawkes Bay 108464
Creative Native, Fremantle 055843
Creative Native, Perth 056455
Creative Nature, San Diego 119497
Creative New Zealand, Toi Aotearoa Arts Council, Auckland 053916
Creative New Zealand, Toi Aotearoa Arts Council, Christchurch 053915
Creative New Zealand, Toi Aotearoa Arts Council, Wellington 053917
Creative Palette, Columbus 115772
Creative Solutions, Villa Park 052311
Creative Spirit Art Centre, Toronto . 006595
Creative Spirit Gallery, Tucson 120118
Creativiteitscentrum Gouden Handen, 's-Heerenberg 029689
Creativity Centre, Coorparoo 094432
Creativity Explored, San Francisco . 119646
Creativity Explored II, San Francisco 119647
Creazioni Fuoco, Roma 076396
Crédence, Issigeac 063220
La Crédence, Paris 065766
Credi Arte, Bucaramanga 098208
Crediorvi, Cartagena 098245
Crédit de l'Or, Lille 063841
Crédit de l'Or, Paris 065767
Crédit du Palet Médailles, Angoulême 060876
Creek, Cherry, Oxted 114207
Creek Antiques, London .. 085233, 130998
Creek Council House Museum, Okmulgee 046656
Creekhouse Gallery, Vancouver ... 097451
Creekside Gallery, Hamilton 096912
Creetown Exhibition Centre, Creetown 039170
Creetown Gem Rock Museum, Creetown 039171
Cregneash Folk Village, Cregneash . 039172
Cregneash Village Folk Museum, Manx National Heritage, Port Saint Mary 040745
Creiche, Jean-Luc, Bazas 061243
Creighton-Davis, Washington 093406, 120277, 123137
Crema, Paola, Firenze 106046
Creman, Jurjen, Amsterdam 128531
Cremona Mdina Arts, Rabat 107449
Cremyll Antiques, Cremyll 084108, 130615
Crescent Arts, Scarborough 040966
Crescent Bend/Armstrong-Lockett House and William P. Toms Memorial Gardens, Knoxville 045035
Crescent City Architecturals, New Orleans 090541
Crescent City Books, New Orleans . 142609
Crescent Collection, Charlotte 087942
Crescent Galleries, Bridgwater 112706
Crescent Galleries, Taunton 114554
Crescent Gallery, New Orleans 117421
Crescent Moon, Saint Paul 092355
Crescent Scents, Seattle 119904
Crescentia-Gedenkstätte, Kaufbeuren 018207
Crescentini, Remo, Roma 127994
Crescenzi, Antonio, Torino 128289
Creski Muzej, Cres 007710
Crespo, J., Madrid 141033
Cress Gallery of Art, Chattanooga .. 042778
Cressever, Ariane, Tarbes 068362
Cressida, Paris 065768
Cresswell, J D M, Turramurra 056745
Cressy, Koroit 136967
Crest Collectables, Eastbourne 084259
Crest Plating, Saint Louis 132745
Crestar Bank Art Collection, Richmond 047413
Crested China Company, Driffield .. 084219
Crested Circle, Dagenham 136205
Crestet-Centre d'Art, Le Crestet ... 012487
Crestline Shunk Museum, Crestline 043215
Creston and District Museum, Creston 005309
Crestwood Antiques, Birmingham .. 087751
Crestwood Coins, Saint Louis 092216
Creswell Crags Museum and Education Centre, Welbeck 041321
Creswick Antiques, Malvern, Victoria 056145
Creswick Historical Museum, Creswick 000957
Creswick Station, Creswick 055724
Crété, Eric, Saint-Hélen 067513
Crété, Guy, Paris 100176
Crétier, François, Vichy 068855
Le Creuset, Charleroi 058142
Creusy, Joël, Lyon 064114
Creusy, J.P., Lyon 064115
Creusy, Rémy, Saint-Étienne 067451
Le Creux de l'Enfer, Centre d'Art Contemporain, Thiers 014929
Creuzberg, Harald, Dernau 125453
Creuze, Raymond, Paris 100177
Creuzevault, Colette, Paris 100178, 138344
Crevoisier, San Antonio 092506
Crewe, Bob, Los Angeles 116748
Crewkerne and District Museum, Crewkerne 039176
Crewkerne Antique Centre, Crewkerne 084111, 130616
CRG Gallery, New York 117811
Cribier, Saint-Paul-de-Vence 101200
Criccieth Castle, Criccieth 039177
Criccieth Gallery, Criccieth 084114, 130617
Crichton Museum, Dumfries 039294
Crick, M.E., London 085234
Cricket Book Collector, Blacktown . 136806
Cricket Gallery, Atlanta 114868
Cricket Hill Gallery, New York 117812
Cricklade Museum, Cricklade 039178
La Criée - Centre d'Art Contemporain, Rennes (Ille-et-Vilaine) 101074
Crimea, Madrid 081284
Criminology Museum, Abbasiya ... 009268
Crimisos, Palermo 127826
Crimson, Bangalore 105603
Crinel, Yves, Paris 124632
Cringle, M. & A., Burnham Market . 083803
Crinoline, Lyon 064116
Cripple Creek District Museum, Cripple Creek 043220
Cripta e Museo di Sant'Anastasio, Asti 023287
Criptonit, Milano 075683
Crisce, Barcelona 080838
Crisostomi, P., Roma 127995
Crisostomi, Paolo, Roma 127996
Crisp, J.W., London 130999
Crispin & Sons, J., London 131000
Crispin, Madeline, London 085235
Cristal, Jakarta 105836
Cristal d'Art, Aiguèze 098777
Cristalarte, Cádiz 110292
Cristall, Elissa, Vancouver 097452

Cristallamp, Milano 075684
Cristea, Alan, London 113564
Cristiani, Giancarlo, Torino 076806
Cristiani, Giancarlo, Torino 076807
Cristiani & Foschini, Bologna 075068
Cristill, Rennes (Ille-et-Vilaine) 101075
Cristin Sistina, Roma 076397
Cristina's Bellas Artes, Panamá City 079526
Cristo, Poissy 066885
Cristobal, Agustin, México 077571
Cristol, Jean-Marc, Labastide-Saint-Pierre 063474
Criswick, New York 117813
Criterion Auction Rooms, London . . 122586
Criterion Books, Vancouver 137726
Critique d'Art, Châteaugiron 135702
Critiques Livres Distribution, Bagnolet 138023
Crivellaro, Lorenzo, Milano 127576
Crkva-Muzej na Oplencu, Oplenac kod Topole 034232
C.R.O.A. Consultores, Madrid 129602
Croatian Heritage Museum, Eastlake 043586
Croce, Ugo, Torino 128290
Crocheted Afghans, Louisville 089971
Crocker, Memphis 090067
Crocker Art Museum, Sacramento . 047588
Crocker House, Mount Clemens . . . 046053
Crockett County Museum, Ozona . . 046782
Crockett Tavern Museum, Morristown 046040
Crockford, Sue, Auckland 108309
Crocq, Guy, Domagné 062700
Croes, Bernard, Paris 124633
Croës, Gisèle, Bruxelles 057900
The Croft, Calgary 096802
Croft, Portree 086295
Croft, Swindon 114540
Croft Castle, Leominster 039985
Croft Wingates, Market Harborough 114058
Crofton Roman Villa, Orpington . . . 040646
Crofts, Peter A., Wisbech 087189
Crohill Gallery, Bicheno 094252
Croisée des Artistes, Maîche 099626
La Croisée des Arts, Albi . 060755, 098807
La Croisée des Temps, Carvin 062004
La Croisée des Temps, Lille 063842
Croisette Antiques, Paris 065769
Croissant de Lune, Landerneau . . . 099421
Croizier, René, Craponne (Rhône) . . 062546
Croizit, Frédéric, Abzac 060657
Crolotte, Dominique, Nancy 124469
Crom Estate, Newtownbutler 040588
Cromados Casamitjana, Barcelona . 129337
Cromarty Antiques, Cromarty 084117
Cromarty Courthouse Museum, Cromarty 039179
The Cromarty Gallery, Cromarty . . . 112924
Crome Gallery & Frame Shop, Norwich 086114, 131328
Cromer Museum, Cromer 039181
Cromford Mill, Cromford 039184
Crompton, Paul H., London 135211
Cromwell Museum, Cromwell 030474
Cromwell Museum, Huntingdon . . . 039785
Cronan, Sandra, London 085236
Crone, Berlin 101835
Crone, Hamburg 103109
Cronin, Frank, Christchurch 079023
Cronos, Milano 075685
Cronosaurio, Villa de Leyva 007637
Cronulla Art, Cronulla 094442
Crook County Museum and Art Gallery, Sundance 048430
Crooked House Gallery, Lavenham . 113354
Crooked Tree Arts Center, Petoskey 046913
Crooked Tree Arts Council, Petoskey 054735
The Crooked Window, Dunster 084235
Cropp, M., Kronberg im Taunus . . . 126156
Cros, Anne, Pézenas 101003
Cros, J. Du, Petworth 086244
Crosby, Cleveland 131955
Crosby Art, Belfast 112610
Crosby County Pioneer Memorial Museum, Crosbyton 043227
Croset, Christian, Nogent-sur-Marne 099877
Cross, Edward, Weybridge 087110, 114674, 131675
Cross, John, Birmingham 083530
Cross, Michael, Dallas 115865
Cross Antiques, Watlington 087056
Cross Art and Books, Kings Cross . . 136965
Cross Art Projects, Kings Cross . . . 094701
Cross Gallery, Dublin 105860
Cross Gallery, Nagoya 106917
Cross Hayes, Chippenham 083981
Cross Keys Antiques, Baltimore . . . 087656
Cross Keys Jewellers, Devizes 084162
Cross Plains Antiques Mall, Nashville 090438
Cross Street Gallery, London 113565
Crosseyed Moose Antique, Fort Worth 088848
Crossing Gate Gallery, Bordon 112671
Crosskeys Art Gallery, Perth 114238
Crossland Furniture, Charlotte 087943, 131870
Crossland & Hydra, Goomeri 055897
Crossley & Scott, Melbourne 094807
Crossman Art Gallery, University of Wisconsin Whitewater, Whitewater 049147
The Crossness Engines, London . . . 040128
Crossover Gallery, Albuquerque . . . 114778
Crossroads Antiques, Prestwick . . . 086314
Crossroads Art Center, Richmond . . 119107
Crossroads Art Market, Calgary . . .058785, 096803
Crossroads Bookshop and Gallery, Wellington 140674
Crossroads Gallery, Wellington 108618
Crossroads Museum, Oyen 006112
Crossroads of America, Bethlehem . 042180
Crosstown Arts, Boston 115165
Crouan, Marguerite, Montussan . . . 064782
Crousel, Chantal, Paris 100179
Crouwel, Amsterdam 128532
Crouzat, Marie-Rose, Millau 064557
Crover Folk Museum, Mount Nugent 022839
Crow & Co., Houston 089064
Crow Canyon Archaeological Center, Cortez 043169
Crow Wing County Historical Museum, Brainerd 042383
Crowder, Houston 132113
Crowder College-Longwell Museum and Camp Crowder Collection, Neosho 046178
Crowell, Providence 119074
Crowley, Yuill, Sydney 095280
Crowley Art Association, Crowley . . 054736
Crowley Art Association and Gallery, Crowley 043231
Crowley Museum, Sarasota 047998
Crown &CO., Los Angeles 132249
Crown, New York 117814
Crown Antique Furniture, Seoul . . . 077364
Crown Antiques, Pittsburgh 091805
Crown Arcade, London 085237
Crown City Hardware, Pasadena . . 132602
Crown & Eagle, Columbus 088401
Crown Fine Arts, Ingleby Barwick . . 113293
Crown Gallery, Bruxelles 096176
Crown Gallery, Newcastle-upon-Tyne 114122
Crown Gardens Museum, Dalton . . 043285
Crown Hill, Seattle 092982
Crown Liquor Saloon, Belfast 038660
Crown Mercantile, Denver 088674
Crown Point Press, San Francisco .119648, 135492
Crown Point State Historic Site, Crown Point 043233
Crown Publishing, New York 135421
Crown Woodcraft, Horsham 130807
Crowninshield-Bentley House, Peabody Essex Museum, Salem 047735
Crows Nest Books, Waikato 140663
Crowsnest Museum, Coleman 005286
Crowyn, P., Bruxelles 057901
Croxteth Hall, Liverpool 040027
Croydon Auction Rooms, Croydon . . 122484
Croydon Museum, Croydon 039186
Croydon Natural History and Scientific Society Museum, Croydon 039187
Crozet, Pierre, Carmaux 061988
CRP, Brescia 075161
Le Cruchon, Haarlem 078450
Crucible Gallery, Mandaluyong 108834
Crucis, Gérard, Bruxelles 137432
Cruck House Antiques, Much Wenlock 086029
Crump, Lucien, Philadelphia 118745
Crump-Padgett, Memphis 090068
Crump-Padgett, Memphis 090069
Crusader Church, Abu Ghosh 022879
Cruttenden's, Haywards Heath 130778
Cruz, Manuel Lopes, Lisboa 079909
Cruz, Mary, Bath 083424, 130351
La Cruz del Sur, Buenos Aires 055197
Cruz del Sur, Buenos Aires 136711
Cruz Mateo, Julian, Madrid 129603
Cruz Reig Fito, Maria, Valencia 081652
Cry for the Moon, Guildford 084538, 130750
The Cry of the Gulls, Fowey 113077
The Crypt - Town Hall Plate Room, Oxford 040658
Crypte Archéologique du Parvis de Notre-Dame, Paris 013579
Crypte Carolingienne de l'Ancienne Abbaye, Flavigny-sur-Ozerain 011823
Cryptoneum, Legenden-Museum, Rostock 019893
Crystal, Minneapolis 090351
Crystal Art Gallery, New York 117815
Crystal Arts Gallery, Kansas City . . . 116563
The Crystal Ball, Annandale 123177
Crystal Brook Heritage Centre, Crystal Brook 000961
The Crystal Ceiling, Haarlem 108056
Crystal City Community Museum, Crystal City 005313
Crystal Clinic, Phoenix 132645
Crystal D., Den Haag 107912
Crystal Dragon, Nashville 090439
Crystal Fine Art, Boston 115166
Crystal House, Manama 057623
Crystal Kingdom, Coonabarabran . . 000946
Crystal Lady, Omaha 091562
Crystal Lake Falls Historical Museum, Barton 042034
Crystal Mountain - Crystal & Mineral Gallery & Museum, Auckland 030434
Crystal Palace Museum, London . . 040129
Crystal River State Archaeological Site, Crystal River 043235
C.S. C.B., Madrid 110476
Csaba Lengyel de Bagota, Budapest 134501
C.S.A.F., Paris 100180
Csalini Libri, Fiesole 134576
C.S.A.O.-Galerie 3a, Paris 100181
Csemadok, Dunajská Streda 140960
Csepel Galéria és Helytörténeti Gyûjtemény, Budapest 021644
Cserno, Amsterdam 077822
Csillár Bazár, Budapest 074675
Csipkeház, Kiskunhalas 021770
Csók, István, Budapest . . . 074676, 105501
Csók István Képtár, Székesfehérvár 021866
Csolt Monostor Középkori Romkert, Vésztő 021921
Csongrádi Múzeum, Tari László Múzeum, Csongrád 021708
Csonth, Istvan, Bamberg 069446
Csontváry Múzeum, Pécs 021815
CSP Editions, Glasgow . . . 113108, 135154
CTK, Bavel 128579
C.T.R, Firenze 127326
C.T.S., Roma 127997
C.T.S. France, Paris 124634
CTS Turner Museum, Elkhart 043660
Čtvrtník, Dobroslav, Praha 123977
Cu4rto Nivel Arte Contemporaneo, Bogotá 098118
Cuadra Lopez, Jose Luis, Barcelona 080839
Cuadrado, Teresa, Valladolid 110850
Cuadro, Cartagena 110297
Cuadro, La Palmas de Gran Canaria 110708
Cuadros, Valencia 110802
Cuadros de Monterrey, Monterrey . 107517
Cuadros Vivos de la Sabana, Corozal 007487
La Cuarenta, Madrid 081285
El Cuarto de San Alejo, Bucaramanga 059866
Cuatro Diecisiete, Madrid 110477
Cuba Aereo, Miami 090162
Cuban Collection Fine Arts, Miami . 117054
Cuban Masters Collection, Miami . . 117055
Cuban Museum of Arts and Culture, Miami 045807
Cubanostalgia, Miami 090163
Cubas Basterrechea, Carmen, Madrid 129604
Cubby Hole Antiques, Portland 091924
Cube, Bowden 094270
Cube Gallery, Bristol 112720
Cuber, Lothar, Köln 103608
Cubeta, C., Castlemaine 055646
Cubic Gallery Ïteza, Kyoto 106891
Cubis Collection, North Sydney 094980
Cubitt Artists Studios, London 113566
Cubus Kunsthalle, Duisburg 016850
Cucchi, Paola, Roma 127998
Cuccia, Vittorio, Palermo 127827
Cucciari, Giuseppe, Roma 127999
Cuccolo, Livio, Torino 140131
Cuchifritos, New York 117816
Cucina, Fabio, Roma 076398, 128000
The Cuckfield Gallery, Cuckfield . . . 112932
Cuckfield Museum, Cuckfield 039188
Cuddle Pot Collectables, Cudal 055733
Cudgewa Antique Shop, Cudgewa . 055734
Cudrio Kystmuseum, Langesund . . 030970
Cudworth, Bath 112573
Cuéllar, Corinne, Zürich 130232
Cuenot, Guy, La Chaux-de-Fonds . . 082301
Cuervo, Medellín 059916
Cueto, Valérie, Paris 100182
La Cueva de Caritas, Rosario 055293
Cugusi, Maurizio, Roma 128001
Cukier, Raymond, Romainville 067200
Čukotskij Okružnoj Kraevedčeskij Muzej, Anadyr' 032981
Culberson County Historical Museum, Van Horn 048744
Culbertson Mansion, New Albany . . 046187
Culbertson Museum, Culbertson . . . 043238
Culinair Historisch Museum De Vleer, Appelscha 029258
Culinair Museum, Amersfoort 029149
Culinary Archives and Museum, Providence 047252
Cullity Gallery, Nedlands 094931
Cullman County Museum, Cullman . 043240
Culloden House Antiques, Vancouver 059348
Culloden Visitor Centre, Inverness . 039806
Cullompton Old Tannery Antiques, Cullompton 084129
Culo, Delphine, Lorient 064002
Culotta, Rosolino, Palermo 076140
Culpeck, Tom, Brüggen, Niederrhein 070070
Culross Palace, Culross 039190
Cult, Wien 095810
Cult Verein zur Förderung aktueller Kunst, Wien 052525
CultiG 7, Mannheim 072417
Cultura 2000 - Kunst im Kuhstall, Kirtorf 103561
Cultura Collection, Cleveland 115699
Cultural Center Hellenic Cosmos, Athinai 021166
The Cultural Center of Fine Arts, Parkersburg 046826

Cultural Center of the Philippines Museo, Pasay 031754
Cultural Heritage Center, Dallas . . . 043265
Cultural Heritage Center Museum, Confederated Tribes and Bands of the Yakama Indian Nation, Toppenish 048583
Cultural Museum, Melaka 027990
Cultural Museum, State University Museum, Kabacan 031677
Cultural Research Institute, Kolkata 022217
Cultural Rights and Protection/Ute Indian Tribe, Fort Duchesne 043913
Culturati Art Gallery, San Diego . . . 119498
Culture and Fine Arts Publishing House, Beijing 133337
Culture Art & Galerie, Leipzig 103861
Culture Art Gallery, New York 117817
Culture Cache Gallery, San Francisco 119649
Culture & Economics, Minden, Westfalen 104077
Cultured Pearl, Portland 091925
Cultureel Centrum van Gogh, Zundert 030402
Cultureel Maçonniek Centrum Prins Frederik, Den Haag 029422
Cultuur-Historisch Museum Sorgdrager, Hollum 029760
Cultuurhistorisch Museum Valkenswaard, Valkenswaard 030251
Cultuurhistorisch Streek- en Handkarrenmuseum De Wemme, Zuidwolde, Drenthe 030399
Cultuurhistorisch Streekmuseum De Acht Zaligheden, Eersel 029531
Culzean Castle and Country Park, Maybole 040439
Cum Museum, Imphal 022168
Cum Tempore, Salzburg 057238
Cumalı Sanat Galerisi, İstanbul 112298
Cumberland Art Conservation, Nashville 132399
Cumberland Art Society, Cookeville 054737
Cumberland County Historical Society Museum, Greenwich 044353
Cumberland County Museum, Amherst 005006
Cumberland Gallery, Chichester . . . 112858
Cumberland Gallery, Nashville 117346
Cumberland Gap National Historical Park, Middlesboro 045837
Cumberland Heritage Village Museum, Cumberland, Ontario 005315
Cumberland House, Regina 006249
Cumberland Museum, Cumberland, British Columbia 005314
Cumberland Pencil Museum, Keswick 039851
Cumberland Science Museum, Nashville 046143
Cumberland Theatre Arts Gallery, Cumberland 043243
Cumberland Toy and Model Museum, Cockermouth 039112
Cumbernauld Museum, Cumbernauld 039193
Cumbria Architectural Salvage, Raughton Head 086329, 131405
Cumbria Auction Rooms, Carlisle . . 122449
Cumbria College of Art and Design, Carlisle 050807
The Cumbrian Antiques Centre, Brampton, Cumbria 083639
Cuming Museum, London 040130
Cummer Museum of Art, Jacksonville 044812
Cumming, A. & Y., Lewes 141724
Cummings, J., Minneapolis 142579
Cumming's Corner, Kansas City . . . 089495
Cummins, James, New York 142646
Cummins, Rob, Dubbo 055761
Cunderdin Municipal Museum, Cunderdin 000963
Cundiff, Bryan, Louisville . 089972, 122947
Cuneo Museum, Vernon Hills 048769
Cunha, Rio de Janeiro 058576
Cunha, Carlos, Porto 080077
Cunha, Ruben, Lisboa 109277
Cunha, Vítor Manuel, Lisboa 140828
Cunha, Walter A., Rio de Janeiro . . 137572
Cuniberti, Beatrice, Firenze 127327
Cunin, Marie-Noëlle, Lacoste 063478
Cunningham, New Orleans 117422
Cunningham, Portland 142786
Cunningham Dax Collection of Psychiatric Art, Parkville, Victoria 001368
Cunnington, Lynette, Woollahra . . . 056862
Cuny, André, Nantes 064920
Cuoccio, Antonio, Milano 075686
Cuoccio, Guiseppe, Milano 075687, 127577
Cuomo, Baltimore 087657
Cuore, Buono, Rio de Janeiro 123702
Cupar and District Heritage Museum, Cupar 005316
Cupboard, Plymouth 142003
Cupboard Antiques, Amersham . . . 083290
Cupboard Collectables, Minneapolis 090352
Cupertino Historical Museum, Cupertino 043247
Cupertino S, Lisboa 109278
Cupid World of Beauty, Ettalong Beach 055807
Cupid's Antiques, Oklahoma City . . 091492
Cupids Museum, Cupids 005317
Cupillard, Grenoble 099303
Cupola House, Egg Harbor 043621
Cuppacumbalong, Tharwa 095328
Cuppalot, Lyons 094748
Cupper, David, Norfolk 091372
La Cúpula, Don Torcuato 055263
Cupuri, Thannhausen 139779
Curá Antiques, London 085238
Curaçao Museum, Curaçao 030416
Curator, New York 136439
Curdnatta Art Gallery, Port Augusta 095080
Curfman Gallery and Duhesa Lounge, Fort Collins 043900
Le Curieux, Saint-Ouen 067758
Curiger, Carl-Rudolf, Uitikon Waldegg 082866, 122354
Curio, Utrecht 140545
Curio Arts, Kathmandu 107578
Curio Books, Hahndorf 136926
Curio-City, Singapore 080452
Curio City, Southend-on-Sea 086654
Curio Corner, Tynemouth 086972
Curio Corner Books, Austin 142216
The Curio Shop, Dublin 074905
Curio Warehouse, Guildford 055923
Curios City, Vancouver 059349
The Curios House, Udaipur 074836
Curios Limited Antiques, Norfolk . . 091373
Curios of Chale, Chale, Isle of Wight 083904
Curiosa, Breda 078088
Curiosa de Markies Roosendaal, Roosendaal 078686
Curiosa, Meubelen & Hebbedingen, Den Haag 078185
Curiosamuseum Nollée, Izenberge . 003541
Curioser & Curioser, Bendigo 055479
Curiosidade's Guatemala, Oklahoma City 091493
Curiosité, Evian-les-Bains 062823
Curiosités, Besançon 061380
Curiosités, Sallanches 068097
Curiosités Marocaine, Rabat 077690
Curiosities, Highgate, Western Australia 055983
Curiosities Shop, Vancouver 059350
Curiosity Corner, Dallas 088497
Curiosity Corner, North Shore 079189
Curiosity Shop, Hawkes Bay 079111
Curiosity Shop, Las Vegas 089562
Curiosity Shop, Nashville 090440
The Curiosity Shop, Saint Sampson 086477
The Curiosity Shop, South Shields . 086645
The Curiosity Shop, Winnipeg 059454
Curiosity Shoppe, Jacksonville 089402
Curious Art Co-Op, Chinderah 094392
Curious Arts, Singapore 109787
The Curious Kids' Museum, Saint Joseph 047641
Curious Sofa, Kansas City 089496
Currahee Military Museum, Virden . 006754
Currency Museum of the Bank of Canada, Ottawa 006099
Currency Press, Redfern 133053
Currier Gallery of Art, Manchester . 045618
Curros, Alberto Cornejo de, Madrid . 110478
Curry Historical Society Museum, Gold Beach 044230
Cursief, Brugge 120713, 137414
Curso de Pintura, Fortaleza 096518
Curtessão, Porto Alegre 058498
Curth, Uwe, Herne 125916
Curti, Paolo, Milano 106202
Curtins, Sankt Moritz 111882
Curtis, Long Melford 085833
Curtis, Edward S., Seattle 119905
Curtis, Lee J. & Eva, München 139501
Curtis Museum, Alton 038500
Curtiss, Louis F., San Diego 092628
Curtze, Dr. Heike, Wien . . 095811, 133188
Curulla, Marco, Cagnes-sur-Mer . . 061891
Curve, Sheffield 114416
Curwen Gallery, London 113567
Curwood Castle, Owosso 046763
Curzon, David, London . . . 085239, 113568, 131001
Cusanus-Geburtshaus, Bernkastel-Kues 016206
Cuscini, Guido, Bologna 075069
Cushing House Museum, Newburyport 046442
Cusimano, Giovanni, Brescia 075162
Cusset, Gérard, Clermont-Ferrand . 099144
Cust Museum, Cust 030475
Custer Battlefield Museum, Garryowen 044153
Custer County 1881 Courthouse Museum, Custer 043252
Custer County Art Center, Miles City 045862
Custer County Historical Society Museum, Broken Bow 042428
Custer Museum, Clayton 042960
Custode, Raymond, Marseille 064345
Custom Art Works, Houston 089065, 116300
Custom by Design, Surry Hills 095249
Custom Collectables, Indianapolis . 089286
Custom Crafted Upholstery, Saint Paul 132766
Custom Engraving, Baltimore 115045
Custom Frame Shop and Gallery, Philadelphia 118746
Custom House Maritime Museum, Newburyport 046443
Custom House Visitor Centre, Dublin 022735
Custom Made Furniture, Salt Lake City 132786
Custom Oil Paintings Reproductions, Houston 116301
Custom Refinishing, Birmingham . . 131833
Custom Refinishing, Omaha 132588
Custom Woodwork and Antiques, New Orleans 132409
Customer Claim Service, Phoenix . . 132646
Customs House Nautical Museum, Robe 001433
Customs Wharf Gallery, Williamstown 095398
Cutelli, Roma 128002
Cutrini, Sabina, Roma 128003
Cutrone, Cleveland 131956
Cutroneo, Giuseppe, Messina 075558
Cuttat, Martine, Paris 100183, 124635
Cutts, Christopher, Toronto 097251
Cuturi, Rudolf Andreas, Linz 133112
Čuvašskij Gosudarstvennyj Chudožestvennyj Muzej, Čeboksary 033061
Čuvašskij Gosudarstvennyj Institut Kultury i Iskusstv, Čeboksary 050628
Čuvašskij Nacionalnyj Muzej, Čeboksary 033062
Cuwo 1801, Pamplona 081514
Cuxhavener Kunstverein, Cuxhaven 053118
Cuyahoga Art Center, Cuyahoga Falls 051216
Cuyler Manor Museum, Uitenhage . 034764
Cuyuna Range Museum, Crosby . . . 043225
Cvetkov, Vladimir, Sofia 058760
CVW Piano Restoration, Jacksonville 132179
CW Exchange, Saint Paul 092356
CWAO News, Port Washington 136440
CWM Galleries, Brisbane 094291
CWM Galleries, Brisbane 094292
Cwmgwili Mill, Carmarthen 083882
CWU Anthropology Department Collection, Ellensburg 043670
Cy Twombly Gallery, Houston 044638
Cybèle, Paris 065770, 133559, 138345
Cybercoins, Pittsburgh 091806
Cybertery Memorials, Nashville . . . 117347
Cybertiques, Louisville 089973
Cyfarthfa Castle Museum and Art Gallery, Merthyr Tydfil 040449
Cygnaeuksen Galleria, Helsinki . . . 009517
Le Cygne Rosé, Paris 065771
Le Cygne Vert, Paris 065772
Cylburn Nature Museum, Baltimore 041977
La Cymaise, Paris 100184
Cymroza Art Gallery, Mumbai 105764
Cynon Valley Museum, Aberdare . . 038437
Cynthia & Wim, Almere 077737
Cypher's & Kallander, Seattle 132933
Cypoly School of Art and Design, Aradippou 049885
Cyprus Academy of Arts, Lemesos . 049887
Cyprus College of Art, Lempa 049889
Cyprus Federation of Associations of Friends of Museums, Lefkosia . . . 052832
Cyprus Folk Art Museum, Lefkosia . 008214
Cyprus Historical Museum, Lefkosia 008215
Cyprus Jewellers Museum, Lefkosia 008216
Cyprus Medieval Museum, Lemesos 008227
Cyprus Museum, Lefkosia 008217
Cyprus National Struggle Museum, Lefkosia 008218
Cyprus Olympic Committee Museum, Lefkosia 008219
Cyr, Raymond, Mar Vista 132313
Cyrette, Winnipeg 097580
Cyrny, H.-J., Moringen 072597
Cyrus Galerie, Hamburg 103110
Cyrus H. McCormick Memorial Museum, Steeles Tavern 048347
Cytrangulo, Julio, Rio de Janeiro . . 058577
Cywaith Cymru. Artworks Wales, Cardiff 054350
Cyx Art, Paris 065773
Cyzer 20th Century Art, London . . . 113569
Czaar Peterhuisje, Zaandam 030360
Czajka, Nowy Dwór Mazowiecki . . . 109034
Czajkowski & Son, Edmund, Woodhall Spa 131711
Czambor, Joachim, Erfurt 070585
Czarina, Monaco 077599
Czarny, Veronika, München 072679
Czarny Butik, Warszawa 109108
Czasostop Artystyczny, Gdynia 108906
Czech Center New York, New York . 046420
Czech Committee of ICOM, Brno . . 052837
Czell, Gertrud, Bamberg 069447
Czempik, Euskirchen 102717
Czernin, Hermann, Puch bei Hallein 123431
Czerny, W., Zweibrücken 074577
Czerwonatis, Gerd, Hamburg 071219, 125806
Czich, Iris, Eisenschmitt 102610
Czichi, Suzanne, Hannover 103269
Czisch, Georg, Aschaffenburg 069194, 125066
Człapa, Tadeusz, Poznań 129061
Czóbel Béla Múzeum, Szentendre . 021880
Czonka, Piotr, Konstancin-Jeziorna . 129024
Czyganowski, Uwe, München 072680
Czymoch, Hans, Berlin 069589

D-Art, Gdynia 108907
D. Art, Ostrava 098398
D-Art, Praha 098426
D & B, Beograd 080392
D & B African Village Art, Houston . 116302
D & B Antiques, New York 090803
D & B Antiques, Omaha . . 091563, 132589
D & D, Ljubljana 080652
D & D, Roma 076399
D D S Antique, New York 132458
D&D Silverware, Warszawa 079743, 109109
D & D Upholstery, San Francisco . . 132876
D-Day Museum and Overlord Embroidery, Portsmouth 040762
D-Day Omaha Musée, Vierville-sur-Mer 015214
D & H Acrylic Designs, Indianapolis 089287
D J B Woodworks, Austin 131796
D & M Antiques, Portland 091926
D M C, Montereau-Fault-Yonne . . . 064676
D & R Fine Art, New York 117818
D. Ralph Hostetter Museum of Natural History, Harrisonburg 044449
D & S, Wien 057396
D & S, Wien 120679
D & T Architectural Salvage, Birkenhead 083524
D137, Sankt-Peterburg 033736
Da, Shun, Shanghai 097905
Da Art Shop, Los Angeles 116749
Da Capo Antiques, Edinburgh 084283, 130677
Da Capo Music, Sydney 137103
Da Hunt, Las Vegas 089563
Da Huo, Shenzhen 097973
Da Jian Wen House, Shenzhen 097974
Da Lozzo, Sydney 095281
Da Luz, Rui, Lisboa 140829
Da Mosto, Venezia 076929
Da Silva, Geneviève, Lazenay 063562
Da Silva, Isabel Lopes, Lisboa 079910
Da Vera, Porto Alegre 096550
Da Vial, Weinsberg 105195
Da Vinci, Bucureşti 109425
Da Vinci, Tuttlingen 105079
Da Vinci Art Alliance, Philadelphia .054738, 118747
Da Vinci Galería de Arte, Bogotá . . . 098119
Da Vinci-Museum, Tongerlo 003800
Da Vinci Restauro, Madrid 129605
D.A. Wurfel Grain Collection, Pinnaroo 001381
daadgalerie, Berlin 016007
DAAP Galleries, Cincinnati 042923
Daatselaar & Godhelp, Amsterdam . 077823
Daatselaar & Godhelp, Utrecht 078792
Al-Dabagh, Jeddah 080360
Al-Dabbas, Mohammed Zuheir, Damascus 083056
Al-Dabbas, Tawfiq, Damascus 083057
Dabbeni, Felice & Angela, Lugano .111662, 135039
Dabberdt, Heike, Kelkheim 071780
Dabdo, Croydon 112927
Dabek, Yolande, Le Mesnil-Esnard . 133479
Dablanc, Jack, Damville 062595
Dablemont, Daniel, Bruay-la-Buissière 061821
Daborn, J.A.P., London 131002
Daborn, Patricia, Karrinyup 123249
Dabren, Lavington 094731
Dąbrowska, Ada, Wrocław 129126
Dąbrowska, Ewa, Sopot 109070
Dabrowski, Berlin 125188
Dača Šaljapina - Gosudarstvennyj Istoriko-kulturnyj Muzej, Kislovodsk 033271
Dacapo Arte Clasico, Alicante 080760
Dach, Strasbourg 068313
Dacić, Ingrid, Tübingen 105072
Daco Verlag, Stuttgart 134409
Dacobra, Tanilba Bay 137105
Dacorum Heritage, Berkhamsted . . 038678
Dacosta Noble, Nelly, Bordeaux . . . 061601
Dacotah Prairie Museum and Lamont Art Gallery, Aberdeen 041559
Dacou Aboriginal Gallery, Adelaide . 055312
Dada, Beograd 080393
D'Adamo & Woltz, Seattle 119906
Dade, Clifford & Roger, Thames Ditton 086880
Dade Battlefield Historic State Park, Bushnell 042532
Dadian Gallery, Wesley Theological Seminary Center for the Arts and Religion, Washington 048893
Dado, Seoul 107218
Dad's Old Book Store, Nashville . . . 142598
Däberitz, T. & V., Bergisch Gladbach 101760
Daegu National Museum, Daegu . . 027473
Daegu National University of Education Museum, Daegu 027474
Daegwallyeong Museum, Gangneung 027487
Dähler, Niklaus, Sulgen 082838
Dählmann & Goldenstein, Westerstede 074373
Daehn, H., Timmendorfer Strand . . 074060
Daehnhardt, Rainer, Lisboa 079911
Dämchen, Thomas, Berlin 069590
Dändorf, Dierhagen 070245
Daensmuseum en Archief van de Vlaamse Sociale Strijd, Aalst 003141
Daeppen, Guillaume, Basel 111173
Daes, Wrocław 079799
Daewoo Art Gallery, Ha Noi 120459
DAF Automobiel Museum, Eindhoven 029538
Daffodil, Skerries 105900
Daffoy-Albuquerque, Martin du, Paris 065774
Daffoy-Albuquerque, Martin du, Paris 065775
Daffoy-Albuquerque, Martin du, Paris 065776
Dag en Zonne, Brugge 057768
Daga, Antonio, Cagliari 106011
Dagali Museum, Geilo 030854
Dagbladmuseum Abraham Verhoevenhuis, Antwerpen 003156
Dagda, Almere 107629
Dagestanskij Gosudarstvennyj Objedinennyj Istoriko-architekturnyj Muzej, Machačkala 033340
Dagestanskij Muzej Izobrazitelnych Iskusstv, Machačkala 033341
Daggett, London . 085240, 113570, 131003
Daghofer, Heinz, Leoben 095643
Daglen, Toledo 132972
Dagmar, North Melbourne 094975
Dagommer, Chantal, Saint-Ouen . . 067759
Dagon Grain Museum, Archaeological Museum of Grain Handling in Israel, Haifa 022920
Dagoneau, Gérard, Paris 124636
Dagot, Sylvie, Montluçon 121076
Dagu Paotai Yi Zhi Museum, Tianjin 007282
Daguenet, Bernard, Niherne 065164
Daguenet, Berthe, Versailles 068798
Dagues-Fouché, Françoise, Montpellier 099753
Dahe Village Yi Zhi Museum, Zhengzhou 007347
Dahesh Museum of Art, New York . 046320
Daheshist Publishing, New York . . . 135422
Daheshite Museum, Beirut 027807
Dahiez, Dr. Anne, Zürich 112058
Dahl, Haugesund 108690
Dahl, København 098547
Dahl, Luzern 111687
Dahl, Heide, Düsseldorf 102484
Dahl, Volker, Ulmet 074156
Dahl Arts Center, Rapid City 047332
Dahlborn, Susanna, Stockholm . . . 129859
Dahle, Halden 079387
Dahlem, Rita, Hützel 103412
Dahling, Oscar, Croydon 084123
Dahlman, Mary, San Antonio 119406
Dahlmüller, Dr. Carlo, Saarbrücken . 104788
Dahlonega Courthouse Gold Museum, Dahlonega 043257
Dahm, Wolfgang, Mannheim 104021
Dahmann, Prof. Dr. Werner, Berlin . 133759
Dahmen, Xanten 074552
Dahringer & Lieb-Dahringer, Muggensturm 072934
Dahua, Chengdu 097698
Dai, Vancouver 123847
Dai Ichi, New York 117819
Dai Nippon Printing, Tokyo 134720
Dai Token Ichi, Tokyo 093798
Daigaku, Osaka 106955
Daigaku, Tokyo 107028
Daigo Fukuryu Maru Exhibition Hall, Tokyo 027154
Daigo-ji Treasure Hall, Kyoto 026710
Daihoon-ji Treasure House, Kyoto . . 026711
Daikakuji Temple Treasure House, Kyoto 026712
Dailey, William, Los Angeles 135378, 142502
Daily-Bul, La Louvière 133288
Daily Planet, Seattle 092983
Daimaru, Tokyo 107029
Daimarufujii, Sapporo 106982
DaimlerChrysler Contemporary, Berlin 016008
Daimonion, Warszawa 140783
Daimyo Tokei Hakubutsukan, Tokyo 027155
Daini &Co., Albert, San Francisco . . 132877
Dairy House Antiques, Semley 086535
Dais, Charkiv 112379
Daishodo, Kyoto 077094
Daiso, Hiroshima 077053
Daisy International Air Gun Museum, Rogers 047522
Daisy Shop, Chicago 088067
Dajmond Klassik, Sankt-Peterburg . 080301
Dajmont Art, Moskva 109502
Dakot, Oakland 118629
Dakota, Lausanne 082541
Dakota County Historical Society Museum, South Saint Paul 048249
Dakota Dinosaur Museum, Dickinson 043466
Dakota Territorial Museum, Yankton 049330
Dakotaland Museum, Huron 044699
Dakovština Museum, Dakovo 007711
DakshinaChitra Museum, Muttukadu 022272
Dal-Paso Museum, Lamesa 045134
Dala Antiktjänst, Stockholm 081938, 129860
Dalälvarnas Flottningsmuseum, Sandviken 036561
Dalahästmuseum, Dala-Järna 036233
Dalancon, Jean, Versailles 068799
Dalane Folkemuseum, Egersund . . 030810
Dalarnas Museum, Falun 036265
Dalbeattie Museum, Dalbeattie . . . 039200
Dalbry Antiques, Canterbury 123204
Dalby Regional Gallery, Dalby 000966
Dalcici, Timişoara 080191
Dale, John, London 085241
Dale, Peter, London 085242
The Dale Gallery, Stanhope 114481
Dale House Antique, Moreton-in-Marsh 086015
Dalecarlia Antik & Auktioner, Falun .081783, 122131
Daled, Bruxelles 133264
Dalemain Historic House, Penrith . . 040687
Dalénmuseet, Stenstorp 036611
Dales Countryside Museum, Hawes 039701
Daleside Antiques, Markington 085944
Dalet, Lucienne, Soucirac 068265
Daleus, Miami 090164
Daley, Minneapolis 117249
Daley, Washington 120278
D'Alfama, Rosa, Lisboa . . 079912, 129150
Dalfling Gallery, Inverurie 113300
D'Alfonso, Maria Felicia, Perugia . . 076232
Dalgaard, Jørgen L., København . . . 060312
Dalgarven Mill, Museum of Ayrshire Country Life and Costume, Kilwinning . . . 039875
Dalhousie Art Gallery, Halifax 005570
Dalhousie Station, Calgary 096804
Dali, Den Haag 078186
Dalian Calligraphy and Painting Gallery, Dalian 097709
Dalian Gallery, Dalian 007054
Dalian Natural History Museum, Dalian 007055
Dalibor, Praha 060119
Dalkeith Arts Centre, Dalkeith 039201
Dalkeith Auctions, Bournemouth . . 122424
Dalla Venezia, Toni, Venezia 128385
Dall'Aglio, Mario, Bolzano 105981
Dallai, Genova 140035
Dallam-Hartley XIT Museum, Dalhart 043259
Dallas, Stella, New York 090804
Dallas Art and Design, Dallas 115866
Dallas Arts Studio, Dallas 115867
Dallas Auction Gallery, Dallas 122872
The Dallas Center for Contemporary Art, Dallas 043266
Dallas Historical Society Museum, Dallas 043267
Dallas Holocaust Memorial Center, Dallas 043268
Dallas Museum of Art, Dallas 043269
Dallas Museum of Natural History, Dallas 043270
Dallas Rare Coins, Dallas 088498
Dallendörfer, H & M, Salzburg 123439
Dallendörfer, Kurt, Salzburg 123440
Dalléra, Catherine, Banon 061189, 098913
The Dalles Art Association Gallery, The Dalles 043280
Dallier, Corinne, Le Poinçonnet 124305
Dallmann, Peter, Bad Feilnbach . . . 125095
Dalmas, Richard, Nice 065066
Dalmau, Carles, Girona 134932
Dalmeny House, South Queensferry 041046
Dalnavert Museum, Winnipeg 006842
Dalnevostočnyj Chudožestvennyj Muzej, Chabarovsk 033082
Dalnevostočnyj Memorialnyj Dom-muzej V.K. Arsenjeva, Primorskij gosudarstvennyj muzej im. V.K. Arsenjeva, Vladivostok 034041
Dalpiaz, Renato, Roma 076400
Dalta & Piccinini, Genova 127446
Dalton, Midge, Palma de Mallorca . 081475
Dalton Centre Museum, Tighish . . . 006571
Dalton Defenders Museum, Coffeyville 043031
Dalton Gallery, Decatur 043348
Dalton Somaré, Milano 106203
Dalva Bros., New York 090805
Dalvi's Art Institute, Kolhapur 050307
Daly House Museum, Brandon 005141
Dalymount, Dublin 127095
Dalype, Oslo 108706
D.A.M., Corte 062487, 099175
Dam, Christian, København 098548
Dam, Christian, Oslo 108707
Dam Mill Antiques, Codsall 084048
Dam Site Museum, Mangla 031389
Damais, Jean, Biarritz 061459
Damani, Köln 071922
Damasco, Gino, Egnach 082350
Damascus Palace, Dubai 083191
Damask Asia, London 113571
Damasquine, Bruxelles 096177
Damasse, Charles, Yerres 069060
Dambeck, Michaela, Passau 104583
Dambourges, Québec 059068
D'Ambra, Raffaele, Napoli 106362
Dambron, Arlette, Schiltigheim 068178
D'Ambrosio, Nicola, Roma 128004
Dambry, Antibes-Juan-les-Pins . . . 060919
La Dame de Malacca, Kuala Lumpur 077499
Dame du Castellet, Le Castellet . . . 099428
Dame e Cavalieri, Milano 075688
D'Amelio & Terras, New York 117820

Damerla Rama Rao Art School, Rajahmundry 050323
Damerla Rama Rao Memorial Art Gallery, Rajahmundry 022316
Les Dames, Paris 065777
Damiano, Agostino, Torino 076808
Damiano, Lina, Cagnes-sur-Mer . . . 061892
Damiano & Macherez, Nice 065067
D'Amico, Camillo, Roma 128005
Damidot, Daniel, Lyon 124351
Damidot, Patrick, Dijon 062652
Damiean, Pierre-Jean, Fabrègues . 124238
Damien, Jean-Philippe, Sancerre . . 068113
Damien, S., Mons 058338
Damioli, Sandro, Basel 082136
Damitot, Daniel, Lyon 124352
Damjanich János Múzeum, Szolnok 021896
Damm, Hamburg 071220
Damm, Helmut, Gescher 070980
Dammann, Detlef, Zwickau 105374, 134480
Dammer, Kurt, Hanau 071370
Dammert, Marco, Düsseldorf 070369
Dammron, Claude, Genève 082418
D'Amodio, Antimo, Napoli 075960
D'Amodio, Antimo, Napoli 075961
Damokles Antiquariaat, Den Haag . 140391
Damon, Yvette, Saint-Martin-de-Ré 067632, 101179
Damongeot, Marie-Claude, Sampans 068108
d'Amore, Valeria e Andrea, Livorno . 106119
Damoutte, Dominique, Vannes (Morbihan) 068717
Damoutte, Gérard, Vannes (Morbihan) 068718
Dampfkornbranntweinbrennerei-Museum, Wildeshausen 020890
Dampflok-Museum, Hermeskeil . . . 017889
Dan, Los Angeles 089737
Dan Andersson Museum, Ludvika . 036435
Dan-Cuthbert Sally, Rose Bay 095157
Dan Flavin Art Foundation Temporary Gallery, Dia Art Foundation, New York 046321
Dan Kook University Museum, Seoul 027547
Dan O'Laurie Canyon Country Museum, Moab 045944
Dan Quayle Center and Museum, Huntington 044675
Dan Winters House - Ancestral Home, Loughgall 040345
Dan-yr-Ogof Showcaves Museum, Abercrave 038436
Al-Dana, Manama 095999
Dana, Helene, Wien 137301
The Dana-Thomas House, Springfield 048283
Danaé, Paris 065778
Danah, Manama 057624
De Danann Antique Centre, Dorchester 084176, 130641
Danant, Jean-Louis, Paris 065779
Danart, Bucureşti 080152, 129220
Dana's Art and Antiques, Braşov . . 080135
Danbury Antiques, Danbury 084133, 130624
Danbury Museum, Danbury 043289
Dance Art, Versoix 111963
Dance Cottage Museum, Ravensthorpe 001423
Dancing Art, Nashville 117348
Dancing Geese Gallery, Tokyo 107030
Dancing Sheep, Cleveland 115700
Dandelion, Philadelphia 091625
Dandelion Books, Dublin 139964
Dando, Andrew, Bradford-on-Avon . 083630
Dandois, Ariane, Paris 065780
Dandois, Ariane, Paris 065781
Dandois, Ariane, Paris 065782
Dandong Museum on the War to resist U.S. Aggression and Aid Korea, Dandong 007061
D'Andrea, Alberto, Roma 076401
Dane, Thomas, London 113572
Dane G. Hansen Memorial Museum, Logan 045364
Danechild, E.E., San Francisco 119650
Danemberg, Arnaldo, Rio de Janeiro 058578
Danenberg, Valérie, Paris 065783
Danese, New York 117821
Danet, Songeons 068261
Danford Collection of West African Art and Artefacts, Birmingham 038729
Danforth Gallery, Portland 047158
Danforth Museum of Art, Framingham 044023
Dang, Geomok, Daegu 077360
Dang, Samkook, Seoul 077365
Dang, Songa, Daegu 107183
Dang, Sunggo, Gwangju 077361
Dang Dynasty, New York 090806
Dangel, Erika, Murrhardt 104387
Dangel, Martina, Blaubeuren 069865
D'Angelo, Antonio, Roma 076402
D'Angelo, Gaetano, Napoli 127761
Danger, B., Vöhringen 074225
L'été Dangereux, Nîmes 138264
Dangol, Kathmandu 107579
Dangoor, Daniella, London 113573
Danhof, J., Brackenheim 069970
Danicourt, Benoît, Paris 065784
Danicourt, Georges, Toulouse 068500
Daniel, Christiane, Paris 065785
Daniel, Christiane, Saint-Hilaire-du-Harcouët 067518, 124904
Daniel, Michel, Saint-Nazaire (Loire-Atlantique) 067684
Daniel Antik, Frederiksberg 060231
Daniel Boone Homestead, Birdsboro 042219
Daniel et Vincent, Paris 065786
Daniel Owen Museum, Mold 040484
Daniel W. Tantoco jr. Collection, Manila 031720
Danièle, B., Paris 065787
Daniëlle, Zeist 078866
Daniel's Antiques, Chicago 088068, 122843
Daniels County Museum and Pioneer Town, Scobey 048050
Daniel's Shop, Strovolos 059966
Danielsen, H., København 060313
Danielson-Kalmarin Huvila, Vääksy 010207
Danielsson, Anders, Ekshärad 122120
Danihelka, Marita, Dorsten 102391
Daninos, Andrea, Firenze 075326
Daninos, Andrea Giovanni, Milano . 075689
Danish Country, Boston 087813
The Danish Cultural Institute, Edinburgh 039383
Danish Immigrant Museum, Elk Horn 043658
Danish National Council of Museums, København 052845
Dank Je de Koekoek, Utrecht 078793
Danker, H., Dublin 074906
Danko, Dr. Waldemar, Lieboch 057148
Dankwardt, M., Leer 072179
Danmar, Stockholm 129861
Danmarks Bogmuseum, København 008961
Danmarks Cykelmuseum, Ålestrup . 008803
Danmarks Fotomuseum, Herning . . 008903
Danmarks Grafiske Museum, Odense 009046
Danmarks Jernbanemuseum, Odense 009045
Danmarks Keramikmuseum, Middelfart 009022
Danmarks Kloster Museum, Ry . . . 009088
Danmarks Mediemuseum, Odense . 009046
Danmarks Tekniske Museum, Helsingør 008896
Dann Antiques, Melksham 085966
D'Anna Antiquariato, Roma 076403, 128006
Dannebrog, København 060314
Dannegger, Köninger & Stebler, Bern 129954
Dannegger, Köninger & Stebler, Fribourg 130018
Dannenberg, Reiner, Berlin 121327
Dannenberg & Ryan, North Adelaide 056354
Danner, F., Appenweier 069179
Danninger, Helmut, Groß Sankt Florian 057042
Danny, L., Hong Kong 097776
Danowski, Marek, Zürich 135084
Danqing Yin Art, Chongqing 097706
Dan's, Houston 132114
Dan's Antiques, Tucson 093220
Dan's Custom Woodworking, Houston 089066
Dans le Temps, Brugny-Vaudancourt 061823
Dans Mon Monde, Nancy 099792
Dan's Place, Albuquerque 087390
Dansk Antik, København 060315
Dansk Billedhunggersamfund, Stouby 052846
Dansk Bogservice, København 137893
Dansk Brandværnshistorisk Museum, Næstved 009024
Dansk Galerie, Paris 065788
Dansk ICOM, The Danish National Committee of the International Council of Museums, Kolding 052847
Dansk Jagt- og Skovbrugsmuseum, Hørsholm 008935
Dansk Kulturhistorisk Museums Forening, Nivå 052848
Dansk Kunst og Antikvitetshandler Union, København 052849
Dansk Landbrugsmuseum, Auning . 008816
Dansk Møbelkunst, København . . . 060316
Dansk Veteranflysamling, Skjern . . 009101
Den Danske Antikvarboghandlerforening, Frederiksberg 052850
Det Danske Filminstitut, København 008962
Det Danske Hedeselskabs Museum, Viborg 009146
Det Danske Kunstindustrimuseum, København 008963
Dansmuseet, Stockholm 036621
Danson Gallery, Orpington 114193
Dantas, Carlos, Noailles 065202
Dante, Padova 106394
Dante, Philadelphia 132613
Le Dantec, Bertrand, Paris 124637
Danter, Susanne, Mainz 126258
Dantica, Amsterdam 107698
Dantikvariát, Praha 137829
Danvers Historical Society Exhibition, Danvers 043293
Danville Museum of Fine Arts and History, Danville 043299
Dany, Laure, Paris 100185
Dany, Lucas, La Baule-Escoublac . . 099374
Dany Antic, Bellot 061338
Dany Art Déco, Saint-Ouen 067760
Danysz, Magda, Paris 100186
Danzi, Angiolo & Cutri, Alessandro, Roma 076404
Danzinger, Maria, Perchtoldsdorf . . 095702
Danzl, Thomas, Nittendorf 126552
Daolio, Mario, Bologna 127142
Dapa, Gean & Merry, Los Angeles . 089738
Dapa International, Timişoara 080192
Dapeng Gucheng Museum, Shenzhen 007259
Daphne's Antiques, Penzance 086211
Dapple-Gray, Saint Louis 092217
Dappon, Cluj-Napoca 140885
Dapsens, Ludovic, Reims 121229
Daqian, Beijing 097649
Dar Al-Bareh Gallery, Manama 057625
Dar Al-Bareh Gallery, Manama 096000
Dar Al-Bareh Gallery, Manama 096001
Dar Al-Ghad Gallery, Manama 096002, 133246
Dar Al-Maaref, Cairo 133435
Dar-es-Salaam National Museum, Dar-es-Salaam 037851
Dar Galereja Naivnogo Iskusstva, Moskva 109503
Dar-Hervey Ely House, Rochester . . 047479
Dar Museum First Ladies of Texas Historic Costumes Collection, Denton 043393
Al-Dara, Manama 096003
Daragnes, Pierre, Biarritz 061460
Daras & Gilbert, Düsseldorf 139008
Darbarhall Museum, Junagadh 022192
Darbre, Florence, Nyon 130133
Darby Houses, Rosehill and Dale House, Coalbrookdale 039103
Darchis, Fabian, Nancy 064866
Darcy's, Lucknow 056119
Dard, Jean, Orléans 121102
Dardamani, Anna, Thessaloniki . . . 074635
Dardel, Benoît de, Neuchâtel 130126
Dardenne, Bruxelles 057902
Dardenne, Bruxelles 057903
Dare, I., Sydney 095282
Dare-Dare, Montréal 096990
Daredevil Hall of Fame, Niagara Falls 006008
Darga & Lansberg, Paris 100187
Dargate, Cleveland 122865
Dargate, Pittsburgh 123056
Dargaville Museum, Dargaville 030477
Daria, Clermont-Ferrand 099145
Daria, Hyderabad 105700
Daries, Valencia 129770
Darilo, Novo Mesto 080667
Darious, Atlanta 114869
Dárius, Budapest 074677
Darius, Galaţi 080183
Darius, New York 090807
Darius, New York 132459
Darjeeling, Manama 096004
Darl At Tifl Museum, Jerusalem . . . 031414
Darlay, Olivier, La Frette-sur-Seine . 063383
Darling, Stockholm 111016
Darling, Lindy, Yallah 095438
Darling Antiques, Chicago 088069
Darling Down's Antique and Art Centre, Toowoomba 056718
Darling Street Books, Rozelle 137076
Darlingford School Heritage Museum, Darlingford 005322
Darlington Art Centre, Darlington . . 039204
Darlington Art Gallery, Darlington . . 039205
Darlington Province Park Pioneer Home, Bowmanville 005124
Darlington Railway Centre and Museum, Darlington 039206
Darl'ys Antiquités, Charleville-Mézières 062156
Darms, Gieri, Ilanz 082507
Darmstädter Münzhandlung, Darmstadt 070180
Darnall's Chance, Upper Marlboro . 048706
Darnas, Daniel, Couzon-au-Mont-d'Or 062541
Darnault, Véronique, Paris 065789
Darnley Fine Art, London 113574
Daros Exhibitions, Zürich 037764
D'Arpino, Rosa Bianca, Roma 076405
Darquenne, Jean, Krombach 139369
Darracq, Bray-sur-Seine 061752
Darre, Cosette, Villepinte 068926
Darreau, Norbert, Mâcon 138187
Darrell, København 060317, 098549
Darrell, Dean, Washington 093407
Darren, K., Columbus 115773
Darrow, New York 090808
Darru, Figtree 094525
D'Ars, Milano 053751, 135895
La Darsena, Modena 075908, 140071
Darshan, Ottawa 097103
Darß-Museum, Ostseebad Prerow . 019531
Dart, Gdańsk 079579, 140718
Dart Antiques & Restoring, Gdańsk . 129008
D'Art en Déco, Rodez 067191
The D'Art Gallery, Dartmouth 112934
D'Arte Mev, Gateshead 113087
Dartenset, Creysse 062567
Dartevelle, P., Bruxelles 057904
Dartford Borough Museum, Dartford 039209
Dartigoeyte, Richard, Castelnau-de-Médoc 062012

Dartington Crystal Glass Museum, Torrington . . . 041233
Dartmoor Bookshop, Ashburton . . . 141389
Dartmoor District Coach House Museum, Dartmoor . . . 000972
Dartmouth Castle, Dartmouth . . . 039210
Dartmouth Fine Art, Totnes . . . 114589
Dartmouth Heritage Museum, Dartmouth . . . 005324
Dartmouth Museum, Dartmouth . . . 039211
Dartmouth Street Gallery, Albuquerque . . . 114779
Darvinovskij Muzej, Moskva . . . 033379
Darwin, Philadelphia . . . 091626
Darwin Gallery, Darwin . . . 094459
Darwin Museum, Home of Chales Darwin, Downe . . . 039279
Darwisch, Rashad, Graz . . . 057008
Dary's, Paris . . . 065790
Darzalas, Varna . . . 096766
Das, Catharina, Roma . . . 076406
Dasar, Forfar . . . 113072
D'Ascanio, Anna, Roma . . . 106513
D'Ascenzi, Gian Carlo, Roma . . . 106514
Daschner, Max, Bamberg . . . 069448
Dåsettunet, Lyngdal . . . 031002
Daspelgruber & Lötsch, Steyr-Gleink . . . 057327
Dasse, Wilfried, Kiel . . . 071824
Dassen, Pieke, Maastricht . . . 108118
Dasser, Prof. Dr. Karl-Ludwig, Köln . 126071
Dassin, West Hollywood . . . 093462
Dassler, Georg, Stuttgart . . . 073968
Dassonvalle, Honfleur . . . 099340
Dat Antiek, Den Haag . . . 128627
Dat lütt Museum, Alt Jabel . . . 015489
Datacolor, Lawrenceville . . . 054739
Datina, Prato . . . 076252
D'Attili, Maria Novella, Roma . . . 076407
Datu Fine Arts, Wishaw . . . 114714
Datura, Chicago . . . 115399
Daubet, Francis, Floirac . . . 062879
Daubisse, Isabelle, Ribérac . . . 067132
Daubitz & Son, Dallas . . . 132004
Daubrée, Valérie, Paris . . . 124638
Daudet, Alain, Toulouse . . 068501, 101340
Dauerausstellung des Missionswerkes, Neuendettelsau . . . 019229
Daugava, Rīga . . . 107318
Daugavas Muzejs, Salaspils . . . 027776
Daugavpils Muzeja, Daugavpils . . . 027672
Daugavpils Muzeja Izstāžu Zāles, Daugavpils . . . 027673
Daugavpils Novadpētniecības un Mākslas Muzejs, Daugavpils . . . 027674
Daugé, Claude, Richelieu . . . 067135
Dauger, Yves, Paris . . . 065791
Daughters of the American Revolution Museum, Washington . . . 048894
Daughters of Utah Pioneers Pioneer Memorial Museum, Salt Lake City 047773
Daulaus, Nice . . . 065068
Daum Museum of Contemporary Art, Sedalia . . . 048101
Daumarie, Jacques, Amphion-les-Bains . . . 098824
Daumas, Jean-Paul, Aigues-Mortes 060679
Daune, Alain, Paris . . . 100188
Dauphin, Singapore . . . 109788
Dauphin, Cedric le, Bruxelles . . . 057905
Le Dauphin Bernard, Paris . . . 065792
Dauphin Publishing, Oxford . . . 135292
Dauphine Street Books, New Orleans . . . 142610
Daura Gallery, Lynchburg College, Lynchburg . . . 045525
Dauriac, Jean-Louis, Dieupentale . . 062629
Dautrait, Daniel, Clermont-Ferrand . 124202
Dautzenberg, Bruno, Köln 071923, 126072
Dauvillier, Middelburg . . . 108139
Dauwe, Christel, Antwerpen . . . 057689
Davaco, Doornspijk . . . 134807
Davaki, Eleni, Iráklion . . . 074623
Davao Museum, Davao . . . 031669
Davaud, Maig, Paris . . . 100189
Dave Antique, Paris . . . 065793
Dave & Bill's Trading Post, Saint Louis . . . 092218
Daveau, Jacqueline, Paris . . . 065794
Daveau, Jean-Michel, Laval (Mayenne) . . . 121028
Daveau, Pierre, Saint-Ouen . . . 124914
Davenham Antique Centre, Davenham . . . 084142
Davenport House Museum, Savannah . . . 048023
Davenport Museum of Art, Davenport . . . 043304
Daventry Museum, Daventry . . . 039214
Daverio, Chrisgeni, Nice . . . 124506
Daves, Tucson . . . 132983
Dave's Antiques, Louisville . . . 089974
Dave's World, Houston . . . 089067
Davi, Timişoara . . . 080193
David, Los Angeles . . . 089739
David, Singapore . . . 080453
David, Bernadette, Langoiran . . . 063516
David, Charles, Providence . . . 119075
David, Francine Marie, Beatenberg . 111235
David, G., Cambridge . . . 141469
David, Jean-Marc, La Trimouille . . . 063455
David, Marie-Christine, Paris . . . 065795
David, Mathias, Paris . . . 065796
David, Philippe, Limey-Remenauville . . . 063876
David & Alfred Smart Museum of Art. Bulletin, Chicago . . . 136441
The David and Alfred Smart Museum of Art, University of Chicago, Chicago . . 042838
David Bradford House, Washington . 048967
David & Charles, Newton Abbot . . . 135286
David Conklin Farmhouse, Huntington . . . 044678
David Crawford House, Newburgh . 046437
David & David, Philadelphia . . . 118748
The David Davis Mansion, Bloomington . . . 042259
David et ses Filles, Paris . . . 065797
David Kakabadze Doma, Tbilisi . . . 015405
David Livingstone Centre, Blantyre . 038767
David Nichols-Captain John Wilson House, Cohasset . . . 043033
David Palombo Museum, Jerusalem 022946
David & Laure Soustiel, Marie-Christine, Paris . . . 065798
Davíd Stefánsson Memorial Museum, Akureyri . . . 021930
David Strawn Art Gallery, Art Association of Jacksonville, Jacksonville . . . 044821
David Winton Bell Gallery, Providence . . . 047253
Daviddi, Farmington . . . 088824, 132068
Davidov, Lina, Paris . . . 100190
Davidowski, F., Almelo . . . 077722
David's, Brampton, Cambridgeshire 083638
Davids, Miami . . . 117056
David's, New Orleans . . . 090542
David's Antiques, Chicago . . . 088070
David's Art, Memphis . . . 116981
Davids Book Exchange, Brighton . . 141436
David's Gallery, Pittsburgh . . . 091807
Davids Samling, København . . . 008964
David's Timeless Treasures, Toorak 056714
Davidsfonds, Leuven . . . 133289
Davidson, Calgary . . . 123741
Davidson, Newcastle-upon-Tyne . . 086064
Davidson, Saint-Ouen . . . 067761
Davidson, Salt Lake City . 092428, 132787
Davidson, Seattle . . . 092984, 119907
Davidson, Carlton, London . . . 085243
Davidson, Greg, Seattle . . . 092985
Davidson, J., Cleveland . . . 142326
Davidson, Maxwell, New York . . . 117822
Davidson, Michael, London . . . 085244
Davidson County Historical Museum, Lexington . . . 045273
Davidson County Museum of Art, Lexington . . . 045274
Davidson & Morgan, London . . . 085245
Davie, Tickhill . . . 114575
Davies, Daryl, Ringwood . . . 114316
Davies, Daryl, Ringwood . . . 135300
Davies & Son, Edmund, Whalley . . .087122, 131678
Davies, Hugh, London . . . 085246
Davies, Jeffrey, San Francisco . . . 092769
Davies, John, Stow-on-the-Wold . . 086746
Davies, John, Stow-on-the-Wold . . 114502
Davies, John, Stow-on-the-Wold . . 131549
Davies, P. H., London . . . 085247, 131004
Davies, Peter, New York . . . 117823
Davies, Phillip, Swansea . . . 114534
Davies, Phillip, Swansea . . . 131566
Davies Antiques, Ormond . . . 056408
Davies & Tooth, London . . . 113575
Davila, Bogotá . . . 123898
Davinci, Vancouver . . . 059351
Davioud, André, Lille . . . 063843, 124316
Davioud, Georges, Lille . . . 063844
Davis, Austin . . . 114972
Davis, Dallas . . . 132005
Davis, Houston . . . 089068
Davis, Long Beach . . . 089630
Davis & Co., Los Angeles . . . 089740
Davis, New Orleans . . . 117423
Davis, Worcester . . . 135525
Davis, A.B., London . . . 085248
Davis, Barbara, Houston . . . 116303
Davis, Caleb, Boston . . . 131845
Davis, E., Nashville . . . 117349
Davis, Gerald, Dublin . . . 105861
Davis, John, New York . . . 117824
Davis, Kenneth, London . . . 085249
Davis, Leslie, Milwaukee . . . 117179
Davis, Meg, Johnson City . . . 116551
Davis, Rachel, Cleveland . 115701, 122866
Davis, Reginald, Oxford . . 086178, 131353
Davis, Roger A., Great Bookham . . .084504, 130744
Davis, Sharyl, San Antonio . . . 092507
Davis Art Center, Davis . . . 043310
Davis Art Gallery, Columbia . . . 043069
Davis & Davis, London . . . 131005
Davis Dominguez, Tucson . . . 120119
Davis & Gardner, New York . . . 090809
Davis & Langdale, New York . . . 117825
Davis Leron, New York . . . 117826
Davis Mardine, Los Angeles . . . 116750
Davis Museum, Wellesley College, Wellesley . . . 049046
Davis Place Antiques, Saint Louis . . 092219
Davishire Interiors, Nashville . . . 090441
Davison Art Center, Wesleyan University, Middletown . . . 045839
Davison Gallery, Holywood . . . 113264
Davos, Marseille . . . 064346
Davoud-Salmani, Bruxelles . . . 057906
Davoy, Coufouleux . . . 062501
Davril, Bogotá . . . 098120
Davy, Michel, Saumur . . . 068149
Dawa, Kathmandu . . . 107580
Dawes, Philip, Royston . . . 086413, 131430
Dawes, Valentyne, Ludlow 085865, 131243
Dawes County Historical Society Museum, Chadron . . . 042695
Dawlish Museum, Dawlish . . . 039215
Dawne, Morgan, Vancouver . . . 097453
Dawo, Udo, Saarbrücken . 073627, 121592
Dawson, Jacksonville . . . 116515
Dawson, Rotorua . . . 108552
Dawson, Stamford . . . 086684
Dawson, Vancouver . . . 123848
Dawson, Douglas, Chicago 088071, 115400
Dawson, Michael, Los Angeles . . . 142503
Dawson, P., Bentley . . . 083488, 130371
Dawson, Phillip, Twickenham . . . 142128
Dawson City Museum, Dawson City 005331
Dawson County Historical Museum, Lexington . . . 045272
Dawson Creek Art Gallery, Dawson Creek . . . 005333
Dawson Creek Station Museum, Dawson Creek . . . 005334
Dawson Folk Museum, Theodore . . 001549
Dawson Springs Museum and Art Center, Dawson Springs . . . 043317
Daxer & Marschall, München . . . 072681
Daxing Xing Du Art Cooperative, Beijing . . . 097650
Day, Alan, Edinburgh . . . 084284
Day, Christopher, Paddington . . . 095023
Day, Dean, Houston . . . 116304
Day, Edward, Toronto . . . 097252
Day, John, Eastbourne . . . 084260, 130668
Day Antiques, Tetbury . . . 086852
Day & Faber, London . . . 113576
Dayan, Paris . . . 065799
Dayboro Shed, Samsonvale . . . 056568
Dayen, Patrick, Paris . . . 121136
Dayer, Stanislas, Châtelaine . . . 111343
Dayi Liu's Manor-House Museum, Chengdu . . . 007041
Daylesford and District Historical Museum, Daylesford . . . 000976
Dayna's Antiques, Jacksonville . . . 089403
Dayrell's Art Gallery, Saint Michael . 096039
Days Gone By Antiques, Kitchener . 058870
Days of Grace, Budleigh Salterton . 083777
Days of Olde Antiques, Ballarat . . . 055429
Daystar Collectibles, Tucson . . . 093221
Dayton Art Institute, Dayton . . . 043320
Dayton Art Institute. Annual Report, Dayton . . . 136442
Dayton Historical Depot Society Museum, Dayton . . . 043328
Dayton Museum of Discovery, Dayton . . . 043318
Dayton Visual Arts Center, Dayton . 043321
Daytona Gallery, Tauranga . . . 108574
Daza, Francisco, Jerez de la Frontera . . . 110391
Dazaifu Tenman-gu Hômotsuden, Dazaifu . . . 026448
Daze Gone By, Gympie . . . 055926
Dazenière, Michel, Boulazac . . . 061682
Dazibao, Montréal . . . 005922
Dazy, Christian, Dijon . . . 099210
Dazy, Christian, Megève . . . 099697
Dazzle, Helmsley . . . 113219
D.B., London . . . 113577
DB Museum im Verkehrsmuseum Nürnberg, Nürnberg . . . 019348
DBL Diffusion, Nice . . . 065069
DC Antiques, Los Angeles . . . 089741
DC Collection, Tucson . . . 093222
DCA Gallery, New York . . . 117827
DCI Gallery, Memphis . . . 116982
DD Starožitnosti, Praha . . . 060120
DDM Auction Rooms, Brigg . . . 122437
DDR-Motorradmuseum, Borna . . . 016348
DDR-Museum im Filmpalast, Malchow, Mecklenburg . . . 018798
De, Beograd . . . 080394
De, Rong, Beijing . . . 097651
De, Rong, Beijing . . . 097652
De Angeli, Giuseppe, Napoli . . . 075962
De Angelis, Antonio, Napoli . . . 075963
De Antoni, Maria Luigia, Padova . . . 076089
De Benedetti, Augusto, Roma . . . 106515
De Bianchi, Luciano, Verona . . . 077000
De Bretts, Moonee Ponds . . . 056248
De Bruin, Marjelle, Milano . . . 075690
De Capola, Mario, Napoli . . . 075964
De Cardenas, Monica, Milano . . . 106204
De Carlo, Massimo, Milano . . . 106205
De Carlo, Massimo, Milano . . . 106206
De Carolis, Massimo, Modena 106348, 127728
De Chhitiz, Kathmandu . . . 107581
De Choses en Choses, Reims . . . 067067
De Colellis, Urbano, Torino . . . 128291
De Crescenzo, Roma . . . 076408
De Crescenzo, Antonio, Roma . . . 076409
De, Dis, Ex, London . . . 136206
De Domenico, Luigi, Messina . . . 075559
De Fazio, Indianapolis . . . 116451
De Ferrari, Renata, Genova 075462, 127447
De Filippis, Domenica, Messina . . . 075560

De Goudron, Laura, Napoli 127762
de Havilland, London 113578
De Hörn, Itzehoe 071645
De Iulio, Adolfo, Genova 075463
De Lancastre, Sebastião, Lisboa . . 079913
De Land Museum of Art, De Land . . 043332
De Lee, Seoul 107219
De Locht - Streekmuseum, Nationaal Asperge- en Champignonmuseum, Horst 029776
De los Viejos Colonos, Bariloche . . . 000134
De Luca, Adele, Roma 076410
De Lullo, Maurizio, Roma 106516
De Marchi, Giuliano, Venezia 128386
De Martini, Cagliari 075205, 140007
De Martini, G. & C., Cagliari 075206
De Martino, Mario, Napoli 127763
De Matteis, Ciro, Napoli 127764
De Matteo, Rosella, Milano 075691
De Mets, Bruxelles 123586
De Mon Temps, Chavanay 062258
De Mores State Historic Site, Bismarck 042237
De Morgan Centre, London 040131
De Palma, Vincenzo, Roma 128007
De Pasquale, Germano, Bologna . . 127143
De Paz, Elisabetta, Livorno 075530
De Pers Koch, Antwerpen 123547
De Piccoli, Claudia, Milano 127578
De Pillis, Alberto, Roma 128008
De Renzo, Raffaele, Napoli 075965
De Rosa, R., Milano 121704
De Ruvo, Franco, Milano 127579
De Salvo, Romolo, Milano 075692
De Sanctis, Sergio, Roma 076411
De Santis, Taranto 128247
De Santis, Fabrizio, Roma 128009
De Santis, Giuseppe, Torino 128292
De Siena, Valter, Roma 128010
De-sign-au, Signau 111904
De Simone, Alessandro, Roma 076412
De Simone, Antonino, Roma 128011
De Smet Depot Museum, De Smet . 043337
De Stefani, Antonio, Genova 075464
De Tudo um Pouco, Porto Alegre . . 058499
De Valera Library and Museum, Ennis 022784
De Venere, Maria Gabriella, Catania 075245
De Vera, San Francisco 119651
De Vera, San Francisco 119652
De Vere, Woodhall Spa 114729
De Witt, Hobart 055992
De Witte Raaf/ The White Raven, Bruxelles 135595
Déa, Paris 100191
Dea, Sofia 096726
DeA-Verlag, Gumpoldskirchen 133084
Deadwax, Chicago 088072
Deaf Smith County Museum, Hereford 044517
Deakin, Montréal 058945
Deakin, Karen, Sydney 056672
Deal Archaeological Collection, Deal 039216
Deal Castle, Deal 039217
Deal Maritime and Local History Museum, Deal 039218
Dealer's Choice, Saint Louis 092220
Dealer's Choice Antiques, Nashville 090442, 122975
Dealers Den, New York 090810
Dean, Minneapolis 117250
Dean, Jeffrey, Philadelphia 091627
Dean Andree, M., New York 117828
Dean Castle, Kilmarnock 039869
The Dean Clough Galleries, Halifax . 039660
Dean Gallery, Edinburgh 039384
Dean Heritage Museum, Soudley . . 041044
Dean Street Antiques, Albury 055329
Deann, Milwaukee 117180
Deans, Thomas, Atlanta 114870
Dean's Antiques, Spalding 086674
Dearborn Historical Museum, Dearborn 043342
Dearing, Tyrone, Woollahra 056863
Deartre, Bologna 127144
Dease, Al, San Diego 092629
Death Valley National Park Visitor Center and Museum, Death Valley 043345
Deaucourt, Pascal, Marseille 124406
Deauville Auction, Deauville 120985
Debaigts, Jacques, Paris 100192
Deballage Antiquités Brocante, Albi-le-Séquestre 093657
Débard, André, Périgny 066719
Debard, Philippe, Mazet-Saint-Voy . 064451
Débarras Bretons, Lorient 064003
Débarras d'Armor, Saint-Vran 068041
Débarras de l'Ouest, Lorient 064004
Debat, Alain, Orthez 065311
El Debate, Buenos Aires 136712
Débatisse, Jean-Pierre, Riorges . . . 067150
Debbas, Viviane, Beirut 077390
Debbia, Roma 076413
Debden Antiques, Debden 084147
Debelleyme, Paris 100193
Debély, Michel, Neuchâtel 082690
Debenham Antiques, Debenham . . 084149
Debeyne, A., Kortrijk 058260
Debladis, Paris 124639
Deblitz, Barbara, Duisburg 102577
DeBolt and District Pioneer Museum, DeBolt 005336
Debonnaire, Philippe, Bernay-Vilbert 061370
Debony, Singapore 109789
Debord, Claudette, Dignac 062631
Debord, Véronique, Tauriac 124951
Debosu, Tokyo 140184
Deboulle, I., Bruxelles 057907
Debras-Bical, Bruxelles 096178
Debray, M., Coignières 062390
Debruille, Luc, Paris 065800
Debs & Co., New York 117829
Dębski, Tadeusz, Warszawa 109110
Deburaux, Patrick, Paris 121137
Debus, Münzenberg 104380
Debusmann, Antje-Kathrin, Solingen 126812
Debutrie, Hugues de la, Marnay . . . 064294
Decade Antiques, Wallasey 087001
Decades Antique Shop, Strovolos . . 059967
Decades Antiques, Canning Vale . . 055622
Decades Collectables, Hamilton . . . 058850
Décades et Lustres, Cruseilles 062578
Décalage, Paris 065801
Decamp, François, Marseille 064347
Décapage de la Maye, Crécy-en-Ponthieu 062551
Décapage Gil, Strasbourg 124944
Décap'Services, Mordelles 064786
Decárdenas, Gijón 081124
Decarlo, Houston 116305
Decatur House Museum, Washington 048895
Decaux, Marc, Vandrimare 068710
Au Décervelé, Caluire-et-Cuire 138062
Deceuninck, Nathalie, Saint-Omer . 067691
Dechamby Horowicz, Caroline, Crans-sur-Sierre 111374
Decharneux, B., Bruxelles 057908
Dechavanne, Muriel, Paris 065802
DeChene, Gene, Los Angeles 142504
Decillo, New York 090811
Decina, Giovanni, Napoli 075966
Deck the Walls, Atlanta 114871
Deck the Walls, Austin 114973
Deck the Walls, Austin 114974
Deck the Walls, Austin 114975
Deck the Walls, Birmingham 115103
Deck the Walls, Cincinnati 115623
Deck the Walls, Fort Worth 116139
Deck the Walls, Houston 116306
Deck the Walls, Jacksonville 116516
Deck the Walls, Jacksonville 116517
Deck the Walls, Louisville 116936
Deck the Walls, Louisville 116937
Deck the Walls, Minneapolis 117251
Deck the Walls, Omaha 118688
Deck the Walls, Pittsburgh 118914
Deck the Walls, Richmond 119108
Deck the Walls, San Antonio 119407
Deck the Walls, San Antonio 119408
Deck the Walls, San Antonio 119409
Deck the Walls, Tampa 120039
Deck the Walls, Tucson 120120
Deck the Walls, Tulsa 120192
Decker, Dr. Bernhard, Frankfurt am Main 070733
Decker, Friedrich, Dresden 125486
Decker, Mike, Luxembourg 077478, 128470
Decker, Rolf, Schwarzheide 126789
Decker, S., Achern 069108
Decker, S. & M., Rheinau 073513
Decker-Heftler, Sylviane de, Paris . 100194
Decker-Lehwald, W., Olpe 073217
Decker-Lehwald & Lehwald, Olpe . . 073218
Decker, Meyerhoff and Pinkard Galleries, Maryland Institute, College of Art, Baltimore 041978
Deckers & Patzer, Berlin 138765
Deckert, Inge & Bernd, Düsseldorf . 070370
Deckmann, Wolfgang, Forchheim, Oberfranken 070715
Deckmann, Wolfgang, München . . . 072682
Declare, Indianapolis 089288
Declerck, Patrick, Douai 120991
Déclic, Luxembourg 107395
Déclic, Luxembourg 107396
Deco, Knokke-Heist 058242
Decó, Verona 077001
Deco 2 Moderne, Saint Louis 092221
Deco 2000, New York 090812
Déco 3003, Cogolin 062383
Deco Art, Dublin 074907
Deco Arte, Cali 098229
Déco Chatelet, Montluçon 064708
Deco Creations, Chicago 115401
Déco-d'Antan, Ars-en-Ré 060994
Deco Days, Vancouver 059352
Déco Deligths, Asnières-sur-Seine . 061009
Deco Deluxe, New York 090813
Deco Design, Stockholm 081939
Deco Etc ., New York 090814
Déco-In, Cosne-Cours-sur-Loire . . . 062489
Deco Jewels, New York 090815
Deco Lighting, New York 090816
Déco Saint-Georges, Paris 065803
Déco Silence, Quimper 067016
Decodence, Christchurch 079024
Decodence, San Francisco 092770
Decodream, Coulsdon 084086
Decollectables, Ranfurly 079227
Decolov, Amsterdam 077824
Decolux Comercio, Fortaleza 096519
Decomania, Milano 075693
Deconinck, Aalst 057660
Decor, Cleveland 136443
Décor, Miami 090165
Decor, Roma 076414
Decor, Pia & Roger, Bellinzona 082189
Le Décor Antic, Bussac 061840
Décor Antic, Perpignan 066741
Decor Art, Dallas 115868
Decor Art Gallery, New York 117830
Decor Art Gallery, New York 117831
Decor Art Gallery, New York 117832
Decor Art Gallery, New York 117833
Decor Art Gallery, New York 117834
Decor Delights, Calgary 096805
Décor et Tradition, Cavaillon 062043
Decor Expo Atlanta, Atlanta 093983
Decor Expo California, Palm Springs 093984
Décor Mobilier, Nice 124507
Decor Splendid, New Orleans 090543
Decora, Wien 057397
Decorables and Antiques, Denver . . 088675
Decoración Gallery, Santiago de Chile 059519
La Decoradora, Alicante 080761
Décorah, Ambilly 060794
Decorama Casa Ciseri, Ronco sopra Ascona 082751
Decorantigo, Porto 080078
Décorantique, Saint-Orens-de-Gameville 067693
Décorantiques, Toulouse 068502
Decorart, Fortaleza 058470
Decorarte, Genova 127448
Decorarte, Rio de Janeiro 058579
Decorasia, Los Angeles 116751
Decoration Homewares, Singapore . 080454
Decorativa, Amsterdam 077825
Decorative and Fine Arts, Oostende 058360
Decorative Antiques, Bishop's Castle 083541
Decorative Antiques, London 085250
Decorative Antiques and Textiles Fair, London 093922
Decorative Arts Center of Ohio, Lancaster 045140
Decorative Arts Museum of Rhodos, Rhodos 021452
Decorative Arts Society, Woodbridge 054351
Decorative Arts Society 1850 to the Present. Journal, Woodbridge 136207
Decorative Arts Society Newsletter, Washington 136444
Decorative Expressions, Atlanta . . . 114872
The Decorative Painter, Wichita . . . 136445
Decorator Source, Tetbury 086853
DeCordova Museum and Sculpture Park, Lincoln 045297
Decoremos Anticuario, Cali 059881
Decorglaz 2000, Madrid 110479
Decoritalia, Prato 127889
Decoro, Chicago 088073
Decoro, Chicago 088074
Decors II, Deal 084143
Decorum, Buffalo 087872
Décorum, Chevanceaux 062281
Decorum, San Francisco 092771
Decorum, Toronto 059172
Decostand, Mandelieu-La Napoule . 099631
Decotiques Antique Refinishing, San Francisco 132878
Decourcelles, Langres 063523
La Découverte, Nantes . . . 099807, 124481
Découvertes Antiquités, Paray-le-Monial 065336
Découvertes Nomades, Marseille . . 064348
Decruyenaere, L., Gent 058178
Decumanus, Napoli 127765
Dedalus, Madrid 141034
Deddington Antique Centre, Deddington 084154
Dede, Roula, Thessaloniki 074636
Dedeystere, P., Sint-Niklaas 058371
Dedham Historical Museum, Dedham 043359
Dedinje, Beograd 080395
Dedry, F., Liège 058293
Dee, Broken Hill 094303
Dee, Raceview 137067
Dee, Atkinson & Harrison, Driffield . 122292
Dee-Jay, Saint Louis 092222
Dee Why Books, Warriewood 137131
Deele, Fröndenberg 070903
Deele, Isernhagen 071638
Deele, Münster 072899
Deeler, Vancouver 059353
Deelers, Vancouver 059354
Deemer, B., Louisville 116938
Deene, R., Gent 137495
Deep Art Gallery, Pune 105825
Deep Sea Adventure and Diving Museum, Weymouth 041356
Deep Water Shark Gallery, Tinonee 095338
Deepe, W., Beckeln 069500
Deepgroove-Antiquariat, Freilassing 139124
Deer Isle-Stonington Historical Society Museum, Deer Isle 043362
Deerberg, Ralf, Minden, Westfalen . 126319
Deere Museum, Moline 045958
Deerfield, Oakland 091414

Deerfield Beach Historical Society Museum, Deerfield Beach 043370
Deerstalker Antiques, Whitchurch, Buckinghamshire 087131
Dee's Antique, Windsor 087181
Deeside Books, Berkhamsted 141408
Defachelle, Michel, Les Attaques . . 063756
Defence Services Museum, Adelaide 000704
Defence Services Museum, Yangon 029075
Défense d'Afficher, Paris 100195
Defeo, L.B., Dordrecht 078299
Defet, Hansfried, Nürnberg 104475
Deffarges, Montvert 064783
Defiance Gallery, Newtown, New South Wales 094955
Defina, Ennio, Venezia 128387
DeFinis, Kevin J., Philadelphia 091628
Definition Press, New York 135423
Défis, Paris 100196, 133560
Defo Gallery, Toronto 097253
Defrawi, Cairo 060436
Defrocourt, Cathy, Bresles 061759
Defuns, Gioni, Trun 111950
Degas Pastel Society, Madisonville . 054740
Degen, Ch., Hollfeld 071564
Degenaar, Amsterdam 077826
Degener, Lilo, Hannover 071391
Degener, Rolf M., Meerbusch 139467
Degenfeld, Regina von, Waibstadt . 074242
Degenhardt, Axel, Bremen 102236
Degenhardt, Gertrude, Mainz 134179
Degenhart, J., Memmingen 072513
Degenhart Paperweight and Glass Museum, Cambridge 042571
Degens, Rotterdam 078712
Degeorge, Charles, Le Boulou 124292
Degheldere, Willy, Brugge 137415
Degioanni, Léopold, Villeurbanne . . 068955
Degkwitz, Prof. Hermann, Hohenfelde 134063
Degli Esposti, Prof. Paola, Bologna . 127145
Deglise, Nicolas, Paris 124640
Degrange, Philippe, Charlieu 062161
Degrazia Gallery in the Sun, Tucson 048632
Degrémont, Madeleine, Clamecy . . 062320
Degrugillier, Hélène, Lagnes 063485
Degutsch, Holger, Stuttgart 139757
Degwitz, Uelzen 074136
Dehaan, Bankstown 094213
Dehennin, Guy, Cotignac 062492
Dehler, Remlingen 073487
Dehner, Georg jun., Bachhagel 069252
Dehoogh, Philadelphia 091629
Deià Museo Arqueológico, Deià . . . 035143
Deichsel, Eckehard, Lemgo 126205
Deichtorhallen Hamburg, Hamburg . 017683
Deicke, U., Süderholz 074019
Deike, Horst, Konstanz 134129
Deile, Bodo & Regina, Dresden 070310
Deiller-Ducatel, Dijon 124219
Deillon & Cie., Daniel, Lausanne . . .082542, 122329
Deillon, Robert, Villeneuve (Vaud) . . 082891
Deilmann, Dietrich & Maureen, Herdecke 071487
Dein, Jens von, Lüneburg 126246
Deinbacher, Andreas, Sankt Pölten . 137252
Deinert, U. & M., Herzebrock-Clarholz 071499
Deines Cultural Center, Russell 047570
Deinhardt, Weinheim, Bergstraße . . 074316
Deininger, Charlotte, Augsburg 125072
Deir ez-Zor Museum, Deir ez-Zor . . 037831
Deiringsen, Soest 073845, 126811
Deitch, New York 117835
Deja View, Portland 142797
Deja Vu, Bruxelles 057909
Déja Vu, Gouda 078384
Déja Vu, Winnipeg 059455
Déjá vu Antik, Stockholm 081940
Deja Vu Antiques, Leigh-on-Sea . . . 084956
Deja Vu Antiques, Shrewsbury 086601
Deja Vu Books, Hobart 136943
Dejans, P., Kortrijk 058261
Dejbjerg Jernalder, Skjern 009102
Deju Art, Carluke 112817
Dejvická Galerie V. Kramáře, Praha 060121, 098427, 120855
Dejwis Bis, Gdańsk 108876
DeKalb Historical Society Museum, Decatur 043349
Dekanatsmuseum, Haus 002025
Dekema State Portrettengalerij, Jelsum 029794
Deketelaere, Oostende 096396
Dekker, Amsterdam 077827
Dekker & Inkelaar, Amsterdam 128533
Dekking-Knap, Delft 128620
Deko Antik, Schneverdingen 073711
Dekora, Baden 082107
Dekoratīvi Lietišķās Mākslas Muzejs, Rīga 027730
Dekorativnoe Iskusstvo, Moskva . . 136053
Dekorator, Warszawa 079744
Del Bono, Domenico Savio, Napoli . 075967
Del Borgo, Giglio, Roma 076415
Del Cerro Gallery, San Diego 119499
Del Conde, Buenos Aires 136713
Del Mestre, Umberto, Torino 128293
Del Monte, Renzo, Roma 128012
Del Norte County Historical Society Museum, Crescent City 043213
Del Prado, Bucaramanga 098209
Del Recuerdo, Buenos Aires 136714
Del Vecchio, Rossano, Milano 127580
Delacour, Puymirol 067002
Delacour, Jean-Claude, La Palme . . 063401
Delacroix, Jean-Arnauld, Paris 065804
Delacroix, Jean-Paul, Saint-Malo (Ille-et-Vilaine) 067610
Delafontaine, Carouge 111332
Delafosse, Wormhout 069056
Delafoy, Jean-Jacques, Paris 065805
Delage, Philippe, Villeurbanne 068956
Delahaye, Didier, Pleurtuit 066854
Delahaye, Isabelle, Paris 065806
Delahaye, Olivier, Chaumont (Haute-Marne) 062247
Delahenty, Olinda 095005
Delahoche, Gérard, Rémerangles . . 067088
Delaine, Rémi, Dole 062697
Delaive, Amsterdam 107699
Delalande, Paris 065807
Delalande, Dominique, Paris 065808
Delamain, Paris 138346
Delamarche, Thierry, Lecousse . . . 063734
Delamare, David, Portland 118990
Delan, Patrick, Pau 066702
Delaney, Los Angeles 089742
Delannoy, Xavier, La Garde-Freinet . 099397
Delano Heritage Park, Delano 043380
Delarce, Paris 065809
Delarue, Alain, Bordeaux 124120
Delarue, Bruno, Paris 100197
Delarue, Dominique, Excideuil 062831
Delarue-Turcat, Paris 124641
Delaunay, Fabrice, Vitry-le-François 069012
Delaune, Francis, Segré 068193
Delaune, Yves, Saumur 068150
Delaveau, Jean-Marc, Saint-Mammès 067618
Delavenne & Lafarge, Paris 121138
Delaware Agricultural Museum, Dover 043489
Delaware and Hudson Canal Museum, High Falls 044533
Delaware Art Museum, Wilmington 049202
Delaware Art Museum Newsletter, Wilmington 136446
Delaware Market, Tulsa 093298
Delaware Museum, Wilmington . . . 049203
Delaware Museum of Natural History, Wilmington 049204
Delaware State Museums, Dover . . 043490
Delawood, Hunstanton . . . 084767, 141683
Delbarre, Fabien, Lille 063845
Delbondo, Leandri, Montevideo . . . 087314
Delbono, Juan, Montevideo 087315
Delbos, Frédéric, Chaumont (Haute-Marne) 062248, 138074
Delbos, Jacques, Paris 065810
Delbos, Jacques, Paris 065811
Delboy, Francoise, Vezin-le-Coquet 068835
Delbridge Museum, Sioux Falls . . . 048189
Delcampo, Ricardo, Miami 090166
Delclaux, Myriam, Aurillac 061074
Déléage, Michel, Yssingeaux 069066
Deleau, Jacques, Carcassonne 120963
Delecaut, M., Charleroi 058143
Delectable Collectibles, Philadelphia 091630
Delectus Books, London 141777
Delehar, Peter, London 085251
DELEIKA, Dinkelsbühl 070253
Delekovec Local History Collection, Delekovec 007712
DeLeon White, Toronto 097254
Delerive, Antoine, Lille 063846
Deletaille, Emile, Bruxelles 057910
Deleu, Vincent, Antwerpen 057690
Deleuil, Huguette, Marignane 064284, 099638
Delfhavens, Rotterdam 108180
Delfi, Padova 076090
Delfi Form, Zwolle 108280
Delfina, London 040132
Delfino, Thierry, Marseille 124407
Delfitto, Alberto, Milano 127581
Delfitto, Mauro, Milano 127582
Delforge, M.-F., Bruxelles 057911
Delfour, Claude, Clermont-Ferrand . 062337
Delftenco, Bruxelles 057912
Delgados, Bendestorf 069518
Delgatie Castle, Turriff 041246
Delh, Richard, Paris 100198
Delhaye, Thierry, Craponne (Rhône) 062547
Delhi Art Gallery, Delhi 105656
Delhi Ontario Tobacco Museum & Heritage Centre, Delhi 005339
Delic, Čačak 109729
Delicias Galeria, Madrid 110480
Delicias Restauración, Madrid 129606
Delight Hamilton, Seattle 119908
Delignières, Jean-Marc, Sailly-sur-la-Lys 067338
Deligny, Marc, Paris 100199
Delille, Francis, Paris 133561
Délire en Formation, Paris 100200
D'Eliso & Tomè, Trieste 128371
Delitz-Kater, Wilma, Hannover 103270
Delius & Co., Berlin 133760
Delius, Cornelia, Bielefeld 069822
Dell, Baesweiler 069434
Dell, Buffalo 087873, 142262
Dell, Detroit 088759
Dell, Klaus-M., Moers 072581
Dell Mill, Isle-of-Lewis 039825
Dell Publishing, New York 135424
Della Porta, Roberto, Roma 128013
Della Toffola, Mauro, Venezia 076930
Della Valle, Roberto, Roma 076416
Dellacasa, Renata, Torino 076809
Dellachá Vaj, Maria Luisa, Torino . . 076810
Dellacherie, Alain, Bergerac 061359
Dell'Aquila, Alfredo, Torino 128294
Dell'Aria, Ignace, Marseille 064349, 099649
Delle Fave, Roberto, Roma 106517
Dellefant, Klaus, Puchheim 073380
Delley, François & Marina, Nyon . . . 082703
Dellière, Christiane, Bellême 061334
Dello Ioio, Napoli 075968
Dello Ioio, Napoli 075969
Dello Ioio, Napoli 075970
Delloye Thoumyre, Anne-Marie, Châteauroux 124192
Dellus, Jacques, Noirmoutier-en-l'Ile 065219
Dellview, San Antonio 092508
Delmar, Hurst Green 084776
Delmar, Saint Louis 142854
DelMar Gallery, Saskatoon 097192
Delmas, Bruguières 061824
Delmas, Jean, Paris 065812
Delmas, Solange, Paris 138347
Delmelle, D., Liège 123649
Delmon, Manama 057626
Delmon, J F, Toulouse 068503
Delmore Gallery, Alice Springs 094136
Deloach, New York 090817
Delobeau & Guffroy, Amiens 120893
Delomosne & Son, North Wraxall . . 086094
Delon, Michel, Malemort-sur-Corrèze 064235
Delor, Nîmes 065174
Delor, Jean-Pierre, Nîmes 065175
Delor, Jean-Pierre, Nîmes 065176
Deloraine Museum, Deloraine 005341
Delorme, Paris 100201
Delorme, Chantal, Milano 075694
Delorme, Daniele, Paris 100202
Delorme, Francis, Avèze (Sarthe) . . 061123
Delorme, Marc, Saint-Ouen 067762
Delorme, Michel, Eaubonne 062758
Delotte, Alain, Montrouge 064780
Delouche, Olivier, Saint-Malo (Ille-et-Vilaine) 067611
Delozier, D.L., Virginia Beach 133009
Delpani, Luciano, Brescia 075163
Delperie, Adrien, Toulouse 068504
Delpero, Antonio, Genova 075465
Delphi Antiques, Dublin 074908
Delphin Verlag, Köln 134100
Delpierre, Philippe, Paris 065813
Delpire, Paris 133562
Delpla, Eric, Saint-Ouen 067763
Delpuech, Charles, Bonnieux 061564
Delray Beach Historical Society Antiques Show, Delray Beach 093985
Delrey, Rio de Janeiro 058580
Delshan Art Gallery, Armadale, Victoria 094162
Delsing, Gerard, Maastricht 078601
Delta, Paris 100203
Delta, Rotterdam 108181
Delta Antiques, İstanbul 083129
Delta - Arte, Donostia-San Sebastián 110332
Delta Blues Museum, Clarksdale . . 042950
Delta Change, Antibes-Juan-les-Pins 060920
Delta County Historical Society Museum, Escanaba 043726
Delta County Museum, Delta 043384
Delta Cultural Center, Helena 044500
Delta Mill and Old Stone Mill Museum, Delta 005342
Delta Museum, Delta 005343
Delta-Phot, Limoges 099503
Delteil, Montréal 137652
Deluermoz, Martine, Ussel 068664
Delusions of Grandeur, Ottawa 097104
Deluxe Junk, Seattle 092986
Delvaille, Olivier, Paris 065814
Delvaulx, L., Bruxelles 123587
Delvaux, Jean-Marc, Paris 121139
Delvigne, Hervé, Ham 063118
Delvoie, M., Maastricht 078602
Dely, Nice 065070
Delzongle, Jean-Paul, Drugeac . . . 062743
Demago, Maribor 109984, 121978
Demak, Sankt-Peterburg 080302
Deman, Nicolas, Paris 100204
Demarchi, Helene, Vaduz 077452
Demarest, Paris 138348
Demartin, Fleury, Colmar 062408
Demary, Rheinbach 073514
Demazières, Sylviane, Courpière . . 062519
Dembinski & Bittner, Kassel 103509
Demenga, Hansruedi, Basel 111174, 129917
Demers, Columbus 131981
Demes, New York 142647
Demessieur, Thomas, Krefeld 072068, 121486
Demetriades, Maria, Athinai 105393

Demetriades Studio, Lemesos 098311
Demetrios, Richmond 132713
Demetrius, Pittsburgh . . . 091808, 132665
Demetzy, London 141778
Demeulemester, Régis, Matignon . . 064424
La Demeure Antique, Colombe 062422
Demeure des Prémontrés, Pagny-sur-Moselle 065325
La Demeure Médiévale, Beaune . . . 061273
Demeyer, N., Gent 058179
DEMHIST-International Committee for Historic House Museums, Milano . 053752
Demi, Seoul 107220
Demi-Lune, Bruxelles 057913
La Demi-Lune, Saint-Lunaire 067595
Demian, Antwerpen 137397
Demigod, Armadale, Victoria 055368
Demille, Melbourne 056185
Demilliere-Vergnais, Laurent, Lyon . 124353
Demir, Ilmiye, Winterthur 082912
Demirjian, Torkom, New York 117836
Demling, Randersacker 073413
Demmer, A., Karlsruhe 071714
Demmler, Schwerin 134391
Demner, M. & H., Wien 057398
Democratic.Art, Madrid 110481
Démons & Merveilles, Paris 100205
Demontrond, Paul, Dannemarie . . . 099195
Demouron, Christine, Biarritz 061461
Demouron, Rémy, Beaune 061274
Demours Antiquités, Paris 065815
Demouzon, Michel, Barberaz 061200
Dempsey, Jacksonville 116518
Demtröder, Ulla, Dortmund 102393
Demun, Saint Louis 119198
Den Hartogh Ford Museum, Hillegom 029744
Den Of Antiquities, Yarra Glen 056897
Den of Antiquity, Calgary . 058786, 123742
Den of Antiquity, Launceston 056088
Den of Antiquity, Los Angeles 089743
Den of Antiquity, Portland 091927
Denbigh, Vancouver 097454
Denbigh Castle Museum, Denbigh . 039222
Denbigh Museum and Gallery, Denbigh 039223
Denburn Antiques, Aberdeen 083235, 130278
Dene Museum, Fort Good Hope . . . 005459
Denecke, S., Haibach, Unterfranken 125782
Denesle, Christian, Rouen 121238
Deneuve, Marie-Odile, Ancretteville-sur-Mer 060833
Deneux, Herve, Paris 065816
Deng, Seattle 119909
Deng Meiyi Shu Cooperative, Wuxi . 098030
Deng Yuan, Shanghai 097906
Dengel-Galerie, Reutte 002525
Denger, E., Alsheim 069143
Dengis, Marc, Bruxelles 096179
Dengleant, Henry, Lunel-Viel 064029
Dengler, Erik, Esslingen 070659
Denham, Warnham 122737
Dénichoir, Châteauneuf 062199
Denijs, P.A., Den Haag 078187
Denis, Francisco, Montigny-sur-Loing 064698
Denis, Jöel, Condé-sur-Noireau . . . 062449
Denis, Laurence, Caen 061865
Denis Antiques, Montréal 058946
Denise, Roma 076417
Denise, François-Henri, Saint-Jouin-de-Blavou 067553
Denise, Pierre, Yerres 069061
Denise Antiques, Cincinnati 088227
Denise Bibro, New York 117837
Deniset, René, Champagnole 124181
Denison, Toronto 097255
Denison University Art Gallery, Granville 044291
Deniston Cottage Antiques, Bungendore 055584
Deniz Müzesi, İstanbul 038088
Denizli Devlet Güzel Sanatlar Galerisi, Denizli 038046
Denkmalhof Arler, Abtenau 001656
Denkmalhof Gererhof, Annaberg . . 001690
Denkmalhof Kösslerhäusl, Großarl . 001967
Denkmalhof Maurerbauernhof, Zederhaus 003064
Denkmalhof Rauchhaus Möllin, Möllin 018970
Denkmalhof Rauchhaus Mühlgrub, Hof bei Salzburg 002051
Denkmalhof Retschow, Retschow . 019804
Denkmalkomplex Saigerhütte Olbernhau-Grünthal mit Technischem Museum und Kupferhammer, Olbernhau 019463
Die Denkmalpflege, München 135756
DenkStätte Weiße Rose am Lichthof der Universität München, Weiße Rose Stiftung, München 019043
Denman Island Museum, Denman Island 005345
Denmark Historical Museum, Denmark 000978
Denneberg, Johann T., Hamburg . . 071221
Denner, G., Maßbach 072472
Dennerle, Pirmasens 139659
Dennett, Clive, Norwich 086115
Denneweg 33 Antiek, Den Haag . . . 078188
Denning, Guildford 084539
Denning & Son, Ron, Russell 128953
Dennis, Margaret, Beaudesert 094222
Dennis, Richard, Shepton Beauchamp 135304
Dennis, Ruud, Minneapolis 132379, 142580
Dennison Railroad Depot Museum, Dennison 043391
Dennler, Guy, Dulverton 084226
Dennos Museum Center of Northwestern Michigan College, Traverse City . . 048598
Denny Ship Model Experiment Tank, Scottish Maritime Museum, Dumbarton 039293
Denoel, Liège 058294
Denoël, Paris 133563
Denova-Tesar, Olga, Paris 124642
Denoyelle, Pascal, Le Cateau-Cambrésis 063593
Denoyelle, Pascal, Paris 065817
Denoyer, Jean-Pierre, Sourzac 068276
Dental Museum, Edmonton 005392
La Dentellière, Paris 065818
Denter, H., Bad Driburg 101637
Denter, M., Lünen 072362
Denter, Marlies, Lünen 072363
Denton, London 085252
Denton, B., Nashville 090443
Denton, Berenice, Nashville 090444
Denton County Historical Museum, Denton 043394
Denuo-A, Warszawa 109111
Denver Art Dealers Association, Denver 054741
Denver Art Museum, Denver 043404
Denver Book Mall, Denver 142385
Denver Institute of Art Conservation, Denver 132033
Denver Museum of Miniatures, Dolls and Toys, Denver 043405
Denver Museum of Nature and Science, Denver 043406
Denver Woodwrights, Denver 132034
Deny, Bernard & Béatrice, Ervy-le-Chatel 062799
Denys-Artus, Philippe, Bruxelles . . . 057914
Denzil Grant, Bury Saint Edmunds .083822, 130490
Denzinger, Herbert, Neustadt an der Weinstraße 073027, 121561, 126544
Deokpojin Educational Museum, Gimpo 027495
DeOro Galería, Bogotá 098121
Deosugung Art Museum, National Museum of Contemporary Art, Seoul 027548
Depaire, Alain, Sauveterre-de-Guyenne 068158
Dep'Art, Saint-Étienne 101147
Départ Musée Ostréophile, Le Château-d'Oléron 012480
Departamento de Artes Plásticas, Facultad de Artes, Universidad Nacional de Cuyo, Mendoza 049602
Departamento de Bellas Artes, Universidad de Caldas, Manizales 049868
Departamento de Bellas Artes, Universidad de Sonora, Hermosillo 050532
Departamento de Escultura e Historia del Arte, Universidad de Sevilla, Facultad de bellas Artes, Sevilla 050733
Departamento de Historia del Arte, Universidad de Santiago de Compostela, Santiago de Compostela 050732
Departamento de Historia del Arte, Universidad de Valencia, Valencia 050736
Departamento de Historia del Arte Diego Velázquez, Instituto de Historia del CSIC, Madrid 050721
Departamento d'Historia de l'Art, Universidad de Barcelona, Barcelona 050711
Departement Archeologie, Kunstwetenschap en Musicologie, Katholieke Universiteit Leuven, Leuven 049713
Departement Architectuur, Audiovisuele en Beeldende Kunsten, Hogeschool Gent, Gent 049699
Departement Architektuur en Beeldende Kunst, Provinciale Hogeschool Limburg, Hasselt 049704
Departement d'Archéologie et d'Histoire de l'Art, Université Catholique de Louvain, Louvain-la-Neuve 049717
Departement des Arts Plastiques et Sciences de l'Art, Université de Provence, Aix-en-Provence 049930
Département des Arts Visuelles, Université de Moncton, Edmundston 049784
Département des arts visuels, Université de Moncton, Moncton 049797
Département d'Histoire de l'Art, Université de Montréal, Montréal 049799
Département d'Histoire de l'Art et de Musicologie, Université de Genève, Genève 050762
Department Architectuur Sint-Lucas, Gent 049700
Department of Advertising Design & Graphic Arts, The City University of New York, New York City College of Technology, Brooklyn 051041
Department of Applied Art, College of Fine Arts, Triruvananthapuram 050330
Department of Architecture, University of Pennsylvania, Philadelphia 051937
Department of Architecture and Landscape Architecture, North Dakota State University, Fargo 051323
Department of Art, Eugene 051309
Department of Art, Raymond 052013
Department of Art, Albright College, Reading 052014
Department of Art, Alma College, Alma 050888
Department of Art, American River College, Sacramento 052065
Department of Art, American University, Washington 052330
Department of Art, Anna Maria College, Paxton 051920
Department of Art, Appalachian State University, Boone 051006
Department of Art, Arkansas State University, State University 052212
Department of Art, Arkansas Tech University, Russellville 052061
Department of Art, Auburn University, Auburn 050927
Department of Art, Augustana College, Rock Island 052048
Department of Art, Austin Peay State University, Clarksville 051150
Department of Art, Ball State University, Muncie 051765
Department of Art, Barat College, Lake Forest 051573
Department of Art, Bay Path College, Longmeadow 051624
Department of Art, Baylor University, Waco 052316
Department of Art, Bethel College, North Newton 051857
Department of Art, Bethel College, Saint Paul 052086
Department of Art, Biola University, La Mirada 051566
Department of Art, Blackburn College, Carlinville 051077
Department of Art, Bloomsburg University, Bloomsburg 050998
Department of Art, Blue Mountain College, Blue Mountain 051000
Department of Art, Bowdoin College, Brunswick 051049
Department of Art, Brescia University, Owensboro 051907
Department of Art, Brigham Young University, Provo 051997
Department of Art, Brigham Young University Idaho, Rexburg 052018
Department of Art, California State University, Turlock 052282
Department of Art, California State University Bakersfield, Bakersfield 050940
Department of Art, California State University, Fullerton, Fullerton . . . 051365
Department of Art, California State University Northridge, Northridge . 051861
Department of Art, California State University Sacramento, Sacramento 052066
Department of Art, Camden County College, Blackwood 050992
Department of Art, Catholic University of America, Washington 052331
Department of Art, Centenary College of Lousiana, Shreveport 052180
Department of Art, Central Connecticut State University, New Britain 051784
Department of Art, Central Michigan University, Mount Pleasant 051760
Department of Art, Central Oregon Community College, Bend 050968
Department of Art, Central Washington University, Ellensburg 051296
Department of Art, Cheyney University of Pennsylvania, Cheyney 051110
Department of Art, Claflin College, Orangeburg 051894
Department of Art, Clarke College, Dubuque 051271
Department of Art, Cleveland State Community College, Cleveland . . 051160
Department of Art, College of Marin, Kentfield 051549
Department of Art, College of New Jersey, Ewing 051317
Department of Art, College of Notre Dame, Belmont 050965
Department of Art, College of Saint Rose, Albany 050875
Department of Art, College of Santa Fe, Santa Fe 052141
Department of Art, College of the Ozarks, Clarksville 051149
Department of Art, College of the Ozarks, Point Lookout 051968
Department of Art, Colorado College, Colorado Springs 051177
Department of Art, Columbia College, Columbia 051183
Department of Art, Columbia State Community College, Columbia . . . 051186
Department of Art, Community College of Rhode Island, Warwick 052326
Department of Art, Contra Costa Community College, San Pablo 052133
Department of Art, Cornell University, Ithaca 051509
Department of Art, Cumberland College, Williamsburg 052378
Department of Art, Cuyahoga Community College, Cleveland 051157
Department of Art, Dallas Baptist University, Dallas 051222
Department of Art, Davis and Elkins College, Elkins 051295

Department of Art, Del Mar College, Corpus Christi 051203
Department of Art, Delta State University, Cleveland 051154
Department of Art, Denison University, Granville 051406
Department of Art, Eastern Illinois University, Charleston 051093
Department of Art, Eastern New Mexico University, Portales 051972
Department of Art, Eastern Washington University, Cheney 051105
Department of Art, Elizabeth City State University, Elizabeth City 051293
Department of Art, Emporia State University, Emporia 051302
Department of Art, Fisk University, Nashville 051778
Department of Art, Florida State University, Tallahassee 052246
Department of Art, Fort Hays State University, Hays 051453
Department of Art, Frostburg State University, Frostburg 051364
Department of Art, Furman University, Greenville 051422
Department of Art, George Washington University, Washington 052332
Department of Art, Georgia Southern University, Statesboro 052214
Department of Art, Georgian Court College, Lakewood 051579
Department of Art, Grace College, Winona Lake 052394
Department of Art, Greensboro College, Greensboro 051416
Department of Art, Greenville College, Greenville 051419
Department of Art, Grinnell College, Grinnell 051428
Department of Art, Hanover College, Hanover 051440
Department of Art, Hardin-Simmons University, Abilene 050866
Department of Art, Harding University, Searcy 052160
Department of Art, Heidelberg College, Tiffin 052261
Department of Art, Hillsdale College, Hillsdale 051465
Department of Art, Hobart and William Smith Colleges, Geneva 051381
Department of Art, Hollins University, Roanoke 052035
Department of Art, Hood College, Frederick 051357
Department of Art, Houston Baptist College, Houston 051480
Department of Art, Huntingdon College, Montgomery 051745
Department of Art, Idaho State University, Pocatello 051967
Department of Art, Indian Hills Community College, Centerville 051089
Department of Art, Indian Hills Community College, Ottumwa 051904
Department of Art, Indiana State University, Terre Haute 052256
Department of Art, Iowa Central Community College, Fort Dodge 051345
Department of Art, Iowa Lakes Community College, Estherville 051307
Department of Art, Jackson State University, Jackson 051514
Department of Art, Jacksonville University, Jacksonville 051520
Department of Art, John Carroll University, Cleveland 051158
Department of Art, Juniata College, Huntingdon 051485
Department of Art, Kauai Community College, Lihue 051607
Department of Art, La Salle University, Philadelphia 051938
Department of Art, Lafayette College, Easton 051282
Department of Art, Lake Forest College, Lake Forest 051574
Department of Art, Lake Michigan College, Benton Harbor 050970
Department of Art, Lambuth College, Jackson 051516
Department of Art, Lander University, Greenwood 051426
Department of Art, Lenoir Rhyne College, Hickory 051461
Department of Art, Long Beach City College, Long Beach 051623
Department of Art, Louisiana College, Pineville 051951
Department of Art, Macalester College, Saint Paul 052087
Department of Art, Manatee Community College, Bradenton 051022
Department of Art, Marshall University, Huntington 051487
Department of Art, Mercer County Community College, Trenton 052270
Department of Art, Mercyhurst College, Erie 051305
Department of Art, Michigan State University, East Lansing 051279
Department of Art, Middle Georgia College, Cochran 051167
Department of Art, Middle Tennessee State University, Murfreesboro 051767
Department of Art, Middlebury College, Middlebury 051705
Department of Art, Mills College, Oakland 051870
Department of Art, Millsaps College, Jackson 051515
Department of Art, Minot State University, Minot 051727
Department of Art, Mississippi College, Clinton 051163
Department of Art, Missouri Southern State College, Joplin 051537
Department of Art, Monmouth University, West Long Branch 052355
Department of Art, Montgomery College, Rockville 052055
Department of Art, Moorhead State University, Moorhead 051750
Department of Art, Moravian College, Bethlehem 050978
Department of Art, Morgan State University, Baltimore 050945
Department of Art, Mount Holyoke College, South Hadley 052191
Department of Art, Mount Olive College, Mount Olive 051758
Department of Art, Mount Union College, Alliance 050887
Department of Art, Muhlenberg College, Allentown 050886
Department of Art, Murray State University, Murray 051768
Department of Art, Newberry College, Newberry 051840
Department of Art, North Carolina Central University, Durham 051277
Department of Art, North Carolina Wesleyan University, Rocky Mount 052056
Department of Art, North Central College, Naperville 051774
Department of Art, North Dakota State College of Science, Wahpeton . . . 052318
Department of Art, North Florida Community College, Madison 051656
Department of Art, North Iowa Area Community College, Mason City . 051688
Department of Art, Northeast Mississippi Community College, Booneville . . 051007
Department of Art, Northeastern Junior College, Sterling 052217
Department of Art, Northwest Missouri State University, Maryville 051686
Department of Art, Northwestern State University of Lousiana, Natchitoches 051780
Department of Art, Oberlin College, Oberlin 051872
Department of Art, Ohio Dominican College, Columbus 051192
Department of Art, Ohio Northern University, Ada 050867
Department of Art, Ohio State University, Columbus 051193
Department of Art, Oklahoma Baptist University, Shawnee 052174
Department of Art, Oregon State University, Corvallis 051206
Department of Art, Ottawa University, Ottawa 051903
Department of Art, Ouachita Baptist University, Arkadelphia 050909
Department of Art, Our Lady of the Lake University, San Antonio 052105
Department of Art, Palm Beach Community College, Lake Worth 051576
Department of Art, Park College, Parkville 051916
Department of Art, Philadelphia Community College, Philadelphia 051939
Department of Art, Pitzer College, Claremont 051142
Department of Art, Portland State University, Portland 051977
Department of Art, Potomac State College, Keyser 051550
Department of Art, Queen's University, Kingston 049793
Department of Art, Quincy University, Quincy 052003
Department of Art, Randolph-Macon Woman's College, Lynchburg 051648
Department of Art, Reed College, Portland 051978
Department of Art, Regis College, Weston 052362
Department of Art, Rhodes College, Memphis 051690
Department of Art, Riverside Community College, Riverside 052033
Department of Art, Rock Valley College, Rockford 052050
Department of Art, Rollins College, Winter Park 052401
Department of Art, Saint Cloud State University, Saint Cloud 052070
Department of Art, Saint Gregory's College, Shawnee 052175
Department of Art, Saint Louis Community College at Forest Park, Saint Louis 052077
Department of Art, Saint Mary's College, Notre Dame 051864
Department of Art, Saint Xavier University, Chicago 051123
Department of Art, Sarah Lawrence College, New York 051815
Department of Art, Seton Hill College, Greensburg 051418
Department of Art, Skagit Valley College, Mount Vernon 051764
Department of Art, Skidmore College, Saratoga Springs 052149
Department of Art, Smith College, Northampton 051858
Department of Art, Southeast Missouri State University, Cape Girardeau 051075
Department of Art, Southeastern Community College, Whiteville 052366
Department of Art, Southern Arkansas University, Magnolia 051663
Department of Art, Southern College of Seventh-Day Adventists, Collegedale 051175
Department of Art, Southern Connecticut State University, New Haven 051791
Department of Art, Southwest Missouri State Univeristy, Springfield 052209
Department of Art, Springfield College in Illinois, Springfield 052205
Department of Art, State University of New York College at Brockport, Brockport 051032
Department of Art, State University of New York College at Geneseo, Geneseo 051380
Department of Art, State University of New York College at Oneonta, Oneonta 051888
Department of Art, Swarthmore College, Swarthmore 052231
Department of Art, Texas Tech University, Lubbock 051645
Department of Art, Texas Wesleyan University, Fort Worth 051351
Department of Art, Thiel College, Greenville 051421
Department of Art, Towson State University, Towson 052268
Department of Art, Trinity University, San Antonio 052106
Department of Art, Union College, Schenectady 052152
Department of Art, Union University, College of Arts and Sciences, Jackson . . . 051517
Department of Art, University at Buffalo, Buffalo 051055
Department of Art, University of Alabama at Birmingham, Birmingham 050989
Department of Art, University of Alaska Anchorage, Anchorage 050899
Department of Art, University of Alaska Fairbanks, Fairbanks 051319
Department of Art, University of Arizona, Tucson 052278
Department of Art, University of Calgary, Calgary 049778
Department of Art, University of California Los Angeles, Los Angeles 051636
Department of Art, University of California Santa Barbara, Santa Barbara . . . 052137
Department of Art, University of Delaware, Newark 051837
Department of Art, University of Hawaii at Manoa, Honolulu 051473
Department of Art, University of Houston, Houston 051481
Department of Art, University of Kansas, Lawrence 051592
Department of Art, University of Kentucky, Lexington 051602
Department of Art, University of La Verne, La Verne 051567
Department of Art, University of Lowell, Lowell 051644
Department of Art, University of Maine, Orono 051898
Department of Art, University of Maryland, College Park 051172
Department of Art, University of Mississippi, University 052291
Department of Art, University of Montana, Missoula 051730
Department of Art, University of Nebraska, Lincoln 051610
Department of Art, University of Nebraska Kearney, Kearney 051545
Department of Art, University of Nevada Las Vegas, Las Vegas 051588
Department of Art, University of North Alabama, Florence 051338
Department of Art, University of North Carolina at Asheville, Asheville . . 050912
Department of Art, University of North Carolina at Greensboro, Greensboro 051417
Department of Art, University of North Carolina at Pembroke, Pembroke . 051924
Department of Art, University of Northern Iowa, Cedar Falls 051086
Department of Art, University of Rhode Island, Kingston 051552
Department of Art, University of San Diego, San Diego 052115
Department of Art, University of Sioux Falls, Sioux Falls 052187
Department of Art, University of South Carolina, Columbia 051184
Department of Art, University of South Dakota, Vermillion 052308
Department of Art, University of Southern Colorado, Pueblo 051998
Department of Art, University of Tampa, Tampa 052248
Department of Art, University of Tennessee at Chattanooga, Chattanooga . . . 051102
Department of Art, University of Texas of Permian Basin, Odessa 051874
Department of Art, University of Toledo, Toledo 052263
Department of Art, University of Tulsa, Tulsa 052280

Department of Art, University of West Florida, Pensacola 051927
Department of Art, University of Wisconsin, Rice Lake 052019
Department of Art, University of Wisconsin Eau Claire, Eau Claire 051283
Department of Art, University of Wisconsin Madison, Madison 051661
Department of Art, University of Wisconsin Oshkosh, Oshkosh 051900
Department of Art, University of Wisconsin Whitewater, Whitewater 052367
Department of Art, University of Wyoming, Laramie 051585
Department of Art, Utah State University, Logan 051621
Department of Art, Valdosta State University, Valdosta 052300
Department of Art, Wake Forest University, Winston-Salem 052398
Department of Art, Wartburg College, Waverly 052340
Department of Art, Washburn University of Topeka, Topeka 052264
Department of Art, Waubonsee Community College, Sugar Grove 052227
Department of Art, Wayland Baptist University, Plainview 051961
Department of Art, Wayne Community College, Goldsboro 051393
Department of Art, Weatherford College, Weatherford 052345
Department of Art, Wellesley College, Wellesley 052347
Department of Art, Wells College, Aurora 050933
Department of Art, West Texas A & M University, Canyon 051074
Department of Art, Western Carolina University, Cullowhee 051213
Department of Art, Western Michigan University, Kalamazoo 051540
Department of Art, Westminster College, Salt Lake City 052100
Department of Art, Wheaton College, Wheaton 052364
Department of Art, Whittier College, Whittier 052368
Department of Art, Wilberfoce University, Wilberforce 052375
Department of Art, Wilkes University, Wilkes-Barre 052376
Department of Art, Williams Baptist College, Walnut Ridge 052322
Department of Art, Winona State University, Winona 052393
Department of Art, York College of Pennsylvania, York 052412
Department of Art, Young Harris College, Young Harris 052413
Department of Art, Youngstown State University, Youngstown 052414
Department of Art and Archaeology, Princeton University, Princeton . . 051990
Department of Art and Architecture, Lehigh University, Bethlehem 050979
Department of Art and Architecture, Northeastern University, Boston . . 051012
Department of Art and Art Education, Delaware State College, Dover . . 051266
Department of Art and Art Education, Indiana University of Pennsylvania, Indiana 051497
Department of Art and Art History, Adelphi University, Garden City 051377
Department of Art and Art History, Albion College, Albion 050878
Department of Art and Art History, Carleton College, Northfield 051860
Department of Art and Art History, Colgate University, Hamilton 051432
Department of Art and Art History, College of Wooster, Wooster 052404
Department of Art and Art History, DePaul University, Chicago 051124
Department of Art and Art History, Dickinson College, Carlisle 051078
Department of Art and Art History, Duke University, Durham 051278
Department of Art and Art History, Florida Southern College, Lakeland 051577
Department of Art and Art History, George Mason University, Fairfax 051320
Department of Art and Art History, Lawrence University, Appleton 050906
Department of Art and Art History, Maple Woods Community College, Kansas City 051543
Department of Art and Art History, Mary Washington College, Fredericksburg 051358
Department of Art and Art History, Mesa Community College, Mesa 051696
Department of Art and Art History, Oakland University, Rochester 052037
Department of Art and Art History, Pomona College, Claremont 051143
Department of Art and Art History, Scripps College, Claremont 051144
Department of Art and Art History, Sonoma State University, Rohnert Park . . . 052057
Department of Art and Art History, Texas Christian University, Fort Worth . . 051352
Department of Art and Art History, University of Alabama in Huntsville, Huntsville 051489
Department of Art and Art History, University of Connecticut, Storrs 052225
Department of Art and Art History, University of Miami, Coral Gables 051202
Department of Art and Art History, University of Missouri Saint Louis, Saint Louis 052078
Department of Art and Art History, University of Nebraska at Omaha, Omaha . . 051885
Department of Art and Art History, University of New Mexico, Albuquerque 050880
Department of Art and Art History, University of Rochester, Rochester 052044
Department of Art and Art History, University of Saskatchewan, Saskatoon 049814
Department of Art and Art History, University of South Alabama, Mobile 051731
Department of Art and Art History, University of Texas at Austin, Austin 050934
Department of Art and Art History, University of Texas at San Antonio, San Antonio 052107
Department of Art and Art History, University of the Pacific, Stockton 052221
Department of Art and Art History, University of the South, Sewanee 052171
Department of Art and Art History, University of Utah, Salt Lake City 052101
Department of Art and Art History, Wayne State University, Detroit 051258
Department of Art and Art History, Western Maryland College, Westminster . . 052361
Department of Art and Art History, Wright State University, Dayton 051230
Department of Art and Art Professions, New York University, New York 051816
Department of Art and Classics, Troy State University, Troy 052272
Department of Art and Design, Charleston 051096
Department of Art and Design, California Polytechnic State University at San Luis Obispo, San Luis Obispo 052129
Department of Art and Design, California State University Fresno, College of Arts, Fresno 051362
Department of Art and Design, California University of Pennsylvania, California 051060
Department of Art and Design, Converse College, Spartanburg 052198
Department of Art and Design, Crowder College, Neosho 051781
Department of Art and Design, Iowa State University, Ames 050894
Department of Art and Design, Montclair State University, Upper Montclair . 052297
Department of Art and Design, Northern Michigan University, Marquette . . 051681
Department of Art and Design, Oklahoma Christian University, Oklahoma City 051877
Department of Art and Design, Pacific Union College, Angwin 050901
Department of Art and Design, Red Deer College, Red Deer 049810
Department of Art and Design, Saginaw Valley State University, University Center 052293
Department of Art and Design, Schoolcraft College, Livonia 051618
Department of Art and Design, Southern Illinois University at Edwardsville, Edwardsville 051288
Department of Art and Design, Southwest Texas State University, San Marcos 052131
Department of Art and Design, University of Alberta, Edmonton 049783
Department of Art and Design, University of Minnesota Duluth, Duluth 051272
Department of Art and Design, University of Wisconsin Stevens Point, Stevens Point 052219
Department of Art and Design, University of Wisconsin Stout, Menomonie 051693
Department of Art and Design, Vancouver Community College, Vancouver . . 049825
Department of Art and Design, West Nottinghamshire College, Mansfield 050847
Department of Art and Design, Winthrop University, Rock Hill 052047
Department of Art and History, Bucknell University, Lewisburg 051599
Department of Art and Industrial Technology, Western State College of Colorado, Gunnison 051429
Department of Art and Music, Assumption College, Worcester 052406
Department of Art and Photography, Phoenix College, Phoenix 051947
Department of Art and Photography, Queensborough Community College, Bayside 050958
Department of Art & Art History, Stanford University, Stanford 052211
Department of Art, Art History and Design, Andrews University, Berrien Springs 050974
Department of Art, Art History and Design, University of Notre Dame, Notre Dame 051865
Department of Art as Applied to Medicine, Johns Hopkins University, Baltimore 050946
Department of Art, College of Arts and Sciences, Gonzaga University, Spokane 052202
Department of Art, College of Liberal Arts, Drew University, Madison 051657
Department of Art, College of the Arts, University of Southern Mississippi, Hattiesburg 051450
Department of Art, Division of Fine Arts, Malone College, Canton 051072
Department of Art, Division of Fine Arts and Humanities, Dickinson State University, Dickinson 051261
Department of Art History, Carleton University, Ottawa 049808
Department of Art History, Dartmouth College, Hanover 051441
Department of Art History, Northwestern University, Evanston 051312
Department of Art History, Pennsylvania State University, University Park . 052295
Department of Art History, State University of New York at Binghamton, Binghamton 050986
Department of Art History, University, Bratislava 050691
Department of Art History, University of Chicago, Chicago 051125
Department of Art History, University of Maryland, College Park 051173
Department of Art History, University of Minnesota, Minneapolis 051724
Department of Art History, University of Nottingham, Nottingham 050851
Department of Art History, University of Saint Thomas, Saint Paul 052088
Department of Art History, University of Wisconsin Madison, Madison 051662
Department of Art History, Villanova University, Villanova 052312
Department of Art History and Archaeology, New York 051817
Department of Art History and Art, Case Western Reserve University, Cleveland 051159
Department of Art History and Visual Arts, Occidental College, Los Angeles . 051637
Department of Art History & Archaeology Visual Resources Collection, New York 046322
Department of Art History, Barnard College, Columbia University, New York . . 051818
Department of Art History, Visual Art and Theory, University of British Columbia, Vancouver 049826
Department of Art History, Visual Arts and Musicology, University of South Africa, Pretoria 050707
Department of Art, Letters and Social Sciences, Polk Community College, Winter Haven 052400
Department of Art, Music and Philosophy, John Jay College of Criminal Justice, New York 051819
Department of Art Practice, University of California Berkeley, Berkeley 050973
Department of Art, School of Fine and Applied Arts, Howard Payne University, Brownwood 051048
Department of Art, School of the Arts, Pacific Lutheran University, Tacoma 052241
Department of Art Theory and Practice, Northwestern University Evanston, Evanston 051313
Department of Arts, Chadron State College, Chadron 051090
Department of Arts, Goddard College, Plainsfield 051960
Department of Arts, Otero Junior College, La Junta 051565
Department of Arts, Rutgers University Newark, Newark 051838
Department of Arts, Slippery Rock University of Pennsylvania, Slippery Rock 052188
Department of Arts, University of Central Oklahoma, Edmond 051287
Department of Arts, University of Minnesota, Minneapolis 051725
Department of Arts, University of New Hampshire, Durham 051276
Department of Arts and Design, Guangzhou University, Guangzhou 049848
Department of Byzantine Museums, Athinai 053664
Department of Commercial Art, Austin Community College, Austin 050935
Department of Communication and Fine Arts, Lubbock Christian College, Lubbock 051646
Department of Communication Design, Fine Art and Photography, Virginia Western Community College, Roanoke . . . 052036
Department of Communications and Visual Arts, University of North Florida, Jacksonville 051521
Department of Creative Art, Purdue University, Hammond 051435
Department of Creative Arts, Stellenbosch 050709
Department of Creative Arts, Muskegon Community College, Muskegon . . 051769
Department of Creative Arts, Siena College, Loudonville 051641
Department of Design, University of Kansas, Lawrence 051593
Department of Design, Housing and Apparel, University of Minnesota, Saint Paul 052089
Department of Display and Design, Langara College, Vancouver 049827
Department of Expressive Arts, Western New Mexico University, Silver City 052182
Department of Fine and Applied Art, Solano Community College, Suisun City . 052228

Department of Fine and Applied Arts, University of Nigeria, Nsukka 050578
Department of Fine and Communication Art, Coppin State College, Baltimore . 050947
Department of Fine and Performing Arts, Chatham College, Pittsburgh 051956
Department of Fine and Performing Arts, Hampton Institute, Hampton 051437
Department of Fine and Performing Arts, Johnson State College, Johnson . 051532
Department of Fine and Performing Arts, Okaloosa-Walton Community College, Niceville 051847
Department of Fine and Performing Arts, Saint Joseph's University, Philadelphia 051940
Department of Fine and Performing Arts, Spring Hill College, Mobile 051732
Department of Fine Art, Chipola Junior College, Marianna 051676
Department of Fine Art, Columbus State University, Columbus 051187
Department of Fine Art, Sul Ross State University, Alpine 050889
Department of Fine Art, University of Reading, Reading 050855
Department of Fine Art, University of Toronto, Toronto 049817
Department of Fine Art, University of Wisconson Platteville, Platteville . 051962
Department of Fine Art, Washington State University, Pullman 051999
Department of Fine Art, West Virginia Wesleyan College, Buckhannon . . 051052
Department of Fine Arts, Alcorn State University, Lorman 051627
Department of Fine Arts, Amherst College, Amherst 050897
Department of Fine Arts, Arcadia University, Glenside 051389
Department of Fine Arts, Auburn University at Montgomery, Montgomery 051746
Department of Fine Arts, Augusta State University, Augusta 050930
Department of Fine Arts, Baltimore City Community College, Baltimore . . . 050948
Department of Fine Arts, Barry University, Miami 051698
Department of Fine Arts, Berkshire Community College, Pittsfield . . . 051959
Department of Fine Arts, Bethany College, Bethany 050976
Department of Fine Arts, Bowie State University, Bowie 051017
Department of Fine Arts, Brandeis University, Waltham 052323
Department of Fine Arts, Butte Community College, Oroville 051899
Department of Fine Arts, Cabrini College, Radnor 052006
Department of Fine Arts, Catholic University of Puerto Rico, Ponce 050615
Department of Fine Arts, Claremont Graduate School, Claremont 051145
Department of Fine Arts, College of our Lady of the Elms, Chicopee 051134
Department of Fine Arts, College of William and Mary, Williamsburg 052379
Department of Fine Arts, Concordia University, Austin 050936
Department of Fine Arts, Daytona Beach Community College, Daytona Beach 051233
Department of Fine Arts, Delgado College, New Orleans 051799
Department of Fine Arts, Ellsworth Community College, Iowa Falls . . 051506
Department of Fine Arts, Georgetown University, Washington 052333
Department of Fine Arts, Georgia Southwestern State University, Americus 050893
Department of Fine Arts, Glenville State College, Glenville 051390
Department of Fine Arts, Gordon College, Barnesville 050953
Department of Fine Arts, Indiana-Purdue University, Fort Wayne 051350
Department of Fine Arts, Inter American University of Puerto Rico, San German 050616
Department of Fine Arts, John C. Calhoun State Community College, Decatur 051237
Department of Fine Arts, Kirkwood Community College, Cedar Rapids 051088
Department of Fine Arts, Lincoln University, Jefferson City 051528
Department of Fine Arts, Lock Haven University, Lock Haven 051620
Department of Fine Arts, Maryville College, Maryville 051687
Department of Fine Arts, Miami University, Hamilton 051433
Department of Fine Arts, Miles Community College, Miles City 051713
Department of Fine Arts, Mississippi Delta Community College, Moorhead . . 051751
Department of Fine Arts, Mount Allison University, Sackville 049812
Department of Fine Arts, New Mexico Highlands University, Las Vegas . . 051589
Department of Fine Arts, Okanagan University College, Kelowna 049792
Department of Fine Arts, Phillips County Community College, Helena 051455
Department of Fine Arts, Porterville Community College, Porterville . . 051973
Department of Fine Arts, Punjab University, Chandigarh 050294
Department of Fine Arts, Rider University, Lawrenceville 051595
Department of Fine Arts, Rockford College, Rockford 052051
Department of Fine Arts, Saint Anselm College, Manchester 051668
Department of Fine Arts, Saint John's University, Jamaica 051523
Department of Fine Arts, Saint Joseph College, West Hartford 052350
Department of Fine Arts, Saint Lawrence University, Canton 051071
Department of Fine Arts, Saint Mary's University, San Antonio 052108
Department of Fine Arts, Saint Peter's College, Jersey City 051531
Department of Fine Arts, Savannah State University, Savannah 052151
Department of Fine Arts, Spokane Falls Community College, Spokane . . . 052203
Department of Fine Arts, State University of New York College at Potsdam, Potsdam 051981
Department of Fine Arts, Syracuse University, Syracuse 052236
Department of Fine Arts, Texas Southern University, Houston 051482
Department of Fine Arts, Trinity College, Hartford 051447
Department of Fine Arts, University of Colorado at Denver, Denver 051250
Department of Fine Arts, University of Colorado Boulder, Boulder 051016
Department of Fine Arts, University of Hong Kong, Hong Kong 049852
Department of Fine Arts, University of New Haven, West Haven 052352
Department of Fine Arts, University of New Orleans Lake Front, New Orleans . 051800
Department of Fine Arts, University of North Carolina at Wilmington, Wilmington 052386
Department of Fine Arts, University of Pennsylvania, Philadelphia 051941
Department of Fine Arts, University of Pittsburgh at Johnstown, Johnstown 051534
Department of Fine Arts, University of the Free State, Bloemfontein 050693
Department of Fine Arts, Vanderbilt University, Nashville 051779
Department of Fine Arts, Waynesburg College, Waynesburg 052343
Department of Fine Arts, Wiley College, Marshall 051683
Department of Fine Arts, Xavier University of Louisiana, New Orleans 051801
Department of Fine Arts, Allen R. Hite Art Institute, University of Louisville, Louisville 051642
Department of Fine Arts and Design, Louisiana State University at Alexandria, Alexandria 050882
Department of Fine Arts, Art History and Humanities, Hofstra University, Hempstead 051456
Department of Fine Arts Gallery, John C. Calhoun State Community College, Decatur 043347
Department of Fine Arts & Mass Communication, Francis Marion University, Florence 051339
Department of Geological Sciences Collection, London 040133
Department of Graphic Communcations, Pennsylvania College of Technology, Williamsport 052380
Department of Graphic Design, Saint Lawrence College, Kingston 049794
Department of Graphic Design, Woodbury University, Burbank 051057
Department of Historical Manuscripts, Tokyo 027156
Department of History in Art, University of Victoria, Victoria 052748
Department of History of Art, Bryn Mawr College, Bryn Mawr 051050
Department of History of Art, Ohio State University, Columbus 051194
Department of History of Art, Potchefstroom University, Potchefstroom 050705
Department of History of Art, Tokyo University, Tokyo 050482
Department of History of Art, University of Edinburgh, Edinburgh 050811
Department of History of Art, University of Michigan, Ann Arbor 050902
Department of History of Art and Architecture, Brown University, Providence 051994
Department of History of Art and Architecture, Harvard University, Cambridge 051063
Department of History of Art and Architecture, University of Pittsburgh, Pittsburgh 051957
Department of Humanities, Chemeketa Community College, Salem 052094
Department of Interior Design, Mount Royal College, Calgary 049779
Department of Language and Visual Arts, Charleston Southern University, Charleston 051094
Department of Liberal Arts and Sciences, Nihon University, Fujisawa 050450
Department of Oriental Art, Nankai University, Tianjin 049858
Department of Semitic Studies Collection, Leeds 039952
Department of Studio Art and Art History, Hamline University, College of Liberal Arts, Saint Paul 052090
Department of the Arts, Rensselaer Polytechnic Institute, Troy 052274
Department of the History of Art, Cornell University, Ithaca 051510
Department of the History of Art, Johns Hopkins University, Baltimore . . . 050949
Department of the History of Art, Yale University, New Haven 051792
Department of the History of Art and Architecture, Dublin 050343
Department of the Treasury Museum, Washington 048896
Department of Visual and Performing Arts, Colorado Mountain College, Vale . 052301
Department of Visual and Performing Arts, Springfield College, Springfield . . 052207
Department of Visual and Performing Arts, University of Colorado, Colorado Springs 051178
Department of Visual Art, Holyoke Community College, Holyoke 051471
Department of Visual Art, Interlochen Arts Academy, Interlochen 051503
Department of Visual Art, Sun Valley Center for the Arts, Sun Valley 052229
Department of Visual Arts, Worcester 052407
Department of Visual Arts, Adams State College, Alamosa 050873
Department of Visual Arts, Asbury College, Wilmore 052388
Department of Visual Arts, California State University San Bernardino, San Bernardino 052113
Department of Visual Arts, Casper College, Casper 051081
Department of Visual Arts, Chowan College, Murfreesboro 051766
Department of Visual Arts, Dowling College, Oakdale 051866
Department of Visual Arts, Dutchess Community College, Poughkeepsie 051983
Department of Visual Arts, Gettysburg College, Gettysburg 051384
Department of Visual Arts, Lakehead University, Thunder Bay 049816
Department of Visual Arts, Loyola University of New Orleans, New Orleans . . . 051802
Department of Visual Arts, McNeese State University, Lake Charles 051571
Department of Visual Arts, Otterbein College, Westerville 052358
Department of Visual Arts, Pensacola Junuior College, Pensacola 051928
Department of Visual Arts, Southeastern Louisana University, Hammond . . 051436
Department of Visual Arts, Texas Lutheran College, Seguin 052169
Department of Visual Arts, Texas Woman's University, Denton 051246
Department of Visual Arts, Ulster County Community College, Stone Ridge . 052223
Department of Visual Arts, University of Dayton, Dayton 051231
Department of Visual Arts, University of North Carolina at Charlotte, Charlotte 051098
Department of Visual Arts, University of Northern Colorado, Greeley 051408
Department of Visual Arts, University of Regina, Regina 049811
Department of Visual Arts, University of Victoria, Victoria 049830
Department of Visual Arts, Weber State College, Ogden 051875
Department of Visual Arts, Yakima Valley Community College, Yakima 052408
Department of Visual Arts, York University, North York 049806
Department of Visual Arts and Humanities, Florida A & M University, Tallahassee 052247
Department of Visual Arts and New Media, State University College at Fredonia, Fredonia 051359
Department of Visual Arts and Technology, San Antonio College, San Antonio 052109
Department of Zoology Museum, Kampala 038216
Departmento de Historia de Arte, Universidad de Murcia, Murcia . . 050729
Departmento de Historia del Arte, Universidad de la Laguna, La Laguna 050718
Departments of Art and Architecture, Pennsylvania State University at New Kensington, New Kensington 051795
Departure Lounge, Burleigh Heads . 094331
DePaul University Art Gallery, Chicago 042839
DePauw University Anthropology Museum, Greencastle 044317
DePauw University Art Center, Greencastle 044318
Depecker, Bernard, Hazebrouck . . . 063140
Depejeteme, Mount Druitt 056279
Depelmann, Langenhagen 103835, 134141
Depen d'Ans, Den Haag 078189
Deperte, Pancrazio, Torino 128295
Dephi Antiques, Montréal 058947
Depieds-Pariente, Paris 065819
D'Epoca, Bologna 075070
D'Epoca di Balmelli, Lugano 082594

Depoid, Henry, Concarneau 099164
Depósito del Automóvil, La Habana 007945
Le Depot, Bruxelles 137433
't Depôt, Maastricht 078603
Depot and Atelier, İstanbul 083130
Dépôt Archéologique, Saint-Thibéry 014553
Dépôt Archéologique du Fort Vauban, Alès 010329
The Depot Arts Space, Auckland . . 108310
Dépot Broc, Béziers 061436
Dépôt de Fouilles Archéologiques, Mailhac 012849
Dépôt de Fouilles Gallo-Romaines et Préhistoriques de Montmaurin, Montmaurin 013185
Dépôt de Jadis, Montargis 064621
Dépôt des Artistes, Levallois-Perret 099479
Dépôt des Equipages, Le Conquet . 063606
Dépot des Islettes, Les Islettes 063768
Dépot du Château, Vincennes 068994
Dépôt-Musée Diocésain, Metz 013040
Depot Museum and Fort Sedgwick Museum, Julesburg 044884
Depot Museum Complex, Condon . . 043127
The Depot Museum Complex, Henderson 044511
Depot Museum of the Mammoth Spring State Park, Mammoth Spring 045611
Depot on Chapel, Windsor, Victoria . 056831
Depot Park Museum, Sonoma 048222
Dépôt Richelieu, Rueil-Malmaison . 067320
Depot Square, Cincinnati 115624
Depot Street Antiques, Columbus . . 088402
Dépôt-Vente, Tarare 068356
Dépot Vente Casino, Hautmont 063136
Dépôt Vente de Coutances, Coutances 062533
Dépot Vente de la Vallée, Chevreuse 062286
Dépôt Vente de Niort, Niort 065194
Dépôt Vente de Paris, Paris 065820
Dépot-Vente du 9ème, Paris 065821
Dépôt Vente du Particulier, Mondeville 064595
Dépôt Vente du Particulier, Paris . . . 065822
Dépôt-Vente la Fouine, Montargis . 064622
Dépot Vente la Réserve, Nîmes . . . 065177
Dépôt Vente Particuliers, Valence (Drôme) 068686
Deppe, Mary, Hannover 071392
Depping, Münster 126495
Deppisch, Wolfgang, Würzburg 074494
Deppner, Market Drayton 085934
Depreciation Lands Museum, Allison Park 041664
DePree Art Center and Gallery, Holland 044572
DePree Art Center & Gallery, Hope College, Holland 051469
Depression Era, Saint Paul 092357
Depression Modern, New York 090818
Depretz, Bernard, Paris . . 100206, 121140
Depretz, Bernard, Paris 124643
Depth of Field, Minneapolis 090353
Depuydt, L., Bruxelles 123588
Deramo, Donald, Pittsburgh 091809
D'Eramo, Walter, Firenze 075327
D'Erasmo, Antonio, Bari 075014
D'Erasmo, Antonio, Bari 075015
Derby, Zürich . . . 082957, 112059, 135085, 141331
Derby Arts, Derby 055750
Derby-Beebe Summer House, Peabody Essex Museum, Salem 047736
Derby City Antique Mall, Louisville . 089975
Derby Industrial Museum, Derby . . 039224
Derby Museum and Art Gallery, Derby 039225
Derby Park Traders Circle, Louisville 089976
Derbylius, Milano 106207
Derbyshire Antiques, Harrogate . . . 084572
Derbyshire Clocks, Glossop 084476, 130731
D'Ercole, Renato, Trieste 128372
Derenzi, Castello de la Plana 110303
Deres, Uwe, Essen 070624
Derhaag, S.H., Maastricht 078604
Déri Múzeum, Debrecen 021709
DeRicci Gallery, Madison 045588
Derigny & Sanson, La Baule-Escoublac 121020
Derigny & Sanson, Saint-Nazaire (Loire-Atlantique) 121249
Dering-Schunk, Elisabeth, Aschaffenburg 101597
Derissi, Chiraz 105843
Derix, Wilhelm, Düsseldorf 125527
Derka, Igor, Bratislava 080603
Derks, Steven, Tucson 120121
Derksen, Arnhem 078049, 121782
Dernier Quartier Général de Napoléon, Genappe 003446
Deroche, San Francisco . . 092772, 123104
Derom, Patrick, Bruxelles 096180
Derouard, Michel & Jacqueline, Antoigné 060931
Derouet, Wolfgang, Timmersiek . . . 074063
Deroussent, Michel, Paris 138349
Deroyan, Armand, Paris . . 065823, 124644
Derrey, Jérémie, Louviers 064018
Derribos Sales, Castello de la Plana 081038
Derrière la Porte, Paris 065824
Derrière la porte, Toulon (Var) 068449
Derrière les Fagots, Clermont-Ferrand 062338
Derrive, Nicole, Hyères 063192
Derry, Benjamin, Paris 100207
Derrymore House, Bessbrook 038687
Derrynane House, Caherdaniel 022698
Dersigny, Patrice, Amiens 124069
Derstroff, Monika M., Oestrich-Winkel 104524
Dert, Martie, Hilversum 128719
Derveaux, Pierre, Aubertin 133452
Derventio, Derby 141552
Dervieux, Denis, Paris 065825
Dervieux, Ferdinand, Avignon 061132
Dervieux, Frédéric, Arles 060971
Dervish, Bellingen 094236
Dervish Pasha Mansion Ethnographical Museum, Lefkoşa 008254
Derwentside Antiques, Belper 083484
Deržavnyj Istoriko-kul'turnyj Zapovidnyk, Kam'janec'-Podil's'kyj 038275
Deržavnyj Istoryko-kul'turnyj Zapovidnyk Pole Poltavskoï Bytvy, Poltava . . . 038376
Deržavnyj Muzej Knigi i Drukarstva Ukraïny, Kyïv 038293
Deržavnyj Muzej Teatral'noho, Muzyčnoho ta Kinomystectva Ukraïny, Kyïv . . 038294
Deržavnyj Muzej Ukraïns'koho Narodnoho Dekorativnoho Mystectva, Kyïv . . 038295
Derzon, David, Milwaukee 090290
Derzypolsky, Dijon 062653
Des 3 Vallées, Saint-Pierre-d'Albigny 067952
Des 4 Moulins, Vallet 068700
Des Lee, Saint Louis 119199
Des Moines Art Center, Des Moines 043424
Des Plaines Historical Museum, Des Plaines 043432
Des Présents du Passé, Courtenay . 062523
Desa, Gdynia 079593, 108908
Desa, Kraków 079628
Desa, Kraków 079629
Desa, Kraków 079630
Desa, Kraków 079631
Desa, Kraków 079632
Desa, Kraków 121890
Desa, Sopot 079707, 109071
Desa Krajowa, Poznań 109045
Desa Unicum, Warszawa 079745
Desa Unicum, Warszawa . 079746, 121903
Desa Unicum Galeria Koszykowa, Warszawa 079747, 109112
Desa Unicum Galeria Staromiejska, Warszawa 079748, 140784
Desa Unicum Galerie Nowy Świat, Warszawa 079749
Desa Unicum Galerie Willa Struvego, Warszawa 079750
Desart, Alice Springs 055337
Desaute, Sylvie, Pont-à-Mousson . . 066907
Desbois, Christian, Paris . 100208, 133564
Desbordes, Jean-Pierre, Huisseau-en-Beauce 063182
Desbrisay Museum and Exhibition Centre, Bridgewater 005150
Descamps, Paris 065826
Descamps, C., Mons 058339
Descamps, Claire, Toulon (Var) 068450
Descant, Toronto 135632
Descarsin, Brienon-sur-Armancon . 099035
Descateaux, Juany, La Rochelle . . . 063429
Desch-Drexler, Pinkafeld 137239
Deschamps, Barcelona . . 080840, 110138
Deschamps, Alain, Theminettes . . . 068382
Deschamps, Jean-Pierre, Montreuil-Bellay 064765
Deschamps, Philippe, Paris 065827
Deschamps, Pierre, Gisors 063006
Deschamps, Sylvie, Harquency . . . 063131
Deschler, Marcus, Berlin 101836
Deschler, Maximilian, München . . . 072683
Deschner, Chemnitz 138962
Deschutes County Historical Society Museum, Bend 042139
Descombes, Genève 141247
Descotis, Pierre-Marie, Vendôme . . 068758
Descours, Michel, Lyon . . 064117, 099552
Descours, Michel, Lyon 138144
Descours, Thierry, Nice 065071
Descubre Museo Interactivo de Ciencia y Tecnología, Aguascalientes 028085
Désert Aride, Saulieu 068143
Desert Art Distributors, Norwood . . 056387
Desert Art Shop, Kalgoorlie 094672
Desert Artisans Gallery, Tucson . . . 120122
Desert Caballeros Western Museum, Wickenburg 049168
Desertina, Chur 135004
Desgans, Patrick, Villegouge 125025
Desha County Museum, Dumas . . . 043525
Desideri, Roma 076418, 128014
Design, Edmonton 096873
Design 18, New York 090819
Design 70, Nice 065072
Design and Art in Greece, Athinai . . 135835
Design and Artists Copyright Society, London 054352
Design & Arts College of New Zealand, Christchurch 050573
Design Austria, Wien 052526
Design Avenue, Almere 077738
The Design Center at Philadelphia University, Philadelphia 046934
Design Center Stuttgart des Landesgewerbeamtes Baden-Württemberg, Stuttgart 020346
Design Centrum České Republiky, Brno 008282
Design Circus Gallery, Jacksonville 116519
Design Connections, Oakland 118630
Design Consortium, Cincinnati 115625
Design Consultancies: Business Ratio Plus, Hampton 136208
Design Council, London 054353
Design de Museu, Rio de Janeiro . . 123703
Design Factory, Oundle 114198
Design Galeria, Wrocław 109214
Design Gallery 1850-1950, Westerham 087097, 131670
Design History Society, Eynsham . . 054354
Design Images, San Francisco 119653
Design in Mind, Chicago 088075
Design Issues, Pittsburgh 136447
Design & Kunst, Dresden 102425
Design Modern, Los Angeles 089744
The Design Museum, Cape Town . . 034577
Design Museum, London 040134
Design Museum Gent, Gent 003452
Design Network Switzerland, Zürich 054178
Design Shop, Louisville 089977
Design Škola Zlín, Vysoká Škola Uměleckoprůmyslová v Praze, Zlín 049896
Design Utopia, Los Angeles 089745
Design Week Action Pack, London . 136209
Design Zentrum Bremen, Bremen . . 102237
Designarts, Chicago 115402
Designated Hatter, Detroit 088760
Designer Antique, Houston 132115
Designer Antiques, Atlanta 087466
Designer Cargo Furniture, Los Angeles 089746
Designer Renaissance, Nashville . . 090445
Designerinnen-Forum e.V., Hamburg 053119
Designers Craft, Tucson 093223
Designers Furniture and Finishing, Pittsburgh 091810, 132666
Designer's Rugs, Los Angeles 089747
Designing Block, Saint Louis 092223
Designmuseo, Helsinki 009518
Designs by Kathryn, Calgary 096806
Designs in Gold, Saint Louis 092224
Designs in Pine, Los Angeles 089748
Designs in Pine, Los Angeles 089749, 132250
Designs UK, Bristol 112721
Designsammlung, Museum für Gestaltung Zürich, Zürich 037765
Designscape Gallerie, Mumbai 105765
Désilets, Pierre, Caen 061866
Desjardins, Claude, Montréal 096991
Desk Doctor, Norfolk 132554
Desloubières, Jean-Marc, Paris . . .065828, 124645
Desmazes, Pézenas 066801
Desmettre, Nadir, Peronne 066728
Desmeules, Jean-François, Pully . . 082732
Desmeules, Jean-Pierre, Genève . . 082419
Desmond Castle, Kinsale 022815
Desmontils, Guy, Vitré 069009
Desmoulin at the Granary, Newbury 114115
Desnoues, Bruno, Paris 124646
Desnoues, Jacques, Bagnolet 061170
Desormeaux, Fort-de-France 140244
Desoto National Memorial, Bradenton 042378
Despalles, Mainz 134180
Despard, Hobart 094640
Desparrain, Christian, Clermont-Ferrand 062339
Despesel, Port-à-Binson 066954
Despesel, Jean, Binson-et-Orquigny 061492
Desprairies, Monique, Saint-Ouen . 067764
Desroches, Bernard, Montréal 096992
Desroches, Brigitte, Montréal 096993
Desroches, Françoise, Paris 124647
Desrues, Gérard, Mont-Dol 064612, 124448
Dessain et Tolra, Paris 133565
Dessapt Editions, Viry-Chatillon . . .101486, 133708
Dessarzin, Jean-Daniel, Colombier . 082323
Dessau- Antik, Dessau, Anhalt 070220
Dessaules, Robert, Paris 065829
Dessaut, Benoît, Armentières 120906
Dessein, Helsinki 060515
Dessemond, J.- P., Aubusson 061046, 124082
Dessers, Hasselt 096310
Dessinee Gallery, Toronto 097256
Destang, Moissac 064578
Destek Reasürans Sanat Galerisi, İstanbul 112299
Desterne, Joëlle, Villeneuve-lès-Avignon 101476
Destillier- und Drogenmuseum, Pernegg 002419
Destina, Eric, Philadelphia 132614
Destiny Studios, Pittsburgh 118915
Destito, Giovanni, Roma 128015
Destito, Saverio, Roma 128016
El Desvan, Barcelona 080841
El Desvan, Ourense 081450
El Desvan de Madrid, Madrid 081286
El Desvan de Olavide, Madrid 081287, 129607
El Desvan de Tendilla, Guadalajara . 081153
Det Hanseatiske Kvarter, Bergen . . 079375

Det Lille Galleri, Stavanger 079499
Details, Indianapolis 116452
Details Art, Tucson 120123
Detalhe, Lisboa 129151
Detašované Pracoviště, Vysoká Škola Uměleckoprůmyslová v Praze, Praha 049892
Détections Loisir, Toulouse 068505
Detering, Houston 142435
Dethlefs, Elmshorn 102616
Dethlefs 6000 Flamweg 7, Hamburg 125807
Dętkoś, Aleksander, Bydgoszcz . . . 108863
Detlefsen-Museum, Glückstadt . . . 017434
Detling International Antiques and Collectors Fair, Detling 093923
Au Détour d'une Promenade, Bonnieux 061565
Détraz, Gérard, Basel 111175
Detre, Oakland 091415
Detroit Antiques Mall, Detroit 088761
Detroit Artists Market, Detroit 043440
Detroit Baseball Card, Farmington . 088825
Detroit Contemporary, Detroit 043441
Detroit Focus Gallery, Detroit 043442
Detroit Focus Quarterly, Detroit . . . 136448
Detroit Historical Museum, Detroit . 043443
The Detroit Institute of Arts, Detroit 043444
Detroit Repertory Theatre Gallery, Detroit 043445
Detroit Science Center, Detroit 043446
Detruche, Anne, Prangins 082730
Detskaja Kartinnaja Galereja, Kyïv . 038296
Detskaja Kartinnaja Galereja, Samara 033714
Detskij Muzej, Čerepovec 033073
Detskij Muzej Buratino-Pinokkio, Moskva 033380
Dettamanti, Daniela, Milano 140050
Detten, Rupert von, Aufseß 125070
Detterer, Martina, Frankfurt am Main 102757
Dettinger Mayer, Lyon 099553
Dettmeyer, Bad Iburg 069305
Dettori, Francesca, Genova 127449
Detursa, Madrid 110482
Deubner, Köln 134101
Deuchar & Son, A.S., Perth 086223
Deuerlein, Thomas, Nürnberg 139602
Deumens, Johan, Heemstede 134814, 140452
Deupoor, E., Bruxelles 137434
Deurbergue, Dominique, Versailles . 068800
Deuschl, Horst, Furth bei Göttweig . 056985
Deuschle, Göppingen 102966
Deuticke, Franz, Wien 133189
Deuticke, Franz, Wien 137302
Deutsch, André, London 135212
Deutsch, Berthold & Sigrid, Jockgrim 071668
Deutsch, Elise, Paris 065830
Deutsch, H. & W., London 085253
Deutsch, Paul Ernst, Wien 057399, 120680
Deutsch, R., Freiburg im Breisgau . 070831
Deutsch, Robert A., Saint Louis . . . 092225
Deutsch-Deutsches Museum Mödlareuth, Museum zur Geschichte der deutschen Teilung, Töpen 020448
Deutsch-Salsedo, Antoine, Paris . . . 065831
Deutschbein, R., Villingen-Schwenningen 105124
Deutsche Arbeitsschutzausstellung, Dortmund 016762
Deutsche Barockgalerie, Städtische Kunstsammlungen, Augsburg . . . 015605
Deutsche Burgenvereinigung e.V., Braubach 053120
Deutsche Exlibris-Gesellschaft e.V., Berlin 053121
Deutsche Gesellschaft für Christliche Kunst e.V., München 053122
Deutsche Gesellschaft für Photographie e.V., Köln 053123
Deutsche Guggenheim, Berlin 016009
Deutsche Mediathek im Filmhaus, Berlin 016010
Deutsche Notaphilie, Frankfurt am Main 070734
Deutsche Numismatische Gesellschaft - Verband der Deutschen Münzvereine e.V., Speyer 053124
Deutsche Raumfahrtausstellung, Morgenröthe-Rautenkranz 018995
Das Deutsche Stickmuster-Museum Celle, Celle 016546
Deutsche Verlags-Anstalt, München 134228
Deutscher Akademischer Austauschdienst - Berliner Künstlerprogramm, Berlin 053125
Deutscher Buchverlag, Oldenburg, Oldenburg 134331
Deutscher Designer Verband e.V., Berlin 053126
Deutscher Designertag e. V., Sektion Design im Deutschen Kulturrat, Hamburg 053127
Deutscher Künstlerbund e.V., Berlin 053128
Deutscher Kunsthandelsverband e.V., Berlin 053129
Deutscher Kunststudenten-Verband, Köln 053130
Deutscher Kunstverlag, München . . 134229
Deutscher-Menzies, Malvern, Victoria 120604
Deutscher Museumsbund e.V., Büro Berlin, Berlin 053131
Deutscher Museumsbund e.V. - Bulletin, Berlin 135757
Arbeitsgemeinschaft der Restauratoren-Museen-Denkmalpflege-Grabungstechnik; Berufsverband staatlich geprüfter RestauratorInnen; Bundesverband Deutscher Diplom-RestauratorInnen; Deutscher Restauratoren Verband; Deutscher Verband Freiberuflicher Restauratoren; Restauratoren Fachverband; Restauratorenverband Sachsen, Bonn 053589, 053589
Deutscher Verein für Kunstwissenschaft e.V., Berlin 053132
Deutscher Verein für Kunstwissenschaft. Zeitschrift, Berlin 135758
Deutscher Verlag für Kunstwissenschaft, Berlin 133761
Deutscher Werkbund, Darmstadt . . 053133
Deutscher Werkbund Baden-Würtenberg, Karlsruhe 053134
Deutscher Werkbund Hessen, Frankfurt am Main 053135
Deutscher Werkbund Nordrhein-Westfalen, Düsseldorf 053136
Deutscher Werkbund Rheinland-Pfalz, Mainz 053137
Deutscher Werkbund Saarland, Saarbrücken 053138
Deutscher Werkbund Sachsen e.V., Dresden 053139
Deutsches Albert-Schweitzer-Zentrum, Archiv, Museum und Forschungsstätte, Frankfurt am Main 017155
Deutsches Apotheken-Museum im Heidelberger Schloß, Heidelberg . 017825
Deutsches Architektur Museum, Frankfurt am Main 017156
Deutsches Automuseum Schloss Langenburg, Langenburg 018503
Deutsches Bauernkriegsmuseum, Böblingen 016292
Deutsches Baumaschinen-Modellmuseum, Weilburg 020724
Deutsches Bergbau-Museum, Bochum 016276
Deutsches Bernsteinmuseum, Ribnitz-Damgarten 019826
Deutsches Bienenmuseum, Weimar, Thüringen 020737
Deutsches Boxsport-Museum, Sagard 019967
Deutsches Brotmuseum, Ulm 020531
Deutsches Buch- und Schriftmuseum der Deutschen Bücherei Leipzig, Leipzig 018564
Deutsches Buchbindermuseum, Mainz 018787
Deutsches Chemie Museum, Merseburg 018914
Deutsches Damast- und Frottiermuseum Großschönau, Großschönau, Sachsen 017581
Deutsches Dampflokomotiv-Museum, Neuenmarkt 019234
Deutsches Drachenmuseum und Stadtmuseum, Museum des Heimatkreises Bischofteinitz/Sudetenland, Furth im Wald 017304
Deutsches Drahtmuseum, Altena . . 015493
Deutsches Edelsteinmuseum, Idar-Oberstein 018044
Deutsches Eichendorff-Museum, Wangen im Allgäu 020670
Deutsches Elfenbeinmuseum Erbach, Erbach, Odenwald 017000
Deutsches Erdölmuseum Wietze, Wietze 020885
Deutsches Fastnachtmuseum, Kitzingen 018276
Deutsches Feld- und Kleinbahnmuseum, Deinste 016660
Deutsches Feuerwehr-Museum, Fulda 017295
Deutsches Film- und Fototechnik Museum, Deidesheim 016658
Deutsches Filmmuseum, Frankfurt am Main 017157
Deutsches Fleischermuseum, Böblingen 016293
Deutsches Fleischermuseum, Sindelfingen 020214
Deutsches Forum für Figurentheater und Puppenspielkunst, Bochum 016277
Deutsches Freimaurermuseum, Bayreuth 015907
Deutsches Gartenbaumuseum Erfurt, Erfurt 017010
Deutsches Glasmalerei-Museum Linnich, Linnich 018663
Deutsches Glockenmuseum, Greifenstein 017520
Deutsches Goldmuseum, Theuern . 020435
Deutsches Goldschmiedehaus, Hanau 017737
Deutsches Harmonikamuseum, Trossingen 020489
Deutsches Hirtenmuseum, Hersbruck 017903
Deutsches Historisches Museum, Zeughaus und Ausstellungshalle Pei-Bau, Berlin 016011
Deutsches Hopfenmuseum, Wolnzach 020975
Deutsches Hugenotten-Museum, Bad Karlshafen 015729
Deutsches Hygiene-Museum, Das Museum vom Menschen, Dresden 016784
Deutsches Jagd- und Fischereimuseum, München 019044
Deutsches Kaltwalzmuseum, Hagen, Westfalen 017622
Deutsches Kartausen-Museum, Buxheim bei Memmingen 016531
Deutsches Kartoffelmuseum Fußgönheim, Fußgönheim 017309
Deutsches Kinderwagenmuseum, Zeitz, Elster 021046
Deutsches Kleingärtnermuseum, Leipzig 018565
Deutsches Klingenmuseum Solingen, Solingen 020236
Deutsches Knopfmuseum, Bärnau . 015858
Deutsches Kochbuchmuseum, Dortmund 016763
Deutsches Korbmuseum, Michelau . 018930
Deutsches Kunst- und Jagdkabinett, München 072684
Deutsches Kunststoff Museum, Düsseldorf 016826
Deutsches Landwirtschaftsmuseum, Stuttgart 020347
Deutsches Landwirtschaftsmuseum Markkleeberg, Markkleeberg 018834
Deutsches Märchen- und Wesersagenmuseum, Bad Oeynhausen 015765
Deutsches Maler- und Lackierer-Museum, Hamburg 017684
Deutsches Medizinhistorisches Museum, Ingolstadt 018071
Deutsches Meeresmuseum, Museum für Meereskunde und Fischerei - Aquarium, Stralsund 020330
Deutsches Museum, München 019045
Deutsches Museum Bonn, Forschung und Technik in Deutschland nach 1945, Bonn 016321
Deutsches Museum - Flugwerft Schleißheim, Museum für Luft- und Raumfahrt, Oberschleißheim 019413
Deutsches Museum für Schulkunst, Hagen, Westfalen 017623
Deutsches Museum - Verkehrszentrum, München 019046
Deutsches Musikautomaten Museum, Zweigmuseum des Badischen Landesmuseums, Bruchsal 016455
Deutsches Orthopädisches Geschichts- und Forschungsmuseum, Frankfurt am Main 017158
Deutsches Panzermuseum Munster, Munster 019164
Deutsches Pferdemuseum, Hippologisches Institut, Verden 020575
Deutsches Phonomuseum, Sankt Georgen im Schwarzwald 019986
Deutsches Pinsel- und Bürstenmuseum, Bechhofen 015929
Deutsches Plakat Museum, Essen . 017062
Deutsches Polizeimuseum, Salzkotten 019974
Deutsches Porzellanmuseum, Hohenberg an der Eger 017969
Deutsches Röntgen-Museum, Remscheid 019795
Deutsches Salzmuseum - Industriedenkmal Saline Lüneburg, Lüneburg 018741
Deutsches Schaustellermuseum, Lambrecht 018469
Deutsches Schiefermuseum Steinach/Thür., Steinach, Thüringen 020298
Deutsches Schiffahrtsmuseum, Bremerhaven 016429
Deutsches Schloss-und Beschlägemuseum, Velbert 020567
Deutsches Schreibmaschinenmuseum, Bayreuth 015908
Deutsches Schuhmuseum, Hauenstein 017802
Deutsches Schustermuseum, Burgkunstadt 016519
Deutsches Segelflugmuseum mit Modellflug, Gersfeld 017387
Deutsches Sielhafenmuseum in Carolinensiel, Wittmund 020932
Deutsches Skimuseum, Planegg . . 019630
Deutsches Spiele-Archiv, Marburg . 018820
Deutsches Spielemuseum, Chemnitz 016554
Deutsches Spielkartenmuseum, Zweigmuseum des Württembergischen Landesmuseums Stuttgart, Leinfelden-Echterdingen 018550
Deutsches Spielzeugmuseum, Sonneberg, Thüringen 020249
Deutsches Sport- und Olympia-Museum, Köln 018304
Deutsches Straßenmuseum, Germersheim 017380
Deutsches Strumpfmuseum, Gelenau, Erzgebirge 017348
Deutsches Tabak- und Zigarrenmuseum, Museum Bünde, Bünde 016494
Deutsches Tabakpfeifenmuseum, Oberelsbach 019387
Deutsches Tanzarchiv Köln, Köln . . 018305
Deutsches Tapetenmuseum, Staatliche Museen Kassel, Kassel 018183
Deutsches Technikmuseum Berlin, Berlin 016012
Deutsches Textilmuseum Krefeld, Krefeld 018396
Deutsches Theatermuseum, München 019047
Deutsches Uhrenmuseum, Furtwangen im Schwarzwald 017308

Deutsches Verpackungs-Museum, Heidelberg 017826
Deutsches Vogelbauer-Museum, Walsrode 020660
Deutsches Weinbaumuseum, Oppenheim 019475
Deutsches Werbemuseum, Düsseldorf 016827
Deutsches Werkzeugmuseum, Historisches Zentrum der Stadt Remscheid, Remscheid 019796
Deutsches Zinnfigurenmuseum, Kulmbach 018440
Deutsches Zollmuseum, Hamburg . 017685
Deutsches Zweirad- und NSU-Museum, Neckarsulm 019196
Deutschheim State Historic Site, Hermann 044520
Deutschl, Walter, Haag 057050
Deutschmann, Kassel . . . 071749, 103510
Deutschordensmuseum Bad Mergentheim, Bad Mergentheim 015750
Deux, Henri, Delft 078143
Deux Aes, Leiden 140476
Les Deux Anges, Paris 100209
Deux Anglès, Flers 099264
Les Deux Ebenistes, Marseille 124408
Les Deux Iles, New York 090820
Les Deux Iles, New York 090821
Les Deux Illes, New York 132460
Les Deux-Mondes, Paris 138350
Les Deux Orphelines, Paris 065832
Deux Rue Antiquités, Caluire-et-Cuire 061911
Deux Rue Antiquités, Villeurbanne . 068957
Deuxièmement, Montréal 058948
Deva, Hartley Wintney 084601
Deva, Marseille 124409
Deva Gallery, New York 117838
DeValera Museum and Bruree Heritage Centre, Bruree 022696
Devar, Minneapolis 117252
Devauchelle, Alain, Paris 124648
Devaud, René, Sarras 068129
DeVaults, Tulsa 093299
Devaux, Alain, Camps-en-Amienois 061929
Devaux, F.J., Bruxelles 123589
Devaux, Hervé, Lyon 064118
Devaux, Jean-Claude, Caen 061867
Devaux, Jean-Luc, Moulins (Allier) . 138224
Devaux, J.F., Charleroi 058144
Deveau, Robert, Toronto 097257
Deveau, Robert, Toronto 120817
Deveaud, Laurent, Bois-le-Roi 061540
Deveaux, Los Angeles 089750
Deveko, Fourmies 062933
Devereaux, Emile, New Orleans . . . 090544
Devereux Antiques, Linden Park . . . 056101
Devic, Auch 061051
Devilé, Leiden 078564
Deville, Mâcon 064203
DeVille, New Orleans 142611
Deville, Saint-Étienne 067452
Deville, Bernard, Bernot 061371
Deville, Bernard, Paris 065833
Devillé, J., Liège 058295
Devilleneuve, Philippe, Tonnerre . . . 121266
Devillers, Bonnières 061563
Devillers, Liège 058296
Devillers, Charlie, Amiens 060812
Devil's Coulee Dinosaur Heritage Museum, Royal Tyrrell Museum of Paleontology, Warner 006764
Devils Tower Visitor Center, Devils Tower 043460
Devin-Hürlimann, Barbara, München 121523
Devisme, Bruno, Amiens 060813
Devisme, Bruno, Flesselles 062873
Devitt, Nial, Leamington Spa 141709
Devivi, Raymond, Saint-Paul-de-Vence 101201
Devizes Museum, Devizes 039235
Devlay, Philippe, Cairo 060437
Devlin, Eric, Montréal 096994
Devo, Brive-la-Gaillarde 061808
Devon, Winn, Seattle 135502
Devon and Cornwall Constabulary Museum, Exeter 039463
Devon Gallery, Vancouver 097455
Devon Guild of Craftsmen, Bovey Tracey Newton Abbot 054355
Devon Guild of Craftsmen Gallery, Bovey Tracey 038797
Devon Pottery Collectors Group, Saint Albans 142028, 054356, 142028, 086437, 086437, 054356
Devonia, Boston 087814
Devonport Antiques, North Shore . . 079190
Devonport Gallery and Arts Centre, Devonport 000979
Devonport Maritime Museum, Devonport 000980
Devons, Judith, Leicester 113372
Devonshire, Cork 074874
Devotional Art, Los Angeles 089751
Devroe, J., Haasrode 137506
Devroede-Missinne, V. & Z., Köln . . 071924, 121470
Devulder, Jean-Marc, Bourges 061724, 124156
Dew, Roderick, Eastbourne 141567
Dewa Roman Experience, Chester . 039060
Dewa San-Zan History Museum, Haguro 026487
Dewards, Greenslopes 094604
Dewart, Bruxelles 096181
Dewart, Bruxelles 096182
Dewasmes, Jean-Charles, Arras . . 060986
Dewazakura Art Museum, Tendo . . 027137
Dewberry Valley Museum, Dewberry 005348
Dewenter, Runhild, Krefeld 126144
Dewey Hotel, Dewey 043461
Dewey Museum, Warminster 041299
Dewi Lewis, Stockport 135305
Dewindt, Bruxelles 057915
DeWitt, Cornell, New York 117839
DeWitt County Historical Museum, Cuero 043237
DeWitt Historical Society Museum, Ithaca 044789
DeWitt Stetten Jr. Museum of Medical Research, Bethesda 042179
DeWitt Wallace Decorative Arts Museum, Williamsburg 049181
Dewsbury Museum, Dewsbury 039237
Dewulf, Patrick, Froidestrees 062948
Dexter Area Museum, Dexter 043464
Dexter Historical Society Museum, Dexter 043463
Dextera, Bilbao 129423
Dey, J.C.A., Marnes-la-Coquette . . 064296
Dey Mansion, Washington's Headquarters Museum, Wayne 049030
Deya Anticuario, Buenos Aires 055198
Deyl, Wolfgang, Salzburg 057239
Dezamy, Jacques-Marie, Niort 121098
Dezign House, Jefferson 044843
Dezuttere, Brugge 057769
DF Gallery, Windsor, Ontario 097557
D'Fab, Brunswick 055571
D.G. Asturias, Oviedo 081458
DG.Art, Paris 100210
DGLM Gallery, Philadelphia 118749
D.H. Lawrence Birthplace Museum, Eastwood 039372
D.H. Lawrence Heritage Centre, Eastwood 039373
Dhaka City Museum, Dhaka 003104
Dhakshini, Bangalore 074767
Dhamapala, Kathmandu 107582
Dharma, Berkeley 135326
Dhénin, Jean, Saint-Loup-de-Naud 067592
Dhenkanal Science Centre, Dhenkanal 022107
Dhennequin, Michèle, Paris 138351
D'Hier à Aujourd'hui, Génolhac 062984
D'Hier à Aujourd'hui, Versailles . . . 068801
D'Hier et Aujourd'hui, Fontainebleau 062897
D'Hier et d'Ailleurs, Annet-sur-Marne 060903
D'Hier et d'Ailleurs, Lagny-sur-Marne 063486
D'Hier et d'Ailleurs, Wambrechies . 069042
D'Hier et d'Aujourdhui, Sisteron . . . 068245
Dhikéos, Pierre, Lyon 099554
Dhoomimal Art Gallery, Delhi 105657, 134513
Dhouailly & Cie., Paris . . . 065834, 138352
Di, Norfolk 091374
Di Baio, Milano 134609
Di Blanco, Avignon 098892
Di Blanco, Montelimar 099741
Di Castro, Alberto, Roma 076419
Di Castro, Alberto, Roma 076420
Di Castro, Angelo, Roma 076421
Di Castro, Leone, Roma 076422
Di Castro, Richard, Roma 076423
Di Castro, Richard, Roma 076424
Di Cave, Giuliana, Roma 140102
Di Ciapetti, Firenze 127328
Di Clemente, Simone, Firenze 075328
Di Colman, Orange 095008
Di Consiglio, Gioia, Roma 076425
Di Domizio, Atlanta 087467
Di Elsden, Yandilla 095443
Di Fani, Aleandro, Roma 128017
Di Gesaro, Angelo, Palermo 106424
Di Giacinto Romani, Tilde, Bologna . 127146
Di Giaimo, Saverio, Napoli 075971
Di Giorno, Giuseppe, Milano 127583
Di Giugno, Catania 075246
Di Giugno, Angela, Catania 127264
Di Iacovo, Rosanna, Roma 076426
Di-Jon, Miami 132338
Di Ka, Changsha 097692
Di Ka, Liuyang 097871
Di Lorenzo, Vincenzo, Napoli 127766
Di Maccio, Sidi Bou Saïd 112256
Di Maggio, Iole Maria, Torino 128296
Di Maio, Andrea, Roma 128018
Di Maio, Felice, Roma . . . 076427, 106518, 128019
Di Maio, Sacha Valentine, Firenze . 127329
Di Marco, Lidia, Roma 076428
Di Marco, Ugo, Roma 076429, 128020
Di Mare, Pasquale, Napoli 075972
Di Maria, Massimiliano, Palermo . . 076141, 127828
Di Mario, Arnaldo, Roma 106519
Di Martino, Antonio, Napoli 075973
Di Mauro, Emilio, Cava dei Tirreni . 134565
Di Méo, Paris 100211
Di Modica, New York 117840
Di Napoli, Raffaele, Napoli 075974
Di Palma 1961, Napoli . . . 075975, 127767
Di Paolo, Bologna 105953
Di Paolo, Domenico, Bologna 075071
Di Parenza, Romano, Roma 076430
Di Parenza, Romano, Roma 076431
Di Parenza, Romano Maria, Roma . 076432
Di Pasquale, Rocco, Bari 075016
Di Pasquale, Vincenzo, Bari 127111
Di Pietrantonio, Alfonso, Roma 128021
Di Pietro, Giulia, Roma 128022
Di Pietro, Tommaso, Roma 128023
Di Roberto, Giorgio, Roma 106520
Di Rollo, Edinburgh 112989
Di Rollo, Edinburgh 112990
Di Salvatore, Marseille 064350
Di Sciascio, Virginia, New York 090822
Di Simone, Antonio, Palermo 127829
Di Stefano, Giuseppe, Palermo 076142
Di Stefano, Ilaria, Roma 076433
Di Summa, Giovanni, Roma 106521
Di Teodoro, Dafne, Bari 075017
Di Tutto, Bogotá 059833
Di Vara, Isabella, Roma 076434
Di Veroli, Paris 100212
Dia Art Foundation, New York 046323
Dia:Beacon, Dia Art Foundation, Beacon 042069
Dia Center for the Arts, Quemado . . 047293
Dia:Chelsea, Dia Art Foundation, New York 046324
Diabira, Carole, Bernay-Saint-Martin 061369
Le Diable Bouilli, Amiens 060814
Diablo Valley College Museum, Pleasant Hill 047087
Diadema, Saratov 080339
Diagram, Nice 065073
Diagram, Nice 065074
Dial a Print, Peterborough 114242
Dial Gallery, Warkworth 114646
Dialog-Verlag, Reinbek 134364
Dialoghi, Biella 134546
Dialogue (Columbus), Columbus . . . 136449
Diamantart, Genève 082420
Diamantmuseum, Antwerpen 003157
Diamantmuseum, Grobbendonk . . . 003480
Diamantschleifermuseum, Brücken 016463
Diamond & Son, Harry, Brighton . . . 083692
Diamond Coin, Indianapolis 089289
Diamond Gallery, Kobe 106876
Diamond Head Gallery, Honolulu . . 116205
Diamond Head Gallery, Honolulu . . 116206
Diamond, Mills & Co., Felixstowe . . 122510
Diamond Sport Cards, Austin 087568
Diamonds on Broadbeach, Broadbeach 055564
Diam'or, Paris 065835
Diana, Kroměříž 060039
Diana Antikvárium, Makó 139937
Dianna's Vault, Saint Louis 092226
Dianpruess, Los Angeles 116752
Diard, Pierre-Olivier, Côte-Saint-André 062491
Diarra, Françoise, Saint-Valery-en-Caux 068030
Dias, Carlos, Lisboa 109279
Dias, Maria L. Gouveia, Lisboa 079914
Dias, Paulo Cesar, Rio de Janeiro . . 058581
Diaspora Vibe Gallery, Miami 117057
Diaspro, Milano 075695
Diaz, Carlos, Wurmbrand 057609
Díaz, Gustavo, Cali 123918
Diaz, Salvador, Madrid 110483
Diaz de Andres, Carlos, A Coruña . . 122024
Díaz Fernández, Francisco Ruíz, Asunción 108797
Diaz Perez, Baldomero, Palma de Mallorca 110675
Díaz y Trancón, Cáceres 129470
Diazo 1, Clermont-Ferrand 099146
Dibit, Norfolk 091375
Dibon, Jean-Luc, Amboise 124066
Dicembre, Carlo, Milano 127584
Dichter bij Dordt, Dordrecht 140410
Dichter- und Stadtmuseum/ Herwegh-Archiv, Liestal 037263
Dichtermuseum Joseph Maria Lutz, Pfaffenhofen an der Ilm 019597
D'Ici et D'Ailleurs, Saint-Jean-de-Luz 101161
Dick, Caroline, Genève 130033
Dick, W., Lütisburg 111657, 135036
Dick & Ambyr's Collectibles, Jacksonville 089404
Dick-Art Galeria Sztuki, Łódź 079667
Dick Institute Museum and Art Gallery, Kilmarnock 039870
Dickel, Hanna, Wuppertal 105349
Dickel, Martin, Hamburg . 071222, 125808
Dickens, C., Atlanta 142201
Dickens Curios, Frinton-on-Sea . . . 084441
The Dickens House Museum, London 040135
Dickens House Museum Broadstairs, Broadstairs 038875
Dickens Libros, Buenos Aires 136715
Dickens Museumtheater, Bronkhorst 029359
Dickens & Rigg, Hong Kong 097777
Dickenson, Alastair, London 085254, 131006
Dicker, Moosdorf 057188

Dickerson, Woollahra 095423
Dickhout, Alkmaar 077711
Dickins, H.C., Bloxham 083565
Dickins, H.C., Bloxham 112669
Dickins, Tom, Ludlow 114005
Dickinson, Berlin 069591
Dickinson, New York 117841
Dickinson, Bernard, Gargrave 084452, 130723
Dickinson, D. & B., Bath 083425
Dickinson, D.E., Mudgee 094917
Dickinson, Simon C., London 113579, 131007
Dickinson County Heritage Center, Abilene 041562
Dickinson Homestead, Amherst . . . 041691
Dickmann, B., Bruchhausen-Vilsen . 102268
Dicks, Marburg 104032
Dickson, José Manuel, Porto 080079
Dickson Mounds Museum, Lewistown 045251
Dickson & Rendall, London 085255
Dickson Store Museum, Spruce View 006504
Dicon, Fuenlabrada 110351
Dicontal, Santiago de Chile 059520
Dicson, Alexandria 060417
Didaktische Ausstellung Urgeschichte, Chur 037019
Didascalies, Aix-en-Provence 060702
Didcot Railway Centre, Didcot 039239
Didi Museum, Abuja 030671
Didier, Corbeil-Essonnes 062468
Didier, New Orleans 090545
Didier, Aaron, Paris 065836
Didier, Aaron, Paris 065837, 100213
Didier, Germain, Paris 100214
Didierjean, Stéphane, Lanvollon . . . 063534
Didimatus, Bollène 061549
Dido Editions, Bristol 112722
Didrichsenin Taidemuseo, Helsinki . 009519
Didsbury and District Museum, Didsbury 005349
Didsbury Antiques, Manchester . . . 085912
Diebold, Juliette, Niederhausbergen 065161
Diebold, Pascal, Semur-en-Auxois .068204, 124931
Dieci Due, Milano 106208
Dieckmann, Gabriele J, Montreux . . 111742
Diederiks, Marcel, Den Haag 121786
Diedrich-Kuehn, Sigrid, Schwalbach am Taunus 126785
Dief- en Duifhuisje, Capelle aan den IJssel 029382
Diefenbaker Canada Centre, University of Saskatchewan, Saskatoon 006416
Diefenbaker Homestead House, Regina 006250
Diefenbaker House, Prince Albert . . 006201
Diego Díaz, José de, Madrid 129608
Diegoni, Christine, Paris 100215
Diego's Gallery, Toronto 097258
Diehl, Hanna, Bergisch Gladbach . . 101761
Diehl, Sibylle, Wettingen . 111987, 130215
Diehl, Volker, Berlin 101837
Diela a Dielka Slovakskych Výtvarnákov, Banská Štiavnica 109904
Diele Galerii, Tallinn 098695
Dielo - The Art Center, Liptovský Mikuláš 109919
Diem, Amsterdam 107700
Diemmeci, Torino 128297
Dienstbier, H. A. sen., Lauf an der Pegnitz 139382
Dieny, Jean-Pierre, Sauxemesnil . . 068159
Diepering Bijlsma, Bergen, Noord-Holland 078063
Dierich, H., Danstedt 070177
Dierick, J.-P., Bruxelles 057916
Dierkes, Kevelaer 103536
Dierking, Köln 071925, 103609
Dierl, Xaver, Waidhaus 074247
Dieruff, Bärbel, Stuttgart 126845
Dies & Das, Salzburg 057240
Diesel, Oakland 142709
Diesenberg, Wilfried, Minden, Westfalen 072547
Dietel, Miami 090167
Dietemann, Toronto 059173
Dieter, Besigheim 069808
Dieter, Norbert, Windesheim 074446
Dieter Roth-Museum, Dieter Roth Foundation, Hamburg 017686
Dieterich, Leipzig 134144
Dieterle, Dr. M., Schenkenzell 073684
Dieth, Volkmar, Lauterach 133109
Dietl-Beissel, M., Naumburg, Saale 072943
Dietrich, Baden-Baden 125125
Dietrich, G., Billerbeck 069846
Dietrich, Horst, Berlin 101838, 133762
Dietrich, Lise, Villach 057341
Dietrichsteinský Palác, Moravské Zemské Muzeum, Brno 008283
Dietro l'Angolo, Bologna 075072
Dietz, Günter, Soyen 134401
Dietz, H ., Erlensee 070604
Dietz, Petra, Heidelberg 071450
Dietz, Sieglinde, Meckenheim, Rheinland 104043
Dietz, Ursula, Holm, Kreis Pinneberg 071566
Dietze, Arndt, Köln 071926
Dietze, R., Leipzig 072202
Dietzel, Berlin 069592, 121328
Dietzel, Meiningen 139472
Dietzen-Seitz, Ute, Trier 126909
Dietzsch, Paul-Uwe, Grasberg 125752
Dietzschold, Conny, Waterloo 095376
Dieutegard, Nice 065075
Dieutegard, Jean-Pierre, Paris 065838, 124649
Dieutegard, Marie-Noëlle, La Fille du Pirate, Paris 065839, 124650
Dieutre, Christophe, Acquigny 060659
Dieutre, Christophe, Le Mesnil-Esnard 063668
Dieutre, Christophe, Rouen 067264
Díez, Buenos Aires 055199
Díez Galería, Rosario 094104
Diez Garcia, Maria Teresa, Valencia 081653
Diez Pérez, José Ramón, Burgos . .081014, 129459
A Diferença, Lisboa 079915
Diferença, Lisboa 109280
Différences, Paris 100216
Different Strokes, Nashville 117350
Dig Impex, Iaşi 140891
Digaro, Claude, Saint-Léonard-de-Noblat 067584
Diggers Antiques, Winnipeg 059456
Diggins, Lauraine, Caulfield North . 055651
Diggs Gallery at Winston-Salem State University, Winston-Salem 049252
Digha Science Centre & National Science Camp, New Digha 022284
Digit Art, Santa Cruz de Tenerife . . . 110739
Digital Art Lab, Holon 022935
Digital Art Museum, Berlin 016013
Digital Design Showcase, Edinburgh 112991
DigitalArt, Frankfurt am Main 102758
DigiTouch Galeria, Berlin 101839
Digterhuset, Farsø 008857
Diguet, Jean-Paul, Barfleur 061208
Dijeau, Olivier, Libourne 063815
Dijeau, Pierre, Les Billaux 063760
Dijeau, René, Rochefort (Charente-Maritime) 121233
Dijecezanski Muzej Zagrebačke Nadbiskupije, Zagreb 007831
De Dijk Te Kijk, Petten 030041
Dike, David, Dallas 088499, 115869, 122873
Dikemark Sykehus Museum, Asker 030745
Dikmayer, Joachim, Berlin 101840, 133763
D'Ilario, Mario, Roma 128024
Dildarian, Louise C., New York 090823
Dilemma, Leuven 096371
Dilemma Artworks, Upper Poppleton 114623
Le Dilettante, Montolieu 138215
Le Dilettante, Paris 133566, 138353
Dilettante, Vex 111969
Diliberto, Palermo 076143
Dillard Mill State Historic Site, Davisville 043316
Dillée, Paris 065840
Dillée, Stéphane, Lisieux 063908
Diller, Johannes, München 072685
Dillhäuser Fachwerkhaus im Tiergarten Weilburg, Weilburg 020725
Dillingham & Co., San Francisco . . 092773
Dillmann, Hilmar, Berlin 125189
Dillon, Dallas 088500
Dillon, Pat, Toronto 059174
Dílna Lochkov, Praha 060122
Dilo - Galerie, Brno 098327
Di'Lorenzo, London 113580
Dilworth, Charlotte 087944
Dilworth, Charlotte 087945
Dima, Paris 100217
Dimadis, Stella, Collingwood 094420
Dimbola Lodge, Freshwater 039526
Dimboola Antiques Centre, Dimboola 055751
Dime a Dance, Milwaukee 090291
Dimensión Centro de Arte, Buenos Aires 094067
Dimension Painting Galeria, Delhi . . 105658
Dimension Plus, Montréal 096995
Dimensions, Taipei 098064
Dimensions Antiques, Houston 089069
Dimitreion Oikima House, Museum of the Sculptor Nikolas, Agios Georgios Nilias 021118
Dimitris Pierides Museum of Contemporary Art, Glyfada 021273
Dimitrova, Z., Pleven 096705
Dimock Gallery, Washington 048897
Dimond & Son, Prospect 123292
Dimondstein, Joshua, Los Angeles . 116753
Din Antik, Stockholm 081941
Dina, Los Angeles 116754
Dinajpur Museum, Dinajpur 003112
Dinallo, West Hollywood 093463
Din'art, Dinard 099229
Dinastia, Lisboa . . 079916, 121927, 136042
Dinbau, Flamatt 122318
Dinc, Abel, Sas van Gent 128826
Diner, Geoffrey, Washington 093408
Diner En Ville, Milano 075696
Dingethal, U., Weil der Stadt 105177
Dingler, Horst, Freiburg im Breisgau 070832
Dingles Steam Village, Lifton 040004
Dingley Dell Gallery, Ipswich 094661
Dingling Museum, Beijing 006984
Dinguidard, Alain, Tourdun 068560
Dingwall Museum, Dingwall 039240
Dini, Daniela, Firenze 075329, 127330
Dini, Stefano, Roma 076435
Dinie's Lampenhaus, Nordhorn . . . 073080
The Dining Room Shop, London . . .085256, 131008
Dinkelacker, Kurt, Lausanne 130067
Dinkelbach, Manfred, Köln 103610
Dinkler, Marina, Berlin 101841
Dinky Toy, Enschede 078369
Dinkytown, Minneapolis 142581
Dinnebier, Gerald, Pleinfeld 073340
Dinnebier, Gerald & Anja, Pleinfeld . 073341
Dinnerware Contemporary Art Gallery, Tucson 048633
Dinolevi, Firenze 075330
Dinosaur Gardens Museum, Ossineke 046742
Dinosaur Isle, Sandown 040956
Dinosaur Museum, Dorchester 039255
Dinosaur Museum, Malabon 031701
The Dinosaur Museum, Saint Louis 047660
Dinosaur Provincial Park, Royal Tyrrell Museum of Palaeontology Field Station, Patricia 006120
Dinosaur Valley State Park, Glen Rose 044204
Dinosauria - Musée des Dinosaures, Espéraza 011735
Dinosaurier-Freilichtmuseum Münchehagen, Rehburg-Loccum 019767
Dinosaurland, Lyme Regis 040364
Dinozzi, Daniela, Livorno 075531
Dinsdale, F.L., Kettering 130840
Dinsmore Homestead History Museum, Burlington 042516
Dintenfass, Terry, New York 117842
Dinter, Jürgen, Köln 139336
Dinter, Jürgen, Schwerin 073772
Diodora, Milano 106209
Diözesan-Museum, Sankt Pölten . . 002616
Diözesanmuseum, Bamberg 015868
Diözesanmuseum, Freising 017244
Diözesanmuseum Eisenstadt, Eisenstadt 001824
Diözesanmuseum Graz, Graz 001928
Diözesanmuseum Linz, Linz 002245
Diözesanmuseum Rottenburg, Rottenburg am Neckar 019926
Diözesanmuseum Sankt Afra, Augsburg 015606
Diözesanmuseum Sankt Ulrich, Regensburg 019745
Diogenes, Nußdorf-Debant 057195
Diogenes, Zürich 135086
Diomedea, Palermo 106425
Dioni, Larnaka 098295
Dionie, Cholargos 105420
Dionis Bennassar, Madrid 110484
Dionizas Poška Hollowed Trunks, Šiauliai Aušros Museum, Bijotai 027846
Dionne Homestead Museum, North Bay 006036
Diop, Baba, Bordeaux 124121
Diorama Bethlehem, Einsiedeln . . . 037058
Diorama Bitva za Dnepr, Dnipropetrovskyj deržavnij istoričnij muzej im Javornic'kogo, Dnipropetrovs'k . . 038256
Diorama der Schalcht bei Rosbach, Reichardtswerben 019769
Diorama Kurskaja Bitva - Belgorodskoe Napravlenie, Belgorodskij Gosudarstvennyj Chudožestvennyj Muzej, Belgorod 033020
Diorama Saint-Bénilde, Saugues-en-Gévaudan 014690
Diorama Šturm Izmaila, Izmaïl 038270
Dioramenschau Altötting, Altötting . 015514
Dios, Margarita de, Madrid 141035
Diósgyőri Vármúzeum, Miskolc . . . 021784
Dip 'n' Strip, Calgary 123743
Dip 'n' Strip, Pittsburgh 132667
Dipartimento di Scienze Archeologiche e Storico Artistiche, Università di Cagliari, Facoltà di Lettere e Filosofia, Cagliari 050356
Dipartimento di Storia dell'Arte, Facoltà di Lettere e Filosofia, Università degli Studi di Roma La Sapienza, Roma 050424
Dipartimento di Storia dell'Arte Medievale e Moderna, Università degli Studi di Roma, Roma 050425
Dipartimento di Storia delle Arti, Pisa 050408
Dipartimento di Storia delle Arti, Università Pisa, Pisa 025261
Dipartimento di Storia delle Arti e Concervazione dei beni Artistici G. Mazzariol, Università Cà Foscari, Venezia 050445
Dipartimento di Storia delle Arti e dello Spettacolo, Università degli Studi di Firenze, Firenze 050367
Dipinti, Bolzano 127195
Dipinti, Enrico, Milano 106210
Dipinti Antichi, Roma 076436
Diplomatic History Museum, Seoul . 027549
Diplomstudiengang Restaurierung, Kunsttechnologie und Konservierungswissenschaften, Technische Universität München, München 050188
Dipressa, Rosina, Torino 128298
Diquero, Yves, Malansac 064233

Diquéro, Yves, Rochefort-en-Terre . 067182
Dirección General de Museos de la Nación, Asunción 053969
Direct Auction, Chicago 122844
De Directiekamer, Middelburg 108140
Direction de Musées de France, Paris 052938
Direction des Musées, Sites et Monuments, Lomé 054244
Direzione Generale per l'Architttura e l'Arte Contemporanee, Roma 053753
Diriwächter, Kurt, Luzern 082622
Dirkedaen, Wilnis 128883
Dirkx, Mariska, Roermond 108163
Dirschedl, Georg, Weinstadt 105197
Dirt Gallery, West Hollywood 120379
Dirting, Michael, Wiesbaden 105251
Dirven, Jan, Schoten 096409
Disa-Antiquités, Lausanne 082543
Disabled Person Art Cooperative, Wuxi 098031
Disagården, Upplandsmuseet, Uppsala 036735
Dischinger Heimatmuseum, Dischingen 016725
Disciples of Christ Historical Society Museum, Nashville 046144
Discount Graphics, San Francisco . 119654
Discover Houston County Visitors Center-Museum, Crockett 043222
Discover Mid-America, Kansas City 136450
Discover Nepal, Kathmandu 107583
Discoveries, Oklahoma City 091494
Discovery, Noosa Heads 056351
Discovery Antiques, Stirling 056634
Discovery Center, Fresno 044079
Discovery Center Museum, Rockford 047498
Discovery Center of Idaho, Boise . . 042289
Discovery Center of Springfield, Springfield 048299
Discovery Center of the Southern Tier, Binghamton 042216
Discovery Center Science Museum, Fort Collins 043901
Discovery Corner, Clayfield 055683
Discovery Creek Children's Museum of Washington DC, Washington 048898
Discovery Harbour, Penetanguishene 006127
The Discovery Museum, Bridgeport 042407
Discovery Museum, Newcastle-upon-Tyne 040547
Discovery Museum History Center, Sacramento 047589
The Discovery Museums, Acton . . . 041576
Discovery Park, Safford 047599
Discovery Place, Charlotte 042756
Discovery Science Center of Central Florida, Ocala 046611
Discovery World - The James Lovell Museum of Science, Economics and Technology, Milwaukee 045887
Diseño Muebles Antiguos, Medellín 059917
Diser 37, København 060318
Dishes From the Past, Fort Worth . . 088849
Dishman Art Gallery, Beaumont . . . 042083
Disjointed, Rotterdam 078713
Disoteo, Mario, Milano 127585
Disparate, Bilbao 080971
Dispela, Los Angeles 089752
La Dispute, Paris 138354
Diss Antiques, Diss 084168, 130635
Diss Museum, Diss 039243
Disselhoff, Los Angeles 089753
Distanza, Leeuwarden 108091
Distil, New York 117843
Distill, Toronto 097259
Distilled Art, Paris 100218
Distillerie du Périgord, Sarlat-la-Canéda 014675
Distinctive African American Art, Salt Lake City 119337
Distinctive Antiques, Claremont . . . 055674
Distinctive Consignments, Richmond 092072
Distinctive Desks, Dunedin 079083
Distinctive Furnishings, New York . . 090824
Distribution Group, Bucureşti 109426
District Archaeological Museum, Dhar 022101
District Ethnographic Museum, Elbasan 000017
District Fine Arts, Washington 120279
District Gallery, Memphis 090070
District Historical Museum, Bérat . . 000011
District Historical Museum, Përmet 000029
District Historical Museum, Vlorë . . 000038
District Museum, Barpeta 022021
District Museum, Darrang 022070
District Museum, Gulbarga 022128
District Museum, Guntur 022130
District Museum, Pillalamari 022298
District Museum, Shimoga 022337
District Museum, Shivpuri 022338
District Museum and Cameronians Regimental Museum, Hamilton . . 039669
District of Columbia Arts Center, Washington 048899
District Science Centre, Dharampur 022102
District Science Centre, Purulia . . . 022312
District Science Centre, Tirunelveli . 022354
District Six Museum, Cape Town . . . 034578
Distrito Arte, A Coruña 110318
Distrito Cu4tro, Madrid 110485
Distrito Cuatro, Donostia-San Sebastián 110333
Dit-Elle, Grignan 138103
Ditchburn & Boxshall, Armadale, Victoria 055369
Ditchling Museum, Ditchling 039244
Ditec, Lisboa 109281
Ditesheim, François, Neuchâtel . . . 111767
Dithmarscher Kunstauktionshaus, Albersdorf 121294
Dithmarscher Landesmuseum, Meldorf 018894
Ditjes en Datjes, Tilburg 078767
Ditt og Datt A/S, Stavanger 079500
Dittmann, A., Daun 070195
Dittmann, Elisabeth, Bergisch Gladbach 101762
Dittmar, Berlin 101842, 133764
Il Ditto Magico, Marseille 124410
Dittrich, Praha 123978
Dittrich, Klaus, Seligenstadt 104883
Dittrick Museum of Medical History, Case Western Reserve University, Cleveland 042990
Ditzoff, Bernard, Coppet 111367
Diva Designz, Oakland 118631
Diva Gallery, Bruxelles 096183
Divadelní Galerie, Uherské Hradiště 098507
Divalco, Mechelen 123662
Divan Edebiyatı Müzesi, İstanbul . . 038089
Divari Kaleva, Helsinki 137936
Divary, Helsinki 137937
Diverse Works, Houston 044639
Diversified, Oklahoma City 132577
Diversified Collectibles, Indianapolis 089290
The Diversion Gallery, Blenheim . . . 078996
Diversity Books, Mordialloc 137005
Diversity Gallery, Saint Louis 119200
Diverso, Amsterdam 077828
Diverssikauppa, Nummi 060617
Divet, Rennes (Ille-et-Vilaine) 067110
Divet, Rennes (Ille-et-Vilaine) 067111
Divet, Rennes (Ille-et-Vilaine) 101076
Divet, Rennes (Ille-et-Vilaine) 101077
Divide County Historical Society Museum, Crosby 043226
La Divine Comédie, Aix-en-Provence 098785
Divine Trash, Miami 090168
Divine Word University Museum, Tacloban 031794
Divinely, Seattle 092987
Divisão de Museus, Patrimônio e Arquivo Histórico, Taubaté 004571
División Museo e Investigaciones Históricas de la Policía Federal, Buenos Aires 000146
Division of Art, Bradley University, Peoria 051929
Division of Art, Florida College, Temple Terrace 052254
Division of Art, Southern Methodist University, Dallas 051223
Division of Art, University of Lethbridge, Lethbridge 049795
Division of Art and Design, Endicott College, Beverly 050980
Division of Art and Design, Purdue University West Lafayete, West Lafayette 052353
Division of Art, Design and Architecture, Judson College, Elgin 051291
Division of Art, School of Fine Arts, Nicholls State University, Thibodaux 052259
Division of Arts, Harrisburg Area Community College, Harrisburg 051443
Division of Arts, Laramie County Community College, Cheyenne 051109
Division of Arts, Russell Sage College, Troy 052275
Division of Arts, Sage Junior College of Albany, Albany 050876
Division of Arts, Western Nebraska Community College, Scottsbluff . . 052153
Division of Arts and Sciences, Concordia University, Mequon 051694
Division of Computer Graphics, Graphic Design and Photography, Sullivan County Community College, Loch Sheldrake 051619
Division of Fine and Performing Arts, Mississippi University for Women, Columbus 051188
Division of Fine Arts, Brevard College, Brevard 051025
Division of Fine Arts, El Camino College, Torrance 052265
Division of Fine Arts, Elmira College, Elmira 051299
Division of Fine Arts, Fullerton College, Fullerton 051366
Division of Fine Arts, Gulf Coast Community College, Panama City 051912
Division of Fine Arts, Judson College, Marion 051679
Division of Fine Arts, Midwestern State University, Wichita Falls 052373
Division of Fine Arts, North Central Texas College, Gainesville 051372
Division of Fine Arts, Oakland City College, Oakland 051871
Division of Fine Arts, Orange Coast College, Costa Mesa 051207
Division of Fine Arts, Sinclair Community College, Dayton 051232
Division of Fine Arts, Truman State University, Kirksville 051555
Division of Fine Arts, University of West Alabama, Livingston 051616
Division of Fine Arts, Wingate University, Wingate 052391
Division of Graphics, La Roche College, Pittsburgh 051958
Division of Humanities and Fine Arts, Illinois Valley Community College, Oglesby 051876
Division of Humanities and Fine Arts, West Shore Community College, Scottville 052155
Division of Humanities & Fine Arts, Saint Norbert College, De Pere 051235
Division of the Arts, Bard College, Annandale-on-Hudson 050905
Divisional Kohima Museum, York . . 041475
Divison of Visual and Performing Arts, Green Mountain College, Poultney 051984
Diwan Dar El Jeld, Tunis 083108
Diwania, Casablanca 107552
Dix, Neuffen 072991
Dix, Axel, Hartmannsdorf 125884
Le Dix-Neuvième, Bruxelles 057917
Dix-Sept, Framlingham 084432
Dixie Gun Works' Old Car Museum, Union City 048697
Dixie's Doll House, Cincinnati 088228
Dixis, New York 117844
Dixon, Midlothian 122964
Dixon, Richmond 123071
Dixon, Charles, London 141779
Dixon, C.J. & A.J., Bridlington 083672
Dixon, John, Auckland 078938
The Dixon Gallery and Gardens, Memphis 045757
Dixon & Harris, New Orleans 090546, 117424
Dixson, Denver 088676
Dixy, Antwerpen 120705
Diyarbakır Devlet Güzel Sanatlar Galerisi, Diyarbakır 038050
Diyarbakır Müzeleri ve Tarihi Kültürel Değerleri, Diyarbakır Arkeoloji Müzesi ve Ziya Gökalp Müze-Evi, Diyarbakır 038051
Dizajn Galerija, Beograd 109687
D.J. & Co., Sutton Coldfield 131564
Djaburov, Bucureşti 080153
Djakarta Museum, Jakarta 022421
Djampel, Santiago de Chile 059521
Djanman, Roosendaal 108168
Djanogly Art Gallery, Nottingham . . 040617
DJT Fine Art, New York 117845
Djuna, Denver 088677
Djursholms Antikvariat, Djursholm . 141092
Djurslands Museum - Dansk Fiskerimuseum, Grenå 008877
Djusa Indianmuseum, Dala Husby . 036232
DK Antiques, New York 090825
D.K. Art Publishing, Los Angeles . . . 135379
DK Project Art, Boston 115167
DKR China Repair Studio, Auckland 128900
DLK Art, New Orleans 117425
DLM, Saint-Laurent-la-Conche 067580
DLM - Deutsches Ledermuseum/ Schuhmuseum Offenbach, Museum für Angewandte Kunst, Ethnologisches Museum, Schuhmuseum und Kunstgalerie, Offenbach am Main 019453
DLT, Philadelphia 132615
D.M., Milano 075697
D.M. Restorations, Weston-super-Mare 087105, 131673
Dmitrenko, Youri, Paris 124651
D.M.S, Saint-Martin-Boulogne 067626
D'n Diestkant, 's-Hertogenbosch . . 108073
DND, Rouen 101114
Dnipropetrovskyj Chudožnij Muzej, Dnipropetrovs'k 038257
DNM Artgroup, Houston 116307
Do, Tokyo 107031
Doa, Alain, Cannes 061941
Doak House Museum, Greeneville . 044321
Dobbie & Roberts, Fenton Barns . . . 084399
Dobbs, John, Sacramento 132733
Dobby, Eric, Orpington 135288
Dobeles Novadpētniecības Muzejs, Dobele 027675
Dober, I., Horstmar 071583
Dobergmuseum/Geologisches Museum Ostwestfalen-Lippe, Museum Bünde, Bünde 016495
Doberschütz, Ute, Stuttgart 126846
Dobes, Heinrich, Petershagen, Weser 073308
Dobi, Marlies & Daniel, Bern 129955
Dobiaschofsky, Bern 122312
Dobkowitz, K., Neustrelitz 073041
Dobler, Renate, Essen 102672
Dobler, Uwe, Augsburg 069221
Doblinger, Ludwig, Wien 137303
Doblougl, Oslo 108708
Dobó István Vármuzeum, Eger 021717
Dobrá Kniha, Praha 137830
O Dobrão, Lisboa 079917
Dobrjanskij Istoriko-kraevedčeskij Muzej, Permskij oblastnoj kraevedčeskij muzej, Dobrjanka 033102
Dobry Styl, Wesola 109208
Dobson Bashford, Christchurch . . . 108392

Dobson's, Abbots Langley 083231
Docal Gonzalez, Maria Estela, Santander 110747
Dochartaigh, B., Dallas 115870
Dock Museum, Barrow-in-Furness . 038604
Dock- och Textilmuseum, Katrineholm 036388
Dock One, Newtown, New South Wales 056338
Dočkal, Dr., Hradec Králové 137783
Docker Street Galleries, Wagga Wagga 095366
Dockmuseum, Gärsnäs 036282
Les Docks de la Rade, Brest 061769
Docks for Antiques, Antwerpen . . . 057691
d.o.c.s. Gallery, New Orleans 117426
The Doctor Vigari Gallery, Vancouver 097456
documenta Archiv für die Kunst des 20. und 21 Jahrhunderts, Kassel 018184
Documentation française, Lyon . . . 138145
Documentation Française, Paris . . . 133567
Documents Magazine, Los Angeles 136451
Dodd, Graeme, Lane Cove 056080, 123253
Dodd, Michael L., Houston 132116
Dodd Cletus, P., Houston 116308
Doddington Hall, Lincoln 040006
Dodds, Mold 122619
Le Dodecaedre, Paris 138355
Dodengang en Oorlogsmuseum, Diksmuide 003404
Dodge & Son, Sherborne . 086576, 131484
Dodge County Historical Museum, Mantorville 045650
Dodge County Historical Society Museum, Beaver Dam 042090
Dodge-Fjeld, New Orleans 090547
Dodier, Philippe, Le Val-Saint-Pere . 063726
Dodin, Roland, Erquy 062797
Dodin, Roland, Pléneuf-Val-André . 066846
Dodington Antiques, Whitchurch, Shropshire 087133
Dodis Shoppe, Vancouver 059355
Dodsland Museum, Dodsland 005354
Dodson, Oklahoma City 118661
Dodsworth, N.J. & C.S., Spennithorne 086677
Döbele, Dresden 102426
Döbele, Ravensburg 104668
Döbele, Ravensburg 104669
Döbler, Rolf-H., Berlin . . . 069593, 125190
Döbritz, Wilhelm M., Frankfurt am Main 070735, 121404
Döderhultarmuseet, Oskarshamn . . 036536
Doehn, Dr. Uwe, Frankfurt am Main 139078
Döhren, Rosemarie von, Radolfzell . 104652
Döllen, Bernhard von, Bad Münstereifel 069332
Dölling & Galitz, Ebenhausen 133901
Dölling & Galitz, Hamburg 134000
Döllinger, Kurt, Markt Erlbach 072460
Dönmez, Galip Bülent, İstanbul 083131
Döpkens, H-J., Berlin 069594
Döppl, Robert, Oberlichtenau 126577
Dörfler, Taura 074045
Dörfler, F., Drackendorf 070302
Dörflihaus-Museum, Spiringen 037586
Dörflinger, A., Freiburg im Breisgau 139108
Dörflinger & Chahin-Dörflinger, Freiburg im Breisgau 139109
Döring, Dinkelscherben 070256
Doering, Abel, Berlin 138766
Doering, Abel, Berlin 138767
Döring, K., Barth 069478
Doerner-Institut, Bayerische Staatsgemäldesammlungen, München 019048
Dörpmuseum Münkeboe, Südbrookmerland 020377
Doerr, Mary, Austin 114976
Dörr & Akin, München 072686
Dörrie & Priess, Hamburg . 103111, 134001
Dörschug, Augsburg 069222
Doesburg, J., Utrecht 078794
Doesburgsch Mosterd- en Azijnmuseum, Doesburg 029486
Dössinger, Franz, München 139502
Dötsch, H.O. & A., Münster 072900
Dofasco Gallery, Dandas Valley School of Art, Dundas 005374
Dog Collar Museum, Maidstone . . . 040387
Dog Eared Books, San Francisco . . 142941
Dog Leap Antiques, Newcastle-upon-Tyne 086065
Dog & Pony Gallery, Birmingham . . 115104
Dogan, Schönecken 104835
Dogan, Enver, Berg, Starnberger See 069529
Dogana d'Arte, Atripalda 023298
Dogenhaus Galerie, Leipzig 103862
Doggerfisher, Edinburgh 112992
Doggett, Ronnie, Louisville 089978
Doggett Street Studio, Newstead . . 094948
The Doghouse, Walsall 087010
Dogon, Berlin 101843
Dogon, Roosendaal 108169
Dogra Art Museum, Jammu 022181
Dogue Bleu, Chamonix-Mont-Blanc 062109
Dohm, Michèle, Pont-à-Mousson . . 066908
Dohnke, Helmut, Geltow 102935
Dohrenbusch, Josef, Mülheim an der Ruhr 134211
Doi Orsi, Milano 075698
Doigts d'Or, Guebwiller 099317
Doison, Christine, Paris 124652
Doka, Tokyo 107032
Dokken, Hol i Hallingdal 030895
Al-Doks, Cairo 060438
Doku Sanat Galerisi, İstanbul 112300
Dokumentačné Centrum Českej Kultúry Martin, Etnografické Múzeum, Martin 034382
Dokumentačné Centrum Rómskej Kultúry Martin, Etnografické Múzeum, Martin 034383
Dokumentarna, Ljubljana . 109955, 129288
Dokumentation des ehemaligen Heilbades, Plastiken-Freilichtmuseum Prof. Knesl, Bad Pirawarth 001733
Dokumentation Obersalzberg - Orts- und Zeitgeschichte, Berchtesgaden . . 015955
Dokumentationraum Georg Matthäus Vischer, Aigen bei Raabs 001666
Dokumentations- und Gedenkstätte, Rostock 019894
Dokumentations- und Informationszentrum, Stadtallendorf 020282
Dokumentations- und Informationszentrum Emslandlager (DIZ), Papenburg . . 019560
Dokumentationsarchiv des österreichischen Widerstandes, Wien 002889
Dokumentationsraum für staufische Geschichte, Göppingen 017445
Dokumentationszentrum Alltagskultur der DDR, Eisenhüttenstadt 016929
Dokumentationszentrum des Landes für die Opfer deutscher Diktaturen, Rostock 019895
Dokumentationszentrum des Landes für die Opfer deutscher Diktaturen, Schwerin 020145
Dokumentationszentrum Prof. Sepp Mayrhuber, Pöchlarn 002435
Dolan, Maxwell, Philadelphia 118750
Dolder, Hans-Rudolf, Hombrechtikon 082499
Doldt, Stefan, Karlsruhe 071715
Dolejschi, Gertrude, Salzburg 057241
Dolenjski Muzej Novo Mesto, Novo Mesto 034509
Dolev, Pamplona 081515
Dolfen, G., Eschweiler 102661
Dolfin, Daniela, Venezia 076931
Dolfus, Paule, Villeurbanne 068958
Dolge, Halberstadt 103058
Dolge, Magdeburg 103986
Dolge, B., Magdeburg 103987
D'Oliver, Palma de Mallorca 081476
Doll, Louisville 135386
Doll, Seoul 107221
Doll and Bear Museum, Manunda . . 001217
Doll Club, Shalford 054357
Doll Gardner Art GAllery, Portland . . 047170
Doll Hospital New York, New York . .090826, 132461
Doll Museum, Tucson 048634
Dollar, Bob, Fort Worth 088850
Dollar Museum, Dollar 039246
Dollenbacher, E., Durmersheim . . . 070488
Dolling, Michael, Glandford 130726
Dollinger, Peter, Luzern 082623
Dolls 4 U, Louisville 089979
Doll's & Bear's at Charlton Court, Long Beach 089631
Dolls, Bears & More, Fresno 088904
Dolls by Jerri, Charlotte 087946
Doll's House, Northleach . 086101, 131323
Dolly Land, London 085257, 131009
The Dolly Mixture, Langbank 039928
Dolly's Antiques, Houston 089070
Dolma Thangka, Kathmandu 107584
Dolmabahçe Sarayı Müzesi, İstanbul 038090
Dølmo Bygdetun, Tolga 031267
Dolnośląskie Stowarzyszenie Artystów Fotografików i Twórców Audiowizualnych, Wrocław 053978
Dolo-Sallard, Annie, Alençon 060765
Dolores Serier, Göteborg 141101
Dolors Junyent, Barcelona 110139
Dolphin Galleries, Honolulu 116207
Dolphin House Gallery, Colyton 112897
Dolphin Quay Antique Centre, Emsworth 084333, 130686
Dolphin Sailing Barge Museum, Sittingbourne 041033
Dolphin Square Antiques, Dorking .084188, 141557
Dolter, Raymond, Wangerland 126967
Dolveck, Christian, Pont-à-Mousson 066909
Dom, Laraia, New York 090827
Dom Aukcyjny Polswiss, Warszawa 121904
Dom Aukcyjny Rempex, Warszawa . 121905
Dom Eskenów, Muzeum Okręgowe w Toruniu, Toruń 032390
Dom Fotografie v Poprade, Poprad . 034410
Dom Gerharta Hauptmanna, Jelenia Góra 031970
Dom Jana Matejki, Muzeum Narodowe w Krakowie, Kraków 032023
Dom Józefa Mehoffera, Muzeum Narodowe, Kraków 032024
Dom Knigi, Sankt-Peterburg 140931
Dom Knigi v Sokolnikach, Moskva . 140904
Dom Książki, Warszawa 140785
Dom Miguel, Porto 080080
Dom-Museum, Fulda 017296
Dom-Museum Bremen, Bremen . . . 016410
Dom-Museum Hildesheim, Hildesheim 017921
Dom-muzej Akademika E.N. Pavlovskogo, Borisoglebskij kraevedčeskij muzej, Borisoglebsk 033042
Dom-muzej L.N. Andreeva, Gosudarstvennyj literaturnyj muzej im. I.S. Turgeneva, Orël 033604
Dom-muzej S.M. Budennogo, Proletarsk 033674
Dom-muzej A.P. Čechova, Gosudarstvennyj literaturnyj muzej, Moskva 033381
Dom-muzej N.N. Chochrjakova, Kirovskij oblastnoj chudožestvennyj muzej im. Viktora i Apollinarija Vasnecovych, Kirov 033260
Dom-Muzej T.N. Chrenikova, Elec . . 033132
Dom-muzej G.V. Čičerina, Tambovskij oblastnoj kraevedčeskij muzej, Tambov 033937
Dom-muzej K.Ė. Ciolkovskogo, Kaluga 033219
Dom-muzej P.P. Čistjakova, Puškin . 033680
Dom-muzej Čudomir, Kazanlăk . . . 004713
Dom-muzej K.I. Čukovskogo, Peredelkino 033641
Dom-muzej M.I. Cvetaevoj, Moskva 033382
Dom-muzej Dekabristov, Kurganskij oblastnoj kraevedčeskij muzej, Kurgan 033315
Dom-muzej F.M. Dostoevskogo, Staraja Russa 033902
Dom-Muzej A.L. Durova, Voronežskij oblastnoj kraevedčeskij muzej, Voronež 034077
Dom-muzej A.A. Dydykina, Gosudarstvennyj muzej palechskogo iskusstva, Palech 033624
Dom-muzej Elin Pelin, Nacionalen Muzej na Bălgarskata Literatura, Bajlovo . . 004623
Dom-muzej E.M. Jaroslavskogo, Jakutskij gosudarstvennyj muzej istorii i kultury narodov severa im. Jaroslavskogo, Jakutsk 033184
Dom-muzej M.N. Ermolovoj, Moskva 033383
Dom-muzej M.V. Frunze, Samarskij oblastnoj istoriko-kraevedčeskij muzej im. P.V. Alabina, Samara 033715
Dom-muzej Gannibalov v Petrovskom, Muzej-zapovednik A.S. Puškina Michajlovskoe, Puškinskie Gory . . 033687
Dom-muzej Generala I.A. Plieva, Vladikavkaz 034035
Dom-muzej N.V. Gogolja, Gorodskaja biblioteka - kulturnyj centr N.V. Gogolja, Moskva 033384
Dom-muzej I.I. Golikova, Gosudarstvennyj muzej palechskogo iskusstva, Palech 033625
Dom-muzej M.B. Grekova, Muzej istorii Donskich kazakov, Novočerkassk 033578
Dom-muzej A.S. Grina, Kirov 033261
Dom-muzej Hamza Hakim-zade Niazy, Kokand 049394
Dom-muzej im. T.N. Granovskogo, Gosudarstvennyj literaturnyj muzej im. I.S. Turgeneva, Orël 033605
Dom-muzej Istorii Molodëžnogo Dviženija, Rjazan 033695
Dom-Muzej P.D. Korina, Gosudarstvennyj muzej palechskogo iskusstva, Palech 033626
Dom-muzej V.G. Korolenko, Gelendžikskij istoriko-kraevedčeskij muzej, Gelendžik 033147
Dom-Muzej I.N. Kramskogo, Ostrogožskij istoriko-chudožestvennyj muzej im. Kramskogo, Ostrogožsk 033620
Dom-muzej P.A. Krasikova, Krasnojarskij kraevoj kraevedčeskij muzej, Krasnojarsk 033293
Dom-muzej Pavla Kuznecova, Chudožestvennyj muzej im. A.N. Radiščeva, Saratov 033853
Dom-muzej V.I. Lenina, Kazan 033230
Dom-muzej V.I. Lenina, Samarskij oblastnoj istoriko-kraevedčeskij muzej im. P.V. Alabina, Samara 033716
Dom-muzej M.Ju. Lermontova, Moskva 033385
Dom-muzej N.S. Leskova, Gosudarstvennyj literaturnyj muzej im. I.S. Turgeneva, Orël 033606
Dom-muzej D.I. Mendeleeva, Boblovo 033036
Dom-muzej M.K. Ammosova, Jakutskij gosudarstvennyj muzej istorii i kultury narodov severa im. Jaroslavskogo, Jakutsk 033185
Dom-muzej N.S. Muchina, Olikjal . . 033595
Dom-muzej N.S. Muchina, Nacionalnyj muzej respubliki Marij Ėl im. T. Evseeva, Joškar-Ola 033201
Dom-muzej Narodnogo Chudožnika V.A. Igoševa, Chanty-Mansijsk 033084
Dom-muzej N.A. Nekrasova, Čudovo 033096
Dom-muzej I.S. Nikitina, Voronežskij oblastnoj literaturnyj muzej im I.S. Nikitina, Voronež 034078
Dom-muzej Osipovych-Vul'f v Trigorskom, Muzej-zapovednik A.S. Puškina Michajlovskoe, Puškinskie Gory . . 033688
Dom-muzej A.N. Ostrovskogo, Moskva 033386

Dom-muzej B.L. Pasternaka, Gosudarstvennyj literaturnyj muzej, Peredelkino 033642
Dom-muzej Penjo Penev, Dimitrovgrad 004664
Dom-muzej Petra Pervogo (Petrovskij Domik), Vologda 034069
Dom-muzej M.M. Prišvina, Gosudarstvennyj literaturnyj muzej Moskva, Dunino 033106
Dom-muzej B.I. Prorokova, Ivanovskij oblastnoj chudožestvennyj muzej, Ivanovo 033169
Dom-Muzej S.V. Rachmaninova, Ivanovka 033168
Dom-Muzej I.E. Repina, Samarskij oblastnoj chudožestvennyj muzej, Žigulevsk 034095
Dom-muzej F.I. Šaljapina, Moskva . 033387
Dom-muzej M.E. Saltykova-Ščedrina, Kirov 033262
Dom-muzej Semji Cvetaevych, Novo-Talicy 033577
Dom-muzej Semji Lopatinych, Stavropol 033908
Dom-muzej Semji Suchanovych, Primorskij gosudarstvennyj muzej im. V.K. Arsenjeva, Vladivostok 034042
Dom-muzej Sestër Nevzorovych, Nižnij Novgorod 033551
Dom-muzej Skulptora A.S. Golubkinoj, Zarajskij Kreml, Zarajsk 034093
Dom-muzej K.S. Stanislavskogo, Muzej Moskovskogo Chudožestvennogo Akademičeskogo teatra, Moskva . 033388
Dom-muzej Tukaevych, Nacionalnyj muzej Respubliki Tatarstan, Košlauč . . . 033285
Dom-muzej Usman Jusupov, Jangi-Jul 049391
Dom-muzej G.I. Uspenskogo, Sjabrenicy 033872
Dom-muzej V.A. Rusanova, Orlovskij oblastnoj kraevedčeskij muzej, Orël 033607
Dom-muzej Ivan Vazov, Sopot 004878
Dom-muzej Konstantin Veličkov, Pazardžik 004769
Dom-muzej Velimira Chlebnikova, Astrachanskaja gosudarstvennaja kartinnaja galereja im. B.M. Kustodieva, Astrachan 033005
Dom-Muzej V.V. Veresaeva, Tula . . . 033971
Dom-muzej N.M. Zinovjeva, Gosudarstvennyj muzej palechskogo iskusstva, Djagilevo 033100
Dom-Muzej N.N. Žukova, Gorodskoj kraevedčeskij muzej, Elec 033133
Dom na Humora i Satirata, Gabrovo 004682
Dom Naščokina, Moskva 109504
Dom-pametnik na Vrach Buzludža, Kazanlăk 004714
Dom Poèta A.N. Širjaevca - Muzej Krestjanskogo Byta, Žigulevsk . . . 034096
Dom Rodzinny Ojca Świętego Jana Pawla II, Wadowice 032408
Dom F.I. Šaljapina - Galereja, Moskva 109505
Dom Sztuki, Gdańsk 108877
Dom und Domschatz Halberstadt, Halberstadt 017644
Dom Uphagena, Muzeum Historyczne Miasta Gdańska, Gdańsk 031906
Dom Urodzenia Fryderyka Chopina, Warszawa 032422
Doma Mungi Gallery, Chiltern 094391
Domaine Cataraqui, Sillery 006473
Domaine de l'Abbé Saunière, Rennes-le-Château 014024
Domaine de l'Hospitalet, Narbonne 013349
Domaine MB, Amsterdam 107701
Domaine National de Chambord, Chambord 011216
Domaines, Toulouse 101341
Domakowski, Lothar, Ostrach 073262
Domani, Christchurch 128920
Domati, Patrizio, Modena 127729
Domberger, Filderstadt . . . 102727, 133929
Dombuchhandlung, Wiener Neustadt 137383
Dome Antiques, London . . 085258, 131010
Domein De Locht, Duffel 003413
Domek Mauretański, Warszawa . . . 109113
Doménat, Brive-la-Gaillarde 061809, 124163
Dômergue, Margaret, Clermont-Ferrand 062340
Domergue & Co., Robert, San Francisco 092774
Domes, Wolfgang, Ochsenfurt 104516
Domgrabungsmuseum, Salzburger Museum Carolino Augusteum, Salzburg . . . 002547
Domik Petra I, Sankt-Peterburg . . . 033737
Domingues, Joaquim Pontes, Lisboa 079918
Domingues da Silva, Marie-Claude, La Destrousse 063364
Dominguez Espinosa, Andres, Madrid 081288
Dominguez Guinaldo, Mario, Salamanca 110734
Dominguez Manteca, Felix Didimo, Getxo 110352
Domini Canes, Tallinn 098696
Dominici Art Edition, Leopoldsdorf bei Wien 133110
Dominicis, Paola, Milano 075699
Dominic's Art Gallery, Hong Kong . . 097778
Dominiiklaste Kloostrimuuseum, Tallinn 009395
Dominik, Königstein im Taunus . . . 126127
Dominikanermuseum Rottweil, Zweigmuseum des Württembergischen Landesmuseums Stuttgart und des Archäologischen Landesmuseums Konstanz, Rottweil 019931
Dominikonų Gatvė Antikvariatas, Vilnius 140230
Dominikowski & Rybarczyk, Wrocław 140805
Dominion Antiques, Toronto 059175
Dominion Books, Auckland 140588
Dominique, Bruxelles 057918
Dominique, C., Pont-Aven 101023
Dominique Antiquités, Saint-Jeoire-Prieure 067552
Domino, Mannheim 072418
Domino Antik, Stockholm 081942
Domino Gallery, Liverpool 113407
Domino Noir, Montréal 123785
Dominović, Zagreb 133401, 137765
Dominus, Bucureşti 109427
Dominus Flevit, Franciscan Custodia di Terra Sancta, Jerusalem 022947
Dominus Z Art, Bucureşti 109428
Domirai, Meersburg 104050
Domizil Antique, Esslingen 070660
Domizil im Berliner Dom, Berlin . . . 016014
Domkammer der Kathedralkirche Sankt Paulus zu Münster, Münster 019142
Dommanovich, Trudica, Großwarasdorf 057047
Dommuseum, Brandenburg an der Havel 016367
Dommuseum, Chur 037020
Dommuseum, Frankfurt am Main . . 017159
Dommuseum zu Salzburg, Salzburg 002548
Domobaal, London 113581
Domont, John, Indianapolis 116453
Domowniski muzej Dešno, Niedersorbisches Heimatmuseum Dissen, Dissen, Niederlausitz 016727
Domschatz, Trier 020478
Domschatz, Würzburg 020994
Domschatz der Sankt Servatius-Stiftskirche, Quedlinburg 019682
Domschatz Sankt Ursen Kathedrale, Solothurn 037573
Domschatz- und Diözesan-Museum Eichstätt, Eichstätt 016909
Domschatz- und Diözesanmuseum, Passau 019569
Domschatz und Museum des Sankt Petri-Domes, Fritzlar 017275
Domschatzkammer, Aachen 015419
Domschatzkammer, Essen 017063
Domschatzkammer, Köln 018306
Domschatzkammer, Minden, Westfalen 018950
Domschatzkammer Sankt Petri, Bautzen 015899
Domschatzkammer und Diözesanmuseum, Osnabrück 019490
Domschatzmuseum, Regensburg . . 019746
Domus, Napoli 075976
Domus, Poznań 109046
Domus, Rozzano 135896
Domus, Vancouver 097457
Domus, Wiesbaden 074398
Domus Antiqua, Milano 075700
Domus Antiqua, Mostra Nazionale di Antiquariato, Civitanova Marche . 093760
Domus Antiqua-Città Dorica, Mostra Nazionale di Antiquariato, Ancona 093761
Domus Arte, Roma 106522
Domus Aurea, Catania 075247
Domus - Casa del Hombre, A Coruña 035123
Domus Galilaeana, Pisa 025262
Domus Mazziniana, Pisa 025263
DoMuS - Museum und Galerie der Gemeinde Schaan, Schaan 027837
Domus Nova, Parma 076204
Domus Romana, Aubechies 003207
Domus Starocie, Warszawa 079751
Domus Varius, Lisboa 109282
Domusvenda, Lisboa 121928
Domvorhalle, Goslar 017480
Domy Brocante, Erquinghem-le-Sec 062796
Don Bank Museum, North Sydney . 001337
Don Books, Invercargill 140635
Don F. Pratt Museum, Fort Campbell 043898
Don Garlits Museum of Drag Racing, Ocala 046612
Don Harrington Discovery Center, Amarillo 041680
Don River Railway Museum, Devonport 000981
Dona, Francesca, Los Angeles 089754
Doña Antigualla, Madrid 081289
Doña Antigualla, Madrid 081290
Dona Taraja, Lisboa 079919
Donabedian Koharig, Michel, Romans-sur-Isère 067202
Donaghue, Chris, San Francisco . . . 142942
Donahue, New York 132462
Donald, Julie, Coburg 094412
Donald Agricultural Museum, Donald 000986
Donald G. Trayser Memorial Museum, Barnstable 042025
Donalda and District Museum, Donalda 005355
Donaldson, E., San Antonio 142886
Donat, Bremen 133842
Donat, Hans-Christoph, Speyer . . . 104932
Donat, Hervé, Strasbourg 068314
Donat-le-Drezen, Simone, Pont-l'Abbé 066926
Donath, Inge, Troisdorf 105068
Donath & Szojda, Berlin 069595
Donath & Szojda, Berlin 125191
Donáti, Budapest 074678
Donati, Giancarlo, Perugia 127875
Donati, Pino & Stefano, Lugano . . . 082595
Donation François Mitterrand, Jarnac 012148
Donation Mario Prassinos, Saint-Rémy-de-Provence 101226
Donato, Colmar 062409
Donato, Niedermorschwihr 065162
Donato, Giuseppe, Roma 128025
Donatzsky, Torben, Gentofte 060249
Donau-Schiffahrts-Museum-Regensburg, Arbeitskreis Schiffartsmuseum Regensburg e.V, Regensburg 019747
Donauhalle, Donaueschingen 016737
Donay, London 085259
Donazione Putti Biblioteca, Raccolta dell'Istituto Ortopedico Rizzoli, Bologna 023418
Donazione Sambo, Palazzo Galatti, Trieste 026136
Doncaster Museum and Art Gallery, Doncaster 039249
Doncaster Sales and Exchange, Doncaster 084173
Dondaine, Claude, Castres 062033
Donderbus, Rotterdam 078714
Dondo, Niš 109733
Dondtai Antique Market, Shanghai . 059736
Done, Ken, Sydney 095283, 133056
Donec'kij Oblasnyj Chudožnij Muzej, Donec'k 038262
Donec'kij Oblasnyj Krajeznavčyj Muzej, Donec'k 038263
Donegal County Museum, Letterkenny 022820
Donegal Historical Society Museum, Rossnowlagh 022854
Donelly & Co., Alan, Perth 056456
Doneux, Kristine, Torino 128299
Dong, Seoul 107222
Dong, Phong, Ha Noi 120460
Dong, Phuong, Ho Chi Minh City . . . 120505
Dong-Bang Gallery, Seoul 107223
Dong-eui University Museum, Busan 027458
Dong Fang, Shanghai 097907
Dong Fang, Shanghai 097908
Dong Fang, Shanghai 097909
Dong-Ho, Seoul 107224
Dong Nai College of Decorative Arts, Bien Hoa 052424
Dong San Bang Gallery, Seoul 107225
Dong Son, Ha Noi 120461
Dong-Suh, Masan 107200
Donga University Museum, Busan . 027459
Dongguk University Museum, Seoul 027550
Dongha Museum, Dongen 029495
Dongjin Irrigation Folk Museum, Gimje 027494
Donglin, Wuxi 098032
Dongshan County Artists Union, Tongling 052794
Dongyi Art, Wuxi 098033
Dongyu Art Gallery, Shenyang 097960
Dongzhang Calligraphy and Painting Gallery, Changshu 097694
Donington Grand Prix Collection, Castle Donington 039010
Donjon, Montréal 137653
Donjon-Château Carondolet, Crupet 003380
Donker, Ad., Rotterdam 134830
Donkersloot, Amsterdam 107702
Donkey Milk House, Key West . . . 044982
Donn, Henry, Whitefield 087136
Donn, Henry, Whitefield 114683
Donn, Henry, Whitefield 131683
Donn, Massimo, Torino 128300
Donna Beam Fine Art Gallery, University of Nevada, Las Vegas, Las Vegas . . . 045182
Dønna Bygdesamling, Dønna 030805
Donna Gallery, Abu Dhabi 112438
Donnaint, Agincourt 124059
Donna's Not Just Antiques, Indianapolis 089291
Donnelly, Adrian, Shrewsbury 086602, 131495
Donnelly Homestead, Lucan 005805
Donnelly River Timber Mill Museum, Donnelly River 000987
Donner, Helsinki 060516
Donner, Johannes, Wegberg 105169
Donner Memorial and Emigrant Trail Museum, Truckee 048622
Donnybrook Art School, Dublin 050344
Dono, Houston 089071
Donohue & Bousquet, Ottawa 059037
Don's Antiques, Jacksonville 089405
Don's Antiques, San Francisco 092775
Don's Auction Barn, Jacksonville . . 122932
Don's Coin Center, Tulsa 093300
Don's Collectables, Seattle 092988
Don's Refinishing Service, Omaha . 132590
Don's Shop, Westerland 074366

Don's Village Coins, San Francisco . 092776
Donskoj Istoriko-kraevedčeskij Muzej, Donskoe 033104
Donson, Theodore B., New York . . . 117846
Donvale Antique Clocks, Donvale . . 055753
Donzé-Van Saanen, Antonia, Lausanne 111613
Donzeau, Dax 120984
Donzella, New York 090828
Donzelli, Roma 134671
Donzelli, Ferdinando, Firenze 106047
Donzelli, Ferdinando, Milano 106211
Doocollect, Madrid 122048
De Doofpot, Den Haag 078190
Dooley, H. & G., Lismore 056105
Doon Heritage Crossroads, Kitchener 005715
Door Art Gallery, Fresno 116173
Door County Maritime Museum, Gills Rock 044192
Door County Maritime Museum, Sturgeon Bay 048407
Door County Museum, Sturgeon Bay 048408
Den Doorbraeck, Amsterdam 077829
Doorten, H., Meppel 128771
Doose, Michael, Hamburg 125809
Doozoo Children's Museum, Grand Junction 044266
Doppelkapelle Sankt Crucis, Landsberg bei Halle, Saale 018480
Doppler, Denis, Rechesy 067046
Doppler, Josef, Ried am Riederberg 057220
D.O.R., Olsberg 073219
Dor Antic, Nice 065076
Dor Art, Vancouver 097458
Doran, M.A., Tulsa 120193
Dorascenzi, Pietro, Roma 128026
Dorate, Ali, Amsterdam 107703
Doratura Su Legno, Roma 076437
Dorau, Gernot, Berlin 069596, 121329
Dorchester Abbey Museum, Dorchester-on-Thames 039262
Dorchester Antiques, Dorchester-on-Thames 084181, 130644
The Dorchester Bookshop, Dorchester 141555
Dorchester County Historical Society Museum, Cambridge 042554
Dordrechts Museum, Dordrecht . . . 029502
Dordtse Antiekhandel, Dordrecht . . 078300
Dore, San Francisco 119655
Doré, Sønderso 098602
Le Doré Brocante, Paris 065841
Dorée, Jacques, Dole 124224
Doreen Young Art Gallery, Great Barrington 044297
Doreth, Georg, Neustadt am Kulm . 126541
Dorety, John, Philadelphia 091631
Dorf- und Fahrradmuseum, Pflückuff 019604
Dorf- und Heimatmuseum, Winterbach bei Schorndorf 020917
Dorfman, Cancún 107464
Dorfman, New York 117847, 135425
Dorfmann, Patricia, Paris 100219
Dorfmuseum, Bad Alexandersbad . . 015643
Dorfmuseum, Bennwil 036921
Dorfmuseum, Birmensdorf 036956
Dorfmuseum, Birr 036957
Dorfmuseum, Bönigen 036961
Dorfmuseum, Bottmingen 036966
Dorfmuseum, Ettingen 037080
Dorfmuseum, Feldbrunnen 037083
Dorfmuseum, Fislisbach 037085
Dorfmuseum, Gahlenz 017313
Dorfmuseum, Görzig 017459
Dorfmuseum, Gontenschwil 037154
Dorfmuseum, Großgörschen 017571
Dorfmuseum, Grube, Holstein 017587
Dorfmuseum, Herrnbaumgarten . . . 002040
Dorfmuseum, Hombrechtikon 037192
Dorfmuseum, Hüntwangen 037195
Dorfmuseum, Katzelsdorf, Leitha . . 002117
Dorfmuseum, Kienberg, Oberbayern 018254
Dorfmuseum, Konolfingen 037216
Dorfmuseum, Langendorf 037231
Dorfmuseum, Nikitsch 002379
Dorfmuseum, Pfaffenweiler 019601
Dorfmuseum, Pöttelsdorf 002449
Dorfmuseum, Rupperswil 037469
Dorfmuseum, Schönbach bei Grimma 020069
Dorfmuseum, Schönwalde am Bungsberg 020086
Dorfmuseum, Schwanden (Glarus) . 037539
Dorfmuseum, Therwil 037628
Dorfmuseum, Wiesen 037707
Dorfmuseum, Zeihen 037746
Dorfmuseum, Ziefen 037750
Dorfmuseum Ahnenhaus, Pliezhausen 019638
Dorfmuseum Alter Forsthof, Wetter, Hessen 020838
Dorfmuseum Altkirchen, Altkirchen 015509
Dorfmuseum Bellach, Bellach 036912
Dorfmuseum Buchenberg, Königsfeld im Schwarzwald 018349
Dorfmuseum Daniel-Martin-Haus, Rauschenberg 019731
Dorfmuseum Deckenpfronn, Deckenpfronn 016653
Dorfmuseum Delligsen, Delligsen . . 016663
Dorfmuseum Dettingen/Iller, Dettingen an der Iller 016695
Dorfmuseum Dietersweiler, Freudenstadt 017251
Dorfmuseum Düppenweiler, Beckingen 015930
Dorfmuseum Düppenweiler, Beckingen 015931
Dorfmuseum Graberhaus, Strengelbach 037611
Dorfmuseum Günzach, Günzach . . . 017596
Dorfmuseum Hanweiler, Städtisches Museum, Winnenden 020912
Dorfmuseum Hausen im Wiesental, Heimathaus des alemannischen Dichters J. P. Hebel, Hausen im Wiesental . 017805
Dorfmuseum Haynrode, Haynrode . 017813
Dorfmuseum Holzburg, Schrecksbach 020098
Dorfmuseum im Greifenhaus, Hausen, Oberfranken 017807
Dorfmuseum Kelter, Marbach am Neckar 018812
Dorfmuseum Kirchbözberg, Unterbözberg 037650
Dorfmuseum Maschwanden, Maschwanden 037316
Dorfmuseum Melihus, Möhlin 037329
Dorfmuseum Mertingen, Mertingen 018917
Dorfmuseum Mönchhof, Mönchhof . 002332
Dorfmuseum Ostheim, Nidderau . . . 019303
Dorfmuseum Poppenweiler, Ludwigsburg, Württemberg 018692
Dorfmuseum Ringenwalde, Ringenwalde bei Templin 019850
Dorfmuseum Roiten, Rappottenstein 002501
Dorfmuseum Schlossweid, Ringgenberg 037456
Dorfmuseum Stove, Stove bei Wismar 020328
Dorfmuseum Tündern, Hameln 017729
Dorfmuseum Weckbach, Weilbach . 020722
Dorfmuseum Weinburg, Weinburg . 002815
Dorfmuseum Wilsenroth, Dornburg, Westerwald 016753
Dorfmuseum Zeissholz, Zeißholz . . 021044
Dorfmuseum Zwingendorf, Zwingendorf 003079
Dorfschulmuseum, Ködnitz 018299
Dorfstube Münchholzhausen, Wetzlar 020839
Doria, Paris 100220
Doria & Lino Santos, Franca, Lisboa 079920
Dorian, Miami 117058
Doric Arts, King's Lynn 113325
Doric House, Flemington 043859
Dorigo, Richard, Zürich . . 082958, 130233
Doris' Place, Saint Louis 092227
Doriti, Maria, Lemesos 098312
Dorking and District Museum, Dorking 039263
Dorking Desk Shop, Dorking 084189
Dorking House Antiques, Dorking . . 084190
Dorman Memorial Museum, Middlesbrough 040460
Dormen, İstanbul 112301
Dormentoni, Romano, Roma 128027
Dorn, Wachtendonk 074234
Dorn, Gertrud, Stuttgart 104971
Dorn, Werner, Weisendorf 074323
Dorn-Schwägerl, Elisabeth, Kerpen, Rheinland 126031
Dornal, Golden Square 055893
Dornburg Galerie, Dornburg, Westerwald 102389
Dornburger Schlösser, Stiftung Weimarer Klassik und Kunstsammlungen, Dornburg, Saale 016752
Dornebusch, A., Düren 070347
Dorner, Aggsbach Dorf 056912
Dorner, Anton, Darmstadt 138973
Dorney Court, Windsor 041413
Dornier, Vincent, Nancy 138231
Dorniermuseum im Neuen Schloß, Meersburg 018871
Dornoch Heritage Museum, Dornoch 039266
Dorobanti, Bucureşti 109429
Dorobell, Castello de la Plana 110304
Doron, Esther, Jerusalem 074999
Dorothea B. Hoover Historical Museum, Joplin 044881
Dorothea C. Witham Gallery, Lewiston 045249
Dorotheum, Bruxelles 120723
Dorotheum, Graz 120662
Dorotheum, Innsbruck . . . 057078, 120665
Dorotheum, Klagenfurt . . . 057105, 120667
Dorotheum, Linz 057155, 120668
Dorotheum, München 121524
Dorotheum, Pasching 057204, 120671
Dorotheum, Praha 060123, 120856
Dorotheum, Salzburg 057242, 120673
Dorotheum, Sankt Pölten 120675
Dorotheum, Vösendorf . . . 057343, 120676
Dorotheum, Wien 057400
Dorotheum, Wien 120681
Dorotheum, Wien 120682
Dorotheum, Wiener Neustadt 120699
Dorothy G. Page Museum, Wasilla . 048977
Dorothy's Antiques, Sheringham . . 086589
Dorothy's House Museum, Cambellcroft 005204
Dorottya Galéria, Budapest 105502
Dorpsmuseum de Kleuskes, Liempde 029868
Dorpsmuseum De Kluis, Eext 029532
Dorpsmuseum in de Drie Snoeken, Oud-Gastel 030019
Dorr, Wiesbaden 074399
Dorrego, Buenos Aires 055200
Dorridge Antiques, Dorridge 084212
Dorrigo Art of the Country, Dorrigo . 094484
Dorrigo Steam Railway and Museum, Dorrigo 000988
D'Orsai, Sebastian, London 085260, 131011
Dorsch, Miami 117059
Dorschel, Klaus, Emmerich 102623
Dorsel, Friederike, Heimbach, Eifel . 103341
Dorset Coin Company, Parkstone . . 086192
Dorset Conservation, Toronto 123829
Dorset County Museum, Dorchester 039256
Dorset Rare Books, Shaftesbury . . . 142055
Dorset Reclamation, Bere Regis . . . 083489
Dorset Teddy Bear Museum, Dorchester 039257
Dorsky, Carol, New York 117848
Dorsky, Marsha, New York 090829
Dorsman, Titus, Amsterdam 140294
Dorta, Antonietta, Miami 117060
Dortmunder Kunstverein e.V, Dortmund 053140
Dortmunder Museumsgesellschaft, Dortmund 053141
Dorval, Claude, Paris 100221
Dorval, Régis, Lille 099485
Dorval Art Gallery and Cultural Centre, Dorval 005357
Dory Shop Museum, Shelburne . . . 006454
Dos Coronas, Barcelona 080842
Dos Hermanos Viejo, Madrid 081291
Dosch, Peter P., Zürich 112060
Dose, Bernd, Lübeck 072323
Doshisha Neesima Memorabilia Room, Kyoto 026713
Dosho-machi Pharmaceutical and Historical Museum, Osaka 026958
Doß, Brigitte, Quickborn 139669
Dossat, Madrid 134940
Dossev, Sofia 096727
Dossier de l'Art, Dijon 135703
Les Dossiers de l'Art Public, La Varenne-Saint-Hilaire 135704
Dossin Great Lakes Museum, Detroit 043447
Dostál, Praha 060124, 123979
Doster, K., Amstetten 101580
Doster, Thomas, Tübingen 074110, 139794
Dot, Genève 111441
Dot Concept, Singapore 109790
Dotart Galeria de Arte, Belo Horizonte 096460
Dots to Nuts, Cleveland 115702
Dotti, Daniel, Roma 140103
Dotzel & Sons, Michael J., New York 132463
Dotzheimer Museum, Wiesbaden . . 020863
Dou, Gerard, Amsterdam 077830
Double Bay Old Books, Double Bay . 136881
Double Dragon II, Honolulu 088945
Double Duck's, Eindhoven 078333
Double Vision Gallery, Los Angeles . 116755
Doublet, Avranches 098904
Doubletake Gallery, Minneapolis . . 117253
Douchet, François, Biéville-Beuville 061482
Les Doucines, Lambres-les-Douai . 063498
Douet, Digosville 062636
Doug, Birmingham 087752
Doug Kerr Vintage Museum, Oaklands 001350
Doughty, John, San Francisco 092777
Douglas, Miami 090169
Douglas, South Deerfield 123121
Douglas, Bobby, Comber 084070
Douglas, David, Indianapolis 116454
Douglas, Gavin, London . . 085261, 131012
Douglas, S., Montréal 096996
Douglas Art Association, Douglas . . 054742
Douglas-Baker, Minneapolis 117254
Douglas Brett Modern Life Designs, San Francisco 119656
Douglas County Historical Society Museum, Superior 048436
Douglas County Museum Complex, Armour 041784
Douglas County Museum of History and Natural History, Roseburg 047541
Douglas Design, Edmonton 096874
Douglas F. Cooley Memorial Art Gallery, Portland 047171
Douglas Hall, Brighton 083693
Douglas Heritage Museum, Douglas, Lanarkshire 039269
Douglas Hyde Gallery, Dublin 022736
Douglas & McIntyre, Vancouver . . . 133330
Douglass, Dallas 115871
Douglass Historical Museum, Douglass 043487
Douillard, Saint-Hilaire-de-Riez . . . 067516
Douillard, Frédéric, Saumur 068151
Douma, Amsterdam 077831, 128534
Douma, A.R., Amsterdam 077832
Douma, M.H., Amsterdam 077833
Doumen County Fine Art Calligraphy Society, Zhuhai 007355
Doumen County Museum, Zhuhai . . 007356

Doumenc, Laurent, Saint-Medard-en-Jalles 067670
Doune Motor Museum, Doune 039270
Doussière, Marseille 124411
Gebr. Douwes, Amsterdam 107704
Douwes, Sint Nicolaasga 128832
Douwes & Edel, London . . 085262, 113582
Dove, San Diego 119500
Dove Cottage and the Wordsworth Museum, Grasmere 039623
Dove House Gallery, Mornington . . . 094884
Dovebid Australasia, Melbourne . . . 120609
Dover-Calais Antiques, Atlanta . . . 087468
Dover Castle, Dover 039273
Dover Museum, Dover 039274
Dover Old Town Goal, Dover 039275
Dover Publications, Mineola 135395
Dover Street Gallery, London 113583
Dover Transport Museum, Whitfield 041373
Doveridge House Antiques, Wolverhampton 087208, 131707
Dovero, Gérard, Marseille 124412
Dovetail Antiques, Peter, Sheffield .086555, 131473
Dovetail Creations, Charlotte 131871
Dovetail Restoration, Atlanta 131767
Dovetails Gallery, Ilfracombe 113287
Dovin Galéria, Budapest 105503
Dow, Fort Worth 116140
Dowd Fine Arts Gallery, State University of New York, Cortland 043173
Dower House Antiques, Kendal 084825
Dowerin District Museum, Dowerin 000989
Dowers, Chester, Cincinnati 122854
Dowie, Robert, Leven 122565
Dowling, Judith, Boston . . 087815, 115168
Dowling & Bray, Looe 085849
Dowling Street Gallery, Dunedin . . .079084, 108430
Down County Museum, Downpatrick 039281
Down Home Antiques, Miami 090170
Down Home Creations, Oklahoma City 091495
Down House, Home of Chales Darwin, Downe 039279
Down Lane Hall Antiques, Tunbridge Wells 086936, 131617
Down Memory Lane, Columbus . . . 088403
Down Memory Lane, Fyshwick 055852
Down Memory Lane, Fyshwick 136911
Down the Lane, Hamilton 058851
Down Town, Paris 100222
Downer, Stella, Waterloo 056807
Downer Ross, Milton Keynes 122618
The Downers Grove Park District Museum, Downers Grove 043500
Downes, Stephen, New York 117849
Downey, Peter, Auckland 078939
Downey Museum of Art, Downey . . 043501
Downhill Castle, Castlerock 039013
Downie, Robert, Whitchurch, Shropshire 142152
Downieville Museum, Downieville . 043502
Downings, Ramsgate 114295
Downpatrick Railway Museum, Downpatrick 039282
Downs Court Galleries, Altrincham . 112503
Downstairs Gallery, Vancouver 097459
Downtown Antiques, West Hollywood 093464
Downtown Antiques Mall, Nashville 090446
Downtown Books, Milwaukee 142567
Downtown Gallery, New Orleans . . . 117427
Downtown Independent Gallery, Los Angeles 116756
Downtown Model Trains, Vancouver 059356
Dow's Books, Aberdeen 141377
The Dowse, Hutt City 030518
Dowse & Son, A.E., Sheffield 122696
Doyen, Yannick, Vannes (Morbihan) 101427
Doyle, Malvern East 056135
Doyle, Rotorua 079229, 128952
Doyle, Stephen F., Providence 092038
Doyle, William, New York . 117850, 122992
D.P. Druck- und Publikations GmbH, München 134230
DPD Svoboda Tone Čufar, Jesenice 109937
DPH Trading, Odense 060396
D.P.M., Brescia 075164, 127213
Dr. Arratta Memorial Museum, Muttaburra 001306
Dr.-Arthur-Lindgens-Jagdmuseum, Schönsee 020085
Dr.-Bauer-Heimatmuseum, Bad Rothenfelde 015777
Dr. Bhau Daji Lad Museum, Mumbai 022261
Dr.-Carl-Haeberlin-Friesen-Museum, Wyk auf Föhr 021031
Dr. Daniel W. Kissam House, Huntington 044679
Dr. Do a Lot, Kumeu 128940
Dr. Eisenbarth- und Heimatmuseum, Oberviechtach 019427
Dr. Engelbert Dollfuß-Museum, Texing 002739
Dr. Francis Medical and Apothecary Museum, Jacksonville 044810
Dr. Giri's Museum, Chennai 022055
Dr. Heins Classic Car Collection, Christchurch 030463
Dr. Henry N. Payne Community Museum, Cow Head 005302
Dr. Hideyo Noguchi Memorial Hall, Inawashiro 026563
Dr. Increase Mathews House, Zanesville 049373
Dr. John Harris Dental Museum, Bainbridge 041948
Dr. Johnson's House, London 040136
Dr. Jose Celso Barbose Museum, Bayamón 032705
Dr. J.'S Baseball Cards, Cleveland .088324, 142336
Dr. Kui-Fang Lai Art Museum, Singapore 034291
Dr. Ljudevit Gaj Museum, Krapina . . 007746
Dr. Norman Bethune Memorial Hall of Tang Xian, Tang Xian 007281
Dr. Park Collection and Gallery, Seoul 027551
Dr. Pepper Museum and Free Enterprise Institute, Waco 048811
Dr. Raj Bali Pandey Puratatva Sangrahalaya, Deoria 022099
Dr. Samuel D. Harris National Museum of Dentistry, Baltimore 041979
Dr. Sun Yat Sen Memorial House, Macau 007181
D.R. Visual Art Center, Nakorn-Chaisri 037915
Dr. V.L. Watson Allied Arts Centre, Dauphin 005327
Dr. William Robinson Plantation, Clark 042948
Dr. Woods House Museum, Leduc . 005761
Draaiorgelmuseum, Assen 029278
Draakoni, Tallinn 098697
Drabinsky, Toronto 097260
Drachenhöhle, Syrau 020393
Drachmanns Hus, Skagen 009092
Drackett, Cincinnati 088229
Dräxler, Dr. Bettina, Wien 123493
Dragehøj Gallerie, Næstved 060394
Dragesco-Cramoisan, Bernard, Paris 065842
The Dragon, South Molton 086640, 131513
Dragon and Fiends Antiques, Hong Kong 059618
Dragon and Fiends Antiques, Hong Kong 059619
Dragon and Friends, Hong Kong . . . 059620
The Dragon and the Phoenix, South Molton 086641
Dragon Antique Furniture, Seoul . . . 077366
Dragon Antiques, Harrogate 084573
Dragon Antiques, Kettering 084834
Dragon Antiques, New York 090830
Dragon Art, Portland 091928, 118991
Dragon Court Antiques, Singapore . 080455
Dragon Culture, Hong Kong 059621
Dragon Culture, Hong Kong 059622
Dragon Era, Shanghai 059737
Dragon Gallery, Ha Noi 120462
Dragon Gate Antique, Hong Kong . . 059623
Dragon House, San Francisco 092778
Dragon House, Singapore 080456
Dragon- og Frihedsmuseet, Holstebro 008923
Dragon & Phoenix, Sunnybank 056649
Dragon Traders, Seattle 092989
La Dragona, Roma 076438
Dragonette, Los Angeles 089755
Dragonette, Patrick, West Hollywood 093465
Dragonflies & Daydreams, Pittsburgh 091811
Dragonfly, Den Haag 078191
Dragonfly Antiques, Louisville 089980
Dragons of Walton Street, London . 085263
Dragør Museum, Dragør 008832
Dragosavljevic, Zoran, Bad Rappenau 069355
Dragus, Mada M., São Paulo 058704
Draheim, Rellingen 073483
Draheim, Michael, Wiesbaden 074400
Drahoš, Ladislav, Rožňava 080636
Drai, Edmond, Le Pian-Medoc 063683
Drai, Guillaume, Bordeaux 061602
Drai, Simon, Bordeaux 061603
Draier Verlag, Friedberg, Hessen . . 133961
Draisienne, Saint-Étienne 067453
Drake House Museum, Plainfield . . 047074
Drake Well Museum, Titusville 048562
Drakensteijn, Amsterdam 077834
Drakesbrook, Waroona 056799
Drammens Museum, Drammen Kunstforening, Drammen 030806
Drammens Museum for Kunst og Kulturhistorie, Fylkesmuseum og Galleri for Buskerud, Drammen 030807
Drangedal Bygdetun, Drangedal . . . 030808
Dranoff, New York 117851
Draper, Jim, Jacksonville 116520
Dratwiński, Jerzy, Poznań 140760
Dráva Múzeum, Barcs 021626
Drawbridge, Saint Paul 092358
Drawe, G., Speyer 073877
Drawing Center, New York 046325
The Drawing Room, Pershore 086218
Drawing Society of Canada, Gabriola Island 052749
The Drawingroom, Chesham 112848
Drawings Collection, Royal Institute of British Architects, London 040137
Drawn From Memory, London 113584
Dray, Jacques, Paris 065843
Draysey, R., London 085264
Drayton Hall, Charleston 042731
Drayton Valley Museum, Drayton Valley 005358
Drazen, Sydney, New York 090831, 122993
Dream, E., San Francisco 119657
Dream a Theme, Detroit 116085
Dream Merchants, Denver 088678
Dream Toys, Bruxelles 057919
Dreamcards, Las Vegas 089564
Dreamhaven Books, Minneapolis . . 142582
The Dreaming Room, San Francisco 092779
Dreamland, Baltimore 087658
Dreamtime Cultural Centre, North Rockhampton 001336
Drechsel, M. & G., Karlsruhe 071716
Drechsel-Selunka, Roswitha, Dresden 125487
Drechsler- und Metalldrücker-Museum, Wendelstein, Mittelfranken 020794
Dreczko, M., Reutlingen 104723
Dred, Scott, Surry Hills 095250
Drees, Bruxelles 096184
Drees, Robert, Hannover 103271
Drefit, Kraków 129034
Dreher, Anselm, Berlin 101844
Drei-Brunnen-Verlag & Co., Plüderhausen 134350
Drei-Königs-Antik, Reutlingen 093715
Drei-Seen-Galerie, Seeham 095759
Dreieich-Museum, Dreieich 016778
Dreier, Wolfgang, Berlin 069597
Dreikronenhaus, Kulturgeschichtliches Museum Osnabrück, Osnabrück . 019491
Dreimäderlhaus, Wien 057401
Dreimol, Uwe, Münster 072901
Dreiseitel, Helmut, Köln 103611
Dreispitz, Thunstetten 111947
Drenewydd Museum, Bute Town . . 038934
Drenth, Almelo 077723
Drenthe's Veste Stedelijk Museum, Coevorden 029386
Drents Museum, Assen 029279
De Drentse Glasbloazer, Dalen 029393
Drescher, Olaf, Berlin 138768
Drescher & Winkelgrund, Kabschütztal 125985
Dresdener Antiquariat, Dresden . . . 138989
Dresdener Kunstauktionshaus, Dresden 121376
Dresdener Kunstblätter, Dresden . . 135759
Dresdner Münzhandlung, Dresden . 070311
Dresdner Rahmenwerkstatt, Dresden 125488
Dresdner Sezession 89 e.V., Dresden 053142
Dreuille, Paris 065844, 124653
Drevet, Saint-Ouen 067765
Drew, Fort Worth 088851
Drew, Simon, Dartmouth 112935
Drew County Historical Museum, Monticello 045999
Drewdale, New York 142648
Dreweatt Neate, Newbury 122626
Drewello, Dr. Rainer, Gräfenberg . . 125749
Drews, Alfons & Augen, Wiesbaden 134458
Drews, Walter, Wien 057402, 137304
Drexler, Louisville 089981
Dreyer, H., Mönchengladbach 072566, 126326
Dreyer, Marc, Thann 068379
Dreyfus, Austin 087569, 131797
Dreyfus, Raymond, Paris . 065845, 100223
Dreyfus, Sophie, Paris 065846
Dreyfuss, Simone Michele, Bari . . . 075018
Dreyfuss, Simone Michele, Bari . . . 075019
Dreyspring, Brigitte, Wiesbaden . . . 127008
Dreysse, Roswitha, Quedlinburg . . . 126669
Driant, Jany, Langres 063524
Driba, Marsa 112251
Dridan, McLaren Vale 094752
Drie Kronen, Alkmaar 077712
De Drie Uilen, Utrecht 078795
Driebe Freight Station, Stroudsburg 048400
Driels Oudheidkundig Museum, Kerkdriel 029808
Driesen, A., Bocholt 069874
Driessen, K., Selfkant 073796
Driessen, P.A.P., Maastricht 128759
Driessen & Schreurs, Genk 058160
Drieux, Pascale, Paris 065847
Drif, Wittenheim 069054
Driffold, Sutton Coldfield . 086801, 114527
Drifting River Museum, Ashville . . . 005033
Driftwood, Cleveland 115703
Driftwood Gallery, Ilfracombe 113288
Drilandmuseum Gronau, Gronau, Westfalen 017551
Drill Hall Gallery, Acton 000699
Drill Hall Market, New Norfolk 056327
Driminagh Castle, Dublin 022737
Dring, C. & K.E., Lincoln 084996
Drinhausen, A., Nümbrecht 073091
Drinhausen, Rolf, Köln 071927
Dri's Phoenix Book Store, Oklahoma City 142725
Drishti, Nagpur 105820
Drisket, Anne-Marie, Liège 058297
Dritsoulas, Serafim, München 072687, 104166, 126369
Dritsoulas, Serafim, Neufahrn 126532
Drive-In Exchange, Baltimore 087659
Drjanovski Manastir Muzej, Drjanovo 004674

Droege, Rudolf, Düsseldorf 070371
Dröge, V., Bad Salzuflen 138702
Dröge, Volker, Bielefeld 138871
Dröll, Gisela, Koblenz 126058
Dröscher, Hamburg 103112
Drogerie-Museum, Weißenstadt . . . 020786
Drogeriemuseum, Frankfurt am Main 017160
Droin, Gérard, Auxonne 120914
Droite, Den Haag 078192
Droitwich Spa Heritage Centre, Droitwich 039284
Dromana and District Museum, Dromana 000990
Dromana Antiques, Dromana 055758
Dromson, Strasbourg 068315, 101285
Dronfield Antiques, Sheffield 086556
Droogdok Jan Blanken, Hellevoetsluis 029718
Droomdeur, Amsterdam 077835
De Droomfabriek, Amsterdam 077836
Drop Dial Antiques, Bolton 083570, 130407
Droschl, Max & Annette, Graz 095521, 133076, 137175
Drostdy Museum, Swellendam 034761
Drostdy Museum, Uitenhage 034765
Droste, Dr. D., Eppelheim 070575
Droste, Dr. Dao, Eppelheim 102632
Droste, Rüdiger von, Andernach . . . 069167
Droste-Museum, Münster 019143
Droste-Museum, Burg Hülshoff, Havixbeck 017812
Droste-Museum im Fürstenhäusle, Meersburg 018872
Droste Verlag, Düsseldorf 133889
Drottningholm Slott, Drottningholm 036236
Drottningholms Teatermuseum, Nacka 036493
Drouant, Paris 100224
Drouart, Paris 100225
Drouet, Juliette, Paris 138356
Drouin, Audincourt 061057
Drouot Art, Paris 121141
Drouot de Richelieu, Paris 121142
Drouot Estimations, Paris 121143
Drouot Montaigne, Paris 121144
Drouot Nord, Paris 121145
Drown, William R., London 131013
Droysen-Keramikgalerie, Berlin . . . 101845
Droz, Genève 135016, 141248
Drtikola, Františka, Příbram 098496
Druckereimuseum, Freienbach 037094
Druckereimuseum, Hatten, Oldenburg 017792
Druckereimuseum, Wildeshausen . 020891
Druckgrafik Kätelhön, Möhnesee . .104084, 134205
DruckKunstHof Dudensen, Neustadt am Rübenberge 134311
Druckmuseum, Darmstadt 016634
Druckmuseum Graz, Graz 001929
Druckwerkstatt im Bethanien, Berlin 101846
Drüner, Dr. Ulrich, Stuttgart 139758
Druivenmuseum, Overijse 003699
Drukkerijmuseum Meppel, Meppel . 029918
Drum & Co., San Francisco 092780
Drum, Denis, Dublin 121663
Drum Barracks Civil War Museum, Wilmington 049201
Drum Castle, Drumoak 039288
Drum Museum Taikokan, Tokyo . . . 027157
Drumheller Dinosaur and Fossil Museum, Drumheller 005360
Drumlanrig Castle, Thornhill, Dumfriesshire 041217
Drumlanrig's Tower, Hawick 039702
Drumlin Farm, Lincoln 045298
Drummer, Matthias, Berlin 138769
Drummond, Hindhead 084690
Drummond, London 085265
Drummond, Nicholas, London 085266, 131014
Drummond Home, Hominy 044589
Drummond Island Historical Museum, Drummond Island 043509
Drummonds Antiques, Auckland . . . 078940
Drumond, Fernanda & Gonzaga, Funchal 109254
Druon, Sylvie, Douchy-les-Mines . . 062729
Drusilla, Baltimore 142223
Društvo Muzejskih Radnika Bosne i Hercegovine, Sarajevo 052697
Društvo Muzejskih Radnika Vojvodine, Novi Sad 054035
Društvo na likovnite umetnici za primeneta umetnost na Makedonija, Skopje . 053849
Društvo Povjesničara Umjetnosti Hrvatske, Zagreb 052817, 135663
Drutt, Helen, Philadelphia 118751
Druvienas Vecā Skola, Druviena . . . 027678
Dry, Dr. Graham, München 134231
Dry Falls Interpretive Center, Coulee City 043190
Dry Mounting, Brilon 102267
Dryden, New York 117852
Dryden and District Museum, Dryden 005366
Dryden Galleries, Providence 119076
Dryphoto, Prato 106473
Drysdale, Bowen Hills 136810
Drysdale, A.F., Edinburgh 084285
Drzażdżyński, Marek, Warszawa . . 129082
Držjavna Chudožestvena Galerija, Plovdiv 004792
D's Antiques, Kansas City 089497
D.S.L, Rennes (Ille-et-Vilaine) 067112
DSM, Saint-Maur-des-Fossés 067658
DSS Coin, Omaha 091564
DSV-Verlag, Hamburg 134002
D.T.A. Galerie, Genk 096279
Du Page County Historical Museum, Wheaton 049135
Du Tam-Tam au Satellite, Angers . . 010389
Duailibe, Fortaleza 096520
Dual Galerija, Novi Sad 109738
Dualchas-Museum Bharraigh Agus Bhatarsaidh, Isle-of-Barra 039822
Dualibe, Fortaleza 096521
Duane Antiques, New York 090832
Duane Reed, R., Saint Louis 119201
Duarte & Martins, Lisboa 121929
Dubach, Langenthal 082523
Dubai Museum, Dubai 038423
Dubard, Dijon 062654
Dubbel, Siegfried, Gevelsberg 070984, 102946
De Dubbele Deur Antiek, Rotterdam 078715, 128818
De Dubbele Palmboom, Historisch Museum Rotterdam, Rotterdam 030078
Dubbert, Nordhorn 073081
Dubbo Antiques, Dubbo 055762
Dubbo Military Museum, Dubbo . . . 000992
Dubbo Museum, Dubbo 000993
Dubbo Regional Gallery, Dubbo . . . 000994
Dube, Saint-Ouen 067766
Dubé, Laurier, Paris 100226, 133568
Dube-Heynig, Dr. Annemarie, München 104167
Dubernet de Garros, Agnès, Cahors 061898
Dubey, Baltimore 087660
Dubinsky, Zürich 112061
Dubio, Den Haag 107913
Dublin Art Metals, Dublin 074909
Dublin Castle, Dublin 022738
Dublin Civic Museum, Dublin 022739
Dublin-Kitzen, Miami 117061
Dublin-Laurens Museum, Dublin . . 043510
Dublin Print Museum, Dublin 022740
Dublin Writers Museum, Dublin . . . 022777
Dubly, Hervé, Saint-Malo (Ille-et-Vilaine) 101171
Dubly, Jacques, Le Castellet 063586
Duboc, Rodolphe, Andé 060834
Dubois, Nantes 064921
Dubois, Paris 065848
Dubois, Adrien, Pertuis 066778
Dubois, Colette, Paris 100227
Dubois, Dominique, Tilques 068421
Dubois, Eric, Paris 065849, 100228
Dubois, Jean-François, Paris 065850
Dubois, Jess E., Denver 115988
Dubois, Michel, Saint-Hilaire-du-Harcouët 067519
Dubois, Nicole, Bias 061480
Dubois, Rémi, Suresnes 068342
Dubois, Rémi, Versailles 068802
Dubois de Marolle, Jean-Claude, Paris 065851
Dubois Rémi, Colombes 062427
Dubouilh, P., Langon 063520
Dubouilh, Patrick, La Reole 063404
Dubouilh, Patrick, Verdelais 068766
Dubourg, Jean-Pierre, Bègles 120923
Dubourg, Jean-Pierre, Bordeaux . . 120941
Dubravcic, Dubravko, Garching bei München 125698
Dubreuil, Bertrand, Bordeaux 124122
Dubrovin Farm Museum, Yisod Hama'ala 023101
Dubuque Museum of Art, Dubuque . 043512
Dubuy, Lucie, Paris 124654
Duc, Minh, Ho Chi Minh City 120506
Duc Minh Art Gallery, Ho Chi Minh City 049535
Ducaat, Doetinchem 078289
El Ducado, Santander 081554, 110748
Ducalerestauro, Venezia . . 076932, 128388
Ducasse, Patrick, Dax 062605
Ducastel, Avignon 098893
Ducate, John, Namur 058350
Ducellier, Hugues, Pithiviers-le-Vieil 121224
Duchange, Roger, Paris 065852
DuChâteau, Bernard, Saint-Ouen . . 067767
Duchâteau, Monique, Paris 124655
Duchatel, Nicolas, Saxon-Sion 068172
Duché d'Uzès, Uzès 015079
Duchemin, Guy, Rouen 067265
Duchemin, Guy, Rouen 067266
Duchêne, Toulouse 138633
Duchenet, Laurent, Caen 061868
Ducheng Museum, Luoyang 007178
Duchenne, Daniel, Compiègne 124207
Ducher, François, Pouilly-sous-Charlieu 066971
Ducher, Jean-Claude, Charlieu 062162
Duchet, Jacques, Pervencheres . . . 066779
Duchoze, Daniel, Rouen 101115
Duck Creek Antique Mall, Cincinnati 088230
Duck Lake Regional Interpretive Centre, Duck Lake 005367
Duckler, Alysia, Portland 118992
Duclerc, André, Sennecey-le-Grand 068210
Duclerc, Marie-Claude, Chalon-sur-Saône 062085
Duclos la Chine, Clermont-Ferrand . 138076
Duco, Breda 107877
Ducos, Marc, Saint-Jean-Mirabel . . 067549
Ducoté, Frédéric-Charles, Lyon . . . 064119
Ducoté, Vincent, Lyon 064120
Ducrocq, Emmanuel, Tournon-sur-Rhône 068563
Ducroz, Michel, Chamonix-Mont-Blanc 062110
Ducroz, Michel, Les Praz-de-Chamonix 063776
Duda, Sonja, Steinheim am Albuch . 073909
Duda, W., Stegen 139742
Dudenhoeffer, Roger, Capestang . . 061966
Dudgeon, Jack, Berwick-upon-Tweed 122408
Dudit, Cholet 062298
Dudley and Mary Marks Lea Gallery, Findlay 043844
Dudley Museum and Art Gallery, Dudley 039290
Dudmaston House, Quatt 040788
Dudouit, François, Honfleur 099341
Dudragne, Vincennes 138662
Le Due Sicilie, Messina 075561
Due Time, Salt Lake City 092429
Dülkener Narrenmuseum, Viersen . 020588
Duell, C., Boston 115169
Dülmer Kunstverein e.V., Dülmen . . 053143
Dümmer-Museum, Lembruch 018604
Dueñas, Teodulo, Bogotá . 059834, 123899
Dünenhaus, Ostseebad Ahrenshoop 104552
Dünnbier, Wolfgang, Großschönau, Sachsen 125770
Dünne, R., Bad Salzuflen 069364
Dünnebacke, Gisela, Düsseldorf . . 102485
Duensing, Elfi, Aschaffenburg 138683
Duensing, Ilse, Gmund 071013
Dür, Adliswil 111109
Dür, Rapperswil, Sankt Gallen 111820
Dür, Wädenswil 111976
Dürbeck, Straubing 104957
Dürbeck, I., Deggendorf 102352
Dürer Verlag, Nürnberg 139603
Düring, Leo, Bad Königshofen 069309
Dürmoser, P.J.H., Millstatt 057182
Dürnberger, Franz, Ihringen 071611
Dürnfelder, Silke, Hannover 125867
Dürr, Worms 074482
Dürr, Bernd, München . . . 072688, 104168, 134232
Dürr, Michel, Carouge 082290
Dürr Hübnerstr 5, Christoph, München 104169
Dürrbeck, Petra & Hubert, Höchstadt an der Aisch 103386
Dürring, Kurt, Basel 111176
Dürrschmidt, M., Großräschen 125769
Dürsteler, Heinz, Zürich 082959
Dürstelerhaus, Ottikon (Gossau) . . . 037408
Dürüst, A., Augsburg 069223
Düsseldorfer Auktionshaus, Düsseldorf 121382
Düsseldorfer Museumsverein e.V., Düsseldorf 053144
Düster, J.B., Essen 070625, 125610
Düsterdieck, Jürgen, Vellmar 126945
Düwal, Eckard, Berlin 138770
Dufaux, Jacques, Morges 082672
Dufey, Serge, Lausanne 130068
Duff, George, Edinburgh 084286
Duff Community Heritage Museum, Duff 005368
Duffar, Nicole, Vichy 068856
Dufferin County Museum, Rosemont 006304
Dufferin Historical Museum, Carman 005230
Duffour, Pierre, Rochefort (Charente-Maritime) 067176, 124879
Duffy, Brian, London 131015
Duffy & Sons, Jimmy, Philadelphia . 118752
Duffy, John, Dublin 121664
Duffy, John, Dunshaughlin 074971
Duffy, Michael, Dublin 074910
Dufillot, Georges, Bordeaux 124123
Dufillot, Georges, Bordeaux 124124
Duflot, Jacques, Angers 060852
Dufor Quercy, Michel, Montauban . . 064633
Dufour, Amiens 098820
Dufour, Alain, Ramatuelle 067034
Dufour, Alain, Saint-Maur-des-Fossés 067659
Dufour, Edmond, Chaumont-sur-Tharonne 062253
Dufour, Eric, Trun 068656
Dufour, Roseline, Saint-Féliu-d'Avall 067472
Dufrasne, Philippe, Bruxelles 057920
Dufreche, Besançon 120927
Dufresne, C., Montréal 096997
Dufresne-Serre, Christine, Genève .082421, 130034
Duftmuseum, Köln 018307
Dufus, Nicolas, Piffonds 066830
Duggan, N.S., Baltimore 087661
Duggan-Cronin Gallery, Kimberley . 034659
Dugger Coal Museum, Dugger 043515
Dugout, Indianapolis 089292
Dugovic, Fresno 088905
Dugrenot, Paris 065853
Dugue, François Xavier, Chatou . . . 062241
Duhamel, Alexis, Béthune 120929

Duhamel, Guillaume, Paris 100229
Duhamel, Laurence, Montigny 064693
Duhme, Osnabrück 073232
Duinat, Saint-Jean-de-Luz 067535
Duivenvoorden, P.H.A., Leiden 128742
Dujardin, Laurent, Marcq-en-Barœul 064273
The Duka, Windsor, Queensland . . . 056830
Dukan, Bangalore 074768
Dukan & Co, Marseille 099650
Duke & Son, Hy., Dorchester 122490
Duke & Son, Hy., Weymouth 122743
Duke, Tom, Dallas 088501
Duke Homestead State Historic Site, Durham 043541
Duke of Cornwall's Light Infantry Museum, Bodmin 038774
Duke University Museum of Art, Durham 043542
Duke University Union Museum and Brown Art Gallery, Durham 043543
Dukek, Ursula, Oberstaufen 073152
Dukel, R.C.T., Leiden 078565
Dukelské Múzeum - Vojenské Múzeum Svidník, Svidník 034438
Duke's Antiques, Kitchener 058871
Dukessa, Vitoria-Gasteiz 110870
Duksung Women's University Art Museum, Seoul 027552
Dukwon Museum of Art, Seoul 027553
Dulce, El Paso 116105
Dulce & Filho, M.H., Porto Alegre . . 096551
Dulcey, Bucaramanga 098210
Duleep Singh Picture Collection, Thetford 041208
Dulitz, Joachim, Guben 103026
Dulkerian, Baltimore 087662
Dullaert, H.W.C., Amsterdam 077837
von Dullak, Karin, Freising 102875
Dulle, Martin, Alsdorf, Rheinland . . 069139
Dulle, Willi, Alsdorf, Rheinland 069140
Dullsville, New York 090833
Dulon Klegman, Paris 100230
Duluth Art Institute, Duluth 043518
Duluth Children's Museum, Duluth . 043519
Dulwich Antiques, Dulwich 055765
Dulwich Art Fair, London 093924
Dulwich Decorative and Fine Arts Society, London 054358
Dulwich Picture Gallery, London . . . 040138
Dům Gustava Mahlera, Jihlava 008410
Dům Pánů z Kunštátu, Moravské Zemské Muzeum, Brno 008284
Dům u Černé Matky Boží, Národní Galerie v Praže, Praha 008599
Dům u Jonáše, Východočeská Galerie, Pardubice 008559
Dům u Kamenného Zvonu, Galerie Hlavního Města Prahy, Praha 008600
Dům u Rytířů, Litomyšl 098382
Dům u Zlatého Prstenu, Galerie Hlavního Města Prahy, Praha 008601
Dům Umění, České Budějovice 008317
Dům Umění, Jihomoravské Muzeum ve Znojmě, Znojmo 008791
Dům Umění Města Brna, Brno 008285
Dumac, London 058881
Dumaine, Le Tronchet 063724
Dumaine, Suzanne, Tulle 068659
Dumaine-Lafare, Bandol 061187
Dumaresq, Rio de Janeiro 058582
Dumartin, Christian, Ligré 063821
Dumartin, Gilles, Chinon 062293
Dumas, Aix-les-Bains 060722
Dumas, La Monnerie-le-Montel . . . 124280
Dumas, André, Lyon 121048
Dumas, François, Beaune 061275
Dumas, Gustave, Nice 124508
Dumas, Jean-Paul, Lyon . 064121, 124354
Dumas, Xavier, Uzès 101396
Dumas-Simart, Paris 100231
Dumbarton House, Washington . . . 048900
Dumbarton Oaks Collections, Harvard University, Washington 048901
Dumesnil, Stéphane, Etretat 124236
Dumez, B., Liège 123650
Dumez Numismatique, Mulhouse . . 064832
Dumfries and Galloway Aviation Museum, Dumfries 039295
Dumfries Museum, Dumfries 039296
Dumins, Frank, Viersen 074210
Dumjahn, Horst-Werner, Mainz 139446
Dumkow, Michael, Winterthur 130221
Dummann, Rüdiger, Wien 057403
Dummer, Julia, Köln 126073
Dumont, Austin 114977
DuMont, Köln 134102
Dumont, Bruno, Aouste 060935
Dumont, Eric, Troyes 101392
Dumont, F., Namur 058351
Dumont, Marcel, Aumale 061065
Dumont, Michel, Fribourg 082377
Dumont, Michel, Mainneville 064219
Dumont, Tancrède & Lô, Caen 120956
DuMont Kunsthalle, Köln 018308
Dumonteil, Andre, Montpellier 138219
Dumonteil, Pierre-Michel, Paris . . . 100232
Dumouchelle, Toledo 120078
DuMouchelle, Lawrence, Detroit . . 122889
Dumoulin, Joël, Condrieu 062456
Dumoussaud, Paris 100233
Dumoussaud, Daniel, Avignon 061133
Dumousset, Patrick, Paris 121146
Dun Laoghaire Institute of Art, Design and Technology, Dun Laoghaire 050347
Duna Galéria, Budapest 105504
Dunaharaszti-Helytörténeti Emléktár, Dunaharaszti 021715
Dunajský, Kežmarok 080614
Dunakapu Téri Régiség Üzlet, Győr . 074737
Dunamelléki Református Egyházkerület Biblia Muzeuma, Budapest 021645
Dunamelléki Református Egyházkerület Ráday Múzeuma, Kecskemét 021756
Dunántúli Képcsarnok, Pécs 074747, 105570
Dunántúli Református Egyházkerület Tudományos Gyűjteményei Múzeum, Pápa 021809
Dunaskin Open Air Museum, Patna . 040675
Dunaway, R., Saint Louis 142855
Dunbar, Marcus, South Queensferry 114453
Dunbar Sloane, Wellington 079322, 121842
Dunbar Town House Museum, Dunbar 039301
Dunblane Museum, Dunblane 039304
Duncan, Louisville 089982, 122948
Duncan, Alan S., Buckie 130471
Duncan, David, New York 090834
Duncan, Jack, York 142177
Duncan, Ken, Matcham 094796
Duncan, Ken, Melbourne 094808
Duncan, Ken, Pokolbin 095075
Duncan, Ken, Sydney 095284
Duncan & Baird, London 135213
Duncan Cottage Museum, Metlakatla 045799
The Duncan Gallery of Art, Stetson University, De Land 043333
Duncan-McAshan Visual Arts Center, Ingram 044757
Duncan of Jordanstone College of Art and Design, Dundee 050810
Duncan of Jordanstone College of Art and Design Exhibition, Dundee 039314
Duncan & Reid, Edinburgh 084287
Duncker, München 072689
Duncker, Alexander, München 134233
Dunconor Workshops, Salida 052096
Dundalek, Peter-Moritz, Göppingen 071027
Dundar Avenue Print Workshop, Vancouver 097460
Dundas Historical Society Museum, Dundas 005375
Dundas Valley School of Art, Dundas 049782
Dundee Art Galleries and Museum Association, Dundee 054359
Dundee Art Society, Dundee 054360
Dundee Art Society, Dundee 112963
Dundee City Council Arts and Heritage, Dundee 039306
Dundee Township Historical Society Museum, Dundee 043530
Dundonian Studio and Gallery, Dundee 094496
Dundurn Castle, Hamilton 005589
Dundy County Historical Society Museum, Benkelman 042143
Dune Art, Cairo 098625
Dunedin Fine Arts and Cultural Center, Dunedin 043531
Dunedin Fine Arts and Cultural Center, Dunedin 051273
Dunedin Historical Society Museum, Dunedin 043532
Dunedin Public Art Gallery, Dunedin 030482
Dunedin Public Libraries Artprint Collection, Dunedin 030483
Dunedoo Country Antiques, Dunedoo 055766
Duner, Göteborg 110908
Dunfermline Museum, Dunfermline 039317
Dung, Peter & Petra, Köln 071928
Dung Bui, Paris 100234
Dungarvan Museum, Dungarvan . . 022781
Dungl, Gustavine, Gars am Kamp . . 137172
Dungog Antiques, Dungog 055767
Dungog Historical Museum, Dungog 000996
Dunguaire Castle, Kinvara 022817
Dunham Massey Hall, Altrincham . . 038501
Dunham Tavern Museum, Cleveland 042991
Dunhill, Cleveland 088325, 131957
Dunhill Museum, London 040139
Dunhuang Literature and Art Publishing House, Lanzhou 133371
Dunilli Arts, Casuarina 055649
Dunimarle Castle, Culross 039191
Dunkel, Helmut, Berlin 069598
Dunkel, Thorsten, Hamm, Westfalen 103243
Dunkeld Antiques, Dunkeld 084233
Dunkeld Cathedral Chapter House Museum, Dunkeld 039322
Dunker & Nellissen, Greven 139154
Dunkers Kulturhus, Helsingborgs Museer, Helsingborg 036332
Dunklin County Museum, Kennett . . 044959
Dunlop Art Gallery, Regina 006251
Dunluce Antiques, Bushmills 083827, 130493
Dunluce House Museum, Kimberley 034660
Dunmore Antiques, Kincardine O'Neill 084847
Dunn & Co, Capes, Manchester . . . 122611
Dunn, Hamish, Wooler . . . 087244, 142172
Dunn, John D. & Francis W., Malvern, Victoria 056146
Dunn, Michael, Tokyo 077241
Dunn, Oliver, Washington 093409
Dunn & Brown, Dallas 115872
Dunn-Seiler Museum, Mississippi State 045930
Dunn & Sonnier, New Orleans 090548
Dunnes, San Jose 132923
Dunnet Pavilion, Castletown 039016
Dunolly Museum, Dunolly 000997
Dunoon and Cowal Museum, Dunoon 039324
Dunree Military Museum, Inishowen 022797
Dunrobin Castle Museum, Golspie . 039600
Duns Area Museum, Duns 039327
Dunsborough Gallery, Dunsborough 094497
Dunsheath, Anah, Auckland 140589
Dunst, Ludwig, Sankt Gallen 130159
Dunstan, Caspar, London 113585
Dunster, K.W., Staines 086680
Dunster Castle, Dunster 039329
Dunvegan Castle, Dunvegan 039330
Dunwell and Community Museum, Weekes 006781
Dunwich Museum, Dunwich 039331
Dunzendorfer, Herwig, Hellmonsödt 095563
Duo, Paris 065854
Duo Antiquités-Brocante, Bruxelles 057921
Duo Yun Xuan, Shanghai 097910
Duodecimo, Gent 123619
Dupard, Yvonne, Pougues-les-Eaux 066967
Dupasquier, Pierre-Alain, Bulle 082281
Dupeux, L'Isle-d'Espagnac 138123
Dupeyron, Claude, Castelmoron-sur-Lot 062011
Dupeyron, Dominique, Orléans 065301
Dupeyroux, Jean, Elbeuf-sur-Seine 120997
Dupierry, Max, Großhansdorf 125763
Dupin, Juliette, Paris 124656
Duplan, Frédéric, Lille 063847
Duplantier, Mireille, Hasparren 063132
Duplessis, Jacques Vigoureux, Vignory 068874, 138659
Dupont, Kortrijk 058262
Dupont, Paris 065855
Dupont, Washington 120280
Dupont, Chantal, Troyes 068646
Dupont, Eric, Paris 100235
Dupont, Jean, Troyes 068647
Dupont, Lucienne, Bergerac 061360
Dupont, Marlène Edith, Montreuil-sous-Bois 124464
DuPont, Polly, Dallas 088502
DuPont, Polly, Dallas 088503
Dupont, Roberte, Troyes 068648
Dupont, Sophie, Paris 065856
Dupont, Thérèse, Fribourg 130019
DuPont-Antiquités, Saint-Ouen 067768
Dupont Gallery, Lexington 045278
DuPont Historical Museum, DuPont 043534
Duprat, Miguel, Saintes 068085
Dupraz, Jean-Baptiste, Fribourg . . . 130020
Dupré, Rob, Amsterdam 077838
Duprez, Monique, Paris 065857
Dupront, Salon-de-Provence 068102
Dupuis, Bernard, Nice 124509
Dupuis, Dominique, Saint-Quentin (Aisne) 124919
Dupuis, Joël, Condette 099170
Dupuis, Joël, Hardelot-Plage 099323
Dupuis, Robert, Berlin 125192
Duputel, Paris 065858, 100236
Dupuy, Honfleur 121015
Dupuy, Daniel, Pujols 066997
Dupuy, Eonnet, Paris 100237
Dupuy, Michèle, Paris 065859
Dura-Strip of Santa Monica, Los Angeles 132251
Durai, Miroslav, Bratislava 129270
Dural Antiques, Dural 055771
Dural Galleries, Dural 094499
Durán, Madrid 081292, 110486
Duran, Madrid 110487
Durán, Madrid 122049
Durán, Fernando, Madrid 081293
Durán, Fernando, Madrid 081294
Durán, Fernando, Madrid 122050
Durán, Fernando, Madrid 122051
Durán, Fernando, Madrid 122052
Durán, Fernando, Madrid 122053
Durán, Fernando, Madrid 141036
Durán, Pedro, Madrid 122054
Durance, G., Nantes 138240
Durand, Calgary 096807
Durand, Brigitte, Saint-Maur-des-Fossés 067660
Durand, Brigitte, Sens 068216
Durand, Gilles, Villeurbanne 068959
Durand, Guy, Montceau-les-Mines . 064664
Durand, Jean-Michel, Menil-la-Tour 064483
Durand-Réville, Françoise, Paris . . . 065860
Durand-Ruel & Cie., Caroline, Paris 100238
Durandot, Denis, Dijon 124220
Durangaldeko Natur Zientzien Museoa, Durango 035156
Durango, Carmen, Valladolid 110851
Durant, Eliane, Saint-Laurent-de-la-Salanque 067576
Durant & Kotek, Bruxelles 057922
Durante, Giovanni, Roma 076439
Durations Gallery, Baltimore 115046
Durban, Caracas 120423
Durban Art, Westbridge 054065

Durban Art Gallery, Durban 034598
Durban Natural Science Museum, Durban 034599
Durban Segnini, Miami 117062
Durbes Pils, Tukums 027785
Ďurčanský, Alexej, Trnava 129284
Durchblick-Galerie, Leipzig 103863
Durden, Memphis 116983
Dureau, Laurence, Bourges 061725
Durero, Gijón 110357
Duret Dujarric, Paris 100239
Durga's Art, Mumbai 105766
Durham, Linda, New York 117853
Durham Art Gallery, Durham 005377
Durham Art Guild, Durham 043544, 054743
Durham Cathedral Treasures of Saint Cuthbert, Durham 039332
Durham Center Museum, East Durham 043559
Durham Heritage Centre and Museum, Durham 039333
Durham Historic Association Museum, Durham 043539
Durham House Antiques Centre, Stow-on-the-Wold 086747
Durham Light Infantry Museum and Durham Art Gallery, Durham 039334
Durham Western Heritage Museum, Omaha 046676
Durie Gallery, Leven 113387
Durier, Limony 063902
Duriez, Alain, Grignan 063078
Durif, Rennes (Ille-et-Vilaine) 067113
Durkee, Michael, Wincanton 131691
Durlacher Fine Art, London 113586
Durot, Charles, Beaurepaire-en-Bresse 061311
Durot, Gilles, Saint-Bris-le-Vineux .067386, 124890
Duroub, Cairo 098626
Durrant, Beccles 122403
Durrell Museum, Durrell 005378
Durrenberger, Henri, Cadouin 099044
Durst, H., Kirchheim unter Teck . . . 071860
Durst, Jean, Paris 065861
Dury, Christian, Nice 099832
Dusable Museum of African-American History, Chicago 042840
Dusan, Wollongong 056841
Dusarduijn, Robert, Amsterdam . . . 077839
Dusart, Jean-Luc, Poitiers 066890
Dusch, Peter, Speyer 073878
Duschl, Alois Franz, Passau 104584
Duse, Leonardo, Brescia 075165
Duseaux, Paris 065862
Duson, Los Angeles 089756
Duss, Martin, Niederrohrdorf 111778
Dussably, Marie-Thérèse, Charolles 062168
Dussi, Paola, Milano 127586
Dussort, Maurice, Beaune 061276
Dussouchaud, Didier, Saint-Junien . 067565
Dust, Las Vegas 116617
Dust Jacket, Cincinnati 142314
Dutch Art, Rotterdam 108182
Dutch Dakota Association Exhibition, Schiphol 030136
Dutch Iris, Baltimore 087663
Dutch Museum Amsterdam, Amsterdam 107705, 134778
Dutch Period Museum, Colombo . . 036131
Dutch Touch Gallery, Philadelphia . . 118753
Dutch Wall Art, Hilversum 108083
Dutchess County Arts Council, Poughkeepsie 054744
Dutel, Jean-Pierre, Paris 138357
Duteurtre, Philippe, Valognes 068701, 125007
Dutilleul, Albi 060756, 098808
Dutilleul, Noel & Giuseppe, Firenze . 075331
Dutko, Jean-Jacques, Paris 065863, 100240
Dutoit, Unterentfelden 130200
Dutrieux, F., Bruxelles 057923
Dutta, Genève 082422, 111442
Duttenhofer, Cincinnati 142315
Dutto, Riccardo, Torino 076811
Dutton, D., Los Angeles 142505
Duval, Jacksonville 089406
Duval, Anne-Sophie, Paris 065864
Duval, Raymonde, Paris 100241
Duval, Robert, Équeurdreville-Hainneville 099250
Duval-Wenta, Simone, Cabourg . . . 099041
Duvall, Atlanta 087469
Duvallier, L. & W., Dublin 074911
Duvauchelle, Frédéric, Bannalec . . 061188
Duvauchelle, Frédéric, Paris 065865
Duveau-Sage, Catherine & Philippe, Paris 065866
Duvert, Martial, Crest 062560
Duvieu, Jacques, Villerville 068935
Duvillard, André, Beaune 061277
Duvillard, Guy, Beaune 061278
Duvillier, Arnaud, Chaumont (Haute-Marne) 120975
Duvivier, Bruxelles 057924
Duvivier, Jacques & Anne, Châtillon (Hauts-de-Seine) 062229
Duwisib Castle, Maltahohe 029087
Dux, Frank, Bath 083426
Duxbury Rural and Historical Society, Duxbury 043550
Duys, Oss 078669
Dvärsätts Auktionsbyrå, Dvärsätt . . 122118
Dvärsätts Auktionsbyrå, Liden 122189
Dvor Trakoščan, Trakoščan 007811
Dvořáček, Kolín 060035
Dvořák, České Budějovice 059998
Dvořák, Jan, Benešov 098323
Dvořáková, Jana, Náchod 060056
Dvorec-Muzej Petra I, Sankt-Peterburg 033738
Dvorec-muzej Petra III, Muzej-zapovednik Oranienbaum, Lomonosov 033332
Dvorec Petra I, Strelna 033915
Dwight D. Eisenhower Library-Museum, Abilene 041563
Dwight Frederick Boyden Gallery, Saint Mary's College of Maryland, Saint Mary's City 047689
Dwór Artusa, Muzeum Historyczne Miasta Gdańska, Gdańsk 031907
Dwór w Dołędze, Muzeum Okręgowego w Tarnowie, Tarnów 032381
Dworek Jana Matejki w Krzesławicach, Kraków 032025
Dworek Wincentego Pola, Muzeum Lubelskiego w Lublinie, Lublin . . . 032127
Dworski, Marijana, Hay-on-Wye . . . 141651
Dwyer, Paul, Melbourne 094809
Dwyer, Sammie, Austin 087570
Dwyer MacAllister Cottage and Museum, Derrynamuck 022726
Dyansen, Boston 115170
Dycheling Antiques, Ditchling 084169
Dycke, München 139503
Dyckman Farmhouse Museum, New York 046326
Dydo, Krzysztof & Ewa Pabis, Kraków 108933
Dyer & Sons, W., Hayle 084636
Dyer Memorial Library, Abington . . 041570
Dyfed Antiques, Haverfordwest . . . 084624
Dyka, Corinne, Nice 065077
Dyke, Peter, Westerham 087098
Dylan, Garches 062966
Dylan, Swansea 142103
Dylan Thomas Boathouse, Laugharne 039937
Dylan's Bookstore, Swansea 142104
Dyma, Walter & Steffen, Rottweil . . 104779
Dyna, Dallas 132006
Dynamic Impressions, Calgary 096808
Dynamic Traders, Milwaukee 090292
Dynamo Arts, Vancouver 097461
Dynasties Antique and Art Gallery, Singapore 080457, 109791
Dynasties Art, Montréal 058949
Dynasty Antique Watch, Hong Kong 059624
Dynasty Antiques Gallery, Hong Kong 059625
Dynasty Art Gallery, Taipei 098065
Dynasty Chinese Antiques, Edmonton 058825
Dynasty Pacific, Göteborg 081801
Dynasty Pacific, Stockholm 081943
Dynasy, Warszawa 109114
Dynon, John, Silverton 095191
Dyrgripen Handelshus, Valbo 122290
Dyroff, Klaus-Peter, Schmiedeberg, Osterzgebirge 126774
Dyrøy Bygdemuseum, Tennevoll . . . 031261
Dyson & Son, Clare 122470
Dyson, D.W., Huddersfield 084747, 130813
Dyson, June, Calgary 058787
Dyte, C.W.E. & R.I., Highbridge 084684
Dyte, John & Colin, Burnham-on-Sea 083808
Dyte, T.M., Highbridge 084685
Dyvelstens Flottningsmuseum, Forshaga 036275
Dyzmann, J., Bleckede 125338
Džambul Historical and Regional Museum, Džambul 027398
Džambulskij Literaturnyj Memorialnyj Muzej, Džambul 027399
DZD Art, Roermond 108164
Dzeržinskij Gorodskoj Kraevedčeskij Muzej, Dzeržinsk 033108
Dziatko, Maciej, Warszawa 109115
Dziersk, Klaus, Söhlde . . . 073842, 126809, 139732
Dzierzynski, Outreau 065317
Dzioba, Edmond, Genay 062978
Dziubas, Renate, Ludwigsburg, Württemberg 072306
DZS, Ljubljana 134896
DZS, Ljubljana 140967
Dzubba, Stefan A., Hamburg 071223
E Antik, Praha 060125
E-Art Group, New York 117854
E. Bindstouw, Viborg 009147
E & C Sales, Tucson 093224
E. de C. Clarke Geological Museum, Crawley 000955
E. Galéria, Kecskemét 105562
The E-gallery, London 113587
E. & J.'s Antiques, Richmond 092073
E-K:s Antik, Göteborg 081802
E & L Furniture, Las Vegas 132213
E & P Libros Antiguos, Madrid 141037
E & S Art Gallery, Louisville 116939
E. St. Julien Cox House, Saint Peter 047712
E Street Gallery, Salt Lake City 119338
E-Werk Freiburg, Hallen für Kunst, Freiburg im Breisgau 017229
E3 Gallery, New York 117855
EAA AirVenture Museum, Oshkosh . 046735
E.A.C, Mios 099724
Eacrett, Sean, Dublin 074912
Eagle Art, Saint Louis 119202
Eagle Consultants, Manama 096005
Eagle Creek Publishing Company, Oklahoma City 135473
Eagle Gallery, Epsom 113029
Eagle Gallery, London 113588
Eagle Historical Society and Museums, Eagle City 043553
Eagle Tavern Museum, Watkinsville 049004
Eaglemont Antiques, Eaglemont . . . 055778
Eagles Antiques, Dallas 088504
Eagle's Dream, Singapore 109792
Eagles Nest, El Paso 088799
The Eagle's Nest, Saint Louis 092228
Eagles Nest Fine Art Gallery, Aireys Inlet 094123
Eagles Nest Odds and Ends, Eagle Heights 055774
The Eakin Gallery, Belfast 112611
Ealing College Gallery, London 040140
EAM-live-Museum Lippoldsberg, Wahlsburg 020621
EAM-live-Museum Wasserkraftwerk Merkenbach, Dillenburg 016710
EAM-live-Museum Wasserkraftwerk Wülmersen, Kassel 018185
EAM-live-Museum Wasserkraftwerk Wülmersen, Trendelburg 020468
Eamonn's Bookshop, Dun Laoghaire 139970
Eandi, Torino 128301
Ear Falls District Museum, Ear Falls 005379
Earist Museum, Manila 031721
Earl, Indianapolis 089293, 122919
Earl, New Orleans 117428
Earle, John, Merewether 094833
The Earle-Harrison House, Waco . . 048812
Earle Wightman Museum, Oyster Bay 046779
Earles, Greg & Frances, Oklahoma City 091496
Earls Barton Museum of Local Life, Earls Barton 039343
Earls Court Gallery, Hamilton 096913
Early American Museum, Mahomet 045598
Early Auctions Company, Milford . . 122965
Early Bird, Nürnberg 139604
Early Days Antiques, Paddington, Queensland 056426
Early Halloween, New York 090835
Early Oak, Knaresborough 084882
Early Works, Austin 114978
Earlystreet, Norman Park 001333
Earlywork, South Fremantle 095199
Earlyworks Museum Complex, Huntsville 044692
It Earmhus en Oud Friese Greidboerderij, Warten 030309
Earsham Hall Pine, Earsham 084239
Earth and Beyond, Salt Lake City . . 119339
Earth Art Studio and Gallery, Panton Hill 095053
Earth Artspace, Auckland 108311
Earth Collectible Toy Mall, Cincinnati 088231
Earth Link Art, Ballarat 094198
Earth Science Museum, Dublin 022741
Earth Sciences Museum, Waterloo . 006772
Earth Spirit Gallery, Albuquerque . . 114780
Earth Water Sky, Portland 118993
Earthsong, Phoenix 136452
Earthworks Gallery, Mount Tamborine 094912
Easatis, Teheran 074841
Easdale Island Folk Museum, Easdale Island 039344
The Easel, Kingston 106812
The Easel Art Gallery, Chennai 105625
Easiaart, Singapore 109793
East and Orient Company, Dallas . . 088505
East and Seaport Museum, Greenport 044328
East and West, Roma 135897
East and West Art, Kew East 094696
East and West Art Gallery, Kew East 056049
East Anglia Transport Museum, Carlton Colville 039000
East Anglian Film Archive, University of East Anglia, Norwich 040604
East Anglian Railway Museum, Colchester 039118
East Art Artworks, Guangzhou 097720
East Art Gallery, Shenyang 097961
East Brunswick Museum, East Brunswick 043558
East Campus Galleries, Valencia Community College, Orlando 046716
East Carlton Steel Heritage Centre, East Carlton 039346
East Coast Museum of Technology, Gisborne 030500
East Collectors, Chicago 088076
East Corner Company, New York . . . 090836
East Coulee School Museum, East Coulee 005380
East Ely Railroad Depot Museum, Ely 043696
East End Arts & Humanities Council, Riverhead 054745
East End Books, Toronto 137704

East End Stores, Kilkenny 074981
East England Arts, Cambridge 054361
East Essex Aviation Society and Museum of the 40's, Saint Osyth 040929
East Gallery, Taipei 098066
East Gippsland Star Auctions, Wy Yung 120660
East Ham Nature Reserve, London . 040141
East Hampton Historical Society Museum, East Hampton 043565
East Hampton Town Marine Museum, East Hampton 043566
East Hants Historical Museum, Maitland 005821
East Hertford District Council, Museum Development, Hertford 054362
The East Hertfordshire Decorative and Fine Arts Society, Knebworth 054363
East Jersey Olde Towne, Piscataway 047036
East Jordan Portside Art and Historical Museum, East Jordan 043573
East Kazakhstan Historical and Regional Museum, Ust-Kamenogorsk 027417
East Lancashire Regiment Museum, Blackburn, Lancashire 038752
East London Museum, East London 034608
East Martello Museum, Key West . . 044983
East Meets West, Los Angeles 089757
East Midlands Museums Service, Colston Bassett 054364
East Point Antiques, Milwaukee . . . 090293
East Poultney Museum, East Poultney 043579
East Riddlesden Hall, Keighley 039836
East Sacramento Gallery, Sacramento 119143
East Side Antiques, Fort Worth 088852
East Side Gallery, Milwaukee 117181
East Side Gallery, Milwaukee 117182
East Side Upholstery, Buffalo 131853
East Somerset Railway, Shepton Mallet 041004
East Street Antiques, Rye 086424
The East Suffolk Decorative and Fine Arts Society, Leiston 054365
East Surrey Museum, Caterham . . . 039021
East Tennessee Discovery Center, Knoxville 045036
East Tennessee Historical Society Museum, Knoxville 045037
East Texas Oil Museum at Kilgore College, Kilgore 044999
East Timorese Cultural Centre Museum Collection, Dili 009168
East Troy Electric Railroad Museum, East Troy 043583
East Village Books and Records, New York 142649
East-West Center, Honolulu 044594
East West Designs, Denver 115989
East West Fine Art Gallery, San Francisco 119658
East-West Gallery, Austin 114979
East West Gallery, London 113589
Eastbourne Antiques Market, Eastbourne 084261
Eastbourne Auction Rooms, Eastbourne 122495
Eastbourne Engraving, Eastbourne . 130669
Eastbourne Fine Art, Eastbourne . . .084262, 130670, 135139
Eastbourne Heritage Centre, Eastbourne 039360
Eastchester Historical Society Museum, Bronxville 042444
Eastend Museum, Eastend 005382
Eastend School Museum, Eastend . 005383
Easterbrook, M.J., Saskatoon 123816
Easterley Gallery, Waikato 108588
Eastern Arizona Museum, Pima . . . 047022
Eastern Art Company, Providence . . 119077
Eastern Art Report, London 135214, 136210
Eastern Arts, New York 117856
Eastern Arts, New York 117857
Eastern Arts Board, Cambridge . . . 054361
Eastern Azarbaijan Province History Museum, Tabriz 022602
Eastern Books, London 141780
Eastern California Museum, Independence 044717
Eastern Curious Company, Penang . 077502
Eastern Discoveries Antiques, Singapore 080458, 129259
Eastern Edge Art Gallery, Saint John's 006364
Eastern Expression, Varsity Lakes . 095362
Eastern Gallery 437 N Wolcott St, Chicago 115403
Eastern Living, Tucson 093225
The Eastern Museum, Derby 039226
Eastern Oregon Museum on the Old Oregon Trail, Haines 044390
Eastern Region Arts Centre, Midland 094844
Eastern Shore Art Association, Fairhope 054746
Eastern Shore Art Center, Fairhope . 043793
Eastern Southland Gallery, Gore . . . 030503
Eastern State Penitentiary Historic Site, Philadelphia 046935
Eastern Suburbs Auctions, Croydon 120579
Eastgate Antiques, Cowbridge 084092
Eastgate Gallery, Chichester 112859
Eastgate Gallery, Cowbridge 112905
Eastgate Gallery, Hawthorn, Victoria 094624, 123238
Eastleigh Museum, Eastleigh 039368
Eastney Beam Engine House, Portsmouth 040763
Eastnor Castle, Ledbury 039947
Easton, Andrea, West Hollywood . . 093466
Easton Farm Park, Easton 039370
Eastside Gallery, Memphis 116984
Eastthorpe, Mirfield 114087
Eastwick, Chicago 115404
Eastwood, Saint Paul 119283
Eastwood House, Glasgow 039552
Easy Art, Mumbai 105767
Easyart.Com, London 113590
Easystrip, Henley-on-Thames 130784
Eaton, Austin 114980
Eaton-Buchan Gallery and Marvin Cone Gallery, Cedar Rapids 042675
Eaton Gallery, London 085267
Eaton Gallery, London . . . 085268, 113591
Eatos Art Collection, Wien 057404
L'Eau Forte, Bordeaux 098990
L'Eau Forte, Lyon 099555
Ebanistería Albaco, Madrid 129609
Ebanite, Albacete 080752
Ebbamåla Bruk, Kyrkhult 036410
Ebbas Hus, Malmö Museer, Malmö . 036455
Ebeling, Bergisch Gladbach 069539
Ebeling, Köln 071929
Ebeling, Monique, Düren 070348
Ebeltoft Antikvariat, Ebeltoft 137864
Ebeltoft Museum, Ebeltoft 008837
Ebenbeck, Edmund O., München . . 126370
Ebene, Paris 065867
Ebène et Sycomore, Gex 062992
Ebène Original, Cannes 099063
Ebenezer Maxwell Mansion, Philadelphia 046936
Ebenhoch, Inge, Feldkirch 056974
Ebenhofer, Leopold, Perg 057207
l'Ebéniste, Nice 124510
Ebeniste, D., New York . . . 090837, 132464
Ebenisteria, Kraków 129035
Ebénisterie & Tradition, Ancenis . . . 060832
Ebénistrie d'Art Campagna, Marseille 124413
Eberhard, Solothurn 082818
Eberhardt & Son, Harry A., Philadelphia 091632
Eberhardt & Son, Harry A., Philadelphia 091633, 132616
Eberhardt, Petra & Wolfgang, Münstermaifeld 104379
Eberhart, Karl, Ermatingen 082358
Eberl, H., Berlin 125193
Ebersdorfer Schulmuseum, Chemnitz 016555
Eberspächer, Helmut, Bruchsal 125401
Ebert, San Francisco 119659
Ebert, Karl-Otto & Monika, Klingenberg am Main 071883
Ebert & Björk, Stockholm 111017
Eberwein, Freiburg im Breisgau . . . 102857
Eberwein, Roswitha, Göttingen 071044
Ebes, Douwma, Melbourne 056186, 094810
Ebeseder, Alois, Wien 137305
Ebinger, Jürgen, Bad Neuenahr-Ahrweiler 069339
Ebinger, Jürgen, Bad Neuenahr-Ahrweiler 069340
Ebinger, Michael, Würzburg 074495
Ebisons & Harounian, New York . . . 090838
Ebisubashi, Osaka 106956
Ebiya, Tokyo 077242
Ebjay, Merbein 056213
Ebland, Verona 106790
Ebner, Heinz Noé, Freiburg im Breisgau 070833, 121412
Ebner von Eschenbach, Kristian, Berlin 069599
Ebony, Dallas 115873
Ebony Elevations, Indianapolis 116455
Ebran, Patrick, Le Havre 063632
Ebreji Latvijā, Rīga 027731
Ebreuil, Royan 067309
Eburne, Paris 065868
E.C. Allison Research Center, San Diego 047819
ECA, Pézenas 066802
E.C.A. France, Paris 100242, 133569
Ecart, Genève 135017
Ec'Art, Ecole-Galerie, Betton 010781
Ecce, Rotterdam 108183
Ecce Homo, Jerusalem 022948
Eccentricities, London 085269
Eccles Community Art Center, Ogden 046628
Eccles Road Antiques, London 085270
Ecclesiastical Collection, Naoussa . 021403
Ecclesiastical Museum, Komotini . . 021334
Ecclesiastical Museum, Mullingar . 022841
Ecclesiastical Museum of Alexandroupolis, Alexandroupolis 021125
Ecclesiastical Museum of the Metropolis of Trikki and Stagoi, Trikala 021512
Eccli, Erika, Salzburg 057243
Eccola, Los Angeles 089758
Echague Cordero, Jorge, Santiago de Chile 059522
Echancrure Galerie, Bruxelles 096185
Echange, Maurice, Brumath 120954
Echarri, Pamplona 081516
Echauguette, Nevers 065009
Echauri, Fermin, Pamplona 081517
Echauri, Fermin, Pamplona 110717
Echauri, Fermin, Pamplona 110718
Echeberria Monteberria, J., Donostia-San Sebastián 110334
Echelle, Strasbourg 068316
Echenard, Michel, Villars-sous-Mont 082888
Echeverri Valasquez, Eduardo, Medellín 098258
Echeverría, Zaragoza 081740
Echizen-No-Sato Museum, Takefu . 027129
Echo, Columbus 088404
Echo, Toledo 093169
Echo Antiques, Reepham . 086345, 131408
Echo Art Deco-Sixties, Zürich 082960
Echo Chamber, Los Angeles 116757
Echo du Passé, Le Havre 138115
Echo Gallery, Washington 120281
Echo Historical Museum, Echo 043600
Echo Home, Tulsa 093301
Echoes, Todmorden 086891, 131596
Echoppe Saint-Guénhaël, Vannes (Morbihan) 101428
Echos d'Art, Ollioules 099887
Echos From the Past, San Antonio . 092509
Echuca Gem Club Collection, Echuca 001005
Echuca Museum, Echuca 001006
Eckardt, Dr. Hans-Georg, Berlin . . . 138771
Eckart, Hans, Altenmarkt im Pongau 123334
Eckart, Karl-Heinz, Ellwangen 070541
Eckel, Dieter K., Köln 139337
Eckel, Friederike, Esslingen 125621
Ecker, Brigitte, Ingolstadt 071624
Ecker, Helmut, Spiegel 082825
Eckers, Willi, Mönchengladbach . . . 139480
Eckert, Indianapolis 116456
Eckert, Agnes, Köln 126074
Eckert, D., Bremen 138944
Eckert, Georges, Luzern 130102
Eckert, Iris, Kampen 103478
Eckert, Karl Josef, Fahrdorf 125626
Eckert & Nolde, Erfurt . . . 070586, 121394
Eckhardt, M., Aglasterhausen 069114
Eckhof-Schirow, Wilma, Sommerhausen 073860
Ecklé, Bruno, Nogent-le-Rotrou . . . 121099
Eckley Miners' Village, Eckley 043601
Eckmann, Christian, Mainz 126259
Eclate, Genève 111443
Eclectic, Abu Dhabi 083171
Eclectic, Beirut 107327
Eclectic Art Gallery, Pittsburgh 118916
Eclectic Attic, Singapore 080459
Eclectica, London 085271
Eclectica, Saint Louis 092229
Eclectique Antiques, New Orleans . 090549
Eclectiques, New York 090839
Eclectiques Antique Mall, Columbus 088405
Eclectors, Houston 089072
Eclips, Nijmegen 108151
Eclipse, Calgary 096809
Eclipse de Mexico, Los Angeles . . . 116758
Ecliptic Gallery, Armadale, Victoria . 094163
Eco Bush Art Gallery, Surfers Paradise 095240
Éco-Musée de la Blanchisserie, Grezieu-la-Varenne 012033
Eco-Musée de la Noix, Castelnaud-la-Chapelle 011143
Éco Musée Vivant de Provence, La Gaude 012269
EcoArt, Wien 095812
Ecodrome Zwolle, Zwolle 030411
Ecole Bohemiarte, Montréal 049800
Ecole Camondo, Paris 049972
Ecole Cantonale d'Art de Lausanne, Lausanne 050766
Ecole Cantonale d'Art du Valais, Sierre 050775
Ecole d'Architecture de Strasbourg, Strasbourg 049988
Ecole d'Art Appliqué, La Chaux-de-Fonds 050760
Ecole d'Art Gérard Jacot, Belfort . . 049936
Ecole d'Art Marseille-Luminy, Marseille 049956
Ecole d'Arts Appliqués, Vevey 050777
École Dentellière, Bailleul 010629
Ecole des Arts, Bruxelles 049687
Ecole des Arts Décoratifs - Ecole Supérieure d'Arts Appliqués, Genève 050763
Ecole des Arts Visuelles, Université Laval, Québec 049809
Ecole des Beaux-Arts, Tamines . . . 049732
Ecole des Beaux-Arts, Galerie des Beaux-Arts, Cherbourg-Octeville 099128
Ecole des Beaux-Arts de Bordeaux, Bordeaux 049938
Ecole des Beaux-Arts de Brest, École Supérieure d'Arts de Brest, Brest . 049940
Ecole des Beaux-Arts de Valenciennes, Valenciennes 049996
Ecole des Beaux-Arts et des Arts Appliqués N. Untersteller, Metz 049958
Ecole des Beaux-Arts Grandjean, Toulon (Var) 049991
Ecole des Buissonnets, Sierre 111901
Ecole du Louvre, Paris 049973

Ecole du Rang II, Authier 005044
Ecole Municipale d'Arts Plastiques, Riom 049985
Ecole Municipale des Beaux Arts, Châteauroux 049944
Ecole Municipale des Beaux-Arts, Mulhouse 049961
Ecole-Musée de Champagny, Champagny 011226
Ecole Nationale d'Art Décoratif, Aubusson 049935
École Nationale de la Photographie, Arles 049934
Ecole Nationale des Arts, Bangui . . 049836
Ecole Nationale des Arts, Port-au-Prince 050278
Ecole Nationale des Beaux-Arts, Tétouan 050550
Ecole Nationale des Beaux-Arts de Bourges, Bourges 049939
Ecole Nationale des Beaux-Arts de Dijon, Dijon 049947
Ecole Nationale des Beaux-Arts de Lyon, Lyon 049955
Ecole Nationale des Chartes, Paris . 049974
Ecole Nationale Superieure d'Art de Cergy, Cergy 049943
Ecole Nationale Supérieure d'Art de Limoges-Aubusson, Limoges 049952
Ecole Nationale Supérieure d'Art de Nancy, Nancy 049962
Ecole Nationale Supérieure des Arts Appliqués Duperré, Paris 049975
Ecole Nationale Supérieure des Arts Décoratifs (Ensad), Paris 049976
Ecole Nationale Supérieure des Arts Visuels de la Cambre, Bruxelles 049688
Ecole Nationale Supérieure des Beaux-Arts, Paris 049977, 133570
Ecole Pilote Internationale d'Art et de Recherche, Villa Arson, Nice 049965
Ecole Régionale des Beaux-Arts, Nantes 049964
Ecole Régionale des Beaux-Arts, Rennes (Ille-et-Vilaine) 049984
Ecole Régionale des Beaux-Arts, Rouen 049986
Ecole Régionale des Beaux-Arts de Caen, Caen 049941
Ecole Régionale des Beaux-Arts de Saint-Étienne, Saint-Étienne 049987
Ecole Régionale des Beaux-Arts et Arts Appliqués, Besançon 049937
Ecole Régionale Supérieure d'Expression Plastique, Tourcoing 049994
Ecole Saint-Luc, Ramegnies-Chin . 049727
Ecole Spéciale d'Architecture, Paris 049978
Ecole Supérieur des Arts Saint-Luc Liège, Liège 049716
Ecole Supérieure d'Art, Cambrai . . . 049942
Ecole Supérieure d'Art, Perpignan . 049982
École Supérieure d'Art d'Aix-en-Provence, Aix-en-Provence 049931
Ecole Supérieure d'Art et de Design, Amiens 049932
Ecole Supérieure d'Art et Design, Reims 049983
Ecole Supérieure d'Art Grenoble, Grenoble 049950
Ecole Supérieure d'Art Visuel, Genève 050764
Ecole supérieure des Arts décoratifs, Strasbourg 049989
École Supérieure des Beaux-Arts, Nîmes 049966
Ecole Supérieure des Beaux-Arts, Toulouse 049992
Ecole Supérieure des Beaux-Arts Ahmed et Rabah-Salim Asselah, Alger 049592
Ecole Supérieure des Beaux-Arts de Casablanca, Casablanca 050549
Ecole Supérieure des Beaux-Arts de Clermont-Ferrand, Clermont-Ferrand 049945
Ecole Supérieure des Beaux-Arts de Montpellier-Agglomération, Montpellier 049959
École supérieure des beaux-arts de Tours, Tours 049995
Ecole Supériure des Beaux-Arts d'Angers, Angers 049933
Ecoles d'Art Americaines de Fontainebleau, Fontainebleau 049949
Ecolver, Barcelona 080843
EcoMare, De Koog 029396
Écomusée, Aspres-sur-Buech 010502
Écomusée, Boigneville 010858
Écomusée, Etel 011751
Ecomusée Agricole du Pays de Fayence, Fayence 011788
Ecomusée d'Alsace, Ungersheim . . 015073
Écomusée d'Alzen, Alzen 010344
Ecomusée d'Arts et Traditions Populaires, Ligny-le-Ribault 012673
Écomusée de Fresnes, Fresnes (Val-de-Marne) 011895
Ecomusée de Hauteluce, Hauteluce 012081
Ecomusée de Keranpercheg, Pont-Aven 013882
Écomusée de la Basse-Seine, Notre-Dame-de-Bliquetuit 013450
Écomusée de la Bourrine du Bois Juquaud, Saint-Hilaire-de-Riez 014328
Ecomusée de la Brenne, Le Blanc . 012464
Ecomusée de la Bresse Bourguignonne, Pierre-de-Bresse 013811
Ecomusée de la Bresse Bourguignonne, Le Vigneron et sa Vigne, Cuiseaux . . 011547
Écomusée de la Cévenne, Saint-Laurent-de-Trèves 014378
Écomusée de la Combe de Savoie, Les Côteaux du Salin, Grésy-sur-Isère 012031
Ecomusée de la Communauté, Ciry-le-Noble 011380
Ecomusée de la Communauté Le Creusot Montceau-les-Mines, Le Creusot . 012488
Écomusée de la Courneuve, La Courneuve 012245
Ecomusée de la Crau, Saint-Martin-de-Crau 014417
Ecomusée de la Ferme de Kervazegan, Pont-l'Abbé 013890
Écomusée de la Ferme de la Forêt, Saint-Trivier-de-Courtes 014556
Ecomusée de la Ferme de l'Espinousse Prat Alaric, Fraisse-sur-Agout 011884
Ecomusée de la Ferme de Roscanvel, Combrit 011441
Ecomusée de la Ferme du Chemin, Parc Naturel Régional de Maine-Normandie, Madré 012841
Écomusée de la Ferme du Moulin Vanneau, Saints-en-Puisaye 014628
Ecomusée de la Ferme et des Vieux Métiers, Lizio 012719
Écomusée de la Forêt d'Orient, Brienne-la-Vieille 010999
Ecomusée de la Forêt Méditerranéenne, Gardanne 011919
Ecomusée de la Forge, Auchy-la-Montagne 010534
Écomusée de la Forge, Menton . . . 013018
Ecomusée de la Gâtine Tourangelle, Rouziers-de-Touraine 014147
Ecomusée de la Grande Lande Marquèze, Sabres 014159
Ecomusée de la Haute-Areuse, Saint-Sulpice, Neuchâtel 037480
Écomusée de la Haute-Beauce, Musée Territoire, Saint-Evariste 006337
Ecomusée de la Lomagne, Miradoux 013070
Ecomusée de la Margeride, Loubaresse 012753
Ecomusée de la Margeride, Ecole de Clémence Fontille, Ruynes-en-Margeride 014157
Écomusée de la Montagne, Germaine 011936
Ecomusée de la Pêche, Thonon-les-Bains 014941
Ecomusée de la Pêche et de la Mer, Capbreton 011103
Ecomusée de la Pomme au Calvados, Le Sap 012562
Écomusée de la Région de Fourmies Trélon en Avesnois, Maison de la Fagne, Trélon 015041
Ecomusée de la région du Viroin, Treignes 003814
Ecomusée de la Sainte-Baume, Plan-d'Aups 013829
Ecomusée de la Tradition Basque Jean Vier, Saint-Jean-de-Luz 014347
Ecomusée de la Truffe, Sorges 014826
Ecomusée de la Vallee d'Aspe, Accous 010266
Ecomusée de la Vallée de l'Aigre, La Ferté-Villeneuil 012259
Ecomusée de la Vallée du Galeizon, Cendras 011170
Ecomusée de la Vie en Altitude, Bénévent-et-Charbillac 010750
Ecomusée de la Vie Montagnarde, Abries 010265
Ecomusée de la Vigne et du Vin, Gradignan 011977
Ecomusée de l'Abeille, Auriac-du-Périgord 010548
Écomusée de l'Abeille, Grateloup . . 012004
Écomusée de l'Abeille, Le Faou . . . 012493
Écomusée de l'Abeille et de la Flore Locale, Faugères 011785
Ecomusée de l'Agriculture, Aigues-Vives 010280
Ecomusée de l'Agriculture, Charmoille-Provenchère 011257
Ecomusée de l'Agriculture Queyrassine, Arvieux-en-Queyras 010495
Écomusée de l'Apiculture, Montargis 013124
Ecomusée de l'Armagnac, Labastide-d'Armagnac 012358
Ecomusée de l'Ile-de-Groix, Ile-de-Groix 012124
Écomusée de l'île d'Ouessant, Maisons du Niou Huella, Ile-d'Ouessant 012129
Ecomusée de Marais Breton Vendéen, La Barre-de-Monts 012200
Ecomusée de Marie Galante, Musée Schœlcher, Grand Bourg 021555
Ecomusée de Montjean, Montjean-sur-Loire 013178
Ecomusée de Plein Air du Quercy, Sauliac-sur-Célé 014693
Ecomusée de Saint-Dégan, Brec'h . 010972
Ecomusée de Saint-Joseph, Fargues-sur-Ourbise 011784
Ecomusée de Saint-Nazaire, Saint-Nazaire (Loire-Atlantique) 014448
Ecomusée de Salazie, Salazie 014631
Ecomusée de Savigny-le-Temple, Savigny-le-Temple 014721
Ecomusée Départemental de la Vendée, Les Épesses 012616
Écomusée des Anciennes Carrières de Pierre Les Capucins, Paris 013580
Ecomusée des Appeaux et de la Faune, Saint-Didier 014256
Écomusée des Boutères-Pilat, Riotord 014054
Ecomusée des Bruneaux, Firminy . . 011817
Écomusée des Deux-Rives, Valleyfield 006683
Ecomusée des Goémoniers et de l'Algue, Plouguerneau 013855
Ecomusée des Houillères de Lorraine, Freyming-Merlebach 011898
Écomusée des Mines de Fer de Lorraine, Aumetz 010544
Ecomusée des Monts d'Arrée, Commana 011442
Ecomusée des Monts d'Arrée, Saint-Rivoal 014528
Ecomusée des Pays de l'Oise, Beauvais 010720
Ecomusée des Pipes Ropp, Baume-les-Dames 010670
Ecomusée des Vallées du Paillon, Contes 011472
Ecomusée d'Hannonville, Hannonville-sous-les-Côtes 012066
Écomusée d'Ichkeul, Bizerte 037948
Ecomusée du Bocage, Sains-du-Nord 014169
Écomusée du Bommelaers Wall, Ghyvelde 011941
Écomusée du Carton, Mesnay 013037
Écomusée du Château-Fort, Saint-Sylvain-d'Anjou 014551
Écomusée du Chemin de Fer en Vendée, Les Épesses 012617
Écomusée du Cheminot Veynois, Veynes 015194
Écomusée du Cognac, Migron 013059
Ecomusée du Commerce et de l'Artisanat, Rochefort (Charente-Maritime) . . 014077
Écomusée du Cuir de la Tannerie Nory, Sainghin-en-Weppes 014168
Écomusée du Domaine de la Petite Couère, Nyoiseau 013464
Écomusée du Haut Pays de la Roya et de la Bevera, Breil-sur-Roya 010974
Écomusée du Larzac, Millau 013060
Ecomusée du Libournais, Montagne 013118
Écomusée du Liège, Gonfaron 011967
Écomusée du Linge, Montcy-Notre-Dame 013150
Ecomusée du Marais Salant, Loix-en-Ré 012731
Ecomusée du Mont-Lozère, Le Pont-de-Montvert 012552
Ecomusée du Montmorillon, Montmorillon 013191
Ecomusée du Moulin de Kerchuz, Saint-Thurien 014555
Écomusée du Moulin de la Sée, Maison de l'Eau et de la Rivière, Brouains . . 011014
Écomusée du Moulin Saint-Martin, Cany-Barville 011102
Ecomusée du Pay de la Cerise de Fougerolles, Fougerolles (Haute-Saône) 011877
Écomusée du Pays de la Roudoule, Puget-Rostang 013962
Ecomusée du Pays de Montfort, Montfort-sur-Meu 013166
Écomusée du Pays de Nied, Gomelange 011963
Ecomusée du Pays de Rennes, Ferme de la Bintinais, Rennes (Ille-et-Vilaine) . 014019
Ecomusée du Pays des Collines, Lahamaide 003566
Écomusée du Paysan Gascon, Toujouse 014969
Écomusée du Pêrche de Saint-Cyr-la-Rosière, Bellême 010741
Écomusée du Phare de Trezien, Plouarzel 013846
Ecomusée du Port Ostréïcole, Maison du Marin et Traditions Populaires, La Teste-de-Buch 012343
Ecomusée du Roannais, Roanne . . . 014064
Ecomusée du Savon, Manosque . . . 012876
Écomusée du Val de Saône, Seurre 014783
Ecomusée du Vernon, Savigny-en-Vernon 014720
Écomusée du Verre de Biot, Biot . . 010808
Ecomusée du Village Breton de Poul-Fetan, Quistinic 013985
Ecomusée Hundisburg, Haldensleben 017650
Ecomusée Industriel de Lochrist-Inzinzac, Musée des Forges, Lochrist-Inzinzac 012723
Ecomusée la Cité des Abeilles, Saint-Faust 014284
Ecomusée la Ferme du Hameau, Bierre-les-Semur 010798
L'Écomusée la Maison de l'Islandais, Gravelines 012008
Écomusée La Vie d'Antan, Esparron-de-Verdon 011734
Ecomusée l'Abeille du Haut-Doubs, Aubonne 010525
Écomusée Le Grain de Sel, Châteauneuf-d'Entraunes 011289
Ecomusée Les Outils de la Vigne et du Vin, Saint-Sulpice-de-Faleyrens 014547
Ecomusée Maison Michaud, Chapelle-des-Bois 011239

Ecomusée Picarvie, Saint-Valéry-sur-Somme 014565
Écomusée Sauvegarde du Vieil Auzon, Auzon 010580
Ecomusée Vivant de la Haie, Châtillon-en-Dunois 011312
Ecomuseo de Guinea, Frontera 035202
Ecomuseo del Habitat Subterráneo de Rojales, Rojales 035713
Ecomuseo della Resistenza, Coazze 023917
Ecomuseo dell'Archeologia Industriale, Schio 025842
Ecomuseo di Archeologia Industriale E. CrumiSre, Villar Pellice 026337
Ecomuseo Los Torres, Lerdo 028387
Ecomuseo - Molino de Zubieta, Zubieta 036119
Ecomuseo Regional Maipú, Maipú . 000420
Ecomuseu, Centro Cultural de Santa Cruz Dr. Antônio Nicolau Jorge, Rio de Janeiro 004338
Ecomuseu da Fazenda Boa Vista, Roseira 004430
Ecomuseu de Itaipu, Foz do Iguaçu 004118
Ecomuseu de les Valls d'Aneu, Esterri d'Aneu 035185
Ecomuseu do Rabeirão do Ilha, Florianópolis 004104
Ecomuseum en Archief van de Boomse Baksteen, Boom 003241
Ecomuseum Simplon, Simplon Dorf 037562
Economical Document Collection, Hikone 026508
Economopoulos Collection, Athinai . 021167
Ecossaise, Saint-Ouen 067769
EcoTarium, Worcester 049305
Ecovillage Centre Africain Reconstitué, Magny-Cours 012844
Écovillage de Lorraine, Ville-sur-Yron 015239
Écovillage Gaulois, Pleumeur-Bodou 013840
ECR Antique Conservation, New York 132465
Ecra Restauraciones, Madrid 129610
L'Ecrin, Marseille 064351
Ecrin, Metz 064528
Ecrin de Clisson, Clisson 062362
Ecritoire, Nantes 064922
Écritures, Commentry 062434
Ecu de France, La Tremblade 063454
L'Ecuelle, Amboise 060797
Ecume des Jours, Bordeaux 061604
Ecume des Temps, Besançon 061381
Ecumes, Paris 100243
Ecurie d'Antan, Orgeval 065284
Ecuries du Seigneur, Le Poët 063686
l'Ecuyer, Bruxelles 096186
Ed Clark Museum of Missouri Geology, Rolla 047528
Ed & Elaine's Custom Interiors, Phoenix 091735
Eda Skans Museum, Åmotfors 036181
La Edad de la Madera y el Bronce, Bogotá 059835
Edams Museum, Edam 029520
Edarcom Europa, Roma 106523
Eddie's Auction, Louisville 122949
Eddie's Furniture, Mount Gambier . 056282
Eddie's Furniture Refinishing, Winnipeg 123865
Eddie's Shoppe, Indianapolis 089294
Eddy, Charenton-le-Pont 062147
Eddy, Paris 065869
Eddy's English Furniture, Brugge . . 057770
Ede, Charles, London 085272
Edecea, Hoorn 134816
Edelbauer, Adolf, Monheim am Rhein 072589
Edelfelt-Vallgren Museo, Porvoon Museo, Porvoo 009992
Edeling, København 060319, 098550
Edelman, New York 117858
Edelman, Catherine, Chicago 115405
Edelman, H. Heather, New York . . . 117859
Edelmann, New York 122994
Edelmann, Nürnberg 104476, 139605
Edelmann, N., Bensheim 069524
Edelstam, Stockholm 081944
Edelsteenslijperij de Steenarend, Eindhoven 029539
Edelstein, Paul, Memphis 116985
Edeltrödel-Antike Möbel, Wettingen 082903
Edelweiss, Houston 089073
Edelweiss, Porto Alegre 096552
Eden, Olomouc 060060
Eden, Matthew, Corsham 084085
Eden Antic, Cannes 061942
Eden Antiques, South Auckland . . .079239, 128956
Eden Camp, Modern History Theme Museum, Malton 040395
Eden Court Art Gallery, Inverness . . 039807
Eden House Antiques, West Auckland 087078, 131662
Eden Killer Whale Museum, Eden . . 001009
Eden Valley Museum, Edenbridge . . 039375
Eden Wharf Antiques, Eden 055788
Edenfeuer, Köln 103612
Edenhurst, West Hollywood 120380
Edenside Gallery, Louisville 116940
Eder, Hans, Hermagor 137190
Eder, Herbert A., München 072690
Eder, Johann, Wiener Neustadt 057595
Eder, K.B., Jüchen 071670, 134073
Eder, Richard & Renate, Linz 095653
Edera, Villeneuve-sur-Lot . 068918, 138661
Ederle, Isabelle, Grenoble 063059
Ederti, Bilbao 110275
Edet, Montreuil-sous-Bois 064767
Edet, Saint-Ouen 067770
Edgar, Paris 100244
Edgar, Paris 100245
Edgar Allan Poe Cottage, Bronx . . . 042435
Edgar Allan Poe House, Philadelphia 046937
Edgar Allan Poe House and Museum, Baltimore 041980
Edgar Allan Poe Museum, Richmond 047414
Edgar County Historical Museum, Paris 046815
Edgar Modern, Bath 112574
The Edge, London 136211
Edge, D., Memphis 116986
Edge City, Auckland 108312
Edge Gallery, Denver 115990
Edge of Glass Gallery, Seattle 119910
Edge of the Cedars State Park, Blanding 042250
Edgerton and District Museum, Edgerton 005386
Edgewater Antique Mall, Chicago . . 088077
Edgewood Coins, Jacksonville 089407
Edgewood Station Antiques, Pittsburgh 091812
Edgware Antiques, Edgware 084272
Ediarte, Napoli 106363
Edicarte, Lisboa 109283
Las Ediciones de Arte, Barcelona . . 134906
Ediciones Encuentro, Madrid 134941
Ediciones Omega, Barcelona 134907
Ediciones Polígrafa, Barcelona 134908
Ediciones Serigráficas, Lima 134853
Ediciones Siruela, Madrid 134942
Ediciones Unión, La Habana 133411
Ediciones y Arte, Asunción 134852
Edicions de l'Eixample, Barcelona . 134909
Edies Bits & Pieces, Birmingham . . 087753
Edies's Antiques, Saint Louis 092230
Edieuropa Gallerie, Roma 106524
Edilan, Madrid 134943, 141038
Ediméta, Vitry-sur-Seine 101488
Edinburgh Architectural Salvage Yards, Edinburgh 084288
Edinburgh Coin Shop, Edinburgh . . 084289
Edinburgh College of Art, Edinburgh 050812
The Edinburgh Gallery, Edinburgh . . 112993
Edinburgh House, Port Lincoln 095092
Edinburgh Printmakers Workshop and Gallery, Edinburgh 039385
Edinburgh Scout Museum, Edinburgh 039386
Edinburgh Square Heritage and Cultural Centre, Caledonia 005178
Edinburgh University Anatomy Museum, Edinburgh 039387
Edinburgh University Collection of Historic Musical Instruments, Edinburgh . . 039388
Edinburgh University Natural History Collections, Edinburgh 039389
Edinburgh University Press, Edinburgh 135140
Edirne Devlet Güzel Sanatlar Galerisi, Edirne 038054
Edish, Houston 089074
Edish, Salt Lake City 092430
Edison, Den Haag 107914
Edison and Ford Winter Estates, Fort Myers 043956
Edison Community College Gallery of Fine Art, Fort Myers 043957
Edison National Historic Site, West Orange 049089
Edison Plaza Museum, Beaumont . . 042084
Edissi, Kitchener 096928, 120804
Edisto Island Historic Preservation Society Museum, Edisto Island 043611
Editart, Genève 111444, 135018
Edith Cowan University Museum of Childhood, Claremont, Western Australia 000921
Edith Elizabeth Antiques, Saint Ives 056561
Edith-Ruß-Haus für Medienkunst, Oldenburg, Oldenburg 019467
Edithburgh Museum, Edithburgh . . . 001011
Edith's Gallery, Hong Kong 097779
Editio Maris, München 134234
Edition A, Ried im Innkreis 133129
Edition Abstracta, Freiburg im Breisgau 133958
Edition Alectri, Köln 134103
Edition Anteros, Seewalchen am Attersee 133163
Edition Aragon, Moers 134209
Edition Ars Antiqua, Hannover 134039
Edition art actuell, Maria Enzersdorf am Gebirge 133117
Edition Artefides, Luzern . 111688, 135043
Edition Augenweide, Bernburg 133820
Edition Balance, Gotha 133981
Edition C, Zürich 135087
Edition Cicero, Velbert 134445
Edition Classic Art, Uster 135072
Edition Curt Visel, Memmingen 134199
Edition de Beauclair, München 134235
Edition des Archives d'Architecture Moderne, Bruxelles 133265
Edition Die Horen, Wirtschaftsverlag NW, Bremerhaven 135760
Edition Divan, Berlin 133765
Edition du Ricochet, Nice 138252
Edition EIKON, Wien 133190
Edition Emma Kunz, Würenlos 135078
Edition Euro Art, Mainz 134181
Edition Fundamental, Köln 134104
Edition Galerie Moderne, Bad Zwischenahn 101718, 133737
Edition Grafic d'Or, Hindelbank 135025
Edition Graph Druckula, Berlin 133766
Edition Graphischer Zirkel, Eichgraben, Niederösterreich 133068
Edition GS, Düsseldorf 133890
Edition Kunst der Comics, Sonneberg, Thüringen 134400
Edition Kunst Heute, Köln 134105
Edition Kunstpodium, München . . . 134236
Edition Lebensretter, Leipzig 134145
Edition Leipzig, Leipzig 134146
Edition Libri Illustri, Ludwigsburg, Württemberg 134164
Edition Lidiarte, Berlin 133767
Édition Lithelle, Ramatuelle 101067, 133693
Edition Maldoror, Berlin 133768
Edition Marguerite, Friedrichsdorf, Taunus 133965
Edition Munich, München . 134237, 139504
Edition Nautilus, Hamburg 134003
Edition Pautsch, Gütersloh 133993
Edition Pittura & Graphica, Celle . . . 133848
edition q, Berlin 133769
Edition Raetia, Bolzano 134557
Edition Reuss, München 134238
Edition Schwarze Seite, Frankenhardt 133932
Edition Solitude, Stuttgart 134410
Edition Spektrum, Regensberg 135060
Edition Stemmle, Thalwil 135071
Edition Tertium, Ostfildern 134337
Edition Tiessen, Neu-Isenburg 134304
Edition und Galerie Erata, Leipzig . .103864, 134147
Edition Va Bene, Klosterneuburg . . . 133104
Edition Waechterpappel, Denkmalschmiede Höfgen, Grimma 133989
Editions, Houston 116309
Editions, Liverpool 113408
Editions 3A, Paris 133571
Editions Alternatives, Paris 133572
Editions Art, Edmonton 096875
Editions Art-Tendance, Los Angeles 116759
Editions Atlantica Séguier, Anglet . . 133447
Editions Atlantica Séguier, Paris . . . 133573
Editions Atlas, Paris 133574
Editions Cahiers d'Art, Paris 133575
Editions Caraibes Marinique, Pointe-à-Pitre 134495
Editions Cartes d'Art, Paris 100246, 133576
Editions Cercle d'Art, Paris 133577
Editions de Grenelle, Paris 133578
Editions de l'Amateur, Paris 133579
Editions d'Ici, Anglet 060870, 133448
Editions du Beau Livre de France, Paris 100247, 133580
Editions du Centre Pompidou, Paris 133581
Editions du Chêne, Paris 133582
Editions du Félin, Paris . . . 133583, 138358
Editions du Griffon, Neuchâtel 111768, 135051
Editions du Jeu de Paume, Paris . . 133584
Editions du Latanier, Saint-Barthélemy 134497
Editions du Maeght Musée, Paris . . 133585
Editions du Marronnier, Montboucher-sur-Jabron 099737
Editions du Moniteur, Paris 133586
Editions du Regard, Paris 133587
Editions du Rocher, Monaco 140262
Editions du Seuil, Paris 133588
Editions Edisud, Aix-en-Provence . . 133444
Editions EFFA, Levallois-Perret 133481
Editions F.B., Paris 100248, 133589
Editions Futura, Paris 100249, 133590
Editions Gadoury, Monaco 077600, 134762
Editions Galilée, Paris 133591
Editions Gallery, Calgary 096810
Editions Gallery, Edmonton 096876
Editions Gallery, Thirroul 095331
Editions Graphiques, Johannesburg 080705
Editions Graphiques Gallery, London 085273, 113592, 141781
Editions Heuwinkel, Carouge 135002
Editions Ides et Calendes, Neuchâtel 135052
Editions Jasor, Pointe-à-Pitre 134496
Editions Limited, Indianapolis 116457
Editions Limited, Indianapolis 116458
Editions Lito-Jesco, Champigny-sur-Marne 133459
Editions Mango, Paris 133592
Editions Martinsart, Baie Mahault . . 134493
Editions Méditerranéennes du Prado, Marseille 133492
Editions Memoire Vivante, Paris . . . 133593
Editions phi, Echternach 134747
Editions Privat, Toulouse 133703
Editions Pygmalion, Paris 133594
Editions Revue Noire, Paris 133595
Editions Rivages, Fouesnant 133470
Editions Saint-Paul, Luxembourg . . 134750

Editions Scriptoria, Chasselay 133460
Editions Stef, Pont-Aven . . 101024, 133691
Editions Textuel, Paris 133596
Editions Traversière, Paris 133597
Editions Yvert & Tellier, Lyon 064122, 133487
Editions Zodiaque, Paris 133598
Editora Cultrix, São Paulo 133305
Editorial Casariego, Madrid 134944
Editorial Fuentemolinos, Madrid . . . 134945
Editorial Gredos, Madrid 134946
Editorial Hermes, México 134759
Editorial Lumen, Barcelona 134910
Editorial Planeta, Barcelona 134911
Editorial Prensa Ibérica, Barcelona . 134912
Editorial Teide, Barcelona 134913
Editoriale Domus, Rozzano 134684
Editoriale Umbra, Foligno 134589
Editout, Paris 100250
Editrice Grafica dei Greci, Roma . . .106525, 134672
Editrice Latina, Roma 106526, 134673
Editrice Vaticana, Città del Vaticano 135527
Editura Academiei Române, Bucureşti 134873
Editura Meridiane, Bucureşti 134874
Edizioni del Cavallino, Venezia 134706, 140150
Edizioni del Museo Pecci Prato, Prato 134663
Edizioni dell'Acquario, Padova 106395
Edizioni dell'Arquata, Foligno 134590
Edizioni Labrarie Siciliane, Santa Cristina Gela 134686
Edizioni L'Altra Riva, Venezia 134707
Edizioni Mediterranee, Roma 134674
Edizioni Poligrafiche Internazionali Cultura ed Arte, Palermo 134648
Edizioni Quattroventi, Urbino 134703
Edizioni San Paolo, Cinisello Balsamo 134569
Edkins, Denis, Bishop Auckland . . . 122418
EDL & Assoc., Atlanta 114873
Edler, J., Porta Westfalica 073355
Edlin, Canberra 055620
Edlin, Andrew, New York 117860
Edlinger, Herta, Klagenfurt 095612
Edmond Antiguedades, Barcelona . 080844
Edmond Historical Society Museum, Edmond 043612
Edmonds, Kent Town 136961
Edmonds, David, London . 085274, 131016
Edmonds Arts Festival Museum, Edmonds 043613
Edmonds South Snohomish County Historical Society Museum, Edmonds 043614
Edmonston House, Vails Gate 048724
Edmonton Antique Warehouse, Edmonton 058826
Edmonton Art Gallery, Edmonton . . 005393
Edmonton Furniture Upholsterers, Edmonton 123758
Edmonton Public Schools Museum, Edmonton 005394
Edmonton Telephone Historical Centre, Edmonton 005395
Edmund Adler-Galerie, Mannersdorf 002276
Edmund Wright House, Adelaide . . . 000705
Edmunds, Andrew, London 085275, 113593
Edmunds, Larry, Los Angeles 142506
Edna Historical Museum, Edna 043615
Edo, Artarmon 055404
Edo-Tokyo Museum, Tokyo 027158
Edo-Tokyo Tatemono-En, Koganei . 026679
Edoardo Villa Museum, Pretoria . . . 034713
Edouard, Josef, Rennes (Ille-et-Vilaine) 101078
Edoya, Tokyo 077243
Edrich, I.D., London 141782
Eds MC- och Motormuseum, Ed . . . 036239
Edsel and Eleanor Ford House, Grosse Pointe Shores 044363
Edu-Prime Training Centre, Singapore 050680
Eduard Bargheer-Haus, Hamburg . . 017687
Eduarda Smiļga Teātra Muzejs, Rīga 027732
Eduarda Veidenbauma Memoriālais Muzejs, Liepa 027704
Eduardo Barón, Letelier, Santiago de Chile 059523
Educatieve Boerderij en Zijdemuseum de Schans, Oud-Gastel 030020
Education Museum, Cairo 009296
Education Museum, Hyderabad . . . 031363
Educational Science Museum, Kuwait 027631
Edurne, Madrid 110488
Eduskuntasalimuseo, Kauhajoki . . . 009677
EDUSP - São Paulo University Press, São Paulo 133306
Edvard Grieg Museum, Paradis 031119
Edventure, Columbia 043078
Edward and Helen Mardigian Museum, Jerusalem 022949
Edward and Marthann Samek Art Gallery, Bucknell University, Lewisburg . . 045241
Edward Dean Museum, Cherry Valley 042795
Edward H. White II Memorial Museum, Brooks Air Force Base 042474
Edward Hopper House, Nyack 046578
Edward M. Bannister Gallery, Rhode Island College, Providence 047254
Edward VIII Antiques, Tyabb 056750
Edwardian Shop, Ipswich 084799
Edwards, Cleveland 088326
Edward's, Johannesburg 110051
Edwards, Seattle 119911
Edwards, Charles, London 085276
Edwards, Christopher, London 085277
Edwards, Clint, Richmond 132714
Edwards, Francis, Hay-on-Wye . . . 141652
Edwards, Francis, London 141783
Edwards, Francis, London 141784
Edwards, Gary, Washington 120282
Edwards, Libby, Portsea 095099
Edwards, Libby, South Yarra 095209
Edwards, Libby, Woollahra 095424
Edwards, Roy, Craigavon 112910
Edwards, Shaw, Hatherleigh 084621
Edwards County Historical Museum, Kinsley 045020
Edward's Jewellers, Liverpool 085024
Edwards Memorial Museum, Chesterfield 042805
Edwin, Jakarta 105837
Edwin & Assoc., Clark, Rochedale . 056538
Edwin A. Ulrich Museum of Art, Wichita State University, Wichita 049152
Edwin Scharff Museum am Petrusplatz, Neu-Ulm 019214
Edwin Wolters Memorial Museum, Shiner 048154
Edwin Young Collection, Salisbury . 040945
Eek, Marth., Skien 121876
Eells-Stow House, Milford 045863
Een Twee Drie, Den Haag 078193
De Eenhoorn, Aalst 057661, 123543
De Eenhoorn, Delft 078144
De Eenhoorn, Venlo 108265
Eera, Milano 075701
Het Eerste Friese Schaatsmuseum, Hindeloopen 029750
Eerste Nederlandse Opel Automuseum, Tijnje 030205
Eesti Ajaloomuuseum, Tallinn 009396
Eesti Arhitektuurimuuseum, Tallinn 009397
Eesti Kirjandusmuuseum, Tartu . . . 009414
Eesti Kunstimuuseum, Tallinn 009398
Eesti Loodusmuuseum, Tallinn 009399
Eesti Meremuuseum, Tallinn 009400
Eesti Muuseumiühing Tallinn, Tallinn 052868
Eesti Muuseumiühing Tartu, Tartu . . 052869
Eesti Muuseumraudtee, Haapsalu . 009357
Eesti Muuseumraudtee Lavassaare Muuseum, Tallinn 009401
Eesti Piimandusmuuseum, Imavere 009366
Eesti Põllumajandusmuuseum, Tõrvandi 009432
Eesti Postimuuseum, Tartu 009415
Eesti Rahva Muuseum, Tartu 009416
Eesti Spordimuuseum, Tartu 009417
Eesti Tarbekunsti- ja Disainimuuseum, Tallinn 009402
Eesti Teatri- ja Muusikamuuseum, Tallinn 009403
Eesti Tervishoiu Muuseum, Tallinn . 009404
Eesti Vabaõhumuuseum, Tallinn . . . 009405
Eewal Galerie, Leeuwarden 108092
EF Antigüedades, Paraná 055289
EF Galéria & Régiségbolt, Budapest 074679, 105505
EFA Museum für Deutsche Automobilgeschichte, Amerang . . 015533
Efes Müzesi, Selçuk 038169
Effa Editions, Paris 100251, 133599
Effe-Erre, Napoli 106364
Effeemme, Torino 128302
Effelsberg, K., Köln 071930
Effigy Mounds Museum, Harpers Ferry 044436
Effler, Elder, Cincinnati 088232
Efinger & Rippel, Berlin 069600
EFMA, Brighton 130442
Efron, Jean, Washington 120283
Efron, Mary, New York 090840
Efté, Paris 100252
EG-atelier, Hilversum 134815
EG Trading Post, Denver 088679
Egam, Madrid 110489
Egan, Sydney 095285
Egan, James, Bungaree 094328
Egarinca, Barcelona 129338
Egart, Georg, Rosenheim 073571
Egawa Museum of Art, Nishinomiya 026921
Ege, Öpfingen 073183
Egea Sanchez, Miguel, Málaga 081420
Egelkamp, T., Bornheim, Rheinland 102207
Egelund, København 098551
Egenolf, Herbert, Düsseldorf 070372, 102486, 139009
Eger, U., Wien 137306
Egerländer-Elbogner Heimatstuben, Illertissen 018050
Egerland-Museum, Marktredwitz . . 018849
Egersund Fayancemuseum, Egersund 030811
Egeskov, Anders, København 060320
Egeskov Veteranmuseum, Kværndrup 009004
Egg, Chicago 115406
Egge Museum, Steinkjer 031238
Egge-Museum Altenbeken, Altenbeken 015497
Egged Museum of Passengers Traffic, Holon 022936
Egger, André, Fribourg . . . 082378, 130021
Egger, Gerhard, Krumpendorf 057133
Egger, Gerry, Zürich 112062
Egger, Jakob, Gerlos 056989
Egger, Ralf, Trausdorf an der Wulka 095770
Egger, S., Neu-Ulm 139584
Eggermann, Gerhard, Steyr 057323
Eggers, M., Wedemark 074289
Eggers, Rüdiger, Sillerup 073819
Eggers, Uwe, Bokel bei Rendsburg . 069907
Eggleston, Ben, Long Marton 085829
Egham Museum, Egham 039430
Egida Antiques, Roma 106527
l'Egide, Bruxelles 057925
Egidius, Amsterdam 140295
d'Églantier, Amsterdam 077840
Eglantine, Beuzeville 061419
Eglau, Otto, Kampen 103479
Egli & Graf, Luzern 141272
Egly Franck, Lutzelhouse 124332
Egnsmuseet Ll. Kolstrupgaard, Aabenraa 008797
EGO Publishers, Sankt-Peterburg . . 134885
Egon Schiele Art Centrum, Český Krumlov 008322
Egon Schiele-Museum, Tulln 002758
Egri Érseki Gyûjteményi Központ Múzeum, Eger 021718
Egri Galéria, Eger 105557
E.G.S., Cantaron 099080
Eguiguren Arte de Hispanoamérica, Buenos Aires 055201
Egyetti, Taipei 098067
Egymalom, Debrecen 139934
Egypt Art, Los Angeles 116760
Egypt Centre, Swansea 041170
Egypt Papyrus Museum, Haram . . . 009336
Egyptian Antique Furniture and Decoration, Cairo 060439
Egyptian Art, Oostende 096397
Egyptian Art Gallery, Manama 096006
The Egyptian Auction Palace, Cairo 120879
Egyptian Center for International Culture, Cairo 098627
Egyptian Museum, Midan-el-Tahrir, Cairo 009297
Egyptian National Railways Museum, Cairo 009298
E.H. Starožitnosti, Praha 060126
Ehbrecht, G. & T., Eicklingen 139033
Ehemalige Benediktinerabtei, Seligenstadt 020183
Ehemalige Synagoge Erfelden, Riedstadt 019835
Ehemalige Synagoge mit Ausstellung Juden auf dem Lande- Beispiel Ichenhausen, Ichenhausen 018042
Ehemaliges Benediktinerinnenstift Göß, Leoben 002223
Ehemaliges Jagdschloß Bebenhausen, Staatliche Schlösser und Gärten Baden-Württemberg, Tübingen 020493
Ehemaliges Postfuhramt, Berlin . . . 016015
Ehemaliges Schlossvorwerk, Bachmann-Museum Bremervörde, Bremervörde 016438
Ehime Bunkakan, Imabari 026559
Ehime-kenritsu Bijutsukan, Matsuyama 026798
Ehime-kenritsu Hakubutsukan, Matsuyama 026799
Ehime-kenritsu Rekishi Minzoku Shiryokan, Matsuyama 026800
Ehlen Marbe, Bert, Sittard 078760
Ehlenbeck, Dorothee, Düsseldorf . . 102487
Ehlers, W., Bornheim, Rheinland . . . 069961
Ehm, Manfred, Hamburg 139173
Ehm Welk-Haus, Bad Doberan 015679
Ehm-Welk-Literaturmuseum, Angermünde 015543
Ehmann, Rudolf, Nürnberg 126561
Ehmer, Erich, München . . 072691, 126371
Ehmke, Edgar, Werder, Havel 126995
Ehnbom, Leni, Lund 081850
Ehnes, Ulrich, Bellheim 101753
Ehns, Mariehamn 060613
Ehrenreiter, Viktor, Niederstuttern . . 123422
Ehrensperger, Dr. Franz & Ingrid, Zürich 112063
Ehrensvärd-Museo, Helsinki 009520
Ehret, Andreas & Gundula, Triebischtal 126906
Ehrhardt, Gustave, Monthou-sur-Bièvre 064689
Ehrhardt, Hans, Künzelsau 072105
Ehrhardt, Heinrich, Madrid 110490
Ehrhardt, Konrad, München 072692
Ehrhart Museum, Antwerp 041749
Ehrhold, Loritta, Berlin 125194
Ehrler, Gerd, Neckarsulm 072955
Ehrler, Rosmarie, Zürich 082961
Ehrli, Viviane, Zürich 112064
Ehrlich & Langwieser, München . . . 121525
Ehrman Mansion, Tahoma 048475
Ehrmann, Fabien, Thionville 068395
Ehrsam, J., Gerbershausen 070971
Ehrsam, Roland, Basel 129918
Ehrt, Jürgen, Esens 125607
Ehrwalder Heimatmuseum, Ehrwald 001812
Ehu, Sendai 106992
Eibel, Münster 072902, 126496
Eibel, Burkhard, Münster 072903

Eiblmeier, Gerhard D., Lenggries . . 126208
Eicha-Museum, Archeologisch Museum voor de Brabantse Kempen, Bergeijk 029309
Eichberg, Helmut & Ursula, Nickenich 073048
Eichelmann, Norbert, Weimar, Thüringen 126978
Eichenberger, Dr. Walter, Beinwil am See 141222
Eichendorff, Mannheim . . 072419, 126272
Eicher, Delhi 105659
Eicher, Fritz, Bad Dürkheim 101638
Eichholz, Jürgen, Kassel 071750
Eichholzer, Werner, Sankt Gallen . .082772, 130160
Eichhorn, J., Langenau, Württemberg 072152
Eichhorn, Reneé, Wien 057405
Eichinger, Georg, Berlin 101847
Eichinger, Max, Ansbach 069174
Eichinger, O., Burglengenfeld 070101
Eichler, Dietmar, Ludwigsburg, Württemberg 126229
Eichler, Helmut, Hausmannstätten . 123380
Eichmayr, Augsburg 069224
Eichold-Heustis Medical Museum of the South, Mobile 045948
Eichsfelder Heimatmuseum, Heilbad Heiligenstadt 017845
Eicken, Elisabeth von, Ostseebad Ahrenshoop 104553
Eickhoff, M. & D., Herford 103356
Eid, Irmgard, Trostberg 074107
Eid, Jichi, Beirut 077391
Eid, Susanna-Isabel, München 126372
Eid & Sengle, Heidelberg 071451
Eidam, Chemnitz 138963
Eidam, Niederwiesa 139596
Eidam, Cornelia, Lichtenau, Sachsen 139413
Eide-Dalrymple Gallery, Augustana College, Sioux Falls 048190
Eidel, P., Neustadt an der Weinstraße 073028
Eidelstedter Heimatmuseum, Hamburg 017688
Eiden, Ludwig, Trier 126910
Eiden, Werner, Hannover 071393
Eiderstedter Heimatmuseum, Sankt Peter-Ording 019994
Eidsberg og Mysen Historielag, Eidsberg 030815
Eidskog Museum, Eidskog 030816
Eidsvold Historical Complex, Eidsvold 001012
Eidsvold Og Eidsvold, Enebakk 121850
Eidsvoll 1814 - Rikspolitisk Senter, Eidsvoll Bygningens Nasjonalhistoriske Samlinger, Eidsvoll Verk 030818
Eidsvoll Bygdemuseet, Eidsvoll Verk 030819
Eidsvollsminnet, Eidsvoll Bygningens Nasjonalhistoriske Samlinger, Eidsvoll Verk 030818
Eifelmuseum, Eifelvereinsmuseum, Mayen 018865
Eifelmuseum Blankenheim, Blankenheim, Ahr 016262
Eiffel, Bruxelles 133266
Eiffel Antique Centre, Singapore . . . 080460
Eigen Art, Dietzenbach 102368
Eigen-Art, Ibbenbüren 071602
Eigen ART, Troisdorf 105069
Eigen Art, Warstein 105163
Eigenart-Verlag, Winterthur 135076
Eigenblut, Neuss 134308
Eigenrauch, Christa, Nördlingen . . . 126553
Eigenschenk, G., Deggendorf 070197
The Eighteen Nineties Society, London 054366
Eighteenth Street Arts Complex, Santa Monica 047986
Eighth Avenue Antique Mall, Nashville 090447
Eigl, Margit, Linz . 057156, 095654, 123408
Eikaasgalleriet, Musea i Jølster, Skei i Jølster 031187
Eikelmann, Burkhard H., Düsseldorf 102488
Eikelmann, Burkhard H., Essen . . . 102673
De Eikenhof, Meppen 128773
Eikens Antikvariat, Bergen 140691
EIKON, Internationale Zeitschrift für Photographie und Medienkunst, Wien 135552
EIKON Gesellschaft der Freunde der Ikonenkunst e.V., Recklinghausen 053145
Eikon Restauri, Roma 128028
Eiktunet Kulturhistorisk Museum, Gjøvik 030857
Eildon Hall Sibbald Memorial Museum, Sutton, Ontario 006542
Eilean Donan Castle Museum, Dornie 039265
Eileen of China, Seattle 092990
Eilers & Hondtong, Hengelo, Overijssel 140457
Eilert, Gerhard, Dresden 138990
Eilert, Gerhard, Meißen 139473
Eilisha's Shoppe, New Farm 056324
Eimer, Christopher, London 085278
Ein-Zich-Artige, Ennepetal 070573
Einari Vuorelan Kirjailijakoti, Keuruu 009701
Einaudi, Giulio, Torino 134690
Einbecker Schreibmaschinenmuseum, Einbeck 016918
Einblick - Minigalerie im Vorhaus, Hallein 095559
Eindhovense Muntenhandel, Eindhoven 078334
Einert, Steffen, Barskamp 069476
Einnolf, Friedeburg, Ostfriesland . . . 070889
Eins und ... Zeitschrift für Kunst und Gestaltung, Stuttgart 135761
Einsiedel, Gräfin, Perchtoldsdorf . . . 057205
Einsiedelei Erzherzog Maximilians des Deutschmeisters, Innsbruck 002078
Einstein, G.W., New York 117861
Einstein-Haus, Bern 036926
Einzmann, Siegfried, Kassel 071751
Eipper, Paul-Bernhard, Eicklingen . . 125578
Eiraku, Kyoto 077095
Eiran Antiikki, Helsinki 060517
Eisei Bunko Museum, Tokyo 027159
Eisel, U., Neu Gaarz 104400
Eisele, Klaus, Kelheim 126024
Eisen, Ulrike, Bickendorf 102106
Eisenacher Münzhandlung, Eisenach 070533
EisenArt, Brackel 069969
Eisenbahn-Museum Lokschuppen Aumühle, Aumühle bei Hamburg 015629
Eisenbahnmuseum, Deutsch Wagram 001775
Eisenbahnmuseum, Eschwege 017050
Eisenbahnmuseum, Falkenberg, Elster 017098
Eisenbahnmuseum, Vienenburg . . . 020585
Eisenbahnmuseum Bayerischer Bahnhof zu Leipzig, Leipzig 018566
Eisenbahnmuseum Bochum-Dahlhausen, Bochum 016278
Eisenbahnmuseum Darmstadt-Kranichstein, Darmstadt 016635
Eisenbahnmuseum Historischer Wasserturm, Bebra 015927
Eisenbahnmuseum Lehmann, Hofheim, Unterfranken 017964
Eisenbahnmuseum Neustadt an der Weinstraße, Neustadt an der Weinstraße 019282
Eisenbahnmuseum - Sammlung Frey, Seifhennersdorf 020178
Eisenbahnmuseum Schwarzenberg, Schwarzenberg, Erzgebirge 020133
Eisenbahnmuseum Strasshof - Das Heizhaus, Strasshof 002721
Eisenbahnmuseum Vienenburg, Bad Zwesten 015843
Eisenberg, Omaha 118689
Eisenberg, G., Düsseldorf 070373
Eisenerzer Krippenhaus, Eisenerz . . 001818
Eisenhammer Dorfchemnitz, Dorfchemnitz bei Sayda 016748
Eisenhoffer, Frédérick, Genève 082423
Eisenhoffer, Frédérick, Rolle 122346
Eisenhower Birthplace, Denison . . . 043389
Eisenhower National Historic Site, Gettysburg 044183
Eisenkunstgußmuseum, Erlebnispark Ziegenhagen, Witzenhausen 020939
Eisenkunstgussmuseum, Stiftung Schleswig-Holsteinische Landesmuseen Schloß Gottorf, Büdelsdorf 016487
Eisenlauer, Karl, Ichenhausen 071604
Eisenmuseum, Ainring 015463
Eisenmuseum, Murau 002346
Eisenuhren- und Antikuhrenmuseum, Steyr 002698
Eisfabrik e.V., Hannover 103272
Eisfeld, L., Göttingen 102976
Eisho, Tokyo 077244
Eisma, Putten 128806
Eismann, Günter, Hamburg 071224
Eisner, Gail, Farmington 116125
Eissner, Frank, Leipzig 134148
Eisstockmuseum, Sankt Georgen im Attergau 002584
Eiteljorg Museum of American Indians and Western Art, Indianapolis 044737
Eittorf, E., Aachen 069083
Eitzenberger, Hans, Hamburg 071225
Eizendo, Tokyo 107033
EJ Designs, Boston 115171
E.K. Antiques, Finedon . . . 084405, 130710
Eka Gallery, Valencia 110803
Ekain Arte Lanak, Donostia-San Sebastián 110335
Ek'Art, Metz 099707
Ekaterina, Moskva 080237
Ekaterinburgskij Muzej Izobrazitelnych Iskusstv, Ekaterinburg 033109
Ekaterininskij Dvorec - Gosudarstvennyj Muzej Carskoje Selo, Puškin 033681
Eke, Sint-Niklaas 058372
Ekeby Qvarn Artspace, Uppsala . . . 111089
Ekegardh, Maastricht 108119
Ekehagens Forntidsby, Åsarp 036202
Ekenäs Museum, Ekenäs 009466
Ekenäs Slott, Linköping 036423
Ekens Bohagstjänst, Lund 081851
Ekenstam, Lena, Svedala 082047
Ekerö Antik, Ekerö 081778
Eketahuna and Districts Museum, Eketahuna 030493
Eketorps Borg, Degerhamn 036234
Ekfrid Township Museum, Appin . . . 005023
Ekhof-Theater, Stiftung Schloss Friedenstein Gotha, Gotha 017489
Al-Ekhtiar, Tawfiq, Damascus 083058
Eklectic, Atlanta 114874
Eklektik, Montréal 058950
Eklektikos, Washington 120284
Ekomuseum Bergslagen, Smedjebacken 036590
Ekomuseum Gränsland och Strømstad Museum, Strømstad 036686
Ekron - The Philistine City and it's Culture, Shiqmim 023061
Eksa, Sofia 123733
Eksi Şark Eserleri Müzesi, İstanbul . 038091
Eksjö Auktionsverk, Eksjö 122121
Eksjö Museum med Albert Engströms Samlingarna, Eksjö 036243
Ekspo-88, Moskva 109506
Ėkspozicija Čelovek. Duša. Duchovnost., Ivanovo 033170
Ėkspozicija Ivanovskaja starina, Ivanovo 033171
Ekstrom & Ekstrom, New York 117862
Ekthesis, Lefkosia 098299
EKZ-Museum Stromhaus Burenwisen, Glattfelden 037151
El Arcón, Panamá City 079527
El-Art, Warszawa 109116
El-Barkai Museum, Khartoum 036147
El Baz, Patrick, Saint-Ouen 067771
El Camino College Art Gallery, Torrance 048586
El Campo Museum of Natural History, El Campo 043626
El-Chimy, Dr. M., Cairo . . . 098628, 133436
El Dorado County Historical Museum, Placerville 047073
El Greco, Concepción 059478
El Greco, Santiago de Chile 123879
El Haddachi, Elhousseine, Torino . . 128303
El Hamed, Samy Abdul, Cairo 124036
El-Ibied Regional Museum, Khartoum 036148
El Marsa, Marsa 112252
El Monte Historical Society Museum, El Monte 043630
El Morro National Monument, Ramah 047320
El Naggar, Houston 089075
El Naggar, Houston 122905
El Ouachni, Ali, Marvejols 064417
El Paso Arts, El Paso 116106
El Paso Coins and Collectible, El Paso 088800
El Paso Holocaust Museum, El Paso 043636
El Paso Import, Dallas 088506
El Paso Import, Tucson 093226
El Paso Import, Tucson 093227
El Paso Import Company, Chicago . 088078
El Paso Museum of Art, El Paso . . . 043637
El Paso Museum of History, El Paso 043638
El Periodico del Arte, Madrid 136084
El Presidio Gallery, Tucson 120124
El Pueblo History Museum, Pueblo . 047276
El Puente, Harsum 134046
El Rancho de Las Golondrinas Museum, Santa Fe 047963
El Shalzi, Walid Ramadan, Roma . . 076440
El-Souk El-Kabin, Alexandria 060418
El Taller Antigüedades y Restauración, Medellín 059918
Elabidi, Nassereddine, Marrakech . 077681
Elabužskij Gosudarstvennyj Istoriko-architekturnyj i Chudožestvennnyj Muzej-zapovednik, Elabuga 033128
Eläinmuseo, Luonnontieteellinen Keskusmuseo, Helsinki 009521
Elaginoostrovskij Dvorec-Muzej Russkogo Dekorativno -Prikladnogo Iskusstva i Interjera XVIII-XX vv., Sankt-Peterburg 033739
Elaine Claire, Louisville 089983
Elaine's Fine Art, New York 117863, 142650
Elaine's Jewel Box, Sacramento . . . 092152
Elam, Carolyn, Nashville 090448
Elam & Assoc., Gary, Dallas 088507
Elam School of Fine Arts, The University of Auckland, Auckland 050570
Elan, Groningen 078413
Elan Design, New York 090841
Eland, Alkmaar 140268
Eland, Jonge, Amsterdam 128535
Elart, Praha 060127
Elas 95, Valladolid 081688
Elazarova, Elena, Sofia 096728
Elbasan Museum, Elbasan 000018
Elbaz, Jacques, Paris 100253
Elbdörfer Galerie, Hamburg 103113
Elbé, Paris 138359
Elbeltagi, Mahmoud M., München . 126373
Elbers, Toronto 059176, 123830
Elbers, Ulrike, Kleve 071875
Elbert Hubbard-Roycroft Museum, East Aurora 043556
Elberton Granite Museum, Elberton 043648
Elbfischerei-Museum, Boizenburg . 016308
Elbogen, Malmö 141127
Elbow Museum, Elbow 005419
Elbschiffahrtsmuseum mit stadtgeschichtlicher Sammlung, Lauenburg 018524
Elbschloss Bleckede, Bleckede . . . 016267
Elbtor Werben, Werben, Altmark . . . 020801
Elca, Madrid 110491
Elca London Gallery, Montréal 096998
Elchlepp, A., Osterode am Harz . . . 073255
Elcho Island Art & Craft, Galiwinku . 055857
Elco, Bremen 102238
Elco Postergalerie, Wilhelmshaven . 105298

Elde, Heilbronn 125906
Elden Antiques, Kirk Deighton 084871
Elder, Charlotte 115284
Elder, Saint Louis 092231
Elder, R., Nashville 142599
Elder Art Gallery, Rogers Center for Fine Arts, Lincoln 045301
Elder Fine Art, North Adelaide 056355
Elder Fine Art, North Adelaide 120620
Eldnäset Flottningsmuseum, Ånge . 036186
Eldon & Choukri, Casablanca 077646, 128511
Eldon House, London 005783
Eldorado Antiques, San Antonio . . . 092510
Eldorado Museum, Eldorado 001013
Eldre Norsk Kunst, Stavanger 079501
Eldred, Robert C., East Dennis 122892
Eldreds, Plymouth 122659
Eldridge, London 085279
Eldridge Street Project, New York . . 046327
Eleanor Barbour Cook Museum of Geology, Chadron State College, Chadron . 042696
Eleanor Roosevelt National Historic Site, Hyde Park 044706
Eleb, Alain, Paris 065870
Eleckij Literaturno-memorialnyj Muzej Pisatelja I.A. Bunina, Gorodskoj kraevedčeskij muzej, Elec 033134
Electa, Milano 134610
Electique, Exeter 084355
Electra Gallery, Waipukurau 108601
Electric Ladyland, The First Museum of Fluorescent Art, Amsterdam 029177
Electric Mountain - Museum of North Wales, Amgueddfa'r Gogledd, Llanberis . 040044
Electric Train Outlet, Saint Louis . . . 092232
Electrical Engineering Museum, Fredericton 005479
The Electrical Industry Museum, Teheran 022610
Electro Antiques, New York 090842
Electro Rádio São João, Lisboa . . . 079921
Electrobroc, Broc 036976
Electroniquel, Gijón 129520
Electrum, Edmonton 096877
El Elefante del Rastro, Madrid 141039
Eleftheriadis Collection, Petra 021429
Eleftherios K. Venizelos Museum, Athinai 021168
Elegance for Hire, Dallas 088508
Elegant Antiques, Paddington, Queensland 056427
Elegant Art Painting Gallery, Hong Kong 097780
Elegant Ceramic Mold, Cleveland . . 115704
Elegant Dollhouse, Sacramento . . . 092153
Elegant Extras, Cleveland 088327
Elegant Findings, Boston 087816
The Elegant Garage Sale, Toronto . . 059177
Elegant International, Delhi 134514
Elegant Junque Shop, Tucson 093228
Elegia, Strasbourg 068317, 138617
Eleker Heimatmuseum, Leimen, Baden 018547
Elektriciteits- en Techniekmuseum, Hoenderloo 029757
Elektrizitätsmuseum, Münchenstein 037353
Elektrizitätszähler-Kabinett, Braunschweig 016383
Elektro Museum, Baden 036867
Elektro-Museum, Hilden 017919
Elektro-Museum Schleswag, Rendsburg 019799
Elektropathologisches Museum, Wien 002890
Elemente, Salt Lake City 092431
Elementos, Bogotá 135662
Elements, Palma de Mallorca 081477
Eléments, Paris 135705
Elements Glass, Portland 118994
Elements of Art, Columbus 115774
Elena Montalto, Venezia 076933
Eleouet, Cathérine, Grenoble 124253
Elephant & Castle, Den Haag 078194
Elephantine Island's Museum, Awan Museum, Aswan 009286
Elephant's Toe, Richmond 092074
Elephant's Toe, Richmond 092075
Elephantsgalore, Virginia Beach . . . 093352
Elet és Irodalom, Budapest 135841
Eleusis, Caen 061869
Eleusis, Firenze 075332
Elevation X, London 113594
Eley, Boston 122421
The Elf Shelf, Las Vegas 089565
Elfenbein-Museum, Michelstadt . . . 018931
Elfenbeinmuseum, Walldürn 020655
Elferink, J., Den Ham 128641
L'Elfo, Bologna 075073, 127147
Elford, Yelverton 114745
Elfred, Lee, San Diego 119501
Elfreth's Alley Museum, Philadelphia 046938
The Elgar Birthplace Museum, Lower Broadheath 040347
Elghanayan, S., New York 090843
Elghanayan, Sina, New York 090844
Elgin Apple Museum, Grabouw 034620
Elgin County Pioneer Museum, Saint Thomas 006394
Elgin Military Museum, Saint Thomas 006395
Elgin Museum, Elgin 039433
Elgin Public Museum, Elgin 043650
Elguabbas, Mohamed, Casablanca . 077647
Elham Valley Bookshop, Canterbury 141482
Elham Valley Railway Museum, Folkestone 039508
Eli Whitney Museum, Hamden 044395
Elia, Alberto S., Buenos Aires 094068
Elian, Lily, Beirut 077392
Elias, Miami 117063
Elias & Esra, Antwerpen 096063
Elia's Restoration, New York 132466
Eliasu Dzimtas Muzejs Zīlēni, Platone 027722
Eliecer, Miranda S., Santiago de Chile 059524
eLightworks, Saint Paul 119284
Elijah Clark Memorial Museum, Lincolnton 045320
Elikases, Thur 123475
Elimäen Kotiseutumuseo ja Koulumuseo, Elimäki 009469
Elimäen Koulumuseo, Elimäki 009470
Elingaard Museum, Fredrikstad Museum, Gressvik 030862
Elins & Eagles-Smith, San Francisco 119660
Eliot, Toronto 137705
Elis, Vaclav, Dresden 125489
Eli's Gallery, Dallas 115874
Elisabet Ney Museum, Austin 041924
Elisabeta, Bucureşti 109430
Elisabeth & Sam, Bruxelles 057926
Elisabethen Antiquitäten, Basel . . . 082137
Elisej, Moskva 080238
Elisengalerie, Aachen 101504
Elitas, Pardubice 060074
Elite Antiques, San Diego 092630
Elite Autographs, Tucson 143029
Elite Upholstery, San Diego 132850
Elitzer, Ernst, Saarbrücken 104789
Eliza Cruce Hall Doll Museum, Ardmore 041766
Eliza Gallery, Mornington 094885
Eliza Jane Antiques, Haberfield . . . 055928
Elizabeth & Son, Ulverston 086981
Elizabeth 260, New York 090845
Elizabeth Anne's Antiques, Gosford 055902
Elizabeth Antiques, Chatswood 055665
Elizabeth Bay House, Elizabeth Bay 001014
Elizabeth Castle, Saint Helier 040912
Elizabeth D. Walters Library, Stroudsburg 048401
Elizabeth Farm, Rosehill 001438
Elizabeth Myers Mitchell Art Gallery, Saint John's College, Annapolis 041741
Elizabeth O'Neill Verner Studio Museum, Charleston 042732
Elizabeth P. Korn Gallery, Drew University, Madison 045583
Elizabeth Perkins House, York 049340
Elizabeth R. Antiques, East Molesey 084248, 130663
Elizabeth Rozier Gallery, Jefferson City 044848
Elizabeth Sage Historic Costume Collection, Bloomington 042262
Elizabeth Slocumb Galleries, Carrol Reece Museum, Johnson City 044865
Elizabeth Street Antiques and Restoration, London 131017
Elizabeth Street Gallery, New York . 090846
Elizabethan House Museum, Great Yarmouth 039632
Elizabethans, Fareham 084381
Elizabeth's Hallmark, New Orleans . 090550
Elizium, Moskva 080239, 109507
Elk Grove Farmhouse Museum, Elk Grove Village 043657
Elk Lake Heritage Museum, Elk Lake 005421
Elk River Area Arts Council, Elk River 054747
Elka, Córdoba 136758
Elkan, Norbert & Birgit van, Marburg 072444
Elke's Galerie, Ehringshausen 102605
Elkhart County Historical Museum, Bristol 042419
Elkoll, Set, Manama 057627, 096007
Elkon, New York 117864
Ella Sharp Museum, Jackson 044795
Ellavale, Pymble 056508
Ellefsen, Uwe, Hamburg 103114
Ellekilde Auktionshus, København . 120869
The Ellen Noel Art Museum of the Permian Basin, Odessa 046624
Ellen Terry Memorial Museum, Tenterden 041199
Ellenberg, Detlef, Flensburg 070699
Ellenor Antiques, Otford 086170
Ellenroad Engine House, Milnrow . . 040471
Ellequadro Documenti, Genova 106090
Eller, Derek, New York 117865
Eller, Peter, Albuquerque 114781
Ellerich, Roland, Remscheid 126713
Ellermann, Heiko, Köln 126075
Ellermeiers Burgmannshof, Baudenkmal und Geigenmuseum, Hardegsen . 017774
Ellerslie Shellfish Museum, Tyne Valley 006674
Elli Riehl-Puppenmuseum, Treffen bei Villach 002754
Ellinga Gallery, Luanda 094050
Ellinghaus, Alfter 069132
Ellingson Car Museum, Rogers 047524
Ellington White Project, Detroit 043448
Elliot Colliery Winding House, New Tredegar 040529
Elliot Lake Nuclear and Mining Museum, Elliot Lake 005424
Elliott, New Orleans 117429
Elliott, New York 090847
Elliott, Saint Paul 132767
Elliott, Singapore 080461
Elliott, Charlotte, Baltimore 087664
Elliott, Samuel, Dublin 074913
Elliott Avedon Museum and Archives of Games, Waterloo 006773
Elliott Gallery, Braunton 112695
Elliott Museum, Stuart 048404
Elliott & Scholz, Eastbourne 084263
Elliott's, Petworth 086245
Ellis, Anita, Avalon 094184
Ellis, Donald, Edinburgh 084290
Ellis, J.R. & R.K., Norwich 141963
Ellis, Ruth, Bendigo 094241
Ellis County Museum, Waxahachie . 049021
Ellisland Farm, Ellisland 039436
Ellison, Beaconsfield 083459
Ellsworth County Museum, Hodgen House Museum, Ellsworth 043683
Ellwanger, Natalie, Kiesen 130054
Ellwart, Lothar, Ronneburg, Thüringen 126730
Ellwood, Southampton 142078
Ellwood House Museum, DeKalb . . 043374
Elm Hill Contemporary Art, Norwich 114162
Elm House Antiques, Merstham . . .085979, 131274
Elm Lodge, London 113595
Elm Tree Antiques, Flaxton 084411
Elman W. Campbell Museum, Newmarket 006007
Elmar Rojas, Guatemala 105477
Elmbridge Museum, Weybridge . . . 041355
Elmby, Hans, København 060321
Elmenwood, Potsdam 104623
Elmenzeh, Casablanca 077648
Elmer, M., Sassenberg 073674
Elmhurst Art Museum, Elmhurst . . . 043686
Elmhurst Historical Museum, Elmhurst 043687
Elmira, Saint Louis 092233
Elmira Railway Museum, Prince Edward Island Museum and Heritage Foundation, Elmira 005425
Elmore, Washington 093410, 133023
Elmore Old Wares, Elmore 055793
Elmore Progress Association Station Museum, Elmore 001015
Elms Lesters Painting Rooms, London 113596
Elmuseet, Danmarks Museum for Elektricitetens Fysik, Teknologi og Kulturhistorie, Bjerringbro 008819
The Elmwood Gallery, Winnipeg . . . 097581
Eloaitta, Kaavin Kotiseutumuseo, Kaavi 009648
Elobu, Apeldoorn 078032
Eloise Pickard Smith Gallery, Santa Cruz 047955
Eloquence, Philadelphia 091634
Elora Spring Antique Show, Elora . . 093624
Elovitz, Albert, Pittsburgh 091813
Eloy-Altmann, Jean-Sébastien, Nice 065078, 124511
Elphinstone Pioneer Museum; Gibsons Maritime Museum, Gibsons 005505
Elrose Heritage Museum, Elrose . . . 005426
Els Encants, Palma de Mallorca . . . 081478
Els Encants Terrenals, Sabadell . . . 081534
Els Llibres del Tirant, Barcelona . . . 140983
Elsberg, Renate van, Bad Oeynhausen 101684
Elschker, K., Leverkusen 072240
Elsener, Werner, Neu Sankt Johann 082686
Elseneur, Paris 065871
Elsenhans, Veith, Freiburg im Breisgau 070834
Elsenzer Heimatstuben, Eppingen . . 016991
Elser, Tilman, Westhofen 127002
Elsewhere Books, San Francisco . . 142943
Első Numizmatikai, Budapest 074680
Elsom, Pamela, Ashbourne 083326
Elspeth, Kangaroo Valley 056032
Elstir, Paris 100254
Elstner, Rudolf, Wien 057406
Elstow Moot Hall, Bedford 038657
Elsworth, June, Beaconsfield 083460
Elten & Elten, Zürich 112065
Eltgen, Dr. Ulrich, Bonn 125351
Eltham Gallery, Eltham 094505
Eltham Palace, London 040142
Elvarheim Museum, Åmli 030725
Elvarts, Ann, Chicago 088079
Elvaston Castle Working Estate Museum, Elvaston 039439
Elvehjem Museum of Art, Madison . 045589
Elverket, Djursholm 110900
Elvick, San Francisco 132879
Elvina, Vence 101439
Elvira, København 060322
Elvira Antikt & Kuriosa, Halmstad . . 081830
Elviras Värld, Stockholm 081945
Elvis History World, Gstatterboden . 001982
Elwert, H.-J., Baden-Baden 101720

Elwert, N.G., Marburg 139459
Elwes & Hanham, London 113597
Elwood Haynes Museum, Kokomo . 045046
ELX Koloniaal Meubel, Eindhoven . . 078335
Ely Books, Ely 141595
Ely Museum, Ely 039441
Elztalmuseum - Regionalgeschichte und Orgelbau, Waldkirch 020643
Em-Dash, Denver 115991
E.M. Violette Museum, Kirksville . . 045022
Emage, Los Angeles 116761
Emailmuseum Gertrude Stöhr, Vorchdorf 002789
Emal, San Diego 092631
Eman, Hamilton 096914
Emanouel Corporation, London 085280
Emanuel Vigeland Museum, Oslo . . 031073
Emar Sanat Galerisi, İstanbul 112302
Emaux d'Art de Longwy, Longwy . . 063991
EMB-Service, Luzern 135044
Emba Museum of Chinese Modern Art, Ashiya 026426
Embassy-Art de Vivre, Luzern 082624
Embden, Antony, Paris 065872
L'Embellie, Jouques 063259
Embellie, Orsay 065310
Emberto, Errico Umberto, Napoli . . 075977
Embling, D.S., Alton 130294
Embom-Garpom Backstugusittarstuga, Liljendal 009825
Embregts, Breda 078089
Embroiderers Guild Museum, Mile End 001262
Embroiderers' Guild Museum Collection, East Molesey 039355
Embroiderers Guild of America, Louisville 054748
Embry & Co., Portland 091929
Embryo, Leuven 096372
Embsay Bolton Abbey Steam Railway, Skipton 041040
Embu, São Paulo 058705
Emel, Bernard, Saint-Baudille-et-Pipet 067372
The Emer Gallery, Belfast 112612
Emerald, Milwaukee 117183
Emerald Art, Magherafelt 114027
Emerald Art Gallery, Emerald 001018
Emerald Art Society, Emerald 052468, 094508
Emerald Bamboo, Seattle 119912
Emerald Bazaar, Emerald 055799
Emerald Empire Arts Association, Springfield 054749
Emerald Museum, Emerald 001019
l'Emeraude, Casablanca 077649
L'Emeraude, Paris 065873
Emeraude, Paris 065874
Emeraude, Paris 065875
Emerge Gallery, Wellington 108619
Emerson, Portland 142787
Emerson Gallery, Clinton 043018
Emery, Etoy 082363
Emett Gallery, Beaminster 112593
EMI Antik, Plzeň 060081
Emigrantmuseet, Kisa 036392
Emigre, Sacramento 136453
Emil A. Blackmore Museum of the American Legion, Indianapolis 044738
Emil Cedercreutzin Museo, Harjavalta 009505
Emil-von-Behring-Ausstellung, Marburg 018821
Emil-von-Behring-Ausstellung, Marburg 018822
Emil Wikström Museo, Valkeakoski 010212
Emīla Dārziņa Muzejs, Jaunpiebalga 027685
Emila Melngaiļa Memoriālais Muzejs, Vidriži 027801
Emile Van Doren Museum, Stedelijk Museum, Genk 003447
Emile Verhaeren Museum, Sint-Amands 003751
Emiliani, Michèle, Dieulefit 099207
Emiliani, Michèle, La Bégude-de-Mazenc 099385
Emilio Aguinaldo Shrine Museum, Kawit 031681
Emilio's Everthing Art, Miami 117064
Emily Carr Arts Centre Museum, Victoria 006739
Emily Carr Institute of Art and Design, Vancouver 049828
Emily Carr Institute of Art & Design, Vancouver 097462
Emily et Nous, Brugge 057771
Emily'S Nook, Donostia-San Sebastián 081080
Emirates Fine Arts Society, Sharjah 054263
Emirates Very Special Arts, Sharjah 038429
Emiyu, Chiba 106836
Emma, Den Haag 078195
Emma Antiquités, Paris 065876
Emma Kunz-Museum, Würenlos . . . 037742
Emmanuel, Camille-Bernard, Paris . 138360
Emmanuelle, d', Liège 096377
Emmanuelli, Antoinette, L'Ile-Rousse 063826
EMMARP, Paris 065877
Emma's, West End 137137
Emma's Antiques, North Fremantle 056361
Emma's Arts Emporium, Pittsburgh 118917
Emmaville Mining Museum, Emmaville 001020
Emmebici, Roma 128029
Emmenegger, Franz, Luzern 082625, 130103
Emmenegger, Oskar, Zizers 130225
Emmerich Kálmán-Gedenkraum, Wien 002891
Emmett Kelly Historical Museum, Sedan 048103
Emminghaus, Hans, Meerbusch . . . 072485
Emócia, Žilina 109927
Emoldurarte, Porto Alegre 096553
Emouna, Deauville 099198
Emperor Arts and Antiques, Manila .079563, 108842
Emperor Maximilian of Mexico Museum, Hardegg 002018
EMPiK Galeria, Łódź 109001
Empire, Düsseldorf 070374
Empire, Słupno 129072
Empire, Tilburg 078768
Empire Antikk, Porsgrunn 079483
Empire Antiques, New Orleans 090551
Empire Area Heritage Group - History Museum, Empire 043702
Empire Auctions, Ottawa 120809
The Empire Company, Alphington . . 055342
Empire Enterprises Antiques, San Diego 092632
Empire Exchange, Manchester 085913
Empire Gallery, New York 117866
Empire State Aerosciences Museum, Glenville 044217
Empire & Virgo, Toronto 097261
Empiric, Los Angeles 116762
Empirical Studies of Arts, Amityville 136454
Empl, Alfons, Landshut 126164
Emporeo, København 060323
Emporia State University Geology Museum, Emporia 043703
Emporio Brasileiro de Arte, São Paulo 058706
Emporium, Houston 089076
Emporium, Nashville 090449
The Emporium, Pontarddulais 086284
Emporium Antique Centre, Lewes . .084980, 141725
Emporium Antique Mall, Saskatoon 059096
Emporium Antique Shop, New York . 090848
The Emporium Antiques, Welling . . 087064
Emporium at Warson Woods, Saint Louis 092234
Emporium Ex V, Nice 065079
Emporium-Merkator Hamburg, Hamburg 071226
Emporos, Greytown 079105
Empreinte, Lille 063848
Empreintes d'Emma, Cran-Gevrier . 099184
Empresa de Conservacion y Restauracion, Elche 129517
Empress Scarlet, West Hollywood . 093467
Emprin, Torino 128304
Emprin-Casabo, Nathalie, Lyon . . . 099556
Empty & Bur, Amsterdam 107706
Empty Walls, Dallas 115875
Empty Walls Dallas Galleria, Dallas 115876
Jürgen Emsbach & Angela Ihden-Emsbach, Koblenz 071891
Emsland-Moormuseum, Geeste . . . 017334
Emslandmuseum Lingen, Lingen . . 018661
Emslandmuseum Schloß Clemenswerth, Sögel 020226
Emsworth Museum, Emsworth 039444
Emu Park Historical Museum, Emu Park 001021
EN Japanese Arts, Los Angeles . . . 089759
En Passant, Amsterdam 077841
En Suite, Apeldoorn 107840
ENAC Section d'Architecture, Lausanne 050767
Enault, Bernard, Valenciennes 121274
Enault, Michèle, Paris 124657
Enbaoui, Casablanca 077650
Encadrements R.D, Reims 124860
Encantada, San Francisco 119661
Los Encantes, Cádiz 081027, 129473
Encantes, A Coruña 081056
Encanto da Freiria, Coimbra 079819
Los Encantos Granadinos, Granada 081142
Encapça, Girona 081133
Encarnacion Matran Bea, Cartagena 110298
Encaustique, Triel-sur-Seine 068629, 138642
Enchanted Aviary, Bury Saint Edmunds 083823
Enchanted Cottage, Cincinnati 088233
Enchanted Light Galleries, Albuquerque 114782
Enchanted Light Gallery, Albuquerque 114783
Enchanted Mansion Doll Museum, Baton Rouge 042043
Enchanted Southwest, Albuquerque 114784
Enchanted What It's Shop, Jacksonville 089408
Enchanted World Doll Museum, Mitchell 045941
Enchantment Antiques, Kenthurst . . 056042
The Enchantry, Birkdale 055505
Enchères Champagne, Mardeuil . . . 121059
Encinas Ayuso, Alberto, Madrid . . . 129611
Encinas Merchan, Angel, Madrid . . 129612
Encontro Marcado Locadora de Livros, Rio de Janeiro 137573
Encore, Farmington 088826
Encore, Miami 132339
L'Encre de Chine, Lausanne 082544
Encuadernacines Hernandez, Zaragoza 129809
Encuadres DM, Santiago de Chile . . 059525
Encuentra, Jacques, Toulouse 124979
Encyclia, Paris 100255
Encyclopaedia Shop, Magill 136987
Encyclopedia World Book, Eaton . . . 136887
End, Karl-Heinz, Erwitte 070605
End-O-Line Railroad Museum, Currie 043249
End of History, New York 090849
End of Steel Heritage Museum, Hines Creek 005618
End of the Row Antiques, Atlanta . .087470, 131768
Endangered Books, Auckland 140590
Endangered Pieces, Portland 091930
Endeavour Antiques, Dunedin 079085
Endeavour Museum, Cessnock 000906
Endele, Elmar, Konstanz 072048
Endemann, Klaus, Kirchheim bei München 126047
Enderby and District Museum, Enderby 005428
Enders, G., Neuburg an der Donau . 072976
Enders Projects Contemporary Fine Arts, Frankfurt am Main 102759
Endhardt, Mechthild, Montevideo . . 131730
Endl, Ulrich, Bad Soden am Taunus 069384
Endlein, Rothenburg ob der Tauber . 073587
Endler, Dr. Franz, Kreuzwertheim . . 072087
Endlich, John, Haarlem 078451
Endre Nemes Múzeum, Pécs 021816
Endres, Detroit 132052
Endres, Helga & Dieter, Uffenheim . 105090
Endres, R., Bad Wildbad 069393
Endrös, Bernhard, Sparneck 073872
Enebakk Bygdetun, Trysil 031291
Enebakk Museet, Enebakk 030823
Enebybergs Antikbod, Enebyberg . . 081779
Enedina, Belo Horizonte 058426
Eneo, Maastricht 108120
Energeia - Museum voor het Industrieel erfgoed Electrabel, Gent 003453
EnergeticA, Museum voor Energietechniek, Amsterdam 029178
Energiemuseum, Fürstenfeldbruck . 017283
Enes, Lisboa 109284
Enes, J., Lisboa 121930
Enes, Z., Cruz Quebrada-Dafundo . . 121919
Enfield Historical Society Museum, Enfield 043709
Enfield Shaker Museum, Enfield . . . 043710
Enforcer Art Gallery, Philadelphia . . 118754
Eng, Ola, Uppsala 141187
Engadiner Museum, Sankt Moritz . . 037503
Engage, The National Association for Gallery Education, London 054367
Engel, Jerusalem 105908
Engel, Leuven 123642
Engel & Co., Stuttgart 139759
Engel, Tel Aviv 105917
Engel, Berthold, Großenlüder 125762
Engel, Fritz, Hamburg 139174
Engel, Gerhard, Ingelheim am Rhein 125969
Engel, Peter, Wiesbaden 074401
Engel, Philippe, Courville-sur-Eure . 062529
Engel, W., Hilden 103374
Engel, Wolfgang, Koblenz 121466
Engel & Hoff, Wien 057407
De Engelbewaarder, Utrecht 078796
Engelbrecht, Alexander, München . .072693, 126374
Engelen, 's-Hertogenbosch 078517
Engelen, Leuven 058273
Engelenburg House Art Collection, Pretoria 034714
Engelhardt, Neukyhna 073000
Engelhorn, Helmut, Wiesloch 105290
Engelhorn, Klaus, Wien 095813
Engeli, Dora, Biel 082257
Engelmann, A., Bellenberg 069513
Engelmann, W., Lahr, Schwarzwald 139373
Engeln Antik, Malmö 081866
O Engenho Antiguidades, Belo Horizonte 096461
Engerbeau, Dominique, La Roche-sur-Yon 063415
Engert, Eschweiler 102662
Engesser, Martin, Zürich . 082962, 130234
Engholm, Kerstin, Wien 095814
Engine House, Dunedin Gasworks Museum Trust, Dunedin 030484
Engine House Project, Chelmsford Museums, Chelmsford 039047
Engine 'n' Tender, London 085281
Engl, Regensburg 104695
England Antiques, Gräfelfing 071074
England & Co, London 113598
Englands Gallery, Leek 084934
Englands Gallery, Leek 113367
Englands Gallery, Leek 130875
Engle, Indianapolis 089295
Englehart and Area Historical Museum, Englehart 005429
Engler, Elsbeth, Langnau am Albis . 111605
Englert, Josef, Erfurt 125597
Englert-Byrne, Amorbach . 069165, 101577
Englich, Ulf, Salzburg 057244

English, Toby, Wallingford 142138
English Accent Antiques, Atlanta . . 087471
English and Continental Antiques, Eye 084368
English Antiques, Antwerpen 057692
English Antiques, El Paso 088801
English Antiques, Knokke-Heist . . . 058243
English Antiques, Rodgau 073553
English Bridge Workshop, Shrewsbury 114431
English-Center-Antiques, Zürich . . . 082963
English Ceramic Circle, Beckenham 054368
English Country Antiques, Uffculme 086978
The English Craftsman, Masterton .079147, 128944
English Galleries, Bruxelles 057927, 123590
English Gallery, Geisenheim 102922
English Heritage, Bridgnorth 083668
English Heritage, London 054369
English Heritage, East Midlands Region, Northampton 054370
English Heritage North West Region, Manchester 054371
English Heritage South East Region, Guildford 039644
English Heritage South West Region, Bristol 038862
English Heritage West Midlands Region, Birmingham 038730
English Heritage Yorkshire Region, York 054372
English Interiors, Den Haag 078196
English Pine Company, Dallas 088509
The English Room, Charlotte 087947
English Rose Antiques, Coggeshall .084050, 130596
English Squirrel Woodcraft, Bacup . 130321
English Traditions, Cincinnati 088234
English Workshop, Knokke-Heist . . 058244
Englishman's Antiques, Charlotte . .087948, 122836
Engman, Fågelmara 122128
Engman, Honolulu 116208
Engrand, Chantal, Mouans-Sartoux 064802
Engraving Art, Linxia 059724
Engraving Print Village Art Museum, Aikawa 026404
Engs, Christianne, West Hollywood . 093468
Engsö Slott, Västerås 036761
Engström, Göran, Stockholm 111018
Engströmsgården, Hult 036351
Enhörningen Antikvariat, Lidingö . . 141117
Enigma, Frome 113083
Enigma, Toronto 097262
Enigma Art Studio, Denver 115992
Het Enigste Winkeltje, Eindhoven . . 078336
Enilem Galerie, Pau 100983
Enisejskij Kraevedčeskij Muzej, Enisejsk 033140
Enjalbert-Bonifassi, Marie-Thérèse, Paris 065878
Enjoy, Roma 076441
Enkhuizer Almanak Museum, Enkhuizen 029560
Enköpings Museum, Enköping 036249
Les Enluminures, Paris 138361
Enmarcaciones Olivar, Tarragona . . 110784
Enmarcados Modernos, Panamá City 079528
Enmarcos, Valdivia 059560
Ennagon, New York 117867
Ennejma Ezzahra-Palais du Baron d'Erlanger, Centre des Musiques Arabes et Méditerranéennes, Sidi Bou Saïd . 037975
Ennistuskoda Kanut, Tallinn 124038
Ennsmuseum Kastenreith, Weyer . . 002841
Ennsthaler, Steyr 137267
Enoagrarimuseum, Castelvetrano . . 023744
Enoch, New Orleans 117430
Enoch Turner Schoolhouse, Toronto 006596
Enook Galleries, Waterloo 006774
Enoteca Regionale del Monferrato, Vignale Monferrato 026325
Enoteca Regionale Permanente la Serenissima, Gradisca d'Isonzo . . 024356
Enrico, Genova 106091
Enrico, Maria, Milano 075702
Enrile Corsini, C., Madrid 129613
Enseñanza Artes Plásticas y Artesanías, Centro Cultural Francisco Eduardo Tresguerras, Celaya 050529
Ensi Gallery, Český Krumlov 098348
Enskede Antik, Enskede 081780
Ensoreanum, Oostende 052668
Enta, Warszawa 109117
Ente Museo Poschiavino, Poschiavo 037421
Entente Cordiale, Warwick 087038
Enterieur Antikvitás, Budapest 074681
Enterprise Collectors Market, Eastbourne 084264
Enterprises Antiques, Portland 091931
Enterprises Antiques, Portland 091932
Entertainment Gallery, New Orleans 117431
Enterzone, Oakland 136455
Enticott, B. J., Hampton 055947
Entlebucher Heimatmuseum, Schüpfheim 037538
Entler-Dvořáková, Praha 098428
Entomological Museum of Fujikyu, Fujiyoshida 026456
Entomological Society Museum, Cairo 009299
Entomologické Oddělení, Národní Muzeum, Praha 008602
Entomology Research Museum, Riverside 047456
Entre Libros, Buenos Aires 136716
Entre Libros, Buenos Aires 136717
Entre Temps, Bordeaux 061605
Entre-Temps, Bourges 061726
Entre Temps, Saint-Ouen 067772
Entre Terre et Mer, Bonnieux 098982
Entre Vents et Marais, Batz-sur-Mer 061222
Entrée des Artistes, Barbizon 098916
L'Entrepôt, Carpentras 061999
L'Entrepôt des Chalets, Roncq 101100
Entrepôt du Troc, Mâcon 064204
Entropia, Wrocław 109215
Entropie, Paris 138362
Entschladen, Claudia, Bamberg . . . 125131
Entzmann & Sohn, Reinhold, Wien .057408, 095815, 137307
Envers Chapin, Toronto 097263
L'Envers du Décor, Azay-le-Rideau . 061151
Enviedart, Paris 100256
Environmental Art Organisation, Stockport 054373
Environmental Education Center, Basking Ridge 042035
Environmentally Friendly Sculpture and Fine Art Show, Beijing 093632
Enwald-Museo, Tuomelan Talo, Maatalousmuseo, Liperi 009831
Enzinger, Sebastian, Salzburg 123441
Enzinger, T., Köln 071931
Eötvös Loránd Emlékkiállítás, Budapest 021646
Eötvös Lorand Tudomanyegyetem, Régészettudomanyi Intézet, Budapest 050281
Eolia, Paris 100257
Eon's Fashion Antique, Pittsburgh . 091814
Eos Verlag, Sankt Ottilien 134379
EP Galerie, Düsseldorf 102489
Epcot, Lake Buena Vista 045099
Epelde, Bilbao 110276
Epema-State, Ijsbrechtum 029789
Ephelides, Auxerre 061103
Ephemer Arts, New York 090850
Ephemer Arts, New York 142651
Ephesos-Museum, Antikensammlung des Kunsthistorischen Museums Wien, Wien 002892
Ephraim Foundation Museums, Thomas Goodletson House, Pioneer School House, Anderson Store Museum, Anderson Barn Museum, Ephraim 043714
Ephrata Cloister, Ephrata 043716
Epicentro, Porto 109370
Epicureo, Cagliari 075207
Epifani, Maurizio, Milano 075703
l'Epigraphe, Lyon 138146
Epigraphical Museum, Athinai 021169
Epigraphy Museum, Department of Antiquities, Tripoli 027832
Epikur, Wuppertal 105350
Epipla, Milano 075704
Época, Badajoz 080775, 129307
D' Epoca, Barcelona 129339
Epoca, Paris 065879, 100258
Epoca Antiquario & Galeria, Fortaleza 058471
Epoca Italiana, Medellín 059919
Epoca Objetos de Arte, Rio de Janeiro 058583
Epoca-Regalos, Madrid 081295
Epocas Antiques, Caracas 093527
Epoche, Parma 076205
Epoha, Beograd 080396
Epok, Stockholm 081946
Epoka Art, Sopot 079708
Epokhe, Breda 078090
Epokia, Täby 082048
Epopea, Paris 100259
Epoque, Basel 082138
Epoque, Château-Thierry 062189
Epoque, Kortrijk 058263
l'Epoque, New York 090851
Epoque, Palermo 076144
l'Epoque Dorée, Bruxelles 057928
Epoques Bleues, Genève 082424
Epoques et Styles, Survilliers 068346
Epp, Franz, Konstanz 072049
Eppe, Christian, Paris 138363
Eppel, Donaueschingen 102383
Epping Forest District Museum, Waltham Abbey 041290
Eppinger, Schwäbisch Hall 134388
Epsilon Fine Art, London 113599
Epsom Art Gallery, Auckland 108313
Eptek National Exhibition Centre, Prince Edward Island Museum and Heritage Foundation, Summerside 006534
Epworth Old Rectory, Epworth 039453
EQ Konservatorsatelje - LAB, Uppsala 129886
Equator Gallery, Boston 115172
Equatorial America, New York 117868
Equey, Bernadette, Fribourg 130022
Equilibrio, Solothurn 141302
Equilibrium, Folkestone 113071
Equine Images, Fort Dodge 136456
Equine Museum, Gwacheon 027499
Equine Museum of Japan, Yokohama 027330
Equinocial Antiguidades, Rio de Janeiro 058584
Equinox Gallery, Vancouver 097463
Equinox Studio Gallery, Enmore . . . 094510
Equinoxe Groupe Artisanat Contemporain, Yvoire 101489
Equipement Culturel Les Pénitents, Gap 062961
Equipo 7, Bilbao 129424
Equipo Patina, Madrid 129614
Equity Art Brokers, New York 117869
Equity Art Brokers, New York 117870
Equrna Gallery, Ljubljana 109956
E.R. Burrowes School of Art, Georgetown 050277
E.R.A., Roma 106528
Era, Toronto 059178
Erard, Patrick, Sauxillanges 124930
Erasmus, Amsterdam 140296
Erasmus Naklada, Zagreb 133402
Erasmushaus, Basel 122303, 141202
Erasmushaus Musik, Stuttgart 139760
Erath, Wolfgang, Ostrach 126603
Erba, Bari 075020
Erbacher Heimatzimmer, Eltville . . . 016951
Erbar, Kurt, Cochem 070150
Erbe, Ulli, Berlin 101848
Erben, Kurt, Wien 057409
Erbguth, Eckhardt, Dabel 102332
Erbland, Pierre, Paris 138364
Erbs-Mailleux, E., Angers 124074
Erbstück, Stade 073886
Ercadi, Eugenio, Roma 128030
Erckens, Fritz, Aachen 069084
Ercoa, Bilbao 129425
Erddig Agricultural Museum, Wrexham 041454
Erdész, Szentendre 074756
Erdgeschichtliches Werksmuseum der ZEAG, Lauffen am Neckar 018529
Erdmann, Erika, Konstanz 139362
Erdmann, Sonja & Walter, Berlin . . . 069601
Erdmannsdörfer, Gisela, Stuttgart . . 104972
Erdölmuseum, Neusiedl an der Zaya 002373
Erdőhegyi, Péter, Budapest 105506
Erdos, John, Singapore 080462
L'Ere du Temps, Genève 082425
Ere du Temps, Sainte-Savine 068079
Eredi, Antonio Esposito, Firenze . . . 075333
Eredi, Tanca, Roma 076442
Eredi, Tanca, Roma 076443
Ereğli Müzesi, Ereğli 038057
Erelöf, Stefan, Stockholm . 081947, 129862
Eremiten-Presse, Düsseldorf 133891
Eren, İstanbul 112303
Erenberg, Fany S. de, Montevideo . 087316
Erenköy İş Sanat Galerisi, İstanbul . 112304
Erents, Almere 077739
Eretz-Israel Museum Tel Aviv, Tel Aviv 023070
Erewash Museum, Ilkeston 039794
't Erf Antiek, Rotterdam . . 078716, 128819
Erfatal-Museum Hardheim, Hardheim 017775
Erfurter Kunstverein e.V., Erfurt . . . 053146
Ergmann-Stracke, Ulla, Siegen 134398
Ergo-Verlag, Berlin 133770
Ergon Verlag, Würzburg 134468
Erhardt, Nina A., Freiberg am Neckar 125668
Erhverv, Frederiksberg 060232
Eric Thomas Galley Museum, Queenstown 001418
Erica Underwood Gallery, Bentley . . 000797
Erich-Bödeker-Gesellschaft für naive Kunst e.V., Hannover 053147
Erich Kästner Museum Dresden, Dresden 016785
Erich Mäder-Glasmuseum, Grünenplan 017588
Erich Maria Remarque-Friedenszentrum, Osnabrück 019492
Erichsen & Kreilos-Erichsen, Freiburg im Breisgau 070835
Erichsens Gaard, Bornholms Museum, Rønne 009076
Erichson, Jörn, Bad Gandersheim . . 125096
Erickson, Arthur W., Portland 091933
Erickson, Dan, Saint Paul 092359
Erickson, Elaine, Milwaukee 117184
Ericsbergs Slott, Mellösa 036476
Ericson, David, Salt Lake City 119340
Erie Art Museum, Erie 043721
Erie Canal Museum, Syracuse 048454
Erie Canal Village, Rome 047533
Erie Historical Museum, Erie 043725
Erie History Center, Erie 043722
Erikas Puppenstube, Bamberg 069449
Eriksbergs Museum, Tranås 036713
Eriksborg Vagnmuseum, Ystad 036804
Eriksdale Museum, Eriksdale 005432
Eriksson, Lloyd, Virserum 122297
Erin House Prints, Burn 112760
Erindale's Antiques, Erindale 055804
Erinnerungsstätte Baltringer Haufen Bauernkrieg in Oberschwaben, Mietingen 018939
Erinnerungsstätte für die Freiheitsbewegungen in der deutschen Geschichte, Rastatt 019713
Erith Museum, Erith 039454
Eritrean Archaeological Museum, Asmara 009355
Erkebispegården, Trondheim 031281

Erkel Ferenc Múzeum, Gyula 021734
Erkenbert-Museum, Frankenthal, Pfalz 017150
Erker-Galerie, Sankt Gallen 111865, 135062, 141292
Erlacher-Bobik, Christa, Graz 057009
Erland Lee Museum, Stoney Creek . 006513
Erlauftaler Feuerwehrmuseum, Purgstall an der Erlauf 002478
Erlbacher, Erika, Wagrain 057344
Erlebniswelt Blockflöte, Fulda 017297
Erlemann, Hartmut, Amsterdam . . . 140297
Erlemann, Hartmut, Eutin 139066
Erlen, Steffisburg 082835
Erler, Berlin 101849
Erler, Hans Jörg, Wien 057410
Erler, Michael, Kitzbühel 057098
Erlichthof, Rietschen 019844
L'Erma, Roma 135898
Erman, A., Paris 100260
Ermasch-Presse-Service, Hamburg 134004
Ermatinger, Clergue National Historic Site, Sault Sainte Marie 006431
Ermes, Potenza 134662
L'Ermete, Roma 106529
Ermini, Bastia 061217
Ermita de San Antonio de la Florida y Museo Panteón de Goya, Madrid 035387
Ermita de San Baudelio de Berlanga, Caltojar 035037
Ermita de Sant Feliu, Xàtiva 036086
Ermitaž, Sankt-Peterburg 129244
Ėrmitaž Antikvarno-juvelirnyj Salon, Nižnij Novgorod 080281
Erna och Victor Hasselblads Fotografiska Centrum, Göteborg 036293
Ernes, E., Liège 058298, 123651
Ernest, Cluj-Napoca 080177, 140886
Ernest and Marion Davis Medical History Museum, Auckland 030435
Ernest Hemingway House Museum, Key West 044984
The Ernest W. Michel Historical Judaica Collection, New York 046328
Ernesta Birznieka-Upīša Muzejs Bisnieki, Zentene 027804
Ernhardt, Holger, Stuttgart 073969
Erni & Fornara-Erni, Simone, Luzern 111689
Ernie Pyle House, Dana 043288
Ernie's Antiques, Jacksonville 089409
Ernst, Konstanz 103755
Ernst, Paderborn 104567
Ernst, Weil der Stadt 105178
Ernst, Albert J., Saarbrücken 073628
Ernst, Manfred, Ronnenberg 126731
Ernst, Rolf-Gerhard, München 126375
Ernst Barlach Gesellschaft e.V., Wedel 053148
Ernst Barlach Haus, Stiftung Hermann F. Reemtsma, Hamburg 017689
Ernst Barlach Museum, Ratzeburg . 019726
Ernst Barlach Museum Wedel, Wedel 020695
Ernst Barlach Stiftung Güstrow, Gertrudenkapelle, Atelierhaus, Ausstellungsforum, Güstrow 017599
Ernst-Bloch-Zentrum, Ludwigshafen am Rhein 018701
Ernst Fuchs-Privatmuseum, Wien . . 002893
Ernst-Haeckel-Haus, Jena 018103
Ernst-Moritz-Arndt-Haus, Stadt Museum Bonn, Bonn 016322
Ernst-Moritz-Arndt-Museum, Garz, Rügen 017330
Ernst Múzeum, Budapest 021647
Ernsta Glika Bībeles Muzejs, Alūksne 027658
Erol Kerim Aksoy Vakfı, İstanbul . . . 054249
Erotic Art Dresden, Dresden 102427
Erotic Art Museum Hamburg, Hamburg 017690
Erotic Museum, Los Angeles 045418
Erotics Gallery, New York 117871
Erotik-Museum, Berlin 016016
Erotisch Museum, Amsterdam 029179
Errance, Paris 133600
Errebi, Firenze 106048
Errico, Umberto, Napoli 075978
Errico, Umberto, Napoli 075979
Errol Station Railway Heritage Centre, Blairgowrie 038763
Ersego, Carla, Brescia 140003
Ersta Diakonimuseum, Stockholm . 036622
Erste Hobby Kunstgalerie, Wien . . . 095816
Erstes Allgäu-Schwäbisches Dorfschulmuseum, Erkheim 017024
Erstes Bayerisches Schulmuseum, Sulzbach-Rosenberg 020383
Erstes Circusmuseum in Deutschland, Preetz, Holstein 019662
Erstes Deutsches Fliesenmuseum, Boizenburg 016309
Erstes Deutsches Historic-Actien-Museum, Kürnbach 018434
Erstes Deutsches Motorroller-Museum, Aschaffenburg 015574
Erstes Deutsches Museum für mechanische Musikinstrumente, Rüdesheim am Rhein 019940
Erstes Deutsches Strumpfmuseum, Gelenau, Erzgebirge 017348
Erstes Deutsches Türmermuseum, Vilseck 020600
Erstes Ethnisches Puppenmuseum der Welt, Zentrum für Außergewöhnliche Museen, Kreuth 018405
Erstes Imaginäres Museum - Sammlung Günter Dietz, Wasserburg am Inn . 020685
Erstes Internationales Wolpertingermuseum, Mittenwald 018958
Erstes Kärntner Handwerksmuseum, Baldramsdorf 001749
Erstes Korkenziehermuseum der Welt, Zentrum für Außergewöhnliche Museen, Kreuth 018406
Erstes Nachttopf-Museum der Welt, München 019049
Erstes Niederbayerisches Automobil- und Motorrad-Museum, Adlkofen 015447
Erstes Niederrheinisches Karneval-Museum, Duisburg 016851
Erstes Oberösterreichisches Schnapsmuseum, Sankt Oswald bei Freistadt 002606
Erstes Österreichisches Friedensmuseum und Heimatstube, Wolfsegg 003060
Erstes Österreichisches Funk- und Radiomuseum, Wien 002894
Erstes Österreichisches Museum für Alltagsgeschichte, Neupölla 002371
Erstes Österreichisches Rettungsmuseum, Hohenems 002055
Erstes Österreichisches Tischler-Museum, Pöchlarn 002436
Erstes Osterhasen Museum der Welt, München 019050
Erstes Schutzengel-Museum der Welt, Zentrum für Außergewöhnliche Museen, Kreuth 018407
Erstes Südburgenländisches Schnapsbrennereimuseum, Kukmirn 002185
Erstes Tiroler Feuerwehrmuseum, Schwaz 002662
Erstes Tiroler Holzmuseum, Wildschönau 003046
Erstes Tretauto-Museum der Welt, München 019051
Erstes Urgeschichtliches Freilichtmuseum der Steiermark, Kulm bei Weiz . . . 002186
Erstes Waldviertler Webereimuseum, Waidhofen an der Thaya 002797
Ertini, Urs-Beat, Zürich 130235
Ertl, Hallstadt 103080
Ertl, Harald, Sandberg 073660
Erud, Birkerød 060213
Ervasti, K., Helsinki 137938
Ervin, S.H., Millers Point 094848
Erwin Museum, Painted Post 046794
Erwin von Kreibig-Museum, München 019052
Eryldene Heritage House, Gordon . . 001071
Erzbergbahn- und Wintersportmuseum, Vordernberg 002792
Erzbischöfliches Diözesanmuseum Köln, Diözesanmuseum Köln, Köln 018323
Erzbischöfliches Diözesanmuseum und Domschatzkammer, Paderborn . . 019548
Erzbischöfliches Dom- und Diözesanmuseum, Wien 002895
Erzgebirgische Volkskunst Ausstellung, Grünhainichen 017590
Erzgebirgische Volkskunststube, Bermsgrün 016199
Erzgebirgischer Spielzeugwinkel, Obereisenheim 019386
Erzgebirgisches Freilichtmuseum, Kurort Seiffen 018448
Erzgebirgisches Heimatmuseum Hospital Sankt Johannis, Sayda 020001
Erzgebirgisches Spielzeugmuseum, Kurort Seiffen 018449
Erzgebirgisches Spielzeugmuseum, Liestal 037264
Erzgebirgsmuseum mit Besucherbergwerk, Annaberg-Buchholz 015549
Erzherzog Franz-Ferdinand Museum, Artstetten 001698
Erzherzog Johann-Dokumentationsstätte, Thernberg 002744
Erzincan Kültür Merkezi, Erzincan . 038058
Erzstollen Silbergründle, Seebach, Baden 020160
Erzurum Arkeoloji Müzesi, Erzurum 038059
Erzurum Kültür Merkezi, Erzurum . . 038060
Erzurum Resim ve Heykel Müzesi, Erzurum 038061
Esau, Ernst-Otto, Lübeck 126241
Esbjerg Kunstmuseum, Esbjerg . . . 008842
Esbjerg Museum, Esbjerg 008843
L'Escabel, Zaragoza 129810
L'Escabelle, Dijon 062655
Escabelle, New York 090852, 132467
La Escalera, Cuenca 110325
L'Escalier d'Argent, Paris 065880
L'Escalier du Commandant, Brest . . 061770
Escande, Jean-Luc, Auch 061052
L'Escapade, Périgueux 100989
Escape Trading, Surfers Paradise . . 095241
L'Escarpolette, Arzon 061004, 098867
Escasso, Braga 079807
Escatllar Soler, Maria, Girona 129522
Escazaux, C., Boissy-Saint-Léger . . 061547
Esch, Heinz Josef, Düsseldorf 070375
Eschenau Summer Press & Eschenau Editions, Knetzgau 134093
Eschenbacher, Erlangen 139047
Eschenburg, Harald, Kiel 139321
Eschmann, Karl-Hermann & Gudrun, Kelkheim 139312
Eschmann, Michael, Griesheim . . . 139155
Eschweiler Kunstverein, Eschweiler 053149
Escobar, Medellín 098259
Escobar, Adriana, Medellín 123931
Escobar Estrada, Guillermo, Medellín 098260
Escola Clàssica de Arte, São Paulo . 049761
Escola d'Art i Diseny de la Diputació, Tarragona 050735
Escola de Artes, Brasília 096491
Escola de Artes Visuais, Rio de Janeiro 049754
Escola de Belas Artes, Universidade Federal da Bahia, Salvador 049756
Escola de Belas Artes, Universidade Federal do Espírito Santo, Vitória 049772
Escola de Belas Artes, Universidade Federal do Rio de Janeiro, Rio de Janeiro 049755
Escola de Belas Artes de São Paulo, São Paulo 049762
Escola de Comunicações e Artes, São Paulo 049763
Escola De Conservació i Restauració d'Obres d'Art, Barcelona 050712
Escola De Conservació i Restauració d'Obres d'Art, Barcelona 129340
Escola de Joalheria Bell Arte, São Paulo 049764
Escola de Música e Belas Artes do Paraná, Curitiba 049747
Escola Municipal de Belles Arts, Lleida 050719
Escola Panamericana de Arte, São Paulo 049765
Escola Superior de Belas Artes de Lisboa, Lisboa 050613
Escola Superior de Disseny, Barcelona 050713
Escola Superior de Disseny, Palma de Mallorca 050730
Escondido Historical Museum, Escondido 043730
Escoural, Lisboa 109285
Escrihuela Adelantado, Jose, Valencia 129771
Escritório de Arte Alto da Bronze, Porto Alegre 058500
Escudero, Madrid 081296, 122055
Escudor, Allez-et-Cazeneuve 060780
Escuela de Arte, Córdoba 049598
Escuela de Arte, Pontificia Universidad Católica de Chile, Santiago de Chile 049839
Escuela de Arte de Madrid, Madrid . 050722
Escuela de Arte y Antiguedades, Madrid 129615
Escuela de Arte y Antigüedades, Madrid 050723
Escuela de Artes Aplicades, Universidad Ignacio Agramonte, Camagüey . . 049880
Escuela de Artes Aplicades, Departamento de Bellas Artes, Universidad del Cauca, Popayán 049870
Escuela de Artes Plásticas, Santiago de los Caballeros 049910
Escuela de Artes Plásticas, La Vega 049914
Escuela de Artes Plasticas de Puerto Rico, San Juan 050617
Escuela de Artes Plásticas y de Bellas Artes, Tuxtla Gutiérrez 050546
Escuela de Artes Visuales, Universidad Autónoma de Nuevo León, Monterrey 050538
Escuela de Bellas Artes, Asunción . 050589
Escuela de Bellas Artes, Concepción 049837
Escuela de Bellas Artes, San Francisco de Macorís 049909
Escuela de Bellas Artes, Universidad Benito Juarez de Oaxaca, Oaxaca 050541
Escuela de Bellas Artes, Universidad Central del Ecquador, Quito 049916
Escuela de Bellas Artes, Universidad de Costa Rica, San José 049876
Escuela de Bellas Artes, Universidad de Querétaro, Querétaro 050544
Escuela de Bellas Artes, Universidad Juarez, Durango 050531
Escuela de Bellas Artes, Universidad Michocana de San Nicolás de Hidalgo, Morelia 050539
Escuela de Bellas Artes, Universidad Veracruzana, Xalapa 050547
Escuela de Bellas Artes General Urquiza, Buenos Aires 049594
Escuela de Dibujo y Pintura, Pamplona 050731
Escuela de Diseño y Artesanías, Morelia 050540
Escuela de Flandes, Granada 081143, 129525
Escuela de Pintura, Pasto 049869
Escuela de Pintura, Dibujo y Cerámica, San José de Mayo 050862
Escuela de Pintura y Artes Plásticas, Universidad del Atlántico, Barranquilla 049862
Escuela Museo de Bellas Artes General Urquiza, Buenos Aires 000147
Escuela Nacional de Artes Plásticas, Universidad Nacional Autónoma de México, México 050534
Escuela Nacional de Artes Plásticas Rafael Rodríguez Padilla, Guatemala . . . 050275
Escuela Nacional de Bellas Artes, Comayagüela 050279
Escuela Nacional de Bellas Artes, Montevideo 050859

Escuela Nacional de Bellas Artes, Santo Domingo . . . 049912
Escuela Nacional de Bellas Artes Manual Belgrano, Buenos Aires . . . 049595
Escuela Nacional de Bellas Artes Prilidiano Pueyredón, Buenos Aires . . . 049596
Escuela Nacional de Bellas Artes San Alejandro, La Habana . . . 049881
Escuela Nacional de Conservación, Restauración y Museografía Manuel del Castillo Negrete, México . . . 050535
Escuela Nacional Superior Autónoma de Bellas Artes, Lima . . . 050592
Escuela Provincial de Bellas Arte, Córdoba . . . 049599
Escuela Provincial de Bellas Artes Fernando Fader, Córdoba . . . 049600
Escuela Regional de Bellas Artes Diego Quispe Tito, Cusco . . . 050591
Escuela Santo Tomás de Aquino, Santa Cruz . . . 049745
Escuela Superior de Arte Carlos Baca Flor, Arequipa . . . 050590
Escuela Superior de Arte Neptali Rincón, Maracaibo . . . 052423
Escuela Superior de Bellas Artes de la Nación Ernesto de la Cárcova, Buenos Aires . . . 049597
Escuela Taller de Artes Plásticas, Quezaltenango . . . 050276
Esculturas y Moldes, Medellín . . . 123932
Esders, Viviane, Paris . . . 100261
Eselsohr, Oldenburg, Oldenburg . . . 139628
Eselstein, Zürich . . . 112066
Esempi del Novecento, Milano . . . 075705
Eseral, Rio de Janeiro . . . 096602
Esglesia de Sant Francesc, Palma de Mallorca . . . 035607
Esie Museum, Esie . . . 030680
Esiew, Singapore . . . 109794
Esk House Arts, Grosmont . . . 113166
Eskape In Time, Esk . . . 055806
Eskbank House, Lithgow . . . 001188
Eskdale Antiques, Sleights . . . 086629
Eskenazi, London . . . 085282
Eskenazi, John, London . . . 085283
Eski İstanbul, Ankara . . . 083109
Eskils Kleine Gallerie, Helsingborg . 110940
Eskilstuna Konstmuseum, Eskilstuna . . . 036252
Eskimo Art, San Francisco . . . 119662
Eskimo Art Gallery, Toronto . . . 097264
Eskimo Museum, Churchill . . . 005270
Eskişehir Atatürk ve Kültür Müzesi, Eskişehir . . . 038062
Eskişehir Devlet Güzel Sanatlar Galerisi, Eskişehir . . . 038063
Eskişehir Müzeleri, Eskişehir . . . 038064
Eskolan Taide- ja Kehysliike, Lahti . 060605
Eskoriatzako Museo Eskola, Eskoriatza . . . 035177
Eslampanah-Kerner, Bruxelles . . . 057929
Eslövs Stadsmuseum, Eslöv . . . 036257
ESMA, El Madania . . . 094048
Esmaili, Dallas . . . 088510
Esmaili, Dallas . . . 132007
Esman, Jacksonville . . . 116521
Esmann, Gabriele, Hildesheim . . . 125929
Esmonpe, Madrid . . . 129616
Espace, Amsterdam . . . 107707
Espace, Delhi . . . 105660
Espace, Montréal . . . 135633
Espace 161, Bruxelles . . . 057930
Espace 36, Galerie d'Art Contemporain, Saint-Omer . . . 101186
Espace 4, Paris . . . 065881, 100262
Espace 54, Cannes . . . 099064
Espace Aïn, Kram . . . 112247
Espace Ambuel, Sion . . . 111907
Espace André Malraux, Colmar . . . 011428
Espace Antiquaires, Clermont-Ferrand . . . 062341
Espace Antiquités, Le Puy-en-Velay 063696
Espace Archéologique Forez-Jarez, Saint-Étienne . . . 014269
Espace Architectural Normand, Crévecœur-en-Auge . . . 011535
Espace Arlaud, Lausanne . . . 037239
Espace Arts Plastiques, Maison du Peuple, Vénissieux . . . 015163
Espace Asie, Genève . . . 111445
Espace Atepa, Paris . . . 100263
Espace Athéna, Binic . . . 061490
Espace Automobiles Matra, Romorantin-Lanthenay . . . 014098
Espace Baroque Tarentaise, Séez . . 014743
Espace Bastides, Monflanquin . . . 013097
Espace BD3D, Bordeaux . 098991, 138038
Espace Beaurepaire, Paris . . . 100264
Espace Brocs'Antiks, Roanne . . . 067169
Espace Châteaudun, Ivry-sur-Seine 099369
Espace Chateaudun, Paris . . . 100265
L'Espace Collections, Lyon . . . 064123
Espace Collections, Quimper . . . 067017
Espace Collections Evreux, Evreux . 062828
Espace Commines, Paris . . . 100266
Espace Commines, Paris . . . 100267
Espace Côte des Arts, Marseille . . . 099651
Espace Courant d'Art, Chevenez . . . 111349
Espace Créativa, Montpellier . . . 099754
Espace Cro-Magnon-Musée et Parc, Thonac . . . 014937
Espace Crous, Rennes (Ille-et-Vilaine) . . . 101079
Espace Culture Paul Doucet, Château-Thierry . . . 011281
Espace Culturel Hippolite-Mars, Équeurdreville-Hainneville . . . 011717
Espace d'Art Contemporain, Demigny . . . 099203
Espace d'Art Contemporain, Marseille . . . 012930
Espace d'Art Contemporain Camille-Lambert, Juvisy-sur-Orge . . . 012189
Espace d'Art Mille Feuilles, Marsa . 112253
Espace de l'Art Concret, Mouans-Sartoux . . . 013256
Espace-de-l'Or, Metz . . . 064529
L'Espace-de-Nesle, Paris . . . 100268
Espace Delille, Nice . . . 099833
Espace des Arts, Le Boulou . . . 012466
Espace des Arts Plastiques, Saint-Dié-des-Vosges . . . 101141
Espace des Saveurs, Herve . . . 003513
Espace des Sciences, Rennes (Ille-et-Vilaine) . . . 014020
Espace d'Exposition Minal, Héricourt . . . 012091
Espace Dhyâna, Gap . . . 099280
Espace du Cheminot, Musée du Chemin de Fer, Nîmes . . . 013419
L'espace Enchère, Lyon . . . 121049
Espace Evasion, Carpentras . . . 099089
Espace Exposition, Centre Culturel Jacques Brel, Thionville . . . 014931
Espace Founoun, Alger . . . 094044
Espace Gallo-Romain, Ath . . . 003203
Espace Gare de l'Est, La Chaux-de-Fonds . . . 111346
Espace Géologique Les Frissons de la Terre, Château-Queyras . . . 011278
Espace Giono, Lalley . . . 012388
Espace Hennessy, Musée de la Tonnellerie, Cognac . . . 011414
Espace Historique de Sword Beach, Hermanville-sur-Mer . . . 012093
Espace Horloger de la Vallée de Joux, Le Sentier . . . 037555
Espace Jean de Joigny, Joigny (Yonne) . . . 012158
Espace Jean Tinguely - Niki de Saint-Phalle, Fribourg . . . 037096
Espace Joseph Besset, Vanosc . . . 015128
Espace-Jouets, Ecomusée des Bruneaux, Firminy . . . 011818
Espace Journal, Gammarth . . . 112246
Espace l'Aurore, Sorens . . . 111924
Espace Lausannoise d'Art Contemporain, Lausanne . . . 037240
Espace Marais d'Anchais, Maillezais . . . 012852
Espace Maritime et Portuaire des Docks Vauban, Le Havre . . . 012505
Espace Minéralogique Minéraux Couleur Nature, Eymoutiers . . . 011769
Espace Mira Phalaina, Montreuil-sous-Bois . . . 013221
Espace Montoise, Le Mans . . . 099446
Espace Multi Collections, Brehal . . 061758
Espace Muséal, Rosheim . . . 014115
Espace Muséal Archéologique, Alba-la-Romaine . . . 010309
Espace Muséal de Beaux-Arts, Fontvieille . . . 011863
Espace Muséal de la Maison du Berger, Châtillon-sur-Saône . . . 011314
Espace Muséal de la Maison du Cordonnier, Châtillon-sur-Saône . . . 011315
Espace Muséal de la Route Romane d'Alsace, Neuwiller-les-Saverne . 013385
Espace Muséal du Four à Pain, Wasigny . . . 015353
Espace Muséal Les Courtinals, Moureze . . . 013275
Espace Musée, Centre d'Information, Freissinières . . . 011887
Espace Musée Sainte-Madeleine, Besançon . . . 010767
Espace Muséographique, Saint-Goazec . . . 014323
Espace Neige et Montagne, Bonneval-sur-Arc . . . 010870
Espace Paragon, Luxembourg . . . 107397
Espace Paroles d'Objets Nègres, Musée Municipal, Blangy-sur-Bresle . . . 010824
Espace Patrimoine le Cœur, Tignes-le-Lac . . . 014956
Espace Paul Rebeyrolle, Eymoutiers 011770
Espace Pepin, Montréal . . . 096999
Espace Photo, Clermont-Ferrand . . . 099147
Espace Pierre Bonnard, Le Cannet . 012477
Espace Pierres Folles, Saint-Jean-des-Vignes . . . 014357
Espace Point Barre, Lille . . . 099486
Espace Saint-Eloi, Valbonne . . . 068678
Espace Saint-François, Lausanne . . 111614
Espace Saint-Martin, Cognac . . . 099158
Espace Salvador Dalí, Paris . . . 013581
Espace Suisse, Strasbourg . . . 101286
L'Espace Temps, Gex . . . 062993
Espace Temps, Paris . . . 100269, 124658
L'Espace Troc 57, Saint-Avold . . . 067367
Espace Véga, Saint-Ouen . . . 101187
L'Espace Vente, Lyon . . . 064124
Espace Verre, Vannes-le-Châtel . . . 015124
Espace Virtuel, Chicoutimi . . . 005266
Espace Wafabank, Casablanca . . . 107553
Espach, Greifensee . . . 111532
Espacio del Arte, Luján . . . 094099
Espacio Distrito Cu4tro, Madrid . . . 110492
Espacio Fortuny, Granada . . . 110373
Espacio Lady Anne, Madrid . . . 081297
Espacio Liquido, Gijón . . . 110358
Espacio Marzana, Bilbao . . . 110277
Espacio Minimo, Madrid . . . 110493
Espacio y Restauro, Zaragoza . . . 129811
Los Espacios Cálidos, Caracas . . . 120424
Espaço Cultural da Marinha, Rio de Janeiro . . . 004339
Espaco Cultural e Galeria Retiro das Artes, Rio de Janeiro . . . 096603
Espaço de São Bento, Lisboa . . . 079922
Espaço dos Anjos, Leopoldina . . . 004189
Espaço Lucio Costa, Brasília . . . 004011
Espaço Museu da Vida, Rio de Janeiro . . . 004340
Espadim, Lisboa . . . 079923
L'Espadon, Paris . . . 065882
Espagne, Nicole, Bruxelles . . . 057931
Espai Lucas, Valencia . . . 110804
Espai Vidre, Barcelona . . . 110140
Espai Visual, Barcelona . . . 110141
Espalter, Madrid . . . 110494
La Española, Buenos Aires . . . 055202
Españoleto, Madrid . . . 129617
Espaxios - Arte Actual, Guatemala . 105478
Espelho da Moda, Luanda . . . 094051
Espelho Design Antiguidades, São Paulo . . . 058707
Esperance Museum, Esperance . . . 001023
Esperluette, Castres . . . 099096
Espersit Ház, József Attila Múzeum, Makó . . . 021778
Espinet, Carmen, Barcelona . . . 110142
Espinosa, José Garcia, Rio de Janeiro . . . 123704
Espinossa, Michel, La Couvertoirade . . . 063358
Espinoza, Oakland . . . 132567
El Espíritu del Mueble, Don Torcuato . . . 055264
Espoir, Colmar . . . 062410
L'Espoir, Paris . . . 065883
Espoon Automuseo, Espoo . . . 009471
Espoon Kaupunginmuseo, Espoo . . 009472
Esposito, Antonio, Napoli . . . 075980
Esposito, Giuseppe, Napoli . . . 075981
Esposito, Giuseppe, Napoli . . . 075982
Esposito, Giuseppe, Napoli . . . 075983
Esposito, Giuseppe, Napoli . . . 075984
Esposito, Giuseppe, Napoli . . . 075985
Esposito Vincenzo, Napoli . . . 127768
Esposizione Forte Airolo, Airolo . . . 036824
l'Esprit de l'Art, Antwerpen . . . 057693
Esprit Decor Gallery, Phoenix . . . 118869
l'Esprit des Lieux, Tournai . . . 096414
Esprit d'Objet les Objets, Saint-Ouen . . . 067773
Esprit d'Uzes, Uzès . . . 068669
Esquerre, Raymond, Toulouse . . . 068506
Esquina, Porto . . . 140865
Esra, Apeldoorn . . . 078033
Essa, Hassan Ali, Muttrah . . . 079515
Essaraya, Tunis . . . 112260
Essem Art Gallery, Mumbai . . . 105768
Essence of Time, Lichfield . . . 084989
Essences de Siècles, Bruxelles . . . 057932
Essences Primitives, Bordeaux . . . 098992
Essential Furniture, Los Angeles . . . 089760
Ėssentukskij Gorodskoj Kraevedčeskij Muzej im. V.P. Špakovskogo, Ėssentuki . 033142
Esser, Günther, Düsseldorf . . . 102490
Esser, Norbert, Köln . . . 071932
Esser & Esser, Köln . . . 071933
Essex, Heathmont . . . 136939
Essex, Richard, Langford, Somerset 084902
Essex Antiques, Winnipeg . . . 059457
Essex Art Association, Essex . . . 054750
Essex Fine Art, Ocean Grove . . . 095000
Essex Gallery, New York . . . 090853
Essex Historical Museum, Essex . . 043733
Essex Police Museum, Chelmsford . 039048
Essex Regiment Museum, Chelmsford . . . 039049
Essex Secret Bunker Museum, Mistley . . . 040480
Essex Shipbuilding Museum, Essex 043734
Essie, London . . . 085284, 131018
Essig Museum of Entomology, University of California, Berkeley, Berkeley . . . 042159
Essler, Siegfried, Bamberg . . . 069450
Essley-Noble Museum, Mercer County Historical Society, Aledo . . . 041629
Esslinger, W., Tuningen . . . 074121
Esslinger Kunstverein, Esslingen . . 053150
Esso, New York . . . 117872
Est Europa Center, Bucureşti . . . 080154
Est-Ouest Auction, Tokyo . . . 121744
El Establo, San Isidro . . . 055299
Estação Ciência / EST CIENC, Reitoria da Universidade de São Paulo / RUSP, São Paulo . . . 004505
Estação da Arte, Fortaleza . . . 096522
Estación Enológica, Haro . . . 035276
Estación Experimental de Zonas Áridas, Almería . . . 034825
Estación Ferrocarril Bejucal, Bejucal . . . 007883
Estades, Michel, Lyon . . . 064125, 099557
Estades, Michel, Saint-Ouen . . . 101188

Estades, Michel, Toulon (Var) 068451, 101319
Estadieu, Aussonne 061083
Estadieu, Portet-sur-Garonne 066958
Estagnié, Solliès-Pont 068259
Le Estampe, Strasbourg 068318
L'Estampe, Tournai 137540
Estampe Ancienne, Grenoble 063060
Estamperia Castells, Barcelona . . . 110143
Estampille, Les Sables-d'Olonne . . 063785
Estampille, Lille 099487
Estampille d'Alpage, Briançon 061788
L'Estampille - L'Objet d'Art, Dijon . . 135706
Estar, Lisboa 134870
Estate Antiques, Las Vegas 089566
Estate Auction, Denver . . . 088680, 122884
Estate Furnishings, Tucson 093229
Estate Furniture, Tulsa 093302
Estate Sale, Atlantic Beach 122803
Estate Silver Company, New York . . 090854
Estates Galleries, New York 117873
Este, Singapore 080463
Esteban, Jbanez, Barcelona 129341
Esteban Pascual, Maria Mercedes, Bilbao 129426
Estela, Tarbes 101307
Estelle, Saint-Rémy-de-Provence . . 101227
Estelle's Antiques, Paddington, Queensland 056428
Estelle's Consignment, Nashville . . 090450
Esterhammer, Innsbruck 095578
Esterházy-Ausstellung, Eisenstadt . 001825
Esterhazy Community Museum, Esterhazy 005433
Esterházy Paláce, Slovenská Národná Galéria, Bratislava 034318
Esterházy-Palota, Sopron 021842
Ester's Gallery, Lockrose 094743
Estes Park Area Historical Museum, Estes Park 043737
Estes Plating, Atlanta 087472, 131769
Estes-Simmons, Atlanta 131770
Estes-Winn Antique Automobile Museum, Asheville 041793
Esteta, Porto 109371
Estetika/Aesthetics, Praha 135666
Estevan National Exhibition Centre, Art Gallery and Museum, Estevan . . . 005435
Estève, Brigitte, Genillé 124247
Esteve, C., Kintzheim 063280
Esteve, Didier, Anduze 060837
Estevez, Austin 114981
Esther M. Klein Art Gallery, Philadelphia 046939
Esther Prangley Rice Gallery, Westminster 049115
The Esther Thomas Atkinson Museum, Hampden-Sydney 044410
Esthete, Bruxelles 096187
Esthetica, Rotterdam 078717
Estiarte, Madrid 110495
Estonian Academy of Arts, Tallinn . . 049922
Estonian Museums Association, Tartu 052870
Estor, Anke, Hamburg 125810
Estorick Collection of Modern Italian Art, London 040143
Estrada, Félix, A Coruña 081057
Estrada Antiguedades, Barcelona . . 080845
Estrada Studios, Dallas 115877
Estrade, Michel, Bordeaux 098993
Estrade Cédric, Saint-Robert 067997
Estrany de la Mota, Barcelona 110144
Estrella, Max, Madrid 110496
Estro, Padova 106396
Estuary Gallery, Leigh-on-Sea 113378
Estucolor, Barcelona 129342
Estudi B2, Barcelona 129343
L'Estudi i Onec, Barcelona 110145
Estudio Anticuario Hom, Madrid . . .081298, 129618
Estudio Arrieta, Bilbao 129427
Estudio la Casilla, Bilbao 129428
Estudio del Angel, México 128503
Estudio Museo Ramoneda, Humahuaca 000362
Estudio San Angel, México 128504
Estudio Técnico de Conservación, Castellón de la Plana 129479
Estudio Urgull, Donostia-San Sebastián 110336
Estudio Urquijo, Bilbao 129429
Estudios de Restauracion Alcazaba, Sevilla 129729
Estudios Italianos em Portugal, Lisboa 136043
Estudios Metodos de la Restauración, Valencia 129772
ESWE Technicum, Wiesbaden 020864
Et Caetera, Paris 065884
E.T.A. Hoffmann-Haus mit Sammlung, Bamberg 015869
Etage, Münster 072904, 126497
Etage 2, Rottweil 104780
Il Etait Une Fois, Sainte-Savine 068080
Etang d'Art, Bages (Aude) 098905
Etat d'Ame, Saint-Jean-de-Monts . 101165
Etat d'Origine, Paris 065885
Etcetera Aesthetic Additions, Chennai 105626
Etcetera Antiques, Denver 088681, 132035
Etcetera Etc Antiques, Seaton 086530
Etchings Art Gallery, Balaclava 055424, 094196
Etelä-Karjalan Museo, Lappeenranta 009801
Etelä-Karjalan Taidemuseo, Lappeenranta 009802
Etelä-Pohjanmaan Maakuntamuseo, Seinäjoki 010070
Etellin, Jean-Claude, Clermont-Ferrand 062342
Etemad, Brian, San Francisco 092781
L'Etendard, Boulogne-sur-Mer 061695
Eterna, Varna 096767
Eternity Antiques, Tuggerah 056740
Ethel, Anne, Hawera 079109
Ethel-20th Century Living, Toronto . 059179
Ethel's, Toronto 059180
Etherton, Tucson 120125
Ethnic Africa, Nairobi 107159
Ethnic Art, Bruxelles 057933
Ethnic Art Gallery, Kathmandu 107585
Ethnic Arts, Calgary 096811
Ethnic Discovery, Singapore 080464
Ethnic Doll and Toy Museum, Canterbury 038981
Ethnic Elegance, Jacksonville 116522
Ethnic Extravaganza, Tampa 120040
Ethnic Homes, Singapore 080465
Ethniki Pinakothiki & Mouseio Alexander Soytzoy, Athinai 021170
Ethnix, New York 117874
Ethno Art, Beograd 093856
Ethno Arts, Elwood 094507
Ethno-Textil-Galerie, Bremen 102239
Ethnoarte, Milano 106212
Ethnographic Museum, Addis Ababa 009439
Ethnographic Museum, Avgorou . . . 008204
Ethnographic Museum, Bérat 000012
Ethnographic Museum, Durrës 000016
Ethnographic Museum, Gjirokastër . 000022
Ethnographic Museum, Port Harcourt 030705
Ethnographic Museum, Assam Institut Guwahati, Guwahati 022135
Ethnographic Museum of Istria, Pazin 007773
Ethnographical Historical Museum of Lárissa, Lárissa 021352
Ethnographical Museum, Aden 049556
Ethnographical Museum, Doha 032758
Ethnographical Museum, Paphos . . 008233
Ethnographical Museum, Turkmenbashi 038212
Ethnographical Museum, Sudan National Museum, Khartoum 036149
Ethnographische Sammlung, Fribourg 037097
Ethnographisches Museum Pöykkölä, Rovaniemi 010042
Ethnographisches Museum Schloss Kittsee, Kittsee 002132
Ethnography Museum, Department of Antiquities, Tripoli 027833
Ethnological and Folklore Museum, Chios 021233
Ethnological Museum, Cairo 009300
Ethnological Museum, Chittagong . 003097
Ethnological Museum, Johannesburg 034647
Ethnological Museum, Pune 022305
Ethnological Museum, Teheran 022611
Ethnological Museum, Sa'd-Abad Museum, Teheran 022612
Ethnological Museum of Hammame-e-Ganj-Ali-Khan, Kerman 022568
Ethnological Museum of Pyrsogianni Stonemasons, Konitsa 021337
Ethnologisches Museum, Staatliche Museen zu Berlin - Stiftung Preußischer Kulturbesitz, Berlin 016017
Ethos, Bologna 105954
Etibank Sanat Galerisi, İstanbul . . . 112305
Etienbled & Jean-Claude Cazenave, Gérard, Paris 065886
Etienne, Danielle, Anières 129898
Etienne, Emmanuel, Riaz 130147
Etienne & Van den Doel, Den Haag . 107915
Etique, Den Haag 128628
Etkin, Argyll, London 141785
Etkin, Jay, Memphis 116987
Etna, Pittsburgh 091815
Etnarref Galerie, Saint-Amand-les-Eaux 101131
Etnogalerija Skrina, Ljubljana 109957
Etnografi Museoa, Arcienaga 034850
Ėtnografičeskij Muzej Kazanskogo Universiteta, Kazanskij gosudarstvennyj universitet, Kazan 033231
Ėtnografičeskij Muzej Narodov Zabajkalja, Ulan-Udė 034000
Ėtnografičeskij Muzej pod Otkrytym Nebom Torum Maa, Chanty-Mansijsk . . . 033085
Ėtnografičeskij Muzej Tavrika, Krymski Kraevedčeskij Muzej, Simferopol . 038393
Etnografické muzeum, Tovačov . . . 008716
Etnografické Múzeum, Slovenské Národné Múzeum, Martin 034384
Etnografický Ústav, Moravské Zemské Museum, Brno 008286
Etnografisch Museum, Antwerpen . 003158
Etnografische Collecties van de Universiteit Gent, Gent 003454
Etnografisk Museum, Universitetets Kulturhistoriske Museer, Oslo . . . 031074
Etnografiska Museet, Statens Museer för Världskultur, Stockholm 036623
Etnografiski Kompleks na Istoričeski Muzej, Vraca 004948
Etnografska Ekspozicija, Pazardžik . 004770
Etnografska Ekspozicija, Svištov . . 004895
Etnografska Ekspozicija Stojova KäsB3ta, Radomir 004809
Etnografska Zbirka, Koprivnički . . . 007739
Etnografska Zbirka Franjevačkog Samostana, Zaostrog 007861
Etnografska Zbirka i Lapidarij Franjevačke Gimnazije, Franciscan Secondary School at Visoko, Visoko 003946
Etnografski Kompleks, Kalipetrovo . 004700
Etnografski Kompleks Starijat Dobrič, Dobrič 004668
Etnografski Muzej, Berkovica 004635
Etnografski Muzej, Dobrič 004669
Etnografski Muzej, Elchovo 004677
Etnografski Muzej, Plovdiv 004791
Etnografski Muzej, Silistra 004830
Etnografski Muzej, Varna 004912
Etnografski Muzej, Zagreb 007832
Etnografski muzej, Burgaski Muzej, Burgas 004649
Etnografski Muzej Crne Gore, Cetinje 034184
Etnografski Muzej Dunavski Ribolov i Lodkostroenie, Tutrakan 004908
Etnografski Muzej Split, Split 007799
Etnografski Muzej Srbije, Beograd . 034147
Etnografski-văzroždenski Kompleks, Kavarna 004710
Etnografya Müzesi, Ankara 038010
Etnografya Müzesi, Konya 038131
Etnološka Muzejska Zbirka, Jasenovo 034197
Etnološko društvo Jugoslavije, Beograd 054036
Etnomuseo dei Monti Lepini, Roccagorga 025455
l'Etoile Royale, New York 090855
Eton Antique Bookshop, Eton 141601
Eton Antiques Partnership, Eton . . . 084341
Eton Art Gallery, Eton 113033
Eton College Natural History Museum, Eton 039458
L'Etourdi, Paris 138365
Etowah Indian Mounds Historical Site, Cartersville 042639
Etruria Industrial Museum, Stoke-on-Trent 041116
Ets Chevalier, Paris 065887
Etta, Claremont 055675
Ettaswir, Tunis 112261
Ettinger, Eleanor, New York 117875
Ettlin, Urs, Sankt Moritz 082791
Etxea, Saint-Jean-de-Luz 067536
Etzel Museum, Tel Aviv 023071
Etzold, S., Leonberg, Württemberg . 072235
Eubie Blake National Jazz Museum and Cultural Center, Baltimore 041981
Eugeen Van Mieghem Museum, Antwerpen 003159
Eugène, Louis-Marie, Le François . 128492
Eugene Field House and Saint Louis Toy Museum, Saint Louis 047661
Eugene Furniture, Cleveland 131958
Eugene Galleries, Boston 087817
Eugene O'Neill National Historic Site, Danville 043295
Eugene V. Debs Home, Terre Haute . 048530
Eugenie-Victoria, Paris 065888
Eugenio e Hijo, Montevideo 087317
Eugster & Urs Brand, Lothar, Appenzell 111123
Eulberg, Bernd, Dornburg, Westerwald 102390
Eule-Art, Flims Waldhaus 111405
Eule-Art, Horn 111561
Eule-Art, Sankt Gallen 111866
Eulenburg, Hamburg 103115
Die Eulenburg, Historisches Museum Rinteln, Rinteln 019851
Eulenschmidt, Rainer, Hamburg . . .103116, 125811
Eulenspiegel Kunstbuchhandlung, Göttingen 139144
Eulenspiegel Museum, Mölln 018971
Euler & Lösch, Saarbrücken 073629
Eulo Telegraph House Gallery, Eulo . 094515
Eumundi Museum, Eumundi 001024
Eunomia, Roma 106530
Euphrat Museum of Art, De Anza College, Cupertino 043248
EURANTICA Antwerp, Antwerpen . . 093601
EURANTICA Brussels, Bruxelles . . . 093602
Eurantik, Woolloongabba 056882
Eurantik, Woolloongabba 056883
Eurasia Antiques, Unley 056767
Eurasian Interiors, San Francisco . . 092782
Euregio Foto-College, Prager Fotoschule Österreich, Neumarkt im Mühlkreis 049642
Euregio-Kunstkreis e.V., Bocholt . . . 053151
Eureka, Bruxelles 057934
Eureka, Cairo 060440
Eureka Antiques, Bowdon 083615
Eureka Antiques & Gallery, Norwood 056388, 094993
Eureka Antwerp, Antwerpen 057694
Eureka Editions, Utrecht 140546
Eureka Fire Museum, Milltown 045875
Eureka Museum, Ballarat 000762

Eureka - Parque de la Ciencia, Mendoza . . . 000430
Eureka Pioneer Museum of McPherson County, Eureka . . . 043754
Eureka School House, Springfield . . 048306
Eureka! The Museum for Children, Halifax . . . 039661
Eurest, Barcelona . . . 129344
Eurl LC, Paris . . . 100270
Euro Antik, Haguenau . . . 063112
Euro Antiques, New York . . . 090856
Euro-Antiques, Ramstein-Miesenbach . . . 073410
Euro Antiquités, Juziers . . . 063275
Euro Art, Bushey . . . 112775
Euro Art 2000, Herzogenrath . . . 103367
Euro-Art-Club, Innsbruck . . . 052527
Euro Arte, Vigo . . . 081701
Euro Artes, Bogotá . . . 059836, 123900
Euro Classics, Columbus . . . 088406
Euro-Collectibles, Hilversum . . . 108084
The Euro Collection, Saint Louis . . . 092235
Euro Dépot-Vente Broc'Antique, Notre-Dame-de-Bondeville . . . 065231
Euro Enterprise, Antwerpen . . . 057695
Euro Exports, Boston . . . 087818
Euro Galeria, Porto . . . 109372
Euro-Galerie KIS, Riedt bei Erlen . . 111834
Euro Graphics, Möhrendorf . . . 104087
EuRo-Kunst, Saarbrücken . . . 104790
Euro Leilões, Lisboa . . . 121931
Euro Orient Arts, Saint-Ouen . . . 067774
Euro-Pacific, Venezia . . . 076934
Euro Pine, Houston . . . 089077
Euro UK Antiques, Wembley . . . 056811
Euroa Fine Books, Euroa . . . 136893
Euroantic, Molesmes . . . 064585
Euroart, Iaşi . . . 080186, 129232
Euroarte, Boston . . . 115173
Eurobroc, Bayonvillers . . . 061241
Eurocaribe, Roma . . . 106531
Eurocenter Sächsische Militärgeschichte, Kossa . . . 018387
Eurocoupes, Illzach . . . 063207
Eurocraft, Chicago . . . 131895
Eurodecor Gallery, Hong Kong . . . 097781
Eurogalerías de Arte Llamas, Bilbao . . . 110278, 129430
Eurogoldor, Bruxelles . . . 057935
Eurographics, Barbing . . . 101736
Euromart, Roma . . . 076444
Euromint, Bochum . . . 069881
Euronumix, Düsseldorf . . . 070376
Europa Antiques, Birmingham . . . 087754
Europa Auktioner, Vallåkra . . . 122291
Europa Books, London . . . 141786
Europa Edizioni, Roma . . . 134675
Európa Galéria - Lex antiquitás, Budapest . . . 074682
Europa-Galerie, Hannover . . . 103273
Europa-Galerie, München . . . 104170
Europa House Antiques, London . . . 085285
Europäische Akademie für Bildende Kunst, Trier . . . 050251
Europäische Antiquitäten- und Sammlerbörse, Sindelfingen . . . 093716
Europäische Glasmalerei- und Krippenausstellung, Schramberg . 020095
Europäische Messe für Junge Kunst, Frankfurt am Main . . . 093717
Europäische Vereinigung bildender Künstler aus Eifel und Ardennen, Prüm . . . 053152
Europäische Werkstatt für Kunst und Kultur im Festspielhaus Hellerau, Dresden . . . 102428
Europäische Zentralgalerie, Frankfurt am Main . . . 102760
Europäischer Kunsthof, Stolberg, Rheinland . . . 073926
Europäischer Skulpturenpark, Willebadessen . . . 020898
Europäisches Brotmuseum, Ebergötzen . . . 016866
Europäisches Industriemuseum für Porzellan und Europäisches Museum für Technische Keramik, Selb . . . 020181
Europäisches Klempner- und Kupferschmiede-Museum, Karlstadt . . . 018175
Europäisches Kulturzentrum Galerie Villa Rolandshof, Remagen . . . 019790
Europäisches Museum für Frieden, Stadtschlaining . . . 002689
Europäisches Spargelmuseum, Schrobenhausen . . . 020100
Europalia International Festival of the Arts, Bruxelles . . . 052669
Europ'Art, Bologna . . . 105955
Europ'Art, Dordrecht . . . 107977
Europart, San Diego . . . 119502
Europ'Art - Foire Internationale d'Art, Genève . . . 093889
Europe Art, Frankfurt am Main . . . 070736
Europe in the Village, Houston . . . 089078
European Accent, Warminster . . . 087027
European Antiquarian Book and Print Fair, Amsterdam . . . 093826
European Antique Market, Louisville . . . 089984, 132293
European Antique Market-Wholesale, Louisville . . . 089985
European Antiques, Auckland . . . 078941
European Antiques, Minneapolis . . . 090354
European Antiques, Seattle . . . 092991
European Antiques Restoration, Chicago . . . 088080, 131896
European Art Garage, Jacksonville . 116523
European Art Importers, Houston . . 116310
European Association of Open Air Museums, Arnhem . . . 053881
European Classic, Cincinnati . . . 088235
European Collaborative for Science, Industry and Technology Exhibitions, Bruxelles . . . 052670
European Confederation of Conservator-Restorers Organisations (ECCO), Bruxelles . . . 052671
European Country Antieks, Saint Louis . . . 092236
European Country Antiques, Saint Louis . . . 092237
European Decorative Arts, New York 090857
European Express, Kansas City . . . 089498
European Federation of Associations of Industrial and Technical Heritage, E-FAITH, Terrassa . . . 054110
European Federation of Funeral Museums, Kassel . . . 053153
European Fine Arts, Preston . . . 086309
European Folkcraft Museum, Kawakami . . . 026642
European Illustration, London . . . 136212
European Interior Designs, Chicago 088081
European Leage of Institutes of the Arts, Amsterdam . . . 053882
European Makers, Amsterdam . . . 107708
European Museum Forum, Bristol . . 054374
European Photography, Göttingen . .133976, 135762
European Pine Imports, Phoenix . . . 091736
European Restorations, New Orleans . . . 132410
European Textile Network, Hannover . . . 053154
European Treasures, Pittsburgh . . . 091816
Européenne de Recherche & Distribution, Paris . . . 065889
Europese Bibliotheek, Zaltbommel . 134841
Europlural, Lancon-Provence . . . 099419
Europ'Occase, Saint-Pierre-des-Corps . . . 067954
Europos Parkas, Vilnius . . . 027862
Eurorestauri, Roma . . . 128031
Eurotrocantic 87, Isle . . . 063215
Eury, Nancy . . . 064867
Eusebia's Antiques, Cleveland . . . 088328
Euskal Arkeologia, Etnografia eta Kondaira Museoa, Bilbao . . . 034984
Eustatia, Utrecht . . . 078797
Eustis Historical Museum, Eustis . . 043757
Euston Hall, Thetford . . . 041209
Euzen, Nicole, Pont-l'Abbé . . . 066927
Eva and Morris Feld Gallery, American Folk Art Museum, New York . . . 046329
Eva Brook Donly Museum, Simcoe . 006476
Eva Faschaunerin-Heimatmuseum, Gmünd, Kärnten . . . 001902
Evaluator, Oak Park . . . 136457
Evan, Lugano . . . 082596, 111663
Evandale Antiques, Evandale . . . 055809
Evangélikus Országos Múzeum, Budapest . . . 021648
Evangelisches Diözesanmuseum, Fresach . . . 001869
Evangelisches Diözesanmuseum, Murau . . . 002347
Evangelisches Diözesanmuseum im Burgenland, Stoob . . . 002716
Evangelisches Museum in Wien, Wien . . . 002896
Evangelisches Museum Oberösterreich, Rutzenmoos . . . 002544
Evangelista Costantino, Napoli . . . 075986
Evans, Miami . . . 117065
Evans, New Orleans . . . 117432
Evans, Oamaru . . . 079201
Evans, Ann, Valley . . . 086993
Evans, Bob, Honiton . . . 084717
Evans, D. D., Mönchengladbach . . . 072567
Evans, Dennis, Saskatoon . . . 097193
Evans, Geoff, London . . . 113600
Evans, Larry, San Francisco . . . 119663
Evans, Lionel, Eagle Heights . . . 055775
Evans, Steven, Treorchy . . . 086915
Evans, W., Bremen . . . 070017
Evans Clarke National, Woodville North . . . 120658
Evans & Evans, Alresford . . . 083276
Evans & Gerst, West Hollywood . . . 093469
Evans-Tibbs Collection, Washington 048902
Evanston Art Center, Evanston . . . 043759
Evanstonia, Chicago . . . 088082, 131897
Evansville Museum of Arts and Science, Evansville . . . 043766
Evarb, Houston . . . 116311
Evêché, Vence . . . 101440
Evelino Antiquario, Rio de Janeiro . 058585
Evelyn Payne Hatcher Museum of Anthropology, Saint Cloud . . . 047624
Evelyn's Antique Chinese Furnitures, San Francisco . . . 092783, 132880
Evelyn's Antiques, Washington . . . 093411
Evénementielle Richelieu, Montréal 097000
Evening Moon, Minneapolis . . . 117255
Évenkijskij Okružnoj Kraevedčeskij Muzej, Tura . . . 033983
Eveno, Pascal, Yerres . . . 069062
L'Eventail, Paris . . . 065890
Eventi e Interventi, Ravenna . . . 135899
Ever Arts, San Francisco . . . 092784
Ever English, Gerrards Cross . . . 113091
Everard, Rosebank . . . 110073
Everarts, Paris . . . 100271
Everett Fine Art, West Buckland . . .087082, 131663
Everglades Fine Art Gallery, Port Macquarie . . . 095093
Everglades Gardens Gallery, Leura . 094736
Evergreen, Sint-Niklaas . . . 096411
Evergreen 2 Antiques, New York . . . 090858
Evergreen Antique, Budapest . . . 074683
Evergreen Antiques, Newtown, Victoria . . . 056342
Evergreen Antiques, Redruth . . . 086343
Evergreen Aviation Museum, McMinnville . . . 045563
Evergreen Books, Fort Worth . . . 142411
Evergreen Books, North Shore . . . 140646
Evergreen Firearms Museum, Belmont . . . 005094
Evergreen Galleries, Evergreen State College, Olympia . . . 046671
Evergreen Gallery, Daventry . . . 112940
Evergreen Gallery, Salt Lake City . . 119341
Evergreen Historic House, Dartmouth . . . 005325
Evergreen House, Johns Hopkins University, Baltimore . . . 041982
Evergreene, Genève . . . 111446
Evergreene, New York . . . 117876
Evergreens, Bezau . . . 056946
Everhart Museum of Natural History, Science and Art, Scranton . . . 048063
Everitt & Rogers, Tiptree . . . 131593
Everley Antiques, Eversley . . . 084350
Everöds Auktioner, Everöd . . . 122126
Evers, Mark, Pittsburgh . . . 091817
Evers, Olaf, Taunusstein . . . 074043
Everson Museum of Art, Syracuse . 048455
Everson Museum of Art Bulletin, Syracuse . . . 136458
Everts, F., Baarn . . . 128574
Every Now & Then, Cincinnati . . . 088236
Everybody's Book Shop, Hawkes Bay . . . 140630
Everything Goes, Phoenix . . . 091737
Evetian & Beck-Arron, Doncaster . . 112950
Evje og Hornnes Museum, Evje . . . 030826
Evleen's Art Studio, Los Angeles . . 116763
Evnur Insaat, İstanbul . . . 083132
Evo, Madrid . . . 129619
Evocation, Saint-Paul-de-Vence . . . 101202
Evolog, Singapore . . . 080466
Evolution Art, Adelaide . . . 094115
Evolution - Prehistoric Art Gallery, Singapore . . . 080467
Evolutionsmuseet, Uppsala Universitet, Uppsala . . . 036736
Evolutionsmuseet, Paleontologi, Uppsala Universitet, Uppsala . . . 036737
Evraiko Mouseio tis Ellados, Athinai 021171
Evro-Art, Moskva . . . 109508
EW Gallery, San Diego . . . 092633
Ewald, Georg, Frankfurt am Main . . 139079
Ewald, Gustav, Würzburg . . . 074496
Ewart Gallery AUC, Cairo . . . 098629
Ewbank Auctioneers, Woking . . . 122756
Ewe, Kiel . . . 071825
Ewelme Cottage, Auckland . . . 030436
Ewha Yoja Taehakkyo Pakmulgwan, Seoul . . . 027554
Ewing, Kathleen, Washington . . . 120285
Ewing Gallery of Art and Architecture, University of Tennessee, Knoxville 045038
Ewings, Norwich . . . 122639
Ex, Amsterdam . . . 077842
Ex-Clou, Neuss . . . 073014, 104421
Ex Convento de Santo Domingo de Guzman, Oaxtepec . . . 028611
Ex-Libris, Gdynia . . . 140724
Ex-Libris, Oyonnax . . . 099893
Ex Libris, Porto Alegre . . . 137564
Ex Libris, Roma . . . 140104
Ex Libris, Toronto . . . 137706
Ex Libris Books, Montréal . . . 137654
Ex Libris Theological Books, Chicago . . . 142286
Exbrayat Guadeloupe, Baie Mahault 139906
Excalibur, Los Angeles . . . 089761
Excalibur Books and Comics, Portland . . . 142798
Excel Art, New York . . . 117877
Excel Art, New York . . . 117878
Excel Shop, Louisville . . . 132294
Excell Blacksmith and Engineering Workshop Museum, Tumby Bay . . 001571
Excelplus Antique, Singapore . . . 080468
Excelsior Coin Gallery, Sacramento 092154
Excelsior Gallery, Columbus . . . 115775
Excelsior House, Jefferson . . . 044844
Excelsior-Lake Minnetonka Historical Museum, Excelsior . . . 043772
Excentury, Milano . . . 075706
Exchange, Fortaleza . . . 096523
The Exchange, Totnes . . . 086905, 142118
Exchange Books, Liverpool . . . 141738
Exchange Bookshop, Dalkey . . . 139957
Exchange Hotel Civil War Museum, Gordonsville . . . 044248
Exclusief Toegepaste Kunst, Alkmaar . . . 107615
Exclusiv Antik und Art, Rorschach . 082752
Exclusivas Europeas, Managua . . . 079367

Exclusive Fine Art, Burton-upon-Trent . . . 112769
Exclusive Fine Art, Houston . . . 116312
Exclusive Lighting Gallery, Milwaukee . . . 090294, 132363
Exclusive Sanat Merkezi, İstanbul . 112306
Exclusive Treasures, Las Vegas . . . 089567
Exe Gallery, Exeter . . . 113038
Executive Book, Southampton . . . 142079
Exécutive Gallery, Toulouse . . . 101342
The Executive Mansion, Frankfort . . 044029
Exedra Books, London . . . 141787
Exercices de Style, Strasbourg . . . 124945
Exeter Rare Books, Exeter . . . 141605
Exhibit 231, Philadelphia . . . 118755
Exhibit A, New York . . . 117879
Exhibit Museum of Natural History, University of Michigan, Ann Arbor 041730
The Exhibition Alliance, Hamilton . . 054751
Exhibition Centre, Lisboa . . . 032628
Exhibition Gallery of the Islamic Dáwah Centre, Bandar Seri Begawan . . . 004612
Exhibition Hall, Ha Noi . . . 049525
Exhibition of the Norwegian-American Historical Association, Northfield . 046550
Exhibition Studies Center, Chicago . 115407
Exhibitionist Gallery of Art, North Perth . . . 094979
Exhibitions International, Leuven . . 133290
Exile, Richmond . . . 092076
Exit, Nowa Sztuka w Polsce, Warszawa . . . 136022
Exit Art, New York . . . 054752, 117880
Exit To Art, Amstelveen . . . 077760
Exler & Co., Frankfurt am Main . . . 102761
Exlibris, Gdynia . . . 140725
Exlibris, Praha . . . 137831
Exlibriswereld, Nederlandse Vereniging voor Exlibris en andere Kleingrafiek, Groenekan . . . 053883
Exmoor Gallery, Dulverton . . . 112960
Exmouth Gallery, Exmouth . . . 113047
Exmouth Museum, Exmouth . . . 039468
Exner, Klaus, Mainburg . . . 072381
Exner, R., Oberstdorf . . . 073155
Exner, W., Wien . . . 095817
Exodus, Mons-en-Barœul . . . 099732
Exodus, Naxxar . . . 077520
Exota, Rotterdam . . . 078718
Exotic Art, Itzstedt . . . 071651
Exotic Art Gallery, Mumbai . . . 105769
Exotiqa II, New York . . . 117881
Expace, Chaponost . . . 099117
De Expeditie, Amsterdam . . . 107709
Experegol, Oviedo . . . 110661
Experience Children's Museum, Erie . . . 043723
Experience Music Project, Seattle . 048079
Experienced Books, Salt Lake City . 142874
Experimenta, Madrid . . . 136085
Experimental Art Foundation, Adelaide . . . 000706
Experimental Art Foundation Booksshop, Adelaide . . . 136769
Experimentarium, Hellerup . . . 008893
Expert Clock Repair, Houston . . . 132117
Expert Restorations, Atlanta . . . 131771
Exploding Head Gallery, Sacramento . . . 119144
Explora Museum, Frankfurt am Main . . . 017161
Explora Science Center and Children's Museum, Albuquerque . . . 041614
Exploration Arts, Calgary . . . 096812
Exploration House, Toronto . . . 059181, 097265, 137707
Exploration Place, Wichita . . . 049153
Exploration Station, A Children's Museum, Boubonnais . . . 042349
Exploration Station, A Children's Museum, Bourbonnais . . . 042357
Explorations, Tucson . . . 093230
Exploratorio, Centro Científico Tecnológico Interactivo, San Isidro . . . 000563
The Exploratorium, San Francisco . 047861
Exploratorium - Kindermuseum Stuttgart und Region, Stuttgart . . . 020348
Explorers Hall, National Geographic Society, Washington . . . 048903
Explorion, Limburgs Science Centrum, Heerlen . . . 029695
Exploris, Raleigh . . . 047311
Explosivos, Lugo . . . 110414
Expo-Arte, Madrid . . . 110497
Expo Display Service, Marcilly-d'Azergues . . . 099635
Expo Haringvliet, Stellendam . . . 030184
Expo-Musée Renault, Boulogne-Billancourt . . . 010907
Expoarte Uadi, Getxo . . . 110353
Expodec, Madrid . . . 110498
Expoint, Budapest . . . 105507
Expol Arte Antiguidade, São Paulo . 058708
Expol-Sources, Hong Kong . . . 097782
Expol-Sources Gallery, Taipei . . . 098068
Expose, Amsterdam . . . 107710
Exposé, Orléans . . . 133506
Exposé, Orléans . . . 135707
Exposició Permanent d'Eines Agrícoles de la Masia de Can Deu, Sabadell . . . 035729
Exposición de Arte, Monterrey . . . 093816
Exposición de Gregorio de Laferrere, Gregorio de Laferrere . . . 000356
Exposición Permanente de Cerámica Indígena, Manizales . . . 007526
Exposición Roberto J. Mouras, Carlos Casares . . . 000263
Exposiciones y Salones Monograficos, Madrid . . . 110499
Expositie 40-45, Blitterswijk . . . 029317
Expositie Versteend Leven, Drouwen . . . 029512
Expositieruimte De Weem, Westeremden . . . 030325
Exposition 1914-1918, Villeneuve-les-Convers . . . 015277
Exposition Apicole Péricard, Beurières . . . 010783
Exposition Archéologique de la Maison de la Cour, Nécropole Mérovingienne, Givrand . . . 011960
Exposition Archéologique Gallo-Romaine, Mandeure . . . 012870
Exposition Artistique et Viticole, Aigues-Mortes . . . 010277
Exposition Arts et Histoire, Mauvezin (Gers) . . . 012981
Exposition Botanique, Villar-d'Arène 015222
Exposition Caillebotte, Yerres . . . 015376
Exposition d'Archéologie Médiévale, Antignac . . . 010433
Exposition d'Art, Saint-Céré . . . 014214
Exposition d'Art et d'Histoire, Pionsat . . . 013822
Exposition d'Art Populaire et Caveau, Caramany . . . 011107
Exposition de Coiffes et Dentelles de Bretagne, Guiclan . . . 012051
Exposition de Cristal Berg, Lemberg 012593
Exposition de Faïences, Desvres . . 011581
Exposition de la Medievale, Evol . . . 011762
Exposition de la Mer, des Arts et de la Culture, Camaret-sur-Mer . . . 011078
Exposition de la Préhistoire, Mazières-en-Mauges . . . 012994
Exposition de la Tour de Castellane, Musée de la Cave des Champagnes de Castellane, Épernay . . . 011703
Exposition de l'Habitat Gallo-Romain, Auch . . . 010529
Exposition de Tapisseries, Felletin . 011796
Exposition des Éditions Tarmeye, Mazet-Saint-Voy . . . 012993
Exposition d'Etains Anciens Arsène Maigne, Gramat . . . 011978
Exposition d'Saint-Romain de la Préhistoire, Saint-Romain . . . 014529
Exposition du Château Fort du Fleckenstein, Lembach . . . 012591
Exposition du Cloître des Cordeliers, Tarascon (Bouches-du-Rhône) . . . 014902
Exposition du Compagnonnage, Pont-de-Veyle . . . 013887
Exposition du Cristal, Hartzviller . . . 012071
Exposition du Fort de l'Estissac, Port-Cros . . . 013915
Exposition du Fort Sainte-Agathe, Porquerolles . . . 013914
Exposition du Jouet en Bois, Arvieux-en-Queyras . . . 010496
Exposition du Mémorial Capétien, Manoir de la Luzerne, Bernières-sur-Mer . . . 010764
Exposition du Moulin à Huile, La Cadière-d'Azur . . . 012211
Exposition du Petit Monde de Pagnol, Musée Marcel Pagnol, Aubagne . . 010507
Exposition for the Design and Management of Interior Environments, Toronto . 093625
Exposition Gadal de Préhistoire et d'Archéologie, Tarascon-sur-Ariège . . . 014905
Exposition Géologique du Gouffre de Proumeyssac, Le Bugue . . . 012474
Exposition Historique, Cahors . . . 011065
Exposition Historique, Odenas . . . 013472
Exposition Historique de l'Armagnac, Condom . . . 011461
Exposition Historique du Château, La Roche-Maurice . . . 012308
Exposition Historique du Monastère, Sauxillanges . . . 014714
Exposition La Guerre de Cent Ans, Saint-Mesmin . . . 014435
Exposition L'Eau dans tous ses États, Saint-Denis-de-Pile . . . 014250
Exposition Minéralogique, Briançon 010991
Exposition Permanente, Aigueperse 010276
Exposition Permanente, Lombez . . . 012732
Exposition Permanente, Thanvillé . . 014925
Exposition Permanente d'Archéologie, Ainvelle . . . 010285
Exposition Permanente d'Art, Bazens . . . 010690
Exposition Permanente d'Art, Brasparts . . . 010964
Exposition Permanente d'Art, Éguilly . . . 011684
Exposition Permanente d'Art Contemporain, Bonnemazon . . . 010868
Exposition Permanente d'Arts Plastiques, Brioude . . . 011006
Exposition Permanente de Documents d'Archives, Bruxelles . . . 003298
Exposition Permanente de la Viticulture, Montalba-le-Château . . . 013120
Exposition Permanente de Peintures, Ploudalmézeau . . . 013848
Exposition Permanente Souvenir du Maréchal Lannes, Lectoure . . . 012584
Exposition Permanente sur la Déportation, Charmes . . . 011256
Exposition Permanente sur les Églises Fortifiées de la Thiérache, Vervins 015190
Exposition Permanente Valence à la Croisée des Chemirs, Valence (Drôme) . . . 015094
Exposition Préhistorique, Choranche . . . 011376
Exposition Préhistorique, Grotte Sous-Marine Cosquer, Marseille . . . 012931
Exposition Ruchon Morin, Le Merlerault . . . 012526
Exposition sur la Parfumerie, Eze . . 011773
Exposition sur la Pierre et la Civilisation du Vin, Saint-Restitut . . . 014525
Exposition sur la Presse Ecrite, Saint-Jean-de-Védas . . . 014353
Exposition sur la Vie Rurale d'Autrefois, Bégard . . . 010732
Exposition sur l'Art Cistercien, Les Abbayes Cisterciennes en Limousin, Bétête 010778
Exposition sur l'Histoire du Textile Choletais, Le Longeron . . . 012513
Exposition Universelle des Vins et Spiritueux, Bandol . . . 010638
Exposition Viticole, Ordonnac . . . 013504
Expositions de Chapelle Sainte-Thècle, Seguret . . . 014746
Expositions du Château, Pierrefonds 013817
Expositions Pipe et Diamant, Saint-Claude . . . 014231
Expostion Grotte Chauvet Pont d'Arc, Vallon-Pont-d'Arc . . . 015110
Exposto, Maria Teresa, Lisboa . . . 079924
Exposure Gallery, Vancouver . . . 006696
Exposure Gallery, Vancouver . . . 097464
Expozee, Lauwersoog . . . 029829
Expozice Asijského Umění Národní Galerie v Praze, Praha . . . 008603
Expozice České Lidové Armády, Vojenské muzea, Praha . . . 008604
Expozice Dominikánský Klášter, Jablonné v Podještědí . . . 008400
Expozice Historického Nábytku 16.-19. a Oděvů 19. Století, Turnov . . . 008726
Expozice Josef Hoffmann, Brtnice . 008300
Expozice Mladý Gustav Mahler a Jihlava, Jihlava . . . 008411
Expozice Řemesel, Moravské Budějovice . . . 008512
Expozícia Historických Hodín, Mestské Múzeum v Bratislave, Bratislava . 034319
Expozícia Meštianskej Bytovej Kultúry, Múzeum v Kežmarku, Kežmarok . 034360
Expozícia Zbraní a Stredovekého Mestského Opevnenia, Mestské Múzeum v Bratislave, Bratislava . . . 034320
Expressions, Calgary . . . 096813
Expressions, Paris . . . 138366
Expressions, Shrewsbury . . . 086603
Expressions Art Gallery, Oakland . . 118632
Expressions Black Art Gallery, Houston . . . 116313
Expressions By Edith, New York . . . 090859
Expressions Gallery, Armadale, Victoria . . . 094164
Expressions in Art, Pittsburgh . . . 118918
Expressions of Culture, Chicago . . . 115408
Expressions of Soul, Bowral . . . 055529
Expressive Therapies Program of Lesley University, Graduate School of Arts and Science, Cambridge . . . 051064
Exquisit Styles, Chicago . . . 115409
Exquisite Art, Pretoria . . . 080733
Exquisite Arts and Antiques, New York . . . 090860
Extence, Leigh C., Shaldon . . . 086547
Extence Antiques, Teignmouth . . . 086835
Exteri-Art, Hawkes Bay . . . 108465
Extra Buch, Berlin . . . 138772
Extrapool, Nijmegen . . . 108152
Extrato Galeria de Arte, Porto Alegre . . . 096554
L'Extreme Orient, Hong Kong . . . 059626
Extrêmes, Bruxelles . . . 057936
Ey, Christa, Viersen . . . 105118, 126950
Eyam Museum, Eyam . . . 039470
Eybergen, Den Haag . . . 078197
Eyck, Ten, Saint Louis . . . 123085
Eye, Candy, Cleveland . . . 115705
Eye, Candy, Denver . . . 115993
Eye, Candy, New York . . . 090861
Eye, Jammie, New York . . . 117882
Eye Blink Studios, Indianapolis . . . 116459
Eye Candy, Sheffield . . . 114417
Eye Cetera, Chicago . . . 115410
Eye Lounge, Phoenix . . . 118870
Eye On the Square, New Orleans . . 117433
Eye Opener Courses, London . . . 050834
Eye Spy, Toronto . . . 059182
Eye. The International Review of Graphic Design, London . . . 136213
Eyebeam, New York . . . 117883
Eyedeal Imports, Minneapolis . . . 117256
Eyemouth Museum, Eyemouth . . . 039471
Eyeneek Youneek, Bobs Farm . . . 094262
Eyes Gallery, Philadelphia . . . 118756
Eyes of the Wild Art Gallery, Minneapolis . . . 117257
Eyes of the Wild Art Gallery, Saint Paul . . . 119285
Eyesong, Yokohama . . . 107141
Eyestorm, New York . . . 117884
Eyestorm-Britart.Com, London . . . 113601
EygenArt Verlag, Kriftel . . . 134133

Eyhorne Manor Laundry Museum, Hollingbourne 039760
Eykelberg, Jan, Antwerpen 096064
Eylül Sanat Galerisi, İstanbul 112307
Eymael, F., Liège 123652
D'Eyncourt, Chertsey 083940, 130549
Eyraud, Emmanuel, Joigny (Yonne) . 063243
Eyre & Greig, London 113602
Eyrie Galleries, Mansfield 114054
Eyvind Johnson-Stugan, Boden . . . 036217
d'Ezaël, Villejuif 125027
Ezair, New York 117885
Ezekiel Harris House, Augusta 041896
Ezra and Cecile Zilkha Gallery, Middletown 045840
Ezra Meeker Mansion, Puyallup . . . 047289
Ezry Gallery, Jerusalem 105909
Ėžvinskij Literaturnyj Muzej, Syktyvkar 033919
F 33, Praha 098429
F & C, Warszawa 109118
F. & F., Perugia 076233
F & F Art, Jihlava 098364
F Rame's Gallery, Knokke-Heist . . . 096333
F8 Fine Art Gallery, Austin 114982
FA Projects, London 113603
Faaborg Museum for Fynsk Malerkunst, Faaborg 008849
Faba Film, Bucureşti 080155
Fabbrica Casa Museo, Albissola Marina 023156
Fabbrica del Lunedí, Napoli 106365
Fabbrini, Carlo, Roma 076445
Fabbrini, Carlo, Roma 076446
Fabbrini, Marcello, Roma 076447
Faber, F., Zülpich 074575
Faber, Johannes, Wien 095818
Faber, Thilo, Rudolstadt 073613
Faber & Faber, Leipzig 134149
Faber & Faber, London 135215
Faber Gotic, Barcelona 110146
Faberge, Madrid 122056
Fabert & Raoult, Meaux . . 064457, 124441
Fabian, Vancouver 123849
Fabian, Daniel, Vaduz 128459
Fabian, F., Stuttgart 126847
Fabian, Frank, Hameln 125854
Fabian & Samuels, Stäfa . 111931, 130185
Fabien, Paris 065891
Fabien, Mathieu, Toulouse 101343
Fabing, Catherine, Toul 068435
Fabio & Max Antichità, Roma 128032
Fabio's Upholstery, Los Angeles . . . 132252
Fabius Frères, Paris 065892, 100272, 138367
Fables, South Fremantle 137087
Fables Antique, Auckland . 078942, 128901
Fables Antiques, Los Angeles 089762
Fabre, Paris 065893
Fabre, Etienne, Peypin 124843
Fabre, Nicole, London 085286
Fabre, Régis, Rochemaure 067186
The Fabric Workshop and Museum, Philadelphia 046940
Fábrica, Asunción 108798
Fabrica, Brighton 038849
La Fabrica, Madrid 110500
Fabricarestauri, Torino 128305
Fabricius-Ház, Soproni Múzeum, Sopron 021843
Fabrik Antique, Bargteheide 069471
Fabrikmuseum der Leonischen Industrie, Roth, Mittelfranken 019908
Fabrikmuseum Johann Nemetz, Wiener Neustadt 003031
Fabrikmuseum Nordwolle, Delmenhorst 016664
Fabrile, Armadale, Victoria 055370
Fabrile, Chicago 115411
Fabris, Giulia, Venezia 076935
Fabrizi, Lionel, Charleville-Mézières 062157
Fabro, Silvia, Milano 127587
Fabry, Paris 124659
Fabry, Forence, Talence 068351
Fabry, Olivier, Bruxelles . . 057937, 123591
Fabry, Robert, Potsdam 073360
Fabulous Fakes, New York 117886
Fabulous Finds, Phoenix 091738
Fabulous Finds, Toronto 059183
Fabulous Frames and Art, Cincinnati 115626
Fabulous Frames and Art, Cincinnati 115627
Fabulous Frames and Art, Cincinnati 115628
Fabus, Paris 065894
Fabyan Villa Museum and Dutch Windmill, Geneva 044162
The Facade, London 085287
Facchinetti, Brescia 075166
Facchini, Silvana, Miami 117066
Facchino, Michele, Tübingen 126919
Face aux Tilleuls, Gavray 062973
Face It Art Gallery, Chicago 115412
Facere, Seattle 092992
Facet Books, Bournemouth 141424
Fach, Joseph, Frankfurt am Main . .070737, 102762, 139080
Fach, Werner R., Frankfurt am Main 139081
Fachbereich Angewandte Kunst Hochschulteil Schneeberg, Westsächsische Hochschule Zwickau, Schneeberg, Erzgebirge 050232
Fachbereich Architektur, Fachhochschule Aachen, Aachen 049999
Fachbereich Architektur, Fachhochschule Biberach, Biberach an der Riß . . . 050032
Fachbereich Architektur, Fachhochschule Bochum, Bochum 050035
Fachbereich Architektur, Fachhochschule Coburg, Coburg 050048
Fachbereich Architektur, Fachhochschule Darmstadt, Darmstadt 050051
Fachbereich Architektur, Fachhochschule Dortmund, Dortmund 050058
Fachbereich Architektur, Fachhochschule Düsseldorf, Düsseldorf 050067
Fachbereich Architektur, Fachhochschule Erfurt, Erfurt 050073
Fachbereich Architektur, Fachhochschule Frankfurt am Main, Frankfurt am Main 050081
Fachbereich Architektur, Fachhochschule Hannover, Nienburg, Weser 050204
Fachbereich Architektur, Fachhochschule Heidelberg, Heidelberg 050126
Fachbereich Architektur, Fachhochschule Kaiserslautern, Kaiserslautern . . . 050137
Fachbereich Architektur, Fachhochschule Karlsruhe, Karlsruhe 050139
Fachbereich Architektur, Fachhochschule Lausitz, Cottbus 050049
Fachbereich Architektur, Fachhochschule Mainz, Mainz 050172
Fachbereich Architektur, Fachhochschule Münster, Münster 050200
Fachbereich Architektur, Fachhochschule Nordostniedersachsen, Buxtehude 050047
Fachbereich Architektur, Fachhochschule Regensburg, Regensburg 050221
Fachbereich Architektur, Fachhochschule Stuttgart - Hochschule für Technik, Stuttgart 050241
Fachbereich Architektur, Fachhochschule Trier, Trier 050252
Fachbereich Architektur, Fachhochschule Wiesbaden, Wiesbaden 050259
Fachbereich Architektur, Georg-Simon-Ohm-Fachhochschule Nürnberg, Nürnberg 050206
Fachbereich Architektur, Hochschule Bremen, Bremen 050045
Fachbereich Architektur, Hochschule für Angewandte Wissenschaften, Hamburg 050110
Fachbereich Architektur, Hochschule für Technik und Wirtschaft des Saarlandes, Saarbrücken 050226
Fachbereich Architektur, Technische Fachhochschule Berlin, Berlin . . . 050016
Fachbereich Architektur, Technische Universität Darmstadt, Darmstadt 050052
Fachbereich Architektur, Universität Gesamthochschule Kassel, Kassel 050147
Fachbereich Architektur, Westsächsische Hochschule Zwickau, Bereich Reichenbach, Reichenbach, Vogtland 050224
Fachbereich Architektur-Design-Kunst, Bergische Universität Wuppertal, Wuppertal 050266
Fachbereich Architektur Hildesheim, Fachhochschule Hildesheim/Holzminden, Hildesheim 050129
Fachbereich Architektur/Innenarchitektur, Fachhochschule Lippe und Höxter, Detmold 050057
Fachbereich Architektur Oldenburg, Fachhochschule Oldenburg/ Ostfriesland/ Wilhelmshaven, Oldenburg, Oldenburg 050213
Fachbereich Architektur/Raum- und Umweltplanung/Bauingenieurwesen, Universität Kaiserslautern, Kaiserslautern 050138
Fachbereich Architektur - Städtebau, Universität-Gesamthochschule Siegen, Siegen 050237
Fachbereich Architektur und Bauingenieurwesen, Fachhochschule Anhalt, Abteilung Dessau, Dessau, Anhalt 050055
Fachbereich Architektur und Bauingenieurwesen, Fachhochschule Augsburg, Augsburg 050003
Fachbereich Architektur und Bauingenieurwesen, Fachhochschule Bielefeld, Minden, Westfalen 050183
Fachbereich Architektur und Bauingenieurwesen, Fachhochschule Würzburg-Schweinfurt-Aschaffenburg, Abteilung Würzburg, Würzburg . . 050263
Fachbereich Architektur und Gestaltung, Fachhochschule Konstanz, Konstanz 050160
Fachbereich Architektur und Stadtplanung, Fachhochschule Koblenz, Koblenz 050152
Fachbereich Architekur, Fachhochschule München, München 050189
Fachbereich Bauingenieurwesen/ Architektur, Hochschule für Technik und Wirtschaft Dresden, Dresden 050061
Fachbereich Bildende Kunst, Fachhochschule Hannover, Hannover 050120
Fachbereich Bildende Kunst, Johannes Gutenberg-Universität Mainz, Mainz 050173
Fachbereich Bildende Kunst, Universität der Künste Berlin, Berlin 050017
Fachbereich Buch und Museum, Hochschule für Technik, Wirtschaft und Kultur Leipzig, Leipzig 050165
Fachbereich Design, Fachhochschule Aachen, Aachen 050000
Fachbereich Design, Fachhochschule Anhalt, Abteilung Dessau, Dessau, Anhalt 050056
Fachbereich Design, Fachhochschule Dortmund, Dortmund 050059
Fachbereich Design, Fachhochschule Düsseldorf, Düsseldorf 050068
Fachbereich Design, Fachhochschule Köln, Köln 050154
Fachbereich Design, Fachhochschule Münster, Münster 050201
Fachbereich Design, Hochschule Niederrhein, Krefeld 050161
Fachbereich Design/Innenarchitektur, Hochschule für Technik, Wirtschaft und Gestaltung Wismar, Wismar 050261
Fachbereich Design, Kunst- und Musikpädagogik, Druck, Bergische Universität-Gesamthochschule Wuppertal, Wuppertal 050267
Fachbereich Design und Medien, Fachhochschule Hannover, Hannover 050121
Fachbereich Edelstein- und Schmuckdesign, Fachhochschule Trier, Idar-Oberstein 050135
Fachbereich Gestaltung, Fachhochschule Augsburg, Augsburg 050004
Fachbereich Gestaltung, Fachhochschule Bielefeld, Bielefeld 050033
Fachbereich Gestaltung, Fachhochschule Darmstadt, Darmstadt 050053
Fachbereich Gestaltung, Fachhochschule für Technik und Wirtschaft Berlin, Berlin 050018
Fachbereich Gestaltung, Fachhochschule Mannheim, Mannheim 050176
Fachbereich Gestaltung, Fachhochschule München, München 050190
Fachbereich Gestaltung, Fachhochschule Wiesbaden, Wiesbaden 050260
Fachbereich Gestaltung, Fachhochschule Würzburg-Schweinfurt-Aschaffenburg, Abteilung Würzburg, Würzburg . . 050264
Fachbereich Gestaltung, Georg-Simon-Ohm-Fachhochschule Nürnberg, Nürnberg 050207
Fachbereich Gestaltung, Hochschule für angewandte Wissenschaften, Hamburg 050111
Fachbereich Gestaltung, Hochschule für Technik und Wirtschaft Dresden (FH), Dresden 050062
Fachbereich Gestaltung - Kunsterziehung, Universität GH Essen, Essen 050078
Fachbereich II Design, Fachhochschule Mainz, Mainz 050174
Fachbereich Islamische Kunstgeschichte und Archäologie, Otto-Friedrich-Universität Bamberg, Bamberg . . 050010
Fachbereich Kunst- , Orient und Altertumswissenschaften, Martin-Luther-Universität Halle-Wittenberg, Halle, Saale 050097
Fachbereich Kunst- und Musikpädagogik, Universität-Gesamthochschule Siegen, Siegen 050238
Fachbereich Kunsterziehung, Pädagogische Hochschule Heidelberg, Heidelberg 050127
Fachbereich Kunstgeschichte, Universität Trier, Trier 050253
Fachbereich Restaurierung, Fachhochschule Erfurt, Erfurt 050074
Fachbereiche Architektur, Design und Innenarchitektur, Hochschule Wismar, Wismar 050262
Fachgebiet Grafik und Malerei, Philipps-Universität, Marburg 050179
Fachgebiet Kunst, Pädagogische Hochschule Karlsruhe, Karlsruhe . 050140
Fachgebiet Restaurierung, Potsdam 050220
Fachhochschul-Studiengang Medientechnik und -design, Hagenberg 049627
Fachhochschul-Studiengang Multi-MediaArt, Techno-Z Fachhochschule, Salzburg 049645
Fachhochschule für Kunsttherapie Nürtingen, Nürtingen 050209
Fachhochschule für Kunsttherapie und Kunstpädagogik und Freie Bildende Kunst, Ottersberg 050215
Fachhochschule Joanneum - Industrial Design, Graz 049621
Fachhochschule Pforzheim, Hochschule für Gestaltung, Technik und Wirtschaft, Pforzheim 050219
Fachhochschule Schwäbisch Gmünd, Schwäbisch Gmünd 050233
Fachmesse für Philatelie und Numismatik, Graz 093577
Fachmesse Gallery, Frankfurt am Main 093718
Fachner, Sigrid, Lippstadt 139417
Fachrichtung Indische Philologie und Kunstgeschichte, Freie Universität Berlin, Berlin 050019
Fachrichtung Kunsterziehung, Universität des Saarlandes, Saarbrücken . . . 050227
Fachrichtung Kunstgeschichte, Universität des Saarlandes, Saarbrücken . . . 050228
Fachschule des Bezirks Oberbayern für Schreiner und Holzbildhauer mit Fachakademie für Holzgestaltung, Garmisch-Partenkirchen 050089
Fachschule für angewandte Malerei und Bildhauerei, Innsbruck 049629

Fachschule für Holzschnitzerei Berchtesgaden, Berchtesgaden . . 050015
Das Fachwerk, Bad Salzuflen 015786
Fachwerkbaumuseum im Ständerbau, Städtische Museen Quedlinburg, Quedlinburg 019683
Facincani, Ennio, Wien 057411
Fackler, Raimund, Traunstein 074077
Facsimile Editions, London 141788
Facsimilia Art & Edition, Darmstadt 102339, 133854
Factoria del Perro Verde, Madrid . . 110501
Factory, Livorno 106120
Factory Fine Art, Modena 106349
Facts and Fiction, Rosebud 137074
Faculdad de Artes, Pontificia Universidad Javeriana, Bogotá 049864
Faculdade de Belas Artes da Universidade do Porto, Porto 050614
Faculdade de Belas Artes de São Paulo, São Paulo 049766
Faculdade Santa Marcelina, Campus II, Itaguera 049748
Facultad de Arquitectura, Universidad de la República, Montevideo 050860
Facultad de Arquitectura y Artes, Universidad Nacional Pedro Henríquez Ureña, Santo Domingo 049913
Facultad de Artes, Universidad Autónoma del Estado de Morelos, Cuernavaca 050530
Facultad de Artes, Universidad Nacional de Colombia, Bogotá 049865
Facultad de Artes y Diseño, Mendoza 049603
Facultad de Bellas Artes, Universidad de Bogotá Jorge Tadeo Lozano, Bogotá 049866
Facultad de Bellas Artes, Universidad de Chile, Santiago de Chile 049840
Facultad de Bellas Artes, Universidad del Atlántico, Barranquilla 049863
Facultad de Bellas Artes, Universidad Nacional de La Plata, La Plata . . . 049601
Facultad de Bellas Artes y Escuels de Artes Plásticas, Universidad de Costa Rica, San José 049877
Faculdade Santa Marcelina, Campus I, Perdizes 049751
Facultas Dombuchhandlung, Melk .133119, 137232
Facultas-Dombuchhandlung, Wien . 137308
Faculté d'Architecture, Université Technique Nationale d'Athènes, Athinai . . . 050271
Faculteit der Kunsten, Akademie voor Beeldende Vorming, Tilburg 050569
Faculty Arts and Humanities, King Abdul Aziz University, Jeddah 050673
Faculty of Architecture, Bangkok . . 050785
Faculty of Architecture, University of Manitoba, Winnipeg 049833
Faculty of Architecture and Planning, Dalhousie University, Halifax 049789
Faculty of Architecture, Landscape and Design, University of Toronto, Toronto 049818
Faculty of Art and Design, Coventry Polytechnic, Coventry 050809
Faculty of Art and Design, Manchester Metropolitan University, Manchester 050845
Faculty of Art, Design and Architecture, Doornfontein 050697
Faculty of Art, Design and Architecture, Technikon Witwatersrand, Johannesburg 050702
Faculty of Art, Design and Communication, RMIT University, Melbourne 049613
Faculty of Arts, Ain Shams University, Cairo 049919
Faculty of Arts, Cairo University, Cairo 049920
Faculty of Arts, Durban University of Technology, Durban 050698
Faculty of Arts, Islamic University of Omdurman, Omdurman 050745
Faculty of Arts, Makerere University, Kampala 050793
Faculty of Arts, University of Alexandria, Alexandria 049917
Faculty of Arts, University of Khartoum, Khartoum 050744
Faculty of Arts, University of Peradeniya, Peradeniya 050742
Faculty of Arts, University of Tabriz, Tabriz 050338
Faculty of Arts and Architecture, University of Brighton, Brighton 050804
Faculty of Arts and Education, University of Plymouth, Exeter 050814
Faculty of Arts and Letters, University of Santo Tomas, Manila 050595
Faculty of Arts and Science, Shiraz University, Shiraz 050337
Faculty of Arts and Sciences, American University of Beirut, Beirut 050519
Faculty of Arts and Social Sciences, University of Malaya, Kuala Lumpur 050526
Faculty of Arts & Education, Benghazi 050520
Faculty of Arts, History and Archaeology, University of Jordan, Amman 050507
Faculty of Decorative Arts, Silpakorn University, Bangkok 050786
Faculty of Fine Arts, Bangkok 050787
Faculty of Fine Arts, Annamalai University, Annamalai Nagar 050291
Faculty of Fine Arts, Aristoteleio Panepistimio Thessalonikis, Thessaloniki 050273
Faculty of Fine Arts, Concordia University, Montréal 049801
Faculty of Fine Arts, Damascus University, Damascus 050784
Faculty of Fine Arts, Maharaja Sayajirao University of Baroda, Vadodara . . 050332
Faculty of Fine Arts, Sri Venkateswara University, Tirupati 050328
Faculty of Fine Arts, University of Teheran, Teheran 050339
Faculty of Fine Arts, University of Travoncore, Triruvananthapuram . 050331
Faculty of Fine Arts and Crafts, Bihar University, Patna 050320
Faculty of Painting, Sculpture and Graphic Art, Bangkok 050788
Faculty of the Built Environment and Design, Cape Technikon, Cape Town 050694
Faculty of Visual Arts, Banaras Hindu University, Varanasi 050333
Fad, Barcelona 110147
FAD Gallery, Melbourne 094811
Faded Fancy, Taranaki 079251
Faded Fines Antiques, Los Angeles 089763
Il Fado, Bologna 127148
Fächerkabinett, Barisch Stiftung, Bielefeld 016234
Fädernegården i Rejpelt, Vörå 010250
Die Fälschergalerie, Leipzig 103865
Fälschermuseum, Ostseebad Binz . 019521
Fængselshiststoriske Museum, Horsens 008931
Faerber, Ahrensburg 101547
Färber, Florian, Traunreut 074073
Faerber, Jorana, Ahrensburg 101548
Färber, Jürgen, Kassel 126015
Färberhaus, Oberstaufen 019421
Färbermuseum, Gutau 001992
Färg och Form, Stockholm 111019
Faes & Faes-Buck, Schlieren 111893
Fässler Söhne, Hermann, Appenzell 082090, 111124, 129899
Fästningsmuseet Karlsborg, Karlsborg 036375
Faethe, Barbara, Berlin 069602
Fåfängans Antik, Göteborg 081803
Fafouille & Grandchamps, Charleroi 137488
Fågelmuseet, Jönköping 036359
Fågelsjö Gammelgård Bortom åa, Los 036434
Faggionato, London 113604
Fagin, Crows Nest, New South Wales 055726
Fagin, N., Chicago 142287
Fagins Antiques, Exeter 084356
Fagioli, Donatella, Roma 128033
Fagus-Gropius-Ausstellung, Alfeld, Leine 015474
FAH Galerie, Maastricht 108121
Faherty, Arty, Market Drayton 085935
Fahey & Klein, Los Angeles 116764
Fahl, J. & S., Freiburg im Breisgau . 139110
Fahl Kro, Hemmet 008900
Fahlbusch, Ludwigshafen am Rhein 072312
Fahlbusch, Ernst, Mannheim 104022
Fahnemann, Berlin 101850
Fahnemann, Berlin 101851
Fahr, Roland, Kranichfeld 126142
Fahrbach, Georg, Köln 071934
Fahrenheit, Denver 142386
Fahrenheit 451, Tilburg 140535
Fahrni, Lünen 126247
Fahrradmuseum, Ybbs 003061
Fahrradmuseum der Fahrrad-Veteranen-Freunde-Dresden 1990, Dresden . 016786
Fahrradmuseum Zumhaus, Feuchtwangen 017114
Fahrzeugmuseum, Frankenberg, Sachsen 017145
Fahrzeugmuseum Marxzell, Marxzell 018857
Fahrzeugmuseum Suhl, Suhl 020380
Fahua Ta Tayuan Museum, Shanghai 007232
Fai Kee, Hong Kong 059627
Faïence d'Antan, Cloyes-sur-le-Loir 062363
Faïencerie Masse, Desvres 062616
Faïences et Emaux, Longwy 012738
Failenschmid, M., Meerbusch 104045
Fain, Eliane, Perpignan 066742
Fainting Couch, Los Angeles 089764
Fair, Anthony, New York 090862
Fair Deal Antiques, Mansfield 085924
Fair for Conservation and Restauration of Art and Architecture, Paris 093658
Fairbanks, H., Nashville . . 090451, 132400
Fairbanks Arts Association, Fairbanks 054753
Fairbanks Gallery, Corvallis 043175
Fairbanks House, Dedham 043360
Fairbanks Museum and Planetarium, Saint Johnsbury 047638
Fairburn Antique Mall, Atlanta 087473
Fairchild, Calistoga 122833
Fairfax, London 085288, 131019
Fairfax, Harriet, Langley Burrell . . . 084904
Fairfax Gallery, Burnham Market . . 112762
Fairfax Gallery, Jacksonville 116524
The Fairfax Gallery, Tunbridge Wells 114610
Fairfax House Museum, York 041476
Fairfax Museum and Visitor Center, Fairfax 043782
Fairfax Publishing, Jacksonville . . . 135370
Fairfield, New York 117887
Fairfield Art Association, Fairfield . . 054754
Fairfield Art Museum, Fairfield 043789
Fairfield City Museum and Gallery, Smithfield 001470
Fairfield County Museum, Winnsboro 049247
Fairfield Museum, Bothwell 005119
Fairfields Manor, Frampton Cotterell 113080
Fairhurst Gallery, Norwich 086116, 131329
Fairlawn Mansion and Museum, Superior 048437
Fairley, Malcolm, London 113605
Fairlie Antique Shop, Fairlie 084373
Fairlook, Seattle 092993, 142985
Fairlynch Museum, Budleigh Salterton 038898
Fairmarket Antique Centre, Lismore 056106
Fairmount, Markham 133315
Fairmount Park Art Association, Philadelphia 054755
Fairport Historical Museum, Fairport 043797
Fairport Marine Museum, Fairport Harbor 043798
Fairview Museum of History and Art, Fairview 043799
Fais Moi une Place dans ta Maison, Biarritz 061462
Faisal, Al-Khobar 080351
Faisan, Strasbourg 101287
Faison, Kim, Richmond 092077
Faisons un Rêve, Bruxelles 057938
Faist Barton, Chicago 115413
Le Fait de Savoir Cyber, Saint-Martin 139908
Fait et Cause, Paris 100273
Faith Trumbull Chapter Museum, Norwich 046565
Faithgrant, Victoria 059437
Faivre-Andrieux-Verdillon, Paris . . . 065895
Faivre-Reuille, Bruno, Paris 065896
Fakenham Antique Centre, Fakenham 084374, 130700
Fakenham Museum of Gas and Local History, Fakenham 039474
Fakkers, Marianne, Alkmaar 107616
Faksimile Verlag, Luzern 135045
Faktoriet, Eskilstuna 036253
Fakultät Architektur, Bauingenieurwesen und Stadtplanung, Brandenburgische Technische Universität Cottbus, Cottbus 050050
Fakultät Architektur, Stadt- und Regionalplanung, Bauhaus-Universität Weimar, Weimar, Thüringen 050256
Fakultät für Architektur, Fachhochschule Köln, Köln 050155
Fakultät für Architektur, Universität Fridericiana zu Karlsruhe, Karlsruhe 050141
Fakultät für Kulturwissenschaft-Institut Kunst, Musik, Gestaltung, Universität Paderborn, Paderborn 050216
Fakultät für Linguistik & Literaturwissenschaft - Abteilung Kunst & Musik, Universität Bielefeld, Bielefeld 050034
Fakultät Gestaltung, Bauhaus-Universität Weimar, Weimar, Thüringen 050257
Fakultät Gestaltung, Fachhochschule Hildesheim/Holzminden/Göttingen, Hildesheim 050130
Fakultät Gestaltung, Institut für Theorie und Geschichte der Gestaltung GTG, Universität der Künste Berlin, Berlin 050020
Fakultet Architektury, Iskusstv i Stroitelstva, Novgorodskij Gosudarstvennyj Universitet im. Jaroslava Mudrogo, Velikij Novgorod 050669
Fakultet Chudožestvennogo Obrazovanija, Voronežskij Gosudarstvennyj Pedagogičeskij Universitet, Voronež 050672
Fakultet Iskusstv, Moskovskij Gosudarstvennyj Universitet im. M.V. Lomonosova, Moskva 050644
Fakultet Iskusstv, Omskij Gosudarstvennyj Pedagogičeskij Universitet, Omsk 050653
Fakultet Iskusstv, Volgogradskij Gosudarstvennyj Pedagogičeskij Universitet, Volgograd 050670
Fakultet Iskusstva, Altajskij Gosudarstvennyj Universitet, Barnaul 050626
Fakultet Iskusstvovedenija i Kulturologii, Uralskij Gosudarstvennyj Universitet, Ekaterinburg 050631
Fakultet Izobrazitelnogo Iskusstva, Rossijskij Gosudarstvennyj Pédagogičeskij Universitet im. A.I. Gercena, Sankt-Peterburg 050660
Fakultet Kultury i Iskusstv, Uljanovskij Gosudarstvennyj Universitet, Uljanovsk 050668
Fakultet Kultury i Iskusstva, Omskij Gosudarstvennyj Universitet, Omsk 050654
Fakultet Technologii i Dizajna, Vjatskij Gosudarstvennyj Gumanitarnyj Universitet, Kirov 050639
Falabrègues, Pascal, Rodez 121234
Falanga, Roma 076448
Falanga, Pasquale, Milano 075707
Falbygdens Museum, Falköping . . . 036263

Falce, Philippe, Beaune 061279
Falch, Hermann, Sankt Gallen 082773
Falchini, Simone, Firenze 075334
Falcieri, Armando, Milano 075708
Falcioni, Moreno, Firenze 127331
Falck, Genève 111447
Falco, Breda 078091
Falcón, Buenos Aires 055203
Falcon, Mercedes, Jerez de la Frontera 081165, 110392
The Falcon Gallery, Wortham 087262, 131717
Falcone, San Jose 092922
Falconer Museum, Forres 039517
Falconnet, Pierre, Menton 064492, 138204
Faleide Skulemuseum, Stryn 031248
Falger-Museum, Elbigenalp 001830
Falia Art, Toronto 097266
Faligowska, Teresa, Wrocław 109216
Falinki, Alain, Orvault 124531
Falk, Christoph, Berlin 133771
Falk, Ragnar, Lund 129846
Falk Art Reference, Madison 135387
Falk & Falk, Zürich 082964, 122364
Falk & Falk, Zürich 122365
Falk & Falk, Zürich 141332
Falk & Falk, Zürich 141333
Falke, Renate, Bleiburg 095478
Falkenberg, Heinz A, Schwedt 073762
Falkenberg, Petra, Düsseldorf 070377, 125528
Falkenbergs Hembygdsmuseum, Falkenberg 036259
Falkenstein, Dr. Klaus, Dinslaken . . 138980
Falkirk Cultural Center, San Rafael . 047920
Falkland Palace and Garden, Falkland 039478
Falkner, Castlemaine 094382
Falknereimuseum, Burg Honenwerten, Werfen 002836
Falkoner Antik, Frederiksberg 060233
Fall River County Historical Museum, Hot Springs 044629
Fall River Historical Society Museum, Fall River 043804
Falla Campos, Maria Eugenia, Madrid 081299
Fallani, Firenze 140015
Fallani &Sons, Long Beach 132224
Fallani Best, Firenze 106049
Falle, John, Saint Helier 086448
The Fallen Angels, Gent . . 058180, 137496
Faller, Dieter, Riehen 130151
Fallet, Micheline Vorbe, Genève . . . 111448
Falleur, Cambrai 099057
Fallingwater - Western Pennsylvania Conservancy, Mill Run 045870
Fallourd, Claude, Saint-Vincent-Sterlanges 068039
Falls Gallery, Wentworth Falls 095386
Falls Road Antiques, Baltimore 087665
Fallwell, M., Nashville 142600
Falmouth Art Gallery, Falmouth . . . 039480
Falmouth Historical Museum, Falmouth 043809
Falon, Las Vegas 116618
Falret, Jérôme, Planioles 066844
Falsi d'Autore, Firenze 127332
Falstadminnet, The Falstad Memorial, Levanger 030981
Falstaff Antiques, Rolvenden 086393
Falsterbo Museum, Falsterbo 036264
Falt, Raymond C., New York 090863, 132468
Faltbootmuseum, Lychen 018765
Falteri, Fiorenza, Firenze 127333
Faltinsky, Rudolf, Braunschweig . . . 069979
Falu Auktionskammare, Falun 122132
Falúas Reales, Aranjuez 034845
Falumúzeum, Hollókő 021741
Falumúzeum, Isaszeg 021745
Falumúzeum, Törökbálint 021908
Falvey, Boston 131846
FAM Galerie, Nijmegen 108153
Famiglietti, Vittorio, Modena 127730
Familie Vrouwenhofje - Hofje van Aerden, Leerdam 029834
Familien Ernsts Samlingers Fond, Assens 008814
Familienmuseum, Schwerin 020146
Familienmuseum Bad Homburg, Bad Homburg v.d.Höhe 015720
Familienmuseum im Altbauernhaus, Göstling an der Ybbs 001916
Familistère de Guise, Guise 012056
Famille des Arts, Université du Québec à Montréal, Montréal 049802
Family Antiques, Manchester 085914
Family Art Gallery, Vancouver 097465
Family Broc, Caen 061870
Family Museum of Arts and Science, Bettendorf 042187
Family Ties, Portland 091934
Family Tree Art Gallery, Baltimore . . 115047
Family Values Antiques, Long Beach 089632
Famine Museum, Strokestown 022862
Famira-Parcsetich, Ursula, Heidelberg 125898
Famous, Amsterdam 077843
Famous French Gallery, Tucson . . . 120126
F.A.N., Feminist Art News, Bedford . 136214
Fan Collector, Clermont-Ferrand . . . 062343
Fan Dali, Shanghai 097911
Fan Dali, Shanghai 097912
Fan Dali, Shanghai 097913
F.A.N. Gallery, Philadelphia 118757
Fan Man, Dallas 132008
Fan Museum, London 040144
Fancelli, Marco, Firenze 127334
Fancies, Toronto 059184
Fancies, Toronto 059185
Fandos y Leonarte, Valencia 110805
Fandrich, B., Berlin 125195
Fandrich, Bernhard, Falkenhagen . . 125627
Fanelli, New York 090864
Fanelli, Piera, Roma 076449
Fanette, Paris 065897
Fanfan des Mûres, Lyon 099558
Fangotto, Palermo 076145
Faninadahen Kosas Guahan, Guam Museum, Adelup 021565
Le Fanion, New York 090865
Fankhänel, Dietrich, Hildesheim . . . 125930
Fanlac, Périgueux 133690
Fanny's Antiques, Reading 086333
Fanø Kunstsamling, Fanø 008853
Fanø Museum, Fanø 008854
Fanø Skibsfarts- og Dragtsamling, Fanø 008855
Fans & Stoves of Five Points, Jacksonville 089410
Fanshawe Pioneer Village, London . 005784
La Fantasia, Roma 076450, 128034
Fantasmak, Paris 138368
Fantastic Art and Image, Hamburg .103117, 134005
Fantastic Fiction, Adelaide 136770
Fantastic Finds, San Antonio 092511
Fantastic French Furniture, San Diego 092634
Fantastic Modern Art Gallery, Beverly Hills 094251
Fantasy Crafts, Manama 057628
Il Fante di Quadri, Napoli 106366
Fantini, Goffredo, New York 090866
Fanuele, Leonardo, Buenos Aires . . 094069
Fapa Ediciones, Barcelona 140984
Faqir Khana Museum, Lahore 031378
Faques, Brighton 083694
Far Corners, Los Angeles 089765
Far East Fine Arts, San Francisco . . 119664
Far East Gallery, Singapore 109795
Far Eastern Antiques and Arts, New York 090867
Far North Art, Alawa 055321
Far North Regional Museum, Kaitaia 030529
Far & Sønn, Oslo 079432
Fara, Maria Ernestina, Roma 106532
Clive Farahar & Sophie Dupré, Calne 141465
Farahbaksh, Houshang, Berlin 069603
Farahnick, Al, Bruxelles 057939
Farahnick, Al, Bruxelles 057940
Farahnick, Philippe-John, Bruxelles 057941
Faraj, Ibrahim, Sharjah 083213
La Farandole, Pont-Sainte-Maxence 066935
Farangis, Yegane, Frankfurt am Main 133940
Faraoni, Luigi, Roma 128035
Farbene, Giorgio, Bolzano 075126
Farbene, S., Bolzano 075127
Farber, Indianapolis 116460
Der Farbkleks, Duisburg 102578
Die Farbpalette, Emden 102618
Farbrother, John, York 131726
Farce, Raleigh 136459
Al-Fardan, Sharjah 112465
Al-Fardan, Ahmed Ibrahim, Manama 096008
Fardel, Le Touquet-Paris-Plage . . . 099458
Fardel, Demanie, Annecy 098840
Fardel, Demanie, Sanary-sur-Mer . 101249
Farel, Aigle 111112
Farella Franck, Marseille 064352
Farelly, Princes Risborough 131398
Farenc, Michel, Le Garric . 063621, 124296
Fares, Saint Louis 132746
Farfouillette, Nice 065080
Fargeaud, Jacques, Saint-Jean-de-Monts 067545
Fargeton, Damien, Lyon 124355
Fargo Air Museum, Fargo 043813
Farha, Cairo 098630
Farhat, Ammar, Sidi Bou Saïd 112257
Farhi, Luc, Paris 065898
Farimagshuset, København 060324
Farina, Prof. Tina, Köln 103613
Farinelli, San Francisco 092785
Faringdon, Arundel 083312, 130305
Fark & Osterheider, Bissendorf 069856
Farleigh House Antiques, Southwold 086669
Farleigh Hungerford Castle, Farleigh Hungerford 039486
Farlow, Peter, London 085289
The Farm, Sturgeon Bay 048409
Farm and Folk Museum, Lanreath . 039931
Farm House Museum, Iowa State University, Ames 041685
Farmaceutická Expozícia, Mestské Múzeum v Bratislave, Bratislava 034321
Farmacevtičeskij Muzej, Moskva . . 033389
Farmacia Conventuale, Venezia . . . 026231
Farmacia Museo Taquechel, La Habana 007946
Farmācijas Muzejs, Rīga 027733
Farmamerica, Waseca 048873
Farmamerica, Minnesota Agricultural Interpretive Center, Janesville . . . 044837
Farmamuseo Sa Potecaria, Villacidro 026332
Farman, P., Paris 065899
Farmer, Andrew, Armadale, Victoria 055371
Farmer Painting Gallery, Shanghai . 097914
Farmer's Arms Hotel Museum, Euroa 001025
Farmers Bank, The Petersburg Museums, Petersburg 046904
Farmers Bank of Rustico, Rustico . . 006314
Farmers Gallery, Leominster 113381
Farmers Gallery, Leominster 141720
Farmer's House, Metulla 023030
The Farmers' Museum, Cooperstown 043137
Farmhouse Antiques, Bolton-by-Bowland 083573
Farmhouse Antiques, Chester 083954
Farmhouse Antiques, Great Houghton 084510
Farmhouse Antiques, Portland 091935
Farmhouse Antiques, Stoke Ferry . .086730, 131546
Farmhouse Collections, Vancouver . 059357
Farming Through the Ages, Whyte Yarcowie 001616
Farmington Historic Home, Louisville 045486
Farmington Museum, Farmington . . 043821
Farmland Museum and Denny Abbey, Waterbeach 041316
Farmlife Centre, Thornhill, Central . 041215
Farnborough Gallery and Bookshop, Farnborough, Hampshire 141610
Farnese, Roma 076451
Farnese, Roma 076452
La Farnesiana Antichitá, Roma 076453
Farnet, Georges, Marseille 064353
Farnham Art Society, Farnham 054375
Farnham Galleries, Simpson College, Indianola 044755
Farnhem Maltings Gallery, Farnham 039489
Farnier, Anne-Marie, Paris 100274
Farningham Pine, Farningham 084393
Farnsworth, John Richard, Münster 126498
Lo Faro, Catania 127265
El Faro, Elche 129518
Il Faro, Firenze 106050
Faro, Artur Lopo, Porto 080081
Faro, Maria José, Porto 109373
El Faro del Fin del Mundo, Buenos Aires 055204
El Faro del Fin del Mundo, Buenos Aires 136718
Farolfi, Pierluigi, Firenze 127335
Farouq Corner Museum, Helwan . . 009339
Farr, Cincinnati 088237
Farradèche, Christian, Hambye . . . 063121
Farradèche, Janine, Chatonrupt-Sommermont 062239
Farrando & Lemoine, Paris 121147
Farrar-Mansur House and Old Mill Museum, Weston 049124
Farrar, Straus & Giroux, New York . . 135426
Farré, Barcelona 140985
Farrel, Lisboa 109286
Farrell, Michael, Seattle 092994
Farrell, Michael, Seattle 092995
Farrelly, Tring 086920, 131609
Farrer, Singapore 080469
Farrington, John, Dublin 074914
Farrington Gallery, Farrington Gurney 113059
Farris, Diane, Vancouver 097466
Farrods, J.D., New York 117888
Farrs Gallery, Woking 114718
Farsetti, Milano 106213
Farsettiarte, Prato 106474
Farsettiarte di Franco Farsetti, Milano 121705
Farsh Museum, Teheran 022613
Farshchian Museum, Sa'd-Abad Museum, Teheran 022614
FART, Černigiv 112376
Farthings, Lynton 085886
Fartygsmagasinet i Stockholm, Stockholm 081948, 122253, 141153
Fartygsmuseet, Göteborgs Maritima Centrum, Göteborg 036294
Faru, Saint Louis 092238, 119203
Faruk, Hanau 103250
Farums Arkiver og Museer, Farums Museer, Farum 008859
Farvan, Charlotte 087949
Farvergården, Kerteminde 008949
Farzin, Dallas 088511
Fasaani, Helsinki 060518
Fasaani, Muijala 060616
Fasanella, Giovanni, Roma 128036
Fasanella, Margherita, Milano 075709
Fasano, Attilio, Napoli 075987
Fasciani, Leonardo, Giubiasco 082475, 130036
Fasciati, Luciano, Chur . . . 082314, 111356, 135005
Fascination Street Gallery, Denver . 088682
Fascino, Padova 127802
Fascino, Rotterdam 108184
Fase 7, Castello de la Plana 110305

Fasel, Oswald, Belfaux 082188
Fashion Design Books, New York . . 142652
Fashion Institute of Technology, State University College of Art and Design, New York 051820
Fashion Museum, Hasselt 003496
Fasone, Placido, Firenze 106051
Fassbender, Ingrid, Chicago 115414
Fassbender, Ingrid, Chicago 115415
Fassbinder- und Weinbaumuseum, Straß im Straßertale 002718
Fassier, Cyrille, Longny-au-Perche . 063984
Fassnacht, Emeran, München 072694, 104171
Fastberg & Söner, Skoghall 122239
Fastnachtmuseum, Nassereith 002351
Fastnachtmuseum Schloß Langenstein, Orsingen-Nenzingen 019482
Fastnachtsmuseum, Herbstein 017881
Fastnachtsmuseum Fasenickl, Kipfenberg 018256
Fastoso, Michele, Milano 127588
Faszinosum, Borna 016349
Fat Chance, Los Angeles 089766
Fat Elvis, Baltimore 087666
Fata Libelli, Paris 138369
Fata Morgana, Saint-Clément-la-Rivière 133697
Fatahillah Museum, Jakarta 022422
F.A.T.E. in Review, Charleston 136460
Fatec, Iserlohn 071631
Fath, Gunter, Salies-de-Béarn 068091
Fath, Martin, Kaiserslautern 071681
Father Marquette National Memorial and Museum, Saint Ignace 047634
Father Pandosy Mission, Kelowna . 005671
Father Time Antiques, Chicago 088083
Father Weyland Gallery, Epworth . . 043719
Fathy, Ibrahim, Cairo 060441
Fathy Tantawi, Cairo 060442
Faton, Dijon 133465
Fattibene, Sabina, Roma 106533
Fatto, Amano, Garmisch-Partenkirchen 070935
Fatto a Mano, Bern 082206
Fattorini, Franco, Roma 128037
Fattorini, Massimo, Firenze 075335
Fattorini, P., Firenze 075336
Fattorini, Remo, Firenze 127336
Fatucchi, Finisio, Milano 127589
Fatzer, B., Zug 141368
Faubourg, Amsterdam . . . 077844, 128536
Faubourg Diffusion, Paris 100275
Faubourg Saint-Gilles, Liège 058299, 123653
Fauchart, Josette, Paris 065900
Fauchatre, Christophe, Campagne-les-Hesdin 061928
Faucher-Touvron, Brigitte & Raphaël, Sainte-Hermine 068065
Fauchet, Bruxelles 057942
Faucheux, Arnaud, Soulge-sur-Ouette 068273
La Faucille d'Or, Paris 065901
Fauconberges, Beccles 083466
Faudou-Fayolle, Chapareillan 124186
Faudree, Charles, Tulsa 093303
Faulconer Gallery at Grinnell College, Grinnell 044359
Fauld Town and Country Furniture, Hereford 130788
Faulkner, Ian, Abingdon 130284
Faulkner County Museum, Conway . 043131
Faulkner House Books, New Orleans 142612
Faulstich-Strümpfler, S., Bremen . . 070018
Faunas, Madrid 110502
Faure, Jean-Jacques, Genève 141249
Fauroux, Philippe, Vic-Fezensac . . .068843, 125022
Faurschou, København 098552
Fauser, Dettingen unter Teck 070237
Fauser, Reutlingen 104724
Fauser, Adolf, Dettingen unter Teck 070238
Fauser, Adolf, Göppingen 071028
Fauske Museum, Fauske 030832
Faust, Arthur, München 104172
Faust-Museum, Knittlingen 018292
Faux Finishes by Clarence, Farmington Hills 088827
Faux-Mouvement, Metz 099708
Fauxtiques, Seattle 092996
Favand, Brigitte, Uzès 068670
Favardin, Patrick, Paris . . 065902, 100276
Favell Museum of Western Art and Indian Artifacts, Klamath Falls 045028
Faverais, Josiane, Craon 062545
Favereaux, Lille 138119
Favero, Fiorenzo & Bellucco, Silvano, Padova 076091
Favorite Things, Denver 088683
Favre, Chaillé-les-Marais 062069
Favre, Christian, Royan 067310
Favre, Daniel, Lyon 064126
Favre, Françoise, Carouge 082291
Favre, Frédéric, Marennes 064281
Favre, Geneviève, Avignon 098894
Favre, Monique, Marans 064254
Favre Antiquité Brocante, Modane . 064572
Favre-Boschung, Christine, Le Tholonet 124310
Favreau, Lucie, Montréal 058951
Favrel, Didier, Vendôme 068759
Favrel, Jean-François, Plancoët . . . 066843
Fawcett Books/Well Spring, New York 135427
Fawick Art Gallery, Baldwin-Wallace College, Berea 042154
Fawkes, Keith, London 141789
Fawley Court Historic House and Museum, Henley-on-Thames 039727
Fay, Hans, Thannhausen 139780
Fay, Pammy, Indianapolis 089296
Fayard, Arthème, Paris 133601
Faye, Henriette, Carcassonne 061975
La Fayence d'Autrefois, Teting-sur-Nied 068377
Faye's Auction Gallery, Richmond . . 123072
Faye's Collectibles, Louisville 089986
Fayet, Reims 067068
Fayette, Gilbert, Villeurbanne 068960
Fayette Art Museum, Fayette 043827
Fayette County Historical Museum, West Union 049102
Fayette County Museum, Washington Court House 048974
Fayette Heritage Museum, La Grange 045065
Fayetteville Museum of Art, Fayetteville 043833
Fayla, Bruxelles 096188
Fayt, I., Nideggen 104439
Fazazz, Christchurch 079025
Fazio, Maria Caterina, Roma 076454
Fazzi, P., Lucca 134598
FB, Auxerre 098883
F.Donald Kenney Museum and Art Study Wing, Saint Bonaventure 047616
Fea, Alessandra, Roma 076455
Fearnley, Nambour 094925
Feast VzW., Berchem 052672
Feathers Gallery, Den Haag 107916
Featherston Gallery, Masterton 108501
Featherston Heritage Museum, Featherston 030494
Featherston Memorabilia Museum, Featherston 030495
Feats of Clay, Austin 114983
Feats of Clay, Columbus 115776
Feature, New York 117889
Featured Wood Gallery, Australind . 094183
Féau & Cie., Paris 065903
Febbraio, Franco, Napoli 075988
Febvre, Gilles, Lyon 099559
Fecarotta, Palermo 076146
Feddi, Abdellah, Casablanca 077651
Fedeli, Andrea, Firenze 127337
Fedelich, Ghylaine, Riom 067149
Feder, Jörg, Germering 139135
Gina Feder & Alexander Zentgraf, Murnau 104384
Federaçao de Amigos de Museus do Brasil, São Paulo 052705
Federaçãon de Amigos dos Museus de Portugal, Lisboa 054003
Federación Argentina de Asociaciones de Amigos de Museos, Buenos Aires 052445
Federación Chilena de Amigos de los Museos, Santiago de Chile 052784
Federación Española de Anticuarios, Madrid 054111
Federación Española de Asociaciones de Amigos de los Museos, Madrid . . 054112
Federación Mexicana de Asociaciones de Amigos de los Museos, México . . 053863
Federal Hall National Memorial, New York 046330
Federal Precious Metals, San Francisco 092786
Federal Reserve Bank of Boston Collection, Boston 042323
Federal Reserve Board Art Gallery, Washington 048904
Federatie Kunstuitleen (FKU), Den Haag 053884
Federation Antiques, Cincinnati . . . 088238
Fédération des Amis des Musées de Belgique, Bruxelles 052673
Fédération des Associations Européennes des Galeries d'Art, Paris 052939
Fédération des Ecomusées et des Musées de Société, Besançon 052940
Fédération des Maisons d'Ecrivain et des Patrimoines Littéraires, Bourges . 052941
Fédération Française des Conservateurs-Restaurateurs, Paris 052942
Fédération Française des Sociétés d'Amis de Musées, Paris 052943
Fédération Hellénique des Amis des Musées, Athinai 053665
Fédération Internationale des Musées du Jouet et de l'Enfance, Moirans-en-Montagne 052944
Federation Lighting and Antiques, Canterbury 055627
Fédération Mondiale des Sociétés d'Amis de Musées, Paris 052945
Fédération Nationale des Experts Professionnels spéc. en Oeuvres d'Art, Paris 052946
Federation of Art Societies, Singapore 034292, 054048, 134891
Federation of Artistic and Culture Organizations of Korea, Seoul . . . 053818
Federation of British Artists, London 054376
Federation of Canadian Artists, Vancouver 052750
Federation of Modern Painters and Sculptors, New York 054756
Federation of Museums and Galleries in Wales, Aberystwyth 054377
Fédération Régionale des Amis des Musées du Nord-Pas de Calais, Dunkerque 052947
Federation Trading, Adelaide 055313
Federazione Italiana delle Associazioni Amici dei Musei, Firenze 053754
Federazione Italiana Mercanti d'Arte, Milano 053755
Federchen Verlag, Neubrandenburg 134305
Federici, Anna, Roma 076456
Federici Antonio, Roma 128038
Federkiel, Gmünd, Niederösterreich 133071
Federseemuseum Bad Buchau, Bad Buchau 015676
Fedora Antiques, Winnipeg 059458
Fedrenes Minne, Hidrasund 030891
La Fée aux Miettes, Paris 065904
Feehan & Co, Cork 074875, 139956
Feekery, Liam & Associates, London 131020
Feeling, Lourmarin 099526
Feering and Kelvedon Local History Museum, Kelevedon 039839
Feerique, Amsterdam 077845
Feet First: The Scholl Story, North Chicago 046520
Fefeye, Liège 058300
Fegan, Dallas 132009
Feheley, Toronto 097267
Feher, Anne-Laure, Paris 124660
Fehérhajó Galéria, Budapest 105508
Fehmarn Antik, Burg auf Fehmarn . 070091
Fehn- und Schiffahrtsmuseum, Rhauderfehn 019815
Fehnmusuem Eiland, Großefehn . . . 017567
Fehringer, Gertrud, Bätterkinden . . . 129906
Fehrle-Choms, C., Schwäbisch Gmünd 104851
Feichter, Bad Gastein 137151
Feichtner & Mizrahi, Wien 095819
Feiden, Margo, New York 117890
Feierabend, W., Zürich 082965
Feiertag, Siegen 139727
Feige, Karin, Glückstadt 071011
Feigen, New York 117891
Feigen, Richard L., New York 090868
Feigl, Anton, Bad Füssing 101645
Feijt, Leiden 078566
Feil, Werner, Hallstadt 125796
Feilchenfeldt, Walter, Zürich 112067
Feilding, Linnet, London 113606
Feilding & District Art Society, Manawatu 053918, 108490
Feille, Clairac 099136
Feinberg, Alan, Washington 120286
Feinberg, Robert, Milwaukee 117185
Feining-Giesinger, Lucia, Altach . . . 095463
Feinman, S.E., New York 117892
Feintes, Joël, Paris 065905
Feira de Arte Contemporânea, Lisboa 093842
Feira de Arte Moderna e Contempoânea - Porto, Leça da Palmeira 093843
Feira de Artes Plásticas e Antiguidades, Batalha 093844
Feira Internacional de Artesanato, Curitiba 093616
Feiss, Muri (Aargau) 082680
Feitian, Anxi 059570
Fejkiel, Jan, Kraków 108934
Fekete-Ház, Móra Ferenc Museum Szeged, Szeged 021858
Fekete Sas Patikamúzeum, Székesfehérvár 021867
Fel, Joseph, Aurillac 061075
Felberturmmuseum, Mittersill 002321
Felbrigg Hall, Norwich 040605
La Felce, Milano 106214
Feld- und Grubenbahnmuseum, Solms 020241
Feld- und Industriebahnmuseum (FIM), Freiland 001865
Feldbaumer, Norberg, Graz 123359
Feldberg, Uwe, Mühlhausen, Thüringen 072605
Feldès, Chantal, Ehnen 128467
Feldhaus, Ulrich, Castrop-Rauxel . . 125425
Feldhausen-Rihm, Johanna, Karlsruhe 125997
Feldherrnhalle, München 019053
Feldman, Marc, Paris 065906
Feldman, Ronald, New York 117893
Feldmann, Moosburg an der Isar . . 072594
Feldmann, David, Onex 122345
Feldmann, D.E., Abensberg 125046
Feldmeijer, Marry, Delft 107887
Feledy-Gyűjtemény - Feledy Ház, Miskolci Galéria, Miskolc 021785
Felekidis, Konst., Kalamaria 105425
Feletin, Thierry, Provins 121227
Felici, Orlando, Roma 128039
Felicie Press, New York 135428
Felicitas-Antiquitäten, Bern 082207
Felicity, Campbell, New York 132469
Felicity of Terrigal, Terrigal 056705
Felisi, Sergio, Parma 076206
Felissimo, New York 090869
Felix, Rosenheim 104763
Felix, Sevilla 081584
Félix, Six-Fours-les-Plages 068246
Felix, Winterthur 130222

Félix, Patrick, Aubais 061027
Félix-Arnaud Huet, Monique de, Paris 065907
Felix Chavez, New York 117894
Felix-Müller-Museum im Zehntspeicher, Neunkirchen am Brand 019257
Felix-Nussbaum-Haus Osnabrück mit Sammlung der Nidersächsischen Sparkassenstiftung, Osnabrück . . 019493
Felix Ravenna: Rivista di Antichita Ravennati, Cristiane e Bizantine, Ravenna 135900
Felix Valle State Historic Site, Sainte Genevieve 047727
Los Feliz Antiques, Los Angeles . . . 089767
Fell, Anthony, Holt, Norfolk 084703
Fell Engine Museum, Featherston . . 030496
Fell Locomotive Museum, Featherston 030496
Fellay Urzua, María Cecilia, Santiago de Chile 059526
Felle, Dr. M., Kempten 103531
Fellenz, Saint Louis 092239
Fellini, Fresno 088906
Fellner, Bernard, Morayfield 123270
Fellner & Scholtz, Oberursel 073163
Fellner von Feldegg, Marie-Luise, Krefeld 103774
Fellows & Sons, Birmingham 122416
Fellows, Maurice, Birmingham 083531, 130390
Fellows of Contemporary Art, Los Angeles 054757
Fellowship of Makers and Researchers of Historical Instruments, London . . 054378
Fells Point Antique Mart, Baltimore . 087667
Felly, Haarlem 078452
Felman, Jacqueline, Paris 100277
Fels, W., Bocholt 069875
Felsberg-Museum, Lautertal, Odenwald 018536
Felsch, Fieberbrunn 056978, 095506
Felsenburg Neurathen, Lohmen, Sachsen 018678
Felsendome Rabenstein, Chemnitz . 016556
Felsengarten Sanspareil mit Morgenländischem Bau, Wonsees 020978
Felsenkeller-Labyrinth im Hirschberg - Brauereimuseum, Beilngries 015938
Felsenmeer-Museum, Hemer 017870
Felsenmuseum, Bernstein, Burgenland 001751
Felsted Studio, Felsted 113064
Felte, Patrick, Vannes (Morbihan) . . 101429
Feltrinelli, Giangiacomo, Milano . . . 134611
Felzmann, Ulrich, Düsseldorf 121383
Fema, Santiago de Chile 059527
Femme Rochas, Cairo 060443
Fenaux, Brigitte, Lons-le-Saunier . . 121039
Fendalton Antiques, Christchurch . . 079026
Fendel, Heinrich & Vera, Gehrden, Hannover 125702
Fene, Valenciennes 068689
Fene, Valenciennes 068690
Fenech, Adrian, San Giljan 107450
Fenelon, Paris 124661
Fenelon Falls Museum, Fenelon Falls 005442
Fenes, Piraeus 105440
Fénestra, Eric, Condom 062453
La Fenetre, Wien 057412
Fenêtre-sur-Cour, Cour-Cheverny . . 062509
Feng, Shenzhen 097975
Fenghua Xikou Museum, Fenghua . 007068
Fenglin Shan Art, Guangzhou 097721
Fengxian Museum, Shanghai 007233
La Fenice, Milano 075710
La Fenice, Roma 076457
La Fenice, Roma 076458
La Fenice-Nottoli, Saint-Paul-de-Vence 067941
Fenichell, Jill, New York 090870
Fenichell-Basmajian, New York . . . 090871
Fenicios, Buenos Aires 055205
Feniks, Ljubljana 080653, 109958
Fenimore Art Museum, Cooperstown 043138
Fenix, Amsterdam 140298
Fenix, Göteborg 110909
Fenix, Miami 117067
Fenix, Stockholm 081949
Fenlan, Olney 131345
Fenland and West Norfolk Aviation Museum, West Walton 041342
Fenner & Co., Tavistock 122721
Fenning, James, Dun Laoghaire . . . 139971
Fenollar Olivert, José, Valencia 081654, 129773
Al-Fenoun Al-Gamila, Cairo 060444
Fens, Amsterdam 077846
Fensch, Seremange-Erzange 068227
Fenske, Edmonton 120802
Fenske, C. G, Kürn 126157
Gershon & Rebecca Fenster Museum of Jewish Art, Tulsa 048652
Fenton Glass Museum, Williamstown 049189
Fenton History Center-Museum and Library, Jamestown 044829
Fenton House, London 040145
Fenton Maclaren, Oakland 091416
Fenway, Boston 115174
Fenway, Boston 131847
Fenwick, Toledo 120079
Fenwick, Toledo 120080
Fenwick, Toledo 120081
Fenwick & Fenwick, Broadway 083757
Fenwick Gallery, Warkworth 114647
Fenyes Adolf Terem, Budapest 105509
Feo Garcia, Maria Teresa, Valencia . 110806
Fer de Lance, Paris 135708
Feral, Jacqueline, Toulouse 068507
Feraud, Patrick, Champtercier 062129
Ferber, Daniel, Daun 125447
Ferber, Lothar, Wettenberg 074377
Ferchaud, Monique, Bordeaux 061606
Ferdinand Domela Nieuwenhuis Museum, Heerenveen 029691
Ferdinando, Steven, Queen Camel . 142011
Fere, Gent 058181
Ferenczy Károly Múzeum, Szentendre 021881
Ferens Art Gallery, Hull City Museum & Art Gallery, Kingston-upon-Hull 039885
Feret, Marc, Paris 124662
Ferfoje Eski, T.D., İstanbul 083133
Ferganskij Oblastnoj Kraevedčeskij Muzej, Fergana 049389
Ferges, Düsseldorf 125529
Ferguson, Cincinnati 088239
Fergusson Gallery, Perth 040696
Feria de Antigüedades, Valencia . . . 093862
Feria de Antigüedades y Galerías de Arte, Madrid 093863
Feria de Arte, La Cumbre 093563
Feria de Arte Contemporáneo, Buenos Aires 093564
Feria de Arte Contemporáneo, México 093817
Feria de Libros, Buenos Aires 136719
Feria de Videoarte en Barcelona, Barcelona 093864
Feria del Arte Contempráneo Sevilla, Sevilla 093865
Feria Internacional de Arte Contemporáneo, Madrid 093866
Feria Internacional de Arte Contemporáneo Marbella, Marbella 093867
Feria Internacional de Arte y Antigüedades, Madrid 093868
Feria Internacional de Arte y Antigüedades, México 093818
Feria Internacional de Artesanias, Córdoba 093565
Feria Internacional del Arte, Valencia 093869
Feria Internacional del Diseño, Diseño, Bogotá 093634
Feria Regional de Antigüedades, Albacete 093870
Férignac, Ateliens, Hautefort 124257
Ferilli, Stuttgart 073970
Feringa Sach - Ortsgeschichte und heimatkundliche Sammlung, Unterföhring 020541
Ferjan, Ljubljana 080654
Ferlini, Bruno, Mons 058340, 137530
Ferlini, Renata, Bologna 127149
Ferma, Barcelona 080846
Fermanagh County Museum at Enniskillen Castle, Enniskillen 039447
Ferme Apicole du Morvan, Rouvray 014145
Ferme aux Abeilles, Saint-Brévin-les-Pins 014204
La Ferme Caussenarde d'Autrefois, Hures-la-Parade 012117
Ferme de Hot Springs, Mohon 064573
Ferme de la Claison, Saint-Étienne-du-Bois 014278
La Ferme des Étoiles, Mauroux . . . 012979
Ferme d'Hier et d'Aujourd'hui, Aviré 010602
Ferme du Château, Beveuge 061420
Ferme du Château, Beveuge 061421
Ferme du Désert-Exposition, Lausanne 111615
La Ferme Marine-Musée de l'Huître et du Coquillage, Cancale 011087
Ferme-Musée à Pans de Bois de Sougey, Montrevel-en-Bresse 013224
Ferme-Musée Barret, Pineuilh 013819
Ferme-Musée de Bray, Sommery . . 014821
Ferme-Musée de la Tonnelière, Courcerault 011509
Ferme-Musée des Frères Perrel, Moudeyres 013258
Ferme-Musée du Contentin, Sainte-Mère-Eglise 014611
Ferme-Musée du Léon, Tréflaouenan 015032
Ferme-Musée du Montagnon, Fournets-Luisans 011882
Ferme-Musée lé Moho dé Soyotte, Musée Arts et Traditions Populaires, Sainte-Marguerite 014602
Fermes-Musée du Pays Horloger, Grand-Combe-Châteleu 011983
Fermette, Epreville 062793
Fermin Garcia, Felipe, Madrid 081300
Fern, Natascha von, München 104173
Fernandes, Paulo, Rio de Janeiro . . 096604
Fernandes & Costa, Carlos, Lisboa . 079925
Fernandez, Zamora 081725
Fernández, Carlos, Santiago de Chile 059528
Fernandez, J., Barcelona 080847
Fernández, Jacinto, Montevideo . . . 122779
Fernández, Jesús Angel, León 081171
Fernández, José, Santiago de Chile 059529
Fernandez, Miguel, Rosières 067225
Fernandez, Salvador, Barcelona . . . 080848
Fernandez Antiguedades, Sevilla . . 081585
Fernandez Battagliese, Isaura, Vigo 081702
Fernández Blanco Libros Antiguos, Buenos Aires 136720
Fernandez de Bobadilla, Teresa, Madrid 129620
Fernandez-Escarzaga, Belen Roiz, Santander 081555
Fernandez Gallart, Manuela, Valencia 081655
Fernandez Lopez, Maria Consuelo, Murcia 081442
Fernandez Muñiz, Maria Jesus, Gijón 110359
Fernando, Pedro, Belo Horizonte . . 096462
Fernbank Museum of Natural History, Atlanta 041855
Fernbank Science Center, Atlanta . . 041856
Fernbrook Gallery, Kurrajong Heights 094720
Ferndown Gallery, Ferndown 113065
Ferner Galleries, Auckland 108314
Ferner Galleries, Auckland 108315
Ferner Gallery, Wellington 108620
Fernhill House, Belfast 038661
Fernie and District Historical Museum, Fernie 005444
Fernlea Antiques, Manchester 085915
Fernwold, Pittsburgh 091818
Féron, Richard, Agon-Coutainville . 060673
Ferozsons, Lahore 108778, 134851, 140711
Ferra, Ray, Los Angeles 089768
Ferracini & Paglia, Bologna 075074
Ferraglia, Parma 076207
Ferraglia, Parma 076208
Ferraguti, Parma 140088
Ferran Cano, Barcelona 110148
Ferran Cano, Palma de Mallorca . . . 110676
Ferrand, Michel, Dammarie 062591
Ferrando, Andrea Armando, Genova 127450
Ferrando, Francesca, Genova 075466
Ferranti, Ugo, Roma 106534
Ferrara, Paris 065908
Ferrara, Jonathan, New Orleans . . . 117434
Ferrara, Rosario, Catania . 075248, 127266
Ferrara, Stefano, Bologna 075075
Ferrari, Clusone 134572
Ferrari, Milano 127590
Ferrari, Saint Louis 092240
Ferrari, Bernard, Nice 065081
Ferrari, Claudia Gian, Milano 106215
Ferrari, Gian-Mario, Mendrisio 082656
Ferrari, Giancarlo, Milano 127591
Ferrari, Giorgio, Roma 076459
Ferrari, Neldo, Modena 127731
Ferrari, Olivier, Châlonvillars 062098
Ferrari Antiquités, Martignargues . . 064413
Ferrari-Auer, Bolzano 134558
Ferrari-Auer, Bolzano 140000
Ferrari Museum, Gotemba 026474
Ferrari Rosetta de Antigüedades, Caracas 093528
Ferrari Sarzábal, Aldo, Montevideo . 122780
Ferraro, Roma 106535
Ferraro, Arturo, Napoli 127769
Ferraroni, Patrizia, Modena 075909
Ferraton, Alain, Bruxelles . 120724, 137435
Ferrazza, Renato, Roma 076460
Ferrazzutti, Pam, Toronto 059186
Ferré, Jacqueline, Ingrandes-sur-Loire 063208
Ferré, Patrick, Saint-Mathurin-sur-Loire 067653
Ferreira, Bruxelles 057943
Matos Ferreira, Lisboa 109287
Ferreira, Oakland 132568
Ferreira, António Almeida, Braga . . 079808
Ferreira, Felismina, Porto 080082
Ferreira, Gilberto M. Teves, Ponta Delgada 129185
Ferreira, Helena Simões, Lisboa . . . 079926
Ferreira, Henrique Meneses, Porto . 080083
Ferreira, João, Cape Town 110023
Ferreira, Luísa & David, Porto 080084
Ferreira, Manuel, Porto . . 121947, 140866
Ferreira, Maria Lurdes, Lisboa 079927
Ferreira, Maria Meira, Lisboa 109288
Ferreira & Manteigas, Lisboa 079928
Ferrer, Bruxelles 120725
Ferrer Carrer, Ramon, Barcelona . . 110149
Ferrer Marcs, Barcelona 110150
Ferrer Martí, Valencia 081656
Ferrería de Mirandaola, Legazpia . . 035324
Ferrero, Nice 099834
Ferrero, K.-C., Chêne-Bourg 082309
Ferrero González, Julia, Burgos . . . 129460
Ferrers, Staunton Harold 114483
Ferret, Georges, Villers-les-Guise . . 068931
Ferret Bookshop, Wellington 140675
Ferretjans, Montevideo 122781
Ferretti, München 104174
Ferretti & Guerrini, Roma 076461
Ferrey, Laurent, Pirey 066835
Ferreyra Lesye y Comp, Córdoba . . 055254
Ferri, Paris 121148
Ferriani & Beccaria, Milano 127592
Ferrien-Marcognet, Eric, Paris 065909
Ferrier, Patrick, L'Isle-sur-la-Sorgue 063934
Ferriere de Lassus, André & Vonia, Chomerac 062303

Ferris, Sacramento 092155
Ferris, Maurice, Oklahoma City . . .091497, 132578
Ferrito, Giancarlo, Palermo 076147
Ferro, Antonino, Palermo 076148
Ferro, Nunzio, Messina 127501
Ferro, Paola, Milano 075711
Ferroni, Montréal 058952
Ferroni, Alice, Genova 127451
Ferrow, David, Great Yarmouth 130748, 141636
Ferrucci, Arnaldo, Roma 076462
Ferruzzi, Balbi Ferruccio, Venezia . . 076936
Ferry, Wargrave 087023, 131650
Ferry, Marcel, Rambervillers 067037
Ferry, Nicole, Paris 100278
Ferry Building Gallery, West Vancouver 006793
Ferry Park Gallery, MacLean, New South Wales 094754
Ferrymead Heritage Park, Christchurch 030464
Fersen, Monaco 077601
Fersini, Massimo, Roma 128040
Fersini, Rocco, Roma 128041
Ferstl, Robert, Karlsruhe . 071717, 125998
Fert-Rifaï, Nathalie, Nyons 065251, 138267
Fertala, Franz, Basberg 069480
Ferzt, Mimi, New York 117895
Fesel, Bernd, Düsseldorf 102491
Fesseler, K., Berlin 125196
Fessler, Paul, Rotthalmünster 126751
Fester, Den Haag 107917
Festetics-Kastély, Keszthely 021765
Festival et Marché Européen des Arts Céramiques, Saint Quentin-la-Poterie 093659
Festival-Institute Museum, Round Top 047555
Festung Kniepaß, Unken 002768
Festung Königstein, Königstein, Sächsische Schweiz 018355
Festung Marienberg mit Fürstenbaumuseum, Würzburg . . 020995
Die Festung Rosenberg - Deutsches Festungsmuseum, Kronach 018414
Festung Wilhelmstein im Steinhuder Meer, Wunstorf 021012
Festungs- und Waffengeschichtliches Museum, Philippsburg 019616
Festungsanlage-Museum Senftenberg, Senftenberg 020189
Festungsmuseum, Salzburger Museum Carolino Augusteum, Salzburg . . . 002549
Festungsmuseum Heldsberg, Sankt Margrethen 037502
Festungsmuseum Reuenthal, Reuenthal 037444
Fethard Park and Folk Museum, Fethard 022787
Fethiye Kültür Merkezi, Fethiye . . . 038067
Fethiye Müzesi, Fethiye 038068
Fetlar Interpretive Centre, Fetlar . . . 039497
Fetoon, Sharjah 112466
Fetsund Lenser Fløtingsmuseum, Fetsund 030833
Fetting & Minx, Berlin 138773
Fettinger, Hannes, Bad Goisern . . . 137152
Fety, F., Bruxelles 057944
Fety, Margaret, Bordeaux 138039
Fetzer, J., Ludwigsburg, Württemberg 139422
Fetzian & Kourd, Athinai 074588
Feuerhelm, Hermann, Bochum 138883
Feuerstätten-Ausstellung im Lausitzer Bergbaumuseum, Hoyerswerda . . 018011
Feuerstein, Karl Heinz, Dornbirn . . . 056961
Feuerstein, Thyl, Berlin 125197
Feuerstein, Wolfgang, Dornbirn . . . 123346
Feuerwehr-Museum Schloß Waldmannshofen, Creglingen . . . 016601
Feuerwehrhistorische Ausstellung, Schmannewitz 020057
Feuerwehrmuseum, Feurwehrverein Stuttgart e.V, Stuttgart 020368
Feuerwehrmuseum, Adligenswil . . . 036816
Feuerwehrmuseum, Bayreuth 015909
Feuerwehrmuseum, Dietzenbach . . 016707
Feuerwehrmuseum, Endingen 037065
Feuerwehrmuseum, Kaufbeuren . . . 018208
Feuerwehrmuseum, Kreuzlingen . . 037219
Feuerwehrmuseum, Lengenfeld, Vogtland 018610
Feuerwehrmuseum, Niederwiesa . . 019314
Feuerwehrmuseum, Perchtoldsdorf 002412
Feuerwehrmuseum, Rehau 019764
Feuerwehrmuseum, Roding 019859
Feuerwehrmuseum, Salem, Baden . 019968
Feuerwehrmuseum, Sankt Florian . 002575
Feuerwehrmuseum, Sayda 020002
Feuerwehrmuseum, Spalt 020258
Feuerwehrmuseum, Stadtprozelten 020288
Feuerwehrmuseum, Steyrermühl . . 002709
Feuerwehrmuseum, Türnitz 002756
Feuerwehrmuseum, Wasserburg am Inn 020686
Feuerwehrmuseum, Wienerbruck . . 003038
Feuerwehrmuseum des Landkreises Harburg, Außenstelle des Freilichtmuseums am Kiekeberg, Marxen 018856
Feuerwehrmuseum Grethen, Parthenstein 019567
Feuerwehrmuseum Hannover, Hannover 017751
Feuerwehrmuseum Kalmbach, Riedbach 019827
Feuerwehrmuseum Kradolf-Schönenberg, Kradolf 037217
Feuerwehrmuseum Lövenich, Erkelenz 017023
Feuerwehrmuseum Musberg, Leinfelden-Echterdingen 018551
Feuerwehrmuseum Ravensburg, Ravensburg 019733
Feuerwehrmuseum Salzbergen, Salzbergen 019970
Feuerwehrmuseum Schleswig-Holstein, Norderstedt 019330
Feuerwehrmuseum Schröttinghausen, Preußisch Oldendorf 019670
Feuerwehrmuseum Winnenden, Winnenden 020913
Feuerwehrmuseum Zeven, Zeven . . 021062
Feuerwehrsmuseum, Tumeltsham . 002764
Feuille d'Acanthe, Thionville 068396, 124955
La Feuille d'Or, Allschwil 129896
Feuille d'Or et Mercure, Paris 124663
Feuilleraie, Vieux-Moulin 068870
Feuillets Libres, Toulouse 101344
Feulner, Richard, Lichtenfels, Bayern 126219
Feurer, Dr. Reto, Obing 139621
Feurstein, Hubert, Schruns 057305
Fevik Auksjonsforretning, Fevik . . . 079384
Février, André, Jouars-Pontchartrain 063255
Février, Laurence, Marboue 064260
Few, Ted, London 085290
Fey, Karlsruhe 071718
Fey, Dr. D., Eutin 070671
Fey, Th., Hittfeld 071535
Fey, Thomas, Hittfeld 125943
Fey-Weidner, Gudrun, Wiesbaden . . 127009
Feycolor, Mäder 095675
FFotogallery, Cardiff 112811, 135133
FH Art Forum, Paris 100279
FH Coin Exchange, New York 090872
Fi Donc, Alkmaar 107617
F.I.A., Dardilly Cedex 062601
FIA Galerie, Amsterdam 107711
Fiakermuseum, Wien 002897
Fiano, Fabrizio, Roma 076463
Fiartega, Vigo 110863
Fibber Mcgee, Seattle 092997
Fiberart Gallery, Saint Ives, Cornwall 114362
Fiberscene, San Francisco 119665
Fibre Arts Studio, Vancouver 097467
La Fibule, Paris 065910
La Fibule, Rabat 077691
Ficara, Santo, Firenze 106052
Ficarra, Fausto, Roma 076464
Fichera & Perkins, New York 090873
Fichet, Jacques, Avèze (Puy-de-Dôme) 061122
Fichtelgebirgsmuseum, Wunsiedel . 021011
Fichter, Aurelio, Frankfurt am Main . 070738
Fichter, Jürgen & Regina, Karlsdorf-Neuthard 071704
Fichtlscherer, Barbara, Müllheim, Baden 126341
Fick Fossil and History Museum, Oakley 046605
Fickels, San Antonio 132811
Ficker, Klaus, Salzburg . . . 057245, 123442
Fidalgo et Fréres, Saint-Ouen 067775
Fidanza, Alberto, Bern 082208
Fiddes & Son, Cardiff 130510
Fiddy's, Osterwald 073257
Fidelo, Edinburgh 112994
Fi.de.v. Casa d'Aste, Roma 121721
Fidia, Brescia 075167, 105997
Fidia Edizioni d'Arte, Lugano 135040
Fidor, Barcelona 080849, 140986
Fidow-Fiddickow, A., Köln 071935
Fidus, Schwülper 139725
Fiebach & Minninger, Köln 103614
Fiebig, Lutz, Miesbach 134202
Fiebig, S., Syke 074035
Fiechter, Münchenstein 130121
Fiedler, Carl, Bremerhaven 102261
Fiedler, Inge, Garbenheim 070928
Fiedler, Karl, Waldstetten 126963
Fiedler, Ulrich, Köln 103615
Fiedler Memorial Museum, Seguin . 048106
Field, San Francisco 142944
Field Dalling Gallery, Field Dalling . 113066
Field Museum, Chicago 042841
Field Museum of Natural History, Chicago 042842
Field of Dreams, Dallas . . 088512, 142367
Field of Dreams, Houston 142436
Field of Dreams, Houston 142437
Field of Dreams, Indianapolis 089297
Field of Dreams, Las Vegas 089568
Field of Dreams, Louisville 089987
Field of Dreams, Norfolk 091376
Field of Dreams, Saint Paul 092360
Field, Staff and Woods, Rochester . 086387
Fieldcote Museum, Ancaster 005011
Fielder, John, Denver 115994
Fielding, Gent 123620
Fielding L. Wright Art Center, Cleveland 042981
Fieldings, Haslingden 084612
Fields, J., New York 117896
Fields, J., New York 117897
Fields Galleries, Tulsa 120194
Fields of Valor, Vancouver 059358
Fieldstone, Dallas 115878
Fier Archaeological Museum, Fier . 000020
Fiera Internazionale d'Arte Moderna e Contemporanea, Milano 093762
Fiera Piacentina di Numismatica, Filatelia e Collezionismo, Piacenza 093763
Fieros Fedros, N., Lefkosia 059953
Fiesta Galerie, Paris 065911
De Fietsenstalling, Den Haag 107918
Fife Folk Museum, Ceres 039027
Fifh, Casablanca 077652
Fifteen Minutes, Minneapolis 090355
Fifteen Ten Antiques, Charlotte 087950
Fifteenth Century Bookshop, Lewes 141726
Fifth Avenue Antiques, Birmingham 087755
Fifth Avenue Antiques, Milwaukee . 090295
Fifth Avenue Antiques, San Diego . . 092635
Fifth Avenue Galleries, Columbus . . 115777
Fifth Class, Atlanta 114875
Fifth Element Pottery, Portland 118995
Fifth Maine Regiment Center, Peaks Island 046853
Fifth Meeting House, Lancaster . . . 045138
Fifth Parallel Gallery, Regina 006252
Fifth Street Antiques, Kansas City . . 089499
Fifties-Sixties, Amsterdam 077847
Fifty Crows, San Francisco 119666
Fifty Five, Göttingen 071045
Fifty-Five Mercer Gallery, New York 117898
Fifty-One Antiques, Toronto 059187
Fifty One Fine Art Photography, Antwerpen 096065
Fig Tree Gallery, Fresno 116174
Figari, Dr. Luisa, Cagliari 127245
Figgis, Moyard 139977
Fighter World, Williamtown 001619
Figl, Anton, Sankt Pölten 057295
Figl, Felice, Linz 095655
Figl, Matthias, Plankenberg 057209
Figueiredo, Carlos Alberto Veiga, Lisboa 140830
Figueiredo, Carlos H.C., Rio de Janeiro 058586
Figueiredo, Luís Boaventura, Lisboa 109289
Figueiredo, Oswaldo, São Paulo . . . 058709
Figueiredo, Rui, Lisboa 079929
Figuière, Geneviève, Lasalle 063544
Figuline, Viroflay 069007
Figuline Antiquités, La Couarde-sur-Mer 063347
Figur, Rainer, Ronnenberg 126732
Figurative Design Group, San Francisco 092787
Die Figuren Gallerie, Klingenberg am Main 103565
Figurencabinett Madamme Lucrezia, Rosegg 002539
Figures de Style, Paris 100280
Fiji Museum, Suva 009450
Le Fil d'Ariane, Antibes-Juan-les-Pins 098849
Le Fil d'Ariane, Toulouse 138634
Le Fil du Bois, Tournai 123672
Fil du Temps, Clermont-Ferrand . . . 138077
Le Fil du Temps, Sanary-sur-Mer . .068112, 124924
Fil Expo, Cournon-d'Auvergne 099181
Filambule, Lausanne 082545
Filaretos, Athinai 074589
Filatelica e Numismatica, Civitanova Marche 093764
La Filature, Anduze 060838
Fildier-Cartophilié, Paris 133602
Fileman, David R., Steyning 086702, 131534
Filene, Washington 120287
Filentroc, Anceaumeville 060831
Filey Museum, Filey 039499
Filial Moskovskogo Gosudarstvennogo Universiteta Kultury i Iskusstv, Naberežnye Čelny 050648
Filial Moskovskogo Gosudarstvennogo Universiteta Kultury i Iskusstv, Norilsk 050651
Filidarte, Palermo 106426
Filigrana, Venezia 128389
Filipiak, Deborah, Buffalo 115254
Filipp, D., Halle, Westfalen 071181
Filippis, Konstantin, Athinai 074590
Filipstads Bergslags Hembygdsgård, Filipstad 036270
Fillaire, Marie-Christine, Mantes-La Jolie 121058
La Fille du Pirate-Dieutegard, Paris 065912, 124664
Filleau, Joël, Belin-Béliet 061331
Les Filles du Calvaire, Paris 100281
Filley, Christopher, Kansas City 089500
Fillipi, B., Seattle 142986
Fillmore County Historical Museum, Fountain 044018
Fillmore Historical Museum, Fillmore 043842
Filloux, Georges, Paris 138370
Film Forum - Film Archives, Collingswood 043048
Film Line Gallery, New York 117899
Film- och Biografmuseet, Säter . . . 036551
Filman Fine Art, Dorking 112953
Filmart, Los Angeles 116765

Filmmuseet, Oslo 031075
Filmmuseet, Regionmuseet i Skåne, Kristianstad 036400
Filmmuseum, Münchner Stadtmuseum, München 019054
Filmmuseum, Museum van Hedendaagse Kunst Antwerpen, Antwerpen 003160
Filmmuseum Bendestorf, Bendestorf 015942
Filmmuseum Berlin, Stiftung Deutsche Kinemathek, Berlin 016018
Filmmuseum Foundation Nederlands, Amsterdam 029180
Filmmuseum Landeshauptstadt Düsseldorf, Düsseldorf 016828
Filmmuseum Potsdam, Potsdam . . 019655
Filmsammlungen Laxenburg, Laxenburg 002211
Filmworks USA, Atlanta 087474
Fils, Françoise, Ecuras 062763
Fils, Gimpel, London 113607
Filsinger, Claus, Neulußheim 073002
The Filson Historical Society Museum, Louisville 045487
Filtzer, Gerald, Barbizon 098917
Filupeit, Harry, Frankfurt am Main . 102763
Fimmers-Van der Cruysse, Brugge . 057772
Fin-Art, Nova Gorica 109997
Fin de Siglo, Buenos Aires 136721
Fina, Gianfranco, Torino 076812
Finacchioli, Rita, Roma 128042
Final Chapter, Tuggeranong 137116
Final Lap, Las Vegas 089569
Final Touch, Indianapolis 116461
Final Touch-Up, Virginia Beach 133010
Finanzgeschichtliche Sammlung der Bundesfinanzakademie, Brühl, Rheinland 016467
Finard, Alain, Paris 065913
Finarte España, Madrid 122057
Finarte Semenzato, Firenze 121685
Finarte Semenzato, Milano 121706
Finarte Semenzato, Napoli 121713
Finarte Semenzato, Roma 121722
Finarte Semenzato, Venezia 121738
Finaz de Villaine, Manuela, Paris . . 065914
Finch, Sandgate 086505, 131454
Finch, Hector, London 085291
Finch, Simon, Holt, Norfolk 141674
Finch, Simon, London 141790
Finch Foundry Working Museum, Okehampton 040637
Finchcocks, Living Museum of Music, Goudhurst 039614
Finches, Saint Louis 092241
Finchingfield Antiques Centre, Finchingfield 084401
Finchley, London 085292, 131021
Finck, Thomas, Quittelsdorf 073400
Finckenstein, Dresden 102429
Find, Los Angeles 089769
Findeisen, Jürgen, Berlin 069604
Finders Keepers, Long Beach 089633
Finders Keepers, Napier 079164
Finder's Keepers, Phoenix 091739
Finders Keepers, Pittsburgh 091819
Finders Keepers, Toronto 059188
Finders Keepers Antiques, Denver . 088684
Finders Keepers Katikati, Katikati . . 079131
Findi, Paris 100282
Findibus, Basel 082139
Findings, Philadelphia 091635
Findlater Museum, Dublin 022742
Findlay, Cynthia, Toronto 059189
Findlay jr., David, New York 117900
Findlay, David, New York 117901
Findley, Peter, New York 117902
Findley, Wally, New York 117903
Findling, Hamburg 139175
Findorff, Ursula, Lüneburg 072356
Finds, Tucson 093231
Fine and Performing Arts Department, Creighton University, Omaha 051886
Fine and Performing Arts Department, Saint Louis University, Saint Louis 052079
Fine and Performing Arts Department, Southwestern Michigan College, Dowagiac 051269
Fine and Performing Arts Department, York College, City University of New York, Jamaica 051524
Fine Antique Restoration, Denver . . 132036
Fine Antiques and More, Las Vegas 089570
Fine Art, Barsinghausen 069474
Fine Art, Granada 110374
Fine Art, Kreuzau 072086
Fine Art, Moskva 109509
Fine Art, Roermond 108165
Fine Art, Saint Louis 119204
Fine Art, Wennigsen 105202
Fine Art Acquisitions, New York . . . 117904
Fine Art Affordables, New York 117905
Fine Art and Antique, Colombo 081758
Fine Art and Artists, Washington . . . 120288
Fine Art and Framing, Jacksonville . 116525
Fine Art Associates, Honolulu 116209
Fine Art Association of Ho Chi Minh City, Ho Chi Minh City 055120
Fine Art by Jane, Long Beach 116668
Fine Art Collectables, Lower Portland 056117
Fine Art Commissions, London 113608
The Fine Art Company, Mumbai . . . 105770
Fine Art & Curios, North Shore 079191
Fine Art Department, Indian River Community College, Fort Pierce . . 051348
Fine Art Department, Ithaca College, Ithaca 051511
Fine Art Department, Joliet Junior College, Joliet 051536
Fine Art Distributors, Alphington . . . 094149
Fine Art Division, Concord College, Athens 050918
Fine Art & Frames, Lytham Saint Annes 114020
Fine Art Gallery, Cannes 099065
Fine Art Gallery, Hong Kong 097783
The Fine Art Gallery, Rochester . . . 114322
Fine Art Gallery, Winnipeg 097582
Fine Art Gallery at Centro Cultural Aztlan, San Antonio 047793
Fine Art Hawaii, Honolulu 116210
Fine Art Images, Richmond 119109
Fine Art Inn, Salt Lake City 119342
Fine Art & Interiors, Norwich 114163
Fine Art Limited, Chicago 115416
Fine Art Living, Chadstone 055659
Fine Art Market Report, Stamford . . 136461
Fine Art Painting Conservation, New Orleans 132411
Fine Art Paper Conservation, Winnipeg 123866
Fine Art Photographics, Arbroath . . 112516
Fine Art Prints on Canvas, San Diego 119503
Fine Art Rentals and Sales, Sacramento 119145
Fine Art Research, Beijing 135651
The Fine Art Resource, Mumbai . . . 105771
Fine Art Restoration, Denver 132037
The Fine Art Society, London 085293, 113609
Fine Art Studios, Eketahuna 108451
Fine Art Trade Guild, London 054379
Fine Art University Exhibition Hall, Ha Noi 049526
Fine Arts, Berlin 101852
Fine Arts, Oostende 096398
Fine Arts, Columbia College, Sonora 052189
Fine Arts and Communications Division, Foothill College, Los Altos 051628
Fine Arts and Humanities Department, Fayetteville State University, Fayetteville 051332
Fine Arts Associates, Los Angeles . 116766
Fine Arts Association, Willoughby . . 054758
Fine Arts Building Gallery, Chicago . 115417
Fine Arts by Todd, Atlanta 114876
Fine Arts Center, East Stroudsburg University, East Stroudsburg 051281
Fine Arts Center for New River Valley, Pulaski 047280
Fine Arts Center Gallery, Maryville College, Maryville 045719
Fine Arts Center of Hot Springs, Hot Springs 044627
Fine Arts Center of Kershaw County, Camden 042581
Fine Arts Collection, Decorah 043357
Fine Arts Collection, Lucay-le-Male 064020
Fine Arts Collection of the Franciscan Monastery, Orebić 007767
Fine Arts Conservation, Chicago . . . 131898
Fine Arts Conservation Group, New York 132470
Fine Arts @ Cypress College, Cypress 051218
Fine Arts Department, Academy of Art College, San Francisco 052122
Fine Arts Department, Allan Hancock College, Santa Maria 052144
Fine Arts Department, Benedict College, Columbia 051185
Fine Arts Department, Benedictine University, Lisle 051613
Fine Arts Department, Bismarck State College, Bismarck 050990
Fine Arts Department, Blue Mountain Community College, Pendleton . . 051925
Fine Arts Department, Boston College, Chestnut Hill 051106
Fine Arts Department, Bucks County Community College, Newton 051845
Fine Arts Department, Burlington County College, Pemberton 051923
Fine Arts Department, Capital University, Columbus 051195
Fine Arts Department, City College of San Francisco, San Francisco 052123
Fine Arts Department, College of Mount Saint Vincent, Riverdale 052029
Fine Arts Department, Community College of Allegheny County, West Mifflin . 052356
Fine Arts Department, Fairleigh Dickinson University, Rutherford 052063
Fine Arts Department, Fort Steilacoom Community College, Tacoma 052242
Fine Arts Department, Gogebic Community College, Ironwood 051507
Fine Arts Department, Haverford College, Haverford 051451
Fine Arts Department, High Point College, High Point 051462
Fine Arts Department, Hill Junior College, Hillsboro 051464
Fine Arts Department, Illinois Central College, East Peoria 051280
Fine Arts Department, Indiana University South Bend, South Bend 052190
Fine Arts Department, Indiana University Southeast, New Albany 051783
Fine Arts Department, Jefferson Community College, Louisville 051643
Fine Arts Department, Kean College of New Jersey, Union 052290
Fine Arts Department, Keystone College, Factoryville 051318
Fine Arts Department, Lakeland Community College, Kirtland 051556
Fine Arts Department, Loyola University of Chicago, Chicago 051126
Fine Arts Department, McLennan Community College, Waco 052317
Fine Arts Department, Manchester Community College, Manchester . 051666
Fine Arts Department, Marymount Manhattan College, New York . . . 051821
Fine Arts Department, Mississippi Valley State University, Itta Bena 051512
Fine Arts Department, Niagara University, Niagara Falls 051846
Fine Arts Department, North Georgia College, Dahlonega 051219
Fine Arts Department, Northwestern Connecticut Community College, Winsted 052395
Fine Arts Department, Ohio Wesleyan University, Delaware 051243
Fine Arts Department, Oral Roberts University, Tulsa 052281
Fine Arts Department, Pace University, Pleasantville 051965
Fine Arts Department, Pearl River Community College, Poplarville . . 051970
Fine Arts Department, Pikeville College, Pikeville 051949
Fine Arts Department, Queens University of Charlotte, Charlotte 051099
Fine Arts Department, Quincy Junior College, Quincy 052004
Fine Arts Department, Regis University, Denver 051251
Fine Arts Department, Saint Francis College, Loretto 051626
Fine Arts Department, Saint Francis Xavier University, Antigonish 049773
Fine Arts Department, Saint Michael's College, Colchester 051171
Fine Arts Department, Santa Barbara City College, Santa Barbara 052138
Fine Arts Department, Seattle University, Seattle 052166
Fine Arts Department, South Plains College, Levelland 051598
Fine Arts Department, State University College at Buffalo, Buffalo 051056
Fine Arts Department, Truett-McConnell College, Cleveland 051153
Fine Arts Department, Tusculum College, Greeneville 051412
Fine Arts Department, University of Arkansas at Little Rock, Little Rock 051614
Fine Arts Department, University of Arkansas at Monticello, Monticello 051748
Fine Arts Department, University of Waterloo, Waterloo 049831
Fine Arts Department, Victoria College, Victoria 052309
Fine Arts Department, Virginia Intermont College, Bristol 051031
Fine Arts Department, Virginia State University, Petersburg 051932
Fine Arts Department, West Hills Community College, Coalinga . . . 051165
Fine Arts Department, Xavier University, Cincinnati 051140
Fine Arts Department Gallery, Xavier University, Cincinnati 042924
Fine Arts Division, Brigham Young University, Laie 051570
Fine Arts Division, Campbellsville College, Campbellsville 051067
Fine Arts Division, Cottey College, Nevada 051782
Fine Arts Division, Middlesex Community College, Middletown 051707
Fine Arts Division, Niagara County Community College, Sanborn 052135
Fine Arts Division, Ventura College, Ventura 052307
Fine Arts Division, Yuba College, Marysville 051685
Fine Arts Exchange, Chicago 115418
Fine Arts Exhibitions, Austin 041925
Fine Arts Express, Dallas 115879
Fine Arts Fund, Cincinnati 115629
Fine Arts Gallery, Al-Khobar 109672
Fine Arts Gallery, Breckenridge . . . 042392
Fine Arts Gallery, Columbus 043100
Fine Arts Gallery, Cypress 043255
Fine Arts Gallery, Korçë 000024
Fine Arts Gallery, Los Angeles 045419
Fine Arts Gallery, New Orleans 046251
Fine Arts Gallery, New York 117906
Fine Arts Gallery, Tiranë 000033
Fine Arts Gallery, Creighton University, Omaha 046677
The Fine Arts Gallery, New Mexico Highlands University, Las Vegas . . 045195
Fine Arts Gallery of New Orleans, New Orleans 117435
Fine Arts Humanities Division, Ohio University - Chillicothe Campus, Chillicothe 051135

Fine Arts Imports, Columbus 088407
Fine Arts International, London 113610
Fine Arts Kraków, Kraków 129036
Fine Arts Museum, Sa'd-Abad Museum, Teheran 022615
Fine Arts Press, Saint Leonards . . . 133055
Fine Arts Section, University of Québec, Trois-Rivières 049824, 097405
Fine Arts Services, Cincinnati 115630
Fine Arts Services, Los Angeles . . . 116767
Fine Arts Society-Indianapolis, Indianapolis 054759
Fine Arts Warehouse, Houston 116314
Fine Arts Work Center, Provincetown 054760
Fine Books Classic, Croydon 136873
Fine Books Oriental, London 141791
Fine China Restoration, Malvern, Victoria 123259
Fine English Antiquités, Bruxelles . . 057945
Fine European Arts Corporation, Miami 117068
Fine Furniture Studio, Warwick 123683
Fine Impressions, Seattle 119913
Fine-Lines Fine Art, Shipston-on-Stour 131492
Fine Paintings, Bruxelles 096189
Fine & Performing Arts, Oakland Community College, Farmington 051326
Fine Pine Antiques, Totnes 086906, 131602
Fine Print Books, Newtown, New South Wales 137031
Fine Refinishing, Albuquerque 131741
Fine Secolo, Firenze 075337
Fine Sporting Art, Lauder 113352
Fine Woodcraft Gallery, Pemberton . 095061
Fine Young Artists, Auckland 078943
Finearts Contra, Berlin 101853
Finecraft Workshop, London 085294, 131022
Finedon Antiques, Finedon 084406
Fineline Gallery, Buffalo 087874
Finer Things, Nashville 117351
Finer Things of Life, Beechworth . . 055463
Finesilver Gallery, San Antonio 119410
Finesse Fine Art, Dorchester 084177
La Finestra, Amsterdam 077848
La Finestra Sull'Arte, Palermo 076149
Fingerhutmuseum, Creglingen 016602
Fingers, Auckland 108316
Finials, Washington 093412
Finial's Unlimited, New York 132471
Fini's Hoeve, Vriezenveen 030294
Finish Line, Las Vegas 132214
Finish Shop, Milwaukee 132364
Finished Look, Memphis 132322
Finishing Touch, Atlanta 131772
The Finishing Touch, Hornchurch . . 113273
Finishing Touch, Milwaukee 090296, 132365
Finishing Touches, Derby 084159
Finishing Touches, Minneapolis . . .090356, 132380
Finishing Traditions, Calgary 123744
Finition de Bois, Montréal 123786
Finitude, Bordeaux 138040
Finizio, Rosario, Napoli 127770
Fink, André & Cecile, Woollahra . . . 056864
Fink, Bob, Virginia Beach 123134
Fink, Josef, Lindenberg im Allgäu . . 134161
Fink, P., Altomünster 069158
Fink, Peter, München 072695
Fink, Ralf-Andreas, Düsseldorf 070378
Fink, Wilhelm, Paderborn 134343
Finkbein, Wolfgang, Gotha 102985, 139150
Finkbeiner, Miriam, Bad Honnef . . . 125103
Finlaggan Centre, Ballygrant 038576
Finlands Svenska Skolmuseum, Munsala 009883
Finlandssvenskt Konstcentrum, Pro Artibus Foundation, Ekenäs 009467
Finlay, K.W., Ciliau Aeron 084013
The Finley House, Wayne 049032
Finnantic, Helsinki 060519, 124044
Finnegan, Chicago 115419
Finnegan, Robin, Darlington 084134
Finnetunet, Grue Finnskog 030867
Finney, Michael, London 141792
Finney County Kansas Historical Museum, Garden City 044139
Finnkroken Bygdemuseum, Tromsdalen 031275
Finnskogsmuseet, Viksjöfors 036793
Finnvedens Auktionsfirma, Hillerstorp 122160
Fins de Siècles et Plus, Bruxelles . . 057946
Finspångs Auktionstjänst, Finspång 122134
Finspångs Slott, Finspång 036273
Finstermacher, Bolzano 075128
Finta Múzeum, Túrkeve 021911
Finuki, Singen, Hohentwiel 073827
Fióka Art, Budapest 105510
Fiol, Xavier, Palma de Mallorca 110677
Fiona & Co., Sacramento 092156
Fior, Jake, London 141793
Fior di Loto, Cagliari 075208
Fiore, Angelo, Roma 128043
Fiore, Carmela, Torino 076813
Fiore, Maria Giuseppina, Roma . . . 076465
Fiore, Mario, Napoli 127771
Fiore, Mario, Roma 076466
Fiore Antichità, Torino 076814
Fiorentini, Enrico, Roma 076467
Fiorentino, Buenos Aires 136722
Fioretto, Firenze 075338
Fiorillo, Marcos Eugenio, Bologna . . 127150
Fiorini, Firenze 075339
Fiorini, Giovanni, Brescia 127214
Fiorini, Umberto, Roma 128044
Il Fiorino, Pisa 076241
Fioroni, Giuseppina, Roma 106536
Fiorucci, Mario, Roma 128045
Fira d'Antiguitats, Colleccionisme i Obres d'Art, Mahón 093871
Fira d'Antiguitats de Mollerussa, Mollerussa 093872
Fira d'Antiguitats i Obres d'Art, Palma de Mallorca 093873
Fira d'Antiquaris i Brocanters, Girona 093874
Firbob & Peacock, Knutsford 113342
Fircks-Huth, Iris, Fuchstal 102892
Firdusi, Chennai 074791
Fire Antiques, Miami 090171
Fire Brigades Museum, Reigate . . . 040818
Fire Brigadesmens Museum, Wellington 030636
Fire Fighting Museum, Toronto 006597
Fire Museum, Kurwongbah 001164
Fire Museum, Minsk 003131
Fire Museum of Maryland, Lutherville 045523
Fire Museum of Memphis, Memphis 045758
Fire Museum of Texas, Beaumont . . 042085
Fire Museum of York County, York . 049347
The Fire Place, Hungerford 084756
Fire Police Museum, Sheffield 040995
Fire Power, the Royal Artillery Museum, London 040146
Fire Service Museum, Hethersett . . 039743
Fire Services Museum of Victoria, East Melbourne 001000
Fire-Works Gallery, Newstead 094949
Fire Works @ Pioneer Square, Seattle 119914
Fire Works @ University Village, Seattle 119915
Fire Works @ Westlake Center, Seattle 119916
Firearms Technology Museum, Orange 001357
Firebird Russian Arts, Bath 112575
Fireborn, Pittsburgh 118919
Fireborne, Portland 091936
Firecracker, San Francisco 092788
Firefighters' Museum of Nova Scotia and National Exhibition Centre, Yarmouth 006888
Firefighting Museum, Chatham, Ontario 005259
Firefly Antiques, Minneapolis 090357
Firehouse Antiques, Tucson 093232
Firehouse Art Center, Norman 046506
Firehouse Art Gallery, Garden City . 044140
Firehouse Gallery, Denver 115995
Firehouse Gallery, Fort Worth 116141
Firehouse Gallery, Oak Bluffs 046579
Firehouse Museum, Ellicott City . . . 043678
Firehouse Museum, Nevada City . . 046181
Firelands Association for the Visual Arts, Oberlin 054761
Firelands Historical Society Museum, Norwalk 046564
Firelight Museum, Leongatha 001182
Fireman's Hall Museum, Philadelphia 046941
Firenze Gallery, Taipei 098069
The Fireplace, London . . . 085295, 131023
Fireside Book Company, Columbus . 142352
Firestone, Eric, Tucson 093233
Firewire Gallery, Totnes 114590
Firino, Carla, Torino 128306
Firinu, Piergiorgio, Torino 134691
Firla, S., Bonn 102178
Firle Place, Firle 039502
Firmani, Giorgio, Roma 128046
Firmenmusemum Novatech, Reutlingen 019806
Firnberg, S., London 131024
Firnkäs-Kuhnt, München 072696
First-Art, Amsterdam 077849
First Art Gallery, Lymington 114014
First Arts and Antiques, Chicago . . . 088084
First at Bat, Buffalo 087875
First Bright, Bruxelles 096190
First Cavalry Division Museum, Fort Hood 043920
First Class, Lohnsburg am Kobernaußerwald 137228
First Coast Trading Post, Jacksonville 089411
First Consolidated School in Minnesota, Saum 048016
The First Division Museum at Cantigny, Wheaton 049136
First Draft, Surry Hills 095251
First Edition Collectibles, Houston . 089079
First Floor Art Gallery, Erevan 094109
First Garden City Heritage Museum, Letchworth 039989
First Glas Galerie, München 104175
First Hussars Citizen Soldiers Museum, London 005785
First Infantry Division Museum, Würzburg 020996
First Light Gallery, Camborne 112785
First Love, Singapore 109796
First Michigan Museum of Military History, Holland 044573
First Missouri State Capitol, Saint Charles 047618
First National Bank of Chicago Art Collection, Chicago 042843
First Nations Art, Albuquerque 114785
First Oriental Rugs of Boston, Boston 087819
First Penny Farthing Museum, Knutsford 039911
First Peoples Art, Vancouver 097468
First Raadsaal Museum, Bloemfontein 034556
First Street Antiques, Milwaukee . . 090297
First Street Gallery, Jacksonville . . 116526
First Street Gallery, New York 117907
First Street Gallery, Vancouver 097469
First Tennessee Heritage Collection, Memphis 045759
First Territorial Capitol of Kansas, Fort Riley 043970
First View, Stourton 114500
First White House of the Confederacy, Montgomery 045994
Firstsite, Colchester 054380
Firstsite at the Minories Art Gallery, Colchester 039119
Fiřt, Karel, Slany 060190
The Firth Gallery, Pickering 114247
Firth Tower Historical Reserve, Matamata 030540
Fiscal Prints, Ferny Creek 055817
Fisch, P., Regensburg 073455
Fischbach, New York 117908
Fischbacher, Paris 138371
Fischbacher, Potsdam 139662
Fischbacher, Anton, Schladming . . . 057304
Fischer, Dr., Baden-Baden 069410
Fischer, Berlin 101854, 133772
Fischer, Bogotá 059837
Fischer, Cleveland 131959
Fischer, Hagen, Westfalen 103045
Fischer, Kaufbeuren 103521
Fischer, Morsum 072598
Fischer, München 072697
Fischer, Ritterhude 073546
Fischer, Stuttgart 104973
Fischer, A., Naunhof bei Grimma . . 072948
Fischer, Albert, Inning am Ammersee 125971
Fischer, Albert, Kaufbeuren 071769
Fischer, Andrea, Stuttgart 126848
Fischer, Andreas, Dresden 070312
Fischer, Arno, Dießen am Ammersee 125462
Fischer, Carsten, Bonn . . . 069917, 125352
Fischer, Christian, Berlin 125198
Fischer, Danielle, Saint-Ouen 067776
Fischer, Dora, Paris 065915
Fischer, E., Frickenhausen, Württemberg 070884
Fischer, E., Kirchenlamitz 071853
Fischer, Frank-Peter, Solingen 073852
Fischer, Friedl, Bamberg 101727
Fischer, Fritz, Gerhardshofen 070974
Fischer, G., Velbert 105110
Fischer, Gabriele, Augsburg 101611
Fischer, Gebhard, Sankt Gallen 111867
Fischer, Gesine, Ludwigsburg, Württemberg 072307
Fischer, Gottfried Michael, Wien . . . 057413
Fischer, H.A., Bern 129956
Fischer, Heide, Oberstdorf 073156
Fischer, Heinz, Osthofen 073261
Fischer, Hermann, Balingen 069436
Fischer, Jacques, Paris . . 065916, 100283
Fischer, Jan, Süderfahrenstedt 126892
Fischer, Jeffrey W.T., Highgate, South Australia 055981
Fischer, Jochen, Bonn 069918
Fischer, Dr. Jürgen, Heilbronn 071471, 103332, 121453
Fischer, Karin, Aachen 133711
Fischer, Klaus, Arnsberg 069181
Fischer, Klaus, Kirchhain 071854
Fischer, Konrad, Düsseldorf 102492
Fischer, Manfred, Braunschweig . . 133837
Fischer, Martina, Schwäbisch Gmünd 126783
Fischer, Michael, Igling 134070
Fischer, Nikolaus, Frankfurt am Main 102764
Fischer, Norbert, Dresden 070313
Fischer, R., Bad Buchau 069273
Fischer, R., Lienen 072247
Fischer, Serge, Montpellier 064739
Fischer, T., Münster 104357
Fischer, Trude & Kuno, Luzern 111690, 122339, 141273
Fischer, Walter, Aich-Assach 056913
Fischer, Bleker & Fischer, Freiburg im Breisgau 102858
Fischer Fine Art, Mouans-Sartoux . . 099774
Fischer & von Koeding-Fischer, Karlsruhe 071719
Fischer-Menshausen, Angelika, Hamburg 125812
Fischer-Reinhardt, Thea, Berlin . . . 101855
Fischer Trendy, Deventer 078274
Fischer- und Webermuseum Steinhude, Steinhude 020310
Fischer-Zöller, Marlies, Düsseldorf . 070379

Fischereimuseum, Neuhausen am Rheinfall . . . 037378
Fischereimuseum, Wassertrüdingen 020691
Fischerplatz-Galerie, Ulm . 074140, 105091, 134436
Fischetti, Carmine, Milano . . . 075712
Fischinger, Markus, Ravensburg . . . 104670
Fischinger, Peter, Stuttgart . . . 073971
Fischinger Heimathaus mit Schimuseum, Fischen im Allgäu . . . 017126
Fischl, Joseph, New York . . . 117909
Fischle, Erwin, Stuttgart . . . 073972
Fischli, Markus, Appenzell . . . 082091
Fischlin & Cie, Nyon . . . 111783
Fischötter, Birgit, Frankfurt am Main . . . 102765
Fish Museum Golden Angel, Damascus . . . 037826
Fish Tales, Fish Creek . . . 136896
Fishbourne Roman Palace and Museum, The Sussex Archaeological Society, Chichester . . . 039069
Fisher, Christchurch . . . 108393, 128921
Fisher, Pittenweem . . . 114251
Fisher, Rozelle . . . 137077
Fisher, Barbara, Cammeray . . . 136844
Fisher, Laura, New York . . . 090874
Fisher Gallery, Los Angeles . . . 045420
Fisher Grove Country School, Frankfort . . . 044038
Fisher Mackenzie, Plymouth . . . 135296
Fisher Museum of Forestry, Harvard University, Petersham . . . 046911
Fisher & Sperr, London . . . 131025, 141794
Fisheries Museum of the Atlantic, Lunenburg . . . 005808
Fisherman's Cottage, Tooradin . . . 001555
Fisherman's Life Museum, Halifax . 005571
Fisherman's Museum, Musgrave Harbour . . . 005972
Fishermen's Life Museum, Jeddore Oyster Ponds . . . 005652
Fishermen's Museum, Hastings . . . 039691
Fishermen's Museum, Pemaquid Point . . . 046862
Fishermen's Museum, Port-de-Grave . . . 006179
Fishers, Auckland 078944, 108317, 128902
Fisher's Upholstery, Jacksonville . . 132180
Fisherton Mill, Salisbury . . . 114389
Fishing Museum, Kibbutz Ein Gev . . 023000
Fishlake Antiques, Fishlake . . . 084409
Fisk University Galleries, Aaron Douglas Gallery and Carl Van Vechten Gallery, Nashville . . . 046145
Fiska- og Náttúrngripasafn Vestmannaeyja, Vestmannaeyjar . . . 021985
Fiskars Museum, Fiskars . . . 009480
Fiske Antiques, Armadale, Victoria . 055372
Fiskemuséet i Kaskö, Kaskinen . . . 009675
Fisken, Austin . . . 087571
Fiskeri- og Søfartsmuseet, Esbjerg . 008844
Fiskerimuseet og Kunstsmie i Sund, Sund i Lofoten . . . 031250
Fiskerimuseet på Hjertøya, Molde . 031028
Fiskerimuseum i Måløy, Måløy . . . 031005
Fissé, Victor, Romanel-sur-Morges . 082750
Fister, Eckental . . . 102595
Fister, Paul, Recourt-le-Creux . . . 067047
Fitch, Michael, Sandgate . . . 086506
Fitch-Febvrel, New York . . . 117910
Fitchburg Art Museum, Fitchburg . . 043848
Fitchburg Historical Society Museum, Fitchburg . . . 043849
Fitchett, Alan, Brighton . . 083695, 130443
Fitoussi, Lucien, La Chapelle-en-Serval . . . 063313
Fittkau, Stefan, Berlin . . . 125199
Fitton Center for Creative Arts, Hamilton . . . 051434
Fitz, Constantin, Schondorf . . . 126778
Fitzgerald, Phoenix . . . 091740
Fitzjohn, London . . . 141795
Fitzkaplan, New York . . . 132472
Fitzpatrick, Richard, Ottawa . . . 137675
Fitzpatrick, Tony, Chicago . . . 135346
Fitzroy, Prospect . . . 056504
Fitzroy Antiques, Ascot Vale . . . 055408
Fitzroy & Everest, Rotterdam . . . 078719, 140518
Fitzroy Gallery, Fitzroy . . . 094532
Fitzsimmons, Chicago . . . 088085
Fitzthum, Andreas, Griesheim . . . 071101
Fitzwilliam Antiques Centre, Peterborough . . . 086231
Fitzwilliam Museum, Cambridge . . 038962
Fiumano, Farmilo, London . . . 113611
Fiumicelli, Stefano, Bologna . . . 075076
La Fiura, Gaetano, Palermo . . . 076150
Ignez Fiuza, Fortaleza . . . 096524
Fiúza, Ceres, Fortaleza . . . 096525
Five Art & Images, Todmorden . . . 114580
Five Broads off Broadway, San Antonio . . . 092512
Five Civilized Tribes Museum, Muskogee . . . 046109
Five Council Museums East Headquarters, Cupar . . . 039196
Five O Seven Antiques, Dallas . . . 088513
Five Owls Bookshop, Richmond, North Yorkshire . . . 142016
Five Story Antique Market, Shanghai . . . 059738
Five Trees, Saint Paul . . . 092361
Five Ways Galleries, Kalorama . . . 094678
Fiver Fiduciaria, Torino . . . 121733
Fizek & Skowron, Poznań . 079687, 121897
Fjärilshuset Haga Tradgard, Stockholm . . . 036624
Fjeld, Ole Jørgen, Oslo . . . 079433
Fjerritslev Bryggeri- og Egnsmuseum, Fjerritslev . . . 008860
Fjordane Forsvarsmuseum, Nordfjordeid . . . 031052
Fjordmuseet, Jyllinge . . . 008945
Fjøsangersamlingene, Fjøsanger . . 030837
Flaccovio, S.F., Palermo . . 134649, 140087
Flach, Stockholm . . . 111020
Flach, Henry, Auma . . . 125081
Flach, Uwe, Gera . . . 070968
Flach, Volker, München . . . 126376
Flachard, Rémi, Paris . . . 138372
Flachmann, Roland, Dresden . . . 125490
Flachs, Peter, München . . . 104176
Flachsmann, Hildegard, Kronberg im Taunus . . . 072092, 103793
Flachsmuseum Wegberg-Beeck, Wegberg . . . 020700
Flade, Jochen, Dresden . . . 125491
Flagler Museum, Palm Beach . . . 046795
Flagstaff Antiques, Cowes 084095, 130612
Flagstaff Gallery, Auckland . . . 108318
Flagstaff House Museum of Tea Ware, Hong Kong . . . 007115
Flagstones Pine, Melton Mowbray .085970, 131273
Flahaut, Michel, Paris . . . 124665
La Flair, Ramstein-Miesenbach . . . 073411
Flais, Gérard, Le Touquet-Paris-Plage . . . 063717
Flajszer, Saint-Ouen . . . 067777
Flak, Paris . . . 065917, 100284, 133603, 138373
Flakkebjerg Skolemuseum, Slagelse . . . 009107
Flamand, Bailleul . . . 061173
Flamary, Jean-Jacques, Aurillac . . . 061076
Flambards Victorian Village and Gardens, Helston . . . 039721
Flame!, The Gasworks Museum of Ireland, Carrickfergus . . . 039006
Flame & Grate, Bristol . . . 083737
Flame Lily Enterprises, Carindale . . 094372
Flame 'n' Grate, Barry . . . 083405
Flame Trees Gallery, Nowa Nowa . . 094995
Flament, Paul-Michel, Brécey . . . 061755
Flamingo Gallery, Las Vegas . . . 045183
Flamingo Street Antiques, Virginia Beach . . . 093353
Flammann, Winfried, Karlsruhe . . . 103488
Flammarion, Lyon . . . 138147
Flammarion, Paris . . . 133604, 138374
Flammarion Centre, Paris . . . 138375
Flanagan, Seattle . . . 092998
Flanagan Valley Campus Art Gallery, Lincoln . . . 045318
Flanagans of Buncrana, Mount Merrion . . . 074995
Flanders, Minneapolis . . . 117258
Flanders, Yokohama . . . 107142
Flanders Antiquity, Gent . . . 058182
Flanders Center, Osaka . . . 026959
Flanders Gallery, Knokke-Heist . . . 058245
Flandes Marcs, Barcelona . . . 110151
Flandrau Science Center, Tucson . . 048635
Flandrin les Trois, Paris . . . 065918
Flaningan, J. Michael, Baltimore . . 087668
Flanquart, C., Agde . . . 060661
Flao, Bernard, Les Ormes-sur-Voulzie . . . 063774
Flapper, Milwaukee . . . 090298
Flash, Bordeaux . . . 061607
Flash Art, Novi Sad . . . 109739
Flash Art Gallery, Sydney . . . 095286
Flash Art International, Milano . . . 135901
Flash Art Italia, Milano . . . 135902
Flash Color Imaging Center, Richmond . . . 119110
Flash Trash Antiques, Camperdown 055616
Flashback, Memphis . . . 090071
Flashback, Northcote . . . 056378
Flashback Antique Mall, San Antonio . . . 132812
Flashbacks, Las Vegas . . . 089571
Flaske-Peters-Samling, Ærøskøbing 008801
Flat Cat Gallery, Lauder . . 084906, 113353
Flat Rock Museum, Flat Rock . . . 005446
Flatanger Bygdemuseum, Flatanger 030838
Flatfile Gallery, Chicago . . . 115420
Flathead Indian Museum, Saint Ignatius . . . 047635
Flatland Gallery, Utrecht . . 108245, 134834
Flaujac, New Orleans . . . 090552
Flava, Bussum . . . 107884
Flavoni, Roma . . . 076468
Flax Art, Chicago . . . 115421
Flaxbourne Settlers Museum, Ward 030629
Flaxman Gallery, Stoke-on-Trent . . 041117
Flaxton Antique Gardens, Flaxton . . 084412
Flea Antique, Atlanta . . . 087475
Flea Antique Depot, Atlanta . . . 087476
The Fleamarket, London . 085296, 131026
Fleck, Ernest, Barcelona . . . 110152
Fleck & Raymond, Marseille . . . 121063
Fleckenstein, Krefeld . . . 103775
Fledderman, T.A., Cincinnati . . . 088240
Fleet, Fort Worth . . . 088853
Fleet, Hamburg . . . 134006
Fleet Air Arm Museum - Concorde, The National Museum of Science & Industry, Yeovilton . . . 041471
Fleet Boston Financial Gallery, Boston . . . 042324
Fleet Galleries, Winnipeg . . . 097583
Fleet Period Furniture, Tecoma . . . 056703
Fleetwood Museum, Fleetwood . . . 039504
Fleichhauer, U., Wünsdorf . . . 139865
Fleischer Museum, Scottsdale . . . 048058
Fleisher & Ollman, Philadelphia . . . 118758
Der Fleißige Biber, Griesheim . . . 071102
Flekkefjord Museum, Flekkefjord . . 030839
Fleming, A., Portsmouth . . 086298, 131393
Fleming, Eris, Bakers Swamp . . . 094193
Fleming Historical Museum, Fleming . . . 043858
Flemming, L., Kenzingen . . . 071796
Flensburger Schiffahrtsmuseum und Rum-Museum, Flensburg . . . 017129
Flesch, Wolfgang, Plettenberg . . . 073342
Flesch, Wolfgang, Plettenberg . . . 073343
Flessenscheepjesmuseum, Enkhuizen . . . 029561
Flesser, Helsingborg . . . 110941
Fleßner, Rastede . . . 073423
Fletcher, H.M., Much Hadham . . . 141949
Fletcher, Leda, Carouge . . . 111333
Fletcher, Michael, New York . . . 117911
Flett, Godalming . . . 113139
La Fleur, Oakland . . . 091417
Fleur de Lis Heritage Centre, Faversham . . . 039493
Fleur de Lys Gallery, London . . . 085297
Fleur de Lys Gallery, London . . . 113612
Fleuraux, Catherine, Peyrehorade . . 066789
Fleurier, Paris . . . 065919
Fleurieu Big Shed, Mount Compass 094901
Le Fleuron, Ableiges . . . 060655
Fleuron, Honfleur . . . 099342
Fleuron, Leiden . . . 140477
Fleurs du Mal, Nîmes . . . 138265
Les Fleurs du Mal, Paris . . . 138376
Fleurs du Sillon, Saint-Malo (Ille-et-Vilaine) . . . 067612
Fleury, Cahir . . . 074870
Fleury, Dublin . . . 074915
Fleury, Benoît, Dives-sur-Mer . . . 062692
Fleury, Michel, Thore-la-Rochette . 068408
Flibusterie, Saint-Tropez . . . 068014
Le Flibustier, Ars-en-Ré . . . 060995
Flick, Peter, Gardelegen . . . 139131
Flick, Stephan, Herxheim bei Landau, Pfalz . . . 125923
Flicker, Portland . . . 118996
Flieger-Flab-Museum, Dübendorf . . 037051
Fliegermuseum, Altenrhein . . . 036834
De Flierefluiter, Oss . . . 078670
Flierl, Berlin . . . 101856
Fligny, Laurence, Paris . . . 065920
Flin Flon Museum, Flin Flon . . . 005448
Flinders Fine Art Gallery, Flinders . . 094549
Flinders Gallery, Townsville . . . 095348
Flinders Lane Gallery, Melbourne . . 094812
Flinders University Art Museum, Adelaide . . . 000707
Flinner, Craig, Baltimore . . 087669, 115048, 142224
Flint, Gregory, Auckland . . . 108319
Flint, J.H., Amsterdam . . . 140299
Flint House, Scotia . . . 048052
Flint Institute of Arts, Flint . . . 043861
Flint Ridge State Memorial Museum, Glenford . . . 044210
Flintham Museum, Flintham . . . 039505
Flintlock Antiques, Stockport . . . 086721
Flipje en Jam Museum Tiel, Tiel . . . 030202
Flipo, Brigitte, Bondues . . . 061552
Flipo, Emmanuel, Pézenas . . . 101004
Flirey Art, Romans-sur-Isère . . . 101099
Flirt, Lisboa . . . 136044
Floating Gallery, Winnipeg . . . 006843
Floating Gallery, Winnipeg . . . 097584
Floating World Gallery, Chicago . . . 115422
Flobert, Thierry, Paris . . . 121149
Le Floch, Cyrillem, Saint-Martin-en-Biere . . . 067647
Flodin, Stockholm . . . 141154
Flöhchen, Burgdorf, Kreis Hannover 070097
Flößer- und Heimatmuseum, Wolfach . . . 020950
Flößer- und Schiffermuseum, Kamp-Bornhofen . . . 018146
Flößerei- und Verkehrsmuseum, Gengenbach . . . 017361
Flößereimuseum, Lychen . . . 018766
Flößermuseum Unterrodach, Marktrodach . . . 018850
Flohnburg, Nordhausen . . . 104463
Flohr-Skade & Skade, Hofstetten . . 103395
Flok, Haarlem . . . 108057
Flood Museum, Johnstown . . . 044872
Flooders Gallery, Ruthven . . . 114331
Floors, Deventer . . . 107967
Floors Castle, Kelso . . . 039841
La Flor, Torino . . . 076815
Flora, Thomas, Innsbruck . 095579, 133090
Flora Twort Gallery, Petersfield . . . 040705
Floravilla Art Gallery, Cow Bay . . . 094435
Floréal, Evreux . . . 062829, 138085
Florence, Chicago . . . 131899

Florence, Pascale, Le Port-Marly . . 063689
Florence 2500 Cedar Springs Rd, Dallas 115880
Florence Art, Marseille 064354
Florence Art Gallery, Firenze 106053
Florence Court House, Enniskillen . 039448
Florence Griswold Museum, Old Lyme 046664
Florence Hawley Ellis Museum of Anthropology, Abiquiu 041571
Florence McLeod Hazard Museum, Columbus 043101
Florence Mine Heritage Centre, Egremont 039432
Florence Museum of Art, Science and History, Florence 043870
Florence Nightingale Museum, Aylesbury 038556
Florence Nightingale Museum, London 040147
Florence Price Pioneer Museum, Florence 043868
Florence Ranch Homestead, Mesquite 045796
Florentin, Linselles 063905, 124329
Florentina Galleries, Glasgow 113109
Les Florentines, Apt 060942
Florés, København 060325
Flores, Krefeld 072069
Flores, New York 090875
Flores & Iva, New York 090876
Florewood State Park, Greenwood . 044355
Florey, Eliane, Sion 111908
Florez Torrez, Guillermo, Ploudiry . . 066866
Florian, Houston 089080
Florianerbahn, Sankt Florian 002576
Florida Adventure Museum, Punta Gorda 047284
Florida Agricultural Museum, Palm Coast 046797
Florida Art Museum Directors Association, Vero Beach 054762
Florida Association of Museums, Tallahassee 054763
Florida Coin and Jewelry, Tampa . . 093121
Florida Fine Art Consignment Gallery, Tampa 120041
Florida Frame and Art, Tampa 120042
Florida Gulf Coast Railroad Museum, Parrish 046828
Florida History Museum, Jupiter . . . 044891
Florida Holocaust Museum, Saint Petersburg 047714
Florida International Museum, Saint Petersburg 047715
The Florida Museum of Hispanic and Latin American Art, Coral Gables 043146
Florida Museum of Natural History, Gainesville 044103
Florida Pastel Association, Hollywood 054764
Florida Printmakers, Tarpon Springs 054765
Florida School of the Arts, Palatka . 051910
Florida State University Museum of Fine Arts, Tallahassee 048478
Florida's Furniture Fixers, Jacksonville 132181
Flories, K., Fort Worth 088854
Florijn, 's-Hertogenbosch 078518
Florilegium, Glebe 136918
Florin, Emmanuel, Le Taillan-Médoc 124309
Florina Museum of Modern Art, Florina 021266
Florissant Valley Historical Society Museum, Florissant 043871
Floristisches Museum, Perchtoldsdorf 002413
FLORIX Multimedia, Firenze 134584
Florke, Randy, New York 090877
Florman, Yvonne, Stockholm 129863
Flormann, Waltraud, Mannheim . . . 072420
La Flosimed, Versailles 068803
Flossoms, Mosman 056264
Fløtermuseet, Osen 031067
Flotow, Ursula, Ottobrunn 139644
Flotsam Camera Collectables, Bentley 055485
Flottmann-Hallen, Herne 017890
Floubuttek, Flou, Ettelbruck 077466
Flour Mill Gallery, Maryborough, Victoria 094794
Flour Mill Museum, Sudbury 006530
Flow Contemporary Art Gallery, London 113613
Flower House Antiques, Tenterden .086843, 131578
Flowerdew Hundred Foundation, Hopewell 044618
Flowers, London 113614
Flowers, New York 117912
Flowers, Angela, London 113615
Flowers Graphics, London 135216
Floyd County Historical Museum, Charles City 042717
Floyd County Museum, New Albany 046185
George Floyd & Mark James, London 085298
Floyd & Rita's, Toronto 059190
Flucher, Maria, Leibnitz 057144
Fluck, Eckhard, Berlin 138774
Fluck, Eckhard, Berlin 138775
Flückiger, René, Thörigen 082847
Flückiger & Fischbach, Zürich 112068
Flügel, M., Köln 103616
Flügen, Thomas, Lörzweiler 126226
Flühmann, Dr. Adrian, Zürich 141334
Flüthe, Reinhold, Telgte 074050
Flughafen Modellschau, Hamburg . 017691
Flugmuseum Aviaticum, Wiener Neustadt 003032
Flugpionier-Gustav-Weißkopf-Museum, Leutershausen 018623
Flumen Diez Martinez, Donostia-San Sebastián 129502
Flur-Galerie, Berlin 016019
Flurgalerie Eisenbart, Magdeburg . . 103988
Fluri, Margrit, Zürich 082966
Flury & Co., Seattle 092999
Flury & Co., Seattle 119917
Flury & Co., Seattle 142987
Flury, Matthias, Höchberg 139270
Fluss & Charlesworth, London 085299
Flusso, New York 117913
Flutlicht, Wien 095820, 133191
Fluweelengrot Valkenburg, Valkenburg, Limburg 030244
Flux, Liège 096378
Fluxion, Omaha 118690
Fluxus-Freunde e.V., Wiesbaden . . . 053155
Fly by Nite Gallery, Chicago 088086
Flyhistorisk Museum, Sola 031205
Flying Arts, Brisbane 094293
Flying Colours Gallery, London 113616
The Flying Cow Project, Bruxelles . . 096191
Flying Cranes Antiques, New York . 090878
Flying Dutchman, Hondarribia 081157
Flying Fish Gallery, South Melbourne 095205, 123305
Flying Goose, Beeston 112605
Flying Pig Precinct, Berry 094248
Flying Shuttles Studio, Providence . 119078
Flyingfrog, Jacksonville 089412
Flynderupgård Museet, Espergærde 008847
Flynn, James, Warminster 114648
Flynn, Norman, Sutton 131561
Flynn, William, Dublin 074916
Flypast Museum of Australian Army Flying, Oakey 001349
Flyway Gallery, Albuquerque 114786
FMR, London 136215
FMR, Paris 133605
FMR artmagazine, Milano 135903
FMR-Gruppo Art'e', Milano 134612
Foam Fotografiemuseum Amsterdam, Amsterdam 029181
Foam Lake Museum, Foam Lake . . 005449
Foata au Passe-Temps, Seine-Port . 068199
Focacci-Wieck, Veronica, Innsbruck 123391
Focal Point Gallery, Southend-on-Sea 041064
Focale-Photographie, Nyon 111784, 141285
Foch, Desvigne, Lyon 138148
Foch Antiquités, Le Creusot 063612
Fochabers Folk Museum, Fochabers 039507
Fochem, Christian, Krefeld 103776
Focke-Museum, Bremer Landesmuseum, Bremen 016411
Focks, Freren 070878
Foco Verde Noe Ciências Cultura e Arte, Belo Horizonte 096463
Focus Galeria de Arte, Rio de Janeiro 096605
Focus Gallery, Chennai 105627
Focus Gallery, London 113617
Focus Gallery, Nottingham 114175
Focus Gallery, San Francisco 119667
Focus on the Past, Bristol 083738
Fodera, New York 132473
Födisch, Helga, Wels 123485
Föglö Museet, Föglö 009481
Foelkel, Th., Köln 071936
Föll, Münster 104358
Fölsing, Gröbenzell 103006
Förde Antik, Flensburg . . . 070700, 125639
Förde Antiquariat, Flensburg 139072
Förde Galerie, Flensburg 070701
Fördergemeinschaft Kunst, Karlsruhe 053156
Fördergemeinschaft Kunst Loschwitz e.V, Dresden 053157
Förderkoje, Berlin 101857
Förderkreis der Leipziger Galerie für Zeitgenössische Kunst, Leipzig . . 053158
Förderkreis der Städtischen Galerie Karlsruhe, Karlsruhe 053159
Förderkreis des Keramikmuseums Westerwald, Montabaur 053160
Förderkreis Schloß Plüschow e.V., Plüschow 053161
Förderkreis Stadtgalerie Saarbrücken, Saarbrücken 053162
Förderkreis zeitgenössischer Kunst Kreis Euskirchen e.V., Euskirchen 053163
Förderverein Aktuelle Kunst, Münster 053164
Förderverein Keramik-Museum Berlin, Berlin 053165
Förderverein Kloster Aldersbach, Aldersbach 053166
Förderverein Künstlerhaus Hooksiel e.V., Hooksiel 053167
Förderverein Kunst und Kultur, Ostseebad Sellin 053168
Förderverein Kunst und Kultur des Bundesverbandes Bildender Künstlerinnen und Künstler Niederbayern/Oberpfalz e.V, Regensburg 053169
Förenade Antik- och Konsthandlare, Linköping 054129
Förg, Roland, Singen, Hohentwiel . . 073828
Förnbacher, Kurt, Freiburg im Breisgau 070836
Förr eller Senare, Stockholm 081950
Förster, Ludwigsburg, Württemberg 072308
Förster, Tamm 074038
Förster, Sabrina, Düsseldorf 102493
Förster, Sabrina, Düsseldorf 102494
Förster & Raab, Köln 126076
Förtsch, Berlin 138776
Förtsch, Bonn 069919
Förtsch, Tobias & Karen, Kronach . . 072089
Főszékesegyházi Kincstár és Könyvtár, Esztergom 021722
Fog, Dan, København 137894
Fogarty, Terrence, Minneapolis 117259
Fogarty, Hojsgaard & Entwistle, Auckland 108320
Fogelmarck, Stockholm 081951
Fogelsangh State, Veenklooster . . . 030260
Fogg, Sam, London 085300
Fogle, Leigh, Jacksonville 116527
Fratelli Fogliato, Torino 106672
Fogola, Torino 134692
El Fogon de los Arrieros, Resistencia 000503
La Foi, Fort-de-France 140245
Foire à la Brocante, Cogolin 062384
Le Foire au Troc, Vezin-le-Coquet . . 068836
Foire aux Antiquités, Barjac 061209
Foire aux Antiquités, Brocante et Fete du Livre Ancien, Albi-le-Séquestre . . 093660
Foire aux Images, Nîmes 138266
Foire d'Art Contemporain de Strasbourg, Strasbourg 093661
Foire des Antiquaires de Belgique, Bruxelles 093603
Foire Internationale Brocante Antiquités de Paris, Le Bourget 093662
Foire Internationale d'Art Contemporain, Bruxelles 093604
Foire Internationale d'Art Contemporain, Paris 093663
Foire Internationale du Livre Ancien, Bruxelles 093605
Foki's, Long Beach 132225
Folavril, Paris 065921
Foldalbruket, Kjøllefjord 030939
Foley, Columbus 115778
Foley, Kel, Miami 094840
Foley, Shannon C., New Orleans . . . 117436
Foley Furniture, Great Malvern 084512
Foley l'Ecuyer, Montréal 058953
Folger, Isolde, Kolitzheim 103751
Folha D'Ouro, Lisboa 129152
La Folie, 's-Hertogenbosch 078519
La Folie des Arts, Montréal 097001
La Folie des Enchanteurs, Les Sables-d'Olonne 099471
Folies Antiques, Torino 076816
Folin Riva, New York 117914
Folini Artecontemporanea, Chiasso 111351
Folio, Bruxelles . . 096192, 123592, 133267
Folio, Gronsveld 128682
Folio Verlag, Bolzano 134559
Folio Verlag, Wien 133192
Foliograph Gallery, Washington . . . 120289
Folk and Country Antiques, Ashbourne 083327
Folk Art and Photography Galleries, High Museum of Art, Atlanta 041857
Folk Art Center, Asheville 041797
Folk Art Finders, Essex 136462
Folk Art Gallery, Zürich 082967
Folk Art Institute, Lefkoşa 008255
Folk Art Messenger, Richmond 136463
Folk Art Museum, Lemesos 008228
Folk Art Museum, Yeroskipos 008235
Folk Art Museum of the Metropolis of Kos, Kos 021341
Folk Art Society of America, Richmond 047415
Folk Museum, Anuradhapura 036127
Folk Museum, Câtel 039020
Folk Museum, Deloraine 000977
Folk Museum, Mbarara 038222
Folk Museum, Mevagissey 040454
Folk Museum, Millom 040467
Folk Museum, Soroti 038224
Folk Museum of Indian Immigration, Moka 028066
Folk Museum of Meguro-ku, Tokyo 027160
Folk Museum of Ota-ku, Tokyo 027161
Folkart Interiors, Vancouver 059359
Folkenborg Museum, Eidsberg og Mysen Historielag, Mysen 031039
Folkens Museum Etnografiska, Statens Museer för Världskultur, Stockholm 036623
Folkes Antiques & Jewellers, Great Yarmouth 084527
Folkestone Museum and Art Gallery, Folkestone 039509
Folkets Hus, Hovmantorp 122164
Folklife Display, Lisnaskea 040021
Folklore and Ethnological Museum of Macedonia and Thrace, Thessaloniki 021491
Folklore Museum, Cairo 009301
Folklore Museum, Karditsa 021307
Folklore Museum, Mysore 022275

Folklore Museum, Pogoniani 021439
Folklore Museum, Thessaloniki . . . 021492
Folklore Museum, Victoria 028040
Folklore Museum, Vitsa 021520
Folklore Museum, Xanthi 021528
Folklore Museum of Avlon, Avlon . . 021218
Folklore Museum of Florina, Florina 021267
Folklore Museum of Thrace, Komotini 021335
Folkloremuseum Florishof, Oostduinkerke 003682
Folklorish Museum, Wuxi 007306
Folkloristisch Museum, Swalmen . . 030192
Folkwang-Museumsverein e.V., Essen 053170
Folldal Bygdetun, Folldal 030843
Folldal Gruver, Folldal 030844
Follens, Hervé, Bapaume 061191
Follett House Museum, Sandusky . . 047929
Folliard, Tory, Milwaukee 117186
Folliasson, Carmen, Paris 100285
Follo Museum, Drøbak 030809
Follot, Jeannine, Gevrey-Chambertin 062989
Folly, New York 090879
Folly Antiques, Clitheroe 084035
Folly Antiques Centre, Petersfield . . 086234
Folsom History Museum, Folsom . . 043880
Folsom Museum, Folsom 043881
Folterkammer mit Heimatmuseum, Pöggstall 002439
Foltermuseum, Burghausen, Salzach 016512
Foltermuseum, Museum für mittelalterliche Rechtsgeschichte, Wien 002898
Foluo Lun Sa, Shenzhen 097976
Fond Régional d'Art Contemporain, Angoulême 010402
Fondaçao-Museu Chissano, Matola 029054
Fondantico, Bologna 075077
Fondatioin Océanographique, Six-Fours-les-Plages 014807
Fondation André Hallet, Bruxelles . . 133268
Fondation Beyeler, Riehen 037451
Fondation Cartier pour l'Art Contemporain, Paris 013582
Fondation Carzou, Manosque 012877
Fondation Charles de Gaulle, Colombey-les-Deux-Eglises 011436
Fondation Cziffra, Senlis 014759
Fondation de Jau, Cases-de-Pène . 011133
Fondation de l'Automobile Marius-Berliet, Lyon 012807
Fondation de l'Hermitage, Lausanne 037241
Fondation Dosne-Thiers, Paris 013583
Fondation du Château de Maintenon, Maintenon 012855
Fondation Dubuffet, Paris 013584
Fondation Dubuffet, Périgny-sur-Yerres 013772
Fondation et Musée René Carcan, Bruxelles 003299
Fondation François-Brochet, Auxerre 010571
Fondation Guerlain, Les Mesnuls . . 012629
Fondation Hergé ASBL, Bruxelles . . 133269
Fondation Herzog, Basel 036883
Fondation La Tène, Hauterive 037180
Fondation Le Corbusier, Paris 013585
Fondation L'Estrée, Espace Culturel, Ropraz 037461
Fondation Louis Moret, Martigny . . 037310
Fondation Maeght, Saint-Paul-de-Vence 014468
Fondation Martin Bodmer, Cologny . 037026
Fondation Neumann, Gingins 037143
Fondation Pierre Gianadda, Martigny 037311
Fondation pour l'Architecture, Bruxelles 003300
Fondation Prouvost, Septentrion, Marcq-en-Barœul 012896
Fondation Rainer Maria Rilke, Sierre 037558
Fondation René Pous, Auterive 010557
Fondation Saner, Stiftung für Schweizer Kunst, Studen 037612
Fondation Sur-la-Velle, Le Noirmont 111780
Fondation Van-Gogh Arles, Arles . . 010469
Fondation Vasarely, Aix-en-Provence 010291
Fondazione Accademia di Belle Arti Pietro Vannucci, Perugia 050407
Fondazione Antonio Mazzotta, Milano 024700
Fondazione Bandera per l'Arte, Busto Arsizio 023554
Fondazione Europea del Disegno, Meina 024660
Fondazione Galleria Gottardo, Lugano 037284
Fondazione M. Minucci, Vittorio Veneto 026354
Fondazione Magnani Rocca, Mamiano di Traversetolo 024590
Fondazione Museo Glauco Lombardi, Parma 025115
Fondazione Palazz Coronini Cronberg, Gorizia 024350
Fondazione Palazzo Albizzini Collezione Burri, Città di Castello 023893
Fondazione Romano nel Cenacolo di Santo Spirito, Firenze 024151
Fondazione T. Balestra, Longiano . . 024526
Fondazione Thyssen-Bornemisza, Castagnola 037001
Fonderie de Cloches, Robecourt . . . 014066
Fondo del Sol, Washington 120290
Fondo Del Sol, Visual Art and Media Center, Washington 048905
Fondo Internacional de Pintura, Barcelona 110153
Fondon, Palma de Mallorca 110678
Fonds Ancien, Manuscrits du Mont Saint-Michel, Avranches 010603
Fonds Ancien de la Bibliothèque Cantonale Jurassienne, Porrentruy 037418
Fonds Régional d'Art Contemporain, Saint-Paul 032765
Foney, E., Houston 116315
Fong, Los Angeles 089770
Fong, D.P., San Jose 119851
Fong, Freddie, San Francisco 119668
Fong, Suzanna, San Francisco 119669
Al Fonoon, Kasr, Cairo 098631
Fons Blavus, Renningen 139689
Fonseca, Maria Cristina, Milano . . . 075713
Font Mascaro, Margarita, Barcelona 129345
La Fontaine, Montevideo 087318
Fontaine, Christophe, Colmar 062411
Fontaine, Danièle, Cherbourg-Octeville 062276
Fontaine, Dominique, Caen 061871
La Fontaine Antiquité, Paris 065922
La Fontaine Charlemagne, Paris . . . 138377
La Fontaine d'Argent, Montluçon . . 064709
Fontaine des Arts, Herblay 099329
La Fontaine des Arts, Sanary-sur-Mer 101250
La Fontaine du Rhône, Genève 111449
La Fontaine du Temps, Fresnay-sur-Sarthe 062941
Fontaliran, Jean-Marc, Montignac . 064692
La Fontana, Paris 100286
Fontana, Alfredo, Roma 128047
Fontana, Marco, Roma 076469
Fontana, Nazzareno, Roma 128048
Fontana, Nicola, Firenze 127338
Fontana, Nicola, Roma 128049
Fontane-Antiquariat, Berlin 138777
Fontanet, Hugues, Cherbourg-Octeville 062277
Fontanez, Marc, Maisons-Laffitte . . 064225
Fontanini, Pietro, Roma 128050
Fontannaz, Serge, Lausanne 130069
La Fonte, Muralto 082678
Fonte d'Abisso Arte, Milano 106216
Fontenele, Fatima, Rio de Janeiro . 096606
Fontenelle, Marly-le-Roi 064290
Fonthill Museum of the Bucks County Historical Society, Doylestown . . . 043503
Fonti e Studi per la Storia di Bologna e delle Province Emiliane e Romagnole, Bologna 135904
Fontvieille Antiquités, Monaco 077602
Fontys Hogeschool voor de Kunsten, Akademie voor Beeldende Vorming, Tilburg 050569
Foo Yong Kong, Kuala Lumpur 107435
Foochow, Hong Kong 059628
Foord-Brown, David, Cuckfield 084126
Foothills Art Center, Golden 051392
Footnote Books, San Diego 142904
Foot's Artworks, Hamilton Island . . 094612
Foot's Artworks, Main Beach 094760
Footscray Community Arts Centre, Footscray 001032
Foott, Andrew, Cheadle Hulme 083913, 130526
For All Seasons, Columbus 088408
For Art Sake Galleries, Newcastle . . 094938
For Decorative Living, London 085301
For Love of the Earth, Esperance . . 094513
For Old Times Sake, Milwaukee . . . 090299
For the Love of Dolls, Dallas 088514
For Your Walls, Louth 114000
Foragers, Christchurch 079027
Forain, Pierre & Suzanne, Annecy-le-Vieux 060900
Foralosso, Jean-Louis, La Murette . 063399
Foralosso, Michel, Voiron . 069026, 125038
Forante, Silvia, Verona 128424
Forbes, M.R., Sacramento 092157
Forbes Antiques, Forbes 055833
Forbes Art Gallery, Forbes 094551
Forbes Collection, New York 046331
Forbes Mill Museum of Regional History, Los Gatos 045477
Forbes Museum, Forbes 001034
Forbes Museum, Tanger 029037
Forbidden Gallery, Dallas 115881
Forbidden Planet, New York 142653
Forcada Fajardo, Francisca, Valencia 081657
Forclaz, Daniel, Grône 082486
Ford, Rita, New York 090880
Ford, Ruth, York 087289
Ford County Historical Society Museum, Paxton 046850
Ford End Watermill, Ivinghoe 039829
Ford Gallery and Slide Collection, Eastern Michigan University, Art Dept., Ypsilanti 049363
Ford Green Hall, Stoke-on-Trent . . . 041118
Ford Museum, Dumalag 031671
Forde Abbey, Chard 039032
Fordholm, Flinders 055831
Fordonskammaren, Solna 122244
Ford's Theatre, Lincoln Museum, Washington 048906
Fordsmith, Denver 088685
Fordyce Joiner's Visitor Centre, Fordyce 039512
Foredown Tower, Portslade-by-Sea 040759
Foreign Affairs, San Antonio 119411
Foreign Affairs, San Antonio 119412
Foreman, Skot, Atlanta 114877
Foreningen af Danske Kunstmuseer, Nivå 052851
Foreningen af Danske Museumsmaend, København 052852
Foreningen af Danske Naturhistoriske Museer, Århus 052853
Foreningen af Danske Naturvidenskabelige Museer, Esbjerg 052854
Foreningen Kunst på Arbejdspladsen, København 052855
Foreningen til Norske Fortidsminnesmerkers Bevaring, Oslo 053940
Forensic Medicine Museum, Bangkok 037875
Forero, Bogotá 098122
Fores Domus, Roma 076470
Foresight International, Omaha . . . 118691
Forest, Laurent, Alès 060772
Forest and Heritage Centre, Geeveston 001052
Forest Art Gallery, Kuranda 094715
Forest Art Gallery, Stafford 114474
Forest Books, Chingford 141521
Forest Books, San Francisco 142945
Forest Books, Uppingham 142134
Forest Books of Cheshire, Alsager . 141386
Forest Books of Cheshire, Manchester 141935
Forest Capital State Museum, Perry 046885
Forest City Gallery, London 096948
Forest Department Utilisation Division Museum, Kampala 038217
Forest Entomology Museum, Bangkok 037876
Forest Gallery, Forestville . 094553, 123225
Forest Gallery, Guildford 113168
Forest Hill Books, London 141796
Forest History Center, Grand Rapids 044280
Forest-Lambton Museum, Forest . . 005451
Forest Lawn Museum, Glendale . . . 044209
Forest Museum, Peshawar 031392
Forest Museum, Soheul 027619
Forest Museum, Taungdwingyi 029070
Forest Park Museum, Perry 046886
Forest Research Institute and College Museum, Dehradun 022073
Forest Sandilands Centre and Museum, Winnipeg 006844
Forestburg and District Museum, Forestburg 005452
Forestier, Antoine & Marie, Saint-Martial-d'Albarède 067624
Forestier, Pierre, Pézenas 066803
Forestry Research Institute Malaysia Museum, Kepong 027956
Forestwood Antique Mall, Dallas . . 088515
Forêt, Patrick, Saint-Dizier 067429
Forêt Verte, Paris 065923
Forever After Books, San Francisco 142946
Forever Amber, Paddington, Queensland 056429
Forever Finishing, Jacksonville 132182
Forever Keepsakes, Saint Louis . . . 119205
Forever Plaza de Mexico, Reynosa . 107518
La Forge, Grandchamp-des-Fontaines 063029, 124252
The Forge Antiques, Coleraine 084062
Forge Antiques, Sandhurst, Kent . .086516, 131457
Forge Gallery, Robin Hoods Bay . . . 114320
Forge Mill Needle Museum and Bordesley Abbey Visitor Centre, Redditch . . . 040814
Forge-Musée d'Etueffont, Etueffont 011758
Forge Museum, Much Hadham 040503
Forge Studio Workshops, Manningtree 131260
The Forges and Manor of Ringwood, Ringwood 047440
Forget, Bernard, Poitiers . 066891, 124847
Forget-me-Knot Antiques, Saint Albans 086438
Forget me not, Christchurch 079028
Forget Me Not, San Jose 092923
Forgotten Shanghai, San Francisco 092789
Forgotten Times, Koorawatha 056064
Forichon, Gisèle, Bessines-sur-Gartempe 061408
Forlaget Cordelia, Skørping 133431
Form 1900, Stockholm 081952
Form Gallery, Albuquerque 087391
Form Gallery, Christchurch 108394
Form Vintage Modern, Oakland . . . 091418
form - Zeitschrift für Gestaltung, Neu-Isenburg 135763
Forma, Moskva 109510
Forma Aktua, Groningen 108035
Forma Studio Gallery, New York . . . 117915
Formanoir & Launoit, Bruxelles . . . 057947
Formargruppen, Malmö 110962
FormArt, Berlin 101858
Formas Plásticas, Barcelona 136086
Formas y Espacios, Bucaramanga . 098211
Format, Kraków 108935
Format, Wrocl^Beaw 136023
Format of Birmingham, Birmingham 083532

Formby, Jeffrey, Moreton-in-Marsh 086016, 141948
Forme d'Art, Las Vegas 116619
Forme Libre, Grenoble 063061
Formenti, Gianni, Padova 127803
Former Glory, Gosport . . . 084488, 130737
Former Glory Country Antiques, Masterton 079148
Former Governors' Mansion, Bismarck 042238
Former Hong Kong and Shanghai Bank Museum, Nagasaki 026860
Formes, Tokyo 107034
Formes, Tokyo 107035
Formliner, Mannheim 072421
Formsammlung der Stadt Braunschweig, Braunschweig 016384
Fornaresio, Giovanni, Torino 106673
Fornaro, Rosalia, Bologna 075078
Fornasier, Alba, Wettolsheim 069049
Forncett Industrial Steam Museum, Forncett Saint Mary 039515
Forneck, Gerd Martin, Höhr-Grenzhausen 071540
Fornès, Le Juch 063642
Forney, Stéphane, Cormondrèche . . 082327
Forney Transportation Museum, Denver 043407
Forngården Hembygdsmuseum, Trollhättan 036717
Forni, Bologna 105956
Fornminnesgården, Eksjö 036244
Forno, Barry, Dunedin 121822
Fornvannen, Stockholm 136109
Foroni, Fausto, Milano 075714
Føroya Fornminnissavn, Tórshavn . 009448
Føroya Náttúrugripasavn, Tórshavn 009449
Forré & Joisten, Engelskirchen 070569
Forres Saleroom, Forres 122513
Forrest, Scott, New York 117916
Forrester Gallery, Oamaru 030556
Forrest's Antiques, Fort Worth 088855
Forsand Bygdemuseum, Forsand . . 030847
Forsblom, Helsinki 098720
Forschungs- und Gedenkstätte Normannenstrasse - Stasi Museum, Berlin 016020
Forschungsarchiv für römische Plastik, Universität zu Köln, Köln 018309
Forschungsinstitut für Kunstgeschichte, Philipps-Universität Marburg, Marburg 050180
Forssan Luonnonhistoriallinen Museo, Forssa 009482
Forst- und Jagdmuseum, Hofgeismar 017960
Forst- und Köhlerhof, Rostock 019896
Forstbotanisches Museum, Technische Universität Dresden, Tharandt . . . 020433
Forster, H. & S., Friedenweiler 139127
Forster & Kaner, Freiburg im Breisgau 139111
Forstliche und Jagdkundliche Lehrschau Grillenburg, Technische Universität Dresden, Grillenburg 017536
Forstmuseum, Reichraming 002514
Forstmuseum Heringen, Heringen, Werra 017885
Forstmuseum im Hochwildpark Karlsberg, Weikersheim 020711
Forsvarsmuseet, Oslo 031076
Forsvarsmuseet på Bornholm, Rønne 009077
Forsviks Industriminnen, Forsvik . . 036276
Forsyth, Dublin 074917
Forsythe, Frank, Cincinnati 088241, 122855
Fort Abercrombie Historic Site, Abercrombie 041558
Fort Amherst Heritage Museum, Chatham 039037
Fort Ancient Museum, Oregonia . . . 046711
Fort Anne, Parks Canada, Annapolis Royal 005016
Fort Atkinson State Historical Park, Fort Calhoun 043896
Fort Beaufort Historical Museum, Fort Beaufort 034613
Fort Beauséjour National Historic Site, Aulac 005040
Fort Bedford Museum, Bedford 042099
Fort Belknap Museum, Newcastle . 046444
Fort Bend Museum, Richmond 047405
Fort Benton Museum of the Upper Missouri, Fort Benton 043889
Fort Bliss Museum, Fort Bliss 043891
Fort Boonesborough Museum, Richmond 047402
Fort Bowie, Bowie 042359
Fort Bridger State Museum, Fort Bridger 043895
Fort Brockhurst, Gosport 039607
Fort Buenaventura, Ogden 046629
Fort Buford State Historic Site, Williston 049191
Fort Calgary, Calgary 005186
Fort Carlton, Regina 006253
Fort Caroline Memorial Museum, Jacksonville 044813
Fort Casey Interpretive Center, Coupeville 043193
Fort Caspar Museum, Casper 042646
Fort-Chambly, Chambly 005241
Fort Charles Maritime Museum, Kingston 026382
Fort Chipewyan Bicentennial Museum, Fort Chipewyan 005454
Fort Christmas, Christmas 042911
Fort Clark Trading Post, Center 042684
Fort Clatsop National Memorial, Astoria 041824
Fort Clinch, Fernandina Beach 043837
Fort Collins Museum, Fort Collins . . 043902
Fort Columbia House Museum, Chinook 042905
Fort Crawford Museum, Prairie du Chien 047219
Fort Croghan Museum, Burnet 042527
Fort Crook Historical Museum, Fall River Mills 043806
Fort Dalles Museum, The Dalles . . . 043281
Fort d'Aubin-Neufchâteau et son Musée, Neufchâteau 003672
Fort Dauphin Museum, Dauphin . . . 005328
Fort Davidson State Historic Site, Pilot Knob 047021
Fort Davis, Fort Davis 043906
Fort de Chartres Museum, Prairie du Rocher 047221
Fort de Seyne, Seyne-les-Alpes . . . 014790
Fort de Vallorbe, Vallorbe 037667
Fort Delaware, Narrowsburg 046134
Fort Delaware Society Museum, Delaware City 043381
Fort Discovery, Augusta 041897
Fort Dix Museum, Fort Dix 043909
Fort Dobbs State Historic Site, Statesville 048340
Fort Dodge Historical Museum, Fort Dodge 043911
Fort Donelson National Battlefield Museum, Dover 043496
Fort Door, Edmonton 096878
Fort Dorsner, Giromagny 011952
Fort Douglas Military Museum, Fort Douglas 043912
Fort Edmonton Park, Edmonton . . . 005396
Fort Edward, Grand-Pré 005537
Fort Erie Historical Museum, Ridgeway 006288
Fort Erie Railroad Museum, Fort Erie 005455
Le Fort et son Musée, Flémalle . . . 003435
Fort Fetterman State Museum, Douglas 043485
Fort Fisher, Kure Beach 045049
Fort Fleur d'Epée, Le Gosier 021556
Fort Frances Museum, Fort Frances 005457
Fort Frederica, Saint Simons Island 047723
Fort Frederick, Big Pool 042198
Fort Garry Horse Regimental Museum, Winnipeg 006845
Fort George, Niagara-on-the-Lake . 006020
Fort George and Buckingham House, Saint Paul 006388
Fort George G. Meade Museum, Fort Meade 043948
Fort George Museum, Elk Point . . . 005422
Fort Gibson Historic Site, Fort Gibson 043917
Fort Glanville, Semaphore Park . . . 001461
Fort Grey and Shipwreck Museum, Saint Peter Port 040935
Fort Hancock Museum, Sandy Hook 047937
Fort Harker Museum, Kanopolis . . . 044910
Fort Hartsuff, Burwell 042531
Fort Hays, Hays 044488
Fort Henry, Kingston 005695
Fort Hill Museum, Hillsboro 044544
Fort Hill - The John C. Calhoun House, Clemson University, Clemson 042975
Fort Huachuca Museum, Fort Huachuca 043921
Fort Hunter Mansion, Harrisburg . . . 044442
Fort Inglish, Bonham 042296
Fort Jackson Museum, Fort Jackson 043923
Fort Jesus Museum, Mombasa 027427
Fort Jones Museum, Fort Jones . . . 043927
Fort Kearney Museum, Kearney . . . 044941
Fort Kearny State Historical Park, Kearney 044942
Fort Kijkduin, Castricum 029384
Fort King George Historic Site, Darien 043302
Fort Klock Historic Restoration, Saint Johnsville 047640
Fort Knox State Historic Site, Stockton Springs 048373
Fort La Reine Museum and Pioneer Village, Portage-la-Prairie 006192
Fort Langley National Historic Site, Fort Langley 005461
Fort Laramie, Fort Laramie 043929
Fort Larned, Larned 045175
Fort Laurens State Memorial, Bolivar 042293
Fort Leaton, Presidio 047228
Fort Leavenworth Historical Museum and Post Museum, Fort Leavenworth . 043937
Fort Leboeuf, Waterford 048982
Fort l'Ecluse, Archéosite Militaire, Leaz 012581
Fort Lee Historic Park and Museum, Fort Lee 043939
Fort Lennox, Saint-Paul-de-Ile-aux-Noix 006390
Fort Lewis Military Museum, Fort Lewis 043944
Fort Ligonier Museum, Ligonier . . . 045290
Fort Loudoun, Chambersburg 042701
Fort Lowell Furniture, Tucson 093234
Fort McAllister, Richmond Hill 047431
Fort MacArthur Museum, San Pedro 047917
Fort McHenry, Baltimore 041983
Fort McKavett State Historic Park, Fort McKavett 043945
Fort Mackinac, Mackinac Island . . . 045551
Fort Macon, Atlantic Beach 041879
Fort Malden, Amherstburg 005007
Fort-Mardi Antiquités, Montévrain . . 064681
Fort Massac, Metropolis 045800
Fort Matanzas, Saint Augustine . . . 047607
Fort Meigs State Memorial, Perrysburg 046888
Fort Mifflin, Philadelphia 046942
Fort Morgan Museum, Fort Morgan 043954
Fort Morgan Museum, Gulf Shores . 044371
Fort Morris, Midway 045857
Fort Mountain, Chattsworth 042784
Fort Muséalisé d'Uxegney, Uxegney 015078
Fort Museum, Fort Macleod 005463
Fort Myers Historical Museum, Fort Myers 043958
Fort N5 - Muzej Istorii Velikoj Otečestvennoj Vojny, Oblastnoj istoriko-chudožestvennyj Muzej, Kaliningrad 033212
Fort Namutoni, Tsumeb 029100
Fort Napoleon, Oostende 003684
Fort Nashborough, Nashville 046146
Fort Necessity National Battlefield, Farmington 043822
Fort Nelson Heritage Museum, Fort Nelson 005467
Fort Nisqually Living History Museum, Tacoma 048464
Fort Normandeau, Red Deer 006241
Fort-Numéro-Un de la Pointe-de-Lévy, Québec 006216
Fort Okanogan, Pateros 046839
Fort Ontario, Oswego 046746
Fort Osage, Sibley 048170
Fort Ostell Museum, Ponoka 006166
Fort Peck Museum, Fort Peck 043961
Fort Pelley and Livingston Museum, Pelly 006124
Fort Phil Kearny, Story 048385
Fort Pike, New Orleans 046252
Fort Pitt Museum, Pittsburgh 047048
Fort Plain Museum, Fort Plain 043965
Fort Point Museum, LaHave 005737
Fort Polk Military Museum, Fort Polk 043966
Fort Pulaski, Savannah 048024
Fort Qu'appelle Museum, Fort Qu'appelle 005468
Fort Queenscliff Museum, Queenscliff 001415
Fort Raleigh, Manteo 045648
Fort Rammekens, Ritthem 030065
Fort Recovery Museum, Fort Recovery 043969
Fort Richardson, Jacksboro 044794
Fort Robinson Museum, Crawford . 043207
Fort Rodd Hill Museum, Victoria . . . 006740
Fort Roosevelt Natural Science and History Museum, Hanford 044422
Fort Saint George Museum, Chennai 022056
Fort Saint James National Historic Site, Fort Saint James 005469
Fort Saint Jean Baptiste, Natchitoches 046163
Fort Saint John-North Peace Museum, Fort Saint John 005470
Fort Saint Joseph, Richards Landing 006276
Fort Saint Joseph Museum, Niles . . 046487
Fort Saint Joseph National Historic Park, Saint Joseph Island 006377
Fort Saint Pierre, Fort Frances 005458
Fort Sam Houston Museum, Fort Sam Houston 043973
Fort San Pedro National Museum, Cebu 031656
Fort Saskatchewan Museum, Fort Saskatchewan 005471
Fort Savannah Museum, Lewisburg 045245
Fort Scott National Historic Site, Fort Scott 043975
Fort Scratchley Museum, Newcastle 001324
Fort Selden State Monument, Radium Springs 047308
Fort Selkirk, Whitehorse 006811
Fort Sidney Museum and Post Commander's Home, Sidney 048172
Fort Sill, Fort Sill 043977
Fort Siloso, Singapore 034293
Fort Sisseton, Lake City 045105
Fort Smith, Fort Smith 043978
Fort Smith Art Center, Fort Smith . . 043979
Fort Smith Museum of History, Fort Smith 043980
Fort Snelling Antiquarian, Saint Paul 142866
Fort Spokane Visitor Center and Museum, Davenport 043306
Fort Stanwix, Rome 047534
Fort Steele Heritage Town, Fort Steele 005473
Fort Stewart Museum, Fort Stewart 043982
Fort Sumner, Fort Sumner 043985
Fort Sumter National Monument, Sullivan's Island 048420
Fort Tejon, Lebec 045226
Fort Ticonderoga, Ticonderoga 048553

Fort Totten State Historic Museum, Pioneer Daughters Museum, Fort Totten . . 043986
Fort Towson Military Park, Fort Towson 043987
Fort Union National Monument, Watrous 049006
Fort Union Trading Post National Historic Site, Williston 049192
Fort Vancouver, Vancouver 048749
Fort Vasquez Museum, Colorado Historical Society Regional Museum, Platteville 047080
Fort Walla Walla Museum, Walla Walla 048834
Fort Walsh, Maple Creek 005829
Fort Ward Museum and Historic Site, Alexandria 041639
Fort Washington, Fort Washington . 043991
Fort Washington Museum, Fort Washington 043993
Fort Washita, Durant 043537
Fort Wayne Firefighters Museum, Fort Wayne 043997
Fort Wayne Museum of Art, Fort Wayne 043998
Fort Wellington, Prescott 006199
Fort Whoop-Up Centre, Lethbridge . 005765
Fort Widley, Portsmouth 040764
Fort Wilkins Historic Complex, Copper Harbor 043143
Fort William Henry Museum, Lake George 045107
Fort Winnebago Surgeons Quarters, Portage 047148
Fort Worth Antiques, Fort Worth . . . 088856
Fort Worth Coin Company, Fort Worth 088857
Fort Worth Museum of Science and History, Fort Worth 044007
Fort Worth Public Library Arts and Humanities, Fort Worth 044008
Fort Yargo, Winder 049233
Fort Zachary Taylor, Key West 044985
Fortaleza de Nuestra Señora de los Angeles de Jagua, Jagua 008030
Fortaleza de San Felipe, Santo Domingo 009155
Forte Rinascimentale, San Leo 025696
Fortebraccio, Firenze 075340
Fortenbacher, Klaus, Crimmitschau 125438
Forteresse-Château, Sainte-Suzanne 014618
Forteresse de Mornas, Mornas 013247
Forteresse de Salses, Salses-le-Château 014654
Fortescue, Birdie, London 085302
Fortifications-de-Québec, Québec . 006217
Fortin, Catherine, Paris 065924
Fortin, Catherine, Saint-Ouen 067778
Fortin, Evelyne, Paris 124666
Fortín San Jerónimo del Boquerón, San Juan 032732
Fortix Ltd, Sharjah 112467
Fortlands Antique, Charleville 074872
Fortmann, Evamarie, Salzburg 057246, 123443
Fortner, Columbus 131982
Fortress of Louisbourg, Louisbourg 005802
Forts Folle Avoine Historic Park, Danbury 043291
Fortuijn, Amsterdam 077850
Fortuna & Co., Firenze 140016
Fortuna, Merano 075545
Fortuna Fine Arts, New York 117917
Fortunate Finds, South Auckland . . 079240
Fortunato, Francesco, Roma 128051
Fortunato, Sebastiano, Milano 127593
Fortune Antiques, New York 090881
Fortune Art Gallery, Pune 105826
Fortune Classics, Leeuwarden 078550
Fortune de Mer, Toulouse 068508
Fortune Green Books, London 141797
Fortune Line, New Orleans 090553, 132412
Fortuny, Madrid 122058
Forty Fifty Sixty, New York 090882
Forty Hall Museum, Enfield 039445
Forty Nine, Manningtree 085923
Forty One Antiques, Heathfield 084642
Forty River Street Antiques, Boston 087820
Forty Seventh Street Silver, New York 090883
Forum, 't Goy-Houten 140428
Forum, Toronto 059191
Forum Alstertal, Hamburg 103118
Forum am Deutschen Museum, München 019055
Forum Antiques, Cirencester 084017, 130580
Forum Arte, Kötzting 103748
Forum Book Art, Hamburg 134007
Forum Cartes et Collections, Nieuil-l'Espoir 138263
Forum d'Art Contemporain, Sierre . 111902
Forum de Artes Antiquario, Rio de Janeiro 058587
Forum de l'Image, Toulouse 101345
Forum der Schweizer Geschichte, Musée Suisse - Schweizerisches Landesmuseum, Schwyz 037542
Forum des Antiquaires, Toulouse . . 068509
Forum des Arts, Aix-en-Provence . . 060703
Forum des Arts, Paris 100287, 133606
Forum des Arts, Rouen 101116
Forum Européen des Conseillers et Consultants de Musée, Bruxelles . 052674
Forum Flüh, Flüh 037090
Forum Fränkischer Hof, Bad Rappenauer Museum, Bad Rappenau 015771
Forum für Angewandte Kunst im Bayerischen Kunstgewerbeverein e.V., Nürnberg 019349
Forum für Kunst, Heidelberg 103319
Forum für Medien und Gestaltung, Bern 036928
Forum Galeria, Łódź 109002
Forum Gallery, Jamestown 044830
Forum Gallery, Los Angeles 116768
Forum Gallery, New York 117918
Forum Gießen, Gießen 017408
Forum Hall, Handwerk-Heimat-Haustüren, Bad Hall 001721
Forum in der Borstei, München . . . 104177
Forum Konkrete Kunst Erfurt, Erfurt 017011
Forum Konkrete Kunst - Peterskirche, Erfurt 017012
Forum Kunst Rottweil e.V., Rottweil 053171, 104781
Forum Kunst Stein, Krems 052528
Forum Marinum, Turku 010162
Forum Museo, Omegna 024995
Forum Prudens, Praha . . . 060128, 098430
Forum Rubigen, Rubigen 111849
Forum Schloß Wolkersdorf, Wolkersdorf im Weinviertel 095977
Forum Schloßplatz, Aarau 036808
Forum Vebikus, Schaffhausen 111887
Forum Yoga Kenkyujo, Tokyo 050483
Forvm, Barcelona 110154
Forvm-Chantal Grande, Tarragona . 110785
Forwarders' Museum, Prescott 006200
Forwoods, Hay-on-Wye 113209
Forzani, Bruno, Milano . . . 075715, 127594
Fos, Zürich 082968
Foscan, Hobart 094641
Foscherari, Bologna 105957
Foschini, Ivan, Genova 127452
Foshan City Museum, Foshan 007069
Fosnes Bygdemuseum, Jøa 030928
Foss Street Galleries, Dartmouth . . 112936
Fossa, Bruno, Capdenac-Gare 061964
Fossa, Enzo, Parma 127850
Fossa Magna Museum, Itoigawa . . 026582
Fossard, Stéphane, Estry 062809
Fossati, Kilchberg, Basel 111579
Fossati, Nerino, Brescia 075168
Fossati, Orazio, Firenze 127339
Fosse Gallery, Stow-on-the-Wold . .086748, 114503
Les Fosses d'Enfer, Maison des Ressources Géologiques de Normandie, Saint-Rémy-sur-Orne 014523
Fossesholm Herregård, Vestfossen . 031333
Fossielenmuseum, Oostkapelle . . . 030001
Fossil Country Museum, Kemmerer 044951
Fossil Grove, Glasgow 039553
Fossil Museum, Fossil 044016
Fossil Station Museum, Russell . . . 047571
Fossilien- und Heimatmuseum, Messel 018920
Fossilienmuseum im Werkforum Rohrbach Zement, Dotternhausen 016775
Fossilienschauraum, Ernstbrunn . . . 001839
Fossils Museum, Byblos 027816
Fossmotunet - Målselv Bygdemuseum, Moen 031022
Foster, Kim, New York 117919
Foster, Marilyn, Jacksonville 089413
Foster, Michael, London 085303
Foster, Paul, London 141798
Foster, Peter, Sydney 056673
Foster, R.L., Denver 115996
Foster, Robert, Newcastle 123022
Foster, Stephen, London 141799
Foster, W.A., London 141800
Foster and District Historical Society Museum, Foster 001038
Foster Caddell's Art School, Voluntown 052315
Foster Gallery, Eau Claire 043596
Foster-Gwin, San Francisco 092790
Foster Road Collectibles, Portland . 091937
Foster & White, Seattle 119918
Foster & White, Seattle 119919
Fosterfields Living Historical Farm, Morristown 046033
Foster's, Albuquerque 131742
Foster's, Rotherham 086407
Fostoria Area Historical Museum, Fostoria 044017
Fota House, Carrigtwohill 022702
Fotevikens Museum, Höllviken 036342
Foth, Freiburg im Breisgau 102859
Foth, Lothar, Osnabrück . . 073233, 126598
Fotheringham Gallery, Stirling 114485
Foti, Salvatore, Roma 128052
Fotland Bygdemølle, Bryne 030796
Fotland Kraftverk, Bryne 030797
Foto en Kunst, Amsterdam 107712
Foto-Gleria Związki Polskich Artystów Fotografików, Kraków 108936
Foto Mida, České Budějovice 133412
Foto-Museum, Essen 017064
Foto-Objektiv, Wien 135553
Foto-Production, Wien 133193
Fotofolio, New York 135429
Fotoforum, Luzern 111691
Fotoforum West, Innsbruck 002079
Fotogalerie Alte Feuerwache, Mannheim 018805
Fotogalerie Friedrichshain, Berlin . . 016021
Fotogalerie in der Fabrik Heeder, Krefeld 103777
Fotogalerie Landesbildstelle, Hamburg 017692
Fotogalerie Münchener Stadtbibliothek, München 104178
Fotogalerie No5, Leeuwarden 108093
Fotogalerie Weinberg, Kefermarkt . 095605
Fotogalerie Wien, Verein zur Förderung künstlerischer Fotografie, Wien . .052529, 095821
Fotografia Video, Bucureşti 136048
Fotografičeskij Muzej Dom Metenkova, Ekaterinburg 033110
Fotograficzny Muzeum Regionalnego w Mielcu, Mielec 032145
Fotografie Forum international, Frankfurt am Main 017162
Fotografijos, Panevėžys 107353
Fotografische Gesellschaft Oberösterreich, Linz 052530
Fotohistorische Sammlung, Penk . . 002411
Fotoinitiative Niederösterreich, Wolkersdorf im Weinviertel 052531
Fotokunst Hannover, Hannover 103274
Fotomuséet i Osby, Osby 036535
Fotomuseet Olympia, Falkenberg . . 036260
Fotomuseum CAMERAMA, Bad Soden am Taunus 015801
Fotomuseum Den Haag, Den Haag . 029423
Fotomuseum im Münchner Stadtmuseum, München 019056
Fotomuseum Provincie Antwerpen, Antwerpen 003161
Fotomuseum Winterthur, Winterthur 037717
Fotoplastikon, Warszawa 032423
La Fototeca, Bologna 127151
Fototeca de Cuba, La Habana 007947
Fototeka, Los Angeles 116769
Fouad, Abdullah, Dammam 121971
Fouasse, Dominique, Toulon (Var) . . 124965
Foucar, Ingeborg, Friedrichsdorf, Taunus 125682
Foucault, Jeanne, Aubigny-sur-Nère 061043
Foucher, Christian, Langoiran 063517
Foucher, Dominique, Le Pellerin . . . 063679
Foucher, Jean-Claude, Bordeaux . .061608, 138041
Foucher, Joël, Peujard 124842
Fouchet, Dijon . . . 062656, 099211, 124221
Fougerolle, Christine, Paris 124667
Fougerouge, Essey 062806
Fougerouge, Christian, Dijon 062657
Fouillis du Livre, Pessac 138570
Le Fouillis du Livre, Vendays Montalivet 138648
Fouilloy, Monique, Clacy-et-Thierret 062311
Le Fouineur, Bruxelles . . . 057948, 137436
Fouineur, Hossegor 063175
Fouineuse, Bayonne 061231
Foulon, Liège 123654
Found, Dallas 088516
Found Collections, Seattle 093000
Found It, Bussum 078131
Found It, Seattle 093001
Found Objects, Seattle 093002
Foundation for Women's Art, London 040148
Founders Gallery, San Diego 047820
Founders Historic Park, Nelson 030547
Founders Room, Museum of the Pioneers, Raanana 023046
Foundling Museum, London 040149
Foundry Gallery, Washington 120291
Founès, Monique de, Lyon 124356
Fountain, Desmond, Hamilton 096418
Fountain Antiques, Honiton 084718
Fountain Art Gallery, Memphis 116988
Fountain Bookstore, Richmond 142827
Fountain Gallery, Port Augusta 095081
Fountain Press, Faringdon 135148
Fountainhead, Seattle 119920
Fouqué, Bernard, Signes 068242
Fouquer, Gérard, Lieurey 063818
Fouquet, Collégien 062394
Fouquet, Paris 065925
Fouquier, Olivier, Les Sièges 063788
Four Banal, Castillon-du-Gard 062020
Four Centuries, New Orleans 090554
Four Continents, Vancouver 059360
Four Corners Antiques, San Francisco 092791
Four Corners Gallery, Kingston 106813
Four Rivers Cultural Center, Ontario 046697
Four Roses Kunst & Antik, Charlottenlund 060217
Four Seasons, Indianapolis 089298
Four Seasons Gallery, Pune 105827
Four Seasons Gallery, Wimborne Minster 087161
Four Solaire, Mont-Louis 013111
Four Star Galleries, Kansas City . . . 116564
Four Star Galleries, Omaha 118692
Four Star Galleries, Omaha 118693
Four Star Galleries, Omaha 118694
Four Wheel Drive Foundation, Clintonville 043020
Four Winds Gallery, Double Bay . . . 094485
Four Winds Gallery, Pittsburgh 091820

Four Winds Gallery, Pittsburgh 091821
Four Winds Gallery, Pittsburgh 118920
Four Winds Gallery, Pittsburgh 118921
Fourbet, Martine, Saint-Jean-du-Gard 067548
Fourcade, Jean-François, Paris . . . 138378
Fourcherot, Josselyn, Le Cellier . . . 063595
Fourcherot, Josselyn, Vertou 068826
Fourchon, Serge, Luc-sur-Mer 064019
Fourcroy, A., Bruxelles 057949
Fouré-Labrot & Bignon, Toulouse . . 121269
Fourment, Christian, Montblanc . . . 064654
Fourmond, Beaune 061280
Fournié Jean-Marc, Moissac 064579
Fournié-Olivié, Jean-Marc, Toulouse 068510
Fournier, Lyon 138149
Fournier, Paris 065926
Fournier, Françoise, Clermont-Ferrand 062344
Fournier, Jean, Paris 100288
Fournier, Michel & Germaine, Pleine-Fougères 066845
Fournier, Nicole, Dance 062597
Fournier, Yolande, Lambesc 063497
Fournier des Corats, Marie-Thérèse, Villeneuve-sur-Lot 068919
Fournier-Guérin, Hélène, Paris 065927
Fourquet, Patrick, Saint-Omer 121250
Fourquier, Stanislas, Paris 138379
Fourteen, 's-Hertogenbosch 108074
Fourth Estate, London 135217
Fourtin, Patrick, Paris 065928
Foust, Charlotte 115285
Fouz Vega, Jesus Manuel, Madrid . 081301
Fov Naif, Viña del Mar 059569
Fővárosi Képtár, Budapest 021649
Fovea, Bruxelles 057950
Fowey River Gallery, Fowey 113078
Fowle, A. & J., London 085304
Fowle, Nicholas, Norwich . 086117, 131330
Fowler, Lorne 136981
Fowler, Anne, Tetbury 086854
Fowler, J.G., Auckland . . . 078945, 128903
Fowler, Robin, Aylesby . . . 083357, 130320
Fowler Museum of Cultural History, Los Angeles 045421
Fox, Bergisch Gladbach 101763
Fox, Brisbane 094294
Fox, Köln 071937
Fox, Manuka 056157
Fox, C., Queenscliff 056512
Fox, J.G., Fordingbridge 130712
Fox, Jon, Moreton-in-Marsh 086017
Fox, Judy, London 085305
Fox, Leonard, New York 142654
Fox, Pearce, Philadelphia 091636
Fox & Co., Q.B., New York 090884
Fox, Ricarda, Essen 102674
Fox and Hen Antiques, Tampa 093122
Fox and Pheasant Antique Pine, White Colne 087134, 131682
Fox Cottage Antiques, Stow-on-the-Wold 086749
Fox Island Historical Society Museum, Fox Island 044021
Fox Lake Historical Museum, Fox Lake 044022
Fox River Trolley Museum, South Elgin 048239
Fox Talbot Museum, Lacock 039916
Foxfire Gallery, Albuquerque 114787
Foxgloves, Chepstow 083936
Foxhall Gallery, Washington 120292
Foxton Canal Museum, Foxton 039521
Foxton Flax Stripper museum, Foxton 030498
Foxton Museum, Foxton 030499
Foxx Galerie, Zürich 112069
Foxy, Denver 088686
Foxy Production, New York 117920
Foye Gallery, Luton 085872, 114008
Foyer Gallery/James Hockey Gallery, Farnham 039490
Foyer Rural, Musée du Bois et de l'Artisanat, Jupilles 012185
Foyle, Londonderry 085824, 131226
Foyle, Londonderry 141923
Foyle Valley Railway Museum, Londonderry 040327
Foynes Flying Boat Museum, Foynes 022788
Fozzato, Lara, Verona 077002
FPS, London 131027
F.R. Szecesszió, Budapest 074684
Fra.Bo.No., Roma 076471
FRAC du Centre, Orléans 013512
FRAC Limousin, Limoges 012690
Fradécor, Gargenville 062969, 124246
Fraenkel, San Francisco 119670
Fränkische Galerie, Zweigmuseum des Bayerischen Nationalmuseums, Kronach 018415
Fränkische Hopfenscheune mit heimatkundlicher Sammlung, Neunkirchen am Sand 019259
Fränkische-Schweiz-Museum, Pottenstein 019660
Fränkisches Bauern- und Handwerkermuseum Kirchenburg Mönchsondheim, Iphofen 018079
Fränkisches Brauereimuseum, Bamberg 015870
Fränkisches Freilandmuseum, Bad Windsheim 015838
Fränkisches Freilandmuseum Fladungen, Fladungen 017127
Fränkisches Museum, Feuchtwangen 017115
Fränkisches Spielzeugmuseum, Gößweinstein 017462
Fränkisches Turmuhrenmuseum, Mistelbach 018956
Fraeylemaborg, Slochteren 030161
Fragment, Amsterdam 134779
Fragmenta Selecta, Amsterdam . . . 140300
Fragments Editions, Paris 133607
Fragne, Paul, Angoulême 060877
Fragonard Anticuario, Valladolid . . . 081689
Frahm, København 098553
Frahm, London 113618
Frahm, Klaus, Owschlag 073278
Fraietta, Raffaele, Roma 128053
Fraise des Bois Antiquités, Plougastel-Daoulas 066868
Fraisse, Pierre, Craponne-sur-Arzon 062549
Fraisse, Pierre, Feurs 062859
Fraisse-Jabot, Tours 121271
Fraissinet, Pierre, Cahors 061899
Fraleigh, Toronto 059192
Framagraphic, Vancouver 097470
Framatic Art Gallery, Singapore . . . 109797
Framboyan, New Orleans 090555
Frame, Madrid 081302, 141040
Frame, Wien 135554
Frame and Art, Dallas 115882
Frame and Art Center, Phoenix 118871
Frame Art, Roxheim 104783
Frame Art Gallery, Kingston 106814
Frame Center and Gallery, Milwaukee 117187
Frame Center Gallery, Kingston . . . 106815
Frame Concepts, Toronto 123831
Frame Factory and Gallery, Tampa . 120043
Frame Gallery, Pittsburgh 047049
Frame Makers Gallery, Atlanta 114878
Frame Merchant and Gallery, Cleveland 115706
Frame 'n Art, Virginia Beach 120219
Frame of Mind, Edmonton 096879
Frame of Mind, Miami 117069
Frame of Mind, Winnipeg 097585
Frame Place and Gallery, El Paso . . 116107
Frame Place and Gallery, Tampa . . 120044
Frame Shop and Art Gallery, Jacksonville 116528
Frame Shop and Gallery, New Orleans 117437
Framed Art Studios, Portland 118997
Framed Memories, Kitchener 096929
Framed to Perfection, Tucson 120127
Framein Place Gallery, Baltimore . . 115049
Framery Art Gallery, Sea Point 110080
The Framery & Gallery, Waikato . . . 108589
Frames and Fantasies, Birmingham 115105
Frames Northern Museum, Creighton 005308
Frames USA and Art Gallery, Miami 117070
Framework Gallery, Dun Laoghaire .105892, 127103
Framework Gallery, London 113619
Frameworks Gallery, Charlotte 115286
Frameworks Gallery, Hamilton 096419
Framgi Dadabhoy Alpaiwalle Museum, Parsi Panchayat Museum, Mumbai 022262
Framing and Art, Charlotte 115287
Framing and Art Matters, Randwick 095114
Framing & Art Centre, Edmonton . . 096880
Framing & Art Centre, Hamilton . . . 096915
Framing & Art Centre, Kitchener . . . 096930
Framing & Art Centre, London 096949
Framing & Art Centre, Saskatoon . . 097194
Framing & Art Centre, Vancouver . . 097471
Framing Concepts and Gallery, El Paso 116108
The Framing Machine & Gallery, Swansea 114535
Framing Place and Gallery, Saint Paul 119286
Framing Place and Gallery, Saint Paul 119287
The Framing Workshop, Bath 112576, 130352
Framingham Historical Society and Museum, Framingham 044024
Frammuseet, Oslo 031077
Framond, Paris 100289
Framtidsantiken Skrot & Korn, Stockholm 081953
Fran Hill Gallery, Toronto 097268
Franc, Ginette, Saint-Blaise 082764
Franc, Isabelle, Villeurbanne 068961
Franc Segent, Marly-le-Roi 064291
Franca, Godofredo, Rio de Janeiro . 058588
Franca, Godofredo, Rio de Janeiro . 096607
Franca Antiguidades e Objetos de Arte, Rio de Janeiro 058589
Franča Trasuna Muzejs Kolnasāta, Sakstagals 027775
Français, Jacky, Vittel 069019
La France, Tampa 093123
France, Sophie, São Paulo 058710
France Afrique, Bayonne 098931
France Création Style, Barbizon . . . 061202
France Création Style, Barbizon . . . 098918
France Création Style, Les Baux-de-Provence 063758
France Expertises Enchères, Montastruc la Conseillère 099734
France Lejeune, Mechelen 096383
France Loisirs Antilles, Fort-de-France 140246
France Tradition, Los Angeles 089771
Francelet-Grosz, Jacqueline, Saint-Pierre-Quiberon 067962
Frances, Lyliane, Chatelaillon-Plage 062215
Francés, Ricardo, Pamplona 081518
Frances Burke Textile Resource Centre, RMIT University, Melbourne 001235
Frances Godwin and Joseph Ternbach Museum, Flushing 043875
Frances Lehman Loeb Art Center, Poughkeepsie 047211
Francesca's Collections, Houston . . 089081
Francesca's Italian Arts and Antiques, Sacramento 092158
Franceschi, Eliseo, Brescia 127215
Franceschi, Severino, Firenze 127340
Franceschini, Roberto, Brescia 075169, 140004
Francescoli, Rosemary, Tavannes . . 082843
Franch-Font, Jean-Yves, Montpellier 099755
Franchi, Angela, Bologna 075079
Franchi, Daniel, Paris 100290
Franchi, Mafalda, Genève 082426
Franchini, Firenze 075341, 140017
Franchini, Stefano, Bologna 127152
Franchino, Gherardo, Torino 128307
Franchitti, Natalina, Genova 127453
Franci, Mario, Roma 076472
Francine, Saint-Tropez 068015
Francis, Annie & Martin, Jacksonville 116529
Francis, C., Providence 119079
Francis, Howard, Stockport 114489
Francis, Karim, Cairo 098632
Francis, Paolo, Croydon 112928
Francis, Peter, Carmarthen 122452
Francis, Peter, Saintfield 086484
Francis Colburn Gallery, Burlington . 042525
Francis Land House, Virginia Beach 048796
Francis Ledwidge Cottage and Museum, Slane 022857
Francis McCray Gallery, Western New Mexico University, Silver City 048175
Francisco Fort Museum, La Veta . . 045079
Francisco Romero, Julian, Valencia 129774
Franck, Gérard & Lydia, Colmar . . . 062412
Franck, Isabelle, Cahuzac-sur-Vere 061902
Franck, Katharina, Münchhausen . . 104351
Franck, Patrick, Couches 062494
Franck, Wolfgang, Hamburg 071227
Franck Cechman, Versailles 068804
Franck & Jean-Pierre, Nice 124512
Franck Laigneau, Paris 065929
Die Franckeschen Stiftungen zu Halle, Halle, Saale 017655
Franco, Cannes 061943
Franco, El Paso 116109
Franco, Nice 065082
Franco, Retford 131413
Franco, Cristian, Badajoz 110098
Franco, Graciela, Buenos Aires 055206
Franco Serrano, Maria del Rosario, Barcelona 110155
Francoarte, Medellín 098261
François, Denis, Paris 065930
François, Marie-Cecile, Bruxelles . . 057951
François, Roger, Gevigney-et-Mercey 062988
François Antiquités, Sedan 068184
Francois & Catherine, Amsterdam . 077851
François & Martine, Villers Semeuse 068932
François-Miron, Paris 100291
Francois Pierre Antiquaire, Martel . 064410
Francoise Cottage, Ulladulla 056758
Franconeri, Palermo 076151
Frandl, Johann, Gundertshausen . . 123375
Frangenberg, Manfred, Lindlar 072273
Frangos, Stratjs, Zürich 082969
Franic, M., Domažlice 060012
Franitza, Frank, Neu-Isenburg 139583
Franjevački Samostan, Fojnica 034192
Frank, Laubach, Hessen 072160
Frank, Paris 100292, 133608
Frank, Anthony, New York 090885
Frank, Günther, Ludwigsburg, Württemberg 134165
Frank, Heinrich, München 139505
Frank, Helga, Gera 102938
Frank, Jean, Mulhouse 064833
Frank, John, Phoenix 091741
Frank, Manfred, Mandern 072411
Frank, Michael, Waiblingen 074239
Frank, Rudolf, München 104179
Frank & Dunya, Seattle 119921
Frank H. McClung Museum, University of Tennessee, Knoxville 045039
Frank-Iniesta, Madrid 081303
Frank Lloyd Wright Home and Studio, Oak Park 046582
Frank Lloyd Wright's Pope-Leighey House, Mount Vernon 046073
Frank Mills Outdoor Mining Machinery Museum, Silverton 006475
Frank Partridge V.C. Military Museum, Bowraville 000824
Frank Phillips Home, Bartlesville . . 042031

Frank Slide Interpretive Centre, Crowsnest Pass 005311
Frank, Zangl & Co., München 072698, 139506
Franke, Kevelaer 071812
Franke, München 072699
Franke, Stuttgart 104974, 139761
Franke, B., Großostheim 071124
Franke, Christian Eduard, Bamberg 069451
Franke, H., Köln 139338
Franke, Dr. J., Wien 057414
Franke, Monika, Münstertal 139577
Franke, R., Dohnsen 070268
Franke & Seij, Rotterdam 140519
Frankel, E. & J., New York 090886
Franken, Dordrecht 078301
Franken, Dordrecht 078302
Franken Antik, Großostheim 071125
Franken & Driessen, Amsterdam . . 128537
Franken Galerie, Kronach 103790
Frankenberger Art Gallery, Charleston 042747
Frankenburger Heimatstube, Frankenburg 001861
Frankenmuth Historical Museum, Frankenmuth 044027
Frankenstein, Peter, Marbach am Neckar 126285
Frankenwaldmuseum, Kronach . . . 018416
Frankfort Area Historical Museum, West Frankfort 049074
Frankfurter Äpfelwein-Museum, Frankfurt am Main 017163
Frankfurter Edition, Berlin 133773
Frankfurter Feldbahnmuseum, Frankfurt am Main 017164
Frankfurter Goethe-Museum mit Goethe-Haus, Frankfurt am Main 017167
Frankfurter Künstlerclub e.V., Frankfurt am Main 053172
Galerie Frankfurter Kunstkabinett Hanna Bekker vom Rath, Frankfurt am Main 102766
Frankfurter Kunstverein e.V., Frankfurt am Main 017165
Frankfurter Kunstverein e.V., Frankfurt/Oder 053173
Frankfurter Münzhandlung, Frankfurt am Main 070739
Frankfurter Numismatische Gesellschaft, Frankfurt am Main 053174
Frankfurter Sportmuseum, Frankfurt am Main 017166
Frankfurter Westend Galerie, Frankfurt am Main 102767
Frankie Antik, Frederiksberg 060234
Franklin, Fulda 102907
Franklin, David, Columbus 088409
Franklin, D.F., Atlanta 131773
Franklin, John, San Diego 092636
Franklin, Lynda, Hungerford 084757
Franklin, N. & I., London 085306
Franklin Arts and Cultural Centre, Pukekohe 030583
Franklin College of Arts and Sciences, Department of Art, University of Georgia, Athens 050916
Franklin County Historical Museum, Pasco 046838
Franklin County Museum, Brookville 042475
Franklin County Old Jail Museum, Winchester 049231
Franklin D. Roosevelt Library-Museum, Hyde Park 044707
Franklin G. Burroughs-Simeon B. Chapin Art Museum, Myrtle Beach 046114
Franklin Historical Society Museum, Franklin 044040
Franklin House, Launceston 001176
The Franklin Institute, Philadelphia . 046943
Franklin Mineral Museum, Franklin 044041
The Franklin Mint, Birmingham . . . 087756
Franklin Mint Museum, Franklin Center 044045
The Franklin Museum, Tucson 048636
Franklin Pierce Homestead, Hillsborough 044549
Franklin Street Gallery, Buffalo 115255
Franklin Town Antiques, El Paso . . . 088802
Frankly Speaking Antiques, Yackandandah 056893
Franks Antique Doll Museum, Marshall 045703
Frank's Coin Shop, Las Vegas 089572
Frank's Coin Shop, Las Vegas 089573
Frank's Coins, Buffalo 087876
Frank's Style Upholstering, Edmonton 123759
Frank's Upholstering Shop, Detroit . 132053
Frank's Used Furniture & Antiques, Port Adelaide 056470
Frankston Auction Mart, Frankston . 120585
Frankston Primary Old School Museum, Frankston 001039
Franky's Galerie, Langenfeld 103834
Fråno Antikbod, Kramfors 122180
Frånö Antikbod, Helsingborg 081831
Frans, London 131028
Frans, London 131029
Fran's Antiques, Virginia Beach . . . 093354
Fran's Fantasies Antiques, Norfolk . 091377
Frans Hals Museum, Haarlem 029653
Frans Walkate Archief/ SNS Historisch Archief, Kampen 029798
Franses, S., London 085307, 131030
Franses, Victor, London . . 085308, 131031
Fransız Kültür Merkezi, İstanbul . . . 112308
Fransk Bokhandel l'Arc Librairie Française, Stockholm 141155
Franske, Elisabeth, Hamburg 134008
Fransson, Landvetter 081844
Fransu-tupa, Himanka 009590
Franta, G., Köln 071938
Frantz, München 072700
Frantz, W. & R., München 072701
Franz, A., Hamburg 071228
Franz, A., Hamburg 103119, 125813
Franz, H., Stuttgart 139762
Franz, Dr. Werner, Augsburg 069225
Franz Jonas-Gedenkraum, Teesdorf 002731
Franz Kafka Librería, Cuernavaca . . 140255
Franz-Liszt-Museum der Stadt Bayreuth, Bayreuth 015910
Franz-Marc-Museum, Kochel am See 018298
Franz Michael Felder-Stube, Schoppernau 002654
Franz Radziwill Haus, Varel 020558
Franz Schmidt Museum, Knappenhof, Perchtoldsdorf 002414
Franz Stelzhamer-Geburtshaus, Pramet 002462
Franz Traunfellner-Dokumentation, Pöggstall 002440
Franz von Stuck Geburtshaus Tettenweis, Tettenweis 020425
Franz Winkelmeier-Gedenkraum, Friedburg 001871
Franz Xaver Gruber-Gedächtnishaus, Ach 001657
Franz Xaver Gruber-Museum, Lamprechtshausen 002194
Franz Zeh-Museum, Heidenreichstein 002026
Franzensburg, Laxenburg 002212
Franzese, Germano, Milano 127595
Franzin & C., Milano 075716
Franzini-Heinen, Arlette, Pont-Sainte-Maxence 066936
Franziskanermuseum, Villingen-Schwenningen 020592
Franzus, Christian, Zwettl, Niederösterreich 057612
Frapin Beauge, Houston 116316
Frasassi- le Grotte, Genga 024290
Frasca, Guglielmo, Roma 128054
La Frascetta, Eching 102594
Frascione, Enrico, Firenze 075342
Frascione, Giulio, Firenze 075343
Fraser, Coldstream 084060, 130602
Fraser, Washington 120293
Fraser, Woodbridge 114727
Fraser, Alex, Vancouver 097472
Fraser, Daphne, Glasgow 130728
Fraser-Fort George Regional Museum, Prince George 006206
Fraser Gifford, Tucson 132984
Fraser Lake Museum, Fraser Lake . 005476
Fraser-Sinclair, South Godstone . . . 131512
Fraserburgh Museum, Fraserburgh . 039524
Fraserorr, Robin, New Orleans 132413
Frasers, Inverness 122550
Frasnetti, Maurice, Cusset 062585
Frass, Doris, Mödling 123420
Frassine, Roberto, Brescia 127216
Fratelli, Casablanca 077653
Fratta, Michele, Milano 127596
Frau Holle Expreß, Hessisch-Lichtenau 017909
Frauchiger, Hans, Othmarsingen . . . 082718
Frauen Kunst Wissenschaft, Marburg 135764
Frauen Museum, Bonn 016323
Frauen Museum Wiesbaden, Wiesbaden 020865
Frauenbad - Zentrum für zeitgenössische Kunst, Baden bei Wien 001744
Frauendorf, Andreas, Dresden 125492
Frauenknecht, München 104180
Frauenkultur, Leipzig 103866
Fraunberger, Georg, Kufstein 123403
Fraunces Tavern Museum, New York 046332
Fraux, Patrice, Lavergne . 063559, 124291
Fray, Jean-Marc, Austin 087572
Frayling-Cork, Alistair J., Wallingford 131640
Frazer, Winnipeg 059459, 123867
Frazer's Museum, Beauval 005087
Freak-Ando, Bologna 075080
Freakatorium, New York 090887
Frearte, Milano 121707
Frebel, Westerland 105225
Frech, Annette, Alzenau 101571
Freckeltons, Loughborough 122605
Freckem, Elke, Bielefeld 069823
Fred, Philadelphia 118759
Fred Antiquités, Jandun 063229
Fred Dana Marsh Museum, Ormond Beach 046723
Fred Harman Art Museum, Pagosa Springs 046791
Fred Jones Jr. Museum of Art, Norman 046507
Fred Light Museum, Battleford 005081
Fred Wolf Jr. Gallery, Philadelphia . 046944
Frede, Den Haag 107919
Frede, Stefan, Münster 126499
Frederic Remington Art Museum, Ogdensburg 046634
Frederichs, Josef, Cloppenburg . . . 125432
Frederick, Milwaukee 117188
Frederick Antique, Fresno 132076
Frederick C. Robie House, Chicago . 042844
Frederick Douglass National Historic Site, Washington 048907
Frederick Gallery, Dublin 105862
Frederick Law Olmsted Historic Site, Brookline 042452
Frederick R. Weisman Art Foundation, Los Angeles 045422
Frederick R. Weisman Art Museum, Minneapolis 045910
Frederick R. Weisman Museum of Art, Malibu 045605
Fredericks & Son, C., London 085309, 131032
Fredericksburg and Spotsylvania National Military Park, Fredericksburg 044056
Fredericksburg Area Museum and Cultural Center, Fredericksburg 044057
Frederickson, Kristen, New York . . . 117921
Frédérik Antiquités, Arc-les-Gray . . 060947
Frederiksberg Antik, Frederiksberg . 060235
Frederiksberg Antikvariat, Frederiksberg 137868
Frederiksbog Antikvariat, Hillerød . . 137874
Frederiksen, Mölln 072559, 121515
Frederikshavn Kunstmuseum- og Exlibrissamling, Frederikshavn . . 008866
Frederiksværk Bymuseum, Frederiksværk 008869
Fredman, Sydney 056674
Fredrick's Antiques and Art Gallery, Ettalong Beach 055808, 094514
Fredrik, Karl, Helsinki 060520
Fredriksdals Friluftsmuseum, Helsingborgs Museer, Helsingborg 036333
Fredriksson, Jan, Kinna 122178
Fredriksson, Ulla, Ludvika 122198
Fredrikstad Museum, Fredrikstad . . 030848
Fred's, Baltimore 087670, 131821
Fred's, Werne 074342
Fred'S Rahmen, Mannheim 126273
Fredtun Antikk, Hafrsfjord 079385
Fredy Brocante, Cabrieres 061851
Fredy's Mechanisches Musikmuseum, Lichtensteig 037260
Free Art School, Helsinki 049924
Free Painters and Sculptors, London 054381, 113620
Free Public Library Collection, New Bedford 046189
Free State Voortrekker Museum, Winburg 034777
Freeborn County Historical Museum, Albert Lea 041608
Freedly, Toledo 143027
Freedman, Matthew, Hove 141681
Freedman Gallery, Albright College, Reading 047344
Freedom House Antiques, New York 090888
Freelance Finishes, Baltimore 131822
Freelancer's News, New York 136464
Freeman, Birmingham 131834
Freeman, Hobart 094642
Freeman, Norwich 141964
Freeman, Philadelphia 123044
Freeman, Roxwell 086412
Freeman, David, Bulleen 120572
Freeman, I. & J., Lefkosia 059954
Freeman, Tip, Miami 090172, 117071, 132340
Freeman, Vincent, London 085310
Freeman & Lloyd, Sandgate 086507
Freeman-Whitehurst, Phoenix 118872
Freemantle, Bernard, Romanel-sur-Lausanne 082749
Freeport Arts Center, Freeport 044071
Freeport Historical Society Museum, Freeport 044074
Freer Gallery of Art, Washington . . . 048908
Freer Gallery of Art Occasional Papers, Washington 136465
Frees, Dirk, Marktschellenberg . . . 072465
Freese, Wilhelmine, Aurich 069244
Freess, Edmond, Roussillon (Vaucluse) 101124
Freestone County Historical Museum, Fairfield 043790
Frefel, Felix, Brunnen 082275
Fregatten Jylland, Ebeltoft 008838
Frégnac, Philippe, Paris 100293
Frégosi, Claire, Marseille 064355
Frehsee, Brigitte, Wiesbaden 105252
Frei, Anton, Kißlegg 126051
Frei, Georges, Toffen 082856
Frei, Marlene, Zürich 112070, 135088
Frei-Nathan, Susan, New York 117922
Freiämter Strohmuseum, Wohlen (Aargau) 037738
Freiberger, Mürzzuschlag 095689
Freibord, Wien 133194, 135555
Freiburger Fasnetmuseum, Freiburg im Breisgau 017230
Freiburger Münzkabinett, Freiburg im Breisgau 070837
Freie Akademie der Künste in Hamburg, Hamburg 050112
Freie Akademie der Künste Mannheim, Mannheim 050177
Freie Akademie der Künste zu Leipzig e.V., Leipzig 050166
Freie Kunstakademie Basel, Basel . 050754

Freie Kunstschule Nürtingen und Freie Akademie, Nürtingen 050210
Freie Universität Teufen, Teufen . . . 050776
Freier, Bernhard, München 072702
Freies Deutsches Hochstift/ Frankfurter Goethe-Museum mit Goethe-Haus, Frankfurt am Main 017167
Freiland-Grenzmuseum Sorge, Sorge, Harz 020256
Freilandmuseum Ammerländer Bauernhaus, Bad Zwischenahn 015844
Freilandmuseum Grassemann Naturpark-Infostelle, Warmensteinach 020679
Freilicht- und Heimatmuseum Donaumoos, Karlshuld 018155
Freilichtmuseum, Bad Tatzmannsdorf 001736
Freilichtmuseum, Diesdorf, Altmark 016700
Freilichtmuseum, Stade 020275
Freilichtmuseum Alt Schwerin, Agrarhistorisches Museum, Alt Schwerin 015490
Freilichtmuseum am Kiekeberg, Rosengarten, Kreis Harburg 019882
Freilichtmuseum am Rätischen Limes, Rainau 019705
Freilichtmuseum Anzenaumühle, Bad Goisern 001716
Freilichtmuseum Apriacher Stockmühlen, Heiligenblut 002031
Freilichtmuseum Beuren, Museum des Landkreises Esslingen für ländliche Kultur, Beuren bei Nürtingen 016213
Freilichtmuseum des Gebirgskrieges, Kötschach-Mauthen 002164
Freilichtmuseum Domäne Dahlem, Stiftung Stadtmuseum Berlin, Berlin 016022
Freilichtmuseum Dorfstube Ötlingen, Weil am Rhein 020715
Freilichtmuseum Ensemble Gerersdorf, Gerersdorf 001891
Freilichtmuseum Erdöl- und Erdgaslehrpfad, Prottes 002472
Freilichtmuseum Finsterau, Mauth . 018863
Freilichtmuseum Frelsdorfer Brink, Frelsdorf 017249
Freilichtmuseum Fürstenhammer, Lasberg 002206
Freilichtmuseum Glentleiten, Großweil 017584
Freilichtmuseum Hammerschmiede, Bad Wimsbach-Neydharting 001739
Freilichtmuseum Handwerkerhaus Stegwagner, Windhaag bei Freistadt 003050
Freilichtmuseum Hessenpark, Neu-Anspach 019209
Freilichtmuseum Himmelreich, Museum Wattens, Volders 002785
Freilichtmuseum Historische Volkskunde Kalte Kuchl, Rohr im Gebirge 002534
Freilichtmuseum Katzensteiner Mühle, Weyer 002842
Freilichtmuseum Klausenhof, Herrischried 017899
Freilichtmuseum Klockenhagen, Klockenhagen 018286
Freilichtmuseum Kugelmühle, Seeham 002673
Freilichtmuseum Ledermühle, Sankt Oswald bei Freistadt 002607
Freilichtmuseum Lehde, Lehde bei Lübbenau 018543
Freilichtmuseum Massing, Massing 018861
Freilichtmuseum Mittelalterliche Bergstadt Bleiberg, Frankenberg, Sachsen . 017146
Freilichtmuseum Mondseer Rauchhaus, Mondsee 002335
Freilichtmuseum Neuhausen ob Eck, Neuhausen ob Eck 019241
Freilichtmuseum Oberlienz, Oberlienz 002384
Freilichtmuseum Ostenfelder Bauernhaus, Zweckverband Museumsverbund Nordfriesland, Husum, Nordsee . . 018034
Freilichtmuseum Pelmberg, Denkmalhof Mittermayer, Hellmonsödt 002035
Freilichtmuseum Petronell, Archäologischer Park Carnuntum, Petronell 002424
Freilichtmuseum Rhöner Museumsdorf, Tann, Rhön 020400
Freilichtmuseum Römersteinbruch, Sankt Margarethen 002597
Freilichtmuseum Römervilla in Brederis, Rankweil 002499
Freilichtmuseum Säge Buch, Buch . 036981
Freilichtmuseum Sägehammer Hofwies, Windhaag bei Freistadt 003051
Freilichtmuseum Scherzenmühle Weidenberg, Weidenberg 020708
Freilichtmuseum Schwebsingen, Bech-Kleinmacher 027868
Freilichtmuseum Spätbronzezeitlicher Hügelgräber, Siegendorf 002676
Freilichtmuseum Stehrerhof - Dreschmaschinenmuseum, Neukirchen an der Vöckla 002361
Freilichtmuseum Tiroler Bauernhöfe, Kramsach 002167
Freilichtmuseum Venetianersäge, Windhaag bei Freistadt 003052
Freilichtmuseum Vorau, Vorau 002788
Freilichtmuseum Wendlandhof, Küsten 018436
Freiligrath Museum, Krone Assmannshausen, Rüdesheim am Rhein 019941
Freimaurer-Museum, Berlin 016023
Freimaurermuseum der Großen Landesloge der Freimaurer von Deutschland, Sankt Michaelisdonn 019991
Freipresse, Bludenz 133061
Freiräume, Bad Großpertholz 133059
Freiraum, Forchtenstein . . 001858, 052532
Freiraum & Landschaft, Schwerin . . 104869
Freiraum - Verein für Kunst und Kultur e.V., Furth im Wald 053175
Freiria Aparicio, Maria Isabel, A Coruña 110319
Freitag, Jörg, Potsdam 126645
Freitag, Werner, Biebertal 125328
Freitag-Badenhausen, L., Reichshof 073477
Freitag-Lévy, Anne, Paris 065931
Freitagsgalerie, Solothurn 111918
Freitas, Bruno, Béziers 061437
Freitas, Francisco Gonçalves, Lisboa 140831
Freitas, Maria Carvalho, Lisboa . . . 109290
Freitas, Raphaël, Maureilhan 064439
Freivogel-Sippel, Nicole, Pforzheim 126627
Frejamuseét, Kil 036390
Fréjaville, Jacques, Gigean 062996
Frelin, Saint-Paul-de-Fenouillet . . . 067937
Freller, Walter, Linz 057157
Fremantle Arts Centre, Fremantle . . 001040
Fremantle History Museum, Fremantle 001041
Fremantle Prison Precinct, Fremantle 001042
Frémeaux & Assoc, Vincennes 068995
Frémont, Pascal, Le Havre 099437
Fremont, Vincent, New York 117923
Fremont Antique Mall, Seattle 093003
Fremont County Pioneer Museum, Lander 045152
Frémontier, Patrick, Paris 065932
French & Co., New York 090889
French, A. & R., London 131033
French, Lily, Saint Paul 092362
French, Peter, Hampton 055948
French, Sherry, New York 117924
French, T. & K., New York 090890
French Accents, Baltimore 087671
French Antique Corner, San Francisco 092792
French Antique Shop, New Orleans 090556
French Antiques, Menora 056209
French Antiques, Minneapolis 090358
French Art Colony, Gallipolis 044126
French Art Network, New Orleans . . 117438
French Azilum, Towanda 048591
French Cable Station Museum in Orleans, Orleans 046722
French Country Imports, Memphis . 090072
French Country Living, Mougins . . . 064804
French Country Road, Cincinnati . . 088242
French Countrystyle, Hale 084552
French Door Antiques, Norfolk 091378
French Heritage Antiques, Mentone 056210
French Heritage Antiques, Ormond . 056409
The French House, London 085311, 131034
The French House, York 087290
French House Decor, Abu Dhabi . . . 083172
French Kings Antiques, West Hollywood 093470
The French Legation Museum, Austin 041926
French Provincial, Mogo 056242
French Provincial Upholstery, Los Angeles 132253
French Quarter, San Jose 092924
French Style, Prahran 056491
French Trading, Queenstown 079223
French Treasures, New York 090891
French Twist, Saint Louis 092242
Frenchman Butte Museum, Frenchman Butte 005490
Frenk, E., Braunschweig 069980
Frenoy, Guy, Flines-lez-Raches . . . 062878
Frenzel, Heroldstatt 071493
Frenzel, Hubertus-Thomas, Rheine . 073520
Frenzel, Peter, München 139507
Fréret, Florent, Soudan 068266
Frerix, Bernd, Duderstadt 125519
Frers, Karl-Gerhard, Bremen 070019
Freschi, Renzo, Milano 075717
Fresco Art, München 104181
Fresen, Dr. Georg, München 104182
Fresh Art, London 093925
Fresh Art, New York 117925
Fresh Art, New York 117926
Fresh Fruit Studio Gallery, Portland . 118998
Fresh Gallery, Dunedin 108431
Freshford House Museum, Bloemfontein 034557
Freshfords Antiques, Freshford 084438
Fresnel, Sophie, Plumetot 066879
Fresno Art Museum, Fresno 044080
Fresno Coin Gallery, Fresno 088907
Fresno Furniture, Fresno 132077
Fresno Metropolitan Museum, Fresno 044081
Freter, Silke, Hagen, Westfalen . . . 071162
Fretex, Oslo 079434
Frettabref Felags Islenskra Safnmanna, Reykjavík 135844
Frettes, François de, Pomport 066902
Freud Museum, London 040150
Freudenheim, Nina, Buffalo 115256
Freudenthal, Peter, Hamburg 103120
Freund, Christian, Mannheim 121509
Freund, Raija, Berlin 101859
Freunde aktueller Kunst e.V., Reinsdorf 053176
Freunde der Dresdner Galerie Neue Meister e.V, Dresden 053177
Freunde der Pinakothek der Moderne, München 053178
Freunde der Schlumper e.V., Hamburg 053179
Freunde des Wallraf-Richartz-Museums und des Museums Ludwig e.V., Köln . 053180
Freunde Historischer Wertpapiere, Wolfenbüttel 074469, 121627
Freunde Mainfränkischer Kunst und Geschichte, Würzburg 053181
Freunde und Förderer des KunstRaum Berlin e.V., Berlin 053182
Freundes- und Fördererkreis der Burg Giebichenstein - Hochschule für Kunst und Design Halle e.V., Halle, Saale . . . 053183
Freundes- und Förderkreis Museum für Kunsthandwerk/Grassimuseum Leipzig e.V., Leipzig 053184
Freundeskreis der Dresdner Porzellansammlung im Zwinger e.V, Dresden 053185
Freundeskreis des Stadtmuseums Düsseldorf e.V., Düsseldorf 053186
Freundeskreis Kunstgewerbemuseum Dresden e.V, Dresden 053187
Freundeskreis zur Förderung der schönen Künste e.V., Rheda-Wiedenbrück . 053188
Freundorfer, Sigrid, New York 117927
Freuville, J., Liège 058301
Frew, Robert, London 141801
Frey, Anne-Sibylle, Basel 082140
Frey, H., Rottweil 139701
Frey, Helmut Leo, Montabaur 072592
Frey, Kayoko, Zürich 112071
Frey, Lothar, Weisenheim am Sand . 126986
Frey, M., Bedburg 069506
Frey, M., Edesheim 102601
Frey, M., Ulm 074141
Frey, Michel, Venelles 068760
Frey, Otto, Cuxhaven 070166
Frey, Simone & Günter, Meiningen . 072501
Frey, Wolfgang, Karlsruhe 125999
Frey & Norris, San Francisco 119671
Freya, Melbourne 056187
Freya, Tacolneston 086819, 131571
Freyburger, Michel, Châtenois 062222
Freyer, Bern 129957
Freyer, Cornelius, Heilbronn 071472, 125907
Fri-Art, Centre d'Art Contemporain, Fribourg 037098
F.R.I. Museums, Dehradun 022073
Friargate Pine and Antiques Centre, Derby 084160
Friary Art Gallery, Lichfield 039998
Frias, Dallas 088517
Frias, Winnipeg 059460
Friazza, Angel Luis, Sevilla 081586
The Frick Art Museum, Pittsburgh . 047050
Frick Collection, New York 046333
Fricke, Dr. Else, Emern 102621
Fricke, M. & R., Düsseldorf 102495
Fricke, Marion & Roswitha, Berlin . 101860
Fricker, A., Meckenbeuren 072479
Fricker, Jürgen H., Dinkelsbühl 070254, 102372
Fricktaler Museum, Rheinfelden . . . 037445
Fričovo Muzeum, Lázně Bělohrad . . 008467
Friday, San Francisco 119672
Friday Street Antique Centre, Henley-on-Thames 084660
Fridrich, Gundelfingen, Breisgau . . 071151
Fridrich, Wiesau 127005
Fridrich, Hans-Peter, Wiesau 074392
Frīdriha Candera Memoriālais Muzejs, Rīga 027734
Friebe, Karin, Mannheim 104023
Friebe, Klaus, Hofheim am Taunus . 071551
Friebes, Wolfgang, Graz 137176
Friebes & Gruber, Graz 137177
Fried, Helene, San Francisco 119673
Friede, Rudolf, Troisdorf 074104
Roswitha Friedelt & Börries Brakebusch, Düsseldorf 125530
Friedenauer Münzstube, Berlin 069605
Friedenshistorisches Museum, Bad Hindelang 015717
Friedensmuseum, Meeder 018867
Friedensmuseum, Remagen 019791
Friedensräume, Museum in Bewegung, Lindau, Bodensee 018652
Friedenszimmer im Schloß Altranstädt, Altranstädt 015524
Friederichsen &Co., Hamburg 139176
Friedhofen, Claudia, Schiffweiler . . 073687
Friedhuber, Eugen, Wels 137278
Friedl, Charlotte, Wildermiening . . . 123540
Friedl, Oskar, Chicago 115423
Friedl, Ursula, Seeheim-Jugenheim 104878
Friedland & Alexandre Rivault, Paule, Paris 100294
Friedlander, David R., Louisville . . .089988, 142530
Friedlandstube Hünfeld, Hünfeld . . . 018020
Friedler, N., Köln 071939
Friedli, Kurt, Netstal 082685
Friedman, Chicago 115424
Friedman, Anita, New York 117928
Friedman, Barry, New York 117929

Friedman, Julia, Chicago 115425
Friedman, Phyllis, Montréal 058954
Friedman, Stephen, London 113621
Friedman, Vallois, New York 117930
Friedmann, Grit Karen, Leipzig 126186
Friedmann, Nando-Martin, Wien . . . 057415
Friedrich, Basel 111177
Friedrich, Barbara & Susanne, Dresden 125493
Friedrich, Helmut, Freudenstadt . . .070881, 102879
Friedrich, J., Dortmund . . 102394, 133870
Friedrich, K., Freiburg im Breisgau . 102860
Friedrich, Klaus, Köln 103617
Friedrich, O., Oldenburg, Oldenburg 073200
Friedrich, Petra, Hannover 125868
Friedrich, Regina, Wildenfels 074437
Friedrich-Eckenfelder-Galerie, Balingen 015861
Friedrich-Engels-Haus, Wuppertal . 021013
Friedrich-Ludwig-Jahn-Gedenkstätte, Lanz 018516
Friedrich-Ludwig-Jahn-Museum, Freyburg 017253
Friedrich-Rückert-Gedächtnisstätte, Coburg 016574
Friedrich & Ungar, München 104183
Friedrich-Wilhelm-Weber-Museum, Bad Driburg 015681
Friedrichson, Thomas, Berlin 125200
Friege, Heinz, Remscheid 104713
Frielich & Deutsch, New York 117931
Frieling, Berlin 133774
Friemann, Peter, Bonn 069920
Friend Art, Tokyo 107036
Friend or Faux, Bungay . . 083781, 130474
Friends Art, Barcelona 110156
Friends Art Gallery, Ha Noi 120463
Friends in the Wild, Saint Louis . . . 092243
Friends of Art, Kansas City 116565
Friends of Bezalel Academy, New York 054766
Friends of French Art, Rancho Palos Verdes 136466
The Friends of Photography at the Ansel Adams Center, San Francisco . . . 047862
Friends of the Arts, Chicago 115426
Friends of the Fan Museum, London 054382
Friends of the Minneapolis Institute of Arts, Minneapolis 054767
The Friends of the Royal Academy, London 054383
Friends of the Tate Gallery, London . 054525
The Friends of the V&A, London . . . 054384
Friends' Preview, Glasgow 136216
Friends' Quarterly (Enfield), Enfield . 136467
Friendship Firehouse, Alexandria . . 041640
Friendship Hill National Historic Site, Point Marion 047110
Friendship Museum, Darhan 029000
Fries, Liesbeth, Bern 082209
Fries, R., Kleinostheim 071872
Fries, Ulrich, Berlin 069606
Fries Landbouw Museum, Exmorra . 029586
Fries Museum, Leeuwarden 029837
Fries Natuurmuseum, Leeuwarden . 029838
Fries Scheepvaart Museum, Sneek 030167
't Friesche Schathuis, Haarlem 078453
Friese, Petra, Solms 126814
Friese-Galerie, Wendländischer Altertumsverein, Lüchow, Wendland 018733
Friesen, Seattle 119922
Friesenecker, H., Lahstedt 072118
Friesenstube Honkenswarf, Langeneß 018508
Friesia Cottage, Dunsborough 055770
Friesisches Heimatmuseum, Freilichtmuseum, Niebüll 019305
Friess, Jean-Pierre, Joigny (Yonne) . 063244
Friess, Jean-Pierre, Joigny (Yonne) . 063245
Friess, Jean-Pierre, Joigny (Yonne) . 124268
Friess, Jean-Pierre, Joigny (Yonne) . 124269
Frieß, Manfred, Augsburg 125073
Friessnig, Leo, Klagenfurt 057106
Frietkotmuseum, Antwerpen 003162
Friez, Marie, Paris 065933
Frieze, London 136217
Frieze Art Fair, London 093926
Frigate Unicorn, Dundee 039307
Friggi, Zeffirino, Verona 128425
Frihedsmuseet, Nationalmuseet, København 008965
Frij, Ole, Dallas 115883
Frijns, Adriaan, Thorn 128840
Frilandsmuseet, Nationalmuseet, Kongens Lyngby 009000
Frilandsmuseet i Maribo, Maribo . . 009018
Frilli, Firenze 106054
Friluftmuseet Hallandsgården, Länsmuseet Halmstad, Halmstad 036324
Friluftmuseet Skansen, Stockholm . 036625
Friluftsmuseet, Jönköping 036360
Friluftsmuseet Gammelgården, Köping 036393
Friluftsmuseet i Apladalen, Värnamo 036759
Friluftsmuseum Färgargården, Norrköpings Stadsmuseum, Norrköping 036499
Fringe, K., Hong Kong 097784
Frings, Brunsbüttel 102277
Frings, T., Titz 074065
Frintrup, Rainer, Bonn 069921
Fripe c'est Chic, Fumay 062949
Frip'ou'net, Saint-Jean-de-Luz 067537
Frippery, New Orleans 090557
Le Fripier, Napoli 075989
Frisch, Dieter, Hamburg 139177
Frisch, Gertrud, München 072703
Frisco, Grou 140438
Frisco Historical Society Museum, Frisco 044086
Frisco Native American Museum and Natural History Center, Frisco . . . 044087
Frisia Museum, Spanbroek 030175
Frisina, Francesco, Torino 128308
Friske, Bardowick 069469
Friske, Anja, Friedeburg, Ostfriesland 070890
Frisso, Z., Brasília 096492
Frist Center for the Visual Arts, Nashville 046147
Frith, Michael, Toowoomba 056719
Frith Street Gallery, London 113622
Fritsch, Beeskow 125143
Fritsch, Georg, Wien 137309
Fritsch, Georg, Wien 137310
Fritsch, Jean-Louis, Sand 068117
Fritsch, U., Rheine 073521
Fritschi, Markus, Rieden 130150
Fritschi, Rolf, Steinmaur 130189
Fritz, Mössingen 104110
Fritz, G. & G., Regensburg 073456
Fritz, Günther, Karlsruhe 071720
Fritz, P., Osnabrück 073234
Fritz-Best-Museum, Kronberg im Taunus 018419
Fritz-Denneville, H., München 104184
Fritz-Denneville, Hildegard, London 085312, 113623, 131035
Fritz Fröhlich-Sammlung im Stift Wilhering, Wilhering 003048
Fritz-Reuter-Literaturmuseum, Reuterstadt Stavenhagen 019805
Fritz-Shaar, Pieterlen 111810
Fritz-Winter-Haus, Galerie für moderne Kunst, Ahlen 015450
Fritz Wotruba-Gedenkraum, Wien . . 002899
Fritzl's Kuchlkredenz, Wien 057416
Fritzøe Museum, Larvik 030972
Fritzsche, Ernst, Berlin 069607
Froaschgass-Museum, Wettenberg 020835
Frobenius-Institut, Johann Wolfgang Goethe-Universität, Frankfurt am Main 050082
Frobisher Thresherman's Museum, Frobisher 005491
Froden, Los Angeles 116770
Frodes, Oslo 079435
Frodsham & Co, Charles, London . . 085313
Fröbelmuseum, Keilhau 018219
Fröhlich, Linz 095656
Fröhlich, Stuttgart 073973
Fröhlich, Hansueli, Sankt Gallen . . . 082774
Fröhlich, Helmut, Wien 137311
Fröhlich, Patrik, Zürich 112072
Das fröhliche Wohnzimmer-Edition, Wien 133195
Frölich, Stuttgart 126849
Frölich, E.J. & M., Enschede 078370
Frölich, Renate, Mainz 126260
Frölich & Kaufmann, Berlin 138778
Froelick Gallery, Portland 118999
Frösåkers Auktioner, Östhammar . . 122222
Froesch, Roger, Singrist . . 068244, 124935
Fröschen, Aachen 069085
Froese, B., Wismar 127025
Frösö Hembygdsmuseum, Frösön . . 036279
Froessel, Pascal, Strasbourg 101288
Frövifors Pappersbruksmuseum, Frövi 036280
The Frog & Mouse Picture, Leicester 113373
Froger, Rochefort (Charente-Maritime) 067177
Frogmore House, Royal Collections, Windsor 041414
Frogtown Books, Toledo 143028
Frohberg, Ulrich, Flonheim 125643
Frohnert, Christine, Köln 126077
Froidl, Christian, Feldafing 125632
Frøksjær, Carsten, København 098554
From Holocaust to Revival Museum, Chof Ashkelon 022901
From Slaveship to Ownership, Denver 115997
From the Hip, Los Angeles 089772
From Times Past, Edmonton 058827
Fromagerie de Démonstration de Gruyères, La Maison du Gruyère, Pringy . . . 037426
Fromaget, Régis, Paris 124668
Fromanger, Jean-Pierre, Paris 065934
Fromantin, Dominique, Paris 065935
Frome Museum, Frome 039528
Froment, Michèle, Vallauris 101415
Fromm, Saarbrücken 073630
Fromm, Bruno, Parsberg 126612
Fromm, Peter, Untermerzbach 074164
Fromme, Suzanne H., Graz 057010, 095522
Fromme, Suzanne H., Pörtschach am Wörther See 057210, 095706
Frommhagen, Eva, Schöneiche bei Berlin 126776
Fronhouse Antiques, Barmouth . . . 083385
Front Gallery, Edmonton 005397
Front Gallery, Edmonton 096881
Front Gate, Indianapolis 089299
Front Porch Antiques, Atlanta 087477
Front Street Museum, Ogallala 046626
The Front Window, San Jose 092925
Fronte Nuovo delle Arti, Venezia . . . 053756
Frontenac County Schools Museum, Kingston 005696
Frontera, Daniela, Córdoba 094096
Fronti di Mare, Propriano . 066986, 101050
Frontier Army Museum, Fort Leavenworth 043938
Frontier Culture Museum, Staunton 048342
Frontier Gallery, Denver 088687
Frontier Gallery, Fort Worth 116142
Frontier Gallery, Houston 116317
Frontier Gallery, Seattle 093004
Frontier Museum, Williston 049193
Frontier Times Museum, Bandera . . 042008
Frontier Village Museum, Jamestown 044832
Frontiers of Flight Museum, Dallas . 043271
Froschauergenossenschaft Züricher Antiquare, Zürich 054179
Froschmuseum, Münchenstein 037354
Froseth, K.M., Minneapolis 090359
Frosio, Gérard, Lausanne 082546
Frøslevlejrens Museum, Padborg . . 009061
Frost, Sydney 056675
Frost & Son, C.R., London 085314, 131036
Frost Antiques, Monmouth 086001, 131281
The Frost Entomological Museum, University Park 048701
Frost & Reed, London 085315, 113624
Frost & Reed, New York 090892
Frosta Bygdemuseet, Frosta 030850
Frosting, Wilhelm, Dortmund 102395
Froula, Barbara, Denver 115998
Frøya Bygdemuseum, Sistranda . . . 031182
Fruch, Jean-Marie, Domremy-la-Pucelle 062712
Frübing, Ruth & Horst, Füssen 070915
Früh, Anna, Karlsruhe . . . 103489, 121461
Früh, Peter, Salem, Baden 126759
Früh-Jenner, Dr. Gustl, München . . 072704
Frühauf, H., Flensburg 070702
Frühauf e.V., Leipzig 053189, 103867
Frühmittelaltermuseum Carantana, Rothenthurn 002542
Frühmorgen, München 134239
Fruehsorge, Berlin 101861
Frühwirth, Wilhelm, Bernstein, Burgenland 137158
Fruhriep, Marianne, Perleberg 104599
Fruitlands Museums, Harvard 044471
Fruitman, C., Bruxelles 057952
Fruitmarket Gallery, Edinburgh 039390
Fruitmarket Gallery, Publishing Department, Edinburgh 135141
Fruitteeltmuseum, Kapelle 029804
Frumas, San Jose 092926
Frutabela, Lisboa 079930
Fry Model Railway, Demesne 022725
Fry Model Railway Museum, Malahide 022832
Fry Public Art Gallery, Saffron Walden 040879
Fryč, J., Liberec 137792
Fryde, Aline, Saint-Ouen 067779
Frydendal, Frederiksberg 060236
Frydman, Renée, Saint-Ouen 067780
Frye & Sohn, Münster . . . 072905, 104359
Frye, Ken, Washington 120294
Frye Art Museum, Seattle 048080
The Fryeburg Fair Farm Museum, Fryeburg 044093
Fryer, Fritz, Ross-on-Wye . 086400, 131426
Fryer Memorial Museum, Munnsville 046089
Frye's Measure Mill, Wilton 049226
Fryksdals-Auktioner, Sunne 122272
Fryoux, Elsie, New Orleans 090558, 132414
Fryś, Agnieszka, Kraków 079633
Frysk Letterkundich Museum, Leeuwarden 029839
Frysk Skildershûs, Leeuwarden . . . 108094
Fryxell Geology Museum, Rock Island 047493
F.S. Antiques, Sheffield . . 086557, 131474
FS & AV Arte Contemporânea, Porto 109374
F.T. Hill Museum, Riverhurst 006294
Fu, Jian, Shenzhen 097977
Fu, Sang, Urumchi 059790
Fu, Xia, Singapore 109798
Fucares, Madrid 110503
Fuchs, Fulda 102908, 125694, 139128
Fuchs, Anja-Renate, Strullendorf . . 126839
Fuchs, Annemarie, Weitra 137277
Fuchs, Anton, Eisingen, Kreis Würzburg 125581
Fuchs, Christel, Sankt Ingbert 073667
Fuchs, Christian, Saalfelden 095713
Fuchs, Daniel, Montevideo 087319
Fuchs, Günter, Bad Münder 138698
Fuchs, Hanspeter & Rosmarie, Trachslau 082859, 130197
Fuchs, Prof. Dr. Heinrich, Wien 133196
Fuchs, Jacques, Nice 124513
Fuchs, Maria, München 126377
Fuchs, Robert, Köln 126078
Fuchs, Willy, München 072705
Fuchs, Wolfgang, Norderstedt 073071
Fuchs-Gerhart, Gertraud, Walchensee 105145
Fuchs & Reposo, Lugano 141268

Fuchsia, Arnhem 107848
Fuchsia Dentelle, Paris 065936
Fuchu-shi Kyodono-mori, Fuchu . . . 026453
Fuchunjiang, Hangzhou 097736
Fucik, Nürnberg 104477
Fuckerrieder, Herta, Wiener Neustadt 095970, 133244
Fuda, Suzhou 097995
Fuego, Tilburg 078769
Führ, Wieland, Naumburg, Saale . .072944, 134301, 139581
Führer, W.T., München 072706
Füldner, Peter, Zemmer 074563
Füllemann, Hans, Lausanne 082547
Füllemann, Hans & Erwin, Schaffhausen 082798
Füllhorn, Sommerhausen 104921
Fündling, Wilhelm, Stade 104940
Fünf-Giebel-Haus, Friedrichstadt . . 017274
La Fuentecilla, Madrid 081304
Fuentes, San Antonio 132813
Fuentes Fortes, Vigo 081703
Fürhacker, Robert, Graz 123360
Fürnkranz, Johann, Wien 057417
Fürst Pückler Museum - Park und Schloß Branitz, Cottbus 016594
Fürst Thurn und Taxis Marstallmuseum, Regensburg 019748
Fürst Thurn und Taxis Schloßmuseum - Museum Kreuzgang, Regensburg 019749
Fürst Thurn und Taxis Zentralarchiv und Hofbibliothek, Regensburg 019750
Städtische Galerie; Fürstbischöfliches Museum, Meersburg 018874
Fürste, Dortmund 102396
Fürstelberger, Hans, Linz 137218
Fürstenbergerhof, Zell am Harmersbach 021048
Fürstengalerie, Fürstenwalde, Spree 102898
Fürstengruft mit russisch-orthodoxer Kirche, Stiftung Weimarer Klassik und Kunstsammlung, Weimar, Thüringen 020738
Fürstenzimmer im Schloß Kirchheim, Kirchheim unter Teck 018267
Fürstlich Esterházy'sche Sammlungen Burg Forchtenstein, Forchtenstein 001859
Fürstlich Fürstenbergisches Schloßmuseum, Donaueschingen 016738
Fürstlich Hohenzollernsche Sammlungen, Sigmaringen 020207
Fürstlich Leiningensche Sammlungen - Heimatmuseum, Amorbach 015536
Fürstlich Ysenburg- und Büdingensches Schloßmuseum, Büdingen 016489
Fürstliches Residenzschloß, Detmold 016688
Fürstliches Schloß mit Gemäldegalerie, Mausoleum, Bückeburg 016483
Fuerte de la Punta del Sauce, La Carlota 000374
Füssl & Jakob, München 104185
Fugger-Museum, Babenhausen, Schwaben 015635
Fuggerei-Museum, Augsburg 015607
Fugitive Art Center, Nashville 046148
Fugitive Art Center, Nashville 117352
Fuglsøcentret, Knebel 008955
Fuheng, Zhuhai 059792
Fuhlrott-Museum, Wuppertal 021014
Fuhr, W., Wiesbaden 074402, 127010
Fuhrer, Hack & Walther, Stuttgart . . 126850
Fuhrmann, Rostock 104765
Fuhrmann, C. & J., Braunschweig . 138920
Fuhrmann, J., Rostock 104766
Fuhrmann, Jürgen, Braunschweig . 138921
Fuiza, Belo Horizonte 058427
Fujairah Museum, Fujairah 038426
Fuji Art Craft, Kyoto 077096
Fuji Art Museum, Fujinomiya 026455
Fuji Fine Arts, Tokyo 077245
Fuji Photo Salon, Osaka 106957
Fuji-Torii, Tokyo 077246
Fuji Visitor Center, Kawaguchiko . . 026640
Fujian Art Cooperative, Fuzhou 052795, 097717
Fujian Fine Arts Publishing House, Fuzhou 133346
Fujian Province Museum, Fuzhou . . 007076
Fujii, T., Honolulu 088946
Fujii Bijutsu Mingeikan, Takayama . 027117
Fujii Saisei-kai Yurinkan, Kyoto . . . 026714
Fujikawa Gakuen, Kyoto Zoukei Geijutsu Gakuin, Kyoto 050460
Fujikawa Galleries, Osaka 106958
Fujikawa Galleries, Tokyo 107037
Fujikeido, Nara 140169
Fujita Museum of Art, Osaka 026960
Fujita-Unkotei, Nara 077159
Fujita Vente, Tokyo 027162
Fujiya, Tokyo 077247
Fukawa, Yokohama 077334
Fukuhara, Tokyo 107038
Fukui, Asahido, Kyoto 077097
Fukui City Natural Science Museum, Fukui 026457
Fukui Fujita Bijutsukan, Fukui 026458
Fukui-ken Togeikan, Miyazaki, Fukui 026823
Fukui-kenritsu Bijutsukan, Fukui . . 026459
Fukui-kenritsu Hakubutsukan, Fukui 026460
Fukunaga, Hiroshima 077054
Fukuoka, Yamato-koriyama 077330
Fukuoka-kenritsu Bijutsukan, Fukuoka 026461
Fukuoka Nichi-do Gallery, Fukuoka 106843
Fukuoka-shi Bijutsukan, Fukuoka . . 026462
Fukuoka-shi Hakubutsukan, Fukuoka 026463
Fukushima-ken Bunka Center, Fukushima 026464
Fukushima-kenritsu Bijutsukan, Fukushima 026465
Fukushima-kenritsu Hakubutsukan, Aizuwakamatsu 026406
Fukuyama Auto and Clock Museum, Fukuyama 026466
Fukuyama-Jo Castle Museum, Fukuyama 026467
Fukuyama Museum of Art, Fukuyama 026468
Fukuzawa Memorial Hall, Nakatsu . 026890
Fulcrand, Bessan 061401
Fulcrand, Jacqueline, Saint-Tropez . 068016
Fulda, Constance, Paris 100295
Fulda Gallery, Salford 114388, 131449
Fuldaer Münze, Ebersburg 070495
Fulford Gallery, Ottawa . . . 059038, 097105
Fulham, London 085316
Full Circle, San Diego 092637
Full Circle Architectural Antiques, Hawthorn, Victoria 055962
Full Circle Gallery, Glasgow 113110
Full Spirit Publishing, Tucson 135516
Fullam, Dublin 074918
Fuller, Clifford, London 131037
Fuller, Ernest, Denver 115999
Fuller, Jeffrey, Philadelphia 118760
Fuller, D'Arch & Smith, London 141802
Fuller Museum of Art, Brockton . . . 042426
Fullerton Museum Center, Fullerton 044094
Fulton, Fresno 088908
Fulton County Historical Museum, Wauseon 049017
Fulton County Historical Society Museum, Rochester 047470
Fulton County Museum, Groversville 044368
Fulton Mansion, Rockport 047510
Fulton Street Art Gallery, New York . 117932
Fultz House Museum, Lower Sackville 005804
Fulwood Gallery, Preston 114287
Fumagalli, Eugenio, Villars-sur-Glâne 130206
Fumagalli, Luigi, Honolulu 116211
Fumelli, Adele Maria, Roma 076473
Fumi, Okegawa 106948
Fumiki, San Francisco 092793
Fumusa, Vincenzo, Milano 127597
Funabashi Bijutsu Gakuin, Funabashi 050451
Funabashi Hakubutsukan, Funabashi 026470
Funaki, Melbourne 094813
Le Funambule, Paris 138380
Function + Art, Chicago 115427
Fund & Arte, Medellín 123933
Fundação Casa de Jorge Amado, Salvador 004436
Fundação Clóuis Salgado - Palácio das Artes, Belo Horizonte 003995
Fundação Cultural Ema Gordon Klabin, São Paulo 004506
Fundação Eva Klabin Rappaport, Rio de Janeiro 004341
Fundação Hansen Bahia, Cachoeira 004029
Fundação Maria Luisa e Oscar Americano, São Paulo 004507
Fundação Memorial da América Latina, São Paulo 004508
Fundação Museu do Zebu Edilson Lamartine Mendes, Uberaba 004589
Fundação Nacional Pró-Memória, Rio de Janeiro 004342
Fundaçao Oscar Niemeyer, Rio de Janeiro 004343
Fundação Ricardo do Espírito Santo Silva, Lisboa 032629
Fundação Ricardo do Espírito Santo Silva, Lisboa 129153
Fundacija Jože Ciuha, Bled 109930
Fundació Antoni Tàpies, Barcelona . 034907
Fundació Barceló, Palma de Mallorca 035608
Fundació Caixa d'Estalvis i Pensions, Serv. Edit., Barcelona 134914
Fundació Emili Vilá, Llagostera 035340
Fundacio Espais, Girona 035228
Fundacio Fita, Girona 035229
Fundació Joan Miró, Barcelona . . . 034908
Fundació la Caixa en las Islas Baleares, Palma de Mallorca 035609
Fundació la Caixa, Revista el treua, Barcelona 136087
Fundació Pilar i Joan Miró, Palma de Mallorca 035610
Fundació Pública Institut d'Estudis Ilerdencs, Fons Bibliogràfic i Documental, Lleida 035345
Fundación Alfredo L. Palacios, Buenos Aires 000148
Fundación Archivo Gráfico y Museo Histórico de la Ciudad de San Francisco y la Región, San Francisco 000559
Fundación Banco Francés, Buenos Aires 000149
Fundación César Manrique, Teguise 035899
Fundación Cultural Otero Pedrayo, Amoeiro 034836
Fundación de Fomento a las Artes, La Paz 003910
Fundación Federico Jorge Klemm, Buenos Aires 000150
Fundación Folch, Barcelona 034909
Fundación Juan March, Madrid . . . 035388
Fundación Municipal de Cultura Luis Ortega Brú, San Roque 035771
Fundacion Museo de la Caricatura Severo Vaccaro, Buenos Aires 000151
Fundacion Privada Espai Guinovart, Agramunt 034782
Fundación Solar Rietti, Buenos Aires 000152
Fundación Yannick y Ben Jakober, Alcúdia 034812
Fundação Cultural do Estado da Bahia, Salvador 133302
Fundatia Galeria de Artă, Cluj-Napoca 109449
Funder, Dover 136884
Fundgrube, Solothurn 082819
Fundgrube, Stockach 073920
Fundgrube für Bücherfreunde, Hamburg 139178
Fundgrube zur Laterne, Sursee . . . 082839
Fundus, Berlin 138779
Fundus, Hamburg 071229
Fundus, Sankt-Peterburg 109618
Der Funduskeller am Wilhelmsplatz, Görlitz 139142
Fundy Geological Museum, Parrsboro 006115
Fune no Kagakukan, Tokyo 027163
Fung, Martin, Hong Kong 059629
Fung, Martin, Hong Kong 059630
Fung, Martin, Hong Kong 059631
Fung, Sabrina, Hong Kong 097785
Funk, Hollis, Chicago 115428
Funk, Robert, Saskatoon . 059097, 123817
Funk, Werner, Grasbrunn 071086
Funk, Wolfgang, Stuttgart 073974
Funk House, Las Vegas 089574
Funkar Art Gallery, Karachi 108773
Funke, Peter, Sundern 074032
Funktionall Art, Minneapolis 117260
Funky Furnishings, Sacramento . . . 092159
Funky Junktion, Whangamata 079361
Funnefoss Industriarbeidermuseum, Årnes 030738
Funque's, Austin 087573
Funtiques, Seattle 093005
Fuoricentro, Roma 106537
Fur Museum, Fur 008871
Furas, Sergio N., Montevideo 087320
Furdyna, Józef, Kraków 129037
Fureai Minatokan, Osaka 026961
Furgadou, Toulouse 068511
Furiko, Fukuoka 077041
Furletti, Belo Horizonte 058428
Furlong Art Gallery, University of Wisconsin-Stout, Menomonie 045777
Furlotti, Alessandra, Milano 075718, 127598, 140051
Furman jr., Donald, Buffalo 087877
Furn Davies, Holt, Wales . 084709, 130799
Furnas-Gosper Historical Society Museum, Arapahoe 041757
Furneaux Museum, Flinders Island . 001031
Furness Abbey, Barrow-in-Furness . 038605
The Furnishing Touch, Tauranga . . .079263, 128965
Furnishings off Foster, Portland . . . 091938
Furniture and Refinishing, Cincinnati 131933
Furniture and Upholstery, Houston . 132118
Furniture Artisans, Philadelphia . . . 132617
Furniture Artist Repair, Miami 132341
Furniture by School Masters, Milwaukee 132366
Furniture Cave, Aberystwyth 083249, 130283
The Furniture Cave, London 085317
Furniture Cave, Preston 123289
Furniture Conservatory, Indianapolis 132154
Furniture Craft Company, Los Angeles 132254
Furniture Craftsman, Cincinnati . . . 131934
Furniture Craftsman, San Antonio . . 132814
Furniture Craftsman, Tucson 132985
Furniture Depot, Denver 088688
Furniture Doctor, Las Vegas 132215
The Furniture Doctor, Vestaburg . . . 133007
Furniture Exchange, Atlanta 087478, 131774
Furniture Haven, Honolulu 088947
Furniture Heaven, Regina 059087
Furniture History Society, Haywards Heath 054385
Furniture History Society, Wahroonga 052469
Furniture Mart, Margate . . 085928, 131262
Furniture Medic, Cleveland 131960
Furniture Medic, Littleton 132220
Furniture Medic, Louisville 132295
Furniture Medic, Memphis 132323
Furniture Medic, Miami 132342
Furniture Medic, Phoenix 132647
Furniture Medic, Sacramento 132734
Furniture Medic, San Antonio 132815
Furniture Now and Then, Albany . . . 055322

Furniture on Consignment, Albuquerque . . . 087392
Furniture Refinishing, Denver . . . 132038
Furniture Renovations Company, London . . . 131038
Furniture Restorables, Saskatoon . . 123818
Furniture Restoration Center, El Paso . . . 132064
Furniture Restorations, Houston . . . 132119
Furniture Revisited, Brunswick . . . 055572
Furniture Revival, Hawthorn, Victoria . . . 055963
Furniture Service, Dunedin . . . 128933
Furniture Shoppe, Norfolk . . . 132555
Furniture Stripping, Kansas City . . . 132208
Furniture Trading Company, Botley, Hampshire . . . 083583
Furniture Vault, London . . . 085318
Furniture Wizards, Winnipeg . . . 123868
Furniture Workshop, San Francisco 132881
Furnitures Friend, Seattle . . . 132934
Furonnet, Jean-Louis, Langon . . . 063521
Furrer, Susi, Zürich . . . 112073
Furrer, Walter J., Brig . . . 129988
Fursdon House, Cadbury . . . 038936
Furstenberg, Paris . . . 100296
Furthmühle, Egenhofen . . . 016889
Furtwengler, Uwe, Baden-Baden . . 069411
Fusa, Marta, Verona . . . 077003
Fusay, Jean-Paul, Reims . . . 124861
Fusban, Daniel, Utting . . . 074175
Fusco, Toni, Aarau . . . 082068
Fuse Magazine, Toronto . . . 135634
Fusebox, Washington . . . 120295
Fushun Calligraphy and Painting Gallery, Fushun . . . 097714
Fushun City Museum, Fushun . . . 007073
Mario Fusi & Alberto Barigazzi, Lugano . . . 082597
Fusiliers London Volunteers' Museum, London . . . 040151
Fusiliers' Museum Lancashire, Bury, Lancashire . . . 038921
Fusiliers Museum of Northumberland, Alnwick . . . 038493
Fusion, Milwaukee . . . 117189
Fusion, Portland . . . 091939
Fusion Fine Arts, Mandurah . . . 094779
Fusions Gallery, Fortitude Valley . . . 001035
Fuso, Tokyo . . . 077248
Fustier, Maxime, Paris . . . 065937
Futierra, Leo, Glasgow . . . 113111
Futselaar, Erna, Amsterdam . . . 107713
Futter, Lothar, Sundern . . . 074033
Futterknecht, Ralf, Stuttgart . . . 126851
Futtsu Oceanographic Museum of Chiba Prefecture, Kimitsu . . . 026651
Futur Antérieur, Bruxelles . . . 057953
Futur Anterieur, Le Touquet-Paris-Plage . . . 063718
Futur Antérieur, Paris . . . 065938
Futur Antérieur, Saint-Ouen . . . 067781
Futura, Paris . . . 100297, 133609
Futurama, Los Angeles . . . 089773
Futurart, Roma . . . 076474, 128055
Futuras Antigüedades, Barcelona . . 080850
Future Antique Furniture, Silverwater . . . 056596
Future Antiques, Saint Louis . . . 092244
Future Visions Books, Houston . . . 142438
Futures Antiques, Norfolk . . . 091379
Futures Past, Dallas . . . 088518
Futurotroc, Chasseneuil-du-Poitou . 062174
Fuxin Calligraphy and Painting Gallery, Fuxin . . . 097716
Fuxin City Museum, Fuxin . . . 007074
Fuyang Museum, Fuyang . . . 007075
Fuyou Lu Auction House, Shanghai .059739, 120842
Fuyou Lu Market, Shanghai . . . 059740
Fuzhou City Hualin Si, Fuzhou . . . 007077
Fuzhou East Art Cooperative, Fuzhou . . . 097718
Fuzhou Painting Gallery, Fuzhou . . . 097719
Fuzoku Hakubutsukan, Kyoto . . . 026715
Fuzzy Art, München . . . 104186
FVSR Kunsthandel, München . . . 072707
Fyansford Antiques, Fyansford . . . 055846
F.Y.B. Arts, Long Beach . . . 116669
Fyfe, Toronto . . . 059193, 123832
Fyndia, Helsinki . . . 060521
Fyns Kunstmuseum, Odense . . . 009047
Den Fynske Landsby, Odense . . . 009048
Fyresdal Bygdemuseet, Fyresdal . . 030851
Fyris Antik, Uppsala . . . 082057
Fyshwick Antique Centre, Fyshwick 055853
Fyson, Jonathan, Burford . . . 083787
Fyvie Castle, Fyvie . . . 039529
G 26, Bern . . . 111249
G. C. Antik Design, København . . . 060326
G Fine Art, Washington . . . 120296
G & G Custom Works, Calgary . . . 123745
G & G Furniture Restorations, Olney 131346
G & G - Górska Glaza, Wrocław . . . 109217
G&G Restaurateurs, 's-Hertogenbosch . . . 128714
G-Gallery, Lemesos . . . 098313
G&H Furniture Repairing, Cincinnati 131935
G + H Verlag, Berlin . . . 133775
G III Antiques, Brugge . . . 057773
G & L Antiques, Wellington . . . 079323
G-Loft, Bruxelles . . . 096193
G-Module, Paris . . . 100298
G & N Lebensart, Wien . . . 095822
G & S, Zemun . . . 109751
G2K, Auckland . . . 108321
GAA Museum, Dublin . . . 022743
De Gaarde, Utrecht . . . 078798
Gaasbeek El-Bar, Amsterdam . . . 077852
Gaasch, Armand, Dudelange . . . 107381
Gaballa, Austin . . . 087574
Gabara, Joan, Picton . . . 079222
Gabarro Art, Sabadell . . . 110728
Gabba Old Wares, Woolloongabba . 056884
Il Gabbiano, Roma . . . 106538
Gabel, Seattle . . . 132935
Gaber, Heinrich, Trier . . . 074090
Gabert, Pascal, Paris . . . 100299
Gabillet, Richard, Tours . . . 068591
Gabinet d'Assessors, Barberà del Vallès . . . 121992
Gabinet Numizmaticzny, Gdańsk . . 079580
Gabinet Numizmatyczny Mennicy Państwowej, Warszawa . . . 032424
Gabinet Prof. K. Sosnowskiego, Ośrodek Muzealny KTG, Kraków . . . 032026
Gabinet Rycin Biblioteki Uniwersyteckiej w Warszawie, Warszawa . . . 032425
Gabinet Rycin Polskiej Akademii Umiejętności w Krakowie, Kraków 032027
Gabinete, Bilbao . . . 080972, 129431
Gabinete de Antigüedades, Madrid . 035389
Gabinete de Arte Minas Contemporânea, Belo Horizonte . . . 096464
Gabinete de Física Experimental Mentora Alsina, Barcelona . . . 034910
Gabinete Numismático de Cataluña, Museu Nacional d'Art de Catalunya, Barcelona . . . 034911
Gabinetto dei Disegni e delle Stampe, Pinacoteca Nazionale, Bologna . . 023419
Gabinetto delle Stampe, Roma . . . 025473
Gabinetto Disegni e Stampe degli Uffizi, Firenze . . . 024152
Gabinetto Disegni e Stampe-Dipartimento di Storia delle Arti dell'Università di Pisa, Pisa . . . 025264
Gabinetto Fotografico, Soprintendenza ai Beni Artistici e Storici, Firenze . . . 024153
Gabinetto Geologico e Botanico Piccinini, Pergola . . . 025158
Gabinetto Nazionale delle Stampe, Roma . . . 025474
Gabinetto Stampe e Disegni, Museo Correr, Venezia . . . 026232
Gabino, Anna, Torino . . . 128309
Gabler, H., Augsburg . . . 069226
Gables, Miami . . . 090173
Gablonzer Archiv Museum, Kaufbeuren . . . 018209
Gablonzer Haus mit Isergebirgsmuseum, Kaufbeuren . . . 018211
Gabonamúzeum, Békéscsaba . . . 021628
Gabor, Toronto . . . 097269
Gaboriaud, Marc, Saint-Ouen . . . 067782
Gaboriaux, Frédéric, Brive-la-Gaillarde . . . 061810
Gaboriaux, Frédéric, Chameyrat . . . 062107
Gaboriaux, J.P., Lyon . . . 064127
Gabory, de, Maule . . . 064426
Gabriel, Footscray . . . 094550
Gabriel, Christophe, Paris . . . 100300
Gabriel, Erich, Wien . . . 095823
Gabriel, Peter, Dresden . . . 125494
Gabrieli, Giovanni, Liebefeld . . . 130081
Gabrielle Salomon-Art Conseil, Paris . . . 100301
Gabriëls, Den Haag . . . 078198
Gabriel's Refinishing, Houston . . . 132120
Gabrielsen, E., Oslo . . . 108709
Gabrius, Milano . . . 106217
Gabrius, New York . . . 135430
Gabus, Pierre-Yves, Montalchez . . .082664, 122342
Gaby's Clocks and Things, Tenterden . . . 086844, 131579
Gaby's Shoppe, Dallas . . . 115884
La Gaceta, La Habana . . . 135664
Gacheon Museum, Incheon . . . 027510
Gachet, Vancouver . . . 097473
Gachnang & Springer, Bern . . . 134991
Gadabout, Toronto . . . 059194
Gadaj, Barbara, Warszawa . . . 129083
Gadda, Eugenio, Milano . . . 127599
Gadebuscher Galerie am Schlossberg, Gadebusch . . . 017311
Gades Art, Roma . . . 106539
Gadesmann, Dr. Detlev, Hannover . 125869
GaDeWe - Galerie des Westens, Bremen . . . 102240
Gadfly Gallery, Dalkeith . . . 094447
Gadfly Online, Charlottesville . . . 136468
Gadient, Manuela, Zürich . . . 112074
Gadiot & Mas, Rotterdam . . . 108185
Gado, Kyoto . . . 106892
Gadow, Hartmut, Itzehoe . . . 071646
Gadow, Hartmut, Puls . . . 073387, 126667
Gadsby's Tavern Museum, Alexandria . . . 041641
Gadsden Arts Center, Quincy . . . 047295
Gadsden Museum, Mesilla . . . 045795
Gadsden Museum of Fine Arts, Gadsden . . . 044101
Gaedigk, Wolfgang, Rellingen . . . 104709
Gaedtke, Hubert, Sonneberg, Thüringen . . . 104926
Gähler, Walter, Glarus . . . 082477
Gael Song, Seattle . . . 093006
Gaelic College of Celtic Arts and Crafts, English Town . . . 005430, 049785
Gällersta Forngård, Örebro . . . 036517
Gaemers, Den Haag . . . 128629
Gäng, Alfred, Osnabrück . . . 073235
Gänshirt, Klaus, Köln . . . 103618
Gaerlich, U., Naumburg, Saale . . . 104390
Gärtner, Berlin . . . 101862
Gärtner, Flammersfeld . . . 070694
Gärtner, Hilden . . . 071515
Gärtner, Schlangenbad . . . 073692
Gärtner, Heinz, Hannover . . . 139232
Gärtner, Magdalene, Aalen . . . 125045
Gaertner, Marlies, Duisburg . . . 070477
Gärtner, Michael, Frankfurt am Main . . . 102768
Gärtner, Walter, Forst, Lausitz . . . 070720
Gärtner- und Häckermuseum, Bamberg . . . 015871
Gaetano, Antonella, Roma . . . 076475
Gaetano, Bruno, Palermo . . . 106427
Gaete García, René, Santiago de Chile . . . 059530
Gätjens, Dieter, Hamburg . . . 139179
Gäubodenmuseum, Straubing . . . 020335
Gävleborgs Läns Auktionskammare, Hamrångefjärden . . . 122153
Gaffé, Daniel, Dieppe . . . 062626
Gaffelaer, Breda . . . 107878
Gaffer, Hong Kong . . . 097786
Gafor, Barcelona . . . 129346
GAG Dépot Vente, Poitiers 066892, 138574
Gagarin, Waasmunster . . . 135596
Gage, Deborah, London . . 085319, 113625
Gagé, Pierre, Cannes . . . 061944, 138065
Gage, Robert, Austin . . . 087575
Gage County Historical Museum, Beatrice . . . 042072
Gaggero & Corbo, Genova . . . 127454
Gagliano, Firenze . . . 127341
Gagliano, Salvatore, Firenze . . . 127342
Gagliardi, London . . . 113626
Gagliardi, Giovanni, Firenze . . . 127343
Gagnaire, Dallas . . . 115885
Gagnaire, Saint-Étienne . . . 124896
Gagnaire, Georges, Marseille . . . 124414
Gagnaire Art Association, Dallas . . . 054768
Gagnon, Clarence, Montréal . . . 097002
Gagosian, London . . . 113627
Gagosian, London . . . 113628
Gagosian, Los Angeles . . . 116771
Gagosian, New York . . . 117933
Gagosian, New York . . . 117934
Gahlberg, Havelaue . . . 103314
GAIA Gallery of Art, Amsterdam . . . 107714
Gaia's Welt, Neumagen-Dhron . . . 104413
Gaibazzi, Cristina, Parma . . . 127851
Gaidu un Skautu Muzejs, Ogre . . . 027717
Gaiffe, Daniel, Champagnole . . . 062115
Gaignon, Claude, Saint-Ouen . . . 067783
Gaildorfer Stadtmuseum im Alten Schloß, Gaildorf . . . 017316
Gaillard, Agathe, Paris . . . 100302
Gaillard, Christian, Paris . . . 124669
Gaillard, Jean-Pierre, La Roche-sur-Yon . . . 063416
Gaillard, Nathalie, Paris . . . 100303
Gailtaler Heimatmuseum-Sammlung Georg Essl, Hermagor . . . 002038
Gaimusho, Gaiko Shiryokan, Tokyo . 027164
Gaineswood, Demopolis . . . 043388
Gainsborough, Oviedo . . . 081459, 110662
Gainsborough Galleries, Calgary . . . 096814
Gainsborough Galleries, Calgary . . . 096815
Gainsborough House Antiques, Tewkesbury . . . 086875, 131587
Gainsborough Old Hall, Gainsborough . . . 039530
Gainsborough's House, Sudbury, Suffolk . . . 041155
Gainsborough's House Review, Sudbury, Suffolk . . . 136218
Gainza, Miami . . . 117072
Gairloch Heritage Museum, Gairloch . . . 039531
Gaisbauer, Aschach an der Donau .056921, 123336
Gajac, Villeneuve-sur-Lot . . . 101477
Gajah, Singapore . . . 109799
Gajdarov, Sofia . . . 137601
Gajendra, Kathmandu . . . 107586
Gajewski, Dariusz, Warszawa . . . 129084
Gajón Mozota, Antonio, Zaragoza . . 141089
Gajowy, Witold, Warszawa . . . 129085
Gakken, Tokyo . . . 134721
Gakki Hakubutsukan, Musashino Ongaku Daigaku, Tokyo . . . 027165
Gakkigaku Shiryôkan, Tachikawa . . 027096
Gaku, New York . . . 132474
Gakuenmae, Nara . . . 106939
G.A.L.A, Gap . . . 099281
Gala, Paris . . . 065939
Gala, Sankt-Peterburg . . . 109619
Gala Galeria, Wrocław . . . 109218
Gala Home Furnishings, San Diego . 092638
Galán, José María, Zaragoza . . . 129812
Galanos, Ioannis, Ilioupoli Athinon . 105423
Galant, Catherine & Patrick, Vaison-la-Romaine . . . 068675
Galantaris, Christian, Paris . . . 138381
Galante, Marie, Bénodet . . . 061350

Galante Antiques, Tyabb 056751
Galarie du Centre, Saint-Lambert . . 006378
Galarie Kir, Oberhausen, Rheinland . 104498
Galarie Original, Nordhorn 104465
Gal'Art, Coimbra 109244
Galashiels Museum, Galashiels . . . 039532
Galateau, Bernard, Paris 121150
Galaxy, Dallas 088519
Galaxy Books, Dunedin 140624
Galbeada, A Coruña 081058
Galbraith, Austin 087576, 131798
La Galcante, Paris 138382
Galchon Mask Museum, Goseong . . 027498
Galea, C., Valletta 107454
Galeano, Bonn 102179
Galeao Antiguidades, Rio de Janeiro 058590
Galearte, Bogotá 098123
Galearte, Lisboa 079931, 121932
Galeie Kunststücke, Halle, Saale . . 103061
Galen Lowe, Seattle 093007
Galena-Jo Daviess County Historical Museum, Galena 044115
Galena Mining and Historical Museum, Galena 044118
La Galera, La Plata 055272
Galerei M, Vrchlabí 098514
Galereja 1000 Stupenej, Tjumen . . 109657
Galereja 102, Sankt-Peterburg 109620
Galereja 2/2, Nižnij Novgorod 109608
Galereja 2000, Ekaterinburg 109468
Galereja 259, Moskva 109511
Galereja 36, Kyïv 112396
Galereja 8 Sov, Sankt-Peterburg . . . 109621
Galereja A & T, Moskva 109512
Galereja A3, Moskva 109513
Galereja AJa, Kursk 109475
Galereja Ajmak, Ufa 109659
Galereja Akademii Chudožestv Rossii, Sankt-Peterburg 109622
Galereja Al'ternativa, Orenburg . . . 109613
Galereja Arbat, Moskva 109514
Galereja Asti, Moskva 109515
Galereja Astrum, Moskva 109516
Galereja Čertanovo, Moskva 109517
Galereja Čingizchan, Ufa 109660
Galereja Elena, Moskva 109518
Galereja FF, Kursk 109476
Galereja Fonda Svobodnogo Russkogo Sovremennogo Iskusstva, Sankt-Peterburg 109623
Galereja Forma, Moskva 109519
Galereja Fortuna, Kyïv 112397
Galereja Forum, Sankt-Peterburg . . 033740
Galereja Fotoimage, Sankt-Peterburg 109624
Galereja Galina, Moskva 109520
Galereja Geoid, Moskva 109521
Galereja Getman, Lviv 112427
Galereja Goroskop, Moskva 109522
Galereja Irena, Kyïv 112398
Galereja Jug, Krasnodar 109474
Galereja Kino, Moskva 109523
Galereja Kino-Fot-703, Sankt-Peterburg 109625
Galereja-klub v Saburovo, Moskva . 109524
Galereja L, Moskva 109525
Galereje Le Vall, Novosibirsk 109609
Galereja Lužniki, Moskva 109526
Galereja M, Kyïv 112399
Galereja-masterskaja Chudožnika G.S. Rajševa, Chanty-Mansijsk 033086
Galereja Meždunarodnogo Universiteta, Moskva 109527
Galereja Milena, Kyïv 112400
Galereja Modern, Novosibirsk 109610
Galereja Morskaja, Odesa 112430
Galereja Moskovskogo Centra Iskusstva, Moskva 109528
Galereja Most, Odesa 112431
Galereja Mucha, Moskva 109529
Galereja na Bastionnoj, Pskov 033675
Galereja na Pesčanoj, Moskva 109530
Galereja na Smolenskoj Naberežnoj, Moskva 080240, 109531
Galereja Navicula Artis, Sankt-Peterburg 109626
Galereja Novyj Passaž, Sankt-Peterburg 033741
Galereja NU, Moskva 109532
Galereja Odoevskogo, Ekaterinburg 033111
Galereja O'K, Kyïv 112401
Galereja Olimp, Kyïv 112402
Galereja OR, Kyïv 112403
Galereja Pan-Ukrainskaja, Dnipropetrovs'k 112385
Galereja Persona, Kyïv 112404
Galereja Pljus, Moskva 109533
Galereja Podsolnuch, Toljatti 109658
Galereja RA, Kyïv 112405
Galereja-salon na Varvarke, Moskva 109534
Galereja Šatc'i, Moskva 109535
Galereja Selskaja Žizn, Sankt-Peterburg 109627
Galereja Sem' Gvozdej, Moskva . . . 109536
Galereja Sojuza Chudožnikov Rossii, Moskva 109537
Galereja Sojuza Tvorčestvo, Moskva 109538
Galereja Šon, Moskva 109539
Galereja Sovremennogo Iskusstva Arka, Vladivostok 034043
Galereja Sovremennogo Iskusstva Artėtaž, Vladivostok 034044
Galereja Sovremennoj Skulptury, Moskva 109540
Galereja Triptich, Kyïv 112406
Galereja UKV, Kyïv 112407
Galereja Ural, Ufa 109661
Galereja Vizit, Moskva 109541
Galereja Vladimir, Charkiv 112380
Galereja Volodimir, Sevastopol 112434
Galereja Vperëd, Moskva 109542
Galereja Vrubel, Omsk 109611
Galereja XL, Moskva 109543
Galereja XL, Moskva 109544
Galereja Zarubežnogo Iskusstva im. Professora M.F. Gabyševa, Jakutsk 033186
Galereja Zoo, Moskva 109545
Galeri Alfa, İstanbul 083134, 141374
Galeri Artist, İstanbul 112309
Galeri Çerçeve, İstanbul 112310
Galéri Luca Marco, Prešov 109922
Galeri Nev, İstanbul 112311
Galeri Oda, İstanbul 112312
Galeri Pago, İstanbul 112313
Galeri Suav ve Küsav, İstanbul 038092
Galeri Ümit Çamaş, İstanbul 112314
Galeri Vinci, İstanbul 112315
La Galería, Buenos Aires 055207
La Galeria, A Coruña 081059
La Galeria, Gersthofen 102944
Galéria, Kecskemét 105563
Galeria, Krzeszowice 108995
La Galeria, Madrid 081305, 110504, 122059
Galeria, Miami 117073
Galeria, Miami 117074
Galeria, Nouméa 108288
Galéria, Poprad 109920
La Galería, Santiago de Chile 097622
La Galeria, Stuttgart 073975
Galeria, Warszawa 109119
Galería 1 2 3, San Salvador 098686
Galeria 10/10, México . . . 107482, 121766
Galeria 11, Poznań 109047
Galeria 111, Lisboa 079932
Galeria 111, Porto 109375
Galeria 1199, São Paulo 058711
Galéria 13, Budapest 105511
Galeria 153, Porto 080085, 109376
Galeria 19, Sopot 109072
Galeria 2000, Kraków 108937
Galeria 2000, Warszawa 109120
Galeria 24 de Outubro, Porto Alegre 096555
Galeria 26, Wrocław 109219
Galeria 28 Poland, Kraków 108938
Galéria 3, Vaison-la-Romaine 101399
Galeria 3 Punt, Barcelona 110157
Galeria 31, Łódź 109003
Galeria 32, Warszawa 109121
Galeria 34 Bis, Warszawa 109122
Galeria 57, Madrid 110505
Galeria 65 A, Lisboa 109291
Galeria 72, Chełm 108864
Galeria 86, Łódź 109004
Galeria 90, Łódź 109005
Galeria A-5, Gdynia 108909
Galería Acquavella, Caracas 120425
Galería Actualidad, Bucaramanga . . 098212
Galeria Aka, Kraków 108939
Galeria Akademii Sztuk Pięknych, Łódź 109006
Galeria Akcji, Warszawa 109123
Galeria Alameda, Vigo 110864
Galeria Alfonso XIII, Madrid 110506
Galeria Alfonso XIII, Madrid 110507
Galeria Alicji, Gdańsk 108878
Galeria Alter Ego, Barcelona 110158
Galeria Alzama, Madrid 110508
Galería Ambar, Bogotá 098124
Galería America, Caracas 120426
Galeria Angel Romero, Madrid 110509
Galeria Angeles Penche, Madrid . . . 110510
Galéria Antika, Košice 080620
Galeria Antika Dorota, Bratislava . . 080604
Galeria Antika Dorota, Bratislava . . 080605
Galeria Antíqua, Porto 080086
Galeria Antique, Kraków 079634
Galeria Antyczna, Nowy Targ 109035
Galéria Ardan, Bratislava 109905
Galeria Argenta, Valencia 110807
Galeria Arqueologia, Madrid 081306
Galeria Arqueologia, Madrid 081307
Galería Arroyo, Buenos Aires 094070
Galería Ars Forum, Caracas 120427
Galeria Art-Deco, Barcelona 080851
Galeria Art-Deco, Barcelona 080852
Galeria Art Petritxol, Barcelona 080853, 110159
Galería Arte Actual, Santiago de Chile 097623
Galería Arte Actual Mexicano, Garza García 107468
Galeria Arte Assinada, Lisboa 079933
Galeria Arte Assinada, Lisboa 109292
Galeria Arte d'Artes, Braga 109238
Galeria Arte e Manifesto, Porto 109377
Galeria Arte Nobre, Porto Alegre . . . 096556
Galería Arte Nuevo, Bogotá 098125
Galería Arte Originales, Medellín . . 098262
Galería Arte y Antigüedades, Maracaibo 093552
La Galeria Arte y Diseño, Granada . 110375
Galeria Arteko, Donostia-San Sebastián 110337
Galeria Artela, Lisboa 109293
Galéria Artemis, Bratislava 109906
Galeria Artemis, Kraków 108940
Galería Artencuentro, Buenos Aires 094071
Galería Artes Alba, Bucaramanga . . 098213
A Galeria Artes Antiquariato, São Paulo 058712
Galería Artesanal de Colombia, Bogotá 098126
Galería Artespacio, Santiago de Chile 097624
Galeria Artfit, Lisboa 109294
Galería Artico, Medellín 098263
Galería Artieri, México 107483
Galería Artificial, Madrid 110511
Galeria Artis, Valencia 110808
Galeria Atlantica, A Coruña 110320
Galeria Autorska, Gdańsk 108879
Galeria Avima, Denia 110328
Galeria Azul, Guadalajara 107471
Galeria B, Gdańsk 108880
Galeria Bałucka, Miejska Galeria Sztuki, Łódź 032107
Galeria Bar Santa Clara, Coimbra . . 109245
Galeria Barata, Lisboa 109295
Galeria Barcelona, Barcelona 110160
Galería Barcelos, Vigo 110865
Galería BAT, Madrid 110512
Galeria Beaskoa, Barcelona 110161
Galería Belarca, Bogotá 098127
Galeria Belarde 20, Madrid 110513
Galeria Belas Artes, Porto Alegre . . 096557
Galeria Belas Artes, Rio de Janeiro . 096608
Galeria Benedito, Málaga 110636
Galeria Benlliure, Valencia 081658, 110809
Galería Bienes Culturales, Victoria de las Tunas 008188
Galeria Bihodo, São Paulo 058713
Galeria Blue Moon, León 107473
Galeria Bonino de Arte, Rio de Janeiro 096609
Galeria Brasil, Oxford 114200
Galeria Bruna, Barcelona 110162
Galeria BWA, Leszno 108998
Galería Café Libro, Bogotá 098128
Galeria Camba, Palma de Mallorca . 110679
Galeria Can Felipa, Barcelona 110163
Galería Canaria de Arte, Santa Cruz de Tenerife 110740
Galeria Canem, Castello de la Plana 110306
Galería Cano, Bogotá 098129
Galería Carlos MuRo, San Miguel de Allende 107519
Galería Carrión Vivar, Bogotá 098130
Galeria Casa Colon, Cancún 107465
Galería Casa Cuadrada, Bogotá . . . 098131
Galería Casa Lamm, México 107484
Galería Casa Negret, Bogotá 098132
Galeria Casar, Alicante 110085
Galeria Catedral, Monterrey 077590
Galería Cedritos, Bogotá 098133
Galeria Cento e Onze, Lisboa 109296
Galeria Cento e Onze, Lisboa 109297
Galeria Centralis, Budapest 105512
Galeria Centre Civic Guinardo, Barcelona 110164
Galeria Centre Civic Pati Llimona, Barcelona 110165
Galeria Centrum, Kraków 108941
Galeria Centrum, Warszawa 109124
Galeria Cervantes, Santander 110749
Galería Charlie, Bogotá 098134
Galeria Charpa, Valencia 110810
Galeria Circulo Art, Palma de Mallorca 081479, 110680
Galería Clásica, Medellín 098264
Galería Clásico, Lima 079551
Galeria el Claustre, Girona 110366
Galeria Clave, Murcia 110648
Galería Clavia, Cartagena 098246
Galeria Collage, Lleida 110402
Galeria Colon, Bilbao 110279
Galeria Comas, Barcelona 110166
Galeria Contrast, Barcelona 110167
Galeria Cortina, Barcelona 080854, 110168
Galéria D, Trnava 109925
Galeria D-Barcelona, Barcelona . . . 110169
Galeria D-Barcelona, Barcelona . . . 110170
Galeria D-Barcelona, Barcelona . . . 110171
Galeria da Arcada, Lisboa 079934
Galeria da Sé, Lisboa 079935
Galería Dacar, Medellín 098265
Galeria d'Art Amat, Lleida 110403
Galeria d'Art Terraferma, Lleida . . . 110404
Galeria d'Arts, Valencia 110811
Galeria das Antas, Porto 080087
Galeria de Artă, Braşov 109413
Galeria de Artă, Cluj-Napoca 109450
Galeria de Artă, Constanţa 109454
Galeria de Artă, Sibiu 109461
La Galería de Arte, La Habana 007948
Galería de Arte, La Serena 097616
Galeria de Arte, Porto Alegre 096558
Galería de Arte, Santiago de Chile . 097625
Galeria de Arte 715, Lima 108803
Galeria de Arte Andre, São Paulo . . 058714
Galeria de Arte Augosto Augusta, São Paulo 096671

Galeria de Arte Brasileira, São Paulo . . . 058715
Galeria de Arte Brasileira, São Paulo . . . 096672
Galeria de Arte Chini, Asunción . . . 108799
Galería de Arte Dalí, Toledo . . . 110789
Galería de Arte de la Escuela Armando Reverón, Barcelona . . . 049438
Galería de Arte de la UCV, Caracas . 049452
Galería de Arte de Santi, Buenos Aires . . . 094072
Galeria de Arte de São Bento, Lisboa . . . 109298
Galería de Arte de Tabasco, Villahermosa . . . 028931
Galería de Arte Diners, Bogotá . . . 098135
Galeria de Arte do Instituto de Artes da Universidade Federal do Rio Grande do Sul, Porto Alegre . . . 004289
Galería de Arte El Callejón, Bogotá . 098136
Galería de Arte el Taller, Medellín . . 098266
Galería de Arte Escuela Zeus, Medellín . . . 098267
Galería de Arte Expo 80, Barranquilla . . . 098088
Galería de Arte Figuras, Cali . . . 098230
Galería de Arte Flagler, Miami . . . 117075
Galeria de Arte Granada Capital, Granada . . . 110376
Galeria de Arte Gravura, Porto Alegre . . . 096559
Galeria de Arte Ipanema, Rio de Janeiro . . . 096610
Galería de Arte Iztapalapa, UAM, México . . . 028425
Galería de Arte Jaguar Despertado, Villahermosa . . . 028932
Galería de Arte Klasse, Panamá City 108786
Galería de Arte Leonardo da Vinci, Buenos Aires . . . 094073
Galería de Arte Metal, Buenos Aires 094074
Galería de Arte Mexicano, México . 107485
Galeria de Arte Moderna, Rio de Janeiro . . . 096611
Galería de Arte Moderna, Museos Universitarios, Sucre . . . 003921
Galeria de Arte Moura Cosme, Lisboa . . . 109299
Galería de Arte Nacional, Caracas . 049453
Galeria de Arte Navona, Lisboa . . . 109300
Galería de Arte Nova, Málaga . . . 110637
Galería de Arte Padre Mariano, Santiago de Chile . . . 097626
Galeria de Arte Porto Feio, Porto . . . 109378
Galeria de Arte Prof. Sylvio Vasconcellos, Belo Horizonte . . . 003996
Galería de Arte Sadco, Bucaramanga . . . 098214
Galería de Arte T-Graba, Cali . . . 098231
Galeria de Arte Tavira, Bilbao . . . 080973, 110280
Galería de Arte Tetracktis, Bogotá . 098137
Galería de Arte Travesia 4, Madrid . 110514
Galeria de Arte UNICAMP, Campinas 004038
Galería de Arte Universal, Santiago de Cuba . . . 008147
Galería de Arte Valentina, Cali . . . 098232
Galeria de Arte Vertice, Guadalajara 107472
Galeria de Arte Via Veneto, Lisboa . 109301
Galería de Arte Virreynal Cusco Art, Lima . . . 108804
Galeria de Arte Virreynal Cusco Art, Lima . . . 108805
Galería de Arte y Antigüedades Imagen, Antofagasta . . . 059474, 097614
Galeria de Arte Ygrego, Lisboa . . . 109302
Galeria de Artes, Belo Horizonte . . . 096465
Galeria de Artes de São Paulo, São Paulo . . . 096673
Galeria de Artes Renoir, Fortaleza . . 096526
Galería de Cinemateca, Montevideo 041503
Galería de Escuela Nacional de Artes Plásticas, Universidad Nacional Autónoma de México, México . . . 028426
Galeria de Exposições Temporárias da CMMP, Macau . . . 007182
Galería de Historia o Museo del Caracol, México . . . 028427
Galería de la Asamblea Legislativa, Barcelona . . . 049439
Galería de la Escuela de Diseño y Artesanias del Instituto Nacional de Bellas Artes, México . . . 028428
Galería de la Escuela Nacional de Artes Plásticas, México . . . 028429
Galería de la Oficina, Medellín . . . 098268
Galería de la Paleta, Bogotá . . . 098138
Galeria de la Raza, San Francisco . 047863
Galería de Lectores-Circulo de Arte, Barcelona . . . 110172
Galería de Marcos, Guatemala . . . 105479
Galeria de Nisi, Roma . . . 106540
La Galería de San Isidro, Lima . . . 108806
Galeria Degas, Bratislava . . . 080606
Galeria Degrau Arte, Porto . . . 109379
Galería del Barrio, Cali . . . 098233
Galería del Bronce, Bogotá . . . 098139
Galería del Centro, Boorowa . . . 055522
Galería del Cerro, Santiago de Chile 097627
Galería del Cisne, Madrid . . . 110515
Galería del Medio Art, Miami . . . 117076
Galería del Museo Anzoátegui, Barcelona . . . 049440
Galería del Pasador, Buenos Aires . 094075
Galería del Paseo, Montevideo . . . 114760
Galería del Sol, Miami . . . 117077
Galería del Sur, UAM Xochimilco, México . . . 028430
Galería Delgado, Madrid . . . 110516
Galeria Der Reiter Kunstraum, Valencia . . . 110812
Galería Di-Marco, Bogotá . . . 098140
Galería Dieciseis, Donostia-San Sebastián . . . 110338
Galería Diez, Madrid . . . 110517
Galería d'Museo, Caracas . . . 120428
Galeria do Claustro, Lisboa 079936, 109303
Galeria Dom Aktora, Gdańsk . . . 108881
Galerie Domplein, Utrecht 078799, 108246
Galería Dos Damas, San Diego . . . 119504
Galería Dr. Miguel Angel Gómez Ventura, Villahermosa . . . 028933
Galería Duque Arango, Medellín . . . 098269
Galería D.V., Donostia-San Sebastián . . . 110339
Galería Eduarte, Medellín . . . 098270
Galeria el Cantil, Santander . . . 110750
Galería el Cerrojo, Medellín . . . 059920
Galería el Circulo Azul, México . . . 107486
Galería El Fanal, Caracas . . . 093529
Galería El Museo, Bogotá . . . 098141
Galería el Socorro, Buenos Aires . . 094076
Galería Enlace Diseño, Bogotá . . . 098142
Galería Episcopal, Zacatecas . . . 028960
Galeria Erotica-Museum für erotische Kunst, Köln . . . 018310
Galería ES Arte, Philadelphia . . . 118761
Galeria Espacio 36, Zamora . . . 110876
Galeria Espaço Arte, Brasília . . . 096493
Galeria Estampa, Madrid . . . 110518
Galeria Estandarte, Madrid . . . 110519
Galería Estil, Valencia . . . 110813
Galería Estilo, Bogotá . . . 098143
Galería Estudio, Donostia-San Sebastián . . . 110340
Galería Eude, Barcelona . . . 110173
Galeria Euroarte, Lisboa . . . 109304
La Galeria Expo Arte, Madrid . . . 110520
Galería Expreso del Arte, Bogotá . . 098144
Galería Fábula, Bogotá . . . 098145
Galeria Facultad de Bellas Artes, San José . . . 007670
Galería Félix, Caracas . . . 120429
Galeria Ferso, Lisboa . . . 109305
Galeria Filomena Soares, Lisboa . . 109306
Galeria Fondo de Arte, Santa Cruz de Tenerife . . . 110741
Galeria Forum, Lima . . . 108807
Galeria Fotograficzna, Wrocław . . . 109220
Galeria Fotografii, Łódź . . . 109007
Galeria Fotografii, Wrocław . . . 109221
Galeria de la Fuente, Bilbao . . . 110281
Galeria G de Artes, Rio de Janeiro . 096612
Galería Galileu, Barcelona 080855, 140987
Galeria G'Arte, Braga . . . 109239
Galería Gemis, Bogotá . . . 098146
Galeria Gestual Artes, Porto Alegre . 096560
Galeria Giart, Girona . . . 110367
Galería Gourmet Pandora, San Salvador . . . 098687
Galería Goya 2, Valencia . . . 110814
Galeria Graça Brandão, Porto . . . 109380
Galeria Graça Brandão, Porto . . . 109381
Galeria Grafiki i Plakatu, Warszawa 109125
Galería Gran Avenida, Bogotá . . . 098147
Galeria Greca, Barcelona . . . 110174
Galería Grifus Negrus, Bogotá . . . 098148
Galeria H2O, Barcelona . . . 110175
Galeria Habitante, Panamá City . . . 108787
Galeria Henry, Lisboa . . . 109307
Galería Hermida, Bogotá . . . 098149
Galeria Hetmańska, Kraków . . . 079635, 108942
Galéria Horný Val, Žilina . . . 109928
Galeria i Ośrodek Plastycznej Twórczości Dziecka, Toruń . . . 032391
Galería IFAL, Instituto Francés de América Latina, México . . . 028431
Galeria III, Porto . . . 109382
Galeria Imperio, São Paulo . . . 058716
Galeria Infantas, Madrid . . . 110521
Galeria Instituto d'Estudis Fotografics da Catalunya, Barcelona . . . 034912
Galeria Italia, Alicante . . . 110086
Galeria J M, Málaga . . . 110638
Galeria JAD, Kalisz . . . 079606, 108918
Galéria Jána Koniarka v Trnave - Kopplov Kaštiel', Trnava . . . 034445
Galeria Janelas Verdes, Lisboa . . . 109308
Galeria Jaume III, Palma de Mallorca . . . 110681
Galeria Joani, Fortaleza . . . 096527
Galeria Jorge Juan, Madrid . . . 110522
Galeria Jorge & Shirley, Lisboa . . . 109309
Galería José María Velasco, México 028432
Galéria Jozefa Kollára, Banská Štiavnica . . . 034306
Galería Kin, México . . . 107487
Galeria Kontynenty, Warszawa . . . 109126
Galeria Krakowskiej Fundacji Hamlet, Kraków . . . 108943
Galeria la Aurora, Murcia . . . 110649
Galería La Bagatela, Bogotá . . . 098150
Galeria la Capella de l'Antic, Hospital de la Santa Creu I Sant Pau, Barcelona 034913
Galería la Cometa, Bogotá . . . 098151
Galería La Consolata, Medellín . . . 098271
Galería la Francia Arte, Medellín . . . 098272
Galería la Quinta, Lima . . . 108808
Galeria la Santa Proyectos Culturales, Barcelona . . . 110176
Galería Latino Americana, La Habana . . . 098293
Galeria Leo, Lisboa . . . 109310
La Galería l'Ermitage, Medellín . . . 098273
Galeria Lipert, Kraków . . . 108944
Galería Los Oficios, La Habana . . . 007949
Galeria Luhian 12, Bucureşti . . . 109431
Galéria M.A. Bazovského, Trenčín . . 034442
Galeria Maeght, Barcelona . . . 110177
Galeria Maes, Madrid . . . 110523
Galeria Majolika, Gdańsk . . . 108882
Galeria Mar, Barcelona . . . 110178
Galeria Mar Gaita, Palma de Mallorca . . . 110682
Galéria Maráky, Bratislava . . . 080607
Galeria Marc3, Barcelona . . . 110179
Galeria Margem, Faro . . . 109250
Galeria Mariacka, Gdańsk . . . 108883
Galéria Marie Medvedckej, Oravská galéria, Tvrdošín . . . 034448
Galeria Marlborough, Madrid . . . 110524
Galeria Mediterrània, Palma de Mallorca . . . 110683
Galeria Mesa, Mesa . . . 045792
Galéria Mesta Bratislavy, Bratislava 034322
Galeria Metropolitana de Barcelona, Barcelona . . . 110180
Galería Metropolitano, México . . . 107488
Galeria Mexicana de Diseño, México . . . 028433
Galeria Międzynarodowego Centrum Kultury, Kraków . . . 032028
Galeria Miejeska Arsenał, Poznań . . 032235
Galeria Millenium, Gdynia . . . 108910
Galeria Minimal, Porto . . . 109383
Galería Minotauro, Caracas . . . 120430
Galería Miro, Bogotá . . . 098152
Galeria Mistral, Kraków . . . 108945
Galeria Mölln, Mölln . . . 072560
Galeria Mölln, Mölln . . . 104088
Galeria Monet, Palma de Mallorca . 110684
Galeria Monet, Palma de Mallorca . 110685
Galeria Montcada, Barcelona . . . 110181
Galeria Monumental, Lisboa . . . 109311
Galería Monumento Histórico Nacional a la Bandera, Rosario . . . 000523
Galeria Multiarte, Fortaleza . . . 096528
Galeria Mun, Madrid . . . 110525
Galería Mundo, Bogotá . . . 098153
Galería Mundo Arte, Medellín . . . 098274
Galería Municipal de Arte Moderno, Barcelona . . . 049441
Galeria Municipal Trem, Faro . . . 032612
Galeria Muntaner, Barcelona . . . 110182
Galeria Muro, Valencia . . . 110815
Galeria na Freta, Warszawa . . . 079752, 109127
Galeria na Każdą Kieszeń, Warszawa . . . 109128
Galeria na Piwnej, Warszawa . . . 079753, 109129
Galeria na Tarczyńskiej, Warszawa . 109130
Galería Nacional, San Juan . . . 032733
Galería Nacional de Arte, Tegucigalpa . . . 021612
Galería Nacional de Bellas Artes, Santo Domingo . . . 009156
Galería Nacional y Museo de los Niños, San José . . . 007671
Galeria Nadir, Valencia . . . 110816
Galeria Nave Diez, Valencia . . . 110817
Galeria Nazareth's, Porto . . . 109384
Galeria Nr 1, Zbigniew, Warszawa . 109131
Galeria Nuevoarte, Sevilla . . . 110769
Galería Obsidiana, Lima . . . 108809
Galeria Okendo, Vitoria-Gasteiz . . . 110871
Galeria Okręgowe, Biała Podlaska . 031824
Galeria Okręgowe, Chełm . . . 031863
Galería OMR, México . . . 107489
Galeria Orfila, Madrid . . . 110526
Galería Oriente, Santiago de Cuba . 008148
Galeria Orizont, Bucureşti . . . 109432
Galeria Osobliwości Este, Kraków . . 079636, 108946
Galeria Ostrołęka, Ostrołęka . . . 109036
Galeria Palatina, Heidelberg . . . 103320, 134049
Galeria Passe-Partout, Lisboa . . . 109312
Galeria Passe-Partout, Lisboa . . . 109313
Galeria Passe-Partout, Lisboa . . . 109314
Galería Pazos, Bogotá . . . 098154
Galeria Pergamon, Barcelona . . . 110183
Galéria Petra Michala Bohúňa, Liptovský Mikuláš . . . 034375
Galería Picasso, Bogotá . . . 098155
Galería Picasso, Medellín . . . 098275
Galeria Pilares, Cuenca . . . 110326
Galeria Pilares, Cuenca . . . 110327
Galeria Pizarro, Valencia . . . 110818
Galeria Plakatów, Warszawa . . . 109132
Galeria Plakatu Astrid, Gdynia . . . 108911
Galeria Plater, Warszawa . 079754, 109133, 121906
Galería Plazuela del Artista, Medellín . . . 098276
Galería Pluma, Bogotá . . . 098156
Galería Pocitos, Montevideo . . . 041504
Galeria pod Rejentem, Kraków . . . 108947
Galéria Poláková, Bratislava . . . 109907
Galeria Polony, Poznań . . . 109048

Galeria Polskiego Plakatu, Warszawa . . . 109134
Galeria Ponto Artes, São Paulo . . . 058717
Galeria Ponto das Artes, Lisboa . . . 109315
Galeria Por Amor à Arte, Porto . . . 109385
Galeria Potocka - Kolekcja Artystów, Kraków . . . 108948
Galería Praxis, México . . . 107490
Galeria Presença, Porto . . . 109386
Galeria Prestige, Caracas . . . 093530
Galeria Pro Arte, Oświęcim . . . 109037
Galeria Profile, Gdynia . . . 108912
Galeria Promocyjna, Warszawa . . . 109135
Galeria Przedmiotu, Kraków . . . 108949
Galeria Puenta, Sopot . . . 109073
Galeria Puerta de Alcala, Madrid . . 110527
Galería Punto Arte, Barcelona . . . 110184
Galeria Quadrado Azul, Porto . . . 109387
Galeria Radwan, Sopot . . . 109074
Galería Rafael, Valladolid . . . 110852
Galeria Ratton Cerâmicas, Lisboa . . 109316
Galería Rembrant, Cali . . . 098234
Galeria Restelo, Lisboa . . . 109317
Galeria Retxa, Ciutadella de Menorca . . . 110310
Galería Reyes Católicos, Salamanca 110735
Galería Río de la Plata, Montevideo 114761
Galería Rodas, Bogotá . . . 098157
Galería Roglan, Barcelona . . . 110185
Galería Rojo y Negro, Bogotá . . . 098158
Galeria Rovira i Monti Se'Leccio, Sabadell . . . 110729
Galeria Rysunku, Toruń . . 079718, 109083
Galeria S, Myślenice . . . 109032
Galeria Safia, Barcelona . . . 110186
Galeria Salduva, Zaragoza . . . 110881
Galería Sam, Bucaramanga . . . 098215
Galería San Antón, Pamplona . . . 110719
Galería San Francisco, Caracas . . . 120431
Galería San Miquel I, San Miguel de Allende . . . 107520
Galeria San Ysidro, El Paso . . . 088803
Galeria São Mamede, Lisboa . . . 109318
Galeria Sardon, León . . . 110398
Galeria SD, Warszawa . . . 109136
Galeria Sen, Madrid . . . 110528
Galeria Sesimbra, Lisboa . . . 109319
Galería Sextante, Bogotá . . . 098159
Galeria Siglo XXI, Lugo . . . 110415
Galeria Siglo XXI, Lugo . . . 110416
Galeria Słowiańska przy Parafii Prawosławnej, Kraków . . . 032029
Galeria Sokoa, Madrid . . . 081308, 110529
Galeria Stary Świat, Warszawa . . . 079755
Galería Studio, Buenos Aires . . . 055208, 094077
Galeria Studio, Warszawa . . . 109137
Galeria Surrealista, Barcelona . . . 080856, 110187
Galeria Sztuka Dawna i Współczesna Antyki, Częstochowa . . . 079573, 108865
Galeria Sztuki, Warszawa . . . 109138
Galeria Sztuki Dawna Synagoga, Muzeum Okręgowego w Nowym Sączu, Nowy Sącz . . . 032174
Galeria Sztuki im. W. i J. Kulczyckich, Muzeum Tatrzańskiego w Zakopanem, Zakopane . . . 032545
Galeria Sztuki Naiwnej & Ludowej, Wrocław . . . 109222
Galeria Sztuki Polskiej XIX w. w Sukiennicach, Muzeum Narodowe w Krakowie, Kraków . . . 032030
Galeria Sztuki TAB, Warszawa . . . 109139
Galeria Sztuki Wozownia, Toruń . . . 032392
Galeria Sztuki Współczesnej, Myślenice . . . 109033
Galeria Sztuki Współczesnej, Przemyśl . . . 109068
Galeria Sztuki Współczesnej, Muzeum Narodowe w Szczecinie, Szczecin 032364
Galeria Sztuki Współczesnej Profil & Galeria Fotografii pf, Centrum Kultury Zamek, Poznań . . . 032236
Galeria Sztukij Współczesnej Związku Polskich Artystów Plastyków, Gdańsk . . . 108884
Galeria T4, Barcelona . . . 110188
Galeria Teatralna, Kraków . . . 108950
Galeria Teatro Nacional Enrique Echandi y Joaquín García Monge, San José . 007672
Galeria Tena'Art, Timişoara . . . 109462
Galéria Teo, Banská Bystrica . . . 109903
Galeria Terracota, Bogotá . . . 098160
Galeria Terranova, Guadalajara . . . 077563
Galeria Testemunhos, Porto . . . 109388
Galeria Thema, Valencia . . . 110819
Galería Thema, Valencia . . . 110820
Galeria Theredoom, Barcelona . . . 110189
Galeria Tolmo, Toledo . . . 110790
Galeria Torre de Anto, Carapinheira 079815
Galeria Torre de Anto, Coimbra . . . 079820
Galeria Torre de Anto, Figueira da Foz . . . 079830
Galeria Torre de Anto, Figueira da Foz . . . 079831
Galeria Towarzyszenia Historyków Sztuki, Kraków . . . 108951
Galeria Trama, Barcelona . . . 110190
Galeria Trazo, México . . . 107491
Galeria Trino Tortosa, Almeria . . . 110094
Galeria Ttopara, Hondarribia . . . 110385
Galeria Tuset, Barcelona . . . 110191
Galéria Typoars, Bratislava . . . 109908
Galeria U-1, Warszawa . . . 109140
Galeria Ubioru, Łódź . . . 109008
Galéria Umelcov Spiša, Spišská Nová Ves . . . 034431
Galéria Umenia, Nové Zámky . . . 034403
Galería Universitaria Artistos, México . . . 028434
Galeria Urbino, Madrid . . . 081309
Galeria Valbom, Lisboa . . . 109320
Galeria Valle Orti, Valencia . . . 110821
Galeria van Gogh, Bilbao . . . 110282
Galeria Veche, Cluj-Napoca . . . 109451
Galería Velázquez, Buenos Aires . . . 094078
Galeria Vena, Warszawa . . . 109141
Galeria Venus, Bilbao . . . 110283
Galeria Vértice, Lisboa . . . 109321
Galería vía Margutta, Córdoba . . . 094097
Galeria Viciana, Valencia . . . 110822
Galeria Victoriei, Braşov . . . 109414
Galeria Vigo, Vigo . . . 110866
Galeria Vincent, Barcelona . . . 110192
Galeria Virtual da Casa das Rosas, São Paulo . . . 004509
Galeria Visor, Valencia . . . 110823
Galeria w Forum, Kraków . . . 108952
Galeria Wiktoria, Kościerzyna . . . 108923
Galeria Władysława Hasiora, Muzeum Tatrzańskiego w Zakopanem, Zakopane . . . 032546
Galeria Xeito, Madrid . . . 110530
Galería y Tienda de Regalos Indues Ganges, Medellín . . . 098277
Galéria Z, Bratislava . . . 109909
Galeria z Rączką, Kraków . . . 108953
Galeria Zaguán, Valencia . . . 110824
Galeria Zamek w Reszlu, Muzeum Warmii i Mazur w Olsztynie, Reszel . . . 032287
Galeria Zapiecek, Warszawa . . . 109142
Galeria Zona Corazon, Columbus . . 115779
Galeria Związku Polskich Artystów Plastyków, Gdańsk . . . 108885
Galeriacuatro, Valencia . . . 110825
Galerías Arte Actual, Santiago de Chile . . . 097628
Galerias Arther, Guadalajara . . . 077564
Galerias de Arte Blubtes, Porto Alegre . . . 096561
Galerias Dom José, Lisboa . . . 079937
Galerias Internacionales de Arte Sebastian, Cancún . . . 107466
Galerías La Granja, México 077572, 107492
Galerías Marquezrios, Caracas . . . 093531
Galerias Net, Amadora . . . 129137
Galerías Pacífico de Centro Cultural Borges, Buenos Aires . . . 000153
Galerías Piazza, Mendoza . . . 094103
Galerias Pina, Faro . . . 109251
Galerias Turisticas, Córdoba . . . 081048
Galerias Vandoma, Porto . . . 080088
Galerias Yela, Lisboa . . . 109322
Galericitra, Kuala Lumpur . . . 107436
La Galerie, Ajaccio . . . 098804
Galerie, Blois . . . 098976
Die Galerie, Bünde . . . 102286
Galerie, Craon . . . 099185
De Galerie, Den Haag . . . 107920
Die Galerie, Detmold . . . 070226
Die Galerie, Dötlingen . . . 102380
Die Galerie, Frankfurt am Main . . . 102769, 133941
Die Galerie, Hiddenhausen . . . 103372
Galerie, Horn . . . 095571
Galerie, Hossegor . . . 099358
Galerie, Hossegor . . . 099359
La Galerie, Les Trois-Ilets . . . 063790
La Galerie, Limoges . . . 099504
Die Galerie, Linz . . . 123409
Die Galerie, München . . . 104187
Die Galerie, Oldenburg, Oldenburg . 104540
Die Galerie, Oldenburg, Oldenburg . 104541
La Galerie, Paris . . . 100304
Die Galerie, Rheinbach . . . 104745
Galerie, Rothenthurm . . . 111848
La Galerie, Saint-Gilles-Croix-de-Vie . . . 101156
La Galerie, Seraincourt . . . 068225
Galerie, Tourgéville . . . 101375
La Galerie, Washington . . . 120297
Die Galerie, Wilhelmshaven . . . 105299
Die Galerie, Worpswede . . . 105330
Galerie 027, Sion . . . 111909
Galerie 10, Karlsruhe . . . 103490
Galerie 10, Wien . . . 095824
Galerie 100, Berlin . . . 016024
Galerie 104, El Jadida . . . 107558
Galerie 10er Haus, Gmunden . . . 095514
Galerie 111, Zürich . . . 082970
Galerie 12, Innsbruck . . . 095580
Galerie 13, Freising . . . 102876
Galerie 13, Sète . . . 101275
Galerie 13 Rue Jacob, Paris . . . 065940
Galerie 130, Paris . . . 065941
Galerie 14, Paris . . . 100305
Galerie 14-16 Verneuil, Paris . . . 100306
Galerie 15, Alès . . . 098813
Galerie 16, Versailles . . . 068805
Galerie 17, Hamburg . . . 103121
Galerie 17, Paris . . . 100307
Galerie 17, Salies-de-Béarn . . . 101244
Galerie 18, Vannes (Morbihan) . . . 101430
Galerie 19, Jena . . . 103447
Galerie 1900, Helsinki . . . 060522
Galerie 1900-2000, Paris . . . 100308
Galerie 1990, Eisenstadt . . . 095502
Galerie 19ème, Limoges . . . 063887
Galerie 2, Schwabach . . . 104849
Galerie 20, Paris . . . 100309
Galerie 2000, Basel . . . 111178
Galerie 2000, Bordeaux . . . 061609
Galerie 2000, Montréal . . . 097003
Galerie 201, Amsterdam . . . 107715
Galerie 2016, Bruxelles . . . 096194
Galerie 2016, Hauterive . . . 111547
Galerie 21, Tours . . . 101378
Galerie 216, Bruxelles . . . 057954
Galerie 22, Pont-Aven . . . 101025
Galerie 25, Siselen . . . 111915, 130179
Galerie 251, Amsterdam . . . 107716
Galerie 26, Paris . . . 100310
Galerie 27, Paris . . . 100311
Galerie 27, Viersen . . . 074211
Galerie 29, Evian-les-Bains . . . 099254
Galerie 29, Münster . . . 104360
Galerie 3, Athinai . . . 105394
Galerie 3, Klagenfurt . . . 095613
Galerie 3, Wien . . . 095825
Galerie 30 Octobre, Paris . . . 065942
Galerie 31, Bastia . . . 098928
Galerie 32, Lyon . . . 099560
Galerie 3.2.1, Zug . . . 112210
Galerie 33, Aachen . . . 101505, 133712
Galerie 33, Essen . . . 102675
Galerie 33, Heidelberg . . . 103321
Galerie 37. Kunst im Museum der Weltkulturen, Frankfurt am Main . 017168
Galerie 39 A, Limoges . . . 099505
Galerie 3K, Rechberghausen . . . 104678
Galerie 4, Cheb . . . 098351
Galerie 40, Wiesbaden . . . 105253
Galerie 41, Monaco . . . 077603, 107527
Galerie 419, Brisbane . . . 094295
Galerie 422, Gmunden . . . 095515
Galerie 43, Paris . . . 100312
Galerie 44, Saint-Sulpice, Vaud . . . 111859
Galerie 45, Riehen . . . 111836
Galerie 46, München . . . 104188
Galerie 48, Saarbrücken . . . 104791
Galerie 49, Angers . . . 060853
Galerie 49, Saumur . . . 101264
Galerie 5, Düsseldorf . . . 102496
Galerie 5020, Salzburg . . . 002550
Galerie 53, Friedrichshafen . . . 070894
Galerie 53, Friedrichshafen . . . 102883
Galerie 53, Paris . . . 100313
Galerie 54, Freiburg im Breisgau . . 102861
Galerie 54, Paris . . . 100314
Galerie 561, Landshut . . . 103825
Galerie 58, Magny-en-Vexin . . . 064213
Galerie 58, Montreux . . . 082667, 111743
Galerie 59, Wuppertal . . . 105351
Galerie 59, Zürich . . . 112075
Galerie 5ünf Sinne, Halle, Saale . . . 103062
Galerie 6, Aarau . . . 111100
Galerie 6, Dijon . . 062658, 099212, 124222
Galerie 60, Feldkirch . . . 095504
Galerie 63, Klosters . . . 111588
Galerie 67, Bern . . . 111250
Galerie 67, Québec . . . 097140
Galerie 7, Lyon . . . 064128
Galerie 73, Bordeaux . . . 061610
Galerie 78, Le Chesnay . . . 099432
Galerie 7ème Avenue, Paris . . . 065943
Galerie 81, Paris . . . 065944
Galerie 82, Bremerhaven . . . 102262
Galerie 88, Kolkata . . . 105739
Galerie 88, Lorsch . . . 103938
Galerie 89, Aarwangen . . . 111106
Galerie 9, Paris . . . 065945, 100315
Galerie 92, Bruxelles . . . 057955
Galerie 93, Saarbrücken . . . 104792
Galerie 96, Bourglinster . . . 107380
Galerie 99, Aschaffenburg . . . 101598
Galerie A & A, Tokyo . . . 107039
Galerie a Muzeum Litoměřické Diecéze, Litoměřice . . . 008479
Galerie A & S, Husum, Nordsee . . . 103414
Galerie AA, Clermont-Ferrand . . . 099148
Galerie AA, Wels . . . 095779, 133170
Galerie AAA, Ostrava . . . 060066, 098399, 120850
Galerie AB, Paris . 065946, 100316, 138383
Galerie Abélard, Sens . . . 101272
Galerie Academia, Salzburg . . . 095718, 133134
Galerie Accord, Marseille . . . 099652
Galerie Action, Sierentz . . . 101276
Galerie Adlergasse, Dresden . . . 102430
Galerie Ägypten, Kufstein . . . 095637
Galerie Afghane, Paris . . . 100317
Galerie Afro-Asiatica, Bremen . . . 102241
Galerie Akzente, Minden, Westfalen 104078
Galerie Albert 1er, Bruxelles . . . 096195
Galerie Albis, Ústí nad Labem . . . 098510
Galerie Albstadt, Albstadt . . . 015466
Galerie Alif Ba, Casablanca . . . 107554
Galerie Alt-Amerika, Stuttgart . . . 104975
Galerie-Alte-Kanzlei, Albstadt . . . 069128
Galerie Alte Kunst Neue Kunst, Marlene, Wien . . . 095826
Galerie Alte Mühle, Würenlos . . . 112010

Galerie Alte & Neue Kunst, Baden-Baden 069412, 101721
Galerie Alte Reichsvogtei, Städtische Sammlungen Schweinfurt, Schweinfurt 020139
Galerie Alte Schmiede, Bochum . . . 102147
Galerie Alte Schmiede, Steinberg-Dörfl 095765
Galerie Alte Schule, Ahrensbök . . . 015455
Galerie Alte Schule, Vils 002779
Galerie Alte Schule Wittstedt, Bramstedt 016363
Galerie Alte Technik, Berlin 069608
Galerie Alte und Neue Kunst, Creglingen 102327
Galerie Altes Rathaus, Worpswede . 020985
Galerie Altes Rathaus Musberg, Leinfelden-Echterdingen 103853
Galerie Altstadt, Krems 057123
Galerie Altstadt, Speyer 104933
Galerie am Abend, München 104189
Galerie am Alten Garten, Siegen . . . 104894
Galerie am Altpörtel, Speyer 104934
Galerie am Bach, Neustadt an der Weinstraße 104427
Galerie am Bach, Obererlinsbach . . 111789
Galerie am Bellevue, Taura 105036
Galerie am Benediktusplatz, Aachen 101506
Galerie am Berg, Kurort Oberwiesenthal 103809
Galerie am Berg, Windischgarsten .057605, 095973
Galerie am Blauen Wunder, Dresden 102431
Galerie am Brasselsberg, Kassel . . 103511
Galerie am Brunnen, Bergisch Gladbach 101764
Galerie am Brunnental, Lauingen . . 103843
Galerie am Carlsplatz, Düsseldorf . . 070380
Galerie am Damm, Dresden 102432
Galerie am Dillberg, Marktheidenfeld 104035
Galerie am Dom, Aachen 101507
Galerie am Dom, Billerbeck 069847
Galerie am Dom, München 104190
Galerie am Dom, Wetzlar 020840
Galerie am Domhof, Zwickau 021085
Galerie am Domplatz, Hamburg . . . 071230
Galerie am Dreieck, Düsseldorf . . . 070381
Galerie am Eichhof, Kiel 103539
Galerie Am Elisengarten, Aachen . . 101508
Galerie am Entenmoos, Bad Waldsee 101710
Galerie Am Finkenbusch, Bocholt . . 102145
Galerie am Fischmarkt, Limburg an der Lahn 103914
Galerie am Fluß, Pegestorf 104592
Galerie am Fürstenhof, Kempten . . 071789
Galerie am Graben, Augsburg 015608
Galerie am Großneumarkt, Hamburg 103122
Galerie am Gsundbrunnen, Burgau, Schwaben 102290
Galerie am Hafen, Glückstadt 102964
Galerie am Hauptplatz, Fürstenfeldbruck 102895
Galerie am Haus der Kunst, München 104191
Galerie am Herzberg, Peine 104594
Galerie am Hinterberg, Zürich 112076
Galerie am Hofgarten, Düsseldorf . . 070382
Galerie am Holzmarkt, Wolfenbüttel 074470
Galerie am Hubertusplatz, Willich . . 105300
Galerie am Johannisplatz, Jena . . . 103448
Galerie am Judenberg, Augsburg . . 101612
Galerie am Kamp, Teterow 020422
Galerie am Kirchplatz, Fiss 095507
Galerie am Kloster, Lorsch 103939
Galerie am Klosterhof, Schalkham . 104818
Galerie am Kreuzplatz, Frauenfeld .082374, 111408
Galerie am Kröpke, Hannover 103275
Galerie am Kugelbühl, Roth, Mittelfranken 104773
Galerie am Leewasser, Brunnen . . . 111311
Galerie am Lindenplatz, Vaduz 107341, 134741
Galerie am Lobkowitzplatz, Wien . . 095827
Galerie Am Märkischen Platz, Rathenow 104659
Galerie am Maintor, Sommerhausen 104922
Galerie Am Markt, Bad Saulgau . . . 015788
Galerie am Markt, Hildesheim 103380
Galerie am Markt, Hofgeismar 017961
Galerie am Markt, Lippstadt 103929
Galerie am Markt, Waldkirch 105149
Galerie am Marktplatz, Büren an der Aare 111315
Galerie am Meer, Varel 105101
Galerie am Meierteich, Bielefeld . . . 102116
Galerie am Michel, Hamburg 103123
Galerie am Mühlentor, Greifswald . . 102993
Galerie am Museum, Flensburg . . . 102729
Galerie am Museum Glasgarten, Frauenau 102845
Galerie am Neuen Palais, Potsdam . 104624
Galerie am Nikolaikirchhof, Leipzig 103868
Galerie am Paradeplatz, Zürich 112077
Galerie Am Park, Kühlungsborn . . . 103803
Galerie am Park, Sankt Gallen 082775, 111868
Galerie am Pfleghof, Tübingen 105073, 134431
Galerie am Platz, Eglisau 111391
Galerie am Prater, Berlin 016025
Galerie am Rathaus, Köln 103619
Galerie am Rathaus, Neuss 104422
Galerie am Rathaus, Nienburg, Weser 104452
Galerie am Rathaus, Röttingen 104759
Galerie am Rathaus, Waldkraiburg . 105150
Galerie am Rathausplatz, Berneck . 111282
Galerie am Ratswall, Bitterfeld 016257
Galerie am Rennweg, Wien 057418
Galerie am Residenzplatz, Passau . 104585
Galerie Am Rex, Wilnsdorf 105303
Galerie am Rotbrunnen, Schopp . . . 104840
Galerie am Sachsenplatz, Leipzig . . 103869
Galerie am Salzbad, Ubstadt-Weiher 074128
Galerie am Salzgries, Wien 095828
Galerie am Samstag, Anzing 101591
Galerie am Schloss, Gottlieben 111528
Galerie am Schloß, Heidelberg 103322
Galerie am Schloß, Senftenberg . . . 020190
Galerie am Schloss, Weimar, Thüringen 105186
Galerie am Schrotturm, Schweinfurt 104860
Galerie am See, Kressbronn am Bodensee 103787
Galerie am See, Potsdam 104625
Galerie am See, Zug 112211
Galerie am Sonnenplatz, Baden-Baden 101722
Galerie am Spalenberg, Basel 111179
Galerie am Springbrunnen, Laßnitzhöhe 095642
Galerie am Stadion, Trier 105058
Galerie am Stadthaus, Bonn 102180
Galerie am Stein, Schärding 095748
Galerie am Steinweg, Passau 104586
Galerie am Stern, Essen 102676
Galerie am Strichweg, Cuxhaven . . 102329
Galerie am Stubentor, Wien 095829, 133197
Galerie am Styg, Safnern 111855
Galerie am Turm, Waiblingen 105139
Galerie am Undertor, Stein am Rhein 082836
Galerie am Wasserturm, Berlin 101863
Galerie am Weinberg, Mainstockheim 072385
Galerie am Weinkeller, Wien 095830
Galerie am Zwillingsbogen, Miltenberg 104072
Galerie Ambiente, Gütersloh 103032
Galerie Ambiente, Kronach 103791
Galerie Ambiente, Wien 057419
Galerie Amicorum, Paris 100318
Galerie Amsterdam, Amsterdam . . . 107717
Galerie an der Aussenalster, Hamburg 103124
Galerie an der Bleiche, Ludwigslust 018708
Galerie an der Börse, Düsseldorf . .070383, 102497
Galerie an der Brenz, Sontheim an der Brenz 104929
Galerie an der Gerbegass, Sempach Stadt 111900
Galerie an der Pinakothek der Moderne, München 104192
Galerie an der Schirn, Frankfurt am Main 139082
Galerie an der Schwebebahn, Dresden 102433
Galerie an der Staatsoper, Hamburg 103125
Galerie Analix Forever, Genève 111450
Galerie Anatome, Paris 100319
Galerie Ange Antoine, Morlaix 099772
Galerie Anima, Paris 100320
Galerie Anima, Waldshut-Tiengen . . 105151
Galerie Anna Paulownahuis, Soest . 030170
Galerie Anne Marie, København . . . 098555
Galerie Anno 1589, Bensheim 101756
Galerie Anno 1900, Wien 057420
Galerie Ansichtssache, Frankfurt am Main 102770
Galerie Antic, Objat 065259
Galerie Antického Umění, Hostinné . 008385
Galerie Anton, Agen 060669, 098769
Galerie Antonigasse, Bremgarten (Aargau) 111306
Galerie Antonína Chittussiho, Ronov nad Doubravou 008669
Galerie Antonins, Nîmes 099865
Galerie AO, Emsdetten 102625
Galerie AP, Brno 098328
Galerie Apé-ro, Illnau 111568
Galerie Apex, Göttingen 102977
Galerie aplanat, Hamburg 103126
Galerie Aquarelle, Biel 111284
Galerie Arcade, Mödling . . 095682, 133120
Galerie Arche, Hameln 103236
Galerie Architektur und Arbeit, Gelsenkirchen 102928
Galerie Architektury Brno, Brno . . . 008287
Galerie Arcturus, Paris 100321
Galerie Arcus, Kommunale Galerie Lichtenberg, Berlin 016026
Galerie argus fotokunst, Berlin 101864
Galerie Ariadne, Wien 095831
Galerie Ariane, Dijon 099213
Galerie Arlette, Lyon 099561
Galerie Arnstein, Weismain 105198
Galerie Ars, Brno 098329
Galerie ARS, Stuttgart 104976
Galerie Arspectus, Neustadt an der Weinstraße 104428
Galerie Art, Biarritz 098962
Galerie Art, Dürnstein, Niederösterreich 095496
Galerie Art 204, Düsseldorf 102498
Galerie Art Aurora, Zürich 112078
Galerie Art Aurora Weisses Schloss, Zürich 112079
Galerie Art Céleste, Bordeaux 098994
Galerie Art Comparaison, Carnac . . 099087
Galerie Art Comparaison, La Baule-Escoublac 099375
Galerie Art Comparaison, Paris 100322
Galerie Art & Craft, Praha 098431
Galerie Art du Temps, Metz 099709
Galerie Art et Culture, Montréal . . . 097004
Galerie Art et Patrimoine, Paris 100323
Galerie Art et Tradition, Honfleur . . 099343
Galerie l'Art Français, Montréal . . . 097005
Galerie Art G, Béziers 098958
Galerie Art-In, Meerane 104044
Galerie Art International, Nancy . . . 099793
Galerie Art K, Paris 100324
Galerie Art Lympia, Nice 065083
Galerie Art-Magazin, Zürich 112080
Galerie art one, Zürich 037766
Galerie Art Rose Azur, Carouge 111334
Galerie Art und Grafik, Wolfsburg . . 105323
Galerie Art und Weise, Heide, Holstein 103317
Galerie Art'7, Nice 099835
Galerie Artcadache, Vallorbe 111959
Galerie Arte, Würzburg 105337
Galerie Arte N, München 104193
Galerie Artelier, Karlsruhe 103491
Galerie Artemisia, Paris 100325
Galerie Artès, Barbizon 098919
Galerie Artgerecht, Eberbach, Baden 102589
Galerie Arthéna, Eguisheim 099246
Galerie Arthu(u)s, Hameln 103237
Galerie Artico, Wiesbaden 105254
Galerie Artigiano, Memmingen 104059
Galerie Artima, Paris 100326
Galerie Artimus, Paris 100327
Galerie Artina, Ebersdorf 095498
Galerie Artis, Darmstadt 102340
Galerie Artis, Villefranche-sur-Mer . 101471
Galerie Artischocke, Bad Schussenried 101697
Galerie Artitude, Montréal 097006
Galerie Artlantis, Bad Homburg v.d.Höhe 101652
Galerie Arts Multiples, Metz 099710
Galerie Asa, Praha 098432
Galerie Asakusa, Marseille 099653
Galerie Aspekte, Waibstadt 074243
Galerie Ateliena 79, Zürich 112081
Galerie & Atelier Altes Rathaus, Heinsberg 103344
Galerie-Atelier Pia, Wolhusen 112007
Galerie Atena, Paris 065947
Galerie Athanor, Marseille 099654
Galerie Atrium ed Arte, Wien 095832
Galerie Au Paon, Avenches 111145
Galerie auf dem Mühlenboden, Teterow 105043
Galerie auf der Treppe, Limburg an der Lahn 103915
Galerie Aufsturz, Berlin 101865
Galerie Augenweide, Münster 104361
Galerie Aujourd'hui, Berlin 101866, 133776
Galerie Aurea, Waiblingen 105140
Galerie Aurika, Frankfurt am Main . 070740
Galerie Aurore, Luxé 099532
Galerie Aurus, Paris 100328
Galerie Austria, Wien 095833
Galerie Azur, Saint-Paul-de-Vence . 101203
Galerie B, Bordeaux 098995
Galerie B, Sinzheim 073838
Galerie B 15, München 104194
Galerie B-312, Montréal 097007
Galerie B des Frankfurter Kunstvereins, Frankfurt/Oder 102842
Galerie B. Vincent, Les Sables-d'Olonne 099472
Galerie B9, Meerbusch 104046
Galerie Bab Rouah, Rabat 107560
Galerie Babylonia, Paris 065948
Galerie Bagnato, Konstanz 103756
Galerie Baguette, Ascot 094177
Galerie Bahnhof, Weidenberg 105174
Galerie Balker Mühle, Leichlingen . 103850
Galerie Bar zur Zinne, Oberrieden . .111790, 130134
Galerie Barbakane, Leipzig 103870
Galerie Barbara, Hradec Králové . . . 098359
Galerie Barbier, Eu 062820
Galerie Basta, Hamburg 103127
Galerie Bayard, Toulouse 101346
Galerie bbs, Bergisch Gladbach . . . 101765
Galerie Beaubourg, Vence 015158
Galerie Beaumontoise, Beaumont-de-Lomagne 061260
Galerie Beauséjour, Paris 065949
Galerie Beethovenstraße, Düsseldorf 102499
Galerie bei der Albertina, Wien 057421, 095834
Galerie bei der Komödie, Augsburg . 101613
Galerie beim Bahnhof, Laa an der Thaya 095639
Galerie beim Rathaus, Wil 111993

Galerie beim Roten Turm, Sommerhausen 104923
Galerie Beim Steinernen Kreuz, Bremen 102242
Galerie beim Steinertor, Krems 095630
Galerie Bel Art, Bad Neuenahr-Ahrweiler 101680
Galerie Bel-Etage, Amsterdam 107718
Galerie Bel Etage, Berlin 101867
Galerie Bel'Art, Stockholm 111021
Galerie Belle Arte, Schwerin 104870
Galerie Bellecour, Lyon 099562
Galerie Belphégor, Étaules 062815
Galerie Belvedere, Singapore 109800
Galerie Benedikta Rejta v Lounech, Louny 008491
Galerie Benjamine, La Trinite-sur-Mer 099411
Galerie Bergam Art, Ellwangen 016944
Galerie Berlin, Berlin 101868
Galerie Berliner Häuser im Siebdruck, Berlin 101869
Galerie Berlioz, Sausset-les-Pins . . 101265
Galerie Bernau, Bernau bei Berlin . . 102097
Galerie Best, Bielefeld 102117
Galerie Bezirksamt Mitte, Berlin . . . 016027
Galerie Bezirkshauptmannschaft Sankt Pölten, Sankt Pölten 095745
Galerie BHAK, Seoul 107226
Galerie Biebertal, Biebertal 016229
Galerie Bild und Rahmen, Schwalbach am Taunus 104856, 134389
Galerie Bildschön, Cottbus 102325
Galerie Bildschön, Heidelberg 071452
Galerie Bildschön, Riesa 104754
Galerie bim Brunne, Dielsdorf 111382
Galerie Binnen, Amsterdam 107719
Galerie Binz 39, Zürich 112082
Galerie Biró, München 104195
Galerie Bismarck, Bremen 102243
Galerie BL, Toulouse 101347
Galerie Blanche, Stockholm 111022
Galerie Blankenese, Hamburg 103128
Galerie Blau-gelbe Zwettel, Waldviertel, Zwettl, Niederösterreich 003075
Galerie Bleiche, Appenzell 111125
Galerie Blickfang, Bielefeld 102118
Galerie Blickfang, Wuppertal 105352
Galerie Blondel, Ostrava 098400
Galerie Bodemannstraße, Gifhorn . . 102959
Galerie Bodenseekreis im Landratsamt, Friedrichshafen 017270
Galerie Bodenseekreis im Roten Haus, Meersburg 018873
Galerie Bohéma, Olomouc 098389
Galerie Bohemiarte, Montréal 097008
Galerie Bohemica, Isernhagen 103442, 134072
Galerie Bona Dea, Cherbourg-Octeville 099129
Galerie Bormes, Bormes-les-Mimosas 099013
Galerie Bornéo, La Varenne-Saint-Hilaire 063464
Galerie Borssenanger, Chemnitz . . . 102307
Galerie Bovary, Musée d'Automates, Ry 014158
Galerie Břetislava Tvaru^BEžka, Opava 098395
Galerie Briand, Royan 101128
Galerie Brötzinger Art e.V., Pforzheim 104603
Galerie Brûlée, Strasbourg 101289
Galerie Bürgerhaus, Schwabach . . . 104850
Galerie Burkartshof, Neukirch, Egnach 111776
Galerie BV, Amsterdam 107720
Galerie C, Amiens 060815, 098821
Galerie - C, Benešov 098324
Galerie C, Sélestat 101268
Galerie C&C, Gevelsberg 102947
Galerie C & C, Schwetzingen 104872
Galerie Cadre, Hagen, Westfalen . . 103046
Galerie Cadr'in, Nouméa 108289
Galerie Caesar, Olomouc . 098390, 137802
Galerie Capazza, Musée Imaginaire du Grand Meaulnes, Nançay 013317
Galerie Capriola, Großostheim 103022
Galerie Carinthia, Klagenfurt 095614, 133099
Galerie Cart, Besançon 098951
Galerie Castiglione, Paris 100329
Galerie Central, Hamburg 103129
Galerie České Plastiky, Praha 098433
Galerie Český Porcelán, Praha 098434
Galerie Chaco, Hamburg 103130
Galerie Chagall, Brno 098330
Galerie Chapelle de la Salamandre, Nîmes 099866
Galerie Charlevoix, Hossegor 099360
Galerie Chez Anne, Traben-Trarbach 105052
Galerie Chmelařovi, Pardubice 060075
Galerie Choiseul, Paris 100330
Galerie Christa, Florstadt 102734
Galerie Christel, Limoges . 063888, 099506
Galerie Christina, Freilassing 102873
Galerie Christine, Saint-Ouen 067784
Galerie Cigarini, Genève 111451
Galerie Cimaise, Senlis 101270
Galerie Cimaise d'Or, Luxembourg . 107398
Galerie Cinq, Genève 082427
Galerie Circa, Rennes (Ille-et-Vilaine) 067114
Galerie Claire, Aesch, Basel-Land . 111110
Galerie Clairefontaine, Luxembourg 107399
Galerie Clairefontaine - Espace 2, Luxembourg 107400
Galerie Classic Art Deco 1930, Düsseldorf 070384
Galerie Classicus, Bissen 107379
Galerie Claude, Köln 071940, 126079
Galerie Claudia, Houston 116318
Galerie Claudiana, Innsbruck 095581
Galerie Clément, Nice 099836
Galerie C.M.C., Paris 065950
Galerie Coiffeur, Leinfelden-Echterdingen 103854
Galerie Collage, Wangerooge 105157
Galerie Colline, Edmundston 005415
Galerie Colombière, Fondettes 062886
Galerie Commercio, Zürich 112083
Galerie Concorde, Mulhouse 099787
Galerie Condillac, Bordeaux 098996
Galerie Connaisseur, Stockholm . . . 111023
Galerie Contact, Böblingen 016294
Galerie Contact, Wien 095835
Galerie Conte, Perpignan 066743
Galerie Contemporaine, Paris 100331
Galerie Contrast, Metz 099711
Galerie Cora, Uzès 101397
Galerie Corridor 23, Berlin 101870
Galerie Côté, Barbizon 098920
Galerie Coup d'Oeil, Saint-Cristol-lès-Alès 067406, 124891
Galerie Cour Carrée, Paris 100332
Galerie Cour Saint-Pierre, Genève . 111452
Galerie Couturier, Paris 100333
Galerie CP, Wiesbaden 105255
Galerie Création Plus, Luxembourg . 107401
Galerie C.R.O.U.S. - Beaux-Arts, Paris 100334
Galerie D, Brno 098331
Galerie da entlang, Dortmund 102397
Galerie Da Vinci, Altenkunstadt . . . 101566
Galerie Daguerre, Photo-Club du Val de Bièvre, Paris 013586
Galerie d'Albertas, Gémenos 099286
La Galerie Danoise, Paris 100335
Galerie d'Antrain, Rennes (Ille-et-Vilaine) 101080
La Galerie d'Architecture, Paris . . . 100336
Galerie d'Arfi, Saint-Sulpice, Vaud . 111860
Galerie d'Armorique, Quimper 101059
Galerie d'Art, Castelsarrasin 062019, 099095
Galerie d'Art, Les Sables-d'Olonne . 099473
Galerie d'Art, Lessines 120766
Galerie d'Art, Nice 099837
Galerie d'Art, Paris 100337
Galerie d'Art, Musee Des Beaux-Arts de Montréal, Montréal 005923
Galerie d'Art, Université de Moncton, Moncton 005895
Galerie d'Art Africain, Céret 062054
Galerie d'Art Alvarès, Draguignan . . 099242
Galerie d'Art Ancien et Moderne, Monaco 077604
Galerie d'Art and Craft, Pézenas . . . 101005
Galerie d'Art Antinea, Marseille . . . 099655
Galerie d'Art Beauséjour, Bir Mourad Rais 094047
Galerie d'Art Contemporain, Chamalières 011204
Galerie d'Art Contemporain, La Seyne-sur-Mer 012338
Galerie d'Art Contemporain, Menton 013019
Galerie d'Art Contemporain, Sarlat-la-Canéda 014676
Galerie d'Art Contemporain Am Tunnel, Luxembourg 027887
Galerie d'Art d'Asie, Bordeaux 061611
Galerie d'Art d'Auteuil, Paris 065951
Galerie d'Art de Créteil, Créteil 011534
Galerie d'Art de Matane, Matane . . 005841
Galerie d'Art d'Esch, Esch-sur-Alzette 027882
Galerie d'Art du Centre Culturel, Sherbrooke, Québec 006460
Galerie d'Art du Château, Bettembourg 027870
Galerie d'Art du Château de Villeneuve, Sablé-sur-Sarthe 101130
Galerie d'Art du Gray d'Albion, Cannes 099066
Galerie d'Art du Parc, Trois-Rivières 006660
Galerie d'Art du Prince Noir, Dinard 099230
Galerie d'Art du Wilson, La Ciotat . . 099390
Galerie d'Art Elysées, Paris 100338
Galerie d'Art et d'Essais, Le Portel . 099452
Galerie d'Art Francais, New Orleans 117439
Galerie d'art la Boucherie, Noyers-sur-Serein 099883
Galerie d'Art Les Amis de l'Art, Monaco 107528
Galerie d'Art l'Union-Vie, Drummondville 005363
Galerie d'Art Moderne, Passavant-la-Rochère 013745
Galerie d'Art Municipale, Baixas . . . 010631
Galerie d'Art Municipale, Oberkorn . 027900
Galerie d'Art Municipale, Rumelange 027901
Galerie d'Art Passé Présent, Aix-en-Provence 098786
Galerie d'Art Royale, Windsor, Ontario 097558
Galerie d'Art Saint-Honoré, Paris . . 100339
Galerie d'Art Saint-Pierre, Vézelay . 101463
Galerie d'Art Salvany, Clermont-Ferrand 099149
Galerie d'Art Stewart Hall, Pointe-Claire 006164
Galerie d'Artisanat d'Art Kalloné, Crémieu 099186
Galerie D'Arts Contemporains, Montréal 097009
Galerie d'Arts Decoratifs, Miami . . . 090174
Galerie Das Da, Zug 112212
Galerie David, Bielefeld 102119
Galerie D'Avignon, Montréal 097010
Galerie D.C., Großmutz 103021
La Galerie de Alliance Française de Manille, Makati 108826
Galerie de Artà, Ploieşti 109460
Galerie de Beaune, Paris 065952
Galerie de Bel Air, Loudun 064009
Galerie de Bel Air, Verrue 068787
Galerie de Bretagne, Quimper 101060
Galerie de Briord, Nantes 099808
Galerie de Cannes, Cannes 099067
Galerie de Catalans Illustres, Barcelona 034914
Galerie de Corbez, Saint-Germain-les-Corbeil 067503
Galerie de Couvaloup, Morges 111753, 141279
Galerie de Dampierre, Dampierre-en-Yvelines 099194
Galerie De Di By, Paris 100340
Galerie de Divonne, Divonne-les-Bains 099237
Galerie de Florence, Paris 100341
Galerie de France, New York 090893
Galerie de France, Paris 100342
Galerie de Guise, Dijon 099214
Galerie de L'Isle, Montréal 097011
Galerie de Joss Joss, Dijon 099215
Galerie de Kerbrest, Guidel 099321
Galerie de la Bièvre, Paris 100343
Galerie de la Bourdonnais, Paris . . . 065953
Galerie de la Cathédrale, Aix-en-Provence 060704
Galerie de la Cathédrale, Marseille . 099656
Galerie de la Cathédrale, Monaco . . 107529
Galerie de la Charité, Lyon 099563
Galerie de la Cité, Penne-d'Agenais 100987
Galerie de la Colombe, Vallauris . . . 101416
Galerie de la Corraterie, Genève . . . 111453
Galerie de la Daurade, Toulouse . . . 101348
Galerie de la Ferme de la Chapelle, Grand-Lancy 111530
Galerie de la Gare, Bayonne 098932
Galerie de la Gare, Molleges 064586
Galerie de la Gare, Nice 065084
Galerie de la Haute Ville, Genève . . 111454
Galerie de la Huchette, Paris 100344
Galerie de la Loge, Lyon 064129
Galerie de la Louve, Gland 082476, 111515
Galerie de la Madeleine, Béziers . . 061438
Galerie de la Madeleine, Béziers . . 098959
Galerie de la Marine, Cherbourg-Octeville 099130
Galerie de la Méditerranée, Les Baux-de-Provence 099467
Galerie de la Méditerranée, Saint-Paul-de-Vence 101204
Galerie de la Mer, Paris 100345
Galerie de la Mer, Pornic 101044
Galerie de la Place, Lyon 099564
Galerie de la Place, Paris 100346
Galerie de la Place Ziem, Beaune . . 098938
Galerie de la Poste, Pont-Aven 101026
Galerie de la Présidence, Paris 100347
Galerie de la Régence, Charleroi . .058145, 120749
Galerie de la Rivière, Saint-Savinien 101232
Galerie de la Rotonde, Paris 100348
Galerie de la Scala, Paris 100349
Galerie de la Sorbonne, Paris 100350
Galerie de la Vielle Fontaine, Sion . 082812
Galerie-de-l'Alpage I, Megève 099698
Galerie de l'Amateur d'Art, Saint-Martin-de-Ré 101180
Galerie de l'Américaine, Villefranche-de-Lauragais 101470
Galerie de l'Ancien Courrier, Montpellier 099756
Galerie de l'Ancienne, Toucy 068431, 101315
Galerie de Lange, Emmen 029559
Galerie de Lara, Litomyšl 098383
Galerie de l'Arcade, Pézenas 066804
Galerie de l'Arche, Ecueille 062761
Galerie de l'Art Erotique, Newstead 094950
Galerie de l'Aspic, Nîmes 099867
Galerie de l'École d'Art, Marseille . . 012932
Galerie de l'École la Chaufferie, Strasbourg 014859
Galerie de l'École Nationale des Beaux-Arts, Nancy 013320
Galerie de l'École Régionale des Beaux-Arts, Nantes 013332
Galerie de l'Ecusson, Montpellier . . 099757
Galerie de l'Elysée, Paris 100351
Galerie de l'Empreinte, Court 111372
Galerie de l'Encadrement, Etampes 099252
Galerie de l'Ermitage, Le Touquet-Paris-Plage 099459
Galerie de l'Estampe, Lyon 064130, 099565
Galerie de l'Estuaire, Honfleur 099344
Galerie de l'Europe, Paris 100352

Galerie de l'Hibiscus, Pont-l'Évêque 101039
Galerie de l'Hôtel de Saulx, Beaune 098939
Galerie de l'Hôtel de Wicque, Pézenas 101006
Galerie de l'Ill, Strasbourg 101290
La Galerie de l'Impasse, Lyon 099566
Galerie de l'Iroise, Douarnenez 099239
Galerie de l'Isle, Montpellier 064740
Galerie de l'Olifant, Paris 100353
Galerie de l'Olympe, Lyon 099567
Galerie de l'Olympe, Perpignan . . .066744, 100990
Galerie-de-l'Orne, Rémalard 067083, 101072
Galerie de l'Université, Lyon 099568
Galerie de l'UQAM, Québec 006218
Galerie de Mai, Penang 107439
La Galerie de Marjac, Saint-Bauzille-de-Putois 067373
Galerie de Messine, Paris 100354
Galerie de Minéralogie, Paris 013587
Galerie de Nemours, Annecy 098841
Galerie de Nesle - Exposition, Paris 013588
La Galerie de Noisy, Noisy-le-Sec . . 013446
Galerie de Normandie, Saint-Vaast-la-Hougue 101237
Galerie de Paléobotanique, Paris . . 013589
Galerie de Pézénas, Pézenas 066805
Galerie de Pontaillac, Royan 101129
Galerie de Pouzauges, Pouzauges . 013934
Galerie de Prêt d'Œuvres d'Art, Bruxelles 096196, 133270
Galerie de Prêt Ville d'Angers, Angers 010390
Galerie de Rue, Rue 111851
Galerie De Ruimte, Eersel 107992
Galerie de Sèze, Lyon 099569
Galerie de Textiles, Paris 100355
Galerie de Varenne, Paris . 100356, 133610
Galerie de Verneuil, Paris 065954
Galerie de Vigreyos, Noailhac 099875
Galerie de Villiers, Le Touquet-Paris-Plage 099460
Galerie de Vinci, Bruxelles 096197
Galerie De Vink, Utrecht . . 078800, 108247
La Galerie d'Egmont, Bruxelles 057956
Galerie Deï Barri, Gassin 099283
Galerie Deichstrasse, Hamburg . . . 103131
Galerie Deichstraße, Holm 103400
Galerie Dekorat, Lübeck 103962
Galerie del'Art, Dinan 099221
Galerie Delta 98, Den Haag 078199
Galerie Demay Debève, Le Touquet-Paris-Plage 099461
Galerie d'Enfer, Bruxelles 096198
Galerie der Begegnung, Verein zur Förderung zeitgenössischer Kunst, Linz 095657
Galerie der Berliner Graphikpresse, Berlin 101871
Galerie der Bezirksbibliothek Rheinhausen, Duisburg 016852
Galerie der Freien Akademie Feldkirchen, Feldkirchen in Kärnten 001851
Galerie der Grünen Akademie, Graz 095523
Galerie der Heimat, Hamm, Sieg . . 103242
Galerie der Hochschule für Graphik und Buchkunst, Leipzig 018567
Galerie der Jenaoptik, Jena 018104
Galerie der Kreissparkasse Esslingen-Nürtingen, Esslingen 102710
Galerie der Künste, Berlin 016028
Galerie der Künstler, München 104196
Galerie der Künstlergruppe Experiment Stuttgart, Stuttgart 104977
Galerie der Küste, Niebüll 104442
Galerie der Kunststudenten, Wien . . 095836
Galerie der Kunstuniversität Linz, Linz 095658
Galerie Der Lichtblick, Obernburg . . 104503
Galerie der Mitte, Linz 002246
Galerie der Sammlung Berthold-Sames, Oberaudorf 019383
Galerie der Sinne, Aschaffenburg . . 101599
Galerie der Sinne (08122) 8213, Erding 102634
Galerie Der Spiegel, Köln . 103620, 134106
Galerie der Stadt, Bad Wimpfen . . . 015830
Galerie der Stadt Backnang, Backnang 015638
Galerie der Stadt Fellbach, Fellbach 017107
Galerie der Stadt Plochingen, Plochingen 019639
Galerie der Stadt Remscheid, Remscheid 019797
Galerie der Stadt Salzburg im Mirabellgarten, Salzburg 002551
Galerie der Stadt Schwaz, Schwaz . 002663
Galerie der Stadt Sindelfingen, Sindelfingen 020215
Galerie der Stadt Stuttgart, Stuttgart 020356
Galerie der Stadt Traun, Traun 002751
Galerie der Stadt Tuttlingen, Tuttlingen 020507
Galerie der Stadt Vöcklabruck, Vöcklabruck 002781
Galerie der Stadt Waiblingen Kameralamt, Waiblingen 020624
Galerie der Stadt Wels, Wels 002826
Galerie der Stadt Wendlingen am Neckar, Wendlingen am Neckar 020796
Galerie der Steine, Arnsberg 101593
Galerie der Volksbank, Lindenberg im Allgäu 103922
Galerie der Volksbank, Weinheim, Bergstraße 105194
Galerie der Zülow-Gruppe, Linz . . . 095659
Galerie des 30, Mazamet 099694
Galerie des 4 Coins, Hauterives . . . 099327
Galerie des Ambassadeurs, Hyères 063193
Galerie des Antiquaires, Saint-Ouen 067785
Galerie des Antiques, Saint-Rémy-de-Provence 101228
Galerie des Arcades, Arcachon 098854
Galerie des Arcades, Noyers-sur-Serein 065243
Galerie des Artistes 2000, Neuchâtel 111769
Galerie des Artistes l'Art dans la Rue, Moulins (Allier) 099781
Galerie des Arts, Lailly-en-Val 099416
Galerie des Arts, New York 117935
Galerie des Arts, Nîmes 099868
Galerie des Arts, Trigance 101387
Galerie des Arts Quotidiens, Paris . . 100357
Galerie des Augustins, Avignon . . .098895, 138020
Galerie des Beaux-Arts, Bordeaux . 010877
Galerie des Beaux Arts, Charleroi . . 058146
Galerie des Bildungshauses Sodalitas, Tainach 002725
Galerie des Chartons, Bordeaux . . . 061612
Galerie des Chartreuses, Gosnay . . 099292
Galerie des Dames, Musée de Cires, Chenonceaux 011346
Galerie des Docks, Nice 099838
Galerie des Ducs, Nevers 099824
Galerie des Estampes, Lille 099488
Galerie des Estampes, Rouen 014122
Galerie des Expositions Pablo Picasso, Denain 011571
Galerie des Franciscains, Saint-Nazaire (Loire-Atlantique) 101184
Galerie des Glariers, Aigle 111113
Galerie des Grands-Augustins, Paris 100358
Galerie des Iles d'Or, Hyères 063194, 124262
Galerie des Jenaer Kunstvereins, Jena 018105
Galerie des Joueries, Saint-Germain-en-Laye 067499
Galerie des Kultur- und Festspielhauses Wittenberge, Wittenberge 020927
Galerie des Kunstvereins Neustadt an der Weinstraße, Neustadt an der Weinstraße 019283
Galerie des Lampes, Paris 065955
Galerie des Landkreises Rügen, Putbus 019679
La Galerie des Laques, Paris 065956
Galerie des Laques, Paris 100359
Galerie des Limonadiers, Vaison-la-Romaine 101400
Galerie des Lumières, Saint-Paul-de-Vence 067942
Galerie des Maîtres Contemporains, Nice 099839
Galerie des Marburger Kunstvereins, Marburg 018823
Galerie des Minimes, Bruxelles . . . 057957
Galerie des Modernes, Paris 100360
Galerie des Ocres, Roussillon (Vaucluse) 101125
Galerie des Orfèvres-Carré Mevel, Paris 100361
Galerie des Ormeaux, Challans 099101
Galerie des Papes, Châteauneuf-du-Pape 099122
Galerie des Peintres, Paris 100362
Galerie des Petits Maîtres, Strasbourg 068319
Galerie des Planches, Montreux . . . 111744
Galerie des Polnischen Instituts Düsseldorf, Düsseldorf 016829
Galerie des Portes Chanac, Tulle . . 101394
Galerie des Quais, Plérin 066848
Galerie des Remparts, Bordeaux . . 098997
Galerie des Remparts, Hyères 099363
Galerie des Remparts, Le Mans . . . 099447
Galerie des Remparts, Vaison-la-Romaine 101401
Galerie des Remparts d'Ainay, Lyon 064131, 099570
Galerie des Sablons, Saint-Malo (Ille-et-Vilaine) 101172
Galerie des Saints-Pères, Paris . . . 100363
Galerie des Sept Collines, Vienne . . 101467
Galerie des Tanneurs, Mulhouse . . . 099788
Galerie des Templiers, Genève 082428, 111455
Galerie des Transports, Marseille . . 012933
Galerie des Trois Pignons, Dijon . . . 062659
Galerie des Tropiques, Papeete . . . 101493
Galerie des Tuileries, Paris 100364
Galerie des Tuiliers, Lyon 099571
Galerie des Vergers, Sion 111910
Galerie des Wantiers, Valenciennes 101413
Galerie Design, Paris 065957
Galerie d'Etraz, Lausanne 111616
Galerie Deux, Tokyo 107040
Galerie d'Exposition, Tours 101379
Galerie d'Exposition d'Art et d'Histoire, Villaries 015229
Galerie d'Exposition de la Direction des Musées, Rabat 029029
Galerie d'Exposition sur la Bourse, Paris 013590
Galerie D.H, Paris 065958
Galerie Dialogue, Paris 100365
Galerie Dida, Graz 095524
Galerie Die Katakombe, Basel 111180
Galerie Die schwarze Treppe, Haigerloch 103054
Galerie Die Treppe, Nürtingen 104494
Galerie Dijk 1, Alkmaar 107618
Galerie DINA4 Projekte, München . . 104197
Galerie-Direkt, Stuttgart 104978
Galerie Documents, Paris 100366
Galerie Domi Nostrae, Lyon 099572
Galerie Dominion, Montréal 005924
Galerie Domino, Praha 098435
Galerie d'Orangerie, Curaçao 108286
La Galerie Dorée, Lyon 099573
Galerie Dorée du Comte de Toulouse, Paris 013591
Galerie d'Orsay, Boston 115175
Galerie Dream On, Paris 065959
Galerie Drei, Dresden 102434
Galerie Drei Könige, Zürich 082971
Galerie Druck & Buch, Tübingen . . .105074, 139795
Galerie Drucksache, Aichtal 101551
Galerie D.S., Paris 065960
Galerie du BAC, Saint-Aubin-Sauges 111856
Galerie du Bastion, Antibes-Juan-les-Pins 010423
Galerie Du Beau, Bornheim, Rheinhessen 102206
La Galerie du Bec, Le Bec-Hellouin 063565, 099423
Galerie du Bellay, Mont-Saint-Aignan 099733
Galerie du Bois d'Amour, Pont-Aven 101027
Galerie du Canal, Limoges 099507
Galerie du Capricorne, Vevey 111965
Galerie du Carlton, Cannes 099068
Galerie du Carré, Versailles 068806
Galerie du Carrois, Zürich 112084
Galerie du Cenacle, Develier 111381
Galerie du Centre, Liège 120767
Galerie du Centre, Paris 100367
Galerie du Chapitre, Rennes (Ille-et-Vilaine) 101081
Galerie du Château, Avenches 111146
Galerie du Château, Biot 098968
Galerie du Château, Vence 101441
Galerie du Château, Espace Graphique, Nice 013393
Galerie du Château, Espace Graphique, Nice 099840
Galerie du Chatel, Senlis 101271
Galerie du Chêne, Lausanne 111617
Galerie du Cheval Blanc, Roanne . . 101095
Galerie du Chevalier et des Collectionneurs, Paris 100368
Galerie du Cirque, Paris 100369
Galerie du Conseil Général du Bas-Rhin, Strasbourg 014860
Galerie du Coq d'Inde, Toulouse . . . 101349
Galerie du Coq d'Inde, Toulouse . . . 101350
Galerie du Cotentin, Cherbourg-Octeville 099131
Galerie du Crescendo, Mougins . . . 099777
Galerie du Cygne, Ferney-Voltaire .062854, 099258
Galerie du Cygne, Paris 100370
Galerie du Cygne d'Etang, Paris . . . 100371
Galerie du Dauphin, Honfleur 099345
Galerie du Dôme, Paris 100372
Galerie du Dourven, Tredrez-Locquemeau 101385
Galerie du Dragon, Mons 096390
Galerie du Dragon, Paris 065961
Galerie du Dragon, Paris 065962
Galerie du Duc Guillaume, Bayeux . 098929
Galerie du Fleuve, Paris 100373
Galerie du Forum, Albi 098809
Galerie du Forum, Monaco 107530
Galerie du Forum, Toulouse 101351
Galerie du Jorat, Mézières 111734
Galerie du Jour, Paris 100374
Galerie du Léman, Paris 100375
Galerie du Limas, Avignon 061134
Galerie du Lion d'Or, North Shore . . 108523
Galerie du Louvre, Montréal 058955, 097012
Galerie du Luberon, Gordes 099290
Galerie du Manoir, Saint-Evarzec . . 101152
Galerie du Marché, Montreux 111745
Galerie du Médoc, Bordeaux 098998
Galerie du Mercadial, Bonifacio . . . 098979
Galerie du Mercadial, Saint-Céré . .067394, 101138
Galerie du Midi, Hamburg 103132
Galerie du Midi, Hamburg 103133
Galerie du Monde, Hong Kong 097787
Galerie du Multiple, Marseille 064356
Galerie du Musée, Dijon 099216
Galerie du Musée, Les Baux-de-Provence 099468
Galerie du Musée, Paris 065963
Galerie du Musée, Paris 100376
Galerie du Musée Montebello, Trouville-sur-Mer 015045
Galerie du Palais, Neuchâtel 082691, 111770
Galerie du Palais des Papes, Avignon 098896

Galerie du Palais Gallien, Bordeaux 098999, 124125
Galerie du Panthéon, Paris 100377
Galerie du Paradis, Lisieux 099511
Galerie du Park Palace, Monaco . . . 077605
Galerie du Passage, Paris 100378
Galerie du Passé, Houdon 063177
Galerie du Pavillon, Bruxelles 057958
Galerie du Perron-Borel, Le Grand-Saconnex 111531
Galerie du Petit Champlain, Québec 097141
Galerie du Petit Michaux, Bar-le-Duc 098914
Galerie du Peyrou, Montpellier 064741
Galerie du Pharos, Avignon 098897
Galerie du Pharos, Marseille 099657
Galerie du Pharos, Saint-Rémy-de-Provence 101229
Galerie du Phonographe, Dinan . . . 099222
Galerie du Phonographe, Dinard . . . 099231
Galerie du Pistolet d'Or, Mons 058341
Galerie du Pont de Corot, Mantes-La Jolie 099634
Galerie du Port, Noirmoutier-en-l'Ile 099880
Galerie du Prado, Marseille 099658
Galerie du Prieuré, Carennac 099086
Galerie du Puits du Bourg, Nevers . 099825
Galerie du Puy Joli, Brantome 099026
Galerie du Quai, Strasbourg 068320, 138618
Galerie du Rhône, Sion . . . 111911, 122351
Galerie du Ruisseau, Paris 065964, 100379
Galerie du Simplon, Vevey 111966
Galerie du Soleil, Tampa 120045
Galerie du Soleil @ International Plaza, Tampa 120046
Galerie du Solstice, Treycovagnes . 111949
La Galerie du Sud, Marseille 099659
Galerie du Sud, Ravensburg 104671
Galerie du Tableau, Marseille 099660
Galerie du Talent, Echallens 111389
Galerie du Théâtre, Besançon 098952
Galerie du Triangle, Bordeaux 099000
Galerie du Triangle, Lyon 099574
Galerie du Verneur, Pont-Aven 101028
Galerie du Vert Galant, Paris 100380
Galerie du Vexin, Vigny 101468
Galerie du Vieux Belfort, Belfort . . . 098948
Galerie du Vieux Chapitre, Meaux . .099695, 138203
Galerie du Vieux Honfleur, Honfleur 099346
Galerie du Vieux Lyon, Lyon 099575
Galerie du Vieux Moulin, Cleres . . . 099137
Galerie du Vieux Pressoir, Onnens . 111802
Galerie du Vieux Saint-Paul, Saint-Paul-de-Vence 101205
Galerie du Vignoble, Saint-Saphorin (Lavaux) 111857
Galerie du Vitrail, Amiens 010367
Galerie du Voisinand, Lutry 111673
Galerie du XXème Siècle, Paris 100381
Galerie Dumont 18, Genève 111456
Galerie Duo, Bochum 102148
Galerie DuPeyrou, Neuchâtel 111771
Galerie Dusseldorf, Mosman Park . . 094897
Galerie D'X, Hamburg 103134
Galerie E, Opfikon 111803
Galerie Eclat, New Orleans 117440
Galerie Ed., Ballens 111158
Galerie Edelsteine, Bad Wörishofen 101715
Galerie Edition Copenhagen, København 098556, 133423
Galerie & Edition GE, Winterthur . . .111997, 135077
Galerie & Editions Aujourd'hui, Meggen 111724, 135049
Galerie Edmond Rostand, Marseille 064357
Galerie Efal, Saint-Dié-des-Vosges . 101142
Galerie Eigen + Art, Berlin 101872
Galerie Eigen und Art, Leipzig 103871
Galerie Einhorn, Schaffhausen 111888
Galerie Einsiedlerhof, Kaiserslautern 103466
Galerie Elbchaussee, Hamburg 103135
Galerie Elbhang, Dresden 102435
Galerie Elfenau, Biel 111285
Galerie Elizabeth LeFort, Cheticamp 005263
Galerie Elle, Liberec 098379
Galerie Emilienplatz, Hagen, Westfalen 103047
Galerie Empreintes, Paris 100382
Galerie-en-Ré, Bois-Colombes 098978
Galerie Entre Cadre, Montréal 097013
Galerie Epreuve d'Artiste, Lille 099489, 133483
Galerie eS, Praha 098436
Galerie Esca et Papiers Libres, Revue d'Art Contemporain, Milhaud 099722
Galerie Eschberg, Saarbrücken . . . 104793
Galerie Espace, Thonon-les-Bains . 101312
Galerie Espacio, Morges 111754
Galerie Esprit Art, La Baule-Escoublac 099376
Galerie Eulenspiegel, Basel 111181
Galerie Eurêka-Espace Montagne, Chambéry 011207
Galerie Europ'Art, Aigues-Mortes . . 098773
Galerie Europeenne, Biel 111286
Galerie Europeenne, Boston 115176
Galerie Europeenne de la Forêt et du Bois, Dompierre (Orne) 011628
Galerie Evrard, Roissy-en-Brie 101098
Galerie Expression Libre, Paris 100383
Galerie Exquisit, Rechtmehring 104679
Galerie F, Bad Nauheim 101674
Galerie F, Dresden 102436
Galerie F, Karditsa 105428
Galerie F5,6 6000 Ludwigstr 7, München 104198
Galerie Faaturuma, Papeete 101494
Galerie Façade, Paris 100384
Galerie Faider, Bruxelles 096199
Galerie Farb, Worb 112008
Galerie Feeling, Toulon (Var) 101320
Galerie Feille, Pézenas 101007
Galerie Felixe Jeneweina, Kutná Hora 008461
Galerie Fernand Léger - Le Crédac, Ivry-sur-Seine 012144
Galerie Fert, Yvoire 101490
Galerie Fichtegasse, Wien 095837
Galerie Figure, Paris 100385
Galerie Finartis, Zug 112213
Galerie Fine Art, Bonn 102181
Galerie Fine Art, Eymet 099255
Galerie Flip-Flop, Hamburg 103136
Galerie Flora, Paris 100386
Galerie Flore, Saint-Brieuc 101135
Galerie Florence-Basset, Flassans-sur-Issole 099262
Galerie Florian, Sceaux 068174
Galerie Fonderie, Toulouse 101352
Galerie Formart, Cuxhaven 102330
Galerie Fortuna, Zürich . . . 082972, 141335
Galerie Forum, Mainz 103998
Galerie Forum Lindenthal, Köln . . . 103621
Galerie Fotohof, Salzburg . 095719, 133135
Galerie Fototreppe 42, Hanau 017738
Galerie Française, München 104199, 134240
Galerie France des Arts, Lillers 099500
Galerie Franck, Paris 100387
Galerie Frankengasse, Zürich 112085
Galerie Franze Kafky, Praha 008605
Galerie Franziskanergasse, Salzburg 095720
Galerie Fred, Lyon 064132
Galerie Freihausgasse, Galerie der Stadt Villach, Villach 002773
Galerie Friedrichstadt, Berlin 101873
Galerie Fuchstal, Fuchstal 102893
Galerie für 1 Tag, Obing 104515
Galerie für angewandte Kunst, München 104200
Galerie für gegenständliche Kunst, Kirchheim unter Teck 103555
Galerie für Gegenwartskunst, Bonstetten 111302
Galerie für Konkrete Kunst, Berlin . . 101874
Galerie für moderne Kunst, Gotha . . 017495
Galerie für zeitgenössische Kunst, Gräfelfing 102987
Galerie für Zeitgenössische Kunst Leipzig, Leipzig 018568
Galerie für Zeitkunst, Bamberg 101728
Galerie Fueterchrippe, Zuckenriet . . 112022
Galerie Fusion, Toulouse 101353
galerie futura, Berlin 101875
Galerie G, Heidelberg 103323
Galerie G, Judenburg 095602
Galerie G, Leonberg, Württemberg . 103905
Galerie G22, La Rochelle 099405
Galerie Gala, Montréal 097014
Galerie Gala Amalvy, Valence (Drôme) 101410
Galerie Gambra, Praha 098437
Galerie Ganesha, Mersch 077486
Galerie Garance, Saint-Germain-en-Laye 101154
Galerie Gaston Gérard, Dijon 099217
Galerie Georges-Goguen, Moncton . 005896
Galerie Gérard, Carcassonne 061976
Galerie Gerbi, Grindelwald 111534
Galerie Gersag Emmen, Emmenbrücke 037064
Galerie Gesellschaft, Berlin 101876
Galerie Ghiglione, Biot 098969
Galerie Gibel, Büron 111318
Galerie Gilgamesh, Paris 065965
Galerie Giovanni, Paris 065966
Galerie Glacis, Graz 057011
Galerie Gloria, Karlovy Vary 098370
Galerie Gloux, Concarneau 099165
Galerie Gmünd, Gmünd, Kärnten . . 001903
Galerie GNG, Paris 100388
Galerie GNG, Verneuil-sur-Avre . . . 101450
Galerie Godot, Praha 098438
Galerie Goethe 53, München 019057
Galerie Goldener Engl, Hall in Tirol . 095557
Galerie Goldturm, Staad 111928
Galerie Gong, Pardubice 098405
Galerie Gora, Montréal 097015
Galerie Gouverneur, Homécourt . . .099330, 133475
Galerie Graal, Toulouse 101354
Galerie Graff, Montréal 097016
Galerie Grand-Rue, Genève 111457, 141250
Galerie Grand Siecle, Taipei 098070
Galerie Grande Fontaine, Sion 111912
Galerie Grand'Rue, Poitiers 101015
Galerie Granero, Bern 111251
Galerie Graphes, Paris 100389
Galerie Grard, Fenin 111404
Galerie Grażyna, Ústí nad Labem . . 098511
Galerie Grenzenlos, Stendal 104951
Galerie Groeneveld, Almelo 107624
Galerie Grüningen, Grüningen 111535
Galerie Grünstraße, Berlin 016029
Galerie Günther Frey, Radenthein . . 002488
Galerie Guislain - États d'Art, Paris . 100390
Galerie Gut Gasteil, Prigglitz 095707
Galerie Hall du Mouggar, Alger 094045
Galerie Hamelin, Honfleur 099347
Galerie Handwerk, München 019058
Galerie Hans Steger, Zeulenroda . . 021059
Galerie Haus 23, Cottbus 016595
Galerie Haus Beda, Bitburg 102140
Galerie Haus Dacheröden, Erfurt . . 017013
Galerie Haus Hegarda, Linz am Rhein 103927
Galerie Haus Hohenzollern, Schlangenbad 073693
Galerie Hausruck, Altenhof am Hausruck 001680
Galerie Heimatverein Zierow e.V., Zierow 021067
Galerie Héritages, Paris 065967
Galerie Hermance, Hermance 111552
Galerie Hermes, Solothurn 111919
Galerie Herwi, Wiesloch 105291
Galerie Hexenhaus, Neuburg an der Donau 104402
Galerie Himmelreich, Magdeburg . . 103989
Galerie Hinter dem Rathaus, Gemeinschaft Wismarer Künstler und Kunstfreunde e.V, Wismar 020920
Galerie HKV, Niederkrüchten 104449
Galerie Hlavního Města Prahy, Praha 008606
Galerie Hlavního Města Prahy, Praha 008607
Galerie Hochmauren, Rottweil 104782
Galerie Hof 12, Amersfoort 107637
Galerie Hofberg 10, Linz 095660
Galerie Hofstetten, Hofstetten-Grünau 002052
Galerie Hoheluft, Hamburg 103137
Galerie Holbein, Lindau, Bodensee . 103919
Galerie Homburg, Homburg 103404
Galerie Hopilliart, Paris 065968
Galerie Horizon, Hermance 111553
Galerie Horizon, Marseille 099661
Galerie Horizon, Marseille 099662
Galerie Hotel Leipziger Hof, Leipzig 103872
Galerie Humus, Lausanne 111618
Galerie I & AC, Graz 095525
Galerie Icon, Berlin 101877
Galerie ID., Carouge 111335
Galerie I.E.M, Antibes-Juan-les-Pins 098850
Galerie IG, Wien 095838
Galerie III, Bussum 107885
Galerie il Quadro, Aachen 101509
Galerie Illusoria, Bern 111252
Galerie Ilsa, Paris 065969
Galerie im 44er Haus, Leonding . . . 002229
Galerie im Adalbert Stifter-Haus, Linz 002247
Galerie im Ainmiller, Landshut 103826
Galerie im Alten Dorf, Münster 104362
Galerie im alten Pfarrhaus, Weilburg 105180
Galerie im alten Rathaus, Homburg 103405
Galerie im Alten Rathaus, Prien . . . 019673
Galerie im Altstadthof, Nürnberg . . 104478
Galerie im Amtshaus, Bad Wurzach 015841
Galerie im Andechshof, Innsbruck . 095582
Galerie im Atelier, Aalen 101534
Galerie im Bahnhof, Bad Freienwalde 101643
Galerie im Bettli, Dübendorf 111387
Galerie im Bildhauerhaus und Skulpturenwanderweg, Einöde . . 001816
Galerie im Bürger- und Gemeindezentrum Hofstetten-Grünau, Hofstetten-Grünau 002052
Galerie im Bürgerhaus, Haigerloch . 017636
Galerie im Bürgerhaus, Neunkirchen, Saar 019261
Galerie im Bürgerspital, Drosendorf an der Thaya 001790
Galerie im Bulgarischen Kulturinstitut, Berlin 101878
Galerie im Coudrayhaus, Bad Berka 015660
Galerie im Cranach-Haus, Lutherstadt Wittenberg 018759
Galerie im Dach, Arlesheim 111130
Galerie im einewelt-haus, Magdeburg 103990
Galerie im Einstein, Berlin 101879
Galerie im Elisabethenhof, Bad Wimpfen 101712
Galerie im Ermelerspeicher, Städtische Museen Schwedt/Oder, Schwedt . 020136
Galerie im ersten Stock, Mödling . . 095683
Galerie im Finnland-Institut, Berlin . 101880
Galerie im Fontanehaus, Berlin 016030
Galerie im Franck-Haus, Marktheidenfeld 018842
Galerie im Ganserhaus, Arbeitskreis 68, Wasserburg am Inn 105165
Galerie im Garten, Mühlacker 072602
Galerie im Gemeinschaftshaus, Berlin 016031
Galerie im Griesbad, Ulm 105092
Galerie im Grund, Ebsdorfergrund . . 102593
Galerie im Haus Knotenbaum, Todtnau 105049
Galerie im Höchhuus, Küsnacht . . . 111598

Galerie im Hörsaalbau, Kustodie der Universität Leipzig, Leipzig 018569
Galerie im Hof, Düsseldorf 102500
Galerie im Hof, Groß-Umstadt 071115, 103016
Galerie im Hof, Zug 112214
Galerie im Hofmannschen Gut, Dittersbach 102379
Galerie im Kehrwiederturm, Hildesheim 017922
Galerie im Kies, Altach 095464
Galerie im Kloster, Magdeburg 103991
Galerie im Kloster, Ribnitz-Damgarten 104751
Galerie im Körnerpark, Kommunale Galerie Neukölln, Berlin 016032
Galerie im Körnerpark, Kommunale Galerie Neukölln, Berlin 016033
Galerie im Kornhauskeller, Ulm . . . 105093
Galerie im Kreishaus, Wetzlar 020841
Galerie im Krottental, Forchheim, Oberfranken 102735
Galerie im Kulturhaus Spandau, Berlin 016034
Galerie im Kunsthaus Erfurt, Erfurt . 017014
Galerie im Kunsthof, Halberstadt . . 103059
Galerie im Kurpark, Bad Steben . . . 101707
Galerie im Lend, Graz 095526
Galerie im Lichtental, Wien 095839
Galerie im Mänihaus, Frutigen 111416
Galerie im Malzhaus, Plauen 019632
Galerie im Nachtwächterhaus, Poysdorf 002455
Galerie im Neuen Kranzler Eck, Berlin 101881
Galerie im Park, Burgdorf 111322
Galerie im Park, Wohlen (Aargau) . . 112003
Galerie im Park, Zürich 112086
Galerie im Polnischen Institut, Leipzig 018570
Galerie im Prediger, Schwäbisch Gmünd 020110
Galerie Im Rahmen, Koblenz 103566
Galerie im Rathaus, Bad Aussee . . . 001707
Galerie im Rathaus Köpenick, Berlin 016035
Galerie im Ratscafe, Bielefeld 102120
Galerie im Rittergut, Niederwiesa . . 104450
Galerie im Rosenhof, Chemnitz . . . 102308
Galerie im Saalbau, Kommunale Galerie Neukölln, Berlin 016036
Galerie im Schauspielhaus, Chemnitz 102309
Galerie im Schlössli, Gontenschwil . 111523
Galerie im Schloß Porcia, Spittal an der Drau 002685
Galerie Im Schloßgarten, Leimen, Baden 103852
Galerie im Schopf, Reinach (Aargau) 111826
Galerie im Seewinkel, Gwatt 111545
Galerie im Stadtmuseum, Städtische Museen Jena, Jena 018106
Galerie im Stadtturm, Gmünd, Kärnten 001904
Galerie im Steinhaus, Zürich 082973
Galerie im Stil, Dresden 102437
Galerie im Taschenbergpalais, Dresden 102438
Galerie im Taxispalais, Innsbruck . . 002080
Galerie im Teisenhoferhof der Malschule Motiv Wachau, Weißenkirchen in der Wachau 002818
Galerie im Theater am Saumarkt, Feldkirch 001846
Galerie im Tor, Emmendingen 016964
Galerie im Traklhaus, Salzburg 002552
Galerie im Troadkasten, Pram 002459
Galerie im Turm, Berlin 016037
Galerie im Turm, Schrobenhausen . 104847
Galerie im Unteren Tor, Bietigheim-Bissingen 102134
Galerie Im Vest, Recklinghausen . . 104681
Galerie im Volkspark, Burg Giebichstein Hochschule für Kunst und Design Halle, Halle, Saale 017656
Galerie im Weytterturm, Straubing . 104958
Galerie im Willy-Brandt-Haus, Berlin 016038
Galerie im Willy-Brandt-Haus, Berlin 016039
Galerie im Wolferlhof, Kötzting 103749
Galerie Image, Wien 095840
Galerie Image In, Mandelieu-La Napoule 099632
Galerie Imago, Bègles 098946
Galerie IMP, Bordeaux 099001
Galerie Impression, München 104201
Galerie in C, Köln 103622
Galerie in de Kerkstraat, Arnhem . . 107849
Die Galerie in der Alten Schule, Kommunale Galerie Treptow, Berlin 016040
Galerie in der alten Villa Hübner, Rostock 104767
Galerie in der Brotfabrik, Berlin . . . 016041
Galerie in der Diele, Nettetal 104397
Galerie in der Druckwerkstatt, Berlin 101882
Galerie in der Fabrik, Burgdorf 111323
Galerie In der Feste, Neckargemünd 104392
Galerie in der Haula, Gurmels 111544
Galerie in der Hauptschule, Ulrichsberg 002766
Galerie in der Hinterstadt, Friedrichstadt 102888
Galerie in der Jahnstrasse, Böblingen 102167
Galerie in der Klosterschule, Glonn . 017431
Galerie in der Kommode, Halle, Saale 103063
Galerie in der Leutenegg, Schönholzerswilen 111895
Galerie in der Prannerstrasse, München 104202
Galerie in der Remise, Radebeul . . 104648
Galerie in der Remise, Tostedt 105050
Galerie in der Scheune, Werneck . . 105215
Galerie in der Schmiede, Pasching . 095701
Galerie in der Waldemai, Schmallenberg 104828
Galerie in der Walpenreute, Stuttgart 104979
Galerie in Eppendorf, Hamburg 103138
Galerie in Riedli, Belp 111238
Galerie in Spirit, Freiburg im Breisgau 102862
Galerie in Touch, Zug 112215
Galerie In'Arts, Genève 111458
Galerie Incontro, Eitorf . . . 102611, 133907
Galerie Incontro, Zürich 112087
Galerie Independenz, Aachen 101510
Galerie Indigo, Martigues 099693
Galerie Individualità, Maur 111722
Galerie Inkatt, Bremen 016412
Galerie Insel, Stuttgart 104980
Galerie Inter Tableaux, Paris 100391
Galerie InterArt, Tutzing 105082
Galerie International, Bochum 102149
Galerie International du Verre, Biot . 098970
Galerie Ippon, Vellinge 082065
Galerie Isartis, Erlangen 102653
Galerie isi, Bad Nauheim 101675
Galerie Isolda, Gießen 102951
Galerie Isshorst, Hamminkeln 103247
Galerie Jacques Cœur, Montpellier . 099758
Galerie J'Aime, Saint-Paul-de-Vence 101206
Galerie Jakubská, Praha 098439
Galerie Jamault, Paris 100392
Galerie Jamborův Dům, Tišnov 008714
Galerie Jánský Vršek, Praha 098440
Galerie Jara, Lyon 099576
Galerie Jaroslava Fragnera, Praha . 008608
Galerie Jaune, Le Mans 099448
Galerie JBK, Praha 098441
Galerie Jean Charles Billy, Le Touquet-Paris-Plage 099462
Galerie Jean Jaurès, Montpellier . . 064742
Galerie Jean Macé, Brest 099028
Galerie Jeanina, Hamburg 103139
Galerie Jeanne, München 104203
Galerie Jeanne d'Arc, Dijon 099218
Galerie Jeannet, Honfleur 099348
Galerie Jerome, København 098557
Galerie Jiřiho Trnky, Unie Výtvarných Umělců, Plzeň 008570
Galerie J.L.P., Bordeaux 061613
Galerie J.M Rousseau, Ars-en-Ré . . 060996
Galerie Joho, Tübingen 105075
Galerie Jolimont, Erlach 111395
Galerie Jouvène, Marseille 099663
Galerie Joy, Zürich 112088
Galerie JPR, Paris 100393, 138384
Galerie Julia L, Passy-en-Valois . . . 066693
Galerie Jupiter, Paris 100394
Galerie Juri, Winterthur 111998
Galerie Justitz, Unhošt 098508
Galerie K, Hannover 103276
Galerie K, Herford 103357
Galerie K., Montreuil-sous-Bois . . . 099767
Galerie k 9, Hannover 103277
Galerie K & S, Berlin 016042
Galerie Kabul Art, Hamburg 071231
Galerie Kaiser, Mayrhofen 095679
Galerie Kaiserstraße, Dortmund . . .102398, 125478
Galerie Kami, Ústí nad Labem 098512
Galerie Kaplička, Hodonín 098358
Galerie Karenina, Wien 095841
Galerie Katja, Landau in der Pfalz . . 103818
Galerie Keller, Zürich 112089
Galerie Kentaro, Studen 111938
Galerie Kerpen, Kerpen, Rheinland . 103533
Galerie Kesselturm, Luzern 111692
Galerie Kiliansmühle, Lünen 103983
Galerie Killeswerk, Stuttgart 104981
Galerie Kleine Komödie, München . 104204
Galerie Klosterformat, Rostock 104768
Galerie Klostermühle, Hude, Oldenburg 103409
Galerie Köln, Köln 121471
Galerie Königsblau, Stuttgart 104982
Galerie Kompromißlos, Dinslaken . . 102375
Galerie Kontraste, Erwitte 102658
Galerie Konzept, Paderborn 104568
Galerie Koráb, Ústí nad Orlicí 098513
Galerie Koralewski, Paris 100395
Galerie Koruna, Hradec Králové . . . 098360
Galerie Krab, Praha 098442
Galerie Kreissprung, Schauren 104819
Galerie Kriens, Kriens 111595
Galerie Kristall 3-D, Oberhausen, Rheinland 104499
Galerie Křižovníků, Praha 008609
Galerie Künstlergruppe adp, Hameln 053190, 103238
Galerie Künstlergruppe Kontra, Hameln 053191, 103239
Galerie KuL - Kunst und Literatur, Bruck an der Mur 095489
Galerie Kulturzentrum Lerchhaus, Eibiswald 001814
Galerie Kunst, Limburg an der Lahn 103916
Galerie Kunst der Gegenwart, Salzburg 002553
Galerie Kunst & Handel, Graz 095527
Galerie Kunst im Gang, Bamberg . . 101729
Galerie Kunstart, Ingelheim am Rhein 103428
Galerie Kunstbrücke Osteuropa, Gesellschaft für Osteuropa-Förderung.e.V, Berlin 016043
Galerie Kunstforum im Alten Haus, Seligenstadt 104884
Galerie Kunstgerecht, Bochum 102150
Galerie Kunsthoken der Stadt Quedlinburg, Quedlinburg 019684
Galerie Kunstlade, Zittau 021071
Galerie Kunstpunkt Berlin, Berlin . . 101883
Galerie Kunststück, Dinslaken 102376
Galerie Kunststück, Leipzig 103873
Galerie Kunststück, Oldenburg, Oldenburg 104542, 134332
Galerie L, Saint-Étienne 101148
Galerie la Belle Angèle, Pont-Aven . 101029
Galerie la Belle Epoque, Beaulieu-sur-Mer 098937
Galerie la Bohème, Zürich 112090
Galerie la Cariatide, La Martyre . . . 099399
Galerie La Cité, Luxembourg 107402, 134751
Galerie La Ferronnerie, Paris 100396
Galerie l.a.-Leipzig Arts, Leipzig . . . 103874
Galerie La Ligne Droite, Genève . . .082429, 111459
Galerie La Martinerie, Amboise . . . 098819
Galerie la Papeterie, Bruxelles 096200
Galerie la Pointe Badine, Vence . . .101442, 138646
Galerie La Poutre, Marseille 064358, 099664, 121064, 124415, 133493
Galerie La Rage, Lyon 099577
Galerie la Ratière, Romont 111845
Galerie la Santoline, Sanary-sur-Mer 101251
Galerie La Serre, Lentillères 133480
Galerie La Serre, Saint-Étienne . . . 101149
Galerie La Signature, Metz 099712
Galerie La Spirale, Vevey 111967
Galerie La Sybille, Paris 100397
Galerie La Toupie, Kröppen 072088
Galerie La Vong, Hong Kong 097788
Galerie Labor 19, Berlin 101884
Galerie Laétitia, Brie-Comte-Robert 099034
Galerie Laforet, Verbier 111960
Galerie Lajarrige, La Baule-Escoublac 063288
Galerie l'Albertine, Nice 065085
Galerie L'Amateur, Lyon 099578
Galerie l'Amour de l'Art, Paris 100398
Galerie Landesbank Baden-Württemberg, Stuttgart 020349
Galerie Landskron, Wien 057422
Galerie Landstrasse, Bludesch 095482
Galerie Lapislazuli, Freiburg im Breisgau 102863
Galerie L'Aquarium, Valenciennes . 015098
Galerie L'Arc en Seine, Paris 100399
Galerie l'Arche, Alès 098814
Galerie Lat die Tied, Nordstrand . . . 104469
Galerie l'Atelier, Le Castellet 099429
Galerie Laterne, Breitenbach 111304
Galerie l'Atmosphére, Männedorf . . 111712
Galerie Latour, Martigny 111720
Galerie Laura, Mandres-les-Roses . 099633
Galerie Lazertis, Zürich . . 082974, 112091
Galerie le 5, Ribérac 101091
Galerie Le Biblion, Toulouse 101355
Galerie le Blason, Ruoms 067330
Galerie le Bouchon, Camaret-sur-Mer 099056
Galerie Le Bréton, Paris 100400
Galerie le Breton, Pont-Aven 101030
Galerie le Cadre, Cahors 099051
Galerie Le Cadre Noir, Paris 100401
Galerie Le Carré, Musée Bonnat, Bayonne 010684
Galerie le Cèdre Rouge, Montréal . . 097017
Galerie Le Cheval de Sable, Paris . . 100402
Galerie le Creuset, Charleroi 096274
Galerie le Deco, Tokyo 107041
Galerie Le Gué, Crevant 099189
Galerie le Lieu, Lorient 099521
Galerie Le Linkin, Perros-Guirec . . . 100998
Galerie Le Minotaure, Paris 100403
Galerie le Patrimoine, Biot 098971
Galerie le Petit Louvre, Avignon . . . 098898
Galerie Le Point, Monaco 107531
Galerie le Point du Jour, Paris 100404
Galerie Le Prestige, Paris 100405
Galerie Le Prestige, Paris 100406
Galerie Le Révèrbère, Lyon 099579
Galerie le Royer, Montréal 097018
Galerie Le Sous-Sol, Paris 100407
Galerie le Sphinx, La Ville-Dieu-du-Temple 099412
Galerie Le Toit du Monde, Paris . . . 100408
Galerie Le Troisième Oeil, Paris . . . 100409
Galerie le Vieux-Bourg, Lonay 111656
Galerie Lebensart, Potsdam 104626
Galerie Leechgasse 24, Graz 095528

Galerie l'Effrontée, Besançon 061382, 098953
Galerie l'Enclume, Bôle 082269
Galerie l'Enfant, Washington 093413
Galerie l'Entracte, Lausanne 111619
Galerie Leonardo da Vinci, Mamer .077483, 107415
Galerie Leonhard, Graz 095529
Galerie Léoni, Marseille 099665
Galerie Les 3 Clefs, Paris 065970
Galerie les Angelots, Fontevraud-l'Abbaye 062910
Galerie les Clevos, Paris 065971
Galerie les Contemporains, Bruxelles 096201
Galerie les Cyclades, Antibes-Juan-les-Pins 098851
Galerie Les Deux-Fontaines, Bursins 111326
Galerie Les Filles du Calvaire, Paris 100410
Galerie les Hirondelles, Coppet 111368
Galerie les Modernes, Montréal . . . 097019
Galerie les Nabis, Caluire-et-Cuire . 099054
Galerie les Oréades, Bagnères-de-Luchon 061165, 098906
Galerie Les Oréades, Toulouse 068512, 101356, 124980
Galerie Les Singuliers, Paris 100411
Galerie les Tournesols, Montbrison . 099738
Galerie les Tournesols, Vichy 101464
Galerie L'Etoile d'Ishtar, Paris 065972
Galerie Leviathan, Bordesholm 102201
Galerie Liberté, Pont-Aven 101031
Galerie Librairie Australienne, Saint-Denis (Seine-Saint-Denis) 101140
Galerie Lichterloh, Wien 057423
Galerie Lichtpunkt, Hamburg 103140
Galerie Lichtung, Leipzig 103875
Galerie Lieve Hemel, Amsterdam . .107721, 134780
Galerie Lifestyle, Ranstadt 104656
Galerie Lindenberg, Basel 111182
Galerie l'Industrielle-Alliance, Montréal 005925
Galerie Lions'Y, Lyon 099580
Galerie Liotard, Genève 111460
Galerie l'Issue, Strasbourg 101291
Galerie Litera, Praha 098443
Galerie Lithoart, Charlottenlund . . . 098522
Galerie LiTo, Detmold 102361
Galerie Litvinov, Litvínov 008486
Galerie LM, Lyon 099581
Galerie LM Art, Trier 105059
Galerie Loc'art, Ollon 111799
Galerie Loft, Paris 100412
Galerie Loïc de Pors-Mellec, Locquirec 099517
Galerie l'Oiseau Bleu, Vertou 101458
Galerie Loisel Grafik, Pörtschach am Wörther See 002448
Galerie l'Orange, Le Havre 099438
Galerie l'Orange, Sainte-Adresse . . 101238
Galerie Louis-Pierre, Leuven 058274
Galerie Louvre, Praha 098444
Galerie Lovers of Fine Arts, Gstaad . 111539
Galerie Ludvika Kuby, Březnice . . . 008279
Galerie Luftschloß, Münster 104363
Galerie Luftschloß, Münster 104364
Galerie Luise, Bielefeld 102121
Galerie Lukas, Bad König 101665
Le Galerie Luministe, Miami 117078
Galerie M, Berlin 016044
Galerie M, Hamburg 103141
Galerie M, Solingen 104916
Galerie M 20, Hamburg 103142
Galerie m Bochum, Bochum 102151
Galerie m Bochum Fotografie, Bochum 102152
Galerie M & K, Jihlava 098365
Galerie M1, Weimar, Thüringen . . . 105187
Galerie Mad, Graz 095530
Galerie Malaval, Lyon 099582
Galerie Malovaný Dům, Třebíč 008719
Galerie Malwerk 2000, Erdweg . . . 102636
Galerie Mana, Wien 095842
Galerie Mani, Berlin 101885
Galerie MANO, Kiel 103540
Galerie Mansarte, Sankt Anton am Arlberg 095740
Galerie Marceau, Paris 100413
Galerie Marco Edition, Bonn 102182, 133828
Galerie Marek, Paris 100414
Galerie Marengo, Angoulême 098832
Galerie Margot, Eindhoven 107998
Galerie Marie-Christine, Bruxelles .057959, 120726
Galerie Marie-Louise, Grenoble . . . 099304
Galerie Marina, Avignon 098899
Galerie Marina, Cassis 099090
Galerie Marine, La Flotte 099394
Galerie Marine, Saint-Malo (Ille-et-Vilaine) 067613
Galerie Marion, Perpignan 066745, 100991
Galerie Maritim, Hamburg 103143
Galerie Marktschlößchen, Halle, Saale 017657
Galerie Marktstätte, Konstanz 103757
Galerie Martagon, Malaucene 099629
Galerie Martine et Thibault de la Chatre, Paris 100415
Galerie Matéo, Grenoble 099305
Galerie Mathilde D., Lyon 099583
Galerie Matignon, Paris 100416
Galerie Matignon 32, Paris 100417
Galerie Max, Nordhausen 104464
Galerie Max 21, Iphofen 103436
Galerie Maxim, Villefranche-sur-Mer 068900
Galerie May, Savigny-sur-Orge 101266
Galerie Mazarine, Nice 065086
Galerie Mazarine, Paris 100418
Galerie Mazur, Kroměříž 098375
Galerie Méditerranée, Bonifacio . . . 098980
Galerie Méduse, Montréal 058956, 097020
Galerie Mémoires, Albi . . . 060757, 098810
Galerie Merci, Kufstein 095638
Galerie Mercure, Paris 065973
Galerie Město Blanska, Blansko . . . 008269
Galerie MG, Paris 065974
Galerie Mia, München 104205
Galerie Michael, Rottach-Egern . . . 104776
Galerie Michel, Paris 100419, 138385
Galerie Michel-Angelo, Montréal . . 097021
Galerie Michelangelo, Las Vegas . . 116620
Galerie Micro, Stockholm 111024
Galerie Milada, Praha 098445
Galerie Millennium, Praha 098446
Galerie Minden, Minden, Westfalen 104079
Galerie Minnepand, Gent 096288
Galerie Mirages, Edinburgh 112995
Galerie Miro, Praha 098447
Galerie mit der blauen Tür, Nürnberg 104479
Galerie Mitte, Dresden 102439
Galerie Mittelstraße, Halle, Saale . . 103064
Galerie Mobile, Bad Wimpfen 101713
Galerie Modena Art, Wien 095843
Galerie modern, Lingen 103925
Galerie Moderne, Bruxelles 120727
Galerie Moderne, Silkeborg 098601
Galerie Moderního Umění, Hradec Králové 098361
Galerie m.o.d.o., Winterthur 111999
Galerie Mönchentor, Rostock 019897
Galerie Momen, Siegen 104895
Galerie Mona Lisa, Paris 100420
Galerie Monaco Fine Arts, Monaco . 107532
Galerie Mondsee, Mondsee 095687
Galerie Mongeon, Portland 091940
Galerie Mont-Blanc, Chamonix-Mont-Blanc 099108, 138070
Galerie Montador, Dieppe 099204
Galerie Montaigne, Monaco 077606
Galerie Montana, Apeldoorn 107841
Galerie Montcalm, Gatineau 005502
Galerie Montgautier, Poitiers 101016
Galerie Montmartre, Monaco 128506
Galerie Morgenland, Hamburg 103144
Galerie Moulay Youssef, Casablanca 077654
Galerie Moulins, Toulouse 068513
Galerie Mozartstraße, Linz 095661
Galerie M.R., Angoulême 098833
Galerie Muda 2, Ursula, Hamburg . . 103145
Galerie Mühlenstrasse, Brühl, Rheinland 102275
Galerie müllerdechiara, Berlin 101886
Galerie Münsterland, Emsdetten . . . 016979
Galerie Municipale, Biscarrosse . . . 061495
Galerie Municipale, Biscarrosse . . . 061496
Galerie Municipale, Montesquieu . . 013156
Galerie Municipale, Vitry-sur-Seine 015323
Galerie Municipale au Palais Montcalm, Québec 006219
Galerie Municipale d'Art Contemporain Julio-Gonzalez, Arcueil 010454
Galerie Municipale du Château d'Eau, Toulouse 014983
Galerie Municipale Eduard Manet, Gennevilliers 011931
Galerie Municipale Renoir, Nice . . . 013394
Galerie Museal, Luxembourg 077479
Galerie-Musée de l'Auberge Champenoise, Moussy 013277
Galerie-Musée Le Petit Chapitre, Fosses-la Ville 003438
Galerie Můstek, Praha 098448
Galerie MXM, Praha 098449
Galerie MY, Jablonec nad Nisou . . . 098363
Galerie N, Dahn 016627
Galerie N, Erbach, Odenwald 102633
Galerie N, Michelstadt 104068
Galerie Nadia B, Dieulefit 099208
Galerie nächst Sankt Stephan, Wien 095844, 133198
Galerie Naja, Le Cap-d'Agde 099424
Galerie Nando, Lausanne 111620
Galerie Nationale d'Art, Dakar 034129
Galerie Nationale de la Tapisserie et de l'Art Textile, Beauvais 010721
Galerie N'Daje, Morges 111755
Galerie Neel, Le Golfe-Juan 099434
Galerie Nei Liicht, Dudelange 107382
Galerie Nepomuk, Kaiserstuhl 111577
Galerie neu & alt, Freudenberg 102877
Galerie Neue Meister, Staatliche Kunstsammlungen Dresden, Dresden 016787
Galerie Neues Rathaus, Wetzlar . . . 105236
Galerie Neunzer, Fürth, Bayern 102900
Galerie Neuve, Grimaud 099314
Galerie New Line, Hohenems 095569
Galerie NKE, Berlin 101887
Galerie No 30, Schwalmstadt 104857
Galerie No. 4, Paris 065975
Galerie No. 9, Praha 098450
Galerie Noa Noa, Papeete 101495
Galerie Noah, Augsburg 101614
Galerie Noctua, Říčany u Prahy . . . 137853
Galerie Nöfa, Wels 095780
Galerie Nöfa, Wels 133171
Galerie Noodlebärg, Basel 111183
Galerie Noord, Groningen 108036
Galerie Nord, Berlin 101888
Galerie Nord-Est, Paris 100421
Galerie Nord-Est, Strasbourg 101292
Galerie Nord-Sam Salzburger-Freilichtskulptur, Salzburg 095721
Galerie Normand, Paris 100422
Galerie Nota Bene, Genève 111461
Galerie Nothburga, Innsbruck 095583
Galerie November, Berlin 101889
Galerie Nový Svět, Praha 098451
Galerie Nr 7, Bad Doberan 101634
Galerie Nuances, Saint-Gilles-Croix-de-Vie 101157
Galerie Nuances et Lumière, Lyon . 099584
Galerie Numero 16, Noordbroek . . . 029970
Galerie O, Schaffhausen 111889
Galerie Oben, Chemnitz . . 102310, 133850
Galerie Oberkampf, Paris 100423
Galerie Objekta, Kreuzlingen 111591
Galerie Objektiv, Berlin 101890
Galerie Objektiv, Köln 103623
Galerie Obkirchen, Sachseln 111854
Galerie Obrist, Essen 102677
Galerie Octobre, Carouge 111336
Galerie of Art, Bad Bentheim 101627
Galerie of Modern Art, Berlin 101891
Galerie Onze, Saint-Paul-de-Vence . 101207
Galerie Opaque, Berlin 101892
Galerie l'Orangerie, Neuchâtel 111772
Galerie Orsel, Paris 100424
Galerie Oskar, Hamburg 103146
Galerie Ost-Art, Berlin 101893
Galerie Ostrov, Praha 098452
Galerie Ovadia, Nancy 099794
Galerie Oviri, Punaauia 101496
Galerie P, Bruxelles 096202
Galerie P, Carouge 111337
Galerie P., Hamburg 103147
Galerie P, Wittingen 105312
Galerie Pablo Picasso, Amsterdam . 107722
Galerie Page, Biarritz 098963
Galerie Palais Starhemberg, Wien . 057424
Galerie Palais Walderdorff, Trier . . . 020479
Galerie Palette Röderhaus, Wuppertal 021015
Galerie Palme, Hamburg 103148
Galerie Palü, Pontresina 111812
Galerie Pankow, Berlin 016045
Galerie Pappelhof, Appenzell 111126
Galerie Parchemine, Montréal 097022
Galerie Parcours, Metz 064530
Galerie Paris-Ispahan, Paris 065976
Galerie Park Art, Marseille 099666
Galerie Parterre, Kommunale Galerie Prenzlauer Berg, Berlin 016046
La Galerie Passage, Tallinn 009406
Galerie Patro, Ostrava 098401
Galerie Páv, Liberec 098380
Galerie Pendo, Zürich 112092
Galerie Peters-Barenbrock im Haus Elisabeth von Eicken, Ostseebad Ahrenshoop 019515
Galerie-PF, Idar-Oberstein 103420
Galerie Pi, København 098558
Galerie Picot-le Roy, Crozon 099191
Galerie Pictures, Aachen 101511
Galerie Pidoux, Meißen 104054
Galerie Pierre, Paris 100425
Galerie Pillango, Berlin 101894
Galerie Pittoresque, Paris 065977
Galerie Place des Arts, Montpellier . 099759
Galerie Plaisance, Paris 100426
Galerie Plak-Art, Frankfurt am Main 102771
Galerie Planie, Reutlingen 104725
Galerie Plein Sud, Les Sables-d'Olonne 099474
Galerie Poesie, Zürich 112093
Galerie Pompadour, Germering 102940
Galerie Port-Maurice, Saint-Léonard 006383
Galerie Portalis, Aix-en-Provence . . 098787
Galerie Porte Avion, Marseille 099667
Galerie Portyč, Písek 008566
Galerie Post, Leipzig 103876
Galerie Prisma, Wien 057425
Galerie Privilège, Biarritz 098964
Galerie Pro Arte, Basel . . . 082141, 111184
Galerie Pro Arte, Bevaix . . 082252, 111283
Galerie Pro Arte, Freiburg im Breisgau 102864
Galerie pro Arte, Hallein 095560
Galerie Pro Arte, Hamburg 103149
Galerie Pro Arte, Wien 095845
Galerie Pro Arte Kasper, Morges . . . 111756
Galerie pro Každého, Ostrava 098402
Galerie pro Radost, Ostrava 098403
Galerie Proarta, Zürich 112094
Galerie Proarta, Zug 112216
Galerie Profil, Cham 016550
Galerie Profil, Weimar, Thüringen . . 105188
Galerie Puce, Barbizon 061203
Galerie Pullach, Pullach 104645
Galerie PurPur, Bad Doberan 101635

Galerie Pygmalion, Saint-Nazaire (Loire-Atlantique) 101185
Galerie Pythéas, Marseille 099668
Galerie Pytheas, Paris 065978
Galerie Q 14, Traunreut 105054
Galerie Quadriga, Leipzig 103877
Galerie Quartier Wörth, Wiesbaden . 105256
Galerie Quattro, Glattfelden 111519
Galerie Quincampoix, Paris 100427
Galerie R, Eindhoven 078337
Galerie Racine, La Ferté-Milon 063373
Galerie Radius, Sankt Gallen 111869
Galerie Rainmühle, Emmenbrücke . 111392
Galerie Raphael, Frankfurt am Main 102772, 133942
Galerie Raugraff, Nancy 099795
Galerie Rauhenstein, Wien 057426
Galerie Réfractaire, Paris 065979
Galerie Refugium, Berlin . 101895, 133777
Galerie Regard, Ajaccio 098805
Galerie Regart, Le Cap-d'Agde 099425
Galerie Reklame, Leonding 095646
Galerie Rema, Montréal 097023
Galerie Remise, Bad Nauheim 101676
Galerie Remise, Berlin 101896
Galerie Renoir, Maastricht 108122
Galerie Repfergasse 26, Schaffhausen 111890
Galerie Rheinland, Solingen 073853
Galerie Riance, Courroux 111371
Galerie Richard Manuel, Paris 100428
Galerie Riehentor, Basel 111185
Galerie Rive Gauche, La Colle-sur-Loup 063342, 099392
Galerie Rive Gauche, Paris 100429
Galerie Römerapotheke, Zürich . . . 112095
Galerie Rondo, Hradec Králové 098362
Galerie Rose, Mosnang 111757
Galerie Roseg, Pontresina 111813
Galerie Rosenbergstrasse, Bern . . . 111253
Galerie Rosengarten, Thun 111945
Galerie Rote Rose, Regensberg . . . 111823
Galerie Rouge, Denver 116000
Galerie Rouge, New Orleans 117441
La Galerie Rouge, Paris 065980
Galerie Roull, Brest 061771
Galerie Route de la Soie, Paris 100430
Galerie Royale, Montréal 097024
Galerie Royale, New Orleans 117442
Galerie Royale, Rochefort (Charente-Maritime) 067178
Galerie Rozehnal, Praha 098453
Galerie Rubikon, Olomouc 098391
Galerie Rudolfinum, Praha 008610
Galerie Ruine, Genève 111462
Galerie Růžový Kopeček, Cheb 098352
Galerie S, Amsterdam 107723
Galerie S 65, Köln 103624
Galerie Saalbach, Saalbach 095712
Galerie Sahara, Rabat 107561
Galerie Saint-Antoine, Bruxelles . . . 057960
Galerie Saint-Antoine, Bruxelles . . . 057961
Galerie Saint-Antoine, Bruxelles . . . 120728
Galerie Saint-Antoine, Bruxelles . . . 120729
Galerie Saint-Benoît, Chambéry . . . 062103
Galerie Saint Charles, Lyon 064133
Galerie Saint Etienne, New York . . . 117936
Galerie Saint-Georges, Lyon 099585
Galerie Saint-Germain, Bussigny-près-Lausanne 111327
Galerie Saint-Germain, Monaco . . . 077607
Galerie Saint-Germain, Segny 101267
Galerie Saint Gilles, Zürich 112096
Galerie Saint-Guénolé, Fouesnant . 062921
Galerie Saint-Hubert, Lyon 099586
Galerie Saint-Jacques, Bruxelles . . . 096203
Galerie Saint-Jacques, Grignan . . . 099312
Galerie Saint Jacques, Toulouse . . . 068514
Galerie Saint-Jean, Genève 082430, 111463
Galerie Saint-Laurent, Plérin 066849, 101012, 124844
Galerie Saint-Leu, Amiens 060816
Galerie Saint-Louis, Saintes 101241
Galerie Saint-Louis, Versailles 068807, 125018
Galerie Saint-Luc, Andernos-les-Bains 098826
Galerie Saint-Luc, Lyon 099587
Galerie Saint-Marceau des Prés, Orléans 099889
Galerie Saint-Martial, Châteauroux . 099124
Galerie Saint-Martin, Bretenoux . . . 061783
Galerie Saint-Martin, Brive-la-Gaillarde 099038
Galerie Saint-Martin, Metz 099713
Galerie Saint-Ménélée, Vichy 068857
Galerie Saint-Merri Art Inuit, Paris . 100431
Galerie Saint-Michel, Bruxelles . . . 057962
Galerie Saint-Michel, Guérande . . . 099319
Galerie Saint-Michel, Nice 065087
Galerie Saint-Nicolas, Remich 107417
Galerie Saint-Paul, Lyon 099588
Galerie Saint-Pierre, Bar-le-Duc . . . 061193
Galerie Saint-Pierre, Limoges 099508
Galerie Saint-Roch, Paris 100432
Galerie Saint-Sauveur, Dinan 099223
Galerie Saint Tropez, Düsseldorf . . . 102501
Galerie Saint-Valérien, Tournus . . . 068568
Galerie Saint-Vincent, Nevers 065010
Galerie Sainte-Barbe, Nevez 099826
Galerie Sainte-Catherine, Honfleur . 099349
Galerie Sainte-Catherine, Quimper . 101061
Galerie Sainte-Catherine, Rodez . . . 101097
Galerie Sainte-Marie, Montluçon . . 064710
Galerie Sala Terrena, Mödling 002324
Galerie Saltiel, Le Castellet 099430
Galerie Samarcande, Paris 065981
Galerie Sambre, Fougères (Ille-et-Vilaine) 099272
La Galerie Samedi, Montfort-l'Amaury 099744
Galerie Samson, Bourges 061727
Galerie San Carlo, Paris . . 065982, 100433
Galerie San Jordy, Rodes 067189
Galerie Sanguine, La Rochelle 099406
Galerie Sankt Barbara, Adrian, Hall in Tirol 095558
Galerie Sankt Georg, Stadtmuseum Gardelegen, Gardelegen 017321
Galerie Sankt Gertrud, København . 098559
Galerie Sankt Johann, Saarbrücken 104794
Galerie Sankt Ulrich, Wien 057427
Galerie Sans Nom, Moncton 005897
Galerie Sanssouci, Potsdam 104627
Galerie Santa Clara, Wiesbaden . . . 105257
Galerie Saphir, Dinard 099232
Galerie Saphir, Paris 100434
Galerie Saqqârah, Gstaad 111540
Galerie Satellite, Paris 100435
Galerie Sattelgut, Neunkirchen-Seelscheid 104418
La Galerie Scandinave, Paris 065983
Galerie Scheune, Nideggen 104440
Galerie Schloss Damtschach, Wernberg 095783
Galerie Schloß Edesheim, Edesheim 102602
Galerie Schloß Lamberg, Steyr 002699
Galerie Schloß Mochental, Ehingen, Donau 102604
Galerie Schloß Neuhaus, Salzburg . 095722
Galerie Schloß Rimsingen, Breisach am Rhein 016400
Galerie Schnitt-art, Schwarzenbach 111897
Galerie Schwarz-Weiss, Osnabrück 104549
Galerie Schwedenkate, Eutin 102721
Galerie Seestrasse 96, Berlingen . . 111239
Galerie Sehens-Wert, Krefeld 072070
Galerie Sehens-wert, Leipzig 072203
Galerie Seiller, Noirmoutier-en-l'Ile . 099881
Galerie Seine 51, Paris 100436
Galerie Severina, Bad Doberan 101636
Galerie Sevogel, Basel 111186
Galerie Shirley, Genève 111464
Galerie Siebzehn, Wädenswil 111977
Galerie Siècles, Beirut 077393
Galerie Sigfrid, Orléans 099890
Galerie Signal Iduna, Dortmund . . . 102399
Galerie Signatur, Laer 103814
Galerie Sigristenkeller, Bülach 111314
Galerie Sillage, Gramat 099293
Galerie Sillage, Paimpol 099894
Galerie Simone, Paris 100437
Galerie Sionnet, Jussy 111576
Galerie Skala, Köln 103625
Galerie Skell, Schmiedeberg, Osterzgebirge 020058
Galerie Skulptura, Wolfenschiessen 112006
Galerie SMA, Carouge 111338
Galerie Soleil, Montréal 097025
Galerie Soleilo, Hampton 094615
Galerie Songe, Montceau-les-Mines 099739
Galerie Sonnenaufgang, Heinsberg . 103345
Galerie Sonnenfels, Wien . 057428, 095846
Galerie Sonnhalde, Grüningen 111536
Galerie Sonnhalde, Zürich 112097
Galerie Sophien-Edition, Berlin 101897
Galerie Spandow, Berlin 101898
Galerie Speicher, Speicher 111926
Galerie Spektrum, Bad Salzuflen . . 101692
Galerie Spektrum, Dortmund 102400
Galerie Spektrum, München 104206
Galerie Spektrum, Sinsheim 104909
Galerie SPHN, Berlin 101899
Galerie Spiekerhof, Münster 104365
Galerie Spitalgasse, Weiden, Oberpfalz 020707
Galerie SR, Paris 100438
Galerie Stadtgraben, Büren an der Aare 111316
Galerie Stadtpark, Krems . 095631, 133107
Galerie Stallburg, Wien 057429
Galerie Stanislas, Paris 065984
Galerie Start, Monaco 107533
Galerie Steinzeit, Aham 101539
Galerie Stephanie Hollenstein, Lustenau 002272
Galerie Stern, Kriens 111596
Galerie Šternberk, Šternberk 008693
Galerie Stift Eberndorf, Eberndorf . . 001800
Galerie Stilbruch, Köln 103626
Galerie Studio 10, Chur 111357
Galerie Stufenbau, Ittigen 111572
Galerie Sud, Bagneux 098909
Galerie Süd, Leipzig 103878
Galerie Sulgenau, Bern 111254
Galerie Sur, Wien 095847
Galerie sur Cour, Paris 100439
Galerie Symbole Art, Montréal 097026
Galerie Synarte, Klagenfurt 095615
Galerie T, Berlin 101900
Galerie T, Middelburg 108141
Galerie t' Elgee, Philadelphia 118762
Galerie Tableau, Berlin . . . 069609, 101901
Galerie Tactile, Genève 111465
Galerie Taisei, Tokyo 027166
Galerie Talbach, Hippach 095565
Galerie Tango, Lutry 111674
Galerie Tannzapfenland, Eschlikon . 111401
Galerie Taube, Berlin 101902
Galerie Templ, Mladá Boleslav 098386
Galerie Teppichkunst, Hattingen . . . 103310
Galerie Terminus, München 104207
Galerie Terra Viva, Saint-Quentin-la-Poterie 014505
Galerie Théma, Bordeaux 099002
Galerie Theodor von Hörmann, Imst 002069
Galerie Théorème, Paris 065985
Galerie Thomas, Paris 100440
Galerie Titanik, Turku 098762
Galerie Torhaus Rombergpark, Dortmund 016770
Galerie Tourbillon, Paris . . 065986, 100441
Galerie Trabant, Wien 095848
Galerie Transit, Mechelen 096384
Galerie Treff, Hamburg 103150
Galerie Trend, Ibbenbüren 103418
Galerie Treppe, Düren 102462
Galerie Triple A, Saint-Saphorin-sur-Morges 111858
Galerie Trittligasse, Zürich 112098
Galerie Turenne, Montréal 097027
Galerie Turquoise, Sidi Bou Saïd . . . 112258
Galerie Tvar, Praha 098454
Galerie Tvrdohlaví, Praha 098455
Galerie Twenty, Biarritz 061463
Galerie Two Rooms, Hamburg 103151
Galerie Uckermark, Templin 105041
Galerie Uenzen 73, Süstedt 105025
Galerie Uhu, Lörrach 103934
Galerie Umění, Karlovy Vary 098371
Galerie Umění, Ostrov nad Ohří . . . 008557
Galerie Uměni Karlovy Vary, Karlovy Vary 008424
Galerie Un Deux Trois, Genève 082431, 111466
Galerie Unart, Villach 095776
Galerie und Edition Artelier, Graz . .095531, 133077
Galerie und Edition Zwettltal-Fessl, Groß Gerungs 095551, 133083
Galerie und Kunst, Berlin 069610
Galerie und Kunsthandel, Trier 105060
Galerie und Weinmuseum Schloß Gamlitz, Gamlitz 001884
Galerie Une, Neuchâtel 111773
Galerie Unie Výtvarný Umělců Teplice, Teplice 008709
Galerie Unikat, Hamburg 103152
Galerie Unikat, Staufen 104946
Galerie Up-Art, Neustadt an der Weinstraße 104429
Galerie Uraeus, Paris 100442
Galerie Utopie, Leysin 111642
Galerie Utrecht, Utrecht 108248
Galerie V, Beverungen 102103
Galerie v Lazarské, Praha 098456
Galerie V & V, Wien 095849
Galerie Valdoria, Vallauris 101417
Galerie Valentin, Brno . . . 098332, 120847
Galerie Van Alom, Berlin 101903
Galerie Vanuxem, Paris 100443
Galerie ve Dvore, Litoměřice 098381
Galerie ve Věži, Mělník 098385
Galerie Vendôme Rive Gauche, Paris 100444
Galerie Venezia, Pirmasens 104608
Galerie Venise-Cadre, Casablanca . 107555
Galerie Verlag Dresden, Radebeul .104649, 134351
Galerie Verre et Bois, Lyon 099589
Galerie Via Art, Praha 098457
Galerie viArtis, Halle, Saale 103065
Galerie Vibrations, Paris 100445
Galerie Vice Versa, Lausanne 111621
Galerie Victor Hugo, Saintes 068086, 101242
Galerie Victor Hugo, Toulouse 068515
Galerie Victoria, København 060327
Galerie Vieille du Temple, Paris . . . 100446
Galerie Vier Jahreszeiten, Hainfeld . 057052
Galerie Village Créole, Les Trois-Ilets 099475
Galerie Vincent, Ottawa 097106
Galerie Viola, Aschaffenburg 101600
Galerie Violetta, Wien 095850
Galerie Vision, Helsinki 098721
Galerie Vista Nova, Zürich 112099
Galerie Vita, Feldbrunnen . 082365, 111402
Galerie Vitesse, Paris 100447
Galerie Vlasta, Praha 098458
Galerie Vltavín, Praha 098459
Galerie Voltaire, Grenoble 099306
Galerie Volubilis, Tanger 077698
Galerie vom P, Hamburg . . 103153, 121425
Galerie Vrais Rêves, Lyon 099590
Galerie Vue-sur-Mer, Dinard 099233
Galerie Výheň, Jihlava 098366
Galerie Vyšehrad, Praha 008611
Galerie Výtvarného Umění, Havlíčkův Brod 008368
Galerie Výtvarného Umění, Hodonín 008374
Galerie Výtvarného Umění, Most . . . 008515
Galerie Výtvarného Umění, Náchod . 008518
Galerie Výtvarného Uměni, Ostrava . 008551

Galerie Výtvarného Umění, Roudnice nad Labem 008670
Galerie W, Paris 100448
Galerie Wagram, Paris 100449
Galerie Waldhof in Birkenwerder, Birkenwerder 016249
Galerie Walfischgasse, Wien 095851
Galerie Walu, Zürich 112100, 122366, 141336
Galerie Wandelbar, Gstaad 111541
Galerie Weberhaus, Weiz 002825
Galerie Weihergut Altstadtgalerie, Salzburg 057247, 095723, 133136
Galerie Weihergut Biberngasse, Salzburg 057248, 095724, 133137
Galerie Weissenseer Freitag, Berlin 101904
Galerie Weisser Elefant, Berlin 101905
Galerie Westend, München 104208
Galerie Westensee, Westensee . . . 105223
Galerie Wickenburg, Wien 095852
Galerie Wildeshausen, Wildeshausen 105296
Galerie Wildlife, Stäfa 111932
Galerie Wittenberg 418, Steckborn . 111934
Galerie Wittenstein, Wuppertal 105353
Galerie WM, Lyon 099591
Galerie Wohnart, Düsseldorf 102502
Galerie Wohnart, Düsseldorf 102503
Galerie Wolfshütt, Essen 102678
Galerie Xenios, Frankfurt am Main . 102773
Galerie XVIIIème XXIème, Pont-Aven 066914
Galerie Ya Zamane, Rabat 077692
Galerie Yan, Quiberon 101052
Galerie Ypsilon, Zürich . . . 112101, 130236
Galerie Z, Landau in der Pfalz 103819
Galerie Z, München 104209
Galerie Z, Norderstedt 104460
Galerie Z Null, Köln 103627
Galerie Zäune 8, Zürich 112102
Galerie ZAK, Fürth, Bayern 102901
Galerie Zeitkunst, Heidenreichstein 095562, 123381
Galerie Zeitlupe, Heidenheim an der Brenz 103328
Galerie Zell am See, Zell am See . . 095981
Galerie Zelle e.V., Reutlingen 053192, 104726
Galerie Zentrum, Wien 095853
Galerie Zentrum, Wien . . . 095854, 133199
Galerie Ziel, Appenzell 111127
Galerie Žlutý Slon, Brno 098333
Galerie Zonzon, Arcachon 098855
Galerie Zoo, Strasbourg 101293
Galerie Züger, Niederteufen 111779
Galerie zum alten Ötztal, Oetz 002398
Galerie zum Burgtor, Rothenburg ob der Tauber 104774
Galerie zum Elephanten, Zurzach . . 112223
Galerie zum Goldrahmen, Murg . . . 104382
Galerie zum Hof, Luzern 082626
Galerie zum kleinen Schwan, Baden 111151
Galerie zum Roten Leuen, Klingnau 111586
Galerie zum Schiff, Zofingen 112016
Galerie zum Strauss, Sankt Gallen . 111870
Galerie zur alten Linde, Villingen-Schwenningen 105125
Galerie zur grünen Tür, Uznach 111957
Galerie zur Hammermühle, Ibach . . 111567
Galerie zur Heubühne, Oberdiessbach 111787
Galerie zur Krähe, Basel 111187
Galerie Zur Krone, Eschenz 082362
Galerie zur Matze, Brig 111307
Galerie zur Münz, Zug 112217
Galerie Zur Stockeregg, Zürich . . . 112103
Galerie zur Uralten Uhr, Rotkreuz . . 082755
Galerie Zweihundert, Berlin 101906
Galerie zwischen den Toren, Xanten 105364
galerie'88, Hanau 103251, 134032
Galerie.be, Bruxelles 096204
Galeriebond Nederland, Amsterdam 053885
Galeriehaus, Nürnberg 019350
Les Galeries de l'Historie, Neuchâtel 037374
Galeries de Paléontologie et d'Anatomie Comparée, Musée National d'Histoire Naturelle, Paris 013592
Galeries des Ducs, Chatenoy-le-Royal 099125
Les Galeries du Fresne, Fresnay-sur-Sarthe 062942, 099275
Galeries du Panthéon Bouddhique du Japon et de la Chine, Paris 013593
Galeries les Alizés, Orléans 099891
Galeries Nationales du Grand Palais, Paris 013594
Galeries Saint-Louis, Bruxelles 057963
Galerieverein, Wendlingen am Neckar 053193
Galerieverein Leonberg e.V., Leonberg, Württemberg 018618, 053194
Galeriewerkstatt am Hirtenturm, Blankenheim, Ahr 102142
Galerii 2, Tallinn 098698
Galerii-G, Tallinn 098699
Galerij C.G., Mechelen 058334
Galerij De Hamer, Apeldoorn 078034
Galerij Goya, Mechelen 096385
Galerij in Situ, Aalst 096047
Galerij Ka, Hasselt 058223
Galerij 't Leerhuijs, Brugge 096115
Galerij S65, Aalst 096048
Galerij ter Gentpoort, Brugge 057774
Galerij Uilenspiegel, Leuven 058275
Galerij Zuid, Antwerpen 096066
Galerija 111, Varna 096768
Galerija 2, Vrhnika 110009
Galerija 56, Ljubljana 109959
Galerija 73, Beograd 109688
Galerija 99, Arandjelovac 109676
Galerija AC, Žalec 110010
Galerija Antuna Augustinčića, Klanjec 007734
Galerija Arheo, Beograd 109689
Galerija Art, Smederevo 109745
Galerija Ata Raj, Sofia 096729
Galerija Avsenik-Hohner, Begunje na Gorenjskem 080645, 109929
Galerija Ažbe, Ljubljana 109960
Galerija Balkon', Burgas 096697
Galerija Bazalt, Beograd 109690
Galerija Benko Horvat, Zagreb 007833
Galerija Bevisa, Bled 109931
Galerija Bevisa, Kranj 109945
Galerija Božidar Jakac, Kostanjevica na Krki 034471
Galerija Centar, Podgorica 109742
Galerija Centăr za Săvremenno Izkustvo, Varna 004913
Galerija Centralnog Kluba Vojske Jugolavije, Beograd 034148
Galerija Contra, Koper 109940
Galerija Dar, Zaprešič 098291
Galerija Denis, Arandjelovac 109677
Galerija Diva, Varna 096769
Galerija Dvor, Tolmin 110007
Galerija Edmond, Sofia . . . 058761, 096730
Galerija Epsilon, Šumen 096758
Galerija Fabris, Beograd 109691
Galerija Fabris, Beograd 109692
Galerija Fara, Škofja Loka 110003
Galerija Freska, Beograd 034149
Galerija Furlan, Ljubljana 109961
Galerija Grad, Ljubljana 109962
Galerija Grafićnog Kolektiva, Beograd 109693
Galerija Harizma, Beograd 109694
Galerija Hlebine-Muzejska Zbirka, Hlebine 007723
Galerija Irida, Sofia 096731
Galerija Jerolim, Stari Grad 007808
Galerija Kamen, Radovljica 110002
Galerija Klovićevi Dvori, Zagreb . . . 007834
Galerija Kos, Ljubljana 109963
Galerija Kozole, Trbovlje 110008
Galerija Kralj, Ljubljana 109964
Galerija Kristina, Sofia 096732
Galerija Kupola, Beograd 109695
Galerija Lala, Ljubljana 109965
Galerija Lazar Vozarević, Sremska Mitrovica 034265
Galerija Leonardo, Sofia 096733
Galerija Likovnih Samorastnikov, Trebnje 034530
Galerija Likovnih Umjetnosti Republike Srpske Banja Slika, Banja Luka . . 003925
Galerija Lina, Ljubljana 109966
Galerija LM, Maribor 109985
Galerija Lorina, Sofia 096734
Galerija Luwigana, Ljubljana 109967
Galerija Majski Zatvor, Sliven 096712
Galerija Matice Srpske, Novi Sad . . 034222
Galerija Media'nox, Maribor 109986
Galerija Meduza, Koper 109941
Galerija Mestne Hiše, Kranj 034472
Galerija Milan Konjović, Sombor . . . 034262
Galerija Milene Pavlović Barilli, Požarevac 034244
Galerija Monmartr, Beograd 109696
Galerija Most, Podgorica 109743
Galerija Mozaik, Celje 109933
Galerija MS, Murska Sobota 109996
Galerija Murska Sobota, Murska Sobota 034506
Galerija Naivnih Slikara, Kovačica . 034203
Galerija Okvir, Celje 109934
Galerija Paleta, Beograd 109697
Galerija Plevna, Škofja Loka 110004
Galerija Portreta Tuzla, Tuzla 003944
Galerija Rafaela, Sofia 096735
Galerija Rampino, Beograd 109698, 140947
Galerija Reprodukcija i Umetničkih Dela, Beograd 034150
Galerija Samoukih Likovnih Umetnika Svetozarevo, Svetozarevo 034272
Galerija Sazdovski, Skopje 107423
Galerija Sebastian, Dubrovnik 007714
Galerija Skrinja, Maribor 109987
Galerija Škuc, Ljubljana 109968
Galerija Slika, Motovun 007759
Galerija Slika Save Sumanovića, Sid 034257
Galerija Slika Umetnickih Predmeta, Beograd 109699
Galerija Snežinka, Prebold 110001
Galerija Sodobne Umetnosti, Celje . 109935
Galerija Sopoćanska Vidjenja, Novi Pazar 034220
Galerija Spektar, Dobrič 096701
Galerija Sqart, Koper 109942
Galerija Srpske Akademije Nauka i Umetnosti, Beograd 034151
Galerija Stara Kapetanija, Zemun . . 109752
Galerija Status, Arandjelovac 109678
Galerija Suluj, Beograd 109700
Galerija Suvremene Umjetnosti, Zagreb 007835
Galerija Sztuki Wozownia, Toruń . . . 109084
Galerija ULUS, Udruženje Likovnih Umetnika Srbije, Beograd 034152
Galerija Ulus-a, Beograd 109701
Galerija Umjetnina, Split 007800
Galerija Umjetnina Narodnog Muzeja Zadar, Zadar 007824
Galerija Valer, Smederevo 109746
Galerija XX, Panevėžys 107354
Galerija Zala, Ljubljana 109969
Galerija Zavjetnih Slika Brodova, Dubrovnik 007715
Galerija Žbona, Koper 109943
Galerija Zebra, Ljubljana 109970
Galerija Zibka, Ljubljana 109971
Galerija Žula, Ljubljana 109972
Galerija Žula 2, Maribor 109988
Galerija Zvono, Beograd 109702
Galerije Sivčeva Hiša, Radovljica . . 034516
Galerila, Werl 105206
Galeriy Unik, Nairobi 107160
Galery 101, Ottawa 097107
Gale's, Dunedin 079086, 121823
Galesburg Civic Art Center, Galesburg 044120
Galetas, Bozel 061741
Galetti Galleria, Milano 075719
Galetti Galleria, Milano 106218
Galetti Galleria, Milano 106219
Galeyrand, Philippe, Saint-Jean-de-Monts 067546, 124907
Galfard, Eric, Paris 100450, 133611
Galia, Bordeaux 099003
Galica, Milano 106220
Galicja, Kraków 140735
Gáliková, Eva, Nové Zámky 129279
Galiläer, M., Giengen an der Brenz . 070988
Galilée, Villarsel-le-Gibloux 082890
Galilee Art School, Singapore 050681
Galimberti, Giovanni, Milano 127600
Galina, Jacksonville 089414
Galindos, Montevideo 087321
Galinier, Marie-Louise, Buzet-sur-Tarn 061843
Galinski, Uwe, Hamburg 071232
Le Galion, Oostende 058361
Le Galion, Paris 065987
Le Galion, Toulon (Var) 068452
Galion Historical Museum, Galion . . 044125
Galitch, Vevey 082880
Galitch, Pierre & Nicole, Neuchâtel . 082692
Gałkowska & Gesing, Kraków 079637
Gall, Didier le, Aigues-Vives 060681
Gall, Ernst, Villmergen 130207
Galla, Bucureşti 109433
Gallagher, Denver 088689, 142387
Gallagher, Norfolk 091380, 123024
Gallagher, R.H.A., Dublin 105863
Gallagher-Christopher, Boston 087821
Gallant, Philip, Baltimore 087672
Gallardo Fuentes, Victoria, Palma de Mallorca 081480
Gallas, Dr. Klaus, München 134241
Gallathe, Ulrich, Löhne 072287
Gallé, Porto 080089
Gallé & C., Rita, Milano 106221
Galle National Museum, Galle 036137
Gallego, Ourense 081451
Gallego, Ourense 081452
Gallego, Berenice, Sevilla 129730
Gallego, Ray, Los Angeles 089774
Gallegos, Robert V., Albuquerque . . 087393
Gallelli Art, Calgary 096816
Gallen-Kallela Museum, Espoo 009473
The Gallereum, Perth 056457
Galleri 1, Göteborg 110910
Galleri 111, Lomma 110952
Galleri 21, Frederiksberg 060237
Galleri 21, Norberg 036496
Galleri 27, Oslo 108710
Galleri 54, Göteborg 036295
Galleri 68, København 060328
Galleri 99, København 098560
Galleri ABCD, Malmö 081867
Galleri ABCD, Malmö 110963
Galleri Amanda, Haugesund 108691
Galleri Amare, Stavanger 079502
Galleri Amare, Stavanger 108755
Galleri Arctandria, Oslo 108711
Galleri Argo, Stockholm 111025
Galleri Asur, Oslo 108712
Galleri Aveny, Göteborg 110911
Galleri BA, Oslo 108713
Galleri Bagdad, Malmö 110964
Galleri Bi-Z, Kristiansand 108695
Galleri Bouhlou, Bergen 108676
Galleri Christian, Bergen 079376
Galleri Cobra, Stockholm 111026
Galleri D 40, Oslo 108714
Galleri Dialog, Stockholm 111027
Galleri Dianahuset, Norrtälje 110985
Galleri Embla, Stockholm 111028
Galleri Eos, Stockholm 111029
Galleri Espolin, Kabelvåg 030929
Galleri Estetica, Malmö 110965
Galleri Ett, Uppsala 111090
Galleri F 12, Forus 108689
Galleri F 15, Moss 108698
Galleri Falkum, Skien 108752
Galleri Ferm, Göteborg 110912

Galleri Final, Malmö 110966
Galleri Fløystad, Arendal 108673
Galleri Format, Oslo 108715
Galleri Futura, Stockholm 111030
Galleri G, Sandnes 108748
Galleri Gl. Lejre, Lejre 098594
Galleri Göteborgs Konstförening, Göteborg 110913
Galleri Graffiti, Oslo 108716
Galleri Grønlund, København 098561
Galleri Gude, Oslo 108717
Galleri Gummeson, Stockholm 111031
Galleri Haaken, Oslo 108718
Galleri Halland, Halmstad 110936
Galleri Hera, Stockholm 111032
Galleri Hillestad, Dølemo 108687
Galleri Hippo, Stockholm 111033
Galleri Hlemmur, Reykjavík 105586
Galleri Inez, Lund 110953
Galleri J2, Oslo 108719
Galleri JMS, Oslo 108720
Galleri K, Oslo 108721
Galleri Katarina, Stockholm 111034
Galleri Klara, Stockholm . . 111035, 134968
Galleri Knabro, København 060329, 098562
Galleri København, København 098563
Galleri Koll, Stavanger 108756
Galleri Konstruktiv Tendens, Stockholm 111036
Galleri LNM, Oslo 108722
Galleri Lora, Stockholm 111037
Galleri Lucidor, Stockholm 111038
Galleri M, Sandnes 079490
Galleri Metallum, Stockholm 111039
Galleri Miva, Malmö 110967
Galleri Mölndal, Mölndal 110984
Galleri Mowestor, Stockholm 111040
Galleri Nobel, Oslo 108723, 121868
Galleri Nørby, København 098564
Galleri Nordens Bilder, Kungälv . . . 110949
Galleri Nygaten 7, Bergen 108677
Galleri Nytorget 13, Stockholm 111041
Galleri Örgryte, Göteborg 110914
Galleri Överkikaren, Stockholm . . . 111042
Galleri Olab, Göteborg 110915
Galleri Opus, Bjärred 110898
Galleri Osebro, Porsgrunn 108743
Galleri Oskar, Helsingborg 110942
Galleri Panorama Art, Stockholm . . 111043
Galleri Paris, Hellvik 108692
Galleri Parken, Bergen 108678
Galleri Pluto Cave Cànem, Stockholm 111044
Galleri Profil, Bergen 108679
Galleri Riga, København 098565
Galleri Rosendal, Rosendal 108744
Galleri Rosengången, Lerum 110950
Galleri s e, Bergen 108680
Galleri Sand, Oslo 108724
Galleri Sankt Erik, Stockholm 111045
Galleri Scandinavia, Göteborg 110916
Galleri Shambala, København 098566
Galleri Siverts, Bergen 108681
Galleri Smiegården, Sandnes 108749
Galleri Sølvberget, Stavanger 108757
Galleri Specta, København 098567
Galleri Steen, Oslo 108725
Galleri Studio 5, Stockholm 111046
Galleri Sulegaarden, Assens 098521
Galleri Svalbard, Longyearbyen . . . 030997
Galleri Svanlunda, Malmö 110968
Galleri Svarta Soffan, Stockholm . . . 111047
Galleri Tendenes, Hundvåg 108694
Galleri Tersæus, Stockholm 111048
Galleri Tonne, Oslo 108726
Galleri Torso, Odense 098599, 133429
Galleri Tre, Kristiansand 108696
Galleri Tvedestrand, Tvedestrand . . 108761
Galleri Udengaard, Malmö 110969
Galleri Urd, Bergen 108682
Galleri Valvet, Malmö 110970
Galleri van Rijn, Stavanger 079503
Galleri Veslemøy, Egersund 108688
Galleri V.H., Göteborg 110917
Galleri Victoria, Halmstad 110937
Galleri Viktoria, Göteborg 110918
Galleri Villvin, Risør 079486
Galleri Vincent, København 098568
La Galleria, London 113629
Galleria, Mumbai 105772
Galleria, Pittsburgh 118922
Galleria 28, Timişoara 109463
Galleria 61, Palermo 106428
Galleria 70, Milano 106222
Galleria 733, Chicago 088087
Galleria 900, Parma 076209
Galleria A, Parma 076210
Galleria AAA, Ascona 111136
Galleria Accademia, Torino 106674
Galleria Accademia Albertina di Belle Arti, Torino 026049
Galleria Aion, Ascona 082098
Galleria Akka, Roma 076476
Galleria Ala Salvatore, Milano 106223
Galleria Alberoni, Piacenza 025204
Galleria Albert IX, Helsinki 098722
Galleria Anfitrite, Lugano 082598
Galleria Anfitrite, Lugano 082599
Galleria Annmari's, Tampere 060624
Galleria Antiquaria, Merano 075546
Galleria Antiques, Atlanta 087479
Galleria Art Alex, Helsinki 098723
Galleria Arte 13, Venezia 106738
Galleria Arte Borgogna, Milano 106224
Galleria Arte Corso, Roma 106541
Galleria Arts & Crafts, Calgary 096817
Galleria Aversa, Torino 106675
Galleria BE'19, Helsinki 098724
Galleria Bellissima, Philadelphia . . . 118763
Galleria Bigli, Milano 075720, 106225, 121708
Galleria Bixio 2, Milano 106226
Galleria Blu, Milano 106227
Galleria Borromeo, Padova 106397
Galleria Bosi, Roma 106542
Galleria Bulevardi 7, Helsinki 098725
Galleria Caldarese, Bologna 105958
Galleria Casa d'Arte, Locarno 111650
Galleria Castiglione, Bologna 105959
Galleria Cavour, Firenze 106055
Galleria Centro Steccata, Parma . . . 106450
Galleria Centro Steccata, Parma . . . 106451
Galleria Ceramica, Betzdorf 102101
Galleria Cherubini, Padova 106398
Galleria Cilea, Napoli 106367
Galleria Ciovasso, Milano 106228
Galleria Civica, Valdagno 026186
Galleria Civica Anna e Luigi Parmiggiani, Reggio Emilia 025411
Galleria Civica d'Arte Contemporanea, Caltagirone 023586
Galleria Civica d'Arte Contemporanea, Suzzara 025979
Galleria Civica d'Arte Contemporanea, Termoli 026009
Galleria Civica d'Arte Moderna, Santhià 025779
Galleria Civica d'Arte Moderna, Spoleto 025938
Galleria Civica d'Arte Moderna e Contemporanea, Torino 026050
Galleria Civica d'Arte Moderna e Contemporanea, Verona 026283
Galleria Colonna, Napoli 106368
Galleria Colonna, Roma 025475
Galleria Comunale d'Arte, Cagliari . 023560
Galleria Comunale d'Arte, Museo Manzoniano, Lecco 024486
Galleria Comunale d'Arte Contemporanea, Arezzo 023235
Galleria Comunale d'Arte Moderna, Bologna 023420
Galleria Comunale d'Arte Moderna, Verucchio 026293
Galleria Comunale d'Arte Moderna e Contemporanea, Roma 025476
Galleria Comunale d'Arte Risorgimento, Imola 024402
Galleria Comunale Santa Croce, Cattolica 023772
Galleria Cons Arc, Chiasso 111352
Galleria Conti, Prato 106475
Galleria Corsini, Firenze 024154
Galleria da Vinci, Ansbach 101587
Galleria Daldiniana, Vezia 111970
Galleria d'Arte, Genova 106092
Galleria d'Arte 2 di Quadri, Bologna 105960
Galleria d'Arte 2000, Milano 106229
Galleria d'Arte 37, Palermo 106429
Galleria d'Arte A. Cefaly, Catania . . 106022
Galleria D'Arte Antica, Baden-Baden 069413
Galleria D'Arte Casana, Freiburg im Breisgau 102865
Galleria d'Arte Centro Storico, Firenze 106056
Galleria d'Arte Cesana, Venezia . . . 121739
Galleria d'Arte Cinquantasei, Bologna 105961
Galleria d'Arte Città Vecchia, Locarno 111651
Galleria d'Arte Contemporanea, Ascoli Piceno 023265
Galleria d'Arte Contemporanea, Cittadella Cristiana, Assisi 023277
Galleria d'Arte Contemporanea L. Spazzapan, Palazzo Torriani, Gradisca d'Isonzo 024357
Galleria d'Arte Contemporanea V. Stoppioni, Santa Sofia 025759
Galleria d'Arte Contini, Venezia . . . 106739
Galleria d'Arte Contini, Venezia . . . 106740
Galleria d'Arte dell'Opera Bevilacqua la Masa, Venezia 026233
Galleria d'Arte Goethe, Bolzano . . . 105982
Galleria d'Arte Internazionale, Venezia 106741
Galleria d'Arte La Stanzina, Firenze 106057
Galleria d'Arte Lelii, Cagliari 106012
Galleria d'Arte Leonardo, Bolzano . . 105983
Galleria d'Arte L'Incontro, Verona . . 106791
Galleria d'Arte L'Occhio, Venezia . . 106742
Galleria d'Arte Moderna, Udine 026162
Galleria d'Arte Moderna, Palazzo Pitti, Firenze 024155
Galleria d'Arte Moderna 31, Napoli . 106369
Galleria d'Arte Moderna A. Discovolo, Bonassola 023475
Galleria d'Arte Moderna Arnoldo Bonzagni, Palazzo Governatore, Cento 023788
Galleria d'Arte Moderna Carlo Rizzarda, Feltre 024087
Galleria d'Arte Moderna Comunale, San Severino Marche 025728
Galleria d'Arte Moderna e Contemporanea, Bergamo 023375
Galleria d'Arte Moderna e Contemporanea R. Guttuso, Bagheria 023314
Galleria d'Arte Moderna F. Montanari, Moncalvo 024785
Galleria d'Arte Moderna Giannoni, Novara 024961
Galleria d'Arte Moderna Moretti, Civitanova Marche 023909
Galleria d'Arte Moderna O. Marchesi, Copparo 023959
Galleria d'Arte Moderna Ricci-Oddi, Piacenza 025205
Galleria d'Arte Ponte Rosso, Milano 106230
Galleria d'Arte Rocca Sforzesca, Imola 024403
Galleria d'Arte Sacra dei Contemporanei, Milano 024701
Galleria d'Arte San Isaia, Bologna . . 105962
Galleria d'Arte Sk, Taranto 106651
Galleria d'Arte Venezia, Venezia . . . 076937
Galleria d'Arte Venezia, Venezia . . . 106743
Galleria d'Arte Vittoriana, Napoli . . . 106370
Galleria Davico, Torino 106676
Galleria dé Fusari - Memoires, Bologna 075081
Galleria de las Islas, Manila 108843
Galleria degli Arazzi, Musei Vaticani, Città del Vaticano 049420
Galleria degli Artisti, Roma 106543
Galleria degli ex Voto del Santuario, Livorno 024507
Galleria degli Uffizi, Firenze 024156
Galleria dei Benci, Firenze 106058
Galleria dei Coronari, Roma 076477
Galleria dei Cosmati, Roma 076478
Galleria dei Cosmati, Roma 121723
Galleria dei Editrice Greci, Roma . . 106544
Galleria dei Masters, Neufahrn 104408
Galleria del Barcon, Milano 106231
Galleria del Corso, Roma 121724
Galleria del Costume, Palazzo Pitti, Firenze 024157
Galleria del Leone, Venezia 106744
Galleria del Maggio, Villa Minozzo . 026330
Galleria del Manifesto, Bolzano . . . 105984
Galleria del Manifesto, Verona 106792
Galleria del Manifesto d'Arte, Bellinzona 111237
Galleria del Mosaico, Chiasso 111353
Galleria del Ponte, Torino 076817
Galleria del Restauro, Cagliari 106013, 127246
Galleria della Pigna, Roma 106545
Galleria della Tartaruga, Roma 106546
Galleria dell'Accademia, Firenze . . 024158
Galleria dell'Accademia di Belle Arti, Napoli 024892
Galleria dell'Accademia Nazionale di San Luca, Roma 025477
Galleria dell'Accademia Tadini, Lovere 024540
Galleria dell'Altabella, Bologna 105963
Galleria delle Stampe Antiche, Catania 075249
Galleria dell'Incisione, Brescia 105998
Galleria Dello Scudo, Verona 106793
Galleria dello Spedale degli Innocenti, Firenze 024159
Galleria dello Stretto, Palermo 106430
Galleria dell'Orologio, Roma 076479
Galleria di Palazzo Bianco, Genova . 024297
Galleria di Palazzo degli Alberti, Prato 025360
Galleria di Palazzo Rosso, Genova . 024298
Galleria di Sorrento, Las Vegas 116621
Galleria Diagramma, Milano 106232
Galleria Dix, Helsinki 098726
Galleria Don Chisciotte, Roma 106547
Galleria Doria Pamphilj, Roma 025478
Galleria Duemila, Mandaluyong . . . 108835
Galleria Duemila, Pasay 108850
Galleria e Mostra del Presepe nel Mondo, Santuario di Montevergine 025784
Galleria Editrice Latina, Roma 106548
Galleria Editrice Latina, Roma 106549
Galleria Emy, Messina 106136
Galleria Enterprise, London 113630
Galleria Estense, Palazzo dei Musei, Modena 024751
Galleria Eustachi, Milano 106233
Galleria Faustini, Firenze 106059
Galleria Ferrari, Maranello 024610
Galleria Fine Art and Graphics, Oakland 118633
Galleria Franco Cancelliere, Messina 106137
Galleria G, Helsinki 060523, 098727
Galleria G. Pedriali, Forlì 024223
Galleria Gianna, Cleveland 115707
Galleria Giorgio Franchetti alla Ca' d'Oro, Venezia 026234
Galleria Giulia, Roma 106550
Galleria Goethe 2, Bolzano 105985
Galleria Goldoni, Livorno 106121
Galleria Guicciardini, Firenze 075344
Galleria I Duchi, Trieste 076891
Galleria Il, San Antonio 119413
Galleria Imperiale, Genova 075467
Galleria L'Incontro, Lugano 111664
Galleria Inter, Turku 060637
Galleria Internacional, Washington . 120298
Galleria Johan S, Helsinki 098728
Galleria La Casa, Vaglio 111958
Galleria La Colomba, Viganello 111971

Galleria La Cornice, Norderstedt . . . 104461
Galleria La Meridiana, Verona 106794
Galleria La Nevera, Gordola 111524
Galleria La Rocca, Torino 106677
Galleria La Sirena, Tucson 120128
Galleria Lapiccirella, Firenze 075345
Galleria Lapidaria, Musei Vaticani, Città del Vaticano 049421
Galleria Le Muse, Messina 106138
Galleria Liberta, Nieder-Olm 104445
Galleria Liguria, Genova 106093
Galleria Luce, Venezia 106745
Galleria M. Rizzi, Sestri Levante . . . 025877
Galleria Magenta, Brescia 105999
Galleria Marieschi, Milano 106234
Galleria Masini, Firenze 106060
Galleria Mentana, Firenze 106061
Galleria Mignanelli, Roma 106551
Galleria Milano, Milano 106235
Galleria Modigliani, Milano 106236
Galleria Mondiale, Surry Hills 095252
Galleria Morone, Milano 106237
Galleria Municipale, Francavilla al Mare 024246
Galleria Museo, Bolzano 105986
Galleria Mystica, Pune 074832
Galleria Narciso, Torino 106678
Galleria Nazionale, Parma 025116
Galleria Nazionale d'Arte Antica, Trieste 026137
Galleria Nazionale d'Arte Antica Palazzo Barberini, Roma 025479
Galleria Nazionale d'Arte Antica Palazzo Corsini, Roma 025480
Galleria Nazionale d'Arte Moderna-Arte Contemporanea, Roma 025481
Galleria Nazionale delle Marche, Palazzo Ducale, Urbino 026173
Galleria Nazionale dell'Umbria, Palazzo dei Priori, Perugia 025165
Galleria Nazionale di Arte Moderna e Contemporanea, San Marino 034110
Galleria Nazionale di Palazzo Spinola, Genova 024299
Galleria Niccoli, Parma 106452
Galleria Nova, Ronco sopra Ascona 111846
Galleria Novelli, Verona 106795
Galleria Nuovo, Lahti 098753
Galleria on Third, New York 117937
Galleria Otso, Espoo 098709
Galleria Pace, Milano 106238
Galleria Palatina, Firenze 024160
Galleria Palazzo Cini, Venezia 026235
Galleria Palladio, Lugano 111665
Galleria Pallavicini, Roma 025482
Galleria Pananti, Firenze 106062
Galleria Perera, Roma . . . 076480, 106552
Galleria Perugi, Padova 106399
Galleria Pinacotheca, Jyväskylän Yliopiston Museo - Kultuurihistoriallinen Osasto, Jyväskylä 009635
Galleria Pinciana, Roma 076481
Galleria Pinocchio, Birchington 083521
Galleria Primavera, Helsinki 098729
Galleria Quadreria Den Hertog, Bari 105930
Galleria Refinishers Too, Seattle . . . 132936
Galleria Regionale d'Arte Moderna e Contemporanea, Sassoferrato . . . 025809
Galleria Regionale della Sicilia, Palermo 025081
Galleria Regionale di Palazzo Bellomo, Siracusa 025901
Galleria Rettori Tribbio 2, Trieste . . 106716
Galleria Rinaldo Carnielo, Firenze . . 024161
Galleria Riviera, Padova 106400
Galleria Romana dell'Ottocento, Roma 076482
Galleria Rusticana, Oslo 079436
Galleria Sabauda, Torino 026051
Galleria San Bernardo, Genova 106094
Galleria San Carlo, Milano 106239
Galleria San Giorgio, Modena 075910
Galleria San Giovanni, Perugia 076234
Galleria San Lorenzo Al Ducale, Genova 106095
Galleria San Nicoló, Venezia 106746
Galleria San Tomaso, Milano 106240
Galleria Sant'Agostino, Torino 106679, 121734
Galleria Sant'Antonin, Venezia 106747
Galleria Santo Stefano, Venezia . . . 106748
Galleria Saskia, Tampere 098759
Galleria Sculptor, Helsinki 098730
Galleria Senato, Milano 106241
Galleria Serego, Verona 106796
Galleria Serodine, Ascona 082099
Galleria Silva, Milano 075721
Galleria Spada, Roma 025483
Galleria Spinetti, Firenze 106063
Galleria Stendhal, Parma 076211
Galleria Storica del Lloyd Triestino, Trieste 026138
Galleria sul Po, Torino 106680
Galleria Taide Apaja, Lohja 098757
Galleria Tecne, Padova 106401
Galleria Tornabuoni, Firenze 106064
Galleria Traghetto, Venezia 106749
Galleria Uusitalo, Helsinki 098731
Galleria Vecchiato, Padova 106402
Galleria Veneziani, Roma 076483
Galleria Verde, Effretikon 111390
Galleria Veronese, New Orleans . . . 117443
Galleria Vesterinen, Helsinki 098732
Galleria Vincent, Napoli 106371
Galleria Vinciana, Milano 106242
Galleria Wanda, Wolverhampton . . . 114725
Gallerie Alegria, Birmingham 115106
Gallerie am Markt, Kirchhain 103552
Gallerie am Rathausmarkt, Viersen . 105119
Gallerie am Schloßberg, Sondershausen 073861
Gallerie Antiques, Hainault 084550, 130753
Gallerie Australis, Adelaide 094116
Gallerie Bella, Athinai 105395
Gallerie dell'Accademia, Venezia . . 026236
Gallerie di Palazzo Leoni Montanari, Vicenza 026308
Gallerie Exclusiv, Plymouth 114258
Gallerie Ganesha, Delhi 105661
Gallerie im Hof, Bad Homburg v.d.Höhe 101653
Gallerie Lavelle, Bangalore 074769
Gallerie l'Orientaliste, Fitzroy North 094542
Gallerie Marin, Appledore, Devon . . 112514
Gallerie Moosgasse, Kempen 103530
Gallerie Phoenix, Montréal 097028
Gallerie Veronique, Enfield 084336, 130687
Gallerie Via Borromei, Milano 106243
Gallerie Zen, Bangalore 105604
Galleries, London 136219
The Galleries, Woking 041427
Galleries America, Las Vegas 116622
Galleries' Association of Korea, Seoul 053819
Galleries at Raven's Nest, Denver . . 116001
Galleries of Fine Arts, Quezon City . 108856
Galleries of Justice, Nottingham . . . 040618
Galleries Primitf, Woollahra 095425
Gallerihuset, København 098569
The Gallery, Abbotsbury 112472
Gallery, Aberdeen 083236, 130279
The Gallery, Al-Harthy 108763
The Gallery, Ardingly 112518
The Gallery, Beer 112602
The Gallery, Blandford Forum 112666
The Gallery, Blenheim 108373
The Gallery, Burnham-on-Sea 112765
The Gallery, Chichester 112860
The Gallery, Clare 112874
Gallery, El Paso 116110
The Gallery, Gateshead 039536
The Gallery, Gisborne 108452
The Gallery, Hamilton 096420
The Gallery, Hampton 113181
The Gallery, Kidderminster 113320
The Gallery, Leek 113368
Gallery, London 113631
Gallery, Los Angeles 116772
The Gallery, Luton 040356
The Gallery, Lynton 114018
The Gallery, Manchester 114042
The Gallery, Mount Victoria 056297
Gallery, New Orleans 117444
The Gallery, New York 117938
Gallery, Oklahoma City 118662
The Gallery, Oundle 114199
The Gallery, Paris 100451
Gallery, Praha 098460
The Gallery, Reigate 086346, 131410
The Gallery, Rhosneigr 114304
The Gallery, Richmond 119111
The Gallery, Saint Helens 114355
Gallery, Vallauris 068698
The Gallery, Vancouver 097474
The Gallery, Virginia Beach 120220
The Gallery, Wentworth 114663
The Gallery, Wymondham 114742
The Gallery, Mercer County Community College, Trenton 048602
Gallery 10, New York 117939
Gallery 10, Washington 120299
Gallery 101, Houston 116319
Gallery 101, Malmö 110971
Gallery 101, Melbourne 094814
Gallery 101, River Falls 047449
Gallery 101.Galerie 101, Ottawa . . . 006100
Gallery 11, Reykjavík 105587
Gallery 113, New York 117940
Gallery 114, Portland 119000
Gallery 117, Long Beach 116670
Gallery 119, Coorparoo 094433
Gallery 12 18, Holmfirth 113253
Gallery 124, Edmonton 096882
Gallery 1250, Chicago 115429
Gallery 13, Epworth 113030
Gallery 13, Hong Kong 097789
Gallery 138, New York 117941
Gallery 14, Chalkida 105419
Gallery 14, Sandwich 114396
Gallery 14, Sutton Coldfield 114528
Gallery 148, Holywood 113265
Gallery 15, Haddington 113173
Gallery 177, Northampton 114152
The Gallery 18, Falmouth 113051
Gallery 181, Iowa State University, Ames 041686
Gallery 185, Halifax 113176
Gallery 19, London 113632
Gallery 2, Chicago 042845
Gallery 2 on Edward, Brisbane 094296
Gallery-2000, Aldershot 112492
Gallery 2000, Baltimore 115050
Gallery 2000, Bonn 102183
Gallery 2000, Seoul 107227
Gallery 2000, West End 095391
Gallery 203, Chicago 115430
Gallery 206 and Foyer Gallery, Missouri Western State College, Saint Joseph 047645
Gallery 21, Bexhill-on-Sea 112633
Gallery 21, Deauville 099199
Gallery 21, Johannesburg 110052
Gallery 210, University of Missouri Saint Louis, Saint Louis 047662
Gallery 218, Milwaukee 117190
Gallery 21+Yo, Tokyo 107042
Gallery 22, Cincinnati 115631
Gallery 23, San Diego 119505
Gallery 23 Antiques, Chalfont Saint Giles 083905
Gallery 25, Fresno 116175
Gallery '25, London 085320, 122587
Gallery 253, Bangkok 112232
Gallery 27, London 113633
Gallery 2700, Virginia Beach 120221
Gallery 286, London 113634
Gallery 3, North Shore 108524
Gallery 31, Nelson 108512
Gallery 312, Chicago 115431
Gallery 33, Coleraine 112892
Gallery 33, Portland 119001
Gallery 33 Downtown, Portland . . . 119002
Gallery 34, Llangollen 113417
Gallery 360, Applecross . . 094157, 123178
Gallery 360, Joondalup . . 094669, 123245
Gallery 360, Minneapolis 117261
Gallery 360, Mount Lawley 094907, 123275
Gallery 360, Subiaco 095230, 123310
Gallery 38, Saint Ives, Cornwall . . . 114363
Gallery 39, Osaka 106959
Gallery 39, Swindon 114541
Gallery 400, Chicago 042846
Gallery 401, Toronto 097270
Gallery 406, Chicago 088088
Gallery 41, Vancouver 059361
Gallery 42, Delhi 105662
Gallery 42, Kirkcaldy 113333
Gallery 42, Tadcaster 114545
Gallery 43, Denver 116002
Gallery 435, Hamilton 096916
Gallery 44, Toronto 006598
Gallery 44, Toronto 097271
Gallery 444, San Francisco 119674
Gallery 460 and Sculpture Park, Green Point 094601
Gallery 47, New York 090894
Gallery 48, Lavenham 113355
Gallery 482, Fortitude Valley 094559
Gallery @ 49, New York 117942
Gallery 515, Atlanta 114879, 142202
Gallery 52, Brailsford 112691
Gallery 53, Cairns 094344
Gallery 53, Hastings 113199
Gallery 532 Soho, New York 090895
Gallery 54, Penola 095063
Gallery 547, Waikato 108590
Gallery 55, Bangkok 112233
Gallery 55, Invercargill 108476
Gallery 56, Salt Lake City 119343
Gallery 56, Stratford 095228
Gallery 57, Cambridge 042558
Gallery 6+, Varna 096770
Gallery 63 Antiques, New York 090896
Gallery 66, Twickenham 114616
Gallery 7, Mumbai 105773, 127086
Gallery 7, Nelson 108513
Gallery 7-18, Hiroshima 106854
Gallery 7000, Tucson 120129
Gallery 702, Saint Paul 119288
Gallery 71, New York 117943
Gallery '72, Omaha 118695
Gallery 757, Winnipeg 097586
Gallery '76, Wenatchee 049056
Gallery 79, Taranaki 108568
Gallery 7916, Los Angeles 116773
Gallery 8, Loganholme 094744
Gallery 8, Varna 096771
Gallery 811, New Orleans 090559, 142613
Gallery 825, West Hollywood 049082
Gallery 83, Banff 112553
Gallery 88, Vancouver 097475
Gallery 888, Toronto 097272
Gallery 9, Los Altos 045409
Gallery 91, New York 117944
Gallery 93, Derby 112944
Gallery A, Chicago 115432
Gallery A, New York 117945
Gallery A and Gallery G, San Pedro . 047918
Gallery Abarth, Yamanakako 027324
Gallery Action, Moskva 109546
Gallery Akasaka, Fukuoka 106844
Gallery Americana, Houston 116320
Gallery Ami, Seoul 107228
Gallery Ann, Gaborone 096449
Gallery Apokalypse, Lefkosia 098300
The Gallery Apparao, Chennai 105628
Gallery Arcturus, Toronto 006599
Gallery Art Beam, Seoul 107229
Gallery Art Center, Columbus 115780
Gallery Art Point, Tokyo 107043
Gallery Art Resource Trust, Mumbai 105774
Gallery Art U, Osaka 106960
Gallery Artsindia, New York 117946

Gallery Association of New York State, Hamilton 054751
Gallery at 4584 Federal Boulevard, San Diego 092639
The Gallery at Blakemere, Blakemere 112664
Gallery at Bristol-Myers Squibb, Princeton 047237
The Gallery at Lakeside, West Thurrock 114670
Gallery at Lands End, San Diego . . . 119506
Gallery at Library Square, Salt Lake City 119344
Gallery at Market East, Philadelphia 118764
Gallery at Midlane, Houston 116321
The Gallery at Newington House, Charlbury 112836
Gallery at Peachtree Hill, Atlanta . . 114880
Gallery at the American Bible Society, New York 046334
Gallery at the Gildenburgh, Peterborough 114243
Gallery at The Rocks, Sydney 095287
Gallery at The Wentworth, Sydney . 095288
Gallery at the Wharf, Coupeville . . . 043194
Gallery at the Willows, Honolulu . . . 116212
The Gallery at UTA, Arlington 041774
Gallery at Ward Centre, Honolulu . . 116213
Gallery at Werribee South, Werribee 095388
Gallery Auctions, Houston 122906
Gallery Aura Soma, Köln 103628
Gallery B, Toledo 120082
Gallery B at the Market, Toledo . . . 120083
Gallery Beaux, Tokyo 107044
The Gallery Beckenham, Beckenham 112598
Gallery Bethlehem, Tauranga 108575
Gallery Bizarre, Double Bay 055755
Gallery Blackheath, Blackheath . . . 094256
Gallery Bouquet, Nagoya 106918
Gallery Bridgetown, Bridgetown . . . 094279
Gallery Cafe, Cleveland 115708
The Gallery Café, Colombo 110894
Gallery Carla, San Francisco 119675
Gallery Celtica, Phoenix 118873
Gallery Chine, Cairo 060445, 098633
Gallery Connexion, Fredericton 005480
Gallery Dalma, Riyadh 080375
Gallery D'art, Lucknow 105746
Gallery Défly, Nice 099841
Gallery Departmental, Gaborone . . . 096450
Gallery Different, London 113635
Gallery East, North Fremantle 094973
Gallery Eastwest, Hong Kong 097790
Gallery Edition 88, Luxembourg . . .107403, 134752
Gallery Editions, Saint Paul 119289
Gallery-ef, Tokyo 107045
Gallery Estitique, Portarlington 095098
Gallery Euro, Seoul 107230
Gallery Europe, Ashford 112528
Gallery Express, Yokohama 107143
Gallery F, Kyoto 106893
Gallery Fifty One, Philadelphia 118765
Gallery Figueroa, Los Angeles 116774
Gallery Focus, Seoul 107231
Gallery for Foreign Art Sveti Kiril i Metodi, Sofia 096736
Gallery Four Seven Nine, Ottawa . . 097108
Gallery Frames, Dallas 115886
Gallery Furniture and Antiques, Chicago 131900
Gallery Fusion, Seoul 107232
Gallery G, Seoul 107233
Gallery Gazelle, Oregon State University, Philomath 047003
Gallery Genesis, Mandaluyong 108836
Gallery Glass, Portland 119003
Gallery Gold, Francistown 096448
Gallery Gondwana Australia, Alice Springs 094137
Gallery Guide, Athinai 135836
Gallery HAM, Nagoya 106919
Gallery Hiro, Tokyo 107046
Gallery Hiyoshi, Yokohama 107144
Gallery Hiyoshi, Yokohama 107145
Gallery Holly Snapp, Venezia 106750
Gallery Holly Snapp, Venezia 106751
Gallery House, Barcelona 110193
Gallery House, Louisville 116941
Gallery Ichiban-cho, Sendai 106993
Gallery ID 8, Baltimore 115051
Gallery II, Bradford 038807
Gallery II, Philadelphia 118766
Gallery II, Western Michigan University, College of Fine Arts, Kalamazoo . 044897
Gallery Ima-Press, Moskva 109547
Gallery in The Square, Hobart 094643
Gallery in the Square, Pittsburgh . . 118923
Gallery in the Sun, De Grazia Foundation, Tucson 048637
Gallery in Wax, Austin 114984
Gallery & Innovations, Toronto 097273
Gallery International, Baltimore . . . 115052
Gallery International, Cape Town . . 110024
Gallery IV, Los Angeles 116775
Gallery J, Bowral 094273
Gallery Joe, Philadelphia 118767
Gallery K, Kingston 106816
Gallery K, London 113636
Gallery K, Washington 120300
Gallery Kaleidoscope, London 113637
Gallery Kaleidoscope, London 131039
Gallery Kobe, Kobe 106877
Gallery Koza, Rhodos 105443
Gallery La, Manchester 114043
Gallery Lambton, Sarnia 006411
Gallery Lavaud, Akaroa 078900
Gallery Leela, Mumbai 105775
Gallery Limited, Milwaukee 117191
Gallery Link International, Sydney . 095289
Gallery Louisiane, New Orleans . . . 117445
Gallery M, Baden 111152
Gallery M, Denver 116003
Gallery M, Oaklands Park 001351
Gallery M E K, Kingston 106817
Gallery Market East, Philadelphia . . 118768
Gallery Medici, Kalk Bay 080722
Gallery Milano, Sendai 106994
Gallery Miro, Cairo 098634
Gallery Miro, Yokohama 107146
Gallery MIZ, Seoul 107234
Gallery Modern, Changwon 107177
Gallery Motomachi, Kobe 106878
Gallery Move Sendai, Sendai 106995
Gallery NAGA, Boston 115177
Gallery New York, Aarau 111101
Gallery New York, Brugg 111309
Gallery Nii, Osaka 106961
Gallery Nine, Cleveland 115709
Gallery Nine, Seoul 107235
Gallery Noor, Manama 096009
Gallery North, Kansas City 116566
Gallery North, Minneapolis 117262
Gallery North, Setauket 048116
Gallery NTK, Croydon 094444
Gallery Oceanic, Dunedin 108432
Gallery of Antique Costume and Textiles, London 085321
Gallery of Antiques and Collectibles, Jacksonville 089415
Gallery of Art, University of Missouri-Kansas City, Kansas City 044918
Gallery of art, Wernigerode 105217
Gallery of Art, Dickinson State University, Dickinson 043467
Gallery of Art, Johnson County Community College, Overland Park 046754
Gallery of Art, University of Northern Iowa, Cedar Falls 042666
Gallery of Arts, London 096950
Gallery of British Columbia Ceramics, Vancouver 006697
Gallery of British Columbia Ceramics, Vancouver 097476
Gallery of Canadian Folk Art, Calgary 058788, 096818
The Gallery of Contemporary Art, Sacred Heart University, Fairfield 043784
Gallery of Contemporary Art, University of Colorado, Colorado Springs 043056
Gallery of Costume, Manchester City Art Gallery, Manchester 040398
Gallery of Fine and Performing Arts, Edison Community College, Fort Myers . . 051347
Gallery of Fine Art, Greenmount . . . 094603
Gallery of Florina Artists, Florina . . 021268
Gallery of Graphic Arts, New York . . 117947
Gallery of History, Las Vegas 089575
Gallery of Holography, Fitzroy North 094543
Gallery of Horyu-ji Treasures, Tokyo National Museum, Tokyo 027167
Gallery of Legends, Las Vegas 089576
Gallery of Modern Art, Glasgow . . . 039554
Gallery of Modern Art, London 113638
Gallery of Modern Greek Art of Kalamata, Kalamata 021293
Gallery of Musical Instruments, Sangeet Natak Akademi, Delhi 022082
Gallery of Naive Art, Zlatar 007862
Gallery of Photography, Dublin 105864
Gallery of Prehistoric Paintings, New York 046335
Gallery of Sculpture Art and Antiquities, Las Vegas 089577, 116623
Gallery of Sports Art, Baltimore . . . 115053
Gallery of Sports Art, Milwaukee . . 117192
Gallery of Stars, Columbus 088410, 142353
Gallery of the Department of Art, Eastern New Mexico University, Portales . 047151
Gallery of the Department of Art and Art History, University of Nebraska, Lincoln 045302
Gallery of the Faculty of Architecture, Bangkok 037877
Gallery of the Municipality of Patras, Patrai 021424
Gallery of the Republic, Austin 114985
Gallery of the Royal Scottish Academy, Edinburgh 039391
Gallery of the Society for Epirot Studies, Ioannina 021278
Gallery of the Society for Macedonian Studies, Thessaloniki 021493
Gallery of the Southwest, San Antonio 119414
Gallery of Traditional Ornamental Art, Minsk 003132
Gallery of Visual Arts, University of Montana, Missoula 045932
Gallery of West Indian Art, Montego Bay 106824
Gallery Off, Nagoya 106920
Gallery Old Town, San Diego 119507
Gallery Oldham, Oldham 040640
Gallery on 43 Street, Pittsburgh . . . 118924
The Gallery On Broadway, Cardiff . . 112812
Gallery on Broadway, San Diego . . . 119508
Gallery On Lock, Hamilton 096917
Gallery On the Bay, Hamilton 096918
Gallery on the Green, London 113639
Gallery on the Net, Harlow 113184
Gallery on the Roof, Regina 006254
Gallery on the Side, Johannesburg . 110053
Gallery on the Square, Johannesburg 110054
Gallery One, Albuquerque 114788
Gallery One, Ellensburg 043671
Gallery One, Hong Kong 059632
Gallery One, Indianapolis 116462
Gallery One, London 113640
Gallery One, Southport 114464
Gallery One Arts, Toronto 097274
Gallery One-Fillmore Plaza, Denver 116004
Gallery One Nine, Swansea 095262
Gallery One One One, University of Manitoba, Winnipeg 006846
Gallery One-Writers Square, Denver 116005
Gallery Ophelia, Los Angeles 116776
Gallery Orbit, Saint Paul 119290
Gallery Persia, Inverness . 084796, 130825
Gallery Plaza, Fresno 116176
Gallery Plus, Los Angeles 116777
Gallery Posters Rambutik, Göteborg 110919
Gallery Q, Tokyo 107047
Gallery Quynh, Ho Chi Minh City . . . 120507
Gallery Rama-Art, Moskva 109548
Gallery Saigon, Ho Chi Minh City . . 120508
Gallery Saint James, Sutton Coldfield 114529
Gallery Savah, Paddington 095024
Gallery Scene, San Diego 119509
Gallery Scene, San Diego 119510
Gallery Sculpturama, Bornem 003243
Gallery Sekiguchi, Tokyo 107048
Gallery Senda, Hiroshima 106855
Gallery Sendai, Sendai 106996
Gallery Senior, Cairo 098635
Gallery Seojong, Seojong 107202
Gallery Services, Birmingham 115107
Gallery Seventeen, Beckenham . . . 112599
Gallery Shop at London Museum, London 096951
Gallery Six, Mona Vale 094870
Gallery Six One One, Toronto 097275
Gallery S.P., Seoul 107236
Gallery Space, Hyderabad 105701
Gallery Stratford, Stratford 006519
Gallery Sumukha, Bangalore 105605
Gallery TE, Amsterdam 107724
Gallery Teneleven, Armadale, Victoria 094165
Gallery the Eastern, Chicago 088089
Gallery Thirty Nine Seventeen, Houston 116322
Gallery Thirty Three, Dunedin 108433
Gallery Tresco, Isles-of-Scilly 113307
Gallery Triangle, Sapporo 106983
Gallery Twenty-Four, Berlin 101907
Gallery Umeda, Osaka 106962
The Gallery Upstairs Torquil, Henley-in-Arden 113227
Gallery Urbis Orbis, Saint Louis . . . 119206
Gallery V, Columbus 115781
Gallery Vetro, San Antonio 119415
Gallery Vietnam, New York 117948
Gallery Vision Studio, Frederiksberg 124015
Gallery W, Sacramento 119146
Gallery West, Alexandria 041642
Gallery West, Claremont 094401
Gallery West, Denver 116006
Gallery West, Tucson 120130
Gallery WM, Amsterdam 107725
Gallery X, Seattle 119923
Gallery XII, Wichita 049154
Gallery Yacou, London 085322
Gallery Z, Providence 119080
Gallery Zen, Portland 091941
Gallesi, Carlo, Bolzano 075129
Gallet, Paris 065988
Gallher, Granada 110377
Galli, Francesca, Parma 076212
Galli Vermigli Giandotti, Firenze . . . 127344
Galliano 6000 Isartorpl 9, München 072708
Gallier House, New Orleans 046253
Gallier's Stripwinkel, Sint-Truiden . 137538
Galligan, Providence 092039
Gallimard, Paris 133612
Gallimard, Paris 138386
Gallimaufry, Blairmore 112663
Gallina, Adriano, Napoli 134642
Gallinari, Jacques, Carouge 082292
Gallini, Milano 075722, 140052
Gallista, San Antonio 119416
Gallmeister, Erxleben 139049
Il Gallo, Pisa 076242
Gallo, Alberto, Venezia 128390
Gallo, Gianni, Roma 076484
Gallo, Mario, Milano 075723
Gallo Pinto, Amsterdam 107726
Gallo-Romeins Museum, Tongeren . 003798
Gallop & Rivers, Crickhowell 084115
Gallori Turchi, Firenze 075346
Gallot Franck, Paray-Vieille-Poste . 065338
Galloway, Newton Stewart 131319
Galloway, Ursula, Soham 131506
Galloway Galleries & Fine Arts Centre, Bowen Hills 055526, 094271

Galloway House and Village, Fond du Lac . . . 043882
Galloway & Porter, Cambridge . . . 141470
Galloway Station Museum, Edson . . 005417
Galluccio, Raffaele, Stuttgart . . . 126852
Gallus, Innsbruck . . . 137196
Gallus, Ljubljana . . . 109973
Gallus, E., Düsseldorf . . . 070385
Galpão de Arte, Fortaleza . . . 096529
Galpón de Campo, Buenos Aires . . . 055209
Galpón del Anticuario, Buenos Aires 055210
Galston Antiques, Galston . . . 055859
Galtebosamlingen, Spydeberg . . . 031216
Galtung, Oslo . . . 108727
Galuchat, Bruxelles . . . 057964
Galvan, Marta, Modena . . . 127732
Galvani, Fabrice, Toulouse . . . 101357
Galvani, Laura, Brescia . . . 075170
Galveston Arts Center, Galveston . . 044130
Galveston County Historical Museum, Galveston . . . 044131
Galvic, Maria, Bochum . . . 069882
Galvin, Sonja & Christoph, Hünibach 111564
Galway Arts Centre, Galway . . . 022789
Galy, Geneviève, Saint-Girons . . . 067506
Galy, Janine, Pau . . . 066703
Gama Art, Bühl, Baden . . . 070081
Gamain, Christian, Nancy . . . 064868
Gambara, Madrid . . . 081310
Gambarini, Malemort-sur-Corrèze . 064236
Gambarini, Vigeois . . . 068872
Gambarini, Catherine, Brive-la-Gaillarde . . . 061811
Gambarini, Catherine, Ussac . . . 068663
Gambart, Jean-Marc, Paris . . . 065989
Gambia National Museum, Banjul . . 015399
Gambit, Praha . . . 098461
Game and Fisheries Museum, Entebbe . . . 038213
Gameiro, Manuel, Lisboa . . . 079938
Gamella, Madrid . 081311, 122060, 141041
Gamella Rodriguez, Luis, Madrid . . 081312
Gamet, Romain, Paris . . . 124670
Gámez López, Armando, Bogotá . . . 133398
Gamila Gallery, Cairo . . . 098636
Gamilarart Gallery, Tamworth . . . 095314
Gamine, Philadelphia . . . 118769
Gaminek, Jörg, Bad Karlshafen . . . 101662
Gamisch & Helmer, Göppingen . . . 071029
Gamla Bankgården, Vrigstad . . . 036801
Gamla Brukets Muséer, Munkfors . . 036491
Gamla Carolina, Göteborg . . . 081804
Gamla Klockor, Stockholm . . . 081954
Gamla Krukmakarverkstaden, Arvika . . . 036199
Gamla Län, Paddington, New South Wales . . . 056416
Gamla Linköping, Linköping . . . 036424
Gamla Skeninge, Skänninge . . . 036573
Gamla Tider, Staffanstorp . . . 081902
Gamla Tiders Antik & Kuriosa, Göteborg . . . 081805
Gamle Bergen Museum, Bergen . . . 030764
Den Gamle By, Danmarks Købstadmuseum, Århus . . . 008806
Den Gamle Gaard, Faaborg . . . 008850
Gamle Hvam Museum, Årnes . . . 030739
Gamle Kvernes Bygdemuseum, Averøy . . . 030751
Gamle Ting, København . . . 060330
Gamle Trehus, Oslo . . . 079437
Gamlehaugen, Paradis . . . 031120
Gamlesmia, Oslo . . . 079438
Gamli, Iundur, Akureyri . . . 105581
Gammel Estrup Jyllands Herregårdsmuseum, Auning . . . 008817
Gammelgården, Sölvesborg . . . 036598
Gammelgården Friluftsmuseet, Bengtfors . . . 036212
Gammelgårdens Antikaffär Le Village, Göteborg . . . 081806
Gammelgruva, Orkla Industrimuseum, Løkken Verk . . . 030991
Gammon, Clarke, Guildford . . . 122530
Gampelen, Claude Daniel, Gampelen . . . 111417
Gamvik Museum 71N, Gamvik . . . 030852
Gan-Song Art Museum, Seoul . . . 027555
Gana, Seoul . . . 107237
Gana-Beaubourg, Paris . . . 100452
Ganada, Broome . . . 055570
Gananoque Museum, Gananoque . . 005493
Ganbara, Pamplona . . . 081519
Gandahus, Vals . . . 037671
Gander, Michael, Hitchin . . . 084693
Gander, Peter, Lienz . . . 137217
Gandhi Centenary Museum, Karimnagar . . . 022200
Gandhi Memorial Museum, Madurai 022249
Gandhi Museum, Bhavnagar . . . 022030
Gandhi Museum, Lucknow . . . 022239
Gandhi National Memorial, Pune . . 022306
Gandhi Sangrahalaya, Patna . . . 022293
Gandhi Smarak Sangrahalaya, Ahmedabad . . . 021990
Gandhi Smarak Sangrahalaya, Barrackpore . . . 022022
Gandhi Smarak Sangrahalaya, Sevagram . . . 022331
Gandini, Jacques, Calvisson . . . 133457, 138064
Gandini, Luigi, Roma . . . 076485
Gandit, Madeleine, Grenoble . . . 063062
Gandy Gallery, Praha . . . 098462
Ganesa Art Gallery, Da Nang . . . 120439
Ganesh, Chennai . . . 105629
Ganesh, Mumbai . . . 105776
Ganesh, Torino . . . 076818
Ganesh, Troyes . . . 068649
Ganesha, Rosengarten, Kreis Harburg . . . 104762
Ganet, Gérard, Paris . . . 138387
Ganexa, Panamá City . . . 050588, 108788
Gang & O'Connell, Chicago . . . 115433
Ganga Government Museum, Bikaner . . . 022043
Gangidori Bijutsukan, Joetsu . . . 026596
Ganglberger, Gebhard, Umhausen . 123480
Gangloff, Mulhouse . . . 138227
Gangloff, Strasbourg . . . 138619
Gangneung Municipal Museum, Gangneung . . . 027488
Gangwon Folk Museum, Cheongil . 027466
Gannon House, Sydney . . . 056676
Gannuso, Ruggiero, Montevideo . . . 087322
Ganondagan State Historic Site, Victor . . . 048780
Gans, Josef, Zeltingen-Rachtig . . . 074562
Gans, Udo, Arnsberg . . . 069182
Gansel, Pfungstadt . . . 073327
Gansel, Horst, Linz . . . 095662
Ganske, M., Oldenburg, Oldenburg . 073201
Gansow, Gido, Buseck . . . 070113
Ganss, Landsberg am Lech . . . 072136
Gansu People's Fine Arts Publishing House, Lanzhou . . . 133372
Gansu Provincial Museum, Lanzhou 007168
Gantner, Benno Michael, Starnberg 126824
Gantner, H., Bonn . . . 069922
Gantois, Cannes . . . 099069
Gaona, Cesar C., Buenos Aires . . . 055211, 120552
Gapp, Nathalie, Charleville-Mézières . . . 062158
Garabelli, Giorgio, Torino . . . 128310
The Garage, Genève . . . 111467
Le Garage, Halle, Saale . . . 103066
Le Garage, Toulouse . . . 101358
Le Garage Antiques, New Orleans . 090560
Garagem de Arte, Porto Alegre . . . 096562
Garai Luca, Bologna . . . 075082
Garakuta-Do, Honolulu . . . 088948
Garaldton Region Museum, Geraldton . . . 001054
Garam, Seoul . . . 107238
Garance, Monpazier . . . 064606
Garance, Paris . . . 065990
Garance, Sainte-Foy-la-Grande . . . 101240
Garanin, Berlin . . . 101908
Garasu, Mudgeeraba . . . 094918
Garattini Malzani, Brescia . . . 127217
Garau, Raimondo, Milano . . . 075724
Garaudel, Guy, Kamen . . . 071689
Garay, Tarbes . . . 068363, 124950
Garbary 48, Poznań . . . 109049
Garbato, Federica, Cagliari . . . 075209
Garbato, Giovanni, Cagliari . . . 075210
Garbe, G., London . . . 131040
Garber, Annemarie, Wolfern . . . 057606
Garber Communications, Blauvelt . . 135331
Garbett, Michael, Bristol . . . 141453
Garbini, Paolo, Lugano . . . 082600
G.A.R.C.E.N. Editions, Paris . . . 133613
Garces, Alonso, Bogotá . . . 098161
Garces, Maria Isabel, Bogotá . . . 098162
Garces Carrascon, Lucia, Zaragoza 081741
Garcia, Grasse . . . 063038
Garcia, Mechelen . . . 137528
García, Palencia . . . 110668
Garcia, Tampa . . . 132951
Garcia, Zamora . . . 081726
García, Hijos de Albaladejo García, Torrevieja . . . 122087
Garcia, Annick, Raincourt . . . 067032
Garcia, Cristobal, Zaragoza . . . 081742
Garcia, Emile, Issoire . . . 063221
Garcia, Gérard, Le Pin-au-Haras . . . 063684
Garcia, Jean, Marseille . . . 064359
Garcia, Jean-Pierre, Portel-des-Corbières . . . 066957
Garcia, José, Saint-Genis-Laval . . . 067487
Garcia, Laurence, Lancon-Provence 063508
García, Leon Jaime, Bogotá . . . 098163
Garcia, Marie-Rose & Victorio, Castres . . . 062034
Garcia, Maud, Paris . . . 065991
Garcia, Rafael, Madrid . . . 110531
Garcia, Victoria, Valencia . . . 081659
Garcia Cabarcos, Carlos, Donostia-San Sebastián . . . 129503
Garcia Cervera, Vicente, Valencia . . 110826
Garcia de Vinuesa Catalan, Pilar, Madrid . . . 129621
Garcia Ferrero, Miguel, Palma de Mallorca . . . 081481
Garcia Gil, Jesus, Valladolid . . . 081690
García Hijos, Barcelona . . . 129347
Garcia-Montes, Louis, Lafrançaise . 063484
Garcia Naharro, Jose Luis, Madrid .081313, 129622
Garcia Reyes, Antonio, La Palmas de Gran Canaria . . . 110709
Garcia Sayes, Fernando, Madrid . . . 081314
Garcia Toldra, Carlos, Terrassa . . . 081627
Garcia Urbina, Alfonso, Stuttgart . . 104983
Garcia Vargas, Agustin, Acapulco . . 128495
Garcia Zalvez, Diego, Girona . . . 081134
Garcin, Michel, Gap . . . 099282
Gard Antikviteter, Oslo . . . 079439
Garda Museum, Dublin . . . 022744
Gardani, Ben, Rotsterhaule . . . 140515
La Garde, Bordeaux . . . 061614
Garde Rail, Seattle . . . 119924
Gardega, New York . . . 117949
Gardella, Mauro, Genova . . . 127455
Gardella, Ombretta, Genova . . . 075468, 127456
Gardelle, Marcel, Pont-du-Château 066922
Garden Art, Hungerford . . . 084758
The Garden Art Gallery, Carrickfergus . . . 112819
Garden Blues, Velleron . . . 068747, 125011
Garden County Museum, Oshkosh . 046734
Garden Court Antiques, San Francisco . . . 092794
Garden Critters, Albuquerque . . . 114789
Garden District Book Shop, New Orleans . . . 142614
Garden Gallery, Apeldoorn . . . 107842
Garden-Gallery, Nice . . . 099842
The Garden Gallery, Southwold . . . 114471
Garden Gallery, Virginia Beach . . . 093355
Garden Gate Antiques, Oklahoma City . . . 091498
Garden Gate Antiques Market of Chestnut Hill, Philadelphia . . . 091637
Garden-Jardin, Paris . . . 065992
Garden of Earthly Delights, Philadelphia . . . 091638
Garden of Eden Art Gallery, London 113641
Garden of Fine Art Kyoto, Kyoto . . . 026716
Garden of the Gulf Museum, Montague . . . 005903
Garden of the Zodiac, Omaha . . . 118696
Garden Park Antiques, Nashville . . . 090452
Garden Park Farm Museum, Alberta Beach . . . 004991
Garden Spot, San Francisco . . . 092795
Garden Suburb Gallery, London . . . 113642
Gardenstone Antiques, San Diego . 092640
Le Gardian du Passé, Aubagne . . . 061024, 124081
Gardin, Danielle, La Sentinelle . . . 063446
Gardiner, Charles, Lurgan . . . 085870
Gardiner, John, Somerton . . . 086637
Gardiner Art Gallery, Stillwater . . . 048360
Gardiner Houlgate, Corsham . . . 122478
Gardner, Kilbarchan . . . 084839
Gardner, Tulsa . . . 143033
Gardner, Martin, Montréal . . . 097029
Gardner, Richard & Janice, Petworth . . . 086246
Gardner, Walter H., London . . . 141803
Gardner Arts Centre, Falmer . . . 039479
Gardner & Barr, New York . . . 117950
Gardner House Museum, Albion . . . 041612
Gardner Museum, Gardner . . . 044145
The Gardner Museum of Architecture and Design, Quincy . . . 047296
Gardner-Pingree House, Peabody Essex Museum, Salem . . . 047737
Gárdonyi Géza Emlékmúzeum, Dobó István Vármuzeum, Eger . . . 021719
Gårdsmuséet, Åre . . . 036190
Garel, Pierre, Riec-sur-Belon . . . 067139
Garelli, Henri, Saint-Tropez . . . 068017
De Garenkoker, Haarlem . . . 078454
Garets, Philippe des, Marolles-en-Hurepoix . . . 064300
Garfield, Pittsburgh . . . 118925
Garfield Farm Museum, Lafox . . . 045093
Garforth Gallery, Market Weighton .085941, 131264
Garganigo, Alice, Zürich . . . 082975
Gargiulo, Giuseppe, Napoli . . . 075990
Gargiulo, Marina, Roma . . . 076486
Gargiulo, Michele, Napoli . 075991, 106372
Gargiulo, Vincenzo, Merano . . . 106132
Gargola, A Coruña . . . 129488
Gargola, Madrid . . . 081315
Gargrave Gallery, Gargrave . . . 084453
Garhi Studio, Delhi . . . 105663
Garibaldi and Meucci Museum, Staten Island . . . 048328
Gariban, İstanbul . . . 083135
Garibay, San Diego . . . 132851
Gariboldi, Milano . . . 106244
De Garilhe, Lyon . . . 124357
Garín, Santiago de Chile . . . 059531
Garland, London . . . 085323
Garland, Merbein . . . 056214
Garlato 5060 Elisabetta, Venezia . . 076938
Garlich, Kurt, Dreieich . . . 070304
Garlin, S., Glun . . . 099289
Garlogie Mill Power House Museum, Garlogie . . . 039534
Garmilla, Jean-Michel, La Rochelle 063430
Garmonija, Sankt-Peterburg . . . 080303
Garmonija Kontrastov, Moskva . . . 109549
Garnavillo Historical Museum, Garnavillo . . . 044148
Garner, John, Uppingham . 086983, 131629
Garner Memorial Museum, Uvalde . 048721
Garnet, Reading . . . 135299
Garnier, Brugge . . . 120714
Garnier, A., Brugge . . . 057775
Garnier, Guy, Valros . . . 068703

Garnier, Jean-Michel, Chartres 138073
Garnier & Cie., Maurice, Paris 100453
Garnier, Serge, Is-sur-Tille 063213
Garnier, Serge, Is-sur-Tille 063214
Garnier, Yves, Toulouse . . 068516, 124981
Garnisionsmuseum Graz, Graz 001930
Garnisonmuseum Nürnberg, Nürnberg 019351
Garnisonsmuseet, Boden 036218
Garo, Montréal 097030
Garo, Gaby & Christian, Knokke-Heist 096334
Gåröströms Industrimuseum, Gnosjö Industrimuseum, Gnosjö 036289
Garofalo, Marco Ubaldo, Milano . . . 127601
Garoli, Milano 127602
Garosi & Mazzoni, Firenze 127345
Garow, Ban, Osaka 106963
Garrard, Ludlow 085866
Garraud, Gilles, Carcassonne 061977
Garrec, Yves le, Inzinzac-Lochrist . . 063210
The Garret, Albury 094131
Garrett, G. & N., Doncaster East . . . 094481
Garrett County Historical Museum, Oakland 046603
Garrett Historical Museum, Garrett . 044151
Garric, Michel, Montpellier 064743
Garrido Martinez, Sergi, Barcelona . 129348
Garrignot, Jérôme, Vichy 068858
Garrigue, Denise, Balaruc-les-Bains 098911
Garrigues, Jean, Forcalquier 062916
Garrigues, Robert, Paris 065993
Garrison, Saint Michael 096040
Garrison Gallery, Historical and Military Museum, Millers Point 001265
Garrone, Annie, Pegomas 100986
Garry, Saint-Ouen 067786
Garst Museum, Greenville 044346
Garstang Fine Art, Garstang 113086
Garstedt, Norderstedt 121562
De Garstkamp, Overasselt 030035
Gartell, Cincinnati 088243
Gartenkunst-Museum Schloss Fantasie, Bayerische Schlösserverwaltung, Eckersdorf 016882
Garter Lane Arts Centre, Waterford . 022870
Garth, Harrogate 084574
Garth, Whixley 087143
Garth's Auctions, Delaware 122879
Garufi, John P., New York 117951
Garvens, Aerzen 069111
Garverimuseet, Simrishamn 036568
Garverimuseet, Volda Bygdetun, Volda 031342
Garvey, Waikato 079288
Gary D.'s, Louisville 089989
Gary-Roche, Paris 065994, 100454
Gary & Wendy, Long Beach 089634
Gary's Antiques, Dallas 088520
Gary's Country Collectables, Mildura 056223
Garyudo, Yokohama 077335
Garza, Frank, Denver 116007
Garzanti, Milano 134613
Garzon, Alvaro, Bogotá . . . 059838, 137758
Gas Light Antique Shoppe, San Antonio 092513
Gas Museum, Kodaira 026675
Gas Pump Heaven, Omaha 091565
Gasan, Seoul 107239
Gasca Ajuria, Julia, Donostia-San Sebastián 129504
Gascon, Rosa, Zaragoza 129813
Gascoyne Junction Museum, Gascoyne Junction 001046
Gasendo, Marui, Osaka 077173
Gaseum, Essen 017065
Gąsior, Jerzy, Wrocław 129127
Gaslight Antiques, Tampa 093124
Gaslight Books, Fyshwick 136912
Gaslight Collectables and Old Books, Burra 055588, 136833
Gaslight Gallery, Chicago 088090
Gaslight & Shadows, San Francisco 092796
Gaso Venus, Nagakute 077143
Gasoline Alley Antiques, Seattle . . . 093008
Gaspar, Donna J., Baltimore 115054
Gaspar, Joan, Barcelona 110194
Gaspar, Joan, Madrid 110532
Gaspard, Marseille 124416
Gasparetto, Jean-Mario, Rolle 082746
Gasparri, Manuela, Livorno 075532, 127493
Gasparrini, C., Roma 076487, 106553
Gasper, Hans, Niederzier 104451
Gasperini, Mario, Roma 128056
Gaspesian British Heritage Village, New Richmond 006000
Gass Forest Museum, Coimbatore . 022063
Gasseling, M.C., Amsterdam 077853
Gasser, Bolzano 075130
Gasser, Haguenau 063113
Gasser, Bruno, Basel 134982
Gasser, Martin, Solothurn 130182
Gasser & Grunert, New York 117952
Gasset-Salembier, Edvige, Vullierens 082895
Gassner, Georg, Bad Hofgastein . . . 123338
Gaßner, Hermann, Ottobrunn 073270
Gassner, Peter, Hamburg 071233
Gasson, Tadley 086821
Gasson, Herbert Gordon, Rye 086425, 131434
Gast & Wodtke, Solingen 126813
Gastaldelli, Giuseppe, Milano 106245
Gastaud, Clermont-Ferrand 099150
Gastaud & Caillard, Paris . 100455, 133614
Gastl, Tübingen 139796
Gaston County Museum of Art and History, Dallas 043260
Gastou, Yves, Paris 065995
Gastown Antique Emporium, Vancouver 059362
Gasu no Kagakukan, Takaishi 027103
Gasu no Kagakukan, Tokyo 027168
Gasworks Arts, Albert Park 094128
Gasworks Arts, Albert Park 094129
Gatčinskij Filial Sankt-Peterburgskogo Gosudarstvennogo Universiteta Technologii i Dizajna, Gatčina . . . 050633
Gatčinskij Kraevedčeskij Muzej - Prioratskij Dvorec, Gatčina 033144
Gatčinskij Literaturno-memorialnyj Muzej-usadba P.E. Ščerbova, Gatčina . . . 033145
The Gate Gallery, Alnwick 112496
The Gate Gallery, Jerusalem 105910
Gate P, Berlin 101909
Gateau, Annick, Artigues-Foulayronnes 060999
Gatehouse Antiques, Macclesfield . 085890
The Gatehouse Gallery, Glasgow . . 113112
Gatekeeper's Museum and Marion Steinbach Indian Basket Museum, Tahoe City 048474
Gatell, Marta, Bilbao 129432
Gately House, East London 034609
Gatermann, Renate, Niendorf, Weser 104455
Gates, B.R., Fort Worth 116143
Gates House, Machiasport 045550
Gates Mills Historical Society Museum, Gates Mills 044156
Gates of Morocco, New York 090897
Gateway Antiques, Burford 083788
Gateway Antiques, Dublin 074919
Gateway Antiques and Art, Denver . 088690
The Gateway Gallery, Dunedin 108434
Gateway Pastel Artists, Saint Louis 054769
Gateway to the Panhandle, Gate . . . 044155
Gatewest, Winnipeg 059461
The Gathering, Cleveland 088329
Gathering, Dallas 088521
A Gathering of the Tribes, New York 136469
Gatherum Books, Uralla 137124
Ágathi, Athinai 105396
Gathy, Hasselt 058224
Gathy, J., Liège 058302
Gatipon-Bachette, Christian, Terraube 068375
El Gatito, Chiba 106837
Gatlyktans Antik, Lund 081852
El Gato Rojo, Bogotá 098164
Gaton Sanchez, Maria Caridad, Valladolid 081691
Gatov Gallery, Long Beach 045379
Gatsch, Steffen, Dresden 125495
Gatti, San Francisco 132882
Gatti, Leonardo, Brescia 127218
Gattinger, Silvia, Passau 104587
Gattis, Nashville 090453
Gattlen, Lausanne 111622
Gatto, Giancarlo, Torino 140132
Gau, Salzgitter 073654
Gaubert, Pierre, Paris 100456
Gauche, B., Bruxelles 123593
Gauchet, Gérard, Montbrison 064656
Gauchet, Gérard, Montbrison 064657
Gauchet, Loïc, Chalain-d'Uzore . . . 062071
Gauchet, Louis, Nice 065088
Gaud & Pirman, Villiers 068988
Gaudard, Reth, Villeurbanne 068962
Gaudet-Blavignac, Marc, Genève . . 111468
Gaudete, Museum voor Volksdevotie, Boxtel 029341
Gaudi, Madrid 110533
Gaudin, Le Havre 099439
Gaudin, Madeleine, Marans 064255
Gaudnek-Museum, Altomünster . . . 015520
Gaudron, Jean, Champagnole 062116
Gaudry, Jacques, Vallan 068697
Gauermann-Museum, Miesenbach . 002312
Gauguin, Rio de Janeiro 096613
Gauhati Medical College Museum, Gauhati 022122
Gaujoux, Carla, Blois 061523
Gaulade, Pinet de, Perpignan 100992
Gauld, Maureen H., Killin 084843
Gauldie, Becca, Abernyte 083247
Gauldie, Becca, Glendoick 084475
Gauldie, Enid, Glendoick 141627
Gaulin & Oestmann, Lübeck 139426
Gaultier, Patrick, Quimper 101062, 138576
Gaumann, Hume 056004
Gauthier, Patrick, Saint-Denis-de-Mailloc 067418, 121242
Gautier, Granville 099297
Gautier, Grenoble 063063
Gautier, Jacques, Paris 100457
Gautier, Jacques, Saint-Félix 067474
Gautier, Laurent, Nice 065089
Gautier, Richard, Niort . . . 099872, 124525
Gautier, Sylvain, Dijon 120988
Gautier, Goxe & Belaisch, Enghien-les-Bains 120998
Gautron, Kostia, Saumur 068152
Gauville, Thierry, Ribaute-les-Tavernes 138583
Gauvin, Serge, Montréal 058957
Gauzy, J.L., Agen 138006
Gavage Longrée, Liège 058303
Gavala Aboriginal Art & Culture, Darling Harbour 055737
Gavallet, Nicole, Paris 124671
Gavar, Paris 100458
Gavardie, Ivana de, Paris 100459
Gavcom, Braşov 080136
Gavilan Community College Art Gallery, Gilroy 044194
Gavin, Alain, Marnac 064293
Gaviolizaal, Helmond 029722
Gaviorno, Lucien, Monaco 107534
Gavriilidis, Efthym., Thessaloniki . . 074637
Gawaz & Schenk, Illertissen 103424
Gawjus Fings, Hawkes Bay 079112
Gawler, Willaston 137138
Gawler Antiques, Gawler 055861
Gawler Museum, Gawler 001047
Gawlik, Andreas, Halle, Saale 071175, 125788
Gawor, Anni, Paderborn 073280
Gawroński i Syn, Gdynia 079594
Gawsworth Hall, Macclesfield 040375
Gaxotte, Porrentruy 111814
Gay, Jean-Philippe, Couchey 062496
Gay 90's Mansion Museum, Barnesville 042023
Gaya Museum, Gaya 022123
Gayan-Sourgen, Jean-Louis & Henri, Dax 062606
Gayaud, Saint-Michel-de-Veisse . . 067675
Gayck, Alexander, Berlin 069611
Gaye, Houston 089082
Gayer, Paul, Baccarat 061155
Gayet, Martine, Dinard 099234
Gaylord & Co., Charles, San Francisco 092797
Gaylord Antiques, Denver 088691
Gaylords, Titchfield 086888
Gayma, Bilbao 080974, 129433
Gayndah Museum, Gayndah 001048
Gayo Museum, Takengon 022523
Gayot, Madeleine, Verdun (Meuse) . 068769
Gayraud, Dominique, Béziers 061439
Gayraud, Jacques, Béziers 061440
Gazado, Daniel, La Coucourde 063353
Gazado, Daniel, Saint-Paul-Trois-Châteaux 067944
Gazai, Nagoya 077148
Gaze & Son, Thomas William, Diss . 122488
Gazebo, Fujisawa 106839
The Gazebo, New York 090898
Gazebo Antiques, Los Angeles 089775
Gazelle Fine Art, Detroit 116086
Gazendam, J.U.R., Groningen 078414
Gazendam, Jur, Tynaarlo 140540
Gazeta Antykwarzyna, Kraków 136024
La Gazette de l'Hôtel Drouot, Paris . 135709
Gazette des Beaux-Arts, Paris 135710
Gazette Gallery, Goomalling 094596
Gazi Müzesi, Samsun 038165
Gaziantep Arkeoloji Müzesi, Gaziantep 038069
Gaziantep Devlet Güzel Sanatlar Galerisi, Gaziantep 038070
Al-Gazirah, Gowhara, Riyadh 080376
Gazirah Museum, Cairo 009302
G.B. Antiques, Lancaster 084898
GB Design, Houston 089083
GCR Art, Miami 117079
Gdańska Galeria Fotografii, Muzeum Narodowe, Gdańsk 031908
Gdańska Galeria Rzeźby, Gdańsk . . 108886
Gdańskie Towarzystwo Przyjaciół Sztuki, Gdańsk 053979
Ge, Changle, Wuxi 098034
Ge, Lianhai, Guangzhou 097722
Ge, Qingliang, Beijing 097653
Ge Li Dai, Hongguang, Beijing 097654
G.E.A., Paris 065996
Geary, J.A., Leeds 084926, 130870
Geazy Vase, Cairo 060446
Geba, Harald, Graz 095532
Gebauer, Berlin 125201
Gebauer, Wolfram, Dresden 070314
Gebecke, Quedlinburg 139667
Gebert, D., Rostock 073578
Gebert, Paul, Schmerikon 082804
Gebert, Ulf, Nürnberg 073102
Gebhardt, Chemnitz 138964
Gebhardt, Margit, Zwickau 127067
Gebirgsjägermuseum, Traditionssammlung der Gebirgstruppe Sonthofen, Sonthofen 020252
Gebken, H., Dötlingen 102381
Geble, Udo, Radolfzell . . . 073402, 121581
Gebrüder-Lachner-Museum, Rain am Lech 019703
Geburtshaus des heiligen Konrad von Parzham, Bad Griesbach im Rottal 015708
Geburtshaus Levi Strauss Museum Jeans und Kult, Buttenheim 016528
Gecko Gallery, Broome 094315
Den Gecroonden Boschboom, 's-Hertogenbosch 078520
Gedächtnisstätte Mida Huber, Landsee 002197
Gedächtnisstätte von Scheidt-Saalfeld, Bad Bergzabern 015657

Geddes, Graham, Armadale, Victoria 055373
Geddes Historic District Village, Geddes 044159
Gede Museum and National Monument, Watamu 027433
Gedenk- und Dokumentationsstätte Opfer politischer Gewaltherrschaft, Frankfurt/Oder 017202
Gedenkräume, Österreichisches Theatermuseum, Wien 002900
Gedenkräume im Schloß Hartheim, Alkoven 001671
Gedenkraum 1945, Hochwolkersdorf 002050
Gedenkstätte Bergen-Belsen, Lohheide 018676
Gedenkstätte Breitenau, Archiv und Ausstellung der Gesamthochschule/Universität Kassel, Guxhagen . . . 017611
Gedenkstätte Buchenwald, Weimar, Thüringen 020739
Gedenkstätte der Luftfahrt, Stölln . . 020322
Gedenkstätte Deutsche Teilung, Marienborn 018831
Gedenkstätte Deutscher Widerstand, Berlin 016047
Gedenkstätte Ehemalige Synagoge, Dorfmuseum Sennfeld, Adelsheim 015445
Gedenkstätte Erfurter Parteitag 1891, Erfurt 017015
Gedenkstätte für C.G. Salzmann und J.C.F. GuthsMuths, Salzmannschule, Schnepfenthal 020065
Gedenkstätte für die Opfer der NS-Euthanasie Bernburg, Bernburg . . 016204
Gedenkstätte für die Opfer politischer Gewaltherrschaft 1945-1989, Magdeburg 018768
Gedenkstätte Goldener Löwe, Eisenach 016921
Gedenkstätte Großbeeren 1813, Großbeeren 017564
Gedenkstätte Hadamar, Hadamar . . 017615
Gedenkstätte in der JVA Wolfenbüttel, Wolfenbüttel 020955
Gedenkstätte Langenstein-Zwieberge, Halberstadt 017645
Gedenkstätte Münchner Platz Dresden, Dresden 016788
Gedenkstätte Museum in der Runden Ecke, Stasi- Macht und Banalität, Leipzig 018571
Gedenkstätte/Museum Seelower Höhen, Seelow 020170
Gedenkstätte Plötzensee für die Opfer des Nationalsozialismus, Berlin 016048
Gedenkstätte Roter Ochse, Halle, Saale 017658
Gedenkstätte Synagoge, Dornum . . 016755
Gedenkstätte und Museum Sachsenhausen, Oranienburg 019478
Gedenkstätte und Museum Trutzhain, Schwalmstadt 020120
Gedenkstätte und Schulmuseum F.E. v. Rochow, Reckahn 019738
Gedenkstätte zum Konzentrationslager im Schloss Lichtenburg, Prettin 019667
Ģederta Eliasa Jelgavas Vēstures un Mākslas Muzejs, Jelgava 027692
Gedexnus, Dietmar, Amsterdam . . . 128538
Het Gedistilleerd Museum, Schiedam 030129
GEDOK-Galerie, Hannover 103278
GEDOK Gemeinschaft der Künstlerinnen und Kunstfreunde, Gruppe Hannover, Hannover 053195
GEDOK Gemeinschaft der Künstlerinnen und Kunstfreunde e.V., Gruppe Sachsen, Leipzig 053196
GEDOK Künstlerinnenforum, Karlsruhe 018159
GEDOK Verband der Gemeinschaft der Künstlerinnen und Kunstförderer e.V., Bonn 053197
Geelen, Amsterdam 077854
Geelong Antiques, Geelong 055864
Geelong Art Society, Geelong 052470, 094576
Geelong Gallery, Geelong 001049
Geelong Heritage Centre, Geelong . 001050
Geelong Naval and Maritime Museum, North Geelong 001335
Geelong Street Antique Centre, Fyshwick 055854
Geels & Co. Koffie- en Theemuseum, Amsterdam 029182
Geels Restauratieatelier, Geel 123617
Geelvinck Hinlopen Huis, Amsterdam 029183
Geerts, Henricus, Alet-les-Bains . . . 060777
Geertsen, Tom, København 060331
Geervliet, Bas, Breda 128604
Geesmann, Franz, Himberg 057059
Geeson Brothers Motor Cycle Museum, South Witham 041051
Geevor Tin Mining Museum, Pendeen 040683
Geffrye Museum, London 040152
El Gegant de la Ciutat, Barcelona . . 110195
Gehain, M., Bruxelles 057965
Gehan, Cairo 060447
Géhan, Hubert, Paimpol 065328
Gehbauer, Fürth, Odenwald 070914
Gehlert, Siegfried, Plauen 073338
Gehrig, Markus, Buchs, Aargau . . . 082279, 129992
Gehrke, Harald, Dresden 070315
Geib, Renate, Ockenheim 139622
Geibel, E., Göttingen 139145
Geidai Bijutsukan, Tokyo Geijutsu Daigaku, Tokyo 027169
Geier, Herbert, Bad Staffelstein, Oberfranken 121307
Geier, Josef, Sankt Gallen 130161
Geigenbau-Museum, Bubenreuth . . 016476
Geigenbaumuseum, Mittenwald . . . 018959
Geiger, Dietramszell 070250
Geiger, Konstanz 103758
Geiger, Ravensburg 073438
Geiger, Leopold, Ebenfurth 056967, 095497
Geiger, Ludwig, Riehen 111837
Geiger, M., Miami 090175
Geiger, R., Kornwestheim 103771
Geijutsu Shinbun Sha, Tokyo 134722
Geijutsu Shincho, Tokyo 135976
Geilenkirchen, P., Stolberg, Rheinland 073927
Geinitz, Jürgen, Alach 125052
Geipel, Katharina, Berlin 125202
Geisel, Gerwin, Detmold 070227
Geisel, Jürgen, Würzburg 074497
Geiseler, Peter, Berlin 125203
Geiselhart, Reutlingen 104727
Geiseltalmuseum der Martin-Luther-Universität, Institut für Geologische Wissenschaften, Halle, Saale 017659
Geisenheyner, Winfried, Münster . . 139563
Geishinsha, Tokyo 107049
Geisinger, Harald, Hamburg 103154
Geisler, Joachim, Xanten 074553
Geisler, Michael, Berlin 125204
Geisler, Ralph, Grünhainichen 071131
Geismar, Dany, Colmar 062413
Geissbühler, Peter, Obernau 082711
Geissbühler-Pitsch, Zofingen 112017
Geissendörfer, Ernst, Rothenburg ob der Tauber 073588
Geissmann, Claudia, Basel 129919
Geiter, Peter, Rottendorf 121590
Geitner, Johann, Velburg 126941
Geja, Maastricht 108123
Gekkeikan Okura Kinenkan, Kyoto . 026717
Gekko Gallery, Utrecht 078801
Gekoski, R.A., London 141804
Gelabert, New York 117953
Gelardini, M.&.C., Roma 106554
Gelbard, Roland, Paris 065997
Das Gelbe Haus, Museum Flims, Flims Dorf 037089
Gelbert, Gundel, Köln 139339
Gelbert, Ralph, Neustadt an der Weinstraße 104430
Gelbgießerei und Nadelmuseum in der Historischen Fabrikanlage Barendorf, Iserlohn 018085
Gelbke, L., Delitzsch 070211
Geldart Gallery, Henbury 113224
Geldermans, Eleonore, Bexbach . . . 125326
Gelders Geologisch Museum, Velp . 030264
Gelders Schuttersmuseum, Didam . 029477
Gelderse Smalspoor Museum, Erlecom 029579
Geldgeschichtliches Museum, Köln 018311
Geldmacher, Eva, Essen 070626
Geldmuseum der Deutschen Bundesbank, Frankfurt am Main 017169
De Gelegenheid, Den Haag 107921
Gelendžikskij Istoriko-kraevedčeskij Muzej, Gelendžik 033148
Gelink, Annet, Amsterdam 107727
Gellé-Lacroix, Laurent, Marseille . . 064360
Gellé-Lacroix, Laurent, Marseille . . 064361
Gellentin, Bernd, Lübeck 072324
Gellert-Museum, Hainichen, Sachsen 017640
Gelli, Giuliana & Marco, Firenze . . . 075347
Gellmann, Leo, Mörfelden-Walldorf 072578
Gellner, Bob, Omaha 091566
Gelmar, Josef, Schwäbisch Gmünd 073738
Gelmar, S., Lauterstein 072172
Geloni, Joseph, Antibes-Juan-les-Pins 060921
Gelos, Moskva . . . 080241, 109550, 121965
Gelot, Philippe, Paris 065998
Gels, Lingen 072278
Gély, Madeleine, Paris 065999
Gély, Monique, Perpignan 066746
Gelysand, Saint-Brice-sous-Forêt . . 101133
Gem Antiques, Maidstone 085895
Gem Antiques, New York 090899
Gem Antiques, Sevenoaks 086541, 131465
Gem Furniture and Antiques, Providence 092040
Gema Art, Praha 098463, 120857, 123980, 133414
Gemälde und Antik AAAAAA, Düsseldorf 070386
Gemäldegalerie, Staatliche Museen zu Berlin - Stiftung Preußischer Kulturbesitz, Berlin 016049
Gemäldegalerie Alte Meister, Staatliche Kunstsammlungen Dresden, Dresden 016789
Gemäldegalerie Alte Meister, Staatliche Museen Kassel, Kassel 018186
Gemäldegalerie Dachau, Dachau . . 016618
Gemäldegalerie der Akademie der Bildenden Künste, Wien 002901
Gemäldegalerie Neue Meister, Staatliche Kunstsammlungen Dresden, Dresden 016787
Das Gemäldehaus, München 072709
Gemäldesammlung, Friedrich-Alexander-Universität Erlangen-Nürnberg, Erlangen 017030
Gemeenschap Beeldende Kunstenaars, Arnhem 053886
Gemeentegrot Valkenburg, Valkenburg, Limburg 030245
Gemeentelijk Archaeologisch Museum, Grobbendonk 003481
Gemeentelijk Archeologisch Museum, Aardenburg 029125
Gemeentelijk Expositiecentrum Aemstelle, Amstelveen 029159
Gemeentelijk Heemkundig Museum, Hoeilaart 003516
Gemeentelijk Heemkundig Museum, Rijkevorsel 003714
Gemeentelijk Historisch Museum Ouder-Amstel, Ouderkerk aan de Amstel 030028
Gemeentelijk Museum, Rekem 003711
Gemeentelijk Museum, Melle 003640
Gemeentelijk Museum Gustaaf de Smet, Deurle 003396
Gemeentelijk Museum 't Oude Slot, Veldhoven 030263
Gemeentelijk Streekmuseum De Veste, Sint-Stevens-Woluwe 003763
Gemeentelijke Academie voor Beeldende Kunsten, Heusden-Zolder 049707
Gemeentelijke Academie voor Beeldende Kunsten, Waasmunster 049738
Gemeentelijke Academie voor schone Kunsten, Arendonk 049677
Gemeentelijke Expositieruimte Kampen, Kampen 029799
Gemeentelijke Kunstacademie, Maldegem 049718
Gemeentelijke Oudheidkamer, Ermelo 029580
Gemeentelijke Oudheidkamer, Geldrop 029597
Gemeentelijke Teken- en Schilderschool, Niel 049724
Gemeentelijke Tekenacademie, Wetteren 049740
Gemeentelijke Tekenschool, Wingene 049741
Gemeentemuseum, Woerden 030344
Gemeentemuseum, Maassluis 029891
Gemeentemuseum, Temse 003785
Gemeentemuseum, Weesp 030318
Gemeentemuseum De Tiendschuur, Weert 030316
Gemeentemuseum Den Haag, Den Haag 029424
Gemeentemuseum Elburg, Elburg . 029551
Gemeentemuseum Helmond, Helmond 029723
Gemeentemuseum Het Hannemahuis, Harlingen 029674
Gemeentemuseum Het Markiezenhof, Bergen op Zoom 029312
Gemeentemuseum 't Behouden Huijs, Terschelling-West 030197
Gemeentemuseum 't Sterkenhuis, Bergen, Noord-Holland 029310
Gemeentemuseum voor Religieuze Kunst Jacob van Horne, Weert 030317
Gemeinde-Heimatmuseum Harsum, Harsum 017780
Gemeinde- und Forstmuseum, Oftersheim 019458
Gemeindegalerie, Wiener Neudorf . 003029
Gemeindegalerie Benzeholz, Meggen 111725
Gemeindemuseum, Krauchthal 037218
Gemeindemuseum, Regensdorf . . . 037439
Gemeindemuseum, Schweiggers . . 002668
Gemeindemuseum Absam, Absam . 001654
Gemeindemuseum im Historischen Rathaus, Seeheim-Jugenheim 020169
Gemeindemuseum Rothus, Oberriet 037393
Gemeinschaft bildender Künstler, Wien 052533
Gemeinschaft Bildender Künstler Straubing e.V., Straubing 053198
Gemeinschaft der Ikonenfreunde, Hannover 053199, 071394, 121444, 125870, 134040
Gemelli, Milano 075725
Gemelli, Flavio, Milano 075726
Gemersko-Malohontské Múzeum, Rimavská Sobota 034418
Gemex, Paris 066000
Gemgold, Amsterdam 077855
Gemi Verlagsgesellschaft, Reichertshausen 134363
Gemica, Roma 076488
Gemica, Roma 076489
Gemini, Maastricht 078605
Gemini, New York 090900
Gemini Galerie, München 104210
Gemini G.E.L., Los Angeles 135380
Gemini G.E.L., West Hollywood 120381
Gemini Trading, Leek 084935
Gemma, Kazan 080208
Gemmala Dauksza, Maria, Düsseldorf 125531
Gemmeren, Belum 069517
Gemmological Association of Great Britain, London 054386
Gemmrig, Berlin 069612
Gems Antiques, Chichester 083973
Gems Display Figures, London 085324

Gems of Africa, Atlanta 114881
Gemst, Montréal 097031
Genadendal Museum, Genadendal . 034615
Genbrugsbøger, Taastrup 137908
Genç Kültür Merkezi, Bingöl 038025
Gence, Danièle, Coustellet 062532
Genchi, Teresa, Bari 075021
Gencor Art Gallery, Auckland Park . 034545
Gendre, Michel, Proissans 066985
Gendrot, Yvon, Languet 063527
Gene Fornby, Örnsköldsvik 036525
Gene Stratton-Porter House, Rome City 047537
Geneen, Lionel, Bournemouth 083597
Generaal Maczek Museum, Breda . 029350
General Adam Stephen House, Martinsburg 045713
General Crook House Museum, Omaha 046678
General Daniel Bissell House, Saint Louis 047663
General Douglas L. McBride Museum, New Mexico Military Institute, Roswell 047552
General Douglas MacArthur Memorial, Norfolk 046497
General George C. Marshall Museum, Zwijndrecht 030409
General Grant National Memorial, New York 046336
General Henry Knox Museum, Thomaston 048546
General Jacob Brown Historical Museum, Brownville 042485
General John J. Pershing Boyhood Home, Laclede 045083
General Lewis B. Hershey Museum, Tri-State University, Angola 041725
General Patton Memorial Museum, Chiriaco Summit 042906
General Patton Memorial Museum, Ettelbruck 027884
General Sterling Price Museum, Keytesville 044998
General Sweeney's Museum, Republic 047382
General Trading, London 085325
General Wait House, Waitsfield 048826
Generalens Blandning, Göteborg . . 081807
Generali Foundation, Wien 002902
Generali Foundation, Wien 133200
Generalić, Josip, Hlebine 098288
Generations, Cincinnati 088244
Generations-Antiques, Buffalo 087878
Generations Antiques, Salt Lake City 092432
Generations Furniture, Tulsa 093304
Generations Rug Gallery, Chicago . . 088091
Generous Miracles Space, New York 117954
Gene's Finishing, Chicago 131901
Genesee Country Village and Museum, Mumford 046082
Genesini, Giorgio, Modena 127733
Genesis, Chicago 115434
Genesis Antiques, New York 090901, 122995
Genesis Art Gallery, Kolkata 105740
Genesis Art Gallery, Portland 119004
Genesis Art Line, New York 117955
Genesis Publications, Guildford . . . 135156
Genette, Daniel, Versailleux 068824
Geneva, Archibald, Louisville 089990
Geneviève, Brice, Cagnes-sur-Mer . 099049
Genghini, Maria Vittoria, Milano . . . 127603
Genghis Khan Furniture, San Diego 092641
Geni, Samuel, Montréal . . 058958, 123787
Genia Schreiber University Art Gallery, Ramat Aviv 023047
Genicot, P., Bruxelles 137437
Genina, Québec 059069
Genji, San Francisco 092798
Genkai, Ljubljana 080655
Genluna Art Gallery, Davao 108817
Gennaro, Piero, Modena 075911
Gennaro, Romano, Napoli 075992
Genner & Co., August, Duisburg . . . 070478
Genner, Gerd, Duisburg 070479
Genninger, Leslie Ann, Venezia 106752
Genninger, Leslie Ann, Venezia 106753
Genolhac, Olivier, Saint-Cristol-lès-Alès 067407
Genootschap Kunstliefde, Utrecht . .053887, 108249
Genossenschaft Pro Sagi, Samstagern 037488
Genre, Diane, New Orleans 090561
Gensing Antiques, Saint Leonards-on-Sea 086464
Gensinger, Elke, Ramstein-Miesenbach 073412
Gensmantel-Keck, Margot, München 072710
Genson, Daniel, Bains-les-Bains . . 061175
Gent, Elisabeth, Bad Neuenahr-Ahrweiler 069341
Gent, Theodor, Braunschweig 069981
Genter, Gebhard, Kehl am Rhein . . . 071774
Genth, D., Dürmentingen 139003
Genthiner 11, Berlin 101910
Gentile, M., Cleveland 115710
Gentile, Mattia, Roma 128057
Gentile, Melissa, Firenze 075348
Gentilhaus, Aschaffenburg 015575
Gentili, Vinicio, Roma 128058
Gentilini, Prof. Giorgio, Firenze 127346
Gentilini, Valter Emilio, Torino 076819
Gentils, Annie, Antwerpen 096067, 133248
Gentle, Rupert, Milton Lilbourne . . . 085994
Gentle Art, Schenefeld 073682
Gentry Antiques, Polperro 086282
Gentse Kunstveilingen en Galerie Sint-John, Gent 120756
Genuine Collection, Miami 117080
Genzkow & Willig, Rosemarie, Hamburg 103155
Geo, Deutsch Schützen 095492
Geo-Ethnics, Tucson 093235
Geo Inn, Oosterbeek 029996
Geochang Museum, Geochang 027491
Géode, Saint-Étienne 101150
Geoffrey Kaye Museum of Anaesthetic History, Melbourne 001236
Geoffroy, Jean-Pierre & Jean-Renaud, Saintes 121255
Geoffroy & Beque, Jean-Renaud & Yves, Royan 121239
Geographical Center Historical Museum, Rugby 047565
Geography Museum, Faizabad 022114
Geoje Museum, Geoje 027492
Geologian museo, Luonnontieteellinen Keskusmuseo, Helsinki 009522
Geologian Tutkimuskeskuksen Kivimuseo, Espoo 009474
Geological Curators' Group, London 054387
Geological Museum, Dublin 022745
Geological Museum, Ho Chi Minh City 049536
Geological Museum, Khartoum 036150
The Geological Museum, Laramie . 045167
Geological Museum, Lucknow 022240
Geological Museum, Mizpe Ramon . 023033
Geological Museum, Teheran 022616
Geological Museum, Gauhati University, Guwahati 022136
Geological Museum, King Saud University, Riyadh 034123
Geological Museum, Museum Africa, Johannesburg 034648
Geological Museum, Prof. Rajneth Memorial Museum, Varanasi 022373
Geological Museum and Art Gallery, University of Exeter, Redruth 040815
The Geological Museum of China, Beijing 006985
Geological Museum of North Wales, Wrexham 041455
Geological Museum of the Institute of Geology, Erevan 000680
Geological Survey and Mines Museum, Department of Geological survey and mines, Entebbe 038214
Geological Survey Museum, Dhaka 003105
Geological Survey Museum, East Perth 001002
Geological Survey Museum, Ipoh . . 027949
Geological Survey Museum, Windhoek 029105
Geologičeskij Muzej, Muzej OAO Poljarnouralgeologija, Vorkuta . . . 034075
Geologičeskij Muzej im. A.A. Černova, Institut geologii Komi naučnogo centra Rossijskoj akademii nauk, Syktyvkar 033920
Geologisch-Mineralogische Ausstellung der Eidgenössischen Technischen Hochschule Zürich, Zürich 037767
Geologisch Museum Hofland, Laren, Noord-Holland 029827
Geologisch-Paläontologisches Museum, Münster 019144
Geologisch-Paläontologisches Museum der Universität Hamburg, Hamburg . . 017693
Geologisch Streek-Museum de IJsselvallei, Olst 029989
Geologische Landessammlung von Vorpommern, Institut für Geologische Wissenschaften, Greifswald 017522
Geologische Sammlung Schloß Kapfenstein, Schloßmuseum, Kapfenstein 002112
Geologisches Freilichtmuseum, Gmünd, Niederösterreich 001907
Geologisches Museum der DSK-Saar, Saarbrücken 019959
Geologisches Museum München, München 019059
Geologisches und Mineralogisches Museum der Christian-Albrechts-Universität, Institut für Geowissenschaften, Kiel 018244
Geologisk Museum, København . . . 008966
Geologisk Museum, Universitets Naturhistoriske Museer, Oslo 031078
Geologo-mineralogičeskij Muzej, Kazan 033232
Geologo-mineralogičeskij Muzej im. A.I. Kozlova, Dal'nevostočnyj gosudarstvennyj techničeskij universitet, Vladivostok 034045
Geology and Geophysics Museum, Roorkee 022321
Geology Department Museum, Aberdeen 038445
Geology Education Museum, Durban 034600
Geology Museum, Amman 027367
Geology Museum, Auckland 030437
Geology Museum, Ha Noi 049527
Geology Museum, Huntington 044683
Geology Museum, Kampala 038218
Geology Museum, Kingston 026383
Geology Museum, Legon 021108
Geology Museum, Lucknow 022241
Geology Museum of the University of Otago, Dunedin 030485
Geology Museum of the University of Stellenbosch, Stellenbosch 034752
GeoMuseum der Universität, Köln . . 018312
Georg, Sophia, Denver 116008
Georg-Büchner-Museum Goddelau, Riedstadt 019834
Georg Elser Gedenkstätte, Königsbronn 018343
Georg-Grabe, Eike, Kassel 139304
Georg Jensen Museum, København 008967
Georg-Kolbe-Museum, Berlin 016050
Georg-Kramann-Heimatmuseum, Nordwalde 019339
Georg-Meistermann-Museum, Städtische Galerie für Moderne Kunst, Wittlich 020931
Georg Papendicks Faschings- und Karnevalsordenmuseum, Bad Reichenhall 015773
Georg Rendl-Museum, Sankt Georgen bei Salzburg 002582
Georg Trakl-Forschungs- und Gedenkstätte, Salzburg 002554
George & Sons, Ottawa 123797
George, F., Birmingham 142238
George, Jill, London 113643
George, N., New York 090902
George, Paul, Spincourt 068282
George A. Spiva Center for the Arts, Joplin 044882
The George Adams Gallery, Victorian Arts Centre, Melbourne 001237
George B. Dorr Museum of Natural History, Bar Harbor 042016
George Bush Presidential Library and Museum, College Station 043044
George C. Marshall Museum, Lexington 045279
The George D. and Harriet W. Cornell Fine Arts Museum, Winter Park 049261
George E. Ohr Arts and Cultural Center, Biloxi 042213
George Eliot Hospital Museum, Nuneaton 040629
George Fraser Gallery, University of Auckland, Auckland 030438
George I. Ashby Memorial Museum, Copper Center 043142
George J. Doizaki Gallery, Los Angeles 045423
George Johnston Tlingit Indian Museum, Teslin 006560
George Meany Memorial Exhibition, Silver Spring 048179
George Museum, George 034616
George Paton Gallery, Victoria 001584
George R. Gardiner Museum of Ceramic Art, Toronto 006600
George Rogers Clark Park Museum, Vincennes 048787
George Street Antiques Centre, Hastings 084617
George Taylor House, Catasauqua . 042655
George the V Antiques, Portland . . . 091942
George W. Brown jr. Ojibwe Museum, Lac du Flambeau 045080
George W. Somerville Historical Library, Chillicothe 042895
George Walter Vincent Smith Art Museum, Springfield 048293
George Washington Birthplace National Monument, Colonial Beach 043051
George Washington Carver House, Diamond 043465
George Washington Carver Museum, Tuskegee Institute 048671
George Washington Masonic National Memorial, Alexandria 041643
George Washington's Ferry Farm, Stafford County 048313
George Washington's Headquarters, Cumberland 043244
George Washington's Mount Vernon, Mount Vernon 046074
Georges, Ambarès-et-Lagrave 060787
Georges, Bordeaux 061615
Georges, Guildford 123233
Georges, Alain, Lyon 099592
Georges, Annick, Chamalières 124178
Georges, Anselme, Marseille 064362
Georgetown Antiques Center, Washington 093414
Georgetown Art Guild, Washington . 054770
Georgetown Art Studio, Washington 120301
Georgetown College Gallery, Georgetown 044173
Georgetown Gallery of Art, Washington 120302
Georgetown Museum, Columbus . . 043103
Georgetown Plating and Polishing, Washington 133024
Georgetown Refinishing, Washington 133025
Georgetown University Art Collection, Washington 048909
Georgi, Peter, Greußen 125754
Georgia Agrirama, 19th Century Living History Museum, Tifton 048555
Georgia Antiques, Pulborough 086317
Georgia Association of Museums and Galleries, Atlanta 054771
Georgia Book Store, Atlanta 142203

Georgia Capitol Museum, Atlanta . . 041858
Georgia Coin and Jewelry, Atlanta . 087480
Georgia Council for the Arts, Atlanta 054772
Georgia Historical Society Museum, Savannah 048025
Georgia Lawyers for the Arts, Atlanta 054773
Georgia Lighting, Atlanta 087481
Georgia Lighting, Atlanta 087482
Georgia Mountains History Museum, Gainesville 044111
Georgia Museum of Art, University of Georgia, Athens 041832
Georgia Museum of Art. Bulletin, Athens 136470
Georgia Museum of Art Newsletter, Athens 136471
Georgia Museum of Natural History, University of Georgia, Athens 041833
Georgia Music Hall of Fame, Macon 045565
Georgia O'Keeffe Museum, Santa Fe 047964
Georgia Salzburger Society Museum, Rincon 047439
Georgia Southern University Museum, Statesboro 048339
Georgia State University Art Gallery, Atlanta 041859
Georgia State University School of Art, Atlanta 050923
Georgia Veterans Memorial Museum, Cordele 043150
Georgiadis Sofoklis, N., Thessaloniki 074638
The Georgian, Lancaster 045141
Georgian Antiques, Christchurch . . 079029
Georgian Antiques, Cork 074876
Georgian Antiques, Edinburgh 084291, 130678
Georgian Antiques and Gallery, Christchurch 079030, 128922
Georgian Cabinets Manufacturers, London 131041
Georgian Gallery, Hasselt 058225
Georgian Gems, Swanage 086808
Georgian Group, London 054388
Georgian House, Bristol 038863
The Georgian House, Edinburgh . . . 039392
Georgian House Antiques, Chipping Norton 083989, 130570
Georgian Museum, Bath 038629
Georgian Reproductions, Houston . . 089084
The Georgian Rooms, Bridlington . . 083673
Georgian State Art Museum, Tbilisi 015406
Georgian State Museum of Oriental Art, Tbilisi 015407
Georgian State Picture Gallery, Tbilisi 015408
Georgian Theatre Royal Museum, Richmond, North Yorkshire 040827
Georgian Village, Kansas City 089501
Georgian Village, London 085326
Georgian Village Antiques Market, London 085327
Georgia's Stone Mountain Park, Stone Mountain 048374
Georgie Lane Antiques, Maleny . . . 056132
Georgie's Gifts, Charlotte 087951
Georgiev, Nedialko, Sofia 137602
Georgikon Majormúzeum, Keszthely 021766
Georgina Pioneer Museum, Keswick 005685
Georgiou, Chr. & A., Larnaka 098296
Georgiou, Iraklis, Athinai 074591
Georgiou Collection, Lindos 021360
Georgiou & Kerr, London 085328
Geosammlung der Technischen Universität Clausthal, Clausthal-Zellerfeld . . . 016568
Geoscience Museum, Pretoria 034715
Geowissenschaftliche Sammlungen, Martin-Luther-Universität Halle-Wittenberg, Halle, Saale 017660
Geowissenschaftliche Sammlungen, TU Bergakademie Freiberg, Freiberg, Sachsen 017220
Geppert, Dieter, Essen 070627
Geppert, Horst, Ederheim 125570
Geppert Rahm, Marth, Frankfurt am Main 070741
Gera Galerie, Gera 102939
Gerätemuseum des Coburger Landes, Ahorn, Kreis Coburg 015454
Gerätesammlung Georg Bauer, Stadtlauringen 020286
Gerätesammlung Koch, Königsberg in Bayern 018342
Gerald E. Eddy Discovery Center, Chelsea 042788
Gerald E. Eddy Geology Center, Chelsea 042788
Gerald R. Ford Library Museum, Grand Rapids 044274
Geraldine, Geraldine 079098
Geraldine's, Portland 091943
Geraldton Regional Art Gallery, Geraldton 001053
Geralka Rural Farm, Spalding 001482
Geraniums Antiques, Tucson 093236
Gerard, Bruxelles 057966
Gerard, Nijmegen 078654
Gérard, Christophe, Rumilly 067329
Gérard, Emond, Montfort-sur-Argens 124451
Gerard, Hubert, Rainville 067033
Gerard, John, Rheinbach 134368
Gérard, Nicole, Paris 066001, 124672
Gérard, Timo, Bremen 125386
Gérardin & Cie., G., Lyon 064134
Gerardo, Vigo 129791
Geraud, Philippe, Honfleur 099350
Gerbe d'Or, Brive-la-Gaillarde 061812
Gerbenzon & Zoon, P., Leeuwarden 078551
Gerber, Kronau 072091
Gerber, Niederhelfenschwil 082701
Gerber, Rosario 055294
Gerber, Almut, Köln 071941, 103629
Gerber, Cyril, Glasgow 113113
Gerber, Daniel, Bern 082210
Gerber, Daniel, Suhr 082837, 130190
Gerber, René, Illkirch-Graffenstaden 063204
Gerber, René, Strasbourg 068321
Gerber, Toni, Bern 134992
Gerber, Waldemar F., Basel 111188, 141203
Gerbereimuseum, Marktschellenberg 018851
Gerbermuseum, Bretten 016445
Gerbeth, Frank, Hof, Saale 071546
Gerbeth, Frank, Schöneck, Vogtland 073714
Gerbino, Francesco, Genova 127457
Gerçek, İstanbul 112316
Gercev, Andrej, Moskva 109551
Gerdau, Angela, Oldenburg, Oldenburg 126591
Gerdsen, Magnus P., Hamburg 103156
Gerduberg Menningarmidstöd, Reykjavík 105588
Gereedschap Museum Mensert, Delft 029405
Geremi, Trieste 076892
Gerencsér, Ildikó, Budapest 074685
Gerencser, Ludwig Lajos, Eisenberg an der Pinka 095501
Gerersdorfer, Wien 095855
Gerg, Magdalena, München 126378
Gerg, Michael, Lenggries 126209
Gerhard, Gerd, Bad Berleburg 101630
Gerhard-Marcks-Haus, Bremen . . . 016413
Gerhardsen, Atle, Berlin 101911
Gerhardt, Michael, Knau 126057
Gerhardt, Renate, Berlin 133778
Gerhart-Hauptmann-Haus, Düsseldorf 016830
Gerhart-Hauptmann-Haus, Kloster, Hiddensee 018287
Gerhart-Hauptmann-Museum, Erkner 017025
Gerhof, Tilburg 078770
Gering, Sandra, New York 117956
Gering, Ulrich, Frankfurt am Main . . 102774
Geri's Antikschöpfli, Cham 082296
Gerlach, Mespelbrunn 126311
Gerlach, A., Tönnhausen 074069
Gerlach, Anita, Thyrow 126901
Gerlach, Birgit, Mönchengladbach . 139481
Gerlach, Günter, Stuttgart 126853
Gerlach Kirner, Kirn 139325
Gerlich, Hermann, Salzburg 095725
Gerling, Bettingen 102099
Gerling, A., Grassau, Chiemgau . . . 071088
Gerloff, Ursula, Braunschweig 125374
Gerly, København 098570
Germa Museum, Department of Antiquities, Germa 027828
Germain, Elisabeth, Aubagne 120907
Germain, Isabelle, Paris 124673
Germain, Jacques, Montréal 097032
Germain, Jacques & Françoise, Boulogne-Billancourt 061686
German, Hassan Yacoub, Valencia .081660, 122088
German, John, Burton-upon-Trent . 122442
German, Michael C., London 085329
German Occupation Museum, Forest 039513
German Underground Hospital, Saint Lawrence 040923
German Village Antiques, Columbus 088411
German Village Furniture, Columbus 088412
Germani, Rossana, Roma 076490
Germanisches Nationalmuseum, Nürnberg 019352
Germann, Zürich 122367
Germantown Historical Society Museum, Philadelphia 046945
Germond, G., Zürich 141337
Germond, Michel, Paris 124674
Gerner Bilderstube, München 104211
Gernhardt, Klaus, Bad Lausick 125107
Gernon House and Blacksmith Shop, Russell 047572
Gerntrup, U., Bückeburg 102283
Gerold, H., Ehrenkirchen 070517
Geroldsecker-Museum im Storchenturm, Lahr, Schwarzwald 018463
Geronimo Berenguer de los Reyes jr. Museum, Cavite 031648
Geronimo Springs Museum, Truth or Consequences 048623
Geronimo's Cadillac, Saint Louis . . 092245
Geronzi, Italo, Torino 076820
Gerringong and District Museum, Gerringong 001056
Gerrit Rietveld Academie, Amsterdam 050552
Gerrit Valk's Bakkerij- en Ijsmuseum, Hellendoorn 029713
El Gerro, Valencia 081661
Gerry's, Portland 132691
Gershel, Marseille 064363
Gerson, D., Antibes-Juan-les-Pins . 060922
Gerst, Hilde, New York 117957
Gerstacker, H. & R., Lauf an der Pegnitz 072168
Gebr. Gerstenberg, Hildesheim 134060
Gerstenlauer, Renate, Lindau, Bodensee 103920
Gerstenlauer, W. & R., Asselfingen . 101607
Gerster, W., Nagold 072941
Gerth, J., Rinteln 073541
Gerth, Uwe, Bad Salzuflen 069365
Gerth, Uwe, Stadthagen 073890
Gerthel, Susanne, Malmö 110972
Gertrude Contemporary Art Spaces, Fitzroy 001028
Gertrude Herbert Institute of Art, Augusta 041898
Gertrude Posel Gallery, Johannesburg 034649
Gertrude Smith House, Mount Airy . 046050
Gertrude Street Artist's Spaces, Fitzroy 094533
Gertrudenhof, Marxzell 072469
Gerullis, Ahlen 101544
Gerusel, E., Bonn 069923
Gerva, Venezia 076939, 128391
Gerva, Venezia 128392
Gerva Deposito Mobili Antiquariato, Venezia 076940, 128393
Gervais, Christian, Avranches 061145
Gervais, Gilbert, Avranches 061146
Gervais, Gilbert, Saint-Martin-des-Champs (Manche) 067640
Gervais Wheels Museum, Alida . . . 004994
Gervis, Daniel, Cannes 099070
Gervis, Daniel, Paris 100460
Gervis, Richard, San Francisco 092799
Gerwert, Idar-Oberstein 103421
Gerwi, Duisburg 102579
GESA Galerie, Aarau 111102
Gesällen Heminredning, Stockholm 081955
Gescheidle, Chicago 115435
Geschichte auf Rädern, Automuseum Melle, Melle 018896
Geschichtlich-heimatkundliche Sammlung, Aschheim 015590
Geschichtliche Begegnungstätte Hachborn, Ebsdorfergrund 016876
Geschichtliches Museum Enns-Donauwinkel, Sankt Valentin 002625
Geschichts- und Kunstverein Aschaffenburg e.V., Aschaffenburg 053200
Geschied- en Oudheidkundig Museum 't Freulekeshuus, Venray 030269
Geschiedkundig Museum Mesen, Mesen 003643
Geschke, Bettina, Hohenkammer . . 125956
Gesellschaft bildender Künstler Österreichs, Wien 052534, 133201
Gesellschaft der Freunde der bildenden Künste, Wien 052535
Gesellschaft der Freunde der Neuen Galerie Graz, Graz 052536
Gesellschaft der Freunde des Museum Haus Cajeth, Heidelberg 053201
Gesellschaft der Freunde junger Kunst, Baden-Baden 053202, 101723
Gesellschaft der Keramikfreunde e.V., Offenbach am Main 053203
Gesellschaft der Künste, Wiesbaden 053204
Gesellschaft der Kunstfreunde Lindau e.V., Wasserburg, Bodensee . 020689, 053205
Gesellschaft der Musikfreunde in Wien, Archiv, Bibliothek und Sammlungen, Wien 002903
Gesellschaft Deutscher Kunsthändler e.V, München 053206
Gesellschaft für Aktuelle Kunst, Bremen 016414
Gesellschaft für Aktuelle Kunst, Bremen 053207
Gesellschaft für Bildende Kunst Trier, Trier 053208
Gesellschaft für Bildende Kunst und Vaterländische Altertümer, Emden 053209
Gesellschaft für fotografische Kunst GFFV e.V., Köln 053210
Gesellschaft für Goldschmiedekunst e.V., Hanau 053211
Gesellschaft für Kunst und Elektronik e.V., Bergisch Gladbach 053212
Gesellschaft für Kunst und Gestaltung e.V., Bonn 053213
Gesellschaft für Kunst und Kultur, Sigmaringen 053214
Gesellschaft für Kunst und Volksbildung, Wien 052537, 133202
Gesellschaft für Moderne Kunst in Dresden e.V, Dresden 053215
Gesellschaft für Schweizerische Kunstgeschichte, Bern . . 054180, 111255
Gesellschaft für vergleichende Kunstforschung, Wien 052538
Gesellschaft von Freunden und Förderern der Kunstakademie Düsseldorf e. V., Düsseldorf 053216
Gesellschaft zur Förderung der norddeutschen Bildhauergruppe Münster e.V., Münster 053217
Gesellschaft zur Förderung Frankfurter Malerei e.V., Frankfurt am Main . . 053218
Gesenkschmiede Lubenbach, Zella-Mehlis 021053
Geser, Gisela, Regensburg 073457
Gesler, Frank & Brigitte, Neckarsulm 072956

Geslin, Patrick, La Chapelle-Janson 063316, 124276
Gessani, Paolo, Roma 128059
Gessinger, Wiesbaden 105258
Gessler, Robert, Friedrichshafen . . . 133966
Gest, Łódź 109009
Gesta, New York 136472
Gestarte, Roma 076491
Gestas & Martine Simorre-Gestas, Jean-Pierre, Pau 066704, 121220
Gesterbyn Kartano - Kirkkonummen Kunnan Museoalue, Kirkkonummi 009713
De Gestlo, Köln 134107
Gestütsmuseum Offenhausen, Gomadingen 017478
Gestures, Saint Kilda, Victoria 056563
Get Art, Seoul 107240
Get Rare, Savigny-sur-Orge 068169
Get Stuffed, London 085330, 131042
Get the Picture, Los Angeles 116778
Getaway Gallery, Columbus 115782
Getchell, Minneapolis 090360
Getchell & Getchell, Minneapolis . . 090361
Gethmann, Berlin 101912
Getty Conservation Institute Newsletter, Los Angeles 136473
Getty Images Gallery, London 113644
Getty Publications, Los Angeles . . . 135381
Gettysburg National Military Park, Gettysburg 044184
Getz, Michael, Washington 093415
Geuer, Grevenbroich 103004
Geukens & de Vil, Knokke-Heist . . . 096335
Geursen, J. & M.I., Richmond, Tasmania 095133
Geurten, Maria, Norwich 114164
Geus, K.H. de, Eindhoven 078338
Geusau, Pia, Wien 123494
Geuthner, Paul, Paris 133615, 138388
Gevaert, Yves, Bruxelles 133271
Gevangenismuseum Veenhuizen, Veenhuizen 030259
Het Geveltje, Middelburg 078637
Gevik, Toronto 097276
Gewehr, Murnau 104385
Gewehr, T., Murnau 104386
Gewehr, Vera Lucia, Porto Alegre . . 058501
Gewerbe-Museum, Spaichingen . . . 020257
Gewerbemuseum, Winterthur 037718
Gewerbemuseum der LGA im Germanischen Nationalmuseum, Nürnberg 019353
Gewerts, Borås 122109
Geyer, E. & C., Bad Aibling 101624
Geyer, Fritz, Plauen 104614
Geymüller, Dr. Johannes von, Essen 102679
Geymüller Schlössel, Sammlung Sobek, Wien 002904
Geyns, S., Bruxelles 057967
Gezira Art Center-Galleries of Fine Arts, Cairo 098637
GFL Fine Art, Nedlands 056320
G.G. Galerie, La Roche-sur-Yon . . . 063417
Ggantija, Xaghra 077547, 107457
Ggantija Prehistoric Temples, Xaghra 028046
G.G.Ice Impex, Bucureşti 109434
GH Art, Atlanta 114882
Ghafari, Sharjah 083214
Ghafary Habibullah, Philadelphia . . 118770
Ghalib Museum, Delhi 022083
Ghalim, Bruxelles 057968
Ghana Armed Forces Museum, Kumasi 021105
Ghana Museums and Monuments Board, Accra 053659
Ghana National Museum, Accra . . . 021098
Ghanassia, Danielle, Paris 100461
Ghandour, Soraya, Beirut 077394
Ghani, Abdul, Jeddah 080361
Ghanimé, Michel, Nantes 124482
Ghar Dalam Cave and Museum, Birzebbuga 028023
Gharb Folklore Museum, Gharb . . . 028024
Gharibi, M., Konstanz 103759
Ghattas, Pierre, Beirut 077395
Ghazarian, Mulhouse 064834
Ghazarian, Mulhouse 064835
Ghazarian, Alain, Benfeld 061344
Ghazni Museum, Ghazni 000002
Ghelfi, Giorgio, Verona 106797
Ghent, Norfolk 091381
Gheorghiu, A., Bucureşti 080156
Gherardi, Cristiano, Roma 076492
Gherardi, Cristiano, Roma 076493
Ghetto Gloss, Los Angeles 116779
Ghiglione, Genova 075469, 121690
Ghini, Aldo, Firenze 127347
Ghinolfi, Andreas, Zürich 082976
Ghio, Dario, Monaco 077608
Ghio, Hervé, Pont-Aven 101032
Ghiordian Knot, New York 090903
Ghiotti, Alain, Buno-Bonnevaux . . . 061837
Ghirardini, Silvana, Torino 076821
Ghislain, Saint-Ouen 067787
Ghislain, Saint-Ouen 067788
Ghislaine, David, Paris 066002
Ghisoni-Giordano, Bruxelles 057969
Ghobadi, M., Göttingen 071046
Ghoniem, Cairo 060448
Ghoochan Museum, Ghoochan 022554
Ghost Dog Gallery, Nashville 117353
G.I. Katsigras Museum, Municipal Gallery of Larrisa, Lárissa 021353
Giacalone, Christian, Zeven 127065
Giaccherini, Riccardo, London 131043
Giacla, Genova 075470
Giacobbo, Bruno, Ossingen 082717
Giacomo lo Bue, Córdoba 094098
Giacomoni, Monaco 128507
Giaconi, Firenze 075349
Giafferi, Paris 121151
Giagnoni, Patrizia Assunta, Cagliari 075211
Giai-Miniet, Daniel, La Bazoge 063293
Giammona, Giuseppe, Palermo . . . 127830
Giampiccolo, Alessandro, Torino . . . 076822
Giancatarina, Maria, L'Isle-sur-la-Sorgue 063935
Giancorrado Fiorin, Roma 076494
Gianferro, Ascenzio, Roma 128060
GianFu Classic Art Museum, Beijing 006986
Giangiacomi, Monaco 128508
Giangiacomo Ottorino, Roma 076495
Giangrossi, Rodolfo, Milano 127604
Giani-Leber, Dr. Claudia, Frankfurt am Main 102775
Il Gianicolo, Perugia 106459
Giannelli, Claudio, Canobbio 082285
Giannetti, Elena, Firenze 127348
Giannini & Marchi, Firenze 127349
Giannotta, Nicolò, Catania 134564
Giannoudis, Sozos, Chalandri 105414
Gianolla, Claudio, Venezia 076941
Giansiracusa, J & L, Preston 123290
Giantomassi & Zari, Roma 128061
Giant's Castle, Marazion 040419
Giant's Causeway and Bushmills Railway, Bushmills 038932
Giants Causeway Visitor Centre, Bushmills 038933
Giaquinto & Turrian, Lausanne 082548
Giard, Fr., Marcq-en-Barœul 138188
Giardini, Pisa 134657
Il Giardino, Trieste 076893
Giardino di Boboli, Firenze 024162
Giardino Storico e Villa Garzoni, Pescia 025191
Giarla's Coin Studio, Boston 087822
Giarraffa, Claudio, Palermo 127831
Giavolucci, Loretta, San Marino . . . 080345
Gibault, Paris 124675
Gibbard, A. & T., Eastbourne 141568
Gibberd, Jane, London 141805
Gibbes Museum of Art, Charleston . 042733
Gibbins, Carol, Houston 089085
Gibbins, Colin, Houston 089086
Gibbins, David, Woodbridge 087217
Gibbons, Stanley, London . 122588, 141806
Gibb's, Manchester 141936
Gibbs, Christopher, London 085331
Gibbs, Paul, Conwy 084077
Gibbs Farm Museum, Falcon Heights 043800
Gibbs Museum of Pioneer and Dakotah Life, Falcon Heights 043801
Gibernau, Barcelona 140988
Giberton, Marie-Claude, Vauvillers . 068739
Gibier, Chantal, Chatellerault 062218
Gibraltar Museum, Gibraltar 021112
Gibran Museum, Gibran National Committee, Bsharri 027815
Gibson, Colin, Newtownards 114145
Gibson, C.R., Norwalk 135471
Gibson, G. 514 E Pike St, Seattle . . 119925
Gibson, John, New York 117958
Gibson, Michael, Atlanta 087483
Gibson, Michael, London 096952
Gibson, Robin, Darlinghurst 094453
Gibson, Roderick, Nantwich 086035
Gibson Barham Gallery, Lake Charles 045101
Gibson Gallery, London 005786
Gibson House, North York 006051
Gibson House Museum, Boston . . . 042325
Gibson-Riley, Houston 116323
Gibson Street Gallery, Cooks Hill . . 094426
Elphinstone Pioneer Museum; Gibsons Maritime Museum, Gibsons 005505
Le Gibus, La Couronne 063357
GIC, Rouen 067267
Gicquel, Pierre, Vouvray 125039
Gidagi, Rotterdam 108186
Gidan Makama Museum, Kano 030692
Giddings, J.C., Wiveliscombe 087197
Giddy Bullfrog Gallery, Red Hill South 095122
Gideon, West Hollywood 120382
Gidiemme, Venezia 106754
Gidts, Amsterdam 077856
Der Giebel, Tangermünde 105031
Gieben, J.C., Amsterdam 134781
Giefarte, Lisboa 109323
Gieling, Marcel, Utrecht 078802
Giellevivi, Milano 075727
Gieraths, Heiko, Gerwisch 125728
Gierek, Joseph, Tulsa 120195
Gierhards, Erwin, Düsseldorf 070387
Gierig, Elmar, Mülheim an der Ruhr 072610
Gierig, Timm, Frankfurt am Main . .102776, 133943
Gierke, Andreas, Boostedt 125366
Gierre Antichitá, Roma 076496
Gierre Antichitá, Roma 076497
Gies, Horst, Essen 125611
Giesberts, Haarlem 078455
Gieschen, U. & B., Lindlar 103923
Giese, Eberhard, Köln 071942
Giese, Ernst, Ivendorf 125981
Giese, Peter, Hamburg 071234
Giese & Schweiger, Wien . 057430, 095856
Giesen, J., Aachen 069086
Giesicke, Dr. Barbara, Badenweiler 069430
Giessen, Julius, Frankfurt am Main 070742
Gießler, M., Hohberg 071555
Gietzelt, Michael, Berlin 069613
Giezendanner, Peter, Bazenheid . . . 082187
Giffard, Patrick, Dieppe 120987
Gifford, Auckland 108322
Gifford-Mead, Nicholas, London . . . 085332
Gift Horse, Cardiff 112813
Gifts for the Soul, Takapuna 108563
Gifu-ken Bijutsukan, Gifu 026473
Gifu-ken Hakubutsukan, Seki 027045
Gifu-ken Toji Shiryokan, Tajimi 027102
Gig Harbor Peninsula Historical Society Museum, Gig Harbor 044188
Gigengack, Gerardus, Hombrechtikon 082500
Gigi's, Birmingham 115108
Giglia, Maria, Roma 128062
Giglio & C., Pasquale, Milano 075728, 121709, 127605
Gigot, R., Bruxelles 123594
Gijon, Francisco, Madrid 129623
Gijselman, Loth, Laren, Noord-Holland 121797
Gil, Claudio, Rio de Janeiro 096614
Gil, Claudio, Rio de Janeiro 096615
Gil, Matt, San Francisco 119676
Gil, Natalia, Valencia 110827
Gil, Verena, Frankfurt am Main 102777
Gil Fernandez, Gregorio, Madrid . . . 129624
Gil Navares, Nemesio, Madrid 081316
Gila County Historical Museum, Globe 044220
Gilan, İstanbul 083136
Gilardi, Silvano, Mendrisio 130117
Gilbach, Gabriele, Essen 125612
Gilbert, Canberra 136846
Gilbert, Detroit 088762
Gilbert, Miami 090176
Gilbert, Miami 132343
Gilbert, Philadelphia 132618
Gilbert, Uppingham 086984
Gilbert, David, Sandgate 086508
Gilbert, John, Robin Hood's Bay . . .086383, 131420
Gilbert, Philip, Horsell . . . 084741, 130806
Gilbert, T., Waldshut-Tiengen 074260
Gilbert Collection, London 040153
Gilbert & Dale, Ilchester 084784
Gilbert House, Atlanta 041860
The Gilbert House Children's Museum, Salem 047749
The Gilbert Stuart Museum, Saunderstown 048018
Gilbert White's House and the Oates Museum, Selborne 040977
Gilbert's Bar House of Refuge, Stuart 048405
Gilbreath, Kay, Houston 089087
Gilchrist, Sacramento 119147
Gilchrist & Gilchrist, Nashville 090454
Gilcraft, Edmonton 123760
Gilcrease Museum, Tulsa 048653
Gild, Katariina, Tallinn 098700
Gilda, Köln 103630
Gildart, Roma 106555
Gilde-Museum, Museumshof, Oldenburg in Holstein 019464
The Gilded Cage Gallery, Calgary . . 096819
Gilded Griffin, Tulsa 093305
Gildehaus Bardowick, Bardowick . . 015887
Het Gildenhuys, Blokzijl 029319
Gilden's Art, San Rafael 135499
Gilder, Tampa 093125
Gilders Tip, Saint Louis 132747
Gildeskål Bygdesamling, Gildeskål . 030855
Gildija Masterov, Sankt-Peterburg . 109628
Gilding, Market Harborough 085937
Gilding Arts, New Orleans 090562, 132415
Gilding Arts and Antiques, Washington 133026
Giles, John, Petworth 086247
Giles, Larry, Saint Louis 092246
Giles, Norman, Dublin 105865
Giles, Sebastian, London 131044
Gilford, Patti, Chicago 115436
Gilgamesh, Portland 091944
Gilgandra Museum, Gilgandra 001057
Gilgen, Batia, Basel 082142
Gilhofer, Wien 137312
Gilhofer, Wien 137313
Gilhofer & Ranschburg, Luzern 141274
Gili, Gustavo, Barcelona 134915
Gilin, Efim, New York 090904
Gilis, Ramatuelle 067035
Gill, Heerlen 078500
Gill, Angelika, Wiesbaden 074403
Gill, David, London 085333, 113645
Gill, David, London 113646
Gillam Community Museum, Gillam 005507
Gillan, Auckland 108323
Gillard, Colette, Champniers 062127
Gillard, Joseph, Plombières-lès-Dijon 066862

Gillardeau, Charles, Brive-la-Gaillarde . . . 120953
Gillardeau, Charles, Paris . . . 066003
Gille, Jean-Pierre, Passy-Grigny . . . 066694
Gille-Stiernet, Bruxelles . . . 096205
Gilleleje Museum, Gilleleje . . . 008872
Gilles, Birgit, Bochum . . . 069883
Gilles, Gilbert, Crest . . . 062561, 124213
Gilles, Thomas, Le Bourg-Saint-Léonard . . . 063575
Gillesgården, Pohja . . . 009981
Gillespie, Houston . . . 089088
Gillespie, Simon, London . . . 131045
Gillespie Museum of Minerals, Stetson University, De Land . . . 043334
Gillet, Michel, Paris . . . 100462
Gillet-Seurat, Anne, Nanterre . . . 121084
Gilli, Joseph-Jean, Trept . . . 068626
Gillian, Toronto . . . 097277
Gillicienne, Charleroi . . . 058147, 096275
Gillies, David, Toronto . . . 059195
Gilligans, Leek . . . 084936
Gillingham, G. & F., London . . . 085334
Gillingham Library Gallery, Gillingham, Kent . . . 039541
Gillingham Museum, Gillingham, Dorset . . . 039540
Gillio, Santa Barbara . . . 092940
The Gillis-Browne Gallery, Harrogate . . . 113190
Gillman, Barbara, Miami . . . 117081
Gillman, Dale, Tulsa . . . 093306
Gillmark, Hertford . . . 130791, 141665
Gillmeister, Peine . . . 104595, 139651
Gillo, John, Dartmouth . . . 112937
Gillot, Raphael, Verviers . . . 123676
Gillot Collin, Paris . . . 066004
Gillott, Chris, Auckland . . . 128904
Gilman, Paul, Liège . . . 058304
Gilman Garrison House, Exeter . . . 043774
Gilman Museum, Hellertown . . . 044504
Gilman Town Hall Museum, Issaquah . . . 044788
Gilmore, Charles, Holywood . . . 113266
Gilmore, Hugh, Philadelphia . . . 142742
Gilmore-CCCA Museum, Hickory Corners . . . 044528
Gilmours, New Plymouth . . . 121828
Gilmozzi, B., München . . . 126379
Gilot, Jean-Pierre, Paris . . . 138389
Gilpin County Arts Association, Central City . . . 054774
Gilpin History Museum, Central City 042690
Gilquin, Jean-Luc, Arcis-sur-Aube . 060954
Gilroy Historical Museum, Gilroy . . . 044195
Gil's Upholstery, Miami . . 090177, 132344
Gilsa, Bettina, Tübingen . . . 126920
Gilstrap Heritage Centre, Newark-on-Trent . . . 040531
Gilt, Portland . . . 091945
Giltwood, Camberwell . . . 055607, 123203
Giltwood, Cheltenham . . . 083919, 130535
Gilty, Unley . . . 123325
G.I.M., Torino . . . 076823
Gimaray, Arlette, Paris . . . 100463
Gimbert, Marc, Saint-Zacharie . . . 068045
Gimel, Jerusalem . . . 105911
Giménez, Edgardo, Don Torcuato . . 055265
Gimle Antikk, Oslo . . . 079440
Gimmick, Amsterdam . . . 077857
Gimsa-Dittmer, Soltau . . . 073859
Ginac, Oliver, Nîmes . . . 065178
Ginac, Romain, Nice . . . 065090
Ginco Gallery, Malvern, Victoria . . . 094776
Giner, Fernando, Madrid . . . 110534
Giner Tronchon, Luis, Valencia . . . 110828
Gingell Littlejohn, Sliema . . . 121762
Ginger, Omaha . . . 118697
Ginger, Omaha . . . 118698
Ginger, G. & D., Ludlow . . . 085867
Ginger Gallery, Bristol . . . 112723
Gingham, Verbier . . . 082873
Gingko Press, Corte Madera . . . 135355
Gingko Press, Hamburg . . . 134009
Gingold, Robert, New York . . . 090905
Gingras Trading Post, Walhalla . . . 048831
Ginhart, Walter, Raubling . . . 104666
Gininger, Ira, Los Angeles . . . 142507
Ginioux, Catherine, Aurillac . . . 061077
Ginja Jar, New Orleans . . . 090563
Ginkgo Museum, Weimar, Thüringen . . . 020740
Ginkgo Projects, Axbridge . . . 112533
The Ginnel, Harrogate . . . 084575
Ginny Williams Family Foundation, Denver . . . 043408
Gino, Sacramento . . . 119148
Ginsberg, Joe, New York . . . 117959
Ginsberg, Nicky, Paddington, New South Wales . . . 056417
Ginsha, Tokyo . . . 107050
Ginsig, Markus, Winkel . . . 082908
Gintzel, Neuburg an der Donau . . . 104403
Ginza Bargins, Palmerston North . . 079214
Ginza Shibuya Gallery, Tokyo . . . 107051
Ginza Shouun, Tokyo . . . 077249
Gioacchini, G., Milano . . . 106246
Giocanti, Hervé, Marseille . . . 124417
Gioffreda, Mariella, Torino . . . 128311
Gioia, Barbara & Giorgio, Torino . . . 128312
Gioie Ed Arti, Verona . . . 077004
Gion Art Gallery, Kyoto . . . 106894
Giordani, Albertino, Bologna . . . 105964
Giordano, Edmonton . . . 096883
Giorgi, Milano . . . 106247
Giorgi, Franco, Firenze . . . 127350
Giorgi, Giorgio, Roma . . . 076498
Giorgione, Ettore, Armadale, Victoria . . . 055374, 123180
Il Giornale dell'Arte, Torino . . . 135905
Giorni, Maria, Firenze . . . 075350, 140018
Giosi, Napoli . . . 106373
Giosi, Dora, Toronto . . . 059196
Giovagnoni, Elisabetta, Roma . . . 106556
Giovanangeli, Ghislaine, Roquevaire 067223
Giovanetti, Marco, Napoli . . . 075993
Giovanna, Nicola, Roveredo . . . 082757
Giovannetti, Cristiana, Roma . . . 128063
De Giovanni Argenteria, Milano . . . 075729
Giovannini, Andrea, Bellinzona . . . 129943
Giovannoni, Enzo, Roma . . . 128064
Giovinazzo, Vincenzo, Torino . . . 128313
Giovine & De Vero, Torino . . . 128314
Gip Art, Postojna . . . 109999
Gipfelmuseum, Ehrwald . . . 001813
Gippsland Art Gallery Sale, Sale . . . 001452
Gippsland Auction House, Traralgon 120648
Gippsland Galleries, Cranbourne . . 094437
Gippsland Heritage Park, Moe . . . 001271
Gipsformerei, Staatliche Museen zu Berlin - Stiftung Preußischer Kulturbesitz, Berlin . . . 016051
Gipsmuseum Oberwiesen, Schleitheim . . . 037527
Gipsoteca, Lucca . . . 024542
Gipsoteca Canoviana e Casa del Canova, Possagno . . . 025344
Gipsoteca del Castello Normanno Svevo, Bari . . . 023335
Gipsoteca F. Jerace, Catanzaro . . . 023767
Gipsoteca Istituto d'Arte, Firenze . . 024163
Gipsoteca M. Guerrisi, Palmi . . . 025101
Giraffe, Ottawa . . . 097109
Giraffe Antiques, Los Angeles . . . 089776
Giraffe Art Africain, Montréal . . . 097033
Girald, Anna, Roma . . . 076499
Giraldi, Fabrizio, Livorno . . . 106122
Giraldi-Delmas, Philippe, Tarascon (Bouches-du-Rhône) . . . 068358
Giran, Christiane, Salin-de-Giraud . 101245
Girand, Christine, Paris . . . 100464
La Girandole, Lyon . . . 064135
Girandole, Metz . . . 064531
Girandole, Saint-Tropez . . . 068018
Girandole, Ville-d'Avray . . . 068880
Girard, Lyon . . . 064136
Girard, André, Paris . . . 100465
Girard, Eric, Brest . . . 061772
Girard, Jacques, Talence . . . 124949
Girard, Jacques, Toulouse . . . 101359
Girard, Jean, Cahors . . . 061900
Girard, Jean-Jacques, Dunkerque . 120996
Girard, Véronique, Paris . . . 066005
Girard, Vincent, Villars . . . 068877
Girard Claudon, Bourg-en-Bresse . .061706, 120949
Girardello, Bruno, Venezia . . . 076942
Girardet, Jacqueline, Paris . . . 066006
Girardet, Robert, Lons-le-Saunier . . 063995
Girardi, Pamela & Ramon, Chermside . . . 094388
Girardi, Renato, Milano . . . 127606
Girardi, Teresita, Buenos Aires . . . 055212
Girardin, Gilbert, Genève . 082432, 111469
Girardot, Stéphane, Saint-Ouen . . . 067789
Giraud, Bordeaux . . . 099004
Giraud, Les Ulis . . . 063791
Giraud, Dominique, Saint-Étienne . .067454, 124897
Giraud, Patrick, Draguignan . . . 062736
Giraud-Badin, Paris . . . 066007, 138390
Giraud, Pissarro & Segalot, New York . . . 117960
Giraud, Pissarro & Ségalot, Paris . . 100466
Girault, Christiane, Saint-Ouen . . . 067790
Girfalco Arte, Firenze . . . 075351, 106065
Giri, Joseph, Long Beach . . . 116671
Girier, Dommartin (Rhône) . . . 062708
Girndt, Uwe, Rheurdt . . . 126719
Girne Kalesi, Girne . . . 008244
Girnus, Andrea & Klaus, Xanten . . . 105365
Girod, Claudia & Mike, Berlin . . . 069614
Giromini, Danièle, Saint-Ouen . . . 067791
Giromini, Danièle B., Paris . . . 066008
Giron, Alain, Selles-sur-Cher . . . 068201
Giron, Christian, Noyers-sur-Cher . . 065242
Giron, Jeanne, Meymac . . . 064548
Giron, Philippe, Saint-Aignan (Loir-et-Cher) . . . 067344
Girotto, Dr. Maria Beatrice, Padova . 127804
Girou, Gilles, Angers . . . 060854
Girou, Gilles, Angers . . . 060855
Giroud, Régine, Luzern . . . 082627
Giroud, Robert, Grenoble . 063064, 099307
Girouette, Crest . . . 099187
Giroux, Frederic, Paris . . . 066009
Gisborne Museum and Arts Centre, Gisborne . . . 030501
Gisborne Steam Park, Gisborne . . . 001058
Gisel, Andi, London . . . 085335
Gisela's Antik-Stube, Fischen im Allgäu . . . 070691
Gisinger, Ferdinand, Dornbirn . . . 056962
Gisler, Hubert, Brunnen . . 082276, 129990
Gisler, Migli, Glarus . . . 082478
Gislöfs Smidesmuseum, Simrishamn . . . 036569
Gismondi, Paris . . . 066010
Gismondi, Jean, Antibes-Juan-les-Pins . . . 060923
Gismondi & Pastor, Monaco . . . 077609, 107535
Gissler-Volm, Ernst H., Badenweiler 138712
Gitanes, Los Angeles . . . 089777
El Gitano, Cali . . . 059882
Gitstappermolen, Vlodrop . . . 030285
Gittel, H., Frankfurt am Main . . . 070743
Gittins & Son, G.J., Caerphilly . . . 083835
Gittins, Kathy, Meifod . . . 114069
Gitton, Thierry, Paris . . . 066011
Giubboni, Prof. Paolo, Perugia . . . 127876
Giubergia, Franco, Torino . . . 076824
Giubergia, Franco, Torino . . . 076825
Giubilo, Trieste . . . 076894
Lo Giudice Giampiero, Roma . . . 076500
Giuliani, Alvaro, Roma . . . 128065
Giunta, Carlo, Roma . . . 076501
Giuratti, Anna Maria, Bologna . . . 075083
Giuriato, Roberto, Padova . . . 127805
Giurleo, Roberto, Firenze . . . 127351
Giuseppe, San Gwann . . . 107451
Giuseppe Emperiale, Santiago de Chile . . . 123880
Giuseppe Upholstering, Milwaukee . 132367
Giust, Silvia, Milano . . . 075730
Giustarini, Alberto, Firenze . . . 075352
Giusti, Luisa Silvia, Prato . . . 127890
Giusti & Bandinelli, Firenze 075353, 127352
Giusti, S. & Podestá, U., Milano . . . 075731
Giustina, S., Padova . . . 127806
Giustina Gallery, Corvallis . . . 043176
Give-Egnens Museum, Give . . . 008873
Givingness, Austin . . . 114986
Givon, Tel Aviv . . . 105918
Giza Zoological Museum, Giza . . . 009331
Gizard, Besançon . . . 061383
Gizard, Antoine, Besançon . . . 061384
Gjecaj, Ilse, Kalsdorf bei Graz . . . 095603
Gjenreisningsmuseet, Hammerfest . 030875
Gjesdal Bygdemuseum, Ålgård . . . 030720
Gjirokastër Museum, National Renaissance Museum, Gjirokastër . . . 000023
Gjotas, Charalambos, Horw 082502, 130047
GJ's Consignment, Miami . . . 090178
G.K. Zhukov Museum, Ulaanbaatar . 029002
Gkikas, Alexandros, Athinai . . . 074592
Glaasker, H. & G., Bokel bei Bremerhaven . . . 102174
Glacier, Zermatt . . . 082926
Glacier National Park Museum, West Glacier . . . 049075
Glade Antiques, High Wycombe . . . 084682
Gladis, Thomas, Stadtroda . . . 126822
Gladius, Jaraiz de la Vera . . . 136088
Gladrags, Edinburgh . . . 084292
Gladstone, Barbara, New York . . . 117961
Gladstone and District Museum, Gladstone . . . 005511
Gladstone Court Museum, Biggar . . 038705
Gladstone Gaol, Gladstone, South Australia . . . 001061
Gladstone Maritime Museum, Gladstone, Queensland . . . 001059
Gladstone Regional Art Gallery and Museum, Gladstone, Queensland . 001060
Gladstone Working Pottery Museum, Stoke-on-Trent . . . 041119
Gladwell & Co, London . . . 085336, 113647
Gläser, Markus, Leipzig . . . 126187
Gläser 5060 Rainer, Rosenhagen . . 073570
Gläsermuseum, Gerersdorf . . . 001892
Glamis Castle, Glamis . . . 039546
Glance Back Bookshop & Gallery, Chepstow . . . 130547, 141506
Glandford Shell Museum, Glandford 039547
Glanmore National Historic Site of Canada, Belleville . . . 005092
Glans, Berith, Stockholm . . . 141156
Glanum, Saint-Rémy-de-Provence . 014514
Glanz, H. & I., Erftstadt . . . 102639
Glanzzeit, Koblenz . . . 071892
Glardon, L., Versoix . . . 082874
Glarner Kunstverein, Glarus . . . 054181
Glas, Ella, Hamburg . . . 125814
Glas Art Scandinavia, Göteborg . . . 110920
Glas-Boden, Malmö . . . 081868
Glas Galerie Linz, Linz . . . 095663
Glas-Museum Marienhütte und Teufelsmoor-Museum und Teufelsmoor-Galerie, Gnarrenburg . . . 017436
Glas- und Keramikmuseum, Großalmerode . . . 017563
Glasbruksmuseet i Surte, Surte . . . 036699
Glaser, Bad Saulgau . . . 069373
Glaser, Anton, Gommersheim . . . 071061
Glaser, W., Crimmitschau . . . 070164
Glaser, Wilhelm, Horb . . . 125962
Glasfachschule, Kramsach . . . 049634
Glasgalerie Hittfeld, Hittfeld . . . 103383
Glasgalerie Hittfeld, Seevetal . . . 104879
Glasgalerie Jacob Bach, Düsseldorf 102504
Glasgow Art Gallery and Museum, Glasgow . . . 039555
Glasgow Auctions, Tauranga . . . 121834
Glasgow Print Studio, Glasgow . . . 039556
Glasgow Print Studio, Glasgow . . . 113114

Glasgow Print Studio, Glasgow 135155
The Glasgow Room, Glasgow 113115
Glasgow School of Art, Glasgow . . . 050817
Glasgow School of Art - Mackintosh Collection, Glasgow 039557
Glasgow Society of Women Artists, Glasgow 054389
Glashaus-Derneburg, Holle 017987
Glashausgalerie, Eisenstadt 095503
Glashütte, Bad Reichenhall 015774
Glashütte Annenwalde, Densow . . . 016671
Glashüttenmuseum des Erzgebirges, Neuhausen, Sachsen 019242
Glasmuseet Ebeltoft, Ebeltoft 008839
Glasmuseum, Frauenau 017209
Glasmuseum, Hergiswil, Nidwalden 037186
Glasmuseum, Immenhausen 018058
Glasmuseum, Warmensteinach . . . 020680
Glasmuseum Alter Hof Herding, Coesfeld 016582
Glasmuseum Boffzen, Boffzen 016305
Glasmuseum Grünenplan, Grünenplan 017589
Glasmuseum Hadamar, Hadamar . . 017616
Glasmuseum Rheinbach, Rheinbach 019821
Glasmuseum Steina, Bad Sachsa . . 015778
Glasmuseum Weisswasser, Weisswasser 020787
Glasmuseum Wertheim, Wertheim . 020818
Glasmuseum Zalto, Nagelberg 002350
Glasow, Gabriele von, Hannover . . . 103279
Glass, Tucson 093237
Glass, Horst, Essen 070628
Glass, Richard, Whaley Bridge 087119
The Glass & Art Gallery, Consett . . . 112901
Glass Art Gallery, New York 117962
Glass Art Gallery, Toronto 097278
Glass Art Society, Seattle 054775
Glass Art Society Journal, Seattle . . 136474
Glass Artists' Gallery, Glebe 094586
Glass Beveling, Indianapolis 132155
The Glass Chick, Albuquerque 114790
Glass Creations, Portland 091946
Glass, Design and Antique Repair, Hapert 128700
Glass Eye Gallery, Seattle 119926
Glass Gallery and Main Gallery, University of Texas at El Paso, Department of Art, El Paso 043639
Glass Garage Gallery, West Hollywood 120383
Glass House Gallery, Truro 114601
Glass Lady, Richmond 092078
Glass Menagerie, Memphis 090073
The Glass Museum, Dunkirk 043533
Glass Museum, Eretz-Israel Museum, Tel Aviv 023072
Glass of Yore, Houston 132121
Glass Onion Studio, Vancouver 097477
Glass Revue, İstanbul 083137
Glass Roots, Denver 088692
Glass Roots Gallery, Richmond 119112
The Glass Stopper, Kingsgrove 056057
Glasschmelzofenbau-Hütte mit Glasausstellung, Plößberg 019641
Glassdrumman Antiques, Tunbridge Wells 086937
Glassell School of Art, Houston 051483
Glasshouse Studio, Seattle 119927
Glassic Art, Las Vegas 116624
Glassic Arts, Los Angeles 116780
Glasslight Gallery, New Orleans . . . 117446
Glassmith, Portland 132692
Glasstetter, Fritz Mario, Basel 082143
Glassworks, Louisville 116942
Glassworks, Seattle 093009
Glassworks 78209, San Antonio . . . 119417
Glassworks 78258, San Antonio . . . 119418
Glastonbury Abbey Museum, Glastonbury 039579
Glastonbury Lake Village Museum, Glastonbury 039580
Glastonbury Museum, Glastonbury . 044198
Glastra, Eddie, Paddington 095025
Glaswerk, Germersheim 102942
Glatzer, Franz, Kierling 057095
Glatzer, Franz, Wien 057431
Glauberg-Museum, Glauburg 017426
Glaza, Tomasz, Gdańsk 108887
Glazar, Annecy 060890
Glazer, George, New York . 090906, 142655
Glazovskij Kraevedčeskij Muzej, Glazov 033149
GLB Création, Jouy (Eure-et-Loir) . .063263, 124272
Gleason, Tim, New York 117963
Glebe House and Gallery, Derek Hill Collection, Church Hill 022710
The Glebe House Museum, Woodbury 049282
Gledel, Claude, Fougères (Ille-et-Vilaine) 062926
Gledel, Gérard, Laval (Mayenne) . . . 063551
Gledel, Philippe, Fougères (Ille-et-Vilaine) 062927
Gledhill, Christchurch 079031, 128923
Gledhill, San Diego 092642
Gledswood Farm Museum and Homestead, Catherine Fields 000903
Gleeson, Terry, Dural 123220
Gleiche, Dr. Rudolf, Kaiserslautern . 071682
Das Gleimhaus, Halberstadt 017646
Gleis 2, Langenhorn 072157
Gleise, Betty, Digne-les-Bains 062633
Glémeau, Raymond, Dinard 099235
Glen, Robert & Julia, Nairobi 107161
Glen Eira City Gallery, Caulfield South 000905
Glen Ewen Community Antique Centre, Glen Ewen 005512
Glen Helen Ecology Institute Trailside Museum, Yellow Springs 049336
Glenara, Boorowa 094267
Glénat, Grenoble 133473
Glénat, Lyon 138150
Glenbow Museum, Calgary 005187
Glencairn Museum, Bryn Athyn . . . 042493
Glencoe and North Lorn Folk Museum, Glencoe 039583
Glencolmcille Folk Village Museum, Glencolmcille 022794
Glencorse, Kingston-upon-Thames . 084865
Glendale, Halifax 113177
Glende, Jürgen, Wandlitz 105155
Glendon Gallery, Glendon College, York University, North York 006052
Glendower State Memorial, Lebanon 045223
Glenelg Antique Centre, Glenelg . . . 055888
Glenelg Art Gallery, Glenelg 094590
Glenelg Fine Art Galleries, Glenelg . 094591
Glenesk Folk Museum, Brechin . . . 038824
Glenesk Folk Museum, Glenesk . . . 039584
Glenfarclas Distillery Museum, Ballindalloch 038573
Glenfiddich Distillery Museum, Dufftown 039292
Glenfinnan Station Museum, Fort William 039519
Glengarry, Paddington, Queensland 056430
Glengarry Pioneer Museum, Dunvegan, Ontario 005376
Glengarry Sports Hall of Fame, Maxville 005846
Glenhyrst Art Gallery of Brant, Brantford 005146
Glenleigh Antiques, Armadale, Victoria 055375
Glenleigh Antiques, Ulverstone 056763
Glenluce Motor Museum, Glenluce . 039585
Glenlyon Gallery, Aberfeldy 112484
Glenn, R., Nashville 090455, 122976
Glenn H. Curtiss Museum, Hammondsport 044407
Glenn House, Cape Girardeau 042612
Glennie & Partners, Fraser, Cirencester 122468
Glenn's Antique Gallery, Nashville . 090456
Glenreagh Memorial Museum, Glenreagh 001066
Glenrhydding Gallery, Otley 114197
Glenross, Holbrook 056002
Glen's Collectibles, Honolulu 088949
Glensheen Historic Estate, Duluth . . 043520
Glentworth Museum, Glentworth . . 005514
Glenview Antiques, Oakland 091419
Glenview Area Historical Museum, Glenview 044215
Glenz, Erbach, Odenwald 070579
Glenz, Rainer, Berlin 069615, 125205
Glerum, Amsterdam 121778
Glesner, Poul H., Hellerup 060253
Glessner House Museum, Chicago . 042847
Gletschergarten, Stiftung Amrein-Troller, Luzern 037295
La Glicina, Don Torcuato 123165
Glimmingehus, Hammenhög 036327
Glims Talomuseo, Espoon Kaupinginmuseo, Espoo 009475
Glineur, Patrice, Saint-Martin-de-Ré 067633
Gliorio, Samuele, Perugia 127877
Global, Groningen 078415
Global Antiques, Las Vegas 089578
Global Art Services, Bruxelles 096206
Global Art Venue, Seattle 119928
Global Arts, Manchester 135281
Global Arts Link, Ipswich 001130
Global d'Co-World Art Gallery, Bruxelles 096207
Global Fine Reproductions, New York 090907
Global Gallery, Paddington 095026
Global Health Odyssey, Atlanta 041861
Global Mail, San Francisco 136475
Global Outlet, Chicago 088092
Global Passages, New York 117964
Global Street Arts, Amsterdam 077858
Global Village, Helensville 079114
Global Works, Murwillumbah 056306
Globalart4u, Glasgow 113116
Glob'Art, Chavennes-près-Renens . 111348
Globart, Rouen 101117
Globe Art Gallery, Hawkes Bay 108466
Globe Books, Seattle 142988
Globe International Book, Chicago . 142288
Globe Poster Printing Corporation, Baltimore 115055
Globe Restoration, Seattle 132937
Globenmuseum der Österreichischen Nationalbibliothek, Wien 002905
Il Globo, Roma 076502
Globus Galerie, Leipzig . . 103879, 134150
Globus Galerie im Europa-Haus, Leipzig 103880
Glocken-Museum, Siegen 020199
Glockenmuseum, Apolda 015561
Glockenmuseum, Laucha, Unstrut . 018519
Glockenmuseum der Glockengiesserei, Innsbruck 002081
Glockenschmiede, Ruhpolding 019951
Gloddfa Ganol Slate Mine, Blaenau Ffestiniog 038757
Glöckner, Claudia, Köln 103631
Gloge, W., Herbrechtingen 103353
Gloggner, Luzern 111693, 122340
Glomdalsmuseet, Elverum 030821
Glommen, Brent, Saint Paul 132768
Glommersträsks Hembygdsmuseum, Glommersträsk 036288
Gloor & Co, Jules, Aarau 111103
Glore Psychiatric Museum, Saint Joseph 047646
Gloria, Lefkosia 098301
Gloria Aguirre Pagazaurtundua, Getxo 081115
Gloria Maris Schelpengalerie, Giethoorn 029610
Gloria Monasterio, Santander 081556
Las Glorias Antiguedades, Barcelona 080857
Gloria's Art Gallery, Omaha 091567, 118699
Glorious Gallery, Toronto 059197
Glory, Los Angeles 089778
Glory Days Antiques, Islington 056015
The Glory Hole, Earl Shilton 084238
The Glory Hole, Oldbury 086156
Glossop Heritage Centre, Glossop . . 039587
Glostrup Antik, Glostrup 060250
Gloth, Gerhard, Hamburg 071235
Glotin, Frédéric, Marseille 124418
Gloucester Antique Centre, Gloucester 084477
Gloucester County Historical Society Museum, Woodbury 049284
Gloucester Folk Museum, Gloucester 001067
Gloucester Folk Museum, Gloucester 039590
Gloucester Lodge Museum, Yanchep 001640
Gloucester Museum, Gloucester . . . 005515
Gloucester Prison Museum, Gloucester 039591
Gloucester Road Bookshop, London 141807
Gloucester School Museum, Gloucester 001068
Gloucestershire Warwickshire Railway, Toddington 041227
Gloux, Josiane, Thourie 068415
Glove Museum, New York 046337
Glover-Baylee & Co, Thornbury . . . 120647
Glowienko-Reinhard, Gisela, Wolfenbüttel 127030
Główna Księgarnia Naukowa im. B. Prusa, Gdynia 140726
Gluckselig, Kurt, New York 090908
Glud Museum, Horsens 008932
Glück, E., Dachau 070168
Glücksspielmuseum, Saxon 037519
Glustin, Saint-Ouen 067792
Glustin, Saint-Ouen 067793
Glyde Gallery, Mosman Park 094898, 123273
Glydon & Guess, Kingston-upon-Thames 084866, 130851
Glyndor Gallery and Wave Hill House Gallery, Bronx 042436
The Glynn Art Association, Saint Simons Island 047724
Glynn Interiors, Knutsford . 084890, 130859
Glynn Vivian Art Gallery, Swansea . 041171
Glyptothèque, Zagreb 007836
G.M Arts, Paris 100467
G.M. Publishing, Atlanta 135322
Gmeiner, Hanny, Dornbirn 056963
GML Fine Art, Saint Paul 119291
GMS Antiques, Baltimore 087673
Der Gmünder, Schwäbisch Gmünd . 104852
Gmünder Kunst & Schmuckauktionshaus, Schwäbisch Gmünd 121597
Gmünder Kunstverein, Schwäbisch Gmünd 053219
Gmurzynska, Zug 112218
Gmurzynska, Krystyna, Köln 103632
Gmyrek, Wolfgang, Düsseldorf 102505
G.N. Chubinashvili Institute of History of Georgian Art, Tbilisi 049998
G.N. Jha Kendriya Sanskrit Vidyapeetha, Allahabad 022003
Gnaccarini, Bologna 105965
Gnadenhutten Historical Park and Museum, Gnadenhutten 044227
Gnägi, Bendicht, Lyss 122341
Gnahs, Eberhard, Völklingen 105127
Gnauck, Anja, Dresden 102440
Gneisenau-Gedenkstätte, Schildau, Gneisenaustadt 020018
Gnoli, Maria Elisabetta, Modena . . .075912, 127734
Gnoss & Horstrup, Oelde 073179
Go Antiques, Columbus 088413
Go Bäng, Bremen 070020
Go-Do, Seoul 107241
GO Gallery, Amsterdam 107728
Goa Science Centre, Panaji 022288
Goanna Gallery, Quindalup 095112
Goanna Hill Gallery, Paringa 095056
Goarnisson-Busson, Emile, Saint-Benoît-des-Ondes 067375
Goat, Billy, Kumara 108487
Gobabis Museum, Gobabis 029080
Gobert, Maria, Meisenthal 064471

Goble, Paul, Brighton 083696
Goclette La Recouvrance, Brest . . . 010982
Godalming Museum, Godalming . . . 039597
Godang, Busan 077358
Godar, Genevieve, Lille 099490
Godard, Mira, Toronto 097279
Godard Desmarest, Paris 066012
Goddard & de Fiddes, West Perth . . 095393
Goddess Gallery, Portland 091947
Godéas, Evelyne, Toulouse 068517
Godeau, Antoine, Paris 121152
Godeccy, Andrzej & Bożena, Łódź . . 079668
Godefroy, Olivier, Cambrai 061919
Godehardt, F., Bochum 102153
Godel & Co., New York 117965
Godement, La Haye-Malherbe 063396
Godfrey, Jemima, Newmarket 086072
Godfrey & Watt, Harrogate 113191
Godfroy, Monique, Vallauris 101418
Godin, Liège 058305
Godolphin, Chagford 083900
Godolphin, Chagford 083901
Godolphin, Chagford 112832
Godon, Lille 138120
Godøy Kystmuseum, Godøy 030858
Gods, Göteborg 081808
Gods Artefacts, Crows Nest, New South Wales 094443
Godson & Coles, London . 085337, 113648
Godwin and Ternbach Museum, Flushing 043875
Göbbel, Nettetal 072963
Göbel, Hannelore, Speyer 073879
Göbl, Arnold, München 072711
Goecke, Christoph, Berlin . 069616, 125206
Goeckler, Bernd H., New York 090909
Göcseji Falumúzeum, Göcseji Múzeum, Zalaegerszeg 021924
Göcseji Múzeum, Zalaegerszeg . . . 021925
Goede, Bremen 102244
Göde, Waldaschaff 074249
De Goede Oude Tijd, Eindhoven . . . 078339
Gödecke, Kerken 071798
Gödecke, Axel, Issum 071641
Goedecker, Harald, München 104212
Goedhuis, London 113649
Goedhuis, New York 117966
Goedkoper, Zutphen 078873
Goeffriault, Alexandre, Montpellier . 138220
Gögler, Roland, Leutkirch im Allgäu 139410
Göhring & Dammeyer, Basel 111189
Goeij, Wim de, Antwerpen 137398
Göke, München 072712
Goeken, Münster 104366
Goeken, Münster 104367
Gölles, Fürstenfeld 056982
Gölles-Valda, Martina, Riegersburg, Steiermark 057227
Göltzschtalgalerie-Nicolaikirche, Auerbach, Vogtland 015598
Gölzhäuser, Kirchhain 103553
Goemanszorg - Streek- en Landbouwmuseum, Dreischor . . . 029509
Göpfert, Sabine, Meiningen 104053
Göppert, J., Freiburg im Breisgau . . 139112
Göreme Açıkhava Müzesi, Nevşehir 038155
Görg, Gerald, Koblenz . . . 103567, 134094
Görg, Jürgen, Boppard 102199
Görg, Kurt, Goldbach, Unterfranken 071059
Görg, Wolfgang, Leipzig . . 072204, 139393
Görigk, Franz-Josef, Duisburg 125560
Goering Institut e.V., München 126380
Goeritz, Flensburg 070703
Görl, Naumburg, Saale 104391
Görlitz, Aribert, Braunschweig 102219
Görög-Római Szobormásolatok Múzeuma, Tata 021903
Görres, Martin, Münster 126500
Görres-Gesellschaft, Sektion für Kunstwissenschaft, Köln 053220
Görsan, İstanbul 112317
Görß, D., Rostock 104769
Görtzen, Xanten 074554
Görtzen, Xanten 127056
Göschenhaus / Seume-Gedenkstätte, Grimma 017537
Göschl, Erich, Krems 057124
Gösken, Anna-Maria, Essen 102680
Gösseln, Anya von, Clonegal 105853
Gösta Serlachiuksen Taidemuseo, Mänttä 009852
Göta Konst, Stockholm 111049
Göteborgs Antik, Göteborg 081809
Göteborg's Antikvariat, Göteborg . . 054130
Göteborgs Konstförening, Göteborg 054131
Göteborgs Konstmuseum, Göteborg 036296
Göteborgs Stadsmuseum, Göteborg 036297
Goetgheluck, Hubert, Caestre 061889
Goethe-Antiquariat, Weimar, Thüringen 139833
Goethe-Gedenkstätte, Friedrich-Schiller-Universität Jena, Jena 018107
Goethe-Gedenkstätte im Amtshaus, Museum der Stadt Ilmenau, Ilmenau 018055
Goethe Institut, Budapest 021650
Goethe Institut, Paris 100468
Goethe-Institut New York - Exhibitions, New York 046338
Goethe-Institut Sydney, Woollahra . 001633
Goethe-Museum Düsseldorf, Anton-und-Katharina-Kippenberg-Stiftung, Düsseldorf 016831
Goethe-Museum Stützerbach mit Museum zur Geschichte des technischen Glases, Stiftung Weimarer Klassik und Kunstsammlungen, Stützerbach . 020340
Goethe-Stube, Bad Berka 015661
Goethe- und Schiller-Archiv, Stiftung Weimarer Klassik und Kunstsammlungen, Weimar, Thüringen 020741
Goethes Gartenhaus 2, Bad Sulza . . 015812
Goethes Gartenhaus - Goethe-Nationalmuseum, Stiftung Weimarer Klassik und Kunstsammlungen, Weimar, Thüringen 020742
Goethes Wohnhaus mit Goethe-Nationalmuseum, Stiftung Weimarer Klassik und Kunstsammlungen, Weimar, Thüringen 020743
Götte, R., Freren 070879
Götter, Walter Max, Hechingen 125893
Götting, H., Münster 072906
Götting, Heinrich, Münster 072907
Göttinger Antiquariat, Göttingen . . . 139146
Göttler, Armin, Wasserburg am Inn . 074283
Göttler, Armin, Wasserburg am Inn . 126970
Göttler, Armin, Wasserburg am Inn . 126971
Göttler, Christine, Wasserburg am Inn 074284
Göttlich, Karin, Dorfgastein 137161
Göttlicher, Helga, Krems 095632
Götz, G., Landau in der Pfalz 072130
Götz, Heinrich, München . 072713, 126381
Götz, Ilse, Stuttgart 104984, 134411
Götz, Karl-Heinz & Doris, Weinstadt 139838
Götz, Kornelius, Oettingen 126586
Götz, Kurt, Karlsruhe 139294
Götz, Rainar, Dresden 102441
Goetz, Silvan, Solothurn 082820
Götz, Ulrike, Berlin 069617, 101913
Götz, Uta, Lappersdorf 103838
Goetz/Fleischack Museum, Potchefstroom 034707
Götzhaber, Dr. Lutz, Essen 139053
Goetzke, Andreas, Oberottmarshausen 126580
Goez, Los Angeles 116781
Goez, Los Angeles 116782
Goffi Carboni, Roma 076503
Goffin, E., Liège 058306
Goffinet, Bernard, Lutterbach 064038
Gofish Gallery, Maylands, Western Australia 094798
Goger, Rüdiger, Osterweddingen . . . 073258
Gogherman, A., Westervoort 128880
Goh, Karin, Bühlertal 102285
Goh, Swar Teck, Singapore 080470
Gohard, Robert, Paris 124676
Goharpour, M., Hamburg . 071236, 125815
Gohltalmuseum, Neu-Moresnet . . . 003671
Goinard, Marie-Claude, La Baule-Escoublac 099377
Goinard, Marie-Claude & Gabriel, Paris 100469
Goins, R.L., Atlanta 114883
Góis, Abel, Funchal 079836
Góis & Ferro, Lisboa 129154
Gojan, Tomasz, Warszawa 129086
Gojun Gallery, Gwangju 077362
Gol Bygdemuseet, Gol 030859
Golan Archaeological Museum, Qatzrin 023045
Gold, Atlanta 087484, 122800
Gold, Fay, Atlanta 114884
Gold, Helmut, Ingelheim am Rhein . 103429
Gold, Vilma, London 113650
Gold and Silver Exchange, Exeter . . 084357
Gold and Silver Lady, Toledo 093170
Gold Art Gallery, București 109435
Gold Cadre, Casablanca 077655
Gold Coast City Art Gallery, Surfers Paradise 001499
Gold Coast Gallery, Chicago 088093
Gold Coast Prepress, Saint Louis . . 119207
Gold Coast Railroad Museum, Miami 045808
Gold & Coin Buyer, Boston 087823
Gold Creek Curiosity Shoppe, Nicholls 056347
Gold Creek Gallery, Nicholls 094963
Gold & Diamond Exchange, Las Vegas 089579
Gold Dragon Gallery, Tampa 120047
Gold Dust Coins, Chicago 088094
Gold Exchange, Las Vegas 089580
Gold Leaf Conservation, Cleveland . 131961
Gold Leaf Restoration, Portland . . . 132693
Gold Mine and Antique Jewelry, New York 090910
Gold Museum, Ballarat 000763
Gold 'n Grape Gallery, Pemberton . . 095062
Gold 'n' Kiwi Antiques, Otorohanga 079207
Gold 'n Silver, Omaha 091568
Gold Rush Jewellers, Bendigo 055480
Gold Rush Numismatics, San Francisco 092800
Gold & Silver Exchange, Great Yarmouth 084528
Gold & Silver Exchange Action, Sacramento 092160
Gold Street Antiques, San Jose . . . 092927
Gold Strike, Chicago 088095
Gold Tech, Buffalo 131854
Gold Touch, Atlanta 131775
Gold Traders, Toronto 059198
Gold Treasury Museum, Melbourne 001238
Gold- und Silberschmiedemuseum, Mülsen, Sankt-Jakob 019027
Gold- und Silberschmiedemuseum, Wien 002906
Goldammer, Breisach am Rhein . . . 069999
Goldberg, West Hollywood 133041
Goldberg, David, New Orleans 090564
Goldberg, Martin, Stade 073887
Goldberg-Museum, Riesbürg 019843
Goldcare, Middlesborough 131277
Goldcoast Auctioneers, Miami 122961
Golden, Caren, New York 117967
Golden, Suzanne, New York 090911
Golden and District Museum, Golden 005518
Golden Art, Brasília 096494
Golden Art, Helsinki 060524
Golden Arts Gallery, Singapore 109801
Golden Ball Tavern Museum, Weston 049121
Golden Bay Museum and Gallery, Golden Bay 030502
Golden Business Company, Antwerpen 057696
Golden Cage, Nottingham 086134
Golden Center, Damascus 083059
Golden Chair, Hampton 055949
Golden City Paddle Steamer Museum, Ballarat 000764
Golden Crust Gallery, Armadale, Victoria 055376
Golden Dragon, Regina 097173
Golden Dragon Museum, Bendigo . 000795
Golden Dynasty Gallery, Chicago . . 088096
Golden Eagle Antiques, Tucson 093238
Golden Era Antiques, Miami 090179
Golden Flower Art Gallery, Pine Creek 095072
Golden Gallery, Miercurea-Ciuc . . . 109459
Golden Gargoyles, Philadelphia . . . 091639
Golden Gate Antiques, San Francisco 092801
Golden Gate Trading, San Francisco 092802
Golden Goose Books, Lincoln 141732
Golden Harvest Antiques, Saint Louis 092247
Golden Hind Museum, Brixham . . . 038871
Golden Hinde Educational Museum, London 040154
Golden Horn, İstanbul 112318
Golden Isles Arts & Humanities Association, Brunswick 054776
Golden Lion, Los Angeles 089779
Golden Lion Antiques, Saint Paul . . 092363
Golden Lion Bazaar, Townsville . . . 056729
Golden Lotus Gallery, Ha Noi 120464
Golden Lotus Gallery, Ho Chi Minh City 120509
Golden Memories of York, York 087291
Golden Oldies, Penkridge 086198
Golden Pacific Arts, San Diego 119511
Golden Peart, Cairo 060449
The Golden Pendulum, Griesheim . . 071103
Golden Ram Gallery, Cincinnati . . . 115632
Golden Saloon, Damascus 083060
Golden Spike National Historic Site, Brigham City 042415
Golden Ta Art Gallery, Wuxi 098035
Golden Tortoise, Bangkok 083096
Golden Triangle, Chicago 088097
Golden Turtle, San Francisco 132883
Golden Wong Enterprise, Singapore 080471
Golden Years Antiques, Kyoto 077098
Goldenbogen, Dr. Sigrud, Dresden . 133876
Goldenes Dachl-Maximilianeum, Innsbruck 002082
Goldenflow Studios, Minneapolis . . 117263
Goldenlands Gallery, Saint Louis . . 119208
Golder Halm, Locarno 111652
Goldesberry, Nancy & Oliver, Houston 116324
Goldfield, West Hollywood 120384
Goldfield Gallery, Portsmouth 114282
Goldfields Aboriginal Art Gallery, Kalgoorlie 094673
Goldfields Arts Centre Gallery, Kalgoorlie 094674
Goldfinger, Lyon 064137
The Goldfish Bowl, Penzance 114232
Goldhorn, M., Groningen 078416
Goldie, Sandra, Montréal 097034
The Goldie Paley Gallery, Moore College of Art and Design, Philadelphia 046946
Golding Young & Co., Grantham . . . 122523
Goldman, Judy Ann, Boston 115178
Goldman, Mary, Los Angeles 116783
Goldmark, Uppingham . . . 114627, 142135
Goldmarkgedenkhaus Deutschkreutz, Deutschkreutz 001778
Gold'n Time, Washington 093416
Goldrach, Alain, New York 132475
Goldsboro Art Center School, Goldsboro 051394
Goldschmidt & Josch, Essen 102681
Goldsmith, Lenham 113380
Goldsmith, Oundle 122644
Goldsmith, Brion, London 096953
Goldsmiths' Hall, London 040155
Goldstein, Houston 116325
The Goldstein Museum of Design, Saint Paul 047697

Goldstream Region Museum, Victoria 006741
Goldthorpe, P., Peasmarsh 114220
Goldtsimmer, Patrice, Nice 124514
Goldwasser, Bernardo, Rio de Janeiro 058591
Goldwasser, Thomas A., San Francisco 142947
Goldwasser & Wilkinson, San Francisco 142948
Goldwater, Auckland 108324
Golem, Denver 116009
Golemoto Staklo, Skopje 135988
Golestan Palace Museum, Teheran . 022617
Golf Antiques, Listowel 074990
Golf Australia House, Melbourne . . 001239
Golf Museum, Far Hills 043810
Golf Museum, Newport News 046469
Golfiana Gallery, London 141808
Golfmuseum, Regensburg 019751
Goliad State Historical Park, Goliad 044242
Goliard, Paul, Espinasse-Vozelle . . .062803, 124234
Goll, Karl H., Zwingenberg, Bergstraße 074584
Gollasch, Werner, Berlin 069618
Goller, E., Frensdorf 070876
Gollnast, Peter, Halle, Saale 103067
Gollner, Christel, Bayreuth 101746
Gollnhuber, Max, Großraming 057046, 123374
Gollong, Frédéric, Saint-Paul-de-Vence 101208
Gollwitzer, Thomas, Landsberg am Lech 072137
Golmard, Dijon 062660
Gołogórski, M., Kraków 108954
Golombeck, Dirk, Petershagen, Weser 073309
Las Golondrinas, Genève . 082433, 111470
Golos, Moskva 134877
Golovanoff, Paris 066013
Het Gols-Station, Winterswijk 030341
Goltz, Bettina von der, Hannover . . . 125871
Goltz, Hans, München 139508
Golubaja Gostinnaja, Sankt-Peterburg 109629
Goluc, Chicago 115437
Golyester, Los Angeles 089780
Goma Laca, Granada 129526
Gomara, Magda de, Madrid 129625
Gomart, México 077573
Gombert, André, Le Blanc-Mesnil . . 063572
Gombert, André, Paris 066014
Gomboc, Ron & Terrie, Middle Swan 094842
Gomensoro, Montevideo 122782
Gomér, Jan, Linköping 122192
Gomér & Andersson, Linköping . . . 122193
Gomersbach, Ellen, Zeist 078867
Dias Gomes, Lisboa 079939
Gomes, Armando Fernandes, Lisboa 129155
Gomes, Hebert, Rio de Janeiro 058592
Gomes, N.V., Porto Alegre 058502
Gomez, Baltimore 115056
Gómez, Bucaramanga 098216
Gomez, Tarragona 081623
Gómez, Cecilia, Bogotá 098165
Gómez, Clara de, Bogotá 098166
Gomez, Emilio, Donostia-San Sebastián 081081
Gomez, Felix, Sevilla 110770
Gómez, Isabel, Madrid 129626
Gomez, Manuel, Perpignan 124838
Gómez, Marco Isaac, Bogotá 123901
Gomez, Victor, Miami 117082
Gómez Benito, Carmelo, Valladolid .081692, 141085
Gomez Costa, Begoña, Madrid 110535
Gomez de Leon, Ernesto Nuñez, Barcelona 080858
Gomez Foundation for Mill House, Marlboro 045691
Gomez Gil, Eduardo Jose, Estepona 081098
Gomez Rodrigo, Jose Maria, Madrid 110536
Gomez Salcedo, Alejandro, Palma de Mallorca 110686
Gomez Turu, Barcelona 080859
Gomez Turu, Josep, Barcelona 110196
Gómez Weiss, La Plata 055273
Gomiti, Nicoló, Firenze 075354
Gomollon Tobajas, Manuel, Zaragoza 110882
Gomringer, B., Mertingen 072524
Gomshall Gallery, Gomshall 039602
Goncalves, Joao, Joué-lès-Tours . . 063257
Gonçalves, João, Porto 129194
Gonçalves, José Pereira, Amadora . 079804
Goncalves, Lobo Joao, Joué-lès-Tours 063258
La Gondolina, Venezia 076943
Gone West Books, Auckland 140591
Gongju Folk Drama Museum, Gongju 027496
Gongju National Museum, Gongju . . 027497
Gongpyeong Art Center, Seoul 027556
Gongsan, Daegu 107184
Gongwangfu Art Cooperative, Beijing 097655
Gonias Monastery, Kolymvari 021332
Gonin, Françoise, Lausanne 135033
Gonin-Flambois, Jean-Philippe, Sainte-Geneviève 068061
Gonnelli, Firenze 075355
Gonnet, Christian, Paris 066015
Gonod, Jean-Bernard, Aurillac 061078
Gonon, Nicole, La Chapelle-de-Guinchay 063312
Gonser, Gero, Münster 072908
Gonsior, S., Hanau 071371
Gontier, Christophe, Saint-Sébastien-sur-Loire 068004
Gonzales Memorial Museum, Gonzales 044244
González, Pamplona 081520
Gonzalez, Rio de Janeiro 096616
González, Cecilia, Lima 108810
Gonzalez, Christopher, Runaway Bay 106833
Gonzalez, Elvira, Madrid 110537
Gonzalez, Jacqueline, Toulouse . . . 068518
Gonzalez, Julio, Valencia 110829
Gonzalez, Maria Pilar, Bilbao 129434
González Angel, Fabiola, Cali 098235
Gonzalez Berlanga, Rodolfo, Madrid 129627
Gonzalez Borjas, Jose Ramon, Sevilla 129731
Gonzalez de la Peña, Beatriz Zamora, Sevilla 129732
Gonzalez Garcia, Ricardo, Getxo . . . 081116
Gonzalez Gonzalez, Miguel Angel, Lleida 110405
Gonzalez Gonzalez, Miguel Angel, Lleida 110406
Gonzalez Rial, Victor, A Coruña 081060
Gonzalo Aurtenechea Urbina, Madrid 081317
Gonzen-Museum, Sargans 037508
Goochland County Museum, Goochland 044245
Good, Daniel, Luzern 141275
Good, Martha, Brisbane 055558
Good, Robert J., Saint Louis 132748
Good, Bad and Ugly, Sacramento . . 092161
Good Day Antiques, Rowlands Castle 086411, 131429
Good Earth Antiques, Buffalo 087879
Good Earth Gallery, Philadelphia . . . 118771
Good Hope Antiques, Beaminster . .083463, 130358
Good Neighbor Thrift Store, Long Beach 089635
Good Old Days, Chicago 088098
Good Old Days, København 060332
Good Old Things, New York 090912
The Good Old Times, Almelo 077724
Good Olde Days, Ockbrook 086153
Good Reading, Benalla 136799
Good Stuff, Albuquerque 087394
Good Stuff, Oklahoma City 091499
The Good, the Bad and the Ugly, Margate 056162
The Good, the Bad and the Ugly, Oakland 091420
Goodacre Engraving, Sutton Bonington 086796
Goodall, Richard, Manchester 114044
Gooday, Debbie, Richmond, Surrey . 086352
Goodbreys, Framlingham 084433
Goodchild, Dallas 088522, 132010
Goode & Co., Thomas, London 085338, 131046
Goodenow, Steve, Honolulu 088950
Goodhue County Historical Society Museum, Red Wing 047355
Goodlad, Anthony D., Chesterfield . 083966
Goodman, Sydney 120642
Goodman, James, New York 117968
Goodman, Marc, Cleveland 088330
Goodman, Marian, New York 117969, 135431
Goodman, Marian, Paris 100470
Goodman Museum, Tyler 048679
Goodnow Museum, Manhattan 045627
The Goods, Brisbane 055559
Goods and Chattels, Mount Gambier 056283
Goods and Chattels, Woolloongabba 056885
Goodsoil Historical Museum, Goodsoil 005520
Goodstuff Consignments, Richmond 092079
Goodwater Gallery, Toronto 097280
Goodwill, Seattle 142989
Goodwin, Edinburgh 084293
Goodwin, Edinburgh 084294
Goodwin & Sons, John, Warwick . .087039, 131652
Goodwin, Loretta, Birmingham 115109
Goodwin, Pamela, Tunbridge Wells . 086938
Goodwood House, Chichester 039070
Goodwood House Antiques, Burswood 055592
Goody, Virginia Beach 093356
Goodyer, Nicholas, London 141809
Goois Museum, Hilversum 029748
Goold Catholic Museum, East Melbourne 001001
Goole Museum and Art Gallery, Goole 039603
Goolen, Wilfried, Aurillac 120911
Goolwa National Trust Museum, Goolwa 001069
Goomeri Antiques, Goomeri 055898
Gooran, Mülheim an der Ruhr 072611
Gooran, Mülheim an der Ruhr 072612
Goors Historisch Museum, Goor . . . 029618
Goose Gallery, Milton on Stour 114085
Goosens, Wilfried, Mechelen 058335
Goosmann, Bad Bergzabern 101629
Goossens, D.&H., Bruxelles 096208, 123595
Goppelt & Lell, Karlsruhe 126000
Àgora, Barcelona 129349
Goralski & Mende, Dresden 070316
Goralsky, Reichstett 101068
Gora's House of Antiques, Ottawa . 059039
Gorba, Therese, Bad Neuenahr-Ahrweiler 101681
Gorcums Museum, Gorinchem 029620
Gordin & Assoc, Victor, Toronto 059199
Gordion Müzesi, Polatlı 038162
Gordon, Geelong 094577
Gordon, Conni, Miami Beach 135394
Gordon, J., Köln 071943
Gordon, Leah, New York 090913
Gordon, Robert, London 085339
Gordon, Roy, Fort Worth 116144
Gordon, Victor, Philadelphia 091640, 123045
Gordon Brown Collection, Ravenshead 040800
Gordon Gallery, Tel Aviv 105919
Gordon Highlanders Museum, Aberdeen 038446
Gordon Museum, London 040156
Gordon Snelgrove Art Gallery, Saskatoon 006417
Gordon's Antiques, Waikato 079289
Gordon's Discoveries, North Perth . 056369
Gore Airforce Museum, Gore 030504
Gore Historical Museum and Hokonui Heritage Research Centre, Gore . . 030505
Gore Place, Waltham 048846
Gorenjski Muzej Kranj, Kranj 034473
Gorepani, Albany 094125
Gorgan Museum, Gorgan 022555
Gorgas House, University of Alabama, Tuscaloosa 048663
Gorge Road Gallery, Dunedin 108435
Gorgi, Mahrajène 112249
Gorgon, New Orleans 117447
La Gorgona, Trieste 128373
Gori Antichitá, Padova 076092
Goriški Muzej, Nova Gorica 034508
Gorky, Paris 066016
Gorlik, Joachim, Kempten 071790
Gorman House Arts Centre, Braddon 000828
Gormleys', Belfast 112613
Gorney, Bravin & Lee, New York . . . 117970
Górnośląski Park Etnograficzny, Chorzów 031874
Gorny & Mosch, Giessener Münzhandlung, München 072714, 121526
Gornyj Muzej, Sankt-Peterburg 033742
Gorodeckij Kraevedčeskij Muzej, Gorodec 033153
Gorodskoj Kraevedčeskij Muzej, Elec 033135
Gorodskoj Muzej Boevoj Slavy, Kaluga 033220
Gorodskoj Muzej Iskusstvo Omska, Omsk 033598
Gorodskoj Muzej Teatralnogo Iskusstva, Omsk 033599
Gorodskoj Vystavočnyj Zal, Petrozavodsk 033659
Gorostarzu, Marie-Odile de, Noailles 065203
Gorring, Tunbridge Wells 142124
Gorring, Tunbridge Wells 142125
Gorringe, Bexhill-on-Sea 122410
Gorringe, Lewes 122566
Gorringe, Lewes 122567
Gorringe, Worthing 122763
Gorringes, Tunbridge Wells 122730
Gorrotxategi Konfiteri Museoa, Tolosa 035929
Gorry, James A., Dublin . . 105866, 127096
Gorry, P.T., Moruya 137007
Gorsium Szabadtéri Múzeum, Székesfehérvár 021868
Gorvitz, Christian, Neuilly-sur-Seine 064992
Goschenhoppen Folklife Museum, Green Lane 044312
Goschler, Salzburg 057249
Gosford Books, Coventry 141541
Gosford Regional Gallery and Arts Centre, Gosford 001073
Goshen Historical Society Museum, Goshen 044251
Goslar, Michele, Bruxelles 057970
Goslarer Münzfreunde e.V., Goslar . 053221
Goslarer Museum, Goslar 017481
Goslarer Zinnfiguren-Museum, Goslar 017482
Goslett, Roland, Richmond, Surrey .086353, 114309, 131414
Gosling, Jenny, Upper Woolhampton 142132
Gospel Music Hall of Fame and Museum, Detroit 043449
Gospodinov, G., Montana 096704
Gosport Museum, Gosport 039608
Goss and Crested China Centre, Horndean 039768
Goss and Crested China Centre, Horndean 136220
Goss and Crested China Centre, Waterlooville 087054
Gossart, Antoine, Paris 066017
Gossens, Thomas, Kevelaer 126034

Gossieaux, Martine, Paris 100471
Gossipgate Gallery, Alston 112501
Gossot, Renée, Dijon 062661
Gost, Jaime, Palma de Mallorca . . . 081482
Goston, Sergio C. A., Rio de Janeiro 096617
Gosudarstevnnyj Istoriko-architekturnyj i Chudožestvennyj Muzej-zapovednik Drevnij Derbent, Derbent 033099
Gosudarstvennaja Kollekcija Unikalnych Muzykalnych Instrumentov, Moskva 033390
Gosudarstvennaja Tretjakovskaja Galerja, Moskva 033391
Gosudarstvennaja Tretjakovskaja Galerja na Krymskom Valu, Moskva 033392
Gosudarstvennyj Biologičeskij Muzej im. K.A. Timirjazeva, Moskva 033393
Gosudarstvennyj Borodinskij Voenno-istoričeskij Muzej-zapovednik, Borodino 033044
Gosudarstvennyj Centralnyj Muzej Musykal'noj Kultury im. M.I. Glinki, Moskva 033394
Gosudarstvennyj Centralnyj Muzej Sovremennoj Istorii Rossii, Moskva 033395
Gosudarstvennyj Centralnyj Teatralnyj Muzej im. Bachrušina, Moskva 033396
Gosudarstvennyj Chudožestvenno-architekturnyj Dvorcovo-parkovyj Muzej-zapovednik Oranienbaum, Lomonosov 033333
Gosudarstvennyj Chudožestvenno-architekturnyj Dvorcovo-parkovyj Muzej-zapovednik Pavlovsk, Pavlovsk . . 033630
Gosudarstvennyj Chudožestvennyj Istoriko-architekturnyj i prirodno-landšaftnyj Muzej-zapovednik Kolomenskoe, Moskva 033397
Gosudarstvennyj Chudožestvennyj Muzej Altajskogo Kraja, Barnaul 033015
Gosudarstvennyj Dom-muzej P.I. Čajkovskogo, Klin 033277
Gosudarstvennyj Ėrmitaž, Sankt-Peterburg 033743
Gosudarstvennyj Geologičeskij Muzej im V.I. Vernadskogo, Moskva 033398
Gosudarstvennyj Istoričeskij Muzej, Moskva 033399
Gosudarstvennyj Istoričeskij Zapovednik Gorki Leninskie, Gorki Leninskie . 033151
Gosudarstvennyj Istoriko-architekturnyj, Chudožestvennyj i Landšaftnyj Muzej-Zapovednik Caricyno, Moskva . . . 033400
Gosudarstvennyj Istoriko-architekturnyj i Etnografičeskij Muzej-zapovednik Kiži, Kiži 033275
Gosudarstvennyj Istoriko-architekturnyj i Etnografičeskij Muzej-zapovednik Kiži, Petrozavodsk 033660
Gosudarstvennyj Istoriko-architekturnyj i Prirodno-landšaftnyj Muzej Zapovednik Izborsk, Izborsk 033178
Gosudarstvennyj Istoriko-Architekturnyj i Prirodnyj Muzej-Zapovednik Monrepo, Vyborg 034089
Gosudarstvennyj Istoriko-chudožestvennyj Dvorcovo-parkovyj Muzej-zapovednik Gatčina, Gatčina 033146
Gosudarstvennyj Istoriko-ėtnografičeskij i Architekturnyj Muzej-zapovednik Staraja Sarepta, Volgograd 034062
Gosudarstvennyj Istoriko-ėtnografičeskij Muzej-zapovednik Šušenskoe, Šušenskoe 033917
Gosudarstvennyj Istoriko-kulturnyj i Prirodnyj Muzej-zapovednik A.S. Griboedova - Chmelita, Chmelita . 033088
Gosudarstvennyj Istoriko-kulturnyj Muzej-zapovednik Moskovskij Kreml, Moskva 033401
Gosudarstvennyj Istoriko-literaturnyj i Prirodnyj Muzej-zapovednik A.A. Bloka, Solnečnogorsk 033892
Gosudarstvennyj Istoriko-literaturnyj Muzej-Zapovednik A.S. Puškina s usadbami Vjazemy i Zacharovo, Bolšie Vjazemy 033039
Gosudarstvennyj Istoriko-memorialnyj Sankt-Peterburgskij Muzej Smolnyj, Sankt-Peterburg 033744
Gosudarstvennyj Istoriko-memorialnyj Zapovednik Rodina V.I. Lenina, Uljanovsk 034004
Gosudarstvennyj Kraevedčeskij Muzej Karakalpakii, Nukus 049398
Gosudarstvennyj Literaturno-memorialnyj Muzej Anny Achmatovoj v Fontannom Dome, Sankt-Peterburg 033745
Gosudarstvennyj Literaturno-memorialnyj Muzej N.A. Dobroljubova, Nižnij Novgorod 033552
Gosudarstvennyj Literaturno-memorialnyj Muzej im. M.Ju. Lermontova, Pjatigorsk 033666
Gosudarstvennyj Literaturno-memorialnyj Muzej N. Ostrovskogo, Soči 033888
Gosudarstvennyj Literaturno-memorialnyj Muzej A.N. Radiščeva, Radiščevo 033691
Gosudarstvennyj Literaturno-memorialnyj Muzej-zapovednik A.P. Čechova, Melichovo 033354
Gosudarstvennyj Literaturno-memorialnyj Muzej-zapovednik N.A. Nekrasova Karabicha, Karabicha 033227
Gosudarstvennyj Literaturnyj Muzej, Moskva 033402
Gosudarstvennyj Literaturnyj Muzej A.M. Gorkogo, Nižnij Novgorod 033553
Gosudarstvennyj Literaturnyj Muzej im. I.S. Turgeneva, Orël 033608
Gosudarstvennyj Memorialnyj Dom-muzej Bulata Okudžavy, Peredelkino . . . 033643
Gosudarstvennyj Memorialnyj Dom-muzej N.A. Rimskogo-Korsakova, Tichvin 033947
Gosudarstvennyj Memorialnyj i Prirodnyj Muzej-zapovednik A.N. Ostrovskogo - Ščelykovo, Ščelykovo 033861
Gosudarstvennyj Memorialnyj i Prirodnyj Muzej-zapovednik I.S. Turgeneva 'Spasskoe Lutovinovo', Spasskoe-Lutovinovo 033898
Gosudarstvennyj Memorial'nyj Istoriko-chudožestvennyj i Prirodnyj Muzej-zapovednik V.D. Polenova, Strachovo 033914
Gosudarstvennyj Memorialnyj Muzej im. A.V. Suvorova, Sankt-Peterburg 033746
Gosudarstvennyj Memorialnyj Muzej Oborony i Blokady Leningrada, Sankt-Peterburg 033747
Gosudarstvennyj Memorialnyj Muzej-usadba V.G. Belinskogo, Literaturnyj muzej Penza, Belinskij 033022
Gosudarstvennyj Moskovskij Muzej Naivnogo Iskusstva, Moskva 033403
Gosudarstvennyj Muzej Detskich Teatrov, Moskva 033404
Gosudarstvennyj Muzej K.A. Fedina, Saratov 033854
Gosudarstvennyj Muzej Iskusstv, Taškent 049406
Gosudarstvennyj Muzej Iskusstv Respubliki Karakalpakstan, Nukus 049399
Gosudarstvennyj Muzej Istorii Aviacii, Sankt-Peterburg 033748
Gosudarstvennyj Muzej Istorii i Kultury Belarusa, Minsk 003133
Gosudarstvennyj Muzej Istorii Kosmonavtiki im. K.Ė. Ciolkovskogo, Kaluga . . . 033221
Gosudarstvennyj Muzej Istorii Kultury i Iskusstva Uzbekistana, Samarkand 049401
Gosudarstvennyj Muzej Istorii Religii, Sankt-Peterburg 033749
Gosudarstvennyj Muzej Istorii Sankt-Peterburga - Petropavlovskij Sobor, Sankt-Peterburg 033750
Gosudarstvennyj Muzej Izobrazitelnogo Iskusstva Rossijskogo Severa, Archangelskij oblastnoj muzej izobrazitelnych iskusstv, Archangelsk 032993
Gosudarstvennyj Muzej Izobrazitelnych Iskusstv Respubliki Kalmykija, Ėlista 033136
Gosudarstvennyj Muzej A.I. Kuprina, Narovčat 033546
Gosudarstvennyj Muzej V.V. Majakovskogo, Moskva 033405
Gosudarstvennyj Muzej-masterskaja Skulptora A.S. Golubkinoj, Moskva 033406
Gosudarstvennyj Muzej Narodnogo Obrazovanija Gruzii, Tbilisi 015409
Gosudarstvennyj Muzej Oborony Moskvy, Moskva 033407
Gosudarstvennyj Muzej Palechskogo Iskusstva, Palech 033627
Gosudarstvennyj Muzej-panorama Stalingradskaja Bitva, Volgograd . 034063
Gosudarstvennyj Muzej Političeskoj Istorii Rossii, Sankt-Peterburg 033751
Gosudarstvennyj Muzej A.S. Puškina, Moskva 033408
Gosudarstvennyj Muzej-Reservat Mangyšlaka Sokrovišča-Zapovedniki Mangyšlaka i Ustyrta, Ševčenko . 027412
Gosudarstvennyj Muzej-Reservat Pamjatniki Drevnego Taraza, Džambul 027400
Gosudarstvennyj Muzej Vadima Sidura, Moskva 033409
Gosudarstvennyj Muzej L.N. Tolstogo, Moskva 033410
Gosudarstvennyj Muzej L.N. Tolstogo, Moskva 033411
Gosudarstvennyj Muzej L.N. Tolstogo Jasnaja Poljana, Jasnaja Poljana (Tula) 033200
Gosudarstvennyj Muzej-usadba Archangelskoe, Archangelskoe . . 032997
Gosudarstvennyj Muzej-usadba P.I. Čajkovskogo, Votkinsk 034085
Gosudarstvennyj Muzej Velikoj Oktjabrskoj Socialističeskoj Revoljucii, Sankt-Peterburg 033751
Gosudarstvennyj Muzej-zapovednik S.A. Esenina, Konstantinovo 033281
Gosudarstvennyj Muzej Zapovednik Petergof, Sankt-Peterburg 033752
Gosudarstvennyj Muzej-zapovednik M.A. Šolochova, Vešenskaja 034031
Gosudarstvennyj Muzej Životnovodstva im Akademika E.F. Liskuna, Moskva . 033412
Gosudarstvennyj Nacionalnyj Muzej Ust-Ordynskogo Burjatskogo Avtonomnogo Okruga, Ust-Ordynsk 034020
Gosudarstvennyj Naučno-issledovatelskij Institut Restavracii, Moskva 129235
Gosudarstvennyj Naučno-issledovatelskij Muzej Architektury im. A.V. Ščuseva, Moskva 033413
Gosudarstvennyj Okružnoj Muzej Prirody i Čeloveka Goroda Chanty-Mansijsk, Chanty-Mansijsk 033087
Gosudarstvennyj Russkij Muzej, Sankt-Peterburg 033753
Gosudarstvennyj Russkij Muzej, Sankt-Peterburg 033754
Gosudarstvennyj Severnyj Morskoj Muzej, Archangelsk 032994
Gosudarstvennyj Vladimiro-Suzdalskij Istoriko-architekturnyj i Chudožestvennyj Muzej-zapovednik, Vladimir 034040
Gosudarstvennyj Voenno-istoričeskij i Prirodnyj Muzej-zapovednik Kulikovo Pole, Tula 033972
Gosudarstvennyj Voenno-istoričeskij Muzej-zapovednik Prochorovskoe Pole, Prochorovka 033673
Gosudarstvennyj Vystavočnyj Zal Zamoskvorec^Bie, Moskva 033414
Got, Frédéric, Barbizon 098921
Got Bears, Oklahoma City 091500
Got to Have It, Cleveland 088331
Gotay, Paul, Salt Lake City 119345
Gothaer Haus der Versicherungsgeschichte, Gotha 017490
Gothaer Kunstforum, Köln 018313
Gotham, New York 142656
Gotham Edicions, Valencia 110830, 134955
Gotham Scenic, New York 117971
Gothic City Collector's Cove, Buffalo 087880
Gothic Fine Arts Gallery, Woodford . 095412
Gothow & Motzke, Berlin 138780
Gothsland, Barcelona 080860, 110197
Gotico Restauraciones, Cáceres . . . 129471
Gotischer Freskenraum, Ostermiething 002403
Gotisches Haus, Kulturstiftung DessauWörlitz, Wörlitz 020944
Gotlands Fornsal med Fenomenalen, Visby 036796
Gotlands Konstmuseum, Visby 036797
Gotlands Naturmuseum, Visby 036798
Gotoh Bijutsukan, Tokyo 027170
Gotta Have Art, Birmingham 115110
Gotta Have It, New York . . 090914, 142657
Gottfried, Esslingen 139061
Gottfried, Schwäbisch Hall 104854
Gottfried, Annemarie, Biedenkopf . . 102108
Gottfried, Birgit, München 104213
Gottfried, G. & A., Kühlungsborn . . . 072102
Gottfried, Walter, Schwerin 139723
Gottfried-August-Bürger-Museum, Molmerswende 018990
Gottfried-Keller-Zentrum, Glattfelden 037152
Gotthelf-Stube, Schriftsteller-Museum, Lützelflüh 037282
Gottlieb Daimler-Gedächtnisstätte, Stuttgart 020350
Gottlieb-Häußler-Heimatmuseum, Filderstadt 017119
Gottmer, Becht, Aramith, Haarlem . 134812
Gottschalch, Erik, København 060333
Gottschalk, Jürgen, Bernau bei Berlin 138868
Gottschalk, Traute, Würzburg 139871
Gottschick & Friedrich, Tübingen . . 105076
Gottsmann, Sandra, Mannheim . . . 126274
Gotty, Denis & Michèle, Agnetz 060672
Gotz, Alexander, London 113651
Goubault, Francis, Paris 124677
Goubert, Claire, Bordeaux 061616
Goudal, Claude, Lyon 099593
Goudard, Laurent, Limoges 063889
Goudemare, S., Paris 138391
De Gouden Eend, Leiden 108100
De Gouden Kroon, Alkmaar 077713
De Gouden Zon, Bergen, Noord-Holland 078064
't Goudmijntje, Breda 078092
't Goudmijntje, Breda 128605
Goudreau Museum of Mathematics in Art and Science, New Hyde Park 046235
Goudriaan, H.O., Haarlem 128689
Gouds Poppentheater en Museum, Gouda 029622
Gougis, Emmanuelle, Bercheres-les-Pierres 061352
Gougis, Emmanuelle, Chartres 062170
Gougis, Philippe, Saint-Denis-en-Val 067421
Gouin, Olivier, Saint-Palais-sur-Mer 067934
Gouin, Pascale, Nantes 064923
Goujon, Jacques, Paris 124678
Goulandris Collection, Athinai 021172
Goulburn Regional Art Gallery, Goulburn 001076
Gould, Newtown, New South Wales 137032
Gould, South Yarra 095210
Gould, Gillian, London 085340
Gould, Hal D., Denver 116010
Gould & Co, Herbert, Holywood . . . 084711
Gould, John, Hawthorn, Victoria . . . 094625
Gould, Juliet, Saint Austell 114350
Gould, Richard, West Hollywood . . . 093471
Gould, Robert, Woollahra 056865
Gould & Gonnermann, London 085341, 131047
Gould Street Art Gallery, Bondi Beach 094264
Goulet, Danièle, Nice 065091
Goulet & de Cazes, Montréal 058959
Goulignac, Agnès, Bordeaux 061617
Gouma, Maria, Nafplion 105434
Goumain, Francis, L'Isle-d'Espagnac 063909
Gounaropoulos Museum of Zografou, Zografou 021534
Goupil, Catherine, Marseille 124419

Goupil, Jacques, Alençon 098812
Gour Nitai, Singapore 080472
Gouriotis Collection, Lárissa 021354
Gourtorbe, Daniel, Miribel 064568
Gous, Julian, Johannesburg 129294
Le Gousset, Durmenach 062755
Gousset, Saint-Étienne . . . 067455, 124898
Gout, Alain, Varagéville 125008
Goutis, Athinai 074593
Gouverneur Historical Association Museum, Gouverneur 044254
Het Gouverneurshuis, Heusden . . . 029743
Gouw, J.ter, Amsterdam 140301
Govan and District Museum, Govan 005524
Govary'S, Barcelona 080861, 110198
Governale, Antonello, Palermo 076152
Governale, Antonello, Palermo 076153
Government Art Collection, London 040157
Government Arts College, Rajahmundry 050324
Government Arts College, Srikakulam 050326
Government Central Museum, Jaipur, Rajasthan 022178
Government College of Art, Chandigarh 050295
Government College of Art and Craft, Kolkata 050311
Government College of Arts and Crafts, Chennai 050296
Government College of Fine Arts, Gwalior 050303
Government Educational Museum, Bulandshahar 022046
Government Educational Museum, Deoria 022100
Government Educational Museum, Etawah 022112
Government House, Sydney 001510
Government House, Winchcombe . . 087168
Government House Museum and Heritage Property, Regina 006255
Government Industrial and Commercial Museum, Kolkata 022218
Government J.T.C. Museum, Faizabad 022115
Government Museum, Ajmer 021996
Government Museum, Alwar 022005
Government Museum, Bharatpur . . 022026
Government Museum, Chennai . . . 022057
Government Museum, Hassan 022151
Government Museum, Jodhpur . . . 022190
Government Museum, Kodagu 022208
Government Museum, Mathura . . . 022255
Government Museum, Mount Abu . 022259
Government Museum, Pudukottai . . 022301
Government Museum, Thiruvananthapuram 022351
Government Museum, Udaipur 022360
Government Museum and Art Gallery, Chandigarh 022051
Government Museum Jhalawar, Jhalawar 022187
Government Museum Vellore, Vellore 022375
Governmental Educational Museum, Muzaffarnagar 022273
Governor Bent Museum, Taos 048496
Governor General's Foot Guards Regimental Museum, Ottawa 006101
Governor Henry Lippitt House Museum, Providence 047255
Governor John Langdon House, Portsmouth 047185
Governor Printz Park, Essington . . . 043735
Governor Ross Plantation, Seaford . 048069
Governor Seay Mansion, Kingfisher 045007
Governor Stephen Hopkins House, Providence 047256
Governor's Gallery, Santa Fe 047965
Governor's Mansion, Columbia 043079
Governor's Mansion, Sacramento . . 047590
Govetosa, Boranga, Padova 076093
Govett-Brewster Art Gallery, New Plymouth 030551
Govi, Alberto, Modena 140072
Govinda, Washington 120303
Govoni, Franco, Bologna 127153
Govreau, Fresno 116177
Gow, Jeremy, Forfar 084426, 130713
Gow Langsford, Auckland 108325
Gow Langsford, Sydney 095290
Gowan, Bud, London 058882
Gowans, Moonah 120613
Gowen, Albuquerque 114791
Gower, Tom, Saint Ives, Cornwall . . 114364
Gower Heritage Centre, Gower 039615
Gowganda and Area Museum, Gowganda 005525
Gowrie, Woollahra 095426
Goy, Renate, Chemnitz 070129
Goya, Madrid 136089
Goya Galleries, Docklands 094478
Goya Galleries, Melbourne 094815
Goya-Girl Press, Baltimore 115057, 135324
Goya Sanat Galerisi, İstanbul 112319
Goyas, Bogotá 098167
Goyert, Köln 103633, 139340
Goyet, Amaury, Paris 066018
Gozi, Stefano, Berlin 069619
Gozo Antiques, Victoria 077544
Gozo Cathedral Museum, Victoria . . 028041
Gozzini, O., Firenze 140019
GP Antiguedades, Guadalajara 077565
G.P.F. Gallery, Newport, Gwent 114135
GPM, Zlonice 060203
Gr 20, Padova 106403
Graaf, de, Nieuwkoop 140504
Graaf-Reinet Museum, Graaff-Reinet 034618
Graaff, R.J. de, Haarlem 128690
Graaham, Barry Joseph, Palma de Mallorca 110687
Graal, Agen 098770
Graal, Moissac 099728
du Graal, Paris 138392
Grabados, Madrid 081318
Grabados y Libros, Madrid 141042
Grabe, Dirk, Düsseldorf 070388
Grabenheinrich, Horst, Gütersloh . . 103033
Graber, Minneapolis 117264
Graber, San Diego 092643
Grabherr, Rosita Ina, Wien 057432
Grabherr-Häfliger, Walter, Lüchingen 082587
Grabinski-Waldeck, Grenoble 063065
Grabkapelle Württemberg, Stuttgart 020351
Grabnegger, Karin, Klagenfurt 057107
Grabner, Ernst, Gmunden 056992
Grabner, Franz, Salzburg 057250
Gråbo Minnenas Museum, Karlskoga 036378
Grabocenter, Antofagasta 059475
Grabow, Ludwig, Berlin 069620
Grabungsmuseum, Langenburg . . . 018504
Grabungsmuseum Kirchhof, Coburg 016575
Grace, El Paso 132065
Grace, Kyoto 077099
Grace & Co., San Francisco 092803
Grace, Sendai 106997
Grace, Ross Nelson, Armadale, Victoria 055377
Grace Campbell Gallery, Prince Albert 006202
Grace Darling Museum, Bamburgh . 038583
Grace Future Heirlooms, New Farm 123277
Grace Hudson Museum and The Sun House, Ukiah 048683
Grace Museum, Abilene 041567
Grace Place, Memphis 090074
Gracefield Arts Centre, Dumfries . . 039297
Graceful Spirit Showcase, Portland . 091948
Graceland, Memphis 045760
Graceys, South Auckland 079241
Gracia de Castro, Pilar, Donostia-San Sebastián 129505
Gracían Prado, C., Santiago de Chile 059532
Graciano, Joseph, Le Havre 063633
Gracie Handpainted Wallpapers, New York 090915
Gracie Mansion, New York 046339
Gracieuse Orient, Montreuil-sous-Bois 064768
Grácio, Rio de Janeiro 096618
Gracis, P.G., Milano 075732
Gracz, Duda, Częstochowa 108866
Gradl & Hinterland, Nürnberg 121564
Gradsign, Singapore 050682
Gradska Chudožestvena Galerija, Berkovica 004636
Gradska Chudožestvena Galerija, Plovdiv 004792
Gradska Chudožestvena Galerija Petko Čurčuliev, Dimitrovgrad 004665
Gradski Archeologičeski Muzej, Chisar 004657
Gradski Archeologičeski Muzej, Nesebăr 004757
Gradski Archeologičeski Muzej, Sandanski 004825
Gradski Istoričeski Muzej, Asenovgrad 004619
Gradski Istoričeski Muzej, Balčik . . 004626
Gradski Istoričeski Muzej, Botevgrad 004642
Gradski Istoričeski Muzej, Čirpan . . 004660
Gradski Istoričeski Muzej, Dalgopol 004662
Gradski Istoričeski Muzej, Jeravna . 004698
Gradski Istoričeski Muzej, Karnobat 004707
Gradski Istoričeski Muzej, Kavarna . 004711
Gradski Istoričeski Muzej, Klisura . . 004726
Gradski Istoričeski Muzej, Lom 004741
Gradski Istoričeski Muzej, Melnik . . 004749
Gradski Istoričeski Muzej, Nova Zagora 004759
Gradski Istoričeski Muzej, Orjachovo 004764
Gradski Istoričeski Muzej, Panagjurište 004765
Gradski Istoričeski Muzej, Peruštica 004775
Gradski Istoričeski Muzej, Samakov 004824
Gradski Istoričeski Muzej, Sevlievo . 004827
Gradski Istoričeski Muzej, Sozopol . 004881
Gradski Istoričeski Muzej, Teteven . 004901
Gradski Istoričeski Muzej Aleko Konstantinov, Svištov 004896
Gradski Istoričeski Muzej Iskra, Kazanlăk 004715
Gradski Muzej, Bjelovar 007700
Gradski Muzej, Foča 034191
Gradski Muzej, Kosovska Mitrovica 034200
Gradski Muzej, Križevci 007749
Gradski Muzej, Požega 007775
Gradski Muzej, Muzej Grada Novog Sada, Sremski Karlovci 034268
Gradski Muzej i Galerija, Bečej 034144
Gradski Muzej Karlovac, Karlovac . . 007732
Gradski Muzej Makarska, Makarska 007755
Gradski Muzej Siska, Sisak 007795
Gradski Muzej Sombor, Sombor . . . 034263
Gradski Muzej Varaždin, Varaždin . . 007816
Gradski Muzej - Városi Muzeum, Subotica 034271
Gradski Muzej Virovitica, Virovitica . 007820
Gradski Muzej Vršac, Vršac 034281
Graduate Program in Art History, Rutgers State University of New Jersey, New Brunswick 051785
Graduate School of Architecture, Columbia University, New York 051822
Graduate School of Figurative Art, New York Academy of Art, New York 051823
Graduate School of Fine Arts, University of Pennsylvania, Philadelphia 051942
Grady, Stewart, Philadelphia 132619
Graeber, Klaus, Wuppertal 121631
Graef, Thomas, Saarbrücken 073631, 104795
Graefe, Lüneburg 103977
Gräfe, K., Dessau, Anhalt 070221
Gräff, A., Karlsruhe 103492
Gräff, Margot, Bad Kreuznach 069315
Gräfliche Sammlungen und Afrikanisches Jagdmuseum, Erbach, Odenwald . 017001
Grähn, Wolfgang, Hamburg 125816
Grähn, Wolfgang, Hamburg 125817
Graeme Park/Keith Mansion, Horsham 044626
Grängesbergsbanornas Järnvägsmuseum, Grängesberg 036310
Grässlin, Bärbel, Frankfurt am Main 102778
Graetz, Frédéric, Liège 137517
Graf, Kandern 071700
Graf, Norderstedt 073072
Graf, Beate, Emmersdorf an der Donau 056972
Graf, Bruno, Hombrechtikon 111557
Graf, Dr. Henriette, München 072715
Graf, Dr. Henriette, Riemerling 073533
Graf, Peter, Pfäffikon (Zürich) 082726
Graf, René, Halle, Saale 103068
Graf, Uwe, Regensburg 126688
Graf, W., Minden, Westfalen 139478
Graf, W., Minden, Westfalen 139479
Graf Harrach'sche Familiensammlung, Rohrau 002535
Graf-Luxburg-Museum, Museen Schloss Aschach, Bad Bocklet 015670
Graf Numismatique, La Rochelle . . 063431
Graf-Pauli, A., Wolfratshausen 074477
Graf & Schelble, Basel 111190
De Grafelijke Torenmolen, Zeddam . 030375
Grafen, Frank, Gevelsberg 070985
von Grafenstein, München 104214
Grafenwald, Hans, Borken, Westfalen 069955
Grafer, Wolf-Dieter, Leutenbach . . . 072238
Graff, Braunschweig 138922
Graff, Montréal 097035, 133318
Graff, A., Charleroi 058148
Graffan, Roger, Ollioules 138268
Graffiti, Verona 077005
Graffiti Bildergalerie, Duisburg 102580
Graffiti Edition, Wien 133203
Graffiti Gallery, Winnipeg 097587
Grafic & Arts, Frankfurt am Main . . 102779
Grafic & Arts, Hamminkeln 103248
Grafic Encadrement, Niort 099873
Grafica, Saint Louis 119209
Grafica Antica, Venezia 106755
Grafica e Arte, Bergamo 134544
Grafica Internazionale, Torino 134693
Grafica Manzoni, Torino 106681
Grafica Portugal, Luanda 094052
Gráficas Estella, Estella 134931
Graficas Santamaria, Vitoria-Gasteiz 134956
Grafička Zbirka Nacionalne i Sveučilišne Knjižnice, Zagreb 007837
Grafički Zavod Hrvatske, Zagreb . . . 133403
Grafiekwinkel Inkt, Den Haag 107922
Grafik-Cabinet Artis, Zell am See . .057610, 137388
Grafik-Design Austria, Wien 133204
Grafik I Väst, Göteborg 110921
Grafik Museum Stiftung Schreiner, Bad Steben 015809
Grafik und Kommunikations-Design, Höhere Lehranstalt für Grafik-Design, Innsbruck 049630
Grafik Verlag, Frankfurt am Main . . 133944
Grafika, Kraków 079638, 140736
Grafika Publishing, Praha 133415
Grafikens Hus, Mariefred 036466
Grafikk Senteret, Oslo 108728
Grafikmuseum, Korsberga 036398
Grafikwerkstatt Dresden in den Technischen Sammlungen, Dresden . 102442, 133877
Grafioteket, Stockholm 111050
Grafisch Atelier Twente, Enschede . 078371
Grafisch Historisch Centrum - Drukkerijmuseum, Etten Leur . . . 029582
Grafisch Musem-Atelier in den Groenen Zonck, Wouw 030355
Grafisch Museum Groningen, Groningen 029637
Grafisch Museum Zutphen, Zutphen 030403
Grafische Sammlung, Museen der Stadt Nürnberg, Nürnberg 019354

Grafisk Skole, Kongelige Danske Kunstakademi, København 049900
Grafiska Institutet, Stockholms Universitet, Stockholm 050749
Grafiska Sällskapet, Stockholm . . . 111051
Den Grafiske Højskole, København . 049901
Grafiti, Gdynia 108913
Grafix, Washington 120304
Grafo, Brescia 134560
Grafos Verlag, Vaduz 134742
Grafschafter, Ohne 073196
Grafschafter Museum im Moerser Schloß, Moers 018982
Grafschaftsmuseum, Wertheim . . . 020819
Grafstein, James, New York 090916
Grafström, Roland, Stockholm 111052
Grafton Galleries, Double Bay 055756
Grafton Museum, Grafton 044256
Grafton Museum of Natural History, Grafton 044257
Grafton Regional Gallery, Grafton . . 001078
Graftons, Market Harborough 085938, 114059
Graglia, Michel, Dijon 062662
Graglia, Michel, Dijon 062663
Graha, Jakarta 105838
Graham, Burghfield Common 130483
Graham, Kembla Heights 094686
Graham, London 085342
Graham, London 113652
Graham, Memphis 090075
Graham, Arthur, Oklahoma City . . . 091501
Graham, Charlton, Nicholls 094964
Graham, Gavin, London . . 085343, 113653
Graham & Sons, James, New York . 117972
Graham, Joss, London 085344
Graham, Neil, Brentwood . 083660, 130434
Graham, Timothy, Twickenham . . . 114617
Graham County Historical Museum, Safford 047600
Graham Gallery, Burghfield Common 112759
Graham & Green, London 085345
Graham-Stewart, M.J., London . . . 113654
Grahame, Milton 094854
Grahame, H.J.O., Westzaan 128882
Grahams of Colchester, Colchester .084056, 130599
Grahn, Minneapolis 132381
Grahn, Patrik, Espoo 060491
Grahn, Volker, Tabarz 105029
Grainbag, Pittsburgh 118926
Graindorge, Sées 068188
Graindorge, Jacky, Sées 068189
Grainger Museum, Parkville, Victoria 001369
Grains Industry Museum, Cabanatuan 031643
Grais, Valérie, Paris 124679
Gramentz, Harms, Putlitz 073388
Grammatopoulou, Yianna, Athinai . . 105397
Grammdorf, Johanna, Aichstetten . 069124
Grammelsbacher, Jochen, Augsburg 069227
Grammes, Beatrix, Frankenthal, Pfalz 102737
Grammophonmuseum, Bad Urach . 015815
Gramolla, Bodo, Essen 102682
Gramophone Records Museum, Cape Coast 021102
The Gramophone Shop, Haarlem . . 078456
Grampian Police Museum, Aberdeen 038447
Grampian Transport Museum, Alford, Aberdeenshire 038482
Grampy, Omaha 091569
Grams, Brita, München 126382
Gramsch, Koblenz 103568
Gramse, K., Köln 071944
Gramzower Heimatstuben, Gramzow 017510
Gran Antique, Don Torcuato 055266
Gran Cala, Barcelona 080862
Gran Mercato dei Mercati di Collezionismo e Antichità, Baganzola 093765
Gran Mercato del'Antico Internazionale, Modena 093766
La Gran Ocasion, Palma de Mallorca 081483
La Gran Ocasion, Palma de Mallorca 081484
Gran Turismo, Wolfenbüttel 105319
Graña Lagoa, Francisco, Vigo 081704, 129792
Granary Collectables, Kendal 084826
Granby Gallery, Bakewell 112537
Grance, Eloïc, Lorette 063997
Grancher, Jacques, Paris 133616
Grand Antique Mall, Cincinnati 088245
Grand Army of the Republic Civil War Museum, Philadelphia 046947
Grand Army of the Republic Memorial and Veteran's Military Museum, Aurora 041912
Grand Art, Kyïv 112408
Grand Art Gallery, Singapore 109802
Grand Arts, Kansas City 116567
Grand Auction Mart, New York 122996
Grand Canyon National Park Museum Collection, Grand Canyon 044259
Grand Central, Montréal 058960
Grand Central Auction, San Francisco 123105
Grand Central Gallery, Boston 115179
Grand Central Station Antiques, San Francisco 092804
Grand Coteau Heritage and Cultural Centre, Shaunavon 006448
Grand County Museum, Hot Sulphur Springs 044631
Grand Encampment Museum, Encampment 043707
Grand Entrances, Sans Souci 056574
Grand Falls Museum, Grand Falls . . 005530
Grand Forks Art Gallery, Grand Forks 005534
Grand Forks County Historical Society Museum, Grand Forks 044260
Grand Gallery, Kansas City 116568
Grand Gulf Military State Park Museum, Port Gibson 047130
Grand Hill Gallery, Saint Paul 119292
Grand Image, Seattle 119929
Grand Island Trader's Cabin, Munising 046088
Grand Lake Area Historical Museum, Grand Lake 044269
The Grand Lodge of Scotland Museum, Edinburgh 039393
Le Grand Magasin, Saint-Rémy-de-Provence 101230
Grand Manan Museum, Grand Manan 005536
Grand Marais Art Colony, Grand Marais 051401
Grand Monde, Paris 124680
Grand Mound History Center, International Falls 044759
Grand Oriental Rugs, Saint Paul . . . 092364
Grand Portage, Grand Marais 044271
Grand Prairie Arts Council, Stuttgart 054777
Grand-Pré National Historic Site of Canada, Grand-Pré 005538
Grand Prix Museum, Macau 007183
Grand Rapids Art Museum, Grand Rapids 044275
Grand Rapids Children's Museum, Grand Rapids 044276
Grand Rapids Kendall College of Art & Design, Ferris State University, Big Rapids 050982
Grand River Gallery, Hamilton 096919
Grand River Historical Society Museum, Chillicothe 042896
Grand Shaft, Dover 039276
The Grand Style Gallery, Baltimore . 115058
Grand Terminal Art Gallery, New York 117973
Grand View Fine Art Gallery, Cleveland 094404
Grand Village of the Natchez Indians, Natchez 046160
Grande Brocante, Besançon 093664
Grande Brocante, Dijon 062664
La Grande Fenêtre, Lyon 138151
La Grande Ile, Bruxelles 057971
Grande Museo, Fabriano 024061
Grande Prairie Museum, Grande Prairie 005539
Grande Victoria Gardens, Saint Paul 092365
Grandfather Clocks, Cincinnati 088246, 131936
Grandfather's Clock Gallery and Clinic, Tulsa 093307, 132997
Grandfather's Clockshop, Ballarat . 055430
Grandfather's Collections, Singapore 080473
Grandi Stazioni, Roma 106557
Grandi Stazioni, Roma 106558
Grandière Frères, Paris 124681
Grandin, Christian, Paris 121153
Grandmaître, Jean-Henri, Châtillon-sur-Marne 062235
Grandmaître, Jean-Henri, Dormans-en-Champagne 062719
Grandma's Attic, Saint Paul 092366
Grandma's Corner, Miami 090180
Grandma's Place, Tampa 093126
Grandma's Things, Jacksonville . . . 089416
Grandma's Top Drawer, Whyalla . . . 056821
Grandmont, Detroit 116087
Grandmother Treasures, Dallas . . . 088523
Grandoni, Carla, Roma 128066
Grandoni, Claudio, Roma 128067
Grandpa Snazzys Hardware, Denver 088693
Grandpa's Antiques, Miami 090181
Grandpa's Antiques, Sacramento . . 092162
Grandpa's Shed, Fitzroy Falls 055826
Les Grands Papiers, Paris 100472
Grandview Antiques, Columbus . . . 088414
Grandview Mercantile Company, Columbus 088415
Grandville & Old Nick, Basel 141204
Granec & Mitteldorf, Augsburg 101615
Graner, Susanne, München 126383
Granero, Bruxelles 096209
Grangärde Hembygdsgården, Grangärde 036313
Grange, Cassel 062005
La Grange, Milano 075733
La Grange, Zaltbommel 078856
Grange, Allan, Landulph 113350
Grange, Gilbert, Dijon 062665
Grange Antiques, Latrobe 056083
Grange aux Affaires, Châteauneuf-les-Martigues 062207
La Grange Aux Arts, Peroy-les-Gombries 066732
La Grange aux Moines, Megève . . . 064464
La Grange Béranger, Musée d'Arts Populaires, Beblenheim 010726
La Grange de Concise, Thonon-les-Bains 068405
Grange de l'Ermitage, Armoy 060976
Grange de Liselotte, Vouzan 069036
Grange des Ongliers, Chandai 062132, 124184
La Grange du Cap Lande, La Teste-de-Buch 063450
Grange Gallery, Saint Saviour 086479, 131446
La Grange Moulin, Les Ardillats . . . 063755
Grange Museum of Community History, London 040158
Grange Notre-Dame, Labastide-d'Armagnac 063472, 124286
Grange Old Style Furniture, Grange 055911
Grange Road Antiques, Glen Huntly 055884
La Grange Saint-Firmin, Nempont-Saint-Firmin 064971
Grangemouth Museum, Grangemouth 039617
Granger, Audes 061056
Granger, Jean-Claude, Dreux 120994
Granger, Jenny, Whitstable 114685
Granger Homestead Society Museum, Canandaigua 042593
Granger House, Marion 045680
Granier, Bielefeld 138872
Granier, C., Löhne 139418
Granier, Didier, Castelnaudary 062016
Granier, Olivier, Valros 068704
Graniou, Christian, Monflanquin . . .064602, 099730
Granit Sanat, İstanbul 112320
Granitabbaumuseum, Königshain . . 018350
Granma Memorial, La Habana 007950
Grannie Used To Have One, Longhaven 085848
Grannies, Framlingham 084434
Grannie's Parlour, Kingston-upon-Hull 084858
Grannona, Portbail 066955
Granny's Antique Furniture Mall, Tucson 093239
Granny's Antiques, Mildura 056224
Granny's Attic, Nottingham 086135
Granny's Attic, Ramsgate 086327
Granny's Attic Antiques, Cootamundra 055717
Granny's Cupboard, Wisbech 087190
Granny's Goodies, Oklahoma City . . 091502
Granny's Jumble Sale, Zaandam . . 078849
Granny's Market, Armadale, Victoria 055378
Granny's Wonders, Oklahoma City . 091503
Granösunds Fiskeläge, Södra Vallgrund 010086
Granoff, Katia, Cannes 099071
Granoff, Katia, Honfleur 099351
Granow, Hans-Dieter, Trier 074091
Grans Lantbruksmuseum, Öjebyn . . 036515
Grant, Droitwich 141560
Grant, New York 117974
Grant, Newcastle, Co. Down 114116
Grant, Andrew, Worcester 122761
Grant, Carl, Barnard Castle 083389, 130336
Grant, Denzil, Drinkstone 084221
Grant, Gary, London 113655
Grant, Jonathan, Auckland 108326, 128905
Grant, Selwyn, New York 117975
Grant Arts Center, San Francisco . . 119677
Grant County Historical Museum, Canyon City 042610
Grant County Historical Museum, Elbow Lake 043649
Grant County Historical Museum, Ephrata 043717
Grant County Museum, Elgin 043651
Grant County Museum, Hyannis . . . 044705
Grant County Museum, Medford . . . 045741
Grant County Museum, Sheridan . . 048148
Grant County Museum, Ulysses . . . 048686
Grant & Gower, Henley 113225
Grant-Humphreys Mansion, Denver 043409
Grant-Kohrs Ranch National Historic Site, Deer Lodge 043364
Grant Medical College Museum, Mumbai 022263
Grant Museum of Zoology and Comparative Anatomy, London 040159
Grant & Shaw, Edinburgh 141579
Grant Street Art Gallery, Ballarat . . . 094199
Grantham, Cleveland 115711
Grantham Clocks, Grantham 084494, 130740
Grantham Furniture Emporium, Grantham 084495
Grantham Museum, Grantham 039620
Granton Centre, National Museums of Scotland, Edinburgh 039394
Grantown Museum, Grantown-on-Spey 039622
Grants, Detroit 132054
Grant's Birthplace State Memorial, Point Pleasant 047111
Grant's Books, Prahran 137058
Grants Contempory Art, Barnard Castle 112558
Grants Pass Museum of Art, Grants Pass 044286
Granviarte, Lisboa 109324

Granville Antiques, Petworth 086248, 131377
Granville Collections, Granville 063032
Granville County Historical Society Museum, Oxford 046771
Granville Gallery, Chicago 115438
Granville Historical Museum, Granville 044292
Granvin Bygdamuseum, Granvin . . . 030860
Grapevine Museum, Chiltern 000916
Grapheo, Roma 128068
Graphes, Paris 100473
Graphia, Sint-Niklaas 052675, 135597
Graphic Art Division, Milwaukee Area Technical College, Milwaukee . . . 051719
Graphic Art Publishing, Miami 135391
Graphic Artists Guild, New York . . . 054778
Graphic Artists Guild's Directory of Illustration, Santa Barbara 136476
Graphic Arts, Tarp 074041
Graphic Arts Department, Oklahoma State University, Okmulgee 051879
Graphic Arts Gallery, Miami 117083
Graphic Communication Department, Mohawk Valley Community College, Utica 052298
Graphic Concepts, Omaha 091570
Graphic Conservation, Chicago 131902
Graphic Design Department, Salt Lake Community College, Salt Lake City 052102
Graphic Design Department, Tunxis Community College, Farmington . 051325
Graphic Design: USA, New York . . . 136477
Graphic Presentations, Philadelphia 118772
Graphic Station Gallery, Kitakyushu 106873
Graphic Studio Gallery, Dublin 105867
Graphic World, Singapore 109803
Graphicom, Sedona 135507
Graphics Division, Western Wisconsin Technical Institute, La Crosse . . . 051561
Graphics Home Gallery, Breda 078093
Graphics Plus Frames, Saint Albans 114344
Graphics World, Maidstone 136221
Graphicstudio, Tampa 135513
Graphigro, Paris 138393
Graphik-Biennale, Stuttgart 093719
Graphik Edition Dornick, Emmerich 133910
Graphik International, Stuttgart . . . 073976
Das Graphik-Kabinett, Hamburg . . . 139180
Graphiker-Verein e.V., München . . . 053222
Graphikmuseum Pablo Picasso Münster, Münster 019145
Graphikpresse, Berlin 101914, 121330
Graphique de France, Noisiel 133505
Graphis, Toronto 097281
Graphis, Woollahra 095427
Graphis Arte, Livorno 134597
Graphis Press, Zürich 135089
Graphische Kunst, Memmingen . . . 135765
Graphische Revue Österreichs, Wien 135556
Graphische Sammlung, Staatliche Museen Kassel, Kassel 018187
Graphische Sammlung, Städtische Kunstsammlungen, Augsburg . . . 015609
Graphische Sammlung am Kunsthistorischen Institut der Universität Tübingen, Tübingen 020494
Graphische Sammlung der Eidgenössischen Technischen Hochschule, Zürich . 037768
Graphische Sammlung der Universität, Erlangen 017031
Graphische Werkstatt im Traklhaus, Salzburg 133138
Graphothek Berlin, Berlin 016052
Grapin, Joël, Thonon-les-Bains . . .068406, 124956
Grappolini, Guidetta, Firenze 075356
Gras, Bonn 069924
Gras, Eric, Romilly-sur-Seine 067206
Grashey, Ursula, Konstanz 103760
Grasiela, Vincennes 068996, 138663
Grasl, Baden bei Wien 133060
Graslin, Nantes 064924
Graslitzer Gedenk- und Informationsraum, Aschaffenburg 015576
Grass, Wien 137314
Grass, Roman, Wien 137315
Grassagården Miljömuseum, Strängnäs 036685
Grasselmühle, Reichenthal 002512
Grassi, P., Hohenberg an der Eger . 071556
Grassi, Peter, Schirnding 073690
Grassimuseum Leipzig, Museum für Kunsthandwerk, Leipzig 018572
Grassin, Jean, Carnac . . . 099088, 133458, 138067
Grassland Gallery, Edmonton 096884
Grassland Gallery, Minneapolis 117265
Grasso, Adriana Gelsomina, Catania 127267
Grassroots, Regina 059088
Gratan Sur, Granada 129527
Grate Expectations, Washington . . . 087051
Gratsos, Constantin, Wien 057433
Il Grattacielo, Livorno 106123
Grattepanche, Pascal, Artres 061003
Grau & Cie., G.A., Hof, Saale 103390
Grau, Gerhard, Hamburg 071237
Grau, Karl-Heinz, Bad Berleburg . . . 069262
Grau Massana, Marta, Barcelona . . 080863
Graue, Herbert, Werther 134453
Graue Mill and Museum, Oak Brook 046580
Grauer'sche Antiquariatsbuchhandlung, Nürnberg 139606
Graupner, S., Siegburg 073804
Grauwert, Hamburg 103157
Grauwin, Nicolas, La Bassée 063282
Grauwinkel & Schön, Siegburg 104889
Grava, Milwaukee 117193
Gravante & Lindemann, Mettmann . 072536
Gravdal, Anne, Sylling 079508
Grave Creek Mound Historic Site, Moundsville 046049
Grave Matters, Cincinnati 142316
Gravelbourg and District Museum, Gravelbourg 005544
Gravensteen Museum voor Gerechtsvoorwerpen, Gent 003455
Graves, Clark, Saint Louis 092248
Graves Art Gallery, Sheffield 040996
Graves-Johnston, Michael, London 141810
Graves Museum of Archaeology and Natural History, Dania Beach 043292
Gravesham Museum, Gravesend, Kent 039625
Graviassy, Sébastien, Toulouse . . . 124982
Gravier, Philippe, Paris 100474
Gravigny, vJosiane, Le Neubourg . . 063673
Gravura, Lisboa 109325, 134871
Gravura Brasileira, Rio de Janeiro . 096619
Gravure, Montréal 133319
Gravure, Paris 133617
Gravy, Sacramento 092163
Gravy, Sacramento 092164
Gravy, Sacramento 132735
Graw, Isabelle, Berlin 133779
Grawe, Schmallenberg 104829
Gray, Cincinnati 115633
Gray, Dunedin 108436
Gray, New York 090917
Gray, Toronto 059200
Gray, Winnipeg 120828
Gray, Alexandra J., Portsmouth . . .086299, 131394
Gray, Julia, New York 090918
Gray, Kimberly Jayne, Dallas 088524
Gray, Laila, Kingsthorpe 084855
Gray, Lenore, Providence 119081
Gray, P. & G., Robe 056535
Gray, R.E., Kitchener 123776
Gray, Richard, Chicago 115439
Gray, Richard, New York 117976
Gray Door, Houston 089089
Gray, Eisdell & Matthews, Springvale 120640
Gray, Eisdell & Timms, Lakemba . . 120599
Gray, Eisdell & Timms, Smithfield . . 120637
Gray Gallery, Quincy 047297
Gray Matters Art Gallery, Dallas . . . 115887
Gray Stone Press and Gallery, Nashville 117354, 135401
Graybar, Craig L., Milwaukee 132368
Graybeal, Atlanta 131776
Graydon, New Farm 094932
Graylings Antiques, Andover 083302
Gray's, Worcester 087254
Gray's, Worcester 087255
Grays Antique Markets, London . . . 085346
Grays Antique Markets, London . . . 085347
Gray's Printing Press, Strabane . . . 041132
Gray's School of Art, The Robert Gordon University, Aberdeen 050799
Grays School of Art Gallery and Museum, Aberdeen 038448
Grayson, Houston 089090
Grayson, Donald & Barbara, Louisville 089991, 142531
Grayson, G.I., Ringwood 056531
Graystone, Portland 119005
Graystone, San Francisco 119678
Grazer Kunstverein, Graz . 001931, 052539
Grazer Stadtmuseum, Graz 001932
Grazia Marotta, Napoli 075994
Alle Grazie, Milano 075734
Gré du Van, Chalon-sur-Saône 062086
Great Acquisitions Book Store, New Orleans 142615
Great Alpine Gallery, Omeo 095006
Great American Antique Mall, Tulsa 093308
Great American Art Works, Cincinnati 115634
Great American Ink, Los Angeles . . 116784
Great American Salvage, New York . 090919
Great Art Gallery, Delhi 105664
Great Atlantic Mapworks Gallery, Saint Just 114379
Great Bardfield Cage, Great Bardfield 039628
Great Bardfield Cottage Museum, Great Bardfield 039629
Great Barn Museum of Wiltshire Rural Life, Avebury 038551
Great Basin Museum, Delta 043385
Great Basin National Park, Baker . . 041951
Great Blacks in Wax Museum, Baltimore 041984
Great Brak River Museum, Great Brak River 034627
Great Brampton House Antiques, Hereford 084668
Great Central Railway Museum, Loughborough 040342
Great Cobar Heritage Centre, Cobar 000933
Great Escape, Louisville . . 089992, 142532
Great Escape, Nashville 142601
Great Escape Book Store, Toronto . 137708
Great Exchange, San Antonio 142887
Great Expectations, Green Bay 044306
Great Expectations, Blackburn, Lancashire 083548, 130404
Great Expectations, Horncastle 084736
Great Expectations, New Orleans . . 090565
Great Expectations, Poole 086287, 131386
Great Expectations Gallery, London 113656
Great Explorations, Saint Petersburg 047716
Great Fish River Museum, Cradock . 034593
Great Gatsby, Atlanta 087485, 122801
Great Grandfathers Bookshop, Leyland 141729
Great Grooms of Dorking, Dorking . 084191
Great Grooms of Hungerford, Hungerford 084759, 130817, 141682
Great Hang-Up, Houston 116326
Great Harbor Maritime Museum, Northeast Harbor 046548
Great Jones, Seattle 093010
Great Lakes Art Studio, Chicago . . . 115440
Great Lakes Art Studio, Chicago . . . 131903
Great Lakes Coin Company, Cleveland 088332
Great Lakes Historical Museum, Tuncurry 001573
Great Lakes Lighthouse Museum, Mackinaw City 045555
Great Lakes Naval Memorial and Museum, Muskegon 046104
Great Lakes Pastel Society, Grand Rapids 054779
Great Lakes Polishing, Cleveland . . 131962
Great Lakes Science Center, Cleveland 042992
Great Laxey Wheel and Mines Trail, Manx National Heritage, Laxey 039940
Great Lord Antiguidades e Objetos, Rio de Janeiro 058593
Great Malvern Antiques, Great Malvern 084513
Great Modern Pictures, New York . . 117977
Great Northern Antiques, Minneapolis 090362
The Great Northern Architectural Antique Co., Tattenhall 086825, 131574
Great Northwest Bookstores, Portland 142799
The Great Oak Bookshop, Llanidloes 141741
Great Orme Tramway, Llandudno . . 040050
Great Plains Art Collection in the Christlieb Gallery, Lincoln 045303
Great Plains Black Museum, Omaha 046679
Great Plains Transportation Museum, Wichita 049155
Great Sandhills Museum, Sceptre . . 006435
Great Sheffield, Sheffield 114418
Great South Land, Drummoyne . . . 094488
Great Stuff, Myrtleford 056308
Great Sydney Antiques Fair, Moore Park 093571
Great Things on High, Columbus . . 115783
Great Valley Museum of Natural History, Modesto 045955
Great Wall Painting and Calligraphy Society, Beijing 097656
Great Walsingham Gallery, Walsingham 114643
Great War Flying Museum, Cheltenham 005262
Great Warrior Aboriginal Art, Berry . 055496
Great Wave, Buffalo 087881
Great West Warehouse, Saskatoon .059098, 120813
Great Western Auctions, Glasgow . . 122516
Great Western Railway Museum, Swindon 041180
Great Yarmouth Museums, Great Yarmouth 039633
Great Zimbabwe Site Museum, Masvingo 049588
Greater Columbus Antique Mall, Columbus 088416
Greater Harvard Area Historical Society, Harvard 044470
Greater Hazleton Historical Society Museum, Hazleton 044497
Greater Lafayette Museum of Art, Lafayette 045088
Greater Loveland Historical Society Museum, Loveland 045503
Greater Manchester Police Museum, Manchester 040399
Greater New Orleans Art League, New Orleans 054780
Greater New Orleans Art League, New Orleans 117448
Greater Philadelphia Book Bank, Philadelphia 142743
Greater Pittsburgh Arts Alliance, Pittsburgh 054781
Greater Port Jefferson Museum, Port Jefferson 047134
The Greater Reston Arts Center, Reston 047384
Greater Sudbury Heritage Museum, Sudbury 006531
Greater Vernon Museum, Vernon, British Colombia 006726
Greb Jagd-Museum, Busswil (Thurgau) 036995
Greca, Barcelona 080864
Greca Trading, Singapore 080474

El Greco, Bogotá 098168
El Greco, Bucureşti 109436
A El Greco, Santiago de Chile 059533
Greco, Eloisa, Messina 075562
Greco-Roman Museum, Alexandria 009275
Gredler, John, New York 090920
Gredt, Léa, Luxembourg 107404
Greef & Jansen-Greef, Bad Arolsen 069257, 125084
The Greek Bookshop, London 141811
Greek Orthodox Museum, Jerusalem 022950
Greeley Square Gallery, New York . . 117978
Green, Austin 131799
Green, Chennai 105630
Green, London 085348
Green, Toronto 059201
Green, Andrew, Portland . 091949, 132694
Green, Arthur, Los Angeles 089781
Green, Essie, New York 117979
Green, Frank, Liverpool 113409
Green & Son, J., Queniborough . . . 086320
Green, Maury, New York 090921
Green, Michael, Harrogate 084576
Green, Richard, London 085349
Green, Richard, London 085350
Green, Richard, London 113657
Green, Richard, London 113658
Green, Richard, London 113659
Green, Ron, Towcester . . . 086911, 131604
Green Apple Books, San Francisco . 142949
Green Art, København 098571
Green Art Gallery, Jumeira 112462
Green Bay Auctions, Auckland 121811
Green Bay Packer Hall of Fame, Green Bay 044307
Green Boutique, Tampa 093127
Green Dolphin Antiques, Boston . . . 087824
Green Door Furniture, Denver 088694
Green Door Gallery, Bellville 110013
Green Door Gallery, Kansas City . . . 116569
Green Dragon Antiques Centre, Wincanton 087163
Green Dragon Museum, Stockton-on-Tees 041111
Green Gables House, Charlottetown 005246
The Green Gallery, Aberfoyle 112485
Green Gallery, Auckland 108327
The Green Gallery, Dublin 105868
Green Gallery, Kram 112248
The Green Gallery, Rhosili 114303
Green Gates Gallery, Nicholson . . . 094966
Green Goat Art Studio, O'Connor . . 095002
The Green Hall Gallery, Craigellachie 112913
Green Hill Center for North Carolina Art, Greensboro 044330
Green Horse Gallery, Bardon 094214
Green House Gallery, Milton 094855
Green Howards Museum, Richmond, North Yorkshire 040828
Green & Hughes, Los Angeles 089782
Green Lane Antiques, Ormskirk . . .086166, 131347
Green Lion Books, Saint Paul 142867
Green Mountain Club, Waterbury Center 048980
Green Palace Museum, Sa'd-Abad Museum, Teheran 022618
Green Palm Gallery, Ha Noi 120465
Green Park Shipbuilding Museum and Yeo House, Prince Edward Island Museum and Heritage Foundation, Port Hill . . . 006184
Green River Museum, Woodbury . . 049283
Green Square Copenhagen, København 060334
Green & Stone, London . . 085351, 131048
Greenan Gallery, Ayr 112534
Greenaway Art Gallery, Kent Town . 094689
Greenaway Gallery, Camberwell . . . 000878
Greenbelt Museum, Greenbelt 044315
Greenberg, Howard, New York 117980
Greenberg Van Doren, Saint Louis . 119210
Greendoor Antiques, Orange 056405
Greene, Drogheda 074887
Greene, Fort Worth 088858
Greene, Barbara, New York 117981
Greene, Michael A., Woollahra 056866
Greene, Naftali, New York 117982
Greene County Historical Museum, Waynesburg 049036
Greene County Historical Society Museum, Xenia 049325
Greene Memorial Museum, Milwaukee 045888
Greene Space Gallery, New York . . . 117983
Greenfield, Milwaukee 090300
Greenfield, Milwaukee 090301
Greenfield & Son, H.S., Canterbury .083863, 130504
Greenfield Historical Society Museum, Greenfield 044327
Greenfield Museum, Greenfield . . . 044326
Greenfield Valley Museum, Greenfield 039637
Greengage Gallery, Chalfont Saint Giles 112834
Greengrass Antiques, Chobham . . . 084000
Greenhill Covenanter's House, Biggar 038706
Greenhill Galleries, Birmingham . . . 112648
Greenhill Galleries, Perth 095066
Greenhill Galleries Adelaide, North Adelaide 094972
The Greenhouse Gallery, Sheffield . 114419
Greenhouse Gallery of Fine Art, San Antonio 119419
Greenoaks Gallery, Launceston . . . 094726
Green's Mill and Science Centre, Nottingham 040619
Greens of Cheltenham, Cheltenham 083920
Greensboro Artists' League, Greensboro 054782
Greensboro Artists' League Gallery, Greensboro 044331
Greensboro Historical Museum, Greensboro 044332
Greenslade, Taylor & Hunt, Taunton 122720
Greensleeves, Aldgate 055335
Greenspond Court House, Greenspond 005547
Greensward Gallery, Oregon State University, Corvallis 043177
Greentown Glass Museum, Greentown 044341
Greenville County Museum of Art, Greenville 044349
Greenville County Museum of Art School, Greenville 051423
Greenville Museum of Art, Greenville 044344
Greenwald, June, Cleveland 088333
Greenwall, Jonathan, Sandgate . . . 086509
Greenway, Dallas 142368
Greenway, Colin, Witney 087192
Greenwich Antiques Market, London 085352
Greenwich Art Society, Greenwich . 054783
Greenwich Borough Museum, London 040160
Greenwich Gallery, London 113660
Greenwich Heritage Centre, London 040160
Greenwich Local History Centre, London 040161
Greenwich Printmakers, London . . . 135218
Greenwich Printmakers Gallery, London 113661
Greenwich Theatre Art Gallery, London 040162
Greenwood, Hamilton 137639
Greenwood, David, Ilkley 113290
Greenwood, Judy, London 085353
Greenwood, W., Burneston 083801, 130484
Greenwood Antique Mall, Seattle . . 093011
Greenwood Books, Seattle 142990
Greenwood County Historical Society Museum, Eureka 043753
Greenwood Great House Museum, Greenwood 026380
Greenwood Military Aviation Museum, Greenwood, Nova Scotia 005549
Greenwood Museum, Greenwood . . 044356
Greenwood Museum, Greenwood, British Columbia 005548
Greenwood Press, London 135219
Greer, New York 117984
Greer, Robin, London 141812
Grefvens, Stockholm 129864
Greger, Malmö 141128
Gregg & Co., Albuquerque 114792
Gregg County Historical Museum, Longview 045398
Greggie, Atlanta 114885, 142204
Gregor, David, Seattle 142991
Gregori, Anna, Verona 128426
Gregorics, Alexander, Oslip 123426
Gregoris, Elena, Brescia 127219
Gregor's Studios, Dallas 088525
Gregory, George, Bath 141397
Gregory, Henry, London 085354
Gregory, Martyn, London 113662
Gregory, Bottley & Lloyd, London . . 085355
Gregory's Antiques and Lights, Fitzroy 055822
Gregory's of Greerton, Tauranga . . . 079264
Greg's Antiques, Cincinnati 088247, 122856
Greg's Antiques, Cleveland 088334
Greg's Refinishing, Milwaukee 132369
Greg's Upholstery, Long Beach 132226
Gregson, Thornleigh 123318
Greifengalerie, Greifswald 102994
Greiff, Dr. Susanne, Winterbach, Kreis Bad Kreuznach 127024
Greim, Dr. Gerhard, Forchheim, Oberfranken 070716, 139073
Greiner, Daniel, Paris 100475
Greinwald, Adelgunde & Manfred, Schliersee 073701
Greinwald, R., Immenstadt 071617
Greis, Christoph & Petra, Öhningen . 104520
Greiser, Olaf, Schriesheim 104846, 139717
Greisinger, Alfred, Baden-Baden . . . 069414
Grekiskt Kulturcentrum, Stockholm 036626
Grelet, Eric, Manosque 064249
Grell-Hansohm, Petra, Kampen . . . 071694
Gremes, Augsburg 069228
Gremese, Roma 134676
Gremi, Barcelona 080865
Gremi d'Antiquaris de Catalunya, Barcelona 054113
Gremi d'Antiquaris i Brocanters de les Comarques Gironines, Girona . . . 054114
Gremi de Llibreters de Vell de Catalunya, Barcelona 140989
Gremillion & Co., Austin 114987
Gremillion & Co., Dallas 115888
Gremillion & Co., Houston 116327
Gremm, T., Mannheim 072422
Grenada National Museum, Saint George's 021554
De Grenadier, Groningen 078417
Grenen Kunstmuseum, Skagen . . . 009093
De Grenen Schuur, Leiden 078567
De Grenen Schuur, Utrecht 078803
Grenette, Sion 111913
Grenfell and District History Museum, Grenfell 001081
Grenfell Community Museum, Grenfell 005550
Grenfell House Museum, Saint Anthony 006325
Grenier, Ajaccio 060739
Le Grenier, Montpellier 064744
Le Grenier, Saint-Denis 080127
Le Grenier, Saint-Nicolas-de-Redon 067687
Le Grenier, Villers-Allerand 068928
Le Grenier, Villuis 068990
Le Grenier Animé, Sainte-Foy-de-Peyrolières 068056
Grenier Antiquité Bar, Blonville-sur-Mer 061531
Le Grenier Antiquités, Quimper 067018
Grenier au Relais, Belfort 061327
Grenier Bovary, Ry 067333
Grenier & Chocolat, New Orleans . . 090566
Le Grenier Crémolan, Crémieu 062557
Grenier d'Adèle, Porto-Vecchio 066960
Grenier d'Alexandre, Saïx 068090
Le Grenier d'Aliénor, Castillon-la-Bataille 062023
Le Grenier d'Aliénor, Sainte-Terre . . 068083
Grenier d'Anaïs, Rennes (Ille-et-Vilaine) 067115
Grenier d'Annick, Gavray 062974
Le Grenier d'Argenteuil, Argenteuil . 060963
Grenier d'Aurelianis, Orléans 065302
Grenier de Bricquebec, Bricquebec 061792
Grenier de Chine, Larmor Plage . . . 063537
Grenier de Françoise, La Roche-Bernard 063407
Grenier de Jupiter, Paris 066019
Le Grenier de la Chapelle, Bruxelles 057972
Le Grenier de la Côte, Morges 082673
Le Grenier de la Reine Margot, Saint-Saturnin 067999
Le Grenier de la Vallée, Salins-les-Thermes 068094
Grenier de l'Autan, Caraman 061967
Grenier de Margot, Saint-Germain-en-Laye 067500
Grenier de Marie, Thierville 068390
Grenier de Montesson, Montesson . 064679
Grenier de Pierrot, Arpajon 060982
Grenier de Recouvrance, Brest 061773, 124161
Grenier de Saint-Léger, Saint-Léger-des-Vignes 067582
Grenier de Sucy, Sucy-en-Brie 068338
Grenier de Thomas, Chaumont (Haute-Marne) 062249
Le Grenier de Valenciennes, Valenciennes 068691
Le Grenier de Vauban, Briançon . . . 061789
Le Grenier de Vulaines, Vulaines . . 069038
Grenier de Xavier, Champs-sur-Yonne 062128
Grenier d'Emilie, Blere 061515
Grenier des Collectionneurs, Épinal 062788
Grenier d'Hélène, Versailles 068808
Le Grenier d'Olivier, Molsheim 064587
Grenier du Cambrésis, Le Cateau-Cambrésis 063594
Le Grenier du Cap, Lege-Cap-Ferret 063736
Grenier du Chapeau Rouge, Montélimar 064673
Le Grenier du Château, La Rochefoucauld 063419
Le Grenier du Chti, Roubaix 067230
Le Grenier du Moulin, Argent-sur-Sauldre 060958
Grenier du Pévèle, Orchies 065280
Grenier du Pévèle, Orchies 065281
Le Grenier du Pilon, Sainte-Maxime 068069
Le Grenier du Pin, Castelnau-le-Lez 062015
Le Grenier du Pin, Lattes 063546
Grenier du Val, Le Val-Saint-Germain 063725
Grenier Lamalgue, Toulon (Var) 068453
Grenier Moretain, Moret-sur-Loing . 064788
Le Grenier Nivernais, Champlemy . 062125
Grenier Picard, Mauregny-en-Haye 064436
Grenier Saint Pierre, Carnac 061991
Grenier Savoyard, Aix-les-Bains . . . 060723
Aux Greniers de l'Espérance, Guise 063110
Les Greniers de Saint-Martin, Saint-Georges-sur-Moulon 067495
Greniers de Sophie, Choisy la Victoire 062296
Les Greniers d'Ici et d'Ailleurs, Megève 064465
Les Greniers du Père Sauce, Rancourt-sur-Ornain 067039
Greniers du Père Sauce, Vandœuvre-lès-Nancy 068708
Grenik, Bicheno 055502
Grenot, Jean-Claude & Marie-Agnès, Urimenil 068660
Grenouillère, La Rochelle 063432
Grenslandmuseum, Dinxperlo 029485
Grenzhuus, Schlagsdorf bei Gadebusch 020033
Grenzland-Galerie, Aachen 101512

Grenzland-Museum Bad Sachsa, Bad Sachsa . . . 015779
Grenzland- und Trenckmuseum, Waldmünchen . . . 020648
Grenzlandheimatstuben des Heimatkreises Marienbad, Neualbenreuth . . . 019217
Grenzlandmuseum, Schnackenburg 020060
Grenzlandmuseum Eichsfeld, Teistungen . . . 020416
Grenzlandmuseum Raabs an der Thaya, Raabs an der Thaya . . . 002485
Grenzlandmuseum Swinmark, Schnega . . . 020064
Grenzmuseum Philippsthal (Werra), Philippsthal, Werra . . . 019618
Grenzmuseum Schifflersgrund, Bad Sooden-Allendorf . . . 015804
Grenzwald-Destillation Museum, Crottendorf . . . 016610
Grerardi, Marina, Roma . . . 128069
Gresham, Crewkerne . . . 141546
Gresham History Museum, Gresham . . . 044357
Grésilières, Marie-Hélène, Villefranche-de-Rouergue . . . 068895
Gresse, Monique, Montpellier . . . 064745
Gressler, Patrick, Ars-en-Ré . . . 060997
Greta Antiques, Greta . . . 055918
Grether, Eberhard, Freiburg im Breisgau . . . 125670
Gretillat, Jean-Claude, Neuchâtel . . 082693
Grétry, Liège . . . 058307
Greul, Aree, Frankfurt am Main . . . 139083
Greulich, Frankfurt am Main . . . 102780
Greulich, Potsdam . . . 073361
Greulich, Achim, Wiesbaden . . . 127011
Greuter, Reinhold, Landeck . . . 057140
Greutert, M.H., Amsterdam . . . 128539
Greuzat, Patrice, Pionsat . . . 066834
Greuze, Jean-Baptiste, Tournus . . . 068569
Grev Wedels Plass Auksjoner, Oslo . 121869
Greve, H., Hamburg . . . 071238
Greve, Karsten, Köln . . . 103634
Grève, Karsten, Paris . . . 100476
Greve, Karsten, Sankt Moritz . . . 111883
Greve, Dr. Werner, Berlin . . . 138781
Greve Museum, Greve . . . 008878
Greven, Köln . . . 134108
Greven, Karel, 's-Hertogenbosch . . 078521
Grevenbroek Museum, Hamont-Achel . . . 003490
Grévendal, J.-L., Bruxelles . . . 057973
Grevesmühlener Mühle, Grevesmühlen . . . 017533
Grewe, R., Bissendorf . . . 069857
Grewe, Theodor, Haltern . . . 071183
Grey Art Gallery, New York University, New York . . . 046340
Grey County Museum, Owen Sound 006108
Grey Dog Trading, Tucson . . . 120131
Grey Goose Studio, Salt Lake City . 119346
Grey Goose Studio @ Trolley Square, Salt Lake City . . . 119347
Grey Gums Gallery, MacLean, Queensland . . . 094755
Grey-Harris & Co, Bristol . . . 083739
Grey Suit, Video for Art & Literature, Adamsdown . . . 136222
Grey Wall Gallery, Tampa . . . 120048
Greyabbey Antiques & Fine Art, Greyabbey . . . 084532, 113161
Greybull Museum, Greybull . . . 044358
Greyer, Margita, Bad Gastein . . . 056927
Greyfriars, Colchester . . . 141530
Greyhound Hall of Fame, Abilene . . 041564
Greystoke, Sherborne . . . 086577
Greystones Antiques, Greystones . . 074978
Greythorn Galleries, Toorak . . . 095341
Greytown Books, Masterton . . . 079149, 140641
Greytown Museum, Greytown . . . 034629
GRG Editions, Paris . . . 138394
Grian, Sankt-Peterburg . . . 080304
Gribaudi, Piero, Torino . . . 134694
Gribaudo, Joseph, Paris . . . 138395
Grice, Alan, Ormskirk . . . 086167, 131348
Grich, Chicago . . . 088099
Gridel, François, Paris . . . 121154
Grieb, Heiner, Enzklösterle . . . 125589
Griebel, Margit & Franz, Bad Neustadt an der Saale . . . 069344
Grieder, Franziska, Zürich . . . 112104
Grieder & von Puttkamer, Berlin . . . 101915
Grier-Musser Museum, Los Angeles 045424
Griese, Volker, Berlin . . . 069621
Grieser, Roland, Deisenhofen . . . 070204
Grieshaber, Gerhard, Sankt Gallen . 082776
Grieshaber, Hans, Zürich . 112105, 141338
Griesinger, Frankfurt am Main . . . 139084
Griesser, Ute, Köln . . . 126080
Grießhaber, Tübingen . . . 105077
Grietje Tump Museum, Landsmeer . 029825
Grife & Escoda, Barcelona . . . 110199
Griff, Budapest . . . 074686
Griffart, Jean-Louis, Bévillers . . . 061422
Griffault, Brigitte, Montauban . . . 064634
Griffe, Rennes (Ille-et-Vilaine) . . . 101082
Griffel, Michael, München . . . 072716
Griffelkunst-Vereinigung Hamburg e.V., Hamburg . . . 053223, 134010
Griffin, Chicago . . . 115441
Griffin, Chicago . . . 115442
Griffin, Dallas . . . 088526
Griffin, Nashville . . . 090457
Griffin, Pittsburgh . . . 091822
Griffin, Max, Richmond . . . 092080
Griffin, Nick & Janet, Leighton Buzzard . . . 084964
Griffin, Simon, London . . . 085356
Griffin, Simon, London . . . 085357
Griffin & Mace, Lewes . . . 084981
Griffins & Gargoyles, Chicago . . . 088100
Griffith, Condong . . . 094422
Griffith & Partners, London . . . 141813
Griffith, Bill, Houston . . . 132122
Griffith Artworks, Nathan . . . 001318
Griffith Cottage Gallery, Griffith . . . 094607
Griffith Gallery, Griffith . . . 094608
Griffith Pioneer Park Museum, Griffith . . . 001082
Griffith Regional Art Gallery, Griffith 001083
Griffith University Gallery, Nathan . . 001318
Griffiths & Co, Worcester . . . 122762
Griffiths, David, London . . . 085358
Griffiths, W. John, Ross-on-Wye . . . 086401
Griffiths Sea Shell Museum and Marine Display, Lakes Entrance . . . 001169
Griffo, Firenze . . . 075357
Griffon, Cleveland . . . 115712
Grifon, Kyïv . . . 112409
Il Grifone, Livorno . . . 075533
Grigoropoulos, Chicago . . . 115443
Grijpma, Groningen . . . 078418
Grijpma & Van Hoogen, Groningen . 078419
Grijse, de, Kortrijk . . . 096369
Grilfeldt, Ole, Westerland . . . 074367
Grili, Marco, Belo Horizonte . . . 058429
Grili, Marco, Belo Horizonte . . . 058430
Grillet, Jeanne, Juzennecourt . . . 063272
Grillon, Hermanville-sur-Mer . . . 063149
Grillon, Paris . . . 100477
Grillon, Vincennes . . . 068997
Grillparzer-Gedenkzimmer, Wien . . 002907
Grima, Barcelona . . . 129350
Grimaldi, Napoli . . . 140078
Grimaldi, Jorge, México . . . 077574
Grimaldi, Vital, Pézenas . . . 066806
Grimaldis, Constantine, Baltimore . 115059
Grimaud, Thierry, Marseille . . . 064364
Grimaud, Thierry, Marseille . . . 124420
Grimaud, Thierry, Marseille . . . 124421
Grimbergen, Lisse . . . 140488
Grimes, Chris, Bristol . . . 083740
Grimes, G. Robert, Saint Louis . . . 132749
Grimes House, Moreton-in-Marsh . 114092
Grimes House Antiques, Moreton-in-Marsh . . . 086018
Grimm, Daniel, Gdynia . . . 129016
Grimm, Jay, New York . . . 117985
Grimm, Rolf, Schramberg . . . 073729
Grimm, Ulrich, Magdeburg . . . 134175
Grimm Rosenfeld, München . . . 104215
Grimme, A., Unterdießen . . . 139811
Grims, Wolfgang, Salzburg . . . 057251
Grimsby Museum, Grimsby . . . 005551
Grimsby Public Art Gallery, Grimsby 005552
Grin, Michel, Lausanne . . . 082549
Grindheim Bygdemuseum, Kollungtveit . . . 030942
Grindsted Museum, Grindsted . . . 008880
Grinnell College Art Gallery, Grinnell 044360
Grinnell Historical Museum, Grinnell 044361
Grinning, Byrd, Cleveland . . . 115713
Grinter Place, Kansas City . . . 044913
Gripes Modeltheatremuseum, Nyköping . . . 036509
Gripsholms Slott, Mariefred . . . 036467
Gris, Jean, Lisboa . . . 079940
Gris, Jean, Lisboa . . . 079941
Gris, Juan, Madrid . . . 110538
Grisard, Francine, Marseille . . . 124422
Grise, Paris . . . 100478, 138396
Grisoni, Andrea, Bologna . . . 075084
Grissom Air Museum, Peru . . . 046894
Grist Mill, Keremeos . . . 005682
Grit, Roma . . . 106559
Gritsch, Imst . . . 123387
Grivot, Jean-François, Chalon-sur-Saône . . . 062087
Grizio, Oostende . . . 058362
Grizolle, Colette, Tours . . . 068592
Grizot, Cyril, Saint-Ouen . . . 067794
Grizzly Bear Prairie Museum, Wanham . . . 006763
Grønboengen Auksjonsforretning, Kongsberg . . . 121853
Groam House Museum, Rosemarkie 040853
Grob, Zürich . . . 130237
Grob, Marianne, Berlin . . . 101916
Grobbel, E., Bad Lippspringe . . . 101669
Grobusch, Aachen . . . 101513
Grobusch, Hannelore, Aachen . . . 069087
Grochal, Kraków . . . 129038
Gród Piastowski w Gieczu, Archeologiczny Muzeum Pierwszych Piastów na Lednicy, Giecz . . . 031932
Grødaland Bygdetun, Jarmuseet, Nærbø . . . 031041
Grodée, Stéphane, Amiens . . . 060817
Grodentz, Wellington . . . 079324
Grodnenski Gosudarstvennyj Istoričeskij Muzej, Grodno . . . 003128
Grodzka Galeria BWA, Lublin . . . 109026
Groeben, Susanne von der, Barcelona . . . 129351
Gröger, Uwe, Tutzing . . . 074124, 126923
Grömansperg, Heide, Wien . . . 137316
Grömling, Max, Karlstadt . . . 071738
Gröna Paletten Galleri, Stockholm . 111053
De Groene Markies, Utrecht . . . 078804
De Groene Schuur, Culemborg . . . 029390
Grönegau-Museum, Melle . . . 018897
Groenenboom, J.C., Zoelen . . . 128887
Groenewoud, Adriaan, Rotterdam . . 078720
Groeningeabdij, Stedelijke Musea Kortrijk, Kortrijk . . . 003558
Groeningemuseum, Stedelijke Musea, Brugge . . . 003269
Groenink Van der Veen, M., Leeuwarden . . . 078552
Grönsöö Slott, Enköping . . . 036250
Groep Interecho, Zandhoven . . . 052676, 133299
Groesser, Omaha . . . 118700
Gröstlinger, Markus, Ungenach . . . 057334
Groesz, M., Alkmaar . . . 077714
Gróf Esterházy Károly Kastély és Tájmúzeum, Pápa . . . 021810
Grofe, Egbert, Geldern . . . 125707
Grofe, Egbert, Kevelaer . . . 126035
Grogan & Co., Dedham . . . 122878
Groh, Germering . . . 133972
Groh, Werner, Volkach . . . 105129
Grohmann, Hans, München . . . 104216
Grolée-Virville, Alain de, Paris . . . 138397
Grolitsch, Gerhild, München . . . 072717
Grollemund, Michel, Biarritz . . . 061464
Grommen, Michel, Liège . 120768, 137518
Grona, Joan, San Antonio . . . 119420
Gronauer Kunstverein, Gronau, Westfalen . . . 053224
Gronchi, Loredana, Verona . . . 077006
Grondin Thibault, Paris . . . 100479
Grondin Thibault, Paris . . . 100480
Gronert, Traunstein . . . 105057
Gronert & Sohn, Kurt, München . . . 104217
Gronert, Ulrich, Berlin . . . 069622
Grong Bygdamuseum, Grong . . . 030865
Gronghe de Cabourg, Cabourg . . . 061848
Groninger Museum, Groningen . . . 029638
Groninger Schaatsmuseum, Sappemeer . . . 030120
Grønlund's Forlag, Maribo . . . 133428
Groot, de, Wiesbaden . . . 105259
Groot, Anneloes, Den Haag . . . 107923
Groot, A.W.J. de, Utrecht . . . 078805
Groot, Barbara de, München . . . 126384
Groot, G. de, Noordeloos . . . 128790
Groot Constantia Manor House and Wine Museum, Constantia . . . 034592
Groot Kasteel van Loppem, Loppem 003615
Groote, de, Antwerpen . . . 057697
Groote, de, Bruxelles . . . 057974
Groote, Zwolle . . . 078888
Grootegoed, Hilversum . . . 078534
Grootfontein Museum Das Alte Fort, Grootfontein . . . 029081
Grootmoeder's Boetiek, Apeldoorn . 078035
Grootmoeders Keukenmuseum, Nijmegen . . . 029959
Groovy, Pittsburgh . . . 091823
Gropius House, Lincoln . . . 045299
Gropler, Wolfgang, Berlin . . . 069623
Groppe, Margareta, Altenstadt, Hessen . . . 125063
Groppler Ulfert, Firenze . . . 127353
Gros, Madrid . . . 122061
Gros, Jean-Pierre, Paris . . . 066020
Gros, Robert, Courmangoux . . . 062516
Gros, Robert, Verjon . . . 068773
Gros, Robert, Villeurbanne . . . 068963
Gros & Delettrez, Paris . . . 121155
Groscaux, Michel, Cricqueboeuf . . . 062570
Grosche, H., Köln . . . 103635
Grosdidier, Claude, Vendargues . . . 068755
Grosell, Peter, København . . . 137895
Grosman, Arnhem . . . 078050
The Grosmont Gallery, Grosmont . . 113167
Grosos, Michel, Villers-Farlay . . . 068929
Gross, Halle, Saale . . . 071176
Groß, Kleinfischlingen . . . 071870
Gross, Barbara, München . . . 104218
Gross, Brian, San Francisco . . . 119679
Groß, D., Ostseebad Binz . . . 073264
Gross, G., Kassel . . . 071752
Groß, Helmi, Kaarst . . . 103463
Gross, Joe, Cleveland . . . 115714
Groß, Norbert, Meckenheim, Pfalz . 072480
Gross, Roger, New York . . . 142658
Gross McCleaf, Philadelphia . . . 118773
Grossbard, Leopoldine, Wien . . . 137317
Grosse Ile Historical Museum, Grosse Ile . . . 044362
Große Kunstschau, Worpswede . . . 020986
Grossen, Grenchen . . . 111533
Grossenbacher, Louise, Zürich . . . 112106
Grossenbacher, S., Münchenstein . 082677
Großer Wappensaal im Landhaus, Klagenfurt . . . 002139
Großheide, A., Osnabrück . . . 073236
Großherzoglich-Hessische Porzellansammlung, Darmstadt . . 016636
Grossi, Pierre-Hélen, Apt . . . 098853
Grossi, Vincenzo, Napoli . . . 075995
Grossi & Lotti, Firenze . . . 127354
Grossman, Chicago . . . 115444
Großmann, B., Schönebeck, Elbe . . 073712

Großmann, Wolfgang, Eberswalde . 070497
Großmitterberger Troadkasten, Laussa 002209
Großschmidt, Marianne, Tulln 137273
Grosstessner, Anna, Neuzeug 057192
Grosvenor, Vancouver 097478
Grosvenor, Brant, Cincinnati 088248
Grosvenor Antiques, Chester 083955, 130558
Grosvenor Fine Art, Auckland 108328
Grosvenor Galleries, Kingston 106818
Grosvenor Gallery, London 113663
Grosvenor House, London 085359, 113664
Grosvenor House Art and Antiques Fair, London 093927
Grosvenor House Interiors, Beaconsfield 083461
Grosvenor Kunama Galleries, Jindabyne 094666
Grosvenor Lodge, London 005787
Grosvenor Museum, Chester 039061
Grosvenor Prints, London . 085360, 131049, 141814
Grosz, Marvin L., Denver 088695
Grote, Welf-W. Freiherr, Worpswede 074486, 127035
Grotemeyer, Petra, Gummersbach . 125775
Groth, Bad Vilbel 133736
Groth, Heinz & Erika, Felsberg 070684
Grothe, Bernd, Berlin 069624
Grothe, Knud, Charlottenlund 098523
Groton Historical Museum, Groton . 044365
Grotowski, Trier 105061, 126911
Grotte de Bédeilhac, Musée de Préhistoire, Tarascon-sur-Ariège 014906
Grotte de Rouffignac, Rouffignac-Saint-Cernin 014136
Grotte et Parc Préhistoriques, Musée Cavernicole, Foissac 011830
Grotte Préhistorique Ornée, Miers . 013058
Grottes de Vallorbe, Vallorbe 037668
Grottes Préhistoriques de Sare-Lezea, Sare 014671
Grotto, Hong Kong 097791
Groudle Glen Railway, Onchan 040645
Ground Zero Designs, Tampa 120049
Groundbirch Museum, Groundbirch 005555
Groundfloor Gallery, Balmain 094204
Grounds & Co, Wisbech 122752
Grounds for Coffee & Antiques, Edmonton 058828
Grounds For Sculpture, Hamilton . . 044397
Group, Bruxelles 096210
Group, Philippe, Antwerpen 057698
Group for Costume and Textile Staff in Museums, Saint Fagans 054390
Group for Directors of Museums, Chester 054391
Group for Education in Museums, Gillingham, Kent 054392
Groupe des Salons Sélectionnés d'Antiquaires, Dijon 052948
Groupement des Amis de Musées de la Région Midi-Pyrénées, Montauban 052949
Groupement des Amis des Musées de la Région Centre, Orléans 052950
Groupement des Antiquaires du Morbihan, Grandchamp 052951
Groupement des Associations d'Amis de Musées de la Région Bretagne, Nevez 052952
Groupement des Associations d'Amis de Musées de la Région Languedoc-Roussillon, Montpellier 052953
Groupement des Associations d'Amis de Musées de la Région Limousin, Limoges 052954
Groupement des Associations des Amis de Musées Région Provence Alpes Côte d'Azur, Toulon (Var) 052955
Groupement National des Entrepreneurs de Restauration de Monuments Historiques, Paris 052956
Groupement Régional des Associations d'Amis de Musées de la Région Ile de France, Paris 052957
Groupement Rhône-Alpes des Amis de Musée, Lyon 052958
Grout Museum of History and Science, Waterloo 048983
Grove, Darwen 084139
The Grove Antiques Centre, Honiton 084719
Grove Farm Gallery, Catfield 112828
Grove Gallery, Saint Paul 119293
Grove Rare Books, Skipton 131502, 142073
Grove Road Antiques, Blenheim . . . 078997
Grove Rural Life Museum, Manx National Heritage, Ramsey, Isle of Man . . . 040792
Grovebrook, Dee Why 055744
Groveland Gallery, Minneapolis . . . 117266
Grover, Ravi, Lucknow 105747
Grover Cleveland Birthplace, Caldwell 042546
Grover M. Hermann Fine Arts Center, Marietta 045671
Grover & Thurston, Seattle 119930
Grovewood Gallery, Asheville 041794
Growrich, Seoul 107242
Growrich, Seoul 107243
The Grub Street Bookshop, Fitzroy . 136901
Grubb Shaft Gold and Heritage Museum, Beaconsfield 000780
Grube, Volker, Hildesheim 125931
Grube Alte Hoffnung Erbstolln, Mittweida 018962
Grubenmann-Sammlung, Teufen . . 037625
Gruber, München 126385
Gruber, A., Altötting 069156
Gruber, Andreas, Pocking 126637
Gruber, Colette, Le Castellet 099431
Gruber, Gerhard, Heilbronn 129258
Gruber, Gertrud, Nänikon 082683
Gruber, Hermann, München 134242
Gruber, Katharina, Klagenfurt 057108
Gruber, Michael, Mengen 104061
Gruca, Wojciech, Gdańsk 129009
Grübel Nombre-Madeira, Alvaro, Wiesbaden 074404
Gruel, Dany, Rennes (Ille-et-Vilaine) 138581
Gruen, Chicago 115445
Grün, A. & M., Püttlingen 073383
Grün, Herbert, Heidelberg 071453
Gruen & Speer, Wiesbaden 105260
Grünauer Wassersportmuseum, Stiftung Stadtmuseum Berlin, Berlin 016053
Grünbichler, Johann, Bad Ischl 056930
Gründ, Paris 133618
Gründer, Braunschweig 138923
Gründler, Ulrich, Hainichen, Sachsen 125786
Grüne, Johann, Kerken 071799
Grüne Galerie, Fränkisch-Crumbach 102736
Grünen, Thomas, Krefeld 072071
Grünert, Osnabrück 073237
Grünes Gewölbe, Staatliche Kunstsammlungen Dresden, Dresden 016790
Grünewald, Sonja, Neuss 104423
Grünewald, Thomas, Waldkirch . . . 126960
Grünwald, Dr. Michael D., München 104219
Grünzig, Mathias, Eppendorf 125590
Gruet Pol, Nantes 124483
Grüttert Uhrenmuseum Bremen, Galerie Juwelier Grüttert, Bremen 016415
Gruetunet Museum, Kirkenær i Solør 030936
Grützner, Ingo, München 126386
Grützner, Paul, Friedrichsdorf, Taunus 070893
Gruia, Christine, Friesoythe 102891
Gruillot, Marie-Françoise, Besançon 061385
Grulier, Courchevel 099179
Grumman Memorial Park, Calverton 042553
Grummer, Heinsberg 071480
Grumps, Los Angeles 089783
Grumpy, Las Vegas 089581
Grund, Andrea, Berlin 125207
Grund, Hendrik, Zeulenroda 074566
Grund, Jeff, Chicago 131904
Grund, Jürgen, Berg, Kreis Ahrweiler 125153
Grundmann, Andreas, Münster 139564
Grundner, Heinz, München 072718
Grundtvigs Mindestuer i Udby, Lundby 009016
Grundy Art Gallery, Blackpool 038755
Grune, Haimhausen 071171
Gruner, Sittard 078761
Grunewald, Klaus, Kansas City 142475
Grunewald, Peter, Essen 070629
Grunow, Dieter, Berlin 069625
Grunschel, K.& R., Siegburg 073805, 104890
Grunspan, Marcel, Paris 066021
Grunspan, Marcel, Paris 066022
Grunt, Vancouver 097479
Grunt Gallery, Vancouver 006698
Grunwald Center for the Graphic Arts, University of California, Hammer Museum of Art and Cultural Center, Los Angeles 045425
Grup 62, Barcelona 134916
Grup d'Art Escola, Barcelona 054116
Grup d'Art Escola, Lleida 110407
Grup d'Art Escola, Tarragona 054115
Grup d'Art Escola, Tarragona 110786
Grupello Verlag, Düsseldorf 133892
Grupo Alternativo Empresarial, Málaga 054117, 110639
Grupo Arte Contemporáneo, México 134760
Gruscht & Krempel, Ulm 074142
Gruse, Andrea, Kamen 071690
Grusenmeyer, K., Bruxelles 057975
Grusenmeyer, Philippe, Boisseron . 061543
Grusenmeyer, Serge, Gent 058183
Grusenmeyer, St., Antwerpen 057699
Gruttmann, Dortmund 102401
Gruvik, Oskarshamn 122225
Gruvmuseet, Sala 036555
Gruyer, Paul, Lentilly 063744
Gryfton Galleries, Ryeish Green . . . 114339
Gryphon Bookshop, New York 142659
Grytøy Bygdetun, Lundenes 031001
Grzelachowski, Detlef, Berlin 069626
Grzimek, Brita, Berlin 069627
GSA Centrum voor Beeldende Kunst, Hilversum 108085
Gschlößl Leithaprodersdorf-Freilichtanlage, Leithaprodersdorf 002218
Gschwendtner, Michael, Stuttgart . . 073977
Gschwendtner, Stefan, Linz 123410
Gschwind & Obertreis, München . . 126387
Gsellmanns Weltmaschine, Edelsbach bei Feldbach 001802
Gselman, Jadranka, Maribor 080661, 109989
GSIS Gallery, Pasay 031755
GSM, Frankfurt am Main 070744
Gstöttner, Friedrich, Salzburg 123444
Gstrein, Gottfried, Zell am Ziller . . . 095983
Gu-Ba-Csó, Budapest 074687
Gu Yue Xuan, Shanghai 059741
Guach, Juan, Palma de Mallorca . . 110688
Guadagno, Gabriella, Bologna 075085
Guadagno, Gabriella, Bologna 075086
Guadagno, Gabriella, Bologna 075087
Guadagno, Gabriella, Bologna 127154
Guadalimar, Madrid 136090
Guadalupe Cultural Arts Center, San Antonio 047794
Guagenti, Luciano, Milano 075735
Guagnini Logarso, Hector H., Buenos Aires 055213
Guainans, Le Castellet 063587
Guainans, Alain, Le Beausset 063564
Guaita, Joan, Palma de Mallorca . . 110689
Gualda Hernandez, Ramon, Granada 081144
Gualtieri, Galatée, Paris 100481
Gualtieri, Galatée, Paris 100482
Guam Museum, Agana 021566
Guanabara, Rio de Janeiro 096620
Guangdong Art Gallery, Guangzhou . 007080
Guangdong Folk Arts and Crafts Museum, Guangzhou 007081
Guangdong Museum, Guangzhou . . 007082
Guangxi Fine Arts Publishing House, Nanning 133377
Guangxi Natural Museum, Nanning 007210
Guangxi Provincial Museum, Guilin . 007093
Guangyi, Wuxi 098036
Guangzhou Ancient Works, Guangzhou 137746
Guangzhou Art Gallery, Guangzhou . 007083
Guangzhou Art Museum, Guangzhou 007084
Guangzhou Artists Gallery, Guangzhou 097723
Guangzhou Liwan District Museum, Guangzhou 007085
Guangzhou Lu Xun Museum, Guangzhou 007086
Guangzhou Museum, Guangzhou . . 007087
Guard House and Soldiers Barracks, Fredericton 005481
Guardadero Blanco y Negro, Medellín 059921
Guardhouse Museum, Tattershall . . 041189
Guardia, Gérard, Le Castellet 063588
El Guardian de lo Pequeño, Madrid . 110539
Guardian Gallery, Los Angeles 116785
Guardian of the East, Singapore . . . 080475
Guardini, Berlin 101917
The Guards Museum, London 040163
Guarisco, Washington 120305
Guarisse, Andre Caruso, Porto Alegre 058503
Guarneri, Severino, Milano 127607
Guarnieri, Rosanna, Parma 106453
Guarracino, Ciro, Napoli . . 075996, 106374, 127772, 140079
Guastalla, Guido, Livorno 106124
Guastalla Arte, Livorno 106125
Guayamurí Antigüedades, Caracas . 093532
Guazzolini, Roma 076504
Guazzolini, Roma 076505
Guckelberger & Co., F.A., Philadelphia 118774
Der Guckkasten, München 139509
Guckloch Galerie, Maur 111723
Gudbrandsdal Krigsminnesamling, Kvam 030964
Gude, Amsterdam 077859
Guedel, Gildas, Paris 066023
Guedj, Didier, Saint-Ouen 067795
Guedot, Bernard, Montpellier 064746
Guée, Jean-Claude, Thury-Harcourt 068417
Gueguen, Jean-Yves, Crozon 062576
Güldaglar, T., Heidelberg 071454
Gülderneyen, Yildirim, Frankfurt am Main 070745
Guelle, Serge, Orléans 065303
Guelman, Moskva 109552
Guelph Civic Museum, Guelph Museums, Guelph 005556
Gün, I., Köln 071945
Guenard-d'Abbadie, Andrée, Toulon (Var) 068454
Gueneau, Jean-Michel, Paris 066024
Güngör Dekorasyon, İstanbul 083138
Guennet, Ventabren 068763
Guénot, Jacqueline, Paris 066025
Günter, Polska Cerkiew 079684
Günter, Anna, Traunkirchen 057332
Günter, Heidemarie, Überlingen . . . 105085
Günter, Stefan, Volkach 074228
Günter Grass-Kulturstiftung Hansestadt Lübeck, Lübeck 018719
Günters, Nordhorn 073082
Günther, Issum 071642
Günther, Albert, Dortmund 125479
Günther, Albert J., Eichstätt 125577
Günther, Dieter, Issum 125979
Guenther, Egon, Johannesburg 080706, 110055
Günther, Dr. Jörn, Hamburg 139181
Günther, Johannes, Offenbach am Main 126587
Günther, Karin, Hamburg 103158
Günther, Knut, Frankfurt am Main . . 070746
Günther, Monika, Hamburg 125818

Guenther, Robert, Milwaukee 117194
Günther, Sabine, Weißenfels 074327
Günther, Wolfgang, Plettenberg . . . 073344
Güntheroth, Claudia, Herzberg (Mark) 139266
Güntheroth, Karl-Friedrich, Meinhard 072499
Guépin, Jean-Jacques, Ruaudin . . . 067317
Gueraiche, Ghodjah, Hydra 055137
Guercio, Joe, Toronto 123833
Guerdener, Victor, Chantemerle-les-Blés 062138
Gueridon, New York 090922
Guérin, Albert, La Baule-Escoublac 099378
Guérin, Guy, Pouance 066964
Guerin, Jean-Claude, Paris 066026
Guérin, Michel, Saint-Dié-des-Vosges 121243
Guérin, Pierre, Nantes 064925
Guérin & Fils, La Baule-Escoublac . 063289
Guerlotté, Philippe, Casteljaloux . . . 062009
Guermeur, Jeannine, Le Faou 063618
Guernsey, New York 122997
Guernsey County Museum, Cambridge 042572
Guernsey Museum and Art Gallery, Saint Peter Port 040936
Guerra, Carmen de la, Madrid 110540
Guerra, Cristina, Lisboa 109326
Guerra, Paolo, Roma 128070
Guerre, Gérard, Avignon . . 061135, 124087
Guerrero, Bogotá 098169
Guerrero, Enrique, México 107493
Guerrero Mancilla, Eugenio, Madrid 129628
Guerrieri, Gianluigi, Roma 076506
Guerrin, Claude, Paris 100483
El Guerro Antiguedades, Valencia . . 081662
Guerrots, François & Chantal des, Heugleville-sur-Scie 063154
Guerta, Madrid 110541
Gürtler, Dietmar, Süßen 134425
Guesne, Pierre, Couptrain 062507
Guess, Fredrick, New Orleans 117449
Guest, G.P. & M.J., Subiaco 056644
Guest, Karen, Beverley . . . 083498, 130375
Guest, Karen, Driffield 084220
Guest, Melissa, Subiaco 123311
Güthinger, R., Tuttlingen 074122
Güttner, Benito, Mittelneufnach . . . 072554
Gützlaf, Wolfgang, Berlin 069628
Guevara, Buenos Aires 055214
Gueyraud Transactions, Laragne-Montéglin 063536
Güzel Sanatlar Müzesi, Girne 008245
Güzelyurt Müzesi, ArKeoloji ve Doğa Müzesi, Güzelyurt 008247
Gufi, Sofia 058762
Guggenberger, Alexander, Wien . . . 057434
Guggenberger, Ilse, Salzburg 057252
Guggenheim Asher, New York 117986
Guggenheim Hermitage Museum, Las Vegas 045184
Guggenheim Museum Bilbao, Bilbao 034985
Guggenheim Museum Soho, New York 046341
Guggisberg, Beat, Zimmerwald . . . 082927
Gugliandolo, Cecilia, Roma 128071
Guglielmetti, Serge, Saint-Cyr-les-Colons 067413
Giuseppe Guglielmi & Sibille Schneider, München 126388
Guhl, Jacques, Montreux 111746
Guicciardi, Marco, Modena 075913
Guichard, Montbellet 064650
Guichard, Guy, Ouzouer-sur-Loire . . 065318
Guichard, Henriette, Paris 124682
Guichard & Juillan, Saint-Brieuc . . . 121241
Guicheney, Philippe, Castelnaudary 062017
Guichoux, François, Carhaix-Plouguer 061987, 124170
Guidarelli, Federico, Roma 128072
Guidarini, Pia, Genova 075471
Guide Emer, Paris 135711
Guide Heritage Centre, London 040164
Guide to National Endowment for the Arts, Washington 136478
Guidi, Guido, Genova 106096
Guidi, Maya, Carouge 111339
Guidi, Silvia, San Marino 129254
Guidieri, Gina, Genova 075472
Guido Gezellemuseum, Stedelijke Musea Brugge, Brugge 003270
Guignard, Caudan 120965
Guignard, Paris 066027
Guignard, Bruno, Rochecorbon 067173
Guignard, Gérard, Saint-Ouen 067796
Guignard, Jean-Louis, Vevey 082881
Guigon, Paris 100484
Guigue, Paris 100485
Guigue, Jean-François & Muriel, Paris 124683
Guigue & Locca, Paris 124684
Guiho, Claude, Varengeville-sur-Mer 068726
Guilbert, Benoît, Paris 138398
Guild Antiques, New York 090923
Guild Art Corporation, Minneapolis . 117267
The Guild Art Gallery, Mumbai 105777
Guild Gallery, Bristol 038864
Guild Gallery at El Con, Tucson 120132
Guild Hall Museum, East Hampton . 043567
Guild House Antiques, Vancouver . . 059363
Guild News, New York 136479
Guild of Antique Dealers and Restorers, Shrewsbury 054393
Guild of Artists, Silvermine Guild Arts Center, New Canaan 054784
Guild of Boston Artists, Boston 054785
Guild of Creative Art, Shrewsbury . . 048167
Guild of Master Craftsmen, Lewes .054394, 135167
Guild of Railway Artists, Warwick . . 054395
Guild of Taxidermists, Glasgow 054396
The Guild of West Midlands Artists and Craftsmen, Lichfield 054397
The Guild Shop, Toronto 097282
La Guilde Graphique, Montréal 052751, 097036
Guilde Royale des Antiquaires de Flandres, Dilbeek 052677
Guilded Salvage Antiques, Minneapolis 090363
Guildford Cathedral Treasury, Guildford 039645
Guildford House Gallery, Guildford . 039646
Guildford Museum, Guildford 039647
Guildhall, Bath 038623
Guildhall, Beverley 038691
Guildhall, Exeter 039464
Guildhall, Leicester 039970
Guildhall, Thaxted 041206
Guildhall Art Gallery, London 040165
Guildhall Galleries, Bury Saint Edmunds 112772
Guildhall Gallery, Poole 114270
Guildhall Gallery, Winchester 041401
Guildhall Museum, Carlisle 038998
Guildhall Museum, Chichester 039071
Guildhall Museum, Rochester 040847
Guildhall Museum, Sandwich 040958
Guildnotes, Englewood 136480
Guilford College Art Gallery, Greensboro 044333
Guilford Courthouse National Military Park, Greensboro 044334
Guilhabert, Françoise, La Rochelle . 063433
Guilhem, Jean-Pierre, Béziers 061441
Guilhemsans, Jean, Ousse 065316
Guilhemsans, Jean, Pau 066705
Guili, Montevideo 087323
Guilin City Museum, Guilin 007094
Guillais, Hubert-Pierre, Paris 066028
Guillard, Patrick, Paris 066029
Guillaume, Paris 100486
Guillaume, Evelyne, Warcq 069043
Guillaume, J.-M., Namur 058352
Guillaumot, Georges, Lyon 121050
Guillaumot, Pierre-Yves, Lyon 121051
Guillebaud, Georges, L'Isle-d'Espagnac 063910
Guillemard, Michel, Dijon 062666
Guillemin, Alain, Romilly-sur-Seine 067207
Guillemin, Jean-Jacques, Tournus . 068570
Guillemin, Michelle, Chalon-sur-Saône 138069
Guillemin, Pascal, Lyon 064138
Guilleminot, Françoise, Villars-le-Pautel 068878
Guillemot, Claude, Paris 100487
Guillemot, Monique, Nantes 064926
Guiller, Medellín 059922
Guiller, Paris 066030
Guillerminet, Pierre, Bourg-en-Bresse 061707
Guillet, Paris 100488
Guillet, Gérard, Lausanne 082550
Guillon-Laffaille, Fanny, Paris 100489, 133619, 138399
Guillot-Renou, Cloyes-sur-le-Loir . . 062364
Guillou, Paris 138400
Guillou, Françoise, Paris 100490
Guilmette, Julie, Firenze 127355
Guimaraes, Rio de Janeiro 058594
Guimaraes, Rio de Janeiro 058595
Guimarães, Alencastro, Porto Alegre 096563
Guimaraes, Maguered P., Belo Horizonte 058431
Guimiot, Philippe, Bruxelles 057976
Guinand, Anse 060909
Guinaudeau, Torfou 101314
Guindani, Adalgisa, Milano 075736
Guindani, Gianna, Milano 127608
Guinevere, London 085361
Guinhut, Daniel, Montrevault 064772
Guinness Archives, London 040166
Guinness Museum of World Records, Niagara Falls 006009
Guinness Storehouse, Dublin 022746
Guinness World of Records Museum, Las Vegas 045185
Guinot, Philippe, Jons 099371
Guiot, Paris 100491
Guiral Barado, Barcelona 080866
Guiraud, Hervé, Bordeaux 124126
Guiraud, Raoul, Paris 066031
Guirrierc, Hervé, Bordeaux 061618
Guisan Aude, La Tour-de-Peilz 130196
Guitar Museo Ex Teresa Arte Actual, México 028435
Guiter, Jean-Luc, Perpignan 066747
Guitine, Evelyne, Saint-Ouen 067797
Guitton, Bernard, Le Lion-d'Angers 063646
Guiyuan Art Cooperative, Shanghai . 097915
Guizhou Provincial Museum, Guiyang 007097
Guizzetti & Collet, Reims 121230
Guizzi, Pietro, Brescia 075171
GUK-Udhus, Lejre 098595
Gukgiwon Taekwondo Museum, Seoul 027557
Gulbenes Vēstures un Mākslas Muzejs, Gulbene 027684
Guldemond, Hermine, Haarlem 078457
Gulden Galeria, Gdańsk 108888
Gulessian, André, Marseille 064365
Gulf Antiques, Abu Dhabi 083173
Gulf Antiques, Manama 057629
Gulf Antiques, Sharjah 083215
Gulf Auctions, Manama . . 057630, 120700
Gulf Beach Art Center, Indian Rocks Beach 044729
Gulf Coast Artworks, Houston 116328
Gulf Coast Exploreum, Mobile 045947
Gulf Coast Museum of Art, Largo . . 045173
Gulf Museum, Port-aux-Basques . . 006173
Gulf of Georgia Cannery, Richmond 006282
Gulf Station Historic Farm, Yarra Glen 001643
Guliker, Emmerich 070561
Gulino, Giovanna, Catania 075250, 127268
Gull Gallery, Merimbula 094835
Gullane Antiques, Guillane 084543
Gullhaugen Setermuseum, Venabygd 031327
Gulli Skoletun, Andebu 030729
Gullia, Carolyn, Atlanta 131777
Gully, Rex, Seaview 086531
Gully Antiques, Boronia 055524
Gumanitarnyj Centr-muzej Tvorčestva Autsajderov, Moskva 033415
Gumbez Manace Literary Ethnographic Museum, Taš-Aryk 027642
Gumer & Co., Louisville 089993
Gumer & Co., Louisville 089994
Gumeracha and District History Centre, Gumeracha 001085
Gumnut Antiques, Gosford 055903
Gumucio, Maria Isabel, Santiago de Chile 123881
Gun O'Clock, Stellenbosch 080749
Gunarsa Museum, Museum Seni Lukis Klasik Bali, Klungkung 022464
Gunda, Zürich 112107
Gundagai Historical Museum, Gundagai 001086
Gunder, Vera, Darmstadt 125443
Gunderman, Anne, Buffalo 115257
Gunderson House, Kenyon 044970
Gundry, Houston 089091
Gunichi, Hiroshima 077055
Gunma-kenritsu Kindai Bijutsukan, Takasaki 027114
Gunma Prefectural Museum of History, Takasaki 027115
Gunn, Lynton 114019
Gunn, Alastair, Culross 130623
Gunn Memorial Library and Museum, Washington 048878
Gunnebo Slott och Trädgårdar, Mölndal 036479
Gunnersbury Park Museum, London 040167
Gunning Antiques, Limerick 074988, 127104
Gunnison County Pioneer and Historical Museum, Gunnison 044372
Gunnison Museum of Natural History, Pawling 046846
Gunston Hall Plantation, Mason Neck 045723
Gunten, Wilfried von, Thun 111946, 130194
Guntermann, Düsseldorf 070389
Guntlisbergen, G., Best 128586
Guntlisbergen, John, Eindhoven . . . 078340
Gunyulgup Galleries, Yallingup 095439
Gunzenhauser, Dr. Alfred Emil Otmar, München 104220
Keith Guo & Liang Ju, San Francisco 119680
Guovdageainnu Gilisillju, Kautokeino Bygdetun, Kautokeino 030935
Gurari, Boston 087825, 142255
Gurgul, Gina & Andrzej Jerzy, Berlin 125208
Gurich, Madrid 081319
Gurievskij Istoriko-Kraevedčeskij Muzej, Guriev 027402
Gurkha Museum, Winchester 041402
Gurlino, Luciano, Torino 128315
Gurriaran, Luis, Madrid 110542
Gurtner, Christian, Wien 123495
Gurtner, Walter & Cornelia, Basel . .082144, 129920
Gurtubay, Madrid 081320
Guruban Tajore Art Gallery, Chennai 105631
Guruda, Delhi 074803
Guruji Bros, Mumbai 105778
Gurusaday Museum, Museum of Bengal Folk Art, Kolkata 022219
Guruve, London 113665
Guseviciaus, Vilnius 128460
Gusewski, Siegfried, Lübeck 126242
Gush Ezyon Museum, Gush Ezyon . 022911
Gusinde, Heike, Leipzig 126188
Gussio, Lucia, Roma 128073
Gustaf-Dalman-Institut für biblische Landes- und Altertumskunde, Greifswald 017523
Gustafson Gallery, Colorado State University, Fort Collins 043903

Gustafsson, Gudrun, Stockholm . . . 081956
Gustafsson & Gyrud, Fengersfors . . 122133
Gustav-Adolf-Gedenkstätte, Lützen 018749
Gustav-Adolf-Museum, Geleithaus, Weißenfels 020780
Gustav-Freytag-Archiv und Museum, Wangen im Allgäu 020671
Gustav-Freytag-Gedenkstätte, Gotha 017491
Gustav III.'s Antikmuseum, Stockholm 036627
Gustav III.'s Paviljong, Solna 036601
Gustav Jeeninga Museum of Bible and Near Eastern Studies, Anderson 041717
Gustav-Lübcke Museum, Hamm, Westfalen 017731
Gustav-Wolf-Kunstgalerie, Östringen 019447
Gustavsbergs Porslinmuseum, Gustavsberg 036316
Guszahn, P. & R., Kirchlengern 071862
Gut, Werner & Mägi, Triengen 082861
Gut Görtz, Görtz 102974
Gut Seekamp der Hans Kock-Stiftung, Kiel 018245
Gut Sonnenschein, Hohenweiden . . 071561
Gut Zernikow, Großwotdersdorf . . . 017585
Gutao Wenming Museum, Beijing . . 006987
Das Gute Buch, Zürich 141339
Gutenberg Al Colosseo, Roma 106560, 140105
Gutenberg-Gedenkstätte, Eltville . . 016952
Gutenberg-Gesellschaft, Internationale Vereinigung für Geschichte und Gegenwart der Druckkunst e.V., Mainz 053225
Gutenberg-Museum, Mainz 018788
Gutenberg Museum, Schweizerisches Museum der graphischen Industrie und der Kommunikation, Fribourg . . . 037099
Guth, Tangermünde 105032
Guth-Maas & Maas, Reutlingen . . . 104728
Gutharc-Ballin, Paris 100492
Guthmann, Steffen, Langenbernsdorf 072154
Guthschmidt, Den Haag 107924
Gutierrez, Eric, Dallas 132011
Gutierrez, Raul, San Antonio 119421
Gutierrez, Véronique, Paris 124685
Gutierrez Carrasquilla, Enrique, Sevilla 129733
Gutlin, London 085362, 131050
Gutman, Jean-Pierre, Versailles . . . 101454
Gutowski, Wiesbaden 121624
Gutschke, Reinhard, Berlin 069629
Gutshaus Steglitz, Berlin 016054
Gutshof Haus Meer, Meerbusch . . . 104047
Gutshof Pinnow, Pinnow bei Angermünde 019620
Guttenberger, Elia, Weinsberg 074321
Guttmann, Max, Helsingør 060256
Guust, den, Breda 078094
Guwahati Medical Museum, Medical College Guwahati, Guwahati 022137
Guwu Xuan Art, Suzhou 097996
Guy, Adam, Bruxelles 137438
Guy, Gerard, Bewdley 083506, 130380
Guy, Jacques, Buchères 061832
Guy, Jean, Mons 064608
Guy Lombardo Museum, London . . 005788
The Guy On Motor, Los Angeles . . . 089784
Guyana Museum, Georgetown 021600
Guyart, Brugge 096116
Guyet, Annick, Rouen 067268
Guyomarc, Noël, Montréal 097037
Guyon, Alain, Besançon 061386
Guyot, Camille, Dinan 062682
Guyot, Gérard, Vanves 068722
Guyot, Marion, Atlanta 114886
Guyot, Thierry, Notre-Dame-du-Pre 065236
Guy's Coins, Chicago 088101
Guzman, Valencia 081663, 110831
GVA Editions, Genève 135019
Gwalia Historical Museum, Leonora 001183
Gwangju Municipal Folk Museum, Gwangju 027502
Gwangju National Museum, Gwangju 027503
Gwanhun Gallery, Seoul 107244
Gwen, Fort Worth 116145
Gwili Steam Railway, Bronwydd . . . 038886
Gwilliam, Edred A.F., Cricklade 084116
Gwinettt Fine Arts Center, Duluth . . 043516
Gwinnett Historical Society Museum, Lawrenceville 045210
Gwinnett History Museum, Lawrenceville 045211
Das Gwölb, Bad Ischl 056931
Gwóźdź, Krzysztof, Poznań 079688, 140761
Gwydir Street Antiques, Cambridge 083846
Gwynby, Cleveland 088335
Gwynedd Education and Culture, Archives, Museums and Galleries, Caernarfon 038941
Gwynfair, Holyhead 084710
Gyard, Christian, Saint-Martin-en-Haut 067648
Gycha, Barbara, Rednitzhembach . . 126685
Gyemyung University Museum, Daegu 027475
Gyeongbo Museum of Paleontology, Namjeong 027534
Gyeongbuk National University Museum, Daegu 027476
Gyeonggi Provincial Museum, Yongin 027625
Gyeongju National Museum, Gyeongju 027505
Gyeongju University Museum, Gyeongju 027506
Gyertyás Antikvitás, Szeged 074753
Gyldenløwe, Oslo 079441
Gyllner, Stockholm 111054
Gympie and District Historical and Gold Mining Museum, Gympie 001090
Gympie Antiques, Gympie 055927, 123234
Gyönygszem Galéria, Pécs 105571
Györ Egyházmegyei Könyvtár es Kincstár, Győr 021730
Gyoĕrffy István Nagykun Múzeum, Karcag 021755
Györy & Osiris, Miami 117084
Gyözö, Farkas, Fertőd 127081
Gyokudo Art Museum, Ome 026950
Gyokuei-do Shoten, Tokyo 140185
Gyokusenji Homotsukan, Kamo, Izu 026617
Gypsy Caravan Antiques, Las Vegas 089582
Gypsy Savage, Houston 089092
Gysbers & Van Loon, Arnhem 140355
It Gysbert Japicxhûs Museum, Bolsward 029323
Gysin, Bob, Zürich 112108
Gyula Derkovits Galéria, Budapest . 021651
Gyzmo Projects, Gent 096289
H. Art Gallery, Antwerpen 096068
H & B Gallery, Minneapolis 090364
H. B. Lamb Early Transport Buggy Museum, Camperdown 000884
H. Earl Clack Museum, Havre 044483
H & G Furniture Restoration, Atlanta 131778
H & L Galerie, Waiblingen 105141
H & M Art Gallery of Harlem, New York 117987
H&M Kunstwinkel, Dordrecht 107978
H & N, Praha 123981
H & R Antiques, Memphis 090076
Hå Bygdemuseum, Varhaug 031319
Hå Gamle Prestegard, Varhaug 031320
Hå gamle prestegard, Varhaug 108762
Ha Noi Fine Arts Association, Ha Noi 055121
Ha Noi Gallery, Ha Noi 120466
Ha Noi Museum, Ha Noi 049528
Ha Noi Studio, Ha Noi 120467
Ha Noi University of Fine Arts, Ha Noi 052426
Ha Noi University of Industrial Design, Ha Noi 052427
Haack, Dr. H., Heidelberg 139250
Haack, Harald, Bochum . . 069884, 102154
Haaf, Franz-Josef, Meckesheim . . .072484, 126299
Haag, Gérard, Zellwiller 069073
Haag, Joachim, München 126389
Haag & Scott, Bad Kreuznach 069316
Haage, Stockholm 081957
Haagen, Los Angeles 116786
Haagen, Harald, Fellbach 070682
Haager Heimatstuben, Haag am Hausruck 001997
Haagmans, Essen 125613
Haags Historisch Museum, Den Haag 029425
Haags Openbaar Vervoer Museum, Den Haag 029426
Haagse Kunstkring, Den Haag 053888, 107925
Haak, Heidi, Wiesbaden 105261
Haaken, Oslo 108729
Haaksman, D.I., Amsterdam 077860
Haan, Marja den, Ter Aar 128517
Haapasalo, Kari, Helsinki 060525
Haardplatenmuseum Klarenbeek, Klarenbeek 029811
Haardt, Anton, New Orleans 117450
Haarlem Antiek, Haarlem 078458
Haas, de, Amsterdam 077861
Gebr. Haas, Bedburg-Hau 138724
Haas, Budapest 105513
Haas, Cicero 131922
Haas, Zürich 112109
Haas, Bruno, Lörrach 134163
Haas, Heinrich, Schaan 077446
Haas, Johann, Wels 137279
Haas, Klaus, Mörlenbach 104107
Haas, Michael, Wiesbaden 074405
Haas, Monika, Bad Kleinkirchheim . 056933
Haas, Otto, London 141815
Haas, Dr. Peter, Teningen 126899
Haas, Raul, Cincinnati 088249
Haas, Reinhold, Randersacker 126678
Haas, Susan P., Seattle 119931
Haas, Tom, Phoenix 118874
Haas, Wolfgang, Berlin 069630
Haas Bowmaker, Steven, Milwaukee 090302
Haas & Fuchs, Berlin 101918
Haas Gallery of Art, Bloomsburg . . . 042271
Haas-Lilienthal House, San Francisco 047864
Haase, Berlin 069631
Haase, Stuttgart 104985
Haase, R., Chemnitz 070130
Haase, Torsten, Neukirchen, Erzgebirge 072998
Haase, Wiebke, Hamburg 125819
Haasler, Alexandra, Jesteburg 103451
Haasner, Brigitte, Wiesbaden 105262
Haastrup Folkemindesamling, Faaborg 008851
La Habana Subastas, Madrid 122062
Habari, Wien 095857
Habashi, Alexandria 060419
Habatat, Chicago 115446
Habbekrats, Gent 058184
Habeck, H.H., Hohenfelde 103397
Habel-Schablitzky, Andrea, Köln . . . 126081
Habelt, Gero, Bonn 138896
Habelt, Dr. Rudolf, Bonn . . 133829, 138897
Haber, Robert, New York 117988
Georg Haber & Joh.L.L. Brandner, Berlin 125209
Georg Haber & Joh.L.L. Brandner, Regensburg 126689
Haber-Feist, Osterhofen 126601
Haberfellner, Gerda, Wien 057435
Haberhauer, Herford 071488
Habermann, Ibi, Innsbruck 095584
Habernicht, Marianne, Trier 074092
Habernickel, K. & A., Much 072601
Habersetzer, Schortens 073727
Habert, Eric & Catherine, Le Passage 063676
Haberzettl, Adolf, Feuchtwangen . . 070685
Haberzettl, Anna-Maria, München . 072719
Habitaat Art and Craft, Mumbai . . . 105779
Habitare, Genova 075473
Habitat, Hamburg 103159
l'Habitat, Indianapolis 089300
Habitat Ancien, Patrimoine Architectural Rural, Montagnac-la-Crempse . . . 013116
Habitat Antiques, Port Macquarie . . 056475
Habite, San Francisco 092805
Habite, San Francisco 092806
Habsburg, Paris 121156
Hachem, Mark, Paris 100493
Hachem, Moussa, Paris 100494
Hachem, Moussa, Paris 100495
Hachette, Paris 133620
Hachidai, Hiroshima 077056
Hachiga Minzoku Bijutsukan, Takayama 027118
Hachijo Municipal Museum, Hachijo 026477
Hachinohe City Museum of Art, Hachinohe 026478
Hachioji-shi Hakubutsukan, Hachioji 026480
Hachiro Yuasa Memorial Museum, Mitaka 026813
Hachmeister, Petershagen, Weser . 139652
Hachmeister, Dr. H., Münster 104368
Hachmeister, W., Petershagen, Weser 073310
Hacı Ömer Sabancı Kültür Merkezi, Adana 037993
Hacıbektaş Müzesi, Nevşehir 038156
Hacienda Art Gallery, Phoenix 118875
Hacienda Buena Vista, Ponce 032719
La Hacienda de Soldeca, Zaragoza . 129814
Hacienda El Paraíso, El Cerrito 007494
Hack, Rainer, Zella-Mehlis 105368
Hacke, Axel, München 126390
Hackelbury, London 113666
Hacker, Roland, Hamburg 071239
Hacker, S., New York 142660
Hackett & Freedman, San Francisco 119681
Hackettstown Historical Society Museum, Hackettstown 044378
Hackhofer, B., Sankt Wendel 139710
Hackler's, Preston 086310
Hackley & Hume Historic Site, Muskegon 046105
Hackner, Klaus, Riedenburg 126720
Hackney House Antiques, Barlow . . 083383
Hackney Museum, London 040168
Hadaka no Taisho Kinenkan, Kyoto . 026718
Hadalhondi, Bilbao 080975, 129435
Hadassa, New York 090924
Hadassa, New York 090925, 132476
Haddad Camano, Andrés, Santiago de Chile 059534
Haddo House, Methlick 040453
Haddon Galleries, Torquay 114584
Haddon Hall, Maastricht 078606
Haddon Hall, Venlo 078834
Haddonfield Museum, Haddonfield . 044379
Haddy, Jeffery, Prahran 056492
H.a.Déco, Fecamp 062850
Hadeland Bergverksmuseum, Grua 030866
Hadeland Folkemuseum, Jaren . . . 030924
Hadeland Glassverks Museum, Hadeland Glassverk, Jevnaker 030926
Haden Hall, Cradley Heath 039162
Haden Hill House, Cradley Heath . . 039163
Hadernverlag, Salzburg 133139
Hadersbeck, Berlin 069632, 121331
Hadersbeck, Potsdam . . . 073362, 121578
Haderslev Museum, Haderslev 008885
Hadfield, G.K., Great Salkeld 084520
Hadiqat al-Asmak Museum, Zamalek 009348
Hadjer, Reynold & Fils, Paris 124686
Hadji Baba Ancient Art, London . . . 085363
Hadjidimou Collection, Athinai 021173
Hadley, New York 090926
Hadley, Peter J., Norwich 141965
Hadley Farm Museum, Hadley 044381

Hadlow Down Antiques, Hadlow Down . . . 084549, 130752
Hadrovský, Josef, Pardubice . . . 098406
Hadsund Egns Museum, Hadsund . 008889
Hadtörténeti Múzeum, Budapest . . 021652
Hadyna, Brno . . . 059978
Hädicke, B., Leipzig . . . 139394
Häffner, P., Gaggenau . . . 070922
Haegang Ceramics Museum, Icheon 027507
Hægebostad Bygdemuseum, Tingvatn . . . 031264
Haegler, Carl, Rehetobel . . . 111825
Hägnan Friluftsmuseet i Gammelstad, Gammelstad . . . 036285
Hähn, Adrian, Essen . . . 102683
Hähnel, R., Bünde . . . 070083
Hähnlein, E., Felsberg . . . 125635
Haeju Historical Museum, Haeju . . . 027434
Häkkilän Museo, Toholampi . . . 010152
Hälleforsnäs Gjuterimuseum, Hälleforsnäs . . . 036318
Hälleviks Fiskemuseum, Sölvesborg 036597
Hällisch-Fränkisches Museum, Schwäbisch Hall . . . 020113
Hällristningsmuseet vid Brunnssalongen, Norrköping . . . 036500
Hälsinge Byrån, Fors . . . 122135
Hälsinglands Museum, Hudiksvall . 036349
Häme-Galleria, Lahti . . . 098754
Hämeen Linna, Hämeenlinna . . . 009489
Hämeen Museo, Tampereen Museot, Tampere . . . 010118
Hämeenkyrön Kotiseutumuseo, Hämeenkyrö . . . 009485
Hämeenlinnan Kaupungin Historiallinen Museo, Hämeenlinna . . . 009490
Hämeenlinnan Puhelinmuseo, Hämeenlinna . . . 009491
Hämeenlinnan Taidemuseo, Hämeenlinna . . . 009492
Hämmerle, Lisi, Bregenz . 095485, 133063
Haendehen, Paulo Roberto, Porto Alegre . . . 058504
Händel-Haus, Musikmuseum der Stadt Halle, Halle, Saale . . . 017661
Häne, Kirchberg (Sankt Gallen) . . . 111583
Haenel, Cape Town . . . 110025
Hänel, Frank, Frankfurt am Main . . 102781
Hänel, Frank, Frankfurt am Main . . 102782
Hänel, Frank, Wiesbaden . . . 105263
Haenel-Pancera-Familienmuseum, Bad Ischl . . . 001722
Haenle, M., Göppingen . . . 071030
Haenle, Otto 07332) 5559, Böhmenkirch . . . 102169
Hänold, Joachim, Berlin . . . 069633
Het Haentje te Paart, Middelburg . . 108142
Haentjens Dekker & Gumbert, Utrecht . . . 134835
Haering, H., Wolfenbüttel . . . 074471
Haering, Jürgen, Freiburg im Breisgau . . . 070838
Häring, Thomas, Leipzig . . . 126189
Härjedalens Fjällmuseum, Jämtlands Läns Museum, Funäsdalen . . . 036281
Härjedalsauktioner, Vemdalen . . . 122293
Härkätien Museo, Renko . . . 010033
Haertel, Karl, Kitzbühel . . . 137202
Härtl, Ulf D., Bamberg . . . 069452
Härtl, Ulf D., Hemhofen . . . 071484
Härtl-Kasulke, Dr. Claudia, Dietzenbach . . . 102369
Härtsfeld-Museum, Neresheim . . . 019200
Härtsfeldbahn-Museum, Neresheim 019201
Haeseleer, Yvette d', Bruxelles . . . 057977, 123596
Hässleholms Auktionskammare, Hässleholm . . . 122148
Häüsler, München . . . 104221
Häuser, Markus, Rottenbach . . . 073606
Häuser, S., Neuenstein, Württemberg . . . 072987
Häuser, Susanne, Öhringen . . . 073177
Häusler, Bischberg . . . 069851
Häusser, Jürgen, Darmstadt . . . 133855
Häusslein, Harald, Schwäbisch Hall 073744
Haeyer, d', Charleroi . . . 058149
Haezeleer, Alain, Stuttgart . . . 139763
Hafemann, Gottfried, Wiesbaden . . 105264
Haferkorn, Inge, Wyk auf Föhr . . . 074549
Haferland, Ulrich, Finsterwalde . . . 125637
Hafez, New York . . . 090927
Haffen, Philippe, Reims . . . 124862
Haffenreffer Museum of Anthropology, Brown University, Bristol . . . 042423
Haffke, Altötting . . . 101570
Haffmans, F.J., Utrecht . . . 078806
Haffmuseum Ueckermünde, Ueckermünde . . . 020519
Haffner, Saint Louis . . . 092249
Haffner, Saint Louis . . . 092250
Haffner, Désiré, Nousseviller-Saint-Nabor . . . 065239
Hafnarborg Art Gallery, Hafnarfjörður . . . 021945
Hafnarhúsið, Listasafn Reykjavíkur, Reykjavík . . . 021960
Hafner, Paul, Sankt Gallen . . . 111871
Hafner, Ueli & Daniele, Bern . . . 082211
Haft Tappeh Museum, Haft Tappeh . 022557
Hafter, Birmensdorf . . . 082265
Hafter, Robert, Zürich . . . 082977, 130238
Haga, Paris . . . 066032
Hagadorn House Museum, Almond . 041667
Hagan, Eggedal . . . 030812
Hagedoorns Plaatse, Epe . . . 029575
Hagedorn, Brigitte, Frankfurt am Main . . . 125647
Hagedorn, M., Detmold . . . 070228
Hagedorn, R., Paderborn . . . 073281
Hagelandse Academie voor Beeldende Kunsten, Aarschot . . . 049675
Hagelin, Stockholm . . . 081958
Hagelmüller, Wolfgang, Hopfgarten im Brixental . . . 137193
Hagelstam, Helsinki . . . 060526, 098733, 120883
Hagelstam, C., Helsinki . . 120884, 137939
Hagemeier, Frankfurt am Main . . . 102783
Hagemoser, Andreas, Berlin . . . 138782
Hagen, Rastede . . . 073424
Hagen, Bert, Castricum . . . 140381
Hagen, Bert & Reiny, Amsterdam . . 077862
Hagen, Bert & Reiny, Amsterdam . . 140302
Hagen, Hans-J., Bayreuth . . . 138721
Hagen, L., Selfkant . . . 104881
Hagen, Richard, Broadway . . . 083758
Hagen, Richard, Broadway . . . 112733
Hagen Aria, London . . . 113667
Hagena & Schulte, Bonn . . . 138898
Hagena & Schulte, Bonn . . . 138899
Hagenauer, Karl, Wien . . . 095858
Hagenbuch, Ernst, Biglen . . . 111292
Hagenburger, Birgit Metall, Großkarlbach . . . 125764
Hagenring e.V. - Bund Bildender Künstler, Hagen, Westfalen . . . 053226
Hager, Gaëlle, Kaltenhouse . . . 063278
Hager, Peter, Steyr . . . 057324
Haggai, Charles, Paris . . . 066033
Haggerty Museum of Art, Milwaukee . . . 045889
The Haggin Museum, Stockton . . . 048371
Haggith, Paul, Holgate . . . 094651
Haghna Museum, Museum Zahal - Beit Eliyahu, Tel Aviv . . . 023073
Hagi Municipal Museum, Hagi . . . 026484
Hagley Hall, Hagley . . . 039653
The Hagley Museum, Wilmington . . 049205
Hagn, Silvia, Neumarkt am Wallersee . . . 095695
Hagner, Louis, Paradiso . . 082720, 130138
Hagondokoff, A.C., Paris . . . 066034
Hagood, Los Angeles . . . 116787
Hagstrom, Judy, Saint Paul . . . 119294
Hahm, Hans-Hugo, Möhrendorf . . . 126323
Hahn, Philadelphia . . . 118775
Hahn, Phoenix . . . 132648
Hahn, Christine, Regensburg . . . 073458
Hahn, Dietrich, Hamburg . . . 103160
Hahn, Gertraud, Erlangen . . . 070597
Hahn, Horst, Köln . . . 126082
Hahn, Margarete, Frielendorf . . . 102889
Hahn, Maria, Berlin . . . 069634
Hahn, Martin, Burgwald . . . 070104
Hahn, Udo, Haßloch . . . 071427
Hahn, Ulrich, Erkrath . . . 125604
Hahndorf Academy Public Art Gallery and Museum, Hahndorf . . . 001091
Hahne, Bernd, Braunschweig . . . 069982
Hahnenberg, Kintzheim . . . 063281
Hahns Peak Area Historical Museum, Clark . . . 042947
Hahoedong Mask Museum, Andong 027447
Hahs Museum, Hattiesburg . . . 044476
Hai, Paris . . . 100496
Hai Ci Tang, Shanghai . . . 059742
Hai Gallery, Dalian . . . 097710
Hai-Ho Upholstery, Windsor, Ontario 123862
Hai Wangcun Antiques Market, Beijing . . . 059575
Hai Yun Ming Hua, Shenzhen . . . 097978
Haida Galleries, Lytham Saint Annes . . . 114021
Haida Gwaii Museum at Qay'llnagaay, Skidegate . . . 006480
Haider, München . . . 104222
Haider, Harald, Purkersdorf . . . 057216
Haiderová, Šárka, České Budějovice . . . 059999
Haidhausen-Museum, München . . . 019060
Haifa Artists Association, Haifa . . . 053720
Haifa City Museum, Haifa . . . 022921
Haifa Museum of Art, Haifa . . . 022922
Haig, Axel, Holcot . . . 113249
Haig Colliery Mining Museum, Whitehaven . . . 041371
Haikun Antique, Shanghai . . . 059743
Haile, Sacramento . . . 119149
Haileybury Heritage Museum, Haileybury . . . 005561
Hailsham Heritage Centre, Hailsham . . . 039655
Hailuodon Kotiseutumuseo Kniivilä, Hailuoto . . . 009498
Haily, Chicago . . . 088102
Haim, Paul, Paris . . . 066035
Haime, Nohra, New York . . . 117989
Haimerl, Bad Tölz . . . 101708
Haimerl, Sigisbert, Königsdorf, Oberbayern . . . 103746
Hain, Gabi, Deggendorf . . . 070198
Hain, Gabriele & Alois, Haslach . . . 095561
Hainan Museum, Haikou . . . 007099
Hainan Photo-Arts Publishing House, Haikou . . . 133350
Haindl, Josef, Langenwang 057142, 123404
Haindl, Josef, Mürzzuschlag . . . 057189
Haines, Los Angeles . . . 116788
Haines, San Francisco . . . 119682
Haines, Robert D., San Francisco . . 142950
Haines Museum, Waukegan . . . 049011
Haiser, Hoyerswerda . . . 103407
Haiti Arts, Tucson . . . 120133
Haiti Images Gallery, New York . . . 117990
Haitian Art Factory, Miami . . . 117085
Haixia Art Cooperative, Tongling . . . 098024
Haiyin, Guangzhou . . . 097724
Haiyun Xuan Gu Dong, Shenzhen . . 097979
Hajdul, Gdańsk . . . 079581, 129010
Hajdusági Múzeum, Hajdúböszörmény . . . 021736
Hajos, Altenweddingen . . . 101569
HaKaren, Singapore . . . 109804
Hakasalmen Huvila, Helsingin Kaupunginmuseo, Helsinki . . . 009523
Hakco, Houston . . . 116329
Hake, Wolfgang, Köln . . . 134109
Hake & Hampp, Leipzig . . . 126190
Hakeney, David, Beverley . . . 083499
Hakeney, David K., Kingston-upon-Hull . . . 084859
Haker, Thomas, Berlin . . . 138783
Hakgojae, Seoul . . . 107245
Hakhamaneshi Museum, Shiraz . . . 022597
Hakodate-shiritsu Hakubutsukan, Hakodate . . . 026488
Hakone-Jinja Homotsuden, Hakone 026491
Hakone Souunzan Bijutsukan, Hakone . . . 026492
Håkonshallen og Rosenkrantztårnet, Bryggens Museum, Bergen . . . 030765
Hakuba Bijutsukan, Hakuba . . . 026494
Hakubutsukan Kenkyu, Tokyo . . . 135977
Hakubutsukan Meiji-Mura, Inuyama 026565
Hakuna Matata, Philadelphia . . . 118776
Hakutosha, Nagoya . . . 106921
Hakutsuru Fine Art Museum, Kobe . 026662
Hal, Marcus, El Paso . . . 116111
Halbach, Celle . . . 102304
Halbach, Rolf, Burgwedel . . . 102295
Halbedel, Salzburg . . . 057253
Halbert, Austin . . . 087577
Halcyon, Richmond . . . 092081
Halcyon, San Francisco . . . 092807
Halcyon, Stockport . . . 086722
Halcyon Days, London . . . 085364
Halcyon Days, London . . . 085365
Halcyon Daze, Mittagong . . . 056237
Halcyon Gallery, Birmingham . . . 112649
Halcyon Gallery, Birmingham . . . 112650
Halcyon Gallery, London . . . 113668
Hald, Volker, Villingen-Schwenningen . . . 074214
Haldemann, Margit, Bern . . . 111256
Halden Historiske Samlinger, Halden . . . 030868
Haldensvassdragets Kanalmuseum, Ørje . . . 031062
Haldimand County Museum, Cayuga . . . 005238
Haldy, Jacques, Montreux . . . 082668
Haldy, Jacques, Montreux . . . 082669
Hale, Patricia H., London . . . 131051
Hale, Robert, London . . . 135220
Hale, William F., Washington . . . 143042
Hale Farm and Village, Bath . . . 042041
Hale School Museum, Wembley Downs . . . 001607
Halem, Clemens von, München . . . 072720
Hales, Robert, London . . . 085366, 122589
Hales, S.J., Bovey Tracey . . . 122428
Halesworth and District Museum, Halesworth . . . 039657
Halewijn Missiaen, Gent . . . 096290
Halewood & Sons, Preston . . . 142008
Haley, Albuquerque . . . 087395
Haley, Pat, Malvern, Victoria . . . 056147, 120605
Haley & Steele, Boston . . . 115180, 122825
Half Back, Dee Why . . . 136878
Half Moon Antiques, Prospect . . . 056505
Half Retro, Bucureşti . . . 080157
Halfa Museum, Wadi Halfa . . . 036158
Halfen, Elsa, Paris . . . 066036
Halff, Harry, San Antonio . . . 119422
Halfmann, Essen . . . 070630
Halfmann, Peter, Duisburg . . . 139026
Halfmoon Antique Mall, San Antonio 092514
Hali, Lidingö . . . 141118
Hali, London . . . 135221
HALI Antique Carpet and Textile Art Fair, London . . . 093928
Hali, The International Magazine of Antique Carpet and Textile Art, London . . . 136223
Haliburton Highlands Museum, Haliburton . . . 005563
Haliburton House Museum, Windsor, Nova Scotia . . . 006828
Haliden, Bath . . . 083427
Halifax Antiques Centre, Halifax . . . 084558
Halifax Citadel, Halifax . . . 005572
Halifax Historical Museum, Daytona Beach . . . 043329
Halifax Police Museum, Halifax . . . 005573
Halifax Property Services, Sandwich . . . 122688
Halikkon Museo, Halikko . . . 009499
Halin Metsäkämppämuseo, Virrat . . 010244
Halina, Warszawa . . . 109143

Halinen, Tampere 060625, 098760
Halk Sanatları Müzesi, Girne 008246
Halkyone, Hamburg 139182
Hall, Dallas 115889
Hall, Anthony C., Twickenham 142129
Hall, Harry, Belfast 141406
Hall, Jacqueline, Tetbury 086855
Hall & Son, Peter, Staveley 131531
Hall, Robert, London 085367
Hall, Thomas, Dallas 115890
Hall-I'Th'-Wood Museum, Bolton . . 038780
Hall & Knight, London 113669
Hall & Knight, New York 117991
Hall of Fame, Buffalo 087882
Hall of Fame and Classic Car Museum, Weedsport 049041
Hall of Fame for Great Americans, Bronx 042437
Hall of Flame - Museum of Firefighting, Phoenix 047008
Hallar Gallery, Kansas City 116570
Hallard, Nigel, Mousehole 114094
Hallaton Museum, Hallaton 039666
Halle Aux Antiquités, Buhl-Lorraine 061834
La Halle aux Oiseaux, Marseillan . . 012925
Halle für Kunst e.V., Lüneburg 018742, 053227
Halle Saint-Pierre Museum, Paris . . 013595
De Hallen, Haarlem 029654
Hallén, Stockholm 141157
Hallen für neue Kunst, Schaffhausen 037522
Haller, H., Pforzheim 073316
Haller, Stephen, New York 117992
Haller, Ursula, München 126391
Haller Akademie der Künste, Schwäbisch Hall 050235
Haller & Evans, Kingston-upon-Hull 122555
Haller Feuerwehrmuseum, Schwäbisch Hall 020114
Hallerbosmuseum, Halle 003484
Hallertauer Heimat- und Hopfenmuseum, Mainburg 018782
Hallertauer Hopfen- und Heimatmuseum, Geisenfeld 017342
Les Halles de la Brocante, Nice . . . 065092
Hallescher Kunstverein, Halle, Saale 053228
Halliday, Swindon 114542
Hallidays Antiques, Dorchester-on-Thames 084182
Hallie Ford Museum of Art, Salem . 047751
Halligans, Auckland 140592
Hallin, Sven, Färnäs 122127
Hallingdal Folkemuseum, Nesbyen . 031050
Halliwell's House Museum, Selkirk . 040980
Hallmark, Brighton 083697
Hallmark, San Diego 092644
Hallockville Museum Farm, Riverhead 047452
Hallplatz Galerie, Zweibrücken 105372
Halls, Shrewsbury 122699
Hall's Bookshop, Tunbridge Wells . . 142126
Hall's Croft, Shakespeare Birthplace Trust, Stratford-upon-Avon 041138
Hallward, Dublin 105869
Hallwylska Museet, Stockholm 036628
Hallynck, Jean-Philippe, Croix 124215
Halm, E.P., Köln 071946
Halmens Hus, Bengtsfors 036213
Halmstads Auktionskammare, Halmstad 122150
Halos, Utrecht 140547
Halosenniemi Museo, Tuusula 010185
Haloux, Félix, Paris 100497
Halpern, Herbert, New Orleans 117451
Halsey Gallery, College of Charleston, Charleston 042734
Halszka-Polonez, Poznań 109050
Haltdalen Bygdetun, Haltdalen 030870
La Halte, Plaisance 066839
Halter, K., Türkheim 074120
Halter, Martin, Bern 129958
Halter, Yves, Rennes (Ille-et-Vilaine) 101083
Halter & Colledani, Luzern 130104
Halton Region Museum, Milton 005872
Haluška, Pavel, Liptovský Mikuláš . 080627
Halwany, Ismat, Beirut 077396
Ham House, Richmond, Surrey 040830
Hama National Museum, Hama . . . 037832
Hamacher, Joachim, Krefeld 126145
Hamada, Cairo 098638
Hamadryade, Paris 066037
Hamaland-Museum und Westmünsterländische Hofanlage, Kreismuseum Borken, Vreden . . . 020611
Hamamatsu City Museum of Art, Hamamatsu 026495
Hamamatsu-shiritsu Hakubutsukan, Hamamatsu 026496
Hamard, Annette, Bar-le-Duc 061194
Hamard, Annette, Bar-le-Duc 061195
Hamard, Annette, Bar-le-Duc 061196
Hamard, Annette, Bar-le-Duc 124091
Hamarøy Bygdetun, Harmarøy 030876
Hamayu, Yokohama 077336
Hambacher Schloss, Neustadt an der Weinstraße 019284
Hambidge Center for the Creative Arts and Sciences, Rabun Gap 047304
Hambleton, Vancouver 097480
Hamblin, John, Yeovil 087283, 131723
Hamburg State Park Museum, Mitchell 045938
Hamburger Antiquariat, Hamburg . . 139183
Hamburger Bahnhof - Museum für Gegenwart Berlin, Staatliche Museen zu Berlin - Stiftung Preußischer Kulturbesitz, Berlin 016055
Die Hamburger Galerie, Hamburg . . 103161
Hamburger Kunsthalle, Hamburg . . 017694
Hamburger Schulmuseum, Hamburg 017695
Hamburger Zimmer, Hamburg 071240
Hameau du Fromage, Cléron 011404
Hameau en Beaujolais, Romanèche-Thorins 014091
Hamecher, Horst, Kassel 139305
Hamel, Corentin, Paris 100498
Hamel, H., Freudenberg 070880
Hamelin, Sébastien, Les Pieux 063775
Hamenstädt, Irene, Kassel 071753
Hamer, Amsterdam 107729
Hamer, Blaricum 134800
Hamer, Bochum 102155
Hamer, Großhansdorf 103020
Hames, Peter, Bideford 141412
Hameslevack, London 113670
Hametner, Stoob 095767
Hamhung Historical Museum, Hamhung 027435
Hamich-Rafensteiner, Ilse, Nördlingen 104456
Hamidèche, Dominique, Lens 063741
Hamill, Boston 115181
Hamilton, Baltimore 142225
Hamilton, Knokke-Heist 058246
Hamilton, New York 117993
Hamilton, Phoenix 132649
Hamilton, Woodbridge 087218
Hamilton & Co, A.D., Glasgow 084465
Hamilton, Anne, Burnham Market . . 083804
Hamilton, Beth, Fairlight 094521
Hamilton, Jane, Tucson 120134
Hamilton, Rosemary, London 131052
Hamilton, Ross, London 085368
Hamilton Art Gallery, Hamilton, Victoria 001096
Hamilton Arteffects, Hamilton, Victoria 094613
Hamilton Artists, Hamilton 096920
Hamilton Billards & Games, Knebworth 084885, 130858
The Hamilton Children's Museum, Hamilton 005590
Hamilton Galleries, London 113671
Hamilton Grange, New York 046342
Hamilton Heritage Museum, Hamilton, Tasmania 001095
Hamilton House, South Berwick . . . 048232
Hamilton House Museum, Clifton . . 043008
Hamilton Hume Museum, Yass 001647
Hamilton Kerr Institute, Cambridge . 130498
Hamilton Library and Two Mile House, Carlisle 042621
Hamilton Low Parks Museum, Hamilton 039669
Hamilton Military Museum, Hamilton 005591
Hamilton & Miller, Camperdown . . . 120575
Hamilton Museum of Steam and Technology, Hamilton 005592
Hamilton Osborne King, Blackrock . 121655
Hamilton Psychiatric Hospital Museum & St. Joseph's Mountain Site, Hamilton 005593
Hamilton & Selway, West Hollywood 120385
Hamilton van Wogener Museum, Clifton 043008
Hamilton's Gallery, London 040169
Haminan Kaupunginmuseo, Hamina 009500
Hamiota Pioneer Club Museum, Hamiota 005599
Hamish, Clark, Woollahra 056867
Hamizgaga Museum, Kibbutz Nachsholim 023014
Hamlin Garland Homestead, West Salem 049098
Hamline University Galleries, Dept of Art, Hamline University, Saint Paul . . . 047698
Hamlyn Lodge, Ollerton . . 086160, 131344
Hamm, Dresden 102443, 138991
Hamm, Lampertheim 072123
Hamm, Gitta, Lindlar 103924
Hamm, Pierre, Benfeld 061345
Hammaslääketieteen Museo, Helsinki 009524
Hammelehle & Ahrens, Köln 103636
Hammer, Augsburg 101616
Hammer, Madrid 122063
Hammer, New York 117994
Hammer, Carl, Chicago 115447
Hammer, Hans-Willi, Bonn 138900
Hammer, Ingo R., Köfering 071898, 126060
Hammer, Juhan, Tallinn 137916
Hammer, Klaus, München 072721
Hammer, Udo, Werbach 074335
Hammer Museum, University of California Los Angeles, Los Angeles 045426
Hammer- und Waffenschmiede-Museum Hexenagger, Altmannstein 015510
Hammerberg, Bob, Seattle 093012
Hammerblow, Tucson 093240
Hammered Design, Denver 116011
Hammerichs Hus, Ærøskøbing 008802
Hammerschmiede und Stockerhof, Neuburg an der Kammel 019226
Hammerstein, Brigitte von, Hamburg 125820
Hammerstein, Hans, München 139510
Hammill, Janet, Thornbury 123317
Hamminoff, Chris, Caen . . 061872, 138060
Hammond, Saint Louis 142856
Hammond, Jeffery, Leominster . . . 084972
Hammond, John, Fürth, Bayern . . . 102902
Hammond, Thomas, Tampa 120050
Hammond Castle Museum, Gloucester 044223
Hammond Hall Antiques, Wagga Wagga 056789
Hammond-Harwood House Museum, Annapolis 041742
Hammond Historical Museum, Hammond 044405
Hammond Museum, North Salem . . 046537
Hamon, Claude, Lampaul-Guimiliau 063506
Hamon, Jacques, Le Havre 099440
Hampden-Booth Theatre Museum, New York 046343
Hampden Junque, Baltimore 087674
Hampden Street Antique, Denver . . 088696
Hampden Trading Company, Great Missenden 084518
Hampe, Susanna, Klosterneuburg . . 057118
Hampel, Dr. Frithjof, Bonn 069925
Hampel, Dr. Frithjof, Köln 071947
Hampel, Holger, München 121527
Hampshire Antiques, Vancouver . . . 059364
Hampshire Contemporary Artists, Lymington 114015
Hampshire Farm Museum, Botley, Hampshire 038792
Hampshire Gallery, Bournemouth . .083598, 130415
Hampshire Gardencraft, Rake 131402
Hampshires of Dorking, Dorking . . . 084192
Hampson Museum, Wilson 049219
Hampstead Museum, London 040170
Hampton, Bentleigh 055484
Hampton Auction Gallery, Belvidere 122813
Hampton, Briggs & Chine, New York 090928
Hampton County Historical Museum, Hampton 044412
Hampton Court Antiques, Hampton . 055950
Hampton Court Emporium, East Molesey 084249
Hampton Court Palace, East Molesey 039356
Hampton Court Palace Antiques, East Molesey 084250, 130664
Hampton Gallery, Tetbury 086856
Hampton House, Richmond 092082
Hampton & Littlewood, Alphington . 122384
Hampton National Historic Site Museum, Towson 048594
Hampton Plantation, McClellanville 045541
Hampton-Preston Mansion, Columbia 043080
Hampton Roads Antique Connection, Norfolk 091382
Hampton Roads Naval Museum, Norfolk 046498
Hampton University Museum, Hampton 044415
Hamptonne Country Life Museum, Saint Lawrence 040924
Hamptons, Antwerpen 057700
Hamptons, Christchurch 084007
Hamptons, Godalming 122522
Hamptons, Great Malvern 122526
Hamptons, Marlborough 122614
Hamura-shiritsu Hakubutsukan, Hamura 026497
Hamzavi, Mohamed, Strasbourg . . . 068322
Han, Bath 083428
Han, Fong, Paris 066038
Han, Kwang, Singapore 080476
The Han Horse, New York 090929
Han Kuk Art Museum, Yongin 027626
Han Mo Xuan, Hong Kong 097792
Han Palace, San Francisco 092808
Hana Cultural Center, Hana, Maui . . 044419
Hana Gallery, Vancouver 059365
Hana Senesh House, Kibbutz Sedot Yam 023021
Hanaire, Madeleine, Paris 124687
Hanak, Los Angeles 089785
Hanall, Buchon 077357
Hanappe, Els, Athinai 105398
Hanart Gallery, Hong Kong 097793
Hanart Gallery, Taipei 098071
Hanart TZ Gallery, Hong Kong 097794
Hanauer Museum, Kehl am Rhein . 018218
Hanausch, Reinhard, Regensburg . . 139683
Hanbat Education Museum, Daejeon 027480
Hanborough Antiques, Long Hanborough 085827
Hanbury Hall, Droitwich 039285
Hanby House, Westerville 049108
Hance, Bruxelles 057978
Hanch Hall, Lichfield 039999
Hancock, Moss Vale 056275
Hancock, Peter, Chichester 083974, 141518
Hancock County Historical Museum, Carthage 042642
Hancock & Harwell, Atlanta 087486
Hancock Historical Museum, Findlay 043845
Hancock Historical Society Museum, Hancock 044420
Hancock House, Hancock's Bridge . 044421

Hancock Museum, Newcastle-upon-Tyne . . . 040548
Hancock Shaker Village, Pittsfield . 047069
Hancocks & Co., London 085369
Hand in Hand, Coldstream 084061
Hand Made, Kühlungsborn 103804
Hand Made Furniture, Atlanta 131779
Hand Made Studio, Vientiane 107313
Hand Workshop Art Center, Richmond 047416
Hand Workshop Art Center, Richmond 119113
Hand Woven Rugs, Los Angeles . . . 089786
Handan Painting Gallery, Handan . . 097732
Handdancer's Art, Louisville 116943
Handel House Museum, London . . . 040171
Handelaren Oude Kunst, Amsterdam 077863
Handels- og Søfartsmuseet paa Kronborg, Helsingør 008897
Handelsgesellschaft für historische Wertpapiere, Wien 120683
Handelskompaniet i Gävle, Gävle . . 081786
Handicrafts Impex Enterprises, Kathmandu 077704
Handke, Peter, Schönermark bei Angermünde 073715
Handley-Hicks, Fort Worth 116146
Handmark Galleries, Battery Point . 094220
Handpress International, Los Angeles 116789, 135382
Handpresse Zwiebelfisch, Köln 134110
Hands Across, Phoenix 091742
Hands on Children's Museum, Olympia 046672
Hands on History, Kingston-upon-Hull 039886
Hands-on House, Children's Museum of Lancaster, Lancaster 045143
Hands On! Regional Museum, Johnson City 044866
Handschriftenabteilung der Landes-, Universitäts- und Murhardschen Bibliothek, Kassel 018188
Handschriftenabteilung der Universitätsbibliothek, Graphische Sammlung, Würzburg 020997
Handsworth Saint Mary's Museum, Sheffield 040997
Handweaving Museum and Arts Center, Clayton 042963
Handweberei Henni Jaensch-Zeymer, Geltow 017359
Handwerk & Gewerbe Museum, Krauschwitz 018393
Handwerker, Helmut, Karlsfeld 139291
Handwerker Gallery of Art, Ithaca . . 044790
Handwerker- und Heimatstube, Gernsbach 017383
Handwerkerstuben, Feuchtwangen . 017116
Handwerksmuseum, Deggendorf . . 016656
Handwerksmuseum am Mühlenberg, Suhlendorf 020382
Handwerksmuseum Dingwerth, Verl 020579
Handwerksmuseum Groß-Gerau, Groß-Gerau 017552
Handwerksmuseum Ovelgönne, Ovelgönne 019546
Handwerksmuseum Rattenberg, Rattenberg, Inn 002506
Handwerksmuseum und Friseurmuseum, Stiftung Stadtmuseum Berlin, Berlin 016056
Hanf-Museum, Berlin 016057
Hanford Mills Museum, East Meredith 043578
Hanft, Harald, Selb 073794
Hang, Hong Kong 059633
Hang, San Francisco 119683
Hang, San Francisco 119684
Hang Art, Mount Lawley 094908
Hang Art, Paris 100499
Hang It, Minneapolis 117268
Hang It, Minneapolis 117269
Hang Ups, Fyshwick 123227
Hang-Ups, Red Hill 095117
Hang Ups of Greytown, Greytown . . 108455
Hanga Ten, London 113672
Hangar-7, Salzburg 002555
Le Hangar des Chineurs, Perros-Guirec 066766
Hangar du Chineur, Dardilly 062600
Hangguk Minsok-chon, Kihung 027523
Hanging Around, Enfield 113021
Hanging Tree Gallery, Albuquerque . 087396
Hangleiter, Hans Michael, Otzberg . 126608
Hangon Rintamamuseo, Karjaa . . . 009666
Hangups Gallery, Omaha 118701
Hangzhou Art Gallery, Hangzhou . . . 097737
Hangzhou Painting Gallery, Hangzhou 097738
Haniel Museum, Duisburg 016853
Hanina, London 113673
Hanisch, Peter, Baden-Baden 121310
Dr. Hanisch & Dr. Trommer, Zwickau 139894
Hanita Museum, Kibbutz Hanita . . . 023006
Hank Snow Country Music Centre, Liverpool 005778
Hankard, Jean-Jacques, Bruxelles . 137439
Hankasalmen Kotiseutumuseo, Hankasalmi 009502
Hanke, Gerhard, Neuss 134309
Hanko Front Museum, Hanko 009503
Hanko Museo, Hanko 009504
Hankook, Seoul 107246
Hanks, Buffalo 087883
Hanks, Steve, Albuquerque 087397
Hanks, W., Austin 087578
Hanley, Jack, San Francisco 119685
Hanley House, Clayton 042961
Hanlim Museum, Daejeon 027481
Hanlin, Hong Kong 059634
Hanlon, Terry, Dallas 088527
Hanmo Art Center, Beijing 097657
Hanna, Birmingham 087757, 142239
Hanna, Fred, Dublin 139965
Hanna Pioneer Museum, Hanna . . . 005601
Hannah & Sisters, Charlotte 087952
Hannah, Catherine, Rotorua 079230
Hannah, Eva, Sydney 095291, 133057
Hannah Lindahl Children's Museum, Mishawaka 045927
Hannah's Art Studio, Miami 117086
Hannak, Gudrun, Murnau 139579
Hannans North Tourist Mine, Kalgoorlie 001140
Hannappel, Thomas, Essen 102684
Hanna's Place, Louisville 089995
Hannes Antik, Valby 060408
Hannes Hus og Fonden Gamle Sønderho, Fanø 008856
Hannoversches Straßenbahn-Museum, Sehnde 020177
Hanns Schell-Collection, Österreichisches Museum für Schloß, Schlüssel, Kästchen, Kassetten und Eisenkunstguß, Graz 001933
Hanover Antiques, Scarborough . . . 086522
Hanover Historical Society Museum, Hanover 044427
Hanover House, Clemson University, Clemson 042976
Hanover Museum, Montego Bay . . . 026394
Hanover Square Gallery, New York . 117995
Hanowski, R., Euskirchen 070668
Hanreich, Bernhard, Pram 123430
Hanrieder-Gedenkraum, Putzleinsdorf 002482
Hanriis Hus, Duved 036238
Hans, Frank, Elsbethen-Glasenstein 123348
Hans, Marcus, Düsseldorf 139010
Hans-Böckler-Geburtshaus, Trautskirchen 020460
Hans Christian Andersen Museum, Odense 009049
Hans Christian Andersens Barndomshjem, Odense 009050
Hans Erni Museum, Hans Erni-Stiftung, Luzern 037296
Hans-Fallada-Gedenkstätte, Berkenbrück bei Fürstenwalde 015977
Hans-Fallada-Haus, Feldberg, Mecklenburg 017104
Hans-Grade-Museum, Borkheide . . 016346
Hans Herr House and Museum, Willow Street 049197
Hans Mauracher-Museum, Graz . . . 001934
Hans Nielsens Hauges Minne, Rolvsøy 031146
Hans Stapelmann, Sankt Wendel . . 104815
Hans-Thoma-Gedächtnisstätte und Vortaunusmuseum, Oberursel . . . 019426
Hans-Thoma-Museum, Bernau, Baden 016200
Hans Trudel-Haus Stiftung, Baden . 036868
Hans van Riessen Museum, Vledderveen 030280
Hanság Múzeum, Mosonmagyaróvár 021795
Hansberg, Peter, Groß Sarau 125760
Hanse, Norbert, Paris 100500
Hanse Galerie, Stralsund 104956
Hanseatic Booth or The Pier House, Symbister 041182
Hanseatische Auktionatoren, Ratekau 121582
Hanseatische Auktionatoren, Westerland 121622
Hanseatische Kunst- und Antiquitätentage, Hamburg 093720
Hanseatische Münzenhandlung, Bremen 070021
Hanseatischer Verlag, Hamburg . . . 134011
Hanseatisches Auktionshaus für Historica, Bad Oldesloe 121305
Det Hanseatiske Museum og Schøtstuene, Bergen 030766
Hansel, Hubert, Stade 126821
Hanselmann, Nikolaus, Stuttgart . . 073978
Hansen, Dr., Berlin 138784
Hansen, Bonn 102184
Hansen, Hennef 103350
Hansen, Honolulu 088951
Hansen, Perpignan 066748
Hansen, B., Mannheim 072423
Hansen, Christian, Berlin 069635
Hansen, Egon, Oslo 079442
Hansen, Ingrid, Washington 120306
Hansen, Jan, Frederiksberg 137869
Hansen, Jens Erik, Frederiksberg . . 124016
Hansen, Martin, Karlsruhe 071721
Hansen Chard Antiques, Pershore .086219, 131371
Hansen-Gerret, Perpignan 066749
Hansen Gerret, Reynès 067127
Hansens, Canberra 055621
Hanses, M. & Wilhelm R., Guderhandviertel 103028
Hansford, Lincoln 084997
Hanshan Tang Books, London 141816
Hanshans, Elisabeth, Lappersdorf . 126172
Hanshin, Ark, Osaka 077174
Hansjakobmuseum im Freihof, Haslach 017786
Hansl, Dieter, Frankfurt am Main . . 102784
Hansmann, C., Bühl, Baden 070082
Hanson, Houston 116330
Hanson, Houston 116331
Hanson, Houston 116332
Hanson, New Orleans 117452
Hanson, San Francisco 119686
Susan Hanson & Paul Weber, Berlin 138785
Hansong Womens College Museum, Seoul 027558
Hanssler, München 104223
Hansson, Malmö 110973
Hansson, Stockholm 081959
Hansson, Wien 137318
Hansson, Elof, Visby 122298
Hanstein, Marlies, Saarbrücken . . . 104796
Hantho Galleri, Haugesund 079388
Hantise, La Ciotat 063332, 124277
Hantke, Jan, Valencia 129775
Hantsch, Claus, Hamburg 071241
Hantverks- och Sjörfartsmuseét på Norra Berget, Medelpads Fornminnesförening, Sundsvall 036691
Hantverksloftet, Simrishamn 036570
Hantverksmuseet, Ängelholm 036170
Hanul cu Tei, Bucureşti 109437
Hanuš & Aufricht, Cheb 060006
Hanusek, Heinz, Nürnberg 073103
Hanwon Art Museum, Seoul 027559
Hanza-Kruger, Szeged 074754
Haos Galerija Beograd, Beograd . . . 109703
Haour, Marie, Paris 124688
Hapart, Philippe, Paris 066039
Ha'Penny Bridge Galleries, Dublin . 074920
Hapetian, J.Z., Lisboa . . . 079942, 129156
Happach, Hans-P., Starnberg 126825
Happy, Alexis de, New York 117996
Happy Angel Antiques, Los Angeles 089787
Happy Art, New Orleans 117453
Happy Days For Old Toys, Amsterdam 077864
Happy Dolphin, Southport 056616
Happy Thought's, Milwaukee 117195
Happy Trails, Houston 142439
HAPU, Wien 095859
Har-Ber Village, Grove 044366
Har-El, Jaffa 134534
Hara Bijutsukan, Tokyo 027171
Hara Castle Memorial Hall, Minamiarima 026805
Hara Museum ARC, Shibukawa . . . 027059
Hara-shobo Japanese Prints, Tokyo 077250
Harajuku, Piga, Tokyo 107052
Harák, Praha 060129
Haralambous, Martin, Hamburg . . . 071242
Sir Harald Art, Venlo 108266
Harare School of Art, Harare 052434
Harari & Johns, New York 117997
Haras National, Strasbourg 014861
Harb, Ingrid, Berlin 069636
Harbeck, Carindale 136847
Harbor, Victor, Victor Harbor 120651
Harbor Branch Oceanographic Institution, Fort Pierce 043962
Harbor Defense Museum of New York City, Brooklyn 042459
Harbor Gallery, Norfolk 118608
Harborne Gallery, Birmingham 112651
Harborough Museum, Market Harborough 040427
Harbott, Sibylle, Münster 126501
Harbottle, Patricia, Gillingham, Dorset 084457
Harbour Antiques, Tewantin 056706
Harbour Cottage Gallery, Kirkcudbright 113335
Harbour Gallery, Dundee 112964
Harbour Gallery, Isles-of-Scilly 113308
Harbour Gallery, Mississauga 005891
Harbour Gallery, Whitstable 114686
Harbour Life Exhibition, Bridport . . . 038840
Harbour Lights Gallery, Porthgain . . 114277
Harbour Museum, Londonderry . . . 040328
Harbour View Gallery, Port-of-Ness 114276
Harboyan, Krikor, Los Angeles 089788
Harcerskie Muzeum Etnograficzne przy Szkole Podstawowej nr 11 w Katowicach, Katowice 031985
Harcourt Antiques, London 085370
Harcourt House Antiques, Harcourt . 055954
Hard 2 Find Toyz, Las Vegas 089583
Hard To Find, Auckland 140593
Hard To Find, Whangarei 140689
Hard To Find Books, Auckland 140594
Hard To Find Books, Auckland 140595
Hardanger, Norheimsund 079405
Hardanger Folkemuseum, Lofthus . 030990
Hardanger Folkemuseum, Utne . . . 031307
Hardcover Haven, Phoenix 142766
Hardeman, G., Leersum 128740
Harder, von, Martinsried 139466
Harder, Jakob, Benken, Sankt Gallen 082192
Harder, Jakob, Kaltbrunn 082511

Harder, Paul, Utrecht 078807
Hardie, Perth 086224
Hardie, Rebecca, London 141817
Hardie, William, Glasgow 113117
Hardin County Historical Museum, Kenton 044969
Harding, Keith, Northleach 086102, 131324
Harding, Yiri, Lisarow 056102
Harding Home and Museum, Marion 045684
Harding Museum, Franklin 044042
Hardner, Gerd, Dresden . . 070317, 138992
Hardom Sädesmagasin och Stenkulla Torp, Loviisa 009840
Hardt, Peter, Radevormwald 073401, 104651
Hardware, London 113674
Hardware Fine Art, Saint Leonards . 095176
Hardwick Hall, Chesterfield 039064
Hardwick Historical Museum, Hardwick 044429
Hardy, Barbara, Trier 126912
Hardy, Barbara, Urbar 126938
Hardy & Co., James, London 085371, 131053
Hardy, Joyce, Hacheston 084544
Hardy Country, Melbury Osmond . . 085965
Hardy's Cottage, Higher Bockhampton 039750
Haremere Hall, Etchingham 039457
Harenberg, Dortmund . . . 102402, 133871
Hareng Saur, Decazeville . 062613, 099201
Hares, Cirencester 084018, 130581
Hare's, Northallerton 114150
Harestanes Countryside Visitor Centre, Ancrum 038508
Haret, Serge le, Huisseau-en-Beauce 063183
Harewood House, Harewood 039670
Harford, Camperdown 055617
Hargesheimer & Günther, Düsseldorf 070390, 121384
Hargesheimer & Günther, Köln 071948
Hari Om, Mumbai 105780
Haring, A., Amsterdam 140303
Haringey Museum, London 040100
Harings, Regina, Nordenham 073067
Hariphunchai National Museum, Lampun 037906
Haris, Warszawa 079756
Haris, Warszawa 079757
Harishin, Kobe 077075
Haritos Gallery, Athinai 105399
Hariya Razna and Ahmed Urabi Museum, Zaqaziq 009350
Harjamäen Sairaalamuseo, Siilinjärvi 010077
Harjukosken Vesimylly, Mikkeli . . . 009871
Harjumaa Muuseum, Keila 009372
Harkányi Galéria, Pécs 105572
Harkins, Brian, London 085372
Harkins, Hammond, Columbus 115784
Harkort, U., Wiesbaden 074406
Harlacher, Manfred, Dillingen an der Donau 125466
Harlan-Lincoln House, Mount Pleasant 046062
Harlan & Weaver, New York 117998
Harland, Tom, North Ferriby 114148
Harlech Castle, Harlech 039671
Harlekin, Neubrandenburg 072972
Harlekin, Schaan 107335
Harlekinäum-Lachmuseum, Wiesbaden 020866
Harlequin, Budapest 105514
Harlequin Antiques, Armadale, Victoria 055379
Harlequin Antiques, Edinburgh 084295
Harlequin Antiques, Grantham 084496
Harlequin Antiques, Nottingham . . .086136, 131336
Harlequin Antiques, Porthcawl 086292, 142006
Harlequin Books, Bristol 141454
Harlequin Books, London 141818
Harlequin Gallery, Lincoln 141733
Harlequin Gallery, London 113675
Harlequin Horse Antiques, Kalamunda 056026
Harleston, Harleston 113182
Harley, Christian Malford 084009
Harley-Davidson en Indian Museum, Raalte 030049
Harley Gallery, Welbeck 041322
Harlinger Aardewerk Museum, Harlingen 029675
Harlinghausen, Barbara, Lengerich, Westfalen 072227
Harlinghausen, Klaus, Osnabrück . . 139638
Harlon, Chicago 088103
Harlow Carr Museum of Gardening, Royal Horticultural Society, Harrogate . . 039676
Harlow Gallery, Kennebec Valley Art Association, Hallowell 044393
Harlow Museum, Harlow 039672
Harlowe, Santiago de Chile 059535
Harmakhis, Bruxelles 057979
Harman, Paul & Nicholas, Dorking .084193, 130646
Harmar Station, Marietta 045672
Harmattan, Fouesnant 062922
Harmatys, Maria, Kraków 140737
Harmel, Berlin 069637
Harmer, H.R., New York 122998
Harmer Johnson, New York 142661
Harmers, London 122590
Harmeyer, M., Bremen 070022
Harmonies, Beir-Mery 134737
Harmonise Fine Art Prints, London . 113676
Harmonium-Art-Museum, Schelle . . 003742
Harmonium-Museum, Liestal 037265
Harmonium-Museum, Sammlung Thein, Hennef 017872
Harmony, Dol-de-Bretagne 062694
Harmony Arts, Ahmedabad 105594
Harmsen, B., Erlangen 070598
Harmssen, Anne, Braunschweig . . . 125375
Harmstorf, Hamburg 103162
Harn Homestead and 1889er Museum, Oklahoma City 046642
Harness, Jack, Marlow 085954
Harness Racing Museum and Hall of Fame, Goshen 044252
Harney County Historical Museum, Burns 042528
Harnisch, Michael, Stuttgart 073979
Harnisch, Michael, Stuttgart 073980
Harold, Sacramento 092165, 132736
Harold Warp Pioneer Village Foundation, Minden 045903
Haroonian, Los Angeles 089789
Haroska, Ulrich, Bad Homburg v.d.Höhe 125099
Harouni, New Orleans 117454
Harper, Poynton 086306, 131396
Harper, York 087292
Harper, Jeff, Wellington 108621
Harper, Martin & Dorothy, Bakewell 083365, 130322
Harper City Historical Museum, Harper 044435
Harper Collins, London 135222
Harper Collins, New York 135432
Harper-James, Montrose . 086003, 131282
Harpers, New Orleans 090567
Harpers Ferry National Historical Park, Harpers Ferry 044437
Harpley, Peter, London 113677
Harraca-Roehl, Paris 100501
Harrassowitz, Otto, Wiesbaden 139849
Harrewyn, Frédéric, Cucq 062580
Harrewyn, Frédéric, Le Touquet-Paris-Plage 063719
Harriann, Minneapolis 132382
Harries, Hamburg 071243
Harriet Beecher Stowe Center, Hartford 044458
Harriet FeBland Art Workshop, New York 051824, 117999
Harringer, Rutzenmoos 057232
Harringer, Alexander, Gmunden . . . 056993
Harrington, Albion 055326
Harrington, Adrian, London 131054, 141819
Harrington, Mark, San Francisco . . 132884
Harrington, Peter, London . 131055, 141820
Harrington Institute of Interior Design, Chicago 051127
Harrington Street Gallery, Chippendale 094393
Harris, Baltimore 087675, 122809
Harris, Fort Worth 088859
Harris, Houston 116333
Harris, Richmond 132715
Harris, San Francisco 119687
Harris, Toronto 097283
Harris, Colin, Eversley 084351
Harris, Elizabeth, New York 118000
Harris, Gene, Marshalltown 122956
Harris, James, Seattle 119932
Harris, Jonathan, London 085373
Harris, Lindsay, London 085374
Harris, Lisa, Seattle 119933
Harris, Lorraine, Colac 055708
Harris, Marlene, Pittsburgh 091824
Harris, Michael, Toronto 059202
Harris, Michael, Winnipeg 059462
Harris, O.K., New York 118001
Harris, Richard, Forster 120584
Harris, Rupert, London 131056
Harris, Thelma, Oakland 118634
Harris Art Gallery, James M. Lykes Maritime Gallery and Hutchings Gallery, Galveston 044132
Harris & Barr, Baltimore . . 087676, 122810
Harris Courtin, Paddington 095027
Harris Exhibit Hall, Oxford 046772
Harris Heritage and Museum, Harris 005605
Harris & Holt, Chester 083956
Harris Museum and Art Gallery, Preston 040778
Harrison, Richmond 092083, 132716
Harrison, Tauranga 108576
Harrison, Vancouver 097481
Harrison, Vancouver 097482
Harrison, Anna, Gosforth, Tyne and Wear 084486, 130735
Harrison, B.P., Regina 123810
Harrison, F., Plymouth 142004
Harrison, John, Aston Tirrold 083346
Harrison County Historical Museum, Marshall 045704
Harrison Galleries, Calgary 096820
Harrison Gray Otis House, Boston . . 042326
Harrison House, Branford 042387
Harrods, London 085375
Harrogate Antique and Fine Art Fair, Harrogate 093929
Harrogate Antique Fair, Harrogate . 093930
Harrogate House, Singapore 080477
Harrogate Pavilions Antiques and Fine Art Fair, Harrogate 093931
Harrop Fold Clocks, Bolton-by-Bowland 083574, 130409
The Harrow Decorative and Fine Arts Society, Pinner 054398
Harrow Museum, Harrow 039681
Harry, Los Angeles 089790
Harry D. Hendren Gallery, Saint Charles 047619
Harry J. Music Museum, Kingston . 026384
Harry Oppenheimer Diamond Museum, Ramat Gan 023049
Harry S. Truman Birthplace State Historic Site, Lamar 045132
Harry S. Truman Home, Independence 044721
Harry S. Truman Library Museum, Independence 044722
Harry S. Truman Little White House Museum, Key West 044986
Harry S. Truman Office and Courtroom, Independence 044723
Harry S. Washbrook Museum, Edam 005385
Harry's Books, Richmond 142822
Harry's Coin Center, Philadelphia . . 091641
Harry's Rare Coins, San Antonio . . . 092515
Harry's Truman Farm Home, Grandview 044282
Hart, Chicago 115448
Hart, Houston 089093
Hart, Houston 089094
Hart, Houston 122907
Hart, Abigail, Kew 123250
Hart, Bob, Jacksonville 089417
Hart, Catherine, Rouen 067269
Hart, David, Mooloolaba 094876
Hart, Edna, Los Angeles 089791
Hart, Julie, Broken Hill 094304
Hart, Kym, Main Beach 094761
Hart, Leonard & Tracy, Houston . . . 116334
Hart, M., Amsterdam 077865
Hart, Penine, New York 090930
Hart-Cam Museum, Hartney 005608
Hart Gallery, Linby 113394
Hart Gallery, London 113678
Hart & Giles, Aylsham 083358
Hart House, Toronto 006601
Hart & Rosenberg, London 085376
Hart-Witzen, Charlotte 115288
Hartan, Thomas, Ahorn, Kreis Coburg 125048
Harté, Florent, Bordères-et-Lamensans 061662
Harten, Beate von, Wien 123496
Harten, Beate von, Wien 123497
Hartenberger, Klaus, Ratzeburg . . . 073434
Hartenbos Museum, Hartenbos . . . 034631
Harter, Eliane, Nice 065093
Harter, Jamil, Montbrison 064658
Harter, Jean, Montbrison 064659
Harter, Monika, Hinterzarten 125940
Harter, Sybille, Schaanwald 107338
Harteveld, Fribourg 141242
Hartford Art School, University of Hartford, West Hartford 052351
Hartford Heritage Auto Museum, Hartford 044465
Hartford House Museum, Manhattan 045628
Hartgen, Stadtbergen 104942
Hartham Park - Underground Quarry Museum, Corsham 039146
Harthan, Angelika, Stuttgart 104986
Hartig, Hans-Christian & Ilse, Goch 071019
Harting, Friedrich, Bremen 102245
Hartistas, Lisboa 129157
Hartl, Ammerbuch 101575
Hartl, Georg L., Bernried, Niederbayern 069806
Hartl, Georg L., München 072722
Hartl, Hans & Sylvia, Poing 104619
Hartland Art Council, Hartland 054786
Hartland Quay Museum, Bideford . . 038701
Hartland Quay Museum, Hartland . . 039682
Hartleben, A., Wien 137319
Hartleib, Michael, Lahr, Schwarzwald 072116
Hartleitner, Walter, Bamberg 125132
Hartlepool Art Gallery, Hartlepool . . 039683
Hartley, Andrew, Ilkley 122549
Hartley, J., Ripley, Surrey 086372
Hartley, John, Petersfield 131374
Hartlich, Petra, Steinberg, Sachsen 073904
Hartman, Columbus 088417
Hartman, Charles A., San Francisco 119688, 142951
Hartman, Zsu Zsi, Subiaco 095231
Hartmanin Mökki, Oripää 009928
Hartmann, Barcelona 110200
Hartmann, Recklinghausen 104682
Hartmann, Saint Louis 092251
Hartmann, E., Homberg, Efze 071574
Hartmann, Frédéric, Toulouse 138635
Hartmann, Heinz-Richard, Karlsruhe 103493
Hartmann, Herbert, Mistelbach an der Zaya 057183
Hartmann, Johannes, Bruchhausen 125399
Hartmann, Michaela, Berlin 101919
Hartmann, N., Berlin 125210

Hartmann, Peter, Nickenich 073049
Hartmann, P.W., Wien 057436, 133205
Hartmann, Robert, Dessau, Anhalt . 125455
Hartmann, Dr. Roland, Sankt Gallen 141293
Hartmann, Sandy, Zürich 130239
Hartmann, Werner W., Düsseldorf . . 102506
Hartmann, H., Aschendorf 069206
Hartmann's, København 060335
Hartnack, Bogen 102173
Hartnell College Gallery, Salinas . . . 047758
Hartnoll, Julian, London . . 085377, 113679
Hartogsohn, Ira, København 060336
Hartskeerl, R.E., Haarlem 128691
Hartsville Museum, Hartsville 044467
Hartung, Gisbert, Weilburg 126976
Hartung, Wolfgang, Raguhn 126675
Hartung & Hartung, München 121528, 139511
Hartung's Auto and License Plate Museum, Glenview 044216
Hartware Medien Kunst Verein, Dortmund 053229
Hartwich, Ostseebad Sellin 104558
Hartwig, Kalchreuth 071686
Hartwig, Bernert, Hamburg 103163
Hartwig, Herbert, München 072723
Hartwig, Robert, Berlin 138786
Hartworks, Dartmouth 112938
Harty, Lela, San Diego 119512
Hartz, Geeveston 094583
Hartz, Saint Louis 119211
Hartz, Jean-Claude, Obernai 065254
Hartzler-Towner Multicultural Museum, Nashville 046149
Harumi, Toronto 097284
Harvard Historical Society Collection, Harvard 044472
Harvard Historical Society Museum, Still River 048357
Harvard House, Shakespeare Birthplace Trust, Stratford-upon-Avon 041139
Harvard Museum of Natural History, Cambridge 042559
Harvard University Art Museums, Fogg Art Museum, Arthur M. Sackler Museum, Busch-Reisinger Museum, Cambridge 042560
Harvard University Semitic Museum, Cambridge 042561
Harvery Art Gallery, Harvey 001098
Harvest, Rose, Irymple 056014
Harvest Home, Bowraville 094274
Harvest Moon, Saint Louis 092252
Harvey & Co., New York 090931
Harvey, Emily, New York 118002
Harvey, James, Clovelly 094407
Harvey, Lola & Barbara, New York . 090932
Harvey, Patricia, London 085378
Harvey, Trevor Victor, Seaforth 095188
Harvey & Co, W.R., Witney 087193, 131701
Harvey, Y. Philippe, Montréal 058961
Harvey County Historical Museum, Newton 046476
Harvey & Gore, London . . 085379, 131057
Harvey Grant Heritage Centre Community Museum, Springdale 006500
Harvey House Museum, Florence . . 043869
Harvey-Lee, Elizabeth, North Aston 086087
Harvey Studio, Nashville 117355
Harvey's Wine Museum, Bristol . . . 038865
Harwath, Arno, Donaueschingen . . 125472
Harwich Antiques Centre, Harwich . 084606
Harwich Maritime Museum and Harwich Lifeboat Museum, Harwich 039687
Harwich Redoubt Fort, Harwich . . . 039688
Harwood, Albuquerque 114793
Harwood Museum of Art of the University of New Mexico, Taos 048497
Haryana Prantiya Puratatva Sangrahalaya, Jhajjar 022186
Hary's Filmkistl, Wien 137320
Harz & Heidorn-Meyer, Syke 074036
Harzenetter, Ludwig, Westerheim bei Memmingen 074363
Harzer Roller-Kanarien-Museum, Sankt Andreasberg 019981
Harzir, Everard de, Bruxelles 057980
Harzmuseum, Wernigerode 020811
Al-Hasam, Abu, Sharjah 083216
Hasan Süzer Etnografya Müzesi, Gaziantep 038071
Hasbach, A.L., Wien 137321
Haschemi Edition Cologne, Köln . . . 134111
Haschtmann, Werner, Frankfurt am Main 102785, 139085
Hase, Grażyna, Warszawa 109144
Hasebe-ya, Tokyo 077251
Hasegawa, Nagoya 106922
Hasegawa Bijutsukan, Tokyo 027172
Haselünner Heimathäuser, Haselünne 017785
Hasemann, R.D., Hannover 139233
Hasenauer, Peter, Saalfelden am Steinernen Meer 123437
Hasenbach, Jorg, Antwerpen 096069
Hasenclever, Michael, München . . . 104224
Hasenkamp, Anne, Rostock 073579
Hasenmuseum, Bubikon 036979
Hasenstab, Aschaffenburg 069195
The Hash Marihuana Hemp Museum, Amsterdam 029184
Hashimoto, Kuraya, Kyoto 077100
Hashimoto Kansetsu Memorial Museum, Kyoto 026719
Hasičské Muzeum, Příbyslav 008658
Hasik, Michael, Solingen 104917
Hasikova, Bratislava 080608
The Haskell County Historical Museum, Sublette 048413
Haslam & Whiteway, London 085380
Haslauer, Hans Jörg, Oberalm 057196
Haslem, Jane, Washington 120307
Haslemere Antiques Market, Haslemere 084607
Haslemere Educational Museum, Haslemere 039690
Haslev Museum, Haslev 008891
Haslinger, Georg, Wien 095860
Haslinger, Quirin, Linz 137219
Haspel jun., Josef, Wien 123498
Haß, Klaus-Michael & Thomas, Berlin 125211
Hassalls Gallery, Eltham 055797
Hassan, Dubai 083192
Hassan, Gilles, Montpellier 138221
Hassan, Pascal, Paris 066040
Hassan, Pascal, Saint-Ouen 067798
Hassan, Roger, Paris 066041
Hassan & Hussein, Cairo 060450
Hassel, Barbara, Frankfurt am Main 125648
Hassel, Barbara, Frankfurt am Main 125649
Hassel, Barbara, Nidderau 126545
Hasselberg, Klaus, Potsdam 126646
Hasselmann, Klaus, Bremen 102246
Hasselmann, Martin, Höslwang . . . 125949
Hasselt Art Galery, Hasselt 096311
Hassett's Uralla Military Museum, Uralla 001579
Hassfurther, Wolfdietrich, Wien . . .057437, 095861, 120684
Hassfurther, Wolfdietrich, Wien . . . 133206
Hassfurther, Wolfdietrich, Wien . . . 137322
Hassler, Christian, Bourron-Marlotte 061734
Hassler, Christian, Moret-sur-Loing 064789
Hassloch, Bad Kissingen 069307
Hassner & Partner, Lübeck 072325
Hassold, B. & R., Augsburg 069229, 138685
Haßold, Robert, Königsbrunn 072032
Hassoldt, J.C, Amsterdam 128540
Haste, Ipswich . . . 084800, 113302, 130828
Hastedt, B., Bremervörde 070057
Hastert, Thomas, Trier 074093
Hasting Valley Fine Art Gallery, Wauchope 095383
Hastings, Roma 076507
Hastings and Rother Decorative and Fine Arts Society, Bexhill-on-Sea 054399
Hastings Antique Centre, Saint Leonards-on-Sea 086465
Hastings Arts, Hastings 113200
Hastings Community Arts Centre, Hastings 030512
Hastings Museum, Hastings 044475
Hastings Museum and Art Gallery, Hastings 039692
Hastings-Western Port Historical Museum, Hastings 001099
Hat Works, Museum of Hatting, Stockport 041108
Hata, Nagasaki 106912
Hatakeyama Collection, Tokyo 027173
Hatay Devlet Güzel Sanatlar Galerisi, Hatay 038074
Hatay Kültür Merkezi, Antakya, Hatay 038014
Hatay Müzesi, Hatay 038075
Hatch, Gideon, London 085381
Hatch-Billops Collections, New York 046344
Hatchards, London 141821
Hatchuel, Paris 138401
Hatfield & Sons, H.J., London 131058
Hatfield House Antiques, Fort Worth 088860
Hatfield I Antikk, Haugesund 079389
Hathaway Ranch Museum, Santa Fe Springs 047981
Hatherleigh Antiques, Hatherleigh . 084622
Hatje Cantz Verlag, Ostfildern 134338
Hatjigeorgiou, Vassili, Quillan 067011
Hatle, Praha 137832
Hatry, Heidelberg 139251
Hatten, Richard de, Poids-de-Fiole . 066882
Hatter, Mad, Auckland 140596
Les Hattes, L'Isle-sur-la-Sorgue . . . 063936
Hatton-Eielson Museum, Hatton . . . 044478
Hatton Gallery, Newcastle-upon-Tyne 040549
Hatton Gallery, Colorado State University, Fort Collins 043904
Hattowska, Grażyna, Kraków 129039
Hatzfeld, Georg von, München 134243
Hatzig, Hermann-Josef, Marburg . . 072445
Haubensack, Hanna, Zürich 141340
Haubrich, Bernd, Trier 074094
Haubs, Markus, München 126392
Hauch, Kirsten, Virum 124035
Hauchs Physiske Cabinet, Sorø Akademis, Sorø 009113
Hauck, Anne, West Hollywood 093472
Hauck, Norma, Rodewald 073551
Hauck, Norma C. & Bernd, Rodewald 134369
Hauck & Aufhäuser, München 072724, 121529
Haucke, Marcus, Berlin . . 101920, 138787
Haucke & Utz, Berlin 125212
Haude & Spener, Berlin 133780
Haudrecy, d', Knokke-Heist 096336
Hauer, Ruth, Hamburg 125821
Haufe & Lutz, Karlsruhe 139295
Haufe & Lutz, Karlsruhe 139296
Haufek-Rull, Elfriede, Mödling 095684
Hauff, Prof. Gottfried, Potsdam 126647
Hauff, Reinhard, Stuttgart 104987
Haug, Hasso R. Maria, Konstanz . . . 126131
Haug, Katrin, Berlin 125213
Haugar Vestfold Kunstmuseum, Tønsberg 031269
Haugesund Billedgalleri, Haugesund 030881
Haugg, Berkheim, Kreis Biberach an der Riß 125158
Haugg, Buxheim bei Memmingen . . 125421
Haughey, Kirkby Stephen 084873
Haughton, Brian, London 085382
Haughton, Stephen, Hawthorn, Victoria 055964, 123239
Haugwitz, Ralph Rüdiger, Berlin . . . 069638
Hauhon Esinemuseo, Hauho 009507
Hauke, Udo, Lützen 126248
Hauke-Sommer, Renate, Geislingen an der Steige 125706
Haukiputaan Koulumuseo, Haukipudas 009508
Haunch of Venison, London 113680
Haunschild, Christine, Penzing 126617
Haunsperger, Ingolstadt 071625
Haupt, Horst, Berlin 069639
Haupt, Paul, Bern 134993
Haupt, Rudolf, Augsburg 069230
Hauptmann, Burkhard, Bamberg . . 069453
Hauptmann, Mike & Hans-Günter, Meißen 139474
Hauptmann & Kampa, Zürich 112110
Hauptstaatsarchiv Stuttgart, Stuttgart 020352
Haurie Vigne, Magdalena, Sevilla . . 110771
Haus am Kleistpark, Kunstamt Schöneberg, Berlin 016058
Haus am Lützowplatz, Berlin 016059
Haus am Waldsee, Berlin 016060
Haus der Auktionen, Frankfurt am Main 121405
Haus der Donauschwaben, Sammlungen heimatlichen Erbes, Sindelfingen . 020216
Haus der Dorfgeschichte Bliesmengen-Bolchen, Mandelbach 018804
Haus der Fotografie, Hannover 017752
Haus der Fotografie - Dr. Robert-Gerlich-Museum, Burghausen, Salzach . . 016513
Haus der Gemälde, Nürnberg 104480
Haus der Geschichte, Bad Harzburger und Schreibenhauer Heimatstube, Burgbergmuseum, Bad Harzburg . 015712
Haus der Geschichte, Lutherstadt Wittenberg 018760
Haus der Geschichte der Bundesrepublik Deutschland, Zeitgeschichtliches Forum Leipzig, Leipzig 018596
Haus der Heimat, Olbernhau 019462
Haus der Heimat Freital, Freital . . . 017247
Haus der Keramik, Wilhelmsburg an der Traisen 095972
Haus der Kulturen der Welt, Berlin . 016061
Haus der Kunst, Graz 095533
Haus der Kunst, Grunbach 071138
Haus der Kunst, München 019061
Haus der Kunst, Nümbrecht 019343
Haus der Kunst, Remshalden 073494, 139687
Haus der Kunst, Waldshut-Tiengen . 105152
Haus der Kunst Sankt Josef, Solothurn 111920
Haus der Landbrandenburg Lottogesellschaft, Potsdam 019656
Haus der Natur, Eichendorf 016904
Haus der Natur, Willingen, Upland . 020901
Haus der Naturfreunde, Duisburg . . 016854
Haus der Ortsgeschichte, Schwäbisch Hall 020115
Haus der Ost- und Westpreußen, Oberschleißheim 019414
Haus der Seidenkultur, Krefeld 018397
Haus der Stadtgeschichte, Offenbach am Main 019454
Haus der Stadtgeschichte, Städtische Museen, Donauwörth 016741
Haus der tausend Bilder, Kiel 071826, 103541
Haus der Völker, Museum für Kunst und Ethnographie, Schwaz 002664
Haus des Gastes mit heimatkundlicher Sammlung, Gößweinstein 017463
Haus des Moores, Heidenreichstein 002027
Haus des Waldes, Köln 018314
Haus-Dorfmark, Bad Fallingbostel . 069281
Haus für Kunst Uri, Altdorf, Uri 036830
Haus für Relief und Halbfiguren von Hans Josephsohn, Stiftung La Congiunta, Giornico 037145
Haus Giersch - Museum Regionaler Kunst, Frankfurt am Main 017170
Haus Kickelhain, Stadtmuseum Mosbach, Mosbach, Baden 018999
Haus Konstruktiv, Zürich 037769
Haus Mährisch-Schönberg, Bad Hersfeld 015715
Haus of Prints & Multiples, Antwerpen 133249
Haus Opherdicke, Holzwickede . . . 018000
Haus Rottels, Neuss 019272
Haus Sandfeld, Wuppertal 074523

Haus Tannenbusch, Dormagen 016749
Haus Ungarn, Berlin 016062
Haus Völker und Kulturen - Ethnologisches Museum, Sankt Augustin 019983
Haus Westland, Mönchengladbach . 018976
Haus Wittgenstein, Bulgarisches Kulturinstitut, Wien 002908
Haus zum Bunten Löwen, Erfurt . . . 102645
Haus zum Geissbock, Zürich 112111
Haus zum Kiel, Museum Rietberg Zürich, Zürich 037770
Haus zum Kirschgarten, Historisches Museum Basel, Basel 036884
Haus zum Palmbaum - Bachausstellung Arnstadt, Arnstadt 015567
Haus zum Stockfisch - Stadtmuseum, Erfurt 017016
Haus zum Torggel, Berneck 036941
Haus zum Wasen, Wagenhausen . . 111980
Hausch, Josef, Fürstenfeldbruck . . 125686
Hauschild, H.M., Bremen 133843
Hausen, Luisa, Euskirchen 070669, 102718
Hausenhäusl, Reit im Winkl 019785
Hauser, München 139512
Hauser, Claudio, Köln 071949
Hauser, Heinz, Schwarzenburg 082805, 122350, 130175
Hauser, Peter, Linz 057158
Hauser, Walter, Lyon 064139
Hauser & Wirth, Henau 111550
Hauser & Wirth, Zürich 112112
Hausgalerie, Müllendorf 095688
Hausjärven Kotiseutumuseo, Hausjärvi 009509
Hausmann & Faust, Freiburg, Elbe . 070817
Hausmühle, Steinbach am Attersee 002694
Hausmuseum Kloster Kreuzlingen, Kreuzlingen 037220
Hausner, D., Leonberg, Württemberg 103906
Hausser, M-P, Soufflenheim 068270
Haußmann, B., Mössingen 126329
Haußmann, Martin, Besigheim 125325
Hauswedell & Co., Dr. Ernst, Stuttgart 134412
Hauswedell & Nolte, Hamburg 121426, 139184
Hauswedell & Nolte, New York 122999
Haut, E., Rheda-Wiedenbrück 073509
Haut-Pavé, Paris 100502
Haut Quartier, Pézenas 138572
Haute Antiques 207, Bruxelles 057981
Haute Ecole d'Art Appliqués de Genève, Genève 050765
Haute Epoque, Flin 062877
Hautecoeur, Paris 100503
Hauteville House, Maison de Victor Hugo Paris, Saint Peter Port 040937
Hautin, Jean-Louis, Cosne-Cours-sur-Loire 120982
Havana Galerie, Zürich 112113
Havana Gallery, Chicago 115449
Havana Gallery, Vancouver 097483
Havant Museum, Havant 039697
Havard Père & Fils, Paris 124689
Havard Père & Fils, Paris 124690
Havard Père & Fils, Paris 124691
Havard, André, Bucéels 120955
Havard & Havard, Cowbridge 084093
Havas, Christophe, Rouen 067270
Havas, Frédéric, Caen 061873
Havayeda Museum, Holon 022937
Havelková, Elena, Mariánské Lázně 137796
Havelkovo Muzeum, Loštice 008488
Havelock Museum, Havelock 030513
Havelocks, Harrogate 084577, 130762
Havemann, Minke, Heinbockel 103343
Haven Antiques, Wainfleet 086998
Haven Art, Sacramento 119150
Het Havenmuseum, Rotterdam 030079
Havenplan's Architectural Emporium, Killamarsh 084841
Havenstein, M., Braderup 069971
Haver, Peter, Blaricum 128590
Haverbeque, Patrick, Marcq-en-Barœul 064274
Haverford Township Historical Society Museum, Havertown 044482
Haverhill and District Local History Centre, Haverhill 039700
Haverhill Historical Museum, Haverhill 044480
Haverhill Public Library Special Collections, Haverhill 044481
Havers, Hamilton, Caversham 130521
Havesdonckhoeve, Museum van Oud Landbouwalaam en Volskhuisraad, Bornem 003244
Havi, Leimuiden 128749
Havilland, de, New York 090933
De Havilland Aircraft Heritage Centre, Mosquito Aircraft Museum, Saint Albans 040882
Havillands, de, Clifton Hill 136862
Havlíček, Znojmo 124010
Havlik, Rudolf, Wien 095862
Havråtunet, Lonevåg 030995
Havre de Grace Decoy Museum, Havre de Grace 044484
Hawaii All-Collectors Show, Honolulu 093986
Hawaii Antique Center, Honolulu . . . 088952
Hawaii Antiques, Art & Collectibles Quarterly, Honolulu 136481
Hawaii Children's Discovery Center, Honolulu 044595
Hawaii Maritime Center, Honolulu . . 044596
Hawaii Museums Association, Honolulu 054787
Hawaii Pacific University Gallery, Honolulu 044597
Hawaiian Antiquities, Honolulu 088953
Hawaiian Art, Indianapolis 116463
Hawaiian Islands Coin, Honolulu . . . 088954
Hawaii's Plantation Village, Waipahu 048825
Hawari, S. & H., München 072725, 126393
Hawera Book Inn, Taranaki 140656
Hawick Museum, Hawick 039703
Hawk, Columbus 115785
Hawk, London 135223
Hawk, Louisville 116944
Hawk, Pittsburgh 118927
Hawke, Kansas City 116571
Hawke House, Bordertown 000816
The Hawker Gallery, Amersham . . . 112507
Hawker Museum, Hawker, South Australia 001100
Hawke's Bay Museum, Napier 030545
Hawkesbury Creative Art Centre, Windsor, New South Wales 095401
Hawkesbury Museum, Windsor, New South Wales 001622
Hawkesbury Valley Auctions, Windsor, New South Wales 120655
Hawkeye Log Cabin, Burlington . . . 042514
Hawkins, J.B., Moss Vale 056276
Hawkins, John, Moss Vale 056277
Hawkins, Mark & David, Brighton . .083698, 141437
Hawkins, Philip, Shaftesbury 131468
Hawkins, Sally, New York 118003
Hawkins & Hawkins, Edinburgh . . . 084296
Hawks Hill Gallery, Kingsley 094705
Hawks Inn, Delafield 043378
Hawks Nest State Park, Ansted . . . 041747
Hawkstrega, Indianapolis 089301
Hawley, Nathan, San Francisco . . . 092809
Hawley Antiques, Beverley 083500, 130376
Hawley Library, Los Angeles 135383
Hawn, W.H., Oklahoma City 091504
Haworth, Binghamton 135329
Haworth, Peter, Beetham . 083477, 130365
Haworth Art Gallery, Accrington . . . 038468
Haws & Co., Denver 116012
Hawthorn, Birmingham 115111
Hawthorn, Gerard, London 085383, 113681, 131059
Hawthorne, Kingston-upon-Hull . . . 130850
Hawthorne Boulevard Books, Portland 142800
Hawthorns Urban Wildlife Centre, Southampton 041056
Hay, Bunbury 094324
Hay, Ashley, Clayfield 055684
Hay Gaol Museum, Hay 001102
Hay House Museum, Macon 045566
Hayashibara Bijutsukan, Okayama . 026940
The Haybarn Antiques, Upper Moutere 079276
Haycraft, Roland, Wallingford 131641
Haydar, Beirut 077397
Hayde, Georg, Feldafing 125633
Haydn-Geburtshaus, Rohrau 002536
Haydn-Gedenkstätte mit Brahms-Gedenkraum, Wien Museum, Wien 002909
Haydn-Haus Eisenstadt, Eisenstadt 001826
Haye, Danielle, Paris 066042
Al-Hayek, Bassam, Damascus 083061
Hayem, François, Paris 066043
Hayes, Burswood 120573
Hayes, Jamie, New Orleans 117455
Hayes, Joseph M., Columbus 088418
Hayes, M., Baltimore 131823
Haygate Gallery, Telford 086838
Haygood, Don & Pola, Glyfada 105422
Hayhurst, Jeanette, London 085384
Hayko Restoration, New York 132477
Hayles, Derek, Maidenhead 141932
Haylett, A.P. & M.A., Outwell 086175
Hayloft Gallery, Palace Stable Heritage Centre, Armagh 038527
The Haymakers Gallery, Hay-on-Wye 113210
Haymar, Busselton 055593
Haymes & Sons, Surry Hills 137098
Haymon, Innsbruck 133091
Hayner Cultural Center, Troy 048620
Haynes, Broadway 112734, 130465
Haynes, Frank, Great Bowden 113150
Haynes, Roger, Leek 084937
Haynes Motor Museum, Sparkford . 041077
Hayo, Châtenois 062223
Hayot, Monelle, Saint-Rémy-en-l'Eau 133699
Hays, Louisville 089996, 122950
Hays, Daniel, Valdivienne 068681
Hay's Gallery, London 113682
Haystack Mountain School of Crafts, Deer Isle 051241
Haystack Mountain School of Crafts Gallery, Deer Isle 043363
Hayungs, H.E., Hamburg 103164
Hayward, Wanganui 121840
Hayward Gallery, London 040172
Hayward Gallery Bookshop, London 141822
Hayworth Art Gallery, Los Angeles . 116790
Hazaël-Massieux, Philippe, Avignon 124088
Hazama Inosuke Museum of Art, Kaga 026602
Hazard Press, Christchurch 134844
ter Hazeborg, Bernhard, Hamburg . 071244
Hazel of Brecon, Brecon 083658
Hazel Sandford Gallery, Clarion University of Pennsylvania, Clarion 042946
Hazelbrook Cottage Antique Centre, Hazelbrook 055970
Hazelhoff, Janna, Groningen 140433
Hazelhurst Regional Gallery and Arts Centre, Gymea 001089
Hazledine, Anthony, Fairford 084372, 130699
Hazlitt, Gooden & Fox, New York . . 118004
Hazlitt, Gooden & Fox, London 085385
Hazor Museum, Ayelet-Hashahar . . 022894
Hazou, Elie, San Diego 119513
Hazrati Museum, Semnan 022594
H.B. Antiquités, Marckolsheim 064268
HB Verlags- und Vertriebsgesellschaft, Hamburg 134012
H.B.S.A. Newsletter, London 136224
HD Antiques, New York 090934
HDM Galerie, Moers 104108
He Xuan, Tian, Singapore 109805
Head, D.R., Weybridge 114675
Head, Peter, Fukuoka 077042
Head House Antiques and Uniques, Louisville 089997
Head-Smashed-In Buffalo Jump, Fort Macleod 005464
Headfooters, Cleveland 115715
Headland Historical Museum, Nambucca Heads 001307
Headlands Center for the Arts, Sausalito 048020
Headley & Menzies, Memphis 090077
Headley-Whitney Museum, Lexington 045258
Headlund Museum, Hugo 044665
Headpress, Manchester 136225
Headrick, Mark, Austin 131800
Headrow Antiques Centre, Leeds . . 084927
Headrow Gallery, Leeds 113364
Heads 'n' Tails, Wiveliscombe 087198, 131703
Healdton Oil Museum, Healdton . . . 044498
Healesville Art Gallery, Healesville . 094628
Healing & Arts Studio, Boston 115182
Healry Gallery, Singapore 080478
Health Adventure, Asheville 041795
Health Museum, Hyderabad 022157
Health Museum, Yangon 029076
Health Museum of Cleveland, Cleveland 042993
Health Science Museum, Hiroshima 026526
Healy, Justin, Malvern 136989
Healy House and Dexter Cabin, Leadville 045220
Heaman's Antique Autorama, Carman 005231
Heanor Antiques Centre, Ilkeston . . 084786
Heape's Antiques, Burnham-on-Sea 083809
Heard Museum, Phoenix 047009
Heard Natural Science Museum, McKinney 045560
Hearn, Pat, New York 118005
Hearst Art Gallery, Saint Mary's College, Moraga 046019
Hearst Books Int., New York 135433
Hearst Castle, San Simeon 047923
Heart, Paris 100504
Heart, Lion, New York 142662
Heart Field Gallery, Nagoya 106923
Heart Of Art, Christchurch 108395
Heart of Diamonds, Miami 090182
Heart of Glass 2003, Greytown 108456
Heart of West Texas Museum, Colorado City 043052
Heart Spoken, Portland 119006
Heart Strings, Trafalgar 056733
Hearthstone Historic House Museum, Appleton 041753
Heartland, Maitland 056126
Heartland Antiques, Jacksonville . .089418, 132183
Heartland - The California Museum of the Heart, Rancho Mirage 047324
Heartland Gallery, Austin 114988
Heartland Mall, Oklahoma City 091505
Heart's Content Cable Station, Heart's Content 005613
Hearts of Oak, Toronto 123834
Heath, Salt Lake City 132788
Heath, A.R, Bristol 141455
Heath, Bob, Parkhurst 120624
Heath, Claudia, Charlotte 115289
Heath, Mike, Newport, Isle of Wight 086077, 131315
Heath-Bullock, Godalming 084480, 130733
Heathcote Antiques, Cross Hills . . . 084121
Heathcote Ball & Co, Leicester 122561
Heather, J.C., Woolpit 087247
Heatherbank Museum of Social Work, Glasgow 039558
Heatherslaw Mill, Cornhill-on-Tweed 039142
Heathfield Antiques & Country Pine, Holt, Norfolk 084704

Heath's Old Wares, Ballina 055441
Heaton Antiques, Bradford 083627
Heaton Hall, Manchester City Art Gallery, Manchester 040400
Heaven, Barrie, Adelaide 055314
Heaven and Earth, Sydney 095292
Heaven & Earth, Sydney 095293
Heaven & Earth Antiques, Edmonton 058829
Heaven Farm Museum, Uckfield . . . 041257
Heaven Hi Originals, Saint Paul . . . 119295
Heaven on Earth, Amsterdam 107730
Heavenly Handbags, Charlotte 087953
The Heavenly One, Singapore 080479
Heaven's Art Gallery, Montego Bay . 106825
Hebbard, Hay-on-Wye 084632
Hebbel-Museum, Wesselburen 020826
Hebbershof, Sonsbeck 104927
Hebecker, Michel, Weimar, Thüringen 105189
Hebei Fine Arts Press, Shijiazhuang 133383
Hebei Museum, Shijiazhuang 007267
Hebei Painting Gallery, Shijiazhuang 097994
Hebei Provincial Museum, Wuhan . 007301
Heberlé, Jean-Jacques, Guebwiller 063090
Heberlein, Weilheim, Oberbayern . . 105182
Heberri, Donostia-San Sebastián . . 129506
Hébert, Serge, Yébleron 069058
Hebezeug-Museum, Witten 020923
Hebler, Bochum 102156
Hebler, Bochum 102157
Hebling, Nadja & K.-H., Schweinfurt 104861
Hebling, R., Gochsheim . . 071023, 125733
Hebraica Judaica, Paris 138402
Hebrew Union College-Jewish Institute of Religion Skirball Museum, Cincinnati 042925
Hebrew University Collections of Natural History, Jerusalem 022951
Hécey, Erna, Luxembourg 107405
Hecher, Gert, Wien 123499
Hecht, A., München 072726
Hecht, P., Emmenbrücke 111393
Hecht, Richard, Dallas 088528
Hecht, Susanne, München 126394
Hecht-Lang, Brigitte, Bad Waldsee . 125120
Heck, Mathias, Chemnitz 125428
Heck, Thomas Leon, Reutlingen . . .073500, 104729, 121586, 139691
Heck, Thomas Leon, Tübingen 121613, 139797
Heck, V.A., Wien 137323
Heckenhauer, J.J., Berlin . 101921, 133781, 138788
Hecker, Maik David, Düsseldorf . . . 125532
Heckington Windmill, Heckington . . 039713
Heckl, Heinrich, Wien 123500
Heckmann, Stuttgart 126854
Heckmann, B., Siegburg 073806
Heckmann, Daniela, Ellwangen . . . 125584
Heckmann, Manfred, Berlin 069640
Heckmann, Pierre, Paris 124692
Heckner, W., Iphofen 071630
Heckscher Museum of Art, Huntington 044680
Heckt, Sönke, Laboe 072109
Hecla Island Heritage Home Museum, Riverton 006297
Hecq, J.-M., Charleroi . . . 058150, 120750
Hedaes Sevira, Paris 100505
Hedberg, O., Bjärtrå 122106
Heddal, Notodden 079406
Heddal, Notodden 121859
Heddal Bygdetun, Notodden 031057
Heddon Museum, Dowagiac 043498
Hedegaard, Søren, København 060337
Hedel, Ansbach 101588
Hedenborg's Antikvariat, Roskilde . 137905
Hédevin, Jean-Pierre, Marck 064265
Hedge, Penny, Whitby 114679
Hedgecoe, Michael, Chobham 130576
Hedgehog Antiques, London 085386
Hediger, M.-Theres, Aachen 101514
Hediger, Thomas, Sankt Gallen 082777
Hedingham Antiques, Sible Hedingham 086611, 131499
Hedley, Peter, Wareham 131647
Hedleys Humpers, Saint-Ouen 067799
Hedley's of Hexham, Hexham 084678, 130793
Hedmarksmuseet og Domkirkeodden, Hamar 030872
Hedon Museum, Hedon 039715
Hedrich, Ruth, Ehringshausen 102606
Hedrick, Natalie, Charlotte 087954
Hedrum Bygdetun, Larvik 030973
Heeb, Iris, Schaan 128457
Heede & Moestrup, København . . .060338, 098572, 133424
Heeke, R., Bocholt 138881
Heel, Königswinter 134128
Heemann, Annette, Münster 072909
Heemerf De Schutsboom, Goirle . . . 029617
Heemkamer Barthold Van Hessel, Aarle Rixtel 029126
Heemken, Frank, Karlsruhe 126001
Heemkundemuseum Beek, Beek . . 029295
Heemkundemuseum Paulus Van Daesdonck, Ulvenhout 030220
Heemkundig Museum, Asse 003202
Heemkundig Museum, Borgerhout . 003242
Heemkundig Museum, Bree 003258
Heemkundig Museum, Ommeren . . 029992
Heemkundig Museum, Tervuren . . . 003790
Heemkundig Museum, Wilrijk 003859
Heemkundig Museum, Zolder 003870
Heemkundig Museum Boekhoute, Boekhoute 003238
Heemkundig Museum Gerard Meeusen, Essen 003426
Heemkundig Museum Sincfala, Knokke 003552
Heemkundig Museum Slag van Lafelt, Vlijtingen 003836
Heemkundig Museum Tempelhof, Beerse 003222
Heemkundig Museum vat het Gaverdomein, Deerlijk 003389
Heemkundig Museum Wetteren, Wetteren 003853
Heemkundig Museum Wissekerke, Kruibeke 003561
Heemkundig Streekmuseum Jan Uten Houte, Etten Leur 029583
Heemmuseum Bystervelt, Schelle . 003743
Heemmuseum De Kaeck, Wommelgem 003861
Heemmuseum de Zuiderkempen, Westerlo 003852
Heemmuseum Die Swane, Heist-op-den-Berg 003505
Heemmuseum Eeklo, Eeklo 003419
Heemschuur Maasland, Heesch . . . 029699
Heemskerk, Gerrit, Amsterdam . . . 107731
Heer, Oslo 108730
Heeramaneck & Son, Mumbai 105781
Heerd, Tucson 093241
Heeren & Co., Pittsburgh 132668
Heeren, Monika von, Rottenbuch, Oberbayern 126745
Héeren, Viviann, Lund 129847
Heeresgeschichtliches Museum im Arsenal, Wien 002910
Heerkens Thijssen, Haarlem 128692
De Heerlijckheid, Middelburg 078638
Hees, Daniel, Mühlacker 126337
Hees, L. van, Saarbrücken 104797
Heeseler, Georg, Krefeld 072072
Heeswyk, J., Ediger-Eller 070507
Hefaistos, Bucureşti 129221
Hefaistos, Děčin 098355
Heffel, Toronto 097285, 120818
Heffel, Vancouver 097484
Heffel Gallery, Vancouver 006699
Heffner, Bratislava 109910
Hegau-Museum, Singen, Hohentwiel 020218
Hegelhaus, Stuttgart 020353
Hegemann, Hagen, Westfalen 103048
Hegenbart, Günther, Wien 057438, 123501
Hegenbart, Werner, Wien 057439
Hegenberg sen., Hans, Essen 070631
Hegetschweiler, Marlène, Ottenbach 111805
Hegge, Oddrun, Fagernes 128987
Heggeli, Oslo 079443
Hegglin, Rorschach 082753
Hegmataneh Museum, Samedan . . 022592
Hegnauer & Schwarzenbach, Bern . 141225
Hegnauer & Schwarzenbach, Bern . 141226
Hegner, Bonn 138901
M. Hegner & J. Pilz, Alfter 138678
Hegyridéki Helytörténeti Gyûjtemény & Kortárs Galéria, Budapest 021653
Hehr, Ralf, Waiblingen 105142
Heian, Houston 089095
Heian, Kyoto 077101
Heian, Kyoto 106895
Heiando, Kyoto 140161
Heibel, Bärbel, Rammsee 073409
Heiber, Winfried, Dresden 125496
De Heibergske Samlinger - Sogn Folkemuseum, Kaupanger 030934
Heickmann, Chemnitz 070131
Heid, Caroline, Sissach 082816
Heide Museum of Modern Art, Bulleen 000859
Heide Museum of Modern Art, Melbourne 001240
Heidefeld & Partner, Krefeld 103778
Heidegalerie, Wels 002827
Heidelberg Motor Museum, Heidelberg 034632
Heidelberger Kunstverein, Heidelberg 017827, 053230
Heidelmann & Hein, Dresden 070318
Heidema, Groningen 078420
Heidemuseum Dat ole Huus, Bispingen 016255
Heidemuseum Rischmannshof Walsrode, Freilichtmuseum, Walsrode 020661
Heidenberg, Lillian, New York 118006
Heidenheimer Verlagsanstalt, Heidenheim an der Brenz 134054
Het Heidenrijck, Nijmegen 078655
Heider Heimatmuseum, Heide, Holstein 017821
Heidi Weber-Museum, Zürich 037771
Heidick, Robert, Riethnordhausen . 073537
Heidi's Attic Wares, Taree 056699
Heidkamp, Ludwig, Düsseldorf 070391, 125533
Heidorn, C., Pinneberg 121575
Heidrich, Ursel, Großwallstadt 071127
Heights Antiques on Yale, Houston . 089096
Heights Gallery, Houston 116335
Heights Station Antiques, Houston . 089097
Heights Theater Antiques, Houston . 089098
Heigl, Traunreut 105055
Heijboer, Anton, Amsterdam 107732
Heijokyuseki Shiryokan, Nara Bunkazaikenkyusho, Nara 026891
Heikintupa, Pohjaslahti 009982
Heikkilä, Helsinki 060527
Heil, Jochen, Frankfurt am Main . . 102786
Heilig, Bruchsal 102271
Heilig, Andreas B., Frankfurt am Main 070747
Heiliggeistkirche, Museen der Stadt Landshut, Landshut 018483
Heilmann, Braderup 102212
Heilmann, Bernhard, Augsburg 069231
Heilongjiang Fine Arts Press, Harbin 133356
Heilongjiang Province Nation Museum, Harbin 007109
Heim, Miami 117087
Heim, Jean-François, Paris 100506
Heim, Philippe, Paris 100507
Heim, Reinhold, Chemnitz 102311
Heimat-Jagdmuseum, Prigglitz . . . 002470
Heimat-Museum, Millstatt 002313
Heimat Museum Amöneburg, Amöneburg 015535
Heimat-Museum Maintal, Maintal . 018785
Heimat-Naturmuseum Untere Havel, Havelberg 017810
Heimat- und Bauernmuseum, Bruck, Oberpfalz 016461
Heimat- und Bergbaumuseum, Lugau, Erzgebirge 018751
Heimat- und Bergbaumuseum, Nentershausen, Hessen 019199
Heimat- und Bergbaumuseum, Reinsdorf 019784
Heimat- und Bienenzuchtmuseum, Orth an der Donau 002401
Heimat und Bildhauer Kern Museum, Forchtenberg 017139
Heimat- und Braueremuseum, Pleinfeld 019635
Heimat- und Braunkohlemuseum, Steinberg, Oberpfalz 020303
Heimat- und Buddelmuseum, Osten 019504
Heimat- und Dorfmuseum Pfaffenwiesbach, Wehrheim 020702
Heimat- und Feuerwehrmuseum, Schauenstein 020006
Heimat- und Floßermuseum Calmbach, Bad Wildbad 015822
Heimat- und Grimmelshausenmuseum, Oberkirch 019393
Heimat- und Hafnermuseum, Heidenheim, Mittelfranken 017844
Heimat- und Handfeuerwaffenmuseum, Kemnath 018228
Heimat-und Handwerkermuseum, Leutershausen 018624
Heimat- und Handwerks Museum Stolberg, Stolberg, Rheinland 020325
Heimat- und Heringsfängermuseum Heimsen, Petershagen, Weser . . . 019593
Heimat- und Humboldtmuseum, Eibau 016900
Heimat- und Industriemuseum, Kolbermoor 018372
Heimat- und Industriemuseum, Wackersdorf 020612
Heimat- und Keramikmuseum, Kandern 018148
Heimat- und Krippenmuseum, Zirl . 003070
Heimat- und Landlermuseum, Bad Goisern 001717
Heimat- und Miedermuseum Heubach, Heubach, Württemberg 017912
Heimat- und Montanmuseum in Schloß Oberkindberg, Kindberg 002123
Heimat- und Naturkunde-Museum Wanne-Eickel, Emschertal-Museum, Herne 017891
Heimat- und Palitzsch-Museum Prohlis, Dresden 016791
Heimat- und Pfarrmuseum, Wildalpen 003042
Heimat- und Posamentermuseum Sissach, Sissach 037569
Heimat- und Rebbaumuseum, Spiez 037584
Heimat- und Schiffahrtsmuseum, Heinsen 017860
Heimat- und Schmiedemuseum, Widdern 020852
Heimat- und Ski-Museum, Braunlage 016379
Heimat- und Torfmuseum, Gröbenzell 017544
Heimat- und Uhrenmuseum, Villingen-Schwenningen 020593
Heimat- und Wallfahrtsmuseum, Xanten 021033
Heimatdiele Kutenholz, Kutenholz . 018452
Heimatecke am Seifenbach, Beierfeld 015936
Heimatgeschichtliche Sammlung des Kirchspiels, Schwabstedt 020108
Heimatgeschichtliches Museum, Modautal 018965
Heimath, H.M., Borken, Westfalen . 133832
Heimathaus, Nesselwang 019206
Heimathaus Alte Mühle, Schladen . 020032
Heimathaus Aying, Aying 015634
Heimathaus Beandhaus, Sankt Johann am Walde 002589
Heimathaus Bevergern, Hörstel . . . 017952

Heimathaus De Theeshof, Schneverdingen 020066
Heimathaus der Stadt Lauingen, Lauingen 018531
Heimathaus der Stadt Warendorf, Warendorf 020678
Heimathaus des Heimatvereins Haslach, Haslach 002020
Heimathaus des Rupertiwinkels und Heimatstube der Sudetendeutschen, Tittmoning 020446
Heimathaus Dingden, Hamminkeln . 017735
Heimathaus Ebensee, Ebensee 001797
Heimathaus Fahringer, Pürgg 002475
Heimathaus Gallneukirchen, Gallneukirchen 001881
Heimathaus Greven Worth, Selsingen 020187
Heimathaus-Handwerkermuseum, Scheidegg 020010
Heimathaus im alten Zollhaus, Kobersdorf 002159
Heimathaus Julbach, Julbach 002108
Heimathaus Königswiesen, Königswiesen 002162
Heimathaus Litzelsdorf, Litzelsdorf . 002260
Heimathaus Mehedorf, Bremervörde 016439
Heimathaus mit Photographiemuseum, Mariazell 002289
Heimathaus Mörbisch, Mörbisch . . 002333
Heimathaus Neuchl-Anwesen, Hohenschäftlarn 017977
Heimathaus Neufelden, Neufelden . 002357
Heimathaus Neukirchen, Neukirchen bei Altmünster 002362
Heimathaus Obernberg am Inn, Obernberg am Inn 002386
Heimathaus Ollershof, Munster . . . 019165
Heimathaus Pfarrkirchen, Pfarrkirchen 019602
Heimathaus Pregarten, Pregarten . . 002466
Heimathaus Raab, Raab 002484
Heimathaus Richard Eichinger und Steinmuseum, Enzenkirchen 001837
Heimathaus Sankt Georgen an der Gusen, Sankt Georgen an der Gusen 002580
Heimathaus Sankt Peter im Sulmtal, Sankt Peter im Sulmtal 002615
Heimathaus Schalchen, Schalchen . 002640
Heimathaus Schörfling, Schörfling am Attersee 002653
Heimathaus Schwanenstadt, Schwanenstadt 002658
Heimathaus Sittensen, Sittensen . . 020225
Heimathaus Sonthofen, Sonthofen . 020253
Heimathaus Spitalskirche/Bürgerspital, Bad Leonfelden 001729
Heimathaus Steinbach am Attersee, Steinbach am Attersee 002695
Heimathaus Stinatz, Stinatz 002712
Heimathaus Ulrichsberg, Ulrichsberg 002767
Heimathaus und Stadtmuseum, Perg 002418
Heimathaus Vöcklabruck, Vöcklabruck 002782
Heimathaus Waidhofen, Waidhofen an der Thaya 002798
Heimathaus Wartenberg an der Krems, Wartberg an der Krems 002808
Heimathaus Wendelstein, Wendelstein, Mittelfranken 020795
Heimathaus Wenigzell, Wenigzell . . 002835
Heimathausanlage Schafstall, Bremervörde 016440
Heimathof Emsbüren, Emsbüren . . 016977
Heimatkabinett Westerholt, Herten 017904
Heimatkundehaus und Münzkabinett, Sankt Marien 002598
Heimatkundesammlung Inzersdorf, Herzogenburg 002041
Heimatkundliche Sammlung, Elzach 016954
Heimatkundliche Sammlung, Heideck 017822
Heimatkundliche Sammlung, Heroldsbach 017895
Heimatkundliche Sammlung, Isen . 018084
Heimatkundliche Sammlung, Pfronten 019611
Heimatkundliche Sammlung, Uznach 037664
Heimatkundliche Sammlung, Haus zum Bären, Richterswil 037447
Heimatkundliche Sammlung Bergendorf, Holzheim bei Rain, Lech 017994
Heimatkundliche Sammlung Burg Rheinfels, Sankt Goar 019987
Heimatkundliche Sammlung des Heimatdienstes Hindelang, Bad Hindelang 015718
Heimatkundliche Sammlung Strick, Bad Mitterndorf 001732
Heimatkundliche Sammlung und Ausstellung, Hermannsburg 017887
Heimatkundliches Museum, Friedeburg, Ostfriesland 017263
Heimatkundliches Museum Medaria, Matrei in Osttirol 002295
Heimatkundliches Museum Wetzlhäusl, Sankt Gilgen 002585
Heimatmuseum, Bad Abbach 015641
Heimatmuseum, Bad Langensalza . 015744
Heimatmuseum, Ebenau 001795
Heimatmuseum, Gehrden, Hannover 017336
Heimatmuseum, Melk 002306
Heimatmuseum, Pritzwalk 019676
Heimatmuseum, Stolberg, Harz . . . 020323
Heimatmuseum, Adelsdorf 015443
Heimatmuseum, Aesch, Basel-Land 036817
Heimatmuseum, Aidlingen 015462
Heimatmuseum, Aken 015464
Heimatmuseum, Allendorf, Lumda . 015480
Heimatmuseum, Allensbach 015482
Heimatmuseum, Angermünde 015544
Heimatmuseum, Annaburg 015552
Heimatmuseum, Arneburg 015565
Heimatmuseum, Arnoldstein 001697
Heimatmuseum, Aßlar 015592
Heimatmuseum, Attiswil 036858
Heimatmuseum, Bad Großpertholz . 001719
Heimatmuseum, Bad Neustadt an der Saale 015762
Heimatmuseum, Bad Radkersburg . 001734
Heimatmuseum, Bad Rodach 015776
Heimatmuseum, Bad Schandau . . . 015790
Heimatmuseum, Bad Vilbel 015819
Heimatmuseum, Belgern 015940
Heimatmuseum, Bernau bei Berlin . 016202
Heimatmuseum, Bernhardsthal . . . 001750
Heimatmuseum, Bezau 001753
Heimatmuseum, Blindheim 016270
Heimatmuseum, Brugg 036977
Heimatmuseum, Buttstädt 016529
Heimatmuseum, Camburg 016543
Heimatmuseum, Crivitz 016608
Heimatmuseum, Dahlen, Sachsen . 016624
Heimatmuseum, Darlingerode 016633
Heimatmuseum, Deutschneudorf . . 016697
Heimatmuseum, Dietenhofen 016704
Heimatmuseum, Dömitz 016732
Heimatmuseum, Domersleben 016735
Heimatmuseum, Donzhausen 037048
Heimatmuseum, Eibelstadt 016901
Heimatmuseum, Elsenfeld 016949
Heimatmuseum, Eltmann 016950
Heimatmuseum, Eppelborn 016990
Heimatmuseum, Ergoldsbach 017021
Heimatmuseum, Falkensee 017101
Heimatmuseum, Falkenstein, Vogtland 017103
Heimatmuseum, Frankenberg, Sachsen 017147
Heimatmuseum, Friedland bei Neubrandenburg 017265
Heimatmuseum, Fügen 001875
Heimatmuseum, Gaaden 001879
Heimatmuseum, Gablitz 001880
Heimatmuseum, Gerstungen 017392
Heimatmuseum, Gleisdorf 001896
Heimatmuseum, Gnas 001914
Heimatmuseum, Grabow, Mecklenburg 017498
Heimatmuseum, Grafenwörth 001922
Heimatmuseum, Gressenberg 001955
Heimatmuseum, Greußen 017531
Heimatmuseum, Grindelwald 037166
Heimatmuseum, Groß-Enzersdorf . . 001962
Heimatmuseum, Großröhrsdorf, Oberlausitz 017578
Heimatmuseum, Großzschepa 017586
Heimatmuseum, Grüningen 037167
Heimatmuseum, Hadersdorf 002000
Heimatmuseum, Haimhausen 017637
Heimatmuseum, Hallau 037175
Heimatmuseum, Haynsburg 017814
Heimatmuseum, Herbrechtingen . . 017879
Heimatmuseum, Hergensweiler . . . 017884
Heimatmuseum, Höpfingen 017951
Heimatmuseum, Holzgau 002061
Heimatmuseum, Immenstaad 018060
Heimatmuseum, Kals am Großglockner 002110
Heimatmuseum, Karlstein am Main 018177
Heimatmuseum, Kematen an der Ybbs 002121
Heimatmuseum, Kirchdorf auf Poel 018262
Heimatmuseum, Kirchham 002128
Heimatmuseum, Kirchschlag 002129
Heimatmuseum, Klipphausen 018285
Heimatmuseum, Kölleda 018300
Heimatmuseum, Krieglach 002179
Heimatmuseum, Kuchl 002183
Heimatmuseum, Küssnacht am Rigi 037226
Heimatmuseum, Langenlois 002198
Heimatmuseum, Langenzersdorf . . 002202
Heimatmuseum, Lengenfeld, Vogtland 018611
Heimatmuseum, Leupahn 018622
Heimatmuseum, Lich 018629
Heimatmuseum, Litschau 002259
Heimatmuseum, Lommatzsch 018683
Heimatmuseum, Luckenwalde 018690
Heimatmuseum, Mank 002275
Heimatmuseum, Marchegg 002278
Heimatmuseum, Markranstädt 018838
Heimatmuseum, Mautern in Steiermark 002299
Heimatmuseum, Mering 018912
Heimatmuseum, Möckmühl 018968
Heimatmuseum, Moosburg an der Isar 018994
Heimatmuseum, Mügeln bei Oschatz 019005
Heimatmuseum, Müllrose 019026
Heimatmuseum, Mureck 002349
Heimatmuseum, Neckargerach . . . 019195
Heimatmuseum, Nellingen 019198
Heimatmuseum, Neukirch, Lausitz . 019244
Heimatmuseum, Neustadt, Sachsen 019295
Heimatmuseum, Niederleis 002374
Heimatmuseum, Niederndorf 002376
Heimatmuseum, Oberhofen 002383
Heimatmuseum, Oberndorf am Neckar 019398
Heimatmuseum, Obertrum am See . 002393
Heimatmuseum, Oederan 019436
Heimatmuseum, Osterwieck 019512
Heimatmuseum, Perleberg 019591
Heimatmuseum, Pfaffstätten 002427
Heimatmuseum, Pfunds 002428
Heimatmuseum, Polling, Kreis Weilheim 019647
Heimatmuseum, Preetz, Holstein . . 019663
Heimatmuseum, Pressbaum 002468
Heimatmuseum, Prieros 019675
Heimatmuseum, Purkersdorf 002481
Heimatmuseum, Radeburg 019698
Heimatmuseum, Radstadt 002489
Heimatmuseum, Rattenberg 019724
Heimatmuseum, Reichenau an der Pulsnitz 019771
Heimatmuseum, Reinach (Basel-Land) 037443
Heimatmuseum, Reuland 003712
Heimatmuseum, Rietz 002531
Heimatmuseum, Rötha 019870
Heimatmuseum, Rothrist 037464
Heimatmuseum, Ruhla 019945
Heimatmuseum, Sandhausen 019978
Heimatmuseum, Sankt Koloman . . 002594
Heimatmuseum, Scheibbs 002645
Heimatmuseum, Schöneiche bei Berlin 020078
Heimatmuseum, Schrems 002656
Heimatmuseum, Schwarzenberg in Vorarlberg 002661
Heimatmuseum, Siget 002677
Heimatmuseum, Sohland 020234
Heimatmuseum, Sternberg 020318
Heimatmuseum, Strausberg 020336
Heimatmuseum, Tarrenz 002729
Heimatmuseum, Taufkirchen an der Pram 002730
Heimatmuseum, Teesdorf 002732
Heimatmuseum, Telfs 002735
Heimatmuseum, Thaya 002743
Heimatmuseum, Traismauer 002747
Heimatmuseum, Treuenbrietzen . . . 020472
Heimatmuseum, Trofaiach 002755
Heimatmuseum, Wald, Zürich 037689
Heimatmuseum, Waldheim 020641
Heimatmuseum, Wartberg im Mürztal 002809
Heimatmuseum, Weisendorf 020769
Heimatmuseum, Weissach im Tal . . 020771
Heimatmuseum, Weißenborn 020774
Heimatmuseum, Wiesenbach, Baden 020879
Heimatmuseum, Wilsdruff 020905
Heimatmuseum, Wippra 020919
Heimatmuseum, Wörgl 003057
Heimatmuseum, Arcun da Tradiziun, Waltensburg 037694
Heimatmuseum, Sammlung Fuchs, Kirchbach 002124
Heimatmuseum, Städtisches Museum, Mülheim an der Ruhr 019021
Heimatmuseum, Zürcher Unterländer Museumsverein, Oberweningen . . 037395
Heimatmuseum Aarburg, Aarburg . 036813
Heimatmuseum Achental, Achenkirch 001659
Heimatmuseum Adelboden, Adelboden 036815
Heimatmuseum Adlhoch-Haus, Altdorf, Niederbayern 015492
Heimatmuseum Aflenz, Aflenz 001663
Heimatmuseum Ahlem, Hannover . 017753
Heimatmuseum Ahlen, Ahlen 015451
Heimatmuseum Ahrbergen, Giesen 017405
Heimatmuseum Aichach, Aichach . 015457
Heimatmuseum Alberschwende, Alberschwende 001670
Heimatmuseum Algermissen, Algermissen 015479
Heimatmuseum Allschwil, Allschwil 036829
Heimatmuseum Alt-Falkenstein, Balsthal 036876
Heimatmuseum Alte Weberstube, Niedercunnersdorf 019309
Heimatmuseum Altenmarkt, Yspertal 003063
Heimatmuseum Alter Pfarrhof, Raisting 019706
Heimatmuseum Altes Rathaus, Angelburg 015541
Heimatmuseum Altes Rathaus, Böhl-Iggelheim 016297
Heimatmuseum Altes Schulhaus, Böhl-Iggelheim 016298
Heimatmuseum Altlichtenwarth, Absdorf 001655
Heimatmuseum Altmannstein, Altmannstein 015511
Heimatmuseum am Kobernaußerwald, Lohnsburg am Kobernaußerwald . 002265
Heimatmuseum am Pfäffikersee, Pfäffikon (Zürich) 037412
Heimatmuseum Amt Blankenstein, Gladenbach 017422

Heimatmuseum Arnold Bärtschi, Dulliken . . . 037052
Heimatmuseum Aschen, Diepholz . 016699
Heimatmuseum Auetal, Auetal 015600
Heimatmuseum Bad Aibling, Bad Aibling . . . 015642
Heimatmuseum Bad Eilsen, Bad Eilsen . . . 015690
Heimatmuseum Bad Endbach, Bad Endbach . . . 015694
Heimatmuseum Bad König, Bad König . . . 015733
Heimatmuseum Bad Laer, Bad Laer 015743
Heimatmuseum Bad Lauterberg, Bad Lauterberg . . . 015746
Heimatmuseum Bad Münder, Bad Münder . . . 015752
Heimatmuseum Bad Oldesloe, Bad Oldesloe . . . 015768
Heimatmuseum Bad Wildungen, Bad Wildungen . . . 015828
Heimatmuseum Balingen, Balingen 015862
Heimatmuseum Bammental, Bammental . . . 015884
Heimatmuseum Baunach, Baunach 015896
Heimatmuseum Beratzhausen, Beratzhausen . . . 015953
Heimatmuseum Berching mit Ritter-v.-Gluck-Archiv, Berching . . . 015954
Heimatmuseum Bergen-Enkheim, Frankfurt am Main . . . 017171
Heimatmuseum Berkatal, Berkatal . 015976
Heimatmuseum Betzenstein, Betzenstein . . . 016212
Heimatmuseum Beuel, Bonn 016324
Heimatmuseum Beutelsbach, Weinstadt . . . 020765
Heimatmuseum Biebesheim, Biebesheim . . . 016230
Heimatmuseum Biebrich, Wiesbaden . . . 020867
Heimatmuseum Bislich, Wesel 020821
Heimatmuseum Blankenau, Hosenfeld . . . 018009
Heimatmuseum Blaubeuren, Blaubeuren . . . 016263
Heimatmuseum Bleicherode, Bleicherode . . . 016268
Heimatmuseum Bockwindmühle, Lebusa . . . 018538
Heimatmuseum Bodenfelde, Bodenfelde . . . 016288
Heimatmuseum Börgerende-Rethwisch, Börgerende . . . 016301
Heimatmuseum Boizenburg, Boizenburg . . . 016310
Heimatmuseum Borgloh, Hilter 017927
Heimatmuseum Boxberg, Boxberg, Baden . . . 016354
Heimatmuseum Brackenheim, Brackenheim . . . 016357
Heimatmuseum Breckerfeld, Breckerfeld . . . 016396
Heimatmuseum Brigachtal, Brigachtal . . . 016450
Heimatmuseum Brüssow, Brüssow 016472
Heimatmuseum Brunsbüttel, Brunsbüttel . . . 016474
Heimatmuseum Bucheggberg, Buchegg . . . 036982
Heimatmuseum Buchenau, Dautphetal . . . 016652
Heimatmuseum Buchenberg, Buchenberg bei Kempten . . . 016478
Heimatmuseum Buchloe, Buchloe . 016481
Heimatmuseum Büddenstedt, Büddenstedt . . . 016486
Heimatmuseum Büderich, Wesel . . 020822
Heimatmuseum Bühl, Baden, Bühl, Baden . . . 016491
Heimatmuseum Bürgeln, Cölbe . . . 016581
Heimatmuseum Burg Stargard, Burg Stargard . . . 016506
Heimatmuseum Burgau, Burgau, Schwaben . . . 016507
Heimatmuseum Calau, Calau 016534
Heimatmuseum Carl Swoboda, Schirgiswalde . . . 020028
Heimatmuseum Charlottenburg-Wilmersdorf, Berlin . . . 016063
Heimatmuseum Crumstadt, Riedstadt . . . 019836
Heimatmuseum Dachwig, Dachwig 016622
Heimatmuseum Dahme, Mark, Dahme, Mark . . . 016626
Heimatmuseum Davos, Davos 037037
Heimatmuseum Debstedt, Langen bei Bremerhaven . . . 018494
Heimatmuseum Delkenheim, Wiesbaden . . . 020868
Heimatmuseum der Albert-Edelmann-Stiftung, Ebnat-Kappel . . . 037054
Heimatmuseum der Deutschen aus Bessarabien, Stuttgart . . . 020354
Heimatmuseum der Gemeinde Dossenheim, Dossenheim . . . 016774
Heimatmuseum der Gemeinde Weißenkirchen, Perschling 002420
Heimatmuseum der Insel Hiddensee, Kloster, Hiddensee . . . 018288
Heimatmuseum der Marktgemeinde Reutte, Reutte . . . 002526
Heimatmuseum der Marktgemeinde Wiggensbach, Wiggensbach 020886
Heimatmuseum der Stadt Bad Tölz, Bad Tölz . . . 015814
Heimatmuseum der Stadt Gernsheim, Gernsheim . . . 017384
Heimatmuseum der Stadt Herrnhut, Herrnhut . . . 017900
Heimatmuseum der Stadt Hückeswagen, Hückeswagen . . . 018016
Heimatmuseum der Stadt Ketzin, Ketzin . . . 018239
Heimatmuseum der Stadt Marsberg, Marsberg . . . 018855
Heimatmuseum der Stadt Murau, Murau . . . 002348
Heimatmuseum der Stadt Neunkirchen, Neunkirchen, Niederösterreich . . 002369
Heimatmuseum der Stadt Northeim, Northeim . . . 019340
Heimatmuseum der Stadt Rerik, Ostseebad Rerik . . . 019532
Heimatmuseum der Stadt Rheinau in Freistett, Rheinau . . . 019820
Heimatmuseum der Stadt Vohenstrauß, Vohenstrauß . . . 020606
Heimatmuseum der Talschaft Lauterbrunnen, Lauterbrunnen . . . 037254
Heimatmuseum des Heimatkreises Scheiflingertal, Scheifling . . . 002647
Heimatmuseum des Landkreises Regensburg, Altenthann . . . 015507
Heimatmuseum des Nordböhmischen Niederlandes, Böblingen . . . 016295
Heimatmuseum Dietzenbach, Dietzenbach . . . 016708
Heimatmuseum Dirlewang, Dirlewang . . . 016724
Heimatmuseum Dölzig, Schkeuditz 020029
Heimatmuseum Dohna, Dohna 016734
Heimatmuseum Dornstetten, Das lebendige Volkskundemuseum, Dornstetten 016754
Heimatmuseum Duderstadt, Duderstadt . . . 016822
Heimatmuseum Durmersheim, Durmersheim . . . 016863
Heimatmuseum Dykhus, Borkum . . 016347
Heimatmuseum Ebenhausen, Oerlenbach . . . 019444
Heimatmuseum Ebermannstadt, Ebermannstadt . . . 016868
Heimatmuseum Ebern, Ebern 016869
Heimatmuseum Ebersbach in der Humboldt-Baude, Ebersbach, Sachsen . . . 016872
Heimatmuseum Echzell, Echzell . . . 016879
Heimatmuseum Egg, Egg . . . 001806
Heimatmuseum Eggenstein-Leopoldshafen, Eggenstein-Leopoldshafen 016893
Heimatmuseum Eichenzell, Eichenzell . . . 016906
Heimatmuseum Eisenbach, Obernburg . . . 019395
Heimatmuseum Elgg, Elgg . . . 037063
Heimatmuseum Ellrich, Ellrich 016939
Heimatmuseum Elsbethen, Elsbethen-Glasenstein . . . 001831
Heimatmuseum Elze, Elze . . . 016955
Heimatmuseum Emskirchen, Emskirchen . . . 016981
Heimatmuseum Epfenbach, Epfenbach . . . 016989
Heimatmuseum Erbenheim, Wiesbaden . . . 020869
Heimatmuseum Eriskirch, Eriskirch 017022
Heimatmuseum Eschenburg, Eschenburg . . . 017047
Heimatmuseum Eschwege, Eschwege . . . 017051
Heimatmuseum Eversberg e.V., Meschede . . . 018918
Heimatmuseum Feuerwehrzeugstätte, Neumarkt am Wallersee . . . 002364
Heimatmuseum Finsterbergen, Finsterbergen . . . 017122
Heimatmuseum Flacht, Weissach, Württemberg . . . 020772
Heimatmuseum Freiamt, Freiamt . . 017218
Heimatmuseum Freigericht, Freigericht . . . 017240
Heimatmuseum Freudenstadt, Freudenstadt . . . 017252
Heimatmuseum Freudenthal, Memmingen . . . 018904
Heimatmuseum Friedewald, Friedewald, Hessen . . . 017264
Heimatmuseum Friedrichsdorf-Seulberg, Friedrichsdorf, Taunus . . . 017267
Heimatmuseum Friedrichshain, Berlin . . . 016064
Heimatmuseum Fronfeste, Limbach-Oberfrohna . . . 018646
Heimatmuseum für Stadt und Kreis Gelnhausen, Gelnhausen . . . 017349
Heimatmuseum für Stadt- und Landkreis, Kirchheimbolanden . . . 018270
Heimatmuseum Fürstenberg/Havel, Fürstenberg, Havel . . . 017280
Heimatmuseum Gadebusch, Gadebusch . . . 017312
Heimatmuseum Gadernheim, Lautertal, Odenwald . . . 018537
Heimatmuseum Garbenheim, Wetzlar . . . 020842
Heimatmuseum Garbsen, Garbsen . 017319
Heimatmuseum Geisa, Geisa 017339
Heimatmuseum Geislingen, Geislingen an der Steige . . . 017344
Heimatmuseum Gemünden, Weilrod 020733
Heimatmuseum Geretsried, Geretsried . . . 017377
Heimatmuseum Gersau, Gersau . . . 037142
Heimatmuseum Gersfeld, Gersfeld . 017388
Heimatmuseum Giesen, Giesen . . . 017406
Heimatmuseum Ginsheim-Gustavsburg, Ginsheim-Gustavsburg . . . 017419
Heimatmuseum Glonn, Glonn 017432
Heimatmuseum Görwihl, Görwihl . . 017458
Heimatmuseum Gößnitz, Gößnitz, Thüringen . . . 017460
Heimatmuseum Graben-Neudorf, Graben-Neudorf . . . 017496
Heimatmuseum Grächen, Grächen . 037157
Heimatmuseum Grafenau Schloß Dätzingen, Grafenau, Württemberg . . . 017502
Heimatmuseum Grafing, Grafing bei München . . . 017507
Heimatmuseum Grafling, Grafling . . 017508
Heimatmuseum Grafschaft Hoya, Hoya . . . 018010
Heimatmuseum Grahhof, Ramsau am Dachstein . . . 002497
Heimatmuseum Gransee, Gransee . 017511
Heimatmuseum Greene, Kreiensen 018401
Heimatmuseum Greversdorf, Geversdorf . . . 017401
Heimatmuseum Grimmen Im Mühlentor, Grimmen . . . 017543
Heimatmuseum Gröbming, Gröbming . . . 001960
Heimatmuseum Grötzingen, Aichtal 015459
Heimatmuseum Großengersdorf, Großengersdorf . . . 001968
Heimatmuseum Großenlüder, Großenlüder . . . 017570
Heimatmuseum Großes Walsertal, Sonntag . . . 002682
Heimatmuseum Großschönau, Großschönau . . . 001979
Heimatmuseum Großseelheim, Kirchhain . . . 018264
Heimatmuseum Günzburg, Günzburg . . . 017597
Heimatmuseum Guntramsdorf, Guntramsdorf . . . 001989
Heimatmuseum Hähnlein, Alsbach-Hähnlein . . . 015485
Heimatmuseum Haiger, Haiger 017631
Heimatmuseum Haiterbach, Haiterbach . . . 017642
Heimatmuseum Hallstadt, Hallstadt 017677
Heimatmuseum Haus Morgensonne, Ostseebad Zingst . . . 019534
Heimatmuseum Hebertsfelden, Hebertsfelden . . . 017815
Heimatmuseum Heidelsheim, Bruchsal . . . 016456
Heimatmuseum Heiligenhafen, Heiligenhafen . . . 017856
Heimatmuseum Heinrich Zoller, Wittelshofen . . . 020922
Heimatmuseum Heuchelheim-Kinzenbach, Heuchelheim, Kreis Gießen 017914
Heimatmuseum Heusenstamm, Heusenstamm . . . 017915
Heimatmuseum Hochzeitshaus, Homberg, Efze . . . 018001
Heimatmuseum Höchstädt an der Donau, Höchstädt an der Donau . . . 017943
Heimatmuseum Hoheneggelsen, Söhlde . . . 020227
Heimatmuseum Hohenroda, Hohenroda . . . 017976
Heimatmuseum Hohenschönhausen, Berlin . . . 016065
Heimatmuseum Hohenwestedt, Hohenwestedt . . . 017983
Heimatmuseum Holzgerlingen, Holzgerlingen . . . 017992
Heimatmuseum Hornburg, Hornburg, Kreis Wolfenbüttel . . . 018008
Heimatmuseum Hossingen, Meßstetten . . . 018922
Heimatmuseum Hüttenberg, Goethehaus Volpertshausen, Hüttenberg 018027
Heimatmuseum Hus tu Löwenberg, Löwenberg . . . 018672
Heimatmuseum Ihringen, Ihringen . 018048
Heimatmuseum im alten Bruderhaus und in der Dechanathofscheune, Altenmarkt im Pongau . . . 001681
Heimatmuseum im Alten Kloster, Erbendorf . . . 017002
Heimatmuseum im alten Marktturm, Fischamend . . . 001856
Heimatmuseum im Alten Pfarrhaus, Hagen am Teutoburger Wald . . . 017620
Heimatmuseum im Alten Rathaus, Bruchköbel . . . 016453
Heimatmuseum im Amonhaus, Lunz . . . 002271
Heimatmuseum im Berchtoldshof, Uhingen . . . 020527
Heimatmuseum im Bürgerhaus Adler Post, Stockach . . . 020319
Heimatmuseum im Fünfeckigen Turm, Neckarbischofsheim . . . 019191
Heimatmuseum im Hartmannhaus, Marktoberdorf . . . 018845
Heimatmuseum im Herrenhaaus, Burghaun . . . 016510
Heimatmuseum im Hintermeierhaus, Donauwörth . . . 016742
Heimatmuseum im Kolb'schen Haus, Bickenbach, Bergstraße . . . 016224
Heimatmuseum im Neuen Spielhaus, Bruchköbel . . . 016454
Heimatmuseum im Oberen Torturm, Lauchheim . . . 018521

Heimatmuseum im Schelfenhaus, Volkach 020608
Heimatmuseum im Schloß, Zörbig . 021076
Heimatmuseum im Unteren Turm, Leutershausen 018625
Heimatmuseum im Vogteigebäude, Hüttlingen 018028
Heimatmuseum im Wachtturm, Geyer 017402
Heimatmuseum im Weserrenaissance Schloß, Bevern, Kreis Holzminden 016215
Heimatmuseum im Wolfschneider-Hof, Taufkirchen, Kreis München 020408
Heimatmuseum in der ehemaligen Schule Hüllhorst, Hüllhorst 018019
Heimatmuseum in der Mühle Gettorf, Gettorf 017400
Heimatmuseum in der Peldemühle, Esens 017055
Heimatmuseum in der Scheune, Mössingen 018986
Heimatmuseum Ingersleben/Neudietendorf, Ingersleben 018066
Heimatmuseum Ittersbach, Karlsbad 018153
Heimatmuseum Kalchofengut, Unken 002769
Heimatmuseum Kappe, Kappe 018150
Heimatmuseum Karlsdorf, Karlsdorf-Neuthard 018154
Heimatmuseum Kastl, Kastl bei Amberg 018205
Heimatmuseum Kaumberg, Kaumberg 002118
Heimatmuseum Kaunertal, Kaunertal 002119
Heimatmuseum Kautzen, Kautzen . 002120
Heimatmuseum Kefenrod, Kefenrod 018217
Heimatmuseum Keltern, Keltern . . . 018227
Heimatmuseum Kirberg, Hünfelden 018024
Heimatmuseum Kirchhain, Kirchhain 018265
Heimatmuseum Kirchheim, Heidelberg 017828
Heimatmuseum Kirchheim, Schwaben, Kirchheim, Schwaben 018266
Heimatmuseum Klösterle, Schönau im Schwarzwald 020068
Heimatmuseum Kloppenheim, Wiesbaden 020870
Heimatmuseum Klosterlangheim, Lichtenfels, Bayern 018631
Heimatmuseum Klus, Klus 037214
Heimatmuseum Königsdorf, Königsdorf, Oberbayern 018348
Heimatmuseum Köpenick, Berlin . . 016066
Heimatmuseum Kösching, Kösching 018360
Heimatmuseum Kohbauernhaus, Köstendorf 002163
Heimatmuseum Kornburg, Nürnberg 019355
Heimatmuseum Kostheim, Mainz-Kostheim 018797
Heimatmuseum Kraiburg am Inn, Kraiburg am Inn 018388
Heimatmuseum Kreuzlingen, Roseneggschulhaus, Kreuzlingen . 037221
Heimatmuseum Kroppenstedt, Kroppenstedt 018423
Heimatmuseum Ladbergen, Ladbergen 018455
Heimatmuseum Lahnau-Waldgirmes, Lahnau 018460
Heimatmuseum Laisa, Battenberg, Eder 015893
Heimatmuseum Lampertheim, Lampertheim 018470
Heimatmuseum Lamspringe, Lamspringe 018471
Heimatmuseum Landau, Landau an der Isar 018473
Heimatmuseum Langelsheim, Langelsheim 018491
Heimatmuseum Langenau, Langenau, Württemberg 018500
Heimatmuseum Langenseifen, Bad Schwalbach 015796
Heimatmuseum Langenselbold, Langenselbold 018511
Heimatmuseum Langenzenn, Langenzenn 018512
Heimatmuseum Laubach, Fridericianum, Laubach, Hessen 018518
Heimatmuseum Lauda-Königshofen, Lauda-Königshofen 018522
Heimatmuseum Lauenau, Lauenau 018523
Heimatmuseum Leeheim, Riedstadt 019837
Heimatmuseum Leer, Leer 018540
Heimatmuseum Leingarten Altes Rathaus Schluchtern, Leingarten 018553
Heimatmuseum Leipheim, Leipheim 018556
Heimatmuseum Lembach, Lembach 002219
Heimatmuseum Lenggries, Lenggries 018614
Heimatmuseum Lengsdorf, Bonn . . 016325
Heimatmuseum Lette, Coesfeld . . . 016583
Heimatmuseum Leuk Stadt, Leuk Stadt 037259
Heimatmuseum Leutershausen, Leutershausen 018626
Heimatmuseum Lichtenberg, Berlin 016067
Heimatmuseum Liebenwalde im historischen Stadtgefängnis, Liebenwalde 018639
Heimatmuseum Lilienthal, Lilienthal 018642
Heimatmuseum Lölling, Lölling . . . 002263
Heimatmuseum Lorch, Lorch, Württemberg 018685
Heimatmuseum Losenstein, Losenstein 002269
Heimatmuseum Luditzer Kreis, Bad Sooden-Allendorf 015805
Heimatmuseum Lübbecke, Lübbecke 018715
Heimatmuseum Lügde, Lügde 018738
Heimatmuseum Lütgendortmund, Dortmund 016764
Heimatmuseum Magstadt, Magstadt 018778
Heimatmuseum Markt Piesting, Markt Piesting 002292
Heimatmuseum Marktl, Marktl, Inn 018844
Heimatmuseum Marner Skatklub von 1873, Marne 018854
Heimatmuseum Maßbach, Maßbach 018859
Heimatmuseum Medenbach, Wiesbaden 020871
Heimatmuseum Meerane, Meerane 018868
Heimatmuseum Meerholz, Gelnhausen 017350
Heimatmuseum Mehrstetten, Mehrstetten 018881
Heimatmuseum Meinhard, Meinhard 018882
Heimatmuseum Mellrichstadt, Mellrichstadt 018899
Heimatmuseum Melsungen, Melsungen 018901
Heimatmuseum-Menton, Teningen . 020421
Heimatmuseum Merkendorf, Merkendorf, Mittelfranken 018913
Heimatmuseum Michelbacher Schlößchen, Alzenau 015527
Heimatmuseum Michelhausen, Michelhausen 002310
Heimatmuseum Miesbach, Miesbach 018938
Heimatmuseum Mindelheim, Mindelheim 018944
Heimatmuseum mit Hugo-Geißler-Saal, Museen der Stadt Tuttlingen, Tuttlingen 020508
Heimatmuseum mit ostdeutscher Heimatstube, Hanerau-Hademarschen 017747
Heimatmuseum mit Raimund von Montecuccoli-Gedenkraum, Hafnerbach 002003
Heimatmuseum Mitte, Berlin 016068
Heimatmuseum Mittelbuchen, Hanau 017739
Heimatmuseum Mitterfels, Mitterfels 018960
Heimatmuseum Moringen, Moringen 018996
Heimatmuseum Münchingen, Korntal-Münchingen 018384
Heimatmuseum Münsingen, Münsingen 019136
Heimatmuseum Nauheim, Nauheim 019183
Heimatmuseum Naumburg, Naumburg, Hessen 019184
Heimatmuseum Naunheim, Wetzlar 020843
Heimatmuseum Naurod, Wiesbaden 020872
Heimatmuseum Neu-Ulm-Pfuhl, Neu-Ulm 019215
Heimatmuseum Neuenwalde, Langen bei Bremerhaven 018495
Heimatmuseum Neukirchen, Neukirchen, Knüllgebirge 019247
Heimatmuseum Neukölln, Museum für Stadtkultur und Regionalgeschichte, Berlin 016141
Heimatmuseum Neunkirchen, Neunkirchen bei Mosbach 019260
Heimatmuseum Neureichenau, Neureichenau 019264
Heimatmuseum Neuried, Neuried, Ortenaukreis 019265
Heimatmuseum Neustadt an der Aisch, Neustadt an der Aisch 019279
Heimatmuseum Neustadtgödens, Sande, Kreis Friesland 019977
Heimatmuseum Nidda, Nidda 019302
Heimatmuseum Nied, Frankfurt am Main 017172
Heimatmuseum Niederaichbach, Niederaichbach 019308
Heimatmuseum Niemes und Prachatitz, Ingolstadt 018072
Heimatmuseum Nordenstadt, Wiesbaden 020873
Heimatmuseum Nüdlingen, Nüdlingen 019342
Heimatmuseum Nürnberg, Nürnberg 019356
Heimatmuseum Nutli-Hüschi, Klosters 037212
Heimatmuseum Obbornhofen, Hungen 018033
Heimatmuseum Obdach, Obdach . . 002381
Heimatmuseum Oberammergau, Oberammergau 019381
Heimatmuseum Oberbichl, Prägarten 002458
Heimatmuseum Oberderdingen, Oberderdingen 019385
Heimatmuseum Obere Mühle, Loßburg 018688
Heimatmuseum Obergünzburg mit Südseesammlung, Obergünzburg 019388
Heimatmuseum Oberndorf am Lech, Oberndorf am Lech 019397
Heimatmuseum Obernfeld, Obernfeld 019400
Heimatmuseum Oberstdorf, Oberstdorf 019423
Heimatmuseum Ochsenfurt, Ochsenfurt 019431
Heimatmuseum Oettingen, Oettingen 019450
Heimatmuseum Ole Schüne, Drakenburg 016776
Heimatmuseum Oltingen-Wenslingen-Anwil, Oltingen 037403
Heimatmuseum Osterhofen, Osterhofen 019508
Heimatmuseum Pabneukirchen, Pabneukirchen 002406
Heimatmuseum Papenburg, Papenburg 019561
Heimatmuseum Peldemühle, Wittmund 020933
Heimatmuseum Persenbeug-Gottsdorf, Persenbeug 002421
Heimatmuseum Pfaffenhausen, Pfaffenhausen 019596
Heimatmuseum Pfarrscheuer, Römerstein 019867
Heimatmuseum Philippsburg, Philippsburg 019617
Heimatmuseum Postbauer-Heng, Postbauer-Heng 019650
Heimatmuseum Prättigau, Grüsch . 037169
Heimatmuseum Pressath, Pressath 019666
Heimatmuseum Prestegg, Altstätten 036836
Heimatmuseum Pretzsch, Pretzsch 019669
Heimatmuseum Prien, Prien 019674
Heimatmuseum Pulkau, Pulkau . . . 002476
Heimatmuseum Rabenstein, Rabenstein an der Pielach 002487
Heimatmuseum Rain am Lech, Rain am Lech 019704
Heimatmuseum Rapperswil, Rapperswil, Sankt Gallen 037434
Heimatmuseum Rauchkate, Zetel . . 021056
Heimatmuseum Rauchstubenhaus Edelschachen, Anger 001689
Heimatmuseum Raunheim, Raunheim 019730
Heimatmuseum Rauschenberg, Rauschenberg 019732
Heimatmuseum Rechnitz, Rechnitz 002509
Heimatmuseum Reiderland, Weener 020698
Heimatmuseum Reilingen, Reilingen 019779
Heimatmuseum Reinheim, Reinheim 019783
Heimatmuseum Reinickendorf, Berlin 016069
Heimatmuseum Reischenau, Dinkelscherben 016720
Heimatmuseum Reiterhaus, Neusalza-Spremberg 019270
Heimatmuseum Reith, Reith im Alpbachtal 002520
Heimatmuseum Reutlingen, Reutlingen 019807
Heimatmuseum Rheinwald, Splügen 037588
Heimatmuseum Rhüden, Seesen . . 020173
Heimatmuseum Riedlingen, Riedlingen 019833
Heimatmuseum Rieneck, Rieneck . 019841
Heimatmuseum Rodenberg, Rodenberg, Deister 019856
Heimatmuseum Rodenstein, Fränkisch-Crumbach 017142
Heimatmuseum Rodewald, Rodewald 019857
Heimatmuseum Römstedthaus, Bergen, Kreis Celle 015965
Heimatmuseum Rötz, Rötz 019872
Heimatmuseum Ronnenberg, Ronnenberg 019879
Heimatmuseum Roßwein, Roßwein 019892
Heimatmuseum Rotenburg, Rotenburg, Wümme 019907
Heimatmuseum Rother Hof, Pottendorf 002451
Heimatmuseum Rothmühle, Rannersdorf 002500
Heimatmuseum Runder Turm, Sigmaringen 020208
Heimatmuseum Sankt Egidien, Sankt Egidien 019985
Heimatmuseum Sankt Laurentius, Dahlenburg 016625
Heimatmuseum Sankt Martin am Wöllmißberg, Sankt Martin am Wöllmißberg 002602
Heimatmuseum Sarnen, Sarnen . . . 037514
Heimatmuseum Schanfigg, Arosa . . 036853
Heimatmuseum Scheeßel, Scheeßel 020008
Heimatmuseum Schermbeck, Schermbeck 020014
Heimatmuseum Schierstein, Wiesbaden 020874
Heimatmuseum Schifferstadt, Schifferstadt 020017
Heimatmuseum Schinznach-Dorf, Schinznach Dorf 037526
Heimatmuseum Schliersee, Schliersee 020047
Heimatmuseum Schlitz, Schlitz . . . 020048
Heimatmuseum Schloß Adelsheim, Berchtesgaden 015956

Heimatmuseum Schloß Brenz, Sontheim an der Brenz . . . 020251
Heimatmuseum Schloß Fels, Fels . . 001852
Heimatmuseum Schloß Hochhaus, Vorchdorf . . . 002790
Heimatmuseum Schloß Pragstein, Mauthausen . . . 002303
Heimatmuseum Schloß Schönebeck, Bremen . . . 016416
Heimatmuseum Schloß Tenneberg, Waltershausen . . . 020664
Heimatmuseum Schloss Wildeck, Zschopau . . . 021079
Heimatmuseum Schloß Wolkenstein, Wolkenstein . . . 020973
Heimatmuseum Schnaittach, Schnaittach . . . 020061
Heimatmuseum Schönau, Günselsdorf . . . 001984
Heimatmuseum Schöneck, Schöneck, Vogtland . . . 020077
Heimatmuseum Schöningen, Schöningen . . . 020084
Heimatmuseum Schulte-Wessels, Neuenhaus . . . 019231
Heimatmuseum Schwalmtal, Niederrhein, Schwalmtal, Niederrhein . . . 020122
Heimatmuseum Schwanfeld, Schwanfeld . . . 020125
Heimatmuseum Schwanheim, Frankfurt am Main . . . 017173
Heimatmuseum Schwarza, Schwarza, Suhl . . . 020129
Heimatmuseum Schwarzbubenland, Dornach . . . 037049
Heimatmuseum Seeg, Seeg . . . 020167
Heimatmuseum Seehof, Buonas . . . 036990
Heimatmuseum Seelze, Seelze . . . 020171
Heimatmuseum Seon, Seon . . . 037556
Heimatmuseum Seßlach, Seßlach . 020192
Heimatmuseum Siebenlehn, Siebenlehn . . . 020193
Heimatmuseum Siegbach, Siegbach . . . 020194
Heimatmuseum Simbach am Inn, Simbach am Inn . . . 020211
Heimatmuseum Spangenberg, Spangenberg . . . 020260
Heimatmuseum Spittel, Büren an der Aare . . . 036985
Heimatmuseum Sprendlingen, Sprendlingen . . . 020270
Heimatmuseum Spycher, Rickenbach (Luzern) . . . 037449
Heimatmuseum Stade, Stade . . . 020276
Heimatmuseum Stadt Bernstadt an der Eigen, Bernstadt auf dem Eigen . . 016210
Heimatmuseum Stadt Nagold-Steinhaus, Nagold . . . 019177
Heimatmuseum Stadt Starnberg, Starnberg . . . 020291
Heimatmuseum Stadt Teltow, Teltow . . . 020419
Heimatmuseum Stadt und Landkreis Neudek im Erzgebirge, Augsburg . 015610
Heimatmuseum Stadtilm, Stadtilm . 020284
Heimatmuseum Stadtsteinach, Stadtsteinach . . . 020289
Heimatmuseum Staufenberg, Staufenberg, Hessen . . . 020295
Heimatmuseum Stein, Stein am Rhein . . . 037605
Heimatmuseum Steinach, Steinbach, Taunus . . . 020302
Heimatmuseum Steinbach, Baden-Baden . . . 015849
Heimatmuseum Steinfischbach, Waldems . . . 020635
Heimatmuseum Steinwiesen, Steinwiesen . . . 020312
Heimatmuseum Steyregg, Steyregg 002708
Heimatmuseum Stockstadt am Main, Stockstadt am Main . . . 020320
Heimatmuseum Strasburg, Strasburg . . . 020332
Heimatmuseum Straub, Gruibingen 017592
Heimatmuseum Stromberg, Stromberg . . . 020338
Heimatmuseum Strümpfelbach, Weinstadt . . . 020766
Heimatmuseum Suhr, Suhr . . . 037614
Heimatmuseum Tambach-Dietharz, Tambach-Dietharz . . . 020395
Heimatmuseum Tannheimer Tal, Tannheim . . . 002728
Heimatmuseum Tempelhof, Berlin . 016070
Heimatmuseum Tiergarten, Berlin . 016071
Heimatmuseum Todtmoos, Todtmoos . . . 020447
Heimatmuseum - Traktoren- und Landmaschinenmuseum, Großengottern . . . 017568
Heimatmuseum Trebur, Trebur . . . 020465
Heimatmuseum Treptow, Berlin . . . 016072
Heimatmuseum Trimmis, Trimmis . 037643
Heimatmuseum Trubschachen, Trubschachen . . . 037644
Heimatmuseum Uelzen mit Gläsersammlung Röver, Uelzen . . 020520
Heimatmuseum Uetze, Uetze . . . 020523
Heimatmuseum und Archiv des Heimatvereins für den Bezirk Steglitz, Berlin . . . 016073
Heimatmuseum und Buchdruckerstube, Beromünster . . . 036943
Heimatmuseum und Dokumentationszentrum zur Deutschen Nachkriegsgeschichte, Wanfried . 020669
Heimatmuseum und Galerie Neue Diele, Jork . . . 018126
Heimatmuseum und Gedenkstätte Bützow, Bützow . . . 016501
Heimatmuseum und Hedwig Courths-Mahler Archiv, Nebra . . . 019190
Heimatmuseum und Karl-August-Forster-Bienenmuseum, Illertissen . . . 018051
Heimatmuseum und Keltenhaus, Ligist . . . 002237
Heimatmuseum und Klöpferhaus, Eibiswald . . . 001815
Heimatmuseum und Klosterruine, Arendsee, Altmark . . . 015564
Heimatmuseum und Naturalienkabinett, Waldenburg, Sachsen . . . 020637
Heimatmuseum und Pfeifenmuseum, Sankt Aegyd am Neuwalde . . . 002572
Heimatmuseum und Sammlung Liechtenstein, Wilfersdorf . . . 003047
Heimatmuseum und Schiele Museum, Neulengbach . . . 002363
Heimatmuseum und Stadtarchiv, Flörsheim am Main . . . 017133
Heimatmuseum und Textil-Schauwerkstatt, Greiz . . . 017526
Heimatmuseum Unterboihingen, Wendlingen am Neckar . . . 020797
Heimatmuseum Unterengadin, Scuol . . . 037545
Heimatmuseum Untergrombach, Bruchsal . . . 016457
Heimatmuseum Usingen, Usingen . 020551
Heimatmuseum Usseln, Willingen, Upland . . . 020902
Heimatmuseum Varel, Varel . . . 020559
Heimatmuseum Velburg, Velburg . . 020570
Heimatmuseum Viernheim, Viernheim . . . 020586
Heimatmuseum Vietze, Höhbeck . . 017946
Heimatmuseum Vilsbiburg - Kröninger Hafnermuseum, Vilsbiburg . . . 020598
Heimatmuseum Vogtturm, Zell am See . . . 003066
Heimatmuseum Vollmers Mühle, Seebach, Baden . . . 020161
Heimatmuseum Wächtersbach, Wächtersbach . . . 020614
Heimatmuseum Waidhofen, Neues Museum, Waidhofen an der Thaya 002799
Heimatmuseum Waidhofen an der Ybbs, Waidhofen an der Ybbs . . . 002801
Heimatmuseum Waldaschaff, Waldaschaff . . . 020629
Heimatmuseum Waldbrunn, Waldbrunn, Westerwald . . . 020632
Heimatmuseum Waldthurn, Waldthurn . . . 020651
Heimatmuseum Walldorf, Mörfelden-Walldorf . . . 018980
Heimatmuseum Waltrop, Waltrop . . 020665
Heimatmuseum Wandsbek, Hamburg . . . 017696
Heimatmuseum Wanna, Wanna . . . 020676
Heimatmuseum Warnemünde, Rostock . . . 019898
Heimatmuseum Wedel, Wedel . . . 020696
Heimatmuseum Weener, Weener . . 020699
Heimatmuseum Weesen, Weesen . 037698
Heimatmuseum Wehlen, Stadt Wehlen . . . 020281
Heimatmuseum Weiler, Schorndorf, Württemberg . . . 020092
Heimatmuseum Weitenung, Bühl, Baden . . . 016492
Heimatmuseum Wemding, Wemding . . . 020792
Heimatmuseum Weng im Innkreis, Weng im Innkreis . . . 002834
Heimatmuseum Wennigsen, Wennigsen . . . 020799
Heimatmuseum Wertach, Wertach . 020817
Heimatmuseum Wertingen, Wertingen . . . 020820
Heimatmuseum Westerhausen, Westerhausen . . . 020828
Heimatmuseum Wettenberg, Wettenberg . . . 020836
Heimatmuseum Wiedenbrück, Rheda-Wiedenbrück . . . 019816
Heimatmuseum Wiedensahl, Kloses heimatgeschichtliche Sammlung, Wiedensahl . . . 020853
Heimatmuseum Wiedlisbach, Wiedlisbach . . . 037705
Heimatmuseum Windeck, Windeck 020908
Heimatmuseum Windischgarsten, Windischgarsten . . . 003056
Heimatmuseum Windmühle Reken, Reken . . . 019787
Heimatmuseum Winterberg im Böhmerwald, Freyung . . . 017256
Heimatmuseum Wißmar, Wettenberg . . . 020837
Heimatmuseum Witten, Witten . . . 020924
Heimatmuseum Wolfratshausen, Wolfratshausen . . . 020960
Heimatmuseum Wolfskehlen, Riedstadt . . . 019838
Heimatmuseum Wommelshausen, Bad Endbach . . . 015695
Heimatmuseum Worben, Worben . . 037741
Heimatmuseum Zarrentin, Zarrentin, Mecklenburg . . . 021038
Heimatmuseum Zehlendorf, Berlin . 016074
Heimatmuseum Zorge, Zorge . . . 021077
Heimatmuseum Zusmarshausen, Zusmarshausen . . . 021082
Heimatmuseum Zwischen Venn und Schneifel, Sankt Vith . . . 003741
Heimatmusuem Bierstatd, Wiesbaden . . . 020875
Heimatsammlung, Sankt Märgen . . 019990
Heimatscheune, Zschepplin . . . 021078
Heimatstätte der Kuhländer, Ludwigsburg, Württemberg . . . 018693
Heimatstube, Altenstadt an der Waldnaab . . . 015505
Heimatstube, Bad Schmiedeberg . . 015792
Heimatstube, Benneckenstein . . . 015947
Heimatstube, Brüel . . . 016464
Heimatstube, Dabel . . . 016616
Heimatstube, Derenburg . . . 016673
Heimatstube, Ditfurt . . . 016728
Heimatstube, Hasselfelde . . . 017788
Heimatstube, Karwe . . . 018178
Heimatstube, Menz . . . 018909
Heimatstube, Quellendorf . . . 019690
Heimatstube, Rehmsdorf . . . 019768
Heimatstube, Schäplitz . . . 020004
Heimatstube, Schochwitz . . . 020067
Heimatstube, Schönwalde bei Tangerhütte . . . 020087
Heimatstube, Spören . . . 020268
Heimatstube, Tanne . . . 020403
Heimatstube, Techentin bei Lübz . . 020410
Heimatstube, Trauenstein . . . 020455
Heimatstube, Vierraden . . . 020587
Heimatstube, Wall . . . 020653
Heimatstube, Heimat- und Förderverein e.V Stapelburg, Stapelburg . . . 020290
Heimatstube 1813 Möckern, Möckern . . . 018967
Heimatstube Abbenrode, Abbenrode 015434
Heimatstube Adlergebirge, Waldkraiburg . . . 020645
Heimatstube Alfeld, Alfeld, Leine . . 015475
Heimatstube Altenau, Altenau, Harz 015496
Heimatstube Altenbrak, Altenbrak . 015500
Heimatstube Am Grevendiek, Sprockhövel . . . 020273
Heimatstube Ansprung, Ansprung . 015559
Heimatstube Arenborn, Oberweser . 019429
Heimatstube Bad Brambach, Bad Brambach . . . 015674
Heimatstube Badenhausen, Badenhausen . . . 015856
Heimatstube Bliedersdorf, Bliedersdorf . . . 016269
Heimatstube Börnecke, Börnecke . 016303
Heimatstube Bredenbeck, Wennigsen . . . 020800
Heimatstube Bühlau, Bühlau . . . 016493
Heimatstube Calbe, Calbe . . . 016536
Heimatstube Crostau, Crostau . . . 016609
Heimatstube Cumlosen, Cumlosen . 016611
Heimatstube Demnitz, Demnitz bei Fürstenwalde . . . 016669
Heimatstube der Deutsch-Reichenauer, Haslach . . . 002021
Heimatstube Der Große Hof, Wienrode . . . 020858
Heimatstube der Stadt Saaz, Roth, Mittelfranken . . . 019909
Heimatstube Dessau-Alten, Dessau, Anhalt . . . 016677
Heimatstube Dreetz, Dreetz bei Neustadt, Dosse . . . 016777
Heimatstube Eime, Eime . . . 016917
Heimatstube Elbingerode, Elbingerode, Harz . . . 016935
Heimatstube Endersbach, Weinstadt . . . 020767
Heimatstube Feldberg, Feldberg, Mecklenburg . . . 017105
Heimatstube Festes Haus Badingen, Badingen bei Gransee . . . 015857
Heimatstube Fischbach, Niedereschach . . . 019310
Heimatstube Frauenwald, Frauenwald . . . 017212
Heimatstube Freest, Freest . . . 017217
Heimatstube Freiwaldau-Bieletal, Kirchheim unter Teck . . . 018268
Heimatstube Fröndenberg, Fröndenberg . . . 017278
Heimatstube für Volkskunst, Podelwitz . . . 019646
Heimatstube Gräfenhain/ Nauendorf, Georgenthal . . . 017367
Heimatstube Groß Nemerow, Groß Nemerow . . . 017556
Heimatstube Großbodungen, Großbodungen . . . 017565
Heimatstube Großraming, Großraming . . . 001975
Heimatstube Gutenberg, Oberostendorf . . . 019406
Heimatstube Hänigsen, Uetze . . . 020524
Heimatstube Haiger, Ehemalige Dorfschmiede, Haiger . . . 017632
Heimatstube Heynitz, Heynitz . . . 017916
Heimatstube Hinternah, Hinternah . 017930
Heimatstube Hohenhameln, Hohenhameln . . . 017971
Heimatstube Hohenzieritz, Hohenzieritz . . . 017984
Heimatstube im Spieker Anno 1754, Tarmstedt . . . 020404
Heimatstube in der Wasserburg, Gerswalde . . . 017393
Heimatstube Langenaubach, Haiger 017633

Heimatstube Lichtenstadt, Zirndorf . 021069
Heimatstube Mederitzsch, Pflückuff 019605
Heimatstube Mühlbach mit Philipp-Neubrand-Gedächtnisstube, Eppingen . . . 016992
Heimatstube Mühlhausen, Villingen-Schwenningen . . . 020594
Heimatstube Münstedt, Lahstedt . . 018465
Heimatstube Neuhaus-Schiernitz, Neuhaus-Schierschnitz . . . 019240
Heimatstube Neunheilingen, Neunheilingen . . . 019256
Heimatstube Offenbach, Mittenaar . 018957
Heimatstube Petznick, Petznick . . . 019595
Heimatstube Podersam-Jechnitz, Kronach . . . 018417
Heimatstube Radegast, Radegast bei Köthen, Anhalt . . . 019699
Heimatstube Röckwitz, Röckwitz . . 019861
Heimatstube Röhrnbach-Kaltenbach, Röhrnbach . . . 019866
Heimatstube Rohrbach, Eppingen . . 016993
Heimatstube Rothenklempenow, Rothenklempenow . . . 019923
Heimatstube Ruhland, Ruhland . . . 019948
Heimatstube Sankt Martin am Tennengebirge, Sankt Martin am Tennengebirge . . . 002601
Heimatstube Schlesien, Kaufbeuren 018210
Heimatstube Schwarzenberg am Böhmerwald, Schwarzenberg am Böhmerwald . . . 002659
Heimatstube Seeheilbad Graal-Müritz, Seeheilbad Graal-Müritz . . . 020168
Heimatstube Sitzenroda, Schildau, Gneisenaustadt . . . 020019
Heimatstube Sperenberg, Sperenberg . . . 020262
Heimatstube Stadt und Landkreis Saaz, Georgensgmünd . . . 017365
Heimatstube Tribsees, Tribsees . . . 020474
Heimatstube Trochtelfingen, Bopfingen . . . 016339
Heimatstube Untere Baranya, Gingen . . . 017417
Heimatstube Usedom, Usedom . . . 020549
Heimatstube Vietmannsdorf, Vietmannsdorf . . . 020590
Heimatstube Wahrenbrück, Wahrenbrück . . . 020623
Heimatstube Warthe, Warthe . . . 020684
Heimatstube Wehrstedt, Bad Salzdetfurth . . . 015783
Heimatstube Wendhausen, Schellerten . . . 020013
Heimatstube Werben, Werben, Altmark . . . 020802
Heimatstube Wiesenburg, Wiesenburg, Mark . . . 020880
Heimatstube Wiesental, Waghäusel 020617
Heimatstube Wilthen, Wilthen . . . 020907
Heimatstube Zwota, Sammlung historischer und neuzeitlicher Zungeninstrumente, Zwota . . . 021097
Heimatstuben, Ellrich . . . 016940
Heimatstuben, Langelsheim . . . 018492
Heimatstuben, Volkmarsen . . . 020610
Heimatstuben, Waldbronn . . . 020630
Heimatstuben der Csávolyer im Beinsteiner Torturm, Waiblingen . . . 020625
Heimatstuben der Stadt, Titisee-Neustadt . . . 020444
Heimatstuben im Arrestturm, Spalt . 020259
Heimatstuben im Oberen Tor, Scheinfeld . . . 020011
Heimatstuben Schlesien, Vilsbiburg 020599
Heimatstuben Weipert und Erzgebirgsschau, Gunzenhausen . . . 017606
Heimatsube, Börgitz . . . 016302
Heimatsube des Harzklub Zweigvereins Bad Suderode, Bad Suderode . . . 015810
Heimatsube Klaushagen, Klaushagen . . . 018278
Heimatsube Staupitz, Pflückuff . . . 019606
Heimatverein Räntzelstecher Güsten Osmarsleben e.V, Güsten . . . 017598
Heimatvertriebenen-Stuben, Traun . 002752
Heimburger, Hanne, Nykøbing Falster . . . 098597
Heimer, Peter, Berlin . . . 069641
Heimerdinger, Debra, San Francisco 119689
Heimeshoff, Essen . . . 102685, 133916
Heimilisidnardarsafnid Halldórustofa, Blönduós . . . 021935
Heimler, Maximilian, Zeitlarn . . . 127057
Heimroth, Alain, Paris . . . 066044
Heimschneidermuseum, Großwallstadt . . . 017583
Heimtali Koduloomuuseum, Heimtali . . . 009362
Hein, Christoph, Dresden . . . 125497
Hein, Gregor, Bitburg . . . 069862
Hein, Jörg, Berlin . . . 125214
Hein, Matthias, Kiel . . . 071827
Hein, R.G., Emmendingen . . . 070559
Heinänen, Helsinki . . . 060528
Heinbrandt, Stockholm . . . 081960, 111055
Heindl, Günter, Heidelberg . . . 125899
Heindl, Josef, Schärding . . . 133160
Heindl, Karin, Oldenburg, Oldenburg 073202
Heine, Hildegard, Köln . . . 126083
Heine, Jutta & Bernd, Dassel . . . 070191
Heine-Haus, Altonaer Museum in Hamburg, Hamburg . . . 017697
Heineken Experience, Amsterdam . 029185
Heinemann, Paul, Starnberg . . . 139740
Heinemann, William, London . . . 135224
Heinen, K., Köln . . . 071950
Heinicke, Hans-Jürgen, Potsdam . . 073363
Heinicke, Thomas, Wickersdorf . . . 127004
Heinikainen, A., Mikkeli . . . 137978
Heinisch, Wieland, Knetzgau . . . 071885
Heinkel, G., Freiburg im Breisgau . . 070839
Heinlein, Christian, Steinbach am Wald . . . 073903
Heinley, Boston . . . 115183
Heino Lubja Kaalumuuseum, Mustvee . . . 009379
Heinolan Kaupunginmuseo, Heinola 009510
Heinonen, Helsinki . . . 124045
Heinrich, G., Bielefeld . . . 069824
Heinrich, Herbert, Rottenburg an der Laaber . . . 126750
Heinrich, Marie-Luce, Köln . . . 071951
Heinrich, Michael, Braunschweig . . 069983
Heinrich, Peter, Hamburg . . . 071245
Heinrich, Peter, Schorndorf, Württemberg . . . 126779
Heinrich-Blickle-Museum, Sammlung gußeiserner Ofenplatten, Rosenfeld . . . 019881
Heinrich-Büssing-Haus, Wolfsburg . 020962
Heinrich Harrer-Museum, Hüttenberg . . . 002066
Heinrich Heine Antiquariat, Düsseldorf . . . 139011
Heinrich-Heine-Institut-Museum, Düsseldorf . . . 016832
Heinrich-Hoffmann-Museum, Frankfurt am Main . . . 017174
Heinrich-Mayer-Haus Elektromuseum, Esslingen . . . 017084
Heinrich-Schliemann-Gedenkstätte, Neubukow . . . 019220
Heinrich-Schliemann-Museum, Ankershagen . . . 015545
Heinrich-Schütz-Haus, Forschungs- und Gedenkstätte im Geburtshaus des Komponisten, Bad Köstritz . . . 015737
Heinrich-Schütz-Haus Weißenfels, Weißenfels . . . 020781
Heinrich-Sohnrey-Archiv und Gedächtnisstätte, Mautturm, Jühnder Schloß, Jühnde . . . 018128
Heinrich Suso Waldeck und Hans Schnopfhagen-Gedenkraum, Sankt Veit im Mühlkreis . . . 002632
Heinrich Vogeler Stiftung Haus im Schluh, Worpswede . . . 020987
Heinrich Zille Museum, Berlin . . . 016075
Heinrichs, Büren, Westfalen . . . 102287
Heinrichs, Bernd, Celle . . . 070124
Sören Heinsohn & David Streichsbier, Hamburg . . . 071246
Heintzelman, Albert, Los Angeles . . 132255
Heinz, Anneli, Hofheim am Taunus . 071552
Heinz, Marcel, Carcès . . . 099085
Heinz & Heinz, Hannover . . . 103280
Heinz & Heinz, Lüneburg . . . 103978
Heinz Nixdorf MuseumsForum, Paderborn . . . 019549
Heinze, Friedrich, Salzburg . . . 095726
Heinze, W., Oldenburg, Oldenburg . 139629
Heinzel, Aberdeen . . . 112478
Heinzel, B., Kassel . . . 103512
Heinzer, Ruth, Schaffhausen . . . 141299
Heinzerling & Achenbach-Heinzerling, Hungen . . . 103413
Heinzl, Luise, Viechtach . . . 074203
Heinzl, Walter, Wien . . . 057440, 123502
Heinzler, Franz X., Inzigkofen . . . 125975
Heinzmann, G., Villingen-Schwenningen . . . 074215
Heirloom, Harrogate . . . 113192
Heirloom, Honolulu . . . 088955
Heirloom Antiques, Winnipeg . . . 059463
Heirloom Doll Museum, Airlie Beach 000720
Heirloom Furniture, Denver 088697, 132039
Heirloom & Howard, West Yatton . . 087091
Heirloom Jewels, Baltimore . . . 087677
Heirlooms, Baltimore . . . 087678
Heirlooms, Coconut Grove . . . 055699
Heirlooms, Dun Laoghaire . . . 074963
Heirlooms, Johannesburg . . . 080707
Heirlooms, Wareham . . . 087019, 131648
Heirlooms, Worcester . . . 087256
Heirlooms International, Tulsa . . . 093309
Heisando, Tokyo . . . 077252, 128449
Heise, T., München . . . 072727
Heisey Museum, Lock Haven . . . 045358
Heisey News, Newark . . . 136482
Heiss, Günther, München . . . 072728
Heiss, Julia, Mainleus . . . 072384
Heiß, Margot, Zapfendorf . . . 074557
Heissler, Willi F. G., Bobenheim am Berg . . . 121348
Heitmann & Zimmermann, Dortmund . . . 102403
Heitmeyer-Löns, Sabine, Havixbeck 125889
Heitsch, Francoise, München . . . 104225
Heitsch, Jörg, München . . . 104226
Heitschl, Christine, Wien . . . 057441
Heitz, Anthony & Daniel, Basel . . . 111191
Heitz-Darmancier, Bourges . . . 120950
Heitzmann, Alain, Beaune . . . 061281
Heitzmann, Jérôme, Chevigny-Saint-Sauveur . . . 062282
Heitzmann, Monique, Chagny . . . 062068
Heitzmann, Patrick, Arc-sur-Tille . . 060948
Heitzmann, Thierry, Mormant . . . 064794
Heiwajima Antique Fair, Tokyo . . . 093799
Heizungsmuseum der Buderus Heiztechnik, Lollar . . . 018682
Heizungsmuseum Wien, Wien . . . 002911
Hejtmanek, Regina, Vitry-sur-Seine 125037
Hekkers & Van Spijker, Deventer . . 128642
De Heksenbal, Breda . . . 078095
De Heksenwaag, Oudewater . . . 030031
Helander, M., Helsinki . . . 120885
Helbing, Hamm, Westfalen . . . 103244
Helbling, Max & Margrit, Benken, Sankt Gallen . . . 082193
Held, Stuttgart . . . 139764
Held, Tönisvorst . . . 126905
Held Joan Museum, Carlton South . 000896
Held-Poage Memorial Home, Ukiah 048684
Ursel Held & Tanja Zielinski, Neustadt in Holstein . . . 073039
Helderse Kunstliga, Den Helder . . .053889, 107965
Helen, Mary, Tucson . . . 120135
Hélen Antiquités, Guecelard . . . 063092
Helen Day Art Center, Stowe . . . 048390
Helen E. Copeland Gallery, Montana State University, Bozeman . . . 042374
Helen King Kendall Memorial Art Gallery, San Angelo . . . 047783
Helen Louise Allen Textile Collection, Madison . . . 045590
Helen of Troy, New York . . . 090935
Helena & Dieb, Lisboa . . . 109327
Helena Rubinstein Pavillon for Contemporary Art, Tel Aviv . . . 023074
Helena Thompson Museum, Workington . . . 041448
Helena's Collectables, Shere . . . 086587
Helene Antiques, Armadale, Victoria 055380
Helen's Depression, San Antonio . . 092516
Helen's Jewelry, Saint Louis . . . 132750
Helen's on Discovery, Helensvale . . 055975
Helensville and District Pioneer Museum, Helensville . . . 030516
Helfertová, Praha . . . 123982
Helfrich, Rödermark . . . 104757
Helfštýn Hrad, Týn nad Bečvou . . . 008728
Helge Ands Kyrkoruin, Visby . . . 036799
Helgheim, Terje Johan, Bergen . . . 121845
Heli, Mannheim . . . 139452
Hélian, Martin, Montpellier . . . 124458
The Helicopter Museum, Weston-super-Mare . . . 041348
Helier, Jean-Luc, Mormant . . . 064795
Heliez, Stephan, Chamalières . . . 062100
Helikon Publishing House, Budapest 134502
Heliloojate Kappide Majamuuseum, Viljandi Muuseumi, Suure-Jaani . . . 009392
Helin, Hauho . . . 060493
Helin, Hauho . . . 060494
Helinä Rautavaaran museo, Espoo . 009476
Héliodore, Saint-Étienne . . . 067456
Helios, Nashville . . . 117356
Helios & Co, Weedon . . . 087059
Helios Arts, Pittsburgh . . . 118928
Helios at the Spinney, Tanworth-in-Arden . . . 114547
Hell, Anton, München . . . 104227
Hell, Dr. Bernhard, München . . . 139513
Hell, Christian, Wolfratshausen . . . 127033
Hell, Claudia, Großgmain . 057043, 123372
Hell, Doris, Großgmain . . . 057044, 123373
Hellbrügge, Dr. Christoph, Ascheberg, Westfalen . . . 125068
Hellenic Antiquities Museum, Melbourne . . . 001241
Hellenic Children's Museum, Athinai . . . 021174
Hellenic Folklore Research Centre, Athinai . . . 021175
Hellenic Museum and Cultural Center, Chicago . . . 042848
Hellenic Theatre Museum and Study Center, Athinai . . . 021176
Hellen's House, Much Marcle . . . 040504
Heller, Madrid . . . 110543
Heller, Madrid . . . 110544
Heller, Omaha . . . 118702
Heller, Douglas, New York . . . 118007
Heller, Joshua, Washington . . . 143043
Heller, M. & H., Sandhausen . . . 073661
Heller, Ottmar, Dannstadt-Schauernheim . . . 125441
Heller, Petra, Bayreuth . . . 069489
Heller, Thomas, Gefrees . . . 070944
Hellfire Gallery, Merivale . . . 094837
Hellhake, Bad Bertrich . . . 069264
Hellhof, Kronberg im Taunus . . . 103794
Helling, Oslo . . . 079444
Helling, Willich . . . 105301
Hellingman Jonker, Amsterdam . . . 077866
Hellman, Monica, Herrliberg . . . 082494
Hellmann, Bad Liebenstein . . . 069322
Hellmann, Kurt, Wien . . . 057442
Hello-Five Antiques, Edmonton . . . 058830
Hellweg-Museum der Stadt Unna, Unna . . . 020537
Hellwig, Lutherstadt Wittenberg . . . 072365
Hellwig, Wuppertal . . . 074524
Hellwig, Prof. Friedemann, Köln . . . 126084
Hellwig, Wilhelm, Wuppertal . . . 074525

Hellwig-Schmid, Regina, Regensburg . . . 104696
Helly Nahmad, New York . . . 118008
Helm, Eberbach, Baden . . . 070491
Helman, Warszawa . . . 079758
Helman, Warszawa . . . 079759
Helman, Warszawa . . . 129087
Helmcken House Pioneer Doctor's Residence, Victoria . . . 006742
Helmdach, G.A., Gelnhausen . . . 125708
Helme Kihelkonnamuuseum, Helme 009363
Helmeke, Jörg, Stendal . . . 104952
Helmerich & Mitchell, Germering . . 102941
Helmering, P., Berlin . . . 069642
Helmeringhausen Museum, Helmeringhausen . . . 029082
Helmersen, Hélène d', Paris . . . 066045
Helmert, Dr. Gunter, Chemnitz . . . 070132
Helmhaus, Zürich . . . 037772
Helmich, Bernd M., Berlin . . . 125215
Helmig, Bielefeld . . . 069825
Helmig, Dissen am Teutoburger Wald . . . 070260
Helming, L. & R., Rheine . . . 073522
Helminger, Hof bei Salzburg . . . 123383
Helmrich, Barbara, Isernhagen . . . 125976
Helms-Museum, Hamburger Museum für Archäologie und die Geschichte Harburgs, Hamburg . . . 017698
Helmshore Textile Museums, Helmshore . . . 039719
Helmsley Bookshop, Helmsley . . . 141655
Helmstedter Freundeskreis für Paramentik und christliche Kunst, Helmstedt . 017864
Helmstetter, Bruno, Schöntal . . . 126777
Helmstetter, Markus, Mörschbach . 072585
Helo, Adriana Carlota, São Paulo . . 096674
Helper, Indianapolis . . . 089302, 122920
Helsingborg Auktionskammare, Helsingborg . . . 122158
Helsingborgs Auktionsverk, Helsingborg . . . 122159
Helsingborgs Idrottsmuseum, Helsingborg . . . 036334
Helsingborgs Ram- & Konsthandel, Helsingborg . . . 081832
Helsingborgs Skolmuseum, Helsingborg . . . 036335
Helsingborgs Slott, Helsingborg . . . 036336
Helsinge Hembygdsmuseum, Vantaa . . . 010221
Helsingin Antiikki, Järvenpää . . . 060599
Helsingin Antikvariaatti, Helsinki . . 137940
Helsingin Automuseo, Helsinki . . . 009525
Helsingin Diakonissalaitoksen Museo, Helsinki . . . 009526
Helsingin Huutokauppakamari, Helsinki . . . 120886
Helsingin Kaupungin Taidemuseo, Mejlahti, Helsinki . . . 009527
Helsingin Kaupungin Taidemuseo, Tennispalatsi, Helsinki . . . 009528
Helsingin Kaupunginmuseo, Helsinki . . . 009529
Helsingin Taidehalli, Helsinki . . . 009530
Helsingin Väestönsuojelumuseo, Helsinki . . . 009531
Helsingin Yliopistomuseo, Helsinki . 009532
Helsingin Yliopistomuseo - Eläinlääketieteen Historian Museo, Helsinki . . . 009533
Helsingin Yliopiston Lääketieteen Historian Laitos ja Museo, Helsinki . . . 009534
Helsingin Yliopiston Maatalousmuseo, Helsinki . . . 009535
Helsingør Bymuseum, Helsingør . . . 008898
Helson Hall, Minnesota State University, Mankato . . . 045643
Helston Folk Museum, Helston . . . 039722
Heltborg Museum, Sydthy Kunst- og Kulturcenter, Hurup Thy . . . 008940
Helth, København . . . 098573
Helvetia Museum, Helvetia . . . 044505
Helytörténeti Gyűjtemény, Budapest 021654
Helytörténeti Múzeum, Pápa . . . 021811
Hemani, Abu Dhabi . . . 083174
Hembygdsgården, Bjurholm . . . 036216
Hembygdsgården i Kristvalla, Nybro 036508
Hembygdsgården Labbas, Storby . . 010098
Hembygdsgården Rots Skans, Älvdalen . . . 036167
Hembygdsmuseet i Korsberga, Korsberga . . . 036399
Hemeleers, Frantz, Bruxelles . . . 057982
Hémery, Francois, Paris . . . 124693
Hémery, François-Paul, Ho Chi Minh City . . . 133042
Hémery, François-Paul, Le Faouët . 124295
Hémery, François-Paul, Paris . . . 124694
Hemingway, New York . . . 118009
Hemingway Museum, Oak Park . . . 046583
Hemken, Helgard, Siegen . . . 073811
Hemlängtan Antikt, Göteborg . . . 081810
Hemmerle, München . . . 072729
Hemmers, Petra, Hannover . . . 125872
Hemmingsen Auksjon, Tromsø . . . 121881
Hemmungen-Kramer, Bayreuth . . . 069490
Hemne Bygdemuseum, Kyrksæterøra . . . 030967
Hemnes Museum, Bjerka . . . 030777
Hempe, R., Vierkirchen . . . 074208
Hempel, Christian, Dresden . . . 125498
Hempel, F.H. Jürgen, Monschau . . . 104115
Hempenius, R., Almelo . . . 077725
Hemphill, Washington . . . 120308
Hemphill, George, Wellington . . . 128974
Hemsedal Bygdatun, Hemsedal . . . 030887
Hemswell Antique Centres, Hemswell Cliff . . . 084653, 130781, 141656
Hemus, Sofia . . . 137603
Henan Fine Arts Publishing House, Zhengzhou . . . 133392
Henan Provincial Museum, Zhengzhou . . . 007348
Henau, Antwerpen . . . 057701
Henaut, Paris . . . 100508
Hendel, Renate, Taufkirchen, Vils . . 105033
Henderson, Louisville . . . 089998, 132296
Henderson, Perth . . . 086225
Henderson, Carol, Fort Worth . . . 116147
Henderson Art & Framing, King's Lynn . . . 113326
Henderson Phillips, Washington . . . 120309
Henderson State University Museum, Arkadelphia . . . 041769
Hendlinger, N., Berlin . . . 125216
Hendon, Brighton . . . 135124
Hendricks, Edmonton . . . 096885
Hendricks, Marc F.J., Meinier . . . 082654
Hendrickson House Museum and Old Swedes Church, Wilmington . . . 049206
Hendrickx-Gourdin, Namur . . . 058353
Hendriks, E.W., Amsterdam . . . 077867
Hendriks, Holger, Hattingen . . . 071431
Hendriks, Twan, Tilburg . . . 108229
Hendrik's Welt, Bad Münstereifel . . 069333
Hendrik's Welt, Nettersheim . . . 072960
Hendrix, Dallas . . . 115891
Hendrycks, Andre, Gent . . . 058185
Heneage, Thomas, London . . . 141823
Héneaux, Marie-Emmanuel, Saint-Brieuc . . . 067383
Henfield Museum, Henfield . . . 039726
Heng, Singapore . . . 109806
Hengesbach, R., Köln . . . 103637
Hengesbach, Rolf, Wuppertal . . . 105354
Hengevoss-Duerkop, Hamburg . . . 103165
Hengistburgmuseum & Volkskundliche Sammlung, Hengsberg . . . 002036
Henham, Martin, London . 085387, 131060
Henhouse, Birmingham . . . 087758
Henie Onstad Kunstsenter, Høvikodden . . . 030914
Henin & Planchar, Bruxelles . . . 057983
Henjes, Ingo, Torgau . . . 074071, 139782
Henk, Budapest . . . 074688
Henke, Heinrich, Passau . . . 139648
Henke, Manfred, Berlin . . . 138789
Henke, Piet, Alkmaar . . . 077715
Henkel, Düsseldorf . . . 070392
Henken, Los Angeles . . . 116791
Henkenjohann & Sander, Bad Aibling . . . 069255
Henki, Ajan, Helsinki . . . 060529
Henle, Stefan, Berlin . . . 101922
Henley Antiques Centre, Henley-in-Arden . . . 084659
Henley Art and Crafts Guild, Reading . . . 054400
Henley Auctions, Mile End . . . 120611
Henley Decorative and Fine Arts, Reading . . . 054401
Henley & Grange Arts Society, Henley Beach . . . 052471, 094633
Henley House Antiques, Rumford . . 086415
Henley-in-Arden Auction Sales, Henley-in-Arden . . . 122540
Henn, Maastricht . . . 108124
Henn, Andreas, Stuttgart . . . 104988
Henn, U., Peine . . . 073300
Henneberg, Horst, Braunschweig . . 138924
Henneberg-Museum, Münnerstadt . 019133
Hennebergisches Museum, Kloster Veßra, Kloster Veßra . . . 018289
Hennecke, Dorsten . . . 125476
Hennemann, Marianne, Bad Homburg v.d.Höhe . . . 101654
Hennen, Christian, Leverkusen . . . 103907
Hennepin History Museum, Minneapolis . . . 045911
Hennessee, Rob, Tampa . . . 123125
Hennessy, Crewkerne . . . 084112
Hennessy, Clive, Vevey . . . 082882
Hennessy & Ingalls, Santa Monica . 135500
Hennig, Birgit, Zerbst . . . 074565
Hennig, Carl Th., Berlin . . . 138790
Hennig, Gerald, Blankenheim, Ahr . 102143
Hennig, Dr. Karl, Hamburg . . . 071247
Hennig, Marie-Louise, Köln . . . 071952
Hennighaus, Dr. L., Aachen . . . 138668
Henning, Enno, Wittmund . . . 074457
Henninger, Karin, Pforzheim . . . 073317
Hennings, Paul, Hamburg . . . 139185
Hennok, Jim A., Toronto . . 097286, 120819
Henoch, New York . . . 118010
Henocq, Sprinkange . . . 077491
Henocque, Marie-Sylvie, Paris . . . 124695
Henot, Marc, Enghien-les-Bains . . . 099248
Henri, Stephan, Condé-sur-Marne . 062448
Henri-Arnaud-Haus - Waldensermuseum, Ötisheim . . . 019449
Henrich, Hella, Schillingen . . . 073688
Henrich, Peter, München . . . 072730
Henrietta's, Jacksonville . . . 116530
Henrik Antiquités, Cannes . . . 061945
Henrik Ibsen Museum, Skien . . . 031189
Henrique & Eduardo, Lisboa . . . 079943
Henriques de Carvalho, Manuel, Lisboa . . . 079944
Henro, New York . . . 090936
Henro, New York . . . 090937
Henry, Pau . . . 100984
Henry, Gene L ., Seattle . . . 093013
Henry, Hubert, Saint-Julien-du-Sault . . . 067557
Henry, Karel & Willis, Marshfield . . 122957
Henry, Ph., Quimper . . . 067019
Henry Art Gallery, University of Washington, Seattle . . . 048081
Henry B. Plant Museum, Tampa . . . 048489
Henry Blogg Lifeboat Museum, Cromer . . . 039182
Henry Clay Frick Estate, Pittsburgh . 047051
Henry County Historical Museum, New Castle . . . 046212
Henry County Museum and Cultural Arts Center, Clinton . . . 043015
Henry-Dunant-Museum, Heiden . . . 037182
Henry Ford Estate, Dearborn . . . 043343
Henry Ford Museum and Greenfield Village, Dearborn . . . 043344
Henry Guest House, New Brunswick 046205
Henry H. Blommel Historic Automotive Data Collection, Connersville . . . 043129
Henry Kendall Cottage and Historical Museum, Gosford . . . 001074
Henry Lawson Centre, Gulgong . . . 001084
Henry Moore Institute, Leeds . . . 039953
Henry S. Reuss Ice Age Visitor Center, Campbellsport . . . 042589
The Henry Sheldon Museum of Vermont Histoy, Middlebury . . . 045833
Henry van de Velde-Gesellschaft, Hagen, Westfalen . . . 053231
Henry van de Velde Museum, Kunstsammlung Chemnitz, Chemnitz . . . 016557
Henry Whitfield State Historical Museum, Guilford . . . 044370
Henry's, Ash . . . 083322
Henry's Antiques, Seattle . . . 093014
Henry's Auktionshaus, Mutterstadt . 121555
Hens, Susanne, Inning am Ammersee . . . 125972
Hensbroek, Harlingen . . . 128705
Henschel, Berlin . . . 133782
Henschel, Edgardo, Buenos Aires . . 136723
Hense, Thomas, Kiel . . . 071828
Hense, Thomas, Kiel . . . 071829
Henseleit Buchholz, Köln . . . 103638
Henseler, Luzern . . . 082628
Henseler, H.A., München . 072731, 104228
Hensellek, Ulla, Friedberg, Hessen . 133962
Henshelwood Gallery, Newcastle-upon-Tyne . . . 114123
Hensing & Döring, Bremen . . . 070023
Hensler, E., Schopfheim . . . 073720
Hensoldt, Rainer, Wetzlar . . . 074381
Hentrich, Berlin . . . 133783
Hentrich, Berlin . . . 138791
Hentrich, L., Mayen . . . 104042
Hentrich, L., Neuwied . . . 073046
R. Hentschel & R. Visser, Bocholt . . 069876
Henty Old Wares, Henty . . . 055978
Henty on the Hill, Olinda . . . 056401
Henz, Johann, Erschwil . . 082360, 130012
Henze, Ernst-Dieter, Norderstedt . . 073073
Henze, M., Halle, Saale . . . 071177
Henze, W. & C., Höxter . . . 103388
Henze & Butkus, Alheim . . 069134, 125057
Henze & Ketterer, Wichtrach . . . 111990
Hepplewhite, Singapore . . . 080480
Heptonstall Museum, Heptonstall . . 039730
Hepworth, Anthony, Bath . . . 083429
Hepworth, Anthony, Bath . . . 112577
Hepworth, Anthony, Bath . . . 112578
Hepworth, Gordon, Newton Saint Cyres . . . 086082
Hepworth, Gordon, Newton Saint Cyres . . . 114142
Her House, London . . . 113683
Her Majesty Customs and Excise National Museum, Liverpool . . . 040028
Her Majesty Tower of London, London . . . 040173
Hera Gallery, Wakefield . . . 048829
Herail, B., Leeds . . . 130871
Herakles, München . . . 072732
Herakles, Pullach . . . 073385
Herakles Numismatics, Charlotte . . 087955
Herald, Marcelline, Eton . . . 084342
Heraldic Museum, Dublin . . . 022747
Heraldry Today, Ramsbury . . . 142012
Heran, Jeanne, Paris . . . 066046
Heras Institute of Indian History and Culture, Mumbai . . . 022264
Heras Tibaida, Maria Luisa de las, Madrid . . . 081321
Herat Museum, Herat . . . 000003
De Heraut, Rotterdam . . . 140520
Herbarium, Department of Plant Sciences, Cambridge . . . 038963
Herbart, Wolfgang, Hannover . . . 125873
Herbelet, Denis, Saint-Memmie . . . 067673
Herbener, Thomas, Neugersdorf . . . 072993
Herber, Frankfurt am Main 070748, 102787
Herbert, London . . . 135225
Herbert, Los Angeles . . . 116792
Herbert, Nürnberg . . . 073104, 126562
Herbert, Paris . . . 066047
Herbert, Ingeborg, Einhausen . . . 070532

Herbert, John, Mühlbeck 139488
Herbert, Sabine, Lüneburg 072357
Herbert and Eileen Bernard Museum, New York 046345
Herbert Art Gallery and Museum, Coventry 039152
Herbert E. Clark Collection of Near Eastern Antiquities, Jerusalem 022952
Herbert F. Johnson Museum of Art, Ithaca 044791
Herbert Hoover National Historic Site, West Branch 049065
Herbert Hoover Presidential Library-Museum, West Branch 049066
Herberta Dorbes Muzejs Senču Putekļi, Ventspils 027797
Herbette, Danièle, Beauval 061314
Herbette, Denis, Doullens 120992
Herbich, Karl, Cebu 079559, 129004
Herbich, Karl, Gernlinden 125724
L'Herbier Déco, Saint-Denis 080128
Herbig, F.A., München 134244
Herbinet, Jacques, Paris 138403
Herbita, Palermo 134650
Herbst, Christiane, Lüneburg 072358
Herbst, Hagen & Holger, Greifswald 071090
Herbst, Krisina, Berlin 125217
Herbst, Thomas, Detmold 121369
Herbstpresse, Wien 133207
Herburger, Heinz, Saarbrücken 104798
Herburger, Heinz, Sankt Ingbert . . .073668, 104811
Hercher, Hans W., Umkirch 074157
Herckenrode, Hasselt 058226
Hercouët, Catherine, Loheac 063976
Herdeiros, José Luís, Lisboa 079945
Herdenkingsbordenmuseum, Lochem 029873
Herdhebaut, Guy, Paris 066048
Herdla Museum, Herdla 030888
Here in the Past, San Diego 092645
Hereford Antique Centre, Hereford .084669, 130789
Hereford City Museum and Art Gallery, Hereford 039733
Hereford Inlet Lighthouse, North Wildwood 046540
Herefordshire Light Infantry Regimental Museum, Hereford 039734
Herendi Porcelánművészeti, Múzeum Alapitvány, Herend 021737
Hereth, Dr. Hans-Jürgen, München . 139514
Hereward, Ely 141596
Hereward Gallery, Bourne 112676
Herforder Kunstverein, Pöppelmann-Gesellschaft e.V., Herford 053232
Herfurthsches Haus, Hainichen, Sachsen 017641
Hergat, Danièle, Bergerac 061361
Herger, Eckhard & Cordula, Hamm, Westfalen 139225
Herget, George, New Orleans 142616
Herholdt Jensen, Nærum 120874
Heriard & Cimino, New Orleans . . . 117456
Héricé, Christophe, Montcaret 064662
Hering, Dirk, Bomlitz 125346
Hering, Jens-Uwe, Hirtstein 071533
Hering, Dr. M. H. Bernd, Fürth, Bayern 125687
Herinneringscentrum Kamp Westerbork, Hooghalen 029768
Heriot-Watt University Museum and Archive, Edinburgh 039395
Héritage, Boulogne-sur-Mer 061696
Héritage, Lyon 064140
Heritage Antique, Baltimore 087679
Heritage Antique Jewellery & Art, Toronto 059203
Héritage Antique Métropolitain, Montréal 058962
Heritage Antiques, Brighton 083699
Heritage Antiques, Calgary 058789
Heritage Antiques, Charlotte 087956
Heritage Antiques, Chichester 083975
Heritage Antiques, Hamilton 058852
Heritage Antiques, London 058883
Heritage Antiques, Mosta 077516
Heritage Antiques, Wem 131660
L'Héritage Antiquité, Québec 059070
Heritage Art and Antiques, Mumbai 074821
Heritage Art Center, Quezon City . . 031774
Heritage Auctions, Swaffham 122718
Heritage Book Shop, West Hollywood 143052
Heritage Books, Ryde 142023
The Heritage Center, Pine Ridge . . . 047026
Heritage Center of Lancaster County, Lancaster 045144
Heritage Centre of Saint Louis Convent, Monaghan 022837
Heritage Collectables and Antiques, Houston 089099
Heritage Collection, Dallas 088529
Heritage Collection Catherina Brand, Ladybrand 034672
Heritage Collections Council, Canberra 052472
Heritage Conservancy, Doylestown . 043504
L'Héritage Contemporain, Québec . 097142
Heritage Custom Furniture, Houston 132123
Heritage Discover Center, Johnstown 044873
Heritage Farm & Village, Western Development Museum, North Battleford 006034
Heritage Farmstead Museum, Plano 047077
Heritage Fine Art, Calgary 096821, 133312
Heritage for the Blind, Miami 090183
Heritage Furniture Restoration, Buffalo 131855
Heritage Furniture Restoration, Regina 123811
Heritage Galleries, Calgary 058790
Heritage Gallery, Ha Noi 093558
Heritage Gallery, Nelson Bay 056322
Heritage Gallery, Singapore 080481
Heritage Gallery, Waikato 079290
Heritage Gift Shop, Tucson 093242
Heritage Hall Museum and Archives, Freeman 044070
Héritage Harwood, Montréal 058963
Heritage Hazenmore, Hazenmore . . 005612
Heritage Hill Museum, Dandenong . 000969
Heritage Hill State Park, Green Bay 044308
Heritage Hjemkomst Interpretive Center, Moorhead 046017
Heritage House, Hamilton 096421
Heritage House Antiques, Auckland 078946
Heritage House Museum, Smiths Falls 006485
Heritage House of Orange County Museum, Orange 046702
Heritage Jewelry, Chicago 088104
Heritage Library and Museum, Anchorage 041713
Heritage Motor Centre, Gaydon . . . 039538
Heritage Museum, Baltimore 041985
Heritage Museum, Idaho Springs . . 044712
Heritage Museum, Kuah 027961
Heritage Museum, Langruth 005746
The Heritage Museum, Clatsop Historical Society, Astoria 041825
Heritage Museum and Potton House, Big Spring 042200
The Heritage Museum at Falfurrias, Falfurrias 043802
Heritage Museum Foundation of Tate County, Senatobia 048111
The Heritage Museum of Fine Arts for Youth, Detroit 043450
Heritage Museum of Northwest Florida, Valparaiso 048740
Heritage Music Repair, Kansas City 132209
Heritage Numismatic Auctions, Dallas 122874
Héritage Oriental, Paris 066049
Heritage Park, Fort McMurray 005465
Heritage Park Folk Museum, Barbados Museum, Saint Phillip 003125
Heritage Park - Historical Village, Calgary 005188
Heritage Park Museum, Terrace . . . 006559
Heritage Plantation of Sandwich, Sandwich 047932
Heritage Restorations, Llanfair Caereinion 085038, 130910
Heritage Restorations, London 131061
Heritage Royal Mail Collection, London 040174
The Heritage Shop, Singapore 080482
The Heritage Society Museum, Houston 044640
Heritage Square Museum, Ontario . 046695
Heritage Trading, Dubai 083193
Heritage Trading Company, Auckland 078947
Heritage Vietnamese Arts and Crafts, Ho Chi Minh City 093560
Heritage Village, Mountain Lake . . . 046075
Heritage Village, Sharonville 048128
Heritage Village Museum, Woodville 049300
Heritage Village - Pinellas County Historical Museum, Largo 045174
Heritage Walk Museum, Escondido 043730
Heritage World Centre, Dungannon . 039320
Héritier, Carmen, Mirmande 099725
Héritier, Maurice, Autun 061088
Heritier, Michelle, Paris 100509
Héritier, Pierre-Antoine, Genève . . . 130035
Heriz, Cincinnati 088250
Herke-Stoß, Bad Waldsee 138707
Herkimer County Historical Society Museum, Herkimer 044519
Herkimer Home, Little Falls 045340
Herkomer-Museum am Mutterturm, Landsberg am Lech 018477
Herles & Rupar, Oberursel 073164
Herlyn, J., Freiburg im Breisgau . . . 070840
Herman, Bruxelles 057984
Herman Son, J., New Orleans 090568
Herman de Cuyper Museum, Willebroek 003857
Herman Ottó Múzeum, Miskolc . . . 021786
Herman Ottó Múzeum, Miskolc . . . 021787
Herman Teirlinckhuis, Beersel 003223
Herman & Wilkinson, Dublin 121665
Hermann, Essen 102686
Hermann, München 072733, 121530
Hermann, Paris 133621
Hermann, Wollombi 123328
Hermann, Arthur, Hamburg 103166
Hermann, Georg Vincent, Dunningen 102587
Hermann, Rudi, Altenmarkt im Pongau 056915
Hermann-Allmers-Haus, Sandstedt 019979
Hermann Broch-Museum, Teesdorf 002733
Hermann-Grima House, New Orleans 046254
Hermann-Grochtmann-Museum Datteln, Datteln 016650
Hermann-Hesse-Höri-Museum, Gaienhofen 017314
Hermann-Hesse-Museum, Calw . . . 016540
Hermann Hesse Museum, Hiroshima 026527
Hermann-Köhl-Museum, Pfaffenhofen an der Roth 019600
Hermann-Oberth-Raumfahrt-Museum, Feucht 017112
Hermann-Simsch, Monika, Frankfurt am Main 070749
Hermanns, Peter, Geilenkirchen . . .070946, 125703
Hermanns, Peter, Übach-Palenberg 126925
Hermanos Cebader, Madrid 129629
Hermanos Garcia, Zaragoza 081743
Hermanovits, Jean-François, Aix-en-Provence 060705
Hermans, Elisabeth, Bruxelles 137440
Hermantier, Dany, Florac 062881
Hermay & Bernar, Hautot-sur-Mer . 063137
Hermeling, E., Arnhem 128568
Hermeneia - Zeitschrift für Ostkirchliche Kunst, Bochum 135766
Hermeneutics of Art, New York 136483
Hermenier, Marcel, Saint-Berthevin 067377
Hermenier, Pascal, La Croixille 063362
Herment, Daniel, Zürich 082978
Herment, Paule et Edouard, Nogent-le-Rotrou 065209
Hermerén, Karin, Landskrona 129843
Hermès, Annemasse 138014
Hermes, La Plata 136759
Hermès, Lyon 099594
Hermes, Salzkotten 073656
Hermes, Elke, Berlin 138792
Hermes, Sabine, Köln 126085
Hermesdorf, K., Trier 074095
Hermet, Paule, Brou 061819
Hermeyer, München 104229
Hermille, Mireille, L'Isle-sur-la-Sorgue 063937
Herminette, Mornant 064796
L'Herminette, Paris 066050
The Hermitage, Ho-Ho-Kus 044560
Hermitage Antiquarian Bookshop, Denver 142388
Hermitage Antiques, Dallas 088530
Hermitage Antiques, Geelong 055865
Hermitage Antiques, Honiton 084720
Hermitage Antiques, London 085388
Hermitage Foundation Museum, Norfolk 046499
Hermitage Gallery, Whitby 114680
Hermitage Gatehouse Museum, Ancaster 005012
The Hermitage - Home of President Andrew Jackson, Hermitage 044522
Hermitage Rooms, London 040175
Hermsen, Wiesbaden 105265
Hernandez, Albuquerque 114794
Hernández, Cali 098236
Hernández, J., Buenos Aires 055215
Hernani, Buenos Aires 055216
Herne Bay Museum and Gallery, Herne Bay 039740
Herning Kunstmuseum, Herning . . . 008904
Herning Museum, Herning 008905
Hernitz, Lilo, München 072734
Herode, Avon 061144
Herodote, Lyon 064141
Heroes and Fantasies, San Antonio 142888
Heroes and Fantasies, San Antonio 142889
Heroes and Fantasies, San Antonio 142890
Heroes and Fantasies, San Antonio 142891
Heroes Aren't Hard to Find, Charlotte 087957
Heroes Collectibles, Houston 089100
Heroes & Fantasies, San Antonio . . 092517
Heroes & Fantasies, San Antonio . . 092518
Herold, Manfred & Christa, Offenbach am Main 073186, 126588
Herold, Rainer, Hamburg 103167
Herold, Rainer, Kampen 103480
Herold, Thessa, Paris 100510
Heron, Cottbus 138968
Heron, Johannesburg 110056
Heron & Son, H.W., Yoxall 087298
Heron Corn Mill and Museum of Papermaking, Beetham 038659
Herons Gallery, Castlemaine 094383
Herons Reef Historic Gold Diggings, Fryerstown 001045
Heros, Vilseck 074220
Herouet, Paris 100511
Herovits, Johann, Goldach 130038
Herøy Bygdesamling, Herøy 030889
Herøy Kystmuseum, Herøy 030890
Herpers, Iris, Gelsenkirchen 125712
Herpin, Hubert, Cannes 061946
Herr, Potsdam 104628
Herr, Arnold, Los Angeles 142508
Herr, Harald, Karlsruhe 134076
Herr, Werner G., Köln 071953, 121472
Herranz Martí, J., Madrid 122064
Herrbach, Bernard, Châtenois 062224, 124194
Herregården Museum, Larvikmuséene, Larvik 030974
Herrenhaus Altenhof, Altenhof 015504
Herrenhausen-Museum, Hannover . 017754

Herrenschmidt, M. & D., Prichsenstadt 073375
Herrera, Dallas 132012
Herrera, Carlos, Los Angeles 089792, 132256
Herrera, Manuel, Caracas 093533
Herréra-Gutierrez, Jean-Claude, Thiers 068389
Herrera de Reyes, Inés, Bogotá . . . 059839
Herrero Arruti, Carlos, Bilbao 129436
Herrero Zurdo, Antonio, Madrid . . . 110545
Herreshoff Marine Museum/America's Cup Hall of Fame, Bristol 042424
Herrett Center for Arts and Science, Twin Falls 048673
Herrgård & Torp, Stockholm 081961
Herriz, Venezia 076944
Herrle, Christine, Erding 102635
Herrlein, Andreas, Frankfurt am Main 070750, 125650
Herrliberger-Sammlung, Museen Maur, Maur 037318
Herrmann, Hamburg 103168
Herrmann, Antonimus, Mertloch . . . 126308
Herrmann, Bärbel, Dresden 070319, 125499
Herrmann, Gunter, Berlin 125218
Herrmann, Hans, Drachselsried . . . 070301
Herrmann, Hellmuth & Sibylle, Schmiedeberg, Osterzgebirge . . . 104830
Herrmann, Peter, Berlin 101923
Herrmann, Roswitha, Dachsberg . . 102333
Herrmann, Thomas, Neumarkt, Oberpfalz 073003, 104414, 139588
Herrmann, Thomas, Wiesbaden . . . 074407
Herrmann-Schmitz, Elfriede, Niederhofen 104447
Herrnhuter Künstlergilde e.V., Herrnhut 053233
Herron Gallery, Indiana University - Purdue University Indianapolis, Indianapolis 044739
Herron & Hill, Memphis 142544
Herron School of Art, Indiana University - Purdue University Indianapolis, Indianapolis 051499
Herrup, Samuel, New York 090938
Herry, Daniel, Beaune 120919
Hers, Rotterdam 108187
Hersche, Urs, Winterthur . 082913, 130223
Herschell Carrousel Factory Museum, North Tonawanda 046538
Herscher, Paris 133622
Herschtritt, Laurent, Paris 100512
Hershey Museum, Hershey 044523
Herstein & Co.), L.A., Baltimore . . .087680, 131824
Hertel, Dieter Emil, Niederzier 073054, 126549
Hertenstein, Axel, Pforzheim 134347
Herter, Clemens, Stuttgart 073981
Hertford Antiques, Hertford 084672
Hertford Museum, Hertford 039742
Hertfordshire Fine Art and Antiques Fair, Hatfield 093932
Hertling, Edmund, Mudershausen . . 139485
Hertling, Michael, Berlin 125219
De Hertogh, C.L., Borsbeek 137412
Hertoghe, Denis, Antwerpen 057702
Hertrich, Bernard, Paris 066051
Herts and Essex Antique Centre, Sawbridgeworth 086520, 131459
Herttoniemen Museo, Helsinki 009536
Hertz, Louisville 116945
Hertz, Cornelius, Bremen . 102247, 133844
Hertzberg Circus Museum, San Antonio 047795
Hertzmann, Paul M., San Francisco 119690
Hervas, Granada 110378
Hervas, Paris 133623
Hervas Paya, Virginia, Murcia 110650
Hervas Rios, Francisco 129297
Hervé, Aline, Saint-Ouen 067800
Hervé, Hugot, Saint-Julien-les-Villas 067563
Hervé, Iseli, Lausanne 130070
Hervé, Jean François, Nancy 124470
Hervé, Jean-Luc, Geneston 062982
Hervé, Jeannine, Paris 124696
Hervé & Dr. Hans Hattinger, Jeannine, Lomener 099518
Hervé & Micheloud, Sion 130177
Hervein, Rosemary, Ramatuelle . . . 067036
Hervey Bay Historical Society Museum, Queensland Museum, Hervey Bay 001104
Hervey Bay Regional Art Gallery, Pialba 001378
Hervieu, Paul, Nice 099843
Hervieu, Paul, Saint-Paul-de-Vence 101209
Hervieux, Jean-Paul, Charmoy 062166
Hervieux, Jean-Paul, Saint-Aubin-sur-Yonne 067366
Hervieux-Motard, Rouen 067271
Hervy, Eric, Villedieu-les-Poêles . . . 068888
Hervy, Fernand, Villedieu-les-Poêles 068889
Hervy, Jacqueline, Courthezon 062525
Herwald, Susan, Cleveland 115716
Herwald, Thomas, Karlsruhe 071722
Herweg, T., Ettenheim 070665
Herweg, Ursula, Leverkusen 072241
Herwick, Egon, Berlin 069643
Herwig, Aalst 096049
Héry, Georges & Jacques, Chalon-sur-Saône 062088
Herzberg-Rebel, Corina, Ebersbach an der Fils 125564
Herzenstreu, Düsseldorf 070393
Herzer, Heinz, München . . 072735, 104230
Herzig & Co, Carl, Wien 095863
Herzliya Museum of Contemporary Art, Herzliya 022933
Herzog, Bamberg 101730
Herzog, Küssnacht am Rigi 130058
Herzog, Bernhard, Salzburg 123445
Herzog, Christiane, Saint-Ouen . . . 067801
Herzog, Enrico, Bahretal 138713
Herzog, Gabriele, Dornbirn 056964
Herzog, Georges, Büren zum Hof . . 111317
Herzog, Helena, Travemünde 074082
Herzog, J., Leichlingen 103851
Herzog, Lucette, Paris . . . 100513, 133624
Herzog, Peter, Basel 082145
Herzog Anton Ulrich-Museum, Kunstmuseum des Landes Niedersachsen, Braunschweig 016385
Herzog August Bibliothek, Wolfenbüttel 020956
Herzogschloss, Celle 016547
Herz'sche Heimatstiftung Hilgerhof, Pittenhart 019629
Heseler, München 104231
Heselmann, Kleve 134092
Heskens, Eindhoven 107999
Hesketh Hubbard Art Society, London 054402
Heskin Hall Antiques, Chorley 084003
Hespe, San Francisco 119691
Hesperus, Hannover 139234
Hess, Neuenstein, Hessen 121559
Hess, New York 132478
Hess, Dietrich, Karlsruhe 103494
Hess, Hanspeter, Hochdorf bei Plochingen 125944
Hess, Hermann, München 126395
Hess, Prof. Manfred, Innsbruck . . .057079, 095585
Hess Divo, Zürich 082979
Hessaby Museum, Teheran 022619
Hesse, Otego 123038
Hesse, Claire, Lyon 124358
Hesse, Isa, Potsdam 126648
Hessel, Alan, Moreton-in-Marsh . . . 131286
Hessel, Elisabeth, Münnerstadt . . . 104352
Hesselbach, Lauenförde 103842
Hessing, Manfred, Münster 072910
Hessische Landes- und Hochschulbibliothek, Darmstadt . 016637
Hessische Landesbibliothek Fulda, Fulda 017299
Hessischer Museumsverband e.V., Kassel 053234
Hessisches Braunkohle Bergbaumuseum, Borken, Hessen 016344
Hessisches Forst-Kulturhistorisches Museum, Biebergemünd 016227
Hessisches Forstmuseum Alte Fasanerie, Hanau 017740
Hessisches Kutschen- und Wagenmuseum, Lohfelden 018675
Hessisches Landesmuseum Darmstadt, Darmstadt 016638
Hessisches Puppenmuseum, Hanau 017741
Hest, Ljubljana 109974
Hest, Ljubljana 109975
Hest, Maribor 109990
Hester Rupert Art Museum, Graaff-Reinet 034619
Hestié Antichitá, Taranto 076748
Hesz, Jürgen, Wels 057351
Hetjens-Museum, Deutsches Keramikmuseum, Düsseldorf 016833
Hétroy, Hugues, Béhen 124096
Hettinger County Historical Society Museum, Regent 047368
Hettmer, V., Burgthann 070103
Hetzel & Klinger, Rosenheim 121589
Hetzler, Max, Berlin 101924
Hetzner, Ingeborg, Ansbach 101589
Heubeck, Nürnberg 139607
Heubeck, Herbert, Ansbach 138681
Heubel, Lothar, Düsseldorf 070394
Heubel, Lothar, Frankfurt am Main . 070751
Heubel, Lothar, Köln 071954
Heuberger, Köln 139341
Heuberger, Christian, Berlin 069644
Heuberger, Roman, Köln 139342
Heuchel, Ute, Stuttgart 126855
Heuer, T., Münster 072911, 126502
Heugas, Michèle, Pau 066706
Heuneburgmuseum, Herbertingen . 017876
Heuner, Jürgen, Neu-Anspach 126525
L'Heure Bleue, Paris 066052
L'Heure Bleue, Rouen 067272
Heureka - The Finnish Science Centre, Vantaa 010222
L'Heureux, Claude, Montréal 058964
Heurich House Museum, Washington 048910
Heurtebise, Dijon 138082
Heusbourg, Brachtenbach 128465
Heuschneider, Ronny, Potsdam . . . 126649
Heusel, Monika, Frankfurt/Oder . . . 070806
Heuser, Christa, Karlsdorf-Neuthard 071705
Heuser Art Center, Peoria 046879
Heuser & Grethe, Dr., Hamburg . . . 121427
Heuser-Mantell, Margret, Düsseldorf 102507
Heuson-Museum im Rathaus, Büdingen 016490
Heuss, Didier, Le Thillot 063709
Heussenstamm Stiftung, Frankfurt am Main 017175
Heuts, M., Köln 071955
Heuts, Dr. Rolf, Hamburg 071248
Heutz, J., Gangelt 070926
Hever Castle and Gardens, Edenbridge 039376
Hevosajoneuvomuseo Ameriikka, Vieremä 010235
Hewitt, Charles, Paddington 095028, 123283, 137037
Hewitt, Muir, Halifax 084559
Hewitt, Sue, Mosman 094891
Hexagon, København 098574, 133425
Hexagone, Aachen 101515
Hexehäusl, Schwetzingen 073778
Hexenbürgermeisterhaus, Städtisches Museum, Lemgo 018605
Hexenmuseum, Riegersburg, Steiermark 002530
Hexenmuseum, Ringelai 019849
Hexenturm, Vicosoprano 037682
Hexter, London 058884
Hey Betty, Pittsburgh 091825
Heybutzki, Gerd, Köln 139343
Heyde, Thomas F., Beeskow 125144
Heydenbluth, E., Barsinghausen . . . 069475
Heyder, Johannes, Wildenfels 074438
Heydthausen, Brigitte, Duisburg . . . 102581
Heyduck, Manfred, Düsseldorf 070395
Heye, Friedrich.W, Unterhaching . . . 134439
Heyer, François, Pfetterhouse 066817
Heykel Atölye/Galeri, İstanbul 112321
Heym-Oliver House, Russell 047573
Heyman, H., Zaltbommel 108270
Heymann, Darmstadt 070181
Heymann, Henrique, Lisboa 109328
Heymans, P.B.W., Den Haag 128630
Heyn, Johannes, Klagenfurt 137203
Heyne, Wilhelm, München 134245
Heytesbury, Farnham 084390
Heyvaert, M., Gent 058186
Heyward-Washington House, Charleston 042735
Heywood, Minneapolis 117270
Heywood, W.O., Whangarei 128983
Heywood Hill, G., London 141824
Hezlett House, Coleraine 039127
HfG-Archiv, Ulmer Museum, Ulm . . 020530
H.G. Albee Memorial Museum, Estherville 043739
HG Art Galleri, Frederiksberg 098526
HGST Antik, Göteborg 081811
H.H. Antique Mall, Toledo 093171
H.H. Maharaja Jayaji Rao Scindia Museum, Gwalior 022142
Hi-Desert Nature Museum, Yucca Valley 049370
Hi Qo, Kingston 106819
Hibberd, H., Philadelphia 142744
Hibbing Historical Museum, Hibbing 044524
Hibel Museum of Art - Jupiter, Jupiter 044892
Hibeletter, Coral Springs 136484
Hibernia-Antiques.com, Dublin 074921
Hibiscus, Modena 075914
Hick, David, Saint Helier 086449
Hick, David, Saint Lawrence 086460
Hickl, Reinhard, Salzburg 057254
Hickman, Miami 132345
Hickmet, David, London 085389
Hickories Museum, Elyria 043698
Hickory Grove Rural School Museum, Ogden 046627
Hickory Museum of Art, Hickory . . . 044526
Hicks, Purdy, London 113684
Hicks Art Center, Newtown 046481
Hicks Gallery, London 113685
Hickson, Lewis E., Gilberdyke 084456
Hicksville Gregory Museum, Hicksville 044529
Hida Minzoku Kokokan, Takayama . 027119
Hida Minzoku-mura, Takayama . . . 027120
Hida Takayama Bijutsukan, Takayama 027121
Hida Takayama Museum, Takayama 027122
Hida Takayama Shunkei Kaikan, Takayama 027123
Hidalgo, Victoria, Madrid 110546
Hidalgo County Historical Museum, Edinburg 043609
Hidalgo Pumphouse Heritage, Hidalgo 044530
Hidde Nijland Museum, Hindeloopen 029751
Hidden House, Whangarei 108659, 128984
Hidden Place, Miami 090184
Hidden Splendor, Salt Lake City . . . 119348
Hidden Splendor, Salt Lake City . . . 119349
Hidden Treasures, Los Angeles 089793
Hidden Treasures, Minneapolis 090365
Hidden Treasures, Philadelphia . . .091642, 132620
Hidden Treasures, Richmond 092084
Hidden Treasures of Tulsa, Tulsa . . 093310
Hiddenite Center, Hiddenite 044531
Hideaway, West Hollywood 093473
Hideaway Antiques, Toronto 059204
Hidell Brooks, Charlotte 115290
Hideout, Hawkes Bay 108467

Hidra, Eivissa 110347
Hidson, Pat, Milwaukee 117196
Hiebl, Hans, München 126396
Hieizan Natural History Museum, Kyoto 026720
Hiekan Taidemuseo, Tampere 010119
Hieke, Dr. Ursula, Wien . . 057443, 095864
Hien, Minh, Ho Chi Minh City 093561
Hienert, Wolfgang, Wien 123503
Hier & Ailleurs, Paris 066053
Hier Aujourd'hui Demain, Paris 066054
Hier Comme Aujourd'hui, Calais . . . 061905
Hier et Ailleurs, Montceau-les-Mines 064665
Hier et Aujourd'hui, Avallon 061118
Hier et Aujourd'hui, Rivière-Salée . . 077554
Hier et Avant Hier Antiguidades, Rio de Janeiro 058596
Hier le Der, Montier-en-Der 064691
Hier pour Demain, Paris 066055
Hierapolis Arkeoloji Müzesi, Denizli 038047
Hiermeier, Karl-Heinz, Eggenfelden 070512
Hieronymus, Dresden 102444
Hieronymus, Ludwigsburg, Württemberg 139423
Hierse, K., Neuenkirchen bei Neubrandenburg 072982
Hiersemann, Anton, Stuttgart 134413
Hietzgern, Hans Jörg, Rossatz 057229
Higashi-Hiroshima-shiritsu Bijutsukan, Higashi-Hiroshima 026503
Higashi Kiyo Gallery, West Hollywood 120386
Higashi-Murayama Municipal Museum of Provincial History, Higashi-Murayama 026504
Higashi-Osaka-shiritsu Kyodo Hakubutsukan, Higashi-Osaka . . . 026505
Higashi-yamate District Historic Preservation Center, Nagasaki . . . 026861
Higdon &Sons, Jo, Tucson 132986
Higgins, Lostwithiel 085852
Higgins, Paris 066056
Higgins, Barbara, South Yarra 056612
Higgins & Sons, Michael D., Tucson 093243
Higgins, Richard, Longnor, Shropshire 131237
Higgins, Sandra, London 113686
Higgins Armory Museum, Worcester 049306
Higgins Art Gallery, West Barnstable 049062
Higgins & Maxwell, Louisville 116946
Higgins Museum, Okoboji 046657
High Cliff General Store Museum, Sherwood 048151
High Desert Museum, Bend 042140
High Museum of Art, Atlanta 041862
High Noon, Los Angeles 089794
High on Art, Armadale, Victoria 094166
High Plains Heritage Center, Great Falls 044300
High Plains Museum, Goodland . . . 044246
High Plains Museum, McCook 045543
High Point Museum, High Point . . . 044534
High Prairie and District Museum, High Prairie 005614
High School Arts of Athen, Athens School of Fine Arts, Athinai 050272
High Street Antiques, Alcester 083257
High Street Book Shop, Hastings . . 141644
High Street Books, Honiton 141675
High Style Deco, New York 090939
High Touch, Manama 096010
High Wire Gallery, Philadelphia 046948
High Wire Gallery, Philadelphia 118777
Highbrow, Winnipeg 137741
Highfields Fine Art, Highfields 094635
Highgate Antiques, Highgate, South Australia 055982
Highgate Fine Art, London 113687
Highland Antiques, Cleveland 088336
Highland Folk Museum, Kingussie . 039896
Highland Folk Museum, Newtonmore 040580
Highland House Museum, Hillsboro 044545
Highland Landscapes, Gairloch . . . 113085
Highland Maple Museum, Monterey 045989
Highland Museum of Childhood, Strathpeffer 041146
Highland Park Antiques, Dallas 088531
Highland Park Gallery, Dallas 115892
Highland Park Historical Museum, Highland Park 044539
Highland Pioneers Museum, Baddeck 005052
Highland Trading Company, Edmonton 058831
Highland Village Living History Museum, Iona 005645
Highlanders of Strathalbyn, Strathalbyn 056636
Highlands, Fort Washington 043994
Highlands Bid & Buy Centre, Mittagong 120612
Highlands Museum and Discovery Center, Ashland 041801
Highlands Museum of the Arts, Sebring 048099
Highlands Vault, Birmingham 087759
Highsmith, David, San Francisco . . 142952
Hightower, Fred, Philadelphia 132621
Highway 65 Antique Mall, Minneapolis 090366, 122969
Highway Antique Mall, Miami 090185
Highway Antiques, Coffs Harbour . . 055702
Highway Galleria, Williams 095397
Highway Gallery, Mount Waverley . . 094916
The Highway Gallery, Upton-upon-Severn 086990
Highway Gallery, Upton-upon-Severn Worcester 114631
Highwic, Auckland 030439
Higuiner, Bruno, Châteauneuf-la-Forêt 062206
Hiihtomuseo, Lahden Kaupunginmuseo, Lahti 009781
Hiiumaa Muuseum, Kärdla 009368
Hijman, D.J., Utrecht 128855
Hikmet, Pinar, İstanbul 083139
Hiko-Antik, Salzburg 057255
Hiko-Antik, Seewalchen am Attersee 057314
Hikobae, Kobe 106879
Hikone Castle Collection, Hikone . . 026509
Al-Hilal, Manama 096011
Hilary, Vincent, Igoville 063202
Hilbe, Innsbruck 057080
Hilbert, Ferdinand, Mettenheim . . . 072532
Hilbert, Franz & Ute, Aachen 069088
Hilbrandt, Katja, Haiger 139158
Hildan & Huldan, Helsinki 060530
Hildebrand, Kashya, New York 118011
Hildebrandt, München 072736
Hildebrandt, Harald, Neuss 139589
Hildebrandt, Petra, Hamburg 139186
Hildebrandt, Sigrun, Berlin 125220
Hildene, Manchester 045623
Hildener Auktionshaus und Kunstgalerie, Hilden 071516, 121455
Hildt, Chicago 115450
Hiles, Kansas City 132210
Hilgemann, Kai, Berlin 101925
Hilgenberg, U., Knüllwald 071886
Hilger, Ernst, Paris 100514
Hilger, Ernst, Wien 095865, 133208
Hilja, Maria, Helsinki 060531
Hilker, Rolf, Werther 074350
Hill, Gdańsk 079582, 140719
Hill, Oklahoma City 132579
Hill, Alan, Sheffield 142060
Hill, David, Kirkby Stephen 084874
Hill, Davis, Omaha 132591
Hill, Erin, Mosman 094892
Hill, Eva-Maria, Remseck 104716
Hill, Eva-Maria, Stuttgart 104989
Hill, J., San Francisco 092810
Hill, Jonathan A., New York 142663
Hill, Laurel, Rokeby 056547
Hill, Marsh, Milwaukee 090303
Hill, Michael, Auckland 078948
Hill, Michael, Queenstown 079224
Hill, Michael, Wellington 079325
Hill, Michael, Whangarei 079363
Hill, Mike, Hamilton 058853, 120803
Hill, Petra & Uwe, Merxheim 104065
Hill, T.S., Dorking 141558
Hill Aerospace Museum, Hill Air Force Base 044540
Hill Country Museum, Kerrville 044975
Hill Cumorah Visitors Center and Historic Sites, Palmyra 046800
Hill Farm Antiques, Leckhampstead 084921, 130867
The Hill Gallery, Tetbury 114563
Hill-Hold Museum, Montgomery . . . 045998
Hill House, Helensburgh 039716
The Hill House, Portsmouth Historical Association, Portsmouth 047198
Hill-Kaspar, Mirjam, Bad Homburg v.d.Höhe 069291
Hill of Tarvit Mansion House, Cupar 039197
Hill Rise Antiques, Richmond, Surrey 086354
Hill-Smith, Sam, Adelaide 094117
Hill-Stead Museum, Farmington . . . 043817
Hill Top, Sawrey 040963
Hill Tribes Museum, Bangkok 037878
Hill & Wang, New York 135434
Hillandale News, Cupar 136226
Hillary House and Koffler Museum of Medicine, Aurora 005042
Hillcrest Gallery, Hampton 094616
Hillcrest Museum, Souris 006493
Hillcroft Furniture, Houston 089101, 132124
Hille, Henning, Bad Bevensen 069266, 121301, 125086
Hillebrand, Wolfgang & Renate, Gauting 070940
Hillegersberg, Rotterdam 078721
Hillel Jewish Student Center Gallery, Cincinnati 042926
Hilleman, Johan Th., Arnhem 078051
Hiller, Erlenbach (Zürich) 111398
Hiller, Joachim, Rottenburg am Neckar 126746
Hiller-König, Werner, Trier 126913
Hillerød Antikvariat, Hillerød 137875
Hillert, G., Sinzheim 126806
Hilleshuis Museum, Rotterdam 030080
Hillforest House Museum, Aurora . . 041915
Hilliard, Kansas City 116572
The Hilliard Society of Miniaturists, Wells 054403
Hilligoss, Chicago 115451
Hillje, S., Oldenburg, Oldenburg . . . 073203
Hillman, New York 090940
Hillmer, L., Nienhagen bei Celle . . . 126551
Hills, J.K., Portland 091950
Hills Antiques, Macclesfield 085891
Hills Native Art, Vancouver 097485
Hills Studio, Kalamunda 094670
Hillsboro Area Historical Society Museum, Hillsboro 044548
Hillsboro Fine Art, Dublin 105870
Hillsboro Museum, Hillsboro 044542
Hillsborough Railway Museum, Hillsborough 005616
Hilltop, Hamilton 058854
Hilltop, Stefani, Fish Creek 094526
Hillview Artspace, Wedmore 114656
Hillview Museum, Bagenalstown . . 022681
Hillwood Art Museum, Long Island University, Brookville 042476
Hillwood Museum, Hillwood Museum Foundation, Washington 048911
Hilmarton Manor Press, Calne 135128, 141466
Hilprecht-Sammlung Vorderasiatischer Altertümer der Friedrich-Schiller-Universität Jena, Jena 018108
Hilscher, München 134246
Hilsenbeck, Pia Maria, Baunatal . . . 125140
Hilt, Basel 111192
Hilt, Basel 111193
Hilton, Roch 114321
Hilton, P.J., London 141825
Hilton Hordern, Cremorne 094440
Hiltunen, Seppo, Helsinki 137941
Himachal State Museum, Shimla . . 022336
Himalaija, Freiburg im Breisgau . . . 070841
Himalayan Vision II, New York 090941
Himangan Kotiseutumuseo, Himanka 009591
Himeji City Museum of Art, Himeji . 026511
Himezaki Lighthouse Museum, Ryotsu 027002
Himiko Oriental Gallery, Stockholm 081962
Himilayan Vision IV, New York 090942
Himley Hall, Himley 039753
Himmel, Frank, Baden-Baden 069415
Himmel och Hav, Norrköping 036501
Himmelein, Karlheinz, Frankfurt am Main 125651
Himmelreich, Beat, Bern . 082212, 129959
Himmighoffen, Frankfurt am Main . 102788
Himovitz, Michael, Sacramento . . . 119151
Hin, Ngaar, Hong Kong 097795
Hince, Kenneth, Prahran . 120628, 137059
Hinchingbrooke House, Huntingdon 039786
Hinchman House, Maria Mitchell Association, Nantucket 046124
Hinckley and District Museum, Hinckley 039754
Hinckley Fire Museum, Hinckley . . . 044554
Hinckley Foundation Museum, Ithaca 044792
Hincz Gyula Állandó Gyűjtemény, Vác 021912
Hind, Paddington, Queensland 056431
Hinderickx & Winderickx, Utrecht . . 140548
Hindevik, Jan, Orrefors 122223
Hindi Sangrahalaya, Allahabad 022004
Hindin, A. & B., New York 090943
Hindley, Marilyn, Townsville 056730
Hindley Museum, Hindley 039755
Hindsight Books, London 141826
Hindsight Books, Waikato 140664
Hines, Judy, Holt, Norfolk . 113259, 130798
Hingerl & Walhöfer, Bernhardswald 069802
Hingley, Richmond 132717
Hings, Toronto 059205
Hingstons, Wilton, Salisbury 087158
Hinkel, Flonheim 070712
Hinkel, Ludwig, Pirmasens 104609
Hinkes, Gerda, Nürnberg 126563
Hinna Antik, Hinna 079391
Hinna Antik, Hinna 079392
Hinner, Klaus, Pfalzfeld 073313
Hinrichs, Klaus, Trier 105062
Hinrichsmeyer, Johannes, Berlin . . 125221
Hinsdale Historical Society Museum, Hinsdale 044557
Hinstorff, Rostock 134373
Hinterglasmuseum, Sandl 002571
Hinterland Art Centre, Landsborough 094724
Hinterlandmuseum Schloss Biedenkopf, Biedenkopf 016231
Hintermayer, Wien 057444, 137324
Hintermayer, Kurt, Salzburg 137243
Hinterreiter, Manfred, Schwertberg . 057309
Hinterschweiger, Friedrich, Murau . 137235
Hintersdorf, Hannelore, Berlin 101926
Hintgen, Joël, Mamer 077484
Hintz, H.-Dieter, Edesheim 070505
Hinz, Jutta, Fredersdorf bei Berlin . 125667
Hiper Ocasion, Palma de Mallorca . 081485
Hipfl, Eva, Zell am See 137389
Hipp, Ed, Dallas 088532
Hipp-Halle, Gmunden 001910
Hippler, Angela, Braunschweig 069984
Hippler, Lothar, Wolfenbüttel 074472
L'Hippocampe, Aigues-Mortes 098774
Hippologické Muzeum, Slatiňany . . 008687
Hirabayashi, New Orleans 132416
Hirado Castle Donjon, Hirado 026514
Hirado Kanko Shiryôkan, Hirado . . . 026515
Hiraide Archaeological Museum, Shiojiri 027073
Hiraizumi Museum, Hiraizumi 026519

Hirakata Gotenyama Art Center, Hirakata 026521
Hiram Blauvelt Art Museum, Oradell 046701
Hiram Smith Octagon House, Neenah 046172
Hirano-go Folk Museum, Hirano Hakabutsukan, Osaka 026962
Hirano Hakabutsukan, Osaka 026963
Hirano Image Library, Hirano Hakabutsukan, Osaka 026964
Hirano Soundscape Museum, Yamato-koriyama 027325
Hirata Kinenkan, Takayama 027124
Hiratsuka Bijutsukan, Hiratsuka . . . 026523
Hiratsuka-shi Hakubutsukan, Hiratsuka 026524
Hiraya Gallery, Manila 108844
Hirbà, Milano 075737, 106248
Hird, Kalgoorlie 094675
Hiret & Nugues, Laval (Mayenne) . . 121029
Hirlam, Gérard, Nice 138253
Hirmer, München 134247
Hirnickel, Elisabeth, Bad Kissingen . 101663
Hiron, Sankt-Peterburg 109630
Hirosaki-shiritsu Hakubutsukan, Hirosaki 026525
Hiroshima Art Club, Hiroshima 053779
Hiroshima Bijutsu, Hiroshima 077057
Hiroshima Bijutsukan, Hiroshima . . 026528
Hiroshima Castle, Hiroshima 026529
Hiroshima Children's Museum, Hiroshima 026530
Hiroshima City Museum of Traditional Provincial Industry, Hiroshima . . . 026531
Hiroshima Heiwa Kinen Shiryokan, Hiroshima 026532
Hiroshima-kenritsu Bijutsukan, Hiroshima 026533
Hiroshima-shi Gendai Bijutsukan, Hiroshima 026534
Hirota, Tatsuo, Tokyo 107053
Hirsch, Miami 117088
Hirsch, New York 090944
Hirsch, Catherine, Paris 066057
Hirsch Nachf., Gerhard, München . .072737, 121531
Hirsch, H., Bedburg 069507
Hirsch & Söhne, Heinz, Bergheim, Erft 069536
Hirsch, Serge, Lyons-la-Forêt 064197, 099621
Hirsch, Siegfried-H., Bamberg 138714
Hirsch, W., Richmond 092085
Hirschbacher Bauernmöbelmuseum, Hirschbach 002045
Hirschberger Heimatstuben, Alfeld, Leine 015476
Hirschfeld, R., Saint Louis 142857
Hirschheydt, Harro von, Wedemark 139827
Hirschi, Peter B., Oberhofen am Thunersee 082710, 141287
Hirschl & Adler, New York 118012
Hirschl Contemporary Art, London . 113688
Den Hirschsprungske Samling, København 008968
Hirschwirtscheuer-Museum für die Künstlerfamilie Sommer, Künzelsau 018431
Hirsel Homestead Museum, Coldstream 039126
Hirsh, London 085390
Hirshhorn Museum and Sculpture Garden, Smithsonian Institution, Washington 048912
Hirsmäen Museoalue, Valkeala . . . 010216
Hirst, London 085391
Hirt, Burg, Spreewald 070095
Hirt, Patrice, La Neuveville 082699
Hirt, Robert & Margrit, Richterswil .111831, 141290
His Galleri, His 108693
His & Hers Collectibles, Houston . . 089102
His Place Too, San Antonio 092519
Hischier, V., Meggen 130116
Hiscock House, Trinity 006653
Hispa-Bel, Bruxelles 057985
Hispanic American Arts, New York . 136485
Hispanic Society of America, New York 046346
Hispanic Society of America, New York 054788
Hispantics, Antwerpen 057703
Histoire Ancienne, Bruxelles 057986
Histoire d'A, Bruxelles 057987
Histoire de l'Art, Paris 135712
Histoire d'un Siècle, Vitré 069010
HistoRail Limousin du Chemin de Fer, Saint-Léonard-de-Noblat 014389
Historia Auktionshaus, Ganderkesee 121415
Historia Hamburg, Hamburg 071249
Historia Verlag, Basel 134983
Historia Verlag, Freiburg im Breisgau 070842, 133959
Historia Verlag, Wolfurt 133245
Historial de la Grande Guerre, Péronne 013779
Historial/Musée de Cire, La Chaise-Dieu 012216
Historiallinen Museo ja Näyttelyhalli, Kokkola 009722
Historic Alexandria Antiques Show, Alexandria 093987
Historic Allaire Village, Allaire 041654
Historic and Ethnic Instrument Collection, Nedlands 001320
Historic Annapolis Antiques Show, Annapolis 093988
Historic Annapolis Foundation, Annapolis 041743
Historic Atlas Coal Mine, East Coulee 005381
Historic Babcock Mill, Odessa 006062
Historic Bath State Historic Site, Bath 042040
Historic Bethany, Bethany 042176
Historic Bethlehem, Bethlehem . . . 042182
Historic Bowens Mills and Pioneer Park, Middleville 045846
Historic Brattonsville, McConnells . 045542
Historic Burlington County Prison Museum, Mount Holly 046059
Historic Camden Revolutionary War Site, Camden 042582
Historic Carson House, Marion 045683
Historic Centennial Village, Greeley 044302
Historic Charleston Foundation, Charleston 042736
Historic Charlton Park Village and Museum, Hastings 044474
Historic Cherry Hill, Albany 041598
Historic Columbia Foundation, Columbia 043081
Historic Columbus Foundation, Columbus 043094
Historic Crab Orchard Museum and Pioneer Park, Tazewell 048511
Historic Cragfont, Castalian Springs 042651
Historic Daniel Boone Home and Boonesfield Village, Lindenwood University, Defiance 043371
Historic Deerfield, Deerfield 043368
Historic District Antique Mall, Phoenix 091743
Historic Dockyard Chatham, Chatham 039038
Historic Edenton State Historic Site, Edenton 043602
Historic Fallsington, Fallsington . . . 043808
Historic Ferryland Museum, Ferryland 005445
Historic Fort Snelling, Saint Paul . . 047699
Historic Fort Steilacoom, Tacoma . . 048465
Historic Fort Stockton, Fort Stockton 043984
Historic Fort York, Toronto 006602
Historic Gardner's Basin, Atlantic City 041881
Historic General Dodge House, Council Bluffs 043191
Historic Georgetown, Georgetown . 044170
Historic Governors' Mansion, Cheyenne 042815
Historic Halifax, Halifax 044392
Historic Hat Creek Ranch, Cache Creek 005175
Historic Heights Antiques, Houston . 089103
Historic Hermann Museum, Hermann 044521
Historic Hope Foundation, Windsor . 049237
Historic House of Fine Art, Yandina . 095444
Historic Houses of Odessa, Delaware, Odessa 046623
Historic Hudson Valley, Tarrytown . . 048504
The Historic Indian Agency House, Portage 047149
Historic Jefferson College, Washington 048966
Historic Kenmore, Fredericksburg . 044058
Historic Landmarks Foundation of Indiana, Indianapolis 044740
Historic Langhorne Museum, Langhorne 045156
Historic Latta Plantation, Huntersville 044671
Historic Liberty Jail Visitors Center, Liberty 045286
Historic Lincoln, Lincoln 045315
Historic London Town, Edgewater . . 043606
Historic Lyme Village, Bellevue 042112
Historic Madison House, Madison . . 045578
Historic Mann House, Concord 043122
Historic Marine, Bruxelles 057988
Historic Markerville Creamery, Markerville 005835
Historic Michie Tavern, Charlottesville 042765
Historic Mill Creek, Mackinaw City . 045556
Historic Morven, New Jersey State Museum, Princeton 047238
Historic Museum of Arkansas, Little Rock 045344
Historic New Harmony, New Harmony 046220
The Historic New Orleans Collection, New Orleans 046255
Historic Newton Home, Decatur . . . 043355
Historic Northampton, Northampton 046544
Historic Occoquan, Occoquan 046614
Historic O'Keefe Ranch, Vernon, British Colombia 006727
Historic Palmyra, Palmyra 046801
Historic Papers, Preding 057214
Historic Pensacola Village, Pensacola 046873
Historic Pithole City, Drake Well Museum, Pleasantville 047093
Historic Pittsford, Pittsford 047070
Historic Preservation Association of Bourbon County, Fort Scott 043976
Historic Renville Preservation Commission Museum, Renville 047380
Historic Resources Centre, Annan . 038512
Historic Richmond Town, Staten Island 048329
Historic Rock Ford, Lancaster 045145
Historic Rosedale, Charlotte 042757
Historic Rugby, Rugby 047566
Historic Saint Mary's City, Saint Mary's City 047690
Historic Sauder Village, Archbold . . 041762
Historic Schaefferstown, Schaefferstown 048040
Historic Scotland, Edinburgh 039396
Historic Shepherdstown Museum, Shepherdstown 048147
Historic Smithfield, Blacksburg . . . 042244
Historic Spanish Point, Osprey 046741
Historic Speedwell, Morristown . . . 046034
Historic Stagville, Bahama 041946
Historic Stewart Farmhouse, Surrey 006538
Historic W.H.C. Folsom House, Taylors Falls 048509
Historic White Pine Village, Ludington 045517
Historic Yale Museum, Yale 006887
Historica, Bremen 070024
Historica Antiquariat, Dresden 138993
Historical and Ethnographical Museum, Mary 038209
Historical and Ethnographical Museum, Turkmenabat 038211
Historical and Ethnological Museum of Cappadocia, Kavala 021321
Historical and Ethnological Museum of Patras, Patrai 021425
Historical and Ethnological Museum of the Mani, Kranae 021347
Historical and Folk Art Museum of Gavalohori, Chania 021227
Historical and Folklore Museum, Kalamata 021294
Historical and Genealogical Society of Indiana County, Indiana 044730
Historical and Natural History Museum of Natick, South Natick 048246
Historical Arms Series, Alexandria Bay 136486
Historical Center for Southeast New Mexico, Roswell 047553
Historical Collection Electronical Engineering, Technische Universiteit Delft, Faculteit ITS, Delft 029406
Historical Design Collection, New York 090945
Historical Electronics Museum, Linthicum 045329
Historical, Folk Art and Natural History Museum of Kozani, Kozani 021346
Historical Investments, Buffalo 087884
Historical Lighting and Design, New York 090946
Historical Materialism, New York . . 090947
Historical Museum, Jerusalem 022953
Historical Museum, Mahébourg . . . 028065
Historical Museum and Pioneer Village, Sundre 006536
Historical Museum at Fort Missoula, Missoula 045933
The Historical Museum at Saint Gertrude, Cottonwood 043183
Historical Museum of Anthiros, Karditsa 021308
Historical Museum of Arta, Arta . . . 021148
Historical Museum of Azogire, Azogire 021219
Historical Museum of Bay County, Bay City 042060
Historical Museum of Cecil County, Elkton 043668
Historical Museum of Crete, Iráklion 021285
Historical Museum of Frederick County, Frederick 044049
Historical Museum of Old Randolph, Randolph 047327
Historical Museum of Palm Beach County, West Palm Beach 049090
Historical Museum of Portitsa, Association The Spirit - To Pneuma, Karditsa . 021309
Historical Museum of Private Schools at the Foreign Settlement, Nagasaki . . . 026862
Historical Museum of Saint James-Assiniboia, Winnipeg 006847
Historical Museum of Southern Florida, Miami 045809
Historical Museum of Talbot County, Easton 043588
Historical Museum of the D.R. Barker Library, Fredonia 044067
Historical Museum of the National Resistance of Rentina, Agrapha, Karditsa 021310
Historical Museum of Uzbekistan M.T. Oibek, Taškent 049407
Historical Portraits, London 113689
Historical Society Museum, Hudson 044663
Historical Society Museum of Carroll County, Westminster 049116
Historical Society Museum of Ocean Grove, New Jersey, Ocean Grove 046617
Historical Society Museum of the Town of Greenwich, Greenwich 044351
Historical Society of Berks County Museum, Reading 047345
Historical Society of Bloomfield Museum, Bloomfield 042251

Historical Society of Kent County Museum, Chestertown 042809
Historical Society of Middletown and the Wallkill Precinct, Middletown 045843
Historical Society of Oak Park and River Forest, Oak Park 046584
Historical Society of Old Yarmouth Museum, Yarmouth Port 049332
Historical Society of Pennsylvania, Philadelphia 046949
Historical Society of Saint Kilda, Saint Kilda, Victoria 001447
Historical Society of Santuit and Cotuit, Cotuit 043187
Historical Village and Pioneer Museum, Willingdon 006826
Historical Woolscour Blackall, Blackall 000808
Historicana, Burlingame 142268
Historické Muzeum, Slavkov u Brna 008688
Historické Muzeum, Národní Muzeum, Praha 008612
Historické Múzeum, Slovenské Národné Múzeum, Bratislava 034323
Historicum, Sargans 037509
Historie, Emmen 078363
Historiekamer Hardenberg, Hardenberg 029669
Historiengewölbe, Rothenburg ob der Tauber 019913
Historik Ambiente, Dietfurt 070248
Historisch-Antiquarischer Verein, Heiden 054182
Historisch Documentatiecentrum voor het Nederlands Protestantisme 1800-Heden, Amsterdam 029186
Historisch Museum, Capelle aan den IJssel 029383
Van Reekum Museum; Historisch Museum Apeldoorn, Apeldoorn 029252
Historisch Museum Arnhem, Arnhem 029264
Historisch Museum de Bevelanden, Goes 029615
Historisch Museum de Scheper, Eibergen 029536
Historisch Museum De Tien Malen, Putten 030047
Historisch Museum Den Briel, Brielle 029357
Historisch Museum Deventer, Deventer 029474
Historisch Museum Ede, Ede 029521
Historisch Museum Grenadiers en Jagers, Oranje Kazerne, Arnhem 029265
Historisch Museum Haarlemmermeer, Hoofddorp 029765
Historisch Museum Hedel, Hedel . . 029685
Historisch Museum Heerenveen, Heerenveen 029692
Historisch Museum Het Kleine Veenlo, Veenendaal 030257
Historisch Museum Het Palthe Huis, Oldenzaal 029986
Historisch Museum Oald Hengel, Hengelo, Overijssel 029727
Historisch Museum Piet Dorenbosch, Boxtel 029342
Historisch Museum Rotterdam Het Schielandshuis, Rotterdam 030081
Historisch Museum 't Oude Huis, Zoetermeer 030392
Historisch Museum Ter Aar, Ter Aar 029124
Historisch Museum Tweestromenland, Beneden Leeuwen 029304
Historisch Museum Warsenhoeck, Nieuwegein 029948
Historisch Museum Wolfheze, Wolfheze 030345
Historisch Museum Zuid-Kennemerland, Haarlem 029655
Historisch Muzeum Hazerswoude, Hazerswoude Dorp 029684
Historisch Openluchtmuseum Eindhoven, Eindhoven 029540
Historisch Pijp en Tabaksmuseum, Sint-Niklaas 003756
Historisch-Technisches Informationszentrum, Peenemünde 019577
Historische Apothekenausstellung, Bremervörde 016441
Historische Arztpraxis, Burgstädt . . 016523
Historische Ausstellung Fragen an die deutsche Geschichte, Deutscher Dom, Berlin 016157
Historische Ausstellung Krupp, Essen 017066
Historische Bibliothek, Städtische Museen Quedlinburg, Quedlinburg 019685
Historische Expositie Klederdracht en Visserijmuseum, Bunschoten Spakenburg 029367
Historische Fahrzeugsammlung, Simmelsdorf 020212
Historische Fraunhofer-Glashütte, Benediktbeuern 015945
Historische Gebirgsmühle mit Bastelkunstwerken, Fischbachau . 017124
Historische Genie Verzameling, Vught 030298
Historische Gerberei, Burg bei Magdeburg 016503
Historische Gesellenherberge, Herbergsmuseum, Blankenburg, Harz 016259
Historische Hammerschmiede, Blaubeuren 016264
Historische Handwerkerstuben, Gingst 017418
Historische Höhler, Stadtmuseum Gera, Gera 017370
Historische Käsküche, Wiggensbach 020887
Historische Kuranlagen und Goethe-Theater Bad Lauchstädt, Bad Lauchstädt . 015745
Historische Lehrsammlung der Feuerwehr Köln, Köln 018315
Historische Lochgefängnisse im Alten Rathaus, Museen der Stadt Nürnberg, Nürnberg 019357
Historische Ochsentretanlage im Brunnenhausmuseum, Schillingsfürst 020022
Historische Ortssammlung, Reigoldswil 037441
Historische Räume des Stadtschlosses, Fulda 017298
Historische Sammlung Bethel, Bielefeld 016235
Historische Sammlung der Audi AG, Ingolstadt 018068
Historische Sammlung Eltville, Eltville 016953
Historische Sammlung im Zeitturm, Mellingen 037324
Historische Sammlung Schloß Hegi, Winterthur 037719
Historische Sammlungen im Gesundheitspark, Bad Gottleuba . 015707
Historische Schlosserei Pelzer, Städtische Museen Jena, Jena 018109
Historische Silbergruben - Schaubergwerk und Museum, Oberzeiring 002396
Historische Spinnerei Gartetal, Gleichen 017429
Historische Turmstuben, Städtisches Museum, Winnenden 020914
Historische Verzameling Aan- en Afvoertroepen, Stroe 030188
Historische Verzameling Cavalerie, Amersfoort 029154
Historische Verzameling Intendance, Bussum 029378
Historische Verzameling Korps Nationale Reserve, Harskamp 029676
Historische Verzameling Luchtdoelartillerie, Ede 029522
Historische Verzameling Militair Geneeskundige Dienst, Loosdrecht 029874
Historische Verzameling Regiment van Heutsz, Arnhem 029266
Historische Weberei, Braunsdorf . . 016395
Historische Wehranlage, Mühlhäuser Museen, Mühlhausen, Thüringen . 019012
Historischer Ausstellungsraum im Heizkraftwerk Moabit, Berlin 016076
Historischer Eisenhammer, Roth, Mittelfranken 019910
Historischer Handblaudruck Wagner, Bad Leonfelden 001730
Historischer Kunstbunker, Museen der Stadt Nürnberg, Nürnberg 019358
Historischer Saal der Fischerzunft, Würzburg 020998
Historischer Schieferbergbau Lehesten, Lehesten, Thüringer Wald 018544
Historischer Straßenbahnhof Leipzig-Möckern, Leipzig 018573
Historischer Verein der Pfalz e.V., Speyer 053235
Historisches Archiv der Stadt Köln, Köln 018316
Historisches Bergamt Bad Wildungen-Bergfreiheit, Bad Wildungen 015823
Historisches Binz Museum, Ostseebad Binz 019522
Historisches Erzbergwerk im Silberbergwerk Bodenmais, Bodenmais 016290
Historisches Feuerwehrmuseum Lüchow-Dannenberg, Dannenberg, Elbe . . 016630
Historisches Heimatmuseum, Östringen 019448
Historisches Kabinett Burgruine Eckartsburg, Eckartsberga 016880
Historisches Kabinett - Sammlung für Bergbaukunde, Modellsammlung, Winkler-Gedenkstätte und Karzer, TU Bergakademie Freiberg, Freiberg, Sachsen 017221
Historisches Käsereimuseum, Altusried 015525
Historisches Museum Aargau, Lenzburg 037256
Historisches Museum am Hohen Ufer, Hannover 017755
Historisches Museum am Strom - Hildegard von Bingen, Bingen am Rhein . . . 016245
Historisches Museum Arbon, Arbon 036849
Historisches Museum Aurich, Aurich 015631
Historisches Museum Bamberg, Museen der Stadt Bamberg, Bamberg 015872
Historisches Museum Basel, Basel . 036885
Historisches Museum Bayreuth, Bayreuth 015911
Historisches Museum Bern, Bern . . 036927
Historisches Museum Bielefeld, Bielefeld 016236
Historisches Museum Blumenstein, Schloß Blumenstein, Solothurn 037574
Historisches Museum Bremerhaven, Morgenstern-Museum, Bremerhaven 016430
Historisches Museum der Pfalz, Speyer 020263
Historisches Museum der Stadt Baden, Baden 036869
Historisches Museum der Stadt Wien, Wien 003017
Historisches Museum des Kantons Thurgau, Frauenfeld 037091
Historisches Museum Dresden, Staatliche Kunstsammlungen Dresden, Dresden 016811
Historisches Museum Frankfurt am Main, Frankfurt am Main 017176
Historisches Museum Hanau, Hanau 017742
Historisches Museum Heiden, Heiden 037183
Historisches Museum im Marstall, Paderborn 019550
Historisches Museum im Spital, Dinkelsbühl 016717
Historisches Museum Luzern, Luzern 037297
Historisches Museum Murten, Murten 037364
Historisches Museum Obwalden, Sarnen 037514
Historisches Museum Olten, Olten . 037399
Historisches Museum Regensburg, Museen der Stadt Regensburg, Regensburg 019752
Historisches Museum Saar, Saarbrücken 019960
Historisches Museum Sankt Gallen, Stiftung Sankt Galler Museen, Sankt Gallen 037491
Historisches Museum Schloß Bad Urach, Bad Urach 015816
Historisches Museum Schloß Gifhorn, Museen des Landkreises Gifhorn, Gifhorn 017414
Historisches Museum Uri, Altdorf, Uri 036831
Historisches Museum Verden, Domherrenhaus, Verden 020576
Historisches Museum Wiedlisbach, Wiedlisbach 037706
Historisches Portfolio, Völklingen . .074226, 139821
Historisches Rathaus, Krempe 018403
Historisches Schmucksteinbergwerk Silberschacht, Bach an der Donau 015637
Historisches Schuhmuseum, Landsberg am Lech 018478
Historisches Silberbergwerk Hella-Glücksstollen, Neubulach 019221
Historisches Silbererzbergwerk Grube Samson und Heimatmuseum, Sankt Andreasberg 019982
Historisches Stadtmuseum, Burghausen, Salzach 016514
Historisches Stadtmuseum Innsbruck, Innsbruck 002083
Historisches Straßenbahn-Depot Sankt Peter, Nürnberg 019359
Historisches Straßenbahndepot, Halle, Saale 017662
Historisches Waffenmuseum im Zeughaus, Überlingen 020515
Historisches Zentrum, Museum für Frühindustrialisierung, Wuppertal 021016
Historisk Museum, Slangerup 009110
Historisk Museum, Universitetets Kulturhistoriske Museer, Oslo . . . 031079
Historiska Museet, Lund 036441
Historiska Museet, Stockholm 036629
Historium de Sedan, Sedan 014741
History, Pittsburgh 091826
History and Legendary Museum, Kuah 027962
History and Natural History Museum, Alger 000040
History and Traditions Museum, Lackland Air Force Base 045082
History Banque, Houston 089104
History Center of the United Methodist Church, Madison 045584
History House, Armadale, Western Australia 000750
History House, Portland 001405
History Merchant, Dallas . 088533, 142369
History Museum, Ahmednagar 021995
History Museum, Rhodes University, Grahamstown 034622
History Museum for Springfield-Greene County, Springfield 048300
History Museum of Saint Paul, Saint Paul 006389
History Museum of the Taiping Heavenly Kingdom in Nanjing, Nanjing 007197
History Museum of Western Virginia, Roanoke 047467
History of Contraception Museum, Toronto 006603
History of Grudziądz, Muzeum w Grudziądzu, Grudziądz 031951
History of Medicine Collections, Durham 043545
History of Photography, Basingstoke 136227
History of Transportation, Western Development Museum, Moose Jaw 005953
History San José, San Jose 047897
History Shop, Wigan 041384
Hit, C., Kullavik 110948

Hita Salamanca, Horacio Perez, Barcelona 080867
Hitachi Kyodo Hakubutsukan, Hitachi 026540
Hitchcocks, Limpley Stoke 113392
Hitchcox, Rupert, Chalgrove 083908
Hitchin Museum and Art Gallery, Hitchin 039756
Hitit, Ankara 083110
Hittite, Toronto 097287
Hittleman, Michael, West Hollywood 120387
Hitzeroth, Dr. Wolfram, Marburg . . . 134192
Hitzler, Dr., Bochum 138884
Hitzler, Franz X., Pfaffenhofen an der Ilm 073311
The Hive, Cambridge 083847
Hiwa Museum for Natural History, Hiwa 026541
Hiwan Homestead Museum, Evergreen 043770
Hixon House, La Crosse 045056
Hiyas ng Bulakan Museum, Malolos 031705
H.J. van de Kamp Museum, Sint Oedenrode 030153
Hjedding Mejerimuseum, Ølgod . . . 009056
Hjemmevaernsmuseet, Holstebro . . 008924
Hjerl Hedes Frilandsmuseum, Vinderup 009151
Hjertholm, Bergen 108683
Hjo Auktionstjänst, Hjo 122161
HK International, Paris 066058
H.L.B. Antiques, Bournemouth 083599
Hlubuček, Ivan, Hradec Králové . . . 060020
Hlucháň, Petr & Chaloupková, Brno 059979
HM Prison Service Museum, Rugby 040866
HMAS Castlemaine - Museum Ship, Williamstown 001617
HMCS Haida, Toronto 006604
HMCS Sackville, Halifax 005574
HMS Belfast, London 040176
HMS Buffalo, Glenelg 001064
HMS Ganges Association Museum, Ipswich 039812
HMS Trincomalee, Hartlepool 039684
HMS Victory, Portsmouth 040765
HMS Warrior 1860, Portsmouth . . . 040766
Ho, Hong Kong 097796
Ho, Cheung, Hong Kong 059635
Ho, Doris, Hong Kong 097797
Ho, Ming, Hong Kong 059636
Ho-Am Art Museum, Yongin 027627
Ho Art Antiques, Singapore 080483
Ho Chi Minh City Fine Arts Museum, Ho Chi Minh City 049537
Ho Chi Minh City University of Fine Art, Ho Chi Minh City 052431
Ho Chi Minh Memorial House, Thua Thien Hue 049552
Ho Chi Minh Museum, Ha Noi 049529
Ho Chi Minh Museum, Ho Chi Minh City 049538
Ho Chi Minh Museum, Thua Thien Hue 049553
Ho Ho, Taichung 098057
Ho Phrakèo, Vientiane 027646
Ho Sam Choi, Hong Kong 059637
Hoa, Sen, Ha Noi 120468
Hoa et B Art, Sélestat 101269
Hoa Mai, Paris 100515
Hoa Sanh, Vancouver 059366
Hoam, Seoul 107247
Hoang, Hac, Ho Chi Minh City 120510
Hoang, Kim, Ho Chi Minh City 120511
Hoard Historical Museum, Fort Atkinson 043887
Hoarders, Auckland 078949
Hoare, Appley, London 085392
Hoare, Bob, Ringmer 086363
Hoare, Oliver, London 113690
Hoare, Peter, Southborough 086653
Hoban, Hindmarsh 055985
Hobart, San Francisco 119692
Hobart Antiques, Hobart 055993
Hobart Heritage Museum, Hobart . . 001105
Hobart Historical Society Museum, Hobart 044561
Hobbies Museum of Fretwork, Dereham 039230
The Hobbit Bookstore, Tanilba Bay . 137106
Hobbit Hill Antiques, Vancouver . . . 059367
Hobbs, Stuart, Horley 130803
Hobbs, Susan, Toronto 097288
Hobbs & Bishops, Hong Kong 059638
Hobbs Parker, Ashford 122392
Hobby, Gdynia 079595
Hobby Lobby, Phoenix 091744
Hobby- och Leksaksmuseum, Stockholm 036630
Die Hobbygallerie, Alfeld, Leine . . . 101556
Hobden, Michael, Battery Point . . . 055455
Hobe, von, Reinbek 104703
Hobe, John & George T., Philadelphia 091643, 132622
Hoberg, Hermann, Düsseldorf 070396
Hobi Sanat Galerisi, İstanbul 112322
Hobin & Blunt, Los Angeles 089795
Hobro Museum, Sydhimmerlands Museum, Hobro 008915
Hobson, Ursula, Philadelphia 091644
Hobsons, Wellington 079326
Hobstar, Ramona 136487
Hochburg-Museum, Emmendingen . 016965
Hoche, Tilmann, Ulm 074143
Hochgerner, Anna, Böheimkirchen . 137159
Hochgesang, Heidrun, Waldalgesheim 126957
Hochhäuser, Mainburg 057173
Hochhauser, Walter, Hofstetten-Grünau 123385
Hochheimer Kunstsammlung, Hochheim am Main 017937
Hochhuth, Walter D., Hamburg 071250, 139187
Hochleitner, C., Schorndorf, Württemberg 073724
Hochleitner, Josef F., Büsingen 121364
Hochman, Irena, New York 118013
Hochmann, Jiří, Praha 060130
Hochofen-Museum Bundschuh, Thomatal 002745
Hochofenmuseum Radwerk IV, Vordernberg 002793
Hochreuther, Max S, Zürich 112114
Hochrheinmuseum, Bad Säckingen 015780
Hochschul-und Landesbibliothek, Fulda 017299
Hochschule der Bildenden Künste Saar, Saarbrücken 050229
Hochschule der Künste Bern, Bern . 050758
Hochschule für Bildende Künste Braunschweig, Braunschweig . . . 050040
Hochschule für Bildende Künste Dresden, Dresden 050063
Hochschule für bildende Künste Hamburg, Hamburg 050113
Hochschule für Gestaltung Offenbach am Main, Offenbach am Main 050212
Hochschule für Gestaltung und Kunst, Basel 050755
Hochschule für Gestaltung und Kunst, Zürich 050778
Hochschule für Grafik und Buchkunst Leipzig, Leipzig 050167, 134151
Hochschullehrgang Museumspädagogik, Kärntner Berufsförderungsinstitut, Klagenfurt 049633
Hochstaffl, Michael, Kufstein 057137
Hochstift Meissen, Meißen 018889
Hock, B., Miami 117089
Hock, Hong, Singapore 109807
Hockaday Museum of Arts, Kalispell 044904
Hockey, Nagoya 077149
Hockey, Garry, Hamilton, Victoria . . 055943
Hockey Hall of Fame, Toronto 006605
Hockin, Keith, Stow-on-the-Wold . . 086750
Hocking Valley Museum of Theatrical History, Nelsonville 046176
Hockley, William, Petworth 086249
Hocky, Rainer, Duisburg 125561
Hodder & Stoughton, London 135226
Hodesh & Assoc., Cincinnati 122857
Hodge, Sarah, Worcester 087257
Hodgen, Judy, Benalla 055473
Hodgepodge, Austin 087579
Hodges, Bill, New York 118014
Hodges, Linda, Seattle 119934
Hodges, William G., Richmond 092086
Hodges Taylor, Charlotte 115291
Hodgeville Community Museum, Hodgeville 005620
Hodgins, Calgary 120799
Hodgkins & Co, Ian, Slad 142074
Hodgkinson, Kenthurst 094691
Hodgson, Alan, Great Shefford 084521
Hodiny & Hubeny, Praha 060131
Hodkins, Ian, Stroud 142096
Hodnet Antiques, Hodnet 084697
Hodsoll, Christopher, London 085393
Höbarth- und Madermuseum der Stadt Horn, Horn 002063
Hoëbeke, Paris 133625
Höberter, Walter, Wien 057445
Höch, Janine, Neusach 095697
Höche, Gabriele, Berlin . . 069645, 138793
Höchsmann, Sven, Neckarwestheim 072957
Höchstetter, Renate, Bamberg 069454
Höchtberger, Hans, München 139515
Höchtl, Johannes Andreas, Krems . 057125
Hoeckhuys, Breda 078096, 128606
Höckner, Walter, Salzburg 057256
Höderath, Ulla & Peter, Bergisch Gladbach 069540
Hoedt, Wolf, Frankfurt am Main . . . 070752
Höfler, Hans, Berlin 125222
Höganäs Museum och Konsthall, Höganäs 036340
Högarps Bymuseum, Vetlanda 036785
Höglinger, Barbara, Gmunden 056994
Höglinger, Wolfgang, Laakirchen . . 057139
Höh, Helmut von der, Hamburg 139188
Höhenberger, Arthur, Augsburg 069232
Höher, Dolores, Feistritz an der Drau 137163
Höhere Abteilung für Kunst und Design, Ortweinschule, Graz 049622
Höhere Bundeslehranstalt für künstlerische Gestaltung, Linz 049636
Höhere Graphische Bundes-Lehr- und Versuchsanstalt, Wien 049650
Höhlenkundemuseum Dechenhöhle, Iserlohn 018086
Höhlenmuseum, Frasdorf 017208
Höhlenmuseum, Obertraun 002392
Höhlenmuseum, Sundlauenen 037616
Höhlenmuseum Eisensteinhöhle, Bad Fischau 001714
Höhlenmuseum in der Lurgrotte, Peggau 002410
Höhlenmuseum Kubacher Kristallhöhle und Freilicht-Steinemuseum, Weilburg 020726
Höhn, Henrike, Berlin 101927
Höhn, M., Sindelfingen 073825
Höhn, Marie, Wien 057446
Höhn, Ulrich, Flonheim 125644
Höhne, Leipzig 103881, 126191
Höhne, Monika & Klaus, Cuxhaven . 102331
Hoek, Groningen 078421, 140434
't Hoekje, Den Haag 078200
Hoekstra, Jubbega 128734
Höland, Karl-Günter, Wernitzgrün . . 126998
Hölder, Doris, Ravensburg 104672
Hölderlinturm, Tübingen 020495
Höllbacher, Erentrud, Salzburg 057257
Hoelle, Christian, Bordeaux 061619
Hoelle, Christian, Villegouge 068904
Höller, Alfred N., Wuppertal 074526
Höller, Hanne, Bielefeld 069826
Höls, Düren 125520
Hölscher, Detlev, Enger 070572
Hölter, Herten 103362
Hölterhoff, Rudolf, Solingen 104918
Höltermann, Klaus, Bremen 070025
Hölty-Stube, Göttingen 139147
Hölz, Christine, Düsseldorf 102508
Hölzer, Birgit Eva-Marie, Uttenreuth 126939
Hölzl, Carl, Wien 137325
Hölzl, Cora, Düsseldorf 102509
Hölzle, Jörg, Ladenburg 126159
Hömberg, Klaus, Arnsberg 101594
Hönigl, Reit im Winkl 104708
Hönsahuset, Lilla, Lund 081853
Höpflinger, Franz, Salzburg 057258, 123446
Hoepfner, Philadelphia 132623
Höpfner, Martin, Großostheim 125766
Hoepli, Ulrico, Milano 134614
Höpner, Gudrun, Herne 125917
Hoeppe, Brigitte, Witzenhausen . . . 134463
Hoeppner, Hans & Marc, Essen . . .102687, 133917
Hörandner, Erwin, Schörfling am Attersee 137260
Hörby Museum, Hörby 036343
Hoermann, Gaby, Deidesheim 070201
Hörner, Hans-Joachim, Wiesbaden . 105266
Hörr, Hanns-Friedrich, Essen 070632
Hörrle, Oskar, Heidelberg . 071455, 121449
Hörschelmann, H.-G., Osnabrück . . 073238
Hörtenbergverlag, Telfs 133166
Hörter, Aschaffenburg 069196
Hörter, Heilbronn 103333
Hösch, Wolfgang, Wörth am Main . . 074463
Hoeschler, Harsewinkel 103304
Hoeschler, Harsewinkel 103305
Hoeve, Victoria, Sittard 108226
Hövel, Barbara von, Kall 125989
Hövelmann, Wesel 074353
Hövelmann, Michael, Bedburg-Hau 069509
Hövels, Wendelin, Dreieich 070305
Hövermann, G., Verden 074191
Hof, Wolfgang, Augsburg 121298
Hof & Hof, Groningen 108037
Hof & Huijser, Amsterdam 107733
Hof ter Lieffebrughe, Gent 058187
Hof van Edens, Zaltbommel 078857
Hof van Hessen, Huissen 029782
Hofbauer, Ken, Las Vegas 116625
Hofeditz, Trendelburg 134429
Hofener, Friedrichshafen 102884
Hofer, London 113691
Hofer, Brigitte, Freistadt, Oberösterreich 056979
Hofer, Christine, Luzern 111694
Hofer, Henri, Cortaillod 082330
Hofer, Herbert, Aschach an der Donau 123337
Hofer, Ingrid, Graz 057012
Hofer, Jürgen, Saarbrücken 073632
Hofer & Sohn, Karl, Wien 057447
Hofer, M., Oberaudorf 073138
Hofer, Dr. Tina, Wien 057448
Hoferick, Frank, Radebeul 126671
Hoff, Ahaus 101540
Hoff, Bernard, Wasselonne 069045
Hoff, Bernard, Wasselonne 069046
Hoff, Markus, Nordhausen 073079
Hoffart, Christine, Höchberg 125948
Hoffeld & Co., Jeffrey, New York . . . 118015
Hoffer, Jean-Jacques, Paris 066059
Hoffinger, Wien 095866
Hoffinger, Wieland, Wien 123504
Hoffman, Portland 119007
Hoffman, E., Columbus 142354
Hoffman, Nancy, New York 118016
Hoffman, Rhona, Chicago 115452
Hoffman, Ronald, New York 090948
Hoffmann, Bad Griesbach im Rottal 101648
Hoffmann, Bruxelles 057989
Hoffmann, Dortmund 070283
Hoffmann, Paris 100516
Hoffmann, Sondershausen 073862
Hoffmann, Weimar, Thüringen 139834
Hoffmann, A., Lienen 072248
Hoffmann, A., Rheine 104749
Hoffmann, Alfons, Bodenmais 069900
Hoffmann, Anne, Bremen 125387
Hoffmann, Claudia, Erlangen 125605

Hoffmann, F., Troisdorf 074105
Hoffmann, Franziska, Kahla, Thüringen 071680
Hoffmann, H., Berlin 069646
Hoffmann, Jan, Helmstedt 125911
Hoffmann, Jürgen, Mutterstadt 126516
Hoffmann, Karl-Josef, Attendorn . . 101608
Hoffmann, Lothar, Ahrensburg 125049
Hoffmann, M., Paderborn 104569
Hoffmann, Monika, Paderborn 104570
Hoffmann, R., Buggingen 070089
Hoffmann, Roland, Paris 066060
Hoffmann, Roland, Saint-Ouen 067802
Hoffmann, Rosa, Koblenz 071893
Hoffmann, U., Usedom 074169
Hoffmann, U. & M., Schwäbisch Gmünd 073739
Hoffmann, Ulrich, Stuttgart 104990
Hoffmann, V., Ludwigshafen am Rhein 072313
Hoffmann Galerie, Zwolle 108281
Hoffmann & Hosemann, Mainz 072391
Hoffmann-Schimpf, Bernd, Mannheim 126275
Michael Hoffmann & Elke Schötzke, Rott 073597
Hoffmann-von-Fallersleben-Museum, Museum zur Geschichte deutscher Dichtung und Demokratie im 19. Jh., Wolfsburg 020963
Hoffmans, Stockholm 081963
Hoffmeister, Braunschweig 138925
Hoffmeister, Wolfenbüttel 139863
Hoffmeister, Eva, Heidelberg 125900
Hoffmeister, Ulrike, Lüdenscheid . . 103972
Hoffmüller, Reimar, Delmenhorst . . 070214
Hoffschult, Heidelberg 139252
Hoffstead II, Negril 106828
Hofft, Joanna, Maastricht 128760
Hofgalerie, Füssen 102906
Hofgarten an der Residenz, München 019062
Hofinger, Andreas, Steinerkirchen an der Traun 123472
Hofinge's Rahmenmuseum, Innsbruck 002084
Hofjagd- und Rüstkammer des Kunsthistorischen Museums, Wien 002912
Hofje Van Gratie, Delft 029407
Hofladen-Antiquariat, Düsseldorf . . 139012
Hofland, Rogier, Amsterdam 128541
Hofmann, Bad Pyrmont 101686
Hofmann, Itzgrund 071648
Hofmann, Luzern 082629
Hofmann, A., Pforzheim 139656
Hofmann, B., München 139516
Hofmann, Dieter, München 139517
Hofmann, Frank, Chemnitz 070133
Hofmann, Gerd, Olbernhau 073197
Hofmann, Gerhard, Neustadt an der Weinstraße 104431
Hofmann, Gunther, Glashütten, Taunus 071005
Hofmann, Harry, Zürich 082980
Hofmann, Jürgen, Heidelberg 071456
Hofmann, P., Oberursel 073165
Hofmann, Rupert, Oberkirch 073149
Hofmann, Theus Patrizia, Jona 111574
Hofmann, Ursula, Nürnberg 126564
Hofmans, J., Antwerpen 057704
Hofmark Antik, Bernhardswald 069803
Hofmarkmuseum, Eggenfelden . . . 016890
Hofmarkmuseum Schloß Eggersberg, Riedenburg 019829
Hofmatt Galerie, Sarnen 111886
Hofmeister, Hans & Emmi, Colmberg 070154
Hofmeister, Margot, Massing 104039
Hofmeister, Sabine, Stuttgart 126856
Hofner, Gerhard, Nürnberg 139608
Die Hofreite, Trebur 074085
Hofsäss, Theo, Freiburg im Breisgau 102866
Hofstätter, Gabriel Maria, Wien 057449
Hofstätter, Ingrid, Wien 095867
Hofstätter, Reinhold, Wien 057450
Hofstätter, Dr. Wolfgang, Wien 057451, 095868
Hofstede, Deventer 078275
Hofsteenge, C., Groningen 078422
Hofstetter, Ried im Innkreis 133130
Hofstetter, E.-J., Rastatt 073420
Hofstetter, Jean-Jacques, Fribourg . 111414
Hofstra Museum, Hempstead 044506
Hofu Tenmangu History Hall, Hofu . 026543
Hofwyl-Broadfield Plantation, Brunswick 042486
Hog Hollow Art Gallery, Saint Louis . 119212
Hog Wild Collectible Toys, Austin . . 087580
Hoga, Benjamin Alexander, San Diego 119514
Hogado, Yokohama 077337
Hogan, Collingwood 094421
Hogarte Deco, Caracas 093534
Hogarth, Paddington 095029
Hogarth's House, London 040177
Hogben, Folkestone 122511
Hoge, Jürgen, Wuppertal 139885
Hogendoorn, Cees, Amsterdam . . . 107734
Hogervorst, M., Dordrecht 078303
Hogeschool voor de Kunsten, Arnhem 050554
Hogger, Hannelore, Uchte 126924
Hogia PC-Museum, Stenungsund . . 036612
Hoglund, Armadale, Victoria 094167
Hoglund, Auckland 108329
Hoglund, Sydney 095294
Hoglund Art, Nelson 108514
Hoglund Art, Nelson 108515
The Hoglund Art, Wellington 108622
Hogue Gallery Waikiki, Honolulu . . . 116214
Hoguet, Anne, Paris 066061
Hoguet, Yves, Amiens 060818
Hohberger Bienenmuseum, Hohberg 017966
Hohemer, Miami 117090
Hohenbalken, Agnes, Wien 123505
Hohenbüchler, Irene, Lienz 133111
Hohenegg, G., Sonthofen 073866
Hohenhof, Museum des Hagener Impulses, Hagen, Westfalen 017624
Hohenlohe & Kalb, Wien 095869
Hohenlohe-Museum, Neuenstein, Württemberg 019235
Hohenloher Freilandmuseum, Schwäbisch Hall 020116
Hohenloher Kunstverein e.V., Langenburg 018505, 053236
Hohenloher Urweltmuseum, Waldenburg, Württemberg 020638
Hohensee, Teja, Hameln 125855
Hohenthal & Bergen, Berlin 101928
Hohenzollerisches Landesmuseum, Hechingen 017817
Hohhaus-Museum, Lauterbach, Hessen 018535
Hohimer, Miami Beach 142562
Hohl, Helmuth, Freistadt, Oberösterreich 056980
Hohl, Marcel, Zürich 130240
Hohlbein, Monika, Salzkotten 073657
Hohls, Hermann, Mönchengladbach 072568
Hohmann, Hamburg 103169
Hohmann, Heiligenhafen 103339
Hohmann, Walsrode 105153
Hohmann, Dieter, Köln 103639
Hohmann, Jürgen, Pulheim 126665
Hoiles-Davis Museum, Greenville . . 044342
Højer Mølle- og Marskmuseum, Højer 008919
Højriis, Susanne, København 098575
HOK Fine Art, Blackrock 121656
Hokamp, Friedrich W., Schlangen . . 134382
Hokkaido Bungakukan, Sapporo . . . 027026
Hokkaido Daigaku Nogakubu Hakubutsukan, Sapporo 027027
Hokkaido Kaitaku Kinenkan, Sapporo 027028
Hokkaido Museum of Literature, Sapporo 027029
Hokkaido Sogo Bijutsu Senmon Gakko, Sapporo 050473
Hokkaidoritsu Asahikawa Bijutsukan, Asahikawa 026422
Hokkaidoritsu Hakodate Bijutsukan, Hakodate 026489
Hokkaidoritsu Kindai Bijutsukan, Sapporo 027030
Hokkaidoritsu Migishi Kotaro Bijutsukan, Sapporo 027031
Hokkaidoritsu Obihiro Bijutsukan, Obihiro 026927
Hokken, Gouda 078385
Hokodate Museum of Art, Hokodate 026545
Hokuetsu Bijutsukan, Nakajo 026889
Hokumouken Kita-mi Bunka, Kita-mi 026656
Hol Bygdemuseum, Hol i Hallingdal 030896
Holasek, Bernd F., Graz 057013
Holasek, Erich, Graz 057014
Holbein, Rijssen 121800
Holburne Museum of Art, Bath 038624
Holden, Ernest, Baltimore 131825
Holden, Hélène, Montréal 058965
Holden, Robert, Craven Arms 112918
Holden, Robert, London 113692
Holden Gallery, Manchester 040401
Holden Historical Society Museum, Holden 005621
Holden Wood Antiques Centre, Haslingden 084613
Holdenhurst Books, Bournemouth . 141425
Holder, H., Bad Krozingen 138697
Holder, H., Schallstadt 139711
Holderried, Bernd, Pfaffenhofen an der Ilm 126623
Holdhus Skulemuseum, Eikelandsosen 030820
Holding, Carole, Saint George's . . . 096437
Holdredge, Long Beach 116672
Holé, Janine, Miribel 064569
Hole, Mark, New York 118017
The Hole-in-the-Wall, Armagh 083308
Holgado de Latorre, Ricardo, Córdoba 129483
Holiday Antique Gift Show, Miami Beach 093989
Holiday Treasures, Birmingham . . . 087760
Holistico, Irene, Caracas 093535
Holladay Art and Antique, Salt Lake City 092433
Die Holländer, Berlin 125223
Holländer-Windmühle, Stove bei Wismar 020329
Holland, Ch., Nohfelden 073065
Holland, Herbert, Wilhelmsburg an der Traisen 057600
Holland, Herbert, Wilhelmsburg an der Traisen 057601
Holland, Lothar, Essen . . . 070633, 121399
Holland, S., Portland 142801
Holland Area Arts Council, Holland . 044574
Holland Art Fair-Den Haag, Den Haag 093827
Holland Art Fair-Utrecht, Utrecht . . . 093828
Holland Art Gallery, Amsterdam . . . 107735
Holland Art Gallery, Den Haag 107926
Holland Art Gallery, Eindhoven 108000
Holland Art Gallery, Rotterdam 108188
Holland Art Group, Eindhoven 053890
Holland Experience, Amsterdam . . . 029187
Holland-Hibbert, Hazlitt, London . . . 113693
Holland Historical Society Museum, Holland 044577
Holland & Holland, London 085394, 141827
Holland House, Louisville 089999
Holland-Imparch Art Publishing, Nijmegen 134825
Holland Land Office Museum, Batavia 042038
Holland & More, Osnabrück 073239
Holland Museum, Holland 044575
Holland Toys, Amsterdam 077868
Hollander, E., Dorking . . . 084194, 130647
Hollander York Gallery, Toronto 097289
Hollands & Assoc., Baltimore 087681
Het Hollands Kaasmuseum, Alkmaar 029131
De Hollandsche Schouwburg, Amsterdam 029188
Hollandsworth, Martin, Saint Louis . 092253
Hollar, Praha 098464
Hollard, Olivier, Damville 062596
Hollenberg Pony Express Station Museum, Hanover 044424
Hollendergaten Antikvariat, Bergen 140692
Holler, Eckart, Chemnitz . . 070134, 125429
Holler Heimatmuseum, Holle 017988
Hollett & Son, R.F.G., Sedbergh . . .086532, 142053
Holleville, Jean-Pierre, Pont-Remy . 066931
Hollevout, Lille 099491
Holliday & Sons, Christchurch 079032, 128924
Holliday, G.P., Christchurch 079033, 128925
Hollingshead, Chris, Teddington . . . 142110
Hollingsworth, Norfolk . . . 091383, 132556
Hollis, Memphis 116989
Hollis, Eric, Los Angeles 116793
Hollis, Susanne, West Hollywood . . 093474
Hollming & Co., V., Helsinki 060532
Hollolan Kotiseutumuseo, Hollola . . 009592
Hollow, Peter, Coburg 123214
Holloway, Edward & Diana, Suckley 086783
Holloway, Elizabeth, Caulfield North 055652
Holloway Book Exchange, London . 141828
Hollufgård - Arkeologi og Landskab, Odense 009051
Hollville, Gérard, Daours 062599
Hollweger, Matthias, Laakirchen . . 137207
Holly Farm Antiques, Rotherham . . 086408
Hollycombe Steam Collection, Liphook 040019
Hollyhock, Kyoto 106896
Hollyhock, West Hollywood 093475
Hollyhock Antiques, Toowoomba . . 056720
Hollytrees Museum, Colchester . . . 039120
Hollywood Antique Showcase, Portland 091951
Hollywood Art Center School, Hollywood 051470
Hollywood Book City, Los Angeles . 142509
Hollywood Bowl Museum, Los Angeles 045427
Hollywood Ceramic Restoration, Portland 132695
Hollywood Classics, Saint Louis . . . 092254
Hollywood Coins, Nashville 090458
Hollywood Dream Factory, Toledo . . 093172
Hollywood Galleries, Hong Kong . . . 059639
Hollywood Guinness World of Records Museum, Los Angeles 045428
Hollywood Heritage Museum, Los Angeles 045429
Hollywood Movie Posters, Los Angeles 116794
Hollywood Poster Company, Los Angeles 116795
Hollywood Poster Exchange, West Hollywood 120388
Hollywood Posters, Denver 116013
Hollywood Square Antiques, Milwaukee 090304
Hollywood Wax Museum, Los Angeles 045430
Hollywoodland, Los Angeles 089796
Holmasto, Helsinki 060533
Holmberg, I., New York 118018
Holmbom, Stockholm 081964
Holme, Peter, Mannheim 134188
Holmes, London 085395, 131062
Holmes, San Jose 119852
Holmes, Andy, Nottingham 141972
Holmes, D., London 085396, 131063
Holmes, David J., Collingswood . . . 142347
Holmes à Court Gallery, East Perth . 001003
Holmes County Historical Society Museum, Millersburg 045872
Holmes-Samsel, San Francisco . . . 092811

Holmestova, Frekhaug 030849
Holmestrand Museum, Holmestrand 030897
Holmgrens Volkswagenmuseum, Pålsboda 036538
Holmöns Båtmuseum, Holmön 036345
Holmsbu Billedgalleri, Holmsbu . . . 030899
Holmsky, Marie de, Paris . 066062, 100517
Holmwood Antiques, Dorking 084195
Holocaust Documentation and Education Center, Miami 045810
Holocaust Memorial Center of Central Florida, Maitland 045600
Holocaust Museum Houston, Houston 044641
Hologrammen 3-D, Amsterdam . . . 107736
Hølonda Skimuseum of Bygdasamling, Gåsbakken 030853
Holowood - Holographiemuseum Bamberg, Bamberg 015873
Holroyd & Co, F.W., Fort William . . . 113074
Holroyd & Co, F.W., Glasgow 113118
Holseybrook, Tampa 132952
Holst, Christian, Todtmoos 126904
Holst, Hans-Jürgen, Groß Rönnau . 071113
Holst Birthplace Museum, Cheltenham 039054
Holst-Jürgensen, Dr. Maren, Oetjendorf 104526
Holstebro Auktioner, Holstebro 120863
Holstebro Kunstmuseum, Holstebro 008925
Holstebro Museum, Holstebro 008926
Holstein, Jürgen, Rothenburg ob der Tauber 126744
Holstentor-Museum, Museen für Kunst und Kulturgeschichte der Hansestadt Lübeck, Lübeck 018720
Holsworthy Museum, Holsworthy . . 039763
Holt, Harris, Charlotte 115292
Holt, John, Houston 089105
Holt & Co., R., London 085397
Holt Antique Centre, Holt, Norfolk . . 084705
Holt Skolemuseum, Tvedestrand . . 031295
Holter, Eberhard, Nürnberg 126565
Holter Museum of Art, Helena 044502
Holtmann, Heinz, Köln . . . 103640, 134112
Holtmann, Heinz, Schüller 104848
Holtreman, João Lopes, Algés 140809
Holtrop-Niessner, B., Bremen 125388
Holtschulte, Recklinghausen 104683
Holtschulte-Urginus, Ingrid, Herten . 103363
Holtz, Albert, Thonon-les-Bains . . . 121265
Holtzman, Karen, Washington 120310
The Holtzman Art Gallery, Towson . 048595
Holub, Reinhard, Lüdenscheid 103973
Holunder Hof, Kelkheim . . 071781, 126025
Holy Defense Museum, Kerman . . . 022567
Holyhead Maritime Museum, Holyhead 039765
Holyland Arts Museum, Bethlehem . 031409
Holyland Exhibition, Los Angeles . . 045431
Holyland Tapestries, Miami 090186
Holyrood Architectural Salvage, Edinburgh 084297
Holyrood Galleries, Newport, Isle of Wight 114136
Holz, Dr. Dagmar, Königswinter . . . 072038
Holz, Françoise, Arles 120905
Holz-Vonderbeck, Offenbach am Main 104529
Holzapfel, Paul, La Ferté-Macé 063371
Holzapfel, Wiliam-Philippe, Bagnoles-de-l'Orne 061168
Holzapfel, William-Philippe, La Ferté-Macé 063372
Holzemer, Shelly, Minneapolis 117271
Holzen, Urs & Pia von, Bubendorf . . 082277
Holzer, Thomas, Emmendingen . . . 070560
Holzer, Werner, Wien 057452
Holzgerätemuseum, Schlüchtern . . 020050
Holzhauer, J., Kamp-Lintfort 071692
Holzhausen, S., Glücksburg, Ostsee 071010
Holzknechtmuseum im Salzkammergut, Bad Goisern 001718
Holzknechtmuseum Ruhpolding, Ruhpolding 019952
Holzknechtmuseum Trübenbach im Naturpark Ötscher-Tormäuer, Wienerbruck 003039
Holzschnitt-Museum Klaus Herzer, Mössingen 018987
Holztechnisches Museum, Rosenheim 019884
Holztreiger, Bela, Rio de Janeiro . . . 058597
Holztriftanlage Mendlingtal, Göstling an der Ybbs 001917
Die Holzwerkstatt, Burghausen, Salzach 125415
Die Holzwerkstatt, Henstedt-Ulzburg 125915
Holzwerkstatt Potsdam, Teltow . . . 126897
Der Holzwurm, Dossenheim 070299
Holzwurm-Museum, Quedlinburg . . 019686
Homan, Cincinnati 131937
Homan, Grace, Austin 087581
Homan, Jim, Albuquerque 087398, 131743
Homburger, Hildegard, Berlin 125224
Home Again, Denver 088698
Home Again, Epping 055803
Home Again, Phoenix 091745
Home and Colonial, Berkhamsted . .083493, 141409
Home and Garden, Toronto 059206
Home Antiquariato, Roma 076508
Home Antiques, Mönchengladbach . 072569
Home Art, İstanbul 083140
Home Art, Vianen 135996
Home Etc., Portland 091952
Home Galéria, Budapest 105515
Home Hook & Ladder Antiques, New Orleans 090569
Home Objet, Paris 066063
Home of 100 Happiness, Singapore 080484
Home of Franklin D. Roosevelt, Hyde Park 044708
Home of History, Rotterdam 030082
Home of Stone, Dodge City 043476
The Home Place, Kansas City 116573
Home Sweet Home, Norderstedt . . 073074
Home Sweet Home, Providence . . . 092041
Home-Sweet-Home, Vandoeuvres . 082871
Home Sweet Home Museum, East Hampton 043568
Homebase Collectibles, Indianapolis 089303
Homenco, São Paulo 058718
Homer Watson Gallery, Kitchener . . 096931
Homer Watson House and Gallery, Kitchener 005716
Homer & Zachary, Virginia Beach . . 133011
Homerville Museum, Homer 044588
Homes, Pubs and Clubs, Coleraine .084063, 130603
Homespun Furniture, Detroit 132055
Homestead Antique Museum, Drumheller 005361
Homestead Clock Repair, Dallas . . . 132013
Homestead Manor, Oklahoma City . 091506
Homestead Museum, Biggar 005100
Homestead National Monument of America, Beatrice 042073
Homestead Park Pioneer Museum, Port Augusta 001393
Homesteader, Oakland 091421
Homestyle, Sacramento 092166
Hometown Connection, Phoenix . . . 091746
Homewood Art Gallery, Birmingham 115112
Homewood Hill Gallery, Kaikoura . . 108482
Homewood House Museum, Johns Hopkins University, Baltimore 041986
Homework, Los Angeles 116796
Homm, Marl, Westfalen 126297
Homm, Hans-Joachim, Oberursel . . 073166
Homm, Peter, Mödling 095685
Homma Museum of Art, Sakata . . . 027019
Homme Debout, Brive-la-Gaillarde . 061813
Hommes et Matières, Paris 066064
Homolka, Martina, Nürnberg 126566
Homolovi Ruins State Park, Winslow 049250
Homs, Llucia, Barcelona 110201
Homs Museum, Homs 037833
Homuth, Inge, Frankfurt am Main . . 102789
Honarhaye Moaser Tehran, Teheran 022620
Honarhaye Tazini - Rakibkhaneh, Isfahan 022562
Honda, New York 118019
Honda Collection Hall, Suzuka 027095
Honda Museum, Kanazawa 026622
Hondenmuseum, Eindhoven 029541
Hondt, Y. de, Brugge 057776
Hone & Son, A.W., Birmingham . . .083533, 130391
Honess, Lymington 114016
Honest, Jon, Salt Lake City 092434
Honey Hive Emporium, Semaphore . 056584
Honeybee Science Center, Tamagawa University, Tokyo 027174
Honeychurch, Seattle 093015
Honeychurch Antiques, Hong Kong . 059640
Honeycombe, K., Framlingham 084435
Honeywood, Hennebont 063143
Honeywood Heritage Centre, London 040178
Hong, Guangzhou 097725
Hong, Choi, Las Vegas 116626
Hong, Hac, Ho Chi Minh City 120512
Hong, Kwong Tai, Hong Kong 059641
Hong-ik University Museum, Seoul . 027560
Hong Kong Gallery Centre, Hong Kong 097798
Hong Kong Heritage Museum, Hong Kong 007116
Hong Kong Museum of Art, Hong Kong 007117
Hong Kong Museum of History, Hong Kong 007118
The Hong Kong Racing Museum, Hong Kong 007119
Hong Kong Railway Museum, Hong Kong 007120
Hong Kong Science Museum, Hong Kong 007121
Hong Kong SDX, Shanghai 097916, 137753
Hong Kong Space Museum, Hong Kong 007122
Hong Kong Visual Arts Centre, Hong Kong 007123
Hong Quang Museum, Hong-Gai . . 049546
Hongkong Craft, Singapore 080485
Hongli Art Guan, Shenzhen 097980
Honglin, Qingdao 097886
Hongmei, Shanghai 059744
Hongsan Museum, Seoul 027561
Honingen, Gouda 108026
Honiton Antique Centre, Honiton . . . 084721
Honiton Antique Toys, Honiton 084722
Honiton Clock Clinic, Honiton 084723, 130801
Honiton Fine Art, Honiton 084724
Honiton Fine Art, Honiton 113267
Honiton Fine Art, Honiton 130802
Honiton Galleries, Honiton 122545
Honiton Lace Shop, Honiton 084725
Honiton Old Bookshop, Honiton . . . 141676
Honkala, Erkki, Helsinki 060534
Honnelaitre, Claude, Paris 124697
Honolulu Academy of Arts, Honolulu 051474
Honolulu Academy of Arts. Journal, Honolulu 136488
Honolulu Academy of Arts Museum, Honolulu 044598
Honolulu Furniture Antiques, Honolulu 088956, 132089
Honolulu Furniture Antiques and Gallery, Honolulu 088957
Honolulu House Museum, Marshall 045700
Honolulu Printmakers, Honolulu . . . 054789
Honor Oak Gallery, London 113694
Honourable Silver Objects Antiquairs, Antwerpen 057705
Honsbeek, P. & J., Den Haag 078201
Honscha, Siegward, Hannover 071395
Honterus, Budapest 121638, 139916
Honts, Jacqui von, San Antonio . . . 119423
Hontza Natur Zientzien Museoa, Durango 035156
Hoo-Hoo International Forestry Museum, Gurdon 044373
Hood, San Diego 092646
Hood Museum of Art, Hanover 044426
Hood River County Historical Museum, Hood River 044614
Hoodoo, Portland 091953
Hoodoo Gallery, Tamworth 095315
Hoog, Antwerpen 135598
Hooge, G. de, Middelburg . 078639, 128774
Hooge Crater Museum, Zillebeke . . 003867
Hoogendam, W., Den Haag 107927
Hoogeveen, Bart, Ter Aar 128518
Hooghuis, Arnhem 107850
Hoogkamp, Amsterdam 140304
Hoogkamp, Amsterdam 140305
Hoogkamp, Amsterdam 140306
Hoogstede, G., Ravenstein 128808
Hoogsteder & Hoogsteder, Den Haag 078202
Hook, Jo Anne, Main Beach 094762
Hooke, Houston 089106
Hooked on Glass, Denver 088699
Hooks-Epstein, Houston 116336
Hooky's Books, Auckland 140597
Hooloways, Banbury 122397
Hoon, Bangkok 083097
Hooper, David & Karol, Leamington Spa 084912
Hoopman, Amsterdam 107737
Hoorn-Ashby, New York 118020
Hoorn's Antiquariaat, Hoorn 140464
Hooshmand, Los Angeles 089797
Hoosier Salon Gallery, Indianapolis . 044741
Hoosier Salon Patrons Association, Indianapolis 054790
Hoot Owl Attic Metaphysical, Atlanta 142205
Hooter, O.J., New Orleans 090570
Hooton Park Exhibition Centre, Ellesmere Port 039435
Hoover Historical Center, North Canton 046519
Hop Farm, Paddock Wood 040667
Hopareboden, Stockholm 081965
Hope, Indianapolis 089304
Hope, R.J., Calgary 096822
Hope and Glory, London 085398
Hope Builders, Columbus 131983
Hope Cottage, Kingscote 001157
The Hope Gallery, Hope Valley 113271
Hope Historical Society Museum, Hope 044615
Hope Lodge and Mather Mill, Fort Washington 043995
Hope Museum, Hope 005623
Hope Water Powered Saw Mill, Peterborough 006138
Hopefulmonster Editore, Torino . . . 134695
Hopetoun House, Sendai 077211
Hopetoun House, South Queensferry 041047
Hopewell Culture National Historic Park, Chillicothe 042898
Hopewell Furnace National Historic Site, Elverson 043695
Hopewell Museum, Hopewell 044617
Hopewell Museum, Paris 046816
Hopf, M., Grünkraut 071132
Hopfen Erlebnis Hof, Altmannstein . 015512
Hopfinger, Wolfgang, Hagenberg im Mühlkreis 137186
Hopi Cultural Museum, Second Mesa 048100
The Hopi Gallery, Albuquerque 114795
Hôpital Notre-Dame de la Rose, Lessines 003578
Hopke, K., Freienhagen 070868
Hopkin & Sons, H., Dublin 074922
Hopkins, Caloundra 094356
Hopkins-Custot, Thomas, Paris . . .066065, 100518
Hoplitschek, Dr. E., Köln 103641

Hopmuseum De Stadsschaal, Poperinge 003704
Hopp Ferenc Kelet-Ázsiai Müvészeti Múzeum, Iparművészeti Múzeum, Budapest 021655
Hopp-Gantner, Maria-Luise, Starnberg 073894
Hoppe, Helmut, Kassel 071754
Hoppe, R., Hoyerswerda 071584
Hoppe, Thomas, Hamburg 125822
Hoppen, Stephanie, London 085399, 113695
Hoppenot, Hubert, Lyon 138152
Hoppenstock, Detlef, Pattensen 139649
Hopper, Pegge, Honolulu 116215
Hoppmann, Andreas, Köln 126086
Hoppstädter, Willi, Mandelbachtal 072410
Hopsewee Plantation, Georgetown 044175
Hopwell, Paul, West Haddon 087087, 131666
Hopwood, Manela & Stacey, Houston 116337
Hopwood, Manela & Stacey, Houston 116338
Hora, Jiří, Náchod 137798
Horace Greeley House, Chappaqua 042714
Horace Young, Cleveland 131963
Horácka Galerie, Nové Město na Moravě 008529
Horácké Muzeum, Nové Město na Moravě 008530
Horaiji-san Shizenkagaku Hakubutsukan, Hourai 026549
Horaiya, Kobe 077076
Horan, Vivian, New York 118021
Horatio Colony House Museum, Keene 044946
Horay, Pierre, Paris 133626
Horch, Karl-Heinz, Bad Bramstedt 101631
Hordago, Saint-Jean-de-Luz 101162
Hordaland Kunstsenter, Bergen 108684
Hordamuseet, Fana 030829
Hordern, David, Aylesbury 130319
Hordern House, Potts Point 137055
Horeau Reynaud, Pierrette, Les Alleuds 063750
Horehronské Múzeum, Brezno 034341
Horhor Sanat Galerisi, İstanbul 112323
Horikawa, Kobe 106880
Horikawa, Michael D., Honolulu 088958
Horim Museum, Seoul 027562
Horisberger-Mattern, Ines, Kaiseraugst 130052
Horizon, Utrecht 121807
Horizon Antiques, Tulsa 093311
Horizon Books, Seattle 142992
Horizon Books, Seattle 142993
Horizon Books, Seattle 142994
Horizon Chimérique, Bordeaux 061620
Horizon Galleries, Broken Hill 094305
Horizon Galleries, New Orleans 117457
Horizon Gallery, Silverton 095192
Horizons Galerie, Bruxelles 096211
Horizons Unlimited Supplementary Educational Center, Salisbury 047763
Horizont, Buenos Aires 135531
Hork, Billy, Chicago 115453
Horka, Chlumec u Ústi nad Labem 098353
Horky, Jan, Fribourg 130023
Horlbeck, Nürnberg 073105
Horley Gallery, Horley 130804
L'Horloge, Touvois 068613
Horn, Düsseldorf 125534
Horn, Poznań 079689
Horn, Anita, Hildesheim 125932
Horn, Edgar, Eastbourne 122496
Horn, Jerry W., Pittsburgh 118929
Horn, Joyce, Houston 089107
Horn, Linda, New York 090949
Horn, Manfred, Hannover 103281
Horn, Penelope, Adelaide 136771
Horn, Simon, London 085400, 131064
Horn, Stefan, Wien 057453
Horn, Traudel, Nürnberg 073106
Hornby Books, Christchurch 140613
Hornby Museum, Hornby 044623
Horncastle Antiques, Motueka 079160
Hornchurch Fine Art Gallery, Hornchurch 113274
Horne, Salt Lake City 119350
Horne, Jonathan, London 085401
Horner, Magherafelt 114028
Horner, Jack, Saint Peters 056565
Horners, North Walsham 122635
Horngacher, François, Genève 082434
Hornické Muzeum OKD, Ostrava 008552
Hornické Muzeum Příbram, Příbram 008657
Hornický Skanzen důl Mayrau, Hornické Muzeum OKD Ostrava, Vinařice u Kladna 008755
Horniman Museum, London 040179
Hornington, Woburn Sands 114717
Hornsbury Mill, Chard 039033
Hornsby, London 131065
Hornsea Museum of Village Life, Hornsea 039769
Hornsey, London 122591
Hornsey, Ripon 086378, 142019
Hornsgatans Antikvariat, Stockholm 141158
Hornsteiner, Michael, Dorfen 125473
Hornung, Anton, Dresden 070320
Horny, Ferdinand, Kirchdorf an der Krems 123399
Horological Workshops, Guildford 084540
Hororata Historic Museum, Darfield 030476
Horowicz, Nathan, New York 090950
Horowitz, Seattle 093016
Horowitz, Glenn, New York 142664
Horrach Moyá, Palma de Mallorca 110690
Horry County Museum, Conway 043132
Hors du Temps, Nîmes 065179
Hors du Temps, Quimperlé 067025
Hors-Série, Bruxelles 137441
Horsch, Bob, Chicago 115454
Horschik & Schultz, Dresden 102445
The Horse and Buggy, Hamilton 140629
Horse Feathers, Indianapolis 089305
Horsefeathers Antiques, Toronto 059207
Horseman, New York 090951, 132479
Horsemanship Museum of Takekoma Shrine, Natori 026907
Horsens Kunstmuseum, Horsens 008933
Horsens Museum, Horsens 008934
Horseshoe Antiques and Gallery, Burford 083789
Horseshoe Bend National Military Park, Daviston 043315
Horseshoe Creek Country Relics, Everton 055810
Horseshoe Gallery, Kelso 113314
Horseshoe Lake Road Antiques, Christchurch 079034
Horsforth Village Museum, Leeds 039954
Horsham Arts Centre, Horsham 039772
Horsham Bookshop, Horsham 141679
Horsham Historical Museum, Horsham 001117
Horsham Museum, Horsham 039773
Horsham Regional Art Gallery, Horsham 001118
Hørsholm Egns Museum, Hørsholm 008936
Horst-Boskamp, ter, Zutphen 078874
Horst-Janssen-Museum, Oldenburg, Oldenburg 019468
Horsten, København 060339
Horster Motorrad-Museum, Gelsenkirchen 017353
Horstmann & Godfrey, Hong Kong 059642
Horswell Art Gallery, Plymouth 114259
Horswill, Helen, West Kirby 087088
Horszowski, Henryk, Wrocław 079800, 121915, 140806
Horta, Bruxelles 120730
Horta, Miguel E., Belo Horizonte 096466
Horta e Costa, Frederico, Lisboa 079946
Horta-Lambeaux Pavilion, Musées Royaux d'Art et d'Histoire, Bruxelles 003301
Horte, Max, Goslar 071063
Horten Bilmuseum, Horten 030907
Hortobágyi Pásztormúzeum, Hortobágy 021744
Horton, Richmond, Surrey 086355
Horton, D., London 085402
Horton, Joe, Nashville 117357
Horton, Robert, Hertford 084673
Horton, Tony, Dallas 115893
Horus, Cairo 098639
Horus, New York 118022
Horváth, Budapest 139917
Horvath, Gmund 071014
Horwarth, Reutlingen 104730
Horwath, Barbara, Bern 111257
Horwich, Joy, Chicago 115455
Horwicz, Nathan, New York 090952
Horyuji Daihozoden Treasure Museum, Ikoma 026556
Horyuji Kondo Hekiga Mosha Tenjikan, Aichi-kenritsu Geijutsu Daigaku, Nagakute 026840
Hosains, London 085403, 141829
Hosan, Busan 107168
Hosang & Schubiger, Allschwil 111115
Hosegood, Alan, Bristol 130456
Hosen Gakuen Tanki Daigaku, Tokyo 050484
Hosfelt, San Francisco 119693
Hoshino, Kyoto 106897
Hoskin, John, Toronto 059208
Hosking, Ballarat 055431
Hosking, Susanne, Leura 056099
Hoskins House, Burlington 042522
Hosko, Saint Paul 119296
Hosokawa, Chizuko, Paris 100519
Hosotte, Georges, Irancy 099367
Hosp, Zell am See 095982
Hosp, Dietmar, Nassereith 095692
Hosp, I. & R., Breisach am Rhein 070000
Hospes, H., Nienhagen bei Celle 073057
Hospice Arts, London 054404
Hospital de los Venerables, Sevilla 035856
Hospital de Quadros, São Paulo 123716
Hospital-Santuario de Nuestra Señora de la Caridad, Illescas 035295
Hospitals and Clinics Medical Museum, University of Iowa, Iowa City 044765
Hospitalsmuseet, Vadstena 036750
Hoss, Tulsa 093312
Hoss, Annette, Kesseling 126032
Hoss & Son, A.W., Seattle 132938
Hoss, Martino, Seattle 119935
Hoss, Marwan, Paris 100520
Hoss & Wollmann, Stuttgart 104991
Hossein, Darmstadt 070182
Hostettler, Ueli, Bern 082213, 111258
Hostis, Guy, Paimpol 065329
Hostrup, Berlin 101929
Hostrup-Pedersen & Johansen, Valby 133434
Hosyokan Byodoin Museum, Uji, Kyoto 027307
Hot Art Framed Prints, Sutton Coldfield 114530
Hot Artz Gallery, Taihape 108562
Hot House Art Gallery, Indianapolis 116464
Hot Property, Toronto 059209
Hot Shops Art Center, Omaha 118703
Hotai, Oakland 132569
Hotbath Gallery, Bath 112579
Hotei, Leiden 078568
Hotei Japanese Prints, Leiden 140478
Hôtel Arturo-Lopez, Neuilly-sur-Seine 013375
Hotel de Paris Museum, Georgetown 044171
Hôtel de Ventes des Chartrons, Bordeaux 120942
Hôtel de Ventes Flagey, Bruxelles 120731
Hôtel de Ventes Newton, Wavre 120790
Hôtel de Ventes Saint-Georges, Toulouse 121270
Hôtel des Encans, Montréal 058966, 097038, 120805
Hôtel des Ventes, Agen 120889
Hôtel des Ventes, Autun 061089, 120912
Hôtel des Ventes, Bernay 120926
Hôtel des Ventes, Chatou 120974
Hôtel des Ventes, Entzheim 120999
Hôtel des Ventes, Lyon 121052
Hôtel des Ventes, Nantes 121087
Hôtel des Ventes, Tours 121272
Hôtel des Ventes Bordeaux Rive Droite, Bordeaux 120943
Hotel des Ventes Couton et Veyrac, Nantes 121088
Hôtel des Ventes du Boischaut, Saint-Amand-Montrond 121240
Hôtel des Ventes Elysée, Liège 120769
Hôtel des Ventes Mobilières, Bayonne 120918
Hôtel des Ventes Mosan, Bruxelles 120732
Hôtel des Ventes Mosan, Liège 120770
Hôtel des Ventes Périgord, Bergerac 120925
Hôtel des Ventes Périgord, Bordeaux 120944
Hôtel des Ventes Saint-Georges, Liège 120771
Hôtel des Ventes Universelles, Saint-Romuald 120812
Hotel Drouot Antiguidades, Rio de Janeiro 058598
Hôtel Groslot, Orléans 013513
Hotel-Museum Arthur Merghelynck, Ieper 003531
Hotelli- ja Ravintolamuseo, Helsinki 009537
Hotelmuseum, Flims Waldhaus 037088
Hotmuseum, Filzmoos 001854
Hotoko Ninomiya Jinja Homotsuden, Odawara 026928
Hotspur, London 085404
Hottelmann-Schmidt, Irene, Bamberg 069455
Hotter, Markus, Innsbruck 057081
Hottowitz, A., Bad Soden am Taunus 069385
Hotz, Manfred, Lindau, Bodensee 072265
Hotz-Behofsits, Rudolf, Oberpullendorf 137238
Hou Shi, Tiang, Singapore 109808
Hou Wang Chinese Temple and Museum, Atherton 000754
Houbraken, J., Veldhoven 128865
Houck, Portland 132696
Houdebert, Jack, Evian-les-Bains 062824
Houdek, J., Praha 123983
Houdini Museum, Scranton 048064
Houf, Thomas, Köln 071956, 126087
Houg, Olivier, Lyon 099595
Hough, Stuart, Paris 066066
Houghton, Mifflin, Boston 135333
Houghton County Historical Museum Society, Lake Linden 045110
Houghton Hall Antiques, Market Weighton 085942, 131265
Houghton Hall Soldier Museum, Houghton 039775
Houis, Lionel, Paimboeuf 065326
Houk, Edwynn, New York 118023
Houldsworth, London 113696
Houle, George J., Los Angeles 089798, 142510
Houllier, Marseille 099669
Hound Dog Antiques, Vancouver 059368
Hourcadette, Pierre, Saint-Jean-de-Luz 067538
Hourian, San Francisco 092812, 132885
Hourrière, Jacques-Denis, Paris 124698
R. Hours & Hugues de Valaurie, Aix-en-Provence 120891
Housatonic Museum of Art, Bridgeport 042408
House & Son, Bournemouth 122425
House, Bernard G., Wells 087068, 131659
House, Howard, Seattle 119936
The House 1860-1925, Monmouth 086002
House Antiques, Birmingham 087761
House Gallery, London 113697
House Gallery, München 104232
House Gallery, Oklahoma City 118663
House in the Horseshoe, Sanford 047941

House Mill, London 040180
House of a Thousand Dolls, Loma . 045367
House of Africa, Chicago 115456
House of Antiquity, Nether Stowey . 141951
The House of Art, Beirut 107328
House of Art, Varna 096772
House of Art Books, New Orleans . . 142617
House of Arts and Letters, Lemesos 098314
House of Bewlay, Hamburg 071251
House of Books, Auckland 078950, 140598
House of Books, Lismore 136977
House of Bottles, Kinglake 001156
House of Bottles and Bottle Museum, Tewantin 001542
House of Castlegate, Knaresborough 113339
House of Cedar, Springwood 056625
House of Christian, Ash Vale 083323
House of Clocks, Ampthill 083296, 130301
House of Color Designs, Las Vegas . 116627
House of Desks, Paddington, New South Wales 056418
House of Dun, Montrose 040493
House of Glass, Houston 089108
House of Hadjigeorgakis Kornesios, Lefkosia 008220
The House of Harriette & John, Austin 087582
House of Heirlooms, San Diego . . . 092647
House of History, Malone 045607
House of Huanghuali, Singapore . . . 080486
The House of Ikat, Auckland 078951
House of International Dolls, Fredericton 005482
House of Lamps, Austin 087583
The House of Lords, Dublin 022748
House of Manannan, Manx National Heritage, Peel 040679
House of Memories, Latchford 005751
House of Memories Museum, Wilson 049220
House of Mirrors, London 085405
House of Music-Parma, Parma 025117
House of Noble Wood, Singapore . . 080487
House of Our Own, Philadelphia . . . 142745
House of Oz, Alice Springs 094138
House of Persian Rugs, Calgary 058791
House of Riches, Cottesloe 055719, 123217
House of Roses, Senator Wilson Home, Deadwood 043340
House of Saint Clair, Bollington . . . 083568
House of Seconds, Louisville 090000
House of Siam Ltd., Bangkok 083098
House of Silver, Pittsburgh 091827
House of Silver, Winnipeg 059464
House of Stapleton Collection, San Diego 092648
House of Steel Antiques, London . . 085406
House of the Binns, Linlithgow 040016
House of the Redtails Gallery, Tucson 048638
House of the Scribe, Almog 022886
The House of the Seven Gables, Salem 047738
House of Wickersham, Juneau 044889
House of Windsor, Mooloolaba 056246
House on Cary, Richmond 092087
House on Crutches Museum, Bishop's Castle 038747
House on the Hill Museums Adventure, Stansted Mountfitchet 041090
The House on the Rock, Spring Green 048277
The House that Moved, Exeter 084358
House Things Antiques, Hinckley . . 084686
Household Cavalry Museum, Windsor 041415
Housesteads Roman Fort and Museum, Hexham 039746
Housing Works, New York 142665
Houston, Old Noarlunga 095004
Houston, William P., Frankfurt am Main 070753
Houston Antique Dealers, Houston . 089109
Houston Antique Dealers Association, Houston 054791
Houston Art Dealers Association, Houston 054792
Houston Center for Photography, Houston 054793
Houston Fine Art Press, Houston . . 135367
Houston Fire Museum, Houston . . . 044642
Houston Glass Company, Houston . 089110
Houston Harte University Center, San Angelo 047784
Houston Museum of Decorative Arts, Chattanooga 042779
Houston Museum of Natural Science, Houston 044643
Houston Numismatic Exchange, Houston 089111
Houston Police Museum, Houston . 044644
Houston Precious Metals, Houston . 089112
Houston Women's Caucus for Art, Houston 054794, 116339
Hout Bay Gallery, Hout Bay 110044
Houthakker, Bernard, Amsterdam . . 077869
De Houtkrul, Alkmaar 128522
Houvet, Christophe, Fontaine-Simon 062894
Høvåg Museum, Høvåg 030912
Hovanec, Jozef, Spišská Nová Ves . 129283
Hovden Jernvinnemuseum, Bykle . . 030800
Hove, Herman ten, Rijssen 128812
Hove Museum and Art Gallery, Hove 039777
Hover, New York 118024
Hovercraft Museum, Gosport 039609
Hoves, Eberhard, Krefeld 103779
Hovingh & Zoon, C., Haarlem 140442
Howald's Erben, Max, Bern 082214
Howard, London 085407
Howard, Stratford-upon-Avon 086775, 131554
Howard, Taipei 098072
Howard, Austin, Miami 117091
Howard, Joe, Los Angeles 116797
Howard, John, Woodstock 087240
Howard, John, Woodstock 087241
Howard, Jonathan, Chipping Norton 083990, 130571
Howard, Patrick, Dublin 074923
Howard, Paul, Indianapolis 132156
Howard B. Owens Science Center, Lanham-Seabrook 045159
Howard & Co, Toronto 059210
Howard County Arts Council, Ellicott City 054795
Howard County Center of African American Culture, Columbia 043068
Howard County Historical Museum, Kokomo 045047
Howard County Historical Society Museum, Ellicott City 043679
Howard-Dickinson House Museum, Henderson 044512
The Howard Gallery, Dorking 084196, 130648
Howard Gardens Gallery, University of Wales Institute, Cardiff 038988
Howard House Antiques, Silvan . . . 056593
Howard House of Artifacts, Old Perlican 006068
Howard Steamboat Museum, Jeffersonville 044850
Howard University Gallery of Art, Washington 048913
Howard University Museum, Washington 048914
Howard W. Cannon Aviation Museum, Henderson 044510
Howards, Baldock 083370, 130324
Howards, Broadway 083759, 130466
Howarth Gallery, Burnley 112766
Howe, Christopher, London 085408
Howeg, Thomas, Zürich . . 112115, 135090, 141341
Howell, Charles, Oldham . 086157, 131342
Howell, Clinton, New York 090953
Howell & Assoc., Linda C., Oklahoma City 118664
Howell, Patti, Austin 087584
Howell Harris Museum, Brecon . . . 038826
Howell Historical Society & Committee Museum, Howell 044658
Howell & Howell, Woollahra 056868
Howell Living History Farm, Titusville 048560
Howeltt, Ruth, Smythesdale 056598
Howes About Antiques, Toronto . . . 059211
Howes Bookshop, Hastings 141645
Howick Contemporary Art, London . 113698
Howick Historical Village, Pakuranga 030567
Howick Museum, Howick 034636
Howisey Brothers, Seattle 132939
Howkins, Peter, Great Yarmouth . . .084529, 130749
Howland House, Plymouth 047095
Howorth, J., Leeds 084928
Howth Harbour Gallery, Howth 105894
Hoxie Gallery, Westerly Public Library, Westerly 049105
Hoxton Books, London 141830
Hoy, Renee, Singapore 080488
Hoyer, A. & O., Jettingen 071664
Hoyer, Heinz-G., Arnsberg 101595
Hoypoloi, Chicago 115457
Hoyt Antiques, Toronto 059212
Hoyt Institute of Fine Arts, New Castle 046214
Hoyt Sherman Place, Des Moines . . 043425
Hozat Kültür Merkezi, Hozat 038076
Hozhoni, Seattle 119937
HP Antiquités, Paris 066067
HP Antiquités, Saint-Ouen 067803
HR Antiquités, Bellac 061332
H.R. MacMillan Space Centre, Vancouver 006700
Hrách, Jiří, Praha 137833
Hrad Roštejn, Muzeum Vysočiny Jihlava, Telč 008707
Hradčany, Praha 060132
Hradecký, Pavel, Liberec 060043
Hrdličkovo Muzeum Člověka, Praha 008613
Hřebíček, Brno 098334
Hron, Otto, Traunreut 074074
Hrozen, České Budějovice 098342
Hruschka, Weil im Schönbuch 105179
Hruška & Hrušková, Písek 060076, 137808
Hrvatska Akademija Znanosti i Umjetnosti, Dubrovnik 049878
Hrvatska Akademija Znanosti i Umjetnosti, Zagreb 049879
Hrvatski Muzej Naivne Umjetnosti, Zagreb 007838
Hrvatski Muzej Pošte i Telekomunikacija, Zagreb 007839
Hrvatski Nacionalni Komitet ICOM, Zagreb 052818
Hrvatski Narodni Zoološki Muzej, Zagreb 007840
Hrvatski Povijesni Muzej, Zagreb . . 007841
Hrvatski Prirodoslovni Muzej, Zagreb 007842
Hrvatski Školski Muzej, Zagreb . . . 007843
Hrvatski Sportski Muzej, Zagreb . . . 007844
Hrvatsko Društvo Likovnih Umjetnika Split, Split 052819
Hrvatsko Društvo Likovnih Umjetnika Varaždin, Varaždin 052820
Hrvatsko Muzejsko Društvo, Zagreb 052821
Hrvatsko Numizmatičko Društvo, Zagreb 052822
HRW Antiques, London 085409
Hryciow, Stefan, Darmstadt 070183
HS Galerie, Heidelberg 071457
HS-Styl, Wrocław 129128
HSR Antiquitäten, Bonn 069926
Hsu, Jeff, Taipei 059796, 098073
HT, Madrid 110547
HTS-Museum, Rødovre 009073
Hu, Xuan, Wuxi 098037
Hu & Hu, Shanghai 059745
Hua Bao, Nanchang 059726
Hua Feng, Beijing 059576
Hua Jia, Hangzhou 059582
Hua Kwan, Singapore 109809
Hua Mei, Seattle 119938
Hua Ren, Beijing 097658
Hua-Ströfer, Hai-Yen, Mannheim . . 126276
Hua Yuan, Dalian 097711
Hua Zhai, Qing, Singapore 109810
Huacheng, Shenzhen 097981
Huachun, Beijing 059577
Huadu, Beijing 097659
Huahan, Beijing 097660
Huai Hong, Paris 066068
Huajing Hua, Shenyang 097962
Huallenz, B., Leibnitz 137214
Huaming, Qingdao 059727
Huan, Les Mureaux 063773
Huan Class Art Gallery, Shanghai . . 097917
Huan Shi Wen Bao, Beijing 097661
Huang, Indianapolis 089306
Huanghe Museum, Zhengzhou 007349
Huangpu Hua Yuan, Shenzhen 097982
Huangpu Painting Gallery, Shanghai 097918
Huangpu Painting Gallery, Shanghai 097919
Huangshan City Museum, Huangshan 007137
Huangshi Municipal Museum, Huangshi 007138
Huanki Cultural Centre, Alofi 030709
Huapai Collectables, Huapai 079117
Huaqiao, Shanghai 059746
Huaqiao, Shanghai 059747
Huasha, Shenzhen 097983
Huashan Literature and Fine Arts Press, Shijiazhuang 133384
Huat & Co., Aik, Singapore 080489
Huaxia Art Cooperative, Beijing . . . 097662
Huayi, Shanghai 059748
Huazhou, Manzhouli 059725
Hub City Collectables, Saskatoon . . 059099
HUB Robeson Galleries, University Park 048702
Hubbard, Ipswich 084801, 130829
Hubbard, Surrey Hills 056650
Hubbard, Andre C., Flatts 123682
Hubbard, John, Blakedown 083559, 130405
Hubbard, Rick, Romsey 086398
Hubbard Museum of the American West, Ruidoso Downs 047567
Hubbardton Battlefield Museum, Hubbardton 044660
Hubbell Trading Post, Ganado 044138
Hubbers Emporium, Invercargill . . . 079127
Hubbuch, Basel 111194
Hubeaux, Liège 058308
Hubei Fine Arts Press, Wuhan 133388
Huber, Einsiedeln 082351
Huber &Co., Frauenfeld 135013
Huber, Andres, Wabern 130209
Huber, Bruno & Susanne, Lommis . 082585
Huber, Carlo, Soulce 111925
Huber, Col. Raymond W., Montpelier 122974
Huber, Franz, Offenburg 134330
Huber, Heidi, Bern 111259
Huber, Herbert & Anne, Burghausen, Salzach 102292
Huber, Inge, München 072738
Huber, Laurent, Paris 124699
Huber, Manfred, Manching 072408, 126271
Huber, P., Norderney 073068
Huber, Dr. Robert, Köln 126088
Huber, Rudger, Mörnsheim 072580
Huber, Ursula, Olten 111800
Huber, Volker, Offenbach am Main .104530, 134326
Huber & Amacker, Aarau 134974
Huber House Gallery, New Orleans . 117458
Huber & Treff, Jena 103449
Hubers & Hawkins, Chandler 094387
Hubert, Boynes 061740
Hubert, Bremen 102248
Hubert, Montréal 058967
Hubert, New York 118025
Hubert, Worpswede 105331
Hubert, Armin, Mannheim 104024

Hubert, Christian, Chevaigne 062280
Hubert, Marie, Caen 061874, 124167
Hubert, Marie, Dreux 062741
Hubert-Kühne, Katrin, Burgdorf ... 129993
Huberte Goote Gallery, Zug 037816
Hubertine, Saint-Triphon 111861
Huberts, Afferden 128520
Hubert's Antiques, Burford 083790
Hubertus, Horst, Seligenstadt 073798
Hubley & Co., F.B., Cambridge 122835
Hubschmid & Bouret, Paris 133627
Hubschraubermuseum, Hubschrauberzentrum Bückeburg, Bückeburg 016484
Huc, Marie-Claude, Toulouse 068519
Hucher, Claude, Tocane-Saint-Apre 068425
Huchet, Patrick, Singapore 080490
La Huchette, Genève 082435
Huckleberry & Chin, Edmonton 058832
Hudcová Dita, Praha 060133
Huddersfield Art Gallery, Huddersfield 039780
Huddersfield Picture Framing Company, Huddersfield 084748, 130814
Huddleston Farmhouse Inn Museum, Cambridge City 042573
Hudební Antikvariat, Ostrava 137806
Hudel, Antoine, Bordeaux 124127
Hudetz-Turm, Wiesent 020882
Hudiksvalls Bruksminnen, Hudiksvall 036350
Hudler, Emil, Dießen am Ammersee 125463
Hudobná Expozícia - Rodný Dom J.N. Hummela, Mestské Múzeum, Bratislava 034324
Hudobné Múzeum, Slovenské Národné Múzeum, Bratislava 034325
Hudson, Jacksonville 142466
Hudson, Oakland 091422
Hudson, J.N., Deniliquin 055749
Hudson Bay Gallery, Virginia Beach 120222
Hudson Bay Museum, Hudson Bay . 005626
Hudson City Antiques, New York ... 090954
Hudson Hills Press, Manchester ... 135389
Hudson Museum, University of Maine, Orono 046726
Hudson Rare Coins, New York 090955
Hudson River Maritime Museum, Kingston 045013
Hudson River Museum of Westchester, Yonkers 049338
The Hudson Valley Antiquer, Rhinebeck 136489
Hudson Valley Art Association, Stamford 054796
Hudson Valley Children's Museum, Nanuet 046127
Hudson's Hope Museum, Hudson's Hope 005627
Hue-Williams, Michael, London ... 113699
Hübens, Theo, Maastricht 108125
Hübert, Jelena, Schwanebeck 073753
Huebmer-Gedächtnisstätte, Naßwald 002352
Hübner, Bielefeld 069827
Hübner, Frankfurt am Main 102790
Hübner, A. & C., Nieblum 073050
Hübner, C., Bad Waldsee 069391
Hübner, Christa, Aichen 069123
Hübner, Christa & Wolfgang, Königsbrunn 072033
Hübner, Heide, Würzburg 074498
Hübner, Rudolf, Wien 057454, 123506
Hück, Joachim, Andernach 069168
Hück, Klaus, Rüsselsheim 073619
Hüffelmann & Schaffrath-Hüffelmann, Aachen 101516
Hügelow, Manfred, Offenbach am Main 104531, 134327
Hühn, G., Goch 071020
Hühn, Jutta, Gevelsberg 102948
Hüll, Dr. Norbert, Köln 121473
Hülls, Dieter von der, Verden 074192
Hülser Heimatstuben, Krefeld 018398
Hülshoff, Frieder, Bochum 069885
Huelsmann, F.K.A., Hamburg 071252, 103170, 139189
Huemul, Buenos Aires 136724
Hünermann, Hete A.M., Düsseldorf . 102510
Hünersdorff, London 141831
Hüning, Bernhard, Münster 072912, 134295, 139565
Hüntelmann, Werlte 105210
Hüntelmann, Werlte 105211
Hüppi, A., Baden-Baden 069416
Hüren, Hans-Joachim, Tönisvorst .. 074067
Hürland, Raymund, München 072739
Hürlimann, Andreas, Zug 083045
Hürlimann, J. & A., Zürich 082981
Hürlimann, Thomas, Zug 112219
Huerta de Rey, La Plata 055274
Huerta de San Vicente, Casa-Museo Federico García Lorca, Granada .. 035249
Hürten, Ulrich, Büsingen 125412
Hürten-Heimatmuseum, Bad Münstereifel 015754
Huertos, Tomas Hernandez, Burgos 081015
Hüsing-Hoge, Bodo-U., Entre-os-Rios 079827
Hüsken, André, Hamburg 071253
Hüsken, Norbert, Würzburg 074499
Huesmann, Ingrid Anna, Langenburg 126167
Hüsstege, 's-Hertogenbosch 108075
Huet, Jean Pierre, Fougères (Ille-et-Vilaine) 062928
Hüter, Friedhelm, Willich 105302
Hütten- und Technikmuseum Ilsenburg, Ilsenburg 018057
Hüttenberger Heimatmuseum, Linden, Hessen 018656
Hüttenmuseum Thale, Thale 020428
Hütter, Trofaiach 137272
Hüttner, München 072740
Hufkens, Xavier, Bruxelles 096212
Hufnagel, E. & W., Lennestadt 072232
Hufschmid, Esther, Zürich 112116
Hufschmiede Museum Frehrking, Neustadt am Rübenberge 019276
Hufschmiedemuseum, Engelhartszell 001833
Hufthamartunet, Storebø 031245
Hug, Aldo, Zürich 130241
Hug, Beat, Colombier 130002
Hug, Reinhard, Rheinberg 073518
Hug & Weber, Genève 111471
Hugelmann, Christian, Muralto 111759
Hugendubel, Heinrich, Kreuzlingen . 135029
Hugendubel, Heinrich, München ... 139518
Hugenotten-Museum, Berlin 016077
Hugenotten-Museum und Heimatmuseum, Stutensee 020342
Huggele, Esslingen 102711
Hugh, Fullarton 094572
Hugh Cash Antiques, Maynooth ... 074994
Hugh Hardinge Book's, Cambridge . 141471
The Hugh Lane Municipal Gallery of Modern Art, Dublin 022749
Hugh Miller's Cottage, Cromarty ... 039180
Hughenden Manor, High Wycombe . 039748
Hughes, Saint Louis 119213
Hughes, Christopher, Worcester ... 114737
Hughes, E., Saint Louis 142858
Hughes, Gordon, Bowral 136814
Hughes, Harriet, Liverpool 130903
Hughes, John, Chippendale 123212
Hughes, Michael, London 085410
Hughes, Paul, Charlotte 115293
Hughes, Ray, Surry Hills 095253
Hughes & Son, Seth, Wrexham 122766
Hughes Day, Judith, New York 118026
Hughes Fine Arts Center, Grand Forks 044261
The Hughes Gallery, Belfast 112614
Hughlin, San Francisco 092813
Hugo, New York 090956
Hugo & Fils, Paris 100521
Hugo Thimig-Gedenkraum, Wien .. 002913
Hugo Wolf-Haus, Perchtoldsdorf .. 002415
Huguenin, Jean-Michel, Paris 100522
Huguenot Historical Society Museum, New Paltz 046268
Huguenot Memorial Museum, Franschhoek 034614
Hugues, Jean, Paris 133628
Huguet Michelle, Fleurance 062876
Huguette, Jean Luc de, Montpellier 064747
Huhehot City Museum, Huhehot ... 007139
Huhn, E., Köln 071957
Huhold, Joachim, Wien 137326
Hui, Hong Kong 097799
Hui, Yang, Singapore 080491
Hui Hua Arts, Chengdu 097699
Hui No'eau Visual Arts Center, Makawao 045603
Huichang County Museum, Huichang 007141
Huihua Group of the Xue Qin Art Cooperative, Beijing 097663
't Huijs Dever, Lisse 029871
Huis-Clos, Paris 100523
Huis de Lalaing, Oudenaarde 003693
Huis Hellemans, Edegem 003418
Huis Marseille, Stichting voor Fotografie, Amsterdam 029189
Huis met de Kogel, Haarlem 078459
Huis Singraven, Denekamp 029467
Het Huis van Alijn, Gent 003456
Huis Verwolde, Laren, Gelderland .. 029826
Huis voor Beeldende Kunst, Utrecht 108250
Huis Zypendaal, Arnhem 029267
Huisgen, Manfred, Neuss 126537
Huisman, Hetty, Amsterdam 134782
Huittisten Museo, Huittinen 009593
Huiyou, Shanghai 097920
Huize Betje Wolff, Middenbeemster 029928
Huize Keizer, Denekamp 029468
Huize Nijenstede, Hardenberg 029670
Huizenga, M.L., Amsterdam 140307
Huizer Klederdrachtmuseum, Huizen 029784
Huizer Museum Het Schoutenhuis, Huizen 029785
Hula, Honolulu 116216
Huldigungssaal und Rathaus, Goslar 017483
Huldreheimen, Bykle 030801
Huleh Valley Regional Prehistoric Museum, Kibbutz Maayan Baruch 023013
Hulihee Palace, Kailua-Kona 044894
Hull and East Riding Museum, Kingston-upon-Hull 039887
Hull Antique Centre, Kingston-upon-Hull 084860
Hull Lifesaving Museum, The Museum of Boston Harbor Heritage, Hull 044668
Hull Maritime Museum, Kingston-upon-Hull 039888
Hull University Art Collection, Kingston-upon-Hull 039889
Hulme, J. Alan, Chester 141509
Hulsch, Carlos, Berlin 101930
Hulsey Gallery, Oklahoma City University, Oklahoma City 046643
Huludao City Museum, Huludao ... 007142
Hum, Göteborg 141102
Humačka Arheološko Zbirka, Franjevački Samostan, Ljubuški 003932
Human Events, Kolkata 135845
Human Horizons Art School, Miami 051699
Human & Rousseau, Cape Town ... 134898
Human Science Museum, Tokai University, Shimizu 027064
Humanities and Social Sciences, Northern Montana College, Havre 051452
Humanities Division, Herkimer County Community College, Herkimer ... 051458
Humber-Bay of Islands Museum, Corner Brook 005293
Humber Estuary Discovery Centre, Cleethorpes 039097
Humbert, Bruno, Oyonnax 065319
Humbert, Dominique, Courtavon ... 062522
Humbert Collection, Münster 019146
Humbi-Humbi, Luanda 094053
Humble, Fyshwick 055855
Humble, Owen, Newcastle-upon-Tyne 086066
Humbleyard Fine Art, London 085411
Humboldt and District Museum and Gallery, Humboldt 005628
Humboldt County Historical Association Museum, Dakota City 043258
Humboldt County Historical Association Museum, Humboldt 044669
Humboldt County Old Settler's Museum, Livermore 045349
Humboldt-Gesellschaft für Wissenschaft, Kunst und Bildung e.V., Mainz ... 053237
Humboldt Historical Museum, Humboldt 044670
Humboldt-Museum Schloß Tegel, Berlin 016078
Humboldt State University Natural History Museum, Arcata 041760
Hume, Dudley, Brighton 083700
Humeurs, Paris 066069
Hummel, Alois, Freiburg im Breisgau 070843
Hummel, Eberhard, Schlüchtern ... 126772
Hummel, Emil, Hofheim, Unterfranken 125951
Hummel, I., Fridolfing 070886
Hummel, Julius, Wien 095870
Hummel, Klaus & Mona, Salem, Baden 073652
Hummel, Richard, Frankfurt am Main 070754
Hummel, Richard, Wiesbaden 074408
Hummer, Edith, Freistadt, Oberösterreich 123352
Humor Graphic, Milano .. 134615, 135906
Humpal Holcombe, Portland 119008
Humpback Rocks Mountain Farm Visitor Center, Waynesboro 049035
Humphrey, Gil, Memphis 090078
Humphrey-Carrasco, London 085412
Humphrey Forum, Minneapolis 045912
Dr. Humpis-Antiquariat, Ravensburg 139678
Hunam, Los Angeles 116798
Hunan Fine Arts Publishing House, Changsha 133343
Hunan Literature and Fine Arts Publishing House, Changsha 133344
Hunan Provincial Museum, Changsha 007030
Hunan Revolutionary Cemetery, Changsha 007031
Hund, Isabella, München 104233
Hundemuseum, Berlin 016079
Hundertmark, Armin, Köln 103642, 134113
Hundertwassershop, Darmstadt ... 102341
Hundörat, Stockholm 141159
Hundred & One Antiques, Toronto .. 059213
Hundsmarktmühle, Thalgau 002741
Hundt, Wesel 074354
Huněk, Jan, Praha 060134
Hunerkada, Islamabad 108769
Hung, Long, Ho Chi Minh City 120513
Hung-Yen Museum, Hung-Yen 049547
Hungarian Folk-Art Museum, Port Orange 047137
Hungarian Heritage Center Museum, New Brunswick 046207
Hungerbühler, Urs, Wald, Zürich ...082897, 130212
Hungerford Arcade, Hungerford ... 084760
Hungry Ghost, Bourton-on-the-Water 083613
Hungry Ghost, London 085413
Hunsche, Licie Fayet, Porto Alegre . 058505
Hunsrück-Museum, Simmern, Hunsrück 020213
Hunt, San Antonio 119424
Hunt, San Francisco 092814
Hunt, Adele, Dallas 088534
Hunt, Daniel, London 113700
Hunt, Stanley, Gainsborough 084448, 130721
Hunt, Stanley, Retford 086349
The Hunt Gallery, Sandwich 114397

Hunt Gallery, Mary Baldwin College, Staunton . . . 048343
Hunt Institute for Botanical Documentation, Pittsburgh . . . 047052
Hunt & Lomas, Cirencester . . . 130582
Hunt-Morgan House, Lexington . . . 045259
The Hunt Museum, Limerick . . . 022822
Hunt Valley Antiques Show, Timonium . . . 093990
Hunter, Louisville . . . 132297
Hunter, Memphis . . . 132324
Hunter, Donald, Cheltenham . . . 130536
Hunter, Jill, Stamford . . . 086685, 131525
Hunter, Moa, Auckland . . . 140599
Hunter, Pat, Fresno . . . 116178
Hunter College Art Galleries, New York . . . 046347
Hunter-Dawson State Historic Site, New Madrid . . . 046243
The Hunter Gallery, Long Melford . . 113988
Hunter House, East Kilbride . . . 039352
Hunter Museum of American Art, Chattanooga . . . 042780
Hunter Street Gallery, Parramatta . . 095058
Hunter-Taylor, Sydney . . . 095295
Hunter Valley Antiques, Branxton . . 055539
Hunter Valley Museum of Rural Life, Scone . . . 001459
Hunter West Gallery, Peterborough . 006139
Hunterdon Historical Museum, Clinton . . . 043017
Hunterdon Museum of Art, Clinton . 043016
Hunterian Art Gallery, Glasgow . . . 039559
Hunterian Museum, Glasgow . . . 039560
Hunterian Museum, London . . . 040181
Hunterian Museum, Zoology Section, Glasgow . . . 039561
Hunters and Collectors Antiques, Mosman . . . 056265
Hunters and Selectors, North Shore 079192
Hunter's Antiques, Seattle . . . 093017
Hunter's Find, Tampa . . . 093128
Hunters Hill Historical Museum, Sydney . . . 001511
Hunter's of Hampton, Hampton . . . 084563
Huntingdon County Museum, Huntingdon . . . 044672
Huntingdon Trading Post, Huntingdon . . . 084771
Huntington, Stow-on-the-Wold . . . 086751
Huntington, Archer M., Austin . . . 114989
Huntington Art Collections, San Marino . . . 047912
Huntington Beach Art Center, Huntington Beach . . . 044687
Huntington Beach International Surfing Museum, Huntington Beach . . . 044688
Huntington County Historical Society Museum, Huntington . . . 044676
Huntington Historical Society Museum, Huntington . . . 044681
Huntington Library, Art Collections and Botanical Gardens. Calendar, San Marino . . . 136490
Huntington Library Press, San Marino . . . 135497
Huntington Museum of Art, Huntington . . . 044684
Huntington Railroad Museum, Huntington . . . 044685
Huntley, Diana, London . . . 085414
Huntly, Campbell . . . 094364
Huntly and Districts Historical Museum, Huntly . . . 001120
Huntly Antiques, Huntly . . . 084773
Huntly House Museum, Edinburgh . 039397
Huntsville Art League, Huntsville . . 054797
Huntsville Museum of Art, Huntsville . . . 044693
Hunziker, Ulrich & Heidi, Zürich . . . 112117
Huon Valley Apple and Heritage Museum, Huonville . . . 001121
Hup Hin, Ipoh . . . 121757
Huppert, Bruno, Forcalquier . . . 062917
Huppertz, Friedrich, Düsseldorf . . . 102511
Huraxdax Verlag, Weilheim, Oberbayern . . . 134449
Hurdal Bygdetun, Hurdal . . . 030916
Hurds, Seattle . . . 093018
Huret, Jean Etienne, Paris . . . 138404
Hurl, Rosemarie & Anthony, Tusmore . . . 056747
Hurley Patentee Manor, Hurley . . . 044696
Hurnall, Marvin, Prahran . . . 056493
Huron City Museums, Port Austin . . 047127
Huron County Museum, Goderich . . 005517
Huronia Museum, Midland . . . 005866
Hurrah's Nest, Austin . . . 087585
Hurricane Valley Heritage Park Museum, Hurricane . . . 044700
Hur's Gallery, Seoul . . . 107248
Hurst, Anthony, Woodbridge . . . 087219, 131708
Hurst, D., London . . . 131066
Hurst, Edward, Salisbury . . . 086493
Hurst, W. Nevin, Hobart . . . 055994
Hurst on First, Vancouver . . . 097486
Hurstmere Antiques, North Shore . . 079193
Hurston, A.J.V., Los Angeles . . . 089799
Hurt & Assoc., Norfolk . . . 118609
Hurta, Houston . . . 089113
Hurtebize, Cannes . . . 061947
Hurtebize, Dominique, Courchevel . 099180
Hurthe, Dieter, Berlin . . . 069647
Hurtigrutemuseet, Stokmarknes . . . 031242
Hurworth Cottage, New Plymouth . . 030552
Hus-Museum, Konstanz . . . 018376
Husa, Tampere . . . 060626
Husarmuseum, Smalands Militarhistoriska Museum, Eksjö . . . 036245
Huseby Bruk, Grimslöv . . . 036314
Huser, Robert, Flawil . . . 082370
Huser, Rose-Marie, Billom . . . 061485
Husi, Heinz, Chippis . . . 082313
Húsipari Múzeum, Budapest . . . 021656
Husitské Muzeum v Táboře, Tábor . 008705
Huskisson Trading Post, Huskisson . 056006
Huskvarna Stadsmuseum, Huskvarna . . . 036353
Huss, Sally, San Diego . . . 119515
Huss, Sally, Tucson . . . 120136
Le Hussard, Metz . . . 064532
Hussard, Jean-Philippe, Paris . . . 066070
Hussenot, Ghislaine, Paris . . . 100524
Hussenot-Desenonges, Bruno, Vierzon . . . 068869
Hussenot Desenonges, Marie-Claude, Nançay . . . 064854
Hussian School of Art, Philadelphia 051943
Hußlein, Richard, Planegg . . . 139660
Husslik-Heimatmuseum, Pöls . . . 002447
Husstege, Haaren . . . 128684
Huste, Dortmund . . . 138981
Huste, Wolfgang, Bad Honnef . . . 069301, 121303, 138693
Husted, Seattle . . . 119939
Huster, V., Baden-Baden . . . 069417
Hut, Manama . . . 096012
The Hut Gallery, Ferntree Gully . . . 094523
Hutchinson, Martha, Philadelphia . . 091645, 132624
Hutchinson Art Association, Hutchinson . . . 054798
Hutchinson Art Center, Hutchinson Art Association, Hutchinson . . . 044702
Hutchinson County Museum, Borger 042311
Hutchinson House Museum, Waupaca . . . 049013
Hutchinson-Scott, Ripon . . . 122669
Hutchison Antiques, Chelmsford . . . 083915, 130528
Huth, Herrenberg . . . 071494
Hutin, Emmanuel, Paris . . . 138405
Hutin, Renaud, Sarlat-la-Canéda . . 068126
Hutong a Roma, Roma . . . 076509
Hutong Gallery, Milano . . . 075738
Hutson Gallery, London . . . 113701
Hutt, Andrew, Kirkcaldy . . . 113334
Hutt Art Society, Wellington . . . 053919
Hutt Street Books, Adelaide . . . 136772
Hutten & Ostermayer, Wackernheim 105136
Hutter, Ira, New York . . . 090957, 123000
Hutter, Stasia, Basel . . . 111195
Hutterer, Jutta, Wiener Neustadt . . 095971
Huttermuseum, Erdweg . . . 017005
Hutto, Houston . . . 132125
Hutton, Leonard, New York . . . 118027
Huvé, Philippe, Saint-Denis-sur-Sarthon . . . 067424
Huvé, Philippe, Sées . . . 068190
Huygens Museum Hofwijck, Voorburg . . . 030289
Huyghe-Cariou, Henri, Tréogat . . . 068625
Huyse Molensloot, Antwerpen . . . 096070
Huysser, d', Bruxelles . . . 096213
Huzette, Jocelyne, Épernay . . . 062783
Hvitträsk, Kirkkonummi . . . 009714
Hwa Kang Museum, Taipei . . . 007368
Hwajeong Museum, Seoul . . . 027563
Hwang, Jason, Portland . . . 091954
HWL-Galerie und Edition, Düsseldorf . . . 102512
Hyacinths, Boston . . . 087826
Hyart & Fils, Compiègne . . . 124208
Hyart, Toronto . . . 097290
Hybrid, London . . . 113702
Hybrid, Seattle . . . 093019
Hyde Art Gallery, Grossmont Community College, El Cajon . . . 043625
Hyde Collection Art Museum, Glens Falls . . . 044213
Hyde Hall, East Springfield . . . 043581
Hyde-n-Seek Antiques, Chicago . . . 088105
Hyde Park Antiques, New York . . . 090958
Hyde Park Art Center, Chicago . . . 042849
Hyde Park Art Center, Chicago . . . 115458
Hyde Park Barracks Museum, Sydney . . . 001512
Hyde Park Jewellery, Sydney . . . 056677
Hyde Park Refinishing, Tampa . . . 132953
Hyde Road Antiques, Paignton . . . 086188, 131358
Hyde & Seek Antiques, San Francisco . . . 092815
Hyder, Jane, Wellington . . . 108623
Hyderabad Museum, Hyderabad . . . 031364
Hydo, Petersham . . . 095069
Hydra Antiques, South Yarra . . . 056613
Hydro Industripark-Museum, Porsgrunn . . . 031122
Hydrobiological Museum, Alexandria . . . 009276
Hyeonchungsa Shrine, Asan . . . 027449
Hyland, Melbourne . . . 136998
Hylleveien, Arendal . . . 079368
Hylteberga Galeri, Skurup . . . 110990
Hylténs Industrimuseum, Gnosjö Industrimuseum, Gnosjö . . . 036290
Hyman, James, London . . . 113703
Hyman and Sons General Store, Gaspé . . . 005497
Hymers Museum, Kakabeka Falls . . 005657
Hymne, Parlow Valley . . . 110067
Hyna, U., Rottach-Egern . . . 104777
Hyogo-ken Togeikan, Kobe . . . 026663
Hyogo-kenritsu Bijutsukan, Kobe . . 026664
Hyogo-kenritsu Rekishi Hakubutsukan, Himeji . . . 026512
Hyperion Antique Centre, Saint Ives, Cambridgeshire . . . 086455, 122679
Hypnos, Paris . . . 100525
Hypocaust, Saint Albans . . . 040883
Hyrax Hill Museum, Hyrax Hill . . . 027420
Hyšpler, Lubomír, Příbram 098497, 137852
Hystory, Trieste . . . 076895
Hythe, Kingston . . . 094706
Hythe Local History Room, Hythe, Kent . . . 039791
Hyun, Seoul . . . 107249
Hyundai, Seoul . . . 107250
Hyundai Art Gallery, Seoul . . . 107251
Hyundai Art Gallery, Seoul . . . 107252
I-20 Gallery, New York . . . 118028
I-35 North Antiques, Kansas City . . 089502
I-40 Antique Mall, Albuquerque . . . 087399
I-44 Antique Mall, Tulsa . . . 093313
I C I, Paris . . . 066071
I Galleriet, Sandnes . . . 108750
I & L Image Corporation, New York . 118029
I Lanzi, Firenze . . . 075358
I Leonarte, Valencia . . . 110832
I-Level, New York . . . 118030
I-Punkt, Sigmaringen . . . 073818
I Remember Mama, Chicago . . . 088106
I Saw Designs, Milwaukee . . . 090305
I Saw It First, Minneapolis . . . 090367
I Segni, Torino . . . 076826
I Thought You Knew, San Francisco 092816
I Tid & Rum, Nacka . . . 081884
Das i-Tüpfelchen, Dortmund . . . 070284
I. Türkiye Büyük Millet Meclisi Binası, Ankara Kurtuluş Savaşı Müzesi, Ankara . . . 038011
i8, Reykjavík . . . 105589
Iaccarino, Francesco, Napoli . . . 075997
Iacoletti, Mariano, Napoli . . . 075998
Ian Kenny, Ian, Hamilton . . . 113180
The Ian Potter Art Museum, University of Melbourne, Melbourne . . . 001242
Iani, Grazia Maria, Genova . . . 075474
Ianira Antique Shop, Lemesos . . . 059960
Iannetti, Pasquale, San Francisco . . 092817, 119694
Ian's Antiques, Oakland . . . 091423
Iavarone, Antonio, Napoli . . . 075999
Iavarone, Domenico, Napoli . . . 127773
Iavarone, Luigi, Napoli . . . 076000
Ibala, Bussum . . . 078132
Ibañez Redondo, Angel, Madrid . . . 129630
Ibara Municipal Denchu Art Museum, Ibara . . . 026550
Ibaraki Daigaku Izura Bijutsu Bunka Kenkyujo, Kitaibaraki . . . 026657
Ibaraki-ken Kindai Bijutsukan, Mito 026815
Ibaraki-ken Rekishikan, Mito . . . 026816
Ibarbia, Elena, Donostia-San Sebastián . . . 129507
Ibars Pallas, Silvia, Barcelona . . . 129352
Ibbett & Mosely, Sevenoaks . . . 122693
Ibel, Rebecca, Columbus . . . 115786
Iberia, Bern . . . 141227
Ibex Gallery, Unterseen . . . 111954
IBRA Collection, International Bee Research Association, Cardiff . . . 038989
Ibrahim, Wien . . . 057455
Ibrahim Hussein Foundation Museum, Pulau Langkawi . . . 028008
Ibresinskij Ėtnografičeskij Muzej pod Otkryrym Nebom, Čuvašskij Nacionalnyj Muzej, Ibresi . . . 033154
Ibsen-museet, Norsk Folkemuseum, Oslo . . . 031080
Ibsenhuset og Grimstad Bymuseet, Grimstad . . . 030863
Ibu, Paris . . . 100526, 133629
Ibunsai, Nara . . . 077160
I.C. Editions, New York . . . 135435
ICA Monthly Bulletin, London . . . 136228
ICAMT International Committee for Architecture and Museums Techniques, Helsinki . . . 052873
Icaro Gallery, Long Beach . . . 116673
ICDAD International Committee for Decorative Arts and Design Museums, Wien . . . 052540
Icebox Gallery, Minneapolis . . . 117272
Icelandic Museums Association, Patreksfjörður . . . 053682
Iceni Village and Museums, Cockley Cley . . . 039115
ICFA International Committee for Fine Art Museums, Ottawa . . . 052752
Ichabod & Crane, Denver . . . 142389
Ichie, Yachiyo . . . 107136
Ichijo-ji Treasure House, Kasai . . . 026631
Ichikawa Municipal Museum, Ichikawa . . . 026552
Ichimai-no-e, Sapporo . . . 077194
Ici, Warszawa . . . 079760
Ickleton Antiques, Saffron Walden . 086431
Icko, Los Angeles . . . 116799

Icks, Horst, Bramsche 125371
Ickworth House, Horringer 039770
ICLM International Committee for Literary Museums, Paradis 053941
ICM, Haarlem 078460
ICMAH International Committee for Archaeology and History Museums, Caen 052959
ICMS International Committee for Museums Security, Los Angeles 054799
ICOFOM International Committee for Museology, München 053238
Icograda Message Board, Bruxelles 135599
ICOM Angola, Luanda 052441
ICOM Arab, Giza 052866
ICOM Argentina, Buenos Aires 052446
ICOM Asia-Pacific Organization, Belconnen 052473
ICOM Australia, Subiaco 052474
ICOM Azerbaijan, Baku 052630
ICOM Bangladesh, Dhaka 052633
ICOM Barbados, Saint Michael 052635
ICOM - Belgian National Comittee, Hornu 052678
ICOM Bénin, Porto-Novo 052693
ICOM Bolivia, La Paz 052696
ICOM Bosnia-Hercegovina, Sarajevo 052698
ICOM Botswana, Gaborone 052701
ICOM Bulgaria, Sofia 052708
ICOM Burkina Faso, Ouagadougou . 052714
ICOM Burundi, Bujumbura 052716
ICOM Cambodia, Phnom Penh 052717
ICOM Cameroon, Yaoundé 052718
ICOM Canada, Ottawa 052753
ICOM Chile, Santiago de Chile 052785
ICOM Chinese National Committee, Beijing 052796
ICOM Comitato Nazionale Italiano, Milano 053757
ICOM Comité Haïtien, Port-au-Prince 053673
ICOM Comité National du Niger, Niamey 053933
ICOM - Comité National Monégasque du Conseil International des Musées, Monaco 053870
ICOM Comité Sénégalais, Dakar . . . 054034
ICOM Comores, Moroni 052810
ICOM Costa Rica, San José 052814
ICOM Côté d'Ivoire, Grand Bassam . 052816
ICOM Cuba, La Habana 052829
ICOM Cyprus, Lefkosia 052833
ICOM du Tchad, N'Djamena 052782
ICOM Ecuador, Guayaquil 052864
ICOM Egypt, Cairo 052867
ICOM Estonia, Tallinn 052871
ICOM Finland, Helsinki 052874
ICOM F.Y.R. Macedonia, Skopje . . . 053850
ICOM Grèce, Athinai 053666
ICOM Guatemala, Guatemala 053672
ICOM Hungary, Budapest 053674
ICOM Iceland, Garðabaer 053683
ICOM India, Kolkata 053696
ICOM International Council of Museums, Deutsches Nationalkomitee, Berlin 053239
ICOM Iran, Teheran 053708
ICOM Ireland, Dublin 053711
ICOM Jamaica, Kingston 053773
ICOM Jordan, Amman 053808
ICOM Kazakhstan, Almaty 053810
ICOM Kenya, Nairobi 053811
ICOM Korea, Seoul 053820
ICOM Kyrgyzstan, Biškek 053829
ICOM Lao, Vientiane 053831
ICOM Latin America and the Caribbean Regional Organization, San Jose . 052815
ICOM Latvijas Nacionāla Komiteja, Tukums 053833
ICOM Liban, Beirut 053837
ICOM Libyan Arab Jamahiriya, Tripoli 053838
ICOM Lietuva, Vilnius 053843
ICOM Luxembourg, Luxembourg . . 053847
ICOM Madagascar, Antananarivo . . 053854
ICOM Malaysia, Kuala Lumpur 053855
ICOM Mali, Bamako 053857
ICOM Maroc, Rabat 053872
ICOM Mauritanie, Nouakchott 053860
ICOM Mauritius, Port Louis 053861
ICOM México, México 053864
ICOM Mongolia, Ulaanbaatar 053871
ICOM Nacionalni Komitet Serbia-Montenegro, Beograd 054037
ICOM Namibia, Windhoek 053873
ICOM National Commitee of Belarus, Minsk 052638
ICOM Nepal, Kathmandu 053875
ICOM Netherlands, Amsterdam . . . 053891
ICOM New Zealand, Rotorua 053920
ICOM News, Paris 135713
ICOM Nigeria, Calabar 053935
ICOM Northern Ireland, Belfast 054405
ICOM Österreichisches Nationalkomitee, Wien 052541
ICOM Oman, Muscat 053962
ICOM Panamá, Panamá City 053967
ICOM Paraguay, Asunción 053970
ICOM Philippines, Manila 053974
ICOM Poland, Poznań 053980
ICOM Portugal, Lisboa 054004
ICOM Qatar, Doha 054011
ICOM Regional Organization for West Africa, Bamako 053858
ICOM República Dominicaine, Santo Domingo 052863
ICOM Republique Congo, Brazzaville 052813
ICOM République Democratique du Congo, Kinshasa 052811
ICOM Romania, Ploieşti 054013
ICOM Schweiz, Conseil International des Musées - Comité National Suisse, Zürich 054183
ICOM Seychelles, Victoria 054046
ICOM Singapore, Singapore 054049
ICOM Slovakia, Bratislava 054052
ICOM Slovenia, Ljubljana 054056
ICOM South Africa, Johannesburg . 054066
ICOM Spain, Madrid 054118
ICOM Sri Lanka, Colombo 054126
ICOM Swaziland, Lobamba 054128
ICOM Sweden, Stockholm 054132
ICOM Tanzania, Dar-es-Salaam . . . 054241
ICOM Thailand, Pathumthani 054242
ICOM Togo, Lomé 054245
ICOM Tunisia, Tunis 054246
ICOM Turkish National Committee, Ulus 054250
ICOM Ukraine, Lviv 054261
ICOM Uruguay, Montevideo 054552
ICOM Uzbekistan, Taškent 055117
ICOM Venezuela, Caracas 055119
ICOM Viet Nam, Ha Noi 055122
ICOM Zambia, Livingstone 055125
ICOM Zimbabwe, Bulawayo 055127
ICOMAC Regional Organization for Central Africa, Kinshasa 052812
ICOMAM International Committee of Museums and Collections of Arms and Military History, Delft 053892
Icon, Albrightsville 087356, 131732
Icon Art Gallery, Picton 108542
Icon Books, Byron Bay 136836
Icon Boulevard 409 First Av S, Seattle 119940
Icon Gallery, Wilmslow 114698
Icon World Studio, Leederville 056093
Iconastas, London 085415
Iconografisch Bureau, Den Haag . . 029427
ICR International Committee for Regional Museums, Ljubljana 054057
Icram, Barcelona 129353
ID Collection, Portland 119009
ID Galerie, Helmond 029724
ID (International Design), New York . 136491
Ida Aalbergin Lapsuudenkoti, Leppäkoski 009820
Ida Green Gallery, Austin College, Sherman 048150
Idaho Association of Museums, Boise 054800
Idaho Museum of Mining and Geology, Boise 042290
Idaho Museum of Natural History, Pocatello 047107
Idaho State Historical Museum, Boise 042291
IDAO Gallery, Chicago 088107
Ida's Idea, Washington 120311
Idea Books, Amsterdam 134783
Idea Books, Milano 134616
Idea-Castellum, Budapest 105516
I.DE.A. - Internationales Designcenter Austria, Schrems 095752, 133161
Idea Scultura, Roma 106561
Idea Studio, Milano 075739
Ideal Baseball Cards, Cincinnati . . . 142317
Ideal Book Store, Yonkers 143055
Ideal Furniture, Austin 131801
Idéal Passion, Marseille 064366
Ideal Upholstery and Furniture, San Francisco 132886
Ideart, Barcelona 129354
Idearte, Pregassona 111817
Ideas and More, Miami 090187
Ideas Galería de Arte, Cali 098237
Idéco, Fontenay-le-Comte 062903
I'Idee, Cincinnati 115635
Idee Arcobaleno, Milano 075740
Idee International, Vilvoorde 123678
Idee nel Tempo, Padova 076094
Idee nel Tempo, Verona 077007
Idées d'Artistes, Paris 100527
Idefix, Montréal 137655
L'Idefix, Montréal 137656
Ideja, Pleven 096706
Idem Editions, Montréal 097039
Idemitsu Bijutsukan, Tokyo 027175
Identity Gallery, Kolkata 105741
Idiom Studio, Wellington 108624
IDL Gallery, Paris 100528
IDL Graphique, Paris 100529
Idle Hour Book Inn, Rotorua 140650
Idle Time Books, Washington 143044
Idojiri Kokokan, Fujimi 026454
Idol House, Hong Kong 097800
Idrottsantikvariatet, Vällingby 141192
Idrottsmuseet, Malmö 036456
Idstedt-Gedächtnishalle, Idstedt . . . 018046
Idube.Co.Uk, Chobham 112866
Idvies Antiques, Letham 084977
Idyllwild Arts Academy, Idyllwild . . . 051495
Iégor, Montréal 120806
Iemmolo, Angelo, Padova 127807
Ien, Amersfoort 107638
I.E.P. Inventaires Estimations & Partages, Paris 066072
Ieri e Oggi, Milano 075741
Ieri e Oggi, Venezia 076945
Iermano Antiquites, Napoli 076001
Iesu, Trieste 076896
IF Museum Innerspaces, Poznań . . 109051
ifa-Galerie Berlin, Institut für Auslandsbeziehungen, Berlin 016080
ifa-Galerie Bonn, Institut für Auslandsbeziehungen, Bonn 016326
ifa-Galerie Stuttgart, Institut für Auslandsbeziehungen, Stuttgart . 020355
IFAR Journals, New York 136492
Iff, Martina, Rattenberg, Inn 057218
Ifield Watermill, Crawley 039169
IG Bildender KünstlerInnen Salzburg, Salzburg 052542
IG Halle Alte Fabrik, Rapperswil, Sankt Gallen 111821
I.G.A., Ramat Gan 134538
Iga Art and Industry Institute, Ueno . 027304
I.G.A. Old Masters, Saint Lawrence 086461
Iga-Ryu Ninja Yashiki, Ueno 027305
Igarskij Kraevedčeskij Kompleks Muzej Večnoj Merzloty, Igarka 033155
Igel, Manya, London 085416, 113704
Iggesunds Bruksmuseum, Iggesund 036355
Iggy's, San Antonio 092520
Igini, Luigi, Roma 128074
Iglesia Caro, Jose de la, Madrid . . . 081322
Iglesia ni Cristo Museum and Gallery, New Era University, Quezon City 031775
Iglińska, Anna, Kraków 108955
Iglinski, Grzegorz, Hamburg 071254
Iglou Art Esquimau, Douai 099238
Ignace Heritage Centre, Ignace . . . 005632
Ignacio Osuna, I., Sevilla 110772
Ignaszewski, Georg, Berlin 125225
Ignatowicz-Woźniakowska, Dorota, Warszawa 129088
Ignaz J. Pleyel Museum, Großweikersdorf 001980
Ignotus Technika, Budapest 139918
Iguana Gallery, Stroud 114514
Ihle, Jürgen, Detmold 125457
Ihle-Wirth, Franziska & Geroon, Fulda 125695
Ihler, Christian, La Garde 063390
Ihn, Seoul 107253
Ihring, Rolf, Berlin 138794
Ihrke, Christine, Berlin 101931
Ii Art Museum, Hikone 026510
II. Türkiye Büyük Millet Meclisi Binası, Cumhuriyet Müzesi, Ankara 038012
Iida-shi Bijutsu Hakubutsukan, Iida 026553
III Wash Design, Houston 116340
Iisakin Jussin Tupa, Kauhava 009679
Iisaku Muuseum, Iisaku 009365
Iittalan Tehtaan Museo, Iittala 009600
Ijff, T., Callantsoog 140380
IJzertoren-Museum Oorlog-Vrede-Vlaamse Ontvoogding, Diksmuide 003405
IK Galerie, Maastricht 108126
Ikaros, Slany 060191, 098500
Ike Taiga Museum of Art, Kyoto . . . 026721
Ikebana Arts, San Jose 119853
Ikeda, Akira, Berlin 101932
Ikeda, Akira, New York 118031
Ikeda 20-seiki Bijutsukan, Ito 026579
Ikeda & Lokker, Tokyo 107054
Ikeder, Bilbao 110284
Ikegami & Takebi, Kyoto 077102
Ikels, Rena, Rellingen 104710
Iklektik Designs, Houston 116341
Iknos, Tartano 128249
IKO Gemeentelijk Instituut voor Kreatieve Opvoeding, Hoogstraten 049708
Ikodespotiko Paleopolio, Lefkosia . . 059955
Ikodinovic & Co., Nenad, Bruxelles . 057990
Ikomayama Uchu Kagakukan, Ikoma 026557
Ikon, New York 090959
Ikon Gallery, Birmingham 038731
Ikon- och Konstföreningen, Stockholm 054133
Ikona Photo Gallery, Venezia 106756
Ikonen Galerie, Berlin 069648
Ikonen-Galerie, Bern 111260
Ikonen Galerie Sophia, Zürich 082982, 112118, 130242
Ikonen-Museum, Museen der Stadt Recklinghausen, Recklinghausen . 019739
Ikonen-Museum der Stadt Frankfurt am Main, Stiftung Dr. Schmidt-Voigt, Frankfurt am Main 017177
Ikonenmuseum, Autenried 015633
Ikonenmuseum Schloß Autenried, Ichenhausen 018043
Ikonos, Burgos 129461
Ikor, Sapporo 106984
Ikra Gallery, London 113705
Ikuno Kobutsukan, Ikuno, Hyogo . . 026558
Il Caminetto, Bologna 105966
Il Etait Une Fois, Beausoleil 061312
Il Etait Une Fois, Paris 066073
Il était une fois, Plaisance-du-Touch 066840
Il Etait Une Fois, Remiremont 067090
Il-Kartell, Tarxien 077535
Il Mauriziano, Reggio Emilia 025412
Il Mercatino, Brugine 121682
Il Pozzo, Modena 075915

Il Tempo, Artonne 061002
Il Tesoro, Ascona 111137
Ilana Goor Museum, Tel Aviv 023075
Ilárraz, Buenos Aires 123155
Ilchester Museum, Ilchester 039792
Ildiko, Malvern, Victoria 056148
Ile au Trésor, Biarritz 061465
Ile aux Antiquités, Victot-Pontfol . . . 068864
Ile aux Trésors, Grenoble . 063066, 138097
Ile aux Trésors, Neufchâtel-en-Bray 064982
Ile de France Antiques, Chicago . . .088108, 131905
Ile du Temps, Libourne 063816
Ile Lettrée, Montolieu 138216
Ilene & Wayne, Honolulu 088959
Iles, Francis, Rochester . . 086388, 114323
Iles, Francis, Rochester 131421
Iles, Francis, Wouldham 114739
Ilfracombe Arts Society, Ilfracombe 054406
Ilfracombe Arts Society, Ilfracombe 113289
Ilfracombe Museum, Ilfracombe . . . 001125
Ilfracombe Museum, Ilfracombe . . . 039793
Ilg, Beatrice, Bern 129960
Ilg, Hansruedi, Zürich 130243
Ilgen, Ursula, Berlin 069649
Ilgner, Jürgen, Melle 072509
İlhami Atalay Sanat Galerisi, İstanbul 112324
Iliad, New York 090960
Ilias, Antonis, Angers 060856, 124075
Ilias Lalaounis Jewelry Museum, Athinai 021177
Ilić, Boza, Prokuplje 109744
Iliev, Köln 103643
Iliev, Rumen, Köln 103644, 134114
Iligan Museum, Iligan 031672
Iliopoulou, Anna, Glyfada 074620
Ilisso, Nuoro 134647
Iliu, Julia, München 139519
Ilja Čavčavadze Memorial Museum, Tbilisi 015410
Ilko, Constanze, Salzburg 057259
Illawarra Museum, Wollongong . . . 001626
Illegaard, Tartu 098704
Illg, Karin, Balingen 069437
Illi, Raymond & Alexandre, Genève .082436, 111472
Illi-Jones, Genève 082437
Illies, Mainz 103999
Illingworth Kerr Gallery, Calgary . . . 005189
Illinois and Michigan Canal Museum, Lockport 045360
Illinois Art Gallery, Chicago 042850
Illinois Artisans and Visitors Centers, Whittington 049151
Illinois Arts Alliance, Chicago 054801
Illinois Association of Museums, Springfield 054802
Illinois Citizen Soldier Museum, Galesburg 044121
Illinois Institute of Art, Chicago 051128
Illinois Railway Museum, Union . . . 048688
Illinois State Museum, Springfield . 048284
Illmer, Osnabrück 104550
Illo Tempore, Bari 127112
Illos, Buffalo 131856
Illum, Miami 090188
Illuminary Art, Toronto 097291
Illuminata Gallery, Houston 116342
Illuminati, Milano 075742
Illusoria-Land, Museum und Galerie für optische Täuschungen und Holographien, Ittigen 037203
Illustrated Gallery, Philadelphia . . . 118778
Illustration 63, Memmingen 135767
Illustration House, New York 090961, 123001
Illustrations and Graphic Design Department, Harcum Junior College, Bryn Mawr 051051
Illustrator, Minneapolis 136493
Illy, Günther, Timelkam 057330
Ilmajoen Museo, Ilmajoki 009602
Ilmatorjuntamuseo, Tuusula 010186
Ilmavoimien Viestikoulun Perinnehuone, Tikkakoski 010147
Ilmenauer Antikmarkt, Ilmenau . . . 071614
Ilmin Museum of Art, Seoul 027564
Ilo, Tallinn 133438, 137917
Ilocaniana Cultural Museum, Magsingal 031693
Iloniemen Pajamuseo, Kuusjoki . . . 009775
L'Ilot Trésors, Paris 066074
Iloulian, John, Los Angeles 089800, 132257
Iloulian, John, West Hollywood 093476
Ils sont fous ces Romains, Ville-d'Avray 068881
Ilse B., Paris 066075
ILTE- Industria Libraria Tipografica Editrice, Moncalieri 134641
Ilulissat Katersugaasiviat, Ilulissat . 021539
Ilumina-Art, Bochum 069886
Ilwaco Heritage Museum, Ilwaco . . 044716
IM Gallery, Singapore 109811
Im Kinsky-Museum, Wien 002914
Im Kinsky-Wiener Kunst Auktionen, Wien 057456, 120685
Im Obersteg, Dr. Markus & Alice, Sankt Gallen 082778
Im Trend, Amberg, Oberpfalz 101573
Imabari City Kono Shiniichi Memorial Culture Hall, Imabari 026560
Imabayashi, Fukuoka 077043
Imafronte, Murcia 136091
Image, Gniezno 108916
Image, Łomianki 109024
Image 54 Gallery, Calgary 096823
Image Art, Gillingham 113093
Image Art, Gillingham 113094
Image Art, Gillingham 135151
Image Arts Etc ., Omaha 118704
Image Arts Etc., San Diego 119516
Image Business, Christchurch 108396, 134845
Image Complete, Denver 116014
Image Direct, Amsterdam 107738
Image Document, Châtillon (Hauts-de-Seine) 062230
Image Document, Paris 066076
Image en Plus, Nîmes 099869
Image et le Livre, Strasbourg 138620
Image Factory, Indianapolis 116465
Image Fine Art & Photography, York 114753
Image Graphics, Oakland 118635
Image in, Gérardmer 062986
Image of Art, Hyderabad 105702
Image One International, Houston . . 116343
Image Reproductions, New York . . . 118032
Image Shed, Halifax 113178
Image Showcase, Albuquerque . . . 114796
Image Visions Gallery, South Yarra . 095211
Imagem, Porto 109389
Imagem Galeria, Fortaleza 096530
Imagen, Panamá City 108789
Imagerie, Den Haag 140392
Imagerie, Lannion 063531
Imagerie d'Epinal, Épinal 133469
Images, London 113706
Les Images, Newtownabbey 114143
Images a Gallery, San Francisco . . . 119695
Images and Frames, Boston 115184
Images Art, Toronto 097292
Images Art Gallery, Bangalore 105606
Images Art Gallery, Kansas City . . . 116574
Images By Woolf, Wellington 108625
Images Corporate Art, New York . . . 118033
Images de la Mer, La Trinite-sur-Mer 063456
Images du Faubourg, Annecy 060891
Images du Passé, Lignieres 063820
Images Fine Art, Pittsburgh 118930
Images for a Canadian Heritage, Vancouver 097487
Images Gallery, Toledo 120084
Images International, Honolulu 116217
Images of Austin and the Southwest, Austin 114990
Images of Nature, Denver 116015
Images of Nature, Las Vegas 116628
Images of Nature, Omaha 118705
Images of Nature, Omaha 118706
Images of the North, San Francisco 119696
Images Under Glass, Minneapolis . . 117273
Images Under Glass, Saint Paul . . . 119297
Images Under Glass, Saint Paul . . . 119298
Imagina-Museo Interactivo Puebla, Puebla 028647
Imaginaciones Arte, Cali 098238
L'Imaginaire, Bruxelles 137442
The Imaginarium, Anchorage 041714
Imaginarium Hands-On Museum, Fort Myers 043959
Imagin'Art, Montréal 097040
Imaginary Places, Philadelphia . . . 118779
Imagination Station Science Museum, Wilson 049223
Imagination Unlimited, Miami 090189
Imagine, Fuchu 077038
Imagine, Luxembourg 107406
Imagine, Maastricht 108127
Imagine Arts Espaces Matières, Bordeaux 099005
Imagine Interiors, Memphis 090079
Imaging Solutions, Richmond 119114
Imagisphere Children's Museum, North Richland Hills 046535
Imago, Amsterdam 107739
Imago, Wernigerode 074344
imago fotokunst, Berlin 101933
Imago Grafica, Perugia 106460
Imago Kunst- und Designschule, Erfurt 050075
Imago Mundi, Buenos Aires 136725
Imago-Verlag, Aichwald 133716
Imaians, Madrid 110548
Imaizumi Museum, Shiozawa 027074
Imari, Porto Alegre 058506
Imari-shi Rekishi Minzoku Shiryokan, Imari 026561
Imasterpiece, Miami 117092
Imatran Kulttuurihistoriallinen Kaupunginmuseo, Imatra 009604
Imatran Taide ja Kehys, Imatra 060596
Imatran Taidemuseo, Imatra 009605
Imavision Gallery, Taipei 098074
Imaxe Gallery, Edmonton 096886
Imbard, Patrick, Paris 066077
Imberman Benson, New York 090962
Imbert, Didier, Paris 100530
Imelda, Knokke-Heist 096337
Imeson Collection, Windsor, Ontario 059440
Imhof, Michael, Petersberg, Kreis Fulda 134345
Imhoff Art Gallery, Saint Walburg . . 006399
Imhoff-Stollwerck-Museum, Museum für Geschichte und Gegenwart der Schokolade, Köln 018317
Imhotep, Buenos Aires 055217
Imig, Harald, Günzburg 125773
Imkamp, M., Bielefeld 069828
Imker- und Heimatmuseum, Wassertrüdingen 020692
Imkereiausstellung Einst-Jetzt, Reidling 002516
Imkereigeschichtliche und bienenkundliche Sammlungen, Celle 016548
Imkereimuseum, Pöggstall 002441
Imkereimuseum, Pramet 002463
Imkereimuseum Grüningen, Wetzikon 037702
Imkerijmuseum Poppendamme, Grijpskerke 029630
IMM Münz Institut, München 072741
L'Immagine, Bari 105931
L'Immagine, Napoli 106375
L'Immagine, Padova 106404
L'Immagine Ritrovata, Bologna 127155
Immendorf, San Francisco 119697
Immig, Anna, Göppingen . 071031, 102967
Immig, Harald, Göppingen 102968
Immigrant City Historical Museum of Lawrence and its People, Lawrence 045209
Immigrant-institutets Museum, Borås 036225
Immigration Museum, Melbourne . . 001243
Immingham Museum, Immingham . 039797
Immler, Georg, Röthenbach, Allgäu . 073565
Immobiliare Restauri, Catania 127269
IMMOCARD, Essen 139054
Immortal Treasures, West Hollywood 093477
Imoberdorf, German, Murten 111763
Imogene Antique and Fine Jewellery, Fitzroy North 055827
Imogene Herbert Historical Museum, Manistique 045635
IMP Jewellery, Toorak 056715
Impact Fine Art Gallery, Buffalo . . . 115258
Impact Livres, Paris 138406
Impact Livres, Paris 138407
Impala, Armadale, Victoria 055381, 123181
l'Impasse, Bruxelles 057991
Impasse Saint-Jacques Antiquités, Bruxelles 057992
Imperato Collection of West African Artifacts, Safari Museum, Chanute 042709
Imperial, Fuengirola 081105
Imperial, Indianapolis 122921, 132157
Imperial and District Museum, Imperial 005634
Imperial Antiques, Armadale, Victoria 055382
Imperial Antiques, Kingston-upon-Hull 084861
Imperial Antiques, Stockport 086723
Imperial Bookshop, Hobart 136944
Imperial Calcasieu Museum, Lake Charles 045102
Imperial Coins, Richmond 092088
Imperial Dream, Honolulu 088960
Imperial Fine Books, New York 142666
Imperial Gallery, Virginia Beach . . . 120223
Imperial Garden, Hong Kong 059643
Imperial Glass and Plywood House, Jaipur, Rajasthan 105721
Imperial Half Bushel, Baltimore . . . 087682
Imperial Oriental Art, New York 090963
Imperial War Museum, London 040182
Imperial War Museum Duxford, Cambridge 038964
Imperial War Museum North, Manchester 040402
Imperial War Museum Review, London 136229
Imperio Antiguedades, Granada . . . 081145
Império dos Sentidos, Porto 080090
Impetus, Stow 136494
Importaciones Pacifico, Los Angeles 116800
Imported Books, Dallas 142370
Impossible Microworld Museum, Bath 038625
Impresa Pouchain, Napoli 127774
Imprésario, Paris 100531
Impresija, Trjavna 096760
Impression, Dunajská Streda 109914
Impressions, Rouen 101118
Impressions, Taipei 098075
Impressions Art Gallery, Regina . . . 097174
Impressions Gallery of Photography, York 041477
Impressions in Leather by Georgie, Milwaukee 117197
Impressions (New York), New York . 136495
Impressions of Daylesford, Daylesford 094465
Imprévu, Chaville 062262
L'Imprévu, Paris 066078
Imprimer, Houston 089114
Imprimerie Nationale, Paris 133630
Imprint (Fairfield), Fairfield 142406
Impronta Restauracion, México . . . 128505
Improta, Enzo, Napoli 127775
Impuls 53, Zürich 112119
Impulse Art, Houston 116344
Impulsion B, Paris 066079

Imran, Singapore 080492
Imrie, Bridge-of-Earn 083664
Imschoot, Gent 133286
Imura Art Museum, Kyoto 026722
In Art We Trust, Miami 117093
In Brief (San Francisco), San Francisco 136496
In Buri National Museum, Sing Buri 037930
In Camera, New York 118034
In de Bolle Baaf, Middelburg 078640
In de Gecroonde Duijvekater, Zaandam 030361
In de Gouden Schmouck Sceer, Maastricht 078607
In de Zevende Hemel, Apeldoorn . . 029253
In den Eenhoorn, Brugge 137416
In Depot 68, Middelburg 108143
In Dreams, Oakland 091424
In Druk, 's-Hertogenbosch 108076
In Fine, Paris 133631
In Flanders Fields Museum, Ieper . . 003532
In focus Galerie am Dom, Köln 103645
In-Frames, Dunfermline 112965
In Graphic Detail, Vancouver 097488
In Her Image Gallery, Portland 119010
In Illo Tempore, Miami 090190
In Period, Winchcombe 087169
IN QUARTO, Marseille 138194
In Site Art, Indianapolis 116466
In-Situ Architectural Antiques, Manchester 085916
In-Situ Architectural Antiques, Manchester 085917
In-Situ Architectural Antiques, Manchester 131256
In 't Paradijs, Maastricht 078608
In The Frame, Blackrock 105847
In the Groove, Baltimore 087683
In the Loupe, Boston 136497
In Visible Culture, Rochester 136498
In Vision, Chicago 115459
In Vogue, Waihi 079278
Inamori, Tenri 077227
Inard, Montesquieu-Volvestre 099742
Inard, Paris 100532
InArt, Glashütten, Taunus 071006
InArt, Glashütten, Taunus 102962
Inarteks, Moskva 080242
In'Arts, Paris 100533
Inasia Art, Singapore 109812
Inatura- Erlebnis Naturschau Dornbirn, Dornbirn 001786
Inauen, André, Zürich 082983
Inauen, Hannes, Sankt Gallen 111872
Inazawa City Oguiss Memorial Art Museum, Inazawa 026564
Het Inboedelhuis, Gouda 078386
Het Inboedelhuis, Gouda 078387
Het Inboedeltje Antiekhal, Breda . . 078097
Incarnat, Grignan 099313
Incarnate Word University of the Arts and Sciences, San Antonio 052110
L'Incartade, Lille . 063849, 099492, 124317
İnce Minare Müzesi, Konya 038132
Inchata, Den Haag 078203
Incheon Metroploitan City Museum, Incheon 027511
Inchmartine Fine Art, Inchture 084791, 130824
Inch's Books, Pickering 142002
INCIBA-Comisión Nacional de Artes Plásticas, Montevideo 054553
Incitti Aldo Cornici, Roma 106562
Inclusion Arts Gallery, Chicago 115460
Incontrart, Genova 106097
Incontro d'Arte, Roma 106563
Incorporateed Society of Valuers and Auctioneers, London 054407
Incredible Art, New York 118035
Incredible Deals, Miami 090191
Incrocci, Marco, Genova 075475
Incubator, London 113707
Incurable Collector, Toronto 097293
Incurável Colecionador, Porto Alegre 058507
Incutti, Lia, Milano 106249
Incutti, Lia, Napoli 106376
Indeco, Seoul 107254
Indeco, Seoul 107255
Independence Coin and Stamp, Charlotte 087958
Independence Hall, Tel Aviv 023076
Independence Hall of Korea, Cheonan 027465
Independence Historical Museum, Independence 044718
Independence National Historical Park, Philadelphia 046950
Independence Seaport Museum, Philadelphia 046951
Independence Visitors Center, Independence 044724
Independent Artisans, Pittsburgh . . 118931
Independent Gallery, London 113708
Inderøy Museums- og Historielag, Inderøy 030919
Index, New York 136499
Index Bookcentre, London 141832
India Arts Museum, Chennai 022058
India International Centre, Delhi . . . 105665
India Street Antiques, San Diego . . 092649
Indian Academy of Fine Arts, Amritsar 050290
Indian Art Gallery, Wädenswil 111978
Indian Art Society, Mumbai 053697
Indian Arts and Crafts Association, Albuquerque 054803
Indian Arts Research Center, Santa Fe 047966
Indian Association for the Study of Conservation of Cultural Property, Delhi 053698
Indian Center Museum, Wichita . . . 049156
Indian Ceramics, Kolkata 135846
Indian City U.S.A., Anadarko 041705
Indian Head Museum, Indian Head . 005636
Indian Hill Historical Society Museum, Cincinnati 042927
Indian Institute of Art in Industry, Kolkata 050312
Indian King Tavern Museum, Haddonfield 044380
Indian Mill Museum State Memorial, Upper Sandusky 048709
Indian Museum, Kolkata 022220
Indian Museum, Lemmer 029864
Indian Museum of Lake County-Ohio, Painesville 046793
Indian Museum of North America, Crazy Horse 043212
Indian Museum of the Carolinas, Laurinburg 045202
Indian Pueblo Cultural Center, Albuquerque 041615
Indian Sculptors' Association, Mumbai 053699
Indian Society of Oriental Art, Kolkata 053700
Indian Springs State Park Museum, Flovilla 043873
Indian Style, West Hollywood 120389
Indian Sun, Houston 116345
Indian Temple Mound Museum, Fort Walton Beach 043989
Indian War Memorial Museum, Delhi 022084
Indiana Basketball Hall of Fame, New Castle 046213
Indiana Historical Society Museum, Indianapolis 044742
Indiana Medical History Museum, Indianapolis 044743
Indiana State Museum, Indianapolis 044744
Indiana Territory Capitol, Vincennes 048788
Indiana Transportation Museum, Noblesville 046492
Indiana University Art Museum, Bloomington 042263
Indiana University Press, Bloomington 135332
Indiana War Memorials Museum, Indianapolis 044745
Indianapolis Art Center, Churchman-Fehsenfeld-Gallery, Indianapolis . 044746
Indianapolis Motor Speedway Hall of Fame Museum, Indianapolis 044747
Indianapolis Museum of Art, Indianapolis 044748
Indianapolis Museum of Art - Columbus Gallery, Columbus 043097
Indianas Antiques, Atlanta 087487, 131780
Indianermuseum, Zürich 037791
Indica, Delhi 105666
L'Indicibile, Firenze 075359
Indicible, Rouen 067273
Indicible, Rouen 067274
Indidjinart Aboriginal Art Gallery, Dubbo 094493
Indien Cinq Nations, Québec 097143
Les Indiennes, Paris 066080
L'Indifférent, Lyon 064142
Indigenart, Fremantle 055844
Indigenart, Subiaco 056645
Indigenous Art, Christchurch 079035
Indigo, Bath 083430
Indigo, Kathmandu 107587
Indigo, London 085417
Indigo, Manningford Bruce 085921
Indigo, Manningford Bruce 085922
Indigo, Minneapolis 090368
Indigo, Philadelphia 091646, 118780
Indigo for Contemporary Art, Saint Andrews 114347
Indigo Uptown, Minneapolis 090369
Indira, Cáceres 081025
Indira Gandhi National Centre for the Arts, Delhi 022085
Individual Artists of Oklahoma, Oklahoma City 046644
Individual Artists of Oklahoma, Oklahoma City 054804
Indo-Cuban Bani Museum, Banes . . 007873
Indonesian Art, Richmond, Victoria . 095137
Indonésie Tropicale, Montgeron . . . 064685
Indre Sør-Troms Distriktsmuseum, Tennevoll 031262
Indruk, Zwolle 140581
Indulgence Antiques, Templestowe . 056704
Indunabor, Bogotá 098170
Industrial and Agricultural Museum, York 049348
Industrial and Commercial Museum, Lahore 031379
Industrial Art, Ha Noi 052428
Industrial Designers Society of America, Dulles 054805
Industrial Heritage Complex, Smiths Falls 006486
Industrial Museum, Nottingham . . . 040620
Industrie Museum Lauf, Lauf an der Pegnitz 018526
Industrie- und Filmmuseum Wolfen, Wolfen 020953
Industrie- und Vorgeschichtemuseum, Freilichtmuseum Himmelreich, Wattens 002810
Industrieel Museum, Sas van Gent . 030121
Industrieel Smalspoor Museum, Erica 029577
Industriemuseum, Limbach-Oberfrohna 018647
Industriemuseum Brandenburg, Brandenburg an der Havel 016368
Industriemuseum Elmshorn, Elmshorn 016948
Industriemuseum Hartha, Hartha bei Döbeln 017782
Industriemuseum Lohne, Lohne, Oldenburg 018679
Industrieviertel-Museum, Museum für Industrie und Arbeitsgeschichte, Wiener Neustadt 003033
Industrimuseet, Kopperå 030951
Industrimuséet C.W. Thorstensons Mekaniska Verkstad, Åmål 036180
Industrion Museum for Industry and Society, Kerkrade 029809
Inecos, Roma 076510
Ineichen, Josef, Rupperswil 130154
Ineichen, Peter, Zürich 122368
Inerdi Studio, Madrid 110549
Ines Art Gallery, Singapore 109813
Infantierie Museum, Harskamp . . . 029677
Infantry and Small Arms School Corps Weapons Collection, Warminster . 041300
Infinito, Sapporo 077195
Infinity Antique Furniture, Hong Kong 059644
Infinity Fine Arts, New York 118036
Infirmary Museum, Saint Ronan's Church Museum and Columba Centre, Isle-of-Iona 039823
Influxfunds, Hong Kong 059645
Info-Musées, Liège 135600
Informationsdienst KUNST, Regensburg 135768
Informationsstelle des Naturparks Fichtelgebirge, Zell, Oberfranken . 021051
Informationszentrum am Wasserstraßenkreuz Minden, Minden, Westfalen 018951
Informationszentrum Schloss Paffendorf, RWE Rheinbraun AG, Bergheim, Erft 015966
Informationszentrum und Heimatsammlung, Zell, Oberfranken 021051
Infozentrum und Elektromuseum, Ansbach 015554
Infusion Art Studio, Tucson 120137
Infusion Design Art Glass Gallery, Tucson 120138
Ingatestone Hall, Ingatestone 039798
Ingbar, Michael F., New York 118037
Ingeborgmuseet, Tangen 031260
Ingebrigt Vik's Museum, Øystese . . 031118
Ingelbrecht, Oslo 079445, 108731
Ingels, F., Gent 123621
Ingels-Humblot, Véronique, Roanne 121232
Inger & Dan, Stockholm 081966
Ingerslev, København 060340
Ingersol, Tonya, Baltimore 115060
Ingersoll Cheese Factory Museum, Ingersoll 005637
Ingiulla, Roma 076511
Ingle, Virginia Beach 093357
Ingle, D.D. & A., Nottingham 086137
Ingleby Gallery, Edinburgh 112996
Inglenook, Harpole 084566
Inglenook, Ramsbury 086324, 131403
Inglett, Susan, New York 118038
Inglett, Susan, New York 118039
Inglewood District Historical Museum, Inglewood 001127
Inglis, Gordon, Edinburgh 084298
Ingrained, Rockingham 056546
Ingram, Toronto 059214
Ingram Gallery, Toronto 097294
Ingrassia, Stefano, Milano 127609
Ingrids Art, Hawkes Bay 108468
Ingrow Loco Museum, Keighley . . . 039837
Ingurugiro Etxea, Azpeitia 034881
Ingušskij Gosudarstvennyj Muzej Kraevedenija im. T.Ch. Malsagova, Nazran 033549
Inherited Arts, Singapore 109814
Inhof, Ryde 123300
Inhofer, E., Regensburg 073459
Inhouse, Toronto 059215
Iniesta Gloria, Moissac 064580
Inishie, Nara 077161
Initial Tree Gallery, San Antonio . . . 119425
Initiative, Sankt-Peterburg 109631
Initiative von Münchner Galerien zeitgenössischer Kunst, München 053240
Iniziative Arte e Cultura, Roma 053758
Injalak Arts & Crafts, Oenpelli 056399
Inje, Den Haag 107928
Injuka, München 072742
Ink Tree, Küsnacht 135030
Inkoart, Kyïv 112410
Inkspecta, Mitcham 094861
Inkt Delft, Delft 107888
Inkworks, Los Angeles 142511

Inland Seas Maritime Museum of The Great Lakes Historical Society, Vermilion 048762
Inland-Water Ecological Laboratory Collection, Jerusalem 022954
Inlibris, Wien 137327
Inlight Art Glass, Buffalo . . 087885, 131857
Inliquid, Philadelphia 118781
Inmaculada Concepcion, Bogotá . . 059840
Inman, Kerry F., Houston 116346
Inman, Raymond P., Brighton 122438
Inn-Galerie, Kufstein 002184
Inn-Museum, Wasserbau- und Schiffahrtstechnische Sammlung, Rosenheim 019885
The Inner Bookshop, Oxford 141983
Inner City Art Gallery, New York . . . 118040
Inner Eye Vision, Leven 113388
Inner Mongolia Museum, Huhehot . 007140
Inner Vision Antiques, Los Angeles . 089801
Innervisions Posters, Seattle 119941
Innisfail and District Historical Museum, Innisfail 001128
Innisfail and District Historical Museum, Innisfail 005639
Inniskeen Folk Museum, Inniskeen . 022799
Innisville and District Museum, Innisville 005640
Innocent Fine Art, Bristol 112724
Innocenti, Ferdinando & Filippo, Firenze 075360, 140020
Innocenti, Roberto, Firenze 075361
Innocenti, Roberto, Firenze 075362
Innovanet, Auckland 108330
Innovative Art Gallery, New York . . . 118041
Innovatum Kunskapens Hus, Trollhättan 036718
Inns of Court and City Yeomanry Museum, London 040183
Innsbrucker Antiquariat, Innsbruck . 137197
Innuit Gallery, London 096954
Innviertler Freilichtmuseum Brunnbauerhof, Andorf 001688
Innviertler Künstlergilde, Ried im Innkreis 052543
Inoue, Tokyo 140186
Inpa Coleções Zoológicas, Manaus . 004204
Inprint, Stroud 142097
Inprints, Seattle 119942
Inquadrature Arte e Cornici, Trieste 106717
A l'Inquet, Carbonne 061968
Inquisitive, Toronto 059216
Inquisitor's Palace, National Museum of Ethnography of Malta, Vittoriosa . 028044
Insa Gallery, Seoul 107256
Insam, Grita, Wien 095871
Insam, Josef & Angelika, Regensburg 073460
Insam, Peter, Regensburg 073461, 126690
Insectarium de Montréal, Montréal . 005926
Insects Museum, Amman 027368
Insel Verlag, Frankfurt am Main . . . 133945
Inselgalerie, Frauenchiemsee 102847
Inselmuseum, Pellworm 019586
Inselmuseum im Alten Leuchtturm, Wangerooge 020675
Inselmuseum Spiekeroog, Spiekeroog 020266
Insensatez, Lisboa 109329
Inshallah Egyptian Imports, Paraparaumu 079219
Insho-Domoto Museum of Fine Arts, Kyoto 026723
Inside, Cleveland 115717
Inside Out, Penkridge 086199
Inside Out, San Antonio 092521
Inside Outside, Houston 089115
Inside Secrets, Portland 091955
Inside Space, London 113709
Insight Art Gallery, Springbrook . . . 095217
Insight Sculpture Gallery, Norwich . 114165
Insights - El Paso Science Center, El Paso 043640
Insite, Marseille 099670
Insolite, Bordeaux 061621
Insolite, Saint-Ouen 067804
Insolite, Troyes 068650
Inspiration Gallery, Memphis 116990
Inspirations, London 113710
Inspirations Gallery, Mildura 094846
Inspire - Hands-on Science Centre, Norwich 040606
Inspires Art Gallery, Oxford 114201
Installation Gallery, San Diego 119517
Installation Gallery Insite, San Diego 047821
Instanbul to Samarkand Gallery, Austin 087586
L'Instant Durable, Clermont-Ferrand 133461
Institut Art et Archéologie de Byzance, Strasbourg 049990
Institut d'Archéologie et d'Histoire de l'Art, Université de Nancy II, Nancy . . . 049963
Institut d'Art Conservation et Couleur, Paris 124700
Institut d'Art Contemporain, Villeurbanne 015297
Institut d'Art Mediéval, Université Paul Valery, Montpellier 049960
Institut d'Arts Visuels, Orléans 049967
Institut de France, Paris 049979
Institut de France, Saint-Jean-Cap-Ferrat 014337
Institut d'Egypte, Cairo 049921
Institut der Künste, Pädagogische Hochschule Freiburg, Freiburg im Breisgau 050087
Institut des Communications Graphiques, Montréal 049803
Institut d'Histoire de l'Art et de Muséologie, Université de Neuchâtel, Neuchâtel 050772
Institut et Musée Voltaire, Genève . 037122
Institut Finlandais, Paris 100534
Institut for Kunsthistorie, Københavns Universitet, København 049902
Institut Français d'Architecture, Cité de l'Architecture et du Patrimoine, Paris 013596
Institut für Ästhetische Bildung und ihre Didaktik, Christian-Albrechts-Universität zu Kiel, Kiel 050149
Institut für Architekturgeschichte, Universität Stuttgart, Stuttgart . . . 050242
Institut für Architekturzeichnen und Raumgestaltung, Technische Universität Carolo-Wilhelmina zu Braunschweig, Braunschweig 050041
Institut für Ausbildung in bildender Kunst und Kunsttherapie, Bochum 050036
Institut für Bau- und Kunstgeschichte, Universität Hannover, Hannover . . 050124
Institut für Baugeschichte, Architekturtheorie und Denkmalpflege, Technische Universität Berlin, Berlin 050021
Institut für Baugeschichte, Architekturtheorie und Denkmalpflege, Technische Universität Dresden, Dresden 050064
Institut für Bildende Künste, Universität Fridericiana zu Karlsruhe, Karlsruhe 050142
Institut für Bildende Künste, Universität Hannover, Hannover 050122
Institut für Bildende Kunst und ihre Didaktik, Universität Flensburg, Flensburg . 050080
Institut für Bildende Kunst und Kunstwissenschaft, Universität Hildesheim, Hildesheim 050131
Institut für Bildnerische Erziehung und Kunstwissenschaft, Akademie der bildenden Künste, Wien 049651
Institut für Buch- und Handschriftenrestaurierung, Bayerische Staatsbibliothek, München 050191
Institut für Byzantinistik, Neugriechische Philologie und Byzantinische Kunstgeschichte, Ludwig-Maximilians-Universität München, München . . 050192
Institut für Darstellen und Gestalten, Universität Stuttgart, Fakultät 1-Architektur+Stadtplanung, Stuttgart 050243
Institut für Darstellung und Gestaltung, Technische Universität Berlin, Berlin 050022
Institut für Designforschung, Oldenburg, Oldenburg 050214
Institut für Elementares Formen, Technische Universität Carolo-Wilhelmina zu Braunschweig, Braunschweig . . . 050042
Institut für Entwerfen und Architektur, Universität Hannover, Hannover . . 050123
Institut für Ethnodesign, Linz 049637
Institut für Gebäudelehre und Entwerfen, Technische Universität Carolo-Wilhelmina zu Braunschweig, Braunschweig . 050043
Institut für Gegenwartskunst, Akademie der bildenden Künste, Wien 049652
Institut für Geschichte und Theorie, FB Architektur, Universität Hannover, Hannover 050124
Institut für Grundlagen der Gestaltung, Universität Fridericiana zu Karlsruhe, Karlsruhe 050143
Institut für Grundlagen der Planung in der Architektur, Universität Stuttgart, Stuttgart 050244
Institut für Grundlagen des Entwerfens, Technische Universität Carolo-Wilhelmina zu Braunschweig, Braunschweig . 050044
Institut für Grundlagen moderner Architektur und Enwerfen, Universität Stuttgart, Stuttgart 050245
Institut für Hermeneutik, Universität Zürich, Zürich 050779
Institut für Kirchenbau und kirchliche Kunst der Gegenwart, Marburg 050181
Institut für Kirchengeschichte, Christliche Archäologie und Kirchliche Kunst, Universität Wien, Wien 049653
Institut für Künste und Medien, Universität Potsdam, Golm 050093
Institut für Künstlerische Gestaltung, Graz 049623
Institut für Künstlerische Gestaltung, Technische Universität Wien, Wien 133209
Institut für Kultur- und Kunstwissenschaften, Humboldt-Universität zu Berlin, Berlin 050023
Institut für Kunst, Katholisch-Theologische Hochschule Linz, Linz 049638
Institut für Kunst, Universität Erfurt, Erfurt 050076
Institut für Kunst, Musik und Literatur, Hochschule Vechta, Vechta 050255
Institut für Kunst, Musik und Sport, Pädagogische Hochschule Ludwigsburg, Ludwigsburg, Württemberg 050171
Institut für Kunst und Handwerk, Lehnin 050164
Institut für Kunst und ihre Didaktik, Universität Dortmund, Dortmund . 050060
Institut für Kunst und Kunsttheorie, Universität zu Köln, Köln 050156
Institut für Kunst- und Musikwissenschaft, Technische Universität Dresden, Dresden 050065
Institut für Kunst und und Kulturwissenschaften, Philosophische und Historische Anthropologie der Kunst, Akademie der bildenden Künste, Wien 049654
Institut für Kunstdokumentation, Forschung und Gemäldebegutachtung, Bad Breisig 050007
Institut für Kunsterziehung, Universität Regensburg, Regensburg 050222
Institut für Kunstgeschichte, Bayerische Julius-Maximilians-Universität Würzburg, Würzburg 050265
Institut für Kunstgeschichte, Erzherzog-Johann-Universität, Graz 049624
Institut für Kunstgeschichte, Friedrich-Alexander-Universität Erlangen-Nürnberg, Erlangen 050077
Institut für Kunstgeschichte, Karl-Franzens-Universität Graz, Graz 049625
Institut für Kunstgeschichte, Leopold-Franzens-Universität Innsbruck, Innsbruck 049631
Institut für Kunstgeschichte, Ludwig-Maximilians-Universität München, München 050193
Institut für Kunstgeschichte, Martin-Luther-Universität Halle-Wittenberg, Halle, Saale 050098
Institut für Kunstgeschichte, Rheinisch-Westfälische Technische Hochschule, Aachen 050001
Institut für Kunstgeschichte, Universität Bern, Bern 050759
Institut für Kunstgeschichte, Universität Fridericiana zu Karlsruhe, Karlsruhe 050144
Institut für Kunstgeschichte, Universität Leipzig, Leipzig 050168
Institut für Kunstgeschichte, Universität Regensburg, Regensburg 050223
Institut für Kunstgeschichte, Universität Salzburg, Salzburg 049646
Institut für Kunstgeschichte, Universität Stuttgart, Stuttgart 050246
Institut für Kunstgeschichte, Universität Wien, Wien 049655
Institut für Kunstgeschichte, Westfälische Wilhelms-Universität Münster, Münster 050202
Institut für Kunstgeschichte, Denkmalpflege und Industriearchäologie, Technische Universität Wien, Wien 049656
Institut für Kunstpädagogik, Johann Wolfgang Goethe-Universität, Frankfurt am Main 050083
Institut für Kunstpädagogik, Justus-Liebig-Universität Gießen, Gießen 050090
Institut für Kunstpädagogik, Ludwig-Maximilians-Universität München, München 050194
Institut für Kunstpädagogik, Universität Leipzig, Leipzig 050169
Institut für Kunstwissenschaft/ Bildende Kunst, Universität Koblenz/Landau, Koblenz 050153
Institut für Kunstwissenschaft/ Bildende Kunst, Universität Koblenz/Landau, Abt. Koblenz, Landau in der Pfalz 050162
Institut für Litaraturwissenschaft, Christliche Kunst und Hymnologie, Karl-Franzens-Universität Graz, Graz 049626
Institut für moderne Kunst, Nürnberg 019360
Institut für Museumskunde, Staatliche Museen zu Berlin - Stiftung Preußischer Kulturbesitz, Berlin 016081
Institut für Neue Technische Form, Darmstadt 016639
Institut für Orientalische Archäologie und Kunst, Martin-Luther-Universität Halle-Wittenberg, Halle, Saale 050099
Institut für Papierrestaurierung, Wien 049657
Institut für Realienkunde des Mittelalters und der Frühen Neuzeit, Österreichische Akademie der Wissenschaft, Krems 049635
Institut für Restaurierung und Konservierung, Fachhochschule Köln, Fakultät für Kulturwissenschaften, Köln 050157
Institut für Technologie der Malerei, Staatliche Akademie der Bildenden Künste, Stuttgart 050247
Institut für textiles Gestalten, Akademie der bildenden Künste, Wien 049658
Institut für Vogelforschung -Vogelwarte Helgoland, Heinrich-Gätke-Halle, Wilhelmshaven 020895
Institut für Wissenschaft und Kunst, Wien 049659
Institut Iskusstv i Dizajna, Udmurtskij Gosudarstvennyj Universitet, Iževsk 050634
Institut l'Homme et le Temps, Centre de Restauration, La Chaux-de-Fonds 129996
Institut National d'Archéologie et des Arts, Tunis 050789
Institut National des Arts, Kinshasa 049873

Institut Néerlandais, Paris 100535
Institut Provincial des Arts et Metiers, Nivelles 049725
Institut Provincial des Arts et Métiers du Centre, La Louvière 049711
Institut Reine Astrid, Arts et Metiers Saint-Luc, Mons 049722
Institut Royal des Sciences Naturelles de Belgique, Bruxelles 003354
Institut Royal du Patrimoine Artistique, Bruxelles 133272
Institut Saint-Luc - Architecture-Urbanisme-Arts Plastiques, Bruxelles 049689
Institut Seni Indonesia Yogyakarta, Jogjakarta 050335
Institut Suisse pour l'Etude de l'Art, Université de Lausanne, Lausanne 050768
Institut Supérieur pour l'Étude du Langage Plastique, Bruxelles 049690, 096214, 133273, 137443
Institut Technique des Arts Plastiques, Lubumbashi 049874
Institut Technologique d'Art, d'Architecture et d'Urbanisme, Tunis 050790
Institut Tessin, Paris 013597
Institut und Museum für Geologie und Paläontologie, Tübingen 020496
Institut Universitaire de formation des maitres, Maxéville 049957
Institut Zeileis, Gallspach 001882
The Institute For American Indian Studies, Washington Green 048976
Institute for Art Research and Documentation, Madison 051655
Institute for Arts and Humanities Education, New Brunswick 051786
Institute for Jewish Studies Gallery, Jerusalem 022955
Institute for the Arts, Rice University, Houston 051484
Institute Menezes Braganza, Panaji 022289
Institute of Aesthetic Studies, Colombo 050741
Institute of Aesthetics and Art History, Graduate School of Letters, Kyoto University, Kyoto 050461
Institute of African Studies Teaching Museum, Legon 021109
Institute of American Indian Arts, Santa Fe 052142
Institute of American Indian Arts Museum, Santa Fe 047967
Institute of Archaeology and Museum Studies, Jos 030689
Institute of Architecture and Art, Baku 049670
Institute of Arts and Crafts, Delhi . . 050299
Institute of Arts and Crafts, Dhaka .003106, 049672
Institute of British Picture Framers, Amersham 054408
Institute of Ceramics, Stoke-on-Trent 054409
Institute of Contemporary Art, Boston 042327
Institute of Contemporary Art, Maine College of Art, Portland 047159
Institute of Contemporary Art, University of Pennsylvania, Philadelphia 046952
Institute of Contemporary Arts, London 040184
Institute of Contemporary Plastic Art Kitakanto, Maebashi 050465
Institute of Design, Illinois Institute of Technology, Chicago 051129
Institute of Fine Arts, New York University, New York 051825
Institute of Fine Arts and Design, Philippine Womens University, Manila 050596
Institute of Geological and Nuclear Sciences, Hutt City 030519
Institute of Jamaica, Kingston 026385
Institute of Meteoritics Meteorite Museum, Albuquerque 041616
Institute Of Modern Art, Judith Wright Centre of Contemporary Arts, Fortitude Valley 001036
Institute of Museum and Liberary Services, Washington 054806
Institute of Nature Study, National Science Museum Tokyo, Tokyo 027176
Institute of Paper Conservation, Upton-upon-Severn 054410
Institute of Texan Cultures, San Antonio 047796
Institute of Visual Arts, University of Wisconsin-Milwaukee, Milwaukee 045890
Institutionen för Konstvetenskap, Stockholms Universitet, Stockholm 050750
Instituto Amatller de Arte Hispánico, Barcelona 034915
Instituto Cultural Cabañas, Guadalajara 028277
Instituto de Arte, Facultad de Humanidades y Educación, Universidad Central, Caracas 052421
Instituto de Artes Gráficas de Oaxaca, Oaxaca 028603
Instituto de Bellas Artes del Magdalena, Santa Marta 049871
Instituto de Bellas Artes, Facultad de Filosofía y Letras, Universidad Nacional del Litoral, Rosario 049604
Instituto de Diseño, Montevideo . . . 050861
Instituto de Investigaciones Arqueológicas y Museo Prof. Mariano Gambier, Albardón 000108
Instituto de Investigaciones Artísticas, Facultad de Arquitectura, Universidad Mayor de San Andrés, La Paz . . . 049743
Instituto de Letras e Artes, Pelotas . 049750
Instituto de Restauración y Conservación Oebén, Madrid 050724, 129631
Instituto de Valencia de Don Juan, Don Juan Institute of Valencia, Madrid 035390
Instituto Departamental de Bellas Artes, Cali 049867
Instituto Europeo di Design, Madrid 050725
Instituto Geográfico Agustín Codazzi, Museo de Suelos de Colombia, Bogotá . . 007412
Instituto Gómez-Moreno de la Fundación Rodríguez-Acosta, Granada 035250
Instituto Hidalguense de Bellas Artes, Pachuca 050543
Instituto Hondureño de Cultura Interamericana, Comayagüela . . . 050280
Instituto Mexicano Norteamericano de Jalisco, Guadalajara 028278
Instituto Moreira Sales, São Paulo . 004510
Instituto Moreira Salles, Belo Horizonte 003997
Instituto Moreira Salles, Poços de Caldas 004286
Instituto Moreira Salles, Centro Cultural IMS - Rio de Janeiro, Rio de Janeiro . . 004344
Instituto Nacional de Bellas Artes y Literatura, México 050536
Instituto Nacional Indigenista, México 050537
Instituto Paulista de Restauro, São Paulo 049767, 133307
Instituto Português de Museus, Lisboa 054005
Instituto Português do Património Arquitectónico e Arqueológico, Lisboa 032630
Instituto Potósino de Bellas Artes, San Luis Potosí 050545
Instituto Regional de Bellas Artes, Orizaba 050542
Instituto Regional de Ucayali, Pucallpa 031585
Instituto Superior de Arte, La Habana 049882
Instituto Zacatecano de Bellas Artes, Zacatecas 050548
Instituts- und Studiensammlung des Instituts für Ur- und Frühgeschichte, Wien 002915
Institutt for Arkeologi, Kunsthistorie og Konservering, Universitetet i Oslo, Oslo 050581
Institutt for Kunsthistorie, Tromsø . . 050584
Institutt for Kunsthistorie, Universitetet i Bergen, Bergen 050579
Institutul de Arheologie şi Istoria Artei, Cluj-Napoca 050623, 134875
Institutul de Arhitectură Ion Mincu, Bucureşti 050618
Institutul de Etnografie si Folclor Constantin Brăilou, Bucureşti 050619
Institutul de Istoria Artei George Oprescu, Bucureşti 050620
Instytut Artystyczno-Pedagogiczny, Toruń 050605
Instytut Historii Architektury i Konserwacji Zabytkow, Kraków 050601
Instytut Historii Sztuki, Kraków 050602
Instytut Historii Sztuki, Warszawa . . 050608
Instytut Historii Sztuki, Wrocław . . . 050611
Instytut Sztuki, Uniwersytet Śląski w Cieszyne, Cieszyn 050598
Instytut Sztuki PAN, Warszawa 050609, 134862
Instytut Zabytkoznawstwa i Konserwatorstwa, Toruń 050606
Intaglio Gallery, Saint Ives 095169
IntAkt - Internationale Aktionsgemeinschaft bildender Künstlerinnen, Wien . . . 052544
Intaria, Madrid 081323
Intarsija, Sankt-Peterburg 129245
Intarta, Knokke-Heist 096338
Intellect, Gent 058188, 137497
Intemporel, Paris 100536
Intemporel, Paris 138408
Intemporel, Saint-Gaudens 067479
Intemporelle, Nantes 064927
Inter Achats Dieuze, Dieuze 062630
Inter African, Silverton 080746
Inter Antiquariaat, Amsterdam 140308
Inter Antiquariaat, Zeist 140577
Inter Art, Berlin 101934
Inter-Art, Helsinki 098734
Inter Art Actuel, Québec 135635
Inter Art Center, Hasselt 096312
Inter Art Galerie, Köln 103646
Inter Art Gallery, New York 118042
Inter Art Ring, Moskva . . . 054021, 109553
Inter Art - Sonsbeek Art and Design, Arnhem 029268
Inter-Atrium, Porto 109390
Inter-Continental, Vancouver 097489
Inter-Fun, Lyon 138153
Inter Galereja Sovremennogo Iskusstva, Moskva 109554
Inter-Livres, Paris 133632
Inter Militaria en Collectibles, Oss . 078671
Inter Prints, Houston 116347
Interaction Designs, Salt Lake City . 132789
Interantik, Achau 056910
Interantiques Limited, Genova 075476
Interart, Genève 111473
Interart, Rotterdam 078722
Het Interbellum, Amsterdam 077870
Interbook, Trier 139788
Interbook International, Schiedam . 140527
Intercisa Múzeum, Dunaújváros . . . 021716
Intercoin, Newcastle-upon-Tyne . . . 086067
Intercol London, London . . 085418, 131067, 141833
INTERCOM International Committee for Museums Management, Castries . 054033
Intercraft Gallery, Sharjah 112468
Intercultural Museum and Art Gallery, Baltimore 041987
Interdruck Galerie, Leipzig 103882
Interessengemeinschaft der Museumsbetreiber, Oberwart 052545
Interessengemeinschaft freier bildender Künstler, Düsseldorf 053241
Interessengemeinschaft niederösterreichischer Museen und Sammlungen, Atzenbrugg 052546
Interfennica, Helsinki 137942
Interforma, Madrid 081324
Intergalerias, Acapulco 107462
Interieur, Budapest 074689
Interieur 13, Gent 058189
Interieur 2000, Judenburg 057092, 123396
Intérieur de Chasse, Paris 066081
Intérieur Design, Marly 130114
Interieurs, New York 090964
Interim Art, London 113711
Interior Angle, Chelmsford 112842
Interior Art Australia, Richmond, Victoria 095138
Interior Details, Louisville 116947
Interior Elements, Nashville 090459
Interior Visions, San Francisco 092818
Intérior's, Le Havre 063634
Interiors Market, Atlanta 087488
Interiors Market, Birmingham 087762
Interiors Marketplace, Charlotte . . . 087959
Interiors Society, Milano 075743
Interlaken Historical Society Museum, Interlaken 044758
Interlibrum, Vaduz 140224
Intermedia Arts Minnesota, Minneapolis 045913
Intermezzo, Cogolin 062385
Intermezzo, Dordrecht 107979
Intermobília, Lisboa 079947
Intermuseum Conservation Association, Oberlin 054807
Internacional Antique, Madrid 081325
Internasjonale Barnekunstmuseet, Oslo 031081
Internasjonalt Kultursenter og Museum, Oslo 053942
Internationaal Exlibriscentrum, Sint-Niklaas 003757
Internationaal Museum 1939-1945, Uithuizen 030215
International, Cairo 060451
International Academy of Media Arts and Sience, Ogaki 050469
International Altex, Madrid 110550
International Antique Books & Coins, Singapore 080493, 140952
International Antique Buyers, New York 090965
International Antique Fair, Nagoya, Aichi 093800
International Antiques, Denver 088700
International Antiques, Norfolk 091384, 132557
International Antiques, Tulsa 093314
International Antiques and Collectables, New York 090966
International Antiquités, Saint-Ouen 067805
International Art and Design Fair, New York 093991
International Art and Frame Gallery, Tampa 120051
International Art Center, Miami 045811
International Art Centre, Auckland .078952, 121812
International Art Designs, Windsor, Ontario 097559
International Art Exchange, New York 118043
International Art Gallery, Nashville . 117358
International Art Gallery, San Francisco 119698
International Art Gallery, Washington 120312
International Art Gallery Saint-Anne, Bruxelles 096215
International Art Group, New York . . 118044
International Art Products, Assendelft 134797
International Art Space, Kellerberrin 094685
International Artexpo New York, New York 093992
International Artists, Phoenix 118876
International Asian Art Fair, New York 093993
International Association for the Fantastic in the Arts Newsletter, Boca Raton . 136500
International Association of Agricultural Museums, Rožnov pod Radhoštěm 052838
International Association of Arts Critics, Skopje 053851
International Association of Astronomical Artists, Lyme Regis 054411
International Association of Astronomical Artists, Orlando 054808

International Association of Custom Museums, Antwerpen 052679
International Association of Dealers in Ancient Art, London 054412
International Association of Libraries and Museums of Performing Arts (SIMBAS), Roma 053759
International Association of Museum Facility Administrators, New York 054809
International Association of Pastel Societies, Falls Church 054810
International Association of Transport and Communication Museums, Ängelholm 054134
International Auctioneers, Genève .054184, 136124
International Bluegrass Music Museum, Owensboro 046759
International Bowling Museum and Hall of Fame, Saint Louis 047664
International Center for Advanced Studies in Art, New York 054811
International Center of Medieval Art. Newsletter, New York 136501
International Center of Photography, New York 046348
International Centre for Expertise of Paintings, Bruxelles 052680
International Centre for the Study of the Preservation and the Restoration of Cultural Property (ICCROM), Roma 053760
International Ceramics Fair, London 093933
International Child Art, Washington . 120313
International Clown Hall of Fame and Research Center, Milwaukee 045891
International Coins Unlimited, Philadelphia 091647
International Committee for Costume Museums, London 054413
International Committee for Egyptology in ICOM - CIPEG, Baltimore 054812
International Committee for Exhibition Exchange, Washington 054813
International Committee for Glass Museums, Corning 054814
International Committee for Monetary Museums, Utrecht 053893
International Committee for Museology, Barcelona 054119
International Committee for Museums and Collections of Modern Art, Helsinki 052875
International Committee for Museums and Collections of Musical Instruments, Trondheim 053943
International Committee for Museums and Collections of Natural History, Frankfurt am Main 053242
International Committee for University Museums and Collections (UMAC), Macquarie 052475
International Company, Chofu 077036
International Confederation, Nairobi 053812
International Confederation of Architectural Museums, Rotterdam 053894
International Congress of Maritime Museums, Essex 054815
International Conservation Services, Chatswood 123211
International Contemporary Art Fair Association, Paris 052960
International Council of African Museums (AFRICOM), Nairobi 053813
International Council of Museums, Andorran National Committee, Aixovall 052440
International Council of Museums ICOM, Paris 052961
International Council of Museums - UK National Committee, London 054414
International Council on Monuments and Sites, Paris 052962
International Crane Foundation Museum, Baraboo 042018
International Cultural Center for Youth in Jerusalem, Jerusalem 022956
International Custom Upolstery, Philadelphia 132625
International Exposition for Sculpture Objects and Functional Art, Chicago 093994
International Fair for Design, Construction and Distribution of Art Derivats, Paris 093665
International Fine Art and Antique Dealers Show, New York 093995
International Fine Art Fair, New York 093996
International Fine Arts College, Miami 051700
International Fine Arts Conservation Studios, Bristol 130457
International Fine Print Dealers Association, New York 054816
International Fox Museum, Summerside 006535
International Furniture, Phoenix . . . 132650
International Furniture Imports, Indianapolis 089307
International Gallery, Pau 100985
International Gallery of African Art, Washington 120314
International Grafik, Frederikshavn . 135671
International Graphics, Eggenstein-Leopoldshafen 133904
The International Guild of Artists, Ilkley 054415
International Hippocratic Foundation of Kos, Kos 021342
International Ice Hockey Federation Museum, Kingston 005697
International Images, Sewickley . . . 048121
International Importers, Sacramento 092167
International Institute for Conservation of Historic and Artistic Works, London 054416
International Institute of Metropolitan Detroit, Detroit 043451
International Interiors, Brighton . . . 083701
International Japanese Print Auctioneers, New York 123002
International Jewish Sports Hall of Fame, Netanya 023039
International Journal of Art and Design Education, Oxford 136230
The International Journal of Arts Management, Montréal 135636
International Motor Racing Research Center, Watkins Glen 049003
International Movement for a New Museology, Zuni 054817
International Museum of Art, El Paso 043641
International Museum of Cartoon Art, Boca Raton 042284
International Museum of Children's Art, Oslo 031082
International Museum of Cultures, Dallas 043272
International Museum of Gay and Lesbian History, Los Angeles 045432
International Museum of Peace and Solidarity, Samarkand 049402
International Museum of Photography and Film, George Eastman House, Rochester 047480
International Museum of Surgical Science, Chicago 042851
International Museum of the Horse, Lexington 045260
International Museum Theatre Alliance, Boston 054818
International Poster Gallery, Boston 115185
International Public Art, New York . . 118045
International Ravissant, New York . 090967
International Review of African American Art, Hampton 136502
International Sculpture Center, Hamilton 044398
International Sewing Machine Collectors' Society, London 054417
International Society for Jewish Art, Mohegan Lake 054819
International Society Of Antique Scale Collectors, Los Angeles 054820
International Society of Appraisers, Seattle 054821
International Society of Copier Artists, Brooklyn 054822
International Society of Libraries and Museums of Performing Arts, Paris 052963
International Society of Marine Painters, Oneco 054823
International Sport Aviation Museum, Lakeland 045122
International Swimming Hall of Fame, Fort Lauderdale 043932
International Tennis Hall of Fame Museum, Newport 046458
International Trading Post, Houston 089116
International Village Gallery, San Francisco 119699
International Visions Gallery, Washington 120315
International Wildlife Museum, Tucson 048639
International Women's Air and Space Museum, Cleveland 042994
International World Of Art Gallery, Dubai 112452
Internationale Akademie für bildende Künste, Niederbipp 050773
Internationale Antikmesse Aabenraa, Rødekro 093643
Internationale Arbeitsgemeinschaft der Archiv-, Bibliotheks- und Graphikrestauratoren - IADA, Göttingen 053243
Internationale Biënnale Antiek, Actuele Kunst en Levensstijl, Kortrijk 093606
Internationale Fachmesse für Ausstellungstechnik, Köln 093721
Internationale Gesellschaft der Bildenden Künste e.V., Berlin 053244
Internationale Gesellschaft für Kunst, Gestaltung und Therapie, Basel . . 054185
Internationale Jugendbibliothek, München 019063
Internationale Kunst- en Antiekbeurs, Brugge 093607
Internationale Kunst- en Antiekbeurs Maastricht, Maastricht 093829
Internationale Kunst- und Antiquitäten-Tage, Berlin 093722
Internationale Kunstbeurs, Amsterdam 093830
Internationale Kunstbeurs 19de, de 20ste en de 21de Eeuw, Gent 093608
Internationale Kunstmesse Art Vienna, Wien 093578
Internationale Kunstmesse Basel, Kunst des 20. und 21. Jahrhunderts, Basel . 093890
Internationale Kunstmesse Zürich, Zürich 093891
Internationale Messe für Editionen, Art Brut, Kunst nach 1980 und Fotografie, Köln 093723
Internationale Messe für Gegenwartskunst, Innsbruck 093579
Internationale Messe für moderne Kunst, Karlsruhe 093724
Internationale Numismatik Messe Berlin-Banknoten- und Wertpapierbörse, Berlin 093725
Internationale Photographieförderung, Gondiswil 054186, 111522
Internationale Puppenausstellung, Sankt Wolfgang im Salzkammergut 002635
Internationale Sammlerausstellung - Welt-Antik - Internationale Münzenmesse, Stuttgart 093726
Internationale Schwarzwälder Antiquitätentage, Villingen-Schwenningen 093727
Internationale Sommerakademie für Bildende Kunst, Salzburg 133140
Internationale Spitzensammlung, Nordhalben 019332
Internationale Tage Boehringer Ingelheim, Ingelheim am Rhein 018064
Internationalen Verkaufsausstellung für wertvolle Autographen, Bücher und Graphik, Berlin 093728
Internationaler Kulturdienst Verlag, München 134248
Internationaler Kunstkritiker-Verband, Sektion Schweiz, Zürich 054187
Internationaler Kunstkritikerverband, Sektion Österreich, Wien 052547
Internationaler Kunstkritikerverband e.V. (AICA), Sektion der Bundesrepublik Deutschland, Köln 053245
Internationales Design Zentrum Berlin e.V., Berlin 053246
Internationales Esperanto-Museum der Österreichischen Nationalbibliothek, Sammlung für Plansprachen, Wien 002916
Internationales FIS Wintersport- und Heimatmuseum, Mürzzuschlag . . 002343
Internationales Haus der Photographie, Hamburg 017699
Internationales Keramik-Museum, Die Neue Sammlung München, Weiden, Oberpfalz 020706
Internationales Luftfahrtmuseum, Villingen-Schwenningen 020595
Internationales Muschelmuseum, Wangerland 020674
Internationales Radiomuseum, Bad Laasphe 015742
Internationales Wind- und Wassermühlenmuseum, Gifhorn . 017415
Internationales Zeitungsmuseum der Stadt Aachen, Aachen 015420
Internazionale d'Arte Contemporanea a Torino, Torino 093767
Internet Auction Group, Pittsburgh . 123057
Internet Auction Service, San Diego 123098
Interni, Milano 075744
Internos Books, London 135227
Interntional Chinese Snuff Bottle Society. Journal, Baltimore 136503
Intersection for the Arts, San Francisco 054824
Intersection for the Arts Gallery, San Francisco 047865
L'Intersigne Livres Anciens, Paris . . 138409
Interspace, Genève 111474
Interstate Wholesalers, Las Vegas .089584, 122938
Intertrus Antiques, New York 090968
Interventi Classensi, Ravenna 135907
Interventia, Den Haag 078204
Intipunku-Art, Amstelveen 107644
Intrepid Sea-Air-Space Museum, New York 046349
Introspect, Dublin 135854
L'Introuvable, Paris 138410
Intrude Gallery, Fitzroy 094534
Inttueri, Rio de Janeiro 096621
Inuit Art Foundation, Ottawa 133321
Inuit Art Quarterly, Ottawa 135637
Inuit Gallery of Vancouver, Vancouver 097490
Invaluable, London 085419
Inventa, Münster 134296
The Invention Factory, Trenton 048603
Inveraray Bell Tower, Inveraray 039801
Inveraray Castle, Inveraray 039802
Inveraray Jail, Inveraray 039803
Inveraray Maritime Museum, Inveraray 039804
Inverbeg Galleries, Alexandria 112494
Inverell Art Society, Inverell 052476, 094660
Inverell Books, Inverell 136951
Inverkeithing Museum, Inverkeithing 039805
Inverness Miners Museum, Inverness 005643
Inverness Museum and Art Gallery, Inverness 039808
Invernizzi, Osvaldo, Zürich 082984
Inversiones en Arte y Naturaleza, Bilbao 110285
Inversiones en Arte y Naturaleza, Madrid 110551
Inversiones en Arte y Naturaleza, Valladolid 110853
Inversiones en Arte y Naturaleza, Zaragoza 110883
Inversiones i Reservats, Barcelona . 122008

Inversora Aranga, Caracas 093536
Investigarte, Roma 076512
Investors Gallery, New York 090969, 123003, 142667
Invetro, Hannover 103282
Invictus Arc, Providence 092042
L'Invitation au Voyage, Perpignan .. 066750
The Inya Gallery of Art, Yangon 107567
Inyaka African Art, Paddington 095030
Inženernyj (Michailovskij) Zamok, Gosudarstvennyj Russkij Muzej, Sankt-Peterburg 033755
IO, Berkeley 136504
Ioannidis, Nik., Piraeus 105441
Ioannidis Collection, Lindos 021361
Ioannidou, Parthena, Thessaloniki . 074639
Ioannina Museum, Ioannina 021279
Iodice, Salvatore, Napoli 127776
Iolani Palace, Honolulu 044599
Iolas, Athinai 134486
Ion Graphics, Chicago 115461
Iona Abbey Museum, Isle-of-Iona .. 039823
Iona Antiques, London 085420
Iona Heritage Centre, Isle-of-Iona .. 039824
Iona House Gallery, Woodstock ... 114731
Ionad Arann Heritage Centre, Aran Islands 022676
Ionad Dualchais Nis, Ness 040521
Ionnina Byzantine Museum, Ioannina 021280
Iook, Dunedin 079087
Iordanova, Lubka, Forcalquier 099270
Iorietti, Carlo, Torino 128316
Iosco County Historical Museum, East Tawas 043582
Iosephus, Lisboa 109330
Iosimi, Giancarlo, Roma 106564
Iowa Aviation Museum, Greenfield . 044325
Iowa Masonic Library and Museum, Cedar Rapids 042676
Iowa Museum Association, Waterloo 054825
Iowa Railroad Historical Museum, Boone 042301
I.P. Stanback Museum, South Carolina State University, Orangeburg 046707
Iparművészeti Múzeum, Budapest . 021657
Ipogeo dei Volumni, Ponte San Giovanni 025310
Ippedico, Guiseppe, Saint-Ouen ... 067806
Ippogrifo, Milano 075745
Ippuku Museum of Art, Asahi 026420
Ipreciation, Singapore 109815
Ipsos Galerie, Soual 068264
Ipswich Art Society, Ipswich 054418
Ipswich Historical Society Museum, Ipswich 044771
Ipswich Museum, Ipswich 039813
Ipswich Transport Museum, Ipswich 039814
Iqbal Museum, Javed Manzil, Lahore 031380
Iquest Children's Museum, Bellevue 042115
Ir-Art, Moskva 109555
Iraan Museum, Iraan 044773
Iraar, Genova 075477, 127458
Iram, Saint-Ouen 067807
Iran Bastan Museum, Teheran 022621
Iran Bazar, Jerusalem 105912
Iran Caligraphers Society, Teheran . 134523
Iranian National Museum of Water, Sa'd-Abad Museum, Teheran 022622
Iraq Natural History Research Centre and Museum, Baghdad 022662
Iraqi Artists Society, Baghdad 053709
Iraqi Museum, Baghdad 022663
Irazu Mendizabal, J.A., Vitoria-Gasteiz 110872
Irbid Archaeological Museum, Yarmouk University, Irbid 027380
Irchel, Buch am Irchel 082278
Irchester Narrow Gauge Railway Museum, Wellingborough 041324
Irea, Braunschweig 125376
Iredell Museum of Arts & Heritage, Statesville 048341
Ireland House Museum, Burlington . 005166
Ireland's Historic Science Centre, Birr 022694
Irene Cullis Gallery, Greensboro ... 044335
Irenka, Frederiksberg 060238
Irg, F., Schwendi 073771
Irgens, Bror, Stockholm 081967
Iriarte, Florida 055269
Irina & Sons, Sofia 096737
Irina's Antiques, San Francisco ... 132887
L'Iris, Milano 075746
Iris and B. Gerald Cantor Art Gallery, Worcester 049307
Iris & B. Gerald Cantor Center for Visual Arts at Stanford University, Stanford .. 048319
L'Iris Blanc, Bordeaux 061622
L'Iris Bleu, Nice 099844
L'Iris Bleu, Paris 066082
Iris Photography Gallery, Parafield Gardens 095054
Irish Academic Press, Dublin 134527
Irish Agricultural Museum, Wexford 022875
Irish American Heritage Museum, East Durham 043560
Irish Antique Dealers Association, Adare 053712
Irish Architectural Archive, Dublin .. 022750
The Irish Art Group, Ballymoney ... 112545
Irish Arts Review, Dublin 135855
Irish Auctioneers and Valuers Institute, Dublin 053713
Irish Historical Picture Company, Dublin 074924
Irish Horse Museum, Tully 022868
Irish International Antique and Fine Art Fair, Dublin 093755
Irish International Arts Centre, Rathkeale 053714
Irish Jewish Museum, Dublin 022751
Irish Labour History Society Museum, Dublin 022752
Irish Linen Centre and Lisburn Museum, Lisburn 040020
Irish Museum of Modern Art, Dublin 022753
Irish Museums Association, Dublin . 053715
Irish Museums Association Newsletter, Dublin 136231
Irish Music Hall of Fame, Dublin ... 022754
Irish Palatine Association Museum, Rathkeale 022850
Irish Professional Conservators' and Restorers' Association, Dublin ... 053716
Irish Steam Preservation Society Museum, Stradbally 022859
Irish Whiskey Corner Museum, Dublin 022767
Irkutskij Architekturno-ėtnografičeskij Muzej Talcy, Irkutsk 033156
Irkutskij Oblastnoj Chudožestvennyj Muzej im. V.P. Sukačeva, Irkutsk 033157
Irkutskij Oblastnoj Kraevedčeskij Muzej, Irkutsk 033158
Irlen, Medellin 123934
Irma Stern Museum of the University of Cape Town, Rosebank 034744
Irmak, Bern 082215, 129961
Irmão, Juazeiro, Rio de Janeiro ... 058599
Irmer, Herten 071495
Iroa, Donostia-San Sebastián 129508
Iroise Collections, Brest 061774
Iron and Steel Museum of Alabama, McCalla 045540
Iron Art, Birmingham 087763
Iron County Museum, Caspian 042649
Iron Creek Museum, Lougheed 005800
Iron Garden, Bridgetown 003120
Iron Gate, Nashville 090460
Iron Horse Design, Albuquerque ... 114797
Iron Mission Museum, Cedar City .. 042664
Iron Mountain Iron Mine, Vulcan ... 048807
Ironbridge Gorge Museum, Ironbridge 039816
Ironbridge Tollhouse, Ironbridge ... 039817
Ironchurch Antiques Centre, Bolton 083571, 130408
Ironcraft of Omaha, Omaha 132592
Ironeyes Gallery, Indianapolis 116467
Ironside Market, San Antonio 092522
Ironton, Denver 116016
Ironwood Area Historical Museum, Ironwood 044775
Ironworld Discovery Center, Chisholm 042907
Iroquois County Historical Society Museum, Watseka 049007
Iroquois Falls Pioneer Museum, Iroquois Falls 005648
Iroquois Indian Museum, Howes Cave 044659
Iroquois Indian Museum Notes, Howes Cave 136505
Irreplaceable Artifacts, New York .. 090970
Irresistibles, Houston 089117
Irrigaray, Bertrand, Jurancon 063267
Irrigaray, Bertrand, Pau 066707
Irrmisch, A., Bad Liebenzell 069323
Irrseer Heimathaus, Sammlung Hans Mairhofer-Irrsee, Zell am Moos .. 003065
Irvine, Washington 120316
Irvine Burns Club Museum, Irvine .. 039819
Irvine Fine Arts Center, Irvine 044776
Irvine Museum, Irvine 044777
Irving, Ruth, One Tree Hill 056403
Irving Arts Center, Irving 044779
Irving E. and Ray Kanner Heritage Museum, North York 006053
The Irving Gallery, Berwick-upon-Tweed 112624
Irving House Historic Centre and New Westminster Museum, New Westminster 006004
Irwin, Anne, Atlanta 114887
Irwin, Rex, Woollahra 056869
Is a Brocante, Nogent-sur-Marne .. 065211
Is Art, Katoomba 094682
Is Kunst Gallery, Oslo 079446
Isaac, John, Albuquerque 087400
Isaac, Sylvia, Heidelberg Heights .. 123240
Isaac Farrar Mansion, Bangor 042011
Isaacs, Louisville 090001
Isaacs, Segovia, Barcelona 110202
Isaacs-Innuit Gallery, Toronto 097295
Isaacs & Isaacs, Louisville 090002
Isaak Kaplan Old Yishuv Coourt Museum, Jerusalem 022957
Isaakevskij Sobor - Memorialnyj Muzej-pamjatnik, Sankt-Peterburg 033756
Isabel Miller Museum, Sitka 048196
Isabella Antiques, Warminster 087028
Isabella Brant Galerij, Antwerpen ..096071, 123548
Isabella M., Modena 075916
Isabella Stewart Gardner Museum, Boston 042328
Isabella's Jewellery, Noosa Heads . 056352
Isabelle, Dijon 062667
Isadora, Beirut 077398
Isadora, Bruxelles 057993
Isadora, Seattle 093020
Isahakians Museum, Erevan 000681
Isanti County Museum, Cambridge . 042568
Isao, Nara 106940
Isart Galerie, München 104234
Isaza, Martha Isabel, Medellín 123935
Isberian, Oscar, Chicago 088109
Isca Gallery, Budleigh Salterton ... 112751
Ischua Valley Historical Society, Franklinville 044046
ISCO, Camberley 135129
ISE Art Foundation, New York 046350
Iseema, Nagoya 077150
Isele, Klaus, Eggingen 133905
Isenbaye Art Gallery and Cultural Troupe, Oshogbo 030700
Isenring, Ersigen 082361, 130013
Isensee, Oldenburg, Oldenburg 134333
Isergebirgs Museum Neugablonz, Kaufbeuren 018211
Iserhardt, Volker, Bad Münster 125114
Isetan Bijutsukan, Tokyo 027177
I.S.F. Exposition, Chassieu 099120
I.S.F. Exposition, Villeneuve-d'Ascq 101473
Isfahan, Cape Town 080681
Isfahan, Essen 070634
Isfara Historical and Regional Museum, Isfara 037840
Isgro & Co., San Francisco 092819
Ishavsmuseet Aarvak, Brandal 030792
Ishibashi Museum of Art and Asian Gallery, Kurume 026705
Ishii, Tokyo 077253
Ishii, David, Seattle 142995
Ishii, Taka, Tokyo 107055
Ishii Chawan Bijutsukan, Hagi 026485
Ishikawa, Sapporo 077196
Ishikawa-kenritsu Bijutsukan, Kanazawa 026623
Ishikawa-kenritsu Dento Sangyo Kogeikan, Kanazawa 026624
Ishikawa-kenritsu Kyodo Shiryokan, Kanazawa 026625
Ishikawa-kenritsu Rekishi Hakubutsukan, Kanazawa 026626
Ishikawa Takuboku Memorial Museum, Tamayama 027134
Ishimaru, Sapporo 140175
Ishimitsu Art Club, Osaka 053780
Ishinomaki Culture Center, Ishinomaki 026575
Isidro, Eduardo Nobre, São João Das Lampas 080121
Ising, Dr., Heubach, Württemberg .. 071505
Isinger Dorfmuseum - Alte Kelter, Tübingen 020497
Isis District Historical Complex, Childers 000912
İskele İon Müzesi, İskele 008249
Iskitimskij Kraevedčeskij Muzej, Novosibirskij oblastnoj kraevedčeskij muzej, Iskitim 033166
Iskusstvo, Moskva 140905
Iskusstvo, Sankt-Peterburg 140932
Iskusstvo - The Russian Art Magazine, Moskva 136054
Isla, Burgos 081016
Isla Center for the Arts at the University of Guam, Mangilao 021568
Islamabad Museum, Islamabad ... 031367
Islamia College Museum, Peshawar 031393
Islamic Art and Architecture, Costa Mesa 136506
Islamic Museum, Abbasiya 009269
Islamic Museum, Amman 027369
Islamic Museum, Cairo 009303
Islamic Museum, Jerusalem 022958
Islamic Museum, Jerusalem 031415
Islamic Museum, Teheran 022623
Islamic Museum, Department of Antiquities, Tripoli 027834
Island Antique Mall, Jacksonville .. 089419
Island Art Galleries, Honolulu 116218
Island Art Galleries, Honolulu 116219
Island Artbiz, Newhaven 094945
Island County Historical Society Museum, Coupeville 043195
Island Fine Arts, Bembridge 112623
Island Mountain Arts Public Gallery, Wells 006785
Island Nantiques, Kingscote 056056
Island Treasures Antique Mall, Honolulu 088961
Island Treasures at the Marina, Honolulu 116220
Isle aux Brocantes, L'Isle-sur-la-Sorgue 063938
Isle d'Avray, Ville-d'Avray 068882
Isle La Motte Historical Society Museum, Isle La Motte 044784
Isle of Wight Courthouse, Smithfield 048203
Isle of Wight Steam Railway and Isle of Wight Railway Heritage Museum, Havenstreet 039698
Isle of Wight Wax Works, Brading .. 038813
Isleford Historical Museum, Isleford 044785
Isles, Andrew, Prahran 137060
Isles of Scilly Museum, Saint Mary's 040927

Islesboro Historical Museum, Islesboro 044786
Islevbro, København 137896
Islington Antiques, Islington 056016
Islington Education Artefacts Library, London 040185
Islington Museum, London 040186
Islip Art Museum, East Islip 043572
Ismailia Museum, Ismailia 009340
Isman-Fänder, Anat, Hamburg 071255
Ismer, Angela, Amelinghausen 069162
Isolresine Edilizie, Bari 127113
Isonkyrön Kotiseutumuseo, Isokyrö 009611
Isopo, Funchal 129144
Isoz, Daniel, Domdidier 082343
İsparta Devlet Güzel Sanatlar Galerisi, İsparta 038078
Israel, Barbara, New York 090971
Israël, B.M., Amsterdam 140309
Israël, B.M., Amsterdam 140310
Israël, B.M-, Egmond aan den Hoef 140414
Israel, Robert, New York 090972
Israel Artists' Association, Jerusalem 053721
Israel Bible Museum, Zefat 023104
Israel Children's Museum, Holon . . 022938
Israel Defense Forces History Museum, Tel Aviv 023077
Israel Goor Theater Archive and Museum, Jerusalem 022959
Israel Museum, Jerusalem, Jerusalem 022960
Israel Museum Products, Jerusalem 134536
Israel National Committee of ICOM, Rishon Le-Zion 053722
Israel Oil Industry Museum, Haifa . . 022923
Israel Railway Museum, Haifa 022924
Israel Theater Museum, Tel Aviv . . . 023078
Israeli Air Force Museum, Hatzerim 022932
Israeli Museum of Photography, Tel Hai 023095
Iss, Dominique, Illkirch-Graffenstaden 063205, 124263
Issaly, François, Cannes 120962
Issaly, Jean-Pierre, Saint-Chamarand 067398
Isseido, Tokyo 140187
Isselbacher, New York 118046
Issert, Catherine, Saint-Paul-de-Vence 101210
Issues, Maastricht 108128
Istana Batu, Kota Bharu 027957
Istanbul Arkeoloji Müzeleri, İstanbul 038093
İstanbul Büyükşehir Belediyesi Karikatür ve Mizah Müzesi, Fatih 038065
İstanbul Devlet Güzel Sanatlar Galerisi, İstanbul 038094
İstanbul Kültür ve Sanat Vakfı, İstanbul 054251
İstanbul Menkul Kıymetler Borsası Sanat Galerisi, İstanbul 112325
İstanbul Sanat Fuarı, İstanbul 093900
Istanbuldream, Roma 106565, 128075
Istituti Culturali ed Artistici, Forlì . . 050373
Istituto Beni Artistici, Bologna 134549
Istituto Centrale per il Restauro, Roma 050426
Istituto Centrale per il Restauro, Sede Distaccata, Roma 050427
Istituto d'Arte di Napoli, Napoli 050398
Istituto della Cultura Arbereshe Giuseppe Gangale, Caraffa 023656
Istituto di Archeologia, Università Cattolica del Sacro Cuore, Milano 050389
Istituto di Cultura Berlin, Berlin 101935
Istituto di Fotografia Alpina Vittorio Sella, Biella 023393
Istituto di Ricerche Per Arte, Antiquariato e Resta, Genova 075478, 127459
Istituto di Storia dell'Arte, Fondazione Giorgio Cini, Venezia 050446
Istituto di Storia dell'Arte, Universita degli Studi di Parma, Parma 050405
Istituto di Storia dell'Arte della Facoltà di Lettere, Torino 050439
Istituto di Storia dell'Arte e di Estetica, Urbino 050442
Istituto di Storia dell'Arte, Facoltà di Lettere, Università degli Studi, Bari 050353
Istituto di Storia dell'Arte, Facoltà di Lettere, Università degli Studi, Milano . . . 050390
Istituto di Storia dell'Arte Medioevale e Moderna, Università Cattolica del Sacro Cuore, Milano 050391
Istituto di Storia dell'Arte Medioevale e Moderna, Università degli Studi, Catania 050360
Istituto di Storia dell'Arte Mediovale e Moderna, Facoltà di Lettere, Università di Trieste, Trieste 050440
Istituto di Storia e di Arte del Lazio Meridionale, Roma 053761
Istituto di Studi Bizantini, Facoltà di Lettere e Filosofia, Università degli Studi di Roma, Roma 050428
Istituto di Studi Romani, Roma 050429
Istituto e Museo di Storia della Scienza, Firenze 024164
Istituto Europeo d'Arte e Cultura, Milano 050392
Istituto Geografico, Novara 134646
Istituto Italiano dei Castelli ONLUS, Roma 025484
Istituto Italiano di Arte Grafiche, Bergamo 050354
Istituto Italiano di Numismatica, Roma 050430
Istituto Italiano di Paleontologia Umana, Roma 025485
Istituto Nazionale d'Archeologia e Storia dell'Arte, Roma 050431
Istituto per la Storia della Resistenza e della Societa Contemporanea nelle Province di Biella e Vercelli, Borgosesia 023492
Istituto per la Storia dell'Arte Lombarda, Cesano Maderno 053762, 134568
Istituto Poligrafico e Zecca dello Stato, Roma 134677
Istituto Statale d'Arte, Galatina 050376
Istituto Statale d'Arte, Nardo 050400
Istituto Statale d'Arte, Parabita 050403
Istituto Statale d'Arte, Poggiardo . . 050409
Istituto Statale d'Arte, Sassari 050435
Istituto Statale d'Arte, Sora 050436
Istituto Statale d'Arte, Urbino 050443
Istituto Statale d'Arte A. Venturi, Modena 050396
Istituto Statale d'Arte Dorso Duro, Venezia 050447
Istituto Statale d'Arte G. Pellegrino, Lecce 050383
Istituto Statale d'Arte per la Ceramica, Grottaglie 050379
Istituto Statale d'Arte per la Ceramica Gaetano Ballardini, Faenza 050363
Istituto Superiore per le Industrie Artistiche-Ceramica, Faenza 050364
Istituto Universitario di Magistero, Fisciano 050371
Istituto Universitario Olandese di Storia dell'Arte, Firenze 050368
Istituto Universitario Orientale di Napoli. Seminario di Studi dell'Europa Orientale. Arte e Litteratura, Napoli 135908
Istituto Veneto di Scienze, Lettere ed Arti, Venezia 050448
Istoki, Belozerskij Istoriko-chudožestvennyj Muzej, Belozersk 033025
Istoria, Beirut 077399
Istoričeskaja Usadba Botik Petra I, Pereslavl-Zalesskij gosudarstvennyj istoriko- architekturnyj i chudožestvennyj muzej-zapovednik, Veskovo 034032
Istoričeski Muzej, Bansko 004628
Istoričeski Muzej, Batak 004631
Istoričeski Muzej, Blagoevgrad 004641
Istoričeski Muzej, Bracigovo 004644
Istoričeski Muzej, Burgas 004650
Istoričeski Muzej, Čiprovci 004658
Istoričeski Muzej, Dimitrovgrad . . . 004666
Istoričeski Muzej, Dobrič 004670
Istoričeski Muzej, Drjanovo 004675
Istoričeski Muzej, Gabrovo 004683
Istoričeski Muzej, Goce Delčev 004689
Istoričeski Muzej, Gorna Orjachovica 004690
Istoričeski Muzej, Ichtiman 004693
Istoričeski Muzej, Isperich 004694
Istoričeski Muzej, Karlovo 004705
Istoričeski Muzej, Loveč 004743
Istoričeski Muzej, Omurtag 004761
Istoričeski Muzej, Petrič 004776
Istoričeski Muzej, Pomorie 004798
Istoričeski Muzej, Popovo 004799
Istoričeski Muzej, Pravec 004802
Istoričeski Muzej, Provadia 004804
Istoričeski Muzej, Razgrad 004813
Istoričeski Muzej, Razlog 004814
Istoričeski Muzej, Svištov 004897
Istoričeski Muzej, Velingrad 004942
Istoričeski Muzej Belogradčik, Belogradčik 004632
Istoričeski Muzej Krastata Kazarma, Vidin 004944
Istoričeski Muzej Pavlikeni, Pavlikeni 004767
Istoričeski Muzej - Preminavane na Ruskite Vojski pri Svištov, Svištov 004898
Istoričeski Muzej Silistra, Silistra . . 004831
Istoričeski Muzej Targovište, Targovište 004900
Istoričeskij Muzej, Tutrakan 004909
Istoričnij Muzej, Dnipropetrovskyj deržavnij istoričnij muzej im Javornic'kogo, Dnipropetrovs'k 038258
Istorijski Muzej Srbije, Beograd . . . 034153
Istoriko-Architekturnyj, Chudožestvennyj i Archeologičeskij Muzej Zarajskij Kreml, Zarajsk 034094
Istoriko-Architekturnyj i Chudožestvennyj Muzej Ivangorodskaja Krepost, Ivangorod 033167
Istoriko-architekturnyj Muzej Kuzneckaja Krepost', Novokuzneck 033580
Istoriko-chudožestvennyj Muzej, Uglič 033997
Istoriko-ėtnografičeskij Muzej Usadba Galskich, Čerepovec 033074
Istoriko-Kraevedčeskij Muzej, Arkalyk 027393
Istoriko-Kraevedčeskij Muzej, Ivanovo 033172
Istoriko-Kraevedčeskij Muzej, Karaganda 027403
Istoriko-Kraevedčeskij Muzej, Temirtau 027415
Istoriko-Kraevedceskij Muzej, Tokmok 027643
Istoriko-Kraevedčeskij Muzej Džezkazgana, Džezkazgan 027401
Istoriko-kraevedčeskij Muzej g. Kronštadta, Kronštadt 033309
Istoriko-Kraevedčeskij Muzej Kattagurgana, Kattakurgan 049393
Istoriko-Kraevedčeskij Muzej Kokčetava, Kokčetav 027404
Istoriko-Kraevedčeskij Muzej Kzyl-Orda, Kzyl-Orda 027405
Istoriko-Kraevedčeskij Muzej Mangyšlaka, Ševčenko 027413
Istoriko-Kraevedčeskij Muzej Ura Tjube, Ura-Tjube 037844
Istoriko-Kraevedčeskij Muzej Vostočnogo Kazachstana, Petropavlovsk 027408
Istoriko-kulturnyj Muzej-zapovednik Idnakar, Glazov 033150
Istoriko-literaturnyj Muzej I.A. Gončarova, Uljanovskij oblastnoj kraevedčskij muzej, Uljanovsk 034005
Istoriko-memorialnyj i Architurno-chudožestvennyj Muzej, Tichvin . . 033948
Istoriko-memorialnyj Kompleks Gerojam Stalingradskoj Bitvy na Mamaevom Kurgane, Volgograd 034064
Istoriko-memorialnyj Muzej M.V. Lomonosova, Lomonosovo 033337
Istoriko-memorial'nyj Muzej Politi̇nych V'jazniv, Ternopil's'kyj oblasnyj krajeznavčyj muzej, Ternopil' 038401
Istoriko-memorialnyj Muzej Semji Fadeevyh-Chan-Blavackij, Dnipropetrovskyj deržavnij istoričnij muzej im Javornic'kogo, Dnipropetrovs'k 038259
Istoriko-memorial'nyj Muzejnyj Kompleks Bobriki, Donskij 033103
Istoriski Muzej, Kruševo 027913
Istoryko-architekturna Pam'jatka-muzej Kyïvska Fortecja, Kyïv 038297
d'Istria, Michel, Paris 066083
Iszatt, Casimir, Heidelberg 071458
IT-Auktion Nordic, Bromma 122114
Ita, Egidio, Innsbruck 123392
Itabashi Kuritsu Bijutsukan, Tokyo . 027178
Itaca, Venezia 106757
Itä-Hämeen Museo, Hartola 009506
Itä-Helsingin Antikvariaatti, Helsinki 137943
Itai Pan, Rio de Janeiro 058600
Ital Reding-Haus, Schwyz 037543
Italarte, Milano 106250
Italarte, Roma 106566
Italarte, Roma 106567
Italarte, Roma 106568
Italarte's, Bogotá 059841, 123902
Italia. Bollettino d'Arte, Roma 135909
Italiaander, Amsterdam 077871
Italian Historical Museum, Carlton South 000897
Italiana Antiquariato, Firenze 075363, 140021
Italy Art Gallery, Los Angeles 116801
Itami-shiritsu Bijutsukan, Itami 026577
Itami-shiritsu Hakubutsukan, Itami . 026578
Itasca Heritage Center Museum, Grand Rapids 044281
Itčan Qala Davlat Muzej Qo'riqxonasi, Chiva 049387
Itel, Martin, Olten 111801
İtfaiye Müzesi, Fatih 038066
Itimuseum, Museo Itinerante de Arte Contemporaneo del Mercosur, Buenos Aires 000154
Itinérante, Château-Gontier 062184
Itinere, A Coruña 110321
Ito, Kyoto 106898
ITO Antiques, Miami 090192
Itojen, Singapore 080494
It's a Blast, Tucson 120139
It's About Time, Westcliff-on-Sea . . 087093
It's Antiques, Miami 090193
It's New to You, Philadelphia 091648
It's Random, New York 118047
Itsukaichi Folk Museum, Itsukaichi . 026586
Itsukushima-jinja Homotsukan, Hatsukaichi 026500
Itsuo Bijutsukan, Ikeda 026555
Itsutsubashikan, Sendai 027046
Ittinger Museum, Warth 037696
Ituna Cultural and Historical Museum, Ituna 005650
Iturralde, Los Angeles 116802
Iturriate, C., Lima 079552
Iturrioz Leza, Roberto, Logroño . . . 081182
Iuliantik, Timişoara 080194
Iupui Cultural Arts Gallery, Indianapolis 044749
Iuric, Emilia, Milano 075747
Iv Cantons, Girona 081135
IVAM Centre Julio González, Valencia 035976
Ivan Dougherty Gallery, University of New South Wales, Paddington 001363
Ivan Franko Museum, Winnipeg . . . 006848
Ivan Meštrović Gallery, Ivan Mestrovič Foundation, Split 007801
Ivana, Dimitrie, Paris 066084
Ivánffy & Uhler, Dallas 115894
Ivanhoe Collectibles Corner, Ivanhoe 056017
Ivano-Frankivs'kyj Chudožnij Muzej, Ivano-Frankivs'k 038266
Ivano-Frankivs'kyj Krajeznavčyj Muzej, Ivano-Frankivs'k 038267
Ivanovskij Oblastnoj Chudožestvennyj Muzej, Ivanovo 033173
Ivanyi, Cherokee 094390

Ivar Aasen-tunet, Hovdebygda 030913
Ivar Lo-Museet, Stockholm 036631
Ivarsson Auktioner, Tibro 122276
I've Been Framed, Miami 117094
I've Been Framed, Tulsa 120196
Iveland og Vegusdal Bygdemuseum, Vatnestrom 031323
Iversen, Leila, Oslo 079447
Ives, John, Twickenham 142130
Ivey-Selkirk, Saint Louis 123086
I.V.K. Rajwade Sanshodhan Mandal Museum, Dhule 022108
Ivorra Segura, Facundo, Alcoy 129299
Ivory Art, Miami 117095
L'Ivre Livre, Foix 138091
Ivy, Lewes 135168
Ivy, Tokyo 077254
Ivy Antiques, Wakefield 079301
Ivy Cottage, San Antonio 092523
Ivy Green, Birthplace of Helen Keller, Tuscumbia 048669
Ivy Hall Antiques, Birr 074860
Ivy House Antiques, Acle 083254
Ivyhale, Tunbridge Wells 086939
Ivy's Antiques, Memphis 090080
Iwaki City Art Museum, Iwaki 026587
Iwakuni Municipal Museum, Iwakuni 026588
Iwalewa Haus, Bayreuth 015912
Iwan de vent nouveau, Jal-el-Dib . . 077427
Iwand-Kussin, Heidrun, Berlin 069650
Iwantja Arts & Crafts, Indulkana Everard 056012
Iwasaki Museum, Yokohama 027331
Iwasaki Museum of Art, Ibusuki . . . 026551
Iwata Senshinkan, Inuyama 026566
Iwata-shi Kyu Mitsukegakko, Iwata, Shizuoka 026591
Iwate-kenritsu Hakubutsukan, Morioka 026830
Iwate Museum of Art, Iwate-kenritsu Bijutsukan, Morioka 026831
IWK - Mitteilungen des Instituts für Wissenschaft und Kunst, Wien . . . 135557
Iynedjian Art, Lausanne 111623
Iynedjian Art, Verbier 111961
Iyoboya Salmon Museum, Murakami 026835
Izaak Walton's Cottage, Shallowford 040991
Izarn, Pascal, Paris 066085
Izaro, Donostia-San Sebastián 141017
Izatt, Michael John, Sotogrande . . . 122086
Izba Muzealna im. Antoniego Krajewskiego, Lanckorona 032088
Izba Regionalna Polskiego Towarzystwa Turystyczno-Krajoznawczego, Sulejów 032346
Izdatelska Kăšta Atlantida, Sofia . . 133309
Izdatelstvo na Balgarskata akademija na naukite, Sofia 133310
Izkustvo, Sofia 135615
Izkustvo i Spomeni, Stara Zagora . .058773, 096757
Izložba na Stari Kotlenski Kilimi, Muzej na Kotlenskite Vazroždenci i Panteon na Georgi S. Rakovski, Kotel 004732
Izložben Kompleks, Veliko Tărnovo . 004932
Izložbena Dvorana Sv. Mihovila, Korčula 007740
Izložbena Zala Sirak Skitnik, Sliven 004834
Izmaïl's'kyj Krajeznavčyj Muzej Pridunav'ja, Izmaïl 038271
Izmaïl's'kyj Muzej O.V. Suvorova, Izmaïl 038272
İzmir Arkeoloji Müzesi, İzmir 038110
İzmir Resim ve Heykel Müzesi, İzmir 038111
Iznik Müzeleri, Iznik Müzesi ve Iznik Ayasofya Müzesi, Iznik 038113
IZO Gallery, London 113712
Izquierdo, Alberto, Montevideo 122783
Izquierdo Ibarra, Juan Carlos, Barcelona 080868
Izstāžu Zāle, Madonas Novadpētniecības un Mākslas Muzejs, Madona 027710
Izumi, Sendai 077212
Izumi, J., Kyoto 077103
Izumo Taisha Shrine Treasure, Taisha 027099
Izumo Taisha Treasure House, Izumo 026595
Izvor, Sofia 096738
Izzo, Giovanna, Napoli 127777
Izzo, Matthew, Philadelphia 118782
J 70, Donostia-San Sebastián 081082
J. & A. Antiques, Bridgend 083665
J & A Brass Polishing, Sacramentosco 132740
J-Arts, Hong Kong 097801
J B M Art Consultancy, South Yarra 056614
J&C Furniture Specialist, New Orleans 132417
J & D Collectibles, Norfolk 091385
J-Delmas, Paris 066086
J & E Antiques, Saint Paul 092367
J. Evetts Haley History Center, Midland 045851
J. F. Schreiber-Museum, Esslingen . 017085
J & G Art, Milano 106251
J & G Gallery, Chichester 112861
J Gallery, Hong Kong 097802
J & H Antiques, Minneapolis 090370
J & H China Repair, Vancouver 123850
J & J Antiques, Fresno . . . 088909, 132078
J J Enmarcaciones, Santiago de Chile 059536
J & J Sportscards & Collectables, Albuquerque 087401
J & K Furniture, Phoenix 091747
Õj Képcsarnok, Budapest 105517
J & L Books, Fort Worth 142412
J L F, Saint-Ouen 067808
J & L New Art, Houston 116348
J & L Refinishing, San Francisco . . 132888
J + M, Leipzig 072205
J & P Fine Art, Zürich 112120
J & P Timepieces, New York 090973, 132480
J. Paul Getty Museum, Los Angeles 045433
J & R Gallery, Tucson 120140
J & V International Trading, New York 132481
J. V. Pianos and Cambridge Pianola, Cambridge 130499
J. Wayne Stark University Center Galleries, College Station 043045
J Z Antiguidades, Porto Alegre 058508
J.A., Castres 062035
Jaafar, André, Paris 124701
Jaap'S Antik, Göteborg 081812
Jabatan Muzium Sabah, Kota Kinabalu 027959
Jabczyński, Paweł, Brzeg Dolny . . . 129005
Al-Jaber, Dubai 083194
Jaberg, Miriam M., Minneapolis . . . 117274
Jabiru Australia, Saint Marys 056564
Jabiru Gallery of Fine Art, Sanctuary Cove 095179
Jablonka, Köln 103647
Jablonka, Köln 103648
Jablonka, Rafael, Köln 103649
Jablonski, Anröchte 069173
Jabłoński, Adam, Warszawa 109145
Jabłoński, Adam, Warszawa 109146
Jabotinsky Museum, Tel Aviv 023079
Jaboulet, Jean-Paul, Brando 061746
Jaca, Milano 134617
Jacazzi, C., Saint-Hilaire-Saint-Florent 067523
Jaccaz, Saint-Julien-en-Genevois . 067558
Jacek, Gdańsk 079583, 140720
Jacek, Bert, Köln 126089
Jacek Malczewski Muzeum, Radom 032279
Jachthuis Sint-Hubertus, Hoenderloo 029758
Jacinto Courthouse, Corinth 043152
Jack, Las Vegas 116629
Jack Heath Art Gallery, University of Natal, Pietermaritzburg 034698
Jack London State Historic Park, House of Happy Walls, Glen Ellen 044201
Jack Lynn Memorial Museum, Horsefly 005625
Jack Miner Museum, Kingsville . . . 005709
Jack R. Hennesey Art Galleries, Saint Clair County Community College, Port Huron 047132
Jack S. Blanton Museum of Art, Austin 041927
Jack the Stripper, Edmonton 123761
Jackdaw Antiques Centres, Henley-on-Thames 084661, 130785
Jackfield Tile Museum, Jackfield . . 039830
Jackie Antiquités, La Celle-Saint-Cloud 063306
Jackiewicz, Ewa & Andrzej, Wrocław 109223
Jackman, Saint Kilda, Victoria 095172
Jackpot, Milwaukee 090306
Jack's, Montréal 058968
Jack's Antiques, Sandringham 056572
Jack's Art, Arnhem 107851
Jack's Art Gallery, New York 118048
Jackson, Atlanta 114888
Jackson, Belmont 120563
Jackson, Birmingham 087764
Jackson, Birmingham 087765
Jackson, Braidwood 055537
Jackson, Dallas 115895
Jackson, Seattle 093021
Jackson, Aaron, New York 090974
Jackson, Allan K.L., Edinburgh 084299
Jackson, B., Atlanta 114889
Jackson, D.T., Saint Louis 092255
Jackson, Lee, London 141834
Jackson, Peter, Brackley 083623
Jackson, Peter, Nottingham 114176
Jackson, Stuart, Toronto . 059217, 097296
Jackson Art Center, Jackson School, Washington 048915
Jackson Artworks, Omaha 118707
Jackson County Historical Museum, Lakefield 045121
Jackson County Historical Museum, Maquoketa 045653
Jackson County Historical Society Museum, Black River Falls 042241
Jackson-Grant, D.M., Teynham . . . 086877
Jackson Hall Gallery, Frankfort 044030
Jackson Hole Historical Museum, Jackson 044808
The Jackson Homestead, Newton . 046477
Jackson Street Gallery, Seattle 093022
Jackson-Washabaugh Historical Museum, Kadoka 044893
Jackson's, Oakland 132570
Jacksons, Stockholm 081968
Jackson's Mill Historic Area, Weston 049125
Jacksonville Fire Museum, Jacksonville 044814
Jacksonville Museum of Modern Art, Jacksonville 044815
Jacmaire & Buteux, Saint-Ouen (Somme) 124915
Jacob, Callian 099053
Jacob, Paris 100537
Jacob, Ann, Atlanta 114890
Jacob, Dietmar, Reichenbach, Vogtland 126706
Jacob, G., Waldmohr 074257
Jacob, Haidelis, Syke 105027
Jacob, John, Woodbridge 142170
Jacob, Rainer, Halle, Saale 103069, 125789
Jacob, René, Grenoble 063067
Jacob, Samuel, Santa Monica 135501
Jacob, Stéphane, Paris 100538
Jacob, Ulrich, Falkenstein, Vogtland 125631
Jacob Breda Bullmuseet, Rendalen 031132
Jacob Kelley House Museum, Hartsville 044468
Jacob Walden House, Walden 048830
Jacobi, Tel Aviv 075003
Jacobs, Buffalo 087886
Jacobs, Cardiff 083872, 130511
Jacobs, A., Aartselaar 123544
Jacobs, F., Bruxelles 057994
Jacobs, Frans, Amsterdam 077872
Jacobs, Hermann, Bremen 102249
Jacobs, Lionel, Richmond, Surrey . 086356
Jacob's Antiques, Brunswick 055573, 120569
Jacobs & Hunt, Petersfield 122655
Jacobs & Uys, Pretoria 110071
Jacobsa, Wolfgang, Nürnberg 073107
Jacobsen, Salt Lake City 132790
Jacobsen, Britta, København 060341
Jacobsen, Margo, Portland 119011
Jacobson, Bernard, London 113713
Jacobson & Howard, New York 118049
Jacobsson, K., Stockholm 122254
Jacomart, Madrid 110552
Jacomet, Nice 124515
Jacomo, Pascale, Paris 124702
Jacono-Muntean, Domenico & Raluca, Wien 137328
Jacotti, Giovanna, Brescia 127220
Jacquard-Stübli, Pratteln 037423
Jacquart, Danielle, Brugge 057777
Jacquelin, Yvette & Pierre, Blanzy . 061508
Jacqueline Casey Hudgens Center for the Arts, Duluth 043516
Jacqueline's Room, Böblingen 069903
Jacquemart, Christiane, Montpellier 064748
Jacquemin, Gérard, Allonzier-la-Caille 060781
Jacquemin, Serge, Presly 066981
Jacques, Houston 089118
Jacques, Oslo 079448
Jacques, Oslo 079449
Jacques, Jason, New York 090975
Jacques Marchais Museum of Tibetan Art, Staten Island 048330
Jacques van Mourik Ruim, Mook . . 029932
Jacqueson, Jean-Guy, Gevrey-Chambertin 062990
Jacquet, Gérard, Lyon . . . 064143, 099596
Jacquet, Gérard, Rugles 067325
Jacquey, Mireille, Paris 066087
Jacquey, Philippe, Besançon 061387
Jacquier, Paul-Francis, Kehl am Rhein 071775
Jacquin, Christiane, Saint-Ouen . . . 067809
Jacquin, Marie-Claude, Grande-Rivière 063030
Jacqulene, Singapore 109816
Jacquot, Patrick, Conflans-en-Jarnisy 062457
Jade, Amsterdam 107740
Jade and Arts Gallery, Hong Kong . . 097803
Jade Antique House, Singapore . . . 080495
Jade Antiquités, Bruxelles 057995
Jadestone, Portland 091956
Jadis, Bath 083431
Jadis, Brive-la-Gaillarde 061814
Jadis, Cerny 062058
Jadis, Dommartin-aux-Bois 062706
Jadis, Lamorlaye 063500
Jadis, Québec 059071
Jadis, Saint-André-de-Sangonis . . . 067355
Jadis, Toulon (Var) 068455
Jadis, Vichy 068859
Jadis Antiquités, Pouillé 066969
Jadis et Naguère, Aubenas 061031
Jadis et Naguère, Bruxelles 057996
Jadis et Naguère, Casablanca 077656
Jadis et Naguère, Deuil-la-Barre . . 062618
Jadis et Naguère, Laissey 063492
Jadis et Naguère, Paris . . 100539, 138411
Jadite, New York 118050
J'Adore, Kansas City 089503
Jaeckin, André, Nancy 099796
Jaeckin, Anne & Just, Paris 100540
Jaeger, F. de, Gent 123622
Jäger, Dr. Johann, Sankt Pölten . . . 057296
Jäger, Julius, Wiesbaden 121625
Jäger, R., Wächtersbach 074235
Jaeger, Dr. Roland, Hamburg 139190
Jäger, Ruthild, Lüneburg 139433
Jäger, Dr. Siegfr., Kelkheim 126026

Jaeger, Winand, Mainz 072392
Jäger, Winand, Mainz 104000
Jägerndorfer Heimatstuben, Ansbach 015555
Jægerspris Slot, Jægerspris 008943
Jäggi, Aeschi 082077
Jäggli, Monica, Massagno 082650
Jael Stichting Mystic Museum, Dronten 029511
Jämtlands Flyg och Lottamuseum, Östersund 036528
Jämtlands Läns Museum, Östersund 036529
Jaenichen, Rita, Grünwald 071135
Jänner, Josef, Schleswig 073696
Jaep, Anne-Marie, Chissay-en-Touraine 062295
Jærmuseet, Nærbø 031042
Järnvägs- och Industrimuseum, Hagfors 036322
Järnvägsmuseet, Regionmuseet i Skåne, Kristianstad 036401
Järvamaa Muuseum, Paide 009385
Järvsö Auktionsbyrå, Järvsö 122168
Jaesche, Paweł Robert, Poznań . . . 079690
Jaeschke, Hildesheim 103381
Jäschke, Jens, Görlitz 071036
Jaeschke, Olaf, Braunschweig 102220, 125377, 138926
Jafe, San Francisco 132889
Jaffa Antigüedades, Lima 079553
Jaffna National Museum, Jaffna . . . 036139
Jaffray, Alan, Melksham 085967
Jaffre, Michel, La Flèche 063378
Jaffrey Civic Center, Jaffrey 044822
JAG, Paris 100541
Jagamarra Collection, Potts Point . . 095102
Jagd- und Falknereimuseum, Riedenburg 019830
Jagd- und Fischereimuseum, Adelsdorf 015444
Jagd- und Fischereimuseum Schloss Tambach, Weitramsdorf 020789
Jagd- und Forstmuseum, Feistritz am Wechsel 001842
Jagd- und Naturkunde Museum, Niederstetten 019311
Jagd- und Naturkundemuseum, Brüggen, Niederrhein 016465
Jagd- und Schloßmuseum Spangenberg, Spangenberg 020261
Jagdhaus Gabelbach, Stiftung Weimarer Klassik und Kunstsammlungen, Ilmenau 018056
Jagdkundemuseum, Dischingen . . . 016726
Jagdmuseum, Buschow 016525
Jagdmuseum, Ellwangen 016945
Jagdmuseum Brandhof, Gollrad . . . 001921
Jagdmuseum Wulff, Dedelstorf . . . 016655
Jagdschau im Jagdschloss Springe, Springe 020271
Jagdschloß Granitz, Ostseebad Binz 019523
Jagdschloß Grunewald, Stiftung Preussische Schlösser und Gärten Berlin-Brandenburg, Berlin 016082
Jagdschloß Paulinzella, Museum zur Geschichte des Klosters sowie zur Forst- und Jagdgeschichte, Rottenbach . 019925
Jagdschoss Letzlingen, Stiftung Schlösser, Burgen und Gärten, Letzlingen . . . 018620
Jager, Hélène, Metz 064533
Jager, Ronald de, Ouderkerk aan de Amstel 128804
Het Jagershuis, Zaandam 078850
Jaggard, Sydney 056678
Jaggedart, London 113714
Jagielski, Wacław, Nowy Sącz 079680
Jagro, Espoo 060492
Jagua, Tampa 132954
Jaguar Daimler Heritage Trust, Allesley 038486
Jahangir Art Gallery, Mumbai 105782
Jahn, Diethelm, Vellmar 126946
Jahn, Fred, München 104235, 134249
Jahn, Karin, Wangerland 105156
Jahn, Lothar, Garbsen 139129
Jahn, Manfred, Berlin 069651
Jahn & Ernst, Scharnebeck 134380
Jahnke Road Antique Center, Richmond 092089
Jahns, Wolfgang, Köln . . . 071958, 103650
Jahr, Ulrich, Hebertsfelden 125892
Jahrbacher, Leoben 057146
Jahrendt, Herbert, Freiburg im Breisgau 070844
Jail Training School Museum, Lucknow 022242
Jailhouse Galleries, Burke Arts Council, Morganton 046025
Jaime's Studio, San Francisco 132890
Jain, Delhi 105667
Jaipur, Los Angeles 089802
Jairos, Bogotá 098171
Jaja, Amsterdam 107741
Jajuta, Singapore 109817
Jakarta History Museum, Jakarta . . 022422
Jakisch, L., Hofgeismar 071550
Jakob, Ernst, Basel 111196
Jakob, Gerhard, Frankfurt am Main 070755
Jakob, Günther, Lichtenfels, Bayern 072246, 126220
Jakob, Karlheinz, Prutting 126663
Jakob, Teo, Bern 082216
Jakob-Grünenwald-Gedächtnisstätte, Ebersbach an der Fils 016870
Jakob-Kocher, Jeannette, Môtier (Vully) 130120
Jakob-Philipp-Hackert Ausstellung, Kulturhistorisches Museum Prenzlau im Dominikanerkloster, Prenzlau . . . 019664
Jakobi, Kurt, Florstadt 070713
Jakobs, Dörthe, Stuttgart 126857
Jakobstads Museum, Jakobstad . . 009614
Jakopičeva Galerija, Ljubljana 109976
Jakovljev, Gordana, March 126289
Jaktvårdsmuseum, Eksjö 036246
Jakubowska, Stefania, Kraków . . . 140738
Jakubowski, Pawel, Warszawa 129089
Jakubowski & de Weydenthal, Paris 124703
Jakutskij Gosudarstvennyj Muzej Istorii i Kultury Narodov Severa im. Jaroslavskogo, Jakutsk 033187
Jala, Cirfontaines-en-Ornois 062306
Jalan, Toronto 059218
Jalan-Jalan, Nashville 090461
Jalance, Valencia 129776
Jalasjärven Museo, Jalasjarvi 009618
Jalkaväkimuseo, Mikkeli 009872
Jallay, Camille, Kleinbettingen 077467
Jallet, Gérard, Varces-Allieres-et-Risset 068725
Jallet, Marie-Christine, Tours 068593
Jallier, Alain, Magny-en-Vexin 064214
Jalna, Little Haywood 085012, 130900
Jalokivi Galleria, Kemi 009689
J.A.M, Saint-Ouen 067810
Jamaat Art Gallery, Mumbai 105783
Jamaica Center for Arts, Jamaica . 044824
Jamaica Folk Museum, Kingston . . 026386
Jamaican People's Museum of Craft and Technology, Spanish Town 026398
Jamalo-Neneckij Okružnoj Kraevedčeskij Muzej im. I.S. Šemanovskogo, Salechard 033710
Jamal's Corner Shop, Chennai 074792
Jamandic, Chester 083957
Jamar, Antwerpen 096072
Jamar, Tracy E., New York 132482
Jamart, Aachen 069089
Jamault, Laurent, La Flotte 099395
Jamault, Philippe, Brest 061775
Jamberoo Antiques, Jamberoo 056018
James, Bangor 112557
James, Dalkey 105854
James, Pittsburgh 118932
James, Angela, Vancouver 059369
James & Son, Anthony, London . . . 085421
James, Anthony, Whimple 087125
James, Brian, Telford 086839, 131577
James, Dominique, Saint-Ouen . . . 067811
James, Joe, Ocho Rios 106832
James, Jonathan, London 085422
James, Joseph, Penrith . . 086203, 131365
James, Julian, Prez-vers-Noréaz . . 130143
James, R.A., Sileby 086620
James, R.A., Tutbury 086958, 131623
James, Renée, Saint-Ouen 067812
James A. Garfield National Historic Site, Mentor 045778
James A. McFaul Environmental Center of Bergen County, Wyckoff 049321
James A. Michener Art Museum, Doylestown 043505
James and Meryl Hearst Center for the Arts, Cedar Falls 042667
James Art, Saskatoon 097195
James Buchanan Foundation for the Preservation of Wheatland, Lancaster 045146
James Colman, London 113715
James Cook Historical Museum, Cooktown 000945
James Dunklin House, Laurens . . . 045201
James E. Lewis Museum of Art, Morgan State University, Baltimore 041988
James Ford Bell Museum of Natural History, University of Minnesota, Minneapolis 045914
James Gilbert Rugby Football Museum, Rugby 040867
James Hall Museum of Transport, Johannesburg 034650
James Hogg Exhibition, Selkirk . . . 040981
James House Museum, Bridgetown 005148
James Howe Gallery, Kean University, Union 048692
James H.W. Thompson House, Bangkok 037879
James II, New York 090976
James J. Hill House, Saint Paul . . . 047700
James J. O'Mara Pharmacy Museum, Saint John's 006365
James Joyce Centre, Dublin 022755
James Joyce Museum, Dublin 022756
James K. Polk Ancestral Home, Columbia 043089
James K. Polk Memorial, Pineville . 047028
James-Krüss-Turm, München 019064
The James Madison Museum, Orange 046705
James Madison's Montpelier, Montpelier Station 046008
James Mitchell Museum, Galway . . 022790
James Mitchell Varnum House and Museum, East Greenwich 043561
James Monroe Museum and Memorial Library, Fredericksburg 044059
James, Murray & Thomson, Woolloongabba 056886
James of Saint Albans, Saint Albans 086439, 142029
James Paterson Museum, Moniaive 040487
James R. Slater Museum of Natural History, Tacoma 048466
James W. Dillon House Museum, Dillon 043472
James Whitcomb Riley Birthplace and Museum, Greenfield 044323
Jamestown Museum, Jamestown . 044834
Jamestown Museum, National Trust of South Australia, Jamestown 001131
Jamestown Settlement, Jamestown-Yorktown Foundation, Williamsburg 049182
Jamestown Visitor Center Museum, Jamestown 044836
Jamet, Geneviève, Clermont-Ferrand 062345
Jamieson Museum, Moosomin 005957
Jamin, Reims 067069
Jamin, Laurent, Enghien-les-Bains . 062777
Jamin, Laurent, Saint-Gratien 067508
Jammes, Paul, Paris 138412
Jammu and Kashmir Academy of Art, Culture and Languages, Srinagar . 050327
Jamshid, Cincinnati 088251
Jamtli Historieland, Jämtlands Läns Museum, Östersund 036530
Jamy Antiquités, Toulon (Var) 068456
Jan Cunen Museum, Oss 030013
J.A.N. Fine Art, London 085423
Jan Karlsgarden, Sund 010102
Jan Kochanowski Muzeum, Jacek Malczewski Muzeum Radom, Czarnolas 031882
Jan Steen Antiquiteiten, Amsterdam 077873
Jan Steen Galerie, Amsterdam 107742
Jan Van Eyck Akademie, Postacademic Institute for Research and Production in Fine Arts, Design and Theory, Maastricht 050564
Jan Van Riebeeckhuis, Culemborg . 029391
Jan Vissermuseum, Museum voor Landbouw, Helmond 029725
Jāņa Akuratera Muzejs, Rīga 027735
Jāņa Jaunsudrabiņa Muzejs Riekstiņi, Neretas Pagasts 027716
Jaņa Rozentāla un Rūdolfa Blaumaņa Muzejs, Rīga 027736
Jāņa Zābera Memoriālais Muzejs, Meirāni 027715
Janalan, Roma 095156
Janani, Bangalore 074770
Janbroers, J.W., Den Haag 140393
Jančík, Jaromír, Opava 098396
Janco-Dada Museum, Ein Hod 022907
Jancou, Marc, New York 118051
Janda, Martin, Wien 095872
Jandolo, Antonio, Roma 076513
Jane Addams' Hull-House Museum, University of Illinois Chicago, Chicago 042852
Jane Austen's House, Chawton . . . 039042
Jane L. and Robert H. Weiner Judaic Museum, Rockville 047513
Jane Neville-Rolfe Gallery, Alpha . . 000742
Jane Voorhees Zimmerli Art Museum, Rutgers State University of New Jersey, New Brunswick 046206
Jane Welsh Carlyle's House, Haddington 039651
Janeček, Václav, Jablonec nad Nisou 060025
Janeiro, Noémia, Lisboa 079948
Janek & Synowie, Marek, Kobylnica 079610, 129023
Jane's Art & Craft, Singapore 080496
Jane's Books, Wellington 140676
Janet Turner Print Museum, California State University-Chico, Chico 042891
Janetschek, Christian, Heidenreichstein 137189
Janfrey, Milwaukee 117198
Janggigot Lighthouse Museum, Pohang 027537
Jangva, Helsinki 098735
Janis Rozentéls Art School, Rīga . . 050515
Janke, Egon, Köln 126090
Janker, A. & R., Würzburg 074500
Janker, B., Beratzhausen 125149
Jankuv, Dávid, Bardejov 080596
Jannin, Jean-Marc, L'Isle-sur-la-Sorgue 063939
Jannis Spyropoulos Museum, Ekali 021252
Le Jannou, Gildas, Perros-Guirec . . 066767
Jannowitz, Juist 071673
Janoray, Charles, New York 118052
Janowitz, Dorsten 070279
Jan's & Co, Los Angeles . 089803, 122945
Jans, Chris, Amsterdam 128542
Jan's Antik, Valby 060409
Jan's Antiques Mall, Long Beach . . 089636
Jan's Art Shop, Teignmouth 114561
Jan's Atellier, Saarbrücken 104799
Jansem, Flora, Paris 100542
Jansen, Fredenbeck 070811
Jansen, Krefeld 072073
Jansen, Miltenberg 104073
Jansen, Philadelphia 091649
Jansen, Alexa, Köln 103651
Jansen, H., Viersen 139816
Jansen, M.F.A., Breda 078098
Jansen, Monika, Kronberg im Taunus 072093

Jansen, Ronald, Weesp 140572
Jansen Collection, Pretoria 034716
Jansonius, Lugano 111666
Jansonius, Morcote 111748
Janssen, Kevelaer 139316
Janssen, Rotterdam 078723
Janßen, Thedinghausen 074056
Janssen, Antje, Bergisch Gladbach . 125157
Janssen, Heinz, Kevelaer . 103537, 126036, 139317
Janssen, Ina, Hamburg 125823
Janssen, Jörg, Geldern 102923
Janssen, L.-A., Paderborn 104571
Janssen, Michael, Köln 103652
Janssen, Rodolphe, Bruxelles 096216
Janssen, Wim, Molenhoek 128779
Janssens, Breda 078099
Janssens, Lenggries 072231
Janssens, J., Wijnegem 123679
Janssens van der Maelen, Francis, Bruxelles 057997
Jansson, Leif, Stockholm 129865
Jansson, Sven, Kalmar 122173
Jantyik Mátyás Múzeum, Békés . . . 021627
Jantzen, Jean-Claude, Nancy 064869
Jantzen, Laurence, Paris 066088
Jantzen, Laurence, Ville-d'Avray . . 068883
Janus, Bruxelles 096217
Janus, Peter, Wuppertal 074527
Janus Interactive, Lyon 064144
Janus Pannonius Múzeum Igazgatòsàga, Pécs 021817
Janus Pannonius Múzeum Természettudományi Osztálya, Janus Pannonius Múzeum, Pécs 021818
Janus Press, Berlin 133784
Janusch, Wasserburg am Inn 105166
Janz, Max, Freiburg im Breisgau . . 070845
Janzen, Gevelsberg 102949
Janzen, Axel, Altensteig 069154
Janzen, Dirk, Hagen, Westfalen . . . 103049
Janzen, Frank, Lilienthal 072252
Janzen, Frank, Lilienthal 126221
Janzen, Gisela, Gescher 102945
Janzen-Köppen, L., Bad Bellingen . 069260
Japan Amateur Art Museum, Ogi . . 026932
Japan Art Academy, Tokyo 050485
Japan Art Dealers Association, Tokyo 053781
Japan Chic, Kobe 077077
Japan-China Peace Negotiations Memorial Hall, Shimonoseki 027067
Japan Folk Art Museum, Osaka . . . 026965
Japan Footwear Museum, Fukuyama 026469
Japan Gallery, New York 118053
Japan Graphic Arts, Tokyo 134723
Japan Print Gallery, London 113716
Japan Publications, Tokyo 134724
Japan Room, Brisbane 094297
Japan Society Gallery, New York . . 046351
Japan Sword, Tokyo 077255
Japan Traditional Craft Center, Tokyo 077256
Japan Ukiyo-e Club, Nagoya 053782
Japanache, West Hollywood 093478
Japanese American National Museum, Los Angeles 045434
Japanese Antiques, Los Angeles . . 089804
Japanese Antiques and Art, San Antonio 092524
Japanese Art Crafts Association, Tokyo 053783
Japanese Art Dealers, New York . . . 118054
Japanese Association of Art Critics, Tokyo 053784
Japanese Association of Museums, Tokyo 053785
Japanese Contemporary Fine Arts Gallery, New York 118055
Japanese Council of Art Museums, Osaka 053786
Japanese Cultural Center of Hawaii, Honolulu 044600
Japanese Gallery, Hiroshima 077058
Japanese Gallery, London 085424
Japanese Gallery, London 085425
Japanese National Committee for ICOM, Tokyo 053787
Japanese Rural Toy Museum, Kurashiki 026697
Japanese Ski Memorial Museum, Joetsu 026597
Japanese Sword and Oriental Antiques, Minneapolis 090371
Japanese Sword Society, San Francisco 054826
Japanese Sword Society of the US Bulletin, Breckenridge 136507
Japanese Works Of Art, Milano . . . 106252
Japanesque, Washington 120317
Japanisches Kulturinstitut, Köln . . . 018318
Japansalon, München 104236
Japantown Art and Media Collection, San Francisco 047866
Japanz Gallery, Christchurch 108397
Japhet, Carl, Paris 066089
Japhet, Christiane & Stéphane, Nice 121094
Japon Antique, Paris 066090
Japonesque Gallery, San Francisco 119700
Jaques, Jean, Philadelphia 118783
Jaques Antique, København 060342
Al-Jarah, Manama 057631
Jarash Archaeological Museum, Jarash 027382
Jarczyński, Ryszard, Swarzędz 079716
Jarden, Kraków 108956
Jardim-Museu Agrícola Tropical, Lisboa 032631
Le Jardin Antique, Sacramento . . . 092168
Le Jardin aux Papillons, Musée Vivant, Vannes (Morbihan) 015125
Jardin de l'Estérel, Castillon-du-Gard 062021
Le Jardin-de-Saint-Julien, Pierrefitte-sur-Sauldre 066825
Jardin de Sculptures et d'Agrumes du Palais, Menton 013020
Jardin d'Ébène, Cliousclat 062361
Le Jardin des Arts, Barbizon 098922
Jardin des Arts, Bergen, Noord-Holland 078065
Le Jardin des Arts, Ris-Orangis . . . 101094
Le Jardin des Arts, Saint-Denis . . . 109411
Jardin des Arts et Encadrements, Honfleur 099352
Jardin des Lettres, Bourges 138054
Jardin des Muses, Saint-Pierre-du-Val 138606
Le Jardin des Papillons, Paris 013598
Jardin du Temps, Lucciana 064022
Le Jardin Ferroviaire, Chatte 011320
Jardinières et Intérieurs, Saint-Ouen 067813
Jardinique, Beech 083474
Jardins, São Paulo 137584
Jardorf, Lina Murel, Holte 098531
Jared's, Tulsa 093315
De Jaren, Breda 078100
Jarman, David, Lewes 141727
Jarmarka Knig po Iskusstvu, Dizajnu i Architekture, Moskva 093848
Jarms, G., Bad Oeynhausen 069346
Jarmuschek & Partner, Berlin 101936
Jarnac, Louis, Yssingeaux 069067
Jarndyce, London 141835
Jarneau, Maryvonne, Granville 063033
Jaroslavskij Chudožestvennyj Muzej - Gubernatorskij Dom, Jaroslavl . . . 033192
Jaroslavskij Istoriko-architekturnyj i Chudožestvennyj Muzej-zapovednik, Jaroslavl 033193
Jaroslavskij Muzej Boevoj Slavy, Jaroslavskij gosudarstvennyj istoriko-architekturnyj muzej-zapovednik, Jaroslavl 033194
Jarovit, Lviv 112428
Jarrell Plantation Georgia, Juliette . 044885
Jarrett, Billy, Dallas 132014
Jarry, Dominique, Saint-Remy-du-Val 067993
Jartunet, Åsgreina 030743
Jarver, Peter, Cairns 094345
Jarver, Peter, Cairns 094346
Jarver, Peter, Cairns 094347
Jarver, Peter, Kuranda 094716
Jarvis, Matlock 141944
Jas, Utrecht 108251
Jas, M., Breda 078101
Jasha's Bohemian Bazaar, Memphis 090081
Jaski, Amsterdam 077874
Jaskula, Jens, Berlin 125226
Jasmine Fine Arts, Singapore 109818
Jason Books, Auckland 140600
Jasper, Federal 094522
Jasper Cultural and Historical Centre, Maple Creek 005830
Jasper Rand Art Museum, Westfield 049110
Jasper-Yellowhead Museum and Archives, Jasper 005651
Jaspers, München 104237
Jasper's Antique Radio Museum, Saint Louis 047665
Jassamine House, Celbridge 074871
Jasu Gallery, Margate 094789
Jász Múzeum, Jászberény 021746
Jatkodd, Los Angeles 116803
Jaton, Christine, Bussigny-près-Lausanne 082283
Jauberthie, Alain, Baladou 061178
Jaud, Georg, Garmisch-Partenkirchen 070936
Jaudel, Marie-Pierre, Paris 066091
Jaudel, Marie-Pierre, Saint-Ouen . . 067814
Jauffroy, Bernard, Royan 067311
Jauker, Hans, Wien 137329
Jaunmoku Pils Muzejs, Tukums . . . 027786
Jaunpils Muzejs, Jaunpils 027686
J.A.V. David Museum, Killarney . . . 005686
Java Antiques, Washington 093417
Java Art, Virginia Beach 120224
Java Books, Jakarta 139953
Java Nook, Toronto 097297
Javaherat, Teheran 022624
Javaheri, Mohammad Bagher, Firenze 127356
Javet, Marc, Genève 082438
Javier Navascues Aoiz, Donostia-San Sebastián 129509
Javogue & Ingall, Miami 117096
Javor, Burgos 081017
Javouhey, Patrick, Beaune 061282
Jawa, Torino 076827
Jawaharlal Nehru State Museum, Itanagar 022176
Jawara, J., New York 118056
Jaworski, Sven & Ingram, Werbach 126993
Jaws Antiques, Toronto 059219
JAX Art Gallery, New Orleans 117459
Jaxquart Antiques, Holywood 084712
Jay, Bruno, La Tronche 063457
Jay, L., Pittsburgh 142774
Gwenda Jay & Dan Addington, Chicago 115462
Jay Books, Edinburgh 141580
Jay I. Kislak Foundation, Miami Lakes 045827
Sri Jayachamarajendra Art Gallery, Mysore 022276
Jayalakshmi & Co., Bangalore 074771
Jayat, Jean, Limoges 099509
Jayer, Sanilhac 068119
Jaylac, Renaud, Toulouse 068520
Jayroe, Dallas 088535
Jay's Antiques, North Petherton . . . 086092
Jay's Place, San Antonio 092525
Jāzepa Vītola Memoriālais Muzejs, Gaujiena 027683
Jazz & Art Galerie, Gelsenkirchen . . 017354
Jazz Galerie, Bonn 102185
Jazz Gallery, New York 118057
Jazzens Museum, Kolbäck 036396
Jazzothèque, Nice 013395
J.B. Antiques, Wimborne Minster . .087162, 131689
J.B. Wallis Museum of Entomology, Winnipeg 006849
J.B.F. Editions d'Art, Paris 100543, 133633
JBL International Antiques, Miami . 090194
J.B.'s Hole in the Wall, Charlotte . . 087960
JC Antiquités, Lacroix-Falgarde . . . 063479
JC Diffusion, Villeurbanne 068964
J.D., Saint-Paul-de-Vence 101211
J.E. Reeves Home and Museum, Dover 043494
Jean, Antoinette, Paris 100544
Jean, Isabelle & Thierry, Aix-en-Provence 060706
Jean, René, Maransin 064256
Jean Art, Seoul 107257
Jean Christophe, Mandelieu-La Napoule 064242
Jean Lafitte National Historical Park and Preserve, New Orleans 046256
Jean-Louis-Antiquités, Caen 061875
Jean P. Haydon Museum, Pago Pago 000081
Jean-Pascal, Bordeaux 124128
Jean-Paul-Museum der Stadt Bayreuth, Bayreuth 015913
Jean Paul Slusser Gallery, University of Michigan, School of Art and Design, Ann Arbor 041731
Jean-Paul-Zimmer in der Rollwenzelei, Bayreuth 015914
Jean-Pierre Antiquités, Lyon 064145
Jean-Pierre Pescatore Collection Villa Vauban, Galerie d'Art de la Ville de Luxembourg, Luxembourg 027888
Jeanette's Collectibles, Saint Louis 092256
Jeanmarie Gallery, New York 118058
Jeanmarie Gallery, New York 118059
Jeanne B. Créations, Casablanca . . 077657
Jeanne et Jeremy, Paris 066092
Jeanneau, Christian, Angers 060857
Jeannelle, Patrice, Paris 066093
Jeannerat, Christian, Neuchâtel . . . 082694
Jeannet, Jean-François, Bourges . . 061728
Jeannette Powell Art Center, Stockton 048372
Jeanrond, H.-J., Saarbrücken 073633
Jean's Accents, Los Angeles 089805
Jean's Military Memories, Great Harwood, Lancashire 084509
Jean's Silversmiths, New York 090977
Jeantet, Jean-Jacques, Balsièges . 061183
Jeck, Eleanor, Tucson 120141
Jedburgh Castle Jail Museum, Jedburgh 039832
Jeff Matthews Memorial Museum, Galax 044114
Jefferds Tavern, York 049341
Jefferson &Co., Los Angeles 132258
Jefferson Barracks, Saint Louis . . . 047666
Jefferson Coin Rarities, New Orleans 090571
Jefferson County Historical Association Museum, Steubenville 048353
Jefferson County Historical Museum, Madison 045579
Jefferson County Historical Museum, Pine Bluff 047024
Jefferson County Historical Society Museum, Port Townsend 047141
Jefferson County Historical Society Museum, Watertown 048994
Jefferson Historical Museum, Jefferson 044845
Jefferson National Expansion Memorial, Saint Louis 047667
Jefferson Patterson Museum, Saint Leonard 047651
Jefferson Telephone Museum, Jefferson 044842
Jefferys, Lostwithiel 122604
Jeffrey & McConnell, San Diego . . . 092650
Jeffries, Catriona, Vancouver 097491
Jeff's 3-D Poster Art, Miami 117097
Jeff's Antiques, Los Angeles 089806

Jegge, Martin, Biel 082258, 129978
Jegun, Antoine, Sénas 068206
Jehangir Art Gallery, Mumbai 022265
Jehl, Philadelphia 118784
Jehle, Mathäus, Eppingen 125591
Jehu, Ron, San Francisco 119701
Jeju-do Folklore and Natural History Museum, Jeju 027514
Jeju Education Museum, Jeju 027515
Jeju Folklore Museum, Jeju 027516
Jeju National University Museum, Jeju 027517
Jēkabpils Vēstures Muzeja Brīvdabas Nodaļa, Jēkabpils 027687
Jēkabpils Vēstures Muzeja Mūzikas Vēstures Nodaļa, Jēkabpils 027688
Jēkabpils Vēstures Muzejs, Jēkabpils 027689
Jekel, Heinrich, Düsseldorf 070397
Jekyll Island Museum, Jekyll Island 044851
Jelanik, Olomouc 060061
Jelínek, Praha 060135
Jelinek, Heinz, Hartberg 137188
Jelinek, Karl, Hainfeld, Niederösterreich 137187
Jellicoe, Colin, Manchester 114045
Jellicoe, Roderick, London 085426
Jellicoe Arts, Nelson 108516
Jellinek, Tobias, Twickenham 086964
Jelly van den Bosch Museum, Roden 030068
Jeltsch, T., Bönnigheim 069904
Jem, Kelmscott 056037
Jem Coins, Fresno 088910
Jemez State Monument, Jemez Springs 044852
Jemo, Villeurbanne 068965
Jems, El Paso 088804
Jena, Tokyo 140188
Jenaer Kunstverein e.V., Jena 053247
Jenbacher Museum, Jenbach 002101
Jendritzko, Anne, Wuppertal 105355
Jenei Béla Betû, Budapest 139919
Jenin, Claude, Lille 124318
Jenior, Winfried, Kassel 134080
Jenisch Haus, Museum für Kunst und Kultur an der Elbe, Hamburg 017700
Jenischek, O., Bergisch Gladbach . 138728
Jenkins-Johnson, Karen, San Francisco 119702
Jenko's, Charlotte 087961
Jenle Museum, Roslev 009085
Jennemann, Dr. S., Isny 103443
Jenner, Le Havre 063635
Jenner Museum, Berkeley 038677
Jennes, M., Antwerpen 137399
Jennie Dean Memorial, Manassas . 045612
Jennings, Paul, Angarrack 083304
Jennings-Brown House Female Academy, Bennettsville 042144
Jennrich, Merzenich 072527
Jennrich, E. & U., Düren 070349
Jenny-Marx-Haus, Museum des Altmarkkreises Salzwedel, Salzwedel 019975
Jennywell Hall Antiques, Crosby Ravensworth 084120
Jens Nielsens & Olivia Holm-Møller Museet, Holstebro 008927
Jens Søndergaard Museet, Lemvig . 009009
Jensen, Auckland 108331
Jensen, Dean, Milwaukee 117199
Jensen, Georg, København 060343
Jensen, Helge, Frederiksberg 137870
Jensen, Leif, Valby 060410, 098603
Jensen, P. Herholdt, Hørsholm 120865
Jensen, Soren, New York 090978
Jensen, Tom, København 060344
Jensen Arctic Museum, Western Oregon University, Monmouth 045965
Jente, Saint Louis 132751
Jentsch, Remplin 073488
Jentsch, Detlef, Gütersloh 071141, 121420
Jentzsch, Carl-Rainer, Adelberg . . . 101538
Jeonju Municipal Museum, Jeonju . 027519
Jeonju National Museum, Jeonju . . 027520
Jeph's Stuff, Portland 091957
Jéquel, Nathalie, Lyon 124359
Jered, San Diego 119518
Jeremiah Lee Mansion, Marblehead 045656
Jeremy, London 085427
Jeremy's, Oxford 086179
Jérez, Jean-Luc, Saint-Julien-de-Lampon 067555
Jeri, Jean, Fontaine-de-Vaucluse . . 062889
Jericho, Oxford 141984
Jericho Historical Society Museum, Jericho Corners 044855
Jerie, Sylvia, München 126397
Jerilderie Doll World Museum, Jerilderie 001133
Jermy, Pete, Ulverstone 137120
Jermy & Westerman, Nottingham . . 141973
Jernander, Bruxelles 057998
Jernander, A., Bruxelles 057999
Jérome, Jean-Luc, Cravant 062550
Jérôme, Jean-Luc, Meung-sur-Loire 064540
Jerome County Historical Society, Jerome 044857
Jerome Galerie, København 060345
Jerome K. Jerome Birthplace Museum, Walsall 041285
Jerome State Historic Park, Jerome 044856
Jeromin, T., Homburg 071576
Jeronymus, 's-Hertogenbosch 078522
Jerrari, Youssef, Casablanca 077658
Jerrye, Ann, Indianapolis 089308
Jerry's Bookshop, Jacksonville . . . 142467
Jerry's Fine Art, Miami 117098
Jerry's Refinishing, Fresno 132079
Jerschewski, Volker, Flensburg . . . 102730
Jersey Antiques, Osborne Park 056412
Jersey Battle of Flowers Museum, Saint Ouen 040931
Jersey City Museum, Jersey City . . 044860
Jersey Heritage Trust, Saint Dominick, Jersey 040906
Jersey Motor Museum, Saint Peter . 040932
Jersey Museum, Saint Helier 040913
Jersey Photographic Museum, Saint Helier 040914
Jersin, Nikki, Denver 088701
Jersin, Nikki, Denver 088702
Jerusalem Artists' House, Jerusalem 022961
Jerusalem Art's, Houston 116349
Jerusalemhaus mit Verwaltung der Städtischen Sammlungen Wetzlar, Wetzlar 020844
Jerxheimer Kunstverein, Jerxheim . 053248
Jeschek, Angelika, Augsburg 069233
Jeschke, Hans-Joachim, Berlin . . .121332, 138795
Jeschke, Greve & Hauff, Berlin 069652, 121333, 138796
Jesenski & Turk, Zagreb 059947
Jesina, Alexander, Bad Aussee 056924
Jesina, Alexander & Claus, Wien . . 057457
Jeske, Norbert, Stollberg, Erzgebirge 073932
Jeske, O., Bevern, Kreis Pinneberg . 069813
Jeske, Wolfgang, Berlin 138797
Jessa, Denise, Montereau-Fault-Yonne 064677, 124449
Jesse, John, London 085428
Jesse, Dr. Jürgen, Bielefeld 069829, 133822
Jesse Besser Museum, Alpena 041668
Jesse James Bank Museum, Liberty 045287
Jesse James Farm and Museum, Kearney 044940
Jesse James Home Museum, Saint Joseph 047647
Jesse Peter Museum, Santa Rosa Junior College, Santa Rosa 047991
Jessie's Art Work, Los Angeles . . . 089807
Jessop, London 085429
Jessy & Raymond's Gallery, Panamá City 108790
Jesteburger Mühle, Jesteburg 071657
Jester Antiques, Tetbury 086857
Jesuitenkolleg, Mindelheim 018945
Jesus Jones and Justice Museum of Art, Los Angeles 045435
Jeta, Singapore 109819
Jetter, Edgar, Vreden 126955
Jeu de l'Oie, Biarritz 061466
Jeu de paume, Paris 013599
Jeudy, I., Tournai 058385
Jeunesse, E R, Paris 138413
Jeunink, Brigitte, Gleize 063009
Jevons, Francis, London . 085430, 131068
Jevrejski Istorijski Muzej, Beograd . 034154
Jewel Antiques, Leek 084938
Jewel Box, Dallas 088536
The Jewel Casket, Dublin 074925
Jewel of Tibel, Toronto 059220
Jewel of Tibet, San Francisco 092820
Jewel Tower, London 040187
The Jewel Tree, Cape Town 080682
Jewell, S. & H., London . . 085431, 131069
Jewell County Historical Museum, Mankato 045640
Jewellery Exchange, Auckland 078953
Jewelry and Coin Center, Buffalo . . 087887
Jewelry Box Antiques, Kansas City . 089504
Jewelry by Mimi, Philadelphia 091650
Jewelry Palace, Las Vegas 089585
Jewett Hall Gallery, Augusta 041904
Jewish Battalions Museum, Ahivil . 022883
Jewish Holocaust Centre, Elsternwick 001016
Jewish Institute for the Arts, Boca Raton 042285
Jewish Museum, London 040188
The Jewish Museum, New York . . . 046352
Jewish Museum Finchley, London . 040189
Jewish Museum of Australia, Gandel Centre of Judaica, Saint Kilda, Victoria . . 001448
Jewish Museum of Florida, Miami Beach 045825
Jewish Museum of Maryland, Baltimore 041989
Jewish Museum of Thessaloniki, Thessaloniki 021494
Jewish Museum Old Synagogue, Cape Town 034584
The Jewish Museum San Francisco, San Francisco 047869
Jewish National Fund House, Museum of Provisional Peoples Council and Administration, Tel Aviv 023080
Jewitt &Co., J.B., Cleveland 131964
Jewry Wall Museum, Leicester 039971
Jeypore Branch Museum, Jaipur, Orissa 022177
Jezebel, Brighton 083702
Jezebel, New Orleans 090572
Jezebel, New York 090979
Jeżewski, Wiesław, Warszawa 129090
Jezler, Peter W., Wallenwil 082899, 130213
JF Galerie, Zürich 112121
J.F. Willumsens Museum, Frederikssund 008868
JFF Fire Brigade & Military Collectables, Bedhampton 083472
J.F.G, Villeurbanne 068966
J.F.H., Aix-en-Provence 060707
Jfj. Lele J. Néprajzi Gyüjteménye, Szeged 021859
JFK Special Warfare Museum, Fort Bragg 043894
J.G.M., Paris 100545
J.H. Antiques, New York 090980
Jhalawar Archaeology Museum, Jhalawar 022188
Jharokha, Delhi 105668
JHS Antiques, Ashbourne 083328
Ji, Zhon, Shenyang 097963
JI Gallery, Los Angeles 089808
Ji Ya, Shenzhen 097984
Jia Friendship Union, Beijing 097664
Jia Society Yiyuan, Beijing 097665
Jiading District Museum, Shanghai 007234
Jian City Museum, Jian 007143
Jiangmen Museum, Jiangmen 007144
Jiangnan, Shanghai 097921
Jiangnan, Wuxi 098038
Jiangnan Gongyuan History Display Center, Nanjing 007198
Jiangning County Museum, Nanjing 007199
Jiangsu, Singapore 080497
Jiangsu Chinese Painting Gallery, Nanjing 097873
Jiangsu Fine Arts Publishing House, Nanjing 133375
Jiangsu Literature and Fine Arts Publishing House, Nanjing 133376
Jianguo Antiques, Shanghai 059749
Jiangxi Fine Arts Publishing House, Nanchang 133374
Jiangyin Art Gallery, Jiangyin 097854
Jiangyin Calligraphy and Painting Gallery, Jiangyin 097855
Jiangyin City Museum, Jiangyin . . . 007145
Jianzhou, Singapore 109820
Jiaonan City Museum, Jiaonan 007147
Jiaozhuang Hu Didao Station, Beijing 006988
Jibac, Tampa 120052
Jibreen, Muscat 079513, 108767
Jidaiya, Kobe 077078
Jie Jie Art, Shanghai 097922
Jihočeské Motocyklové Muzeum, České Budějovice 008318
Jihočeské Muzeum v Českých Budějovicích, České Budějovice 008319
Jihomoravské Muzeum ve Znojmě, Znojmo 008792
Jikjiseongbo Museum, Gimcheon . . 027493
Jilin City Wenmiao Museum, Jilin . . 007148
Jilin Museum, Changchun 007022
Jilin Natural Museum, Changchun . 007023
Jilin Revolutionary Museum, Changchun 007024
Jillin Fine Arts Publishing House, Changchun 133341
Jillings, Doro & John, Newent 086070, 131307
Jim Clark Room, Duns 039328
Jim Gatchell Museum, Buffalo 042508
Jim Savage Art Gallery and Museum, Sioux Falls 048191
Jim & Shirley's Antiques, Long Beach 089637
Jim Thorpe Home, Yale 049328
Jimenez, Christine, Pougues-les-Eaux 066968
Jiménez, Javier, Madrid 081326
Jiménez Alvárez, Carmen Maria, La Laguna 129542
Jimenez Garcia, Mario, Madrid 141043
Jimmie Rodgers Museum, Meridian 045786
The Jimmy Stewart Museum, Indiana 044731
Jimnette, Pretoria 080734
Jimo City Museum, Jimo 007149
Jimpy's Antiques, Nelson 079175
Jim's Antiques, Phoenix . . 091748, 132651
Jim's Shop, Fresno 132080
Jin, Kitakyushu 106874
Jin, Tokyo 077257
Jin, Rong Zhai, Taiyuan 098005
Jin Apple Art Gallery, Shanghai . . . 097923
Jin Contemporary Shi Museum, Shenyang 007254
Jin Hing, Los Angeles 089809
Jin Jing Art Gallery, Conghua 097707
Jinan City Museum, Jinan 007151
Jinan Painting Gallery, Jinan 097857
Jinan Revolutionary Mausoleum of Fallen Heroes, Jinan 007152
Jindra, Gerhard, Wuppertal 074528
Jindu, Suzhou 097997
Jing Niao, Shenyang 097964
Jing Zhai Arts, Tianjin 098010
Jingdezhen Porcelain Museum, Jingdezhen 007159
Jingdu Art Cooperative, Beijing . . . 097666
Jingu Museum of Antiquities, Ise . . 026569

Jingu Nogyokan, Ise 026570
Jingyi, Beijing 097667
Jinjiuhuang, Shanghai 059750
Jinju National Museum, Jinju 027522
Jinlong, Taiyuan 098006
Jinpra, Tokyo 077258
Jinsenko, K.B., Kobe 077079
Jinshan Museum, Shanghai 007235
Jinshi Art Guan, Handan 097733
Jinta Desert Art Gallery, Sydney 095296
Jinxi Yingchun New Year Picture Factory, Tianjin 098011
Jinyu Art, Shanghai 097924
Jinze Xuan Art Center, Shenzhen 007260
Jinze Xuan Art Center, Shenzhen 097985
Jinzhou District Museum, Dalian 007056
Jitensha Bunka, Tokyo 027179
Jitensha Hakubutsukan Saikuru Senta, Sakai 027012
Jitter, Bug, Salt Lake City 092435
Jiulio's Furniture Restoration, Memphis 132325
Jivoult, Boris, Vesoul 121283
Jixian Display Center, Jixian 007163
Jiya, Shanghai 059751
Jízdárna Pražskeho Hradu, Praha 008614
JJ Antiek, Zaandam 078851
J.J. Jackson Memorial Museum, Weaverville 049038
JJNT Antiques, Portland 091958
J.J.'s Collectables, Oklahoma City 091507
J.K. MacCarthy Museum, Goroka 031436
J.L. Runebergin Koti, Porvoo 009993
J.L. Shellshear Museum of Comparative Anatomy and Physical Anthropology, Sydney 001513
JLG, Veigne 068743
Ójlipótvárosi Klub Galéria, Budapest 105518
Jllien, Andy, Zürich 112122
JLM Antiquités, Paris 066094
JLM Négoce, Lyon 064146
JLP, Orvault 138270
JLP-Antik, Bratislava 080609, 129271
JLT, Le Bouscat 063577
J.M. Antiquités, Paris 066095
JM Arts, Paris 100546
J.M. Davis Arms and Historical Museum, Claremore 042941
JM Galleries, Pittsburgh 118933
JM Modern, San Francisco 092821
JMB Diffusion, Nice 065094
J.M.F, Saint-Rémy-de-Provence 067988
JMJ, Créteil 062565
JMK Artwork, Mount Gravatt 056285
J.M.L. Lente Editions, Cormeilles-en-Parisis 133462
JMP Sonorisation, Venelles 101444
JMS Gallery, Philadelphia 118785
JMW Gallery, Boston 087827
J.M.W. Turner House, London 040190
J.N. Antiques, Redbourn 086338
Jo, Seoul 107258
Jo An, 's-Hertogenbosch 078523
Jo-An Fine Art Gallery, New York 118060
Joaillerie, Lille 063850
Joalheria, Giam & Carlos, Rio de Janeiro 058601
Joana Village, Mandelieu-La Napoule 064243
Joanin, Pau 066708
Joanne & Vicenta, Paris 100547
Jo@Ann's Antiques, Houston 089119
Joanny, Castres 120964
Joanny, Jacques, Albi 120892
Joan's Antiques, Littlehampton 085016
Joan's on Miller, North Sydney 094981
Joan's Ridge Street Art Gallery, North Sydney 094982
Joao, Manuel, La Primaube 063402
Joao, Manuel, Rodez 067192
Joas, G., Deißlingen 070206
Joas, K., Korb 072054
Jobst, Alois, Weilheim, Oberbayern 105183
Jocham, Anna, Sankt Gallen 082779
Jochum, Hans-Peter, Berlin 101937
Jochum & Tissi, Berlin 101938
Joconde's Kabinet, Den Haag 107929
Jodaline, Austin 114991
Jodd, Berlin 101939
Jodie's Gallery, Charlotte 115294
Jødisk Museum, Trondheim 031282
Þjóðmenningarhúsið, Reykjavík 021961
Jodrell Bank Science Centre and Arboretum, Macclesfield 040376
Joe and Emily Lowe Art Gallery, Syracuse 048456
Joe Kubert School of Cartoon and Graphic Art, Dover 051268
Joe Upholstry, New York 132483
Joe Weatherly Museum, Darlington 043303
Jöchler, J., Landeck 137209
Joeë, Erhart, Hoheneich 095567
Jöhle, H., Vöhrenbach 074224
Joel, Leonard, South Yarra 120638
Joel and Lila Harnett Print Study Center, University of Richmond, Richmond 047417
Joella's House of Antiques, Omaha 091571, 123035
Jönköpings Läns Museum, Jönköping 036361
Jöns, Karen, Wohlde 074465
Jöns, M. & M., Laatzen 072107, 103810
Joensen, Helgi, Stavanger 079504
Joensuun Taidemuseo, Joensuu 009621
Jörg-Metzler-Stube, Ravenstein 019737
Joe's Coin Shop, Long Beach 089638
Joe's Cooperative Antiques, Omaha 091572
Joe's Furniture, Los Angeles 089810
Joest-Landwers, Amelie von, München 126398
Joetsu-shiritsu Hakubutsukan, Joetsu 026598
Jofa, Phoenix 118877
Joffo, Roby, Paris 066096
Joffr'Antiq', Aix-en-Provence 060708
Jogglejoint Gallery, Regina 059089, 097175
Johan Nygaardsvold Museum, Hommelvik 030902
Johann-Baptist-Graser-Schulmuseum, Bayreuth 015915
Johann-David-Köhler-Haus, Zweigstelle des Museums der Stadt Colditz, Colditz 016585
Johann-Friedrich-Böttger und die Geschichte der Porzellanmanufaktur Meissen, Schleiz 020035
Johann-Friedrich-Danneil-Museum, Museum des Altmarkkreises Salzwedel, Salzwedel 019976
Johann Jacobs Museum, Sammlung zur Kulturgeschichte des Kaffees, Zürich 037773
Johann Köleri Muuseum, Vastemõisa 009434
Johann Michael Haydn-Gedenkstätte, Salzburg 002556
Johann-Sebastian-Bach-Museum, Bach-Archiv Leipzig, Leipzig 018563
Johann Ulrich Steiger-Freilichtmuseum, Zurzach 037822
Johanna Museet, Skurup 036585
Johanna-Spyri-Museum im Alten Schulhaus, Hirzel 037190
Johannes, Helsinki 137944
Johannes, B., Bessenbach 069809
Johannes Brahms-Museum, Mürzzuschlag 002344
Johannes-Buchhandlung, München 139520
Johannes-Gutenberg-Buchhandlung, Mainz 139447
Johannes Jørgensens Mindestuer, Svendborg 009122
Johannes Larsen Museet, Kerteminde 008950
Johannes Linnankosken Nuoruudenkoti, Askola 009462
Johannes-Molzahn-Centrum für Documentation und Publication, Kassel 018189
Johannes Stegmann Art Gallery, Bloemfontein 034558
Johannesburg Art Gallery, Johannesburg 034651
Johannesen, Jens P., København 060346
Johannesen, Jens Peter, Værløse 060405
Johannesgalerie, Eisenach 070534
Johanniter-Museum, Krautheim, Jagst 018394
Johanniter- und Maltesermuseum, Heitersheim 017861
Johannitermuseum, Bubikon 036980
Johannsen, Chr., Husum, Nordsee 071598
Johannsen, Dirk, Ockholm 073171
Johannsen, Harry J., Saint Paul 092368
Johannsen, W., Büdelsdorf 070080
Johannsson, Ingvar, Malmö 081869
Johansson, Lars Y., Stockholm 081969
Johansson, Per-Anders, Aplared 122099
Johansson, Sven, Reftele 122230
Johen, Singapore 080498
Johenneken, Uwe, Bonn 069927
John, C., London 085432, 131070
John, Carolin, Hamburg 125824
John A. Hermann jr. Memorial Art Museum, Bellevue 042113
John A. Logan College Museum, Carterville 042641
The John A. Noble Collection, Staten Island 048331
John Abbott II House, Hamilton 044399
The John and Mable Ringling Museum of Art, State Art Museum of Florida, Sarasota 047999
John B. Davis Gallery of Fine Art, Pocatello 047108
John Brown Farm, Lake Placid 045113
John Brown House, Osawatomie 046732
John Brown House, Providence 047257
John Brown Wax Museum, Harpers Ferry 044438
John Buchan Centre, Tweedoale 041250
John Bunyan Museum, Bedford 038658
John Burroughs Memorial, Roxbury 047562
John Creasey Museum, Salisbury 040946
John Curtin Collection, Bentley 000798
John Day Fossil Beds National Monument, Kimberly 045001
John Deere House, Dixon 043473
John Dony Field Centre, Bushmead 038930
John E. and Walter D. Webb Museum of Vintage Fashion, Island Falls 044783
John E. Conner Museum, Kingsville 045019
John E. Weatherhead Gallery, University of Saint Francis, Fort Wayne 043999
John Elliott Classics Museum, Hobart 001106
John F. Kennedy Presidential Library-Museum, Boston 042329
John Fisher Memorial Museum, Kingston 005698
John Fitzgerald Kennedy House, Brookline 042453
John Furlong Gallery, University of Wisconsin-Stout, Menomonie 045777
John G. Blank Center for the Arts, Michigan City 045828
John G. Diefenbaker Replica Law Office, Wakaw 006760
John G. Johnson Collection, Philadelphia Museum of Art, Philadelphia 046953
John G. Neihardt Center, Nebraska State Historical Society, Bancroft 042007
John G. Voigt House, Plymouth 047104
John Gershom-Parkington Collection of Timekeeping Instruments, Bury Saint Edmunds 038924
John Gorrie Museum, Apalachicola 041750
John Greenleaf Whittier Home, Whittier Home Association, Amesbury 041689
John H. Vanderpoel Art Association, Chicago 054827
John H. Vanderpoel Art Gallery, Chicago 042853
John Hancock Warehouse, York 049342
John Hansard Gallery, University of Southampton, Southampton 041057
The John Harris/Simon Cameron Mansion, Dauphin County Museum, Harrisburg 044443
John Hastie Museum, Strathaven 041145
John Humphrey House, Swampscott 048446
John Hutchings Museum of Natural History, Lehi 045233
John J. Harvey Fireboat Collection, New York 046353
John J. McDonough Museum of Art, Youngstown 049361
John James Audubon Museum, Henderson 044507
John Jarrold Printing Museum, Norwich 040607
John Jay French House, Beaumont 042086
John Jay Homestead, Katonah 044935
John Kane House, Pawling 046847
John King Workshop Museum, Pinxton 040715
John Knox's House, Edinburgh 039398
John Labatt Visual Arts Centre, University of Western Ontario, London 049796
John McDouall Stuart Museum, Dysart 039340
John Mariani Art Gallery, Greeley 044303
John Marshall House, Richmond 047418
John Maxine Belger Center, University of Missouri-Kansas City, Kansas City 044918
John Michael Kohler Arts Center, Sheboygan 048136
John Moore Countryside Museum, Tewkesbury 041203
John Muir's Birthplace, Dunbar 039302
John P. Barclay Memorial Gallery, Pittsburgh 047053
John Paul Jones Birthplace Museum, Arbigland 038517
John Paul Jones House Museum, Portsmouth 047186
John Paynter Gallery and Police Station Museum, Newcastle 001325
The John Q. Adams Center for the History of Otolaryngology - Head and Neck Surgery, Alexandria 041644
John R. Jackson House, Winlock 049243
John R. Park Homestead, Harrow 005607
John Rains House, Rancho Cucamonga 047321
John Ralston Museum, Mendham 045771
John Rivers Communications Museum, Charleston 042737
John Rylands Library, Manchester 040403
John S. Barry Historical Society Museum, Constantine 043130
John Sinclair Railway Collection, Killingworth 039868
John Slade Ely House, New Haven 046223
John Smart House, Medina County Historical Society, Medina 045747
The John Southern Gallery, Dobwalls 039245
John Stark Edwards House, Warren 048859
John Street Studio, Oban 114182
John Strong Mansion, Addison 041579
John Sydnor's 1847 Powhatan House, Galveston 044133
John-Wagener-Haus Sievern, Langen bei Bremerhaven 018496
John Ward House, Peabody Essex Museum, Salem 047739
John Weaver Sculpture Museum, Hope 005624
John Wesley Powell Memorial Museum, Page 046790
John Woolman Memorial, Mount Holly 046060
John Wornall House Museum, Independence 044725
Johndandy, Toronto 097298
Johnen & Schöttle, Köln 103653
Johnny's Auktioner, Arvika 122101
Johns, Derek, London 085433, 113717
John's Antiques, Chicago 088110, 131906
John's Antiques, Saint Louis 092257
John's Antiques, Saint Paul 092369

John's Art and Antiques, Baltimore . 087684
John's Book Shop, Mosman 137009
John's Corner, Petworth 086250
John's Furniture Repair, Saskatoon 123819
The Johns Hopkins University Archaeological Collection, Baltimore 041990
Johnson, Chicago 088111
Johnson, Edmonton 096887
Johnson, Edmonton 096888
Johnson, Long Beach 132227
Johnson, Memphis 090082, 132326
Johnson, Seattle 093023
Johnson, West Hollywood 120390
Johnson & Sons, Arthur, Nottingham 122641
Johnson, David, San Antonio 092526
Johnson, Ernest, Ottawa 059040
Johnson, Eron, Denver 088703
Johnson & Son., G., Boston 131848
Johnson, Howard, Saint Louis 132752
Johnson, Jan, Montréal 137657
Johnson, Lucy, London 085434
Johnson, Margot, New York 090981
Johnson, Marybeth, Chicago 115463
Johnson, Matthew R., Seattle 093024
Johnson, Pat, Houston 089120
Johnson, Peter, Penzance 086212, 131369
Johnson & Sons, Rex, Birmingham . 083534
Johnson, Robert, Brasília 058462
Johnson, Robert R., San Francisco . 092822
Johnson, R.S., Chicago 115464
Johnson, Sam, Los Angeles 142512
Johnson, Samuel, Armadale, Victoria 094168
Johnson, Sarah, San Francisco . . . 132891
Johnson, Steve, Newcastle-upon-Tyne 086068
Johnson, William E., Dallas 115896
Johnson Atelier, Mercerville 045784
Johnson Collection of Photographs, Movies and Memorabilia, Safari Museum, Chanute 042710
Johnson County Historical Society Museum, Coralville 043149
Johnson County Historical Society Museum, Tecumseh 048513
Johnson County Historical Society Museum, Warrensburg 048865
Johnson County History Museum, Franklin 044039
Johnson County Museums, Shawnee 048133
Johnson Ferry House Museum, Titusville 048561
Johnson-Feugère, Dun-le-Palestel .062745, 099243
Johnson Gyr, New York 118061
Johnson Hall, Johnstown 044870
Johnson Heritage Post, Grand Marais 044272
Johnson-Humrickhouse Museum, Coshocton 043180
Johnson & Johnson, Seattle 093025
Johnson, Walker & Tolhurst, London 085435, 131071
Johnson Willard, E., Oklahoma City 118665
Johnson's, Leek 084939
Johnsons, Maastricht 128761
Johnssen, Carol, München 104238
Johnston, Dublin 074926
Johnston, Hunters Hill 094654
Johnston, Mayen 072476
Johnston, Pittsburgh 118934
Johnston & Shine, Tampa 093129
Johnstone, Saint Paul 092370
Johnstown Historical Society Museum, Johnstown 044871
Johyun, Busan 107169
Joigny, Renaud de, Nantes 124484
Joint Jacky, Saint-Quentin (Aisne) . 067974
Joint Publishing, Hong Kong 133363
Joint Venture Antiques, Saint Louis 092258
Jojo's Place, Vancouver 059370
Jojo's Treasures, Fort Worth 088861
Jojuma! Electronic Art Gallery, El Paso 116112
Joka Sortti, Turku 060638
Jókai Memorial Room, Budapest . . 021658
Jókai Mór Emlékmúzeum, Mór Jókai Memorial Museum, Balatonfüred . 021621
Jokioisten Museorautatie ja Kapearaidemuseo, Jokioinen 009623
Jokioisten Naulamuseo, Jokioinen . 009624
Jokioisten Pappilamuseo, Jokioinen 009625
Jokkmokks Stencenter, Jokkmokk . 036367
Joli, Memphis 116991
Joliat, André, Dübendorf 082344
Joliat, André, Zürich 082985
Joliet Area Historical Museum, Joliet 044875
Jolivet, François-Pierre, Angers . . . 120897
Jolly Farm Antiques, Villers-sur-Mer 068933
Jølstramuseet, Vassenden 031322
Joly, Alain, La Frette 063382
Joly, Claude, Ligueil 063822
Joly, Marc, Belfort 061328
Joly, Patrick, Thezy-Glimont 068386
Joly Antiquités, Namur 058354
Jolyon Warwick James, Woollahra . 056870
Jomain, Marie-Claire, Orange 065275
Jomamo, Palma de Mallorca 081486
Jomier, Daniel, Meaulne 064454
Jon, New Orleans 090573
Jonard, Robert, Paris 138414
Jonas, Cortaillod 111370
Jonas, Marburg 134193
Jonas, Paris 066097, 100548
Jonas, Doris, Andernach 138680
Jonathan Hager House and Museum, Hagerstown 044384
Jonathan Swift Gallery, Carrickfergus 112820
Jonckers, Sittard 078762
Jonckheere, de, Paris 100549
Jones, Gräfelfing 071075
Jones, London 085436, 131072
Jones, New York 090982
Jones, Stockholm 141160
Jones, Alan, Okehampton 086155
Jones, Alan & Margaret, Auckland . 078954
Jones, Cameron, New Orleans 117460
Jones, Casey, Louisville 090003
Jones, Christopher, Flore 084415
Jones, Christopher, London 085437
Jones & Co., Clark, New York 090983
Jones, C.V., Ballarat 055432, 094200
Jones, Dave & Pamela, Yarrahapinni 095448
Jones, Elfed, Colwyn Bay 141537
Jones, Helen, Sacramento 119152
Jones, Herb, Norfolk 118610
Jones, Howard, London 085438
Jones, Jane E., Dallas 115897
Jones, Kevin, Dublin 074927
Jones, Louis & Susan, Norfolk 118611
Jones, Louis & Susan, Norfolk 118612
Jones, Louis & Susan, Virginia Beach 120225
Jones, Michael, Northampton 086097
Jones, Paul, Clayfield 055685
Jones, Peter, London 085439
Jones, Robert, San Antonio 092527
Jones, Solomon, Indianapolis 089309
Jones, Solway, Los Angeles 089811
Jones, Stella, New Orleans 117461
Jones, Steven, Beaumaris 112595
Jones, Tiffany, Buderim 055577
Jones Center for Contemporary Art, Austin 041928
Jones & Howell, Atlanta 131781
Jones & Jones, San Antonio 092528
The Jones Museum of Glass and Ceramics, Sebago 048096
Jonesborough-Washington County History Museum, Jonesborough 044880
Jong, de, Amsterdam 077875
Jong, de, Eindhoven 078341
Jong, A. de, Utrecht 128856
Jong, Anne de, Berlicum 128584
Jong, Harry, Amsterdam 077876
Jong, Leo de, Rotterdam 108189
Jong, R.F.G.J. de, Den Haag 078205
Jong, Ria, Amsterdam 077877
Jong, Sophie, Alkmaar 107619
Jongbloed & Zoon, A., Leiden 140479
Jonge, Jon de, Mount Nelson 094910
Jonge, Maartje de, Amsterdam . . . 077878
Jongen, Henri, Liège 123655
Jongeneel, Pieter-Pierre, Bergen, Noord-Holland 107865
Jongert & Jongert, Amsterdam 107743
Jongh, Matthys de, Zutphen 140579
Jonina, Maastricht 078609
Joniskeit, Reiner D., Stuttgart 104992
Jonker, Bert, Zwolle 128890
Jonker, Henk, Egmond Binnen 128660
Jonkers, Christian, Henley-on-Thames 141658
Jonny's Antiques, Toronto 059221
Jono Bugailiškio, Vilnius 107360
Jonquet, Etienne, Paris 121157
Jonson Gallery, University of New Mexico Art Museum, Albuquerque 041617
Jonsson, K.A., Stockholm 129866
Jonsson, Stig, Leksand 081845
Joods Historisch Museum, Amsterdam 029190
Joods Museum van Deportatie en Verzet, Mechelen 003632
Joodse Schooltje, Leek 029830
Joongang, Daegu 107185
Joongang University Museum, Seoul 027565
Joop, Den Haag 107930
Joorde, Gerd, Dortmund 102404
Joos, Ursula, Würzburg 127039
Joost, Lioba, Wolfenbüttel 127031
Joosten, Yolanda, Arnhem 128569
Jopie Huisman Museum, Workum . 030349
Jorba, Mogoda 122074
Jorcas, Buenos Aires 094079
Jordan, Denver 088704
Jordan, New York 118062
Jordan, Potsdam 104629
Jordan, Helmut, Stockelsdorf 126837
Jordan, Ingrid, Wilnsdorf 105304
Jordan, James A., Lichfield 084990, 130893
Jordan, Maximilian, Hollabrunn . . . 137192
Jordan, Sigrid, Kassel 071755
Jordan, Stefan, München 072743
Jordan, T.B. & R., Stockton-on-Tees 086728, 114490, 131544
Jordan Archaeological Museum, Amman 027370
Jordan-Fahrbach, Eva, Braunschweig 125378
Jordan Folklore Museum, Amman . 027371
Jordan Historical Museum of the Twenty, Jordan 005655
Jordan Museum of Popular Tradition, Amman 027372
Jordan National Gallery of Fine Arts, Amman 027373
Jordan Natural History Museum, Irbid 027381
Jordan Schnitzer Museum of Art, Eugene 043742
Jordans, Anke, Köln 126091
Jorde, Ursula, München 072744
Jordi, Peter & Ursula, Wabern 130210
Jordi, Rosa, La Bisbal d'Empordà . . 081006
Jordi Ramos, Barcelona 129355
Jordis & Sohn, Salzburger Handdrucke, Salzburg 133141
Jorge B. Vargas Museum and Filipiana Research Center, University of the Philippines, Quezon City 031776
Jorge Barlin National Monument, Baao 031621
Jorgensen, Dublin 105871
Joris, E.E., Breda 078102
Jorissen, Gisela, Ratingen 073427
Jorissen, P.C., Dordrecht . 078304, 140411
Jorns, Markus, Unterseen 082867
Joroisten Kotiseutumuseo, Joroinen 009626
Joron-Derem, Christophe, Paris . . . 121158
Jorvik Museum, York 041478
Jos, Amsterdam 107744
Jos, Fritz, Münster 072913, 139566
Jo's Gallery, Detroit 116088
Jos National Museum and Museum of Traditional Nigerian Architecture, Jos 030690
Jósa András Múzeum, Nyíregyháza 021803
Josán, Valencia 129777
Jose, Mary, College Park 123215
Jose Antonio, Sevilla 081587
Jose Drudis-Biada Art Gallery, Los Angeles 045436
Jose P. Laurel Memorial Museum, Manila 031722
José P. Laurel Monument Museum, Santo Tomas 031786
José Rizal Shrine Museum, Calamba 031645
José Rizal Shrine Museum, Dapitan 031666
José Rizal Shrine Museum, Manila . 031723
Josef Kainz-Gedenkraum, Wien . . . 002917
Josef Weinheber-Museum, Kirchstetten 002130
Josefine-Weihrauch-Heimatmuseum, Neudenau 019227
Joseloff Gallery, University of Hartford, Hartford Art School, West Hartford 049076
Joselsson, Delft 078145
Joseph, Ehrenhausen 095500
Joseph, West Hollywood 093479
Joseph, Paul, Las Vegas 116630
Joseph, R.N., New York 090984
Joseph, Robert, Cincinnati 115636, 142318
Joseph A. Cain Memorial Art Gallery, Corpus Christi 043164
The Joseph A. Callaway Archaeological Museum, Louisville 045488
Joseph A. Driscoll Art Gallery, Brockton 042427
Joseph A. Tallman Museum, Cherokee 042790
Joseph Brant Museum, Burlington . 005167
Joseph D. Carrier Art Gallery, Toronto 006606
Joseph Haydn-Museum, Eisenstadt 001826
Joseph Manigault House, Charleston 042738
Joseph Misson-Gedenkstätte, Mühlbach am Mannhartsberg 002340
Joseph Moore Museum, Richmond . 047399
Joseph Parry's Cottage, Merthyr Tydfil 040450
Joseph & Pearce, London 085440
Joseph Priestley House, Northumberland 046559
Joseph Schneider Haus, Kitchener . 005717
Joseph Smith Historic Center, Nauvoo 046166
Josephraj, Austin 114992
Joseph's Antique Repair, Los Angeles 132259
Joseph's Antiques, Kansas City . . . 089505
Joseph's Oriental Rug, Indianapolis 089310
Josephski, Joschi, Vilgertshofen . . 105123
Jose's Rare Coins, Cleveland 088337
Josette's Antiques, Las Vegas 089586
Josh, Birmingham 115113
Josh, Debenham 084150
Joshi Bijutsu Daigaku, Tokyo 050486
Josiah Quincy House, Quincy 047302
Joslowitzer Heimatstube, Zwingendorf 003080
Joslyn Art Museum, Omaha 046680
Joslyn News, Omaha 136508
Josnin, Paris 124704
Jossaume, Jack, Nice 065095
Josseaud, A.P., Haarlem 128693
Josselin-Vecten, Alain, Belloy 061339
Jost, Leonhard, Backnang 125082
Jost House Museum, Sydney 006547
Jot Galeria, Kołobrzeg 108922
Jottier, M., Sint-Niklaas 058373

Jottos Museum-Workshop, Erevan . 000682
Jouan, Paris 124705
Joubert, Paris 066098
Joubert, Anne, Hallivillers 124256
Joubert, Jean-Pierre, Paris 100550, 133634
Joubier, Gérard, Quimperlé 067026
Jouets Passion, Liège 058309
Jouffroy, Concarneau 062443
Jouglar, William, Saint-Sauveur . . . 101231
Jouhate, Marie-Annette, Saint-Yrieix-sous-Aixe 068044, 138609
Jouissance, Pittsburgh 091828
Joumana, Dubai 112453
Jourdain, Mennecy 064486
Jourdain, Mildrède, Bordeaux 061623
Jourdan, Franck, Gaillon-sur-Montcient 062955
Jourdan-Bachman Pioneer Farm, Austin 041929
Le Journal des Arts, Paris 135714
Journal für Kunstgeschichte, Karlsruhe 135769
Journal of Aesthetics and Art Criticism, Cincinnati 136509
Journal of Canadian Art History, Montréal 135638
Journal of Contemporary Art, New York 136510
Journal of Decorative and Propaganda Arts, Miami Beach 136511
Journal of Design History, Oxford . . 136232
Journal of Early Southern Decorative Arts, Winston-Salem 136512
Journal of Education in Museums, Gillingham, Kent 136233
Journal of Egyptian Archaeology, London 136234
Journal of Multicultural and Cross-Cultural Research in Art Education, Columbus 136513
Journal of Museum Education, Washington 136514
Journal of Regional Criticism, Colorado Springs 136515
Journal of Social Theory in Art Education, Reston 136516
The Journal of Stained Glass, London 136235
Journal of the History of Collections, Oxford 136236
Journal of the Tokyo National Research Institute of Cultural Properties (Deparment of Performing Arts), Tokyo 135978
Journal of the Warburg and Courtauld Institutes, London 136237
The Journal of the William Morris Society, London 136238
Journée Professionelles Internationales de l'Antiquités et de la Brocante, Lille 093666
Journée Professionelles Internationales de l'Antiquités et de la Brocante, Lyon 093667
Journée Professionelles Internationales de l'Antiquités et de la Brocante, Montpellier 093668
Journet, Jean-Claude, Chambéry . . 062104
Journey East, Singapore 080499
Journey Museum, Rapid City 047333
Journeyman Antiques Centre, East Molesey 084251
Journey's End, Toronto 059222
Journey's End Cottage and Laishley House, Onehunga Fencible, Auckland . . . 030440
Journiac, Gilles, La Chapelle-sur-Oudon 063322
Journiac, Luc, Segré 068194
Journiac, Luc, Segre 068195
Jours Anciens, Paris 138415
Jousse, Paris 100551
Jousseaume, Dominique & François, Paris 138416
Joutsan Kotiseutumuseo, Joutsa . . 009627
Joutsen, Taina, Helsinki 137945
Jouvène, Cassis 099091
Jouvent, Madeleine, Toulouse 068521
Jouvent, Mady, Alvignac 060785
Jouvent, Michel, Rignac 067144
Jovanovic, Wuppertal 074529
Jovanović, Zeljko, Beograd 109704
Jovenart, Madrid 110553
Jovinas, San Francisco 132892
Jovis, Berlin 133785
Joy, Lillebonne 063873
Joyas de Ocasion, Madrid 081327
Joyas Tucumán, Buenos Aires 055218
Joyas Vitorio, Montevideo 087324
Joyce, Paris 100552
Joyce, Lincoln, Leatherhead 113359
Joyce, Thomas J., Chicago 142289
Joyce & Co., Roma 134678
Joyce-Royce, Antwerpen 137400
Joyerot, Gagny 124244
The Joyo Geibun Center, Mito 026817
Joy's Antique, Pittsburgh 091829
Joys Antiques, Wellington 079327
Joysmith, Memphis 116992
Jozef Gregor Tajovský Pamätný Dom, Tajov 034440
Jozefien, Antwerpen 096073
Jozefowski, Maciej, Korschenbroich 072059, 103772
József Attila Emlékmúzeum, Attila József Memorial Museum, Balatonszárszó 021622
József Attila Múzeum, Makó 021779
Jozsefvarosi Kiallitoterem, Budapest 105519
JP Antik, Audun-le-Roman 061059
JP Antik, Beuvillers 061416
JP Art Galerie, Cannes 099072
JP Art Gallery, Beijing 097668
J.P. Art International, Paris 100553
JPC, Clamart 062316
J.P.C., Lyon 133488, 138154
J.P.L.D., Paris 066099
J.R. Toys and Model Car Gallery, Dallas 088537
JRB Art at the Elms, Oklahoma City 118666
JRM International, Singapore 109821
JRS Fine Art, Providence 119082
JS Design, Bergen op Zoom 078070
JSC, Paris 100554
JSL Fine Art, San Francisco 119703
J.T. Wilson Museum of Human Anatomy, Sydney 001514
Ju, Xinjia, Shenzhen 097986
J.U. Polimski Muzej, Berane 034175
Juan Alberto, Rosario 055295
Juan Luna Shrine Museum, Badoc . 031625
Juanas Cerrada, Fernando, Madrid . 110554
Juanes, Juan de, Alicante 110087
Juaniquet, Jean, Toulouse 068522, 138636
Juanita Studio Gallery, Austinmer . . 094182
Juaristi Larragon, Maria Pilar, Barcelona 129356
Jubb, Margaret R., Bristol 083741
Jubilee, Houston 089121
Jubilee Antiques, Tottenhill 086909
Jubilee Hall Antiques Centre, Lechlade 084918
Jubilee Photographica, London . . . 085441
Jubilee Terrace Antiques, Bardon . . 055448
Jucileia, Patricio, Porto Alegre 058509
Jud & Co., Felix, Hamburg 139191
Judah L. Magnes Museum, Berkeley 042162
The Judah P. Benjamin Confederate Memorial at Gamble Plantation, Ellenton 043674
Judaica, Amstelveen 077761
Judaica Classics by Doina, New York 090985
Judaica Museum of Central Synagogue, New York 046354
Judaica Museum of the Hebrew Home for the Aged at Riverdale, Bronx 042438
Judd, Desmond, Cranbrook 122482
Judd Street Books, London 141836
Judenbad, Wetterau Museum Friedberg, Friedberg, Hessen 017261
La Juderia, Sevilla 081588
Judge Roy Bean Visitor Center, Langtry 045158
The Judge's Lodging, Presteigne . . 040777
Judges' Lodgings, Lancaster 039920
Judiska Museet i Stockholm, Stockholm 036632
Judith, Barcelona 080869
Judith Basin County Museum, Stanford 048321
Judy's Antiques, Las Vegas 089587
Judy's Antiques, Philadelphia 091651
Jüdische Galerie Berlin, Berlin 016083
Jüdische Gedenkstätte und ehemalige Synagoge, Wallhausen, Württemberg 020659
Jüdisches Kulturmuseum, Augsburg 015611
Jüdisches Kulturmuseum und Synagoge, Veitshöchheim 020565
Jüdisches Kulturzentrum, Fulda . . . 017300
Jüdisches Museum, Dorsten 016757
Jüdisches Museum, Frankfurt am Main 017178
Jüdisches Museum, Göppingen . . . 017446
Jüdisches Museum, München 019065
Jüdisches Museum Berlin, Berlin . . 016084
Jüdisches Museum der Schweiz, Basel 036886
Jüdisches Museum der Stadt Wien, Wien 002918
Jüdisches Museum Emmendingen, Emmendingen 016966
Jüdisches Museum Franken in Fürth, Fürth, Bayern 017288
Jüdisches Museum Franken in Schnaittach, Schnaittach 020062
Jüdisches Museum Georgensgmünd, Georgensgmünd 017366
Jüdisches Museum Hohenems, Hohenems 002056
Jüdisches Museum im Raschi-Haus, Worms 020980
Jüdisches Museum Rendsburg und Dr.-Bamberger-Haus, Stiftung Schleswig-Holsteinische Landesmuseen Schloß Gottorf, Rendsburg 019800
Jühe, Warendorf 105162
Jülich, A., Speyer 139736
Jülich, Alfred, Speyer 073880
Jülich, Klaus, Kirchhain 071855
Juen, Christian, Innsbruck 057082
Jünemann, Klaus, Hannover 103283
Juenemann, Robert, Porto Alegre . . 058510
Jünger, Waldshut-Tiengen 074261
Jünger, Andrea, Baden bei Wien . . . 095472
Jürgens, G., Schloß Holte-Stukenbrock 104827
Jürgens, K. u. V., Freiburg im Breisgau 102867
Jürgens, U., Quedlinburg 139668
Jürgens, Ulrich, Blomberg, Lippe . . 138880
Juers, Westerland 074368
Juette, Christian, Saint-Pern 067950
Jüttemeier, Sven, Recklinghausen . 126683
Jüttner, Dr. Angelika, Wien 095873
Jüttner, Paul, Wernigerode 139841
Juffa, Bad Staffelstein, Oberfranken 069387
Juffermans, Utrecht 078808
Juffermans, Utrecht 108252
Juffermans, Utrecht 140549
Jugal Kishore, Chennai 074793
Jugendhuset, Varde Museum, Varde 009138
Jugendkunstschule Pankow, Berlin 016085
Jugendkunstschule Pankow, Berlin 050024
Jugendmuseum Schöneberg, Berlin 016086
Jugendstil, Beograd 080397
Jugendstilmuseum Reissenweber, Brühl, Baden 016466
Jugglers Gallery, Foster 094563
Jugoslovenska Galerija Umetnickih Dela, Beograd 034155
Juhani Ahon Museo, Iisalmi 009598
Juhás, Banská Štiavnica 080595
Juhokusti, Lahti 060606
Juilien, Bernard, Camiers 061925
Juillard, Marcel, Mortagne-au-Perche 064799
Juillard, Pascal, Saint-Ouen 067815
Juillerat, Claude, Hyèvre-Paroisse . 063199
Juillet, Michel, Sévrier 068238
Juju's Gallery, Atlanta 114891
Juke Box Classic, Malakoff 064231
The Jukebox Collection, Sissach . . 037570
Jukkasjärvi Museet, Jukkasjärvi . . 036368
Jukurrpa Artists, Alice Springs 055338
Jukurrpa Artists, Alice Springs 094139
Jularbodens Antik & Auktion, Krylbo 081842, 122184
Julémont, Paul, Leuven 058276
Jules, Den Haag 078206
Juli, Christiane, Perpignan 066751
Julia, Bydgoszcz 140714
Julia, James D., Fairfield 122894
Julia A. Purnell Museum, Snow Hill 048208
Julia C. Butridge Gallery, Austin . . . 041930
Julia Gallery, Taipei 098076
Julian Antiques, Hurstpierpoint 084779
Julian Antiques, New York 090986, 132484
Julian Armytage, Crewkerne 084113
Julian Ashton Art School, Sydney . . 095297
Julian H. Sleeper House, Saint Paul 047701
Juliana Gallery, Seoul 107259
Julian's Contemporary Art, Cleveland 115718
JuliArt, Toronto 097299
Julia's Art Studio, Windsor, Ontario 097560
Julie, François, Paris 066100
Julien, Anne, Paris 100555
Julien-Laferrière, Eric, Paris 066101
Julienne, Patrick, Saint-Grégoire . . 067511
Juliette, Bordeaux 124129
Juliette Gordon Low Birthplace, Savannah 048026
Julio, Jean, Prades 066976
Julistemuseo, Lahden Kaupunginmuseo, Lahti 009782
Julita Sveriges Lantbruksmuseums, Julita 036369
Julius, Helsinki 135675
Julius Gordon Africana Centre, Riversdale 034740
Jullié, Pierre, Mazamet 064445
Jullien, Bernard, Paris 066102
Jumalon Museum and Art Gallery, Cebu 031657
Jumbo's, Timaru 079269
Jumeau Yves, Tarascon (Bouches-du-Rhône) 068359
Juming Museum, Taipei 007369
Jumoke, Surry Hills 056652
Jumpoff, Madrid 110555
Jun, Philadelphia 118786
Junagadh Museum, Junagadh 022193
Juncal Piñon, Carlos, Pontevedra . . 081533
Junck, Rossella, Venezia 076946
Junction Antiques, Guildford 055924
Junction City Historical Society Museum, Junction City 044887
Junction Cottage, Pontypool 040732
Jundt Art Museum, Gonzaga University, Spokane 048274
June, West Hollywood 120391
Juneau-Douglas City Museum, Juneau 044890
Junee Historical Museum, Junee . . 001135
Juneja Art Gallery, Jaipur, Rajasthan 105722
Jung, Kaiserslautern 103467
Jung, Heinrich, Ginsheim-Gustavsburg 070999
Jung, K., Aachen 138669
Jung, Marlise, München 072745
Jung, Peter, Mellingen 126303
Jungara Gallery, Port Douglas 095085
Jungbauer, Dr. Rainer, Straubing . . 073937
Junge Kunst, Frechen 135770
Junge Kunst, Wolfsburg . . 020964, 053249
Das Junge Museum, Bottrop 016351
Jungersted & Brostrøm, Frederiksberg 098527
Junghanns, R., Bad Salzuflen 101693

Junghans, Karl, Berlin . . . 069653, 133786, 138798
Jungi, Rudolph, Zürich 082986
Jungle Art, Paris 100556
Jungle Bookshop, Port Douglas . . . 137049
Jungle Studio, New York 118063
Jungmann, Eric, Sarrebourg 068131
Jungmun Folklore Museum, Seogwipo 027540
Jungschläger, Dordrecht . 078305, 128648
Jungsong, Seoul 107260
Jungsteinzeitliche Grabhügel, Sarmenstorf 037512
Jungvirtová, Jiřina, České Budějovice 060000
Jungwirth-Müller, Hildegard, Tulln . 137274
Junho Ontwerpen, Den Haag 128631
Juniata College Museum of Art, Huntingdon 044673
Junion, Moskva 109556
Het Junior, Nieuw Buinen 140501
Junior Museum, Troy 048618
Junior Museum, Newark Museum, Newark 046423
The Junior Museum of Bay County, Panama City 046808
JuniorMuseum im Ethnologischen Museum, Staatliche Museen zu Berlin - Stiftung Preußischer Kulturbesitz, Berlin . . 016087
Juniper Arts, Christchurch 108398
Juniset-Art, Moskva 080243
Junk, Amsterdam 140311
The Junk Box, London 085442
Junk 'n Treasures, Chicago 088112
The Junk Shop, London . . 085443, 131073
Junken-Warnecke, A., Wedel 126973
Junker & Partner, Wien 057458
Junketeria, Fort Worth 088862
Junktion, New Bolingbroke 086048
Junktiques, Calgary 058792, 123746
Junle, Singapore 109822
Junma, Shanghai 097925
Juno, Brugge 057778
Juno, Eynsham 130698
Juno, New York 118064
Juno Design, Dunoon 112967
Junqua-Lamarque, Alain, Pau 066709
Junque, Houston 089122
The Junque Cellar, Edmonton 058833
Junque Shop, Detroit 088763
Junqueira 220, Lisboa 129158
Junta Nacional de Arqueología y Etnología, La Habana 052830
Junten Gakuen Design Academy, Tokyo 050487
Juntiques Fifth Avenue, Jacksonville 089420
Jura-Bauernhof-Museum, Hitzhofen 017936
Jura Buch, Saarbrücken 139704
Jura-Museum, Willibaldsburg, Eichstätt 016910
Juran & Co., Alexander, London . . . 085444
Juraschek, Helmut, Lauben 126174
Jurecko, Dr. Pavol, Frankfurt am Main 070756
Jurgeleit, H., Wegberg 074291
Jurica Nature Museum, Benedictine University, Lisle 045331
Jurídica Yny, Buenos Aires 136726
Jurinskij Istoriko-chudožestvennyj Muzej, Jurino 033207
Juris & Perl, Venezia 106758
Jurisch, Salzwedel 104807
Jurjeveckij Kraevedčeskij Muzej, Muzej goroda Jurjevca, Jurjevec 033208
Jurk, M., Lutherstadt Wittenberg . . 139436
Jurka, Rob, Amsterdam 107745
Jūrmalas Pilsētas Muzejs, Jūrmala 027696
Juro Antiques, Worcester 087258
Jurrissen, M., Zutphen 121809
Jury Moreau, Geneviève, Digoin . . . 062635
Jus Afrika Imports, Tampa 120053
Jussi Björlingmuseet, Borlänge . . . 036228
Just, Düsseldorf 102513
Just, Andreas, Mommenheim 126332
Just, F., Niederkassel 104448
Just, H., Milwaukee 142568
Just a Second, London 085445
Just a Second Variety, Philadelphia 091652
Just Antiques, Midland 056222
Just Art, Fochabers 113070
Just Bearly New Orleans, Cincinnati 088252
Just Because, Denver 088705
Just Books, Tampa 143022
Just Books, Truro 142122
Just Browsing, Blenheim . 078998, 140607
Just Clicked Photo Gallery, Hamilton 096422
Just Dandy, Seattle 093026
Just Desks, London 085446
Just Fine Art, Coleraine 112893
Just Frames and Art, Cleveland . . . 115719
Just Glass, Alston 083283
Just Imagine, Russell 108557
Just Like Grandma's, Tulsa 093316
Just Painting, Meopham 114078
Just Pictures, Saint Louis 119214
Just Plain Positive, Philadelphia . . . 118787
Just Plane, Auckland 078955
Just Scottish Gallery, Edinburgh . . . 112997
Just Stuff, Oakleigh 056396
Just the Thing, Westbury 114671
Juste à Côté, Lyon 099597
Juste Autrement, Saint-Julien-en-Genevois 067559
Justeau, La Boisse 063294
Justice, George, Lewes 130889
Justice and Police Museum, Sydney 001515
Justin & Burks, Portland 091959
Justin Smith Morrill Homestead, Strafford 048391
Justina M. Barnicke Gallery, Hart House, University of Toronto, Toronto . . . 006607
Justine & Marco, New York 090987
Justinus-Kerner-Haus, Weinsberg . 020763
Justinus Mulle-Museum, Sankt Veit an der Glan 002627
Justis, Martha, Jacksonville 122926
Justuff, Louisville 090004
Justum, Nelly, Cucuron 062582
Justus, Solna 081896
Justus Brinckmann Gesellschaft, Hamburg 053250
Jusupov, Sankt-Peterburg 109632
Jusupovskij Dvorec, Sankt-Peterburg 033757
Jusupovskij Sad, Sankt-Peterburg . 080305
Juszczak, Janusz, Poznań 129062
Jute Museum, Kolkata 022221
Jutheau, Vivane, Paris 121159
De Jutter, Delft 078146
't Jutterke, Breda 078103
Jutulheimen Bygdemuseum, Museet i Nord-Gudbrandsdalen, Vaagaa 031309
Jutz, Susanne, Celle 102305
Jutzi, Volker, Röhrmoos 126728
Juuan Pitäjänmuseo, Juuka 009630
Juvan Museo, Juva 009632
Juvelir Torg-A, Moskva 080244
Juxtapoz, San Francisco 136517
J.V. Snellmanin Kotimuseo, Kuopio . 009759
JW Auction Sales, Winnipeg 120829
J.W. Parmely Historical Home Museum, Ipswich 044772
Jydepotten, Frederiksberg 060239
Jydsk Antikvariat, Århus 137862
Jym, Paris 066103
Jysk Automobilmuseum, Gjern 008874
Jyväskylän Lyseon Museo, Jyväskylä 009636
Jyväskylän Näkövammaisten Koulun Museo, Jyväskylä 009637
Jyväskylän Taidemuseo, Jyväskylä . 009638
Jyväskylän Vanha Antikvariaatti, Jyväskylä 137968
Jyväskylän Yliopiston Museo - Keski-Suomen Luontomuseo, Jyväskylä 009639
Jyväskylän Yliopiston Museo - Kulttuurihistoriallinen Osasto, Jyväskylä 009640
K & A, Kassel 071756
K-An Co, Hong Kong 097804
K & B Arts, Chicago 115465
K-B Sales, Fort Worth 088863
K & C Agencies, Greenacre 055912
K & D, Schöneiche bei Berlin 134386
K D Antiques, Chester 083958
K-D Did It, Portland 091960
K & G - Keshishian, İstanbul 083141
K & G Old Orchard Antique Mall, Toledo 093173
K Galerie, München 104239
K Gallery, Bratislava 109911
K Gallery, Bruxelles 096218
K & K Galerie, Freudenstadt 102880
K & K-Museum, Türnitz 002757
K & K Restoration, San Antonio . . . 132816
K & K Schmuckhandel, Wien 057459
K-Konservator, Göteborg 129839
K Livres, Aix-en-Provence 138007
K + M Kunst, Düsseldorf 070398
K & P Collectibles, Indianapolis . . . 089311
K-Pro Galerie, Brno 098335, 120848
K. Restorations, London 131074
K20 Kunstsammlung am Grabbeplatz, K20K21 Kunstsammlung Nordrhein-Westfalen, Düsseldorf 016834
K21 Kunstsammlung im Ständehaus, K20K21 Kunstsammlung Nordrhein-Westfalen, Düsseldorf 016835
K4, Lisboa 129159
K4 Galerie, Saarbrücken 104800
KA, Burgas 096698
Ka-Do-Ha Indian Village Museum, Murfreesboro 046093
Ka Lui, Puerto Princesa 108852
Kaaber, København 137897
Kaan Zamaan, Kerikeri 108486
Kaandy Gallery, South Fremantle . . 095200
Kaarinan Antikka, Turku 137995
Kaarinan Koulumuseo, Littoinen . . . 009832
Kaarlelan Kotiseutumuseo, Kokkola 009723
Kaasboerderijmuseum de Weistaar, Maarsbergen 029884
Kaasmuseum Bodegraven, Bodegraven 029320
Kaaswaag Gouda, Gouda 029623
Kaatsmuseum, Franeker 029589
Kaatza Station Museum, Lake Cowichan 005739
Kaban ng Hiyas ng Lungsod ng Mandaluyong, Mandaluyong 031708
Kabanadze, Boris, Berlin 125227
Kabardino-Balkarskij Gosudarstvennyj Muzej Izobrazitelnych Iskusstv, Nalčik 033539
Kabarnet Museum, Kabarnet 027421
Kabat Wrobel, Toronto 097300
Kabayan National Museum, Kabayan 031678
Kabel & Lang, Darmstadt 070184
Kabella, Wolfgang, Paderborn 073282
Kabinet, Sankt-Peterburg 136055
Kabinet 18, Almere 107630
Kabinet České Grafiky, Praha 098465
Kabinet Grafike HAZU, Zagreb 007845
Kabinett, Bern 111261
Kabinett, Zürich 112123
Kabinett für aktuelle Kunst, Bremerhaven 102263
De Kabinetten van de Vleeshal, Middelburg 029920
Kaboom, New Orleans 142618
Kaboom, Virginia Beach 093358
Al-Kabra, Al-Khobar 080352
Kabul Antique Center, Manila 079564
Kabul Museum, Kabul 000004
Kabuth, Markus, Gelsenkirchen . . . 102929
Kachchh Museum, Bhuj 022041
Kachelmuseum De Drie Kronen, Boekel 029321
Kachinas, Navaho, Albuquerque . . . 114798
Kachler, Walldorf, Baden 074264
Kacprzak, Isabella, Berlin 101940
Kaczmarczyk, Roman, Kraków 079639
Kaczmarek, Triberg 074088
Kaczorowski, Philippe, Nantes 121089
Kádáns, Den Haag 107931
Kadavý, Milan, Praha 123984
Kadel, W., Kampen 071695
Kaden, Jutta, Dresden 070321
Kadenz, Mülheim an der Ruhr 104130
Kadgien, Kitzingen 139327
Kadi, Bruxelles 058000
Kadıköy Belediyesi Kültür Merkezi, İstanbul 112326
Kadın Eserleri Kütüphanesi ve Bilgi Merkezi, İstanbul 054252
Kadina Antiques, Kadina 056025
Kadina Heritage Museum, Kadina . . 001137
Kadlec, David, Indianapolis 116468
Kadman Numismatic Pavilion, Eretz-Israel Museum, Tel Aviv 023081
Kadoff & Sander, Arzl im Pitztal . . . 056920
Kadrinoff, Léré 063747
Kadrinoff, Alain, Saint-Ouen 067816
Kadrissime, Saint-Raphaël 101223
Kaede, Kamakura 106864
Käfer, Hubert, Kronberg im Taunus . 103795
Käfer, Susanne M., Gutach, Schwarzwaldbahn 125777
Käfer, Wilfried, Marburg 072446
Käferstein, Martin, Kleinmachnow . 126052
Kähler, Cordula, Frankfurt am Main 125652
Kähler, Ingrid, Hamburg 071256
Kähler-Abs, E., Greifswald 102995
Källaren, Eslöv 141094
Kämmer, N. & H., Deidesheim 070202
Kämpf, Basel 111197
Kämpf, Waltraud, Bad Windsheim . 069397
Kaempfer, Friedel & Horst, Erftstadt 102640
Kämpfert, Gerald, Halle, Saale 139160
Kärntner Bauernmöbelsammlung, Maria Saal 002283
Kärntner Druck- und Verlagsgesellschaft, Klagenfurt 133100
Kärntner Freilichtmuseum, Maria Saal 002284
Kärntner Landesausstellung, Klagenfurt 133101
Kärntner Landesgalerie, Klagenfurt 002146
Kärsämäen Kotiseutumuseo, Kärsämäki 009650
Kaes, Antonia, Holler 125957
Kaesemann, Barbara, Engelskirchen 102626
Käser, Hans, Metzingen 126312
Käserei und Glasmalerei, Schlierbach 095750
Käsewelt Schleedorf, Schleedorf . . 002649
Käsi- ja Taideteollisuusmessut, Tampere 093648
Kaess-Weiss, Gudrun, Stuttgart . . . 104993
Kaesser, Monika, Wien 057460
Käthe-Kollwitz-Museum Berlin, Berlin 016088
Käthe Kollwitz Museum Köln, Köln . 018319
Käthe Kruse-Poppenmuseum, Den Helder 029462
Käthe-Kruse-Puppen-Museum, Städtische Museen, Donauwörth 016743
Käufeler, M., Sursee 111940
Kafe, Chicago 115466
Kaffeekannenmuseum, Schöppenstedt 020088
Kafka's Kafe, Miami Beach 142563
Kafsack, Margareta, Paderborn . . . 073283
De Kaft, Leuven 137510
Kagaku Gijutsukan, Japan Science Foundation, Tokyo 027180
Kagan, Alona, New York 118065
Kagan, Beverlee, Miami 090195
Kaganczuk, Berlin 069654
Kagaribi, Osaka 077175
Kagawa-ken Bunka Kaikan, Takamatsu 027104
Kagedo, Seattle 119943
Kagoshima-ken Bunka Center, Kagoshima 026603

Kagoshima-kenritsu Hakubutsukan, Kagoshima . . . 026604
Kagu no Hakubutsukan, Tokyo . . . 027181
Kahala, Honolulu . . . 088962
Kahan, Jane, New York . . . 118066
Kahitsukan - Kyoto Museum of Contemporary Art, Kyoto . . . 026724
Kahl, Bad Kösen . . . 069313
Kahl, d., Naumburg, Saale . . . 072945
Kahl, Dieter, Berlin . . . 101941, 138799
Kahl, Günter, Saal . . . 104785
Kahl, Kerstin & Holger, Rudolstadt . 073614
Kahler, Rudolf & Ingeborg, Selb . . . 073795
Kahlhammer, Maria Saal . . . 057176
Kahmen, Dr. Hartmut, Rheinbach . . 073515
Kahn, Strasbourg . . . 101294
Kahn, Helen R., Montréal . . . 137658
Kahnert, Ulrich, Solingen . . . 073854
Kahoku, Sendai . . . 106998
Kahramanmaraş Devlet Güzel Sanatlar Galerisi, Kahramanmaraş . . . 038114
Kahramanmaraş Müzesi, Kahramanmaraş . . . 038115
Kahutara Canoes and Taxidermy Museum, Featherston . . . 030497
Kai Heng Yueyang, Shanghai . . . 097926
Kai See, Hong Kong . . . 097805
Kai Zhi, Wuxi . . . 098039
Kaiblinger, Siegfried, Sankt Leonhard am Forst . . . 095744
Kaieji Buddhist Temple Site Museum, Sennan . . . 027054
Kaien, Sandnes . . . 079491
Kaifeng Municipal Museum, Kaifeng 007164
Kaigado, Tokyo . . . 107056
Kaikodo, New York . . . 090988, 118067
Kaikohe Pioneer Village and Museum, Kaikohe . . . 030527
Kaikoura District Museum, Kaikoura 030528
Kaim, A., Köln . . . 071959
Kaim, Reinhold, Speyer . . . 073881
Kaimes Smithy, Edinburgh 084300, 130679
Kain, Irena, Riehen . . . 111838
Kainuun Museo, Kajaani . . . 009651
Kairė-Dešin, Vilnius . . . 107361
Kairos Antigüedades, Buenos Aires 055219
Kaisendo Museum, Kaminoyama . . 026614
Kaiser, Hilden . . . 103375
Kaiser, Weimar, Thüringen . . . 074308
Kaiser, Anne, Chur . . . 082315, 111358
Kaiser, C., Baden-Baden . . . 069418
Kaiser, Egon, Oberscheinfeld . . . 126581
Kaiser, G., Friesenheim, Baden . . . 070899
Kaiser, Jessika, Dietzenbach . . . 102370
Kaiser, R., Landsberg am Lech . . . 072138
Kaiser, Rüdiger, Frankfurt am Main . 070757
Kaiser Franz-Josef-Museum für Handwerk und Volkskunst, Baden bei Wien . 001745
Kaiser-Mühlecker, Johann, Gerersdorf . . . 123355
Kaiser-Schumann, Berlin . . . 138800
Kaiserappartements, Sisi Museum und Silberkammer, Wien . . . 002919
Kaiserburg Nürnberg, Germanisches Nationalmuseum, Nürnberg . . . 019361
Kaiserdom-Museum, Königslutter . 018352
Kaisergruft, Wien . . . 002920
Kaiserliche Hofburg zu Innsbruck, Innsbruck . . . 002085
Kaiserliches Hofmobiliendepot, Museen des Mobiliendepots, Wien . . . 002921
Kaiserpfalz mit Sankt Ulrichskapelle, Goslar . . . 017484
Kaiserpfalz Salzburg, Bad Neustadt an der Saale . . . 015763
Kaiserpfalzruine, Verwaltung der Staatlichen Schlösser und Gärten Außenstelle Steinau/Gelnhausen, Gelnhausen 017351
Kaisersaal Schwarzburg, Thüringer Landesmuseum Heidecksburg Rudolstadt, Schwarzburg . . . 020131
Kaiserstühler Heimatmuseum, Endingen . . . 016983
Kaiserstühler Weinbaumuseum, Vogtsburg . . . 020605
Kaiservilla, Bad Ischl . . . 001723
Kaitseväe Ühendatud Õppeasutuste Muuseum, Tartu . . . 009418
Kaivolan Museo, Laitila . . . 009794
Kaivopuiston Antiikki, Helsinki . . . 060535
Kaizen Gallery, Broadstairs . . . 112731
Kaizen International, Rochester . . 086389, 131422
Kajaanin Taidemuseo, Kajaani . . . 009652
Kaji, Kyoto . . . 077104
Kaji Aso Studio Gallery Nature and Temptation, Boston . . . 042330
Kake Tribal Heritage Foundation, Kake . . . 044895
Kakh-e-Rejat Va Ebrat & Mellat, Teheran . . . 022625
Kakiemon, Tokyo . . . 077259
Kaklamanou, Chalandri . . . 105415
Kakurin-ji Treasure House, Kakogawa . . . 026608
Kala, Santeny . . . 068122
Kala Art Institute, Berkeley . . . 042160
Kala Bharati Art Foundation, Mumbai . . . 053701
Kala Bharati Art School, Mumbai . . 050315
Kala Bhavana College of Fine Arts and Crafts, Santiniketan . . . 050325
Kala Kendra, Dehradun . . . 050297
Kala Mandir Art Gallery, Hyderabad 105703
Kala Niketan, Kolhapur . . . 050308
Kaláb, Dr. Bedřich, Kroměříž . . . 060040
Kalae, Montréal . . . 058969
Kalahari-Oranje Museum, Upington 034768
Kalajoen Kalastusmuseo, Kalajoki . 009654
Kalajoen Kotiseutumuseo, Kalajoki . 009655
Kalakriti, Hyderabad . . . 105704
Kalakruti, Chennai . . . 105632
Kalamahavidyalya Government College of Fine Arts, Indore . . . 050306
Kalamazoo Aviation History Museum, Kalamazoo . . . 044898
Kalamazoo Institute of Arts, Kalamazoo . . . 044899
Kalamazoo Valley Museum, Kalmazzo Valley Community College, Kalamazoo . . 044900
Kalamunda History Village, Kalamunda . . . 001138
Kalan Torppa, Kauhava . . . 009680
Kaland, Björn, Bergen . . . 128986
Kalannin Kotiseutumuseo, Kalanti . 009656
Kalantiaw Shrine Museum, Batan . . 031630
Kalao, La Coucourde . . . 063354
Kalart, San Francisco . . . 119704
Kalash, Lemesos . . . 059961
Kalaupapa Historical Park, Kalaupapa . . . 044901
Kalberg, Gerd, Halberstadt . . . 125787
Kalcher, Margarita, Salzburg . . . 057260
Kaldas, Johanna, Frankfurt am Main . . . 102791
Kaldenbach, Hans-Jürgen & Wenke, Neckarsulm . . . 126520
Kaldewey Press, New York . . . 135436
Kaleden, Miami . . . 090196
Kaleidoscope, Kansas City . . . 044919
Kaleidoscope, Phoenix . . . 118878
Kaleidoscope, Richmond . . . 092090
Kaleidoskop, Zürich . . . 141342
Kaleidoskop Galerie, Pfungstadt . . . 104606
Kalejdoskop, Åhus . . . 136110
Kaleko Mølle, Faaborg . . . 008852
Kalenbach, Philipp, Albstadt . . . 138676
Kalesse, B., Haynsburg . . . 071438
Kalfas, Barbara, Kraków . . . 129040
Kalfayan, Arsen & Roupen, Athinai . 105400
Kalfayan, Arsen & Roupen, Thessaloniki . . . 105447
Kalfhues, Laer . . . 072113
Kalfon, Guy, Paris . . . 066104
Kalfon, Guy, Paris . . . 066105
Kalfon, Patrick, Saint-Ouen . . . 067817
Kalgoorlie Galleries, Kalgoorlie . . . 094676
Kali-Bergbaumuseum Volpriehausen, Uslar . . . 020552
Kalidoscope Gallery, Calgary . . . 096824
Kaligos & Co., N., Thessaloniki . . . 105448, 134492, 139903
Kalihi-Palama Culture and Arts Society, Honolulu . . . 054828
Kalil & Lauar, Belo Horizonte . . . 096467
Kaliman, Paddington . . . 095031
Kalina, Regen . . . 104688
Kalinčeva Kăšta, Trjavna . . . 004902
Kaliningradskaja Chudožestvennaja Galereja, Kaliningrad . . . 033213
Kaliningradskij Oblastnoj Istoriko-chudožestvennyj Muzej, Kaliningrad . . . 033214
Kaliningradskij Oblastnoj Kraevedčeskij Muzej, Kaliningrad . . . 033215
Kalinka Antique Gallery, Bondi . . . 055518
Kalinowski, Moorabbin . . . 094879
Kalipong Art Gallery, Mumbai . . . 105784
Kalisch, Beate, Düsseldorf . . . 070399
Kalix Antik, Kalix . . . 081840
Kalix Flottningsmuseum, Kalix . . . 036370
Kaliya, Paris . . . 066106
Kalkaska County Historical Museum, Kalkaska . . . 044905
Kalke, Klaus, Wien . . . 095874
Kalkmann, Hans-Werner & Jens, Bad Salzdetfurth . . . 101690
Kalkuhl, Hans, Sternberg . . . 104954
Kalle, Malmö . . . 081870
Kallenaution Kievari, Korkeakoski . . 009732
Kallensee & Sohn, Kurt, Potsdam . . 126650
Kaller-Kimche, R., New York . . . 118068
Kalligramm, Berlin . . . 138801
Kalligraphie Edition, Hardheim . . . 134045
Kallinger, Hofkirchen, Bayern . . . 125954
Kallinger, Johannes, Regensburg . . 126691
Kallinger, Dr. Winfried, Wien . . . 057461
Kallion, Helsinki . . . 060536
Kallion, Helsinki . . . 060537
Kallion, Helsinki . . . 137946
Kallioniemi, Taivalkoski . . . 010111
Kallisté, Paris . . . 100557
Kallisté 21, Paris . . . 100558
Kallmann-Museum, Ismaning . . . 018092
Kallmeyer, Seelze . . . 134394
Kalman, Crane, London . . . 113718
Kalmar Antiques, Sydney . . . 056679
Kalmar Konstmuseum, Kalmar . . . 036371
Kalmar Läns Museum, Kalmar . . . 036372
Kalmar Sjöfartsmuseum, Kalmar . . 036373
Kalmar Slott, Kalmar . . . 036374
Kalmyckaja Gosudarstvennaja Kartinnaja Galereja, Ėlista . . . 033137
Kalmyckij Respublikanskij Kraevedčeskij Muzej im. Prof. N.N. Palmova, Ėlista . . . 033138
Kalncempju Pagasta Novadpētniecības Muzejs Ates Dzirnavās, Kalncempji . . . 027700
Kalnjali, Hyderabad . . . 074809
Kalos, Barcelona . . . 110203
Kalos, Taipei . . . 098077
Kalo's Antiquariato, Messina . . . 075563, 140037
Kalousek, Praha . . . 098466
Kalpa de Boer, Amsterdam . . . 107746
Kalpers, Marie-Josette, Liège . . . 058310
Kals, Burkhard, Kirchberg in Tirol . . 057096
Kalt, F., Riedlingen . . . 073531
Kalt-Zehnder, Zug . . . 135108
Kalteis, Walter, Krems . . . 057126
Kaltenbach, Klaus, Marburg . . . 139460
Kaltenstadler, Hann Münden . . . 071373
Kalthoff, Jürgen, Essen . . . 102688
Kalundborg og Omegns Museum, Kalundborg . . . 008947
Kalusche, Dr. Bernd, Frankfurt am Main . . . 139086
Kalusche, Dr. Bernd, Leipzig . . . 139395
Kalusky, K.-J., Verden . . . 074193
Kalusteneuvos, Helsinki . . . 060538
Kałużny, Antoni, Kraków . . . 129041
Kalužskij Filial Moskovskogo Gosudarstvennogo Universiteta Kultury i Iskusstv, Kaluga . . . 050636
Kalužskij Oblastnoj Chudožestvennyj Muzej, Kaluga . . . 033222
Kalužskij Oblastnoj Kraevedčeskij Muzej, Kaluga . . . 033223
Kalvolan Kunnan Kotiseutumuseo, Iittala . . . 009601
Kalymnios, John, New York . . . 118069
Kam-Ho, Edmonton . . . 058834
Kamaaina, Honolulu . . . 132090
Kamada Local Museum, Sakaide . . 027017
Kamakura Gallery, Kamakura . . . 106865
Kamakura Gallery, Kamakura . . . 106866
Kamakura Garo, Kamakura . . . 106867
Kamakura Kindai Bijutsukan, Kamakura . . . 026609
Kamakura Kokuhokan, Kamakura . . 026610
Kamakuragu Homotsu Chinretsujo, Kamakura . . . 026611
Kamali, New York . . . 090989
Kaman, Tampa . . . 120054
Kamčatskij Oblastnoj Kraevedčeskij Muzej, Petropavlovsk-Kamčatskij . . . 033655
Kamčatskij Voenno-istoričeskij Muzej, Petropavlovsk-Kamčatskij . . . 033656
Kamea Kawiarnia Galeria, Poznań . 109052
Kameja, Samara . . . 080286
Kameleon, Warszawa . . . 109147
Kamelot, Philadelphia . . . 123046
Kamen, Leo, Toronto . . . 097301
Kamena Gallery, Edmonton . . . 096889
Kamenný Dům, Okresní muzeum v Kutné Hoře, Kutná Hora . . . 008462
Kameo, Tokyo . . . 107057
De Kamer, Breda . . . 078104
Kamera- und Fotomuseum Leipzig, Leipzig . . . 018574
Kameralehti, Helsinki . . . 135676
Kamernyj Šaljapinskij Zal, Nacionalnyj Kulturnyj Centr Kazan, Kazan . . . 033233
Kames, Brodick and Whiting Bay . . 083765
Kami no Hakubutsukan, Tokyo . . . 027182
Kamienica Hipolitów, Kraków . . . 032031
Kamienica Szołayskich, Muzeum Narodowe w Krakowie, Kraków . . . 032032
Kamiina Museum, Ina . . . 026562
Kamińska-Samek, Krystyna, Kraków . . . 140739
Kaminski House Museum, Georgetown . . . 044176
Kamiss, Houston . . . 089123
Kamiya Bijutsukan, Handa . . . 026499
Kaml, Isabella, Kammern im Liesingtal . . . 123397
Kamloops Art Gallery, Kamloops . . . 005658
Kamloops Museum, Kamloops . . . 005659
Kamm, Bettina, München . . . 126399
Kamm, Erika, Ennenda . . . 082354
Kamm, Hans-Rudolf, Mollis 082662, 130119
Kamm, Joanna, Berlin . . . 101942
Kammann, Rolf, Bremen . . . 070026
Kammari, Alexandran, Helsinki . . . 060539
Kammer, Renate, Hamburg . . . 103171
Kammerer, Christina, Erlangen . . . 070599
Kammerer, Jutta, Graz . . . 095534
Kammerer, S., Bietigheim-Bissingen . . . 102135
Kammerhofgalerie der Stadt Gmunden, Gmunden . . . 001911
Kammerhofmuseum Ausseerland, Bad Aussee . . . 001708
Kammerhofmuseum der Stadt Gmunden, Gmunden . . . 001912
Kammerlander, Walter, Dornbirn . . . 056965
Kammermann, Werner, Kriens . . . 082518, 130055
Kamniški Muzej, Kamnik . . . 034466
Kamoliddin Bekhzad National Insitute of Arts and Design, Academy of Arts of Uzbekistan, Taškent . . . 052417
Kamon Antiques, Tokyo . . . 077260
Kamotzke, Eva-Maria, Rheda-Wiedenbrück . . . 104740
Kamp-Lintforter Münzfreunde, Kamp-Lintfort . . . 053251
Kamper, Maria, München . . . 134250
Kamper, Maria, Pischeldorf, Kärnten 133126

Kamper Tabaksmuseum, Kampen . 029800
Kampf, Heinz Hubertus, Muri bei Bern . . . 082681, 141281
Kamphaeng Phet National Museum, Kamphaeng Phet . . . 037900
Kamphans, T., Beelen . . . 069511
Kamphof, Günter, Willich . . . 127021
Kamphuis, J., Zwolle . . . 108282
Kampintorin Antikvariaatti, Helsinki 137947
Kampl, Mathias, Berlin . . . 101943
Kampl, Mathias, München . . . 104240
Kampmann, Henrik, København . . . 098576
Kampmann-Wilsker, Ralf, Münster . 126503
Kamps, Lüdenscheid . . . 139430
Kampschulte, Ingrid, Friedrichsthal 125683
Kamsack and District Museum, Kamsack . . . 005663
Kamthieng House, Bangkok . . . 037880
Kan, Sendai . . . 077213
Kan, Toyo, Tokyo . . . 077261
Kan Kan Kyo Art Gallery, Tokyo . . . 107058
Kana Art, Beograd . . . 080398
Kanabec History Center, Mora . . . 046018
Kanagawa-kenritsu Kanazawabunko Museum, Yokohama . . . 027332
Kanagawa Kenritsu Kindai Bijutsukan, Hayama . . . 026501
Kanagawa-kenritsu Rekishi Hakabutsukan, Yokohama . . . 027333
Kanagawa Prefectural Gallery, Yokohama . . . 027334
Kanai-machi Hakabutsukan, Kanai . 026620
Kanal- och Sjöfartsmuseet, Motala . 036488
Kanalgalleriet, Notodden . . . 108700
Kanalmuseet, Trollhättan . . . 036719
Kanalmuseet Skantzen, Hallstahammar . . . 036323
Al-Kananah, Dubai . . . 083195
Kanatzer, Fort Worth . . . 132071
Kanazawa Bijutsu Kogei Daigaku, Kanazawa . . . 050454
Kanazawa-shiritsu Nakamura Kinen Bijutsukan, Kanazawa . . . 026627
Kanda Kotetsudo, Tokyo . . . 077262
Kandahar Museum, Kandahar . . . 000007
Kandeil, Cairo . . . 060452
Kandeloos Museum, Kojoor . . . 022576
Kandelous Museum, Kandelous . . . 022564
Kandiyohi County Historical Society Museum, Willmar . . . 049195
Kandler, Toulouse . . . 101360
Kandos Bicentennial Industrial Museum, Kandos . . . 001141
Kandy National Museum, Kandy . . . 036140
Kandyan Antiques, Colombo . . . 081759
Kandyan Antiques, Colombo . . . 081760
Kane, Boston . . . 115186
Kane, Marie, Virginia Beach . . . 120226
Kane, Paul, Dublin . . . 105872
Kanebo Museum of Textiles, Osaka 026966
Kaneesha Art Gallery, Ahmedabad . 105595
Kaneesha Boutique, Ahmedabad . . 105596
Kanegendo, Sendai . . . 077214
Kanekichi, Nagoya . . . 077151
Kaneko, Yokohama . . . 140213
Kanel, Gilbert, Savigneux . . . 068166
Kanel, Marie-José, Saint-Étienne . . 067457
Kaner & Kaner, Freiburg im Breisgau . . . 139113
Kanev, Den Haag . . . 107932
Kanfer, Larry, Minneapolis . . . 117275
Kang Da, Shanghai . . . 059752
Kang Da, Shanghai . . . 059753
Kang Weon Folk Museums, Chunchon . . . 027470
Kang Xicao Museum, Beijing . . . 006989
Kanga Books, Chifley . . . 136858
Kangaroo House, Hurstbridge . . . 094656
Kangaroo Island Gallery, Kingscote . 094704
Kangasalan Museo, Kangasala . . . 009657
Kangaslammin Koti- ja Koulumuseo, Kangaslampi . . . 009659
Kangasniemen Museo, Kangasniemi . . . 009660
Kangomar, Kraków . . . 079640
Kangourou, Pulnoy . . . 066998
Kanhistique, Ellsworth . . . 136518
Kania, Bad Füssing . . . 101646
Kanizsai Dorottya Múzeum, Mohács 021793
Kankaanpään Kaupunginmuseo, Niinisalo . . . 009904
Kankakee County Historical Society Museum, Kankakee . . . 044908
Kanlungan ng Sining, Manila . . . 108845
Kannada Research Institute Museum, Dharwar . . . 022106
Kanne & Kruike, Rotterdam . . . 078724
Kannen, Elisabeth, Mönchengladbach . . . 104093
Kannenberg-Rentschler, Manfred, Berlin . . . 138802
Kannengießer, Ute, Wien . . . 123507
Kannonkosken Kotiseutukokoelma, Kannonkoski . . . 009662
Kannuksen Museo, Kannus . . . 009663
Kanon Auktioner, Nacka . . . 122217
Kansai, Osaka . . . 106964
Kansainvälinen Kahvikuppimuseo, Posio . . . 009999
Kansainvälinen Pullomuseo, Sonkajärvi . . . 010094
Kansallis-Osake-Pankin Rahanäyttely, Helsinki . . . 009538
Kansallispukukeskus, Suomen Käsityönmuseo, Jyväskylä . . . 009641
Kansas African American Museum, Wichita . . . 049157
Kansas Aviation Museum, Wichita . 049158
Kansas Barbed Wire Museum, La Crosse . . . 045054
Kansas City Art Institute, Kansas City . . . 051544
Kansas City Artists Coalition, Kansas City . . . 054829, 116575, 135372
Kansas City Collectibles, Kansas City . . . 089506
Kansas City Legends, Kansas City . 089507
Kansas City Museum/Science City at Union Station, Kansas City . . . 044920
Kansas Cosmosphere and Space Center, Hutchinson . . . 044703
Kansas Health Museum, Kansas Learning Center for Health, Halstead . . . 044394
Kansas Museum of History, Topeka 048581
Kansas Museums Association, Topeka . . . 054830
The Kansas Teachers' Hall of Fame, Dodge City . . . 043477
Kansas Watercolor Society, Hutchinson . . . 054831
Kanshin-ji Reihokan, Kawachi-Nagano . . . 026638
Kant, Praha . . . 137834
Kant, Renate, Singapore . . . 129260
Kant- en Textielcentrum, Diest . . . 003402
Kanta Museum Argungu, Argungu . 030674
Kantcentrum, Brugge . . . 003271
Kante, Mariana, Bruxelles . . . 058001
Kantelberg, Jill, Toronto . . . 059223
Het Kantenhuis, Amsterdam . . . 029191
Kantipur Art Gallery, Kathmandu . . . 107588
De Kantlijn, Bredevoort . . . 140369
Kantmuseum, Olsene . . . 003680
Kantmuseum, Uithuizen . . . 030216
Kantner, Hermann, Wien . . . 137330
Kantokorpi, Otso, Helsinki . . . 137948
Kantonales Fischereimuseum Mettlen, Netstal . . . 037370
Kantonales Museum Altes Zeughaus, Wehrhistorisches Museum, Solothurn . . . 037575
Kantonales Museum für Urgeschichte, Zug . . . 037818
Kantonsmuseum Baselland, Liestal 037267
Kantor, Los Angeles . . . 116804
Kantor, Jacques, Paris . . . 066107
Kantz Aranyozó, Budapest . . . 127075
Kanuma Municipal Art Museum of Kawakami Sumio, Kanuma . . . 026629
Kanumis, Lyon . . . 064147
Kanzeon-ji Treasure House, Dazaifu 026449
Kanzler, Wilhelm, Hof bei Salzburg . 123384
Kao Chong, Trang . . . 037938
Kao Luang, Nakhon Si Thammarat . 037912
Kao Ta Phet, Sukhothai . . . 037932
Kao Yai, Saraburi . . . 037929
Kapenguria Museum, Kapenguria . . 027422
Kaperdalen Samemuseum, Midt-Troms Museum, Senja . . . 031180
Kapfer, Niederwaldkirchen . . . 057193
Kapfhamer, Ingrid, Aichach . . . 138675
Kaphammel, Thomas, Braunschweig . . . 102221
Kaphammel, Thomas, Goslar . . . 102982
Kapinos, Michael, Berlin . . . 101944
Kapiolani Community College, University of Hawaii, Honolulu . . . 051475
Kapitän Tadsen Museum, Langeneß 018509
Kapiteinshuis Pekela, Nieuwe Pekela . . . 029947
Kapiti Coast Museum Waikanae, Wellington . . . 030637
Kaplan, Austin . . . 087587, 131802
Kaplan, Stockholm . . . 122255
Kaplan & Son, Alec, Germiston . . . 080697
Kaplan & Son, Alec, Johannesburg . 080708
Kaplan, Howard, New York . . . 090990
Kaplan, Leo, New York . . . 090991
Kaplan, Leo, New York . . . 118070
Kaplanstöckl, Hohenzell . . . 002058
Kaple Sv. Kříže, Praha . . . 008615
Kapoor, New York . . . 118071
Kapopoulos, Eyag., Athinai . . . 074594
Kaposvar Historic Site, Our Lady of Assumption Church Museum, Esterhazy . . . 005434
Kappa, Roma . . . 134679
Kappa Pi International Honorary Art Fraternity, Cleveland . . . 054832
Kappatos Gallery, Athinai . . . 105401
Kappaun, Ursula, Leibnitz . . . 137215
Kappel, Günther jun., Bad Mitterndorf . . . 056937
Kappel, Manfred, Salzburg 057261, 123447
Kappeler, Urs, Tafers . . . 130192
Kappelhoff, Herbert, Emmerich . . . 070562
Kappelsberger, Stefan, Graz . . . 057015, 123361
Kappenstein, Christoph, Jülich . . . 071672
Kappler, Chris, Seattle . . . 093027
Kappler, Doris, Darmstadt . . . 102342
Kapucijnenmuseum, 's-Hertogenbosch . . . 029732
Kapunda Museum, Kapunda . . . 001143
Kapusta, Matej, Kremnica . . . 129276
Kapuzinerturm, Radstadt . . . 002490
Kar Art Nostalgia, Helsinki . . . 060540
Kara, Paris . . . 066108
Karačaevo-Čerkesskij Istoriko-kul'turnyj i Prirodnyj Muzej-Zapovednik, Čerkessk . . . 033079
Karacolskij Istoričeskij Kraevedčeskij Muzej, Karacol . . . 027638
Karajian, Jean, New York . . . 090992
Karakalpakskij Istoričeskij Muzej, Nukus . . . 049400
Karakter, Amsterdam . . . 077879
Karam, Jorge Alberto, Porto Alegre . 096564
Karaman Müzesi, Karaman . . . 038116
Karambamba & Attalidou, Lefkosia . 098302
Karamea Centennial Museum, Karamea . . . 030530
Karan Art Gallery, Jaipur, Rajasthan 105723
Karascho, Essen . . . 102689
Karasek, Brigitte W., Geretsried . . . 070973
Karasek-Museum, Seifhennersdorf 020179
Karatay Çini Eserler Müzesi, Konya . 038133
Karatchoff, Paris . . . 100559
Karatepe-Aslantaş Açıkhava Müzesi, Osmaniye . . . 038161
Karau, Horst, Westensee . . . 074359
Karausz, Daniel, Montevideo . . . 087325
Karava, Maria, Athinai . . . 074595
Karavanserai, Maastricht . . . 078610
Karbstein, Peter, Düsseldorf . . . 121385
Karby Gård Konstcentrum, Täby . . . 036702
Kard Bar Prints & Posters, Newcastle-upon-Tyne . . . 114124
Kardamyla Cultural Centre of Michael and Stamatia Xylas, Ano Kardamyla . . 021136
Karden-und Heimatmuseum, Katsdorf . . . 002116
Kare Sanat Galerisi, İstanbul . . . 112327
Kare Shelley Railroad Museum, Boone . . . 042302
Kareem, Atlanta . . . 114892
Karekla, Frankfurt am Main . . . 125653
Karekla, Frankfurt am Main . . . 125654
Karel, Marel, Niddatal . . . 139595
Karelskij Gosudarstvennyj Kraevedčeskij Muzej, Petrozavodsk . . . 033661
Karen Blixen Museet, Rungsted Kyst . . . 009087
Karen Blixen Museum, Nairobi . . . 027428
Karen's Collectible Dolls, Miami . . . 090197
Karen's Creative Centre, Singapore 050683
Karen's Gifts, Louisville . . . 090005
Karen's Photo Restoration, Houston 132126
Kareńska, Anna, Poznań . . . 109053
Karepa Kalame Talumuuseum, Vihula . . . 009435
Kareum - Gamla Bilsalongen, Sparreholm . . . 036607
Karges, William A., West Hollywood 120392
Kargl, Georg, Wien . . . 095875
Kargopolskij Gosudarstvennyj Istoriko-Architekturnyj i Chudožestvennyj Muzej, Kargopol . . . 033228
Karhulan Lasimuseo, Karhula . . . 009664
Kari, Kenetti, Helsinki . . . 098736
Kariandusi Prehistoric Site Museum, Gilgil . . . 027419
Karibil Cottage, Griffith . . . 055920
Karich, S., Üxheim . . . 074139
Karijoen Kotiseutumuseo, Karijoki . 009665
Karikatürcüler Derneği Sanat Galerisi, İstanbul . . . 112328
Karikatur und Cartoon Museum Basel, Basel . . . 036887
Karikaturmuseum Krems, Krems . . 002171
Karin, Klesper, Jesteburg . . . 103452
Karins Antik Stube, Kerpen, Rheinland . . . 071803
Karioth, J., Berlin . . . 125228
Karjaan Museo, Karjaa . . . 009667
Karjalainen Kotitalo, Imatra . . . 009606
Karjalan Kotiseutumuseo, Mynämäki . . . 009889
Karjalan Portti, Imatra . . . 060597
Karkkila Högforsin Työläismuseo, Karkkila . . . 009668
Karkmann, Lamstedt . . . 072126
Karl, Helmut, Stephanskirchen, Simssee . . . 126835
Karl Drerup Fine Arts Gallery, Dept of Fine Arts, Plymouth State College, Plymouth . . . 047102
Karl-Ernst-Osthaus-Bund, Hagener Kunstverein, Hagen, Westfalen . . 053252
Karl Ernst Osthaus-Museum der Stadt Hagen, Hagen, Westfalen . . . 017625
Karl Ernst von Baeri Muuseum, Tartu . . . 009419
Karl & Faber, München . . . 072746, 121532, 139521
Karl Heinrich Waggerl-Haus, Wagrain . . . 002796
Karl Hofer-Gesellschaft, Freundeskreis der Universität der Künste Berlin, Berlin . . . 053253
Karl-Marx-Buchhandlung, Berlin . . 138803
Karl-Marx-Haus, Trier . . . 020480
Karl-May-Haus, Hohenstein-Ernstthal . . . 017978
Karl-May-Museum, Radebeul . . . 019696
Karl Pollender-Stadtmuseum, Karl-Pollender-Stadtmuseum, Werne . 020810
Karl Ristikivi Majamuuseum, Tartu . 009420
Karl-Seckinger-Ausstellung, Karlsruhe . . . 018160
Karl the Twelfth Sweedish Antiques, West Hollywood . . . 093480

Karl-Wagenplast-Museum, Schwaigern . . . 020119
Karla Antik, Stockholm . . . 081970
Kārļa Skalbes Muzejs, Vecpiebalga 027796
Kārļa Ulmaņa Pikšas, Bērze . . . 027665
Karlebo Museum, Kokkedal . . . 008996
Karlie, Philadelphia . . . 118788
Karlinger-Schmiede, Unterweißenbach . . . 002771
Karlovarské Muzeum, Karlovy Vary . 008425
Karlovské Muzeum, Velké Karlovice 008746
Karlshamns Museum, Karlshamn . . 036376
Karlskoga Konstförening, Karlskoga 054135
Karlskoga Konsthall, Karlskoga . . . 036379
Karlsruher Radierpresse, Karlsruhe 134077
Karlsson, Leo, Frankfurt am Main . . 070758
Karlsson, Magnus, Stockholm . . . 111056
Karlucci, Saint Paul . . . 092371, 132769
Karma, Cairo . . . 098640
Karma, Den Haag . . . 107933
Karmal-Skillington, Nashville . . . 090462
Karmazyn, Kraków . . . 079641
Karmøy Fiskerimuseum, Vedavågen 031324
Karmsund Folkemuseum, Haugesund . . . 030882
Karnataka Chitrakala Parishath, Bangalore . . . 050292, 105607
Karnataka Government Museum and Venkatappa Art Gallery, Bangalore 022015
Karnevalmuseum, Mönchengladbach . . . 018977
Karnowsky, Merry, Los Angeles . . . 116805
Karol Plicka Múzeum, Slovenské Národné Múzeum, Blatnica . . . 034314
Karoline Antikt, Oslo . . . 079450
Karos, Milwaukee . . . 090307
Karowski, M., Rosbach . . . 104760
Karp, J. Louis & Phyllis T., Cincinnati . . . 088253, 122858
Karp, Jules, New York . . . 090993
Karpa, L., Roßla . . . 073577
Karpatendeutsches Museum, Karlsruhe . . . 018161
Karpf, Helmut, Wiener Neustadt . . . 057596
Karpisek, Yves, Ceyras . . . 062064
Karrasburg Museum Coswig, Coswig bei Dresden . . . 016592
Karrenbauer, Carlo, Konstanz . . . 121484
Karrenmuseum, Essen . . . 003427
Karrer, Jürgen, Berlin . . . 069655
Kars Devlet Güzel Sanatlar Galerisi, Kars . . . 038117
Kars Kültür Merkezi, Kars . . . 038118
Kars Müzesi, Kars . . . 038119
Karsch, Jörg-Peter, Wielenbach . . . 074389
Karsenty, Jean-Louis, Paris . . . 100560
Karst, Jean, Schaan . . . 077447, 107336, 128458
Karst, Michael, Heide, Holstein . . . 071440
Karst- und Höhlenkundliche Abteilung, Naturhistorisches Museum Wien, Wien . . . 002922
Karsten, L., Bielefeld . . . 138873
Karstens, Mike, Münster . . . 104369
Karstmuseum Heimkehle, Uftrungen . . . 020526
Karstulan Kotiseutumuseo, Karstula 009670
Kartäusermuseum Tückelhausen, Ochsenfurt . . . 019432
Kartause Aggsbach, Aggsbach Dorf 001665
Kartause Gaming, Gaming . . . 001883
Karthaus-Prüll Museen des Bezirksklinikums Regensburg, Regensburg . . . 019753
Kartinnaja Galereja A.A. Plastova, Uljanovskij oblastnoj chudožestvennyj muzej, Uljanovsk . . . 034006
Kartinnaja Galereja K. Vasiljeva, Kazan . . . 033234
Kartinnaja Galereja Pejzažej P.M. Grečiškina, Stavropol . . . 033909
Kartinnaja Galereja Respubliki Adygeja, Majkop . . . 033349
Kartinnaja Galerija im. P.I. Šolochova, Borisoglebsk . . . 033043
Kartiny-Baget-Antikvariat, Moskva . 080245
Kartiny-Baget-Antikvariat, Moskva . 080246
Kartnaller, Anton, Innsbruck . . . 057083
Das Kartoffelmuseum, München . . 019066
Karttulan Kotiseutumuseo, Karttula 009671
Kartynna Galereja, Kam'janec'-Podil's'kyj . . . 038276
Kartynna Galereja, Volyns'kyj Krajeznavčyj Muzej, Luc'k . . . 038328
Karvian Museo, Karvia . . . 009673
Karwah, Toronto . . . 097302
Kary, Al, Fortaleza . . . 096531
Karyes-Protaton, Agion Oros . . . 021116
Kaş Galerisi, İstanbul . . . 112329
Kasagi, Kamakura . . . 106868
Kaschenbach, Peter, Trier . . . 105063
Kasden, Los Angeles . . . 089812
Kasel, Chicago . . . 088113, 131907
Kashba, Amsterdam . . . 077880
Kashima-jingu Treasure House, Kashima, Ibaraki . . . 026635
Kashishian, Long Beach . . . 089639
Kashma House, Nelson . . . 079176
Kashmir Art Emporium, Manama . . 096013
Kashmir Art Palace, Chennai . . . 074794
Kashmir Carpets, Hyderabad . . . 074810
Kashya, Hildebrand, Genève . . . 111475
Kasimir's, Brugge . . . 057779
Kaškadarinskij Kraevedčeskij Muzej, Karši . . . 049392
Kaskarots, Ciboure . . . 062305
Kaskines Collection, Lindos . . . 021362
Kaskö Hembygdsmuseum, Kaskinen . . . 009676
Kasmin, Paul, New York . . . 118072
Kaspar, Toronto . . . 097303
Kaspari, Nürnberg . . . 104481
Kasper, Dr. Alfons, Bad Schussenried . . . 133735
Kasper, Ralf, Kiel . . . 071830
Kasperek, Iris, Konstanz . . . 103761
Kaspers & Co., Arnhem . . . 078052
Kaspers, Ralf, Düsseldorf . . . 102514
Kasr Tin Hinan, El Madania . . . 055134
Kass, Bertrand, Innsbruck . . . 095586
Kass Galéria, Szeged . . . 021860
Kass Meridian, Chicago . . . 115467
Kassai, R. & P., New York . 090994, 132485
Kassàk, Budapest . . . 134503
Kassák Museum, Budapest . . . 021659
Kasseler Kunstverein e.V., Kassel . . 053254
Kassl, Günther, Brückl . . . 137160
Kaßler, Winfried, Langenhagen . . . 072156
Kast, Thomas, Röfingen . . . 073558
Kăšta-muzej Akademik Dončo Kostov, Nacionalen Selskostopanski Muzej Sofia, Lokorsko . . . 004740
Kăšta-muzej Aleksandăr Mutafov, Sozopol . . . 004882
Kăšta-muzej Angel Kănčev, Trjavna 004903
Kăšta-muzej Angel Karalijčev, Dom na Detskata Kniga, Sofia . . . 004845
Kăšta-muzej Asen Razcvetnikov, Draganovo . . . 004672
Kăšta-muzej Asen Zlatarov, Chaskovo . . . 004655
Kăšta-muzej Bojan Chonos, Vidin . . 004945
Kăšta-muzej Canko Cerkovski, Bjala Čerkva . . . 004639
Kăšta-muzej Chadži Dimităr, Okrăžen Istoričeski Muzej, Sliven . . . 004835
Kăšta-muzej Christo Botev, Kalofer 004701
Kăšta-muzej Christo G. Danov, Istoričeski Muzej, Plovdiv . . . 004793
Kăšta-muzej Christo i Ivan Michailovi, Michajlovgrad . . . 004753
Kăšta-muzej Christo Smirnenski, Nacionalen Muzej na Bălgarskata Literatura, Sofia . . . 004846
Kăšta-muzej Dimcho Debeljanov, Koprivštica . . . 004727
Kăšta-muzej Dimităr Blagoev, Bankja . . . 004627
Kăšta-muzej Dimităr Blagoev, Sofia 004847
Kăšta-muzej Dimităr Dimov, Nacionalen Muzej na Bălgarskata Literatura, Sofia . . . 004848
Kăšta-muzej Dimitar Pešev, Istoričeski Muzej, Kjustendil . . . 004721
Kăšta-muzej Dimităr Poljanov, Karnobat . . . 004708
Kăšta-muzej Dobri Čintulov, Sliven . 004836
Kăšta-muzej Dobri Voinikov, Šumen 004888
Kăšta-muzej Došo Mihajlov, Babuk . 004621
Kăšta-muzej Emilijan Stanev, Veliko Tărnovo . . . 004933
Kăšta-muzej Ĕrdan Ĕovkov, Žeravna 004953
Kăšta-muzej Geo Milev, Stara Zagora . . . 004883
Kăšta-muzej Georgi Benkovski, Koprivštica . . . 004728
Kăšta-muzej Georgi Damianovo, Georgi Damianovo . . . 004688
Kăšta-muzej Georgi Dimitrov, Kovačevci . . . 004736
Kăšta-muzej Iljo Vojvoda, Istoričeski Muzej, Kjustendil . . . 004722
Kăšta-muzej Ivan Lazarov, Nacionalna chudožestvena galerija, Sofia . . . 004849
Kăšta-muzej Ivan Vazov, Berkovica 004637
Kăšta-muzej Ivan Vazov, Nacionalen muzej na bălgarskata literatura, Sofia . . 004850
Kăšta-muzej Lamartine, Plovdiv . . . 004794
Kăšta-muzej Ljuben Karavelov, Koprivštica . . . 004729
Kăšta-muzej Mitko Palauzov, Okrăžen muzej Gabrovo, Gabrovo . . . 004684
Kăšta-muzej na Slivenskija Bit ot 19 Vek, Sliven . . . 004837
Kăšta-muzej Neofit Rilski, Bansko . 004629
Kăšta-muzej Nikola Ĕnkov Vapcarov, Bansko . . . 004630
Kăšta-muzej Nikola P. Karadžchata, Bradvari . . . 004645
Kăšta-muzej Nikola Parapunov, Razlog . . . 004815
Kăšta-muzej Nikola Vapcarov, Nacionalen Muzej na Bălgarskata Literatura, Sofia . . . 004851
Kăšta-muzej Panaët Chitov, Okrăžen istoričeski muzej, Sliven . . . 004838
Kăšta-muzej Panaët Volov, Šumen . 004889
Kăšta-muzej Pančo Vladigerov, Šumen . . . 004890
Kăšta-muzej Pejo Javorov, Nacionalen Muzej na Bălgarskata Literatura, Sofia . . . 004852
Kăšta-muzej Pejo K. Javorov, Čirpan . . . 004661
Kăšta-muzej Petko i Pencho Slavejkovi, Nacionalen Muzej na Bălgarskata Literatura, Sofia . . . 004853
Kăšta-muzej Rajna Knjaginja, Panagjurište . . . 004766
Kăšta-muzej Rusi Čorbadži, Žeravna . . . 004954
Kăšta-muzej s Dom-pametnik Jordan Jovkov, Dobrič . . . 004671
Kăšta-muzej Sava Filaretov, Žeravna . . . 004955
Kăšta-muzej Slavejkovi, Trjavna . . . 004904
Kăšta-muzej Stanislav Dospevski, Pazardžik . . . 004771
Kăšta-muzej Stojan i Vladimir Zaimovi, Pleven . . . 004780
Kăšta-muzej Svetoslav Obretenov, Provadia . . . 004805
Kăšta-muzej Todor Kableškov, Koprivštica . . . 004730
Kăšta-muzej Vasil Kolarov, Šumen . 004891
Kăšta-muzej Zachari Stojanov, Medven . . . 004748
Kăšta-muzej Zachari Stojanov, Ruse 004819
Kastamonu Devlet Güzel Sanatlar Galerisi, Kastamonu . . . 038120
Kasteel Achtendries, Gent . . . 003457
Kasteel Amerongen, Amerongen . . 029146
Kasteel Ammersoyen, Ammerzoden 029157
Kasteel Beauvoorde, Wulveringem . 003863
Kasteel Cannenburch, Vaassen . . . 030243
Kasteel De Doornenburg, Doornenburg . . . 029498
Kasteel de Haar, Collectie Th. Baron Van Zuylen Van Nijevelt Van de Haar, Haarzuilens . . . 029662
Kasteel Doorwerth, Doorwerth . . . 029499
Kasteel Duivenvoorde, Voorschoten 030291
Kasteel Groeneveld, Baarn . . . 029288
Kasteel Heeswijk, Heeswijk-Dinther 029701
Kasteel Heeze - Collectie H.N.C. Baron Van Tuyll Van Serooskerken Van Heeze en Leende, Heeze . . . 029703
Kasteel Hernen, Hernen . . . 029730
Kasteel Het Hijenhuis, Hannema-de Stuers Fundatie, Heino . . . 029711
Kasteel Hoensbroek, Hoensbroek . . 029759
Kasteel Huis Doorn, Doorn . . . 029496
Kasteel Middachten, De Steeg . . . 029400
Kasteel-Museum Sypesteyn, Loosdrecht . . . 029875
Kasteel Ooidonk, Deinze . . . 003390
Kasteel Radboud, Medemblik . . . 029911
Kasteel Rosendael, Rozendaal . . . 030112
Kasteel van Beersel, Beersel . . . 003224
Kasteel van Bornem, Bornem . . . 003245
Kasteel van Gaasbeek, Gaasbeek . . 003441
Kasteel van Horst, Sint-Pieters-Rode . . . 003762
Kasteel van Leeuwergem, Zottegem 003872
Kasteel van Wijnendale, Torhout . . . 003801
Kasteelmuseum Slot van Laarne, Laarne . . . 003565
Kasteelruïne Valkenburg, Valkenburg, Limburg . . . 030246
Kasteeltoren IJsselstein, IJsselstein . 029790
Kaštela Gradski Muzej, Kaštel Lukšić . . . 007733
Kastélymúzeum, Fertőd . . . 021726
Kasten, Dr. Friedrich W., Mannheim 104025
Kasten, Gabriele, Grömitz . . . 103009
Kasten & Kisten, Dordrecht . . . 078306
Kastens, F., Stuhr . . . 139747
Kastern, Hannover 071396, 121445, 139235
The Kasteyev State Museum of Arts of the Republic of Kazakhstan, Almaty . . 027390
Kaštiel a Kysuce Galéria, Oščadnica 034405
Kastleholm Castle, Sund . . . 010103
Kastner, Honolulu . . . 116221
Kastner, Thekla, München . . . 139522
Kastoria Byzantine Museum, Kastoria . . . 021317
Kastrupgaardsamlingen, Kastrup . . 008948
Kasuga Taisha, Nara . . . 026892
Kasumisou, Tokyo . . . 077263
Kasuo, Iwamura Pierre, Valognes . . 101425
Kasvimuseo, Turku . . . 010163
Kasvimuseo, Luonnontieteellinen Keskusmuseo, Helsinki . . . 009539
Kat, Gilles, Beaulieu-sur-Mer . . . 061256
Katachi, Hamburg . . . 071257
Katamatite Museum, Katamatite . . 001144
Katanning Historical Museum, Katanning . . . 001145
Katarina-Antikvariatet, Stockholm . 141161
Katarina Kuriosa, Stockholm . . . 081971
Kate, Hemswell Cliff . . . 084654
Kate, Joyce, Seattle . . . 119944
Kate-Antik, Ferch . . . 139071
The Kate Chopin House and Bayou Folk Museum, Cloutierville . . . 043024
Katebi, G., Köln . . . 071960
Katedra Výtvarné Výchovny, České Budějovice . . . 049890
Katedralna Zbirka, Hvar . . . 007725
Katelman, Omaha . . . 091573, 132593
Kateri Galleries, National Shrine of the North American Martyrs, Auriesville . . . 041907
Kates, Mary, Auckland . . . 078956
Kathan, Erwin, Tettnang . . . 105045
Kathareze, Tilburg . . . 108230
Katharina-Luther-Stube, Torgau . . . 020451
Katharinas Puppenhaus, Pleystein . 019636
Katharine House Gallery, Marlborough . . . 085948
Katharine House Gallery, Marlborough . . . 114061
Katharine House Gallery, Marlborough . . . 141942
Katherine Art Gallery, Katherine . . . 094680

Katherine Mansfield Birthplace, Wellington . . . 030638
Katherine Museum, Katherine . . . 001146
Katherine Nash Gallery, University of Minnesota, Minneapolis . . . 045915
Katherine's Collection, Dallas . . . 088538
Kathmandu - Hot Spring in the Art Museum, Yuzawa . . . 027352
Kathree Häusle, Dettenhausen . . . 016693
Kathryn's Antiques, Portland . . . 091961
Kathy's Antiques, Long Beach . . . 089640
Katia, Genova . . . 106098
Katia, Paris . . . 066109
Katiane, Saint-Céneri-le-Gérei . . . 101136
Katina Paxinou Museum, Athinai . . 021178
Katir, Maria, Rosenheim . . . 073572
Kati's Antik, Falkenstein, Vogtland . 070675
Katlin, Auckland . . . 078957
Kato, Kyoto . . . 077105
Kato, Kyoto . . . 106899
Kato, Seto . . . 077222
Kato, Tokyo . . . 107059
Katona József Múzeum, Kecskemét 021757
Katona József Múzeum, Kecskemét 021758
Katona József Múzeum, Dept of History of Medicine, Kecskemét . . . 021759
Katonah Museum of Art, Katonah . . 044936
Katong, Singapore . . . 080500
Katoomba Antiques, Katoomba . . . 056035
Katoomba Fine Art, Katoomba . . . 094683
Katori-jingu Treasure House, Sawara . . . 027042
Katrineholms Hembygdsmuseet, Kristineholm . . . 036405
Kats, Rotterdam . . . 078725
Katschtaler Heimatmuseum, Rennweg . . . 002522
Katsushika Hokusai Bijutsukan, Tsuwano . . . 027298
Katsushika-ku Kyoiku Shiryokan, Tokyo . . . 027183
Katt, Elliot, Los Angeles . . . 142513
Katten Kabinet, Amsterdam . . . 029192
Kattenburg, Rob, Amsterdam . . . 077881, 140312
Kattlunds Museigård, Havdhem . . . 036330
Katumuseo, Helsingin Kaupunginmuseo, Helsinki . . . 009540
Katwijks Museum, Katwijk aan Zee 029806
Katxibatxes, Donostia-San Sebastián . . . 081083
Katy's Art Gallery, Indianapolis . . . 116469
Katz, Atlanta . . . 114893
Katz, Boston . . . 115187
Katz, Allie, Tampa . . . 093130
Katz, Anne, Bruchköbel . . . 102270
Katz, Daniel, London . . . 113719
Katz, David, Basel . . . 111198
Katz, David, Sankt Moritz . . . 111884
Katz, Holly, New York . . . 118073
Katz, Karla, New Orleans . . . 090574
Katz Morris, New York . . . 118074
Katzbichler, Bernd, Wiesenfelden . . 139858
Katzen, C.Y., Washington . . . 120318
Katzenmeyer, Günther, Feldkirch . . 056975
Katzenmuseum, Traunstein . . . 020456
Katzer, Wolfgang, Augsburg . . . 069234
Kauai Children's Discovery Museum, Kapaa . . . 044933
Kauai Museum, Lihue . . . 045291
Kauba, Indianapolis . . . 116470
Kauffelt, Matthias, Mannheim . . . 126277
Kauffman Gallery, Shippensburg . . . 048155
Kauffman Museum, North Newton . 046529
Kauffmann, Nördlingen . . . 104457
Kauffmann, Gudrun, Möttingen . . . 104112
Kauffmann, Gudrun, München . . . 104241
Kaufman, Tel Aviv . . . 075004
Kaufman, Inna, Amsterdam . . . 107747
Kaufman, Sam, Los Angeles . . . 089813
Kaufmann, Toulouse . . . 068523
Kaufmann, Alwin, Vandans . . . 057337
Kaufmann, Elisabeth, Zürich . . . 112124
Kaufmann, Martin, Castrop-Rauxel . 125426
Kaufmann, Rainer & J., Sulzburg . . 074030
Kaufmann, Stefan, Grünstadt . . . 071133
Kaufmannsmuseum des Heimatvereins Haslach, Haslach . . . 002022
Kauhajoen Museo, Kauhajoki . . . 009678
Kauhavanmuseo, Kauhava . . . 009681
Kaul & Streibel, Gerabronn . . . 070970
Kaulbach-Haus, Museum Bad Arolsen, Bad Arolsen . . . 015645
Kaulbachatelier, Ohlstadt . . . 019459
Kaulitz, S., Magdeburg . . . 072370
Kaun, Kurt, Sankt Florian . . . 057286
Kaunislehdon Talomuseo, Hyrynsalmi . . . 009596
Kauno Galerija, Kaunas . . . 107346
Kauno Langas, Kaunas . . . 107347
Kauno Langas, Kaunas . . . 107348
Kauno Paveikslų, Kaunas . . . 107349
Kaupel, Jürgen, Recklinghausen . . 073444
Kaupp, Karlheinz, Sulzburg . . . 121611
Kauppamakasiini, Helsinki . . . 137949
Kauppilan perinnetalo, Humppila . . 009594
Kauppilan Umpipiha, Laitila . . . 009795
Kauppilanmäen Museo, Valkeakoski 010213
Kauri Books, Birkenhead . . . 140606
The Kauri Museum, Matakohe . . . 030539
Kaurilan Koulumuseo, Tohmajärvi . . 010150
Kausl, Wilhelm, Wien . . . 137331
Kaustisen Kotiseutumuseo, Kaustinen . . . 009683
Kausynoé, Bruxelles . . . 058002
Kautsch, Veronica, Michelstadt . . . 104069
Kauttuan Tehtaan Museo, Kauttua . 009685
Kautz, Willi, Pforzheim . . . 073318
Kautzsch & Sohn, Klein Dahlum . . . 071868
KavaDo, Dortmund . . . 102405
Kavalet, Varna . . . 096773
Kavalierhaus Gifhorn- Museum für bürgerliche Wohnkultur, Museen des Landkreises Gifhorn, Gifhorn . . . 017416
Kavanagh, Kevin, Dublin . . . 105873
Kavanagh Antiques, Montréal . . . 058970
Kaw Mission, Council Grove . . . 043192
Kawaguchi-ko Motor Museum, Narusawa . . . 026905
Kawaguchi Tibetan Collection, Sendai . . . 027047
Kawaguchiko Bijutsukan, Kawaguchiko . . . 026641
Kawai Kanjiro's House, Kyoto . . . 026725
Kawakami, Gasendo, Kyoto . . . 106900
Kawamura Memorial Museum of Art, Sakura . . . 027021
Kawanabe Kyosai Memorial Museum, Warabi . . . 027317
Kawartha Settlers' Village, Bobcaygeon . . . 005107
Kawasaki, Kyoto . . . 077106
Kawasaki Municipal Industrial and Cultural Museum, Kawasaki . . . 026644
Kawasaki-shi Shimin Hakubutsukan, Kawasaki . . . 026645
Kawasaki-shiritsu Nihon Minkaen, Kawasaki . . . 026646
Kawhia Regional Museum Gallery, Kawhia . . . 030531
Kawilihan Art Gallery, Mandaluyong 108837
Kawsara Fall, Amsterdam . . . 077882
Kay, Frances, San Diego . . . 119519
Kay, Gary, Armadale, Victoria . . . 055383
Kay & Assoc., Hanna, San Francisco . . . 119705
Kay, Susan, San Francisco . . . 119706
Kay Kee, Hong Kong . . . 059646
Kayafas, Boston . . . 115188
Kaye, Anne, Providence . . . 092043
Kaye, Lita, Lyndhurst . . . 085883
Kayes, Chester . . . 083959, 130559
Kayes, Pretoria . . . 080735
Kayo, San Francisco . . . 142953
Kay's Antiques, Claremont . . . 080689
Kay's Antiques, Tulsa . . . 093317
Kayser, Isny . . . 103444, 125978
Kayser, Enrico, Marburg . . . 072447
Kayser, Jean-Huber, Nancy . . . 064870
Kayseri Arkeoloji Müzesi, Kayseri . . 038124
Kayseri Devlet Güzel Sanatlar Galerisi, Kayseri . . . 038125
Kayu, Hohenlinden . . . 071558
Kazakov, Köln . . . 071961
Kazama, Pizançon . . . 066836
Kazanläshka Roza, Gradski istoričeski muzej, Kazanläk . . . 004716
Kazanskaja Gosudarstvennaja Akademija Iskusstv i Kultury, Kazan . . . 050637
Kazanskaja Starina, Kazan . . . 080209
Kazantzakis Museum, Iráklion . . . 021286
Kazari, Prahran . . . 056494
Kazari, Richmond, Victoria . . . 056527
Kazarian, Eschweiler . . . 102663
Kaze, Osaka . . . 106965
Kazemattenmuseum, Oosterend . . . 029997
Kazemattenmuseum Kornwerderzand, Kornwerderzand . . . 029820
Kazerooni, Manama . . . 057632
Kazmine, Michelle, Montceau-les-Mines . . . 099740
Kazuaki Iwasaki Space Art Gallery, Ito . . . 026580
Kazuo County Museum, Chaoyang . 007037
Kazuo Kotera, Kyoto . . . 077107
K.B. Books, San Diego . . . 142905
K.B. Books, San Diego . . . 142906
KBCC Art Gallery, Kingsborough Community College, Brooklyn . . . 042460
K.B.M. Antiquités, Paris . . . 066110
K.C. Antiques, Darwen . . . 084140
KCM Auctions, Seattle . . . 123113
KD Coins, Cincinnati . . . 088254
KdF-Museum, Ostseebad Binz . . . 019524
Ke, Chua, Beijing . . . 097669
K.E. Kivirikon Lintu- ja Nisäkäskokoelma, Helsingin Yliopisto, Helsinki . . . 009541
Ke-Shan, Taipei . . . 098078
Kealley's Gemstone Museum, Nannup . . . 001308
Kearm, Kraków . . . 079642
Kearney, John Walter, Chicago . . . 115468
Kearney & Sons, T.H., Belfast . . . 083480, 130367
Kearney Area Children's Museum, Kearney . . . 044943
Kearney County Historical Museum, Minden . . . 045904
Kearney Mansion Museum, Fresno . 044082
Kearny Cottage, Perth Amboy . . . 046891
Keating, Michael, San Francisco . . . 119707
Keating, Nevill, London . . . 113720
Keats Gallery, Shanklin . . . 114408
Keats House, London . . . 040191
Keats-Shelley House, Roma . . . 025486
De Kebof, Zwolle . . . 078889
Kebon Binatang Taman Sari, Bandung . . . 022386
Keck, Deggingen . . . 125449
Keck, Siegfried, Dillingen an der Donau . . . 102371
Keckler & Donovan, Seattle . . . 119945
Kecskeméti Képtár és Tóth Menyhért Emlékmúzeum, Kecskemét . . . 021760
Kedah Royal Museum, Alor Setar . . 027944
Kedah State Art Gallery, Alor Setar . 027945
Kedzie Coins, Chicago . . . 088114
Kędzierski, Ryszard, Wrocław . . . 140807
Kee & Co., Cheong, Singapore . . . 080501
Kee, Hung, Hong Kong . . . 059647
Kee, Meng Cheng, Singapore . . . 109823
Keeble, Sherborne . . . 086578
Keeble's, Ottawa . . . 059041
Keegan, Peter, Dublin . . . 127097
Keel, Birmingham . . . 131835
Keel, Magdolna, Killwangen . . . 135028
Keel Row, North Shields . . . 141958
Keeler Tavern Museum, Ridgefield . 047435
Keene, San Antonio . . . 119426
Keene, Barry, Henley-on-Thames . . 113233
Keene, Barry M., Henley-on-Thames . . . 084662, 130786
Keens, Surbiton . . . 114523
Keepsakes, Innerleithen . . . 084794
Keepsakes, Regina . . . 097176
Keepsakes, Saint Louis . . . 092259
Keepsakes & Kollectibles, Houston . 089124
De Keersmaeker, Sint-Niklaas . . . 058374
Keeser, Dr. Dorothea, Hamburg . . . 134013
Keetmanshoop Museum, Museum Association of Namibia, Keetmanshoop . . . 029083
Keevil, Frances, Woollahra . . . 095428
Kegel, Gerhard, Buchholz in der Nordheide . . . 102280
Kegel-Konietzko, Boris, Hamburg . . 071258
Kegelmann, P. Michael, Frankfurt am Main . . . 070759, 121406
Kegworth Museum, Kegworth . . . 039834
Kehayoff, Gina, München . . . 134251
Kehoe, Lesley, Melbourne . . . 056188
Kehr, Theodor, Bremen . . . 070027
Kehrein, Bruno, Düsseldorf . . . 139013
Kehrein, Peter, Neuwied . . . 139591
Kehrer Verlag Heidelberg, Heidelberg . . . 134050
Kehwa, Amsterdam . . . 077883
Kehwa Art, Amsterdam . . 107748, 134784
Kehys ja Kultaus, Turku . . . 060639
Kehysaitta, Turku . . . 060640
Kei, Amersfoort . . . 107639
Kei, Wing, Hong Kong . . . 059648
Kei Fujiwara Art Museum, Bizen . . . 026435
Kei Mino, Tokyo . . . 077264
Keiflin, Roger, Saint-Raphaël . . . 101224
Keigado, Fukuoka . . . 077044
Keighley and Worth Valley Light Railway Museum, Keighley . . . 039837
Keighley and Worth Valley Railway Museum, Haworth . . . 039708
Keijzer & Zoon, J., Sint Maartensvlotbrug . . . 128830
Keijzer, T. de, Amersfoort . . . 107640
Keiko, Boston . . . 115189
Keiko Abiko, Barcelona . . . 110204
Keikyän Kotiseutumuseo, Keikyä . . 009686
Keil, New Orleans . . . 090575
Keil, H.W., Broadway . . . 083760, 130467
Keil, John, London . . . 085447
Keil, Dr. Robert, Wien . . . 057462, 095876, 120686
Keilhacker, Ludwig P., Taufkirchen, Vils . . . 126895
Keillor House Museum, Dorchester . 005356
Keinath & Decurtins, R., Zürich . . . 082987
Keio Gallery, Tokyo . . . 107060
Keip, Goldbach, Unterfranken . . . 133978, 139148
Keir Memorial Museum, Kensington 005678
Keishodo, Kamiya, Osaka . . . 077176
Keitele-Museo, Suolahti . . . 010106
Keitelman, Maurice, Bruxelles . . . 096219
Keith Harding's World of Mechanical Music, Northleach . . . 040598
Keith Haring Gallery, New York . . . 118075
Keith National Trust Museum, Keith 001147
De Keizerin, Eindhoven . . . 078342
Kekäläinen, Reijo & Tuula, Imatra . . 060598
Kékfestő Múzeum, Pápa . . . 021812
Keladi Museum, Keladi . . . 022202
Kelantan Malay Arts and Crafts, Kelantan . . . 077496
Kelderman, Oss . . . 140511
Kelet, Bruxelles . . . 096220
Kelham Island Museum, Sheffield . 040998
Kelifa, Gilles, Marseille . . . 124423
Kell House Museum, Wichita Falls . 049166
Kellenberger, Eric, Blonay 111300, 141235
Kellenberger & Graf, Zürich . . . 130244
Keller, Bautzen . . . 138719
Keller, Dinkelsbühl . . . 070255
Keller, Donauwörth . . . 102384
Keller, Kandern . . . 071701
Keller, C., Weimar, Thüringen . . . 105190
Keller, Dany, München . . . 104242
Keller, Dieter, Luzern . . . 082630, 111695, 130105
Keller, Fritz, Stuttgart . . . 073982, 139765
Keller & Assoc., Kelsey, Tampa . . . 120055

Keller, Robert, Berlin 101945
Keller, Robert, Kandern 103484
Keller, Roman, Neuenhof 130129
Keller, Sonja & Ernst, Basel 082146
Keller, Tracy, New Farm 094933
Keller, W., Soden 073840
Keller & Greene, Los Angeles 116806
Kellergalerie - Büchergilde Wiesbaden, Wiesbaden 105267, 139850
Kellergedenkstätte Krippen, Stadtverwaltung Bad Schandau, Bad Schandau 015791
Kellermann, Detlef, Aachen 069090
Kellermuseum, Falkenstein 001840
Kellermuseum Das Preßhaus, Großkrut 001974
Kellerviertel Heiligenbrunn, Freilichtmuseum, Heiligenbrunn . 002033
Kellerweßel, Karl, Grevenbroich . . . 071098
Kelley, Atlanta 087489
Kelley, Cincinnati 115637
Kelley, San Antonio 119427
Kelley, Anthony, New Orleans 117462
Kelley House Museum, Mendocino . 045772
Kellhammer, Bernhard, Thyrnau . . . 126900
Kellie Castle, Pittenweem 040719
Kellie's Antiques, Brisbane 055560
Kelliher and District Heritage Museum, Kelliher 005669
Kellnberger, Otto, München 072747
Kellner, Gottfried, Theresienfeld . . . 057329
Kellner, Hans, München 126400
Kellner, Karel, Coorparoo 123216
Kellner, Michael, Hamburg 134014
Kello, Charles, Norfolk 118613
Kellogg Historical Society Museum, Kellogg 044948
Kellokosken Sairaalan Museo, Kellokoski 009688
Kellross Heritage Museum, Leross . 005763
Kellum, Ulla, København 098577
Kelly, Albuquerque 131744
Kelly, Saint Louis 092260
Kelly, Alison, Armadale, Victoria . . . 094169
Kelly, Frank R., Sheffield 086558
Kelly, June, New York 118076
Kelly, Nevin J., Washington 120319
Kelly, Sean, New York 118077
Kelly Antiques, Rodley 086392
Kelly Gallery, Glasgow 039562
Kelly-Griggs House Museum, Red Bluff 047351
Kelly-Randall, Cleveland 115720
Kelly's Refinishing, Jacksonville . . . 132184
Kellyville Antiques, Kellyville 056036
Kelmscott, Baltimore 142226
Kelmscott House Antiques, Waikato 079291
Kelmscott Manor, Kelmscott 039840
Kelnhof-Museum, Bräunlingen 016358
Kelowna Art Gallery, Kelowna 005672
Kelowna Museum, Kelowna 005673
Kelsey, Ken, Auckland 128906
Kelsey Museum of Ancient Archaeology, Ann Arbor 041732
Kelso Decorative Arts & Antiques, Kelso 084820
Kelso Decorative Arts & Antiques, Kelso 113315
Kelso House, Kent 044965
Kelso Museum and Turret Gallery, Kelso 039842
Kelsterbacher Museum für Porzellan, Kelsterbach 018225
Kelston Fine Arts, Bath 112580
Kelten-Keller, Zürich 112125
Keltenmuseum, Hallein 002013
Keltenmuseum Gracarca, Sankt Kanzian 002593
Keltenmuseum Hochdorf/Enz, Eberdingen 016864
Kelter- und Weinbaumuseum, Niederstetten 019312
Kelterborn, Etta & Klaus, Schortens 073728
Keltisch-Römisches Museum, Manching 018803
Kelton House Museum, Columbus . 043108
Kelvedon Hatch Secret Nuclear Bunker, Kelvedon Hatch 039843
KEM Art Studio, New York 118078
Kemajuan Kraftangan Malaysia, Rawang 028011
Kembery, Bath 083432, 130353
Kemble, Hereford 113237
Kemble, Rodney F., Glusburn 130732
Kemenani, Sonja, Iserlohn 071632
Kemeny, Ulrike, Wangen im Allgäu . 074274
Kemerer Museum of Decorative Arts, Bethlehem 042183
Kemerovskaja Gosudarstvennaja Akademija Iskusstv i Kultury, Kemerovo 050638
Kemerovskij Istoriko-architekturnyi Muzej Krasnaja Gorka, Kemerovo 033255
Kemerovskij Oblastnoj Kraevedčeskij Muzej, Kemerovo 033256
Kemerovskij Oblastnoj Muzej Izobrazitelnych Iskusstv, Kemerovo 033257
Kemijärven Kotiseutumuseo, Kemijärvi 009694
Kemin Kirjadivari, Kemi 137970
Kemin Museo, Kemi 009690
Kemin Taidemuseo, Kemi 009691
Kemin Työläismuseo, Kemi 009692
Keminmaan Museo, Keminmaa . . . 009695
Kemmer, Eberhard, Hamburg 139192
Kemmerich, M., Lindlar 072274
Kemp, I., Bonn 069928
Kemp & Assoc., Karl, New York . . . 090995
Kemp, Melville, Nottingham 086138, 131337
Kemp, Peter, London 085448, 131075
Kemp-McCarthy Memorial Museum, Rowe 047558
Kempa, Bodo, Berlin 069656, 125229
Kempe-Wolter, Freia, Gräfelfing . . . 071076
Kempeleen Kotiseutumuseo, Kempele 009696
Kempenaar, Haarlem 078461
Kemper Museum of Contemporary Art, Kansas City 044921
Kempf, Stephan J., Zürich 082988, 112126, 141343
Kempin, Hermann, Hannover 103284
Kempisch Bosmuseum W. Vandenbroucke, Essen 003425
Kempisch Museum, Brecht 003256
Kempner, Jim, New York 118079
Kemps, Bristol 083742
Wiebke Kemps & Andreas Schäfer, Berlin 125230
Kempsey Antiques, Kempsey 056039
Kempsey Historical and Cultural Museum, Kempsey 001149
Kempton Old Books, Kempton 136958
Ken, Chicago 115469
Ken Domon Museum of Photography, Sakata 027020
Ken et Dy, Salon-de-Provence 101248
Ken Lochhead Gallery Publications, Haddington 135157
Kenal, Roman, Edmonton 058835
Kenan, Avi, Antwerpen 096074
Kendal Museum, Kendal 039845
Kendal Studios Antiques, Kendal . . 084827
Kendall, Miami 142556
Kendall, Beryl, London . . . 085449, 113721
Kendall Campus Art Gallery, Miami-Dade Community College, Miami 045812
The Kendall College Mitchell Museum of the American Indian, Evanston 043760
Kendall College of Art and Design, Ferris State University, Grand Rapids . . . 051405
Kendall Gallery, Grand Rapids 044277
Kendall Whaling Museum, Sharon . 048126
Kendall's, Cowes 112908
Kenderdine Art Gallery, Saskatoon . 006418
Kendle Green Antiques, Albury 055330
Kendons, Ingatestone 084793
Kendzia, Klaus D., Hamburg 121428
Keng Seng, Hong Kong 137748
Kenilworth Historical Society Museum, Kenilworth 044952
Kenji Igarashi Memorial Museum, Tokyo 027184
Kenji Taki Gallery, Nagoya 106924
Kenji Taki Gallery, Tokyo 107061
Kenkeleba, New York 118080
Kenmore Gallery, Kenmore 094688
Kenmore Plantation and George Washington's Ferry Farm, Fredericksburg 044058
Kennard, Salt Lake City 092436
Kennebunkport Historical Museum, Kennebunkport 044955
Kennedy, Boston 115190
Kennedy, Dallas 088539
Kennedy, Dublin 105874
Kennedy, London 085450, 131076
Kennedy, Miami 117099
Kennedy, New York 118081
Kennedy, Sacramento 092169
Kennedy, Teheran 074842
Kennedy, Fred, Atlanta 087490
Kennedy, Peter, Woking 142162
Kennedy, Robin, Canterbury 055628
Kennedy, Robin, Richmond, Surrey . 086357
Kennedy-Douglass Center for the Arts, Florence 043865
Kennedy House, Selkirk 006438
Kennedy Museum of Art, Athens . . 041838
Kennedy Park Gallery, Düsseldorf . . 102515
Kennedy Wolfenden & Co., Belfast . 074859
Kennedy Wolfenden, Portrush 086297, 131391
Kenner, T. & B., Steißlingen 073911
Kennerknecht, Immenstadt 071618
Kennesaw Civil War Museum, Kennesaw 044957
Kennesaw Mountain National Battlefield Park, Kennesaw 044958
Kennet and Avon Canal Trust Museum, Devizes 039234
Kenneth, Haymarket 094626
Kennis, Dirk, Antwerpen 057706
Kenny, Ian, Strathaven 114511
Kenny, Paul, Botany 055525
The Kenny Gallery, Galway 105893
Kenny's Antiques, Hamlyn Heights . 055944
Kennys Bookshop, Galway 139973
Kenny's Coins, Oklahoma City 091508
Kenny's Collectibles, Austin 087588
Keno, Leigh, New York 090996
Keno City Mining Museum, Keno City 005675
Kenosha County Museum, Kenosha 044960
Kenosha Public Museum, Kenosha . 044961
Kenoz, Cairo 098641
Kenrick, Saint Louis 092261
Kenritsu Kagakukan Joetsu, Joetsu 026599
Ken's, Firenze 106066
Ken's Antique and Fine Art, Singapore 080502
Ken's Antiques, Pittsburgh 091830
Ken's Gallery, Fort Worth 116148
Kensington, Barcelona 080870
Kensington, Sevilla 081589
Kensington, Tokyo 077265
Kensington Antiques, Ascot Vale . . 055409
Kensington Art Gallery, Norwood . . 094994
Kensington Church Street Antique Centre, London 085451
Kensington Church Street Antique Dealers Association, London 054419
Kensington Gallery, Calgary 096825
Kensington House Collections, Richmond 092091
Kensington Road Antiques, Norwood 056389
Kensoon, Singapore 080503
Kent, New York 118082
Kent, Cheslava, Mordialloc 123271
Kent, J., Wallasey 122735
Kent, Jonathan, Los Angeles 116807
Kent and East Sussex Railway, Tenterden 041200
Kent and Sharpshooters Yeomanry Museum, Edenbridge 039377
Kent Antiques, Kent Town 056041
Kent Art Association, Kent 044963, 054833
Kent Battle of Britain Museum, Hawkinge 039705
Kent Campus Museum and Gallery, Jacksonville 044816
Kent Collector, Plattsburgh 136519
Kent-Delord House Museum, Plattsburgh 047084
Kent House Antiques, Haverfordwest 084625
Kent & Kent, Hobart 055995
Kent Police Museum, Chatham 039039
Kent Potters Gallery, Maidstone . . . 114031
Kent State University Art Galleries, Kent 044966
Kent State University Museum, Kent 044967
Kent-Stone, Dallas 088540
Kent & Sussex Gold Refiners, Tunbridge Wells 086940, 131618
Kentdale Antiques, Tunbridge Wells 086941, 131619
Kenthurst Galleries, Kenthurst 094692
Kentmere House, York 114754
Kenton, Portland 091962
Kenton, J., Brooklyn 122830
Kentshire, New York 090997
Kentuck Museum and Art Center, Northport 046556
Kentuckiana Pastel Society, Louisville 054834
Kentucky Association of Museums, Murray 054835
Kentucky Derby Museum, Louisville 045489
Kentucky Folk Art Center, Morehead 046022
Kentucky Guild of Artists and Craftsmen, Berea 054836
Kentucky Historical Society Museum, Frankfort 044031
Kentucky Military History Museum, Frankfort 044032
The Kentucky Museum, Western Kentucky University, Bowling Green 042366
Kentucky Museum of Arts and Design, Louisville 045490
Kentucky New State Capitol, Frankfort 044033
Kentucky Railway Museum, New Haven 046230
Kentucky Woodworks, Louisville . . 132298
Kenulf Fine Arts, Stow-on-the-Wold 086752
Kenulf Fine Arts, Stow-on-the-Wold 114504
Kenulf Fine Arts, Stow-on-the-Wold 131550
Kenwood, Cincinnati 115638
Kenwood, London 040192
Kenworthy, Latrobe 056084
Keny, Columbus 115787
Kenya Museum Society, Nairobi . . . 053814
Kenyon, Gerald, Dublin 074928
Kenz, Casablanca 077659
Kenz, Casablanca 107556, 128512
Kenzen, G., Rothenburg ob der Tauber 073589
Keogh & Riehlman, New York 118083
Keokuk Art Center, Keokuk 044971
Keokuk River Museum, Keokuk . . . 044972
Keown, John T., Tulsa 120197
Képcsarnok, Budapest 105520
Képcsarnok, Budapest 105521
Képcsarnok - Gulácsy Lajos Terem, Szeged 021861
Le Képi Rouge, Paris 066111
Kepler, Weil der Stadt 139828
Kepler, Herwig, Hollabrunn 057067
Kepler-Gedächtnishaus, Museen der Stadt Regensburg, Regensburg 019754
Keplermuseum, Weil der Stadt 020720
Keppel, Haarlem 078462
't Keppeltje, Doetinchem 078290
Képzőművészek Gulácsy Lajos, Budapest 021660
Ker, David, London 113722
Ker, Iliz de, Perros-Guirec . 066768, 100999
Ker, Maria, Guérande 063099

Keramaikos, Arnhem 107852
Kerameiki Techni, Piraeus 135837
Kerámevo, Amersfoort 107641
Keramiek, Utrecht 135997
Keramiek Studio, Enschede 108020
Keramiekcentrum Tiendschuur, Tegelen 030193
Keramik-Galerie zum Kobold, Gossau (Sankt Gallen) 111526
Keramik Kabinett Dießen, Dießen am Ammersee 133864
Keramik Magazin/Ceramics Magazine, Frechen 135771
Keramik-Museum, Bürgel 016498
Keramik-Museum, Triengen 037642
Keramik-Museum Berlin, Berlin . . . 016089
Keramik Museum Mettlach, Mettlach 018926
Keramikatelier, Hesperange 107388
Keramikgalerie Terra Rossa, Leipzig 103883
Keramikkunst Bayreuth e.V., Bayreuth 053255
Keramikmuseum, Frechen 017213
Keramikmuseum, Württembergisches Landesmuseum Stuttgart, Ludwigsburg, Württemberg 018694
Keramikmuseum Schloss Obernzell, Zweigmuseum des Bayerischen Nationalmuseums, Obernzell 019403
Keramikmuseum Staufen, Badisches Landesmuseum Karlsruhe, Staufen 020293
Keramikmuseum Westerwald, Deutsche Sammlung für Historische und Zeitgenössische Keramik, Höhr-Grenzhausen 017948
Keramisch Atelier, Utrecht 108253
Keramisch Museum Goedewaagen, Nieuw Buinen 029942
Keramos, Offenbach am Main 135772
Keramos, Paris 124706
Keramos, Paris 124707
Keramos, Pune 074833
Kerang Antiques, Kerang 056043
Keranroue, Hyacinthe, Paris 124708
Keraudren, Marie, Trégastel 068619
Keravan Museo, Kerava 009697
Keravan Taidemuseo, Kerava 009698
Kerber, Bielefeld 133823
Kerbyville Museum, Kerby 044974
Kerčskij Gosudarstvennyj Istoriko-Kulturnyj Zapovednik, Kerč 038279
Kerdour, Michel de, Québec 097144
Kerdrain, Lionel, Meudon 064539
Kerebel, Alain, Temae, Moorea 101497
Kerényi Jenő Emlékmúzeum, Ferenczy Múzeum, Szentendre 021882
Keresztény Múzeum, Esztergom . . . 021723
Kerhir, Laurent, Auray 061069
Kerkhof, W., Dordrecht . . . 078307, 128649
Kerkmuseum, Sint-Niklaas 003758
Kerkmuseum Janum, Janum 029793
Kerkonkosken Myllymuseo, Rautalampi 010028
Kerl, J., Weißenburg in Bayern 074326
Kerler, G., Lorch, Württemberg 072301
Kerler, Heinrich, Ulm 139808
Kerley, Geelong 120588
Kerlikowsky, Dr. Horst, München . . 072748
Kerlin, Dublin 105875
Kerlin Gallery, Belfast 112615
Kerls, Ingo, Bremen 070028
Kermani, Deira 083180, 112445
Kermanshah, New York 090998
Kermer, André, Leipzig 103884
Kermes, Madrid 129632
Kermes, Roma 128076
Kermis- en Circusmuseum Steenwijk, Steenwijk 030180
Kern, Rosemarie, Bad Wimpfen . . . 069395
Kern County Museum, Bakersfield . 041955
Kernaghan, Bryan, Southport 142084
Kerner, Cecil, Bruxelles 058003
Kerner, Claude, Elbeuf-sur-Seine . . 062772
Kernstock-Museum, Bruck an der Lafnitz 001768
Kërpeeva Kašta, Kotel 004733
Kerr, Jacksonville 089421
Kerr, Albertina, Portland 091963
Kerr, Jody, Oklahoma City 091509
Kerr, Louella, Glebe 136919
Kerr, Louella, Petersham 137048
Kerr, Norman, Cartmel 141495
Kerr, Thomas, London 085452
Kerr Place, Onancock 046685
Kerrobert and District Museum, Kerrobert 005684
Kerry Anne's Fine Arts, Kew 056045
Kerry Anne's Fine Arts, Toorak 056716
The Kerry Bog Village Museum, Glenbeigh 022793
Kerry County Museum, Tralee 022864
Kers, Apeldoorn 078036
Kersa, Kerava 137971
Kerschbaum, Wilfried, Berlin 069657
Kerschbaumer-Gugu, Armin, Stein an der Enns 137265
Kerschberger, Th., Regensburg . . . 073462
Kerschhackl, Josef, Ortenburg 073225
Kerseboom, Willem, Bergen, Noord-Holland 078066
Kershaw County Historical Society Museum, Camden 042583
Kerson, New York 090999
Keršovani, Otokar, Rijeka 133399
Kersten, Kraków 108957
Kersten, R., Hamminkeln 071366
Kersting, Jolanthe, Immenhausen . 125967
Kerteminde Egnens Museer, Kerteminde 008951
Kertesz, San Francisco 119708
Kesälahden Museo, Kesälahti 009700
Keshett, Melbourne 056189
Keshishian, London 085453
Keski-Suomen Ilmailumuseo, Tikkakoski 010148
Keski-Suomen Museo, Jyväskylä . . 009642
Keski-Suomen Sairaanhoitopiirin Sairaalamuseo, Jyväskylä 009643
Keski-Suomen Tieliikennemuseo, Kintaus 009712
Keskin, B., Eutingen 070673
Keskiner Antika, İstanbul 083142
Keskisuomalaisen Museo, Jyväskylä 009644
Kesmarky, Jutta, Sankt Gilgen 057291
Kesner, Jan, Los Angeles 116808
Kessel, Dieter, Bonn 102186
Kesselmark, Christiane, Cancale . . 099058
Kessler, Annette, Stuttgart 126858
Kessler, K., Östringen 073185
Kessler, Marina, Miami 117100
Kessler, Randall, Omaha 132594
Keßler, Thomas, Burkardroth 125418
Kessler Ford, Ashburton 083336
Kesteloot, Bruxelles 058004
Kestemont, Bruxelles 058005
Kesting, Maria, Kassel 071757
Kestler, Gerhard, Korneuburg 137205
Kestner Gesellschaft, Hannover . . .017756, 053256
Kestner-Museum, Hannover 017757
Kestrel, Vancouver 137727
Keswick Bookshop, Keswick 141691
Keswick Museum and Art Gallery, Keswick 039852
Keta's Antiques, Toledo 093174
Ketelbuters, R., Bruxelles 096221
Ketley, Carol, London 085454
Kett, Ulrich, Kierspe 103549
Kéttemplom, Kecskemét 105564
Ketterer, Hamburg 071259, 121429, 139193
Ketterer, Lausanne 122330
Ketterer Kunst, München . 072749, 121533, 139523
Ketterer-Haus-Museum, Biberach, Baden 016223
Kettle River Museum, Midway 005868
Kettle's Yard, Cambridge 038965
Kettle's Yard House and Gallery, Cambridge 141472
Kettlewell, Piers, Paisley 131360
Kettumäen Ulkomuseo ja Kotiseututalo, Kuusankoski 009771
Kettumäki, Aaro, Tampere 060627
Ketz, Hans-Jürgen, Münster 139567
Keuck, Bad Harzburg 069286
Keuken, Lehrte 072186
Keul & Sohn, Wiesbaden . 074409, 105268
Keulen, Köln 126092
Keulenaer, Fanny de, Reims 067070
Keulenaer, G. de, Gent 096291
Keumho Museum of Art, Seoul 027566
Keumsan, Seoul 107261
Keune, Sabine, Duisburg 139027
Keup, Regensburg 121584
Keuper, Klaus, Bispingen 069854
Keuruun Kotiseutumuseo, Keuruu . . 009702
Keuruun Museo, Keuruu 009703
Keussen, E., Ortenberg, Baden 073224
Keuster, de, Antwerpen 120706
Kev Rohrlach Technology and Heritage Museum, Tanunda 001534
Kever, Hermann, Varel 074182
Keverne, Roger, London . . 085455, 131077
Kevin's Book Nook, Springwood . . . 137090
Kevin's Collectibles, Charlotte 087962
Kevorkian Carning, Paris 066112
Kew & Cie, Hong Kong 059649
Kew Bridge Steam Museum, Kew . . 039857
Kew Gallery, Kew 094695
Kew Historical Museum, Kew 001151
Kew Palace Museum of the Royal Botanic Gardens, Kew 039858
Kewaunee County Historical Museum, Kewaunee 044980
Keweenaw County Historical Society Museum, Eagle Harbor 043554
Kewenig, Köln 103654
Kewriosity, Kew 056046
Key, Houston 132127
Key, Houston 132128
Key, Sarah, Cambridge 141473
Key Antiques, Chipping Norton 083991
Key Antiques, Tugun 056741
The Key to It All, Phoenix 091749
Key West Company, Tokyo 077266
Key West Lighthouse Museum, Key West 044987
Key West Museum of Art and History, Key West 044988
Keya Gallery, New York 118084
Keyes, Siegrid, Stuttgart 126859
Keymer Son & Co, Brasted 083650
Keys, Aylsham 122393
Keys & Sons, Indianapolis 089312, 132158
Keyser, Annette de, Antwerpen 096075
Keyser, W. de, Antwerpen 057707
Keystone, Cleveland 142325
Keystone, Coalville 084040
Keystone, Singapore 080504
Keystone Area Museum, Keystone . 044995
Keystone Furniture, Indianapolis . . . 089313
Keystone Pioneer Museum, Roblin . 006299
K.F.C., Bristol 112725
kforum - Verein für zeitgenössische Kunst und Kulturvernetzung, Wien 052548
KG Books, New Farm 137025
KGM-Atelje, Zaprešič 098292
K.G.O., Zagreb 098289
Kgosi Bathoen II (Segopotso) Museum, Kanye 003952
K.H. Renlundin Museo, Kokkola . . . 009724
Khachatrians Museum, Erevan 000683
Khai, Singapore 080505
Khairalla, Camille, Beirut 077400
Khairallah, Ghida, Baabda 107324
Khajana Buildings Museum, Hyderabad 022158
Al-Khaleej, Zahrat, Manama 057633, 096014
Khalid, Marrakech 077682
Khalid, Singapore 080506
Khalifa's House Museum, Omdurman 036156
Khalif's House Museum, Khartoum . 036151
Khalkhal Museum, Khalkhal 022572
Khallouf, Faddoui, Joué-lès-Tours . 124271
Khama III Memorial Museum, Serowe 003955
Khami Ruins Site Museum, Bulawayo 049576
Khamoddost, Freudenstadt 125676
Khan, Matthias, Wiesloch 105292
Khan, Shaker Bin Murad, Muttrah . . 079516
Khan El-Khalily, Alexandria 060420
Khanate, Portland 091964
Khatchikian, Jacques, Croignon . . . 062571
Khayam, Souffelweyersheim 068268
Khayats, Beirut 134738
Khazana, Minneapolis 117276
Khedr, Krikor, Damascus 083062
Khépri, Paris 066113
Khersones Museum of History and Archeology, Sevastopol 038389
Khiching Museum, Khiching 022205
Khim Art, Sartrouville 068137
KHM-Gemälderestaurierung im Naturhistorischen Museum Wien, Wien 123508
Khoja, Manama 057634
Khorassan Natural History Museum, Shahid Beheshti Collage, Mashad 022582
Khot-la-Cha, Vancouver 097492
Khoy Museum, Khoy 022575
KHR Antik, Mainhardt 072382
Khris, Saint Louis 119215
Khushbu Art Gallery, Pune 105828
Kiama Art Society, Kiama . 052477, 094697
Kiang, Marilyn, Atlanta 114894
Kiangan National Museum, Kiangan 031682
Kiasma Nykytaiteen Museo, Helsinki 009542
Kibbutz Art Gallery, Tel Aviv 023082
Kibbutz Negba Museum, Kibbutz Negba 023015
Kibi Archaeological Collection, Soja 027086
Kibler, Alain, Haguenau 063114
Kibo Art Gallery, Marangu 037855
KIBO Gallery, Seattle 119946
Kicherer, Leni, Maulbronn 104040
Kichline, H., Atlanta 087491
Kick Gallery, Northcote 094990
KickArts, Cairns 094348
Kicken, Berlin 101946
Kicken, Rudolf, Aachen 101517
Kidder Smith, Boston 115191
Kidderminster Railway Museum, Kidderminster 039860
Kidding Awound, Toronto 059224
Kidner, George, Lymington 122608
Kidogo Arthouse, Fremantle 094569
Kids Can Press, Toronto 133324
Kidspace Children's Museum, Pasadena 046832
Kidwelly Industrial Museum, Kidwelly 039862
Kiebler, Kurt, Bad Wurzach 125123
Kiecken Duthoit, Dunkerque 062750
Kiefel, Gütersloh 133994
Kiefer, Eva, Salzburg 123448
Kiefer, Hans, Basel 129921
Kiefer, Mariele, Bad Kreuznach 069317
Kiefer, Peter, Pforzheim . . 121573, 139657
Kieferle, Albert, Möglingen 126322
Kiefernrausch 6000 Tarpenbek Str 51, Hamburg 071260
Kiehle Gallery, Saint Cloud State University, Saint Cloud 047625
Kiehns, Dannstadt-Schauernheim . 070175
Kiek in beim Turm, Lemgo 072223
Kiekeboe, Gent 137498
Kiekebusch, Jörg, Wunstorf 105345, 134472
't Kiekenkot, Gent 058190
Kieker, Ute, Berlin 069658
't Kiekhuus, Wolvega 030346
Kiel, A., Düsseldorf 139014
Kiel, Albert, Darmstadt 070185

Kieler Stadt- und Schiffahrtsmuseum, Kiel 018246
Kiene, Hansjoachim, Solingen 139734
Kienel, Anton, Imst 057070, 095573
Kiener, Chantal, Paris 100561
Kiener, Martin, Zürich 082989, 130245
Kiener Antiquité, Paris 066114
Kienhorst, Breda 078105
Kienhorst, Groningen 078423
Kiennast, Julius, Gars am Kamp . . . 137173
Kienzle, Andr. Claus, Augsburg 125074
Kienzle & Gmeiner, Berlin 101947
Kiepert, Berlin 138804
Kierlinger Heimatmuseum, Kierling 002122
Kiernan, Mosman Park 056270
Kierondino, Groningen 078424
Kieselbach, Budapest 074690, 105522
Kieser, Andrea, Augsburg 125075
Kießling, Berlin 069659
Kiev Museum of Western and Oriental Art, Kyïv 038314
Kievartcentr, Kyïv 112411
Kievskaja Galereja, Kyïv 112412
Kiezelbach, Budapest 105523, 121639
Kihniön Museo, Kihniö 009705
Kii Fudoki-No-Oka Museum, Wakayama 027314
Kiido, Tokyo 077267
Kiihtelysvaaran Museo, Kiihtelysvaara 009706
Kiikalan Kotiseutumuseo, Kiikala . . 009707
Kiikoisten Kotiseutumuseo, Torpparimuseum/Esinemuseo, Kiikoinen 009708
Kiimingin Museo, Kiiminki 009709
Kiippa, Tapani, Helsinki 098737
Kijarat Kiadó, Budapest 134504
Kijk en Luister Museum, Bennekom 029305
Kijk- en Luistermuseum, Bant 029291
Kijkoor, Hilversum 108086
KiK - Kultur im Kloster, Klostermarienberg 002153
Kikava Sanat Evi, Samsun 083169
Kikel, A., Bodman-Ludwigshafen . . 069902
Kikkermuseum, Den Haag 029428
Kikori, Nishitokyo 077170
Kiku, San Francisco 092823
Kikuchi-Rekishikan, Kikuchi 026650
Kikusui Handicraft Museum, Kawanishi 026643
Kikuta, Sendai 106999
Kikuya, Kyoto 077108
Kilátó, Budapest 105524
Kilback Brothers, Vancouver 123851
Kilby Historic Store and Farm, Harrison Mills 005606
Kilchmann, Peter, Zürich 112127
Kilcock Art Gallery, Kilcock 105897
Kildonan, Winnipeg 123869
Kildonan Museum, Kildonan 039864
Kile Sanat Galerisi, İstanbul 112330
Kilens Hembygdsgård, Sideby 010073
Kili, Lyon 138155
Kilian, Bad Kreuznach 101667
Kilian, Francis, Strasbourg 101295
Kilian, Hans, Marburg 072448
Kilian, Mechthild, Großkarolinenfeld 133990
Mechthild Kilian & Helmut Lachmann, Großkarolinenfeld 071121
Kiliansboden, Lund 081854
The Kilim Warehouse, London 085456, 131078
Kilin, Singapore 109824
Kiliński, Jacek, Warszawa 109148
Kilkee Heritage Gallery, Kilkee 022803
Kilkivan Historical Museum, Kilkivan 001153
Kill City Crime Books, Prahran 137061
Killarney Centennial Museum, Killarney 005687
Killen, David, New York 091000
Killen, David, New York 091001
Killen 5060 David, New York 118085
Killer, München 072750
Killhope, the North of England Lead Mining Museum, Weardale 041318
Killin Gallery, Killin 084844
Kilmacolm Antiques, Kilmacolm . . .084845, 130844
Kilmainham Gaol and Museum, Dublin 022757
Kilmallock Museum, Kilmallock . . . 022811
Kilmaurs Historical Society Museum, Kilmaurs 039872
Kilmister, Masterton 128945
Kilmorack Gallery, Beauly 112594
Kilmore Old Wares, Kilmore 056053
Kilmore Quay Maritime Museum, Kilmore Quay 022812
Kilmore Quay Maritime Museum, Wexford 022876
Kilsyth's Heritage, Kilsyth 039874
The Kilvert Gallery, Clyro 112881
Kilwinning Abbey Tower, Kilwinning 039876
Kim, Hong Kong 059650
Kim, Leong, Singapore 080507
Kim, Long Seng, Singapore 080508
Kim, San, Singapore 129261
Kim, Thye Lee, Singapore 080509
Kim, Yung Hee, New York 118086
Kim 3, Los Angeles 089814
Kim 3, San Francisco 092824
Kim Gallery, Murcia 081443, 110651
Kimba and Gawler Ranges Historical Society Museum, Kimba 001154
Kimball Art Center, Park City 046819
Kimball House Museum, Battle Creek 042055
Kimbell, Patsy, Buderim 055578
Kimbell Art Museum, Fort Worth . . . 044009
Kimbell Art Museum, Publications Department, Fort Worth 135360
Kimber & Son, Malvern . . 085905, 131251
Kimberley, Bilbao 080976
Kimberley, Melbourne 094816
Kimberley Heritage Museum, Kimberley 005688
Kimberley Mine Museum, Kimberley 034661
Kimberly Crest House, Redlands . . . 047359
Kimberly's Fine Art, Dallas 115898
Kimble County Historical Museum, Junction 044886
Kimcherova, New York 091002
Kimchi Field Museum, Pulmuone Gimchi Museum, Seoul 027567
Kime, Robert, Marlborough 085949
Kimga, Yokohama 107147
Kimin, Singapore 080510
Kimjack, Calgary 058793
Kimmel, Frankfurt am Main 133946
Kimmerich, Horst, Düsseldorf 102516
Kimmich, Klaus, Köln 103655
Kimmich, Wilhelm, Lauterbach, Schwarzwald 103845
Kimo Bruks Museum and Gallery, Oravais 009924
Kimpfbeck, J., Nersingen 104395
Kimpton, K., San Francisco 119709
Kimura, Kyoto 077109
Kimura, San Francisco 119710
Kimzey Miller, Seattle 119947
Kin, Lai Mau, New York 091003
Kin, Shing, Hong Kong 059651
Kin Fat, Hong Kong 059652
Kin Liou, Gérard, Paris 066115
Kina NZ, Taranaki 108569
Kina Slott, Drottningholm 036237
Kincaid Museum, Kincaid 005689
Kincová, Zlín 098515
Kind, Phylis, New York 118087
Kindbom & Co, Olof, Karlsborg 122175
Kindel, Hans-Peter, Erfurt 070587
Kinder-Akademie Fulda Werkraummuseum, Fulda 017301
Kinder Fine Arts, Christchurch 108399
Kinder-Knürstl-Museum, Götzis . . . 001918
Kinder- und Jugendgalerie Sonnensegel, Brandenburg an der Havel 016369
Kinder- und Jugendmuseum München, München 019067
Kinder- und Jugendmuseum Prenzlauer Berg, Berlin 016115
Kindergarten Museum, Groß Glienicke 017554
Kindergartenmuseum, Bruchsal . . . 016458
Kinderkunsthal Villa Zebra, Rotterdam 030083
Kinderkunstschule Goldfisch, Leipzig 050170
Kindermann, Berlin 125231
Kindermann, Thomas, Wiebelsdorf . 074384
Kindermuseum, Frankfurt am Main 017179
Kindermuseum, Schaufenster, Schule und Kinderkunst e.V., Wuppertal 021017
Kindermuseum, Staatliche Kunsthalle Karlsruhe, Karlsruhe 018162
Kindermuseum Hamburg, Hamburg 017701
Kindermuseum Zoom, Wien 002923
Kindersley Plains Museum, Kindersley 005690
Kinderwagenmuseum, Nieuwolda . 029954
Kinderwagens van toen, Dwingeloo 029514
Kinderweltmuseum, Vöcklamarkt . . 002783
Kindheitsmuseum, Marburg 018824
Kindheitsmuseum, Schönberg, Holstein 020070
Kindler, München 134252
Kindler, Matthias Johannes Andreas, Graz 057016, 120663
Kindler-Lambertz, Maria, Groß Wittensee 103018
Kinenkan Mikasa, Yokosuka 027344
Kinet, J., Bruxelles 058006
Kineya, Tokyo 077268
King, Cleveland 115721
King, Fort Worth 088864
King, Houston 089125
King, Houston 122908
King, New York 091004
King, Salt Lake City 119351
King, San Antonio 092529
King & Co., San Francisco 119711
King, Wymondham, Norfolk 087276
King, A., San Antonio 092530, 123095
King, Ann, Bath 083433
King, David, New York 118088
King, David, New York 118089
King, David, New York 118090
King, David H., Dallas 088541
King, Erika, Miami 117101
King, Henry, New York 118091
King, John, London 085457
King, John K., Detroit 142402
King, John K., Ferndale 142407
King, Kevin, Dunedin 128934
King, Laurence, London 135228
King, N.I., Chicago 088115
King, Peter, Ti Tree 056710
King, Philip, Auckland 128907
King, Roger, Dallas 088542
King, Roger, Hungerford 084761
King & Chasemore, Midhurst 122617
King County Arts Commission Gallery, Seattle 048082
King George VI Art Gallery, Port Elizabeth 034705
King Griffin, San Diego 119520
King Hooper Mansion, Marblehead . 045657
King Island Historical Museum, Currie 000965
King John's Castle, Limerick 022823
King Kamehameha V - Judiciary History Center, Honolulu 044601
King Mac Craw, Trappes 068616
King Manor, Jamaica 044825
King-Prime Gallery, Bangalow 094210
King Richard's, Atlanta 087492
King Saud University Museum, Riyadh 034124
King Seaman School Museum, River Herbert 006293
King Sejong The Great Memorial Exhibition, Seoul 027568
King-Smith & Nutter, Stow-on-the-Wold 086753
King Street Antiques, Toledo 093175
King Street Curios, Melksham 085968
King Street Curios, Tavistock 086832
King Street Gallery, Darlinghurst . . . 094454
King Street Gallery, Newcastle, Staffordshire 114119
King Street Gallery, Newtown, New South Wales 094956
King Township Historical Museum, King City 005691
King Tut, San Diego 119521
King Tut Egyptian Imports, Tampa . 093131
Kingaroy Art Gallery, Kingaroy 001155
Kinge, Samy, Paris 100562
Kingfisher Gallery, Cowbridge 112906
Kinglake Gallery, Kinglake 094700
Kingman County Historical Museum, Kingman 045009
Kingman Museum of Natural History, Battle Creek 042056
Kingman Tavern Historical Museum, Cummington 043245
King's, Canterbury 112801
Kings Art Gallery, Vancouver 097493
King's Cottage Antiques, Leamington Spa 084913
Kings County Museum, Hampton . . 005600
Kings County Museum, Kentville . . 005681
Kings Court Antiques, Ngaruawahia 079184
King's Court Galleries, Dorking 084197
King's Court Galleries, Dorking 112954
King's Court Galleries, Dorking 141559
King's Court Galleries, London 085458, 141837
Kings Fireplaces, Antiques & Interiors, Cardiff 083873, 130512
King's Gallery, London 113723
King's House Antiques, Birmingham 087766
Kings Landing Historical Settlement, Prince William 006211
King's Lynn Arts Centre, King's Lynn 039877
King's Lynn Museum, King's Lynn . 039878
King's Mill Antique Centre, Burnley 083812, 130485
King's Mill Visitor Centre, Wrexham 041456
Kings Mountain National Military Park, Blacksburg 042242
King's Own Royal Regiment Museum, Lancaster 039921
King's Own Scottish Borderers Regimental Museum, Berwick-upon-Tweed . . 038683
King's Own Yorkshire Light Infantry Regimental Museum, Doncaster . 039250
The Kings Park of Art, Amsterdam . 107749
Kings Quair, Aberdeen 141378
Kings Road Gallery, London 113724
The King's Royal Hussars Museum, Winchester 041403
Kings Weston Roman Villa, Bristol . 038866
Kingsbridge Auction Sales, Kingsbridge 122553
Kingsbury Watermill Museum, Saint Albans 040884
Kingsclere Old Bookshop, Kingsclere 141694
Kingsgate Gallery, London 040193
Kingsland Homestead, Queens Historical Society, Flushing 043876
Kingsley & Co., Barnard Castle 083390
Kingsley & Co, Wirral 122751
Kingsley Plantation, Jacksonville . . 044817
Kingsmount, Toronto 097304
Kingston, Boston 115192
Kingston, Moorabbin 094880
Kingston, Richard J., Henley-on-Thames 084663, 141659
Kingston Antiques, Fitzroy North . . . 055828
Kingston Antiques Market, Kingston-upon-Thames 084867, 130852, 141695
Kingston Archaeological Centre, Kingston 005699
Kingston Fire Department Museum, Kingston 005700

Kingston Galleries, Hull 113280
Kingston Gallery, Kingston 113328
Kingston Mills Blockhouse, Elgin . . 005420
Kingston Museum, Kingston-upon-Thames 039893
Kingston Pioneer Museum, Kingston 001159
Kingstone, Honolulu 088963
Kingsway Auction Rooms, Lytham Saint Anne's 122609
Kinistino District Pioneer Museum, Kinistino 005711
Kinizsi Vármúzeum, Nagyvázsony . . 021799
Kinkade, Fort Worth 116149
Kinkade, Thomas, Atlanta 114895
Kinkade, Thomas, Broadway 112735
Kinkade, Thomas, Dallas 115899
Kinkade, Thomas, Edinburgh 112998
Kinkade, Thomas, Fresno 116179
Kinkade, Thomas, Glasgow 113119
Kinkade, Thomas, Greenhithe 113159
Kinkade, Thomas, Indianapolis 142455
Kinkade, Thomas, Jacksonville . . . 116531
Kinkade, Thomas, Louisville 116948
Kinkade, Thomas, Minneapolis 117277
Kinkade, Thomas, New Orleans . . . 117463
Kinkade, Thomas, New York 118092
Kinkade, Thomas, Oklahoma City . . 118667
Kinkade, Thomas, Oklahoma City . . 142726
Kinkade, Thomas, Portland 119012
Kinkade, Thomas, San Diego 119522
Kinkade, Thomas, Solihull 114445
Kinkade, Thomas, Toronto 097305
Kinkaide, Thomas, Kansas City . . . 116576
Kinkead, James W., Memphis 132327
Kinkel, J., Kerzenheim 071810
Kinky Beaux Arts, Stuttgart 135773
Kinler, New Orleans 132418
Kinlough Folk Museum, Kinlough . . 022814
Kinnear, Glenreagh 055892
Kinneil Museum and Roman Fortlet, Bo'ness 038785
Kinney Pioneer Museum, Clear Lake 042967
Kinnulan Kotiseutumuseo, Kinnula . 009711
Kinokuniya, Tokyo 107062
Kinokuniya, Tokyo 140189
Kinreizuka Archaeological Collection, Kisaradu 026653
Kinross Museum, temporary closed, Kinross 039898
Kinsale Regional Museum, Kinsale . 022816
Kinsella, Edge Hill 055789
Kinsey Marable, New York 142668
Kinsman, Robinson, Toronto 097306
t'Kint de Roodenbeke, Harold, Bruxelles 058007, 096222
Kinter, Prof. Klaus & Jutta, Remshalden 104717
Kintolai, Adelaide 094118
Kintolai Gallery, Adelaide 094119
Kinzel & Bode, Braunschweig 069985
Kinzelt, Karina, Cottbus 125435
Kinzelt, Karina, Peitz 126615
Kioskshop Berlin, Berlin 016090
Kiosques, Toulon (Var) 138626
Kiosques, Toulon (Var) 138627
Kipling, Houston 116350
Kipling District Historical Society Museum, Kipling 005712
Kipp, Jürgen, Mainz 139448
Kipp, Manfred, Lengerich, Westfalen 072228
Kipp, P.J., Utrecht 128857
Kipp Gallery, Indiana University of Pennsylvania, Indiana 044732
Kippert, Bruno, Erlangen 070600
Kipping, Venlo 078835
Kipton, New York 091005, 118093
Király, Gabriella, Aszód 105483
Ķirbižu Meža Muzejs, Viļķene 027803
Kirby, R., Acrise 083255
Kirche am Hohenzollernplatz, Berlin 016091
Kirchengeschichtliches Museum in der Pfalzkapelle, Bad Wimpfen 015831
Kirchenhäusl, Sankt Oswald bei Freistadt 002608
Kirchenmuseum, Ernen 037073
Kirchenmuseum, Marienhafe 018832
Kirchenmuseum in der Pfarrei, Gengenbach 017362
Kirchenschatz, Bremgarten (Aargau) 036970
Kirchenschatz, Glarus 037148
Kirchenschatz des Chorherrenstiftes, Beromünster 036944
Kirchenschatz im Sankt Fridolinsmünster, Bad Säckingen 015781
Kirchenschatz-Museum, Baden . . . 036870
Kirchenschatz-Museum Sankt Martin, Altdorf, Uri 036832
Kirchenschatz Sankt Pelagius Kirche, Bischofszell 036959
Kirchhoff, J., Kiel 071831
Kirchmeyer, Bitschwiller-les-Thann 061502
Kirchner, Rainer, Dortmund 070285, 138982
Kirchner, Rainer, Essen . . 102690, 139055
Kirchner, S., Keitum 071777
Kirchner Museum Davos, Davos Platz 037039
Kirchwehm, Gudrun, Berlin 101948
Kirikiño, Bilbao 080977
Kırıkkale Kültür Merkezi, Kırıkkale . 038126
Kirillo-Belozerskij Istoriko-Architekturnyj i Chudožestvennyj Muzej-Zapovednik, Kirillov 033259
Kirisits, Werner, Stubenberg 057328
Kirium, Helsinki 098738
Kiriyama Gallery, Tokyo 107063
Kirja- ja Lehtilinna, Kuopio 137975
Kirja- ja Paperikonservointi, Mikkeli 124055
Kirjakaruselli, Kauhava 137969
Kirjapaja, Helsinki 133441
The Kirk, Surry Hills 095254
Kirk Ports Gallery, North Berwick . . 086088
Kirkaldy Testing Museum, London . 040194
Kirkcaldy Museum and Art Gallery, Kirkcaldy 039899
Kirkgate, Thirsk 131591
Kirkham House, Paignton 040671
Kirkkomuseo, Mikkeli 009873
Kirkland, Leumeah 094734
Kirkland, David, Wellington 079328, 128975
Kirkland Fine Arts Center-Perkinson Gallery, Decatur 043351
Kirkleatham Museum, Redcar 040812
Kirklees Collection of Photographs, Huddersfield 039781
Kirkonkylän Museo, Suodenniemi . . 010105
Kirkpatrick, Jim R., Houston 089126
Kirkpatrick Mostert, Jeanie, Houston 089127
Kirkpatrick Science and Air Space Museum at Omniplex, Oklahoma City 046645
Kirk's Kards, Cleveland 088338
Kirkuk Museum, Kirkuk 022667
Kirkwood, Vancouver 137728
Kirms-Krackow-Haus, Stiftung Weimarer Klassik und Kunstsammlungen, Weimar, Thüringen 020744
Kiron, Paris 100563
Kirovograds'kyj Chudožno-memorial'nyj Muzej O. Osmorkina, Kirovograd . 038280
Kirovograds'kyj Literaturno-memorial'nyj Muzej M.L. Kropyvnyc'kogo, Kirovograds'kyj oblasnyj krajeznavčyj muzej, Kirovograd 038281
Kirovograds'kyj Literaturnyj Muzej, Kirovograd 038282
Kirovograds'kyj Muzej Musyčnoï Kul'tury im. Karolja Šymanovs'kogo, Kirovograd 038283
Kirovograds'kyj Oblasnyj Chudožnij Muzej, Kirovograd 038284
Kirovograds'kyj Oblasnyj Krajeznavčyj Muzej, Kirovograd 038285
Kirovskij Oblastnoj Chudožestvennyj Muzej im. Viktora i Apollinarija Vasnecovych, Kirov 033263
Kirovskij Oblastnoj Kraevedčeskij Muzej, Kirov 033264
Kirriemuir Gateway to the Glens Museum, Kerriemuir 039849
Kirrmann, J., Karlsruhe . . 071723, 103495
Kirsch, Wien 057463
Kirsch, Alfred, München 072751
Kirschner, Renate, Gundelfingen an der Donau 103036
Kırşehir Devlet Güzel Sanatlar Galerisi, Kırşehir 038127
Kırşehir Müzesi, Kırşehir 038128
Kirst, Siegfried, Wunstorf 074517
Kirsten, Beedenbostel 069510
Kirsten, Seattle 119948
Kirsten Flagstad Museum, Hedmarksmuseet og Domkirkeodden, Hamar 030873
Kirsten Kjærs Museum, Frøstrup . . 008870
Kirsten's Antik, København 060347
Kirsti Rauman Museo, Rauma 010022
Kirtland Temple Historic Center, Kirtland 045024
Kirton Antiques, Kirton 084878
KIS Galerie, Amsterdam 107750
Kis Géza Ormánság Múzeum, Sellye 021839
Kisa, Tokyo 077269
Kiscelli Múzeum, Budapest 021661
Kisfaludy Emlékmúzeum, Sümeg . . 021852
Kisgaléria, Győr 105558
Kish, New York 118094
Kishon, Sara, Tel Aviv 105920
Kiskon Kotiseutumuseo, Kisko 009715
Kiskun Múzeum, Kiskunfélegyháza . 021768
Kisler Rosenvald, Paris 066116
Kislovodskij Istoriko-kraevedčeskij Muzej Krepost', Kislovodsk 033272
Kismet, San Jose 119854
Kismit, Toledo 120085
Kiss, Szeged 105577
Kiss, Ilona, Budapest 134505
Kiss, Marlène & Andreas, Cham . . . 070128
Kiss My Art, Totnes 114591
Kiss Pál Múzeum, Tiszafüred 021907
Kißler, Sabine, Köln 126093
Kistefos-museet, Jevnaker 030927
Kistemann, Berlin 138805
Kistler, Lyss 082643, 111711
Kistner, E. & R., Nürnberg 139609
Kistner, Erwin & Rolf, Nürnberg . . . 139610
Kisumu Museum, Kisumu 027423
Kit & Caboodle, Toronto 059225
Kit Carson Historic Museums, Taos 048500
Kit Carson Historical Society Museum, Kit Carson 045026
KIT Kindermuseum, Tropenmuseum, Amsterdam 029193
KIT Tropenmuseum, Amsterdam . . . 029194
Kita, Kyoto 077110
Kita, Lille 063851
Kita, Yamato-koriyama 107138
Kita Garo, Sapporo 106985
Kita-kamakura Museum, Kamakura 026612
Kitajskij Dvorec-muzej, Muzej-zapovednik Oranienbaum, Lomonosov 033334
Kitakami Municipal Museum, Kitakami 026658
Kitakyushu-shiritsu Bijutsukan, Kitakyushu 026660
Kitale Museum, Kitale 027424
Kitano Bijutsukan, Nagano 026843
Kitano Temman-gu Treasure House, Kyoto 026726
Kitazawa, Tokyo 140190
Kitazawa Bijutsukan, Suwa 027093
Kitchen Witch Country Furnishings, Toronto 059226
Kitchenaid, Columbus 131984
Kitchener, Hamilton 058855
Kitchener Gallery, Auckland 108332
Kitchener-Waterloo Art Gallery, Kitchener 005718
Kitchener-Waterloo Art Gallery, Kitchener 096932
Kiteen Kotiseutumuseo, Kitee Local History and Crafts Museum, Kitee 009716
Kiten Art, Langenbach, Kreis Freising 072153, 134140
Kithur Rani Channamma Memorial Museum, Kittur 022206
Kitimat Centennial Museum, Kitimat 005720
Kitovras, Moskva 109557
Kitsap Museum, Bremerton 042396
Kitsch, Montréal 058971
Kitsch, Emely, Oslo 079451
Kitsch und Kunst, Heilbronn 071473
Kitsos Makris Folk Art Center, Volos 021522
Kitte no Hakubutsukan, Tokyo 027185
Kittel, Michael, Rosengarten, Württemberg 126735
Kittelberger, Pittsburgh 091831
Kittelsenhuset, Berg-Kragerø Museum, Kragerø 030953
Kittelty, Ballarat 120562
Kittery Historical and Naval Museum, Kittery 045027
Kittilän Kotiseutumuseo, Kittilä 009717
Kittilbu Utmarksmuseum, Østre Gausdal 031116
Kittiwake Gallery, Eyemouth 113048
Kittredge Art Gallery, University of Puget Sound, Tacoma 048467
Kittrell & Riffkind, Dallas 115900
Kittson County History Center Museum, Lake Bronson 045098
Kitwanga Fort, Queen Charlotte . . . 006233
Kitz-Art, Kitzbühel 095607
Kitzbüheler Antiquitäten- und Sammlermesse, Kitzbühel 093580
Kitzig, Erdmann, Wennigsen 126991
Kitzig & Erdmann, Hemmingen 125912
Kitzinger, J., München 139524
Kiuruveden Kotiseutumuseo, Kiuruvesi 009718
Kivikauden Kylä, Saarijärvi 010053
Kivimuseo, Luonnontieteellinen Keskusmuseo, Helsinki 009543
Kivimuseo, Tampereen Museot, Tampere 010120
Kiwanis Club Antiques Show, Old Greenwich 093997
Kiwanis Van Slyke Museum Foundation, Caldwell 042544
Kiya, Yokohama 077338
Kiyoharu Shirakaba Museum, Nagasaka 026856
Kiyosato Museum of Photographic Arts, Takane 027109
Kiyose-shi Kyodo Hakubutsukan, Kiyose 026661
Kızıltoprak Sanat Galerisi, İstanbul . 112331
Kizljarskij Kraevedčeskij Muzej im. P.I. Bagrationa, Dagestanskij gosudarstvennyj objedinennyj istoriko-architekturnyj muzej, Kizljar 033276
Kjær, Viborg 137911
Kjær, Flemming, København 060348
Kjarvalsstaðir, Listasafn Reykjavíkur, Reykjavík 021962
Kjempen, Oslo 079452
Kjerringøy Gamle Handelssted, Nordland Fylkesmuseet, Bodø 030783
Ajå Kjøp & Arbys Eiendom, Oslo . . . 079453
KJT Art Factory, Houston 116351
kjubh Kunstverein, Köln 053257
K.K. Gallery, Pickering 114248
Klaavola Museo, Tuusula 010187
Klaber & Klaber, London . . 085459, 131079
Klabisz, Marian, Warszawa 129091
Klabund, Hannover 139236
Klabunde, Bernd, München 072752
Klæbu Bygdemuseum, Klæbu 030940
Kläppgården Hembygdsmuseum, Harads 036329
Klag, A., Duchroth 070338
Klagsbrun, Nicole, New York 118095
Klaipėdos Galerija, Klaipėda 107351
Klaipėdos Paveikslų Galerija, Klaipėda 107352
Klamath County Museum, Klamath Falls 045029
Klamath Falls Art Association, Klamath Falls 054837

Klamath National Forest Interpretive Museum, Yreka 049365
Klange, Osaka 106966
Klapka, Georg, Budapest 121640
Klapka György Múzeum, Komáron . 021775
Klaproth, Bernd, Hagen, Westfalen . 071163
Klar, Manfred, Berlin 069660
De Klare Lijn, Leiden 078569
De Klare Lijn, Leiden 078570
Klaricová, Kateřina, Praha 098467
Klaschewski, Jürgen, Bleicherode . 069867
Klasema, Bergen op Zoom 078071
Klasing, U., Lemgo 072224
Klášter Sv. Anežky České, Národní Galerie v Praže, Praha 008616
Klašter Sv. Jiří, Národní galerie v Praze, Praha 008617
Klau, S., Holdenstedt 139278
Klauk, W. & K., Celle 070125
Klaus, Bucureşti 080158
Klaus, Dietmar, Marienberg 072456
Klaus, Kurt, Lübeck 072326
Klaus, Vollmar, Bad Salzuflen 138703
Klaus-Groth-Museum und Neue Museumsinsel Lüttenheid, Heide, Holstein 017821
Klaus Jantzen, Hamburg 071261
Klaushenke, Joachim Josef, Seeth-Ekholt 126794
Klausner, Louisville 116949
Klausnitzer, Andrea, Dresden 102446
Klavdianos, Angelique, Kifissia 105430
Klaver, H.A.M., Amsterdam 077884
't Klavertje, Antwerpen 057708
Klax-Galerie für Kinderkunst, Berlin 101949
Klayman, Leon, New York 135437
Kleanthous Antiques, London 085460
Kléber, Béziers 061442
Kleber, H. & B., Jestetten 139289
Kléber Broc Antic, Dunkerque 062751
Klee, Hong Kong 097806
Klee, Brigitte, Darmstadt 102343
Klee, Erwin, Wiesbaden 074410
Klee, Karl-Heinz, Wasungen 074287
Klees & Cursiefen, Hünxe 071589
Kleff, Jacques, Erbach, Odenwald . 070580
Kleffmann, Meinolf, Lennestadt . . . 126211
Klefing, Nordhorn 073083
Klefisch, Köln 071962, 121474
Klei, Hong Kong 097807
Kleidt, Stephanie, München 126401
Kleihues, Sigrid, Berlin 069661
Kleijn, Harderwijk 128703
Kleijn, Alexander, Zutphen 078875
Kleijn & Zoon, W., Rijswijk, Zuid-Holland 128813
Kleim, Obernai 065255
Klein, Chicago 115470
Klein, Essen 102691, 125614
Klein, Leverkusen 072242
Klein, Stuttgart 073983
Klein, West Hollywood 120393
Klein, A., Raesfeld 073405
Klein, André, Sainte-Colombe-sur-Seine 068052
Klein, Beat A., Bern 082217
Klein, Bertrand, Mulhouse 064836
Klein, Dominique, Bayonne 061232
Klein, Erhard, Bad Münstereifel . . . 101673
Klein, Eric, Nice 065096
Klein, Erich & Anneliese, Neu-Ulm . 072969
Klein, François, Paris 124709
Klein, Fritz, Hannover 071397
Klein, G. & E., Achim 101537
Klein, H., Köln 071963
Klein, Isabelle, Paris 066117
Klein, Isabelle, Toulouse 068524
Klein, J. Alex, Adenau 069109
Klein, K., Bernried, Niederbayern . . 069807
Klein, K.-H., Nidda 139593
Klein, Katharina, Pirmasens 104610
Klein, Lysiane, Pézenas 066807
Klein, Martina, Wörrstadt 074461
Klein, Michel, Saint-Ouen 067818
Klein, Prof. Dr. Peter, Hamburg 125825
Klein, Peter, Wörrstadt 074462
Klein, Robert, Boston 115193
Klein, Stefan, Augsburg 069235
Klein, Stéfan, Beblenheim 061318
Klein, Toan, Toronto 097307
Klein, Ulrike, Remagen 126711
Klein, Werner, Köln 103656
Klein 14 Stichting, Rotterdam 108190
Klein Beekman, Zwolle 078890
Klein Chrétien, Lemberg 063739
Klein Kras, Arnhem 078053
Klein, Lawrence & Tan, North Shore 079194, 128948
Klein Museum, Mobridge 045954
Klein-Reesink, Hamminkeln 139226
Klein Saab Museum d'Oude Bolneus, Woerden 030343
Klein & Scholer, Merzig 072529
Klein Vredenburg Gallery, Paarl . . . 080725
Klein Westphal, C., Amsterdam . . . 077885
Klein & Zwickmann, Peter, Bonn . . . 069929
Kleinbauer, Dieter, Merseburg . . . 072521
Kleindiek, Birger, Duisburg 102582
Kleindienst, Matthias, Leipzig 103885, 134152
Kleindienst, Susanne, Sulz 126894
Kleine, J., Gummersbach 071146
Kleine Duitse Antiquariaat, Bredevoort 140370
Die Kleine Galerie, Billerbeck 102136
Die kleine Galerie, Braunschweig . . 102222
Kleine Galerie, Den Haag 107934
Kleine Galerie, Ebersbach an der Fils 102591
Kleine Galerie, Eberswalde 102592
Die Kleine Galerie, Neunkirchen, Siegerland 104419
Kleine Galerie, Paderborn 073284
Kleine Galerie, Regensburg 104697
Kleine Galerie, Sankt Martin , Pfalz 104812
Kleine Galerie, Venezia 076947
Kleine Galerie, Waiblingen 105143
Die Kleine Galerie, Wien 002924
Kleine Galerie Bad Waldsee, Bad Waldsee 101711
Kleine Galerie Eckes, Nieder-Olm . . 104446
Kleine Galerie im Hühnerstall, Krummin 103800
Kleine Humboldt-Galerie, Humboldt-Universität, Berlin 016092
De Kleine Kunsthandel, Heerlen . . . 078501
Der Kleine Kunstladen, Regensburg 073463
Das Kleine Museum, Gelsenkirchen 017355
Kleine Schloßgalerie Weiher, Ahorntal 101545
Das kleine Spielzeugmuseum, Baden-Baden 015850
Kleinehelleforth-Kaunitz, Verl 074197
Kleiner, Gottfried, Ober-Ramstadt . . 126573
Kleiner Prinz, Aschau im Chiemgau 069204
Kleiner Prinz, Baden-Baden 069419
Kleinert, D., Berlin 069662
Kleinert-Nicolas, Isabelle, Paris . . . 124710
Kleines Bücherhaus, Zürich 141344
Kleines Guß-Museum, Selfkant . . . 020182
Kleines Heimatmuseum Windmühle, Werdum 020806
Kleines Kirchengeschichtsmuseum Sankt Gumbertus, Evang.-Luth. Pfarramt Illesheim, Illesheim 018052
Kleines Kunsthaus am Schloß, Quedlinburg 073397
Kleines Museum am Hafen, Romanshorn 037459
Kleines Museum - Kinder der Welt, Frankfurt/Oder 017203
Kleines Plakatmuseum, Bayreuth . . 015916
Kleines Stuck-Museum, Freiburg im Breisgau 017231
Kleines technisches Museum, Baden 036867
Kleingärtner, Lothar, Natendorf 121557
Kleingalerie Dependenze, Stans . . . 111933
Kleinhaarhuis, Almelo 077726
Kleinhans, S., Lörrach 072292
Kleinheinrich, Dr. Josef, Münster . . 134297
Kleinhenz, Hans-Dieter, Ludwigshafen am Rhein 072314, 103949, 121503
Kleinjan, Willem, Utrecht 078809
Kleinman, Dick, Cleveland 115722
Kleinöder, R., Düsseldorf 070400
Kleinschmidt, I., Bonn 102187
Kleinskulpturen Biennale, Stuttgart 093729
Kleinsorge, R., Köln 071964
Kleinwächter, Helma, Rosbach 104761
Kleio, Haarlem 078463
Kleisen, Jacqueline, Amsterdam . . 077886
Kleiss, Riedlingen 104752
Kleiss & Polzer, Riedlingen 104753
Kleist, Idstein 071608, 103422
Kleist-Museum, Kleist-Gedenk- und Forschungsstätte e.V., Frankfurt/Oder 017204
Klement, Anna, Neulengbach 137237
Klement, Manfred, Schwerin 134392
Klement & Kaye, Hamburg 071262
Klement & Kaye, Hamburg 071263
Klemettimuseo, Kuortane 009765
Klemke, Hilmar M., Düsseldorf 102517
Klemm, Heidelberg 103324
Klemm, Holger, Hochheim am Main 125945
Klemm, Kristin, Saarbrücken 126756
Klemm Gallery, Siena Heights University, Adrian 041580
Klemme, Bad Salzuflen 101694
Klemmer, Gerd, Dortmund 070286, 125480
Kleopatra, Duisburg 070480
Kleplisch, Raphaël, Brunoy 061826
Klepner, Melbourne 056190
Klepp Bygdemuseum, Kleppe 030941
Klepper Museum, Rosenheim 019886
Klerksdorp Museum, Klerksdorp . . . 034669
Klesel, Gerhard, Bleicherode 069868
Klesper, Karin, Jesteburg 071658
Kless, Elvira, Dresden 125500
Klette, Jürgen, Berlin 138806
Klettgau-Museum, Waldshut-Tiengen 020650
Klevering, Amsterdam 077887
Klevering, Amsterdam 077888
Klevfos Industrimuseum, Ådalsbruk 030712
Kley, Werner, Hamm, Westfalen . . . 134029
KLH Gallery, Newtown, New South Wales 094957
Klick Kindermuseum Hamburg, Hamburg 017702
Klickitat County Historical Society Museum, Goldendale 044236
Kliemchen, Franz & Doris, Wuppertal 074530
Klier, Alois, Frankfurt am Main 102792
Klier, Heinz, Rosenheim 073573
Klijn, Johan, Den Haag 128632
Klim, Toronto 133325
Klim, Wolfgang, Falkenstein 056973
Klimas, Hans-Detlef, Baden-Baden 069420
Klimaty, Warszawa 109149
Klimbacher, Dietmar, Imst 095574
Klimetzek, Stuttgart 073984
Klimp, de, Venlo 078836
Klin, Poznań 109054
Klincker, D., Kastorf 071768
Klincker, Dieter, Kastorf 126020
Klincksieck & Cie., Paris . 133635, 138417
Kline, Eric, Santa Monica 142972
Kline Creek Farm, Winfield 049241
Kling, Alfred, Leutkirch im Allgäu . . 072239
Kling, Hendrik, Stuttgart 073985
Klingender, Marlies, Berlin 069663
Klingenschmid, Margit, Hall in Tirol 057053
Klinger, Nieblum 104441
Klinger, Dietmar, Passau 134344
Klinger, Eberhard, Görlitz 102973
Klinger, Johannes, Aschau im Chiemgau 101604
Klinger, Karin, Nürnberg 073108
Klinger, Klaus, Frechen 070809
Klinger, Udo, Lützelbach 072364
Klinghammer, Esther, Köln 103657, 126094
Klinghoffer, Andrea, Ermatingen . . . 082359
Klinghoffer, Charlotte Daniela, Salenstein 122347
Klingner, Bruxelles 058008
Klingspor-Museum, Offenbach am Main 019455
Klinker, Leslie John, Frespech 062946
Klinkhamer, Groningen 078425
Klinkhammer, Ruth, Bornheim, Rheinland 125370
Klinkhoff, Walter, Montréal 097041
Klinskoe Muzejnoe Obedinenie, Klin 033278
Klio 1, Pleven 058757, 137598
Klio Buchhandlung und Antiquariat, Zürich 141345
KLIO Deutsche Gesellschaft der Freunde und Sammler kulturhistorischer Zinnfiguren e.V., Frickingen 053258
Klismos, Parma 127852
Klis'sche Buchhandlung, Hohenstein-Ernstthal 139276
Klitgaard, Søren, København 060349
Klittich-Pfankuch, Adelheid, Braunschweig . . 102223, 121354, 138927
Klix, Ulrich, Berlin 069664
Kljuev, Nikolaj, Moskva 080247
KLM Enterprises, Dallas 088543
Kloane Galerie im Gwölb, Zwettl, Niederösterreich 095984
Klobassa, Martin, Wien 123509
Kloboučnické Muzeum, Nový Jičín . 008536
Klocke, Alois, Viersen 074212
Klocker, Dr. Hubert, Wien 095877
Klöckner, Heinz, Köln 103658
Klöckner, Stefan, Gelnhausen 125709
Klöden, Kurt, Neuss 104424
Klöpfer, Gerda, Darmstadt 070186
Klöppelmuseum und Heimatkundliche Sammlung, Abenberg 015435
Kloess, Werner, Wien 057464
Klöter, Peter, Grafenau, Württemberg 071079, 121418
Klöttschen, H., Berlin 069665
Kloiber, Berta, Neuhaus am Klausenbach 137236
Kloidt-Haus, VG Buch- und Pressehandel, Essen 139056
Klokkengieterij Museum, Heiligerlee 029705
Klokkengieterijmuseum, Vries 030293
De Klokkenkamer, Groningen 078426
Klokkenmuseum, Frederiksoord . . . 029591
Klokkenmuseum, Hechtel 003504
Klokkenmuseum van de Sint-Martinusbasiliek, Halle 003485
Klokkergården Bygdetun Lyngdal Misjonsmuseum, Lyngdal 031003
Klokowski, Magdeburg 072371
't Klokske, Deventer 078276
Klomp, Nijmegen 078656
Klompenmuseum De Platijn, Best . . 029313
Klompenmuseum Gebr. Wietzes, Eelde 029526
Klompenmuseum 't Oale Ambacht, Goor 029619
Klompenmuseum 't Schöpke Enter, Enter 029572
De Klomphoek, Beilen 029299
Klondike Gold Rush National Historical Park, Seattle 048083
Klondike National Historic Sites, Dawson City 005332
Klondyke, Almere 140270
Klonk, Dieter, München 126402
Kloonen, Raamsdonksveer 128807
De Kloosteresch, Almelo 107625
Klopfenstein, M., Ebersbach bei Döbeln 070494
Klopfenstein, Marianne, Döbeln . . . 070262
Klopfer, Herbert, Sankt Gallen 082780, 130162
Klopfermühle mit Mühlenmuseum, Lengenfeld, Vogtland 018612
Klopstock Museum, Städtische Museen Quedlinburg, Quedlinburg 019687

Klose, Bielefeld 102122
Klose, Essen 102692
Klose, Dieter, Mainz 104001
Klose, Gustav, Hamburg . . 071264, 125826
Klose, Ilka, Würzburg 105338
Klose, D., Bad Wünnenberg 069401
Kloster Altenberg, Königsberger Diakonissen-Mutterhaus der Barmherzigkeit, Solms 020242
Kloster Ebstorf, Ebstorf 016877
Kloster-Galerie, Uetersen 105089
Kloster Hadmersleben, Hadmersleben 017618
Kloster Irsee, Irsee 018082
Kloster Isenhagen, Hankensbüttel . 017748
Kloster Lüne, Lüneburg 018743
Kloster Mariensee, Neustadt am Rübenberge 019277
Kloster Medingen, Bad Bevensen . . 015668
Kloster-Museum, Sankt Märgen . . . 019990
Kloster Sankt Marienberg, Helmstedt 017865
Kloster Seeon, Seeon 020172
Kloster Walsrode, Walsrode 020662
Kloster Wienhausen, Wienhausen . . 020857
Kloster zum Heiligen Kreuz, Kulturhistorisches Museum Rostock, Rostock 019899
Klosteranlage mit Klostermuseum, Maulbronn 018862
Klosterbräu Brauereimuseum, Irsee 018083
Klosterfelde, Berlin 101950
Klostergalerie, Fürstenfeldbruck . . . 102896
Klostergalerie, Zehdenick 021041
Klosterkirche Blaubeuren, Blaubeuren 016265
Klosterkirche Himmelpfort, Bredereiche 016397
Klosterlund Museum og Naturcenter, Engesvang 008840
Klostermann, K., Brand-Erbisdorf . . 069974
Klostermann, Rudolf, Havixbeck . . . 125890
Klostermühlenmuseum, Thierhaupten 020436
Klostermuseum, Müstair 037360
Klostermuseum, Muri (Aargau) 037362
Klostermuseum, Roggenburg 019874
Klostermuseum der Benediktiner-Abtei, Ottobeuren 019542
Klostermuseum der Sankt Josefskongregation, Ursberg 020547
Klostermuseum Disentis, Disentis . 037047
Klostermuseum Heggbach, Maselheim 018858
Klostermuseum Hirsau, Calw 016541
Klostermuseum in der Pfarrkirche Sankt Magnus, Bad Schussenried 015793
Klostermuseum Jerichow, Jerichow 018119
Klostermuseum Sankt Georgen, Stein am Rhein 037606
Klosterruine Memleben, Memleben 018902
Klostersammlung der Benediktinerabtei, Michaelbeuern 002308
Klostertal-Museum, Dalaas 001774
Klostertunet, Sunnhordland Folkemuseum, Halsnøy Kloster 030869
Klostervalvet Antik, Stockholm 081972
Klotz, Aschaffenburg 069197
Klotz, Carol, Atlanta 087493
Klotz, Christa, Passau 104588
Klotz, Ferdinand, Landau in der Pfalz 072131
Klotz, François, Obernai 065256
Klotz, Martine, Paris 124711
Klotz, Uta, Köln 103659
Klotz & Sirmon, New York 118096
Klotzer, Mira & Dieter, New York . . . 132486
Kluane Museum of Natural History, Burwash Landing 005173
Klub, Szczecin 109082
Klubbslaget, Lyrestad 122202
Kluckert, Torsten H., Berlin 125232
Kluckow, Alan, Sunningdale 114521
Klucznik Galeria, Gdańsk 108889
Klüber, Weinheim, Bergstraße 074317
Klügel, Walter, Wien 137332
Klügel, Walter, Wien 137333
Klümann, Hans-Gerd, Rheine 073523
Klün, Anja, Ludwigsburg, Württemberg 126230
Klüser, Bernd, München 104243
Kluge, Hedehusum 103316
Kluge, Eduard von, Zürich 082990, 130246
Kluger, Claudia, Kassel 126016
Klughammer, Markt Indersdorf 126294
Kluizenaar, M. de, Leiden 078571
Klukas, Martina, Bietigheim-Bissingen 069845
Klun, Ernesto, Dallas 088544
Klute, Felix, Schmallenberg 073705
Kluuvin Galleria - Glogalleriet, Helsingin Kaupungin Taidemuseo, Helsinki . 009544
Klyne Esopus Historical Society Museum, Ulster Park 048685
KM-Antik, Kirchardt 071852
KM Art, Milwaukee 117200
Kmetty Múzeum, Ferenczy Múzeum, Szentendre 021883
Knaap, Nancy, Oosterlittens 128800
Knall, Stockholm 111057
Knapp, E.L., Louisville 090006
Knapp, Gerhard, Perchtoldsdorf . . . 057206
Knapp, Jeanine-Natacha, Genève . . 111476
Knapp, Reinhard & Karola, Reichenbach, Kreis Birkenfeld Nahe 073474
Knappogue Castle, Quin 022847
Knapstein, Sundern 074034
Knaresborough Castle and Old Courthouse Museum, Knaresborough 039908
Knauf, Martina, Weitersbach 105201
Knauf-Museum, Iphofen 018080
Knaus, Albrecht, München 134253
Knaus, Bernhard, Mannheim 104026, 134189, 139453
Knaus, Petra, Heilbronn 125908
Knauß, Maren, Helgoland . 071483, 139260
Knebel, Sven, Regensberg 135061
Knebworth House, Knebworth 039910
Knecht, Alfred, Karlsruhe 103496
Knecht & Wrzal, Neuchâtel 130127
Kneehill Historical Museum, Three Hills 006563
Kneer, Ekkehard, Munderkingen . . . 126515
Kneidinger, Thomas, Linz 123411
Kneifel, Cloppenburg 138967
Kneipp-Museum, Bad Endbach . . . 015696
Kneisel, Bernd, Aschaffenburg 069198
Knepper, G. & K.-H., Güntersberge . 071139
Kner Nyomdaipari Múzeum, Gyomaendrőd 021729
Knežev Dvor, Cavtat 007708
Knick, Recklinghausen 104684
Knick and Knack, Bangalore 074772
Knickknack, Phoenix 091750
Knickl, Erika, München 072753
Knicks Knacks Emporium, Sutton-on-Sea 086804
Knie, Rolf, Rapperswil, Sankt Gallen 111822
Kniebel, Eva, Nürnberg 073109
Kniele, A., Erbach, Odenwald 070581
Knieß, Uwe, Berlin 069666
Knife River Indian Villages National Historic Site, Stanton 048322
Knight, Houston 089128
Knight, Singapore 109825
Knight & Sons, B.R., Saint Ives, Cambridgeshire 086456
Knight, Darren, Waterloo 095377
Knight Museum of High Plains Heritage, Alliance 041662
Knights of Columbus Museum, New Haven 046224
Knightsbridge, Tampa 093132
Knightsbridge Auctions, Loganholme 120603
Knightsbridge Coins, London 085461
Knightsbridge Gallery, Newent 114130
Knigočej, Moskva 140906
Knijff, Zeist 078868
De Knipoog, Gouda 078388
Knippschild-Strätz, Christa, Lübeck 139427
Knirim, Ingrid, Münster 072914
Knittel, Frieder, Konstanz 103762
Knižnaja Lavka, Sankt-Peterburg . .080306, 140933
Knižnaja Lavka Architektora, Moskva 140907
Knižnaja Lavka Pisatelej, Moskva . . 140908
Knižnaja Lavka Vostokoveda, Moskva 140909
Knižny Magazin N60, Sankt-Peterburg 140934
Knižnyj Aukcion v Centralnom Dome Literatorov, Moskva 121966
Knjeižna Starinarna, Radovljica . . . 140971
Knjižara i Antikvarijat Srpske Književne Zadruge, Beograd 140948
Knobel, Marie-Claire, Lausanne . . . 082551
Knobkerry, New York 091006
Knoblach, Dirk, Berlin 125233
Knobloch, Stephan, Frankfurt am Main 125655
Knobloch, Wolfgang, Waldbronn . . . 126958
Knock Folk Museum, Knock 022819
Knock Gallery, Crathie 112917
Knock on Wood, Montréal 123788
Knockengorroch, Castle Douglas . . 112824
Knockreer House, Killarney 022807
Knödgen, Hugo, Koblenz 071894
Knoedler & Co., New York 118097
Knödler, A., Blumberg 069872
Knöll, Friederike, Wien 057465
Knöll, Niklaus, Basel 111199
Knöll, Niklaus, Basel 129922
Knöll, Niklaus, Bern 111262, 129962
Knöll, Thomas, Basel 082147, 111200, 129923
Knöpper, Birgit, Amsterdam 128543
Knörle-Jahn, Cornelia, München . . 126403
Knoester, Den Haag 078207
Knol, Reinier, Leeuwarden 108095
Knole, Sevenoaks 040986
Knoll, Backnang 101622, 125083
Knoll, Hans, Budapest 134506
Knoll, Hans, Dillingen, Saar 125467
Knoll, Hans, Wien 095878, 133210
Knollmayer, Othmar, Tulln . 057333, 123479
Knollwood, New York 091007
Knoor, Heimer, Issum 071643, 125980
Knop, Klaus, Görlitz 071037
Knopek, Köln 071965
Knopf, Alfred A., New York 135438
Knopf, Heinrich, Moosach 104120
Knopp, Klaus, Ohlsdorf 057202
Knops, C.J.M., Munstergeleen 128780
Knops, Michel, Sittard 108227
Knott House Museum, Tallahassee . 048479
Knous, Bill & Sue, Denver 088706
Knowles, Beverley, London 113725
Known Space Books, Adelaide 136773
Knox, Denver 116017
Knox County Historical Society Museum, Edina 043608
Knox County Museum, Benjamin . . 042142
Knox County Museum, Knoxville . . . 045030
Knox's Headquarters State Historic Site, Vails Gate 048725
Knoxville Museum of Art, Knoxville . 045040
Knud Rasmussens Hus, Hundested 008939
Knudaheio - Garborgheimen, Undheim 031303
Knudsen, Lars, Millfield 094849
Knüttel, Kurt & Maria, Königstein im Taunus 126128
Knuf, Frits, Vendôme 138649
Knuht, A., Berlin 069667
Knust, Sabine, München 104244
Knuth, Potsdam 139663
Knuts, Bruxelles 058009
Knutsford Antiques Centre, Knutsford 084891, 130860
Knutsford Heritage Centre, Knutsford 039912
Knutsson, Stockholm 081973
Knutsson, Bo, Vänersborg 082063
Knyrim, Brigitte, Regensburg 104698
Knysna Museum, Knysna 034670
K.O. Braun Museum, Ludwigshafen am Rhein 018702
Ko Kwok Yau, Hong Kong 059653
Kō-Zen, Montréal 097042
KOA Art Gallery, University of Hawaii, Kapiolani Community College, Honolulu 044602
Koala Country Commodities, Port Macquarie 056476
Koan Collection, Hadano 026483
Kobariški Muzej, Kobarid 034467
Kobe Fashion Museum, Kobe 026665
Kobe Maritime Museum, Kobe 026666
Kobe-shiritsu Hakubutsukan, Kobe . 026667
Kobelius, E., Lassan 126173
København Museum for Moderne Kunst, København 008969
Københavns Auktioner Chr. Hee's Eftf., København 120870, 137898
Københavns Bymuseum, København 008970
Kober, Köln 071966
Kober, Wertheim 105220
Koberstein, Dr. A.B., Singen, Hohentwiel 126802
Koberstein, E., Kleinostheim 071873
Kobie, Bilbao 136092
Kobijutsu Kaito, Kyoto 077111
Kobijutu Sanshi-bo, Toyo, Kyoto . . . 077112
Koblischeck, Bernd, Wörrstadt 105316
Koblitz, Helga, Lüneburg 072359
Kobo, Seattle 119949
Kobo Aya, Yokohama 077339
Kobold, Josef, Vilsbiburg 074219
Kobrine, Danièle, Paris 066118
Kobrinski Voenno-istoričeski Muzej im. A.V. Suvorova, Kobrin 003129
Kobrossi, Mouna, Jounieh 107330, 140220
Kobs, Detlef, Ausacker 069246
Kobsik, Meersburg 072491
Kocábek, Praha 060136
Kocaeli Devlet Güzel Sanatlar Galerisi, İzmit 038112
Kocal, A., Sandhausen 073662
Koch, Berlin 138807
Koch, Den Haag 128633
Koch, Stenungsund 110994
Koch, Stockerau 137269
Koch, Wolfenbüttel 074473
Koch, Anette von, Stockholm 081974
Koch, Beate, Freiberg, Sachsen . . . 102851
Koch, Carla, Amsterdam 107751
Koch, Frank, Weinstadt . . 074322, 126984
Koch, Friedrich, Neuburg an der Donau 126530
Koch, Horst, Idar-Oberstein 071606
Koch, Ingrid, München 139525
Koch, Jean-Marie, Schlierbach 068179
Koch, Jochen, Reichartshausen . . . 126704
Koch, Jürgen, Berlin 138808
Koch, Jürgen, Berlin 138809
Koch, Jürgen, Hannover 103285
Koch, Matthias, Duderstadt 070339
Koch, Michael, Minden, Westfalen . 126320
Koch, Peter, Suhl 126893
Koch, Richard, Münster 072915
Koch, Robert, San Francisco 119712
Koch, Silvia, Berlin 125234
Koch, Ursula, Windelsbach 074444
Koch, Ute & Heike, Warstein 105164
Koch, Walter, Hannover 103286
Koch, Waltraud, Graz 057017
Koch, Wilfried, Frankfurt am Main . 102793
Koch & Englert, Gießen 102952
Achim Koch & Cornelia Glemser, Ravensburg 104673
Koch & Kesslau, Berlin 101951
Koch-McErlain, New York 091008
Koch & Unthan, Essen 102693
Koch-Westenhoff, Margot, Lübeck . 103963
Kochan, Pat, Dallas 115901
Kochan, W., Bremen 138945
Kochanek, Frank, Gelsenkirchen . . 070956

Kocher & Allemann, Selzach 111899
Kocher-Benzing & Co., Dr. Frieder, Stuttgart 139766
Kochi-ken Kaitokukan, Kochi 026671
Kochi-kenritsu Bijutsukan, Kochi . . 026672
Kochinian Ovanes, Los Angeles . . . 116809
Kochukyo, Tokyo 077270
Kočí, Tomáš, Ústí nad Labem 124008
Kocken, Willi, Kevelaer . . . 071813, 103538
Kockisch, Dieter, Rabenau, Sachsen 126670
Kockler, Paul, Le Luc 063649
Kocsis-Seger, Illes, Stuttgart 126860
Kodai Orient Hakubutsukan, Tokyo . 027186
Kodai Yuzenen, Kyoto 026727
Kodak Gallery Hiroshima, Hiroshima 026535
Kodály Zoltán Emlékmúzeum, Budapest 021662
Kodansha International, Tokyo 134725
Kodisjoen Kotiseutumuseo, Kodisjoki 009719
Koditek, Ursula, Emmerich 102624
Kodner, Saint Louis 092262
Kodner, Saint Louis 092263
Kodner, Saint Louis 119216
Kodner, Saint Louis 119217
Kodo, Seoul 107262
Kodric, Friederike, Salzburg 057262
Kodymý, Miroslav, Praha 123985
Koe, Lilian, Petaling Jaya 134754
Kö Galerie, Düsseldorf 102518
Kö-Galerie am Kaisergarten, Siegen 104896
Köbelin, Rainer, München 139526
Köberich, A. & H., Rabenau, Hessen 139671
Köberle, Ulrich, Überlingen 074133
Köcher, Berlin 125235
Koechlin, Dr., Basel 141205
Köck, Rückersdorf 057231
Köck, Günter Frank, München 104245, 126404
Köckert, Anne Marie, Bad Homburg v.d.Höhe 069292
Köhl, Peter H., Saarbrücken 139705
Köhler, Ottobrunn 104561
Köhler, Wittlich 105314
Köhler, Christian, Mönchengladbach 104094
Köhler, Josef, Erwitte 070606
Köhler, Kai, Warnau 074280
Köhler, Renate, Ulm 074144
Köhler, S., Rhauderfehn 104737
Köhlereimuseum, Hasselfelde 017789
Köhn, J., Eching 070499
Köhn, Joachim, Neufahrn 072988
Köhnlein, Werner, Reutlingen 104731
Köhrmann, G., Oldenburg, Oldenburg 073204
Koek, H., Beverwijk 128587
Kölle, Rolf, Ulm 074145
Koeller, Frédéric, Beure 061415
Köllermann, Iris, Ahlen 069116
Kölling, Torsten, Burg bei Magdeburg 070093
Köllisch, Nürnberg 073110
Köllner, Franziska M., Leipzig 103886
Kölner Münzkabinett, Köln 071967
Kölner Münzstube, Köln 071968
Kölner Museums-Bulletin, Berichte und Forschungen aus den Museen der Stadt Köln, Köln 135774
Kölner Museumszeitung, Köln 135775
Kölner Weinmuseum, Köln 018320
Kölnischer Kunstverein, Köln 018321
Kölnischer Kunstverein, Köln 053259
Kölnisches Stadtmuseum, Museen der Stadt Köln, Köln 018322
Kölpin, H., Veltheim 074189
Koelsch, Houston 116352
Kölsch, Hans-Werner, Wuppertal . . 105356
Koeltz, Sven, Königstein im Taunus 139358
Kölzer, Arnold, Mastershausen 072473
Koenders, M.C.J., Voorthuizen 128874
Köndgen, Heinrich, Wuppertal 139886
Koendo, Iida, Tokyo 077271
Koenen, Hans-Gerd, Xanten 074555
Koenig, Bruxelles 058010
König, Darmstadt 102344
König, Münster 104370
König, Overijse 133295
Koenig, Pézenas 066808
König, Soest 073846
König, Andreas, Vetschau, Spreewald 126948
König, B & R., Ebersdorf bei Coburg 070496
König, Christine, Wien 095879
König, Edmund von, Dielheim 133863
König, Gisela, Stuttgart 126861
König, Hartmut, Markee 139465
Koenig, Hermann, Stuhr 073947
König, Johann, Berlin 101952
König, Johann, Waldfischbach-Burgalb 074254
Koenig, K.-H., Fürstenau 070906
König, Katrin, Berlin 125236
Koenig, Leo, New York 118098
König, M., Leichlingen 072189
König, Manfred, München 126405
König, Marianne, Rednitzhembach . 139681
König, O., Overath 073274
Koenig, Peter, Zürich 130247
König, R., Döbeln 070263
König, Ursula, Hanau 103252
König, W., Altdorf, Pfalz 069146
König, Walther, Berlin 138810
König, Walther, Berlin 138811
König, Walther, Bonn 138902
König, Walther, Dresden 138994
König, Walther, Düsseldorf 139015
König, Walther, Frankfurt am Main . 139087
König, Walther, Frankfurt am Main . 139088
König, Walther, Köln 134115, 139344
Koenig, Walther, London 141838
König, Walther, München 139527
König, Walther, Münster 139568
König, Walther, Nürnberg 139611
König, Wolfgang, Rhodt 073529
König Ludwig II.-Museum, Herrenchiemsee 017896
Königsbaum, Ane, Norderstedt 073075
Königshaus am Schachen und Alpengarten, Garmisch-Partenkirchen 017325
Königspesel, Hallig Hooge 017676
Königspfalz Freilichtmuseum, Tilleda 020441
Koenigstein, Prof. Georg, Klosterneuburg 133105
Koenitz, Martin, Dresden 138995
Koenitz, Martin, Leipzig 139396
Könizer Galerie, Köniz 111589
Könnecke, Möser 072586
Könner, Neustadt am Rübenberge . 073020
Könyv & CD Antikvárium, Budapest 139920
Könyvesbolt & Antikvárium, Szolnok 139943
Köpings Museum, Köping 036394
Koepp, Jeanne, Berlin 101953
Köppe, Dr. Rainer, Limbach-Oberfrohna 072253
Köppen, Bernd, Berlin 125237
Körbel, Maria, Wien 057466
Körber, A., Stephanskirchen, Simssee 073915
Koerner, Ann, New Orleans 090576
Körner, Ralf, Olsberg 126595
Koerner, Valentin, Baden-Baden . . .133739, 138709
Körnig, Uwe, Frankfurt am Main . . . 139089
Köröndi, Budapest 105525
't Körrefke, Maastricht 078611
Körs, Wilhelm, Düsseldorf 102519
Körtgen, Rendsburg 104718
Kössl, Ried im Innkreis . . . 057221, 133131
Kössner, Leopold, Litschau 137227
Köster, D.C.H., Kiel 071832
Köster, H., Hilden 071517
Köster, Hubert, Braunschweig 069986
Kösters, Wilhelm, Münster 072916
Koestler, B., München . . . 072754, 104246
Koether, Mario, Falkenstein, Vogtland 070676
Koether, Mario, Falkenstein, Vogtland 070677
Koetser, David, Zürich 112128
Het Koetshuis, Den Haag 029429
Koetsudo, Tokyo 107064
Koetz, Walter, Köln 103660
Köyhän Maalarin Kehys- ja Taidekauppa, Tampere 060628
Köyliön Torpparimuseo, Tuiskula . . 010158
Középkori O-Zsinagóga, Soproni Múzeum, Sopron 021844
Közlekedési Múzeum, Budapest . . . 021663
Központi Bányászati Múzeum, Sopron 021845
Központi Kohászati Múzeum, Miskolc 021788
Koffie- en Theemuseum, Amsterdam 029195
Koffie- en Winkelmuseum, Pieterburen 030042
Koffie Verkeert, Rotterdam 108191
Koffiebanderij De Gulden Tas, Bree . 003259
Koffler Centre School of Visual Arts, Toronto 049819
Koffler Gallery, Toronto 006608
Kofmel, Walter, Deitingen 130005
Kofukuji Kokuhokan, Nara 026893
Kogado, Tokyo 077272
Kogal, Bern 111263
Kogando, Osaka 077177
Køge Museum, Køge 008994
Kogei Murata, Tokyo 107065
Kogire Kai Auction, Kyoto 121742
Koglin, Matthias, Hamburg 071265
Kogoj, Oskar, Miren 109995
Kogoj, Oskar, Žalec 110011
KOH Art Gallery, New York 118099
Kohan Densitograph, Tokyo 134726
Kohán Múzeum, Gyula 021735
Kohdo Bijutsu Kyokai, Chofu 053788
Kohl, Georg, Rosenheim 073574
Kohl, Marie-Luise, Aachen 101518
Kohl Children's Museum, Wilmette . 049198
Kohlbacher, Peter, Saarbrücken . . . 073634
Kohler, Rorschach 111847
Kohler, Villingen-Schwenningen . . . 074216
Kohler, Christine, Winterthur 082914, 122357
Kohler, Douglas B., Columbus 088419
Kohler, M., Meilen 111726
Kohlhammer, W., Stuttgart 134414
Kohli, Christine, Saanen 082760
Kohli, Emil, Saanen 082761
Kohlmann, Dres. Matthias & Thomas, Gräfelfing 071077
Kohlpoth, Offenbach am Main 073187
Kohlross, A., Haiger 071170
Kohlweyer, W., Braunschweig 138928
Kohn, Barmstedt 069472
Kohn, Francine, Saint-Ouen 067819
Kohn, Marc-Arthur, Paris 121160
Kohn, Michael, Los Angeles 116810
Kohok, Tain-l'Hermitage 101306
Kohr, Adolf, Bamberg 138715
Kohtla Kaevanduspark-muuseum, Ida 009364
Kohut, Darina, Bern 111264
Kohut, Jan Maciej, Torino . 076828, 128317
Kohut Maciej, Jan, Torino 128318
Koine, Napoli 106377
Koine, Roma 128077
Koinz, Pittsburgh 091832
Koita, Mory, Milano 075748
Koizumi Yakumo Kinenkan, Matsue 026785
Koj, W., Einbeck 070529
Kok & Zoon, Bilthoven 128588
Kok & Zoon, A., Amsterdam 140313
Koke, Danette, New York 118100
Koke'e Natural History Museum, Kauai 044937
Kokemäen Maatalousmuseo, Kokemäki 009720
Kokemäen Ulkomuseo, Kokemäki . 009721
Kokerbeck, Bielefeld 069830
Kokerbeck, Bielefeld 069831
Kokerbeck, Bielefeld 102123
Kokerei Zollverein, Essen 017067
Kokh-Wosnitza, Tatiana A., Dienheim 125461
Kokka, Tokyo 135979
Kokkie, Haarlem 078464
Koko, New York 091009
Kokodo, Sendai 077215
Kokodo, Sendai 140179
Kokon, New York 118101
Kokon, Tilburg 108231
Kokopelli, Mönchengladbach 104095
Kokorian & Co., Wien 057467
Kokoro, Paris 066119
Kokot, Elżbieta, Gniezno 079603
Kokubunji Cultural Exhibition Center, Kokubunji 026682
Kokubunji-shi Bunkazai Hozonkan, Kokubunji 026683
Kokugado, Tokyo 077273, 128450
Kokugakuin University Archaeological Collection, Tokyo 027187
Kokuritsu Kagaku Hakubutsukan, Tokyo 027188
Kokuritsu Kokusai Bijutsukan, Suita 027088
Kokuritsu Minzokugaku Hakubutsukan, Minpaku, Suita 027089
Kokuritsu Rekishi Minzoku Hakubutsukan, Sakura 027022
Kokuritsu Seiyo Bijutsukan, Tokyo . 027189
Kokusai Bijutsu Renmei Nihon linkai, Tokyo 053789
Kola, Anja L., Boston 115194
Kolaitis, Giannis, Patrai 074626
Kolans, Belo Horizonte 096468
Kolar, N., Slovenj Gradec 110006
Kolarik, Walter, Linz 137220
Kolarik, Walter & Gudrun, Wien . . . 137334
Kolarin Kunnan Kotiseutumuseo, Sieppijärvi 010074
Kolawski, K., Leipzig 103887
Kolb, Baden-Baden 069421
Kolb, München 072755
Kolb, Anne-Jacqueline, Bern 129963
Kolb, Erwin, Wetzikon 141310
Kolb, Gerhard, Lauterach 123407
Kolb, Hartwig W., Lohr am Main . . . 103937
Kolb, Martin Arnulf, Wien 057468
Kolb, Wolfgang, Ulm 074146
Kolb, Wolfgang & Sylvia, Stiefenhofen 073918
Kolbe, Hildegard, Urbar 074166
Kolbenheyer-Archiv und Gedenkstätte, Geretsried 017378
Kolbien, R. & M., Garbsen 102914, 133968
Kolbinger, Alfred, Regensburg 126692
Koldo Mitxelena Kulturunea Erakustaret, Donostia-San Sebastián 035149
Kolekcjoner, Poznań 079691
Kolen, F., Montevideo 087326
Kolhammer, Alfred, Klosterneuburg 057119
Kolhammer, Alfred, Wien 057469
Kolhapur Museum, Kolhapur 022210
Kolibius-Best, Gudrun, Herdecke . . 103354
Kolin, B., Zug 112220
Kolinda Gallery, Alstonville 094150
Kolisch, Heinz, Wien 137335
Kolk Raamatuantikvariaat, Tallinn . . 137918
Kolkmann, Stephan, Coesfeld 070151
Kollar, A.J., Seattle 119950
Kollectible Kingdom, Las Vegas . . . 089588
Kollector's Kastle, Tucson 093244
Kolledž Iskusstv, Meždunarodnyj Vostočno-Evropejskij Universitet, Iževsk . . . 050635
Kolleg für Grafik-Design, Linz 049639
Kollegium der Restauratoren, Berlin 125238
Kollekcija, Sankt-Peterburg 080307
Kollekcija Drevnostej, Moskva 080248
Kollekcioner, Sankt-Peterburg 080308
Kollekcioner-M, Sankt-Peterburg . . 080309
Kollektion Lindenau, Leipzig 103888
Koller, Budapest 105526
Koller, Genève . . . 082439, 111477, 122323

Koller, München 121534
Koller, Schaan 121754
Koller, Zürich 082991
Koller, Zürich 112129, 122369, 141346
Koller, Andrea, Iserlohn 071633
Koller-Piskernik, Dr. Elke, Sankt Gallen 082781
Kollmann, Annette, Leonberg, Württemberg 126214
Kollmann, Armin, Osterholz-Scharmbeck 126602
Kollmann, Kurt, Breddorf 125382
Kollmann & Sachtlebe, Halle, Saale 103070
Kollmeier, Beate, Essen 102694
Kollschegg, Uwe, Ahrensburg 069120
Kollwitz & Klinger, Dresden 133878
Kolly, Michel, Marly 082646
Kolmanová, Eva, Poděbrady 123968
Kolmanskop Museum, Kolmanskop 029084
Koło Galeria, Gdańsk 108890
Kolodziejski-Zieba, Wieslaw-M., Roding 126724
Kolomoki Mounds State Park Museum, Blakely 042249
Kolonaki, Antwerpen 057709
Koloniaal, Antwerpen 057710
Kolonija, Moskva 109558
Kolouch, Vlastimil, Ústí nad Labem . 060200
Kolpings- und Handwerksmuseum im Faltertor, Dettelbach 016692
Kolska Auktioner, Kolsva 122179
Kolta, Kyïv 112413
Koltermann, H., Schnega 073710
Kolthek, F., Amsterdam 077889
Kolthoon, Amsterdam 077890
Kolton, Ursula, Weinstadt 126985
Kolumba, Diözesanmuseum Köln, Köln 018323
Komagata Jukichi Bijutsu Kinenkan, Nagaoka 026846
Komárek, Pavel, Praha 123986
Komatsu Hitoshi Art Museum, Kyoto 026728
Komatsu Shiritsu Hakubutsukan, Komatsu 026685
Komatzki, Feldmeilen 111403, 141240
Komi-Permjackij Okružnoj Kraevedčeskij Muzej im. Subbotina-Permjaka, Kudymkar 033313
Komi Respublikanskij Istoriko-Kraevedčeskij Muzej, Syktyvkar 033921
Komimarkt, Basel 082148
Komis Meblowy, Warszawa 079761, 129092
Komiyama, Tokyo 140191
Kommandør Chr. Christensen's Hvalfangst Museum, Sandefjord 031166
Kommissiehuis Kanapee, Amersfoort 077747
Kommissionshaus Sankt Andrä, Salzburg 057263
Die Kommode, Stuhr 073948
Kommödchen, Bad Lauterberg 069320
Kommödchen, Hünxe 071590
Das Kommödchen, Neustadt am Rübenberge 073021
Kommunale Galerie, Darmstadt . . . 016640
Kommunale Galerie, Kunstamt Charlottenburg-Wilmersdorf, Berlin 016093
Kommunale Galerie Gelsenkirchen, Gelsenkirchen 017356
Kommunale Galerie im Leinwandhaus, Frankfurt am Main 017180
Komoka Railway Museum, Komoka 005724
Komorowska-Sławiec, Anna, Warszawa 129093
Komperon Kotiseutumuseo, Viinijärvi 010239
Kompleksi Monumental i Lidhjes Shqiptare të Prizrenit, Prizren 034250
Komponierstube Gustav Mahlers, Steinbach am Attersee 002696
Komposch, Helmut, Altach 056914
Økomuseum Grenseland, Sarpsborg 031174
Kon-Tiki Museum, Oslo 031083
Konak, İstanbul 083143
Konark, Kolkata 074816
Koncz & Társa, Balatonfüred 074654
Kondeyne & Borgemeister, Inga, Berlin 101954
Kondo-Tchouko, Eyoutekebiye, Les Abymes 074644
Kondo Yuzo Memorial Museum, Kyoto 026729
Kondor Gallery, Silverwater 095194
Kondorosi, J., Rothenburg 130153
Kondos Art Gallery, Sacramento City College, Sacramento 047591
Kondras, John, New York 132487
Koneczny, P., London 131080
Konfeksjonsmuseet, Romsdalsmuseet, Molde 031029
Kong Shu Ming, Hong Kong 059654
Det Kongelige Akademi for de skønne Kunster, København 049903
Den Kongelige Mønt- og Medaillesamling, Nationalmuseet, København 008971
Den Kongelige Mynts Museum, Kongsberg 030944
Det Kongelige Nordiske Oldskriftselskab, København 052856
Kongenhus Mindeparks Museum, Viborg 009148
Konginkankaan Kotiseutumuseo, Konginkangas 009728
Kongkan, Busan 107170
Kongkan, Busan 107171
Kongosho-ji Treasure House, Ise . . 026571
Kongsberg Ski Museum, Department of Norwegian Mining Museum, Kongsberg 030945
Kongsberg Våpenfabrikks Museum, Kongsberg 030946
Kongshantang, Beijing 097670
Kongsvinger Festningsmuseum, Kongsvinger 030949
Konietzko, Julius, Hamburg 071266
Konigorski, Gabriele, Kleve 071876
De Koningshoek, Amsterdam 077891
't Koningshof, Deventer 078277
Koninklijk Militair Historisch Museum, Armamentarium, Delft 029408
Koninklijk Museum voor Schone Kunsten Antwerpen, Antwerpen 003163
Koninklijk Nederlands Leger- en Wapenmuseum, Armamentarium, Delft 029408
Koninklijk Oudheidkundig Genootschap, Amsterdam 029196
Koninklijk Paleis te Amsterdam, Amsterdam 029197
Het Koninklijk Penningkabinet, Leiden 029848
Koninklijk Tehuis voor Oud-Militairen en Museum Bronbeek, Arnhem 029269
Koninklijke Academie van Beeldende Kunsten, Den Haag 050555
Koninklijke Academie voor Beeldende Kunsten, Mechelen 049719
Koninklijke Academie voor Schone Kunsten, Antwerpen 049676
Koninklijke Academie voor Schone Kunsten, Dendermonde 049695
Koninklijke Academie voor Schone Kunsten, Kortrijk 049710
Koninklijke Hoofdgilde Sint-Sebastiaan, Brugge 003272
Koninklijke Kring voor Oudheidkunde, Letteren en Kunst van Mechelen, Mechelen 052681
Koninklijke Kunstkring Heikracht, Lommel 052682
Koninklijke Maatschappij voor Dierkunde van Antwerpen, Antwerpen 003164
Koninklijke Vlaamse Academie van België voor Wetenschappen en Kunsten, Bruxelles 052683
Konishi, Los Angeles 089815
Konjušenny Muzej -Muzej Avtomobil'nogo Transporta, Sankt-Peterburg 033758
Konkol, Steffen, Rathmannsdorf . . . 073425
Konkursbuch, Tübingen 134432
Konneveden Kotiseutumuseo, Konnevesi 009729
Konoha, Tokyo 107066
Konopatzki, C. & K.-H., Braunschweig 069987
Konouz, Manama 057635
Konrad, Winnipeg 123870
Konrad, Anton H., Weißenhorn 134452
Konrad jun., Gustav, Moosthenning 072595
Konrad, Nils, Ellhofen 070538
Konrad, Renate, Wien 057470
Konrad-Falz, Wolfgang, Hildesheim 125933
Konradsburg Ermsleben, Ermsleben 017042
Konros, Sankt-Peterburg 121969
Konschak, M. & I, Schwangau 073755
Konservointikeskus, Jyväskylä 124054
Konserwacja Dziel Sztuki, Pozłotnictwo, Warszawa 129094
Konst-, Design- och Antikvitetsmässa i Stockholm, Nacka 093883
Konst i Lund, Lund 110954
Konst Världen och Disajn, Stockholm 136111
Konstandoglou Collection, Athinai . 021179
Konstantinovskij Dvorec, Sankt-Peterburg 033759
Konstanzer Atelier, Bötzingen 069905
Konstfack, Hägersten 050747
Konstföreningen Aura Krognoshuset, Lund 054136, 110955
Konstfrämjandet, Örebro 054137
Konstfrämjandet i Västerbotten, Umeå 054138, 111087
Konstfrämjandet Skåne, Malmö . . .054139, 110974
Konstgalleri Svenska Bilder, Stockholm 111058
Konsthistorisk Tidskrift, Stockholm 136112
Konsthistoriska Sällskapet, Institut for Konstvetenskap, Stockholm 054140
Konstlagningsspecialisten, Malmö . 129850
Konstmuseum, Lund 036442
Konstmuseum Gösta Werner och Havet, Simrishamn 036571
Konstmuseum Gösta Werner och Rådhusets Konsthall, Örnsköldsvik 036526
Konstnärernas Riksorganisation, Stockholm 054141
Konstnärshuset, Stockholm 054142, 111059
Konstperspektiv, Malmö 136113
Konstsalongen, Helsinki 060541
Konstsamlingarna, Uppsala Universitet, Uppsala 036738
Konstvetenskapliga Institutionen, Göteborg 050746
Konstvetenskapliga Institutionen, Uppsala Universitet, Uppsala 050753
Kontainer, Los Angeles 116811
Kontakt Impex, Poznań 079692
Konteksty. Polska Sztuka Ludowa, Warszawa 136025
Kontextverlag, Berlin 133787
Kontiolahden Museo, Kontiolahti . . 009730
Kontrast Galerie, Wohlen (Aargau) . 112004
Kontur, Wien 135558
Konventmuseum der Barmherzigen Brüder, Wien 002925
Konvolut, Roma 140106
Konya Devlet Güzel Sanatlar Galerisi, Konya 038134
Konz & Peterek, Aschaffenburg . . . 069199
Konzeptgalerie buepa.com, Berlin .101955, 133788
Konzert, Franz, Innsbruck 057084
Konzett, Philipp, Graz 095535
Koo, Alfred, Singapore 080511
Koo de Kir Art, Boston 115195
Koochiching County Historical Society Museum, International Falls 044760
Kooiman, P., Ottoland 128802
kooio, Innsbruck 135559
Kooistra, E., Amsterdam 077892
Kook, Petra, Werl 105207
Kook Museum, Jerusalem 022962
Kookaburra Antiques, Cairns 055597
Kookaburra Books, Battery Point . . 136793
Kookaburras Gallery, Bonny Hills . . 094265
Kookmin College Museum, Seoul . . 027569
Kool, A.W. de, Dordrecht 107980
Kool Braun, Negril 106829
Kool Kitchens, Pittsburgh 091833
Kool Kollectables, Las Vegas 089589
Kool Toiz Collectibles, El Paso 088805
Koolau, Honolulu 116222
Koolen, Françoise, Venterol 101447
Kools, C., Amsterdam 128544
Koompartoo, San Gwann 077526
Koop, Oldenzaal 128795
Koop, Heinz, Papenburg 073291
Koop, Sigrid, Bochum 069887
Koop, Wolfgang, Düsseldorf 139016
Koopjes Bazar, Almelo 077727
Koopkunst, Rotterdam 108192
Koopman, London 085462
Koopmans-De Wet House Museum, Iziko Museums of Cape Town, Cape Town 034579
Koorda Museum, Koorda 001160
Koorenman, Leiden 078572
Koori Kullas, Goulburn 055908
Koorie, Melbourne 056191
Koorie Heritage Trust Cultural Centre, Melbourne 056192
Koorn, P., Alkmaar 077716
Koornmarktspoort, Kampen 029801
Kootenai Brown Pioneer Village, Pincher Creek 006153
Kootenay Gallery of Art, History and Science, Castlegar 005234
Kootenay School of Art, Nelson . . . 049805
Kooymans, Den Haag 078208
Kop, Arnhem 078054, 128570
Kop van Zuid, Rotterdam 108193
Kopatz-Baumann, Sigrun, Homburg 129279
Kopecká, Hradec Králové 123956
Kopeikin, Paul, Los Angeles 116812
De Koperen Bol, Enschede 078372
Kopermolen, Vaals 030242
Koperslagersmuseum Van der Beele, Horst 029777
Kopetz, Hanny, Bayreuth . 069491, 138722
Kopiergerätemuseum, Wien 002926
Kopitzki, Bernau bei Berlin 069798
Kopitzki, Michael, Bernau bei Berlin 069799, 125322
Koplin del Rio, West Hollywood . . . 120394
Kopp, Bad Homburg v.d.Höhe 069293
Kopp, Saarbrücken 073635
Kopp, Annette, Großmaischeid 071122, 125765
Kopp, Rainer, Berlin 069668
Koppány, László, Budapest 105527
Kopparberget Gruvmuseum, Falun . 036266
Koppe, Markus, Nordstemmen 073087
Koppel, Alan, Chicago 115471
Koppelwiser, Schwerin 073773
Koppen, Bussum 078133
Koppius, Bernd, Altenburg, Thüringen 069149
Koprikorn, Varna 096774
Kopriva, Manfred, Krems . 095633, 133108
Kopsendal, Malden 128768
Het Koptisch Museum, Ruinerwold . 030114
Kor Gallery, Kitchener 096933
Koraalberg, Antwerpen 096076
Korablinskij Kraevedčeskij Muzej, Korablino 033282
Koralewski, Paris 100564
Korallen- und Heimatmuseum, Nattheim 019181
Korb, Magdeburg 072372
Korb, Heinrich, Linz 137221
Korber, Ralph, Berlin 069669
Korbmacher, C., Burg bei Magdeburg 070094
Korbmacher-Museum, Malsfeld . . . 018802
Korçë Museum, Korçë 000025
Korczak, Mariusz, Łódź 109010
Kordegarda, Warszawa 109150
Kordeuter, Zürich 082992
Korea Antique Company, Seoul 077367
Korea Art Auction, Seoul 121750
Korea Art Gallery, Busan 107172

Korea Art Gallery, Seoul 107263
Korea Craft Artist Association, Seoul 053821
Korea Culture and Art Foundation, Seoul 053822
Korea Maritime University Museum, Busan 027460
Korea University Museum, Seoul . . 027570
Korea War Memorial, Seoul 027571
Korean Agricultural Museum, Seoul 027572
Korean Art Gallery, Pyongyang 027437
Korean Central Ethnographic Museum, Pyongyang 027438
Korean Central Historical Museum, Pyongyang 027439
Korean Culture And Arts Foundation, Venezia 106759
Korean Culture Library, Los Angeles 142514
Korean Fine Arts Association, Seoul 053823
Korean Furniture Museum, Seoul . . 027573
Korean International Art Fair, Seoul 093808
Korean Magazine Museum, Seoul . 027574
Korean Museum, Los Angeles 045437
Korean Museum Association, Seoul 053824
Korean Museum Association, Seoul 053825
Korean Museum of Contemporary Clothing, Seoul 027575
Korean National Committee for the International Council of Museums (ICOM), Seoul 053826
Korean National University of Arts, Seoul 050512
Korean Professional Artists Association, Seoul 053827
Korean Revolutionary Museum, Pyongyang 027440
Korean Ski Museum, Ganseong . . . 027490
Korean War Veterans National Museum, Tuscola 048667
Koreana Art and Antiques, New York 091010
Koreana Folkcraft, Seoul 077368
Koreck & Langenbacher, Füssen . . 125692
Korecký, Dr. Miroslav, Praha 060137, 098468
Korekawa Archaeological Museum, Hachinohe 026479
Koreman, Frans, Amsterdam 128545
Koren en Pel Molen De Eendracht, Anjum 029249
Koren en Pelmolen De Noordstar, Noordbroek 029971
Korenke, H., Frankfurt am Main . . . 139090
Korenmolen de Hoop, Hellendoorn . 029714
Korenmolen de Hoop, Klarenbeek . . 029812
Korenmolen de Phenix, Nes 029939
Korenmolen de Zandhaas, Santpoort 030118
Korenwolf, Herkenbosch 140458
Koreshan Historic Site, Estero 043736
Korhonen, Pekka, Jyväskylä 060601
Koridon, J.G.M., Almelo 077728
Koriyama City Museum of Art, Koriyama 026688
Korkea Vuoren Antiikki, Helsinki . . . 060542
Korn, Harry, Handschuheim 063123
Korn, M.E., London 141839
Kornby, Cairns 055598, 136838
Korne, H., Rheinbach 073516
Kornelius-Galerie, Aachen 101519
Kornfeld & Cie., Bern 111265, 122313, 134994, 141228
Kornfeld & Cie., Zürich 112130
Kornhamnstorgs Antikvariat, Stockholm 141162
Kornhaus Georgenthal-Klosterruinen, Georgenthal 017368
Kornhaus-Museum, Weiler-Simmerberg 020728
Kornhausforum, Bern 036928
Kornowski, Dr. Gerhard, Flensburg . 125640
Kornschütte, Luzern 037298
Kornye, Dallas 088545, 115902
Kornye, Fort Worth 116150
Koroit Antiques, Koroit 056066
Koroneou, Eleni, Athinai 105402
Koronowicz, Mark, Prahran 056495

Koroška Galerija Likovnih Umetnosti, Slovenj Gradec 034522
Koroški Muzej Ravne na Koroškem, Ravne na Koroškem 034517
Korper, Olga, Toronto 097308
Korpilahden Kotiseutumuseo, Korpilahti 009733
Korppoon Kotiseutumuseo, Korppoo 009734
Korsch, A., Gilching 133975
Korsgren, Eric & Stefan, Stockholm 081975
Korsnäs Hembygdsmuseum, Korsnäs 009735
Korsør By- og Overfartsmuseum, Korsør 009002
Kort & Bilder, Hägersten 134959
Kortárs Művészeti Múzeum - Ludwig Múzeum Budapest, Budapest . . . 021664
Kortás Galéria, Debrecen . 074729, 105556
Kortás Galéria, Kecskemét 105565
Korte, Klaus, Hamburg 071267
Kortedala Museum, Göteborg 036298
Kortelisy Historical Museum, Kortelisy 038290
Kortesjärven Museo, Kortesjärvi . . . 009737
Kortforlaget, Oslo 108732
Korth, A., Krummhörn 072098
Korth, Benedikt, Köln 071969
Kortjakje, Nijmegen 078657
Kortländer, Karin, München 072756
Kortmann, U. & E., Nordkirchen . . . 104468
Kortright Centre Museum, Woodbridge 006881
Korttien Talo, Hämeenlinna 009493
Kortum, Leipzig 072206
Koru-Kivi Antiques, Helsinki 060543
Koru NZ Art, Dunedin 108437
Korvenkylän Nuorisoseuran Museo, Muhniemi 009879
Korvensuun Museo, Mynämäki 009890
Korvensuun Voimalaitos- ja Konepajamuseo, Mynämäki 009891
Koryo Museum of Art, Kyoto 026730
Koryo Taehakyo Pakmulgwan, Seoul 027576
Korytowski, Peter, Ratingen 104661
Koryu-ji Reihoden, Kyoto 026731
Korzelius, Thomas, New York 118102
Kosak, Christine, Baden bei Wien . . 095473
Kosanji Temple Museum, Toyota, Hiroshima 027293
Kosbab, Tom, Tetenbüll 105042
Koschatmuseum, Klagenfurt 002140
Kościańska-Orth, Zofia, Kraków . . .079643, 140740
Kosciuszko-Museum, Solothurn . . . 037576
Kosensky, Prof. Hugo, Neu-Purkersdorf 123421
Kosetsu Bijutsukan, Kobe 026668
Koshare Indian Museum, La Junta . 045072
Kosian, Silvia, Wien 095880
Kosido, Ruse 096709
Kosig, Detlef, Berlin 069670
Kosken Kotiseutumuseo, Koski 009738
Koskenniskan Mylly- ja Kievarimuseo, Tuupovaara 010183
Koskowski, B., Dornum 070276
Koslowski & Müller, Chemnitz 138965
Kośmicki, Michał, Poznań 129063
Kosmos, Warszawa 140786
Kosnowski, Andrzej J., Warszawa . 140787
Kosowski, Włodzimierz, Warszawa . 129095
Kossär, Alexander, Graz 057018
Kossann, Roger, Bremen 125389
Kossert, Oschatz 073226
Kossuth Lajos Emlékmúzeuma, Magyar Nemzeti Múzeum, Monok 021794
Kossuth Lajos Tudomamyegyetem, Debrecen 050286
Kossuth Múzeum, Cegléd 021706
Kost, Gabriela, Hamburg 071268
Kostabi, New York 118103
Kostallet Antikt & Kuriosa, Helsingborg 081833
Kostede Museum für Überlebenskunst, Kamen 018142

Kostel, Paris 100565
Koster, Hans & Ria, Amsterdam . . . 077893
Kostercraft, North Richmond 056372
Kostia, Jacques, Lyon 124360
Kostorek, Radoslav, Olomouc 060062
Kostoulakos, Peter, Lowell 132312
Kostromskoj Gosudarstvennyj Istoriko-architekturnyj Muzej-zapovednik, Kostroma 033286
Kostromskoj Gosudarstvennyj Obedinennyj Chudožestvennyj Muzej, Kostroma 033287
Kostrzewa, Bernard, Blénod-les-Toul 061513, 124103
Kostüm-Museum im neuen Schloß Schleißheim, Bayerisches Nationalmuseum, Oberschleißheim 019415
Kostuummuseum De Gouden Leeuw, Noordhorn 029973
Koszta József Múzeum, Szentes . . . 021890
Kotalla, Ralf, Haigerloch 125783
Koterba, Edward, Los Angeles 132260
Kotikadun Mainio, Helsinki 060544
Kotiseutumuseo, Jurva 009629
Kotiseutumuseo Lukkarin Puustelli, Loppi 009839
Kotiseutumuseo Muina, Rauma . . . 010023
Kotiseutumuseo Pellava ja Sahti Lammin Ajokalumuseo, Lammi 009798
Kotiseututalo, Noormarkku 009909
Kotitaidenäyttely Halmeila, Lahti . . 098755
Kotkaniemi - Presidentti P.E. Svinhufvudin koti, Luumäki 009845
Koto-ku Fukagawa Edo Siryokan, Tokyo 027190
Kotobuki, München 104247
Kotohira-gu Museum, Kotohira 026689
Kotsu Hakubutsukan, Tokyo 027191
Kotsu Kagaku Hakubutsukan, Osaka 026967
Kotte, Kaufering 139311
Kottmann, Renate, Oberstaufen . . . 104506
Kottmeier, Hans-Jörg, Trier 074096, 139789
Kotuku Gallery, Whataroa 108671
Kotulova Dřevěnka, Muzeum Těšínska, Havířov 008365
Kotzebue Museum, Kotzebue 045048
Kotzev, Atanas, Nittendorf 073062
Kotzinger, H., Glonn 102963
Kotziok, Roman, München 134254
Kougea, Eleni, Athinai 105403
Kougeas, Ioannis, Athinai 139897
Koukodo, Tokyo 077274
Koukos, Nikol., Thessaloniki 105449
Koulumuseo, Helsingin Kaupunginmuseo, Helsinki 009545
Kourion Museum, Episkopi 008205
Kouros, New York 118104
Kourosh, Berlin 101956
Kourtidis, Ioan E., Athinai 074596
Kousbroek, Rudy, Arnhem 107853
Kouseiroudoushou Sangyo Anzen Gijutsukan, Tokyo 027192
Koušek, Zdeněk, Praha 123987
Kouvolan Lukusoppi, Kouvola 137973
Kouvolan Taidemuseo, Kouvola . . . 009744
Kova, Witka & Dr. Lázló, Hamburg .134015, 139194
Kovac, Marie-Anne, Villette 082892
Kovacek, Peter, Wien 095881
Kovacek, Regine & Michael, Wien . . 095882
Kovacek & Zetter, Wien . . 057471, 095883
Kovacs, Brigitta, Wien 057472
Kovács, Endréné, Budapest 074691
Kovacs, Patrick, Wien 057473
Kovács Margit Kerámiagyűjtemény, Ferenczy Múzeum, Szentendre . . . 021884
Kovács Margit Múzeum, Győr 021731
Kovan, Duisburg 102583
Kovář, Pavel, Praha 060138
Kovčeg, Moskva 109559, 134878
Kovčeg, Odesa 112432
Koveks 91, Sofia 096739
Kovels on Antiques and Collectibles, Pepper Pike 136520

Kovjoki Museo, Uusikaarlepyy 010191
Kowal, Jean-Michel, Roanne 067170
Kowal, Karl-Heinz, Schwalmstadt . . 126786
Kowall, Heinrich, Mödling 057185
Kowallik, Brigitta, Neuss 139590
Kowalska, Krystyna, Wrocław 109224
Kowalski, Andrzej, Warszawa 129096
Kowasa, Barcelona 110205, 140990
Kowloon Antique Arts and Crafts, Hong Kong 059655
Kown Young Ok, Roma 076514
Koyama, Tomio, Tokyo 107067
Koyama Keizo Art Museum, Komoro 026687
Koyanagi, Tokyo 107068
Koyasan Reihokan, Koya 026690
Koyman, Toronto 097309
Koyoen Pastel Society, Nishinomiya 053790
Koyunoglu Müzesi, Konya 038135
Koz, Mandurah 094780
Kozak, Philippe, Valenciennes 068692
Kozáková, Eva, Praha 137835
Kozan, Chicago 115472
Kozierowski, Alexander, Linz 095664
Kozin, Chiba 106838
Kozloff & Meaders, Pittsburgh 091834
Kozminsky, Melbourne . . . 056193, 094817
Kozu Kobunka Museum, Kyoto 026732
De Kraal, Venlo 078837
De Kraal, Venlo 078838
Kraay, Aalst 128516
Krabb, Herbert, Kuchl 057135
De Krabbedans, Eindhoven 108001
Kracer, Miami 117102
Kracheel, Klaus, Nürnberg 121565
Kracher, Wolfgang, Fürstenfeld 137171
Kracht, Hermann, Wolfsburg 105324
Kracke, Bremen 125390
Krächan, Klaus, Quierschied 073399
Kraeckel-Hansum, Thomas, Hildesheim 125934
Krähmer, Claudia & Andree, Köln . .071970, 126095
Krämer, Eisenheim 070536
Kraemer & Cie., Paris 066120
Krämer, Anton, Mitterteich 072556
Krämer, Karl, Stuttgart 134415
Krämer, Lukas, Köln 126096
Krämer, Michael, Meiningen 072502
Kraemer & Hansen, Osnabrück 139639
Kränz, Regine, Hamburg 125827
Kränzl, Göppingen 102969
Kräter, Ida & Isolde, Bern 082218
Krätzer, Hermann, Hannover 071398, 125874
Krätzler, W. Mona, München 072757
Kräuchi, Werner, Solothurn 082821
Kräutermuseum - Naturpark Jauerling Wachau, Maria Laach am Jauerling 002281
Kräutler, Anton, Koblach . . 057120, 123401
Kraevaja Detskaja Kartinnaja Galereja, Vladivostok 034046
Kraevedčeskij Muzej, Samarkand . . 049403
Kraevedčeskij Muzej Čirčika, Čirčik 049388
Kraevedčeskij Muzej Evrejskoj Avtonomnoj Oblasti, Birobidžan 033032
Kraevedčeskij Muzej g. Lomonosova, Lomonosov 033335
Kraevedčeskij Muzej g. Puškina, Puškin 033682
Kraevedčeskij Muzej g. Puškino, Puškino 033686
Kraevedčeskij Muzej Namangana, Namangan 049397
Kraevedčeskij Muzej Novgorodskogo Rajona, Velikij Novgorod 034025
Kraevoj Muzej Istorii Literatury, Iskusstva i Kultury Altaja, Barnaul 033016
Krafft, Anthony, Pully 135058
Kraft, Salt Lake City 092437
Kraft, Alfred, Spiegelau 104938
Kraft, Christina, Gotha 102986
Kraft, Konrad, Bockhorn, Oberbayern 125342
Kraft, Mavis, Tanunda 056696

Kraft, Stuart, Dallas 115903
Kraft, Thomas, Perg 123427
Kraft, Vera von, Knokke-Heist 096339, 123640
Kraft & Lieberman, Chicago 115473
Jean-Claude Kraftchik & Thierry Tramblay, Paris 100566
Kraftwerkmuseum Löntsch, Netstal 037371
Krages, Ulrike, Hamburg 071269
Krahforst, J., Datteln 070194
Krahnstöver, Matthias, Kohren-Sahlis 126129
Krahuletz-Museum, Eggenburg . . . 001808
Krainer, Harald, Karlstetten 123398
Krajanské Múzeum MS Bratislava, Bratislava 034326
Krajčírik, L'ubomír, Levoča 129277
Krajnja Chata, Luc'k 112425
Krajská Galerie, Galerie moderniho umění, Hradec Králové 008388
Krajská Galerie Výtvarného Umeni ve Zlíně, Zlín 008786
Krajské Múzeum, Prešov 034414
Krajské Muzeum Cheb, Cheb 008328
Krajské Muzeum Sokolov, Sokolov . 008691
Krak, Martina, Zossen 105371
Kråkö Båtbyggarmuseum, Kråkö . . 009748
Krakow, Barbara, Boston 115196
Krakowska, Ewa, Poznań 109055
Krakowska, Krystyna, Kraków 108958
Krakowski Antykwariat Naukowy, Kraków 140741
Kråksundet notnaust Sjøbruksmuseum, Tustna 031294
Kral, Oakland 118636
Kral, Anton, Berndorf 137157
Kral, Bretislav, Bergen, Chiemgau . 069531
Kral, Markus Johann, Hörsching . . . 057063
Kral, Werner, Baden bei Wien 056939
Kralingsmuseum, Rotterdam 030084
Krall, Artur & Marion, Bad Saulgau . 069374
Královsky Letohradek, Praha 008618
Kram, Halmstad 110938
Krambuvika Bygdemuseum, Tennevoll 031263
Kramer, Minneapolis 117278
Kramer, D., Offenburg 139624
Kramer, E., Offenburg 139625
Kramer, Edith, Wackersberg 105137
Kramer, Karin, Berlin 133789
Kramer, Waldemar, Frankfurt am Main 133947
Kramer, Wilhelm, Volkmarsen 074231
The Kramer House, Baltimore 115061
Kramm, Günter, Hamburg 071270
Kramm, Hans, Düsseldorf 125535
Krammer, Erich, Wien 137336
Kramp, Lemgo 072225
Krampitz, Hans-Jochen, Bremen . . 070029
Krampitz, Peter, Flensburg 070704
Krampitz, Peter, Flensburg 070705
Krampl, Reinhard, Weißkirchen in Steiermark 057348
Krampus, Trieste 076897
Kramski, M., Burgdorf, Kreis Hannover 102291
Kranefuß von Both, Theres, Neuss . 126538
Kranenburg, A., Borken, Westfalen . 102204
Kranendonk, Amsterdam 077894
Kranich, Zürich 130248
Kranich & Kurmann, Zürich 112131
Das Kranichhaus, Museum des alten Landes Hadeln, Otterndorf 019537
Kranister, Klosterneuburg 095626
Krankenhaus-Museum am Zentralkrankenhaus Bremen-Ost, Bremen 016417
Krankenhausgalerie, Castrop-Rauxel 102300
Krankenhausmuseum, Nürnberg . . 019362
Krannert Art Museum, University of Illinois, Champaign 042704
Krans, J., Drachtstercompagnie . . . 128653
Kranz, Edith, Hennef 103351
Kranz & Sohn, Kristina, Braunschweig 069988, 121355
Kranz, M., Beckum 069504
Kranz, Manfred, Frankfurt am Main 070760
Kranzbühler, Gero, Osnabrück 073240
Krapohl, Ulrich, Heikendorf 125904
Kras, Ulft 128852
Krasl Art Center, Saint Joseph 047642
Krāslavas Vēstures un Mākslas Muzejs, Krāslava 027701
Krasnodarskij Chudožestvennyj Muzej im. F.A. Kovalenko, Krasnodar 033290
Krasnodarskij Gosudarstvennyj Istoriko-archeologičeskij Muzej-zapovednik, Krasnodar 033291
Krasnodarskij Gosudarstvennyj Universitet Kultury i Iskusstv, Krasnodar 050641
Krasnodarskij Vystavočnyj Zal, Krasnodar 033292
Krasnojarskij Chudožestvennyj Muzej im. V.I. Surikova, Krasnojarsk 033294
Krasnojarskij Gorodskoj Vystavočnyj Zal, Krasnojarsk 033295
Krasnojarskij Istoričeskij Muzej Memorial Pobedy, Krasnojarsk 033296
Krasnojarskij Kraevoj Kraevedčeskij Muzej, Krasnojarsk 033297
Krasnojarskij Kulturno-istoričeskij Muzejnyj Kompleks, Krasnojarsk 033298
Krasnokamskaja Kartinnaja Galereja, Krasnokamsk 033303
Krasnokamskij Kraevedčeskij Muzej, Krasnokamsk 033304
Krasnoturinskij Kraevedčeskij Muzej, Krasnoturinsk 033305
Krasnye Palaty XVII Veka, Moskva .080249, 109560
Krass, Rosario 094105
Krasser, Dr. Alexander, Wernberg . .057359, 095784
Kraszewski-Museum, Stadtmuseum Dresden, Dresden 016792
Kratochvíl, Josef, Klatovy . 060034, 123960
Kratz &Co., Dr. E. J., Hamburg 071271
Kraus, Nashville 117359
Kraus, Barbara, Øyslebø 108742
Kraus, Carole, New York 118105
Kraus, E., Overath 073275
Kraus, Gérard, Versailles 068809
Kraus, H.P., New York 142669
Kraus, Jürgen, Pirmasens 073330
Kraus, M., Hemhofen 071485
Kraus, Monika & Jörg-Rudolf, Hörsching 057064
Kraus, Sylvia, Santiago de Chile . . . 059537
Kraus, Werner, München 072758
Kraus & Silbernagel, Berlin 121334
Krause, Almere 077740
Krause, Iola 135368
Krause, Helmut, Mörfelden-Walldorf 072579, 126327
Krause, Hermann, Köln . . 103661, 139345
Krause, Joachim, Mannheim 139454
Krause, Jochen, Bielefeld 069832
Krause, Oliver, Berlin 125239
Krause, Oskar, Pfäffikon (Zürich) . .111808, 135057
Krause, Peter-Jörg, Berlin 101957
Kraushaar, New York 118106
Kraushaar, Gaby, Düsseldorf 102520
Krausmann, Walter, Ried im Innkreis 057222
Krauß, Dennis, Perleberg 073307
Krauß, Rudolf, Oelsnitz, Vogtland . . 073181
Krauß, Sylvia, Stuttgart 126862
Krauß, U., Ulm 139809
Krausz, Ron, München 072759
Kraut, Roztoky u Prahy 124006
Kraut, Michael, Bleiburg . . 056948, 095479
Krautgartner, Karin, Ried im Innkreis 057223
Krauts, Frankfurt am Main 070761
Kravets Wehby, New York 118107
Krawarik, Wien 057474
Krawczyk, Edmund, Lublin 079678
Kraxenberger, R., Erharting 070593
Kray, Oakland 132571
Krazie Gal's Kloset, Jacksonville . . 089422
Krbušek, Jaroslav, Praha 098469
Krchňavý, Telč 060195
Kreations Gallery, Rosebud 095160
Kreativo, Cancún 107467
Kreatum Interieur, Genk 058161
Krebber & Schmid, Werne 105214
Krebs, Witten 074454
Krebs, Bianka, Fürth, Bayern 102903
Krebs, D., Königswinter 072039
Krebs, D., Visselhövede 074221
Krebs, Elisabeth, Wien 123510
Krebs, Karin, Bremen 070030
Krebs & Co., Karl Heinz, Bremen . . 133845
Krebs, Martin, Bern 111266
Krebs, Roswitha, Witten 074455
Krebs, Thekla, Hamburg 125828
Krebsen, København 098578
Krebser, Thun 082851, 141305
Kreckovic, L. & E., London 085463, 131081
The Kreeger Museum, Washington . 048916
Krefelder Kunstmuseen, Kaiser Wilhelm Museum, Museum Haus Lange, Museum Haus Esters, Krefeld 018399
Krefelder Kunstverein e.V., Krefeld . 053260
Kreft, I., Spenge 104930
Kreft, Sylvia, Chemnitz 102312
Dieter Kreft & Lilo Kreft-Hirschinger, Dahn 102336
Kregl, Renate, Kirchberg-Thening . .057097, 137201
Kreijmborg, E.H.M., Amsterdam . . . 077895
Kreil, München 104248
Kreinberg, Sidney, Cleveland 088339, 131965
Kreis, J., Battenberg, Eder 069483
Kreis Feuerwehrmuseum Lohmen, Lohmen bei Güstrow 018677
Kreis-Heimatmuseum, Bad Frankenhausen 015698
Kreis- und Heimatmuseum, Bogen . 016306
Kreis- und Stadtmuseum, Dieburg . 016698
Kreis- und Universitätsmuseum Helmstedt, Helmstedt 017866
Kreisagrarmuseum, Dorf Mecklenburg 016747
Kreischer, Anton, Bad Schönborn . . 069375
Kreischer, Jürgen, Ubstadt-Weiher . 074129
Kreisgalerie, Dahn 016628
Kreisgalerie, Mellrichstadt 018900
Kreisheimatmuseum, Helmstedt . . . 017866
Kreisheimatmuseum, Luckenwalde 018690
Kreisheimatmuseum, Demmin 016668
Kreisheimatmuseum, Frankenberg, Eder 017143
Kreisheimatmuseum, Grimma 017538
Kreisheimatmuseum Striediecks Hof, Museum Bünde, Bünde 016496
Kreisheimatmuseum Weißes Haus, Rotenburg an der Fulda 019906
Kreisheimatstube, Ellzee 016947
Kreisheimatstuben Riederau, Dießen am Ammersee 016702
Kreisler, Madrid 110556
Kreisler, Lesley, Taranaki 108570
Kreismuseum, Blankenheim, Ahr . . 016262
Kreismuseum, Neuwied 019298
Kreismuseum, Oschersleben 019489
Kreismuseum, Osterburg 019505
Kreismuseum, Rathenow 019720
Kreismuseum Bad Liebenwerda, Bad Liebenwerda 015749
Kreismuseum Bitterfeld, Bitterfeld . 016258
Kreismuseum der Heimatvertriebenen, Seligenstadt 020184
Kreismuseum Finsterwalde, Finsterwalde 017123
Kreismuseum Geilenkirchen, Geilenkirchen 017338
Kreismuseum Gräfenhainichen, Oranienbaum 019476
Kreismuseum Heinsberg, Heinsberg 017859
Kreismuseum Herzogtum Lauenburg, Ratzeburg 019727
Kreismuseum Jerichower Land, Genthin 017364
Kreismuseum Lodron-Haus, Mühldorf am Inn 019009
Kreismuseum Oranienburg, Oranienburg 019479
Kreismuseum Peine mit Kreisarchiv, Peine 019581
Kreismuseum Prinzeßhof, Itzehoe . . 018099
Kreismuseum Schönebeck, Schönebeck, Elbe 020074
Kreismuseum Senftenberg, Senftenberg 020189
Kreismuseum Syke, Syke 020390
Kreismuseum Torgau - Schloß Hartenfels, Torgau 020453
Kreismuseum Walderbach, Walderbach 020640
Kreismuseum Wewelsburg, Büren, Westfalen 016497
Kreismuseum Wittenberg, Prettin . . 019668
Kreismuseum Zons, Dormagen 016750
Kreitz, J., Bad Homburg v.d.Höhe . . 069294
Kreitz-Matthies, B., Karlsruhe 071724, 139297
Krekel, Elisabeth, Mengerskirchen . 104062
Krell'sche Schmiede, Wernigerode . 020812
Kreloufi, Gilbert, La Varenne-Saint-Hilaire 063465
Kremecek, Jaroslav, Zürich 112132
Kremer, Hugo, Ankum 069169
Kremer, Karl, Osnabrück 073241
Kremer, Margret, Spangdahlem . . . 073871
Kremer, Rainer, Düsseldorf 070401
Kremer, U., Paderborn 073285
Kremmer'n Antikk, Helleland 079390
Krempel, Ralf, Groitzsch bei Pegau . 103011
Krempien, Silke, Schwerin 126790
Kremser Künstlervereinigung Kremser Kreis, Krems 052549
Kremstaler Raritäten, Micheldorf . . 057180
Křenek, Karel, Dobřichovice 137779
Křenek, Karel, Praha 098470, 137836
Krenzer, Meerbusch 072486
Kréo, Paris 100567
Krepl, Karin, Ulm 126930
Kreps, Andrew, New York 118108
Kresge Art Museum, East Lansing . 043574
Kresky, Ellen, Grebenhain 133987
Kress, Michael, Birstein 125335
Kress, Willi, Brugg 129989
Kressibucher, Beat, Aadorf 082067
Kretschmann, Buchholz in der Nordheide 125407
Kretz, Pascal et Carine, Beaugency 061251
Kretzschmann, Hannelore, Velten . . 126947
Werner Kreuder & Wilhelm Heidi, Obertshausen 073160
Kreusel, T., Spaichingen 073867
Kreussel, Lutz-Peter, Kulmbach . . . 139372
Kreuter, Björn, Stockholm 081976
Kreutz, B., Ediger-Eller 070508
Kreutz, Inge, Aschaffenburg 069200
Kreutzer, Joachim, Saarbrücken . . . 073636
Kreutzer & Ernst, Pohlheim 126640
Kreutziger, A. Caroline, Worpswede 105332
Kreuz, Gerhard, Wien 123511
Kreuz-Verlag, Stuttgart 134416
Kreuzberg Museum, Berlin 016094
Kreuzer, Maria, Amorbach 101578
Kreuzstadelmuseum, Türkenschlacht-Gedenkraum, Mogersdorf 002334
Krevsky, George, San Francisco . . . 119713
Krichel, Mönchengladbach 072570
Krichel, B., Zornheim 074573
Kricheldorf, Volker, Freiburg im Breisgau 070846
Krick, Würzburg 134469
Kriebel, Michael, Stuttgart 126863
Krief, Paris 100568
Krieg, Hans-Peter, Oberwil 082713, 111795
Krieg, Jens, Berlin 069671
Krieger, Stephanie, New York 091011
Krieger-Stahlmann, Essen 125615
Krieghoff, Dietrich, Bremen 070031

Kriegler, Bad Aussee 056925
Krienke, Christine, Wiesbaden 127012
Krienke, Kendra, New York 118109
Kriivari, Rovaniemi 137986
Krijgsman & Minderman, Den Haag 078209
Krikl, Andreas, Wien 137337
Kriminal- und Foltermuseum Henke, Brandenburg an der Havel 016370
Kriminalmuseet, Trondheim 031289
Kriminalmuseum der Kantonspolizei Zürich, Zürich 037774
Krimmel, Karin, Köln 126097
Krings, Antonio, Köln 071971
Krings-Ernst, Dr. Thomas, Köln 103662
Krins, Werner, Poppholz 073354
Krinzinger, Dr. Ursula, Wien 095884, 133211
Krippenmuseum, Glattbach 017425
Krippenmuseum, Telgte 020417
Krippensammlung, Großraming . . . 001976
Krippenstube-Heimatstube, Plößberg 019642
Krips, Maximilian, Köln 103663
Kris, Kiel 071833
Krisal, Carouge 111340
Krischke, Dragan, Berlin 069672
Krishtie, Bangalore 074773
Krišjāņa Barona Muzejs, Rīga 027737
Krispen, Houston 089129
Krißler, Ursula, Kirchheim unter Teck 126049
Kristall Galerie, Überlingen 105086
Kristall-Museum, Obergesteln 037387
Kristalle und Edle Steine Turracher Höhe, Ebene Reichenau 001796
Kristallgrotte, Guttannen 037172
Kristallmuseum, Guttannen 037173
Kristallmuseum, Viechtach 020581
Kristallmuseum Riedenburg, Riedenburg 019831
Kristalmuseum 't Los Hoes, Borculo 029328
Kristensen, Jette, Brøndby Strand . 060214
Kristianhus Motormuseum, Vik i Sogn 031336
Kristiansand Kanonmuseum, Kristiansand 030956
Kristiansands Auksjons-Forretning, Kristiansand 121854
Kristina, Sofia 096740
Kristinehamns Auktionskammare, Kristinehamn 122181
Kristinehamns Konstmuseum, Kristinehamn 036403
Kristinehamns Museum, Kristinehamn 036404
Kristiregi Galleries, Las Piñas 108851
Kristi's Selections, Antwerpen 057711
Kristjan Raud Museum, Eesti Kunstimuuseum, Tallinn 009407
Kristjonsson, Bragi, Reykjavík 074760, 121648, 139945
Kristof, Erika, Gersfeld 102943
Kristoffersen, M., Malmö 110975
Kriterion Società di Restauro Scientifico e Manutenzione, Bologna 127156
Kritik, München 135776
Kritische Berichte, Marburg 135777
Krivoriz'kyj Krajeznavčyj Muzej, Kryvyj Rig 038291
Křížek, Miroslav, Praha 123988
Krkonošské Muzeum, Jilemnice . . . 008414
Krkonošské Muzeum, Vrchlabí 008761
Krkonošské Muzeum, Památník Zapadlých vlastenců, Paseky nad Jizerou . . . 008562
Kro, de, Dordrecht 128650
Krobath & Wimmer, Wien 095885
Krøderbanen, Krøderen 030963
Kröger, Wedel 134448
Kröger, Christian, Löhne 126225
Kröger, Edzard, Horst 071582
Kröger, Hinrich, Berlin 101958
Kröger, Roland, Herford 071489
Kröhs, R., Weimar, Thüringen 139835
Kröll, Rafaela, Tutzing 074125
Kröller-Müller Museum, Otterlo . . . 030015
Kröner, Geisenhausen 102921
Kröpeliner Heimatstube, Kröpelin . . 018413
Kröpeliner Tor, Rostock 019900
Kroes, Anna-Marie, Amsterdam . . . 077896
Krogmann, H., Lohne, Oldenburg . . 072300
Krohn, Ebenhausen 070490
Krohn, Katharina, Basel 111201
Krohn, Richard M., Süderbrarup . . . 074018
Krojer, Landshut 103827
Kroker, Torsten, Straubing 073938
Kroker & Walsch, Stuttgart 073986
Kroma, Saint Louis 119218
Krombholz, Köln 103664
Krombholz & Schnake, Bergheim, Erft 133743
Kronacher Kunstverein, Kronach . . . 053261
Kronans Mynt, Göteborg 081813
Kronberger Antiquariat, Kronberg im Taunus 139371
Kronberger Haus, Historisches Museum, Frankfurt am Main 017181
Kronbloms Kök, Örebro 036518
Kronborg Slot, Helsingør 008899
Krone, Bätterkinden 111156
Krone, Leichlingen 139385
Krone, Zürich 112133
Krone, H., Leichlingen 139386
Krone, U., Euskirchen 139065
Krone Antik, København 060350
Kronenberg, Basel 122304, 141206
Kronis, Dimitri, Paris 138418
Kronobergs Lantbruksmuseum, Alvesta 036175
Kronthaler, Thomas Rudolf, Fügen . 056981
Kronwitter, Straubing 073939
Krookilan Kotiseutualue, Raisio . . . 010016
De Kroon, Zeist 078869
Kroos, Brenda, Cleveland 115723
Kropáček, Petr, Písek 060077
Kropshofer, Nenzing 095693
Krosna, Moskva 109561
Krosse, Winfried, Erfurt 139045
Kroumova, Galia, Milano 106253
Kroumova, Galia, Roma 106569
Kroupa, Ernst K., Wien 057475
Kroyer, Helmut, Hamburg 071272
Kru-Kü-Ku-Krei Kleine Galerie, Krumpendorf 095636
Krudttaarnsmuseet, Frederikshavn . 008867
Krüge-Museum, Creußen 016605
Krüger, Düsseldorf 102521
Krüger, Hamburg 071273
Krüger, Korbach 072055
Krueger, Saint Louis 119219
Krüger, C. L., Dortmund . . 102406, 138983
Krüger, Christiane, Rödermark 104758
Krüger, D., Vechelde 074183
Krüger, Frank, Rheinsberg 073528
Krüger, Karl-Heinz, Kassel 071758
Krüger, Klaus, Salzburg 057264
Krüger, O. & E., Emsbüren 070566
Krüger, Patrick Urs, Saarbrücken . .073637, 126757
Krüger, Peter, Berlin 069673
Krüger, Stefan, Köln 139346
Krüger, Wolfgang, Leipzig 072207
Krügersches Haus, Museum Gesthacht, Geesthacht 017335
Krümmel, Gerd, Fleestedt 070695
Krüzner, Marco, Krefeld 072074
Krug, Klaus, Gau-Algesheim 070938
Krug, Manfred, Betzdorf 069811
Krug, Sonja, München 126406
Kruger, Bredevoort 140371
Kruger Museum, Pretoria 034717
Kruger y Tejada, Madrid 081328
Krugier, Ditesheim & Cie., Genève . 111478
Kruidentuin de Groene Kruidhof, Elburg 029552
Kruiermuseum, Balen 003211
Kruimel, Nico, Bussum 078134
't Kruithuis, Alkmaar 077717
Kruj, Andor, Budapest 074692
Kruk, Gerry, Calgary 058794
Kruk, W., Poznań 079693
Krul, René, Nieuw Vennep 140503
Krumbiegel, Karin, Kaarst 071675
Kruml, Pierluigi, Trieste 140145
Krumpendorfer Künstler Kultur Kreis, Kru-Kü-Ku-Krei, Krumpendorf 052550
Krumpeter, Christian, Lübeck 072327
Kruna, Beograd 109705
Krunk, Sankt-Peterburg 109633
Krupan, München 104249
Krupicka, Frank Rainer, Kaiserslautern 103468
Krupinski, B., Waldkirch 074255
Krupp, H. Gerhard, Weinbach 105192
Krupp, Nicolas, Basel 111202
Kruppa, S., Auhagen 069242
Kruså Antikvitets Lager, Kruså 060393
Kruschel, Andreas, Radebeul 104650
Kruse, Auburn 122804
Kruse, D., Dipperz 070258
Kruse, Eva, Söhren 073843
Kruse, Günter, Flensburg 102731
Kruse House Museum, West Chicago 049069
Krusemark-Camin, Elke, Mühlheim am Main 072608
Krusenbaum, Carl, Bochum 069888
Kruska, Herbert, Essen 102695
Kruydt, La Baule-Escoublac 063290
Kruzina, Antoine, Sin-le-Noble 068243
Krymski Respublikanskij Kraevedčeskij Muzej, Simferopol 038394
Krypta 182, Kunstverein Bergisch Gladbach, Bergisch Gladbach 015968
Krypte en Schatkamer van de O.L.V. Basiliek, Halle 003486
Kryptemuseum onder de Sint-Hermeskerk, Ronse 003728
Krzisnik, Milan, Werbach 074336
Krzysztof Kawenczynski Muzeum, Trzcianne 032399
Krzyżanowski, Kraków 140742
Krzyzanowski, U. & M., Waldhufen . 139824
K's, Frankfurt am Main 102794
K.S. Art, New York 118110
K's Selection, Chiba 077035
Ksan Historical Village and Museum, Hazelton 005610
Księgarnia Naukowa, Gdańsk 140721
K.T. Art, New York 118111
Ktema, L'Isle-sur-la-Sorgue 063940
Ku Lou, Hung, Hong Kong 059656
Ku Yan Hua Wu, Shenyang 097965
Kuala Lumpur College of Art, Kuala Lumpur 050527
Kuala Lumpur Craft Museum, Kuala Lumpur 027969
Kuballe, Reinhard, Osnabrück 139640
Kubalu Skolas Muzejs, Dundaga . . . 027679
Kube, Jan K., München . . 072760, 121535
Kube, Jan K., Sugenheim . 074026, 121610
Kubera, Nice 065097
Kubeš, Dobruška 060010
Kubias, Emmendingen 102622
Kubicki, Józef, Warszawa 140788
Kubin-Haus, Wernstein am Inn 002840
Kubinyi Ferenc Múzeum, Nógrádi Megyei Múzeum, Szécsény 021857
Kubis, Bodo, Gelsenkirchen 070957
Kubo, Itsuo, São Paulo 096675
Kuboso Memorial Museum of Arts, Izumi 026592
Kubowicz, Maria i Piotr, Warszawa . 109151
Kubus Hannover, Hannover 017758
Kuc & Kozicka, Berlin 069674, 125240
Kucera, Christian, Duisburg 070481
Kucera, Greg, Seattle 119951
Kuch, Angelika, Plüderhausen 126636
Kuckei + Kuckei, Berlin 101959
Kuckó, Eger 074732
Kuckuck, Soest 104912
Kuczynski, Paulo, São Paulo 058719
Kuddnäs Z. Topeliusksen Lapsuudenkoti, Z. Topelius Barndomshem, Uusikaarlepyy 010192
Kudełko, Robert, Zabierzów 129136
Kudlek, Martin, Köln 103665
Kudos Gallery, Paddington 095032
Kübelbeck, Sylvia, Schaan 077448
Kübler, Hella, Wilhelmsdorf, Württemberg 127019
Kübli, Astrid, Basel 082149, 129924
Kübli, Josua, Basel 082150
Kügelgenhaus, Museum der Dresdner Romantik, Dresden 016793
Kügler, Bernhard, Lenggries 126210
Kühl, Christoph, Hannover 103287
Kühling, Anton, Augsburg . 069236, 121299
Kühn, Berlin 101960
Kühn, Hans, Osterode am Harz 073256
Kühn, Harald, Alheim 101558
Kühn, Marianne, Köln 103666
Kühn, V. & E., Lilienthal 103911
Kühn & Watolla 6000 Rosenthaler Str 40, Berlin 069675
Kühne, D., Hünxe 071591
Kühne, Frank, Dresden . . . 070322, 102447
Kühne, Franz, Hedingen 141258
Kühnemuth, Reinhard, Berlin 125241
Kühner, G., Schleusingen 073699
Kühner, W., Rümmingen 073618
Kuehnert, Houston 122909
Kühnert, Ruth, Sebnitz 104874
Kühr, Manfred, Münchberg 072623
Küker, Bernd & Karin, Stadt Wehlen 104941
Kümmel, Duderstadt 070340
Kümmel, Lüdenscheid 072346
Künker, München 072761
Künker, Fritz Rudolf, Osnabrück . . .073242, 121571
Künstler, München 135778
Die Künstler aus Gugging, Klosterneuburg 052551
Künstler der Filder, Filderstadt 053262
Künstlerbahnhof Ebernburg, Bad Münster 015753
Künstlerbund Dresden, Dresden . . . 053263
Künstlerbund Graz, Graz 052552
Künstlerbund Klosterneuburg, Klosterneuburg 052553
Künstlerbund Mecklenburg und Vorpommern e.V. im BBK, Schwerin 053264
Künstlerbund Steinburg e.V., Itzehoe 053265
Künstlerbund Tübingen e.V., Tübingen 053266
Künstlerei 68 e.V., Nürnberg 053267, 104482
Künstlerforum Bonn, Bonn 016327
Künstlergarten Alfred Kurz, Lichtenau 002233
Künstlergemeinschaft, Thun 054188
Die Künstlergilde, Esslingen 053268, 102712, 135779
Künstlergilde Buslat e.V., Neulingen, Enzkreis 053269, 104412
Künstlergilde Hechingen, Hechingen 053270
Künstlergilde Salzkammergut, Traunkirchen 052554
Künstlergilde Ulm, Ulm 053271
Künstlergilde Wels, Wels 052555
Künstlergruppe Ebenfurth, Ebenfurth 052556
Künstlergruppe Experiment Stuttgart e.V., Stuttgart 053272
Künstlerhaus, Freienbach 111409
Künstlerhaus, Hohenossig 103398, 134064
Künstlerhaus 188 e.V., Halle, Saale 103071
Künstlerhaus Berlin, Berlin 101961
Künstlerhaus Bethanien, Berlin . . .016095, 133790
Künstlerhaus Bremen, Bremen 102250
Künstlerhaus des Berufsverbandes Bildender Künstler Niederbayern, Passau 053273
Künstlerhaus Dortmund, Dortmund .053274, 102407
Künstlerhaus Exter, Übersee 020518
Künstlerhaus Graz, Graz 001935
Künstlerhaus Hamburg, Hamburg . . 103172

Künstlerhaus Hooksiel, Hooksiel . . . 018004
Künstlerhaus Lenz, Gladenbach . . . 017423
Künstlerhaus Marktoberdorf, Kunst- und Kulturstiftung Dr. Geiger-Haus, Marktoberdorf . . . 018846
Künstlerhaus mit Galerie, Göttingen 017465
Künstlerhaus mit Galerie e.V., Göttingen . . . 102978
Künstlerhaus Palais Thurn und Taxis, Bregenz . . . 095486
Künstlerhaus S11, Solothurn . . . 111921
Künstlerhaus Schloß Balmoral, Bad Ems . . . 015692
Künstlerhaus Schloss Wiepersdorf, Wiepersdorf bei Jüterbog . . . 020860
Künstlerhaus Stuttgart, Stuttgart . .053275, 104994
Künstlerhaus Ulm, Ulm . . . 105094
Künstlerhaus Walter Helm, Aschaffenburg . . . 015577
Künstlerhaus Wien, Wien . . . 002927
Künstlerhausgalerie, Karlsruhe . . . 103497
Künstlerinnenhof Die Höge e.V, Bassum . . . 101742
Künstlerkeller, Annweiler . . . 101585
Künstlerkreis Ortenau - Neue Galerie im Artforum, Offenburg . . . 104532
Künstlerverband-Nachrichten österreichischer Bildhauer, Wien . 135560
Künstlerverband österreichischer Bildhauer, Wien . . . 052557
Künstlerverein Malkasten, Düsseldorf . . . 053276
Künstlervereinigung Kärnten, Villach . . . 052558
Künstlervereinigung Maerz, Linz . . . 052559
Künstlerzeche Unser Fritz 2/3, Herne . . . 103359
Künzle, Fredy, Lichtensteig . . . 130080
Küpper, Eugen, Münster . . . 139569
Küppers, Illerkirchberg . . . 071612
Küppers Historisches Biermuseum, Historische Braustätte und Küppers Galerie alter Bierreclame, Köln . . 018324
Kürbismühlenmuseum, Preding . . . 002464
Kürkman, Garo, İstanbul . . . 135112
Küsten-Museum der Stadt Wilhelmshaven, Wilhelmshaven . . . 020896
Küstenmuseum, Juist . . . 018133
Küster, Limburg an der Lahn . . . 072258
Kütahya Devlet Güzel Sanatlar Galerisi, Kütahya . . . 038141
Kufa Gallery, London . . . 040195
Kufa Gallery, London . . . 113726
Kufsteiner Kunstverein, Kufstein . . . 052560
Kugel, Irmhild, Duisburg . . . 070482
Kugel, Jacques, Paris . . . 066121, 100569
Kugler, Innsbruck . . . 095587
Kuhl-Linscomb, Houston . . . 089130
Kuhl-Linscomb, Houston . . . 089131
Kuhlberg, Brigitte von, Berlin . . . 069676
Kuhlemann, Katharina, Bad Homburg v.d.Höhe . . . 125100
Kuhler, Amsterdam . . . 107752
Kuhlmann, Dieter & Margot, Oberhausen, Rheinland . . . 139616
Kuhlmann, Heinrich, Münster . . . 072917
Kuhlmann, L., Bielefeld . . . 138874
Kuhlmann King Historical House and Museum, Boerne . . . 042287
Kuhlow, G., Aachen . . . 069091
Kuhmalahden Kotiseutumuseo, Kuhmalahti . . . 009753
Kuhmoisten Kotiseutumuseo, Kuhmoinen . . . 009756
Kuhn, Anne-Grit, Gera . . . 125717
Kuhn, Claude, Basel . . . 111203
Kuhn, Karl-Josef, Düsseldorf . . . 102522
Kuhn, Nick, Bath . . . 083434
Kuhnert, Dieter, San Francisco . . . 132893
Kuhnke, Siegfried, Fischen am Ammersee . . . 070690
Kuhnke, Siegfried, Pähl . . . 073290
Kuhsen, K., Esslingen . . . 070661
Kuijper, Breda . . . 078106
Kuiper, M., Meerssen . . . 128769
Kuivaniemen Kotiseutumuseo, Kuivaniemi . . . 009757
Kujaku, Sendai . . . 107000
Kujumzian, Dicki, München . . . 072762
Kuk, Moskva . . . 109562
K.u.k. Hausmuseum, Weyregg am Attersee . . . 002844
Kukje Gallery, Seoul . . . 027577
Kukkola Fiskemuseum, Haparanda . 036328
Kuknip Minsok Pakmulgwan, Seoul 027578
Kulay-Diwa Art Galleries, Parañaque . . . 108848
Kulbach, Gregor, Dötlingen . . . 125471
Kulbach, Richart, Heidelberg . . . 139253
Kulbackens Museum, Västervik . . . 036770
Kulbrock, H.-Jürgen, Oberhausen, Rheinland . . . 073146
Kulcsar, Peter, Wien . . . 057476
Kuldīgas Novada Muzejs, Kuldīga . . 027702
Kulhus anno 1769, Værløse . . . 060406
Kulik Art Inuit, Québec . . . 097145
KULIMU, Zeitschrift für Kunst & Literatur & Musik, Lappersdorf . . . 135780
Kulíšek, Dr. Ladislav, Znojmo . . . 060206
Kuljabskij Istoriko-Kraevedčeskij Muzej, Kuljab . . . 037841
Kulkukirja, Tampere . . . 137991
Kulla Gunnarstorps Mölla, Helsingborg . . . 036337
Kullaan Kotiseutumuseo, Kullaa . . . 009758
Kullängsstugan, Askersund . . . 036204
Kullagårdens Auktioner, Hökerum . . 122163
Kullhagen, Uppsala . . . 082058
Kulli, Susanna, Zürich . . . 112134, 135091
Kulma-Antikvari, Mikkeli . . . 137979
Kulø, Erry, Oslo . . . 108733
Kulstrunk, Gabriele, Baden . . . 111153
Kulta Galleria Ailio, Jyväskylä . . . 098751
Kultamuseo Tankavaara, Tankavaara . . . 010141
Kultaraami, Lahti . . . 060607
Kulthaus, Haigerloch . . . 103055
Kulttuurien Museo, Helsinki . . . 009546
Kultur Bahnhof Eller, Düsseldorf . . . 016836
Kultur-Gut-Museum, Aigen-Schlägl 001668
Kultur-Historisches Museum Grenchen, Grenchen . . . 037163
Kultur im Bären, Alter Mostkeller, Häggenschwil . . . 111546
Kultur- und Kommunikationszentrum Lagerhalle Osnabrück, Osnabrück 019494
Kultur- und Militärmuseum, Grafenwöhr . . . 017506
Kultur- und Stadthistorisches Museum Duisburg, Duisburg . . . 016855
Kultura Weekly, Sofia . . . 135616
Kulturama, Museum des Menschen, Zürich . . . 037775
Kulturamt Mitte, Berlin . . . 016096
Kulturamt Neukölln, Berlin . . . 016097
Kulturas Books, Washington . . . 143045
Kulturbryggarna, Malmö . . . 141129
Kulturbunker Mülheim, Köln . . . 018325
Kulturelles Forum im Freiherr-vom-Stein-Haus, Langenfeld . . . 018510
Kulturen Zivot, Skopje . . . 135989
Kulturerbe Hallstatt, Hallstatt . . . 002016
Kulturforum Alte Post, Neuss . . . 019273
Kulturforum Burgkloster, Lübeck . . 018721
Kulturgården på Lassfolk, Lillby . . . 009827
Kulturgeschichtliches Museum Bügeleisenhaus, Hattingen . . . 017795
Kulturgeschichtliches Museum Osnabrück, Osnabrück . . . 019495
Kulturgeschichtliches Museum Wurzen mit Ringelnatzsammlung, Wurzen . . . 021024
Kulturhaus der Otto-Hellmeier-Stiftung, Raisting . . . 019707
Kulturhistorische Sammlung, Frankenmarkt . . . 001863
Kulturhistorische Sammlung, Iphofen . . . 018081
Kulturhistorische Sammlung, Landesmuseum Joanneum, Graz . 001936
Kulturhistorisches Museum Barockhaus, Städtische Sammlungen für Geschichte und Kultur Görlitz, Görlitz . . . 017453
Kulturhistorisches Museum der Hansestadt Stralsund, Stralsund . . . 020331
Kulturhistorisches Museum Franziskanerkloster, Städtische Museen Zittau, Zittau . . . 021072
Kulturhistorisches Museum Kaisertrutz/ Reichenbacher Turm, Städtische Sammlungen für Geschichte und Kultur Görlitz, Görlitz . . . 017454
Kulturhistorisches Museum Magdeburg, Magdeburg . . . 018769
Kulturhistorisches Museum Prenzlau im Dominikanerkloster, Prenzlau . . . 019665
Kulturhistorisches Museum Schloss Köthen, Köthen, Anhalt . . . 018363
Kulturhistorisches Museum Schloß Merseburg, Merseburg . . . 018915
Kulturhistorisk Museum, Randers . . 009063
Kulturhistoriska Museet i Bunge, Farösund . . . 036267
Kulturhistoriska Museet 'Kulturen i Lund', Lund . . . 036443
De Kulturhistoriske Samlinger, Bergen . . . 030767
Kulturhuset, Stockholm . . . 036633
Kulturinstitut in der Italienischen Botschaft, Berlin . . . 016098
Kulturmühle Lützelflüh, Stiftung Jolanda Rodio, Lützelflüh . . . 037283
Kulturni Centar Ivan Napotnik, Velenje . . . 034534
Kulturno Prosvetni Centar Bela Crkva-Muzejska Jedinica, Bela Crkva . . 034145
Kulturno-vystavočnyj Centr Raduga, Samara . . . 033717
Kulturno-vystavočnyj Centr Raduga, Uljanovsk . . . 034007
Kulturnyj Centr Kazan, Kazan . . . 033235
Kulturnyj Centr-muzej V.S. Vysockogo, Moskva . . . 033416
Kulturos Barai, Vilnius . . . 140231
Kulturraum Galerie, Speyer . . . 104935
Kulturspeicher im Schamuhn Museum, Uelzen . . . 020521
Kulturwerk des Berufsverbandes Bildender Künstler Berlins, Berlin . . . 053277
Kulturwerk des Berufsverbandes Bildender Künstler Niederbayern e.V, Fürstenzell . . . 053278
Kulturwissenschaftliche Fakultät, Universität Bayreuth, Bayreuth . . . 050014
Kulturzentrum der Aktion Lebensqualität, München . . . 019068
Kulturzentrum Hans-Reiffenstuel-Haus, Pfarrkirchen . . . 019603
Kulturzentrum Kolvenburg, Billerbeck . . . 016244
Kulturzentrum Ostpreußen, Ellingen, Bayern . . . 016937
Kulturzentrum Schloß Bonndorf, Bonndorf im Schwarzwald . . . 016338
Kulturzentrum Sinsteden des Kreises Neuss, Landwirtschaftsmuseum und Skulpturenhallen Ulrich Rückriem, Rommerskirchen . . . 019877
Kulunkian, Charles, Saint-Yrieix-la-Montagne . . . 068043
Kulunkian, Stéphane, Garat . . . 062965
Kulunkian-Joumier, Marie-Geneviève, Saint-Cybardeaux . . . 067409
Kuma Museum of Art, Kuma . . . 026691
Kumagai Morikazu Museum, Tokyo 027193
Kumaki, Tokyo . . . 077275
Kumamoto Castle, Kumamoto . . . 026692
Kumamoto International Folk Art Museum, Kumamoto . . . 026693
Kumamoto-kenritsu Bijutsukan, Kumamoto . . . 026694
Kumamoto-shiritsu Hakubutsukan, Kumamoto . . . 026695
Kumano Nachi Taisha Treasure House, Nachikatsuura . . . 026839
Kumar, Jain-Virendra, Delhi . . . 074804
Kumar, Jain-Virendra, Delhi . . . 074805
Kumar, Jain-Virendra, Delhi . . . 105669
Kumar, Jain-Virendra, Delhi . . . 105670
Kumar, Jain-Virendra, Delhi . . . 134515
Kumar, Prakash, Bangalore . . . 074774
Kumar, Sushil, Hyderabad . . . 074811
Kumaya Bijutsukan, Hagi . . . 026486
Kumbu Kumbu, Nairobi . . . 107162
Kume Bijutsukan, Tokyo . . . 027194
Kumer, Navin, New York . . . 118112
Kumf, Toronto . . . 097310
Kumlehn, Inge, Sandhausen . . . 126761
Kummer, Beat, Bern . . . 082219
Kummer, Wolfram, Pattensen . . . 126614
Kumon, Los Angeles . . . 116813
Kumpf, Daniela, Wiesbaden . . . 074411
Kumps, L., Antwerpen . . . 057712
Kumquat, San Francisco . . . 119714
Kumra & Co., Singapore . . . 080512
Kumutat, Axel, Stuttgart . . . 073987
K'Un Sun, Bogotá . . . 059842
Kunac, Stan, München . . . 104250
Kunaicho Sannomaru Shozokan, Tokyo . . . 027195
Kunewälder Heimatstube, Leimen, Baden . . . 018548
Kungajaktmuseet, Vargön . . . 036783
Kungang Mei Ye Art Galley, Shanghai . . . 097927
Kungl. Akademien för de fria Konsterna, Stockholm . . . 054143
Kungl. Konsthögskolan, Stockholm . 050751
Kungl. Myntkabinettet, Sveriges Ekonomiska Museum, Stockholm 036634
Kungl. Vitterhets Historie och Antikvitets Akademien, Stockholm . 050752, 054144
Kungliga Akademien för de Fria Konsterna, Stockholm . . . 036635
Kungsbacka Auktionsverk, Kungsbacka . . . 122186
Kungshöjds Restaurering & Konservering av Antika Möbler, Göteborg . . . 129840
Kungsholmens Antik och Kuriosa, Stockholm . . . 081977
Kungsstugan och Cajsa Wargs Hus, Örebro . . . 036519
Kungsudden Local Museum, Kungsör . . . 036409
Kungurskij Kraevedčeskij Muzej, Kungur . . . 033314
Kunisaki-machi Rekishi Minzoku Shiryokan, Kunisaki . . . 026696
Kunitachi Bijutsu Kenkyujo, Kokubunji . . . 050456
Kunj Art Gallery, Karachi . . . 108774
Kunja-Urgench Historical Site Museum, Keneurgench . . . 038206
Kunkel, Hans-Joach., Herne . . . 125918
Kunozan Toshogu Museum, Shizuoka . . . 027079
Kunsch, Berlin . . . 125242
Kunshan Calligraphy and Painting Gallery, Kunshan . . . 097867
Kunshan Painting Gallery, Kunshan . 097868
Die Kunskamer, Cape Town . . . 080683
Kunst & Co., Amstelveen . . . 107645
Kunst, Christchurch . . . 108400
Kunst & Ko., Eindhoven . . . 108002
Kunst, Tallinn . . . 133439
Kunst ab Werk, Miltach . . . 104071
Kunst Adelt, Maastricht . . . 134822
Kunst-aktuell, Reinharz . . . 135781
Kunst am Kö, Augsburg . . . 101617
Kunst am Wall, Bremen . . . 102251
Kunst & Antiek Journaal, Schiedam 135998
Kunst & Antiekrevue, Den Haag . . . 135999
Kunst & Antiquitätenmesse Leipzig, Leipzig . . . 093730
Kunst Archiv Darmstadt, Darmstadt 016641
Kunst auf der Zugspitze, Garmisch-Partenkirchen . . . 017326
Kunst aus Nordrhein-Westfalen, Ministerium für Städtebau und Wohnen, Kultur und Sport des Landes Nordrhein-Westfalen, Aachen . . . 015421
Kunst & Beterschap, Amsterdam . . 107753
Kunst-Buero, München . . . 104251
Kunst-Bulletin, Zürich . . . 136125

Kunst & Cultuur, Bruxelles 135601
Kunst der Zeit, Leipzig 072208
Kunst-Design & Antiquitäten, Hermagor 057058
Kunst en Antiekbeurs 's-Hertogenbosch, 's-Hertogenbosch 093831
Kunst- en Antiekbeurs van de Lage Landen, Amsterdam 093832
Kunst en Vliegwerk, Leiden 108101
Kunst für Alle, Monschau 104116
Kunst Galerie Am Rathaus, Emden . 070552
Kunst Galerie Am Rathaus, Emden . 102619
Kunst Halle in der Villa Kobe, Halle, Saale 017663
Kunst i Skolen, Oslo 079454
Kunst im Alten Schützenhaus, Zofingen 037755
Kunst im Arte Pietra, Paderborn ... 104572
Kunst im Bild, Halle, Saale 103072
Kunst im Burggrafiat, Alzey 101572
Kunst im Carré, Berlin 101962
Kunst im Keller, Halle, Saale 103073
Kunst im Rahmen, München 104252
Kunst im Raum, Bielefeld 102124
Kunst im Schloss Untergröningen, Abtsgmünd 015438
Kunst im Tal, München 104253
Kunst-in-Ahoy, Rotterdam 093833
Kunst in der Klinik, Bad Krozingen . 015740
Kunst in der Schranne, Feuchtwangen 102726
Kunst in der Zehntscheune, Bad Homburg v.d.Höhe 101655
Kunst in Frankfurt e.V., Frankfurt am Main 053279
Kunst in Herrenhausen, Hannover . 093731
Kunst in Holz, Hamburg 134016
Kunst in Huis, Antwerpen 096077
Kunst in Huis, Arnhem 107854
Kunst in Huis, Bruxelles 096223
Kunst In Opdracht, Almere 053895
Kunst in Opdracht, Almere 077741
Kunst & Interiør, Oslo 079455
Kunst-Kabinett Usedom, Benz 015951
Kunst Klubben, Oslo 108734
Kunst Konsum, Miesbach 072544
De Kunst Kringloop, Bussum 078135
Kunst & Kultur, Stuttgart 135782
Kunst Kultur X, Tauberbischofsheim 135783
Kunst & Kunst, Eindhoven 108003
Kunst & Kunst, Groningen 078427
Kunst Kurier, Köln 135784
Kunst & Kuriosa, Heidelberg 121450
Kunst Mammern, Mammern 111717
Kunst-Museum Ahlen, Theodor F. Leifeld-Stiftung, Ahlen 015452
Kunst-Oase, München 072763
Kunst-Oase, München 104254
Kunst oder Reklame, München 104255
Kunst og Antikviteter, Kristiansand . 079397
Kunst og Håndverksmessen, Lillestrøm 093838
Kunst og Kultur, Oslo 136014
Kunst og Museums, Nivå 135672
Kunst Parterre, Viersen .. 105120, 134446
Kunst & Primitives, Berlin 101963
Kunst & Psyche, Wien 133212
Kunst & Raum, Düsseldorf 102523
Kunst Raum, Wien 095886
Kunst Raum Goethestraße, Linz ... 002248
Kunst Raum Riehen, Riehen 037452
Kunst Raum Saite Galerie, Dresden 102448
Kunst-Stück, Leipzig 103889
Kunst und Antiquitäten, Bonn 069930
Kunst und Antiquitäten, Hinterbrühl 057060
Kunst und Antiquitäten am Breiteweg, Bern 082220
Kunst und Antiquitäten an der Lahn, Limburg an der Lahn 072259
Kunst und Antiquitäten Ausstellung, Baddeckenstedt 093732
Kunst und Antiquitäten Ausstellung, Wotersen 093733
Kunst und Antiquitäten Galerie, Zell am See 057611
Kunst- und Antiquitäten-Messe Bonn, Bonn 093734
Kunst- und Antiquitäten-Messe Hannover, Hannover 093735
Kunst- und Antiquitäten-Messe München, München 093736
Kunst- und Antiquitäten-Messe Ostsee, Wangels 093737
Kunst- und Antiquitäten-Messe Sylt, Kampen 093738
Kunst und Antiquitäten München, München 093739
Kunst- und Antiquitätentage, Braunschweig 093740
Kunst-und Auktionshaus, Emsdetten 121393
Kunst- und Auktionshaus Schloß Hagenburg, Hagenburg 121422
Kunst- und Ausstellungshalle der Bundesrepublik Deutschland Bonn, Bonn 016328
Kunst und Bild, Berlin 133791
Kunst und Form e.V., Berlin 053280
Kunst und Gesellschaft, Marl, Westfalen 053281
Kunst und Grafik Kabinett, Nürnberg 073111, 104483, 139612
Kunst- und Heimathaus, Paderborn 019551
Kunst- und Heimatmuseum, Lorch, Rheingau 018684
Kunst und Kirche, Darmstadt 135785
Kunst und Kirche, Kremsmünster .. 135561
Kunst und Kirche, Wien 057477
Kunst und Kledage, Rostock 104770
Kunst und Kommunikation e.V., München 053282
Kunst- und Kulturkontakt Perchtoldsdorf, Perchtoldsdorf 052561
Kunst- und Kulturkreis Rastede, Rastede 053283
Kunst- und Kulturpädagogisches Zentrum der Museen in Nürnberg, Nürnberg 053284
Kunst- und Kulturverein Kappeln e.V., Kappeln 053285
Kunst- und Kunstgewerbeverein Pforzheim e.V., Pforzheim 053286
Kunst und Literatur-Verein Lahn-Dill e.V., Sinn 053287
Kunst und Museum, Hollfeld 017989
Kunst- und Museumsbibliothek, Museen der Stadt Köln, Köln 018326
Kunst- und Museumskreis, Bad Essen 053288
Kunst- und Museumsverein Starnberger See e.V., Feldafing 053289
Kunst- und Museumsverein Wuppertal e.V., Wuppertal 021018, 053290
Kunst und Rahmen, Frankfurt am Main 102795, 125656
Kunst und Rahmen, Mannheim 126278
Kunst und Rahmen, Stuttgart 073988
Kunst und Stein, Bern 136126
Kunst und Unterricht, Seelze 135786
Kunst und Werk, Greven 103002
Kunst & Vliegwerk, Hilversum 078535
Kunst & Vorm, Dordrecht 078308
Kunst Werk, Herford 103358
Kunst & Werk, Ingelheim am Rhein 103430
Kunst - Werk, Utrecht 108254
Kunst-Werkstatt, Rheda-Wiedenbrück 104741
Kunst Wien - Messe für zeitgenössische Kunst, Wien 093581
Kunst-Wirk-Raum, Recklinghausen 104685
Kunst Zeit, Berlin 101964
Kunst zur Zeit, Mönchengladbach .. 135787
Kunstacademie De Lei, Stedelijke Academie voor Beeldende Kunst, Leuven ... 049714
Kunstadapter, Frankfurt am Main .. 102796
Kunstakademie Düsseldorf, Düsseldorf 050069
Kunstakademie Münster, Hochschule für Bildende Künste, Münster 050203
Kunstakademiet i Trondheim, Norges Teknisk-Naturvitenskapelige Universitet, Trondheim 050585
Kunstakademiets Bibliotek, København 008972
Kunstamt Tempelhof-Schöneberg, Berlin 016099
Kunstatelier Carte Blanche, Hasselt 096313
Kunstauktionen Nächst Sankt Sebald, Nürnberg 121566
Kunstauktionshaus an der Frauenkirche, Dresden 121377
Kunstauktionshaus Leipzig, Leipzig 121494
Kunstauktionshaus Schloß Ahlden, Ahlden 121292
Kunstausstellung des Rothenburger Künstlerbundes, Rothenburg ob der Tauber 019914
Kunstausstellung Stift Herzogenburg, Herzogenburg 002042
Kunstbahnhof, Herrnhut 017901
Kunstbank, Galerie der Senatsverwaltung für Wissenschaft, Forschung und Kultur, Berlin 016100
Kunstbeeld, Amsterdam 136000
Kunstbehandlung Müller Str 40, München 072764
Kunstberg, Landsberg am Lech ... 072139
Kunstbibliothek, Staatliche Museen zu Berlin - Stiftung Preußischer Kulturbesitz, Berlin 016101
Kunstblick - Galerie im Internet, Adnet 095461
Der Kunstblitz, Wuppertal 135788
Kunstbuch Anzeiger, Königstein im Taunus 135789
Kunstbüro Berlin, Berlin 101965
Kunstbunker Tumulka, München .. 019069
De Kunstcaemer van Blijkshof, Deventer 107968
Kunstcentralen, Oslo 053944
Kunstcentrum Aktueel, Gent 120757
Kunstcentrum De Waagh, Oldenzaal 029987
Kunstcentrum II Ventuno, Hasselt .. 096314
Kunstcentrum Pand Paulus, Schiedam 030130
Kunstcentrum Zaanstad, Zaandam . 134840
Kunstchronik, Nürnberg 135790
Kunstdienst der Evangelischen Kirche, Berlin 053291
Kunstenaarscentrum De Fabriek, Eindhoven 029542
Kunstetagen-Galerie, Remscheid .. 104714
Kunstevent Antwerpen, Antwerpen . 093609
Kunstevent Dortmund, Dortmund .. 093741
Kunstevent Zuid-Nederland, Eindhoven 093834
Kunstfabrik am Flutgraben, Berlin . 016102
Kunstförderverein Schöningen, Schöningen 053292, 104836
Kunstförderverein Surealismus Aktuelle e.V., Hohenösen 053293
Kunstförderverein Weinheim e.V., Weinheim, Bergstraße 053294
Kunstforeningen GL Strand, København 008973, 052857
Kunstforum Arabellapark, München 019070
Kunstforum Bâloise, Basel 036888
Kunstforum Berliner Volksbank, Berlin 101966
Kunstforum Ebendorf, Wien 002928
Kunstforum Gummersbach, Bergisch Gladbach 053295
Kunstforum Halberstadt e.V., Halberstadt 053296
Kunstforum in der Grundkreditbank, Berlin 016103
Kunstforum, International, Ruppichteroth 135791
Kunstforum Montafon, Schruns ...052562, 095753
Kunstforum Ostdeutsche Galerie, Regensburg 019755
Kunstforum Rheinhessen, Essenheimer Kunstverein e.V, Essenheim 053297
Kunstforum Seligenstadt e.V., Seligenstadt 053298
Kunstforum Waldviertel e.V., Schrems 052563
Kunstforum Weil der Stadt, Weil der Stadt 053299
Kunstforum Wien, Wien 002855
Kunstfreunde Ahrensburg e.V., Ahrensburg 053300
Kunstgalerie, Bad Hersfeld 069287
Kunstgalerie am Schloß, Essen ... 102696
Kunstgalerie Francesco, Bad Kissingen 101664
Kunstgalerie Meduna, Wien 095887
Kunstgalerie Siena, Vilnius 107362
Kunstgalerie Vaqué, Jona 111575
Kunstgalerie Zebracode, Berlin 101967
Kunstgalerij R.B., Genk 096280
Kunstgalleriet URD, Bergen 108685
Kunstgarten, Aarwangen 111107
Kunstgeschichte aktuell, Wien 135562
Kunstgeschichte I, insbes. für Mittelalterliche Kunstgeschichte, Otto-Friedrich-Universität Bamberg, Bamberg 050011
Kunstgeschichte II, insbes. für Neuere und Neueste Kunstgeschichte, Otto-Friedrich-Universität Bamberg, Bamberg .. 050012
Kunstgeschichtliche Gesellschaft zu Berlin, Berlin 053301
Kunstgeschichtliches Institut, Albert-Ludwigs-Universität Freiburg, Freiburg im Breisgau 050088
Kunstgeschichtliches Institut, Johann Wolfgang Goethe-Universität, Frankfurt am Main 050084
Kunstgeschichtliches Institut, Johannes Gutenberg-Universität Mainz, Mainz 050175
Kunstgeschichtliches Institut, Philipps-Universität, Marburg 050182
Kunstgeschichtliches Institut, Ruhr-Universität Bochum, Bochum 050037
Kunstgeschichtliches Seminar, Humboldt-Universität zu Berlin, Berlin 050025
Kunstgeschichtliches Seminar, Universität Hamburg, Hamburg 050114
Kunstgeschichtliches Seminar und Kunstsammlung, Georg-August-Universität Göttingen, Göttingen . 050092
Kunstgesellschaft Grenchen, Grenchen 054189
Kunstgesellschaft Luzern, Luzern .. 054190
Kunstgewerbemuseum, Staatliche Kunstsammlungen Dresden, Dresden 016794
Kunstgewerbemuseum, Staatliche Museen zu Berlin - Stiftung Preußischer Kulturbesitz, Berlin 016104
Kunstgewerbemuseum im Schloß Köpenick, Staatliche Museen zu Berlin - Stiftung Preußischer Kulturbesitz, Berlin .. 016126
Kunstgriff, Leipzig 103890
Kunstgroep Nederland, Amsterdam 053896
Kunstgußmuseum Hirzenhain, Hirzenhain 017932
Kunstgußmuseum Lauchhammer, Lauchhammer 018520
Kunstgut Döbele, Dettelbach 102362, 121371
Kunsthal Rotterdam, Rotterdam ... 030085
Kunsthal Sint-Pietersabdij, Gent ... 003458
Kunsthalle 3, Innsbruck 095588
Kunsthalle am Goetheplatz, Stadtmuseum Weimar, Weimar, Thüringen 020745
Kunsthalle Barmen, Von der Heydt-Museum, Wuppertal 021019
Kunsthalle Basel, Basel 036889
Kunsthalle Bern, Bern 036929
Kunsthalle Bielefeld, Bielefeld 016237
Kunsthalle Bremen, Bremen 016418
Kunsthalle Bremerhaven, Bremerhaven 016431
Kunsthalle Darmstadt, Darmstadt .. 016642
Kunsthalle der Europäischen Kunstakademie, Trier 020481
Kunsthalle der Hypo-Kulturstiftung, München 019071
Kunsthalle Dominikanerkirche, Osnabrück 019496
Kunsthalle Dresden im Art'otel Dresden, Dresden 016795
Kunsthalle Düsseldorf, Düsseldorf . 016837

Kunsthalle Erfurt im Haus zum Roten Ochsen, Erfurt . . . 017017
Kunsthalle Exnergasse, Wien . . . 002929
Kunsthalle Faust, Hannover . . . 017759
Kunsthalle Fridericianum, Kassel . . 018190
Kunsthalle Gießen, Gießen . . . 017409
Kunsthalle Göppingen, Göppingen . 017447
Kunsthalle im Schloss, Isny . . . 018094
Kunsthalle in Emden, Stiftung Henri und Eske Nannen und Schenkung Otto van de Loo, Emden . . . 016958
Kunsthalle Jesuitenkirche, Aschaffenburg . . . 015578
Kunsthalle Koblenz, Koblenz . . . 018293
Kunsthalle Krems, Krems . . . 002172
Kunsthalle Leoben, Leoben . . . 002224
Kunsthalle Lingen, Lingen . . . 018662
Kunsthalle Loppen, Loppem . . . 003616
Kunsthalle Mannheim, Mannheim . 018806
Kunsthalle Neumarkt, Neumarkt, Oberpfalz . . . 019252
Kunsthalle Nürnberg, Nürnberg . . . 019363
Kunsthalle Palazzo, Liestal . . . 037266
Kunsthalle Prisma, Arbon . . . 036850
Kunsthalle Rostock, Rostock . . . 019901
Kunsthalle Sankt Gallen, Sankt Gallen . . . 037492
Kunsthalle Sankt Moritz, Sankt Moritz . . . 037504
Kunsthalle Sparkasse Leipzig, Leipzig . . . 018575
Kunsthalle T3, Dresden . . . 102449
Kunsthalle Tirol, Hall in Tirol . . . 002008
Kunsthalle Tübingen, Tübingen . . . 020498
Kunsthalle Vierseithof, Luckenwalde . . . 018691
Kunsthalle Wien, Wien . . . 002930
Kunsthalle Wien, Projekt Space, Wien . . . 002931
Kunsthalle Wil, Wil . . . 037709
Kunsthalle Wilhelmshaven, Wilhelmshaven . . . 020897
Kunsthalle Winterthur, Winterthur . . 037720
Kunsthalle Würth, Schwäbisch Hall 020117
Kunsthalle Ziegelhütte, Appenzell . . 036845
Kunsthalle zu Kiel, der Christian-Albrechts-Universität, Gemäldegalerie und Grafische Sammlung, Kiel . . . 018247
Kunsthalle Zürich, Zürich . . . 037776
Kunsthallen, København . . . 008974
Kunsthallen, København . . . 120871
Kunsthallen Brandts Klaedefabrik, Odense . . . 009052
Kunsthandel, Mannheim . . . 135792
Kunsthandel Lange Gasse, Wien . . . 057478
Kunsthandel Venlo, Venlo . . . 078839
Kunsthandelsverband der Schweiz, Association des Commerçants d'Art de la Suisse, Zürich . . . 054191
Kunsthandlerforeningen af 1943, Slagelse . . . 052858
Kunsthandlung Christine, Bamberg . 069456
Kunsthandlung in der Marktstraße, Erfurt . . . 070588
Kunsthandlung Prinz Albert, Coburg 070146
Kunsthandwerk & Design, Frechen . 135793
Kunsthandwerk und Plastik Sammlung, Staatliche Museen Kassel, Kassel 018191
Kunsthaus, Grenchen . . . 037164
Kunsthaus, Wien . . . 057479
Kunsthaus Adlerstraße, Stuttgart . . 073989
Kunsthaus am Friesenpark, Delmenhorst . . . 102354
Kunsthaus am Museum, Trier . . . 139790
Kunsthaus am Museum der Schwalm, Schwalmstadt . . . 073750
Kunsthaus Apolda Avantgarde, Apolda . . . 015562
Kunsthaus Baselland, Muttenz . . . 037366
Kunsthaus Benrath, Düsseldorf . . . 070402
Kunsthaus Bregenz, Bregenz . . . 001762
Kunsthaus Bregenz, Bregenz . . . 133064
Kunsthaus Burg Obernberg, Obernberg am Inn . . . 057199
Kunsthaus Centre PasquArt, Biel . . 036949
Kunsthaus City, Hamburg . . . 071274
Kunsthaus Dresden, Städtische Galerie für Gegenwartskunst, Dresden . . . 016796
Kunsthaus Eckernförde, Eckernförde . . . 102596, 139030
Kunsthaus Erfurt e.V., Erfurt . . . 053302
Kunsthaus Essen, Essen . . . 017068
Kunsthaus Fürstenstraße, Rottach-Egern . . . 073599
Kunsthaus Gahlberg-Strodehne e.V., Potsdam . . . 053303
Kunsthaus Glarus, Glarus . . . 037149
Kunsthaus Glarus, Glarus . . . 111516
Kunsthaus Graf, Klagenfurt . . . 095616
Kunsthaus Graz, Graz . . . 001937
Kunsthaus Hamburg, Hamburg . . . 017703
Kunsthaus Hannover, Hannover . . . 103288
Kunsthaus Hinter den Zäunen, Schöneck, Hessen . . . 134384
Kunsthaus Hohenlockstedt, Arthur Boskamp-Stiftung, Hohenlockstedt . . . 017973
Kunsthaus Horn, Horn . . . 095572
Kunsthaus in Stade, Stade . . . 020277
Kunsthaus Kaiserslautern, Kaiserslautern . . . 103469
Kunsthaus Kannen, Münster . . . 019147
Kunsthaus Kaufbeuren, Kaufbeuren 018212
Kunsthaus Kloster Gravenhorst, Hörstel . . . 017953
Kunsthaus Langenthal, Langenthal . 111604
Kunsthaus Lübeck, Lübeck . . . 103964
Kunsthaus Magdeburg, Magdeburg 072373
Kunsthaus Mettmann, Mettmann . . 018927
Kunsthaus Meyenburg, Nordhausen 019333
Kunsthaus Mürzzuschlag, Mürzzuschlag . . . 002345
Kunsthaus Mürzzuschlag, Verlagsabteilung, Mürzzuschlag . . . 095690, 133122
Kunsthaus Nordwalde, Nordwalde . 104470
Kunsthaus Nova, München . . . 072765
Kunsthaus Nürnberg, Nürnberg . . . 019364
Kunsthaus Oberkassel, Düsseldorf . 070403
Kunsthaus Raskolnikoff, Dresden . . 102450
Kunsthaus Ratingen, Ratingen . . . 104662
Kunsthaus Richterswil, Richterswil . 111832
Kunsthaus Sankt Alban, Basel . . . 111204
Kunsthaus Santa Fé, San Miguel de Allende . . . 107521
Kunsthaus Schenefeld, Schenefeld . 073683
Kunsthaus Stadt Bocholt, Bocholt . . 016271
Kunsthaus Strodehne, Strodehne . . 104959
Kunsthaus Tacheles, Berlin . . . 101968
Kunsthaus Verden, Verden . . . 074194
Kunsthaus Zürich, Zürich . . . 037777
Kunsthaus Zug, Zug . . . 037817
Kunsthaus zur Linde, Naters . . . 082684
KunstHausWien, Wien . . . 002932
Kunsthistoriker aktuell, Wien . . . 135563
Kunsthistorisch Instituut, Leiden . . . 050562
Kunsthistorisch Instituut - Afdeling Kunstgeschiedenis, Katholieke Universiteit, Nijmegen . . . 050566
Kunsthistorische Arbeitsblätter, Köln . . . 135794
Kunsthistorische Gesellschaft Wien, Wien . . . 052564
Kunsthistorisches Institut, Christian-Albrechts-Universität zu Kiel, Kiel 050150
Kunsthistorisches Institut, Eberhard-Karls-Universität Tübingen, Tübingen . . 050254
Kunsthistorisches Institut, Freie Universität Berlin, Berlin . . . 050026
Kunsthistorisches Institut, Ruprecht-Karls-Universität Heidelberg, Heidelberg 050128
Kunsthistorisches Institut, Universität zu Köln, Köln . . . 050158
Kunsthistorisches Institut, Universität Zürich, Zürich . . . 050780
Kunsthistorisches Institut der Universität Bonn, Bonn . . . 050038
Kunsthistorisches Institut in Florenz, Max-Planck-Institut, Firenze . . . 050369
Kunsthistorisches Museum, Admont 001660
Kunsthistorisches Museum, Seckau 002670
Kunsthistorisches Museum im Palais Harrach, Wien . . . 002933
Kunsthistorisches Museum, Verlagsabteilung, Wien . . . 133213
Kunsthistorisches Museum Wien, mit MVK und ÖTM, Wien . . . 002934
Kunsthistorisches Seminar, Universität Basel, Basel . . . 050756
Kunsthistorisches Seminar und Kustodie, Friedrich-Schiller-Universität Jena, Jena . . . 050136
Kunsthochschule Berlin-Weißensee, Berlin . . . 050027
Kunsthochschule für Medien Köln, Köln . . . 050159
Kunsthochschule Kassel, Studiengänge Bildende Kunst, Kunstwissenschaft, Kunstpädagogik, Product Design und Visuelle Kommunikation, Kassel . 050148
Kunsthof Bad Salzelmen, Schönebeck, Elbe . . . 020075
Kunsthof Zürich, Hochschule für Gestaltung und Kunst, Zürich . . . 037778
Kunsthøgskolen in Bergen, Bergen . 050580
Het Kunsthuis, Almere . . . 107631
Kunsthuis 1927, Emmen . . . 108014
Kunsthuis Marc Chagall, Amsterdam . . . 107754
Kunsthuset, Oslo . . . 108735
Kunstigalerii, Narva . . . 009380
Kunstindustrimuseet, Nasjonalmuseet for Kunst, Oslo . . . 031084
KunsTirol, Innsbruck . . . 135564
Kunstjahr, Regensburg . . . 135795
Kunstkabinett, Regensburg . . . 104699
Kunstkabinett am Rheintor, Rees . . 104687
De Kunstkamer, Gouda . . . 108027
Kunstkamera, Sankt-Peterburg . . . 033774
Kunstkammer der Pfarrkirche Sankt Georg, Bocholt . . . 016272
Kunstkammer des Innsbrucker Servitenkloster, Innsbruck . . . 002086
Kunstkanzlei, Wien . . . 095888
Kunstkaten Ahrenshoop, Ostseebad Ahrenshoop . . . 019516
Kunstkaufhaus Leipzig, Leipzig . . . 103891
Kunstkeller, Liestal . . . 111644
Kunstkeller Annaberg, Annaberg-Buchholz . . . 015550
Kunstkeller Bern, Bern . . . 111267
Kunstklause, Bern 082221, 111268, 129964
Kunstkontor Westnerwacht, Regensburg . . . 104700
Kunstkreis freischaffender Maler, Bielefeld . . . 053304
Kunstkreis-Galerie, Lauda-Königshofen . . . 103840
Kunstkreis Hameln, Gesellschaft zur Förderung der bildenden Künste e.V., Hameln . . . 053305
Kunstkreis Landshut, Landshut . . . 053306
Kunstkreis Lauda-Königshofen e.V., Lauda-Königshofen . . . 053307
Kunstkreis Niederrhein, Emmerich . 053308
Kunstkreis Schenefeld e.V., Schenefeld, Bezirk Hamburg . . . 053309
Kunstkreis Südliche Bergstraße, Wiesloch . . . 053310
Kunstkring Jacques Gorus, Antwerpen . . . 052684, 096078
Kunstmagasinet, Frederiksberg . . . 135673
Het Kunstmagazijn, Dordrecht . . . 107981
Kunstmanifest - Kunstbüro, Pinkafeld . . . 133125
Kunstmarkt.com, Krefeld . . . 135796
Kunstmesse Dresden, Dresden . . . 093742
Kunstmesse München, München . . 093743
Kunstmesse Salzburg, Bergheim . . 093582
Kunstmesse Schwetzingen, Schwetzingen . . . 093768
Kunstmuseet Køge Skitsesamling, Køge . . . 008995
Kunstmuseum, Sankt Gallen . . . 037493
Kunstmuseum, Solothurn . . . 037577
Kunstmuseum, Städtisches Museum, Mülheim an der Ruhr . . . 019022
Kunstmuseum Basel, Öffentliche Kunstsammlung Basel, Basel . . . 036890
Kunstmuseum Bayreuth mit Tabakhistorischer Sammlung, Bayreuth . . . 015917
Kunstmuseum Bern, Bern . . . 036930
Kunstmuseum Bonn, Bonn . . . 016329
Kunstmuseum Celle mit Sammlung Robert Simon, Celle . . . 016549
Kunstmuseum des Kantons Thurgau, Warth . . . 037697
Kunstmuseum Dr. Krupp, Privatmuseum für moderne Kunst und Ausstellung zur Schloßgeschichte, Weinbach . . . 020759
Kunstmuseum Düsseldorf im Ehrenhof, Düsseldorf . . . 016841
Kunstmuseum Heidenheim, Heidenheim an der Brenz . . . 017840
Kunstmuseum Hohenkarpfen, Hausen ob Verena . . . 017806
Kunstmuseum Kloster Unser Lieben Frauen, Magdeburg . . . 018770
Kunstmuseum Liechtenstein, Vaduz 027841
Kunstmuseum Luzern, Luzern . . . 037299
Kunstmuseum Nörvenich, Museum Arno Breker, Sammlung Europäische Kunst, Nörvenich . . . 019324
Kunstmuseum Olten, Olten . . . 037400
Kunstmuseum Stuttgart, Stuttgart . 020356
Kunstmuseum Thun, Thun . . . 037629
Kunstmuseum Winterthur, Winterthur . . . 037721
Kunstmuseum Wolfsburg, Wolfsburg . . . 020965
Kunstnachrichten, Zürich . . . 136127
Kunstnerforbundet, Oslo . . . 053945
Kunstnerforeningen af 18. November, København . . . 052859
Kunstnernes Informasjonskontor, Oslo . . . 108736
Kunstobjekt Berlin e.V., Berlin . . . 053311
Kunstogenblik, Gent . . . 058191
Kunstpanorama im Bourbaki, Luzern . . . 037300
Kunstpaviljoen, Nieuw Roden . . . 029943
Kunstpaviljongen, Høvik . . . 079393
Kunstpavillon, München . . . 019072
Das Kunstplakat, Steinach . . . 135565
Kunstpreis-Jahrbuch, München . . . 135797
De Kunstproeverij, Groningen . . . 108038
Kunstpunkt, Darmstadt . . . 102345
Kunstpunkt, Emden . . . 102620
Kunstpunkt-Edewecht, Edewecht . . 070506
Kunsträume, Zermatt . . . 112014
Kunstrat im Deutschen Kulturrat, Bonn . . . 053312
KunstRaum, Bayreuth . . . 101747
Kunstraum, Essen . . . 102697
Kunstraum, Stuttgart . . . 104995
KunstRaum, Trier . . . 105064
Kunstraum, Thurgauische Kunstgesellschaft, Kreuzlingen . . 111592
Kunstraum 3, Köln . . . 103667
Kunstraum Aarau, Aarau . . . 036809
Kunstraum Alter Wiehrebahnhof, Freiburg im Breisgau . . . 017232
Kunstraum Baden, Baden . . . 036871
Kunstraum Berlin, Berlin . . . 016105
Kunstraum Bruxelles, Bruxelles . . . 003302
Kunstraum Dornbirn, Dornbirn . . . 001787
Kunstraum Düsseldorf, Düsseldorf . 016838
Kunstraum Eching, Eching . . . 016878
Kunstraum Eppendorf, Hamburg . . . 103173
Kunstraum Falkenstein, Hamburg . . 103174
Kunstraum Farmsen, Hamburg . . . 017704
Kunstraum Fuhrwerkswaage, Köln . 018327
Kunstraum Hebel_121, Basel . . . 111205
Kunstraum Innsbruck, Innsbruck . .002087, 133092
Kunstraum Klosterkirche, Traunstein . . . 020457
Kunstraum Kreuzberg/Bethanien, Berlin . . . 016106
Kunstraum Leoben, Leoben . . . 095644
Kunstraum Mühlenstraße, Lübeck . 103965
Kunstraum München, München . .019073, 053313
Kunstraum neue Kunst, Hannover . . 017760

Kunstraum Neuruppin, Neuruppin . . 019267
Kunstraum Notkirche, Essen 017069
Kunstraum Sankt Virgil, Salzburg . . 002557
Kunstraum Schloss Buchberg, Verein zur Förderung konstruktiver Kunst, Gars am Kamp 052565, 095509, 133070
Kunstraum Stein am Rhein, Stein am Rhein 111935
Kunstraum Universität Lüneburg, Lüneburg 103979
Kunstraum69, Hanau 103253
kunstraumno.10, Mönchengladbach 104096
Kunstreich am Pergamon-Museum, Berlin 069677
Kunstring Folkwang e.V., Essen . . . 053314
Kunstsalon Wolfsberg, Zürich 112135
Kunstsammlung der Universität Göttingen, Göttingen 017466
Kunstsammlung der Universität Leipzig, Leipzig 018561
Kunstsammlung des Benediktinerstifts Seitenstetten, Seitenstetten 002674
Kunstsammlung des Herzoglichen Georgianums, München 019074
Kunstsammlung Gerhard Schreiber, München 072766
Kunstsammlung im Schloß Rheinstein, Trechtingshausen 020466
Kunstsammlung Lorenzkapelle Rottweil, Rottweil 019932
Kunstsammlung Neubrandenburg, Neubrandenburg 019218
Kunstsammlung Robert Spreng, Reiden 037440
Kunstsammlung Sankt Nicolai-Kirche, Kalkar 018140
Kunstsammlung und Kupferstichkabinett der Martin-Luther- Universität Halle-Wittenberg, Halle, Saale 017664
Kunstsammlung Villa Schüpbach, Steffisburg 037603
Kunstsammlung Volpinum, Wien . . 002935
Kunstsammlungen, Staatliches Museum Schwerin, Schwerin 020147
Kunstsammlungen Böttcherstraße, Paula Modersohn-Becker Museum & Museum im Roselius-Haus, Bremen 016419
Kunstsammlungen Chemnitz, Chemnitz 016558
Kunstsammlungen der Ruhr-Universität Bochum, Bochum 016279
Kunstsammlungen der Stadt Limburg, Limburg an der Lahn 018648
Kunstsammlungen der Veste Coburg, Coburg 016576
Kunstsammlungen des Stiftes Kremsmünster, Kremsmünster . . . 002176
Kunstsammlungen Palais Schwarzenberg, Wien 002936
Kunstsammlungen und Graphische Sammlung, Furth bei Göttweig . . 001878
Kunstsammlungen Zwickau, Städtische Museen Zwickau, Zwickau 021086
Kunstschacht Katernberg, Essen . . 017070
Kunstschatulle, Aschersleben 069207
Kunstscheune, Plattenburg 104613
Kunstscheune Barnstorf, Ostseebad Wustrow 104559
KunstSchnitt, Passau 104589
Kunstschule, Mistelbach an der Zaya 049641
Kunstschule A. Khan-Leonhard, Schluchsee 050231
Kunstschule Alsterdamm Hamburg, Internationale Schule für Graphik-Design, Hamburg 050115
Kunstschule Bad Essen, Bad Essen 050008
Kunstschule für Malerei, freie und angewandte Grafik, Düsseldorf . . 050070
Kunstschule im Kolping-Bildungswerk, Stuttgart 050248
Kunstschule Rödel, Mannheim 050178
Kunstschule Rostock, Rostock 050225
Kunstschule Wandsbeck, Hamburg . 050116
Kunstseminar-Galerie, Luzern 111696
Kunstshop Has, Zürich . . . 082993, 141347
Kunstsjop, Bergen op Zoom 078072
Kunststätte Bossard, Jesteburg . . . 018120
Kunststätte Kuenburg, Payerbach . . 002408
Der Kunststall, Dahlem 102335
Kunststation Kleinsassen, Hofbieber 103391
Kunststiftung Baden-Württemberg, Stuttgart 020357
Kunststiftung Dr. Hans-Joachim und Elisabeth Bönsch, Uhingen 020528
Kunststiftung Poll, Berlin 016107
Kunststube, Drosendorf an der Thaya 001791
Die Kunststube, Giengen 102950
Kunststube, Wien 057480
Kunststübchen am Teich, Neustadt, Hessen 073037
Kunststück Galerie, Hamburg 103175
Kunststücke, Linz 095665, 123412
Kunsttempel, Kassel 103513
kunsttermine.de, Stuttgart 135798
Kunsttijdschrift Vlaanderen, Tielt, West-Vlaanderen 135602
Kunsttreppe Roesti, Winterthur 112000
't Kunstuus, Heinkenszand 029709
Kunstverein Aalen e.V., Aalen 053315
Kunstverein ACUD, Berlin 053316
Kunstverein Ahlen e.V., Ahlen 053317
Kunstverein Amstetten, Amstetten . 052566
Kunstverein Arnsberg e.V., Arnsberg 053318
Kunstverein Arthaus, Ahaus 053319
Kunstverein Augsburg, Augsburg . . . 053320
Kunstverein Aurich e.V, Aurich 053321
Kunstverein Bad Aibling, Bad Aibling 053322, 101625
Kunstverein Bad Salzdetfurth, Bad Salzdetfurth 015784, 053323
Kunstverein Baden, Baden bei Wien 052567, 095474
Kunstverein Bamberg, Bamberg . . . 053324
Kunstverein Baselland, Muttenz . . . 054192
Kunstverein Bayreuth, Bayreuth . . . 053325
Kunstverein Bergisches Land, Wipperfürth 053326
Kunstverein Bergneustadt, Bergneustadt 053327, 101768
Kunstverein Biberach e.V., Ummendorf 053328
Kunstverein Biel, Biel 054193
Kunstverein Binningen, Binningen . 054194
Kunstverein Bochum, Bochum 053329
Kunstverein Braunschweig, Braunschweig 053330
Kunstverein Braunschweig e.V., Braunschweig 016386
Kunstverein Bremerhaven von 1886, Bremerhaven 053331
Kunstverein Bretten, Bretten 053332
Kunstverein Bruchsal, Karlsruhe . . . 053333
Kunstverein Buttermarkt, Köln 053334, 103668
Kunstverein Buxtehude, Buxtehude 053335
Kunstverein Celle e.V., Celle 053336
Kunstverein Coburg, Coburg 053337, 102319
Kunstverein Darmstadt, Darmstadt . 053338
Kunstverein Das Damianstor, Bruchsal 053339
Kunstverein Deggendorf, Deggendorf 053340
Kunstverein der Diözese Rottenburg-Stuttgart, Bad Buchau 053341
Kunstverein der Stadt Glauchau, Glauchau 053342
Kunstverein Dillingen im Alten Schloß, Dillingen, Saar 053343
Kunstverein Donauwörth, Donauwörth 053344
Kunstverein Ebersberg, Ebersberg . 053345
Kunstverein Eisenturm Mainz, Mainz 053346
Kunstverein Eislingen, Eislingen . . . 053347
Kunstverein Ellwangen, Ellwangen . 053348
Kunstverein Elmshorn, Elmshorn . .053349, 133909
Kunstverein Elsterpark, Leipzig . . . 053350
Kunstverein Emmerich, Emmerich . 053351
Kunstverein Emsdetten, Emsdetten 053352
Kunstverein Erlangen, Erlangen . . . 053353
Kunstverein Etting-Pfaffenwinkel e.V., Polling, Kreis Weilheim 053354
Kunstverein Feldberger Land, Feldberg, Mecklenburg 053355
Kunstverein Flensburg, Flensburg . . 053356
Kunstverein Freiburg, Freiburg im Breisgau 053357
Kunstverein Friedberg, Friedberg, Hessen 053358
Kunstverein Friedrichshafen, Friedrichshafen 053359
Kunstverein Friedrichstadt, Berlin . .016108, 053360
Kunstverein für die Rheinlande und Westfalen, Düsseldorf 016839
Kunstverein für die Rheinlande und Westfalen e.V., Düsseldorf 053361, 133893
Kunstverein für Stadt und Landkreis Böblingen e.V., Stuttgart 053362
Kunstverein Ganderkesee, Ganderkesee 053363
Kunstverein Gauting, Gauting 053364
Kunstverein Gelderland, Geldern . .017347, 053365
Kunstverein Gelsenkirchen, Gelsenkirchen 053366
Kunstverein Germersheim, Germersheim 053367
Kunstverein Giannozzo, Verein zur Förderung der aktuellen plastischen Kunst, Berlin 053368
Kunstverein Gifhorn, Gifhorn 053369
Kunstverein Göppingen, Göppingen 053370
Kunstverein Göttingen e.V, Göttingen 053371
Kunstverein Grafschaft Bentheim, Neuenhaus 019232, 053372
Kunstverein Greven e.V., Greven . . . 053373
Kunstverein Gundelfingen, Gundelfingen, Breisgau 053374
Kunstverein Hannover, Hannover . .017761, 053375
Kunstverein Harburger Bahnhof, Hamburg 053376
Kunstverein Hattingen, Hattingen . . 053377
Kunstverein Heidenheim e.V., Heidenheim an der Brenz 053378
Kunstverein Heilbronn, Heilbronn . .017849, 053379
Kunstverein Hildesheim, Hildesheim 053380
Kunstverein Hochrhein, Bad Säckingen 053381
Kunstverein Hof, Hof, Saale 017956, 053382
Kunstverein Horn, Horn 052568
Kunstverein Hürth, Hürth 053383
Kunstverein Husum, Schobüll 053384
Kunstverein Ibbenbüren, Ibbenbüren 053385
Kunstverein in Bremen e.V., Bremen 053386
Kunstverein in Erftstadt e.V., Erftstadt 053387
Kunstverein in Hamburg e.V, Hamburg 017705, 053388
Kunstverein Ingolstadt, Ingolstadt . .018073, 053389
Kunstverein Jülich e.V., Jülich 053390
Kunstverein Jura, Neumarkt, Oberpfalz 053391
Kunstverein Kärnten, Klagenfurt . . .002141, 052569
Kunstverein Kaponier Vechta e.V., Vechta 053392
Kunstverein Kehdingen, Freiburg, Elbe 053393
Kunstverein Kehl-Hanauerland e.V., Kehl am Rhein 053394
Kunstverein Kirchheim unter Teck, Kirchheim unter Teck 053395
Kunstverein Kirchzarten e.V., Kirchzarten 053396
Kunstverein KISS-Kunst im Schloss Untergröningen e.V., Abtsgmünd . 053397
Kunstverein Köln rechtsrheinisch e.V., Köln 018328, 053398
Kunstverein Konstanz e.V., Konstanz 018377, 053399
Kunstverein Kornwestheim e.V., Kornwestheim 053400
Kunstverein Kreis Güterloh e.V., Gütersloh 053401
Kunstverein Langenhagen, Langenhagen 053402
Kunstverein Leimen '81 e.V., Leimen, Baden 053403
Kunstverein Lingen e.V., Lingen . . . 053404
Kunstverein Lippstadt e.V., Lippstadt 053405
Kunstverein Litfas, Wien . . 052570, 133214
Kunstverein Ludwigsburg e.V., Ludwigsburg, Württemberg 053406
Kunstverein Ludwigshafen am Rhein e.V., Ludwigshafen am Rhein 053407
Kunstverein Lübbecke, Lübbecke . . 053408
Kunstverein Lüneburg e.V., Lüneburg 053409
Kunstverein March e.V., March 053410
Kunstverein Mittleres Kinzigtal, Haslach 053411
Kunstverein München, München . .019075, 053412
Kunstverein Münsterland, Coesfeld 053413
Kunstverein Museum Schloß Morsbroich e.V., Leverkusen 053414
Kunstverein Neckar-Odenwald e.V., Mosbach, Baden 053415
Kunstverein Neuhausen e.V., Neuhausen auf den Fildern 053416
Kunstverein Neustadt am Rübenberge e.V., Neustadt am Rübenberge 053417
Kunstverein Neustadt an der Weinstraße e.V., Neustadt an der Weinstraße . 053418
Kunstverein Nordenham e.V., Nordenham 053419
Kunstverein Nümbrecht e.V., Nümbrecht 053420
Kunstverein Oberaargau, Langenthal 054195
Kunstverein Oberhausen e.V., Oberhausen, Rheinland 053421
Kunstverein Oberwallis, Brig 054196
Kunstverein Oerlinghausen e.V., Oerlinghausen 053422
Kunstverein Osterholz, Osterholz-Scharmbeck 053423
Kunstverein Ostseebad Kühlungsborn, Kühlungsborn 053424, 103805
Kunstverein Paderborn e.V., Paderborn 053425
Kunstverein Panitzsch, Panitzsch . .053426, 104580
Kunstverein Paradigma, Linz 052571, 095666
Kunstverein Passau e.V., Passau . . 053427
Kunstverein Passau- Sankt Anna-Kapelle, Passau 019570
Kunstverein Pikanta e.V., Leipzig . . 053428
Kunstverein Plauen-Vogtland e.V, Plauen 053429
Kunstverein Radolfzell e.V., Radolfzell 053430
Kunstverein Rastatt e.V., Rastatt . . . 053431
Kunstverein Region Heinsberg e.V., Heinsberg 053432
Kunstverein Reutlingen, Hans Thoma-Gesellschaft, Reutlingen 019808, 053433
Kunstverein Ribnitz-Damgarten e.V., Ribnitz-Damgarten 053434
Kunstverein Röderhof, Röderhof . . . 053435
Kunstverein Rosenheim, Rosenheim 053436, 134370
Kunstverein Rügen e.V., Rambin, Rügen 053437
Kunstverein Ruhr e.V., Essen 017071, 053438
Kunstverein Salzgitter e.V., Salzgitter 053439
Kunstverein Sankt Gallen, Sankt Gallen 054197
Kunstverein Schaffhausen, Schaffhausen 054198
Kunstverein Schieder-Schwalenberg, Schieder-Schwalenberg 053440
Kunstverein Schopfheim e.V., Schopfheim 053441

Kunstverein Schorndorf e.V., Schorndorf, Württemberg 053442
Kunstverein Schwäbisch Hall, Schwäbisch Hall 053443
Kunstverein Schwarzwald-Baar-Heuberg, Hausen ob Verena 053444
Kunstverein Schwerte, Schwerte . .020153, 053445
Kunstverein Schwetzingen, Schwetzingen 053446
Kunstverein Siegen, Siegen 053447
Kunstverein Speyer, Speyer 020264
Kunstverein Speyer e.V., Speyer . . . 053448
Kunstverein Springhornhof e.V., Neuenkirchen, Lüneburger Heide .019233, 053449
Kunstverein Südsauerland, Olpe . . . 053450
Kunstverein Talstrasse, Halle, Saale 017665, 053451
Kunstverein Tauberbischofsheim, Tauberbischofsheim 053452
Kunstverein Teterow, Teterow 053453
Kunstverein Trier Junge Kunst e.V., Trier 053454
Kunstverein Tübingen e.V., Tübingen 053455
Kunstverein Uelze, Lüneburg 053456
Kunstverein Uelzen, Uelzen 053457
Kunstverein Ulm, Ulm 053458
Kunstverein Unna, Unna 053459
Kunstverein Uri, Altdorf, Uri 054199
Kunstverein Veritas, Wien 052572
Kunstverein Viernheim e.V., Viernheim 053460
Kunstverein Villa Streccius Landau e.V., Landau in der Pfalz 053461
Kunstverein Wallisellen, Wallisellen 054200
Kunstverein Weiden, Weiden, Oberpfalz 020707
Kunstverein Weiden e.V., Weiden, Oberpfalz 053462
Kunstverein Wesseling, Wesseling . 053463
Kunstverein Wien-Alte Schmiede, Wien 052573
Kunstverein Wilhelmshöhe Ettlingen, Ettlingen 053464
Kunstverein Wiligrad, Lübstorf 053465
Kunstverein Winterthur, Winterthur . 054201
Kunstverein Wolfenbüttel, Wolfenbüttel 053466
Kunstverein Wolfsburg, Wolfsburg . 053467
Kunstverein Würzburg e.V., Würzburg 053468
Kunstverein Xanten, Xanten 053469
Kunstverein zu Frechen e.V., Frechen 017214, 053470
Kunstverein zu Rostock, Rostock . . 053471
Kunstvereinigung Wasgau, Dahn . . 053472
Kunstvereniging Diepenheim, Diepenheim 029478, 053897
Kunstverkehr, Verein für kulturelle Interaktion und Information, Wien 052574, 133215
Kunstverket Galleri, Oslo 079456
Kunstverlag Weingarten, Weingarten, Württemberg 134451
Kunstverlag Würzburg, Würzburg . . 134470
Kunstweb, Rotterdam 078726
Kunstwerk, Köln 018329, 053473
Das Kunstwerk, Wien 057481, 120687
Die Kunstwerkstatt, Stuttgart 126864
Kunstwerkstatt, Tulln 095774
Kunstwerkstatt, Ulm 105095
Kunstwerkstatt Rehalp, Zürich 112136
Kunstwerkstatt Wuppertal, Wuppertal 074531
Kunstwissenschaftler- und Kunstkritiker-Verband e.V., Berlin 053474
Kunstzaken, Genk 096281
Kunstzeit, Sankt Gallen 082782
Kunstzeitung, Regensburg 135799
Kunstzentrum Koppelschleuse, Meppen 104064
Kuntsin Taidekokoelma, Vaasa 010200
Kuny Domokos Múzeum, Tata 021904
Kunz, Vreny, Uster 082869, 130201
Kunz-Werle, A., Häusern 071161
Kunze, Claus, Dresden 138996
Kunze, Gerhard, Berlin 125243
Kunze, Lilli E., Düsseldorf 070404
Kunze-Kania, I., Karlsbad 071703
Kuo, Georg, Berlin 069678
Kuo, Jean, Berlin 069679
Kuo, Veronika, Fürstenwalde, Spree 070909
Kuokkalan Museoraitti, Lempäälä . . 009816
Kuopion Korttelimuseo, Kuopio 009760
Kuopion Luonnontieteellinen Museo, Kuopion Kulttuurihistoriallinen Museo, Kuopio 009761
Kuopion Taidemuseo, Kuopio 009762
Kuparas, Vilnius 107363
Kupf, Linz 133113
Kupferberg-Museum, Mainz 018789
Kupfergraben Verlagsgesellschaft, Berlin 133792
Kupferschmiede-Museum, Tangermünde 020398
Kupferstich-Kabinett, Staatliche Kunstsammlungen Dresden, Dresden 016797
Kupferstichkabinett, Akademie der bildenden Künste, Wien 002937
Kupferstichkabinett, Öffentliche Kunstsammlung Basel, Basel 036891
Kupferstichkabinett - Sammlung der Zeichnungen und Druckgraphik, Staatliche Museen zu Berlin - Stiftung Preußischer Kulturbesitz, Berlin 016109
Kupina, Moskva 080250
Kupina, Moskva 080251
Kupitz, Marie, Köln 126098
Kupno, Pyrzyce 079704
Kupperman, Amsterdam 077897
Kuppinger, Lothar, Hockenheim . . . 125947
Kupser, Dr., Ansbach 101590
Kupšina, Jiří, Kolín 060036
Kur Gallery, Donostia-San Sebastián 110341
Kur-und Stadtmuseum, Bad Ems . . 015693
Kura, Auckland 108333
Kura, Waikato 108591
Kura Gallery, Wellington 030639
Kuralan Kylämäki, Turku 010164
Kuramayama Museum, Kyoto 026733
Kuranda Arts Cooperative, Kuranda 094717
Kurashiki Archaeological Museum, Kurashiki 026698
Kurashiki City Art Museum, Kurashiki 026699
Kurashiki Geijutsu Kagaku Daigaku, Kurashiki 050459
Kurashiki Mingeikan, Kurashiki . . . 026700
Kuraya, Sakai 077191
Kuraya, San Francisco 092825
Kurayoshi Museum, Kurayoshi 026703
Kurdi, Talal, Jeddah 080362
The Kurdish Museum, Brooklyn . . . 042461
Kure Bijutsukan, Kure 026704
Kurek, Stanislaw, Bonn . . 102188, 125353
Kurella, Annette, Sinzing 126808
Kurer, Bernadette, Sankt Gallen . . . 130163
Kurfis, Josef, Ascona 111138
Kurfner, Michael, München 072767
Kurfürst, K., Offenburg 073189
Kurfürstliches Freihaus, Stadt- und Kulturgeschichtliches Museum, Torgau 020452
Kurfürstliches Gärtnerhaus, Bonn . . 016330
Kurganskij Oblastnoj Chudožestvennyj Muzej, Kurgan 033316
Kurganskij Oblastnoj Kraevedčeskij Muzej, Kurgan 033317
Kuri, Wolfgang, Augsburg 069237
Kurikan Museo, Kurikka 009767
Kurimanzutto, México 107494
Kuriosa & Antik, Saarbrücken 073638
Kuriosamässan, Inredning, Prylar och Samlarobjekt, Stockholm 093884
Kuriositet & Antikk, Stavanger 079505
Kurita, Paris 066122
Kurita, Paris 066123
Kurita Bijutsukan, Ashikaga 026424
Kurmann, André, Biberist 082255
Kurmann, André & Paulette, Solothurn 082822
Kurmuseum, Bad Tatzmannsdorf . . 001737
Kurmuseum Bad Wildungen, Bad Wildungen 015824
Kurmuseum des Österreichischen Moorforschungsinstituts, Bad Wimsbach-Neydharting 001740
Kurnikova Hiša, Tržič 034531
Kuroda Kinenshitsu, Tokyo 027196
Kurofune, Tokyo 077276
Kurowski, Weißwasser 074329
Kurpfälzische Münzhandlung, Mannheim 072424, 121510, 126279
Kurpfälzisches Museum der Stadt Heidelberg, Heidelberg 017829
Kurrajong Antique Centre, Kurrajong 056071
Kurrer, Mölln 072561
Kursiv - eine Kunstzeitschrift, Graz . 135566
Kurskaja Kartinnaja Galereja im. A.A. Denejki, Kursk 033318
Kurskij Gosudarstvennyj Oblastnoj Kraevedčeskij Muzej, Kursk 033319
Kurskij Gosudarstvennyj Oblastnoj Muzej Archeologii, Kursk 033320
Kurt, Andreas, Murnau 072937
Kurt-Tucholsky-Gedenkstätte, Rheinsberg 019823
Kurta, Axel, Berlin 138812
Kurtej, Miloš, Kutná Hora . 060041, 098376
Kurth, Bernhard & N., Spiegel 082826
Kurth, Hanspeter, Laupen, Bern . . . 082527
Kurth, K., Dormagen 102387
Kurts, Lisa, Memphis 116993
Kurt's Furniture Stripping, Buffalo . 131858
Merve Kurttepeli & Barbara Ther, İstanbul 083144
Kurukshetra Panorama & Science Centre, Kurukshetra 022233
Kurun Ulkomuseo, Kuru 009768
Kurun Warun, Pomona 056467
Kurz, Wien 057482
Kurz, Birgit, Stuttgart 126865
Kurz, Lothar, Lenting 103904
Kurz, Rainer, Oberaudorf 139615
Kurz Rainer (08033) 91499, Rohrdorf 139694
Kurze, G., Benz 101758
Kurze, H., Gütersloh 103034
Kurzemes Hercogu Kapenes, Rundāles Pils Muzejs, Jelgava 027693
Kurzreuther, Christa, Monheim am Rhein 072590
Kurzweg, Beckum 069505
Kusabue, Nagoya 106925
Kuschel, Joachim, Burgwedel 070109, 125416
Kuschel, Karin, Hamburg 071275
Kuser Farm Mansion, Hamilton . . . 044400
Kushiro Art Museum, Hokkaido, Kushiro 026707
Kushiro City Museum, Kushiro 026708
Kushner & Taylor, New York 118113
Kusmikim, Amsterdam 077898
Kusseneers, Paul, Lier 096380
Kustannus Oy Taide Art Publishers, Helsinki 133442
Kustavin Kotiseutumuseo, Kustavi . 009769
Kuster, 's-Hertogenbosch 078524
Kuster, Hugo, Sankt Gallen 082783
Kustom Korners, Pittsburgh 118935
Kuszelevic, Henri, Saint-Ouen 067820
Kuszelewic, Henri, Paris 066124
Kutaisskij Gosudarstvennyj Muzej Istorii i Etnografii, Kutaisi 015403
Kutas, Wien 057483
Kutjarra Arts, Alice Springs 094140
Kutscha, Maria, Salzburg 095727
Kutschen-, Schlitten- und Wagenmuseum Rottach-Egern, Rottach-Egern . . . 019924
Kutschen- und Heimatmuseum, Sillian 002680
Kutschen- und Schlittenmuseum, Großraming 001977
Kutschenmuseum, Augustusburg . . 015624
Kutschenmuseum, Gaildorf 017317
Kutschenmuseum, Laa an der Thaya 002189
Kutschenmuseum, Ludwigslust . . . 018709
Kutschenmuseum, Neustadt, Dosse 019290
Kutschenmuseum, Historisches Museum Basel, Basel 036892
Kutschenmuseum Hessisches Landgestüt, Dillenburg 016711
Kutschensammlung, Eigeltingen . . . 016915
Kutschensammlung Robert Sallmann, Amriswil 036840
Kuttig, Falkenstein, Vogtland 139068
Kutynski, Piet, Tilburg 078771
Kutz-Leitner, Ellengard, Linz 057159
Kuurojen Museo, Helsinki 009547
Kuurstra, J.J., Amsterdam 134785
Kuusamon Kotiseutumuseo, Kuusamo 009770
Kuusiston Kartano, Kuusisto 009774
Kuvataideakatemia, Helsinki 049925
Kuwait Auction Hall, Safat 121751
Kuwait National Museum, Kuwait . . 027632
Kuwasawa Design Kenkyujo, Tokyo 050488
Kuybyshev Republican Memorial Museum, Kzyl-Orda 027406
Kuyper, Bubb, Haarlem . . . 121791, 140443
Kuzbik, Joëlle, Montcenis 064668
Kvadrat, Omsk 109612
Kvadrat, Sankt-Peterburg 109634
Kvæfjord Museum, Harstad 030877
Kvæven Bygdetun, Tjørhom 031266
Kvam Bygdemuseum, Norheimsund 031055
Kvariaatti Antikvaarinen Kiirjakauppa, Turku 137996
Kvarkens Båtmuseum, Malax 009855
Kvarnbacken Prylmuseum, Sandviken 036562
Kvarnbackmuseet i Harrström, Korsnäs 009736
Kvevlax Hembygdsmuseum, Kvevlax 009776
Kvikmyndasafn Islands, Hafnarfjörður 021946
Kvindemuseet i Danmark, Århus . . 008807
Kviteseid Bygdetun, Kviteseid 030966
KW Institute for Contemporary Art, Kunst-Werke Berlin e.V., Berlin 016110
Kwa Muhle Museum, Durban 034601
Kwa Zulu Natal Technikon Sculpture Department, Durban 050699
Kwade, Alexander, Hannover 071399
Kwagiulth Museum, Quathiaski Cove 006214
Kwak, Los Angeles 089816, 132261
Kwang Fu, Taipei 133395
Kwangdong College Museum, Gangneung 027489
Kwartijn, Amsterdam 107755
't Kwartje, Mechelen 137529
Kwartler, Alice, New York 091012
Kweichow Provincial Museum, Kueiyang 007165
Kwidzinski, Kasimir J., Spechbach . 126818
Kwinitsa Station Railway Museum, Prince Rupert 006208
Kwok, Singapore 080513
KX., Hamburg 017706
Kyaratei, Narita 077169
Kyburz, Rudolf, Schindellegi 082802
Kyffhäuser-Denkmal, Bad Frankenhausen 015699
Kyïv State Institute of Fine Arts, Kyïv 050796
Kyïvs'kyj Literaturno-memOorial'nyj Budinok-muzej Tarasa Ševčenka, National Taras Shevchenko Museum, Kyïv . 038298
Kyïvs'kyj Literaturno-memorial'nyj Budinok-muzej M. Ryl's'kogo, Kyïv 038299
Kyïvs'kyj Literaturno-memorial'nyj Budinok-muzej M. Zan'kovec'koï, Kyïv . . . 038300
Kyïvs'kyj Literaturno-memorial'nyj Muzej-kvartyra P. Tyčyny, Kyïv 038301
Kyïvskyj Muzej Puškina, Kyïv 038302

Kyïvs'kyj Muzej Rosijs'koho Mystectva, Kyïv . . . 038303
Kyle, Francis, London . . . 113727
Kyle and Carrick District Library and Museum, Ayr . . . 038559
Kylia Arte, Bucaramanga . . . 098217
Kymenlaakson maakuntamuseo, Kotka . . . 009741
Kymmel, Peter, Oderwitz . . . 073173
Kyneton Museum, Kyneton . . . 001165
Kyngston House Museum, Saint Albans . . . 040885
Kynigalakis Dimitris, S., Galatsi . . . 074619
Kynologisches Museum, Wien . . . 002938
Kyodo Gangu-kan, Takayama . . . 027125
Kyösti- ja Kalervo Kallion Museo, Nivala . . . 009906
Kyoko chirathivat, Bangkok . . . 112234
Kyomo, Nueva Andalucía . . . 122076
Kyongju University Museum, Kyongju . . . 027527
Kyongnam College Museum, Masan 027529
Kyoto Antique Center, Kyoto . . . 077113
Kyoto Arashiyama Music Box Museum, Kyoto . . . 026734
Kyoto Bazaar, Kyoto . . . 077114
Kyoto Bisho, Kyoto . . . 077115
Kyoto City Archaeological Museum, Kyoto . . . 026735
Kyoto City Dohda Senior High School of Arts, Kyoto . . . 050462
Kyoto Daigaku Bungakubu Hakubutsukan, Kyoto . . . 026736
Kyoto Daigaku Sougou Hakubutsukan, Kyoto . . . 026737
Kyoto-fu Kyoto Bunka Hakubutsukan, Kyoto . . . 026738
Kyoto Gion Oil Lamp Museum, Kyoto . . . 026739
Kyoto Kokuritsu Hakubutsukan, Kyoto . . . 026740
Kyoto Kokuritsu Kindai Bijutsukan, Kyoto . . . 026741
Kyoto Mingei Kan, Kyoto . . . 026742
Kyoto Museum for World Peace, Kyoto . . . 026743
Kyoto Museum of Traditional Crafts - Fureaikan, Kyoto . . . 026744
Kyoto Prefectural Museum, Kyoto . . 026745
Kyoto-shi Bijutsukan, Kyoto . . . 026746
Kyoto-shi Seishonen Kagaku, Kyoto 026747
Kyoto-shiritsu Geijutsu Daigaku, Kyoto . . . 050463
Kyoto Shoin, Kyoto . . . 140162
Kyoto Yuzen Bunka Kaikan, Kyoto . . 026748
Kyoto Zokei Geijutsu Daigaku, Kyoto . . . 050464
Kypriotis & Sia, E., Glyfada . . . 074621
Kyrgyz State Museum of Fine Arts G. Aitiyev, Biškek . . . 027634
Kyriazopoulos Collection, Thessaloniki . . . 021495
Kyrios Books, Nottingham . . . 141974
Kyrou Collection, Athinai . . . 021180
Kyser-Hollingsworth, Washington . . 093418
Kystmuseet Hvaler, Vesterøy . . . 031332
Kystmuseet i Nord-Trøndelag, Rørvik . . . 031151
Kystmuseet i Øygarden, Rong . . . 031148
Kystmuseet i Sogn og Fjordane, Florø . . . 030841
Kystmuseet i Sør-Trøndelag, Hitra . 030892
Kystmuseet Staværingen, Stadsbygd . . . 031218
Kysucka Galéria, Čadca . . . 034343
Kysucke Múzeum, Čadca . . . 034344
Kyu Aoyama Bettei, Otaru . . . 026994
Kyukodo, Sendai . . . 077216
Kyunghee University Museum, Seoul . . . 027579
Kyungin Museum of Fine Art, Seoul 027580
Kyungsung Museum, Busan . . . 027461
Kyusei Atami Art Museum, Atami . . 026430
Kyushu, Fukuoka . . . 106845
Kyushu Rekishi Shiryokan, Dazaifu . 026450
Kyyjärven Kotiseutumuseo, Kyyjärvi 009777
KZ-Gedenk- und Begegnungsstätte, Ehemalige Außenstelle des Konzentrationslagers Neuengamme, Ladelund . . . 018456
KZ-Gedenkstätte - Dachau, Dachau 016619
KZ-Gedenkstätte Flossenbürg, Flossenbürg . . . 017135
KZ-Gedenkstätte Husum-Schwesing, Schwesing . . . 020155
KZ-Gedenkstätte Mauthausen, Mauthausen . . . 002304
KZ-Gedenkstätte Mittelbau-Dora, Nordhausen . . . 019334
KZ-Gedenkstätte Neuengamme, Hamburg . . . 017707
KZ-Gedenkstätte und Zeitgeschichte-Museum Ebensee, Ebensee . . . 001798
L. and CO, Saint-Cyr-en-Pail . . . 067411
L Art, Kyïv . . . 112414
L & B Antiquitäten, Essen . . . 070635
L & B Antiquitäten, Essen . 070636, 121400
L & B Viewing Room, Portland . . . 119013
L & L Antiklädchen, Merchweiler . . 072519
L & L Arts, New York . . . 118114
L & L Coins, Denver . . . 088707
L. Lange's Ovnmuseum, Svendborg 009123
L & M Antiques, Tampa . . 093133, 132955
L & N Productions, Philadelphia . . . 118789
L & R Antiques, Houston . . . 089132
L & R Antiques, Houston . . . 089133
L & S Coins, Jacksonville . . . 089423
La Baule Auction, La Baule-Escoublac . . . 121021
La Belle Epoque, Châteaudun . . . 062192
La Boheme Gallery, Macclesfield . . 114024
La Brea Antique Collection, Los Angeles . . . 089817
La Butte aux Cailles, Paris . . . 066125
La-di-da, Stratford-upon-Avon . . . 131555
L.A. Galerie, Frankfurt am Main . . . 102797
La Galerie d'Art, Bowness-on-Windermere . . . 112686
La Hougue Bie Museum, Saint Helier . . . 040915
La Hune Brenner, Paris . . . 100570
La Loie Fuller, Paris . . . 066126
La Malle des Indes, Metz . . . 099714
L.A. Mayer Museum for Islamic Art, Jerusalem . . . 022963
La Parete, Wien . . . 057484, 123512
La Petite Galerie, Tampa . . . 093134
La Raza-Galeria Posada, Sacramento . . . 047592
La Rocca, Leonardo, Palermo . . . 106431
La Salle University Art Museum, Philadelphia . . . 046954
La Trobe Street Gallery, Melbourne . 094818
La Trobe University Art Museum, Melbourne . . . 001244
La Vetrata, Roberto, Roma . . . 106570
La vie des musées, Liège . . . 135603
Laade, Hansjürgen, Meerbusch . . . 072487
Laage, Salomon, Paris . . . 100571
Laakes, W., München . . . 072768
Laarman, J.H., Hardenberg . . . 128702
Laat, H. de, 's-Hertogenbosch . . . 078525
Laatzen, Hermann, Hamburg . . . 139195
The Lab, San Francisco . . . 047867
Labadie, Charles, Saint-Jean-de-Luz . . . 101163
Labaëre, Dourges . . . 124226
Laban, Jean-Michel, Oloron-Sainte-Marie . . . 065267
Laband Art Gallery, Los Angeles . . . 045438
Labarbe, Marc, Toulouse . . . 101361
Labarre A, Saint-Germain-Lembron 067502
L'Abat Jour de Charme, Trouville-sur-Mer . . . 068636
Labatut, Paris . . . 100572
Labbé, Armel, La Chartre-sur-le-Loir . . . 063326
Label 2-4-DIX, Montluçon . . . 099747
Labet, Michel, Étiolles . . . 062816
Labeyrie, Alain, Bordeaux . . . 124130
Labeyrie, Pascal, Bordeaux . . . 124131
Labiche, Nicole, Montaure . . . 064642
Labiche, Nicole, Rouen . . . 067275
Il Labirinto, Milano . . . 140053
Labirynt, Kraków . . . 108959
Labirynt 2 BWA, Lublin . . . 109027
Labirynt II, Kraków . . . 108960
Labisch, Hubert, Unterpleichfeld . . . 126934
Labonne, Albert-Claude, La Réole . 063405
Labor Fruit, Los Angeles . . . 116814
Laboratário de Ensino de Ciências, Faculdade de Filosofia, Ciências e Letras de Ribeirão Preto, Ribeirão Preto . 004325
Il Laboratorio, Milano . . . 127610
Il Laboratorio, Roma . . . 128078
Laboratorio Antiquariato, Milano . . 127611
Laboratório de Anatomia e Identificação de Madeiras, Manaus . . . 004205
Laboratorio de Conservacion y Restauracion, Barcelona . . . 129357
Laboratório de Demonstração do Instituto de Fisica, Intituto de Fisica / IF, São Paulo . . . 004511
Laboratorio de Restauracion y Enmarcacion, Barcelona . . . 129358
Laboratorio del Gerva, Venezia . . . 128394
Laboratorio di Restauro, Brescia . . 127221
Laboratorio di Restauro, Genova . . 127460
Laboratorio di Restauro, Genova . . 127461
Laboratorio di Restauro, Milano . . . 127612
Laboratorio di Restauro, Milano . . . 127613
Laboratorio di Restauro, Modena . . 127735
Laboratorio di Restauro Santo Stefano, Bologna . . . 127157
Laboratorio Restauri d'Arte, Trieste 128374
Laboratorios Dopla, Sevilla . . . 129734
Laboratorios Dopla, Sevilla . . . 129735
Labour of Love, Jacksonville . . . 132185
Labrada, Cali . . . 098239
Labrador Heritage Museum, Happy Valley . . . 005603
Labrador Straits Museum, L'Anse-au-Loup . . . 005021
Labråten, Asker Museum, Valstads samlinger, Hvalstad . . . 030918
Labre, Michael, Sassey . . . 068140
Labriffe, M., Marcq-en-Barœul . . . 064275
Labriola, Phoenix . . . 091751
Labriola, J., Phoenix . . . 091752
Labrouche, Montendre . . . 064675
Labrouche, Line & Michel, Messac . 064513
Labry, Dominique-Mathieu, Montpeyroux . . . 064761
Laburnum, Poole . . . 086288, 131387
Laburnum Antiques, Richmond . . . 092092
Laburnum Cottage Antiques, Eye . . 084369
Labus, Oberhausen, Rheinland . . . 104500
Labyrint, Praha . . . 133416, 135667
Labyrinth, Valletta . . . 077539
Labyrinth Kindermuseum Berlin, Berlin . . . 016111
Labyrinthos, Firenze . . . 135910
Lac, Hong, Ho Chi Minh City . . . 120514
Lac, Isabelle du, Toulouse . . . 068525
Lac Cardinal Regional Pioneer Village Museum, Grimshaw . . . 005554
Lac La Hache Museum, Barkerville 005067
Lac LaRonge Museum, LaRonge . . 005748
L.A.C. Lieu d'Art Contemporain, Sigean . . . 014799
Lac Qui Parle County Historical Museum, Madison . . . 045582
Lac Sainte-Anne and District Pioneer Museum, Sangudo . . . 006410
Lacam, Nice . . . 065098
Lacan, Strasbourg . . . 101296
Lacarin, Madeleine, Montluçon . . . 064711
Lacaze, Alain, Québec . . . 097146
Lacaze, Bernard, Paris . . . 066127
L'Accent Sud, Saint-Tropez . . . 068019
Laccroix, Jean-Claude, Lorient . . . 064005
Lace Antiguidades, Rio de Janeiro . 058602
Lace House Museum, Black Hawk . 042240
Lace Museum, Sunnyvale . . . 048432
Lacerte, Madeleine, Québec . . . 097147
Lacewing Fine Art, Winchester . . . 114704
Lacey, Stephen, London . . . 113728
Lacey Historical Society Museum, Forked River . . . 043885
Lach, G., Kraków . . . 129042
Lachaert, Sofie, Tielrode . . . 096413
Lachapelle, New York . . . 091013
Lachaux, Alain, Beaune . . . 061283
Lachaux, Jean-Christophe, Paris . . 066128
Lachaux, Jean-Pierre, Beaune . . . 061284
Lachenaud, Jean-Luc, Tours . . . 101380
Lacher-Biene, Silvia, Müllheim, Baden . . . 072619
Lachin, Venezia . . . 076948
Lachin, Venezia . . . 076949
Lachin, Venezia . . . 076950
Lachman, Dušan, Praha . . . 123989
Lachmann, Alex, Köln . . . 103669
Lachmayr, Hannes, Adnet . 056911, 123332
Lachmuth, Wolfgang, Schopfheim . 073721
Lacidogna, Michele, Torino . . . 076829
Lackey, Oklahoma City . . . 091510
Lackey, David, Houston . . . 089134
Lackey, Hugh, San Antonio . . . 092531
Lackham Museum of Agriculture and Rural Life, Lacock . . . 039917
Lackmann, Sabine, Essen . . . 070637
Lackmann-Wisskirchen, L., München . . . 072769
Lackner, G., Salzburg . . . 057265
Lackner, Martin, Köln . . . 071972
Lackus, H., Kraichtal . . . 072062
Lacombe, Claudine, Auneau . . . 061066
Lacombe, Eric, Bordeaux . . . 120945
Lacombe, Jean-Pierre, Rodez . . . 067193
Lacote, Philippe, Beaune . . . 061285
Lacour, Guy, Goven . . . 063026
Lacour, Jean-Marc, Bruz . 061829, 124165
Lacour, Jean-Marie, L'Isle-sur-la-Sorgue . . . 063941
Lacour, Josette, Genève . . . 082440
Lacour, Pierre, Fourdrain . . . 062932
Lacourbas, Hélène et Romain, Bellenaves . . . 061335
Lacourière & Frelaut, Paris 100573, 133636
Lacourt, Maurice, Charmes . . . 062164
The Lacquer Chest, London . . . 085464
Lacquerware Museum, Pagan . . . 029066
Lacrimosa, Osaka . . . 077178
Lacroix, Québec . . . 097148
Lacroix, Alexandre, Paris . . . 100574
Lacroix, Serge, Saint-Julien-en-Genevois . . . 067560
The Lacrosse Museum and National Hall of Fame, Baltimore . . . 041991
Lacruz, Valencia . . . 129778
Lacueva, Eduardo, Buenos Aires . . 136727
Lacy, London . . . 085465, 113729
Lacy, West Hollywood . . . 120395
Lacy Scott & Knight, Bury Saint Edmunds . . . 122443
Lacy Scott & Knight, Stowmarket . . 122714
Lacydon, Marseille . . . 099671, 133494
Laczkó Dezsoě Múzeum, Veszprém 021919
Ladakh, Delhi . . . 105671
Ladbyskibsmuseet, Kerteminde . . . 008952
Ladenburger Spielzeugauktion, Ladenburg . . . 121489
Laderer, Pittsburgh . . . 118936
Ladeuille, Roger, Lamorlaye . . . 063501
Ladevèze, Michel, Cormeilles . . . 062477
Ladew Manor House, Monkton . . . 045961
Ladner, Hubert & Helma, Urbar . . . 074167
Ladoucette, Marc de, Paris . . . 100575
Ladron de Guevara, José Manuel, Dresden . . . 070323
Lads, Osaka . . . 106967
Ladson, Malvern, Victoria . . . 123260
Ladue Antique Galleries, Saint Louis . . . 092264
Lady and the Tramp Antiques Mall, Saint Paul . . . 092372
Lady Cant Bis, Antwerpen . . . 057713
Lady Denman Maritime Museum, Huskisson . . . 001124
Lady Di Régiségbolt, Budapest . . . 074693
Lady Franklin Gallery, Lenah Valley 001181

Lady Jane, Rotterdam 078727
Lady L, Bad Nenndorf 069338
Lady Lever Art Gallery, Port Sunlight 040747
Lady Matilda Gallery, Nana Glen . . . 094926
Lady of the Lake, Austin 087589
Lady of the Sea Gallery, Norfolk . . . 091386
Lady Piú, Torino 076830
Lady Steptoe, Orange 056406
Lady Waterford Gallery, Berwick-upon-Tweed 038684
Lady Wilson Museum, Dharampur . 022103
Ladybug, San Diego 119523
Ladybug Books, Seattle 142996
Ladysmith Railway Museum, Ladysmith 005735
Läänemaa Muuseum, Haapsalu . . . 009358
Lääninkivalteri Aschanin Talo, Heinola 009511
Läckö Slott, Lidköping 036417
Lähetysmuseo, Helsinki 009548
Lækkert, Bærre, Oslo 079457
Lämmermann, Astrid, Rödermark . . 126727
Lände, Kressbronn am Bodensee . . 018404
Längelmäen Kirkkomuseo, Längelmäki 009778
Längelmäen Pellavamuseo, Länkipohja 009779
Länsmuseet Gävleborg, Gävle 036283
Länsmuseet Halmstad, Halmstad . . 036325
Länsmuseet Västernorrland, Härnösand 036319
Länsmuseet Varberg, Varberg 036778
Lärisch, Hedwig, Berlin 069680
Lærken, Nykøbing Falster 098598
Læsø Museum, Læsø 009005
Läzer, Weimar, Thüringen 105191
Lafarge, Jean-Pierre, Cognac 062378
Lafaurie, Bénédicte de, Paris 066129
Lafay, Benoît, Lyon 124361
Lafayette, Cleethorpes 141523
Lafayette, Saint-Ouen 067821
Lafayette Antics, Paris 066130
Lafayette College Art Gallery, Easton 043589
Lafayette Miners Museum, Lafayette 045087
Lafayette Museum - Alexandre Mouton House, Lafayette 045090
Lafayette Museum Association, Lafayette 054838
Lafayette Natural History Museum, Lafayette 045091
Lafayette Ragsdale, Memphis 116994
Lafeara, Manama 096015
Laffanour, François, Paris 100576
Lafferty, Tampa 093135
Laffitte, Jeanne, Marseille 138195
Lafite, Céline, Paris 124712
Lafitte, Christchurch 112870
Lafitte, Claude, Montréal 097043
Laflamme Galleries, Calgary 096826
Lafleur, Amiens 060819
Lafon, Didier, Brunoy 061827
Lafon, François, Le Puy-en-Velay . . 121033
Lafon, Josée, Saint-Pierre-d'Oléron 067956
Lafond, Pittsburgh 118937
Lafond, Pittsburgh 118938
Lafond, Bernard, Régnié-Durette . . 067048
Lafont, Jorge A., Baradero 055143
Laforge, Pierre, Saint-Maximin-la-Sainte-Baume 067668, 124911
Lafosse, Jean, Pontaubert 066939
Lafougère, Patricia, Bordeaux 061624
Lafougère, Patricia, Bordeaux 061625
Lafourcade, Antonio y Eduardo Roman, Madrid 129633
Lafourcade, Yannick, Tours 068594
Lafouresse, Jean-Bruno, Bayonne . 061233
Lafouresse, Jean-Bruno, Bayonne . 061234
Lafouresse, Jean-Bruno, Bayonne . 124093
Lafouresse, Jean-Bruno, Bayonne . 124094
Lafreniere & Pai, Ottawa 097110
Lagan Lookout Centre, Belfast 038662
Laganà, Salvatore, Reggio Calabria 127898
Laganda, Johann Josef, Unterach am Attersee 057336
Laganland Bilmuseum, Lagan 036411
Lagard, Buenos Aires 094080
Lagarde, Fabrègues 062835
Lagarde, Hugues, Brin-sur-Seille . . 061802
Lagazio, Valparaiso 059563, 097634
Lågdalsmuseet, Museum for Kongsberg, Numedal and Øvre-Eiker, Kongsberg 030947
Lage, Madrid 081329
L'âge d'Or, Saint-Gaudens 067480
L'Age d'Or, Valenciennes 068693
Lagénie, Françoise, Paris 124713
Das Lager, Freiburg im Breisgau . . 070847
Lagerquist, Evelyn & Kay, Atlanta . . 114896
Laget, Guy, Ambronay 060801
Laget, Guy, Ambronay 060802
Laget, Léonce, Paris 138419
Laget, Yves, Valence (Drôme) 101411
Laghzaoui, Mohamed, Genève 111479
Lagier, Annie, L'Isle-sur-la-Sorgue . 099513
Lagier, Gilbert, Orange 065276
Lagier, Jean-Fr., Chartres 124189
Lagière, Jacques, Issoire 124265
Lagios, Kostas, Agia Paraskeri Attikis 105377
Lagnel-Tastemain, Caen 061876
Lago, R., Montevideo 087327
Lago, R., Punta del Este 087354
Lagorio, Marco, Brescia 106000
Lagrain, P., Gent 123623
Lagrand, C., Bruxelles 058011
Lagrand, Marc, Paris 066131
Lagrange, André, Beauzelle 061317
Lagrange-Choux, Monique, Marseille 064367
Lagravère, Nicole, Bracieux 061743
Lagravinese, Leonardo, Roma 076515, 128079
Lagrille, Marc, La Guerche-de-Bretagne 063395
Laguardia and Wagner Archives, Long Island City 045387
Laguna, Seattle 093028
Laguna Art Museum, Laguna Beach 045095
Lahaina, San Francisco 119715
Lahaina Arts Society, Lahaina 054839
Lahaina Restoration Foundation, Lahaina 045096
Laham, Rio de Janeiro 058603
LaHave Islands Marine Museum, LaHave 005738
Lahcen, Eva, Saarbrücken 104801
Lahden Antikvaarinen Kirjakauppa, Lahti 137976
Lahden Historiallinen Museo, Lahden Kaupunginmuseo, Lahti 009783
Lahden Kaupunginmuseo, Lahti . . . 009784
Lahden Kuvastin ja Taidesoppi, Lahti 060608
Lahden Taidemuseo, Lahden Kaupunginmuseo, Lahti 009785
Lahm, Wilhelm, Düsseldorf 070405
Lahmi, Claude, L'Isle-sur-la-Sorgue 063942
Lahoda, Gernot, Zell am See 137390
Lahore Art Gallery, Lahore 108779
Lahore Arts Council, Lahore 053964
Lahore Fort Museum, Lahore 031381
Lahore Museum, Lahore 031382
Lahoreau, Patrick, Pezou 066814
Lahovari, Bucureşti 109438
Lahrichi, Rabat 077693
Lahrichi, Rabat 107562
Lahumière, Paris 100577, 133637
Lai, Vientiane 107314
Lai, C.C., Toronto 059227, 097311
Lai, Sandro, Cagliari 075212
Lai Chi Kok, Hong Kong 059657
Laibstain, Harry, Norfolk 091387
Laick, Jean & Marcelle, Dol-de-Bretagne 062695
Laidhay Croft Museum, Dunbeath . 039303
Laidlaw, Chicago 131908
Laidley District Historical Village, Laidley 001166
Laigle, Elisabeth, Roquebilliere . . . 067216
Laihian Kirkkomuseo, Laihia 009792
Laihian Museo, Laihia 009793
Laik, Bad Ems 101639
Laïk, Jean-Marc, Koblenz 103569, 134095
Laimbacher, Karl, Appenzell 082092
Laimer Schlößl, München 072770
Laine, Henri, Nantes 124485
Lainé, Pascal, Avignon 098900
Lainé, Pascal, Gordes 099291
Laing, Shayna, Montréal 097044
Laing Art Gallery, Newcastle-upon-Tyne 040550
Laing Museum, Newburgh 040539
Laiptai, Šiauliai 107356
Lair, Christian, Falaise 062837
L'Air d'Antan, Neuville-sur-Sarthe . 065000
Lairaud, Jean-Pierre, Bordeaux . . . 061626
L'Aire, Saint-Pierre-d'Eyraud 067955
Lairgate Galleries, Beverley 112629
Laitinen, Pekka L., Tampere 060629
Lajba, John E., Omaha 118708
Lajoix, Anne, Paris 066132
Lajoix, Anne, Paris 066133
Lakdiva Gallery, Palmerston 095051
Lake, Lake 084893
Lake, A. & R., Cloppenburg 102318
Lake, D & E, Toronto 097312
Lake, Daniel, Gillingham, Kent 130725
Lake, Randall, Salt Lake City 119352
Lake Austin Fine Arts, Austin 114993
Lake Bathurst Cottage Collectables, Braidwood 055538
Lake Broadwater Natural History Museum, Dalby 000967
The Lake Champlain Maritime Museum, Vergennes 048761
Lake Country Museum, Okanagan . 006066
Lake Country Pastel Society, White Bear Lake 054840
Lake County Discovery Museum, Wauconda 049009
Lake County Historical Museum, Tavares 048508
Lake County Historical Society Museum, Kirtland Hills 045025
Lake County Historical Society Museum, Mentor 045779
Lake County Historical Society Museum, Two Harbors 048676
Lake County Museum, Lakeport . . . 045125
Lake Daylesford Book Barn, Daylesford 136877
Lake Erie Nature and Science Center, Bay Village 042064
Lake Forest-Lake Bluff Historical Society Museum, Lake Forest 045106
The Lake Gallery, Waikato 108592
Lake George Historical Association Museum, Old Country Courthouse, Lake George 045108
Lake Guernsey Museum, Guernsey 044369
Lake Hopatcong Historical Museum, Landing 045153
Lake Hopatcong Historical Museum, Landing 045154
Lake House Arts Centre, Auckland . 030441
Lake House Bookshop, Colombo . . 141090
Lake Jackson Mounds Archaeological Park, Tallahassee 048480
Lake Macquarie City Art Gallery, Booragul 000815
Lake Malawi Museum, Mangochi . . 027940
Lake Meredith Aquatic and Wildlife Museum, Fritch 044088
Lake of the Red Cedars Museum, Cedar Lake 042672
Lake of the Woods County Museum, Baudette 042058
Lake of the Woods Museum, Kenora 005676
Lake Placid-North Elba Historical Society Museum, Lake Placid 045114
Lake Russell Gallery, Emerald Beach 094509
Lake Saint Louis Historical Society Museum, Montréal 005927
Lake Shore Railway Museum, North East 046525
Lake State Rare Coin, Saint Paul . . 092373
Lake Superior Maritime Visitors Center, Duluth 043521
Lake Superior Railroad Museum, Duluth 043522
Lake Tabourie Museum, Lake Tabourie 001168
Lake Taupo Museum and Art Gallery, Taupo 030597
Lake Waccamaw Depot Museum, Lake Waccamaw 045116
Lake Wales Depot Museum, Lake Wales 045117
Lakeeren, Mumbai 105785
Lakeland Antiques Art Gallery, Ambleside 083288
Lakeland Antiques Art Gallery, Grasmere 084499, 113147
Lakeland Motor Museum, Grange-over-Sands 039616
Lakeman, Oscar, Miami 117103
Lakes Antiques Gallery, Grasmere .084500, 141631
Lakes District Museum, Arrowtown 030423
Lakes District Museum, Burns Lake 005172
Lakes Entrance Art and Print Gallery, Lakes Entrance 094722
Lakeshore Gallery, Milwaukee 117201
Lakeside Interiors Classic, Berlin . . 069681
Lakeside Interiors Country, Berlin . . 069682
Lakeside Joondalup Bookshop, Joondalup 136954
Lakeside Museum, Bulyea 005162
Lakeside Studio, Lakeside 045126
Lakeside Treasures, Chicago 088116
Lakeview Furniture Refinishing, Hamilton 123771
Lakeview Museum of Arts and Sciences, Peoria 046880
Lakewood, Dallas 088546
Lakewood Antiques Market, Atlanta 087494
Lakewood Lighting, Dallas 132015
Lakewood's Heritage Culture and the Arts Galleries, Lakewood 045128
Laks, New York 091014, 132488
Lakshana, Bangalore 105608
Lakshana, Chennai 105633
Lakshana, Hyderabad 105705
Lakshana, Hyderabad 105706
Lal Antik, Ankara 083111
Lalanne, Jean-Claude, Paris 066134
Lalbagh Fort Museum, Dhaka 003107
Lalbaltry, Gilbert, Saint-Ouen 067822
Laleham Antiques, Laleham 084894
Laligant, Patricia, New York 118115
Lalique, Paris 133638
Lalit Kala Akademi, Delhi . 050300, 105672
Lalla Wool Shed Gallery, Launceston 094727
Lallak & Tom, Chicago 115474
Lallemand, Honfleur 099353
Lallier, Fontenay-le-Fleury 062905
Lallouz, Samuel, Montréal 097045
Lally & Co., J.J., New York 118116
Lalmi, Hachemi, Herzeele 063153
L'Altra, Lugano 082601
Laluque, Claude, Saint-Ouen 067823
L.a.M., Torino 076831
Lam, Maria, Hong Kong 059658
Lam, Yuet Wah, Hong Kong 059659
Lam Chak Leung, Hong Kong 059660
Lam Dong Museum, Lam Dong . . . 049548
LAM-Librairie, Art et Musée, Ouagadougou 137614
Lama Arts, Kathmandu 107589
Lama-Verlag, Dießen am Ammersee 133865
Lamanai Archaeological Site, Lamanai 003883

Lamantia jr., James R., New Orleans 117464
Lamar Dodd Art Center, La Grange . 045062
Lamarche, Patrick, Benfeld 061346
Lamarche, Patrick, Strasbourg 068323
Lamarche-Barral, Virginie, Lyon . . . 124362
Lamare, Frédéric, Fontaine-Heudebourg 062890
Lamare, Pierre, Saint-Aquilin-de-Pacy 067361
Lamarkeez, Manama 096016
Lamas Bolaño, Barcelona 110206
Lamasat, Jdeideh 077429
Lamasat, Manama 057636
Lamazza, Francesco, Hannover . . . 125875
Lamb, Alexander, Vancouver 059371
Lamb, Beris & Cheryl, Wolverhampton 087209
Lamb, Jerry, Portland 091965
Lamb, Roger, Stow-on-the-Wold . . 086754
Lamb Arcade, Wallingford 087004, 131642
Lambay, Howth 105895
Lambda Rising Bookstore, Baltimore 142227
Lambert & Son, Woodbridge 087220
Lambert, Dorrian, Lincoln . 084998, 130897
Lambert, J.-F., Bruxelles 058012
Lambert, James, La Ferté-Gaucher 063369
Lambert, Jeanine, Paris 066135
Lambert, Lambert, Paris 066136
Lambert, Michel, Marseille 138196
Lambert, Philippe, Saint-Maur-des-Fossés 067661
Lambert, William M., Oklahoma City 091511
Lambert, Yvon, New York 118117
Lambert, Yvon, Paris 100578
Lambert-Barnett, G., Paris 124714
Lambert & Foster, Tenterden 122724
Lambert-Pelco, Paul E., Columbus . 088420
Lambert Rouland, Paris 100579
Lamberth, Espergærde . . . 133420, 137865
Lambertini, Ezio, Bologna 127158
Lambertini, Leandro, Bologna 127159
Lambertini, Villiam, Bologna 127160
Lamberty, London 085466
Lambertz-Abraham, Karin, Düsseldorf 070406
Lambiek, Amsterdam 107756
Lambing Flat Museum, Young 001651
Lambrays, Wadebridge 122733
L'Ambre Humeur, Paris 066137
Lambrecht, Christoph, Herschbach . 125922
Lambrecht, Wolfram, Steinebach an der Wied 126832
Le Lambrequin, Rosiers-d'Egletons 067227
Lambrich, Christiane, Mainz 072393
Lambropoulos Collection, Polygyros 021441
Lamb's Ears, Birmingham 087767
Lambton Heritage Museum, Grand Bend 005529
L'Ame des Objets, Beaujeu 061252
Lamere, Houston 116353
Lameris, Gouda 078389
Lameris Frides, Amsterdam 077899
Lamers, Dortmund 102408
Lamers, Dortmund 102409, 133872
Lamers, Hannover 071400
Lamers, A. & W., Düsseldorf 102524
Lamers, Günther, Hannover 071401
Lamers, W.M., Winterswijk 128884
L'Ami des Arts, Paris 100580
Lamine, Guy, Hirson 063159
Lamm, Bad Wildungen 069394
Lammek, Oldenburg, Oldenburg . . . 139630
Lammel, Manfred, Nettersheim . . . 104396
Lammers, Köln 071973
Lammertse, Matthijs, Amsterdam . 128546
Lammi, J., Helsinki 060545
Lamnek, Nadja, Kelsterbach 103528
Lamon, Cathy, Castres 099097
Lamont, Evesham 113036
Lamont, London 085467
The Lamont Gallery, Phillips Exeter Academy, Exeter 043775
Lamort, Anne, Paris 138420
Lamot, Bruxelles 058013, 096224
Lamouille, Bernard, Ville-la-Grand . 068885
Lamouret, Patrick, Nantes 064928
Lamoureux Ritzenhoff, Montréal . . . 097046
The Lamp Gallery, Ripley, Surrey . . 086373
Lamp Post Antiques, Jacksonville . 089424
Lamp Post Gallery, Portland 119014
Lamp Repair 'n Shade Studio, Tampa 132956
Lamp Restorations, Botany 123192
Lampa, Daniel F., Plaidt 104611
Lampade, Roma 076516
Lampasiak, Martin, Herborn, Hessen 071486
Lampe à Huile, Flers 062872
La Lampe d'Aladin, Marrakech 077683
La Lampe d'Aladin, Marseille 064368
Lampenmuseum, Geel 003443
Lampenmuseum, Wezemaal 003855
Lampi-Museo, Liminka 009829
Lamplighter, Columbus 131985
Lamplighters, Portland 132697
Lampronti, Carlo, Roma 076517
Lampronti, Cesare, Roma 076518
Lampronti, Giulio, Roma 076519
Lampronti-Lebole, Milano 075749
Lamps & Lighting, San Antonio . . . 092532
Lamsa, Riyadh 080377
Lamson, Ho Chi Minh City 120515
Lamu Museum, Lamu 027425
Lamus, Kraków 079644
Lamus, Kraków 079645
Lamus, Kraków 129043
Lamus, Poznań 140762
Lamus, Warszawa 079762
Lamus, Warszawa 079763, 121907
Lamus, Warszawa 140789
Lamus, Warszawa 140790
L'Amusée, La Gacilly 063385
Lamutov Likovni Salon, Kostanjevica na Krki 109944
Lamy, Véronique, Le Titre 063713
Lamyantic, Vouillé 069030
L'an 1767, Thenon 068384
L'An 1920, Annecy 060892
Lan Sang, Tak 037937
Lanai, México 077575, 107495
Lanan, Berry 055497
Lanark Gallery, Lanark 113346
Lanark Museum, Lanark 039918
Lancaster, Auckland 078958
Lancaster, Oklahoma City 091512
Lancaster, Toowoomba 056721
Lancaster Antique Toy and Train Collection, Portsmouth Museums, Portsmouth 047199
Lancaster City Museum, Lancaster . 039922
Lancaster County Art Association, Strasburg 054841
Lancaster County Museum, Lancaster 045147
Lancaster Historical Society Museum, Lancaster 045139
Lancaster Leisure Park Antiques, Lancaster 084899
Lancaster Maritime Museum, Lancaster 039923
Lancaster Museum/Art Gallery, Lancaster 045136
Lancaster Museum of Art, Lancaster 045148
Lancastrian Antiques & Co, Lancaster 084900
Lancefield, David M., Sandgate . . . 086510
Lancefield Court House Museum, Lancefield 001170
Lancelot Hill Antiques, Bowral 055530
Lancer Centennial Museum, Lancer 005743
Lancioni, Francesco, Bologna 075088
Lancz, Patrick, Bruxelles 096225
Land, Janne, Wellington . . 079329, 108626
Land-Art, Dannstadt-Schauernheim 070176
Land- en Tuinbouwmuseum, Etten-Leur 029584
Land of the Beardies History House Museum, Glen Innes 001063
Land of Was, San Antonio 092533
Het Land van Strijen, Strijen 030187
Het Land van Thorn/ Panorama Thorn, Thorn 030199
Landau, Robert, Montréal 097047
Landberg & Co, Leif, Mellerud 122212
Landbouw- en Juttersmuseum Swartwoude, Buren, Friesland 029370
Landbouwmuseum Erve Niehof, Diepenheim 029479
Landbouwmuseum Leiedal, Bissegem 003234
Landbrugs- og Interiørmuseet, Farsø 008858
Landbrugsmuseet Melstedgård, Gudhjem 008883
Landbrugsmuseet Skarregaard, Nykøbing Mors 009036
Landbruksmuseet for Møre og Romsdal, Vikebukt 031337
Landeau, Alain, Paris 066138
Landelle, Françoise, Paris 066139
Landells, Keith, New Orleans 132419
Landen, Rupert, Reading 086334
Landenberger, Jürgen, Nürtingen . . 073131
Landenberger, Ulrich, Hechingen . . 125894
Landenberger, Viola, Esslingen 125622
Lander & Partner, Forbach, Baden . 070714
Lander, Truro 114602
Landers, Ross, El Paso 088806
Landes-Feuerwehrmuseum, Stendal 020315
Landesbergbaumuseum Baden-Württemberg, Sulzburg 020387
Landesbibliothek Oldenburg, Oldenburg, Oldenburg 019469
Landesfachschule für Keramik und Ofenbau, Stoob 049647
Landesfeuerwehrmuseum Meetzen Mecklenburg-Vorpommern, Meetzen 018878
Landesgalerie Oberösterreich, Oberösterreichische Landesmuseen, Linz 002249
Landesgeschichtliche Sammlung der Schleswig-Holsteinischen Landesbibliothek, Kiel 018248
Landesgremium Wien des Handels mit alter und moderner Kunst, Antiquitäten sowie Briefmarken und Numismatika, Wien 052575
Landeskirchliches Museum, Ludwigsburg, Württemberg 018695
Landesmuseum für Kunst und Kulturgeschichte, Stiftung Schleswig-Holsteinische Landesmuseen Schloss Gottorf, Schleswig 020039
Landesmuseum für Kunst und Kulturgeschichte Oldenburg, Schloß, Augusteum und Prinzenpalais, Oldenburg, Oldenburg 019470
Landesmuseum für Natur und Mensch, Oldenburg, Oldenburg 019471
Landesmuseum für schaumburg-lippische Geschichte, Landes- und Volkskunde, Bückeburg 016485
Landesmuseum für Technik und Arbeit in Mannheim, Mannheim 018807
Landesmuseum für Vorgeschichte, Landesamt für Archäologie, Dresden 016798
Landesmuseum für Vorgeschichte Sachsen-Anhalt, Halle, Saale 017666
Landesmuseum Joanneum, Referate Zoologie, Botanik, Geologie und Paläontologie, Mineralogie, Graz . 001938
Landesmuseum Kärnten, Klagenfurt 002142
Landesmuseum Koblenz, Staatliche Sammlung technischer Kulturdenkmäler, Koblenz 018294
Landesmuseum Mainz, Mainz 018790
Landesmuseum Schloß Tirol, Tirolo di Merano 026024
Landesrabbiner Dr. I.E. Lichtigfeld-Museum, Michelstadt 018932
Landesschau Äthiopien, Neulingen, Enzkreis 019249
Landesverband Berliner Galerien e.V., Berlin 053475
Landesverband der Kunst- und Antiquitätenhändler Baden-Württemberg e.V., Mannheim 053476
Landesverband Deutscher Auktionatoren für Rheinland und Westfalen e.V., Hilden 053477
Landesverband Galerien in Baden Württemberg e.V, Grafenau, Württemberg 053478
Landeszeughaus, Landesmuseum Joanneum, Graz 001939
Landfall, Chicago 135347
Landgate Books, Rye 142026
Landherr, Detlef, Berlin 125244
Landik & Měchura, Praha 123990
Landini, Renato, Milano 075750
Landis, Alan, Sydney 056680
Landis Valley Museum, Lancaster . 045149
Landjunk, Arthur, Hamburg 121430
Landlmuseum Sulzbürg, Mühlhausen, Oberpfalz 019010
Landlord's Manor House Museum, Dayi 007063
Landman, Santiago, Santiago de Chile 059538
Landmark Art, Mumbai 105786
Landmark Forest Heritage Park, Carrbridge 039005
Landmark Gallery, Cairns 094349
Landmark Gallery, Winnipeg 097588
Landmark Park, Dothan 043481
Landmaschinenmuseum - Sammlung Speer, Rimbach bei Eggenfelden 019845
Landole Italiano, Barcelona 129359
Landré, G.N., Amsterdam 140314
Landrieux, Pierre & Didier, Paris . . . 066140
Landrock, Stefan, Aindling 101552
Landrock-Granoff, Katia, Paris 100581
Landrot, Paris 100582
Landry, Montréal 058972
Landry, L.A., Essex 122893
Landry, L.A., South Essex 123122
Lands Museum, Dokka 030804
Landscape America, Chicago 115475
Landscape Research, Exeter 136239
Landscapes of the Holy Land Park, Eretz-Israel Museum, Tel Aviv 023083
Landschaftsinformationszentrum (LIZ) Hessisches Kegelspiel Rasdorf, Rasdorf 019712
Landschaftsmuseum, Seligenstadt . 020185
Landschaftsmuseum Angeln, Langballig 018490
Landschaftsmuseum der Dübener Heide, Bad Düben 015684
Landschaftsmuseum der Kulmregion, Pischelsdorf in Steiermark 002433
Landschaftsmuseum im Schloß Trautenfels, Steiermärkisches Landesmuseum Joanneum, Trautenfels 002753
Landschaftsmuseum Obermain, Kulmbach 018441
Landschaftsmuseum Schönhengstgau, Göppingen 017448
Landschaftsmuseum Westerwald, Hachenburg 017614
Landschloss Pirna-Zuschendorf-Botanische Sammlungen, Pirna 019625
Landschulmuseum Göldenitz, Göldenitz bei Rostock 017444
Landskron, Gabi, Regensburg 126693
Landskrona Konsthall, Landskrona . 036412
Landskrona Museum, Landskrona . 036413
Landstingsmuseet, Örebro 036520
Landstrich, Schärding 135567
Landt, Frederiksberg 137871
Landtau, Auka, Böklund 102170
Landtechnik-Museum Gut Steinhof, Braunschweig 016387
Landtechnikmuseum, Leiben 002216
Landtechnisches Museum Burgenland, Sankt Michael im Burgenland . . . 002605
Landwehr, Hans-Jürgen, Kassel . . . 139306
Landwehr, Heinrich, Langenargen . 126165
Landwehr, Stephan, Berlin 101969, 125245

Landwirtschaftliches Museum und Pfarrer Franz Engel-Museum, Prinzendorf 002471
Landwirtschaftliches Museum Wetzlar, Wetzlar 020845
Landwirtschafts- und Heimatmuseum, Karben 018152
Landwirtschaftsmuseum, Rhede, Ems 019819
Landwirtschaftsmuseum, Weil am Rhein 020716
Landwirtschaftsmuseum Hof Espe, Bad Berleburg 015663
Landwirtschaftsmuseum Lüneburger Heide, Museumsdorf Hösseringen, Suderburg 020376
Landwirtschaftsmuseum Schloss Ehrental, Klagenfurt 002143
Landy, New York 118118
Lane, London 085468
Lane, Stockbridge 086713
Lane, André, Châteauroux 120972
Lane, Eileen, New York 091015
Lane, Neil, Los Angeles 089818
Lane, Neil C., New York 132489
Lane, Peter, Woollahra 056871
Lane, Russell, Warwick 087040
Lane & Son, W.H., Penzance 122651
Lane Community College Art Gallery, Eugene 043743
Lane County Historical Museum, Dighton 043468
Lane County Historical Museum, Eugene 043744
The Lane Gallery, Auckland 108334
Lane Gallery, Manchester 114046
Lane House, Roseburg 047542
The Lane Place, Crawfordsville . . . 043209
Lanecki, Arthur, Montréal 123789
Laneri, Lucia, Roma 076520
Lanes Armoury, Brighton 083703
Lanesfield School, Edgerton 043604
The Laneside Gallery, Coleraine . . . 112894
Laney, Philip, Great Malvern 122527
Laney College Art Gallery, Oakland . 046594
Lang, Shanghai 097928
Lang, Wien 095889
Lang, Dominique, Dudelange 107383
Lang, Franz, Aschenberg 137150
Lang, Franz, Schwäbisch Gmünd . . 139719
Lang, H., Ludwigsburg, Württemberg 103944
Lang, Helmut R., Rennerod 139688
Lang, Helmut R., Wiesbaden 105269, 139851
Lang, J.M., New York 091016
Lang, Katarina, Wien 057485
Lang, Manfred, Grafenwörth 095517
Lang, Marco, Dresden . . . 070324, 125501
Lang, Marion E., Indianapolis 089314
Lang, Paul, Zürich 082994
Lang, Siegfried & Ernestine, Traunstein 074078
Lang, Thomas, Hanau 103254
Lang-Levin, Chicago 088117
Lang Pioneer Village, Keene 005668
Lang-Vollmuth, Axel, Langheckerhof 072158
Lang Water Powered Grist Mill, Peterborough 006140
Långasjö Auktionskammare, Emmaboda 122122
Långbans Gruvby, Filipstad 036271
Langbeinmuseum, Hirschhorn, Neckar 017931
Lange, Bayonne 061235
Lange, Bremen 070032
Lange, de, Emmen 078364
Lange, Halver 071185
Lange, Kierspe 071847
Lange, Siegburg 104891
Lange, B., Wathlingen 074288
Lange, Dietmar, Paderborn 073286
Lange, G., Troistorrents 082863
Lange, Gerd & Hilde, Greding 102992
Lange, Gerhard, Hamburg 071276
Lange, H., Tarnow 074040
Lange, H.-J., Twist 139804
Lange, Juliane, Karlsruhe 126002
Lange, L., Hannover 139237
Lange, Ludwig, Berlin 101970
Lange, Peter, Stockholm 134969
Lange, Dr. Petra, Berlin 101971
Lange, Ursula, Berlin 069683
De Lange IJzeren Brug, Dordrecht . 078309
Lange & Lange, Hamm, Westfalen . 071362
Lange & Springer, Berlin 138813
Langeberg, Zutphen 078876
Långedrags Konst, Västra Frölunda 111096
Långelanda Tingshus, Årjäng 036191
Langelands Museum, Rudkøbing . . 009086
Langeloh, Elfriede, Weinheim, Bergstraße 074318
L'Angelus, Paris 066141
Langemann, M., München 104256
Langen, Patricia, Bonn 125354
Langen,Müller & Herbig, München . 134255
Langenbach, Dr. H., Freiburg im Breisgau 070848
Langenbach, Uli, Siegen 104897
Langenberg, Amsterdam 107757
Langenfeld, D., Burgwald 070105
Langenhof, de, Zwolle 108283
Langenholt, Thomas, München . . . 126407
Langer, Martin, Roth, Mittelfranken 126743
Langer, Robert, Saarbrücken 073639
Langer, Udo, Pogeez 073350
Langer, Wolfgang, Zürich 141348
Långeruds Auktionskammare, Kristinehamn 122182
Langeveer, Haarlem 108058
Langeweg & Langeweg, Tilburg . . .078772, 128843
Langewiesche, Karl Robert, Königstein im Taunus 134127
Langewiesche-Brandt, Ebenhausen 133902
Langford, London 085469, 131082
Langford, J. & R., Llangollen 085039
Langgadå 62, Sandnes 079492
Langhagen & Harnisch, Hamburg . . 071277
Langham and District Heritage Village Museum, Langham 005744
Langham Cultural Centre Galleries, Kaslo 005666
Langhans, Praha 060139
Langheinz, F., Darmstadt 102346
Langhoff, Nils, Bad Wiessee 125121
Långholmens Fängelsemuseum, Stockholm 036636
Langhorne Place Antiques, Oklahoma City 091513
Het Langhuis, Zwolle 108284
Langi Morgala Museum, Ararat . . . 000747
Langingkoski Imperial Fishing Lodge, Kotka 009742
Langlade, Emmanuel, Paris 121161
Langlade County Historical Society Museum, Antigo 041748
Langlet, Jean-Marie, Cambrai 061920
Langley, Rochester 086390, 131423
Langley Centennial Museum and National Exhibition Centre, Fort Langley . . 005462
Langlois, Danièle, Amiens 138011
Langlois, Marie-Pierre, Saint-Ouen . 067824
Langlois Antiquités, Louhans 064010
Langlois Tapisseries, Blois 061524
Langloy, Brigit, Lyon 099598
Langmann Uno, Vancouver 097494
Langobardenwerkstatt Zethlingen, Zethlingen 021058
Langohr, J.-F., Liège 058311
Langolo, Las Vegas 116631
Langotsky, Gamba, New York 118119
Langsdorfer Heimatmuseum, Lich . 018630
Langstaff, Edward, Bruxelles 123597
Langston, B., Jacksonville 089425
Langston, B., Jacksonville 089426
Langston, B., Jacksonville 122927
Langston, B., Jacksonville 122928
Langston, Tom, San Jose 092928
Langton, Sheffield 086559
Langton, Sheffield 086560
Langton Matravers Museum, Langton Matravers 039930
Langton Street Gallery, London . . .085470, 113730
Lanham, Louisville 132299
Lanhydrock, Bodmin 038775
Lanier Mansion, Madison 045580
Lanier Museum of Natural History, Buford 042509
Lanier's Refinishing, Denver 132040
Lanigan and District Heritage Centre, Lanigan 005747
Lanik, Atlanta 114897
Lani's Antiques, Tampa 093136
Lankershim Art Gallery, Los Angeles 116815
Lankes, Heinz-Dieter, Döhlau 070264, 121372
Lankes, Heinz-Dieter, Hof, Saale . . 071547
Lankes & Spaan, Eilsbrunn 133906
Lankester, Saffron Walden 086432, 142027
Lanman Museum, Framlingham . . . 039523
Lann, Henri le, Poitiers 066893
Lanna Museum, Lampang 037903
Lannan, Boston 087828
Lannards, Billingshurst 083515
Lannaud, T., Portbail 066956
Lanneau, Léon, La Chapelle-Basse-Mer 099389
Lannel, Brionne 061804
Lanni, Massimo, Roma 076521
Lannier, Monique, Tours 068595
Lanninger, Günther, Meckenheim, Pfalz 072481
Lannino, Giovanni, Palermo 127832
Lanno Antichitá, Napoli 076002
Lannody, São Paulo 096676
Lannoo, Tielt, West-Vlaanderen . . . 133297
Lansch, Perl 073306
Lansdown Antiques, Bath 083435
Lansdowne Auction Galleries, Lansdowne 122936
Lansing Art Gallery, Lansing 045162
Lansing Manor House Museum, North Blenheim 046517
Lansing Veterans Memorial Museum, Lansing 045160
Lansquenet, Lille 063852
De Lantaarn, Den Haag 078210
Lantbruksmuseum, Ingatorp 036356
Lanteiron, Marie-Agnès, Monflanquin 064603
Lantern, Dublin 074929
Lantern Bryn Mawr Bookshop, Washington 143046
Lantern Gallery of Fine Art, Elgin . . 113015
Lanterna Magica, Genova 075479
La Lanterna Magica, Torino 076832
La Lanterne, Bayeux 061227
Lanterne de Hans, Grasse 063039
Lanting, Shanghai 097929
Lanting, Shanghai 097930
Lantsoght, Alphonse, Paris 100583
Lanz, Dr. Hubert, München 072771, 121536
Lanza, San Francisco 132894
Lanzani, Gaëtan, Paris 124715
Lanzenberg, Fred, Bruxelles 096226
Lanzhou City Museum, Lanzhou . . . 007169
Lanzone 16, Milano 075751
Lao, Miao, New York 091017
Lao Gallery, Vientiane 107315
Laoag Museum, Vigan 031806
Laocheng Xian Art Academy, Shanghai 049856
Laocheng Xian Painting and Calligraphy Association, Shanghai 052797
Laocoonte, Madrid 129634
Laorden Garzon, Maria Dolores, Madrid 129635
Laoshan Art Cooperative, Qingdao . 097887
LAPADA Autumn Antiques and Fine Art Fair, Cheltenham 093934
Lapalus, Jean-Pierre, Meursanges . 064543
Lapchin, Marc, Lyon 124363
Lapczyna, Kornelia, Essen 070638
LaPelle, Rodger, Philadelphia 118790
Lapeyre, Françoise, Brive-la-Gaillarde 061815
Lapeyrière, Catherine, Champcevinel 099110
Lapham-Patterson House, Thomasville 048548
Lapidarij - Klaustar Samostana Sv. Domenika, Trogir 007812
Lapidario Civico, Gradisca d'Isonzo 024358
Lapidario Comunale, Osimo 025024
Lapidarium, Neustadt am Main . . . 019275
Lapidarium, Sankt Gallen 037494
Lapidarium, Berlinische Galerie, Berlin 016112
Lapidarium - Historische Grenzsteinsammlung, Niederstetten 019313
Lapierre, Dunedin 108438
Lapierre, Thierry, Challes les Eaux . 062075
Lapin Maakuntamuseo, Rovaniemi . 010043
Lapin Metsämuseo, Rovaniemi 010044
Lapin Tl. Kotiseutumuseo, Lappi . . . 009808
Lapinlahden Taidemuseo ja Eemil Halosen Museo, Halosten Museosäätiö, Lapinlahti 009800
Lapis Box, Vancouver 059372
Lapis Fine Art, London 113731
Lápiz-Revista Internacional de Arte, Madrid 136093
Laplace, Bertrand, Rouen 067276
Lapointe, Edith, Vigoulet-Auzil 068875
Laporta del Rio, Antonio, Madrid . . 129636
Laporte, Nicole, Soyaux 068281
Laporte, Patrice, Paris 066142
Lapoutre, Utrecht 140550
Lappa Valley Steam Railway, Newquay 040571
Lappan, Oldenburg, Oldenburg 134334
Lappstaden, Arvidsjaur 036197
Laprugne, Jean-Pierre, Paris 066143
Lapworth Museum of Geology, Birmingham 038732
Laqua, Carsten, Berlin . . . 101972, 138814
Lar, Donostia-San Sebastián 081084
L.a.R., Roma 076522
L.A.R.A., Genova 127462
Lara, Elida, Barranquilla 098089
Lara, Isabel, Madrid 081330
Lara Arte, Roma 106571
Laramie Plains Museum, Laramie . 045168
Larasati, Jakarta 121652
Larasati, Singapore 121654
L'Arcadia, Livorno 106126
Larchmere Antiques, Cleveland . . . 088340
Larchmont Historical Society Museum, Mamaroneck 045610
Lårdal Bygdemuseum, Høydalsmo . 030915
Lardanchet, Paris 138421
Lardanchet, Henri, Lyon 138156
Lardenois, Pierre, Forest 062918
Lardeux, Joël, Crosmieres 062574
Laredo Children's Museum, Laredo 045172
LaReido, Kerava 060603
The Large Art Company, Baltimore . 115062
Large Print Book, Denver 142390
Largeaud, André & Jacqueline, Paris 100584
Largeault, Didier, Paris 066144
L'Argile, Sancerre 068114
Largs Museum, Largs 039933
Lari, Rossella, Firenze 127357
Larimer Exchange, Denver 088708
Larini, Anna Maria, Parma 127853
Larivière, Romain, Paris 100585
Lark, Asheville 135320
Lark Lane Motor Museum, Liverpool 040029
Larking-Coste, Marc, Paris 124716
Larks, Ballater 112540
L'Armada, Loupian 064013
Les Larmes d'Éros, Paris . 100586, 133639, 138422

Larnaca District Archaeological Museum, Larnaka 008208
Larnaca District Museum, Larnaka . 008209
Larne Museum, Larne 039934
Laroche, Gabrielle, Paris 066145
Laroche, Gabrielle, Paris 066146
Laroche, Yves, Montréal 097048
Laroche & Denis, Québec 097149
Laros, Hermann Josef, Trier 126914
Laroy, Houston 089135, 132129
Larrea, Martínez 055282, 123170
Larrea Fernandez-Valdes, Julian, Madrid 081331
Larrieu, André, Martigues 064415
Larrison, Indianapolis 089315
Larrivet, Jean-Philippe, Camblanes-et-Meynac 061916
Larrouilh, Ginou, Biarritz 098965
Larruy, Ramon, Vitoria-Gasteiz 081719
Larrybane and Carrick-A-Rede, Ballycastle 038575
Larry's Antiques, Buffalo 087888
Larry's Antiques, Virginia Beach . . . 093359
Larry's Fabrication's, New Orleans . 132420
Larry's Place, Houston 089136
Lars Noak Blacksmith Shop, Larsson/ Ostlund Log Home & One-Room Capitol School, New Sweden 046274
Larsen, Exeter 136894
Larsen, Jesper, Frederiksberg 060240, 124017
Larsmo Hembygdsmuseum, Larsmo 009811
Larson Gallery, Yakima Valley Community College, Yakima 049326
Larsson, Stockholm 129867
Larsson, Regina, Siselen 135068
L'Art au Zénith, Nyons 099884
L'Art Décor, Mereglise 064500
L'Art du Temps, La Rochelle 063434, 099407
L'Art du Temps, Paris 066147
L'Art et la Manière, Lattes 099422
L'Art, l'Objet et le Goût, Paris 100587
L'art Lonnes, Bremen 102252
L'Artiste, Chamalières 124179
L'Artistica, Girona 110368
Larue, Chantal, Colombes 062428
Larunda, Timişoara 080195
Larvik Sjøfartsmuseum, Larvikmuséene, Larvik 030975
Larwood, Roderick, Larling 130863
Larz Anderson Auto Museum, Brookline 042454
Las Casas Gil, Manuel Enrique de, Zaragoza 129815
Las Cruces Museum of Natural History, Las Cruces 045178
Las Luces, Buenos Aires 136728
Las Vegas Antique Jewelry and Watch Show, Las Vegas 093998
Las Vegas Antique Slot Machine, Las Vegas 089590
Las Vegas Art Museum, Las Vegas . 045186
Las Vegas International Scouting Museum, Las Vegas 045187
Las Vegas Natural History Museum, Las Vegas 045188
Las Venus, New York 091018
LaSalle County Historical Society Museum, Utica 048716
Lasalle-Sia College of the Arts, Singapore 050684
Lasarettimuseo, Turku 010165
Lasartis, Paris 066148
Lasbleiz, Roger, Melesse 064472
Lascaux II, Fac-similé de Lascaux, Montignac 013173
Lasch, Mark, Mainz 072394
Lasch, Traudi, Schwerin 104871
Laserow, Malmö 081871
Lasés, Amsterdam 107758
Lashburn Centennial Museum, Lashburn 005750
Lashenden Air Warfare Museum, Headcorn 039710
Lasher, Neil, London 131083
Laski, Gérard, Paris 066149
Laski, Stanislas, Saint-Ouen 067825
Laskowska, Marta, Gdańsk 079584
Laskowski i Syn, Piastów 079683
Laslo, Madrid 110557
Lasnier, Jean-Pascal, Latresne 063545
Lassa & Scalese, Genova 075480
Lassacher, E. & L., Ramingstein . . . 123432
Lassaletta Delclos, Ignacio, Barcelona 110207
Lassaletta Delclos, Ignacio, Barcelona 110208
Lassalle, Judith, London . 085471, 131084
Lassandro, Maria Vita, Cagliari 075213
Lassaner Mühle, Lassan 018517
Lassaussois, Chartres 062171
Lassco, London 085472
Lassen, Honolulu 116223
Lassen, Las Vegas 116632
Lassen Museum Waikiki, Honolulu . 044603
Lasserie, M., Paris 066150
Lasseron, Olivier, Paris 121162
Lasserre, Denis, Colmar 062414
Lasserre-du-Rozel, Gérard, Bénodet 061351
Lassetters, Fyshwick 094573
Lassiter, Joie, Charlotte 115295
Lassnig, Alexander, Oberalm 123423
Lasso de la Vega, Alvaro, Málaga . . 081421
Lassus, Catherine, Bordeaux 061627
Last Century Antiques, Innerleithen 084795
Last Century Shoppe, Midhirst 079154
The Last Chance Saloon, London . . 113732
Last Frontier Antique Furniture Restorers, Tucson 132987
The Last Hurrah, Bibra Lake 136803
Last Indian Raid Museum, Oberlin . 046606
The Last Post Book Shop, Wagga Wagga 137126
Last Roundup, Phoenix 091753
Last Touch, Gharghur 107444
Lasta, Moskva 098388
Lastenmuseo, Helsingin Kaupunginmuseo, Helsinki 009549
Lastentarhamuseo, Helsinki 009550
Lasting, A., Artarmon 055405
Lasting Impressions, San Antonio . . 092534
Lasting Impressions Gallery, Kenilworth 094687
Lastrucci, Francesco, Prato 076253
Lata Dwudzieste Lata Trzydzieste, Kraków 108961
Latchford, K. & R., Cheltenham . . . 083921
Late Bloomers, New York 091019
Late Bloomers Treasures, Tampa . . 093137
The Late Joy's, Houston 089137
L'Atelier, Thoiry 068400
L'Atelier Brocante, Cannes 061948
L'Atelier du Care, Cairo 098642
Latemse Verkoopzaal, Sint-Martens-Latem 120788
Laténium, Parc et Musée d'Archéologie de Neuchâtel, Hauterive 037181
Lateral, Barcelona 136094
Laterna Antika, Hannover 071402
Laterna Magica, Helsinki . 098739, 137950
Laterna-Magica, Marne 072467
Laterna Magica, München 134256
DIE Laterne, Ovelgönne 073273
Latgales Kultūtvēstures Muzejs, Rēzekne 027727
Latham, Lionel, Genève 082441
Latham, Polly, Boston 087829
Latham, R.H., Tarleton 086822
Lathière, Andrée, Le Blanc 063570
Latin American Art Association, Miami 054842
Latin American Art Museum, Miami 045813
Latin American Cultural Center Museum, Koyang 027525
Latin Art Broker, Los Angeles 116816
Latin Inspiration, Northampton 114153
Latin Sun, Los Angeles 116817
Latina, Asunción . 079531, 108800, 128998
Latino Art Gallery, Philadelphia 118791
Latino Artists Group, Minneapolis . .054843, 117279
Latitude 53, Edmonton 005398
Latitude 53, Edmonton 096890
Latitudes, Houston 116354
Latona, Saltsjö-Duvnas 110987
Latorre, Fernando, Madrid 110558
Latorre, Fernando, Zaragoza 110884
Latragna, Franco, Aschaffenburg . . 101601
Latrobe Bicycle Race Club Museum, Latrobe 001173
Latrobe Court House Museum, Latrobe 001174
Latrobe Regional Gallery, Morwell . 001288
Latrobe Street College of Art and New Media, Melbourne 049614
Latroc-Ant, Ascoux 061007
Lattelekom Muzejs, Rīga 027738
Lattemann, Reinhard, Mühltal 104127
Lattimer, Leona, Vancouver 097495
De Lattre, Paris 138423
Lattre, Dominique de, Saint-Ouen .101189, 138603
Latude, Hugues de, Gardouch 138093
Latus, Urs, Erlangen 125606
Latvian Centre for Contemporary Art, Rīga 027739
Latvian History Museum, Toronto . . 006609
Latvian Museum, Rockville 047514
Latvian Museum, Wayville 001605
Latvian Museum Council, Rīga 053834
Latvijas Arhitektūras Muzejs, Rīga . 027740
Latvijas Biškopības Vēstures Muzejs, Bebri 027663
Latvijas Dabas Muzejs, Rīga 027741
Latvijas Etnogrāfiskais Brīvdabas Muzejs, Rīga 027742
Latvijas Fotogrāfijas Muzejs, Rīga . 027743
Latvijas Kara Muzejs, Rīga 027744
Latvijas Ķīmijas Vēstures Muzejs, Rīga 027745
Latvijas Kultūras Muzejs Dauderi, Rīga 027746
Latvijas Lauksaimniecības Universitātes Muzejs, Jelgava 027694
Latvijas Mākslas Akadēmija, Rīga . 050516
Latvijas Mākslas Akadēmija - Restaurācijas Nodaļas, Rīga 050517
Latvijas Muzeju Asociācija, Rīga . . 053835
Latvijas Okupācijas Muzejs, Rīga . . 027747
Latvijas Republikas Meliorācijas un Zemkopības Muzejs, Mālpils 027714
Latvijas Sporta Muzejs, Rīga 027748
Latvijas Ugunsdzēsības Muzejs, Rīga 027749
Latvijas Universitātes Botānikas Muzejs, Rīga 027750
Latvijas Universitātes Ģeologijas Muzejs, Rīga 027751
Latvijas Universitātes Skaitļošanas Tehnikas un Informatikās Muzejs, Museum of the History of Science and Technologies of thr University of Latvia, Rīga 027752
Latvijas Universitātes Vēstures Muzejs, Rīga 027753
Latvijas Universitātes Zoologijas Muzejs, Rīga 027754
Latvijas Vēstures Muzejs, Rīga 027755
Latzer, Josef, Kreuzlingen 111593
Latzko, H., Marxzell 072470
Lau, Helga, Sindelfingen 104906
Lauaxeta, Bilbao 080978
Laub, Claudia, Los Angeles 116818
Laubbach, Ostrach 104551
Laube, August, Zürich 141349
Lauber, M.R., Bad Endorf 125090
Lauber, Wolfgang, Bad Endorf 125091
Laubinger, K.-D., Delbrück 070207
Laubinger, Rudolf, Osnabrück 073243
Laubry, Jean-Paul, Le Chatelet-en-Brie 063599
Laucirica, Carlos, Bilbao 080979
Laucournet, Dominique, Paris 138424
Laudal Museum, Marnardal Museum, Marnardal 031010
Laudenbach, Helmuth, Berg, Starnberger See 069530
Laudenbacher, Konrad, München . . 126408
Lauder & Howard, East Freemantle 055782
Lauder Museum, Amityville 041699
Lauderdale House, London 040196
Laudoueneix, Pierre, L'Isle-sur-la-Sorgue 063943
Laue, Georg, München 072772
Laue, J.G., München 072773
Lauenburgischer Kunstverein e.V., Mölln 053479
Lauer, H.-Dieter, Freisen 070872
Lauer, Klaus, Saarbrücken 073640
Lauer, Klaus, Zweibrücken 074578
Laufener Stiftsschatz, Laufen, Salzach 018528
Laug, Herford 139262
Laug, Rüdiger, Herford 139263
Laughing at the Sun Art Gallery, Austin 114994
The Laughing Hippo, Townsville . . . 095349
Laughing Horse Gallery, Byron Bay . 094338
Laughing Ogre, Columbus 088421
Laughlin, Seattle 119952
Laughlin, Kenneth, Philadelphia . . . 091653
Laughlin, Spencer, Minneapolis . . . 132383
Laugier, Jacques, Beaulieu-sur-Mer 061257
Lauk, Waiblingen 074240
Lauksaimniecības Tehnikas Muzejs Kalēji, Talsi 027782
Laumann, Dülmen 133882
Laumeier, Saint Louis 119220
Laumeier Sculpture Park and Museum, Saint Louis 047668
Laumière, Paris 138425
Launceston Steam Railway, Launceston 039938
Lauper, Allschwil 111116
L'Aur-en-Toi, Champs-sur-Yonne . . 099115
Laura, Luigi, Monaco 077610
Laura, Luigi Anton, Monaco 077611
Laura and Paul Mesaros Galleries, Morgantown 046027
Laura Ann Antiques, Indianapolis . . 089316
Laura Antiques, Vancouver 059373
Laura Brocante, Yutz 069068
Laura Ingalls Wilder Museum, Burr Oak 042529
Laura Ingalls Wilder Museum, Walnut Grove 048841
Laura Ingalls Wilder-Rose Wilder Lane Historic Home and Museum, Mansfield 045646
Laura Korpikaivo Tammisen Käsityömuseo, Lappeenranta 009803
Laura Rocca, Torino 076833
Laura Secord Homestead, Niagara Falls 006010
Lauraine Designs, Miami 132346
Laurans, Joël, Maumusson 064434, 124439
Laurantica, Toulon (Var) 068457
Laura's Collectibles, Milwaukee . . . 090308
Laure, Edouard, Saint-Ouen 067826
Laure A. Sprague Art Gallery, Joliet 044876
Laurel and Hardy Museum, Ulverston 041261
Laurel Antiguedades, Sevilla 081590
Laurel Hill Antiques, Providence . . . 092044
The Laurel Museum, Laurel 045196
Laurella, Hyères 063195
Laurelwood, Memphis 116995
Laurelwood, San Jose 092929
Lauren Rogers Museum of Art, Laurel 045199
Laurence, London 085473
Laurence C. Jones Museum, Piney Woods 047030
Laurencier, Bordeaux 138042
Laurencier, Patrick, Bordeaux 138043
Laurencin, Lyon 099599
Laurens, Albuquerque 087402
Laurens, Whitstable 087140, 131684
Laurens, Marie Helene, Venezia . . . 076951
Laurent, Brigitte, Pazayac 066718, 124837

Laurent, Brigitte, Terrasson-Lavilledieu 068374, 124952
Laurent, Corentin, Pleuven 066857
Laurent, Corentin, Quimper 067020
Laurent, Danièle, Niort 065195
Laurent, Fronçois, Vic-le-Comte . . . 068845
Laurent, Guy, Vichy 068860, 121284
Laurent, Jacques, L'Isle-sur-la-Sorgue 063944
Laurent, Jean-Claude, Ennordres . .062778, 124230
Laurent, Juliette, Paris 100588
Laurent, Patrick, Mougins 064805
Laurent, Serge, Paris 100589
Laurent Hubert Musée, Orbey 013500
Laurent-Lasson, Eric, Paris 124717
Laurentin, Antoine, Paris 066151
Laures, Georges, Luxembourg 107407
Lauretta, Michel, Mandelieu-La Napoule 064244, 124384
Lauri, Bruno, Villeparisis 068925
Lauri Viidan Museo, Tampere 010121
Laurie, James & Mary, Minneapolis 142583
Laurie, John, London 085474, 131085
Laurie, Peter, London 085475
Laurier House, Ottawa 006102
Laurie's, Pittsburgh 091835
Laurin, Zürich 112137
Laurin, Claire M., Aix-en-Provence . 098788
Laurin, Didier, Lannion 063532
Laurin, Guilloux, Buffetaud & Tailleur, Paris 121163
Laurinmäen Torpparimuseo, Janakkala 009619
Laurino, Giusi, Napoli 106378
Lauriol, Simone, Saint-Hippolyte-du-Fort 067524
Lauriston Castle, Edinburgh 039399
Lauritz, Malmö . . . 110976, 122209, 129851
Laursen, Birthe, Paris 100590
Laursen, Per Michael, Humlebæk . . 124024
Laury-Bailly, Paris 066152
Lausanne, Rio de Janeiro 096622
Lausecker, Claude, Champigny-sur-Marne 062124
Lausitzer Bergbaumuseum Knappenrode, Hoyerswerda 018012
Lausmann, M., Hann Münden 125860
Lausmann, Manfred, Schwalmstadt 126787
Lauta, Varna 096775
Lauterbach, Hans, Berlin . 069684, 101973
Lauterbach, R.-P., Göttingen 071047
Lauth, Werner, Ludwigshafen am Rhein 103950, 126235
Lauth, Werner, Mannheim 072425, 126280
L'Authie, Tigny-Noyelle 068419
Lautier, Claude, Vetheuil 068831
Lautner, Mainz 104002
Lauxtermann, Britta, Osnabrück . . . 126599
Lava Beds National Monument, Tulelake 048650
Laval, Alain, Souillac 068272
Laval, Didier, Levroux 063806
Lavalier, New York 091020
Lavanchy, Evian-les-Bains 062825
Lavanchy, Thonon-les-Bains 068407
Lavanchy, Henri, Evian-les-Bains . . 062826
Lavande, Saint-Paul-de-Vence 101212
Lavanttaler Heimatmuseum, Eitweg 001829
Lavanttaler Heimatmuseum, Wolfsberg, Kärnten 003058
Lavanttaler Obstbaumuseum, Sankt Paul 002612
Lavarino, Maria Teresa, Torino 076834
Lavda, Anastasia, Athinai 105404
Laveen, Sydney 056681
Lavelli, Guéret 063100, 138105
Låven Antik, Skien 079494
Lavender, Boston 087830
Lavender, Maldon 056130
Lavender, D.S., London 085476
Lavender, Lida, London 085477
Lavender Bay Gallery, North Sydney 094983
Lavender Blue, Dartmouth 112939
Lavender Hill, Philadelphia 091654
Lavender Passion Gallery, Longwood 094745
Lavender & Roses, Den Haag 078211
Lavenham Contemporary, Lavenham 113356
Lavergne, Bertrand de, Paris 066153
Laverroux, Jean-Pierre, Clermont-Ferrand 062346
Lavest, Georges, Clermont-Ferrand 062347
Lavezzo, New York 091021
Lavian, Joseph, London . . 085478, 131086
Lavian Kotiseutumuseo, Lavia 009813
Lavignes-Bastille, Paris 100591
Lavigueur, Marc-André, Québec . . . 123805
Lavilgrand, François, Montlhéry . . . 064703
Lavín, Bilbao 080980
Lavirotte, Philippe, Chalon-sur-Saône 062089
Lavka Antikvara, Sankt-Peterburg . 080310
Lavka Antikvara, Sankt-Peterburg . 080311
Lavka Chudožnikov, Sankt-Peterburg 109635
Lavka knigoljuba, Moskva 140910
Lavka Starevščika, Sankt-Peterburg 080312
Lavocat Insignes Militaires, Prades-le-Lez 066977
Le Lavoir de Mougins, Mougins . . . 013259
Lavorazione Antica del Cuoio, Torino 128319
Lavradio de Radios, Rio de Janeiro . 058604
Lavrille, J., Gent 123624
Lavy, Bernard, Bons-en-Chablais . . 061567
Lavy, Corinne, La Roche-sur-Foron . 063410
Law Enforcement Museum, Roselle 047543
Law Uk Folk Museum, Hong Kong . 007124
Lawen, Ferdinand, Briedel 125398
Lawes, Anne, Neuenstadt 072985
Lawford, Suzanne, Rushcutters Bay 056559
Lawler-Taylor, Birmingham 115114
Lawn, Lincoln 040007
Lawn Heritage Museum, Lamaline . 005741
Lawndale, Philadelphia 091655
Lawniczak, Lüdinghausen 072351
Lawrence, Kansas City 116577
Lawrence, Vancouver 137729
Lawrence, Bob, London . . 085479, 131087
Lawrence, Brad J., Erskineville . . . 055805
Lawrence, David, Virginia Beach . . 093360
Lawrence & Sons, F.G., Redhill 086342
Lawrence, Hermann, Schwanewede 073754
Lawrence, Martin, Boston 115197
Lawrence County Gray House Museum, Ironton 044774
Lawrence County Historical Museum, Bedford 042096
Lawrence Gallery, Portland 119015
Lawrence Hall of Science, University of California, Berkeley 042161
Lawrence House Museum, Launceston 039939
Lawrence House Museum, Maitland 005822
Lawrence L. Lee Scouting Museum, Manchester 045619
Lawrence & Scott, Seattle 093029
Lawrence Wilson Art Gallery, Crawley 000956
Lawrences, Bletchingley 122419
Lawrences, Crewkerne 122483
Lawrens & Cie., Paris 066154
Lawry, John, Malvern East 094774
Law's Artland, Hong Kong 059661
Laws Railroad Museum, Bishop . . . 042232
Lawson, Albuquerque . . . 087403, 131745
Lawson, Cambridge 141474
Lawson, Dallas 115904
Lawson, Hurst Green 084777
Lawson, San Francisco 119716
Lawson & Co, E.M., East Hagbourne 141565
Lawson, Enid, London 113733
Lawson, F. & T., Richmond, Surrey . 086358
Lawson, Keith, Scratby 086524
Lawson, Peter, Townsville 095350
Lawsons, Sydney 120643
Lawton, Hughes 136949
Lawton Gallery, University of Wisconsin-Green Bay, Green Bay 044309
Laxa, Tilo, Rüdenhausen 073617
Laxfield and District Museum, Laxfield 039942
Lay, David, Penzance 122652
Lay, Kenneth, Prahran 056496
Le Lay, Philippe, Châteaulin 062196
Lay-Bonnot, Madeleine, Nice 065099
Layan, Roselyne, Montauban 138211
Layard, Siegrid, Sielbeck 073817
Layland Museum, Cleburne 042973
Laymance, Houston 116355
Layne, A.C., Carlisle 130516
Layr, Sieglinde, Gars am Kamp 095510
Layug, Budji, Makati 108827
Laywood, Anthony W., Knipton 141701
Lazar, Beograd 109706
Lazareth, Annick, Mesigny 064510
Lazaro Montelongo, Maria Magdalena, Santa Cruz de Tenerife 110742
Lazarovici, Bernard, Saint-Ouen . . . 067827
Laz'art Déco, Lyon 064148
Laz'art Déco, Lyon 064149
Lazartigues, Josiane, Nérac 064973
Lazarus, David, Hartley Wintney . . . 084602
Lazarus, Julie, Fort Worth 116151
Lazer, Buffalo 087889
Lazerhead, Louisville 116950
Lazic, Rubens, Saint-Ouen 067828
Lazoukine, Deauville 099200
Lazrak, Khadija, Casablanca 077660
Lazuli, de, Paris 124718
Lazulum, Marseille 124424
Lazy Daisies, Hazel Grove 113216
Lazzarato, Giovanni, Padova 076095
Lazzareschi, Riccardo, Livorno 127494
Lazzarini, Alain, Le Ban-Saint-Martin 063563
Lazzarini Restauri, Torino . 076835, 128320
Lazzaro, Vivioli & Figli, Genova 075481
Lazzaro By Corsi, Milano 106254
Lazzeri, Filippo, Firenze 127358
Lazzoni, Chantal, Saint-Étienne . . . 067458
LBB, Schwaigern 073747
LB's Antiques, Dallas 088547
LBW Gallery, Indianapolis 116471
L.C. Bates Museum, Hinckley 044553
LCE School of Arts and Design, Singapore 050685
L.D. Brinkman Art Foundation, Kerrville 044976
L.D. Upholstery and Refinishing, Edmonton 123762
LDM-Múzeum Andreja Sládkoviča Krupina, Krupina 034370
Le, Xuan, Ho Chi Minh City 120516
Le Bihan, Gildas, Carnoët 061995
Le Bihan, Jacques, Paris 066155
Le Bouffo, Magdeleine, Loudéac . . 099524
Le Bric a Brac, Negril 106830
Le Brun, Guy, Livarot 099515
Le Calonnec, Pierre & René, Pleurtuit 066855
Le Cam, Françoise & Philippe Belhache, Nantes 064929
Le Chanjour Marais, Paris 066156, 100592
Le Cheval Blanc, Ury 068662
Le Clerc, Bruxelles 058014
Le Coz, Gilbert, Pommerit-le-Vicomte 066898
Le Dean, David-Pierre, Nantes 064930
Le Fell, Jean-Marie, Paris 100593, 138426
Le Floch, Ludovic, Tousson 068612
Le Fuel de L'Espée, Paris 066157
Le Gaillard & Associés, Alain de, Paris 100594
Le Gatti, Jean-Pierre, Bruxelles . . . 120733
Le Goff, François-Xavier & Sylvie, Pléneuf-Val-André 066847
Le Gouil, Dominique, Asnières-sur-Seine 061010
Le Hénant, Paris 066158
Le Houelleur, Guy, Deauville 120986
Le-Lay, Philippe, Locronan 063974
Le Mans, Wendover 114662
Le Mouël, Jean-Marie, Paris 121164
Le Musée du Champagne, Le Mesnil-sur-Oger 012528
Le Nost, Alain, Paimpol 099895
Le Paon Artistic Circle, Singapore . . 050686
Le Point Fortifié Hillmann, Colleville-Montgomery 011419
Le Puy Collection, Le Puy-en-Velay 063697
Le Roy, Bianca, La Varenne-Saint-Hilaire 063466
Le Roy, Sabine, Lisieux 099512
Le Roy House and Jell-o Gallery, Le Roy 045217
Le Scaphandre, Paris 066159
Le Sueur Museum, Le Sueur 045218
Le Vesconte, Peter, Saint Helier . . . 086450
Le Wenshu Hua Fang, Tianjin 098012
Lea, Klaus, München 104257
Lea, Rocky, Bairnsdale 094189
Lea County Cowboy Hall of Fame and Western Heritage Center, Hobbs . 044562
Leach, Derek, Cincinnati 088255
Leach, Elizabeth, Portland 119016
Leader, Tampa 093138
Leadhills Miners' Library Museum, Leadhills 039943
Leadon, Eric, Las Vegas 116633
Léadouze, Alexandre, Cannes 099073
Leadouze, Alexandre, Paris 100595
Leaf Galleries, Maidstone 114032
Leaf Rapids National Exhibition Centre, Leaf Rapids 005758
Léage, François, Paris 066160
Leah's Gallery, New York 091022
Leah's Gallery, New York 091023
Leakey, Charles, Inverness 141689
Léal, Eduardo, Blois 061525
Leal Antiquario, Rio de Janeiro 058605
Leali, Alberto, Roma 128080
Leali, Alessio, Roma 128081
Leali, Andrea, Roma 128082
Leali, Angelo, Roma 128083
Leaming's Run Garden and Colonial Farm, Cape May Court House 042616
Leamington Spa Art Gallery and Museum, Leamington Spa 039944
Leamingtons Little Auction House, Waikato 121837
Leanin' Tree Museum of Western Art, Boulder 042353
Leapfrog Studio, Mooloolaba 094877
Leaping Rabbit, Ottawa 059042
Learmonth Museum, Learmonth . . . 001180
Learsy, Miami 090198
Leather Bucket, Philadelphia 091656
Leather Museum, Haram 009337
Leather Museum, Gerberei Museum, Swakopmund 029097
Leatherhead Museum of Local History, Leatherhead 039945
Leatherland, P.D., Reading 086335
Leatherstocking Brush & Palette Club, Cooperstown 054844
Leavenworth County Historical Society Museum, Leavenworth 045222
Leavin, Margo, West Hollywood . . . 120396
Lebaillif, Daniel, Le Breuil-en-Auge 063579
Lebanon' Marine Wildlife Museum with Collection of Murex, Jdeidet El-Metn 027818
LeBaron, Sacramento 119153
Lebas, François, Issoudun 063223
Lebas, François, Saint-Georges-sur-Arnon 067493
Lebbing, F.G., Amsterdam 077900
Lebeer Hossmann, Bruxelles 133274
Lebeer & Hossmann, Hamburg 134017
Lebell Residence, Kristiinankaupunki 009750
Lebende Galerie, Graz 001940
Lebendes Textilmuseum, Groß Siegharts 001965
Lebendiges Museum, Bad Wildungen 015825

Lebensart, Grüna, Sachsen 071129
Lebert, San Francisco 092826
Lebert, Jean-Claude, Gondrecourt-le-Château 063013
Lebesgue, Vincent, Laroque-des-Arcs 063540
Leblanc, Christian, Lyon 124364
Leblanc, Danièle, Wiege-Faty 069050
Leblay, Bernard, Clermont-Ferrand . 124203
Leblond, Les Vans 063794
Lebole, Nicoletta, Roma 076523
Lebon, Baudoin, Paris 100596
Lebourg, A., Le Havre 124300
Lebourg, Marie-Nicole, Dinard 062687
Lebouteiller, Jacky, Vire 069002
Lebouteiller, Joël, Mesnil-Clinchamps 064512
Lebouteiller, Joël, Saint-Sever-Calvados 068008
Lebovic, Josef, Paddington 095033
Lebra, François, Nice 065100
Lebraly, Guy, Cannes 124169
Lebreton, Alain, Bonneville-sur-Touques 061562
Lebreton, Alain, Deauville 062608
Lebriz Sanat Galerisi, İstanbul 112332
Lebrun, Paris 066161, 124719
Lebrun, Adrienne, Paris 066162
Lebrun, Adrienne, Sartilly 068136
Lebrun, Jean, Lisieux 121038
Lebrun, Marie-Thérèse, Saint-Honoré 067525
Lebsack, Linda, Denver 142391
Lebzelterei- und Wachsziehereimuseum, Pfaffenhofen an der Ilm 019598
Leccese, P., Köln 103670
Leccese, Pasquale, Milano 106255
Leccese, Pasquale, Milano 106256
Lecchi, Jeannine, Paris 124720
Lecerf, Acquigny 060660
Lecerf, Rouen 133696
Lechelt, R. & A., Elster 102617
Lechevallier, Coutances 062534
Lechfeldmuseum, Königsbrunn . . . 018346
Lechflößermuseum, Lechbruck am See 018539
Lechlade Arcade, Lechlade 084919
Lechleitner, Herwig, Braz 056949
Lechler, Stuttgart 139767
Lechmere, Malvern 141933
Lechner, Gérard, Bourgoin-Jallieu . 061732
Lechner, Karl-U., Holm-Seppensen . 071567
Lechner, Rene, Mönchengladbach . 072571
Lechner, Rupert, Wien 057486
Lechthaler, Herbert, Ampaß 056917
Leckie, Maldon 094766
Leclerc, Prahran 056497
Leclerc, Simbach am Inn 073820
Leclerc, Alain, Villeneuve-sur-Lot . . 125030
Leclerc, Marie-Sylvie, Manosque . . 121057
Leclerc Franck, Le Translay 063721
Leclercq, Denise, Prouzel 066987
Leclercq, Jamy, Martainneville 064407
Leclercq, Jean-Louis, Amiens 060820
Leclercq de Lescure, Bernard, Lille 124319
Lecoeur, Jean, Saint-Michel-Chef-Chef 067674
Lecointre-Drouet, Paris 138427
Lecomte, Alain, Paris 100597
Lecomte, Bernard, Paris . . 100598, 138428
Lecomte, Daniel, Héric 063147
Lecomte, Max, Château-Gontier . . . 062185
Lecomte-Durouil, Marc, Toulon (Var) 101321
Leconey, Elizabeth, Dallas 088548
Leconte, Jean-Marc, Paris 066163
Leconte, Pierre, Veyreau 068833
Lecourt, Gilbert, Pleine-Fougerès . . 101011
Lecourt, Gilbert, Saint-Malo (Ille-et-Vilaine) 101173
Lecourtois, Jean-Jacques, Carentan 061985
Lectori Salutem, Weesp 140573
Les Lectures d'Ysengrin, Bordeaux . 138044
Lecuire, Pierre, Paris 133640
Lécuyer, Vincent, Paris 100599
L.E.D.A., Paris 066164
Leda Décors, Gambais 062957
Leda Decors, Saint-Ouen 067829
Ledaal Museum, Stavanger 031224
Leder, Hugo, Geltendorf 125713
Leder, Jutta, Wolfratshausen 074478
Lederman, Geo, New York 091024, 142670
Ledermann, Burggen 070099
Ledermann, Charles, Laronxe 063539
Ledermann, Leo, Locarno 111653, 130086
Ledeur, Jean-Paul, Paris 124721
Ledford & Ledford, Oklahoma City .091514, 132580
Ledoux, M., Miami 142557
Ledra, Lefkosia 059956
Ledri School of Art and Design, Lefkosia 049886
Ledru, Guy, Livarot 063967
Ledru, Servane, Nantes 064931
Leduc, Sylvia, Saint-Ouen 067830
Lee, Hong Kong 097808
Lee, Los Angeles 089819
Lee, A., London 131088
Lee, Diane, Oklahoma City 091515
Lee, Fred, Hong Kong 059662
Lee, Harvey, Jacksonville 116532
Lee, Hwaik, Seoul 107264
Lee, Hyun, Daegu 107186
Lee, J. Morton, Hayling Island 113213
Lee, Jacques, Paris 124722
Lee, Jain, Buffalo 087890
Lee, James K., King's Lynn 084849
Lee, Janie C., Houston 116356
Lee, Kwong Tin, Hong Kong 059663
Lee, Lori, Ivybridge 113310
Lee, Lothar & Marianne, Berlin 069685
Lee, Lothar & Marianne, Berlin 069686
Lee, Ron, Las Vegas 116634
Lee, Sabina, Los Angeles 116819
Lee, Tom, Memphis 090083
Lee, Vincent, Hong Kong 097809
Lee, Y., Los Angeles 116820
Lee Chapel and Museum, Lexington 045280
Lee Conklin Antique Organ History Museum, Hanover 044425
Lee County Historical Society Museum, Loachapoka 045357
Lee-Fendall House, Alexandria 041645
Lee Kong Chian Art Museum, Singapore 034295
Lee Po Gallery, Hong Kong 097810
Lee Verre, Elena, Montréal 097049
Leeber Corgan, Sharon, Dallas 115905
Leech, John, Auckland 108335
Leeds Industrial Museum, Leeds Museums and Galleries, Leeds 039955
Leeds Metropolitan University Gallery, Leeds 039956
Leeds Museums and Galleries Review, Leeds 136240
Leedy, Sherry, Kansas City 116578
Leedy-Voulke's Art Center, Kansas City 044922
Leeflang Oude Dingen, Den Haag . . 078212
Leegenhoek, J. O. & H., Paris 100600
Leek Antiques Centre, Leek 084940, 130876
Leek Art Gallery, Leek 039966
Leek Old Books, Leek 141714
Leelanau Historical Museum, Leland 045234
Leemark, Christchurch 079036
Lees, London 131089
Lees & Sons, M., Worcester 087259
Lees, Michael Scott, Bungendore . . 094330
Lees, Michael Scott, Jindabyne . . . 094667
Lee's Antiques, Clitheroe 084036
Lee's Comm. Art Institute, Kuala Lumpur 050528
Leest, Den Haag 140394
Leetz, Elke, Woltersdorf bei Erkner . 105326
Leeuw, Jef Theo de, Ekeren 096277, 133284
Lefa, Dresden 102451
Lefakis, Chalandri 105416
Lefakis, Néa Kifissia 105436
Lefèbvre & Fils, Paris 066165
Lefebvre, Arnaud, Paris 100601
Lefebvre, Eric, Saint-Pryvé-Saint-Mesmin 138607
Lefèbvre, Jacques, Montebourg . . . 064670
Lefèbvre, Marc, Paris 066166, 138429
Lefèbvre, Michel, Versailles 101455, 138653
Lefèbvre, Véronique, Beaucamps-Ligny 061249
Lefebvre & Petrenko, Paris 100602
Lefèvre, Saint-Maur-des-Fossés . . 067662
Lefèvre, Blandine, Paris 066167
Lefevre, Blandine, Saint-Ouen 067831
Lefevre, François, Bazoches-les-Hautes 061247
Lefevre, Jean-Claude, Mayenne . . . 064442
Lefèvre, Nicolas, Granville 063034
Lefèvre, Pierre-Yves, Paris 121165
Lefèvre, Romain, Gisors 063007
Lefèvre, Romain, Vesly 068827
Lefèvre, Valérie, Conty 062465
Lefèvre, W. & V., Kortrijk 058264
Lefferts Homestead, Brooklyn 042462
Leffingwell House Museum, Norwich 046566
Leffler, Toledo 093176
Leffler, Toledo 093177
Lefkowicz, Edward J., Providence . 142816
Lefor-Openo, Paris 100603
Leforestier, Alain, Forges-les-Eaux . 062920
Lefranc, Frédéric, Auxerre 120913
Lefranc, Monique-Valérie, Marmande 064292
Lefrançois, F.J., Bordeaux 061628
Left Bank Art Consultants, Surry Hills 056653
Left Bank Art Gallery, Greymouth . . 030506
Left Bank Artists Co-Op, Beechworth 094227
Left Bank Books, Saint Louis 142859
Left Bank Books, Seattle 142997
Left Bank Gallery, Norfolk 118614
Left Gallery, Toronto 097313
Lefteris Kanakakis Gallery, Rethymnon 021449
Leg Laki, Edit, Pécs 105573
Legabilleux, Jean-Paul, Parville . . . 066692
Legacies Antiques, Vancouver 059374
Legacies Limited, Milwaukee 090309
Legacy, New York 091025
Legacy, Panamá City 108791
Legacy, Shannon 079236
Legacy Antiques, Athinai 074597
Legacy Antiques, Cleveland 088341
Legacy Antiques, Dallas 088549
Legacy Art, Saint Paul 119299
Legacy Artworks, Boston 115198
Legacy Furniture, Milwaukee 090310
Legacy Gold, Dallas 088550
Legacy Home Collections, Singapore 080514
Legacy Limited, Seattle 119953
Legacy's Antiques, San Diego 092651
Legal Book Store, Los Angeles 142515
Legart, Perugia 127878
Legaspi City Museum, Legaspi 031684
Legat-Verlag, Tübingen 134433
Legault, Pouance 101048
Legend Antiques, Oakland 091425
Legend Press, Artarmon 133044
Legenda, Budapest 139921
La Légende, Nice 065101
La Légende, Nice 065102
Légende des Siècles, Besançon . . . 061388
La Légende des Siècles, Lyon 064150
Legends Concert Posters, Portland . 119017
Legends in Time, Toledo 093178
Legends of Art, Las Vegas 116635
Legends of Hollywood, Omaha 118709
Legends of the Game Baseball Museum, Arlington 041775
Leger, Malmö 110977
Leger, Helmut, München . 104258, 134257
Léger, Joël, Le Havre 063636
Legg & Son, E.C., Cirencester 130583
Legg, Michael, Dorchester 084178
Legg of Dorchester, Bere Regis . . . 083490
Legg of Dorchester, Dorchester . . .084179, 130642
Legge, Dublin 105876
Legge, Redfern 095127
Legge, Christopher, Oxford 086180, 131354
Legge, Elisabeth, Toronto . 059228, 137709
Legge, Joan, Salt Lake City 092438
Legge, Joy, Subiaco 056646
Leggett, Arthur, Toronto 097314
Légier, Nathalie, L'Isle-sur-la-Sorgue 063945
Legiewicz, Dinslaken 070257
Legislative Building Art Galleries, Regina 006256
Leglaive, Jacques, La Ferté-sous-Jouarre 063375, 138111
Legnaghi, Mattea, Verona 128427
Legot-Thisse, Bruxelles . . 058015, 123598
Legra Gallery, Leigh-on-Sea 113379
Legrado Garcia, Jose Maria, Madrid 129637
Legrand, Alain, Paris 124723
Legrand, Claudine, Paris 100604
Legrand, Jean-Luc, Cormainville . . 062475
Legrand, Nadine, Armentières 098860
Legros, Martine, Saint-Martin-de-Ré 067634
Legroux, Pascale, Fontenay-le-Comte 124240
Legue, Jacques, Bondy 061555
Lehalle, Paris 100605
Lehár-Schlößl, Schikaneder-Schlößl, Wien 002939
Lehár-Villa, Bad Ischl 001724
Lehembre, Philippe, Marcilly-la-Campagne 064263
Lehembre, Philippe, Verneuil-sur-Avre 068780
Leher, Alfred, Landshut 072143
Lehigh County Historical Society Museum, Allentown 041659
Lehigh University Art Galleries/Museum, Zoellner Arts Center, Bethlehem . 042184
Lehle, Kolbermoor 103750
Lehman, Claude, Paris 066168
Lehman College Art Gallery, Bronx . 042439
Lehmann, Dortmund 070287
Gebr. Lehmann, Dresden 102452
Lehmann, D., Köln 139347
Lehmann, Heinz, Stans 082833
Lehmann, J., Chemnitz . . 070135, 121366
Lehmann, Jens, Lehrte 126179
Lehmann, Prof. Jirina, Hildesheim . 125935
Lehmann, Marc, Lausanne 082552
Lehmann, Monika, Hamburg 103176
Lehmann, Uwe, Groß Glienicke . . . 071111
Lehmann, Volker, Lutherstadt Wittenberg 072366
Lehmann, Leskiw & Schedler, Toronto 097315
Lehmann Maupin, New York 118120
Lehmann-Özyurt, Stephan, Varel . . 139813
Lehmeier, Andrea & Roland, Pyrbaum 073389
Lehmkuhl, Thomas, Steinfurt 126833
Lehmmuseum, Gnevsdorf 017438
Lehn, Joseph, Baltimore 087685
Lehner, Seitenstetten 137263
Lehner, Hermann, Linz 095667
Lehner, Ilse, Wien 057487
Lehner, Maria, Wolfsberg im Schwarzautal 095975
Lehner, Nikolaus, Altdorf, Niederbayern 125061
Lehnert, Rüdiger, Wincheringen . . . 127022
Lehnert & Landrock, Cairo 133437
Lehr, Dr. Irene, Berlin 121335

Lehr, Karl, Darmstadt 138974
Lehr, Maria, Trier 105065
Lehr- und Schaubergwerk Frisch Glück, Johanngeorgenstadt 018125
Lehr- und Schaubergwerk Herkules Frisch Glück, Beierfeld 015937
Lehrstuhl für Bildnerische Gestaltung, Rheinisch-Westfälische Technische Hochschule Aachen, Aachen 050002
Lehrstuhl für Bildnerisches Gestalten, Technische Universität München, München 050195
Lehrstuhl für Kunst, Pädagogische Hochschule Schwäbisch Gmünd, Schwäbisch Gmünd 050234
Lehrstuhl für Kunsterziehung, Universität Passau, Passau 050217
Lehrstuhl für Kunstgeschichte, Technische Universität München, München . . 050196
Lehrstuhl für Kunstgeschichte, Universität Augsburg, Augsburg 050005
Lehrstuhl für Kunstgeschichte und Christliche Archäologie, Philosophische Fakultät, Universität Passau, Passau 050218
Lehrstuhl für Kunstgeschichte und Professur für Kunsterziehung, Katholische Universität, Eichstätt 050072
Lehrstuhl für Kunstpädagogik, Universität Augsburg, Augsburg 050006
Lehrstuhl für Kunstpädagogik und Kunstdidaktik, Otto-Friedrich-Universität Bamberg, Bamberg 050013
Lehrstuhl für Restaurierung, Kunsttechnologie und Konservierungswissenschaft, Technische Universität München, München . . 050197
Lehrstuhl Kunst, Pädagogische Hochschule Weingarten/ Fakultät II, Weingarten, Württemberg 050258
Lehrstuhl Kunsterziehung, Friedrich-Alexander-Universität Erlangen-Nürnberg, Nürnberg 050208
Lehtimäen Museo, Lehtimäki 009814
Lehuard, Jacques, Jonquières-Saint-Vincent 063248
Lehuard, Ludovic, Nîmes 065180
Lei Cheng Uk Han Tomb Museum, Hong Kong Museum of History, Hong Kong 007125
Leia Livraria, São Paulo 137585
Leibelt, Ulrich, München 126409
Leiber, Mario & Waltraud, Hinzert-Pölert 071530
Leibfried, Fr., Sindelfingen 073826
Leibovici, Laura Eliette, Biarritz . . . 098966
Leib'sches Haus, Abteilung Stadtgeschichte und Volkskunde, Oberhessisches Museum und Gail'sche Sammlungen, Gießen 017410
Leibzig-Biland, Marly 130115
Leica Galerija Praha, Praha 008619
Leica Gallery, New York 118121
Leica Stammbaum und Museum, Solms 020243
Leicester Antiques Warehouse, Leicester 084948
Leicester Art Books, London 141840
Leicestershire CCC Museum, Leicester 039972
Leicestershire Museums, Arts and Records Service, Glenfield 054420
Leicestershire Pastel Society, Leicester LE4 4LD 054421
Leicht, Markus, Mainz 126261
Leichter, Danica, Frankfurt am Main 070762
Leida, Wageningen 134838, 140567
Leidel, Herbert, München 104259
Leidelmeijer, Amsterdam 077901
Leidens, Ursula, Menden 104060
Leidl, Monika, München 139528
De Leidse Wagenmaker, Leiden . . . 128743
Leif's Custom Upholstery, Vancouver 123852
Leigh, Jamie, Oldbury West Midlands 114185
Leigh, Laurie, Oxford 086181
Leigh Gallery Books, Southend-on-Sea 142082
Leigh Heritage Centre, Leigh-on-Sea 039981
Leigh Jewellery, Leigh, Lancashire . 084953
Leigh Yawkey Woodson Art Museum, Wausau 049015
Leighton Art Gallery, Weymouth . . . 114677
Leighton Buzzard Railway, Leighton Buzzard 039983
Leighton Foundation Collection, Calgary 005190
Leighton Hall, Carnforth 039003
Leighton House Museum, London . 040197
Leighton-Morris, Johannesburg . . . 080709
Leijon, Ulf, Uppsala 129887
Leijser, Margot, Arnhem 078055
Leilivende, Amadora 121916
A Leiloeira, Lisboa 121933
A Leiloeira, Porto 121948
Leiloeira Corte Real, Porto 080091, 121949
A Leiloeira Invicta do Norte, Porto . 121950
Leilões União, Porto 121951
Leimarel Museum and Research Centre, Imphal 022169
Leimberger, Hanns, Bodenmais . . . 102165
Leinen & Lavendel, Lübeck 072328
Leinen- und Spitzenmuseum Haigerseelbach, Haiger 017634
Leineweber-Museum, Rheda-Wiedenbrück 019817
Leingruber, Rolf, Basel . . . 082151, 129925
Leinorte, Porto 121952
Leinster, Dublin 105877
Leinweber, Dr. J., Marburg 139461
Leinz, Gabriele, Bonn 125355
Leipold, Günther, Fulda 070917
Leipziger Antiquariat, Leipzig 139397
Leipziger Antiquariatsmesse, Leipzig 093744
Leipziger Grafikbörse e.V., Leipzig .053480, 103892
Leipziger Jahresausstellung e.V., Leipzig 053481
Leipziger Münzhandlung und Auktion, Leipzig 072209, 121495
Leipziger Verlagsgesellschaft, Leipzig 134153
Leirfjord Bygdesamlinger, Leirfjord . 030976
Leiria & Nascimento, Lisboa 079949
Leiria & Nascimento, Lisboa 079950
Leiria & Nascimento, Lisboa 079951
Leiria & Nascimento, Lisboa 121934
Leiria & Nascimento, Lisboa 121935
Leiria & Nascimento, Lisboa 121936
Leiria & Nascimento, Porto 080092, 121953
Leiris, Louise, Paris 100606, 133641
Leirvika Bygdesamling, Foldereid . . 030842
Leis, Karl, Karlsruhe 071725
Leis, Ulla, Mömbris 072563
Leiser-Hofmann & Conen, Karlstein am Main 071740
Leismann, Hedwig, Sankt Wendel . 104816
Leiss, Hilde, Hamburg 103177
Leissle, Peter, München 139529
Leiston Trading Post, Leiston 084965
Leisure Art Gallery, Singapore 109826
Leisure Painter, Tenterden 136241
Leitch Collieries, Crowsnest Pass . . 005312
Leitenmeier, Franz, Augsburg 125076
Leith Gallery, Edinburgh 112999
Leith Hall, Huntly 039788
Leitheimer Schloß-Museum, Kaisheim 018138
Leithenmühle, Windhaag bei Freistadt 003053
Leithner, Klaus, Hamburg 103178
Leitner-Szapary, Barbara, Wolfsbach 123541
Lejbzon & Co., Olek, New York 132490
Lejeune Uselding, Stanislas, Bruxelles 058016
Lejre Forsøgscenter, Lejre 009008
LEK Taululiike, Turku 060641
Leka Bygdemuseum, Leka 030977
Lekon, Essen 102698
Leks, Paris 138430
Leksaksmuseet, Stockholm 036637
Leksbergs Skolmuseum, Vadsbo Museum, Mariestad 036472
Leksvik Bygdesamling, Leksvik . . . 030979
Lela Harty School of Arts, San Diego 052116
Leland, Kippie L. & Ted, Nashville . . 090463
Leland, Perry H., San Francisco . . . 092827
Lelandais, Marcel, Bourseul 061735
Leleu, Gérald, Leubringhen 063797
Lelievre, Jean-Marie, Athies-sous-Laon 061015
Lellouche, Abraham Guy, Paris 066169
Lelong, Argenteuil 098858
Lelong, New York 118122
Lelong, Paris 100607, 133642
Lelong, Zürich 112138, 135092
Lelouch, Jean-Marc, Paris 066170
Leloup, Hélène & Philippe, Paris . . . 100608
Lemaire, Amsterdam 077902
Lemaire, Bruxelles 058017
Lemaire, André, Paris 066171
Lemaire, André, Paris 066172
Lemaire, Bernard, Tours 124999
Lemaire, Chantal, Alençon 060766
Lemaire, Dominique, Toufflers 068434
Lemaire, Régis, Moulins (Allier) . . . 064815
Lemaitre, Olivier, Paris 066173
Lemaître d'Estève de Bosch, M.H., Saint-Ouen-de-Thouberville 067930
Lemand, Claude, Paris 100609
Lemarchand, Philippe, Saint-Sauveur-le-Vicomte 068003
Lemarié, Jean, Notre-Dame-du-Touchet 065237
Lemarie, Sylvie, Brive-la-Gaillarde . 138058
Lemasson, Gaetan, Roquebilliere . . 067217
Lemaster, Austin 087590, 131803
Lemay, Los Angeles 116821
Lemazo, Jean-Claude, Dole 062698
Lembaga Muzium Negeri, Pulau Pinang 028009
Lembcke, Wolfgang, Ammersbek . . 069163
Lemberg, Andreas, Venezia 106760
Lemberg-Richtermeier, Ilona M., Berlin 125246
Lembessi, Antoinette, Paris 066174
Lemburg, Hamburg 071278
Lemcke, Karin, Schleswig 073697
Lemee House, Natchitoches 046164
Lemeni, Valentin, Vandœuvre-lès-Nancy 068709
Lemercier, Philippe, Laval (Mayenne) 063552
Lemhi County Historical Museum, Salmon 047767
Lemieux, André, Québec 097150
Lemin Kotiseutumuseo, Lemi Heritage Museum, Lemi 009815
Lemke, M., Berlin 069687
Lemke, Olaf, Berlin 069688, 101974
Lemkow, Sara & Rachel, Ely 084326
Lemmer, Eva, Peißenberg 104598
Lemmers, S.C., Lisse 140489
Lemoine, Arras 060987
Lemoine, Catherine, Villegouge . . . 125026
Lemoine, J., Paris 100610
Lemoine, Stanislas, Caen 061877
Lemoine, Yves, Dolus-le-Sec 062699
Lemon Grass Arts, Singapore 080515
Lemon Hill Mansion, Philadelphia . . 046955
Lemon Pie, Virginia Beach 093361
Lemon Sky, Los Angeles 116822
Lemon Sky, Miami 117104
Lemon Street Gallery, Dublin 105878
The Lemon Street Gallery, Truro . . . 114603
Lemon Tree Antiques, Art & Books, Fort Worth 088865, 142413
Lemonnier, Bruxelles 058018, 120734
Lemonnier Frères, Versailles 068810
Lemousse, Michel, Guignen 063105
LeMoyne Art Foundation, Tallahassee 048481
Lempart, Renate, Hamburg 139196
Lempertz, Basel 122305
Lempertz, Berlin 101975, 121336
Lempertz, Brooklyn 122831
Lempertz, Bruxelles 120735
Lempertz, Buenos Aires 120553
Lempertz, Frankfurt am Main 121407
Lempertz, Hamburg 121431
Lempertz, Köln . . 071974, 103671, 121475
Lempertz, München 121537
Lempertz, Tokyo 121745
Lempertz, Valparaíso 120837
Lempertz, Versailles 121278
Lempertz, Matthias, Bonn 138903
Lempio & Ern, Wiehl 074388
Lemun Kotiseutumuseo, Lemu 009819
Lemuria Gallery, Philadelphia 118792
Lemvig Museum Vesterhus, Lemvig 009010
Leña Gomariz, Córdoba 081049
Lenaerts, D., Antwerpen 123549
LenArt, Sankt-Peterburg 109636
Lenbachmuseum, Schrobenhausen 020101
Lencastre, Isabel, Porto 080093
Lencquesaing, Hughes de, Boulogne-Billancourt 061687
Lendemar, Pia, Berlin 125247
Lendl, Eugen, Graz 095536
Lendo & Pintando, Brasília 137552
Lenduce, Basel 111206
Lenfant, Fernand, Launois-sur-Vence 063548
Lengenfelder, Dr. Helga, München . 134258
Lengerer, Albstadt 101553
Lengertz, Lund 141122
Lenggenhager, Hans, Neuhausen am Rheinfall 082697
Lengil, Porto Alegre 058511
Lengler, Josef Maria, Chur 129999
Lenglet, Christine, Paris 066175
Lenhart, San Jose 119855
Leni, M., Chicago 088118
Lenin-Museo, Tampere 010122
Lenk, Michael, Wels 137280
Lenk, Norbert, Seybothenreuth 126798
Lenkų Meno Galerija, Vilnius 107364
Lennard Antiques, Sible Hedingham 086612
Lennart, Wormer 134839
Lennon, Francis, Manchester 135282
Lennon School of Art and Design, Lemesos 049888
Lennox, Parramatta 095059, 123284
Lennox, Karen, Chicago 115476
Lennox and Addington County Museum and Archives, Napanee 005984
Lennoxlove House, Haddington . . . 039652
Lenoir & Assoc., San Antonio 119428
Lenoir, Jean-Marc, Chécy 062265
Lenoir-Retaud, Bernadette, Cruzilles-les-Mepillat 062579
Lenorman, Mathieu, Paris 066176
Lenormand, Jacques, Paris 066177, 121166
Lenormand, Xavier, Paris 066178
L'Enrajolada Casa-Museu Santacana, Martorell 035476
Lensen, O.J., Voorburg 128872
Lensfire, Toronto 097316
Lentini, Vincenzo, Palermo 127833
Lentjou, Christina, Kifissia 105431
Lenton, A., Leicester 141718
Lentos Kunstmuseum Linz, Wolfgang-Gurlitt-Museum, Linz 002250
Lentulo, Flavio, Genova 127463
The Lentz Center for Asian Culture, Lincoln 045304
Lenvik Bygdemuseet, Finnsnes . . . 030834
Lenz, Milwaukee 117202
Lenz, Andreas, Coburg 070147
Lenz, Axel, Singen, Hohentwiel . . .073829, 121600
Lenz, Horst, Wennigsen 126992
Lenz, Kurt, Murnau 072938
Lenzen, Düsseldorf 139017
Lenzi, Raffaela, Palermo 076154

Lenziemill Archive Store, Cumbernauld . . . 039194
Lenzy, Houston . . . 089138
Leo, New York . . . 091026
Leo, Vincenzo, Palermo . . . 127834
Leo & Coppi, Berlin . . . 101976
Leobon, Frédéric, Cholet . . . 062299
Leodina Antiguidades, Belo Horizonte . . . 058432
Leoframes, Brighton . . . 130444, 141438
Leominster Antiques Market, Leominster . . . 084973
Leominster Folk Museum, Leominster . . . 039986
Leon, Atlanta . . . 114898
León, Bilbao . . . 129437
Leon, Miami . . . 090199
Leon, Washington . . . 133027
Léon, Albert de, Paris . . . 066179
Leon, F., Los Angeles . . . 132262
Léon, Philippe, Plouigneau . . . 066877
Leon Apacible Historical Landmark Museum, Taal . . . 031791
Leon Art, Nienburg, Weser . . . 104453
León Campos, Guatemala . . . 105480
Léon & Claverie, Paris . . . 066180
Leona, Madrid . . . 110559
Leona Paegles Memoriālais Muzejs, Vidriži . . . 027802
Leonard, Nashville . . . 132401
Leonard, Roma . . . 076524
Leonard, Antoine, Zoersel . . . 123680
Leonard, C.M., New York . . . 091027
Leonard, M., Charleville-Mézières . 062159
Leonard, Marjorie, Enniskillen . . . 113024
Leonard & Bina Ellen Art Gallery, Montréal . . . 005928
Leonardis, Oberursel . . . 104512
Leonardis, David, Chicago . . . 115477
Leonardo, Lausanne . . . 111624
Leonardo, Omaha . . . 118710
Léonardo, Paris . . . 100611
Leonardo, Skopje . . . 107424
Leonardo: Art, Science & Technology, Cambridge . . . 136521
Leonardo da Vinci Society Newsletter, London . . . 136242
Leonardof, Bogotá . . . 059843
LeonArt, Basel . . . 111207
Leondar, Knokke-Heist . . . 096340
Leone, Rio de Janeiro . . . 096623
Il Leone, Roma . . . 106572
Leone, Giacinto, Taranto . . . 076749
Leone, Pasquale, Napoli . . . 076003
Leone & C., Antonino, Messina . . . 075564
Leong & Sons, Seow Kok, Singapore . . . 080516
Leong Thin Lien, Penang . . . 077503
Leonhardi, Bad Füssing . . . 101647
Leonhardi-Museum, Dresden . . . 016799
Leonhardi-Museum Aigen, Bad Füssing . . . 015704
Leonhardt, Görlitz . . . 071038, 125736
Leonhardt, Ludwigshafen am Rhein 072315
Leonhardt, Jochen, Ibbenbüren . . . 121458
Leonhardt, Klaus, Würzburg . . . 074501, 121628
Leonhardt, Monika, Rehlingen-Siersburg . . . 073472
Leonhardt, Wolfgang, Weilheim, Oberbayern . . . 074305
Léoni, Saint-Galmier . . . 101153
Leoni, Lilia, Roma . . . 076525
Leopaldi, Donato, Torino . . . 128321
Leopard Books, Bristol . . . 141456
Leopold, Kansas City . . . 116579
Léopold d'Or, Agen . . . 060670
Leopold Figl-Museum, Michelhausen . . . 002311
Leopold-Hoesch-Museum Düren, Düren . . . 016823
Leopold Museum, Wien . . . 002940
Léopoldi-Ansaldi, Bastia . . . 061218
Leopold's Antikvariat, Stockholm . . 081978, 141163
Leorbide Contratas, Donostia-San Sebastián . . . 129510
Leo's Antiques, Houston . . . 089139
Leow, Singapore . . . 080517
Lepage, Claudine, Châteaudun . . . 062193
Lepage, Raymond, Paris . . . 124724
Lepape, Claude, Nancy . . . 064871
Lepavec, Alain, Paris . . . 124725
Lepeintre, Isabelle, Fribourg . . . 111415
Leperre, Carole, Reims . . . 067071
Lepert & Scheler, Paris . . . 138431
Lépic, Lausanne . . . 111625
Lepic, Paris . . . 100612, 133643, 138432
Lepic, Roland, Paris . . . 066181
L'Epicerie, Tourrettes-sur-Loup . . . 068573
Lepikon Torppa, Pielavesi . . . 009969
Lepina, Juan, Vigo . . . 081705
Leporatti, Alessandro, Pisa . . . 076243
Lepoultel, Philippe, Heugueville-sur-Sienne . . . 063155
Lepoutre et Fils, Roubaix . . . 067231
Lepoutre, André, Hardelot-Plage . . 063126
Leppävirran Kotiseutumuseo, Leppävirta . . . 009821
Lepramuseet Sant Jørgens Hospital, Bergen . . . 030768
Lepre, Aurelio, Palermo . . . 106432
Leprévost, Claude, Isneauville . . . 063219
Lepri, Amedeo, Firenze . . . 127359
Leprince, Christian, Paris . . . 100613
Leptis Magna Museum, Department of Antiquities, Leptis Magna . . . 027829
Lerch, Lauf an der Pegnitz . . . 072169
Lerch, Robert M., New York . . . 091028
Lerch, Dr. Tom, Berlin . . . 125248
Lerchenfeld, Ingrid Freifrau von, München . . . 072774
Lerchenfeld, Ingrid Freifrau von, München . . . 072775
Lerchl, Klaus, Lippstadt . . . 126224
Lereec, Elizabeth, Saint-Malo (Ille-et-Vilaine) . . . 067614
Lérein, Guy & Claude, Ancy-le-Franc . . . 098825
Lerendu, Alain, Marcey-les-Greves 064261
Lermer, Michael J., München . . . 126410
Lermontovskij Gosudarstvennyj Muzej-zapovednik Tarchany, Lermontovo 033325
Lerner, Leonardo, Buenos Aires . . . 136729
Lernon, Rouen . . . 101119
Leroux, Philippe, Nice . . . 065103
Leroux, Régis, Thiberville . . . 068387
Leroy, Nancy . . . 121083
Leroy, Alain, Paris . . . 121167
Leroy, Dominique, Paris . . . 133644
Leroy, Olivier, Bondues . . . 061553
Leroy and District Heritage Museum, Leroy . . . 005764
Lerverk Galleri, Göteborg . . . 110922
Lervoire, Thénac . . . 068383
Les Antiquitees, Roma . . . 076526
Les Chances de L'Art, Bolzano . . . 105987
Les Images, Ballymena . . . 112544
Les Liles, Barcelona . . . 080871
Les Vieilles Choses, Saint-Hilaire-du-Harcouët . . . 067520, 124905
Lesage, Montpellier . . . 099760
LesArt e.V., Überregionaler Verein lesbischer Künstlerinnen und für kunstinteressierte Lesben, Köln . . . 053482
Lesbian Herstory Educational Foundation, Brooklyn . . . 042463
Lesch, Inge, Freiburg im Breisgau . 070849
Leschevin, Christophe, Lille . . . 063853
Leschevin, Sabine, Lille . . . 063854
Lescomère, François, Yvrac . . . 069071
Lescop de Moy, Antoine, Paris . . . 066182
Lescoules, Christian, Albi . . . 060758
Lescouzères, Rousseau, Bazas . . . 061244
Lescroart, Marcel, Toucy . . . 068432
Lescure Collections, Mazamet . . . 064446
Lescureux, Christian, Amiens . . . 060821
Lescureux, Christian, Amiens . . . 060822
Leseratte, Braunschweig . . . 138929
Lesiak, Krzysztof, Warszawa . . . 129097
Lesieur & Le Bars, Le Havre . . . 121030
Lesieutre, Paris . . . 066183
Lesigne, Michel, Orval . . . 065312
Lesja Bygdatun, Museet i Nord-Gudbrandsdalen, Lesja . . . 030980
Lesjöforsmuseum, Lesjöfors . . . 036414
Leske, W., Einbeck . . . 070530
Leslie Hill Open Farm, Ballymoney . 038581
Leslie & Leslie, Haddington 084546, 122531
Leslie-Lohman Gay Art Foundation, New York . . . 046355
Leslie's, Seattle . . . 093030
Leslie's Collectibles, Long Beach . . 089641
Lesnícke a Drevárske Múzeum, Zvolen . . . 034454
Lesnické, Myslivecké a Rybářské Muzeum, Národní Zemědělské Muzeum Praha, Hluboká nad Vltavou . . . 008373
Lesotho National Museum, Maseru 027822
Lesourd, Lucien, Talmont-Saint-Hilaire . . . 068353
Lespès, Annie, Auch . . . 061053
Lespinasse, Bry-sur-Marne . . . 061830
Lespinasse, François, Rouen . . . 101120
L'Esprit du Cap, Lege-Cap-Ferret . . 063737
Lessentin, Heinz, Hannover 103289, 125876
L'Essenza, Lugano . . . 082602
Lessing-Museum, Kamenz . . . 018144
Lessirard, Marie-Louise, Chandai . . 062133
L'Estanco, Tassin-la-Demi-Lune . . . 068367
Lester, M., Albuquerque . . . 114799
Lester-Garland Premises, Trinity . . . 006654
Lestijärven Kotiseutumuseo, Lestijärvi . . . 009822
Lestrade, Michel, Toulouse . . . 138637
L'Estrange, Christchurch . . . 108401
Lestranger, Paris . . . 100614
Lestranger, Saint-Rémy-de-Provence . . . 067989
Lesueur, Patrice, Villefranche-de-Rouergue . . . 138660
Lesueur County Historical Museum, Elysian . . . 043700
Leszczyłowski, Jan, Sopot . . . 079709
Letecké Muzeum, Historický Ústav Armády České Republiky, Praha . . . 008620
Letellier, Jean, Paris . . . 066184
Leterreau, Briec, Rennes (Ille-et-Vilaine) . . . 101084
Letham, Ponsonby . . . 108545
Lethbridge Community College Gallery, Lethbridge . . . 005766
Lethert, Peter & Sybille, Bad Münstereifel . . . 069334
Lethgau, Lübeck . . . 103966
Łętocha i Nowosielski, Kraków . . . 140743
Letortu, Janine, Paris . . . 066185
Letostruj, Sofia . . . 058763
Letostruj, Sofia . . . 137604
Let's Collect Devon Pottery Magazine, Saint Albans . . . 136243
Let's Dish, Austin . . . 087591
Let's Go Antiquing!, New Orleans . . 090577
Let's Talk Antiques, Daytona Beach 122877
Letschert, Peter, Ransbach-Baumbach . . . 073414
Letson, Petra, Erlensee . . . 102656
Lett, Michael, Auckland . . . 108336
Letter a Gallery, Whittlesey . . . 114690
Le Lettere, Firenze . . . 134585
Letterkundig Museum en Kinderboekenmuseum, Den Haag 029430
Letters Bookshop, Toronto . . . 137710
Lettick, Gail, New York . . . 091029
Lettl-Atrium, Museum für surreale Kunst, Augsburg . . . 015612
La Lettre Écarlate, Paris . . . 138433
La Lettre Volée, Bruxelles 096227, 133275
Lettrée, Anne, Paris . . . 100615
Letty's Antiques, Leicester . . . 084949
Letz, Tom, Pirna . . . 126633
Lëtzebuerger Artisten Center - Salon de Printemps, Luxemburg . . . 093812
Letzelter, Doris, Baltmannsweiler . . 069441
Leu, Zürich . . . 082995
Leu, Kerstin & Holger, München . . . 104260
Leu, Michael, San Francisco . . . 119717
Leuchten & Hammes, Mönchengladbach . . . 072572
Leuchter, Ruth, Düsseldorf . . . 102525
Leudet, Christian, Le Bec-Hellouin . 063566
Leuenberg, M., Berlin . . . 138815
Leuenberger, Zürich . . . 082996
Leuenberger, Zürich . . . 112139
Leuenberger, Zürich . . . 130249
Leuenberger, Roland, Wangen bei Olten . . . 130214
Leupi, Ascona . . . 111139
Leupi, Nottwil . . . 111781
Leupolt, Fred, Templin . . . 074054
Leura Fine Woodwork Gallery, Leura . . . 094737
Leuro-Arte, Málaga . . . 110640
Lev, London . . . 085480, 131090
Levanger Museum, Levanger . . . 030982
Levasseur, Noyon . . . 065245
Levasseur, Paris . . . 100616
Levé, François, Paris . . . 066186
Levecher, Michel, Juziers . . . 063276
Leveillé, Jean-Claude, Pacy-sur-Eure . . . 065323, 124533
Léveilley, Jean-Pierre, Angers . . . 060858
Leven Antiques, Ulverstone . . . 056764
Levende Grafisk Museum, Skjeberg 031194
Levene, M.P., London . . . 085481
Levent, Alain, Athies-sous-Laon . . . 061016
Leventis Municipal Museum of Nicosia, Lefkosia . . . 008221
Lévêque, André, Montlouis-sur-Loire . . . 124452
Leveque, Claude, Fresnes . . . 062943
Lever, Vancouver . . . 059375
Levere Memorial Temple, Evanston 043761
Leverenz & Ritter, Hamburg . . . 071279
Leverett Historical Museum, Leverett . . . 045239
Levers, Wollongong . . . 095405, 123329
Levesque, Paris . . . 066187
Levesque, Jeanne, Paris . . . 066188
Lévi, Liana, Paris . . . 133645
Levi, Sara, Tel Aviv . . . 105921
Levi Coffin House, Fountain City . . . 044019
Levin, Betty, New York . . . 118123
Levin, Inger, Göteborg . . . 081814
Levin Fine Arts Gallery, Levin Manawatu . . . 108488
Levina-Swannet, Toulon (Var) . . . 068458
Levine, Diana, Boston . . . 115199
Levine & Assoc., Elizabeth, New York . . . 118124
Levine, Leona, Norwich . . 086118, 131331
Levine Museum of the New South, Charlotte . . . 042758
Levionnais, Marie-Jeanne, Blainville-sur-Orne . . . 061505
Levis, Calgary . . . 120800
Levison, Don, San Francisco . . . 092828
Levitske Brothers, Pittsburgh . . . 142775
Levoir, Rose, Paris . . . 124726
Levy, Rio de Janeiro . . . 058606
Lévy, Albert-Bernard, Paris . . . 066189
Levy, Claudia, Santiago de Chile . . . 059539
Lévy, Etienne, Paris . . . 066190, 124727
Lévy, Gérard, Paris . . . 066191
Lévy, Jacques, Paris . . . 100617
Lévy, Johann, Paris . . . 100618
Lévy, Luc, Montpellier . . . 124459
Levy, Michael, Long Beach . . . 116674
Levy, Pierre, Paris . . . 100619
Levy, Richard, Albuquerque . . . 114800
Levy, Stan, New Orleans . . . 090578
Levy, Thomas, Hamburg . . . 103179
Levy, Wendy J., Manchester . . . 114047
Lévy-Alban, Sylvain, Paris . . . 066192
Levy & Dean, New York . . 091030, 118125
Levy Gallery, Moore College of Art and Design, Philadelphia . . . 046956
Lew Chin Chuan & Co., Kuala Lumpur . . . 121759

Lewandowski, Jean-Pierre, Blanzy . 061509
Lewcock, John, Ely 141597
Lewendon, Nedlands 056321
Lewerentz, Sigrid, Kamen 103476
Lewes Antiques Centre, Lewes . . .084982, 130890
Lewes Book Centre, Lewes 141728
Lewes Castle and Barbican House Museum, Lewes 039993
Lewes Clock Shop, Lewes 084983, 130891
Lewes Historical Society Museum, Lewes 045240
Lewin, Bruce R., New York 118126
Lewin, David & Harriett, London . . . 085482
Lewin, Henri, Paris 066193
Lewin, Henri, Saint-Ouen 067832
Lewis, Miami 117105
Lewis, Omaha 118711
Lewis & Fils, Paris 124728
Lewis, Toronto 059229
Lewis, Doris, Los Angeles 089820
Lewis, Guy, Den Haag 107935
Lewis, H., Baltimore 115063
Lewis, Ivor & Patricia, Peterborough 086232
Lewis, Julianne, Kew 056047
Lewis, M. & D., London 085483
Lewis, M. & D., London 085484
Lewis, M. & D., London 085485
Lewis, Michael, Bruton 083774
Lewis, Michael, Bruton 112749
Lewis, Michael, Bruton 141460
Lewis, Michael & Amanda, Wellington 087067, 131658
Lewis, Richard, New Orleans 117465
Lewis, Sandra, Kasendorf 071741
Lewis and Clark Center, Saint Charles 047620
Lewis Collection, Cambridge 038966
Lewis County Historical Museum, Chehalis 042786
Lewis County Historical Society Museum, Lowville 045511
Lewis County Historical Society Museum, Lyons Falls 045537
Lewis Elton Gallery, Guildford 039648
Lewis, James and Nellie Stratton Gallery, Stephens College, Columbia 043070
Lewis & Lloyd, London 085486
Lewis Textile Museum, Blackburn, Lancashire 038753
Lewisham Local Studies Centre, London 040198
Lewistown Art Center, Lewistown . . 045253
Lewitt, New York 118127
Lewitzka, Victor Harbor 095363
Lewitzki, Celle 070126
Lewitzki, Robert, Celle 070127
Lewry, David C.E., Gosport 130738
Lex, Hans, Bad Endorf 101642
Lex, Horst & Hinrika, Weyarn 105237
Lexa a Syn, Litoměřice 060047
Lexington Art, New York 118128
Lexington Art League, Lexington . . 054845
Lexington Children's Museum, Lexington 045261
Lexington County Museum, Lexington 045276
Lexington Historical Society Exhibition, Lexington 045269
Lexxicon.com, Newman 136522
Ley, Joe & Sheila, Louisville 090007, 122951
Leye, Bernard de, Bruxelles 058019
Leyendecker, Santa Cruz de Tenerife 110743
Leyendecker, Horst, Karlsruhe 126003
Leyer, R., Kaarst 071676
Leyh, Michael, Rothenburg ob der Tauber 104775
Leyrolles, D., Liège 123656
Leyrolles, Jean-Marie, Rodez 067194
Leyshon, M., Columbus 142355
Lézard, Paris 066194
Lézards de la Table, Saint-Ouen . . . 067833
Lézarts, Cap-d'Ail 099081
LFL Gallery, New York 118129
L.G. Antique Restoration, Los Angeles 132263
LG Objetos de Arte, São Paulo 058720
LGC Arte Hoje, Rio de Janeiro 096624
Lgovskij Gosudarstvennyj Kraevedčeskij Muzej, Lgov 033326
Lgovskij Literaturno-memorialnyj Muzej A.P. Gajdara, Lgov 033327
Lgovskij Literaturno-memorialnyj Muzej N.N. Aseeva, Lgov 033328
Lhalia, Rio de Janeiro 096625
L'Harmattan, Paris 138434
L'Héritier, Pont-Aven 101033
Lhermitte, Paris 138435
Lhomme, Liège 120772
Lhomme, Liège 137519
L'Homme-de-Plume, Saint-Ouen . . 067834
Lhoste, Eric, Pau 066710
Lhotte, Nicole, Nancy 064872
L'Huillier, Thierry, Houilles 063179
Li Bros., Shanghai 059754
Li Bros., Shanghai 059755
Li, An, Singapore 109827
Li, Bab, Singapore 109828
Li, Bai, Singapore 080518
Li, Hing, Los Angeles 089821
Li, H.K., Vancouver 097496
Li, Huo, Wuxi 098040
Li, L., Albuquerque 087404
Li Vigni, Pietro, Palermo 076155
Li Xian Jun Former Residence, Nanjing 007200
Li Yun Ge, Shanghai 097931
Li Zong Ren Display Center, Guilin . 007095
Liagre, Hugues, L'Isle-Jourdain . . . 063912
Liagre, Hugues, L'Isle-Jourdain . . . 063913
Liaigre, Jacqueline, Gençay 062979
Lian Lian, Wuxi 098041
Liancourt, Paris 124729
Liane and Danny Taran Gallery, Saidye Bronfman Centre for the Arts, Montréal 005929
Liangzhu Cultural Museum, Hangzhou 007103
Liao, Philadelphia 091657
Liao Jincheng Yuan, Beijing 006990
Liaoning Art Gallery, Shenyang 007255
Liaoning Calligraphy and Painting Gallery, Dalian 097712
Liaoning Fine Arts Publishing House, Shenyang 133382
Liaoning Museum, Shenyang 007256
Liaoning Painting Gallery, Shenyang 097966
Liaoning Provincial Museum, Chinchow 007048
Liaoyang City Museum, Liaoyang . . 007171
Li.Arte Giotto, Palermo 106433
Lib Lab, Lisboa 079952
Libbrecht, A., Gent 058192
Libby, Cincinnati 088256
Libby, John A., Toronto 097317
Libby Museum, Wolfeboro 049276
Libelle, Basel 141207
Libelle, Basel 141208
Liber Antiquus, Washington 143047
Libera Accademia di Belle Arti, Fondazione Trossi-Uberti, Livorno 050385
Liberace Museum, Las Vegas 045189
Liberal Art Program, Laurinburg . . . 051590
Liberal Arts Department, Gloucester County College, Sewell 052173
Liberal Arts Division, Elgin Community College, Elgin 051292
Liberal Arts Division, Northeast Community College, Norfolk 051848
Liberal Arts Division, Saint Louis Community College at Florissant Valley, Ferguson 051334
Liberal Arts Gallery, Detroit 116089
Libería Anticuaria Astarloa, Bilbao . 141010
Liberman, Anne-Marie, Mazères (Ariège) 064449
Liberman, Rachel, Paris 066195
Libermann, Bruxelles 058020
Libert, Paris 121168
La Liberté, Clermont-Ferrand 062348
Liberty, Kortrijk 058265
Liberty, London 085487
Liberty Books, Christchurch 140614
Liberty Books, Christchurch 140615
Liberty Books, Christchurch 140616
Liberty Coins, Minneapolis 090372
Liberty County Museum, Chester . . 042800
Liberty Hall, Frankfort 044034
Liberty Hall Historic Center, Lamoni 045135
Liberty Hall Museum, Union 048693
Liberty Investments, Gent 096292
Liberty Kunsthandel, Rotterdam . . .078728, 128820
Liberty Memorial Museum of World War One, Kansas City 044923
Liberty Village Arts Center and Gallery, Chester 042801
Liberty's, Deauville 062609
Libertyville-Mundelein Historical Society Museum, Libertyville 045288
Libra Antiques, Bournemouth 083600
Libra Antiques, London 085488
Libra Auctioneers, Bangalore 074775, 121649
Il Libraio, Vicenza 140153
Libraire Antiquaire, Montréal 058973
Les Libraires entre les Lignes, Paris 138436
Librairie A la Recherche du Passé, Sarzeau 138613
Librairie à Micita, Bordeaux 138045
Librairie Ancienne, Metz . 064534, 138206
Librairie Ancienne, Paris 138437
Librairie Andante, Paris 138438
Librairie Arcade, Osaka 140170
Librairie Ardennaise, Redu 137536
Librairie Art des Jardins, Sauliac-sur-Célé 138615
Librairie Arte, Bruxelles 137444
Librairie aux Belles Images, Rabat . 140264
Librairie aux Livres d'Alésia, Paris . 138439
Librairie Bonaparte, Paris 138440
Librairie Book Shop, New Orleans . 142619
Librairie Brocante du Palais, Nantes 138241
Librairie Chevalier Paul, Toulon (Var) 138628
Librairie Compact, Montréal 137659
Librairie d'Argences, Paris 138441
Librairie de la Seine, Paris 138442
Librairie de la Tour, Vichy 138658
Librairie de l'Abbaye, Paris 138443
Librairie de l'Amateur, Strasbourg . 138621
Librairie de l'Ameublement et de la Décoration, Paris 138444
Librairie de l'Avenue, Saint-Ouen . . 138604
Librairie de l'Escurial, Nice 138254
Librairie de Montbel, Paris 138445
Librairie de Sèvres, Paris . 066196, 138446
Librairie Denis, Tours 138641
Librairie des Alpes, Grenoble 138098
Librairie des Alpes, Paris 138447
Librairie des Arts et Métiers, Lormaye 138125
Librairie des Canuts, Lyon 138157
Librairie des Carrés, Versailles 138654
Librairie des Eléphants, Bruxelles . .120736, 137445
Librairie des Galeries, Bruxelles . . . 137446
Librairie des Galeries Nationales du Grand Palais, Paris 138448
Librairie des Hautebises, Grenoble . 138099
Librairie des Nouveautés, Lyon 138158
Librairie des Pyrénées, Bayonne . . 138025
Librairie des Terreaux, Lyon 138159
Librairie Diamond, Montréal 137660
Librairie Diogène, Lyon 138160
Librairie du Bât d'Argent, Lyon 138161
Librairie du Camée, Paris 138449
Librairie du Change, Lyon 138162
Librairie du Château de Villeneuve, Vence 138647
Librairie du Cygne, Paris 138450
Librairie du Lycée, Lyon 138163
Librairie du Métro, Lyon 138164
Librairie du Miroir, Mons 137531
Librairie du Musée d'Art Moderne de la Ville de Paris, Paris 138451
Librairie du Musée des Beaux-Arts, Nantes 138242
Librairie du Musée des Beaux-Arts, Rouen 138588
Librairie du Musée d'Orsay, Paris . . 138452
Librairie du Musée du Louvre, Paris 138453
Librairie du Musée du Moyen-Age, Paris 138454
Librairie du Musée du Petit Palais, Paris 138455
Librairie du Musée Matisse, Nice . . 138255
Librairie du Nouveau Monde, Québec 137682
Librairie du Planetarium, Bruxelles . 137447
Librairie du Spectacle Garnier Arnoul, Paris 138456
Librairie Edition Guénégaud, Paris .133646, 138457
Librairie Epigrammes, Paris 138458
Librairie Epsilon, Paris 138459
Librairie et Documentation de l'Auto Moto-Avion-Train, Paris 138460
Librairie Expérience, Lyon 138165
Librairie Farfouille, Paris 138461
Librairie Footnotes, Montréal 137661
Librairie Godot de Mauroy, Paris . . . 138462
Librairie Gourmande, Paris 138463
Librairie Henner, Paris 138464
Librairie Henri-Julien, Montréal . . . 137662
Librairie Impériale, Arras 138015
Librairie Jakin, Bayonne . . 098933, 138026
Librairie Jules Verne, Paris 138465
Librairie La Bourse, Lyon 138166
Librairie La Gryffe, Lyon 138167
Librairie La Porte Étroite, Paris 138466
Librairie la Procure-Léo, Lyon 138168
Librairie l'Arc Franco-Suédoise, Stockholm 141164
Librairie L'Arnaqueur, Paris 138467
Librairie le Moniteur, Lyon 138169
Librairie Le Petit Prince, Paris 138468
Librairie Le Temps Retrouvé, Strasbourg 138622
Librairie Les Arcades, Paris 138469
Librairie Les Beaux Livres, Monaco 140263
Librairie Lyonnaise, Lyon 138170
Librairie Maitre Albert, Paris 138470
Librairie Mazarine, Paris 138471
Librairie Mécanique, Lyon 138171
Librairie Méridiés, Lyon 138172
Librairie Monte Cristo, Paris 138472
Librairie Nicaise, Paris 138473
Librairie Notre-Dame, Grenoble . . . 138100
Librairie Nouvel Age, Montréal 137663
Librairie Occitania, Toulouse 138638
Librairie Oriens, Paris 138474
Librairie Orientale Samuelian, Paris 138475
Librairie Pages Volantes, Paris 138476
Librairie Paris-Musées, Paris 138477
Librairie Picasso, Paris 138478
Librairie Pont-Neuf, Paris 138479
Librairie Puce, Paris 138480
Librairie Réunion des Musées Nationaux, Lyon 138173
Librairie Romain, Paris 138481
Librairie Saint-Pierre, Bordeaux . . . 138046
Librairie sur le Parc, Montréal 137664
Librairie Ulysse, pays et voyages, Paris 138482
Librairie Uniformologique International, Paris 138483
Librairie Vers et Prose, Paris 138484
Librantica, Libramont 093610
Library and Collection of the Worshipful Company of Clockmakers, London 040199
Library Cafe, Seattle 142998
Library Drawings Collection, London 040200
Library of the Greek Orthodox Patriarchate of Alexandria and All Africa, Alexandria 009277

Libre Art, Santiago de Chile 097629
Libre Boek, Warffum 140569
Le Libre Regard, Agde 098767
Libreria Albertina, Torino 140133
Libreria Anticuaria, Valencia 141077
Librería Anticuaria de México, Puebla 140260
Librería Anticuaria de México, Toluca 140261
Librería Anticuaria Studio, Barcelona 140991
Librería Anticuaria Studio, Barcelona 140992
Libreria Antiquaria, Bologna 139988
Libreria Antiquaria Docet, Bologna . 139989
Libreria Antiquaria Giulio Cesare, Roma 076527, 140107
Libreria Antiquaria Palatina, Firenze 140022
Libreria Antiquaria Piemontese, Torino 140134
Libreria Antiquaria Sant'Agostino, Roma 140108
Libreria Antiquaria Umberto Saba, Trieste 140146
Libreria Balague, Barcelona 140993
Librería Bonaire, Valencia 141078
Librería Castalia, México 140256
Libreria Dante Alighieri, Torino 140135
Librería de Avila, Buenos Aires 136730
Librería de la Escalinata, Madrid . . 141044
Librería del Ayer, Buenos Aires 136731
Libreria del Porcellino, Firenze 140023
Libreria delle Occasioni, Roma 140109
Libreria Ed Oggettistica Avalon, Genova 075482
Librería el Foro, Buenos Aires 136732
Librería el Jagüel, Buenos Aires . . . 136733
Librería el Túnel, Buenos Aires 136734
Librería Errata, Bogotá . . . 059844, 137759
Librería Fabre, Barcelona 140994
Libreria Facultades, Valencia 141079
Librería El Filobiblión, Madrid 141045
Librería Goya, Barcelona 140995
Librería Gulliver, Madrid 141046
Librería Helena de Buenos Aires, Buenos Aires 136735
Libreria Il Putto, Torino 140136
Libreria Incunable, A Coruña 141014
Libreria La Fenice, Brescia 140005
Libreria Laia, Valencia 141080
Libreria L'Archivolto, Milano 140054
Librería Lux, Alicante 140976
Libreria Maxtor, Valladolid 141086
Librería Mosca Hns, Montevideo . . 142184
Librería Nacional, La Plata 136760
Libreria Naturalistica, Bologna 139990
Libreria Ogarde, Madrid 141047
Libreria Roges, Mataró 141063
Libreria Sansoviniana, Biblioteca Nazionale Marciana, Venezia 026237
Libreria Selvaggio, Barcelona 140996
Librería Solar del Bruto, Puente Tocinos-Murcia 141069
Libreria Tara, Roma 076528, 140110
Libreria Universal, Asunción 140712
Libreria Vitorio, Madrid 141048
Libreria Vobiscum, Alicante 140977
Libresso - Antiquariat in der Universität, Hamburg 139197
Libretto, Langnau im Emmental . . . 141262
De Librije, Edam 140412
Libris, Tampere 137992
Libris Antikvariatet, Stockholm 141165
Libropiel, Madrid 141049
Libros el Glyptodon, Buenos Aires . 136736
Libros la Cueva, Buenos Aires 136737
Libros Lenzi, La Plata 136761
Libros Lord Byron, Buenos Aires . . . 136738
Libros Madrid, Madrid 141050
Libros Romo, Madrid 141051
Libya Antiqua. Annual of the Department of Antiquities of Libya, Roma 135911
Licandro, Gianfranco, Wien 095890
Licastro, Francesco, Roma 106573
Liceo Artistico, Cassino 050358
Liceo Artistico, Frosinone 050375
Liceo Artistico, Latina 050381
Liceo Artistico Statale, Lecce 050384
Liceo Artistico Statale, Taranto 050437
Lices Antiquités, Rennes (Ille-et-Vilaine) 067116
Licheng District Museum, Jinan . . . 007153
Lichfield County Antiques Show, Kent 093999
Lichfield Heritage Centre, Lichfield . 040000
Lichtdruck-Kunst Leipzig e.V., Leipzig 018576, 053483
Lichtdruck-Werkstatt-Museum, Dresden 016800
De Lichte Gaard, Utrecht 140551
Lichtenberg, München 134259
Lichtenburg Museums and Art Gallery, Kultuurhistories, Diamant Delwers en Landboumuseum, Lichtenburg . . 034673
Lichtentaler Pfarrmuseum, Wien . . 002941
Lichter, Dr. Walter, Metterich 072533
Lichterfelder Antiquariat, Berlin . . . 138816
Lichtfuß, J., Köln 139348
Lichtlstall, Kitzbühel 057099
Lichtungen, Graz 135568
Lichtzone, Groningen 108039
Licking County Art Association, Newark 054846
Licking County Art Association Gallery, Newark 046426
Licking County Historical Museum, Newark 046427
Licorne, Antony 060933
La Licorne, Beirut 077401
Licorne, Bordeaux 061629
La Licorne, Clermont-Ferrand 062349
La Licorne, Landas 063509
La Licorne, Neaufles-Saint-Martin . 064969
La Licorne, Paris 066197
Licorne, West Hollywood 093481
La Licorne Bleue, Flavigny-sur-Ozerain 099263
Licorne Saint-Antoine, Castanet-Tolosan 062008
Licorne Saint-Antoine, Egletons . . . 062764
Lidia, Cluj-Napoca 080178
Lidköpings Konstförening, Lidköping 054145
Lidköpings Konsthall, Lidköping . . . 036418
Lidlbauer, Walter, Traun 057331
Lidman, Malmö 081872
Lidon, Patrick, Orléans 065304
Lids, Saint Louis 092265
Lidtke, Kurt, Seattle 119954
Lie, K., Nienhagen bei Celle 073058
Liebaert, Thierry, Roncq 067213
Liebe, Luda, Monheim am Rhein . . 104113
Liebel, Detlef, Rheinfelden 130145
Liebenberger Geschichtsmuseum, Liebenberg 018637
Liebenberger Schloß Museum, Liebenberg 018638
Liebens, Piet, Mechelen 123663
Liebenswertes aus alter Zeit, Bernkastel-Kues 069804
Lieber & Sohn, Dr., Dresden 070325, 125502
Lieber, Gebr., Rippien 073545
Lieber, Ian, London 085489
Liebermann House, Nahariya 023034
Liebermann-Villa, Berlin 016113
Lieberuks, U., Naumburg, Saale . . . 072946
Liebetrau, Katharina, Bonn 125356
Liebhardt, Michael, Velburg 126942
Liebhart, Henrik, Dreieich 070306
Liebig-Museum, Gießen 017411
Liebisch, Marc, Dorsten 070280
Liebler, K., Daun 070196
Liebrecht, Juliane, Köln 126099
Liebscher, Gerd, Zepernick 074564
Liebsohn, Daniel, México 077576
Liechtenstein Museum, Die Fürstlichen Sammlungen, Wien 002942
Liechtenstein Schloss Wilfersdorf, Wilfersdorf 003047
Liechtensteinische Kunstgesellschaft, Vaduz 053839
Liechtensteinische Kunstschule, Eschen 050522
Liechtensteinische Landesbibliothek, Vaduz 027842
Liechtensteinische Staatliche Kunstsammlung, Vaduz 027841
Liechtensteinisches Landesmuseum, Vaduz 027843
Lied Discovery Children's Museum, Las Vegas 045190
Liedenpohjan Museo, Virrat 010245
Lieder, Roland, Lutherstadt Wittenberg 072367
Liedermann, Krems 057127
Liedermann, Erich, Rohrendorf bei Krems 057228
Liedigk, Thomas, Hamburg 103180
Liedmeier-Stein, Münster 072918
Liedon Vanhalinna, Vanhalinna 010220
Lief, West Hollywood 093482
Lieh, Hsin Hang, Singapore 080519
Liehrmann, Liège 096379
Liekam, Claudia, Hamburg 103181
Liemers Museum, Zevenaar 030383
Lien, Ha Noi 120469
Lien, Ha Noi 120470
Lien, Minneapolis 142584
Liepājas Muzeja, Liepāja 027705
Liepājas Muzeja Izstāžu Zāles, Liepāja 027706
Liepājas Vēstures un Mākslas Muzejs, Liepāja 027707
Lier Bygdetun, Tranby 031272
Lierheimer, H., Niedereschach 073053
Lierne museer, Nordli 031053
Liers, Dr. D., Berlin 125249
Lierz, Manfred, Hennef 125914
Liesch, Jens, Langenleuba-Niederhain 126170
Liesegang, Karl, Schleswig 139713
Liesenberg, W., Freiburg im Breisgau 070850
Lieser, Wolf, Berlin 101977
Lietuvos Aido, Vilnius 107365
Lietuvos Dailes Muziejus, Vilnius . . 027863
Lietuvos Nacionalinis Muziejus, Vilnius 027864
Lietzmann, Rüdiger, Berlin 069689
Le Lieu, Québec 097151
Lieu d'Art Contemporain, Colomiers 011437
Lieu Historique National de Côteau-du-Lac, Côteau-du-Lac 005300
Lieu Historique National de Sir Wilfrid Laurier, Ville des Laurentides 006753
Lieu Historique National des Forges du Saint-Maurice, Trois-Rivières . . . 006661
Lieu Historique National du Canada de la Bataille-de-la-Ristigouche, Pointe-à-la-Croix 006161
Lieu Historique National du Commerce de la Fourrure, Lachine 005731
Lieu Historique National du Manoir-Papineau, Montebello 005904
Lieutaud, James, Toulon (Var) 068459
Lieutenant General Ashton Armoury Museum, Victoria 006743
Lieve Hemel, Amsterdam 107759
Life, Colchester 112889
Life Art, Zürich 112140
Life Gallery, Manama 096017
Lifeboat House, Margate 040422
Lifeboat Museum, Barmouth 038594
Lifeline, Cairns 136839
Lifeline, Lutwyche 136982
Lifeline, Toowoomba 137111
Lifetime Gallery, West Hollywood . . 093483
Lifton, Judy, Cleveland 115724
Liga Nieuw Beelden, Leiden 108102
Ligeard, Catherine, Goult 063022
Ligems, Kuala Lumpur 107437
Liger, Jean-Philippe, Orléans 065305
Liger, Jean-Philippe, Yèvre-le-Chatel 069063
Liget, Budapest 105528
Liggett, Tulsa 120198
Liggieri, Roberto, Padova 076096
Lighezzolo, Robert, Le Lardin-Saint-Lazare 063644, 124303
Light & Art, Innsbruck 095589
Light Factory, Charlotte 042759
Light Factory, Charlotte 115296
Light Flight, Seattle 119955
The Light Gallery, Leamington Spa . 084914
Light House Gallery, Tokyo 107069
Light Infantry Museum, Winchester 041404
Light Opera Gallery, San Francisco . 119718
Light Power, Boston 087831, 131849
Light Square Gallery, Adelaide 000708
Light Street Gallery, Baltimore 115064
Lightart, Neukloster 072999
Lighthouse Antiques, Miami 090200
Lighthouse Gallery, Mamble 114037
Lighthouse Gallery, Tequesta 048528
Lighthouse Glass, New Orleans . . . 117466
Lighthouse Images, Saint Paul 119300
Lighthouse Keepers Cottage, Carnarvon 000901
Lighthouse Poole Centre for the Arts, Poole 040738
Lighthouse Rockart Gallery, Tewantin 095327
Lightner Museum, Saint Augustine . 047608
Lights, Camera, Action United Kingdom, Nottingham 141975
Lightship Museum and Naval Shipyard Museum, Portsmouth Museums, Portsmouth 047200
Lightstorm Photo Gallery, Berry . . . 094249
Lightview Gallery, Baltimore 087686
Lightworks, Minneapolis . 090373, 132384
Lightworks Magazine, Birmingham 136523
Ligija, Kazan 080210
Lignan Fine Arts Publishing House, Guangzhou 133348
Lignarium, Madrid 129638
Ligne Art Sud, Montolieu . 064726, 099748
Ligne Claire, Mons 137532
La Ligne Droite, Genève 082442
Ligne Treize, Carouge 111341
Ligneau, Thierry, Paris 066198
Lignier, Guy, Boulogne-sur-Mer . . . 099020
Lignier, Guy, Hardelot-Plage 099324
Lignum, Prato 127891
Ligozat, André, Gap 062962
Ligozat, André, Gap 062963
Ligüerre, Zaragoza 129816
Liguerre, Pablo, Zaragoza 081744, 129817
Liguori Editore, Napoli 134643
Liinelot, Helsinki 060546
Liisa's Antiikki, Helsinki 060547
Liisa's Antiikki, Helsinki 060548
Lijiang Publishing House, Guilin . . . 133349
Lijn 3, Den Haag 107936
Lik, Peter, Cairns 094350
Lik, Peter, San Francisco 119719
Lik, Peter, Sydney 095298
Like Before, Cagliari 075214
Likha Antiques and Crafts Inc., Manila 079565
Liki Rossii, Sankt-Peterburg 134886
Likin, Sandanski 096711
Likion Ton Ellinidon Collection, Rethymnon 021450
Likovni Klub Scena Crnjanski, Beograd 109707
Lil, Los Angeles 116823
Lil-Tob-Lou, Los Angeles 089822
Lila Chrif, Casablanca 077661
Lila Laden, Bonn 069931
L'Ile au Trésor, Annecy 060893
L'Ile au Trésor, Saint-Dizier 067430
Lile & Lav, Beograd 109708
Lilfords, New Milton 114114
Lili Marleen, New York 091031
Lilian, Andrée, Riehen 111839
Lilian's Fine Collectables, Toronto . 059230
Lilias Lane, Nelson 079177
Lilienhof, Lilienthal 018643

Liliesleaf Gallery, Rosebank 110074
Liliput, Köln 139349
Liljendal Hembygdsmuseum, Liljendal 009826
Liljevalchs Konsthall, Stockholm . . 036638
Lilla Antikurmakeriet, Malmö 081873
Lilla Bukowskis, Stockholm 122256
Lilla Galleriet, Göteborg 110923
Lilla Galleriet Helsingborg, Helsingborg 110943
De Lille Antikstuv, Kiel 071834
Lille Heddinge Rytterskole, Rødvig Stevns 009074
Lillebonne, Nancy 099797
Lillehammer Kunstmuseum, Lillehammer 030983
Lillesand By-og Sjøfartsmuseum, Lillesand 030987
Lillian and Albert Small Jewish Museum, Washington 048917
Lillian and Coleman Taube Museum of Art, Minot 045924
Lillian Stevenson Nursing Archives Museum, Saint John's 006366
Lillie Art Gallery, Milngavie 040470
Lilliput, Pittsburgh 091836, 132669
Lilliput Antique Doll and Toy Museum, Brading 038814
Lillklara-Grafik, Stockholm 111060
Lillooet District Museum, Lillooet . . 005773
Lillstreet Art Center, Chicago 115478
Lilly's Art, Boston 115200
Lil's Treasure, Mulgoa 056301
Lily White, Portland 091966
Lilydale Antique Centre, Lilydale . . 056100
Lily's Antiques, Maryborough, Queensland 056165
Lily's Antiques, Pittsburgh 091837
Lim, Ben, Calgary 058795, 096827
Lim, Dae, Seoul 107265
Lim, Raywin, Whitianga 079365
Lim, Woo, Seoul 107266
Lima Hembygdsgård, Lima 036420
L'Image-en-Provence, Marseille . . . 099672
Limassol District Museum, Lemesos 008229
Limassol Municipal Art Gallery, Lemesos 008230
Limb, R.R., Newark-on-Trent 086051
Limbažu Muzejs, Limbaži 027708
Limberlost State Historic Site, Geneva 044163
Limburg, Den Haag 078213
Limburgs Miniatuurmuseum, Sint Geertruid 030149
Limburgs Museum, Venlo 030267
Limburgs Openluchtmuseum Eynderhoof, Nederweert Eind 029937
Lime Tree Antiques, Burwash 130486
Lime Tree Gallery, Stanhope 114482
Limelight Gallery, Surry Hills 095255
Limerick City Gallery of Art, Limerick 022824
Limerick Museum, Limerick 022825
Limesmuseum, Tulln 002759
Limesmuseum Aalen, Zweigmuseum des Archäologischen Landesmuseums Baden-Württemberg, Aalen 015428
Limfjordsmuseet, Løgstør 009013
Limhamns Auktionsbyrå, Trelleborg 122280
Limhamns Museum, Malmö 036457
Liming Fine Arts Gallery, Qingdao . . 097888
Limingan Kotiseutumuseo, Liminka 009830
Limited, London 135229
Limited Additions, New York 091032
Limited Edition Contemporary Graphics, Pershore 114236
Limited Edition Graphics, London . . 113734
Limited Edition Mint, Philadelphia . 091658
Limited Editions, Ashburton 140584
Limited Editions, Mobberley 085997, 131280
LIMN Gallery, San Francisco 119720
Limner, New York 118130
Limol, H., Denzlingen 070217
Limol, Hippolyte von, Denzlingen . . 070218
Limongelli, Michelangelo, Torino . . 128322
L'Impérial, Nice 099845
Limpsfield Watercolours, Limpsfield 084994, 113393, 130894
Lin, Peter, Los Angeles 132264
Lin, Polly, Los Angeles 089823
Lin Art, Košice 080621
Lin San Zhi Art Display Center, Zhujiang 007358
Lina & Terry's Antiques, Bonn 069932
Linan Museum, Hangzhou 007104
Linard, Eric, La Garde-Adhemar . . . 099396
Linardi & Risso, Montevideo 142185
Linares, Palma de Mallorca 081487
Linares Muñoz, Antonio, Sevilla . . . 081591
Lina's Antiques, Fresno 088911
Linc, San Francisco 119721
Linckersdorff, von, Berlin 069690
Linckersdorff, Stefan, München . 072776
Linckh, Andrea, Stuttgart 126866
Lincoln, Buffalo 087891
Lincoln Antique Mall, Chicago 088119
Lincoln Arts Council, Lincoln 054847
Lincoln Avenue Antiques, Chicago . 088120
Lincoln Cathedral Treasury, Lincoln 040008
Lincoln Children's Museum, Lincoln 045305
Lincoln County Historical Museum, Davenport 043307
Lincoln County Historical Society Museum, Lincoln 045295
Lincoln County Historical Society Museum, North Platte 046534
Lincoln County Historical Society Museum of Pioneer History, Chandler 042708
Lincoln County Museum, Hugo 044665
Lincoln County Pioneer Museum, Hendricks 044514
Lincoln Home, Springfield 048285
Lincoln Homestead, Springfield . . . 048291
Lincoln Log Cabin, Lerna 045237
Lincoln Memorial Shrine, Redlands 047360
The Lincoln Museum, Fort Wayne . . 044000
Lincoln Parish Museum, Ruston . . . 047576
Lincoln Park Book Shop, Chicago . . 142290
Lincoln Park Historical Museum, Lincoln Park 045319
Lincoln School of Art and Design, University of Lincoln, Lincoln 050822
The Lincoln-Tallman Restorations, Janesville 044838
Lincoln Tomb, Springfield 048286
Lincoln Train Museum, Gettysburg . 044185
Lincolns House, Los Angeles 089824
Lincoln's New Salem Historic Site, Petersburg 046901
Lincolnshire Fine Arts, Grimsby . . . 113165
Lincolnshire Road Transport Museum, Lincoln 040009
Lind, David, Louisville 116951
Lind, Gregory, San Francisco 119722
Linda, Singapore 109829
Linda Loves Lace, San Antonio 092535
Lindale Art Gallery, Paraparaumu . . 108540
Lindart, Birmingham 115115
Lindas, Mallow 074993
Linda's Antiques, Kinsale . 074985, 139975
Lindås Skulemuseum, Isdalstø 030922
Linda's Treasures, Dallas 088551
Lindberg, B. & M., Helsinki 060549
Lindberg & Persson, Björkö 141091
Lindberg & Persson, Täby 141182
Linde, de, Aalst 057662
Linde, Lübeck 103967
Linde Auktionstjänst, Lindesberg . . 122190
Linde-Schöpfli, Winterthur 082915
Lindemann, Dülmen 070344
Lindemann, Dorothea, Algermissen 125056
Lindemann, Felix, Altenrhein 111117
Lindemann, Max, Hamburg 103182
Lindemann, Oliver, Hamburg 103183
Lindemann, Winfried, Schermbeck . 073685
Lindemanns, H., Stuttgart 139768
Linden, Bilambil 094253
Linden, Hannover 139238
Linden, Tampa 120056
Linden, Peter, Blackrock 074863
Linden Art Center, Birmingham 115116
Linden House Antiques, Leominster 084974, 130886
Linden House Antiques, Stansted Mountfitchet 086694
Linden-Museum Stuttgart, Staatliches Museum für Völkerkunde, Stuttgart 020358
Linden - Saint Kilda Centre for Contemporary Arts, Saint Kilda, Victoria 001449
Lindenau-Museum, Altenburg, Thüringen 015501
Lindenauer, Isak, San Francisco . . . 092829
Lindenberg, Rotterdam 140521
Lindencrone, Hellerup 124020
Lindenfelser Museum, Lindenfels, Odenwald 018659
Lindengalerie, Essen 102699
Linder, Fritz, Horn 057068
Linder, Gisèle, Basel 111208
Linder, Lars, Hedesunda 122155
Linder, Peter, Grainau 102990
Linder, Reinhard, Gummersbach . . 071147
Lindesbergsmuseum, Lindesberg . . 036422
Lindesnes Bygdemuseum, Sør-Audnedal 031208
Lindfield Parvise Museum, Haywards Heath 039709
Lindhberg, Kjell, Limhamn 081847
Lindholm, Ashausen 069210
Lindholm Høje Museet, Nørresundby 009030
Lindig, Nürnberg 104484
Lindigtmühle am Lindenvorwerk, Kohren-Sahlis 018369
Lindinger + Schmid, Regensburg . . 134360
Lindisfarne Priory, Holy Island 039764
The Lindisfarne Room, Gateshead . 113088
Lindisfarne Wine and Spirit Museum, Berwick-upon-Tweed 038685
Lindkvist & Sjöberg, Stockholm . . . 081979
Lindner, Stuttgart 073990
Lindner, Wien 095891
Lindner, Andreas, Wien 057488
Lindner, H., Callenberg 070118
Lindner, H., Eichstätt 139032
Lindner, Hans, Mainburg 139441
Lindner, Johannes, Radebeul 126672
Lindner, Konrad, Bernried, Niederbayern 125324
Lindner, Kornelia, Radebeul 126673
Lindner, Minni, Cunnersdorf bei Kamenz 102328
Lindner, Minni, Schönteichen 104838
Lindner, Ramon, Essen 070639
Lindner, Walter, Berlin 133793
Lindorf, Hans-Karl, Kiel 071835
Lindquist, Solveig, Helsinki 124046
Lindsay, Albuquerque 087405
Lindsay, Den Haag 140395
Lindsay, London 113735
Lindsay, Duff, Columbus 115788
Lindsay, Lillian, Oberon 056398
Lindsay, Robert, Melbourne 094819
Lindsay, Burns & Co., Perth 122653
Lindsay Gallery, Lindsay 005775
Lindsay Wildlife Museum, Walnut Creek 048840
Lindsay's Antiques, Invercargill . . . 079128
Lindsell Art Gallery, Lindsell 113400
Lindsey, Albuquerque 087406
Lindsey, Nashville 090464
Lindsey Antiques, North Berwick . . 086089
Lindsey Court Antiques, Horncastle 084737
Lindskoug, Mats, Lund 129848
Lindstrand-Bengtsson, Ginger, Mjölby 122213
Lindströms, Kenth, Stockholm 081980
Lindtner, Johann, Salzburg 123449
The Line Gallery, Linlithgow 113401
La Linea d'Ombra, Roma 140111
Lineart, Offenbach am Main 134328
Lineaverde, Vomero 135912
Linecker, Leopold, Schalchen 137258
Lines, D. & J., Wychbold . 087273, 131721
Linga Longa, Tirau 108586
Lingard, London 085490
Lingard, Ann, Rye 086426
Lingbeek & Van Daalen, Amsterdam 128547
Lingelsheim, Eckhard von, Lübeck . 139428
Lingenauber, Eckard, Düsseldorf . . 070407
Lingenauber, Eckard, Paris 100620
Lingiardi, Alba, Milano 127614
Lingier-Sermeus, Gent . . . 058193, 096293
Lingnan Hua Pai Memorial Hall, Guangzhou 007088
Lingtong Exhibition, Changzhou . . . 007035
Lingyuan City Museum, Lingyuan . . 007172
Linhart, Henrich, Košice 080622
Lini, Cristiano, Milano 127615
Linija-Art, Moskva 109563
Link, E., Fridingen 070885
Link, M., Brühl, Rheinland 070073, 102276
Linka, Israël, Amsterdam 107760
Linke, Dietmar, Potsdam 126651
Linke, Friedr.-A., Goslar 125746
Linke, Günter, Berlin 138817
Linke, Stefan, Düsseldorf . 070408, 125536
Linkowski, Giorgio A., Zürich 112141
Links for International Promotion of the Arts, Chicago 115479
Linley Sambourne House, London . 040201
Linlithgow Palace, Linlithgow 040017
Linlithgow Story, Linlithgow 040018
Linn County Historical Museum and Moyer House, Brownsville 042481
Linn County Historical Society Museum, Cedar Rapids 042677
Linn County Museum, Pleasanton . . 047089
Linn-Sui, Torino 106682
Linnan Museo ja Ortodoksinen Kirkkomuseo, Olavinlinna 009922
Linnanmäen Museo, Helsinki 009551
Linnartz, H., Köln 071975
Linné, Uppsala 111091
Linneborn, Berlin 101978
Linnémuseet, Uppsala 036739
Linnenschmidt'sche Vormals Landesherrliche Mühle zu Venne, Ostercappeln 019507
Linner, Adolf, Wien 137338
Linnés Hammarby, Uppsala 036740
Linnés Råshult, Älmhult 036165
Linnhoff, Birgit, Honigsee 125961
Linnhoff, Simmert & Freitag, Kiel . . 126041
Linnig, Elisabeth, Darmstadt 133856
Linnoitus- ja Kotiseutumuseo, Luumäki 009846
Linnoitusmuseo, Hanko 009504
Liño - Revista de Arte, Oviedo 136095
Linossier, Gilles, Paris 066199
Lins, Gebhard, Feldkirch 137164
Lins, Ursula, Schleswig 126768
Linschoten, J., Utrecht 078810
Linscott, King River 094699
Linsolas-Chaux, Bernard & Véronique, Bellevesvre 061337
Linsolite, Liège 058312, 137520
Linssen, Venlo 078840
Linssen, H.J.C., Venlo 078841
Linssen, P.H.A., Venlo 078842
Linssen, P.H.A., Venlo 078843
Lint, Milano 134618
Lintner, Fritz, Spit Junction 056622
Lintner, Joachim M., Salzburg 057266
Linton & Assoc., Richard, Frankston 094565
Linton and District Museum, Linton 001185
Linton Court Gallery, Settle 114403
Linton & Shaw, Subiaco 095232
Lintong County Museum, Xian 007315
Lintow, Joachim, Schönhagen 073716
Linwood Community Arts Centre, Christchurch 108402
Linz, Peer, Amsterdam . . . 107761, 140315
Linzen, H.J., Heinsberg 071481

LinzGenesis, Linz 002251
Il Liocorno, Torino 128323
Lion, Roland, Gignac 062998
Lion and Eagle, San Antonio 092536
Lion Antiques, Pershore 086220
Lion Bazaar, Wellington 079330
Lion Books, Bewdley 141411
Le Lion d'Argent, Lyon 064151
Lion d'Or, Rotterdam 078729
Lion Fine Arts, Hay-on-Wye 084633
Lion Gallery, Leominster 113382
Lion Gallery, Penrith 114225
The Lion Gallery and Bookshop, Knutsford 084892, 113343, 130861, 141702
Le Lion Qui Nous Regarde, Fontvieille 099269
Lion Saint Book's, Hereford 141663
Lion Salt Works, Northwich 040599
Lionel, François, Nœux-les-Mines . 065206
Lionel Wendt Art Gallery, Colombo . 036132
Liongoren Art Gallery, Quezon City . 108857
Lionheart Gallery, Louisville 116952
The Lions Mark, Vancouver 059376
Lions-Trend, Bern 082222
Liova, Paris 066200
Lipah, Herbert, München 072777
Lipan, Ljubljana 109977
Lipanjepuntin, Trieste 106718
Lipeckij Oblastnoj Kraevedčeskij Muzej, Lipeck 033329
Lipicai Múzeum, Szilvásvárad 021894
Lipitch, Michael, Barnet 083394
Lipitch, Peter, London 085491
Lipizzaner Museum, Wien 002943
Lipp, Karl M., München 134260
Lippische Gesellschaft für Kunst e.V., Detmold 053484
Lippische Landesbibliothek, Detmold 016689
Lippischer Künstlerbund, Detmold . 053485
Lippisches Landesmuseum, Detmold 016690
Lippl, Alois, Viechtach 074204
Lips, Claudia, Köln 103672
LIPS Slotenmuseum, Dordrecht . . . 029503
Lipschitz, Cape Town 110026
Lipton, Honolulu 122902
Lipton, William, New York 091033
Liptovské Múzeum, Ružomberok . . 034420
Liquid Paper Correction Fluid Museum, Santa Fe 047968
Liquid Paper Museum, Nambe 046121
Lire Entre les Vignes, Paris 100621
Lire et Chiner, Colmar 138079
Lire et Relire, Montréal 137665
Liron Pean Reynald, Saint-Julien-sur-Calonne 067564
Lis, Claire, Plaisance-du-Touch . . . 066841
Lis, Gilles, Perthes 066775
LIS Art Restoration, New York 132491
Lis Tes Ratures, Nantes 138243
Lisa J, Kingswinford 113330
Lisabeth, P., Brugge 057780
Lisboa 20, Lisboa 109331
Lisbon Historical Society Museum, Lisbon 045330
Lischa Line, Nice 065104
Lischka-Elfenspeich, Berlin 069691
Liselund Gamle Slot, Borre 008824
Lisht, Rio de Janeiro 058607
Lishui County Museum, Nanjing . . . 007201
Lishui County Museum, Zaicheng . . 007344
Liška, Praha 060140
Lisker, Gal, Genova 075483
Lisle Station Park, Lisle 045332
Lismed, Lisboa 121937
Lismore Regional Art Gallery, Lismore 001186
Lison, F., Bretten 070058
Liss, Toronto 097318
Liss, L., Montreuil-sous-Bois 064769
Liss Ohayon, Josephine, Toronto . . 059231
Lissauer, H.M., Elwood 055798
Lisse, Heinsberg 103346
Lisson Gallery, London 113736
The List, Edinburgh 136244
List, Monika, Stuttgart 126867
List, Thomas, Berlin 125250
List & Francke, Meersburg 139469
List-Petersen, Husum, Nordsee . . . 071599
Lista Museum, Vanse 031316
Listaháskóli Íslands, Reykjavík 050288
Listasafn Así, Àsmundarsalur, Reykjavík 021963
Listasafn Einars Jónssonar, Reykjavík 021964
Listasafn Kópavogs - Gerðasafn, Kópavogur 021953
Listasafn Sigurjóns Ólafssonar, Reykjavík 021965
Listasafn Íslands, Reykjavík 021966
Liste-The Young Art Fair, Basel 093892
Lister, West Perth 056816
Lister Calder Gallery, Subiaco 095233
Listidjan, Reykjavík 074761
Liszt Ferenc Emlékmúzeum és Kutatóközpont, Budapest 021665
Liszthaus - Goethe-Nationalmuseum, Stiftung Weimarer Klassik und Kunstsammlungen, Weimar, Thüringen 020746
Lisztmuseum, Raiding 002492
Lit, Oklahoma City 118668
Lit Sing Kwang Chinese Temple, Innisfail 001129
Lit Verlag, Münster 134298
Litaraturny muzej Janki Kupaly, Minsk 003134
Litcham Village Museum, Litcham . 040022
Litchfield, Saratoga 095183
Litchfield Historical Society Museum, Litchfield 045333
Literair Museum, Hasselt 003497
Literárna Expozícia - Múzeum Janka Jesenského, Mestské Múzeum v Bratislave, Bratislava 034327
Literárne a Hudobné Múzeum, State Scientific Library Banská Bystrica, Banská Bystrica 034301
Literary Documentation Centre H.B. Yasin, Jakarta 022423
Literary History Museum, Minsk . . . 003135
Literate Veteran, Cleveland 142337
Literatur- und Heimatmuseum Altaussee, Altaussee 001676
Literaturarchiv Sulzbach-Rosenberg, Sulzbach-Rosenberg 020384
Literature, Theatre and Music Museum, Rïga 027756
Literaturhaus, Magdeburg 018771
Literaturhaus München, München . 019076
Literaturium / Micro Hall Art Center, Edewecht 016885
Literaturmuseum Brecht-Weigel-Haus, Buckow, Märkische Schweiz 016482
Literaturmuseum im Baumbachhaus, Meininger Museen, Meiningen . . . 018883
Literaturmuseum Theodor Storm, Heilbad Heiligenstadt 017846
Literaturno-chudožestvennyj Muzej M. Cvetaevoj, Nacionalnyj muzej respubliki Baškortostan, Usen-Ivanovskoe . . 034018
Literaturno-chudožestvennyj Muzej-usadba Prijutino, Vsevoložsk 034087
Literaturno-Memoralnyj Muzej N.A Ostrovskogo, Šepetovka 038384
Literaturno-Memorialnyj Muzej A.A. Achmatovoï, Slobidka Šelechivs'ka 038396
Literaturno-Memorialny Muzej Lesi Ukrainky, Volynskyj Krajeznavčyj Muzej, Kolodjažne 038286
Literaturno-memorial'nyj Budinok-muzej M. Bulgakova, Kyïv 038304
Literaturno-memorialnyj Dom-Muzej D.N. Mamina-Sibirjaka, Municipalnyj objedinennyj muzej pisatelej Urala, Ekaterinburg 033112
Literaturno-memorial'nyj Dom-Muzej F.M. Rešetnikova, Municipalnyj objedinennyj muzej pisatelej Urala, Ekaterinburg 033113
Literaturno-memorialnyj Dom-muzej Sulejmana Stalskogo, Ašaga-Stalsk 033000
Literaturno-memorialnyj Muzej O.S. Puškina ta P.I. Čajkovskogo, Kam'janka . . 038277
Literaturno-memorialnyj Muzej F.M. Dostoevskogo, Novokuzneck 033581
Literaturno-memorialnyj Muzej F.M. Dostoevskogo, Sankt-Peterburg . 033760
Literaturno-memorialnyj Muzej Vasilija Erošenko, Starooskolskij kraevedčeskij muzej, Staryj Oskol 033906
Literaturno-memorialnyj Muzej F.A. Abramova, Verkola 034030
Literaturno-memorialnyj Muzej M. Gorkogo, Samara 033718
Literaturno-memorialnyj Muzej im. A.M. Gorkogo, Nacionalnyj Muzej Respubliki Tatarstan, Kazan 033236
Literaturno-memorialnyj Muzej Ivana Franko, Lviv 038342
Literaturno-Memorial'nyj Muzej M. Eminesku, Černivec'kyj krajeznavčyj muzej, Černivci 038240
Literaturno-memorial'nyj Muzej Puškina, Odes'kyj literaturnyj muzej, Odesa 038366
Literaturno-memorialnyj Muzej Stancionnyj Smotritel, Vyra 034091
Literaturno-memorialnyj Muzej M.M. Zoščenko, Sankt-Peterburg 033761
Literaturno-mystec'kyj Muzej, Chmel'nyc'kyj 038253
Literaturno-teatralnyj Muzej N.M. Djakonova, Syktyvkar 033922
Literaturnyj Lviv Peršoï Polovyny XXst, Lvivs'kyj istoryčnyj muzej, Lviv . . 038343
Literaturnyj Muzej, Krasnojarsk . . . 033299
Literaturnyj Muzej, Penza 033631
Literaturnyj Muzej Abakumcevo, Gosudarstvennyj literaturno-memorialnyj muzej-zapovednik N.A. Nekrasova Karabicha, Abakumcevo 032971
Literaturnyj Muzej Alisher Navoj, Taškent 049408
Literaturnyj Muzej Andižana, Andižan 049383
Literaturnyj Muzej-centr K.G. Paustovskogo, K.G. Paustovski Museum-Centre of Literature, Moskva 033417
Literaturnyj Muzej Goroda Nalčik, Nacionalnyj Muzej Kabardino-Balkarskoj Respubliki, Nalčik 033540
Literaturnyj Muzej G. Guliama iz Fergana, Kokand 049395
Literaturnyj Muzej im. K.V. Ivanova, Čeboksary 033063
Literaturnyj Muzej Instituta Russkoj Literatury, Rossijskaja Akademija Nauk, Sankt-Peterburg 033762
Literaturnyj Muzej Literatura Chersonščina, Oblasnyyj krajeznavčyj muzej, Cherson 038248
Literaturnyj Muzej Literaturnoe Pridneprovje, Dnipropetrovskyj deržavnij istoričnij muzej im Javornic'kogo, Dnipropetrovs'k 038259
Literaturnyj Muzej F.I. Tjutčeva, Brjanskij gosudarstvennyj obedinennyj kraevedčeskij muzej, Ovstug 033623
Litho Galerie, Amsterdam 107762
Lithographie, Paris 100622
Lithographiesteinarchiv und druckhistorische Werkstätte, München 019077
Lithos, Venezia 128395
Lithuanian Artists' Association, Vilnius 053844
The Lithuanian Museum, Chicago . . 042854
Lithuanian Museum-Archives of Canada, Mississauga 005892
Lithuanian Museums Association, Vilnius 053845
Lithuanian State Museum, Vilnius . . 027865
Lito Offset Nacional, México 134761
Litografia Tucano, Rio de Janeiro . . 096626
Litografia Tucano, Rio de Janeiro . . 096627
Litra, Paris 138485
Litsch, Helmut, Köln 103673
Litschi, Rudolf, Wil 082906
Litt, David, Ampthill 083297
Litterae, Genova 127464
Litterer, Heinz & Renate, Wiesenbach, Baden 105287
Little Antique Shop, Nashville 090465
Little Antique Shop, New York 091034
Little Balkans Review, Pittsburgh . . 136524
Little Bighorn Battlefield Museum, Crow Agency 043230
Little Bits, Gisborne 079101
Little Black Pearl, Chicago 115480
The Little Brick House, Vandalia . . . 048751
Little & Brown, Boston 135334
Little, Brown & Co., London 135230
Little Cavern, Beatles-Museum, Biebelnheim 016225
Little Collectables, Congleton 084073
Little Compton Historical Society Museum, Little Compton 045337
Little Cowboy Bar and Museum, Fromberg 044089
Little English, Memphis 090084
Little Falls Historical Museum, Little Falls 045341
The Little Gallery, Hamilton 096423
Little Gallery, Hawkes Bay 108469
The Little Gallery, Johannesburg . . 110057
The Little Gallery, Pittenweem 086272
The Little Gallery, Pittenweem 114252
Little Gallery, Prince Albert 006203
The Little Gallery, Saint-Emilion . . . 101144
Little Gallery, Singapore 109830
Little Gem, Shrewsbury . . 086604, 131496
Little Holland House, London 040202
Little House Heirloom Gallery, Birmingham 087768
Little House on the Parking Lot, Toronto 059232
Little Houses, Dunkeld 039323
Little Jem's, Penzance 086213
Little Ladies, Chicago 088121
Little Lane Books, Camden 136843
Little London Gallery, Holloway . . . 113250
Little Lu, San Francisco 092830
Little Malop Gallery, Geelong 094578
Little Moreton Hall, Congleton 039132
Little Museum, Tewkesbury 041204
Little Nemo, Torino 106683, 140137
Little Nest of Treasures, New York . 091035
Little Norway, Blue Mounds 042274
Little Paddocks Art Gallery, Timaru . 108582
Little Paris Antiques, Los Angeles . . 089825
Little Picture Gallery.Com, Greenford 113156
Little Prairie Heritage Museum, Chetwynd 005265
Little Red School House Museum, Weyauwega 049131
Little Red Schoolhouse-Living Library, Beloit 042130
Little River Gallery, Christchurch . . 108403
Little School Museum, Lockeport . . 005782
The Little Strawberry Gallery, Bristol 112726
Little Studio, San Antonio 119429
Little Summerhouse, Miami 132347
Little Sweets Museum, Hirano Hakabutsukan, Osaka 026968
Little Theatre Antiques Centre, Jesmond 084814, 130835
Little Things, Las Vegas 089591
Little Traverse Historical Museum, Petoskey 046914
Little Treasures, Caulfield North . . . 055653
Little Treasures, Caulfield North . . . 055654
Little Treasures, Dornoch 084211
Little Treasures, Pretoria 080736
Little Van Gogh, Bruxelles 096228
Little White Barn, Jacksonville 142472
Little White House, Warm Springs . 048852
Little White Schoolhouse, Ripon . . . 047443

Little White Schoolhouse, Truro . . . 006669
Little World Museum of Man, Inuyama . . . 026567
Littlebury Antiques, Saffron Walden 086433, 131435
Littlehampton Museum, Littlehampton . . . 040024
Littlejohn, New York . . . 118131
Littleton, Maurine, Washington . . . 120320
Littleton Historical Museum, Littleton . . . 045348
Littman Gallery, Portland State University, Portland . . . 047172
Littmann, Basel . . . 111209
Littmann Kulturprojekte, Münchenstein . . . 111758
Litvich, Judith, San Francisco . . . 119723
Litvin, Salt Lake City . . . 092439
Litwin, Fred, Washington . . . 093419
Litwinschuh, Manfred & Renate, Weiskirchen . . . 074324
Liuhe County Display Center, Liucheng . . . 007175
Liuksialan Maatalousmuseo, Liuksiala . . . 009833
Liv An Amzer, Ploudalmézeau . . . 066865
Livani, Athinai . . . 134487
Livarot Troc, Livarot . . . 063968
Live-Art, Lippstadt . . . 072282
Livellini, Luigi, Verona . . . 128428
Lively Set, New York . . . 091036
Liven, Isai, Köln . . . 071976, 126100
Livengood, Los Angeles . . . 089826
Liverpool Academy of Art, Liverpool 050823
Liverpool Academy of Art, Liverpool 113410
Liverpool Museum, Liverpool . . . 040030
Liverpool School of Art and Design, Liverpool John Moores University, Liverpool . . . 050824
Liverpool Scottish Regimental Museum, Liverpool . . . 040031
Liverpool Street Gallery, Surry Hills 095256
Liverpool University Press, Liverpool . . . 135170
Livesey, Scott, Armadale, Victoria . 055384
Livesey Museum for Children, London . . . 040203
Livia de Alencar Chaucs, Barcellos, Porto Alegre . . . 096565
Livia Furniture Finishing, Miami . . . 132348
Livinec, Gauducheau & Jézéquel, Rennes (Ille-et-Vilaine) . . . 121231
Livinec, Pincemin & Gauducheau, Fougères (Ille-et-Vilaine) . . . 121007
Living, Waldenburg, Württemberg . 074252
Living Art Gallery, Chippendale . . . 094394
Living Art Gallery, Portland . . . 123064
The Living Arts and Science Center, Lexington . . . 045262
Living Arts of Tulsa, Tulsa . . . 120199
Living Desert Art Gallery, Broken Hill . . . 094306
Living History Farms Museum, Urbandale . . . 048715
Living In The Past, Ballarat . . . 055433
Living Legacy, Calgary . . . 096828
The Living Museum, Springfield . . . 136525
Living Museum at Tulsa Zoo, Tulsa . 048654
Living Prairie Museum, Winnipeg . . 006850
The Living Room, New Orleans . . . 117467
Living Spring Publishing, Seattle . . 135503
Living Stone, Den Haag . . 107937, 134805
The Living Store, Salzburg . . . 095728
Living with Art, Amsterdam . . . 136001
Living Word National Bible Museum, Aledo . . . 041630
Livingston, Thomas, San Francisco 092831
Livingston Arts Department, Rutgers State University of New Jersey, New Brunswick . . . 051787
Livingston County Historical Society Museum, Geneseo . . . 044161
Livingston Depot Center, Livingston 045352
Livingstone, Den Haag . . . 107938
Livingstone, Neil, Dundee . . . 084229
Livingstone and Stanley Memorial, Tabora . . . 037860
Livingstone Museum, National Museum of Zambia, Livingstone . . . 049568
Livonijas Ordeņa Pils Tornis, Tukums . . . 027787
Livraghi, Pietro, Milano . . . 127616
Livraria Académica, Porto . . . 140867
Livraria Alfarrabista, Coimbra . . . 140813
Livraria Alfarrabista, Lisboa . . . 140832
Livraria Amadeu, Belo Horizonte . . 137544
Livraria Amadeu, Belo Horizonte . . 137545
Livraria Antiquária do Calhariz, Lisboa . . . 140833
Livraria Antiquario, Fortaleza . . . 137559
Livraria Antiquario, Rio de Janeiro . 137574
Livraria Artes e Letras, Lisboa . . . 140834
Livraria AZ do Livro, Lisboa . . . 140835
Livraria Barateira, Lisboa . . . 140836
Livraria Bizantina, Lisboa . . . 140837
Livraria Brasileira, Rio de Janeiro . . 137575
A Livraria do Messias, São Paulo . . 137586
Livraria Dom Pedro V, Lisboa . . . 140838
Livraria e Sebo Horizonte, Belo Horizonte . . . 137546
Livraria Elcla Boavista, Porto . . . 140868
Livraria Histórica e Ultramarina, Lisboa . . . 140839
Livraria João do Rio, Rio de Janeiro 137576
Livraria Kaleidoscópio, Porto Alegre 137565
Livraria Leitura Livros Novos e Usados, Belo Horizonte . . . 137547
Livraria Leonardo, Rio de Janeiro . . 137577
Livraria Maria de Historias, Rio de Janeiro . . . 137578
Livraria Mosaico, Porto Alegre . . . 137566
Livraria Olisipo, Lisboa . . . 140840
Livraria Pindorama, Brasília . . . 137553
Livraria Santo Santo Piamarta, Fortaleza . . . 137560
Le Livre, Salleboeuf . . . 068099, 138612
Livre à Lili, Lyon . . . 138174
Livre Comme l'Air, Nantes . . . 138244
Livre et Passion, Redu . . . 137537
Livre Mon Ami, Paris . . . 138486
Le Livre Penseur, Auray . . . 138017
Livres d'Antan, Paris . . . 138487
Livres d'Autrefois, Angoulême . . . 138013
Livres Sans Frontières, Paris . . . 138488
Livresse, Feytiat . . . 138086
Livrustkammaren, Stockholm . . . 036639
Liwan, Casablanca . . . 077662
Lixia Qidong Art, Jinan . . . 097858
Lixin, Hang, Singapore . . . 080520
Liyang Art Gallery, Shenyang . . . 097967
Liz, Bern . . . 082223
Liz, Utrecht . . . 108255
Lizan, New York . . . 118132
Lizardi-Harp, West Hollywood . . . 120397
Lizauli Cultural Village, Lizauli . . . 029085
Lizène, Jacques, Liège . . . 133292
Lizhor Gallery, Bogotá . . . 098172
Lizzadro Museum of Lapidary Art, Elmhurst . . . 043688
Lizzani, Luca, Roma . . . 076529
Lizzi, Enrico, Merano . . . 075547
Lizzie's Place, South Brisbane . . . 056605
Ljósmyndasafn Reykjavíkur Grófarhús, Reykjavík . . . 021967
Ljudmilova, Cvetanka, Gorna Orjachovica . . . 096703
Ljungbergmuseet, Ljungby . . . 036427
Ljungby Gamla Torg Hembygdsmuseum, Ljungby . . . 036428
Ljusdals Auktioner, Ljusdal . . . 122196
Ljusdalsbygdens Museum, Ljusdal . 036429
Ljusterö Hembygdsmuseum, Ljusterö . . . 036430
Ljuva Hem, Trelleborg . . . 082052
LKAB Gruvmuseum, Kiruna . . . 036391
LL Worldwide Art Industry, Amsterdam . . . 107763
LLAC Sala d'Exposicions, Tarragona . . . 081624, 141073
Lladro Collectors Society, New York 054848
Lladro Museum, New York . . . 046356
Llanberis Lake Railway, Llanberis . 040045
Llancaiach Fawr Living History Museum, Nelson . . . 040519
Llandudno Museum and Art Gallery, Llandudno . . . 040051
Llangollen Motor Museum, Llangollen . . . 040063
Llangollen Railway, Llangollen . . . 040064
Llanidloes Museum, Llanidloes . . . 040066
Llanishen Antiques, Cardiff . . . 083874
Llanyrafon Farm, Cwmbran . . . 039198
Llarenas, La Palmas de Gran Canaria . . . 081504
Llechwedd Slate Caverns, Blaenau Ffestiniog . . . 038758
Lleonart Claraso, Jaime, Barcelona 110209
Llewellyn, Alexander, London . . . 113737
Llewellyn, Alexander, London . . . 131091
Lleyn Historical and Maritime Museum, Nefyn . . . 040518
Llibrería Al Tossal, Valencia . . . 141081
Llibreria Antiquària Catedral, Tarragona . . . 141074
Llibreria Canuda, Barcelona . . . 122009, 140997
Llibreria Gabernet, Barcelona . . . 140998
Lloan, Janine, Montréjeau . . . 064763
Llobet Germans, Barcelona . . . 129360
La Llonja, Palma de Mallorca . . . 035611
Llorenc Coll Gelado, Girona . . . 110369
Llorente, Madrid . . . 081332
Lloret, B., Toulouse . . . 101362
La Llorona, Chicago . . . 115481
Lloyd, Brisbane . . . 136820
Lloyd, John, Ditchling Common . . . 130636
Lloyd, John, London . . . 131092
Lloyd, Michael, Llandysul . . . 085035
Lloyd, Robert, New York . . . 091037
Lloyd, Robin, Ross-on-Wye 086402, 131427
Lloyd-Davies, Sue, Carmarthen . . . 141493
Lloyd George Museum and Highgate, Llanystumdwy . . . 040069
Lloyds, London . . . 122592
Lloyd's Nelson Collection, London . 040204
Lloyd's of Kew, Kew . . . 141692
Lluch Fluxa Rossello, Maria de, Palma de Mallorca . . . 110691
Llywernog Silver-Lead Mine Museum, Ponterwyd . . . 040731
L.M., Torino . . . 076836
LM Escritório de Arte, Fortaleza . . . 096532
L.M.A France, Paris . . . 066201
LMB Arts, London . . . 113738
LMS Galerija, Rīga . . . 107319
LnD Outlet, Koblenz . . . 071895
Lo, Napoli . . . 106379
Lo, Saint Louis . . . 092266
Lo, Alvin, New York . . . 091038
Lo, K.S., Hong Kong . . . 097811
Lo Biondo, Salvatore, Palermo . . . 076156
Lo Scrigno, Parma . . . 076213
Lo Scrigno, Trieste . . . 076898
Loango, Strasbourg . . . 101297
Loas, Nice . . . 099846
Lobasso, Giuseppe, Milano . . . 127617
Lobato Ranger, Oscar, Barcelona . . 080872
Lobaumuseum, Wien . . . 002944
Lobdengau-Museum, Ladenburg . . 018458
Lobel, New York . . . 091039
Lobel, Christian, Nice . . . 099847
Lober, Valette Thierry, Limoges . . . 063890
Lobera Amann, Jose, Bilbao . . . 129438
Lobis, Klaipėda . . . 140228
L'Objet, Noirmoutier-en-l'Ile . . . 099882
Lobkovicky Palác, National Museum, Praha . . . 008621
Lobo, Albuquerque . . . 087407
Lobstein, Alain, Paris . . . 124730
Local and Maritime Museum, Newhaven . . . 040557
Local Antiquities Museum, Chitradurga . . . 022062
Local Color Gallery, Nashville . . . 117360
Local Colors Artworks, Salt Lake City . . . 119353
Local History Collection, Aberfoyle Park . . . 000695
Local History Museums, Durban . . . 034602
Local Images Art Gallery, Penola . . 095064
Local Museum, Ashkelon . . . 022891
Local Museum, Bhanpura . . . 022025
Local Museum, Kibbutz Maabarot . 023012
Local Museum, Kibbutz Sasa . . . 023019
Local Studies Collection, Marrickville . . . 001222
Localbahnmuseum, Tiroler Museums Bahnen, Innsbruck . . . 002088
Localbahnmuseum Bayerisch Eisenstein, Bayerisch Eisenstein . . . 015903
Locastro, Matteo, Genova . . . 127465
Locatelli, Alain, Lyon . . . 064152
Location One, New York . . . 118133
Locci, Luciano, Roma . . . 128084
Loch, Silvia, Eschwege . . . 139051
The Loch Ewe Gallery, Bridport . . . 112707
Loch Fyne Gallery, Tarbert . . . 114548
Loch Gallery, Toronto . . . 097319
Loch & Mayberry, Winnipeg . . . 097589
Loch Ness 2000 Exhibition, Drumnadrochit . . . 039286
Lochaber, Fort William . . . 113075
Locher, Erika, Luzern . . . 082631
Locher, René, Horw . . . 082503
Lochhead, Ken, Haddington . . . 113174
Lochmann, Hans-Rudolf, Neustadt an der Weinstraße . . . 073029
Lochmann, W., Karlsruhe . . . 071726
Lochte, Alfred, Hamburg . 103184, 134018
Lochtenberg, L.M., Hilversum . . . 078536
Lochwinnoch Community Museum, Lochwinnoch . . . 040071
Lociuro, Alberto, Roma . . . 076530
Lock jr., John H., Philadelphia . . . 091659
Lock, Wilma, Sankt Gallen . . . 111873
Lock Museum of America, Terryville 048536
Locke & Assoc., Suzy, Oakland . . . 118637
Locke & England, Leamington Spa . 122559
Locke Street Antiques, Hamilton . . 058856
Locke Street Interiors, Hamilton . . . 058857
Lockehaven Schoolhouse Museum, Enfield . . . 043711
Lockerbie Street Home of James Whitcomb Riley, Indianapolis . . . 044750
Locke's Distillery Museum, Kilbeggan . . . 022801
Lockhouse-Friends of the Delaware Canal, New Hope . . . 046233
Lockner, Hermann P., Würzburg . . . 074502
Lockport Gallery, Illinois State Museum, Lockport . . . 045361
Locks, Marian, Philadelphia . . . 118793
Locksmith, A., Chicago . . . 115482
Locksmith, Charles, New York . . . 091040
Lockwood & Co, Airport West . . . 120558
Lockwood-Mathews Mansion Museum, Norwalk . . . 046562
Loco Gringo Studio, Dallas . . . 115906
Lococo Fine Art, Saint Louis . . . 135484
Locus Gallery, Saint Louis . . . 119221
Locus Solus, Napoli . . . 106380
Locus Solus, Paris . . . 100623
Locust Grove, Louisville . . . 045491
Locust Grove, Samuel Morse Historic Site, Poughkeepsie . . . 047212
Locust Lawn and Terwilliger House, Gardiner . . . 044143
Loder, York . . . 056906
Lodewijk, Eindhoven . . . 078343
Lodewijk, M.J., Den Haag . . . 078214
Lodge, Ballyduff . . . 074858
Lodge, Fenny, Bletchley . . . 112668
Lodge Antiques, Robe . . . 056536
Lodge Antiques, Rosedale . . . 056551
Lodi, Roberto, Modena . . . 075917
Lodi Junior, Silvano, Milano . . . 106257
Lodiana, Nice . . . 065105
Lodolo Pasialis, Rita, Roma . . . 106574
Lodrini, Rosa, Brescia . . . 075172

Loë-Galerie, Chur 111359
Loe-Van, Singapore 109831
Loe-Van, Singapore 109832
Loeb, Albert, Paris 100624
Löber, Alois, Faulbach 070680
Löber, Heidi E., Stuttgart 073991
Löbig, Richard, Dieburg 125460
Löblein, Peter, Bamberg 069457
Loecher, Roger P., Denver 088709
Löcker, Erhard, Wien 133216, 137339
Loeckx, Gent 058194, 120758
Lödöse Museum, Lödöse 036432
Loeffel, Tobias, Basel 111210, 129926
Löffelsend, Rolf & Angelika, Düsseldorf 125537
Löffler, Kirchheim unter Teck 139324
Löffler, Maria, Renchen 073496
Löffler, Stefan, Kronach 126154
Löfgren, Stockholm 081981
Löfstad Slott Museum, Östergötlands Museum, Norrköping 036502
Löhe-Zeit-Museum, Neuendettelsau 019230
Loehr, Dorothea, Frankfurt am Main 102798
Löhr, H., Alfter 069133
Löhrl, Mönchengladbach 104097
Löhrl, Christa & Dietmar, Mönchengladbach 104098
L'Oeil Nu, Alès 098815
Loek Kok, Haarlem 078465
Lönnströmin Taidemuseo, Rauma . . 010024
Loeper, Gabriele von, Hamburg . . . 103185
Loerakker, Amsterdam 107764
Lörcher, Margot, Aystetten 138691
Loës, de, Genève . 082443, 111480, 141251
Loes & Reinier, Deventer 107969
Lösch, Erich, Monsheim 121516
Loescher, Johannes, Köln 126101
Lösekrug, Berlin 069692
Lösekrug, Berlin 069693
Loest-Militzki, Leipzig 139398
Lötschentaler Museum, Kippel 037211
L'Oeuvre Copiée, Paris 100625
Lövångers Sockenmuseum, Lövånger 036433
Lövei, Jánosné, Miskolc 139939
Lövgren, Gustav, Strömsnäsbruk . . 122266
Lövsbergsauktionerna, Mjölby 122214
Löw Fine Art, Seltisberg 082806
Loewe, München 104261
Löwe, Claus-Dieter, Ottendorf-Okrilla 073267
Löwe, Edmund, München 072778
Loewe, Oskar, Recklinghausen 139679
Löwel, Stockach 073921
Löwen-Drogerie und Museum, Oelsnitz, Vogtland 019443
Löwenburg, Kassel 018192
Loewinstein, Avner, Frankfurt am Main 070763
Loewinstein, Avner, Frankfurt am Main 070764
Lofanta, Kaunas 140226
Lofoten Krigsminnemuseum, Svolvær 031255
Lofotmuseet, Kabelvåg Fiskerimuseum, Kabelvåg 030930
Loft, Cincinnati 115639
Loft Antiques, Ballyboughhal 074857
Loft Antiques, Minneapolis 090374
Loft Art, Siegen 104898
Loft Art Gallery, Guckheim 103027
Loft Art Gallery, Kreuztal 103788
Loft Gallery, Hillsborough 113243
Log Cabin Antiques, Austin 087592
Log Cabin Museum, Murray Harbour 005971
Log Cabin Train Shop, Pittsburgh . . 091838
Log Cabin Village, Fort Worth 044010
The Log Farm, Nepean 005992
Log of Mystic Seaport, Mystic 136526
Logan, Ottawa 059043
Logan Art Gallery, Logan 001191
Logan County Historical Society Museum, Bellefontaine 042105
Logan County Museum, Paris 046813
Logan Museum of Anthropology, Beloit 042132
Loganberry Books, Cleveland 142338
Logans, Washington 093420
Logello, Allemand, Montfavet 064682
Logemann, L., Bremen 070033
L.o.G.G. Lights, Tynemouth 086973
Logge dell'Orafo, San Marino 109669
La Loggia, Brescia 075173
Logie Steading Art Gallery, Dunphail 112969
Logisoft, Oslo 121870
Loglio, Ivano, Torino 128324
Logos, Warszawa 140791
Loh, Lüneburg 139434
Lohaus, Stella, Antwerpen 096079
Lohéac, Landerneau 063511
Lohgerber-, Stadt- und Kreismuseum, Dippoldiswalde 016722
Lohilammen Museo, Sammatti 010061
Lohjan Museo, Lohja 009834
Lohl, Dieter, Göttingen 102979
Lohmann, A., Emsdetten 070567
Lohmann, Günther, Halle, Westfalen 139162
Lohmann, M., Bergen, Kreis Celle . 069532
Lohmann, Michael, Timmendorfer Strand 074061
Lohmann, Michael, Timmendorfer Strand 074062
Lohner, A., Inchenhofen 071620
Thomas Lohr & Martina Hahn, Thomas, Mainz 072395
Lohrbacher Heimatstuben, Mosbach, Baden 019000
Lohri, Andreas, Zug 130275
Lohse, Henri, Berlin 125251
Lohtajan Kotiseutumuseo, Lohtaja . 009836
Loi, Cristina, Cagliari 075215
Loi, Katia, Cagliari 127247
Loïc, Monnier, Chinon 062294
Loidl, Matthias, Unterreit . 134440, 139812
Loimaan Kotiseutumuseo, Loimaa . 009837
Lois E. Woods Museum, Norfolk . . . 046500
Loiseau, Pornichet 066952
L'Oiseau Bleu, Pont-Aven 101034
Loiseau & Schmitz, Saint-Germain-en-Laye 121246
Loison, Lyon 064153
Loison, Savasse 068163
Loizillon, Dominique, Compiègne . . 120980
Łój, Bogusław, Warszawa 129098
Loja da Calçada, Lisboa 079953
Loja das Colecções, Lisboa 140841
Loja do Atalaia, Lisboa 079954
Loja do Atalaia, Lisboa 079955
Loja do Colecionador, Rio de Janeiro 058608
Lojas de Antiguidades Vila Real, São Paulo 058721
Lojkásková, Věra, Český Těšín 060005, 137776
Lok Virsa Museum, National Institute of Folk and Traditional Heritage, Islamabad 031368
Lokaal 01, Antwerpen 096080
Lokaal 01, Breda 107879
De Lokeend, Breda 078107
De Lokeend, Venlo 078844
Løkken 6, Stavanger 079506
Løkken Museum, Løkken 009015
Lokmuseet, Grängesberg 036310
Lola Gallery, San Francisco 119724
Loldia, Constanţa 080180
Loleo, Mauro, Genova 127466
Loliée, Bernard, Paris 138489
Lolland-Falsters Stiftsmuseum, Maribo 009019
Lolland-Falsters Traktor- og Motormuseum, Eskildstrup 008846
Lolli, Dino, Prato 076254
Lollichon, François, Fay-de-Bretagne 062846
Lollipop, San Francisco 092832
Lom Bygdamuseum, Museet i Nord-Gudbrandsdalen, Lom 030993
Lomakovskij Muzej Starinnych Avtomobilej i Motociklov, Moskva 033418
Lombard, Honiton 084726
Lombard, Stepney 095224
Lombard Antiques, Newark-on-Trent 086052
Lombard-Fried, New York 118134
Lombard Historical Museum, Lombard 045368
Lombard Korona, Saratov 080340
Lombardi, Alessandro, Roma 076531
Lombardi, Enrico, Roma 106575
Lombart, Marcel, Le Havre 063637
Lombart, Marcel, Le Havre 063638
Lombrail-Teucquam, Paris 121169
L'Ombre Bleue, Fougères (Ille-et-Vilaine) 099273
Lometsch, Kassel 139307
Lomillo, Florentino, Burgos 129462
Lommedalsbanen, Rykkinn 031156
Lomonds Gallery, Gateside 113090
Lomonosov, Deventer 140407
Lompoc Museum, Lompoc 045370
Lompoc Valley Historical Society Museum, Lompoc 045371
Lon C. Hill Home, Harlingen 044432
Lonardini, Franco, Brescia 127222
London Antique Gallery, London . . .085492, 131093
London Antique Shop, Auckland . . . 078959
London Antiquités, La Baule-Escoublac 063291
London Antiquités, Saint-Nazaire (Loire-Atlantique) 067685
London Art Fair, London 093935
London Borough of Bromley Museum, Orpington 040647
London Brass Rubbing Centre, London 040205
The London Brass Rubbing Centre in Washington D.C., Gaithersburg . . 044113
London Canal Museum, London . . . 040206
London Chelsea Book Fair, London . 093936
The London Cigarette Card, Somerton 122702
London Coin, London 058885
London Contemporary Art, Oslo . . . 079458
London Court Antiques, Perth 056458
London Desvan, Sevilla 081592
London Federation of Museums and Art Galleries, London 054422
London Film School, London 050835
London Fine Arts, Singapore 109833
London Fire Brigade Museum, London 040207
London Frameworks, Dubai 112454
London Gallery, Bruxelles 058021
London Gallery, Detroit 088764
London Gallery, Tokyo 107070
London House, Harrogate . 084578, 130763
London-House, München 072779
London House Antique Centre, Moreton-in-Marsh 086019
London House Antiques, Westerham 087099, 131671
London House Oriental Rugs and Carpets, Boston Spa 083582, 130412
London Institute Gallery, London . . 040208
London Irish Rifles Regimental Museum, London 040209
London & Kent, London 122593
London Market, Lyon 064154
London Militaria Market, London . . 085493
London Motorcycle Museum, Greenford 039638
London Museum of Archaeology, London 005789
London Museums and Galleries Marketing Association, London 054423
London Original Print Fair, London . 093937
London Picture Centre, London . . . 113739
London Regional Children's Museum, London 005790
London Road Antiques, Edinburgh . 084301
London Scottish Regimental Museum, London 040210
London Sewing Machine Museum, London 040211
London Shop, Royan 067312
London Silver Vaults, London 085494
London Street Projects, Los Angeles 116824
London Toy and Model Museum, London 040212
Londonderry Mines Museum, Londonderry 005794
Londoño, María Teresa, Medellín . . 123936
Londoño Villegas, Mario, Medellín . 059923
London's Transport Museum, London 040213
Lone Star Coins, San Antonio 092537
Lone Star Flight Museum/Texas Aviation Hall of Fame, Galveston 044134
Lone Star Pastel Society, Amarillo . 054849
Lone Star Toys, Dallas 088552
Lone Star Trains, San Antonio 092538
Long, New York 118135
Long, Bao, New York 091041
Long, Meredith, Houston 116357
Long, Michael D., Nottingham 086139
Long, Stephen, London 085495
Long, Timothy, Sevenoaks 131466
Long, Van, Ha Noi 120471
Long, Van, Hue 120546
Long Beach Antique and Collectible Mall, Long Beach 089642
Long Beach Arts, Long Beach 116675
Long Beach Arts, Long Beach 116676
Long Beach Museum of Art, Long Beach 045380
Long Branch Historical Museum, Long Branch 045386
The Long Curve Gallery, Chipping Campden 112864
Long Eaton Town Hall, Long Eaton . 040332
Long Fang Ge, Nanjing 097874
Long Island Children's Museum, Garden City 044141
Long Island Culture History Museum, Commack 043113
Long Island Maritime Museum, West Sayville 049100
Long Island Museum of American Art, History and Cariages, Stony Brook 048377
Long Island Museum of Science and Technology, Garden City 044142
Long Lost Friends, Houston 142440
Long Melford Antique Centre, Long Melford 085834
Long & Ryle, London 113740
Long Shop Museum, Leiston 039984
Long Warehouse, Coalbrookdale . . 039104
Long Wenge, Tianjin 098013
Long Wenge, Tianjin 098014
Longaberger, Saint Louis 092267
Longaberger, Saint Louis 092268
Longanesi, Milano 134619
Longari, Nella, Milano 075752
Longbai, Shanghai 059756
Longboat Key Center for the Arts, Longboat Key 045395
Longchamp, Olivier, Fribourg 130024
Longdale Craft Centre and Museum, Ravenshead 040801
Longden, George, Macclesfield . . . 141929
Longelin, Michel, Saint-Laurent-Blangy 067574
Longfellow, Portland 142802
Longfellow-Evangeline State Historic Site, Saint Martinville 047685
Longfellow National Historic Site, Cambridge 042562
Longfellow's Wayside Inn Museum, South Sudbury 048250
Longford Antiques, Longford 056114
Longgang Ke Jia Folklorish Museum, Shenzhen 007261
Longhorn, San Antonio 092539
Longhorn Museum, Pleasanton . . . 047091
Longhu Painting and Calligraphy Association, Beijing 052798

Longhua Mausoleum of Fallen Heroes, Shanghai . . . 007236
Longleat House, Warminster . . . 041301
Longman, Harlow . . . 135158
Longmire, London . . . 085496
Longmont Museum, Longmont . . . 045397
Longo, Angelo, Ravenna . . . 134665
Longo, Christine, Grézet-Cavagnan 063077
Longo, Franco, Milano . . . 127618
Longo, Luigi, Vevey . . . 082883
Longo, Sergio, São Paulo . . . 096677
Longo, Vittorio, Milano . . . 075753
Longquanyi District Museum, Chengdu . . . 007042
Longreach Power House Museum, Longreach . . . 001193
Longridge Gallery, Longridge . . . 113993
Longstreet Farm, Holmdel . . . 044581
Longtemps, Antan, Paris . . . 066202
Longue Vue House, New Orleans . . 046257
Longuestre Franck, Brest . . . 061776
Longuet, Bernard, Saint-Vincent . . . 068036
Longueville, Daniel, Maisons-Laffitte . . . 064226
Longview Museum of Fine Art, Longview . . . 045399
Longwood, Salt Lake City . . . 092440
Longwood Center for the Visual Arts, Farmville . . . 043826
Longyear Museum, Chestnut Hill . . 042810
La Lonja, Ayuntamiento de Zaragoza, Zaragoza . . . 036100
Lonnie's Art, El Paso . . . 116113
Lonsdale, Toronto . . . 097320
Lonsdale, Elaine, Hemswell Cliff . . . 141657
Lonsdale Antiques, Southend-on-Sea . . . 086655
Lonsdale Antiques, Vancouver . . . 059377
Lonsdale Quay Native Arts, Vancouver . . . 097497
De Looier Antiek Centrum, Amsterdam . . . 077903
Look, Almaty . . . 107155
Look, Wildeshausen . . . 105297
Look, John, Boston . . . 087832
Look Art Gallery, Helmsley . . . 113220
Look Galerie und Edition, Krefeld . . 103780, 134131
Look Gallery, Minneapolis . . . 117280
Look Out Discovery Centre, Bracknell . . . 038801
Looking Glass 1950's and Carnival Memorabilia, Saint Louis . . . 092269
Looking Glass of Bath, Bath . . . 083436, 130354
Looking Glass Toy Company, Portland . . . 132698
Loomes, Brian, Pateley Bridge . . . 086193
Loomes, Robert B., Stamford . . . 131526
Les Looms Gallery, New York . . . 091042
Loong, Singapore . . . 080521, 129262
Loong, Thng, Singapore . . . 080522
Loop, Melbourne . . . 094820
Loop, Toronto . . . 097321
Loop Museum and Art Center, Seagraves . . . 048071
Loosduins Museum De Korenschuur, Den Haag . . . 029431
Loose, Ingeborg, Altenholz . . . 069152
Loose, R., Den Haag . . . 140396
Loosen-Dellemann, Kurt, Mönchengladbach . . . 104099
Loosveldt, Oostende . . . 096399
Loot, Oakland . . . 091426
Looze, A. de, Rotterdam . . . 078730
Lopard-Dessolin, Mâcon . 064205, 121056
Lopburi, Bath . . . 083437
Lopburi, Singapore . . . 080523
Lopdell House Gallery, Auckland . . 030442
Lopdell House Gallery, Auckland . . 108337
Lopera, Verona . . . 128429
Lopes, Anabela Oliveira, Lisboa . . . 079956
Lopes, Benedito Gilberto Almeida, São Paulo . . . 137587
Lopes, Luís, Lisboa . . . 079957
Lopes, Marciano, Fortaleza . . . 058472
Lopes, Tania Maria Weckerle, Porto Alegre . . . 096566
López, Madrid . . . 129639
Lopez, Florence, Paris . . . 066203
López, Javier, Madrid . . . 110560
Lopez, Javier, Madrid . . . 110561
Lopez, Jean-François, Nîmes . . . 065181
Lopez, Joaquin & Tony, Miami . . . 117106
Lopez, Nola, New York . . . 118136
López, Ricardo, Medellín . . . 059924
Lopez, Yvette, Chêne-Bourg . . . 082310, 122316
Lopez Island Historical Museum, Lopez Island . . . 045402
Lopez-Linares, Madrid . . . 081333
Lopez-Linares, Madrid . . . 081334
Lopez Memorial Museum, Pasig . . . 031762
Lopez Morales, Enrique, Zaragoza . 129818
López Quiroga, Ramón, México . . . 107496
Lopez Rey, Francisco Javier, A Coruña . . . 110322
López Salgado, Fred, Bogotá . . . 123903
Lopez Villa, Jose, Madrid . . . 081335
Lopiccolo, Stephen, New York . . . 132492
Łopieńska-Lipczyk, Anna, Warszawa . . . 129099
Lopinski, Michel, Argelès-sur-Mer . 124078
Lopreito Anticuario, Buenos Aires . . 055220
Loquens Gallery, Cheltenham . . . 083922, 130537
Loqui Delfa, Torino . . . 076837
L'Or du Temps, Pamiers . . 099896, 124535
Lora Robins Gallery of Design from Nature, University of Richmond, Richmond . . . 047419
Lorandi, Franco, Milano . . . 127619
Lorang, Robert, Bamberg . . . 138716
L'Orange Bleue, Coutances . . . 062535
L'Orangerie-de-la Motte, Saint-Quentin-la-Motte-Croix-au-Bailly . . . 067978
Lorant, Eva, Vallauris . . . 101419
Lorcan O' Neill, Roma . . . 106576
Daniela Lorch & Jürgen Schulz-Lorch, Sigmaringen . . . 126801
Hans-Martin Lorch & Dr. Reinhold Seidel, Berlin . . . 101979
Lord, Alan, Folkestone . . . 084418
Lord, Michael H., Milwaukee . . . 117203
Lord Frontenac, Napier . . . 079165
Lord Howe Island Museum, Lord Howe Island . . . 001195
Lord Ponsonby Antiques, Auckland . 078960
Lord Selkirk Settlement, Charlottetown . . . 005247
Lord Strathcona's Horse Museum, Calgary . . . 005191
Lordereau, Serge, La Chaise-Dieu . 063307
Lore, Milwaukee . . . 136527
Lore Degenstein Gallery, Selinsgrove . . . 048108
Loreau, Ludovic, Nantes . . . 124486
Loreau, Pierre, Riec-sur-Belon . . . 067140
Lorelei, Amsterdam . . . 140316
Lorelei, Bruxelles . . . 096229
Loreley Galerie, Oberwesel . . . 104514
Lorene's Antiques, Tampa . . . 093139
Lørenskog Bygdemuseum, Skårer . 031184
Lorentz, Thomas, Gröbenzell . . . 071105, 125755
Lorentzon, Stockholm . . . 111061
Lorenz, Burghausen, Salzach . . . 102293
Lorenz, Toronto . . . 059233
Lorenz, Toronto . . . 059234, 097322
Lorenz, Dieter, Düsseldorf . . . 070409
Lorenz, Gerhard & Monika, Lindberg . . . 072269
Lorenz, Hans, Jüchen . . . 071671
Lorenz, Ingrid, Frankfurt am Main . 139091
Lorenz, Kristen, Berlin . . . 138818
Lorenz, Lutz, Chemnitz . . . 125430
Lorenz, Nancy, New York . . . 132493
Lorenz, Ute, Erfurt . . . 125598
Lorenz-Haramus, Georg, München . 072780
Dr. Lorenz & Meyer, Cloppenburg . . 121367
Lorenz & Müller, München . . . 139530
Lorenzelli, Milano . . . 106258
Lorenzen, Brigitte, Gelting . . . 102934
Lorenzer, Anna-Barbara, Eigeltingen . . . 125579
Lorenzi, Flávio José de, Porto Alegre . . . 058512
Lorenzi & Meier, Zürich . . . 130250
Lorenzini, Donatella, Milano . . . 127620
Lorenzo, Dennis de, New York . . . 118137
Lorenzo State Historic Site, Cazenovia . . . 042662
Lorette, Jean-Paul, Nancy . . . 064873
Lorgère, Hervé, Paris . . . 066204
Lori, Marco, Milano . . . 106259
Lorient Collections, Lorient . . . 064006
Lorin & Kristy, Singapore . . . 109834
Loriot, Jean-Claude, Fitilieu . . . 062866
Lorizon, Paris . . . 100626
Lorke, Edo, Trier . . . 074097
Lorn Museum, Ledaig . . . 039946
Lorne Antiques, Lorne . . . 056115
Lorne Scots Regimental Museum, Brampton . . . 005133
Lornoy, A., Bruxelles . . . 058022
Lornyon, Budapest . . . 074694
Lorra, G., Marl, Westfalen . . . 072466
Lorrai, Eric, Marseille . . . 064369
Lorraine, Genk . . . 058162
Lorraine's Antiques and Collectables, Yarragon . . . 056901
Lorraine's Collectibles, Saint Louis . 092270
Lorre, Zwolle . . . 078891
Lorrie, Albuquerque . . . 087408
Lortal, Jean, Saint-Mandé . . . 067619
Lorthois, Catherine, Confolens . . . 062460
Los Alamos County Historical Museum, Los Alamos . . . 045408
Los Angeles Antiques, Los Angeles 089827
Los Angeles Antiques Show, Santa Monica . . . 094000
Los Angeles Art Association, West Hollywood . . . 054850
Los Angeles Art Exchange, Los Angeles . . . 116825
Los Angeles Artcore, Los Angeles . . 116826
Los Angeles Artcore Center, Los Angeles . . . 116827
Los Angeles Asian and Tribal Art Show, Santa Monica . . . 094001
Los Angeles Center for Photographic Studies, Los Angeles . . . 045439
Los Angeles Contemporary Exhibitions, Los Angeles . . . 045440
Los Angeles County Museum of Art, Los Angeles . . . 045441
Los Angeles Craft and Folk Art Museum, Los Angeles . . . 045442
Los Angeles Fine Art Gallery, West Hollywood . . . 120398
Los Angeles Interior Design and Antiques Show, Santa Monica . . . 094002
Los Angeles Maritime Museum, San Pedro . . . 047919
Los Angeles Modernism Show, Santa Monica . . . 094003
Los Angeles Municipal Art Gallery, Los Angeles . . . 045443
Los Angeles Museum of the Holocaust, Los Angeles . . . 045444
Los Angeles Photo Group, Los Angeles . . . 054851, 116828
Los Angeles Print Fair, Los Angeles 094004
Los Angeles Printmakers Society, South Pasadena . . . 054852
Los Angeles Rugs and Antiques, Los Angeles . . . 089828
Los Angeles Stripping and Finishing Center, Los Angeles . . . 132265
Los Angeles Valley College Art Gallery, Valley Glen . . . 048739
Los Cachorros, Buenos Aires . . . 136739
Los Mexicanos, Hamburg . . . 103186
Los Nogales Museum, Seguin . . . 048107
Los Tintoretto's, Bucaramanga . . . 098218
Loscorpione, Bari . . . 127114
Loseley House, Guildford . . . 039649
Losenscky, Monika, Westerstede . . 074374
Losert, Günter, Marktredwitz . . . 072463
Loški Muzej, Škofja Loka . . . 034521
Lossiemouth Fisheries and Community Museum, Lossiemouth . . . 040338
Lossnitzer, Carin, Coburg . . . 125433
Lost and Found Books, Indianapolis 142456
Lost Art, Cincinnati . . . 131938
Lost City Art, Washington . . . 120321
Lost City Art, Washington . . . 120322
Lost City Arts, New York . . . 091043
Lost City Museum, Overton . . . 046755
Lost Dutchman, Indianapolis . . . 089317
Lost Eras Antiques, Chicago . . . 088122
Lost & Found Antiques, Oakland . . . 091427
Lost & Foundry Antiques, New Orleans . . . 090579
The Lost Gallery, Strathdon . . . 114512
Lost Nation Casting, New Orleans . 117468
Lost World of Wonders, Milwaukee . 090311
Lostalot-Dutel, de, Valence (Drôme) 121273
Lostwithiel Museum, Lostwithiel . . 040339
Lot Antique, Cahors . . . 061901
Lotempio Antiques, Buffalo 087892, 131859
Løten Bankmuseum, Løten . . . 030999
Loth, Mainz . . . 072396, 121508
Lotherton Hall, Leeds Museums and Galleries, Aberford . . . 038456
Lothon, Mireille, Coulombs . . . 062503
Lothringer 13, München . . . 019078
Lotos, Wien . . . 057489
Lots of Furniture Antiques, Dallas . . 088553
Lots Road Auctions, London . . . 122594
Lotsabooks, Waikato . . . 140665
Lotta Galleria, Kuopio . . . 098752
Lottan Torppa, Lokalahti . . . 009838
Lotte Gallery, Seoul . . . 107267
Lotte Glob, Altnaharra . . . 112502
Lotte World Folk Museum, Seoul . . 027581
Lottermann & Söhne, Mannheim . . 072426
Lotti, Dallas . . . 115907
Lottin, Henriette, Ommeél . . . 065269
Lotton, Chicago . . . 115483
Lotus, Bangkok . . . 083099
Lotus Antiquities, Los Angeles . . . 089829
Lotus Art Gallery, Ho Chi Minh City . 120517
Lotus Collection, San Francisco . . . 092833
Le Lotus d'Eze, Eze . . . 099257
Lotus Galerie, Den Haag . . . 107939
Lotus Gallery, Austin . . . 087593
The Lotus Gallery, Bath . . . 112581
Lotus Gallery, Salt Lake City . . . 092441
Lotus Gallery, Surfers Paradise . . . 095242
Lotus House, Los Angeles . . . 116829
Lotz, Edeltraud & Ulrich, Esslingen . 102713
Lotz, L., Holzheim, Rhein-Lahn-Kreis . . . 071570
Lotz, P.G. de, London . . . 141841
Lotz, Stefan & Marion, Flensburg . . 125641
Lou, Meggie, Long Beach . . . 089643
Lou Carreyrou, Villefranche-du-Périgord . . . 068897
Lou Holtz and Upper Ohio Valley Hall of Fame, East Liverpool . . . 043576
Lou Solei, Lavey-Village . . . 111636
Loubatières, Francis, Portet-sur-Garonne . . . 133692
Loudean, Memphis . . . 090085
Louden-Henritze Archaeology Museum, Trinidad State Junior College, Trinidad . . . 048612
Loudoun Mansion, Philadelphia . . . 046957
Loudoun Museum, Leesburg . . . 045230
Lough Cutra Castle Antiques, Gort . 074976
Louhisaaren Kartanolinna, Askainen 009461
Loui, P., Krummsee . . . 103801
Louie, Harry F., San Francisco . . . 132895
Louie's Rock-n-Reels, Albuquerque 087409
Les Louis, Peymeinade . . . 066787
Louis, Françoise, Cogolin . . . 062386
Louis, James, Domme . . . 062711
Louis, René, Caen . . . 061878
Louis' Antiques, Wembley . . . 056812

Louis Couperus Museum, Den Haag 029432
Louis d'Or, Monaco 077612
Louis E. May Museum, Fremont . . . 044076
Louis H. and Lena Firn Grover Museum, Shelbyville 048143
Louis Philippe, Nantes . . . 064932, 099809
Louis Spohr-Gedenk- und Forschungsstätte, Museum der Geschichte des Violinspiels, Kassel 018193
Louis Tussaud Wax Museum, København 008975
Louis Tussaud's Waxworks Museum, Niagara Falls 006011
Louisa County Historical Museum, Louisa 045480
Louisa's Antiques, Hobart 055996
Louisburg College Art Gallery, Louisburg 045481
Louise Wells Cameron Art Museum, Wilmington 049213
Louisiana Arts and Science Center, Baton Rouge 042044
Louisiana Association of Museums, Baton Rouge 054853
Louisiana Auction Exchange, Baton Rouge 122812
Louisiana Children's Museum, New Orleans 046258
Louisiana Country Music Museum, Marthaville 045710
Louisiana Museum of Modern Art, Humlebæk 008938
Louisiana Naval War Memorial U.S.S. Kidd, Baton Rouge 042045
Louisiana Old State Capitol, Center for Political and Governmental History, Baton Rouge 042046
Louisiana State Exhibit Museum, Shreveport 048159
Louisiana State Museum, New Orleans 046259
Louisiana State Museum, Patterson 046844
Louisiana State University Museum of Art, Baton Rouge 042047
Louisiana Tech Museum, Ruston . . 047577
Louistine, Ottawa 123798
Louisville Antique Mall, Louisville . . 090008
Louisville Science Center, Louisville 045492
Louisville Slugger Museum, Louisville 045493
Louisville Visual Art Association, Louisville 054854
Louisville Visual Art Museum, Louisville 045494
Louly, Cairo 060453
Lounais-Hämeen Museo, Forssa . . 009483
Lounge Gallery, London 113741
Loup de Sable, Rouen 067277
Loupret, Patrick, Saint-Sever (Landes) 068009, 124920
Loupý, Miroslav, Jilemnice 060030
Lourdel, Hervé, Paris 100627
Lourdes Carcedo, Burgos 110290
Loureiro, Bilbao 080981
Loureiro, Leonardo, Porto Alegre . . 096567
Loureiro Rodriguez, Nelson Manuel, Milano 127621
Louro, Porto 080094
Louro, Maria Sousa, Braga 079809
L'Ours Sam, Montapas 064620
Louth Museum, Louth 040346
Louvencourt, Anaury (de), Paris . . . 100628
Louvre, Montevideo 087328
Louvre, Teheran 074843
Le Louvre des Antiquaires, Paris . . 066205
Le Louvre French Antiques, Dallas . 088554
Louvre Gallery, Los Angeles 089830
Louvre Gallery, Los Angeles 089831
Louvre Gallery, Los Angeles 132266
Louvre's Gallery, Picnic Bay 095070
Louwman Collection - Het National Automobilmuseum, Raamsdonksveer 030051
Loux Bazar, Cairo 060454
Lovački Muzej, Zagreb 007846
Lovart, Montreuil-sous-Bois 099768
Love, Fresno 132081
Love, David, Harrogate 084579
Love, Richard H., Chicago 115484
Love Field Antique Mall, Dallas 088555, 142371
Love Lane Antiques, Nantwich 086036
Love Saves the Day, New York 091044
Lovegrove, Karyn, Los Angeles 116830
Loveland Museum and Gallery, Loveland 045502
Lovely Lane Museum, Baltimore . . 041992
Lovers Lane Antique Market, Dallas 088556
Loves Auction Rooms, Perth 122654
Loves Auctioneers, Richmond 120811
Lovett, Houston 089140
Lovett, Palm Beach 095049
Lovett, Tulsa 120200
Loviisan Kaupungin Museo, Loviisa 009841
Lovriner Stube, Donauwörth 016744
Low, Michael, Forres 084427
Low, Rebecca, Fort Worth 116152
Lowak, J., Austin 114995
Lowe, Atlanta 114899
Lowe & Sons, Chester 083960
Lowe, Los Angeles 116831
Lowe, Loughborough 085854, 131239
Lowe, Santa Monica 119869
Lowe, James, New York 142671
Lowe, Lynn Rae, Tucson 120142
Lowe, Michael, Cincinnati 115640
Lowe, William Fraser, London 131094
Lowe Art Museum, University of Miami, Coral Gables 043147
Lowe & Butcher, London 131095
The Lowe Gallery at Hudson Guild, New York 046357
Lowell Damon House, Wauwatosa . 049018
Lowell National Historical Park, Lowell 045506
Lowell Telecommunications Corporation Museum, Lowell 045507
Lowenstein, Diana, Miami 117107
Lower, Graham, Flimwell 084413
Lower Cape Fear Historical Society Museum, Wilmington 049214
Lower Columbia College Fine Arts Gallery, Longview 045400
Lower East Side Tenement Museum, New York 046358
Lower Fort Garry, Selkirk 006439
Lower House Fine Antiques, Redditch 086341, 131406
Lower Methil Heritage Centre, Lower Methil 040348
Lower Nupend Gallery, Malvern . . . 114036
Lowes Court Gallery, Egremont . . . 113014
Lowestoft and East Suffolk Maritime Museum, Lowestoft 040350
Lowestoft Museum, Lowestoft 040351
Lowewood Museum, Hoddesdon . . 039759
Lowndes County Museum, Valdosta 048729
Lowood Antiques, Lowood 056118
Lowrence, West Hollywood 093484
The Lowry Gallery, Salford 040942
Lowy, Julius, New York 132494
Loxton District Historical Village, Loxton 001198
Loy, Rastede 104658
Loy, Versmold 074199
Loy, Dieter, Bad Rothenfelde 069360
Loyal Edmonton Regiment Military Museum, Edmonton 005399
Loyal Heights Upholstery Shop, Seattle 132940
Loyal Upholstery Shop, Philadelphia 132626
Loyalist Cultural Centre, Bath 005076
Loyalist House Museum, Saint John 006353
Loyer & Fils, Poissy 066886
Loyola, Salt Lake City 092442
Lozano, Málaga 081422
Lozano, Oscar, México 077577
Lozicarte, San Marino 109670
Lozinguez, Marie-José, Ambert . . . 060792
Ložinský, Aleš, Praha 123991
L.P. Antiques, Walsall 087011
LP Décoration Inter, Tournai 058386
LR Galeria de Arte, Brasília 058463
LRB Antiquities, Brahma Lodge . . . 055535
LS Antiquariaat, Amsterdam 140317
LS Art Curators of Collections, Genève 111481
L.S. Raheja School of Art, Mumbai . 050316
LT Antiques, Baltimore 087687
LTG Gallery, Delhi 105673
Lu, Ee Ge, Singapore 080524
Lu Ju Troupe Xiyuan Art Gallery, Jinan 097859
Lu Xun Museum In Shaoxing, Shaoxing 007253
Lubano, Bordeaux 061630
Lubbe, E., San Francisco 142954
Lubbock Art Association, Lubbock . 054855
Lube, San Antonio 119430
Lube, San Antonio 119431
Luber Galerias, Santander 110751
La Luberonne, Saint-Michel-l'Observatoire 124912
Lubespére, Le Castera 063590
Lubespére, Pierrette, Le Castera . . 063591
Lubicki, Estelle, Paris 066206
Lubie, Castres 062036
Lubin, Jocelyne, Moissac 064581
Lublin, Mary, New York 118138
Lubovnianske Múzeum - Hrad, Stará Lubovňa 034433
Lubovniansky Skanzen, Stará Lubovňa 034434
Lubrano, Gaetano, Roma 076532
Lubrano, Michel, Paris 124731
Lubuskie Muzeum Wojskowe w Zielonej Górze z/s w Drzonowie, Letnica . . 032099
Luca, Lingen 134162
Luca, Zaltbommel 108271
Luca, Frédéric de, Paris 100629
Lucan Antique Show, Lucan 093626
Lucarelli, Irma, Roma 128085
Lucas, Aldbourne 130286
Lucas &Son, Las Vegas 132216
Lucas, Noordhorn 128791
Lucas, Fay, London 085497
Lucas, G.C., Indianapolis 116472
Lucas, Gilles, Pierrelaye 066828
Lucas, Joël, Beauvoir-sur-Mer 061315, 124095
Lucas, Klaus, Sommerhausen 126815
Lucas, Philippe, Lyon 064155, 138175
Lucas, Phyllis, New York 091045
Lucas Palomo, Jose Andres, Madrid 129640
Lucca, Barcelona 080873
Lucca, Lucien, Saint-Ouen 067835
Lucchetti, Virgilio, Roma 128086
Lucchini, Anna Maria, Milano 127622
Lucchini, Aristodemo, Roma 076533
Lucci, I., Torino 128325
Lucciola, Tucson 093245
Luce, Brett, Paris 066207
Luce, Jean-Marc, Crest . . 062562, 124214
Luce & Dintorni, Roma 128087
Luce Gallery, Cornell College, Mount Vernon 046072
Lucente, Antonio, Torino 128326
Le Lucernaire, Paimpol 065330
Lucero, Eduardo, Los Angeles 116832
Luchetta, Daniele, Venezia 106761
Luchmann, Roland, Berlin 125252
Luchou Museum, Luchou 007176
Luchsinger, Hans, Riehen 082743
Luchtvaart Museum Texel, De Cocksdorp 029395
Luchtvaart Museum Twenthe, Enschede 029565
Lucia, Gino, Roma 128088
Lucian, Ene, Brügge, Holstein 070068
Luciani, Lidia, Roma 076534
Lucidi & Pietropaoli, Roma 128089
Lucido, Bad Nenndorf 101678
Lucien-Paris, Nogent-sur-Marne . . 121100
Luciferlag im Kunsthaus Lübeck, Lübeck 134171
Lucinda, Baltimore 115065
Lucioli, Laura, Firenze 127360
Lucioni, Irela y Mario, Lima 079554
Luck, J., Ladbergen 072110
Luck, Rainer, Rosenheim 126737
Luckhard Museum - The Indian Mission, Sebewaing 048097
Luckhurst, Bruce, Bethersden 050802, 130374
Luckhurst, J., Sandgate . . 086511, 131455
Luckman, Coventry 084090, 141542
Luckow, Kai H., Düsseldorf 125538
Lucks, München 072781
Lucky Dog Antiques, Portland 091967
Lucky Draw, Fort Worth 116153
Lucky Find, London 058886
Lucky Find, Saint Paul 092374
Lucky Seven Antiques, Providence . 092045
Lucky Strike Oldwares, Dunolly . . . 055769
Lucky Village, San Antonio 092540
Lucky Village, San Antonio 092541
Luckystar, Milwaukee 117204
Luco Arrue, Pedro Jaime, Valparaíso 059564
Lucoff, K., Los Angeles 116833
Lucrèce, Paris 100630
Lucretius, Bucureşti 140880
Lucullus, New Orleans 090580
Lucullus, New Orleans 090581
Lucy Craft Laney Museum of Black History, Augusta 041899
Lucy Maud Montgomery Birthplace, Charlottetown 005248
Lucy's Attic, Milwaukee 090312
Luda Bērziņa Memoriālais Muzejs, Jūrmala 027697
Ludescher, Gabriele, Krefeld 072075
Ludi-Bretscher, Esther, Neuchâtel . . 141283
Ludion, Gent 133287
Le Ludion, Paris 066208
Ludlow, Paris 066209
Ludlow Museum, Shropshire County Museum, Ludlow 040354
Ludolf Backhuysen Gesellschaft, Kunstverein in Ostfriesland e.V., Emden 053486
Ludopassion, Toulon (Var) 068460
Ludorff, Düsseldorf 102526
Ludvig, Budapest 105529
Ludvika Gammelgård och Gruvmuseum, Ludvika 036436
Ludwig, Rio de Janeiro 058609
Ludwig, Andrea & Verena, Walzenhausen 082900
Ludwig, Bernd, Hohenstein, Untertaunus 139277
Ludwig, Eberhard, München 126411
Ludwig, Franz, Holzminden 071572
Ludwig, Günter, Oberasbach 073136
Ludwig, Jürg, Zizers 082928
Ludwig, Martin, Kulmbach 103807
Ludwig, Rolf, Berlin 138819
Ludwig-Doerfler-Galerie, Schillingsfürst 020023
Ludwig-Forum für Internationale Kunst, Aachen 015422
Ludwig Galerie Schloß Oberhausen, Oberhausen, Rheinland 019390
Ludwig-Gebhard-Museum, Tiefenbach, Oberpfalz 020439
Ludwig-Harms-Haus, Ausstellung und Veranstaltungshaus des Ev.-luth. Missionswerkes in Niedersachsen, Hermannsburg 017888
Ludwig Museum im Deutschherrenhaus, Koblenz 018295
Ludwig-Roselius-Museum für Ur- und Frühgeschichte, Worpswede 020988
Ludwig-Thoma-Haus, Tegernsee . . 020411
Ludwig Wittgenstein-Dauerausstellung, Kirchberg am Wechsel 002126
Ludwika, Sopot 079710
Ludzas Novadpētniecības Muzejs, Ludza 027709
LÜ 14 Antik, Ahrensbök 069118
Lübbe, Bergisch Gladbach 133744

Lübeck, Goch . . . 071021
Lübking, Dorothea, Minden, Westfalen . . . 072548, 104080
Lüchinger, Sankt Gallen . . . 141294
Lück, Laatzen . . . 072108
Lück, Mannheim . . . 126281
Lück, Astrid-Thekla, Malente . . . 072407, 104016
Lücke, Schweinfurt . . . 139722
Lücker, R., Kinheim . . . 071849
Lüddecke, Wilhelm, Chemnitz . . . 070136
Lüdemann, I., Rotenburg, Wümme . 073584
Lüder, Groß Vollstedt . . . 103017
Lüderitz Museum, Lüderitz . . . 029086
Lüders, Axel, Hamburg . . . 139198
Lüdin, Paul, Basel . . . 082152, 111211
Lüdtke, Monika, Bad Münder . . . 125111
Lüers, Günter, Lauterecken . . . 072171
Lüffe, Friedrich-Wilhelm, Bamberg . 069458
Lühikese Jala Galerii, Tallinn . . . 098701
Lühl, Jan & Hélène, Paris . 066210, 100631, 138490
Lühr, Ernst, Oldenburg, Oldenburg . 073205
Lührs, Joachim, Hamburg 071280, 139199
Luen Chai, Hong Kong . . . 059664
Luen Chai, Hong Kong . . . 059665
Lüngen, L., Ehingen, Donau . . . 070515
Lüngen, L., Uttenweiler . . . 074174
Lüpnitz, Berlin . . . 138820
Lüscher, Werner, Basel . . . 129927
Lüssi, Martin, Steckborn . . . 082834
Lütge, Cape Town . . . 110027
Lüth, H.-H., Schobüll . . . 104834
Lüthi, Beat, Basel . . . 082153, 129928
Lüthi, Beat, Bern . . . 082224
Lüthi, Beat, Bern . . . 082225
Lüthi, Monika, Bern . . . 129965
Lüthi, Paul, Biel . . . 111287
Lüthi, Ursula, Bern . . . 082226, 129966
Lüthy, Solothurn . . . 141303
Lütke, Manfred, Leverkusen . . . 072243
Lütt Galerie, Fahrdorf . . . 102723
Lüttfring, B., Bocholt . . . 069877
Lüttgens, Hubert, Aachen . . . 069092
Lüttgens, Klaus, Aachen . . 069093, 125041
Lüttje Koophus, Emden . . . 070553
Lüttmerding, Laszlo, München . . . 072782
Lützau, R. von, Celle . . . 138960
Luez, Beauvais . . . 120920
Lüzinyan Evi, Lefkoşa . . . 008256
Luffman, J., Haslington . . . 084615
Luftfahrt-Museum Laatzen-Hannover, Laatzen . . . 018453
Luftfahrt- und Technik-Museumspark, Merseburg . . . 018916
Luftfahrtausstellung im Alten Straßenbahndepot, Brandenburg an der Havel . . . 016371
Luftfahrttechnisches Museum, Rothenburg, Oberlausitz . . . 019921
Luftwaffenmuseum der Bundeswehr, Berlin . . . 016114
Lugan, Xavier, Lafitte-sur-Lot . . . 063482
Lugans'kyj Chudožnij Muzej, Lugans'k . . . 038331
Lugans'kyj Oblasnyj Krajeznavčyj Muzej, Lugans'k . . . 038332
Lugauer, Carina, München . . . 139531
Lugdunumis, Lyon . . . 064156
Lugert, Peter, Frankfurt am Main . . 133948
Luggage Store, San Francisco . . . 047868
Lugger, Hans, Treglwang . . . 123477
Lughien, Amsterdam . . . 107765
Lugley Street Antiques, Newport, Isle of Wight . . . 086078, 131316
Lugmair, Hans, Wien . . . 137340
Lugmair, Hans, Wien . . . 137341
Lugo & Poiesi, Verona . . . 077008
Lugouqiao Display Center, Beijing . 006991
Luguet, Didier, Montdidier . . . 064669
Luh, W., Trossingen . . . 074106
Luhr, K.-H., Köln . . . 071977
Luhring, Augustine, New York . . . 118139
Luiéve Galeria Arte, Funchal . . . 109255
Luigi, San-Pawl-Il-Bahar . 077529, 128479
Luigi Antiquités, Voiron . . . 069027
Luis E. Peña G. Collection, Santiago de Chile . . . 006927
Luis Muñoz Rivera Museum, Barranquitas . . . 032704
Luiscius, 's-Hertogenbosch . . . 140460
Luisenhütte, Balve . . . 015867
Lujain, Damascus . . . 083063
Luka, Praha . . . 098471
Lukacs & Donath, Roma . . . 076535
Lukas, K., Cuxhaven . . . 070167
Lukas, S., Brno . . . 123951
Lukas Verlag, Berlin . . . 133794
Luke's Antiques, Birmingham . . . 087769
Lula B.'s Antique Mall, Dallas . . . 088557
Lulay, Armin, Schwieberdingen . . . 073780
Luleå Auktionsverk, Luleå . . . 122199
Lullaby, Indianapolis . . . 116473
Lullingstone Roman Villa, Eynsford . 039472
Lulu & Lavigne, Toronto . . . 059235
Lum and Abner Museum and Jot 'Em Down Store, Pine Ridge . . . 047025
Lumb & Sons, Charles, Harrogate . . 084580
Lumbard, Jean, New York . . . 118140
Lumen, Venlo . . . 078845
Lumen Travo, Amsterdam . . . 107766
Lumgair, Irene, San Diego . . . 119524
Lumière, Tokyo . . . 077277
Lumière de l'Oeil, Paris . . 066211, 124732
Lumina Gallery, Malvern, Victoria . . 094777
Luminaires Anciens, Vannes (Morbihan) . . . 068719
Luminaires de Prestige, Fontenay-le-Comte . . . 099268, 124241
Lumma & Nistahl, Ronnenberg . . . 073568, 126733
Lummis Home El Alisal, Los Angeles . . . 045445
Lumsden Heritage Museum, Lumsden . . . 005806
Lun Yee Association, New York . . . 054856, 118141
Luna, Amsterdam . . . 077904
Luna, New York . . . 118142
Luna, Nottingham . . . 086140
Luna, Josue, São Paulo . . . 058722
La Luna Casa y Arte, San Salvador . 098688
Luna Collectibles, Jacksonville . . . 089427
Luna Creazioni, Venezia . . . 076952
Luna Hernandez, Francisco, Málaga 081423
Luna House Museum, Lewiston . . . 045247
Luna Mimbres Museum, Deming . . 043387
La Luna nel Pozzo, Venezia . . . 076953
Lunacy, Philadelphia . . . 091660
Lunadei, Franco, Roma . . . 076536
Lund Bygdemuseum, Moi . . . 031027
Lund & Lund, Klampenborg . . . 098532
Lundar Museum, Lundar . . . 005807
Lundberg, Börje, Rimforsa . . . 122231
Lundell, P., Nykvarn . . . 081888, 122220
Lundgren, Stockholm . . . 081982
Lundin, A., København . . . 060351
Lundmark, Täby . . . 111086
Lundquist, Sten E., Göteborg . . . 141103
Lunds, Victoria . . . 120827
Lunds Konsthall, Lund . . . 036444
Lunds Konsthandel, Lund . . . 081855
Lunds Universitets Antikmuseum, Lund . . . 036445
Lundströmska Gården, Sigtuna . . . 036565
Lundvall, Regina, Stockholm . . . 129868
Lundy's Lane Historical Museum, Niagara Falls . . . 006012
Lune, Pierre de, Liège . . . 058313
Luneau, Michel & Sophia, Pont-Saint-Martin . . . 101040
Lunel, Annie, Beaumont-sur-Sarthe 061264
Lunel, Patrick, Douains . . . 062727
Lunenburg Art Gallery, Lunenburg . 005809
Lung, Robert, Reichenau, Baden . . 126705
Lungauer Heimatmuseum Tamsweg, Tamsweg . . . 002726
Lungauer Landschaftsmuseum, Mauterndorf . . . 002301
Luniddi, Ettore, Roma . . . 128090
Luniver & Co, Montréal . . . 097050
Luniverre Gallery, Paris . . . 100632
L'Univers, Le Mans . . . 063659
Lunkenheimer, Mainz . . . 104003
Lunn, London . . . 085498, 131096
Lunsford, Stephen, Vancouver . . . 137730
Lunt Roman Fort, Baginton . . . 038563
Lunwerg, Madrid . . . 134947
Luohan, Paris . . . 066212
Luonnonhistoriallinen Museo, Porvoo . . . 009994
Luonnontieteellinen Museo, Luonnontieteellinen Keskusmuseo, Helsinki . . . 009552
Luontomuseo, Kokkola . . . 009725
Luontotalo Arkki, Satakunta Museo, Pori . . . 009985
Luopioisten Museo, Luopioinen . . . 009843
Luopioisten Torpparimuseo, Luopioinen . . . 009844
Luostarinmäen Käsityöläismuseo, Turku . . . 010166
Luotsitupa, Uusikaupunki . . . 010195
Luoyang City Folklorish Museum, Luoyang . . . 007179
Luoyang City Museum, Luoyang . . . 007180
Lupe Gallery, London . . . 113742
Luper, T.C., Richmond . . . 119115, 123073
Luperini, Beatrice, Verona . . . 077009
Lupi, Monica, Firenze . . . 075364
Lupi, Monica, Firenze . . . 075365
Lupin, Arsène, Montréal . . . 058974
Lupo, Palermo . . . 106434
Luppo, Antwerpen . . . 057714
Lupton Square Gallery, Honley . . . 113269
Lupu, Jean, Paris . . . 066213
Luquet, Roger, Saint-Maurice-l'Exil 067665
Lura Watkins Museum, Middleton . 045838
Lure Me In, Minneapolis . . . 090375
Lurens, Loviisa . . . 009842
Lurie, Gertrude, Basel . . . 082154
Lury, Thérèse, Fontenais . . . 082372
Lusa, Patricia, Buenos Aires . . . 055221
Lusaka National Museum, Lusaka . 049571
Luscious Conceptions, Windsor . . . 114709
Luseland and Districts Museum, Luseland . . . 005810
Lusenhop, David, Cincinnati . . . 142319
Lusetti, Luca, Brescia . . . 075174
Lush, Auckland . . . 108338
Lush, Jacksonville . . . 089428
Lusher, Nicholas, Hamilton . . . 096424
Lushun Museum, Dalian . . . 007057
Lushun Snakes Dao Natural Museum, Dalian . . . 007058
Lushun Su Jun Mausoleum of Fallen Heroes, Dalian . . . 007059
L'Usine, Menton . . . 064493
Lusk, David, Memphis . . . 116996
Lussan, Régine, Paris . . . 100633
Lust, B.N.J., Amsterdam . . . 077905
Lustinger, H., München . . . 072783
Lusto-Suomen-metsämuseo ja metsätietokeskus, Punkaharju . . . 010004
Lustr'Antic, Saint-Quentin (Aisne) . . 067975
Lustre, Auckland . . . 078961
Lustyk, Louisville . . . 116953
Lutèce, Narbonne . . . 064964
Lutèce, Paris . . . 066214
Lutèce, Paris . . . 138491
Lutèce, Saint-Pierre-Eglise . . . 067958
Lutece, San Francisco . . . 119725
Lutet Toti, Saint-Maur-des-Fossés . 124910
Luther, Heidrun, Dinslaken 102377, 133867
Luther, H.M., New York . . . 091046
Luther, Michael, London . . . 085499
Luther, Reinhard, Duisburg . . . 102584
Luther, Tracy, Saint Paul . . . 123090
Luther Burbank Home, Santa Rosa . 047992
Luther-Stube Mansfeld, Mansfeld, Südharz . . . 018811
Lutheran Brotherhood Gallery, Minneapolis . . . 045916
Lutherhaus, Eisenach . . . 016922
Lutherhaus Wittenberg, Stiftung Luthergedenkstätten in Sachsen-Anhalt, Lutherstadt Wittenberg . . . 018761
Lutherkirche und Lutherzimmer im Dorfgemeinschaftshaus, Möhra . . 018969
Lutherstube, Möhra . . . 018969
Lutnia, Łódź . . . 109011
Luton Museum and Art Gallery, Luton . . . 040357
Luttár, Budapest . . . 105530
Lutterbeck, H., Ennigerloh . . . 102629
Lutterworth, Cambridge . . . 135132
Lutz, Delft . . . 107889
Lutz, A., Windeck . . . 139859
Lutz, Alexandra & Egon, Trier . . . 126915
Lutz, Edmond, Zürich . . . 082997, 130251
Lutz, G., Eckersdorf . . . 125568
Lutz, Hans-Rudolf, Zürich . . . 135093
Lutz, Martin, Schrobenhausen . . . 126780
Lutz, Yvan, Trouville-sur-Mer . . . 068637
Lutz Children's Museum, Manchester . . . 045615
Lutz Custom Upholstery, Fresno . . . 132082
Lutz Mountain Meeting House, Moncton . . . 005898
Lutz & Thalmann, Zürich . . . 112142
Lutze, Bernd, Friedrichshafen . . . 102885
Luusuan Kylämuseo, Luusua . . . 009847
Luvane, Walsall . . . 114642
Luvian Kotiseutumuseo, Luvia . . . 009848
Lux, Koblenz . . . 121467
Lux, Münster . . . 072919
Lux, Neuleiningen . . . 104411
Lux, Kenneth, New York . . . 118143
Lux Art, Köln . . . 103674
Luxford, Rosedale . . . 056552
Luxl, Peter, Wien . . . 057490
Luxor Gallery, Caracas . . . 093537
Luxor Museum of Ancient Art, Al-Uqsur . . . 009271
Luxor Trading, Houston . . . 089141
Luz, Denver . . . 116018
Luz, Jan de, New York . . . 091047
Luz, Manfred, Ammerbuch . . . 101576
Luz, Paula, Braga . . . 079810
La Luz de Jesus, Los Angeles . . . 116834
Luz Gallery, Makati . . . 079560, 108828
Luza Acht, Lübben . . . 103955
Luza Acht, Lübbenau . . . 103957, 121504
Luzán, Bremen . . . 102253
Luzerne County Historical Museum, Wilkes-Barre . . . 049174
Luzernische Glasmalerei, Luzern . . 111697
Álvarez García, Félix, León . . . 081172
Álvarez Rojo, Berango . . . 129418
Lvivs'ka Galereja Mystectv, Lviv . . . 038344
Lvivs'kyj Istoryčnyj Muzej, Lviv . . . 038345
Lvivs'kyj Muzej Istorii Religii, Lviv . 038346
L.V.S. Antiquités, Paris . . . 066215
Lyall, Alexander, Long Melford . . . 085835, 131229
Lycée Technique des Arts et Métiers, Luxembourg . . . 050524
The Lyceum - Alexandria's History Museum, Alexandria . . . 041646
Lyceum Antique Store, Shanghai . . 059757
Lydd Town Museum, Lydd . . . 040362
Lydia, Kriz-Binarova, Wien 095892, 123513
Lydia Koidulu Memoriaalmuuseum, Pärnu . . . 009383
Lydiard Antiques, Ballarat . . . 055434
Lydiard Furniture and Antiques, Ballarat . . . 055435
Lydiard House, Swindon . . . 041175
Lydia's Jewelry, San Francisco . . . 092834
Lydon, Chicago . . . 115485
Lye Antique Furnishings, Lye . . . 085874
Lyet, J.P, Villeurbanne . . . 068967
Lyktan, Lund . . . 141123
Lyle, Selkirk . . . 135302
Lyle-Tapley Shoe Shop and Vaughn Doll House, Peabody Essex Museum, Salem . . . 047740
Lylyn Viestivarikon Museo, Lyly . . . 009849

Lyman Allyn Museum of Art, New London 046238
Lyman House Memorial Museum, Hilo 044551
Lyme Academy College of Fine Arts, Old Lyme 051880
Lyme Art Association, Old Lyme . . . 054857
Lyme-Bay Auction Galleries, Seaton 122690
Lyme Hall, Disley 039241
Lyme Regis Philpot Museum, Lyme Regis 040365
Lymington Antiques Centre, Lymington 085878, 141928
Lyn and Exmoor Museum, Lynton . . 040368
Lynch, Florence, New York 118144
Lynch, John, Norfolk 142705
Lynch, Mary, Colchester 130600
Lynch, Merrill, Dallas 088558
Lynchburg Fine Arts Center, Lynchburg 045526
Lynchburg Museum System, Lynchburg 045527
Lyndale House Antiques, Minneapolis 090376
Lynden, San Francisco 119726
Lynden Pioneer Museum, Lynden . . 045531
Lyndhurst, Tarrytown 048505
Lyndhurst Antiques Centre, Lyndhurst 085884
Lyndon, Louisville 090009
Lyndon B. Johnson National Historical Park, Johnson City 044869
Lyndon Baines Johnson Museum, Austin 041931
Lyndon House Art Center, Athens . . 041834
Lynette, Long Beach 089644
Lyngby Antikvariat, Kongens Lyngby 137904
Lynge & Søn, København 137899
Lynn Canyon Ecology Centre, North Vancouver 006044
Lynn Lake Mining Town Museum, Lynn Lake 005811
Lynn Museum, Lynn 045533
Lynnhaven House, Association for the Preservation of Virginia Antiquities, Virginia Beach 048797
Lynnwood Arts Centre, Simcoe 006477
Lyon, Kansas City 116580
Lyon, Oliver, Malmesbury 085901
Lyon, Richard, Hurstpierpoint 135161, 141686
Lyon County Historical Society Museum, Marshall 045701
Lyon County Museum, Emporia . . . 043704
Lyon Scène Productions, Villeurbanne 101482
Lyonel-Feininger-Galerie, Quedlinburg 019688
Lyonnet, Aline, Saint-Didier-au-Mont-d'Or 067426
Lyons Corner House, Northwood . . 114158
The Lyons Redstone Museum, Lyons 045534
Lyra, Amsterdam 077906
La Lyre, Rabat 077694
Lys Antique, Antibes-Juan-les-Pins 060924
Le Lys Antique, Louhans 064011
Lys Art - Kunsthandel Schloss Lilienhof, Berlin 069694
Lys d'Or, Cogolin 062387
Le Lys d'Or, Grenoble 063068
Lyse Antic, Saint-Lye 067597
Lysekils Auktionsbyrå, Lysekil 122203
Lysoňkovi, Stanislav a Marta, Brno . 059980
Lyth Arts Centre, Lyth 040369
Lytham Hall, Lytham Saint Anne's . 040370
Lytham Heritage Centre, Lytham Saint Anne's 040371
Lytham Lifeboat Museum, Lytham Saint Anne's 040372
Lytham Saint Annes Art Society, Lytham Saint Anne's 054424
Lytham Windmill Museum, Lytham Saint Anne's 040373
Lythe Cottage Antiques, Lythe 085889
Lyttelton Historical Museum, Christchurch 030465
Lyttleton Gallery, North Melbourne . 094976
Lytton Museum, Lytton 005812
Lyytikäinen, Lahti 060609
Lyytikäinen, Jorma, Helsinki 124047
Lyzon, Nashville 117361
M.., Kraków 108962
M., Agnès, Rueil-Malmaison 067321
M-Ars, Kranj 109946
M-Art Arnhem, Arnhem 107855
M-Art Prestige, Maribor . . 080662, 109991, 129290
M & B Antiques, Kansas City 089508
M B Antiquités, Marseille 064370
M B G Antiques, Newark-on-Trent .086053, 131300
M. Christina Geis Gallery, Georgian Court College, Lakewood 045129
M & D Furniture, London 131097
M de G, Paris 066216
M F Husain's Museum of Art and Cinema, Hyderabad 022159
M G Artes, Fortaleza 058473
M & G Upholstery, Houston 132130
M% Gallery, Cleveland 115725
M & K, Praha 098472
M K Art Foundation, Ahmedabad . . 105597
M L Vende Tutti, Madrid 129641
M & M, Barcelona 129361
M & M, Edmonton 058836
M&M, Vrhnika 080669
M & M Antiques, Blackheath 055509
M & M Books, Calgary 137624
M & M Coins, Buffalo 087893
M-Oriental Art, Los Angeles 116835
M & P Antiek, Rotterdam 078731
M & S Antiquitäten, Ahrensburg . . .069121, 125050
M & S Curio Shop, Houston 089142
M&S Rare Books, Providence 142817
M & S Sales, Miami 090201
M. Sarians Museum, Erevan 000684
M. & V. Anticuario, Medellín 059925
M & W Graphics, New York 118145
M16 Studios, Fyshwick 094574
Ma, C.L., Hong Kong 059666
Ma Bohème, Orcet 065279
Ma Boutique, Toulon (Var) 068461
Ma Maison, Paris 066217
Ma Maison de Papier, Bruxelles . . . 137448
Ma Tasse de Thé, Vitry-le-François 069013
Maack, Salt Lake City 119354
Maali, Mia, Henley Brook 094634
Maanmittausmuseo, Helsinki 009553
Maarten van Rossum Museum, Zaltbommel 030372
Maas, Aalsmeer 140265
Al-Maas, Sharjah 083217
Maas- en Scheepvaartmuseum, Maasbracht 029888
Maas en Waal, Druten 128654
Maas en Waals Museum 1939-1945, Winssen 030339
The Maas Gallery, London 085500
Maas Gallery, London 113743
Maaser, Klaus, Wuppertal 105357
Maasland, Maastricht 140494
Maaß, Jörg, Berlin 101980
Maaß, Maria, Lübeck 072329
Maassen, Ralf-Dieter, Blieskastel . . 125339
Maatilamuseo Luhdinsola, Naantali 009894
Mabee-Gerrer Museum of Art, Shawnee 048135
Mabel Larson Fine Arts Gallery, Austin Peay State University, Clarksville 042955
Mabel's, Cleveland 131966
Mabillon, Aix-en-Provence 098789
Måbødalen Kulturlandskapsmuseum, Eidfjord 030814
Mabry-Hazen House, Knoxville 045041
M.A.C, Paris 066218
Mc Buffers, Cleveland 131967
The Mac Gallery, Dallas 115908
Mac Humble, Bradford-on-Avon . . . 083631
McAdams, Alice, New York 091048
McAdams, Christopher, Oakland . . . 132572
Macalester College Art Gallery, Saint Paul 047702
McAllen International Museum, McAllen 045539
McAllister House Museum, Colorado Springs 043057
McAnthony, Fort Worth 116154
Macari, Ernesto, Roma 128091
MacArthur, Ballarat 094201
Macassar, Dijon 062668
Macau Artes Antigas, Rio de Janeiro 058610
Macau Museum of Art, Macau 007184
Macau Wine Museum, Macau 007185
Macaulay Heritage Park, Picton . . . 006147
Macaulay Museum of Dental History, Charleston 042739
McAuley, Currajong 094446
McAuley, Marjorie, Greyabbey 084533
McBains, Exeter 084359
McBride, Albuquerque 131746
Mcbride, Austin 087594
McBride, J. Michael, Omaha 118712
McBride, Will, Berlin 133795
MacBride Museum, Whitehorse . . . 006812
McBurnie & Cutler, Toronto 137711
McCabe, Gerard, Adelaide 055315
Maccacaro, Egidio, Verona 077010
McCaig Museum, Oban 040635
McCall, Betsy, Denver . . . 088710, 132041
McCalls, Aberdeen 083237
McCalls, Aberdeen 083238
MacCallum More Museum, Chase City 042772
McCallum Museum, Sibley 048169
McCallum's Museum, Dauphin 005329
McCanse, Stephen, Toronto 097323
MacCarone, New York 118146
McCarron, Paul, New York 118147
McCarthy, Cork 074877
McCarthy, Ian, Clutton . . . 084039, 130591
McCarthy, Patrick, Los Angeles . . . 116836
McCartneys, Ludlow 122607
McCarty, Philadelphia 091661
McCaughen & Burr, Saint Louis . . . 119222
Macchi, Pisa 106467
Macchiaroli, Gaetano, Napoli 134644
McClain, David, Chicago 088123
McClain & Co., Robert, Houston . . . 116358
McClellan, Judith, Houston 089143, 122910
McClelland, Camberwell 094359
McClelland, Joshua, Melbourne . . . 056194
McClelland Gallery, Langwarrin . . . 001172
McClelland & Stewart, Toronto 133326
Macclesfield Silk Museum, Macclesfield 040377
McClure, Tulsa 132998
McClurg Mansion, Westfield 049112
McColl Shiraz, Charlotte 115297
McCollum-Chidester House Museum, Camden 042574
McCone County Museum, Circle . . . 042933
MacConnal-Mason, London 085501, 113744, 131098
McConnell Mansion, Moscow 046046
McCool, Richmond 119116
McCord and District Museum, McCord 005814
McCord Museum, Montréal 005930
McCormack, R. & C., Dublin 074930
McCormick, Anne, Potts Point 056483
McCormick, Thomas, Chicago 115486
McCormick, Tim, Woollahra 056872, 137143
McCormick Gallery, Midland College, Midland 045852
McCoy, Sacramento 123079
McCoy, Mary Helen, Birmingham . . 087770
McCoy House, Lewistown 045254
McCrae, McCrae 094749
McCrae Homestead Museum, McCrae 001199
McCrae House, Guelph Museums, Guelph 005557
McCrossin's Mill Museum, Uralla . . 001580
McCulloch, John, Felixstowe 084396
McCulloch Campbell, Eden 094503
Macculloch Hall Historical Museum, Morristown 046035
McCulloch House Museum and Hector Exhibit Centre, Pictou 006149
McCullough, Theresa, London 113745
McCully, Honolulu 088964
McCune, Stephen, San Antonio . . . 132817
McCutchen Overland Inn, McCutchenville 045545
McCutcheon, John, Columbus 115789
McDade Museum, McDade 045546
MacDonald, Gosforth, Tyne and Wear 084487, 130736
Macdonald, Newcastle-upon-Tyne . 114125
McDonald, San Francisco 142955
MacDonald, Donald, Glasgow 141623
McDonald, Joy, London . . 085502, 131099
Macdonald, Magdalene, Rüthen . . . 104784
McDonald, Mary, Albuquerque 114801
McDonald, Rosemary, Surry Hills . . 123312
Macdonald Stewart Art Centre, Guelph 005558
Das McDonald's Junior-Tüten & Pin Museum, Wiener Neustadt 003034
McDonnell, Bridget, Carlton South . 094375
McDonnell, Derek, Potts Point 056484
McDonnell, Nadia, Hampton 055951
McDonnell, Stephen, Dun Laoghaire 074964
McDonough, Pittsburgh 091839
McDougal, A., New York 118148
McDougall Mill Museum, Renfrew . 006271
Macdougalls, Breakish 122431
McDowell, Rosalie, Denver 088711
McDowell House and Apothecary Shop, Danville 043298
Macé, Andrée, Paris 066219
Macé, Christophe, Biarritz 061467
Macé, Roland, Verneuil-sur-Avre . . 068781
Mace, Victor, Milton 094856
Macedo, Manoel, Belo Horizonte . . 096469
Macedon Historical Society Museum, Macedon 045547
Macedonian Museum of Contemporary Art, Thessaloniki 021496
McElwain, Saint Louis 119223
McEvoy & Assoc., John, San Francisco 119727
McEwan, Ballater . 083373, 130325, 141390
McEwan, Garry, Saint Kilda, Victoria 095173
McFadden, Tulsa 093318
McFaddin-Ward House, Beaumont . 042087
McFarland Historical Society Museum, McFarland 045548
McFarland House, Niagara Falls . . . 006013
Macfarlane, Salt Lake City 092443
McFee, Indianapolis 116474
McGahan, Sean, Dublin 074931
McGahern, Ottawa 137676
McGaw, Bruce, West Nyack 135523
McGeary, Bruxelles 096230
McGill-Duncan, Castle Douglas . . . 112825
McGillis Pioneer Home, Saint Victor 006398
McGilloway Gallery, Londonderry . . 113987
McGilvery, Laurence, La Jolla 135374
McGinnis, Cheryl, New York 118149
McGinnis, John, Louisville 090010, 122952
McGlinn, Jack, Philadelphia 091662
McGlynn, Mike, Bunratty 074867
MacGowan, Saskatoon 059100
McGrath, B.J., Bathurst 055453
McGrath, Earl, New York 118150
McGrath & Braun, Denver 116019
McGraw-Hill, Maidenhead 135278
McGraw-Hill, New York 135439
Macgregor, Saint Andrews 122677
MacGregor, Nicola Ann, Firenze . . . 127361
Macgregor Museum, Harare 049581

McGregor Museum and Duggan Cronin Gallery, Kimberley 034662
McGregor Wright, Wellington 108627, 128976
McGriff, Dallas 088559
McGroarty Cultural Art Center, Tujunga 048649
McGuire, Houston 116359
McGuire, San Francisco 092835
Macha, Mary, Subiaco 056647
Avelar Machado, Lisboa 140842
Machado, Rio de Janeiro 058611
Machado, Rio de Janeiro 058612
Machado de Jesus, Lisboa 121938
McHale, Gaines, Baltimore 087688
McHale, Michael J., Baltimore 087689
Machan Museum, La Grange 045063
Machan Museum, Lagrange 045094
McHardy, London 113746
MacHenry, Newtownabbey 086085
McHenry County Historical Society Museum, Union 048689
McHenry Museum, Modesto 045956
Macheret, Michel, Langres 063525
Macheret, Yannick & Michel, Paris . 066220
Macherez, Catherine, Nice 065106
Machida-shiritsu Hakubutsukan Machida City Museum, Machida 026778
Machida-shiritsu Kokusai Hanga Bijutsukan, Machida 026779
Machin Chouette, Québec 059072
Machine-Age Corporation, Boston . 087833
Machine Age Gallery, Geelong 055866
Machine Age Modern, Toronto 059236
Machine Age Wonders, Vancouver . 059378
MACHmit! Museum für Kinder, Berlin 016115
Macho, Wolfgang, Wien 057491
Machoi, Monika, Schönow 073717
Machoïr-Bailly, Versailles 121279
Machold, Bremen 070034, 125391
Machon, Antonio, Madrid 110562
McHugh, Richmond 132718
Macias, Christina, Honolulu 116224
Macias, Christina, Honolulu 116225
Macias, Manuel, Madrid 110563
Macia's Photography, Los Angeles . 116837
Macik, Paula, Charlotte 087963
McIlreavy, Alan & Fiona, Buderim . . 136831
MacInnes, Don, Wellington 079331
McIntire Department of Art, University of Virginia, Charlottesville 051100
Macintosh, Patrick & Elona, Sherborne 086579
McIntosh County Historical Society Museum, Ashley 041814
McIntosh Gallery, Kingussie 113331
McIntosh Gallery, London 005791
McIntyre Gallery, Regina 097177
McIntyre Street Gallery, Regina . . . 006257
Macio, Bordeaux 099006
McIvor, John & Fran, New Lambton 056326
Mack, Houston 132131
Mack, Seattle 119956
Mack, Christian, Gordes 063018
Mack, David, Branksome . 083645, 130429
Mack, D.J. & S.A., Carlton, New South Wales 055632
Mack, E.A., Baltimore 087690
Mack, Eva, Stuttgart 104996
Mack, Toni, Eglfing 125571
Maçka Mezat, İstanbul 112333
Maçka Mezat, İstanbul 122380
Maçka Sanat Galerisi, İstanbul 112334
McKay, Unley 056768
McKay, Hamish, Wellington 108628
McKay, J., New Town 137027
McKays Museum, Bowsman 005125
Macke, A., Hannover 103290
McKechnie Institute, Girvan 039543
McKee, Casino 055641
Mackenbach, J.P., Den Haag 078215
McKenna & Co., London 085503
McKenna, North Adelaide 056356
McKenzie, Claremont 094402
McKenzie, New York 118151
MacKenzie, Regina 097178
McKenzie, J.W., Ewell 141603
McKenzie, Robert, Cannon Hill 055624
Mackenzie and District Museum, Mackenzie 005815
MacKenzie Art Gallery, Regina 006258
MacKenzie Heritage Printery Museum, Queenston 006234
Mackenzie House, Toronto 006610
Mackenzie King Estate, Ottawa . . . 006103
Mackenzie & Smith, Ludlow 085868, 131244
Mackenzie Thorpe Arthaus, Richmond, North Yorkshire 114305
Mackey, Denver 116020
Mackey, Houston 116360
McKinley Museum and McKinley National Memorial, Canton 042607
McKinn, Austin 087595
McKinney Avenue Antique Market, Dallas 088560
McKinnon, Karen, Charlotte 087964
McKinnon & Gibbons, Deloraine . . . 055746
McKissick Museum, University of South Carolina, Columbia 043082
Macklin, Terence, Whitstable 114687
Macklin and District Museum, Macklin 005816
Macklowe, New York 091049
McKnight, Michael, Tampa 093140
Mackowitz, Felix, Innsbruck 123393
Macktown Living History Site and Whitman Trading Post, Rockton 047512
McLain & Brash, Pittsburgh 132670
Mclaine, Mark, Toronto 059237
Mclaren, Houston 089144
MacLaren Art Centre, Barrie 005069
Maclaren Roberts, Mosman 094893
McLarty Treasure Museum, Vero Beach 048772
Maclaurin Art Gallery, Ayr 038560
MacLean, London 113747
McLean-Alanreed Area Museum, McLean 045561
McLean County Art Association, Bloomington 054858
McLean County Arts Center, Bloomington 042260
McLean County Historical Society Museum, Washburn 048875
McLean County Museum of History, Bloomington 042261
McLean Mill, Port Alberni 006169
McLean Museum and Art Gallery, Greenock 039640
McLeavey, Peter, Wellington 079332
Macleay Museum, Sydney 001516
McLellan Galleries, Glasgow 039563
McLeod, Braidwood 094276
McLeod, Paddington, New South Wales 056419
MacLeod, Vancouver 137731
McLoughlin, Paul & Linda, Strathalbyn 056637
McLurg Museum, Wilkie 006820
McMahon, Gene, Seattle 119957
McMahons, Keith, Seaford 056581
MacMaison, New Orleans 090582
McManus Galleries, Dundee 039308
McMaster Museum of Art, Hamilton 005594
McMichael, Richmond 123074
McMichael Canadian Art Collection, Kleinburg 005722
Mcmillan, Omaha 091574
McMinn County Living Heritage Museum, Athens 041841
McMorland, J&J, Gourock 113142
McMullen Museum of Art, Boston College, Chestnut Hill 042811
McMullens, Los Angeles 089832
McMurray, Avoca 094185
McMurtrey, Houston 116361
McNamara House Museum, Victoria 048782
McNaught, Hamilton 096921
McNaughtan, Edinburgh 141581
McNee, Tracey, Glasgow 113120
McNeill, Radlett 114292
MacNiles, Buenos Aires 055222
McNoon, Los Angeles 089833
Macon, Jacques, Ferrières (Loiret) . 062857
Macon, Jacques, Montargis 064623
Macon County Museum Complex, Decatur 043352
Macondo, Pittsburgh 118939
Macoun, Dietrich, Hamburg 071281, 103187, 125829
MacPheadris/Warner House, Portsmouth 047187
McPhee, G.D., Prahran 056498
McPheeters, Richard, Tulsa 093319
McPherson & Co, Kingston 135373
McPherson, R. & G., London 085504, 131100
McPherson College Gallery, McPherson 045571
McPherson County Old Mill Museum, Lindsborg 045327
McPherson Museum, McPherson . . 045572
MacPherson's Mill and Farm Homestead, New Glasgow 005998
McPhillips Street Gallery, Winnipeg 097590
McQuade, Kilbarchan 084840
McRae, Neil, Auchterarder 112532
MacRobert Gallery, Stirling 041104
Macroom Museum, Macroom 022831
Macrorie House Museum, Pietermaritzburg 034699
Macrorie Museum, Macrorie 005817
Macrosun, Saint Louis 119224
Macrosun, Saint Louis 119225
Mac's Antique Car Museum, Tulsa . 048655
Macsai, Janos, Budapest 127076
McSpadden & Haskell, Chicago . . . 088124
McSwain, Charlotte 087965, 131872
McSweeney, Gerald, Midleton 139976
MacSwiney Memorial Museum, Kilmurry 022813
McTague, Harrogate 084581
McTague of Harrogate, Harrogate . . 113193
McTear, Glasgow 122517
Macula, Paris 133647, 135715
Macula, Santa Cruz de Tenerife . . . 110744
McWane Center, Birmingham 042224
McWhirter, London 085505
Mad Art, Saint Louis 119226
Mad Dog and the Pilgrim Booksellers, Lander 142480
MAD Gallery, Lancefield 094723
Mad Parade, Chicago 088125
Madaba, Paris 100634
Madaba Archaeology Museum, Ajloun 027358
Madaire, Thierry, Sainte-Agathe-la-Bouteresse 068047
Madalyn, Norfolk 091388
Madam Brett Homestead, Beacon . 042070
Madame Tussaud's, London 040214
Madame Tussaud's Amsterdam, Amsterdam 029198
Madame Tussaud's Wax Museum, New York 046359
Madames, Mice & More, Indianapolis 089318
Madang Museum, Yomba 031437
Madara Nacionalen Istoriko-archeologičeski Rezervat, Madara 004746
Madcap Antiques, Toronto 059238
Maddermarket Antiques, Norwich . 086119
Maddick, Chicago 115487
Maddi's Gallery, Charlotte 115298
Made By Hand, Ashbourne 112524
Made From Australia Galleries, Deakin 094469
Made Gallery, Carlton North 094374
Made in France, Houston 089145
Made in France, Nashville 090466
Made in Japan, Hyde Park 056008
Made in Nippon, Auckland 078962
Made in the Murray Mallee, Swan Hill 056660
Madec, Eliane, Fécamp 121004
Madel, Pierre, Paris 066221
La Madeleine, Bouin 061681
La Madeleine, Cabourg 061849
La Madeleine, Abri sous Roche Archéosite d'un Village Troglodytique, Tursac 015067
Madeline Island Historical Museum, La Pointe 045074
Mader, Milwaukee 117205
Mader, Brigitta, Wien 057492
Madera County Museum, Madera . . 045574
Maderas Gallery, Tucson 120143
Madert, Mehring 104052
Madhavan Nair Foundation, Edapally 022109
Madhouse, Rotorua 108553
Madhouse Fun Furnishings, Buffalo 087894
Madhya Pradesh Tribal Research and Development Institute, Bhopal . . . 022034
Madison, Atlanta 114900
Madison Art Center, Madison 045591
Madison Avenue Antique Mall, Memphis 090086
Madison Avenue Galleries, Toledo . 093179
Madison Children's Museum, Madison 045592
Madison County Historical Museum, Edwardsville 043618
Madison County Historical Society Museum, Winterset 049263
Madison Historical Society Museum, Madison 045575
Madison-Morgan Cultural Center Collection, Madison 045577
Madison Press Books, Toronto 133327
Madliger-Schwab, Zürich 141350
Madoi, Alessandro, Parma 127854
Madonas Novadpētniecības un Mākslas Muzejs, Madona 027711
Madonna House Pioneer Museum, Combermere 005289
Madonna Massimo, Palermo 076157
Madoura, Vallauris 101420
Madras Christian College Museum, Chennai 022059
Madres Dominicanas - Monasterio Sancti Spiritus, Toro 035937
Madrières, Olivier, Laguepie 063489
Madrigal Center, Muntinlupa 108846
La Madrileña, Madrid 081336
Madureira, Maria, Porto Alegre 096568
Madurodam, Den Haag 029433
Mäder, Bern 082227
Mäder, Franz, Basel 111212, 134984
Maeder & Studer, Biel 111288
Mädi's Antiquitätenlädeli, Thun . . . 082852
Maeght, Montrouge 099770, 133500
Maeght Musée, Paris 013600
Maegle, Rudolf, Wien 095893, 137342
Mährisch-Schlesisches Heimatmuseum, Klosterneuburg 002155
Maejima Memorial Museum, Joetsu 026600
Maek, Hyang, Daegu 107187
Maek, Hyang, Daegu 107188
Mäkelänkadun Antikvariaatti, Helsinki 137951
Mäkilän Taidemakasiini, Turku 060642
Mälsåkers Slott, Stallarholmen 036609
Mäntsälän Kotiseutumuseo, Mäntsälä 009850
Mäntyharjun Museo, Mäntyharju . . 009853
Mäntyviidan Kijakauppa, Helsinki . . 137952
Märchenhain Gföhl, Gföhl 001893
Märchenhaus und Heimatmuseum Ottenschlag, Ottenschlag 002405
Märchenofen, Fachmuseum Gußeiserne Öfen/Feuerstättenmuseum, Neu-Ulm 019216
Maere, Jan de, Bruxelles . 058023, 096231
Märkisches Museum, Kulturforum Witten, Witten 020925
Märkisches Museum, Stiftung Stadtmuseum Berlin, Berlin 016116

Märkisches Ziegelei-Museum Glindow, Glindow . . . 017430
Märklin-Museum, Göppingen . . . 017449
Maertzdorf, Doetinchem . . . 078291
März, Ladenburg . . . 103812
Maerz, Leipzig . . . 103893
Maerz, Linz . . . 095668
Maerzgalerie, Leipzig . . . 103894
Maes, Knokke-Heist . . . 096341, 123641
Maese, Lewis, Houston . . . 089146
Mästerby Antik, Stockholm . . . 081983
Mätzelt, R., Hörstel . . . 071542
Mafe, São Paulo . . . 096678
Maffart, Guy, Rennes (Ille-et-Vilaine) . . . 067117, 124874
Maffei, São Paulo . . . 096679
Maffeis, Giacomo, Milano . . . 127623
Maffeischächte der Grube Auerbach-Nitzlbuch, Bergbau-und Industriemuseum Ostbayern, Auerbach, Oberpfalz . . 015597
Maffra Sugarbeet Museum, Maffra . 001203
Maffucci, Manuel, Lugano . . . 130093
Mafikeng Museum, Mafikeng . . . 034676
Mafra & Mafra, Lisboa . . . 129160
Maga Magò, Trieste . . . 140147
Magadanskij Oblastnoj Kraevedčeskij Muzej, Magadan . . . 033344
Magan Sangrahalaya Samiti, Wardha . . . 022377
Magana Gallery, Windsor, Ontario . . 097561
Magapa, Granada . . . 129528
Magasin, Duisburg . . . 070483
Le Magasin, Haarlem . . . 078466
Magasin - Centre National d'Art Contemporain, Grenoble . . . 012017
La Magasin de Cadres, Lille . . . 063855, 124320
Magasin Eclair, Angers . . . 060859
Le Magasin Pittoresque, Nice . . . 138256
Magatani, Tokyo . . . 107071
El Magatzem, La Bisbal d'Empordá 081007
Het Magazijn, Amsterdam . . . 077907
Het Magazijn, Gent . . . 058195
Magazin Etalon, Bucureşti . . . 080159
Magazine, Asheville . . . 136528
Magazine, San Francisco . . . 142956
The Magazine Antiques, New York . 136529
Magazine Arcade Antiques, New Orleans . . . 090583
Magazine Street Gallery, New Orleans . . . 117469
Magazinpresse Verlag, München . . 134261
Magazinul Colectiilor, Bucureşti . . . 080160
Magazyn Artystyczny, Warszawa . . 136026
Magazyn MM, Warszawa . . . 079764
Magazzino d'Arte Moderna, Roma . 106577
Il Magazzino di Aristide, Milano . . . 075754
Magdalen Museum, Wainfleet . . . 041271
Magdalene Gallery, Taunton . . . 114555
Magdalenen-Verlag, Holzkirchen, Oberbayern . . . 134065
Magdeburger Antiquariat, Magdeburg . . . 139439
Magdeburger Museen, Direktion, Magdeburg . . . 018772
Magdeburská Kasárna, Terezín . . . 008712
Magd.factor, Sellingen . . . 134833
Magdzik, Ingolf, Rostock . . . 073580
Magellan Trading, Tucson . . . 093246
Magenta, Florida . . . 135532
Magenta, Nijmegen . . . 108154
Magenta, Palermo . . . 106435
Magenta, Roermond . . . 108166
Magenta Fine Arts, West Kirby . . . 114668
Magers & Quinn, Minneapolis . . . 142585
Magersfontein Battlefields Museum, McGregor Museum, Kimberley . . . 034663
Mages, Christian de, Nice . . . 065107
Mages, Otto, Rottach-Egern . . . 073600
Magevney House, Memphis . . . 045761
Maggia, Giovanni, Verona . . . 077011
Maggie May's, North Shields . . . 086093, 131321
Maggie's Book Bazaar, Highgate Hill . . . 136940
Maggies Place, Columbus . . . 088422
Il Maggiolino, Bari . . . 075022
Maggiore, Bologna . . . 105967
Maggs Bros., London . . . 141842
Maggs, John, Falmouth . . 130701, 141609
Maggs, Philip, Petworth . . . 086251
Magg's Shipping, Liverpool . . . 085025
Al-Maghraby, Khan, Cairo . . . 098643
Magi, Milano . . . 106260
Magi, Cezar, New Orleans . . . 117470
Magia Imagem, Lisboa . . . 109332
Magic Art Corporation, Pretoria . . . 080737
Magic Changes, Schaumburg . . . 136530
Magic Dragon, Los Angeles . . . 116838
Magic Faces, Buffalo . . . 115259
Magic Flute Artworks, Lower Swanwick . . . 114001
Magic House-Saint Louis Children's Museum, Saint Louis . . . 047669
Magic Lantern Castle Museum, San Antonio . . . 047797
Magic Lanterns, Saint Albans . . . 086440
Magic Moments, Albuquerque . . . 087410
Magic of Quimper, Littlehampton . . 085017
Magic Oriental Antiques, Abu Dhabi 083175
Magic Shop, Columbus . . . 088423
Magica, Beograd . . . 109709
Le Magicien, Orchies . . . 065282
La Magie du Verre, La Tour-de-Peilz 111948
Magill Antiques and Art Gallery, Magill . . . 056121
Magin, Bruxelles . . . 123599
Magin, Claudia, Wien . . . 123514
Magis, J.-J., Paris . . . 138492
Magistrati, Sandro, Milano . . . 127624
Magistri, Roma . . . 076537, 128092
Magli, Ettore, Bologna . . . 127161
Maglio, Alfredo, Torino . . . 128327
Magliocchetti, Roma . . . 128093
Magloire, Philippe & Claude, Paris . 066222
Magna, Coimbra . . . 109246
Magna Gallery, Oxford . . . 086182, 141985
La Magnanerie du Coudray, Maison de la Soie d'Anjou, Le Coudray-Macquard . . . 012485
Magnanerie Muséalisée de la Roque, Molezon . . . 013086
Magne, Michel, Rouen . . . 138589
Magne, René, Saint-Julien-de-Jordanne . . . 067554
The Magnes Museum, Berkeley . . . 042162
The Magnes Museum, San Francisco . . . 047869
Magnes News, Berkeley . . . 136531
Magnet, Mönchengladbach . . . 072573
Magnet, Wilfried, Völkermarkt . . . 095777, 133168
Magnet, Wilfried, Wien . . . 095894
Magnetawan Historical Museum, Magnetawan . . . 005818
Magnifico, Albuquerque . . . 114802
Magnin, François, Paris . . . 138493
Magnino, Mondeville . . . 064596
Magnität, Braunschweig . . . 069989
Magnitogorskaja Kartinnaja Galereja, Magnitogorsk . . . 033346
Magnitogorskij Kraevedčeskij Muzej, Magnitogorsk . . . 033347
Magnolia Editions, Oakland . . . 135472
Magnolia Grove-Historic House Museum, Greensboro . . . 044329
Magnolia Manor Museum, Cairo . . . 042543
Magnolia Mound Plantation, Baton Rouge . . . 042048
Magnolia Plantation, Charleston . . . 042740
Magnolias, Houston . . . 116362
Des Magnolias comme Autrefois, Paris . . . 066223
Magnoni, Massimo, Roma . . . 128094
Magnum Ars, Moskva . . . 080252, 109564, 129236, 140911
Magnus Dagestad Museet, Voss Folkemuseum, Voss . . . 031344
Magnus Edizioni, Fagagna . . . 134574
Magnussen, E.G., Nordhackstedt . . 073078
Magnussen's, Bergen . . . 079377
Magoffin Home, El Paso . . . 043642
Magome Studio, Tokyo . . . 128451
Magpie, Hinckley . . . 084687
Magpie, Windsor, Ontario . . . 059441
Magpie Antiques, Long Melford . . . 085836
Magpie Antiques, Swansea 086812, 131567
Magpie Auctions, Port Adelaide . . . 120626
Magpie Books, Fremantle . . . 136908
Magpie Gallery, Uppingham . . . 114628
Magpie Jewellers and Antiques, Evesham . . . 084352
Magpies, Rushden . . . 086417
Magpie's Nest, Salt Lake City . . . 092444, 119355
Magsingal National Museum, Magsingal . . . 031694
Magus, Frankfurt am Main . . . 070765
Magus, Seattle . . . 142999
Maguy, Laurent, Font-Romeu-Odeillo-Via . . . 062888
Magvető Könyvkiad, Budapest . . . 134507
Magyar Elektrotechnikai Múzeum, Budapest . . . 021666
Magyar Építészeti Múzeum, Budapest . . . 021667
Magyar Földrajzi Gyűjtemény, Érd . . 021720
Magyar Fotográfiai Múzeum, Kecskemét . . . 021761
Magyar Fotográfusok Háza, Budapest . . . 105531
Magyar-Francia Galéria, Budapest . 105532
Magyar Iparművészeti Egyetema, Budapest . . . 050282
Magyar Képzőművészek és Iparművészek Szövetsége, Budapest . . 021668, 053675
Magyar Kepzőművészeti Egyetem, Budapest . . . 050283
Magyar Kereskedelmi és Vendéglátóipari Múzeum, Budapest . . . 021669
Magyar Környezetvédelmi és Vízügyi Múzeum, Esztergom . . . 021724
Magyar Mezőgazdasági Múzeum, Budapest . . . 021670
Magyar Múzeumok, Budapest . . . 135842
Magyar Naiv Művészek Múzeuma, Katona József Múzeum, Kecskemét . . . 021762
Magyar Nemzeti Galéria, Budapest . 021671
Magyar Nemzeti Múzeum, Budapest . . . 021672
Magyar Numizmatikai Társulat, Budapest . . . 053676
Magyar Olajipari Múzeum, Zalaegerszeg . . . 021926
Magyar Ortodox Múzeum, Miskolc . 021789
Magyar Régészeti és Művészettörténeti Társulat, Budapest . . . 053677
Magyar Természettudományi Múzeum, Budapest . . . 021673
Magyar Tudományos Akadémia, Budapest . . . 050284
Magyar Vegyészeti Múzeum, Várpalota . . . 021915
Magyarországi Régiségkiállítás és Vásár, Budapest . . . 093752
Maha Al Saqqa Center - Palestinian Folk Museum, Bethlehem . . . 031410
Maha Wirawong National Museum, Nakhon Ratchasima . . . 037911
Mahaboudha Art Centre, Kathmandu . . . 107590
Mahaffie Stagecoach Stop and Farm, Olathe . . . 046658
Mahaki, Kawakawa . . . 108484
Mahakoshal Art Gallery, Raipur . . . 022314
Mahakoshal Fine Arts College, Raipur, Madhya Pradesh . . . 050322
Mahal, Martina, Hünstetten . . . 139281
Mahana Gallery, Gisborne . . . 108453
Mahaney, Louisville . . . 132300
Mahant Ghasidas Memorial Museum, Raipur . . . 022315
Mahara Gallery, Paraparaumu . . . 108541
Maharaja Banaras Vidya Mandir Museum, Varanasi . . . 022374
Maharaja Fate Singh Museum, Vadodara . . . 022365
Maharaja Sawai Man Singh II Museum, Jaipur, Rajasthan . . . 022179
Maharaja's Emporium, Montréal . . . 058975
Mahatma Gandhi Hindi Sangrahalaya, Kalpi . . . 022195
Mahatma Gandhi Memorial College Museum, Udupi . . . 022362
Mahatma Gandhi Museum, Mangalore . . . 022253
Mahatma Gandhi Museum, Verulam 034770
Mahatma Phule Vastu Sangrahalaya, Pune . . . 022307
Mahaux, Bruxelles . . . 058024
Mahaux, Pierre, Bruxelles . . . 058025
Mahboubian, London . . . 085506
Mahé, Gérard, Saint-Ouen . . . 067836
Mahé, Joël, Châteaudun . . . 062194
Mahe, Ros, Moustiers-Sainte-Marie . . . 064820, 099782
Mahérault, Pascal, Lagny-sur-Marne . . . 063487
Maherault, Pascal, Vaires-sur-Marne . . . 068674
Mahgoub, Mostafa Hassan, Alexandria . . . 060421
Mahieu, Jouarre . . . 138108
Mahieu, Paris . . . 124733
Mahl, Lesley, Schwelm . . . 073769
Mahla & Co., Pittsburgh . . . 091840
Mahler, Launceston . . . 056089
Mahler, Irene, Seattle . . . 119958
Mahler, Jakob, Badenweiler . . . 069431
Mahler, Norbert, Schwarzach am Main . . . 073756
Al-Mahmood, Manama . . . 057637
Al-Mahmood, Manama . . . 096018
Mahn, Rainer, Leipzig . . . 126192
Mahn- und Gedenkstätte Düsseldorf, Düsseldorf . . . 016840
Mahn- und Gedenkstätte Isenschnibber-Feldscheune, Gardelegen . . . 017322
Mahn- und Gedenkstätte Ravensbrück, Stiftung Brandenburgische Gedenkstätten, Fürstenberg, Havel . . . 017281
Mahn- und Gedenkstätte Steinwache, Stadtarchiv Dortmund, Dortmund . 016765
Mahn- und Gedenkstätte Wernigerode, Wernigerode . . . 020813
Mahn- und Gedenkstätten Wöbbelin, Wöbbelin . . . 020943
Mahogany Inn, Mahogany Creek . . 001204
Mahogany Shop, San Diego . . . 132852
Mahoney, Geelong . . . 094579
Mahoney & Weekly, Buffalo . . . 142263
Mahonia, Helsinki . . . 060550
Mahringer, Gottfried, Wien . . . 057493
Mahtra Talurahvamuuseum, Juuru . 009367
Mai, Ha Noi . . . 120472
Mai, Ho Chi Minh City . . . 120518
Mai, Sint-Niklaas . . . 096412
Mai, Stuttgart . . . 126868
Mai 36 Galerie, Zürich . . . 112143
Mai Hien & Ahn Khanh, Ha Noi . . . 120473
Maia, Alice R. Silva, Funchal . . . 079837
Maia, Ana Paula Silva, Lisboa . . . 079958
Maia, L.F., Dallas . . . 122875
Maia, Paulo Silva, Porto . . . 080095
Maia, Philip, Dallas . . . 088561
Maibaum, Walter, New York . . . 118152
Maici Nonoi, Philadelphia . . . 091663
Maidens & Foster, Hawkes Bay . . . 121825
Maidhof Bros., San Diego . . . 092652
Maidstone Library Gallery, Maidstone . . . 040388
Maidstone Museum and Bentlif Art Gallery, Maidstone . . . 040389
Maiensäss, Lenzerheide . . . 082574
Maier, München . . . 072784
Maier, A., Ellwangen . . . 070542
Maier, B., Kirchheim am Neckar . . . 071858
Maier, Bernhard, Ellwangen . . . 102613
Maier, Ernst, Lengenfeld bei Krems 057145
Maier, Frieder, Nürtingen . . . 139614
Maier, I., Neuburg an der Donau . . . 072977
Maier, Josef, Innsbruck . . . 095590

Maier, Konrad, Schwäbisch Gmünd 104853
Maier, Lothar, Bruchsal 070066
Maier, Manfred, Heidenheim an der Brenz 071468
Maier, R., Pforzheim 073319
Maier, René, Saint-Rémy-de-Provence 067990
Maier, Thomas, Olbernhau 073198
Maier & Co., Thomas, Stuttgart . . . 073992
Maier, Werner, Vandans . . 057338, 123481
Maier Hahn, Kiki, Düsseldorf 102527
Maier-Mangold, N., Hüttisheim 071595
Maier Museum of Art, Randolph-Macon Woman's College, Lynchburg 045528
Maigret, Thierry de, Paris 121170
Maihaugen, De Sandvigske Samlinger, Lillehammer 030984
Maillard, Julie, Paris 100635
Maillard, Olivier, Villard-de-Lans . . 068876
Maillard, Valérie, Chatenoy-le-Royal 062227
Maille, Bernard, Paris 138494
Maillon Manquant, Rouen 067278
Mailly, Chantal, Versailles 068811
Mailors Flat Antiques, Mailors Flat . 056122
Mailout, Chesterfield 136245
Maimana Museum, Maimana 000008
Main, C. & K.M., Green Hammerton 084531
Main Access Gallery, Winnipeg 097591
Main Art Gallery, Department of Art, California State University, Fullerton 044095
Main Art Tree, Pacific Paradise 095011
Main Centre Heritage Museum, Main Centre 005820
Main d'Or, Arzon 098868
Main Fine Art, Glasgow 113121
Main Furniture, Hamilton 058858
Main Gallery of Henry Street Settlement, New York 046360
Main Line Art Center, Haverford . . . 044479
Main Place for Antiques, San Antonio 092542
Main Point Books, Edinburgh 141582
Main Street Collectors Mall, Portland 091968
Main Street Gallery, Hahndorf 094610
Main Street Gallery, Minneapolis . . 117281
Main Street Gallery, Montville 094871
Mainardi, Livorno 127495
Mainart, Philadelphia 132627
Maine Antique Digest, Waldoboro . . 136532
Maine Art Gallery, Wiscasset 049269
Maine Association of Museums, Augusta 054859
Maine Coast Artists, Rockport 054860
Maine College of Art, Portland 051974
Maine Durieu, Paris 100636
Maine Historical Society Museum, Portland 047160
Maine Maritime Museum, Bath . . . 042039
Maine Photographic Workshops, Rockport College, Rockport 052053
Maine State Museum, Augusta 041905
Mainetti, Pully 111819
Mainetti, Mirko, Milano 106261
Mainfränkisches Museum Würzburg, Würzburg 020999
Mainguet, Nicole, Soleil d'Orient, Clermont-Ferrand 062350
Mainhill Gallery, Ancrum 112510
Mainhill Gallery, Jedburgh 084810
Maini & Veli, Helsinki 060551
Mainichi Art Collection, Nagoya . . . 026880
Mainieri, Giuseppe, Milano 075755
The Mainland Museum of Texas City, Texas City 048540
Mainly Books, Northbridge 137035
Maino, Maria Paola, Roma 106578
Mainstream Publishing Company, Edinburgh 135142
Maintal-Steigerwald-Museum, Knetzgau 018291
Maio & Partner, Lahr, Schwarzwald 072117
Maio, Michel de, Ippling 063211
Maioli, Alberto, Cernusco sul Naviglio 134567
Maiquez, Tampa 093141
Mair, Ursula, Salzburg 123450
Mairangi Arts Centre, Auckland . . . 030443
Le Maire, Liège 058314
Mairie, Champagné 099109
Maironis Lithuanian Literature Museum, Kaunas 027847
Mairose, Rösrath 073561
De Mais, Getxo 081117
Maisa, Cairo 098644
Maisel, Albuquerque 114803
Maisel's Brauerei- und Büttnerei-Museum, Privatbrauerei Gebr. Maisel, Bayreuth 015918
Maisenbacher, Christoph, Trier 105066, 134430
La Maison, Bourne End . . 083590, 130413
La Maison, London 085507
La Maison, Memphis 090087
Maison, M.A., Saint Paul 092375
Maison, Michel, Seattle 093031
Maison 14, Washington 093421
Maison A. Ravier, Morestel 013235
Maison André-Benjamin-Papineau, Laval 005754
Maison André Derain, Chambourcy . 011218
Maison Antique, Catania 075251
Maison Arthur, Clermont-Ferrand . . 099151
Maison-Atelier Foujita, Villiers-le-Bacle 015303
Maison Berckheim du Parc Anglais de Schoppenwihr, Ostheim 013526
Maison Beys, Saint-Ouen 067837
Maison Bibelot, Firenze . . 075366, 121686
Maison Blanche, Singapore 080525
La Maison Bleue, Chinon 099134
Maison Buttin-de Loës, Grandvaux . 037162
Maison Chaussavoine, Brece 061753
Maison Communale Gérard Philippe, La Garde 012264
La Maison Couleur du Temps, Venas 015155
Maison Creole Eureka, Moka 028067
Maison d'Abraham Mazel à Falguières, Mialet 013056
La Maison d'Amandine, Bruxelles . . 058026
Maison d'Art, Monaco 077613
Maison D'Art, Toowoomba 056722
La Maison d'Art, Us 101395
Maison d'Art Alsacienne, Strasbourg 101298
Maison d'Art Montegrappa, Bologna 075089
Maison d'Auguste Comte, Paris . . . 013601
Maison Daumm, Saint-Ouen 067838
La Maison d'Aure, Musée Paysan - Arts et Traditions Populaires, Sailhan . . . 014165
Maison de Balzac, Paris 013602
Maison de Boua Kang Bung, Luang Prabang 027644
La Maison de Charrier, Valbonne . . 068679
Maison de Famille, Montargis 064624
Maison de Géologie de Haute-Alsace, Sentheim 014765
Maison de Gergovie, La Roche-Blanche 012306
Maison de Jean Monnet, Bazoches-sur-Guyonne 010691
La Maison de Jules, Gassin 099284
Maison de la Baie, Courtils 011517
Maison de la Baie du Mont Saint-Michel, Vains 015086
Maison de la Bible, Lyon 138176
Maison de la Broderie, Villers-Outréaux 015292
Maison de la Canne, Les Trois-Ilets 028057
La Maison de la Chicorée, Orchies . 013502
Maison de la Dentelle, Urçay 015074
Maison de la Dernière Cartouche, Bazeilles 010689
La Maison de la Dordogne Quercynoise, Souillac 014835
Maison de la Faïence, Badonviller . 010617
Maison de la Faïence, Musée de la Céramique, Desvres 011582
Maison de la Faune, Murat (Cantal) 013302
Maison de la Fonderie, Vrigne-aux-Bois 015343
Maison de la Forêt, Bon-Secours . . 003239
Maison de la Forêt de Miers, M.F. du Pestre, Pleaux 013835
La Maison de la Forêt et du Bois, Ecomusée de la Bresse, Saint-Martin-en-Bresse 014425
Maison de la Lentille du Berry, Chouday 011377
Maison de la Loire, Montlouis-sur-Loire 013180
Maison de la Magie Robert-Houdin, Blois 010844
Maison de la Manufacture d'Armes Blanches, Klingenthal 012194
Maison de la Mariée, Saint-Joachim 014362
Maison de la Mer, Courseulles-sur-Mer 011511
Maison de la Metallurgie et de l'Industrie de Liège, Liège 003585
Maison de la Meunerie, Nieul-sur-l'Autise 013416
Maison de la Musique Mécanique, Mirecourt 013076
Maison de la Nature, Eze 011774
Maison de la Nature, Paris 013603
Maison de la Nature et de l'Oiseau, Neuville-sur-Ailette 013382
Maison de la Négritude et des Droits de l'Homme, Champagney 011224
Maison de la Pêche à Pied et Anciennes Salines, Vains 015086
Maison de la Pétanque, Vallauris . . 015104
Maison de la Pierre de Volvic, Volvic 015334
Maison de la Pierre et du Ciment, Montalieu-Vercieu 013121
Maison de la Pisciculture, Sizun . . . 014809
Maison de la Poesie, Montréal 097051
Maison de la Pomme et de la Poire, Barenton 010653
Maison de la Pomme et Forge, Sainte-Opportune-la-Mare 014615
Maison de la Poste, Montréal 005931
Maison de la Réserve Naturelle du Lac de Remoray, Labergement-Sainte-Marie 012363
Maison de la Résistance, Chasseneuil-sur-Bonnieure 011271
Maison de la Rivière, Châteauneuf-sur-Sarthe 011294
Maison de la Rivière, Chinon 011363
Maison de la Rivière, de l'Eau et de la Pêche, Sizun 014810
Maison de la Rivière et du Pêcheur, Saint-Georges-de-Montaigu 014300
Maison de la Sainte-Victoire, Saint-Antonin-sur-Bayon 014188
Maison de la Science, Liège 003586
Maison de la Terre Cuite, Les Rairies 012631
Maison de la Thiérache, Liart 012663
Maison de la Treille, Sion 111914
Maison de la Vallée d'Ossau, Laruns 012434
Maison de la Vigne, Essoyes 011742
Maison de l'Abbé Grégoire, Embermenil 011692
Maison de l'Abeille et du Miel, Riez 014044
Maison de l'Air, Paris 013604
Maison de l'Amandier, Saint-Rémy-de-Provence 014515
Maison de l'Amérique Latine, Paris 100637
Maison de l'Antiquité, Moncé-en-Belin 064591
Maison de l'Araire, Yzeron 015383
Maison de l'Archéologie des Vosges du Nord, Niederbronn-les-Bains 013415
Maison de l'Ardoise, Rimogne 014050
Maison de l'Argile, Ateliers Thérèse Neveu, Aubagne 010508
La Maison-de-L'Autographe, Paris . 138495
Maison de l'Automate, Lunas 064026
La Maison de l'Eau, Mallièvre 012868
Maison de l'Eau et de la Pêche, Besse-en-Chandesse 010775
Maison de l'Eau et de la Pêche, Neuvic (Corrèze) 013376
Maison de l'Eclusier, Saint-Malo-de-Guersac 014407
Maison de l'Energie, Eguzon 011685
Maison de l'Environnement et de la Chasse, Centres de Découverte de la Nature, Sault (Vaucluse) 014696
Maison de l'Espace Vert, Nancy . . . 013321
Maison de l'Etain, Villedieu-les-Poêles 015242
La Maison de l'Etameur, Toulouse . 101363
Maison de l'Éventail, Bèze 010787
Maison de l'Histoire de la Terre de Gorze, Gorze 011973
Maison de l'Industrie - Exposition Permanente, Saint-Berthevin 014198
Maison de l'Olivier, Le Val 012571
Maison de Louis Pasteur, Arbois . . . 010445
Maison de Louise, Les Quatre-Routes-du-Lot 063777
La Maison de l'Ours, Saint-Lary-Soulan 014375
Maison de l'Outil et de la Pensée Ouvrière, Troyes 015049
Maison de Marie-Louise, Samoens 068107
La Maison de Maud, Le Puy-en-Velay 063698, 099455
Maison de Nicolas Ledoux, Château de Bénouville, Bénouville 010751
Maison de Nostradamus, Salon-de-Provence 014649
Maison de Pays, Bage-le-Chatel . . 010618
Maison de Pays, Mornant 013246
Maison de Pays, Pont-sur-Sambre . 013899
Maison de Pays, Sainte-Marie-aux-Mines 014604
Maison de Pays, Seuilly 014781
Maison de Pays, Tourzel-Ronzieres 015026
Maison de Pays du Haut Verdon, Beanvezer 010694
Maison de Pays du Haut-Verdon, Beauvezer 010724
Maison de Poupée, Paris 066224
Maison de Provence, Atlanta 087495
Maison de Provence, New Orleans . 090584
Maison de Robert Schuman, Scy-Chazelles 014737
La Maison de Russie, Aix-les-Bains 060724
Maison de Sainte Marie-Madeleine-Postel, Barfleur 010654
Maison de Troglodytique Seigneuriale, Turquant 015065
La Maison de Van Gogh, Auvers-sur-Oise 010566
Maison de Victor Hugo, Paris 013605
Maison de Victory, Le Lavandou . . . 063645
La Maison dell'Antico Arredo, Modena 075918
Maison d'Elsa Triolet et Louis Aragon, Saint-Arnoult-en-Yvelines 014190
Maison d'Émile Zola, Musée de l'Affaire Dreyfus, Medan 012996
Maison Départementale de l'Innovation, Clermont-Ferrand 011395
Maison d'Erasme, Bruxelles 003303
Maison des Abeilles, Brignoles 011002
Maison des Amis du Blanc, Le Blanc 012465
Maison des Ancêtres de Bossuet, Seurre 014784
Maison des Archers, Musée de la Villemarque et des Traditions Bretonnes, Quimperlé 013980
Maison des Artisans, Angers 010391
Maison des Artisans & Créateurs, Espace Saint-Eloi, Séez 014744
Maison des Artisans d'Art, Sarzeau 101260
Maison des Arts, Chexbres 111350, 135003
Maison des Arts, Malakoff 012862
Maison des Arts, Saint-Martin 105470
Maison des Arts, Tunis 037984
Maison des Arts, Tunis 112262
Maison des Arts et du Vin, La Réole 012298

Maison des Arts et Tradition Populaires de la Landes Médocaine, Carcans . . 011110
Maison des Arts Ruraux, Saint-Germain-de-Marencennes 014306
Maison des Beaux-Arts, Rablay-sur-Layon 013986
Maison des Chapais, Saint-Denis . . 006334
Maison des Châteaux Forts, Obersteinbach 013471
Maison des Cinq Sens, Paris 013606
Maison des Compagnons du Devoir du Tour de France, Strasbourg 014862
Maison des Deux Marines, Briare . . 010995
Maison des Esclaves, Gorée 034133
Maison des Etangs, Saint-Viâtre . . . 014569
Maison des Fortifications, Maubeuge 012970
Maison des Fromages d'Auvergne, Egliseneuve-d'Entraigues 011683
Maison des Jardies-Musée Léon Gambetta, Centre des Momuments Nationaux, Sèvres 014787
Maison des Johnnies, Roscoff 014109
Maison des Liqueurs de l'Auzonnet, Saint-Florent-sur-Auzonnet 014288
Maison des Marais, Marchesieux . . 012887
Maison des Minéraux, Crozon 011540
Maison des Paludiers, Saille 014166
Maison des Papillons, Saint-Tropez 014559
Maison des Rochers, Graufthal 012006
Maison des Sirènes et des Siréniens, Réserve Géologique de Haute-Provence, Castellane 011138
Maison des Sports Bretons, Berrien 010765
Maison des Traditions, La Chapelle-des-Marais 012225
Maison des Traditions Agricoles et Artisanales, L'Abattoir, Avallon . . 010583
La Maison des Tupiniers, Lyon 099600
Maison des Ventes, Saint-Gaudens 067481
Maison Design, Salt Lake City 092445
Maison d'Histoire Locale, Cocheren 011413
Maison Dieu, Faversham 039494
Maison Dieu, Ospringe 040648
Maison dite de la Duchesse Anne, Morlaix 013241
Maison d'Offwiller, Offwiller 013475
Maison d'Ossau, Musée du Parc National, Arudy 010494
Maison du 15ème Antiquités, Nogent-l'Artaud 065207
La Maison du Bal, Los Angeles 089834
Maison du Bison d'Europe, Sainte-Eulalie-en-Margeride 014595
La Maison du Blé et du Pain, Echallens 037055
Maison du Buronnier, Laveissière . . 012453
La Maison du Cadre, Paris 100638
Maison du Calvet, Montréal 005932
La Maison du Cerf, Ligny-le-Ribault 012674
Maison du Chanoine, Treigny 015038
Maison du Cheval, Corlay 011483
Maison du Collectionneur, Bordeaux 061631
La Maison du Collectionneur, Paris . 066225
Maison du Comté, Poligny 013870
Maison du Gabardan, Gabarret 011909
Maison du Haut-Rhône, Centre Culturel, Seyssel 014796
Maison du Kochersberg, Truchtersheim 015058
La Maison du Lac, Les Salles-sur-Verdon 012641
Maison du Lac, Musée Avifaune du Lac de Grandlieu, Saint-Philbert-de-Grand-Lieu 014478
Maison du Lauzeron, Champclause 011227
Maison du Lin, Routot 014144
Maison du Littoral, Perros-Guirec . . 013794
La Maison du Livre, Leura 136975
Maison du Livre, de l'Image et du Son, Arthothèque, Villeurbanne 015298
Maison du Livre et de l'Affiche, Chaumont (Haute-Marne) 011324
Maison du Luthier-Musée, Jenzat . 012157
Maison du Miel, Volvic 015335
Maison du Mont Aiguille Vercors-Trièves, Chichilianne 011359
Maison du Pain d'Alsace, Sélestat . 014748
Maison du Parc, Sorèze 014825
Maison du Parc et des 4 Montagnes, Autrans 010559
Maison du Parc National des Ecrins, Vallouise 015114
Maison du Parc Naturel Régional de Camargue, Saintes-Maries-de-la-Mer 014625
Maison du Parc Naturel Régional de Lorraine, Bisping 010815
Maison du Parc Naturel Régional de Maine-Normandie, Carrouges 011131
Maison du Parc Naturel Régional des Ballons des Vosges, Munster 013301
Maison du Parc Naturel Régional des Vosges du Nord, La Petite-Pierre . 012294
Maison du Parc Naturel Régional du Luberon, Musée de Paléontologie, Apt 010440
Maison du Patrimoine, Blanquefort . 010831
Maison du Patrimoine, Lampaul-Guimiliau 012396
Maison du Patrimoine, Le Crès 012486
Maison du Patrimoine, Le Relecq-Kerhuon 012558
Maison du Patrimoine, Lesterps . . . 012649
Maison du Patrimoine, Marsannay-la-Côte 012924
Maison du Patrimoine, Sarcelles . . 014669
Maison du Patrimoine, Villard-de-Lans 015227
Maison du Patrimoine, Wimmenau . 015365
Maison du Patrimoine, Musée de Matour, Matour 012969
Maison du Patrimoine de Saint-Chef, Saint-Chef 014218
Maison du Patrimoine d'Oloron et du Haut Béarn, Oloron-Sainte-Marie 013490
Maison du Patrimoine et Ilsle, Crémieu 011531
Maison du Patrimoine Historique du Donezan, Rouze 014146
Maison du Patrimoine Maritime, Camaret-sur-Mer 011078
Maison du Pays des Étangs, Tarquimpol 014913
Maison du Pays Roussillonnais, Roussillon (Isère) 014141
Maison du Pays Welche, Fréland . . 011893
La Maison du Père Mousset, Vrigny 015344
Maison du Platin, La Flotte 012263
Maison du Portal, Levens 012652
Maison du Protestantisme, Nîmes . 013420
Maison du Recteur et de la Paroisse, Loqueffret 012744
Maison du Recteur et des Pilhaoueriens, Loqueffret 012745
Maison du Rhône, Givors 011959
Maison du Roi, Musées de la Ville de Bruxelles, Bruxelles 003304
Maison du Roy, Saint-Antonin-Noble-Val 067359
Maison du Sabot Neufchâtelois, Neufchâtel-en-Saosnois 013370
Maison du Saint-Curé, Ars-sur-Formans 010490
Maison du Saint-Nectaire, Saint-Nectaire 014449
Maison du Sauvetage, Grand-Fort-Philippe 011984
Maison du Seigle, Menessaire 013011
Maison du Spectacle La Bellone, Bruxelles 003305
Maison du Terroir, Saint-Martin-Lacaussade 014426
Maison du Val de Villé, Albé 010312
Maison du Vieil Alby, Albi 010318
Maison du Viet Nam, Paris 100639
Maison du Vieux-Zinal, Zinal 037754
Maison du Vin, Tilburg 030206
Maison Dumulon, Rouyn-Noranda . 006312
Maison et Atelier de Jean-François Millet, Barbizon 010648
Maison et la Tour de Mélusine, Vouvant 015341
Maison Etienne, Nantes 064933
Maison Européenne de la Photo, Paris 013607
La Maison Fassier, Rémalard 067084
La Maison Française, West Hollywood 093485
Maison Francis Jammes, Orthez . . 013524
Maison Gerard, New York 091050
Maison Guillaume de Rubroek, Rubrouck 014150
Maison Hamel-Bruneau, Sainte-Foy 006403
Maison Henri IV, Cahors 011066
Maison Historique de Léon et Jeanne Blum, Jouy-en-Josas 012174
Maison Ideale, San Francisco 092836
Maison J.A. Vachon, Sainte-Marie . 006405
Maison Jacques Prévert, Omonville-la-Petite 013492
Maison Jean-Giono, Manosque . . . 012878
Maison Jean-Vilar, Bibliothèque Nationale de France, Avignon 010589
Maison Jeanne d'Arc, Orléans 013514
Maison la Laurière, Québec 097152
Maison Lamontagne, Rimouski . . . 006291
Maison Lansyer, Loches (Indre-et-Loire) 012721
Maison Levanneur, Chatou 011318
Maison Littéraire de Victor Hugo, Bièvres 010801
Maison Louis-Hippolyte Lafontaine, Boucherville 005121
La Maison Lune de Miel, Antony . . . 060934
Maison Maillou, Québec 006220
Maison & Maison, Houston 089147
Maison Marc, Saint-Ouen 067839
Maison Marie Henry, Clohars-Carnoët 011409
Maison Médard-Bourgault, Saint-Jean-Port-Joli 006347
Maison-Musée de Charles Maurras, Martigues 012962
Maison-Musée de Jeanne Jugan, Cancale 011088
Maison-Musée de Kerlard, Ile-de-Groix 012125
Maison-Musée de la Nature, Marcillé-Robert 012894
Maison-Musée de la Vie d'Autrefois et des Métiers, La Pesse 012293
Maison-Musée des Arômes, Montguers 013170
Maison-Musée des Charcot, Neuilly-sur-Seine 013374
Maison-Musée des Sciences, Lettres et Arts de Cholet et de sa Région, Cholet 011372
Maison-Musée du Parc Naturel Régional du Haut-Jura, Lajoux 012387
Maison-Musée du Sabotier, Ecomusée de la Brière, La Chapelle-des-Marais . . 012226
Maison-Musée du Vigneron de Champagne, Saint-Imoges 014335
Maison-Musée Ted Jacobs, Les Cerqueux-sous-Passavent 012615
Maison-Musée Vivant des Papillons Exotiques, Hunawihr 012113
Maison Natale de Claude Gellée, Chamagne 011203
Maison Natale de Jean Giraudoux, Bellac 010738
Maison Natale de Jeanne d'Arc, Domremy-la-Pucelle 011633
Maison Natale de Jeanne d'Arc et Centre d'Interprètation, Domremy-la-Pucelle 011634
Maison Natale de la Religieuse Sophie Barat, Joigny (Yonne) 012159
Maison Natale de Saint-Vincent-de-Paul, Saint-Vincent-de-Paul 014572
Maison Natale du Brave Crillon, Fidèle Compagnon d'Henri IV, Murs 013308
Maison Natale du Maréchal Foch, Musée du Maréchal Foch, Tarbes 014909
Maison natale Sainte Therese, Alençon 010324
Maison Nationale Bonaparte, Ajaccio 010303
Maison Nationale de la Pêche et de l'Eau, Ornans 013521
Maison Neumann, Metz 099715
Maison Philippe, Paris 066226
Maison Philippe, Pézenas 066809
Maison Philippe T, La Queue-en-Brie 063403
Maison Renaud, Troyes 068651
Maison Res Rara, Den Haag 078216
Maison Rouge, Fondation Antoine de Galbert, Paris 013608
Maison Rurale de l'Outre-Forêt, Kutzenhausen 012196
Maison Saint-Dominique, Fanjeaux 011782
Maison Saint-Vincent, Villepreux . . 101479
Maison Sergeur, Douai 062725
Maison-Souvenir de George Sand, Nohant-Vic 013438
Maison Stendhal, Grenoble 012018
Maison Tavel, Genève 037123
Maison Traditionnelle de la Boucherie, Limoges 012691
Maison V Collections, Vancouver . . 059379
Maison Vauban, Musée du Maréchal de Vauban, Saint-Léger-Vauban 014388
Maison Vincent Van Gogh, Cuesmes 003381
Maison Visinand, Centre Culturel, Montreux 037334
Maison Zina, Chéraga 055133
Maisonnette, Hamburg 071282
Maisonneuve, Adrien, Paris 133648
Maisonneuve, Alain, Paris 066227
Maisonneuve, Grégoire, Paris 100640
Maisonneuve, Jean, Paris 133649, 138496
Les Maisons de Bouteilles, Cap-Egmont 005216
Maisternia Sens, Kyïv 112415
Maitland Art Center, Maitland 045601
Maitland City Art Gallery, Maitland . 001206
Maitland Historical Museums, Maitland Historical Museum, Telephone Museum, Historic Waterhouse Residence Museum, Maitland 045602
Maitland Museum, Maitland, South Australia 001207
Maitre, Jean-Jacques, Bignoux . . . 061483
Les Maitres Anciens, Québec 059073
Les Maitres Argenteurs, Paris 124734
Maîtres de Forme Contemporains, Bruxelles 096232
La Maîtrise, Hasselt 058227
Maiwald, Klaus, Langen in Hessen . 072150
Maja, Gdańsk 108891
Majesteit, Rotterdam 078732
Majestic Auction, Saint Paul 123091
Majestic Coins, Salt Lake City 092446
Majesty Promotional Products, San Diego 092653
Majewska, Maria, Łódź 140753
Majewski, Zdzisław, Wołomin 109209
Majlath, Judith, Wien 057494
Al-Majlis, Dubai 112455
Majmua Art Gallery, Karachi 108775
Majnabbe, Göteborg 110924
Majo, Denia 081069
The Major General Frederick Funston Boyhood Home and Museum, Iola 044764
Major John Bradford House, Kingston 045012
Majorana, Gian Paolo, Brescia 106001
Majorelle Museum, Marrakech 029026
Majori, Hasselt 058228
Majorstuen, Oslo 140702
Majuscules, Marseille 064371
Mak, A., Dordrecht 121789
MAK Art Society, Wien 052576
MAK Center for Art and Architecture, Pearl M. Mackey Apartment House, Los Angeles 045446
MAK Center for Art and Architecture, Schindler House, West Hollywood 049083
MAK - Österreichisches Museum für angewandte Kunst/ Gegenwartskunst, Wien 002945
MAK Verlag, Wien 133217
Makasiinimuseo, Talomuseo, Koulumuseo, Polvijärvi 009983
Makassar, Bochum 069889

Makassar, France, Paris 066228
Makatka, Warszawa 079765
Make It Big, Philadelphia 118794
Make Magazine, London 136246
Make - The Organization for Women in the Arts, London 054425
Makedonsko Archeološko Društvo - Zavod i Muzej Prilep, Prilep 027915
Makerere Art Gallery, Makerere University, Kampala 038219
Makers, Milano 075756
Makers on Mair, Ballarat 094202
Maket, Michel, Paris 066229
Makhoul, Claudine Varan Keutnedjian, São Paulo 058723
Makk, Honolulu 116226, 135364
Makler, Paul Todd & Hope, Philadelphia 118795
Mako, Gene, Los Angeles 116839
Makonde African Arts, Wembley . . . 114660
Makonde Art Museum, Bammental . 015885
Makoschey, G., Bad Essen 069280
Makoveć, J., Wien 123515
Makovský, Zdeněk, Plzeň 137811
Makowski, Moers 072582
Makowski, Prichsenstadt 073376
Makowski, K., Warszawa 129100
Maksim Bogdanovich Literature Museum, Minsk 003136
Makta, Sofia 096741
Maktabi & Sons, Ali, Beirut 077402
Maktabi & Sons, Hassan, Beirut . . . 077403
Maktabi, Iwan, Beirut 077404
Mała Galeria, Warszawa 109152
Mala Galerija, Moderna Galerija, Ljubljana 034481
Malá Sova, Praha 137837
Malabar Farm State Park, Lucas . . 045516
Malacañan Palace Presidential Museum, Manila 031724
Malacca Museums Corporation, Malacca 027988
Malafaia, Rio de Janeiro 058613
Malagoli, Rosa, Modena 075919
Malahide Antiques, Malahide 074992
Malahide Castle, Malahide 022833
Malaika, Almere 107632
Malaise, V., Bruxelles 058027
Malakološki Muzej, Makarska 007756
Malanda Antiques, Malanda 056128
Malatesta, Brescia 075175
Malatya Devlet Güzel Sanatlar Galerisi, Malatya 038142
Malatya Müzesi, Malatya 038143
Malatya Sabancı Kültür Merkezi, Malatya 038144
Malausséna, Simone, Nice 065108
Malavasi, Milano 140055
Malavolta, Cesare, Roma 128095
Malavoy, Brigitte, Paris 124735
Malay Art Gallery, Singapore 109835
Malay Ethnographic Museum, University of Malaya, Kuala Lumpur 027970
Malaysian Youth Museum, Melaka . 027991
Malazgirt Kültür Merkezi, Malazgirt 038145
Malbasa, Strasbourg 068324
Malbert, Chicago 115488
Malbork, Montréal 097052
Malbos, Charles, Avignon 061136
Malbrunot, Paris 066230
Malchers, Anne, Bergisch Gladbach 101766
Malco, Helsinki 060552
Malcolm, Christian T., New York . . . 118153
Malcolm, Franklin, Chicago 088126
Malcolm's No. 1, Sherburn-in-Elmet 122698
Malda Museum, Malda 022251
Malden Public Library Art Collection, Malden 045604
Maldis, Vilnius 107366, 140232
Maldon and District Agricultural and Domestic Museum, Goldhanger . . 039599
Maldon Antiques and Collectors Market, Maldon 085899
Maldon District Museum, Maldon . . 040392
Maldon Museum, Maldon 001208
Maldon's Old Grain Store Antiques, Maldon 056131
Maldoror, Toulouse 101364
Malé Máslovické Muzeum Másla, Vodochody 008759
Malek Museum, Teheran 022626
Maleny Antiques, Maleny 056133
Maleny Art Gallery, Maleny 094770
Malerisalongen, Hafrsfjord 079386
Måleriyrkets Museum, Stockholm . 036640
Malermuseum Wetzikon, Wetzikon . 037703
Malerschulen Baden-Leesdorf, HTL Baden, Malerschule Leesdorf, Baden bei Wien 049619
Malerskole 1, Kongelige Danske Kunstakademi, København 049904
Malerskole 2, Kongelige Danske Kunstakademi, København 049905
Malerskole 3, Kongelige Danske Kunstakademi, København 049906
Malerstübchen Willingshausen, Willingshausen 020904
Malesa, Jeffery, Sorrento 095197
Malesherbes, Paris 066231
Malet, Montmorency 064719
Malgrati, Elena, Milano 127625
Malibu Galleries, Omaha 118713
Malibu Galleries, Omaha 118714
Malibu Gallery, Minneapolis 117282
Malibu Lagoon Museum, Malibu . . . 045606
La Malice, Freiburg im Breisgau . . . 102868
Malichin, Hildegard, Baden-Baden . 101724
Malignon, Josiane, Paris 066232
Malik & Son, David, London 085508
Malik, Gisela, Lübeck 072330
Malika, Québec 123806
Målilla Hembygdspark, Målilla 036450
Målilla Motormuseum, Målilla 036451
Målilla Sanatoriums Museum, Målilla 036452
Maling Road Antique Market, Canterbury 055629
Malingarte, Amadora 079805
Malingue, Daniel, Paris 100641
Malinka, Köln 071978, 126102
Malinowski, Gerhard, Hamburg . . . 139200
Malinowski, Mark, Laatzen 126158
Malinowski, Zdzisław, Gdynia 079596
Malissa, Houston 142441
Malits, Ewald, Guntramsdorf 057049
Malke, München 072785
Malki Museum, Banning 042012
Malkia, Tucson 120144
Malkia, Tucson 120145
The Mall Antiques Arcade, London . 085509
Mall Galleries, London 040215
Mall of Saint Paul, Saint Paul 092376
Malla Bleikvasslis Samlinger, Bleikvasslia 030781
Mallaig Heritage Centre, Mallaig . . 040393
Mallala and Districts Historical Museum, Mallala 001209
Mallalieu Motor Museum, Christ Church 003121
Mallams, Cheltenham 122459
Mallams, Oxford 122646
Mallarmé, Charenton-le-Pont 062148
Mallawy Museum, Mallawy 009341
La Malle à Bart, Bart 061213
La Malle Anglaise, Cormeilles 062478
La Malle Anglaise, Pont-d'Ouilly . . . 066921
La Malle Anglaise, Rennes (Ille-et-Vilaine) 067118
La Malle au Trésor, Lausanne 082553, 130071
La Malle aux Chimères, Châteauneuf 062200
Malle aux Idées, Niort 065196
Malle aux Trésors, Blois 061526
La Malle aux Trésors, Bruxelles . . . 058028
Malle Cauchoise, Gonneville-la-Mallet 063016
Malle du Martroi, Orléans 138269
Malle Pietje, Zutphen 078877
Malle Poste, Annecy 060894
Mallee, Billabong 094254
Mallek, Kay, Tucson 093247
Mallet, Edith, Montrond-les-Bains . 064775
Mallet, Marco Antonio Serveira, São Paulo 058724
Mallett & Son, London . . . 085510, 113748
Mallett, Mosman 056266
Mallett, New York 091051
Mallett at Burdon House, London . . 085511
Mallette & Assoc., Cincinnati 088257, 122859
Malleville, Étienne, Rouen 067279
Malliaris, A., Thessaloniki 139904
Mallon, J.M., Indianapolis 116475
Mallory & Sons, San Diego 092654
Mallory & Sons, E.P., Bath 083438
Mallory-Neely House, Memphis . . . 045762
La Malmaison, Cannes 011095
Malmede, P., Frechen 102848
Malmin Taide ja Kehys, Helsinki . . . 060553
Malmö Auktionsbyrå, Åkarp 122095
Malmö Konsthall, Malmö 036458
Malmö Konstmuseum, Malmö 036459
Malmö Museer, Malmö 036460
Malmska Gården, Jakobstads Museum, Jakobstad 009615
Malo Deux, Leiden 078573
Maloberti-Miermont, Marie-Claude, Courpière 062520
Malojaroslaveckaja Gorodskaja Kartinnaja Galereja, Malojaroslavec 033350
Malojaroslaveckij Istoriko-kraevedčeskij Muzej, Malojaroslavec 033351
Malojaroslaveckij Muzej Voennoj Istorii 1812 Goda, Malojaroslavec 033352
Malojaroslaveckij Muzejno-vystavočnyj Centr, Malojaroslavec 033353
Malokarpatské Múzeum v Pezinku, Pezinok 034406
Malombra, Vicenza 140154
Malone, Begoña, Madrid 110564
Les Malouines, Charleroi 096276
Malouinière-Musée, Saint-Malo (Ille-et-Vilaine) 014408
Malouvier, Le Havre 099441
Malouvier, Rouen 067280
Malovat, Chicago 115489
Malow, P., Nossentiner Hütte 073090
Malrait, Marthe, Paris 066233
Målselv Bygdemuseum, Midt-Troms Museum, Moen 031023
Malt House Antiques, Narbeth 086039
Malt House Antiques, Stow-on-the-Wold 086755
Malta National Committee of ICOM, Valletta 053859
Maltby, Winchester 114705
Malten, Helga, Dortmund 102410
Maltepe, İstanbul 112335
Maltese Cross Antiques, Christchurch 079037
Malteser-Museum Mailberg, Mailberg 002273
Malthouse Antiques, Bridgnorth . . .083669, 130437
Malthouse Antiques, Dorking 084198
Malthouse Antiques Centre, Alcester 083258
Malthouse Arcade, Hythe, Kent . . . 084780
Maltinti, Bruno, Milano . . . 075757, 127626
Malton, Cincinnati 115641
Malton Antique Market, Malton . . . 085903
Malton Museum, Malton 040396
Maltwood Art Museum and Gallery, Victoria 006744
Malu, Maastricht 078612
Malungs Hembygdsgård, Malung . . 036465
Malura-Museum, Unterdießen 020540
Malvaux, Bertrand, Nantes 064934
Malvern Antiques, Malvern, South Australia 056138
Malvern Antiques and Collectors Fair, Malvern 093938
Malvern Artists' Society, Malvern, Victoria 094778
Malvern Bookshop, Great Malvern . 141633
Malvern Link Antiques Centre, Malvern 085906, 131252
Malvern Museum, Great Malvern . . 039631
Malvern Studios, Great Malvern . . .084514, 130746
Malvisi, Stefania, Parma 127855
Maly, Severin, Paris 100642
Malynowsky, Daniel J, Montréal . . . 058976
MAMA Showroom for Media and Moving Art, Rotterdam 108194
Mamco, Musée d'Art Moderne et Contemporain, Genève 037124
Mamie Doud Eisenhower Birthplace, Boone 042303
Mamma Kunsthuis, Brugge 096117
Mammana, Gudrun, Kaufbeuren . . . 103522
Mammoth Site of Hot Springs, Hot Springs 044630
Man and His Work Center in Memory of S. Avitsur, Eretz-Israel Museum, Tel Aviv 023084
Man and Telecommunication Museum, Edmonton 005400
Man and the Living World Museum, Ramat Gan 023050
Man Arte, Paris 100643
Man at Arms, Lincoln 136533
Man From Snowy River Folk Museum, Corryong 000951
Man in the Galilee Museum, Kibbutz Ginosar 023005
MAN Museum, Augsburg 015613
Man of Ross Gallery, Ross-on-Wye . 114325
Man Po, Hong Kong 059667
Manahil Art Works, Manama 096019
Manaia Gallery, Waikato 108593
Manama Auction Center, Manama . 120701
Manao, Argentan 060959
Manart, Zürich 112144
Manassas Museum System, Manassas 045612
Manassas National Battlefield Park, Manassas 045613
Manasse, Pierugo, Roma 076538
Manassero, Gianvittorio, Torino . . . 128328
Manastirli Palace and Nilometer, Cairo 009304
Manastirski Muzej, Cetinje 034185
Manatee Village Historical Park Museum, Bradenton 042379
Manawatu Auctions, Palmerston North 079215, 121830
Manawatu Upholstery, Manawatu . . 128941
Manca, Mérignac (Gironde) 064504
Manceaux, Jean-Denis, Reims 124863
Mancebo, São Paulo 058725
Mancheron, Roger, Paris 066234
Manchester Antique Company, Stockport 086724
Manchester Art Gallery, Manchester 040404
Manchester Craftsmen's Guild, Pittsburgh 047054
Manchester Historic Association Museum, Manchester 045620
Manchester Historical Society Museum, Manchester 045616
Manchester House Antiques Centre, Chipping Norton 083992
Manchester Jewish Museum, Manchester 040405
Manchester Museum, Manchester . 040406
Manchester Museum of Transport, Manchester 040407
Manchester United Museum and Tour Centre, Manchester 040408
Manchester University Medical School Museum, Manchester 040409
Manchester University Press, Manchester 135283
Manchini, Marta, Asunción 108801, 128999
Mancina, Saverio, Autun 061090
Mancini, Carla, Perugia 127879
Mancini, Letizia & Alessandra, Roma 106579
Mancini, Simone, Perugia 127880
Mancino, Ivana, Palermo 127835

Mancuso, Dionisia, Roma 128096
Mancuso, Gianpaolo, Trieste 128375
Mancy, Jean-Luc, Meaulne 064455
Mandal Auksjonsforretning, Mandal 121857
Mandal Bymuseum, Mandal 031006
Mandal Kunstforening, Mandal 053946
Mandal og Opplands Folkemuseum, Mandal 031007
Mandalá, Giuseppa, Palermo 076158
Mandala Fine Arts, Hong Kong 059668
Mandallaz, Michel, Le Vivier-sur-Mer 063733
Mandarin, Hong Kong 059669
Mandarin, Seattle 093032
Mandarin Antik, Stockholm 081984
Mandarin Antique, Atlanta 087496
Mandarin Gallery, Otford . 086171, 131349
Mandarin Oriental Fine Arts, Hong Kong 097812
Mandel, Ludwig, Landshut 072144
Mandell, Norwich 131332
Mandells Gallery, Norwich 114166
Mander and Mitchenson Theatre Collection, London 040216
Manderley Manor, Toronto 059239
La Mandigotte, Royan 067313
Mandi's Gallery, Sacramento 119154
Mandl, Helmut, München 126412
Mandos, Ron, Rotterdam 108195
Mandos-Feldmann, Westerstede . .105232, 134455
Mandra, Rodolphe, Presly 066982
Mandragora Verlag, Münster 104371, 126504, 134299
Mandragore, Prades 124853
Mandrake, Seattle 093033, 132941
Mandt, Petra, Köln 126103
Mandurah Community Museum, Mandurah 001212
Manduras, John, Jerrabomberra . . 094665
Mané-Katz Museum, Haifa 022925
Manecke, F., Tecklenburg 074046
Al-Maneei, Mohammed Abdulrahman, Riyadh 080378
Maneesi Sotamuseo, Helsinki 009554
Le Manége, Paris 066235
Manège des Hogues, Saint-Léonard (Seine-Maritime) 067585
Manège du Temps, Orgeval 065285
Manelli, Saint-Maur-des-Fossés . . .101181, 133698
Manenstegell, Bathmen 128578
Manenstegell, Deventer 128643
Manera, East Freemantle 055783
Manes, Francesco, Napoli 127778
Manescau, Raymonde, Avignon . . . 061137
Manetstötter, Karlheinz, Maisach . . 104013
Manetti & Masini, Firenze 127362
Manevy, Madeleine, Paris 066236
Manfred, K. Breitenstein, Vorderweidenthal 105132
Manfred, Neumann, Molchow 126330
Mang, Thomas, Bürmoos . 056955, 123344
Mang, Wolfgang, Saarbrücken 139706
Mangalam, Paris 066237, 100644
Mangano, Giuseppe, Bari 127115
Mangapps Farm Railway Museum, Burnham-on-Crouch 038906
Mangel, Benjamin, Philadelphia . . . 118796
Mangesius, Yvonne, Bad Arolsen . . 069258
Manggha Centrum Sztuki i Techniki Japońskiej, Muzeum Narodowe w Krakowie, Kraków 032033
Mangia, Giovanna Maria, Roma . . . 128097
Mangili Bartolacci, Carlo, Brescia . . 075176
Mangin, Charlotte, Mirepoix 064564
Mangin, Stéphane, Paris 066238
Mångkulturellt Centrum, Tumba . . . 036722
Manglam Arts, Jaipur, Rajasthan . . . 105724
Manglano Gil, Matilde, Madrid . . . 129642
Manglano Gil, Matilde, Madrid 129643
Mangold, Leipzig 103895
Manhattan Art, New York 118154
Manhattan Art Gallery, New York . . 118155
Manhattan Arts and Antiques Center, New York 091052
Manhattan Arts Center, Manhattan . 045629
Manhattan Arts Interntional, New York 136534
Manhattan Books, New York 142672
Manhattan Frame and Art, New York 118156
Manhattan Galeria, Łódź 109012
Manhattan Gallery, Nottingham . . . 114177
Manhattan Shoppes, Tampa 093142
Manhattan West Timeless Jewelry, Denver 088712
Manheim, Ida, New Orleans 090585
Manhyia Museum, Kumasi 021106
Mania, Kay, Hessisch Oldendorf . . .071502, 125925
Manial Palace Museum, Cairo 009305
Manic, Paris 066239, 124736
Manicó, Mercato, Catania 075252
Manifesta, Torino 076838
Manigand Mobilier, Saint-Cyr-sur-Menton 067415
Maniitsup Katersugaasivia, Sukkertoppen Museum, Maniitsoq 021541
Manila Galería, Medellín 098278
Manila Police Department Museum and Gallery, Manila 031725
Manilla Historical Royce Cottage Museum, Manilla 001213
Maningrida Arts & Culture, Winnellie 056836
Manion, Ashbourne 083329
Maniototo Early Settlers Museum, Naseby 030546
Manipulator, Düsseldorf 135800
Manipur State Museum, Imphal . . . 022170
Manipur University Museum, Canchipur 022049
Manisa Devlet Güzel Sanatlar Galerisi, Manisa 038146
Manisa Müzesi, Manisa 038147
Manisa Salihli Kültür Merkezi, Salihli/Manisa 038164
Maniscalco, Santo, Catania 127270
Manistee County Historical Museum, Manistee 045634
Manitoba Agricultural Hall of Fame, Brandon 005142
Manitoba Agricultural Museum, Austin 005043
Manitoba Amateur Radio Museum, Brandon 005143
Manitoba Automobile Museum, Elkhorn 005423
Manitoba Children's Museum, Winnipeg 006851
Manitoba Electrical Museum, Winnipeg 006852
Manitoba Museum of Man and Nature, Winnipeg 006853
Manitoba Printmakers Association, Winnipeg 052754
Manitoba Sports Hall of Fame and Museum, Winnipeg 006854
Manitou Pioneer Museum, Neilburg 005989
Manitoulin Historical Society Museum, Gore Bay 005522
Manjimup Timber Museum, Manjimup 001214
Manjiya, Osaka 140171
Manjusha Museum, Dharmasthala . 022104
Manko, Hans-Werner, Wiesbaden . . 074412
Manks, Hong Kong 059670
Manley, Ashleigh, Surfers Paradise . 095243
Manley, Brett, Armadale, Victoria . .055385, 123182
Manley, J., Eton 084343, 130690
Manly Art Gallery and Museum, Manly 001215
Manly Collectables, Manly 056151
Manly Gallery, Manly 094781
Gebr. Mann, Berlin 133796
Mann, New Orleans 090586
Mann & Sons, David, Cranleigh . . . 130614
Mann, John, Canonbie . . . 083854, 130500
Mann, Mina, New York 091053
Mann, Robert, New York 118157
Mann, Stephanie, Köln 071979
Mann, Thomas, New Orleans 117471
Mann-Simons Cottage, Columbia . . 043083
Manna, Den Haag 078217
Manna, Emilia, Napoli 076004
Manna Gum Gallery, Dromana 094487
Manneken-Pis-Museum, Geraardsbergen 003474
Mannenzaal van het Sint Pieters en Bloklands Gasthuis, Amersfoort . . 029150
Mannerheim Museo, Helsinki 009555
Mannerheimintien Antiikki, Helsinki 060554
Manners, E. & H., London 085512
Manneschi, Rovigo, Firenze 127363
Mannhardt & Ruhdorfer, Rottach-Egern 073601
Mannheimer Kunstverein e.V., Mannheim 053487
Mannies Arts, Kathmandu 107591
Manning, K., San Francisco 142957
Manning, Oliver, Canterbury 130505
Manning, Shedd, Atlanta 131782
Manning Regional Art Gallery, Taree 001537
Manninger, Karl, Pöcking 126638
Manningham Gallery, Doncaster . . . 094480
Manno Art Museum, Osaka 026969
Mannsfeld, Colmar 099161
Mannum Old Wares and Curios, Mannum 056155
Del Mano, Los Angeles 116840
Mano, Jose M. de la, Madrid 081337, 110565
Mano Tonnerre, Paris 100645
Manoel Theatre and Museum, Valletta 028030
Le Manoir, Rabat 077695, 107563
Manoir Automobile, Lohéac 012729
Manoir de Folie Vallée, Pont-de-l'Arche 066919
Manoir de Folie Vallée, Rouen 067281
Manoir de Kernault, Mellac 013003
Manoir de la Ville de Martigny, Martigny 037312
Manoir de Veygoux, Scénomusée des Combrailles, Charbonnières-les-Varennes 011245
Manoir de Villers, Saint-Pierre-de-Manneville 014483
Manoir du Huis Bois-Maison P.N.R. du Boulonnais, Le Wast 012580
Manoir Leboutillier, Anse-au-Griffon 005020
Manoir Mauvide-Jenest, Saint-Jean 006345
Manolaki, Thessaloniki 105450
Manor Antiques, Gravesend, Kent . . 084502
Manor Antiques, Wilstead 087155
Manor Barn, Skipton 086625
The Manor Bindery, Fawley 130707
Manor Cottage Heritage Centre, Southwick 041072
Manor Farm, Bursledon 038913
Manor Farm Antiques, Standlake . . 086692
Manor Fine Arts, Banbridge 112549
Manor Gallery, Gravesend 113149
Manor House, Cardiff 130513
Manor House, Donington-le-Heath . 039253
Manor House, Sandford Orcas 040953
Manor House Antique Mall, Indianapolis 089319
Manor House Antiques, Blackheath 055510
The Manor House Antiques, Brasted 083651
Manor House Antiques, Fishguard . 084408
Manor House Antiques, Sacramento 092170, 132737
Manor House Gallery, Cheltenham .112845, 130538
Manor House Museum, Kettering . . 039856
Manor House Museum and Art Gallery, Ilkley 039795
Manor Museum, Manor 005826
Manorism, Atlanta 087497
Manos, Denver 116021
Manos Faltaits Museum, Euboea . . 021258
Las Manos Gallery, Chicago 115490
Las Manos Magicas, Houston 116363
Manou, Ronchamp 067210
Manrique, Martin, Los Angeles 132267
Manroy, Antwerpen 057715
Le Mans Collections, Le Mans 063660
Mansa Mussa, New York 091054
La Mansarda, Medellín 059926
La Mansarde, Dampierre-en-Yvelines 062593
Mansart Rémy, Bruxelles 058029
Mansell, G., Hoylake 084745
Mansell, William C., London 131101
Manser & Son, F.C., Shrewsbury . .086605, 131497
Mansfeld-Museum Hettstedt, Hettstedt, Sachsen-Anhalt 017911
Mansfelder Bergwerksbahn e.V., Benndorf 015946
Mansfeldgalerie im Kulturhaus, Lutherstadt Eisleben 018754
Mansfield, Deloraine 055747
Mansfield, Louise, Stillorgan 105901
Mansfield Art and Antiques, Christchurch 079038
Mansfield Art Center, Mansfield . . . 045647
Mansfield Costume Study Centre, Colchester 039121
Mansfield Fine Arts Guild, Mansfield 054861
Mansfield Gallery, Mansfield 094785
Mansfield Historical Society Museum, Storrs 048383
Mansfield Museum and Art Gallery, Mansfield 040418
Mansfield Park Gallery, Glasgow . . 113122
Mansfield State Historc Site, Mansfield 045645
Manship House Museum, Jackson . 044797
Manshodo, Hiroshima 077059
Mansion, Gracie, New York 118158
Mansion Antique House, Singapore 080526
La Mansión del Fraile, Bucaramanga 059867
Mansion House, Warkworth 030630
Mansions, Lincoln 084999
Manske, D., Bernburg 069800
Mansky, Claudia, Rotenburg an der Fulda 073583
Manson, Edward, Woodbridge 087221, 131709
Manson, Yves, La Flèche 121023
Mansour, Cairo 098645
Mansour Bros., Damascus 083064
Mansour, London 085513, 113749
Mansour, Ahmed, Cairo 098646
Al-Mansour Gallery, Cairo 098647
Manten, W., Vreeland 128875
Manthey, Berlin 069695
Manthey, Cornelia, Hamburg 139201
Manthey, Gerhard, Kiel 071836
Mantiques, New York 091055
Mantiques Modern, New York 091056
Mantler, Maria, Ziersdorf 137391
Mantler, Wolfgang, Wien 137343
Manton, F.T., Uxbridge 131634
Mantoux-Gignac, Paris 100646
Mantovani, Le Lavandou 099445
Mantra, Torino 106684
Mantu, N., Galaţi 109456
Mantua, Isidoro, Torino 140138
Manu, Breda 078108
Manu Arte, Jesteburg 071659
Manualidades, La Paz 096441
Manuel L. Quezon Memorial Shrine Museum, Quezon City 031777
Manuelian, Georges, Nice 065109
Manuella, Nice 065110
Manujlivs'kyj literaturno-memorialnyj Muzej O.M. Gor'kogo, Verchnja Manujlivka 038411
Manuka, Fisher 055819
Manumedia, Graz 133078
Manurewa Community Arts Centre, Auckland 030444
Manus, Männedorf 135048
Manus, Magnus, Amsterdam 107767

Manusardi, Marina, Milano 075758
Manuscribe, Tucson 143030
Manuscript, Rotterdam . . 121802, 140522
Manuscript Museum, Bibliotheca Alexandria, Alexandria 009278
O Manuscrito Histórico, Lisboa 140843
Manwarning, M.G, Bristol 141457
Manx Museum, Manx National Heritage, Douglas, Isle of Man 039268
Many, I., Chicago 115491
Manyara Museum, Manyara 037854
Manyung Gallery, Mount Eliza 094902
Manzanal, Donostia-San Sebastián 129511
Manzano, Juan B., Sevilla 081593
Manzke, Holger, Potsdam 126652
Manzo, Oklahoma City . . . 091516, 132581
Manzoni Villa, Musei Civici, Lecco . 024487
Mao Dun Former Residence, Beijing 006992
The Map House of London, London 141843
Map World, London 085514
Mapes, David W., Vestal 123132
Mapes, Shirley K., Omaha 142729
Maple Antiques, Surbiton 086792
Maple Leaf Furniture Refinishing, Toronto 123835
Maple Ridge Art Gallery, Maple Ridge 005832
Maple Ridge Museum, Maple Ridge 005833
Maple Street Book Shop, New Orleans 142620
Maple Sugar Museum, Art Gallery and Pioneer Home, Sundridge 006537
Maple Syrup Museum, Saint Jacobs 006343
Maple Valley Historical Museum, Maple Valley 045652
Maples, Mosta 077517
Maplewood Antique Mall, Saint Louis 092271
Mappa Mundi and Chained Library, Hereford 039735
Il Mappamondo, Milano 106262
Mappamundi, Knokke-Heist 096342, 137509
Maps, Prints & Books, Brecon 141431
Mapungubwe Museum, Pretoria . . . 034718
Maqdisi, Damascus 083065
Maqueda Abreu, Maria Luisa, Granada 110379
La Mar, Denia 081070
Mar Pau, Viña del Mar 097635
Mára, Erlangen 070601
Mára! SunArt Verlag, Meppen 134200
Marabini, Bologna 105968
Marafini, Iliadora, Roma 128098
Maragall, Barcelona 080874, 110210, 122010, 134917
Maragheh Museum, Maragheh 022579
Marais, Jean-Claude, Pezou 066815
Marais Des Cygnes Memorial Historic Site, Pleasanton 047090
Maralt, Kyra, Berlin 101981
Maramec Museum, The James Foundation, Saint James 047636
Maramigi, Rosanna, Roma 128099
Marangon Da Soaxe, Venezia 128396
Marani, Ferny Creek 055818
Marani, Roma 076539
Maraninchi, Marseille 124425
Marante, Amsterdam 140318
Maraş Ikon Müzesi, Gazimağusa . . 008237
Marat Art, Bratislava 109912
Maratha History Museum, Deccan College, Pune 022308
Marathon County Historical Society Museum, Wausau 049016
Maraut, Michèle & Didier, Saint-Jean-Cap-Ferrat 067527
Maraux, Patrick, Nevers 065011
Maravillas Irujo Montaner, Barcelona 080875
Marazzi, Gian Luca, Parma 127856
Marazzi, Loris, Venezia 106762
Marbach, Mulhouse 099789
Marbach, Jean, Mulhouse 064837
Mårbacka Manor, Home of Selma Lagerlöf, Östra Ämtervik 036532
Marbeau, Paris 100647
Marbella, New York 118159
Marbella, David, New Orleans 090587
Marble Arts, Richmond 092093
Marble Hill Gallery, Twickenham . . . 086965
Marble Hill House, Twickenham . . . 041251
Marble Historical Museum, Marble . 045655
Marble Moon, Glenelg 094592
Marble Mountain Community Museum, West Bay 006791
Marble Palace, Houston 089148
Marble Palace Art Gallery and Zoo, Kolkata 022222
Marble Springs State Historic Farmstead Governor John Sevier Memorial, Knoxville 045042
Marblehead Arts Association, Marblehead 054862
Marblehead Historical Museum and J.O.J. Frost Folk Art Gallery, Marblehead 045658
Marborough, Hong Kong 097813
La Marbrerie, Lille 063856
Marbrier, Thierry, Mauregny-en-Haye 064437
Marbs, U., Baden-Baden 069422
Marburger Kunstverein e.V., Marburg 053488
Marburger Universitätsmuseum für Kunst und Kulturgeschichte, Marburg . . 018825
Marc, Fougères (Ille-et-Vilaine) . . . 062929
Marc, Jean-Louis, Paris 100648
Marc, Philip, Chantenay Saint-Imbert 062139
Marc Chagall Galeria de Arte, Rio de Janeiro 096628
Marc Chagall Galerie, Amsterdam . 107768
Marc Chagall Kunsthuis, Amsterdam 029199
Marca d'Acqua, Milano 140056
Marca Puig, Maria Teresa, Barcelona 080876
Marcar'art, Albi 060759
Marcazzan, Fabien, Monferran-Saves 064600
Marce, Jean Philippe, Montpellier . 124460
Marceau, Paris 066240
Marceau, Frédéric, Saint-Genis-les-Ollières 067488
Marcel-Ordas, Lyon 138177
Marcela M. Agoncillo Historical Museum, Taal 031792
Marcelin, Franck, Aix-en-Provence . 060709
Marcella Sembrich Opera Museum, Bolton Landing 042295
Marcellus Historical Society Museum, Marcellus 045661
Marcelo H. del Pilar Museum, Malolos 031706
Marcelpoil, Jeanne, Saint-Just 067568
Marcel's Antik Shop, Basel 082155
Marcet Books, London 141844
March, Brigitte, Stuttgart 104997
March, Danielle, Paris 100649
March, David & Sally, Abbots Leigh 083232
March, Tomas, Valencia 110833
March and District Museum, March 040420
March Ballester, Antonio Maria, Barcelona 080877, 110211
March Field Museum, Riverside . . . 047457
March-Museum, Vorderthal 037686
Marchal, Christiane, Paris 066241
Marchal, Étienne, Paris 066242
Marchan, F., Gent 137499
Marchand, Fréderic, Paris 066243
Marchand, Joséphine, Villeurbanne 068968
Marchand, Nathalie, Beaune 061286
Marchand, Nathalie, Paris 066244
Marchand, P.J., Rotterdam 128821
Marchand d'Art, Belo Horizonte . . . 096470
Marchand d'Oubli, Paris 066245
Marchand d'Oublis, Arnay-le-Duc . . 060979
Marchandet, Pascale, Paris 121171
Les Marchands du Design, Bordeaux 061632
Marchant, Mark, Coggeshall 084051, 130597
Marchant & Son, S., London 085515, 131102
Le Marche, Norfolk 091389
Le Marché, Tokyo 077278
Marche, Eric, La Croix-Saint-Leufroy 063361
Marché aux Puces du Canal, Villeurbanne 068969
Le Marche Biron, Saint-Ouen 067840
Marché d'Art, Fortaleza 058474
Marché Dauphine, Saint-Ouen 067841
Marché des Antiquaires, Vallauris . . 068699
Marché des Antiquités, Saint-Étienne 067459
Marché Jules Vallès, Saint-Ouen . . 067842
Marché Paul Bert, Walincourt-Selvigny 069040
Marches à Suivre, Paris 066246
Marches du Palais, Aix-en-Provence 060710
Marchese, Antonio, Prato 106476
Marchese, Paola, Bologna 127162
Marchesi, Maurizio, Bologna 127163
Marchetti, Roma 106580
Marchetti & Fontanini, Brescia 127223
Marchewka, Edmond, Mairé-Levescault 064221
Marchfeldmuseum, Weikendorf . . . 002813
Marchgraber, Erwin, Marchtrenk . . 057174
Marchi, Roberto, Roma 106581
Marchi Nerio, Andrea, Genova 127467
Marchin, Simonetta, Roma 106582
Marchió, Fabrizio, Merano 075548
Marchis-Mouren, Jean-François, Frankfurt am Main 070766
Marchisio, Felice, Torino 128329
Marchland-Wurm, Lassee 095641
Marchpane, E.W., London 141845
Márcia & Molduras, Belo Horizonte 096471
Marciana, Venezia 076954
Marciana, Venezia 076955
Marciana, Venezia 076956
Marciano, Gilbert, Montréal 058977
Marciano, Mickael, Paris 100650
Marcilhac, Félix, Paris 100651
Marcina Galeria, Poznań 109056
Marckle Myers, New York 091057
Marclay-Naef, Marie-Noëlle, Ollon . 082715
Marco, San Diego 119525
Marco Polo, Torino 076839
Marco Polo, Valencia 081664
Marco Polo Antiquités, Marrakech . 077684
Marco Polo Gold Buyers, New York . 091058
Marcoe, Leonard, Winnipeg 097592
Marcoff, Hasselt 058229
Marcolino, Arnaud, Rio de Janeiro . 123705
Marcombo, Barcelona 134918
Marcon, Bucureşti 080161
Marcon, Charles, Polignac 066896
Marcon, Paul, Cussac-sur-Loire . . . 062584
Marcon, Robert, Le Puy-en-Velay . . 063699
Marcon, Robert, Saint-Paulien 067947
Marconcini, Romano, Pisa 076244
Marconi, Gio, Milano 134620
Marcoola Antiques, Marcoola 056160
Marcorama, Panamá City 108792
Marcos, Miguel, Barcelona 110212
Marcos, Miguel, Zaragoza 110885
Marcos de Matos Bicalho, Antônio, Belo Horizonte 058433
Marcos Museum, Batac 031629
Marcos y Cuadros, Antofagasta . . . 059476
Marcos y Cuadros, Santiago de Chile 059540
Marcou, Marcel, Lyon 064157
Marcoux, Sandra, Mably 064200
Marcoz, Boston 087834
Marcq Antiquités, Marcq-en-Barœul 064276
Marcum, Louisville 116954
Marcum, Paris 066247
Marcus, Paris 100652
Marcus, Curt, New York 118160
Marcus, Johannes, Amsterdam . . .077908, 128548, 140319
Marcus Galleries, Birmingham 112652
Marcy's Things, Milwaukee 090313
Mardfeld, Samuel, Franconville . . . 062935
Mardfeld, Samuel, Saint-Ouen 067843
Mardfeld, Samuel, Saint-Ouen 067844
Mardi Gras Arts, Saint Louis 092272
Mardi Gras Gallery, New Orleans . . 117472
Mardi Gras Museum, Biloxi 042211
Mardin Müzesi, Mardin 038148
Mardjan, Paris 066248
Mardom-shenasi-ye Kavir, Nayin . . 022587
De Mare, Leiden 108103
Marec, Yves, Le Folgoët 063620
Maréchal, Alexis, Bordeaux 061633
Maréchal, B., Saint-Martin-du-Mont 067645
Marechal, Frans, Brugge 137417
Maréchal, Jacques, Rouen 067282
Maréchaux, Paris 066249
Mareeba District Rodeo Museum, Mareeba 001219
Mareeba Heritage Museum, Mareeba 001220
Marek, Warszawa 109153
Marek, West Hollywood 120399
Marek i Art, Warszawa 079766
Marel, Karel, Friedberg, Hessen . . . 139126
Marella, Milano 106263
Marelle, Bruno, Rouen 067283
Marelli, Omaha 118715
Marelli, Roberto Gaetano, Milano . . 075759
Maren Gallery, México 107497
Marengo, Marco, Genova 127468
Mares, Hans, Hilden 071518
Marescalchi, Bologna 105969
Marescalchi, Monaco 107536
Maresch-Engelbrecht, Manon, München 126413
Maretti, Monaco 107537
Marêve, Collobrières 062396
Marêve, Collobrières 062397
Marfé Gioielli, Napoli 076005
Marg, Mumbai 135847
Marg Publications, Mumbai 134520
Margam County Park, Port Talbot . . 040749
Margaree Salmon Museum, North East Margaree 006041
Margaret Fort Trahern Gallery, Clarksville 042956
Margaret Harvey Gallery, Saint Albans 040886
Margaret Harwell Art Museum, Poplar Bluff 047122
Margaret Hutchinson Compton Gallery, Cambridge 042563
Margaret Laurence Home, Neepawa 005987
Margaret Mansion Arts, Hong Kong 059671
The Margaret Mitchell House and Museum, Atlanta 041863
Margaret River Galleries, Margaret River 094788
Margaret Thatcher Projects, New York 046361
Margaret Trowell School of Industrial and Fine Art, Kampala 050794
Margarete-Steiff-Museum, Giengen an der Brenz 017403
Margaretha Museum, Laag Keppel . 029824
Margaret's Antiques, Wellington . . . 079333
Margaret's Cupboard, Denver 088713
Margaron, Alain, Paris 100653
Margas Antik-Laden, Kerpen, Rheinland 071804
Margate Caves, Margate 040423
La Marge, L'Isle-sur-la-Sorgue . . . 138124
Margetić, Beograd 109710
Margherita, Taranto 076750
Margie, L., Basel 082156
Margie's Menagerie, Indianapolis . . 089320
Marginessi, Kyïv 112416
Marginiai, Vilnius 107367
Margo, Adair, El Paso 116114
Margo, Thierry, Paris 138497

Margolet, Baltimore 087691
Margolis, Nancy, New York 118161
Margot's Galerie, Westerstede 105233
Margren, Stockholm 111062
Margret-Knoop-Schellbach-Museum, Körle 018359
Margrove - South Cleveland Heritage Centre, Boosbeck 038787
Marguerat, Bernard & Marialyne, Genève 082444
Marguerite d'Youville Museum, Montréal 005933
Marguet, Michel, Lausanne 082554
Margutta 102, Roma 106583
Margutta 83, Roma 128100
Margy's Antiquetates Azure, Berwick 055500
Mari-jo, Volkach 105130
Mari Valles, Maria Isabel, Barcelona 110213
Maria Antik, Stockholm 081985
Maria de Lisitzin Fine Art and Historical Museum, Porvoo 009995
Maria del Valle Quintana Dominguez, Madrid 110566
Maria Luisa Marchesi, Modena . . . 075920
Maria Martinez Museum, Santa Fe . 047969
Mariadevadassan, Joseph, Pantin . 065335
Mariager Museum, Mariager 009017
Mariah's Antiques, Vancouver 059380
Marialust, Apeldoorn 107843
Marian and Religious Museum, Brooklyn 042464
Mariani, Antonio, San Francisco . . . 092837
Mariani, Antonio, San Francisco . . . 092838
Mariani, Antonio, San Francisco . . . 132896
Mariani, Claudio, San Francisco . . . 092839
Mariani, Claudio, San Francisco . . . 092840
Mariani, Claudio, San Francisco . . . 132897
Mariani, Claudio, San Francisco . . . 132898
Mariani, Giuseppe, Roma 106584
Mariani, Luigi, Milano 127627
Mariani, Piero, Roma 128101
Marianini, Foresto, Firenze 127364
Marianist, Saint Louis 119227
Mariann Galéria, Győr 105559
Marianna Kistler Beach Museum of Art, Kansas State University, Manhattan 045630
Marianna-Lee County Museum, Marianna 045663
Marianna's Fine Arts, Saint Louis . . 119228
Marianne, Châtenois 062225
Marianne Antiquités, Vauréal 068738
Mariano, João, Lisboa 079959
Mariano Rodríguez Gallery, La Habana 007951
Marian's Collection, Surry Hills 056654
Mariantiquités, Sainte-Savine 068081
Mariaplans & Lindegrens Antikvariat, Göteborg 141104
Maria's Antik Boutique, Mainz 072397
Marias Antikvariat, Hanko 137925
Maria's Antiques, Virginia Beach . . 093362
Marias Museum of History and Art, Shelby 048141
Mariaschin, Shirley, New York 091059
Maricastaña, Tandil 055305
Maridadi, C.C., Pretoria 080738
Marie, Daniel, Rémalard 067085
Marie, Marc, Nice 065111
Marie-Andrée, Olivet 065263
Marie Antoinette, Toronto 059240
Marie-Hélène, Rouen 067284
Marie Hull Gallery, Hinds Community College, Raymond 047341
Marie-Pierre Antiquités, Beaune . . . 061287
Marie Rawdon Museum, Matjiesfontein 034678
Marie Tak van Poortvliet Museum, Domburg 029494
Marie-Tortue, Compiègne 062438
Marie Walsh Sharpe Art Foundation, Space-Program, New York 046362
Mariefreds Hembygdsmuseum, Mariefred 036468
Mariehamns Glas & Ramaffär, Mariehamn 060614
Mariehamns Konsthandel, Mariehamn 060615
Mariella Antichitá, Bologna 075090
Mariemont, Cincinnati 088258
Marien-Antiquariat, Berlin 138821
Marienglashöhle Friedrichroda, Friedrichroda 017266
Marier, Buenos Aires 094081
Maries Antiques & Pianos, Clane . . 074873
Marie's Treasures, San Antonio . . . 092543
Mariestads Industrimuseum, Vadsbo Museum, Mariestad 036473
Marietta House Museum, Glenn Dale 044211
Marietta Museum of History, Marietta 045666
Marigorri, Donostia-San Sebastián . 081085
Marije, Tilburg 078773
Marika Kotopouli Museum, Zografou 021535
Marika's Antique Shop, Boston 087835
Mariko, Denver 116022
Marília de Dirceu Antiguidades, Belo Horizonte 058434
Marilla Historical Society Museum, Marilla 045674
Marimeks, Veliko Tărnovo 096780
Marimon, Marisa, Ourense 110656
Marín, Medellín 059927
Marín, F., Burgos 081018, 129463
Marin, Gérard, Saint-Maurice 067664
Marin Almellones, Miguel Angel, Sevilla 129736
Marin County Watercolor Society, Corte Madere 054863
Marin History Museum, San Rafael . 047921
Marin Museum of the American Indian, Novato 046575
Marin Orts, Elena, Alicante 080762
Marin Society of Artists, Ross 054864
Marina, Los Angeles 089835
Marina Gallery, Port Douglas 095086
Marine Art Gallery, New York 118162
Marine Art Gallery, Padstow 114211
Marine Arts Gallery, Toronto 097324
Marine Corps Art Collection, Washington 048918
Marine d'Autrefois, Paris . 066250, 124737
Marine-Ehrenmal und Technisches Museum U 995, Laboe 018454
Marine Fine Arts, Terrey Hills 095326
Marine Gallery, Busan 107173
The Marine Gallery, Cowes 112909
The Marine Gallery, Scarborough . . 114400
Marine House, Beer 112603
Marine Museum at Fall River, Fall River 043805
Marine-Museum Limburg, Limburg an der Lahn 018649
Marine Museum of Manitoba, Selkirk 006440
Marine Museum of the Great Lakes, Kingston 005701
Marine Museum of Upper Canada, Toronto 006611
Marine Sciences Museum, Mayagüez 032718
Marine Transportation Museum, Ogi 026933
Marine & Wildlife, Lincoln 113399
Marineland Ocean Museum, Marineland 045675
Marinella Sanesi, Milano 075760
Marinelli, Strasbourg 101299
Marinelli, Flavio, Cagliari 127248
Marinelli, Lorenzo, Torino 128330
Marinemuseet, Horten 030908
Marinemuseum, Den Helder 029463
The Mariners' Museum, Newport News 046470
Mariners' Park Museum, Milford . . 005870
Marinesse, Henri, Groslay 063087
Marinette County Historical Museum, Marinette 045676
Maringalleriet, Stockholm 111063
Maringer, Dr. Karl-Heinz, Sankt Pölten 095746
Marini, Alessio, Roma 076540
Marini, Ruben, Firenze 127365
Mariniersmuseum, Rotterdam 030086
Marinius, Göteborg 081815
Marinmuseum, Karlskrona 036383
Marino, Firenze 127366
Marino, Emanuela, Roma 128102
Marino, Massimiliano, Genova 127469
Marino, Pierre, Lausanne . 082555, 130072
Marino Affaitati, Gabriele, Milano . . 127628
Marino Meubles, Valette-du-Var . . . 125006
Marinosci, Cosimo, Torino 128331
Marinov, Emil, Kjustendil 058756
Marinov, Emil, Šumen 137609
Cornelia Marinowitz & Udo Storz, Cornelia, Singen, Hohentwiel 126803
Mario Lanza Museum, Philadelphia 046958
Marion, Perpignan 100993
Marion, Josiane, La Bresse 063297
Marion County Historical Society Museum, Marion 045685
Marion County Historical Society Museum, Salem 047752
Marion Heritage Center, Marion . . . 045681
Marion Koogler McNay Art Museum, San Antonio 047798
Marion Public Library Museum, Marion 045678
Marion Scott Gallery, Vancouver . . . 006701
Marionettmuseet, Stockholm 036641
Marion's, Iron Acton 113303
Mario's Antique Shop, Philadelphia 091664
Marios Galerie, Schweinfurt 104862
Mariotti, Franco, Firenze 075367
Mariposa County Gallery, Los Angeles 045447
Mariposa Gallery, Albuquerque 114804
Marischael, Nicolas, Paris 124738
Marischal Museum, Marischal College, University of Aberdeen, Aberdeen 038449
Marit, Antwerpen 057716
Maritiem Buitenmuseum; Openlucht Binnenvaartmuseum, Rotterdam . 030079
Maritiem en Jutters Museum, Oudeschild 030030
Maritiem Museum Rotterdam, Rotterdam 030087
Maritiem Shop, Antwerpen 057717
Maritim Antik, Hamburg 071283
Maritime and Industrial Museum, Swansea 041172
Maritime and Seafood Industry Museum, Biloxi 042212
Maritime Antiques, København 060352
Maritime Archaeology Museum, Melaka 027992
Maritime Art Association, Summerside 052755
Maritime Command Museum, Halifax 005575
Maritime Heritage Centre, Bristol . . 038868
Maritime Heritage Exhibition, Fort Victoria Museum, Yarmouth 041465
Maritime Heritage Prints, Boston . . 087836
Maritime Museum, Cohasset 043034
The Maritime Museum, Dublin 022758
Maritime Museum, Low Head 001196
Maritime Museum, Melaka 027993
Maritime Museum, Port Victoria . . . 001403
Maritime Museum, Ramsgate 040793
Maritime Museum, Singapore 034294
Maritime Museum, Vittoriosa 028045
Maritime Museum for East Anglia, Great Yarmouth 039634
Maritime Museum of Andros, Andros 021133
Maritime Museum of British Columbia, Victoria 006745
Maritime Museum of Macau, Macau 007186
Maritime Museum of Monterey, Monterey 045982
Maritime Museum of Tasmania, Hobart 001107
Maritime Museum of the Atlantic, Halifax 005576
Maritime Museum of Thera (Santorini), Oia 021411
Maritime Museum of Townsville, Townsville 001562
Maritime Museum Zierikzee, Zierikzee 030388
Maritime Prints, Stoke-sub-Hamdon 114495
Maritime Replicas America, Miami . 090202
Maritime Tradition Museum, Piraeus 021431
Mariu s Comercio de Antiguidades, Rio de Janeiro 058614
Marjan, Vancouver 059381
Marjankov, Bohumil, Litoměřice . . . 137793
La Marjolaine, Breteuil-sur-Iton . . . 061786
Marjorie Kinnan Rawlings Historic State Park, Cross Creek 043228
Mark, London . . . 085516, 113750, 131103
Mark, Oederan 073174
Mark, I., Chicago 115492
Mark Hall Cycle Museum, Harlow . . 039673
Mark Twain Birthplace Museum, Stoutsville 048387
Mark Twain Home and Museum, Hannibal 044423
Mark Twain House, Hartford 044459
Marka Mesat Antika, İstanbul 083145
Markarian, Cincinnati 088259
Markarydsortens Hembygdsmuseum, Markaryd 036475
Markau, Heinz, Bippen 125334
Markbygdens Auktionsjänst, Fritsla 122136
Markefka, Gusti & Manfred, Mühldorf am Inn 104126
Markel, Kathryn, New York 118163
Marker Museum, Marken 029909
Markert, Julia, Firenze 127367
Market-Antiques, Dallas 088562
Market-Antiques, Dallas 088563
Market-Antiques, Dallas 088564
Market-Antiques, Dallas 088565
Market-Antiques, Fort Worth 088866
Market-Antiques, Houston 089149
The Market Antiques, San Antonio . 092544
Market Art, Houston 116364
Market Books, Whangarei 140690
Market Central, Memphis 090088
Market Coins, Seattle 093034
Market Collectibles, Seattle 093035
Market Cross Gallery, Debenham . . 112943
The Market Cross Gallery, Sturminster Newton 114518
Market Deeping Antiques, Market Deeping 085932
Market Five Gallery, Washington . . 120323
Market Gallery, Culture Division, City of Toronto, Toronto 006612
Market Graphics, Seattle 119959
Market House, Burnham Market . . . 083805
Market House Gallery, Marazion . . . 114055
Market Lavington Village Museum, Market Lavington 040429
Market Street Mews, Penryn 114227
Market the Champion Village, Houston 089150
Marketplace Antiques Gallery, Detroit 088765
Markey, Lawrence, New York 118164
Markfield Beam Engine and Museum, London 040217
Markgräfler Museum Müllheim, Müllheim, Baden 019025
Markgräfliches Opernhaus, Bayreuth 015919
Markgraf, Gunzenhausen 103037
Markgrafenmuseum Ansbach, Ansbach 015556
Markham & Son, E.J., Colchester . .084057, 130601
Markham Museum and Historic Village, Markham 005836
Marki, Brian, Portland 119018
De Markies, Breda 078109

Markies, J., Forest Row 084425
Markiewicz, Paris 100654
Markiza, Beograd 080399
Markoff, Youri, Sablonnières 067336
Markov, W., Bonn 138904
Marks, Anthony, London 085517
Marks, B. J. & S., Oldham 086158
Marks, Barrie, London 141846
Marks, Matthew, New York 118165
Marks, Matthew, New York 118166
Marks, Percy, Sydney 056682
Mark's Antique Tubs, New Orleans . 090588
Mark's Book Barn, Turrella 137117
Mark's China Pottery, Fresno 132083
Marks-Hirshfeld Museum of Medical History, Herston 001103
Marks & Marks, Denver 116023
Marksteiner, Frank, Reutlingen 104732
Markt Einersheimer Heimatstuben, Markt Einersheim 018839
Markt- und Schaustellermuseum, Essen 017072
't Marktje, Den Haag 078218
Markus, New York 091060
Markus, M., Lingen 103926
Markvardsen, Charlotte, Roskilde . . 060398
Markwalder, Beatrice, Würenlos . . . 082921
Markworth, Nidda 139594
Marland's Grand Home, Ponca City 047117
Marlboro County Historical Museum, Bennettsville 042145
Marlboro Gold Arts, Cork 074878
Marlboro Museum, Marlboro 045692
Marlborough, Buenos Aires 094082
Marlborough, Monaco 107538
Marlborough, New York 118167
Marlborough, New York 118168
Marlborough, Santiago de Chile . . . 097630
Marlborough Antiques, Milton 056228, 123266
Marlborough Fine Art, London 113751
Marlborough Gallery, Blenheim . . . 108374
Marlborough Parade Antique Centre, Marlborough 085950, 131269
Marlborough Rare Books, London . . 141847
Marle Place Gallery, Brenchley 112697
Marletta, Pino, Firenze 127368
Marlière, Hélène, Saint-Tropez 068020
Mårlind, Göteborg 110925
Marlipins Museum, Shoreham-by-Sea 041015
Marlo, Philadelphia 142746
Marlo Galeria, Wrocław 109225
Marlow Antique Centre, Marlow . . . 085955
Marlowe Books, Canterbury 141483
Marly, Biel 082259
Marma Gully Antiques, Murtoa 056305
Marmar, Madrid 110567
Marmaras, Timotheos, Athinai 074598
Marmet, Peter, Igis 082506
Marmoles Carrigarc, Barcelona . . . 129362
Marmor Galerie, Gauting 102920
Marmorbad, Kassel 018194
Marmori, Elisabetta, Roma 076541
Marmormuseum, Adnet 001662
Marnardal Museum, Marnardal . . . 031011
Marney, Patrick, Long Melford 085837, 131230
Marnier, Edward, Shepton Mallet . . 086573
Marninart, Washington 120324
Marnix, Mechelen 123664
Maroc, Marseille 099673
Marokunst, Rotterdam 078733
Marona, Helsinki 060555
Maronie, Kyoto 106901
Maronne, Elisabeth, Bordeaux 138047
Marotta, Lou, New York 091061
Marotte, Nancy 064874
La Marotte, Nyon 082704
Die Marotte, Schweinfurt 073766
Marotte, Pascal, Passenans 124836
Marotte de Foucade, Boulogne-sur-Mer 061697
Marotti, Silvio, Montevideo 087329, 142186
Marotti, Silvio, Punta del Este 142189
Marouchian, Kevork, München 072786
Maroun, Salloum, Paris 066251
Maroux, Simone, Corbigny 062471
Marprieh, Bilbao 129439
Marquage, Marseille 099674
Marquand, Seattle 135504
Marquard, Rotterdam 078734
Marquardsen, H., Breklum 070004
Marquardt, Bernd-Olaf, Berlin 069696
Marquardt, Curt, Ottersberg 073269
Marquardt, Dieter, Vechelde 105105
Marquardt, Martin, Ludwigsburg, Württemberg 126231
Marquardt, Nikki Diana, Paris 100655
Marquardt, U., München 104262
Marquart, Belm 069515, 125146
Marque, Blakehurst 136808
Marque, Edouard de la, Paris 066252
Marqueria Esart, La Paz 096442
O Marquês, Lisboa 079960
Marques, Jaime Silva, Lisboa 079961
Marquès, Magin, Bedoin 098945
Marques, Maria E., Amadora 109236
Marques, Maxime, Aubagne 138016
Marques, Paulo Tavares, Lisboa . . . 079962
Marques, Silvia, Bilbao 080982
Marquet, Karine, Paris 100656
Marquetabla, Bucaramanga 098219
Marquetería y Galería Acropólis, Bucaramanga 098220
Marqueterie d'Art, Saverne 068165
Marquette, Cincinnati 115642
Marquette, Frédéric, Abbeville 060652
Marquette, Frédéric, Cocquerel . . . 062374
Marquette County History Museum, Marquette 045695
Marquette County Museum, Westfield 049113
Marquez, Laura, Madrid 110568
Marquis, Épinal 121000
Marquis, Los Angeles 116841
Le Marquis de Carabas, Boissy-la-Rivière 061546
Marquisat de Pont-Croix, Musée du Patrimoine, Pont-Croix 013885
Marquistoir, Paris 066253
Marquit, Andrea, Boston 115201
Marquois, Jacky, Niort . . . 065197, 124526
Marr, Iain, Beauly 083464
Marra & Carbone, Roma . . 076542, 128103
Marrakech Interieur, Köln 071980
Marrari, Enrico, Roma 076543
Marrassé, Philippe, Saint-Hilaire-de-Lusigna 067515
Marrero, La Palmas de Gran Canaria 110710
Marrett House, Standish 048317
Marri, Tito, Prato 127892
Marrin & Sons, G. & D.I., Folkestone 084419, 130711, 141616
Marringhurst Pioneer Park Museum, Pilot Mound 006151
Marriott, Corinda 136868
Marriott, Stafford 137091
Marriott, Strathpine 137093
Marriott, Michael, London 085518, 131104
Marro, Ferdinando, Tübingen 074111
Marrone, München 072787
Marrone, Oscar, Roma 128104
Marry, Lyon 124365
Marryat, Richmond, Surrey 086359, 131415
M'Ars, Moskva 109565
Mars Gallery, Chicago 115493
Marsa, Kobarid 109938
Marsaleix, Christian, Bordeaux 124132
Marsaleix, Pierre, Paris 124739
Marsam, Rabat 107564
Marsault, Biarritz 061468
Marschall, Volker, Düsseldorf 102528
Marschke, Raymond, Alsdorf, Sieg . 069141
Marschner, B., Leipzig 072210
Marschollek, Nicolle, Groningen . . . 078428
Marschpoort Kunst en Antiek, Zutphen 078878
Marsden, Barrett, London 113752
Marsden, Franck, Hardinghen 063128
Marsden, Jane J., Atlanta 087498
Marsden Galleries, Bathurst 094218
Marsden Hall Antiques, Taupo 079255
Marse Taltavull, Maria Amor, Barcelona 110214
Marseille Collections, Marseille . . .064372, 138197
Marsel, Beograd 109711
Marsh, Indianapolis 122922
Marsh, Gerald E., Winchester 087174, 131696
Marsh Art Gallery, Richmond 047425
Marshall, London 085519, 131105
Marshall, San Antonio 092545
Marshall, Clifford, Atlanta 131783
Marshall & Co., Frank R., Knutsford 122558
Marshall, Kevin, Kingston-upon-Hull 084862
Marshall, Lyne, Tallegalla 095312
Marshall, Nancy, New York 091062
Marshall Arts, Memphis 116997
Marshall County Historical Museum, Holly Springs 044578
Marshall County Historical Museum, Plymouth 047094
Marshall County Historical Society Museum, Warren 048858
Marshall County Museum, Marshalltown 045707
Marshall Field's, Chicago 088127
Marshall M. Fredericks Sculpture Museum, Saginaw Valley State University, University Center 048699
Marshall Seifert, Dunedin 108439
Marshalls of Wells, Wells 087069
Marsilio, Venezia 134708
Marsilius, Speyer 139737
La Marsillargue, Avignon 061138
Marsjandisen, Oslo 079459
Marsol, Milano 075761
Marstal Søfartsmuseum, Marstal . . 009021
Marstallmuseum, München 019079
Marsteen, Geelong 055867
Marston, Abingdon 135114
Marston, Petworth 086252, 131378
Marston, Luce, Washington 093422
Marston House, San Diego 047822
Marszalec-Milanowska, Katarzyna, Gdańsk 108892
Marszand, Warszawa 109154
Mart Saare Majamuuseum, Viljandi Muuseumi, Suure-Jaani 009393
Martano, Torino 106685
Martayan Lan, New York 142673
M'Arte, Milano 106264
Marteau, Thierry, Bonneuil Matours 061560
Martel, Thierry, Goult 124251
Martel Greiner, Paris 100657
Martel Maides, Saint Peter Port . . . 122682
Martella, Francesco, Roma 076544
Martella, Michele, Milano 127629
Martelli, Giorgio, Roma 128105
Martelli & d'Addato, Bologna 105970
Martelli Castaldi, Napoli 127779
Martello d'Arte, Palermo 076159
Martelot, Gisèle, Sainte-Marie-du-Mont 068066
Marten River Logging Museum, Marten River 005837
Martens, Gent 096294
Martens, Monica, Aardenburg 128519
Martensson, Järpen 122167
Martha Berry Museum, Rome 047532
Martha's Mixture, Richmond 092094, 132719
Martha's Vineyard Historical Society Exhibition, Edgartown 043603
Marti, Barcelona 129363
Marti Carbonell, Carlos, Barcelona . 129364
Martial, Philippe, Paris 124740
Martin & Co., Birmingham 130392
Martin & Co, Cheltenham 083923
Martin, Los Angeles 116842
Martin, Montpellier 064749
Martin & Co., Norfolk 118615
Martin, Reims 124864
Martin, Saint Louis 092273
Martin, Alain Georges, Roma 076545
Martin, Ambrosio, Miami 117108
Martin, Chantal, Toulouse 124983
Martin, Christophe & Sylvain, Chauffailles 062243
Martin, Christopher H., Dallas 115909
Martin, C.J., London 085520
Martin, Clorinde, Paris 100658
Martin, Daniel, Chatellerault 062219
Martin, Didier, Aucamville 124083
Martin, Florence, Paris 066254
Martin, Gail, New York 118169
Martin, Georges, Vence 068752
Martin, Günter, Bürgstadt 070087
Martin, Guy, Paris 138498
Martin, J., Indianapolis 116476
Martin, Jean, Paris 124741
Martin, Jean Claude, Chavanoz . . . 124196
Martin, Jean-Pierre, Bourg-Saint-Maurice 061715
Martin, John, London 113753
Martín, Juan, México 107498
Martin, Lawrence, New York 118170
Martin, Lawrence, San Francisco . . 119728
Martin, Lous, Delft 107890
Martin, Maria, Bram-le-Lauragais . 061745
Martin, Maria, Madrid 110569
Martin, Mary-Anne, New York 118171
Martin, Michael, Heinsberg 071482
Martin, Michael, San Francisco . . . 119729
Martin, Michel, Quiberon 101053
Martin, Olivier, Montréal 097053
Martin, Olivier, Montréal 097054
Martin, Patrice, Saint-Étienne-de-Chigny 067470
Martin, Patrice, Souppes-sur-Loing 068274
Martin, Paul, Marlborough 085951
Martin, Peter, Clayfield 055686
Martin, Peter J., Eton 084344, 130691
Martin, Richard, Gosport . 084489, 130739, 141630
Martin, Richard, Paddington 095034
Martin, Robert, Paris 066255
Martin, Robin, London 085521
Martin, Steve, New Orleans 117473
Martin, Tatjana, Sissach 111916
Martin, Ted, Toronto 097325
Martin, Thierry, Nantes 064935
Martin, Tony, Looe 085850
Martin, Vance, San Francisco 119730
Martin, Yvona, Berlin 069697
Martin and Osa Johnson Safari Museum, Chanute 042711
Martin-Anselme, Moncontour-de-Bretagne 064594
Martin Art Gallery, Allentown 041660
Martin Benka Múzeum, Martin 034385
Martin-Caille, Bruno, Paris 100659
Martin-Caille Matignon, Paris 100660
Martin & Chausselat, Versailles . . . 121280
Martin County Historical Museum, Stanton 048323
The Martin D'Arcy Museum of Art, Loyola University Museum of Medieval, Renaissance and Baroque Art, Chicago 042855
Martin du Louvre, Paris 100661
Martin du Nord- de Bouvet, Sainte-Geneviève-des-Bois 121254
Martin & G. Chausselat, J., Versailles 121281
Martin-Gropius-Bau, Berlin 016117
Martin Hernandez, Jose Manuel, Salamanca 081538
Martin-Lauterburg-Stiftung, Schloss Jegenstorf, Bern 036931
Martin & Lawrence, New Orleans . .117474, 122979

Martin Ledesma, Miguel Juan, Madrid 081338
Martin Lorente, Mariano, Madrid . . 129644
Martin Luther King jr. Center for Nonviolent Social Change, Atlanta 041864
Martin Luther King jr. National Historic Site and Preservation District, Atlanta . 041865
Martin Luthers Geburtshaus, Stiftung Luthergedenkstätten in Sachsen-Anhalt, Lutherstadt Eisleben 018755
Martin Luthers Sterbehaus, Stiftung Luthergedenkstätten in Sachsen-Anhalt, Lutherstadt Eisleben 018756
Martin-Malburet, Marc, Paris 100662, 138499
Martin Museum of Art, Waco 048813
Martin of London, Los Angeles 089836
Martin of Melbourne, Armadale, Victoria 055386
Martin of Melbourne, Armadale, Victoria 123183
Martin & Parke, Farnborough, Hampshire 084384, 141611
Martin & Pole, Wokingham 122757
Martin-Quick, Wolverhampton 087210
Martin Rodriguez, Jose Luis, Salamanca 081539
Martin Saenz, Francisco, Málaga . . 081424
Martin Sanchez, Ricardo Antonio, Madrid 110570
Martin & Stein, Sydney 056683
Martin Street Antiques, Gardenvale 055860
Martin Van Buren Historic Site, Kinderhook 045003
Martín Villena, Ignacio, Granada . . . 141021
Martin-von-Wagner-Museum der Universität Würzburg, Antikensammlung und Neuere Abteilung mit Graphischer Sammlung, Würzburg 021000
Martin-Zambito, Seattle 119960
Martinarte, Torino 106686
Martinborough Gallery, Martinborough 108498
Martinčoková-Husárová, Katarína, Košice 129275
Martine, Dudelange 077464
Martine Encadrement, Viry-Chatillon 101487
Martinelli, Elisa, Modena 106350
Martinelli, Castaldi & Co., Napoli . . 127780
Martines, Luca, Torino 128332
El Martinete, Málaga 081425
Martinetti, Gerard, Toulon (Var) 124966
Martinez, Madrid 081339
Martínez, Montevideo 087330
Martinez, Alfredo, Miami 117109
Martinez, Antonio Gil, Sevilla 081594
Martinez, Didier, Paris 138500
Martínez, Eugenio, Barcelona 129365
Martínez, Félix, Valencia 129779
Martinez, Guy, Amboise 060798
Martinez, J., Edinburgh 084302
Martinez, Jean-Claude, Paris 100663
Martinez, José, Lyon 099601
Martinez, Lorenzo, Madrid 081340
Martínez, Luis Fernando, Barranquilla 098090
Martinez, M., Liège 058315, 120773
Martinez-Aldama y Hervas, Josefina, Madrid 110571
Martinez Antiquité, Saint-Gratien . . 067509
Martinez-Barbeito Manovel, Beatriz, A Coruña 129489
Martínez Charry, Octavio, Bogotá . . 123904
Martinez-Fleurot, Paris . . . 066256, 138501
Martínez García, Antonio, Cádiz . . . 129474
Martinez Romero, M., Valencia 110834
Martinez Rueda, Barcelona 129366
Martinez Sanchez, M.L., Madrid . . . 110572
Martinho, Ricardo P. Ferreira, Lisboa 140844
Martini, Roma 076546
Martini, Brigitte, Landsberg am Lech 072140
Martini, Fabrizio, Livorno 075534
Martini, Giovanni, Padova 076097
Martini, Laurent, Paris 066257
Martini, Mario, Roma 128106
Martini, Roland, Lafox 063483
Martini Girl Art Gallery, Atlanta 114901
Martini & Ronchetti, Genova 106099
Editions de la Martinière, Paris 133650
Martinis, Marika de, Flims Waldhaus 111406
Martinoja, Angelo, Roma 076547
Martinos, Eleni, Athinai 074599
Martinot, Alain, Paris 066258
Martinot, Savignat & Antoine, Cergy-Pontoise 120966
Martinot, Savignat & Antoine, Pontoise 121226
Martins, Fortaleza 096533
Martins, Ana P. Silva, Lisboa 079963
Martins, Henri, Venette 125013
Martins, João Moura, Porto 080096
Martins, João, Setúbal 109406
Martins, Manuel Murteira, Lisboa . . 079964
Martins, Manuel L. Murteira, Lisboa 079965
Martins, Manuel L. Murteira, Lisboa 079966
Martins Antikhandel, Göteborg 081816
Martinsart, Romorantin-Lanthenay . 133694
Martinus, Werner, Gräfelfing 125748
Martinustoren, Losser 029879
Martlesham Antiques, Martlesham . 085957
Martock Gallery, Martock 114065
Marton Historic Village Museum, Marton 030534
Martorano, Paolo M., Milano 075762
Martorell Museum, Barcelona 034928
Martre, Caroline, Pont-l'Abbé 066928
Marttilan Kirkkomuseo, Marttila . . . 009861
Marttilan Kotiseutumuseo, Marttila . 009862
Marty, Claude, Désandans 062614
Marty, Laure, Toulouse 068526
Marty, Wilfrid, Toulouse 101365
Marty-Parrot, Nathalie, Zürich 130252
Marty & Pat's Art Gallery, Fort Worth 116155
Martyn Ferenc Gyűjtemény, Janus Pannonius Múzeum, Pécs 021819
Martyrologiczny Punkt Upamiętnienia - Rotunda, Zamość 032552
Martyr's Memorial at Sports City, Amman 027374
Martyrs' Shrine, Midland 005867
Marue Ohno Shoten, Tokyo 077279
Marugame Bijutsukan, Marugame . 026781
Marugame Genichiro-Inokuma, Marugame 026782
Marugan de Santos Santi, Saint-Ouen 067845
Marugan Perez, Miguel Angel, Palencia 081461
Marui, Hiratsuka 077049
Marukiya, Kobe 077080
Maruku Arts, Ayers Rock 055418
Marull Dalmau, Jesus Maria, Barcelona 080878, 129367
Marulla, Giuseppe, Roma 128107
Marullo, Edvige, Roma 076548
Marumo, Claude, Paris 100664
Marunaka, Hiroshima 077060
Marunouchi, Jain, New York 118172
Marusho, Kadoma 106862
Maruyo, Nagoya 077152
Maruzen, Tokyo 140192
Marvelous Arts & Antiques of China, Vancouver 059382
Marvin, San Marino 080346
Marvin Newton House, Brookfield . 042447
Marvol Museum, Kuilsriver 034671
Marv's Collectibles Plus, Portland . . 091969
Marway, Winnipeg 059465
Marwen Foundation, Chicago 042856
Marx, Frankfurt am Main 139092
Marx, Etienne, Compiègne 062439
Marx, Heather, San Francisco 119731
Marx, Klaus-Günter, Düsseldorf . . . 070410
Marx, M., Lengerich, Westfalen . . . 072229
Marx Antik, Düsseldorf 070411
Marx & Saunders, Chicago 115494
Marxhausen Art Gallery, Seward . . . 048120
Mary and Leigh Block Museum of Art, Northwestern University, Evanston 043762
Mary Ann's Antiques, Denver 088714
Mary Arden's House and the Countryside Museum, Shakespeare Birthplace Trust, Stratford-upon-Avon 041140
Mary Ball Washington Museum, Lancaster 045151
Mary Brogan Museum of Art and Science, Tallahassee 048482
Mary Catherine's Antiques, Columbus 088424
Mary MacKillop Pilgrimage Centre, Fitzroy 001029
Mary Mackillop Place Museum, North Sydney 001338
Mary McLeod Bethune House, Washington 048919
Mary March Regional Museum and Logging Exhibition, Grand Falls-Windsor . . 005532
Mary Moffat Museum, Griquatown . 034630
Mary Place Gallery, Paddington . . . 095035
Mary Porter Sesnon Art Gallery, Santa Cruz 047956
Mary Queen of Scots' House, Jedburgh 039833
Mary Rose Museum, Portsmouth . . 040767
Mary Todd Lincoln House, Lexington 045263
Mary Washington College Galleries, Fredericksburg 044060
Mary Washington House, Fredericksburg 044061
Maryborough Art Society, Maryborough, Queensland 052478, 094791
Maryborough Station Antique Emporium, Maryborough, Victoria 056167
Maryfield Museum, Maryfield 005838
Maryhill Museum of Art, Goldendale 044237
Maryland Arms Collectors Association, Baltimore 054865
Maryland Art Place, Baltimore 041993
Maryland Art Place, Baltimore 115066
Maryland Association of History Museums, Annapolis 054866
Maryland College of Art and Design, Silver Spring 052183
Maryland Federation of Art, Annapolis 054867
Maryland Historical Society Museum, Baltimore 041994
Maryland Institute Museum, College of Art Exhibitions, Baltimore 041995
Maryland Pastel Society, Riderwood 054868
Maryland Printmakers, Savage 054869
Maryland Science Center, Baltimore 041996
Marymont Plantation Antique Shop, Nashville 090467
Marymoor Museum of Eastside History, Redmond 047363
Maryol, Johannesburg 110058
Maryol, Rosebank 110075
Maryport Maritime Museum, Maryport 040430
Mary's Attic, Virginia Beach 093363
Mary's Book Exchange, Tampa 143023
Mary's Imports, Jacksonville 089429
Mary's Stuff, Chicago 088128
Mary's Swap Meet, Oklahoma City . 091517
Mary's Upholstery, Memphis 090089, 132328
Marysa, Paris 066259
Maryse, Trouville-sur-Mer 068638
Marystown Museum, Marystown . . 005839
Marywood University Art Galleries, Scranton 048065
Marzano, Roberto, Roma 076549
Marzee, Nijmegen 108155
Marzellus-Buchhandlung, Köln 139350
Marzocco, Firenze 140024
Marzoll, Cornelia, Neustadt an der Weinstraße 073030
MAS, Amsterdam 077909
Mas, Christian, Saint-Barthélemy . . 105468
Mas, Colette, Paris 100665, 138502
Mas, Yannick, Bordeaux 099007
Mas, Yves, Paris 066260
Mas d'Antic, Valencia 081665
Mas de Bony, Marsillargues 064404
Mas de Curebourg, L'Isle-sur-la-Sorgue 063946
Le Mas des Arnaud, Saint-Martin-de-Crau 101178
Mas des Chevaliers, Les Baux-de-Provence 063759
Mas Maury, André, Pescadoires . . . 066780
Mas Muntaner, Palma de Mallorca . 081488
Mas Oliveras, Santiago, Barcelona . 140999
Mas Suárez, Elvira, A Coruña 081061, 141015
Masa Art, Miami 117110
Masago, Osaka 106968
Masaki Art Museum, Osaka 026970
Masamune, Saron, Osaka 077179
Masanek, H.-Peter, Kirrweiler 071864
Masanek, Hans-Peter, Neustadt an der Weinstraße 073031
Masao Koga Museum, Tokyo 027197
Masar, Vero de, Wien 095895
Masarykovo Muzeum, Hodonín 008375
Mascal, Castellarano 134563
Mascalchi, Mariapia, Prato 076255
Maschenmuseum, Stadtverwaltung Albstadt, Museumsamt, Albstadt . 015467
Mascherino, Roma 106585
Il Mascherone, Palermo 076160
Maschio, Fernand, Vercia 125014
Maschke, Walter, Calw 125423
Masciantonio, Gabriele, Verona . . . 128430
Masclef, Amiens 060823
Mascot, New York 118173
Masen, S., Maastricht 078613
Maser, Pittsburgh 118940
Masfrand, Denis, Lomme 063979
Masha, Prieto, Madrid 110573
Mashiko Sankokan, Mashiko 026783
Mashrabia, Cairo 098648
Al-Mashrabia, Manama 057638
Masi, Antonio, Milano 075763
Masi, Lamberto, Palermo 076161
Masi, Ninetta, San Marino 080347
Masi, Rosario, Torino 076840
Masia Museu Can Magarola, Alella . 034816
Masiero, Pietro, Milano 127630
Masini, Buenos Aires 055223
Masini, Amel, Paris 124742
Masini, Francesco, Firenze 127369
Masini, Stefania, Firenze 075368
Masip Pascual, Jose, Barcelona . . . 080879
Masis-Metna, Genève 082445
Maske, Siegfried, Behrensdorf 101751
Maskell & Co., Don, San Francisco . 119732
Maskerade, Rotterdam 078735
Maskun Museo, Masku 009863
Maslak McLeod, Toronto 097326
Maslak McLeod, Toronto 097327
Maslan, Michael, Seattle . 093036, 143000
Maslewski, K. & R., Kirchheim unter Teck 071861
Masliah, Guy, Saint-Ouen 067846
Maslin, Betty, Murchison 056303
La Masmédula Galería, México . . . 107499
Mason, Cincinnati 088260
Mason, Darwin 094460
Mason, Dublin 074932
Mason, Fresno 116180
Mason, Kings Park 094702
Mason, New Orleans 117475
Mason, David, Toronto 137712
Mason, D.J., Tunbridge Wells 086942
Mason, Harry, Brighton . . 083704, 130445
Mason, Ian, Ballarat 136790
Mason, Jane, North Shore 108525
Mason, Paul, London 085522
Mason, Paul, London 113754
Mason, Paul, London 131106
Mason County Museum, Mason . . . 045721
Mason County Museum, Maysville . 045730
Mason Gray Strange, Kilkenny 120596

The Masonic Library and Museum of Pennsylvania, Philadelphia 046959
Masonic Temple, Hobart 001108
Masonry Museum Vånevik and Näset, Påskallavik 036539
Måsøy Museum, Havøysund 030884
Al-Masri, Mohammed Bassam, Damascus 083066
Mass Gallery, Fitzroy North 094544
Mass Moca, North Adams 046511
Massachusetts Antiques Cooperative, Waltham 093373
Massachusetts College of Art, Boston 051013
Massachusetts Historical Society Museum, Boston 042331
Massacre Rocks State Park Museum, American Falls 041683
Massalme, Dr. Elisabeth, Sankt Michaelisdonn 104813
Massarella, Saltaire 114391
Massarelli, Pedro H., São Paulo . . . 096680
Massaroni, Rosina, Roma 076550
Massbay Antiques, Danvers 136535
Masse, Vincent, Troyes 068652
Masseguin Lou Brocantou, Mende . 064478
Massenet, Aliette, Paris 066261
Massey, Saint Louis 123087
Massey & Son, D.J., Alderley Edge . 083260
Massey & Son, D.J., Macclesfield . . 085892
Massey Area Museum, Massey . . . 005840
Massias, Jacques, Nantes 064936
Massicot, Rennes (Ille-et-Vilaine) . . 101085
Massieu, Martine, Champeaux-et-la-Chapelle-Pommier 062117
Massillon Museum, Massillon 045724
Massimiliani, Marco, Roma 106586
Massin, Paris 133651
Massin-Dumartin, Christian, Paris . 066262
Massingham, Roy, Brasted 083652
Massnes Villmarksmuseum, Bjordal 030778
Massol, Jacques, Paris 100666
Masson, Paris 066263
Masson, Andrée, Villeurbanne 068970
Masson, Jean, Cucq 062581
Masson, Philippe, Jaunay-Clan . . . 063238
Le Masson Brunot, Paris 124743
Masson, Pictet & Boissonnas, Zürich 130253
Massone, Giuseppe, Torino 076841
Massot, Régis, Changé 062134
Massoud, Mervet, Cairo 098649
Massow, Dagmar von, Berlin 069698
Massua-Educational Museum on the Holocaust, Tel Yitzhak 023097
Mastelinck, Jean-Pierre, Avesnes-le-Comte 061121
Master, Amsterdam 077910
Master Drawings Association, New York 135440
Master Drawings Quarterly, New York 136536
Master Framers, Saint Paul 132770
Master Mirror's, Modena 106351
Master Rug Gallery, Los Angeles . . 089837
Masterpaintings, Rotterdam 078736
Masterpeach, Kenmare 110065
Masterpiece, Hobart 055997
Masterpiece Gallery, Cincinnati . . . 115643
Masterpiece Gallery, Toronto 097328
Masterpiece Gallery, Vancouver . . . 097498
Masterpieces Antiques, Cincinnati . 088261
Masters Art, Barcelona 110215
Masters Art, Palma de Mallorca . . . 110692
Masters Art, Palma de Mallorca . . . 110693
Masters Art Gallery, New York 118174
Masters Gallery, Calgary 096829
Masters Gallery, Woodend 095410
Masterworks, Oakland 118638
The Masterworks Foundation Collection, Hamilton 003900
MasterWorks Gallery, Auckland . . . 108339
MasterWorks Gallery, Auckland . . . 108340
Masterworks Gallery, Tampa 120057
Masterworks of New Mexico, Albuquerque 114805
Mastny & Dietrichstein, Wien 057495
Mastracci, Pittsburgh 091841
Mastrigt & Verheul, Den Haag 107940
Mastro, Beppe, Cagliari 127249
Mastroberardino, Emanuele, Taranto 128248
Mastruzzi, Umberto, Roma 128108
Masuch & Schnell, Braunschweig . 133838
Masuhr, Ch., Bernkastel-Kues 069805
Masur Museum of Art, Monroe 045969
Masure, Arnaud, Châteaulin 062197
Masuya, Hiroshima 077061
Masuzawa, Sapporo 077197
Mata-Hari Antiques, Singapore 080527
Mata Saralegui, Jose Manuel, Donostia-San Sebastián 081086
Mata Valles, Teresa, Barcelona 080880
Mataatua Gallery, Whakatane 108657
Matagorda County Museum, Bay City 042061
Matahari, Napier 079166
Matanza, Miami 090203
Matarazzo, Gesualdo, Catania 075253
Matarrese, Cosimo, Torino 128333
Matchbox Road Museum, Newfield 046450
Matchboxmuseum Latent, Prinsenbeek 030044
Matchimawas National Museum, Songkhla 037931
Matei, Soltau 104920
Matei, Elvira, Bucureşti 080162
Matenadaran, Erevan 000685
Mateo e Hijo, Rafael, Sevilla 129737
Mateos Osorio, Antonio, Málaga . . . 141062
Materazzo, Michele, Bologna 127164
Materia, Québec 097153
Materia. Revista d'Art, Barcelona . . 136096
Material, Stockholm 136114
Material Culture, Philadelphia 091665
Materialis Verlag, Frankfurt am Main 133949
Materiały Starożytne, Warszawa . . . 136027
Matériaux d'Antan, Aix-en-Provence 060711
Matern, Lorsch 103940
Matern, Christiana, Salzburg 057267, 095729, 137244
Materna, Daniel, Vancouver 097499
Materne, Hans-Jürgen, Dortmund . 070288
Maternus, Erfstadt 139041
Maters & Begeer, Franeker 128669
Mateu, Montserrat, Taller Editorial, Barcelona 134919
Mateus, Joaquim Cunha, Porto 080097
Mateyka, Marsha, Washington 120325
Mathaf, London 085523, 113755
Mathé, Villeurbanne 068971
Mathé, Frédéric, Lyon 064158
Mathé, Lucile, Nice 065112
Mathé, Monique & Jean, Sens 068217
Mathematikum, Gießen 017412
Mathematisch-Physikalischer Salon, Staatliche Kunstsammlungen Dresden, Dresden 016801
Mathes, Barbara, New York 118175
Mathes, Rudolf, München 139532
Mathes, Siegfried, Neumarkt, Oberpfalz 073004
Matheson Museum, Gainesville . . . 044104
Mathew & Sons, Klujian, Chicago . . 088129
Mathews, Gloria, Omaha 091575
Mathewson, Tracy, Warkworth 108606
Mathias, Ph., Daisendorf 070173
Mathias Ham House, Dubuque 043513
Mathies, Bad Driburg 125087
Mathieson, Tom, Ramsgate 056517
Mathieu, Besançon 061389
Mathieu, Lyon 099602
Mathieu, Alain, Champeix 062118
Mathieu, Jean-Claude, Dommartin-aux-Bois 062707
Mathieu, Marie-France, Etival-Clairefontaine 062817
Mathieu, Patrick, Chatillon-sur-Loire 062234
Mathieu Coron, Andrée, Augea 098876
Mathis, Jean-Louis, Bléré 138032
Mathisen, Bjørn, Oslo 079460
Matignon, Chicago 115495
Matignon Fine Art, Paris 100667
Matignon Saint-Honoré, Paris 100668
Matilda Antiques, Long Jetty 056112
Matilda Art Rentals, Sydney 056684
Matilda Prints, Sydney 056685
Matilda Roslin-Kalliolan Kirjailijakoti, Merikarvia 009866
Matilda's Antique Centre, North Fremantle 056362
Matinais, Herbignac 063144
Mativet, Georges, Paris 124744
Matiz, Belo Horizonte 058435
Matiz Arte Galeria, Belo Horizonte . 096472
Matlock Antiques and Collectables Centre, Matlock 085964
Matlosz & Co., W., Phoenix 091754, 132652
Matong Memories, Matong 056169
Matopos National Park Site Museums, Bulawayo 049577
Matos, Maria Oliveira, Setúbal 109407
Matousek, Peter, Oberteuringen . . . 073158
Mátra Múzeum, Gyöngyös 021728
Matre & Penley, Atlanta 114902
Matriart, Toronto 135639
Matrica Múzeum, Százhalombatta . 021856
Matrixarts, Sacramento 047593
Mats Kuriosa, Malmö 081874
Matschnig, Wien 057496
Matsell, Brian, Derby 084161
Matsqui Sumas Abbotsford Museum, Abbotsford 004984
Matsudo Museum, Matsodo 026784
Matsui, Nara 106941
Matsukyu, Kyoto 077116
Matsumoto, Osaka 077180
Matsumoto, K., San Jose 119856
Matsumoto Folk Arts Museum, Matsumoto 026791
Matsumoto-shiritsu Hakubutsukan, Matsumoto 026792
Matsumura, Tokyo 140193
Matsunaga Memorial Hall, Odawara 026929
Matsuoka Museum of Art, Tokyo . . 027198
Matsushima, Sendai 077217
Matsushima Kanrantei Museum, Matsushima 026796
Matsushita Art Museum, Aira 026405
Matsuura Shiryo Hakubutsukan, Hirado 026516
Matsuyama, Sapporo 106986
Matsuyama Municipal Shiki Kinen Museum, Matsuyama 026801
Matsuzaki, Yokohama 077340
Matt, Frederic, Dommartin (Rhône) . 062709
Matt, Dr. Hansjakob von, Zürich . . .082998, 141351
Matt, J., Schopfheim 073722
Matt, Serge, San Francisco 092841, 132899
Matt, Sibylle von, Stans 130186
Matta, John, New Orleans 132421
Mattancherry Palace Museum, Kochi 022207
Mattapoisett Museum and Carriage House, Mattapoisett 045726
The Mattatuck Museum of the Mattatuck Historical Society, Waterbury 048979
Mattawa and District Museum, Mattawa 005844
Mattei, Milano 075764
Mattei, Valentina, Roma 128109
Matteoli, Daniele, Firenze 127370
Matter, Willy, Weissenburg 082902
Mattern, Charles, Saint-Ouen 067847
Mattern, Thomas, Limburgerhof . . . 126222
Matteuzzi, Bologna 139991
Matthew, New York 091063
Matthew, Clayton & Brown, New Orleans 122980
Matthews, Tampa 120058
Matthews, Richard, Auckland 078963
Matthews, William, Denver 116024
Matthews Museum of Maine Heritage, Union 048691
Matthias, J., Houston 116365
Matthias, Ralf, Berlin 069699
Matthies, Joachim D., Hamburg . . . 071284
Matthiesen, London 085524, 113756
Matthijsse, Thijs, Middelburg 128775
Matthys, Bruxelles 058030
Mattiello, Corinna, Venezia 128397
Mattila, Robert W., Seattle 143001
Mattioli, Gérard, Guebwiller 063091
Mattioli, Manuela, Bologna 127165
Mattioli, Paola, Roma 128110
Mattisrud Småbruksmuseum, Løten 031000
Mattix, D.H., Chicago 115496
Mattke, Jörg, Lübeck 072331
Matton, Bochum 102158
Mattress Factory Museum, Pittsburgh 047055
Matt's, London 135231
Matt's Museum, Lawtell 045214
Mattson, E. Christian, Baltimore . . . 142228
Mattssous Mynt, Uppsala 082059
Mattye, Houston 089151
Mattye Reed African Heritage Center, Greensboro 044336
Matuizos Manto, Vilnius 140233
Maturango Museum of the Indian Wells Valley, Ridgecrest 047433
Maturen, Antonio Esteban, Zaragoza 081745, 129819
Matusalen, Salamanca 081540
Matuschek, B., Taunusstein 105034
Matuschka, Sophie Gräfin von, Wiesbaden 127013
Mátyás Király Múzeum, Magyar Nemzeti Múzeum, Visegrád 021922
Matyó Múzeum, Mezőkövesd 021782
Matzat, Brigitte, Ludwigsfelde 103948
Matzke, Helga, Grünwald 071136
Mauad, Juan, Omar & Michel, Montevideo 122784
Maubach, Katarina, Dresden 125503
Maubach, Magdalene & Susanne, Goch 125732
Maubert, Jean-Marie, Hiers-Brouage 063156
Maubrie, Gabrielle, Paris 100669
Mauch, Brigitte, Göppingen 102970
Mauchard, François, Tendon 068371
Maud Railway Museum, Maud 040438
Maude I. Kerns Art Center, Eugene . 043745
Maude Kerns Art Center School, Eugene 051310
Maudet, Bruno, Tours 101381, 125000
Maudrich, Wilhelm, Wien 137344
Maudrux-Miniconi, Marie-France, Alata 060742
Maud's Attic, Ipswich 084802
Maué, Michael, Lüneburg 072360
Mauer-Design, Ettlingen 133925
Mauermuseum - Museum Haus am Checkpoint Charlie, Berlin 016118
Mauersberg, R., Nienburg, Weser . . 073056
Mauersberger-Museum, Großrückerswalde 017580
Maui Gallery, Westport 108655
Mauilotus Asian Arts Gallery, Minneapolis 117283
Maul, Georg, Köln 126104
Maulbecker, Heiko & Marianne, Köln 103675
Maulberger, Kampen 103481
Maulberger, München 104263
Mauléon, Cordes-sur-Ciel 099173
Maulet, Didier, Paris 124745
Maune, J., Saint Louis 092274
Maunier & Noudel-Denian, Toulon (Var) 121267
Maunoury Dufour, Jacqueline, Chablis 062066
Mauny, Philippe, Mortagne-sur-Gironde 064801

Maupas, Catherine, Montoire-sur-le-Loir . . . 064725
Maupilier, Belz . . . 061342
Maupilier et Fils, Les Clayes-Sous-Bois . . . 063762
Maupin, Constance, Paris . . . 066264
Maupin, Frédéric, Boulogne-sur-Mer . . . 061698
Maupin, Olivier, Jargeau . . . 124267
Maurel, Guy, Orange . . . 065277
Maurel Franck, Montescot . . . 064678
Mauren, Gisela, Köln . . . 071981
Maurer, Küsnacht . . . 111599
Maurer, A. & F., Buchs, Zürich . . . 111313
Maurer, Annette M., Barcelona . . . 129368
Maurer, Annette M., Madrid . . . 129645
Maurer, Eduard, Alchenflüh . . . 082078
Maurer, Fritz, Stuttgart . . . 126869
Maurer, H.-J. & R., Bretzfeld . . . 070059
Maurer, Peter, Pfeffingen . . . 130140
Maurer, R., Düsseldorf . . . 070412
Maurer, Ruth, Zürich . . . 112145
Maurer, W., Gmund . . . 071015
Maurer, Wolfgang, München . . . 104264
Maurermuseum und Dachdeckermuseum, Langenlois . . . 002199
Mauri Ora Gallery, Kaikoura . . . 108483
Mauriac, Rony, Larressore . . . 063542
Maurice, London . . . 131107
Maurice Antiquités, Saint-Étienne . 067460
Maurienne, La Chambre . . . 063308
Maurier, Frédérique, Paris . . . 124746
Mauries, Denis, Coulomby . . . 062505
Maurin, Paul, Paris . . . 066265
Maurin, Raymond, Arles . . . 060972
Mauritianum, Naturkundliches Museum, Altenburg, Thüringen . . . 015502
Mauritius Postal Museum, Port Louis . . . 028070
Maurits Galerie, Utrecht . . . 108256
Mauritshuis, Koninklijk Kabinet van Schilderijen, Den Haag . . . 029434
Mauro Bi, Torino . . . 076842
Mauron, Pierre, La Teste-de-Buch .063451, 124284
Mauroner, Mario, Salzburg 095730, 133142
Maury, Bernard, Crouttes-sur-Marne . . . 062575
Maury, P.C., Paris . . . 124747
Maury, Pierre, Paris . . . 124748
Maus, Kampen . . . 071696
Maus, Phillip, Groß Nordende . . . 071112, 125758
Maus, Phillip, Hamburg . . . 071285
Maus Park Antiques, Toronto . . . 059241
Mausefallen-Museum, Neroth . . . 019202
Mausefallen- und Galerie der Stillen Örtchen, Güntersberge . . . 017595
Mauthe, Markus, Langenargen . . . 103830
Mauthner, Manfred, Baden bei Wien 056940
Mauve, Paris . . . 066266
Mauz, Elisabeth, Albstadt . . . 101554
Mauzoleum Walki i Męczeństwa 1939-1945, Muzeum Niepodległości w Warszawie, Warszawa . . . 032426
Mava, Singapore . . . 109836
Mavec & Co., J., New York . . . 091064
Mavelle, Thierry, Reims . . . 124865
Maverick, Atlanta . . . 114903
Maverick, Cincinnati . . . 142320
Mave's Gallery, Stow-on-the-Wold . 114505
Mavie, Aubagne . . . 061025
Mawer & Son, Thomas, Lincoln . . . 122572
Mawr-Vassar, Bryn, Pittsburgh . . . 142776
Maws, Telford . . . 114562
Maws Gallery, Bridgnorth . . . 112701
Maws Gallery, Ironbridge . . . 113304
Max, Erich, Döhlau . . . 070265
Max Ernst Museum, Brühl, Rheinland . . . 016468
Max et Isa, Megève . . . 064466
Max Euwe Centrum, Amsterdam . . 029200
Max Galerie d'Art, Nice . . . 099848
Max-Klinger-Gedenkstätte, Naumburg, Saale . . . 019185
Max-Kommerell-Gedenkstätte, Münsingen . . . 019135
Max-Reger-Gedächtniszimmer, Brand, Oberpfalz . . . 016365
Max Studio, Venezia . . . 106763
Maxa, Martin, Banská Bystrica . . . 080594
Maxfield House Antiques, Warminster . . . 087029
Maxhütten-Museum, Bergen, Chiemgau . . . 015962
Maxi Livres, Lyon . . . 138178
Maxies Antiikki, Helsinki . . . 060556
Maxim, Prato . . . 076256
Maxim-Gorki-Gedächtnisstätte, Seebad Heringsdorf . . . 020164
Maxime, Marie, Paris . . . 066267
Maxime Brocante, Bressuire . . . 061760
Maximilian, Peguera . . . 122081
Maximilian-Gesellschaft e.V., Stuttgart . . . 053489
Maximilian Verlag, München . . . 134262
Maximilianmuseum, Städtische Kunstsammlungen, Augsburg . . . 015614
Maximiliansanlagen mit Friedensengel, München . . . 019080
Maximo Art, Albuquerque . . . 114806
Maxine's, Saint-Ouen . . . 067848
Maxoly, Miami . . . 117111
Maxwell, Roleystone . . . 095154
Maxwell, San Francisco . . . 119733
Maxwell, Helen, Braddon . . . 094275
Maxwell & Dockrees, Woodford . . .087228, 122760
Maxwell Museum of Anthropology, Albuquerque . . . 041618
Maxwelton House Museum, Moniaive . . . 040488
Maxwood, Cape Town . . . 080684, 129292
May & Son, Andover . . . 122388
May, Aschaffenburg . . . 133724
May, Megève . . . 099699
May, Seoul . . . 107268
May, Taipei . . . 098079
May, Ilona, Benshausen . . . 125147
May, J.E., Amsterdam . . . 077911
May, K.H., Amsterdam . . . 077912
May, Lilian A., Gauting . . . 125700
May, Maggie, Denver . . . 088715
May, Marita, Daun . . . 102351
May, Monika, Marburg . . . 126287
May, Thierry, Fontainebleau . . . 062898
May Antique Center Mall, Oklahoma City . . . 091518
May-Lüllemann, Christa, Wiesbaden . . . 074413
May Moré, Madrid . . . 110574
May Museum and Park, Farmville . 043825
May Natural History Museum and Museum of Space Exploration, Colorado Springs . . . 043058
May Street Gallery, Saint Peters . . . 095177
Maya, Maastricht . . . 078614
Maya Plastik Sanat Galerisi, İstanbul . . . 112336
Maya Polsky Gallery, Chicago . . . 115497
Mayan, E., New York . . . 118176
Mayart, Enschede . . . 108021
Mayborn Museum, Waco . . . 048814
Mayer & Co., Klosterneuburg . . . 137204
Mayer, Tamm . . . 105030
Mayer, Wien . . . 137345
Mayer, B.H., Buffalo . . . 087895
Mayer, Bridgette, Philadelphia . . . 118797
Mayer, Christine, München . . . 104265
Mayer, Claus-Peter, Regenstauf . . . 126703
Mayer, Dr. Gunter, Gunskirchen . . . 133085
Mayer, Hannelore, Stuttgart . . . 104998
Mayer, Hans, Düsseldorf . . . 102529
Mayer, Harald, Tübingen . . . 074112
Mayer, Helga, Ostseebad Prerow . . 104556
Mayer, Joachim, Göttingen . . . 071048
Mayer, Kuno, Bregenz . . . 056950
Mayer, Ludwig, Jerusalem . . . 139979
Mayer, Mirko, Köln . . . 103676
Mayer, Nadja & Martin, Simbach am Inn . . . 073821
Mayer, Norbert, Neustadt an der Weinstraße . . . 104432
Mayer, Oswald, Kreimbach-Kaulbach . . . 103786
Mayer, Peter, Oberndorf bei Salzburg . . . 123425
Mayer, Richard H., Bamberg . . . 101731
Mayer, Susanne, Freiberg, Sachsen 125669
Mayer, Trace, Louisville . . . 090011
Mayer, U. & S., Göttingen . . . 071049
Mayer, Wahrmut, Schöneck, Hessen . . . 134385
Mayer, Willi, Langenenslingen . . . 126168
Mayer, Y. & D., New York . . . 091065
Mayer-Jung, Paul G., Jagsthausen . 071652
Mayer & Mayer, Stuttgart . . . 073993
Mayerhofer, Gabriele, Krumpendorf 057134
Mayerling, Paris . . . 066268
Mayer'sche Hofkunstanstalt, München . . . 126414
Mayes Hilary, Saint Ives, Cornwall . 114365
Mayfair & Co., New York . . . 091066
Mayfair Antiques, Dorking . . . 084199
Mayfair Antiques, Otley . . 086173, 131351
Mayfair Antiques, Tampa . . . 093143
Mayfair Galleries, Moorabbin . . . 120615
Mayfair Gallery, London . . . 085525
Mayfair Gallery, West Hollywood . . 093486
Mayfayre, North Shore . . . 121829
The Mayfield Gallery, Bournemouth 112681
Mayflower Antiques, London . . . 085526
Mayflower Gold Mill, Silverton . . . 048181
Mayflower Society Museum, Plymouth . . . 047096
Mayhem, New York . . . 091067
Mayibuye Centre Collection, University of the Western Cape, Bellville . . . 034551
Maylands Antiques, Maylands, South Australia . . . 056172
Maylis, Tours . . . 068596
Maymont, Richmond . . . 047420
Maynard, Mark, London . . . 085527
Mayne Gallery, Kingsbridge . . . 113327
Mayne Island Museum, Mayne Island . . . 005847
de Mayo, Paris . . . 066269
Mayor, Gudrun, Carouge . . . 141237
Mayor Gallery, London . . . 113757
Mayoral, Manuel, Barcelona 080881, 110216
Mayorcas, London . . . 131108
Mayorga, Saint-Jean Pied-de-Port . 101166
Maypole, Charlotte . . . 087966
Mayr, Hans, Kreuth . . . 126151
Mayr, Rudolf, München . . . 072788
Mayr, Stephan, Sistrans . . 057315, 123470
Mayr, Thomas, Singen, Hohentwiel . 104908
Mayrberger, Ute, Neusiedl am See . 057191
Mayrhans, Tübingen . . . 139798
Mayrhofer, Horst, Breitenfurt . . . 056953
Mayrhofer, Max, Obernberg am Inn 057200
Mayrhofer, Monika E., Zell am Moos 095980
Mayrische Musikalienhandlung, Salzburg . . . 137245
Mayrl, Kelkheim . . . 071782, 126027
Mays, Maggie, Buxton . . . 083829
Maysa, Cairo . . . 098650
Maysbury, Elsternwick . . . 055795
Maysnow, Boston . . . 115202
Mayte Muñoz, Barcelona . . . 110217
Mayuyama & Co., Tokyo . . . 077280
Mayville Area Museum of History and Genealogy, Mayville . . . 045731
Mayville Historical Society Museum, Mayville . . . 045733
Mazaleyrat, Daniel, Pont-sur-Yonne 066937
Mazanec, Martin, Litoměřice . . . 060048
Mazar-i-Sharif Museum, Mazar-i-Sharif . . . 000009
Mazar Islamic Museum, Al-Mazar . 027360
Mazarin, Albi . . . 060760
Mazarin, Toulon (Var) . . . 101322
Mazarine, Montréal . . . 097055
Mazarine, Nice . . . 065113
Mazarini, Lyon . . . 099603
Mazda Creative, Nagpur . . . 105821
Maze, Jonathan, Auckland . . . 128908
Mazeau, Edith, Périgueux . . . 066723
Mazelle, Sven Walter, Spielberg . . .057317, 095761
Mazenaud, Fabien, Bû . . . 061831
Mazerand, Joseph, Massaguel . . . 064419
Mazet, Daniel, Voulangis . . . 069031
La Mazière, Cordes-sur-Ciel . . . 062473
Mazières, Serge, Nice . . . 065114
Mazo, Alain, Paris . . . 133652
Mazo Lebouc, Paris . . . 100670, 138503
Mazomanie Historical Society Museum, Mazomanie . . . 045734
Mazot, Annecy . . . 060895
Mazot-Musée de Plan-Cerisier, Martigny . . . 037313
Mazot Savoyard, Combloux . . . 062432
Mazoyer, Hugues, Clermont-Ferrand . . . 062351
Mazuel, Jacques, Savigny-sur-Orge 068170
Mazuel, Jacques, Savigny-sur-Orge 068171
Mazure, Florence, Bordeaux . . . 061634
Mazurier, Myriam, Jonzac . . . 063250
Mazza, David, Baltimore . . . 131826
Mazza, Erminio, Torino . . . 128334
Mazzanti, Claudio, Bologna 075091, 127166
Mazzara, Riehen . . . 111840
Mazzella Di Bosca, Paul, Marseille . 124426
Mazzini-Gedenkstätte, Grenchen . . 037165
Mazzitelli, Riccardo, Roma . . . 076551
Mazzola, Gustavo, Milano . . . 106265
Mazzoleni, Torino . . . 106687
Mazzoleni Arte, Milano . . . 075765
Mazzoli, Emilio, Modena . . . 106352
Mazzolini, Maria Grazia, Roma . . . 128111
Mazzon Bruna, Venezia . . . 076957
Mazzone, Enrico, Torino . . . 076843
Mazzoni, Cristina, Bologna . . . 075092
Mazzoni, Fabrizio, Firenze . . . 075369
Mazzoni, Gabriele, Bologna . . . 127167
Mazzoni, Pietro, Roma . . . 076552
Mazzotta, Gabriele, Milano . . . 134621
Mazzú, Francesco, Messina 075565, 127502
Mazzù, Francesco, Messina . . . 127503
Mazzucchi, Venezia . . . 106764
MB Antigüedades, Buenos Aires . . . 055224
MB-Art, Stuttgart . . . 104999
MB Galerie, Kaufbeuren . . . 103523
Mbantua Gallery, Alice Springs . . . 094141
MBD, Waikato . . . 128967
MBRC, San Diego . . . 092655
MC Art, London . . . 113758
MC Collectables, Indianapolis . . . 089321
M.C. Mehta Gallery, Ahmedabad . . 021991
MC-Museum Gyllene Hjulet, Surahammar . . . 036697
MCC Museum, London . . . 040218
McCaffrey, Victoria, South Yarra . . . 123307
McClelland, Whangarei . . . 108660
McClelland, Whangarei . . . 108661
McClenaghan, North Shore . . . 079195
McCormack, Wellington . . . 108629
McCrostie & Co, Christchurch . . . 079039
MCD-Antik, Dessau, Anhalt . . . 070222
McDonnell, Bridget, Carlton, Victoria . . . 094377
MCF Antiques, Waikato . . . 079292
MCK-Bilder, Oberhausen, Rheinland 104501
McKearney, Hawkes Bay . . . 079113
McKenzie, Kenneth, Malvern East . 056136
M.C.M. Antiquités, Bourg-en-Bresse . . . 061708
MCM Antiquités, Montauroux . . . 064644
M.C.N. Antiques, London . . . 085528
McPherson, Auckland . . . 108341
MCS, Jacksonville . . . 132186
mda, Museum Documentation Association, Cambridge . . . 054426
M.D.C.A., Paris . . . 100671
MDG Fine Arts, London . . . 113759

MDI Gallery, Philadelphia 118798
Mdina, Valletta 077540
MDM, Warszawa 079767, 109155
M.D.'s Auction, Kirkaldy 122556
Me, Bowdoinham 136537
Meacci Freisleben, Firenze 075370
Mead, Mount Martha 056292
Mead Art Museum, Amherst 041692
Mead Gallery, Coventry 039153
Meade County Historical Society Museum, Meade 045735
Meadow, M., San Francisco 092842
Meadow Brook Art Gallery, Rochester 047471
Meadow Brook Hall, Rochester . . . 047472
Meadow Creek Galleries, Saint Paul 119301
Meadow Farm Museum, Glen Allen 044199
Meadow Garden Museum, Augusta 041900
Meadow Lake Museum, Meadow Lake 005848
Meadowcroft Museum of Rural Life, Historical Society of Western Pennsylvania, Avella 041942
Meadowgate Antiques, Dallas 088566
Meadowlands Gallery, Banff 112554
Meadowlands Museum, Rutherford 047578
Meadows Antiques, Edinburgh 084303
Meadows Lamp Gallery, Edinburgh . 084304
Meadows Museum, Dallas 043273
Meadows Museum of Art, Centenary College, Shreveport 048160
Meadows & Passmore, Brighton . . . 130446
Meadowtide, Bartestree 112562
Meaford Museum, Meaford 005849
Meagan, Miami 090204
Meagher County Historical Association Castle Museum, White Sulphur Springs 049144
Meakk, Roosendaal 078687
Meandar, Zagreb 133404
Meandr, Moskva 080253
Meanskinisht Museum, Kitwanga . . 005721
Measham Museum, Measham 040440
Meath Archaeological and Historical Museum, Trim 022865
Méaux-Rougemont, Andrée, Annonay 098846
Meb-Art, Strzelin 129074
MEB Sanat Galerisi, İstanbul 112337
Mebel, Singapore 080528
M.E.C. Art Gallery, Delhi 105674
M.E.C. Art Gallery, Delhi 105675
Meca,Angi & Detrás del Rollo, Murcia 110652
La Mécanique, Haarlem 078467
Mecano Catalunya, L'Hospitalet de Llobregat 129538
La Mecedora, Estepona 081099
Il Mecenate, Milano 075766
Mécène, Paris 138504
Meceras, Montevideo 114762
Mecha Arte y Porcelana, La Paz . . . 096443
Mechanical Music and Doll Collection, Chichester 039072
Mechanical Music Museum and Bygones, Cotton 039148
Mechanische Schau-Werkstätte, Rehau 019765
Mechanisches Musikmuseum, Sursee 037617
Méchiche, Frédéric, Paris 100672
Méchiche, Jean-Luc, Paris 066270, 100673
Meck, Renate, Berlin 069700
Meckenstock, Düsseldorf 125539
Mecking, J. Garvin, New York 091068
Mecklenburg, Werner Christian, München 104266, 126415
Mecklenburger Antik-Diele, Neustrelitz 073042
Mecklenburgisches Orgelmuseum, Malchow, Mecklenburg 018799
Mecklenburgisches Volkskundemuseum Schwerin, Freilichtmuseum Schwerin-Mueß, Schwerin 020148
Meckum, Günter, Idar-Oberstein . . . 071607
Mecoen, Moissac 064582
Mecosta County Historical Museum, Big Rapids 042199
Mecrom & Holey, Feldkirchen, Niederbayern 070681
Mecseki Banyászati Múzeum, Pécs 021820
Meda, Massimo, Milano 106266
Médailles du Travail, Marseille 064373
Médaillier Municipal, Bordeaux . . . 010878
Medal of Honor Museum of Military History, Chattanooga 042781
Medalhão Galeria de Arte, Brasília . 096495
Medalių, Vilnius 107368
Mede, Robert, Toronto 097329
Medea, Rotterdam 108196
Medea, Winnipeg 097593
Medeja, Minsk 096042
Medelhavsmuseet, Stockholm 036642
Medelpads Auktionsservice, Sundsvall 122269
Medeltidsmuseet, Stockholm 036643
Meden en Perzen, Dordrecht 078310
Medgyessy Múzeum, Debrecen . . . 021710
Média, Neuchâtel 135053
Média 3000, Paris 100674
Media And Moving Art, Rotterdam . 108197
Media & Communications Department, Holland College, Charlottetown . . 049780
Media Rare Gallery, Los Angeles . . 116843
Media Xchange 123, Saint Paul . . . 092377
Mediaevalia, Roma 135913
Medialia Gallery, New York 118177
Médiart, Paris 100675
Medic, Houston 132132
Medical Art Society, London 054427
Medical Artists Association of Great Britain, Stotfold 054428
Medical Arts Gallery, Los Angeles . . 116844
Medical College Museum, Vadodara 022366
Medical History Museum, Hobart . . 001109
Medical History Museum, Melbourne 001245
Medical Museum, Amman 027375
Medicea, Dogana 080342
Medici, Solothurn 111922
Medici, Giovanni, Roma 076553
Medici Fine Arts, Los Angeles 116845
Medici Gallery, London 113760
Medici House, Zürich 112146
The Medici Society, London 135232
Medicine and Pioneers Museum, Menahimiya 023028
Medicine Hat Museum and Art Gallery, Medicine Hat 005851
Medicine Man Gallery, Tucson 093248, 120146
Medicinhistoriska Museet, Göteborg 036299
Medicinhistoriska Museet, Linköping 036425
Medicinhistoriska Museet, Lund . . . 036446
Medicinhistoriska Museet, Vänersborg 036755
Medicinhistoriska Museet Eugenia, Stockholm 036644
Medicinsk-Historisk Museum, København 008976
Médicis, Besançon 098954
Médicis, Paris 066271
Médicis, Paris 100676
Médicis, Zürich 112147
Medienhaus für Kunst und Kultur, Hannover 103291
Medieval Art, London 085529
Medika Gallery, Blyth 094261
Medina, Tunis 112263
Medina, Luis A., Bogotá 098173
Medina-Bi, Donostia-San Sebastián 129512
Medina Cobo, Carmen, Donostia-San Sebastián 081087
Medina Gallery, Barnstaple 083396
Medinabeitia, Isabel, Bilbao 080983
Mediodía Vidrio y Restauración, Madrid 129646
Mediolanum, Milano 140057
Medisch Farmaceutisch Museum de Griffioen, Delft 029409
Meditalia Edizioni, Roma . 106587, 134680
Meditativ Art Galerie, Krefeld 103781
La Mediterranea Arte, Napoli 106381
Mediterranean Art, Palma de Mallorca 110694
Medium Modernes Antiquariat, Münster 139570
Medizin- und Pharmaziehistorische Sammlung Kiel der Christian-Albrechts-Universität, Kiel 018249
Medizinhistorische Sammlung der Ruhr-Universität Bochum, Institut für Geschichte der Medizin, Bochum . 016280
Medizinhistorische Sammlungen, Chemnitz 016559
Medizinhistorisches Museum, Institut für Geschichte der Medizin der Universität Wien, Wien 002946
Medizinhistorisches Museum, Universität Zürich, Zürich 037779
Medlar, San Antonio 092546
Međnarodni Grafični Likovni Centar, Ljubljana 034482
Medranda Abenza, Justo, Madrid . . 129647
Medrese Müzesi, Akşehir 038000
Medu, Atlanta 142206
Medunarodna Izložba Umetnosti, Novi Sad 093857
Medusa, Hamburg 071286
La Medusa, Palermo 076162
Medusa Antik, Stockholm 081986
Medway Heritage Centre, Chatham 039040
Medway Towns Gallery, Rochester . 040848
Medzinárodná Výstava Výtvarného Umenia, Bratislava 093859
Mee, Seoul 107269
Mee-Mee's & Makin's, Saint Louis . 092275
Meed, Kansas City 132211
Meehan, M.E., New York 091069
Meeker County Museum and G.A.R. Hall, Litchfield 045335
Meeker Home Museum, Greeley . . 044304
Meekins & Co., Fort Worth 088867
Meeks & Co, F., Birmingham 083535, 130393
Meeky, Jennifer, Nhill 056345
Meemelink, Jan, Den Haag 140397
Sri Meenakshi Sundaresvara Temple Museum, Madurai 022250
Meenen, Lilienthal 139414
Meeniyan Art Gallery, Meeniyan . . . 094801
Meent Art, Hilversum 108087
Meer, J. ter, Hoge Hexel . . 078547, 128723
Meeraner Kunstverein, Meerane . . . 053490
Meerbuscher Kunstauktionshaus, Meerbusch 072488, 121511
Meerhemmuseum, Gent 003459
Meerrettichmuseum, Baiersdorf . . . 015859
Meert, Jef, Knokke 137508
Meert & Rihoux, Bruxelles 096233
Meesters, Hans, Amsterdam 107769
Meeteetse Museums, Meeteetse . . 045750
The Meeting House, Ilminster 113291
Meezkeret-Batia Museum, Meezkeret-Batia 023027
Mefisto, Praha 123992
Méga Troc 63, Aigueperse 060677
Megan Fox, Kelly, New York 118178
Megaride Antichitá, Napoli 076006
Megarry's and Forever Summer, Blackmore 083550
Megart, Kraków 129044
Megarte, Paris 100677
Meg'Arts Galerie, Milly-la-Forêt . . . 099723
Megaw & Hogg, Adelaide . 055316, 123174
Megaw & Hogg, Unley 120650
Megerian, New York 091070
Megginch Castle, Errol 039455
Meghalaya State Museum, Shillong 022333
Megisti Museum, Kastellorizo 021316
Megna, Fabio Massimo, Roma 076554
Megson, Susan, New York 118179
Meguro Gajoen Bijutsukan, Tokyo . . 027199
Meguro Kiseichukan, Tokyo 027200
Meguro Museum of Art, Tokyo 027201
Mehler-Koch, M., Juist 103460
Mehlis, Jens, Plauen 121576
Mehlkopf, O., Aachen 069094
Mehlman, Justine, Washington . . . 093423
Mehmet Kamil Keskiner, İstanbul . . 083146
Mehner, Holger, Marienberg 072457
Mehr am Meer, Wangerland 074276
Mehran, West Hollywood 093487
Mehrangarh Museum, Jodhpur 022191
Mehrbrey & Hohner, Regensburg . . 073464
Mehrhoff, Cincinnati 088262, 131939
Mehrholz, U., Remagen 104711
Mehringer, Ernst, Spitz 057320
Mehs, Peter, Düsseldorf 139018
Mehta, Mumbai 074822
Mehu, New York 118180
Mei, Cham, Hong Kong 059672
Mei Lian, Roma 076555
Mei Qi, Shanghai 097932
Mei Xie, Changshu 097695
Meichle, Erich, Salzburg 057268
Meier, Aerzen 069112
Meier, Anthony, San Francisco 119734
Meier, Anton, Genève 111482
Meier, Astrid, Castrop-Rauxel 102301
Meier, Bernard, Kapellen . 058235, 123639
Meier, Christophe, Bruyères le Châtel 124164
Meier, Corina, Kammerstein 125991
Meier, David, San Antonio 132818
Meier, Erich-Franz, Hannover 125877
Meier, Fabian, Liebefeld 082576
Meier, Gisela, München 072789
Meier, H., Gutenzell-Hürbel 071155
Meier, Dr. Helmut, Arth 111132
Meier, Horst Dieter, Freiburg im Breisgau 102869
Meier, Jack, Houston 116366
Meier, Michael Th., Bad Münder . . . 125112
Meier, Peter, Wien 095896
Meier-Za, E., Oftringen . . . 082714, 130135
Meier-Za, E., Zofingen 082929
Meierhofer, Arnulf, Salzburg 123451
Meierhoff, Kansas City 089509
Meierimuseet, Institutt for næringsmiddelfag, Ås 030740
Meierische Museumboerderij, Heeswijk-Dinther 029702
Meigle Gallery, Meigle 114070
Meigle Museum of Sculptured Stones, Meigle 040441
Meignen, Christian, Gent 123625
Meigniez, A., Morges 122344
Meigs County Museum, Pomeroy . . 047116
Meijer, Amsterdam 128549
Meijer, Utrecht 108257
Meijerimuseo, Saukkola 010064
Meijerink & Zoon, G.A., Enschede . . 128667
Meijerink, T., Sebaldeburen 128828
Meijerink & Frohn, Deventer 107970
Meiji, Tokyo 107072
Meiji-Daigaku Keiji Hakubutsukan, Tokyo 027202
Meiji-Daigaku Kouko Hakubutsukan, Tokyo 027203
Meiji-Daigaku Shouhin Hakubutsukan, Tokyo 027204
Meiji Jingu Homotsuden, Tokyo . . . 027205
Meiji Memorial Picture Gallery, Tokyo 027206
Meiji Shobo, Tokyo 140194
Meile, Urs, Luzern 111698
Meili, Herbert, Horgen 111558
Meindl, P., Eichelsdorf, Unterfranken 070518
Meindl, P., Hofheim, Unterfranken .071554, 125952
Meindl & Sulzmann, Wien 137346
Meinema, A., Enschede 078373
Meiner, M.F., Hamburg 103188
Meiners, Enschede 078374
Meinhold & Reucker, Berlin 101982
Meininger Museen, Schloss Elisabethenburg, Meiningen 018884

Meintzinger, Frickenhausen am Main 070883
Meir Dizengoff Museum, Tel Aviv 023085
Meire, Belo Horizonte 058436
Meire, Jean-Marie & Dominique, Brugge 057781
Meirelles, Maurício, Belo Horizonte 058437, 123690
Meirelles, Miguel, Malvern, Victoria 123261
Meisel, Louis K. & Susan P., New York 118181
Meisinger, Helmut, Stadl-Paura 057321, 123471
Meiso, Sendai 107001
Meissen Galerie, Berlin 101983
Meißener Porzellan-Sammlung Stiftung Ernst Schneider, Zweigmuseum des Bayerischen Nationalmuseums, Oberschleißheim 019416
Meissl, Gerhard, Bad Sauerbrunn 123339
Meissl, Gerhard, Rohrbach bei Matterburg 123435
Meissl, Michaela & Walter, Wien 095897
Meißner, Hamburg 103189, 134019
Meissner, Praha 060141, 137838
Meissner, Bruno, London 113761
Meißner, Karl-Heinz, München 104267
Meissner, Kurt, Zürich 082999, 112148
Meissner & Neumann, Praha 060142, 120858
Meißner Porzellan-Kabinett, Bad Soden am Taunus 015802
Meissonnier, Henri, Mende 121071
Meister, M., Ludwigsburg, Württemberg 072309
Meister-Götz, Brigitte, Hettstadt 103370
Meisterhäuser, Dessau, Anhalt 016678
Meisterschule für Bildhauerei, Akademie der bildenden Künste, Wien 049660
Meisterschule für Bildhauerei, Akademie der bildenden Künste, Wien 049661
Meisterschule für Medailleurkunst und Kleinplastik, Akademie der bildenden Künste, Wien 049662
Meisterschule für Restaurierung und Konservierung, Akademie der bildenden Künste, Wien 049663
Meisterschule für Tapisserie, Akademie der bildenden Künste, Wien 049664
Le Meitour, Portland 091970, 119019
Meiwald, München 104268
Meixner, A., Würzburg 139872
Meixner, Wolfgang, Hausen bei Brugg 082492
Meja, Renate, Wenden 074333
Méjanès, Claude, Auzits 061113
Mejean, Christine & Gilles, Perpignan 066752
Mejerimuseet vid Korsholms Lantbruksskolor, Vaasa 010201
Mejía, José Manuel, Medellín 059928
Mejia, Roxana, Medellín 059929
Mejía Vallejo, Roxana, Medellín 059930
Mejlby Kunsthaus, Lintrup 009012
Mekaanisen Musiikin Museo, Varkaus 010227
Mekanik, Antwerpen 096081, 137401
Mekong Gallery, Singapore 109837
Mel Fisher Maritime Heritage Museum, Key West 044989
La Mela e il Serpente, Padova 076098
Melaleuca Gallery, Anglesea 094153
Melanchthon-Antiquariat, Lutherstadt Wittenberg 139437
Melanchthonhaus Bretten, Bretten 016446
Melanchthonhaus Wittenberg, Stiftung Luthergedenkstätten in Sachsen-Anhalt, Lutherstadt Wittenberg 018762
Melanide, Palermo 076163
Melanin, Baltimore 115067
Mélanson, Chantal, Annecy 098842
Melberg, Jerald, Charlotte 115299
Melbourne, London 085530, 131109
Melbourne Affordable Art Show, Carlton South 093572
Melbourne Antique Prints and Maps, Camberwell 055608
Melbourne Art Fair, Melbourne 093573
Melbourne Clocks Museum, Hampton 001097
Melbourne Contemporary Arts, Melbourne 114071
Melbourne Fine Art Gallery, Melbourne 056195
Melbourne Fine Art Gallery, Melbourne 094821
Melbourne Hall, Melbourne 040442
Melbourne Museum, Carlton South 000898
Melbourne Museum of Printing, Footscray 001033
Melbourne Studio of Painting and Drawing, Fitzroy 094535
Melbourne Tank Museum, Narre Warren North 001315
Melbourne's Living Museum of the West, Maribyrnong 001221
Melcher, Dirk, Monheim am Rhein 072591
Melchior, F., Merseburg 072522
Melchior, Karin, Kassel 103514
Melchiori, Anna, Genova 127470
Melco, Düsseldorf 070413
Melco, Mönchengladbach 072574
Meldal Bygdemuseum, Trøndelag Folkemuseum, Meldal 031015
Meldrum House, Whangarei 079364
Melelli, Firenze 075371
Melelli, Fernando, Trieste 076899
Melet, Laurent, Macornay 064209
Melet & Cassie, New York 091071
Meletta, Eric, München 072790
Melford Fine Arts, Long Melford 113989
Melford Hall, Long Melford 040335
Melfort and District Museum, Melfort 005855
Melgarejo Peñuela, Alonso, Bucaramanga 098221
Melgosa Sanchez, Martin Sergio, México 107500
Méli-Mélo, Minneapolis 090377
Meli-Melo, Montréal 097056
Méli-Mélo, Saint-Macaire 067598
Meli-Melo Artist's Alliance, Hong Kong 052799
Melicharovo Městské Muzeum, Unhošt 008734
Melina, Möhlin 082660, 111735
Melindre, São Paulo 058726
Mélior, Marseille 124427
Melissa Publishing House, Athinai 134488
Mellado, San Lorenzo de El Escorial 129718
Mellado Lopez, Jose Antonio, Badalona 129308
Mellat Museum, Sa'd-Abad Museum, Teheran 022627
Mellemværftet, Nordmøre Museum, Kristiansund 030960
Meller, Ingo, Köln 071982
Mellerstain House, Gordon 039605
Mellette House, Watertown 048997
Melli Museum, Teheran 022628
Mellier, Jean-Louis, Castillon-la-Bataille 062024
Mellilän Museoriihi, Mellilä 009864
Melling, K., Burnley 112767
Mellinger, Stuttgart 134417
Mellon Financial Corporation's Collection, Pittsburgh 047056
Mellors & Kirk, Nottingham 122642
Mellow, Honolulu 088965
Melnick House Gallery, Ascot 083319
Melnick House Gallery, Ascot 112521
Melnick House Gallery, Ascot 130309
Meloche, Monique, Chicago 115498
Mélodie du Temps, Paris 066272
Melody Art, Alresford 112500
Melody Art Studio, Tugun 095353
Melody's Antique, Chester 083961
Meloni, Mauro, Cagliari 127250
Melori & Rosenberg, Venezia 106765
Melori & Rosenberg, Venezia 106766
La Meloria, Livorno 075535
Meloun, Karel, Klášterec nad Ohří 098374
Meløy Bygdemuseum, Ørnes 031063
Melrose Abbey Museum, Melrose 040444
Melrose Courthouse Museum, Melrose 001252
Melrose House, Pretoria 034719
Melrose Lightspace, Los Angeles 116846
Melrose Plantation Home Complex, Melrose 045752
Melrose Vintage, Phoenix 091755
Mel's Antiques, Baltimore 087692
Mel's Antiques, Kitchener 058872
Melse & Rietema, Groningen 078429
Melsheimer, Hubertus, Köln 071983
Melson, R., Kiel 071837
Melting Art, Limoges 063891
Melton, London 085531
Melton Antiques, Woodbridge 087222
Melton Art Reference Library Museum, Oklahoma City 046646
Melton Carnegie Museum, Melton Mowbray 040445
Melton Park Gallery, Oklahoma City 118669
Meltzer, Neal, New York 118182
Melusine, Asnières-sur-Seine 061011
Melville, Paris 066273
Melville, Donald, Takapuna 079248
Melville Discovery Centre, Applecross 000744
Melville Heritage Museum, Melville 005858
Melville Railway Museum, Melville 005859
Melvin Art Gallery, Florida Southern College, Dept. of Art, Lakeland 045123
Melvin B. Tolson Black Heritage Center, Langston 045157
Melwood Photography Gallery, Pittsburgh 118941
Melzer, Angelika, Lüdenscheid 139431
Mem-Erie Historical Museum, Erie 043720
Members Calender, New York 136538
Membrado, Buenos Aires 055225
Meme et Moi, Los Angeles 089838
Mémin, Gilles, Le Mans 063661
Memlingmuseum Sint Janshospitaal, Stedelijke Musea Brugge, Brugge 003273
Memme-Taadi Kamber, Karksi 009371
Memmel, Fritz, Speyer 073882
Memmo & Freschi, New York 118183
Mémoire de la Nationale 7, Piolenc 013820
Mémoire de Saumon, Petite Camargue Alsacienne, Saint-Louis-la-Chaussée 014396
Mémoire d'Enfance, Cannes 061949
Mémoire du Livre, Paris 138505
Mémoire du Rhin, Petite Camargue Alsacienne, Saint-Louis-la-Chaussée 014397
La Mémoire du Temps, Bruxelles 058031
Mémoire du Temps, Byblos 077425
Mémoires, Rouen 138590
Memoires Antiguidade, Rio de Janeiro 058615
Mémoires de Grande-Synthe, Maison du Patrimoine, Grande-Synthe 011987
Mémoires de Grenier, Vincennes 068998
Mémoires de Greniers, Fargues-Saint-Hilaire 062839
Les Mémoires d'Obersoultzach, Obersoultzbach 013470
Memola, Angela, Bologna 105971
Memorable Sports Autographs, Las Vegas 142482
Memorable Treasures, Atlanta 114904
Memorear Antiguidades, Rio de Janeiro 058616
Mémorial Caen-Normandie, Caen 011052
Memorial Day Museum of Waterloo, Waterloo 048988
Memorial de Sergipe, Aracaju 003966
Mémorial de Vendée, Musée du Logis de la Chabotterie, Saint-Sulpice-le-Verdon 014549
Mémorial des Guerres en Indochine, Fréjus 011888
Mémorial des Soldats de La Nouvelle France, Le Château-d'Oléron 012481
Mémorial d'Évocation Vaudois et Huguenot, La Roque-d'Anthéron 012332
Memorial di Imigração Ucraniana, Curitiba 004079
Memorial do Imigrante, Departamento de Museus e Arquivos, São Paulo 004512
Mémorial du Maréchal Leclerc de Hauteclocque et de la Libération de Paris et Musée Jean Moulin, Paris 013609
Memorial Galleries, Houston 116367
Memorial Geroïčnoï Oboroni Odesi - 411 Beregova Linija, Odes'kyj istoriko-krajeznavčyj muzej, Odesa 038367
Memorial Goethe, Sessenheim 014776
Memorial Hall Museum, Deerfield 043369
Memorial Hall of the Zunyi Conference, Zunyi 007362
Memorial JK, Brasília 004012
Memorial Library and Art Gallery, Saskatoon 006419
Memorial Museum, Ada 041577
Memorial Museum B.P. Hasdeu, Câmpina 032823
Memorial Museum King Tribhuvan, Kathmandu 029114
Memorial Museum of the Kanto Earthquake Disaster, Tokyo 027207
Memorial Museum of the Peasant Movement Institute by Comrade Mao Zedong, Guangzhou 007089
Memorial Museum of the War of Liberation, Pyongyang 027441
Memorial Pengisytiharan Kemerdekaan, Melaka 027994
Memorial Picture Gallery, Tokyo 107073
Memorial Pontes de Miranda da Justiça do Trabalho em Alagoas, Maceió 004193
Memorial Sultan Tidore Museum, Tidore 009172
Memorial Tancredo Neves, São João Del Rei 004482
Memorial Union Art Gallery, Corvallis 043178
Memorial Union Art Gallery, Davis 043311
Memorial Union Gallery, Fargo 043814
Memorial Union Gallery, Tempe 048518
Memorial War Museum, Bathurst 005077
Memorialen Kompleks Balova Shuma, Gavril Genovo 004687
Memorialmuseum Friedrich Fröbel, Oberweißbach 019428
Memorialnaja Gvardejskaja Krasnoznamënnaja Podvodnaja Lodka S-56 1939 g., Voenno-istoričeskij Muzej Tichookeanskogo Flota, Vladivostok 034047
Memorialnaja Muzej-kvartira N.A. Nekrasova, Sankt-Peterburg 033763
Memorialno-chudožestvennyj Dom-muzej Vladimira Aleksandroviča Serova, Tverskaja oblastnaja kartinnaja galereja, Emmaus 033139
Memorialno-literaturnyj Muzej A.P. Bondina, Ekaterinburg 033114
Memorial'nyj Budinok-muzej A.A. Kocky, Užgorod 038405
Memorial'nyj Budinok-muzej F.F. Manajla, Užgorod 038406
Memorial'nyj Budinok-muzej Tarasa Ševčenka, Kyïv 038305
Memorial'nyj Budinok-muzej V. Dalja, Muzej istorii ta kjl'tury mista Lugans'ka, Lugans'k 038333
Memorialnyj Chudožestvennyj Muzej Valentina Aleksandroviča Serova v Domotkanovo, Tverskaja oblastnaja kartinnaja galereja, Krasnaja Nov' 033289
Memorialnyj Dom-muzej Akademika S.P. Koroleva, Moskva 033419
Memorialnyj Dom-muzej Akademika A.A. Uchtomskogo, Rybinskij gosudarstvennyj istoriko-architekturnyj i chudožestvennyj muzej-zapovednik, Rybinsk 033706
Memorialnyj Dom-muzej Akademika I.M. Vinogradova, Velikie Luki 034023
Memorialnyj Dom-muzej S.T. Aksakova, Nacionalnyj muzej Respubliki Baškortostan, Ufa 033990

Memorialnyj Dom-Muzej M.V. Biškek, Biškek 027635
Memorialnyj Dom-muzej Gercena, Moskva 033420
Memorialnyj Dom-muzej I.I. Levitana, Plesskij gosudarstvennyj istoriko-architekturnyj i chudožestvennyj muzej-zapovednik, Ples 033668
Memorialnyj Dom-muzej P.D. Korina, Moskva 033421
Memorialnyj Dom-muzej Marko Vovčok, Nalčik 033541
Memorialnyj Dom-muzej Mažita Gafuri, Ufa 033991
Memorialnyj Dom-muzej im. N.G. Slavjanova, Permskij oblastnoj kraevedčeskij muzej, Perm 033647
Memorialnyj Dom-muzej G.V. Plechanova, Lipeck 033330
Memorialnyj Dom-muzej Podpolnaja Tipografija Permskogo Komiteta RSDRP 1906 g., Permskij oblastnoj kraevedčeskij muzej, Perm 033648
Memorialnyj Dom-muzej I.P. Požalostina, Rjazanskij Oblastnoj Chudožestvennyj Muzej im. I.P. Požalostina, Solotča 033893
Memorialnyj Dom-Muzej P.P. Bažova, Municipalnyj objedinennyj muzej pisatelej Urala, Ekaterinburg 033115
Memorialnyj Dom-Muzej I.I. Šiškina, Gosudarstvennyj muzej izobrazitelnych iskusstv Respubliki Tatarstan, Elabuga 033129
Memorialnyj Dom-muzej L.V. Sobinova, Jaroslavskij gosudarstvennyj istoriko-architekturnyj i chudožestvennyj muzej-zapovednik, Jaroslavl 033195
Memorialnyj Dom-muzej Uljanovych, Astrachanskij Muzej-zapovednik, Astrachan 033006
Memorialnyj Dom-muzej A.A. Vaneeva, Gosudarstvennyj istoriko-ėtnografičeskij muzej-zapovednik Šušenskoe, Ermakovskoe 033141
Memorialnyj Dom-muzej Viktora i Apolinarija Vasnecovych, Kirovskij Oblastnoj Chudožestvennyj Muzej im. V.M. i A.M. Vasnecovych, Rjabovo 033694
Memorialnyj Dom-muzej V.M. Vaznecova, Gosudarstvennaja Tretjakovskaja galereja, Moskva 033422
Memorialnyj Dom-muzej N.E. Žukovskogo, Orechovo 033603
Memorialnyj Istoriko-biografičeskij Dom-muzej Akademika N.V. Melnikova, Muzej istorii i kultury Srednego Prikamja, Sarapul 033850
Memorialnyj Kompleks G. Tukaja, Nacionalnyj muzej Respubliki Tatarstan, Novyj Kyrlaj 033594
Memorialnyj Kompleks 'Vorošilovskaja Batareja', Voenno-istoričeskij Muzej Tichookeanskogo Flota, Vladivostok 034048
Memorialnyj Literaturnyj Muzej F.M. Dostoevskogo, Semey 027409
Memorialnyj Muzej Abu Ali Ibn Sina, Afčona 049381
Memorialnyj Muzej Akademikov A.E. i B.A. Arbuzovych, Kazan 033237
Memorialnyj Muzej-dača A.S. Puškina, Puškin 033683
Memorialnyj Muzej Jurija Gagarina, Gagarin 033143
Memorialnyj Muzej-kabinet M.V. Frunze, Ivanovo 033174
Memorialnyj Muzej Karima Chakimova, Nacionalnyj muzej Respubliki Baškortostan, Ufa 033992
Memorialnyj Muzej I.S. Ključnikova-Palantaja, Joškar-Ola 033202
Memorialnyj Muzej Kosmonavtiki, Moskva 033423
Memorialnyj Muzej-kvartira A.A. Šogencukova, Nalčik 033542
Memorialnyj Muzej-kvartira Aktërov Samojlovych, Sankt-Peterburgskij Muzej Teatralnogo i Muzykalnogo Iskusstva, Sankt-Peterburg 033764
Memorialnyj Muzej-Kvartira S.M. Kirova, Vladikavkaz 034036
Memorialnyj Muzej-kvartira P.K. Kozlova, Institut Estestvoznanija i Techniki Rossijskoj Akademii Nauk, Sankt-Peterburg 033765
Memorialnyj Muzej-kvartira G.M. Kržižanovskogo i V.V. Starkova, Minusinskij Regionalnyj Kraevedčeskij Muzej im. N.M. Martjanova, Minusinsk 033359
Memorialnyj Muzej-kvartira I.P. Pavlova, Institut Fiziologii im. I.P. Pavlova Rossijskoj Akademii Nauk, Sankt-Peterburg 033766
Memorialnyj Muzej-kvartira A.S. Puškina, Gosudarstvennyj Muzej A.S. Puškina, Moskva 033424
Memorialnyj Muzej-kvartira Rimskogo-Korsakova, Sankt-Peterburg 033767
Memorialnyj Muzej-kvartira M.S. Spiridonova, Čeboksary 033064
Memorialnyj Muzej-kvartira Vadima Alekseeviča Kozina, Magadan . . . 033345
Memorialnyj Muzej-kvartira A.M. Vasnecova, Gusadrstvennaja Tretjakovskaja galereja, Moskva . 033425
Memorialnyj Muzej-laboratorija A.S. Popova, Kronštadt 033310
Memorialnyj Muzej Licej, Nacionalnyj Muzej Puškina, Puškin 033684
Memorial'nyj Muzej-majsternja Teodizii Briž, Lvivs'ka Galereja Mystectv, Lviv . 038347
Memorialnyj Muzej A.G. Malyškina, Mokšan 033363
Memorialnyj Muzej-Masterskaja Skulptora S.T. Konenkova, Moskva 033426
Memorialnyj Muzej Alii Moldagulovoj, Geroiny Sovetskogo Sojuza, Aktöbe 027388
Memorial'nyj Muzej Mychajla Gruševskogo u Lvovi, Lviv 038348
Memorial'nyj Muzej N.I. Beloborodova, Tula 033973
Memorialnyj Muzej B.L. Pasternaka, Nacionalnyj muzej Respubliki Tatarstan, Čistopol 033091
Memorialnyj Muzej A.S. Popova, Sankt-Peterburg 033768
Memorialnyj Muzej A.S. Popova - Izobretatelja Radio, Krasnoturinskij kraevedčeskij muzej, Krasnoturinsk 033306
Memorialnyj Muzej N.M. Prževalskogo, Prževalsk 027640
Memorialnyj Muzej A.N. Skrjabina, Moskva 033427
Memorialnyj Muzej-usadba Akademika I.P. Pavlova, Rjazan 033696
Memorialnyj Muzej-usadba Chudožnika N.A. Jarošenko, Kislovodsk 033273
Memorialnyj Muzej-usadba M.P. Musorgskogo, Naumovo 033548
Memorial'nyj Muzej V. Ivasjuka, Černivci 038241
Memorialnyj Muzej-zapovednik N.A. Rimskogo-Korsakova Ljubensk-Večaša, Pljussa 033671
Memorialul Ipoteşti-Centrul Naţional de Studii Mihai Eminescu, Ipoteşti . . 032885
Memories, Bramley 083636
Memories, Great Dunmow 084506
Memories, Rochester 086391
Memories, Sheffield 142061
Memories, Vancouver 059383
Memories Antiques, San Diego 092656
Memories from Yvonne, Regina . . . 059090
Memories in Glass, Tulsa 093320
Memories of Old Antiques, Houston 089152
Memories of Vail, Denver 116025
Memories of Yesteryear, Torquay . . 056727
Memories Old & New, Jacksonville . 089430
Memorijalna Galerija Djure Tiljka, Komiža 007736
Memorijalna Galerija Veliša Lekovića, Bar 034142
Memorijalna Zbirka Antuna Masle, Dubrovnik 007716
Memorijalna Zbirka Eugena Kumičića, Brseč 007704
Memorijalni Centar Josip Broz Tito, Beograd 034158
Memorijalni Muzej Džuro Jakšić, Srpska Crnja 034269
Memorijalni Muzej Gavrila Principa u Obljaju, Bosansko Grahova 003930
Memorijalni Muzej u Goši, Smederevska Palanka 034260
Memorijalni Muzeji Bela Crkva i Stolice, Krupanj 034209
Memorijalnyj Budinok-muzej D. Javornic'kogo, Dnipropetrovskyj deržavnij istoričnij muzej im Javornic'kogo, Dnipropetrovs'k 038260
Memory House Antiques, San Francisco 092843
Memory Lane, Sowerby Bridge 086672
Memory Lane, Wellington 079334
Memory Lane Antique, Los Angeles 089839
Memory Lane Antiques, Ascot Vale .055410, 123186
Memory Lane Antiques, Great Bookham 084505
Memory Lane Antiques, London . . . 058887
Memory Lane Antiques, Lower Stondon 085858
Memory Lane Antiques, Pomona . . 056468
Memory Lane Antiques, Regina . . 059091
Memory Lane Antiques, San Jose . 092930
Memory Lane Antiques, Sidcup . . . 086614
Memory Lane Antiques Centre, Ripley, Derbyshire 086371
Memory Lane Collection, Goodwood 055895
Memory Lane Museum at Seattle Goodwill, Seattle 048084
Memory Lane Photographics, Hastings 094617
Memory Lane Upholstery, Calgary . 123747
Memory Market, Oklahoma City . . . 091519
Memoryville USA, Rolla 047529
Mempel, Dagmar, Vieselbach 105122
Memphis, Cairo 060455
Memphis Antique Market, Memphis 090090
Memphis Belle B17 Flying Fortress, Memphis 045763
Memphis Brooks Museum of Art, Memphis 045764
Memphis Coin Gallery, Memphis . . 090091
Memphis College of Art, Memphis . 051691
Memphis College of Art Gallery, Memphis 045765
Memphis Pink Palace Museum, Memphis 045766
Memphis Plating Works, Memphis . 132329
Menage A Trois, Christchurch 079040
Ménager, Benoît, Mûrs-Erigné 064848
La Ménandière, Alpe-d'Huez 060784
Menard, Henri, Marseille 064374
Ménard, Hervé, La Chapelle-Saint-Mesmin 063320
Menard Art Museum, Komaki 026684
Menardi, Uta, Leiden 078574
Menarini, Giampiero, Bologna 139992
Menart, Aude, Monpazier 099731
Menat, Roma 076556
Menat, Roma 076557
Mencendorfa Nams, Rīga 027757
Menches, Viktor, Bergisch Gladbach 069541
Menczer Museum of Medicine and Dentistry, Hartford 044460
Mende, Karlsruhe 139298
Mende, B. & F., Havixbeck 103315
Mende, P., Eimeldingen 070527
Mende-Kohnen, Susanne, Wiesbaden 127014
Mendel, Berlin 138822
Mendel Art Gallery, Saskatoon 006420
Mendelianum - Památník Gregora Mendela, Moravské Zemské Muzeum, Brno 008288
Mendelssohn-Haus, Leipzig 018577
Mendes, São Paulo 137588
Mendes, São Paulo 137589
Mendès, Martial, Toulouse 068527
Mendes-Fernandes, Maria, Paris . . 066274
Mendez, Vezin-le-Coquet 125021
Méndez, Marvia, Caracas 093538
Mendez, Oscar, Barcelona 129369
Mendl, Reinhard, Bad Reichenhall . 069356
Mendo, Amsterdam 107770
Mendocino Art Center, Mendocino . 051692
Mendocino Art Center Gallery, Mendocino 045773
Mendocino County Arts Council, Boonville 054870
Mendocino County Museum, Willits 049194
Mendoza, Caracas 120432
Mendoza Rodriguez, Hector, Bogotá 059845
Mendoza Rodriguez, Hector, Bogotá 059846
Menec, Helsinki 137953
Menegaz, Claudio, Roma 076558
Meneghel, Susanne, Wien 057497
Menem, Alex, Paris 100678
Ménendez, Claude, Fontiers-Cabardès 062911
Ménendez, Pierre, Fontiers-Cabardès 062912
Menez, Marie-Françoise, Aurillac . . 061079
Menezes, Gessy Geyer De, Porto Alegre 096569
Menezes, Roberto, Miami 090205, 132349
Meng, Singapore 129263
Mengelmoes, Arnhem 078056
Menges, A., Oldenburg, Oldenburg . 073206
Menges & Söhne, Aloys, Hannover . 071403
Menges, Axel, London 135233
Mengès, Christophe, Monbalen . . . 064589
Mengès, Gérard, Monbalen 064590
Menhir, Bern 141229
Menikos, Menikou, Pafos 059965
The Menil Collection, Houston 044645
Menim Restorations, Langport 130862
Las Meninas, Barcelona 080882
Las Meninas, Barcelona 080883
Menine, Millau 064558
Měnínská Brána, Muzeum města Brna, Brno 008289
Menka-s Antiques, Clifton Hill . . . 055694
Menke, Friedhelm, Bielefeld 102125
Menke, Hermann-Anton, Lindau, Bodensee 103921
Menke, K., Lippstadt 121501
Menkhaus, Antonius, Georgsmarienhütte 102937
Mennello Museum of American Folk Art, Orlando 046717
Mennickheim, Kassel 126017
Mennink, L.J., Amsterdam 077913
Mennonite Heritage Center, Harleysville 044431
Mennonite Heritage Museum, Goessel 044229
Mennonite Heritage Museum, Rosthern 006309
Mennonite Heritage Village, Steinbach 006508
Mennonite Library and Archives Museum, North Newton 046530
Mennour, Kamel, Paris 100679
Menocal, Nina, México 107501
Menominee County Heritage Museum, Menominee 045775
Menomonee Falls Antiques, Milwaukee 090314
Menories Antiguidades, Rio de Janeiro 058617
Menotti, Baden bei Wien 095475
Menotti, Croix 062572
Menozzi, Mauro, Modena 127736
Menrad, W., Ladenburg . . 072111, 103813
Menrva, Foggia 127429
Mensch, Bernd, Hamburg 103190
Menschik, Rosemarie Franziska, Mauerkirchen 095678
Mensing, Berlin 101984
Mensing, Hamburg 103191
Mensing, Hannover 071404
Mensing, Westerland 105226
Mensing, Josef, Düsseldorf 070414
Mensing, Josef, Hamm, Westfalen . 103245
Mensing, Josef, Mülheim an der Ruhr 072613

Mensing & Büsching, Telgte 074051
Menssen, Norderstedt 104462
Menßen, J., Esens 070614
Mensura, Roma 076559
Mentalvårdsmuseet Säter, Säter . . . 036552
Mentel, Kisdorf 071866
Mentges, Charlotte, Senheim 104887
Menth, Maria, München 104269
Menth, Ralf, Würzburg 074503
Mentlhof-Bergbauernmuseum, Heiligenblut 002032
Mentor Graham Museum, Blunt . . . 042278
Mentougou Huayang Antique, Beijing 059578
Mentougou Museum, Beijing 006993
Menu, Jean, Saint-Calais 067387
Menuiserie au Fil du Temps, Evaux et Menil 062822
Menuiserie Claude, Giromagny 124250
Menyea, Los Angeles 089840
Menzel, Goslar 071064
Menzel, Lübeck 072332
Menzel, Wien 057498
Menzel, Hermann, Hamburg 071287
Menzel, Manfred, Bad Honnef 069302
Menzel, Michael, Salzburg 057269
Menzel, Nils, Berlin 069701
Menzel-Dach - Seminar für künstlerisch-ästhetische Praxis, Humboldt-Universität zu Berlin, Berlin 050028
Menzer Heimatstube, Stechlin 020296
Menzerath, A., Simmerath 073822
Menzoyan, Marc, Saint-Andeol-le-Château 067351
Meopham Windmill, Meopham 040446
Mephisto, Unna 139810
Mephisto Antiquariat, Paderborn . . 139646
Meppeler Expositie Centrum, Meppel 029919
Meppener Kunstkreis e.V., Meppen 053491
Mer et Découvertes, Bonifacio 061557
La Mer les Bateaux, Noirmoutier-en-l'Ile 065220
Mer Terre et Soleil, Sète 068235
Meråker Bygdemuseum, Meråker . 031016
Meramec Antiques, Saint Louis . . . 092276
Merano Arte - Casa Editrice, Merano 134600
Merano Arte - Kunst Meran, Merano 024668
Merc & Cia, Sevilla 081595
Mercadante, Antonio, Torvilliers . . . 068430
Mercadé, Richard, Céret 062055
Mercader, Houston 089153
El Mercader de Venecia, Badalona . 080776
El Mercadillo de Salado, Sevilla . . . 081596
Mercado, Brasília 096496
Mercado das Pulgas Antiguidades, Rio de Janeiro 058618
Mercado de las Pulgas, Buenos Aires 055226
Mercado de las Pulgas, Buenos Aires 055227
Mercado de Tesouros de Objetos Antigos, Rio de Janeiro 058619, 123706
Mercado del Mueble Usado, La Plata 055275
Mercado Negro Antiguidades, Porto Alegre 058513
Mercado Puerta de Toledo, Madrid . 110575
Mercador da Sé, Lisboa 079967
Il Mercante, Napoli 076007
Il Mercante, Roma 076560
Mercantic, Sant Cugat del Vallès . . 122083
Mercati Dr. Traiano, Roma 025487
Al Mercatino, Milano 075767
Mercatino dell'800 e del '900, Napoli 076008
Mercatino dell'Usato, Bologna 075093
Mercato, Roberto, Claro 082322
Il Mercato dell' Arte e News, Brugine 135914
Mercato dell'Antiquariato, Brescia .075177, 140006
Mercato d'Epoca, Miami 090206
Mercator, Utrecht 140552
Mercator, Zürich 112149
Mercator Graventoren-Watermolen, Rupelmonde 003734
Mercator Museum, Sint-Niklaas . . . 003759
Mercatorfonds, Antwerpen 133250
Mercator's World, Eugene 136539
Mercatu Arte, Belo Horizonte 096473
La Merced, Bilbao 080984, 129440
Merced County Courthouse Museum, Merced 045782
Mercedes-Benz Museum, Stuttgart 020359
Mercer, Noel, Long Melford 085838
Mercer, Thomas, London 085532
Mercer Art Gallery, Harrogate 039677
Mercer County Genealogical and Historical Society Museum, Princeton 047236
Mercer County Historical Museum, Celina 042682
Mercer County Museum, Mercer . . 045783
Mercer Gallery, Rochester 047481
Mercer Museum of the Bucks County Historical Society, Doylestown . . . 043506
Mercer Street Books and Records, New York 142674
Mercer Union - Centre for Contemporary Visual Art, Toronto 006613
Merchant Adventurers' Hall, York . . 041479
Merchant House Antiques, Honiton . 084727
Merchant House Antiques, Ipswich . 084803
The Merchant of Welby, Welby 056810
Merchants House Antique, Ross-on-Wye 086403, 131428
Merchant's House Museum, New York 046363
Merchant's House Museum, Plymouth 040722
Merchat, Gérard, Besançon 061390
Mercier, Chantal, Clermont-Ferrand 062352
Mercier, Gaëtan, Aubigny-sur-Nère 061044
Mercier, Jean-Marie, Biarritz 061469
Mercier, Jean-Yves, Cholet 062300
Mercier, Josiane, Saint-Geniez-d'Olt 067485
Mercier, Michel, Marseille 064375
Mercier & Cie., Patrick, Lille 121035
Mercier & Kalck, Paris 121172
Mercier Press, Cork 134526
Merck hoe Sterck, Rotterdam 128822
Mercorelli, Fabrizio, Roma 128112
Mercure, Toulon (Var) 068462
Mercuri, Giuseppe, Roma 128113
Mercuri & Talarico, Roma 128114
Mercurio, Milano 106267
Mercurio, Th., Levallois-Perret 063802
Mercurio Arte, Palermo 106436
Mercurius, Almelo 077729
Mercury, London 085533
Mercury Bay and District Museum, Whitianga 030660
Mercury Gallery, Boston 115203
Mercury Signs, Houston 116368
Merdøgård, Arendal 030736
Mere Antiques, Topsham 086898
Mere Museum, Mere 040447
Meredith, Baltimore 115068
Meredith Gallery, Baltimore 041997
Merello, Massimo, Genova 075484
Merenwijk, Leiden 108104
Mereside Books, Macclesfield 131248, 141930
Merge, Auckland 108342
Mergel, Albert, Wiesbaden 105270
Mergemeier, Düsseldorf . . 102530, 125540
Mergenthaler, Gerd, Wiesloch 074431
Mergenthaler, Walter, Arnstein 138682
Mergozzi, Ursula, Bern 129967
Mergus, Melle 134198
Meri-Valentino, Sofia 137605
Meriden Historical Society Museum, Meriden 045785
Meridian art Verlag, Selm 134396
Meridian Galerie, Zürich 112150
Meridian Gallery, San Francisco . . . 119735
Meridian Gallery at Artstore, Boston 112675
Meridian International Center - Cafritz Galleries, Washington 048920
Meridian Museum of Art, Meridian . 045787
Meridian Street Antiques, Indianapolis 089322
La Meridiana, Messina 106139
Meridiana, Milano 075768
Meridiana Restauri, Firenze 127371
Meridiani, Torino 076844
La Meridienne, Haarlem 078468
La Méridienne Antique, Rabat 077696, 128513
Meriër, Thierry, Paris 100680
Merigot, Bordeaux 124133
Merijärven Kotiseutumuseo, Merijärvi 009865
Merikarvian Kalastusmuseo, Merikarvia 009867
Merimiehen Koti, Uusikaupunki . . . 010196
Merimiehenkotimuseo, Pohjois-Pohjanmaan Museo, Oulu 009932
De Merindol, Pretoria 080739
Merino, Monsheim 104117
Merino, Edouard 93506581, Monaco 077614
Meritalon Museo, Salo 010060
Merivale Fine Art, Christchurch . . . 108404
Meriwether Lewis Dredge Museum, Brownville 042484
Meriwether Lewis National Monument, Hohenwald 044567
Merkator 1, Varna 137612
Merkel, Rudolf, Erlangen 139048
Merkelbach-Museum, Höhr-Grenzhausen 017949
Merkl, Thomas, Bretten 125396
Merklappenmuseum, Dieteren 029482
Merkle, Den Haag 107941
Merkle, Stuttgart 105000, 134418
Merkle, Thierry, Strasbourg 124946
Merkz, Peter, Bad Homburg v.d.Höhe 125101
Merle, Bernadette, Beaumont-sur-Grosne 061262
Merle, Irma, Alsfeld 101563
Merlet, Alain-Claude, Saint-Martin-Petit 067651
Merlet, Odette, Barbezieux-Saint-Hilaire 061201
Merlin, Singapore 109838
Merlin, Tetbury 086858
Merlin, Jean-Michel, Paris 066275
Merlin Gallery, Swindon 114543
Merlin-Lochet, Aix-en-Provence . . . 060712
Merlin Verlag, Vastorf 105104, 134443
Merlins Antiques, Carmarthen 083883
Merlin's Books, Tampa 143024
Merlo, Norfolk 091390, 132558
Mermal Books, Bangkok 141370
Mermier, Jean-Eric, Allaman 082081, 129894
Mermier, Jean-Eric, Vésenaz 082876, 130203
Mermod, Patrick, Les Arcs 063754
Mermoz, Paris 066276
Mermoz-Santo Micali, Paris 066277
Meroni, Daniele Mario, Milano 127631
Meroogal House, Nowra 001346
Merowe Museum, Merowe 036155
Merredin Military Museum, Merredin 001257
Merredin Railway Station Museum, Merredin 001258
Merrepen Arts, Daly River 055736
The Merrick Art Gallery, New Brighton 046200
Merrifield, Tom, London 113762
Merrill, Detroit 116090
Merrill, Duane E., South Burlington . 123119
Merrill & Assoc., Todd, New York . . 091072
Merrill Historical Museum, Merrill . 045789
Merrill & Johnson, Denver 116026
Merrill Museum, Carrollton 042630
Merrill-West, Carmel 135343
Merrin, New York 118184
Merrion, London 135234
The Merriscourt Gallery, Churchill . . 112871
Merritt Museum of Anthropology, Oakland 046595
Merriwa Colonial Museum, Merriwa 001259
Merry, Robert, Saint Louis 123088
Merry Old England, Frankfurt am Main 070767
Merry Old England, Garmisch-Partenkirchen 070937, 121416
Merry Old England, Kelkheim 071783
Merry's, Northampton 122636
Merryvale Antiques, Pittsburgh 091842
Mersch, Eckhard, Wien 123516
Mersea Island Museum, West Mersea 041341
Mersey Lane Antiques, Gore 079102
Merseyside Maritime Museum, Liverpool 040032
Mersin Müzesi, Mersin 038149
Merson, Paris 066278
Merten, Bornheim, Rheinland 069962
Mertens, Merzen 072525
Mertens, Friedhelm, Köln 103677
Mertens, Sabine, Solingen 134399
Mertens & Pomplun, Berlin 138823
Mertes-Schön, Eva, Bonn 125357
Mertinat, Harald, Wuppertal 074532
Mertins, Jürgen, Dortmund 133873
Mertins, Till, Berlin 125253
Merton Abbey Mills, London 122595
Merton & Simpson, New York 118185
Meru Museum, Meru 027426
Merv, Dinmore 055752
Merve, Berlin 133797
Les Merveilles d'Alice, Saint-Ouen . 067849
Les Merveilles de la Mer, Jdeidet El-Metn 027818
Merville Antiques & Fine Art, Newtownabbey 086086
Mervyn Quinlan Museum, Benenden 038674
Merwin House Tranquility, Stockbridge 048364
Mery's Galerie, Huttwil 111566
Merz, Edinburgh 113000
Merz, Hannover 139239
Merz, Ulrike, München 126416
Merz Akademie, Hochschule für Gestaltung Stuttgart, Stuttgart 050249
M.E.'s Gallery, Houston 116369
Mesa Southwest Museum, Mesa . . 045793
Mesa Street Antique Mall, El Paso . 088807
Mesa Verde National Park Museum, Mesa Verde 045794
La Mésangère, Liège 058316
Mesaoo, Hamburg 103192
Mesaric, Alfred, Hartberg 057056
Meschke, Bärbel & Ralf, Obermachtal 126578
Mese-Fischer, Del, Meisterschwanden 111730
Mesecke, Bernd, Kollmar 103752
Meseguer Jordan, Madrid 110576
Meseke, A., Eime 070526
Meshkinshahr Museum, Meshkinshahr 022585
Mesiti, Barbara, Torino 128335
Mesmer, Hanspeter, Basel 082157, 111213
Mesnier, Jacques, La Cluse-et-Mijoux 063340
Mesnier-Jelstrup, Marie-Christine, Aix-en-Provence 098790
Mesnil, Lucien, Saint-Ursanne 082767
Mesnil aux Abeille, Beautheil 010719
Mesnil mon Temps, Le Mesnil-Esnard 063669
Mesogée, Marseille 135716
Mesolithic Museum, Abinger Common 038467
Messageot, Charles-Henri, Versailles 068812
Messageot, Charles-Henri, Voisins-le-Bretonneux 069029
Messager, Michele, Saint-Brieuc . . 067384

Messages, Washington 136540
Méssaggio, Célestin, Les Andelys . .063752, 099465
Messe für Kunst und Antiquitäten Hofburg Wien, Wien 093583
Messe für Kunst und Antiquitäten Residenz Salzburg, Salzburg 093584
Messengers, Bicester 122411
Messer, Stephen, Clewer, Windsor . 130590
Messerermuseum, Steinbach an der Steyr 002697
Messerli, Marcel, Bern 082228
Messerschmidt, Thomas, Flensburg 070706
Messiez-Poche, Thierry, Toulouse . 124984
Messina, Francesco, Milano 106268
Messina, Orazio, Milano 127632
Messina Museum, Messina 034679
Messina & Wagner, München 104270
Messineo-Wyman, New York 118186
Messink, Apeldoorn 128564
Messiqua, Marcia, New York 091073
Messmer, Otto, München 104271
Messner Mountain Museum Dolomites, Cibiana di Cadore 023875
Messner Mountain Museum Juval, Castelbello 023708
Messori, Roncaglia Giancarlo, Modena 075921
Messum, David, London . . 113763, 131110
Messum, David, Marlow 114062
Mest 50-tal, Farsta 081784
Mestdach, Knokke-Heist 058247
Mestdagh, Patrick, Bruxelles 058032, 137449
Mestna Galerija, Soštanj 034525
Mestna Galerija Ljubljana, Ljubljana 034483
Mestni Muzej Idrija, Idrija 034464
Mestni Muzej Ljubljana, Ljubljana . 034484
Mesto Pechati, Moskva 136056
Mestre Ubach, Barcelona 110218
Městská Galerie, Městské Muzeum a Galerie, Polička 008583
Městská Galerie Art Club, Týn nad Vltavou 008729
Městská Galerie Josefa Lieslerova, Kadaň 008419
Městská Galerie Karla Havlíčka, Kadaň 008420
Městská Galerie Špejchar, Chomutov 008334
Městská Galerie v Zámeckém Parku, Veselí nad Moravou 008752
Mestská Výstavná Sieň Barónka Kežmarok, Kežmarok 034361
Městské Muzeum, Aš 008261
Městské Muzeum, Bílovec 008268
Městské Muzeum, Budyně nad Ohří 008304
Městské Muzeum, Bystřice nad Pernštejnem 008305
Městské Muzeum, Čáslav 008307
Městské Muzeum, Čelákovice 008311
Městské Muzeum, Česká Třebová . 008316
Městské Muzeum, Chotěboř 008336
Městské Muzeum, Chrast u Chrudimě 008338
Městské Muzeum, Chrastava 008339
Městské Muzeum, Dačice 008345
Městské Muzeum, Dobruška 008350
Městské Muzeum, Františkovy Lázně 008359
Městské Muzeum, Frenštát pod Radhoštěm 008360
Městské Muzeum, Horažďovice . . . 008379
Mestské Múzeum, Ilava 034358
Městské Muzeum, Jesenice u Rakovníka 008406
Městské Muzeum, Klobouky u Brna 008439
Městské Muzeum, Kožlany 008450
Městské Muzeum, Králíky 008452
Městské Muzeum, Lanškroun 008466
Městské Muzeum, Ledeč nad Sázavou 008469
Městské Muzeum, Letohrad 008471
Městské Muzeum, Mnichovo Hradiště 008509
Městské Muzeum, Moravská Třebová 008511
Městské Muzeum, Nejdek 008521
Městské Muzeum, Nepomuk 008524
Městské Muzeum, Nové Město nad Metují 008531
Městské Muzeum, Nové Strašecí . . 008533
Městské Muzeum, Nový Bydžov . . . 008535
Městské Muzeum, Počátky 008577
Městské Muzeum, Přelouč 008654
Městské Muzeum, Přibyslav 008659
Městské Muzeum, Protivín 008662
Městské Muzeum, Radnice u Rokycan 008664
Městské Muzeum, Rýmařov 008680
Mestské Múzeum, Sabinov 034423
Městské Muzeum, Sadská 008681
Městské Muzeum, Sedlčany 008682
Městské Muzeum, Skuteč 008684
Městské Muzeum, Slapanice 008686
Městské Muzeum, Strážnice 008697
Městské Muzeum, Stříbro 008698
Městské Muzeum, Úpice 008735
Městské Muzeum, Valašské Klobouky 008740
Městské Muzeum, Velká Bíteš 008744
Městské Muzeum, Veselí nad Moravou 008753
Městské Muzeum, Vimperk 008754
Městské Muzeum, Volyně 008760
Městské Muzeum, Žamberk 008773
Městské Muzeum, Zbiroh 008776
Mestské Múzeum, Zlaté Moravce . . 034453
Městské Muzeum, Jihomoravské Muzeum Znojmo, Moravský Krumlov 008513
Městské Muzeum, Městské Muzeum a Galerie, Polička 008584
Městské Muzeum, Okresní muzeum Kroměřížska, Holešov 008377
Městské Muzeum a Galerie, Břeclav 008278
Městské Muzeum a Galerie, Dvůr Králové nad Labem 008358
Městské Muzeum a Galerie, Hlinsko v Čechách 008371
Městské Muzeum a Galerie, Hořice v Pokrkonoší 008380
Městské Muzeum a Galerie, Lomnice nad Popelkou 008487
Městské Muzeum a Galerie, Svitavy 008703
Městské Muzeum a Galerie, Vodňany 008758
Městské Muzeum a Galerie J. Karse, Velvary 008750
Městské Muzeum a Galerie Otakara Spaniela a Josefa Wágnera, Jaroměř 008404
Městské Muzeum a Galerie T.F. Simona, Železnice 008782
Městské Muzeum a Památník Jakuba Jana Ryby, Rožmitál pod Třemšínem . . 008673
Městské Muzeum Antonína Sovy, Pacov 008558
Mestské Múzeum Filakovo, Filakovo 034353
Městské Muzeum Klenotnice, Nová Paka 008527
Mestské Múzeum Michala Tillnera, Malacky 034380
Mestské Múzeum Poltár, Poltár . . . 034409
Mestské Múzeum Rajec, Rajec 034417
Mestské Múzeum v Bratislave, Bratislava 034328
Městské Muzeum v Kralupech nad Vltavou, Kralupy nad Vltavou 008454
Městské Muzeum v Mariánských Lázních, Mariánské Lázně 008498
Městské Muzeum v Železném Brodě, Železný Brod 008783
Městské Vlastivědné Mudruňkovo Muzeum, Říčany u Prahy 008666
Městské Vrbasovo Muzeum, Ždánice 008778
Mesuret, Claude, Lesparre-Médoc . 063796
Mesureur, Karine, L'Isle-sur-la-Sorgue 063947
Mesuroscope, Douai 011639
Met Room, Barcelona 110219
Meta-Aesthetix, Port Melbourne . . . 095096
La Métairie, Paris 066279
Metais, Claude, Compiègne 124209
Métais, Henri, Rouen 067285, 138591
Metal, Warszawa 109156
Metal Art, Birmingham 131836
Metal Art Company, San Francisco . 132900
Metal Art Studio, New York 091074, 132495
The Metal Arts Guild, Toronto 097330
The Metal Gallery, London 113764
Metal Maddness Art Gallery, Salt Lake City 119356
Metallmuseum, Tullnerbach-Lawies 002763
Metamora Courthouse, Metamora . 045797
Metamorforse, Amsterdam 140320
Metamorphis, Ashburton 112527
Metamorphosis Church Museum, Metéora 021379
Metaphores, Nijmegen 078658
Metaphysical Book Store Center, Denver 142392
Metára, Rio de Janeiro 096629
Metaux Précieux, Aix-en-Provence . 060713
Métaux Précieux, Carpentras 062000
Metaxas Collection, Iráklion 021284
Métayer, Jean-Jacques, Mérignac (Charente) 064502
Métayer, Marie-Antoinette, Paris . . 066280
Metcalfe - Hofmann, Deal 112941
Metchosin School Museum, Victoria 006746
Meteorite Museum of the Center for Meteorite Studies, Tempe 048519
Meteorkrater-Museum, Steinheim am Albuch 020306
Methe, Reiner, Ringgau 073538
Methil Heritage Centre, Methil 040452
Methmann & Co., Hamburg 071288
Methner, Berlin 125254
Methodist Church Museum - a Laura Ingalls Wilder Site, Spring Valley 048278
Metier, Bradford 054429
Les Métiers d'Antan, Musée d'Art et de Traditions Populaires, Monêtier-les-Bains 013096
Metiers d'Art Sant Roch, Céret 011175
Les Métiers du Champagne, Musée de la Cave des Champagnes de Castellane, Épernay 011704
Metin Sanat Galerisi, İstanbul 112338
Metis, Amsterdam 107771
Metlewicz, Dr. Thomasz, Wien 057499
Metodo, Parma 127857
Métra, Raoul, Autun 061091
Metras, Rene, Barcelona 110220
Métraux, Raynald, Lausanne 111626
Metro 5 Gallery, Armadale, Victoria 094170
Metro Antiques, New York 091075
Metro Antiques, Philadelphia 091666
Metro Art, New York 118187
Metro Art, New York 118188
Metro Arts, Brisbane 000839
Metro Furniture, Mumbai 074823
Metro Pictures, New York 118189
Metro Retro, Dallas 088567
Metrocoins, Pirmasens 073331
Metroform, Tucson 120147
Metrolina Antiques, Charlotte 087967
Metronom, Barcelona 110221
Metrònom, Fundació Rafael Tous d'Art Contemporani, Barcelona 034916
Metropolart, Paris 100681
Metropole Gallery, Folkestone 039510
Metropolis, Bordeaux 061635
Métropolis, Lyon 099604
Métropolis, Paris 066281, 100682
Metropolis M, Utrecht 136002
Metropolitan Antique Gallery, Denver 088716
Metropolitan Antiques, New York . . 091076
Metropolitan Antiques, New York . . 091077
Metropolitan Arts Institute, Phoenix 051948
Metropolitan Gallery, Austin 114996
Metropolitan Garage Door, Milwaukee 090315
Metropolitan Home, Vancouver 059384
Metropolitan Museum of Art, New York 046364
Metropolitan Museum of Art Bulletin, New York 136541
Metropolitan Museum of Art Journal, New York 136542
Metropolitan Museum of Art, Special Publications, New York 135441
Metropolitan Museum of Manila, Manila 031726
Metropolitan Pavilion, New York . . . 091078
Metropolitan Police Historical Museum, London 040219
Metropolitan Toronto Police Museum and Discovery Centre, Toronto 006614
Metropolitana Leiloeira, Porto 121954
Métrot, André, Paris 066282
Métrot, André, Paris 066283
Mets, Jan, Amsterdam 134786
Metsämuseo, Helsinki 009556
Metsers, G.L., Den Haag 107942
Metta, Madrid 110577
Mettchen, Dieter, Darmstadt 070187
Mettelsiefen, Dieter, Berlin 138824
Mettlach Steinzeugsammler e.V., Rehlingen-Siersburg 053492
Metz, Hilde, Antwerpen 096082
Metz, J. & M., Heidelberg . 071459, 121451
Metz Collection, Pierrevillers 066829
Metz de Benito, München 072791
Metz-Noblat, Bertrand de, Nancy . . 064875
Metze, Manfred, Blankenrath 125336
Metzen, T., Tübingen 074113
Metzgalerie, Koblenz 103570
Metzger, Elisabeth, Augsburg 125077
Metzger, Jean-Pierre, Prunières . . . 066993
Metzger, Marcel, Pouancé 066965
Metzger, Marcel, Pouancé 066966
Metzger, S., Graben-Neudorf 071072
Metzner, Bernd, Seevetal 104880
Metzner, Eberhard, Mainz . 072398, 126262
Metzner & Menacher, München . . . 126417
Meubles & Cie, Orvault 124532
Les Meubles d'Antan, Mehun-sur-Yèvre 064469
Meubles d'Art, Pully 082733
Meubles d'Art Chartres, Ribérac . . . 067133
Meubles d'Autrefois, Augy 061062
Meubles d'Autrefois, Besançon . . . 061391
Meubles Décennies 30'a 70', Québec 059074
Meubles d'Hier et d'Aujourd'hui, Poilley 066883
Meubles et Objets en Périgord, Piegut-Pluviers 066823
Meubles la Merisière, Fréjus 062938
Meubles Oubliés, Québec 123807
Meubles Ray, Québec 059075
Meubles Style Restauration, Bonne 124107
Meubl'Occase, Montpellier 064750
Meugnier, Jean-Louis, Cordes-sur-Ciel 062474
Meulen, ter, Dordrecht 078311, 128651
Meunier, Franck, Ferney-Voltaire . . 099259
Meunier, Jacqueline, Saint-Martin-de-Gurson 067627
Meunier, Jean-Jacques, Jarnac . . . 063234
Meunier, Marie-Yolande, Toulouse . 124985
Meunier, Patrice, Bordeaux 124134
Meunier, Philippe, Paris 066284
Le Meur, Dijon 138083
Meurer, Koblenz 103571
Meurier, Jocelyne, Nîmes 065182
Meuron, Anita, Honolulu 116227
Meurs, I.J.A., Leiden 140480
Meusburger, Marlis, München 072792
Meuschel, Konrad, Bad Honnef . . . 138694
Meussling, Anna-Maria, Plötzky . . . 126635
Mevagissey Fine Art, Mevagissey . . 114079
Mevel, Claude le, Lille 063857
Mével, Jacques, Ploulech 066878
Mével, Jacques, Trébeurden 068617
Mevel, Jean-Pierre, Toulon (Var) . . . 068463
Mevlânâ Müzesi, Konya 038136
Mevlevi Tekke Müzesi, Lefkoşa . . . 008257

Mewes, Lübeck 072333
Mewes, Axel, Hamburg 103193
Mewes, Werner, Ulm 074147
Mews, Dallas 088568
Mews, Dallas 088569
Mews Antique Emporium, Holt, Norfolk 084706
Mexic-Arte Museum, Austin 041932
Mexican Fine Arts Center Museum, Chicago 042857
Mexican Gallery, Dallas 115910
The Mexican Museum, San Francisco 047870
Mey, Irmelin, Kiel 071838
Mey, Jürgen, Geldern 102924
Meyburg, Klaus-J., Hamburg 071289
Meyenburg-Museum, Nordhausen . 019333
Meyer, Artlenburg 069187
Meyer, Marseille 099675
Meyer, Paris 100683
Meyer, Recklinghausen 073445
Meyer, Alexander, Sankt Martin, Pfalz 073673
Meyer, Bernard, Strasbourg 124947
Meyer, Björn, Garbsen 070929
Meyer, Claude, Paris 066285
Meyer, Dr. Claus-Peter, Aachen . . . 069095
Meyer, Don, Dallas 088570
Meyer, Ernst, Hunzenschwil 082504
Meyer, Françoise, Hamburg 071290
Meyer, H. Jürgen, Lüneburg 103980
Meyer, Harry, Hamburg 071291
Meyer, Heinrich A., Saarbrücken . . 104802
Meyer, Helmut, Aurich 069245
Meyer, Irin von, Hamburg 125830
Meyer, Jean-Claude, Paris 066286
Meyer, Joe, Fulenbach 082384
Meyer, Jutta, Lüneburg 103981
Meyer, K., Nümbrecht 073092
Meyer, Karlheinz, Karlsruhe 103498
Meyer, Marion, Paris 100684
Meyer, Martin, Nürnberg 126567
Meyer, Michel, Nice 138257
Meyer, Michel, Paris 066287
Meyer, Rainer F., Berlin 138825
Meyer, Thomas, Regensburg 139684
Meyer, Thomas V., San Francisco . . 119736
Meyer, Ulrich, Oedheim 073175
Meyer, Werner, Cloppenburg 070143
Meyer Boswell, San Francisco 142958
Meyer-Buhr, Ute, Nürnberg 126568
Meyer & Deubert, Neustadt an der Weinstraße 104433
Meyer-Dommert, M., Berlin 125255
Meyer-Ellinger, Herbert, Frankfurt am Main 102799
Meyer Kainer, Wien 095898
Meyer-Lindenberg, Reinhard, Lehrte 072187
Meyer Zafra, Paris 100685
Meyerdiercks, Peter, Hamburg 071292
Meyerdierks, Gabriele, Bad Sooden-Allendorf 101704
Meyerovich, San Francisco 119737
Meyerowitz, Ariel, New York 118190
Meyer's Antik, København 060353
Meyer's Laden, Erftstadt 139042
Meyniel, Georges, Laval (Mayenne) 063553
Meynier, Maria-Hélène, Toulouse . .068528, 124986
Meyrat, Sonia, Genève 111483
Meyring, Carl-Ulrich, Sankt Augustin 104809, 134378
Meysenburg, Ulrich F., Essen 139057
Meysenburg, Ulrich-Ferdinand, Essen 133918
Meysey-Thompson, Sarah, Woodbridge 087223
Meža Muzejs Boju Pilī, Aizpute 027656
Mézaute, Michel, Lalinde 063493
Meždunarodna Restavracija, Ruse . 096710
Meždunarodnaja Cudožestvennaja Jarmarka, Moskva 093849
Meždunarodnaja Vystavka Architektury i Sredovovo Disajna, Moskva 093850
Meždunarodnaja Vystavka-Prodaža Zivopisi, Grafiki, Skulptury i Izdelij Dekorativno-Prikladnogo Iskusstva, Perm 093851
Meždunarodnyj Centr-Muzej im. N.K. Rericha, Moskva 033428
Meždunarodnyj Muzejno-vystavočnyj Centr, Primorskij gosudarstvennyj muzej im. V.K. Arseneva, Vladivostok 034049
Mèze, Yoland, Tavel 068368
Mézerac, Arnaud de, Arromanches-les-Bains 098866
Mezinárodní Veletrh Poštovních Známek, Mincí, Telefonních Karet, Minerálů a Sběratelství, Praha 093636
Mezquita Catedral de Córdoba, Córdoba 035112
Mezzacqui, Tino, Modena 140073
Mezzani, G., Verona 106798
Mezzani, Giuseppe, Verona 077012
Mezzanin, Wien 095899
Mezzanine, Cleveland 088342
La Mezzanine, Montréal 097057
Mezzomonaco, Pascal, Lyon 124366
MFA Circle Gallery, Maryland Federation of Art, Annapolis 114840
MFA City Gallery, Maryland Federation of Art, Baltimore 115069
MFF, Saint-Paul-de-Vence 101213
MFK Mund- und Fußmalende Künstler Verlag, Stuttgart 134419
M.G. Publicité, Paris 138506
MGJ Jewellers, Wallingford 087005
MGM Galeria, Warszawa 109157
MGM Münzgalerie München, München 072793
M.G.R. Exports, Bruton 083775
MGS & NSI, Minneapolis 090378
MH, Châteaurenard 062210
M.H. de Young Memorial Museum, Fine Arts Museums of San Francisco, San Francisco 047871
Mhiripiri, Minneapolis 117284
Mhiripiri Gallery, Edina 043607
Mi, Alma, Los Angeles 089841
Mi, Alma, Los Angeles 089842
Mia, Taman Melawati 107440
MIA Gallery, Chicago 115499
Mia Lou, Philadelphia 118799
Mia Mia Gallery, Templestowe 095323
Mialkas, G., Magdeburg 072374
Miami Art Museum, Miami 045814
Miami Auction Gallery, Miami 122962
Miami Beach Antique Jewelry and Watch Show 094005
Miami Beach Fantasy, Miami 090207
Miami Books, Miami 142558
Miami Children's Museum, Miami . 045815
Miami Contemporary Art Fair, Miami 094006
Miami County Museum, Peru 046895
Miami Gold Coins, Miami 090208
Miami Mid-Century, Miami 090209
Miami Museum, Miami 005863
Miami Museum of Science, Miami . 045816
Miami Shores Antiques, Miami 090210
Miami Twice, Miami 090211
Miami University Art Museum, Oxford 046773
Miami Watercolor Society, Miami . . 054871
Miandoab Museum, Urmieh 022648
Miani, Adriano, Venezia 128398
Miano, Guido, Milano 134622
Mianposhteh Palace Museum, Bandar-Anzali 022549
Miasskij Kraevedčeskij Muzej, Miass 033355
Miazzo, Lucia, Milano 127633
Mibedo, Paris 066288
Mica Troc, Saint-Grégoire 067512
Micawber Antiques, Bridgnorth . . . 083670
Miccinesi, Livio, Firenze 127372
Miceli, Roberta, Roma 128115
Micello, Luigi, Rolle 082747
Michael, Dr., North Tamborine 056377
Michael, Portland 119020
Michael, San Francisco . . 092844, 119738
Michael, Alan, Virginia Beach 120227
Michael, Dan, Paris 066289
Michael, Heike, Betzdorf 069812
Michael, Judith, Corbridge 084083
Michael, S., Larnaka 059950
Michael Bruce Cottage Museum, Kinnesswood 039897
Michael C. Carlos Museum, Emory University, Atlanta 041866
Michael C. Rockefeller Arts Center Gallery, Fredonia 044068
Michael Davitt National Memorial Museum, Straide 022861
Michael-Ende-Museum, München . 019081
Michael Faraday's Laboratory and Museum, London 040220
Michael og Anna Anchers Hus og Saxilds Gaard, Skagen 009094
Michael Pacher-Haus, Sankt Wolfgang im Salzkammergut 002636
Michaelis Collection, Cape Town . . 034580
Michaelis School of Fine Art, University of Cape Town, Cape Town 050695
Michaels, México 077578
Michaels, J., Minneapolis 132385
Michaels, Lawrence, Milwaukee . . 117206
Michael's Antique Clocks, Oklahoma City 091520, 132582
Michael's Antiques, Birmingham . . 087771
Michael's Antiques, New York 091079
Michaels Bookshop, Ramsgate 142013
Michael's China Porcelain, Seattle . 132942
Michael's Old Books, Oklahoma City 142727
Michael's Rug Gallery, Baltimore . . 087693
Michaelsen, Anke-Friedericke, Berlin 069702
Michaelsen, Prof. Hans, Berlin 125256
Michail-Lombardo, New York 118191
Michajlovskij Istoričeskij Muzej, Rjazanskij istoriko-architekturnyj muzej-zapovednik, Michajlov 033356
Michajlovskoe - Gosudarstvennyj Memorialnyj Istoriko-literaturnyj i Prirodno-landšaftnyj Muzej-Zapovednik A.S. Puškina, Puškinskie Gory . . . 033689
Michalak, Goch 071022
Michalak, T., Gdynia 129017
Michalakakos, Michalis, Athinai . . . 074600
Michalko, Praha 123993
Michallek, Alain, Reugny 067125
Michallon, René, Le Paradou 099451
Michalopoulos, James, New Orleans 117476
Michalovský, Tibo, Košice 080623
Michałowska, Marzena, Warszawa . 129101
Michalská, Praha 060143
Michalski, Passau 073295
Michaud, Nevers 121092
Michaud, Henry-François, Reims . . 067072
Michel, Albin, Paris 133653
Michel, Claude, Lausanne 130073
Michel, Gerd, Würzburg 074504
Michel, Hélène et Eric, Saint-Saturnin-les-Avignon 068000
Michel, Jean, La Chaux-de-Fonds .082302, 129997
Michel, Klaus, Gießen 070990
Michel, Leo, Milano 075769
Michel, Leo, Milano 075770
Michel, Lotti, Biel 111289
Michel, Luc, Paris 124749
Michel, Marie-Claude, Bordeaux . . 061636
Michel, Perle, Saint-Amand-Montrond 067347
Michel, Raymond, Champs-sur-Marne 099114
Michel, Robert, Nice 124516
Michel, Romuald, Ellhofen 070539
Michel Antiquités, Meylan 064547, 124446
Michel Brouillet House and Museum, Vincennes 048789
Michelaine, Aigues-Mortes 098775
Michelangeli, Sergio, Roma 128116
Michelangelo, Brescia 121681
Michelangelo, La Paz 058398, 123685
Michelangelo Refinishing Company, New York 132496
Michelangelo Refinishing Company, New York 132497
Michele, C., Los Angeles 089843
Michelet, Antibes-Juan-les-Pins . . 060925
Michelet-Huot, Jacques, Reims . . . 067073
Micheletti, Colette, Arles 060973
Michelham Priory, Hailsham 039656
Michelis, U., Gifhorn 070996
Michell Moder, Santiago de Chile . . 059541
Michelotti, Marseille 099676, 124428
Michelotti, Claudio, Parma 076214
Michelotti, Marzia, Roma 076561
Michels, B., Kempten 071791
Michelsen, Christian, Wald, Zürich . 082898
Michelsen, Selma, Køge 098591
Michelson Museum of Art, Marshall 045705
Micheluzzi, Venezia 076958
Michi, Houston 089154
Michiels, J., Bruxelles 058033
Michielssen, P., Knokke-Heist 058248
Michigan Avenue Antiques, Detroit .088766, 122890
Michigan Avenue Art Gallery, Chicago 115500
Michigan Chapter Gallery, National Conference of Artists, Detroit 043452
Michigan Guild of Artists and Artisans, Ann Arbor 054872
Michigan Historical Museum, Lansing 045163
Michigan Hot Glass Workshop Studio, Detroit 116091
Michigan Maritime Museum, South Haven 048242
Michigan Museums Association, Lansing 054873
Michigan Sports Hall of Fame, Detroit 043453
Michigan State Trust for Railway Preservation, Owosso 046764
Michigan State University Museum, East Lansing 043575
Michigan Street Antique Center, Indianapolis 089323
Michigan Transit Museum, Mount Clemens 046054
Michitsch, Elisabeth, Wien 057500, 095900
Michl, Regensburg 073465
Michot, M., Brugge 057782
Michotte, J.L., Bruxelles 137450
Michoutouchkine Pilioko Foundation, Port Vila 049415
Micioni, Ginardo, Roma 128117
Mickelson, Washington 120326
Mickey's Autograph Arena, Indianapolis 142457
Mick's Place, Gent 058196
Mickyz Curios, Opotiki 079205
Miclescu, Alexander, Frankfurt am Main 070768
Mico INAFCA Museum, Kingston . . 026387
Micovna, Praha 008622
Micro-Musée de la Lessive, Seyne-les-Alpes 014791
Micro-Musée de l'École, Seyne-les-Alpes 014792
Micro-Musée de l'Ex-Colonie Pénitentiaire, Mettray 013039
Micro-Musée du Tailleur, Seyne-les-Alpes 014793
Micro Rolled Thread, Chicago 088130
Micromusée, La Trinité 028055
Micromusée Archéologique, Padirac 013533
Micromusée de la Légion Etrangère, Douzillac 011653
Micromusée de la Maison de Retraîte Jeanne Pierretée Carnot, Nolay . . 013447
Micromusée de Marcel Proust, Cabourg 011041
Micromusée du Village Ardéchois, Pailhares 013534
Micromusée Républicain, Villars-les-Blamont 015231

Micus, Herbert, Siegburg 073807
Mid-AM Antique Appraisers Association Newsletter, Springfield 136543
Mid-America Air Museum, Liberal . 045284
Mid America Antique Center, Milwaukee 090316
Mid-America Arts Alliance and Exhibits USA, Kansas City 054874
Mid America Print Conseil, New Albany 054875
Mid-America Science Museum, Hot Springs 044628
Mid Atlantic Air Museum, Reading . 047346
Mid-Atlantic Association of Museums, Baltimore 054876
Mid-Atlantic Center for the Arts, Cape May 042614
Mid Century Design, Auckland 078964
Mid-Century Design, San Diego . . . 092657
Mid Century Modern, Atlanta 087499
Mid-Century Modern, Toronto 059242
Mid-City Coins, Saint Louis 092277
Mid-Continent Railway Museum, North Freedom 046527
Mid Cornwall Galleries, Saint Blazey Gate 114351
Mid Hampshire Railway Museum, Alresford 038496
Mid-Hudson Children's Museum, Poughkeepsie 047213
Mid-Richmond Historical Museum, Coraki 000947
Mid-South Coin Company, Memphis 090092
Mid-States Coin, Tulsa 093321
Mid-Town Specialties, Sacramento 092171
Mid-Valley Art Leaugue, Glendora . 054877
MidAmerica Pastel Society, Overland Park 054878
Mida's Touch, Memphis 090093
Middelfart Museum, Middelfart . . . 009023
Middendorpshuis, Den Ham 029460
Middione, Angelo, Torino 128336
Middle Border Museum of American Indian and Pioneer Life, Mitchell 045942
Middle East Public Auction, Riyadh . 121972
Middle Eastern Culture Centre in Japan, Mitaka 026814
Middle Kingdom, Ottawa 059044
Middle Lake Museum, Middle Lake 005865
Middle Park Fine Art Gallery, Middle Park 094841
Middleborough Historical Museum, Middleborough 045830
The Middlebury College Museum of Art, Middlebury 045834
Middlebury Historical Society Museum, Wyoming 049322
Middleham Antiques, Middleham . . 085984
Middlesbrough Art Gallery, Middlesbrough 040461
Middlesex Canal Collection, Center for Lowell History, Lowell 045508
Middlesex County Historical Society Museum, Middletown 045841
Middlesex University, Art and Design Learning Resources, London 050836
Middleton, Arthur, London 085534
Middleton, Bobbie, Tetbury 086859
Middleton Place Foundation, Charleston 042741
Middleton Top Engine House, Middleton-by-Wirksworth 040463
Middletown Antiques, Louisville . . . 090012
Middletown Fine Arts Center, Middletown 045844
Middletown Valley Historical Society Museum, Middletown 045842
Middleville Museum, Lanark 005742
Midgård Miljø, København 060354
Midhurst, Matfen 085962, 114067
Midiri, Francesco, Milano 075771
Midland Air Museum, Baginton 038564
Midland Arts, Indianapolis 116477
Midland Arts and Antiques Market, Indianapolis 089324
Midland Center for the Arts, Midland 051710
Midland County Historical Museum, Midland 045848
Midland County Historical Museum, Midland 045853
Midland Motor Museum, Bridgnorth 038831
Midland Pictures, Birmingham 112653
Midland Railway Centre, Ripley, Derbyshire 040837
Midland Warplane Museum, Warwick 041304
Midlands Art Centre, Birmingham . . 038733
Midlands Art Centre, Birmingham . . 054430
Midlands Federation of Museums and Art Galleries, Telford 054431
Midland's Fine Furniture, Omaha . .091576, 132595
Midmarch Arts Press, New York . . . 135442
Midnight Pickle, Jacksonville 089431
Mido, Wittlich 139860
Midoma, New York 118192
Midorikawa Yoishi Shashin Bijutsukan, Okayama 026941
Midpoint Gallery, Omaha 118716
Midsomer Norton and District Museum, Radstock 040789
Midt-Telemark Auksjonsforretning, Bø i Telemark 079382
Midtown Antiques, New York 091080
Midtown Art Center, Houston 044646
Midtown Artist Market, Memphis . . 116998
Midtown Collectibles, Tulsa 093322
Midtown Galleries and Auction, Memphis 090094, 122958, 132330
Midtown Gallery, Nashville 117362
Midtsønderjyllands Museum, Gram 008876
Midttunet, Skei i Jølster 031188
Midway Museum, Midway 045858
Midway Used and Rare Books, Saint Paul 142868
Midway Village and Museum, Rockford 047499
Midwest Art History Society, Dearborn 054879
Midwest Coin COompany, Saint Louis 092278
Midwest Money, Saint Louis 092279
Midwest Museum Bulletin, Elkhart . 136544
Midwest Museum of American Art, Elkhart 043661
Midwest Old Settlers and Threshers Association Museum, Mount Pleasant 046063
Midwestern Arts and Antiques, Chicago 088131
Midwinter, Richard, Market Drayton 085936
Midwood, Charlotte 087968
Mie-kenritsu Bijutsukan, Tsu 027294
Mie-kenritsu Hakubutsukan, Tsu . . 027295
Miedler, Hans, Wien 057501
Miedler-Ludi, Ursula, Gstaad 082489
Międzynarodowe Centrum Sztuki, Poznań 109051
Miegunyah Pioneer Women's Memorial House Museum, Bowen Hills 000821
Miehseler, F., Zülpich 074576
Miejska, Wrocław 109226
Miejska Galeria Sztuki, Częstochowa 108867, 121885
Miejska Galeria Sztuki, Łódź 032108
Miejskie, Łódź . . .079669, 109013, 140754
Mielcarek-Kulak, Warszawa 129102
Miele, Frank J., New York 118193
Miele-Museum, Gütersloh 017602
Mielenz, Gerhard, Hannover 071405
Mieli, David, Roma 076562
Mieli, Ruben, Roma 076563
Mielke, M., Hannover 139240
Mielke, Thomas, Hannover 139241
Miellerie des Gorges de la Loire, Roche-la-Molière 014071
Miers, J. & P., Mogo 094866
Miervalda Ķemera Muzejs, Jūrmala 027698
Mies-Pilsner-Heimatmuseum, Dinkelsbühl 016718
Mies van der Rohe Haus, Berlin . . . 016119
Mieszkanie-Pracownia Kazimiery Iłłakowiczówny, Biblioteka Raczyńskich, Poznań 032237
Miethe, H., Borken, Westfalen 069956
Miethe, Uwe, Chemnitz 070137
Miettinen, Arto, Tampere 060630
Mietto, Marco Emiliano, Milano . . . 127634
Le Mieux Galleries, New Orleans . . 117477
Migaldi, Federico, Prato 127893
Migale, Nice 099849
Migard, Riquewihr 067151, 101093
Migart, Praha 098473
Migge, U., Worpswede 139864
Migliorini & Co, Claudio, Firenze . . . 127373
Migliorini, Lorenzo, Firenze 127374
Migneco, Franzina Cinzia, Palermo . 076164
Mignerot, Jean-Philippe, Paris 066290
Mignon, Haßloch 103307
Mignot, Saint-Sébastien-sur-Loire . 068005
Migration Museum, Adelaide 000709
Migros Museum für Gegenwartskunst, Zürich 037780
Miguaise, Jean-Paul, Provins 066991
Miguaise, Jean-Paul, Voulton 069032
Miguel Malvar Museum, Santo Tomas 031787
Miguelenea, Pamplona 081521
Miguet Frères, Paris 066291
Miguet, Maité, Saint Anatoly 124887
Mihálka, Budapest 074695
Mihkli Talumuuseum, Saaremaa Museum, Kihelkonna 009373
Miho Museum, Shigaraki 027063
Mihrab, Vancouver 059385
Mijabi, Warszawa 079768, 109158
Mijangos, Alberto, San Antonio 119432
Mijiza, Chicago 115501
Mijn Winkeltje, Haarlem 078469
Mijndert, Oegstgeest 128793
Mikado, Claude, Toulon (Var) 068464
Mikaélian, Edouard, Grenoble 063069
Mikaeloff, Robert, Monaco 077615
Mikaeloff, Robert, Paris 100686
Mikaeloff, Yves, Paris 066292
Mike & Társa, Budapest 139922
Mike & Schneider, Berlin . 069703, 125257
Mikel, Thomas, Klagenfurt 095617
Mike's Antiques, Detroit 088767
Mike's Antiques, Tulsa 093323
Mike's Art, Louisville 116955
Mikes Polishing, Austin 131804
Mikes World of Books, Hamilton . . . 137640
Mikeska, J., Bad Homburg v.d.Höhe 069295
Miki Gallery, Tokyo 107074
Mikkeli, Tartu 098705
Mikkelin Taidemuseo, Mikkeli 009874
Mikki, F., Knokke-Heist 096343
Miklautsch, Markus, Klagenfurt . . .057109, 095618
Miklautz, Bad Kleinkirchheim 056934
Miklautz, Gmünd, Kärnten 056990
Miklautz, Heinz, Spittal an der Drau 057319
Miklin-Kniefacz, Silvia, Wien 123517
Mikołajczyki, Kraków 108963
MIKST, Kyïv 112417
Mikumi Museum, Mikumi 037856
Mil, Warszawa 109159
Mil Objetos, Fortaleza 058475
Mil Objetos, Fortaleza 058476
Mila, Buenos Aires 055228
Milagros 1530 Post Alley, Seattle . . 119961
Milam, Houston 142442
Milam County Historical Museum, Cameron 042584
Milan, Fresno 132084
Milan, Hong Kong 059673
Milan, Houston 089155
Milán, Montevideo 122785
Milan Gallery, Fort Worth 116156
Milan Historical Museum, Milan . . . 045860
Milanese & Son, San Francisco . . . 132901
Milani, Francesco, Giubiasco 111514
Milano, Warszawa 109160
Milano, Eugène, Paris 066293
Milano, Stefano, Roma 128118
Milano International Modern Arts Show, Milano 093769
Milano Internazionale Antiquariato, Milano 093770
Milano Model and Toy Museum, Elmhurst 043689
Milanoarte, Milano 075772
Mil'Art, Poznań 109057
Milarte, Milano 106269
Milas Kültür Merkezi, Milas 038150
Milas Müzesi, Milas 038151
Milazzo, Santo, Catania 127271
Milazzotto, Antonino, Firenze 127375
Milbrado, Timişoara 080196
Milchpintli, Rubigen 111850
Milchwirtschaftliches Museum, Kiesen 037209
Milden Community Museum, Milden 005869
Mildenhall, Brighton, Victoria 055551
Mildenhall and District Museum, Mildenhall, Suffolk 040464
Mildenhall Antiques, Brighton, Victoria 136817
Mildenhall Antiques, Mildenhall, Suffolk 085989
Mildred M. Mahoney Silver Jubilee Dolls' House Gallery, Fort Erie 005456
Mildred's, Minneapolis 090379
Mildred's Antiques, Edmonton 058837
Mildura Arts Centre, Mildura 001261
Milefsky, Lee, Baltimore . . 087694, 115070
Mileham, Tom, Buffalo 087896
Milenario, Logroño 081183
Milenium, Beograd 109712
Milenium Unic Art, Bucureşti 080163
Milenković, Dragan, Beograd 109713
Miles, Kinross 084870, 130854
Miles, New York 118194
Miles, Round Corner 095162
Miles, Anna, Auckland 108343
Miles, Archie, Gosforth, Cumbria . . 141629
Miles, Roy, London 113765
Miles and District Historical Village Museum, Miles 001263
Miles B. Carpenter Museum, Waverly 049020
Miles Mineral Museum, Eastern New Mexico University, Portales 047152
Miles, Wynn & Cato, London 085535, 113766
Milesi, Bruno, Le Vaudioux 063727
Milestone Antiques, Easingwold . . . 084240
Milestone Antiques, Lichfield 084991
Milestone Publications, Rowlands Castle 135301
Milestones: Hampshire's Living History Museum, Basingstoke 038611
Milevské Muzeum, Milevsko 008504
Milford, Dunedin 108440
Milford, Dunedin 108441
Milford Galleries, Auckland 108344
Milford Haven Antiques, Milford Haven 085990
Milford Haven Museum, Milford Haven 040465
Milford Historical Museum, Milford . 045866
Milford Historical Society Museum, Milford 045864
Milford Museum, Milford 045865
Milhes, Bruno, Toulouse 124987
Mili Weber-Haus, Sankt Moritz 037505
Milic, Zoran, Ljubljana 129289
Le Milieu du Monde, Saint-Paul-de-Vence 101214
Milieu Educatie Centrum, Eindhoven 029543
Milieucentrum De Grote Rivieren, Heerewaarden 029693
Il Milione, Milano 106270
Militär-Stüble, Nendeln 077445
Militär- und Jagdgeschichtliche Sammlung, Staatliche Museen Kassel, Bad Wildungen 015826
Militärgeschichtliche Ortssammlung, Schnifis 002652

Militärgeschichtliches Museum, Ardagger . . . 001694
Militärhistorisches Museum der Bundeswehr, Dresden . . . 016802
Militair Historisch Museum De Veteraan, Eefde . . . 029525
Militaire Luchtvaart Museum, Soesterberg . . . 030172
Militaria-Archiv, Ulm . . . 074148
Militaria Barcelona, Barcelona . . . 080884
Militarial Musée Mémorial pour la Paix, Boissezon . . . 010861
Military Academy Museum, Seoul . 027582
Military Arms and Collectibles, San Diego . . . 092658
Military Aviation Museum, Tangmere . . . 041185
Military Best, Jacksonville . . . 089432
Military Bookman, New York . . . 142675
Military Bookroom, Malvern, Victoria . . . 136990
Military Collectables, San Antonio . 092547
Military Collectible Items Wanted, Detroit . . . 088768
Military Communications and Electronics Museum, Kingston . . . 005702
Military Curios, Gloucester . . . 084478
Military Heritage Museum, Lewes . 039994
Military Heritage Tours, Longford . . 022827
Military Historians Museum, Westbrook . . . 049103
Military History Bookshop, Hythe, Kent . . . 141687
Military Medal Museum, San Jose . 047898
Military Museum, Aden . . . 049557
Military Museum, Cairo . . . 009306
Military Museum, El-Alamein . . . 009328
Military Museum, Macau . . . 007187
Military Museum, Sanaa . . . 049561
Military Museum, Teheran . . . 022629
Military Museum, Ulaanbaatar . . . 029003
Military Museum, Jamaica Defence Force Museum, Kingston . . . 026388
Military Museum Fort, Bloemfontein 034559
Military Museum of Devon and Dorset, Dorchester . . . 039258
Military Museum of Southern New England, Danbury . . . 043290
Military Parade Bookshop, Marlborough . . . 141943
Military Vehicle Museum, Newcastle-upon-Tyne . . . 040551
Military Veterans Museum, Oshkosh 046736
Militos, Alimos . . . 134481, 139895
Militz, Ernst, Kamen . . . 125990
Miljømuseet Dokken, Karmsund Folkemuseum, Haugesund . . . 030883
Milk Creek Crossing, Portland . . . 091971
Milk Gallery & Spotty Dog Design, Wellington . . . 108630
The Mill, Haarlem . . . 078470
The Mill, Haarlem . . . 078471
Mill, Philadelphia . . . 118800
Mill Antiques, Sleaford . . . 086627, 131503
Mill Antiques of Bibury, Bibury . . . 083507
Mill Creek Antiques, Nashville . . . 090468
Mill Farm Antiques, Disley 084166, 130634
The Mill Gallery, Coverack . . . 112903
Mill Gallery, Ermington . . . 084338, 130688
Mill Green Museum and Mill, Hatfield . . . 039696
Mill Grove, The Audubon Wildlife Sanctuary, Audubon . . . 041894
Mill House Antiques, Goudhurst . . . 084491
Mill House Cider Museum and Dorset Collection of Clocks, Owermoigne 040652
Mill House Gallery, Parbold . . . 114219
Mill Lane Antiques, Woodford Green 087229
Mill Race Historical Village, Northville . . . 046560
Mill Street Studio, Clare . . . 094398
Mill Studio, Moniaive . . . 114088
Mill Trail Visitor Centre, Alva . . . 038502
Millan, Cádiz . . . 081028
Millard, Omaha . . . 091577
Millard, Jon, Louisville . . . 116956
Millard Fillmore House, East Aurora 043557
Mill'Broc, Guignes . . . 063106
Millbrook, Baltimore . . . 087695
Millbrook Antiques, Las Vegas . . . 089592
Millchell, Fort Worth . . . 088868
Millcreek Antiques, Cincinnati . . . 088263
Mille et Une Feuilles, Beaune . . . 138027
Mille Facettes, Paris . . . 066294
Millefiori, Villeneuve-sur-Lot . . . 068920
Millénaires, Cogolin . . . 062388
Millenium-Antikvarnica, Herceg-Novi . . . 080410
Millenium Fine Arts, Roma . . . 106588
Millennic Glass, Kansas City . . . 116581
Millennium, Dallas . . . 088571
Millennium Art Gallery, New York . . 118195
Millennium Art Gallery, Philadelphia 118801
Millennium Art Gallery, Vancouver . 097500
Millennium Centre Antiques, Tunbridge Wells . . . 086943, 131620
Millennium Decorative Arts, Washington . . . 093424
Millennium Galleries, Sheffield . . . 040999
Millenniumi Földalatti Vasúti Múzeum, Budapesti Közlekedési Részvénytársaság, Budapest . . . 021674
Miller, Cincinnati . . . 115644
Miller, Dallas . . . 088572
Miller, Kansas City . . . 116582
von Miller, München . . . 104272
Miller, Paris . . . 066295
Miller, Tulsa . . . 093324
Miller, Virginia Beach . . . 120228
Miller, Austin T., Columbus . . . 088425
Miller, D., New York . . . 132498
Miller, Duncan R., London . . . 085536
Miller, Duncan R., London . . . 085537
Miller, Duncan R., London . . . 113767
Miller, Duncan R., London . . . 113768
Miller, James, Wooler . . . 087245
Miller, Janie, North Sydney . . . 056375
Miller, Jason S., Miami . . . 117112
Miller, Johannes von, Bad Wiessee . 125122
Miller, John, Newcastle . . . 094939
Miller, Laurence, New York . . . 118196
Miller, Maggie, Bovey Tracey . . . 112685
Miller, Marc, Tucson . . . 120148
Miller, Maritta von, Frankfurt am Main . . . 102800
Miller, Marlene, Sorrento . . . 056604
Miller, Mary Frances, Charlotte . . . 087969
Miller, Max, Houston . . . 089156
Miller, Nick, Cullompton . . . 084130
Miller, Percy, London . . . 113769
Miller, Peter, Chicago . . . 115502
Miller, Robert, New York . . . 118197
Miller, Ron, Los Angeles . . . 089844
Miller, Simone, Burtenbach . . . 125420
Miller, Susan, San Francisco . . . 119739
Miller, Thomas N., Newcastle-upon-Tyne . . . 122629
Miller, Virginia, Miami . . . 117113
Miller & Arney, Washington . . . 093425
Miller Art Center, Springfield . . . 048307
Miller Art Museum, Sturgeon Bay . . 048410
Miller Bakehouse Museum, Palmyra 001365
Miller & Block, Boston . . . 115204
Miller-Cory House Museum, Westfield . . . 049111
Miller House Museum, Hagerstown 044385
Miller Museum of Geology, Kingston 005703
Miller & Vivante, New York . . . 118198
Milleroses-Mohler & Schmeissner, Pully . . . 082734
Millers, Ringwood . . . 086366
Millers, Frantz, Tournon-sur-Rhône 068564, 124998
Millescamps, Henri-Pierre, Périgueux . . . 138569
Millesgården, Lidingö . . . 036416
Millet, Martínez . . . 055283
Millet, Saint-Martin-du-Mont . . . 067646
Millet, Jean-Claude, La Charité-sur-Loire . . . 063325
Millet, René, Paris . . . 100687
Millet, Roger, Torce-en-Vallee . . . 068428
Millet and District Museum, Millet . 005871
Millgate Museum, Newark-on-Trent 040532
Millgate Pine and Antiques, Thirsk . 086882
Millhouse Art Society Gallery, Milton . . . 094857
Milliard, Jacques, Montréal . . . 058978
Milliarede Besch, Lyon . . . 121053
Milliat, Robert, Rive-de-Gier . . . 067157
Millicent, Los Angeles . . . 116847
Millicent, Pittsburgh . . . 091843
The Millicent Gallery, Millicent . . . 094850
Millicent National Trust Museum, Millicent . . . 001266
Millicent Rogers Museum of Northern New Mexico, Taos . . . 048498
Milliken Gallery, Converse College, Spartanburg . . . 048262
Millington, K.L. & J., Lepton . . . 084976
Milliyet Sanat Dergisi, İstanbul . . . 136139
Millmount Museum and Tower, Drogheda . . . 022729
Millner, Arthur, London . . . 085538
De Millo Fine Art, Monaco . . . 077616
Millon & Associés, Mathias, Paris . . 121173
Millon-Garnier, Christelle, Chalon-sur-Saône . . . 062090
Millord, Crécy-la-Chapelle . . . 062553
Millpool Gallery, Mousehole . . . 114095
Mills, Boston . . . 115205
Mills, Cork . . . 074879
Mills, Honolulu . . . 088966
Mills, Robert, Bristol . . . 083743
Mills, Robert H., Philadelphia . . . 091667
Mills, Rocky, Indianapolis . . . 116478
Mills Antiques, Cullompton . . . 084131
Mills College Art Museum, Oakland 046596
Mills County Museum, Glenwood . . 044218
Mills Mansion State Historic Site, Staatsburg . . . 048312
Mills Observatory Museum, Dundee 039309
Millside Antique Restoration, Harlow . . . 130758
Millstreet Local Museum, Millstreet 022836
Millwall FC Museum, London . . . 040221
Millwheel Gallery, Minehead . . . 114086
Millwood Gallery, Wellington . . . 108631
Millyard Gallery, Uppermill . . . 114625
Milmo-Penny, Dominic, Dublin . . . 105879
Milne, John, Aberdeen . . . 122382
Milne, T., London . . . 141848
Milne Bay Military Museum, Toowoomba . . . 001557
Milner House, Chatham, Ontario . . . 005260
Milnthorpe & Daughters, Mary, Settle . . . 086537
Milo, New York . . . 118199
Milo, Seattle . . . 119962
Milone, Giovanni, Torino . . 076845, 134696
Milou, Atlanta . . . 087500
Milou, Perry, Philadelphia . . . 118802
Milpitas, San Jose . . . 092931
Milrose, I., Mettmann . . . 072537
Milstain, Marc, Bruxelles . . . 096234
Miltgen, Michel, Echternach . . . 077465
Milton, Jacksonville . . . 089433, 132187
Milton, Lionel, New Orleans . . . 117478
Milton Antiques, Blandford Forum .083560, 130406
The Milton Art & Craft Gallery, Banchory . . . 112551
Milton Blacksmith Shop Museum, Milton . . . 005873
Milton Historical Museum, Milton . . 045882
Milton Holgate, Ripon . . . 086379
Milton House Museum, Milton . . . 045883
Milton J. Rubenstein Museum of Science and Technology, Syracuse . . . 048457
Milton Keynes Gallery, Milton Keynes . . . 040473
Milton Keynes Museum, Milton Keynes . . . 040474
Milton's Cottage, Chalfont Saint Giles . . . 039029
Milwaukee Art Museum, Milwaukee 045892
Milwaukee Auction Galleries, Milwaukee . . . 122967
Milwaukee County Historical Society Museum, Milwaukee . . . 045893
Milwaukee Institute of Art and Design, Milwaukee . . . 051720
Milwaukee Public Museum, Milwaukee . . . 045894
Milwaukee Underground Ink, Milwaukee . . . 117207
Milwaukee Very Special Art Center, Milwaukee . . . 045895
Milwaukee's Finest Antique Store, Milwaukee . . . 090317
Milwaukie Antique Mall, Portland . . 091972
Milwe, Maria-Helene von der, Aachen . . . 101520
Milwee, Frank, Washington . . . 093426
Milz, Franz, Füssen . . . 133967
Mimax-Inn Gallery, Singapore . . . 109839
Mimbridge Antiques Centre, Chobham . . . 084001
Mimer, Stockholm . . . 141166
Mimesi, Firenze . . . 127376
Mimi, Chicago . . . 115503
Mimì, Venezia . . . 128399
Mimi Fifi, London . . . 085539
Mimi's African Art Gallery, Minneapolis . . . 117285
Mimi's Baz'Art, Obernai . . . 065257
Mimi's Memories, Jacksonville . . . 089434
Mimi's Memories, Jacksonville . . . 089435
Min, Daegu . . . 107189
Min, Ngai, San Francisco . . . 119740
Mina Andreina, Torino . . . 128337
Minaaz Art Gallery, Hyderabad . . . 105707
Minami-aoyama Green Gallery, Tokyo . . . 107075
Minami-yamate District Historic Preservation Center, Nagasaki . . . 026863
Minaret, Philippe, Paris . . . 100688
Minarini, Roberto, Torino . . . 128338
Miñarte, Málaga . . . 081426, 129706
Minassian, Dominique, Marennes . . 064282
Minatogawa, Kobe . . . 077081
Minatoya, Tokyo . . . 107076
Minault, Rene, Ayl . . . 069247
Mind and Matter Gallery, White Rock . . . 006809
Mindata, Bath . . . 135118
Mindener Museum für Geschichte, Landes- und Volkskunde, Minden, Westfalen . . . 018952
Mindener Museum für Geschichte, Landes- und Volkskunde, Minden, Westfalen . . . 018953
Minder, Daniel, Zürich . . . 130254
Mindermann, Rolf, Juist . . 071674, 103461
Mindermann, Uwe, Norderney . . . 073069
Minds Eye, Wellington . . . 140677
Mindy, Los Angeles . . . 116848
Mine d'Argent Saint-Barthélemy, Sainte-Marie-aux-Mines . . . 014605
La Mine-Image, Musée de la Mine, La Motte-d'Aveillans . . . 012289
Mine Sanat Galerisi, İstanbul . . . 112339
Mine Témoin d'Alès, Alès . . . 010330
Minelli, Giuseppe, Genova . . . 127471
Miner, A., Seattle . . . 119963
Minera Lead Mines, Minera . . . 040477
Mineral and Gem Geological Museum, Parrsboro . . . 006116
Mineral and Lapidary Museum of Henderson County, Hendersonville . . . 044513
Mineral County Museum, Superior . 048435
Mineral Museum, University of Montana, Butte . . . 042535
Mineral- och Gruvmuseet, Holsbybrunn . . . 036348
Mineral Resources Divisional Museum, Dodoma . . . 037853
Mineralenexpositie De Siersteen, Oostwold, Leek . . . 030004

Mineralien-Fossilien-Bergbau, Privat-Museum Helmut und Monika Steininger, Langenlois 002200
Mineralien-Fossilien-Museum, Neckartenzlingen 019197
Mineralien-Kabinett der TU Braunschweig, Braunschweig 016388
Mineralien Museum, Seedorf (Uri) . 037548
Mineralien-Museum Andreas Gabrys, Lam 018468
Mineralien-Museum Zirbenhof, Ebene Reichenau 001796
Mineralien-Sammlung, Hohenwarth 017982
Mineralien- und Heimatmuseum, Pleystein 019637
Mineralienmuseum, Einsiedeln 037059
Mineralienmuseum, Freisen 017242
Mineralienmuseum Essen, Museen der Stadt Essen, Essen 017073
Mineralienmuseum Pforzheim-Dillweißenstein, Pforzheim 019607
Mineraliensammlung, Lauingen . . . 018532
Mineralienschau, Afritz 001664
Mineralienschau, Vohenstrauß 020607
Mineralogical Museum of Harvard University, Cambridge 042564
Mineralogical Museum of Kamarzia, Attica 021217
Mineralogical Museum of Lavrion, Lavrion 021355
Mineralogičeskij Muzej, Geologičeskij institut Kol'skogo naučnogo centra RAN, Apatity 032987
Mineralogičeskij Muzej im. A.E. Fersmana Rossijskoj Akademii Nauk, Moskva 033429
Mineralogičeskij Muzej im. A.V. Sidorova, Irkutsk 033159
Mineralogisch-Geologisch Museum, Delft 029410
Mineralogisch-Geologische Gesteins-Sammlung, Schwarzenfeld 020135
Mineralogisch Museum, Grou 029647
Mineralogisch Museum, Academy for Mineralogy, Merksem 003641
Mineralogisch-Petrografische Sammlungen der Eidgenössischen Technischen Hochschule, Zürich 037781
Mineralogisch-petrographische Sammlung der Universität Leipzig, Leipzig . . 018578
Mineralogische Sammlung, Oberthal, Saar 019425
Mineralogische Sammlung, Friedrich-Alexander-Universität Erlangen-Nürnberg, Erlangen 017032
Mineralogische Schau- und Lehrsammlung, Tübingen 020499
Mineralogisches Museum der Philipps-Universität Marburg, Marburg . . . 018826
Mineralogisches Museum der Universität, Würzburg 021001
Mineralogisches Museum der Universität Bonn, Bonn 016331
Mineralogisches Museum der Universität Hamburg, Hamburg 017708
Mineralogisches Museum (Kristalle und Gesteine), Universität Münster, Münster 019148
Mineralogisches Museum Oberkirchen, Freisen 017243
Mineralogy Museum, Bangkok 037881
Mineralogy, Petrography and Volcanology Museum, Catania 023761
Mineraloška Zbirka Rudnika Trepča, Stari Trg 034270
Mineraloško-Petrografski Muzej, Zagreb 007847
Mineralovodskij Kraevedčeskij Muzej, Mineral'nye Vody 033357
Miners Foundry Cultural Center, Nevada City 046182
Minerva, The International Review of Ancient Art and Archaeology, London 136247
Minerva Antik, Malmö 081875
Minerva Editrice, Assisi 134542
Minerva International, Staufenberg, Hessen 134402
Minerva Quilt Centre, Llanidloes . . . 113418
Minerva Restauri, Milano 127635
Minerva's Antiques, Birmingham . . 087772
Minerve, Toulon (Var) 068465
Minervini, Giorgio, Roma 076564
Mines d'Asphalte de la Presta, Travers 037640
Mines de Sel de Bex, Bex 036946
Minet Frères, Bruxelles 137451
Ming, Cincinnati 115645
Ming, Hong Kong 097814
Ming, Honolulu 088967
Ming, Johannesburg 080710
Ming, New York 091081
Ming, Shenzhen 097987
Ming, Yu, New York 091082
Ming-Ching, Singapore 080529
Ming Direct, Waikato 079293
Ming Direct, Weikato 079309
Ming Gallery, Louisville 090013
Ming Qing Antiques, Shanghai 059758
Ming Shu Wangling Museum, Chengdu 007043
Ming Things, Ottawa 059045
Ming Tong, Lille 099493
Mingardi, Gianfranco, Brescia 127224
Mingazzini, Michela, Roma 076565
Mingboy, Singapore 080530
Mingcheng Yuan Shi Museum, Nanjing 007202
Mingei, Atlanta 087501
Mingei, Charenton-le-Pont 062149
Mingei International Museum, San Diego 047823
Mingenback Art Center Gallery, Lindsborg 045328
Mingenew Museum, Mingenew . . . 001267
Mingus, Praha 137839
Minh, Chau, Ha Noi 120474
Minhang, Shanghai 097933
Minhauzena Muzejs, Dunte 027680
Minhwa, Paris 066296
Mini Antik, København 060355
Mini-Château, Amboise 010356
Mini-Mint of Tucson, Tucson 093249
Mini-Musée Architectural, Charnat . 011258
Mini-Musée de l'Ossuaire, Pleyben 013842
Mini Musée des Miniatures, Sospel 014828
Mini Print International de Cadaqués, Cadaqués 093875
Mini Rastro Casavella, Vigo 081706
Miniaci, Venezia 106767
Miniatura e Art Minori in Campania, Napoli 135915
Miniaturbuchverlag Leipzig, Garching bei München 133969
Miniature English Village and Brass Rubbing Centre, Flaxton 001030
Miniature Magic, Austin 087596
Miniatures, Lyon 124367
Miniaturpark Klein-Erzgebirge, Oederan 019437
Miniatuur Walcheren, Middelburg . . 029921
Miniatuurstad, Antwerpen 003165
Minigallery.Co.Uk, Thornton Heath . 114572
Minilista, F., Miami 117114
Minimal, Wien 057502, 133218
Minimundus, Klagenfurt 002144
Minimuseum, Groningen 029639
Mining Industry House, National Museum of Australia, Braddon 000829
The Mining Museum, Platteville . . . 047081
Minion, Kyoto 077117
Miniota Municipal Museum, Miniota 005878
Minischeepvaartmuseum, Ouwerkerk 030033
Minisink Valley Historical Society Museum, Port Jervis 047135
Minjasafn Austurlands, Egilsstadir . 021940
Minjasafn Egils Ólafssonar, Patreksfjörður 021956
Minjasafnid Burstarfelli, Vopnafjörður 021986
Minjasafnida á Akureyri, Akureyri . . 021931
Minkoff, Genève 135020
Minkoff, Paris 133654
Minlaton National Trust Museum, Minlaton 001268
Minna Street Gallery, San Francisco 119741
Minnaert, Alain, Hasselt 123638
Minnamoora, Wanniassa 056798
Minneapolis College of Art and Design, Minneapolis 051726
Minneapolis College of Art and Design Gallery, Minneapolis 045917
Minneapolis Institute of Arts, Minneapolis 045918
Minneapolis Institute of Arts. Annual Report, Minneapolis 136545
Minneapolis Institute of Arts. Bulletin, Minneapolis 136546
Minneapolis Print and Drawing Fair, Minneapolis 094007
Minneapolis Uptown Antiques, Minneapolis 090380
Minnedosa and District Museum, Minnedosa 005879
Minnenas Bod, Göteborg 081817
Minnesota Air National Guard Exhibition, Saint Paul 047703
Minnesota Association of Museums, Minneapolis 054880
Minnesota Children's Museum, Saint Paul 047704
Minnesota Historical Society Museum, Saint Paul 047705
Minnesota Museum of American Art, Saint Paul 047706
Minnesota Pioneer Park Museum, Annandale 041737
Minnesota Transportation Museum, Saint Paul 047707
Minnette, Los Angeles 089845
Minnick, Honolulu 132091
Minnie's Thirteen Forty One, Jacksonville 089436
Minnilusa Pioneer Museum, Rapid City 047334
Minni's Kunsttruhe, Mittenwald . . . 072555
Minnucci, Maria Luisa, Roma 106589
Mino, Alain, Beinheim . . . 061322, 124097
Mino, Alvaro, Roma 076566
Minobusan Homotsukan, Minobu . . 026807
Minoletti, Gianfranco, Genova 075485, 127472
Minolta Photo Space Hiroshima, Hiroshima 026536
Minor, Jutta, Forchheim, Oberfranken 125646
Minoriten Galerien, Graz 095537
Minority Arts Resource Council Studio Art Museum, Philadelphia 046960
Minot, Paris 066297
Minot Art Association, Minot 054881
Minotaur, Toulouse 138639
Le Minotaure, Alger 055131
Minotauro, Roma 076567, 128119
Minouche, Marin-Epagnier 111718
Minowa Museum, Minowa 026808
Minsky, Paris 100689
Minssen, Ile-Tudy 099365
Minster Abbey, Minster 040478
Minster Abbey Gatehouse Museum, Sheerness 040992
Minster Books, Wimborne Minster .131690, 142158
Minster Gate Bookshop, York 131727, 142178
Mint, Franklin, Las Vegas 089593
Mint Museum, Osaka 026971
Mint Museum Membernews, Charlotte 136547
Mint Museum of Art, Charlotte 042760
Mint Museum of Craft and Design, Charlotte 042761
Mintage, Mumbai 105787
Minten, Kees, Beers bij Cuyk 128581
Mintmaster, Atlanta 087502
Minto Museum, Minto 005880
Minton, Damien, Newcastle 094940
Minton, Joseph, Dallas 088573
Minton Museum, Stoke-on-Trent . . 041120
Mintrop, Bernhard, Hattingen 125886
Mintsas, Theodoros, Athinai 074601
Les Minuscules, Marseille 064376
Minusinskaja Chudožestvennaja Kartinnaja Galereja, Minusinsk 033360
Minusinskij Regionalnyj Kraevedčeskij Muzej im. N.M. Martjanova, Minusinsk 033361
Minute Man National Historical Park, Concord 043118
Minymaku Arts, Amata 055343
Miqueleiz, Pamplona 081522, 141068
Mir, Sankt-Peterburg 140935
Mir Dizajna/ World of Design, Sankt-Peterburg 136057
Mir-Emad Calligraphy Museum, Sa'd-Abad Museum, Teheran 022630
Mir i Muzej, Tula 136058
Mir Iskusstv, Moskva 080254
Mir Iskusstv, Vinnycja 112437
Mir Russki, Linlithgow 085007
Mira Antique, Bucureşti 080164
Mira Fine Art Gallery, Melbourne . . 056196
Mirabeau, Houston 089157
Mirabeau, Paris 100690, 124750
Mirabella, Giacomo, New York 132499
Mirabella, Patrizia, Napoli 076009
Mirabilia, Roma 106590
Miracle Metal, Cleveland 131968
Miracle of America Museum, Polson 047115
Mirada, Kassel 103515
Mirage, Douglas 136548
Mirage Art Gallery, Delhi 105676
Mirage Studio, Cleveland 115726
Miraglia, Salvador, Lyon 138179
Mirakhore, Esther, Les Acacias . . . 082076
Miralles Guillen, Vicente H., Valencia 129780
Miramar Zeemuseum, Vledder 030277
Miramichi Natural History Museum, Miramichi 005881
Miramon Kutxaespacio de la Ciencia, Donostia-San Sebastián 035150
Miramont, Céline, Les Ternes 063789
Miramont Castle Museum, Manitou Springs 045636
Miranda, Dino, Roma 076568
Miranda, Jorge, Paris 124751
Miranda, Roberto, San Isidro 055300
Miranda Libreria, Madrid 141052
Miranda Libros, Madrid 141053
Mirandas, Carmen, Salt Lake City . 092447
Mirande, Bernard, Fortaleza 096534
Mirani, Bucureşti 080165
Mirari, Windsor, Ontario 097562
Miras, Moskva 109566
Miras, Ufa 109662
Mirasaka Peace Museum of Art, Mirasaka 026809
Mirate, Francesco, Venezia 076959
Mire, New Orleans 090589
Mirehouse, Keswick 039853
Mirer, Rudolf, Zernez 112015
Mirer, Thomas, Obersaxen Affeier . 111791
Mireuksa Temple Museum, Iksan . . 027508
Mireya, Buenos Aires 136740
Miri & Giangravé, Venezia 106768
Miriam and Ira D. Wallach Art Gallery, New York 046365
Miriam Switching Post, Saint Louis 092280
Mirishet, Bergen, Noord-Holland . . 078067
Mirkovich, N., Houston 116370
Miro, Ljubljana 080656, 109978
Miro, Isabel, Madrid 081341
Miro, Victoria, London 113770
Miro 464, Sofia 058764
Miro Art, Kortrijk 058266
Miroir aux Alouettes, Genève 082446
Miroir de Fief, Orgeval 065286
Miroir des Maîtres, Genève 111484
Miroirs & Meubles, Hilversum 078537
Miroiterie, Villefranche-sur-Saône . 068902
Miroiterie Pays, Mâcon 064206
Miromesnil Fine Art, Paris 100691

Miron, Paris . . . 066298
Miron Antic, Nice . . . 065115
Miroonamu, Daegu . . . 107190
Mirou, Lille . . . 063858
Mirowicz, Adam, Poznań . . . 140763
Mirror and District Museum, Mirror 005883
Mirror Fair, New York . . . 091083
Mirror Image, Dallas . . . 115911
Mirror Mirror, New Orleans . . . 090590
Mirrow, Southsea . . . 142086
Mirski, Boris, Boston . . . 115206
Miru, Karlsruhe . . . 071727
Mirus, Wiesbaden . . . 074414
Mirvish, David, Toronto . . . 137713
Miryang Municipal Museum, Miryang . . . 027531
Miscellanea, Mumbai . . . 105788
Miscellanea, San Diego . . . 092659
Miscellanées, Lille . . . 063859
Miscellaneous, Montevideo . . . 087331
Miscellaneous, Punta del Este . . . 087355
Miscellany Antiques, Great Malvern 084515
Mischell, Hans H., Köln . . . 071984
Mischkind, Raphaël, Lille . 099494, 124321
Miscio, Giorgio, Roma . . . 128120
Mise en Page, Lyon . . . 138180
Mise en Valeur du Site Archéologique, Barzan . . . 010660
Mis'en Scène 40, Tours . . . 068597
Miser, Saint Louis . . . 092281
Mishima Taisha Treasure House, Mishima . . . 026811
Mishkan Le'Omanut, Ein Harod . . . 022906
Misia, Paca, Montevideo . . . 087332
Misia Arte, Bari . . . 075023
Misijné Múzeum Nitra, Nitra . . . 034397
Misirloglou, Christos, Frankfurt am Main . . . 139093
Misjonsmuseet, Stavanger . . . 031225
Misjonsmuseet på Fjellhaug, Oslo . 031085
Mis'ka Chudožna Galereja im. S.I. Vasyl'kivs'kogo, Charkiv . . . 038245
Miskolci Galéria - Rákóczi-ház, Miskolc . . . 021790
Misley, Mauro, Trieste . . . 128376
Misora Hibari Memorial House, Kyoto . . . 026749
Misrachi, México . . . 107502
Misrachi, Alberto, México . . . 107503
Misrachi, Alberto, México . . . 107504
Miss Baltimore Agency, New York . . 091084
Miss Edna's Antiques, New Orleans 090591
Miss Elany, Long Eaton . . . 085826
Missa, Yongin . . . 107312
Missal, Birgit, Hamburg . . . 071293
Missal, Gisela, Wenningstedt . . . 074334
Missenbeck, Graz . . . 123362
Misseri, Andrea & Palombi, Alessandro, Roma . . . 076569
Missiemuseum Steyl, Steijl . . . 030182
Missillier, Philippe, Lyon . . . 064159
Missillier, Philippe, Lyon . . . 064160
The Missing Link, New York . . . 091085
Mission, Cliff, San Diego . . . 123099
Mission and Folklore Museum, Polanica Zdrój . . . 032231
Mission Antiques, Portland . . . 091973
Mission Art, Pécs . . . 074748, 105574
Mission Bell Museum, Coweta . . . 043202
Mission Cultural Center for Latino Arts, San Francisco . . . 047872
Mission Gallery, San Diego . . . 092660
Mission Gallery, Swansea . . . 041173
The Mission House, Stockbridge . . 048365
Mission Houses Museum, Honolulu 044604
Mission Inn Museum, Riverside . . . 047458
Mission Mill Museum, Salem . . . 047753
Mission Museum, Mission . . . 005885
Mission Oak Shop, San Francisco . . 092845
Mission Oak Shop, Seattle . . . 093037
Mission San Carlos Borromeo del Rio Carmelo, Carmel . . . 042627
Mission San Diego de Alcala, San Diego . . . 047824
Mission San Juan Capistrano Museum, San Juan Capistrano . . . 047906
Mission San Luis Obispo de Tolosa, San Luis Obispo . . . 047907
Mission San Luis Rey Museum, Oceanside . . . 046620
Mission San Miguel, San Miguel . . . 047916
Missionart, Miskolc . . . 105566
Missionary Museum, Amathole Museum, King William's Town . . . 034668
Missionary Museum of the N.G. Kerk, Stellenbosch . . . 034753
Missions-Ethnographisches Museum St. Gabriel, Mödling . . . 002325
Missions-Museum der Pallottiner Limburg, Limburg an der Lahn . . . 018650
Missionsmuséet, Vårgårda . . . 036780
Missionsmuseum, Sankt Ottilien . . 019993
Missionsmuseum, Schwarzach am Main . . . 020130
Missionsmuseum Bug, Bamberg . . 015874
Missionsmuseum der Mariannhiller Missionare, Würzburg . . . 021002
Missionsmuseum der Spiritaner Knechtsteden, Dormagen . . . 016751
Missionsmuseum des päpstlichen Missionswerks der Kinder in Deutschland, Aachen . . . 015423
Missirlakis, Madrid . . . 129648
Missisquoi Museum, Stanbridge East . . . 006506
Missisquoi Valley Historical Society Museum, North Troy . . . 046539
Mississagi Strait Lighthouse Museum, Meldrum . . . 005853
Mississippi Art Colony, Stoneville . . 054882
Mississippi Baptist Historical Commission Museum, Clinton . . . 043014
Mississippi County Historical Society Museum, Charleston . . . 042723
Mississippi Crafts Center, Ridgeland 047436
Mississippi Governor's Mansion, Jackson . . . 044798
Mississippi Museum of Art, Jackson 044799
Mississippi Museum of Natural Science, Jackson . . . 044800
Mississippi Museums Association, Natchez . . . 054883
Mississippi Petrified Forest Museum, Flora . . . 043863
Mississippi River Museum, Dubuque . . . 043514
Mississippi River Museum at Mud Island River Park, Memphis . . . 045767
Mississippi University for Women Museum, Columbus . . . 043102
Mississippi Valley Textile Museum, Almonte . . . 004999
Mississipppi Agriculture and Forestry/ National Agricultural Aviation Museum, Jackson . . . 044801
La Missive, Besançon . . . 061392
Mißler, Herbert, Peiting . . . 073304
Missouri Coin, Saint Louis . . . 092282
Missouri Historical Society Museum, Saint Louis . . . 047670
Missouri Mouse, Saint Paul . . . 092378
Missouri Museums Association, Kansas City . . . 054884
Missouri State Museum, Jefferson City . . . 044849
Missouri Town 1855, Lees Summit . 045229
Misteckij Kurin, Kyïv . . . 112418
Misteckij Ljoch, Kyïv . . . 112419
Mister Daves, Winnipeg . . . 059466
Mister Poster, Indianapolis . . . 116479
Mister R's, San Francisco . . . 132902
Mister Thrifty Book Shop, Sydney . . 137104
Misterek, Uwe, Jever . . . 071667
The Mistletoe Gallery, Masham . . . 114066
Místní Muzeum, Kopidlno . . . 008443
Místní Muzeum, Libáň . . . 008472
Místní Muzeum, Městec Králové . . . 008500
Místní Muzeum, Mladá Vožice . . . 008508
Místní Muzeum, Netvořice . . . 008526
Místní Muzeum, Muzeum Dr. Otakara Kudrny, Netolice . . . 008525
Mistral, La Bégude-de-Mazenc . . . 099386
Mistrali, Emilio, Parma . . . 076215
Mistretta, Diana, Palermo . . . 076165
Misty's Antiques, Portland . . . 091974
Misura Su Misura, Messina 075566, 127504
Misuraca, Prof. Donatello, Roma . . 128121
MIT-List Visual Arts Center, Cambridge . . . 042565
The MIT Museum, Cambridge . . . 042566
M.I.T. Press, Cambridge . . . 135341
The MIT Press, London . . . 135235
Mita, Tokyo . . . 107077
Mitchell, Cockermouth . . . 122474
Mitchell, Jacksonville . . . 116533
Mitchell, Algus, New York . . . 118200
Mitchell, Algus, New York . . . 118201
Mitchell, Anthony, Nottingham . . . 086141, 131338
Mitchell, Brett, Cleveland . . . 115727
Mitchell, Christina, Milton . . . 094858
Mitchell, Duncan, Aldridge . . . 112493
Mitchell & Son, John, London . . . 113771, 131111
Mitchell, L.K., Richmond . . . 132720
Mitchell, Mike, Washington . . . 120327
Mitchell, Paul, London . . . 085540
Mitchell, Sally, Tuxford . . . 086961, 114615
Mitchell, Suzanne, New York . . . 118202
Mitchell, T.J., Dublin . . . 074933, 127098
Mitchell County Historical Museum, Osage . . . 046731
Mitchell Gallery of Flight, Milwaukee . . . 045896
Mitchell House, Maria Mitchell Association, Nantucket . . . 046125
Mitchell-Innes & Nash, New York . . 118203
Mitchell Museum at Cedarhurst, Mount Vernon . . . 046071
Mitchell Museum of the American Indian, Evanston . . . 043763
Mitchell's, Blackburn, Lancashire . . 083549
Mitchell's Refinishing, Buffalo . . . 131860
Miter Box, Cincinnati . . . 115646
Mitered Corner, Seattle . . . 119964
Mithos, Milano . . . 075773
Mitnitzky, Joaquim, Rio de Janeiro . 058620
Mito, Warszawa . . . 109161
Mito Geijutsukan Gendai Bijutsu Center, Mito . . . 026818
Mitochu, Tokyo . . . 077281
Mito's Antigüedades, Caracas . . . 093539
Mitre Box, Baltimore . . . 115071
Mitre Box, San Francisco . . . 119742
Mitre House Antiques, Ludlow . . . 085869
Mitropoličji Palaty - Muzej Drevnerusskogo Iskusstva, Jaroslavskij chudožestvennyj muzej, Jaroslavl . . . 033196
Mitschkowski, H., Bremen . . . 070035
Mitsubishi Automobile Gallery, Okazaki . . . 026946
Mitsukoshi Art Gallery, Yokohama . . 107148
Mitsukoshi Gallery, Tokyo . . . 107078
Mitsukuni and Nariaki Tokugawa Memorial Collection, Mito . . . 026819
Mitsumura, Tokyo . . . 134727
Mittamuseo, Virrat . . . 010246
Mitteilungen der Gesellschaft für Vergleichende Kunstforschung in Wien, Wien . . . 135569
Mitteilungen der Österreichischen Numismatischen Gesellschaft, Wien . . . 135570
Mittelalterliches Foltermuseum, Rüdesheim am Rhein . . . 019942
Mittelalterliches Kriminalmuseum, Rothenburg ob der Tauber . . . 019915
Mittelalterliches Museum, Wien Museum, Wien . . . 002968
Mittelhessische Druck- und Verlagsgesellschaft, Gießen . . . 133973
Mittelmoselmuseum im Barockhaus Böcking, Traben-Trarbach . . . 020454
Mittelrhein-Museum, Koblenz . . . 018296
Mittelschwäbisches Heimatmuseum Krumbach, Krumbach, Schwaben 018424
Mittelsten-Scheid, Vivica, Wuppertal . . . 127050
Mittendorf, K.-H., Vienenburg . . . 074206
Mittendorf, Karl-Heinz, Goslar . . . 071065
Mittentzwey, M., Mannheim . . . 072427
Mitter, Josef, Wien . . . 057503
Mitter, Josef, Wien . . . 057504, 123518
Mitterand, Edward, Genève . . . 111485
Mitteregger, Dieter, Lavamünd . . . 137213
Mittermüller, Andreas, Kolbermoor . 126130
Mitz, Frances, Paris . . . 121174
Mitzlaff, Otto von, Wächtersbach . . 074236
Mitzpe Revivim Museum, Kibbutz Revivim . . . 023017
Miu, Singapore . . . 109840
Miura Arts, Tokyo . . . 107079
Mix, Buffalo . . . 087897
Le Mix, Pittsburgh . . . 091844
Mix, Toronto . . . 135640
Mix Media Gallery, Jacksonville . . . 116534
Mixa, Otmar, Wien . . . 137347
Mixed Company, Philadelphia . . . 091668
Mixed Greens, New York . . . 118204
Mixed Media, Las Vegas . . . 116636
Mixed Media, Portland . . . 136549
Mixed Media Art Gallery, San Diego 119526
Mixed Media Gallery, Columbus . . . 115790
Mixografia Gallery, Los Angeles . . . 116849
Mixture Gallery, Houston . . . 116371
Miyagi-ken Bijutsukan, Sendai . . . 027048
Miyagi Michio Memorial Hall, Tokyo 027208
Miyakonojo City Museum of Art, Miyakonojo . . . 026822
Miyakoya, Kyoto . . . 077118
Miyandoab Museum, Miyandoab . . 022586
Miyashita, Sapporo . . . 106987
Miyawaki, Ichiro, Kyoto . . . 106902
Miyazaki, Kobe . . . 106881
Miyazaki-ken Sogo Hakubutsukan, Miyazaki, Miyazaki-ken . . . 026826
Miyazaki-kenritsu Bijutsukan, Miyazaki, Miyazaki-ken . . . 026827
Miyoshi, Kobe . . . 077082
Miyuki, Tokyo . . . 107080
Mizar, Roma . . . 076570
Mizel Museum of Judaica, Denver . 043410
Mizener, Hamilton . . . 058859
Mizener, Toronto . . . 059243
Mizon, Maree, Paddington . . . 095036
Mizue, Tokyo . . . 135980
Mizuhomachi Kyodo Shiryokan, Mizuho . . . 026828
Mizunami-shi Kaseki Hakubutsukan, Mizunami . . . 026829
Mizuno, West Hollywood . . . 120400
Mizuno Old Ceramics House, Miyazaki, Fukui . . . 026824
Mizzi, Marsa . . . 077514
M.J. Decoarts, Philadelphia . . . 118803
M.J. Photos, Philadelphia . . . 118804
Mjellby Konstmuseum, Halmstad . . 036326
MJM Art Gallery, New York . . . 118205
MJM Arte Antigo, São Paulo . . . 123717
MJM Global Arts, Bruxelles . . . 058034
Mjölby Hembygdsgård, Mjölby . . . 036477
Mjs Antiques, Tauranga . . . 079265
M.J.'s Bookshop, Boronia . . . 136809
M.K. Čiurlionis National Museum of Art, Kaunas . . . 027848
MK Galerie, Rotterdam . . . 108198
MK Kunst Galerie, Mülheim an der Ruhr . . . 104131
MKG Art Management, Houston . . . 116372
Mkrtchyan, A.H., Erevan . . . 094110
MLA West Midland, Regional Council for Museums, Libraries and Archives, Birmingham . . . 054432
Mladinska Knjiga, Ljubljana . . . 134897, 140968
Mladost, Zagreb . . . 133405
MLD, Saint-Ouen . . . 067850
Mleczko, Andrzej, Kraków . . . 108964
M.L.H.A. Shop, New York . 091086, 132500
MM Galerie, Grebenstein . . . 102991

MM-Kunstverlag, Flensburg 133930
M.M.C., Saint Louis 136550
MNAC Publications, Barcelona 134920
MNK Art, Thônex 082848
MO-Art Gallery, Amsterdam 077914
Mo Lan, Beijing 097671
Mo Yuan Ge, Beijing 097672
MOA Bijutsukan, Atami 026431
Moanalua Gardens Foundation, Honolulu 044605
Moat Park Heritage Centre, Biggar . 038707
Moatti, Alain, Paris 100692
Moatti, Emmanuel, New York 118206
Moatti, Emmanuel, Paris 100693
Moaven Al- Molk Museum, Kermanshah 022571
Moba, Bruxelles 096235
Mobach Keramiek Museum, Utrecht 030228
Mobèche, Pablo, La Tine 082854
Mobilart C & R, Montréal 123790
Mobile Home, London 113772
Mobile Medical Museum, Mobile . . 045948
Mobile Museum of Art, Mobile 045949
Mobile Städtische Galerie im Museum Folkwang, Essen 017074
Mobiles Kindermuseum im Freizeitheim Vahrenwald, Hannover 017762
Mobili & Oggetti della Nonna, Roma 076571
Mobilia, Kangasala 009658
Mobilier, New York 091087
Mobilier des Vallées de l'Himalaya, Aussois 061082
Mobilier et Décoration, Paris 124752
Mobilus, Strasbourg 124948
Mobius, Boston 115207
Mobius Gallery, Boston 042332
Mobles Monthy, Sabadell 110730
Mobydick Antiquités, Saint-Malo (Ille-et-Vilaine) 067615
Moca London, London 113773
Mocenni, M., Den Haag 078219
MoCHA, London 040222
Mock, Wolfgang, Seebruck 104877
Mockbeggar Plantation, Bonavista . 005115
Mockler, Stephen, Berchtesgaden . 125150
Mocza, Renate, Wien 123519
Moda, Buffalo 087898
Moda, San Francisco 092846
Modalen Skulemuseum, Modalen . . 031020
Mode Moderne, Philadelphia 091669
Model House Gallery, Llantrisant . . 040067
Model Railway Museum, Matlock . . 040433
Modelbouwmuseum, Wassenaar . . 030311
Modell Äldre, Stockholm 081987
Modellbahnmuseum-Muggendorf, Wiesenttal 020883
Modelleisenbahnmuseum Die Bahnschranke, Wiesenttal 020883
Modello, A., Paris 100694
Modell's Restoration, New Orleans . 132422
Modemuseum, Münchner Stadtmuseum, München 019082
Modemuseum, Württembergisches Landesmuseum Stuttgart, Ludwigsburg, Württemberg 018696
Modemuseum Provincie Antwerpen, Antwerpen 003166
Modenantiquaria e Mostra Mercato di Antiquariato per Parchi, Giardini e Ristrutturazioni, Modena 093771
Moder Nena, Santiago de Chile . . . 059542
Modern & Antique Clock Repair, Dallas 132016
Modern Art, Coesfeld 102322
Modern Art, Lübbecke 103953
Modern Art, Mechelen 096386
Modern Art, Tokyo 107081
Modern Art Criticism, Farmington Hills 136551
Modern Art Gallery, Hadres 095553
Modern Art Gallery, Karlsruhe 103499
Modern Art Gallery, Los Angeles . . . 116850
Modern Art Gallery, Singapore 109841
Modern Art Museum of Fort Worth, Fort Worth 044011
Modern Art Oxford, Oxford 040659
Modern Art Oxford Bookshop, Oxford 141986
Modern Art Plakatgalerie, Frankfurt am Main 102801
Modern Art Products, Hong Kong . . 097815
Modern Art Research Institute, Academy of Arts of the Ukraine, Kyïv 050797, 135113
Modern Artifacts, San Francisco . . . 092847
Modern Artists Gallery, Whitchurch, Berkshire 114682
Modern at Sundance Square, Fort Worth 116157
Modern Day, Miami 132350
Modern Design Furniture, Luqa . . .077513, 128475
Modern Done Upholstery, Vancouver 123853
Modern Gallery, Hyderabad 105708
Modern Graphics, Rastatt 104657
Modern House, Cleveland 088343, 115728
Modern Hut, Houston 089158
Modern Magyar Képtár I, Janus Pannonius Múzeum, Pécs 021821
Modern Magyar Képtár II, Janus Pannonius Múzeum, Pécs 021822
Modern Masters Gallery, San Francisco 119743
Modern Mural Arts Institute, Atami . 106834
Modern Painters, London 136248
Modern Painting & Framing, Ottawa 097111
Modern Primitive Gallery, Atlanta . . 114905
Modern Studio, Bruxelles 058035
Modern Time Antique, Vancouver . . 059386
Modern Times, Chicago 088132
Modern Woodworking, Louisville . . 132301
Moderna Galerija, Ljubljana 034485
Moderna Galerija, Podgorica 034241
Moderna Galerija, Zagreb 007848
Moderna Galerija Rijeka - Muzej Moderne i Suvremene Umjetnosti, Museum of Modern and Contemporary Art, Rijeka 007779
Moderna Möbelklassiker, Malmö . . 081876
Moderna Museet, Stockholm 036645
Moderna Museet Butik, Stockholm .134970, 141167
Moderna Ravagnan, Venezia 106769
Modernaire, Oakland 091428
Moderne, Amsterdam 107772
Moderne Antiques, Los Angeles . . . 089846
Moderne Galerie im Weinstadtmuseum Krems, Krems 002173
Moderne Gallery, Philadelphia 091670, 118805, 142747
Modernes Antiquariat, Halle, Saale . 139161
Modernes Antiquariat, Hannover . . 139242
Modernica, Los Angeles 089847
Modernica, New York 091088
Modernism, Saint-Ouen 067851
Modernism, San Francisco 119744
Modernism, A Century of Art and Design, New York 094008
Modernism Gallery, Miami 090212
The Modernist, New York 136552
Il Modernista, Bologna 127168
Modernista, Praha 060144
Modernpast, San Francisco 092848
Modernt & Antikt, Järfälla 081839
Modersitzki, Wehrheim 074296
Modes, Erich, München 072794
Modes & Dugardyn, Bruxelles 058036
Modesammlung, Wien Museum, Wien 002947
Modeschauraum des Historischen Museums der Stadt Wien, Wien Museum, Wien 002947
Modesta, Waltershausen . 074271, 126964
Modestie, Deauville 062610
Modified Art, Phoenix 047010
Modique Antiques, Vancouver 059387
Modjopahit, Amsterdam 140321
Modoc County Historical Museum, Alturas 041673
Modschiedler, Hamburg 071294
Modub'Art, Paris 100695
Modulo, Lisboa 109333
Modulo, Porto 109391
Modulverlag, Wien 133219
Modus, Paris 100696
Modus, Rotterdam 108199
Modus Vivendi, Carentan 061986
Modus Vivendi Gallery, Lemesos . . 098315
Moe Historical Museum, Moe 001272
Moebel Angèle, Bartenheim 061214
Möbelberget Auktions- & Styckegodslager, Storvik 122263
Möbelgruppen, Hägersten 081829
Der Möbelhof, Lehrberg 072185
Möbelindustrimuseum i Virserum, Virserum 036795
Möbelkällaren, Enskede 081781
Möbelkonservator, Stockholm 081988, 129869
Die Möbelschmiede, Hilden 071519
Möbeltjänst, Malmö 081877
Möbius, Klaus-Jürgen, Büdingen . . 102284
Möcking, Ingo, Bielefeld 125329
Mödlinger Künstlerbund, Mödling . . 052577
Mödlinger Stadtverkehrsmuseum, Mödling 002326
Mögelin, Wiesbaden 105271
Möglich, J., Wetzlar 139845
Möglich, Joachim, Aßlar 138684
Möhkön Ruukki, Ilomantsin Museosäätiö, Möhkö 009878
Möhlmann, Dr. Horst & Dagmar, Ratingen 104663
Möhring, Dortmund 070289
Moeken, Nordhorn 104466
Möllenhoff, Irmgard, Porta Westfalica 073356
Möllenkamp, Eva, Nordkirchen 126557
Möller, Kassel 139308
Möller, Ostercappeln 073254
Möller, Waibstadt 074244
Moeller, Achim, New York 118207
Möller, Dieter H., Werder, Havel . . . 074337
Möller, Frank-C., Hamburg 071295
Möller, Harald, Hohenkirchen, Holstein 071557
Möller, J., Dortmund 070290, 102411
Möller, Rico, Michendorf 126316
Möller, Thomas, Berlin 125258
Möller, Ulrike-S., Rostock 104771
Moeller & Rotermund, Hamburg . . .071296, 103194
Möllering, Beate, München 104273
Möllers, Dr. Doris, Münster 072920
Möllers, K., Birkenau 102139
Möllner Museum Historisches Rathaus, Mölln 018972
Mölndals Museum, Mölndal 036480
Mömken, Heinz-Günther, Schweinfurt 073767
Mönchehaus-Museum für moderne Kunst Goslar, Goslar 017485
Mönchguter Museen im Ostseebad Göhren, Göhren, Rügen 017443
Mönchhof Galerie, Kilchberg, Zürich 111580
Möndel, Bernhard, Maikammer . . . 072380
Mönikes, F. jun., Steinheim, Westfalen 073910
Mönkemöller, E., Bielefeld 138875
Moens, Romain, Lovendegem 123660
Mönter, Konrad, Meerbusch 104048, 139468
Moerchen, Anne, Hamburg 103195
Mörfelden Museum, Mörfelden-Walldorf 018981
Mörgeli, Zürich 112151, 130255
Mörikehaus Ochsenwang, Bissingen an der Teck 016256
Mörmann, Elmar, Rothenburg ob der Tauber 073590
Mörrums Auktionsbyrå, Asarum . . . 122102
Mörsbacher Museum, Mörsbach . . 018985
Mörth, Sylvia & Adolf, Wien 137348
Moervarststede, Wachtebeke 003838
Moes, Anny, Bar-le-Duc 061197
Mösch & Marianne Baumann, Kuno, Balgach 111157
Mösenbacher, E.F., Den Haag 128634
Moesgaard, Skodsborg 060402
Moesgaard, J., Kampen 071697
Moesgård Museum, Højbjerg 008916
Moesker, Papenburg 073292
Mösl, Kristina, München 126418
Möwe, Heusenstamm 071508
Möwe Bay Museum, Möwe Bay . . . 029088
Moffarts, Benoît de, Bruxelles 058037
Moffat Museum, Moffat 040482
Moffatt-Ladd House, Portsmouth . . 047188
Moffett, Richard, San Francisco . . . 119745
Mogador, Aubagne 098869
Mogador, Bruxelles 058038
Mogens & Angelo, København 060356
Moghul, Adelaide 055317
Mogliani, Lamanon 099417
Mohan, Kathmandu 107592
Mohanjeet, Paris 100697
Mohapp, Emmerich, Graz 123363
Moharic, Megève 099700
Mohave Museum of History and Arts, Kingman 045008
Moheban & Son, Abraham, New York 091089
Moheda Skolmuseum, Moheda . . . 036483
Mohler, Basel 082158, 141209
Mohler, Philipp, Liestal . . . 111645, 130082
Mohn, Johan Albert, Bergen 079378
Mohomed, Carimo, Lisboa 140845
Mohonk Preserve, Gardiner 044144
Mohr, Arno, Offenbach an der Queich 073188
Mohr, Heinz, Wiesbaden 139852
Mohr, I., Hirschberg 071532
Mohr, I., Schriesheim 073733
Mohr, M., Itzehoe 071647
Bernhard Mohr & Gabriele Kübler-Mohr, Herdwangen-Schönach 103355
Mohr & Suckel, Lindau, Bodensee . 072266
Mohrmann, Edgar, Hamburg 121432
Mohzee, London 113774
Moin, Seoul 107270
Moin, Seoul 107271
Moinard, Gérard, La Rochelle 063435
Moinat, Genève 082447
Moinat, Charles-Emile, Rolle 082748
Moinat, H.C., Amsterdam 140322
Moineau, Nadine, Nantes 099810
Moinet, Civray 062307
Moir Street Books, Hawthorn, Victoria 136937
Moira, London 085541
Moira Furnace, Moira 040483
Moirandat, Alain François, Basel . . 141210
Mõisaküla Muuseum, Mõisaküla . . 009378
Moisan, Martine, Paris 100698
Moisan, Richard, Cannes 099074
Moisan, Richard, Vallauris 101421
Moisburger Mühlenmuseum, Außenstelle des Freilichtmuseums am Kiekeberg, Moisburg 018988
Moisel, W., Allmersbach 069137
Moissinac, Alain, Aurillac 061080
Moisson, Dominique & Valentin, Doué-la-Fontaine 062731, 124225
Moissonnier, Laurent, Clessé 062359
Moissonnier, Laurent, Pommiers . . 066899
Al-Moiz, Sharjah 083218
Mojahid, Casablanca 077663
Mojahid, Casablanca 077664
Mojavari, Abdullah, Köln 103678
Mojraghi, Mauro & Music, Steven, Parma 106454
Mok, Cheung, Hong Kong 059674
Mok Am Museum of Art, Koyang . . 027526
Moka Buddhist Museum, Gangcheon 027484
Mokichi Saito Museum, Kaminoyama 026615
Mokka-Antiquitäten, Mettmann . . . 072538
Mokkumto, Seoul 107272

Mokrzycki, Stanisław, Gdańsk 129011
Moksha, Stockholm 111064
Mokum, Amsterdam 107773
Mokuzo-gan Gallery, Odawara 026930
Mol, Conny, Amsterdam 077915
Mola- het Provinciaal Molenmuseum, Wachtebeke 003839
Molard, Aline, Brégnier-Cordon . . . 061756
Molarum, Stockholm 081989
Molayem, Albert, Roma 076572
Moldai Studios, Keighley 113312
Moldenhauer, A., Ostseebad Prerow 104557
Molding Art, Pittsburgh 091845
Moldurarte, Zaragoza 110886
Moldurarte, Zaragoza 110887
Molduras & Pardini, Belo Horizonte 096474
Molduseg, Bogotá 098174, 123905
Mole Hall Antiques, Aldeburgh 083259
Mole Hole, Birmingham 087773
Moleiro, Barcelona 134921
Molen & Art Garage, Tallinn 098702
Molen-, Bakkerij- en Stoommuseum, Essen 003428
Molen De Vriendschap, Weesp 030319
Molen van Frans Expositie, Mander (Tubbergen) 029906
Molen van Sloten, Amsterdam 029201
Molenaars, Breda 107880
Molenmuseum, Koog aan de Zaan . 029818
Molenmuseum, Lommel 003612
Molenmuseum, Centrum voor Molinologie, Sint-Amands 003752
Molenmuseum de Assumburg, Nieuw Vossemeer 029945
Molenmuseum De Valk, Leiden . . . 029849
Molenmuseum De Wachter, Zuidlaren 030398
Molerhiisli, Hausach 017803
Molermuseet, Nykøbing Mors 009037
Molero, V., Granada 129529
Molesworth Gallery, Dublin 105880
Molhant, V., Brugge 123567
Moli d'en Gaspar, Lluchmajor 035359
Molica, Giuseppe, Roma 106591
Molina, Gabriel, Madrid 141054
Molina, Juan, Arévalo 129305
Molina, Pedro, Bogotá 059847
Molina Art, Valladolid 110854
Molina Art, Valladolid 110855
Molinari, Modena 075922
Molinari, Cristina, Genova 127473
Molinari, Prof. Paola, Parma 127858
Molinaro, Livia, Versailles 068813
Moline, Florian, Nîmes 065183
Molínek, Jan, Rychnov nad Kněžnou 060189, 137854
Molkerei-Museum, Bernbeuren . . . 016203
Moll, Evert, Amsterdam 128550
Molland, Leek 084941
Mollbrink, Uppsala 111092
Molle, Gilbert, Lyon 064161
De Mollegangen, Bergen op Zoom . 107870
Mollenhoff, Rolf, Aubenas 061032
Møller, København 060357
Mollet, Grigny 063080
Mollnar, Wien 057505
Molloy, Dallas 132017
Molloy, Southport 086657
Molly Brown House Museum, Denver 043411
Molmar, Pamplona 110720
Molnar, Bergen op Zoom 078073
Molnar, Atila, Stuttgart 073994
Molnár, László, Eger 074733
Molnár C. Pál Müteremmuzeum, Budapest 021675
Molong Historical Museum, Molong 001273
Mølsteds Museum, Dragør 008833
Molteno Museum, Molteno 034681
Moltke-Gedächtnisstätte, Museum der Stadt Parchim, Parchim 019563
Moltkerei Werkstatt, Köln 103679
Moluks Historisch Museum, Utrecht 030229
Molwitz-Stube, Mitterteich 018961
Mom & Pop Antiques, Washington . 093427
Le Moma, Casablanca 077665
M.O.M.A., New York 136553
Momentoes, Chennai 105634
Momentum, Berlin 101985
Mommers, Ascona 082100
Mommers, Davos Platz 082337
Mommers, Sankt Gallen 082784
Momoyama Art Museum, Kyoto . . . 026750
Mompart, Michel, Donzenac 062716
Mompesson House, Salisbury 040947
Mom's Ole Stuff, Kansas City 089510
Momu Galleries, Houston 116373
Momus, Atlanta 114906
Mon D'Art, Galați 109457
Mon Grenier, Alès 060773
Mon-Jam Arts, Deal 112942
Mon State Museum, Mawlamyine . 029062
Mon Style à Moi, Bruxelles 058039
Mona and Don's Antiques, Austin . .087597, 131805
Mona Lisa, Bottrop 102208
Mona Lisa, Viersen 105121
Mona Vale Aero Nautical Museum, Mona Vale 001274
Monacensia-Literaturarchiv und Bibliothek, München 019083
Monachesi, Luce, Roma 106592
Monaco, Vincenzo, Napoli 076010
Monaco Art Show, Monaco 093821
Monaco Modern Art Museum, Monaco 028990
Monaghan County Museum, Monaghan 022838
El Monaguillo, Pamplona 081523
Monalisa, Erkrath 102650
Monalisa Art Gallery, New York 118208
Monalisa Art Studio, Chicago 115504
Monarch Antiques, Saint Leonards-on-Sea 086466, 131442
Monarch Books, London 135236
Monarch Coin Corporation, Salt Lake City 092448
Monarch Collectibles, Houston 089159
Monarch Collectibles, San Antonio . 092548
Monarch Gallery, Greenock 113160
Monarch Historical Museum, Williamtown 001620
Monaro, Lydia, Montréal 097058
Monart Saint Vital, Winnipeg 097594
Monash Gallery of Art, Wheelers Hill 001613
Monash University Museum of Art, Clayton 000925
Monasterio, Madrid 081342
Monasterio, Madrid 081343
Monasterio de Dominicas, Quejana 035687
Monasterio de la Cartuja, Sevilla . . 035857
Monasterio de la Encarnación, Madrid 035391
Monasterio de la Encarnación, Osuna 035576
Monasterio de la Santa Cruz, Sahagún 035736
Monasterio de las Descalzas Reales, Madrid 035392
Monasterio de Nuestra Señora de Guadelupe, Guadelupe 035266
Monasterio de Nuestra Señora de la Piedad, Casalarreina 035063
Monasterio de San Juan de los Reyes, Toledo 035917
Monasterio de San Lorenzo de El Escorial, San Lorenzo de El Escorial 035761
Monasterio de San Millán de Suso, San Millán de Suso 035768
Monasterio de San Pedro, San Pedro de Cardeña 035769
Monasterio de San Pedro de Cardeña, Castrillo del Val 035072
Monasterio de Sant Cugat, Sant Cugat del Vallès 035778
Monasterio de Santa Catalina, Arequipa 031457
Monasterio de Santa Clara, Zafra . . 036093
Monasterio de Santa Clara de Tordesillas, Tordesillas 035932
Monasterio de Santa María, Ripoll . 035706
Monasterio de Santa María, Santa María de Huerta 035803
Monasterio de Santa María, Sobrado 035880
Monasterio de Santa María de la Rábida, Palos de la Frontera 035628
Monasterio de Santa María la Real, Nájera 035537
Monasterio de Santa María San Salvador, Cañas 035040
Monasterio de Santes Creus, Santes Creus 035815
Monasterio San Juan de Duero, Sección Medieval del Museo Numantino, Soria 035885
Monasterio Santa María la Real de las Huelgas, Museo de Ricas Telas, Burgos 035002
Monasterio Santo Espíritu, Gilet . . . 035226
Monasterium De Wijngaard, Brugge 003274
Monastery of Saint Catherine, Gebel Katherîna 009329
Monastery of the Archangel Michael Panormitis, Chora 021236
Monastery of the Evangelistria, Skopelos 021470
Monastery of the Panagia Xenia, Almyros 021126
Monastery of the Taxiarchs, Aigion . 021124
Monastery of the Zoodochos Pigi or Agia, Batsi 021220
Monberg, Morten, Vedbæk 060412
Monbrison, Alain de, Paris 066299
Monbrison, Naïla de, Paris 100699
Moncada, Fernando, Lisboa 079968
Moncada, Francisco Cabral, Lisboa 079969
Moncada, Francisco Xavier, Lisboa . 079970
Moncada, Francisco Xavier, Lisboa . 079971
Moncada, Isabel Cabral, Lisboa . . . 079972
Moncada, Miguel Cabral, Lisboa . . 079973
Monchy, de, Zutphen 108277
Monclus Rodriguez, Enrique, Madrid 081344
Moncton Museum, Moncton 005899
Moncur Gallery, Boissevain 005110
Mondadori, Arnoldo, Verona 134709
Mondak Heritage Historical Museum and Art Gallery, Sidney 048171
Monde à l'Envers, Chevreuse 062287
Le Monde Antiques, Dallas 088574
Le Monde de Belibaste, Épopée Cathare, Villerouge-Termenès 015288
Le Monde de Gonor, Plan-d'Orgon . 066842
Le Monde des Abeilles, Villeneuve-de-Berg 015270
Le Monde du Voyage, Saint-Ouen . . 067852
Mondial Art, Bougival 061673
Mondial Art, Paris 100700
Mondial Art Exchange, Saint-Ouen . 067853
Mondiart, Napoli 106382
Mondo Arte, Roma 135916
Mondo Cane, New York 091090
Il Mondo dell'Arte, Roma 106593
Il Mondo dell'Arte, Roma 106594
Il Mondo dell'Arte, Roma 106595
Il Mondo dell'Arte, Roma 106596
Il Mondo Stijl, Den Haag 078220
Mondolfio, Namia, Caracas 120433
Mondriaanhuis - Museum voor Constructieve en Concrete Kunst, Amersfoort 029151
Mondseer Antiquitäten- und Sammlermesse, Mondsee 093585
Moneghini, Gian Pietro, Brescia . . . 127225
Monemvasia Archeological Collection, Monemvasia 021384
Monestir de Cura, Randa 035691
Monet, Shepton Mallet 114425
Monet, Shepton Mallet 114426
Monet, Skopje 107425
Moneta, Warszawa 079769
Moneta Nova, Bremen 070036
Monetti, Antonio, Napoli 127781
Monetto, Grimaud 099315
Money Museum, Kingston 026389
Money Museum, Teheran 022631
money trend, Wien 135571
Monfregola, Emilio & Doris, Riehen 111841
Mongers, Hingham 084691
Mongerson, Chicago 115505
Mongin, Robert, Paris 066300, 100701
Mongolian National Modern Art Gallery, Ulaanbaatar 029004
Mongolian Theatre Museum, Ulaanbaatar 029005
The Monhegan Museum, Monhegan 045960
Monica, Leuven 058277
Monier, Murrhardt 104388
Monier, Patrice, Nice 124517
Monin, Trevoux 068627
Monin, Villeurbanne 068972
Monin, Anne Marie, Paris . 066301, 100702
Monin, Jacques, Lyon 064162
Monini, Massimo, Toulouse 068529
Monis alte Stube, Südlohn 074022
Mõniste Muuseum, Kuutsi 009377
Monks' Dormitory Museum, Durham 039335
Monkwearmouth Station Museum, Sunderland 041157
Monleon, Lenore, New York 091091
Monluc, Gérard, Paris 066302
Monmouth County Historical Museum, Freehold 044069
Monmouth Museum, Lincroft 045321
Monna Lisa, Vechta 105107
La Monna Lisa Galería de Arte, Cali 098240
Monnaie d'Or, Paris 066303
Les Monnaies de Lyon, Paris 066304
Les Monnaies de Notre-Dame, Lyon 064163
Monnaies Médailles 17, La Rochelle 063436
Monnaies Médailles 17, La Rochelle 063437
Monnais, Montréal 058979
Monnet, François, Clermont-Ferrand 124204
Monney, Daniel, Fribourg 141243
Monnier, Murrhardt 072939, 134300
Monnier, Bernard, La Valette-du-Var 063459
Monnier, Corinne de, Le Havre 099442
Monnier, Frédéric, Busy 061841
Le Monnier, Philippe, Strasbourg . . 068325
Le Monnier, Philippe, Strasbourg . . 068326
Monnier, Raymond, Lyon 064164
Monnier, Virginie, Besançon 061393
Monnier, Wilhelmina, Le Pré-Saint-Gervais 063693
Monnier-Debroux, Jacqueline, Quingey 067028
Monnin, Patrick, Chambéry 062105
Monnot, Nolay 065226
Monocacy National Battlefield, Frederick 044050
Monografie Muzeum Narodowego w Poznaniu, Poznań 136028
Monogrammit, Houston 089160
Monopteros Fine Art, Chesham . . . 112849
Monotype Guild of New England, Chatham 054885
Monreal & Poppen, Bonn 102189
Monro, London 085542, 131112
Monroe, Tampa 132957
Monroe County Heritage Museum, Monroeville 045975
Monroe County Historical Museum, Monroe 045971
Monroe County Historical Society, Bloomington 042264
Monroe County Local History Room and Library, Sparta 048261
Monroe Historical Society Museum, Monroe 045966
Mons Breidvik Galleries, Norheimsund 031056
Mons-Montmartre, Mons 123666
Møns Museum, Stege 009117
Monsalve, Madrid 129649
Monsantic.com, Mons 120780
Monseau, Claude, Bordeaux 061637

Monsenhor, Braga 079811, 129140
Monserrato Arte, Roma 076573
Monsignor Hawes Priest House Museum, Mullewa 001295
Monsignor Yatco Ecclesiastical Museum, Batangas 031631
Monsone, Andrea, Roma 076574
Monsoon, Düsseldorf 070415
Monsoon Traders, Woodside 056849
Monsù Pingon, Torino 140139
Mont De Lancey Historical Museum, Wandin 001592
Mont-Martre, Eindhoven 078344
Mont Orgueil Castle, Gorey 039606
Mont Vert, Apeldoorn 078037
Montafoner Heimatmuseum Schruns, Schruns 002657
Montafoner Tourismusmuseum Gaschurn, Gaschurn 001888
Montage, Castleton 112827
Montage, Nelson 114112
Montage, Wellington 079335
Montage Gallery, Baltimore 115072
Montagnac, Marion, Arpajon 060983
Montagnani, Mario, Genova 075486
Montagnon, Jeanney Sylvie, Montbéliard 099735
Montagu Museum, Montagu 034682
Montague Museum, Montague 045976
Montaigne, Chantilly 062141
Montaigne, Yves, Lamorlaye 063502
Montalto, Attilio, Catania 075254
Montalvo Center for the Arts, Saratoga 048003
Montana Auto Museum, Deer Lodge 043365
Montana Historical Society Museum, Helena 044503
Montanari, Aurora, Modena 075923
Montanaro-Visconteum, C & A, Roma 076575
Montanini, Gian Paolo, Parma 140089
Montanmuseum, Gußwerk 001991
Montanmuseum, Hieflau 002043
Montansier, Versailles 068814
Montaperto, Angelo L., New York . . 132501
Montariol, Jacqueline, Condom . . . 062454
Montarras, Jean Francois, Raon-l'Etape 067043
Montauban Numismatique, Montauban 064635
Montauk, Clermont 042978
Montauk Point Lighthouse Museum, Montauk 045977
Montaut, Bordeaux 099008, 124135
Montaut, Denis, Bordeaux 133455, 138048
Montauti, Siegfried, Nice . 099850, 124518
Montavoci, Marco, Milano 127636
Montázs, Miskolc 105567
Montbarbon, Toulon (Var) 138629
Montbel, Eric de, Paris 100703
Montcada Taller, Barcelona 110222
Montcades Dos, Palma de Mallorca 081489
Montchaud, André, Provins 066992
Montclair, Oakland 091429, 123028
Montclair Art Museum, Montclair . . 045978
Montclair Art Museum. Bulletin-Newsletter, Montclair 136554
Montclair Art School, Montclair . . . 051740
Montclair Historical Society Museum, Montclair 045979
Montclair State University Art Galleries, Upper Montclair 048708
Monte-Carlo Antiquités, Monaco . . 077617
Monte-Carlo International Fine Art and Antiques Fair, Monaco 093822
Monte Clark, Vancouver 097501
Monte Clark Gallery, Toronto 097331
Monte L. Bean Life Science Museum, Provo 047273
Monte Titano Arte, San Marino 109671
Monte Wade, San Antonio 119433
Monteblanco Galería, Medellín 098279
Montecatini, Concepción 097615
Montelatici, Sirio, Firenze 127377
Montemaggi, Linda K., New York . . 142676
Montemayor, Barcelona 080885
Montemayor Fortea, Julian, Barcelona 080886, 110223
Montenegro Antiguedades, Madrid . 081345
Monter, Robert, Saint-Amand-Montrond 067348
Monterey Art Gallery, South Auckland 108560
Monterey History and Art Association, Monterey 054886
Monterey History and Art Association Museum, Monterey 045983
Monterey Museum of Art, Monterey 045984
Monterey Museum of Art News, Monterey 136555
Monterey State Historic Park, Monterey 045985
Montero Gomez, Juan, La Palmas de Gran Canaria 110711
Montero Rodriguez, Teresa, Cáceres 081026, 122019
Montes, Luisa, Donostia-San Sebastián 081088
Montet, Champagne-au-Mont d'Or . 062114
Monteverde, A., Montevideo 142187
Monteverdi Car Collection, Schweizer Automuseum, Binningen 036954
Montezuma, Erftstadt 102641
Montezuma Galerie, Hürth 103411
Montezuma Galerie, Köln 103680
Montfort, Feldkirch 056976, 137165
Montfort, Vaison-la-Romaine 101402
Montfort-Museum, Tettnang 020426
Montgomery, San Francisco 119746
Montgomery, W.H.C., Greyabbey . . 113162
Montgomery County Historical Society Center, Dayton 043322
Montgomery County Historical Society Museum, Rockville 047515
Montgomery Gallery, Claremont . . . 042938
Montgomery Museum and Lewis Miller Regional Art Center, Christiansburg 042910
Montgomery Museum of Fine Arts, Montgomery 045995
Montgomery Street Antique Mall, Fort Worth 088869
Montgomery's Inn, Etobicoke 005438
Montheillet, Pierre, Lyon 099605
Montheillet Pierre, Lyon 099606
Monthly Art Magazine, Tokyo 135981
Monti, Firenze 127378
Monti, Piero, Roma 128122
Monti, Roberto, Modena 106353
Montialoux, Jacques, Saint-Pargoire 067935
Monticello, Norfolk 091391, 132559
Monticello, Portland 091975
Monticello Gallery, Dallas 115912
Monticello, Home of Thomas Jefferson, Charlottesville 042766
Monticello Railway Museum, Monticello 046000
Montleau, Gérald de, La Rochefoucauld 063420
Montleau, Gérald de, Paris 100704
Montmartre, Den Haag 078221
Montoriol, Esther, Barcelona 110224
Montorsi, Mirco, Modena 127737
Montoya Antiguedades, Madrid . . . 081346
Montoya Jimenez, Enrique, Madrid . 081347
Montpelier Cultur Arts Center, Laurel 045197
Montpellier Clocks, Cheltenham . . .083924, 130539
Montpellier Mansion, Laurel 045198
Montpellier Mews, Harrogate 084582
Montpellier Numismatique, Montpellier 064751
Montre, Alicante 080763
Montrose, Albury 055331
Montrose Air Station Museum, Montrose 040494
Montrose County Historical Museum, Montrose 046010
Montrose Museum and Art Gallery, Montrose 040495
Montserrat, New York 118209
Montserrat, Jean-Pierre, Limoux . . 063903
Montserrat College of Art, Beverly . 050981
Montshire Museum of Science, Norwich 046571
Montville Antiques, Montville 056245
Montville Township Historical Museum, Montville 046013
Monty's, Fortitude Valley 055838
Montys, Pantin 099897
Montys, Paris 100705
Monty's Moorabbin Auctions, Moorabbin 120616
Monum, Paris 133655
Monumen Nasional, Jakarta 022424
Monument Lefebvre, Memramcook 005860
Monumental Brass Society, Stratford Saint Mary 054433
Monumenti Antichi, Medioevali e Moderni, Roma 025488
Monumenti Musei e Gallerie Pontificie, Città del Vaticano 049422
Monumento a Cristo Rey, Belalcázar 007400
Monumento Arqueológico de Chavín, Huari 031521
Monveneur, Francis, Saint-Georges-de-Reneins 067490
Monvoisin, Lille 124322
Monzani, Massimiliano, Modena . . 075924
Monzel, Th., Essenbach 070657
Monzon, Uria, Ciboure 099135
Mood Indigo, New York 091092
Moods, Mechelen 096387
Moody & Assoc., Birmingham 115117
Moody, Houston 116374
Moody County Museum, Flandreau . 043856
Moody Mansion Museum, Galveston 044135
Moog jr., Henry B., Atlanta 087503
Mooi Per Stuk, Amsterdam 077916
Mooie Dingen, Groningen 108040
Mooij, Utrecht 078811
Mook, Seoul 107273
Sree Moolam Shastyabdapurti Memorial Institute, Thiruvananthapuram . . . 022352
Moon, Michael, Whitehaven 142153
Moon Gate, Singapore 080531
Moon & Star Antiques, Cleveland . . 088344
Moon-Stone Gallery, Paris 066305
Moonah Arts Centre, Moonah 001275
Moonee Ponds Antiques, Moonee Ponds 056249
Mooney, J.R., San Antonio 119434
Mooney, Riro D., Duxford 084237
Moongate Oriental Antiques and Gallery, Armadale, Victoria 055387
Moonlight Antiques, Miami 090213
Moonraker Gallery, Fowey 113079
Moonta Antiques, Moonta 056251
Moonta Mines Museum, Moonta . . 001276
Moonta National Trust Museum, Moonta 001277
Moor, Alain de, Bischoffsheim 061498
Moor, Christian, Vichy 068861
Moor, Edith, Genève 082448
Moor Antiques, Ashburton 083337
Moor-Galerie, Friedhelm, Hille 103382
Moor Hall Antiques, Chester 083962, 130560
Moor Street Art Gallery, Fitzroy 094536
Moor- und Fehnmuseum, Barßel . . 015891
Moor- und Torfmuseum, Heidenreichstein 002027
Moorabbin Air Museum, Cheltenham 000910
Moorabbin Air Museum, Moorabbin 001279
Moorabool Antique Galleries, Geelong 055868
Moore, Birmingham 115118
Moore, Toronto 097332
Moore, Carl, Houston 089161
Moore, D.C., New York 118210
Moore, E., Tulsa 132999
Moore, Elizabeth, New York 118211
Moore, Eric T., Hitchin 141668
Moore, Jack, Trawden . . . 086912, 131605
Moore, Marcus, Stanton-upon-Hine Heath 086696, 131529
Moore, Sigrid, Stuttgart 073995
Moore, T., Ottawa 059046
Moore, Widney, Portland 119021
Moore, Allen & Innocent, Cirencester 122469
Moore College of Art and Design, Philadelphia 051944
Moore County Historical Museum, Dumas 043526
Moore Home, Lerna 045238
Moore Museum, Mooretown 005952
Mooreichensammlung Johann Weber, Göppingen 017450
Mooren, Francine, Liège 058317
Moores & Son, Walter, Market Harborough 085939
Moores Creek National Battlefield, Currie 043250
Moorfoot Contemporary Art, Amisfield 112508
Moorhead, Patrick, Brighton 083705
Moorland, Uppermill 142133
Moorman, Memphis 090095, 132331
Moormuseum Moordorf, Südbrookmerland 020378
Mooroopna Hospital, Mooroopna . . 001280
Moorside Books, Clitheroe 141526
Moorthamers, Paris 138507
Moorthamers, Louis, Bruxelles 137452
Moos, Toronto 097333
Moose, Jeffrey, Seattle 119965
Moose Factory Centennial Museum, Kirkland Lake 005713
Moose Jaw Museum and Art Gallery, Moose Jaw 005954
Moosehorn Heritage Museum, Moosehorn 005956
Moosim, Chongju 107180
Moot Hall Museum, Aldeburgh 038471
Mope, Sevilla 081597, 129738
Mopsi, Den Haag 078222
Mor, Giovanna & C., Brescia 075178
Mora, Marie, Salzburg 137246
Mora, Migliore, Palermo 076166
Mora, William, Richmond, Victoria . 095139
Móra Ferenc Emlékház, Kiskunfélegyháza 021769
Móra Ferenc Múzeum, Szeged 021862
Mora Rodriguez, Lluis, Barcelona . . 080887
Mora & Upham, London . . 085543, 131113
Morabito, Catania 106023
A Morada, Lisboa 079974
Morada, Porto 080098
Moraes, Eurema Fatima Gallo, Porto Alegre 096570
Moraes, Julio, São Paulo 123718
Moraes, Luciano Diniz de, Brasília . 096497
Moraes, Oliveira & Oliveira, Brasília 096498
Morain, Gilbert, Callian 061909
Morales, David, New York 118212
Moran, Miami 132351
Moran, San Antonio 092549
Moran, Joe, Regina 097179
Moran, John, Pasadena 123042
Moran Open-air Museum, Namyangju 027536
Morand, Chantal, Genève 082449
Morand, Corinne, Lalinde 063494
Morand, Richard & Ludovic, Paris . . 121175
Morandell, A. & T., Bolzano 105988
Morandi, Rita, Porto Alegre 096571
Morange Candas, Arras 060988
Morantes, Bucaramanga 059868
Morard, Claude, Nyon . . . 082705, 111785
Moras Fuente, Jesús, Madrid 141055
Morassutti, Amistani, Padova 076099
Morassutti, Amistani, Padova 127808
Morassutti, Amistani, Padova 127809

Morat-Institut für Kunst und Kunstwissenschaft, Freiburg im Breisgau . . . 017233
Morate, Cuenca . . . 081066
Morate Tornero, Manuel, Valladolid 081693
Morate Tornero, Manuel, Valladolid 081694
Morate Tornero, Manuel, Valladolid 129789
Morate Tornero, Manuel, Valladolid 129790
Morato Esmaltador, Barcelona . . . 129370
Moravec, Vít, Brno . . . 123952
Moravian Museum, Pudsey . . . 040784
Moravian Museum of Bethlehem, Bethlehem . . . 042185
Moravská Galerie Brno - Místodrzitelsky Palác, Brno . . . 008290
Moravská Galerie Brno - Pražákův Palác, Brno . . . 008291
Moravské Zemské Muzeum, Brno . 008292
Morawa, Wien . . . 095901
Morawa, Wien . . . 137349
Morawa, Wien . . . 137350
Morawa, Wien . . . 137351
Morawa Old Police Station Museum, Morawa . . . 001281
Moray, Dunedin . . . 108442
Mørch, Jan, Oslo . . . 079461, 128993
Morchard Bishop Antiques, Morchard Bishop . . . 086005
Morcos, Patrick, Paris . . . 066306
Morcrette, Daniel, Luzarches . . . 133485, 138127
Mord + Totschlag, Braunschweig . . 138930
Mordecai Historic Park, Raleigh . . . 047312
Morden and District Museum, Morden . . . 005959
Mordialloc Historical Society Museum, Mentone . . . 001254
Mordoch, Lélia, Paris . . . 100706
Mordovskij Muzej Izobrazitelnych Isskustv im. S.D. Érzi, Saransk . . . 033844
Mordovskij Respublikanskij Kraevedčeskij Muzej, Saransk . . . 033845
More Gallery, Philadelphia . . . 118806
More & More Antiques, New York . . 091093
More Nucci, Milano . . . 075774, 127637
... More Stars, Portland . . . 091976
Moreau, Saint-Ouen . . . 067854
Moreau, Tours . . . 068598
Moreau, Annette, Saint-Hilaire-de-Riez . . . 067517
Moreau, B. Freiherr von, Bad Tölz . 125117
Moreau, Catherine Philomène, Paris 066307
Moreau, Jean-Luc, Paris . . . 066308
Moreau, P., Verviers . . . 123677
Moreau-Billy, Danielle, La Baule-Escoublac . . . 099379
Moreau-Billy, Danielle, La Baule-Escoublac . . . 099380
Moreau-Guionneau, Ginette, Bergerac . . . 061362
Moreaux-Jouannet, Isabelle, Aix-les-Bains . . . 124061
Moree Gallery, Moree . . . 094881
Moree Plains Gallery, Moree . . . 001282
Morefield, Port Macquarie . . . 095094
Moreira, Fernando, Paris . . . 124753
Moreira & Galveias, Lisboa . . . 109334
Moreira & Galveias, Lisboa . . . 109335
Morel, Viriat . . . 069005
Morel, Christophe, Paris . . . 121176
Morel, Dury, Lyon . . . 064165
Morel, Henri, Champigny-en-Beauce . . . 062122
Morel, Jean, Bihorel-Lés-Rouen . . . 138031
Morel, Laurent, Neuchâtel . . . 130128
Morel, Olivier, Paris . . . 124754
Morel de Westgaver, Alain & Evelyne, Bruxelles . . . 120737, 137453
Moreland, Brunswick . . . 120570
Morell, Jim, Cleveland . . . 088345
Morelli, Jean, Orange . . . 065278
Morelli, Sandro, Firenze . . . 075372
Morelli Antichitá, Napoli . . . 076011
Morena-Kalopisi, Chalandri . . . 074617
Moreno, San Antonio . . . 132819
Moreno, Antonio - Hijo, Salamanca 081541
Moreno, Leticia, Cali . . . 059883
Moreno Alaix, Carlos, Bogotá . . . 098175
Moreno Herrera, Carmen Rosa, Roma . . . 106597
Moreno Sanchez, Antonio Jose, Córdoba . . . 081050
Moreno Sanz, Juan Salvador, Badalona . . . 080777
Morera Alvarez, Isabel, Toledo . . . 110791
Morera Soler, Francisco, Sabadell .081535, 129713
Morero, Jean-Claude, Cruis . . . 062577
Moreschi, Martin, Ohlsbach . . . 073194
Moréteau, Paule, Lyon . . . 124368
Moreton, C.S., Inchture . . . 084792
Moreton, Rex, Newport, Gwent . . . 131312
Moreton Street Gallery, London . . .085544, 113775
Moreton's Harbour Museum, Moreton's Harbour . . . 005961
Moretti, Firenze . . . 075373
Moretti, Montevideo . . . 114763
Moretti, Alfredo, Prato . . . 076257
Moretti, Attilio, Roma . . . 076576
Moretti, Ferdinando, Roma . . . 128123
Moretti, Raymonde, Paris . . . 124755
Morettini, Ortensia, Roma . . . 128124
Moreux, Paris . . . 066309
Morey & Sons, William, Bridport . . . 122436
Morf, Angela, Lausanne . . . 082556
Morfi, Lemesos . . . 098316
Morgama, Madrid . . . 110578
Morgan, Chicago . . . 115506
Morgan, Kansas City . . . 116583
Morgan, New York . . . 118213
Morgan, Norfolk . . . 091392
Morgan, Omaha . . . 091578
Morgan, Pittsburgh . . . 118942
Morgan, Alexander, Epping . . . 113028
Morgan, Bob, Louisville . . . 132302
Morgan, Jeff, Hawker, South Australia . . . 094619
Morgan, Linda, New York . . . 091094
Morgan, R., Ringwood . . . 086367
Morgan Roberts, Jean, Conwy . . . 112902
Morgan Row Museum, Harrodsburg 044451
Morgan Street Gallery, Auckland . . 108345
Morgan-West, New Orleans . . . 117479
Morgana, Cairo . . . 098651
Morgand, Evelyne, Mereville . . . 064501
Morgans Auctions, Belfast . . . 122406
Morge, Jean-Jacques, Chevrainvilliers . . . 062284
Morgenland, Düsseldorf . . . 070416
De Morgenster, Tilburg . . . 078774
Morgenstern, Miami . . . 090214
Morgenstern, Stralsund . . . 139745
Morgenstern, Thun . . . 141306
Morgenstern, Claude, Saint-Mandé 067620
Morgulis, Michael, Buffalo . . . 115260
Mori, Gianni, Parma . . . 076216
Mori, Hanae, Tokyo . . . 077282
Mori, Ryozo, Sapporo . . . 140176
Mori Bijitsukan, Tokyo . . . 027209
Mori Gallery, Sydney . . . 095299
Mori Hokokai Hakubutsukan, Hofu . 026544
De Moriaan Antiek, Leiden . . . 078575
Moriah, Cleveland . . . 135353
Moriah, New York . . . 091095
Moriah, New York . . . 091096
Moriani, Milena, Pisa . . . 106468
Moriarty, Madrid . . . 110579
Moriarty, Salt Lake City . . . 092449
Moriarty Historical Museum, Moriarty . . . 046029
Morigi & Figlio, G., Bologna . . . 127169
Morija Museum, Morija . . . 027823
The Morikami Museum and Japanese Gardens, Delray Beach . . . 043383
Morikuma, Saitama . . . 077190
Morillas, Donostia-San Sebastián . . 129513
Morillon, Lyon . . . 099607
Morin, Jacques, Saint-Brieuc . . . 067385
Morin, Jean, Plougonven . . . 066869
Morin, Jean-Yves, Sainte-Pience . . 068075
Morin, Michel André, London . . . 085545
Morin, Pierre Stéphane, Isle . . . 063216
Morin, Thierry, Lyon . . . 064166
Morin-Pitel, Emmanuelle, Paris . . . 100707
Morini, Lucio, Brescia . . . 075179
Morioka City Local Hall, Morioka . . 026832
Morioka Hashimoto Museum of Art, Morioka . . . 026833
Morion, Helsinki . . . 060557
Morisco, Federico, Roma . . . 128125
Morisco, Gianfranco, Roma . . . 076577
Morishita Bijutsukan, Hinase . . . 026513
Morisot, Patrick, Colombey-les-Belles . . . 062429
Morita, Tokyo . . . 077283
Moritz, E., Goslar . . . 071066
Morlan Gallery, Lexington . . . 045264
Morley, David, Twickenham . . . 086966
Morley, Patrick & Gillian, Warwick . 087041
Morley & Co, Robert, London 085546, 131114
Morley College, London . . . 050837
Morley Gallery, London . . . 040223
Morley Gallery, London . . . 113776
Morlock, Barbara, Schenefeld . . . 104821
Mormon Visitors Center, Independence . . . 044726
Mormors Skattkista, Stockholm . . . 081990
Mormors Spegel, Stockholm . . . 081991
Mornet-Tristan, Colette, Oloron-Sainte-Marie . . . 065268
Morning Glory Antiques, Kansas City . . . 089511
Morning Mountain Arts, Berry . . . 055498
Morning Star Antiques, Tucson . . . 093250
Morning Star Traders, Tucson . . . 120149
Morningside Antiques, Albuquerque 087411
Morningside Antiques, Miami . . . 090215
Morningside Art, Houston . . . 116375
Morningside Gallery, Edinburgh . . . 113001
Morningside Nature Center, Gainesville . . . 044105
Mornington Peninsula Regional Gallery, Mornington . . . 001285
Moro de Venecia, Valencia . . . 081666
Moron, Marseille . . . 064377
Moroni, Rebecca, Genova . . . 127474
Moroni, Renzo, Roma . . . 076578
Moroni, Umberto, Roma . . . 076579
Morosini, Padova . . . 076100
Moroten, Stockholm . . . 081992
Morpeth Art Studio, Morpeth . . . 094887
Morpeth Gallery, Morpeth . . . 094888
Morpeth Trading Post, Morpeth . . . 056261
Morph, Denver . . . 116027
Morphets, Harrogate . . . 122536
Morphett's Enginehouse Museum, Burra . . . 000867
Morpurgo, J.M., Amsterdam . . . 077917
Morrab, Truro . . . 114604
Morrab Studio, Penzance . . . 114233
Morrin, Dublin . . . 074934
Morrin Museum, Morrinsville . . . 030542
Morring, Robert, Atlanta . . . 087504
Morrinsville Antiques, Morrinsville . 079156
Morris, Södertälje . . . 141135
Morris, Alfred James, Southampton . 086650, 114457, 122703, 131517
Morris, Cavin, New York . . . 118214
Morris, Chris, Sassafras . . . 056576
Morris, Darlene, Tucson . . . 093251
Morris, Frances, Enniskillen . . . 113025
Morris, Ian, Chesterfield . . . 083967
Morris, M.A.J., Burton-upon-Trent .083815, 141464
Morris, Peter, Bromley . . . 083767
Morris, Robert Lee, New York . . . 118215
Morris and District Centennial Museum, Morris . . . 005963
Morris and Helen Belkin Art Gallery, University of British Columbia, Vancouver . . . 006702
Morris Belknap Gallery, Dario Covi Gallery and SAL Gallery, Louisville . . . 045495
Morris & Bricknell, Ross-on-Wye . . 122670
Morris-Butler House Museum, Indianapolis . . . 044751
Morris Graves Museum of Art, Eureka . . . 043752
Morris-Jumel Mansion, New York . . 046366
Morris Marshall & Poole, Llanidloes 122576
Morris Marshall & Poole, Montgomery . . . 122621
Morris Marshall & Poole, Newtown, Powys . . . 122633
The Morris Museum, Morristown . . 046036
Morris Museum of Art, Augusta . . . 041901
Morrison, D., Portland . . . 142803
Morrison, David J., Christchurch . . 128926
Morrison, Guy, London . . . 113777
Morrison, Jan, Bristol . . . 083744
Morrison & Son, Robert, York . . . 087293
Morrison, Thomas, Dallas 088575, 132018
Morrison Museum of the Country School, Islay . . . 005649
Morrison & West, Lyttelton . . . 079139
Morristown Antiques Show, Morristown . . . 094009
Morristown National Historical Park, Morristown . . . 046037
Morro Bay State Park Museum of Natural History, Morro Bay . . . 046043
Morrow Mountain State Park Museum, Albemarle . . . 041606
Mors Doré, Paris . . . 124756
Morsak, Grafenau, Niederbayern . . 133984
Morse Museum, Morse . . . 005965
Morse Road Antique Center, Columbus . . . 088426
Morseburg, West Hollywood . . . 120401
Morsink, Jan, Amsterdam . . . 077918
Morsink, Saskia, Enschede . . . 078375
Morskoj Muzej, Karelskij morskoj istoriko-kulturnyj centr i morskoj klub Poljarnyj Odissej, Petrozavodsk . . . 033662
Morskoj Muzej-Akvarium, Tichookeanskogo naučno-issledovatelskogo instituta rybnogo chozjajstva i okeanografii (TINRO), Vladivostok . . . 034050
Morslands Historiske Museum, Nykøbing Mors . . . 009038
Morten, Eric J., Manchester . . . 141937
Mortgage, Portland . . . 119022
Morthland, Sarah, New York . . . 118216
Mortier-Valat, Joëlle, Paris . . . 100708
Mortimer, Brian, Exeter . . . 084360
Mortlake Antiques, Kaber . . . 130837
Morton, Fort Worth . . . 088870
Morton & Co, Timaru . . . 079270
Morton, Betty, London . . . 113778
Morton, Ian, Düsseldorf . . . 070417
Morton, John, Dublin . . . 074935
Morton, Louis C., Guadalajara . . . 077566
Morton, Louis C., México . . . 077579
Morton, Louis C., Monterrey . . . 077591
Morton Grove Historical Museum, Morton Grove . . . 046044
Morton Homestead, Prospect Park . 047247
Morton House Museum, Benton Harbor . . . 042150
Morton J. May Foundation Gallery, Maryville University, Saint Louis . . . 047671
Morton Lee, J., Hayling Island . . .084637, 113214
Morton Museum of Cooke County, Gainesville . . . 044112
Morton Square Antiques, Nashville . 090469
Morueco Rodriguez, Luis, Madrid . . 081348
Morus-Verlag, Berlin . . . 133798
Morvan, Alain, München . . . 072795
Morven, Timaru . . . 079271
Morven Gallery, Barvas . . . 112565
Morven Historical Museum, Morven 001287
Morven Park Museum, Leesburg . . 045231
Morvillo, Pasquale, Napoli . . . 076012
Morwellham Quay Historic Port & Copper Mine, Tavistock . . . 041193
Mory-Wydeven, Ann M., Milwaukee 117208

Mo's Gallery, Tucson 120150
Mosaic Gallery, Amman 027376
Mosaic Planet, Blackheath 055511
Mosaic (St. Petersburg), Saint Petersburg 136556
Mosaico Gal Arte, Porto Alegre 096572
Mosaicon, Locarno 130087
Mosaïque, Briançon 099033
Mosaique Gallery, Chicago 115507
Mosaïque Gallo-Romaine, Amou . . 010374
Mosarm, Liège 058318
Mosburger, Marburg 072449
Mosca, Duilio, Roma 128126
Moscatelli, Claudio, London 131115
Moschakeion, International Museum of Marine Research, Moschato 021385
Moscow Art Magazine, Moskva . . . 136059
Moscow Business Plaza Gallery, Moskva 109567
Mosebach, Rainer, Halle, Saale . . . 071178
Mosebacke, Stockholm 081993
Mosel-Antiquariat, Traben-Trarbach 139783
Mosel & Tschechow, München 104274, 134263
Moseley Emporium, Birmingham . .083536, 130394
Moser, Graz 133079, 137178
Moser, İstanbul 083147
Moser, Adolf, Salzburg 123452
Moser, Charlotte, Genève 111486
Moser, Michael, Osnabrück 073244
Moser, Paul, Mittelbiberach 072553
Moser, Roland, Landshut 139376
Moser, Ulrich, Graz 137179
Moser, Walter, Wien 057506
Moser & Klang, Stockholm 081994
Moser & Raschke, Leipzig 072211
Moses, Dallas 115913
Moses, New York 118217
Moses, Dexter, Croydon Park 055732
Moses, Manuel, München 126419
Moses, Manuel, München 126420
Moses, Nancy, Philadelphia 118807
Moses Lake Museum and Art Center, Moses Lake 046048
Moses Myers House, Norfolk 046501
Moses Saidian, Teheran 074844
Mosie & Midge, Baltimore 087696
Moskat, Walter, Wolfurt 057608
Moskovitz, Ira, New York 091097
Moskovskaja Gosudarstvennaja Kartinnaja Galereja A. Šilova, Moskva 033430
Moskovskaja Gosudarstvennaja Specializirovannaja Škola Akvareli Sergeja Andrijaki, Moskva 050645
Moskovski Dom Knigi, Moskva 140912
Moskovskij Akademičeskij Chudožestvennyj Licej, Rossijskaja Akademija Chudožestv, Moskva 050646
Moskovskij Dom Fotografii, Moskva 033431
Moskovskij Dom Skulptorov, Moskva 109568
Moskovskij Dvor Art-Agentstvo, Moskva 109569
Moskovskij Gosudarstvennyj Muzej S.A. Esenina, Moskva 033432
Moskovskij Gosudarstvennyj Universitet Kultury i Isskustv, Chimki 050630
Moskovskij Gosudarstvennyj Vystavočnyj Zal Malyi Manež, Moskva 033433
Moskovskij Literaturnyj Muzej-Centr K.G. Paustovskogo, Moskva 033434
Moskovskij Muzej-usad'ba Ostankino, Moskva 033435
Mosman Art Gallery, Mosman 094894
Mosnier, Laure, Montpellier 124461
Mosoblrestavracija, Moskva 129237
Mo.Sor., Napoli 127782
Mosquera, Panamá City 108793
Moss, Cheltenham 141503
Moss, New Orleans 090592
Moss & Co., Washington 093428
Moss, A., London 085547
Moss, Alan, New York 091098
Moss, Brendan M., Vancouver 059388
Moss, Ralph & Bruce, Baldock 083371
Moss, Sydney L., London 085548
Moss, Tobey C., Los Angeles 116851
Moss End Antique Centre, Warfield . 087021
Moss Mansion Museum, Billings . . 042205
Moss-Thorns Gallery of Arts, Hays . 044489
Mossakowski, Marek, Warszawa . . 079770
Mossakowski, Marek, Warszawa . . 079771
Mossakowski, Marek, Warszawa . . 140792
Mossakowski, Marek, Warszawa . . 140793
Mossbank and District Museum, Mossbank 005966
Mosses Pottery, Bennettsbridge . . . 022693
Mossette, Fresno 088912
Mossman Gallery, Mossman 094900
Most, Bamberg 069459
Most, Peter, Berlin 125259
Most Čerez Stiks - Pons per Styx, Muzej Nonkonformistskogo Iskusstva, Sankt-Peterburg 033769
Mostert, Dorothy, Houston 089162
Mostly Bali, New York 091099
Mostly Bears, Tucson 093252
Mostly Boxes, Eton 084345, 130692
Mostly Movables, Toronto 059244
Mostly Posters, Boston 115208
Mostmuseum, Neumarkt im Mühlkreis 002366
Mostmuseum, Sankt Leonhard am Forst 002596
Mostmuseum und Heimathaus, Sankt Marienkirchen an der Polsenz . . . 002599
Mostra Archeologica G. Venturini, San Felice sul Panaro 025674
Mostra Cabriniana, Codogno 023920
Mostra Cartografica, Mendatica . . . 024664
Mostra Culturale di Apicoltura, Dopolavoro Gruppo Enichem, Porto Marghera 025330
Mostra d'Arte ed Antiquariato, Kunst- und Antiquitätenausstellung, Bolzano . 093772
Mostra degli Antichi Mestieri di Calabria, Tropea 026155
Mostra dei Pupi Siciliani, Teatro Stabile dell'Opera, Caltagirone 023587
Mostra della Civiltà Contadina, Lavello 024480
Mostra della Civiltà Contadina, Massa Marittima 024637
Mostra della Civiltà Contadina e Pastorale, Avezzano 023308
Mostra della Giudaica e Raccolta di Minerali, Laino Borgo 024445
Mostra di Antiquariato e d'Arte e Salone delle Stampe e dei Libri Antichi, Forlì 093773
Mostra di Cimeli del Risorgimento, Salemi 025632
Mostra di Modernariato, Antichità e Collezionismo, Napoli 093774
Mostra di Palazzo Farnese, Museo delle Carrozze, Piacenza 025206
Mostra Etnografica Museo Contadino della Piana, Capannori 023639
Mostra Europea d'Arte Antica, Genova 093775
Mostra Internazionale di Modernariato, Antichità e Collezionismo, Baganzola 093776
Mostra Internazionale di Modernariato, Antichità e Collezionismo, Baganzola 093777
Mostra Mercato Antiquari Milanesi, Milano 093778
Mostra Mercato d'Arte Contemporanea, Artisti e Associazioni in Fiera, Forlì 093779
Mostra Mercato d'Arte Contemporanea Cremona, Cremona 093780
Mostra Mercato d'Arte e Antiquariato, Milano 093781
Mostra Mercato d'Arte Moderna, Forlì 093782
Mostra Mercato d'Arte Moderna e Contemporanea, Vicenza 093783
Mostra Mercato dell'Antiquariato, Piacenza 093784
Mostra Mercato di Arte e Antiquariato, Padova 093785
Mostra Mercato Internazionale d'Arte Contemporanea, Bologna 093786
Mostra Mineraria Permanente, Sutri 025975
Mostra Nazionale di Antichità, Baganzola 093787
Mostra Nazionale di Pittura Contemporanea, Marsala 024621
Mostra Permanenta P. Mariani, Istituto Internazionale di Studi Liguri, Bordighera 023479
Mostra Permanente del Costume Arbereshe, Vaccarizzo Albanese 026180
Mostra Permanente del Presepio, Muggia 024885
Mostra Permanente della Biblioteca Estense, Modena 024752
Mostra Permanente della Ceramica, ex Convento dei Carmelitani, San Lorenzello 025699
Mostra Permanente della Civiltà Contadina, Montefoscoli 024845
Mostra Permanente della Cultura Materiale, Levanto 024499
Mostra Permanente della Resistenza, Lugo 024556
Mostra Permanente della Resistenzo, Massa Marittima 024638
Mostra Permanente della Tradizione Mineraria, Tarvisio 025991
Mostra Permanente di Paleontologia, Chiesa di San Tommaso, Terni 026010
Mostra Permanente di Xilografie di Pietro Parigi, Firenze 024165
Mostra Permanente Le Carrozze d'Epoca, Roma 025489
Mostre e Musei, Napoli 135917
Mostviertelmuseum Haag, Haag, Niederösterreich 001998
Mostviertler Bauernmuseum, Amstetten 001686
Mosul Museum, Mosul 022668
Mosvik Museum, Mosvik 031038
Mot, J., Bruxelles 096236
Motala Museum, Motala 036489
Motel Court Antiques, Seattle 093038
Mother Hubbard's Cupboard, Manwatu 128943
Mother Wouldn't Like It?, Sandy Bay 056573
Motherwell Heritage Centre, Motherwell 040500
Motherwell Homestead, NHS of Canada, Abernethy 004986
Moti, Delhi 105677
Motion Picture Arts Gallery, New York 091100
Motive, Haarlem 108059
Motley, Richmond 123075
Moto, Tokyo 107082
Moto Moto Museum, Mbala 049574
Motoki, Mitaka 077141, 140167
Motoori Norinaga Memorial Hall, Matsusaka 026795
Motor Books World, Camberwell . . 136841
Motor Car Museum of Japan, Futatsunashi 026471
Motor Museum, Filching 039498
Motor Museum, Ramsgate 040794
Motor-Sport-Museum Hockenheimring, Hockenheim 017939
The Motorboat Museum, Basildon . 038608
Motorcycle Hall of Fame Museum, Pickerington 047016
Motorcycle Haven, Adelaide River . 000719
Motormuseet, Strømmen 031247
Motorola Museum, Schaumburg . . . 048041
Motorrad-Museum, Augustusburg . 015625
Motorrad Museum, Ibbenbüren . . . 018039
Motorrad-Museum Krems-Egelsee, Krems 002174
Motorrad-Veteranen- und Technikmuseum, Großschönau, Sachsen 017582
Motorradmuseum, Gossau (Sankt Gallen) 037156
Motorradmuseum, Michelstadt 018933
Motorradmuseum, Neunkirchen, Niederösterreich 002370
Motorradmuseum, Sammlung Waldmann, Sulz 002724
Motown Historical Museum, Detroit 043454
Motsu-ji Storage House, Hiraizumi . 026520
Motta, Federico, Milano 134623
Motta, Luigi, Milano 075775
Motte, Alexandre, Dinard 099236
Motte, Dominique, Dinard 062688
Motte, Rémy, Villeneuve-d'Ascq . . . 068912
Motte-Barrois, Marie-Christine, Marcq-en-Barœul 064277
Motte,Jean-Pierre y Otro, Valencia . 110835
Mottier, Alexandre, Genève 111487
Mottin, Jean-Marie, Caligny 061907
Mottola, Dario, Milano 075776
Motts Military Museum, Groveport . 044367
Mottys, Broke 055565
Motueka District Museum, Motueka 030543
Motyw, Warszawa 109162
Motz, Anton, Deggendorf 125448
Moucheron, Joël, Chalons-en-Champagne 062096
Mouchez, Paris 124757
Moudgalya Antiques, Bangalore . . . 074776
Moudy Exhibition Hall, Fort Worth . . 044012
Mouël-Chouffot, Lucienne, Anglet . 120898
Le Mouel Enchères, Anglet 060871, 120899
Moufflet, Jane, Los Angeles 116852
Moufflet, Jane, Saint-Ouen 067855, 138605
Moufflet, Pascal, Nice 065116
Moufflet, Pascal, Nice 065117
Moufflet Antikk, Oslo 079462
Mougenot, Patricia, Le Thillot 063710
Mougin, Paris 100709
Mougin-Berthet, Paris 066310
Mougins, Pierre de, Paris 100710
Mougins Antiquités, Mougins 064806
Mougins Art Prestige, Mougins 099778
Mouhtar Ashrafi Museum, Taškent . 049409
Moulagensammlung des Universitätsspitals und der Universität Zürich, Zürich 037782
Moulart, E., Bruxelles 058040
Moulart, Thierry, Bruxelles 123600
Moulay, Ismaïl, Rabat 107565
Mould, Anthony, London 113779
Mouldings, C.C., Albuquerque 087412
Mouldsworth Motor Museum, Mouldsworth 040502
Mouliart, Madrid 110580
Moulierac, Jean-Marie, Nice 121095
Mouliet, Olivier, Jarret 063235
Le Moulin, Plan-les-Ouates 082727
Moulin à Musique Mécanique, Mormoiron 013244
Le Moulin à Papier de Brousses, Brousses-et-Villaret 011015
Moulin à Papier Vallis-Clausa, Fontaine-de-Vaucluse 011837
Moulin à Vent de 1802, Boeschepe 010855
Moulin à Vent Gaillardin, Chapelon . 011240
Moulin de Beaumont, Beaumont . . 005085
Moulin de la Brocante, Juziers 063277
Moulin de la Croix, Saint-Thomas-de-Conac 014554
Le Moulin de la Pleugère, Saint-Ouen-de-Sécherouvr 067929
Moulin de l'Epinette, Angles 060865
Moulin de Mérouvel, L'Aigle 063491
Moulin de Nouvet, Courville-sur-Eure 062530
Moulin de Traou-Meur-Écomusée, Pleudaniel 013837
Moulin de Vauboyen, Bièvres 098967, 133453
Moulin Doisy, Denain 011572
Moulin du Vieux Guingamp, Bégard 061320
Moulin Fleming, LaSalle 005749
Moulin Légaré, Saint-Eustache 006335
Moulin Maître Marcel, Sainte-Agathe-en-Donzy 014579
Moulin-Musée de la Brosserie, Saint-Félix 014285
Moulin-Musée de La Roche, La Possonnière 012297
Moulin-Musée Le Rotrou, Vaas 015082

Moulin Pomper, Baden 061160
Moulin Rouge, Portland 091977
Les Moulins, Sagy 014163
Moulins, Toulouse 101366
Moulins Souterrains du Col-des-Roches, Le Locle 037275
Moullec, Gabriel, Rosnoen 067228
Moulton, Mosman 094895
Moundarren, Millemont 133498
Moundbuilders State Memorial and Museum, Newark 046428
The Mount, Woore 087248, 142173
Mount Airy Museum of Regional History, Mount Airy 046051
The Mount Antiques Centre, Carmarthen 083884, 130517
Mount Barker Antiques, Mount Barker 056278
Mount Bruce Pioneer Museum, Masterton 030536
Mount Clare Museum House, Baltimore 041998
Mount Dandenong Antiques Centre, Olinda 056402, 123282
Mount Desert Island Historical Museum, Somesville 048221
Mount Dora Center for the Arts, Mount Dora 046057
Mount Edgcumbe House, Cremyll .. 039173
Mount Ephraim Prints, Tunbridge Wells 114611
Mount Ephraim Prints, Tunbridge Wells 142127
Mount Falcon Estates, Ballina 074856
Mount Holyoke College Art Museum, South Hadley 048240
Mount Kembla Collectables and Old Wares, Mount Kembla 056287
Mount Kenya Art Galleries, Nanyuki 107166
Mount Laura Homestead Museum, Whyalla Norrie 001615
Mount Manaia Art Gallery, Whangarei 108662
Mount Mary College Costume Museum, Milwaukee 045897
Mount Morgan Historical Museum, Mount Morgan 001292
Mount Pleasant, Philadelphia Museum of Art, Philadelphia 046961
Mount Pleasant Antiques Centre, Market Weighton 085943, 131266
Mount Pleasant Furniture, Vancouver 059389
Mount Pleasant Historical Society Museum, Mount Pleasant 046066
Mount Prospect Historical Society Museums, Mount Prospect 046069
Mount Pulaski Courthouse, Mount Pulaski 046070
Mount Royal College Gallery, Calgary 005192
Mount Rushmore National Memorial, Keystone 044996
Mount Saint Vincent University Art Gallery, Halifax 005577
Mount Stewart House, Newtownards 040586
Mount Street Gallery, Brecon 112696, 141432
Mount Vernon Hotel Museum, New York 046367
Mount Vernon Museum of Incandescent Lighting, Baltimore 041999
Mount Victoria and District Historical Museum, Mount Victoria 001293
Mount Victoria Antiques and Book Shop, Mount Victoria 056298, 137015
Mount Wachusett Community College Art Galleries, Gardner 044146
Mount Washington Museum, North Conway 046522
Mountain Art, Llanberis 113413
Mountain Bookstore, Hamilton 137641
Mountain Farm Museum, Cherokee 042792
Mountain Gateway Museum, Old Fort 046663
Mountain Heritage Center, Cullowhee 043241
Mountain Life Museum, London ... 045373
Mountain Mills Museum, Saint Catharines 006329
Mountain Peaks Antiques, Salt Lake City 092450
Mountain-Plains Museums Association, Durango 054887
Mountain Resort Museum, Chengde 007038
Mountain View Doukhobor Museum, Grand Forks 005535
Mountain View Furniture Centre, Stratford 079247
Mountain View Gallery, Highfields . 094636
Mountain View Gallery, Port Moody 006186
Mountain View Museum, Olds 006069
Mountaineering Museum, Darjeeling 022069
Mountbatten Exhibition, Romsey .. 040852
Mounted Branch Museum, East Molesey 039357
Mountfitchet Castle and Norman Village, Stansted Mountfitchet 041091
Mourad, Cairo 098652
Mourad, Samir, Kilchberg, Zürich .. 111581
Mourad-Bachmann, Samir, Zürich . 083000
Mouradian, Hélène, Paris 100711
Mouret, Gilbert, Marseille . 064378, 124429
Mourier, Vibeke, Frederiksberg 060241
Mourlot, J.L, Marseille 099677
Mourmans, Knokke-Heist 096344
Mouseio Akropoleos, Athinai 021181
Mouseio Ellinikis Laïkis Technis, Athinai 021182
Mouseio Ellinikis Paidikis Tehnis, Athinai 105405
Mouseio Ethnikon Archaiologikon, Athinai 021183
Mouseio Isrorias tis Ellinikis Endymasias, Athinai 021184
Mouseio Istorias Laografias Aharnon, Athinai 021185
Mouseio Kerameikos, Athinai 021186
Mouseio Kompologiou, Nafplion ... 021401
Mouseio Laikon Organon, Athinai .. 021187
Mouseio Mpenaki, Athinai 021188
Mouseio Trenon, Athinai 021189
Mouseio Vorre, Paiania 021414
Mouseion, Paris 066311
Mouseion Goulandri Fysikis Istorias, Kifissia 021325
Mousley Museum of Natural History, Yucaipa 049368
Moussa Castle Museum, Beiteddine 027813
Moussé, Claude, Toulouse 124988
Mousseau, Séverine, Chef-Boutonne 062266
Mousset, Daniel, Lyon 124369
Moussion, Paris 100712
Moust, J., Brugge 057783
Moustache & Trottinette, Montpellier 138222
Moutain Lodge Pottery and Art School, Newport 050348
Mouthon, Sylvain, Faverges 062842
Mouton, Michel, Lanester 063513
Mouvances, Paris 100713
Mouvements Modernes, Paris 066312
Mouysset, Francine, Rodez 067195
Mouzannar, Pierre, Beirut 077405
Moveis, Alvinus, Rio de Janeiro ... 058621
Movelanjos, Rio de Janeiro 058622
Movements in the Arts, Westport .. 136557
Movie Arts Posters, San Jose 119857
The Movie Museum, Owosso 046765
The Movie Poster Art Gallery, London 113780
Movie Shop, Norwich 086120, 141966
Movieland Wax Museum of the Stars, Niagara Falls 006014
Movilla, Leichhardt 123254
Movimiento Artistico del Rio Salado, Phoenix 054888
Moving Image Centre, Auckland ... 108346
Mowbray Gallery, Port Douglas 095087
Mowhay Gallery, Trebetherick 114597
Moxham Antiques, Bradford-on-Avon 083632
Moxiang Ge Art Cooperative, Changshu 097696
Moy, Saint-Malo (Ille-et-Vilaine) ... 121247
Moy, J., London 131116
Moy, Jakob Graf von, Salzburg 057270
Moy Antique Pine, Moy 086027
Moy Antiques, Moy 086028
Moyano, Barcelona 080888
Moyano 21, Madrid 081349
Moyard, Morges 082674
Moyon-Avenard, Nantes 099811
Moyse's Hall Museum, Bury Saint Edmunds 038925
Mozart Antiquités, Paris 066313
Mozart Figarohaus, Wien Museum, Wien 002948
Mozart-Gedenkstätte im Bezirksgericht, Sankt Gilgen 002586
Mozart Wohnhaus, Salzburg 002558
Mozarthaus, Augsburg 015615
Mozarts Geburtshaus, Salzburg ... 002559
Mozimúzeum, Kaposvár 021751
MPA Studio, Winnipeg 097595
Mpellos, Agios Dimitrios 105378
MPF Gallery, Philadelphia 118808
MPG Contemporary, Boston 115209
MPG Town Gallery, Odiongan 031751
MPLS Numisatics, Minneapolis ... 090381
MPM Dizajn, Ohrid 107420
MPP 83, Pleven 123729
MPR International Committee for Museums Marketing and PR, Malmö 054146
Mr Antiguedades, Estepona 081100
Mr. George, Luzern 082632
Mr. Lucky, San Francisco 092849
Mr. Paint Stripper, Los Angeles 132268
Mr Pickwicks Trading Company, Christchurch 079041, 140617
Mr. Yeste, Barcelona 080889, 129371
Mramornyj Dvorec, Gosudarstvennyj Russkij Muzej, Sankt-Peterburg 033770
Møre Auksjonsforretning, Tornes I Romsdal 121880
Mronz, Ute, Köln 103681
Mróz, Jerzy, Łódź 109014
Mrozek, Jerzy Emanuel, Rimsting .. 126723
Mrs Mills Antiques, Ely 084327
Mrugalla, Peter, Regensburg 073466
MRW Antiguidades, Rio de Janeiro . 058623
MS Art, Praha 098474
Ms. B Art Gallery, Oklahoma City .. 118670
MS Libros, Buenos Aires 136741
MSA Limited, Saint Louis 092283
MSC Forsyth Center Galleries, Texas A & M University, College Station 043046
M.S.M., Cagliari 075216
Msvar, Tampa 093144
MTB Coins, New York 091101
Mtengatenga Postal Museum, Namaka 027942
MTG Boutique, Sion 082813
MU - De Witte Dame, Eindhoven .. 108004
Mucciaccia, Lucio, Roma 106598
Muccioli, Detroit 116092
Much, Ado, Atlanta 087505
Much Galerie, Nantes 099812
Much Wenlock Museum, Much Wenlock 040505
Mucha, La Rochelle 063438
The Muchnic Gallery, Atchison 041830
Muci, Caracas 120434
Muciaccia, Massimo, Roma 106599
Muck, Stefan, Köln 126105
Muckenhofer, Robert, Trieben 123478
Muckenhuber, Franz, Linz 057160
Muckenthaler Cultural Center Gallery, Fullerton 044096
Muckleburgh Collection, Weybourne 041353
Muckross House Gardens and Traditional Farms, Killarney 022808
Műcsarnok, Budapest 021676
Mudac-Musée de Design et d'Arts Appliqués Contemporains, Lausanne 037242
Mudanya Mutareke Evi Müzesi, Mudanya 038152
Mudde, A.M., Haarlem 078472
MudFire Pottery Center, Atlanta ... 114907
Mudfish Pottery, Albuquerque 114807
Mudgee Colonial Inn Museum, Mudgee 001294
Mudhead, Denver 116028
Mudhead, Denver 116029
Mü-Terem, Budapest 074696, 105533, 121641
La Mueblería, Medellín 059931
Muebles Baque, Barcelona 080890
Muebles la Ganga, Fuengirola 081106
Muebles Usados el Callejón, Medellín 059932
Muebles y Ceramicas Colombia, Barranquilla 123888
Mück, Brombachtal 070062
Mück, Meerbusch 104049
Mück, Sabina Mia, Wien 095902
Mühl, Regensburg 073467
Mühl jun., Dieter, Kempten 139315
Mühlan, Adelheid & Michael, Landau in der Pfalz 139374
Mühlbauer, Franz, Rosenheim 126738
Mühlbauer, Peter, Pocking 073348
Mühlbauer, Siegfried, Regensburg . 126694
Mühlbauer, Stephan, Regensburg .. 126695
Mühlberger, Gudrun, Pichl bei Wels 123428
Mühlberger, Michael, Zapfendorf .. 074558
Mühlburger, Werner, Lienz 057150
Die Mühle, Eberswalde 016874
Mühle Laar, Zierenberg 021066
Mühle Oberneuland, Bremer Landesmuseum für Kunst-und Kulturgeschichte, Bremen 016420
Mühlen- und Landwirtschaftsmuseum, Jever 018121
Mühlen- und Landwirtschaftsmuseum, Westfehmarn 020831
Mühlenbeck, Holger, Wuppertal ... 074533
Mühlenbein-Schelkle, Berlin 125260
Mühlenberg, Burghard, Braunschweig 069990, 121356
Das Mühlendorf, Ottenhöfen 019536
Mühlenfachmuseum, Aurich 015632
Mühlenhof-Freilichtmuseum Münster, Münster 019149
Mühlenmuseum, Pfullingen 019612
Mühlenmuseum, Sontra 020254
Mühlenmuseum, Vehlefanz 020564
Mühlenmuseum, Woldegk 020949
Mühlenmuseum, Zechlin Dorf 021039
Mühlenmuseum Brüglingen, Münchenstein 037355
Mühlenmuseum Haren (Ems), Haren 017776
Mühlenmuseum Katzbrui, Apfeltrach 015560
Mühlenmuseum Mitling-Mark mit Sammlung Omas Küche, Westoverledingen 020832
Mühlerama, Museum in der Mühle Tiefenbrunnen, Zürich 037783
Mühlfeld & Stohrer, Frankfurt am Main 102802
Mühlhaus, Alena, Wiesbaden 105272
Mühlhausen, Rudolf, Salzburg 095731
Mühlich & Neumann, Berlin 125261
Mühling, Amberg, Oberpfalz 101574
Mühlschlegel, Bärbel G., Taunusstein 105035
Mühlviertler Keramikwerkstätte Hafnerhaus, Leopoldschlag 002231
Mühlviertler Kulturgütermuseum, Sankt Johann am Wimberg 002590
Mühlviertler Schlossmuseum Freistadt, Freistadt, Oberösterreich 001868
Mühlviertler Vogelkundeweg, Gutau 001993
Mühlviertler Waldhaus, Windhaag bei Freistadt 003054

Mülheimer Kunstverein e.V., Mülheim an der Ruhr 053493
Mülhens-Molderings, Barbara, Köln 126106
Müllauer, Thomas Franz, Krems . . . 057128
Müller, Aschaffenburg . . . 101602, 125067
Müller, Chemnitz 070138
Müller, Deutsch Evern 070242
Müller, Hamburg 071297
Müller, Neuss 073015
Müller, Rendsburg 104719
Müller, Reutlingen 104733
Müller, Würzburg 105339
Müller's Söhne, Alfred, Bern 082229, 129968
Müller, Alfred Otto, Köln . . 103682, 126107
Mueller, André, Kindsbach, Pfalz . . 071848
Müller, Andreas, Glashütten, Taunus 139139
Müller, Andreas, Sinn 073832, 126804
Müller, Artur, Kirchhain 071856
Müller, Bärbel, Großpösna 103023, 133991
Müller, Barbara, Chemnitz 125431
Mueller, Ceridwen, London 131117
Müller, Christian, Großpösna 133992
Müller, Christine, Leipzig 126193
Müller, Dorit, Bad Nauheim 069337
Müller, Dorothea, Xanten 139891
Müller, E., Oberkirch 073150
Müller, Elfriede, Salzwedel 073659
Müller, Eva, Grünwald 103024
Mueller, Evelyn, Biebergemünd . . . 102107
Müller, E.W., Kiel 071839
Müller's Nachf., Ferdinand Rudolf, Wien 137352
Müller, Franz Xaver, Würzburg 139873
Müller, Fritz, Landshut 121490
Müller, Gabriele, Horw 130048
Müller, Gerhard, Essen 125616
Müller, Günter, Augsburg 069238
Müller, H.-J., Heiligenhaus 103340, 134056
Müller, H.-J., Leonberg, Württemberg 072236
Müller, Hans, Olsberg 073220
Müller, Harald, Antweiler 069176
Müller, Heidrun & Bernd, Gladbeck . 071001
Müller, Helmut, Bad Mergentheim . 125108
Müller, Henry, Winterthur 141313
Müller, Herman & Frederik, Sint-Niklaas 058375
Müller, Hubertus, Zwickau 074579
Müller, Jakob, Esslingen 070662
Müller, Johannes, Bern 082230
Müller, Johannes, Salzburg 137247
Müller, Josef, Bad Tölz 138706
Müller, Karl, München 126421
Müller, Karl-Heinz, Brühl, Rheinland 125404
Müller, Karlheinz, Villmar . 074218, 121618, 126951, 139818
Müller, Karsten, Berlin . . . 069704, 138826
Müller, Klaus, Göttingen 071050
Müller, Klaus, Landau in der Pfalz . .126162, 139375
Müller, Lars, Baden 134979
Müller, M., Leipzig 072212
Müller, Manfred, Kempten 071792
Müller, Manfred, Morbach 072596
Müller, Manfred, Tengen 074055
Müller, Mark, Zürich 112152
Müller, Max, Chemnitz 138966
Müller, Meike, Ratingen 073428
Müller, Monika, Viechtach 074205
Müller, Monika & Dietmar, Velbert . 105111
Müller, Otto, Salzburg 133143
Müller, P., Dietzenbach 070251
Müller, R., Chemnitz 070139
Müller, Reinhardt, Bad Langensalza 125106
Müller, Reinhold, Mainz 072399
Müller Nachf., Robert A., Isernhagen 139285
Müller, Rudolf, Saarbrücken 073641
Müller, Sigrid & Johannes, Stuttgart 121605
Müller, Sonja, Gelnhausen 125710
Müller, Stefan, Düsseldorf 139019
Müller, Stefan, Mönchengladbach . 139482
Müller, Thomas, Kelkheim 126028
Müller, Thomas, Schaffhausen 141300
Müller, Thomas 6000 Alexanderpl 2, Berlin 125262
Mueller, Dr. Ulrich, Köln 071985
Müller, W., Bonn 069933
Müller, Walter, Neusäß 073012
Müller, Werner, Flums Hochwiese . . 111407
Müller, Werner, München 126422
Müller, Willi, Hamburg 125831
Mueller Bhavan, Max, Bangalore . . 105609
Müller-Feldmann, Annemarie, Bad Neuenahr-Ahrweiler 138701
Müller-Göbel, Anne-Sybill, Berlin . . 125263
Müller & Gräff, Stuttgart 139769
Müller & Kiepenheuer, Hanau 134033
Müller-Kögler, Klaus, Mainaschaff . 134176
Herbert Müller & Marie-Rose Müller-Rembeck, Oy-Mittelberg 104564
Müller-Pröls, Herbert, Pettstadt . . . 126622
Mueller-Roth, Dieter & Christine, Stuttgart 105001
Müller & Schindler, Stuttgart 134420
Müller-Schneevoigt, Friedrich, Neckargerach 139582
Müllertz, Birte, Charlottenlund 060218
Müllner, Helmut, Graz 123364
Mülstroh, Klaus, Heinsberg 103347, 134057
Münch, Mainz-Kastel 126268
Münch, Rainer, Gutenstetten 071154
Münchau, Melanie, Köln 126108
München Kereskedohaz, Miskolc . . 074742
Münchhausen-Erinnerungszimmer und Heimatmuseum, Bodenwerder . . . 016291
Münchhausen-Museum, Bodenwerder 016291
Münchmeyer, Hohen Neuendorf . . . 103396
Münchner Antiquitätenmarkt e.V., München 053494
Münchner Feuerwehrmuseum, München 019084
Münchner Förderkreis Indonesischer Bilderkunst, München 053495
Münchner Luft, Garching bei München 102915
Münchner Puppenmuseum, München 019085
Münchner Secession, Künstlervereinigung, Haus der Kunst, München 053496
Münchner Stadtmuseum, München 019086
Münchner Tiermuseum, München . 019087
Mündel, Ferry, Wien 095903, 133220
Mündener Kulturring e.V., Hann Münden 053497
Münger, Esther, Burgdorf 111324
Münkel & Brettschneider, Eiterfeld . 125582
Münker, Duisburg 102585
Münkwitz, Michael, Rostock 126741
Das Münster, Regensburg 135801
Münstersches Kunst- und Auktionshaus, Münster 121554
Münter-Haus, Murnau 019167
Münz Zentrum Rheinland, Solingen 073855, 121601
Münzen Revue, Regenstauf 135802
Münzen-und Medaillen-Galerie, Köln 071986
Der Münzen- und Medaillensammler, Freiburg im Breisgau 135803
Münzenetage, Stuttgart 073996
Münzenloher, Franz, Dorfen 070273, 125474
Münzensammlung, Landesmuseum Joanneum, Graz 001941
Münzer, Adolf, Basel 082159
Münzkabinett, Sankt Veit an der Glan 002628
Münzkabinett, Staatliche Kunstsammlungen Dresden, Dresden 016803
Münzkabinett, Staatliche Museen zu Berlin - Stiftung Preußischer Kulturbesitz, Berlin 016120
Münzkabinett der Preussag AG, Hannover 017763
Münzkabinett Frankfurt am Main, Frankfurt am Main 070769
Münzkabinett im Stadtarchiv Mainz, Mainz 018791
Münzkabinett und Antikensammlung der Stadt Winterthur, Winterthur 037722
Münzkabinett und Archäologische Lehrsammlung der Universität Rostock, Institut für Altertumswissenschaften, Rostock 019902
Münzmuseum, Bad Iburg 015727
Münzprägestätte - Alte Münze, Hall in Tirol 002009
Müri, Charles-Louis, Biel 111290
Müri, Matthias, Zürich 083001
Müritz-Museum, Waren 020677
Mues, Hans-D., Orsfeld 104548
Müser, Monika, Düsseldorf 070418
Müsers, Köln 103683
Müßler, Thomas, Limbach-Oberfrohna 072254
Muestra Arqueológica, Armenia . . . 007391
Muestra Arqueológica, Montenegro 007550
Muestra Arqueológica, Quimbaya . . 007594
Muestra Arqueológica Colección Rosmary, Colosó 007486
Muestrario Arqueológico de Amazonas, Chachapoyas 031486
Muestra's, Valencia 110836
Müthing, Bernhard, Billerbeck 125332
Müveszettörteneti Ertesitö, Budapest 135843
Muga, Nagoya 106926
Mugal India, Jaipur, Rajasthan 105725
Mugart, Donostia-San Sebastián . . 110342
Mugavero, Aachen 069096
Mugele, Werner, Fichtenau 125636
Muggenthaler, Margit, München . . . 072796
Mughal Art Corner, Mumbai 074824
Mughal Museum, Lahore 031383
Muğla Devlet Güzel Sanatlar Galerisi, Muğla 038153
Muğla Kültür Merkezi, Muğla 038154
Mugler, Nicole, Paris 066314
Mugnier, Yves, Paris 100714
Muguet-Lhermine, Daniele, Paris . . 124758
Muhammadi, London 141849
Muhl, Gerd, Gessertshausen 125729
Muhlack, Werner, Siegen 126800
Muhle, Felix, Leonberg, Württemberg 126215
Muhoksen Kotiseutumuseo, Muhos 009880
Muhr, Claus-Maria, Wels 057352
Mui, Hiroshima 077062
Muiderslot, Muiden 029933
Muijsers, P.R., Tilburg 108232
Muir, Patrick, Kingston 077031
Muir, Robert, Nedlands 137022
De Muizon & Le Coënt, Senlis 121260
de Muizon & Le Coënt, Chantilly . . . 120969
Muizwijk, Waddinxveen 128878
Mújica, Santiago de Chile 097631
Muka Gallery, Auckland 108347
Muka Studio, Auckland . . 108348, 134843
Mukai, Kobe 106882
Mukaishima Marine Biological Station, Mukaishima 026834
Mukashi & Mukashi, Sapporo 077198
Mukhopadhyay, K.L., Kolkata 134517
Mukhtar Museum, Giza 009332
Mukti Juddha Museum, Dhaka 003108
Mulberry, Pittsburgh 091846
Mulberry Heights Antiques, Birmingham 087774
Mulberry House, Vancouver 059390
Mulberry Phospate Museum, Mulberry 046080
Mulcahy, Dallas 115914
Mulch, Wetzlar 074382
Mulder, Frederick, London 085549, 113781, 141850
Mulet, Jean-François, Hyères 063196
Mulet, Pilar, Madrid 110581
Mulford House and Farm, East Hampton 043569
Mulgara Gallery, Yulara 095459
Mulgi Külamuuseum, Halliste 009360
Mulgrave Art Gallery, Mulgrave . . . 094919
Mulgrave Settlers Museum, Gordonvale 001072
Mulherin, Katharine, Toronto 097334
Mulholland, Susan, Tucson 120151
Mulier & Mulier, Knokke-Heist 096345
Mulitze, Traute, Linden, Hessen . . . 072270
Mull, Seema, Frankfurt am Main . . 133950
Mull Art Gallery, Frankfurt am Main 102803
Mull Museum, Tobermory 041226
Mulla, Berlin 069705, 121337
Mullach Ban Folk Museum, Mullach Ban 040506
Mullan Gallery, Belfast 112616
Mullen, Robin, Guildford 113169
Mullenders, Georges, Liège 058319
Mullendorff, Antwerpen 057718
Muller, Almelo 077730
Muller, Forbach 062915
Muller, Claude, Esch-sur-Alzette . . 128468
Muller, Frederik, Bergum 140361
Muller, Jean-François, Appoigny . . 060938
Muller, Jean-François, Appoigny . . 060939
Muller, Nicolas, Nice 065118
Muller, Roland, Strasbourg 068327
Muller, Rudolph H., El Paso 088808
Muller von Rohrbach, Jean, Lausanne 130074
Mulligan, Richard, West Hollywood . 093488
Mullingar Military Museum, Mullingar 022842
Mullion Gallery, Mullion 114100
Mullis, Robert, Swindon 131569
Mullvaden, Stockholm 141168
Mulorz, Schwerte 073775
Mulot, Saint-Gilles-Croix-de-Vie . . . 101158
Mulsant, Yves, Brie-Comte-Robert . 061794
Multatuli Museum, Amsterdam . . . 029202
Multi Art International, Bonn 069934
Multi Colour Museum, Middelburg . 029922
Multi-druck Verlag, Neusäß 134307
Multi Dutch, Amsterdam 077919
Multi Studio, Brasília 096499
Multian Kotiseutumuseo, Multia . . . 009881
Multiart, Verona 128431
Multicollection, Angers 060860
Multicolor, Madrid 081350, 141056
Multicultural Arts, Ottawa 097112
Multicultural Heritage Centre, Stony Plain 006514
Multigestion Puerto Mont, Getxo . . 110354
Multigestion Puerto Mont, Hondarribia 110386
Multigraphic, Venezia 106770
Multimarcos, Santiago de Chile . . . 059543
Multimedia Arte Contemporanea, Brescia 106002
Multipel 13, Knokke-Heist 096346
Multipla de Arte, São Paulo 096681
Multiple Art, Hamburg 103196
Multiple Box, Waterloo 095378
Multiple Box Hamburg, Hamburg . . 103197
Multiple Choice, Amsterdam 107774
Multiple Design, Huizen . . 108089, 134817
Multiple Impressions, New York . . . 118218
Multiplicidad, Madrid 110582
Multnomah, Portland 091978
Mulvane Art Museum, Topeka 048582
Mulzer, Georg, Lautrach . . 072173, 126178
Mummery, Andrew, London 113782
Munakata Prints Museum, Kamakura 026613
Munakata Shiko Kinenkan, Aomori . 026416
Munakata Taisha Shinpōkan, Genkai 026472
Munari, René, Grenoble 138101
Muncaster Castle, Ravenglass 040797
Muncaster Watermill, Ravenglass . . 040798
Munce Art Center, Zionsville 049377
Munch-museet, Oslo 031086
Munchs Hus, Åsgårdstrand 030742
Muncie Children's Museum, Muncie 046085
Mundaring Arts Centre, Mundaring . 094921
Munden, Norfolk 132560

The Mundesley Gallery, Mundesley 114102
Mundo Antiguo, Montevideo 087333
El Mundo de Carmen, Caracas 093540
El Mundo de la Ceramica, Baranquilla 123887
El Mundo de la Moneda, México . . .077580, 121767
O Mundo do Livro, Lisboa . 109336, 140846
El Mundode Muñecas, Icod de los Vinos 035291
Mundt, Henry A.W., Chicago 131909
Mundt, Thomas, Fürth, Bayern 125688
Mundubbera and District Historical Museum, Mundubbera 001298
Mundulla National Trust Museum, Bordertown 000817
Mundy, C.W., Indianapolis 116480
Mundy, Ewan, Glasgow 084466
Mundy, Ewan, Glasgow 113123
Mundy, Ewan, Glasgow 130729
Muné, Mercédès, Saint-Quentin (Aisne) 121252
Muñeca, Barniz de, Alcalá de Henares 080753, 129298
Muñecas, Madrid 122065
Munganbana Aboriginal Art Gallery, Cairns 094351
Municipal Art Gallery, Thessaloniki . 021497
Municipal Art Gallery of Xanthi, Xanthi 021529
Municipal Art Society, New York . . . 046368
Municipal Art Society of New York, New York 054889
Municipal d'Arts Plastiques, La Menuiserie, Choisy-le-Roi 011370
Municipal Gallery of Athens, Athinai 021190
Municipal Gallery of Corfu, Corfu . . 021241
Municipal Gallery of Herakleion, Iráklion 021287
Municipal Gallery of Lamia, Lamia . 021350
Municipal Gallery of Livadia, Livadia 021363
Municipal Gallery of Piraeus, Piraeus 021432
Municipal Gallery of Rhodes, Rhodos 021453
Municipal Gallery of Samos, Samos 021458
Municipal Gallery of Volos, Volos . . 021523
Municipal Museum, Alexandria . . . 009279
Municipal Museum, Baoji 006959
Municipal Museum, Dimona 022903
Municipal Museum, Jiuquan 007162
Municipal Museum Gwalior, Gwalior 022143
Municipal Museum of Kavala, Kavala 021322
Municipality Museum, Hebron 031412
Municipalnaja Chudožestvennaja Galereja g. Kostromy, Kostroma 033288
Municipalnyj Objedinennyj Muzej Pisatelej Urala, Ekaterinburg 033116
Municipialnyj Muzej Anna Achmatova - Serebrjannyj vek, Sankt-Peterburg 033771
Municypal'nyj Muzej Pryvatnych Kollekcij im. O. Bleščunova, Odesa 038368
Munk, Werner, Günzburg 103029
Munkácsy Mihály Múzeum, Békéscsaba 021629
Munkeborg, Nacka 081885
Munkinseudun Galleria, Helsinki . . 098740
Munkkiniemen Antiikkipuuseppä, Helsinki 060558
Munnuisten Museo, Mynämäki 009892
Muñoz, Jose, Estepona 081101
Muñoz Antiguedades, Málaga 081427
Muñoz Jimenez, Alfredo, Estella . . . 122025
Muñoz Turégano, Valencia 081667
Munro, Vera, Hamburg 103198
Munroe, Victoria, Boston 115210
Munro's Mill Antique Centre, Tamworth 056693
Munsala Hembygdsmuseum, Munsala 009884
Munsin Museum, Masan 027530
Munson-Williams-Proctor Arts Institute Museum of Art, Utica 048719
Munson-Williams-Proctor Institute. Bulletin, Utica 136558
Munster Literature Centre, Cork . . . 022721
Munt- en Penningkabinet van de Provincie Limburg, Tongeren 003799
Munt- en Penningkabinet van de Spaar- en Voorschotbank, Surhuisterveen . . 030189
Muntadas Pascual, Maria Isabel, Barcelona 129372
Munteanu, Marcela, Frankfurt am Main 125657
Munting Museo Ng Namayan, Mandaluyong 031709
De Muntkoerier, Apeldoorn 136003
Muntwisselkantoor, Apeldoorn 078038
Munves, Barbara R., New York 091102
Munz, Ottweiler 104563
Munzi, Gabriella, Roma 076580
Muonion Kotiseutumuseo, Muonio . 009885
Le Mur Vivant, London 113783
Mura Clay Gallery, Newtown, New South Wales 094958
Mura-Todesco, Béatrice, Dijon 062669
Murad, Mohammed Isam, Damascus 083067
Murakami Folk Museum, Murakami 026836
Murakami Hojido, Tokyo 077284
Muraki, Ebetsu 077037
Mural da História, Lisboa 129161
Muramooto, Akiko, Hong Kong 059675
Murari, Max, Villeneuve-sur-Lot . . . 068921
Murarka's Art Gallery, Kolkata 105742
Murat, Pamplona 081524
Murat-David, Philippe, Paris 066315
Murata & Friends, Berlin 101986
Murauchi Art Museum, Hachioji . . . 026481
Al-Murbati, Manama 057639
Murch, Jill, Moonta 094878
Murchison Falls National Park Museum, Murchison Falls 038223
Murchison Museum, Murchison . . . 030544
Murchison Settlement Museum, Mullewa 001296
Murdaca, Natale, Milano 127638
Murder by the Book, Cranston 142358
Murder by the Book, Denver 142393
Murder by the Book, Houston 142443
Murder by the Book, Portland 142804
Murder Ink, New York 142677
Murdocca, Vincenzo, Roma 128127
Murdoch & Barclay, Moorabbin . . . 123269
Murdoch & Barclay, South Yarra . . . 123308
Murdoch McLennan, Auckland 078965
Muré, Robert, Toulouse . . 068530, 124989
Mureau, Dreux 124228
Murer, Milano 075777
Murgtäler Dorfmuseum, Forbach . . 017136
Murgtal-Museum, Forbach 017136
Murias Numismatica, A Coruña . . . 081062
Murie Museum, Kelly 044949
Muriel, Boris, West Hollywood 120402
Murilla Shire Art Gallery, Miles 001264
Murillo, Edmonton 123763
Murillo, Lisboa 109337
Murmanskij Oblastnoj Chudožestvennyj Muzej, Murmansk 033534
Murmanskij Oblastnoj Kraevedčeskij Muzej, Murmansk 033535
Les Murmures du Temps, Crémieu . 062558
Murney Tower Museum, Kingston . . 005704
Muroran-shi Seishonen Kagakukan, Muroran 026837
Muros Vivos, Bucaramanga 098222
Murphy, Los Angeles 132269
Murphy, Jan, Fortitude Valley 094560
Murphy, Jennifer, Charlotte 115300
Murphy, Michael, Tampa 120059
Murphy, Roger, Kingston 056058
Murphy's Loft, Cleveland 115729
Murr, Gabriele, Bamberg 069460
Murr, Gertrud & Roland, Bamberg . . 138717
Murr, Renate, Esslingen 139062
Murray, David, New York 091103
Murray, Graeme, Edinburgh 135143
Murray, Guy, New York 118219
Murray, John, London 135237
Murray, Kevin, Armadale, Victoria . . 055388
Murray, Mark, New York 118220
Murray Hill Art, Cleveland 115730
Murray & Kennett, Horsham 141680
Murray-Lindsay Mansion, Lindsay . 045325
Murray's Motorcycle Museum, Laxey 039941
Murray's Museum of History, Neepawa 005988
Murrell Home, Park Hill 046821
Murrell Home, Tahlequah 048473
Murrer, Werner, München 126423
Murrumburrah-Harden Historical Museum, Murrumburrah 001300
Murrurundi Museum, Murrurundi . . 001301
Mursia, Ugo, Milano 134624
Murston House, Geelong 094580
Murtada, Abdul Khaliq Najwani, Muttrah 079517
Murtaugh, Delgany 074885
Murtoa Water Tower - Concordia Collage Museum, Murtoa 001302
Murtovaaran Talomuseo, Valtimo . . 010217
Murtuz, Moskva 109570
Musa, Milano 075778
Musa, Milano 075779
Musa, Laura, Roma 128128
La Musa Antichità, Lugano 082603
Musa Fine Art, Newcastle-upon-Tyne 114126
Músaem Cathrach Na Gaillimhe, Galway 022791
Músaem Corca Dhuibhne, Corca Dhuibhne Regional Museum, Ballyferriter . . 022687
Musafir-Khana, Cairo 009307
Musardière, Renescure 067093
Musashimurayama City Rekishi Minzoku Shiryo-kan, Musashimurayama . . 026838
Musashino Bijutsu Daigaku, Tokyo . 050489
Musashino Museum, Kodaira 026676
Al-Musbahi, Jeddah 080363
Muscarelle Museum of Art, Williamsburg 049183
Muscariello, Mario, Napoli 076013
Muscariello, Pasquale, Napoli 127783
Muscariello, Vincenzo, Napoli 076014
Muscat Gate Museum, Muscat 031347
Muscatine Art Center, Muscatine . . 046103
Muschel- und Schneckenmuseum, Norden 019325
Muschelkalkmuseum Hagdorn, Ingelfingen 018063
Muschi & Licheni, Trieste 076900
Muschter, A., Berlin 069706
Musci, Antonio, Roma 128129
Le Muse, Milano 075780
Muse Art Gallery, Philadelphia 046962
Muse Gallery, Philadelphia 118809
The Muse Galley, Milawa 094845
Muse Studio, Point Lonsdale 095073
Muse X Editions, Los Angeles 135384
Museactron, Maaseik 003619
Muséal Adolphe Pégoud, Montferrat 013161
Museam na Oileran, Aran Islands . . 022677
Musée, Châteaurenard 011297
Musée, Cransac 011525
Musée, Cruzy 011544
Musée, Kampong Thom 004968
Musée, Le Landeron 037229
Musée, Laragne-Montéglin 012424
Musée, Moyen 013287
Musée, Orainville 013495
Musée, Quiberon 013971
Musée, Tauriers 014915
Musée, Champagne J.M. Gobillard, Hautvillers 012084
Musée, Société des Amis du Musée, Ville-d'Avray 015234
Musée 1900, Arpaillargues-et-Aureillac 010479
Musée 1900, Cauterets 011161
Musée 2ème Guerre Mondiale, Ambleteuse 010352
Musée 39-45, Roscoff 014110
Musée 40-44, Monceau-Imbrechies 003648
Musée à Flot, Bordeaux 010879
Musée à Flot de l'Escorteur d'Escadre, Musée Naval Maillé Brézé, Nantes 013333
Musée à Flot du Galion, Plouharnel 013858
Musée à la Ferme de Rome, Bézu-la-Forêt 010793
Musée à la Mémoire des Combattants et de Victimes de Guerre, Mâcon 012838
Musée a la Recherche du Temps Perdu, Bricquebec 010997
Musée A la Rencontre des Vieux Métiers, Bouray-sur-Juine 010914
Musée Abbaye d'Airvault, Airvault . 010288
Musée-Abbaye de Charroux, Charroux 011262
Musée-Abbaye Saint-Germain, Auxerre 010572
Musée Abbé Deletoille, Fondation Boudenoot, Fruges 011905
Musée Abbé Jules Lemire, Vieux-Berquin 015216
Le Musée Acadien, Caraquet 005218
Musée Acadien, Cheticamp 005264
Musée Acadien, Gloucester 005516
Musée Acadien, Prince Edward Island Museum and Heritage Foundation, Miscouche 005884
Musée Acadien, Université de Moncton, Moncton 005900
Musée Acadien de Pubnico-Ouest, West Pubnico 006792
Musée Acadien du Québec, Bonaventure 005112
Musée Accous-Fermiers Basco-Béarnais, Accous 010267
Musée Adam Mickiewicz, Paris . . . 013610
Musée Adolphe Hardy, Dison 003410
Musée Adrien Mentienne, Bry-sur-Marne 011025
Musée Adzak, Paris 013611
Musée Aéronautique, La Baule-Escoublac 012204
Musée Aérorétro, Albon 010322
Musée Africain, Ile-d'Aix 012122
Musée Africain, Lyon 012808
Musée Africain de Namur, Namur . . 003661
Musée Agathois, Agde 010268
Musée Agricole, Coffrane 037024
Musée Agricole, Villy-le-Maréchal . 015307
Musée Agricole Bras de Brosne, Marles-sur-Canche 012910
Musée Agricole de Brullioles ou la Cadole, Brullioles 011018
Musée Agricole de la Haute Hesbaye, Liernu 003606
Musée Agricole Départemental Marcel-Mouilleseaux, Botans 010900
Musée Agricole des Ruralies, Prahecq 013942
Musée Agricole du Château de Didonne, Semussac 014755
Musée Agricole du Parlement, Gap . 011917
Musée Agricole du Verdus, Freyssenet 011900
Musée Agricole-Ferme des Aïeux, Plélo 013836
Musée Agricole Paysan, Vallon-Pont-d'Arc 015111
Musée Agricole Vivant, Bissey-la-Pierre 010816
Musée Agro-Pastoral d'Aussois, Aussois 010556
Musée Airborne, Sainte-Mère-Eglise 014612
Musée Al Mathaf El Lubnani, Musée du Liban Féodal, Beiteddine 027814
Musée Alain-Fournier et Jacques-Rivière, La Chapelle-d'Angillon 012223
Musée Albert André, Bagnols-sur-Cèze 010626
Musée Albert Schweitzer, Gunsbach Village 012059
Musée Albert Schweitzer, Kaysersberg 012190
Musée Alésia, Alise-Sainte-Reine . . 010335

Musée Alexandre Dumas, Villers-Cotterêts . . . 015289
Musée Alexandre-Louis Martin, Carnières . . . 003362
Musée Alexis Forel, Morges . . . 037340
Musée Alfred Bonnot, Chelles . . . 011341
Musée Alfred de Vigny, Champagne-Vigny . . . 011223
Musée Alice Taverne, Ambierle . . . 010351
Musée Alphonse Daudet, Beaucaire 010695
Musée Alphonse Daudet, Fontvieille 011864
Musée Alphonse Daudet, Saint-Alban-Auriolles . . . 014170
Musée Alpin, Chamonix-Mont-Blanc . . . 011219
Musée Alpin d'Anzère, Musée des Bisses, Anzère . . . 036844
Musée Alsacien, Haguenau . . . 012063
Musée Alsacien, Strasbourg . . . 014863
Musée America-Gold Beach, Ver-sur-Mer . . . 015169
Musée Amora, Musée de la Moutarde Amora, Dijon . . . 011601
Musée Amphoralis, Musée des Potiers Gallo-Romains, Sallèles-d'Aude . . 014640
Musée Anatole Le-Braz, Saint-Brieuc . . . 014206
Musée André Abbal, Carbonne . . . 011109
Musée André Dunoyer-de-Ségonzac, Boussy-Saint-Antoine . . . 010950
Musée André-Marie Ampère, Musée de l'Électricité, Poleymieux-au-Mont-d'Or . . . 013869
Musée Angladon, Avignon . . . 010590
Musée Animalier, Cheraute . . . 011349
Musée Animalier, Ville-sous-Anjou . 015236
Musée Animé des Arts et Traditions Populaires, Serralongue . . . 014771
Musée-Animé du Jouet et des Petits Trains, Colmar . . . 011429
Musée Animé du Tissage, Arles-sur-Tech . . . 010474
Musée Animé du Vin et de la Tonnellerie, Chinon . . . 011364
Musée Anne de Beaujeu, Moulins (Allier) . . . 013268
Musée Annexe de Youkounkoun, Youkounkoun . . . 021597
Musée Antoine Brun, Sainte-Consorce . . . 014589
Musée Antoine Lécuyer, Saint-Quentin (Aisne) . . . 014501
Musée Antoine Vivenel, Compiègne 011448
Musée Antoine Wiertz, Musées Royaux des Beaux-Arts de Belgique, Bruxelles 003306
Musée Août 1944, La Bataille de la Poche de Falaise, Falaise . . . 011780
Musée Apicole, Nedde . . . 013361
Musée Apicole, Le Monde Merveilleux des Abeilles, Le Mesnil-sous-Jumièges . . . 012527
Musée-Aquariophile, Dunkerque . . 011665
Musée Aquarium, Bergerac . . . 010755
Musée-Aquarium du Laboratoire Arago, Banyuls-sur-Mer . . . 010643
Musée-Aquarium Marin du Roc, Granville . . . 011989
Musée Archéologique, Aigues-Mortes . . . 010278
Musée Archéologique, Andilly-en-Bassigny . . . 010382
Musée Archéologique, Antibes-Juan-les-Pins . . . 010424
Musée Archéologique, Auzances . . 010578
Musée Archéologique, Bagnols-en-Forêt . . . 010625
Musée Archéologique, Banassac . . 010636
Musée Archéologique, Bezouce . . . 010792
Musée Archéologique, Bray-sur-Seine . . . 010970
Musée Archéologique, Brignon . . . 011004
Musée Archéologique, Brumath . . . 011020
Musée Archéologique, Champagnole . . . 011225
Musée Archéologique, Charleroi . . . 003365
Musée Archéologique, Châteaurenard (Loiret) . . . 011300
Musée Archéologique, Châtelais . . . 011305
Musée Archéologique, Chirac . . . 011367
Musée Archéologique, Corseul . . . 011490
Musée Archéologique, Couffy . . . 011498
Musée Archéologique, Cutry . . . 011556
Musée Archéologique, Delme . . . 011570
Musée Archéologique, Dijon . . . 011602
Musée Archéologique, Ensisheim . . 011693
Musée Archéologique, Entrains-sur-Nohain . . . 011696
Musée Archéologique, Escolives-Sainte-Camille . . . 011726
Musée Archéologique, Fontaine-Française . . . 011844
Musée Archéologique, Gafsa . . . 037954
Musée Archéologique, Gouzeaucourt . . . 011976
Musée Archéologique, Jonzac . . . 012166
Musée Archéologique, Jujurieux . . . 012181
Musée Archéologique, Kassba . . . 029022
Musée Archéologique, La Villeneuve-au-Châtelot . . . 012351
Musée Archeologique, L'Aigle . . . 012382
Musée Archéologique, Laissac . . . 012386
Musée Archéologique, Larache . . . 029023
Musée Archéologique, Le Thoureil . 012567
Musée Archéologique, Lectoure . . . 012585
Musée Archéologique, Loupiac . . . 012764
Musée Archéologique, Magalas . . . 012842
Musée Archéologique, Magnac-Laval . . . 012843
Musée Archéologique, Martizay . . . 012964
Musée Archéologique, Marvejols . . 012966
Musée Archéologique, Monségur . . 013105
Musée Archéologique, Montbard . . 013133
Musée Archéologique, Montseret . . 013232
Musée Archéologique, Mormoiron . 013245
Musée Archéologique, Murol . . . 013305
Musée Archéologique, Nages-et-Solorgues . . . 013316
Musée Archéologique, Namur . . . 003662
Musée Archéologique, Nîmes . . . 013421
Musée Archéologique, Palaja . . . 013538
Musée Archéologique, Panossas . . 013544
Musée Archéologique, Petit-Bersac 013801
Musée Archéologique, Peyriac-de-Mer . . . 013803
Musée Archéologique, Pithiviers-le-Vieil . . . 013824
Musée Archéologique, Pons . . . 013878
Musée Archéologique, Prades . . . 013937
Musée Archéologique, Prunoy . . . 013961
Musée Archéologique, Quarante . . . 013969
Musée Archéologique, Rabat . . . 029030
Musée Archéologique, Saint-Bonnet-de-Joux . . . 014200
Musée Archéologique, Saint-Gilles-du-Gard . . . 014320
Musée Archéologique, Saint-Macaire . . . 014401
Musée Archéologique, Saint-Martin-de-Bromes . . . 014416
Musée Archéologique, Saint-Pal-de-Mons . . . 014462
Musée Archéologique, Saint-Paulien . . . 014475
Musée Archéologique, Sainte-Agnès . . . 014580
Musée Archéologique, Saverne . . . 014715
Musée Archéologique, Simiane-Collongue . . . 014801
Musée Archéologique, Sollières-Sardières . . . 014816
Musée Archéologique, Soulosse-sous-Saint-Élophe . . . 014842
Musée Archéologique, Soyons . . . 014846
Musée Archéologique, Strasbourg . 014864
Musée Archéologique, Suippes . . . 014885
Musée Archéologique, Tarare . . . 014900
Musée Archéologique, Tétouan . . . 029040
Musée Archéologique, Therouanne . 014926
Musée Archéologique, Vachères . . . 015083
Musée Archéologique, Vaison-la-Romaine . . . 015088
Musée Archéologique, Vienne-en-Val . . . 015213
Musée Archéologique, Villemagne-l'Argentière . . . 015260
Musée Archéologique, Villeneuve-d'Ascq . . . 015263
Musée Archeologique, Grottes d'Azé, Azé . . . 010613
Musée Archéologique, Le Trésor d'Eauze, Eauze . . . 011675
Musée Archéologique, Musée de la Boulangerie, Blaye . . . 010835
Musée Archéologique, Musée de Saint-Bazeille, Sainte-Bazeille . . . 014585
Musée Archéologique, Musées Municipaux, Saintes . . . 014620
Musée Archéologique Armand Viré, Luzech . . . 012803
Musée Archéologique Blasimon, Musée Municipal de Blasimon, Blasimon 010833
Musée Archéologique d'Argentomagus, Saint-Marcel (Indre) . . . 014412
Musée Archéologique de Djemila, Sétif . . . 000070
Musée Archéologique de la Basse-Meuse, Oupeye . . . 003698
Musée Archéologique de la Porte du Croux, Nevers . . . 013388
Musée Archéologique de la Région de Breteuil, Breteuil . . . 010988
Musée Archéologique de l'Institut Catholique, Toulouse . . . 014985
Musée Archéologique de l'Université Americaine, Beirut . . . 027808
Musée Archéologique de Makthar, Makthar . . . 037963
Musée Archéologique de Rom-Sainte-Soline, Rom . . . 014090
Musée Archéologique de Sfax, Sfax 037972
Musée Archéologique de Site, Liffol-le-Grand . . . 012668
Musée Archéologique de Thésée-la-Romaine, Thésée-la-Romaine . . . 014927
Musée Archéologique de Touraine, Tours . . . 015015
Musée Archéologique de Viuz-Faverges, Faverges . . . 011786
Musée Archéologique Départemental, Jublains . . . 012178
Musée Archéologique Départemental, Saint-Bertrand-de-Comminges . . . 014199
Musée Archéologique Départemental du Val-d'Oise, Guiry-en-Vexin . . . 012054
Musée Archeologique du Cap Bon, Nabeul . . . 037969
Musée Archéologique du Château Féodal, Bressieux . . . 010977
Musée Archéologique du Gâtinais, Montargis . . . 013125
Musée Archéologique du Minervois, Olonzac . . . 013489
Musée Archéologique du Théâtre de Guelma, Guelma . . . 000065
Musée Archéologique d'Uxellodunun, Vayrac . . . 015148
Musée Archéologique - Eglise Saint-Laurent, Grenoble . . . 012019
Musée Archéologique et d'Art Populaire, Saint-Goussaud . . . 014324
Musée Archéologique et de Paléontologie, Minerve . . . 013067
Musée Archéologique et d'Histoire Locale, Saint-Prix . . . 014499
Musée Archéologique et Historique, Clichy . . . 011407
Musée Archéologique et Historique, Loupian . . . 012766
Musée Archéologique et Historique, Proupiary . . . 013955
Musée Archéologique et Historique Cantonal de Gimont, Gimont . . . 011949
Musée Archéologique et Historique de la Vigne, Lieu-dit Kitterlé, Guebwiller 012040
Musée Archéologique et Historique du Comte de Logne, Vieuxville . . . 003830
Musée Archéologique et Historique Municipal, Bibliothèque André Malraux, Ermont . . . 011719
Musée Archéologique et Lapidaire, Aix-les-Bains . . . 010300
Musée Archéologique et Lapidaire, Blois . . . 010845
Musée Archéologique et Missionnaire, Saxon-Sion . . . 014730
Musée Archéologique Gallo-Romain, Jonvelle . . . 012163
Musée Archéologique Gallo-Romain, Revel-Tourdan . . . 014036
Musée Archéologique Henri Prades, Lattes . . . 012436
Musée Archéologique - Hôtel de Sade, Saint-Rémy-de-Provence . . . 014516
Musée Archéologique Hôtel Dieu, Cavaillon . . . 011163
Musée Archéologique Jean Régnier, Mont-Saint-Vincent . . . 013115
Musée Archéologique Le Cloitre, Elne . . . 011688
Musée Archéologique Léon Alègre, Bagnols-sur-Cèze . . . 010627
Musée Archéologique Ludna, Saint-Georges-de-Reneins . . . 014301
Musée Archéologique Mariste de Puylata, Lyon . . . 012809
Musée Archéologique Municipal, Pelissanne . . . 013762
Musée Archéologique Municipal de Fréjus, Fréjus . . . 011889
Musée Archéologique Parat, Arcy-sur-Cure . . . 010455
Musée Archéologique Régional d'Orp-le-Grand, Orp-le-Grand . . . 003692
Musée Archeologique René Galloux, Musées du Donjon, Montrichard . . . 013226
Musée Archéologique Géologique et Ethnologique des Vans, Les Vans . 012643
Musée Archipélitude, Saint-Pierre . 034105
Musée-Archives de Saint-Pierre, Saint-Pierre . . . 034106
Musée Ardeche d'Autrefois, Thueyts . . . 014950
Musée Ardoisien, Saint-Julien-Mont-Denis . . . 014371
Musée Ariana, Musée Suisse de la Céramique et du Verre, Genève . . 037125
Musée Aristide-Maillol, Banyuls-sur-Mer . . . 010644
Musée Armand Charnay, Charlieu . . 011252
Musée Arménien de France, Nourhan Fringhian Foundation, Paris . . . 013612
Musée Arouane, Wendake . . . 006789
Musée Art du Chocolat, Lisle-sur-Tarn . . . 012711
Musée Art et Culture, Lescar . . . 012645
Musée Art et Histoire, Penne-d'Agenais . . . 013769
Musée Art Paysan, Villeneuve-de-Berg . . . 015271
Musée Arteum, Châteauneuf-le-Rouge . . . 011291
Musée Arthur Batut, Labruguiere . . 012367
Musée Arthur Bonnet, Saint-Jean-d'Angély . . . 014339
Musée Arthur Le-Duc, Musée du Château, Torigni-sur-Vire . . . 014965
Musée Arthur Rimbaud, Charleville-Mézières . . . 011249
Musée Artisanal Animé, Les Loges-Marchis . . . 012625
Musée Artisanal et Rural d'Arts, Ars 010489
Musée Arts d'Afrique et d'Asie, Vichy . . . 015204
Musée Arts et Histoire, Bormes-les-Mimosas . . . 010897
Musée-Atelier Calixa-Lavellée, Calixa-Lavallée . . . 005202
Musée Atelier d'Automates, Lusigny-sur-Barse . . . 012795
Musée-Atelier de la Cristallerie des Papes, Fontaine-de-Vaucluse . . . 011838
Musée-Atelier de Poterie, Neuvic-sur-l'Isle . . . 013379
Musée-Atelier de Poupées Francépoque, Nances-Lac d'Aiguebelette . . . 013318
Musée-Atelier du Cuivre, Villedieu-les-Poêles . . . 015243
Musée-Atelier du Cuivre et de l'Argent, Paris . . . 013613

Musée-Atelier Werner Lichtner-Aix, Sérignan-du-Comtat 014767
Musée Atger, Montpellier 013200
Musée Athois, Ath 003204
Musée Au fil du papier, Musée Municipal de Pont-à-Mousson, Pont-à-Mousson 013879
Musée Au Filament Rouge, Perrefitte 037410
Musée Aubois d'Histoire de l'Éducation, Troyes 015050
Musée Auguste Rodin, Paris 013614
Musée Augustin-Bernard, Bourbon-l'Archambault 010919
Musée Auto Moto Vélo, Châtellerault 011306
Musée Auto-Retro, Trooz 003816
Musée Automobile, Genève 037126
Musée Automobile, La Clayette 012237
Musée Automobile, Saint-Germain-Laval 014311
Musée Automobile, Saint-Jacques 006344
Musée Automobile Bellenavois, Bellenaves 010742
Musée Automobile de la Sarthe, Le Mans 012517
Musée Automobile des Voitures des Chefs d'Etat, Sauvigny-Le-Bois 014713
Musée Automobile Espera Sbarro, Pontarlier 013900
Musée aux Dominicaines, Espace Culturel des Dominicaines, Pont-l'Évêque 013893
Musée Baccarat, Baccarat 010615
Musée Baccarat, Paris 013615
Musée Baillet-Latour, Latour 003572
Musée Bajén-Vega, Monesties 013094
Musée Balzac, Saché 014160
Musée Bamilike, Dschang 004975
Musée Barbey d'Aurévilly, Saint-Sauveur-le-Vicomte 014536
Musée Barbier-Mueller, Genève 037127
Musée Baron Gérard, Bayeux 010679
Musée Baron Martin, Gray 012013
Musée Baroncelli, Saintes-Maries-de-la-Mer 014626
Musée Barrois, Bar-le-Duc 010646
Musée Barthélemy-Thimonnier de la Machine à Coudre et du Cycle, Amplepuis 010375
Musée Bartholdi, Colmar 011430
Musée-Base V 3 de Mimoyecques, Landrethun-le-Nord 012402
Musée Basque et de l'Histoire de Bayonne, Bayonne 010685
Musée Bastien Lepage, Montmédy 013186
Musée Bastion Saint-André, Antibes-Juan-les-Pins 010425
Musée Baud, L'Auberson 036860
Musée Baudy, Giverny 011954
Musée Bayard et de la Chevalerie, Pontcharra 013904
Musée Béarnais, Pau 013747
Musée Beauceron du Grand Breau, Tivernon 014962
Musée Beaulne, Coaticook 005280
Musée Benoist, Le Gavre 012498
Musée Benoît de Puydt, Bailleul 010630
Musée Benoît XIII, Châteaurenard 011298
Musée Bernadette, Lourdes 012767
Musée Bernadotte, Pau 013748
Musée Bernard Buffet, Paris 013616
Musée Bernard Buffet, Shizuoka 027080
Musée Bernard d'Agesci, Niort 013427
Musée Bernard Palissy, Lacapelle-Biron 012368
Musée Bert Flint, Agadir 029017
Musée Bert Flint, Marrakech 029024
Musée-Bibliothèque A.-Albert, Briançon 010992
Musée-Bibliothèque de l'Histoire du Protestantisme, Musée du Pasteur, Joigny (Yonne) 012160
Musée-Bibliothèque François Pétrarque, Fontaine-de-Vaucluse 011839
Musée-Bibliothèque Humaniste, Sélestat 014749
Musée-Bibliothèque Pierre-André Benoît, Alès 010331
Musée Bigouden, Pont-l'Abbé 013891
Musée Bigourdan du Vieux Moulin, Bagnères-de-Bigorre 010620
Musée Bijoux de Braque, Saint-Dié-des-Vosges 014258
Musée Biochet-Brechot, Caudebec-en-Caux 011154
Musée Boleslaw Biegas, Paris 013617
Musée Bon-Pasteur, Québec 006221
Musée Bonaparte, Auxonne 010576
Musée Bonaventure Fieullien, Regniowez 014001
Musée Bonnat, Bayonne 010686
Musée Bonnevallais, Bonneval 010869
Musée Bossuet, Meaux 012995
Musée Botanique, Conakry 021590
Musée Botanique de Wakombo, M'Baiki 006900
Musée Bouchard, Paris 013618
Musée Boucher-de-Perthes, Abbeville 010263
Musée Bouilhet-Christofle, Paris 013619
Musée Bourbonnais, Moulins (Allier) 013269
Musée Bourbonnais de Vesse à Bellerive, Bellerive-sur-Allier 010743
Musée Bourdelle, Paris 013620
Musée Bourgeon-Jallieu, Bourgoin-Jallieu 010943
Musée Bourguignon Perrin de Puycousin, Tournus 015010
Musée Bres Marcel, Saint-Léger-près-Troyes 014386
Musée Breton, Quimper 013973
Musée Briard et de la Crypte Mérovingienne, Jouarre 012169
Musée Bruno Danvin, Saint-Pol-sur-Ternoise 014489
Musée Bruxellois de la Gueuze, Bruxelles 003307
Musée Bruxellois de l'Industrie et du Travail, Bruxelles 003308
Musée Buffon, Montbard 013134
Musée-Cabinet Lafaille, La Rochelle 012316
Musée Cadou, Louisfert 012763
Musée Calbet, Grisolles 012038
Musée Calvet, Avignon 010591
Musée Calvin, Noyon 013459
Musée Camarguais, Arles 010470
Musée Camille Lemonnier, Bruxelles 003309
Musée Campagnard Agricole, Fillières 011815
Musée Campagnard du Haut-Beaujolais, Saint-Christophe-la-Montagne 014225
Musée Campanaire, L'Isle-Jourdain 012708
Musée Campanaire Bollée, Saint-Jean-de-Braye 014343
Musée Campredon, Maison René Char, L'Isle-sur-la-Sorgue 012709
Musée Canadien de la Poste, Gatineau 005503
Musée Canadien des Civilisations, Gatineau 005504
Musée Cantini, Marseille 012934
Musée Cantonal d'Archéologie, Musées Cantonaux du Valais, Sion 037563
Musée Cantonal d'Archéologie et d'Histoire, Lausanne 037243
Musée Cantonal de Géologie, Lausanne 037244
Musée Cantonal de Zoologie, Lausanne 037245
Musée Cantonal des Beaux-Arts, Musées Cantonaux du Valais, Sion 037564
Musée Cantonal des Beaux-Arts de Lausanne, Lausanne 037246
Musée Cantonal d'Histoire, Musées Cantonaux du Valais, Sion 037565
Musée Cantonal d'Histoire Militaire, Musées Cantonaux du Valais, Saint-Maurice 037478
Musée Cantonal d'Histoire Naturelle, Musées Cantonaux du Valais, Sion 037566
Musée Cappon, Marans 012881
Musée Cappuis-Fähndrich, Develier 037043
Musée Carnavalet - Histoire de Paris, Paris 013621
Musée Casa Catalana de la Cultura, Céret 011176
Musée Casa De Les Alberes, Argelès-sur-Mer 010458
Musée Casimir Delavigne, Pressagny-l'Orgueilleux 013949
Musée Castral, Wintzenheim 015366
Musée Catalan des Arts et Traditions Populaires, Casa Pairal Joseph Deloncle, Perpignan 013785
Musée Catalan d'Histoire, Salses-le-Château 014655
Musée Caverne du Dragon, Oulches-la-Vallée-Foulon 013529
Musée Cavernicole, Blanot 010830
Musée Cavernicole, Prignac-et-Marcamps 013951
Musée Cavernicole de la Grotte de Balme, La Balme-les-Grottes 012197
Musée Cavernicole de la Grotte de la Vache, Alliat 010339
Musée Cavernicole de la Grotte de Thais, Saint-Nazaire-en-Royans 014447
Musée Cavernicole de la Grotte des Planches, Arbois 010446
Musée Cavernicole de la Grotte d'Osselle, Roset-Fluans 014113
Musée Cavernicole de Marquay, Marquay 012917
Musée C.C. Olsommer, Veyras 037681
Musée Célestin Freinet, Bonnut 010873
Musée Celte - Gallo Romain, Musée Krumacker, Seltz 014751
Musée-Centre Charles Péguy, Orléans 013515
Musée Centre Culturel, Vichy 015205
Musée Centre d'Art et de Littérature, L'Echelle 012582
Musée-Centre d'Arts Plastiques Chanot, Clamart 011385
Musée-Centre de Documentation Alfred Desmasures, Hirson 012105
Musée Centre de l'Alchimie, Tiffauges 014955
Musée-Centre de l'Imaginaire Arthurien, Concoret 011456
Musée Centre Historique des Sapeurs-Pompiers, Firminy 011819
Musée Centre Jean Rostand, Pouydesseaux 013932
Musée Centre National Jean Moulin, Bordeaux 010880
Musée Cernuschi, Musée des Arts de l'Asie de la Ville de Paris, Paris 013622
Musée Césaire Phisalix, Mouthier-Haute-Pierre 013280
Musée César-Filhol, Annonay 010416
Musée Cévenol, Le Vigan (Gard) 012578
Musée-Chalutier Le Kifanlo, OCEAM, Les Sables-d'Olonne 012636
Musée Champenois de l'Imprimerie, Musée de la Cave des Champagnes de Castellane, Épernay 011705
Musée Champollion, Figeac 011812
Musée-Chapelle Bellini, Cannes 011096
Musée-Chapelle Saint-Blaise-des-Simples, Milly-la-Forêt 013064
Musée Charbonneau-Lassay, Loudun 012756
Musée Charles Cros, Fabrezan 011777
Musée Charles de Bruyères, Remiremont 014015
Musée Charles de Gaulle, Lille 012677
Musée Charles Léandre, Salle d'Exposition, Domfront 011625
Musée Charles-Louis Philippe, Cérilly 011179
Musée Charles Milcendeau-Jean Yole, Soullans 014841
Musée Charles-Portal, Cordes-sur-Ciel 011480
Musée Charles VII, Pôle de la Porcelaine, Mehun-sur-Yèvre 012999
Musée Charlier, Bruxelles 003310
Musée Charolais du Machinisme Agricole, Neuvy-Grandchamp 013384
Musée-Château, Grignan 012036
Musée-Château, La Ferté-Saint-Aubin 012255
Musée-Château, Le Plessis-Macé 012546
Musée-Château, Malesherbes 012865
Musée-Château, Montmort-Lucy 013194
Musée-Château, Montreuil-Bellay 013219
Musée-Château, Senonches 014763
Musée-Château, Château de Ville-d'Avray, Ville-d'Avray 015235
Musée Château Abbaye de Cassan, Roujan 014139
Musée Château d'Aigremont, Awirs 003208
Musée Château d'Annecy et Observatoire Régional des Lacs Alpins, Annecy 010411
Musée-Château de Bourdeilles, Bourdeilles 010923
Musée-Château de Cheverny, Contres 011473
Musée-Château de Fontaine-Henry, Fontaine-Henry 011845
Musée-Château de Haute-Goulaine, Haute-Goulaine 012078
Musée-Château de la Garnache, La Garnache 012267
Musée-Château de la Pioline, Aix-en-Provence 010292
Musée-Château de La Verrerie, Oizon 013484
Musée Château de la Vigne et du Vin, Boën-sur-Lignon 010851
Musée-Château de Montremy, Dieue-sur-Meuse 011588
Musée-Château de Pommard, Pommard 013873
Musée-Château de Pyrénée, Lourdes 012768
Musée-Château de Raguin, Chazé-sur-Argos 011337
Musée-Château de Rochebrune, Etagnac 011745
Musée-Château de Saint-Germain-de-Livet, Saint-Germain-de-Livet 014305
Musée-Château de Saint-Ouen, Saint-Ouen 014457
Musée-Château des Adhémar, Montélimar 013153
Musée-Château des Evêques de Monistrol, Monistrol-sur-Loire 013099
Musée Château des Princes de Ligne et Musée Lapidaire, Antoing 003149
Musée-Château des Roures, La Bastide-de-Virac 012201
Musée-Château d'Espeyran, Saint-Gilles-du-Gard 014321
Musée Château du Bucheneck, Soultz-Haut-Rhin 014843
Musée-Château du Moine Sacristain, Aurec-sur-Loire 010547
Musée-Château du Riau, Villeneuve-sur-Allier 015281
Musée-Château Saint-Brisson, Saint-Brisson-sur-Loire 014210
Musée Chaussures Humeau, La Salle-et-Chapelle-Aubry 012335
Musée Chemtou, Jendouba 037957
Musée Chintreuil, Pont-de-Vaux 013886
Musée Christhi, Capvern-les-Bains 011106
Musée Christian-Dior, Granville 011990
Musée Ciotaden, La Ciotat 012235
Musée Claude Bernard, Fondation Marcel Merieux, Saint-Julien-en-Beaujolais 014369
Musée Claude Chappe, Brûlon 011019
Musée Claude Debussy, Saint-Germain-en-Laye 014308
Musée Claude Monet, Giverny 011955
Musée Claude Nicolas Ledoux Saline Royale, Arc-et-Senans 010450
Musée Clément Ader, Muret 013304
Musée Cloître Roman Saint-André-le-Bas, Vienne 015208
Musée Cognacq-Jay, Paris 013623
Musée Cointreau, Saint-Barthélemy-d'Anjou 014195

Musée Colette, Saint-Sauveur-en-Puisaye . . . 014535
Musée Collection Ferroviaire, Miramas . . . 013071
Musée Colombophile, Bouvignies . . 010952
Musée Colombophile du Mont-Valérien, Suresnes . . . 014887
Musée Communal, Bouvignes . . . 003250
Musée Communal, Clérac . . . 011391
Musée Communal, Xhoris . . . 003864
Musée Communal d'Archéologie, d'Art et d'Histoire, Nivelles . . . 003678
Musée Communal de Folklore Léon Maes, Mouscron . . . 003658
Musée Communal de Huy, Huy . . . 003528
Musée Communal de la Pierre de Sprimont, Sprimont . . . 003780
Musée Communal de la Résistance et de la Déportation, Vénissieux . . . 015164
Musée Communal de la Ville de Braine-le-Comte, Braine-le-Comte . . . 003255
Musée Communal de Woluwe-Saint-Lambert, Bruxelles . . . 003311
Musée Communal des Traditions Populaires Locales, Cussac-Fort-Médoc . . . 011552
Musée Communal du Comte de Jette, Bruxelles . . . 003312
Musée Communal Georges Mulpas, Elouges . . . 003420
Musée Communal Herstalien d'Archéologie et de Folklore, Herstal . . . 003512
Musée Communal Robert Tatin, Cossé-le-Vivien . . . 011493
Musée Comtadin, Carpentras . . . 011124
Musée Comtois, Besançon . . . 010768
Musée Condé, Chantilly . . . 011236
Musée Condorcet, Ribemont . . . 014040
Musée Conrad-et-Marcel-Schlumberger, Crévecœur-en-Auge . . . 011536
Musée Conservatoire, Mauriac . . . 012977
Musée-Conservatoire d'Arts et Traditions Populaires, Villefagnan . . . 015247
Musée-Conservatoire de la Dentelle, Luxeuil-les-Bains . . . 012796
Musée-Conservatoire de la Savonnerie Marius-Fabre, Salon-de-Provence 014650
Musée Conservatoire de la Vie Agricole et Rurale, Ecomusée des Pays de l'Oise, Hétomesnil . . . 012099
Musée Conservatoire de la Vie Agricole et Rurale d'Autrefois, Gimont . . . 011950
Musée Conservatoire de l'Agriculture, Chartres . . . 011264
Musée-Conservatoire de l'Outil, Brecy-Brières . . . 010973
Musée Conservatoire des Cépages, Saint-Ilpize . . . 014334
Musée-Conservatoire des Productions Fruitières, Saint-Jean-d'Arvey . . . 014340
Musée Conservatoire du Matériel Agricole, Droyes . . . 011662
Musée-Conservatoire du Patrimoine, La Garde-Freinet . . . 012266
Musée Conservatoire Ethnologique de Haute-Provence, Mane . . . 012871
Musée-Conservatoire International de la Plaisance, Bordeaux . . . 010881
Musée Conservatoire Maritime et Rural, Narbonne . . . 013350
Musée-Conservatoire Nationale de la Typographie, Paris . . . 013624
Musée Constantin Meunier, Musées Royaux des Beaux-Arts de Belgique, Bruxelles . . . 003313
Musée Corneille, Rouen . . . 014123
Musée Créatif du Tissage, Louhossoa . . . 012762
Musée Crozatier, Le Puy-en-Velay . 012555
Musée Curie, Paris . . . 013625
Musée Curtius, Liège . . . 003587
Musée da Guine Portugesa, Bissau . 021598
Musée d'Abeche, Abeche . . . 006902
Musée d'Allard, Montbrison . . . 013143
Musée d'Allauch, Allauch . . . 010336
Musée d'Anatomie Delmas-Orfila-Rouvière, Paris . . . 013626
Musée d'Anatomie Lesbres-Tagand de l'Ecole Vétérinaire de Lyon, Marcy-l'Étoile . . . 012898
Musée d'Andernos, Maison Louis David, Andernos-les-Bains . . . 010380
Musée d'Ansembourg, Liège . . . 003588
Musée d'Antan, Aigremont . . . 010274
Musée d'Antan, La Léchère . . . 012282
Musée d'Anthropologie, Kinshasa . . 007653
Musée d'Anthropologie Préhistorique, Monaco . . . 028991
Musée Dapper, Paris . . . 013627
Musée d'Aquitaine, Bordeaux . . . 010882
Musée Dar Ayed, Ksar Hellal . . . 037960
Musée Dar Bourguiba, Tunis . . . 037985
Musée Dar-Chraiet, Tozeur . . . 037982
Musée Dar-El-Annabi, Sidi Bou Saïd 037976
Musée Dar-Hammamet, Hammamet . . . 037955
Musée Dar-Si-Said, Marrakech . . . 029025
Musée d'Archéologie, Battambang . 004966
Musée d'Archéologie, Béjaïa . . . 000051
Musée d'Archéologie, Capdenac-le-Haut . . . 011104
Musée d'Archéologie, Carignan . . . 011120
Musée d'Archéologie, Gorée . . . 034134
Musée d'Archéologie, Houffalize . . 003523
Musée d'Archéologie, Izernore . . . 012145
Musée d'Archéologie, Le Pègue . . . 012541
Musée d'Archéologie, Séverac-le-Château . . . 014786
Musée d'Archéologie, Tournai . . . 003805
Musée d'Archéologie Bargoin, Clermont-Ferrand . . . 011396
Musée d'Archéologie de l'Université du Québec à Trois-Rivières, Trois-Rivières . . . 006662
Musée d'Archéologie, du Costume, d'Art et Traditions Populaires, Saint-Jean-de-Maurienne . . . 014350
Musée d'Archéologie du Jura, Lons-le-Saunier . . . 012741
Musée d'Archéologie et de Géologie, Rougemont . . . 014137
Musée d'Archéologie et de Sciences Naturelles, Douai . . . 011640
Musée d'Archéologie et d'Ethnologie, Villeneuve (Alpes-de-Haute-Provence) . . . 015262
Musée d'Archéologie et d'Histoire Locale, Loury . . . 012784
Musée d'Archéologie et d'Histoire Locale, Denain . . . 011573
Musée d'Archéologie et Folklore, Musée Communal, Verviers . . . 003824
Musée d'Archéologie Industrielle, Vaulx . . . 003822
Musée d'Archéologie Méditerranéenne, Marseille . . . 012935
Musée d'Archéologie Précolombienne et de Préhistoire de la Martinique, Fort-de-France . . . 028053
Musée d'Archéologie Préhistorique de l'Université de Liège, Liège . . . 003589
Musée d'Archéologie Sublacustre, Musée des Lacs, Sanguinet . . . 014664
Musée d'Archéologie Tricastin, Saint-Paul-Trois-Châteaux . . . 014472
Musée d'Archéologieque, Saint-Ciers-sur-Gironde . . . 014226
Musée d'Archéologique, Saint-Raphaël . . . 014508
Musée d'Archéologique, d'Arts et d'Folklorique Al-Kaçabah, Tanger 029038
Musée d'Archéologique Municipal, Martres-Tolosane . . . 012965
Musée d'Architecture - La Loge, Bruxelles . . . 003314
Musée d'Arenberg, Rebecq . . . 003710
Musée d'Argonne, Varennes-en-Argonne . . . 015133
Musée d'Armes Anciennes, La Cluse-et-Mijoux . . . 012238
Musée d'Armes-Citadelle de Dinant, Dinant . . . 003408
Musée d'Armes de Liège, Liège . . . 003590
Musée d'Armes du Bordj Nord, Fèz 029020
Musée d'Armes et d'Historie Militaire, Tournai . . . 003806
Musée d'Armes et Objets Anciens, Sonvilier . . . 037582
Musée d'Arromanches, Musée du Débarquement, Arromanches-les-Bains . . . 010488
Musée d'Art, Toulon (Var) . . . 014972
Musée d'Art Africain, Dakar . . . 034130
Musée d'Art Africain Religieux, Gentinnes . . . 003472
Musée d'Art Américain, Giverny . . . 011956
Musée d'Art Ancien, Montpeyroux . 013214
Musée d'Art Ancien, Musées Royaux des Beaux-Arts de Belgique, Bruxelles 003315
Musée d'Art Brut, Beauchastel . . . 010698
Musée d'Art Contemporain, Dunkerque . . . 011666
Musée d'Art Contemporain, La Croix Blanche, Noyers-sur-Serein . . . 013457
Musée d'Art Contemporain, MAC, Marseille . . . 012936
Musée d'Art Contemporain de la Brenne, Espace Art Brenne, Concremiers . 011457
Musée d'Art Contemporain de Lyon, Lyon . . . 012810
Musée d'Art Contemporain de Montréal, Montréal . . . 005934
Musée d'Art Contemporain du Château de Veauce, Veauce . . . 015149
Musée d'Art Contemporain en Plein Air le Cyclop, Milly-la-Forêt . . . 013065
Musée d'Art Contemporain et d'Histoire Locale, Chaumont (Yonne) . . . 011329
Musée d'Art Contemporain et Moderne, Fondation Deutsch, Belmont-sur-Lausanne . . . 036919
Musée d'Art Contemporain - FAE, Pully . . . 037428
Musée d'Art de Joliette, Joliette . . . 005653
Musée d'Art de Mont-Saint-Hilaire, Mont-Saint-Hilaire . . . 005902
Musée d'Art de Saint-Laurent, Saint-Laurent . . . 006380
Musée d'Art Differencie, Liège . . . 003591
Musée d'Art et d'Archéologie, Aire-sur-l'Adour . . . 010287
Musée d'Art et d'Archéologie, Aurillac . . . 010551
Musée d'Art et d'Archéologie, Laon 012421
Musée d'Art et d'Archéologie, Senlis . . . 014760
Musée d'Art et d'Archéologie, Soulac-sur-Mer . . . 014839
Musée d'Art et d'Archéologie, Hôtel Fouquet, Château-Gontier . . . 011276
Musée d'Art et d'Archéologie, Musée Municipal, Hyères . . . 012120
Musée d'Art et d'Archéologie de l'Université d'Antananarivo, Antananarivo . . . 027928
Musée d'Art et d'Artisanat, Corsavy 011489
Musée d'Art et de Folklore Régional, Fessy . . . 011809
Musée d'Art et de Tradition Populaire, Bazoges-en-Pareds . . . 010693
Musée d'Art et de Traditions Populaires André Abet, Saint-Laurent-de-Cerdans . . . 014376
Musée d'Art et des Traditions Populaires, Sizun . . . 014811
Musée d'Art et d'Histoire, Cernay . . 011183
Musée d'Art et d'Histoire, Saint-Pol-sur-Ternoise . . . 014489
Musée d'Art et d'Histoire, Belfort . . 010735
Musée d'Art et d'Histoire, Bergues . 010760
Musée d'Art et d'Histoire, Bulgnéville . . . 011029
Musée d'Art et d'Histoire, Château-sur-Allier . . . 011280
Musée d'Art et d'Histoire, Chaumont (Haute-Marne) . . . 011325
Musée d'Art et d'Histoire, Cholet . . 011373
Musée d'Art et d'Histoire, Dreux . . . 011660
Musée d'Art et d'Histoire, Eymet . . . 011768
Musée d'Art et d'Histoire, Firmi . . . 011816
Musée d'Art et d'Histoire, Fribourg . 037100
Musée d'Art et d'Histoire, Frontignan . . . 011904
Musée d'Art et d'Histoire, Genève . 037128
Musée d'Art et d'Histoire, Grézolles 012034
Musée d'Art et d'Histoire, Kaysersberg . . . 012191
Musée d'Art et d'Histoire, Ligny-en-Barrois . . . 012672
Musée d'Art et d'Histoire, Livry-Gargan . . . 012718
Musée d'Art et d'Histoire, Montferrer . . . 013162
Musée d'Art et d'Histoire, Mouthiers-sur-Boême . . . 013281
Musée d'Art et d'Histoire, Narbonne 013351
Musée d'Art et d'Histoire, Nice . . . 013396
Musée d'Art et d'Histoire, Oisy-le-Verger . . . 013483
Musée d'Art et d'Histoire, Poissy . . 013865
Musée d'Art et d'Histoire, Ravel . . . 013995
Musée d'Art et d'Histoire, Rueil-Malmaison . . . 014153
Musée d'Art et d'Histoire, Saint-Denis (Seine-Saint-Denis) . . . 014253
Musée d'Art et d'Histoire, Saint-Julien-du-Sault . . . 014368
Musée d'Art et d'Histoire, Schirmeck . . . 014734
Musée d'Art et d'Histoire, Thorens-Glières . . . 014944
Musée d'Art et d'Histoire, Villefranche-sur-Mer . . . 015253
Musée d'Art et d'Histoire, Villespassans . . . 015296
Musée d'Art et d'Histoire, Maison d'Armande Béjart, Meudon . . . 013044
Musée d'Art et d'Histoire, Musées Municipaux, Rochefort (Charente-Maritime) . . . 014078
Musée d'Art et d'Histoire Alfred-Douët, Saint-Flour (Cantal) . . . 014290
Musée d'Art et d'Histoire de Baugé, Baugé . . . 010668
Musée d'Art et d'Histoire de la Chapelle Notre-Dame, Luz-Saint-Sauveur . 012801
Musée d'Art et d'Histoire de Langres, Langres . . . 012409
Musée d'Art et d'Histoire de l'Avranchin, Avranches . . . 010605
Musée d'Art et d'Histoire de Lisieux, Lisieux . . . 012703
Musée d'Art et d'Histoire de Provence, Grasse . . . 011996
Musée d'Art et d'Histoire de Puisaye, Villiers-Saint-Benoît . . . 015305
Musée d'Art et d'Histoire de Toul, Toul . . . 014970
Musée d'Art et d'Histoire des Côtes d'Armor, Saint-Brieuc . . . 014207
Musée d'Art et d'Histoire du Judaïsme, Paris . . . 013628
Musée d'Art et d'Histoire du Pays Blayais, Blaye . . . 010836
Musée d'Art et d'Histoire Local, Pezens . . . 013807
Musée d'Art et d'Histoire Louis Senlecq, L'Isle-Adam . . . 012707
Musée d'Art et d'Histoire Neuchâtel, Neuchâtel . . . 037375
Musée d'Art et d'Histoire Roger Rodière, Montreuil-sur-Mer . . . 013223
Musée d'Art et d'Histoire Romain Rolland, Clamecy . . . 011387
Musée d'Art et d'Industrie, Quintin . 013984
Musée d'Art et d'Industrie, Saint-Étienne . . . 014270
Musée d'Art et d'Industrie - La Piscine, Roubaix . . . 014121
Musée d'Art et Historique, Montbéliard . . . 013140
Musée d'Art et Tradition Populaire, Lamballe . . . 012392
Musée d'Art et Traditions Populaires, Binic . . . 010807
Musée d'Art et Traditions Populaires, Nancy . . . 013322
Musée d'Art et Traditions Populaires, Sidi Boulbaba . . . 037978
Musée d'Art Haïtien, Port-au-Prince 021602
Musée d'Art Islamique, Marrakech . 029026

Musée d'Art Islamique du Ribat, Monastir . . . 037968
Musée d'Art Islamique Raqqada, Kairouan . . . 037958
Musée d'Art Juif, Paris . . . 013629
Musée d'Art Juif J.C.-Katz, Colmar . 011431
Musée d'Art Local, Oisemont . . . 013481
Musée d'Art Militaire, Vincey . . . 015312
Musée d'Art Moderne, Belfort . . . 010736
Musée d'Art Moderne, Saint-Étienne . . . 014271
Musée d'Art Moderne, Troyes . . . 015051
Musée d'Art Moderne, Musées Royaux des Beaux-Arts de Belgique, Bruxelles 003316
Musée d'Art Moderne de la Ville de Paris, Paris . . . 013630
Musée d'Art Moderne des Templiers, Collioure . . . 011422
Musée d'Art Moderne et Contemporain, Strasbourg . . . 014865
Musée d'Art Moderne et Contemporain, Les Abattoirs, Toulouse . . . 014986
Musée d'Art Moderne et d'Art Contemporain, Liège . . . 003592
Musée d'Art Moderne et d'Art Contemporain, Nice . . . 013397
Musée d'Art Moderne Grand-Duc Jean, Luxembourg . . . 027889
Musée d'Art Moderne Jean Peské, Collioure . . . 011423
Musée d'Art Moderne Lille Métropole, Villeneuve-d'Ascq . . . 015264
Musée d'Art Moderne Méditerranéen, Cagnes-sur-Mer . . . 011060
Musée d'Art Moderne Richard Anacréon, Granville . . . 011991
Musée d'Art Naïf, Lasne-Chapelle-Saint-Lambert . . . 003570
Musée d'Art Naif, Nice . . . 013398
Musée d'Art Nègre, Yaoundé . . . 004981
Musée d'Art Néo-Byzantin, Montréal . . . 005935
Musée d'Art Oriental Asiatica, Biarritz . . . 010794
Musée d'Art Polonais, Montrésor . . 013218
Musée d'Art Populaire, Le Monastier-sur-Gazeille . . . 012530
Musée d'Art Populaire, Sauveterre-de-Rouergue . . . 014710
Musée d'Art Populaire Africain, Besançon . . . 010769
Musée d'Art Populaire des Mangettes, Saint-Étienne-du-Bois . . . 014279
Museé d'Art Populaire du Hauran, Museé d'Antiquites de Bosra, Bosra . . . 037825
Musée d'Art Populaire Marocain, Tétouan . . . 029041
Musée d'Art Populaire Régional, Château des Ducs de Bretagne, Nantes . . . 013334
Musée d'Art Populaire Religieux, Saint-Julien-Molhesabate . . . 014370
Musée d'Art Religieux, Blois . . . 010846
Musée d'Art Religieux, Castelnau-Magnoac . . . 011141
Musée d'Art Religieux, Marsal . . . 012922
Musée d'Art Religieux, Vermand . . . 015179
Musée d'Art Religieux, Wellington, Prince Edward Island . . . 006784
Musée d'Art Religieux et d'Art Mosan, Liège . . . 003593
Musée d'Art Roger Quilliot, Clermont-Ferrand . . . 011397
Musée d'Art Rustique, Musée Edouard Wolff, Vianden . . . 027903
Musée d'Art Sacré, Bergerac . . . 010756
Musée d'Art Sacré, Bourbon-l'Archambault . . . 010920
Musée d'Art Sacré, Dijon . . . 011603
Musée d'Art Sacré, Entrevaux . . . 011700
Musée d'Art Sacré, Gramat . . . 011979
Musée d'Art Sacré, Hambye . . . 012065
Musée d'Art Sacré, Le Monêtier-les-Bains . . . 012532
Musée d'Art Sacré, Le Val . . . 012572
Musée d'Art Sacré, Saint-Béat . . . 014196
Musée d'Art Sacré, Saint-Cirq-Lapopie . . . 014228
Musée d'Art Sacré, Saint-Michel-l'Observatoire . . . 014442
Musée d'Art Sacré, Senez . . . 014758
Musée d'Art Sacré, Viviers-en-Ardèche . . . 015325
Musée d'Art Sacré, Trésor de la Cathédrale Notre-Dame, Paris . . . 013631
Musée d'Art Sacré à la Cathédrale Russe de 1912, Nice . . . 013399
Musée d'Art Sacré Copte et Byzantin Scete, Le Revest-les-Eaux . . . 012560
Musée d'Art Sacré de Fourvière, Lyon . . . 012811
Musée d'Art Sacré de la Cathédrale Saint-Siffrein, Carpentras . . . 011125
Musée d'Art Sacré de Loukine, Arsonval . . . 010491
Musée d'Art Sacré du Gard, Pont-Saint-Esprit . . . 013896
Musée d'Art Sacré - Francis Poulenc, Rocamadour . . . 014067
Musée d'Art Sacré Occidental, Le Revest-les-Eaux . . . 012561
Musée d'Art Singulièr Raymond Reynaud, Sénas . . . 014757
Musée d'Arte Sacré, Lorgues . . . 012746
Musée d'Artillerie, Caudeval . . . 011156
Musée d'Artisanat Monuments en Allumettes et Sciences Naturelles, Fontet . . . 011860
Musée d'Arts Africains, Langonnet . 012408
Musée d'Arts et de Traditions Populaires, Amélie-les-Bains-Palalda . . . 010363
Musée d'Arts et de Traditions Populaires, Augirein . . . 010541
Musée d'Arts et de Traditions Populaires, Aurice . . . 010549
Musée d'Arts et de Traditions Populaires, Bonifacio . . . 010865
Musée d'Arts et de Traditions Populaires, Cervione . . . 011187
Musée d'Arts et de Traditions Populaires, Lavaufranche . . . 012451
Musée d'Arts et de Traditions Populaires, Oisly . . . 013482
Musée d'Arts et de Traditions Populaires, Palinges . . . 013540
Musée d'Arts et de Traditions Populaires, Poncé-sur-le-Loir . . . 013876
Musée d'Arts et de Traditions Populaires, F. Arnaudies, Saint-Paul-de-Fenouillet . . . 014466
Musée d'Arts et de Traditions Populaires, Musée André Voulgre, Mussidan . 013310
Musée d'Arts et d'Histoire, Hesdin . 012097
Musée d'Arts et d'Histoire, Sainte-Maure-de-Touraine . . . 014607
Musée d'Arts et d'Histoire de la Poterne, Preuilly-sur-Claise . . . 013950
Musée d'Arts et d'Histoire du Donjon, Niort . . . 013428
Musée d'Arts et Traditions Populaires, Cancale . . . 011089
Musée d'Arts et Traditions Populaires, La Guérinière . . . 012276
Musée d'Arts et Traditions Populaires, Marmoutier . . . 012915
Musée d'Arts et Traditions Populaires, Montmaur . . . 013184
Musée d'Arts et Traditions Populaires, Troo . . . 015044
Musée d'Arts et Traditions Populaires, Yssingeaux . . . 015378
Musée d'Arts et Traditions Populaires de Castellane et du Moyen Verdon, Castellane . . . 011139
Musée d'Arts et Traditions Populaires Paul Reclus, Domme . . . 011627
Musée d'Arts et Traditions Rurales, Saint-Alban-Auriolles . . . 014171
Musée d'Arts Populaires, Asco . . . 010501
Musée d'Arts Populaires, Briançonnet . . . 010994
Musée d'Arts Populaires, Gramat . . 011980
Musée d'Arts Populaires, Laroque-des-Albères . . . 012428
Musée d'Arts Populaires de l'Argonne, Braux-Sainte-Cohière . . . 010969
Musée d'Arts Populaires de Lille-Sud, Lille . . . 012678
Musée d'Arts Religieux, Verdelais . . 015170
Musée d'Assier, Feurs . . . 011810
Musée Daubigny, Auvers-sur-Oise . 010567
Musée Dauphinois, Grenoble . . . 012020
Musée d'Automates, Courtillers . . . 011516
Musée d'Automobiles en Miniature - Den Dinky, Vianden . . . 027904
Musée David et Alice Van Buuren, Bruxelles . . . 003317
Musée d'Aylmer, Aylmer . . . 005049
Musée de Abris, Albert . . . 010314
Musée de Bagnes, Le Châble . . . 037005
Musée de Baie Comeau, Baie Comeau . . . 005054
Musée de Basse-Navarre et des Chemins de Saint-Jacques, Institut Culturel Basque, Saint-Palais (Pyrénées-Atlantiques) . . . 014463
Musée de Bataille, Mutzig . . . 013312
Musée de Béjaïa, Béjaïa . . . 000052
Musée de Bible et Terre Sainte, Paris . . . 013632
Musée de Bibracte, Saint-Léger-sous-Beuvray . . . 014387
Musée de Biot, Musée d'Histoire et de Céramique Biotoise, Biot . . . 010809
Musée de Boîtes à Musique et Automates, Sainte-Croix . . . 037481
Musée de Bonoua, Bonoua . . . 007688
Musée de Borda, Dax . . . 011564
Musée de Botanique, Lausanne . . . 037247
Musée de Bouteilles Anciennes et Originales, Saint-Christophe-des-Bardes . . . 014223
Musée de Bouxwiller et du Pays de Hanau, Bouxwiller . . . 010953
Musée de Bretagne, Rennes (Ille-et-Vilaine) . . . 014021
Musée de Brou, Bourg-en-Bresse . 010926
Musée de Butemo, Butemo . . . 007650
Musée de Cahors Henri-Martin, Cahors . . . 011067
Musée de Calès, Lamanon . . . 012391
Musée de Calligraphie et Epigraphie Arabe, Damascus . . . 037827
Musée de Carouge, Carouge . . . 036998
Musée de Centre International de l'Automobile, Pantin . . . 013545
Musée de Cerdagne, Sainte-Léocadie . . . 014600
Musée de Cerdagne d'Eyne, Eyne . . 011771
Musée de Cervières, Cervières . . . 011186
Musée de Charlevoix, Pointe-au-Pic 006163
Musée de Charroux et de son Canton, Charroux-d'Allier . . . 011263
Musée de Château, Durtal . . . 011673
Musée de Château Guillaume, Lignac . . . 012669
Musée de Châtillon-Coligny, Châtillon-Coligny . . . 011311
Musée de Chauny, Chauny . . . 011330
Musée de Cherchell, Cherchell . . . 000055
Musée de Cherves en Mirebalais, Cherves-Mirebeau . . . 011354
Musée de Chine, Bruxelles . . . 003318
Musée de Circonscription Archéologique, Sétif . . . 000071
Musée de Cire, Waterloo . . . 003844
Musée de Cire de l'Historial, Sainte-Anne-d'Auray . . . 014583
Musée de Cire et Salle de Documents Historiques, Perros-Guirec . . . 013795
Musée de Cire-Historial de la Haute-Auvergne, Aurillac . . . 010552
Musée de Cires, Historial des Princes de Monaco, Monaco . . . 028992
Musée de Cognac, Cognac . . . 011415
Musée de Cohennoz, Cohennoz . . . 011418
Musée de Constantine, Constantine 000057
Musée de Cosne, Cosne-Cours-sur-Loire . . . 011492
Musée de Cotonou, Cotonou . . . 003889
Musée de Cox, Cox . . . 011524
Musée de Dar-El-Jamaï, Meknès . . 029027
Musée de Diamare, Maroua . . . 004978
Musée de Djemila, Djemila . . . 000060
Musée de Dol, Dol-de-Bretagne . . . 011620
Musée de Domaine de Lacroix-Laval, Marcy-l'Étoile . . . 012899
Musée de Drummond Castle, Ile-de-Molène . . . 012126
Musée de Enchanteurs, Antrain-sur-Couesnon . . . 010435
Musée de Figurines Végétales, Basse-Pointe . . . 028052
Musée de Folklore, Nismes . . . 003675
Musée de Folklore, Tournai . . . 003807
Musée de Folklore de la Chée, Heiltz-le-Maurupt . . . 012087
Musée de Folklore et d'Histoire Armand Pellegrin, Ancienne Ecole Communale des Garçons, Opheylissem . . . 003690
Musée de Folklore Flamand Jeanne Devos, Wormhout . . . 015371
Musée de France de Berck-sur-Mer, Berck-sur-Mer . . . 010754
Musée de Fresques, Blain . . . 010821
Musée de Géologie, Lozanne . . . 012789
Musée de Géologie, Saint-Avit-Senieur . . . 014194
Musée de Geologie, Sainte-Foy . . . 006404
Musée de Géologie Botanique, La Bourboule . . . 012207
Musée de Germigny et Grange Germignonne, Germigny-des-Prés 011937
Musée de Glozel, Ferrières-sur-Sichon . . . 011804
Musée de Grenoble, Grenoble . . . 012021
Musée de Groesbeeck de Croix, Namur . . . 003663
Musée de Hottemme, Durbuy . . . 003414
Musée de Jean Chouan, Saint-Ouen-des-Toits . . . 014458
Musée de Jouet et da la Poupée Ancienne, L'Isle-sur-la-Sorgue . . . 012710
Musée de Jouques, Jouques . . . 012172
Musée de Jules Gounon-Loubens, Loubens-Lauragais . . . 012754
Musée de Kabgayi, Kabgayi . . . 034101
Musée de Kamouraska, Kamouraska . . . 005662
Musée de Kerhinet, Saint-Lyphard . 014400
Musée de la Baleine, Port-la-Nouvelle . . . 013919
Musée de la Bande Dessinée, Musée Municipal, Angoulême . . . 010403
Musée de la Banderette, Travers . . 037641
Musée de la Banque Nationale de Belgique, Bruxelles . . . 003319
Musée de la Barrique, Moulis-en-Médoc . . . 013273
Musée de la Base Secrète de V 2, Eperlecques . . . 011702
Musée de la Basilique et des Thermes Romains, Arlon . . . 003198
Musée de la Bataille, Fontenoy-en-Puisaye . . . 011857
Musée de la Bataille, Rocroi . . . 014084
Musée de la Bataille de Tilly sur Seulles 1944, Tilly-sur-Seulles . . . 014959
Musée de la Bataille des Ardennes, Wiltz . . . 027909
Musée de la Bataille du 6 Août 1870, Woerth . . . 015370
Musée de la Bataille Mai-Juin 1940, Semuy . . . 014756
Musée de la Batellerie, Conflans-Sainte-Honorine . . . 011464
Musée de la Batellerie, Offendorf . . 013473
Musée de la Batellerie de l'Ouest, Redon . . . 013998
Musée de la Batellerie et du Plan Incliné, Saint-Louis-Arzviller . . . 014395
Musée de la Batterie de Merville, Merville-Franceville-Plage . . . 013036
Musée de la Beate, Marlhes . . . 012911
Musée de la Bécane à Grand-Père, Sault-lès-Rethel . . . 014695
Musée de la Bendrologie, Manéga . 004959
Musée de la Bière, Armentières . . . 010476
Musée de la Bière, Stenay . . . 014849
Musée de la Blanchardière, Flers . . 011824

Musée de la Blanchisserie Artisanale Joseph Gladel, Craponne (Rhône) 011527
Musée de la Bohème, Yviers 015382
Musée de la Boissellerie, Bois-d'Amont 010859
Musée de la Boite à Biscuits, Opheylissem 003691
Musée de la Bonneterie, Troyes . . . 015052
Musée de la Bonneterie et du Negoce de la Toile, Quevaucamps 003707
Musée de la Boulangerie, Bonnieux 010872
Musée de la Boulangerie Rurale, La Haye-de-Routot 012278
Musée de La Bouteille, Saint-Emilion 014265
Musée de la Brasserie, Saint-Dizier 014263
Musée de la Brasserie, C.B.B. Museum, Bruxelles 003320
Musée de la Bresse, Saint-Cyr-sur-Menton 014245
Musée de la Broderie, Fontenoy-le-Château 011859
Musée de la Cabane des Bangards, Thann 014922
Musée de la Cadillac, Saint-Michel-sur-Loire 014444
Musée de la Camargue, Arles 010470
Musée de la Caricature, La Cassagne 012213
Musée de la Casse, Orcières 013503
Musée de la Castre, Cannes 011097
Musée de la Cavalerie, Saumur . . . 014699
Musée de la Cave, Damery 011560
Musée de la Cave des Champagnes de Castellane, Épernay 011706
Musée de la Céramique, Digoin . . . 011596
Musée de la Céramique, Lezoux . . . 012660
Musée de la Céramique, Rouen . . . 014124
Musée de la Céramique Architecturale, Auneuil 010545
Musée de la Céramique d'Andenne, Andenne 003146
Musée de la Céramique et de l'Ivoire, Musée Municipal de Commercy, Commercy 011446
Musée de la Céramique Saint-Jean-l'Aigle, Longwy 012739
Musée de la Cervoise, du Gruyt et des Bières Mediévales, Anthisnes . . . 003148
Musée de la Chalosse, Montfort-en-Chalosse 013164
Musée de la Chapellerie, Espéraza . 011736
Musée de la Chapellerie, Le Somail 012564
Musée de la Charronnerie, Brienne-la-Vieille 011000
Musée de la Chartreuse et Fondation Bugatti, Molsheim 013088
Musée de la Chasse, Rance 003709
Musée de la Chasse, Chambord . . . 011217
Musée de la Chasse, Musée de la Faune, Boutenac 010951
Musée de la Chasse, de la Vénerie et de la Protection de la Nature, Lavaux-Sainte-Anne 003573
Musée de la Chasse et de la Nature, Baurech 010674
Musée de la Chasse et de la Nature, Foix 011831
Musée de la Chasse et de la Nature, Paris 013633
Musée de la Chasse et de la Venerie, Villiers-le-Duc 015304
Musée de la Châtaigne, Pied-de-Borne 013810
Musée de la Châtaigneraie, Joyeuse 012177
Musée de la Châtaigneraie, Saint-Gervais-sur-Mare 014316
Musée de la Chaumière, Audierne . 010537
Musée de la Chemiserie et de l'Elégance Masculine, Argenton-sur-Creuse . 010463
Musée de la Chimie, Jarrie 012149
Musée de la Chouannerie et des Guerres de l'Ouest, Plouharnel 013859
Musée de la Cigarette, Dijon 011604
Musée de la Citadelle, Bitche 010817
Musée de la Citadelle, Sisteron . . . 014804
Musée de la Citadelle Militaire, Verdun (Meuse) 015173
Musée de la Civilisation, Québec . . 006222
Musée de la Civilisation Gallo-Romaine, Lyon 012812
Musée de la Cloche, Sévrier 014789
Musée de la Cloches et de Sonnailles, Espace Campanaire André Malraux, Hérépian 012090
Musée de la Cochonnaille, Tourzel-Ronzieres 015027
Musée de la Coiffe, Blesle 010839
Musée de la Coiffe et Broderies de Touraine, Rochecorbon 014075
Musée de la Coiffe et du Costume Oléronnais, Le Grand-Village-Plage 012500
Musée de la Comédie, Preignac . . . 013947
Musée de la Commanderie, Viaprès-le-Petit 015199
Musée de la Communication en Alsace, Poste-Diligences-Télécoms, Riquewihr 014056
Musée de la Compagnie des Indes, Port-Louis 013920
Musée de la Compagnie Nationale du Rhône, Lyon 012813
Musée de la Compagnie Royale des Anciens Arquebusiers de Visé, Visé 003834
Musée de la Comtesse de Ségur, Aube 010512
Musée de la Conciergerie, Paris . . . 013634
Musée de la Confiture, Pau 013749
Musée de la Confrérie de l'Immaculée-Conception, Bastia 010664
Musée de la Confrérie des Vignerons, Vevey 037676
Musée de la Conscription, Strasbourg 014866
Musée de la Conserverie Le Gall, Loctudy 012725
Musée de la Construction Navale, Noirmoutier-en-l'Ile 013441
Musée de la Contrefaçon, Paris . . . 013635
Musée de la Corbillière, Mer 013025
Musée de la Cordonnerie, Alby-sur-Chéran 010323
Musée de la Correrie, Saint-Pierre-de-Chartreuse 014479
Musée de la Corse, Corte 011491
Musée de la Course Automobile, Romorantin-Lanthenay 014098
Musée de la Course Landaise, Bascons 010661
Musée de la Course Landaise, Pomarez 013871
Musée de la Coutellerie, Nogent-en-Bassigny 013434
Musée de la Coutellerie, Thiers . . . 014930
Musée de la Création Franche, Bègles 010733
Musée de la Crèche, Chaumont (Haute-Marne) 011326
Musée de la Crèche, Chaumont (Haute-Marne) 099126
Musée de la Crèche Provençale, Cavaillon 011164
Musée de la Crêpe Dentelle des Crêpes Bretonnes, Quimper 013974
Musée de la Cristallerie, Saint-Louis-les-Bitche 014398
Musée de la Cristallière, Charmeil . 011255
Musée de la Cuisine, Drummondville 005364
Musée de la Curiosité et de la Magie, Paris 013636
Musée de la Dame aux Camélias, Gacé 011910
Musée de la Dentelle, Caudry 011158
Musée de la Dentelle, Chamalières-sur-Loire 011206
Musée de la Dentelle, Marche-en-Famenne 003625
Musée de la Dentelle, Mirecourt . . . 013077
Musée de la Dentelle à la Main, Arlanc-en-Livradois 010467
Musée de la Dentelle au Point d'Alençon, Alençon 010325
Musée de la Dentelle du Puy-la-Galerie, Le Puy-en-Velay 012556
Musée de la Déportation, Labourse 012365
Musée de la Déportation et de la Résistance, Tarbes 014910
Musée de la Diligence, Riquewihr . 014057
Musée de la Distillerie, Pierre Guy, Pontarlier 013901
Musée de la Distillerie Combier, Saumur 014700
Musée de la Douane et des Frontières, Hestrud 012098
Musée de la Draperie, Vienne 015209
Musée de la Fabuloserie, Dicy 011584
Musée de la Faculté de Médecine, Strasbourg 014867
Musée de la Faïence, Samadet . . . 014656
Musée de la Faiënce, Sarreguemines 014684
Musée de la Faïence, Forges-les-Eaux 011867
Musée de la Faïence, Marseille . . . 012937
Musée de la Faïence, Montereau-Fault-Yonne 013155
Musée de la Faïence, Géo Martel, Longfosse 012734
Musée de la Faïence et de la Poterie, Ferriére-la-Petite 011802
Musée de la Faïence et des Arts de la Table, Samadet 014656
Musée de la Faïence Jules Verlingue, Quimper 013975
Musée de la Faïencerie de Gien, Gien 011942
Musée de la Faïencerie de Quimper H.-B. Henriot, Quimper 013976
Musée de la Famille, Chasselay . . . 011270
Musée de la Faucillonnaie, Vitré . . . 015320
Musée de la Faune, La Chapelle-d'Abondance 012222
Musée de la Faune, Lanhélin 012412
Musée de la Faune Alpine, Servoz . 014775
Musée de la Faune et de la Nature, Séez 014745
Musée de la Faux, Pont-Salomon . . 013898
Musée de la Fédération Nationale de Spéléologie, Revel 014034
Musée de la Ferme, Musée Municipal, Blangy-sur-Bresle 010825
Musée de la Ferme d'Antan, Jugon-lès-Lacs 012179
Musée de la Ferme d'Antan, Ploudiry 013849
Musée de la Ferme et des Vieux Métiers, Bosquentin 010899
Musée de la Ferronnerie et des Métiers Annexes, Francheville 011885
Musée de la Fête Foraine, Plancher-les-Mines 013830
Musée de la Fève et de la Crèche, Musée des Arts et Traditions Populaires, Blain 010822
Musée de la Figurine, La Grande-Fosse 012272
Musée de la Figurine, Toulon (Var) . 014973
Musée de la Figurine, Tulette 015059
Musée de la Figurine Historique, Compiègne 011449
Musée de la Figurine Historique, Château de Mongaston, Charre 011261
Musée de la Figurine Historique et du Jouet Ancien, Le Val 012573
Musée de la Filature, Angoustrine-Villeneuve 010409
Musée de la Flore et de la Faune du Haut Bugey, Hotonnes 012110
Musée de la Foire, Saint-Ghislain . . 003735
Musée de la Folie Marco, Barr 010657
Musée de la Fondation Jean-Dubuffet, Périgny-sur-Yerres 013772
Musée de la Fontaine et de l'Eau, Genval 003473
Musée de la Forêt, Saugues-en-Gévaudan 014691
Musée de la Forêt, Spa 003777
Musée de la Forêt Ardennaise, Renwez 014026
Musée de la Forge, Berlise 010761
Musée de la Forge, Ittre 003537
Musée de la Forge et des Sapeurs-Pompiers, Saint-Germain-l'Herm . 014315
Musée de la Fortification, Auxonne . 010577
Musée de la Fortification Cuirassée, Villey-le-Sec 015302
Musée de la Fraise et du Patrimoine, Plougastel-Daoulas 013851
Musée de la Fraise et du Terror Wépionnais, Wépion 003850
Musée de la Franc-Maçonnerie, Musée du Grand Orient de France, Paris . . . 013637
Musée de la France Protestante de l'Ouest, Monsireigne 013106
Musée de la Gaspésie, Gaspé 005498
Musée de la Gendarmerie, Melun . . 013006
Musée de la Gendarmerie, Toamasina 027936
Musée de la Géologie et de l'Archéologie, Musée Municipal, Blangy-sur-Bresle 010826
Musée de la Glace, Mazaugues . . . 012986
Musée de La Glacerie, La Glacerie . 012270
Musée de la Goubaudière, Cholet . . 011374
Musée de la Grande Forge, Buffon . 011026
Musée de la Grange aux Outils, Chens-sur-Léman 011348
Musée de la Grenouillère, Maison Joséphine, Croissy-sur-Seine . . . 011539
Musée de la Grosse Forge, Aube . . 010513
Musée de la Grosse Horloge, La Rochelle 012317
Musée de la Grotte de Cougnac, Payrignac 013759
Musée de la Grotte des Huguenots, Vallon-Pont-d'Arc 015112
Musée de la Guerre, Calais 011074
Musée de la Guerre, Fromelles 011903
Musée de la Guerre 1939-45, Pourrain 013931
Musée de la Guerre au Moyen Âge, Castelnaud-la-Chapelle 011144
Musée de la Guerre de 1870, Gravelotte 012010
Musée de la Guerre de Vendée, Les Sables-d'Olonne 012637
Musée de la Halte du Pèlerin, Larressingle 012431
Musée de la Hardt, Fessenheim . . . 011807
Musée de la Haute-Auvergne, Saint-Flour (Cantal) 014291
Musée de la Haute Sûre, Martelange 003630
Musée de la Houille Blanche et de ses Industries, Lancey 012397
Musée de la Kasbah, Rabat 029031
Musée de la la Faune des Pyrénées, Nébias 013360
Musée de la Laine, Verviers 003825
Musée de la Lauze, Annoisin-Châtelans 010415
Musée de la Lavande, Cabrières-d'Avignon 011045
Musée de la Lavande, Montguers . . 013171
Musée de la Lavande, Saint-Remèze 014509
Musée de la Légion Étrangère, Aubagne 010509
Musée de la Liberation, Aywaille . . 003209
Musée de la Libération, Cherbourg-Octeville 011350
Musée de la Libération 15 Août 1944, Le Muy 012538
Musée de la Libération de la Normandie, Surrain 014890
Musée de la Liberté, Quineville . . . 013981
Musée de la Ligne Koningshooikt-Wavre, Chaumont 003373
Musée de la Ligne Maginot, Bambiderstroff 010635
Musée de la Ligne Maginot, Entrange 011697
Musée de la Ligne Maginot, Hatten 012074
Musée de la Ligne Maginot, Hunspach 012115
Musée de la Ligne Maginot, La Ferté-sur-Chiers 012257

Musée de la Ligne Maginot, Lembach . . . 012592
Musée de la Ligne Maginot, Fort de Fermont, Longuyon . . . 012737
Musée de la Ligne Maginot Alpine, Sainte-Agnès . . . 014581
Musée de la Ligne Maginot des Alpes, Sospel . . . 014829
Musée de la Ligne Maginot Immerhof, Association du Petit Ouvrage, Hettange-Grande . . . 012100
Musée de la Lunette, Morez . . . 013237
Musée de la Lutherie et de l'Archèterie Françaises, Mirecourt . . . 013078
Musée de la Machine à Vapeur, Arc-en-Barrois . . . 010449
Musée de la Machine Agricole, Saint-Loup . . . 014399
Musée de la Machine Agricole, Vroncourt . . . 015345
Musée de la Machine Agricole et à Vapeur, Ambert . . . 010348
Musée de la Machine de Guerre, Espalion . . . 011728
Musée de la Maille, Riorges . . . 014053
Musée de la Main, Fondation Claude Verdan, Lausanne . . . 037248
Musée de la Mairie de Crécy, Crécy-la-Chapelle . . . 011529
Musée de la Maison de Retraite, Couilly-Pont-aux-Dames . . . 011499
Musée de la Maison de Tartarin, Tarascon (Bouches-du-Rhône) . . . 014903
Musée de la Maison Sauvagnarde, Sauvain . . . 014708
Musée de la Maison s'Kleenderfel, Weyersheim . . . 015362
Musée de la Maison Traditionelle du Queyras, Saint-Véran . . . 014567
Musée de la Marine, Etaples . . . 011748
Musée de la Marine, Grasse . . . 011997
Musée de la Marine, Saint-Brévin-les-Pins . . . 014205
Musée de la Marine de la Seine, Caudebec-en-Caux . . . 011155
Musée de la Marine de Loire, Châteauneuf-sur-Loire . . . 011293
Musée de la Marine et de l'Économie de Marseille, Marseille . . . 012938
Musée de la Médaille Miraculeuse, La Vie de Sainte Catherine Labouré, Lourdes . . . 012769
Musée de la Médecine, Bruxelles . . 003321
Musée de la Médecine Légale, Strasbourg . . . 014868
Musée de la Mémoire de la Vigne et du Vin, Saint-Pierre-de-Mézoargues . . . 014484
Musée de la Mémoire des Murs et d'Archéologie Locale, Verneuil-en-Halatte . . . 015183
Musée de la Mémoire du Royans, Rochechinard . . . 014072
Musée de la Mémoire et de la Paix, Clerval . . . 011406
Musée de la Mémoire Paysanne, Estissac . . . 011743
Musée de la Mer, Biarritz . . . 010795
Musée de la Mer, Cannes . . . 011098
Musée de la Mer, Gorée . . . 034135
Musée de la Mer, Havre-Aubert . . . 005609
Musée de la Mer, Iles-de-la-Madeleine . . . 005633
Musée de la Mer, Le Grau-du-Roi . . 012502
Musée de la Mer, Paimpol . . . 013535
Musée de la Mer, Centre National de Recherches Océanographiques, Nosy-Bé . . . 027935
Musée de la Mer de Rimouski, Pointe-au-Père . . . 006162
Musée de la Mer des Faluns, Doué-la-Fontaine . . . 011647
Musée de la Mer OCEAM, Les Sables-d'Olonne . . . 012638
Musée de la Métallurgie, Bogny-sur-Meuse . . . 010856
Musée de la Météorite, L'Aigle . . . 012383
Musée de la Météorologie, Valleraugues . . . 015108
Musée de la Meunerie, Bannegon . 010641
Musée de la Meunerie, Beaumont-sur-Sarthe . . . 010712
Musée de la Meunerie, Braine-le-Château . . . 003254
Musée de la Meunerie, Challain-la-Potherie . . . 011193
Musée de la Meunerie, Huisseau-sur-Mauves . . . 012112
Musée de la Meunerie, Le Breuil . . 012471
Musée de la Meunerie, Saint-Michel-Mont-Mercure . . . 014443
Musée de la Meunerie, Moulin à Eau, Courtelevant . . . 011515
Musée de la Meunerie et de la Boulangerie, Angrie . . . 010410
Musée de la Mine, Brassac-les-Mines . . . 010965
Musée de la Mine, Champagnac-les-Mines . . . 011222
Musée de la Mine, Houdeng-Aimeries . . . 003522
Musée de la Mine, La Machine . . . 012285
Musée de la Mine, Nœux-les-Mines 013433
Musée de la Mine, Saint-Étienne . . 014272
Musée de la Mine, Sainte-Maime . . 014601
Musée de la Mine, Villar-Saint-Pancrace . . . 015225
Musée de la Mine, Puits de Mine Hély d'Oissel, Gréasque . . . 012016
Musée de la Mine de Cap Garonne, Le Pradet . . . 012554
Musée de la Mine de Cuivre et de Soufre, Saint-Pierre-de-la-Palud . . . 014481
Musée de la Mine, de la Verrerie et du Chemin de Fer, Epinac . . . 011712
Musée de la Mine et de Meunerie-Moulin de Marcy, Le Molay-Littry . . . 012529
Musée de la Mine et des Hommes, Blanzy . . . 010832
Musée de la Mine et des Techniques Minières, Giromagny . . . 011953
Musée de la Mine Lucien-Mazars, Aubin . . . 010524
Musée de la Mine Marcel Maulini, Ronchamp . . . 014101
Musée de la Mine, Musée de la Clouterie, Musée du Gazomètre, Fontaine-l'Evêque . . . 003437
Musée de la Mine - Tissage, Histoires Jean-Marie Somet, Villars (Loire) . . . 015232
Musée de la Miniature, Saint-Sauves-d'Auvergne . . . 014533
Musée de la Mode, Avallon . . . 010582
Musée de la Mode, Marseille . . . 012939
Musée de la Mode et du Textile, Union Centrale des Arts Décoratifs, Paris 013638
Musée de la Mode Retrovée, Digoin 011597
Musée de la Moineaudière, Xonrupt-Longemer . . . 015375
Musée de la Moisson, Sagy (Magny-en-Vexin) . . . 014164
Musée de la Monnaie de Paris, Paris . . . 013639
Musée de la Montagne et de la Forêt, La Haut-du-Them . . . 012277
Musée de la Montagne Saint-Pierre, Lanaye . . . 003567
Musée de la Montre Droz-Flores, Villers-le-Lac . . . 015290
Musée de la Mosaïque et des Émaux, Briare . . . 010996
Musée de la Mosaique Gallo-Romaine, Sorde-l'Abbaye . . . 014822
Musée de la Moto, Marseille . . . 012940
Musée de la Moto, Savigny-les-Beaune . . . 014723
Musée de la Motocyclette, Entrevaux . . . 011701
Musée de la Musique, Anduze . . . 010384
Musée de la Musique, Cité de la Musique, Paris . . . 013640
Musée de la Musique de Ouagadougou, Ouagadougou . . . 004962
Musée de la Musique et des Instruments, Musée Municipal, Blangy-sur-Bresle . . . 010827
Musée de la Musique Mécanique, Crillon-le-Brave . . . 011537
Musée de la Musique Mécanique, Haubourdin . . . 012076
Musée de la Musique Mécanique, Les Gets . . . 012622
Musée de la Mytiliculture, Esnandes . . . 011727
Musée de la Mytiliculture, Pénestin 013765
Musée de la Nacre et de la Tabletterie, Méru . . . 013033
Musée de la Naissance de l'Aviation Suisse, Avenches . . . 036864
Musée de la Natation, Chissey-les-Mâcon . . . 011369
Musée de la Nativité, Lourdes . . . 012770
Musée de la Nature, Ettelbruck . . . 027885
Musée de la Nature, Sivry . . . 003771
Musée de la Nature et de la Chasse, Thuir . . . 014952
Musée de la Navigation Fluviale/ Ascenseur à Bateaux, Arques (Pas-de-Calais) 010483
Musée de la Pailletterie, Amilly . . . 010371
Musée de la Papeterie, Puymoyen . 013967
Musée de la Papeterie-Canson et Montgolfier, Davézieux . . . 011563
Musée de la Parfumerie, Bastia . . . 010665
Musée de la Parfumerie, Paris . . . 013641
Musée de la Parfumerie Fragonard, Grasse . . . 011998
Musée de la Parfumerie Fragonard, Paris . . . 013642
Musée de la Parfumerie Galimard, Grasse . . . 011999
Musée de la Parfumerie Molinard, Grasse . . . 012000
Musée de la Parole, Bastogne . . . 003215
Musée de la Paysannerie, Cholet . . 011374
Musée de la Paysannerie, Baguer-Morvan . . . 010628
Musée de la Pêche, Beauchastel . . 010699
Musée de la Pêche, Concarneau . . 011453
Musée de la Pêche et de la Nature, APNLE, Levallois-Perret . . . 012651
Musée de la Pelote Basque, Saint-Étienne-de-Baigorry . . . 014274
Musée de la Pelote Basque, Sare . . 014672
Musée de la Percée d'Avranches, Avranches . . . 010604
Musée de la Perle, Papeete . . . 015393
Musée de la Petite Bergère, Bartres 010659
Musée de la Petite Gare, Olonne-sur-Mer . . . 013487
Musée de la Pétrification, Savonnières . . . 014729
Musée de la Pharmacie, Tence . . . 014917
Musée de la Pharmacie Albert Ciurana, Montpellier . . . 013201
Musée de la Photographie, Charleroi . . . 003366
Musée de la Photographie, Mougins 013260
Musée de la Photographie, Port Louis . . . 028071
Musée de la Pierre, Antoing . . . 003150
Musée de la Pierre, Muno . . . 003660
Musée de la Pierre, Trambly . . . 015029
Musée de la Pierre, Vézelay . . . 015196
Musée de la Pierre à Fusil, Luçay-le-Male . . . 012791
Musée de la Pierre à Fusil, Meusnes . . . 013048
Musée de la Pierre et du Marbre, Basècles . . . 003212
Musée de la Pierre et Site des Carrières, Maffle . . . 003622
Musée de la Pierre Philosophale, Issoire . . . 012137
Musée de la Pince, Montecheroux . 013152
Musée de la Planète Métal, Hagondange . . . 012062
Musée de la Plongée, Espalion . . . 011729
Musée de la Pointe Saint-Mathieu, Plougonvelin . . . 013852
Musée de la Poire Tapée, Rivarennes . . . 014061
Musee de la Pomme, Bourg-Saint-Maurice . . . 010928
Musée de la Pomme et du Cidre, Pleudihen-sur-Rance . . . 013838
Musée de la Pomme et du Cidre, Vaudeurs . . . 015142
Musée de la Pomme et du Cidre et des Métiers Traditionnels, Rosay . . . 014108
Musée de la Porcelaine, Couleuvre . 011502
Musée de la Porcelaine, Saint-Yrieix-la-Perche . . . 014577
Musée de la Porte, Tubize . . . 003817
Musée de la Porte de Bourgogne, Mouzon . . . 013285
Musée de la Porte de Hal, Bruxelles 003322
Musée de la Porte de Thann, Cernay . . . 011183
Musée de la Poste, Amélie-les-Bains-Palalda . . . 010364
Musée de la Poste, Paris . . . 013643
Musée de la Poste, Prunelli-di-Fium'Orbu . . . 013959
Musée de la Poste, Saint-Flour (Cantal) . . . 014292
Musée de la Poste des Pays de Loire, Nantes . . . 013335
Musée de la Poste et des Techniques de Communication de Basse-Normandie, Caen . . . 011053
Musée de la Poste et des Voyages, Amboise . . . 010357
Musée de la Poterie, Nospelt . . . 027898
Musée de la Poterie, Saint-Emilion . 014266
Musée de la Poterie, Saint-Jean-de-Fos . . . 014345
Musée de la Poterie, Vallauris . . . 015105
Musée de la Poterie de Grès, Betschdorf . . . 010780
Musée de la Poterie du Sartre, Saint-Alban-Auriolles . . . 014172
Musée de la Poterie et de la Céramique, Sadirac . . . 014161
Musée de la Poudrerie Nationale, Association des Amis du Parc Forestier National de Sevran, Vaujours . . . 015144
Musée de la Poupée, Aubeterre-sur-Dronne . . . 010516
Musée de la Poupée, La Côte-d'Aime . . . 012240
Musée de la Poupée, Le Beausset . 012463
Musée de la Poupée, Montbrison . . 013144
Musée de la Poupée, Paris . . . 013644
Musée de la Poupée Ancienne, Cerisiers . . . 011180
Musée de la Poupée et des Jouets Anciens, Guérande . . . 012043
Musée de la Poupée et du Jouët, Wambrechies . . . 015349
Musée de la Préhistoire, Coux-et-Bigaroque . . . 011522
Musée de la Préhistoire, Jemeppe-sur-Sambre . . . 003546
Musée de la Préhistoire, Le Mas-d'Azil . . . 012523
Musée de la Prehistoire, Rânes . . . 013991
Musée de la Préhistoire, Saint-Flovier . . . 014293
Musée de la Préhistoire, Saint-Porchaire . . . 014491
Musée de la Préhistoire, Solesmes . 014815
Musée de la Préhistoire, Cavernes Préhistoriques de Goyet, Gesves . 003477
Musée de la Préhistoire Charentaise, La Rochefoucauld . . . 012313
Musée de la Préhistoire du Vercors, Vassieux-en-Vercors . . . 015138
Musée de la Préhistoire en Wallonie, Flémalle . . . 003436
Musée de la Préhistoire L'Age des Garrigues, Viols-le-Fort . . . 015314
Musée de la Préhistoire-Le Cairn, Centre Archéologique de Recherche sur le Néolithique, Saint-Hilaire-la-Forêt 014331
Musée de la Préhistoire/Paléontologie, Peyzac-le-Moustier . . . 013805
Musée de la Préhistorique, Mozet . 003659
Musée de la Première Guerre Mondiale, Villeneuve-les-Convers . . . 015277
Musée de la Princerie, Verdun (Meuse) . . . 015174

Musée de la Principauté de Stavelot-Malmedy, Stavelot 003781
Musée de la Protohistoire, Beynac et Cazenac 010786
Musée de la Protohistoire, Saint-Martin-de-Fressengeas 014418
Musée de la Prune et du Pruneau, Lafitte-sur-Lot 012376
Musée de la Publicité, Paris 013645
Musée de la Radio, Cornol 037034
Musée de la Radio, Villers-le-Lac . . 015291
Musée de la Radio et du Phonographe, Lanobre 012415
Musée de la Radio Galletti, Saint-Maurice-de-Rotherens 014431
Musée de la Radio Les Années 30, Saint-Victor-sur-Arlanc 014570
Musée de la Radiodiffusion et Télévision Belge, Bruxelles 003323
Musée de la Reddition, Reims 014004
Musée de la Régence, Ensisheim . . 011694
Musée de la Reine Bérengère, Le Mans 012518
Musée de la Reliure, Beaumesnil . . 010709
Musée de La Remise, Gex 011940
Musée de la Réparation Navale, Marseille 012941
Musée de la Reproduction du Son, Saint-Fargeau 014282
Musée de la Résistance, Auch 010530
Musée de la Résistance, Cabanès (Aveyron) 011039
Musée de la Résistance, Limoges . 012692
Musée de la Résistance, Mussy-sur-Seine 013311
Musée de la Résistance, Saint-Connan 014236
Musée de la Résistance, Sospel . . . 014830
Musée de la Résistance, Varennes-Vauzelles 015134
Musée de la Résistance Bretonne, Saint-Marcel (Morbihan) 014413
Musée de la Résistance d'Anterrieux de la 7éme Cie et des Maquis du Réduit de la Truyère, Anterrieux 010422
Musée de la Résistance, de l'Internement et de la Déportation, Chamalières . . 011205
Musée de la Résistance du Mont Mouchet, Auvers (Haute-Loire) 010564
Musée de la Résistance en Morvan, Saint-Brisson (Nièvre) 014209
Musée de la Résistance en Vercors, Vassieux-en-Vercors 015139
Musée de la Résistance en Zone Interdite, Denain 011574
Musée de la Résistance et de la Bataille du 19 Juin 1940, Chargé 011247
Musée de la Résistance et de la Déportation, Lyon 012806
Musée de la Résistance et de la Déportation, Agen 010270
Musée de la Résistance et de la Déportation, Angoulême 010404
Musée de la Résistance et de la Déportation, Besançon 010770
Musée de la Résistance et de la Déportation, Grenoble 012022
Musée de la Résistance et de la Déportation, Montauban 013128
Musée de la Résistance et de la Déportation, Centre Régional d'Histoire de la Résistance, Castelnau-le-Lez . 011140
Musée de la Résistance et de la Déportation en Picardie, Fargniers 011783
Musée de la Résistance et Déportation, Blois 010847
Musée de la Résistance et des Anciens Combattants, Floing 011828
Musée de la Résistance Henri Queuille, Neuvic (Corrèze) 013377
Musée de la Résistance Nationale, Champigny-sur-Marne 011228
Musée de la Révolution Française, Vizille 015327
Musée de la Rose et des Arts, Les Rosiers-sur-Loire 012633
Musée de la Roue Tourne, La Mothe-Achard 012288
Musée de la Route, Mons 003649
Musée de la Rubanerie Cominoise, Comines 003376
Musée de la Sahla, Audun-le-Tiche 010540
Musée de la Schlitte, Barr 010658
Musée de la Schlitte et des Métiers du Bois, Muhlbach-sur-Munster 013289
Musée de la Science-Fiction, de l'Utopie et des Voyages Extraordinaires, Maison d'Ailleurs, Yverdon-les-Bains 037743
Musée de la Scierie Ariel-Vincent, Sainte-Croix-aux-Mines 014590
Musée de la Seconde Guerre Mondiale, Avranches 010604
Musée de la Seconde Guerre Mondiale, Digne-les-Bains 011590
Musée de la Seconde Guerre Mondiale, Message Verlaine, Tourcoing 015006
Musée de la Seconde Guerre Mondiale Roger Bellon, Conlie 011465
Musée de la Sénatorie, Guéret 012045
Musée de la Serrure, Musée Bricard, Paris 013646
Musée de la SNSM, Ile-de-Molène . 012127
Musée de la Société Archéologique de Corseul, Plancoët 013831
Musée de la Société Archéologique et Historique de la Charente, Angoulême 010405
Musée de la Société de l'Histoire du Protestantisme Français, Paris . . 013647
Musée de la Société d'Histoire et d'Archéologie, Musée de Briord, Briord 011005
Musée de la Soie, Jujurieux 012182
Musée de la Soie, Monoblet 013101
Musée de la Soierie, Charlieu 011253
Musée de La Source, Valignat 015102
Musée de la Station Biologique, Roscoff 014111
Musée de la Statue Religieuse, Lourdes 012771
Musée de la Straize, Gy-en-Sologne 012060
Musée de la Symbolique Militaire, Vincennes 015309
Musée de la Taillanderie, Nans-sous-Sainte-Anne 013331
Musée de la Tapiserie et des Arts du Tissu, Tournai 003808
Musée de la Tapisserie, Enghien . . 003422
Musée de la Tapisserie Contemporaine, Angers 010392
Musée de la Tapisserie de Bayeux, Bayeux 010680
Musée de la Targette, Neuville-Saint-Vaast 013381
Musée de la Terre, Rambervillers . . 013987
Musée de la Terre Ardèchoise, Privas 013954
Musée de la Terre et du Bois, Saint-George 037475
Musée de la Thiérache, Vervins . . . 015191
Musée de la Toinette, Murat-le-Quaire 013303
Musée de la Tonnellerie, Generac . . 011927
Musée de la Tonnellerie, Musée Municipal, Chécy 011339
Musée de la Tonnellerie Animée, Vergèze 015178
Musée de la Tonnellerie et du Vin, Aloxe-Corton 010342
Musée de la Tour, Coucy-le-Château-Auffrique 011496
Musée de la Tour, Histoire et Traditions Locales, Antibes-Juan-les-Pins . . 010426
Musée de la Tour aux Puces, Thionville 014932
Musée de la Tour Carelot, Avensan . 010585
Musée de la Tour Carrée, Rosans . . 014107
Musée de la Tour de l'Abbaye, Jouarre 012170
Musée de la Tour de l'Orle d'Or, Semur-en-Auxois 014752
Musée de la Tour des Echevins, Luxeuil-les-Bains 012797
Musée de la Tour d'Honneur, Lesparre-Médoc 012647
Musée de la Tour du Brau, Les Baux-de-Provence 012606
Musée de la Tour du Moulin, Marcigny 012893
Musée de la Tour Romaine, Arlon . . 003199
Musée de la Tour Salamandre, Beaumont 003218
Musée de la Tradition Champenoise, Musée de la Cave des Champagnes de Castellane, Épernay 011707
Musée de la Tradition de la Brigade des Sapeurs-Pompiers de Paris, Paris 013648
Musée de la Tradition de la Brigade des Sapeurs-Pompiers de Paris, Paris 013649
Musée de la T.S.F., Charleville-Mézières 011250
Musée de la Tuile, Blajan 010823
Musée de la Tuilerie, Malbrans 012864
Musée de la Vallée, Jausiers 012154
Musée de la Vallée d'Aure, Ancizan 010377
Musée de la Vallée de la Creuse, Eguzon 011686
Musée de la Vallée de l'Ubaye, Barcelonnette 010650
Musée de la Vallée du Lot, Ecomusée de la Vallee d'Aspe, Villeneuve-sur-Lot 015282
Musée de la Vallée et de la Faïencerie, Rarecourt 013992
Musée de la Vannerie, Cadenet . . . 011048
Musée de la Vannerie, Remilly-sur-Lozon 014014
Musée de la Vannerie, Villaines-les-Rochers 015219
Musée de la Vannerie et de l'Artisant, Vallabrègues 015103
Musée de la Vannerie L'Osarium, Le Mayet-en-Montagne 012524
Musée de la Vénerie et des Spahis, Senlis 014761
Musée de la Verrerie, Blangy-sur-Bresle 010828
Musée de la Verrerie, Veauche 015150
Musée de la Verrerie, Atelier du Souffleur de Verre, Saint-Galmier 014295
Musée de la Vie, Bidon 010797
Musée de la Vie Artisanale, Ambachtenmuseum, Ham-sur-Heure 003488
Musée de la Vie Bourguignonne Perrin-de-Puycousin, Dijon 011605
Musée de la Vie d'Autrefois, Marchin 003628
Musée de la Vie d'Autrefois, Vandré 015123
Musée de la Vie d'Autrefois, Vivoin . 015326
Musée de la Vie en Bassin Minier, Escaudain 011723
Musée de la Vie Lensoise, Lens . . . 003576
Musée de la Vie Locale et de la Coutellerie, Gembloux 003445
Musée de la Vie Monastique, Centre d'art Sacré, Saint-Hilaire-du-Harcouët . 014329
Musée de la Vie Paysanne, Musees Gaumais, Dampicourt 003388
Musée de la Vie Populaire, Soumagne 003776
Musée de la Vie Réginal des Rièzes et des Sarts, Cul-des-Sarts 003383
Musée de la Vie Régionale, Cerfontaine 003364
Musée de la Vie Romantique, Hôtel Schefffer-Renan, Paris 013650
Musée de la Vie Rural, Monflanquin 013098
Musée de la Vie Rurale, Chasteix . . 011272
Musée de la Vie Rurale, Mont-Saint-Jean 013113
Musée de La Vie Rurale, Saint-Quentin-Fallavier 014503
Musée de la Vie Rurale, Steenwerck 014848
Musée de la Vie Rurale, Tusson . . . 015069
Musée de la Vie Rurale, Musée Municipal, Desaignes 011580
Musée de la Vie Rurale Condruze, Fondation Christian Blavier, Nandrin 003670
Musée de la Vie Rurale d'Huissignies, Huissignies 003526
Musée de la Vie Rurale en Wallonie, Saint-Hubert 003736
Musée de la Vie Rurale et Forestière, Saint-Michel-en-Thiérache 014440
Musée de la Vie Rurale Li Vîle Grègne, Erezée 003424
Musée de la Vie Rurale Régionale, Saint-Maurin 014433
Musée de la Vie Wallonne, Liège . . 003594
Musée de La Vieille École, Pernes-les-Fontaines 013776
Musée de la Vieille Forge, Denazé . 011576
Musée de la Vieille Pharmacie, Apothicairerie, La Rochefoucauld 012314
Musée de la Vieille Pharmacie, Moutiers-Saint-Jean 013282
Musée de la Vieille Prune, Distillerie Louis Roque, Souillac 014836
Musée de la Vigne, La Roche-Vineuse 012312
Musée de la Vigne, Verzenay 015192
Musée de la Vigne Benoit-Raclet, Musée Dèpartemental du Compagnonnage, Romanèche-Thorins 014092
Musée de la Vigne et de la Vie Rurale, Plauzat 013834
Musée de la Vigne et du Patrimoine, Brioude 011007
Musée de la Vigne et du Terroir, Saint-Pourçain-sur-Sioule 014494
Musée de la Vigne et du Vin, Aigle . 036821
Musée de la Vigne et du Vin, Ansouis 010420
Musée de la Vigne et du Vin, Aubière 010520
Musée de la Vigne et du Vin, Buzet-sur-Baise 011038
Musée de la Vigne et du Vin, Cérons 011185
Musée de la Vigne et du Vin, Curtil-Vergy 011549
Musée de la Vigne et du Vin, Gigondas 011945
Musée de la Vigne et du Vin, Gruissan 012039
Musée de la Vigne et du Vin, Le Mesnil-sur-Oger 012528
Musée de la Vigne et du Vin, Lézignan-Corbières 012659
Musée de la Vigne et du Vin, Lods . 012728
Musée de la Vigne et du Vin, Loupiac 012765
Musée de la Vigne et du Vin, Mareau-aux-Près 012901
Musée de la Vigne et du Vin, Onzain 013493
Musée de la Vigne et du Vin, Pierreclos 013812
Musée de la Vigne et du Vin, Prayssas 013945
Musée de la Vigne et du Vin, Vaux-en-Beaujolais 015146
Musée de la Vigne et du Vin d'Anjou, Saint-Lambert-du-Lattay 014374
Musée de la Vigne et du Vin de Franche-Comté, Arbois 010447
Musée de la Vigne-Moulin du Haut-Benauge, Gornac 011972
Musée de la Vilaine Maritime, La Roche-Bernard 012305
Musée de la Villa Romaine de Pully, Pully 037429
Musée de la Ville de Saint-Quentin-en-Yvelines, Montigny-le-Bretonneux 013176
Musée de la Ville de Saverne, Saverne 014716
Musée de la Ville de Strasbourg, Strasbourg 014869
Musée de la Ville d'Eaux, Spa 003778
Musée de la Viscose, Échirolles . . . 011678
Musée de la Viticulture, Barizey . . . 010656
Musée de la Viticulture, Durban-Corbières 011671
Musée de la Viticulture, Lhomme . . 012662
Musée de la Viticulture, Mirepeisset 013079
Musée de la Viticulture, Montlouiș-sur-Loire 013181
Musée de la Viticulture, Santenay . 014667
Musée de la Viticulture et des Arts Populaires, Portel-des-Corbières . 013924

Musée de la Viticulture et Renaissance du Vignoble, Contz-les-Bains 011474
Musée de la Voie Sacrée, Souilly . . 014838
Musée de la Voiture à Cheval, Les Épesses 012618
Musée de la Voiture de Course, Savigny-les-Beaune 014724
Musée de la Voiture Hippomobile et de la Citadelle de Bourg, Bourg-sur-Gironde 010931
Musée de la Volaille de Bresse, Romenay 014096
Musée de l'Abbaye, Echternach . . . 027879
Musée de l'Abbaye, Lacaune 012369
Musée de l'Abbaye de Bourgueil, Bourgueil 010944
Musée de l'Abbaye de Clairvaux, Ville-sous-la-Ferté 015237
Musée de l'Abbaye de Port-Royal, Magny-lès-Hameaux 012846
Musée de l'Abbaye de Saint-Mathieu, Plougonvelin 013853
Musée de l'Abbaye d'Orval, Villers-devant-Orval 003831
Musée de l'Abbaye Romane, La Sauve-Majeure 012336
Musée de l'Abbaye Saint-Vigor, Cérisy-la-Forêt 011181
Musée de l'Abbaye Sainte-Croix, Les Sables-d'Olonne 012639
Musée de l'Abeille, Château-Richer 005255
Musée de l'Abeille, Québec 006223
Musée de l'Abeille, Tilff 003796
Musée de l'Abeille et de la Cire, Toulouse 014987
Musée de l'Abeille et du Braconnage, Salbris 014632
Musée de l'Abeille Vivante, Vitré . . 015321
Musée de l'Abri, Hatten 012075
Musée de l'Absinthe, Auvers-sur-Oise 010568
Musée de l'Academie de la Val d'Isère, Moutiers (Savoie) 013283
Musée de l'Accordéon, Montmagny 005905
Musée de Lachine, Lachine 005732
Musée de l'Aéronautique de Nancy-Essey, Tomblaine 014963
Musée de l'Affiche de la Carte Postale et de l'Art Graphique, Toulouse 014988
Musée de l'Agriculture Auvergnate, Coltines 011439
Musée de l'Agriculture Catalane, Saint-Michel-de-Llotes 014436
Musée de l'Agriculture de Montagne, Saint-Paul-sur-Ubaye 014471
Musée de l'Aile Delta, Athis-Mons . 010506
Musée de l'Air et de l'Espace, Le Bourget (Seine-Saint-Denis) 012470
Musée de l'Alambic, Quimper 013977
Musée de l'Alambic, Saint-Desirat . 014255
Musée de l'Albanais, Rumilly 014156
Musée de l'Algérie Française, Perpignan 013786
Musée de l'Alta Rocca, Lévie 012655
Musée de l'Amérique Française, Québec 006224
Musée de l'Amour et des ses Traditions, Oger 013476
Musée de l'Ancien Collège des Jésuites, Reims 014005
Musée de l'Ancien Évêché-Patrimoine, Grenoble 012023
Musée de l'Ancien Havre, Le Havre 012506
Musée de l'Ancienne Abbaye, Stavelot 003781
Musée de l'Ancienne Abbaye de Landévennec, Landévennec 012399
Musée de l'Ancienne Cathédrale, Noyon 013460
Musée de l'Ancienne Chartreuse de la Verne, Collobrières 011424
Musée de L'Ancienne Forge, Pesmes 013797
Musée de l'Arc de Triomphe, Paris . 013651
Musée de l'Archéologie, Céret 011177
Musée de l'Archerie Traditionnelle, Ayssenes 010609
Musée de l'Archiconfrérie Notre-Dame de la Miséricorde, Musée Jean Giraudoux, Pellevoisin 013764
Musée de l'Ardenne, Charleville-Mézières 011251
Musée de l'Ardoise, Renazé 014017
Musée de l'Ardoise, Trélazé 015039
Musée de l'Ardoise, Couvent des Carmélites, Fumay 011907
Musée de l'Areuse, Boudry 036967
Musée de l'Argonne, Sainte-Menehould 014610
Musée de l'Arles et Provence Antiques, Arles 010471
Musée de l'Armagnac, Condom . . . 011462
Musée de l'Arme Blanche et Conservatoire de l'Épée, France-Lames, Monistrol-sur-Loire 013100
Musée de l'Armée, Alger 000041
Musée de l'Armée, Paris 013652
Musée de l'Armée des Alpes, Sospel 014831
Musée de l'Armée Russe, Paris . . . 013653
Musée de l'Armée Secrète dans la Loire, Estivareilles 011744
Musée de l'Art Africain, Sailly 014167
Musée de l'Art Campanaire, Labergement-Sainte-Marie 012364
Musée de l'Art Culinaire, Fondation Auguste Escoffier, Villeneuve-Loubet 015279
Musée de l'Art Forain et de la Musique Mécanique, Raymond D'Ys, Conflans-en-Jarnisy 011463
Musée de l'Art Wallon, Liège 003595
Musée de l'Artillerie, Draguignan . . 011656
Musée de l'Artisanat et des Traditions Rurales, Brebotte 010971
Musée de l'Artisanat Rural Ancien, Tigy 014957
Musée de l'Assistance Publique, Bruxelles 003324
Musée de l'Assistance Publique-Hôpitaux de Paris, Paris 013654
Musée de l'Association des Marches Folkloriques de l'Entre-Sambre-et-Meuse, Gerpinnes 003476
Musée de l'Atelier de Rosa Bonheur, Thomery 014935
Musée de l'Atelier de Xaintonge, Pont-l'Abbé-d'Arnoult 013892
Musée de l'Attelage, Marquillies . . 012918
Musée de l'Attelage et du Cheval, Sérignan (Hérault) 014769
Musée de l'Audiovisuel, Montarcher 013123
Musée de l'Auditoire, Joinville (Haute-Marne) 012162
Musée de l'Auditoire, Sainte-Suzanne 014619
Musée de l'Auld Alliance Franco-Écossaise, Aubigny-sur-Nère 010522
Musée de l'Automate et de la Robotique, Souillac 014837
Musée de l'Automobile, Martigny . . 037314
Musée de l'Automobile, Muriaux . . 037363
Musée de l'Automobile, Orgon 013507
Musée de l'Automobile, Plan-les-Ouates 037415
Musée de l'Automobile, Valençay . . 015092
Musée de l'Automobile, Velaine-en-Haye 015152
Musée de l'Automobile Ancienne, Buis-sur-Damville 011028
Musée de l'Automobile de Vendée, Talmont-Saint-Hilaire 014894
Musée de l'Automobile du Mans, Le Mans 012517
Musée de l'Automobile Française, Collection Philippe Charbonneaux, Reims 014006
Musée de l'Automobile La Belle Époque, Pont-l'Évêque 013894
Musée de l'Automobile Miniature, Fontenay-sur-Mer 011855
Musée de l'Automobile Miniature et des Poupées Anciennes, Nointel (Oise) 013439
Musée de l'Automobile Sportive, Sanary-sur-Mer 014661
Musée de l'Automobiliste, Mougins 013261
Musée de l'Avallonnais, Avallon . . . 010584
Musée de l'Aventure Industrielle, Apt 010441
Musée de l'Aviation, Savigny-les-Beaune 014725
Musée de l'Aviation, Warluis 015352
Musée de l'Aviation Charles Noetinger, Perpignan 013787
Musée de l'Aviation Légère de l'Armée de Terre, Dax 011565
Musée de l'Eau, Pont-en-Royans . . 013889
Musée de l'Eau de Vie et des Vieux Métiers, Valognes 015115
Musée de l'Échevinage, Saintes . . . 014621
Musée de l'Eclairage, Dinant 003409
Musée de l'Éclairage, Liège 003596
Musée de l'École, Bourges 010935
Musée de l'Ecole, Bruxelles 003325
Musée de l'École, Carcassonne . . . 011112
Musée de l'Ecole, Chartres 011265
Musée de l'École, Châtelus (Allier) . 011308
Musée de l'Ecole, Echery 011677
Musée de l'École, Saint-Étienne-de-Tinée 014275
Musée de l'École, Saint-Remy 014512
Musée de l'Ecole, Villeneuve-d'Ascq 015265
Musée de l'Ecole 1900, Saint-Martin-des-Olmes 014423
Musée de l'Ecole Biblique et Archéologique Française, Jerusalem 031416
Musée de l'École d'Autrefois, Pontis 013908
Musée de l'Ecole de Nancy, Nancy . 013323
Musée de l'Ecole et de la Mine, Harnes 012068
Musée de l'Ecole Jules Ferry, Aubeterre-sur-Dronne 010517
Musée de l'École Nationale d'Art Décoratif, Aubusson 010526
Musée de l'Ecole Navale, Lanvéoc-Poulmic 012420
Musée de l'Ecole Rurale, Trégarvan 015033
Musée de l'École Rurale d'Auvergne, Messeix 013038
Musée de l'Ecologie des Rives de l'Adour, Orist 013510
Musée de l'Église de Lorris, Lorris . 012751
Musée de l'Eglise Notre-Dame, Montréal 005936
Musée de l'Électricité, Dijon 011606
Musée de l'Elysée, Lausanne 037249
Musée de l'Empéri, Salon-de-Provence 014651
Musée de l'Enfance, Alger 000042
Musée de l'Enfance École de la Vie, Cannes 011099
Musée de l'Entité de Walcourt, Walcourt 003840
Musée de l'Ephèbe, Agde 010269
Musée de l'Epicerie et des Commerces, Lignerolles 012671
Musée de l'Escrime Charles Debeur, Bruxelles 003326
Musée de l'Espace, Kourou 015389
Musée de l'Estérel, Les Adrets-de-l'Estérel 012597
Musée de l'Établissement des Constructions Navales de Ruelle, Ruelle 014155
Musée de l'Etang de Thau, Bouzigues 010955
Musée de l'Evéché, Sion 037567
Musée de l'Evêché, Verdun (Meuse) 015175
Musée de l'Eventail, Paris 013655
Musée de l'Evolution du Style Plantagenêt, Angers 010393
Musée de l'Habitat Ancien, Bessans 010774
Musée de l'Habitat Rural en Pays d'Aigues, La Tour-d'Aigues 012345
Musée de l'Habitat Rural Passé et des Traditions, La Garnache 012268
Musée de l'Heure et du Feu, Villerest 015287
Musée de l'Histoire de France, Paris 013656
Musée de l'Histoire de France à travers son Armée, Montet et Bouxal 013158
Musée de l'Histoire de la Forêt d'Ardenne, Saint-Hubert 003737
Musée de l'Histoire de la Médecine, Vandœuvre-les-Nancy 015122
Musée de l'Histoire de la Médecine de Toulouse, Toulouse 014989
Musée de l'Histoire de la Poterie, Bouconville-Vauclair 010903
Musée de l'Histoire de la Poterie, La Chapelle-des-Pots 012227
Musée de l'Histoire de l'Abbaye, Saint-Sauveur-le-Vicomte 014537
Musée de l'Histoire de l'Emigration Percheronne au Canada, Tourouvre 015012
Musée de l'Histoire des Bastides et de l'Evolution de l'Habitat, Bassoues 010663
Musée de l'Histoire du Costume, Scey-sur-Saône-et-Saint-Albin 014733
Musée de l'Histoire du Fer, Jarville . 012150
Musée de l'Histoire du Feu, Musée des Sapeurs-Pompiers, Campuzan . . . 011086
Musée de l'Histoire et de la Vie Salmiennes, Vielsalm 003828
Musée de l'Histoire Paysanne, Maraye-en-Othe 012882
Musée de l'Histoire Vivante Parc Montreau, Montreuil-sous-Bois 013222
Musée de l'Histore Estudiantine, Assens 036857
Musée de l'Historie de Montpellier, Montpellier 013202
Musée de l'Historire de Rosny, Rosny-sous-Bois 014118
Musée de l'Holographie, Paris 013657
Musée de l'Homme, Paris 013658
Musée de l'Homme de Néandertal, La Chapelle-aux-Saints 012220
Musée de l'Homme et de l'Industrie, Le Creusot 012489
Musée de l'Homme et de sa Montagne, Sainte-Croix-Vallée-Française . . . 014591
Musée de l'Hôpital, Musée Saint-Roche et de la Pharmacie, Yssingeaux 015379
Musée de L'Hôpital Général de Dijon, Dijon 011607
Musée de l'Hôpital Psychiatrique, Brumath 011021
Musée de l'Horlogerie, Pesmes . . . 013798
Musée de l'Horlogerie, Saint-Nicolas-d'Aliermont 014451
Musée de l'Horlogerie Ancienne, Fougères (Ille-et-Vilaine) 011873
Musée de l'Horlogerie du Haut-Doubs, Morteau 013253
Musée de l'Horlogerie et de l'Emaillerie, Genève 037129
Musée de l'Horlogerie et du Décolletage, Cluses 011411
Musée de l'Hospice Comtesse, Lille 012679
Musée de l'Hospice Saint-Roch, Issoudun 012138
Musée de l'Hôspital, Apothicairerie, La Rochefoucauld 012314
Musée de l'Hôtel Bellevue, Bruxelles 003327
Musée de l'Hôtel de Barral, Soissons 014813
Musée de l'Hôtel de Berny, Amiens 010368
Musée de l'Hôtel de Vermandois, Senlis 014762
Musée de l'Hôtel de Ville, Hondschoote 012106
Musée de l'Hôtel-Dieu, Beaune . . . 010713
Musée de l'Hôtel-Dieu, Mantes-La Jolie 012880
Musée de l'Hôtel-Dieu, Porrentruy . 037419
Musée de l'Hôtel Sandelin, Saint-Omer 014454
Musée de l'Huître, Marennes 012903
Musée de Lignan et du Canton de Créon, Lignan-de-Bordeaux 012670
Musée de l'Iguanodon, Bernissart . 003232
Musée de l'Ile de France, Sceaux . . 014731
Musée de l'Image Populaire, Pfaffenhoffen 013808
Musée de l'Imagerie Publicitaire sur le Chocolat, Pontlevoy 013910

Musée de l'Images, Épinal 011713
Musée de l'Impression sur Etoffes, Mulhouse 013292
Musée de l'Imprimerie, Billom 010806
Musée de l'Imprimerie, Bordeaux . . 010883
Musée de l'Imprimerie, Association Pro Arte Graphica, Nantes 013336
Musée de l'Imprimerie, Cabinet des Estampes, Bruxelles 003328
Musée de l'Imprimerie de Lyon, Lyon 012814
Musée de l'Industrie Régionale de la Chaussure, Saint-André-de-la-Marche 014181
Musée de l'Infanterie, Montpellier . 013203
Musée de l'Insigne et de la Symbolique Militaire, Vincennes 015310
Musée de l'Insolite, Cabrerets 011042
Musée de l'Insolite, Font-Romeu-Odeillo-Via 011835
Musée de l'Insolite, Manent Max, Loriol-sur-Drôme 012748
Musée de l'Institut de Géologie et de Géoscience de Rennes, Rennes (Ille-et-Vilaine) 014022
Musée de l'Institut du Monde Arabe, Paris 013659
Musée de l'Invasion Aéroportée, 1944 Pegasus-Bridge, Bénouville 010752
Musée de l'île d'Oleron Aliénor d'Aquitaine, Saint-Pierre-d'Oléron 014485
Musée de l'Âne, Venosc 015165
Musée de l'Océanie, Saint-Symphorien-sur-Coise 014552
Musée de Lodève, Lodève 012727
Musée de l'Œuf et de l'Icône, Banne 010640
Musée de l'Œuvre, Avignon 010592
Musée de l'Œuvre de la Madeleine, Vézelay 015197
Musée de l'Oeuvre Notre-Dame, Strasbourg 014870
Musée de l'Olivette, Sorède 014824
Musée de l'Olivier, Les Baux-de-Provence 012607
Musée de l'Olivier, Nyons 013465
Musée de l'Opéra, vichy 015206
Musée de l'Opéra National de Paris, Paris 013660
Musée de l'Opinel, Saint-Jean-de-Maurienne 014351
Musée de l'Optique, Biesheim 010799
Musée de l'Optométrie, Institut et Centre d'Optométrie, Bures-sur-Yvette . . 011031
Musée de l'Or, Jumilhac-le-Grand . 012183
Musée de l'Oratoire Saint-Joseph, Montréal 005937
Musée de l'Ordre de la Libération, Paris 013661
Musée de l'Ordre de Malte, Bardonnex 036877
Musée de l'Orfevrerie Boilhet-Christofle, Saint-Denis (Seine-Saint-Denis) . 014254
Musée de l'Orfevrerie de la Communaute Française, Château de Seneffe, Seneffe 003746
Musée de l'Ostrévant, Bouchain . . . 010901
Musée de Lourdes, Lourdes 012772
Musée de l'Ours des Cavernes, Entremont-le-Vieux 011699
Musée de l'Outil, Espezel 011737
Musée de l'Outil, Turquant 015066
Musée de l'Outil à la Ferme, Juvigné 012187
Musée de l'Outil des Métiers du Bois, Montjoie-Saint-Martin 013179
Musée de l'Outil et de la Vie au Village, Saint-Privat-des-Près 014497
Musée de l'Outil et des Métiers, Tinténiac 014961
Musée de l'Outil et des Vieux Métiers, La Celle-Guenand 012214
Musée de l'Outil, la Forge Médiévale, Wy-Dit-Joli-Village 015373
Musée de l'Outillage Agricole et Viticole du Château Aney, Cussac-Fort-Médoc 011553
Musée de l'Outillage Artisanal Rural et Bourguignon, Cruzille-en-Mâconnais 011543
Musée de l'Outillage et des Techniques Traditionnelles de la Taille de Pierre, Coucouron 011495
Musée de Louvain-la-Neuve, Louvain-la-Neuve 003617
Musée de Luluabourg, Luluabourg . 007659
Musée de l'Uniforme Legionnaire, L'Institution des Invalides, Puyloubier 013965
Musée de l'Uniforme Militaire Français et du Vieux Bourbon, Bourbon-Lancy . . 010915
Musée de l'Union Compagnonnique des Devoirs Unis, Compagnons du Tour de France, Nantes 013337
Musée de l'Université de Fianarantsoa, Fianarantsoa 027934
Musée de l'Université de Tuléar, Tuléar 027938
Musée de l'Uranium, Lachaux 012372
Musée de Machines Agricoles Miniatures, Guerlesquin 012048
Musée de Mahdia, Mahdia 037962
Musée de Maison-Alfort, Maisons-Alfort 012856
Musée de Maquettes, Animées sur les Ateliers, Métiers et Scènes de Jadis, Vallon-en-Sully 015109
Musée de Marine, Faranui 015390
Musée de Maroua, Maroua 004979
Musée de Matériel Agricole, Saint-Laurent-des-Autels 014379
Musée de Matériel Viticole, Saint-Laurent-des-Autels 014380
Musée de Matière Médicale, Paris . 013662
Musée de Mayombe, Kinshasa 007654
Musée de Mbandaka, Mbandaka . . 007661
Musée de Megève, Megève 012997
Musée de Melun, Melun 013007
Musée de Miellerie, Miellerie des Butineuses, Saint-Saturnin-les-Avignon 014532
Musée de Millau, Millau 013061
Musée de Minéralogie, Strasbourg . 014871
Musée de Minéralogie de l'Ecole des Mines de Paris, Paris 013663
Musée de Minéralogie et de Géologie, Musées de l'Université, Bruxelles 003329
Musée de Miniatures, Brantôme . . . 010962
Musée de Miquelon, Miquelon 034104
Musée de Mobilier Breton, Saint-Vougay 014575
Musée de Modèles Réduits, La Rochelle 012318
Musée de Modélisme, Savigny-les-Beaune 014726
Musée de Montmartre, Paris 013664
Musée de Monuments d'Allumettes et d'Artisanat, La Réole 012299
Musée de Morlaix et Maison du 9 Grand Rue, Morlaix 013242
Musée de Moulages, Strasbourg . . 014872
Musée de Musiques, L'Auberson . . 036861
Musée de Natitingou, Natitingou . . 003890
Musée de Nogent, Nogent-sur-Marne 013436
Musée de Normandie, Caen 011054
Musée de Notre-Dame-de-Paris, Paris 013665
Musée de Ouadane, Nouakchott . . . 028062
Musée de Paléontologie, La Voulte-sur-Rhône 012353
Musée de Paléontologie, Menat . . . 013008
Musée de Paléontologie, Villers-sur-Mer 015293
Musée de Paléontologie, Sciences de la Terre, Villeurbanne 015299
Musée de Paléontologie Christian Guth, Chilhac 011360
Musée de Paléontologie Humaine de Terra Amata, Nice 013400
Musée de Palmyra, Palmyra 037834
Musée de Payerne et Abbatiale, Payerne 037409
Musée de Pays de Seine-et-Marne, Saint-Cyr-sur-Morin 014248
Musée de Peinture, Rodilhan 014088
Musée de Peinture Contemporaine, Vars 015135
Musée de Peinture J. Drevon, Saint-Jean-de-Bournay 014342
Musée de Peinture Louis Français, Plombières-les-Bains 013844
Musée de Peinture Mario Prassinos, Saint-Rémy-de-Provence 014517
Musée de Peintures Contemporaines Hors du Temps, Pierrefeu (Alpes-Maritimes) 013814
Musée de Peyne, Laurède 012439
Musée de Picardie, Amiens 010369
Musée de Pierre Corneille, Le Petit-Couronne 012542
Musée de Plein Air, Landerneau . . . 012398
Musée de Plein Air, Parakou 003892
Musée de Plein Air, Seurre 014785
Musée de Plein Air, Maison pour Tous, Gueugnon 012050
Musée de Plein Air, Parc Préhistorique, Saint-Vallier-de-Thiey 014566
Musée de Plein Air de Rothéneuf, Rothéneuf 014120
Musée de Plein Air des Maisons Comtoises, Nancray 013319
Musée de Plein Air du Quercy Cuzals, Cahors 011068
Musee de Plein de Cherchell, Cherchell 000056
Musée de Pont-Aven, Pont-Aven . . 013883
Musée de Pont-Saint-Esprit, Saint-Paulet-de-Caisson 014473
Musée de Pontarlier, Pontarlier 013902
Musée de Préhistoire, Aurignac . . . 010550
Musée de Préhistoire, Coulmiers . . 011503
Musée de Préhistoire, Echternach . 027880
Musée de Préhistoire, Kinshasa . . . 007655
Musée de Préhistoire Amédée Lemozi, Cabrerets 011043
Musée de Préhistoire des Gorges du Verdon, Quinson 013982
Musée de Préhistoire d'île-de-France, Nemours 013363
Musée de Préhistoire et d'Art Populaire, Violay 015313
Musée de Préhistoire James Miln-Zacharie le Rouzic, Carnac 011122
Musée de Préhistoire Libanaise, Beirut 027809
Musée de Préhistoire Mésolitique L. Coulonges, Sauveterre-la-Lémance 014712
Musée de Préhistoire Régionale, Menton 013021
Musée de Provins et du Provinois, Provins 013956
Musée de Pully, Pully 037430
Musée de Radio France, Paris 013666
Musée de Région Auguste Chabaud, Graveson 012011
Musée de Rome, Caen 011055
Musée de Rouget de Lisle, Donation André Lançon, Lons-le-Saunier 012742
Musée de Royan, Royan 014148
Musée de Saint-Boniface, Saint-Boniface 006327
Musée de Saint-Gengoux-le-Royal, Saint-Gengoux-le-National 014298
Musée de Saint-Germain-Laval, Saint-Germain-Laval 014312
Musée de Saint-Gervais, Saint-Gervais-sur-Mare 014317
Musée de Saint-Martin, Saint-Martin 021562
Musée de Saint-Maurin, Saint-Maurin 014433
Musée de Saint-Paul, Saint-Paul-de-Vence 014469
Musée de Saint-Pierre-Jolys, Saint-Pierre-Jolys 006392
Musée de Sainte-Anne, Sainte-Anne-de-Beaupré 006402
Musée de Sainte-Sigolène, Écomusée La Fabrique, Sainte-Sigolène 014617
Musée de Salon et de la Crau, Salon-de-Provence 014652
Musée de Sarreguemines, Sarreguemines 014684
Musée de Sciences Naturelles, Vevey 037677
Musée de Sétif, Sétif 000072
Musée de Sismologie et Magnétisme Terrestre, Strasbourg 014873
Musée de Site, Digne-les-Bains . . . 011591
Musée de Site, Sare 014673
Musée de Site Le Bazacle, Toulouse 014990
Musée de Skikda, Skikda 000074
Musée de Sologne, Cheverny 011357
Musée de Sologne, Moulin du Chapitre, Romorantin-Lanthenay 014099
Musée de Sonis, Bataille du 2 Décembre 1870, Loigny-la-Bataille 012730
Musée de Soueida, Soueida 037835
Musée de Sousse, Sousse 037979
Musée de Souvigny, Souvigny 014845
Musée de Spéléologie, Ecomusée du Gouffre, Fontaine-de-Vaucluse . . 011840
Musée de Statues d'Enfants, Musée Schoenenberger, Les Mages 012626
Musée de Sucy, Sucy-en-Brie 014883
Musée de Suresnes René Sordes, Suresnes 014888
Musée de Surréalisme, Vaux-le-Pénil 015147
Museé de Tabarka, Tabarka 037980
Musée de Tahiti et des Iles-Te Fare Iamanaha, Punaauia 015395
Musée de Tauroentum, Saint-Cyr-les-Lecques 014244
Musée de Tautavel-Centre Européen de la Préhistoire, Tautavel 014916
Musée de Tazoult, Tazoult 000075
Musée de Temouchent, Ain Temouchent 000039
Musée de Tessé, Le Mans 012519
Musée de Tiemcen, Tiemcen 000077
Musée de Tigran, Champvoux 011232
Musée de Timgad, Timgad 000078
Musée de Tipasa, Tipasa 000079
Musée de Tissage, Chauffailles . . . 011321
Musée de Tlemcen, Tlemcen 000080
Musée de Tourisme et d'Artisanat, Lys-Saint-Georges 012837
Musée de Traditions Populaires et d'Archéologie, Chauvigny 011331
Musée de Uahuka, Uahuka 015396
Musée de Vavoua, Vavoua 007692
Musée de Ventabren, Musée Archéologique La Calade, Ventabren 015167
Musée de Verrières-le-Buisson, Verrières-le-Buisson 015186
Musée de Vieux Cormeilles, Cormeilles-en-Parisis 011486
Musée de Vieux-la-Romaine, Vieux-la-Romaine 015217
Musée de Vieux Sallèles, Sallèles-d'Aude 014641
Musée de Voitures Anciennes et Sellerie, Menetou-Salon 013013
Musée de Voitures Hippomobiles Anciennes, Tour-en-Sologne 015003
Musée de Vulliod Saint-Germain, Pézenas 013806
Musée de Waterloo, Waterloo 003845
Musée de Zoologie Auguste Lameere, Bruxelles 003330
Musée de Zoologie de l'Université de Liège, Liège 003597
Musée d'Eben, Eben-Emael 003415
Musée d'Egyptologie, Villeneuve-d'Ascq 015266
Musée d'El-Oued, El-Oued 000063
Musée Delphinal, Beauvoir-en-Royans 010725
Musée d'Enfidaville, Enfidaville . . . 037953
Musée d'Ennery, Paris 013667
Musée Denoix, Maîtres Liquoristes à Brive depuis 1839, Brive-la-Gaillarde . . 011011
Musée Dentaire de Lyon, Lyon 012815
Musée d'Entrecasteaux, Entrecasteaux 011698

Musée Départemantal des Sapeurs-Pompiers de l'Orne, Bagnoles-de-l'Orne . . . 010624
Musée Départemental, Pontécoulant . . . 013906
Musée Départemental Albert-Kahn, Boulogne-Billancourt . . . 010908
Musée Départemental Alexandre Franconie, Cayenne . . . 015387
Musée Départemental Breton, Quimper . . . 013978
Musée Départemental d'Archéologie, Hastingues . . . 012073
Musée Départemental d'Archéologie, Montrozier . . . 013229
Musée Départemental d'Art Ancien et Contemporain, Épinal . . . 011714
Musée Départemental d'Art Contemporain de Rochechouart, Rochechouart . 014073
Musée Départemental d'Art Religieux, Sées . . . 014742
Musée Départemental d'Art Religieux Contemporain, Saint-Pierre-de-Chartreuse . . . 014480
Musée Départemental d'Art Religiux, Digne-les-Bains . . . 011592
Musée Départemental de Flandre, Musée d'Art et d'Histoire, Cassel . . . 011135
Musée Départemental de la Montagne, Le Haut-du-Them . . . 012503
Musée Départemental de la Poupée et du Jouët, Nontron . . . 013449
Musée Départemental de la Préhistoire, Le Grand-Pressigny . . . 012499
Musée Départemental de la Résistance, Le Teil . . . 012565
Musée Departemental de la Résistance et de la Déportation, Forges-les-Eaux . . . 011868
Musée Départemental de la Résistance et de la Déportation, Lorris . . . 012752
Musée Départemental de la Résistance et de la Déportation, Manneville-sur-Risle . . . 012873
Musée Départemental de la Résistance et de la Déportation, Tulle . . . 015060
Musée Départemental de la Résistance et de la Déportation de l'Ain et du Haut-Jura, Nantua . . . 013348
Musée Départemental de la Résistance et de la Déportation Jean Philippe, Toulouse . . . 014991
Musée Départemental de la Tapisserie, Aubusson . . . 010527
Musée Départemental de la Vigne et des Pressoirs, Champlitte . . . 011229
Musée Départemental de l'Abbaye de Saint-Riquier, Saint-Riquier . . . 014526
Musée Départemental de l'École Publique, Chevregny . . . 011358
Musée Départemental de l'École Publique, Saint-Clar-de-Lomagne . . . 014230
Musée Départemental de l'Éducation, Saint-Ouen-l'Aumône . . . 014459
Musée Départemental de l'Oise, Beauvais . . . 010722
Musée Départemental de Préhistoire, Solutré-Pouilly . . . 014819
Musée Départemental de Préhistoire Corse, Sartène . . . 014687
Musée Départemental de Saint-Antoine, Saint-Antoine-l'Abbaye . . . 014185
Musée Départemental del'Ariège, Château des Comtes de Foix, Foix . . . 011832
Musée Départemental des Antiquités de la Seine-Maritime, Rouen . . . 014125
Musée Départemental des Arts et Traditions Populaires de la Haute-Loire et du Massif Central, Saint-Didier-en-Velay . . . 014257
Musée Départemental des Arts et Traditions Populaires du Perche, Saint-Cyr-la-Rosière . . . 014242
Musée Départemental des Hautes-Alpes, Gap . . . 011918
Musée Départemental des Sapeurs-Pompiers, Sciez . . . 014736
Musée Départemental des Sapeurs-Pompiers du Val-d'Oise, Osny . . . 013525
Musée Départemental Dobrée, Nantes . . . 013338
Musée Departemental du Textile, Lavelanet . . . 012454
Musée Départemental Georges de La-Tour, Vic-sur-Seille . . . 015202
Musée Départemental Hébert, La Tronche . . . 012348
Musée Départemental Ignon-Fabre, Mende . . . 013009
Musée Départemental Jérôme-Carcopino, Aléria . . . 010328
Musée Départemental Maurice Denis, Saint-Germain-en-Laye . . . 014309
Musée Départemental Pascal Paoli, Morosaglia . . . 013249
Musée Départemental Stéphane Mallarmé, Vulaines-sur-Seine . . . 015346
Musée Dermatologique, Paris . . . 013672
Musée des 4 Saisons, Generagues . 011928
Musée des Abénakis, Odanak . . . 006061
Musée des Affiches Léonetto-Cappiello, Épernay . . . 011708
Musée des Ailes Anciennes, Colomiers . . . 011438
Musée des Alambics, Saint-Romain-de-Benet . . . 014530
Musee des Allues, Maison Bonnevie, Meribel . . . 013028
Musée des Alpilles, Saint-Rémy-de-Provence . . . 014518
Musée des Amis de Castrum Vetus, Châteauneuf-les-Martigues . . . 011292
Musée des Amis de Montmélian, Montmélian . . . 013187
Musée des Amis de Thann, Thann . 014923
Musée des Amis du Vieux Corbie, Corbie . . . 011478
Musée des Amis du Vieux Donzère, Donzère . . . 011635
Musée des Amis du Vieux Guérigny, Guérigny . . . 012047
Musée des Amis du Vieux Lormont, Lormont . . . 012749
Musée des Amis du Vieux Montrichard, Musees du Donjon, Montrichard . 013227
Musée des Amis du Vieux Nolay, Nolay . . . 013448
Musée des Amis du Vieux Saint-Étienne, Saint-Étienne . . . 014273
Musée des Amoureux, Werentzhouse . . . 015360
Musée des Anciens Canadiens, Saint-Jean-Port-Joli . . . 006348
Musée des Anciens Combattants, Carcans . . . 011111
Musée des Anciens Enfants de Troupe, Autun . . . 010560
Musée des Anciens Outils Agricoles, Saint-Mathurin . . . 014429
Musée des Années 30, Boulogne-Billancourt . . . 010909
Musée des Antiquités de Volubilis, Moulay Driss . . . 029028
Musée des Antiquités Nationales, Saint-Germain-en-Laye . . . 014310
Musée des Archives, Saint-Hubert . 003738
Musée des Archives, Villeneuve-la-Comptal . . . 015272
Musée des Archives de l'Etat à Namur, Namur . . . 003664
Musée des Archives Départementales de l'Aveyron, Conseil Général de l'Aveyron, Rodez . . . 014085
Musée des Armées et du Souvenir, Clerval . . . 011406
Musée des Armes, Tulle . . . 015061
Musée des Arômes de Provence, Saint-Rémy-de-Provence . . . 014519
Musée des Arômes et du Parfum, Graveson . . . 012012
Musée des Art et Tradition, Reulle-Vergy . . . 014033
Musée des Arts Africains, Océaniens, Amérindiens, Marseille . . . 012942
Musée des Arts Anciens du Namurois, Namur . . . 003665
Musée des Arts Asiatiques, Nice . . 013401
Musée des Arts Contemporains de la Communauté Française, Hornu . . 003520
Musée des Arts Décoratifs, Lausanne . . . 037242
Musée des Arts Décoratifs, Bordeaux . . . 010884
Musée des Arts Décoratifs, Lyon . . 012816
Musée des Arts Décoratifs, Marseille . . . 012943
Musée des Arts Décoratifs, Paris . . 013668
Musée des Arts Décoratifs, Saumur 014701
Musée des Arts Décoratifs, Strasbourg . . . 014874
Musée des Arts Décoratifs de Montréal, Montréal . . . 005938
Musée des Arts Décoratifs et de la Modernité, Gourdon (Alpes-Maritimes) . . . 011974
Musée des Arts Décoratifs Sabatier d'Espeyran, Montpellier . . . 013204
Musée des Arts et de l'Enfance, Fécamp . . . 011790
Musée des Arts et des Sciences, Sainte-Croix . . . 037482
Musée des Arts et des Traditions Bamboun, Foumban . . . 004976
Musée des Arts et d'Histoire, Locronan . . . 012724
Musée des Arts et Metiers, Paris . . 013669
Musée des Arts et Métiers de la Vigne et du Vin, Moulis-en-Médoc . . . 013274
Musée des Arts et Tradition Apicoles, Fontan . . . 011851
Musée des Arts et Traditions, Tozeur . . . 037983
Musée des Arts et Traditions Béarnaises, Salies-de-Béarn . . . 014635
Musée des Arts et Traditions de la Haute-Vézère, Treignac . . . 015036
Musée des Arts et Traditions Populaires, Auxi-le-Château . . . 010575
Musée des Arts et Traditions Populaires, Baume-les-Messieurs . . . 010671
Musée des Arts et Traditions Populaires, Cherves-Mirebeau . . . 011355
Musée des Arts et Traditions Populaires, Djerba . . . 037951
Musée des Arts et Traditions Populaires, Ermont . . . 011720
Musée des Arts et Traditions Populaires, Esse . . . 011738
Musée des Arts et Traditions Populaires, Gaillac . . . 011912
Musée des Arts et Traditions Populaires, Laval-Roquecezière . . . 012447
Musée des Arts et Traditions Populaires, Le Sel-de-Bretagne . . . 012563
Musée des Arts et Traditions Populaires, Marignane . . . 012907
Musée des Arts et Traditions Populaires, Monbazillac . . . 013091
Musée des Arts et Traditions Populaires, Montmorin . . . 013193
Musée des Arts et Traditions Populaires, Saint-Arnoult-en-Yvelines . . . 014191
Musée des Arts et Traditions Populaires, Saint-Esprit . . . 028058
Musée des Arts et Traditions Populaires, Wattrelos . . . 015358
Musée des Arts et Traditions Populaires, Abbaye de Valbonne, Valbonne . . 015090
Musée des Arts et Traditions Populaires, Musée Municipal, Bressuire . . . 010978
Musée des Arts et Traditions Populaires, Positifs de Moules à Gâteaux, La Petite-Pierre . . . 012295
Musée des Arts et Traditions Populaires Dar Ben Abdallah, Tunis . . . 037986
Musée des Arts et Traditions Populaires de la Haute-Loire, Lavaudieu . . . 012450
Musée des Arts et Traditions Populaires de la Vallée de la Cère, Arpajon-sur-Cère . . . 010481
Musée des Arts et Traditions Populaires de Moyenne Provence, Draguignan . 011657
Musée des Arts et Traditions Populaires du Québec, Trois-Rivières . . . 006666
Musée des Arts et Traditions Populaires et des Arts Appliqués, Moissac . . . 013084
Musée des Arts Patrimoine et des Traditions, Nanteuil-en-Vallée . . . 013346
Musée des Arts Populaires, Reillanne . . . 014003
Musée des Arts Populaires et Traditions, Alger . . . 000043
Musée des Arts Populaires et Traditions, Sfax . . . 037973
Musée des Arts Traditionnels, Tétouan . . . 029042
Musée des Ateliers de l'Art du Fer, Livarot . . . 012717
Musée des Attelages de la Belle Epoque, Saint-Martin-du-Lac . . . 014424
Musée des Attelages, de la Carrosserie et du Charronnage, Vonnas . . . 015338
Musée des Augustines de l'Hôpital Général de Québec, Québec . . . 006225
Musée des Augustins, Toulouse . . . 014992
Musée des Automates, La Rochelle 012319
Musée des Automates, Neuilly-sur-Seine . . . 013375
Musée des Automates, Saint-Pourçain-sur-Besbre . . . 014493
Musée des Automates, Sauclières . 014689
Musée des Automates et Maison Enchantée, Amboise . . . 010358
Musée des Avelines, Musée Muicipal de Saint-Cloud, Saint-Cloud . . . 014234
Musée des Ballons, Musée des Montgolfières, Balleroy . . . 010633
Musée des Batailles, Montesquieu-des-Albères . . . 013157
Musée des Bateliers de la Dordogne, Port-Sainte-Foy . . . 013922
Musée des Beaux-Arts, Agen . . . 010271
Musée des Beaux-Arts, Angers . . . 010394
Musée des Beaux-Arts, Arras . . . 010485
Musée des Beaux-Arts, Beaune . . . 010714
Musée des Beaux Arts, Beirut . . . 027810
Musée des Beaux-Arts, Béziers . . . 010788
Musée des Beaux-Arts, Blois . . . 010848
Musée des Beaux-Arts, Brest . . . 010983
Musée des Beaux-Arts, Caen . . . 011056
Musée des Beaux-Arts, Carcassonne . . . 011113
Musée des Beaux-Arts, Chambéry . 011208
Musée des Beaux-Arts, La Chaux-de-Fonds . . . 037012
Musée des Beaux-Arts, Dijon . . . 011608
Musée des Beaux-Arts, Dole . . . 011621
Musée des Beaux-Arts, Gaillac . . . 011913
Musée des Beaux-Arts, Kinshasa . . 007656
Musée des Beaux-Arts, La Ferté-Macé . . . 012250
Musée des Beaux-Arts, La Rochelle 012320
Musée des Beaux-Arts, Lille . . . 012680
Musée des Beaux-Arts, Le Locle . . 037276
Musée des Beaux-Arts, Lyon . . . 012817
Musée des Beaux-Arts, Marseille . . 012944
Musée des Beaux-Arts, Menton . . . 013022
Musée des Beaux-Arts, Mirande . . . 013073
Musée des Beaux-Arts, Montbard . 013135
Musée des Beaux-Arts, Nancy . . . 013324
Musée des Beaux-Arts, Nantes . . . 013339
Musée des Beaux-Arts, Nîmes . . . 013422
Musée des Beaux-Arts, Orléans . . . 013516
Musée des Beaux-Arts, Pau . . . 013750
Musée des Beaux-Arts, Quimper . . 013979
Musée des Beaux-Arts, Reims . . . 014007
Musée des Beaux-Arts, Rouen . . . 014126
Musée des Beaux-Arts, Strasbourg 014875
Musée des Beaux-Arts, Tourcoing . 015007
Musée des Beaux-Arts, Tournai . . . 003809
Musée des Beaux-Arts, Tours . . . 015016
Musée des Beaux-Arts, Valenciennes . . . 015099
Musée des Beaux-Arts, Vannes (Morbihan) . . . 015126
Musée des Beaux-Arts, Villeneuve-sur-Yonne . . . 015284
Musée des Beaux-Arts, Musée Municipal, Angoulême . . . 010406
Musée des Beaux-Arts, Musées Municipaux, Saintes . . . 014622
Musée des Beaux-Arts, Villa Steinbach, Mulhouse . . . 013293

Musée des Beaux-Arts Charleroi, Charleroi . . . 003367
Musée des Beaux-Arts de Bordeaux, Bordeaux . . . 010885
Musée des Beaux-Arts de Dunkerque, Dunkerque . . . 011667
Musée des Beaux-Arts de la Ville de Mons, Mons . . . 003650
Musée des Beaux-Arts de Montréal, Montréal . . . 005938
Musée des Beaux-Arts de Sherbrooke, Sherbrooke, Québec . . . 006461
Musée des Beaux-Arts Denys Puech, Rodez . . . 014086
Musée des Beaux-Arts et Arts Décoratifs Raymond Ritter, Morlanne . . . 013243
Musée des Beaux-Arts et Céramique, Verviers . . . 003826
Musée des Beaux-Arts et d'Archéologie, Troyes . . . 015054
Musée des Beaux-Arts et d'Archéologie, Besançon . . . 010771
Musée des Beaux-Arts et d'Archéologie, Libourne . . . 012664
Musée des Beaux-Arts et d'Archéologie, Rennes (Ille-et-Vilaine) . . . 014023
Musée des Beaux-Arts et d'Archéologie, Vienne . . . 015210
Musée des Beaux-Arts et d'Archeologie Joseph Déchelette, Roanne . . . 014065
Musée des Beaux-Arts et de la Dentelle, Alençon . . . 010326
Musée des Beaux-Arts et de la Dentelle, Calais . . . 011075
Musée des Beaux-Arts et d'Histoire, Saint-Lô . . . 014393
Musée des Beaux-Arts Jules Chéret, Nice . . . 013402
Musée des Bêtises de Cambrai, Cambrai . . . 011083
Musée des Blasons, Saint-Jean-de-Veleriscle . . . 014354
Musée des Blindés, Saumur . . . 014702
Musée des Bois Jolis, Ecomusée de la Région de Fourmies, Felleries . . . 011795
Musée des Bois Sculptes, Cancale . 011090
Musée des Bories, Gordes . . . 011968
Musée des Bujoliers, Saint-Cezaire 014215
Musée des Calèches, Apremont-sur-Allier . . . 010439
Musée des Camions de Brasserie, Romedenne . . . 003727
Musée des Canadiens Nord-Bourguignons, Sainte-Colombe-sur-Seine . . . 014587
Musée des Canonniers Sédentaires de Lille, Lille . . . 012681
Musée des Carrosses, Versailles . . 015187
Musée des Caves de la Cantrie, Saint-Fiacre-sur-Maine . . . 014286
Musée des Champs, Saint-Ségal . . 014538
Musée des Chantiers de Jeunesse, Châtel-Guyon . . . 011303
Musée des Charmettes, Chambéry . 011209
Musée des Chartrons, Bordeaux . . . 010886
Musée des Chasseurs à Pied, Charleroi . . . 003368
Musée des Chasseurs Alpins, Villefranche-sur-Mer . . . 015254
Musée des Chemins de Fer Belges, Bruxelles . . . 003331
Musée des Civilisations, Saint-Just-Saint-Rambert . . . 014373
Musée des Civilisations de Côte d'Ivoire, Abidjan . . . 007685
Musée des Civilisations de L'Europe et de la Méditerranée, Marseille . . . 012945
Musée des Coiffes, Fresnay-sur-Sarthe . . . 011894
Musée des Coiffes d'Anjou, Les Ponts-de-Cé . . . 012630
Musée des Collections Historiques de la Préfecture de Police, Paris . . . 013670
Musée des Commerces Anciens, Doué-la-Fontaine . . . 011648
Musée des Contenants Vinaires, Pouzols-Minérvois . . . 013935
Musée des Corbières, Sigean . . . 014800
Musée des Costumes, Carcassonne 011114
Musée des Couronnes de Mariées, Vacheresse-les-Basses . . . 015084
Musée des Cultures Guyanaises, Cayenne . . . 015388
Musée des Cultures Légumières et ses Réserves, La Courneuve . . . 012246
Musée des Cultures Taurines, Nîmes . . . 013423
Musée des Curiosités Horlogères, Puidoux . . . 037427
Musée des Débuts de l'Aviation, Douzy . . . 011654
Musée des Demineurs, Lepuix . . . 012596
Musée des Dirigeables, Beauvais . . 010723
Musée des Distilleries Limougeaudes, Limoges . . . 012693
Musée des Docks Romains, Marseille . . . 012946
Musée des Eaux de Vie, Fougerolles (Haute-Saône) . . . 011878
Musée des Eaux de Vie, Lapoutroie 012423
Musée des Egouts de Paris, Paris . . 013671
Le Musée des Enfants- Het Kindermuseum, Bruxelles . . . 003332
Musée des Engins de Travaux Publics, Mallemort . . . 012867
Musée des Enrôles de Force, Dudelange . . . 027877
Musée des Épaves Sous-Marines, Commes . . . 011447
Musée des Équipages, Maincy . . . 012854
Musée des Évolutions, Maison de Pays, Bousies . . . 010948
Musée des Fagnes, Roly . . . 003726
Musée des Faïences Anciennes de la Tour d'Aigues, La Tour-d'Aigues . . . 012346
Musée des Faïences de Varages, Varages . . . 015129
Musée des Faïences E. Tessier et de Faïencerie d'Art de Malicorne, Malicorne-sur-Sarthe . . . 012866
Musée des Feuillardiers, Chalus . . . 011202
Musée des Flûtes du Monde, Bollène . . . 010863
Musée des Fontaines Salées, Saint-Père-sous-Vezelay . . . 014477
Musée des Forges, Brocas-les-Forges . . . 011013
Musée des Fossiles, Montceau-les-Mines . . . 013147
Musée des Francs et de la Famenne, Marche-en-Famenne . . . 003626
Musée des Galvachers, Anost . . . 010418
Musée des Glacières, Strasbourg . . 014876
Musée des Glaciers, Lourtier . . . 037280
Musée des Goemoniers, Plouguerneau . . . 013856
Musée des Grenouilles, Estavayer-le-Lac . . . 037077
Musée des Grottes Préhistoriques de Gargas, Aventignan . . . 010586
Musée des Guerres de Vendée, Le Pin-en-Mauges . . . 012544
Musée des Guerres de Vendée, Saint-Florent-le-Vieil . . . 014287
Musée des Haudères, Les Haudères 037178
Musée des Hospices Civils de Lyon, Lyon . . . 012818
Musée des Illustres, Lectoure . . . 012586
Musée des Industries du Viemeu, Friville-Escarbotin . . . 011901
Musée des Industries Hydro-Électriques, Allemont-Vaujany . . . 010337
Musée des Instruments de Musique, L'Aigle . . . 012384
Musée des Instruments de Musique, Musées Royaux d'Art et d'Histoire, Bruxelles . . . 003333
Musée des Instruments de Musique à Vent, La Couture-Boussey . . . 012247
Musée des Ivoires, Yvetot . . . 015380
Musée des Jacobins, Morlaix . . . 013242
Musée des Jacobins, Saint-Sever (Landes) . . . 014542
Musée des Jacobins, Musée d'Auch, Auch . . . 010531
Musée des Jallouli, Sfax . . . 037974
Musée des Jasseries des Monts du Forez, Saint-Anthème . . . 014184
Musée des Liqueurs Cherry-Rocher, La Côte-Saint-André . . . 012242
Musée des Machines Agricoles Anciennes, Montigny-le-Gannelon . . . 013177
Musée des Maisons d'Autrefois, Brennilis . . . 010976
Musée des Majorettes, Saint-Quentin-Fallavier . . . 014504
Musée des Maladies de la Peau, Paris . . . 013672
Musée des Manufactures de Dentelles, Retournac . . . 014030
Musée des Maquettes, Forges-les-Eaux . . . 011869
Musée des Maquettes, Saint-Privat-des-Près . . . 014498
Musée des Marais Salants, Batz-sur-Mer . . . 010667
Musée des Mariniers, Batellerie et Folklore Touraine-Anjou, Chouzé-sur-Loire 011378
Musée des Mariniers du Rhône, Serrières . . . 014773
Musée des Marionnettes, Aubeterre-sur-Dronne . . . 010518
Musée des Materiaux du Centre de Recherche sur les Monuments Historiques, Paris . . . 013673
Musée des Médailles et Vieux Courseulles, Courseulles-sur-Mer . . . 011512
Musée des Meilleurs Ouvriers de France, Bourges . . . 010936
Musée des Merveilles, Tende . . . 014919
Musée des Métiers de France, Argent-sur-Sauldre . . . 010459
Musée des Métiers de la Pierre, Saint-Beauzély . . . 014197
Musée des Métiers du Bois, Labaroche . . . 012357
Musée des Métiers et des Légendes de la Forêt d'Orléans, Loury . . . 012784
Musée des Métiers et Traditions Paysannes, Argy . . . 010466
Musée des Métiers Ruraux, Eternoz 011752
Musée des Mille et une Racines, Cornimont . . . 011487
Musée des Minéralogie, Université Louis Pasteur, Strasbourg . . . 014877
Musée des Minéraux et de la Faune des Alpes, Le Bourg-d'Oisans . . . 012467
Musée des Minéraux et des Fossiles, Rougemont . . . 037465
Musée des Minéraux et Fossiles des Ardennes, Bogny-sur-Meuse . . . 010857
Musée des Mines d'Argent des Gorges du Fournel, L'Argentière-la-Bessée . 012427
Musée des Mines de Fer de Lorraine, Neufchef . . . 013371
Musée des Missions, Plouguerneau 013857
Musée des Moulages, Lyon . . . 012819
Musée des Moulages, Montpellier . 013205
Musée des Moulins, Aram, Villeneuve-d'Ascq . . . 015267
Musée des Musiques Populaires, Montluçon . . . 013182
Musée des Oiseaux, Douzens . . . 011652
Musée des Ostensions et de la Religon Populaire, Esse . . . 011739
Musée des Oudaïa, Rabat . . . 029032
Musée des Outil d'Hier, Chauvirey-le-Vieil . . . 011332
Musée des Outils Agraires, Châteaurenard . . . 011299
Musée des Outils du Bois et de la Vie Paysanne, Bligny-sur-Ouche . . . 010841
Musée des Outils du Terroir Normand, Caugé . . . 011159
Musée des Outils et Appareils Ménagers, Merceuil . . . 013027
Musée des Papes, Grand-Anse . . . 005527
Musée des Papeteries Canson et Montgolfier, Annonay . . . 010417
Musée des Papillons, Fuveau . . . 011908
Musée des Papillons, Saint-Chély-d'Apcher . . . 014219
Musée des Parachutistes, Pau . . . 013751
Musée des Patenôtriers, Brain-sur-Allonnes . . . 010958
Musée des Peintres de l'Ecole de Murol, Murol . . . 013306
Musée des Peintres du Pays, Saint-Cyprien . . . 014240
Musée des Pénitents, Villar-Saint-Pancrace . . . 015226
Musée des Pénitents Blancs, Marsac-en-Livradois . . . 012920
Musée des Petits Hommes en Pyrénées, Arreau . . . 010486
Musée des Petits Métiers de la Ferme, Wervicq-Sud . . . 015361
Musée des Petits Meubles Bretons, Plozevet . . . 013862
Musée des Pioneers, Saint-André-Avelin . . . 006321
Musée des Plans-Reliefs, Paris . . . 013674
Musée des Plantes Médicinales et de la Pharmacie, Musées de l'Université Libre de Bruxelles, Bruxelles . . . 003334
Musée des Pompiers, Wasquehal . . 015354
Musée des Pompiers, Centre de Secours Principal, Fontainebleau . . . 011847
Musée des Postes et Telecommunications, Luxembourg . . . 027890
Musée des Poupées, Collection Rohan, Josselin . . . 012168
Musée des Poupées d'Antan, Maisons-lès-Chaource . . . 012860
Musée des Poupées Pascalines, Commana . . . 011443
Musée des Rangers, Grandcamp-Maisy . . . 011985
Musée des Records, La Tour-Blanche . . . 012344
Musée des Religions, Nicolet . . . 006025
Musée des Réserves Naturelles de la Haute-Savoie, Sallanches . . . 014639
Musée des Roulottes Anciennes, Saintes-Maries-de-la-Mer . . . 014627
Musée des Santons Animés, Maussane-les-Alpilles . . . 012980
Musée des Santons des Baux, Les Baux-de-Provence . . . 012608
Musée des Santons Di-Landro, Aubagne . . . 010510
Musée des Sapeurs Pompiers, Bièvres . . . 010802
Musée des Sapeurs-Pompiers, Fessenheim . . . 011808
Musée des Sapeurs-Pompiers, Saverne . . . 014717
Musée des Sapeurs-Pompiers, Thônes . . . 014938
Musée des Sapeurs-Pompiers de France, Montville . . . 013234
Musée des Sapeurs-Pompiers du Grand Lyon, Lyon . . . 012820
Musée des Sciences, Laval (Mayenne) . . . 012443
Musée des Sciences Naturelles, Orléans . . . 013517
Musée des Sciences Naturelles, Vaudreuil . . . 006721
Musée des Soeurs de Sainte-Anne, Lachine . . . 005733
Musée des Soeurs Grises de Montréal, Montréal . . . 005939
Musée des Soldats du Feu, Wambrechies . . . 015350
Musée des Sous-Stations R.A.T.P., Paris . . . 013675
Musée des Souvenirs Napoléoniens et des Archives du Palais, Monaco . . . 028993
Musée des Spahis, La Horgne . . . 012280
Musée des Spahis, Valence (Drôme) 015095
Musée des Suisses à l'Etranger, Pregny-Chambésy . . . 037425
Musée des Suisses dans le Monde, Pregny-Chambésy . . . 037425
Musée des Tanneurs, Montargis . . . 013126
Musée des Tanneurs et des Ciriers, Maringues . . . 012908
Musée des Tapisseries, Aix-en-Provence . . . 010293
Musée des Techniques Faïencières, Sarreguemines . . . 014685

Musée des Techniques Fromagères, Saint-Pierre-sur-Dives 014486
Musée des Technologies Ferroviaires, La Seyne-sur-Mer 012339
Musée des Télécommunications, Perros-Guirec 013796
Musée des Télécommunications et de la Poste, Bordeaux 010887
Musée des Télécommunications Rhône-Alpes, Lyon 012821
Musée des Télécoms, Pleumeur-Bodou 013841
Musée des Téléphones de Genève, Plan-les-Ouates 037416
Musée des Temps Barbares, Marle . 012909
Musée des Terre-Neuvas et de la Pêche, Fécamp 011791
Musée des Timbres et des Monnaies, Monaco 028994
Musée des Tisserands Mayennais, Ambrières-les-Vallées 010362
Musée des Tissus, Lyon 012822
Musée des Toiles Peintes, Colombier 037028
Musée des Tourneurs, Aiguines . . . 010282
Musée des Tradition de l'île, Noirmoutier-en-l'Ile 013442
Musée des Traditions, Les Avanchers-Valmorel 012602
Musée des Traditions Agricoles du Ségala, Pradinas 013941
Musée des Traditions Bugistes, Saint-Rambert-en-Bugey 014507
Musée des Traditions Comtadines, Pernes-les-Fontaines 013777
Musée des Traditions du Ban-de-la-Roche, Neuviller-la-Roche 013383
Musée des Traditions du Vieux Dirinon, Dirinon 011619
Musée des Traditions et Arts Normands, Martainville-Epreville 012958
Musée des Traditions et Arts Populaires, Meylan 013049
Musée des Traditions et Arts Populaires, Maison de Pauline, Gréoux-les-Bains 012028
Musée des Traditions et des Barques du Léman, Saint-Gingolph 037476
Musée des Traditions Locales, Plounéour-Trez 013860
Musée des Traditions Locales, Sainte-Maxime 014608
Musée des Traditions Populaires, Collonges-la-Rouge 011425
Musée des Traditions Populaires, Saint-Gilles-du-Gard 014322
Musée des Traditions Populaires, Saint-Hilaire-en-Lignière 014330
Musée des Traditions Populaires, Mémoire des Olonnes, Olonne-sur-Mer . . . 013488
Musée des Traditions Populaires Cap Al Campestre, Lherm 012661
Musée des Traditions Populaires de la Frasse, Araches-les-Carroz 010443
Musée des Traditions Populaires Marius Audin, Beaujeu 010705
Musée des Traditions Religieuses de la Haute-Loire, Musée de Saint-Didier, La Séauve-sur-Semène 012337
Musée des Traditions Rousselandes, Les Rousses 012634
Musée des Traditions Rurales et Artisanales, Revel-Tourdan 014037
Musée des Traditions Stéphanoises, Saint-Étienne-de-Tinée 014276
Musée des Traditions Vésubiennes, Saint-Martin-Vésubie 014428
Musée des Traditions Vigneronnes, Le Caveau Bugiste, Vongnes 015337
Musée des Tramway et Autobus, Luxembourg 027891
Musée des Tramways à Vapeur et des Chemins de Fer Secondaires Français, Butry-sur-Oise 011036
Musée des Transmissions, Suresnes 014889
Musée des Transports, Bavinchove . 010677
Musée des Transports, Pithiviers-le-Vieil 013825
Musée des Transports, du Tourisme et des Communications, Toulouse 014993
Musée des Transports en Commun du Pays de Liège, Liège 003598
Musée des Transports Urbains, Colombes 011434
Musée des Trophées de Chasse, La Chapelle-Glain 012228
Musée des Troupes Aéroportées, Sainte-Mère-Eglise 014612
Musée des Troupes de Marine, Fréjus 011890
Musée des Troupes de Montagne, Grenoble 012024
Musée des Ursulines, Mâcon 012839
Musée des Ursulines, Québec 006226
Musée des Ursulines, Trois-Rivières 006663
Musée des Ustensiles de Cuisine Anciens, Saint-Denis-la-Chevasse 014251
Musée des Vallées Cévenoles, Acropolis Museum Montpellier, Saint-Jean-du-Gard 014359
Musée des Vieilles Automobiles, Canet-en-Roussillon 011091
Musée des Vieilles Landes, Lit-et-Mixe 012716
Musée des Vieilles Pierres, Chazay-d'Azergues 011336
Musée des Vieux Métiers, Ardes-sur-Couze 010456
Musée des Vieux Métiers, Melgven 013002
Musée des Vieux Métiers, Saissac . 014630
Musée des Vieux Métiers et des Eaux-de-vie, Dabo 011557
Musée des Vieux Métiers et des Traditions Populaires, Sainte-Croix-Volvestre 014592
Musée des Vieux Outils, Auterive . . 010558
Musée des Vieux Outils, Fourcés . . 011880
Musée des Vieux Outils Noël-Morard, Caromb 011123
Musée des Vieux Outils Vignerons, Aragon 010444
Musée des Vieux Tacots, Les Riceys 012632
Musée des Vieux Tracteurs, Sainte-Geneviève (Meurthe-et-Moselle) . 014598
Musée des Vins de Touraine, Tours . 015017
Musée des Voitures Anciennes, Landivisiau 012400
Musée des XVIes Jeux Olympiques d'Hiver, Albertville 010315
Musée Despiau Wlérick, Mont-de-Marsan 013110
Musée d'Estavayer, Estavayer-le-Lac 037078
Musée d'Ethnographie, Conches . . 037031
Musée d'Ethnographie, Genève . . . 037130
Musée d'Ethnographie, Le Mans . . 012520
Musée d'Ethnographie, Neuchâtel . 037376
Musée d'Ethnographie Corse, Bastia 010666
Musée d'Ethnographie de l'Université de Bordeaux II, Bordeaux 010888
Musée d'Ethnographie et d'Histoire de Conflans, Albertville 010316
Musée d'Evreux, Evreux 011763
Musée d'Exposition des Fouilles Archéologiques, Javols 012155
Musée d'Eysses, Villeneuve-sur-Lot 015283
Musée d'Hippone, Annaba 000050
Musée d'Histoire, Besançon 010773
Musée d'Histoire, La Chaux-de-Fonds 037013
Musée d'Histoire, La Neuveville . . . 037380
Musée d'Histoire, Obernai 013468
Musée d'Histoire, Ouidah 003891
Musée d'Histoire 1939-1945 L'Appel de la Liberté, Fontaine-de-Vaucluse . . . 011841
Musée d'Histoire Contemporaine, Bibliothèque de Documentation Internationale Contemporaine, Paris 013676
Musée d'Histoire de la Médecine, Paris 013677
Musée d'Histoire de la Médecine et de la Pharmacie, Lyon 012823
Musée d'Histoire de la Ville de Luxembourg, Luxembourg 027892
Musée d'Histoire de la Ville et d'Ethnographie du Pays Malouin, Saint-Malo (Ille-et-Vilaine) 014409
Musée d'Histoire de Marseille, Marseille 012947
Musée d'Histoire des PTT d'Alsace, Poste-Diligences-Télécoms, Riquewihr . 014056
Musée d'Histoire des Sciences, Genève 037131
Musée d'Histoire d'Orainville, Orainville 013496
Musée d'Histoire du 20e Siècle, Estivareilles 011744
Musée d'Histoire et d'Archéologie, La Sarre 005729
Musée d'Histoire et d'Archéologie, Longjumeau 012735
Musée d'Histoire et d'Archéologie, Seclin 014739
Musée d'Histoire et d'Archéologie, Vannes (Morbihan) 015127
Musée d'Histoire et d'Archéologie, Warneton 003843
Musée d'Histoire et d'Archéologie de Die et du Diois, Musée de France, Die . . 011585
Musée d'Histoire et d'Archéologie de la Chartreuse, Molsheim 013089
Musée d'Histoire et d'Archéologie des Baux de Provence, Les Baux-de-Provence 012609
Musée d'Histoire et d'Archéologie René Bauberot, Châteauponsac 011295
Musée d'Histoire et d'Art, Mirande . 013074
Musée d'Histoire et d'Arts Populaires, Pellafol-le-Vieux 013763
Musée d'Histoire et de la Nature, Jougne 012171
Musée d'Histoire et de Tamnow, Amnéville-les-Thermes 010372
Musée d'Histoire et de Traditions Populaires, Azincourt 010614
Musée d'Histoire et de Traditions Populaires, Gaspé 005499
Musée d'Histoire et des Arts Décoratifs, Tournai 003810
Musée d'Histoire et d'Ethnographie, Aneho 037940
Musée d'Histoire et Traditions Populaires, L'Oudon-Notre-Dame-de-Fresnay 012755
Musée d'Histoire Local, Maubourguet 012972
Musée d'Histoire Locale, Viarmes . 015200
Musée d'Histoire Locale, Belin-Beliet 010737
Musée d'Histoire Locale, Cagnes-sur-Mer 011061
Musée d'Histoire Locale, Deuil-la-Barre 011583
Musée d'Histoire Locale, Mouans-Sartoux 013257
Musée d'Histoire Locale, Saint-Paul-de-Vence 014470
Musée d'Histoire Locale, Saint-Renan 014524
Musée d'Histoire Locale, Savigny-sous-Mâlain 014728
Musée d'Histoire Locale et des Traditions, Fréjus 011891
Musée d'Histoire Locale et des Vieux Métiers, Saint-Ciers-sur-Gironde . 014227
Musée d'Histoire Locale et Traditions Populaires, Arts et Traditions Populaires, Olargues 013485
Musée d'Histoire Maritime, Le Conquet 012484
Musée d'Histoire Médiévale, Châtel-sur-Moselle 011304
Musée d'Histoire Militaire, La Cluse-et-Mijoux 012238
Musée d'Histoire Militaire à Bandera, Ajaccio 010304
Musée d'Histoire Militaire A. Henriot, Montréjeau 013217
Musée d'Histoire Naturell, Auxerre . 010573
Musée d'Histoire Naturelle, Le Mans 012521
Musée d'Histoire Naturelle, Aix-en-Provence 010294
Musée d'Histoire Naturelle, Amiens 010370
Musée d'Histoire Naturelle, Angers 010395
Musée d'Histoire Naturelle, Baume-les-Messieurs 010672
Musée d'Histoire Naturelle, Besançon 010772
Musée d'Histoire Naturelle, Chambéry 011210
Musée d'Histoire Naturelle, La Chaux-de-Fonds 037014
Musée d'Histoire Naturelle, Eloyes . 011691
Musée d'Histoire Naturelle, Fribourg 037101
Musée d'Histoire Naturelle, Gray . . 012014
Musée d'Histoire Naturelle, La Rochelle 012321
Musée d'Histoire Naturelle, Nantes 013340
Musée d'Histoire Naturelle, Perpignan 013788
Musée d'Histoire Naturelle, Rouen . 014127
Musée d'Histoire Naturelle, Saint-Léger-les-Mélèzes 014385
Musée d'Histoire Naturelle, Saint-Michel (Gers) 014441
Musée d'Histoire Naturelle, Aquarium, Amnéville-les-Thermes 010373
Musée d'Histoire Naturelle, Vivarium, Dijon 011609
Musée d'Histoire Naturelle de Mons, Mons 003651
Musée d'Histoire Naturelle de Toulon, Toulon (Var) 014974
Musée d'Histoire Naturelle et de Géologie, Lille 012682
Musée d'Histoire Naturelle et de la Préhistoire, Nîmes 013424
Musée d'Histoire Naturelle et d'Ethnographie, Colmar 011432
Musée d'Histoire Naturelle et d'Histoire Locale, Musée Municipal, Elbeuf-sur-Seine 011687
Musée d'Histoire Naturelle et Vivarium, Tournai 003811
Musée d'Histoire Naturelle Gabriel-Foucher, Bourges 010937
Musée d'Histoire Naturelle Philadelphe Thomas, Gaillac 011914
Musée d'Histoire Paul Mirat, Sauveterre-de-Béarn 014709
Musée d'Histoire Urbaine de Bergerac, Bergerac 010757
Musée d'Histore Naturelle Victor-Brun, Montauban 013129
Musée d'Homme, Porto-Novo 003893
Musée d'Horlogerie du Locle, Le Locle 037277
Musée d'Huez et de l'Oisans, L'Alpe-d'Huez 012390
Musée Dicks, Vianden 027905
Musée d'Iconographie Historique, Onoz 003681
Musee d'Ifri, Ifri 000066
Musée d'Initiation à la Nature de Normandie, Caen 011057
Musée d'Initiation à la Préhistoire, Tamnies 014896
Musée d'Institut National de Archéologique d'El-Jem, El-Jem 037952
Musée d'Instruments Anciens et d'Archives au Conservatoire de Musique, Museum für Musikinstrumente und Archiv des Musikkonservatoriums, Luxembourg 027893
Musée d'Intérêt National du Tabac, Bergerac 010758
Musée Diocésain d'Art Religieux, Bayeux 010681
Musée Diocésain d'Art Sacré, Moulins (Allier) 013270
Musée Diocésain et Trésor de la Cathédrale Saint-Aubain, Namur 003666
Musée Diocésan d'Art Religieux, Lille 012683
Musée-Diorama du Pèlerinage du 19 Mars, Espaly-Saint-Marcel 011732
Musée d'Istres, Istres 012142
Musée d'Ixelles, Bruxelles 003335
Musée d'Izieu Mémorial des Enfants Juifs Exterminés, Izieu 012146

Musée d'Métiers et Traditions du Pays d'Olliergues, Olliergues 013486
Musée Dobrée, Nantes 013341
Musée Docteur Joseph Fau, Conques 011467
Musée Domaine de Gourjade, Castres 011150
Musée Domaine de Samara, La Chaussée-Tirancourt 012233
Musée Don Bosco, Duekoue 007689
Musée Donation Suzy-Solidor, Cagnes-sur-Mer 011062
Musée Donjon, Ballon 010634
Musée d'Orange, Culture Espace, Orange 013497
Musée d'Orbe, Orbe 037404
Musée d'Orbigny-Bernon, La Rochelle 012322
Musée d'Orgues de Kermesse, Bruxelles 003336
Musée d'Orsay, Paris 013678
Musée d'Orstom, Antananarivo . . . 027929
Musée Doubrère, Marciac 012890
Musée d'Ourthe-Ambléve, Musée Communal, Comblain-au-Pont . . . 003375
Musée d'Outil, Champoulet 011231
Musée d'Outillage Agricole Miniature, Caden 011047
Musée d'Outillage Paysan, Jonvelle 012164
Musée d'Sacré, Mours-Saint-Eusèbe 013276
Musée du 11 Septembre 1709, Musée de la Bataille de Malplaquet, Bavay . . . 010675
Musée du 18 Novembre 1939, Téboursouk 037981
Musée du Bailles, Nismes 003676
Musée du Bain Rituel Juif, Bischheim 010812
Musée du Barreau de Paris, Paris . . 013679
Musée du Bas Saint-Laurent, Rivière-du-Loup 006298
Musée du Bassin Houiller Lorrain, C.C.S.T.I., Petite-Rosselle 013802
Musée du Bateau, Douarnenez 011642
Musée du Bateau, Douarnenez 011643
Musée du Bateau-Lavoir Le Saint-Julien, Laval (Mayenne) 012444
Musée du Batha, Fèz 029021
Musée du Batiment, Moulins 013267
Musée du Béret, Nay 013359
Musée du Berry, Bourges 010938
Musée du Biterrois, Béziers 010789
Musée du Bizarre, Lavilledieu 012457
Musée du Blé au Pain, Pierreclos . . 013813
Musée du Blé et du Pain, Ecomusée de la Bresse Bourguignonne, Verdun-sur-le-Doubs 015176
Musée du Bocage Normand, Saint-Lô 014394
Musée du Bois, Aubonne 036862
Musée du Bois, Seyssel 014797
Musée du Bois de Maredret-Galerie A la Fontaine, Maredret 003629
Musée du Bois et de la Forêt, La Chaise-Dieu 012217
Musée du Bois et de l'Outil, Montgobert 013169
Musée du Bonbon Haribo, Uzès . . . 015080
Musée du Bonsaï, Châtenay-Malabry 011309
Musée du Bouchardais, L'Ile-Bouchard 012675
Musée du Bouton-Château d'Ambleville, Ambleville 010354
Musée du Breuil, Bourbon-Lancy . . 010916
Musée du Breuil de Saint-Germain, Langres 012410
Musée du Bronze d'Inverness, Inverness 005644
Musée du Bûcheron, Grandes-Piles 005541
Musée du Bugey-Valmorey, Lochieu 012722
Musée du Café Gondrée, Bénouville 010753
Musée du Calvados et des Métiers Anciens de Pont-l'Évêque, Pont-l'Évêque . 013895
Musée du Calvaire de Pontchateau, Pontchâteau 013905
Musée du Camembert, Vimoutiers . 015308
Musée du Camp d'Internement, Le Vernet 012577
Musée du Camp-Romain, Saint-Jean-de-Vieux 014355
Musée du Canal, Cleden-Poher . . . 011390
Musée du Canal, Ecuisses 011682
Musée du Canal de Berry, Audes-Reugny 010536
Musée du Canal du Duc de Berry, Dun-sur-Auron 011664
Musée du Canal du Midi, Revel . . . 014035
Musée du Capitellu, Ajaccio 010305
Musée du Cardinal Verdier, Lacroix-Barrez 012374
Musée du Carmel, Libourne 012665
Musée du Cartonnage et de l'Imprimerie, Valréas 015121
Musée du Casque de Combat, Saint-Vincent-sur-Jabron 014573
Musée du Centenaire, Bischwiller . 010813
Musée du Centre de Recherches sur les Monuments Historiques, Paris . . . 013680
Musée du Cerf-Volant, Perrigny-lès-Dijon 013793
Musée du Chablais, Thonon-les-Bains 014942
Musée du Champignon, Saumur . . . 014703
Musée du Chanvre, Bligny-sur-Ouche 010842
Musée du Charroi Rural, Salmiech . 014648
Musée du Châtaignier, Marrons et Champignons, Villefranche-du-Périgord 015252
Musée du Château, Aubenas 010514
Musée du Château, Baugé 010669
Musée du Château, Dinan 011615
Musée du Château, Flers 011825
Musée du Château, Fougères (Ille-et-Vilaine) 011874
Musée du Château, Laas 012354
Musée du Château, Noirmoutier-en-l'Ile 013443
Musée du Château, Roquebrune-Cap-Martin 014103
Musée du Château, Siorac-en-Périgord 014803
Musée du Château de Cassaigne, Cassaigne 011134
Musée du Château de Dourdan, Dourdan 011650
Musée du Château de Flaugergues, Montpellier 013206
Musée du Château de Franchimont, Theux 003792
Musée du Château de la Guignardière, Avrillé 010608
Musée du Château de la Louviere, Montluçon 013183
Musée du Château de Lunéville, Lunéville 012793
Musée du Château de Mascarras, Garlin 011924
Musée du Château de Mesnières-en-Bray, Neuchatel-en-Bray 013367
Musée du Château de Pontécoulant, Pontécoulant 013906
Musée du Château de Vincennes, Vincennes 015311
Musée du Château de Vitré, Vitré . . 015322
Musée du Château des Comtes de Marchin, Modave 003645
Musée du Château des Ducs de Wurtemberg, Montbéliard 013141
Musée du Château d'Henri IV, Nérac 013364
Musée du Château d'Oigny-en-Valois, Oigny-en-Valois 013479
Musée du Château du Marais, Le Val-Saint-Germain 012575
Musée du Château du Prince Noir, Arcizans-Avant 010453
Musée du Château et des Anciennes Écuries, Montbard 013136
Musée du Château-Fort, Ecaussinnes-Lalaing 003417
Musée du Château Fort-Liberia, Villefranche-de-Conflent 015248
Musée du Château Paul Pastre, Marsillargues 012955
Musée du Château Ramezay, Montréal 005940
Musée du Château Saint-Jean, Nogent-le-Rotrou 013435
Musée du Châtillonnais, Châtillon-sur-Seine 011317
Musée du Chemin de Fer, Apremont-la-Forêt 010438
Musée du Chemin de Fer Miniature, Clécy 011388
Musée du Cheminot, Ambérieu-en-Bugey 010347
Musée du Cheval, Gondrecourt-le-Château 011965
Musée du Cheval, La Ferté-Saint-Aubin 012256
Musée du Cheval, La Sarraz 037517
Musée du Cheval, Saumur 014704
Musée du Cheval, de la Vie Rurale et du Tabac, Thuillies 003793
Musée du Cheval en 1900, Cussac-Fort-Médoc 011554
Musée du Cheval et de l'Attelage, Obernai 013469
Musée du Chien, Villeneuve-les-Convers 015278
Musée du Chocolat, Barcelonnette . 010651
Musée du Cidre, Montaure 013131
Musée du Cidre, Saint-Jean-des-Champs 014356
Musée du Cidre Breton, Alain Bourvon, Argol 010464
Musée du Cidre du Pays d'Othe, Eaux-Puiseaux 011674
Musée du Cinéma, Bruxelles 003337
Musée du Cinéma, Cine-Chaplin, Nismes 003677
Musée du Cinéma Henri Langlois, Paris 013681
Musée du Cinquantenaire, Musées Royaux d'Art et d'Histoire, Bruxelles 003338
Musée du Circuit de Spa-Francorchamps, Stavelot 003782
Musée du Cirque, Vatan 015140
Musée du Cirque, Wasquehal 015355
Musée du Clocher, Haute-Rivoire . . 012079
Musée du Cloître, Tulle 015062
Musée du Cloître Notre-Dame en Vaux, Châlons-en-Champagne 011197
Musée du Clos-Lucé, Demeure de Léonard de Vinci, Amboise 010359
Musée du Clou, Saint-Cornier-des-Landes 014237
Musée du Collège Bourget, Rigaud . 006290
Musée du College de Lévis, Lévis . . 005771
Musée du Colombier, Alès 010332
Musée du Colombier, Sarniguet . . . 014677
Musée du Commerce International et de la Vie Quotidienne des Armateurs, Négociants et Corsaires, Troissereux 015043
Musée du Commissariat de l'Armée de Terre, Montpellier 013207
Musée du Compagnonnage, Bordeaux 010889
Musée du Compagnonnage, Paris . 013682
Musée du Compagnonnage, Tours . 015018
Musée du Coquillage, Le Lavandou 012512
Musée du Coquillage, Papara 015391
Musée du Corps de la Cavalerie Française 1940, Jandrain-Jandrenouille . . . 003544
Musée du Corps Franc Pommpiès, Castelnau-Magnoac 011142
Musée du Costume, Château-Chinon 011273
Musée du Costume, Le Portel 012553
Musée du Costume Breton, Sainte-Anne-d'Auray 014584
Musée du Costume Civils, La Chapelle-Caro 012221
Musée du Costume Comtadin, Pernes-les-Fontaines 013778
Musée du Costume Comtois, Montgesoye 013168
Musée du Costume et de la Dentelle, Musées de la Ville de Bruxelles, Bruxelles 003339
Musée du Costume Militaire, Manoir de Sainte-Mesme, Sainte-Mesme . . 014613
Musée du Costume Provençal, Solliès-Ville 014817
Musée du Costume Savoyard, Bourg-Saint-Maurice 010929
Musée du Costume Trégor-Goëlo, Paimpol 013536
Musée du Coticule, Vielsalm 003829
Musée du Couteau de Laguiole, Laguiole 012380
Musée du Crest-Cherel, Ugine 015071
Musée du Crime, Bruxelles 003340
Musée du Cristal, Bayel 010678
Musée du Crozet, Le Crozet 012491
Musée du Cuir et de la Tannerie, Château-Renault 011279
Musée du Cuir et du Parchemin, Levroux 012657
Musée du Cuivre, Cerdon 011172
Musée du Cwarmê, Malmedy 003623
Musée du Débarquement à Utah Beach, Sainte-Marie-du-Mont 014606
Musée du Débarquement en Provence, Toulon (Var) 014975
Musée du Désert, Mialet 013057
Musée du Dessin et de l'Estampe Originale, Gravelines 012009
Musée du Docteur Faure, Musée Municipal, Aix-les-Bains 010301
Musée du Dolder, Riquewihr 014058
Musée du Donjon, Rouen 014128
Musée du Donjon de la Toque, Huriel 012118
Musée du Faouët, Le Faouët 012494
Musée du Felicien, Argentine 010462
Musée du Fer, Reichshoffen 014002
Musée du Fer à Repasser, Longwy . 012740
Musée du Fer Blanc Ancien et Moderne, Saint-Arcons-d'Allier 014189
Musée du Fer et de la Métallurgie Ancienne, Saint-Hubert 003739
Musée du Fer et des Traditions Catalanes, Prades 013938
Musée du Fer et du Chemin de Fer, Vallorbe 037669
Musée du Fer et du Fil, Dompierre (Orne) 011629
Musée du Feu Adjudant-Chef Gérard, Châlons-en-Champagne 011198
Musée du Feutre, Mouzon 013286
Musée du Fil de Soie, Vierzon 015215
Musée du Fjord, La Baie 005725
Musée du Flacon à Parfum, La Rochelle 012323
Musée du Florentinois, Saint-Florentin 014289
Musée du Florival, Guebwiller 012041
Musée du Foie Gras, Frespech 011897
Musée du Foie Gras, Roquettes . . . 014106
Musée du Foie Gras et des Traditions Populaires, Samatan 014657
Musée du Folklore, Ittre 003538
Musée du Folklore, Sainte-Enimie . 014593
Musée du Folklore, Musée du Boubonnais, Moulins (Allier) 013271
Musée du Folklore et de la Vie Montoise, Mons 003652
Musée du Football en France - Musée du Sport, Paris 013683
Musée du Fort de Huy, Huy 003529
Musée du Fort de la Pompelle, Reims 014008
Musée du Fort de Vaux, Vaux-devant-Damloup 015145
Musée du Fort d'Embourg, Musée sur les Deux Guerres Mondiales, Embourg 003421
Musée du Fort Saint-Jean, Saint-Jean 006346
Musée du Fort Vauban, Ambleteuse 010353
Musée du Fossile, Lion-sur-Mer . . . 012701
Musée du Frère André, Montréal . . 005941
Musée du Fromage, Laye 012460
Musée du Fromage, Saint-Marcellin 014414
Musée du Fromage de la Chèvrerie, Noirmoutier-en-l'Ile 013444

Musée du Gabarier, Saint-Simon (Charente) 014545
Musée du Gemmail, Lourdes 012773
Musée du Gemmail, Art de Lumière, Tours 015019
Musée du Général Thys, Dalhem . . 003384
Musée du Grand-Lens, Lens 037255
Musée du Grand Saint-Bernard, Le Grand-Saint-Bernard 037160
Musée du Granit, Bécon-les-Granits 010728
Musée du Granit, Saint-Michel-de-Montjoie 014437
Musée du Graveur Oscar Roty, Jargeau 012147
Musée du Grenier du Roy Louis XIII, Villemur-sur-Tarn 015261
Musée du Grès, Saint-Amand-en-Puisaye 014175
Musée du Groupe Jovinien de Résistance Bayard, Musée de Joigny, Joigny (Yonne) 012161
Musée du Guesclin, Châteauneuf-de-Randon 011288
Musée du Hard Rock Café, Paris . . 013684
Musée du Haut-Richelieu, Saint-Jean-sur-Richelieu 006350
Musée du Haut-Rouergue, Laguiole 012381
Musée du Haut-Val-d'Arly, Megève 012998
Musée du Huchier, Poucharramet . . 013927
Musée du Jamais Vu, Puymaurin . . 013966
Musée du Jeu Ancien, Saint-Hilaire-de-Brethmas 014326
Musée du Jeu de l'Oie, Collection Dietsch, Rambouillet 013988
Musée du Jouet, Bruxelles 003341
Musée du Jouet, Canet-en-Roussillon 011092
Musée du Jouet, Clervaux 027873
Musée du Jouet, Moirans-en-Montagne 013082
Musée du Jouet, Poissy 013866
Musée du Jouet Ancien Atlantrain, Saint-Just-Luzac 014372
Musée du Jouet Ancien Automobile, Rocamadour 014068
Musée du Jouet et de l'Enfant, Ferrières 003434
Musée du Jus de Fruit, Espace Muséographique les Pressoirs de Provence, Saint-Andiol 014180
Musée du Lac de Paladru, Maison d'Art et d'Histoire des Trois Vals, Charavines 011242
Musée du Lac Léman, Nernier 013366
Musée du Lait, Belvedere 010747
Musée du Lait, Montebourg 013151
Musée du Lait et des Traditions, Saint-Étienne-de-Tinée 014277
Musée du Lapidaire, Lamoura 012395
Musée du Lavage et du Repassage, Verneuil-en-Bourbonnais 015182
Musée du Lavandin, Musée Aromes, Carennac 011118
Musée du Léman, Nyon 037384
Musée du Léon, Lesneven 012646
Musée du Libertaire, Fontenay-les-Briis 011854
Musée du Liège, Maureillas-las-Illas 012976
Musée du Liège et du Bouchon, Mezin 013055
Musée du Littoral et de des Fours à Chaux, Regnéville-sur-Mer 013999
Musée du Livre, Beaune 138028
Musée du Livre, Langres 012411
Musée du Livre, de la Pierre et du Verre, Conches-en-Ouche 011454
Musée du Livre et Cabinets de Donations de la Bibliothèque Royale de Belgique, Bruxelles 003342
Musée du Loup, Le Cloître-Saint-Thégonnec 012483
Musée du Louvre, Paris 013685
Musée du Luxembourg, Paris 013686
Musée du Lycée Militaire de Saint-Cyr, Saint-Cyr-l'École 014243
Musée du Machinisme Agricole, Bourbon-Lancy 010917
Musée du Machinisme Agricole, Neuvic (Corrèze) 013378
Musée du Machinisme Agricole, Prissac 013953
Musée du Machinisme Agricole, Revest-Saint-Martin 014038
Musée du Machinisme Agricole, Tullins-Fures 015063
Musée du Machinisme Agricole et du Cheval de Trait de 1830 à nos Jours, Juvigny-sous-Andaine 012188
Musée du Maïs, Laas 012355
Musée du Maïs, Morlaàs 013239
Musée du Malgré-Tout, Treignes . . 003815
Musée du Manoir, Saussey 014707
Musée du Manoir d'Argentelles, Villebadin 015240
Musée du Maquettisme, de la Fonderie et de la Moulerie, Musée Municipal, Blangy-sur-Bresle 010829
Musée du Marbre et de la Pierre Bleue, Bellignies 010744
Musée du Maréchal Lannes, Mareuil-sur-Belle 012904
Musée du Maréchal Murat, Labastide-Murat 012361
Musée du Mariage et de ses Traditions, Oger 013476
Musée du Marineland, Antibes-Juan-les-Pins 010427
Musée du Mas de la Pyramide, Saint-Rémy-de-Provence 014520
Musée du Matériel Agricole, La Villeneuve-les-Convers 012352
Musée du Mémorial de Sidi Ferruch, Port-Vendres 013923
Musée du Mémorial du Martyr Juif Inconnu, Paris 013687
Musée du Mémorial National de la Déportation, Natzwiller 013356
Musée du Meuble Normand, Villedieu-les-Poêles 015244
Musée du Miel, Lobbes 003610
Musée du Miel et de l'Abeille, Gramont 011981
Musée du Mineur, Ensisheim 011695
Musée du Mineur, La Grand-Combe 012271
Musée du Modèle Réduit, Varces . . 015132
Musée du Monde Rural, Rettel 014031
Musée du Monde Souterrain, Han-sur-Lesse 003491
Musée du Monde Souterrain et Historique de la Spéléologie Française, Saint-Remèze 014510
Musée du Mont Corbier, Saint-Jean-de-Maurienne 014352
Musée du Mont-de-Piété et de la Condition des Soies, Avignon 010593
Musée du Mont-Repais, La Caquerelle 036997
Musée du Mont Riant, Alger 000044
Musée du Moteur, Saumur 014705
Musée du Moulin, Saint-Jean-Saint-Nicolas 014361
Musée du Moulin, Wissant 015368
Musée du Moulin à Eau, Eschviller . 011725
Musée du Moulin à Eau et de la Boulangerie, Harzé 003495
Musée du Moulin à Marée, Trégastel 015034
Musée du Moulin de Boly, Lourdes . 012774
Musée du Moulin Roupeyrac, Durenque 011672
Musée du Moulins des Bouillons, Gordes 011969
Musée du Mouton et de la Bergerie Nationale, Rambouillet 013989
Musée du Mouvement National, Tunis 037987
Musée du Mur de l'Atlantique, Audinghen 010539
Musée du Mur de l'Atlantique, Ouistreham 013527
Musée du Navigateur Flottant, La Goelette, Saint-Joseph-de-Sorel 006376
Musée du Nord de la Vendée, Montaigu (Vendée) 013119
Musée Du Nougat Arnaud Soubeyran, Montélimar 013154
Musée du Nouveau Monde, La Rochelle 012324
Musée du Noyonnais, Noyon 013461
Musée du Pain, Uhlwiller 015072
Musée du Pain Bouilli et du Four Communal, Villar-d'Arène 015223
Musée du Pain d'Épices d'Alsace et des Douceurs, Gertwiller 011938
Musée du Palais, Foumban 004977
Musée du Palais de la Reine, Antananarivo 027930
Musée du Palais des Evêques, Saint-Lizier 014392
Musée du Palais du Dey, Casbah, Alger 000045
Musée du Palais Royal, Phnom Penh 004969
Musée du Panache Gascon, Termes-d'Armagnac 014920
Musée du Panorama de la Vie de Sainte-Bernadette, Lourdes 012775
Musée du Panthéon National Haïtien, Port-au-Prince 021603
Musée du Papier Chiffon, Muzillac . 013314
Musée du Papier Le Nil, Musée Municipal, Angoulême 010407
Musée du Papier Peint, Museum of Wall Paper, Rixheim 014063
Musée du Papillon, Orgerus 013505
Musée du Papillon et des Arts Africains, Aubeterre-sur-Dronne 010519
Musée du Papogay, Rieux-Volvestre 014043
Musée du Para, Orléans 013518
Musée du Parchemin et de l'Enluminure, Duras 011670
Musée du Parchemin et du Sceau, Saint-Omer 014455
Musée du Passé Agricole de Beauvechain, Beauvechain 003220
Musée du Pastel, Magrin 012848
Musée du Pastis, Aubagne 010511
Musée du Patrimoine, Néris-les-Bains 013365
Musée du Patrimoine, Roquebrune-sur-Argens 014104
Musée du Patrimoine, Maison du Patrimoine, Six-Fours-les-Plages . 014808
Musée du Patrimoine André Cane, Beaulieu-sur-Mer 010706
Musée du Patrimoine de l'Isle Crémieu, Hières-sur-Amby 012102
Musée du Patrimoine des Pères de Bétharram, Lestelle-Bétharram . . 012648
Musée du Patrimoine du Canton de Giat, Voingt 015329
Musée du Patrimoine et de la Dentelle, Chantilly 011237
Musée du Patrimoine et des Pratiques Locales, Jouy (Eure-et-Loir) 012176
Musée du Patrimoine Montagnard, Nages 013315
Musée du Patrimoine Religieux et des Croyances Populaires, Moustey . . 013278
Musée du Patrimoine Rural, Dompierre (Orne) 011630
Musée du Pays, Ussel 015076
Musée du Pays Brignolais, Brignoles 011003
Musée du Pays d'Albe, Sarralbe . . . 014678
Musée du Pays de Caux, Yvetot . . . 015381
Musée du Pays de Luchon, Bagnères-de-Luchon 010623
Musée du Pays de Retz, Bourgneuf-en-Retz 010942
Musée du Pays de Sarrebourg, Sarrebourg 014683
Musée du Pays de Thônes, Thônes . 014939
Musée du Pays du Der, Sainte-Rémy-en-Bouzemont 014616
Musée du Pays et du Vignoble de Reuilly, Reuilly (Indre) 014032
Musée du Pays et Val de Charmey, Charmey (Gruyère) 037009
Musée du Pays Rabastinois, Monesties 013095
Musée du Pays Vaurais, Lavaur . . . 012452
Musée du Peigne et de la Plasturgie, Oyonnax 013532
Musée du Peintre Gustave Stoskopf, Brumath 011022
Musée du Père Jean-Marie de la Mennais, Ploërmel 013843
Musée du Perigord, Périgueux 013773
Musée du Petit Bateau et des Aventures de la Mer, Canet-en-Roussillon 011093
Musée du Petit Lourdes, Lourdes . . 012776
Musée du Petit-Palais, Avignon . . . 010594
Musée du Pétrole, Merkwiller-Pechelbronn 013032
Musée du Pétrole, Parentis-en-Born 013549
Musée du Peuple Haïtien, Port-au-Prince 021604
Musée du Phare de Cordouan, Le Verdon-sur-Mer 012576
Musée du Phonographe et de la Musique Mécanique, Sainte-Maxime 014609
Musée du Phonographe et de Musique Mécanique, Limoges 012694
Musée du Pilori, Niort 013429
Musée du Poète Racan, Aubigné-Racan 010521
Musée du Poids Lourd et des Véhicules Anciens, Mondoubleau 013093
Musée du Poitier Gallo-Romain, Blicquy 003235
Musée du Pousse-Rapière, Saint-Puy 014500
Musée du Premier Empire, Musée Noisot, Fixin 011821
Musée du Président Jacques Chirac, Sarran 014680
Musée du Présidial, Musée et Moulin de Castelnaudary, Castelnaudary . . . 011146
Musée du Prieuré, Charolles 011259
Musée du Prieuré, Harfleur 012067
Musée du Prieuré, Ecomusée du Creusot-Montceau, Perrecy-les-Forges . . . 013792
Musée du Prieuré d'Amilhac, Servian 014774
Musée du Prieuré de Graville, Le Havre 012507
Musée du Prophète Djouman Mihin, Vavoua 007693
Musée du Protestantisme Dauphinois, Le Poët-Laval 012549
Musée du Protestantisme en Haut Languedoc, Société de l'Histoire du Protestantisme Français, Ferrières (Tarn) 011805
Musée du Québec, Québec 006228
Musée du Quercorb, Puivert 013963
Musée du Radar Allemand, Douvres-la-Délivrande 011651
Musée du Rail, Cajarc 011071
Musée du Rail, Dinan 011616
Musée du Rail Bressan Bress'Pulmann, Louhans 012759
Musée du Ranquet, Clermont-Ferrand 011398
Musée du Regiment GG.FF., Firenze 024166
Musée du Regourdou, Montignac . . 013174
Musée du Rethélois e du Porcien, Rethel 014028
Le Musée du Rêve, Paris 100715
Musée du Revermont, Treffort-Cuisiat 015031
Musée du Rhum, Sainte-Marie 028061
Musée du Rhum, Sainte-Rose 021563
Musée du Rocher des Fourches, Cornus 011488
Musée du Roi de Cuba, Mushenge . 007662
Musée du Rouergue, Espalion 011730
Musée du Rouergue Arts Métiers, Salles-la-Source 014647
Musée du Roy Soleil, Mont-Louis . . 013112
Musée du Royal 22e Régiment, Québec 006227
Musée du Sable, Collège Jean-Monnet, Le Château-d'Olonne 012482
Musée du Sabot, Buironfosse 011027
Musée du Sabot, Etang-sur-Arroux . 011747
Musée du Sabot, La Haye-de-Routot 012279

Musée du Sabot, Porcheresse 003706
Musée du Sabotier, Le Brugeron ... 012472
Musée du Sabotier, Soucht 014834
Musée du Safran, Boynes 010957
Musée du Santon, Generagues 011929
Musée du Santon, Le Val 012574
Musée du Santon, Pierrefeu-du-Var 013815
Musée du Santon, Marseille 012948
Musée du Santon et des Traditions de Provence, Fontaine-de-Vaucluse . 011842
Musée du Santons, Gréoux-les-Bains 012029
Musée du Sapeur-Pompier, Bouzigues 010956
Musée du Sapeur-Pompier, Mulhouse 013294
Musée du Sapeur Pompier, Espace Martin Ducros, Saint-Hippolyte-du-Fort . 014332
Musée du Sapeurs-Pompiers, Ille-sur-Têt 012132
Musée du Saut du Tarn, Saint-Juéry 014363
Musée du Savignéen, Savigné-sur-Lathan 014719
Musée du Sceau Alsacien, La Petite-Pierre 012296
Musée du Schlittage et de la Forêt, Le Hohwald 012511
Musée du Scribe, Saint-Christol-lès-Alès 014221
Musée du Second-Empire, Ancienne Boulangerie, Bitche 010818
Musée du Sel, Marsal 012923
Musée du Sel, Salies-de-Béarn ... 014636
Musée du Séminaire, Consolation-Maisonettes 011471
Musée du Séminaire de Saint-Hyacinthe, Saint-Hyacinthe 006342
Musée du Séminaire de Sherbrooke, Sherbrooke, Québec 006462
Musée du Septennat de François Mitterrand, Château-Chinon 011274
Musée du Service de Santé des Armées, Paris 013688
Musée du Silex, Eben-Emael 003416
Musée du Site Balnéaire, Dinard .. 011618
Musée du Site de l'Outil au Moutier-d'Ahun, Ahun 010273
Musée du Ski, Besse-en-Chandesse 010776
Musée du Ski, Exposition Parc des Ecrins, Briançon 010993
Musée du Ski et du Bobsleigh, Les Rousses 012635
Musée du Souvenier, Seillans 014747
Musée du Souvenier du Combattant, Chalon-sur-Saône 011194
Musée du Souvenir, Guer 012042
Musée du Souvenir, Soulac-sur-Mer 014840
Musée du Souvenir 1914-1918, Ablain-Saint-Nazaire 010264
Musée du Souvenir-Arts et Traditions Mullem-William, Cheminon 011343
Musée du Souvenir du Génie, Angers 010396
Musée du Souvenir du Prytanée Militaire, La Flèche 012260
Musée du Souvenir Général Estienne, Berry-au-Bac 010766
Musée du Souvenir Leersois, Leers 012587
Musée du Souvenir Militaire de Lyon, Lyon 012824
Musée du Souvenir Militaire de Thiérache, Martigny 012960
Musée du Souvenir Pierre de Bourdeille, Saint-Crépin-de-Richemont 014239
Musée du Suaire et du Pèlerinage, Cadouin 011050
Musée du Tacot, Cléron 011405
Musée du Tapis d'Art, Musée Bargoin, Clermont-Ferrand 011399
Musée du Téléphone, Maison de la Communication, Nancy 013325
Musée du Téléphone Narbonne, Narbonne 013352
Musée du Temple de Minerve, Tebessa 000076
Musée du Temps, Besançon 010773
Musée du Temps des Baigneurs, Cordemais 011479
Musée du Temps et de l'Art Religieux, Ceillac 011168
Musée du Temps Passé, Sainte-Agnès 014582
Musée du Temps qui Passe, Carquefou 011129
Musée du Terrain d'Aviation de Conde-Vraux, Vraux 015342
Musée du Terroir, Villeneuve-d'Ascq 015268
Musée du Terroir Bressan, Montpont 013215
Musée du Terroir de Peille, Peille .. 013760
Musée du Terroir des Clots, Mizoën-en-Oisans 013081
Musée du Terroir et de la Volaille, Romenay 014097
Musée du Terroir Hérissonnais, Hérisson 012092
Musée du Terroir Marseillais, Marseille 012949
Musée du Terroir Saint-Dalmas, Valdeblore 015091
Musée du Terroire, Conches-en-Ouche 011455
Musée du Textile, Cholet 011375
Musée du Textile des Vosges, Ventron 015168
Musée du Textile et de la Vie Sociale, Ecomusée de la Région Fourmies-Trélon, Fourmies 011881
Musée du Textile et du Peigne en Corne, Lavelanet 012455
Musée du Textilen, Labastide-Rouairoux 012362
Musée du Thé, Mariage Frères, Paris 013689
Musée du Théâtre, Couilly-Pont-aux-Dames 011500
Musée du Théâtre de Toone, Bruxelles 003343
Musée du Théâtre Forain et Musée Archéologique, Artenay 010492
Musée du Théâtre Royal de Toone, Bruxelles 003344
Musée du Tire-Bouchon, Ménerbes 013010
Musée du Tissage et de la Soierie, Bussières 011033
Le Musée du Tisserand Dauphinois, La Batie-Montgascon 012202
Musée du Touage et Canal de Saint-Quentin, Riqueval 014055
Musée du Touquet, Le Touquet-Paris-Plage 012568
Musée du Tour Automatique et d'Histoire de Moutier, Langdrehautomaten- und Geschichtsmuseum, Moutier 037349
Musée du Tour de France, Arvieux-en-Queyras 010497
Musée du Train, Clairac 011382
Musée du Train à Vapeur, Sainte-Foy-l'Argentière 014597
Musée du Train et de la Miniature, Musée de la Vie Rurale, Saint-Sauves-d'Auvergne 014534
Musée du Train et des Equipages Militaires, Tours 015020
Musée du Train et du Jouet, Arpaillargues-et-Aureillac 010480
Musée du Transport Urbain Bruxellois, Bruxelles 003345
Musée du Travail, Montfermeil 013159
Musée du Travail Charles Peyre, Montfermeil 013160
Musée du Trégor, Guimaec 012052
Musée du Tribunal Révolutionnaire, Tinchebray 014960
Musée du Trièves, Mens 013016
Musée du Trompe L'Oeil, Béziers .. 010790
Musée du Trophée des Alpes, La Turbie 012349
Musée du Val-de-Cher, Selles-sur-Cher 014750
Musée du Val-du-Grâce, Paris 013690
Musée du Valois, Vez 015195
Musée du Valois et de l'Archerie, Ecomusée des Pays de l'Oise, Crépy-en-Valois 011532
Musée du Vélo, Cormatin 011485
Musée du Vélo, Fenneviller 011798
Musée du Vélo, Labastide-d'Armagnac 012359
Musée du Vélo, Periers 013771
Musée du Vélo et de la Moto, Domazan 011623
Musée du Vélocipède, Cadouin 011051
Musée du Veneur, Céré-la-Ronde .. 011174
Musée du Ver à Soie, La Soie Vivante, Montreuil-Bellay 013220
Musée du Verre, Blaye-les-Mines .. 010837
Musée du Verre, Liège 003599
Musée du Verre, Sars-Poteries 014686
Musée du Verre Art et Technique, Charleroi 003369
Musée du Verre chez Val-Saint-Lambert Château, Seraing 003748
Musée du Verrier, Saint-Prex 037479
Musée du Vieaux Château, Bricquebec 010998
Musée du Vieil Aix, Aix-en-Provence 010295
Musée du Vieil Argenteuil, Argenteuil 010461
Musée du Vieil Auvillar, Auvillar ... 010569
Musée du Vieil Eygalières, Eygalières 011766
Musée du Vieux-Baulmes, Baulmes 036910
Musée du Vieux-Bex, Bex 036947
Musée du Vieux Biarritz, Musée Historique, Biarritz 010796
Musée du Vieux Bourg, Mimizan .. 013066
Musée du Vieux Brest, Brest 010984
Musée du Vieux-Château, Collections d'Art Naïf, Laval (Mayenne) 012445
Musée du Vieux-Cimetière, Soignies 003773
Musée du Vieux Clairac, Clairac 011383
Musée du Vieux Courseulles, Courseulles-sur-Mer 011513
Musée du Vieux Figeac, Figeac ... 011813
Musée du Vieux Granville, Granville 011992
Musée du Vieux Honfleur, Honfleur . 012107
Musée du Vieux-Lamballe et du Penthièvre, Lamballe 012392
Musée du Vieux Lambesc, Lambesc 012394
Musée du Vieux L'Arbresle, L'Arbresle 012425
Musée du Vieux Marseille, Marseille 012950
Musée du Vieux Mazeres, Mazères (Ariège) 012989
Musée du Vieux Merville, Merville . 013035
Musée du Vieux-Monthey, Monthey 037332
Musée du Vieux Montpellier, Montpellier 013208
Musée du Vieux-Montreux, Montreux 037335
Musée du Vieux-Moudon, Moudon . 037347
Musée du Vieux Moulin, Villar-Loubière 015224
Musée du Vieux Moulin à Vent, Maves 012983
Musée du Vieux Moulin à Vent, Vensac 015166
Musée du Vieux Moulin de Pierre, Hauville 012085
Musée du Vieux Nîmes, Nîmes 013425
Musée du Vieux Nimy, Mons 003653
Musée du Vieux-Pays, Le Châble .. 037006
Musée du Vieux Pays, Dieulouard .. 011589
Musée du Vieux-Pays d'Enhaut, Château-d'Oex 037011
Musée du Vieux Pérouges, Pérouges 013781
Musée du Vieux-Phare, Matane ... 005842
Musée du Vieux Plassac, Plassac .. 013833
Musée du Vieux Pommiers, Pommiers-en-Forez 013874
Musée du Vieux Pressoir et de la Vigne, Coulanges-la-Vineuse 011501
Musée du Vieux Saint-Chamas, Saint-Chamas 014217
Musée du Vieux-Saxon, Saxon 037520
Musée du Vieux Toulon, Toulon (Var) 014976
Musée du Vieux Toulouse, Toulouse 014994
Musée du Vieux-Tréport, Le Tréport 012570
Musée du Vieux Vélo, Trois-Fontaines 015042
Musée du Vieux Warcq, Warcq 015351
Musée du Vigneron, Buxy 011037
Musée du Vigneron, Chaumont-le-Bois 011327
Musée du Vigneron, Les Marches .. 012627
Musée du Vigneron, Cave Vinicole du Vieil Armand, Wuenheim 015372
Musée du Vigneron Paul Coulon et Fils, Rasteau 013993
Musée du Vignoble et des Vins d'Alsace, Kientzheim 012192
Musée du Vignoble Montluçonnais, Domérat 011624
Musée du Vignoble Nantais, Le Pallet 012539
Musée du Village, Moknine 037967
Musée du Village, Saint-Sorlin-d'Arves 014546
Musée du Vin, Brem-sur-Mer 010975
Musée du Vin, Cheignieu-la-Balme 011340
Musée du Vin, Ehnen 027881
Musée du Vin, Luri 012794
Musée du Vin, Nangy 013330
Musée du Vin, Nissan-lez-Ensérune 013431
Musée du Vin, Paris 013691
Musée du Vin, Saint-Hilaire-de-Loulay 014327
Musée du Vin, Cave Brotte, Châteauneuf-du-Pape 011290
Musée du Vin dans l'Art, Pauillac .. 013755
Musée du Vin de Bourgogne, Beaune 010715
Musée du Vin de Bourgogne, Beaune 010716
Musée du Vin de Cahors et de la Table Lotoise, Cahors 011069
Musée du Vin de Champagne Piper-Heidsieck, Reims 014009
Musée du Vin de la Batellerie et de la Tonnellerie, Bergerac 010759
Musée du Vin et de la Mirabelle, Bruley 011017
Musée du Vin et de la Tonnellerie, Clermont-Soubiran 011403
Musée du Vin et du Pèlerinage de Saint-Jacques de Compostelle, Pomerol 013872
Musée du Vitrail, Gordes 011970
Musée du Vivarais Protestant, Pranles 013943
Musée du Zinc, Montpellier 013209
Musée Ducal, Bouillon 003249
Musée Duhamel du Monceau, Pithiviers-le-Vieil 013826
Musée d'Unterlinden, Colmar 011433
Musée Dupleix et Amas, Landrecies 012401
Musée Duplessis, Carpentras 011126
Musée Dupuytren, Collections d'Anatomie Pathologique, Paris 013692
Musée d'Utique, Utique 037989
Musée d'Uxellodunum, Martel 012959
Musée Dynamique, Dakar 034131
Musée d'Yverdon-les-Bains et sa Région, Yverdon-les-Bains 037744
Musée E. Chenon, Château-Meillant 011277
Musée Eclaté d'Arts et de Traditions Populaires, Cardaillac 011117
Musée Éclaté de la Sidérurgie en Bourgogne du Nord, Sainte-Colombe-sur-Seine 014588
Musée-École, Centre d'Etudes et des Patrimoines, Saint-Christophe-en-Brionnais 014224
Musée-Ecole de Broderie, Cilaos .. 032760
Musée-Ecole de la Perrine, Laval (Mayenne) 012446
Musée-École du Grand Meaulnes, Épineuil-le-Fleuriel 011715
Musée Écologique Vanier, Laval ... 005755
Musée EDF Electropolis, L'Aventure de l'Electricité, Mulhouse 013295
Musée Edgar Melik, Cabriès 011046

Musée Edgard Clerc, Musée Précolombien, Le Moule 021557
Musée Edith Piaf, Paris 013693
Musée Edmond Rostand, Cambo-les-Bains 011081
Musée Edouard Barthe, Montblanc . 013142
Musée Edouard Branly, Paris 013694
Musée Edouard Mahé, Retiers 014029
Musée Éducatif de Préhistoire, Villeneuve-la-Comtesse 015273
Musée Éducatif d'Entomologie de Levens, Levens 012653
Musée Église Catholique de l'Assomption, Rosenwiller 014112
Musée Emile Aubry, Béjaïa 000053
Musée Emile Chéron, Châteaumeillant 011287
Musée Émile Guillaumin, Musée du Folklore, Ygrande 015377
Musée Émile Jean, Villiers-sur-Marne 015306
Musée Émile Verhaeren, Honnelles 003518
Musée Emile Villez, Guines 012053
Musée Emir Abdelkader, Miliana . . 000067
Musée Emmanuel de la Villéon, Fougères (Ille-et-Vilaine) 011875
Musée en Herbe, Paris 013695
Musée en Piconrue, Bastogne 003216
Musée en Plein Air de Sculptures Contemporaines, Étiolles 011754
Musée en Plein Air du Sart-Tilman, Centre d'Animation et d'Intégration des Arts Plastiques de la Communauté française de Belgique, Liège 003600
Musée Entomologique, Musée des Papillons, Saint-Quentin (Aisne) . . 014502
Musée Ernest Cognacq, Saint-Martin-de-Ré 014420
Musée Ernest Renan, Tréguier 015035
Musée Espace Bérenger Saunière, Rennes-le-Château 014025
Musée Espéranto a Gray, Gray 012015
Musée Estève, Bourges 010939
Musée et Atelier d'Art Animalier, La Chapelle-Thouarault 012230
Musée et Centre de Transmission de la Culture Daniel Weetaluktuk, Inukjuak 005641
Musée et du Vieux Chinon, Chinon . 011365
Musée et Exposition Archéologiques, Luzy 012804
Musée et Maison des Vins, Bandol . 010639
Musée et Parc Archéologiques de Montauban, Buzenol 003361
Musée et Pavillon Flaubert, Croisset 011538
Musée et Salon Permanent de l'Automobile de Sport Prestige et Collection, Chauffailles 011322
Musée et Site Archéologiques de Nice-Cimiez, Nice 013403
Musée et Sites Archéologiques de Saint-Romain-en-Gal-Vienne, Saint-Romain-en-Gal 014531
Musée et Temple des Bastides, Labastide-d'Armagnac 012360
Musée et Trésor de l'Hospice, Bourg-Saint-Pierre 036968
Musée Ethnographique, Chefchaouen 029018
Musée Ethnographique, Porto-Novo 003894
Musée Ethnographique, Tétouan . . 029043
Musée Ethnographique de l'Olivier, Cagnes-sur-Mer 011063
Musée Ethnographique du Donjon, Niort 013430
Musée Ethnographique du Peuple Basque, Isturitz 012143
Musée Ethnographique Regional, Bouar 006899
Musée Ethnologique Intercommunal du Vermandois, Vermand 015180
Musée Ethnolopique Provincial, Tshikappa 007663
Musée Etienne-Jules Marey, Beaune 010717
Musée Étienne Martin, Noyal-sur-Vilaine 013455
Musée Etival dans le Temps, Ferme-Musée, Etival-Clairefontaine 011755
Musée Eugène Boudin, Honfleur . . . 012108
Musée Eugène Burnand, Moudon . . 037348
Musée Eugène Farcot, Sainville . . . 014629
Musée Eugène le Roy et Vieux Métiers, Montignac 013175
Musée Européen de Sculptures Contemporaines en Plein Air, Launstroff 012437
Musée-Expo de la Grange aux Abeilles, Giffaumont-Champaubert 011944
Musée Expo Forêt, Gérardmer 011934
Musée Exposition la Voiture à Travers les Âges, Chamblanc 011213
Musée Extraordinaire Georges-Mazoyer, Ansouis 010421
Musée Fabre, Montpellier 013210
Musée Fantastique de la Bête du Gévaudan, Saugues-en-Gévaudan 014692
Musée Fayet, Béziers 010791
Musée Féerie des Coquillages, Granville 011993
Musée Fenaille, Rodez 014087
Musée-Ferme Conservatoire Bigourdane, Péré 013770
Musée-Ferme d'Antan, Saint-Fargeau 014283
Musée Ferme d'Autrefois et Matériel Artisanal, Musée Hunault Joseph, Thourie 014949
Musée Ferme de la Patte d'Oie, Le Plessis-Patte-d'Oie 012547
Musée-Ferme des Castors du Chili, Musée de la Faune et Traditions du Béarn, Arzacq-Arraziguet 010500
Musée-Ferme Georges Ville, Paris . 013696
Musée Fernandèl, Carry-le-Rouet . . 011132
Musée Ferroviaire, Bize-Minervois . 010820
Musée Ferroviaire, Connerré 011466
Musée Ferroviaire, Longueville 012736
Musée Ferroviaire, Saint-Sulpice (Loir-et-Cher) 014550
Musée Ferroviaire de Saint-Géry, Saint-Géry 014318
Musée Ferroviaire et des Vieilles Gares, Guîtres 012057
Musée Ferroviaire La Lorraine en Périgord, Excideuil 011765
Musée Fesch, Ajaccio 010306
Musée Flaubert et d'Histoire de la Médecine, Rouen 014129
Musée Fleury, Lodève 012727
Musée Flottant-Architecture Navale, Audierne 010538
Musée Folklorique de Ghardaïa, Ghardaïa 000064
Musée Folklorique et Viticole à Possen, Bech-Kleinmacher 027869
Musée-Fondation Alexandra David Néel, Digne-les-Bains 011593
Musée-Fondation Arp, Clamart 011386
Musée-Fondation Bemberg, Toulouse 014995
Musée-Fondation Louis Jou, Les Baux-de-Provence 012610
Musée Fondation Musée Volti, Villefranche-sur-Mer 015255
Musée Fondation Royale d'Albanie, La Chapelle-d'Angillon 012224
Musée-Fort de Leveau, Feignies . . . 011794
Musée Fort de Sucy, Sucy-en-Brie . 014884
Musée Fort Lagarde, Prats-de-Mollo-la-Preste 013944
Musée Fougou, Montpellier 013211
Musée Fournaise, Chatou 011319
Musée Fragonard de l'Ecole Nationale Vétérinaire d'Alfort, Maisons-Alfort 012857
Musée Français - 1e Armée Française Mai 1940, Cortil-Noirmont 003378
Musée Français de la Brasserie, Saint-Nicolas-de-Port 014453
Musée Français de la Carte à Jouer, Issy-les-Moulineaux 012140
Musée Français de la Photographie, Bièvres 010803
Musée Français de la Spéléologie, Courniou-les-Grottes 011510
Musée Français de Spéléologie, Gagny 011911
Musée Français des Phares et Balises, Ile-d'Ouessant 012130
Musée Français du Chemin de Fer, Mulhouse 013296
Musée Francis Jammes, Hasparren 012072
Musée Francisque Mandet, Riom . . 014051
Musée Franco-Américain, Sommepy-Tahure 014820
Musée Franco-Tchécoslosvaque, Darney 011561
Musée François Desnoyer, Saint-Cyprien 014241
Musée François Flori Ricordi Vividi Antichi Niulinchi, Calacuccia 011072
Musée François Guiguet, Corbelin . 011476
Musée François Mauriac, Saint-Maixant (Gironde) 014405
Musée François-Mauriac, Vemars . 015154
Musée François Pilote, La Pocatière 005727
Musée François-Pompon, Saulieu . 014694
Musée Frédéric Japy, Beaucourt . . 010701
Musée Frédéric Mistral, Maillane . . 012850
Musée Friry, Remiremont 014016
Musée Fromages et Patrimoine, Ambert 010349
Musée Gadagne, Musée Historique de Lyon et Musée International de la Marionnette, Lyon 012825
Musée-Galerie Alexis et Gustave Adolf Mossa, Nice 013404
Musée-Galerie de la Mine de Fer de Framont, Grandfontaine (Bas-Rhin) 011988
Musée Galerie Honoré Camos, Bargemon 010655
Musée-Galerie Marcel Baudou, Sainte-Eulalie 014594
Musée-Galerie Raoul Dufy, Nice . . . 013405
Musée Gallé-Juillet, Musée Municipal, Creil 011530
Musée Galliéra, Musée de la Mode de la Ville de Paris, Paris 013697
Musée Gallo-Romain, Berneau 003231
Musée Gallo-Romain, Biesheim . . . 010800
Musée Gallo-Romain, Périgueux . . . 013774
Musée Gallo-Romain, Rumes 003732
Musée Gallo-Romain, Musée des Potiers de Portout, Chanaz 011234
Musée Gallo-Romain d'Aoste, Aoste 010437
Musée Gallo-Romain de Tauroentum, Saint-Cyr-sur-Mer 014247
Musée Gallo-Romain d'Octodure, Martigny 037315
Musée Gantner, La Chapelle-sous-Chaux 012229
Musée Gardanne Autrefois, Gardanne 011920
Musée Garinet, Châlons-en-Champagne 011199
Musée Garret, Vesoul 015193
Musée Gaspar, Arlon 003200
Musée Gaston Fébus, Associaton Escole Gastou Fébus, Mauvezin (Hautes-Pyrénées) 012982
Musée Gaston Grégor, Musée d'Arts et d'Histoire, Salles-d'Angles 014646
Musée Gatien-Bonnet, Lagny-sur-Marne 012378
Musée Gauguin, Le Carbet 028056
Musée Gay-Lussac, Saint-Léonard-de-Noblat 014390
Musée General Leclerc, Alençon . . 010327
Musée Géo Charles, Échirolles 011679
Musée Géologique, Conakry 021591
Musée Géologique, Dakar 034132
Musée Géologique, La Charguia . . . 037961
Musée Geologique, Vernet-les-Bains 015181
Musée Géologique du Rwanda, Kigali 034102
Musée Géologique et Paléontologique, Langé 012404
Musée Géologique Fossiles Préhistoire, Neuil 013372
Musée Geologique Sengier-Cousin, Jadotville 007651
Musée Géologique ULP, Université Louis Pasteur, Strasbourg 014877
Musée George Sand et de la Vallée Noire, La Châtre 012232
Musée Georges Borias, Uzès 015081
Musée Georges Clemenceau, Paris 013698
Musée Georges Labit, Toulouse . . . 014996
Musée Georgette Lemaire, Angoulême 010408
Musée Gilles-Villeneuve, Berthierville 005096
Musée Girodet, Montargis 013127
Musée Girouxville, Girouxville 005509
Musée Goethe, Sessenheim 014777
Musée Goetz-Boumeester, Villefranche-sur-Mer 015256
Musée Gorsline, Bussy-le-Grand . . 011035
Musée Goupil, Bordeaux 010890
Musée Goupil, Conservatoire de l'Image Industrielle, Bordeaux 010891
Musée Goya, Castres 011151
Musée Granet, Aix-en-Provence . . . 010296
Musée Grétry, Liège 003601
Musée Greuze, Tournus 015011
Musée Grévin, Paris 013699
Musée Grévin, Saint-Jean-de-Luz . 014348
Musée Grévin, Historial des Ducs de Bourgogne, Dijon 011610
Musée Grévin de la Provence, Salon-de-Provence 014653
Musée Grévin de Lourdes, Lourdes 012777
Musée Grobet-Labadié, Marseille . . 012951
Musée Grotte de Limousis, Limousis 012699
Musée Gruérien, Bulle 036989
Musée Guerre et Paix en Ardennes, Novion-Porcien 013454
Musée Guillaume Apollinaire, Stavelot 003783
Musée Guillion, Musée Départemental du Compagnonnage Pierre-François Guillon, Romanèche-Thorins 014093
Musée Gustave Moreau, Musée National, Paris 013700
Musée Gyger, Vallorbe 037670
Musée-Hameau de Sculptures XIXe s, Fransèches 011886
Musée Hansi, Riquewihr 014059
Musée Hardy, Clécy 011389
Musée Harmas Jean-Henri Fabre, Sérignan-du-Comtat 014768
Musée Haut Savoyard de la Résistance, Bonneville 010871
Musée Haviland, Limoges 012695
Musée Hector Berlioz, La Côte-Saint-André 012243
Musée Henri-Barre, Thouars 014948
Musée Henri Boez, Maubeuge 012971
Musée Henri Chapu, Le Mée-sur-Seine 012525
Musée Henri Dupuis, Saint-Omer . . 014456
Musée Henri Giron, Le Vigan (Lot) . 012579
Musée Henri IV, Saint-Sulpice-de-Faleyrens 014548
Musée Henri Malartre, Rochetaillée-sur-Saône 014082
Musée Henri Mathieu, Bruyères . . . 011024
Musée Henri Ughetto, Lyon 012826
Musée Henry Clews, Mandelieu-La Napoule 012869
Musée Henry de Monfreid, Ingrandes (Indre) 012134
Musée Héritage, Saint-Albert 006320
Musée Héritage, Saint-Pierre 034107
Musée Hermès, Paris 013701
Musée Hippomobile, Saint-Michel-des-Andaines 014438
Musée Historial, Mazères (Gironde) 012990
Musée Historial du Vieux Pessac, Pessac 013799
Musée Historie Locale, Marchiennes 012889
Musée Historique, Abomey 003887

Musée Historique, Antananarivo . . . 027931
Musée Historique, Bapaume 010645
Musée Historique, Basse-Rentgen . 010662
Musée Historique, Bessé-sur-Braye 010777
Musée Historique, Bort-les-Orgues . 010898
Musée Historique, Bourail 030418
Musée Historique, Carhaix-Plouguer 011119
Musée Historique, Cellettes 011169
Musée Historique, Cérisy-la-Forêt . 011182
Musée Historique, Chalençon 011192
Musée Historique, Châtillon-sur-Saône 011316
Musée Historique, Clervaux 027874
Musée Historique, Elne 011689
Musée Historique, Fénetrange 011797
Musée Historique, Fondremand . . . 011833
Musée Historique, Gourdon (Alpes-Maritimes) 011975
Musée Historique, Haguenau 012064
Musée Historique, La Couvertoirade 012248
Musée Historique, Laroquebrou . . . 012429
Musée Historique, Le Chambon-sur-Lignon 012479
Musée Historique, Mont-Saint-Michel 013114
Musée Historique, Mulhouse 013297
Musée Historique, Peyrusse-le-Roc 013804
Musée Historique, Strasbourg 014878
Musée Historique, Institut National des Jeunes Aveugle, Paris 013702
Musée Historique 1814, Essises . . . 011741
Musée Historique Charles Le Moyne, Longueuil 005796
Musée Historique d'Abomey, Abomey 003888
Musée Historique de Gorée, Gorée . 034136
Musée Historique de Graffiti Anciens, Marsilly 012956
Musée Historique de la Citadelle, Belle-Ile-en-Mer 010739
Musée Historique de la Faïence, Moustiers-Sainte-Marie 013279
Musée Historique de la Laub, Bischwiller 010814
Musée Historique de la Ligne Maginot Aquatique, Sarralbe 014679
Musée Historique de la Médecine Scientifique et des Pratiques Populaires, Beauchastel 010700
Musée Historique de la Poterie, Wismes 015367
Musée Historique de la Réformation, Genève 037132
Musée Historique de la Tour de la Chaîne, La Rochelle 012325
Musée Historique de Lausanne, Lausanne 037250
Musée Historique de l'Hydraviation, Biscarrosse 010811
Musée Historique de l'Ile-de-Sein, Ile-de-Sein 012128
Musée Historique de Saint-Gilles-les-Hauts, Saint-Paul 032766
Musée Historique de Saint-Pierre, Saint-Pierre 028059
Musée Historique de Troyes et de la Champagne, Troyes 015053
Musée Historique de Verfeil, Verfeil 015177
Musée Historique de Vevey, Vevey . 037678
Musée Historique de Villèle, Saint-Gilles-les-Hauts 032764
Musée Historique du Bailliage de Rouffach, Rouffach 014134
Musée Historique du Centre-Var, Le Luc 012514
Musée Historique du Château, Langoiran 012407
Musée Historique du Cidre, La Duretière, Melleray-la-Vallée 013005
Musée Historique du Domaine National, Saint-Cloud 014235
Musée Historique du Groupe Lorraine, Reims 014010
Musée Historique du Madawaska, Edmundston 005416
Musée Historique du Papier, Ambert 010350
Musée Historique du Papier, Couze-et-Saint-Front 011523
Musée Historique du Papier, Saint-Jean-de-Côle 014344
Musée Historique du Port, La Rochelle 012326
Musée Historique et Archéologique, Montségur 013231
Musée Historique et Archéologique de l'Orléanais, Orléans 013519
Musée Historique et de la Pêche, Talmont-sur-Gironde 014895
Musée Historique et des Porcelaines, Nyon 037385
Musée Historique et Diorama 1914-1918, Souchez 014833
Musée Historique et Erckmann-Chatrian, Phalsbourg 013809
Musée Historique et Lapidaire, Isle-Aumont 012135
Musée Historique et Lapidaire, Morlaàs 013240
Musée Historique et Logis Thiphaine, Le Mont-Saint-Michel 012534
Musée Historique et Militaire, Freyming-Merlebach 011899
Musée Historique et Militaire, Huningue 012114
Musée Historique et Militaire, Mémorial du Finistère, Brest 010985
Musée Historique et Préhistorique Van den Steen, Jehay-Amay 003545
Musée Historique Local, Mougins . . 013262
Musée Historique Valdec-de Lessart, Portets 013926
Musée Hofer-Bury, Lavérune 012456
Musée Horlogerie Automates Yves Cupillard, Morteau 013254
Musée Horreum Romain, Narbonne 013353
Musée Horta, Bruxelles 003346
Musée Hospitalier, Charlieu 011254
Musée Hospitalier - Apothicairerie, Hôtel-Dieu, Bourg-en-Bresse 010927
Musée Hospitalier et Apothicairerie, Louhans 012760
Musée-Hôtel Bertrand, Châteauroux 011302
Musée-Hôtel de Beaumont, Valognes 015116
Musée Hôtel de la Dentelle, Brioude 011008
Musée Hôtel de Ville, Thann 014924
Musée-Hôtel Granval-Caligny, Valognes 015117
Musée Hôtel Lallemand, Bourges . . 010940
Musée-Hôtel Le Vergeur, Reims . . . 014011
Musée Humoristique Albert Dubout, Palavas-les-Flots 013539
Musée Huperel de l'Histoire Cathare, Minerve 013068
Musée Huppy Autrefois, Huppy 012116
Musée Hyacinthe Rigaud, Perpignan 013789
Musée Hydrogéologique, Chaudfontaine 003372
Musée Ianchelevici, La Louvière . . . 003564
Musée Ianchelevici, Maisons-Laffite 012858
Musée Impérial de la Miniature, Musée Atelier de Soldats de Plomb, Les Barils 012603
Musée in Situ des Bains Romains, Aix-les-Bains 010302
Musée Industriel Corderie Vallois, Notre-Dame-de-Bondeville 013451
Musée Industriel du Val-de-Travers, Fleurier 037087
Musée Industriel et d'Ethnologie, Lille 012684
Musée Ingres, Montauban 013130
Musée Ingres: Bulletin, Montauban 135717
Musée Intercommunal d'Histoire et d'Archéologie, Louvres 012787
Musée International d'Art Naïf, Vicq 015207
Musée International d'Arts Modestes, Sète 014779
Musée International de Akum, Bamenda 004972
Musée International de la Chasse, Gien 011943
Musée International de la Chaussure, Romans-sur-Isère 014095
Musée International de la Croix-Rouge et du Croissant-Rouge, Genève 037133
Musée International de la Faune, Argelès-Gazost 010457
Musée International de la Faune, Québriac 013970
Musée International de la Marionnette, Bruxelles 003347
Musée International de la Parfumerie, Grasse 012001
Musée International de l'Automobile, Le Grand-Saconnex 037159
Musée International de l'Etiquette, Aigle 036822
Musée International de Mobilier Miniature, Vendeuvre 015160
Musée International des Hussards, Tarbes 014911
Musée International des Polices et des Gendarmeries, Charvieu-Chavagneux 011269
Musée International d'Horlogerie, Institut l'Homme et le Temps, La Chaux-de-Fonds 037015
Musée International du Carnaval et du Masque, Binche 003233
Musée International du Coquillage, Saint-Barthélemy 021560
Musée International du Long Cours Cap Hornier, Saint-Malo (Ille-et-Vilaine) 014410
Musée International du Menu Gastronomique, Nointel (Oise) . . . 013440
Musée International du Trans-Manche, Escalles 011722
Musée International, Pétanque et Boules, Saint-Bonnet-le-Château 014201
Musée Isérables, Isérables 037200
Musée Ivan Tourguéniev, Bougival . 010905
Musée J. Armand Bombardier, Valcourt 006681
Musée J.-E. Blanche, Offranville . . 013474
Musée J.-F. Leyraud, La Roche-sur-le-Buis 012309
Musée Jacquaire, Ferrières (Tarn) . 011806
Musée Jacquemart-André, Fontaine-Chaalis 011836
Musée Jacquemart-André, Paris . . 013703
Musée Jacques Warminski, Saint-Georges-des-Sept-Voies 014302
Musée Jadis Allevard, Allevard-les-Bains 010338
Musée-Jardin d'Art Contemporain, Bitche 010819
Musée-Jardin Paul-Landowski, Boulogne-Billancourt 010910
Musée J.B. Mathon et André Durand, Neufchâtel-en-Bray 013369
Musée Jean-Aicard, La Garde 012265
Musée Jean Aicard, Solliès-Ville . . 014818
Musée Jean-Charles Cazin, Samer . 014658
Musée Jean-Claude Colin, Association Art Culture Amitié, Saint-Bonnet-le-Troncy 014202
Musée Jean Cocteau, Menton 013023
Musée Jean de la Fontaine, Château-Thierry 011282
Musée Jean Farkas, Baden 010616
Musée Jean Gabin, Mériel 013029
Musée Jean-Henri Fabre, Saint-Léons 014391
Musée Jean-Honoré Fragonard, Grasse 012002
Musée Jean-Hotte, Saint-Eustache 006336
Musée Jean-Jacques Rousseau, Genève 037134
Musée Jean-Jacques Rousseau, Montmorency 013190
Musée Jean-Jacques Rousseau, Môtiers 037344
Musée Jean-Lurçat, Angers 010397
Musée Jean Lurçat, Saint-Laurent-les-Tours 014383
Musée Jean Macé, Beblenheim . . . 010727
Musée Jean-Marie Souplet, Musée Minéralogique et Paléontologique, Engis 003423
Musée Jean-Mermoz, Aubenton . . . 010515
Musée Jean-Moulin, Paris 013704
Musée Jean-Philippe Marchand, Marsais 012921
Musée Jean-Racine, La Ferté-Milon 012253
Musée Jean Tua, Genève 037135
Musée Jeanne d'Aboville, La Fère . 012249
Musée Jeanne d'Arc, Chinon 011366
Musée Jeanne d'Arc, Rouen 014130
Musée Jeanne d'Arc, Sainte-Cathérine-de-Fierbois 014586
Musée Jenisch, Musée des Beaux-Arts de Vevey et Cabinet Cantonal des Estampes, Vevey 037679
Musée Joachim du Bellay, Liré 012702
Musée Johannique, Vaucouleurs . . 015141
Musée Joseph Abeilhe, Marciac . . . 012891
Musée Joseph Denais, Beaufort-en-Vallée 010703
Musée Joseph Durand, Saint-Clément-des-Baleines 014232
Musée Joseph Lhoménède, Frugières-le-Pin 011906
Musée Joseph-Vaylet, Espalion . . . 011731
Musée Jouenne, Saint-Rémy-de-Provence 014521
Musée Jourdain, Morez 013238
Musée Judéo-Alsacien, Bouxwiller . 010954
Musée Juif Comtadin, Cavaillon . . . 011165
Musée Juin 1944, L'Aigle 012385
Musée Jules Desbois, Parçay-les-Pins 013547
Musée Jules Destrée, Charleroi . . . 003370
Musée Jules Romains, Saint-Julien-Chapteuil 014366
Musée Jules Verne, Nantes 013342
Musée Jungle des Papillons Vivants, Antibes-Juan-les-Pins 010428
Musée Jurassien d'Art et d'Histoire, Delémont 037042
Musée Jurassien des Arts, Moutier . 037350
Musée Jurassien des Sciences Naturelles, Porrentruy 037420
Musée Juste Pour Rire, Montréal . . 005942
Musée K. Raphaël, Vavoua 007694
Musée Kateri Tekakwitha, Kahnawake 005656
Musée Kaysone Phomvihane, Vientiane 027647
Musée Kio-Warini, Loretteville 005799
Musée Kwok-On, Paris 013705
Musée La Diana, Montbrison 013145
Musée la Faïencerie, Ancy-le-Franc 010379
Musée La Ferme Forézienne, Saint-Bonnet-les-Oules 014203
Musée la Magie des Automates, Lans-en-Vercors 012416
Musée La Main et l'Outil, Pannes . . 013543
Musée La Maison du Passé, Royat-les-Bains 014149
Musée la Maison du Pêcheur et Le Hope, Saint-Gilles-Croix-de-Vie 014319
Musée la Muse, Mérindol 013031
Musée la Perçée du Bocage 1944, Saint-Martin-des-Besaces 014422
Musée La Pouponnière, Bourg-Charente 010924
Musée La Sagne, La Sagne 037474
Musée la Taille de Pierre, Saint-Antoine-l'Abbaye 014186
Musée la Vie des Jouets, Mauleon . 012974
Musée la Villa Aurélienne, Fréjus . . 011892
Musée Labasso, Bangassou 006897
Musée l'Abeille Vivante, Le Faouët . 012495
Musée Labenche d'Art et d'Histoire, Brive-la-Gaillarde 011012
Musée Lacordaire, Recey-sur-Ource 013997
Musée Lacoune, Lacaune 012370
Musée Laennec, Nantes 013343
Musée Lamartine, Mâcon 012840
Musée Lambinet, Versailles 015188

Musée Lamothe-Cadillac, Saint-Nicolas-de-la-Grave . . . 014452
Musée Langlois, Beaumont-en-Auge . . . 010711
Musée Languédocien, Montpellier . 013212
Musée Laperouse, Albi . . . 010319
Musée Lapidaire, Avignon . . . 010595
Musée Lapidaire, Baume-les-Messieurs . . . 010673
Musée Lapidaire, Cabasse . . . 011040
Musée Lapidaire, Carpentras . . . 011127
Musée Lapidaire, Lalouret-Laffiteau 012389
Musée Lapidaire, Léhon . . . 012589
Musée Lapidaire, Riez . . . 014045
Musée Lapidaire, Saint-Germain-Laval . . . 014313
Musée Lapidaire, Saint-Guilhem-le-Désert . . . 014325
Musée Lapidaire, Villeveyrac . . . 015300
Musée Lapidaire, Palais des Archevêques, Narbonne . . . 013354
Musée Lapidaire de la Cité, Carcassonne . . . 011115
Musée Lapidaire de l'Abbaye, Savigny (Rhône) . . . 014727
Musée Lapidaire de l'Abbaye Saint-Pierre, Maillezais . . . 012853
Musée Lapidaire de Mozac, Mozac . 013288
Musée Lapidaire de Saint-Pierre, Vienne . . . 015211
Musée Lapidaire du Cloître de l'Ancienne Cathédrale, Vaison-la-Romaine . . 015089
Musée Lapidaire Municipal, Saint-Sever (Landes) . . . 014543
Musée Lapidaire Paléochrétien, Toulx-Sainte-Croix . . . 015000
Musée Larrey, Beaudean . . . 010702
Musée L'Art en Marche Hauterives Art Brut, Neuve Invention, Hauterives . . . 012082
Musée L'Art en Marche Lapalisse Art Brut, Lapalisse . . . 012422
Musée Laurier, Victoriaville . . . 006751
Musée Lautrecois, Lautrec . . . 012442
Musée Le Chafaud, Percé . . . 006132
Musée Le Corbusier, Pessac . . . 013800
Musée Le Grenier de l'Histoire, Lèves . . . 012654
Musée Le Jacquemart, Langeac . . . 012405
Musée Le Masque en Liberté, Nibelle . . . 013391
Musée le Mémoire d'Oyé, Oyé . . . 013531
Musée Le Minerve, Yzeures-sur-Creuse . . . 015384
Musée Le Mont-Saint-Michel, Le Mont-Saint-Michel . . . 012535
Musée Le Palais des Naïfs, Bages (Pyrénées-Orientales) . . . 010619
Musée Le Patrimoine du Sapeur-Pompier, Beaune . . . 010718
Musée Le Petit Louvre, La Pacaudière . . . 012292
Musée le Petit Mont-Saint-Michel, Saint-Marcan . . . 014411
Musée Le Pionnier, Saint-Malo . . . 006385
Musée Le Secq des Tournelles - Musée de la Ferronnerie, Rouen . . . 014131
Musée le Soum, Saint-Véran . . . 014568
Musée le Temple du Soleil, Saint-Michel-en-l'Herm . . . 014439
Musée Leblanc-Duvernoy, Auxerre . 010574
Musée Leclerc Briant, Épernay . . . 011709
Musée Lecoq, Museum d'Histoire Naturelle, Clermont-Ferrand . . . 011400
Musée Lella Hadria, Midoun . . . 037966
Musée Lénine, Paris . . . 013706
Musée Léon de Smet, Deurle . . . 003397
Musée Léon Dierx, Saint-Denis . . . 032762
Musée Léon Marès, Lovagny . . . 012788
Musée Léon Perrin, Môtiers . . . 037345
Musée Les Amis de l'Outil, Bièvres 010804
Musée Les Ateliers du Bois, Vadencourt . . . 015085
Musée les Retrouvailles, Saint-Jean-Port-Joli . . . 006349
Musée les Sources d'Hercule, Musée Archéologique de Site Gallo-Romain, Deneuvre . . . 011577
Musée les Thermes d'Antonin, Carthage . . . 037949
Musée Libertador du Général San Martin, Boulogne-sur-Mer . . . 010912
Musée Ligier Richier, Saint-Mihiel . 014445
Musée Lillet, Podensac . . . 013863
Musée Littéraire Victor Hugo, Vianden . . . 027906
Musée Local, Boën-sur-Lignon . . . 010852
Musée Local, Brandenbourg . . . 027872
Musée Local, Weiler-la-Tour . . . 027908
Musée Local d'Art, Eze . . . 011775
Musée Local de Préhistoire, Sceaux-du-Gatinais . . . 014732
Musée Loïc Raison, Cruas . . . 011542
Musée Lombard, Doullens . . . 011649
Musée Longines, Saint-Imier . . . 037477
Musée Lorrain, Nancy . . . 013326
Musée Lou Férouil, Gilette . . . 011946
Musée Louis Braille, Coupvray . . . 011506
Musée Louis Cornu, Wassigny . . . 015356
Musée Louis-Hemon, Peribonka . . . 006133
Musée Louis Jou, Les Baux-de-Provence . . . 012611
Musée Louis Jourdan, Saint-Paul-de-Varax . . . 014467
Musée Louis-Lacrocq, Guéret . . . 012046
Musée Louis Lutaud, Ferrière-la-Grande . . . 011801
Musée Louis Pasteur, Strasbourg . . 014879
Musée Louis Pergaud, Belmont . . . 010745
Musée Louis Philippe, Eu . . . 011759
Musée Louis-Vouland, Avignon . . . 010596
Musée Louise Cottin, Vigneulles-lès-Hattonchâtel . . . 015218
Musée Louise Weiss, Saverne . . . 014718
Musée Louison Bobet, Saint-Méen-le-Grande . . . 014434
Musée Lucien Roy, Beure . . . 010782
Musée Luxembourgeois, Arlon . . . 003201
Musée Maçonnique de la Grande Loge de France, Paris . . . 013707
Musée Mado Robin, Yzeures-sur-Creuse . . . 015385
Musée Magie des Abeilles, Villechauve . . . 015241
Musée Maginot de Rohrbach-Fort Casso, Rohrbach-les-Bitche . . . 014089
Musée Magnanerie, Vallon-Pont-d'Arc . . . 015113
Musée Magnelli, Musée de la Céramique, Vallauris . . . 015106
Musée Magnin, Dijon . . . 011611
Musée Mai Juin 1940, Margut . . . 012906
Musée Maillol, Fondation Dina Vierny, Paris . . . 013708
Musée Mainssieux, Voiron . . . 015331
Musée Mairie, Le Pont-de-Beauvoisin . . . 012550
Musée-Maison d'Art Contemporain Chaillioux, Fresnes (Val-de-Marne) . . . 011896
Musée-Maison de Chateaubriand, Châtenay-Malabry . . . 011310
Musée-Maison de Clemenceau, Saint-Vincent-sur-Jard . . . 014574
Musée Maison de George Sand, Gargilesse-Dampierre . . . 011922
Musée-Maison de la Baleine, Luc-sur-Mer . . . 012790
Musée Maison de la Brique, Saint-Martin-d'Aubigny . . . 014415
Musée Maison de la Dame de Brassempouy, Brassempouy . . . 010968
Musée-Maison de la Nature, A. Caron, Samer . . . 014659
Musée-Maison de la Nature et de l'Estuaire de l'Orne, Sallenelles . . . 014642
Musée Maison de la Soie, Saint-Hippolyte-du-Fort . . . 014333
Musée-Maison de la Vie Rurale, La Flocellière . . . 012261
Musée Maison de l'Armateur, Le Havre . . . 012508
Musée-Maison de l'Aspre, Arts et Traditions Populaires, Thuir . . . 014953
Musée-Maison de l'Erdre, Nantes . . 013344
Musée Maison de l'Huître, Gujan-Mestras . . . 012058
Musée-Maison de Sainte-Thérèse, Lisieux . . . 012704
Musée-Maison d'Ecole, Montceau-les-Mines . . . 013148
Musée Maison Déodat Roché, Maison du Catharisme, Arques (Aude) . . . 010482
Musée-Maison des Amis de la Forêt, Mervent . . . 013034
Musée-Maison des Arts des Hauts-Cantons, Bédarieux . . . 010729
Musée-Maison des Canuts, Lyon . . 012827
Musée-Maison des Dentelles et du Point d'Argentan, Argentan . . . 010460
Musée-Maison des Milelli, Propriété des Bonaparte, Ajaccio . . . 010307
Musée-Maison des Pierreux, Massangis . . . 012968
Musée Maison des Templiers, Musée Art et Tradition du Pays de Salers, Salers . . . 014634
Musée-Maison des Tresses et des Lacets, La Terrasse-sur-Dorlay . . . 012342
Musée-Maison des Vanniers, Feytiat . . . 011811
Musée-Maison du Café, Vieux-Habitants . . . 021564
Musée-Maison du Canal, Fégréac . 011793
Musée-Maison du Jardinier, Gétigné . . . 011939
Musée-Maison du Pain, Commeny . 011445
Musée-Maison du Parc National et de la Vallée, Luz-Saint-Sauveur . . . 012802
Musée-Maison du Parc National et du Val d'Azun, Arrens-Marsous . . . 010487
Musée-Maison du Parc Naturel Régional de la Montagne de Reims, Pourcy . . 013930
Musée Maison du Pays, Moisdon-la-Rivière . . . 013083
Musée-Maison du Paysan, Touvois . 015028
Musée-Maison du Pêcheur, La Chevrolière . . . 012234
Musée-Maison du Petit Poitou, Chaillé-les-Marais . . . 011190
Musée Maison du Potier, Le Fuilet . 012497
Musée-Maison du Saumon et de la Rivière, Brioude . . . 011009
Musée-Maison du Terroir, Châteauponsac . . . 011296
Musée-Maison du Verre, Meisenthal . . . 013001
Musée-Maison Lohobiague dite Maison Louis XIV, Saint-Jean-de-Luz . . . 014349
Musée-Maison Marcel Proust, Maison de Tante Léonie, Illiers-Combray . . . 012133
Musée Maison Mathelin, Bastogne . 003217
Musée-Maison Natale de Jean de Lattre de Tassigny, Mouilleron-en-Pareds . . 013264
Musée-Maison Natale du Maréchal Jourdan, Limoges . . . 012696
Musée-Maison Natale Gustave Courbet, Ornans . . . 013522
Musée-Maison Paternelle de Bernadette, Lourdes . . . 012778
Musée Maison Robert-Doisneau, Gentilly . . . 011932
Musée Maison Saint-Gabriel, Montréal . . . 005943
Musée Malraux, Le Havre . . . 012509
Musée M'Am Jeanne, Fontenoy-en-Puisaye . . . 011858
Musée Manoir de Kerazan, Loctudy 012726
Musée-Manoir de la Touche, Nantes . . . 013345
Musée Manoir de Vains, Vains . . . 015087
Musée-Manoir des Évêques de Lisieux, Deauville . . . 011566
Musée-Manoir des Sciences, Réaumur . . . 013996
Musée Maraîchin, Sallertaine . . . 014644
Musée Marc-Aurèle Fortin, Montréal . . . 005944
Musée Marc Deydier, Cucuron . . . 011545
Musée Marc Leclerc, La Ménitré . . 012286
Musée Marc Mureau, Restigné . . . 014027
Musée Marcel Cachin, Choisy-le-Roi . . . 011371
Musée Marcel Collet, Musée d'Histoire et d'Archéologie, Loverval . . . 003618
Musée Marcel de Marcheville, Romorantin-Lanthenay . . . 014100
Musée Marcel-Lenoir, Montricoux . 013228
Musée Marcel Sahut, Volvic . . . 015336
Musée Marchiennois d'Histoire et d'Archéologie Industrielle, Marchienne-au-Pont . . . 003627
Musée Maréchal Joffre, Rivesaltes . 014062
Musée Marguerite-Audoux, Aubigny-sur-Nère . . . 010523
Musée Marguerite Bourgeoys, Montréal . . . 005945
Musée Marguerite de Bourgogne, Tonnerre . . . 014964
Musée Marguerite Yourcenar, Saint-Jans-Cappel . . . 014336
Musée Marial de Beauraing, Beauraing . . . 003219
Musée Marie Laurencin, Chino . . . 026444
Musée Marie-Rose Durocher, Longueuil . . . 005797
Musée-Marinarium du Haut Lavédan, Pierrefitte-Nestalas . . . 013816
Musée Marine et Montagne, Mons (Var) . . . 013104
Musée Maritime, Camaret-sur-Mer 011079
Musée Maritime, Carantec . . . 011108
Musée Maritime, Le Mont-Saint-Michel . . . 012536
Musée Maritime à Flot France I, La Rochelle . . . 012327
Musée Maritime Chantereyne, Cherbourg-Octeville . . . 011351
Musée Maritime de l'Ile de Tatihou, Saint-Vaast-la-Hougue . . . 014561
Musée Maritime de l'île de Tatihou, Saint-Vaast-la-Hougue . . . 014562
Musée Maritime de Regnéville, Les Fours à Chaux, Regnéville-sur-Mer . . . 014000
Musée Maritime du Québec, L'Islet 005777
Musée Maritime, Fluvial et Portuaire, Rouen . . . 014132
Musée Maritime Islais, Port-Joinville . . . 013918
Musée Maritime La Rochelle, La Rochelle . . . 012328
Musée Maritime l'Esvale et Ostréicole, La Tremblade . . . 012347
Musée Marius Barbeau, Saint-Joseph-de-Beauce . . . 006375
Musée Marmottan Claude Monet, Paris . . . 013709
Musée Marsa El-Kharez, El-Kala . . 000061
Musée Marsil, Saint-Lambert . . . 006379
Musée Martin Duby, Auriol . . . 010554
Musée Massey, Tarbes . . . 014912
Musée Matheysin, La Mure-d'Isère 012291
Musée Mathurin Méheut, Lamballe 012393
Musée Matisse, Le Cateau-Cambrésis . . . 012478
Musée Matisse, Nice . . . 013406
Musée Maurice Beaumont, Musée du Cobattant de Haute-Soane, Luxeuil-les-Bains . . . 012798
Musée Maurice Carême, Bruxelles . 003348
Musée Maurice-Dufresne, Azay-le-Rideau . . . 010612
Musée Maurice et Eugénie de Guérin, Andillac . . . 010381
Musée Maurice Genevoix, Saint-Denis-de-l'Hôtel . . . 014249
Musée Maurice Gottlob, Espace Culturel, Mougins . . . 013263
Musée Maurice Poignant, Bourg-sur-Gironde . . . 010932
Musée Maurice Ravel, Montfort-l'Amaury . . . 013165
Musée Maxime Mabilleau, Saumur . 014706
Musée Médiéval, Brain-sur-Allonnes . . . 010959
Musée Medieval, Serralongue . . . 014772
Musée Médiumnique Fernand Desmoulin, Brantôme . . . 010963
Musée Mémoires de la Terre et Horizons Cathares, Mazamet . . . 012984

Musée Mémoires du Moyen Âge, Carcassonne 011116
Musée Mémorial 1914-1918, Wattwiller 015359
Musée Memorial Alain, Mortagne-au-Perche 013250
Musée-Mémorial de la Bataille de l'Atlantique, Camaret-sur-Mer . . . 011080
Musée Mémorial de la Bataille de Normandie, Bayeux 010682
Musée Mémorial de la Bataille de Verdun, Fleury-devant-Douaumont 011826
Musée Mémorial de la Ligne Maginot du Rhin, Marckolsheim 012895
Musée-Mémorial de la Résistance et de la Déportation, Metz 013041
Musée Mémorial des Combat de la Poche de Colmar, Turckheim 015064
Musée Mémorial du Général de Gaulle, Bayeux 010683
Musée-Mémorial du Linge, Orbey . 013501
Musée Mémorial Maginot de Haute-Alsace, Mémorial de Haute-Alsace, Uffheim 015070
Musée-Mémorial National du Débarquement en Provence (1944), Toulon (Var) 014977
Musée Memorial Omaha Beach, Saint-Laurent-sur-Mer 014384
Musée Mer et Désert, Maison de l'Eau, Villerville 015295
Musée Michel Braibant, Conservatoire des Arts et Métiers du Livre, Montolieu 013196
Musée Militaire, Bordeaux 010892
Musée Militaire, Cambrai 011084
Musée Militaire, Clères 011393
Musée Militaire, Colombier 037029
Musée Militaire, Mer 013026
Musée Militaire, saint-maixent-l'École 014406
Musée Militaire, Veckring 015151
Musée Militaire, Villeneuve-Loubet . 015280
Musée Militaire de Bure, Bure-Tressange 011030
Musée Militaire de Thiaucourt, Thiaucourt 014928
Musée Militaire des Gloires et Souvenirs du Périgord, Périgueux 013775
Musée Militaire du 12e Régiment Blindé du Canada, Trois-Rivières 006664
Musée Militaire du Fort, Douaumont 011645
Musée Militaire du Souvenir, Dompierre-sur-Mer 011632
Musée Militaire Faller, Mars-la-Tour 012919
Musée Militaire Genevois, Cologny . 037027
Musée Militaire Ligne Mareth, Mareth 037965
Musée Militaire National, Manouba 037964
Musée Militaire Vaudois, Morges . . 037341
Musée Mine, Cagnac-les-Mines . . . 011058
Musée Mineralexpo, La Bourboule . 012208
Musée Minéralogique, Nîmes 013426
Musée Minéralogique d'Asbestos, Asbestos 005030
Musée Minéralogique de la Société Industrielle, Mulhouse 013298
Musée Minéralogique de l'École des Mines d'Alès, Alès 010333
Musée Minéralogique du Dolon, Chanas 011233
Musée Minéralogique du Morvan, La Grande-Verrière 012273
Musée Minéralogique et Minier de Thetford Mines, Thetford Mines 006562
Musée Minéralogique et Paléontologique, Saint-Pierre-de-la-Palud 014482
Musée Minéralogique et Paléontologique de Guerledan, Saint-Gelven 014297
Musée Mini-Trains-Lyonnais, Lyon . 012828
Musée Miniatures et Poupées, Gréoux-les-Bains 012030
Musée Missionnaire, Pontmain 013911
Musée Mistorique, Jaulny 012153
Musée Mnemosina, Prunelli-di-Fium'Orbu 013960
Musée Moissan, Paris 013710
Musée Mondial du Rugby, Avignonet-Lauragais 010600
Musée Monetaire Cantonal, Lausanne 037251
Musée Monsieur Pigneau de Behaine, Origny-en-Thiérache 013509
Musée Montagnard, Les Houches . . 012623
Musée Montagnard du Lavedan, Aucun 010535
Musée Montebello, Galerie du Musée, Trouville-sur-Mer 015046
Musée Montenot Agricole et Archéologique, Genay 011926
Musée Moralès, Port-de-Bouc 013916
Musée Morice Lipsi, Rosey 014114
Musée Moto du Douhet, Le Douhet . 012492
Musée-Moulin à Vent de Rairé, Sallertaine 014645
Musée Moulin Cézanne, Le Tholonet 012566
Musée-Moulin de Guerin, Saint-Julien-Chapteuil 014367
Musée-Moulin de l'Espine, Fougax-et-Barrineuf 011872
Musée Moulin de Maupertuis, Donzy 011636
Musée-Moulin de Pierre, Artenay . . 010493
Musée-Moulin du Papé Malaval, Tornac 014966
Musée Municipal, Espace Culturel, Mougins 013263
Musée Municipal, Saint-Germain-Laval 014312
Musée Municipal, Toul 014970
Musée Municipal, Amboise 010360
Musée Municipal, Barentin 010652
Musée Municipal, Bernay 010762
Musée Municipal, Bourbonne-les-Bains 010921
Musée Municipal, Châlons-en-Champagne 011200
Musée Municipal, Chartres 011266
Musée Municipal, Châtellerault . . . 011307
Musée Municipal, Conques 011468
Musée Municipal, Coutances 011519
Musée Municipal, Cusset 011555
Musée Municipal, Diekirch 027875
Musée Municipal, Digne-les-Bains . 011594
Musée Municipal, Dudelange 027878
Musée Municipal, Ferrette 011800
Musée Municipal, Forcalquier 011866
Musée Municipal, Gerberoy 011935
Musée Municipal, Hazebrouck 012086
Musée Municipal, Hennezel-Clairey 012089
Musée Municipal, La Charité-sur-Loire 012231
Musée Municipal, La Réole 012300
Musée Municipal, La Roche-sur-Yon 012311
Musée Municipal, Le Monastier-sur-Gazeille 012531
Musée Municipal, Lons-le-Saunier . 012743
Musée Municipal, Louhans 012761
Musée Municipal, Mauriac 012978
Musée Municipal, Mazan 012985
Musée Municipal, Nuits-Saint-Georges 013463
Musée Municipal, Pierrelatte 013818
Musée Municipal, Saint-Amand-les-Eaux 014176
Musée Municipal, Saint-Antonin-Noble-Val 014187
Musée Municipal, Saint-Calais 014211
Musée Municipal, Saint-Dié-des-Vosges 014259
Musée Municipal, Saint-Dizier 014264
Musée Municipal, Semur-en-Auxois 014753
Musée Municipal, Villandraut 015220
Musée Municipal, Vire 015315
Musée Municipal, Musée de l'Hôtel de Ville, Richelieu 014041
Musée Municipal, Musée du Jardin Jean Rostand, Lillebonne 012688
Musée Municipal A. Danicourt, Péronne 013780
Musée Municipal A.G. Poulain, Vernon 015184
Musée Municipal Albert Marzelles, Marmande 012912
Musée Municipal Alfred Canel, Pont-Audemer 013881
Musée Municipal Ancienne Abbaye Saint-Léger, Soissons 014814
Musée Municipal Apt, Apt 010442
Musée Municipal Auguste Grasset, Varzy 015136
Musée Municipal Auguste Jacquet, Beaucaire 010696
Musée Municipal Bar-sur-Seine, Bar-sur-Seine 010647
Musée Municipal Berck-sur-Mer, Berck-sur-Mer 010754
Musée Municipal Bourbon-Lancy, Bourbon-Lancy 010918
Musée Municipal Châteaubriant, Châteaubriant 011284
Musée Municipal d'Archéologie, Roquefort-sur-Soulzon 014105
Musée Municipal d'Archéologie et du Vin de Champagne, Épernay 011710
Musée Municipal d'Archéologique, Murviel-les-Montpellier 013309
Musée Municipal d'Art et d'Histoire, Colombes 011435
Musée Municipal d'Art Moderne, Céret 011178
Musée Municipal d'Art Naïf, Nantillé 013347
Musée Municipal d'Art Naïf, Noyers-sur-Serein 013458
Musée Municipal d'Arts Asiatiques, Toulon (Var) 014978
Musée Municipal d'Avranches, Avranches 010605
Musée Municipal de Cambrai, Musée des Beaux-Arts, Cambrai 011085
Musée Municipal de Civray, Civray . 011381
Musée Municipal de Draguignan, Draguignan 011658
Musée Municipal de la Chartreuse, Douai 011641
Musée Municipal de la Poterie, La Chapelle-aux-Pots 012219
Musée Municipal de la Toile de Jouy, Jouy-en-Josas 012175
Musée Municipal de la Vie Sauvage, Le Bugue 012475
Musée Municipal de l'École de Barbizon - Auberge Ganne, Barbizon 010649
Musée Municipal de l'Évêché, Limoges 012697
Musée Municipal de Louviers, Louviers 012786
Musée Municipal de Millau, Millau . 013062
Musée Municipal de Mokolo, Mokolo 004980
Musée Municipal de Montmorillon, Montmorillon 013192
Musée Municipal de Moret, Moret-sur-Loing 013236
Musée Municipal de Pithiviers, Pithiviers-le-Vieil 013827
Musée Municipal de Préhistoire, Fismes 011820
Musée Municipal de Préhistoire, Les Matelles 012628
Musée Municipal de Préhistoire Régionale, Saint-Pons-de-Thomières 014490
Musée Municipal de Saint-Barthélemy, Saint-Barthélemy 021561
Musée Municipal de Saint-Gaudens, Saint-Gaudens 014296
Musée Municipal de Saint-Maur, La Varenne-Saint-Hilaire 012350
Musée Municipal de Sault, Sault (Vaucluse) 014697
Musée Municipal de Vendôme, Vendôme 015161
Musée Municipal Département Jouet, Les Bains Douches, La Ferté-Macé . . 012251
Musée Municipal d'Ernée, Ernée . . 011721
Musée Municipal des Beaux-Arts, Valence (Drôme) 015096
Musée Municipal des Beaux Arts et d'Histoire Naturelle, Châteaudun . 011286
Musée Municipal des Capucins, Coulommiers 011504
Musée Municipal des Fossiles, Tourtour 015024
Musée Municipal d'Étampes, Etampes 011746
Musée Municipal d'Histoire et d'Archéologie, Harnes 012069
Musée Municipal d'Orbec, Orbec . . 013499
Musée Municipal d'Ossau, Musée du Parc National, Arudy 010494
Musée Municipal du Château, Musée Delarue, Gannat 011915
Musée Municipal du Peigne, Art et Traditions, Ezy-sur-Eure 011776
Musée Municipal du Présidial, Bazas 010688
Musée Municipal Frédéric Blandin, Nevers 013389
Musée Municipal Gautron du Coudray, Marzy 012967
Musée Municipal Georges Turpin, Musée d'Art et d'Histoire, Parthenay 013744
Musée Municipal Joseph Jacquiot, Montgeron 013167
Musée Municipal Marcel Migrenne, Guise 012056
Musée Municipal Max Claudet, Salins-les-Bains 014637
Musée Municipal Méditerranéen de Cassis, Cassis 011136
Musée Municipal Nicolas Poussin, Les Andelys 012598
Musée Municipal Paul Lafran, Saint-Chamas 014217
Musée Municipal Robert Dubois-Corneau, Brunoy 011023
Musée Municipal Saint-John-Perse, Pointe-à-Pitre 021558
Musée Municipal Saraleguinea, Guéthary 012049
Musée Municipal Urbain-Cabrol, Villefranche-de-Rouergue 015251
Musée Municipal Vendôme, Naveil . 013358
Musée Municipale, Lay-Saint-Christophe 012459
Musée Municipale, Mont-de-Lans . 013108
Musée Municipale, Saint-Laurent-d'Olt 014381
Musée Municipale, Villefranche-de-Lonchat 015249
Musée Nader, Port-au-Prince 021605
Musée Namesokanjik, Lac Mégantic 005730
Musée Napoleon, Ligny 003607
Musée Napoléon Ier et Tresors des Eglises, Brienne-le-Château 011001
Musée Napoléonien, Ajaccio 010308
Musée Napoléonien, Ile-d'Aix 012123
Musée Napoléonien d'Art et d'Histoire Militaire, Fontainebleau 011848
Musée Napoléonien du Château de Grosbois, Boissy-Saint-Léger . . . 010862
Musée Natiocional des Deux Victoires, Mouilleron-en-Pareds 013265
Musée National, Beirut 027811
Musée National, Moroni 007649
Musée National, N'Djamena 006903
Musée National, Porto-Novo 003895
Musée National Adrien Dubouché, Limoges 012698
Musée National Ahmed Zabana - Demaeght Museum, Oran 000068
Musée National Auguste Rodin, Villa des Brillants, Meudon 013045
Musée National Barthélémy Boganda, Bangui 006898
Musée National Cirta, Constantine . 000058
Musée National d'Archéologie de Sétif, Sétif 000073
Musée National d'Art Brassicole et Musée de la Tannerie, Wiltz 027910
Musée National d'Art Moderne, Paris 013711
Musée National de Burkina Faso, Ouagadougou 004963
Musée National de Carthage, Carthage 037950

Musée National de Céramique, Sèvres 014788
Musée National de Conakry, Conakry 021592
Musée National de Géologie, Antananarivo 027932
Musée National de Gitega, Gitega . 004965
Musée National de Guinée, Conakry 021593
Musée National de Kananga, Kananga 007652
Musée National de la Céramique, Safi 029035
Musée National de la Coopération Franco-Américaine, Blérancourt 010838
Musée National de la Légion d'Honneur et des Ordres de Chevalerie, Paris . . 013712
Musée National de la Marine, Brest 010986
Musée National de la Marine, Paris 013713
Musée National de la Marine, Port-Louis 013921
Musée National de la Marine, Rochefort (Charente-Maritime) 014079
Musée National de la Marine, Saint-Tropez 014560
Musée National de la Marine, Toulon (Var) 014979
Musée National de la Renaissance, Ecouen 011680
Musée National de la Résistance, Bruxelles 003349
Musée National de la Résistance, Esch-sur-Alzette 027883
Musée National de la Voiture et du Tourisme, Compiègne 011450
Musée National de l'Assurance Maldie, Lormont 012750
Musée National de l'Éducation, Rouen 014133
Musée National de l'Orangerie, Paris 013714
Musée National de Lubumbashi, Lumumbashi 007660
Musée National de Monaco, Collection de Galéa, Monaco 028995
Musée National de Nouakchott, Nouakchott 028063
Musée National de Phnom Penh, Phnom Penh 004970
Musée National de Préhistoire, Les Eyzies-de-Tayac-Sireuil 012621
Musée National de Préhistoire et d'Ethnographie du Bardo, Alger . . 000046
Musée National de Sarh, Sarh 006905
Musée National de Yaoundé, Yaoundé 004982
Musée National d'Enéerune, Site et Archéologique, Nissan-lez-Ensérune 013432
Musée National des Antiquités, Alger 000047
Musée National des Arts Asiatiques Guimet, Paris 013715
Musée National des Arts d'Afrique et d'Océanie, Paris 013716
Musée National des Arts et Traditions, Libreville 015397
Musée National des Arts et Traditions Populaires, Paris 013717
Musée National des Beaux-Arts d'Alger, Alger 000048
Musée National des Beaux-Arts du Québec, Québec 006228
Musée National des Châteaux de Malmaison et de Bois-Préau, Rueil-Malmaison 014154
Musée National des Châteaux de Versailles et de Trianon, Versailles 015189
Musée National des Douanes, Bordeaux 010893
Musée National des Ecoles Préparatoires de l'Armée de Terre, Autun 010560
Musée National des Granges de Port Royal, Magny-lès-Hameaux 012847
Musée National des Mines Fer Luxembourgeoisie, Rumelange . . 027902
Musée National des Monuments Français, Paris 013718
Musée National des Prisons, Fontainebleau 011849
Musée National d'Histoire et d'Art, Luxembourg 027894
Musée National d'Histoire Militaire, Diekirch 027876
Musée National d'Histoire Naturelle, Nationalmuseum für Naturgeschichte, Luxembourg 027895
Musée National du Bardo, Bardo . . 037946
Musée National du Château de Compiègne - Musée du Second Empire, Musée de la Voiture et du Tourisme, Compiègne 011451
Musée National du Château de Fontainebleau, Fontainebleau . . . 011850
Musée National du Château de Pau, Musée Henri IV, Pau 013752
Musée National du Congo, Brazzaville 007664
Musée National du Costume, Grand Bassam 007690
Musée National du Djihad, Alger . . 000049
Musée National du Foie Gras, Thiviers 014934
Musée National du Gabon, Libreville 015398
Musée National du Mali, Bamako . . 028019
Musée National du Marbre, Rance . 003709
Musée National du Moudjahid, El Madania 000062
Musée National du Moyen Age, Paris 013719
Musée National du Niger, Niamey . . 030667
Musée National du Papier, Malmedy 003624
Musée National du Rwanda, Butare 034100
Musée National du Scoutisme en France, Thorey-Lyautey 014946
Musée National du Sport, Paris . . . 013720
Musée National du Togo, Lomé . . . 037942
Musée National Ernest Hébert, Paris 013721
Musée National Eugène Delacroix, Paris 013722
Musée National Fernand Léger, Biot 010810
Musée National Jean-Jacques Henner, Paris 013723
Musée National Lao, Vientiane 027648
Musée National Message Biblique Marc Chagall, Nice 013407
Musée National Nasserdine Dinet, Bou Saada 000054
Musée National Picasso La Guerre et la Paix, Vallauris 015107
Musée National Suisse, Prangins . . 037422
Musée National Suisse de l'Audiovisuel, Montreux 037336
Musée Naval, Monaco 028996
Musée Naval de Nice, Nice 013408
Musée Naval de Sarcelles, Sarcelles 014670
Musée Naval et Napoléonien, Antibes-Juan-les-Pins 010429
Musée Naval Fort Balaguier, La Seyne-sur-Mer 012340
Musée N'Djamena, N'Djamena 006904
Musée Nicéphore Niépce, Chalon-sur-Saône 011195
Musée Nicholas Ibrahim Sursock, Beirut 027812
Musée Nissim de Camondo, Union Centrale des Arts Décoratifs, Paris 013724
Musée No.4 Commando, Ouistreham 013528
Musée Notre Dame, Le Folgoët . . . 012496
Musée Notre-Dame, Musée du Gemmail, Lourdes 012779
Musée Notre Dame de la Pierre, Ecomusée de la Vallee d'Aspe, Sarrance . . . 014681
Musée Numismatique J. Puig, Perpignan 013790
Musée Nungesser et Coli, Etretat . . 011757
Musée Oberlin, Waldersbach 015347
Musée-Observatoire de la Vallée d'Anjou, Saint-Mathurin-sur-Loire 014430
Musée Océanien de Cuet, Montrevel-en-Bresse 013225
Musée Océanographique, Arcachon 010451
Musée Océanographique, Bonifacio 010866
Musée Océanographique, Kingersheim 012193
Musée Océanographique, L'Ile-Rousse 012676
Musée Océanographique/Aquariophilie, Saint-Macaire 014402
Musée Océanographique Dar-El-Hout de Salammbô, Salammbô 037970
Musée Océanographique de l'Odet, Ergué-Gabéric 011718
Musée Océanographique de Monaco, Monaco 028997
Musée Olivier-de-Serres, Mirabel (Ardèche) 013069
Musée Ollier, Les Vans 012644
Musée Olympique Lausanne, Lausanne 037252
Musée Omaha Beach, Saint-Laurent-sur-Mer 014384
Musée Organistrum et des Vielles à Roues du Périgord Noir, Belvès 010748
Musée Ornithologique Charles Payraudeau, La Chaize-le-Vicomte 012218
Musée Ostréicole, Bourcefranc-le-Chapus 010922
Musée Ostréicole, Étaules 011750
Musée Ostréicole, Saint-Trojan-les-Bains 014557
Musée P. Dubois-A. Boucher, Nogent-sur-Seine 013437
Musée P.-J. Redouté et de l'Illustration Botanique, Saint-Hubert 003740
Musée Pablo Casals, Prades 013939
Musée Paderewski, Morges 037342
Musée Palais Lascaris, Musée des Arts et Traditions Populaires du Pays Niçois, Nice 013409
Musée Palaisien du Hurepoix, Palaiseau 013537
Musée Paléo-Écologique, Marchamp 012885
Musée Paléochrétien de Saint-Seurin, Bordeaux 010894
Musée Paléontologique, Aguessac . 010272
Musée Paléontologique du Gouffre de la Face, Larche 012426
Musée-Palombière, Près de l'Aire de Repos de l'Autoroute, Le Mas-d'Agenais 012522
Musée Parc de la Droséra, Jeansagnière 012156
Musée Passé Simple, Pleudihen-sur-Rance 013839
Musée Pasteur, Dole 011622
Musée Pasteur, Paris 013725
Musée Pasteur, Calmette et Guérin, Lille 012685
Musée Pastoral le Monde Paysan d'Autrefois, Saint-Pé-de-Bigorre . 014476
Musée Patrimoine et Traditions, Montferrier 013163
Musée Paul Arbaud, Aix-en-Provence 010297
Musée Paul Charnoz, Musée de la Faïence, Paray-le-Monial 013546
Musée Paul Dini, Villefranche-sur-Saône 015258
Musée Paul Dupuy, Toulouse 014997
Musée Paul-Emile Victor, Centre Polaire, Prémanon 013948
Musée Paul Gauguin, Papeete 015394
Musée Paul Gauguin, Pont-Aven . . . 013884
Musée Paul Géradin, Jodoigne 003547
Musée Paul-José Gosselin, Saint-Vaast-la-Hougue 014563
Musée Paul Raymond, Pont-Saint-Esprit 013897
Musée Paul Valéry, Sète 014780
Musée Paul Voivenel, Capoulet-Junac 011105
Musée Paysan, Clion-sur-Seugne . . 011408
Musée Paysan, Le Grand-Village-Plage 012501
Musée Paysan de Bourgogne Nivernaise, La Celle-sur-Loire 012215
Musée Paysan de la Save, Espaon . 011733
Musée Paysan du Moulin Neuf, Saint-Diéry 014262
Musée Paysan du Sundgau, Oltingue 013491
Musée Paysan et Artisanal, La Chaux-de-Fonds 037016
Musée Pedagogique, Rouen 014133
Musée Percheron, Mortagne-au-Perche 013251
Musée Petiet, Limoux 012700
Musée Peugeot, Sochaux 014812
Musée Peynet, Antibes-Juan-les-Pins 010430
Musée Picassiette, Chartres 011267
Musée Picasso, Antibes-Juan-les-Pins 010431
Musée Picasso, Paris 013726
Musée Pierre-Bayle, Carla-Bayle . . 011121
Musée Pierre Borrione, Aime-en-Tarentaise 010284
Musée Pierre Boucher, Trois-Rivières 006665
Musée Pierre de Luxembourg, Villeneuve-lès-Avignon 015276
Musée Pierre Fauchard, Musée d'Art Dentaire, Paris 013727
Musée Pierre Gaudin, Puteaux 013964
Musée Pierre-Loti, Musées Municipaux, Rochefort (Charente-Maritime) . . 014080
Musée Pierre Marly, Paris 013728
Musée Pierre Mondanel, Musée de la Batellerie, Pont-du-Château 013888
Musée Pierre Noël, Saint-Dié-des-Vosges 014260
Musée Pierre Salvi, Viarmes 015200
Musée Pierre Tauziac, Montcaret . . 013146
Musée Pierre Vigne, Boucieu-le-Roi 010902
Musée Pigeard, Magny-en-Vexin . . 012845
Musée Pillon, Chaumont-en-Vexin . 011323
Musée Pincé, Angers 010398
Musée Pissarro, Pontoise 013912
Musée-Placard d'Erik Satie, Paris . 013729
Musée Place-Royale, Québec 006229
Musée Pobe Mengao, Mengao 004960
Musée Pointe des Chênes, Sainte-Anne 006401
Musée Pol Mara, Gordes 011971
Musée Pontois, Le Pont-de-Beauvoisin 012551
Musée Populaire des Arts et Métiers, Noyant 013456
Musée Portuaire, Dunkerque 011668
Musée Postal, Bruxelles 003350
Musée Postal, Rabat 029033
Musée Postal, Tunis 037988
Musée Postal d'Aquitaine, Saint-Macaire 014403
Musée Poveal, Battambang 004967
Musée-Préau des Accoules, Marseille 012952
Musée Préfectoral de Boké, Boké . . 021589
Musée Préfectoral de Kissidougou, Kissidougou 021594
Musée Préfectoral de Koundara, Koundara 021595
Musée Préfectoral de N'Zerekore, N'Zerekore 021596
Musée Préhistorique, Grotte, Marsoulas 012957
Musée Préhistorique Charles Nardin, Sainte-Foy-la-Grande 014596
Musée Préhistorique du Tumulus de Barnenez, Plouezoch 013850
Musée Préhistorique et de Peinture, Montaut 013132
Musée Préhistorique Finistérien, Penmarch 013767
Le Musée Privé, Paris 100716
Musée-Privé de Cire, Albi 010320
Musée Privé de la Documentation Ferroviaire-Mupdofer, Bruxelles . . 003351
Musée Privé de la Grande Guerre 14-18, Essigny-le-Grand 011740
Musée Privé Saint-Jean l'Aigle, Herserange 012095
Musée-Promenade Marly-le-Roi, Louveciennes 012785
Musée Protestant de la Grange de Wassy, Wassy 015357
Musée Provençal des Transports Urbains et Régionaux, La Barque 012199

Musée Provençal du Costume et du Bijou, Grasse 012003
Musée Provençal et Folklorique Taradeau, Les Arcs 012600
Musée Provincial de Douala, Douala 004974
Musée Provincial de la Forêt, Namur 003667
Musée Provincial du Houet, Bobo-Dioulasso 004956
Musée Provincial du Poni, Gaoua . . 004957
Musée Provincial du Sanmatenga, Kaya 004958
Musée Provincial Félicien Rops, Namur 003668
Musée Pyrénéen, Lourdes 012780
Musée Pyrénéen de Niaux, Niaux . . 013390
Musée Québécois de Culture Populaire, Trois-Rivières 006666
Musée Quentovic, Etaples 011749
Musée Rabelais, Seuilly 014782
Musée Raimu, Cogolin 011416
Musée Rambolitrain, Rambouillet . . 013990
Musée Raoul Dastrac, Collection d'Arts et de Traditions Populaires, Aiguillon 010281
Musée Rath, Genève 037136
Musée Raymond Lafage, Lisle-sur-Tarn 012712
Musée Raymond Peynet, Brassac-les-Mines 010966
Musée Raymond Poincaré, Sampigny 014660
Musée Raymond Rochette, Saint-Sernin-du-Bois 014539
Musée Réattu, Arles 010472
Musée Reflet, Iguerande 012121
Musée Regards sur le Passé, Hourtin 012111
Musée Régimentaire les Fusiliers de Sherbrooke, Sherbrooke, Québec 006463
Musée Regional, Kisangani 007658
Musée Régional André Grenard Matsoua, Kinkala 007665
Musée Régional Bieth d'Abengourou, Abengourou 007684
Musée Régional Charles Combes, Bingerville 007686
Musée Regional d'Argenteuil, Saint-André-d'Argenteuil 006322
Musée Régional d'Armes, Mutzig . . 013313
Musée Régional d'Arts et de Traditions Popoulaires, Grimaud 012037
Musée Régional d'Auvergne, Riom . 014052
Musée Regional de Beyla, Beyla . . . 021588
Musée Régional de Bondoukou, Bondoukou 007687
Musée Régional de Fouras, Fouras . 011879
Musée Régional de Géologie Pierre Vetter, Decazeville 011568
Musée Régional de la Côte-Nord, Sept-Iles 006442
Musée Régional de la Poterie bas Normande, Ger 011933
Musée Régional de la Résistance et de la Déportation, Thionville 014933
Musée Regional de la Vigne et du Vin, Montmélian 013188
Musée Régional de l'Air, Groupement Préservation Patrimoine Aéronautique, Marcé 012883
Musée Régional de l'Alsace Bossue, Sarre-Union 014682
Musée Régional de l'Orléanais, Beaugency 010704
Musée Régional de Préhistoire, Orgnac-l'Aven 013506
Musée Régional de Rimouski, Rimouski 006292
Musée Régional de Sikasso, Sikasso 028021
Musée Régional de Sokadé, Sokadé 037943
Musée Régional de Vaudreuil-Soulanges, Vaudreuil 006722
Musée Régional de Zinder, Zinder . 030668
Musée Régional des Arts de la Table, Ancien Hospice Saint-Pierre du XVIIe s, Arnay-le-Duc 010477
Musée Régional des Arts et Traditions Populaires, Kef 037959
Musée Régional des Mines et des Arts de Malartic, Malartic 005823
Musée Régional des Savanes, Dapaong 037941
Musée Régional des Télécommunications en Flandres, Marcq-en-Barœul . . 012897
Musée Régional d'Ethnologie du Nord/Pas-de-Calais, Béthune 010779
Musée Régional d'Histoire et d'Archéologie, Visé 003835
Musée Régional d'Histoire et d'Artisanat du Val-de-Travers, Môtiers 037346
Musée Régional d'Histoire et d'Ethnographie, Fort-de-France . . 028054
Musée Régional du Cerel, Toamasina 027937
Musée Régional du Chemin de Fer, Rosny-sous-Bois 014119
Musée Régional du Chemin de Fer Nord-Pas-de-Calais, Denain 011575
Musée Régional du Cidre et du Calvados, Valognes 015118
Musée Régional du Machinisme Agricole, La Ferté-Milon 012254
Musée Régional du Sahel, Gao 028020
Musée Régional du Timbre et de la Philatélie, Le Luc 012515
Musée Régional du Vieux-Coppet, Coppet 037033
Musée Régional Dupuy-Méstreau, Saintes 014623
Musée Régional Ex-Dixième Riaom, Thiès 034138
Musée Régional Ma-Loango Diosso, Pointe-Noire 007666
Musée Régional Peleforo Gbon Coulibaly, Korhogo 007691
Musée Relais du Cheval de Trait Comtois, Levier 012656
Musée Religieux d'Art Franciscain, Nice 013410
Musée Religieux Franco-Canadien, Tours 015021
Musée Remenber 39-45, Léhon . . . 012590
Musée Remise aux Outils Champenois, Dormans-en-Champagne 011637
Musée Renaudot, Loudun 012757
Musée René Davoine, Charolles . . . 011260
Musée Renoir, Cagnes-sur-Mer . . . 011064
Musée Républicain, Touet-sur-Var . 014968
Musée Requien, Avignon 010597
Musée Rétromobile Drouais, Dreux 011661
Musée Rêve Auto-Jeunesse, Mosnac 013255
Musée Ribauri, Lasne-Chapelle-Saint-Lambert 003571
Musée Rignault, Saint-Cirq-Lapopie 014229
Musée Riquet et du Canal du Midi, Centre Pierre-Paul Riquet, Avignonet-Lauragais 010601
Musée Rizla Croix, Mazères-sur-Salat 012992
Musée Rochelais d'Histoire Protestante, La Rochelle 012329
Musée Rodava, Cercle d'Histoire et d'Archéologie, Rêves 003713
Musée Rodriguez Huguette, Saint-Macaire 014404
Musée Roger Thières, Payrac 013758
Musée Rolin, Musées Municipaux, Autun 010561
Musée Romain, Avenches 036865
Musée Romain, Caudeval 011157
Musée Romain, Lausanne 037253
Musée Romain, Nyon 037386
Musée Romand de la Machine Agricole, Gingins 037144
Musée Ronsard, La Riche 012304
Musée Rosine Perrier, Villargondran 015228
Musée Roux, Villefranche-sur-Mer . 015257
Musée Royal de l'Armée et d'Histoire Militaire, Koninklij Museum van het Leger en de Krijgsgeschiedenis, Bruxelles 003352
Musée Royal de Mariemont, Morlanwelz-Mariemont 003657
Musée Royaume de l'Horloge, Villedieu-les-Poêles 015245
Musée Roybet Fould, Courbevoie . . 011508
Musée Rude, Dijon 011612
Musée Rupert de Chièvres, Poitiers 013867
Musée Rural, Doyet 011655
Musée Rural, Foucherans 011871
Musée Rural, Saint-André-d'Embrun 014182
Musée Rural, Écomusée des Monts du Forez, Usson-en-Forez 015077
Musée Rural Berry-Marche, Boussac 010949
Musée Rural d'Arts et Traditions Populaires La Combà, Autrafé, La Combe-de-Lancey 012239
Musée Rural d'Auris-en-Oisans des Choses d'Autrefois, Auris-en-Oisans 010555
Musée Rural de la Sologne Bourbonnaise, Beaulon 010708
Musée Rural des Art Populaires, Laduz 012375
Musée Rural du Bois, Coupiac 011505
Musée Rural du Porzay, Plomodiern 013845
Musée Rural du Porzay, Saint-Nic-Pontrez 014450
Musée Rural Jurassien, Les Genevez 037141
Musée Ruzo, Montreux 037337
Musée Sabatier d'Eyspéran, Montpellier 013213
Musée Saharien de Ouargla, Ouargla 000069
Musée Sahut, Simiane-Collongue . . 014802
Musée Saint-Brieux, Saint-Brieux . . 006328
Musée Saint-Étienne, Honfleur 012109
Musée Saint-François-Régis, La Louvesc 012283
Musée Saint-Georges, Saint-Georges, Manitoba 006339
Musée Saint-Jacques, Moissac . . . 013085
Musée Saint-Jean, Anneyron 010414
Musée Saint-Jean, Corbeil-Essonnes 011475
Musée Saint-Jean, La Rochette (Savoie) 012331
Musée Saint-Joachim, La Broquerie 005726
Musée Saint-Joseph, Saint-Joseph 006374
Musée Saint-Loup, Troyes 015054
Musée Saint-Martin, Tours 015022
Musée Saint-Raymond, Musée des Antiques de Toulouse, Toulouse 014998
Musée Saint-Remi, Reims 014012
Musée Saint-Rémy, Cuesmes 003382
Musée Saint-Sauveur Nibelle Autrefois, Nibelle 013392
Musée Saint-Simon, La Ferté-Vidame 012258
Musée Saint-Vic, Saint-Amand-Montrond 014177
Musée Sainte-Catherine-Laboure, Fain-les-Moutiers 011778
Musée Sainte-Croix, Poitiers 013868
Musée Sainte-Jeanne-Antide-Thouret, Sancey-le-Long 014662
Musée Sainte-Marie, Church Point . 005269
Musée Salésien, Annecy 010412
Musée Salies, Musée des Beaux-Arts, Bagnères-de-Bigorre 010621
Musée Salle Documentaire, Coucy-le-Château-Auffrique 011497
Musée Santons du Monde, Huilerie, Clermont-l'Hérault 011401
Musée Sarret de Grozon, Arbois . . . 010448
Musée Saturnin Garimond, Fons . . . 011834
Musée Savoisien, Chambéry 011211
Musée Sbeïtla, Sbeïtla 037971
Musée Schiller-Goethe, Châlons-en-Champagne 011201
Musée Schœlcher, Pointe-à-Pitre . . 021559
Musée Scientifique de Boukoko, M'Baiki 006901
Musée Scolaire de Hautepierre, Strasbourg 014880
Musée Scout Baden-Powell, Sisteron 014805
Musée Sculpture sur Bois, Lans-en-Vercors 012417
Musée Sellier, Cogolin 011417
Musée Serret, Saint-Amarin 014178
Musée Sherlock Holmes, Lucens . . 037281
Musée Sidi Bou Saïd, Sidi Bou Saïd 037977
Musée Sidi Med Ben Abdellah, Essaouira 029019
Musée Sidi Zitouni, Houmt Souk . . . 037956
Musée Simon-Segal, Aups 010546
Musée Site Départemental d'Archéologie de Bavay, Bavay 010676
Musée Skolig al Louarn, Skolig al Louarn, Plouvien 013861
Musée Sobirats, Carpentras 011128
Musée Sonvilier, Sonvilier 037583
Musée Souleïado Charles Demery, Musée du Tissu Provençal, Tarascon (Bouches-du-Rhône) 014904
Musée Sous-Glaciaire, La Grave . . 012274
Musée Sous Marin Pays Lorient, Lorient 012747
Musée Souterrain de l'Outillage Ancien, Chacé 011189
Musée Spadois du Cheval, Spa . . . 003779
Musée Spectacle de Musiques du Monde, Montoire-sur-le-Loir 013195
Musée Stendhal, Grenoble 012025
Musée Sterna de l'Armée et des Trois Guerres, Seynod 014795
Musée Stewart au Fort de Ile Sainte-Hélène, Montréal 005946
Musée Suffren et du Vieux Saint-Cannat, Saint-Cannat 014212
Musée Suisse, Landesmuseum Zürich, Zürich 037784
Musée Suisse de la Figurine Historique, Morges 037343
Musée Suisse de la Machine à Coudre, Fribourg 037102
Musée Suisse de la Marionette, Fribourg 037103
Musée Suisse de la Mode, Yverdon-les-Bains 037745
Musée Suisse de l'Appareil Photographique, Vevey 037680
Musée Suisse de l'Audiovisuel - Audiorama, Montreux 037338
Musée Suisse de l'Orgue, Schweizer Orgelmuseum, Roche 037457
Musée Suisse de Spéléologie, Chamoson 037008
Musée Suisse du Jeu, La Tour-de-Peilz 037638
Musée Suisse du Sel, Aigle 036823
Musée Suisse du Vitrail, Romont . . 037460
Musée Sundgauvien, Altkirch 010343
Musée sur l'Archéologie et l'Histoire du Pays d'Ancenis, Ancenis 010376
Musée sur l'Artillerie, la Cavalerie et l'Infanterie, Seclin 014740
Musée sur l'Ordre de Malte, Compesières 037030
Musée Talleyrand, Saint-Chéron . . . 014220
Musée Tancrède, Hauteville-la-Guichard 012083
Musée Tavet-Delacour, Pontoise . . . 013913
Musée Tchantchès - Musée de la République Libre d'Outre-Meuse, Liège 003602
Musée Technique des Poudres, Association des Amis du Parc Forestier National de Sevran, Vaujours 015144
Musée Terrasse, Viverols 015324
Musée Territorial de Nouvelle-Calédonien, Nouméa 030419
Musée Terrus, Elne 011690
Musée Textile de Haute-Alsace, Husseren-Wesserling 012119
Musée Théâtre Antique, Vienne . . . 015212
Musée Théophile Jouglet, Anzin . . . 010436
Musée Thimonnier Doyen, Saint-Germain-au-Mont-d'Or 014304
Musée Thomas-Henry, Cherbourg-Octeville 011352
Musée Tibétain, La Boulaye 012206
Musée Toffoli, Charenton-le-Pont . . 011246
Musée Toulouse-Lautrec, Albi 010321
Musée Toulouse-Lautrec, Naucelle . 013357

Musée Tour de la Lanterne, La Rochelle ... 012330
Musée Tour Saint-Michel, Guérande 012044
Musée Tradition et Modernité, Verbier ... 037673
Musée Traditions et Vie, Châtillon-sur-Chalaronne ... 011313
Musée Traditions Verrieres, Eu ... 011760
Musée Trésor d'Église, Art Sacré de la Cathédrale Saint-Étienne, Metz .. 013042
Musée-Trésor d'Eglise de la Cathédrale Sainte-Croix, Orléans ... 013520
Musée Trio et du Vieil Outil Hastière, Hastière ... 003502
Musée Troglodytique, Louresse ... 012782
Musée Troglodytique de la Fosse, Dénezé-sous-Doué ... 011579
Musée Une Halte sur le Chemin de Saint-Jacques, Ecomusée de la Vallée d'Aspe, Borce ... 010874
Musée Urbain Tony Garnier, Lyon .. 012829
Musée Utrillo-Valadon, Sannois ... 014665
Musée Valaisan de la Vigne et du Vin, Walliser Reb- und Weinmuseum, Sierre ... 037559
Musée Valentin Haüy, Paris ... 013730
Musée Valery Stuyver, Seraing-le-Château ... 003749
Musée Van Œveren, Bourgueil ... 010945
Musée Vauban, Neuf-Brisach ... 013368
Musée Vauban et de la Fortification dans les Alpes, Mont-Dauphin ... 013107
Musée Vendéen, Fontenay-le-Comte ... 011853
Musée Verger Tarin, Autun ... 010562
Musée Verlaine, Juniville ... 012184
Musée Vert, Le Mans ... 012521
Musée Victor Aubert, Maule ... 012973
Musée Victor Charreton, Bourgoin-Jallieu ... 010943
Musée Victor Hugo, Villequier ... 015286
Musée Vigneron, Vendres ... 015162
Musée Villa Tamaris Pacha, La Seyne-sur-Mer ... 012341
Musée-Village des Automates, Saint-Cannat ... 014213
Musée-Village Gallo-Romain de Chênehutte-les-Tuffeaux, Chênehutte-Trêves-Cunault ... 011344
Musée Villageois d'Orgon, Orgon .. 013508
Musée Villeneuvien, Villeneuve-sur-Yonne ... 015285
Musée Villien, Musée de la Société Archéologique, Avesnes-sur-Helpe ... 010587
Musée Vini-Viticole, Chambolle-Musigny ... 011214
Musée Vini-Viticole, Volnay ... 015333
Musée Vini-Viticole Gallo-Romain, Beaucaire ... 010697
Musée Vissoie, Vissoie ... 037684
Musée Viticole, Cerdon ... 011173
Musée Viticole, Saint-Yzans-de-Médoc ... 014578
Musée Viticole, Verdigny ... 015172
Musée Viticole Charles Bernard, Fixin ... 011822
Musée Vivant de Bujumbura, Bujumbura ... 004964
Musée Vivant de la Faisanderie, Milly ... 013063
Musée Vivant de la Forge, Seyne-les-Alpes ... 014794
Musée Vivant de la Laine et du Mouton, Saint-Pierreville ... 014487
Musée Vivant de la Métairie de Crampet, Mazères (Gironde) ... 012991
Musée Vivant de la Meunerie, Cales 011076
Musée Vivant de la Meunerie, Wimille ... 015364
Musée Vivant de la Mine, Auchel .. 010533
Musée Vivant de la Moisson, Rochehaut ... 003719
Musée Vivant de la Passementerie, Jonzieux ... 012167
Musée Vivant de la Plante Aquatique, Limal ... 003608
Musée Vivant de la Polyculture, Lucey ... 012792
Musée Vivant de l'Abeille, Corbeny . 011477
Musée Vivant de l'Abeille, Valensole 015100
Musée Vivant de l'Apiculture Gâtinaise, Châteaurenard (Loiret) ... 011301
Musée Vivant de l'Arbre, Fontaine-les-Coteaux ... 011846
Musée Vivant de l'Oie, Collonges-la-Rouge ... 011426
Musée Vivant Denon, Chalon-sur-Saône ... 011196
Musée Vivant des Vieux Métiers, Argol ... 010465
Musée Vivant d'Histoire Naturelle, Nancy ... 013327
Musée Vivant du Cheval, Chantilly . 011238
Musée Vivant du Cheval de Trait et de l'Attelage, Pradelles ... 013936
Musée Vivant du Cinéma, Lyon ... 012830
Musée Vivant du Cochon, Chambonas ... 011215
Musée Vivant du Parchemin et de l'Enluminure, Miramont-de-Guyenne ... 013072
Musée Vivant du Roman d'Aventures, Jassans-Riottier ... 012151
Musée Vivant du Textile - Écomusée du Moulinage, Chirols ... 011368
Musée Vivant et Historique du Chemin de Fer à Voie Etroite, Rillé ... 014049
Musée Vivant et Historique du Train Historique du Lac de Rillé, Rillé .. 014048
Musée Vivant Européen du Cirque, Piolenc ... 013821
Musée Vivant Médiéval, Murol ... 013307
Musée Voland, Cerny ... 011184
Musée Vosgien de la Brasserie, Ville-sur-Illon ... 015238
Musée Vulcanologique Franck-Arnold-Perret, Saint-Pierre ... 028060
Musée Wagon de l'Armistice, Compiègne ... 011452
Musée Wellington, Waterloo ... 003846
Musée Westercamp, Wissembourg . 015369
Musée Yan' Dargent, Saint-Servais . 014540
Musée Yani Faux, Orbais-l'Abbaye . 013498
Musée Yves Brayer, Cordes-sur-Ciel 011481
Musée Yves Brayer, Les Baux-de-Provence ... 012612
Musée Zadkine, Les Arques ... 012601
Musée Zadkine, Paris ... 013731
Musée Zervos, Préfiguration de la Fondation Zervos, Vézelay ... 015198
Musée Ziem, Martigues ... 012963
Musée Zoologique de l'Université Louis Pasteur et de la Ville de Strasbourg, Strasbourg ... 014881
Muséem d'Histoire Naturelle, Marseille ... 012953
Museen Alte Bischofsburg, Wittstock, Dosse ... 020935
Museen der Stadt Bad Kösen, Romanisches Haus, Kunsthalle, Käthe-Kruse-Puppenmuseum, Bad Kösen ... 015736
Museen für Kunst und Kulturgeschichte der Hansestadt Lübeck - Verwaltung, Lübeck ... 018722
Museen im Alten Rathaus, Bürkel-Galerie, Scherenschnitt-Kabinett, Schuhmuseum, Pirmasens ... 019621
Museen im Kulturzentrum, Historisches Museum Rendsburg/ Druckmuseum, Rendsburg ... 019801
Museen im Rathaus, Perchtoldsdorf 002416
Museen im Wehrturm, Perchtoldsdorf ... 002417
Museerne i Fredericia, Fredericia .. 008861
Musées, Montréal ... 052756
Musées de la Cour d'Or, Metz ... 013043
Musées de La Poëslerie et de la Dentelle, Villedieu-les-Poêles ... 015246
Musées de la Réole, Musée Militaire, Automobile, Ferroviaire et d'Agricole, La Réole ... 012301
Musées de l'Horlogerie Pater, Langueville ... 003569
Musées de Sens, Sens ... 014764
Musées Départementaux Albert Demard, Champlitte ... 011230
Musées Départementaux de la Guadeloupe, Pointe-à-Pitre ... 053670
Musées des Colombiers Cauchois, Oherville ... 013477
Musées des Technique et Cultures Comtoises, Salins-les-Bains ... 014638
Musées et Collections Publiques de France, La Lettre des Musées, Paris ... 135718
Musées et Société en Wallonie, Namur ... 052685
Musées Gaumais, Virton ... 003833
Musées Royaux d'Art et d'Histoire, Bruxelles ... 003353
Musées Universitaire, Kinshasa ... 007657
Museet Ett Hem, Turku ... 010167
Museet Færgegaarden, Jægerspris . 008944
Museet for Dansk Bladtegning, København ... 008977
Museet for Fotokunst, Odense ... 009053
Museet for Holbæk og Omegn, Holbæk ... 008920
Museet for Religiøs Kunst og Bodil Kaalund Samlingerne, Lemvig ... 009011
Museet for Samtidskunst, Roskilde 009078
Museet for Samtidskunst, Nasjonalmuseet for Kunst, Oslo ... 031087
Museet for Thy og Vester Hanherred, Thisted ... 009129
Museet for Varde By og Omegn, Varde ... 009139
Museet Holmen, Løgumkloster ... 009014
Museet i Mælandsgården, Skudeneshavn ... 031197
Museet Kvarnen, Konstgalleri och Ferlinmuseum, Filipstad ... 036272
Museet Kystens Arv, Stadsbygd ... 031218
Museet Malmahed, Malmköping .. 036453
Museet Näktergalen, Vimmerby ... 036794
Museet på Gudhjem Station, Gudhjem ... 008884
Museet på Koldinghus, Kolding ... 008997
Museet på Sønderborg Slot, Sønderborg ... 009112
Museet på Sønderskov, Brørup ... 008828
Museet Psykiatrisk Hospital i Århus, Risskov ... 009072
Museet Tikøb Frysehus, Tikøb ... 009130
Museet ved Sct. Ansgar Kirke, København ... 008978
Museet ved Trelleborg, Slagelse ... 009108
Musehum.BL, Liestal ... 037267
Musei Anatomici, Modena ... 024753
Musei Capitolini, Roma ... 025490
Musei Civici, Lecco ... 024488
Musei Civici, Reggio Emilia ... 025413
Musei Civici, Castello Visconteo, Pavia ... 025139
Musei Civici agli Eremitani, Padova 025050
Musei Civici e Pinacoteca L. Sturzo, Caltagirone ... 023588
Musei Civici - Museo della Città, Monza ... 024875
Musei Civici Veneziani, Venezia ... 026238
Musei Comunali di Roma. Bollettino, Roma ... 135918
Musei del Castello Scaligero, Malcesine ... 024584
Musei della Civiltà Contadina del Friuli Imperiale, Aiello del Friuli ... 023137
Musei della Cultura Popolare Radana, San Benedetto Po ... 025654
Musei e Gallerie d'Italia, Roma ... 135919
Musei, Gallerie, Gabinetto Stampe e Archivio Fotografico, Roma ... 025491
O Musei Moveis Antigos, São Paulo 058727
Musei Provinciali di Gorizia, Gorizia 024351
Musei Sistini del Piceno, San Benedetto del Tronto ... 025649
Museifartyget Pommern, Mariehamn ... 009859
Museion - Museo d'Arte Moderna e Contemporanea, Bolzano ... 023467
Museion Versand, Berlin ... 069707
Museisällskapet Jädraås-Tallås Järnväg, Jädraås ... 036357
Museispårvägen Malmköping, Malmköping ... 036454
Museo, Helsinki ... 135677
Museo, Roma ... 135920
Museo 13 de Marzo, Pinar del Río . 008089
Museo 9 de Abril, Santa Clara ... 008137
Museo A. Binda, Cittiglio ... 023902
Museo A. Cassioli, Asciano ... 023262
Museo A. Colocci, Jesi ... 024430
Museo A. e C. Gaffoglio, Rapallo .. 025392
Museo a la Bandera y Santuario de la Patria, Iguala de la Independencia 028342
Museo A. Lia, La Spezia ... 024438
Museo A. Murer, Falcade ... 024075
Museo A. Ricci dei Minerali Elbani, Rio nell'Elba ... 025438
Museo Abarth, Marietta ... 045667
Museo Abel Santamaría, La Habana 007952
Museo Abel Santamaria, Santa Clara ... 008138
Museo Abraham González, Vicente Guerrero ... 028924
Museo Acacia, La Habana ... 007953
Museo Academia de Historia Leonardo Tascón, Buga ... 007461
Museo Activo del Pago de los Arroyos, Rosario ... 000524
Museo Ada e Giuseppe Marchetti, Fumone ... 024259
Museo Adolfo López Mateos, Atizapán de Zaragoza ... 028113
Museo Aeronáutico, Baradero ... 000132
Museo Aeronáutico, Montevideo .. 041505
Museo Aeronautico, Padova ... 025051
Museo Aeronautico Caproni di Taliedo, Roma ... 025492
Museo Aeronautico Caproni di Taliedo, Vizzola Ticino ... 026359
Museo Aeronáutico Colonel Luis Hernan Paredes, Maracay ... 049502
Museo Aeronáutico Torreón de Gando, Museo del Aire, Telde ... 035902
Museo Aeronautico y del Espacio, Quito ... 009230
Museo Aerospaziale Monte di Apollo, Perugia ... 025166
Museo Africano, Roma ... 025493
Museo Africano, Verona ... 026284
Museo Africano Mundo Negro, Madrid ... 035393
Museo Afro Antillano, Panamá City . 031421
Museo Agrario Tropicale, Istituto Agronomico per l'Oltremare, Firenze ... 024167
Museo Agrarista de Tzurúmutaro, Pátzcuaro ... 028637
Museo Agricolo, Ronco Briantino .. 025594
Museo Agricolo Alto Adige, Lana .. 024451
Museo Agricolo Brunnenburg, Landwirtschaftsmuseum, Tirolo di Merano ... 026025
Museo Agricolo della Civiltà Contadina L. Carminati, San Giuliano Milanese 025693
Museo Agricolo e del Vino Ricci Curbastro, Capriolo ... 023653
Museo Agricolo e Museo dell'Arte Conciaria, Castelfranco Veneto ... 023717
Museo Agro-Forestale San Matteo, Erice ... 024054
Museo Agro-Pastorale dell'Area Ellenofona, Istituto Ellenofono, Bova Marina . 023505
Museo Agrumario, Reggio Calabria . 025406
Museo al Aire Libre, Buenos Aires . 000155
Museo Alberto Arvelo Torrealba, Barinas ... 049444
Museo Alcázar de Colón, Santo Domingo ... 009157
Museo Aldrovandiano, Musei di Palazzo Poggi, Bologna ... 023421
Museo Alejandro Galvis, Tona ... 007625
Museo Alejandro Otero, Caracas .. 049454
Museo Alejo Carpentier, Camagüey 007892
Museo Alessandro Minuziano, San Severo ... 025732
Museo Alessi, Enna ... 024048
Museo Alfieriano, Asti ... 023288
Museo Alfonsiano, Pagani ... 025071

Museo Alfredo Ramírez de Arellano & Rosello, San Germán 032726
Museo All'Aperto di Storia dell'Agricultura, Sassari 025801
Museo Almacén El Recreo, Chivilcoy 000275
Museo Almafuerte, La Plata 000383
Museo Alpino Duca degli Abruzzi, Courmayeur 023990
Museo Alpino e Archeologico, Aosta 023216
Museo Alta Valle Scrivia, Sezione Etnologica, Valbrevenna 026185
Museo Altar de la Patria, Ixcateopan de Cuauhtémoc 028345
Museo Alternativo Remo Brindisi, Comacchio 023936
Museo Alto Bierzo, Bembibre 034971
Museo Amano, Lima 031543
Museo Ambientale del W.W.F., Centro di Educazione Ambientale, Orbetello 024999
Museo Ambientalistico Madonita, Polizzi Generoso 025297
Museo Ambiente Cubano, Gibara . . 007928
Museo Amedeo Bocchi, Parma 025118
Museo Americanista, Lomas de Zamora 000407
Museo Americanistico Federico Lunardi, Genova 024300
Museo Amparo, Puebla 028648
Museo Anatomia Veterinaria, Napoli 024893
Museo Anatomico, Pisa 025265
Museo Anatómico, Valladolid 035996
Museo Anatomico, Dipartimento di Scienze Biomediche, Siena 025884
Museo Anatomico G. Tumiati, Ferrara 024101
Museo Andrés Avelino Cáceres, Lima 031544
Museo Andrés Cué, Amancio 007868
Museo Anenecuilco, Ayala 028117
Museo Angel Orensanz y Artes de Serralbo, Sabiñánigo 035732
Museo Antártico, Montevideo 041506
Museo Antica Miniera di Talco Brunetta, Cantoira 023635
Museo Antiguo Colegio de San Ildefonso, México 028436
Museo Antiguo Cuartel de Caballería del Ejército Español, Camagüey 007893
Museo Antiguo Palacio de la Medicina Mexicana, México 028437
Museo Antiguo Palacio del Arzobispado, México 028474
Museo Antimperialista, Nueva Gerona 008074
Museo Antiquarium Archeologico, Falerone 024076
Museo Antiquarium Etrusco, Colle di Val d'Elsa 023924
Museo Antón, Candás 035041
Museo Antoniano, Padova 025052
Museo Antonio Lussich, Punta Ballena 041548
Museo Antonio Maceo, San Pedro . 008126
Museo Antonio Raimondi, La Merced 031539
Museo Antonio Ricaurte, Villa de Leyva 007638
Museo Antrológico, Ceretė 007482
Museo Antropología e Historia, Universidad Autónoma de Tamaulipas, Victoria 028927
Museo Antropologia e Historia Valle de Sula, San Pedro Sula 021611
Museo Antropológico, Museos Universitarios, Sucre 003922
Museo Antropológico, Universidad del Tolimo, Ibagué 007517
Museo Antropológico de Antofagasta, Antofagasta 006907
Museo Antropológico de Iquique, Iquique 006916
Museo Antropológico de Tunja, Tunja 007629
Museo Antropológico del Banco Central, Guayaquil 009205
Museo Antropológico Montané, La Habana 007954
Museo Antropológico Reina T. de Araúz, Panamá City 031422
Museo Antropológico Shuar, Quito . 009231
Museo Antropológico Tairona, Santa Marta 007604
Museo Antzetik Ta Jtelum, Zinacantán 028982
Museo Anzoátegui, Pamplona 007562
Museo Aperos de Labranza, Lerdo . 028388
Museo Apistico, Bologna 023422
Museo Apistico Didattico, Bregnano 023512
Museo A.R. Giorgi, Reggiolo 025418
Museo Archeologica, Savignone . . . 025819
Museo Archeologico, Acqualagna . . 023115
Museo Archeologico, Amelia 023191
Museo Archeologico, Arborea 023227
Museo Archeologico, Artena 023260
Museo Archeologico, Bonorva 023477
Museo Archeologico, Caltanissetta . 023590
Museo Archeologico, Camaiore . . . 023595
Museo Archeologico, Carassai 023658
Museo Archeologico, Castello di Godego 023729
Museo Archeologico, Castiglione della Pescaia 023748
Museo Archeologico, Cecina e Marina 023780
Museo Archeologico, Cesena 023813
Museo Archeologico, Dorgali 024037
Museo Archeologico, Enna 024049
Museo Archeologico, Faenza 024066
Museo Archeologico, Fermo 024093
Museo Archeologico, Follonica 024214
Museo Archeologico, Frosinone . . . 024255
Museo Archeologico, Gropello Cairoli 024370
Museo Archeologico, Isola della Scala 024423
Museo Archeologico, Lentini 024494
Museo Archeologico, Marianopoli . . 024616
Museo Archeologico, Milano 024702
Museo Archeologico, Molfetta 024774
Museo Archeologico, Monopoli 024794
Museo Archeologico, Ostiglia 025034
Museo Archeologico, Palazzuolo sul Senio 025078
Museo Archeologico, Pontecagnano 025311
Museo Archeologico, Povegliano Veronese 025348
Museo Archeologico, Priverno 025371
Museo Archeologico, Pula 025373
Museo Archeologico, Rocca di Mezzo 025452
Museo Archeologico, San Miniato . 025715
Museo Archeologico, Santa Severina 025757
Museo Archeologico, Santadi 025761
Museo Archeologico, Santorso 025782
Museo Archeologico, Scansano . . . 025833
Museo Archeologico, Teramo 026003
Museo Archeologico, Varallo Pombia 026206
Museo Archeologico, Venafro 026225
Museo Archeologico, Ventotene . . . 026273
Museo Archeologico, Veroli 026280
Museo Archeologico, Villasimius . . 026338
Museo Archeologico, Galleria d'Arte Moderne e Contemporanea, San Gimignano 025678
Museo Archeologico, Gruppo Archeologico Cavriana, Cavriana 023779
Museo Archeologico al Teatro Romano, Verona 026285
Museo Archeologico Antiquarium Arborense, Palazzo Parpaglia, Oristano 025009
Museo Archeologico Antonio Santarelli, Forlì 024224
Museo Archeologico Aquaria, Soncino 025915
Museo Archeologico Attrezzato e Cattedrale di San Zeno, Pistoia 025272
Museo Archeologico B. Antonucci, Pietrasanta 025229
Museo Archeologico Baglio Anselmi, Marsala 024622
Museo Archeologico Civico, Forlimpopoli 024234
Museo Archeologico Comprensoriale, Teti 026019
Museo Archeologico Comunale, Vicchio 026305
Museo Archeologico Comunale di Artimino, Carmignano 023665
Museo Archeologico dei Campi Flegrei, Bacoli 023312
Museo Archeologico del Finale, Finale Ligure 024134
Museo Archeologico del Territorio, Palazzo Cipoletti, Cupra Marittima 024015
Museo Archeologico del Territorio - Antiquarium Suasanum, San Lorenzo in Campo 025700
Museo Archeologico del Territorio di Populonia, Piombino 025252
Museo Archeologico della Badia, Licata 024500
Museo Archeologico della Lucania Occidentale, Padula 025070
Museo Archeologico della Sabbia, Gavardo 024280
Museo Archeologico dell'Abruzzo, Crecchio 023991
Museo Archeologico dell'Agro Nocerino, Nocera Inferiore 024944
Museo Archeologico dell'Alto Adige, Bolzano 023468
Museo Archeologico dell'Alto Canavese, Cuorgnè 024014
Museo Archeologico dell'Antica, Alife 023174
Museo Archeologico dell'Antica Calatia, Maddaloni 024573
Museo Archeologico dell'Antica Capua, Santa Maria Capua Vetere 025751
Museo Archeologico dell'Arte della Lana, Consorzio Sistena Museale Valle de Liri, Arpino 023255
Museo Archeologico di Belriguardo, Voghiera 026362
Museo Archeologico di Casteggio, Casteggio 023701
Museo Archeologico di Morgantina, Aidone 023136
Museo Archeologico di Naxos, Giardini Naxos 024338
Museo Archeologico di Sepino, Sepino 025857
Museo Archeologico di Tarquinia. Materiali, Roma 135921
Museo Archeologico di Vallecamonica, Cividate Camuno 023906
Museo Archeologico di Villa Sulcis, Carbonia 023660
Museo Archeologico e Antiquarium, Sala Consilina 025631
Museo Archeologico e Antiquarium Nazionale, Formia 024236
Museo Archeologico e d'Arte della Maremma, Grosseto 024373
Museo Archeologico e della Ceramica, Montelupo Fiorentino 024850
Museo Archeologico e della Collegiata, Casole d'Elsa 023695
Museo Archeologico e della via Flaminia, Cagli 023558
Museo Archeologico e Paleontologico, Asti 023289
Museo Archeologico e Paleontologico di Farneta, Cortona 023978
Museo Archeologico e Pinacoteca, Musei di Palazzo Farnese, Piacenza 025207
Museo Archeologico e Pinacoteca Comunale, Palazzo Trinci, Foligno 024213
Museo Archeologico e Storico Aristico, Palazzo Traversa, Bra 023508
Museo Archeologico ed Etnografico, Ittireddu 024427
Museo Archeologico Eoliano, Lipari 024504
Museo Archeologico Etneo, Adrano 023123
Museo Archeologico Etnografico, Paulilatino 025137
Museo Archeologico F. Milizia, Oria 025004
Museo Archeologico G. Allevi, Offida 024986
Museo Archeologico G. Cilnio Mecenate, Arezzo 023236
Museo Archeologico G. Moretti, San Severino Marche 025729
Museo Archeologico G. Rambotti, Desenzano del Garda 024027
Museo Archeologico Girolamo Rossi, Ventimiglia 026271
Museo Archeologico Ibleo, Ragusa . 025385
Museo Archeologico Isidoro Falchi, Vetulonia 026298
Museo Archeologico Iulium Carnicum, Zuglio 026377
Museo Archeologico Lametino, Lamezia Terme 024448
Museo Archeologico Liutprando, San Giovanni in Persiceto 025689
Museo Archeologico Lomellino, Gamboló 024272
Museo Archeologico Lomellino, Garlasco 024277
Museo Archeologico Lucus Feroniae, Capena 023641
Museo Archeologico Luigi Donini, San Lazzaro di Savena 025694
Museo Archeologico Medievale, Attimis 023299
Museo Archeologico Michele Janora, Irsina 024415
Museo Archeologico Nazionale, Adria 023124
Museo Archeologico Nazionale, Aquileia 023223
Museo Archeologico Nazionale, Cagliari 023561
Museo Archeologico Nazionale, Campli 023615
Museo Archeologico Nazionale, Capaccio 023638
Museo Archeologico Nazionale, Cassino 023698
Museo Archeologico Nazionale, Chieti 023860
Museo Archeologico Nazionale, Chiusi Città 023871
Museo Archeologico Nazionale, Cividale del Friuli 023904
Museo Archeologico Nazionale, Crotone 024005
Museo Archeologico Nazionale, Eboli 024042
Museo Archeologico Nazionale, Firenze 024168
Museo Archeologico Nazionale, Gioia del Colle 024344
Museo Archeologico Nazionale, Manfredonia 024597
Museo Archeologico Nazionale, Mantova 024600
Museo Archeologico Nazionale, Metaponto 024684
Museo Archeologico Nazionale, Napoli 024894
Museo Archeologico Nazionale, Parma 025119
Museo Archeologico Nazionale, Quarto d'Altino 025376
Museo Archeologico Nazionale, Sperlonga 025933
Museo Archeologico Nazionale, Spoleto 025939
Museo Archeologico Nazionale, Taranto 025988
Museo Archeologico Nazionale, Venezia 026239
Museo Archeologico Nazionale, Venosa 026269
Museo Archeologico Nazionale, Viterbo 026348
Museo Archeologico Nazionale del Melfese, Melfi 024662
Museo Archeologico Nazionale della Sibaritide, Cassano allo Jonio . . . 023696
Museo Archeologico Nazionale delle Marche, Ancona 023197
Museo Archeologico Nazionale dell'Umbria, Perugia 025167
Museo Archeologico Nazionale di Cosa, Orbetello 025000

Museo Archeologico Nazionale di Luni, Ortonovo . . . 025019
Museo Archeologico Nazionale di Metaponto, Bernalda . . . 023382
Museo Archeologico Nazionale di Palestrina, Palestrina . . . 025097
Museo Archeologico Nazionale e Antiquarium Statale, Locri . . . 024516
Museo Archeologico Nazionale Etrusco, Cerveteri . . . 023807
Museo Archeologico Nazionale Etrusco, Siena . . . 025885
Museo Archeologico Nazionale Etrusco, Tuscania . . . 026160
Museo Archeologico Oliveriano, Pesaro . . . 025174
Museo Archeologico per la Preistoria e Protostoria del Tigullio, Chiavari . 023846
Museo Archeologico Provinciale, Potenza . . . 025345
Museo Archeologico Provinciale, Salerno . . . 025634
Museo Archeologico Provinciale, Palazzo Ateneo, Bari . . . 023336
Museo Archeologico Provinciale F. Ribezzo, Brindisi . . . 023528
Museo Archeologico Regionale, Agrigento . . . 023132
Museo Archeologico Regionale, Aosta . . . 023216
Museo Archeologico Regionale, Gela . . . 024286
Museo Archeologico Regionale, Santa Croce Camerina . . . 025745
Museo Archeologico Regionale A. Salinas, Palermo . . . 025082
Museo Archeologico Regionale Paolo Orsi, Siracusa . . . 025902
Museo Archeologico Remo Fumagalli, Novara . . . 024962
Museo Archeologico San Giovanni in Compito, Savignano sul Rubicone 025818
Museo Archeologico Sentinate, Sassoferrato . . . 025810
Museo Archeologico Statale, Altamura . . . 023177
Museo Archeologico Statale, Arcevia . . . 023229
Museo Archeologico Statale, Ascoli Piceno . . . 023266
Museo Archeologico Statale, Cingoli 023881
Museo Archeologico Statale, Teano 025994
Museo Archeologico Statale, Urbisaglia . . . 026178
Museo Archeologico Statale V. Capialbi, Vibo Valentia . . . 026303
Museo Archeologico Statale V. Laviola, Amendolara . . . 023192
Museo Archeologico Tifernum Mataurense, Sant'Angelo in Vado . . . 025765
Museo Archeologico Villa Abbas, Sardara . . . 025788
Museo-Archivio di Fotografia Storica, Roma . . . 025494
Museo Archivio Sacrario di Storia Patria, Bagheria . . . 023315
Museo-Archivo de Falset y Comarca, Falset . . . 035187
Museo Arciprestal, Morella . . . 035524
Museo Arcivescovile, Ravenna . . . 025396
Museo Areneo de Estudios Históricos de Nueva Pompeya, Buenos Aires . . 000156
Museo Argentino de Ciencias Naturales Bernardino Rivadavia, Buenos Aires . . . 000157
Museo Argentino de Motos Antiguas, Mendoza . . . 000431
Museo Armando Reverón, Caracas . 049455
Museo Armando Reverón, Macuto . 049500
Museo Armería 9 de Abril, La Habana . . . 007955
Museo Arqueològic, Gandía . . . 035211
Museo Arqueològic Municipal, Vallada . . . 035992
Museo Arqueològic Municipal Cal Guimerà, El Vendrell . . . 036022
Museo Arqueológica de Mongua, Mongua . . . 007548
Museo Arqueológical Rafael Larco Herrera, Lima . . . 031545
Museo Arqueológico, Aguilares . . . 000107
Museo Arqueológico, Alcalá de Henares . . . 034799
Museo Arqueológico, Almuñécar . . 034829
Museo Arqueológico, Aranzazu . . . 007389
Museo Arqueológico, Cacabelos . . . 035014
Museo Arqueológico, La Carolina . . 035057
Museo Arqueológico, Cartago . . . 007480
Museo Arqueológico, Curumaní . . . 007491
Museo Arqueológico, Gata de Gorgos . . . 035217
Museo Arqueológico, Granada . . . 030664
Museo Arqueológico, Gualeguaychú 000358
Museo Arqueológico, Inzá . . . 007520
Museo Arqueológico, La Tebaida . . 007524
Museo Arqueológico, Manizales . . . 007527
Museo Arqueológico, Nerja . . . 035541
Museo Arqueológico, Novelda . . . 035545
Museo Arqueológico, Oiba . . . 007559
Museo Arqueológico, Osuna . . . 035577
Museo Arqueológico, Paéz . . . 007560
Museo Arqueológico, Pasca . . . 007566
Museo Arqueológico, Puerto Berrío . 007590
Museo Arqueológico, Puerto de la Cruz . . . 035681
Museo Arqueológico, Sagunto . . . 035735
Museo Arqueológico, Salamina . . . 007601
Museo Arqueológico, Santa Cruz de Tenerife . . . 035794
Museo Arqueológico, Sogamoso . . . 007616
Museo Arqueológico, Tafí del Valle . 000625
Museo Arqueológico, Universidad Estatal de Cuenca, Cuenca . . . 009186
Museo Arqueológico Adán Quiroga, San Fernando del Valle de Catamarca 000554
Museo Arqueológico Alejandro Pezzia Aseretto, La Angostura . . . 031536
Museo Arqueológico Alto Maestrazgo, Benasal . . . 034974
Museo Arqueológico Atahualpa, Ibarra . . . 009216
Museo Arqueológico Calima, Calima . . . 007475
Museo Arqueológico Carlos Aiiercado, Esmeraldas . . . 009200
Museo Arqueológico Casa de Madame Augustín, Santa Marta . . . 007605
Museo Arqueológico Casa del Marqués de San Jorge, Bogotá . . . 007413
Museo Arqueológico Chiametlán, Rosario . . . 028691
Museo Arqueológico Chimica, Istituto de Cultura de El Copey, El Copey . . . 007497
Museo Arqueológico Comarcal, Palacio de Rubalcaba, Orihuela . . . 035566
Museo Arqueológico, Costumbrista y Naturalista, Güimar . . . 035270
Museo Arqueológico Cuicuilco, México . . . 028438
Museo Arqueológico de Ancash, Huaraz . . . 031519
Museo Arqueológico de Apaxco, Apaxco . . . 028107
Museo Arqueológico de Asturias, Oviedo . . . 035584
Museo Arqueológico de Õbeda, Õbeda . . . 034965
Museo Arqueológico de Cajamarca y Museo Médico, Cajamarca . . . 031471
Museo Arqueológico de Campeche, Campeche . . . 028127
Museo Arqueológico de Cancún, Cancún . . . 028135
Museo Arqueológico de Chasicó, Chasicó . . . 000272
Museo Arqueológico de Ciudad Guzmán, Guzmán . . . 028312
Museo Arqueológico de Comayagua, Comayagua . . . 021608
Museo Arqueológico de Comitán, Comitán de Domínguez . . . 028180
Museo Arqueológico de Guacarí, Guacarí . . . 007507
Museo Arqueológico de la Ciudad, Emiliano Zapata . . . 028239
Museo Arqueológico de la Costa Grande, Zihuatanejo . . . 028980
Museo Arqueológico de la Plana Baja, Burriana . . . 035011
Museo Arqueológico de La Serena, La Serena . . . 006918
Museo Arqueológico de la Universidad Nacional del Altiplano, Pucara . . . 031586
Museo Arqueológico de Lagos de Moreno, Lagos de Moreno . . . 028378
Museo Arqueológico de Martins Sarmento, Guimarães . . . 032619
Museo Arqueológico de Mazatlán, Mazatlán . . . 028407
Museo Arqueológico de Muzo, Muzo . . . 007552
Museo Arqueológico de Nextlalpan, Nextlalpan . . . 028597
Museo Arqueológico de Puerto Esperanza, Puerto Esperanza . . . 000488
Museo Arqueológico de Salta, Salta 000536
Museo Arqueológico de Tepeapulco, Tepeapulco . . . 028816
Museo Arqueológico de Tilcara, Tilcara . . . 000634
Museo Arqueológico de Tizatlán, Tizatlán . . . 028846
Museo Arqueológico de Tonalá, Tonalá, Chiapas . . . 028879
Museo Arqueológico de Tula Jorge R. Acosta, Tula de Allende . . . 028892
Museo Arqueológico de Venustiano Carranza, Venustiano Carranza . . 028918
Museo Arqueológico de Xochimilco, México . . . 028439
Museo Arqueológico d'Eivissa i Formentera, Eivissa . . . 035160
Museo Arqueologico del Banco Central de Bahia, Bahia de Carácluez . . . 009177
Museo Arqueológico del Centro de Estudios Histórico Sociales Julio Espejo Nuñez, Jauja . . . 031534
Museo Arqueológico del Cerro de la Estrella, México . . . 028440
Museo Arqueológico del Cesar, Valledupar . . . 007635
Museo Arqueológico del Huila, Neiva . . . 007554
Museo Arqueológico del Instituto de Arqueología y Etnología, Mendoza 000432
Museo Arqueológico del Sinú, Tierralta . . . 007624
Museo Arqueológico del Soconusco, Tapachula . . . 028785
Museo Arqueológico Dr. Román Piña Chan, Tenango del Valle . . . 028806
Museo Arqueológico e Histórico de Andahuaylas, Andahuaylas . . . 031456
Museo Arqueológico Etnológico Municipal, Guardamar de Segura . . . 035268
Museo Arqueológico Frederico Galvez Durand, Huancayo . . . 031513
Museo Arqueológico Guamuhaya, Trinidad . . . 008178
Museo Arqueológico Horacio Urteaga, Cajamarca . . . 031472
Museo Arqueológico I.B. Niguel de Mañara, San José de la Rinconada . . . 035758
Museo Arqueológico José Casinelli, Santa Inés . . . 031593
Museo Arqueologico José María Morante de la Universidad Nacional de San Augustín de Arequipa, Arequipa . . . 031458
Museo Arqueológico Juan Sepúlveda y Museo Eduardo Ruiz, Uruapán . . . 028904
Museo Arqueológico Julio César Cubillos, Cali . . . 007465
Museo Arqueológico Julio César Cubillos, San Agustín . . . 007602
Museo Arqueológico La Bagatela, Villa del Rosario . . . 007642
Museo Arqueológico La Merced, Cali . . . 007466
Museo Arqueológico Luis G. Urbina, México . . . 028441
Museo Arqueológico Marco Fidel Micolta, Guamo . . . 007512
Museo Arqueológico Mesoamericano, Tijuana . . . 028839
Museo Arqueológico Municipal, Alcúdia . . . 034813
Museo Arqueológico Municipal, Cartagena . . . 035059
Museo Arqueológico Municipal, Cehegín . . . 035077
Museo Arqueológico Municipal, Crevillente . . . 035133
Museo Arqueológico Municipal, Elda . . . 035170
Museo Arqueológico Municipal, Jerez de la Frontera . . . 035307
Museo Arqueológico Municipal, Lorca . . . 035362
Museo Arqueológico Municipal, Marchena . . . 035470
Museo Arqueológico Municipal, Montoro . . . 035522
Museo Arqueológico Municipal, Santaella . . . 035809
Museo Arqueológico Municipal, Castell de Dénia, Dénia . . . 035146
Museo Arqueológico Municipal, Iglesia de la Soledad, Caravaca de la Cruz . . . 035051
Museo Arqueológico Municipal Alejandro Ramos Folqués, Elche . . . 035165
Museo Arqueológico Municipal Antonio Ballester, Callosa de Segura . . . 035034
Museo Arqueológico Municipal Camilo Visedo Molto, Museu d'Alcoi, Alcoi . . . 034808
Museo Arqueológico Municipal Cayetano Mergelina, Yecla . . . 036091
Museo Arqueológico Municipal de Obulco, Porcuna . . . 035669
Museo Arqueológico Municipal José María Soler, Villena . . . 036069
Museo Arqueológico Municipal Precolombino, Benalmádena . . . 034973
Museo Arqueológico Municipal y Museo Municipal Miguel Justino Ramírez, Piura . . . 031583
Museo Arqueológico Nacional, Madrid . . . 035394
Museo Arqueológico Nacional Brüning, Lambayeque . . . 031540
Museo Arqueológico Padre Martín Recio, Estepa . . . 035183
Museo Arqueológico Pío P. Díaz, Cachi . . . 000254
Museo Arqueológico Poblado de la Hoya, Laguardia . . . 035314
Museo Arqueológico Provincial, Palencia . . . 035595
Museo Arqueológico Provincial, Badajoz . . . 034884
Museo Arqueológico Provincial, Huesca . . . 035286
Museo Arqueológico Provincial, Ourense . . . 035579
Museo Arqueológico Provincial, San Salvador de Jujuy . . . 000594
Museo Arqueológico Provincial, Sevilla . . . 035858
Museo Arqueológico Provincial Andalgalá, Andalgalá . . . 000113
Museo Arqueológico Provincial Condor Huasi (interim), Belén . . . 000137
Museo Arqueológico Provincial-MARQ, Alicante . . . 034819
Museo Arqueológico Regional Anibal Montes, Río Segundo . . . 000520
Museo Arqueológico Regional de Ancash, Ancash . . . 031455
Museo Arqueológico Regional Guane, Floridablanca . . . 007502
Museo Arqueológico Regional Inca Huasi, La Rioja . . . 000393
Museo Arqueológico R.P. Gustavo Le Paige S.J., San Pedro de Atacama . . . 006926
Museo Arqueológico San Miguel de Azapa, Arica . . . 006909
Museo Arqueológico y Colonial, Fuerte Quemado . . . 000348
Museo Arqueológico y Etnográfico Soler Blasco, Jávea . . . 035305
Museo Arqueológico y Etnológico Córdoba, Consejería de Cultura Junta de Andalucia, Córdoba . . . 035113

Museo Arqueológico y Etnológico de Granada, Granada 035251
Museo Arqueológico y Paleontológico de Guane, Barichara 007395
Museo Arqueológico y Paleontológico Municipal, Rojales 035714
Museo Arqueológico y Termas Romanas, Caldes de Montbui 035029
Museo Arqueoloógico y Etnográfico, Ibarra 009217
Museo Arqueolóxico e Histórico, A Coruña 035124
Museo Arquidiocesano, Santiago de Cuba 008149
Museo Arquidiocesano de Arte Religioso, Pamplona 007563
Museo Arquidiocesano de Arte Religioso de Popayán, Popayán 007582
Museo Arquitectura de Trinidad, Trinidad 008179
Museo Art Nouveau-Art Deco, Fundación Manuel Ramos Andrade, Salamanca 035739
Museo Arte Visuales Alejanoro Otero Mavao, Caracas 049454
Museo Artes Decorativo, Gibara . . . 007929
Museo Artes Plásticas, Pinar del Río 008090
Museo Artes y Costumbres Populares Alto Guadalquivir, Cazorla 035076
Museo Artesanal de Gualaceo, Gualaceo 009203
Museo Arti e Mestieri di un Tempo, Cisterna d'Asti 023889
Museo Arti e Tradizioni Popolari del Gargano Giovanni Tancredi, Monte Sant'Angelo 024819
Museo Artístico de Roncesvalles, Roncesvalles 035719
Museo Artistico della Bambola, Suvereto 025977
Museo Artistico Industriale F. Palizzi, Istituto d'Arte di Napoli, Napoli 024895
Museo Arturo Michelena, Caracas . 049456
Museo Astronomico Copernicano, Roma 025495
Museo Astronomico e Geofisico, Modena 024754
Museo Atelier Antonio Ortiz Echagüe, Carro Quemado 000265
Museo Audiovisual, Caracas 049457
Museo Augustín Landívar, Cuenca . 009187
Museo Augusto Righi, Montese . . . 024863
Museo Aurelio Castelli, Siena 025886
Museo Aurelio Espinosa Polit, Cotocollao 009184
Museo Aurelio Espinoza Pólit, Quito 009232
Museo Aurelio Marena, Bitonto . . . 023406
Museo Austral de Pintura Primitiva Moderna Naif, Esquel 000343
Museo Auto d'Ecopa, San Marino . . 034111
Museo Azuayo del Folklore, Cuenca 009188
Museo Badia di San Gemolo, Valganna 026192
Museo Bagatti Valsecchi, Milano . . 024703
Museo Bahía de los Angeles, Ensenada 028243
Museo Balaa Xte Guech Gulal, Teotitlán del Valle 028813
Museo Balear Ciencies Naturals, Sóller 035881
Museo Balmes, Vic 036028
Museo Balseros del Mar del Sur, Salango 009262
Museo Baluarte de Santiago, Veracruz 028919
Museo Banco Central de Reserva del Perú, Lima 031546
Museo Banco del Pacifico, Guayaquil 009206
Museo Bandini, Fiesole 024121
Museo Bardini, Firenze 024169
Museo Baroffio e del Santuario del Sacro Monte sopra Varese, Varese 026212
Museo Barovier e Toso, Venezia . . . 026240
Museo Barracco, Roma 025496
Museo Beata P. Morosini, Albino . . 023152
Museo Beato Angelico, Vicchio 026306
Museo Beato Angelo, Acri 023121
Museo Belgraniano, La Plata 000384
Museo Belisario Porras, Panamá City 031423
Museo Bellapart, Santo Domingo . . 009158
Museo Bello Piñeio, Ferrol 035190
Museo Benedettino Nonantolano e Diocesano di Arte Sacra, Nonantola 024952
Museo Benigno Malo, Cuenca 009189
Museo Benito Hortiz, Sancti-Spíritus 008127
Museo Benito Juárez, José Azueta . 028365
Museo Benito Juárez, Casa del Benemérito de las Américas, La Habana 007956
Museo Berenziano, Cremona 023995
Museo Bernabé de las Casas, Mina 028549
Museo Bernardino Caballero, Asunción 031441
Museo Bernardo de Muro, Tempio Pausania 025999
Museo Bernardo Martínez Villegas, Bácum 028121
Museo Bernardo Samper Sordo, Bogotá 007414
Museo Bersano delle Contadinerie e Stampe antiche del Vino, Nizza Monferrato 024941
Museo B.Gigli, Recanati 025403
Museo Biblioteca Comunale, Etroubles 024060
Museo, Biblioteca e Archivio, Museo Civico, Bassano del Grappa 023352
Museo Biblioteca Municipal Cesar Fernández Navarro, Santa Fé 000600
Museo Biblioteca Nueva Cádiz y Casa Natal de Juan Bautista Arismendi, Nueva Cádiz 049508
Museo Biblioteca Palacio Postal, México 028442
Museo Biblioteca Palafoxiana, Puebla 028649
Museo Biblioteca Pape, Monclova . 028555
Museo Biblioteca Rosauro Rosa Acosta, Pampatar 049509
Museo Bicknell, Bordighera 023480
Museo Bicocchi, Pomarance 025300
Museo Bodoniano, Parma 025120
Museo Bodoniano. Bolletino, Parma 135922
Museo Bolívariano, Caracas 049458
Museo Bolivariano de Arte Contemporáneo, Fundación Museo Bolivariano, Santa Marta 007606
Museo Bologna-Buonsignori, Siena 025887
Museo Boncompagni Ludovisi per le Arti Decorative, Roma 025497
Museo Borromeo, Isola Bella 024421
Museo Botanico, Buenos Aires 000158
Museo Botánico, Córdoba 000290
Museo Botánico, Montevideo 041507
Museo Botánico, Tuxtla Gutiérrez . . 028895
Museo Botanico Cesare Bicchi, Lucca 024543
Museo Botanico della Lessinia, Fumane 024258
Museo Bottacin, Padova 025053
Museo Bottega della Tarsia Lignea, Sorrento 025926
Museo Brandolini e Giol, Oderzo . . . 024981
Museo Brembano di Scienze Naturali, San Pellegrino Terme 025722
Museo C. Nivola, Orani 024998
Museo Ca' la Ghironda, Bologna . . . 023423
Museo Cabrera, Ica 031525
Museo Cabriniano, Sant'Angelo Lodigiano 025766
Museo Cacique Balata, La Cumbre . 000376
Museo Calabozo de Hidalgo, Chihuahua 028153
Museo Calabrese di Etnografia e Folklore R. Corso, Palmi 025102
Museo Camillo Leone, Vercelli 026275
Museo Camilo Egas del Banco Central, Quito 009233
Museo Camón Aznar, Zaragoza . . . 036101
Museo Campagna G. Bruno, Campagna 023612
Museo Campamento Irritila, San Pedro 028749
Museo Camuno e Biblioteca Civica, Breno 023513
Museo Canario, Las Palmas de Gran Canaria 035623
Museo Canonica, Roma 025498
Museo Canonicale, Verona 026286
Museo Cantábrico, Comillas 035107
Museo Cantonale d'Arte, Lugano . . 037285
Museo Cantonale di Storia Naturale, Lugano 037286
Museo Capilla Alfonsina, México . . 028443
Museo Capitán Juan de Zevallos, Valle Hermoso 000652
Museo Capitolare, Atri 023296
Museo Capitolare, Cagliari 023562
Museo Capitolare, Ortona 025016
Museo Capitolare, Cattedrale di San Rufino, Assisi 023278
Museo Capitolare delle Antichità Corfiniesi, Corfinio 023966
Museo Capitolare di Arte Sacra, Gravina di Puglia 024366
Museo Capitolare di San Lorenzo, Chiostro di San Lorenzo, Perugia 025168
Museo Cappella di Santa Fina, San Gimignano 025677
Museo Cappella San Severo, Napoli 024896
Museo Cappuccini Emiliani, Reggio Emilia 025414
Museo Capuaniano, Mineo 024744
Museo Cardenal Crisanto Luque, Tenjo 007623
Museo Carducci - Biblioteca e Casa, Bologna 023424
Museo Carlo Venturini, Massa Lombarda 024634
Museo Carlos Emilio Grijalva, Tulcán 009265
Museo Carlos Torres Barraza, Valentín Gómez Farías 028906
Museo Carnico delle Arti Popolari Michele Gortani, Tolmezzo 026041
Museo Carozzi, Seriate 025859
Museo Casa, Valverde del Camino . 036018
Museo Casa Alejandro de Humboldt, La Habana 007957
Museo Casa Blanca, San Juan 032734
Museo Casa Busoni, Empoli 024044
Museo Casa Cautiño, Guayama . . . 032714
Museo Casa Clautana E. Borsatti, Claut 023915
Museo Casa Colonial, Pamplona . . . 007564
Museo Casa Cultural Alfonso López Pumarejo, Honda 007515
Museo Casa de Africa, La Habana . 007958
Museo Casa de Agustín Arrieta, Puebla 028650
Museo Casa de Asia, La Habana . . 007959
Museo Casa de Benalcazar, Quito . . 009234
Museo Casa de Bernardo A. Houssay, Buenos Aires 000159
Museo Casa de Bolívar, Academia de Historia de Santander, Bucaramanga 007457
Museo Casa de Carmen Montilla, La Habana 007960
Museo Casa de Carranza, Cuatrocienegas 028199
Museo Casa de Carranza, México . . 028444
Museo Casa de Colón, Las Palmas de Gran Canaria 035624
Museo Casa de Cultura de Ixtlán, Ixtlán del Río 028350
Museo Casa de Dulcinea, Museo del Santa Cruz, El Toboso 035914
Museo Casa de Hidalgo La Francia Chiquita, San Felipe 028714
Museo Casa de la Bola, México . . . 028445
Museo Casa de la Cultura, Montemorelos 028559
Museo Casa de la Cultura de Barichara, Barichara 007396
Museo Casa de la Cultura de Cuacutecuta, Instituto de Cultura de Norte Santander, Cuacutecuta 007488
Museo Casa de la Cultura de Pensilvania, Pensilvania 007576
Museo Casa de la Cultura Luis Camacho Rueda, Socorro 007615
Museo Casa de la Moneda, Madrid . 035405
Museo Casa de la Moneda, Mariquita 007532
Museo Casa de la Obrapía, La Habana 007961
Museo Casa de la Orfebrería, La Habana 007962
Museo Casa de la Plomada, Vallecillo 028912
Museo Casa de la Poesía, La Habana 007963
Museo Casa de la Tecnología, Monterrey 028560
Museo Casa de la Troya, Santiago de Compostela 035818
Museo Casa de León Trotsky, México 028446
Museo Casa de los Mártires, La Habana 007964
Museo Casa de Morelos, Ecatepec de Morelos 028233
Museo Casa de Morelos, Morelia . . 028574
Museo Casa de Policarpa Salavarrieta, Guaduas 007509
Museo Casa de Puerto Rico y Sala del Tabaco, La Habana 007965
Museo Casa de Ramón López Velarde, Jerez de García Salinas 028360
Museo Casa de Ricardo Rojas, Buenos Aires 000160
Museo Casa de Sais Montes de Oca Hermanos, Pinar del Río 008091
Museo Casa de Sucre, Quito 009235
Museo Casa de Yrurtia, Buenos Aires 000161
Museo Casa de Zela, Tacna 031598
Museo Casa del Agua, Tehuacán . . 028801
Museo Casa del Alfeñique, Puebla . 028651
Museo Casa del Deán, Puebla 028652
Museo Casa del Diego, Celaya 028140
Museo Casa del Dr. Mora, Comonfort 028183
Museo Casa del Duca, Venezia 026241
Museo Casa del Fundador Ponzalo Suárez Rendón, Tunja 007630
Museo Casa del General Alvaro Obregón, Huatabampo 028329
Museo Casa del Libertador Simón Bolívar, La Habana 007966
Museo Casa del Maestro José Márquez Figueroa, Puebla 028653
Museo Casa del Marques de Aguayo y Museo Municipal, Mazapil Zacatecas 028406
Museo Casa del Padre, Orselina . . . 037407
Museo Casa Diego Rivera, Guanajuato 028299
Museo Casa Dr. Belisario Domínguez, Comitán de Domínguez 028181
Museo Casa Estudio Diego Rivera y Frida Kahlo, México 028447
Museo Casa Francisco Villa, Hidalgo del Parral 028322
Museo Casa Fundación Oswaldo Guayasamín, La Habana 007967
Museo Casa Galimberti, Cuneo . . . 024011
Museo Casa José Lezama Lima, La Habana 007968
Museo Casa Mata, Matamoros 028404
Museo Casa Maya, Cancún 028136
Museo Casa Mosquera, Popayán . . 007583
Museo Casa Murillo, Sevilla 035859
Museo Casa Natal de Antonio Maceo, Santiago de Cuba 008150
Museo Casa Natal de Calixto Garcia, Holguín 008022
Museo Casa Natal de Camilo Cienfuegos, La Habana 007969
Museo Casa Natal de Carlos Manuel de Céspedes, Bayamo 007877
Museo Casa Natal de Celia Sanchez Manduley, Media Luna 008064
Museo Casa Natal de Cervantes, Alcalá de Henares 034800

Museo Casa Natal de Frank País, Santiago de Cuba . . . 008151
Museo Casa Natal de Hermanos Ameijeiras, Pueblo Viejo . . . 008102
Museo Casa Natal de Ignacio Agramonte, Camagüey . . . 007894
Museo Casa Natal de Isabel la Católica, Madrigal de las Altas Torres . . . 035445
Museo Casa Natal de José María Heredia, Santiago de Cuba . . . 008152
Museo Casa Natal de José Martí, La Habana . . . 007970
Museo Casa Natal de Morelos, Morelia . . . 028575
Museo Casa Natal de Pedro Martínez Brito, Ciego de Avila . . . 007905
Museo Casa Natal de Serafín Sánchez, Sancti-Spíritus . . . 008128
Museo Casa Natal General Santander, Villa del Rosario . . . 007643
Museo Casa Natal Juan Manuel Márquez, La Habana . . . 007971
Museo Casa Natale di Giotto, Vicchio . . . 026307
Museo Casa Natale di San Pio X, Riese Pio X . . . 025426
Museo Casa Natale di Tiziano Vecellio, Pieve di Cadore . . . 025231
Museo Casa Natale G. D'Annunzio, Pescara . . . 025183
Museo Casa Natale Giacomo Puccini, Lucca . . . 024544
Museo Casa Negret, Popayán . . . 007584
Museo Casa Padilla, San Miguel de Tucumán . . . 000579
Museo Casa Paoli, Ponce . . . 032720
Museo Casa Pascoli, Barga . . . 023333
Museo Casa Rafael Núñez, Cartagena . . . 007476
Museo Casa Roig, Humacao . . . 032717
Museo Casa Rossini, Pesaro . . . 025175
Museo Casa Ruth Lechuga, México 028448
Museo Casa Studio F. Melani, Pistoia . . . 025273
Museo Casa Walser, Macugnaga . . 024570
Museo Casabianca, Malo . . . 024587
Museo Casartelli, Como . . . 023942
Museo Casita Blanca de Agustín Lara, Boca del Río . . . 028125
Museo Castello Masegra, Sondrio . 025918
Museo Castillo de la Fortaleza de Ansite, Santa Lucía . . . 035801
Museo Castillo El Macho, Peñiscola 035648
Museo Castillo Serrallés, Ponce . . . 032721
Museo Catedral, Palma de Mallorca 035612
Museo Catedral de La Plata, La Plata . . . 000385
Museo Catedralicio, Almería . . . 034826
Museo Catedralicio, Badajoz . . . 034885
Museo Catedralicio, Baeza . . . 034890
Museo Catedralicio, Burgo de Osma 035000
Museo Catedralicio, Burgos . . . 035003
Museo Catedralicio, Cádiz . . . 035020
Museo Catedralicio, Ciudad Real . . 035095
Museo Catedralicio, Cuenca . . . 035137
Museo Catedralicio, Eivissa . . . 035161
Museo Catedralicio, Guadix . . . 035267
Museo Catedralicio, Jaén . . . 035301
Museo Catedralicio, León . . . 035326
Museo Catedralicio, Lleida . . . 035346
Museo Catedralicio, Málaga . . . 035451
Museo Catedralicio, Ourense . . . 035580
Museo Catedralicio, Salamanca . . . 035740
Museo Catedralicio, Santo Domingo de la Calzada . . . 035836
Museo Catedralicio, Segovia . . . 035844
Museo Catedralicio, Sigüenza . . . 035873
Museo Catedralicio, Tortosa . . . 035948
Museo Catedralicio, Zamora . . . 036095
Museo Catedralicio, Iglesia Catedral, Palencia . . . 035594
Museo Catedralicio de La Seo de Zaragoza, Zaragoza . . . 036102
Museo Catedralicio de Tui, Tui . . . 035959
Museo Catedralicio Diocesano, Ciudad Rodrigo . . . 035099
Museo Catedralicio-Diocesano, León . . . 035327
Museo Catedralicio Diocesano, Pamplona . . . 035630
Museo Catedralicio-Diocesano, Valencia . . . 035977
Museo Catedralico y Giralda, Sevilla 035860
Museo Católica de Santa María, Cercado . . . 031484
Museo Católico Peninsular, Mérida . 028410
Museo Cavour, Santena . . . 025778
Museo Cemento Rezola, Donostia-San Sebastián . . . 035151
Museo Centrale del Risorgimento, Roma . . . 025499
Museo Centrale dell'Istituto Storico della Resistenza, Imperia . . . 024410
Museo Centro Cultural Pachamama, Amaicha del Valle . . . 000112
Museo Centro de Cultura Mayo de El Júpare Blas Mazo, Huatabampo . . . 028330
Museo Centro de la Imagen, México 028449
Museo Centro Studi A.G. Barrili, Carcare . . . 023662
Museo Centro Taurino Potosino, San Luis Potosí . . . 028728
Museo Ceramoteca, Salamanca . . . 028694
Museo Cerlogne, Saint Nicolas . . . 025627
Museo Cerralbo, Madrid . . . 035395
Museo Cerro de la Campana, Santiago Suchilquitongo . . . 028769
Museo Cerro de los Huizaches, San Pablo Huixtepec . . . 028748
Museo Cervi, Gattatico . . . 024279
Museo Chairama, Santa Marta . . . 007607
Museo Charcas, Universidad Boliviana Mayor, Sucre . . . 003923
Museo Chavin de Huantar, Martínez 000429
Museo Chiaramonti e Braccio Nuovo, Musei Vaticani, Città del Vaticano . . . 049423
Museo Chihuahuense de Arte Contemporáneo, Chihuahua . . . 028154
Museo Chileno de Arte Precolombino, Santiago de Chile . . . 006928
Museo Chorro de Maita, Yaguajay . 008197
Museo Christiano, Cividale del Friuli 023905
Museo Ciénaga de San Pedro, Madera . . . 028396
Museo Ciencias Naturales, Nueva Gerona . . . 008075
Museo Ciencias Naturales Carlos de la Torre, Sancti-Spíritus . . . 008129
Museo Ciudades del Mundo, La Habana . . . 007972
Museo Civici Veneziani. Bollettino, Venezia . . . 135923
Museo Civico, Bagnacavallo . . . 023317
Museo Civico, Aci Castello . . . 023113
Museo Civico, Agrigento . . . 023133
Museo Civico, Airola . . . 023138
Museo Civico, Alatri . . . 023143
Museo Civico, Amalfi . . . 023185
Museo Civico, Apice . . . 023220
Museo Civico, Argenta . . . 023241
Museo Civico, Ariano Irpino . . . 023245
Museo Civico, Asolo . . . 023275
Museo Civico, Atina . . . 023294
Museo Civico, Avola . . . 023311
Museo Civico, Baranello . . . 023327
Museo Civico, Bardonecchia . . . 023331
Museo Civico, Barga . . . 023334
Museo Civico, Belluno . . . 023363
Museo Civico, Bisacquino . . . 023400
Museo Civico, Bolzano . . . 023469
Museo Civico, Borgo Velino . . . 023490
Museo Civico, Cabras . . . 023556
Museo Civico, Campagnano di Roma . . . 023613
Museo Civico, Campochiaro . . . 023622
Museo Civico, Caprino Veronese . . 023652
Museo Civico, Casale Monferrato . . 023680
Museo Civico, Casamicciola Terme 023687
Museo Civico, Castel Bolognese . . . 023702
Museo Civico, Castelleone . . . 023726
Museo Civico, Castelnovo Bariano . 023732
Museo Civico, Castelnuovo Scrivia . 023739
Museo Civico, Castelraimondo . . . 023740
Museo Civico, Castroreale . . . 023755
Museo Civico, Centuripe . . . 023791
Museo Civico, Champdepaz . . . 023833
Museo Civico, Cittadella . . . 023899
Museo Civico, Collelongo . . . 023930
Museo Civico, Conversano . . . 023957
Museo Civico, Cori . . . 023967
Museo Civico, Cosenza . . . 023981
Museo Civico, Crema . . . 023992
Museo Civico, Crotone . . . 024006
Museo Civico, Cuneo . . . 024012
Museo Civico, Erba . . . 024051
Museo Civico, Feltre . . . 024088
Museo Civico, Ferentino . . . 024092
Museo Civico, Foggia . . . 024208
Museo Civico, Fondi . . . 024220
Museo Civico, Fornovo San Giovanni . . . 024239
Museo Civico, Fratta Polesine . . . 024251
Museo Civico, Fucecchio . . . 024257
Museo Civico, Gangi . . . 024274
Museo Civico, Gibellina . . . 024340
Museo Civico, Guardiagrele . . . 024387
Museo Civico, Iesi . . . 024396
Museo Civico, Larciano . . . 024467
Museo Civico, Larino . . . 024469
Museo Civico, Licata . . . 024501
Museo Civico, Lodi . . . 024518
Museo Civico, Lucignano . . . 024551
Museo Civico, Maddaloni . . . 024574
Museo Civico, Magliano Sabina . . . 024577
Museo Civico, Manerbio . . . 024596
Museo Civico, Mattinata . . . 024653
Museo Civico, Mazara del Vallo . . . 024654
Museo Civico, Medicina . . . 024658
Museo Civico, Mirandola . . . 024748
Museo Civico, Monsampolo del Tronto . . . 024799
Museo Civico, Montelparo . . . 024849
Museo Civico, Noto . . . 024957
Museo Civico, Osimo . . . 025025
Museo Civico, Patrica . . . 025132
Museo Civico, Pegognaga . . . 025150
Museo Civico, Pescia . . . 025192
Museo Civico, Piedimonte . . . 025223
Museo Civico, Pieve di Cento . . . 025236
Museo Civico, Pistoia . . . 025274
Museo Civico, Pizzighettone . . . 025285
Museo Civico, Pontecorvo . . . 025314
Museo Civico, Putignano . . . 025374
Museo Civico, Ragogna . . . 025383
Museo Civico, Riva del Garda . . . 025447
Museo Civico, Rovereto . . . 025608
Museo Civico, San Bonifacio . . . 025657
Museo Civico, San Ferdinando di Puglia . . . 025675
Museo Civico, San Gimignano . . . 025679
Museo Civico, San Severo . . . 025733
Museo Civico, Sansepolcro . . . 025743
Museo Civico, Santa Giusta . . . 025747
Museo Civico, Siena . . . 025888
Museo Civico, Susa . . . 025970
Museo Civico, Taverna . . . 025993
Museo Civico, Tolfa . . . 026040
Museo Civico, Trevignano Romano . 026118
Museo Civico, Trinitapoli . . . 026149
Museo Civico, Troia . . . 026153
Museo Civico, Vasanello . . . 026218
Museo Civico, Viterbo . . . 026349
Museo Civico, Convento degli Agostinianoi Scalzi, Cerchio . . . 023794
Museo Civico, Convento Gesuitico, Salemi . . . 025633
Museo Civico, Museo dell'Artigianato e del Lavoro Contadino, Andreis . . . 023203
Museo Civico, Palazzo Aumale, Terrasini . . . 026016
Museo Civico, Palazzo Borea d'Olmo, Sanremo . . . 025741
Museo Civico, Palazzo Comunale, Rieti . . . 025427
Museo Civico, Palazzo Comunale, Sesto Calende . . . 025871
Museo Civico, Palazzo De Simoni, Bormio . . . 023495
Museo Civico, Palazzo Ducale, San Cesario di Lecce . . . 025663
Museo Civico, Palazzo Verbania, Luino . . . 024558
Museo Civico, Palazzo Zagarese, Rende . . . 025420
Museo Civico, Pinacoteca Comunale, Nocera Umbra . . . 024945
Museo Civico, Pinacoteca della Resistenza, Caldarola . . . 023581
Museo Civico, Raccolta del Giocattolo G. Superti Furga, Canneto sull'Oglio . 023630
Museo Civico, Raccolta Oglio-Chiese, Canneto sull'Oglio . . . 023631
Museo Civico, Sez. Archeologica, Biella . . . 023394
Museo Civico, Sezione Archeologia e Storia Naturale, Finale Emilia . . . 024131
Museo Civico, Sezione Archeologica, Bojano . . . 023411
Museo Civico, Sezione Paleontologica, Bojano . . . 023412
Museo Civico, Villa Colloredo Mels, Recanati . . . 025404
Museo Civico, Villa Pallavicino, Busseto . . . 023551
Museo Civico A. Giacomelli, Montagnana . . . 024806
Museo Civico A. Klitsche de la Grange, Allumiere . . . 023175
Museo Civico A. Parazzi, Viadana . . 026299
Museo Civico A. Tubino, ex Convento degli Agostiniani, Masone . . . 024629
Museo Civico A.E. Baruffaldi, Badia Polesine . . . 023313
Museo Civico Ala Ponzone, Cremona . . . 023996
Museo Civico Albano, Albano Laziale . . . 023146
Museo Civico Alta Val Brembana, Valtorta . . . 026204
Museo Civico Antiquarium, Nettuno 024933
Museo Civico Antiquarium Platina, Piadena . . . 025212
Museo Civico Antonino Olmo e Gipsoteca, Savigliano . . . 025815
Museo Civico Antonio Cordici, Erice 024055
Museo Civico Archeologica e Quadreria, Monterubbiano . . . 024862
Museo Civico Archeologico, Angera 023205
Museo Civico Archeologico, Anzio . 023214
Museo Civico Archeologico, Arona . 023252
Museo Civico Archeologico, Barbarano Romano . . . 023328
Museo Civico Archeologico, Bergamo . . . 023376
Museo Civico Archeologico, Bologna . . . 023425
Museo Civico Archeologico, Camerino . . . 023599
Museo Civico Archeologico, Canosa di Puglia . . . 023633
Museo Civico Archeologico, Casalmaggiore . . . 023682
Museo Civico Archeologico, Castelfranco Emilia . . . 023714
Museo Civico Archeologico, Castelleone di Suasa . . . 023727
Museo Civico Archeologico, Castro dei Volsci . . . 023754
Museo Civico Archeologico, Castrovillari . . . 023757
Museo Civico Archeologico, Cavaion Veronese . . . 023775
Museo Civico Archeologico, Cologna Veneta . . . 023934
Museo Civico Archeologico, Concordia Sagittaria . . . 023952
Museo Civico Archeologico, Fiesole 024122
Museo Civico Archeologico, Gazzo Veronese . . . 024285
Museo Civico Archeologico, Gottolengo . . . 024354
Museo Civico Archeologico, Grotte di Castro . . . 024380

Museo Civico Archeologico, Latronico . . . 024478
Museo Civico Archeologico, Marciana . . . 024612
Museo Civico Archeologico, Massa Marittima . . . 024639
Museo Civico Archeologico, Mel . . . 024661
Museo Civico Archeologico, Mondragone . . . 024791
Museo Civico Archeologico, Montalto Marche . . . 024810
Museo Civico Archeologico, Nepi . . 024931
Museo Civico Archeologico, Nicotera . . . 024937
Museo Civico Archeologico, Norma 024954
Museo Civico Archeologico, Padria . 025069
Museo Civico Archeologico, Pitigliano . . . 025280
Museo Civico Archeologico, Portoferraio . . . 025334
Museo Civico Archeologico, Ramacca . . . 025387
Museo Civico Archeologico, Remedello . . . 025419
Museo Civico Archeologico, Roccagloriosa . . . 025454
Museo Civico Archeologico, Rosignano Marittimo . . . 025601
Museo Civico Archeologico, Rutigliano . . . 025621
Museo Civico Archeologico, Salò . . 025640
Museo Civico Archeologico, Santa Marinella . . . 025756
Museo Civico Archeologico, Sarteano . . . 025797
Museo Civico Archeologico, Tolentino . . . 026033
Museo Civico Archeologico, Treia . . 026104
Museo Civico Archeologico, Verucchio . . . 026294
Museo Civico Archeologico, Palazzo Lucerna di Rová, Bene Vagienna . 023367
Museo Civico Archeologico Arsenio Crespellani, Bazzano . . . 023359
Museo Civico Archeologico C. Cellini, Ripatransone . . . 025439
Museo Civico Archeologico della Val Tenesi, Manerba del Garda . . . 024595
Museo Civico Archeologico di Fregellae, Ceprano . . . 023793
Museo Civico Archeologico e Paleobotanico, Perfugas . . . 025157
Museo Civico Archeologico e Pinacoteca, Chiomonte . . . 023867
Museo Civico Archeologico Eno Bellis, Oderzo . . . 024982
Museo Civico Archeologico Etnologico, Modena . . . 024755
Museo Civico Archeologico F. Saverio Majellaro, Bisceglie . . . 023401
Museo Civico Archeologico Genna Maria, Villanovaforru . . . 026336
Museo Civico Archeologico Goffredo Bellini, Asola . . . 023274
Museo Civico Archeologico L. Fantini, Monterenzio . . . 024859
Museo Civico Archeologico M. Petrone, Vieste . . . 026320
Museo Civico Archeologico O. Nardini, Velletri . . . 026221
Museo Civico Archeologico P. Giovio, Como . . . 023943
Museo Civico Archeologico Paleoambientale, Budrio . . . 023540
Museo Civico Archeologico 'Romualdi', Notaresco . . . 024956
Museo Civico Archeologico Sa Domu Nosta, Senorbì . . . 025856
Museo Civico Archeologico Trebula Mutesca, Palazzo Comunale, Monteleone Sabino . . . 024847
Museo Civico Archeologico U. Granafei, Mesagne . . . 024679
Museo Civico Archeologico Ugo Granafei di Mesagne. Testi e Monumenti, Roma . . . 135924
Museo Civico Arecheologico delle Acque, Chianciano Terme . . . 023838
Museo Civico Aufidenate, Castel di Sangro . . . 023704
Museo Civico Aufidenate De Nino, Alfedena . . . 023167
Museo Civico B. Romano, Termini Imerese . . . 026008
Museo Civico Belliniano, Catania . . 023762
Museo Civico Borbonico, Salle . . . 025639
Museo Civico C. G. Nicastro, Bovino 023507
Museo Civico C. Verri, Biassono . . . 023392
Museo Civico Casa Cavassa, Saluzzo . . . 025643
Museo Civico Castel Nuovo, Napoli . 024897
Museo Civico Castello Ursino, Catania . . . 023763
Museo Civico Chiusa, Convento dei Cappuccini, Chiusa . . . 023868
Museo Civico Craveri di Storia Naturale, Bra . . . 023509
Museo Civico D. dal Lago, Valdagno 026187
Museo Civico d'Arte, Modena . . . 024756
Museo Civico d'Arte, Palazzo Ricchieri, Pordenone . . . 025324
Museo Civico d'Arte Antica, Torino . 026052
Museo Civico d'Arte Contemporanea, Albissola Marina . . . 023157
Museo Civico d'Arte Contemporanea U. Apollonio, San Martino di Lupari . 025706
Museo Civico d'Arte Industriale e Galleria Davia Bargellini, Bologna . . . 023426
Museo Civico dei Villaggi Scomparsi, Villa Estense . . . 026329
Museo Civico del Castello, Conegliano . . . 023954
Museo Civico del Marmo, Carrara . 023673
Museo Civico del Risorgimento, Bologna . . . 023427
Museo Civico del Risorgimento, Palazzo dei Musei, Modena . . . 024757
Museo Civico del Risorgimento e della Resistenza, Bergamo . . . 023380
Museo Civico del Sigillo, La Spezia 024439
Museo Civico del Territorio, San Daniele del Friuli . . . 025671
Museo Civico della Carta, Cairate . . 023572
Museo Civico della Ceramica, Nove 024971
Museo Civico della Cultura Materiale, Roseto degli Abruzzi . . . 025600
Museo Civico della Laguna Sud, ex Chiesa di San Francesco, Chioggia . . . 023866
Museo Civico della Media Valle del Liri, Sora . . . 025922
Museo Civico della Navigazione Fluviale, Battaglia Terme . . . 023358
Museo Civico della Torre, Treviglio . 026117
Museo Civico della Val Fiorentina Vittorino Cazzetta, Selva di Cadore . . . 025847
Museo Civico delle Armi L. Marzoli, Brescia . . . 023517
Museo Civico delle Arti e Tradizioni Popolari, Micigliano . . . 024685
Museo Civico delle Centuriazioni Romane Padovana, Borgoricco . . . 023491
Museo Civico delle Ceramiche, Santo Stefano di Camastra . . . 025781
Museo Civico delle Civiltà in Polesine, Rovigo . . . 025614
Museo Civico delle Scienze, Pordenone . . . 025325
Museo Civico di Archeologia Ligure, Genova . . . 024301
Museo Civico di Arona, Arona . . . 023253
Museo Civico di Arte Contadina, Romagnese . . . 025590
Museo Civico di Arte Moderna, Mombercelli . . . 024782
Museo Civico di Belle Arti, Lugano . 037287
Museo Civico di Belriguardo, Voghiera . . . 026362
Museo Civico di Merano - Stadtmuseum Meran, Merano . . . 024669
Museo Civico di Numismatica, Etnografia e Arti Orientali, Torino . . . 026053
Museo Civico di Palazzo Te, Mantova . . . 024601
Museo Civico di Paleontologia, Empoli . . . 024045
Museo Civico di Paleontologia e Archeologia, Ugento . . . 026167
Museo Civico di Paleontologia e Paletnologia, Borgosesia . . . 023493
Museo Civico di San Francesco, Montefalco . . . 024834
Museo Civico di San Francesco, Montone . . . 024873
Museo Civico di Santa Maria della Consolazione, Ex Convento dei Domenicani, Altomonte . . . 023180
Museo Civico di Schifanoia, Ferrara 024102
Museo Civico di Scienze Naturali, Faenza . . . 024067
Museo Civico di Scienze Naturali, Lovere . . . 024541
Museo Civico di Scienze Naturali, Voghera . . . 026360
Museo Civico di Scienze Naturali E. Caffi, Bergamo . . . 023377
Museo Civico di Scienze Naturali ed Archeologia della Valdinievole, Pescia . . . 025193
Museo Civico di Storia Naturale, Carmagnola . . . 023664
Museo Civico di Storia Naturale, Casalnuovo Monterotaro . . . 023684
Museo Civico di Storia Naturale, Chies d'Alpago . . . 023858
Museo Civico di Storia Naturale, Cittanova . . . 023901
Museo Civico di Storia Naturale, Crocetta del Montello . . . 024002
Museo Civico di Storia Naturale, Ferrara . . . 024103
Museo Civico di Storia Naturale, Milano . . . 024704
Museo Civico di Storia Naturale, Morbegno . . . 024880
Museo Civico di Storia Naturale, Taino . . . 025984
Museo Civico di Storia Naturale, Trieste . . . 026139
Museo Civico di Storia Naturale, Venezia . . . 026242
Museo Civico di Storia Naturale, Verona . . . 026287
Museo Civico di Storia Naturale del Liceo Glassico N. Machiavelli, Lucca . . 024545
Museo Civico di Storia Naturale del Salento, Calimera . . . 023585
Museo Civico di Storia Naturale Giacomo Doria, Genova . . . 024302
Museo Civico di Vignola, Vignola . . 026326
Museo Civico di Villa Rathgeb, Abano Terme . . . 023106
Museo Civico di Zoologia, Roma . . . 025500
Museo Civico Didattico di Scienze Naturali, Pinerolo . . . 025244
Museo Civico Didattico Gian Andrea Irico, Trino . . . 026150
Museo Civico Diocesano, Tropea . . 026156
Museo Civico Diocesano G. B. Leopardi, Penne . . . 025154
Museo Civico Diocesano La Castellina, Norcia . . . 024953
Museo Civico Don Queirolo, Vado Ligure . . . 026181
Museo Civico e Antiquarium, Latina 024475
Museo Civico e Archeologico, Locarno . . . 037272
Museo Civico E. Barba, Gallipoli . . . 024271
Museo Civico e d'Arte Sacra, Palazzo dei Priori, Colle di Val d'Elsa . . . 023925
Museo Civico e della Ceramica, Cerreto Sannita . . . 023801
Museo Civico e Diocesano d' Arte Sacra, Montalcino . . . 024808
Museo Civico e Foro Romano, Assisi . . . 023279
Museo Civico E. Nardi, Poggio Mirteto . . . 025294
Museo Civico e Pinacoteca, Sassoferrato . . . 025811
Museo Civico e Pinacoteca, Urbania 026169
Museo Civico e Pinacoteca, Palazzo Malatestiano, Fano . . . 024078
Museo Civico e Pinacoteca A. Vernarecci, Palazzo Ducale Corte Alta, Fossombrone . . . 024244
Museo Civico e Pinacoteca Basilio Cascella, Pescara . . . 025184
Museo Civico e Pinacoteca E. Lancerotto, Noale . . . 024942
Museo Civico e Pinacoteca G. de Nittis, Barletta . . . 023348
Museo Civico e Pinacoteca P.F. Crociani, Montepulciano . . . 024855
Museo Civico e Risorgimentale Don Giovanni Verità, Modigliana . . . 024770
Museo Civico e Teatro e Serbatoio Romano, Falerone . . . 024077
Museo Civico Etno-Antropologico, Petralia Sottana . . . 025200
Museo Civico Etnografico, Atri . . . 023297
Museo Civico Etnografico, Casale di Scodosia . . . 023679
Museo Civico Etnografico, Stanghella . . . 025945
Museo Civico Etnografico C.G. Franchini, Oleggio . . . 024991
Museo Civico Etnografico La Lessinia, Bosco Chiesanuova . . . 023499
Museo Civico Etnografico M.G. Fontana, Sappada . . . 025785
Museo Civico F. Bodini, Gemonio . . 024289
Museo Civico F. de Rocco, San Vito al Tagliamento . . . 025734
Museo Civico F. L. Belgiorno, Modica . . . 024768
Museo Civico F. Rittatore Von Willer, Farnese . . . 024081
Museo Civico Fedrigo, Sona . . . 025914
Museo Civico Filippo Meli, Ciminna 023879
Museo Civico Fossili, Besano . . . 023385
Museo Civico G. Sutermeister, Legnano . . . 024492
Museo Civico G. Ugonia, Brisighella 023531
Museo Civico G. Zannato, Montecchio Maggiore . . . 024829
Museo Civico Gaetano Filangieri, Napoli . . . 024898
Museo Civico-Galleria di Palazzo Pretorio, Prato . . . 025361
Museo Civico G.B. Adriani, Cherasco . . . 023836
Museo Civico Geo-Speleologico, Garessio . . . 024276
Museo Civico Geologia e Etnografia, Predazzo . . . 025368
Museo Civico Giacomo Rodolfo, Carignano . . . 023663
Museo Civico Giovanni Fattori, Livorno . . . 024508
Museo Civico Giulio Ferrari, Carpi . . 023669
Museo Civico Gonzaga, Novellara . . 024972
Museo Civico Guiseppe Fiorelli, Lucera . . . 024550
Museo Civico Il Correggio, Correggio . . . 023972
Museo Civico L. Mallé, Dronero . . . 024041
Museo Civico Luigi Bailo, Treviso . . 026120
Museo Civico Luigi Dalla Laita, Ala . 023139
Museo Civico M. Trucco, Albisola Superiore . . . 023155
Museo Civico Mambrini, Galeata . . 024265
Museo Civico Marinaro Gio-Bono Ferrari, Camogli . . . 023611
Museo Civico Marinaro U. Mursia, Milano . . . 024705
Museo Civico Medievale, Bologna . 023428
Museo Civico Messapico, Alezio . . . 023166
Museo Civico Naturalistico, Maserada sul Piave . . . 024628
Museo Civico Naturalistico dei Monti Prenestini, Capranica Prenestina . 023647
Museo Civico Naturalistico Severo Sini, Villa d'Almè . . . 026328
Museo Civico Orientale Santa Cardu, Cagliari . . . 023563
Museo Civico Ornitologico, Lonato . 024523
Museo Civico Ornitologico e di Scienze Naturali Luigi Scanagatta, Varenna . . . 026210
Museo Civico P. A. Garda, Ivrea . . . 024428

Museo Civico P. Mortara, Canneto sull'Oglio 023632
Museo Civico P. Rosario, Ascoli Satriano 023272
Museo Civico Padre Michele Jacobelli, Casalvieri 023685
Museo Civico Paleontologico, Macerata Feltria 024569
Museo Civico per la Preistoria del Monte Cetona, Cetona 023830
Museo Civico Pietro Lotti, Ischia di Castro 024416
Museo Civico-Pinacoteca, Palazzo Chiericati, Vicenza 026309
Museo Civico Pio Capponi, Terracina 026015
Museo Civico Polivalente, Mistretta 024749
Museo Civico Preistorico, Pofi 025289
Museo Civico Rocca Flea, Gualdo Tadino 024383
Museo Civico Rogadeo, Bitonto . . . 023407
Museo Civico Speleo-Archeologico, Nuoro 024977
Museo Civico Storico Archeologico, Leno 024493
Museo Civico Storico Artistico, Antrodoco 023212
Museo Civico Storico ed Etnografico, Primaluna 025370
Museo Civico Storico-Etnografico, Ripatransone 025440
Museo Civico U. Formentini, La Spezia 024440
Museo Civicodi Scienze Naturali, Randazzo 025389
Museo Civicodi Storia Naturale, Stazzano 025946
Museo Civiltà Lavoro Contadino e Artigiano, Pagnacco 025072
Museo Clarisse Coulombie de Goyaud, Ituzaingó 000367
Museo Clemente Rospigliosi, Pistoia 025275
Museo Coahuila y Texas, Monclova 028556
Museo-Colección Específico Militar El Desnarigado, Ceuta 035086
Museo Colombiano de Informática, Bogotá 007415
Museo Colonial, Antigua 021570
Museo Colonial, El Tocuyo 049489
Museo Colonial de Acolman, Acolman 028083
Museo Colonial del Conde de Sierra Gorda, Santander Jiménez 028766
Museo Colonial e Histórico, Complejo Museográfico Enrique Udaondo, Luján 000411
Museo Coltzin, Culiacán 028212
Museo Comandancia La Plata, Santo Domingo 008171
Museo Comarcal, Zalduondo 036094
Museo Comarcal da Fonsagrada, A Fonsagrada 035196
Museo Comarcal Durán y Sanpere, Cervera 035081
Museo Comarcal Reus, Reus 035695
Museo Comarcal Velezano Miguel Guirao, Vélez Rubio 036020
Museo Come Eravamo, Borgamanero 023481
Museo Comercial, Hellín 035277
Museo Comité Olímpico, México . . 028450
Museo Communale Antiquarium, Atena Lucana 023293
Museo Comparativo de Biología Marina, Viña del Mar 006950
Museo Complesso della Collegiata, Castiglione Olona 023752
Museo Comunal de Chañar Ladeado, Chañar Ladeado 000270
Museo Comunal Pedro Bargero, Emilio Bunge 000338
Museo Comunal Regional de San Guillermo, San Guillermo 000562
Museo Comunale, Montaione 024807
Museo Comunale, Monte San Savino 024818
Museo Comunale, Nova Ponente . . 024958
Museo Comunale, Paria a Mare . . . 025110
Museo Comunale, Roggiano Gravina 025461
Museo Comunale, Vico Equense . . . 026316
Museo Comunale A. Mendola, Favara 024086
Museo Comunale Archeologico, Viddalba 026319
Museo Comunale d'Arte Moderna di Ascona, Ascona 036854
Museo Comunale della Ceramica, Cutrofiano 024021
Museo Comunale della Manifattura Chini, Borgo San Lorenzo 023488
Museo Comunale della Valle dei Nuraghi, Torralba 026084
Museo Comunale della Valle del Sarno, Sarno 025792
Museo Comunale E. Durio, Civiasco 023903
Museo Comunale La Malaria e la sua Storia, Pontinia 025318
Museo Comunale Storico, Acquaviva delle Fonti 023118
Museo Comunale Trappeto Maratea, Vico del Gargano 026315
Museo Comunidad Las Terrazas, San Cristobal 008120
Museo Comunitario, Mineral del Monte 028551
Museo Comunitario, Puente de Ixtla 028677
Museo Comunitario Altagracia de Arauz, Ensenada 028244
Museo Comunitario Amuzgo de Xochistlahuaca, Xochistlahuaca . . 028951
Museo Comunitario Colonia Vicente Guerrero, Colonia Vicente Guerrero 028175
Museo Comunitario Concuemitl, Cuencamé 028203
Museo Comunitario Coronela Amelia La Güera Robles, Xochipala 028950
Museo Comunitario Crónica y Arte Agropecuario de la Sierra Gorda, Landa de Matamoros 028381
Museo Comunitario Cuarenta Casas, Valentín Gómez Farías 028907
Museo Comunitario de Antropología e Historia, Apatzingán 028106
Museo Comunitario de Atoyac, Atoyac 028115
Museo Comunitario de Carrillo Puerto, Alvaro Obregón 028101
Museo Comunitario de Ciudad Lerdo, Lerdo 028389
Museo Comunitario de Estación Coahuila, Mexicali 028418
Museo Comunitario de Historia de San José de Gracia, San José de Gracia . . . 028717
Museo Comunitario de Huitzapula, Huitzapula 028338
Museo Comunitario de Ixtlahuacán, Ixtlahuacán 028349
Museo Comunitario de la Ballena, La Paz 028373
Museo Comunitario de la Sal, Armería 028112
Museo Comunitario de Las Varas, Compostela 028184
Museo Comunitario de Pejelagartero, Huimanguillo 028336
Museo Comunitario de Pipillola, Españita 028252
Museo Comunitario de San Andrés Mixquic, México 028451
Museo Comunitario de San Nicolás Zoyatlán, San Nicolás Zoyatlán . . 028746
Museo Comunitario de Santa Eulalia, Santa Euralia 028763
Museo Comunitario de Santa Martha, Mulegé 028588
Museo Comunitario de Tototepec, Tototepec 028891
Museo Comunitario de Villa Regina, Villa Regina 000672
Museo Comunitario de Xalisco, Xalisco 028945
Museo Comunitario de Xolalpan, Ixtacamaxtitlán 028347
Museo Comunitario del Valle de Guadalupe, Ensenada 028245
Museo Comunitario el Asalto a las Tierras, Mexicali 028419
Museo Comunitario El Rosario, El Rosario 028238
Museo Comunitario Felipe Carrillo Puerto, Motul 028586
Museo Comunitario Francisco I. Madero, Francisco I. Madero, Coahuila . . . 028255
Museo Comunitario General Francisco Villa, Durango 028225
Museo Comunitario Hicupa, Tehuacán 028802
Museo Comunitario Hitalulu, San Martín Huamelulpan 028738
Museo Comunitario Huitza Chilin, San Pedro 028750
Museo Comunitario Iluikatlachiyalistli, Yahualica 028954
Museo Comunitario Ismael Girón González, Pánuco, Zacatecas 028633
Museo Comunitario Itzmal Kauil, Izamal 028351
Museo Comunitario Ji, Ocosingo . . 028615
Museo Comunitario Jna Niingui, San Miguel Tequixtepec 028743
Museo Comunitario Joyonaque, Tuxtla Gutiérrez 028896
Museo Comunitario Juan García Aldama de la Comunidad Cucapá, El Mayor Indígena 028236
Museo Comunitario Kumkuy Ys Untzi, Copainalá 028187
Museo Comunitario Maika, Poanas . 028646
Museo Comunitario Note Ujía, Santa María Asunción Tlaxiaco 028764
Museo Comunitario Nu-kuiñe, Cuquila 028218
Museo Comunitario Raramuri, Guachochi 028270
Museo Comunitario Rubén Jaramillo, Tlaquiltenango 028859
Museo Comunitario Serafín Olarte, Papantla 028634
Museo Comunitario Shan-Dany, Santa Ana del Valle 028756
Museo Comunitario sin Paredes Colonia Orizaba, Mexicali 028420
Museo Comunitario Snuuvico, San Juan Mixtepec Juxtlahuaca 028726
Museo Comunitario Tejamen, Nuevo Ideal 028601
Museo Comunitario Tzakualli, Zacualpan 028971
Museo Comunitario Unidad Indígena Emiliano Zapata, Hueyapan de Ocampo 028334
Museo Comunitario Unión y Progreso, Cuatrocienegas 028200
Museo Comunitario Xiximes, Gómez Palacio 028266
Museo Comunitario Xolalpan Calli, Hueyapan 028333
Museo Comunitario Ya Nfädi Yu Nohño Los Conocimientos de los Otomíes, Tolimán 028867
Museo Comunitario Yucu-Iti, Santa María Yucu-Iti 028765
Museo Comunitario Ze Acatl Topiltzin Quetzalcoatl, Tepoztlán 028830
Museo Concha Ferrant, La Habana . 007973
Museo Conchiliologico e della Carta Moneta, Bellaria Igea Marina 023362
Museo Contadino, Lana 024450
Museo Contadino, Montalto Pavese 024812
Museo Contadino, Varese Ligure . . 026216
Museo Contadino della Bassa Pavese, San Cristina e Bissone 025670
Museo Contalpa de Nombre de Dios, Nombre de Dios 028600
Museo Contemporáneo al Aire Libre, Aracena 034844
Museo Contisuyo, Moquegua 031574
Museo Convento de San Diego, Quito 009236
Museo Convento de Santa Clara, Salamanca 035741
Museo Convento del Desierto de la Candelaria, Ráquira 007595
Museo Convento Santo Ecce Homo, Sutamarchán 007622
Museo Conventual, Medina de Pomar 035483
Museo Conventual de Santa Paula, Sevilla 035861
Museo Cooperativo Eldorado, Eldorado 000335
Museo Coronel Félix Luque Plata, Guayaquil 009207
Museo Correale di Terranova, Sorrento 025927
Museo Correr, Venezia 026243
Museo Costumbres Populares Pedro Antonio de Alarcón, Capileira 035050
Museo Costumbristá, La Paz 003911
Museo Costumbrista de Sonora, Alamos 028097
Museo Coyug-Curá, Pigüé 000474
Museo Criollo de los Corrales, Buenos Aires 000162
Museo Cristero Ing. Efrén Quezada, Encarnación de Díaz, Jalisco 028242
Museo Cristero Señor Cura Cristóbal Magallanes, Totatiche 028888
Museo Cristóbal Mendoza, Trujillo . 049514
Museo Cruz Herrera, La Línea de la Concepción 035335
Museo Cuadra de Bolívar, Caracas . 049459
Museo Cuartel de Emiliano Zapata, Tlaltizapán 028854
Museo Cuartel Zapatista, México . . 028452
Museo Cultura Antigua Ribera del Bernesga, Cuadros 035136
Museo Cultura e Musica Popolare dei Peloritani, Messina 024680
Museo Cultura y Tradición de Jalcomulco, Jalcomulco 028353
Museo Cultural del Instituto Geografico Militar, Quito 009237
Museo Cultural Iijdio Guaranga, Guaranga 009204
Museo D. Agostinelli, Roma 025501
Museo d' Arte e Scienza, Fondazione Goffried Matthaes, Milano 024706
Museo D. Chalonge, Erice 024056
Museo da Citania de Santa Tegra, A Guardia 035269
Museo da Terra de Melide, Melide . 035489
Museo Dannunziano del Vittoriale, Il Vittoriale degli Italiani, Gardone Riviera 024275
Museo Dantesco, Ravenna 025397
Museo d'Art Contemporani, Elche . 035166
Museo d'Arte, Giulianova 024347
Museo d'Arte, Tenero 037623
Museo d'Arte Antica, Milano 024707
Museo d'Arte C. Barbella, Chieti . . . 023861
Museo d'Arte Contemporanea, Torino 026054
Museo d'Arte Contemporanea D. Formaggio, Teolo 026002
Museo d'Arte Contemporanea di Villa Croce, Genova 024303
Museo d'Arte d'Ammobigliamento, Stupinigi 025961
Museo d'Arte e Ammobiliamento, Nichelino 024936
Museo d'Arte e Archeologia I. Mormino, Fondazione Banco di Sicilia, Palermo 025083
Museo d'Arte e Storia Antica Ebraica, Casale Monferrato 023681
Museo d'Arte G. Bargellini, Pieve di Cento 025237
Museo d'Arte Mendrisio, Mendrisio 037325
Museo d'Arte Moderna, Brescia . . . 023518
Museo d'Arte Moderna, Gazoldo degli Ippoliti 024283
Museo d'Arte Moderna, Lugano . . . 037288
Museo d'Arte Moderna, Tertenia . . . 026018
Museo d'Arte Moderna e Contemporanea, Museo Ottocento, Filippo de Pisis e Michelangelo Antonioni, Ferrara . 024104

Museo d'Arte Moderna e Contemporanea di Trento e Rovereto, Palazzo delle Albere, Trento . . . 026107
Museo d'Arte Moderna L. Répaci, Palmi . . . 025103
Museo d'Arte Moderna M. Rimoldi, Cortina d'Ampezzo . . . 023976
Museo d'Arte Moderna Pagani, Castellanza . . . 023721
Museo d'Arte Nuoro, Nuoro . . . 024978
Museo d'Arte Orientale, Palazzo Pesaro, Venezia . . . 026244
Museo d'Arte Orientale Edoardo Chiossone, Genova . . . 024304
Museo d'Arte P. Pini, Milano . . . 024708
Museo d'Arte Pietro Cavoti, Galatina . . . 024264
Museo d'Arte Preistorica, Pinerolo . 025245
Museo d'Arte S. Pertini, Savona . . . 025825
Museo d'Arte Sacra, Baiardo . . . 023324
Museo d'Arte Sacra, Camaiore . . . 023596
Museo d'Arte Sacra, Chiaramonte Gulfi . . . 023840
Museo d'Arte Sacra, Colle di Val d'Elsa . . . 023926
Museo d'Arte Sacra, Faenza . . . 024068
Museo d'Arte Sacra, Gradoli . . . 024361
Museo d'Arte Sacra, Montespertoli . 024866
Museo d'Arte Sacra, Ponzone . . . 025320
Museo d'Arte Sacra, San Casciano in Val di Pesa . . . 025662
Museo d'Arte Sacra, San Gimignano . . . 025680
Museo d'Arte Sacra, San Giovanni in Persiceto . . . 025690
Museo d'Arte Sacra, Tavarnelle Val di Pesa . . . 025992
Museo d'Arte Sacra, Viterbo . . . 026350
Museo d'Arte Sacra, Palazzo Corboli, Asciano . . . 023263
Museo d'Arte Sacra, Palazzo Mediceo, San Leo . . . 025697
Museo d'Arte Sacra Cardinale Agnifili, Chiesa di Santa Maria della Neve, Rocca di Mezzo . . . 025453
Museo d'Arte Sacra della Insigne Collegiata di San Lorenzo, Montevarchi . . . 024867
Museo d'Arte Sacra della Marsica, Celano . . . 023785
Museo d'Arte Sacra della Santa Maria Assunta, Gallarate . . . 024267
Museo d'Arte Sacra della Val d'Arbia, Buonconvento . . . 023545
Museo d'Arte Sacra L. Acquarone, Lucinasco . . . 024552
Museo d'Arte Sacra San Marco, Mombaroccio . . . 024779
Museo d'Arte Sacro San Martino, Alzano Lombardo . . . 023184
Museo d'Arti e Mestieri Antichi, Montelupone . . . 024851
Museo das Mariñas, Betanzos . . . 034980
Museo das Peregrinacións, Santiago de Compostela . . . 035819
Museo David Paltán, San Gabriel . . 009264
Museo David Paltan, Tulcán . . . 009266
Museo David Ramírez Lavoignet, Misantla . . . 028552
Museo de Abancay, Abancay . . . 031454
Museo de Academia de San Carlos, Universidad Nacional Autónoma de México, México . . . 028453
Museo de Acaponeta, Acaponeta . . 028078
Museo de Aduanas y Puerto, Buenos Aires . . . 000163
Museo de Aeronáutica y Astronáutica, Madrid . . . 035396
Museo de Aguascalientes, Aguascalientes . . . 028086
Museo de Ahumada, Villa Ahumada y Anexas . . . 028929
Museo de Akil Uyotoch Cah, Akil . . 028096
Museo de Albacete, Albacete . . . 034792
Museo de Alfarería Tradicional Vasca, Elosu . . . 035172
Museo de Almería, Almería . . . 034827
Museo de Ambiente Histórico Cubano, Santiago de Cuba . . . 008153
Museo de Ameca, Vetagrande . . . 028922
Museo de América, Madrid . . . 035397
Museo de Anatomía, México . . . 028454
Museo de Animales Venenosos, Buenos Aires . . . 000164
Museo de Antioquia, Medellín . . . 007535
Museo de Antofagasta, Antofagasta 006908
Museo de Antropología, Ibarra . . . 009218
Museo de Antropología, Tecolotlán . 028797
Museo de Antropología, Universidad del Atlántico-Facultad de Ciencias Humanas-Departamento de Historia, Barranquilla . . . 007398
Museo de Antropología, Universidad Nacional de Córdoba, Córdoba . . . 000291
Museo de Antropología de Tenerife - Casa de Carta, La Laguna . . . 035316
Museo de Antropología de Xalapa, Universidad Veracruzana, Xalapa . 028941
Museo de Antropología e Historia, Fundación Lisandro Alvarado, Maracay . . . 049503
Museo de Antropología e Historia de Allende, Allende . . . 028099
Museo de Antropología e Historia de Santiago Papasquiaro, Santiago Papasquiaro . . . 028768
Museo de Antropología e Historia Natural Los Desmochados, Casilda . . . 000266
Museo de Antropología y Ciencias Naturales, Concordia . . . 000286
Museo de Anzoátegui, Barcelona . . 049442
Museo de Armas, Montevideo . . . 041508
Museo de Armas de la Nación, Buenos Aires . . . 000165
Museo de Armería de Alava, Vitoria-Gasteiz . . . 036080
Museo de Arqueología, Acapulco de Juárez . . . 028080
Museo de Arqueología, La Habana . 007974
Museo de Arqueología, Ixtepec . . . 028348
Museo de Arqueología Colonial Rodolfo I. Bravo, Cafayate . . . 000255
Museo de Arqueología de Alava, Vitoria-Gasteiz . . . 036081
Museo de Arqueología de Córdoba, Córdoba . . . 028188
Museo de Arqueología de la Universidad Nacional de Trujillo, Trujillo . . . 031605
Museo de Arqueología de la Universidad Nacional de Tucumán, San Miguel de Tucumán . . . 000580
Museo de Arqueología de León, León . . . 028384
Museo de Arqueología de Occidente de México, Universidad de Guadalajara, Guadalajara . . . 028279
Museo de Arqueología e Historia Natural de Yungay, Yungay . . . 031616
Museo de Arqueología El Chamizal, Juárez . . . 028367
Museo de Arqueología Josefina Ramos de Cox del Instituto Riva-Agüero, Universidad Católica del Perú, Lima . . . 031547
Museo de Arqueología Samuel Humberto Espinoza Lozano, Huaytará . . . 031522
Museo de Arqueología y Antropología, Universidad Nacional Mayor de San Marcos, Lima . . . 031548
Museo de Arqueología y Etnografía, Sinarcas . . . 035876
Museo de Arquitectura, Caracas . . . 049460
Museo de Arquitectura Leopoldo Rother, Universidad Nacional de Colombia, Bogotá . . . 007416
Museo de Arte Abstracto Español, Fundación Juan March, Cuenca . . 035138
Museo de Arte Abstracto Manuel Felguérez, Zacatecas . . . 028961
Museo de Arte Alberto Mena Caamaño, Quito . . . 009238
Museo de Arte Alvar y Carmen T. de Carrillo Gil, México . . . 028455
Museo de Arte Americano de Maldonado, Maldonado . . . 041494
Museo de Arte Colonial, Antigua . . . 021570
Museo de Arte Colonial, Bogotá . . . 007417
Museo de Arte Colonial, Caracas . . 049461
Museo de Arte Colonial, Mérida . . . 049505
Museo de Arte Colonial, Morelia . . . 028576
Museo de Arte Colonial, Quito . . . 009239
Museo de Arte Colonial de la Habana, Casa Conde Bayona, La Habana . . . 007975
Museo de Arte Colonial de Palacio Valle Iznaga, Sancti-Spíritus . . . 008130
Museo de Arte Colonial de San Francisco, Santiago de Chile . . . 006929
Museo de Arte Colonial Pedro de Osma, Lima . . . 031549
Museo de Arte Contemporáneo, Bahía Blanca . . . 000124
Museo de Arte Contemporáneo, Bogotá . . . 007418
Museo de Arte Contemporáneo, Cusco . . . 031497
Museo de Arte Contemporáneo, Montevideo . . . 041509
Museo de Arte Contemporáneo, Panamá City . . . 031424
Museo de Arte Contemporáneo, Santiago de Chile . . . 006930
Museo de Arte Contemporaneo, Sevilla . . . 035862
Museo de Arte Contemporaneo, Valdivia . . . 006944
Museo de Arte Contemporáneo, Museo del Museo de Santa Cruz, Toledo . . . 035918
Museo de Arte Contemporáneo Alfredo Zalce, Morelia . . . 028577
Museo de Arte Contemporáneo Ateneo de Yucatán, Mérida . . . 028411
Museo de Arte Contemporáneo de Caracas Sofía Imber, Caracas . . . 049462
Museo de Arte Contemporáneo de Chihuahua, Chihuahua . . . 028155
Museo de Arte Contemporáneo de Monterrey, Monterrey . . . 028561
Museo de Arte Contemporáneo de Oaxaca, Oaxaca . . . 028604
Museo de Arte Contemporáneo de Puerto Rico, San Juan . . . 032735
Museo de Arte Contemporáneo Fra Angélico, La Plata . . . 000386
Museo de Arte Contemporáneo Francisco Narvárez, Porlamar . . . 049512
Museo de Arte Contemporáneo Internacional Rufino Tamayo, México . . . 028534
Museo de Arte Contemporáneo José María Moreno Galván, La Puebla de Cazalla . . . 035313
Museo de Arte Contemporáneo Moderno de Ibagué, Ibagué . . . 007518
Museo de Arte Contemporáneo Ángel Zárraga, Durango . . . 028226
Museo de Arte Contemporáneo Número 8, Aguascalientes . . . 028087
Museo de Arte Contemporáneo Pajar de Agustín, Valle de Hecho . . . 036012
Museo de Arte Coro y Museo Alberto Henríquez, Falcón . . . 049490
Museo de Arte Costarricense, San José . . . 007673
Museo de Arte de Caguas, Caguas . 032709
Museo de Arte de Lima, Lima . . . 031550
Museo de Arte de Matanzas, Matanzas . . . 008056
Museo de Arte de Mazatlán, Mazatlán . . . 028408
Museo de Arte de Orizaba y del Estado de Veracruz, Orizaba . . . 028621
Museo de Arte de Pereira, Pereira . 007578
Museo de Arte de Ponce, Ponce . . . 032722
Museo de Arte de Puerto Rico, San Juan . . . 032736
Museo de Arte de Querétaro, Querétaro . . . 028683
Museo de Arte de Sinaloa, Culiacán 028213
Museo de Arte e Historia, Durango . 035157
Museo de Arte e Historia, Universidad Nacional Mayor de San Marcos, Lima . . . 031551
Museo de Arte e Historia Casa de Los Celis, Valencia . . . 049517
Museo de Arte e Historia de la Ciudad Jorge y Elisa, Instituto de Cultura de Norte de Santander, Cuacutecuta . . . 007489
Museo de Arte e História de Los Toldos, Los Toldos . . . 000409
Museo de Arte Eduardo A. Minnicelli, Río Gallegos . . . 000512
Museo de Arte en Ciudad Juárez, Instituto Nacional de Bellas Artes, Juárez . 028368
Museo de Arte Español, Buenos Aires . . . 000166
Museo de Arte Francisco Oller, Bayamón . . . 032706
Museo de Arte Gauchesco La Recova, San Antonio de Areco . . . 000546
Museo de Arte Gráficas Juan Pablos, México . . . 028456
Museo de Arte Guillermo Ceniceros, Durango . . . 028227
Museo de Arte Habana, La Habana . 007976
Museo de Arte Hispanoamericano Isaac Fernández Blanco, Buenos Aires . 000167
Museo de Arte, Historia y Cultura Casa Alonso, Vega Baja . . . 032753
Museo de Arte Industrial, Montevideo . . . 041510
Museo de Arte Italiano, Lima . . . 031552
Museo de Arte José Luis Bello y González, Puebla . . . 028654
Museo de Arte José Luis Bello y Zetina, Puebla . . . 028655
Museo de Arte Latinoamericano de Buenos Aires, Buenos Aires . . . 000168
Museo de Arte Moderno, Buenos Aires . . . 000169
Museo de Arte Moderno, Cuenca . . 009190
Museo de Arte Moderno, Mérida . . 049506
Museo de Arte Moderno, México . . 028457
Museo de Arte Moderno, Santo Domingo . . . 009159
Museo de Arte Moderno de Barranquilla, Barranquilla . . . 007399
Museo de Arte Moderno de Bogotá, Bogotá . . . 007419
Museo de Arte Moderno de Bogotá II, Bogotá . . . 007420
Museo de Arte Moderno de Bucaramanga, Bucaramanga . . . 007458
Museo de Arte Moderno de Cartagena, Cartagena . . . 007477
Museo de Arte Moderno de Durango, Gómez Palacio . . . 028267
Museo de Arte Moderno de la Ciudad de Buenos Aires, Buenos Aires . . . 000170
Museo de Arte Moderno de Medellín, Medellín . . . 007536
Museo de Arte Moderno del Estado de México, Toluca . . . 028868
Museo de Arte Moderno Jesús Soto, Ciudad Bolívar . . . 049483
Museo de Arte Moderno La Tertulia, Cali . . . 007467
Museo de Arte Moderno Ramírez Villamizar, Pamplona . . . 007565
Museo de Arte Olga Costa, Guanajuato . . . 028300
Museo de Arte Oriental, Ávila . . . 036034
Museo de Arte Popular Americano, Santiago de Chile . . . 006931
Museo de Arte Popular de la Universidad, Puebla . . . 028656
Museo de Arte Popular de la Universidad Nacional San Cristóbal de Huamanga, Humanga . . . 031524
Museo de Arte Popular de Quinua, Quinua . . . 031589
Museo de Arte Popular de San Bartolo de Coyotepec, San Baltazar Chichicapan . . . 028706
Museo de Arte Popular del Instituto Riva-Agüero, Universidad Católica del Perú, Lima . . . 031553
Museo de Arte Popular Petare, Caracas . . . 049463
Museo de Arte Popular Poblano y Museo de Artesanías, Puebla . . . 028657
Museo de Arte Popular Tlajomulco, Tlajomulco de Zúñiga . . . 028851
Museo de Arte Popular Venezolano, Juangriego . . . 049496
Museo de Arte Prehispánico, Mascota . . . 028402

Museo de Arte Prehispánico Carlos Pellicer, Tepoztlán 028831
Museo de Arte Prehispánico de México Rufino Tamayo, Oaxaca 028605
Museo de Arte Religioso, Cartagena 007479
Museo de Arte Religioso, La Habana 007977
Museo de Arte Religioso, Huaquechula 028328
Museo de Arte Religioso, Parita . . . 031434
Museo de Arte Religioso Colonial, Comayagua 021609
Museo de Arte Religioso Colonial, Panamá City 031425
Museo de Arte Religioso Concepción, Riobamba 009258
Museo de Arte Religioso Convento de San Francisco, Cajamarca 031473
Museo de Arte Religioso de Girón, Girón 007506
Museo de Arte Religioso de la Catedral, Lima 031554
Museo de Arte Religioso de la Catedral de San Nicolás, Rionegro 007597
Museo de Arte Religioso de Monguí, Monguí 007549
Museo de Arte Religioso de Piura, Piura 031584
Museo de Arte Religioso de Santa Mónica, Puebla 028658
Museo de Arte Religioso Ex Convento Franciscano, Huejotzingo 028331
Museo de Arte Religioso Juan de Tejeda, Córdoba 000292
Museo de Arte Religioso Julio Franco Arango, Duitama 007492
Museo de Arte Religioso la Concepción, Baños 009179
Museo de Arte Religioso Porta Coeli, San Juan 032737
Museo de Arte Religioso Presbítero Antonio María Franco, Supía 007621
Museo de Arte Religioso Santo Domingo de Porta Coeli, San Germán 032727
Museo de Arte Religioso Tiberio de J. Salazar y Herrera, Parroquia de la Catedral de Sonsón, Sonsón 007618
Museo de Arte Religioso y Colonial, Cali 007468
Museo de Arte Sacra das Clarisas, Monforte de Lemos 035507
Museo de Arte Sacra de Iria Flavia, Padrón 035590
Museo de Arte Sacra de Santa Clara, Allariz 034821
Museo de Arte Sacra de Santa María do Campo, A Coruña 035125
Museo de Arte Sacra de Vilanova, Lourenzá 035364
Museo de Arte Sacro, Calatayud . . . 035027
Museo de Arte Sacro, Castrojeriz . . 035074
Museo de Arte Sacro, Chihuahua . . 028156
Museo de Arte Sacro, Huete 035288
Museo de Arte Sacro, Osuna 035578
Museo de Arte Sacro, Santiago de Compostela 035820
Museo de Arte Sacro de La Rioja, La Rioja 000394
Museo de Arte Sacro de Santiago de Galdar, Gáldar 035208
Museo de Arte Sacro San Francisco, Salta 000537
Museo de Arte Universidad Nacional de Colombia, Bogotá 007421
Museo de Arte Virreinal de Taxco, Taxco de Alarcón 028787
Museo de Arte y Artesanía de Linares, Linares 006919
Museo de Arte y Diseño Contemporáneo, San José 007674
Museo de Arte y Tradiciones Populares, Bogotá 007422
Museo de Artes Decorativas de Palacio Salcines, Guantánamo 007935
Museo de Artes e Industrias Populares, Pátzcuaro 028638
Museo de Artes Gráficas, Bogotá . . 007423
Museo de Artes Plásticas, Madonado 041492
Museo de Artes Plásticas Eduardo Sívori, Buenos Aires 000171
Museo de Artes Populares, Tepic . . 028825
Museo de Artes Visuales Aramara, Tepic 028826
Museo de Artes y Artesanías Enrique Estrada Bello, Santo Tomé 000619
Museo de Artes y Costumbres Populares, Bornos 034995
Museo de Artes y Costumbres Populares, Combarro 035106
Museo de Artes y Costumbres Populares, Sevilla 035863
Museo de Artes y Costumbres Populares, Fundacón Unicaja, Málaga 035452
Museo de Artes y Costumbres Populares, Museo Monográfico del Castro de Viladonga, Pedrafita do Cebrero . . 035642
Museo de Artes y Costumbres Populares e internacional de Arte Naif, Jaén . . 035302
Museo de Artes y Tradiciones Populares, Espinal 007498
Museo de Artes y Tradiciones Populares, Madrid 035398
Museo de Artes y Tradiciones Populares de Ráquira, Ráquira 007596
Museo de Artes y Tradiciones Populares de Tlaxcala, Tlaxcala 028860
Museo de Artesanía Iberoamericana, La Orotava 035575
Museo de Artesanias Cefa, Quito . . 009240
Museo de Artesanías del Mundo, Silvia 007611
Museo de Artesanías Tradicionales Folklóricas, Corrientes 000318
Museo de Atoyac, Atoyac de Alvarez 028116
Museo de Autos y del Transporte Humberto Lobo Villarreal, Monterrey 028562
Museo de Ayutla, Ayutla de los Libres 028118
Museo de Bahía de Cochinos, Playa Girón 008100
Museo de Baracoa, Baracoa 007874
Museo de Barquisimeto, Barquisimeto 049445
Museo de Batopilas, Francisco I. Madero, Coahuila 028256
Museo de Belas Artes da Coruña, A Coruña 035126
Museo de Bellas Artes, Badajoz . . . 034886
Museo de Bellas Artes, Córdoba . . . 035114
Museo de Bellas Artes, Lincoln . . . 000405
Museo de Bellas Artes, Luján 000412
Museo de Bellas Artes, Mahón 035446
Museo de Bellas Artes, Valencia . . . 035978
Museo de Bellas Artes, Viña del Mar 006951
Museo de Bellas Artes Agustin Araujo, Treinta y Tres 041557
Museo de Bellas Artes Bonaerense, La Plata 000387
Museo de Bellas Artes Ceferino Carnacini, Villa Ballester 000658
Museo de Bellas Artes Claudio León Sempere, Burzaco 000253
Museo de Bellas Artes de Alava, Vitoria-Gasteiz 036082
Museo de Bellas Artes de Asturias, Oviedo 035585
Museo de Bellas Artes de Caracas, Caracas 049464
Museo de Bellas Artes de Castellón, Castellón de la Plana 035068
Museo de Bellas Artes de Coronel Pringles, Coronel Pringles 000316
Museo de Bellas Artes de Granada, Granada 035252
Museo de Bellas Artes de la Boca, Buenos Aires 000172
Museo de Bellas Artes de Santander, Santander 035811
Museo de Bellas Artes de Sevilla, Sevilla 035864
Museo de Bellas Artes de Toluca, Toluca 028869
Museo de Bellas Artes Departamental de San José, San José de Mayo 041555
Museo de Bellas Artes Domingo Faustino Sarmiento, Mercedes 000440
Museo de Bellas Artes Franklin Rawson, San Juan 000569
Museo de Bellas Artes Juan Yapari, Posadas 000479
Museo de Bellas Artes Laureano Brizuela, San Fernando del Valle de Catamarca 000555
Museo de Bellas Artes Octavio de la Colina, La Rioja 000395
Museo de Bermejillo, Bermejillo . . . 028124
Museo de Betancuria, Betancuria . . 034979
Museo de Bomberos, Madrid 035399
Museo de Bordados Paso Blanco, Lorca 035363
Museo de Buenos Aires, Tacotalpa . 028778
Museo de Burgos, Burgos 035004
Museo de Cáceres, Cáceres 035015
Museo de Cádiz, Cádiz 035021
Museo de Calcos y Esculturas Compardas, Buenos Aires 000173
Museo de Campeche, Campeche . . 028128
Museo de Caracas, Caracas 049465
Museo de Carruajes, Madrid 035400
Museo de Carruajes de Sevilla, Sevilla 035865
Museo de Casa Popenoe, Antigua . 021571
Museo de Caza Benito Albarrán, Zapopan 028973
Museo de Centro Cultural Recoleta, Buenos Aires 000174
Museo de Cera, Guadalajara 028280
Museo de Cera, Madrid 035401
Museo de Cera de la Ciudad de México, México 028458
Museo de Cera de la Villa, México . 028459
Museo de Cera de Tijuana, Tijuana . 028840
Museo de Cerámica Contemporánea Luis García Romo, Las Navas de la Concepción 035540
Museo de Cerámica de la Cartuja, Salteras 035751
Museo de Cerámica La Peñuela, Chinchilla de Monte-Aragón 035088
Museo de Cerámica Ruíz de Luna, Museo del Santa Cruz, Talavera de la Reina 035888
Museo de Cerámica y Bellas Artes Julián de la Herreria, Asunción 031442
Museo de Cerámica y Loza Popular, Falcón 049491
Museo de Chilecito, Chilecito 000273
Museo de Chusis de Sechura, Sechura 031594
Museo de Ciencia, Cuernavaca . . . 028204
Museo de Ciencia y Técnica, Buenos Aires 000175
Museo de Ciencia y Tecnología del Estado de Veracruz, Xalapa 028942
Museo de Ciencias, Caracas 049466
Museo de Ciencias, Huánuco 031516
Museo de Ciencias Antropológicas y Naturales, Santiago del Estero . . . 000615
Museo de Ciencias de Ensenada, Ensenada 028246
Museo de Ciencias Explora, León . . 028385
Museo de Ciencias Morfológicas, Rosario 000525
Museo de Ciencias Naturales, Asunción 031443
Museo de Ciencias Naturales, Pamplona 035631
Museo de Ciencias Naturales, Panamá City 031426
Museo de Ciencias Naturales, Pontevedra 035666
Museo de Ciencias Naturales, Salta 000538
Museo de Ciencias Naturales, Toluca 028870
Museo de Ciencias Naturales, Utrera 035966
Museo de Ciencias Naturales, Valverde de la Virgen 036017
Museo de Ciencias Naturales, Villafranca del Bierzo 036063
Museo de Ciencias Naturales, Universidad Nacional San Antonio Abad, Cusco 031498
Museo de Ciencias Naturales Augusto G. Schulz, Resistencia 000504
Museo de Ciencias Naturales Bartolomé Mitre, Córdoba 000293
Museo de Ciencias Naturales Carlos de la Torre, Holguín 008023
Museo de Ciencias Naturales de Alava, Vitoria-Gasteiz 036083
Museo de Ciencias Naturales de Oberá, Oberá 000458
Museo de Ciencias Naturales de Tenerife, Santa Cruz de Tenerife 035795
Museo de Ciencias Naturales del Colegio de San José, Medellín 007537
Museo de Ciencias Naturales del Departamento San Cristóbal, San Cristóbal 000553
Museo de Ciencias Naturales Dr. Amado Bonpland, Corrientes 000319
Museo de Ciencias Naturales e Historia, Instituto Superior del Profesorado Antonio Ruiz de Montoya, Posadas 000480
Museo de Ciencias Naturales Federico Carlos Lehmann, Cali 007469
Museo de Ciencias Naturales Luma, Tanti 000630
Museo de Ciencias Naturales Rvdo. P. Antonio Scasso, Colegio Don Bosco, San Nicolás de los Arroyos 000588
Museo de Ciencias Naturales Tomás Romay, Santiago de Cuba 008154
Museo de Ciencias Naturales y Antropológicas Juan Cornelio Moyano, Mendoza 000433
Museo de Ciencias Naturales y Antropológicas Prof. Antonio Serrano, Paraná 000463
Museo de Ciencias Naturales y Misional del Colegio San José, Esperanza 000340
Museo de Ciencias y Antropología, Cartago 007481
Museo de Ciudad Bolívar, Ciudad Bolívar 049484
Museo de Ciudad Real, Ciudad Real 035096
Museo de Ciudades Hermanas, Guadalajara 028281
Museo de Coamo, Coamo 032713
Museo de Cochoapa, Ometepec . . . 028620
Museo de Cocula es El Mariachi, Cocula 028166
Museo de Colexiata do Sar, Santiago de Compostela 035821
Museo de Colón, Colón 028173
Museo de Conkal, Conkal 028186
Museo de Cosautlán de Carvajal, Cosautlán de Carvajal 028192
Museo de Coscomatepec, Coscomatepec de Bravo 028193
Museo de Cuajinicuilapa, Cuajinicuilapa 028197
Museo de Cuenca, Cuenca 035139
Museo de Cultura Popular Angel Gil Hermidas, Villahermosa 028934
Museo de Cultura Popular Costa Rica, Heredia 007668
Museo de Cultura Populares del Estado de México, Toluca 028871
Museo de Culturas Populares, Durango 028228
Museo de Culturas Populares de Chiapas, San Cristóbal de las Casas 028708
Museo de Culturas Populares de San Luis Potosí, San Luis Potosí 028729
Museo de Culturas Populares e Indígenas, Obregón 028612
Museo de Culturas Populares e Indígenas de Sonora, Hermosillo 028316
Museo de Descubrimiento, Montevideo 041511
Museo de Dibujo Castillo de Larrés, Sabiñánigo 035733
Museo de Ejército Oriental, Holguín 008024
Museo de Emiliano Zapata, Emiliano Zapata 028240
Museo de Escuela de Educación Técnica Número 1, Dolores 000327

Museo de Escultura al Aire Libre, Leganés . . . 035323
Museo de Escultura Jacinto Higueras, Santisteban del Puerto . . . 035835
Museo de Escultura Novarro Santafé, Villena . . . 036070
Museo de Escultura Octavio Vicent, Jijona . . . 035309
Museo de Esculturas Luis Perlotti, Buenos Aires . . . 000176
Museo de Etnografía, Quito . . . 009241
Museo de Etnohistoria de Suyo, Suyo . . . 031597
Museo de Farmacia, Burgos . . . 035005
Museo de Farmacia, Llivia . . . 035355
Museo de Farmacia, Peñaranda de Duero . . . 035647
Museo de Farmacia Militar, Madrid 035402
Museo de Ferrocarriles en Miniatura Werner Dura, La Falda . . . 000377
Museo de Filatelia de Oaxaca, Oaxaca . . . 028606
Museo de Filigrana de Cobre, La Esperanza . . . 031537
Museo de Firmat, Firmat . . . 000346
Museo de Física de la Universidad Nacional de La Plata, La Plata . . . 000388
Museo de Física Recreativa, Puebla 028659
Museo de Fósiles y Minerales, Igea 035292
Museo de Frank País, Holguín . . . 008025
Museo de Gendarmería Nacional, Buenos Aires . . . 000177
Museo de General Zaragoza, General Zaragoza . . . 028264
Museo de Geología, Universidad de Caldas, Manizales . . . 007528
Museo de Geología de la UNAM, México . . . 028460
Museo de Geología del IPN, México 028461
Museo de Geología Dr. Jenaro González Reyna, Universidad Michoacana, Morelia . . . 028578
Museo de Geología y Paleontología, Neuquén . . . 000456
Museo de Geología y Suelos, Armenia . . . 007392
Museo de Gomellano, Gumiel de Hizán . . . 035275
Museo de Granjita Siboney, Santiago de Cuba . . . 008155
Museo de Guadalajara, Guadalajara 035264
Museo de Guadalupe, Guadalupe . . 028293
Museo de Guamúchil de Salvador Alvarado, Guamúchil . . . 028297
Museo de Heráldica Alavesa, Mendoza . . . 035491
Museo de Herrera, Panamá City . . . 031427
Museo de Historia de Ciencias Naturales, Chuquimarca . . . 031493
Museo de Historia de Ensenada, Ensenada . . . 028247
Museo de Historia de Higueras, Higueras . . . 028323
Museo de Historia de la Medicina, Bogotá . . . 007424
Museo de Historia de la Medicina y de la Cirugía Vincente A. Risolía, Universidad Buenos Aires, Buenos Aires . . . 000178
Museo de Historia de la Minería de Santa Rosalía, Mulegé . . . 028589
Museo de Historia de Lampazos de Naranjo y las Armas Nacionales, Lampazos de Naranjo . . . 028380
Museo de Historia de Linares, Linares . . . 028393
Museo de Historia de Panamá, Panamá City . . . 031428
Museo de Historia de Tabasco, Villahermosa . . . 028935
Museo de Historia de Tenerife y Archivo Insular, La Laguna . . . 035317
Museo de História del Deporte, Sala Polivalente Ramón Font, La Habana . . . 007978
Museo de Historia del Transporte, Guadalupe . . . 028294
Museo de Historia Económica, Bogotá . . . 007425
Museo de Historia Mexicana, Monterrey . . . 028563
Museo de Historia Natural, Alta Suiza . . . 007386
Museo de Historia Natural, Bogotá . 007426
Museo de Historia Natural, Guatemala . . . 021578
Museo de Historia Natural, Manizales . . . 007529
Museo de Historia Natural, Mérida . 028412
Museo de Historia Natural, México . 028462
Museo de Historia Natural, Panamá City . . . 031429
Museo de Historia Natural, Pereira . 007579
Museo de Historia Natural, Popayán 007585
Museo de Historia Natural, Puebla . 028660
Museo de Historia Natural, Santiago de Compostela . . . 035822
Museo de História Natural, Tunja . . 007631
Museo de Historia Natural, Villahermosa . . . 028936
Museo de Historia Natural, Zapotlán del Rey . . . 028977
Museo de Historia Natural, Universidad Autónoma de Baja California Sur, La Paz . . . 028374
Museo de Historia Natural, Universidad Industrial de Santander, Bucaramanga . . . 007459
Museo de Historia Natural Alfredo Dugès, Universidad de Guanajuato, Guanajuato . . . 028301
Museo de Historia Natural de Concepción, Concepción . . . 006912
Museo de Historia Natural de El Salvador, San Salvador . . . 009352
Museo de Historia Natural de la Universidad Antenor Orrego, Trujillo . . . 031606
Museo de Historia Natural de San Pedro Nolasco, Santiago de Chile . . . 006932
Museo de Historia Natural de Valparaíso, Valparaíso . . . 006947
Museo de Historia Natural del Ateneo Fuente, Universidad Autónoma de Coahuila, Saltillo . . . 028696
Museo de Historia Natural del Paraquay, Asunción . . . 031444
Museo de Historia Natural Dr. Manuel M. Villada, Universidad Autónoma del Estado de México, Toluca . . . 028872
Museo de Historia Natural Dr. Manuel Martínez Solórzano, Universidad Michoacana, Morelia . . . 028579
Museo de Historia Natural Dr. Ricardo S. Vadell, Suipacha . . . 000623
Museo de Historia Natural Felipe Poey, La Habana . . . 007979
Museo de Historia Natural Javier Prado, Universidad Nacional Mayor de San Marcos, Lima . . . 031555
Museo de Historia Natural José Vilet Brullet, Mexquitic . . . 028545
Museo de Historia Natural Regional, Universidad Juárez del Estado de Durango, Lerdo . . . 028390
Museo de Historia Natural Valle de la Prehistoria, Santiago de Cuba . . . 008156
Museo de Historia Natural Víctor Vaca Aguinaga, Lambayeque . . . 031541
Museo de Historia Reginal San Lorenzo y Galería del Libertador General San Martín, San Lorenzo . . . 000574
Museo de Historia Regional de Pánuco, Pánuco, Veracruz . . . 028632
Museo de Historia Regional de Sabinas Hidalgo, Sabinas Hidalgo . . . 028693
Museo de Historia Regional de Tristán Suárez, Trisán Suárez . . . 000645
Museo de Historia Republicana, Tegucigalpa . . . 021613
Museo de Historia y Artesanía de la Colonial Tovar, Colonia Tovar . . . 049485
Museo de História y Ciencias Naturales, Lobería . . . 000406
Museo de Historia y Cultura Casa Pedrilla, Cáceres . . . 035016
Museo de Histórico, Tunja . . . 007632
Museo de Hostotipaquillo, Hostotipaquillo . . . 028324
Museo de Hualpén, Concepción . . . 006913
Museo de Huelva, Huelva . . . 035285
Museo de Imáges de la Semana Santa en Popayán, Popayán . . . 007586
Museo de Insectos de la Universidad de Costa Rica, San José . . . 007675
Museo de Instituto Antártico Argentino, Buenos Aires . . . 000179
Museo de Instituto Magnasco, Gualeguaychú . . . 000359
Museo de Instituto Nacional de Estudios de Teatro, Buenos Aires . . . 000180
Museo de Instrumentos Musicales, Buenos Aires . . . 000181
Museo de Instrumentos Musicales Pablo Traversari, Quito . . . 009242
Museo de Intendencia, Madrid . . . 035403
Museo de Jaén, Jaén . . . 035303
Museo de Jala, Jala . . . 028352
Museo de Jamapa, Jamapa . . . 028357
Museo de la Abadía del Sacro-Monte, Granada . . . 035253
Museo de la Academia de Infantería, Toledo . . . 035919
Museo de la Acuarela del Estado de México, Toluca . . . 028873
Museo de la Administración Federal de Ingresos Públicos, Buenos Aires . 000182
Museo de la Alhambra, Granada . . . 035254
Museo de la Amistad México-Cuba, Tuxpan de Rodríguez Cano . . . 028893
Museo de la Antigua Estación Ferroviaría, Teocelo . . . 028809
Museo de la Artesanía Tradicional Juan Alfonso Carrizo, La Plata . . . 000389
Museo de la Asegurada, Colección Arte Siglo XX, Alicante . . . 034820
Museo de la Aviación Naval, Bahía Blanca . . . 000125
Museo de la Basílica de Guadalupe, México . . . 028463
Museo de la Basílica de Santa María, Elche . . . 035167
Museo de la Basílica Nuestra Señora de la Candelaria, Candelaria . . . 035042
Museo de la Batalla de Vitoria, Vitoria-Gasteiz . . . 036084
Museo de la Caña de Azúcar, El Cerrito . . . 007495
Museo de la Canción Yucateca, Mérida . . . 028413
Museo de la Capilla Real, Granada . 035255
Museo de la Caricatura, México . . . 028464
Museo de la Casa de Acuerdo de San Nicolás, San Nicolás de los Arroyos . . . 000589
Museo de la Casa de Cultura de Tepeapulco, Tepeapulco Hidalgo . 028818
Museo de la Casa de Cultura de Zacapú, Zacapu . . . 028959
Museo de la Casa de Gobierno, San Miguel de Tucumán . . . 000581
Museo de la Casa de la Cultura, Pinchote . . . 007581
Museo de la Casa de la Cultura, San Luis Potosí . . . 028730
Museo de la Casa de la Cultura Ecuatoriana, Quito . . . 009243
Museo de la Casa de la Cultura Martín Gamarra, Gamarra . . . 007503
Museo de la Casa de la Independencia, Asunción . . . 031445
Museo de la Casa de la Música Mexicana, México . . . 028465
Museo de la Casa de las Artesanías del Estado de Chihuahua, Bocoyna . . 028126
Museo de la Casa del Risco, México 028466
Museo de la Casa del Teatro, Buenos Aires . . . 000183
Museo de la Casa Histórica de la Independencia Nacional, San Miguel de Tucumán . . . 000582
Museo de la Casa Nacional de la Moneda, Potosí . . . 003919
Museo de la Casa Rosada, Buenos Aires . . . 000184
Museo de la Catedral, Astorga . . . 034870
Museo de la Catedral, Cusco . . . 031499
Museo de la Catedral, Granada . . . 035256
Museo de la Catedral, Murcia . . . 035529
Museo de la Catedral, Trujillo . . . 031607
Museo de la Catedralico de Santiago de Compostela, Santiago de Compostela . . . 035823
Museo de La Cerería, Tlayacapan . . 028864
Museo de la Charrería, México . . . 028467
Museo de la Ciencia y el Cosmos, La Laguna . . . 035318
Museo de la Ciencia y el Juego, Bogotá . . . 007427
Museo de la Ciudad, Buenos Aires . 000185
Museo de la Ciudad, Campeche . . . 028129
Museo de la Ciudad, Guadalajara . . 028282
Museo de la Ciudad, Melilla . . . 035490
Museo de la Ciudad, Mérida . . . 028414
Museo de la Ciudad, Paraná . . . 000464
Museo de la Ciudad, Quito . . . 009244
Museo de la Ciudad, Salta . . . 000539
Museo de la Ciudad, Tecate . . . 028796
Museo de la Ciudad, Victoria . . . 000655
Museo de la Ciudad, Vinaròs . . . 036075
Museo de la Ciudad de Chetumal, Chetumal . . . 028148
Museo de la Ciudad de Colón, Colón . . . 000279
Museo de la Ciudad de Córdoba, Córdoba . . . 028189
Museo de la Ciudad de Irapuato, Irapuato . . . 028344
Museo de la Ciudad de La Habana, La Habana . . . 007980
Museo de la Ciudad de León, León . 028386
Museo de la Ciudad de México, México . . . 028468
Museo de la Ciudad de Píritu, Píritu 049510
Museo de la Ciudad de Querétaro, Querétaro . . . 028684
Museo de la Ciudad de San Francisco, San Francisco . . . 000560
Museo de la Ciudad de Santiago de Compostela, Santiago de Compostela . . . 035824
Museo de la Ciudad de Sombrerete, Sombrerete . . . 028776
Museo de la Ciudad de Tepatitlan de Morelos, Tepatitlán de Morelos . . 028814
Museo de la Ciudad de Veracruz, Veracruz . . . 028920
Museo de la Ciudad Tuxtlán, Tuxtla Gutiérrez . . . 028897
Museo de la Clandestinidad, Nueva Gerona . . . 008076
Museo de la Colegiata, Medinaceli . 035487
Museo de la Colegiata, Colegiata-Parroquia de San Bartolomé Apóstol, Belmonte . . . 034970
Museo de la Colegiata de la Coruña, A Coruña . . . 035127
Museo de la Colegiata de Santa Juliana y Claustro, Santillana del Mar . . . 035831
Museo de la Colegiata San Luis, Villagarcía de Campos . . . 036064
Museo de la Colonia Siete de Marzo, Juan Aldama . . . 028366
Museo de la Colonización, Esperanza . . . 000341
Museo de la Comisión Provincial de Monumentos, León . . . 035328
Museo de la Comunidad de Agua Blanca, Puerto López . . . 009229
Museo de la Comunidad de Chordeleg, Chordeleg . . . 009182
Museo de la Constitución, Guáimaro . . . 007931
Museo de la Coria, Trujillo . . . 035955
Museo de la Cueva del Señor del Calvario, México . . . 028469
Museo de la Cultura de Albán, Albán . . . 007384
Museo de la Cultura Huasteca, Tampico . . . 028783
Museo de la Cultura José Arens Berg, Sullana . . . 031596
Museo de la Cultura Maya, Chetumal . . . 028149

Museo de la Cultura Potosina, San Luis Potosí 028731
Museo de la Dirección Nacional del Antártico, Buenos Aires 000186
Museo de la Diversidad Biológica y Cultural del Pacífico, Quibdó 007593
Museo de la E.E.M. Número 3, Colegio Nacional, Dolores 000328
Museo de la Electricidad, Caracas . 049467
Museo de la Electricidad, Lima . . . 031556
Museo de la Encarnación, Corella . 035120
Museo de la Energía, Embalse 000337
Museo de la Escuela General de Policía, Madrid 035404
Museo de la Escuela Normal Alejandro Carbo, Córdoba 000294
Museo de la Escultura Mexica Eusebio Dávalos, Acatitlán 028081
Museo de la Estampa, Cuitzeo 028211
Museo de la Estampa del Estado de México, Toluca 028874
Museo de la Estampa y del Diseño Carlos Cruz Diez, Caracas 049468
Museo de la Evangelización, Huejotzingo 028332
Museo de la Fabrica nacional de Moneda y Timbre, Madrid 035405
Museo de la Facultad de Ciencias Naturales y del Instituto Miguel Lillo, San Miguel de Tucumán 000583
Museo de la Familia Dominicana Siglo XIX, Santo Domingo 009160
Museo de la Farmacia Dra. D'Alessio Bonino, Buenos Aires 000187
Museo de la Farmacia Hispana, Madrid 035406
Museo de la Fauna, Aguascalientes 028088
Museo de la Fauna de Veracruz, Xalapa 028943
Museo de la Fauna y Ciencias Naturales, Monterrey 028564
Museo de la Ferrería de La Pradera, Subachoque 007620
Museo de la Fotografía, Rafaela . . . 000495
Museo de la Fotografía, Fototeca del INAH, Pachuca 028624
Museo de la Fuerza de Aviación Naval, Callao 031476
Museo de la Fuerza de Submarinos, Callao 031477
Museo de la Fundación Duque de Lerma, Toledo 035920
Museo de la Fundación Guayasamin, Quito 009245
Museo de la Fundación John Boulton, Caracas 049469
Museo de la Gaita, Fundación Municipal de Cultura, Educación y Universidad Popular, Gijón 035221
Museo de la Gráfica de la Historia Social de Taxco Siglo XX, Taxco de Alarcón . 028788
Museo de la Guardia Civil, Madrid . 035407
Museo de la Guerra de Castas, Felipe Carrillo Puerto 028254
Museo de la Guerra Hispano-Cubano-Norteamericana, Santiago de Cuba 008157
Museo de la Historia de la Cultura José de Obaldia, David 031418
Museo de la Historia de Ponce, Ponce 032723
Museo de la Historia y la Tradición, Panamá City 031430
Museo de La Huaxteca, Amatlán de los Reyes 028102
Museo de la Huerta de Almoradi, Almoradi 034828
Museo de la Iglesia, Oviedo 035586
Museo de la Iglesia de la Compañía de Jesús, Ica 031526
Museo de la Iglesia de San Pedro, Chucuito 031489
Museo de La Imagen, Vista Alegre . 008196
Museo de la Independencia, Dolores Hidalgo 028223
Museo de la Indumentaria Mexicana Luis Márquez Romay, México 028470
Museo de la Industria Azucarera, Abel Santamaría 007864
Museo de la Inmaculada Concepción, Cuenca 009191
Museo de la Insurgencia, Rincón de Romos 028689
Museo de la Isla de Cozumel, Cozumel 028196
Museo de la Labranza, Francisco I. Madero, Hidalgo 028259
Museo de la Lealtad Republicana, Chihuahua 028157
Museo de la Lucha Clandestina, Nueva Gerona 008077
Museo de la Lucha Clandestina, Santiago de Cuba 008158
Museo de la Lucha Estudiantil Jesús Suárez Gayol, Camagüey 007895
Museo de la Lucha Obrera, Cananea 028133
Museo de la Luz, México 028471
Museo de la Máquina Agrícola, Esperanza 000342
Museo de la Máscara, Morelia 028580
Museo de la Medicine, Cuenca 009192
Museo de la Memoria, Cuacutecuta 007490
Museo de la Memoria, Tlaxcala . . . 028861
Museo de la Minería, San Juan de Guadalupe 028721
Museo de la Minería del Estado de México, El Oro 028237
Museo de la Minería José de la Borda, Taxco de Alarcón 028789
Museo de la Minería y de la Industria de Asturias, San Martín del Rey 035763
Museo de la Moneda, Caracas 049470
Museo de la Muerte, San Juan del Río 028722
Museo de la Música Alejandro García Caturla, Santa Clara 008139
Museo de la Música Grabada, Zapotlanejo 028978
Museo de la Música Rodrigo Prats, Santa Clara 008140
Museo de la Nacionalidad, Panamá City 031431
Museo de la Naturaleza de Cantabria, Cabezón de la Sal 035012
Museo de la No Intervención Fuerte de Loreto, Puebla 028661
Museo de la Paeria, Lleida 035347
Museo de la Palabra, Villa Adelina . 000657
Museo de la Parroquia de Gámbita, Gámbita 007504
Museo de la Partitura Historica, Rosario 000526
Museo de la Patagonia Dr. Francisco P. Moreno, Bariloche 000135
Museo de la Pintura Mural y Museo Manuel Gamio, Teotihuacán 028810
Museo de la Piratería, Santiago de Cuba 008159
Museo de La Plata, La Plata 000390
Museo de la Platería, Taxco de Alarcón 028790
Museo de la Pluma, México 028472
Museo de la Policía del Chaco, Resistencia 000505
Museo de la Policía Federal Argentina, Buenos Aires 000188
Museo de la Policía Preventiva de la Ciudad de México, México 028473
Museo de la Provincia de Granma, Bayamo 007878
Museo de la Provincia El Dorado, El Dorado 031509
Museo de la Psicología Experimental Argentina Horacio G. Piñero, Buenos Aires 000189
Museo de la Purísima Concepción, Celaya 028141
Museo de La Quemada, Guadalupe 028295
Museo de la Radiodifusión, Puebla . 028662
Museo de la Real Academia de Bellas Artes de la Purísima Concepción, Valladolid 035997
Museo de la Real Academia de Bellas Artes de San Fernando, Madrid 035408
Museo de la Real Capilla, Arenas de San Pedro 034853
Museo de la Real Colegiata, Roncesvalles 035720
Museo de la Real Plaza de Toros de Sevilla, Sevilla 035866
Museo de la Recoleta, Yanahuara . . 031615
Museo de la Reconquista, Orihuela 035567
Museo de la Reconquista, Tigre . . . 000631
Museo de la Región de Ansenuza Aníbal Montes, Miramar 000446
Museo de la Reincorporación, Tacna 031599
Museo de la Resistencia Indígena, Ixcateopan de Cuauhtémoc 028346
Museo de la Revolución, La Habana 007981
Museo de la Revolución, Nueva Gerona 008078
Museo de la Revolución, Casa Hermanos Aquiles Serdán, Puebla 028663
Museo de la Revolución de San Pedro, San Pedro 028751
Museo de la Rioja, Logroño 035361
Museo de la Sal, Zipaquirá 007647
Museo de la Salle, Dasmariñas . . . 031668
Museo de la Santa Iglesia Catedral, Ávila 036035
Museo de la Secretaria de Hacienda y Credito Publico Antiguo Palacio del Arzobispado, México 028474
Museo de la Selva Juan Forster, Miramar 000447
Museo de la Sep, México 028475
Museo de la Sidra Copa de Oro, San Andrés Cholula 028705
Museo de la Sociedad Amigos de Laguardia, Laguardia 035315
Museo de la Soledad, Oaxaca 028607
Museo de la Solidaridad Salvador Allende, Santiago de Chile 006933
Museo de la Técnica de Euskadi, Barakaldo 034897
Museo de la Tortuga, Ecomuseo de Colola, Aquila 028110
Museo de la Universidad Nacional Hermilio Valdizán, Huánuco 031517
Museo de la Vera Cruz, Caravaca de la Cruz 035052
Museo de la Vida Animal Herpetario, Puebla 028664
Museo de la Vida Rural, L'Espluga de Francolí 035179
Museo de la Villa de Ahome, Ahome 028092
Museo de Laca, Chiapa de Corzo . . 028150
Museo de Lagos de Moreno, Lagos de Moreno 028379
Museo de Las Americas, Denver . . 043412
Museo de Las Américas, San Juan . 032738
Museo de las Artes, Universidad de Guadalajara, Guadalajara 028283
Museo de las Artes Populares Cidap, Cuenca 009193
Museo de las Artes Populares de Jalisco, Guadalajara 028284
Museo de las Atarazanas, Santo Domingo 009161
Museo de las Aves de México, Saltillo 028697
Museo de las Californias, Los Cabos 028395
Museo de las Californias, Tijuana . . 028841
Museo de las Casas Reales, Santo Domingo 009162
Muséo de Las Conceptas, Cuenca . 009194
Museo de las Culturas, Cotacahi . . 009183
Museo de las Culturas, Saltillo 028698
Museo de las Culturas Aborígenes, Cuenca 009195
Museo de las Culturas Afromestizas, Cuajinicuilapa 028198
Museo de las Culturas de la Huasteca Potosina Tamuantzán, Valles 028913
Museo de las Culturas de Oaxaca, Oaxaca 028608
Museo de las Culturas de Occidente, Colima 028168
Museo de las Culturas del Norte, Monte Verde 028558
Museo de las Culturas Prehispánicas, Puerto Vallarta 028679
Museo de las Culturas Prehispánicas de Durango, Durango 028229
Museo de las Encartaciones, Sopuerta 035884
Museo de las Estelas Mayas, Campeche 028130
Museo de las Excavaciones de Torralba, Ambrona 034834
Museo de las Leyendas, Guanajuato 028302
Museo de las Luchas Obreras, Manzanillo 008050
Museo de las Miniaturas Poblanas, Palmar de Bravo 028630
Museo de las Misiones Jesuitas, Loreto 028394
Museo de las Momias, Guanajuato . 028303
Museo de las Muñecas, Píritu 049511
Museo de las Parrandas de Remedios, Remedios 008109
Museo de las Pinturas Rupestres de San Ignacio, Pueblo de San Ignacio . . 028676
Museo de las Reales Atarazanas, Valencia 035979
Museo de las Revoluciones Mariano Jiménez, San Luis Potosí 028732
Museo de las Telecomunicaciones, Madrid 035409
Museo de las Telecomunicationes, México 028476
Museo de las Termas Públicas de Caesaraugusta, Zaragoza 036103
Museo de las Tradiciones Potosinas, San Luis Potosí 028733
Museo de l'Enginyeria de Catalunya, Barcelona 034917
Museo de León, León 035329
Museo de Lluc, Escorca 035176
Museo de los Altos de Chiapas, San Cristóbal de las Casas 028709
Museo de los Andes, Socha 007614
Museo de los Asentamientos, Federación 000345
Museo de los Bomberos, Guayaquil 009208
Museo de los Bomberos, Matanzas 008057
Museo de los Caminos, Astorga . . . 034871
Museo de los Combates contra los Bandidos, Trinidad 008180
Museo de los Combatientes del Morro de Arica, Lima 031557
Museo de los Concilios y de la Cultura Visigoda, Museo del Santa Cruz, Toledo 035921
Museo de los Condestables de Castilla, Medina de Pomar 035484
Museo de los Corporales, Museo Diocesano, Daroca 035141
Museo de los Corrales Viejos de Parque de los Patricios, Buenos Aires 000190
Museo de los Llanos, Guanare 049493
Museo de los Metales, Cuenca 009196
Museo de los Molinos de Gregorio Prieto, Valdepeñas 035967
Museo de los Niños, Bogotá 007428
Museo de los Niños Abasto, Buenos Aires 000191
Museo de los Niños Barrilete, Córdoba 000295
Museo de Los Niños de Caracas, Caracas 049471
Museo de los Orishas, Asociacion Cultural Yoruba de Cuba, La Habana 007982
Museo de los Pioneros, Río Gallegos 000513
Museo de Málaga, Sección de Arqueología, Málaga 035453
Museo de Málaga, Sección de Bellas Artes, Málaga 035454
Museo de Maní y Museo del Convento San Miguel Arcángel, Maní 028398
Museo de Marionetas, Bogotá 007429
Museo de Medicina Legal y Ciencas Forenses, Bogotá 007430
Museo de Medicina Maya, San Cristóbal de las Casas 028710

Museo de Medicina Tradicional y Herbolaria, Cuernavaca 028205
Museo de Medicina Tropical Carlos J. Finlay, La Habana 007983
Museo de Medios de Comunicación, Resistencia 000506
Museo de Menorca, Mahón 035447
Museo de Mercedes, Mercedes . . . 041497
Museo de Metrología, Tres Cantos . 035953
Museo de Mexticacan, Mexticacán . 028546
Museo de Mier y Noriega, Mier y Noriega 028548
Museo de Minerales del Instituto Geofísico, Universidad Javeriana, Bogotá . . . 007431
Museo de Minerales y Fósiles, Zumárraga 036124
Museo de Mineralogía, Universidad Autónoma de Hidalgo, Pachuca . . 028625
Museo de Mineralogía, Universidad de Guanajuato, Guanajuato 028304
Museo de Mineralogía Dr Miguel Romero Sánchez, Tehuacán 028803
Museo de Mineralogía y Geología Dr. Alfredo Stelzner, Córdoba 000296
Museo de Mineralogía y Geología Ing. Luis Silva Ruelas, Universidad Michoacana, Morelia 028581
Museo de Minería de la Compañía Real del Monte, Pachuca 028626
Museo de Minería e Historia de Cosala, Cosalá 028191
Museo de Miniaturas, Huaraz 031520
Museo de Mitos y Leyendas, Tafí del Valle 000626
Museo de Momias de Celaya, Celaya 028142
Museo de Monseñor Ramón Ibarra y González, Puebla 028665
Museo de Motivos Argentinos José Hernández, Buenos Aires 000192
Museo de Murcia, Sección de Arqueología, Murcia 035530
Museo de Murcia, Sección de Bellas Artes, Murcia 035531
Museo de Museos Colsubsidio, Bogotá 007432
Museo de Navajas y Curiosidades del Mundo, Puebla 028666
Museo de Navarra, Pamplona 035632
Museo de Nosa Señora da Antiga, Monforte de Lemos 035508
Museo de Nuestra Raíz Africana, San Juan 032739
Museo de Nuestra Señora del Rosario, Talpa de Allende 028782
Museo de Numismática, Museos del Banco Central de Costa Rica, San José . 007676
Museo de Numismática del Estado de México, Toluca 028875
Museo de Odontología, México . . . 028477
Museo de Oro del Perú y Armas del Mundo, Lima 031558
Museo de Oro Precolombino, Museos del Banco Central de Costa Rica, San José 007677
Museo de Oxolotán, Tacotalpa 028779
Museo de Palencia, Palencia 035595
Museo de Paleontología, Delicias . . 028220
Museo de Paleontología de Guadalajara, Guadalajara 028285
Museo de Paleontología de la Preparatoria, Apaxtla de Castrejón 028108
Museo de Paleontología de Rincón Gallardo, General Cepeda 028263
Museo de Paleontología Eliseo Palacios Aguilera, Tuxtla Gutiérrez 028898
Museo de Paracho, Paracho 028636
Museo de Patología, Buenos Aires . 000193
Museo de Pericos, Culiacán 028214
Museo de Piedra y Artesanía Canaria, Ingenio 035296
Museo de Pintura, Sant Pol de Mar . 035787
Museo de Piria, Piriápolis 041547
Museo de Pontevedra, Pontevedra . 035667
Museo de Prehistoria e Arqueoloxía de Vilalba, Vilalba 036046
Museo de Prehistoria y Paleontología, Orce 035564
Museo de Prehistoria y Servicio de Investigación Prehistórica, Valencia 035980
Museo de Pungarabato, Pungarabato 028682
Museo de Ra Regoles, Cortina d'Ampezzo 023977
Museo de Relojes, Colección de Reloxos, A Coruña 035128
Museo de Reproducciones Artísticas, Bilbao 034986
Museo de Reproducciones de El Greco, Yecla 036092
Museo de Rocas, Yaiza 036090
Museo de Ruiz, Ruiz 028692
Museo de SADAIC Vincente López y Planes, Buenos Aires 000194
Museo de Salamanca, Salamanca . 035742
Museo de San Antolín, Tordesillas . 035933
Museo de San Esteban, Salamanca 035743
Museo de San Esteban Tetelpa, Zacatepec de Hidalgo 028969
Museo de San Isidro, Madrid 035410
Museo de San Jerónimo, Cusco . . . 031500
Museo de San José María de Yermo y Parres, Puebla 028667
Museo de San Juan, San Juan 032740
Museo de San Juan Raya, Zapotitlán Salinas 028976
Museo de San Juan Tlacotenco, San Juan Tlacotenco 028727
Museo de San Lorenzo Tenochtitlán, Texistepec 028838
Museo de San Miguel, Tlaxiaco . . . 028863
Museo de San Pablo, San Pablo Huitzo 028747
Museo de San Pedro, Navolato 028596
Museo de San Pedro, San Pedro Lagunillas 028753
Museo de Santa Clara, Bogotá 007433
Museo de Santa Cruz, Toledo 035922
Museo de Santa Monica, Panay . . . 031752
Museo de Santiago de los Caballeros, Antigua 021572
Museo de Sayula Juan Rulfo, Sayula 028773
Museo de Segóbriga, Museo de Cuenca, Saelices 035734
Museo de Segovia, Segovia 035845
Museo de Semana Santa, Orihuela . 035568
Museo de Semana Santa, Zamora . 036096
Museo de Sitio Arqueologico el Mongote Real Alto, Guayaquil 009209
Museo de Sitio Arqueológico Kuntur Wasi, San Pablo 031592
Museo de Sitio Boca de Potrerillos, Mina 028550
Museo de Sitio Casa de Juárez, Oaxaca 028609
Museo de Sitio Castillo de Teayo, Castillo de Teayo 028139
Museo de Sitio Complejo Arqueológico de Sillustani, Atuncolla 031464
Museo de Sitio de Cacaxtla, Nativitas 028593
Museo de Sitio de Cempoala, Cempoala 028143
Museo de Sitio de Chalcatzingo, Chalcatzingo 028145
Museo de Sitio de Chan Chan, Trujillo 031608
Museo de Sitio de Chichen Itza, Timun 028843
Museo de Sitio de Chinchero, Urubamba 031611
Museo de Sitio de Cholula, San Pedro Cholula 028752
Museo de Sitio de Coatetelco, Coatetelco 028165
Museo de Sitio de Comalcalco, Comalcalco 028179
Museo de Sitio de El Tajín, Papantla 028635
Museo de Sitio de El Zapotal, Ignacio de la Llave 028341
Museo de Sitio de Higueras, Vega de Alatorre 028916
Museo de Sitio de Ingapirca, Azogues 009176
Museo de Sitio de la Pampa Galeras, Quinua 031590
Museo de Sitio de La Venta, Huimanguillo 028337
Museo de Sitio de la Zona Arqueológica de Tzintzuntzan, Tzintzuntzan 028903
Museo de Sitio de Monte Albán, Oaxaca 028610
Museo de Sitio de Narihualá, Catacaos 031483
Museo de Sitio de Ocuilan, Ocuilan 028619
Museo de Sitio de Pachacamac, Lima 031559
Museo de Sitio de Palenque Alberto Ruz Lhuillier, Palenque 028629
Museo de Sitio de Paracas Julio C. Tello, Pisco 031581
Museo de Sitio de Pomona, Tenosique de Pino Suárez 028808
Museo de Sitio de Puruchuco, Lima 031560
Museo de Sitio de Querétaro, Querétaro 028685
Museo de Sitio de San Isidro, Tembladera 031604
Museo de Sitio de San Lorenzo Tenochtitlán, Tenochtitlán 028807
Museo de Sitio de San Miguel Ixtapan, San Miguel Ixtapan 028742
Museo de Sitio de Sipán, Zaña 031617
Museo de Sitio de Tenayuca, Tlalnepantla 028852
Museo de Sitio de Teotihuacán, Teotihuacán 028811
Museo de Sitio de Toniná, Ocosingo 028616
Museo de Sitio de Tres Zapotes, Santiago Tuxtla 028770
Museo de Sitio de Túcume, Campo 031481
Museo de Sitio de Uxmal, Santa Elena 028762
Museo de Sitio de Wari, Wari 031612
Museo de Sitio de Xochicalco, Xochicalco 028949
Museo de Sitio de Xochitecatl, Nativitas 028594
Museo de Sitio Degollado Jalisco, Degollado 028219
Museo de Sitio del Campo de la Alianza, Tacna 031600
Museo de Sitio del Claustro de Sor Juana, México 028478
Museo de Sitio del Rumicucho, San Antonio 009263
Museo de Sitio El Algarrobal, El Algarrobal 031508
Museo de Sitio El Torreoncito, Torreón 028882
Museo de Sitio Huaca El Dragón, La Esperanza 031538
Museo de Sitio Ocotelulco, Totolac . 028889
Museo de Sitio Polyforum Siqueiros, México 028479
Museo de Sitio San Agustín, Juárez 028369
Museo de Sitio Talavera, México . . 028480
Museo de Sitio Tecpan, México . . . 028481
Museo de Sitio Wari, Ayacucho . . . 031466
Museo de Sitio Wari Willca, Huancayo 031514
Museo de Siyasa, Cieza 035091
Museo de Suelos, Universidad Nacional Amazónica, Iquitos 031530
Museo de Susticacán, Susticacán . 028777
Museo de Tabar, Tabar - Urraul Bajo 035887
Museo de Tacuichamona, Culiacán 028215
Museo de Tahdziú, Tahdziú 028780
Museo de Tapalpa, Tapalpa 028786
Museo de Tapices, Oncala 035559
Museo de Tarlac, Tarlac 031800
Museo de Taximaroa, Hidalgo 028321
Museo de Tecnología Aeronáutica y Espacial, Córdoba 000297
Museo de Telecomunicaciones, Buenos Aires 000195
Museo de Telefonía, Delicias 028221
Museo de Tepeticpa, Tepeticpa . . . 028820
Museo de Terra Santa, Santiago de Compostela 035825
Museo de Texcalyacac, Texcalyacac 028836
Museo de Tlahualilo, Tlahualilo de Zaragoza 028849
Museo de Tlalancaleca, San Matías Tlalancaleca 028739
Museo de Tlapa, Tlapa de Comonfort 028855
Museo de Tlayacapan, Tlayacapan . 028865
Museo de Todos los Santos, La Paz 028375
Museo de Totolapan, Totolapan . . . 028890
Museo de Tradiciones Populares de Aguadas, Aguadas 007382
Museo de Trajes Regionales de Colombia, Bogotá 007434
Museo de Transportes, Complejo Museográfico Enrique Udaondo, Luján 000413
Museo de Tudela, Tudela 035957
Museo de Ulía, Montemayor 035518
Museo de Urología, Buenos Aires . . 000196
Museo de Valladolid, Valladolid . . . 035998
Museo de Velardeña, Velardeña . . . 028917
Museo de Ávila, Ávila 036036
Museo de Xiutetelco, Xiutetelco . . . 028948
Museo de Xochitepec, Xochitepec . 028952
Museo de Xolalpancalli, Zacapoaxtla 028958
Museo de Yautepec, Yautepec 028955
Museo de Zamora, Zamora 036097
Museo de Zaragoza, Zaragoza 036104
Museo de Zaragoza, Sección Cerámica, Zaragoza 036105
Museo de Zaragoza, Sección de Etnología, Zaragoza 036106
Museo de Zaragoza, Secciones de Arqueología y Bellas Artes, Zaragoza 036107
Museo de Zoología, Universidad de Córdoba, Córdoba 000298
Museo de Zoología Alfonso L. Herrera, México 028482
Museo de Zoología Juan Ormea, Universidad Nacional de La Libertad, Trujillo 031609
Museo de Zurbarán, Marchena 035471
Museo degli Affreschi G.B. Cavalcaselle, Verona 026288
Museo degli Alpini, Bassano del Grappa 023353
Museo degli Alpini, Savignone 025820
Museo degli Arazzi delle Madrice, Marsala 024623
Museo degli Argenti, Ariano Irpino . 023246
Museo degli Argenti, Museum of Silver, Firenze 024170
Museo degli Argenti Contemporanei, Sartirana Lomellina 025798
Museo degli Arredi Sacri, Santuario di Santa Maria delle Rupi, Castel Sant'Elia 023706
Museo degli Attrezzi Agricoli, Suno . 025969
Museo degli Attrezzi Agricoli Ferretti Florindo, Sefro 025845
Museo degli Ex Voto, Viterbo 026351
Museo degli Indios dell'Amazonia, Assisi 023280
Museo degli Insetti, Bisegna 023403
Museo degli Scavi, Piuro 025282
Museo degli Strumenti della Riproduzione del Suono, Roma 025502
Museo degli Strumenti Musica Populare Sardi, Tadasuni 025980
Museo degli Strumenti Musicali, Istituto Musicale Arcangelo Corelli, Cesena 023814
Museo degli Strumenti Musicali Meccanici, Savio 025821
Museo degli Strumenti Musicali Meccanici, Sestola 025875
Museo degli Studenti e della Goliardia, Bologna 023429
Museo degli Usi e Costumi della Gente di Romagna, Santarcangelo di Romagna 025773
Museo degli Usi e Costumi della Gente Trentina, San Michele all'Adige . . 025713
Museo degli Usi e Costumi della Valle di Goima, Zoldo Alto 026375
Museo degli Usi e Costumi delle Genti dell'Etna, Giarre 024339

Museo dei Bambini Explora, Roma . 025503
Museo dei Benedettini, Pontida . . . 025317
Museo dei Bozzetti, Pietrasanta . . . 025230
Museo dei Bronzi Dorati, Pergola . . 025159
Museo dei Burattini, Mantova 024602
Museo dei Burattini e delle Figure, Cervia 023808
Museo dei Cappuccini, Bassano del Grappa 023354
Museo dei Combattenti, Soncino . . 025916
Museo dei Costumi della Partita a Scacchi, Marostica 024620
Museo dei Costumi e Tradizioni locali, Gurro 024395
Museo dei Cuchi, Roana 025450
Museo dei Damaschi, Lorsica 024538
Museo dei Ferri Battuti e Galleria d'Arte Moderna Carlo Rizzarda, Feltre . . 024089
Museo dei Ferri Chirurgici, Pistoia . 025276
Museo dei Ferri Taglienti, Scarperia 025836
Museo dei Fossili, Meride 037327
Museo dei Fossili, Vestenanova . . . 026297
Museo dei Fossili, Zogno 026372
Museo dei Fossili Don Giuseppe Mattiacci, Serra San Quirico 025861
Museo dei Fossili e dei Minerali, Smerillo 025907
Museo dei Fossili e di Storia Naturale, Montefalcone Appennino 024835
Museo dei Fossili e Minerali del Monte Nerone, Apecchio 023219
Museo dei Fossili e Mostra dei Funghi, Pioraco 025256
Museo dei Grandi Fiumi, Rovigo . . . 025614
Museo dei Legni Processionali, Petriolo 025202
Museo dei Magli, Ponte Nossa 025309
Museo dei Minerali e della Miniera, Oltre il Colle 024994
Museo dei Minerali Elbani, Rio Marina 025437
Museo dei Navigli, Milano 024709
Museo dei Parati Sacri, Montemarano 024853
Museo dei Reperti Bellici e Storici della Guerra 1915-1918, Capovalle . . . 023646
Museo dei Reperti della Civiltà Contadina, Alberobello 023151
Museo dei Soldati del Montello, Nervesa della Battaglia 024932
Museo dei Soldatino e della Figurina Storica, Calenzano 023582
Museo dei Tasso e della Storia Postale, Camerata Cornello 023598
Museo dei Trasporti, Ranco 025388
Museo dei Trombini di Lessinia, San Bortolo 025658
Museo dei Vigili Urbani, Cosenza . . 023982
Museo del Agua y del Suelo, Viedma 000656
Museo del Aire, Madrid 035411
Museo del Alcázar, Toledo 035923
Museo del Almudín, Xàtiva 036087
Museo del Ambiente Histórico Cubano, Santiago de Cuba 008160
Museo del Area Fundacional, Mendoza 000434
Museo del Ateneo de Bellas Artes, Sucre 003924
Museo del Automóvil, Buenos Aires 000197
Museo del Automóvil, México 028483
Museo del Automóvil, Montevideo . 041512
Museo del Automóvil, Complejo Museográfico Enrique Udaondo, Luján 000414
Museo del Automóvil Club Argentino, Buenos Aires 000198
Museo del Automóvil de Santa Teresita, Santa Teresita 000614
Museo del Automóvil Puebla, Puebla 028668
Museo del Automovilismo Juan Manuel Fangio, Balcarce 000129
Museo del Azulejo, Montevideo . . . 041513
Museo del Azulejo, Onda 035560
Museo del Azulejo Francés, Madonado 041493
Museo del Banco Central, Cuenca . 009197
Museo del Banco Central, Loja 009222
Museo del Banco Central, Riobamba 009259
Museo del Banco Central de Manta, Manta 009225
Museo del Banco Provincia de Córdoba, Córdoba 000299
Museo del Bandolero, Ronda 035721
Museo del Baroffio e del Sacro Monte, Metamusa, Gallarate 024268
El Museo del Barrio, New York 046369
Museo del Barro, Asunción 031446
Museo del Battistero, Albenga 023148
Museo del Beisbol, Caracas 049472
Museo del Bigallo, Firenze 024171
Museo del Bijou, Casalmaggiore . . 023683
Museo del Biroccio Marchigiano e Museo Beltrami, Filottrano 024129
Museo del Blat y de la Pagesia, Cervera 035082
Museo del Borgo, Amato 023190
Museo del Bosco, Sovicille 025930
Museo del Botijo, Villena 036071
Museo del Bracciante Artigiano, Berra 023383
Museo del Brigante, Sonnino 025920
Museo del Café, San Cristóbal de las Casas 028711
Museo del Calzado, Elda 035171
Museo del Calzado El Borceguí, México 028484
Museo del Calzado y Ciencias Naturales, Arnedo 034859
Museo del Camino Real de Hecelchakan, Hecelchakán 028314
Museo del Camoscio, Opi 024997
Museo del Campesino, Xochitepec . 028953
Museo del Camposanto Vecchio e dell'Opera, Pisa 025266
Museo del Canal Interoceanico de Panamá, Panamá City 031432
Museo del Cañamo, Callosa de Segura 035035
Museo del Canasto Cafetero y Muestra Arqueológica de la Cultura Quimbaya, Filandia 007499
Museo del Capoluogo, Castelbellino 023707
Museo del Cappello, Alessandria . . 023163
Museo del Cappello, Montappone . . 024813
Museo del Capriolo, Bisegna 023404
Museo del Capriolo, San Donato Val di Comino 025673
Museo del Carajo, Cali 007470
Museo del Carbón, Lenguazaque . . 007525
Museo del Carmen, México 028485
Museo del Carmen, Villa de Leyva . 007639
Museo del Carmen de Maipú, Santiago de Chile 006934
Museo del Carnaval, Santiago de Cuba 008161
Museo del Carro y Aperos de Labranza, Tomelloso 035930
Museo del Carruaje El Tacu, Villa General Belgrano 000667
Museo del Cartel José P.H. Hernández, Río Grande 032724
Museo del Casin, Bagni di Lucca . . 023319
Museo del Castagno, Pescaglia . . . 025182
Museo del Castello, Fumone 024260
Museo del Castello Colleoni Porto, Thiene 026020
Museo del Castello di Porciano, Stia 025949
Museo del Castello di San Giusto e Lapidario Tergestino, Trieste 026140
Museo del Castello di Sarre, Sarre . 025793
Museo del Castello e della Città, Piombino 025253
Museo del Castello Scaligero, Torri del Benaco 026092
Museo del Castillo de Peralada, Peralada 035650
Museo del Cattedrale, Ferrara 024105
Museo del Cavallo Giocattolo, Grandate 024363
Museo del Cenacolo di Andrea del Sarto a San Salvi, Firenze 024172
Museo del Cenedese, Vittorio Veneto 026355
Museo del Centro Caprense Ignazio Cerio, Capri 023650
Museo del Centro Cultural de Villasarracino, Villasarracino 036067
Museo del Centro Cultural Joaquín Arcadio Pagaza, Valle de Bravo 028909
Museo del Centro Cultural La Cantera, Jonacatepec 028363
Museo del Centro Cultural Patio de los Ángeles, Guadalajara 028286
Museo del Centro Cultural Sor Juana Inés de la Cruz, Tepetlixpa 028821
Museo del Centro Cultural Universitario Quinta Gameros, Universidad Autónoma de Chihuahua, Chihuahua 028158
Museo del Centro Cultural Zacualpan, Comala 028176
Museo del Centro de Estudios de la Revolución Mexicana, Jiquilpan . . 028362
Museo del Centro de Historia de Tuluá, Tuluá 007626
Museo del Centro de Investigación Arqueológica de Ancón, Lima . . . 031561
Museo del Centro Histórico, San Juan del Río 028723
Museo del Centro Studi, Albissola Marina 023158
Museo del Ceppo, Pistoia 025276
Museo del Cervo Sardo, Sinnai 025899
Museo del Chiodo, Forno di Zoldo . 024238
Museo del Chocolate, Astorga 034872
Museo del Cielo, Villa Carlos Paz . . 000660
Museo del Cine, Durango 028230
Museo del Cine Pablo C. Ducrós Hicken, Buenos Aires 000199
Museo del Cine y la Fotografía, Puebla 028669
Museo del Cinema, Milano 024710
Museo del Cioccolato, Norma 024955
Museo del Círculo de Bellas Artes, Pozoblanco 035672
Museo del Círculo de Estudios Ferroviarios del Uruguay, Montevideo 041514
Museo del Cobre, Bogotá 007435
Museo del Colegio Costa y Llobera, Port de Pollença 035671
Museo del Colegio Médico de Santiago, Santiago de Compostela 035826
Museo del Colegio Nacional Amauta, Chupaca 031491
Museo del Colegio Nacional Justo José de Urquiza, Paraná 000465
Museo del Colegio Nacional Pedro Vicente Maldonado, Riobamba 009260
Museo del Colegio Padres Franciscanos, Ontinyent 035563
Museo del Colegio Stella Maris, Atacames 009175
Museo del Collezionista d'Arte, Fondazione Goffried Matthaes, Milano 024706
Museo del Coltello Sardo, Arbus . . . 023228
Museo del Combattente, Modena . . 024758
Museo del Conservatorio die Napoli, Napoli 024899
Museo del Convento de La Merced, Mantas 031573
Museo del Convento de los Descalzos, Lima 031562
Museo del Convento de San Francisco, Lima 031563
Museo del Convento de Santa Catalina, Cusco 031501
Museo del Convento de Santa Clara, Carrión de Los Condes 035058
Museo del Convento de Santa Õrsulas, Salamanca 035744
Museo del Convento de Santo Domingo, Cusco 031502
Museo del Convento di San Francesco, Susa 025971
Museo del Corallo, Ravello 025394
Museo del Corallo, Torre del Greco . 026087
Museo del Costume Arbereshe, Frascineto 024250
Museo del Costume e della Tradizione Nostra Gente, Guardiagrele 024388
Museo del Costume Farnesiano, Gradoli 024362
Museo del Costume R. Piraino, Palermo 025084
Museo del Costume Tradizionale, Grosio 024371
Museo del Cuale, Puerto Vallarta . . 028680
Museo del Danza, La Habana 007984
Museo del Deporte, Cienfuegos . . . 007909
Museo del Deporte, Holguín 008026
Museo del Deporte, Pabellón de Arteaga 028623
Museo del Deporte Pierre de Coubertin, La Falda 000378
Museo del Desierto, Saltillo 028699
Museo del Disco, Zipacón 007646
Museo del Doctor Olavide, Madrid . 035412
Museo del Duomo, Città di Castello 023894
Museo del Duomo, Fidenza 024117
Museo del Duomo, Guardiagrele . . 024389
Museo del Duomo, Massa 024631
Museo del Duomo, Milano 024711
Museo del Duomo, Ravello 025395
Museo del Duomo, Udine 026163
Museo del Duomo, Valenza 026190
Museo del Ejército, Madrid 035413
Museo del Ejército y Fuerza Aérea Bethlemitas, México 028486
Museo del Ejército y Fuerza Aérea Mexicanos Cuartel Colorado, Guadalajara 028287
Museo del Ejidatario, Guasave 028310
Museo del Emigrante Canario, Teguise 035900
Museo del Estado, Morelia 028582
Museo del Estado de Mérida, Mérida 049507
Museo del Este, Monte Caseros . . . 000450
Museo del Ex Convento de Culhuacán, México 028487
Museo del Falegname T. Sana-Onlus, Almenno San Bartolomeo 023176
Museo del Ferro e della Ghisa, Ex Officine Meccaniche Ilva, Follonica 024215
Museo del Ferrocarril, Aguascalientes 028089
Museo del Ferrocarril, Guadalajara . 028288
Museo del Ferrocarril, Monterrey . . 028565
Museo del Ferrocarril, Torreón 028883
Museo del Ferrocarril de Madrid, Madrid 035414
Museo del Festero, Villena 036072
Museo del Fin del Mundo, Ushuaia . 000648
Museo del Fiore, Acquapendente . . 023116
Museo del Folklore e dei Poeti Romaneschi, Roma 025535
Museo del Folklore e delle Tradizioni Popolari, Caltanissetta 023591
Museo del Foro Caesaraugusta, Ayuntamiento de Zaragoza, Zaragoza 036108
Museo del Foro d'Augusto, Roma . . 025504
Museo del Fossile del Monte Baldo, Brentonico 023514
Museo del Foto Gabinetto die Fisica, Università Urbino, Urbino 026174
Museo del Frer, Chiaverano 023853
Museo del Fuerte de San Felipe, Bacalar 028120
Museo del Fuerte de San Juan de Ulúa, Veracruz 028921
Museo del Fungo e di Scienze Naturali, Boves 023506
Museo del Gaucho y de la Moneda, Montevideo 041515
Museo del General Toribio Ortega, Coyame 028194
Museo del Giocattolo, Palermo 025085
Museo del Giocattolo, Sezze 025880
Museo del Gioco del Pallone a Bracciale e Tamburello, Santarcangelo di Romagna 025774
Museo del Grabado Español Contemporáneo, Marbella 035468
Museo del Grano, Cerignola 023797
Museo del Hombre, Tegucigalpa . . . 021614

Museo del Hombre Dominicano, Santo Domingo . . . 009163
Museo del Hombre en el Universo, Sopó . . . 007619
Museo del Hombre y su Entorno, Caleta Olivia . . . 000256
Museo del Humor, San Antonio de los Baños . . . 008117
Museo del Indio, Los Toldos . . . 000410
Museo del Indio de Puerto Rico, San Juan . . . 032741
Museo del Indio y del Gaucho, Tacuarembó . . . 041556
Museo del Instituto Americano del Arte, Cusco . . . 031503
Museo del Instituto de Investigaciones Antropológicas, México . . . 028488
Museo del Instituto Nacional de Cultura, Arequipa . . . 031459
Museo del Int. Presepio in Miniatura Guido Colitti, Campobasso . . . 023619
Museo del Istmo, La Línea de la Concepción . . . 035336
Museo del Jade, San José . . . 007678
Museo del Jazz G. Dagnino, Genova 024305
Museo del Juguete Tradicional Mexicano, San Francisco de los Romo . . . 028715
Museo del Lago Gutiérrez, Bariloche . . . 000136
Museo del las Comunicaciones de Mar del Plata, Mar del Plata . . . 000423
Museo del Lavoro, Castelmagno . . . 023730
Museo del Lavoro, Follonica . . . 024216
Museo del Lavoro Contadino, Brisighella . . . 023532
Museo del Lavoro Contadino, Campobello di Mazara . . . 023621
Museo del Lavoro e della Civiltà Rurale, Palaia . . . 025073
Museo del Lavoro e della Tradizioni Popolari della Versilia Storica, Seravezza . 025858
Museo del Lavoro Povero e della Civiltà Contadina, Livraga . . . 024513
Museo del Lazio Meridionale, Palazzo di Bonifacio VIII, Anagni . . . 023195
Museo del Legno, Cantù . . . 023636
Museo del Libro, Madrid . . . 035415
Museo del Libro, San Javier . . . 000565
Museo del Libro Antiguo, Antigua . . 021573
Museo del Limarí, Ovalle . . . 006922
Museo del Lino, Pescarolo . . . 025188
Museo del Litoral Boliviano, La Paz 003912
Museo del Lupo Appenninico, Centro di Visita del Parco d'Abruzzo, Civitella Alfedena . . . 023913
Museo del Maglio, Breganze . . . 023511
Museo del Malcantone, Curio . . . 037036
Museo del Mantecado, Estepa . . . 035184
Museo del Mar, Cádiz . . . 035022
Museo del Mar, La Barra . . . 041491
Museo del Mar, Mazatlán . . . 028409
Museo del Mar, San Pedro del Pinatar . . . 035770
Museo del Mar, Santa Pola . . . 035808
Museo del Mar, Universidad de Oriente, Boca de Río . . . 049446
Museo del Mar El Rodadero, Santa Marta . . . 007608
Museo del Mar Mundo Marino, Santa Marta . . . 007609
Museo del Mare, Furci Siculo . . . 024261
Museo del Mare, Ischia Ponte . . . 024417
Museo del Mare, Nard . . . 024926
Museo del Mare, Pesaro . . . 025176
Museo del Mare, Piombino . . . 025254
Museo del Mare, Pizzo . . . 025286
Museo del Mare, Pollica . . . 025299
Museo del Mare e della Costa M. Zei, Sabaudia . . . 025623
Museo del Ámbar de Chiapas, San Cristóbal de las Casas . . . 028712
Museo del Médico, Santa Fé . . . 000601
Museo del Medio Ambiente, Valencia . . . 035988
Museo del Medioevo e del Rinascimento, Sorano . . . 025925
Museo del Melonero, Villaconejos . 036058
Museo del Menù, Bolgheri . . . 023413
Museo del Merletto, Offida . . . 024987
Museo del Merletto, Venezia . . . 026245
Museo del Milagroso, Buga . . . 007462
Museo del Modellismo Storico, Voghiera . . . 026363
Museo del Molino de Papel, México 028489
Museo del Monasterio de San Joaquín y Santa Ana, Valladolid . . . 035999
Museo del Monasterio de Santa Isabel, Valladolid . . . 036000
Museo del Monasterio de Santa María de la Vid, La Vid . . . 036031
Museo del Monasterio de Tulebras, Tulebras . . . 035961
Museo del Monastero della Beata Filippa Mareri, Petrella Salto . . . 025201
Museo del Mondo Contadino, Savoca . . . 025822
Museo del Motociclo, Rimini . . . 025431
Museo del Motociclo Moto Guzzi, Mondello del Lario . . . 024790
Museo del Mundo, Buenos Aires . . 000200
Museo del Niño, Albacete . . . 034793
Museo del Niño, San Juan . . . 032742
Museo del Niño, Santa Ana del Valle . . . 028757
Museo del Niño Globo mi Ciudad Pequeña, Guadalajara . . . 028289
Museo del Niño Papalote, México . . 028490
Museo del Observatorio Astronómico Nacional, Madrid . . . 035416
Museo del Opera Omnia R. Musa e Pinacoteca Parmigiani, Bedonia . . 023360
Museo del Oppidum de Iruña, Iruña de Oca . . . 035298
Museo del Origen, Santiago Ixcuintla . . . 028767
Museo del Oro, Ipiales . . . 007522
Museo del Oro, Banco de la República, Bogotá . . . 007436
Museo del Oro Calima, Cali . . . 007471
Museo del Oro Nariño, Pasto . . . 007567
Museo del Oro Quimbaya, Armenia 007393
Museo del Oro Quimbaya, Manizales . . . 007530
Museo del Oro y Metales Preciosos, La Paz . . . 003913
Museo del Paesaggio, Castelnuovo Berardenga . . . 023734
Museo del Paesaggio, Museo Storico e Artistico del Verbano, Pallanza . . . 025099
Museo del Paesaggio e Museo Storico Artistico, Verbania Pallanza . . . 026274
Museo del Paesaggio Storico dell'Appennino, Firenzuola . . . 024203
Museo del Palacio de Bellas Artes, México . . . 028491
Museo del Palacio Nacional, Guatemala . . . 021579
Museo del Palazzo del Podestà e Gipsoteca Libero Andreotti, Pescia . . . 025194
Museo del Pane, Sant'Angelo Lodigiano . . . 025767
Museo del Papiro, Siracusa . . . 025903
Museo del Parco Nazionale Gran Paradiso, Noasca . . . 024943
Museo del Parque Abel Santamaría Cuadrado, Santiago de Cuba . . . 008162
Museo del Parque Nacional Los Alerces, Villa Futalaufquen . . . 000666
Museo del Pasado Cuyano, Mendoza . . . 000435
Museo del Patriarca, Valencia . . . 035981
Museo del Patrimonio Histórico, Aguas Argentinas, Buenos Aires . . . 000201
Museo del Patrimonio Industriale, Bologna . . . 023430
Museo del Patrimonium, Sutri . . . 025976
Museo del Periodismo Bonaerense, Capilla del Señor . . . 000260
Museo del Periodismo y las Artes Gráficas, Guadalajara . . . 028290
Museo del Pianoforte Antico, Ala . . 023140
Museo del Piccolo Regio, Torino . . . 026055
Museo del Pizzo al Tombolo, Rapallo . . . 025391
Museo del Po, Museo Civiltà Contadina e Artigina, Monticelli d'Ongina . . . 024870
Museo del Po e Young Museum, Revere . . . 025422
Museo del Policía, Monterrey . . . 028566
Museo del Presepe, Modena . . . 024759
Museo del Presepio, Dalmine . . . 024024
Museo del Presepio Tipologico Internazionale, Roma . . . 025505
Museo del Primer Supremo Tribunal de Justicia de la Nación, Ario de Rosales . . . 028111
Museo del Profumo, Milano . . . 024712
Museo del Pueblo, Guanajuato . . . 028305
Museo del Pueblo, Pirané . . . 000476
Museo del Pueblo de Asturias, Gijón 035222
Museo del Pueblo-Hospital, Quiroga 028687
Museo del Pueblo Maya Dzibilchaltún, Chablekal . . . 028144
Museo del Puerto de Ingeniero White, Ingeniero White . . . 000364
Museo del Real Seminario de Bergara, Bergara . . . 034976
Museo del Recuerdo de la Academia Mexicana de la Lengua, México . . 028492
Museo del Reggimento Giovani Fascisti, Ponti sul Mincio . . . 025316
Museo del Regio Esercito Italiano, Orta . . . 025013
Museo del Retablo, Burgos . . . 035006
Museo del Retrato Hablado, México 028493
Museo del Río Magdalena, Honda . 007516
Museo del Risorgimento, Brescia . . 023519
Museo del Risorgimento, Castelfidardo . . . 023710
Museo del Risorgimento, Genova . . 024306
Museo del Risorgimento, Imola . . . 024404
Museo del Risorgimento, Lucca . . . 024546
Museo del Risorgimento, Massa Marittima . . . 024640
Museo del Risorgimento, Santa Maria Capua Vetere . . . 025752
Museo del Risorgimento, Solferino . 025912
Museo del Risorgimento, Villafranca 026333
Museo del Risorgimento, Musei di Palazzo Farnese, Piacenza . . . 025208
Museo del Risorgimento Aurelio Saffi, Forlì . . . 024225
Museo del Risorgimento Duca d'Aosta, Museo delle Ceroplastiche e quartiere feudale, Sanluri . . . 025739
Museo del Risorgimento e della Resistenza, Ferrara . . . 024106
Museo del Risorgimento e della Resistenza, Vicenza . . . 026310
Museo del Risorgimento e Raccolte Storiche, Milano . . . 024713
Museo del Risorgimento F. Tanara, Langhirano . . . 024454
Museo del Risorgimento L. Musini, Fidenza . . . 024118
Museo del Risorgimento Vittorio Emanuele Orlando, Palermo . . . 025086
Museo del Risorgmento e Resistenza R. Giusti, Mantova . . . 024603
Museo del Ron, Santiago de Cuba . 008163
Museo del Ron Havana Club, La Habana . . . 007985
Museo del Rubinetto e della sua Tecnologia, San Maurizio D'Opaglio . . . 025710
Museo del Sacrario, Asiago . . . 023273
Museo del Sacro dell'Alta Val Trebbia, Ex Convento degli Agostiniani, Montebruno . . . 024823
Museo del Sale, Paceco . . . 025044
Museo del Samán, Guacarí . . . 007508
Museo del Sannio, Benevento . . . 023368
Museo del Santuario de la Virgen de Agua Santa, Baños . . . 009180
Museo del Santuario del Santissima Crocifisso, Borgo a Buggiano . . . 023485
Museo del Santuario di Crea, Serralunga di Crea . . . 025862
Museo del Santuario di Montevergine, Mercogliano . . . 024677
Museo del Santuario di Santa Maria Santissima della Fontenuova, Monsummano Terme . . . 024802
Museo del Seminario Conciliar de Nueva Caceres, Naga . . . 031749
Museo del Seminario Diocesano, Gabinete Ciencias Naturales, Burgos . . . 035007
Museo del Seminario Vescovile, Rovigo . . . 025615
Museo del Sidecar, Cingoli . . . 023882
Museo del Siglo XIX, Bogotá . . . 007437
Museo del Sottosuolo P. Parenzan, Instituto Sperimentale di Biologia, Latiano 024472
Museo del Sovrano Ordine Militare dei Cavalieri di Malta, Roma . . . 025506
Museo del Sud-Ovest Americano, Cuveglio . . . 024023
Museo del Tabaco Herminio, Caguas . . . 032710
Museo del Tamburo Parlante, ex Convento di San Francesco, Montone . . . 024874
Museo del Tango Roberto Firpo, Salto . . . 000543
Museo del Tasso, Roma . . . 025507
Museo del Teatro, Almagro . . . 034824
Museo del Teatro, Cesena . . . 023815
Museo del Teatro, Faenza . . . 024069
Museo del Teatro, Teatro Nuovo, Spoleto . . . 025940
Museo del Teatro Argentina, Roma . 025508
Museo del Teatro Colón, Buenos Aires . . . 000202
Museo del Teatro dell'Aquila, Fermo 024094
Museo del Teatro G. Borgatti, Cento 023789
Museo del Teatro Municipale, Piacenza . . . 025209
Museo del Teatro Romagnolo, Forlì . 024226
Museo del Teatro y la Música de Córdoba Cristobal de Aguilar, Córdoba . . . 000300
Museo del Teclado, Caracas . . . 049473
Museo del Tejido Sedero Valenciano, Art Major de la Seda, Valencia . . . 035982
Museo del Templo Mayor, México . . 028494
Museo del Tequila, Tequila . . . 028833
Museo del Territorio, Foggia . . . 024209
Museo del Territorio, Longiano . . . 024527
Museo del Territorio, Riccione . . . 025425
Museo del Territorio, San Severino Marche . . . 025730
Museo del Territorio, Museo Civico, Finale Emilia . . . 024132
Museo del Territorio Biellese, Biella 023395
Museo del Territorio dell'Alta Valle dell'Aulella, Casola in Lunigiana . 023692
Museo del Territorio F.R. Fazio, Roccapalumba . . . 025458
Museo del Tesoro, Lodi . . . 024519
Museo del Tesoro del Duomo, Berceto . . . 023372
Museo del Tesoro del Duomo, Monza . . . 024876
Museo del Tesoro del Duomo, Rieti 025428
Museo del Tesoro del Duomo, Veroli 026281
Museo del Tesoro della Cattedrale, Anagni . . . 023196
Museo del Tesoro della Cattedrale, Aosta . . . 023217
Museo del Tesoro della Cattedrale, Savona . . . 025826
Museo del Tesoro della Cattedrale di San Lorenzo, Genova . . . 024307
Museo del Tesoro Santuario della Misericordia, Savona . . . 025827
Museo del Tessile, Convento di Santa Maria, Chieri . . . 023854
Museo del Tessile e della Tradizione Industriale, Busto Arsizio . . . 023555
Museo del Tessuto, Prato . . . 025362
Museo del Traje, La Rioja . . . 000396
Museo del Traje en Tabasco, Villahermosa . . . 028937
Museo del Transporte, Garza García 028260
Museo del Transporte Guillermo José Schael, Caracas . . . 049474
Museo del Transporte Terrestre, Santiago de Cuba . . . 008164
Museo del Trattore Agricolo, Senago . . . 025849
Museo del Tricolore, Reggio Emilia . 025415

Museo del Turismo dell'Alta Pusteria, Villabassa 026331
Museo del Vajont, Longarone 024525
Museo del Valle de Tehuacán, Tehuacán 028804
Museo del Valle de Xico, Valle de Chalco 028910
Museo del Vetro, Venezia 026246
Museo del Vicino Oriente, Facoltà di Scienze Umanistiche, Roma 025509
Museo del Vidrio, Monterrey 028567
Museo del Vidrio, San Ildefonso . . . 035756
Museo del Villaggio, Fraz Gudon, Chiusa 023869
Museo del Vino, Caldaro 023578
Museo del Vino, Villafamés 036061
Museo del Vino, Fondazione Lungarotti, Torgiano 026042
Museo del Vino, Museo de Vilafranca-Museu del Vi, Vilafranca del Penedès 036042
Museo del Vino e della Donna, Ciliverghe 023878
Museo del Vino Juan Carcelén, Jumilla 035310
Museo del Virrey Ezpeleta, Guaduas 007510
Museo Deleddiano, Nuoro 024979
Museo della Accademia Ligustica di Belle Arti, Biblioteca di Storia dell'Arte, Genova 024308
Museo della Antica Civiltà Locale, Bronte 023533
Museo della Badia Benedettina, Cava dei Tirreni 023774
Museo della Badia di San Salvatore, Vaiano 026183
Museo della Barca Lariana, Pianello del Lario 025215
Museo della Basilica, Gandino 024273
Museo della Basilica, Grotte di Castro 024381
Museo della Basilica, Santa Maria degli Angeli 025753
Museo della Basilica di San Marco, Venezia 026247
Museo della Basilica di San Michele Arcangelo, Monte Sant'Angelo . . . 024820
Museo della Basilica di San Nicola, Bari 023337
Museo della Basilica di San Pancrazio, Roma 025510
Museo della Basilica di San Venanzio, Camerino 023600
Museo della Basilica di Santa Maria del Colle, Pescocostanzo 025198
Museo della Basilica di Santa Maria della Passione, Milano 024714
Museo della Basilica Patriarcale Santa Maria degli Angeli, Assisi 023281
Museo della Battaglia, San Martino della Battaglia 025705
Museo della Battaglia, Vittorio Veneto 026356
Museo della Battaglia del Senio, Alfonsine 023169
Museo della Battaglia di Marengo, Alessandria 023164
Museo della Battaglia di Marengo, Spinetta Marengo 025937
Museo della Battaglia di San Martino, Desenzano del Garda 024028
Museo della Biblioteca Maldotti, Guastalla 024390
Museo della Bilancia, Campogalliano 023623
Museo della Bonifica, Argenta 023242
Museo della Bonifica, San Donà di Piave 025672
Museo della Calzatura, Sant'Elpidio a Mare 025777
Museo della Calzatura d'Autore di Rossimoda, Strá 025954
Museo della Calzatura P. Bertolini, Vigevano 026323
Museo della Canape e della Vita Contadina, Bentivoglio 023370
Museo della Canzone e della Riproduzione Sonora, Vallecrosia 026197
Museo della Carrozza, Macerata . . 024564
Museo della Carta, Amalfi 023186
Museo della Carta e della Filigrana, Fabriano 024062
Museo della Carta e della Filigrana, Pioraco 025257
Museo della Cartolina S. Nuvoli, Isera 024419
Museo della Casa Carnica, Prato Carnico 025367
Museo della Casa Carsica, Monrupino 024798
Museo della Casa Contadina, Bolognetta 023463
Museo della Casa Contadina, Corciano 023962
Museo della Casa Fiorentina Antica, Firenze 024173
Museo della Casa Trevigiana, Treviso 026121
Museo della Casina delle Civette, Roma 025511
Museo della Cattedrale, Bari 023338
Museo della Cattedrale, Barletta . . 023347
Museo della Cattedrale, Chiusi Città 023872
Museo della Cattedrale, Fossano . . 024242
Museo della Cattedrale, Monopoli . 024795
Museo della Centuriazione, Cesena 023816
Museo della Ceramica, Ascoli Piceno 023267
Museo della Ceramica, Bassano del Grappa 023355
Museo della Ceramica, Castellamonte 023719
Museo della Ceramica, Fiorano Modenese 024136
Museo della Ceramica, Patti 025135
Museo della Ceramica, Salerno . . . 025635
Museo della Ceramica, Vietri 026321
Museo della Ceramica A. Ribezzi, Latiano 024473
Museo della Ceramica del Castello, Salerno 025636
Museo della Ceramica di Castelli, Palazzo Comunale, Castelli 023728
Museo della Certosa, Certosa di Pavia 023804
Museo della Certosa, Serra San Bruno 025860
Museo della Chiesa di San Francesco, Mercatello sul Metauro 024674
Museo della Chiesa di San Lorenzo, Portovenere 025343
Museo della Città, Ancona 023198
Museo della Città, Aquino 023226
Museo della Città, Udine 026164
Museo della Città, Musei Comunali, Rimini 025432
Museo della Città e del Territorio, Monsummano Terme 024803
Museo della Civiltà Contadina, Cortaccia 023975
Museo della Civiltà Contadina, Acri 023122
Museo della Civiltà Contadina, Aliano 023172
Museo della Civiltà Contadina, Amandola 023188
Museo della Civiltà Contadina, Andrate 023202
Museo della Civiltà Contadina, Ateleta 023292
Museo della Civiltà Contadina, Barolo 023349
Museo della Civiltà Contadina, Bastiglia 023357
Museo della Civiltà Contadina, Borghi 023482
Museo della Civiltà Contadina, Borgo San Lorenzo 023489
Museo della Civiltà Contadina, Calvisano 023594
Museo della Civiltà Contadina, Castelfranco Emilia 023715
Museo della Civiltà Contadina, Cavenago d'Adda 023778
Museo della Civiltà Contadina, Cervia 023809
Museo della Civiltà Contadina, Copparo 023960
Museo della Civiltà Contadina, Curtatone 024019
Museo della Civiltà Contadina, Fabriano 024063
Museo della Civiltà Contadina, Figline Valdarno 024126
Museo della Civiltà Contadina, Filottrano 024130
Museo della Civiltà Contadina, Guardia Piemontese 024385
Museo della Civiltà Contadina, Loret Aprutino 024530
Museo della Civiltà Contadina, Maierato 024579
Museo della Civiltà Contadina, Mairano 024582
Museo della Civiltà Contadina, Mombaroccio 024780
Museo della Civiltà Contadina, Montechiaro d'Acqui 024830
Museo della Civiltà Contadina, Montefiore dell'Aso 024840
Museo della Civiltà Contadina, Novellara 024973
Museo della Civiltà Contadina, Perdifumo 025156
Museo della Civiltà Contadina, Roscigno 025597
Museo della Civiltà Contadina, San Nicola La Strada 025718
Museo della Civiltà Contadina, Sappada 025786
Museo della Civiltà Contadina, Sassocorvaro 025807
Museo della Civiltà Contadina, Serrastretta 025865
Museo della Civiltà Contadina, Sesto Fiorentino 025872
Museo della Civiltà Contadina, Spinetoli 025936
Museo della Civiltà Contadina, Teggiano 025995
Museo della Civiltà Contadina, Todi 026029
Museo della Civiltà Contadina, Torre Pallavicina 026089
Museo della Civiltà Contadina, Verdello 026277
Museo della Civiltà Contadina, Zibello 026371
Museo della Civiltà Contadina, Concento di San Francesco, Moio della Civitella 024773
Museo della Civiltà Contadina, Istituto Agrario A. Motti, Castelnovo no' Monti 023733
Museo della Civiltà Contadina, Pastorale, Artigianale e della Miniera, Seui . 025878
Museo della Civiltà Contadina, Villa Smeraldi, Bentivoglio 023371
Museo della Civiltà Contadina A. Marsiano, Niscemi 024939
Museo della Civiltà Contadina D. Bianco, Sammichele di Bari 025647
Museo della Civiltà Contadina del Cilento, Montecorice 024833
Museo della Civiltà Contadina del Mendrisiotto, Stabio 037590
Museo della Civiltà Contadina dell'Alto Monferrato e della Bassa Langa, Castagnole delle Lanze 023700
Museo della Civiltà Contadina e Artigianale d'Enza, Montecchio Emilia 024828
Museo della Civiltà Contadina e della Canapa G. Romagnoli, Argelato . . 023240
Museo della Civiltà Contadina e Tradizioni Popolari, Tuglie 026158
Museo della Civiltà Contadina ed Artigiana, Monterosso Calabro 024860
Museo della Civiltà Contadina ed Artigiana, Cripta Chiesa San Filippo, Ripatransone 025441
Museo della Civiltà Contadina Friulana, Farra d'Isonzo 024082
Museo della Civiltà Contadina in Val Vibrata, Controguerra 023956
Museo della Civiltà Contadina L. Rubat, Piscina 025271
Museo della Civiltà Contadina Masseria Lupoli, Crispiano 024001
Museo della Civiltà Contadina nell'Area, Montefalcone di Val Fortore 024836
Museo della Civiltà Contadina Valle dell'Aniene, Roviano 025613
Museo della Civiltà del Lavoro, Campiglia Marittima 023614
Museo della Civiltà Locale, Buseto Palizzolo 023549
Museo della Civiltà Locale, Raccolta d'Arte di San Francesco, Trevi 026115
Museo della Civiltà Messapica, Poggiardo 025290
Museo della Civiltà Montanara, Sestola 025876
Museo della Civiltà Romana, Roma 025512
Museo della Civiltà Rupestre, Zungri 026378
Museo della Civiltà Rurale, Altamura 023178
Museo della Civiltà Rurale del Vicentino, Malo 024588
Museo della Civiltà Salinara, Cervia 023810
Museo della Civiltà Solandra, Malé . 024585
Museo della Civiltà Valligiana, Fortezza di Bardi, Bardi 023330
Museo della Civitella, Chieti 023862
Museo della Collegiata, Chianciano Terme 023839
Museo della Collegiata, Chiostro della Chiesa dell'Assunta, Castell'Arquato 023722
Museo della Collegiata, Stiftsmuseum Innichen, San Candido 025659
Museo della Collegiata di Santa Maria a Mare, Maiori 024581
Museo della Collegiata di Sant'Andrea, Empoli 024046
Museo della Collezione Gambarotta, Piozzo 025258
Museo della Comunità Ebraica, Venezia 026248
Museo della Comunità Ebraica Carlo e Vera Wagner, Trieste 026141
Museo della Confraternita della Misericordia, Anghiari 023207
Museo della Congregazione Mechitarista dei Padri Armeni, Venezia 026249
Museo della Corte, Porto Viro 025333
Museo della Croce Rossa Italiana, Campomorone 023624
Museo della Cultura Alpina del Comelico, Comelico Superiore 023940
Museo della Cultura Arbereshe, San Paolo Albanese 025720
Museo della Cultura Marinara, Tortoreto Lido 026096
Museo della Cultura Mezzadrile, Scuola Elementare, Morro d'Alba 024883
Museo della Cultura Popolare, Grosseto 024374
Museo della Cultura Popolare e Contadina, Carrega Ligure 023677
Museo della Donna, Angrogna 023209
Museo della Donna E. Ortner, Merano 024670
Museo della Esposizione Permanente, Milano 024715
Museo della Farmacia Picciola, Trieste 026142
Museo della Figurina, Modena 024760
Museo della Figurina di Gesso e dell'Emigrazione, Coreglia Antelminelli 023965
Museo della Filigrana, Campo Ligure 023616
Museo della Flora, Fauna e Mineralogia, Auronzo di Cadore 023303
Museo della Fondazione Giovanni Scaramangà di Altomonte, Trieste 026143
Museo della Fondazione Horne, Palazzo Corsi, Firenze 024174
Museo della Fondazione Mandralisca, Cefalù 023782
Museo della Fondazione Querini Stampalia, Venezia 026250
Museo della Fondazione Ugo da Como, Lonato 024524

Museo della Fotografia Storica e Contemporanea, Fondazione Italiana per la Fotografia, Torino 026056
Museo della Frutticoltura Adofo Bonvicini, Massa Lombarda 024635
Museo della Gente dell'Appennino Pistoiese, Cutigliano 024020
Museo della Gente Senza Storia, Altavilla Irpina 023179
Museo della Geotermia, Pomarance 025301
Museo della Grancia, Serre di Rapolano 025868
Museo della Guerra, Castel del Rio . 023703
Museo della Guerra, Il Vittoriale degli Italiani, Gardone Riviera 024275
Museo della Guerra Adamellina, Spiazzo 025934
Museo della Guerra Bianca, Temù . 026001
Museo della Guerra Bianca, Vermiglio 026278
Museo della Linea Gotica, Montefiore Conca 024838
Museo della Liquirizia, Rossano . . . 025604
Museo della Liuteria, Arpino 023256
Museo della Macchina da Scrivere P. Mitterhofer, Schreibmaschinenmuseum P. Mitterhofer, Parcines 025109
Museo della Magnifica Comunità di Cadore, Pieve di Cadore 025232
Museo della Mail Art, Montecarotto 024825
Museo della Marineria dell'Alto e Medio Adriatico, Cesenatico 023827
Museo della Marionetta, Torino . . . 026057
Museo della Miniera, Cesena 023817
Museo della Miniera, Massa Marittima 024641
Museo della Miniera, Prata di Pordenone 025355
Museo della Miniera, Schilpario . . . 025840
Museo della Miniera Aurifera della Guia, Macugnaga 024571
Museo della Miniera di Zolfo di Cabernardi, Sassoferrato 025812
Museo della Misericordia, Collezione dell'Arciconfraternita della Misericordia, San Miniato 025716
Museo della Montagna, Macugnaga 024572
Museo della Nave Romana, Comacchio 023937
Museo della Nostra Terra, Pieve Torina 025240
Museo della Paglia e dell'Intreccio D. Michalacci, Signa 025897
Museo della Pesca, Caslano 036999
Museo della Pesca, Magione 024576
Museo della Pesca e delle Civiltà Marinara, Museo delle Anfore - Antiquarium Truentinum, San Benedetto del Tronto 025650
Museo della Pietà Popolare, Molfetta 024775
Museo della Pietra Serena, Firenzuola 024204
Museo della Pievania, Corciano . . . 023963
Museo della Pieve, Sant'Ambrogio di Valpolicella 025764
Museo della Pieve di San Pietro, Prato 025363
Museo della Pieve di Staggia, Poggibonsi 025292
Museo della Pipa, Gavirate 024282
Museo della Plastica, Pont Canavese 025305
Museo della Preistoria, Celano 023786
Museo della Preistoria della Tuscia, Valentano 026189
Museo della Propositura di San Pietro, Montecatini Val di Nievole 024827
Museo della Regina, Cattolica 023773
Museo della Repubblica Partigiana, Montefiorino 024842
Museo della Resistenza e del '900, Imola 024405
Museo della Resistenza e della Civiltà Contadina, Pietrabruna 025226
Museo della Resistenza e del Folclore Valsabbino, Pertica Bassa 025161
Museo della Rocca, Cesena 023818
Museo della Rocca, Dozza 024039
Museo della Sanità e dell'Assistenza, Bologna 023431
Museo della Santa, Bologna 023432
Museo della SAT, Trento 026108
Museo della Scuola, Bolzano 023470
Museo della Scuola, Pramollo 025353
Museo della Scuola Grande dei Carmini, Venezia 026251
Museo della Seta Abegg, Garlate . . 024278
Museo della Sindone, Torino 026058
Museo della Società di Esecutori di Pie Disposizioni, Siena 025889
Museo della Società di Studi Patri, Gallarate 024269
Museo della Società Geografica Italiana, Roma 025513
Museo della Società Storia del Novese, Novi Ligure 024974
Museo della Specola, Bologna 023433
Museo della Stampa, Jesi 024431
Museo della Stampa, Soncino 025917
Museo della Tarsia, Rolo 025463
Museo della Tecnica e del Lavoro MV Agusta, Samarate 025645
Museo della Tecnica e del Lavoro MV Augusta, Trequanda 026114
Museo della Tecnologia Contadina, Santu Lussurgiu 025783
Museo della Terza Armata, Padova . 025054
Museo della Tipografia, Città di Castello 023895
Museo della Tonnara, Milazzo 024738
Museo della Tonnara, Stintino 025953
Museo della Torre, Albino 023153
Museo della Val Codera, Novate Mezzola 024970
Museo della Val d'Agri, Sant'Arcangelo 025772
Museo della Val Gardena, Union di Ladins, Ortisei 025015
Museo della Val Venosta, Sluderno . 025906
Museo della Valchiavenna, Chiavenna 023851
Museo della Valle, Cavargna 023777
Museo della Valle Cannobina, Gurro 024395
Museo della Valle Intelvi, Lanzo d'Intelvi 024457
Museo della Via Ostiense, Roma . . 025514
Museo della Vicaria di San Lorenzo, Zogno 026373
Museo della Villa Bettoni, Bogliaco . 023410
Museo della Vita, Castelmagno . . . 023731
Museo della Vita Contadina, Castelnuovo Don Bosco 023737
Museo della Vita Contadina in Romagnolo, Russi 025619
Museo della Vita e del Lavoro della Maremma Settentrionale, Cecina e Marina 023781
Museo della Vita e delle Tradizioni Popolari Sarde, Nuoro 024980
Museo della Vite e del Vino, Carmignano 023666
Museo della Vite e del Vino, Rufina . 025618
Museo della Viticoltura, Prarostino . 025354
Museo della Xilografia, Carpi 023670
Museo della Zampogna, Mostra Pernamente di Cornamuse Italiane e Stranicre, Scapoli 025834
Museo della Zisa, Palermo 025087
Museo dell'Abazia di San Colombano, Bobbio 023409
Museo dell'Abbazia, Casamari-Veroli 023686
Museo dell'Abbazia, Castiglione a Casauria 023747
Museo dell'Abbazia, ex Refettorio Monastico, San Benedetto Po . . . 025655
Museo dell'Abbazia di Farfa, Fara Sabina 024080
Museo dell'Abbazia di San Nilo, Grottaferrata 024377
Museo dell'Abbazia di Santa Maria in Sylvis, Sesto al Reghena 025870
Museo dell'Accademia d'Arte C. Scalabrino, Montecatini Terme 024826
Museo dell'Accademia di Belle Arti, Perugia 025169
Museo dell'Accademia di Sant'Anselmo, Musée de l'Académie Saint-Anselme, Aosta 023218
Museo dell'Accademia Etrusca, Cortona 023979
Museo dell'Accademia Ligustica di Belle Arti, Genova 024309
Museo dell'Accademia Nazionale Virgiliana, Mantova 024604
Museo dell'Aeronautica G. Caproni, Trento 026109
Museo dell'Agricoltura e del Mondo Rurale, San Martino in Rio 025707
Museo dell'Agro Falisco, Civita Castellana 023908
Museo dell'Agro Veientano, Formello 024235
Museo dell'Alta Val Venosta, Curon Venosta 024018
Museo dell'Alto Medioevo, Roma . . 025515
Museo dell'Apicoltura, Renon 025421
Museo dell'Apicultura, Gruppo la Cappelletta, Abbiategrasso 023110
Museo dell'Arciconfraternita, Tolentino 026034
Museo dell'Arciconfraternita dei Genovesi, Cagliari 023564
Museo dell'Ardesia, Cicagna 023876
Museo dell'Arredo Contemporaneo, Russi 025620
Museo dell'Arte Classica, Sezione di Archeologia, Roma 025516
Museo dell'Arte Contadina, Marciana 024613
Museo dell'Arte del Cappello, Ghiffa 024336
Museo dell'Arte del Vino, Staffolo . . 025944
Museo dell'Arte della Seta, Catanzaro 023768
Museo dell'Arte della Tornitura del Legno, Pettenasco 025203
Museo dell'Arte e della Tecnologia Confetteria, Sulmona 025963
Museo dell'Arte Mineraria, Iglesias . 024398
Museo dell'Arte Sacra, Aldino 023162
Museo dell'Arte Serica e Laterizia, Malo 024589
Museo dell'Arte Votiva, Cesena . . . 023819
Museo dell'Artigianato Tessile e della Seta, Reggio Calabria 025407
Museo dell'Attore Napoletano, Napoli 024900
Museo dell'Automobile, San Martino in Rio 025708
Museo dell'Automobile Carlo Biscaretti di Ruffia, Torino 026059
Museo dell'Automobile e della Tecnica, Farra d'Isonzo 024083
Museo dell'Automobile L. Bonfanti, Romano d'Ezzelino 025591
Museo dell'Aviazione, Rimini 025433
Museo dell'Avifauna Appenninica, Sarnano 025789
Museo delle Anime dei Defunti, Roma 025517
Museo delle Armi, Terni 026011
Museo delle Armi Antiche, Martinsicuro 024625
Museo delle Armi Antiche, Offagna . 024984
Museo delle Armi Antiche, San Marino 034112
Museo delle Armi Antiche e Fortezza Medievale, Acquaviva Picena . . . 023119
Museo delle Armi, Armature e Strumenti di Tortura, Ischia Ponte 024418
Museo delle Armi e del Martello, Sarnano 025790
Museo delle Armi e delle Uniformi, Urbisaglia 026179
Museo delle Armi Moderne, San Marino 034113
Museo delle Arti e delle Tradizioni, Treviso 026122
Museo delle Arti e delle Tradizioni di Puglia, Latiano 024474
Museo delle Arti e delle Tradizioni Popolari, Canepina 023628
Museo delle Arti e delle Tradizioni Popolari, Sassoferrato 025813
Museo delle Arti e Tradizioni Popolari, Civitanova Marche 023910
Museo delle Arti e Tradizioni Popolari, Correggio 023973
Museo delle Bilance e dei Pesi, Monterchi 024858
Museo delle Carrozze, Catanzaro . . 023769
Museo delle Carrozze, Firenze 024175
Museo delle Carrozze, Napoli 024901
Museo delle Carrozze, Trani 026098
Museo delle Carrozze dell'Ottocento, Verona 026289
Museo delle Centuriazioni, Granze . 024364
Museo delle Ceramiche, Forlì 024227
Museo delle Ceramiche, Tolentino . 026035
Museo delle Ceramiche Abruzzesi, Loreto Aprutino 024535
Museo delle Cere, Roma 025518
Museo delle Cere Anatomiche Luigi Cattaneo, Università di Bologna, Dep. Anatomia Umana e Fisiopatologia, Bologna 023434
Museo delle Cere - Strumenti di Tortura, San Marino 034114
Museo delle Civiltà Contadina, San Pellegrino in Alpe 025721
Museo delle Contadinerie, Costigliole d'Asti 023988
Museo delle Cripte, Santa Maria degli Angeli, Poggiardo 025291
Museo delle Culture del Mondo, Museum of the Cultures of the World, Genova 024310
Museo delle Culture Extraeuropee, Castagnola 037002
Museo delle Culture Extraeuropee Dinz Rialto, Rimini 025434
Museo delle Curiosità, San Marino . 034115
Museo delle Due Guerre Mondiali, Loro Piceno 024537
Museo delle Erbe, Teggiano 025996
Museo delle Erbe, Veroli 026282
Museo delle Ferrovie, Monserrato . 024801
Museo delle Ferrovie in Sardegna, Cagliari 023565
Museo delle Genti d'Abruzzo, Pescara 025185
Museo delle Genti di Montagna, Palazzuolo sul Senio 025079
Museo delle Grigne, Esino Lario . . . 024058
Museo delle Guerre, Grassobbio . . . 024365
Museo delle Icone, Palazzo Pretorio, Peccioli 025149
Museo delle Marionette, Campomorone 023625
Museo delle Miniere, Valle Aurina . 026195
Museo delle Mummie, Chiesa di San Stefano, Ferentillo 024091
Museo delle Mura, Roma 025519
Museo delle Musiche dei Popoli, Museum of Folk Music, Genova 024311
Museo delle Navi e Antiche Carte Geografiche, Università Bologna, Bologna 023435
Museo delle Navi Romane, Fiumicino 024205
Museo delle Navi Romane, Nemi . . 024930
Museo delle Origini, Roma 025520
Museo delle Palafitte, Molina di Ledro 024778
Museo delle Pentole nella Storia, Rozzano 025616
Museo delle Porcellane, Firenze . . . 024176
Museo delle Rimembranze, Cosenza 023983
Museo delle Scienze della Terra e del Lavoro Contadino, Piandimeleto . 025213
Museo delle Sinopie, Opera della Primaziale Pisana, Pisa 025267
Museo delle Statue Menhir, Laconi . 024444
Museo delle Statue - Stele Lunigianesi, Pontremoli 025319
Museo delle Tavolette di Biccherna, Siena 025890
Museo delle Terme, Bagni di Lucca 023320
Museo delle Terre Marchigiane, San Lorenzo in Campo 025701

Museo delle Tradizioni Agroalimentari della Sardegna, Siddi 025882
Museo delle Tradizioni ed Arti Contadine, Picciano 025221
Museo delle Tradizioni Locali, Zoppè di Cadore 026376
Museo delle Tradizioni Popolari, Città di Castello 023896
Museo delle Tradizioni Popolari, Offida 024988
Museo delle Tradizioni Popolari, San Vito di Cadore 025736
Museo delle Trame Mediterranee, Gibellina 024341
Museo delle Truppe Alpine Mario Balocco, Biella 023396
Museo delle Valli, Comacchio 023938
Museo delle Valli d'Argenta, Argenta 023243
Museo delle Valli Valdesi, Torre Pellice 026091
Museo dell'Emigrante Casa Giannini, Favale di Malvaro 024085
Museo dell'Emigrazione G.B. Scalabrini, Francavilla Angitola 024247
Museo dell'Energia Elettrica, Brescia 023520
Museo dell'Enoteca Regionale Piemontese, Grinzane Cavour 024369
Museo dell'Homo Salvadego, Cosio Valtellino 023986
Museo dell'Illustrazione, Ferrara . . 024107
Museo dell'Immagine, Cesena 023820
Museo dell'Informazione, Senigallia 025851
Museo dell'Ingegno e della Tecnologia Preindustriale, Colorno 023935
Museo dell'Intreccio Mediterraneo, Castelsardo 023741
Museo dell'Istituto di Anatomia Patologica, Padova 025055
Museo dell'Istituto di Patologia del Libro, Roma 025521
Museo dell'IstitutoCentral di Patologia, Roma 025522
Museo dello Sbarco, Anzio 023215
Museo dello Sbarco Alleato, Nettuno 024934
Museo dello Scalpellino Povese, Pove del Grappa 025347
Museo dello Scarpone e della Scarpa Sportiva, Montebelluna 024821
Museo dello Sfilato Siciliano, Chiaramonte Gulfi 023841
Museo dello Spazzacamino, Santa Maria Maggiore 025754
Museo dello Studio, Bologna 023436
Museo dell'Occhiale, Pieve di Cadore 025233
Museo dell'Olio, Cisano 023888
Museo dell'Olio in Sabina, Castelnuovo di Farfa 023736
Museo dell'Olivo, Imperia 024411
Museo dell'Olivo e dell'Olio, Torgiano 026043
Museo dell'Ombrello e del Parasole, Gignese 024343
Museo dell'Opera, Borgo a Buggiano 023486
Museo dell'Opera del Duomo, Orvieto 025021
Museo dell'Opera del Duomo, Perugia 025170
Museo dell'Opera del Duomo, Prato 025364
Museo dell'Opera del Santuario, Basilica di San Nicola, Tolentino 026036
Museo dell'Opera di Santa Croce, Firenze 024177
Museo dell'Opera di Santa Maria del Fiore, Firenze 024178
Museo dell'Opera di Santa Niccolao, Fraz Buggiano Castello, Buggiano 023543
Museo dell'Opera Metropolitana, Siena 025891
Museo dell'Opificio delle Pietre Dure, Firenze 024179
Museo dell'Orologio da Torre G.B. Bergallo, Tovo San Giacomo 026097
Museo dell'Orso, Villavallelonga . . . 026339
Museo dell'Osservatorio, Monte Porzio Catone 024814
Museo dell'Osservatorio Astronomico di Capodimonte, Napoli 024902
Museo dell'Uomo, Serrapetrona . . . 025864
Museo dell'Uomo, Susegana 025973
Museo dell'Uomo e dell'Ambiente, Terra del Sole 026014
Museo dell'Utensileria, Lanzo Torinese 024458
Museo Demantropologico, Sez. di Arte Orafa, Cervaro 023806
Museo Demoantropologico, Pastena 025131
Museo Demologico dell'Economia, del Lavoro e della Storia Sociale Silana, San Giovanni in Fiore 025687
Museo Départemental A. Demard, Le-Haut-du-Them-Château-Lambert 012504
Museo Depero, Rovereto 025609
Museo des Orígenes, La Habana . . 007986
Museo di Anatomia, Facoltà di Medicina Veterinaria,, Camerino 023601
Museo di Anatomia Comparata, Bologna 023437
Museo di Anatomia Comparata Battista Grassi, Università di Roma, La Sapienza, Roma 025523
Museo di Anatomia Patologica, Roma 025524
Museo di Anatomia Patologica C. Taruffi, Bologna 023438
Museo di Anatomia Patologica Veterinaria, Ozzano dell'Emilia 025041
Museo di Anatomia Umana, Torino . 026060
Museo di Anatomia Umana, Università Napoli, Napoli 024903
Museo di Anatomia Umana Normale, Istituto di Anatomia Umana, Parma 025121
Museo di Anatomia Umana Normale, Università Bologna, Bologna 023439
Museo di Anatomia Veterinaria, Napoli 024904
Museo di Antichita, Collezioni Archeologiche, Torino 026061
Museo di Antichità Etrusche e Italiche, Roma 025525
Museo di Antonio da Sangallo il Giovane, Montefiascone 024837
Museo di Antropologia, Università Bologna, Bologna 023440
Museo di Antropologia, Università di Napoli, Napoli 024905
Museo di Antropologia Criminale, Torino 026062
Museo di Antropologia ed Etnografia, Padova 025056
Museo di Antropologia ed Etnografia, Torino 026063
Museo di Antropologia ed Etnologia, Firenze 024180
Museo di Antropologia G. Sergi, Università Roma, Roma 025526
Museo di Apicoltura Guido Fregonese, Piavon di Oderze 025216
Museo di Archeologia, Pavia 025140
Museo di Archeologia Sacra e Profana, Roma 025527
Museo di Archeologia Urbana e dei Commerc Antichi, Lanciano 024452
Museo di Architettura, Casa di Biagio Rossetti, Ferrara 024108
Museo di Architettura Militare, Bologna 023441
Museo di Arte Cinese ed Etnografico, Centro Internazionale Arte, Cultura & Società, Parma 025122
Museo di Arte Contadina, Montegallo 024846
Museo di Arte Contemporanea, Stia 025950
Museo di Arte Contemporanea e del Novecento, Monsummano Terme . 024804
Museo di Arte e Giacimenti Minerari, Facoltà di Ingegneria, Latina 024476
Museo di Arte e Storia delle Miniere, Massa Marittima 024642
Museo di Arte e Tradizione Contadina, Olevano di Lomellina 024993
Museo di Arte Medioevale e Moderna, Palazzo Bruno Ciocchi, Arezzo . . . 023237
Museo di Arte Moderna e Contemporanea di Trento e Rovereto, Rovereto 025610
Museo di Arte Religiosa, Oleggio . . 024992
Museo di Arte Sacra, Agnone 023127
Museo di Arte Sacra, Bientina 023398
Museo di Arte Sacra, Castrovillari . . 023758
Museo di Arte Sacra, Longiano 024528
Museo di Arte Sacra, Sabbioneta . . 025624
Museo di Arte Sacra, Saracena . . . 025787
Museo di Arte Sacra, Suvereto 025978
Museo di Arte Sacra, Vibo Valentia . 026304
Museo di Arte Sacra del Castello, Genga 024291
Museo di Arte Sacra Diocesano, Ripatransone 025442
Museo di Arte Sacra San Giuseppe, Rogliano 025462
Museo di Arti Decorative della Fondazione Pietro Accorsi, Torino 026064
Museo di Auto e Moto d'Epoca, Vigolzone 026327
Museo di Bevagna, Bevagna 023389
Museo di Biologia Marina, Porto Cesareo 025329
Museo di Biologia Marina, Instituto Talassografico, Taranto 025989
Museo di Biologia Marina, Università Bologna, Fano 024079
Museo di Blenio, Lottigna 037279
Museo di Botanica, Museo di Storia Naturale, Firenze 024181
Museo di Capodimonte, Palazzo Reale di Capodimonte, Napoli 024906
Museo di Casa Vasari, Arezzo 023238
Museo di Castelgrande, Historical Museum, Bellinzona 036916
Museo di Castelvecchio, Verona . . . 026290
Museo di Chimica, Roma 025528
Museo di Cimeli Storico Militari, Chiaramonte Gulfi 023842
Museo di Civiltà Contadina, Castelnuovo Calcea 023735
Museo di Civiltà Preclassiche della Murgia Meridionale, Ostuni 025038
Museo di Collodi e Pinocchio, Pescia 025195
Museo di Criminologia Medievale, San Gimignano 025681
Museo di Criminologico, Roma 025529
Museo di Cultura Contadina, Oriolo 025007
Museo di Cultura Contadina dell'Alta Val Trebbia, Convento degli Agostiniani, Montebruno 024824
Museo di Cultura Popolare, Egna . . 024043
Museo di Dipinti Sacri Ponte dei Greci, Venezia 026252
Museo di Ecologia e Storia Naturale, Marano sul Panaro 024611
Museo di Etnografico e Antropologia Giovanni Podenzana, La Spezia . . 024441
Museo di Etnomedicina, Collezione A. Scarpa, Piazzola sul Brenta 025220
Museo di Etnomedicina A. Scarpa, Università Genova, Genova 024312
Museo di Etnopreistoria, Napoli . . . 024907
Museo di Fisica, Bologna 023442
Museo di Fisica-Dipartimento di Scienze Fisiche, Napoli 024908
Museo di Fossili, Ronca 025593
Museo di Geologia, Camerino 023602
Museo di Geologia, Napoli 024909
Museo di Geologia, Università Roma, Roma 025530
Museo di Geologia e Paleontologia, Firenze 024182
Museo di Geologia e Paleontologia, Pavia 025141
Museo di Geologia e Paleontologia, Torino 026065
Museo di Geologia e Paleontologia, Università Padova, Padova 025057
Museo di Informatica e Storia del Calcolo, Pennabilli 025151
Museo di Leventina, Giornico 037146
Museo di Merceologia, Roma 025531
Museo di Milano, Palazzo Morando, Milano 024716
Museo di Minerali e Fossili, Montefiore Conca 024839
Museo di Mineralogia, Massa Marittima 024643
Museo di Mineralogia, Palermo . . . 025088
Museo di Mineralogia, Università Roma, Roma 025532
Museo di Mineralogia, di Petrologia e Geologia, Università Modena, Modena 024761
Museo di Mineralogia e Paleontologia, Finale Emilia 024133
Museo di Mineralogia e Paleontologia, Saint Vincent 025629
Museo di Mineralogia e Petrografia, Pavia 025142
Museo di Mineralogia e Petrografia, Università Parma, Parma 025123
Museo di Mineralogia e Petrografia L. Bombicci, Università Bologna, Bologna 023443
Museo di Mineralogia e Petrologia, Università Padova, Padova 025058
Museo di Mineralogia L. De Prunner, Università Cagliari, Cagliari 023566
Museo di Muggia e del Territorio, Muggia 024886
Museo di Nostra Signora di Bonaria, Cagliari 023567
Museo di Palazzo Altieri, Oriolo Romano 025008
Museo di Palazzo d'Arco, Mantova . 024605
Museo di Palazzo De Vio, Gaeta . . . 024262
Museo di Palazzo della Penna, Perugia 025171
Museo di Palazzo Ducale, Mantova 024606
Museo di Palazzo Fortuny, Venezia . 026253
Museo di Palazzo Gamilli, Nocera Umbra 024946
Museo di Palazzo Mirto, Palermo . . 025089
Museo di Palazzo Mocenigo, Centro Studi di Storia del Tessuto e del Costume, Venezia 026254
Museo di Palazzo Pepoli Campogrande, Bologna 023444
Museo di Palazzo Piccolomini, Pienza 025224
Museo di Palazzo Pretorio, Certaldo 023803
Museo di Palazzo Reale, Napoli . . . 024910
Museo di Palazzo Reale Genova, Genova 024313
Museo di Palazzo Strozzi, Firenze . . 024183
Museo di Palazzo Vecchio, Firenze . 024184
Museo di Paleobotanica ed Etnobotanica dell'Orto Botanico, Napoli 024911
Museo di Paleontologia, Milano . . . 024717
Museo di Paleontologia, Modena . . 024762
Museo di Paleontologia, Napoli . . . 024912
Museo di Paleontologia, Roma 025533
Museo di Paleontologia dell'Accademia Federiciana, Catania 023764
Museo di Paleontologia e di Mineralogia, Valdagno 026188
Museo di Paleontologia e Mineralogia, Campomorone 023626
Museo di Paleontologia e Paletnologia, Maglie 024578
Museo di Paleontologia e Speleologia E.A. Martel, Carbonia 023661
Museo di Paleontologia G. Buriani, San Benedetto del Tronto 025651
Museo di Paletnologia, Polignano a Mare 025296
Museo di Pantelleria, Pantelleria . . 025106
Museo di Peppone e Don Camillo, Brescello 023516
Museo di Pittura Murale, Prato 025365
Museo di Prali e della Val Germanasca, Prali 025351
Museo di Preistoria e del Mare, Trapani 026100
Museo di Preistoria e Protostoria della Valle del Fiume Fiora, Manciano 024592
Museo di Preistorico e Paleontologico, Sant'Anna d'Alfaedo 025770
Museo di Rievocazione Storica, Mondavio 024788

Museo di Rocca Fregoso, Sant'Agata Feltria 025763
Museo di Rodoretto, Prali 025352
Museo di Roma, Roma 025534
Museo di Roma in Trastevere, Roma 025535
Museo di San Domenico, Bologna . 023445
Museo di San Francesco, Aversa . . 023307
Museo di San Francesco, Montella . 024848
Museo di San Giuseppe, Bologna . . 023446
Museo di San Marco, Firenze 024185
Museo di San Mercuriale, Forlì 024228
Museo di San Michele, Sagrado . . . 025626
Museo di San Petronio, Presso Basilica San Petronio, Bologna 023447
Museo di San Pietro, Assisi 023282
Museo di Santa Cecilia, San Lazzaro di Savena 025695
Museo di Santa Chiara, Camerino . 023603
Museo di Santa Maria degli Angioli, Lugano 037289
Museo di Santa Maria delle Grazie, San Giovanni Valdarno 025692
Museo di Santa Maria di Castello, Genova 024314
Museo di Santa Restituta, Lacco Ameno 024443
Museo di Sant'Agostino, Genova . . 024315
Museo di Sant'Antonino, Piacenza . 025210
Museo di Santo Stefano, Bologna . . 023448
Museo di Scienza dela Terra, San Gemini 025676
Museo di Scienza della Terra, Università Bari, Bari 023339
Museo di Scienze Archeologiche e d'Arte, Padova 025059
Museo di Scienze della Terra U. Baroli, Crodo 024003
Museo di Scienze Naturale e Umane, L'Aquila 024460
Museo di Scienze Naturali, Belvi . . 023366
Museo di Scienze Naturali, Bolzano 023471
Museo di Scienze Naturali, Brescia 023521
Museo di Scienze Naturali, Cesena . 023821
Museo di Scienze Naturali, Città della Pieve 023890
Museo di Scienze Naturali, Malnate 024586
Museo di Scienze Naturali, Rosignano Marittimo 025602
Museo di Scienze Naturali, Musei Universitari, Pavia 025143
Museo di Scienze Naturali, Università Camerino, Camerino 023604
Museo di Scienze Naturali del Collegio, Lodi 024520
Museo di Scienze Naturali Don Bosco, Alassio 023142
Museo di Scienze Naturali L. Paolucci, Offagna 024985
Museo di Scienze Naturali Tommaso Salvadori, Fermo 024095
Museo di Sculture Iperspaziali, Bomarzo 023473
Museo di Speleologia, Borgo Grotta Gigante 023487
Museo di Speleologia e Carsismo A. Parolini, Valstagna 026202
Museo di Speleologia Vincenzo Rivera, L'Aquila 024461
Museo di Stato, San Marino 034116
Museo di Storia Contemporanea, Milano 024718
Museo di Storia, d'Arte e d'Antichità Don Florindo Piolo, Serravalle Sesia . . 025867
Museo di Storia della Fisica, Padova 025060
Museo di Storia della Fotografia Fratelli Alinari, Firenze 024186
Museo di Storia della Medicina, Roma 025536
Museo di Storia dell'Agricoltura, Cesena 023822
Museo di Storia dell'Agricoltura, Urbania 026170
Museo di Storia dell'Agricoltura e della Pastorizia, Morano Calabro 024879
Museo di Storia delle Mezzadria, Senigallia 025852
Museo di Storia e Arte, Musei Provinciali di Gorizia, Gorizia 024352
Museo di Storia e Civiltà, Medesano 024657
Museo di Storia e Cultura Contadina, Genova 024316
Museo di Storia e Cultura della Val del Biois, Vallada Agordina 026194
Museo di Storia Locale, Velturno . . 026224
Museo di Storia Naturale, Cremona 023997
Museo di Storia Naturale, Follonica 024217
Museo di Storia Naturale, Macerata 024565
Museo di Storia Naturale, Merate . . 024673
Museo di Storia Naturale, Perugia . 025172
Museo di Storia Naturale, Piacenza 025211
Museo di Storia Naturale, Saint Pierre 121728
Museo di Storia Naturale, Senna Lodigiana 025855
Museo di Storia Naturale, Stroncone 025960
Museo di Storia Naturale, Sulmona 025964
Museo di Storia Naturale, Dipartimento per lo studio del Territorio e le sue Risorse, Genova 024317
Museo di Storia Naturale, Invertebrati, Parma 025124
Museo di Storia Naturale, Vertebrati, Parma 025125
Museo di Storia Naturale A. Orsini, Ascoli Piceno 023268
Museo di Storia Naturale A. Stoppani, Venegono Inferiore 026227
Museo di Storia Naturale Aquilegia, Assemini 023276
Museo di Storia Naturale del Cilento, Laureana Cilento 024479
Museo di Storia Naturale della Lunigiana, Aulla 023302
Museo di Storia Naturale della Maremma, Grosseto 024375
Museo di Storia Naturale dell'Accademia dei Fisocritici, Siena 025892
Museo di Storia Naturale Don Bosco, Torino 026066
Museo di Storia Naturale e del Territorio, Calci 023576
Museo di Storia Naturale e dell'Uomo, Carrara 023674
Museo di Storia Naturale Faraggiana-Ferrandi, Novara 024963
Museo di Storia Naturale S. Ferrari, Bedonia 023361
Museo di Storia Naturale - Sez Mineralogia, Firenze 024187
Museo di Storia Naturale - Sez Zoologica La Specola, Università Firenze, Firenze 024188
Museo di Storia Naturali e Archeologia, Montebelluna 024822
Museo di Storia Quarnese, Quarna Sotto 025375
Museo di Strumenti del Conservatorio Statale di Musica Giuseppe Verdi, Torino 026067
Museo di Torcello, Venezia 026255
Museo di Tradizioni Popolari e del Costume d'Epoca, San Pietro Avellana 025724
Museo di Val Verzasca, Sonogno . . 037581
Museo di Vallemaggia, Giumaglio . . 037147
Museo di Valmaggia, Cevio 037004
Museo di Villa Beatice d'Este, Cinto Euganeo 023886
Museo di Villa Cagnola, Gazzada . . 024284
Museo di Villa Carlotta, Tremezzo . . 026105
Museo di Villa Faraggiana, Albissola Marina 023159
Museo di Vita Artigiana e Contadina, Scarperia 025837
Museo di Vita Cappuccina, Convento di Santa Caterina di Portoria, Genova 024318
Museo di Vita Quotidiana e Lavoro in Villa, Orgiano 025001
Museo di Zoologia, Bari 023340
Museo di Zoologia, Modena 024763
Museo di Zoologia, Napoli 024913
Museo di Zoologia, Università Bologna, Bologna 023449
Museo di Zoologia, Università Roma, Roma 025537
Museo di Zoologia e Mineralogia, Siddi 025883
Museo di Zoologia Pietro Doderlein, Università Palermo, Palermo 025090
Museo di Zoologico, Università Catania, Catania 023765
Museo di Zoologico e di Anatomia, Università Torino, Torino 026068
Museo Diacesano, Enna 024050
Museo Didáctico Antonini, Nasca . . 031576
Museo Didáctico Artiguista, Maldonado 041495
Museo Didáctico de Prehistoria, Alba de Tormes 034790
Museo Didattico, Morimondo 024882
Museo Didattico, Niscemi 024940
Museo Didattico, Villa Adriana, Tivoli 026027
Museo Didattico Archeologico, Laterza 024471
Museo Didattico d'Arte e Vita Preistorica, Capo di Ponte 023643
Museo Didattico del Mare, Napoli . . 024914
Museo Didattico della Riserva Regionale Incisioni Rupestri, Ceto 023829
Museo Didattico della Scuola Medica Salernitana, Salerno 025637
Museo Didattico della Seta, Como . 023944
Museo Didattico delle Maioliche, Istituto Statale d'Arte, Grottaglie 024378
Museo Didattico Giuseppe Pellizza, Istituto Giuseppe Pellizza, Volpedo 026364
Museo Didattico Zoologico, Oria . . . 025005
Museo Diefenbach, Capri 023651
Museo Diego Aragona Pignatelli Cortes, Napoli 024915
Museo Diego Rivera Anahuacalli, México 028495
Museo Diffuso, I Luoghi dell'Anima, Pennabilli 025152
Museo Dillmann S. Bullock, Angol . 006906
Museo d'Interesse Locale, Crespadoro 024000
Museo Diocesà, Tarragona 035891
Museo Diocesano, Pamplona 035630
Museo Diocesano, Acerenza 023111
Museo Diocesano, Agrigento 023134
Museo Diocesano, Albenga 023149
Museo Diocesano, Andria 023204
Museo Diocesano, Ariano Irpino . . . 023247
Museo Diocesano, Ascoli Piceno . . 023269
Museo Diocesano, Bari 023341
Museo Diocesano, Benevento 023369
Museo Diocesano, Bisceglie 023402
Museo Diocesano, Brugnato 023535
Museo Diocesano, Cassano allo Jonio 023697
Museo Diocesano, Castelvecchio Subequo 023743
Museo Diocesano, Catanzaro 023770
Museo Diocesano, Ciudad Real . . . 035097
Museo Diocesano, Córdoba 035115
Museo Diocesano, Cuenca 035140
Museo Diocesano, Empoli 024047
Museo Diocesano, Fermo 024096
Museo Diocesano, Gaeta 024263
Museo Diocesano, Gerace 024332
Museo Diocesano, Gubbio 024391
Museo Diocesano, Jaca 035299
Museo Diocesano, Jesi 024432
Museo Diocesano, Lamezia Terme . 024449
Museo Diocesano, Lanciano 024453
Museo Diocesano, Lanusei 024455
Museo Diocesano, Lleida 035348
Museo Diocesano, Mantova 024607
Museo Diocesano, Mazara del Vallo 024655
Museo Diocesano, Melfi 024663
Museo Diocesano, Milano 024719
Museo Diocesano, Nola 024948
Museo Diocesano, Osimo 025026
Museo Diocesano, Ourense 035581
Museo Diocesano, Palencia 035596
Museo Diocesano, Piazza Armerina 025217
Museo Diocesano, Pitigliano 025281
Museo Diocesano, Pordenone 025326
Museo Diocesano, Recanati 025405
Museo Diocesano, Salamanca 035745
Museo Diocesano, Salerno 025638
Museo Diocesano, San Miniato . . . 025717
Museo Diocesano, Santa Lucia del Mela 025748
Museo Diocesano, Sant'Agata de'Goti 025762
Museo Diocesano, Sassari 025802
Museo Diocesano, Squillace 025943
Museo Diocesano, Sulmona 025965
Museo Diocesano, Trani 026099
Museo Diocesano, Tudela 035958
Museo Diocesano, Urbania 026171
Museo Diocesano, Valle del Espíritu Santo 049518
Museo Diocesano, Vallo della Lucania 026198
Museo Diocesano, Velletri 026222
Museo Diocesano, Chiesa Cattedrale, Capua 023654
Museo Diocesano, Chiesa del Gesù, Cortona 023980
Museo Diocesano, Oratorio della Misericordia, Sarzana 025799
Museo Diocesano, Palazzo Rospigliosi, Pistoia 025277
Museo Diocesano, Palazzo Vescovile, Imola 024406
Museo Diocesano, Palazzo Vescovile, Pienza 025225
Museo Diocesano, Palazzo Vescovile, Spoleto 025941
Museo Diocesano, Vecchio Episcopio, Ancona 023199
Museo Diocesano A. Bernareggi, Bergamo 023378
Museo Diocesano Albani, Urbino . . 026175
Museo Diocesano Antonio Bergamaschi, Pennabilli 025153
Museo Diocesano-Catedralicio, Segorbe 035838
Museo Diocesano-Catedralicio, Valladolid 036001
Museo Diocesano-Catedralicio, Catedral y Antiguo Palacio Episcopal, Barbastro 034899
Museo Diocesano Catedralicio de Arte Sacro, Orihuela 035569
Museo Diocesano d'Arte Sacra, Alghero 023170
Museo Diocesano d'Arte Sacra, Brescia 023522
Museo Diocesano d'Arte Sacra, Caltanissetta 023592
Museo Diocesano d'Arte Sacra, Grosseto 024376
Museo Diocesano d'Arte Sacra, Nicotera 024938
Museo Diocesano d'Arte Sacra, Orte 025014
Museo Diocesano d'Arte Sacra, Pinerolo 025246
Museo Diocesano d'Arte Sacra, Piteglio 025279
Museo Diocesano d'Arte Sacra, Rossano 025605
Museo Diocesano d'Arte Sacra, Scaria 025835
Museo Diocesano d'Arte Sacra, Treviso 026123
Museo Diocesano d'Arte Sacra, Trivento 026152
Museo Diocesano d'Arte Sacra A. Luciani, Vittorio Veneto 026357
Museo Diocesano d'Arte Sacra Santa Apollonia, Venezia 026256
Museo Diocesano de Arte Antiguo, Sigüenza 035874
Museo Diocesano de Arte Religioso Nuestra Señora del Cisne, Loja 009223
Museo Diocesano de Arte Sacro, Bilbao 034987
Museo Diocesano de Arte Sacro, Moguer 035500

Museo Diocesano de Arte Sacro, Las Palmas de Gran Canaria 035625
Museo Diocesano de Arte Sacro, Teruel 035909
Museo Diocesano de Huesca, Huesca 035287
Museo Diocesano de San Sebastián, Donostia-San Sebastián 035152
Museo Diocesano de Tui, Tui 035960
Museo Diocesano della Basilica del Crocefisso, Amalfi 023187
Museo Diocesano dell'Arredo Sacro, Bertinoro 023384
Museo Diocesano di Arte Sacra, Chiavari 023847
Museo Diocesano di Arte Sacra, Genova 024319
Museo Diocesano di Arte Sacra, Lodi 024521
Museo Diocesano di Arte Sacra, Palermo 025091
Museo Diocesano di Arte Sacra, Santa Severina 025758
Museo Diocesano di Arte Sacra, Sarsina 025795
Museo Diocesano di Arte Sacra, Susa 025972
Museo Diocesano di Arte Sacra, Palazzo Vescovile, Volterra 026367
Museo Diocesano di Arte Sacra del Duomo, Arezzo 023239
Museo Diocesano di Arte Sacra di Italo Bolano, Marina di Campo 024618
Museo Diocesano di Arte Sacra San Gregorio Barbarigo, Padova 025061
Museo Diocesano di Santo Stefano, Firenze 024189
Museo Diocesano e Catedralicio de Lugo, Lugo 035366
Museo Diocesano e Catedralicio Santos Sancristobal, Mondoñedo 035505
Museo Diocesano e Collezione dei Presepi, Bressanone 023527
Museo Diocesano e Gallerie del Tiepolo, Palazzo Patriarcale, Udine 026165
Museo Diocesano e Oratorio di San Bernardino, Siena 025893
Museo Diocesano e Tesoro della Cattedrale, Troia 026154
Museo Diocesano Inercomunale di Arte Sacra, Castignano 023753
Museo Diocesano Intercomunale di Arte Sacra, Comunanza 023951
Museo Diocesano Intercomunale di Arte Sacra, Grottammare 024379
Museo Diocesano Intercomunale di Arte Sacra, Monteprandone 024854
Museo Diocesano Intercomunale di Arte Sacra, Ripatransone 025443
Museo Diocesano Intercomunale di Arte Sacra, Rotella 025606
Museo Diocesano Lucas Guillermo Castillo, Falcón 049492
Museo Diocesano Regina Coeli, Santillana del Mar 035832
Museo Diocesano San Pietro, Teggiano 025997
Museo Diocesano Teatino, Chiesa di San Domenico, Chieti 023863
Museo Diocesano Tridentino, Trento 026110
Museo Diocesano y Cedralicio, Calahorra 035024
Museo División del Norte, Canutillo 028137
Museo División del Norte, Lerdo . . . 028391
Museo do Humor, Fene 035189
Museo do Mosteiro de San Paio de Antealtares, Santiago de Compostela 035827
Museo do Moucho, Cerceda 035080
Museo do Pobo Galego, Santiago de Compostela 035828
Museo Doctor Francia, Yaguarón . . 031453
Museo Documental, Guernica y Luno 035271
Museo Documentario della Città, Gradisca d'Isonzo 024359
Museo Doganale Svizzero, Schweizerisches Landesmuseum, Gandria 037107
Museo Dolomythos di San Candido, San Candido 025660
Museo Dolores Olmedo Patiño, México 028496
Museo Domenicani, Taggia 025981
Museo Don Pio Palla, Leonessa . . . 024495
Museo Doña Rosario, Santiago de Cuba 008165
Museo Donazione Luxoro, Genova . 024320
Museo Donazione U. Mastroianni, Arpino 023257
Museo Donizettiano, Bergamo 023379
Museo Dr. Atl, Pihuamo 028642
Museo Dr. José Gómez Panaco, Balancán 028122
Museo Duca di Martina, Villa Floridiana, Napoli 024916
Museo Ducati, Bologna 023450
Museo Dupré, Fiesole 024123
Museo e Archivio Capitolare, Assisi 023283
Museo E. Bernardi, Padova 025062
Museo e Biblioteca della Resistenza, Sansepolcro 025744
Museo e Centro Culturale Marco Scacchi, Convento di Santa Chiara, Gallese 024270
Museo e Certosa di San Martino, Napoli 024917
Museo e Chiostri Monumentali di Santa Maria Novella, Firenze 024190
Museo E. Galessi, Montevarchi 024868
Museo E. Leandro, San Cesario di Lecce 025664
Museo e Pinacoteca Civica, Alessandria 023165
Museo e Pinacoteca Civica del Broletto, Novara 024966
Museo e Pinacoteca Civici, Vasto . . 026219
Museo e Pinacoteca Comunali, Palazzo dei Consoli, Gubbio 024392
Museo e Pinacoteca della Basilica di San Paolo, Roma 025538
Museo e Pinacoteca della Città, Todi 026030
Museo e Pinacoteca della Comunità di Fiemme, Cavalese 023776
Museo e Pinacoteca delle Arti Epizephiri, Palazzo Nieddu del Rio, Locri 024517
Museo e Pinacoteca Diocesana, Palazzo Arcivescovile, Camerino 023605
Museo e Pinacoteca Nazionale di Palazzo Mansi, Lucca 024547
Museo e Pinacoteca S. Gentili, San Ginesio 025685
Museo E. Renzi, Coriano 023968
Museo E. Treccani, Milano 024720
Museo e Villaggio Africano, Basella di Urgnano 023351
Museo Ebraica di Roma, Roma 025539
Museo Ebraico, Asti 023290
Museo Ebraico, Bologna 023451
Museo Ebraico, Ferrara 024109
Museo Ebraico, Firenze 024191
Museo Ebraico, Livorno 024509
Museo Ebraico, Merano 024671
Museo Ebraico, Soragna 025923
Museo Ebraico, Venezia 026257
Museo Ecclesiastico, Caorle 023637
Museo Ecuatoriano de Ciencias Naturales, Quito 009246
Museo Eduardo Carranza, Villavicencio 007645
Museo-Eerola, Tuulos 010182
Museo Efrain Martínez Zambrano, Popayán 007587
Museo Egipcio, Montevideo 041516
Museo Egizio, Torino 026069
Museo El Cañón, Puerto Boniato . . . 008103
Museo El Castillo Diego Echavarría, Medellín 007538
Museo El Centenario, Garza García . 028261
Museo El Chapulín, Saltillo 028700
Museo El Hombre y la Naturaleza, San Juan 000570
Museo El Hurón Azul, La Habana . . . 007987
Museo El Jonotal, Playa Vicente, Veracruz 028644
Museo El Minero, Santa Bárbara . . 028759
Museo El Pariancito, San Luis Potosí 028734
Museo El Piñero, Nueva Gerona . . . 008079
Museo El Polvorín, Monclova 028557
Museo El Reencuentro, Darregueira 000325
Museo El Remate, Comala 028177
Museo El Sol de las Botellas, Barcelona 049443
Museo Elder, Las Palmas de Gran Canaria 035626
Museo Elías Nandino, Cocula 028167
Museo Elisarion, Minusio 037328
Museo elle Arti e Tradizioni Contadine, Roccasecca dei Volsci 025459
Museo elle Genti delle Valli di Lanzo, Ceres 023795
Museo Emidiano, Chiesa di Sant'Emidio, Agnone 023128
Museo Emilia Ortiz, Tepic 028827
Museo Emilio Greco, Catania 023766
Museo Emilio Greco, Palazzo Soliano, Orvieto 025022
Museo Enologico Grasso, Milazzo . . 024739
Museo Entomológco Mariposas del Mundo, San Miguel 000578
Museo Epper, Ascona 036855
Museo Erbario, Dipertimento di Biologia Vegetale, Roma 025540
Museo Eritreo Bottego, Parma 025126
Museo Ermita de Santa Elena, Necrópolis Romana Siglos I Y II, Irún 035297
Museo Ernest Hemingway, San Francisco de Paula 008122
Museo Ernesto Laroche, Montevideo 041517
Museo Escolar de Ciencias Naturales Carlos A. Merti, San Antonio de Areco . . 000547
Museo Escolar de Pusol, Elche 035168
Museo Escolar de Sitio de la Matamba, Jamapa 028358
Museo Escolar María Goretti, Pasto 007568
Museo Escolar y Comunitario de Acamalín, Xico 028946
Museo Escultórico de Geles Cabrera, México 028497
Museo Español de Arte Contemporaneo, Madrid 035417
Museo Específico de la Academia de Artillería, Segovia 035846
Museo Específico de la Academia de Caballería, Valladolid 036002
Museo Especifico de la Academia de Ingenieros, Hoyo de Manzanares . 035284
Museo Específico de la Academia General Militar, Zaragoza 036109
Museo Específico de la Brigada Paracaidista, Alcalá de Henares . . 034801
Museo Específico de la Legión, Ceuta 035087
Museo Estatal de Culturas Populares, Monterrey 028568
Museo Estatal de Patología, Puebla 028670
Museo Estudio Diego Rivera, México 028498
Museo Ethnográfico, Florencia 007500
Museo Ethnográfico de las Obras Misionales Pontificias, Buenos Aires 000203
Museo Ethnohistórico, Soatá 007613
Museo Etiopico G. Massaia, Frascati 024248
Museo Etnico-Agricolo-Pastorale ed Artigiano, Alcamo 023160
Museo Etnico Arbereshe, Civita . . . 023907
Museo Étnico de los Seris, Hermosillo 028317
Museo Étnico de los Yaquis, Obregón 028613
Museo Etnico della Civiltà Salentina Agrilandi Museum, Brindisi 023529
Museo Etno-Antropologico, Calatafimi 023575
Museo Etno-Antropologico, San Cipirello 025666
Museo Etno-Antropologico, San Mauro Castelverde 025711
Museo Etno-Antropologico, Scaletta Zanclea 025831
Museo Etno-Antropologico della Terra di Zabut, Sambuca di Sicilia 025646
Museo Etno-Antropologico della Valle del Belice, Gibellina 024342
Museo Etno-Antropologico delle Madonie, ex Convento de Padri Cappuccini, Geraci Siculo 024334
Museo Etnobotánico, Tuluá 007627
Museo Etnográfico, Albán 007385
Museo Etnográfico, Alcubilla del Marqués 034811
Museo Etnografico, Aprica 023222
Museo Etnografico, Aritzo 023250
Museo Etnográfico, Arteta 034867
Museo Etnográfico, Atauta 034874
Museo Etnografico, Bomba 023474
Museo Etnográfico, Cajamarca 031474
Museo Etnográfico, Castrojeriz 035075
Museo Etnografico, Collinas 023932
Museo Etnografico, Faeto 024074
Museo Etnografico, Fossalta di Portogruaro 024240
Museo Etnografico, Fratta Polesine 024252
Museo Etnográfico, Grado 035241
Museo Etnográfico, Grandas de Salime 035261
Museo Etnográfico, Inzá 007521
Museo Etnografico, Lusevera 024561
Museo Etnográfico, Madruga 008042
Museo Etnografico, Malborghetto Valbruna 024583
Museo Etnografico, Montodine 024872
Museo Etnografico, Novalesa 024960
Museo Etnografico, Novara di Sicilia 024969
Museo Etnografico, Oneta 024996
Museo Etnografico, Ortonovo 025020
Museo Etnografico, Ossimo Superiore 025029
Museo Etnografico, Parma 025127
Museo Etnografico, Ponte in Valtellina 025307
Museo Etnográfico, Quintana Redonda 035689
Museo Etnografico, Roccalbegna . . 025456
Museo Etnográfico, Rollamienta . . . 035716
Museo Etnográfico, Romanillos de Medinaceli 035717
Museo Etnográfico, Santa Lucía . . . 008146
Museo Etnografico, Schilpario 025841
Museo Etnográfico, Torreandaluz . . 035938
Museo Etnografico, Trebisacce 026103
Museo Etnográfico, Tuxtla Gutiérrez 028899
Museo Etnografico Africo, Bari 023342
Museo Etnográfico Andrés Barbero, Asunción 031447
Museo Etnografico Antico Mulino ad Acqua Licheri, Fluminimaggiore 024206
Museo Etnografico Archeologico, Palau 025074
Museo Etnografico Castello D'Albertis, Museum of the Cultures of the World, Genova 024310
Museo Etnografico Cerginolano, Cerignola 023798
Museo Etnografico Civiltà Contadina, Forlì 024229
Museo Etnográfico Comarcal de la Sierra y la Campiña Sur, Azuaga 034883
Museo Etnografico Comunale, Premana 025369
Museo Etnografico Coumboscuro della Civiltà Provenzale in Italia, Sancto Lucìa de Coumboscuro 025738
Museo Etnográfico da Limia, Vilar de Santos 036053
Museo Etnográfico de Amurrio Felix Murga, Amurrio 034840
Museo Etnográfico de Cantabria, Muriedas 035535
Museo Etnográfico de Colombia, Bogotá 007438
Museo Etnográfico de los Valles de Campoo, Canduela 035043
Museo Etnográfico de Oyón-Oion, Oyón 035588

Museo Etnografico dei Cimbri, Selva di Progno . . . 025848
Museo Etnografico del Cansiglio Servadei, Tambre . . . 025985
Museo Etnografico del Carretto Siciliano, Terrasini . . . 026017
Museo Etnografico del Cologio Nacional Mejia, Quito . . . 009247
Museo Etnografico del Coumboscuro, Monterosso Grana . . . 024861
Museo Etnografico del Ferro, Bienno . . . 023397
Museo Etnografico del Pinerolese e Museo del Legno, Pinerolo . . . 025247
Museo Etnografico del Ponente Ligure, Cervo . . . 023811
Museo Etnografico della Civiltà Contadina, Marianopoli . . . 024617
Museo Etnografico della Cultura Contadina, Morigerati . . . 024881
Museo Etnografico della Lunigiana, Villafranca in Lunigiana . . . 026334
Museo Etnografico della Piana del Dragone, Volturara Irpina . . . 026370
Museo Etnografico della Provincia die Belluno, Cesiomaggiore . . . 023828
Museo Etnografico della Trinità, Botticino . . . 023503
Museo Etnografico della Val Varatella, Toirano . . . 026031
Museo Etnografico della Valle, Ultimo . . . 026168
Museo Etnografico della Valle Brembana, Zogno . . . 026374
Museo Etnografico dell'Alta Valle Seriana, Ardesio . . . 023232
Museo Etnografico dell'Etna, Linguaglossa . . . 024503
Museo Etnografico di Servola, Trieste . . . 026144
Museo Etnografico di Sorrentini, Patti . . . 025136
Museo Etnografico Don Luigi Pellegrini, Castiglione di Garfagnana . . . 023751
Museo Etnográfico e da Historia de San Paio de Narla, Friol . . . 035200
Museo Etnografico e del Folklore Valsesiano, Borgosesia . . . 023494
Museo Etnografico e della Cultura Materiale, Aquilonia . . . 023225
Museo Etnografico e della Stregoneria, Triora . . . 026151
Museo Etnografico e di Scienze Naturali, Torino . . . 026070
Museo Etnografico e Tradizioni Contadine Borgo Antico, Torricella Sicura . . . 026094
Museo Etnografico Extremeño González Santana, Olivenza . . . 035554
Museo Etnografico Francesco Bande, Sassari . . . 025803
Museo Etnografico G. Carpani, Lizzano in Belvedere . . . 024514
Museo Etnografico Galluras, Luras . 024560
Museo Etnográfico Huichol Wixarica, Zapopan . . . 028974
Museo Etnografico I Zuf, Vione . . . 026343
Museo Etnografico Il Cicle della Vita, Quartu Sant'Elena . . . 025377
Museo Etnográfico Juán B. Ambrosetti, Buenos Aires . . . 000204
Museo Etnografico La Steiva, Piverone . . . 025284
Museo Etnográfico Leonés Ildefonso Fierro, León . . . 035330
Museo Etnográfico Madre Laura, Medellín . . . 007539
Museo Etnográfico Miguel Angel Builes, Medellín . . . 007540
Museo Etnográfico Municipal Dámaso Arce, Olavarría . . . 000459
Museo Etnográfico Olimio Liste, San Cristovo de Cea . . . 035754
Museo Etnográfico Piedad Isla, Cervera de Pisuerga . . . 035083
Museo Etnografico Romagnolo Benedetto Pergoli, Forlì . . . 024230
Museo Etnográfico Rural, Valderrueda . . . 035970
Museo Etnográfico Rural y Comarcal, Prioro . . . 035679
Museo Etnografico San Domu de is Ainas, Armungia . . . 023251
Museo Etnográfico Santa Rosa de Ocopa, Concepción . . . 031494
Museo Etnografico Siciliano Giuseppe Pitrè, Palermo . . . 025092
Museo Etnográfico Sotelo Blanco, Santiago de Compostela . . . 035829
Museo Etnografico sulla Lavorazione del Legno, San Vito di Leguzzano . . . 025737
Museo Etnográfico Textil Pérez Enciso, Plasencia . . . 035656
Museo Etnografico Tiranese, Madonna di Tirano . . . 024575
Museo Etnografico Tiranese, Tirano 026022
Museo Etnografico U. Ferrandi, Novara . . . 024964
Museo Etnografico Vallivo, Val Masino . . . 026184
Museo Etnográfico y Archivo Histórico Enrique Squirru, Azul . . . 000123
Museo Etnográfico y Colonial Juan de Garay, Santa Fé . . . 000602
Museo Etnohistórico de Ayabacara, Ayabacara . . . 031465
Museo Etnológico, Barca . . . 034900
Museo Etnológico, Bejis . . . 034968
Museo Etnológico, Bielsa . . . 034981
Museo Etnológico, Boltaña . . . 034994
Museo Etnológico, San Juan de Plan . . . 035760
Museo Etnológico, Sechura . . . 031595
Museo Etnológico Aljibes de Gasparito, Rojales . . . 035715
Museo Etnológico Casa Mazo, Valle de Hecho . . . 036013
Museo Etnológico de Amazonas, Puerto Ayacucho . . . 049513
Museo Etnológico de la Diputación, Castellón de la Plana . . . 035069
Museo Etnológico de la Huerta, Alcantarilla . . . 034802
Museo Etnológico de Morella y del Meastrazgo, Morella . . . 035525
Museo Etnológico de Navarra Julio Caro Baroja, Ayegui . . . 034876
Museo Etnológico de Ribadavia, Casa da la Fundación Martínez Vázquez, Ribadavia . . . 035701
Museo Etnologico della Apuane, Massa . . . 024632
Museo Etnológico Misional C.M.F., Santa Isabel . . . 009354
Museo Etnologico Missionario, Castelnuovo Don Bosco . . . 023738
Museo Etnológico Popular, Fuensanta . . . 035204
Museo Etnolólogico Anselmo Buil, Blecua . . . 034991
Museo Etnomusicale I Gigli di Nola, Nola . . . 024949
Museo Etrusco, Asciano . . . 023264
Museo Etrusco, Chiusi Città . . . 023873
Museo Etrusco, San Gimignano . . . 025682
Museo Etrusco Gasparri, Piombino . 025255
Museo Etrusco Gasparri, Populonia 025323
Museo Etrusco M. Guarnacci, Palazzo Desideri-Tangassi, Volterra . . . 026368
Museo Etrusco Ranuccio Bianchi Bandinelli, Colle di Val d'Elsa . . . 023927
Museo Ettore Pomarici Santomasi, Gravina di Puglia . . . 024367
Museo Evaristo Valle, Gijón . . . 035223
Museo Evocativo y de Bellas Artes Osvaldo Gasparini, San Antonio de Areco . 000548
Museo Ex Convento Agustino de San Pablo, Yuriria . . . 028957
Museo Ex Convento Agustino Siglo XVI, México . . . 028499
Museo Ex-Convento de San Juan Bautista, Tlayacapan . . . 028866
Museo Ex Convento del Carmen, Guadalajara . . . 028291
Museo Ex Hacienda San Gabriel de Barrera, Guanajuato . . . 028306
Museo Ex Templo de San Agustín, Zacatecas . . . 028962
Museo Ex Voto di Santa Maria della Portella, Cervara di Roma . . . 023805
Museo Ex Votos Sr. de la Misericordia, Tepatitlán de Morelos . . . 028815
Museo Exposición El Hombre, Bogotá . . . 007439
Museo-Exposición Permanente Diocesano, Albarracín . . . 034794
Museo Extremeño e Iberoamericano de Arte Contemporáneo, Badajoz . . . 034887
Museo F. Assetto, Frontino . . . 024253
Museo F. Renzi, Borghi . . . 023483
Museo F. Renzi, San Giovanni in Galilea . . . 025688
Museo F.A. Marcucci, Ascoli Piceno 023270
Museo Fallero, Valencia . . . 035983
Museo Farallón Dillon, Ballenita . . . 009178
Museo Farmacéutico, Matanzas . . . 008058
Museo Farmacobotánica, Buenos Aires . . . 000205
Museo Faryluk, Aristóbulo del Valle 000117
Museo Felisa Rincón de Gautier, San Juan . . . 032743
Museo Félix de Jesús, México . . . 028500
Museo Fernán Félix de Amador, Luján . . . 000415
Museo Fernando García, Canelones 041490
Museo Ferrocarrilero, Empalme . . . 028241
Museo Ferrovario, Stazione di Trieste Campo Marzio, Trieste . . . 026145
Museo Ferroviario, Alcázar de San Juan . . . 034804
Museo Ferroviario, Tacna . . . 031601
Museo Ferroviario, Stazione Ferroviaria, Cuneo . . . 024013
Museo Ferroviario de Gualeguaychú, Gualeguaychú . . . 000360
Museo Ferroviario del Verbano, Luino . . . 024559
Museo Ferroviario Piemontese, Savigliano . . . 025816
Museo Ferroviaro, Bogotá . . . 007440
Museo Ferrucciano, Gavinana . . . 024281
Museo Ferrucciano, San Marcello Pistoiese . . . 025702
Museo Filatélico del Banco de la República, Medellín . . . 007541
Museo Filemón Gutiérrez Ramírez, Ameca . . . 028103
Museo Filipe Santiago Gutiérrez, Toluca . . . 028876
Museo Fin de la Tierra, Francisco I. Madero, Coahuila . . . 028257
Museo Finca El Abra, Siguanea . . . 008176
Museo Fiorentino di Preistoria, Firenze . . . 024192
Museo Fioroni, Legnago . . . 024490
Museo Fittile, Ripatransone . . . 025444
Museo Florencio de la Fuente, Huete . . . 035289
Museo Florencio Molina Campos, Moreno . . . 000452
Museo Florentino Ameghino, Bolívar . . . 000140
Museo Folklórico, La Rioja . . . 000397
Museo Folklórico Araucano de Cañete Juan A. Ríos M., Cañete . . . 006910
Museo Folklórico Provincial, San Miguel de Tucumán . . . 000584
Museo Folklórico Regional de Humahuaca, Humahuaca . . . 000363
Museo Fomento Cultural Banamex, México . . . 028501
Museo Fondazione C. Faina e Museo Civico Palazzo Faina, Orvieto . . . 025023
Museo Fondazione Famiglia Piccolo di Calanovella, Capo d'Orlando . . . 023645
Museo-Fondazione P. Conti, Fiesole 024124
Museo Forestal de la Policía Ecológica, Jesús María . . . 031535
Museo Forestale C. Siemoni, Poppi 025321
Museo Fortaleza de San Carlos de la Cabaña, La Habana . . . 007988
Museo Fotográfico, Calarcá . . . 007464
Museo Fotográfico de Nanchital, Nanchital de Lázaro Cárdenas del Río . . . 028592
Museo Fournier de Naipes de Alava, Vitoria-Gasteiz . . . 036085
Museo Fragua Martiana, La Habana 007989
Museo Francescano, Roma . . . 025541
Museo Francescano Padre Aurelio Menin, Convento Francescano, Chiampo . 023837
Museo Francescano - Raccolta d'Arte, Convento di San Francesco, Gubbio . . . 024393
Museo Francesco Borgogna, Vercelli . . . 026276
Museo Francesco Cilea, Palmi . . . 025104
Museo Francisco Campos, Guayaquil . . . 009210
Museo Francisco Goitia, Zacatecas 028963
Museo Francisco Huerta Rendón en la Casona Universitaria, Guayaquil . 009211
Museo Francisco Javier Sauza, Tequila . . . 028834
Museo Francisco José de Caldas, Bogotá . . . 007441
El Museo Francisco Oller y Diego Rivera, Buffalo . . . 042505
Museo Francisco Sarabia, Lerdo . . 028392
Museo Franco Azzinari, Altomonte . 023181
Museo Franco Lázaro, Chiapa de Corzo . . . 028151
Museo Franz Mayer, México . . . 028502
Museo Fray Bernardo Padilla, Acámbaro . . . 028075
Museo Frey Pedro Bedón, Ibarra . . . 009219
Museo Frida Kahlo, Casa Azul, México . . . 028503
Museo Frissel de Arte Zapoteca, Universidad de las Américas, Santa Ana del Valle . . . 028758
Museo Friulano di Storia Naturale, Udine . . . 026166
Museo Fuentes de Loreto y Guadelupe, Palmar de Bravo . . . 028631
Museo Fuerte Conde de Mirasol de Vieques, Institute of Puerto Rican Culture, Vieques . . . 032754
Museo Fuerte de la Loma, Victoria de las Tunas . . . 008189
Museo Fuerte Independencia, Tandil . . . 000628
Museo Fundación Díaz Caneja de Arte Contemporaneo, Palencia . . . 035597
Museo Fundación Estero Beach, Ensenada . . . 028248
Museo Fundación Naum Komp, Buenos Aires . . . 000206
Museo G. Arcucci, Ariano Irpino . . . 023248
Museo G. Filangieri, San Potito Sannitico . . . 025725
Museo G. Manzù, Ardea . . . 023231
Museo G. Marconi, Pontecchio Marconi . . . 025313
Museo G. Scarabelli, Imola . . . 024407
Museo G. Spontini, Maiolati Spontini . . . 024580
Museo G. Whitaker, Marsala . . . 024624
Museo Gabriel García Márquez, Aracataca . . . 007388
Museo Gabriel Mateus, Sabanagrande . . . 007600
Museo Gabriela Mistral de Vicuña, Vicuña . . . 006949
Museo Galego de Arte Contemporánea Carlos Maside, Arès . . . 034856
Museo Galego do Xoguete, Allariz . 034822
Museo Galería Manuel Lepe, Puerto Vallarta . . . 028681
Museo Galleria di Villa Borghese, Roma . . . 025542
Museo Garibaldino, Caprera . . . 023648
Museo Garibaldino, Genova . . . 024321
Museo Garibaldino della Campagna dell'Agro Romano per la Liberazione di Roma 1867, Mentana . . . 024666
Museo Gauchesco Ricardo Güiraldes, San Antonio de Areco . . . 000549
Museo G.B. Filippa, Rimella . . . 025430
Museo G.D. Cassini, Perinaldo . . . 025160
Museo Gemológico, Bogotá . . . 007442

Museo General, Yanahuanca 031614
Museo General Belgrano, Buenos Aires 000207
Museo General de Arequito, Arequito 000116
Museo General Francisco Villa, San Juan del Río 028724
Museo General Ignacio Zaragoza, Puebla 028671
Museo General Lavalle, General Pinto 000354
Museo General Porfirio Rubio, Landa de Matamoros 028382
Museo Geo-Paleontologico, Ferrara 024110
Museo Geográfico Einstein, San Juan 000571
Museo Geologico, Castell'Arquato . 023723
Museo Geológico, Laspaules 035320
Museo Geológico de la Universidad Nacional de Ingeniería del Perú, Lima 031564
Museo Geológico del Seminario, Barcelona 034918
Museo Geológico del Uruguay, Montevideo 041518
Museo Geologico e Paleontologico G. Capellini, Bologna 023452
Museo Geologico G.G. Gemmellaro, Palermo 025093
Museo Geológico José Royo y Gómez, Bogotá 007443
Museo Geológico Marino Arce Herrera, Bucaramanga 007460
Museo Geológico Petrolero, Universidad Surcolombiana, Neiva 007555
Museo Geominero, Madrid 035418
Museo Geopaleontologico Alto Aventino, Arielli 023249
Museo Geopaleontologico Cava Bomba, Cinto Euganeo 023887
Museo Geopaleontologico dei Fossili della Lessinia, Velo Veronese 026223
Museo Geopaleontologico del Castello, Lerici 024496
Museo Geopaleontologico Naturalistico Antropico e Ornitologico Brancaleoni, Piobbico 025251
Museo Germán Guglielmetti, Benito Juárez 000138
Museo Gianmaria da Tusa, Cefalù . 023783
Museo Giannettino Luxoro, Genova 024322
Museo Gianni Visentin, Carpané di San Nazario 023667
Museo Giovanni Antonio Sanna, Museo Nazionale Archeologico ed Etnografico, Sassari 025804
Museo Giovanni Boldini, Palazzo Massari, Ferrara 024111
Museo Gli Orsanti, Compiano 023949
Museo Gonzalo Carrasco, Otumba . 028622
Museo Gráfico de la Mujer Guerrenese, Chilpancingo 028161
Museo Gran Casino, Bayamo 007879
Museo Gran Mariscal de Ayacucho, Cumaná 049488
Museo Gregoriano Egizio, Musei Vaticani, Città del Vaticano 049424
Museo Gregoriano Etrusco, Musei Vaticani, Città del Vaticano 049425
Museo Gregoriano Profano, Musei Vaticani, Città del Vaticano 049426
Museo Gregorio Aguilar Barea, Chontales 030663
Museo Gregorio Prieto, Valdepeñas 035968
Museo Guillermo Perez Chiriboga del Banco Central, Quito 009248
Museo Guillermo Spratling, Taxco de Alarcón 028791
Museo Gustavo de Maeztu, Estella . 035182
Museo Hacienda San Pedro, Universidad Autónoma de Nuevo León, General Zuazua 028265
Museo Hans Multscher e Museo Civico, Vipiteno 026344
Museo Hendrik Christian Andersen, Roma 025543
Museo Herbario de la Facultad de Ciencias, México 028504
Museo Hermanas Giralt, Cienfuegos 007910
Museo Hermann Hesse, Montagnola 037331
Museo Hermanos López Rayón, Tlalpujahua 028853
Museo Hermanos Nacif Weiss, Rivadavia 000521
Museo Hermenegildo Galeana, Tecpan de Galeana 028799
Museo Hermila Domínguez de Castellanos, Comitán de Domínguez 028182
Museo Hidalgo, Salamanca 028695
Museo Hidráulico del Sistema de Drenaje Profundo, México 028505
Museo Hidráulico los Molinos del Río Segura, Murcia 035532
Museo Historia de las Ciencias Carlos J. Finlay, La Habana 007990
Museo Historia del Ferrocarril de Antioquia, Medellín 007542
Museo Historia Municipal, Antilla . . 007870
Museo Historiador Hernández Galiano, Tostado 000637
Museo Histórica Ex Convento de Tepoztlán, Tepoztlán 028832
Museo Histórico, El Carmen de Bolívar 007493
Museo Histórico, Pinar del Río 008092
Museo Historico, Riobamba 009261
Museo Historico, San Antonio de los Baños 008118
Museo Histórico, Zapala 000675
Museo Histórico Andrés Avelino Cáceres, Ayacucho 031467
Museo Histórico Andrés Avelino Cáceres, Huamanga 031510
Museo Histórico Anton García de Bonilla, Ocaña 007558
Museo Histórico Arqueológico, Doña Mencia 035148
Museo Histórico Arqueológico Guillermo Magrassi, Mar del Plata 000424
Museo Histórico, Arqueológico y de Arte Pedro Balduín, San Pedro de Jujuy 000592
Museo Histórico-Artístico, Cuacos de Yuste 035135
Museo Historico Bae Calderon, Guayaquil 009212
Museo Histórico BBVA, Bilbao 034988
Museo Histórico Casa de la Convención de Rionegro, Rionegro 007598
Museo Historico Casa de los Tratados, Cuenca 009198
Museo Histórico, Colonial y de Bellas Artes y Museo de Ciencias Naturales Regional Mesopotámico, Mercedes 000441
Museo Histórico Comunal, Villa Trinidad 000673
Museo Histórico Comunal de San Genaro Norte, San Genaro Norte 000561
Museo Histórico Comunal y de la Colonización Judía Rabino Aaron H. Goldman, Moisés Ville 000449
Museo Histórico Conventual San Carlos, San Lorenzo 000575
Museo Histórico Cultural Juan Santamaría, Alajuela 007667
Museo Histórico de 26 de Julio, Santiago de Cuba 008166
Museo Histórico de Acapulco, Fuerte de San Diego, Acapulco 028079
Museo Histórico de Antioquia, Palacio de la Cultura Rafael Uribe Uribe, Medellín 007543
Museo Histórico de Arenaza, Arenaza 000115
Museo Histórico de Arrecifes, Arrecifes 000119
Museo Histórico de Arte, Morón . . . 000454
Museo Histórico de Ayotzinapa, Tixtla de Guerrero 028845
Museo Histórico de Cañuelas, Cañuelas 000259
Museo Histórico de Cartagena Casa de la Inquisición, Academia de la Historia de Cartagena de Indias, Cartagena . . 007478
Museo Histórico de Cera, Buenos Aires 000208
Museo Histórico de Chacamarka, Chacamarka 031485
Museo Historico de Ciego de Avila, Ciego de Avila 007906
Museo Histórico de Corrientes Manuel Cabral de Mayo y Alpoín, Corrientes 000320
Museo Histórico de Entre Ríos Martiniano Leguizamón, Paraná 000466
Museo Histórico de Guachinango, Guachinango 028269
Museo Histórico de Guatraché, Guatraché 000361
Museo Histórico de la Casa de la Cultura, Ambalema 007387
Museo Histórico de la Ciudad, Torreón 028884
Museo Histórico de la Ciudad, Valencia 035984
Museo Histórico de la Ciudad de Buenos Aires Brigadier-General Cornelio de Saavedra, Buenos Aires 000209
Museo Histórico de la Colonia San Carlos, San Carlos Centro 000552
Museo Histórico de la Dirección General Impositiva, Buenos Aires 000210
Museo Histórico de la Educación Tecnológica en México, Chilpancingo 028162
Museo Histórico de la Honorable Cámara de Diputados de la Nación, Buenos Aires 000211
Museo Histórico de la Iglesia, Buenos Aires 000212
Museo Histórico de la Policía de la Provincia de Misiones, Posadas 000481
Museo Histórico de la Policía National, Bogotá 007444
Museo Histórico de la Prefectura Naval Argentina, Tigre 000632
Museo Histórico de la Provincia, Santiago del Estero 000616
Museo Histórico de la Provincia de Catamarca, San Fernando del Valle de Catamarca 000556
Museo Histórico de la Revolución Mexicana, Chihuahua 028159
Museo Histórico de La Rioja, La Rioja 000398
Museo Histórico de la Sierra Gorda, Jalpan 028356
Museo Histórico de Laborde, Laborde 000399
Museo Histórico de Múzquiz, Múzquiz 028590
Museo Histórico de Navarro, Navarro 000455
Museo Histórico de Osorno, Osorno 006921
Museo Histórico de Palma Soriano, Palma Soriano 008083
Museo Histórico de Ranchos, Ranchos 000499
Museo Histórico de Requena y su Comarca, Requena 035694
Museo Histórico de Reynosa, Reynosa 028688
Museo Histórico de San Francisco, Santa Fé 000603
Museo Histórico de San Miguel de Allende, San Miguel de Allende 028740
Museo Histórico de San Nicolás de los Garza, San Nicolás de los Garza . 028745
Museo Histórico de Sargadelos, Cervo 035085
Museo Historico del Norte, Salta . . 000540
Museo Histórico del Oriente de Morelos, Cuautla 028201
Museo Histórico del Regimiento de Granaderos a Caballo General San Martín, Buenos Aires 000213
Museo Histórico del Transporte Carlos Hillner Decoud, Quilmes 000492
Museo Historico Dr. Rafael Angel Calderón Guardia, San José 007679
Museo Histórico Etnológico, Llosa de Ranes 035358
Museo Histórico Ex Aduana de Ciudad Juárez, Juárez 028370
Museo Histórico Ferroviario Escribano Alfredo Rueda, Rueda 000533
Museo Histórico Franciscano, San Salvador de Jujuy 000595
Museo Histórico Fuerte Barragan, Ensenada 000339
Museo Histórico Fuerte de San José el Alto, Campeche 028131
Museo Histórico General Julio de Vedia, 9 de Julio 000105
Museo Histórico Hipólito Unanue, Ayacucho 031468
Museo Histórico José Hernández-Chacra Pueyrredón, Villa Ballester 000659
Museo Histórico Judío y del Holocausto Tuvie Maizel, México 028506
Museo Histórico La Casona de Santa Rosa, Liberia 007669
Museo Histórico La Gallareta Forestal, La Gallareta 000379
Museo Histórico Local, Puente Genil 035680
Museo Histórico Manuel A. Moreira, Laboulaye 000400
Museo Histórico Mexicano de Cananea, Cananea 028134
Museo Histórico Militar, Asunción . . 031448
Museo Histórico Militar Real Felipe, Callao 031478
Museo Histórico Minero Don Felipe de Borbón y Grecia, Madrid 035419
Museo Histórico Municipal, Baena . 034889
Museo Historico Municipal, Bahía Blanca 000126
Museo Histórico Municipal, Cádiz . . 035023
Museo Histórico Municipal, Cañete de las Torres 035045
Museo Histórico Municipal, Fuente Tójar 035206
Museo Histórico Municipal, Ocotlán 028617
Museo Histórico Municipal, Salto . . 041552
Museo Histórico Municipal, San Fernando 035755
Museo Histórico Municipal, Taxco de Alarcón 028792
Museo Histórico Municipal Alfredo E. Múlgura, General Belgrano 000351
Museo Histórico Municipal Andrés A. Roverano, Santo Tomé 000620
Museo Histórico Municipal Brigadier General Juan Martín de Pueyrredón, San Isidro 000564
Museo Histórico Municipal de Armstrong, Armstrong 000118
Museo Histórico Municipal de Cañada de Gómez, Cañada de Gómez 000258
Museo Histórico Municipal de Écija, Ecija 035158
Museo Histórico Municipal de Guanabacoa, Guanabaoa 007932
Museo Histórico Municipal de Luque, Luque 000418
Museo Histórico Municipal de Pergamino, Pergamino 000470
Museo Histórico Municipal de Regla, Regla 008108
Museo Histórico Municipal de Villa Gesell, Villa Gesell 000668
Museo Histórico Municipal General Levalle, General Levalle 000352
Museo Histórico Municipal Guillermo Zegarra Meneses, Arequipa 031460
Museo Histórico Municipal Hércules J. Rabagliati, Ramallo 000498
Museo Histórico Municipal Juan Lavalle, Baradero 000133
Museo Histórico Municipal La Para, La Para 000380
Museo Histórico Municipal Monte Grande, Monte Grande 000451
Museo Histórico Municipal Víctor E. Míguez, Mercedes 000442
Museo Histórico Municipal Villa Clara, Villa Clara 000662
Museo Histórico Municipal Villa del Rosario, Villa del Rosario 000665
Museo Histórico Municipal y Colección de Arte Precolombino Arminio Weiss, Rafaela 000496

Museo Historico Munipal, Montilla . 035521
Museo Histórico Nacional, Buenos Aires 000214
Museo Histórico Nacional, Santiago de Chile 006935
Museo Histórico Nacional Casa del Virrey Liniers, Alta Gracia 000110
Museo Histórico Nacional del Cabildo de Buenos Aires y de la Revolucion de Mayo, Buenos Aires 000215
Museo Histórico Nacional Luis A. de Herrera, Montevideo 041519
Museo Histórico Naval, Cienfuegos 007911
Museo Histórico Naval Central, México 028507
Museo Histórico Policial de La Plata, La Plata 000391
Museo Histórico Provincial, Cienfuegos 007912
Museo Histórico Provincial, Sancti-Spíritus 008131
Museo Histórico Provincial Agustín V. Gnecco, San Juan 000572
Museo Histórico Provincial Brig. Estanislao López, Santa Fé 000604
Museo Histórico Provincial Colonel Manuel José Olascoaga, Chos Malal 000277
Museo Histórico Provincial de Guantánamo, Guantánamo 007936
Museo Histórico Provincial de Rosario Dr. Julio Marc, Rosario 000527
Museo Histórico Provincial Marqués de Sobremonte, Córdoba 000301
Museo Histórico Regional, Alpachiri 000109
Museo Histórico Regional, Gualeguay 000357
Museo Histórico Regional - Casa Garcilaso Cusco, Cusco 031504
Museo Histórico Regional de Ayacucho, Ayacucho 000122
Museo Histórico Regional de Gaiman, Gaiman 000349
Museo Histórico Regional de la Colonia San José, San José 000566
Museo Histórico Regional De la Isla, Isla del Cerrito 000366
Museo Histórico Regional de Magallanes, Punta Arenas 006924
Museo Histórico Regional de Río Cuarto, Río Cuarto 000510
Museo Histórico Regional de Tacna, Tacna 031602
Museo Histórico Regional de Urdinarrain, Urdinarrain 000647
Museo Histórico Regional de Villa La Angostura, Villa La Angostura . . . 000669
Museo Histórico Regional Ex Cuartel de la Compañía Fija, Ensenada 028249
Museo Histórico Regional Gabriel Campomar Cervera, Salliqueló . . 000535
Museo Histórico Regional Ichoalay, Resistencia 000507
Museo Histórico Regional Municipal de Magdalena, Magdalena 000419
Museo Histórico Regional Pablo Argilaga, Santo Tomé 000621
Museo Histórico Regional Padre Francisco Cremasco, Villa Concepción del Tío 000663
Museo Histórico San Ignacio de Loyola, San José 000567
Museo Histórico Sanmartíniano, Mendoza 000436
Museo Histórico Sarmiento, Buenos Aires 000216
Museo Histórico y Antropológico de la Universidad Austral de Chile, Valdivia 006945
Museo Histórico y Arqueológico, Belén de Umbría 007401
Museo Histórico y Arqueológico, Charalá 007483
Museo Histórico y de la Tradiciones Populares de la Boca, Buenos Aires 000217
Museo Histórico y Natural de Lavalle, Lavalle Villa Tulumaya 000404
Museo Histórico y Regional Pico Truncado, Pico Truncado 000473
Museo Histórico y Tradicional de Barracas al Sud, Avellaneda 000120
Museo Históricos del Banco de la Provincia de Buenos Aires, Buenos Aires . . 000218
Museo Hotel Marquetá, Mariquita . 007533
Museo Houssay de Historia de la Ciencia y Técnología, Universidad Buenos Aires, Buenos Aires 000219
Museo Huehuetla-tolli, Comala . . . 028178
Museo Hunucmá de Sisal, Hunucmá 028339
Museo I Luoghi del Lavoro Contadino, Buscemi 023548
Museo I. Nievo, Fossalta di Portogruaro 024241
Museo I. Salvini, Cocquio Trevisago 023918
Museo Iberoamericano de Arte Moderno de Popayán, Popayán 007588
Museo Ibleo delle Arti e Tradizioni Popolari S.A. Guastella, Modica 024769
Museo Iconográfico, Itaugua 031452
Museo Iconográfico del Quijote, Guanajuato 028307
Museo Ideale Leonardo Da Vinci, Vinci 026341
Museo Iglesia del Salvador, Oña . . . 035558
Museo Ignacio Zuloaga, Pedraza de la Sierra 035643
Museo Igneológico del Cuerpo Ofical de Bomberos, Bogotá 007445
Museo Il Giardino dell'Arte, Portoferraio 025335
Museo Illichiano, Castell'Arquato . . 023724
Museo Iloilo, Iloilo 031673
Museo Immaginario, Domodossola . 024036
Museo in Erba, Bellinzona 036917
Museo In Situ, Museo Civico, Sulmona 025966
Museo Inca de la Universidad Nacional San Antonio Abad, Cusco 031505
Museo Independencia, Córdoba . . . 000302
Museo Indiano, Università Bologna, Bologna 023453
Museo Indígena de Colombia Ethnia, Bogotá 007446
Museo Indígena de Guatavita, Guatavita 007513
Museo Indígena Regional Enin, Mitú 007546
Museo Indigenista, Esquel 000344
Museo Indigeno, San José 007680
Museo Industrial de Santa Catarina El Blanqueo, Santa Catarina 028760
Museo Inés Mercedes Gómez Álvarez, Universidad Ezequiel Zamora, Guanare 049494
Museo Instituto Cultural México Israel, México 028508
Museo Insular de la Palma, Santa Cruz de la Palma 035792
Museo Inter-étnico de la Amazonía, Florencia 007501
Museo Interactivo de Ciencia, Tecnología y Medio Ambiente Sol del Niño, Mexicali 028421
Museo Interactivo de Ciencias, Paraná 000467
Museo Interactivo de Ciencias, Parque de las Ciencias, Granada 035257
Museo Interactivo de Ciencias Naturales, Ituzaingó 000368
Museo Interactivo del Centro de Ciencias de Sinaloa, Culiacán 028216
Museo Interactivo del Medio Ambiente, México 028509
Museo Interactivo El Rehilete, Pachuca 028627
Museo Interactivo La Avispa, Chilpancingo 028163
Museo Interattivo delle Scienze, Foggia 024210
Museo Internacional de Arte Contemporáneo, Arrecife 034862
Museo Internacional de Arte Naïf, Jaén 035304
Museo Internazionale del Folklore e Civiltà Contadina, Atina 023295
Museo Internazionale del Presepio, Morrovalle 024884
Museo Internazionale della Campana, Agnone 023129
Museo Internazionale della Caricatura, Tolentino 026037
Museo Internazionale della Croce Rossa, Castiglione delle Stiviere 023749
Museo Internazionale della Fisarmonica, Castelfidardo 023711
Museo Internazionale delle Ceramiche, Faenza 024070
Museo Internazionale delle Marionette A. Pasqualino, Palermo 025094
Museo Internazionale dell'Etichetta, Cupramontana 024017
Museo Internazionale dell'Immagine Postale, Belvedere Ostrense 023365
Museo Internazionale di Burattini e Marionette, L'Aquila 024462
Museo Interparroquial de Alaejos, Alaejos 034789
Museo Interparroquial de Arte Sacro, Iglesia de Santa María de Mediavilla, Medina de Rioseco 035485
Museo Irineo Germán, Azoyú 028119
Museo Irpino, Avellino 023305
Museo Irureta, Tilcara 000635
Museo Isabel Rubio, Isabel Rubio . . 008029
Museo Isidro Fabela, Atlacomulco . 028114
Museo It Akean, Kalibo 031679
Museo Italgas, Torino 026071
Museo Italiano della Ghisa, Chiesa di Santa Maria delle Lacrime, Longiano . . . 024529
Museo Italoamericano, San Francisco 047873
Museo Ittico, Pescara 025186
Museo Ittico Augusto Capriotti, San Benedetto del Tronto 025652
Museo Ixchel del Traje Indigena, Guatemala 021580
Museo Jacinto Jijón y Caamaño, Quito 009249
Museo Jacobo Borges, Caracas . . . 049475
Museo Jarocho Salvador Ferrando, Tlacotalpan 028848
Museo Jesuítico de Sitio, Yapeyú . . 000674
Museo Jesuitico Nacional de Jesus María, Córdoba 000303
Museo Jesútico Nacional de Jesús María, Jesús María 000369
Museo J.M. Cruxent, Los Teques . . 049499
Museo Jorge Eliécer Gaitán, Puerto Gaitán 007591
Museo Jorge Pasquini López, San Salvador de Jujuy 000596
Museo José Antonio Páez, Acarigua 049436
Museo José Celso Barbosa, Bazamón 032707
Museo José de Jesús Almaza, Xicoténcatl 028947
Museo José Fernando Ramírez, Durango 028231
Museo José Guadalupe Posada, Aguascalientes 028090
Museo José Luis Cuevas, Colima . . 028169
Museo José Luis Cuevas, México . . 028510
Museo José Manuel Estrada, Suipacha 000624
Museo José María Luis Mora, Ocoyoacac 028618
Museo José María Morelos y Pavón, Cuautla 028202
Museo José María Velasco, Toluca . 028877
Museo José Martí, La Habana 007991
Museo José Natividad Correa Toca Teapa, Teapa 028794
Museo José Serra Farré, La Riba . . 035699
Museo José y Tomás Chávez Morado, Silao 028775
Museo Jovellanos, Pinacoteca Municipal, Gijón 035224
Museo Juan Carlos Iramaín, San Miguel de Tucumán 000585
Museo Juan Lorenzo Lucero, Pasto 007569
Museo Juan Manuel Blanes, Montevideo 041520
Museo Juan Pablo Duarte, Santo Domingo 009164
Museo Juan Zorrilla de San Martín, Montevideo 041521
Museo Juárez del Jardín Borda, Cuernavaca 028206
Museo Juárez e Historia de Mapimí y Ojuela, Mapimí 028401
Museo Juarista de Congregación Hidalgo, Entronque Congregación Hidalgo . 028250
Museo Judío de Buenos Aires Dr. Salvador Kibrick, Buenos Aires 000220
Museo Julio Romero de Torres, Córdoba 035116
Museo Kan Pepen, Teabo 028793
Museo Kartell, Noviglio 024975
Museo Ken Damy di Fotografia Contemporanea, Brescia 023523
Museo L. Ceselli, Subiaco 025962
Museo L. Garaventa, Chiavari 023848
Museo L. Minguzzi, Milano 024721
Museo la Antigua Casa del Agua, Hunucmá 028340
Museo La Casa del Libro, San Juan 032744
Museo La Chole, Petatlán 028640
Museo La Cinacina, San Antonio de Areco 000550
Museo La Flor de Jimulco, Torreón . 028885
Museo La Fudina, Comelico Superiore 023941
Museo La Isabelica, Santiago de Cuba 008167
Museo La Pesca, Benito Juárez . . . 028123
Museo La Vieja Estación, María Teresa 000428
Museo La Vigía, Matanzas 008059
Museo-Laboratorio, Vernio 026279
Museo Laboratorio del Tessile, Soveria Mannelli 025929
Museo Laboratorio di Archeologia, Monsampolo del Tronto 024800
Museo Laboratorio di Arte Contemporanea, Università La Sapienza, Roma . . . 025544
Museo Ladino di Fassa, Pozza di Fassa 025349
Museo Ladino-Fodom, Livinallongo del Col di Lana 024506
Museo Laguna del Caimán, Tlahualilo de Zaragoza 028850
Museo Lapidario, Ferrara 024112
Museo Lapidario, Urbino 026176
Museo Lapidario del Duomo, Novara 024965
Museo Lapidario del Duomo di Sant' Eufemia, Grado 024360
Museo Lapidario e del Tesoro del Duomo, Modena 024764
Museo Lapidario Estense, Modena . 024765
Museo Lapidario Maffeiano, Verona 026291
Museo Lapidario Marsicano, Avezzano 023309
Museo Lara, Ronda 035722
El Museo Latino, Omaha 046681
Museo Lázaro Galdiano, Madrid . . . 035420
Museo Legislativo los Sentimientos de la Nación, México 028511
Museo Leonardiano, Vinci 026342
Museo Leoniano, Carpineto Romano 023672
Museo Lítico de Pukara, Pukara . . . 031588
Museo Local de Acámbaro, Dolores Hidalgo 028224
Museo Local de Antropología e Historia de Compostela, Compostela 028185
Museo Local de Valle de Santiago, Valle de Santiago 028911
Museo Local Tuxteco, Santiago Tuxtla 028771
Museo Locale, Termeno 026006
Museo Lodovico Pogliaghi, Santa Maria del Monte, Varese 026213
Museo Lombardo di Storia dell'Agricoltura, Sant'Angelo Lodigiano 025768
Museo López Claro, Santa Fé 000605
Museo Lorenzo Coullaut-Valera, Marchena 035472
Museo Loringiano, Málaga 035455
Museo Los Amantes de Sumpa, Guayaquil 009213

Museo Luciano Rosero, Pasto 007570
Museo Lucio Balderas Márquez, Landa de Matamoros 028383
Museo Luigi Varoli, Cotignola 023989
Museo Luis A. Calvo, Agua de Dios 007381
Museo Luis Alberto Acuña, Villa de Leyva 007640
Museo Luis Donaldo Colosio, Francisco I. Madero, Coahuila 028258
Museo M. Antonioni, Ferrara 024113
Museo Madres Benedictinas, Sahagún 035737
Museo Maestro Alfonso Zambrano, Pasto 007571
Museo Malacologico, Erice 024057
Museo Malacologico delle Argille, Cutrofiano 024022
Museo Malacologico Piceno, Cupra Marittima 024016
Museo Malvinas Argentinas, Río Gallegos 000514
Museo Manuel de Falla, Alta Gracia 000111
Museo Manuel Ojinaga, Manuel Ojinaga 028399
Museo Manuela Sáenz, Quito 009250
Museo Manzoniano, Lesa 024497
Museo Manzoniano, Milano 024722
Museo Marcelo López del Instituto Hellen Keller, Córdoba 000304
Museo Marcha del Pueblo Combatiente, La Habana 007992
Museo Marchigiano del Risorgimento G. e D. Spadoni, Macerata 024566
Museo Marciano, Venezia 026258
Museo Marcos Redondo, Pozoblanco 035673
Museo María Augusta Urrutia, Quito 009251
Museo Mariano, La Habana 007993
Museo Mariano Acosta, Ibarra 009220
Museo Mariano Matamoros, Jantetelco 028359
Museo Maridiaz, Pasto 007572
Museo Marinaro Tommasino-Andreatta, San Colombano Certenoli 025668
Museo Marino d'Arte Sacra Contemporanea, Comacchio 023939
Museo Marino de Tecolutla, Tecolutla 028798
Museo Marino Marini, Firenze 024193
Museo Marino Marini, Pistoia 025278
Museo Marino Marini, Galleria d'Arte Moderna, Milano 024723
Museo Mario Abreu, Maracay 049504
Museo Mario Praz, Roma 025545
Museo Marítimo de Asturias, Gozón 035240
Museo Marítimo de Ushuaia y Presidio, Ushuaia 000649
Museo Marítimo del Cantábrico, Santander 035812
Museo Marítimo-Ecológico Malvín, Montevideo 041522
Museo Marítimo Torre del Oro, Sevilla 035867
Museo Marítimo y Naval de la Patagonia Austral, Río Gallegos 000515
Museo Marsiliano, Bologna 023454
Museo Martín Gusinde, Puerto Williams 006923
Museo Martin Perez, Montevideo . . 041523
Museo Martínez de Compañon, Tambogrande 031603
Museo Martini di Storia dell'Enologia, Chieri 023855
Museo Martini di Storia dell'Enologia, Pessione 025199
Museo Mascagnano, Livorno 024510
Museo Maschera, Folklore e Civiltà Contadina, Acerra 023112
Museo Massó, Bueu 034998
Museo Maurice Minkowski, Buenos Aires 000221
Museo Máximo Gómez, La Habana . 007994
Museo Medardo Burbano, Pasto . . . 007573
Museo Medardo Rosso, Barzio 023350
Museo Mediceo della Petraia e Giardino, Firenze 024194
Museo Melezet, Bardonecchia 023332
Museo Melia Cayo Coco y Museo Tryp Colonial, Cayo Coco 007903
Museo Memoria Coronel Leoncio Prado, Callao 031479
Museo Memorial 12 de Septiembre, La Habana 007995
Museo Memorial 26 de Julio, Victoria de las Tunas 008190
Museo Memorial Antonio Guiteras Holmes, Pinar del Río 008093
Museo Memorial El Morrillo, Matanzas 008060
Museo Memorial Ernesto Che Guevara, Santa Clara 008141
Museo Memorial José Martí, La Habana 007996
Museo Memorial La Demajagua, Manzanillo 008051
Museo Memorial Los Malagones, Moncada 008069
Museo Memorial Mártires de Barbados, Victoria de las Tunas 008191
Museo Memorial Vicente García, Victoria de las Tunas 008192
Museo Memorias de Yucundé, San Pedro y San Pablo Teposcolula 028754
Museo Memorie Pollentine, Pollenza 025298
Museo Merano, Merano 024669
Museo Mercantile, Bolzano 023472
Museo Mercedes Sierra de Pérez El Chico, Bogotá 007447
Museo Meteorológico Nacional Dr. Benjamín A. Gould, Córdoba 000305
Museo Metropolitano, Buenos Aires 000222
Museo Metropolitano de Monterrey, Monterrey 028569
Museo Michelangelo, Caprese 023649
Museo Michoacano de las Artesanías, Morelia 028583
Museo Miguel Álvarez del Toro, Tuxtla Gutiérrez 028900
Museo Militar de Colombia, Bogotá 007448
Museo Militar de Menorca, Es Castell 035064
Museo Militar Regional, A Coruña . . 035129
Museo Militar Regional, Castell de San Carlos, Palma de Mallorca 035613
Museo Militar Regional de Burgos, Burgos 035008
Museo Militar Regional de Canarias, Santa Cruz de Tenerife 035796
Museo Militar Regional de Sevilla, Museo Naval de San Fernando, Sevilla . . 035868
Museo Mille Voci e Mille Suoni, Bologna 023455
Museo Mineralogico, Bortigiadas . . 023497
Museo Mineralogico, La Paz 003914
Museo Mineralogico, Valle Aurina . . 026196
Museo Mineralogico Campano, Vico Equense 026317
Museo Mineralogico e Naturalistico, Bormio 023496
Museo Mineralogico e Paleontologico delle Zolfare, Caltanissetta 023593
Museo Mineralogico Permanente, Carro 023678
Museo Mineralógico Prof. Manuel Tellechea, Mendoza 000437
Museo Mineralógico Salón Tulio Ospina, National University of Colombia, Medellín 007544
Museo Mineralogico Sardo, Iglesias 024399
Museo Mineralógico y Antropológico, Ibagué 007519
Museo Minerario Alpino, Cogne . . . 023923
Museo Minero, Gallarta 035210
Museo Minero, La Unión 035964
Museo Minero de Riotinto, Minas de Riotinto 035495
Museo Minero Ferrería de San Blas, Sabero 035731
Museo Minimo, Corigliano Calabro . 023969
Museo Miniscalchi Erizzo, Verona . . 026292
Museo Mirador de Quistococha, Iquitos 031531
Museo Miscellaneo Galbiati, Brugherio 023534
Museo Misional de Nuestra Señora de Regla, Chipiona 035090
Museo Missionario, Loreto 024531
Museo Missionario, Padova 025063
Museo Missionario Cinese e di Storia Naturale, Lecce 024482
Museo Missionario delle Grazie, Santuario della Madonna delle Grazie, Rimini 025435
Museo Missionario Etnologico, Musei Vaticani, Città del Vaticano 049427
Museo Missionario Francescano, Fiesole 024125
Museo Mitre, Buenos Aires 000223
Museo Moesano, San Vittore 037489
Museo Mohicca, Mohicca 028554
Museo Molino Nant Fach, Trevelin . 000643
Museo Molino Papelero de Capellades, Capellades 035049
Museo Monasterio Santa María La Real de Vileña, Villarcayo 036066
Museo Monástico Medival y de Farmacia, Santo Domingo de Silos 035837
Museo Monográfico Aquis Querquernis, Bande 034894
Museo Monográfico de Cástulo, Linares 035334
Museo Monográfico de Clunia, Peñalba de Castro 035646
Museo Monográfico de El Cigarralejo, Mula 035527
Museo Monográfico de la Alcudia, Elche 035169
Museo Monográfico de la Colonia Celsa, Museo de Zaragoza, Velilla de Ebro 036021
Museo Monográfico de la Villa Romana de la Olmeda, Saldaña 035747
Museo Monográfico de Tiermes, Montejo de Tiermes 035517
Museo Monográfico del Azafrán, Monreal del Campo 035512
Museo Monográfico del Castro de Viladonga, Castro de Rei 035073
Museo Monográfico y Necrópolis Púnica de Puig des Molins, Eivissa 035162
Museo Mons Juan Sinforiano Bogarin, Asunción 031449
Museo Monseñor José Fagnano, Río Grande 000518
Museo Montemartini, Roma 025546
Museo Monumento al Deportato, Carpi 023671
Museo Morandi - Collezioni Comunali d'Arte, Palazzo Accursio, Bologna 023456
Museo Morando Bolognini, Sant'Angelo Lodigiano 025769
Museo Morelos, Carácuaro 028138
Museo Multidisciplinario del Colegio La Salle, Lima 031565
Museo Mundocaña, Cali 007472
Museo Mundocaña, Palmira 007561
Museo Municipal, Alcázar de San Juan 034805
Museo Municipal, Algeciras 034818
Museo Municipal, Alzira 034833
Museo Municipal, Amposta 034837
Museo Municipal, Antequera 034842
Museo Municipal, Aroche 034861
Museo Municipal, Ayllón 034877
Museo Municipal, Cabra 035013
Museo Municipal, Calatayud 035028
Museo Municipal, Ciego de Avila . . . 007907
Museo Municipal, Consuegra 035108
Museo Municipal, Forcall 035197
Museo Municipal, Holguín 008027
Museo Municipal, Iquitos 031532
Museo Municipal, Jérica 035308
Museo Municipal, Mier 028547
Museo Municipal, Nerva 035543
Museo Municipal, Ourense 035582
Museo Municipal, Palma del Río . . . 035620
Museo Municipal, Pavias 035641
Museo Municipal, Pizarra 035655
Museo Municipal, El Puerto de Santa María 035684
Museo Municipal, Requena 035694
Museo Municipal, Reus 035696
Museo Municipal, Sancti-Spíritus . . 008132
Museo Municipal, Tárrega 035897
Museo Municipal, Valdepeñas 035969
Museo Municipal, Vélez-Málaga . . . 036019
Museo Municipal, Zuheros 036120
Museo Municipal, Museo de la Ciudad, Carmona 035056
Museo Municipal Alex Urquiola, El Salvador 008114
Museo Municipal Arco Ajújar, Medina de Rioseco 035486
Museo Municipal Barão de Santo Angelo, Rio Pardo 004425
Museo Municipal Cabildo de Montevideo, Montevideo 041524
Museo Municipal Carmen Funes, Plaza Huincul 000477
Museo Municipal Casa de Alfaro, Montecristi 009226
Museo Municipal C.I.P.A.S., Salto . . 000544
Museo Municipal de 10 de Octubre, La Habana 007997
Museo Municipal de Abreus, Abreus 007865
Museo Municipal de Aguada de Pasajeros, Aguada de Pasajeros 007866
Museo Municipal de Alto Songo y La Maya, Alto Songo 007867
Museo Municipal de Amancio, Amancio 007869
Museo Municipal de Arqueología y Etnología, Segorbe 035839
Museo Municipal de Arqueología y Etnología, Villajoyosa 036065
Museo Municipal de Arte, Rauch . . . 000500
Museo Municipal de Arte Angel María de Rosa, Junín 000371
Museo Municipal de Arte Decorativo Firma y Odilo Estévez, Rosario 000528
Museo Municipal de Arte Juan Carlos Castagnino, Mar del Plata 000425
Museo Municipal de Arte Moderno, Cuenca 009199
Museo Municipal de Arte Moderno de Mendoza, Mendoza 000438
Museo Municipal de Artes Plásticas, Avellaneda 000121
Museo Municipal de Artes Plásticas, Olavarría 000460
Museo Municipal de Artes Plásticas, Rivera 041550
Museo Municipal de Artes Plásticas Pompeo Boggio, Chivilcoy 000276
Museo Municipal de Artes Visuales, Concordia 000287
Museo Municipal de Artes Visuales, Quilmes 000493
Museo Municipal de Artes Visuales, Santa Fé 000606
Museo Municipal de Arucas, Arucas 034868
Museo Municipal de Báguano, Báguano 007871
Museo Municipal de Bahía Honda, Bahía Honda 007872
Museo Municipal de Baraguá, Baraguá 007875
Museo Municipal de Bartolomé Masó, Bartolomé Masó 007876
Museo Municipal de Bayamo, Bayamo 007880
Museo Municipal de Baza, Baza . . . 034963
Museo Municipal de Bellas Artes, Bahía Blanca 000127
Museo Municipal de Bellas Artes, Godoy Cruz 000355
Museo Municipal de Bellas Artes, La Calera 000373
Museo Municipal de Bellas Artes, La Paz 000381
Museo Municipal de Bellas Artes, Pergamino 000471
Museo Municipal de Bellas Artes, San Nicolás de los Arroyos 000590
Museo Municipal de Bellas Artes, Tandil 000629
Museo Municipal de Bellas Artes, Xàtiva 036088

Museo Municipal de Bellas Artes, Antiguo Convento de San Francisco, Santa Cruz de Tenerife 035797
Museo Municipal de Bellas Artes de Campana, Campana 000257
Museo Municipal de Bellas Artes de Valparaíso, Valparaíso 006948
Museo Municipal de Bellas Artes Dr. Genaro Perez, Córdoba 000306
Museo Municipal de Bellas Artes Dr. Genaro Pérez, Río Cuarto 000511
Museo Municipal de Bellas Artes Dr. Urbano Poggi, Rafaela 000497
Museo Municipal de Bellas Artes Juan B. Castagnino, Rosario 000529
Museo Municipal de Bellas Artes Juan Manuel Blanes, Montevideo 041525
Museo Municipal de Bellas Artes Lucas Braulio Areco, Posadas 000482
Museo Municipal de Bellas Artes Prof. Amelio Ronco Ceruti, Metán 000444
Museo Municipal de Bolivia, Bolivia 007884
Museo Municipal de Boyeros, La Habana 007998
Museo Municipal de Buey Arriba, Buey Arriba 007885
Museo Municipal de Cabaiguán, Cabaiguán 007886
Museo Municipal de Cabana, Cabana 031469
Museo Municipal de Cacomun, Cacomun 007887
Museo Municipal de Caibarién, Caibarién 007888
Museo Municipal de Caimanera, Caimanera 007889
Museo Municipal de Calahorra, Calahorra 035025
Museo Municipal de Calasparra, Calasparra 035026
Museo Municipal de Calimete, Calimete 007891
Museo Municipal de Camajuaní Hermanos Vidal Caro, Camajuaní 007897
Museo Municipal de Campechuela, Campechuela 007898
Museo Municipal de Candelaria, Candelaria 007899
Museo Municipal de Carlos Manuel de Céspedes, Carlos Manuel de Céspedes 007901
Museo Municipal de Cauto Cristo, Cauto Cristo 007902
Museo Municipal de Cerámica, Paterna 035640
Museo Municipal de Chambas, Chambas 007904
Museo Municipal de Chincha, Chincha Alta 031488
Museo Municipal de Ciencias, Bahía Blanca 000128
Museo Municipal de Ciencias Naturales, El Real de la Jara 035692
Museo Municipal de Ciencias Naturales Carlos Ameghino, Mercedes 000443
Museo Municipal de Ciencias Naturales Carlos Darwin, Punta Alta 000491
Museo Municipal de Ciencias Naturales Lorenzo Scaglia, Mar del Plata . . 000426
Museo Municipal de Cifuentes, Cifuentes 007913
Museo Municipal de Ciro Redondo, Ciro Redondo 007914
Museo Municipal de Colón José R. Zulueta, Colón 007916
Museo Municipal de Consolación del Sur, Consolación del Sur 007917
Museo Municipal de Contramaestre, Contramaestre 007918
Museo Municipal de Corralillo, Corralillo 007919
Museo Municipal de Cruces, Cruces 007920
Museo Municipal de Cueto, Cueto . 007922
Museo Municipal de Cumanayagua, Cumanayagua 007923
Museo Municipal de El Trébol, El Trébol 000334
Museo Municipal de Eldorado, Eldorado 000336
Museo Municipal de Esmeralda, Esmeralda 007924
Museo Municipal de Etnografía, Villadiego 036059
Museo Municipal de Etnología, Castellón de la Plana 035070
Museo Municipal de Florencia, Florencia 007925
Museo Municipal de Florida, Florida 007926
Museo Municipal de Fomento, Fomento 007927
Museo Municipal de Gibara, Gibara 007930
Museo Municipal de Guamá, La Plata 008099
Museo Municipal de Guane, Guane 007933
Museo Municipal de Guantánamo - Antigua Cárcel, Guantánamo 007937
Museo Municipal de Guayaquil, Guayaquil 009214
Museo Municipal de Guisa, Guisa . . 007938
Museo Municipal de Habana del Este, La Habana 007999
Museo Municipal de Historia, Necolí 007553
Museo Municipal de Historia del Arte, Montevideo 041526
Museo Municipal de Historia Malitzín de Huiloapan, Huiloapan de Cuauhtémoc 028335
Museo Municipal de Historia Natural, General Alvear 000350
Museo Municipal de Historia Natural, San Rafael 000593
Museo Municipal de Historia y Arqueología, González 028268
Museo Municipal de Historia y Arqueología, Rivera 041551
Museo Municipal de Huaytará, Huaytará 031523
Museo Municipal de Imías, Playitas y Cajobabo, Cajobabo 007890
Museo Municipal de Jagüey Grande, Jagüey Grande 008031
Museo Municipal de Jesús Menéndez, Jesús Menéndez 008034
Museo Municipal de Jiguaní, Jiguaní 008035
Museo Municipal de Jovellanos Domingo Mujica, Jovellanos 008038
Museo Municipal de la Ciudad de Carcarañá, Carcarañá 000261
Museo Municipal de la Ciudad de Rosario, Rosario 000530
Museo Municipal de la Ciudadela, Ciutadella de Menorca 035100
Museo Municipal de la Construcción, Montevideo 041527
Museo Municipal de la Lisa, La Habana 008000
Museo Municipal de La Sierpe, La Sierpe 008175
Museo Municipal de La Yaya, La Yaya 008201
Museo Municipal de Lajas, Lajas . . 008039
Museo Municipal de Lomas de Zamora, Lomas de Zamora 000408
Museo Municipal de Los Arabos Clotilde García, Los Arabos 008040
Museo Municipal de Los Palacios, Los Palacios 008041
Museo Municipal de Madrid, Madrid 035421
Museo Municipal de Maisí, Maisí . . 008043
Museo Municipal de Majagua, Majagua 008044
Museo Municipal de Majibacoa, Majibacoa 008045
Museo Municipal de Manatí Jesús Suárez Gayol, Manatí 008046
Museo Municipal de Manicaragua, Manicaragua 008047
Museo Municipal de Mantua, Mantua 008048
Museo Municipal de Manuel Tames, Manuel Tames 008049
Museo Municipal de Manzanillo, Manzanillo 008052
Museo Municipal de Marianao, La Habana 008001
Museo Municipal de Martí, Martí . . 008053
Museo Municipal de Mayarí, Mayarí 008063
Museo Municipal de Media Luna, Media Luna 008065
Museo Municipal de Minas, Minas . 008066
Museo Municipal de Minas de Matahambre, Minas de Matahambre 008067
Museo Municipal de Moa, Moa 008068
Museo Municipal de Morón, Morón 008070
Museo Municipal de Najasa, Sibanicú 008173
Museo Municipal de Nazca y Casa Museo María Reiche, Nazca 031577
Museo Municipal de Niceto Pérez, Niceto Pérez 008071
Museo Municipal de Niquero, Niquero 008072
Museo Municipal de Nuevitas, Nuevitas 008082
Museo Municipal de Palma Soriano, Palma Soriano 008084
Museo Municipal de Pedro Betancourt, Pedro Betancourt 008086
Museo Municipal de Perico, Perico . 008087
Museo Municipal de Pilón, Pilón . . . 008088
Museo Municipal de Pintura, Villadiego 036060
Museo Municipal de Placetas, Placetas 008098
Museo Municipal de Poblado de Jimaguayú, Jimaguayú 008036
Museo Municipal de Ponteareas, Ponteareas 035665
Museo Municipal de Porteña, Porteña 000478
Museo Municipal de Prehistoria, Gandía 035212
Museo Municipal de Primero de Enero, Primero de Enero 008101
Museo Municipal de Quemado de Güines, Quemado de Güines 008105
Museo Municipal de Rafael Freyre, Rafael Freyre 008106
Museo Municipal de Ranchuelo, Ranchuelo 008107
Museo Municipal de Río Cauto, Río Cauto 008110
Museo Municipal de Rodas, Rodas . 008111
Museo Municipal de Sagua de Tánamo, Sagua de Tánamo 008112
Museo Municipal de Sagua la Grande, Sagua la Grande 008113
Museo Municipal de San Cristobal, San Cristobal 008121
Museo Municipal de San Juan y Martínez, San Juan y Martínez 008123
Museo Municipal de San Luis 29 de Abril, San Luis 008124
Museo Municipal de San Miguel del Padrón, La Habana 008002
Museo Municipal de San Telmo, Donostia-San Sebastián 035153
Museo Municipal de Sandino, Sandino 008135
Museo Municipal de Santa Cruz del Sur, Santa Cruz del Sur 008145
Museo Municipal de Santo Domingo, Santo Domingo 008172
Museo Municipal de Sibanicú, Sibanicú 008174
Museo Municipal de Sierra de Cubitas, Cubitas 007921
Museo Municipal de Taguasco, Taguasco 008177
Museo Municipal de Trinidad, Trinidad 008181
Museo Municipal de Unión de Reyes Juan G. Gómez, Unión de Reyes 008183
Museo Municipal de Urbano Noris, Urbano Noris 008184
Museo Municipal de Varadero, Varadero 008185
Museo Municipal de Vedado, La Habana 008003
Museo Municipal de Venezuela, Venezuela 008186
Museo Municipal de Vertientes, Vertientes 008187
Museo Municipal de Vigo Quiñones de León, Vigo 036033
Museo Municipal de Viñales Adela Azcuy Labrador, Pinar del Río 008094
Museo Municipal de Yaguajay, Yaguajay 008198
Museo Municipal de Yara, Yara 008199
Museo Municipal de Yateras, Yateras 008200
Museo Municipal del Cerro, La Habana 008004
Museo Municipal del Deporte, San Fernando del Valle de Catamarca 000557
Museo Municipal del III Frente, Santiago de Cuba 008168
Museo Municipal Dr. Rodolfo Doval Fermi, Sastre 000622
Museo Municipal Dreyer, Dreyer . . . 031507
Museo Municipal Eduard Camps Cava, Guissona 035274
Museo Municipal Elisa Cendrero, Ciudad Real 035098
Museo Municipal Emilio Daudinot, San Antonio del Sur 008119
Museo Municipal Fernando García Grave de Peralta, Puerto Padre 008104
Museo Municipal Forte de San Damián, Ribadeo 035702
Museo Municipal Francisco Javier Balmaseda, Santa Clara 008142
Museo Municipal Histórico Fotográfico de Quilmes, Quilmes 000494
Museo Municipal Histórico Regional Almirante Brown, Bernal 000139
Museo Municipal Histórico Regional Santiago Lischetti, Villa Constitución 000664
Museo Municipal Ignacio Balvidares, Puan 000485
Museo Municipal IV Centenario, Pinos 028643
Museo Municipal Jatibonico, Jatibonico 008033
Museo Municipal Jerónimo Molina, Jumilla 035311
Museo Municipal Jesús González Herrera, Matamoros 028405
Museo Municipal Jesús H. Salgado, Teloloapan 028805
Museo Municipal José A. Mulazzi, Tres Arroyos 000640
Museo Municipal José Manuel Maciel, Coronda 000314
Museo Municipal José Reyes Meza, Altamira 028100
Museo Municipal Juan M. Ameijeiras, El Salvador 008115
Museo Municipal Lino Enea Spilimbergo, Unquillo 000646
Museo Municipal Los Guachimontones y Museo de Arquitectura Prehispánica, Teuchitlán 028835
Museo Municipal Manuel Torres, Marín 035474
Museo Municipal Marceliano Santa María, Burgos 035009
Museo Municipal Mariano Benlliure, Crevillente 035134
Museo Municipal Mateo Hernández, Béjar 034967
Museo Municipal Nueva Gerona, Nueva Gerona 008080
Museo Municipal Paula Florido, 25 de Mayo 000104
Museo Municipal Precolombino y Colonial, Montevideo 041528
Museo Municipal Primeros Pobladores, San Martín de los Andes 000577
Museo Municipal Punta Hermengo, Miramar 000448
Museo Municipal Quetzalpapalotl, Teotihuacán 028812
Museo Municipal Ramón María Aller Ulloa, Lalín 035319
Museo Municipal Roberto Rojas Tamayo, Colombia 007915
Museo Municipal Rosendo Arteaga, Jobabo Dos 008037

Museo Municipal Sala Dámaso Navarro, Petrer . . . 035653
Museo Municipal Ulpiano Checa, Colmenar de Oreja . . . 035104
Museo Municipal Victorio Macho, Palencia . . . 035598
Museo Municpal Dr. Santos F. Tosticarelli, Casilda . . . 000267
Museo Mural Diego Rivera, México 028512
Museo Mural Homenaje a Benito Juárez, México . . . 028513
Museo Muratoriano, Modena . . . 024766
Museo Musicale d'Abruzzo, Archivio F.P. Tosti, Ortona . . . 025017
Museo Na-Bolom, San Cristóbal de las Casas . . . 028713
Museo Nacional Casa Guillermo Valencia, Popayán . . . 007589
Museo Nacional Centro de Arte Reina Sofía, Madrid . . . 035422
Museo Nacional David J. Guzmán, San Salvador . . . 009353
Museo Nacional de Aeronáutica, Buenos Aires . . . 000224
Museo Nacional de Agricultura, Universidad Autónoma Chapingo, Texcoco de Mora . . . 028837
Museo Nacional de Antropología, Bogotá . . . 007449
Museo Nacional de Antropología, Madrid . . . 035423
Museo Nacional de Antropología, México . . . 028514
Museo Nacional de Antropología, Montevideo . . . 041529
Museo Nacional de Antropología, Arqueología e Historia del Perú, Lima . . . 031566
Museo Nacional de Arqueología, La Paz . . . 003915
Museo Nacional de Arqueología Marítima, Centro Nacional de Investigaciones Arqueológicas Submarinas, Cartagena . . . 035060
Museo Nacional de Arqueología y Etnología, Guatemala . . . 021581
Museo Nacional de Arquitectura, Madrid . . . 035424
Museo Nacional de Arquitectura, México . . . 028515
Museo Nacional de Arte, La Paz . . . 003916
Museo Nacional de Arte, México . . 028516
Museo Nacional de Arte Decorativo, Buenos Aires . . . 000225
Museo Nacional de Arte Fantástico, Córdoba . . . 028190
Museo Nacional de Arte Hispanomusulmán, Granada . . . 035258
Museo Nacional de Arte Moderno, Guatemala . . . 021582
Museo Nacional de Arte Oriental, Buenos Aires . . . 000226
Museo Nacional de Arte Popular, Mérida . . . 028415
Museo Nacional de Arte Romano, Mérida . . . 035492
Museo Nacional de Artes Decorativas, La Habana . . . 008005
Museo Nacional de Artes Decorativas, Madrid . . . 035425
Museo Nacional de Artes Decorativas de Santa Clara, Santa Clara . . . 008143
Museo Nacional de Artes e Industrias Populares, México . . . 028517
Museo Nacional de Artes Visuales, Montevideo . . . 041530
Museo Nacional de Bellas Artes, Buenos Aires . . . 000227
Museo Nacional de Bellas Artes, La Habana . . . 008006
Museo Nacional de Bellas Artes, Montevideo . . . 041531
Museo Nacional de Bellas Artes de Santiago de Chile, Santiago de Chile . . . 006936
Museo Nacional de Bellas Artes y Antigüedades, Asunción . . . 031450
Museo Nacional de Camilo Cienfuegos, Sancti-Spíritus . . . 008133
Museo Nacional de Caza, Riofrío . . 035704
Museo Nacional de Cerámica y de las Artes Suntuarias González Martí, Valencia . . . 035985
Museo Nacional de Ciencias Naturales, Madrid . . . 035426
Museo Nacional de Colombia, Bogotá . . . 007450
Museo Nacional de Costa Rica, San José . . . 007681
Museo Nacional de Culturas Populares, México . . . 028518
Museo Nacional de Escultura, Valladolid . . . 036003
Museo Nacional de Etnografía y Folklore, La Paz . . . 003917
Museo Nacional de Ferrocarriles Mexicanos, Puebla . . . 028672
Museo Nacional de Historia, Guatemala . . . 021583
Museo Nacional de Historia, Castillo de Chapultepec, México . . . 028519
Museo Nacional de Historia Colonial, Omoa . . . 021610
Museo Nacional de Historia de la Medicina Eduardo Estrella, Quito . . . 009252
Museo Nacional de Historia Natural, Guatemala . . . 021578
Museo Nacional de Historia Natural, La Habana . . . 008007
Museo Nacional de Historia Natural, Santiago de Chile . . . 006937
Museo Nacional de Historia Natural y Antropología, Montevideo . . . 041532
Museo Nacional de la Acuarela, México . . . 028520
Museo Nacional de la Alfabetización, La Habana . . . 008008
Museo Nacional de la Cerámica, La Habana . . . 008009
Museo Nacional de la Cerámica, Tonalá, Jalisco . . . 028880
Museo Nacional de la Ciencia y la Tecnología, Madrid . . . 035427
Museo Nacional de la Cultura Peruana, Lima . . . 031567
Museo Nacional de la Dirección Regional del Banco Central del Ecuador, Quito . . . 009253
Museo Nacional de la Estampa, México . . . 028521
Museo Nacional de la Histórico del Traje, Buenos Aires . . . 000228
Museo Nacional de la Máscara, San Luis Potosí . . . 028735
Museo Nacional de la Música, La Habana . . . 008010
Museo Nacional de la Revolución, México . . . 028522
Museo Nacional de las Culturas, México . . . 028523
Museo Nacional de las Intervenciones, México . . . 028524
Museo Nacional de las Telecomunicaciones, Bogotá . . . 007451
Museo Nacional de los Ferrocarriles Mexicanos, México . . . 028525
Museo Nacional de Nicaragua, Managua . . . 030665
Museo Nacional de Panamá, Panamá City . . . 031433
Museo Nacional de Reproducciones Artísticas, Madrid . . . 035428
Museo Nacional de San Carlos, México . . . 028526
Museo Nacional de Virreinato, Tepotzotlán . . . 028829
Museo Nacional del Cobre, Salvador Escalante . . . 028704
Museo Nacional del Grabado, Buenos Aires . . . 000229
Museo Nacional del Hombre, Buenos Aires . . . 000230
Museo Nacional del Ministerio del Interior, La Habana . . . 008011
Museo Nacional del Petróleo, Comodoro Rivadavia . . . 000281
Museo Nacional del Petróleo Samuel Schneider Uribe, Barrancabermeja . . . 007397
Museo Nacional del Prado, Madrid . 035429
Museo Nacional del Sombrero, Aguadas . . . 007383
Museo Nacional del Títere, Huamantla . . . 028325
Museo Nacional Justo José de Urquiza, Concepción del Uruguay . . . 000284
Museo Nacional Mariano, Chiquinquira . . . 007484
Museo Nacional Tihuanacu, La Paz 003918
Museo Nacional y Centro de Estudios Históricos Ferroviarios, Buenos Aires . . . 000231
Museo Nacional y Centro de Investigación de Altamira, Santillana del Mar . . 035833
Museo Nacional y Zoológico La Aurora, Guatemala . . . 021584
Museo Nahim Isaias, Guayaquil . . . 009215
Museo Nájerillense, Nájera . . . 035538
Museo Napoleónico, La Habana . . . 008012
Museo Napoleonico, Rivoli Veronese . . . 025449
Museo Napoleonico, Roma . . . 025547
Museo Napoleonico, Tolentino . . . 026038
Museo Napoleonico G. Antonelli, Arcole . . . 023230
Museo Natural, Pensilvania . . . 007577
Museo Natural de Historia y Geografía, Santo Domingo . . . 009165
Museo Natural Dr. Carlos A. Marelli, Colón . . . 000280
Museo Naturali e Appennino, Revi nel Lazio . . . 025423
Museo Naturalistica-Archeologico, Vicenza . . . 026311
Museo Naturalistico, Champdepraz 023834
Museo Naturalistico, L'Aquila . . . 024463
Museo Naturalistico, Lesina . . . 024498
Museo Naturalistico, Pescasseroli . 025189
Museo Naturalistico, Picinisco . . . 025222
Museo Naturalistico, Portoferraio . . 025336
Museo Naturalistico, Instituto Sacra Famiglia, Chieri . . . 023856
Museo Naturalistico Archeologico M. Locati, Lama dei Peligni . . . 024447
Museo naturalistico del Frignano, Pavullo nel Frignano . . . 025148
Museo Naturalistico del Lago, Montepulciano . . . 024856
Museo Naturalistico del Parco, San Romano di Garfagnana . . . 025726
Museo Naturalistico della Riserva Naturale Orientata di Onferno, Gemmano . . 024287
Museo Naturalistico della Vallata del Bidente, Bagno di Romagna . . . 023322
Museo Naturalistico e della Civiltà Contadina, Berceto . . . 023373
Museo Naturalistico F. Minà Palumbo, Convento Badia, Castelbuono . . . 023709
Museo Naturalistico G. Zanardo, Tambre . . . 025986
Museo Naturalistico Libero Gatti, Copanello . . . 023958
Museo Naturalistico Missionario, Chiusa Pesio . . . 023870
Museo Naturalistico N. De Leone, Penne . . . 025155
Museo Naturalistico O. Perini, Borca di Cadore . . . 023478
Museo Naturalistico P. Barrasso, Caramanico Terme . . . 023657
Museo Naucalpan de la Cultura Tlatilca, Naucalpan de Juárez . . . 028595
Museo Naval, Catia la Mar . . . 049481
Museo Naval, Madrid . . . 035430
Museo Naval, Montevideo . . . 041533
Museo Naval de Cartagena, Cartagena . . . 035061
Museo Naval de Ferrol, Ferrol . . . 035191
Museo Naval de Ilo, Ilo . . . 031528
Museo Naval de la Nación, Tigre . . 000633
Museo Naval de la Zona Marítima del Cantábrico, Ferrol . . . 035191
Museo Naval de Viña del Mar, Viña del Mar . . . 006952
Museo Naval del Perú, Callao . . . 031480
Museo Naval del Puerto de la Cruz, Puerto de la Cruz . . . 035682
Museo Naval Puerto Belgrano, Puerto Belgrano . . . 000486
Museo Navale, Genova . . . 024323
Museo Navale, Napoli . . . 024918
Museo Navale Archeologico N. Lamboglia, La Maddalena . . . 024434
Museo Navale Didattico, Milano . . . 024724
Museo Navale Internazionale del Ponente Ligure, Imperia . . . 024412
Museo Navale O. Zibetti, Caravaggio . . . 023659
Museo Navale Romano, Albenga . . 023150
Museo Nazionale, Ravenna . . . 025398
Museo Nazionale, Reggio Calabria . 025408
Museo Nazionale Archeologico, Chieti . . . 023864
Museo Nazionale Archeologico, Civitavecchia . . . 023912
Museo Nazionale Archeologico, Ferrara . . . 024114
Museo Nazionale Archeologico, Sarsina . . . 025796
Museo Nazionale Archeologico, Tarquinia . . . 025990
Museo Nazionale Archeologico di Egnazia, Fasano-Savelletri . . . 024084
Museo Nazionale Archeologico di Vulci, Canino . . . 023629
Museo Nazionale Atestino, Este . . . 024059
Museo Nazionale Cagliari, Cagliari . 023568
Museo Nazionale Concordiese, Portogruaro . . . 025340
Museo Nazionale d'Abruzzo, L'Aquila . . . 024464
Museo Nazionale d'Arte Medievale e Moderna, Matera . . . 024651
Museo Nazionale d'Arte Orientale, Roma . . . 025548
Museo Nazionale degli Strumenti Musicali, Roma . . . 025549
Museo Nazionale degli Strumenti per il Calcolo, Università di Pisa, Pisa . . 025268
Museo Nazionale del Bargello, Firenze . . . 024195
Museo Nazionale del Cinema, Torino . . . 026072
Museo Nazionale del Cinema, Fondazione M.A. Prolo - F.I.A.F., Torino . . . 026073
Museo Nazionale del Palazzo di Venezia, Roma . . . 025550
Museo Nazionale del Risorgimento Italiano, Torino . . . 026074
Museo Nazionale del San Gottardo, Airolo . . . 036825
Museo Nazionale della Attività Subacquee, Marina di Ravenna . . . 024619
Museo Nazionale della Certosa, Calci . . . 023577
Museo Nazionale della Fotografia, Brescia . . . 023524
Museo Nazionale della Montagna Duca degli Abruzzi, Torino . . . 026075
Museo Nazionale della Residenza Napoleonica, Portoferraio . . . 025337
Museo Nazionale della Residenza Napoleonica dei Mulini, Portoferraio . . . 025338
Museo Nazionale della Scienza e della Tecnica Leonardo da Vinci, Milano 024725
Museo Nazionale della Siritide, Policoro . . . 025295
Museo Nazionale dell'Agro Picentino, Pontecagnano . . . 025312
Museo Nazionale dell'Alta Val d'Agri, Grumento Nova . . . 024382
Museo Nazionale dell'Antartide F. Ippolito, Genova . . . 024324
Museo Nazionale dell'Arma della Cavalleria, Pinerolo . . . 025248
Museo Nazionale delle Arti e Tradizioni Popolari, Roma . . . 025551
Museo Nazionale delle Arti Naïves C. Zavattini, Luzzara . . . 024562
Museo Nazionale delle Paste Alimentari, Roma . . . 025552

Museo Nazionale dell'Età Neoclassica in Romagna, Faenza 024071
Museo Nazionale di Canossa N. Campanini, Ciano d'Enza 023874
Museo Nazionale di Casa Giusti, Monsummano Terme 024805
Museo Nazionale di Castel Sant'Angelo, Roma 025553
Museo Nazionale di Palazzo Reale, Pisa 025269
Museo Nazionale di San Matteo, Lungarno Mediceo, Pisa 025270
Museo Nazionale di Santa Maria delle Monanche e Paleolitico, Isernia . . 024420
Museo Nazionale di Villa Guinigi, Lucca 024548
Museo Nazionale Domenico Ridola, Matera 024652
Museo Nazionale Etrusco di Villa Giulia, Roma 025554
Museo Nazionale Etrusco Pompeo Aria, Marzabotto 024626
Museo Nazionale Ferroviario, Stazione Pietrarsa, Napoli 024919
Museo Nazionale Garibaldino, La Maddalena 024435
Museo Nazionale Jatta, Ruvo di Puglia 025622
Museo Nazionale Preistorico ed Etnografico Luigi Pigorini, Roma 025555
Museo Nazionale Romano-Terme di Diocleziano, Roma 025556
Museo Néstor, Las Palmas de Gran Canaria 035627
Museo Nezahualcóyotl Acomiztli, Nezahualcóyotl 028598
Museo ng Bangko Sentral ng Pilipinas, Manila 031727
Museo ng Batangas, Lipa 031686
Museo ng Buhay Pilipino, Nayong Pilipino, Pasay 031756
Museo ng Kalinangang Pilipino, Manila 031728
Museo ng Kalinangang Pilipino, Pasay 031757
Museo ng Katipunan, Lipa 031687
Museo ng Makati, Makati 031698
Museo ng Manila, Manila 031729
Museo ng Rebolusyon, San Juan . . 031782
Museo Ángel Barrios, Granada 035259
Museo Ñiace, Tepelmeme de Morelos 028819
Museo Nicanor Piñole, Gijón 035225
Museo Ñico Lopez, Bayamo 007881
Museo Nicola Antonio Manfroce, Palmi 025105
Museo Niño Minero, Vetagrande . . . 028923
Museo Norace, Rosignano Marittimo 025603
Museo Norawa, Guachochi 028271
Museo Normanno-Bizantino, San Marco d'Alunzio 025703
Museo Notarial Argentino, Universidad Notarial Argentina, Buenos Aires . 000238
Museo Novarese d'Arte e Storia R. Fumagalli, Novara 024966
Museo Nuestra Señora de Carrodilla, Luján de Cuyo 000416
Museo Nuestro Pueblo y Museo Etnográfico de Tecpatán, Tecpatán 028800
Museo Nueva Cádiz, La Asunción . . 049497
Museo Numantino, Soria 035886
Museo Numismático, La Habana . . 008013
Museo Numismático del Banco Continental, Arequipa 031461
Museo Numismático del Banco Naciónal, Buenos Aires 000232
Museo Numismático del Banco Wiese, Lima 031568
Museo Numismatico della Zecca, Roma 025557
Museo Numismático Dr. José Evaristo Uriburu, Buenos Aires 000233
Museo Nuovo - Museo del Conservatori, Roma 025558
Museo Obispo Fray José Antonio de San Alberto, Córdoba 000307
Museo Obispo Vellosillo, Ayllón . . . 034878
Museo Ocarina e degli Strumenti in Terracotta, Budrio 023541
Museo Ochoa, Valencia 035986
Museo Odontológico Dr. Jorge E. Dunster, Corrientes 000321
Museo O'Higginiano y de Bellas Artes de Talca, Talca 006942
Museo Omar Huerta Escalante, Jonuta 028364
Museo Omero, Ancona 023200
Museo Oncativo, Oncativo 000461
Museo Onsernonese, Loco 037278
Museo Ora Ton, Chamula 028146
Museo Oraziano, Palazzo Baronale, Licenza 024502
Museo Orazio Comes, Portici 025328
Museo Organologico Didattico, Cremona 023998
Museo Organológico Folklórico Musical, Bogotá 007452
Museo Oriental, Valladolid 036004
Museo Orientale, Tagliacozzo 025982
Museo Orlando Binaghi, Círculo Criollo El Rodeo, Moreno 000453
Museo Ornitológico, Aragua 049437
Museo Ornitologico, Poppi 025322
Museo Ornitologico, Chiesa di San Francesco, San Gimignano 025683
Museo Ornitologico C. Beni, Stia . . 025951
Museo Ornitologico e di Scienze Naturali, Ravenna 025399
Museo Ornitologico Naturalistico S. Bambini, Pietralunga 025227
Museo Ornitológico Patagónico, El Bolsón 000332
Museo Ornitologico U. Foschi, Forlì 024231
Museo Orve, Chaupimascos 031487
Museo Oscar Fernandez Morera, Sancti-Spíritus 008134
Museo Oscar María de Rojas, Cárdenas 007900
Museo Ossenvanza, Museo Missionario d'Arte Cinese, Bologna 023457
Museo Ostetrico, Bologna 023458
Museo Ostetrico, Padova 025064
Museo Ostiense, Ostia Antica 025032
Museo Ostiense, Scavi di Ostia, Roma 025559
Museo Othoniano, San Luis Potosí . 028736
Museo P. Calderini, Varallo Sesia . . 026207
Museo P. Canonica, Roma 025560
Museo P. Vagliasindi, Randazzo . . . 025390
Museo Pablo Bush Romero, Puerto Aventura 028678
Museo Pablo Casals, San Juan 032745
Museo Pablo Gargallo, Zaragoza . . 036110
Museo Pablo Serrano, Zaragoza . . . 036111
Museo Padiglione delle Carozza, Museo Storico, Città del Vaticano 049428
Museo Padre Coll, Buenos Aires . . . 000234
Museo Paisa, Caicedonia 007463
Museo Palacio de Don Pedro I, Astudillo 034873
Museo-Palacio de Fuensalida, Toledo 035924
Museo Palacio de la Canal, San Miguel de Allende 028741
Museo-Palacio del Emperador Carlos V, Cuacos de Yuste 035135
Museo Palatino, Roma 025561
Museo Palatino, Roma 025562
Museo Palazzina Storica, Peschiera del Garda 025190
Museo Palenteológico de la Laguna, Torreón 028886
Museo Paleocristiano, Aquileia 023224
Museo Paleomarino, Museo di Biologia Marina & Paleontologia, Reggio Calabria 025409
Museo Paleontologico, Amandola . . 023189
Museo Paleontologico, Bova 023504
Museo Paleontologico, Fluminimaggiore 024207
Museo Paleontologico, L'Aquila . . . 024465
Museo Paleontológico, Mariquita . . 007534
Museo Paleontológico, Miño de Medinaceli 035496
Museo Paleontologico, Mondaino . . 024786
Museo Paleontologico, Monfalcone 024792
Museo Paleontologico, Montevarchi 024869
Museo Paleontológico, Pinar del Río 008095
Museo Paleontológico, Universidad Nacional de Colombia, Villa de Leyva 007641
Museo Paleontologico Archeologico V. Caccia, San Colombano al Lambro 025667
Museo Paleontológico, Arqueológico e Histórico de la Ciudad de Deán Funes, Deán Funes 000326
Museo Paleontológico Egidio Feruglio, Trelew 000638
Museo Paleontologico M. Gortani, Portogruaro 025341
Museo Paleontologico Parmense, Parma 025128
Museo Paleontologico S. Lai, Ceriale 023796
Museo Paleontológico - Sala Longinos Navás, Zaragoza 036112
Museo Paleontológico y Petrolero Astra, Comodoro Rivadavia 000282
Museo Paleoveneto, Pieve di Cadore 025234
Museo Pambata, Manila 031730
Museo Pampeano de Chascomús, Chascomús 000271
Museo Pampeano del Pergamino, Pergamino 000472
Museo Pantaleón Panduro, Tlaquepaque 028857
Museo Parigino a Roma, Roma 025563
Museo Parlamentario, Buenos Aires 000242
Museo Parma Gemma, Casarza Ligure 023688
Museo Parque de Esculturas, Montevideo 041534
Museo Parque de la Cristianía, Chapala 028147
Museo Parrocchiale, Bionaz 023399
Museo Parrocchiale, Campo Tures . 023618
Museo Parrocchiale, Castell'Arquato 023725
Museo Parrocchiale, Challand Saint Victor 023831
Museo Parrocchiale, Chambave . . . 023832
Museo Parrocchiale, Champorcher . 023835
Museo Parrocchiale, Fié 024120
Museo Parrocchiale, Gressoney Saint Jean 024368
Museo Parrocchiale, La Salle 024437
Museo Parrocchiale, Mogliano Marche 024771
Museo Parrocchiale, Ornavasso . . . 025011
Museo Parrocchiale, Ponte Buggianese 025306
Museo Parrocchiale, Saint Vincent . 025630
Museo Parrocchiale, San Marco d'Alunzio 025704
Museo Parrocchiale, Sarre 025794
Museo Parrocchiale, Valgrisenche . 026193
Museo Parrocchiale, Valtournenche 026205
Museo Parrocchiale d'Arte Sacra, Dozza 024040
Museo Parrocchiale del Santuario del Santissimo Crocifisso, Buggiano . 023544
Museo Parrocchiale della Chiesa Collegiata, Mercatello sul Metauro 024675
Museo Parrocchiale della Propositura di San Martino, Lastra a Signa 024470
Museo Parrocchiale di Arte Sacra, Valstrona 026203
Museo Parrocchiale di Arte Sacra, Chiesa di San Maurizio, Ponte in Valtellina . 025308
Museo Parrocchiale e Museo P. Mascagni, Bagnara di Romagna 023318
Museo Parrocchiale Madonna dei Raccomandati, Gessopalena 024335
Museo Parrocchiale San Giacomo, Massignano 024648
Museo Parrocchiale San Pietro Martire, Venezia 026259
Museo Parroquial, La Almunia de Doña Godina 034830
Museo Parroquial, Alquezar 034831
Museo Parroquial, El Barco de Ávila 034962
Museo Parroquial, Benabarre 034972
Museo Parroquial, Bocairente 034992
Museo Parroquial, Celanova 035079
Museo Parroquial, Cervera de Pisuerga 035084
Museo Parroquial, Ecija 035159
Museo Parroquial, Espejo 035178
Museo Parroquial, Ezcaray 035186
Museo Parroquial, Hondarribia 035281
Museo Parroquial, Madrid 035431
Museo Parroquial, Miranda del Castañar 035497
Museo Parroquial, Paradas 035634
Museo Parroquial, Pastrana 035639
Museo Parroquial, Roda de Isábena 035711
Museo Parroquial, San Sebastián del Oeste 028755
Museo Parroquial, Santa Gadea del Cid 035800
Museo Parroquial, Santa María del Campo 035806
Museo Parroquial, Segovia 035847
Museo Parroquial Colegiata de San Miguel, Aguilar de Campoo 034786
Museo Parroquial de Arte Religioso, Turmequé 007634
Museo Parroquial de Arte Sacro y Etnología, Anso 034841
Museo Parroquial de Monterroso, Monterroso 035519
Museo Parroquial de San Cosme y San Damián, Covarrubias 035132
Museo Parroquial de San Félix, Girona 035230
Museo Parroquial de San Martiño de Mondoñedo, Foz 035199
Museo Parroquial de San Martiño de Mondoñedo, San Martiño de Mondoñedo-Foz 035764
Museo Parroquial de Santa Eulalia, Paredes de Nava 035637
Museo Parroquial de Zurbarán, Marchena 035473
Museo Parroquial San Pedro, Cisneros 035092
Museo Parroquial Santa María del Salvador, Chinchilla de Monte-Aragón 035089
Museo Parroquial Santa María La Real, Xunqueira de Ambia 036089
Museo Participativo de Ciencias, Buenos Aires 000235
Museo Particular Los Abuelos, Franck 000347
Museo Partigiano, Carpasio 023668
Museo Partigiano Alfredo Di Dio, Ornavasso 025012
Museo Patio del Moro, Guaduas . . . 007511
Museo Patio Herreriano, Museo de Arte Contemporáneo Español, Valladolid 036005
Museo Patria Chica de Mohamed Diaz, Realicó 000502
Museo Pavese di Scienze Naturali, Pavia 025144
Museo Pecharromán, Pasarón de la Vera 035638
Museo Pedagógico Carlos Stuardo Ortiz, Santiago de Chile 006938
Museo Pedagógico Ciencias Naturales Jesús María Hernando, Valladolid 036006
Museo Pedagógico de Arte Infantil, Madrid 035432
Museo Pedagógico de Historia del Arte, Caracas 049476
Museo Pedagógico José Pedro Varela, Montevideo 041535
Museo Pedrin Troya, San Nicolás de Bari 008125
Museo Pedro Ara, Córdoba 000308
Museo Pedro Coronel, Zacatecas . . 028964
Museo Pedro Luro, Dolores 000329
Museo Penitenciario Argentino, Buenos Aires 000236
Museo Peñón Blanco, Peñón Blanco 028639
Museo per la Matematica - Giardino di Archimede, Priverno 025372
Museo per la Storia dell'Università di Pavia, Pavia 025145

Museo per l'Arte e l'Archeologia del Vastese, Gissi 024345
Museo Pérez Comendador-Leroux, Hérvas 035280
Museo Perrando, Sassello 025806
Museo Petatlán, Petatlán 028641
Museo Peten Ak, Valladolid 028908
Museo Petrográfico del Servicio Nacional de Geología y Minería, Quito 009254
Museo Picasso, Buitrago del Lozoya 034999
Museo Piersanti, Matelica 024649
Museo Pietro Canonica, Stresa 025957
Museo Pietro della Vedova, Rima San Giuseppe 025429
Museo Pietro Micca e dell'Assedio, Torino 026076
Museo-Pinacoteca, Visso 026347
Museo Pinacoteca A. Salvucci, Seminario Vescovile, Molfetta 024776
Museo-Pinacoteca Comunale, Mogliano Marche 024772
Museo-Pinacoteca de Arte Contemporáneo, Zarzuela del Monte 036117
Museo Pinacoteca dell'Arte dei Bambini, Smerillo 025908
Museo - Pinacoteca San Francesco, San Marino 034117
Museo Pinacoteca Santa Casa, Palazzo Apostolico, Loreto 024532
Museo Pintor Antonio Rodríguez Luna, Montoro 035523
Museo Pio Clementino, Musei Vaticani, Città del Vaticano 049429
Museo Pio Collivadino, Banfield . . . 000131
Museo Pio Cristiano, Musei Vaticani, Città del Vaticano 049430
Museo Pío del Río Ortega, Valladolid 036007
Museo Pio IX, Senigallia 025853
Museo Pio X, Chiesa Parrocchiale, Salzano 025644
Museo Planetario, Garza García . . . 028262
Museo Plaza de Revolución General Antonio Maceo, Santiago de Cuba 008169
Museo Plebano, Agno 036819
Museo Poblano de Arte Virreinal, Puebla 028675
Museo Polare Etnografico Silvio Zavatti, Fermo 024097
Museo Poldi Pezzoli, Milano 024726
Museo Policial, Ávila 036037
Museo Polifacético Regional Vottero, Laguna Larga 000401
Museo Polivalente, Chiaramonte Gulfi 023843
Museo Polivalente, Vittoria 026352
Museo Polivalente de Palmira, Palmira 008085
Museo Pomposiano, Codigoro 023919
Museo Ponchielliano, Paderno Ponchieli 025047
Museo Popol Vuh, Guatemala 021585
Museo Popoli e Culture, Milano . . . 024727
Museo Popular de Arte Contemporáneo, Villafamés 036062
Museo Porfirio Corona Covarrubias, El Grullo, Jalisco 028235
Museo Posta de Yatasto, Metán . . . 000445
Museo Postal Cubano, La Habana . 008014
Museo Postal Eduardo Santos, Bogotá 007453
Museo Postal y Filatélico del Perú, Lima 031569
Museo Postal y Telegráfico, Madrid 035433
Museo Postal y Telegráfico Doctor Ramon J. Carcano, Buenos Aires 000237
Museo Postale e Telegrafico della Mitteleuropa, Trieste 026146
Museo Postale, Filatelico-Numismatico, San Marino 034118
Museo Prehistórico, Villa de Leyva . 007640
Museo Prehistórico de Tepexpan, Tepexpan 028822
Museo Preistorico, Paceco 025045
Museo Preistorico Balzi Rossi, Ventimiglia 026272
Museo Preistorico dell'Isolino, Museo Civico di Varese, Biandronno 023391
Museo Preistorico e Archeologico A.C. Blanc, Viareggio 026301
Museo Preistorico e Lapidario, Verucchio 026295
Museo Preistorico N. Lamboglia e Val Varatello, Palazzo Marchese, Toirano 026032
Museo Presidente José Evaristo Uriburu, Salta 000541
Museo Presidio Modelo, Nueva Gerona 008081
Museo Privado de Arqueología Regional Julio Gironde, Carmen de Patagonés 000264
Museo Prof. Arturo Reyes Viramontes, Jalpa 028354
Museo Prof. Dr. Juan Augusto Olsacher, Zapala 000676
Museo Prof. Moisés Sáenz Garza, Apodaca 028109
Museo Prof. Ricardo Vega Noriega, San Ignacio 028716
Museo Profano, Città del Vaticano . 049431
Museo Progressivo d'Arte Contemporanea, Livorno 024510
Museo Provincial, Ciego de Avila . . 007908
Museo Provincial, Lugo 035367
Museo Provincial, Museo de Teruel, Teruel 035910
Museo Provincial Arqueológico Eric Boman, Santa María de Catamarca 000610
Museo Provincial de Arqueología Wagner, Santiago del Estero 000617
Museo Provincial de Artes de La Pampa, Santa Rosa 000611
Museo Provincial de Bellas Artes, Corrientes 000322
Museo Provincial de Bellas Artes, Salta 000542
Museo Provincial de Bellas Artes Dr. Pedro E. Martínez, Paraná 000468
Museo Provincial de Bellas Artes Emiliano Guiñazu - Casa de Fader, Luján de Cuyo 000417
Museo Provincial de Bellas Artes Emilio A. Caraffa, Córdoba 000309
Museo Provincial de Bellas Artes Ramón Gómez Cornet, Santiago del Estero 000618
Museo Provincial de Bellas Artes Rene Brusau, Resistencia 000508
Museo Provincial de Bellas Artes Rosa Galisteo de Rodríguez, Santa Fé . 000607
Museo Provincial de Bellas Artes Timoteo Eduardo Navarro, San Miguel de Tucumán 000586
Museo Provincial de Ciencias Naturales Dr. Angelo Gallardo, Rosario 000531
Museo Provincial de Ciencias Naturales Florentino Ameghino, Santa Fé . . 000608
Museo Provincial de Ciencias Naturales y Oceanográfico, Puerto Madryn . . . 000489
Museo Provincial de Historia Natural de La Pampa, Santa Rosa 000612
Museo Provincial de Holguín La Periquera, Holguín 008028
Museo Provincial de la Historia de Pinar del Río, Pinar del Río 008096
Museo Provincial de Matanzas, Matanzas 008061
Museo Provincial de Villa Clara y Museo Municipal, Santa Clara 008144
Museo Provincial do Mar, San Ciprian-Concello de Cervo 035753
Museo Provincial Don Emilio Bacardí Moreau, Santiago de Cuba 008170
Museo Provincial Dora Ochoa de Masramón, San Luis 000576
Museo Provincial General Vicente García, Victoria de las Tunas 008193
Museo Provincial Ignacio Agramonte, La Vigía 008195
Museo Provincial José María Morante, Arequipa 031462
Museo Provincial Mario Brozoski, Puerto Deseado 000487
Museo Provincial y Parroquial, Piña de Campos 035654
Museo Provinciale, Catanzaro 023771
Museo Provinciale, Chieti 023865
Museo Provinciale Campano, Capua 023655
Museo Provinciale d'Arte Contempranea, Crotone 024007
Museo Provinciale della Caccia e della Pesca, Racines 025381
Museo Provinciale della Vita Contadina, San Vito al Tagliamento 025735
Museo Provinciale delle Miniere, Racines 025382
Museo Provinciale delle Miniere, Vipiteno 026345
Museo Provinciale delle Tradizioni Popolari Abbazia Cerrate, Lecce 024483
Museo Provinciale di Storia Naturale, Foggia 024211
Museo Provinciale di Storia Naturale, Livorno 024511
Museo Provinciale Sigismondo Castromediano, Lecce 024484
Museo Pucciniano, Torre del Lago Puccini 026088
Museo Pueblo de Luis, Trelew 000639
Museo Puertorriqueño del Deportes, Salinas 032725
Museo Quattroruote, Rozzano 025617
Museo Quevedo Zornoza, Zipaquirá 007648
Museo Quezaltenango, Quezaltenango 021587
Museo Quinta Amalia Simoni, Camagüey 007896
Museo Quinta Casa de Juan Montalvo, Ambato 009173
Museo Quinta de San Pedro Alejandrino, Fundación Museo Bolivariano, Santa Marta 007610
Museo Quinta Juan Leon Mera, Ambato 009174
Museo R. Campelli, Palazzo Comunale, Pievebovigliana 025242
Museo R. Cassolo, Mede 024656
Museo R. Cuneo, Savona 025828
Museo R. De Cesare, Spinazzola . . 025935
Museo Rabelo, La Habana 008015
Museo-Raccolta di Fisica, Bari 023343
Museo Radiofónico de la Ciudad de Boulogne, Boulogne 000141
Museo Rafael Coronel, Zacatecas . 028965
Museo Rafael Escriña, Santa Clara de Saguier 000599
Museo Raíces, Jesús María 007523
Museo Raíces de Satevó, Satevó . . 028772
Museo Ralli, Marbella 035469
Museo Ralli, Punta del Este 041549
Museo Ralli, Santiago de Chile 006939
Museo Ramón Gaya, Murcia 035533
Museo Ramón López Velarde, México 028527
Museo Ramón Pérez Fernández, Rivadavia 000522
Museo Ramos Generales, Villa María 000670
Museo Ratti dei Vini d'Alba, La Morra 024436
Museo Rauzi, Palmira 000462
Museo Rayo, Roldanillo 007599
Museo Real Colegiata de San Isidoro, Panteón, Biblioteca, Museo, Claustro, León 035331
Museo Recoleto, Quezon City 031778
Museo Regional, Chichicastenango 021574
Museo Regional, San Juan Bautista Tuxtepec 028719
Museo Regional Amazónico, Iquitos 031533
Museo Regional Aníbal Cambas, Posadas 000483
Museo Regional Carlos Funes Derieul, Coronel Dorrego 000315
Museo Regional Castelli, Castelli . . 000268
Museo Regional Cayetano Alberto Silva, Venado Tuerto 000653
Museo Regional Comunitario Altepepialcalli, México 028528
Museo Regional Cuauhnáhuac, Cuernavaca 028207
Museo Regional Daniel Hernández Morillo, Huancavelica 031512
Museo Regional de Acambay, Acambay 028076
Museo Regional de Actopán, Actopán 028084
Museo Regional de Aldama, Aldama 028098
Museo Regional de Antropología, Resistencia 000509
Museo Regional de Antropología Carlos Pellicer Cámara, Villahermosa . . . 028938
Museo Regional de Antropología e Historia de Baja California Sur, La Paz . . . 028376
Museo Regional de Antropología J. Jesús Figueroa Torres, Sayula 028774
Museo Regional de Arqueología, Huamanga 031511
Museo Regional de Arqueología de Junín, Chupaca 031492
Museo Regional de Arqueología de Tuxpan, Tuxpan de Rodríguez Cano 028894
Museo Regional de Arqueología Maya, Ciudad de Copán 021607
Museo Regional de Arte e Historia, Jerez de García Salinas 028361
Museo Regional de Arte Popular La Huatápera, Uruapán 028905
Museo Regional de Atacama, Copiapó 006915
Museo Regional de Campeche, Campeche 028132
Museo Regional de Casma Max Uhle, Casma 031482
Museo Regional de Chiapas, Tuxtla Gutiérrez 028901
Museo Regional de Ciencias Naturales Tomás Santa Coloma, Tres Arroyos 000641
Museo Regional de Cinco Saltos, Cinco Saltos 000278
Museo Regional de Claromecó, Balneario Claromecó 000130
Museo Regional de Cuetzalan, Cuetzalán 028210
Museo Regional de Durango y Museo del Niño, Universidad Juárez, Durango 028232
Museo Regional de Guadalajara, Guadalajara 028292
Museo Regional de Guanajuato Alhóndiga de Granaditas, Guanajuato 028308
Museo Regional de Guerrero, Chilpancingo 028164
Museo Regional de Hidalgo, Pachuca 028628
Museo Regional de Historia, Universidad de Sonora, Hermosillo 028318
Museo Regional de Historia de Aguascalientes, Aguascalientes . . 028091
Museo Regional de Historia de Colima, Colima 028170
Museo Regional de Historia de Tamaulipas, Victoria 028928
Museo Regional de Ica María Reiche Gross Newman, Ica 031527
Museo Regional de Iguala, Iguala de la Independencia 028343
Museo Regional de Iquique, Iquique 006917
Museo Regional de la Araucania, Temuco 006943
Museo Regional de la Cerámica, Tlaquepaque 028858
Museo Regional de la Ciudad de La Paz, La Paz 000382
Museo Regional de la Laguna, Torreón 028887
Museo Regional de las Culturas Occidente, Guzmán 028313
Museo Regional de Mascota, Mascota 028403
Museo Regional de Nayarit, Tepic . . 028828
Museo Regional de Nuevo León, Monterrey 028570
Museo Regional de Pigüé, Pigüé . . 000475
Museo Regional de Pintura José Antonio Terry, Tilcara 000636

Museo Regional de Prehistoria y Arqueología de Cantabria, Santander 035813
Museo Regional de Puebla, Puebla . 028673
Museo Regional de Querétaro, Querétaro 028686
Museo Regional de Río Verde, Río Verde 028690
Museo Regional de Sacanta, Sacanta 000534
Museo Regional de San Carlos, San Carlos 041553
Museo Regional de San Martín, Moyobamba 031575
Museo Regional de Sinaloa, Culiacán 028217
Museo Regional de Sonora, Hermosillo 028319
Museo Regional de Telecomunicaciones Tomás Guzmán Cantú, La Paz . . . 028377
Museo Regional de Tierra Caliente, Coyuca de Catalán 028195
Museo Regional de Tlaxcala, Tlaxcala 028862
Museo Regional de Yucatán, Mérida 028416
Museo Regional del Valle del Fuerte, Ahome 028093
Museo Regional Doctor Leonardo Oliva, Ahualulco de Mercado 028094
Museo Regional Dr. Adolfo Alsina, Carhué 000262
Museo Regional Dr. Federico Escalada, Río Mayo 000519
Museo Regional Dr. José Luro, Pedro Luro 000469
Museo Regional El Fuerte, El Fuerte 028234
Museo Regional Francisco Mazzoni, Maldonado 041496
Museo Regional Guayupe de Puerto Santander, Puerto Santander 007592
Museo Regional Histórico y de Ciencias Naturales, Coronel Pringles 000317
Museo Regional Huasteco, Valles . . 028914
Museo Regional José G. Brochero, Santa Rosa de Río Primero 000613
Museo Regional Las Varillas, Las Varillas 000403
Museo Regional Lázaro Cárdenas, Tlapehuala 028856
Museo Regional Luciano Márquez, Zacatlán 028970
Museo Regional Malargüe, Malargüe 000421
Museo Regional Maracó, General Pico 000353
Museo Regional Michoacano, Morelia 028584
Museo Regional Municipal de El Calafate, El Calafate 000333
Museo Regional Particular Epifanio Saravia, Santa Catalina 000598
Museo Regional Patagónico, Comodoro Rivadavia 000283
Museo Regional Potosino, San Luis Potosí 028737
Museo Regional Provincial Padre Manuel Jesús Molina, Río Gallegos 000516
Museo Regional Rescate de Raíces, Ahualulco de Mercado 028095
Museo Regional Rincón de Vida, Villa Mirasol 000671
Museo Regional Rufino Muñiz Torres, Ocampo 028614
Museo Regional Rumi Mayu (Río de Piedra), Sanagasta 000597
Museo Regional Salesiano de Rawson, Rawson 000501
Museo Regional Salesiano Maggiorino Borgatello, Punta Arenas 006925
Museo Regional Trevelin, Trevelin . 000644
Museo Regional Valcheta, Valcheta 000651
Museo Regional Valparaíso, Valparaíso 028915
Museo Regional y de Arte Marino, Puerto San Julián 000490
Museo Regionale, Messina 024681
Museo Regionale A. Pepoli, Trapani 026101
Museo Regionale della Centovalli e del Pedemonte, Intragna 037199
Museo Regionale della Ceramica, Caltagirone 023589
Museo Regionale della Ceramica, Convento di San Francesco, Deruta 024025
Museo Regionale di Camarina, Ragusa 025386
Museo Regionale di Scienze Naturali, Saint Pierre 025628
Museo Regionale di Scienze Naturali, Affiliation Regione Piemonte, Torino 026077
Museo Religioso de Guatavita, Guatavita 007514
Museo Religioso Santo Domingo, Bolivar 009181
Museo Religioso y Colonial de San Francisco, Cali 007473
Museo Renacimiento Indígena, Huamuxtitlán 028327
Museo Renato Brozzi, Palazzo Comunale, Traversetolo 026102
Museo Retrospectivo de Farmacia y Medicina, El Masnou 035478
Museo Richard Ginori della Manifattura di Doccia, Sesto Fiorentino 025873
Museo Ripley, México 028529
Museo Risorgimentale, Montichiari 024871
Museo Risorgimentale, Pieve di Cadore 025235
Museo Rivarossi dei Treni in Miniatura, Como 023945
Museo Roberto M. Arata, Universidad Notarial Argentina, Buenos Aires . 000238
Museo Roberto Noble, Buenos Aires 000239
Museo Roca, Buenos Aires 000240
Museo Rocsen, Nono 000457
Museo Rodolfo Valentino, Castellaneta 023720
Museo Rognoni Salvaneschi, Novara 024967
Museo Romano, Tortona 026095
Museo Romántico, Madrid 035434
Museo Romántico, Montevideo . . . 041536
Museo Romántico, Trinidad 008182
Museo Rómulo Raggio, Vicente López 000654
Museo Ron Arehucas, Arucas 034869
Museo Rosendo Mejica, Iloilo 031674
Museo Rosminiano, Stresa 025958
Museo Rubén Herrera, Saltillo 028701
Museo Rudolf Stolz, Sesto in Pusteria 025874
Museo Runa de Antropología, Tafí del Valle 000627
Museo Rural, Pozorrubio de Santiago 035674
Museo Rural de la Posta de Sinsacate, Jesús María 000370
Museo S. Fancello, Dorgali 024038
Museo Sa Domu De Donna Nassia, Lotzorai 024539
Museo Sac-be, Yaxcabá 028956
Museo Sacrario delle Bandiere, Roma 025564
Museo Sacrario Galileo Ferraris, Livorno Ferraris 024512
Museo Sacro, Città del Vaticano . . . 049432
Museo Sacro, Santuario della Madonna del Rosario, Pompei 025302
Museo Sacro de Caracas, Caracas . 049477
Museo Sacro de la Catedral, San Miguel de Tucumán 000587
Museo Sacro - Tesoro di Sant'Ambrogio, Milano 024728
Museo Sala, San Juan Bautista Tuxtepec 028720
Museo Sala de Arte, Universidad Autónoma de Baja California, Tijuana 028842
Museo Sala de Arte Moderno, Juchitán de Zaragoza 028371
Museo Sala de Arte Público David Alfaro Siqueiros, México 028530
Museo Sala de Exposición Banco Central de Esmeraldas, Esmeraldas 009201
Museo-Sala de los Símbolos Patrios, Hermosillo 028320
Museo Salesiano, Huancayo 031515
Museo Salesiano Ceferino Namuncura, Córdoba 000310
Museo Salvatore Ferragamo, Firenze 024196
Museo Salzillo, Murcia 035534
Museo San Antonio de Padua, Córdoba 000311
Museo San Francisco, Teruel 035911
Museo San Giuseppe da Copertino, Osimo 025027
Museo San Gregorio de Polanco, San Gregorio de Polanco 041554
Museo San José el Mogote, San José el Mogote 028718
Museo San Juan de la Cruz, Úbeda 034966
Museo San Juan de Letrán, Chucuito 031490
Museo San Juan en la Historia, San Juan del Río 028725
Museo San Miguel del Padrón, La Habana 008016
Museo San Miguel Teotongo, México 028531
Museo San Nicolò, Militello in Val di Catania 024742
Museo San Roque, Buenos Aires . . 000241
Museo Santa Barbara, Mammola . . 024591
Museo Santa Clara la Real, Tunja . . 007633
Museo Santa Iglesia Catedral, Plasencia 035657
Museo Sant'Andrea, Clusone 023916
Museo-Santuario de San Pedro Claver, Cartagena 007479
Museo Santuario Nuestra Señora Natividad del Guayco, La Magdalena 009224
Museo Santuarios Andinos de la Universidad Católica de Santa María, Arequipa 031463
Museo Sardo di Antropologia ed Etnografia, Università di Monserrato, Cagliari 023569
Museo Sardo di Geologia e Paleontologia D. Lovisato, Università Cagliari, Cagliari 023570
Museo Schaferrer, Oxapampa 031579
Museo Scientifico L. Guidi, Osservatopio Vauepio, Pesaro 025177
Museo Scout-Guía, Madrid 035435
Museo Scuola Odin-Bertot, Angrogna 023210
Museo Sefardí, Toledo 035925
Museo Selinuntino, Castelvetrano . 023745
Museo Sella e Mosca, Alghero 023171
Museo Senador Domingo Faustino Sarmiento, Buenos Aires 000242
Museo Senen Mexic, Acatlán de Osorio 028082
Museo Serfín de Indumentaria Indígena, México 028532
Museo Servando Cabrera Moreno, La Habana 008017
Museo Severino Pose, Montevideo . 041537
Museo Siciliano delle Tradizioni Religiose, San Salvatore di Fitalia 025727
Museo Siderúrgico de Colombia, Nobsa 007556
Museo Silvanus G. Morley y de las Estelas, El Petén 021575
Museo Silvestre Vargas, Tecalitlán . 028795
Museo Simón Bolívar, Bolívar 034993
Museo Sinagoga de Santa María la Blanca, Toledo 035926
Museo Sistino Vescovile, Montalto Marche 024811
Museo Sito Arqueológico Guayabo de Turrialba, Turrialba 007683
Museo Social Argentino de Universidad, Buenos Aires 000243
Museo Sol y Mar, Matanzas 008062
Museo Soldati della Battaglia, San Biagio di Callalta 025656
Museo Sor María de Jesús de Agreda, Agreda 034784
Museo Sorolla, Madrid 035436
Museo Soumaya, México 028533
Museo Speleopaleontologico, Genga 024292
Museo Speologico, Sgonico 025881
Museo Sperimentale d'Arte Contemporanea Muspac, L'Aquila 024466
Museo Statale, Anghiari 023208
Museo Statale, Mileto 024741
Museo Staur s di Arte Sacra Contemporanea, Isola del Gran Sasso 024422
Museo Stibbert, Firenze 024197
Museo Storia Memoria, Sossano . . 025928
Museo Storico, Lugano 037290
Museo Storico, Montese 024864
Museo Storico, Voghera 026361
Museo Storico-Aeronautica Militare, Bracciano 023510
Museo Storico Alfa Romeo, Arese . 023233
Museo Storico Aloisiano, Castiglione delle Stiviere 023750
Museo Storico Alpino, Antrodoco . . 023213
Museo Storico Archeologico, Cicagna 023877
Museo Storico Archeologico, Segni 025846
Museo Storico Archeologico del Territorio, Bagni di Lucca 023321
Museo Storico Archeologico dell'Antica Nola, Convento delle Canossiane, Nola 024950
Museo Storico Archeologico G. Gabetti, Dogliani 024032
Museo Storico Artistico, Cassino . . 023699
Museo Storico Artistico, Tesoro, Città del Vaticano 049433
Museo Storico Badogliano, Bari . . . 023344
Museo Storico C. Levi, Aliano 023173
Museo Storico C. Musazzi, Parabiago 025107
Museo Storico Cappuccino, Convento dei Cappuccini, Camerino 023606
Museo Storico Casa del Senato, Pinerolo 025250
Museo Storico Civico Cuggionesie, Cuggiono 024009
Museo Storico D. Foschi, Forlì 024232
Museo Storico degli Spaghetti, Pontedassio 025315
Museo Storico degli Truppe Alpini, Trento 026111
Museo Storico dei Bersaglieri, Roma 025565
Museo Storico dei Granatieri di Sardegna, Roma 025566
Museo Storico dei Vigili del Fuoco, Mantova 024608
Museo Storico del Castello di Miramare, Trieste 026147
Museo Storico del Combattente, Paderno Dugnano 025046
Museo Storico del Forte, Osoppo . . 025028
Museo Storico del Mutuo Soccorso, Pinerolo 025249
Museo Storico del Nastro Azzurro, Salò 025641
Museo Storico del Risorgimento della Società Economica, Chiavari 023849
Museo Storico del Soldatino M. Massacesi, Bologna 023459
Museo Storico del Teatro Argentina, Roma 025567
Museo Storico del Trotto, Civitanova Marche 023911
Museo Storico del Vetro e della Bottiglia J.F. Mariani, Montalcino 024809
Museo Storico dela Caccia e del Territorio, Cerreto Guidi 023800
Museo Storico della Brigata Sassari, Sassari 025805
Museo Storico della Città, Bergamo 023380
Museo Storico della Didattica, Roma 025568
Museo Storico della Fanteria, Roma 025569
Museo Storico della Filarmonica Sestrese, Genova 024325
Museo Storico della Guardia di Finanza, Roma 025570
Museo Storico della Guerra 1915-1918, Roana 025451
Museo Storico della Liberazione di Roma, Roma 025571

Museo Storico della Linea Gotica, Auditore 023300
Museo Storico della Motorizzazione Militare, Roma 025572
Museo Storico della Resistanza S. Maneschi, Neviano degli Arduini . 024935
Museo Storico della Resistenza, Stazzema 025947
Museo Storico della Tappezzeria, Bologna 023460
Museo Storico dell'Antichità, Cesena 023813
Museo Storico dell'Arma dei Carabinieri, Roma 025573
Museo Storico dell'Arma del Genio, Roma 025574
Museo Storico dell'Arte Sanitaria, Roma 025575
Museo Storico delle Armi, Civitella del Tronto 023914
Museo Storico delle Poste e Telecomunicazioni, Roma 025576
Museo Storico delle Saline, Margherita di Savoia 024614
Museo Storico dell'Oro Italiano, Silvano d'Orba 025898
Museo Storico di Architettura Militare, Roma 025577
Museo Storico Dittico Alto Livenza, Sacile 025625
Museo Storico e Topografico, Firenze Com'era, Firenze 024198
Museo Storico Etnografico, Bruscoli 023538
Museo Storico Etnografico, Sampeyre 025648
Museo Storico-Etnografico, Sanluri 025740
Museo Storico Etnografico della Bassa Valsesia, Romagnano Sesia 025589
Museo Storico Etnografico delle Alpi Liguri, Mendatica 024665
Museo Storico Etnografico Naturalistico, Chiesa in Valmalenco 023859
Museo Storico G. Garibaldi, Como . 023946
Museo Storico in Trento Onlus, Trento 026112
Museo Storico Italiano della Guerra, Rovereto 025611
Museo Storico Italo-Ungherese, Vittoria 026353
Museo Storico Lisotti Maria, Gradara 024355
Museo Storico Michele Ghislieri, Vicoforte 026318
Museo Storico Militare, Comun Nuovo 023950
Museo Storico Militare e Sacrario die Redipuglia, Fogliano Redipuglia . . 024212
Museo Storico Militare Umberto I, Turate 026159
Museo Storico Minerario, Perticara . 025162
Museo Storico Minerario di Perticara, Novafeltria 024959
Museo Storico Multimediale B. d'Alviano, Alviano 023183
Museo Storico Navale, Venezia . . . 026260
Museo Storico Nazionale di Artiglieria, Torino 026078
Museo Storico Novarese Aldo Rossini, Novara 024968
Museo Storico Perugina, Perugia . . 025173
Museo Storico Vaticano, Città del Vaticano 049434
Museo Stradivariano, Museo Civico Ala Ponzone, Cremona 023999
Museo Strumenti Musicali, Ravenna 025400
Museo Sudtirolese della Frutticoltura, Lana 024451
Museo Sveviano, Trieste 026148
Museo T. Nuvolari, Mantova 024609
Museo Taller de Escultura, Victoria de las Tunas 008194
Museo Taller del Moro, Museo del Santa Cruz, Toledo 035927
Museo Taller Luis Nishizawa, Toluca 028878
Museo Tamayo Arte Contemporáneo, México 028534
Museo Taminango de Artes y Tradiciones Populares de Nariño, Pasto 007574
Museo Tarike, Chihuahua 028160
Museo Taurino, Cali 007474
Museo Taurino, Córdoba 035117
Museo Taurino, Hellín 035278
Museo Taurino, Huamantla 028326
Museo Taurino, La Línea de la Concepción 035337
Museo Taurino, Madrid 035437
Museo Taurino, Salamanca 035746
Museo Taurino, County council of Valencia, Valencia 035987
Museo Taurino Conde de Colombi, Alcalá de Guadaira 034797
Museo Taurino de Bogotá, Bogotá . 007454
Museo Taurino de la Plaza de Acho, Lima 031570
Museo Taurino de la Real Maestranza de Caballería de Ronda, Ronda 035723
Museo Taurino de Mijas, Mijas 035494
Museo Taurino José Vega, Gerena . 035220
Museo Taurino Municipal, Antequera 034843
Museo Teatrale alla Scala, Milano . 024729
Museo Teatrale del Burcardo, Roma 025578
Museo Teatrale presso il Teatro Verdi, Pisa 025259
Museo Teatro La Casa de los Títeres, Monterrey 028571
Museo Tecnico Navale, La Spezia . . 024442
Museo Técnico Pedagógico de la Región de Pasco, San Juan 031591
Museo Tecnologia, Cultura e Civiltà Contadina, Guardia Lombardi . . . 024384
Museo Tecnológico Aeroespacial, Las Higueras 000402
Museo Tecnológico de la Comisión Federal de Electricidad, México 028535
Museo Tecnológico Ingeniero Eduardo Latzina, Buenos Aires 000244
Museo Telefónico Victoria, México . 028536
Museo Templete de los Heros Nacionales, Colegio Militar Eloy Alfaro, Quito . 009255
Museo Tenderi, Masaya 030666
Museo Teniente José Azuela, Zihuatanejo 028981
Museo Teo, Milano 135925
Museo Teodoro Ramos Blanco, La Habana 008018
Museo Tepeapulco, Tepeapulco . . . 028817
Museo Teresiano, Alba de Tormes . 034791
Museo Teresiano, Ávila 036038
Museo Teresiano Monasterio de la Encarnación, Ávila 036039
Museo Territoriale del Lago di Bolsena, Bolsena 023464
Museo Territoriale dell'Agro Foronovano, Torri in Sabina 026093
Museo Tesoro Basilica di San Francesco, Assisi 023284
Museo-Tesoro Catedralicio, Lugo . . 035368
Museo-Tesoro Catedralicio, Toledo . 035928
Museo-Tesoro de la Basílica de la Macarena, Sevilla 035869
Museo-Tesoro de la Cofradía de la Expiración, Málaga 035456
Museo Tesoro de la Santina, Cangas de Onis 035047
Museo-Tesoro de la Santina, Covadonga 035131
Museo Tesoro del Tempio della Beata Vergine, Reggio Emilia 025416
Museo-Tesoro del Templo del Cristo del Gran Poder, Sevilla 035870
Museo Tesoro della Collegiata di San Lorenzo, Canonica di San Lorenzo, Chiavenna 023852
Museo Tesoro dell'Arcivescovado, Cosenza 023983
Museo-Tesoro Parroquial, Arcos de la Frontera 034851
Museo Tesoro Parroquial, Lebrija . . 035322
Museo-Tesoro Parroquial de Santiago, Orihuela 035570
Museo Tetetzontlilco, Tizayuca 028847
Museo Textil La Trinidad, Santa Cruz Tlaxcala 028761
Museo Thermalia, Museu d'Història, Caldes de Montbui 035030
Museo Thyssen-Bornemisza, Madrid 035438
Museo Timoteo L. Hernández, Villaldama 028940
Museo Tipologico del Presepe, Macerata 024567
Museo Tlallán, Tala 028781
Museo Tohue, Vicente Guerrero, Durango 028926
Museo Toma de Zacatecas o Cerro de la Bufa, Zacatecas 028966
Museo Tomaskitla, Epazoyucan . . . 028251
Museo Tomochic, Vicente Guerrero 028925
Museo Tonallán, Tonalá, Jalisco . . . 028881
Museo Tonatiuh, Zempoala 028979
Museo Torlonia, Roma 025579
Museo Tornambe de la Universidad Nacional de San Juan, San Juan . 000573
Museo Torre di Porta Romana, Gubbio 024394
Museo Torres García, Montevideo . 041538
Museo Torricelliano, Faenza 024072
Museo Toti dal Monte, Pieve di Soligo 025239
Museo Towi, Guachochi 028272
Museo Tradicional Ik Al Ojov, Zinacantán 028983
Museo Tradicionalista El Rancho, Chacabuco 000269
Museo Transumanza e Costume Abruzzese Molisano, Sulmona 025967
Museo Tribunal de la Santa Inquisición y del Congreso, Lima 031571
Museo Tridentino di Scienze Naturali, Palazzo Sardagna, Trento 026113
Museo Túenl Casa Parker, Angangueo 028104
Museo Tuscolano, Frascati 024249
Museo U Gumbu, Cervo 023812
Museo Ucraniano, Apóstoles 000114
Museo Universitario, Cochabamba . 003908
Museo Universitario, Medellín 007545
Museo Universitario, Pasto 007575
Museo Universitario, Universidad Autónoma de Baja California, Mexicali 028422
Museo Universitario Alejandro Rangel Hidalgo, Nogueras 028599
Museo Universitario Antigua Casa de los Muñecos, Puebla 028674
Museo Universitario Contemporáneo de Arte, México 028537
Museo Universitario de Arqueología de Manzanillo, Manzanillo 028400
Museo Universitario de Artes, Mendoza 000439
Museo Universitario de Artes Populares, Colima 028171
Museo Universitario de Ciencias, Universidad Autónoma de Zacatecas, Zacatecas 028967
Museo Universitario de Ciencias y Artes, Roma, México 028538
Museo Universitario de Paleontología, México 028539
Museo Universitario de San Carlos, Guatemala 021586
Museo Universitario del Chopo, México 028540
Museo Universitario Florentino y Carlos Ameghino, Rosario 000532
Museo Universitario Lariab de Historia Antigua de la Huaxteca, Tamuín . . 028784
Museo Universitario Pio López Martínez, Cayey 032712
Museo Universitario y Museo de Anatomía General, Universidad Nacional Daniel Alcides Carrión, Yanacancha 031613
Museo Univérsitas, El Cerrito 007496
Museo Urdaneta Histórico Militar, Maracaibo 049501
Museo Usina Vieja, San Antonio de Areco 000551
Museo V. Venturi, Loro Ciuffenna . . 024536
Museo Valdese, Rorà 025595
Museo Valdese della Balziglia, Massello 024647
Museo Valencià d'Història Natural, Valencia 035988
Museo Valenzuela, Valenzuela 031804
Museo Vallerano Bregagliotto, Stampa 037594
Museo Vallivo, Valfurva 026191
Museo Valtellinese di Storia e Arte, Sondrio 025919
Museo Vanvitelliano, Caserta 023690
Museo Vasariano di San Croce, Bosco Marengo 023501
Museo Vasco de Gastronomía, Laudio 035321
Museo Vasco de Historia de las Ciencias y de la Medicina, Leioa 035325
Museo Vasco del Ferrocarril, Azpeitia 034882
Museo Vásquez Fuller, Otavalo 009227
Museo Vela, Ligornetto 037269
Museo Vesuviano G. B. Alfano, Pompei 025303
Museo V.G. Rossi, Santa Margherita Ligure 025749
El Museo Viajero, Buenos Aires . . . 000245
Museo Víctor Alejandro Jaramillo, Ibarra 009221
Museo Víctor Manuel, La Habana . . 008019
Museo Vilal Visconti Venosta, Grosio 024372
Museo Villa dei Cedri, Bellinzona . . 036918
Museo Villa Medicea, Cerreto Guidi 023800
Museo Villa Medicea, Poggio a Caiano 025293
Museo Villa Urania-Antiche Maioliche di Castelli, Fondazione Paparella Treccia-Devlet, Pescara 025187
Museo Villa Urpo, Siivikkala 010078
Museo Virgen de la Portería, Ávila . 036040
Museo Virgen de Zapopan, Zapopan 028975
Museo Virgiliano, Virgilio 026346
Museo Virreinal de Zinacantepec, San Miguel Zinacantepec 028744
Museo Virtual de Artes el Pais, Montevideo 041539
Museo Vitaliano Zuccardi, Sincelejo 007612
Museo Vivo della Scienza, Napoli . . 024920
Museo Vostell-Malpartida de Cáceres, Malpartida de Cáceres 035459
Museo V.S. Breda, Padova 025065
Museo Vulcanologico dell'Osservatorio Vesuviano, Ercolano 024052
Museo Wakuatay, Playas de Rosarito 028645
Museo Weilbauer, Quito 009256
Museo Wifredo Lam, La Habana . . . 008020
Museo Wilhelm Schmid, Brè sopra Lugano 036969
Museo Xochiltepec, Magdalena . . . 028397
Museo Xólotl, San Bartolo Tenayuca 028707
Museo Xul Solar, Buenos Aires 000246
Museo y Archivo Dardo Rocha, La Plata 000392
Museo y Archivo Histórico de San Nicolás, Primer Combate Naval Argentino, San Nicolás de los Arroyos 000591
Museo y Archivo Histórico Localista Almirante Guillermo Brown, Adrogué 000106
Museo y Artesanía el Molino, Agüimes 034785
Museo y Biblioteca Blanco Acevedo, Montevideo 041540
Museo y Biblioteca de la Literature Porteña, Buenos Aires 000247
Museo y Biblioteca Leoncio Prado, Huánuco 031518
Museo y Centro Cultural AGADU, Montevideo 041541
Museo y Centro Cultural Victoria Ocampo, Mar del Plata 000427
Museo y Centro Estudios Históricos de la Facultad de Odontología, Buenos Aires 000248
Museo y Jardin Botánico Profesor Atilio Lombardo, Montevideo 041542

Museo y Monumento Histórico Las Bóvedas, Uspallata . . . 000650
Museo y Parque Arqueológico de Obando, Obando . . . 007557
Museo y Parque Historico de Caparra, San Juan . . . 032746
Museo y Parque Libres del Sur, Dolores . . . 000330
Museo y Parque Nacional, Montenegro . . . 007551
Museo Yacimiento Romano, Cartagena . . . 035062
Museo Yoloxúchitl, Cuernavaca . . . 028208
Museo Zabaleta, Quesada . . . 035688
Museo Zacatecano, Zacatecas . . . 028968
Museo Zambiano, Castelfidardo . . . 023712
Museo Zoloxúchitl, Zacualpan . . . 028972
Museo Zoologico, Padova . . . 025066
Museo Zoologico Cambria, Messina 024682
Museo Zoologico César Domìnguez Flores, Tuxtla Gutiérrez . . . 028902
Museo Zoológico Dámaso A. Larrañaga, Montevideo . . . 041543
Museo Zoologico degli Vertebrati, Avellino . . . 023306
Museo Zoologico dell'Istituto Nazionale per la Fauna Selvatica, Ozzano dell'Emilia . . . 025042
Museo Zoologico G. Scarpa, Treviso 026124
Museo Zucchi Collection, Milano . . 024730
Museo Zuloaga, Segovia . . . 035848
Museo Zumalacárregui, Ormaiztegi 035573
Museoalus Sigyn, Turku . . . 010168
Museográfica Antonio Martínez, La Roda . . . 035710
Museogràfica de la Parròquiad l'Assumpció, Montesa . . . 035520
Museográfica de la villa, Camporrobles . . . 035038
Museokeskus Vapriikki, Tampere . . 010123
Museokylä Kalluntalo, Laukaa . . . 009812
Museologia Scientifica, Firenze . . . 135926
Museological Review, Leicester . . . 136249
Museon, Den Haag . . . 029435
Museon Arlaten, Arles . . . 010473
Museonder, Otterlo . . . 030016
Muséoparc de Découverte des Tourbières et du Cezallier, Saint-Alyre-ès-Montagne . . . 014173
Muséoparc de la Ferme de l'Aurochs, Menétrux-en-Joux . . . 013014
Muséoparc de la Préhistoire, Saint-Vrain . . . 014576
Muséoparc du Soleil et du Cosmos, Les Angles . . . 012599
Muséoparc La Petite Ferme Provençale, Antibes-Juan-les-Pins . . . 010432
Museos Arqueológico, Portoviejo . . 009228
Museos de la Universidad Nacional de Cajamarca, Museo Herramientas Andinas, Museo de Zoología, Museo Botánico, Museo Entomológico, Museo de Geología, Museo de Fitología, Cajamarca . . 031475
Museos del Gaucho y de la Moneda, Montevideo . . . 041544
Museos Integrales de Antofagasta de la Sierra y Laguna Blanca, San Fernando del Valle de Catamarca . . . 000558
Muséoscope du Lac, Rousset . . . 014140
Muséosite Cavernicole de la Grotte de la Madeleine, Saint-Remèze . . . 014511
Muséosite de l'Amphithéâtre Gallo-Romain, Lillebonne . . . 012689
Muséosite du Volcan à Ciel Ouvert, Saint-Ours-les-Roches . . . 014461
Muséosite Gallo-Romain, Pithiviers-le-Vieil . . . 013828
Museotalo Warpunen, Anjalankoski 009457
Muses Galantes, Paris . . . 138508
Museu Académico de Coimbra, Coimbra . . . 032595
Museu Aeroespacial, Rio de Janeiro 004345
Museu Afro-Brasileiro, Salvador . . . 004437
Museu Afro Brasileiro de Sergipe, Laranjeiras . . . 004185
Museu Agrícola Tropical, Lisboa . . . 032631
Museu Alfredo Andersen, Curitiba . 004080
Museu Alfredo Varela, Jaguarão . . . 004159
Museu Amsterdam Sauer de Pedras Preciosas, Rio de Janeiro . . . 004346
Museu Anchieta Ciencias Naturais, Porto Alegre . . . 004290
Museu Angelo Agostini / Casa de Cultura Laura Alvim, Rio de Janeiro . . . 004347
Museu Aníbal Ribeiro Filho, Paranaguá . . . 004260
Museu Anjos Teixeira, Sintra . . . 032691
Ao Museu Antiguidade, São Paulo . 123719
Museu Antoniano, Lisboa . . . 032632
Museu Antonino, Faro . . . 032613
Museu Antonio Granemann de Souza, Curitibanos . . . 004095
Museu Antonio Lago, Rio de Janeiro . . . 004348
Museu Antonio Parreiras, Niterói . . 004241
Museu Antropológico, Coimbra . . . 032596
Museu Antropológico, Goiânia . . . 004124
Museu Antropológico Caldas Júnior, Santo Antônio da Patrulha . . . 004468
Museu Antropológico Diretor Pestana, Ijuí . . . 004143
Museu Antropológico do Instituto Superior de Cultura Brasileira, Rio de Janeiro . . . 004349
Museu Antropológico do Rio Grande do Sul, Porto Alegre . . . 004291
Museu Arquediocesano Dom Joaquim, Brusque . . . 004028
Museu Arqueològic, Ponts . . . 035668
Museu Arqueològic Comarcal, Banyoles . . . 034895
Museu Arqueològic de l'Esquerda, Roda de Ter . . . 035712
Museu Arqueològic i Paleontològic, Baldomar . . . 034892
Museu Arqueològic i Paleontològic, Moià . . . 035501
Museu Arqueològic Municipal, Els Prats de Rei . . . 035677
Museu Arqueologic Municipal, La Vall d'Uixo . . . 035991
Museu Arqueológico, Lagoa Santa . 004180
Museu Arqueológico, Lisboa . . . 032633
Museu Arqueológico, Oliva . . . 035552
Museu Arqueológico de Sambaqui Joinville, Joinville . . . 004166
Museu Arqueológico de São Miguel de Odrinhas, Câmara Municipal de Sintra, Sintra . . . 032692
Museu Arqueológico e Etnológico António Tomás Pires, Elvas . . . 032608
Museu Arqueológico e Lapidar do Infante D. Henrique, Faro . . . 032614
Museu Arquidiocesano de Mariana, Mariana . . . 004212
Museu Arquivo Histórico da Santa Casa, Belém . . . 003986
Museu Arquivo Histórico Florense, Flores da Cunha . . . 004103
Museu Arxiduc Lluís Salvador d'Austria de son Marroig, Deià . . . 035144
Museu-Arxiu Arbocenc, L'Arboç . . . 034848
Museu Arxiu Comarcal, Moià . . . 035502
Museu-Arxiu de Santa María de Mataró, Mataró . . . 035481
Museu Arxiu de Vilassar de Dalt, Vilassar de Dalt . . . 036055
Museu-Arxiu Municipal, Tortosa . . . 035949
Museu-Arxiu Municipal de Calella, Calella . . . 035033
Museu-Arxiu Parroquial, Canet de Mar . . . 035044
Museu-Arxiu Tomàs Balvey i Bas, Cardedeu . . . 035053
Museu Banespa, São Paulo . . . 004513
Museu Barão de Mauá, Mauá . . . 004217
Museu Barrau, Santa Eulària del Río . . . 035798
Museu Bi Moreira, Lavras . . . 004186
Museu-Biblioteca da Fundacão de Casa de Bragança, Vila Viçosa . . . 032701
Museu Biblioteca Fundació Mauri, La Garriga . . . 035215
Museu Botânico Dr. João Barbosa Rodrigues, São Paulo . . . 004514
Museu Calmon Barreto, Araxá . . . 003972
Museu Calouste Gulbenkian, Lisboa 032634
Museu Câmara Cascudo, Natal . . . 004234
Museu Capela Santa Luzia, Vitória . 004605
Museu Capitular, Lleida . . . 035349
Museu Capitular de la Catedral de Girona, Girona . . . 035231
Museu Carlos Costa Pinto, Salvador 004438
Museu Carlos Reis, Torres Novas . . 032697
Museu Carmen Miranda, Rio de Janeiro . . . 004350
Museu Carpológico do Jardim Botânico do Rio de Janeiro, Rio de Janeiro . . . 004351
Museu Casa Alphonsus de Guimaraens, Mariana . . . 004213
Museu Casa Cel. Joaquim Lacerda, Lapa . . . 004182
Museu Casa da Hera, Vassouras . . 004597
Museu Casa d'Areny-Plandolit, Ordino . . . 000084
Museu Casa de Benjamin Constant, Rio de Janeiro . . . 004352
Museu Casa de Portinari, Brodowski . . . 004027
Museu Casa de Rui Barbosa, Rio de Janeiro . . . 004353
Museu Casa de Rui Barbosa, Salvador . . . 004439
Museu Casa do Anhanguera, Santana de Parnaíba . . . 004464
Museu Casa do Pontal, Rio de Janeiro . . . 004354
Museu Casa do Sertão, Universidade Estadual de Feira de Santana, Feira de Santana . . . 004101
Museu Casa dos Contos, Ouro Preto 004250
Museu Casa Fritz Alt, Joinville . . . 004167
Museu Casa Guignard, Ouro Preto . 004251
Museu Casa Guimarães Rosa, Cordisburgo . . . 004070
Museu Casa Pedro Américo, Areia . 003976
Museu Casa Rull, Sispony . . . 000086
Museu-Casa Verdaguer, Museu d'Història de la Ciutat, Vallvidrera . . . 036016
Museu Castro Alves, Salvador . . . 004440
Museu Cau Ferrat, Sitges . . . 035877
Museu Central das Forças Armadas, Luanda . . . 000094
Museu Cerdà, Puigcerdà . . . 035686
Museu Ceroplástico Augusto Esteves, Faculdade de Medicina / FM, São Paulo . . . 004515
Museu Civico-Religioso Padre Cicero, Juazeiro do Norte . . . 004170
Museu Clarà, Barcelona . . . 034919
Museu Claretiano, Vic . . . 036029
Museu Codorniú, Sant Sadurní d'Anoia . . . 035789
Museu Comajoan Fauna del Montseny, Santa María de Palautordera . . . 035804
Museu Comarcal, Tárrega . . . 035898
Museu Comarcal de Berga, Berga . 034975
Museu Comarcal de la Conca de Barberà, Montblanc . . . 035513
Museu Comarcal de la Garrotxa, Olot . . . 035555
Museu Comarcal de l'Anoia, Igualada . . . 035293
Museu Comarcal de l'Horta Sud, Torrente . . . 035944
Museu Comarcal de Manresa, Manresa . . . 035464
Museu Comarcal Salvador Vilaseca, Reus . . . 035697
Museu Comendador Ananias Arruda, Baturit . . . 003985
Museu Comendador Jos' Dias de Andrade, Arceburgo . . . 003975
Museu Comercial, Belo Horizonte . . 058438
Museu Comercial e Arqueológico do Sindicato dos Empregados, Maceió . . . 004194
Museu Comunitário, Ipumirim . . . 004144
Museu Comunitário, Itapiranga . . . 004151
Museu Condes de Castro Guimarães, Cascais . . . 032590
Museu Corina Novelino, Sacramento . . . 004433
Museu Coritiba Football Club, Curitiba . . . 004081
Museu Cosme Bauça, Felanitx . . . 035188
Museu Criminal, Academia de Polícia Dr. Coriolano Nogueira Cobra / ACADEPOL, São Paulo . . . 004516
Museu D. João VI, Rio de Janeiro . . 004355
Museu D. Lopo de Almeida, Abrantes . . . 032570
Museu da Abolição, Centro de Referência da Cultura Afro-Brasileia, Recife . 004311
Museu da Agua da Epal, Lisboa . . . 032635
Museu da Agua Manuel da Maia, Lisboa . . . 032635
Museu da Arte Brasileira, Maceió . . 004195
Museu da Arte Pierre Chalita, Maceió . . . 004196
Museu da Associação Nacional dos Veteranos, São João Del Rei . . . 004483
Museu da Bacia do Paraná, Maringá . . . 004215
Museu da Borracha, Rio Branco . . . 004327
Museu da Brigada Militar, Porto Alegre . . . 004292
Museu da Cachaça, Paty do Alferes 004266
Museu da Casa Brasileira, São Paulo . . . 004517
Museu da Casa da Cultura de Teresina, Teresina . . . 004578
Museu da Cerâmica de Sacavém, Loures . . . 032659
Museu da Cidade, Campinas . . . 004039
Museu da Cidade, Lisboa . . . 032636
Museu da Cidade, São Paulo . . . 004518
Museu da Cidade de Recife, Recife 004312
Museu da Companhia Independente do Palácio Guanabara, Rio de Janeiro . . . 004356
Museu da Companhia Paulista, Jundiá . . . 004177
Museu da Cultura e Arte Popular, João Pessoa . . . 004164
Museu da Curia Metropolitana, Porto Alegre . . . 004293
Museu da Educação e do Brinquedo, São Paulo . . . 004519
Museu da Eletricidade, Rio de Janeiro . . . 004357
Museu da Energia, Itu . . . 004154
Museu da Escola de Engenharia, Rio de Janeiro . . . 004358
Museu da Escola de Minas Gerais, Belo Horizonte . . . 003998
Museu da Escola Naval, Rio de Janeiro . . . 004359
Museu da Escravatura, Museum of Slavery, Luanda . . . 000095
Museu da Estrada de Ferro Madeira-Mamoré, Porto Velho . . . 004307
Museu da Estrada de Ferro Sorocabana, Sorocaba . . . 004568
Museu da Faculdade de Direito, Faculdade de Direito da Universidade de São Paulo, São Paulo . . . 004520
Museu da Faculdade de Odontologia, Araraquara . . . 003970
Museu da Família Colonial, Blumenau . . . 004007
Museu da Farmáciada Santa Casa da Misericórdia do Rio de Janeiro, Rio de Janeiro . . . 004360
Museu da Fauna, Rio de Janeiro . . 004361
Museu da Fazenda Federal, Rio de Janeiro . . . 004362
Museu da Força Expedicionária Brasileira, Rio de Janeiro . . . 004363
Museu da Fundação Nacional de Saúde, Brasília . . . 004013
Museu da Gravura, Curitiba . . . 004082
Museu da Gravura Brasileira, Bagé 003979
Museu da Imagem, Campinas . . . 004040
Museu da Imagem, Franca . . . 004119
Museu da Imagem e do Som, Campo Grande . . . 004046
Museu da Imagem e do Som, Rio de Janeiro . . . 004364

Museu da Imagem e do Som de Alagoas, Maceió 004197
Museu da Imagem e do Som de Campinas, Campinas 004041
Museu da Imagem e do Som de Campos, Campos dos Goitacazes 004052
Museu da Imagem e do Som de Cascavel, Cascavel 004060
Museu da Imagem e do Som de Curitiba, Curitiba 004083
Museu da Imagem e do Som de e da Imprensa da Bahia, Salvador 004441
Museu da Imagem e do Som de Goiás, Goiás 004130
Museu da Imagem e do Som de Piracicaba, São Paulo 004521
Museu da Imagem e do Som de Resende, Resende 004323
Museu da Imagem e do Som de Santa Catarina, Florianópolis 004105
Museu da Imagem e do Som de São Paulo, São Paulo 004522
Museu da Imagem e do Som de Taubaté, Taubaté 004572
Museu da Imagem e do Som do Ceará, Fortaleza 004114
Museu da Imagem e do Som do Pará, Belém 003987
Museu da Imagem e do Som do Paraná, Curitiba 004084
Museu da Imigração, Departamento de Museus e Arquivos, São Paulo . . . 004512
Museu da Imigração, Santa Bárbara d'Oeste 004456
Museu da Imprensa, Brasília 004014
Museu da Inconfidência, Ouro Preto 004252
Museu da Liga dos Combatentes da Grande Guerra, Lisboa 032637
Museu da Limpeza Urbana - Casa de Banhos de Dom João VI, Rio de Janeiro 004365
Museu da Literatura, São Paulo . . . 004523
Museu da Loucura, Barbacena 003982
Museu da Música Portuguesa, Estoril 032609
Museu da Pessoa, São Paulo 004524
Museu da Polícia Civil, Polícia Civil do Estado do Rio de Janeiro, Rio de Janeiro 004366
Museu da Polícia Militar de Pernambuco, Recife 004313
Museu da Porcelana Senhor Adelino dos Santos Gouveia, Pedreira 004269
Museu da Quinta das Cruzes, Funchal 032616
Museu da Rainha Dona Leonor, Beja 032583
Museu da Regiao Flâviense, Chaves 032593
Museu da República, Rio de Janeiro 004367
Museu da Revolução, Maputo 029046
Museu da Santa Casa da Misericórdia, Coimbra 032597
Museu da Secção de Tecnologia do Serviço Florestal, Rio de Janeiro 004368
Museu da Terra e da Vida, Mafra . . 004202
Museu da Universidade Federal do Pará, Belém 003988
Museu da Venrável Ordem Terceira de São Francisco da Penitência, Rio de Janeiro 004369
Museu Darder d'Història Natural, Banyoles 034896
Museu d'Arqueología de Catalunya, Barcelona 034920
Museu d'Arqueologia de Catalunya, Olèrdola 035550
Museu d'Arqueologia de Catalunya-Empúries, L'Escala 035175
Museu d'Arqueologia de Catalunya Girona, Girona 035232
Museu d'Arqueología de Catalunya Ullastret, Ullastret 035963
Museu d'Arqueològia Submarina, Pals 035629
Museu d'Arquitectura de la Real Càtedra Gaudí, Barcelona 034921
Museu d'Art, Cadaqués 035018
Museu d'Art, Girona 035233
Museu d'Art Casa Turull, Sabadell . 035727
Museu d'Art Contemporani, Pego . . 035644
Museu d'Art Contemporani, Conjunt Monumental la Cartoixa, Valldemosa 036009
Museu d'Art Contemporani de Barcelona, Barcelona 034922
Museu d'Art Contemporani de Mallorca, Sa Pobla 035659
Museu d'Art Contemporani d'Eivissa, Eivissa 035163
Museu d'Art Espanyol Contemporani, Fundación Juan March, Palma de Mallorca 035614
Museu d'Art Frederic Marès, Montblanc 035514
Museu d'Art Matern, Sant Vicenç dels Horts 035790
Museu d'Art Modern, Tarragona . . . 035892
Museu d'Art Modern del MNAC, Barcelona 034923
Museu d'Art Modern 'Jaume Morera, Lleida 035350
Museu d'Art Popular, Horta de Sant Joan 035282
Museu das Alfaias da Paróquia da Cachoeira, Cachoeira 004030
Museu das Armas, Lapa 004183
Museu das Bandeiras, Goiás 004131
Museu das Comunicações, Lisboa . 032638
Museu das Monções, Porto Feliz . . 004305
Museu das Reduções, Ouro Preto . . 004253
Museu de Alberto Sampaio, Guimarães 032620
Museu de Anatomia Humana Prof. Dr. Alfonso Bovera, Instituto de Ciências Biomédicas / ICB, São Paulo 004525
Museu de Anatomia Veterinária Prof. Dr. Plínio Pinto e Silva, São Paulo . . . 004526
Museu de Angra do Heroísmo, Angra do Heroísmo 032578
Museu de Antropologia do Vale do Paraíba, Jacareí 004158
Museu de Armas Ferreira da Cunha, Petrópolis 004278
Museu de Armas Major Lara Ribas, Florianópolis 004106
Museu de Arqueologia e Artes Populares, Paranaguá 004261
Museu de Arqueologia e Etnologia, Salvador 004442
Museu de Arqueologia e Etnologia da Universidade de São Paulo, São Paulo 004527
Museu de Arte, Belém 003989
Museu de Arte, Goiânia 004125
Museu de Arte, Joinville 004168
Museu de Arte, Londrina 004190
Museu de Arte Antiga, Instituto Feminino da Bahia, Salvador 004453
Museu de Arte Assis Chateaubriand, Campina Grande 004036
Museu de Arte Brasileira, São Paulo 004528
Museu de Arte Contemporâea, Jataí 004161
Museu de Arte Contemporânea, Feira de Santana 004102
Museu de Arte Contemporânea da Universidade de São Paulo, São Paulo 004529
Museu de Arte Contemporânea de Niterói, Niterói 004242
Museu de Arte Contemporânea de Pernambuco, Olinda 004247
Museu de Arte Contemporânea de Serralves, Fundação de Serralves, Porto 032677
Museu de Arte Contemporônea, Curitiba 004085
Museu de Arte da Bahia, Salvador . 004443
Museu de Arte da Pampulha, Belo Horizonte 003999
Museu de Arte da Universidade Fedral do Ceará, Fortaleza 004115
Museu de Arte de Santa Catarina, Florianópolis 004107
Museu de Arte de São Paulo Assis Chateaubriand, São Paulo 004530
Museu de Arte do Paranà, Curitiba . 004086
Museu de Arte do Rio Grande do Sul Aldo Malagoli, Porto Alegre 004294
Museu de Arte e Cultura Canjira, Itaobim 004150
Museu de Arte e Cultura Popular Coordenação de Cultura, Cuiabá . 004075
Museu de Arte e História, Natal . . . 004235
Museu de Arte e História Racioppi, Belo Horizonte 004000
Museu de Arte e Histórico, Jaboticabal 004157
Museu de Arte Mágica e Ilusionismo João Peixoto dos Santos, São Paulo . . . 004531
Museu de Arte Moderna, Resende . 004324
Museu de Arte Moderna da Bahia, Salvador 004444
Museu de Arte Moderna de São Paulo, São Paulo 004532
Museu de Arte Moderna do Rio de Janeiro, Rio de Janeiro 004370
Museu de Arte Popular, Lisboa 032639
Museu de Arte Popular da Fortaleza dos Reis Magos, Natal 004236
Museu de Arte Religiosa, Vitória . . . 004606
Museu de Arte Sacra, Rio de Janeiro 004371
Museu de Arte Sacra, Salvador . . . 004445
Museu de Arte Sacra, São Cristóvão 004475
Museu de Arte Sacra, São João Del Rei 004484
Museu de Arte Sacra, São Luís 004492
Museu de Arte Sacra, São Paulo . . 004533
Museu de Arte Sacra, São Sebastião 004562
Museu de Arte Sacra, Taubaté 004573
Museu de Arte Sacra da Catedral-Basílica, Salvador 004446
Museu de Arte Sacra da Universidade, Coimbra 032598
Museu de Arte sacra de Angra dos Reis, Angra dos Reis 003961
Museu de Arte Sacra de Boa Morte, Goiás 004132
Museu de Arte Sacra de Iguape, Iguape 004142
Museu de Arte Sacra de Santos, Santos 004469
Museu de Arte Sacra do Carmo / Paróquia do Pilar, Ouro Preto 004254
Museu de Arte Sacra do Estado de Alagoas, Marechal Deodoro 004211
Museu de Arte Sacra do Pará, Belém 003990
Museu de Arte Sacra Dom Ranulfo, Maceió 004198
Museu de Arte Sacra Padre Roberto Barbalho, Recife 004314
Museu de Artes Plásticas, Taubaté . 004574
Museu de Artes Plásticas Quirino da Silva, Mococa 004220
Museu de Artes Sacras Iria Josepha da Silva, Mococa 004221
Museu de Artes Visuais, São Luís . . 004493
Museu de Artes Visuais Ruth Schneider, Passo Fundo 004262
Museu de Astronomia e Ciências Afins, Rio de Janeiro 004372
Museu de Aveiro, Aveiro 032580
Museu de Azambuja, Azambuja . . . 032581
Museu de Badalona, Badalona 034888
Museu de Belas-Artes, Cataguases 004062
Museu de Bellvís, Bellvís 034969
Museu de Biodiversidade do Cerrado, Uberlândia 004590
Museu de Biologia Prof. Mello Leitão, Santa Teresa 004463
Museu de Bonecos e Ventrílocos, São Paulo 004534
Museu de Carlos Machado, Ponta Delgada 032669
Museu de Carrosses Fúnebres, Barcelona 034924
Museu de Cartão, São Paulo 004535
Museu de Cera, Barcelona 034925
Museu de Cera, Binissalem 034990
Museu de Cerámica, Barcelona . . . 034926
Museu de Ceràmica de Manises, Manises 035462
Museu de Ciência e Técnica da Escola de Minas, Ouro Preto 004255
Museu de Ciência e Tecnologia, Salvador 004447
Museu de Ciências da Terra - DNPM, Rio de Janeiro 004373
Museu de Ciências Naturais, Guarapuava 004136
Museu de Ciências Naturais, Porto Alegre 004295
Museu de Ciências Naturais, Recife 004315
Museu de Ciências Naturais, Triunfo 004584
Museu de Ciências Naturais PUC Minas, Belo Horizonte 004001
Museu de ciències Naturals, Costitx 035130
Museu de Ciències Naturals, Lleida 035351
Museu de Ciències Naturals, Onda . 035561
Museu de Ciències Naturals de Barcelona, Institut de Cultura Barcelona, Barcelona 034927
Museu de Comunicação Social Hipólito José da Costa, Porto Alegre 004296
Museu de Corrente, Corrente 004072
Museu de Coses del Poble, Collbató 035103
Museu de Curiositats Marineres, Vilanova i la Geltrú 036049
Museu de Documentos Especiais, Praia 006896
Museu de Esportes Mané Garrincha, Rio de Janeiro 004374
Museu de Etnografia do Lobito, Lobito 000092
Museu de Etnografia e História, Porto 032675
Museu de Evora, Evora 032610
Museu de Ex-votos do Senhor do Bonfim, Salvador 004448
Museu de Farmácia, São Paulo . . . 004536
Museu de Física, Coimbra 032599
Museu de Folclore Édison Carneiro, Rio de Janeiro 004375
Museu de Folclore Saul Martins, Vespasiano 004599
Museu de Francisco Tavares Proença Júnior, Castelo Branco 032592
Museu de Gavà, Gavà 035218
Museu de Gelida, Gelida 035219
Museu de Geociências, São Paulo . 004537
Museu de Geociências da Universidade de Brasília, Brasília 004015
Museu de Geologia, Barcelona 034928
Museu de Geologia, Maringá 004216
Museu de Geologia, Porto Alegre . . 004297
Museu de Geología, Sant Celoni . . . 035776
Museu de Geológia, Paleontológia e Mineralógia, Luanda 000096
Museu de Geología Valenti Masachs, Manresa 035465
Museu de Granollers, Granollers . . . 035262
Museu de Granollers-Ciències Naturals, Granollers 035263
Museu de Grão Vasco, Viseu 032703
Museu de Historia da Ocupação Colonial e da Resistencia, Maputo 029047
Museu de História e Ciências Naturais, Além Paraíba 003957
Museu de História Natural, Belo Horizonte 004002
Museu de História Natural, Campinas 004042
Museu de História Natural, Coimbra 032600
Museu de História Natural, Crato . . 004074
Museu de História Natural, Maputo 029048
Museu de História Natural, Porto . . 032676
Museu de História Natural Prof. Antonio Pergola, Atibaia 003978
Museu de Homem do Norte, Manaus 004206
Museu de Homem Sergipano, Aracaju 003967
Museu de Imagem e do Som de Pernambuco, Recife 004316
Museu de Images do Inconsciente, Rio de Janeiro 004376
Museu de Índio, Uberlândia 004591

Museu de Instrumentos de Cálculo Numérico, São Carlos 004474
Museu de José Malhoa, Caldas da Rainha 032587
Museu de la Catedral, Barcelona . . 034929
Museu de la Ciencia de la Fundació la Caixa, Barcelona 034930
Museu de la Ciència i de la Tècnica de Catalunya, Terrassa 035907
Museu de la Ciutat, Valls 036015
Museu de la Farmàcia Catalana, Barcelona 034931
Museu de la Festa, Casal de Sant Jordi, Alcoy 034810
Museu de la Fusta, Areu 034857
Museu de la Música, Barcelona . . . 034932
Museu de la Noguera, Balaguer . . . 034891
Museu de la Pedra i de l'Estable, Guimerà 035272
Museu de la Pesca, Palamós 035592
Museu de la Piel, Igualada 035294
Museu de la Vall de Lord, Sant Lorenç de Morunys 035786
Museu de la Vila, Vilar-Rodona 036054
Museu de l'Acordió, Arsèguel 034863
Museu de l'Adet, Torelló 035934
Museu de l'Aigua Colleció Gavarró, Vilanova del Camí 036047
Museu de Lamego, Lamego 032624
Museu de l'Aquarella, Fundació J. Martínez Lozano, Llança 035342
Museu de l'Automòbil, Barcelona . . 034933
Museu de Leiria, Leiria 032625
Museu de l'Empordà, Figueres 035192
Museu de les Arts Decoratives, Barcelona 034934
Museu de les Arts Escèniques, Barcelona 034935
Museu de les Arts Gràfiques, Barcelona 034936
Museu de l'Estampació de Premià de Mar, Premià de Mar 035678
Museu de L'Hospitalet de Llobregat, L'Hospitalet de Llobregat 035283
Museu de l'Institut de Criminología, Barcelona 034937
Museu de l'Institut Paleontològic Miquel Crusafont, Sabadell 035728
Museu de l'Instituto Botánico, Barcelona 034938
Museu de Llaberia, Tivissa 035913
Museu de Llavaneres, Sant Andreu de Llavaneres 035775
Museu de Lloret de Mar, Lloret de Mar 035357
Museu de Malacología Cau del Cargol, Vilassar de Dalt 036056
Museu de Mallorca, Palma de Mallorca 035615
Museu de Manacor, Manacor 035460
Museu de Marinha, Lisboa 032640
Museu de Mataró, Mataró 035482
Museu de Medallística Enrique Giner, Nules 035547
Museu de Medicina, Curitiba 004087
Museu de Minerais e Rochas, Uberlândia 004592
Museu de Mineralogia, Congonhas . 004066
Museu de Mineralogia Luiz Englert, Porto Alegre 004298
Museu de Montgrí i del Baix Ter, Torroella de Montgrí 035946
Museu de Montserrat, Monistrol de Montserrat 035509
Museu de Nampula, Nampula 029055
Museu de Nossa Senhora da Glória do Outeiro, Rio de Janeiro 004377
Museu de Odontologia Dr. Solon de Miranda Galvão, Natal 004237
Museu de Odontología Professor Salles Cunha, Rio de Janeiro 004378
Museu de Olaria, Barcelos 032582
Museu de Ornitologia, Goiânia 004126
Museu de Ovar, Ovar 032667
Museu de Paleontologia, Monte Alto 004224
Museu de Patologia do Instituto Oswaldo Cruz, Rio de Janeiro 004379
Museu de Pedras Ramis Bucair, Cuiabá 004076
Museu de Pesca, Santos 004470
Museu de Poblet, Monestir de Poblet 035506
Museu de Polícia Militar, São Paulo 004538
Museu de Pré-História Professora Márcia Angelina Alves, Perdizes 004275
Museu de Prehistòria i de les Cultures de València, Valencia 035989
Museu de Relógio Prof. Dimas de Melo Pimenta, São Paulo 004539
Museu de Rocafort, El Pont de Vilomara i Rocafort 035664
Museu de Roque Gameiro, Minde . . 032662
Museu de Rua Alto Paraná Ontem e Hoje, Alto Paran 003958
Museu de Rubí, Rubí 035724
Museu de Sal de Josep Arnau, Cardona 035054
Museu de Sant Joan de Mediona, Mediona 035488
Museu de Sant Pol de Mar, Sant Pol de Mar 035788
Museu de Santo André, Santo André 004467
Museu de São Roque, Lisboa 032641
Museu de Saúde Pública Emílio Ribas, São Paulo 004540
Museu de Serralves, Fundação de Serralves, Porto 032677
Museu de Sertão, Petrolina 004277
Museu de Setúbal - Convento de Jesus - Galeria de Arte Quinhentista, Setúbal 032688
Museu de Telecomunicações, Rio de Janeiro 004380
Museu de Torrebesses, Torrebesses 035939
Museu de Torrellebreta, Malla 035458
Museu de Torroja, Torroja del Priorat 035947
Museu de Tradições do Nordeste, Brasília 004016
Museu de Valldoreix, Sant Cugat del Vallès 035779
Museu de Valores, Rio de Janeiro . 004381
Museu de Valores do Banco Central do Brasil, Brasília 004017
Museu de Venâncio Aires, Venâncio Aires 004598
Museu de Vilafranca-Museu del Vi, Vilafranca del Penedès 036043
Museu de Zoologia, São Paulo 004541
Museu de Zoologia de Barcelona, Institut de Cultura Barcelona, Barcelona . . . 034927
Museu d'Eines Antigues, Torregrossa 035941
Museu d'Eines del Camp Masia de Can Deu, Sabadell 035729
Museu d'Eines del Pagès, Sant Climent de Llobregat 035777
Museu del Bast, Llaberia-Tivissa . . 035339
Museu del Blat, Taradell 035889
Museu d'El Bruc, El Bruc 034997
Museu del Calcat Antic, Barcelona . 034939
Museu del Camp, Vilabella 036041
Museu del Càntir, Argentona 034858
Museu del Castell de Odna, Onda . . 035562
Museu del Ferrocarril, Vilanova i la Geltrú 036050
Museu del Joguet de Catalunya, Figueres 035193
Museu del Monestir de Santa María de L'Estany, L'Estany 035181
Museu del Montsec, Artesa de Segre 034866
Museu del Montsià, Amposta 034838
Museu del Pagès, Castelldans 035066
Museu del Pagès, Linyola 035338
Museu del Pagès, Torroella de Fluvià 035945
Museu del Pastor, Fornells de la Muntanya 035198
Museu del Perfum, Barcelona 034940
Museu del Prat, El Prat de Llobregat 035675
Museu del Temple Expiatori de la Sagrada Familia, Barcelona 034941
Museu del Vidre, Algaida 034817
Museu del Volcans, Olot 035556
Museu dels Autòmats, Barcelona . . 034942
Museu dels Raiers, El Pont de Claverol 035663
Museu des Comunicações Marechal Rondon, Ji-Paran 004163
Museu d'Etnografia d'Eivissa, Santa Eulària del Río 035799
Museu d'Etnologia, Pego 035645
Museu d'Història, Sabadell 035730
Museu d'Història Casa Castellarnau, Tarragona 035893
Museu d'Història de la Ciudad, Sant Feliu de Guíxols 035781
Museu d'Història de la Ciutat, Barcelona 034943
Museu d'Història de la Ciutat, Girona 035234
Museu d'Historia de Nules, Nules . . 035548
Museu d'Historia de Tarragona Pretori Romà, Pretorio Romano, Tarragona 035894
Museu di Arte Contemporânea, Americana 003959
Museu Diocesà de Barcelona, Barcelona 034944
Museu Diocesà de Girona, Girona . . 035235
Museu Diocesà de Mallorca, Palma de Mallorca 035616
Museu Diocesa de Menorca, Ciutadella de Menorca 035101
Museu Diocesá d'Urgell, La Seu d'Urgell 035850
Museu Diocesà i Comarcal, Solsona 035882
Museu Diocesà i Comarcal, Secció Etnogràfica, Solsona 035883
Museu Diocesano de Arte Sacra, Funchal 032617
Museu do Ar, Alverca do Ribatejo . . 032575
Museu do Automóvel, Arte & História, São Francisco de Paula 004477
Museu do Banco de Crédito Real de Minas Gerais, Juiz de Fora 004172
Museu do Bonde, Rio de Janeiro . . 004382
Museu do Brinquedo, Faculdade de Educação / FE, São Paulo 004542
Museu do Café, Luanda 000097
Museu do Café Cel. Francisco Schmidt, Ribeirão Preto 004326
Museu do Cangaço, Triunfo 004585
Museu do Caramulo, Caramulo . . . 032588
Museu do Carnaval, Rio de Janeiro 004383
Museu do Carnaval Hilton Silva, Florianópolis 004108
Museu do Carro Eléctrico, Porto . . . 032678
Museu do Ceará, Fortaleza 004116
Museu do Chiado, Museu Nacional de Arte Contemporânea, Lisboa 032642
Museu do Círio de Nazaré, Betém . 004006
Museu do Colégio Mauá, Santa Cruz do Sul 004457
Museu do Colono, Santa Leopoldina 004458
Museu do Congo, Carmona 000089
Museu do Diamante, Diamantina . . 004096
Museu do Dundu, Chitato 000090
Museu do Estado da Bahia, Salvador 004449
Museu do Estado de Pernambuco, Recife 004317
Museu do Estado do Pará, Belém . . 003991
Museu do Eucalipto, Rio Claro 004328
Museu do Expedicionário, Curitiba . 004088
Museu do Gás, Rio de Janeiro 004384
Museu do Homem, Curitiba 004089
Museu do Homem do Nordeste, Recife 004318
Museu do Índio, Florianópolis 004109
Museu do Índio, Lagoa Seca 004181
Museu do Índio, Manaus 004207
Museu do Indio, Rio de Janeiro . . . 004385
Museu do Instituto Arqueológico, Histórico e Geográfico Pernam Bucano, Recife 004319
Museu do Instituto Butantan, São Paulo 004543
Museu do Instituto de Antropologia Câmara Cascudo, Natal 004238
Museu do Instituto Geografico e Historico da Bahia, Salvador 004450
Museu do Instituto Histórico, Carpina 004058
Museu do Instituto Histórico e Geográfico Brasileiro, Rio de Janeiro 004386
Museu do Instituto Histórico e Geográfico de Alagoas, Maceió 004199
Museu do Instituto Histórico e Geográfico do Rio Grande do Norte, Natal 004239
Museu do Instituto Oceanográfico, Instituto Oceanográfico / IO, São Paulo . . . 004544
Museu do Jardim Botânico, Rio de Janeiro 004387
Museu do Mamulengo, Olinda 004248
Museu do Mar - Rei D. Carlos, Cascais 032591
Museu do Minstério do Trabalho, Brasília 004018
Museu do Monumento Nacional aos Mortos da Segunda Guerra Mundial, Rio de Janeiro 004388
Museu do Ouro, Sabará 004432
Museu do Piauí, Teresina 004579
Museu do Pio XII, Novo Hamburgo . 004246
Museu do Pioneiro, Malange 000101
Museu do Porto de Belém, Belém . . 003992
Museu do Porto do Rio, Rio de Janeiro 004389
Museu do Primeiro Reinado, Rio de Janeiro 004390
Museu do Rádio, Juiz de Fora 004173
Museu do Reino do Koongo, Mbanza Koongo 000102
Museu do Santuário de Nossa Senhora da Abadia, Amares 032577
Museu do Seridó, Caicó 004033
Museu do Sol, Penápolis 004272
Museu do STF, Brasília 004019
Museu do Superior Tribunal de Justiça, Brasília 004020
Museu do Telephone, Rio de Janeiro 004391
Museu do Theatro Municipal, São Paulo 004545
Museu do Trem, Rio de Janeiro . . . 004392
Museu do Trem, São Leopoldo 004490
Museu do Trem da Cidade de Recife, Recife 004320
Museu do Tribunal de Justiça do Estado de São Paulo, São Paulo 004546
Museu do Tropeiro, Castro 004061
Museu do Vaqueiro, Morada Nova . 004229
Museu do Vinho, Videira 004603
Museu Dom Avelar Brandão Vilela, Teresina 004580
Museu Dom Diogo de Souza, Bagé . 003980
Museu Dom Inocencio, Campanha . 004035
Museu Dom João VI, Rio de Janeiro 004393
Museu Dom José, Sobral 004567
Museu Dom Vital, Recife 004321
Museu dos Baleeiros, Lajes do Pico 032623
Museu dos Inhamuns, Tauá 004570
Museu dos Teatros do Rio de Janeiro, Rio de Janeiro 004394
Museu dos Transportes, Coimbra . . 032601
Museu dos Transportes Públicos Gaetano Ferolla, São Paulo 004547
Museu Dr. José Faibes Lubianca, Porto Alegre 004299
Museu e Arquivo Histórico, Itu 004155
Museu e Arquivo Histórico do Centro Cultural Banco do Brasil, Rio de Janeiro 004395
Museu e Arquivo Histórico Municipal, Guapor 004135
Museu e Arquivo Municipal, Bom Jesus 004009
Museu e Arquivo Público Municipal de Campo Belo, Campo Belo 004044
Museu e Biblioteca do Instituto Geográfico e Histórico do Amazonas, Manaus . 004208
Museu e Biblioteca Pública Pelotense, Pelotas 004271

Museu e Laboratório Mineralógico e Geológico, Lisboa 032643
Museu Ecologia, Nanuque 004231
Museu Educativo Gama d'Eça, Santa Maria 004460
Museu Egipci de Barcelona, Barcelona 034945
Museu Els Cups, Montbrió del Camp 035515
Museu Eng. António de Almeida, Porto 032679
Museu Enric Monjó, Vilassar de Mar 036057
Museu Episcopal de Vic, Vic 036030
Museu-Escola Esacro do Estado da Paraiba, João Pessoa 004165
Museu Estadual do Carvão, Arroio dos Ratos 003977
Museu Etnogràfic Andino-Amazònic, Barcelona 034946
Museu Etnogràfic de Ripoll, Ripoll . 035707
Museu Etnográfico da Sociedade de Geografia de Lisboa, Lisboa 032644
Museu Etnográfico e Arqueológico do Dr. Joaquim Manso, Nazaré 032663
Museu Etnografico Nacional, Bissau 021599
Museu Etnològic de Barcelona, Barcelona 034947
Museu Etnològic de Dénia, Dénia . . 035147
Museu Etnologic de Guadalest, Casa Típica del Segle XVIII, Guadalest 035265
Museu Etnològic de Muro, Secció Etnologia Museu de Mallorca, Muro 035536
Museu Etnològic del Montseny La Gabella, Arbúcies 034849
Museu Etnologic d'Era Val d'Aran, Vielha 036032
Museu Etnològic i Arqueològic, Juneda 035312
Museu Etnologic Moli del Dalt, Sant Lluis 035785
Museu Etnològic Municipal, Torrella 035943
Museu Eugênio Teixeira Leal, Salvador 004451
Museu Farmàcia de l'Hospital de Santa Catarina, Girona 035236
Museu Farroupilha, Triunfo 004586
Museu Fazenda, Nanuque 004232
Museu Ferreira de Almeida, Nampula 029056
Museu Ferroviário de Pires do Rio, Pires do Rio 004285
Museu Florestal Octávio Vecchi, São Paulo 004548
Museu Folclorico da Divisão de Discoteca e Biblioteca de Música de São Paulo, São Paulo 004549
Museu Frederic Marès, Barcelona . 034948
Museu Frei Galvão, Guaratinguetá . 004138
Museu Futbol Club Barcelona President Núñez, Barcelona 034949
Museu Gabinet Postal, Barcelona . . 034950
Museu Geológico, Lisboa 032645
Museu Geológico da Bahia, Salvador 004452
Museu Geológico Valdemar Lefèvre, São Paulo 004550
Museu Getúlio Vargas, São Borja . . 004472
Museu Goiano Zoroastro Artiaga, Goiânia 004127
Museu Guido Straube, Curitiba 004090
Museu Gustavo Barroso, Fortaleza . 004117
Museu H. Stern, Rio de Janeiro . . . 004396
Museu Henriqueta Catharino, Instituto Feminino da Bahia, Salvador 004453
Museu Hernández Mora-Hernández Mora, Mahón 035448
Museu Hipólito Cabaço, Alenquer . . 032573
Museu Històric de la Seu, Manresa 035466
Museu Històric Municipal, Riudoms 035709
Museu Historic Municipal de Ca l'Arra, Barcelona 034951
Museu Historic Municipal de Polinyà, Polinyà 035661
Museu Histórico, Cambé 004034
Museu Histórico, Divinópolis 004097
Museu Histórico, Igarassu 004140
Museu Histórico, Lavras 004187
Museu Histórico, Londrina 004191
Museu Histórico, Nova Ponte 004244
Museu Histórico, Pará de Minas . . . 004259
Museu Histórico, Rio Pomba 004426
Museu Histórico, São Francisco do Sul 004478
Museu Histórico, São Paulo 004551
Museu Histórico, Sertanópolis 004565
Museu Histórico, Siqueira Campos . 004566
Museu Histórico Abílio Barreto, Belo Horizonte 004003
Museu Histórico Aurélio Dolabella, Santa Luzia 004459
Museu Histórico Bárbara Heliodora, São Gonçalo do Sapucaí 004481
Museu Histórico Beato José de Anchieta, Pedreira 004270
Museu Histórico Casa do Imigrante, Bento Gonçalves 004005
Museu Histórico Corália Venites Maluf, Sacramento 004434
Museu Histórico Cultural, Rio do Sul 004423
Museu Histórico da Cidade, Brasília 004021
Museu Histórico da Cidade do Rio de Janeiro, Rio de Janeiro 004397
Museu Histórico da Imigração Japonesa no Brasil, São Paulo 004552
Museu Histórico da Universidade Federal, Viçoasa 004601
Museu Histórico de Araxá - Don Beja, Araxá 003973
Museu Histórico de Brejo Madre de Deus, Brejo Madre de Deus 004026
Museu Histórico de Jataí Francisco Honório de Campos, Jataí 004162
Museu Histórico de Sergipe, São Cristóvão 004476
Museu Histórico de Witmarsum, Palmeira 004258
Museu Histórico Desembargador Edmundo Mercer Júnior, Tibagi 004583
Museu Histórico do Corpo de Bombeiros Militar do Estado do Rio de Janeiro, Rio de Janeiro 004398
Museu Histórico do Exército e Forte de Copacabana, Rio de Janeiro 004399
Museu Histórico do Piaú, Teresina . 004581
Museu Histórico do Senado Federal, Brasília 004022
Museu Histórico Dona Mariana Joaquina da Costa, Vespasiano 004600
Museu Histórico Dr. Sellmann Nazareth, São José do Rio Preto 004487
Museu Histórico e Artístico, Quitandinha 004309
Museu Histórico e Artístico do Maranhão, São Luís 004494
Museu Histórico e de Artes, Santana do Ipanema 004465
Museu Histórico e de Ordem Geral Plínio Travassos dos Santos, Rebeirão Preto 004310
Museu Histórico e Diplomático do Itamaraty, Rio de Janeiro 004400
Museu Histórico e Geográfico de Monte Sião, Monte Sião 004227
Museu Histórico e Geográfico de Poços de Caldas, Poços de Caldas 004287
Museu Histórico e Geral da Cidade de São Vicente, São Vicente 004564
Museu Histórico e Pedagógico, Mococa 004222
Museu Histórico e Pedagógico Conselheiro Rodrigues Alves, Guaratinguetá . . 004139
Museu Histórico e Pedagógico Dr. Washington Luís, Batatais 003984
Museu Histórico e Pedagógico Fernão Dias Paes, Penápolis 004273
Museu Histórico e Pedagógico Marechal Cândido Rondon, Araçatuba 003969
Museu Histórico e Pedagógico Monteiro Lobato, Taubaté 004575
Museu Histórico e Pedagógico Pe. Manoel da Nóbrega, São Manuel 004495
Museu Histórico e Pedagógico Prof. Lourenço Filho, Porto Ferreira . . . 004306
Museu Histórico e Pedagógico Zequinha de Abreu, Santa Rita do Passa Quatro 004462
Museu Histórico Farroupilha, Piratini 004284
Museu Histórico Kiyoshi Takano, Ura 004595
Museu Histórico Militar, Maputo . . . 029049
Museu Histórico Muncipal José Chiachiri, Franca 004120
Museu Histórico Municipal, Carangola 004055
Museu Histórico Municipal, Dois Irmãos 004098
Museu Histórico Municipal, Montenegro 004228
Museu Histórico Municipal, Telêmaco Borba 004577
Museu Histórico Municipal e da Imigração Italiana Oswaldo Samuel Massei, São Caetano do Sul 004473
Museu Histórico Municipal Tuany Toledo, Pouso Alegre 004308
Museu Histórico Nacional, Rio de Janeiro 004401
Museu Histórico Pedagógico Conselheiro Dr. João da Silva Carrão, Americana . 003960
Museu Histórico Pedagógico Índia Vanuíre, Tupã 004587
Museu Histórico Prof. Carlos de Silva Lacaz, Faculdade de Medicina / FM, São Paulo 004553
Museu Histórico Professor Jos' Alexandre Vieira, Palmas 004257
Museu Histórico Regional, Apucarana 003964
Museu Histórico Regional, Itambacuri 004148
Museu Histórico Regional, Passo Fundo 004263
Museu Histórico Tenente Coronel PM Augusto de Almeida Garrett, Curitiba 004091
Museu Histórico Visconde de São Leopoldo, São Leopoldo 004491
Museu Homo Sapiens, Nanuque . . . 004233
Museu i Centre d'Estudis de l'Esport Dr. Melcior Colet, Barcelona 034952
Museu i Centre d'Estudis Juniperians, Petra 035652
Museu I Fons Artistic, Porreres 035670
Museu i Necròpolis Paleocristians, Museu Nacional Arqueològic de Tarragona, Tarragona 035895
Museu Imperial, Petrópolis 004279
Museu Inaldo de Lyra Neves-Manta, Academia Nacional de Medicina, Rio de Janeiro 004402
Museu Instrumental, Lisboa 032646
Museu Integrado de Roraima, Boa Vista 004008
Museu Internacional de Arte Naïf do Brasil, Rio de Janeiro 004403
Museu Jaguaribano, Aracati 003968
Museu João Pedro Nunes, São Gabriel 004480
Museu Joaquim José Felizardo, Porto Alegre 004300
Museu José Bonifácio, São Paulo . . 004554
Museu Julio de Castilhos, Porto Alegre 004301
Museu Krekovic, Palma de Mallorca 035617
Museu la Granja, Espai Cultural, Mogoda 035498
Museu Lasar Segall, São Paulo . . . 004555
Museu Leprológico, Curitiba 004092
Museu Local Arqueològic, Artesa de Lleida 034865
Museu Local d'Artesania Terrissaire, Verdú 036025
Museu Luso-Hebraico de Albraão Zacuto, Tomar 032695
Museu Maçônico Mário Verçosa, Manaus 004209
Museu Malinverni Filho, Lages 004178
Museu Manolo Hugué, Mas Manolo, Caldes de Montbui 035031
Museu Marès de la Punta, Arenys de Mar 034854
Museu Mariano Procópio, Juiz de Fora 004174
Museu Maricel de Mar, Sitges 035878
Museu Marítim de Barcelona, Barcelona 034953
Museu Mazzaropi, Taubaté 004576
Museu Memória do Bixiga, São Paulo 004556
Museu Meridional, Porto Alegre . . . 004302
Museu Metropolitano de Arte, Curitiba 004093
Museu Militar, Barcelona 034954
Museu Militar, Coimbra 032602
Museu Militar de Lisboa, Lisboa . . . 032647
Museu Militar do Forte do Brum, Recife 004322
Museu Mineiro, Belo Horizonte 004004
Museu Mineralógico da Escola de Minas, Ouro Preto 004256
Museu Mineralógico e Geológico, Secção do Museu de História Natural, Coimbra 032603
Museu Moacir Andrade, Manaus . . 004210
Museu Mollfulleda de Mineralogía, Arenys de Mar 034855
Museu Monàstic, Vallbona de les Monges 036008
Museu Monografic de Pol Lèntia, Museo Monográfico de Pllentia, Alcúdia . 034814
Museu Monogràfic del Castell de Llinars, Llinars del Vallés 035353
Museu Monográfico de Conimbriga, Condeixa-a-Nova 032607
Museu Monstruário de Manica, Manica 029045
Museu Muncipal de Victor Graeff, Victor Graeff 004602
Museu Municipal, Vilassar de Dalt . 036055
Museu Municipal, Alcochete 032572
Museu Municipal, Alcover 034809
Museu Municipal, Barbacena 003983
Museu Municipal, Cachoeira do Sul 004032
Museu Municipal, Caxias do Sul . . . 004064
Museu Municipal, Conquista 004067
Museu Municipal, Garibaldi 004123
Museu Municipal, Guimerà 035273
Museu Municipal, Itambaracá 004149
Museu Municipal, Llagostera 035341
Museu Municipal, Llivia 035356
Museu Municipal, Manlleu 035463
Museu Municipal, Missal 004219
Museu Municipal, Molins de Rei . . . 035503
Museu Municipal, Nova Lisboa 000103
Museu Municipal, Palafrugell 035591
Museu Municipal, Paulínia 004267
Museu Municipal, Pedras Grandes . 004268
Museu Municipal, Pinhel 032668
Museu Municipal, Rafelcofer 035690
Museu Municipal, Riudecanyes . . . 035708
Museu Municipal, Rolândia 004428
Museu Municipal, Rosário de Oeste 004429
Museu Municipal, Sant Feliu de Guíxols 035782
Museu Municipal, São João Del Rei 004485
Museu Municipal, Tona 035931
Museu Municipal, Tossa de Mar . . . 035950
Museu Municipal, Uberlândia 004593
Museu Municipal, Visconde do Rio Branco 004604
Museu Municipal Abade Pedrosa, Santo Tirso 032685
Museu Municipal Adão Wolski, Contenda 004069
Museu Municipal Adolfo Eurich, Turvo 004588
Museu Municipal Alípio Vaz, Cataguases 004063
Museu Municipal Amadeo de Souza-Cardoso, Amarante 032576
Museu Municipal Atílio Rocco, São José dos Pinhais 004489
Museu Municipal Can Xifreda, Sant Feliu de Codines 035780
Museu Municipal Capitão Henrique Jos' Barbosa, Canguçu 004053

Museu Municipal d'Agramunt, Agramunt . . . 034783
Museu Municipal David Canabarro, Sant'Anna do Livramento . . . 004466
Museu Municipal de Antônio Prado, Antônio Prado . . . 003962
Museu Municipal de Arqueologia, Monte Alto . . . 004225
Museu Municipal de Arqueologia, Silves . . . 032690
Museu Municipal de Arte e História, Nova Era . . . 004243
Museu Municipal de Chaves, Chaves . . . 032593
Museu Municipal de Costums, Oropesa del Mar . . . 035574
Museu Municipal de la Pagesia, Castellbisbal . . . 035065
Museu Municipal de Náutica, El Masnou . . . 035479
Museu Municipal de Óbidos, Óbidos 032664
Museu Municipal de Pallejà, Pallejà 035599
Museu Municipal de Pollença, Pollença . . . 035662
Museu Municipal de Portalegre, Portalegre . . . 032670
Museu Municipal de Santarém, Santarém . . . 032683
Museu Municipal de São José dos Campos, São José dos Campos . . . 004488
Museu Municipal de Viana do Castelo, Viana do Castelo . . . 032698
Museu Municipal Deolindo Mendes Pereira, Campo Mourão . . . 004049
Museu Municipal do Folclore, Penápolis . . . 004274
Museu Municipal do Funchal (História Natural), Funchal . . . 032618
Museu Municipal do Seixal Núcleo Sede, Seixal . . . 032687
Museu Municipal Domingos Battistel, Nova Prata . . . 004245
Museu Municipal Dr. José Formosinho, Lagos . . . 032622
Museu Municipal Dr. Santos Rocha, Figueira da Foz . . . 032615
Museu Municipal Elisabeth Aytai, Monte Mor . . . 004226
Museu Municipal Embaixador Hélio A. Scarabôtolo, Marília . . . 004214
Museu Municipal Francisco Manoel Franco, Itaúna . . . 004153
Museu Municipal Francisco Veloso, Cunha . . . 004077
Museu Municipal Guilleries, Sant Hilari Sacalm . . . 035783
Museu Municipal Joan Pal i Gras, Llinars del Vallés . . . 035354
Museu Municipal Joaquim de Bastos Bandeira, Perdões . . . 004276
Museu Municipal Josep Aragay, Breda . . . 034996
Museu Municipal Karl Ramminger, Mondaí . . . 004223
Museu Municipal Les Maleses, Montcada i Reixac . . . 035516
Museu Municipal Miquel Soldevila, Prats de Lluçanès . . . 035676
Museu Municipal Napoleão Joele, São Sebastião de Paraíso . . . 004563
Museu Municipal Oswaldo Russomano, Bragança Paulista . . . 004010
Museu Municipal Padre Antônio Ribeiro Pinto, Urucânia . . . 004596
Museu Municipal Pedro Laragnoit, Miracatu . . . 004218
Museu Municipal Pedro Nunes, Alcácer do Sal . . . 032571
Museu Municipal Polinucleado de Tomae, Tomar . . . 032696
Museu Municipal Prof. Hugo Daros, Gramado . . . 004134
Museu Municipal Quinta do Conventinho, Loures . . . 032660
Museu Municipal Vicenç Ros, Martorell . . . 035477
Museu Municipal Visconde de Guarapuava, Guarapuava . . . 004137
Museu Municipal Wenceslau Braz, Itajubá . . . 004146
Museu Municipal Wülson Jehovah Lütz Farias, Frederico Westphalen . . . 004122
Museu Nacional, Rio de Janeiro . . . 004404
Museu Nacional, São Tomé . . . 034121
Museu Nacional Arqueològic de Tarragona, Tarragona . . . 035896
Museu Nacional da Ciência e da Técnica, Coimbra . . . 032604
Museu Nacional da Moeda, Maputo 029050
Museu Nacional d'Art de Catalunya, Barcelona . . . 034955
Museu Nacional de Antropologia, Luanda . . . 000098
Museu Nacional de Arqueologia, Benguela . . . 000087
Museu Nacional de Arqueologia, Lisboa . . . 032648
Museu Nacional de Arte, Maputo . . 029051
Museu Nacional de Arte Antiga, Lisboa . . . 032649
Museu Nacional de Belas Artes, Rio de Janeiro . . . 004405
Museu Nacional de Etnologia, Lisboa . . . 032650
Museu Nacional de Geologia, Maputo . . . 029052
Museu Nacional de História Natural, Lisboa . . . 032651
Museu Nacional de História Natural, Luanda . . . 000099
Museu Nacional de Imigração e Colonização, Joinville . . . 004169
Museu Nacional de l'Automòbil, Encamp . . . 000082
Museu Nacional de Machado de Castro, Coimbra . . . 032605
Museu Nacional de Soares dos Reis, Porto . . . 032680
Museu Nacional do Mar - Embarações Brasileiras, São Francisco do Sul . 004479
Museu Nacional do Teatro, Lisboa . 032652
Museu Nacional do Traje, Lisboa . . 032653
Museu Nacional dos Coches, Lisboa 032654
Museu Naval de Amazônia, Belém . 003993
Museu Naval e Oceanográfico, Rio de Janeiro . . . 004406
Museu Navio Comandante Bauru, Rio de Janeiro . . . 004407
Museu Nossa Senhora Aparecida, Aparecida . . . 003963
Museu Numismático e Filatélico, Rio de Janeiro . . . 004408
Museu Numismático Português, Lisboa . . . 032655
Museu O Mundo Ovo de Eli Heil, Florianópolis . . . 004110
Museu Oceanográfico, Setúbal . . . 032689
Museu Oceanográfico do Valo do Itajaí, Universidade do Valo do Itajaí, Itajaí . . . 004145
Museu Oceanográfico Prof. Eliézer de C. Rios, Rio Grande . . . 004424
Museu Oswaldo Aranha, Alegrete . . 003956
Museu Padre Joseph Cornellius Maria Demam, Coronel Fabriciano . . . 004071
Museu Padre Júlio Maria, Russas . . 004431
Museu Palácio Nacional da Ajuda, Lisboa . . . 032656
Museu Paleontológic, Museo de Ciencias Naturales, Valencia . . . 035990
Museu Paleontologic Juna Cano Forner, San Mateo . . . 035767
Museu Paraense Emílio Goeldi, Belém . . . 003994
Museu Paranaense, Curitiba . . . 004094
Museu Paroquial de Óbidos, Óbidos 032665
Museu Parque Malwee, Jaraguá do Sul . . . 004160
Museu Parraquial de Sant Julià, Campos . . . 035039
Museu Parroquial, Altafulla . . . 034832
Museu Parroquial, Calonge de Mar . 035036
Museu Parroquial, Castellò d'Empúries . . . 035067
Museu Parroquial, Llanera de Ranes . . . 035343
Museu Parroquial, Santa Pau . . . 035807
Museu Parroquial, Vinaixa . . . 036074
Museu Parroquial de Santa Joan Baptista, Deià . . . 035145
Museu Parroquial Palau Solitar, Palau de Plegamans . . . 035593
Museu Parroquialí, Vimbodí . . . 036073
Museu Particular de Armas de Arlindo Pedro Zatti, Porto Alegre . . . 004303
Museu Patríco Corrêa da Câmara, Bagé . . . 003981
Museu Pau Casals, El Vendrell . . . 036023
Museu Paulista da Universidade de São Paulo, São Paulo . . . 004557
Museu Paulo Firpo, Dom Pedrito . . 004099
Museu Paulo Machado de Carvalho, São Paulo . . . 004558
Museu Pedro Ludovico, Goiânia . . . 004128
Museu Perrot Moore d'Art Grafic Europeu, Cadaqués . . . 035019
Museu Picasso, Barcelona . . . 034956
Museu Pinacoteca, Igarassu . . . 004141
Museu-Poblat Ibèric, Tornabous . . . 035935
Museu Postal d'Andorra, Ordino . . . 000085
Museu Postal e Telegráfico da ECT, Brasília . . . 004023
Museu Professor Hugo Machiado da Silveira, Patrocínio . . . 004265
Museu Rafael Bordalo Pinheiro, Lisboa . . . 032657
Museu Regional, Vitória da Conquista . . . 004608
Museu Regional Abade de Baçal, Bragança . . . 032586
Museu Regional D. Bosco, Campo Grande . . . 004047
Museu Regional da Fauna e Flora do Itatiaia, Itatiaia . . . 004152
Museu Regional da Huila, Lumbango . . . 000100
Museu Regional d'Artá, Artá . . . 034864
Museu Regional de Arqueologia D. Diogo de Sousa, Braga . . . 032584
Museu Regional de Cabinda, Cabinda . . . 000088
Museu Regional de Olinda, Olinda . 004249
Museu Regional de São João Del Rei, São João Del Rei . . . 004486
Museu Regional do Alto Uruguai, Erechim . . . 004100
Museu Regional do Planalto Central, Huambo . . . 000091
Museu Regional Dr. Alípio de Araújo Silva, Rio Preto . . . 004427
Museu Regional Olívio Otto, Carazinho . . . 004057
Museu Republicano Convenção de Itu, Universidade de São Paulo, Itu . . 004156
Museu Restauraçao, Lisboa . . . 032658
Museu Rocaguinarda, Oristà . . . 035572
Museu Romàntic Can Llopis, Sitges 035879
Museu Romantic Can Papiol, Vilanova i la Geltrú . . . 036051
Museu Romàntic Delger, Caldes de Montbui . . . 035032
Museu Romântico da Quinta da Macieirinha, Porto . . . 032681
Museu Rural e do Vinho do Concelho, Cartaxo . . . 032589
Museu Sacro da Igreja de São Sebastião, Araxá . . . 003974
Museu Sacro São José de Ribamar, Aquiraz . . . 003965
Museu Salles Cunha, Rio de Janeiro 004409
Museu São João Batista, Caratinga 004056
Museu São Norberto, Pirapora do Bom Jesus . . . 004283
Museu Sargento Edésio de Carvalho, Sousa . . . 004569
Museu Sentronà, Tiana . . . 035912
Museu Sitio Arqueológico Casa dos Pilões, Rio de Janeiro . . . 004410
Museu Solar Monjardim, Vitória . . . 004607
Museu Taurí de la Monumental, Barcelona . . . 034957
Museu Teatro, Rio de Janeiro . . . 004411
Museu Técnico-Científicio do Instituto Oscar Freire, Faculdade de Medicina / FM, São Paulo . . . 004559
Museu Tempostal, Salvador . . . 004454
Museu Teresa Bernardes Adami de Carvalho, Sant Antônio do Monte . 004455
Museu Territorial do Amapá, Macapá . . . 004192
Museu Textil i d'Indumentaria, Barcelona . . . 034958
Museu Théo Brandão de Antropologia de Folclore, Maceió . . . 004200
Museu Theodormiro Carneiro Santiago, Itajubá . . . 004147
Museu Tinguí-Cuera, Araucária . . . 003971
Museu Torre Balldovina, Santa Coloma de Gramenet . . . 035791
Museu-Tresor Parroquial, Olot . . . 035557
Museu-Tresor Parroquial, Verdú . . . 036026
Museu Universitário, Campinas . . . 004043
Museu Universitário de Arte, Uberlândia . . . 004594
Museu Universitário Gama Filho, Rio de Janeiro . . . 004412
Museu Universitário Professor Oswaldo Rodrigues Cabral, Florianópolis . . 004111
Museu Valencia del Joguet, Ibi . . . 035290
Museu Vallhonrat, Rubí . . . 035725
Museu Víctor Balaguer, Vilanova i la Geltrú . . . 036052
Museu Victor Bersani, Santa Maria . 004461
Museu Victor Meirelles, Florianópolis . . . 004112
Museu Viladomat d'Escultura, Escaldes-Engordany . . . 000083
Museu Villa-Lobos, Rio de Janeiro . 004413
Museu Vivo da Memória Candanga, Brasília . . . 004024
Museu von Martius, Teresópolis . . . 004582
Museu Zé Didor, Campo Maior . . . 004048
Museu Zoobotânico Augusto Ruschi, Passo Fundo . . . 004264
Museu Zoológico, Coimbra . . . 032606
Museum, Bagheria . . . 023316
Museum, Coswig, Anhalt . . . 016591
The Museum, Greenwood . . . 044356
Museum, Mühlacker . . . 019007
The Museum, Newton Stewart . . . 040577
Museum, Zofingen . . . 037756
Museum 15, Bezirksmuseum Rudolfsheim-Fünfhaus, Wien . . . 002949
Museum 1806, Cospeda . . . 016590
Museum 1915-1918, Kötschach-Mauthen . . . 002165
Museum 1940-1945, Dordrecht . . . 029504
Museum 3. Dimension, Dinkelsbühl 016719
Museum '40-'45, Slochteren . . . 030162
Museum Abdij Mariënlof, Kerniel . . 003551
Museum Abdij van Egmond, Egmond Binnen . . . 029535
Museum Abdijkerk, Thorn . . . 030200
Museum Abodiacum, Denklingen . . 016670
Museum Abri Satriamandala, Jakarta . . . 022425
Museum Abtei Liesborn, Museum des Kreises Warendorf, Wadersloh . . . 020613
Museum Adam Malik, Jakarta . . . 022426
Museum Adorf, Adorf, Vogtland . . . 015448
Museum Affandi - Museum Seni, Yogyakarta . . . 022532
Museum Africa, Johannesburg . . . 034652
Museum Agios Nikolaos, Agios Nikolaos . . . 021120
Muséum Agricole et Industriel de Stella Matutina, Piton-Saint-Leu . . . 032761
Museum Aguntum, Dölsach . . . 001785
Museum Ald Slot, Wergea . . . 030320
Museum Alpin, Pontresina . . . 037417
Museum Alte Brettersäge, Rappottenstein . . . 002502
Museum Alte Burg Penzlin, Penzlin bei Waren . . . 019589
Museum Alte Kirche, Reken . . . 019788
Museum Alte Lateinschule Großenhain, Großenhain, Sachsen . . . 017569
Museum Alte Münze, Stolberg, Harz 020323

Museum Alte Pfefferküchlerei, Weißenberg 020773
Museum Alte Post, Pirmasens 019622
Museum Alte Schmiede, Wien 002950
Museum Alte Textilfabrik, Weitra . . 002822
Museum Altes Bad Pfäfers, Bad Ragaz 036866
Museum Altes Bürgerhaus, Stolberg, Harz 020324
Museum Altes Gymnasium, Städtische Sammlungen Schweinfurt, Schweinfurt 020140
Museum Altes Land, Jork 018127
Museum Altes Rathaus, Gerolzhofen 017386
Museum Altomünster, Altomünster . 015521
Museum Alzey, Alzey 015528
Museum am Burghof, Lörrach 018670
Museum am Dannewerk, Museet ved Danevirke, Dannewerk 016632
Museum am Elbberg, Checkpoint Harry, Boizenburg 016311
Museum am Lindenbühl, Mühlhäuser Museen, Mühlhausen, Thüringen . 019013
Museum am Lindenplatz, Weil am Rhein 020717
Museum am Markt, Schiltach 020026
Museum am Markt / Schubarts Museum, Aalen 015429
Museum am Mühlturm, Isny 018095
Museum am Odenwaldlimes, Elztal 016956
Museum am Ostwall, Dortmund . . . 016766
Museum am Schölerberg, Natur und Umwelt-Planetarium, Osnabrück . 019497
Museum am Thie, Göttingen 017467
Museum Amandinhuis, Herk-de-Stad 003511
Museum Amden, Amden 036838
Museum Amelinghausen, Amelinghausen 015531
Museum Amstelkring, Amsterdam . 029203
Museum Amtspforte Stadthagen, Stadthagen 020283
Museum an der Krukenburg, Bad Karlshafen 015730
Museum Anatomicum, Marburg . . . 018827
Museum Anatomicum, Rīga 027758
Museum Anatomy FK UI, Jakarta . . 022427
Museum, Ancient Synagogue and Necropolis, Beit Shearim 022899
Museum and Archives of Georgia Education, Georgia College and State University, Milledgeville 045871
Museum and Art Gallery, Burdwan . 022047
Museum and Art Gallery, Forfar . . . 039514
Museum and Art Gallery, Hooghly . . 022154
Museum and Art Gallery, Letchworth 039990
Museum and Art Gallery, Newport, Gwent 040563
Museum and Art Gallery, Nuneaton 040630
Museum and Art Gallery, Universiti Teknologi Mara, Shah Alam 028014
Museum and Art Gallery Leicester, Leicester 039973
Museum and Art Gallery of the Northern Territory, Darwin 000975
Museum and Arts Center in the Sequim Dungeness Valley, Sequim 048115
Museum and Exhibition Design Group, London 054434
Museum Anna Nordlander, Skellefteå 036579
Museum Anna Paulowna, Breezand 029354
Museum Appenzell, Appenzell 036846
Museum-Aquarium de Nancy, Nancy 013328
Museum Arbeitswelt Steyr, Steyr . . 002700
Museum Arnold Vander Haeghen, Gent 003460
Museum-Art Collection of the National Bank, Athinai 021191
Museum Artha Suaka, Jakarta 022428
Museum Åsättra, Ljusterö 036431
Museum Asia Africa, Bandung 022387
Museum Asimbugo, Bima 022401
Museum Asmat, Jakarta 022429
Museum Aspern-Essling 1809, Wien 002951
Museum Asserajah El Hasyimiah Palace, Bengkalis 022398
Museum Association of Aotearoa New Zealand, Museums Aotearoa, Wellington 053921
Museum Association of Arizona, Phoenix 054890
Museum Association of Israel, Rishon Le-Zion 053723
Museum Association of Montana, West Glacier 054891
Museum Association of New York, Troy 054892
Museum Association of Newfoundland and Labrador, Saint John's 052757
Museum Astros, Astros 021151
The Museum at Drexel University, Philadelphia 046963
Museum at Mountain Home, Johnson City 044867
Museum at the Fashion Institute of Technology, New York 046370
Museum at the Site of the First National Congress of the Communist Party of China, Shanghai 007237
The Museum at Warm Springs, Warm Springs 048853
Museum Auerbach, Auerbach, Vogtland 015599
Museum auf Abruf, Wien 002952
Museum auf dem Burghof, Springe 020272
Museum auf der Burg, Raron 037436
Museum auf der Osterburg, Weida . 020705
Museum Bad Abbach, Bad Abbach . 015641
Museum Bad Füssing, Bruckmann-Haus, Bad Füssing 015705
Museum Bad Orb, Bad Orb 015769
Museum Baden, Solingen 020237
Museum Bärengasse, Zürich 037785
Museum Bahari, Jakarta 022430
Museum Bahnhof Bexbach, Bexbach 016217
Museum Bakkerij Mendels, Middelstum 029926
Museum Balanga, Palangkaraya . . 022483
Museum Bangga & Lore, Poso 022496
Museum Bargteheide, Bargteheide . 015888
Museum Barockschloß Rammenau, Rammenau 019708
Museum Barsinghausen, Barsinghausen 015890
Museum Batara Guru, Palopo 022487
Museum Batara Guru, Pare-Pare . . 022489
Museum Batik, Pekalongan 022490
Museum Batik, Yogyakarta 022533
Museum Bayerisches Vogtland, Hof, Saale 017957
Museum Bebinghehoes, Exloo 029585
Museum Beeckestijn, Velsen Zuid . 030265
Museum Beelden aan Zee, Den Haag 029436
Museum - Begegnung der Kulturen, Krenglbach 002178
Museum bei der Kaiserpfalz, Ingelheim am Rhein 018065
Museum beim Markt - Angewandte Kunst seit 1900, Badisches Landesmuseum Karlsruhe, Karlsruhe 018163
Museum beim Solenhofer Aktien-Verein, Maxberg 018864
Museum Bellerive, Zürich 037786
Museum Bergér, Eichstätt 016911
Museum Berggruen - Picasso und seine Zeit, Staatliche Museen zu Berlin - Stiftung Preußischer Kulturbesitz, Berlin 016121
Museum Bergsdorf, Bergsdorf 015975
Museum Berlin-Karlshorst, Berlin . . 016122
Museum Berliner Arbeiterleben, Berlin 016123
Museum Bernhard Brühl, Landsberg bei Halle, Saale 018481
Museum Bevrijdende Vleugels, Best 029314
Museum Bickel, Walenstadt 037690
Museum Biologi UGM, Yogyakarta . 022534
Museum Bischofsheim, Bischofsheim bei Rüsselsheim 016252
Museum Bischofszell, Bischofszell . 036960
Museum Blaafarveværket, Åmot i Modum 030726
Museum Blauer Anger, Bergen, Chiemgau 015963
Museum Blindenwerkstatt Otto Weidt, Jüdisches Museum Berlin, Berlin . 016124
Museum Bochum, Kunstsammlung, Bochum 016281
Museum Bockwindmühle, Falkenhain bei Wurzen 017100
Museum Böhl-Iggelheim, Böhl-Iggelheim 016297
Museum Böhl-Iggelheim, Böhl-Iggelheim 016298
Museum Boerhaave, Leiden 029850
Museum Boijmans Van Beuningen, Rotterdam 030088
Museum Bookshop, London 141851
Museum Boutique Intercontinental, New York 118221
Museum Bramberg Wilhelmgut, Bramberg 001760
Museum Brawijaya, Malang 022469
Museum Bredius, Den Haag 029437
Museum Brigade en Garde Prinses Irene, Oirschot 029982
Museum Briner und Kern, Winterthur 037723
Museum Broeker Veiling, Broek op Langedijk 029358
Museum Bruder Klaus, Sachseln . . 037472
Museum Brückenkopf, Stadtgeschichtliches Museum Jülich, Jülich 018129
Museum Bürgstadt, Bürgstadt 016499
Museum Bundo Kandung, Bukittinggi 022408
Museum Buntes Holz im Postgut am Altmarkt, Hohenstein-Ernstthal . . 017979
Museum Buren en Oranje, Buren, Gelderland 029372
Museum Burg Abenberg, Haus Fränkischer Geschichte Klöppelmuseum, Abenberg 015436
Museum Burg Bederkesa, Bad Bederkesa 015650
Museum Burg Brome, Brome 016451
Museum Burg Eisenhardt, Belzig . . 015941
Museum Burg Falkenstein, Stiftung Schlösser, Burgen und Gärten des Landes Sachsen-Anhalt, Pansfelde 019559
Museum Burg Frankenberg, Aachen 015424
Museum Burg Freyenstein, Freyenstein 017255
Museum Burg Golling, Golling an der Salzach 001920
Museum Burg Heidenreichstein, Heidenreichstein 002028
Museum Burg Hohnstein, Hohnstein 017985
Museum Burg Kriebstein, Kriebstein 018411
Museum Burg Linn, Krefeld 018400
Museum Burg Mylau, Mylau 019172
Museum Burg Posterstein, Posterstein 019651
Museum Burg Pottenstein, Pottenstein 019661
Museum Burg Querfurt, Querfurt . . 019691
Museum Burg Ramsdorf, Velen . . . 020571
Museum Burg Ranis, Ranis 019710
Museum Burg Ronneburg, Ronneburg, Hessen 019878
Museum Burg Scharfenstein, Scharfenstein 020005
Museum Burg Stein, Hartenstein bei Zwickau 017781
Museum Burg Stickhausen, Detern 016686
Museum Burghalde, Lenzburg 037257
Museum Buurt Spoorweg, Haaksbergen 029649
Museum Caledon River, Smithfield . 034750
Museum California Center for the Arts Escondido, Escondido 043731
Museum Camera, Braunschweig . . 016389
Museum Cards, Amersfoort 134766
Museum Casa Anatta, Casa Selma und Klarwelt der Seligen, Ascona 036856
Museum de Casteelse Poort, Wageningen 030303
Museum Castellum, Mainz-Kastell . 018796
Museum Catharijneconvent, Utrecht 030230
Museum Ceuclum, Cuijk 029389
Museum Charlotte Zander, Bönnigheim 016299
Museum Cheann A'Loch, Ballallan . 038571
Museum Chill Donnan, Kildonan . . . 039865
Museum Chora, Amorgos 021129
Museum Chornhuus, Gränichen . . . 037158
Museum Chris Van Niekerk, Boshof 034567
Museum Collection and Old Pharmacy of the Friars Minor, Dubrovnik 007717
Museum Computer Network, National Office, Laguna Beach 054893
Museum Connection Die, Cape Town 034581
Museum Constant Permeke, Jabbeke 003543
Museum Council, Moskva 054022
Museum Daerah Bangkalan, Bangkalan 022393
Museum Daerah Blambangan, Banyuwangi 022397
Museum Daerah Sumenep, Sumenep 022513
Museum Dara Yuanti, Sintang 022509
Museum de 5000 Morgen, Hoogeveen 029766
Museum De Bres, Ruisbroek, Antwerpen 003731
Museum de Burghse Schoole, Burgh-Haamstede 029374
Museum De Cateraars, Groningen . 029640
Museum De Cruquius, Cruquius . . . 029387
Museum De Doornboom, Hilvarenbeek 029745
Museum de Géologie Provençale, La Roque-d'Anthéron 012333
Museum de Gevangenpoort, Den Haag 029438
Museum De Ghulden Roos, Roosendaal 030074
Museum De Goudse Glazen - Sint Janskerk, Gouda 029624
Museum De Grutterswinkel, Leeuwarden 029840
Museum De Helpoort, Maastricht . . 029894
Museum de Historische Drukkerij, Maastricht 029895
Museum De Kijkuit, Merksem 003642
Museum De Kluis, Boekel 029322
Museum De Koloniehof, Frederiksoord 029592
Museum de Koperen Knop, Hardinxveld-Giessendam 029672
Museum de Maurits 1940-1945, Doesburg 029487
Museum De Moriaan, Gouda 029625
Museum De Paviljoens, Almere . . . 029141
Museum De Roode Tooren, Museum voor Stad en Ambt Doesburg, Doesburg 029488
Museum De Schilpen, Maasland . . 029890
Museum de Speeltoren, Monnickendam 029930
Museum de Stratemakerstoren, Nijmegen 029960
Museum de Striid tsjin it Wetter, Wommels 030348
Museum de Timmerwerf, De Lier . . 029397
Museum de Trije Gritenijen, Grou . . 029648
Museum de Valkhof, Hellendoorn . . 029715
Museum de Verzamelaar, Zuidhorn . 030397
Museum De Vier Quartieren, Museum van het Brabantse Volksleven 1800-1950, Oirschot 029983
Museum De Waag, Deventer 029474
Museum De Wieger, Deurne 029470
Museum de Zwarte Tulp, Lisse 029872
Museum Delfzijl, Delfzijl 029417
Museum der 50er Jahre, Zusmarshausen 021081

Museum der Anthropologie, Universität Zürich-Irchel, Zürich 037787
Museum der Arbeit, Hamburg 017709
Museum der Barbarossastadt Gelnhausen, Gelnhausen 017352
Museum der bildenden Künste Leipzig, Leipzig 018579
Museum der Brotkultur, Ulm 020531
Museum der Cistercienserinnen-Abtei Lichtenthal, Baden-Baden 015851
Museum der Deutschen Binnenschifffahrt Duisburg-Ruhrort, Duisburg 016856
Museum der Deutschen Spielzeugindustrie, Neustadt bei Coburg 019288
Museum der deutschen Sprachinselorte bei Brünn, Erbach, Donau 016998
Museum der Dinge-Werkbundarchiv, Berlin 016125
Museum der Donauschwaben, Herbrechtingen 017880
Museum der Elbinsel Wilhelmsburg, Hamburg 017710
Museum der Freiwilligen Feuerwehr, Laxenburg 002213
Museum der Gemeinde, Straß im Straßertale 002718
Museum der Gewerkschaft Agrar-Nahrung-Genuß, Wien 002953
Museum der Göttinger Chemie, Göttingen 017468
Museum der Grafschaft, Barmstedt 015889
Museum der Grafschaft Mark, Altena 015494
Museum der Granitindustrie, Bischheim, Sachsen 016250
Museum der Heimatvertriebenen, Stadtmuseum Wels-Burg, Wels .. 002828
Museum der heimischen Tierwelt, Feuerwehrhaus, Nabburg 019173
Museum der Hermann-Lietz-Schule, Spiekeroog 020267
Museum der historischen Waschtechnik, Ostbevern 019503
Museum der Katakombenstichting, Valkenburg, Limburg 030247
Museum der Klosterruine mit Lapidarium, Rüeggisberg 037466
Museum der Kommunikations- und Bürogeschichte, Bamberg 015875
Museum der Kulturen Basel, Basel . 036893
Museum der Landschaft Hasli, Meiringen 037321
Museum der Marktgemeinde Sankt Johann in Tirol, Sankt Johann in Tirol ... 002592
Museum der Mechitharisten-Congregation, Wien 002954
Museum der Moderne Salzburg, Salzburg 002560
Museum der Natur, Gotha 017492
Museum der Natur und Umwelt Cottbus, Cottbus 016596
Museum der Oberzent, Beerfelden, Odenwald 015934
Museum der RaumKunst aus Renaissance, Barock und Rokoko, Staatliche Museen zu Berlin - Stiftung Preußischer Kulturbesitz, Berlin 016126
Museum der Schildbürger, Schildau, Gneisenaustadt 020020
Museum der Schwalm, Schwalmstadt 020121
Museum der Schweizer Kapuzinerprovinz, Sursee 037618
Museum der schweizerischen Luftwaffe, Dübendorf 037051
Museum der Seefahrt, Geiselhöring 017341
Museum der Staatlichen Porzellan-Manufaktur Meissen, Meißen ... 018890
Museum der Stadt Alfeld (Leine), Alfeld, Leine 015477
Museum der Stadt Aue, Aue, Sachsen 015596
Museum der Stadt Bad Berleburg, Bad Berleburg 015664
Museum der Stadt Bad Gandersheim, Bad Gandersheim 015706
Museum der Stadt Bad Ischl, Bad Ischl 001725
Museum der Stadt Bad Neuenahr-Ahrweiler, Bad Neuenahr-Ahrweiler 015760
Museum der Stadt Bad Staffelstein, Bad Staffelstein, Oberfranken 015807
Museum der Stadt Bensheim, Bensheim 015950
Museum der Stadt Bludenz, Bludenz 001758
Museum der Stadt Boppard, Boppard 016342
Museum der Stadt Borna, Borna ... 016350
Museum der Stadt Butzbach im Solms-Braunfelser Hof, Butzbach 016530
Museum der Stadt Calw, Calw 016542
Museum der Stadt Colditz, Colditz . 016586
Museum der Stadt Dommitzsch, Dommitzsch 016736
Museum der Stadt Dorsten, Dorsten 016758
Museum der Stadt Ehingen, Ehingen, Donau 016896
Museum der Stadt Eschborn, Eschborn 017046
Museum der Stadt Ettlingen, Ettlingen 017091
Museum der Stadt Fürstenfeld, Fürstenfeld 001876
Museum der Stadt Füssen, Füssen . 017291
Museum der Stadt Gladbeck, Gladbeck 017420
Museum der Stadt Gmünd, Gmünd, Kärnten 001905
Museum der Stadt Güstrow, Güstrow 017600
Museum der Stadt Hagenow, Hagenow 017629
Museum der Stadt Kapfenberg, Kapfenberg 002111
Museum der Stadt Köflach, Köflach 002161
Museum der Stadt Korneuburg, Korneuburg 002166
Museum der Stadt Kraichtal, Kraichtal 018390
Museum der Stadt Lahnstein im Hexenturm, Lahnstein 018461
Museum der Stadt Lahr, Villa Jamm im Stadtpark, Lahr, Schwarzwald ... 018464
Museum der Stadt Langen, Langen in Hessen 018497
Museum der Stadt Lauffen am Neckar, Lauffen am Neckar 018530
Museum der Stadt Lennestadt, Lennestadt 018616
Museum der Stadt Leoben, Leoben 002225
Museum der Stadt Lienz, Lienz ... 002235
Museum der Stadt Ludwigsfelde, Ludwigsfelde 018700
Museum der Stadt Lünen, Gesindehaus Schloß Schwansbell, Lünen 018747
Museum der Stadt Miltenberg und Porzellansammlung Kreis Dux, Miltenberg 018943
Museum der Stadt Mittweida Alte Pfarrhäuser, Mittweida 018963
Museum der Stadt Nauen, Nauen .. 019182
Museum der Stadt Neu-Isenburg Haus zum Löwen, Neu-Isenburg 019210
Museum der Stadt Neustadt an der Weinstraße, Neustadt an der Weinstraße 019285
Museum der Stadt Neustrelitz, Neustrelitz 019296
Museum der Stadt Neutraubling - Ortsgeschichtliche Dokumentation, Neutraubling 019297
Museum der Stadt Parchim, Parchim 019564
Museum der Stadt Pasewalk und Künstlergedenkstätte Paul Holz, Pasewalk 019568
Museum der Stadt Pegau, Pegau .. 019579
Museum der Stadt Poysdorf, Poysdorf 002456
Museum der Stadt Ratingen, Ratingen 019721
Museum der Stadt Rüsselsheim, Rüsselsheim 019944
Museum der Stadt Schkeuditz, Schkeuditz 020030
Museum der Stadt Schopfheim, Schopfheim 020091
Museum der Stadt Schwartau, Bad Schwartau 015797
Museum der Stadt Schwaz, Schwaz 002665
Museum der Stadt Sinsheim, Sinsheim 020221
Museum der Stadt Steyr, Steyr 002701
Museum der Stadt Troisdorf, Troisdorf 020487
Museum der Stadt Villach, Villach . 002774
Museum der Stadt Vils, Vils 002780
Museum der Stadt Waiblingen, Waiblingen 020626
Museum der Stadt Weinheim, Weinheim, Bergstraße 020762
Museum der Stadt Wolgast, Wolgast 020970
Museum der Stadt Worms, Worms . 020981
Museum der Stadt Zerbst mit Sammlung Katharina II., Zerbst 021055
Museum der Stadtwerke, Pirmasens 019623
Museum der Trauerarbeitsplätze, Institut für Philosophie und Gruppendynamik, Klagenfurt 002145
Museum der Wahrnehmung, Graz . 001942
Museum der Weltkulturen, Frankfurt am Main 017182
Museum der Westlausitz Kamenz, Kamenz 018145
Museum der Winterthur-Versicherungen, Winterthur 037724
Museum Dermbach, Dermbach ... 016674
Museum des Augustiner-Chorherrenstifts, Reichersberg 002513
Museum des Blindenwesens, Wien 002955
Museum des Chorherrenstifts Klosterneuburg, Klosterneuburg .. 002156
Museum des ehemaligen Kreises Stuhm/Westpr., Bremervörde 016442
Museum des Haager Landes, Haag, Oberbayern 017612
Museum des Handwerks Bremerhaven-Wesermünde in Bederkesa, Bad Bederkesa 015651
Museum des Heimatkundlichen Vereins, Scheßlitz 020015
Museum des Historischen Vereins Freising, Freising 017245
Museum des Instituts für gerichtliche Medizin, Wien 002956
Museum des Kreises Plön mit norddeutscher Glassammlung, Plön 019640
Museum des Landes Glarus, Näfels 037368
Museum des Landkreises Schönebeck, Schönebeck, Elbe 020074
Museum des Nötscher Kreises, Nötsch im Gailtal 002380
Museum des Oberbergischen Kreises, Nümbrecht 019344
Museum des Ohrekreises, Wolmirstedt 020974
Museum des Sciences naturelles de Belgique, Bruxelles 003354
Museum des Todesmarsches im Belower Wald, Wittstock, Dosse 020936
Museum des Vereins für Heimatkunde im Landkreis Birkenfeld, Birkenfeld, Nahe 016247
Museum des Veterinäramtes, Wien 002957
Muséum des Volcans, Aurillac 010553
Museum des Wiener Männergesang-Vereins, Wien 002958
Museum des Zisterzienserstifts mit Margret Bilger-Galerie, Schlierbach 002651
Museum Dewantara Kirti Griya, Yogyakarta 022535
Museum Dharma Wiratama, Yogyakarta 022536
Muséum d'Histoire Naturelle, Autun 010563
Muséum d'Histoire Naturelle, Bagnères-de-Bigorre 010622
Muséum d'Histoire Naturelle, Blois . 010849
Muséum d'Histoire Naturelle, Chartres 011268
Muséum d'Histoire Naturelle, Genève 037137
Muséum d'Histoire Naturelle, Grenoble 012026
Muséum d'Histoire Naturelle, Le Havre 012510
Muséum d'Histoire Naturelle, Lyon . 012831
Muséum d'Histoire Naturelle, Neuchâtel 037377
Muséum d'Histoire Naturelle, Nice . 013411
Muséum d'Histoire Naturelle, Saint-Denis 032763
Muséum d'Histoire Naturelle, Troyes 015055
Muséum d'Histoire Naturelle, Fauniscope, Gras 011995
Muséum d'Histoire-Naturelle, Museum Parc Emanuel Liais, Cherbourg-Octeville 011353
Muséum d'Histoire Naturelle de Bordeaux, Bordeaux 010895
Muséum d'Histoire Naturelle de la Ville de Bayonne, Bayonne 010687
Muséum d'Histoire Naturelle de Toulouse, Toulouse 014999
Muséum d'Histoire Naturelle de Tours, Tours 015023
Museum Dhondt-Dhaenens, Deurle 003398
Museum Diergeneeskunde, Utrecht 030231
Museum Dingolfing-Herzogsburg, Dingolfing 016716
Museum Diponegoro, Magelang ... 022466
Museum Directors Federation, Wellington 053922
Museum Dirgantara Mandala, Yogyakarta 022537
Museum Dom Benoît, Notre-Dame-de-Lourdes 006056
Museum Dorestad, Wijk bij Duurstede 030332
Museum Dorf, Wittenbach 037735
Museum Dorpsbehoud Papendrecht, Papendrecht 030039
Museum Dr. Guislain, Gent 003461
Museum du Coquillage, Les Sables-d'Olonne 012640
Museum du Parc Tsimbazaza, Antananarivo 027933
Museum Duin en Bosch, Castricum 029385
Museum Echt, Echt 029519
Museum Eckernförde, Eckernförde . 016881
Museum Education for Letchworth Museum and Hitchin Museum, Hitchin 039757
Museum Education Roundtable, Washington 054894
Museum een Eeuw Landelijk Leven, Museum voor Oude Ambachten, Torhout 003802
Museum ehemalige Klöppelschule Tiefenbach, Tiefenbach, Oberpfalz 020440
Museum Eisenhüttenwerk Peitz, Peitz 019585
Museum Elisabeth Weeshuis, Culemborg 029392
Museum en oud Kempisch Dorp, Heist-op-den-Berg 003506
Museum Enschedé, Haarlem 029656
Museum Ensorhuis, Oostende 003685
Museum Ephraim-Palais, Stiftung Stadtmuseum Berlin, Berlin 016127
Museum Erwin Rehmann, Laufenburg 037235
Museum Erzgebirgische Volkskunst Buntes Holz im Postgut am Altmarkt, Hohenstein-Ernstthal 017979
Museum Ethnographers Group, Edinburgh 054435
Museum Europäischer Kulturen, Staatliche Museen zu Berlin - Stiftung Preußischer Kulturbesitz, Berlin 016128
Museum Expressiver Realismus, Kißlegg 018274
Museum Fahrzeug-Technik-Luftfahrt, Bad Ischl 001726
Museum Falak-ol-Aflak, Khorram-Abaad 022573
Museum Falsters Minder, Nykøbing Falster 009034

Museum Félix de Boeck, Drogenbos 003412
Museum Festung Dresden - Kasematten, Dresden . . . 016804
Museum 't Fiskershúske, Moddergat . . . 029929
Museum Flavia Solva, Wagna . . . 002795
Museum Flederwisch, Furth im Wald . . . 017305
Museum Flehite Amersfoort, Amersfoort . . . 029152
Museum för Utombordsmotorer, Varberg . . . 036779
Museum Folkwang Essen, Essen . . 017075
Museum for African Art, Long Island City . . . 045388
Museum for Beduin Culture, Kibbutz Lahav . . . 023011
Museum for Contemporary Arts, Baltimore . . . 041976
Museum for Textiles, Toronto . . . 006615
Museum for the Victims of Political Repression, Ulaanbaatar . . . 029006
Museum for Zone-Redningskorpsets, Holbæk . . . 008921
Museum Fort Kijkduin, Den Helder . 029464
Museum Forum der Völker, Völkerkundemuseum der Franziskaner, Werl . . . 020807
Museum Franz Gertsch, Burgdorf . . 036991
Museum Franz Schubert und sein Freundeskreis, Atzenbrugg . . . 001705
Museum Freriks, Winterswijk . . . 030342
Museum Frerikshuus, Aalten . . . 029123
Museum Freudenthaler Glassammlung, Weißenkirchen im Attergau . . . 002817
Museum-Freundschaften, Ostseebad Binz . . . 019525
Museum Friedhof Ohlsdorf, Hamburg . . . 017711
Museum Friedrichshagener Dichterkreis, Berlin . . . 016129
Museum Friesenheim, Ludwigshafen am Rhein . . . 018703
Museum für Abgüsse Klassischer Bildwerke, München . . . 019088
Museum für aktuelle Kunst, Groß-Umstadt . . . 017561
Museum für Angewandte Kunst, Frankfurt am Main . . . 017183
Museum für Angewandte Kunst, Gera . . . 017371
Museum für Angewandte Kunst, Museen der Stadt Köln, Köln . . . 018330
Museum für Antike Schiffahrt des Römisch-Germanischen Zentralmuseums, Mainz . . . 018792
Museum für Archäologie, Frauenfeld . . . 037092
Museum für Archäologie und Volkskunde, Kösching . . . 018361
Museum für Astronomie und Technikgeschichte, Staatliche Museen Kassel, Kassel . . . 018180
Museum für bäuerliche Arbeitsgeräte, Imst . . . 002070
Museum für bäuerliche Arbeitsgeräte des Bezirks Oberfranken, Bayreuth . . 015920
Museum für bäuerliche und sakrale Kunst, Ruhpolding . . . 019953
Museum für bäuerliches Handwerk und Kultur, Wilhelmsdorf, Württemberg . . . 020894
Museum für Bergedorf und die Vierlande, Museum für Hamburgische Geschichte, Hamburg . . . 017712
Museum für bergmännische Volkskunst Schneeberg, Schneeberg, Erzgebirge . . . 020063
Museum für Beschirrung und Besattelung, Hufbeschlag und Veterinär-Orthopädie, Wien . . . 002959
Museum für bildende Kunst im Landkreis Neu-Ulm, Nersingen . . . 019203
Museum für Billard- und Kaffeehauskultur, Wien . . . 002960
Museum für Blasmusikinstrumente, Kürnbach . . . 018435
Museum für Bodenschätzung, Eickendorf . . . 016914
Museum für Brauereigeschichte, Burghausen, Salzach . . . 016515
Museum für das Fürstentum Lüneburg, Lüneburg . . . 018744
Museum für deutsche Fernsehgeschichte, Wiesbaden . . . 020876
Museum für die Archäologie des Eiszeitalters, Neuwied . . . 019299
Museum für Dithmarscher Vorgeschichte, Albersdorf . . . 015465
Museum für dörfliche Alltagskultur Rubenheim, Gersheim . . . 017389
Museum für Druck, Mosbach, Baden . . . 019001
Museum für Druckkunst, Leipzig . . 018580
Museum für Eisenkunstguß, Hirzenhain . . . 017933
Museum für Energiegeschichte(n), Avacon AG, Hannover . . . 017764
Museum für Film- und Fototechnik, Deidesheim . . . 016658
Museum für Forst- und Jagdwirtschaft, Groß Schönebeck . . . 017560
Museum für Fotokopie, Mülheim an der Ruhr . . . 019023
Museum für Frühgeschichte des Landes Niederösterreich, Traismauer . . . 002748
Museum für Frühislamische Kunst, Bamberg . . . 015876
Museum für Gegenwartskunst, Öffentliche Kunstsammlung Basel, Basel . . . 036894
Museum für Gegenwartskunst Siegen, Siegen . . . 020200
Museum für Geologie und Paläontologie am Geowissenschaftlichen Zentrum der Universität Göttingen, Göttingen . 017469
Museum für Gestaltung Basel, Basel . . . 036895
Museum für Gestaltung Zürich, Zürich . . . 037788
Museum für Glaskunst, Lauscha . . 018534
Museum für Hamburgische Geschichte, Hamburg . . . 017713
Museum für Haustierkunde Julius Kühn, Halle, Saale . . . 017667
Museum für historische Wehrtechnik, Röthenbach an der Pegnitz . . . 019871
Museum für Höchster Geschichte, Frankfurt am Main . . . 017184
Museum für Höhlenkunde, Laichingen . . . 018466
Museum für Holographie, Esens . . . 017054
Museum für Holographie und neue Medien, Pulheim . . . 019677
Museum für Holzhandwerke, Sinzig, Rhein . . . 020224
Museum für Indische Kunst, Staatliche Museen zu Berlin - Stiftung Preußischer Kulturbesitz, Berlin . . . 016130
Museum für Industrie- und Technikgeschichte, Frankfurt am Main . . . 017185
Museum für islamische Fliesen und Keramik, Tegernsee . . . 020412
Museum für Islamische Kunst, Staatliche Museen zu Berlin - Stiftung Preußischer Kulturbesitz, Berlin . . . 016131
Museum für Jagdtier- und Vogelkunde des Erzgebirges, Augustusburg . . . 015626
Museum für Kaffeetechnik, Emmerich . . . 016971
Museum für Kartographie, Gotha . . 017493
Museum für klösterliche Kultur, Bad Wurzach . . . 015842
Museum für Kloster- und Heimatgeschichte, Harsefeld . . . 017779
Museum für Kommunikation, Bern . 036932
Museum für Kommunikation Berlin, Berlin . . . 016132
Museum für Kommunikation Frankfurt, Frankfurt am Main . . . 017186
Museum für Kommunikation Hamburg, Hamburg . . . 017714
Museum für Kommunikation Nürnberg im Verkehrsmuseum, Nürnberg . . . 019365
Museum für Konkrete Kunst, Ingolstadt . . . 018074
Museum für Kunst in Steatit, Frankfurt am Main . . . 017187
Museum für Kunst und Gewerbe Hamburg, Hamburg . . . 017715
Museum für Kunst und Kulturgeschichte der Stadt Dortmund, Dortmund . . . 016767
Museum für Kutschen, Chaisen, Karren, Zweigmuseum des Württembergischen Landesmuseums Stuttgart, Heidenheim an der Brenz . . . 017841
Museum für Lackkunst, Münster . . 019150
Museum für ländliches Kulturgut, Landwirtschaft, Forsten und Jagd, Ulrichstein . . . 020535
Museum für Landtechnik und Landarbeit, Emmerthal . . . 016975
Museum für landwirtschaftliche Geräte, Grafenwörth . . . 001923
Museum für Literatur am Oberrhein, Karlsruhe . . . 018164
Museum für Luftfahrt und Technik, Wernigerode . . . 020814
Museum für Magie und Hexenverfolgung, Penzlin bei Waren . . . 019589
Museum für mechanische Musik und Volkskunst, Haslach . . . 002023
Museum für Medizin-Meteorologie, Museum Dürnhof, Zwettl, Niederösterreich . . . 003076
Museum für Militär- und Zeitgeschichte, Kolitzheim . . . 018373
Museum für Mineralogie und Geologie, Staatliche Naturhistorische Sammlungen Dresden, Dresden . . . 016805
Museum für moderne Kunst, Cremlingen . . . 016604
Museum für Moderne Kunst Frankfurt am Main, Frankfurt am Main . . . 017188
Museum für Modernes Glas, Kunstsammlungen der Veste Coburg, Rödental . . . 019862
Museum für Mühlenbautechnik, Syrau . . . 020394
Museum für Musikautomaten, Sammlung Dr. hc H. Weiss-Stauffacher, Seewen . . . 037550
Museum für Naive Kunst, Bönnigheim . . . 016299
Museum für Natur und Umwelt, Lübeck . . . 018723
Museum für Naturkunde, Chemnitz 016560
Museum für Naturkunde, Dortmund 016768
Museum für Naturkunde, Magdeburg . . . 018773
Museum für Naturkunde der Humboldt-Universität zu Berlin, Berlin . . . 016133
Museum für Naturkunde der Stadt Gera, Gera . . . 017372
Museum für Naturkunde des Zittauer Landes, Städtische Museen Zittau, Zittau . . . 021073
Museum für Naturkunde und Völkerkunde Julius Riemer, Städtische Sammlungen, Lutherstadt Wittenberg . . . 018763
Museum für Naturkunde und Vorgeschichte, Dessau, Anhalt . . . 016679
Museum für Neue Kunst, Städtische Museen Freiburg, Freiburg im Breisgau . . . 017234
Museum für Neue Kunst, ZKM Karlsruhe Zentrum für Kunst- und Medientechnologie, Karlsruhe . . . 018165
Museum für Niederrheinische Sakralkunst, Kempen . . . 018229
Museum für Nummernschilder, Verkehrs- und Zulassungsgeschichte, Großolbersdorf . . . 017575
Museum für Österreichische Zeitgeschichte, Scharnstein . . . 002642
Museum für Ostasiatische Kunst, Museen der Stadt Köln, Köln . . . 018331
Museum für Ostasiatische Kunst, Staatliche Museen zu Berlin - Stiftung Preußischer Kulturbesitz, Berlin . . . 016134
Museum für Outsiderkunst, Schleswig . . . 020040
Museum für Photographie, Braunschweig . . . 016390
Museum für Puppentheater, Sammlung Fritz Fey jun., Lübeck . . . 018724
Museum für Rechtsgeschichte, Pöggstall . . . 002442
Museum für Regionalgeschichte und Volkskunde, Stiftung Schloss Friedenstein Gotha, Gotha . . . 017494
Museum für römische Funde, Mainhardt . . . 018784
Museum für Sächsische Fahrzeuge, Chemnitz . . . 016561
Museum für Sächsische Volkskunst, Staatliche Kunstsammlungen Dresden, Dresden . . . 016806
Museum für Sakrale Kunst und Liturgie, Heidelberg . . . 017830
Museum für schlesische Landeskunde im Haus Schlesien, Königswinter . . . 018356
Museum für Schnitzkunst und Kulturgeschichte, Oberammergau 019381
Museum für Schuhproduktion und Industriegeschichte, Hauenstein . 017802
Museum für Seenotrettungsgeräte, Neuharlingersiel . . . 019239
Museum für Sepulkralkultur, Kassel 018195
Museum für Sozialkunde und Geschichte des Möbels, Gleisdorf . . . 001897
Museum für Stadtgeschichte, Alpirsbach . . . 015484
Museum für Stadtgeschichte, Breisach am Rhein . . . 016401
Museum für Stadtgeschichte, Neuenburg am Rhein . . . 019228
Museum für Stadtgeschichte, Augustinermuseum, Freiburg im Breisgau . . . 017235
Museum für Stadtgeschichte Dessau, Dessau, Anhalt . . . 016680
Museum für Stadtgeschichte im Adam-und-Eva-Haus, Paderborn . . . 019552
Museum für Stadtgeschichte und Volkskunde, Heppenheim . . . 017874
Museum für Thüringer Volkskunde Erfurt, Erfurt . . . 017018
Museum für Tierkunde, Staatliche Naturhistorische Sammlungen Dresden, Dresden . . . 016807
Museum für Uhren und mechanische Musikinstrumente, Oberhofen am Thunersee . . . 037389
Museum für Uhren und Schmuck, Frankfurt am Main . . . 017189
Museum für Unterwasserarchäologie, Archäologisches Landesmuseum Mecklenburg-Vorpommern, Saßnitz . . . 019999
Museum für Ur- und Frühgeschichte, Freiburg im Breisgau . . . 017236
Museum für Ur- und Frühgeschichte, Stillfried . . . 002711
Museum für Ur- und Frühgeschichte, Wieselburg an der Erlauf . . . 003041
Museum für Ur- und Frühgeschichte, Willibaldsburg, Eichstätt . . . 016912
Museum für Ur- und Frühgeschichte Thüringens, Weimar, Thüringen . . 020747
Museum für Urgeschichte, Koblach 002160
Museum für Urgeschichte des Landes Niederösterreich, Asparn an der Zaya . . . 001702
Museum für Urgeschichte(n), Zug . . 037818
Museum für verfolgte Kunst-Israel, Ashdod . . . 022890
Museum für Verkehr und Technik, Berlin . . . 016135
Museum für visuelle Kommunikation, Köln . . . 018332
Museum für Völkerkunde, Frankfurt am Main . . . 017182
Museum für Völkerkunde, Burgdorf 036992
Museum für Völkerkunde, Wien . . . 002961
Museum für Völkerkunde, Witzenhausen . . . 020940
Museum für Völkerkunde der Universität Kiel, Kiel . . . 018250
Museum für Völkerkunde Hamburg, Hamburg . . . 017716
Museum für Völkerkunde zu Leipzig/ Grassimuseum, Leipzig . . . 018581
Museum für Volkskultur in Württemberg, Württembergisches Landesmuseum Stuttgart, Waldenbuch . . . 020636

Museum für Volkskultur Spittal an der Drau, Spittal an der Drau 002686
Museum für Volkskunst, Sammlung Hagenlocher, Meßstetten 018923
Museum für Vor- und Frühgeschichte, Gunzenhausen 017607
Museum für Vor- und Frühgeschichte, Langenau, Württemberg 018501
Museum für Vor- und Frühgeschichte, Staatliche Museen zu Berlin - Stiftung Preußischer Kulturbesitz, Berlin . . 016136
Museum für Vor- und Frühgeschichte, Stiftung Saarländischer Kulturbesitz, Saarbrücken 019961
Museum für Vor- und Frühgeschichte - Archäologisches Museum, Frankfurt am Main 017152
Museum für Vor- und Frühgeschichte sowie Stadtgeschichte, Egeln 016888
Museum für Waage und Gewicht, Stadtverwaltung Balingen, Stadt Archiv, Balingen 015863
Museum für Waffentechink, Ausrüstung, Auszeichnungswesen, Vilshofen . 020601
Museum für Wattenfischerei, Wremen 020990
Museum für Weinbau und Stadtgeschichte, Edenkoben 016883
Museum für Weinkultur, Deidesheim 016659
Museum für Wohnkultur des Historismus und des Jugendstils, Hilterfingen . 037188
Museum für Zeitgenössische Glasmalerei, Langen in Hessen 018498
Museum für zeitgenössische Metallplastik, Sankt Pantaleon 002611
Museum Furthmühle, Pram 002460
Museum G. Frey des Entomologischen Instituts, Tutzing 020511
Museum & Galerie Rob Mohlman, Venhuizen 030266
Museum Galgenhaus, Stiftung Stadtmuseum Berlin, Berlin 016137
Muséum Gallery, Albi 098811
Museum Garching an der Alz, Garching an der Alz 017320
Museum Gasteiger-Haus, Utting . . . 020554
Museum Gayo, Aceh Tengah 022378
Museum Gedong Kirtya, Singaraja . 022508
Museum Gedung Arca, Gianyar . . . 022416
Museum Gedung Joang '45, Jakarta 022431
Museum-Gemaal de Hoogte, Nieuwolda 029955
Museum Gensungen, Felsberg 017111
Museum Geologi, Bandung 022388
Museum Geologie/Paläontologie, Heidelberg 017831
Museum Georg Schäfer, Schweinfurt 020141
Museum Gesigt van't Dok, Hellevoetsluis 029719
Museum Gevaert-Minne, Sint-Martens-Latem 003755
Museum Geyerhammer, Scharnstein 002643
Museum GGZ-Drenthe, Assen 029280
Museum Goa Bala Lompoa, Sungguminasa 022514
Museum Goch, Museum für Kunst und Kulturgeschichte, Goch 017439
Museum Godshuis Belle, Ieper 003533
Museum Göltzsch, Rodewisch 019858
Museum Goldener Steig, Waldkirchen, Niederbayern 020644
Museum Gottfried Silbermann, Frauenstein 017211
Museum Graphia, Urbino 026177
Museum Griesheim, Griesheim 017535
Museum Grootseminarie, Brugge . . 003275
Museum Grossauheim, Hanau 017743
Museum Großklein, Hallstattmuseum, Großklein 001972
Museum Großkrotzenburg, Großkrotzenburg 017574
Museum Gülden Creutz, Worbis . . . 020979
Museum Gula, Klaten 022463
Museum Gunnar-Wester-Haus, Städtische Sammlungen Schweinfurt, Schweinfurt 020142
Museum Gustavianum, Uppsala . . . 036741
Museum Haldensleben, Haldensleben 017651
Museum Halle, Halle, Westfalen . . . 017675
Museum Hameln, Hameln 017730
Museum Haus Cajeth, Heidelberg . . 017832
Museum Haus Löwenberg, Gengenbach 017363
Museum Haus Ludwig für Kunstausstellungen, Saarlouis . . . 019965
Museum Haus Martfeld, Schwelm . 020144
Museum Havezate Mensinge, Roden 030069
Museum Hedendaagse Grafiek en Glaskunst, Vledder 030278
Museum Heimathaus Irmintraut, Ottersberg 019540
Museum Heimathaus Münsterland, Telgte 020418
Museum Heineanum, Museum für Vogelkunde, Halberstadt 017647
Museum Helferhaus, Heimat- und Kunstverein, Backnang 015639
Museum Henriette Polak, Zutphen . 030404
Museum Heraldiek Benelux, Temse 003786
Museum Herbarium Bogoriensis, Bogor 022403
Museum - Herberg de Ar, Westerbork 030323
Museum Herisau, Herisau 037187
Museum Herzogsburg, Braunau am Inn 001761
Museum Hessenstube, Baunatal . . 015897
Museum Het Alaam, Genk 003448
Museum het Catharina Gasthuis, Gouda 029626
Museum Het Groot Graffel, Warnsveld 030307
Museum Het Oude Raadhuis, Megen 029916
Museum Het Paleis, Den Haag 029439
Museum Het Petershuis, Gennep . . 029604
Museum Het Prinsenhof, Delft 029411
Museum Het Rembrandthuis, Amsterdam 029204
Museum Het Schip, Amsterdam . . . 029205
Museum het Tramstation, Schipluiden 030138
Museum Het Valkhof, Nijmegen . . . 029961
Museum Het Verscholen Dorp, Vierhouten 030272
Museum Heylshof, Worms 020982
Museum Highlights, Wickenburg . . 136559
Museum Historische Verzameling Nederlandse Politie, Zaandam . . . 030362
Museum Höxter-Corvey, Höxter . . . 017954
Museum Hoffmann'sche Sammlung, Kohren-Sahlis 018370
Museum Hofmühle, Immenstadt . . . 018061
Museum Hohenau an der March, Hohenau an der March 002054
Museum Hohenzollern in Franken, Kulmbach 018442
Museum Hraček, Praha 008623
Museum HSF, Hannema-de Stuers Fundatie, Zwolle 030412
Museum Huelsmann, Kunstgewerbesammlung der Stadt Bielefeld/ Stiftung Huelsmann, Bielefeld 016238
Museum Hüsli- Sammlung Schwarzwälder Volkskunst, Grafenhausen 017503
Museum Huize Bareldonk, Berlare . 003229
Museum Humanum, Waldkirchen . . 002805
Museum Huta Bolon Simanindo, Pematangsiantar 022492
Museum Huta Bolon Simanindo, Samosir 022499
Museum Huthaus Einigkeit, Brand-Erbisdorf 016364
Museum Huthaus Zinnwald, Galerie Ewald Schönberg, Altenberg, Erzgebirge 015499
Museum Iancheleviсi, Goudriaan . . 029629
Museum Idar-Oberstein, Idar-Oberstein 018045
Museum Illingen, Illingen 018053
Museum Ilz, Ilz 002068
Museum im Adler, Benningen 015949
Museum im alten Brauhaus, Homberg, Ohm 018002
Museum im Alten Rathaus, Bad Brückenau 015675
Museum im Alten Rathaus, Mönchberg 018975
Museum im Alten Rathaus, Neckargemünd 019193
Museum im Alten Rathaus, Schmitten 020059
Museum im Alten Rathaus, Waghäusel 020618
Museum im Alten Schloß, Altensteig 015506
Museum im Alten Schloß, Neckarbischofsheim 019192
Museum im Ammes Haus, Hatzfeld 017801
Museum im Amtshausschlüpfla, Erlangen 017033
Museum im Astorhaus, Walldorf, Baden 020654
Museum im Ballhaus, Imst 002071
Museum im Bellpark, Kriens 037224
Museum im Bierlinghaus, Bad Bayersoien 015649
Museum im Blaahaus am Unteren Römerweg, Kiefersfelden 018242
Museum im Bock, Leutkirch im Allgäu 018627
Museum im Boyneburgischen Schloß, Sontra 020255
Museum im Dorf, Wittingen 020930
Museum Im Dorf, Außenstelle des Heimatmuseums Reutlingen, Reutlingen 019809
Museum im ehemaligen Augustiner-Chorherrenstift, Herrenchiemsee . 017897
Museum im Franck-Haus, Marktheidenfeld 018843
Museum im 'Fressenden Haus' - Burgkasten Weißenstein, Regen . 019742
Museum im Frey-Haus, Brandenburg an der Havel 016372
Museum im Fürstenstöckl, Ebenau . 001795
Museum im Goetz-Haus, Leipzig . . 018582
Museum im Goldschmiedehaus, Ahlen 015453
Museum im Gotischen Haus, Bad Homburg v.d.Höhe 015721
Museum im Greuterhof, Islikon . . . 037201
Museum im Grünen Haus der Marktgemeinde Reutte, Reutte . . 002526
Museum im Heimathaus, Traunstein 020458
Museum im Herrenhaus, Hausach . 017804
Museum im Hof, Sankt Pölten 002617
Museum im Hollerhaus, Dietfurt . . . 016706
Museum im Jost-Sigristen-Haus, Ernen 037074
Museum im Kirchhoferhaus, Stiftung Sankt Galler Museen, Sankt Gallen 037495
Museum im Klösterle, Peiting 019584
Museum im Kloster Grafschaft, Schmallenberg 020055
Museum im Kloster - Museum des Landkreises Osnabrück, Bersenbrück 016211
Museum im Koffer, Kinder- und Jugendmuseum Nürnberg, Nürnberg 019366
Museum im Kornhaus, Rorschach . 037463
Museum im Kräuterkasten, Albstadt 015468
Museum im Kreuzgang, Museen der Stadt Landshut, Landshut 018484
Museum im Kulturspeicher, Würzburg 021003
Museum im Lagerhaus, Sankt Gallen 037496
Museum im Ledererhaus, Purgstall an der Erlauf 002479
Museum im Malhaus, Wasserburg, Bodensee 020690
Museum im Markgrafen-Schloss, Stadtgeschichtliche Sammlung und Fotomuseum Hirsmüller, Emmendingen 016967
Museum im Marstall, Winsen, Luhe 020916
Museum im Mesnerhaus, Pfaffenhofen an der Ilm 019599
Museum im Pflegschloss, Schrobenhausen 020102
Museum im Prediger, Schwäbisch Gmünd 020111
Museum im Rathaus Möhringen, Museen der Stadt Tuttlingen, Tuttlingen . . 020509
Museum im Ritterhaus, Offenburg . 019456
Museum im Ritterhaus, Osterode am Harz 019511
Museum im Römerbad, Heidenheim an der Brenz 017842
Museum im Schäferhaus, Wahlsburg 020622
Museum im Schafhof Bayerns Landwirtschaft seit 1800, Freising 017246
Museum im Schlößle, Freiberg am Neckar 017219
Museum im Schloß, Frohburg 017279
Museum im Schloss, Porzellanmanufaktur Fürstenberg, Fürstenberg, Weser . 017282
Museum im Schloß Bad Pyrmont, Bad Pyrmont 015770
Museum im Schloß Lützen, Lützen . 018750
Museum im Schloß Wolfenbüttel, Stadtmuseum, Wolfenbüttel 020957
Museum im SchmidtHaus, Nabburg 019174
Museum im Schottenstift, Wien . . . 002962
Museum im Schulhaus, Niederrohrdorf 037382
Museum im Seelhaus, Bopfingen . . 016340
Museum im Stadtpark, Grevenbroich 017532
Museum im Stadtturm, Groitzsch bei Pegau 017549
Museum im Stasi-Bunker, Museum in der Runden Ecke, Machern 018767
Museum im Steinhaus, Bad Wimpfen 015832
Museum im Steintor, Anklam 015546
Museum im Steintorturm, Brandenburg an der Havel 016373
Museum im Stockalperschloß, Brig 036974
Museum im Strumpferhaus, Oberstaufen 019422
Museum im Tabor, Feldbach 001844
Museum im Thomas Legler-Haus, Diesbach 037044
Museum im Trafohaus, Leipzig 018583
Museum im Troadkostn zu Giem, Feldbach 001845
Museum im Tuchmacherhaus, Thammhausen 020432
Museum im Turmhof, Steckborn . . . 037601
Museum im Umweltschutz-Informationszentrum Oberfranken mit Kinder-Erlebnis-Museum, Bayreuth 015921
Museum im Vorderen Schloss, Mühlheim an der Donau 019018
Museum im Wasserwerk, Berliner Wasserbetriebe, Berlin 016138
Museum im Wehener Schloss, Taunusstein 020409
Museum im Wittelsbacher Schloss Friedberg, Friedberg, Bayern 017260
Museum im Zendenrathaus, Ernen . 037075
Museum im Zeughaus, Vechta 020563
Museum im Zeughaus, Tiroler Landesmuseum Ferdinandeum, Innsbruck 002089
Museum im Zwinger, Goslar 017486
Museum in Black, Los Angeles 045448
Museum in de Stiftkerk, Thorn 030201
Museum in de Veenen, Vinkeveen . 030273
Museum in den Halven Maen, Rockanje 030066
Museum in der Adler-Apotheke, Eberswalde 016875
Museum in der Alten Schule, Efringen-Kirchen 016887
Museum in der Burg, Bad Driburg . 015682

Museum in der Burg, Coppenbrügge . . . 016588
Museum in der Burg Zug, Zug . . . 037819
Museum in der Fronfeste, Neumarkt am Wallersee . . . 002365
Museum in der Gaststätte Scherrerwirt, Markt Piesting . . . 002293
Museum in der Kaiserpfalz, Paderborn . . . 019553
Museum in der Majolika-Manufaktur, Badisches Landesmuseum Karlsruhe, Karlsruhe . . . 018166
Museum in der Präparandenschule, Höchberg . . . 017941
Museum in der Remise, Bad Harzburger und Schreibenhauer Heimatstube, Burgbergmuseum, Bad Harzburg . 015712
Museum in der Scheuergasse, Zwingenberg, Bergstraße . . . 021093
Museum in der Wegscheid, Ternberg . . . 002737
Museum in Kochi Park, Kochi . . . 026673
Museum in Memory of Lu Xun, Beijing . . . 006994
Museum in Progress, Wien . . . 002963
Museum in Schweizer Hof, Bretten . 016447
Museum in 't Houtenhuis, De Rijp . 029398
Museum in the Community, Hurricane . . . 044701
The Museum in the Park, Stroud . . 041152
Museum Indonesia, Jakarta . . . 022432
Museum Industrieforum, Steyr . . . 002702
Museum Industriekultur, Osnabrück 019498
Museum Industriekultur mit Motorradmuseum, Museen der Stadt Nürnberg, Nürnberg . . . 019367
Museum Innviertler Volkskundehaus und Galerie der Stadt Ried, Ried im Innkreis . . . 002527
Museum Insel Hombroich, Neuss . . 019274
Museum International, Oxford . . . 136250
Museum Internationales Baum Archiv, Winterthur . . . 037725
Museum Istana Mangkunegaran, Surakarta . . . 022518
Museum Istana Sultan Ternate, Maluku Utara . . . 009171
Museum Istana Sultan Ternate, North Malaku . . . 022480
Museum Istant Siak Sri Indapura, Bengkalis . . . 022399
Museum It Kokelhûs van Jan en Sjut, Earnewald . . . 029518
Museum Jacobs van den Hof, Amersfoort . . . 029153
Museum Jagd und Wild auf Burg Falkenstein, Falkenstein, Oberpfalz . . . 017102
Museum Jagdschloß Kranichstein, Stiftung Hessischer Jägerhof, Darmstadt . 016643
Museum Jakob Smits, Mol . . . 003646
Museum Jamu Nyonya Menir, Semarang . . . 022503
Museum Jan Boon, De Rijp . . . 029399
Museum Jan Cunen, Oss . . . 030013
Museum Jan Heestershuis, Schijndel . . . 030134
Museum Jan Lont, Hippolytushoef . 029754
Museum Jan van der Togt, Amstelveen . . . 029160
Museum Jannink, Enschede . . . 029566
Museum Jerusalem Panorama Kreuzigung Christi, Altötting . . . 015515
Museum Joang '45, Medan . . . 022473
Museum Joang '45, Surabaya . . . 022515
Museum Jordanbad, Eppingen . . . 016994
Museum Josephine Baker, Castelnaud-la-Chapelle . . . 011145
Museum Joure, Joure . . . 029795
Museum Judengasse, Jüdisches Museum, Frankfurt am Main . . . 017190
Museum Judenplatz Wien, Wien . . . 002964
Museum Viadrina; Museum Junge Kunst, Frankfurt/Oder . . . 017206
Museum Junkerhaus, Lemgo . . . 018606
Museum Kaiser Franz Joseph I. und die Jagd, Neuberg an der Mürz . . . 002355
Museum Kalimantan Tengah, Palangkaraya . . . 022484
Museum Kalt-Heiß, Deckenpfronn . 016654
Museum Kameleon Dorp en Museum Hans Brinker, Terherne . . . 030194
Museum Kaprun, Kaprun . . . 002113
Museum Kartause Astheim, Volkach 020609
Museum Kartini, Jepara . . . 022459
Museum Kartini Rembang, Rembang . . . 022498
Museum Kasper, Norrtälje . . . 036505
Museum Kasteel Wijchen, Wijchen . 030330
Museum Katendrecht, Rotterdam . . 030089
Museum Katharinenhof mit Mühlenturm und Stadtscheune, Kranenburg, Niederrhein . . . 018392
Museum Kebangkitan Nasional, Jakarta . . . 022433
Museum Kebudayaan dan Kemajuan Asmat, Irian Jaya . . . 022419
Museum Kebun Binatgang Semarang, Semarang . . . 022504
Museum Kebun Raya Bogor, Bogor . 022404
Museum Kedokteran, Jakarta . . . 022434
Museum Kellinghusen, Kellinghusen . . . 018223
Museum Kempenland, Eindhoven . . 029544
Museum Kempenland, Lommel . . . 003613
Museum Kendil Riau, Tanjungpandan . . . 022525
Museum Kennemerland, Beverwijk 029315
Museum Kepolisian Negara Republik Indonesia, Jakarta . . . 022435
Museum Kereta, Ambarawa . . . 022381
Museum Kerkschat Sint-Katharinakerk, Maaseik . . . 003620
Museum Khan, Hadera . . . 022912
Museum Kinderwereld, Roden . . . 030070
Museum Kindheit und Jugend, Stiftung Stadtmuseum Berlin, Berlin . . . 016139
Museum Kirche zum Heiligen Kreuz, Städtische Museen Zittau, Zittau . 021074
Museum Kitzbühel, Kitzbühel . . . 002133
Museum Kleines Klingental, Sammlung Basler Münsterskulpturen, Kloster Klingental, Basel . . . 036896
Museum Kleines Schloß, Blankenburg, Harz . . . 016260
Museum Klingelbeutel, Gaukönigshofen . . . 017332
Museum Klösterli, Ettiswil . . . 037081
Museum de Klompenmaker, Keijenborg . . . 029807
Museum Kloster Asbach, Bayerisches Nationalmuseum München, Rotthalmünster . . . 019930
Museum Kloster Bentlage, Städtische Museen Rheine, Rheine . . . 019822
Museum Kloster Hude, Sammlung zur Klostergeschichte, Hude, Oldenburg . . . 018015
Museum Kloster Stift zum Heiligengrabe, Heiligengrabe . . . 017855
Museum Kloster Ter Apel, Ter Apel . 029250
Museum Kloster Zeven, Zeven . . . 021063
Museum Kloster Zinna, Kloster Zinna . . . 018290
Museum Knoblauchhaus, Stiftung Stadtmuseum Berlin, Berlin . . . 016140
Museum Knochenstampfe, Zwönitz 021094
Museum Kölner Karnevalsorden, Köln . . . 018333
Museum Komodo, Jakarta . . . 022436
Museum Kranenburgh, Bergen, Noord-Holland . . . 029311
Museum Kraton Kasepuhan, Cirebon . . . 022411
Museum Kraton Yogyakarta, Yogyakarta . . . 022538
Museum Kremayr, Ybbsitz . . . 003062
Museum Kriminal-Mabak, Jakarta . 022437
Museum Kruijsenhuis, Oirschot . . . 029984
Museum Kuenburggewölbe, Werfen 002837
Museum Künstlerkolonie, Institut Mathildenhöhe, Darmstadt . . . 016644
Museum Küppersmühle, Duisburg . 016857
Museum Kulturgeschichte der Hand, Wolnzach . . . 020976
Museum Kunst-Kultur-Kellerromantik, Schleinbach . . . 002650
Museum Kunst Palast mit Sammlung Kunstakademie und Glasmuseum Hentrich, Düsseldorf . . . 016841
Museum Der Kunststall, Dahlem . . 016623
Museum Kura Hulanda, Curaçao . . 030417
Museum Kurhaus Kleve, Ewald Mataré-Sammlung, Kleve . . . 018280
Museum Kutschen-Wagen-Karren, Museen der Stadt Gescher, Gescher . . . 017394
Museum La Bangenge, Pare-Pare . 022489
Museum La Diligence, Heerlen . . . 029696
Museum La Truaisch, Sedrun . . . 037547
Museum Lambert Van Meerten, Delft . . . 029412
Museum Lammert Boerma, Borgercompagnie . . . 029334
Museum Langenargen/ Bodensee, Langenargen . . . 018499
Museum Langenthal, Langenthal . . 037232
Museum Langes Tannen, Uetersen . 020522
Museum Langmatt, Stiftung Langmatt Sidney und Jenny Brown, Baden . 036872
Museum Laufental, Laufen . . . 037234
Museum Lauriacum, Enns . . . 001835
Museum Laxenburg, Laxenburg . . . 002214
Museum Le Mayeur, Sanur . . . 022500
Museum Leben am Meer, Esens . . . 017055
Museum Lettergieten 1983, Westzaan . . . 030326
Museum Leuchtenburg, Seitenroda 020180
Museum Lindengut, Historischer Verein Winterthur, Winterthur . . . 037726
Museum Lindwurm, Stein am Rhein 037607
Museum Liner Appenzell, Appenzell 036847
Museum Lionardo da Vinci Ideale, Karlskrona . . . 036384
Museum Löffingen, Löffingen . . . 018669
Museum Löwenburg, Christoph Merian Stiftung, Ederswiler . . . 037056
Museum Loka Budaya, Jayapura . . 022457
Museum London, London . . . 005792
Museum Ludwig, Museen der Stadt Köln, Köln . . . 018334
Museum Ludwig in der Halle Kalk, Köln . . . 018335
Museum Maagdenhuis, Antwerpen . 003167
Museum Maarssen, Maarssen . . . 029886
Museum Malerwinkelhaus, Marktbreit . . . 018841
Museum Malikusaleh, Aceh Utara . 022380
Museum Management and Curatorship, Kidlington . . . 136251
Museum Mandala Bakti, Semarang 022505
Museum Mandala Wangsit Siliwangi, Bandung . . . 022389
Museum Manggala Wanabakti, Jakarta . . . 022438
Museum Mannersdorf, Mannersdorf 002277
Museum Mayer van den Bergh, Antwerpen . . . 003168
Museum Mechanischer Musikinstrumente, Zweigmuseum des Badischen Landesmuseums, Bruchsal . . . 016455
Museum mechanischer Musikinstrumente, Königslutter . . . 018353
Museum Meerenberg, Bloemendaal 029318
Museum Meermanno-Westreenianum, Den Haag . . . 029440
Museum Megalopolis, Megalopolis . 021371
Museum Mengeringhausen, Bad Arolsen . . . 015646
Museum Menkemaborg, Uithuizen . 030217
Museum Mensch und Natur, München . . . 019089
Museum Mesdag, Van Gogh Museum Amsterdam, Den Haag . . . 029441
Museum Militer, Jakarta . . . 022439
Museum Mini Korem, Sintang . . . 022510
Museum Mistra, Mystras . . . 021392
Museum Mobil, Bandung . . . 022390
Museum Modern Art, Hünfeld . . . 018021
Museum Moderner Kunst Kärnten, Klagenfurt . . . 002146
Museum Moderner Kunst Stiftung Ludwig Wien, Wien . . . 002965
Museum Moderner Kunst - Stiftung Wörlen, Passau . . . 019571
Museum Modest Huys, Zulte . . . 003875
Museum Mödling, Mödling . . . 002327
Museum Moorseer Mühle, Nordenham . . . 019327
Museum Morsbroich, Leverkusen . . 018628
Museum MPU Tantular, Surabaya . . 022516
Museum Münster, Münster . . . 037358
Museum Municipal, Beira . . . 029044
Museum Musica, Stadskanaal . . . 030176
Museum Nagele, Nagele . . . 029936
Museum Nan Eilean, Sgoil Lionacleit, Benbecula . . . 038672
Museum Nan Eilean, Steornabhagh, Stornoway . . . 041127
Museum Nanning Hendrik Bulthuis, Leeuwarden . . . 029841
Museum Nasional, Jakarta . . . 022440
Museum National, Civic Square . . . 135541
Muséum National d'Histoire Naturel Arboretum de Chèvreloup, Rocquencourt . . . 014083
Muséum National d'Histoire Naturelle, Paris . . . 013732
Museum National d'Histoire Naturelle, Rabat . . . 029034
Muséum National d'Histoire Naturelle du Val Rameh, Menton . . . 013024
Museum Natur und Mensch, Greding . . . 017515
Museum near the Ming Tombs, Changping . . . 007028
Museum Necca and New England Center for Contemporary Art, Brooklyn . . . 042456
Museum Nederlandse Cavalerie, Amersfoort . . . 029154
Museum Negeri Bali, Denpasar . . . 022412
Museum Negeri Djawa Timur, Surabaya . . . 022516
Museum Negeri Jambi, Jambi . . . 022456
Museum Negeri Java Tengah, Semarang . . . 022506
Museum Negeri Jawa Barat, Bandung . . . 022391
Museum Negeri Kalimantan Barat, Pontianak . . . 022495
Museum Negeri Kalimantan Timur Mulawarman, Tenggarong . . . 022527
Museum Negeri Lampung, Bandarlampung . . . 022385
Museum Negeri Maluku Siwa Lima, Ambon . . . 009167
Museum Negeri Nusa Tenggara Barat, Mataram . . . 022472
Museum Negeri of Aceh, Banda Aceh . . . 022384
Museum Negeri of Bengkulu, Bengkulu . . . 022400
Museum Negeri of Irian Jaya, Jayapura . . . 022458
Museum Negeri of La Galigo, Ujungpanang . . . 022530
Museum Negeri of Lambung Mangkurat, Banjarbaru . . . 022395
Museum Negeri Propinsi Nusa Tenggara Timur, Kupang . . . 022465
Museum Negeri Propinsi Sumatera Selatan Balaputra Dewa, Palembang . . . 022485
Museum Negeri Sulawesi Tenggara, Kendari . . . 022462
Museum Negeri Sulawesi Utara, Manado . . . 022470
Museum Negeri Sumatera Barat, Padang . . . 022481
Museum Negeri Sumatera Utara, Medan . . . 022474
Museum Negeri Timor-Timur, Dili . . 009169
Museum Nekara, Selayar . . . 022501
Museum Neue Mühle, Erfurt . . . 017019
Museum Neuhaus, Biel . . . 036950
Museum Neukirchen-Vluyn, Neukirchen-Vluyn . . . 019248
Museum Neukölln, Museum für Stadtkultur und Regionalgeschichte, Berlin . . 016141
Museum Neuruppin, Neuruppin . . . 019268

Museum News, Washington 136560
Museum Nicolaihaus, Stiftung Stadtmuseum Berlin, Berlin 016142
Museum Nienburg, Nienburg, Weser 019315
Museum Niesky, Niesky 019317
Museum Nikolaikirche, Stiftung Stadtmuseum Berlin, Berlin 016143
Museum No 1, Richmond, Surrey . . 040831
Museum Nordenham, Nordenham . 019328
Museum NordJura, Weismain 020770
Museum Nostalgie der 50er Jahre, Burgpreppach 016521
Museum Notes (Providence), Providence 136561
Museum Nusantara, Museum voor het Indonesisch Cultuurgebied, Delft . 029413
Museum Ober-Ramstadt, Ober-Ramstadt 019380
Museum Oberes Donautal, Heimatmuseum Fridingen, Fridingen 017259
Museum Oculorum, Buenos Aires . . 000249
Museum Oedenhof, Wittenbach . . . 037736
Museum of Aboriginal Affairs, Gombak 027948
Museum of Acre, Acre 022880
Museum of African American Art, Los Angeles 045449
The Museum of African Tribal Art, Portland 047161
Museum of Afro-American History, Boston 042333
Museum of Afro-American History, Brookline 042455
Museum of Amana History, Amana . 041677
Museum of Ambleside, Ambleside . 038505
Museum of American Architecture and Decorative Arts, Houston 044647
Museum of American Financial History, New York 046371
Museum of American Folk Art, New York 046283
Museum of American Frontier Culture, Staunton 048344
Museum of American Glass at Wheaton Village, Millville 045876
Museum of American Historical Society of Germans from Russia, Lincoln . . . 045306
Museum of American Political Life, University of Hartford, West Hartford 049077
Museum of American Presidents, Strasburg 048395
Museum of Anatomy, Glasgow 039564
Museum of Anatomy of the Department of Anatomy, Athinai 021192
Museum of Ancient and Modern Art, Penn Valley 046870
Museum of Ancient Artifacts, Chicago 042858
Museum of Ancient Culture, Kilmartin 039871
Museum of Animal Husbandary and Veterinary, Assam Veterinary College, Guwahati 022138
Museum of Anthracite Mining, Ashland 041812
Museum of Anthropology, Chico . . . 042892
Museum of Anthropology, Denver . . 043413
Museum of Anthropology, Fullerton 044097
Museum of Anthropology, Lawrence 045204
Museum of Anthropology, Pullman . 047282
Museum of Anthropology, Tempe . . 048520
Museum of Anthropology, Vancouver 006703
Museum of Anthropology, Winston-Salem 049253
Museum of Anthropology, Northern Kentucky University, Highland Heights 044537
Museum of Anthropology, University of Michigan, Ann Arbor 041733
Museum of Anthropology, University of Missouri, Columbia 043071
Museum of Anthropology and Archaeology, Pretoria 034720
Museum of Antique Armour Helmets and Swords, Kyoto 026751
Museum of Antiquities, Alnwick . . . 038494
Museum of Antiquities, Jamnagar . 022182
Museum of Antiquities, Newcastle-upon-Tyne 040552
Museum of Antiquities, Saskatoon . 006421
Museum of Appalachia, Norris 046510
Museum of Aqaba Antiquities, Aqaba 027379
Museum of Archaeological Site Moenjodaro, Dokri 031360
Museum of Archaeology, Durham . . 039336
Museum of Archaeology, Legon . . . 021110
Museum of Archaeology, Vadodara . 022367
Museum of Archaeology and Ethnology, Burnaby 005170
Museum of Archaeology and History, National Museum of Ireland Ard-Mhúsaem na hÉireann, Dublin 022759
Museum of Archaeology, Classics and Oriental Studies, Liverpool 040033
Museum of Army Flying, Middle Wallop 040457
Museum of Army Transport, Beverley 038692
Museum of Art, Fort Lauderdale . . . 043933
Museum of Art, Pullman 047283
Museum of Art, Rhode Island School of Design, Providence 047258
Museum of Art, University of Maine, Orono 046727
Museum of Art and Archaeology, Dharwad 022105
Museum of Art and Archaeology, Mysore 022277
Museum of Art and Archaeology, University of Missouri-Columbia, Columbia . 043072
Museum of Art and History, Santa Cruz 047957
Museum of Arthropoda, Pune 022309
Museum of Arts and Crafts, Lucknow 022243
The Museum of Arts and Sciences, Daytona Beach 043330
Museum of Arts and Sciences, Macon 045567
Museum of Arts Downtown Los Angeles, Los Angeles 045450
Museum of Asian Art, Corfu 021242
Museum of Audio Visual Technology, Wellington 030640
Museum of Automobile History, Syracuse 048458
Museum of Automobiles, Morrilton . 046030
Museum of Aviation, Paraparaumu . 030572
Museum of Aviation at Robins Air Force Base, Warner Robins 048855
Museum of Bad Art, Dedham 043361
Museum of Banknotes of the Ionian Bank, Corfu 021243
Museum of Barnstaple and North Devon, Barnstaple 038602
Museum of Bath at Work, Bath 038626
Museum of Belize, Belize City 003881
Museum of Berkshire Aviation, Woodley 041437
Museum of Biloxi, Biloxi 042211
Museum of Biloxi, Biloxi 042212
Museum of British Road Transport, Coventry 039154
The Museum of Broadcast Communications, Chicago 042859
Museum of Bronx History, Bronx . . 042440
Museum of Byzantine Culture, Thessaloniki 021498
Museum of Cannock Chase, Hednesford 039714
Museum of Cape Breton Heritage, North East Margaree 006042
Museum of Carousel Art and History, Sandusky 047930
Museum of Casts and Archeological Collection, Thessaloniki 021499
Museum of Central Australia, Alice Springs 000736
Museum of Central Connecticut State University, New Britain 046201
Museum of Ceramics, East Liverpool 043577
Museum of Ceramics at East Liverpool, East Liverpool 043577
Museum of Childhood, Boscombe . 038790
Museum of Childhood, Dublin 022760
Museum of Childhood, Edinburgh . . 039400
Museum of Childhood, Masterton . . 030537
Museum of Childhood, Sudbury, Derbyshire 041154
Museum of Childhood, Toronto 006616
Museum of Childhood at Bethnal Green, London 040224
Museum of Childhood Memories, Beaumaris 038648
Museum of Children's Art, Oakland 046597
Museum of Chinese in the Americas, New York 046372
Museum of Chungju National University, Chungju 027472
Museum of Church History and Art, Salt Lake City 047774
Museum of Citrus County History-Old Courthouse, Inverness 044762
The Museum of Clallam County Historical Society, Port Angeles 047124
Museum of Classical Archaeology, Adelaide 000710
Museum of Classical Archaeology, Cambridge 038967
Museum of Clock and Watch Making, Prescot 040775
Museum of Coast and Anti-Aircraft Artillery, Green Point 034628
Museum of Coastal History, Saint Simons Island 047725
Museum of Communication, Bo'ness 038786
Museum of Conceptual Art, San Francisco 047874
Museum of Connecticut History, Hartford 044461
Museum of Contemporary Art, Chicago 042860
Museum of Contemporary Art, Fort Collins 043905
Museum of Contemporary Art, Miami 045817
Museum of Contemporary Art, Washington 048921
Museum of Contemporary Art, West Hollywood 049084
Museum of Contemporary Art, Basil and Elise Goulandris Foundation, Andros 021134
Museum of Contemporary Art Denver, Denver 043414
Museum of Contemporary Art Los Angeles, Los Angeles 045451
Museum of Contemporary Art San Diego - Downtown, San Diego 047825
Museum of Contemporary Art San Diego - La Jolla, La Jolla 045068
Museum of Contemporary Art Sapporo, Sapporo 027032
Museum of Contemporary Art Sydney, Sydney 001517
Museum of Contemporary Articrafts, Teheran 022632
Museum of Contemporary Canadian Art, North York 006054
Museum of Contemporary Greek Painters, Amfissa 021128
The Museum of Contemporary Photography, Columbia College Chicago, Chicago 042861
Museum of Contemporary Religious Art, Saint Louis 047672
Museum of Contemporary Sculpture, Tokyo 027210
Museum of Cosmetology, Chicago . 042862
Museum of Costume, Bath 038627
Museum of Costume, National Museums of Scotland, New Abbey 040523
Museum of Costume and Textiles, Nottingham 040621
Museum of Country Life, National Museum of Ireland Ard-Mhúsaem na hÉireann, Castlebar 022705
Museum of Craft Folk Art, San Francisco 047875
Museum of Cretan Ethnology, Vori . 021525
Museum of Cultural and Natural History, Central Michigan University, Mount Pleasant 046064
Museum of Cycladic and Ancient Greek Art, Athinai 021193
Museum of Daejeon History, Daejeon 027482
Museum of Dartmoor Life, Okehampton 040638
Museum of Datong, Datong 007062
The Museum of Death, Los Angeles 045452
Museum of Death, San Diego 047826
Museum of Decorative Art, Chicago 042863
Museum of Decorative Arts, Athinai 021194
Museum of Decorative Arts and History, National Museum of Ireland Ard-Mhúsaem na hÉireann, Dublin 022761
Museum of Decorative Painting and Decorative Arts Collection, Wichita 049159
Museum of Delphic Celebrations of Angelos and Eva Sikellianou, Athinai 021195
Museum of Dentistry, Liverpool . . . 040034
Museum of Dionysios Solomos and Eminent Zakynthians, Zakynthos 021531
Museum of Discovery and Science, Fort Lauderdale 043934
Museum of Domestic Design and Architecture MODA, Middlesex University, Barnet 038597
Museum of Dr. Sun Yat-Sen, Zhongshan 007352
Museum of Early Southern Decorative Arts, Winston-Salem 049254
Museum of Early Trades and Crafts, Madison 045585
Museum of East Anglian Life, Stowmarket 041131
Museum of East Asian Art, Bath . . . 038628
The Museum of East Texas, Lufkin . 045519
Museum of Education, Elbasan . . . 000019
Museum of Education, Korçë 000026
Museum of Electricity, Christchurch 039086
Museum of English Rural Life, Reading 040807
Museum of Engravings and Graphic Arts, Athinai 021196
Museum of Entertainment, Whaplode 041362
Museum of Epirot Folk Art, Metsovon 021381
Museum of Ethnography and Folklore, Eretz-Israel Museum, Tel Aviv . . . 023086
Museum of Ethnology and Folk Art, Ratnapura 036141
Museum of Eton Life, Eton 039459
Museum of Exploration, Survey and Land Settlement, Adelaide 000711
Museum of Farming Life, Ellon 039437
Museum of Farnham, Farnham 039491
Museum of Fine Art, Lugansk 038334
Museum of Fine Arts, Beijing 006995
Museum of Fine Arts, Boston 042334
Museum of Fine Arts, Chandigarh . . 022052
Museum of Fine Arts, Hobart 001110
The Museum of Fine Arts, Houston . 044648
Museum of Fine Arts, Missoula . . . 045934
Museum of Fine Arts, Nanchang . . . 007192
Museum of Fine Arts, Santa Fe 047970
Museum of Fine Arts, Springfield 048294
Museum of Fine Arts, Tbilisi 015411
Museum of Fine Arts and Cultural Center, Alexandria 009280
Museum of Fine Arts Bulletin, Houston 136562
Museum of Fine Arts Saint Petersburg, Florida, Saint Petersburg 047717
Museum of Fire, Edinburgh 039401
Museum of Flight, Seattle 048085
Museum of Flight, National Museums of Scotland, North Berwick 040589
Museum of Florida History, Tallahassee 048483
Museum of Freemasonry, London . . 040225
Museum of Fulham Palace, London 040226
Museum of Garden History, London 040227

Museum of Gems and Minerals, Ratnapura . . . 036142
Museum of Geology, Edmonton . . . 005401
Museum of Geology, South Dakota School of Mines and Technology, Rapid City . . . 047335
Museum of Glass, International Center for Contemporary Art, Tacoma . . . 048468
Museum of Greek Musical Instruments, Thessaloniki . . . 021500
Museum of Gujarat Vidyasabha, Ahmedabad . . . 021992
Museum of Hartlepool, Hartlepool . 039685
Museum of Health and Medical Science, Houston . . . 044649
Museum of Health Care, Kingston . 005705
Museum of Historical Archaeology, Kingston . . . 026390
Museum of Historical Geology and Geological Survey of Pakistan, Quetta . . . 031398
Museum of Historical Philips Products, Eindhoven . . . 029545
Museum of History and Art, Morehead City . . . 046024
Museum of History and Art, Ontario 046694
Museum of History and Ethnography Negeri, Melaka . . . 027995
Museum of History and Industry, Seattle . . . 048086
Museum of History, Anthropology and Art, San Juan . . . 032747
Museum of Holography, Chicago . . 042864
Museum of Human Sciences, Harare . . . 049582
Museum of Hygiene, Cairo . . . 009308
Museum of Icons and Art Objects, Gangtok . . . 022117
Museum of Independent Telephony, Abilene . . . 041565
Museum of Indian Arts and Culture, Santa Fe . . . 047971
Museum of Indian Culture, Allentown . . . 041661
Museum of Industry, Stellarton . . . 006509
Museum of Inhaca Island, Maputo . 029053
Museum of Installation, London . . . 040228
Museum of Instruments, Royal College of Music, London . . . 040229
Museum of International Children's Art, Santa Cruz . . . 047958
Museum of International Folk Art, Santa Fe . . . 047972
Museum of International Friendship, Beijing . . . 006996
Museum of Irish Transport, Killarney . . . 022809
Museum of Iron and Darby Furnace, Coalbrookdale . . . 039105
Museum of Islamic Art, Cairo . . . 009309
Museum of Islamic Ceramic, Gezira Art Center, Cairo . . . 009310
Museum of Island History, Newport, Isle of Wight . . . 040567
Museum of Islay Life, Port Charlotte 040743
Museum of Isle of Wight Geology, Sandown . . . 040956
Museum of Israeli Art, Ramat Gan . 023051
Museum of Istrian History, Pula . . . 007777
Museum of Japanese Sword Fittings, Tokyo . . . 027211
Museum of Jewish Art, Kiryat Banot, Jerusalem . . . 022964
Museum of Jewish Heritage - A Living Memorial to the Holocaust, New York . . . 046373
Museum of Kent Life, Sandling . . . 040955
Museum of Kerala History, Edapally 022110
Museum of Komotini, Komotini . . . 021336
Museum of Korea Indigenous Straw and Plant, Seoul . . . 027583
Museum of Korean Buddhist Art, Seoul . . . 027584
Museum of Korean Commercial History, Yongin . . . 027628
Museum of Korean Embroidery, Seoul . . . 027585
Museum of Korean Traditional Music, Seoul . . . 027586
Museum of Lakeland Life, Kendal . 039846
Museum of Lancashire, Preston . . . 040779
Museum of Latin American Art, Long Beach . . . 045381
Museum of Lead Mining, Wanlockhead . . . 041293
Museum of Lighting, Edinburgh . . . 039402
Museum of Lillydale, Lilydale . . . 001184
Museum of Lincolnshire Life, Lincoln . . . 040010
Museum of Liverpool Life, Liverpool 040035
Museum of Local Crafts and Industries, Burnley . . . 038907
Museum of Local History, Hastings . 039693
Museum of Local History and Industry, Llandrindod Wells . . . 040047
Museum of Local Life, Worcester . . 041443
Museum of London, London . . . 040230
Museum of London, Publications Department, London . . . 135238
Museum of Long Island Natural Sciences, Stony Brook . . . 048378
Museum of Macao, Macau . . . 007188
Museum of Malawi, Blantyre . . . 027939
Museum of Man in the Sea, Panama City . . . 046809
Museum of Mankind, London . . . 040231
Museum of Marine Life of Cyprus, Aghia Napa . . . 008202
Museum of Maroccan Arts, Tanger . 029039
Museum of Maryland History, Maryland Historical Society, Baltimore . . . 042000
Museum of Medical Equipment, Bangkok . . . 037882
Museum of Medical History, Shanghai . . . 007238
Museum of Medical Sciences, Hong Kong . . . 007126
Museum of Mental Health Services, Toronto . . . 006617
Museum of Methodism, London . . . 040232
Museum of Migrating People, Bronx 042441
Museum of Military and Naval History, San Juan . . . 032748
Museum of Military Intelligence, Intelligence Corps Museum and Medmenham Collection, Chicksands . . . 039075
Museum of Mineralogy, Petrology and Geology, Zografou . . . 021536
Museum of Mobile, Mobile . . . 045950
Museum of Modern Art, Oxford . . . 040659
Museum of Modern Art, Cairo . . . 009311
The Museum of Modern Art, Machynlleth . . . 040381
Museum of Modern Art, New York . 046374
Museum of Modern Art in Queens, Long Island City . . . 045389
Museum of Modern Art, Publications Department, New York . . . 135443
Museum of Mohamed Mahmoud Khalil and his wife, Giza . . . 009333
Museum of Mongolian Ethnography, Ulaanbaatar . . . 029007
The Museum of Museums, Waregem . . . 003842
Museum of Nahariya, Nahariya . . . 023035
Museum of NaJu Pears, Naju . . . 027533
Museum of Natural History, Northern Flagship Institution, Pretoria . . . 034731
Museum of Natural History, Jerusalem . . . 022965
Museum of Natural History, Marshall . . . 045702
Museum of Natural History, Providence . . . 047259
The Museum of Natural History, Stevens Point . . . 048354
Museum of Natural History, National Museum of Ireland Ard-Mhúsaem na hÉireann, Dublin . . . 022762
Museum of Natural History, University of Illinois at Urbana-Champaign, Urbana . . . 048712
Museum of Natural History, University of Oregon, Eugene . . . 043746
Museum of Natural History, University of the Philippines Los Baños, Los Baños 031689
Museum of Natural History and Historical Photography, Polygyros . . . 021442
Museum of Natural Science, Baton Rouge . . . 042049
Museum of Natural Sciences, Saskatoon . . . 006422
The Museum of Naval Firepower, Gosport . . . 039610
Museum of Nebraska Art, Kearney . 044944
Museum of Nebraska History, Lincoln . . . 045307
Museum of Neon Art, Los Angeles . 045453
Museum of Net Manufacture, Dorset . . . 039267
Museum of New Hampshire History, Concord . . . 043124
Museum of New Mexico, Santa Fe . 047973
The Museum of Newport History, Newport . . . 046459
Museum of Ningxia Autonomous Region of the Hui Nationality, Yinchuan . . . 007340
Museum of North Carolina Minerals, Spruce Pine . . . 048311
Museum of North Craven Life, Settle . . . 040985
Museum of North Idaho, Coeur d'Alene . . . 043030
Museum of Northern Arizona, Flagstaff . . . 043851
Museum of Northern British Columbia, Prince Rupert . . . 006209
Museum of Northern History at the Sir Harry Oakes Château, Kirkland Lake . . . 005714
Museum of Northwest Art, La Conner . . . 045052
Museum of Northwest Colorado, Craig . . . 043205
Museum of Nottingham Lace, Nottingham . . . 040622
The Museum of Nursing, Camperdown . . . 000885
The Museum of Nursing History, Philadelphia . . . 046964
Museum of Orient and East Marion History, Orient . . . 046712
Museum of Our National Heritage, Van Gorden-Williams Library and Archives, Lexington . . . 045270
The Museum of Outdoor Arts, Englewood . . . 043712
Museum of Oxford, Oxford . . . 040660
Museum of Paleontology, University of California at Berkeley, Berkeley . . 042163
Museum of Palestinian Popular Heritage, Al-Bireh . . . 031405
Museum of Pathology, Sydney . . . 001518
Museum of Pedagogics, Kaunas . . . 027849
Museum of Peoples and Cultures, Provo . . . 047274
Museum of Philippine Art, Manila . . 031731
Museum of Philippine Political History, Manila . . . 031732
Museum of Photographic Arts, San Diego . . . 047827
Museum of Pioneer Settlement, Kibbutz Yifat . . . 023023
Museum of Piping, Glasgow . . . 039565
Museum of Post and Telecomunication Mokhaberat, Teheran . . . 022633
Museum of Postindependence Athens, Athinai . . . 021197
Museum of Prehistory, Haifa . . . 022929
Museum of Prehistory, Jerusalem . 022966
Museum of Prehistory, Shaar Hagolan . . . 023059
Museum of Primitive Art and Culture, Peace Dale . . . 046852
Museum of Primitive Methodism, Englesea Brook, Crewe . . . 039174
Museum of Printing History, Houston . . . 044650
Museum of Psalms, Jerusalem . . . 022967
Museum of Radio and Technology, Huntington . . . 044686
Museum of Rail Travel, Keighley . . . 039838
Museum of Reading, Reading . . . 040808
Museum of Regional and Mediterranean Archaeology, Nir-David . . . 023040
Museum of Religious History, Ulaanbaatar . . . 029008
Museum of Richmond, Richmond, Surrey . . . 040832
Museum of Robotics, Orinda . . . 046713
Museum of Roman Antiquities, Rabat . . . 028028
Museum of Rugby, Twickenham . . . 041252
Museum of Rural Industry, Sticklepath . . . 041100
Museum of Rural Life, Denton . . . 043392
Museum of Russian Culture, San Francisco . . . 047876
Museum of Sacred Art, Macau . . . 007189
Museum of Sacred Icons, Athinai . . 021198
Museum of Saint Albans, Saint Albans . . . 040887
Museum of Samoa, Apia . . . 034108
Museum of Science, Boston . . . 042335
Museum of Science and History of Jacksonville, Jacksonville . . . 044818
Museum of Science and Industry, Chicago . . . 042865
Museum of Science and Industry, Tampa . . . 048490
Museum of Science and Industry in Manchester, Manchester . . . 040410
Museum of Science and Technology, Accra . . . 021099
Museum of Science and Technology, Pretoria . . . 034721
Museum of Science at the Toledo Zoo, Toledo . . . 048568
Museum of Scotland, National Museums of Scotland, Edinburgh . . . 039403
Museum of Scottish Country Life, National Museums of Scotland, East Kilbride . . . 039353
Museum of Scottish Lighthouses, Fraserburgh . . . 039525
Museum of Sculpture and Figurines of Loukia Georganti, Athinai . . . 021199
Museum of Seminole County History, Sanford . . . 047939
Museum of Sex, New York . . . 046375
Museum of Shanxi Province, Taiyuan . . . 007278
Museum of Shells of the Greek Seas, Néa Moudiana . . . 021409
Museum of Shops, Eastbourne . . . 039361
Museum of Site, Most I, Hong Kong 007127
Museum of Site, Most II, Hong Kong 007128
Museum of Smuggling History, Ventnor . . . 041268
Museum of South East Alberta, Etzikom . . . 005439
Museum of South Somerset, Yeovil 041470
Museum of South Yorkshire Life, Doncaster . . . 039251
Museum of Southern African Rock Art, Museum Africa, Johannesburg . . 034653
Museum of Southern History, Jacksonville . . . 044819
The Museum of Southern History, Sugarland . . . 048417
Museum of Southwestern Biology, Albuquerque . . . 041619
Museum of Spanish Colonial Art, Santa Fe . . . 047974
Museum of Speed, Pendine . . . 040685
Museum of Submarine Telegraphy, Porthcurno . . . 040753
Museum of Surveying, Lansing . . . 045164
Museum of Sussex Archaeology, Lewes . . . 039995
Museum of Sydney, Sydney . . . 001519
Museum of Taxes, Jerusalem . . . 022968
Museum of Telecommunications, Néa Kifissia . . . 021407
Museum of Television and Radio, Beverly Hills . . . 042194
Museum of Television and Radio, New York . . . 046376
Museum of Texas, Waco . . . 048815
Museum of Texas Tech University, Lubbock . . . 045513

Museum of the 40's, Point Clear Bay . . . 040727
Museum of the Agricultural College and Research Institute, Coimbatore . . 022064
Museum of the Albemarle, Elizabeth City . . . 043653
Museum of the Alphabet, Jaars Summer Institute of Linguistics, Waxhaw . 049022
Museum of the American Hungarian Foundation, New Brunswick 046207
Museum of the American Numismatic Association, Colorado Springs . . . 043059
Museum of the American Piano, New York . . . 046377
Museum of the American Quilter's Society, Paducah . . . 046787
Museum of the Bedford Historical Society, Bedford . . . 042097
Museum of the Berkeley Springs, Berkeley Springs . . . 042167
Museum of the Big Bend, Alpine . . 041669
Museum of the Cape Fear Historical Complex, Fayetteville . . . 043834
Museum of the Cariboo Chilcotin, Williams Lake . . . 006822
Museum of the Central Marine Fisheries Research Station, Mandapam Camp . . . 022252
Museum of the Chado Research Center, Kyoto . . . 026752
Museum of the Cherokee Indian, Cherokee . . . 042793
Museum of the Cherokee Strip, Oklahoma Historical Society, Enid . . . 043713
Museum of the Chinese People's Revolutionary Military Affairs, Beijing . . . 006997
Museum of the Chinese Revolution, Beijing . . . 007000
Museum of the City of Athens, Vouros-Eutaxias, Athinai . . . 021200
Museum of the City of Lake Worth, Lake Worth . . . 045118
Museum of the City of New York, New York . . . 046378
Museum of the City of New York. Annual Report, New York . . . 136563
Museum of the College of Engineering, Chennai . . . 022060
The Museum of the Confederacy, Richmond . . . 047421
Museum of the Contemporary Art, Lake Worth . . . 045120
Museum of the Cultural Palace of National Minorities, Beijing . . . 006998
Museum of the Cumbraes, Millport . 040468
Museum of the Dog, Saint Louis . . . 047673
Museum of The Duke of Wellington's Regiment, Halifax . . . 039662
Museum of the Faculty of Arts, Alexandria . . . 009281
Museum of the former Residence of Comrade Mao Zedong at Shaoshan, Shaoshan . . . 007252
Museum of the former Residence of Premier Zhou En-Lai, Huaian . . . 007136
Museum of the Franciscan Convent, Jerusalem . . . 022969
Museum of the Fur Trade, Chadron . 042697
Museum of the Geological Sciences, Blacksburg . . . 042245
Museum of the George and Nefeli Giabra Pierides Collection, Bank of Cyprus Cultural Foundation, Lefkosia . . . 008222
Museum of the Great Plains, Lawton . . . 045215
Museum of the Grove of the Village Shrine, Hirano Hakabutsukan, Osaka 026972
Museum of the Guangxi Province, Nanning . . . 007211
Museum of the Gulf Coast, Port Arthur . . . 047126
Museum of the Highwood, High River . . . 005615
Museum of the Historical Society of Trappe, Collegeville, Perkiomen Valley, Trappe . . . 048596
Museum of the History and Art of the Holy City of Missolonghi, Mesolongion 021375
Museum of the History of Azerbaijan, Baku . . . 003083
Museum of the History of Children's Games and Books, Myrina . . . 021390
Museum of the History of Cypriot Coinage, Lefkosia . . . 008223
Museum of the History of Education, Leeds . . . 039957
Museum of the History of Medicine, Cairo . . . 009312
Museum of the History of Revolution, Lhasa . . . 007170
Museum of the History of Science, Oxford . . . 040661
Museum of the History of Science, Sydney . . . 001520
Museum of the History of Tel Aviv-Yafo, Tel Aviv . . . 023087
Museum of the History of Termurids, Taškent . . . 049410
Museum of the History of the Salt Industry, Zigong . . . 007361
Museum of the History of the University of Athens, Athinai . . . 021160
Museum of the History of Tiberias and the Lake Kinnereth, Tiberias . . . 023099
Museum of the Holmesdale Natural History Club, Reigate . . . 040819
Museum of the Holy Trinity Church of Ethiopia, Addis Ababa . . . 009440
The Museum of the Home, Pembroke . . . 040681
Museum of the Hudson Highlands, Cornwall-on-Hudson . . . 043160
Museum of the Imperial Palace of Manchu State, Changchun . . . 007025
Museum of the Institute of African Studies, Ibadan . . . 030682
Museum of the Institute of African Studies, Oshogbo . . . 030701
Museum of the Institute of History and Philology, Academia Sinica, Taipei 007370
Museum of the Iron Age, Andover . . 038510
Museum of the Isles, Armadale . . . 038525
Museum of the Jewellery Quarter, Birmingham . . . 038734
Museum of the Jimmy Carter Library, Atlanta . . . 041867
Museum of the Korean Cultural Center, Los Angeles . . . 045454
Museum of the Liangshan Autonomous Prefecture of the Yi Nationality, Xichang . . . 007330
Museum of the Linxia Autonomous Region, Linxia . . . 007173
Museum of the Llano Estacado, Plainview . . . 047076
Museum of the Manchesters, Ashton-under-Lyne . . . 038542
Museum of the Mausoleum of King Nanyue, Guangzhou . . . 007090
Museum of the Medical College, Mysore . . . 022278
Museum of the Merchant Marine, Piraeus . . . 021433
Museum of the Metropolis of Messinia, Kalamata . . . 021295
Museum of the Mid-Suffolk Light Railway, Wetheringsett . . . 041352
Museum of the Mountain Man, Pinedale . . . 047027
Museum of the Moving Images, London . . . 040233
Museum of the Nagasaki Heavy Industries, Nagasaki . . . 026864
Museum of the National Center of Afro-American Artists, Boston . . . 042336
Museum of the National Center of Afro-American Artists, Roxbury . . . 047560
Museum of the North American Indian Travelling College, Cornwall . . . 005297
Museum of the Northamptonshire Regiment, Northampton . . . 040594
Museum of the Northern Great Plains, Fort Benton . . . 043890
Museum of the Olive and Greek Olive Oil, Spárti . . . 021477
Museum of the Order of Saint John, London . . . 040234
Museum of the People's Assambly, Cairo . . . 009313
Museum of the Percy Tenantry Volunteers 1798-1814, Alnwick . . . 038495
Museum of the Plains Indian, Browning . . . 042477
Museum of the Red River, Idabel . . 044710
Museum of the Regiments, Calgary 005193
Museum of the Revolution, Nanchang . . . 007193
Museum of the Revolution, Yanan . . 007334
Museum of the Rockies, Bozeman . 042375
Museum of the Royal College of Physicians, London . . . 040235
Museum of the Royal College of Surgeons, London . . . 040181
Museum of the Royal College of Surgeons of Edinburgh, Edinburgh . . . 039404
Museum of the Royal Historical Society of Queensland, Brisbane . . . 000838
Museum of the Royal Leicestershire Regiment, Leicester . . . 039974
Museum of the Royal Military School of Music, Twickenham . . . 041253
Museum of the Royal National Lifeboat Institution, Eastbourne . . . 039362
Museum of the Royal Pharmaceutical Society of Great Britain, London . 040236
Museum of the Royal Regiment of Canada, Toronto . . . 006618
Museum of the Royal Thai Air Force, Bangkok . . . 037883
Museum of The Royal Westminster Regiment Historical Society, New Westminster . . . 006005
Museum of the Sacrifice of the People of Kalavryta, Kalavryta . . . 021299
Museum of the Sarvajanik Wachanalaya, Nasik . . . 022283
Museum of the Shwenawdaw Pagoda, Bago . . . 029057
The Museum of the South Dakota State Historical Society, Pierre . . . 047018
Museum of the Southern Jewish Experience, Jackson . . . 044802
Museum of the Southwest, Midland 045854
Museum of the Statesman Eleftherios Venizelos and the Corresponding Historical Period, Leshi Fileleytheron, Athinai . . . 021201
Museum of the Struggle for National Liberation, Tiranë . . . 000034
Museum of the Tujia and Miao Autonomous Prefecture in Western Hunan, Jishou . . . 007161
Museum of the Underground Prisoners-Acre, Acre . . . 022881
Museum of the University of Connecticut Health Center, Farmington . . . 043818
Museum of the Waxhaws and Andrew Jackson Memorial, Waxhaw 049023
Museum of the Weathersfield Historical Society, Weathersfield . . . 049037
Museum of the Welsh Woollen Industry, Llandysul . . . 040053
Museum of the Western Jesuit Missions, Hazelwood . . . 044496
Museum of the Western Prairie, Altus . . . 041674
Museum of the Weston Historical Society, Weston . . . 049122
Museum of the White Mountains of Samaria, Chania . . . 021228
Museum of the Worcestershire Regiment, Worcester . . . 041444
Museum of Traditional Custumes, Alor Gajah . . . 027943
Museum of Transport, Glasgow . . . 039566
Museum of Transport and Technology, Auckland . . . 030445
Museum of Transportation, Brookline . . . 042454
Museum of Transportation, Saint Louis . . . 047674
Museum of Transportation and Rural Industries, Boyanup . . . 000825
Museum of Tropical Queensland, Townsville . . . 001563
Museum of Ukrainian Arts and Culture, Edmonton . . . 005402
Museum of Unearthed Artifacts, Nagasaki . . . 026865
Museum of Vertebrate Zoology, University of California, Berkeley . . . 042164
Museum of Veterinary, Agricultural University, Guwahati . . . 022139
Museum of Victorian Reed Organs and Harmoniums, Shipley . . . 041013
Museum of Victorian Whitby, Whitby 041365
Museum of Vintage Fashion, Lafayette . . . 045086
The Museum of Vision, San Francisco . . . 047877
Museum of Visual Science and Optometry, Waterloo . . . 006775
Museum of Vítkovice, Ostrava 008553
Museum of Waldensian History, Valdese . . . 048727
Museum of Waterpower, Okehampton . . . 040637
Museum of Wellington, City and Sea, Wellington . . . 030641
Museum of Welsh Life, Saint Fagans . . . 040907
Museum of Western Australian Sport, Claremont, Western Australia . . . 000922
Museum of Western Colorado, Grand Junction . . . 044267
Museum of Witchcraft, Cornwall . . 039143
Museum of Wonders, Imbil . . . 001126
Museum of Woodcarving, Shell Lake . . . 048144
Museum of Woodwork and Ornamental Turning, Ashburton . . . 030427
Museum of Worcester Porcelain, Worcester . . . 041445
Museum of Works by Theophilos, Mytilini . . . 021395
Museum of Works by Theophilos, Varia Lesbos . . . 021516
Museum of Yachting, Newport 046460
Museum of Yarmouth History, Yarmouth . . . 049331
Museum of Yarmukian, Kibbutz Shaar Hagolan . . . 023022
Museum of York County, Rock Hill . 047488
Museum of Yorkshire Dales Lead Mining, Earby . . . 039341
Museum of Yunnan Province, Kunming . . . 007167
Museum of Zoology, Edmonton . . . 005403
Museum of Zoology, University of Massachusetts, Amherst . . . 041693
Museum of Zoology, University of Michigan, Ann Arbor . . . 041734
Museum Okręgowe im. Stanisława Staszica, Piła . . . 032220
Museum Omega, Biel . . . 036951
Museum on the History of Blindness, Watertown . . . 048993
Museum on the Mound, Edinburgh . 039405
Museum on the Seam, Jerusalem . 022970
Museum onder de N.H. Kerk, Elst . . 029557
Museum Onze-Lieve-Vrouw ter Potterie, Stedelijke Musea Brugge, Brugge 003276
Museum Oorlog en Vrede, Breda . . 029351
Museum Orvelte, Orvelte . . . 030009
Museum Oskar Reinhart am Stadtgarten, Winterthur . . . 037727
Museum Ostdeutsche Galerie, Regensburg . . . 019755
Museum Osterzgebirgsgalerie im Schloß, Dippoldiswalde . . . 016723
Museum Otto Ludwig, Eisfeld . . . 016933
Museum Otzberg, Sammlung zur Volkskunst in Hessen, Otzberg . . . 019545
Museum Oud-Asperen, Asperen . . . 029275
Museum Oud Overschie, Rotterdam 030090
Museum Oud-Rijnsburg, Rijnsburg . 030061
Museum Oud Soest, Soest . . . 030171
Museum Oud Vriezenveen, Vriezenveen . . . 030295
Museum Oud Westdorpe, Westdorpe . . . 030322
Museum Oude Boekdrukkunst, Almen . . . 029140

Museum Pachten, Dillingen, Saar 016715
Museum Palagan, Ambarawa 022382
Museum Palthehof, Nieuwleusen 029953
Museum Pancacsila Sakti, Jakarta 022441
Museum Pangeran Diponegoro, Yogyakarta 022539
Museum Papageorgiou, Limenaria 021358
Museum Papiermühle Homburg, Triefenstein 020475
Museum Passeier - Andreas Hofer, San Leonardo in Passiria 025698
Museum Pater Valentinus Paquay-Heilig Paterke, Hasselt 003498
Museum Paul Delvaux, Sint-Idesbald 003754
Museum Paul Tétar Van Elven, Delft 029414
Museum Pemda Balige, Balige 022383
Museum Pemirintah Daerah Grobogan, Purwodadi Grobogan 022497
Museum Pendidikan Islam, Yogyakarta 022540
Museum Perjuangan, Bogor 022405
Museum Perjuangan, Yogyakarta 022541
Museum Perjuangan Bukit Barisan, Medan 022475
Museum Pers, Surakarta 022519
Museum Pers Antara, Jakarta 022442
Museum Petersberg, Petersberg bei Halle, Saale 019592
Museum Pfleggerichtshaus, Abfaltersbach 001653
Museum Pfleggerichtshaus, Schloss Anras, Anras 001691
Museum Plagiarius, Berlin 016144
Museum Plantin-Moretus, Antwerpen 003169
Museum Pos & Giro, Bandung 022392
Museum Prabu Geusan Ulun, Yayasan Pangeran Sumedang, Sumedang 022512
Museum Practice, London 136252
Museum Presidency, Bloemfontein 034560
Museum Professionals Group, Salford 054436
Museum Pugung Ulago Sembah, Donggala 022415
Museum Pura Mangkunegara, Surakarta 022520
Museum Purbakala Mojokerto, Mojokerto 022477
Museum Purbakala Trowulan, Mojokerto 022478
Museum Puri Lukisan, Foundation Ratna Wartha, Ubud 022529
Museum Quality Finishes, New York 046379
Museum Quality Finishes, New York 091104
Museum Quintana - Archäologie in Künzing, Künzing 018433
Museum Raabe-Haus, Eschershausen 017048
Museum Rade am Schloß Reinbek, Sammlung Rolf Italiaander, Hans Spegg, Reinbek 019780
Museum Radio-Wereld, Diever 029483
Museum Radya Pustaka, Surakarta 022521
Museum Raesfeld, Raesfeld 019701
Museum Ratna Wartha, Gianyar 022417
Museum Regiunal, Savognin 037518
Museum Regiunal Surselva Casa Carniec, Ilanz 037198
Museum Reich der Kristalle, Mineralogische Staatssammlung München, München 019090
Museum Reichenau, Reichenau, Baden 019772
Museum Reichenfels, Hohenleuben 017972
Museum Rekor Indonesia, Srondol 022511
Museum Rekor Indonesia Jamu Jago, Semarang 022507
Museum Reksa Artha, Jakarta 022443
Museum Rietberg Zürich, Villa Wesendonck, Zürich 037789
Museum Rijn- en Binnenvaart, Antwerpen 003170
Museum Rijswijk Het Tollenshuis, Rijswijk, Zuid-Holland 030064
Museum Roemervilla, Bad Neuenahr-Ahrweiler 015761
Museum Römervilla, Grenzach-Wyhlen 017529
Museum Rolf Werner, Seebad Bansin 020163
Museum Rufferdinge, Landen 003568
Museum Ruman Bolon, Pematang 022491
Museum Rupelklei, Terhagen 003787
Museum Sacrum, Tiel 030203
Museum Saet en Cruyt, Andijk 029247
Museum Saigerhütte Olbernhau-Kupferhammer, Olbernhau 019463
Museum Salzbütte, Huttwil 037196
Museum Sankt Blasien, Sankt Blasien 019984
Museum Sankt Ingbert, Sankt Ingbert 019988
Museum Sankt Wendel, Mia-Münster-Haus, Sankt Wendel 019996
Museum Saoraja Lapawowoi, Watampone 022531
Museum Sarganserland, Sargans 037510
Museum Sasmita Loka, Yogyakarta 022542
Museum Sasmita Loka A. Yani, Jakarta 022444
Museum Satria Mandala, Jakarta 022445
Museum Scheveningen, Den Haag 029442
Museum Schietkamp-Harskamp, Harskamp 029678
Museum Schloß Ahrensburg, Ahrensburg 015456
Museum Schloß Bernburg, Bernburg 016205
Museum Schloß Burgk, Burgk 016518
Museum Schloss Colditz, Colditz 016586
Museum Schloß Delitzsch, Delitzsch 016661
Museum Schloß Ehrenstein, Ohrdruf 019460
Museum Schloß Erla, Sankt Valentin 002626
Museum Schloss Fasanerie, Hessische Hausstiftung, Eichenzell 016907
Museum Schloss Friedrichsfelde, Stiftung Stadtmuseum Berlin, Berlin 016145
Museum Schloß Glücksburg, Römhild 019868
Museum Schloss Hardenberg, Velbert 020568
Museum Schloss Hellenstein, Heidenheim an der Brenz 017843
Museum Schloss Herzberg, Herzberg am Harz 017906
Museum Schloß Hohenlimburg, Hagen, Westfalen 017626
Museum Schloß Hundshaupten, Egloffstein 016894
Museum Schloß Klippenstein, Radeberg 019695
Museum Schloß Kuckuckstein, Liebstadt 018641
Museum Schloss Kyburg, Kyburg 037227
Museum Schloss Lembeck, Dorsten 016759
Museum Schloss Lichtenberg, Fischbachtal 017125
Museum Schloss Luisium, Kulturstiftung DessauWörlitz, Dessau, Anhalt 016681
Museum Schloß Molsdorf, Molsdorf 018991
Museum Schloss Moritzburg, Moritzburg 018997
Museum Schloß Moritzburg, Zeitz, Elster 021047
Museum Schloss Moyland, Sammlung van der Grinten, Joseph Beuys Archiv des Landes Nordrhein-Westfalen, Bedburg-Hau 015933
Museum Schloss Netzschkau, Netzschkau 019208
Museum Schloß Neu-Augustusburg, Weißenfels 020782
Museum Schloss Neuenburg, Freyburg 017254
Museum Schloss Oberschwappach, Knetzgau 018291
Museum Schloß Pöllau, Pöllau 002445
Museum Schloß Ratibor, Roth, Mittelfranken 019911
Museum Schloß Rheinsberg, Rheinsberg 019824
Museum Schloß Rochlitz, Rochlitz 019854
Museum Schloß Rochsburg, Lunzenau 018753
Museum Schloß Schwarzenberg, Schwarzenberg, Erzgebirge 020134
Museum Schloß Steinheim, Hanau 017744
Museum Schloss Waldegg, Feldbrunnen 037084
Museum Schloß Weesenstein, Müglitztal 019006
Museum Schloß Wetzdorf, Glaubendorf 001895
Museum Schloß Wilhelmsburg, Schmalkalden 020053
Museum Schmelzra, Scuol 037546
Museum Schnütgen, Museen der Stadt Köln, Köln 018336
Museum Schöngrabern, Hollabrunn 002059
Museum Schokland, Ens 029564
Museum School, Arkansas Arts Center, Little Rock 051615
Museum Schwab, Museum für Urgeschichte und Archäologie, Biel 036952
Museum Schwarzes Ross, Hilpoltstein 017926
Museum Schweizer Hotellerie und Tourismus, Zürich 037790
Museum Science and Technology, Jakarta 022446
Museum Sejarah Mesjid Banten, Bogor 022406
Museum Seni, Denpasar 022413
Museum Seni, Jakarta 022447
Museum Seni, Medan 022476
Museum Seni, Padang 022482
Museum Seni Rupa dan Keramik, Jakarta 022448
Museum Sensenwerk, Deutschfeistritz 001777
Museum Sepakat Segenap, Aceh Tenggara 022379
Museum Services Australia, Pymble 123293
Museum Simalungun, Pematangsiantar 022493
Museum Sint Bernardushof, Aduard 029128
Museum Sint Sellian, Sellingen 030145
Museum Siwa Lima, Ambon 009167
Museum Skänninge Rådhus, Skänninge 036574
Museum Slag bij Heiligerlee, Heiligerlee 029706
Museum Slag der Zilveren Helmen, Halen 003483
Museum Slager, 's-Hertogenbosch 029733
Museum Smallingerland, Drachten 029508
Museum Smidt van Gelder, Antwerpen 003171
Museum Soltau, Soltau 020245
Museum Sono Budoyo, Yogyakarta 022543
Museum Sonyine Malige, Halmahera Tengah 009170
Museum Spaans Gouvernement, Maastricht 029896
Museum Specken, Bad Zwischenahn 015845
Museum SPUR Cham, Cham 016551
Museum Stad Appingedam, Appingedam 029260
Museum Stadt Bad Hersfeld, Bad Hersfeld 015716
Museum Stadt Königsberg, Duisburg 016858
Museum Stammertal, Unterstammheim 037657
Museum Stapelen, Boxtel 029343
Museum Stedhûs Sleat, Sloten 030164
Museum Steinarbeiterhaus, Hohburg 017967
Museum Steinmetzhaus, Eggenburg 001809
Museum Stellingwerff-Waerdenhof, Hasselt 003499
Museum Stemmler, Schaffhausen 037523
Museum Stichting van het Rotterdamsche Tramweg Maatschappij, Ouddorp 030022
Museum Stift Admont, Admont 001660
Museum Stift Börstel, Berge bei Quakenbrück 015961
Museum Stoffels Säge-Mühle, Hohenems 002057
Museum Stoomdepot, Rotterdam 030091
Museum Stoomgemaal Winschoten, Winschoten 030336
Museum Studies, Chicago 136564
The Museum Studio and Arts Centre, Nairobi 027429
Museum Suaka Budaya, Surakarta 022522
Museum Subak Bali, Kediri 022461
Museum Sudirman, Magelang 022467
Museum Sulawesi Tengah, Palu 022488
Museum Sumpah Pemuda, Jakarta 022449
Museum Suriname, Amsterdam 029206
Museum Sursilvan, Trun 037645
Museum Swaensteyn, Voorburg 030290
Museum Synagoge Gröbzig, Gröbzig 017545
Museum Synthese, München 019091
Museum 't Coopmanshûs, Franeker 029590
Museum 't Gevang, Doetinchem 029490
Museum 't Kniphof, Essen 003429
Museum 't Nieuwhuys Hoegaarden, Hoegaarden 003514
Museum 't Schilderhuis, Driebergen-Rijsenburg 029510
Museum Takstil, Jakarta 022450
Museum Taman Laut Ancol, Jakarta 022451
Museum Taman Prasati, Jakarta 022452
Museum Taruna Akbari Udarat, Magelang 022468
Museum Tegernseer Tal, Tegernsee 020413
Museum-Telefonzentrale, Magden 037306
Muséum Testut Latarjet, Médicine et d'Anatomie de Lyon, Lyon 012832
Museum Theo Jans, Klarenbeek 029813
Museum Theo Kerg, Schriesheim 020099
Museum Thonet, Stuhlmuseum, Frankenberg, Eder 017144
Museum Tinguely, Basel 036897
Museum Tni A.L. Loka Jala Carana, Surabaya 022517
Museum Ton Schulten, Ootmarsum 030005
Museum Trading Association, Worcester 054295
Museum Transgariep, Philippolis 034696
Museum Tre Kronor, Stockholm 036646
Museum - Treasures from the National Archives, Kew 039859
Museum Trustee Association, Washington 054895
Museum Trusteeship, Washington 136565
Museum Tugu Nasional, Jakarta 022453
Museum Tysmans, Houthalen 003525
Museum und Archiv der Stadt Gronau (Leine), Gronau, Leine 017550
Museum und Besucherbergwerk, Goslar 017487
Museum und Besucherbergwerk der Graphit Kropfmühl AG, Hauzenberg 017809
Museum und Galerie der Stadt, Schwabmünchen 020107
Museum und Kunstsammlung Schloß Hinterglauchau, Glauchau 017428
Museum und Schatzkammer des Deutschen Ordens, Wien 002966
Museum und Stiftung Anton Geiselhart, Münsingen 019137
Museum U.P.T. Balitung, Tanjungpandan 022526
Museum Uranbergbau, Schlema 020036
Museum Uslar, Uslar 020553
Museum Valkenheide, Maarsbergen 029885
Museum Van Bommel Van Dam, Venlo 030268
Museum van de Abdij van Roosenberg, Waasmunster 003837
Museum van de Boerenkrijg, Berlare 003230
Museum van de Kanselarij der Nederlandse Orden, Apeldoorn 029254
Museum van de Koninklijke Marechaussee, Buren, Gelderland 029373
Museum van de Kruisbooggilde Sint-Joris, Brugge 003277
Museum van de Onze-Lieve-Vrouwkerk, Brugge 003278

Museum van de Sint-Jakobskerk, Antwerpen 003172
Museum van de Stichting Bisdom van Vliet, Haastrecht 029663
Museum van de Twintigste Eeuw, Hoorn 029771
Museum van de Willebroekse Vaart, Willebroek 003858
Museum van Deinze en de Leiestreek, Deinze 003391
Museum van Egmond, Egmond aan Zee 029533
Museum Van Gerwen-Lemmens, Valkenswaard 030252
Museum van Hedendaagse Kantwerken, Sint-Truiden 003767
Museum van Hedendaagse Kunst, Gent 003469
Museum van Hedendaagse Kunst Antwerpen, Antwerpen 003173
Museum Van Hemessen, Woubrugge 030353
Museum van het Abtenhuis, Geraardsbergen 003475
Museum van het Ambacht, Den Haag 029443
Museum van het Groot Begijnhof, Sint-Amandsberg 003753
Museum van het Heilig Bloed, Baseliek van het Heilig Bloed, Brugge 003279
Museum van het Kamp van Beverlo, Leopoldsburg 003577
Museum van het Nederlandse Uurwerk, Zaandam 030363
Museum van het Vlaams Studentenleven, Leuven 003579
Museum van Knipkunst, Westerbork 030324
Museum van Lien, Fijnaart 029588
Museum Van Loon, Amsterdam 029207
Museum van Zwerfstenen in de Rosmolen, Zeddam 030376
Museum Veeteelt en K.I., Beers bij Cuyk 029298
Museum Veluwezoom, Doorwerth 029500
Museum Verbindingsdienst, Ede 029523
Museum Vermessen in Bayern - von der Messlatte zur Antenne, München 019092
Museum Viadrina; Museum Junge Kunst, Frankfurt/Oder 017206
Museum Victoria, Melbourne Museum, Carlton South 000899
Museum Viechtach, Viechtach 020582
Museum Villa Haiss, Museum für Zeitgenössische Kunst, Zell am Harmersbach 021049
Museum Villa Rot - Kunstsammlung Hoenes-Stiftung, Burgrieden 016522
Museum Villa Rustica, Möckenlohe 018966
Museum Villa Sarabodis, Gerolstein 017385
Museum Villa Stahmer, Georgsmarienhütte 017369
Museum Villa Stuck, München 019093
Museum Village, Monroe 045972
Museum Vlaamse Minderbroeders, Sint-Truiden 003768
Museum Vleeshuis, Antwerpen 003174
Museum Vliegbasis Deelen, Deelen 029403
Museum Volunteers of the Philippines, Dasmariñas 053975
Museum von Abgüssen und Originalsammlung, Institut für Klassische Archäologie der Universität, Innsbruck 002090
Museum voor Anesthesie Verantare, Antwerpen 003175
Museum voor Communicatie, Den Haag 029444
Museum voor de Geschiedenis van de Wetenschappen, Gent 003462
Museum voor de Oudere Technieken, Grimbergen 003479
Museum voor Figuratieve Kunst de Buitenplaats, Eelde 029527
Museum voor Folklore, Zottegem 003873
Museum voor Geschiedenis van de Geneeskunde, Gent 003463
Museum voor Hedendaagse Kunst, 's-Hertogenbosch 029734
Museum voor Heem- en Oudheidkunde, Kontich 003555
Museum voor Heem- en Volkskunde, Wenduine 003849
Museum voor Heemkunde Almelo, Almelo 029137
Museum voor het Kruideniersbedrijf, Utrecht 030232
Museum voor het Radiozendamateurisme Jan Corver, Budel 029364
Museum voor Industriele Archeologie en Textiel, Gent 003464
Museum voor Keramiek Pablo Rueda Lara, Rotterdam 030092
Museum voor Kerkelijke Kunst, Workum 030350
Museum voor Kerkelijke Kunst Sint-Carolus, Antwerpen 003176
Museum voor Klederdracht en Oud Speelgoed, Warnsveld 030308
Museum voor Moderne Kunst, Arnhem 029270
Museum voor Moderne Kunst Oostende (PMMK), Oostende 003686
Museum voor Naaldkunst, Wedde 030315
Museum voor Natuur- en Wildbeheer, Nederlands Jachtmuseum, Doorwerth 029501
Museum voor Plaatselijke Geschiedenis, Nieuwpoort 003674
Museum voor Religieuze Kunst, Uden 030213
Museum voor Schone Kunsten, Oostende 003687
Museum voor Schone Kunsten Gent, Gent 003465
Museum voor Sierkunst en Vormgeving, Gent 003452
Museum voor Stenen Voorwerpen, Gent 003470
Museum voor Torhouts Aardewerk, Torhout 003803
Museum voor Valse Kunst, Vledder 030279
Museum voor Volkskunde, Dendermonde 003393
Museum voor Volkskunde, Stedelijke Musea Brugge, Brugge 003280
Museum voor Vrede en Geweldloosheid, Amsterdam 029208
Museum voor Zuid- en Noord-Beveland, Goes 029615
Museum Voswinckelshof, Dinslaken 016721
Museum Vrolik, Amsterdam 029209
Museum Waemena, Irian Jaya 022420
Museum Wald und Umwelt, Ebersberg 016873
Museum Waldhof, Bielefelder Kunstverein e.V., Bielefeld 016239
Museum Wanua Paksinanta, Manado 022471
Museum Wasseralfingen, Aalen 015430
Museum Wasseramt, Halten 037177
Museum Wasserburg, Kunst- und kulturgeschichtliche Sammlungen der Stadt, Wasserburg am Inn 020687
Museum Wasserburg Anholt, Isselburg 018098
Museum Wateringhuis, Lommel 003614
Museum Watersnood 1953, Ouwerkerk 030034
Museum Wattens, Wattens 002811
Museum Wayang, Jakarta 022454
Museum West, San Francisco 119747
Museum West, San Jose 119858
Museum Wierdenland, Ezinge 029587
Museum Wiesbaden, Wiesbaden 020877
Museum Wildberg, Wildberg, Württemberg 020888
Museum Willem van Haren, Heerenveen 029692
Museum Willet-Holthuysen, Amsterdam 029210
Museum Wolfhalden, Wolfhalden 037739
Museum Wolfram von Eschenbach, Wolframs-Eschenbach 020959
Museum Woning voor antieke Horlogerie, Mechelen 003633
Museum Würth, Künzelsau 018432
Museum Wurzen mit Ringelnatzsammlung, Wurzen 021024
Museum Wustrow, Wustrow, Niedersachsen 021029
Museum Wuyts-Van Campen en Baron Caroly, Lier 003603
Museum Yadnya, Tangawi 022524
The Museum Yamato Bunkakan, Nara 026894
Museum Year, Boston 136566
Museum Yerseke, Yerseke 030358
Museum Yogya Kembali, Yogyakarta 022544
Museum Zahal, Hakirya 022931
Museum Zeitreise Mensch, Cortaccia 023975
Museum Zella-Mehlis, Zella-Mehlis 021054
Museum Ziegelei Lage, Westfälisches Industriemuseum, Lage, Lippe 018459
Museum Zitadelle, Stadtgeschichtliches Museum Jülich, Jülich 018130
Museum zu Allerheiligen, Schaffhausen 037524
Museum zum Anfassen, Ostseebad Binz 019526
Museum Zum Arabischen Coffe Baum, Stadtgeschichtliches Museum Leipzig, Leipzig 018584
Museum zum Schiff, Laufenburg 037236
Museum zur brandenburg-preußischen Geschichte/ Zinnfigurenmuseum, Gusow 017609
Museum zur Dresdner Frühromantik im Kügelgen-Haus, Museum der Dresdner Romantik, Dresden 016793
Museum zur Geschichte der Juden in Kreis und Stadt Heilbronn, Obersulm 019424
Museum zur Geschichte Hohenheims, Stuttgart 020360
Museum zur Geschichte von Christen und Juden, Laupheim 018533
Museum zur Kloster- und Stadtgeschichte, Steinheim an der Murr 020307
Museum zur Ronmühle, Schötz 037536
Museum Zwaantje Hans Stockman's Hof, Schoonebeek 030140
Museumboerderij, Leens 029833
Museumboerderij, Paasloo 030038
Museumboerderij, Staphorst 030179
Museumboerderij de Karstenhoeve, Ruinerwold 030115
Museumboerderij de Tip, Herveld 029741
Museumboerderij de Zwemkolk, Markelo 029907
Museumboerderij Erve Hofman, Hellendoorn 029716
Museumboerderij Eungs Schöppe, Markelo 029908
Museumboerderij Gilde Koat, Zeddam 030377
Museumboerderij New Greenwich Village, Zuidwolde, Drenthe 030400
Museumboerderij Scholten, Den Ham 029461
Museumboerderij Tante Jaantje, Callantsoog 029381
Museumboerderij Vreeburg, Schagen 030124
Museumboerderij Wendezoele, Ambt-Delden 029143
Museumboerderij Westfrisia, Hoogwoud 029769
Museumbrief, Antwerpen 135604
Museumbrouwerij de Hemel, Nijmegen 029962
Museumbrouwerij De Roos, Hilvarenbeek 029746
Museumgemaal Caners, 's-Hertogenbosch 029735
Museumhaven Zeeland, Zierikzee 030389
'T Museumke, Handel 029667
Museumkelder Derlon, Maastricht 029897
Museumkerk Sint Pieter, Rekem 003711
Museumleven, Antwerpen 135605
Museummolen, Schermerhorn 030128
Museummolen de Nieuwe Palmboom, Schiedam 030131
Museummolen Jan Pol, Dalen 029394
Museumproject AZG, Groningen 029641
Museums Abashirikangoku, Abashiri 026401
Museums Alaska, Anchorage 054896
Museums and Galleries Disability Association, Hove 054437
Museums and Study Collection, Central Saint Martins College of Art and Design, London 040237
Museums Association, London 054438
Museums Association of India, Delhi 053702
Museums Association of Namibia, MAN, Windhoek 053874
Museums Association of Nigeria, Lagos 053936
The Museums Association of Pakistan, Karachi 053965
Museums Association of Saskatchewan, Regina 052758
Museums Association of the Caribbean, Bridgetown 052636
Museums at Stony Brook, Stony Brook 048377
Museums Australia, Civic Square 052479
Museums-Everten Johanne Dan, Ribe 009066
Museums-Gutshof Sonnekalb, Kleinheringen 018279
Museums in Essex Committee, Chelmsford 054439
Museums Journal, London 136253
Museums-Journal, Berichte aus den Museen, Schlössern und Sammlungen in Berlin und Potsdam. Zugleich 'Berliner Museen, 6. Folge', Berlin 135804
Museums Newsletter aktuell, Köln 135805
Museums North, Northern Federation of Museums and Art Galleries, Hartlepool 054440
Museums of Filipinana and Rizaliana, Sampaloc 031780
The Museums of Oglebay Institute, Wheeling 049140
Museums of South Lanarkshire, Ferniegair 039496
Museums- und Kunstverein Osnabrück e.V., Osnabrück 053498
Museums Weapons Group, Leeds 054441
Museums Yearbook, London 136254
Museumsakademie, Berlin 050029
Museumsanlage Kulturstiftung Landkreis Osterholz, Osterholz-Scharmbeck 019509
Museumsbahn Steyrtal, Steyr 002703
Museumsberg Flensburg, Städtische Museen und Sammlungen für den Landesteil Schleswig, Flensburg 017130
Museumsbibliothek, Stiftung Luthergedenkstätten in Sachsen-Anhalt, Lutherstadt Eisleben 018757
Museumsboerderij Oud Noordwijk, Noordwijk, Zuid-Holland 029974
Museumsbygningen Kunstautioner, København 120872
Museumscenter Hanstholm, Hanstholm 008890
Museumschip Mercuur, Den Haag 029445
Museumsdorf Bayerischer Wald, Tittling 020445
Museumsdorf Cloppenburg, Niedersächsisches Freilichtmuseum, Cloppenburg 016572
Museumsdorf Düppel, Stiftung Stadtmuseum Berlin, Berlin 016146
Museumsdorf Krumbach, Krumbach 002182
Museumsdorf und Technisches Denkmal, Baruth, Mark 015892
Museumsdorf Volksdorf mit Spiekerhus, Hamburg 017717
Museumseisenbahn Payerbach-Hirschwang, Hirschwang 002046
Museumseisenbahn Schwalm-Knüll, Fritzlar 017276
Museumsfeuerschiff Amrumbank/Deutsche Bucht, Emden 016959

Museumsfreunde Münnerstadt e.V., Münnerstadt 053499
Museumsfriedhof Tirol, Kramsach . 002168
Museumsgalerie, Altomünster 015522
Museumsgalerie Allerheiligenkirche, Mühlhäuser Museen, Mühlhausen, Thüringen 019014
Museumsgården, Læsø 009006
Museumsgesellschaft, Zürich 054202
Museumshäuschen, Krebes 018395
Museumshof, Bad Oeynhausen . . . 015766
Museumshof, Neuruppin 019269
Museumshof, Rahden 019702
Museumshof, Roßtal 019891
Museumshof am Sonnenlück, Heimatmuseum Erkner, Erkner . . 017026
Museumshof auf dem Braem, Museen der Stadt Gescher, Gescher 017395
Museumshof Emmerstedt, Helmstedt 017867
Museumshof Ernst Koch, Silstedt . . 020210
Museumshof Ernst Koch, Wernigerode 020815
Museumshof-Galerie, Oldenburg in Holstein 019465
Museumshof Historischer Moorhof Augustendorf, Gnarrenburg 017437
Museumshof Lerchennest - Friedrich-der-Große-Museum, Sinsheim 020222
Museumshof und Heimatmuseum, Meisdorf 018887
Museumskirche Sankt Katharinen, Museen für Kunst und Kulturgeschichte der Hansestadt Lübeck, Lübeck 018725
Museumskunde, Berlin 135806
Museumsland Donauland Strudengau, Mitterkirchen 002318
Museumslandschaft Deilbachtal, Essen 017076
Museumslogger AE7 Stadt Emden, Emden 016960
Museumsmühle Hasbergen, Delmenhorst 016665
Museumsmühle mit heimatkundlicher Sammlung, Varel 020560
Museumsnytt, Oslo 136015
Museumspädagogische Beratung, Staatliche Museen Kassel, Kassel 018196
Museumspädagogische Gesellschaft e.V., Köln 053500
Museumspark, Rüdersdorf bei Berlin 019939
Museumspoorlijn Star, Stadskanaal 030177
Museumsscheune, Bachmann-Museum Bremervörde, Bremervörde 016443
Museumsscheune Fränkische Schweiz, Hollfeld 017990
Museumsscheune Kremmen, Kremmen 018402
Museumsschiff FMS Gera, Bremerhaven 016432
Museumsschiff Mannheim des Landesmuseums für Technik und Arbeit, Mannheim 018808
Museumsschiff STÖR, Holzminden . 017996
Museumsstadl, Bernried, Niederbayern 016207
Museumsstiftung Post und Telekommunikation, Bonn 016332
Museumsstube, Eisgarn 001828
Museumsstube Obermeiser, Calden 016537
Museumstjenesten, Viborg 052860
Museumstoomtram Hoorn-Medemblik, Hoorn 029772
Museumsverband, Verband österreichischer Museen, Galerien, Schau- und Studiensammlungen, Pram 052578
Museumsverband Baden-Württemberg e.V., Esslingen 053501
Museumsverband des Landes Brandenburg e.V., Potsdam 053502
Museumsverband für Niedersachsen und Bremen e.V., Hannover . 053503, 135807
Museumsverband in Mecklenburg-Vorpommern e.V., Güstrow 053504
Museumsverband Sachsen-Anhalt e.V., Bernburg 053505
Museumsverband Schleswig-Holstein e.V., Rendsburg 053506
Museumsverband Thüringen e.V., Gera 053507
Museumsverbund Südniedersachsen e.V., Göttingen 053508
Museumsverein Aachen, Aachen . . 053509
Museumsverein Düren e.V., Düren . 053510
Museumsverein für das Fürstentum Lüneburg, Lüneburg 053511
Museumsverein Hameln e.V., Hameln 053512
Museumsverein Kassel e.V., Schloß Wilhelmshöhe, Kassel 053513
Museumsverein Mönchengladbach e.V, Mönchengladbach 053514
Die Museumswelt, Wiener Neustadt 003035
Museumszentrum Lorsch, Lorsch . . 018686
Museumszentrum-Rehau, Rehauer,-Schlesicher,-Ascher Heimatstuben und Roßbacher Weberstuben, Rehau . 019766
Museumvisie, Amsterdam 136004
Museumwerf 't Kromhout, Amsterdam 029211
Museumwinkel Albert Heijn, Zaandam 030364
Museumwoning de Kiefhoek, Rotterdam 030093
Museus de História Natural e Etnologia Indígena, Centro de Ensino Superior, Academia SVD, Juiz de Fora 004175
Musexpo, Clairfayts 011384
Muséyé Chay-e Lahijan, Lahijan . . . 022577
Muséyé Honarha-ye Melli, Teheran 022634
Muséyé Kerman, Kerman 022568
Muséyé Mardom Shenassi, Teheran 022635
Musgrave Bickford, Crediton 084107
Mushakoji Saneatsu Memorial Hall, Chofu 026447
Musiani, Nicoletta, Bologna 075094
Music Box of Zami Museum, Metula 023029
The Music House, Acme 041575
Music Lovers, Cincinnati 142321
Music Museum, Rīga 027759
Musica Kremsmünster, Musikinstrumentenmuseum, Kremsmünster 002177
Musical Box Society International Museum, Norwalk 046563
Musical Instruments Museum, Jerusalem 022971
Musical Museum, London 040238
Musical Museum of Macedonia, Thessaloniki 021501
Musical Treasures, Los Angeles . . . 089848
Musical Wonder House, Wiscasset . 049270
Mus'ign, Bad Essen 015697
Mus'ign - Anthologie Quartett Designmuseum, Preußisch Oldendorf 019671
Musik-Antiquariat, Zentralantiquariat Leipzig, Leipzig 139399
Musik- und Wintersportmuseum, Klingenthal 018284
Musikantiquariat zum Grossen C, Oberried 139620
Musikhistorische Sammlung Jehle, Albstadt 015469
Musikhistorisk Museum og Carl Claudius' Samling, København 008979
Musikinstrumenten-Ausstellung des Händel-Hauses, Halle, Saale 017668
Musikinstrumenten-Museum, Markneukirchen 018837
Musikinstrumenten-Museum, Staatliches Institut für Musikforschung-Stiftung Preußischer Kulturbesitz, Berlin . . 016147
Musikinstrumenten-Museum der Universität Leipzig (Interim), Leipzig 018585
Musikinstrumenten- und Puppenmuseum, Goslar 017488
Musikinstrumentenmuseum, Sankt Gilgen 002587
Musikinstrumentenmuseum, Münchner Stadtmuseum, München 019094
Musikinstrumentenmuseum Lißberg, Ortenberg, Hessen 019485
Musikinstrumentensammlung, Friedrich-Alexander-Universität Erlangen-Nürnberg, Erlangen 017034
Musikinstrumentensammlung der Universität, Göttingen 017470
Musikinstrumentensammlung Hans und Hede Grumbt Wasserburg Haus Kemnade, Hattingen 017796
Musikmuseet, Stockholm 036647
Musikmuseum, Historisches Museum Basel, Basel 036898
Musikvariatet, Oslo 140703
Musin, Genevieve, Larressingle . . . 063541
MuSiS - Verein zur Unterstützung der Museen und Sammlungen in der Steiermark, Graz 052579
Muskee, Thim, Groningen 078430
Muskegon County Museum, Muskegon 046106
Muskegon Museum of Art, Muskegon 046107
Muskogee War Memorial Park and Military Museum, Muskogee 046110
Muskoka Antique Show, Port Carling 093627
Muskoka Heritage Place, Huntsville 005630
Muskoka Lakes Museum, Port Carling 006175
Musolff, Claudia, Münster 126505
Musolini, Tommaso, Torino 134697
Musquodoboit Railway Museum, Musquodoboit Harbour 005973
Mussallem, Jacksonville 089437
Mussallem, Phoenix 091756
Mussard, C.A, Nyon 141286
Mussard, Nathalie, Paris 066316
Musselshell Valley Historical Museum, Roundup 047557
Musselwhite, Carol, Wilton, Salisbury 087159
Mussenden & Son, G.B., Bournemouth 083601
Mußler, Peter-Paul, Wiesbaden 074415
Musta Taide, Helsinki 135678
Mustafa Kamil Museum, Cairo 009314
Mustansiriya School Collections, Baghdad 022664
The Mustard Seed Gallery, Cleethorpes 112875
Mustard Shop Museum, Norwich . . 040608
Mustialan Maataloushistoriallinen Museo, Mustiala 009886
Musuemsverein Bahnhofmuseum e.V, Benneckenstein 015948
Musumeci, Quart 134664
Musumeci, Vincenzo, Catania 127272
Muswellbrook Regional Arts Centre, Muswellbrook 001304
Muszyńska, Magdalena, Gdynia . . . 079597
Muszyński, Marcin, Poznań 129064
Mutare Museum, Mutare 049589
Mutascio Ronconi, Verona 077013
MUTEC Museo Pinacoteca Comunale, Barletta 023348
Mutel, René, Oullins 065315
Muthesius-Gesellschaft e.V., Gesellschaft zur Förderung der bildenden Künste der Muthesius-Hochschule, Kiel 053515
Muthesius-Hochschule, Fachhochschule für Kunst und Gestaltung, Kiel 050151
Mutlu Sanat Odasi, İstanbul 112340
Mutscher, Hartmut & Eva, Neißeaue 126522
Mutsen en Poffermuseum Sint-Paulusgasthuis, Sint Oedenrode . 030154
Muttart Art Gallery, Calgary 005194
Mutter Museum, College of Physicians of Philadelphia, Philadelphia 046965
Mutterbusch, Hamminkeln 071367
Muttner, Le Landeron 130060
Muttner, Marcel, Le Landeron 082522
Muttonchop, Petworth 142001
Mutua Museum, Imphal 022171
Muurhuizen Antiek, Amersfoort . . . 077748
Muuri, R., Helsinki 060559
Muurlan Kotiseutumuseo, Muurla . . 009887
Muurtooi, Arnhem 078057
Muurtooi, Arnhem 107856, 128571
Muurtooi, Leeuwarden 078553
Muuruveden Kotiseutumuseo, Muuruvesi 009888
Muuseum, Tartu 009421
Muwayire, Edward, Cape Town . . . 110028
Muze-ha, Edare-ye Koll-e Ganjine-ha va Namayeshgah, Teheran 135850
Muzeal Conacul Bellu, Urlaţi 032965
Muzeal de Istorie, Târgovişte 032945
Muzealnictwo, Warszawa 136029
Muzeen Kat Kooperativna Pečatnica Rabotnik, Veliko Tărnovo 004934
Muzeen Kat Parva Socialističeska Sbirka, Veliko Tărnovo 004935
Muzei Geroïčnoï Oborony i Vyzvolennja Sevastopolja, Sevastopol 038387
Muzei Permskogo Gosudarstvennogo Universiteta, Perm 033649
Muzej, Pliska 004787
Muzej 700 let - Landskrona, Nevskoe Ustje, Nienšanc, Sankt-Peterburg 033772
Muzej A Muzy ne Molčali, Sankt-Peterburg 033773
Muzej A.A. Kiseleva, Tuapse 033969
Muzej Afričke Umetnosti-Zbirka Vede i Dr. Zdravka Pečara, Zbirka Vede i Dr. Zdravka Pečara, Beograd 034156
Muzej Aleksandăr Stambolijski, Slavovica 004833
Muzej Aleksandăr Stambolijski, Sofia 004854
Muzej Al'manachu Rusalki Dnistrovoï, Lvivs'ka Galereja Mystectv, Lviv . 038349
Muzej Alpinizma, Turizma i Istorii Kurorta Teberda, Teberda 033945
Muzej Antropologii i Etnografii im. Petra Velikogo (Kunstkamera), Sankt-Peterburg 033774
Muzej AO Petrozavod, Sankt-Peterburg 033775
Muzej Archeologii, Institut jazyka, literatury i istorii Komi naučnogo centra Rossijskoj akademii nauk, Syktyvkar 033923
Muzej Archeologii i Etnografii, Dal'nevostočnyj gosudarstvennyj universitet, Vladivostok 034051
Muzej Archeologii i Ėtnografii, Otdel Narodov Ufimskogo Naučnogo Centra Rossijskoj Akademii Nauk, Ufa . . 033993
Muzej Archeologii i Ėtnografii, Syktyvkarskij gosudarstvennyj universitet, Syktyvkar 033924
Muzej Archeologii Moskvy, Moskva 033436
Muzej Archeologii Prikamja, Perm . 033650
Muzej 'Archeologija, Ėtnografija i Ėkologija Sibiri' Kemerovskogo Gosudarstvennogo Universiteta, Kemerovo 033258
Muzej Architektury Byta Narodov Nižegorodskogo Povolžja, Nižnij Novgorod 033554
Muzej Architektury i Archeologii Vez Burana, Čujsk 027637
Muzej Architektury i Stroitelstva, Samara 033719
Muzej-Archiv D.I. Mendeleeva, Sankt-Peterburg 033776
Muzej Arsenal - Muzej Velikoj Otečestvennoj Vojny, Voronežskij oblastnoj kraevedčeskij muzej, Voronež 034079
Muzej Aviacii Severa, Archangelsk . 032995
Muzej Avtogravov imeni Imperatora Nikolaja Vtorogo, Novosibirsk 033585
Muzej Avtomobilnogo Transporta, Joint Stock Company Avtoprogress, Kursk 033321
Muzej Baki Urmanče, Kazan 033238
Muzej Belišče, Belišče 007697
Muzej Boevogo i Trudovogo Podviga 1941-1945, Saransk 033846
Muzej Boevoj Slavy, Astrachanskij Muzej-zapovednik, Astrachan 033007
Muzej E.A. Boratynskogo, Nacionalnyj muzej Respubliki Tatarstan, Kazan 033239
Muzej Bosanske Krajine, Banja Luka 003926
Muzej Bratjev Tkačevych, Brjanskij oblastnoj chudožestvennyj muzej, Brjansk 033052
Muzej Brdovec, Savski Marof 007787

Muzej Brjanskij Les, Brjansk 033053
Muzej Budva, Budva 034179
Muzej V.I. Čapaeva, Čuvašskij Nacionalnyj Muzej, Čeboksary 033065
Muzej Carskoselskaja Kollekcija, Puškin 033685
Muzej Cerkov Dekabristov, Oblastnoj kraevedčeskij muzej im. A.A. Kuznecova, Čita 033094
Muzej Cerkov Petra i Pavla, Tjumen 033949
Muzej Cetinjske Krajine, Sinj 007793
Muzej Chrama Christa Spasitelja, Moskva 033437
Muzej Cirkovogo Iskusstva, Sankt-Peterburg 033777
Muzej-čitalnja N.V. Fëdorova, Moskva 033438
Muzej-čitalnja na Nacionalnych Jazykach, Penza 033632
Muzej Čovek i negovoto Zdrave, Varna 004914
Muzej V.I. Dalja, Moskva 033439
Muzej Dekabristov, Minusinsk 033362
Muzej Dekabristov, Moskva 033440
Muzej Dekabristov - Dom Trubeckogo, Irkutsk 033160
Muzej Dekabristov - Dom Volkonskich, Irkutskij oblastnoj kraevedčeskij muzej, Irkutsk 033161
Muzej Dekorativno-prikladnogo Iskusstva, Sankt-Peterburgskaja Gosudarstvennaja Chudožestvenno- promyšlennaja Akademija, Sankt-Peterburg 033778
Muzej Dekorativno-prikladnogo Iskusstva Urala, Čeljabinsk 033069
Muzej Dekoratyvno-prykladnogo Mystectva, Sums'kyj chudožnij muzej im. N. Onac'kogo, Sumy 038398
Muzej Derevjannogo Zodčestva Malye Karely, Archangelsk 032996
Muzej Detskogo Tvorčestva, Sankt-Peterburg 033779
Muzej Detstva A.M. Gorkogo - Domik Kaširina, Gosudarstvennyj Literaturnyj Muzej A.M. Gorkogo, Nižnij Novgorod 033555
Muzej-Diorama Orlovskaja Nastupatelnaja Operacija, Orlovskij oblastnoj kraevedčeskij muzej, Orël 033609
Muzej Diplomatičeskogo Korpusa, Vologda 034070
Muzej Dom Mašarova, Tjumenskij oblastnoj kraevedčeskij muzej im. I.Ja. Slovcova, Tjumen 033950
Muzej Dominikanskog Samostana, Bol 007702
Muzej Družba na Narodite ot 1944 g., Varna 004915
Muzej A.A. Durova, Taganrogskij gosudarstvennyj literaturnyj i istoriko-architekturnyj muzej-zapovednik, Taganrog 033930
Muzej Durylina S.N., Korolev 033283
Muzej Dvorec A.D. Menšikova, Gosudarstvennyj Ėrmitaž, otdel istorii russkoj kultury, Sankt-Peterburg . 033780
Muzej Ekslibrisa, Moskva 033441
Muzej Emfiedžieva Kăšta, Istoričeskij Muzej, Kjustendil 004723
Muzej Etnografičeskogo Kostjuma na Kuklach, Moskva 033442
Muzej Ėtnografii, Istorii i Kultury Narodov Baškortostana, Ufa 033994
Muzej-Filial Nadi Ruševoj, Tuvinskij Respublikanskij Kraevedčeskij Muzej im. Aldan Maadyr, Kyzyl 033323
Muzej Filiki Eterija, Odes'kyj istoriko-krajeznavčyj muzej, Odesa 038369
Muzej Ford i Bălgarija, Sofia 004855
Muzej Franjevačkog Samostana, Rovinj 007784
Muzej Franjevačkog Samostana Košljun, Punat 007778
Muzej Gabdulla Tukaja, Nacionalnyj muzej Respubliki Tatarstan, Kazan 033240
Muzej-Galerija Kavadarci, Kavadarci 027912
Muzej Geologii, Čeljabinskij oblastnoj kraevedčeskij muzej, Čeljabinsk . 033070
Muzej Geologii Centralnoj Sibirii, Krasnojarsk 033300
Muzej Geologii, Nefti i Gaza, Tjumenskij oblastnoj kraevedčeskij muzej im. I.Ja. Slovcova, Tjumen 033951
Muzej Georgi Velčev, Varna 004916
Muzej Get'manstva, Kyïv 038306
Muzej Glavna Kvartira na Ruskata Armija 1877-1878, Pordim 004800
Muzej A.M. Gorkogo, Moskva 033443
Muzej Goroda Jurjevca, Jurjevec . . 033209
Muzej Goroda Penzy, Penzenskij gosudarstvennyj obedinennyj kraevedčeskij muzej, Penza 033633
Muzej Gorodskaja Duma, Tjumenskij oblastnoj kraevedčeskij muzej im. I.Ja. Slovcova, Tjumen 033952
Muzej Gosudarstvennogo Akademičeskogo Bolšogo Teatra Rossii, Moskva . . 033444
Muzej Gosudarstvennogo Akademičeskogo Malogo Teatra, Moskva 033445
Muzej Gosudarstvennogo Akademičeskogo Marijnskogo Teatra Opery i Baleta, Sankt-Peterburg 033781
Muzej Gosudarstvennogo Akademičeskogo Teatra Opery i Baleta imeni Mussorgskogo, Sankt-Peterburg . 033782
Muzej Gosudarstvennogo Centralnogo Teatra Kukol pod Rukovodstvom Narodnogo Artista S.V. Obrazcova, Moskva 033446
Muzej Gosudarstvennogo Prirodnogo Nacionalnogo Parka Losinogo Ostrova, Moskva 033447
Muzej Grada, Šibenik 007791
Muzej Grada Beograda, Beograd . . 034157
Muzej Grada Koprivnice, Koprivnica 007737
Muzej Grada Novog Sada, Novi Sad 034223
Muzej Grada Perasta, Perast 034234
Muzej Grada Rijeke, Rijeka 007780
Muzej Grada Splita, Split 007802
Muzej Grada Trogira, Trogir 007813
Muzej Grada Zagreba, Zagreb 007849
Muzej Grada Zenice, Zenica 003948
Muzej Gradostroitelstva i Byta Taganroga, Taganrogskij gosudarstvennyj literaturnyj i istoriko-architekturnyj muzej-zapovednik, Taganrog 033931
Muzej Grebnych Vidov Sporta, Moskva 033448
Muzej Hamza Hakim-Žade Niazy, Fergana 049390
Muzej Hercegovine, Mostar 003933
Muzej Hrvatske Književnosti i Kazališne Umjetnosti, Zagreb 007850
Muzej Hrvatskih Arheoloških Spomenika, Split 007803
Muzej Hvarske Baštine, Hvar 007726
Muzej i Galerija Bitola, Bitola 027911
Muzej i Obščestvennyj Centr Mir, Progress, Prava Čeloveka im. Andreja Sacharova, Moskva 033449
Muzej I.A. Bunina, Gosudarstvennyj literaturnyj muzej im. I.S. Turgeneva, Orël 033610
Muzej Igora Stravinskogo, Ustyloog 038404
Muzej Igorja Talkova, Moskva 033450
Muzej im. S.M. Kirova, Sankt-Peterburg 033783
Muzej im. B.M. Kustodieva, Kostromskij gosudarstvennyj obedinennyj chudožestvennyj muzej, Ostrovskoe 033622
Muzej im. N.A. Ostrovskogo, Moskva 033451
Muzej-institut Semji Rerichov, Sankt-Peterburg 033784
Muzej Instituta Biologii Morja, Dal'nevostočnoe otd. Rossijskoj Akademii Nauk, Vladivostok 034052
Muzej Internacionalnoj Družby, Saransk 033847
Muzej Iskusstva Narodov Vostoka, Moskva 033452
Muzej Istične Bosně, Tuzla 003945
Muzej Istorii Aksaja, Aksaj 032974
Muzej Istorii Architektury i Architekturnogo Obrazovanija Sibiri, Novosibirskaja architekturno-chudožestvennaja akademija, Novosibirsk 033586
Muzej Istorii Architektury i Promyšlennoj Techniki Urala, Ekaterinburg 033117
Muzej Istorii Burjatii im. M.N. Changalova, Ulan-Udė 034001
Muzej Istorii Dal'nevostočnoj Morskoj Akademii im. G.I. Nevel'skogo, Vladivostok 034053
Muzej Istorii Doma XIX-XX vekov, Tjumen 033953
Muzej Istorii Ekaterinburga, Ekaterinburg 033118
Muzej Istorii g. Stavropolja, Stavropol 033910
Muzej Istorii Goroda Irkutska, Irkutsk 033162
Muzej Istorii Goroda Joškar-Oly, Joškar-Ola 033203
Muzej Istorii Goroda-Kurorta Soči, Soči 033889
Muzej Istorii Goroda Nabereżnye Čelny, Nacionalnyj muzej respubliki Tatarstan, Nabereżnye Čelny 033538
Muzej Istorii Goroda Šlisselburga, Šlisselburg 033873
Muzej Istorii Goroda Tjumeni, Tjumenskij oblastnoj kraevedčeskij muzej im. I.Ja. Slovcova, Tjumen 033954
Muzej Istorii i Kultury Goroda Votkinska, Votkinsk 034086
Muzej Istorii i Kultury Moskovskogo Rajona, Nižnij Novgorod 033556
Muzej Istorii i Kultury Srednego Prikamja, Sarapul 033851
Muzej Istorii Izučenija i Osvoenija Evropejskogo Severa, Apatity . . . 032988
Muzej Istorii Jaroslavlja, Jaroslavskij gosudarstvennyj istoriko-architekturnyj i chudožestvennyj muzej-zapovednik, Jaroslavl 033197
Muzej Istorii Kamnereznogo i Juvelirnogo Iskusstva, Ekaterinburg 033119
Muzej Istorii Kazanskogo Universiteta, Kazanskij gosudarstvennyj universitet, Kazan 033241
Muzej Istorii Kolskich Saamov, Murmanskij Oblastnoj Kraevedčeskij Muzej, Lovozero 033338
Muzej Istorii Kraja, Belozersk 033026
Muzej Istoriï Kyjeva, Kyïv 038307
Muzej Istorii Milicii, Sankt-Peterburg 033785
Muzej Istoriï Mista Chmel'nyc'kogo, Chmel'nyc'kyj 038254
Muzej Istoriï Mista Dniprodzeržins'ka, Dniprodzeržins'k 038255
Muzej Istoriï Mista Kolomyï, Kolomija 038287
Muzej Istorii Moskovskogo Metropolitena, Moskva 033453
Muzej Istorii Moskvy, Moskva 033454
Muzej Istorii Narodnych Chudožestvennych Promyslov, Nižnij Novgorod 033557
Muzej Istorii OAO Gaz, Nižnij Novgorod 033558
Muzej Istorii OAO Nižegorodskij Televizionnyj Zavod im. V.I. Lenina, Nižnij Novgorod 033559
Muzej Istorii Orenburga, Orenburg . 033614
Muzej Istorii Osvoenija i Razvitija Norilskogo Promyšlennogo Rajona, Norilsk . . 033575
Muzej Istorii Otečestvennogo Predprinimatelstva, Moskva 033455
Muzej Istorii Pečati Sankt-Peterburga, Sankt-Peterburg 033786
Muzej Istorii Permskogo Rajona, Perm 033651
Muzej Istorii Peterburgskoj Konservatorii, Sankt-Peterburg 033787
Muzej Istorii Političeskoj Policii Rossii - Gorochovaja 2, Gosudarstvennyj muzej političeskoj istorii Rossii, Sankt-Peterburg 033788
Muzej Istorii Političeskoj Ssylki, Bratskij gorodskoj objedinennyj muzej istorii osvoenija Angary, Bratsk 033048
Muzej Istorii Politssylki v Jakutii, Jakutskij gosudarstvennyj muzej istorii i kultury narodov severa im. Jaroslavskogo, Jakutsk 033188
Muzej Istorii Poljarnych Olimpiad, Murmanskij Oblastnoj Kraevedčeskij Muzej, Murmansk 033536
Muzej Istorii Priokskogo Rajona, Nižnij Novgorod 033560
Muzej Istorii Prosveščenija Komi Kraja, Syktyvkarskij Gosudarstvennyj Universitet, Syktyvkar 033925
Muzej Istorii Razvitija Mediciny, Astrachanskij muzej-zapovednik, Astrachan 033008
Muzej Istorii Razvitija Mosenergo, Moskva 033456
Muzej Istorii Revoljucionno-demokratičeskogo Dviženija 1880-1890 gg, Sankt-Peterburg 033789
Muzej Istorii Rossijskogo Gosudarstvennogo Pedagogičeskogo Universiteta im A.I. Gercena, Sankt-Peterburg 033790
Muzej Istorii Rybnoj Promyšlennosti Dagestana, Machačkala 033342
Muzej Istorii Sankt-Peterburgskogo Universiteta, Sankt-Peterburg . . . 033791
Muzej Istoriï Sevastopol's'koï Červonoprapornoï Komsomol'skoï Organiiacii, Muzei geroïčnoï oborony i vyzvolennja Sevastopolja, Sevastopol 038388
Muzej Istorii Svjazi Respubliki Tatarstan, Kazan 033242
Muzej Istoriï ta Kul'tury Mista Lugans'ka, Lugans'k 038335
Muzej Istorii Teatrov Dagestana, Dagestanskij gosudarstvennyj objedinennyj istoriko-architekturnyj muzej, Machačkala 033343
Muzej Istorii Turizma, Sankt-Peterburg 033792
Muzej Istorii UVD Kalužskoj Oblasti, Kaluga 033224
Muzej Istorii Vojsk Moskovskogo Voennogo Okruga, Moskva 033457
Muzej Istorije Jugoslavije, Beograd 034158
Muzej Istoryčnych Koštovnostej Ukraïny, Kyïv 038308
Muzej Ivana Gončara, Kyïv 038309
Muzej Ivanovskogo Sitca, Ivanovo . 033175
Muzej Izobrazitel'nych Iskusstv, Ašgabat 038202
Muzej Izobrazitelnych Iskusstv, Astana 027394
Muzej Izobrazitelnych Iskusstv, Komsomolsk-na-Amure 033279
Muzej Izobrazitelnych Iskusstv, Rostov-na-Donu 033702
Muzej Izobrazitelnych Iskusstv im. A.S. Puškina, Moskva 033458
Muzej Izobrazitelnych Iskusstv Karelii, Petrozavodsk 033663
Muzej Izobrazitelnyh Iskusstv Respubliki Marij Ėl, Joškar-Ola 033204
Muzej Jantarja, Kaliningrad 033216
Muzej Jesenice, Jesenice 034465
Muzej Jevreja Bosne i Hercegovine, Sarajevo 003937
Muzej Jovana Jovanovića-Zmaja, Sremska Kamenica 034264
Muzej Jugoslavenska Kinoteka, Beograd 034159
Muzej Junye Zaščitniki Rodiny, Kurskij gosudarstvennyj oblastnoj kraevedčeskij muzej, Kursk 033322
Muzej K. Ė. Ciolkovskogo, Aviacii i Kosmonavtiki, Kirov 033265
Muzej Kajuma Nasyri, Nacionalnyj muzej Respubliki Tatarstan, Kazan 033243
Muzej Kăkrinsko Chanče, Kăkrina . 004699
Muzej Karamzinskaja Obščestvennaja Biblioteka, Uljanovsk 034008
Muzej Kazanskoj Chimičeskoj Školy, Kazanskij gosudarstvennyj universitet, Kazan 033244
Muzej Keramiki i Usadba Kuskovo XVIII Veka, Moskva 033459
Muzej Kino, Moskva 033460

Muzej Kirovskogo Zavoda, Sankt-Peterburg 033793
Muzej Kizyl-Arvata, Kizyl-Arvat 038207
Muzej Klassičeskogo i Sovremennogo Iskusstva, Moskva 033461
Muzej Kliničke Psihijatrijske Bolnice Vrapče, Zagreb 007851
Muzej V.O. Ključevskogo, Penza . . . 033634
Muzej Knigi, Rossijskaja gosudarstvennaja biblioteka, Moskva 033462
Muzej Kninske Krajine, Knin 007735
Muzej Književnosti i Pozorišne Umjetnosti Bosne i Hercegovine i Galerija MAK, Sarajevo 003938
Muzej A. Kolcova, Voronežskij oblastnoj literaturnyj muzej im I.S. Nikitina, Voronež 034080
Muzej Kolju Fičeto, Drjanovo 004676
Muzej Konevodstva, Moskva 033463
Muzej Konspiritavnaja Kvartira Simbirskoj Gruppy RSDRP 1904-1906, Uljanovskij oblastnoj kraevedčskij muzej im. I.A. Gončarova, Uljanovsk 034009
Muzej Korčula, Korčula 007741
Muzej Košek, Moskva 033464
Muzej Kosova, Priština 034248
Muzej Kraevedenija, Jalta 038273
Muzej Kraevedenija g. Elabuga, Gosudarstvennyj istoriko-architekturnyj i chudožestvennnyj muzej-zapovednik, Elabuga 033130
Muzej Krajine Negotin, Negotin . . . 034215
Muzej Krapinskog Pračovjeka, Krapina 007747
Muzej Krejsera Avrora, Centralnyj Voenno-morskoj muzej, Sankt-Peterburg . 033794
Muzej-krepost Baba Vida, Vidin . . . 004946
Muzej Krestovosdviženskaja Cerkov, Palech 033628
Muzej Kriminalistiki, Alktajskij gosudarstvennyj universitet, Barnaul 033017
Muzej-kripta Aleksandăr Nevski, National Art Gallery, Sofia 004856
Muzej Kronštadtskaja Krepost, Kronštadt 033311
Muzej Kronštadtskogo Morskogo Zavoda, Kronštadt 033312
Muzej Krutickoe Podvore, Moskva . 033465
Muzej Krylova, Tulskij muzej izobrazitelnych iskusstv, Tula 033974
Muzej Kukol i Detskoj Knigi Strana Čudes, Municipalnyj objedinennyj muzej pisatelej Urala, Ekaterinburg 033120
Muzej Kulturne Istorije, Požarevac . 034245
Muzej Kul'turnoï Spadščyny, The Museum of Cultural Heritage, Kyïv 038310
Muzej Kultury Astrachani, Astrachanskij muzej-zapovednik, Astrachan . . . 033009
Muzej Kupečeskogo Byta, Ekaterinburg 033121
Muzej-kvartira Alliluevych, Gosudarstvennyj istoriko-memorialnyj muzej Smolnyj, Sankt-Peterburg 033795
Muzej-kvartira A.M. Gorkogo, Moskva 033466
Muzej-kvartira I.I. Brodskogo, Research Museum of the Russian Academy of Arts, Sankt-Peterburg 033796
Muzej-kvartira A.S. Čaplygina, Sankt-Peterburg 033797
Muzej-kvartira M.I. Cvetaevoj v Bolševo, Korolev 033284
Muzej-kvartira Dirižëra N.S. Golovanov, Moskva 033467
Muzej-kvartira F.M. Dostoevskogo, Gosudarstvennyj literaturnyj muzej, Moskva 033468
Muzej-kvartira Elizarovych, Sankt-Peterburg 033798
Muzej-kvartira A.B. Goldenvejzera, Moskva 033469
Muzej-kvartira A.M. Gorkogo, Gosudarstvennyj Literaturnyj Muzej A.M. Gorkogo, Nižnij Novgorod 033561
Muzej-kvartira G.D. Krasilnikova, Nacionalnyj muzej Udmurtskoj Respubliki im. K. Gerda, Iževsk 033179
Muzej-kvartira A.I. Kuindži, Muzej Rossijskoj Akademii Chudožestv, Sankt-Peterburg 033799
Muzej-kvartira L. Lapcuja, Jamalo-Neneckij okružnoj kraevedčeskij muzej im. I.S. Šemanovskogo, Salechard 033711
Muzej-kvartira Lunačarskogo, Moskva 033470
Muzej-kvartira V.S. Mejercholda, Moskva 033471
Muzej-kvartira Naziba Žiganova, Nacionalnyj muzej Respubliki Tatarstan, Kazan 033245
Muzej-kvartira V.I. Nemiroviča-Dančenko, Muzej Moskovskogo Chudožestvennogo Akademičeskogo Teatra, Moskva . 033472
Muzej-kvartira A. Puškina, Vserossijskij Muzej Puškina, Sankt-Peterburg . 033800
Muzej-kvartira A.D. Sacharova, Nižnij Novgorod 033562
Muzej-kvartira F.I. Šaljapina, Sankt-Peterburgskij Muzej Teatralnogo i Musykalnogo Iskusstva, Sankt-Peterburg 033801
Muzej-kvartira T.G. Ševčenko, Muzej Rossijskoj Akademii Chudožestv, Sankt-Peterburg 033802
Muzej-Kvartira Ju.P. Spegalskogo, Pskov 033676
Muzej-kvartira K.A. Timirjazeva, Moskva 033473
Muzej-kvartira A.N. Tolstogo, Moskva 033474
Muzej-kvartira A.T. Tvardovskij v Smolenske, Smolenskij Muzej-Zapovednik, Smolensk 033876
Muzej-kvartira V. Tytova, Muzej istoriï ta kul'tury mista Lugans'ka, Lugans'k 038336
Muzej-kvartita Musa Džalilja, Nacionalnyj muzej Respubliki Tatarstan, Kazan 033246
Muzej Lavka Čechovych, Taganrogskij gosudarstvennyj literaturnyj i istoriko-architekturnyj muzej-zapovednik, Taganrog 033932
Muzej-ledokol Angara, Irkutskij oblastnoj kraevedčeskij muzej, Irkutsk 033163
Muzej-ledokol Bajkal, Angarsk 032986
Muzej V.I. Lenina, Gosudarstvennyj istoričeskij muzej, Moskva 033475
Muzej Lesi Ukraïnki, Kyïv 038311
Muzej Ličnych Kollekcij, Moskva . . 033476
Muzej Literaturnaja Žizn' Urala XIX Veka, Municipalnyj objedinennyj muzej pisatelej Urala, Ekaterinburg 033122
Muzej Literaturnoj Žizni Jaroslavskogo Kraja, Gosudarstvennyj muzej-zapovednik N.A. Nekrasova - Karibicha, Jaroslavl 033198
Muzej Literatury Burjatii im. Choca Namsaraeva, Ulan-Udė 034002
Muzej Ljudske Revolucije Slovenj Gradec, Slovenj Gradec 034523
Muzej Ljudske Revolucije Trbovlje, Trbovlje 034529
Muzej M.V. Lomonosova, Muzej Antropologii i Etnografii im. Petra Velikogo, Sankt-Peterburg 033803
Muzej-majsternja I.P. Kavaleridze, Museum-workshop of I. Kavaleridze, Kyïv . 038312
Muzej A.S. Makarenko, Moskva . . . 033477
Muzej Marcialnye Vody, Karelskij gosudarstvennyj kraevedčeskij muzej, Petrozavodsk 033664
Muzej Mecenatov i Blagotvoritelej Rossii, Moskva 033478
Muzej Medjimurja, Čakovec 007706
Muzej Meteorologii Glavnoj Geofizičeskoj Observatorii im. A.I. Voejkova, Sankt-Peterburg 033804
Muzej Meterologičeskaja Stancija Simbirska, Gosudarstvennyj zapovednik Rodina V.I. Lenina, Uljanovsk 034010
Muzej Miniaturnych Kukol Malenkij Mir, Semipalatinsk 033865
Muzej Mir Vody Sankt-Peterburga, Sankt-Peterburg 033805
Muzej Mirovogo Okeana, Kaliningrad 033217
Muzej Mologskogo Kraja, Rybinskij gosudarstvennyj istoriko-architekturnyj i chudožestvennyj muzej-zapovednik, Rybinsk 033707
Muzej Mordovskoj Kultury, Saransk 033848
Muzej Morskogo Flota, Mintrans RF, Moskva 033479
Muzej Morskogo Flota Dal'nevostočnogo Morskogo Parochodstva, Vladivostok 034054
Muzej Moskovskogo Chudožestvennogo Akademičeskogo Teatra, Moskva . 033480
Muzej Moskovskoj Konservatorii, Moskva 033481
Muzej Moslavine, Kutina 007752
Muzej Muzykalnoj i Teatralnoj Kultury na Kavkazskich Mineralnyh Vodach, Kislovodsk 033274
Muzej Muzykalnych Instrumentov, Sankt-Peterburg 033806
Muzej M.V. Lisenka, Kyïv 038313
Muzej Mystectv imeni Bogdana ta Varvari Chanenkiv, Kyïv 038314
Muzej Mystectva Davnoï Ukraïns'koï Knigi, Lvivs'ka Galereja Mystectv, Lviv . 038350
Muzej na Aviacijata, Krumovo 004738
Muzej na Bivolarstvoto i Konevădstvoto, Nacionalen Selskostopanski Muzej Sofia, Šumen 004892
Muzej na Blejskem Gradu, Bled . . . 034458
Muzej na Chudožestvenata Akademija, Sofia 004857
Muzej na Chudožestvenite Zanajati i Priložnite Izkustva, Trojan 004907
Muzej na Grad Skopje, Skopje 027917
Muzej na Gradskij Bit Oslekova Kăšta, Koprivštica 004731
Muzej na Gradskija Bit, Isoričeski Muzej Ruse, Ruse 004820
Muzej na Ikonata v Carkvata Sv. Nikolai, Pleven 004781
Muzej na Kotlenskite Vazroždenci i Panteon na Georgi S. Rakovski, Kotel 004734
Muzej na Makedonija - Arceološki, Etnološki i Istoriski, Skopje 027918
Muzej na Ministerstvoto na Vnatrešnite raboti, Sofia 004858
Muzej na Morskoto Stopanstvo, Nacionalen Voenno-morski Muzej, Varna 004917
Muzej na Mozaikite, Devnja 004663
Muzej na Naroden Teatar Ivan Vazov, Sofia 004859
Muzej na Narodnata Opera, Sofia . . 004860
Muzej na Poklonnoj, Moskva 033482
Muzej na Rezbarskoto i Zografsko Izkustvo, Trjavna 004905
Muzej na Rodopskija Karst, Čepelare 004652
Muzej na Rudodobiva i Minnoto Delo, Madan 004745
Muzej na Septemvrijskoto Văstanie, Michajlovgrad 004754
Muzej na Sovremenata Umetnost Skopje, Skopje 027919
Muzej na Tekstilnata Industrija, Nacionalen Politechničeski Muzej Sofia, Sliven 004839
Muzej na Tetovskiot Kraj, Tetovo . . 027926
Muzej na Văzraždaneto, Varna 004918
Muzej na Văzroždeneto i Nacionalno-osvoboditelnite Borbi, Elena 004678
Muzej na Văzroždenskata Ikona, Okrăžen Istoričeski Muzej, Varna 004919
Muzej Nacionalnoj Kultury, Kulturnyj Centr Kazan, Kazan 033247
Muzej Naivne Umetnosti, Sid 034258
Muzej Najdavniših Pamjatok Lvova, Lvivs'ka Galereja Mystectv, Lviv . 038351
Muzej Narodne Osvoboditve, Maribor 034499
Muzej Narodne Revolucije, Rijeka . . 007780
Muzej Narodnogo Chudožnika Rossii A.I. Morozova, Ivanovskij oblastnoj chudožestvennyj muzej, Ivanovo . 033176
Muzej Narodnogo Dekorativnogo Mystectva, Oblasnyj istoryčnyj muzej im. V. Tarnovs'kogo, Černigiv 038231
Muzej Narodnogo Derevjannogo Zodčestva Vitoslavlicy, Velikij Novgorod 034026
Muzej Narodnogo Iskusstva, Moskva 033483
Muzej Narodnogo Mystectva Slobožanščyny, Charkivs'kij Chudožnij Muzej, Charkiv 038246
Muzej Narodnogo Obrazovanija Oblasti, Penza 033635
Muzej Narodnogo Tvorčestva, Penza 033636
Muzej Narodnogo Tvorčestva, Uljanovsk 034011
Muzej Narodnoho Mystectva Gucul'ščini ta Pokuttja im. J. Kobryns'koho, Kolomija 038288
Muzej Narodnoï Architektury i Pobutu u Lvovi, Lviv 038352
Muzej Narodnoï Architektury ta Pobutu Ukraïny, Kyïv 038315
Muzej Narodnoj Grafiki, Moskva . . . 033484
Muzej Narodnoje Obrazovanie Simbirskoj Gubernii v 70-80 gody 19 veka, Gosudarstvennyj zapovednik Rodina V.I. Lenina, Uljanovsk 034012
Muzej Narodnych Muzykalnych Instrumentov Kazachstana, Almaty 027391
Muzej Narodov Vostočnogo Kazachstana, Ust-Kamenogorsk 027418
Muzej Nauke i Tehnike, Beograd . . 034160
Muzej Nekropol' Demidovych i Vystavočnyj Zal Tulskij Metall, Tula 033975
Muzej-nekropol Literatorskie Mostki, Gosudarstvennyj muzej gorodskoj skulptury, Sankt-Peterburg 033807
Muzej N.G. Rubinstejna, Moskva . . 033485
Muzej Nikole Tesle, Beograd 034161
Muzej Nižegorodskaja Radiolaboratorija, Radiolabaratory Museum, Nižnij Novgorod 033563
Muzej Nižegorodskij Ostrog, Nižegorodskij gosudarstvennyj istoriko-architekturnyj muzej-zapovednik, Nižnij Novgorod 033564
Muzej Nižegorodskoj Intelligencii, Nižnij Novgorod 033565
Muzej Nonkonformistskogo Iskusstva, Sankt-Peterburg 033808
Muzej Novejše Zgodovine Celje, Celje 034462
Muzej Novejše Zgodovine Slovenije, Ljubljana 034486
Muzej 'Novoj Akademii Izjaščnych Iskusstv', Sankt-Peterburg 033809
Muzej Obščestva Krasnogo Kresta Rossii, Moskva 033486
Muzej Obščestva Sporta Dinamo-Moskva, Moskva 033487
Muzej Obščestvennogo Pitanija, Moskva 033488
Muzej Ochotovedenija, Irkutskaja Selskochozjajstvennaja Akademija, Irkutsk 033164
Muzej Ochoty i Rybolovstva, Moskva 033489
Muzej Oktjabrskogo Vooružennogo Vosstanija, Voronežskij oblastnoj kraevedčeskij muzej, Voronež . . . 034081
Muzej Oleksi Dovbuša, Ivano-Frankivs'kyj Krajeznavčyj Muzej, Ivano-Frankivs'k 038268
Muzej Orijentalnih Rukopisa, Prizren 034251
Muzej Osvoboždenieto na Pleven 1877, Pleven 004782
Muzej Palechskogo Remesla, Palech 033627
Muzej-Pamjatnik Chram Voskresenija Christova (Spas na Krovi), Sankt-Peterburg 033810
Muzej-panorama Borodinskaja Bitva, Moskva 033490
Muzej Parka Iskusstv na Krymskoj Naberežnoj, Moskva 033491
Muzej-Parochod Svjatitel Nikolaj, Krasnojarskij kraevedčeskij muzej, Krasnojarsk 033301
Muzej Pejzaža, Plesskij gosudarstvennyj istoriko-architekturnyj i chudožestvennyj muzej-zapovednik, Ples 033669

Muzej Pidpil'nyj ta Partizans'kyj Ruch na Mykolaïvščyn Mykolaïvščyni u Roki Velikoï Vitčyznjanoï Vijny 1941-1945 rr, Mykolaïv 038361
Muzej Pisanka, Kolomija 038289
Muzej Pisatelej-orlovcev, Gosudarstvennyj literaturnyj muzej im. I.S. Turgeneva, Orël 033611
Muzej Pisatelja A.P. Bibika, Mineral'nye Vody 033358
Muzej po Istorii Stroitelstva Gidroelektričeskogo Zavoda v Nurke, Nurek 037842
Muzej Podviga Ivana Susanina, Susanino 033916
Muzej Poėta S. Orlova, Belozersk . . 033027
Muzej Pograničnoj Ochrany, Moskva 033492
Muzej Ponišavlja Pirot, Pirot 034237
Muzej Pozorišne Umetnosti Srbije, Beograd 034162
Muzej Prezidentskogo Centra Kultury Respubliki Kazachstan, Astana . . 027395
Muzej Prigorja, Sesvete 007790
Muzej Primenjene Umetnosti, Beograd 034163
Muzej Priroda Morja i eë Ochrana, Institut biologii morja, Dal'nevostočnoe otd. Rossijskoj Akademii Nauk, Vladivostok 034055
Muzej Prirody, Čerepovec 033075
Muzej Prirody Burjatii, Ulan-Udė . . . 034003
Muzej S.S. Prokofjeva, Moskva . . . 033493
Muzej A.S. Puškina, Toržok 033967
Muzej A.S. Puškina v Bernove, Tverskoj gosudarstvennyj obedinennyj muzej, Bernov 033029
Muzej Radio im. A.S. Popova, Ekaterinburg 033123
Muzej Radničkog Pokreta i Narodne Revolucije, Novi Sad 034224
Muzej Radničkog Pokreta i NOB za Slavoniju i Baranju, Slavonski Brod 007797
Muzej Rafail Popov, Madara 004747
Muzej Ras, Novi Pazar 034221
Muzej Rečnog Brodarstva, Beograd 034164
Muzej Rečnogo Flota, Volžskaja Gosudarstvennaja Akademija Vodnogo Transporta, Nižnij Novgorod 033566
Muzej Remesla, Architektury i Byta, Kaluga 033225
Muzej Republike Srpske, Banja Luka 003926
Muzej Revoljucii, Moskva 033494
Muzej Revoljucionnogo Dvizenija, Altanbulag 028999
Muzej-riznica Stare Srpske Pravoslavne Crkve, Sarajevo 003939
Muzej Rossijskoj Akademii Chudožestv, Sankt-Peterburg 033811
Muzej Rudarstva i Metalurgije, Bor . 034177
Muzej Rumănski Voin, Voenno-istoričeski Muzej Pleven, Pordim 004801
Muzej Russko-Armjanskoj Družby, Rostovskij oblastnoj muzej kraevedenija, Rostov-na-Donu 033703
Muzej Russkoj Pesni im. A. Averkina, Sasovo 033860
Muzej Sakral'noï Skul'ptury XVIII st. - Tvorčist' Ivana Pinzelja, Lvivs'ka Galereja Mystectv, Lviv 038353
Muzej Salicha Sajdaševa, Nacionalnyj muzej Respubliki Tatarstan, Kazan 033248
Muzej M.E. Saltykova-Ščedrina, Tverskoj gosudarstvennyj obedinennyj muzej, Tver 033984
Muzej Samocvety Bajkala, Sljudjanka 033875
Muzej Šarifa Kamala, Nacionalnyj muzej Respubliki Tatarstan, Kazan 033249
Muzej Savremene Likovne Umetnosti, Novi Sad 034225
Muzej Savremene Umetnosti, Beograd 034165
Muzej Sceničeskogo Iskusstva im. V.Ė. Mejercholda, Penza 033637
Muzej Seljackih Buna, Muzeji Hrvatskog Zagorja, Gornja Stubica 007722
Muzej Semejstvo Obretenovi, Ruse . 004821
Muzej Semji Benua, Gosudarstvennyj Muzej Zapovednik Petergof, Sankt-Peterburg 033812
Muzej Simbirskaja Čuvašskaja Škola - Kvartira I.Ja. Jakovleva, Gosudarstvennyj zapovednik Rodina V.I. Lenina, Uljanovsk 034013
Muzej Simbirskaja Klassičeskaja Gimnazija, Gosudarstvennyj zapovednik Rodina V.I. Lenina, Uljanovsk 034014
Muzej Skulptury, Sankt-Peterburg . 033813
Muzej Skulptury S.T. Konenkova, Smolenskij Muzej-Zapovednik, Smolensk . . . 033877
Muzej Slavonije Osijek, Osijek 007769
Muzej Slivenski Zatvor, Sliven 004840
Muzej Smolenščina v Gody Velikoj Otečestvennoj Vojny 1941 -1945, Smolenskij Muzej-Zapovednik, Smolensk 033878
Muzej Smolenskij Len, Smolenskij Muzej-Zapovednik, Smolensk 033879
Muzej Snovidenij Zigmunda Frejda, Sankt-Peterburg 033814
Muzej Sovremennogo Iskusstva Evrejskoj Avtonomnoj Oblasti, Birobidžan . . 033033
Muzej Sovremennogo Izobrazitelnogo Iskusstva im. A.A. Plastova, Uljanovsk 034015
Muzej Sovremennoj Istorii i Kultury Severnoj Osetii, Vladikavkaz 034037
Muzej Spasskaja Cerkov, Tjumenskij Oblastnoj Kraevedčeskij Muzej im. I.Ja. Slovcova, Tjumen 033955
Muzej Sporta v Lužnikach, Moskva . 033495
Muzej Srema, Sremska Mitrovica . . 034266
Muzej Srpske Pravoslavne Crkve, Beograd 034166
Muzej Srpske Pravoslavne Crkve, Dubrovnik 007718
Muzej Štab-kvartira V.K. Bljuchera, Tjumenskij oblastnoj kraevedčeskij muzej im. I.Ja. Slovcova, Tjumen 033956
Muzej Stara Livnica, Zastava Namenski Proizvodi, Kragujevac 034204
Muzej Staražytna Belaruskaj Kultury, Minsk 003137
Muzej Staryj Anglijskij Dvor, Moskva 033496
Muzej-studija Radioteatra, Gosteleradiofond, Moskva 033497
Muzej Sudnobuduvannja ta Flotu, Mykolaïv 038362
Muzej A.V. Suvorova, Velikij Novgorod 034027
Muzej Suvremene Umjetnosti, Museum of Contemporary Art, Zagreb 007852
Muzej Svjazi Amurskoj Oblasti, Blagoveščensk 033035
Muzej S.I. Taneeva v Djutkovo, Zvenigorod 034098
Muzej Andreja Tarkovskogo, Muzej goroda Jurjevca, Jurjevec 033210
Muzej Teatra, Sankt-Peterburg 033815
Muzej Teatra Operetty, Moskva . . . 033498
Muzej Teatralnoj Kukly A.A Veselova, Voronež 034082
Muzej A.K. Tolstogo, Brjanskij gosudarstvennyj obedinennyj kraevedčeskij muzej, Krasnyj Rog 033308
Muzej L.N. Tolstogo na stancii Lev Tolstoj, Gosudarstvennyj muzej L.N. Tolstogo, Stancija Lev Tolstoj 033900
Muzej Tomaža Godca, Gorenjski Muzej Kranj, Bohinjska Bistrica 034459
Muzej Tropinina i Moskovskich Chudožnikov ego Vremeni, Moskva 033499
Muzej Tul'skie Samovary, Tula 033976
Muzej Tul'skij Kreml', Tula 033977
Muzej Turopolja, Velika Gorica 007818
Muzej Tverskogo Byta, Tverskoj gosudarstvennyj obedinennyj muzej, Tver 033985
Muzej u Arandjelovcu, Arandjelovac 034140
Muzej u Smederevu, Smederevo . . 034259
Muzej Uezdnogo Goroda, Nacionalnyj muzej Respubliki Tatarstan, Čistopol . . . 033092
Muzej Ulcinj, Ulcinj 034276
Muzej Unikalnych Kukol, Moskva . . 033500
Muzej Uralskogo Gosudarstvennogo Techničeskogo Universiteta, Ekaterinburg 033124
Muzej-usadba A.T. Bolotova, Dvorjaninovo 033107
Muzej-usadba V.E. Borsova-Musatova, Chudožestvennyj muzej im. A.N. Radiščeva, Saratov 033855
Muzej-usadba N.G. Černyševskogo, Saratov 033856
Muzej- Usadba F.M. Dostoevskogo Darovoe, Darovoe 033098
Muzej-usadba N.A. Durovoj, Elabuz^skij muzej-zapovednik, Elabuga 033131
Muzej-usadba M.I. Glinki, Novospasskoe 033591
Muzej-usadba im. N.K. Rericha, Izvara 033183
Muzej-usadba Izmajlovo, Gosudarstvennyj istoričeskij muzej, Moskva 033501
Muzej-usadba L.N. Tolstogo Nikol'skoe Vjazemskoe, Nikol'skoe-Vjazemskoe 033550
Muzej-usadba Muranovo im. F.I. Tjutčeva, Lugovskoe 033339
Muzej-usadba Ostafjevo Russkij Parnas, Ostafjevo 033619
Muzej-usadba poėta D. Venevitinova, Novoživotinnoe 033593
Muzej-usadba I.E. Repina, Repino . 033692
Muzej-usadba Roždestveno, Roždestveno 033705
Muzej-usadba V.I. Surikova, Krasnojarsk 033302
Muzej-usadba A.V. Suvorova, Končanskoe-Suvorovskoe 033280
Muzej-usadba A.N. Tolstogo, Literaturno-memorialnyj muzej M. Gorkogoo, Samara 033720
Muzej-Usadba L.N. Tolstogo v Chamovnikach, Gosudarstvennyj muzej L.N. Tolstogo, Moskva 033502
Muzej-usadba A.T. Tvardovskij na Chutore Zagorje, Smolenskij gosudarstvennyj muzej-zapovednik, Zagorje 034092
Muzej V Mire Skazok, Smolenskij Muzej-Zapovednik, Smolensk 033880
Muzej Vasil Levski, Karlovo 004706
Muzej Vasil Levski, Istoričeski Muzej, Loveč 004744
Muzej Văzraždane i Učreditelno Săbranie, Veliko Tărnovo 004936
Muzej Văzroždenski Ikoni, Radomir 004810
Muzej Velenje, Velenje 034535
Muzej Vereščaginych, Čerepovec . . 033076
Muzej Vjatskie Narodnye Chudožestvennye Promysly, Kirov 033266
Muzej Vladimira Raevskogo, Bogoslovka 033038
Muzej Vody, Moskva 033503
Muzej Vojniško Văstanie 1918, Radomir 004811
Muzej Volyns'koj Ikony, Volyns'kyj Krajeznavčyj Muzej, Luc'k 038329
Muzej Voskovych Figur, Sankt-Peterburg 033816
Muzej Vydatnych Dijačiv Ukraïns'koï Kul'tury - Lesi Ukraïnki, Mychajla Staric'koho, Mikoli Lisenka, Panasa Saksagans'koho, Kyïv 038316
Muzej Vyzvol'nych Zmagan' Prikarpats'koho Kraju, Ivano-Frankivs'kyj Krajeznavčyj Muzej, Ivano-Frankivs'k 038269
Muzej za Istorija na Medicinata, Varna 004920
Muzej za Istorija na Varna, Varna . . 004921
Muzej za Umjetnost i Obrt, Zagreb . 007853
Muzej-zapovednik Abramcevo, Abramcevo 032972
Muzej-zapovednik Dmitrovskij Kreml, Dmitrov 033101
Muzej-zapovednik Kazanskij Kreml, Kazan 033250
Muzej-zapovednik Pisatelja S.T. Aksakova, Aksakovo 032975
Muzej Zavoda Crvena Zastava, Kragujevac 034205
Muzej Zavoda Moskvič, Moskva . . . 033504
Muzej Zdravoochranenija, Sankt-Peterburg 033817
Muzej Železnodorožnoj Techniki, Sankt-Peterburg 033818
Muzej Zemlevedenija Moskovskogo Gosudarstvennogo Universiteta M.V. Lomonosova, Moskva 033505
Muzeji i Galerije Podgorica, Podgorica 034242
Muzeji Radovljiške Občine, Begunje na Gorenjskem 034457
Muzeji Radovljiške Občine, Kropa . . 034475
Muzejno-vystavočnyj Centr, Dal'negorsk 033097
Muzejno-vystavočnyj Centr, Ivanovo 033177
Muzejno-vystavočnyj Centr - Diorama, Kirovskij oblastnoj kraevedčeskij muzej, Kirov 033267
Muzejno-vystavočnyj Centr Ego, Sankt-Peterburg 033819
Muzejno-vystavočnyj Centr Tul'skie Drevnosti, Gosudarstvennyj voenno-istoričeskij i prirodnyj muzej-zapovednik Kulikovo Pole, Tula 033978
Muzejno-vystavočnyj Kompleks, Moskovskaja Gosudarstvennaja Specializirovannaja Škola Akvareli Sergeja Andrijaki, Moskva 033506
Muzejno-vystavočnyj Kompleks Volokolamskij Kreml, Volokolamsk 034074
Muzejnyj Kompleks Tomskogo Politechničeskogo Universiteta, Tomsk 033962
Muzejnyj Kulturno-vystavočnyj Kompleks, Dnipropetrovs'k 038261
Muzejska Zbirka, Imotski 007728
Muzejska Zbirka, Knić 034199
Muzejska Zbirka, Rogoška Slatina . 034520
Muzejska Zbirka Franjevačkog Samostana, Imotski 007729
Muzejska Zbirka Jastrebarsko, Jastrebarsko 007730
Muzejska Zbirka Kapucinskog Samostana, Karlobag 007731
Muzejska Zbirka Krapina i Okolica, Krapina 007748
Muzejska Zbirka Laško, Laško 034476
Muzejska Zbirka NOB, Zagorje 034539
Muzejska Zbirka pri Narodnoj Biblioteki Dimitrije Tucović, Čajetina 034182
Muzejski Dokumentacijski Centar, Zagreb 007854
Muzejsko Društvo na Makedonija, Skopje 053852
Muzejsko Društvo SR Crne Gore - Cetinje, Cetinje 054038
Muzejsko Društvo Srbije, Beograd . 054039
Muzeju Vestnesis, Rīga 135985
Muzéo, Villeurbanne 068973
Muzerelle, Claude, Rochefort-en-Terre 067183
Muzerelle, Claude, Rochefort-en-Terre 067184
Muzeu Historik Fier, Fier 000021
Muzeu i Filmit Shkodër, Shkodër . . 000031
Muzeu i Shkencave Natyrore, Tiranë 000035
Muzeul Arheologic Adamclisi, Adamclisi 032767
Muzeul Arheologic Sarmizegetusa, Muzeul Civilizaţiei Dacice şi Romane Deva, Sarmizegetusa 032929
Muzeul Arhitecturii Populare din Gorj, Muzeul Judeţean Gorj, Bumbeşti-Jiu 032819
Muzeul Arta Iemnului, Wooden Art Museum, Câmpulung Moldovenesc 032827
Muzeul Banatului, Timişoara 032957
Muzeul Banatului Montan, Reşiţa . . 032924
Muzeul Brăilei, Brăila 032787
Muzeul Bran, Bran 032788
Muzeul Breslelor, Muzeul National Secuiesc S.F. Gheorghe, Tîrgu Secuiesc . . . 032958
Muzeul Câmpiei Băileştitor, Băileşti 032779
Muzeul Castelul Corvinestilor, Hunedoara 032873
Muzeul Civilizaţiei Dacice şi Române, Deva 032854

Muzeul Colecţiilor de Artă, Bucureşti . . . 032795
Muzeul Cornel Medrea, Muzeul Municipiului Bucureşti, Bucureşti . . . 032796
Muzeul Curtea Veche, Palaţul Voievodal, Bucureşti . . . 032797
Muzeul de Arheologie, Săveni . . . 032931
Muzeul de Arheologie Callatis Mangalia, Mangalia . . . 032890
Muzeul de Arheologie Olteniţa, Olteniţa . . . 032901
Muzeul de Arheologie şi Etnografie, Corabia . . . 032846
Muzeul de Artă, Braşov . . . 032790
Muzeul de Artă, Drobeta-Turnu Severin . . . 032858
Muzeul de Artă, Iaşi . . . 032875
Muzeul de Artă, Medgidia . . . 032891
Muzeul de Artă, Târgovişte . . . 032946
Muzeul de Artă, Târgu Jiu . . . 032948
Muzeul de Artă, Tulcea . . . 032960
Muzeul de Artă Constanţa, Constanţa . . . 032842
Muzeul de Artă Craiova, Craiova . . . 032849
Muzeul de Artă Dinu şi Sevasta Vintilă, Topalu . . . 032959
Muzeul de Artă Piatra-Neamţ, Complexul Muzeal Judetean Neamţ, Piatra-Neamţ . . . 032908
Muzeul de Artă Populară, Constanţa 032843
Muzeul de Artă Populară, Ploieşti . . 032913
Muzeul de Artă Populară Prof. Dr. Nicolae Minovici, Bucureşti . . . 032798
Muzeul de Artă Populară şi Etnografie, Tulcea . . . 032961
Muzeul de Artă şi Artă Populară, Calafat . . . 032821
Muzeul de Artă Vizuală, Galaţi . . . 032866
Muzeul de Etnografie Braşov, Braşov . . . 032791
Muzeul de Etnografie Piatra-Neamţ, Complexul Muzeal Judetean Neamţ, Piatra-Neamţ . . . 032909
Muzeul de Etnografie şi a Regimentului de Graniţă, Caransebeş . . . 032831
Muzeul de Etnografie şi Artă Populară, Reghin . . . 032923
Muzeul de Etnografie şi Artă Populară Orăştie, Orăştie . . . 032906
Muzeul de Istorie, Bicaz . . . 032782
Muzeul de Istorie, Oneşti . . . 032902
Muzeul de Istorie, Târgu Jiu . . . 032949
Muzeul de Istorie a Evreilor din România, Bucureşti . . . 032799
Muzeul de Istorie al Moldovei, Iaşi . 032876
Muzeul de Istorie Augustin Bunea, Blaj . . . 032784
Muzeul de Istorie, Etnografie şi Artă Plastică, Lugoj . . . 032887
Muzeul de Istorie Gherla, Gherla . . . 032869
Muzeul de Istorie Locală şi Etnografie, Brad . . . 032786
Muzeul de Istorie Naţională şi Archeologie, Constanţa . . . 032844
Muzeul de Istorie Naturală din Sibiu, Muzeul Naţional Brukenthal, Sibiu . . . 032935
Muzeul de Istorie Naturală Iaşi, Universităţii Iaşi, Iaşi . . . 032877
Muzeul de Istorie şi Arheologie, Tulcea . . . 032962
Muzeul de Istorie şi Artă Roman, Roman . . . 032925
Muzeul de Istorie şi Etnografie, Târgu Neamţ . . . 032955
Muzeul de Istorie Sighişoara, Sighişoara . . . 032938
Muzeul de Istorie Turda, Turda . . . 032964
Muzeul de Istorie Valea Hârtibaciului, Agnita . . . 032768
Muzeul de Mineralogie Baia Mare, Baia Mare . . . 032777
Muzeul de Ştiinte Naturale, Complexul Muzeal Judeţean Neamţ, Piatra-Neamţ . . . 032910
Muzeul de Ştiinţele Naturii, Dorohoi 032856
Muzeul de Ştiinţele Naturii, Focşani 032863
Muzeul de Stiinţele Naturii, Roman . 032926
Muzeul de Ştiinţele Naturii Aiud, Aiud . . . 032769
Muzeul de Şttiinte Naturale, Institutul de Cercetări Eco-Muzeale, Tulcea . . 032963
Muzeul Doftana, Doftana . . . 032855
Muzeul Dunării de Jos, Călăraşi . . . 032822
Muzeul Etnografic, Vatra Dornei . . . 032968
Muzeul Etnografic al Moldovei, Iaşi 032878
Muzeul Etnografic al Transilvaniei, Cluj-Napoca . . . 032835
Muzeul Etnografic Ioan Tugui, Câmpulung Moldovenesc . . . 032828
Muzeul Etnografic Lupşa, Lupşa . . . 032888
Muzeul Etnografic Tehnici Populare Bucovinene, Rădăuţi . . . 032919
Muzeul Grănicieresc Năsăudean, Năsăud . . . 032896
Muzeul Haáz Rezsö, Odorheiu Secuiesc . . . 032900
Muzeul Hrandt Avakian, Muzeul Naţional de Artă al României, Bucureşti . . . 032800
Muzeul în Aer Liber, Negreşti-Oaş . 032898
Muzeul Judeţean Alexandru Ştefulescu, Târgu Jiu . . . 032950
Muzeul Judeţean Argeş, Piteşti . . . 032912
Muzeul Judeţean Bistriţa-Năsăud, Bistriţa . . . 032783
Muzeul Judeţean Botoşani, Botoşani . . . 032785
Muzeul Judeţean Buzău, Buzău . . . 032820
Muzeul Judeţean de Artă, Ploieşti . 032914
Muzeul Judeţean de Etnografie, Slatina . . . 032940
Muzeul Judeţean de Istorie, Galaţi . 032867
Muzeul Judeţean de Istorie, Complexul Muzeal Judetean Neamţ, Piatra-Neamţ . . . 032911
Muzeul Judeţean de Istorie Braşov, Braşov . . . 032792
Muzeul Judeţean de Istorie şi Arheologie Iulian Antonescu Bacău, Bacău . . 032776
Muzeul Judeţean de Istorie şi Arheologie Prahova, Ploieşti . . . 032915
Muzeul Judeţean de Istorie şi Artă, Slatina . . . 032941
Muzeul Judeţean de Istorie şi Artă Zalău, Zalău . . . 032969
Muzeul Judeţean de Istorie Teleorman, Alexandria . . . 032772
Muzeul Judeţean de Ştiinţele Naturii Prahova, Ploieşti . . . 032916
Muzeul Judeţean Ialomiţa, Slobozia 032942
Muzeul Judeţean Maramureş, Baia Mare . . . 032778
Muzeul Judeţean Mureş, Târgu Mureş . . . 032951
Muzeul Judeţean Mureş-Secţia de Artă, Târgu Mureş . . . 032952
Muzeul Judeţean Mureş-Secţia de Etnografie şi Artă Populară, Târgu Mureş . . . 032953
Muzeul Judeţean Mureş-Secţia de St^Biinţele Naturii, Târgu Mureş . 032954
Muzeul Judeţean Satu Mare, Satu Mare . . . 032930
Muzeul Judeţean Ştefan cel Mare, Vaslui . . . 032967
Muzeul Judeţean Teohari Antonescu, Giurgiu . . . 032870
Muzeul Judeţean Vâlcea, Râmnicu Vâlcea . . . 032921
Muzeul K.H. Zambaccian, Muzeul Naţional de Artă al României, Bucureşti . . 032801
Muzeul Literaturii Române, Iaşi . . . 032879
Muzeul Maramureşului, Sighetu Marmaţiei . . . 032937
Muzeul Marinei Române, Constanţa 032845
Muzeul Memorial Ady Endre, Oradea . . . 032903
Muzeul Memorial Avram Iancu, Avram Iancu . . . 032774
Muzeul Memorial Bojdeuca Ion Creangă, Iaşi . . . 032880
Muzeul Memorial Emil Isac, Cluj-Napoca . . . 032836
Muzeul Memorial George Coşbuc, Coşbuc . . . 032848
Muzeul Memorial George Enescu, Dorohoi . . . 032857
Muzeul Memorial Gheorghe M. Tattarascu, Bucureşti . . . 032802
Muzeul Memorial Iosif Vulcan, Oradea . . . 032904
Muzeul Memorial Liviu Rebreanu, Năsăud . . . 032897
Muzeul Memorial Nicolae Grigorescu, Câmpina . . . 032824
Muzeul Memorial Octavian Goga, Ciucea . . . 032833
Muzeul Memorial Petöfi Sándor, Coltau . . . 032840
Muzeul Mihai Eminescu, Iaşi . . . 032881
Muzeul Militar Naţional, Bucureşti . 032803
Muzeul Mineritului, Petroşani . . . 032907
Muzeul Municipal, Huşi . . . 032874
Muzeul Municipal, Râmnicu Sărat . 032920
Muzeul Municipal Câmpulung, Câmpulung . . . 032825
Muzeul Municipal Câmpulung-Secţia de Etnografie şi, Artă Populară, Câmpulung . . . 032826
Muzeul Municipal Curtea de Argeş, Curtea de Argeş . . . 032852
Muzeul Municipal de Istorie, Roşiorii de Vede . . . 032927
Muzeul Municipal Dej ş Galeria de Artă, Dej . . . 032853
Muzeul Municipal Ioan Raica Sebeş, Sebeş . . . 032932
Muzeul Municipal Medias, Mediaş . 032892
Muzeul Municipiului Bucureşti, Bucureşti . . . 032804
Muzeul National al Literaturii Române, Bucureşti . . . 032805
Muzeul Naţional al Petrolului, Ploieşti . . . 032917
Muzeul Naţional al Pompierilor, Bucureşti . . . 032806
Muzeul Naţional al Satului, Bucureşti . . . 032807
Muzeul Naţional al Unirii, Alba Iulia 032771
Muzeul Naţional Brukenthal, Sibiu . 032936
Muzeul Naţional Cotroceni, Bucureşti . . . 032808
Muzeul Naţional de Artă al României, Bucureşti . . . 032809
Muzeul Naţional de Artă Cluj-Napoca, Cluj-Napoca . . . 032837
Muzeul National de Arte Plastice, Chişinău . . . 028984
Muzeul National de Etnografie si Istorie Naturala, Chişinău . . . 028985
Muzeul National de Istorie a Moldovei, Chişinău . . . 028986
Muzeul Naţional de Istorie a României, Bucureşti . . . 032810
Muzeul Naţional de Istorie a Transilvaniei, Cluj-Napoca . . . 032838
Muzeul Naţional de Istorie Naturala Grigore Antipa, Bucureşti . . . 032811
Muzeul Naţional George Enescu, Bucureşti . . . 032812
Muzeul Naţional Peleş, Sinaia . . . 032939
Muzeul National Secuisec, Sfântu Gheorghe . . . 032933
Muzeul Nicolae Iorga, Vălenii de Munte . . . 032966
Muzeul Obiceiurilor Populare din Bucovina, Gura Humorului . . . 032872
Muzeul Olteniei, Craiova . . . 032850
Muzeul Orăşanesc Fălticeni, Fălticeni . . . 032862
Muzeul Orăşenecs de Istorie şi Etnografie, Beiuş . . . 032781
Muzeul Orăşenesc, Carei . . . 032832
Muzeul Orăşenesc, Lipova . . . 032886
Muzeul Orăşenesc, Tecuci . . . 032956
Muzeul Orăşenesc de Istorie, Aiud . 032770
Muzeul Orăşenesc Molnar Istvan, Cristuru Secuiesc . . . 032851
Muzeul Pedagogic Republican, Chişinău . . . 028987
Muzeul Primei Şcoli Româneşti din Scheii Braşovului, Braşov . . . 032793
Muzeul Regiunii Porţilor de Fier, Drobeta-Turnu Severin . . . 032859
Muzeul Romanaţiului, Caracal . . . 032829
Muzeul Romanaţiului Secţia de Artă Plastică, Caracal . . . 032830
Muzeul Sătesc, Cornu . . . 032847
Muzeul Secuiesc al Ciucului, Miercurea-Ciuc . . . 032893
Muzeul Ştiinţei şi Tehnicii Ştefan Procopiu, Iaşi . . . 032882
Muzeul Tăranului Român, Bucureşti 032813
Muzeul Ţării Crişurilor, Oradea . . . 032905
Muzeul Tării Oaşului, Negreşti-Oaş . 032899
Muzeul Tarisznyás Márton, Gheorghieni . . . 032868
Muzeul Taru Făgărasuliu, Făgăraş . 032861
Muzeul Teatrului, Iaşi . . . 032883
Muzeul Teatrului Naţional, Bucureşti . . . 032814
Muzeul Tehnic Prof. Ing. Dimitrie Leonida, Bucureşti . . . 032815
Muzeul Theodor Aman, Muzeul Municipiului Bucureşti, Bucureşti . . . 032816
Muzeul Theodor Pallady, Muzeul Naţional de Artă al României, Bucureşti . . . 032817
Muzeul Tiparului şi al Cărţii Vechi Româneşti, Târgovişte . . . 032947
Muzeul Unirii, Iaşi . . . 032884
Muzeul Vasile Pârvan, Bârlad . . . 032780
Muzeul Vrancei, Focşani . . . 032864
Muzeul Zoologic al Universităţii Babeş-Bolyai, Cluj-Napoca . . . 032839
Muzeum, Bzenec . . . 008306
Muzeum, Koszalin . . . 032019
Muzeum, Zábřeh na Moravě . . . 008772
Muzeum 1 Pułku Strzelców Podhalańskich Armii Krajowej, Muzeum Diecezjalnego w Tarnowie, Szczawa . . . 032362
Muzeum 24 Pułku Ułanów, Muzeum Regionalnego w Kraśniku, Kraśnik 032071
Muzeum 600-lecia Jasnej Góry, Częstochowa . . . 031885
Muzeum 7 Pułku Ułanów Lubelskich, Mińsk Mazowiecki . . . 032148
Muzeum a Galerie, Okresní vlastivědné muzeum Přerov, Hranice . . . 008391
Muzeum a Galerie Litomyšl, Litomyšl . . . 008482
Muzeum a Galerie Orlických Hor, Rychnov nad Kněžnou . . . 008679
Muzeum a Galerie Severního Plzeňska, Kralovice . . . 008453
Muzeum a Pojizerská Galerie, Semily . . . 008683
Muzeum Adwokatury Polskiej, Warszawa . . . 032427
Muzeum Afrykanistyczne im. Dr. Bogdana Szczygła, Olkusz . . . 032188
Muzeum Akademii Medycznej, Poznań . . . 032238
Muzeum Akademii Sztuk Pięknych, Warszawa . . . 032428
Muzeum Aloise Jiráska, Hronov . . . 008392
Muzeum Aloise Jiráska a Mikoláše Alše, Praha . . . 008624
Múzeum Andreja Kmet'a, Slovenské Národné Múzeum, Martin . . . 034386
Muzeum Andrzeja Struga, Muzeum Literatury w Warszawie, Warszawa . . . 032429
Muzeum Antického Sochařství a Architektury Litomyšl, Litomyšl . . 008483
Muzeum Antonína Dvořáka, Praha . 008625
Muzeum Archeologiczne, Gdańsk . . 031909
Muzeum Archeologiczne, Gniew . . . 031939
Muzeum Archeologiczne, Poznań . . 032239
Muzeum Archeologiczne, Muzeum Miejskie Wrocławia, Wrocław . . . 032514
Muzeum Archeologiczne i Etnograficzne, Łódź . . . 032109
Muzeum Archeologiczne Środkowego Nadodrza, Świdnica . . . 032354
Muzeum Archeologiczne w Biskupinie, Gąsawa . . . 031903
Muzeum Archeologiczne w Krakowie, Kraków . . . 032034
Muzeum Archeologiczne w Krakowie, Oddział w Nowej Hucie, Kraków . 032035

Muzeum Archeologiczno-Historyczne, Głogów 031935
Muzeum Archidiecezjalne, Katowice 031986
Muzeum Archidiecezjalne, Poznań . 032240
Muzeum Archidiecezjalne, Przemyśl 032261
Muzeum Archidiecezjalne, Szczecin 032365
Muzeum Archidiecezjalne, Wrocław 032515
Muzeum Archidiecezjalne Lubelskie, Lublin 032128
Muzeum Archidiecezjalne w Krakowie, Kraków 032036
Muzeum Archidiecezjalne w Oliwie, Gdańsk 031910
Muzeum Archidiecezji Łódzkiej, Łódź 032110
Muzeum Archidiecezji Warszawskiej, Warszawa 032430
Muzeum Architektury, Wrocław . . . 032516
Muzeum Armii Krajowej, Kraków . . 032037
Muzeum Armii Poznań, Wielkopolskie Muzeum Walk Niepodległościowych w Poznaniu, Poznań 032241
Muzeum Azji i Pacyfiku, Warszawa . 032431
Múzeum Bábkarských Kultúr a Hračiek Hrad Modrý Kameň, Slovenské Národné Múzeum, Modrý Kameň 034394
Múzeum Bábkarských Kutúr a Hračiek Hrad Modrý Kameň, expozícia Dolná Strhová, Dolná Strehová 034348
Muzeum Bedřicha Hrozného, Lysá nad Labem 008494
Muzeum Bedřicha Smetany, Praha . 008626
Muzeum Benátky nad Jizerou, Benátky nad Jizerou 008264
Muzeum Beskidzkie im. A. Podżorskiego, Muzeum w Cieszynie, Wisła 032497
Muzeum Beskyd Frýdek-Místek, Frýdek-Místek 008361
Muzeum Betlémů, Karlštejn 008428
Muzeum Biblioteki Kórnickiej, Polish Academy of Sciences, Kórnik . . . 032014
Muzeum Biblioteki Publicznej Warszawa-Bielany, Warszawa 032432
Muzeum Bicyklů, Rokycany 008667
Muzeum Biograficzne Władysława Orkana, Muzeum im. Wł. Orkana w Rabce, Poręba Wielka 032234
Muzeum Bitwy Grunwaldzkiej, Muzeum Warmii i Mazur w Olsztynie, Stębark 032341
Muzeum Bitwy Legnickiej, Muzeum Miedzi w Legnicy, Legnickie Pole 032096
Muzeum Blansko, Blansko 008270
Muzeum Bolesława Prusa, Bolesława 031846
Muzeum Bolesława Prusa, Nałęczów 032160
Muzeum Borów Tucholskich, Tuchola 032400
Muzeum Boskovicka, Boskovice . . . 008272
Muzeum Boženy Němcové, Česká Skalice 008314
Muzeum Bratří Čapků, Malé Svatoňovice 008496
Muzeum Broni Pancernej, Poznań . 032242
Muzeum Bučovice, Muzeum Vyškovska, Bučovice 008302
Muzeum Budownictva Ludowego, Sanok 032307
Muzeum Budownictwa i Techniki Wiejskiej, Muzeum w Gorzowie Wielkopolskim, Bogdaniec 031845
Muzeum Budownictwa Ludowego - Park Etnograficzny w Olsztynku, Olsztynek 032193
Muzeum Byłego Obozu Zagłady w Chełmnie nad Narem, Chełmno 031865
Muzeum Byłego Obozu Zagłady w Sobiborze, Muzeum Pojezierza Łęczyńsko-Włodawskiego, Sobibór 032323
Muzeum Cechu Rzemiosł Skórzanych im. Jana Kilińskiego, Warszawa 032433
Muzeum Ceramiki, Bolesławiec . . . 031848
Muzeum Ceramiki Kaszubskiej Neclów, Chmielno 031867
Múzeum Červený Kameň, Slovenské Národné Múzeum, Častá 034345
Múzeum Červený Kláštor, Červený Kláštor 034346
Muzeum České Hudby, Národní muzeum, Praha 008627
Muzeum Českého granátu, Třebenice 008718
Muzeum Českého Krasu v Berouně, Beroun 008266
Muzeum Českého Krasu v Berouně - pobočka muzeum v Žebráku, Žebrák 008781
Muzeum Českého Porcelánu, Klášterec nad Ohří 008435
Muzeum Českého Ráje, Turnov . . . 008727
Muzeum Chodska, Domažlice 008353
Muzeum Cystersów, Wąchock 032407
Muzeum Częstochowskie, Częstochowa 031886
Muzeum Czynu Niepodległościowego, Kraków 032038
Muzeum Czynu Partyzanckiego, Muzeum Okręgowego w Piotrkowie Trybunalskim, Polichno 032233
Muzeum Czynu Powstańczego, Muzeum Śląska Opolskiego w Opolu, Leśnica 032097
Muzeum Czynu Zbrojnego Pracowników Huty im. Tadeusza Sendzimira, Kraków 032039
Muzeum Dawnego Kupiectwa, Świdnica 032355
Muzeum Diecezjalne, Płock 032226
Muzeum Diecezjalne, Siedlce 032310
Muzeum Diecezjalne, Tarnów 032382
Muzeum Diecezjalne Sztuki Kościelnej, Sandomierz 032303
Muzeum Diecezjalne Sztuki Religijnej, Lublin 032129
Muzeum Diecezjalne w Opolu, Opole 032198
Muzeum Diecezji Pelpińskiej, Pelplin 032217
Muzeum Dom Urbańczyka, Chrzanów 031876
Muzeum Dom Wincentego Witosa, Wierzchosławice 032496
Muzeum Dr. Aleše Hrdličky, Humpolec 008395
Muzeum Dr. Bohuslava Horáka, Rokycany 008668
Muzeum Dr. Bohuslava Horáka, Pobočka vodni hamr Dobřív, Dobřiv 008349
Muzeum Drukarstwa Warszawskiego, Muzeum Historyczne Warszawy, Warszawa 032434
Muzeum Dworek Zabytkowy, Stryszów 032343
Muzeum Dworu Polskiego, Plochocin 032225
Muzeum Dzieje i Kultura Żydów, Muzeum Historyczne Miasta Krakowa, Kraków 032040
Muzeum Emeryka Hutten-Czapskiego, Muzeum Narodowe w Krakowie, Kraków 032041
Muzeum Emila Zegadłowicza, Wadowice 032409
Muzeum Energetyki Jeleniogórskiej, Szklarska Poręba 032374
Muzeum Etnograficzne, Toruń 032393
Muzeum Etnograficzne, Muzeum Narodowe w Poznaniu, Poznań 032243
Muzeum Etnograficzne, Muzeum Narodowe w Wrocławiu, Wrocław 032517
Muzeum Etnograficzne, Ziemi Kujawskiej i Dobrzyńskiej, Włocławek 032502
Muzeum Etnograficzne im. Franciszka Kotuli, Muzeum Okręgowego w Rzeszowie, Rzeszów 032300
Muzeum Etnograficzne im. Seweryna Udzieli, Kraków 032042
Muzeum Etnograficzne w Oliwie, Muzeum Narodowe go w Gdańsku, Gdańsk 031911
Muzeum Etnograficzne w Zielonej Górze z Siedzibą w Ochli, Ochla 032182
Muzeum Etnograficzny, Muzeum Okręgowego w Tarnowie, Tarnów 032383
Muzeum Ewolucji Instytutu Paleobiologii PAN, Warszawa 032435
Muzeum Farmacji, Warszawa 032436
Muzeum Farmacji, Collegium Medicum Uniwersytetu Jagiellońskiego, Kraków 032043
Muzeum Feliksa Nowowiejskiego, Barczewo 031817
Múzeum Ferdiša Kostku, Stupava . . 034435
Muzeum Filumenistyczne, Bystrzyca Kłodzka 031859
Muzeum Fojtství, Kopřivnice 008444
Muzeum-Fort VII, Oddział Muzeum Historii Ruchu Robotniczego w Poznaniu, Poznań 032244
Muzeum - Františkánský klaster, Kadaň 008421
Muzeum Fryderyka Chopina, Towarzystwo im. Fryderyka Chopina, Warszawa 032437
Muzeum Fryderyka Chopina w Żelazowej Woli, Sochaczew 032326
Muzeum G. Casanovy, Duchcov . . . 008355
Muzeum Gazownictwa, Paczków . . 032214
Muzeum Gazownictwa, Sobótka . . . 032324
Muzeum Gazownictwa przy Gazowni Warszawskiej, Warszawa 032438
Muzeum Geologiczne, Instytutu Nauk Geologicznych PAN, Kraków 032044
Muzeum Geologiczne, Instytutu Nauk Geologicznych Uniwersytetu Wrocławskiego, Wrocław 032518
Muzeum Geologiczne, Wydziału Geologii, Geofizyki i Ochrony Środowiska AGH, Kraków 032045
Muzeum Geologiczne Obszaru Górnośląskiego Instytutu Geologicznego, Sosnowiec 032331
Muzeum Geologiczne Państwowego Instytutu Geologicznego, Warszawa 032439
Muzeum Geologiczne Uniwersytetu Szczecińskiego, Szczecin 032366
Muzeum Geologii Złóż im. Czesława Poborskiego, Politechnika Śląska, Gliwice 031933
Muzeum Górnictwa i Hutnictwa Kopalina Złota, Złoty Stok 032564
Muzeum Górnictwa i Hutnictwa Rud Żelaza, Muzeum Częstochowskiego, Częstochowa 031887
Muzeum Górnictwa Podziemnego, Nowa Ruda 032166
Muzeum Górnictwa Węglowego, Zabrze 032540
Muzeum Górnicze, Bogatynia 031844
Muzeum Górnośląskie, Bytom 031860
Muzeum Gross-Rosen, Wałbrzych . 032412
Muzeum Henryka Sienkiewicza, Wola Okrzejska 032509
Muzeum Henryka Sienkiewicza w Oblęgorku, Muzeum Narodowe w Kielcach, Oblęgorek 032181
Muzeum Historických Motocyklů, Kašperské Hory 008430
Muzeum Historii Fotografii, Kraków 032046
Muzeum Historii Fotografii im. Prof. Władisława Bogackiego, Krakowskie Towarzystwo Fotograficzne, Kraków 032047
Muzeum Historii Katowic, Katowice 031987
Muzeum Historii Medycyny i Farmacji, Szczecin 032367
Muzeum Historii Miasta, Zduńska Wola 032557
Muzeum Historii Miasta, Muzeum Narodowe w Szczecinie, Szczecin 032368
Muzeum Historii Miasta Łodzi, Łódź 032111
Muzeum Historii Miasta Lublina, Muzeum Lubelskiego w Lublinie, Lublin . . . 032130
Muzeum Historii Miasta Poznania, Muzeum Narodowe w Poznaniu, Poznań . . 032245
Muzeum Historii Młynarstwa i Wodnych Urządzeń Przemysłu Wiejskiego w Jaraczu, Muzeum Narodowe Rolnictwa i Przemysłu Rolno-Spożywczego w Szreniawie, Jaracz 031961
Muzeum Historii Polskiego Rucha Ludowego, Piaseczno koło Gniewa 032218
Muzeum Historii Polskiego Ruchu Ludowego, Warszawa 032440
Muzeum Historii Polskiego Ruchu Ludowego w Warszawie, Oddział w Sandomierzu, Sandomierz 032304
Muzeum Historii Przemysłu, Opatówek 032194
Muzeum Historii Włocławka, Muzeum Ziemi Kujawskiej i Dobrzynskiej, Włocławek 032503
Muzeum Historii Żdów Polskich, Warszawa 032441
Muzeum Historyczne, Muzeum Okręgowego w Białymstoku, Białystok 031827
Muzeum Historyczne, Muzeum Okręgowego w Ostrołęce, Przasnysz 032260
Muzeum Historyczne Miasta Gdańska, Gdańsk 031912
Muzeum Historyczne Miasta Krakowa, Kraków 032048
Muzeum Historyczne Miasta Krakowa - Oddział Pomorska, Kraków 032049
Muzeum Historyczne Miasta Starego Warszawy, Warszawa 032442
Muzeum Historyczne Miasta Tarnobrzega, Tarnobrzeg 032380
Muzeum Historyczne - Pałac w Dukli, Dukla 031899
Muzeum Historyczne w Sanoku, Sanok 032308
Muzeum Historyczne w Wrocławiu, Muzeum Miejskie Wrocławia, Wrocław . . . 032519
Muzeum Historyczno-Archeologiczne, Ostrowiec Świętokrzyski 032206
Muzeum Historyczno-Etnograficzne, Chojnice 031869
Muzeum Hlavního Města Prahy, Praha 008628
Muzeum Hodin, Šternberk 008694
Muzeum Hrnčířstvi a Keramiky, Kostelec nad Černými lesy 008447
Muzeum Husitstvi, Žlutice 008790
Muzeum Hymnu Narodowego, Muzeum Narodowe w Gdańsku, Nowy Karczma 032173
Muzeum i Instytut Zoologi PAN, Warszawa 032443
Muzeum Ignacego Jana Paderewskiego i Wychodźstwa Polskiego w Ameryce, Muzeum Narodowe w Warszawie, Warszawa 032444
Muzeum im. Adama Mickiewicza w Śmiełowie, Muzeum Narodowe w Poznaniu, Żerków 032558
Muzeum im. Aleksandra Świętochowskiego, Gołotczyzna 031942
Muzeum im. Anny i Jarosława Iwaszkiewiczów w Stawisku, Podkowa Leśna 032230
Muzeum im. Edmunda Bojanowskiego w Grabonogu, Grabonóg 031949
Muzeum im. Jana Dzierzona, Kluczbork 032006
Muzeum im. Jana Kasprowicza, Inowrocław 031958
Muzeum im. Jana Nikodema Jaronia, Olesno 032187
Muzeum im. Jerzego Dunin-Borkowskiego, Krośniewice 032075
Muzeum im. J.G. Herdera w Morągu, Oddział Muzeum Warmii i Mazur w Olsztynie, Morąg 032151
Muzeum im. Kazimierza Pułaskiego, Warka-Winiary 032416
Muzeum im. Michąla Kajki w Ogródku, Muzeum Okręgowego w Suwałkach, Ogródek 032184
Muzeum im. Nałkowskich, Wołomin 032511
Muzeum im. Orła Białego, Skarżysko-Kamienna 032317
Muzeum im. Oskara Kolberga, Muzeum Wsi Radomskiej w Radomiu, Przysucha 032265
Muzeum im. prof. Władysława Szafera, Ojców 032185
Muzeum im. Stanisława Noakowskiego, Muzeum Ziemi Kujawskiej i Dobrzyńskiej, Nieszawa 032165
Muzeum im. Stanisława Staszica, Muzeum Okręgowego w Zamościu, Hrubieszów 031956

Muzeum im. Wiktora Stachowiaka, Trzcianka ... 032398
Muzeum im. Władysława Orkana, Rabka ... 032277
Muzeum im. Władysława St. Reymonta, Muzeum Okręgowego w Żyrardowie, Lipce Reymonotowskie ... 032104
Muzeum im. Wojciecha Kętrzyńskiego, Kętrzyn ... 031996
Muzeum Instrumentów Muzycznych, Muzeum Narodowe w Poznaniu, Poznań ... 032246
Muzeum Inżynierii Miejskiej, Kraków ... 032050
Muzeum Jáchymovského Hornictví a Lázeňství, Jáchymov ... 008403
Muzeum Jana Ámoše Komenského, Uherský Brod ... 008733
Muzeum Jana Cybisa, Muzeum Śląska Opolskiego w Opolu, Głogówek .. 031936
Muzeum Jana Kasprowicza, Stowarzyszenia Przyjaciół Twórczości J.Kasprowicza, Zakopane ... 032547
Múzeum Janka Krála, Liptovský Mikuláš ... 034376
Muzeum Jeseník, Jeseník ... 008407
Muzeum Jihovýchodní Moravy, Zlín 008787
Muzeum Jindřicha Jindřicha, Domažlice ... 008354
Muzeum Jindřicha Simona Baara, Klenčí pod Čerchovem ... 008437
Muzeum Jindřicho Hradecka, Jindřichův Hradec ... 008416
Múzeum J.M. Petzvala, Slovenské Technické Múzeum Košice, Spišská Béla ... 034428
Muzeum Josefa Dobrovského a pamětní síň Jaroslava Kvapila, Chudenice ... 008343
Muzeum Józefa Ignacego Kraszewskiego, Romanów ... 032293
Muzeum Juliana Fałata, Oddział Muzeum Okręgowego w Bielsku-Białej, Bystra ... 031858
Muzeum Kamieni Szlachetnych, Polanica Zdrój ... 032232
Muzeum Kamienica Łozińskich, Muzeum Narodowe, Kraków ... 032051
Muzeum Kamienica Orsettich w Jarosławiu, Jarosław ... 031963
Muzeum Karkonoskie, Jelenia Góra 031971
Muzeum Karola Szymanowskiego, Muzeum Narodowe w Krakowie, Zakopane 032548
Muzeum Karykatury, Warszawa ... 032445
Muzeum-Kaszubski Park Etnograficzny w Wdzydzach Kiszewskich, Wdzydze Kiszewskie ... 032488
Muzeum Kaszubskie, Kartuzy ... 031984
Muzeum Kaszubskie, Kościerzyna . 032016
Muzeum Katedralne Jana Pawła II, Kraków ... 032052
Muzeum Katolickiego Uniwersytetu Lubelskiego im. Ks. Władzińskiego, Lublin ... 032131
Muzeum Katyńskie, Warszawa ... 032446
Muzeum Keramiky, Bechyně ... 008262
Múzeum Keramiky, Holíč ... 034356
Muzeum Kinematografii, Łódź ... 032112
Muzeum Klasztorne OO Cystersów, Szczyrzyc ... 032372
Muzeum Klimkovice, Klimkovice .. 008438
Muzeum Knihy, Národní muzeum Praha, Žďár nad Sázavou ... 008779
Muzeum Kolei Wąskotorowej, Sochaczew ... 032327
Muzeum Kolei Wąskotorowej w Wenecji, Muzeum Ziemi Pałuckiej w Żninie, Wenecja ... 032491
Muzeum Kolejnictwa, Warszawa .. 032447
Muzeum Kolekcji im. Jana Pawła II, Fundacji Carroll Porczyńskich, Warszawa ... 032448
Muzeum Komenského v Přerově, Přerov ... 008655
Muzeum Kornela Makuszyńskiego, Muzeum Tatrzańskiego w Zakopanem, Zakopane ... 032549
Muzeum Kościuszkowskie Dworek Zacisze, Miechów ... 032140
Muzeum Kouřimska, Kouřim ... 008448
Muzeum Kowalstwa w Warszawie, Warszawa ... 032449
Muzeum Krajky, Prachatice ... 008590
Muzeum Krajky, Vamberk ... 008743
Muzeum Krnov, Muzeum v Bruntále, Krnov ... 008458
Muzeum Kroměřížska, Kroměříž ... 008459
Muzeum Krupka, Regionální muzeum v Teplicích, Krupka ... 008460
Muzeum Książąt Czartoryskich, Muzeum Narodowe w Krakowie, Kraków .. 032053
Muzeum Książki Artystycznej, Łódź 032113
Múzeum Kultúry Karpatských Nemcov, Slovenské Národné Múzeum, Bratislava ... 034329
Muzeum Kultury Łemkowskiej w Zyndranowej, Tylawa ... 032403
Muzeum Kultury Ludowej, Kolbuszowa ... 032008
Muzeum Kultury Ludowej, Węgorzewo ... 032489
Muzeum Kultury Ludowej, Muzeum Okręgowego w Pile, Osiek nad Notecią ... 032203
Múzeum Kultúry Maďarov na Slovensku, Slovenské Národné Múzeum, Bratislava ... 034330
Muzeum Kultury Szlacheckiej, Łopuszna ... 032122
Muzeum Lachów Sądeckich im. Zofii i Stanisława Chrząstowskich, Sądecki Park Etnograficznego w Nowym Sączu, Podegrodzie ... 032229
Muzeum Lasu i Drewna przy Lesnym Zakładzie Doświadczalnym SGGW, Rogów ... 032290
Muzeum Lat Szkolnych Stefana Żeromskiego, Kielce ... 031998
Muzeum Latarnia Morska, Władysławowo ... 032500
Muzeum Łazienki Krolewskie, Warszawa ... 032450
Múzeum Letectva Košice, Slovenské Technické Múzeum, Košice ... 034364
Muzeum Lidových Staveb, Kouřim . 008449
Muzeum Literackie Henryka Sienkiewicza, Poznań ... 032247
Muzeum Literackie im. Józefa Czechowicza, Muzeum Lubelskiego w Lublin, Lublin ... 032132
Muzeum Literatury im. Adama Mickiewicza, Warszawa ... 032451
Muzeum Literatury im. Jarosława Iwaszkiewicza, Muzeum Okręgowego w Sandomierzu, Sandomierz ... 032305
Muzeum Litovel, Litovel ... 008485
Muzeum Lotnictwa Polskiego, Kraków ... 032054
Muzeum Loutkářských Kultur, Chrudim ... 008341
Muzeum Łowiectwa i Jeździectwa, Warszawa ... 032452
Muzeum Lubelskie, Lublin ... 032133
Múzeum Ludovita Štúra, Modra ... 034393
Muzeum Ludowych Instrumentów Muzycznych, Szydłowiec ... 032379
Múzeum Madarskej Kultúry a Podunajska, Komárno ... 034363
Muzeum Małego Miasta, Bieżuń ... 031837
Muzeum Marie Gardavské, Kojetín . 008440
Muzeum Marii Dąbrowskiej, Warszawa ... 032453
Muzeum Marii Konopnickiej, Muzeum Okręgowego w Suwałkach, Suwałki ... 032350
Muzeum Marii Konopnickiej w Żarnowcu, Jedlicze ... 031968
Muzeum Marii Skłodowskiej-Curie, Warszawa ... 032454
Muzeum Martyrologiczne w Żabikowie, Luboń ... 032137
Muzeum Martyrologii, Bielsk Podlaski ... 031832
Muzeum Martyrologii Alianckich Jeńców Wojennych, Żagań ... 032543
Muzeum Martyrologii i Walki Radogoszcz, Łódź ... 032114
Muzeum Martyrologii Pod Zegarem, Muzeum Lubelskiego w Lublinie, Lublin ... 032134
Muzeum Martyrologii (Sonnenburg), Słońsk ... 032319
Muzeum Martyrologii Wielkopolan w Forcie VII, Wielkopolskiego Muzeum Historycznego w Poznaniu, Poznań ... 032248
Muzeum Marynarki Wojennej, Gdynia ... 031926
Muzeum Mazowieckie w Płocku, Płock ... 032227
Muzeum Mazowsza Zachodniego, Gabinet Pisarza Pawła Hulki-Lasowskiego, Żyradów ... 032567
Muzeum Mazurskie, Muzeum Warmii i Mazur w Olsztynie, Szczytno ... 032373
Muzeum Města Brna, Brno ... 008293
Muzeum Města Ústí nad Labem, Ústí nad Labem ... 008737
Muzeum Městské Ústí nad Orlicí, Ústí nad Orlicí ... 008738
Muzeum Miar - Zbiory Metrologiczne Głównego Urzędu Miar, Warszawa 032455
Muzeum Miasta Gdyni, Gdynia ... 031927
Muzeum Miasta i Rzeki Warty, Warta ... 032486
Muzeum Miasta Jaworzna, Jaworzno ... 031967
Muzeum Miasta Kołobrzegu, Muzeum Oręża Polskiego, Kołobrzeg ... 032010
Muzeum Miasta Ostrowa Wielkopolskiego, Ostrów Wielkopolski ... 032205
Muzeum Miasta Pabianice, Pabianice ... 032213
Muzeum Miasta Zgierza, Zgierz ... 032559
Múzeum Michala Greisigera, Spišská Béla ... 034429
Muzeum Miedzi, Legnica ... 032095
Muzeum Miejskie, Nowa Sól ... 032169
Muzeum Miejskie, Świętochłowice . 032357
Muzeum Miejskie, Zabrze ... 032541
Muzeum Miejskie, Muzeum Okręgowego w Ostrołęce, Wyszków ... 032538
Muzeum Miejskie im. Maksymiliana Chroboka, Ruda Śląska ... 032294
Muzeum Mikołaja Kopernika, Frombork ... 031902
Muzeum Mikołaja Kopernika, Muzeum Okręgowego w Toruniu, Toruń ... 032394
Muzeum Militariów Arsenał Miejski, Muzeum Miejskie Wrocławia, Wrocław ... 032520
Muzeum Mineralogiczne, Szklarska Poręba ... 032375
Muzeum Mineralogiczne, Instytutu Nauk Geologicznych Uniwersytutu Wrocławskiego, Wrocław ... 032521
Muzeum Mineralogicznego Uniwersytetu Wrocławskiego, Wrocław ... 032522
Muzeum Misyjne, Czerna ... 031883
Muzeum Misyjne, Krosno ... 032076
Muzeum Misyjne Misjonarzy Oblatów MN, Święty Krzyż ... 032358
Muzeum Misyjno-Etnograficzne, Seminarium Duchownego Księży Werbistów, Pieniężno ... 032219
Muzeum Mladaboleslavska, Mladá Boleslav ... 008506
Muzeum Młynarstwa Powietrznego, Bęsia ... 031823
Muzeum Mohelnice, Mohelnice ... 008510
Muzeum Morskie, Muzeum Narodowe w Szczecinie, Szczecin ... 032369
Muzeum Motocyklů, Lesná u Znojma ... 008470
Muzeum Motoryzacji, Otrębusy ... 032210
Muzeum Motoryzacji Automobilklubu Wielkopolski, Poznań ... 032249
Muzeum Nadwiślański Park Etnograficzny, Babice ... 031815
Muzeum Nadwiślańskie, Kazimierz Dolny ... 031990
Muzeum Narodowe, Gdańsk ... 031913
Muzeum Narodowe, Szczecin ... 032370
Muzeum Narodowe, Biblioteka Czartoryskich, Kraków ... 032055
Muzeum Narodowe Rolnictwa i Przemysłu Rolno-Spożywczego, Uzarzewo .. 032405
Muzeum Narodowe Rolnictwa i Przemysłu Rolno-Spożywczego w Szreniawie, Komorniki ... 032012
Muzeum Narodowe w Kielcach, Kielce ... 031999
Muzeum Narodowe w Krakowie, Kraków ... 032056
Muzeum Narodowe w Poznaniu, Galeria Malarstwa i Rzeźby, Poznań ... 032250
Muzeum Narodowe w Poznaniu, Oddział w Rogalinie, Rogalin ... 032288
Muzeum Narodowe w Warszawie, Warszawa ... 032456
Muzeum Narodowe we Wrocławiu, Wrocław ... 032523
Muzeum Narodowe Ziemi Przemyskiej, Przemyśl ... 032262
Muzeum Niepodległości, Warszawa 032457
Muzeum Nikifora, Galeria Sztuki Romanówka, Krynica ... 032081
Múzeum Obchodu, Bratislava ... 034331
Múzeum Obchodu, Ilava ... 034359
Muzeum Oceanograficzne Mir, Gdynia ... 031928
Muzeum Oddział im. Albina Makowskiego, Chojnice ... 031870
Muzeum Odona Bujwida, Kraków .. 032057
Muzeum Okręgowe, Biała Podlaska 031825
Muzeum Okręgowe, Bielsko-Biała . 031835
Muzeum Okręgowe, Ciechanów ... 031878
Muzeum Okręgowe, Konin ... 032013
Muzeum Okręgowe, Krosno ... 032077
Muzeum Okręgowe, Nowy Sącz ... 032175
Muzeum Okręgowe, Ostrołęka ... 032204
Muzeum Okręgowe, Piotrków Trybunalski ... 032223
Muzeum Okręgowe, Rzeszów ... 032301
Muzeum Okręgowe, Sandomierz .. 032306
Muzeum Okręgowe, Sieradz ... 032314
Muzeum Okręgowe, Suwałki ... 032351
Muzeum Okręgowe, Tarnów ... 032384
Muzeum Okręgowe, Zamość ... 032553
Muzeum Okregowe, Żyradów ... 032568
Muzeum Okręgowe, Tarnów Oddział - Dwór w Dołędze, Zaborów ... 032539
Muzeum Okręgowe im. Leona Wyczółkowskiego, Bydgoszcz ... 031855
Muzeum Okręgowe w Chełmie, Chełm ... 031864
Muzeum Okręgowe w Lesznie, Leszno ... 032098
Muzeum Okręgowe w Toruniu, Toruń ... 032395
Muzeum Okręgowe Zabytków Techniki, Drogownictwa przy Rejonie Dróg Publicznych w Tarnowie, Tarnów . 032385
Muzeum Okręgowe Ziemi Kaliskiej, Kalisz ... 031976
Muzeum Okręt Błyskawica, Gdynia . 031929
Muzeum Olomučanské Keramiky, Olomučany ... 008544
Muzeum Oręża Polskiego, Kołobrzeg ... 032011
Muzeum Oświatowe, Szkolne Schronisko Młodzieżowe Muzeum Oświatowe w Puławach, Puławy ... 032272
Muzeum Oświaty w Bydgoszczy, Bydgoszcz ... 031856
Muzeum Pałac w Wilanowie, Warszawa ... 032458
Muzeum Pamiątek po Janie Matejce Koryznówka, Nowy Wiśnicz ... 032179
Muzeum Pamięci Narodowej, Kraków ... 032058
Muzeum Pamięci Narodowej lata 1939 - 1956, Kielce ... 032000
Muzeum Papiernictwa, Duszniki Zdrój ... 031900
Muzeum Parafialne, Pakość ... 032215
Muzeum Parafialne, Widawa ... 032492
Muzeum Parafialne, Filia Muzeum Diecezjalnego w Tarnowie, Bobowa ... 031841
Muzeum Parafialne, Filia Muzeum Diecezjalnego w Tarnowie, Iwkowa ... 031960

Muzeum Parafialne, Filia Muzeum Diecezjalnego w Tarnowie, Rzepiennik Strzyżewski . . . 032299
Muzeum Parafialne, Filia Muzeum Diecezjalnego w Tarnowie, Tropie 032397
Muzeum Parafialne, Muzeum Diecezjalne w Tarnowie, Dobra . . . 031895
Muzeum Parafialne, Muzeum Diecezjalnego w Tarnowie, Grybów . . . 031954
Muzeum Parafialne, Muzeum Diecezjalnego w Tarnowie, Krynica . . . 032082
Muzeum Parafialne, Muzeum Diecezjalnego w Tarnowie, Złota . . . 032562
Muzeum Parafialne im. Jana Wnęka w Odporyszowie, Muzeum Diecezjalnego w Tarnowie, Odporyszów . . . 032183
Muzeum Parafialne im. Ks. Edwarda Nitki, Filia Muzeum Diecezjalnego w Tarnowie, Paszyn . . . 032216
Muzeum Pedagogiczne, Gdańsk . . . 031914
Muzeum Piastów Śląskich, Brzeg . . 031852
Muzeum Pienińskie im. Józefa Szalaya, Muzeum Okręgowego w Nowym Sączu, Szczawnica . . . 032363
Muzeum Pierwszych Piastów na Lednicy, Lednogóra . . . 032093
Muzeum Piśmiennictwa i Muzyki Kaszubsko-Pomorskiej, Wejherowo . . . 032490
Muzeum Plakatu w Wilanowie, Muzeum Narodowe w Warszawie, Warszawa . . . 032459
Muzeum Początków Państwa Polskiego, Gniezno . . . 031941
Muzeum Poczty i Telekomunikacji, Wrocław . . . 032524
Muzeum Poczty i Telekomunikacji Oddział w Gdańsku, Gdańsk . . . 031915
Muzeum Podhalańskie PTTK, Nowy Targ . . . 032177
Muzeum Podkrkonoší, Trutnov . . . 008725
Muzeum Pojezierza Łęczyńsko-Włodawskiego, Włodawa . . . 032507
Múzeum Polície Slovenskej Republiky, Bratislava . . . 034332
Muzeum Politechniki Warszawskiej, Warszawa . . . 032460
Muzeum Polná, Polná . . . 008587
Muzeum Północno-Mazowiecke, Łomża . . . 032121
Muzeum Polskiej Wojskowej Służby Zdrowia, Łódź . . . 032115
Muzeum Południowego Podlasia, Biała Podlaska . . . 031825
Muzeum Pomorza Środkowego, Słupsk . . . 032321
Muzeum Porcelánu Pirkenhammer, Březová u Karlových Var . . . 008280
Muzeum Powstania Chochołowskiego, Chochołów . . . 031868
Muzeum Powstania Warszawskiego, Muzeum Historycznego Miasta Starego Warszawy, Warszawa . . . 032461
Muzeum Pożarnictwa, Alwernia . . . 031812
Muzeum Pożarnictwa, Lidzbark . . . 032101
Muzeum Pożarnictwa Ziemi Olkuskiej, Olkusz . . . 032189
Muzeum Pożarnicze, Dział Muzeum w Przeworsku, Przeworsk . . . 032263
Muzeum-Pracownia Literacka Arkadego Fiedlera, Puszczykowo . . . 032275
Muzeum Prawa i Prawników Polskich, Katowice . . . 031988
Muzeum Prof. Josepha Wittiga, Nowa Ruda . . . 032167
Muzeum Prostějovska, Prostějov . . 008661
Muzeum Prowincji oo Bernardynów, Leżajsk . . . 032100
Muzeum Prywatne Diabła Polskiego Przedpiekle, Warszawa . . . 032462
Muzeum Przemysłu, Muzeum Techniki, Warszawa . . . 032463
Muzeum Przemysłu i Techniki, Muzeum w Wałbrzychu, Wałbrzych . . . 032413
Muzeum Przemysłu Naftowego w Bóbrce, Chorkówka . . . 031872
Muzeum przy Zakładach Metalowych im. Hipolita Cegielskiego, Poznań . . . 032251
Muzeum Przyrodnicze, Jelenia Góra 031972
Muzeum Przyrodnicze, Muzeum Nadwiślańskie, Kazimierz Dolny . 031991
Muzeum Przyrodnicze, Nadmorski Park Krajobrazowy, Władysławowo . . . 032501
Muzeum Przyrodnicze Babiogórskiego Parku Narodowego, Zawoja . . . 032555
Muzeum Przyrodnicze Bieszczadzkiego Parku Narodowego, Ustrzyki Dolne . . . 032404
Muzeum Przyrodnicze Instytutu Systematyki i Ewolucji Zwierząt, Kraków . . . 032059
Muzeum Przyrodnicze Karkonoskiego Parku Narodowego, Jelenia Góra . . . 031973
Muzeum Przyrodnicze Uniwersytetu Łódzkiego, Łódź . . . 032116
Muzeum Przyrodnicze Uniwersytetu Wrocławskiego, Wrocław . . . 032525
Muzeum Przyrodnicze Wolińskiego Parku Narodowego im. Prof. Adama Wodziczki, Międzyzdroje . . . 032144
Muzeum Przyrodniczo-Leśne, Białowieża National Park, Białowieża . . . 031826
Muzeum Przyrodniczo-Leśne Słowińskiego Parku Narodowego, Smołdzino . . 032322
Muzeum Przyrodniczo-Leśne Świętokrzyskiego Parku Narodowego, Święty Krzyż . . . 032359
Muzeum Puszczy Kampinoskiej, Kampinos . . . 031980
Muzeum Reformacji Polskiej, Muzeum Okręgowego w Suwałkach, Mikołajki . . . 032147
Muzeum Regionalne, Barlinek . . . 031819
Muzeum Regionalne, Bełchatów . . . 031822
Muzeum Regionalne, Biecz . . . 031831
Muzeum Regionalne, Biłgoraj . . . 031838
Muzeum Regionalne, Brodnica . . . 031851
Muzeum Regionalne, Brzeziny . . . 031853
Muzeum Regionalne, Cedynia . . . 031862
Muzeum Regionalne, Chojnów . . . 031871
Muzeum Regionalne, Człuchów . . . 031890
Muzeum Regionalne, Głogówek . . . 031937
Muzeum Regionalne, Iłża . . . 031957
Muzeum Regionalne, Jarocin . . . 031962
Muzeum Regionalne, Jasło . . . 031964
Muzeum Regionalne, Jawor . . . 031966
Muzeum Regionalne, Kościan . . . 032015
Muzeum Regionalne, Kozienice . . . 032021
Muzeum Regionalne, Krasnystaw . . 032074
Muzeum Regionalne, Kutno . . . 032086
Muzeum Regionalne, Lubań . . . 032125
Muzeum Regionalne, Łuków . . . 032138
Muzeum Regionalne, Miechów . . . 032141
Muzeum Regionalne, Międzychód . 032142
Muzeum Regionalne, Mielec . . . 032146
Muzeum Regionalne, Nowe Miasto nad Pilicą . . . 032171
Muzeum Regionalne, Ojców . . . 032186
Muzeum Regionalne, Opoczno . . . 032196
Muzeum Regionalne, Ostrzeszów . . 032207
Muzeum Regionalne, Pińczów . . . 032222
Muzeum Regionalne, Pułtusk . . . 032274
Muzeum Regionalne, Pyzdry . . . 032276
Muzeum Regionalne, Radomsko . . 032282
Muzeum Regionalne, Siedlce . . . 032311
Muzeum Regionalne, Sławków . . . 032318
Muzeum Regionalne, Środa Śląska 032334
Muzeum Regionalne, Sucha Beskidzka . . . 032345
Muzeum Regionalne, Szczecinek . . 032371
Muzeum Regionalne, Szydłów . . . 032378
Muzeum Regionalne, Wągrowiec . . 032411
Muzeum Regionalne, Wiślica . . . 032498
Muzeum Regionalne, Wronki . . . 032535
Muzeum Regionalne, Filia Muzeum Okręgowego w Koninie, Słupca . . 032320
Muzeum Regionalne, Muzeum Lubelskiego w Lublinie, Kraśnik . . . 032072
Muzeum Regionalne, Muzeum Lubelskiego w Lublinie, Łęczna . . . 032091
Muzeum Regionalne, Muzeum Lubelskiego w Lublinie, Lubartów . . . 032126
Muzeum Regionalne, Muzeum w Międzyrzeczu, Pszczew . . . 032266
Muzeum Regionalne, Muzeum Ziemi Bydgoskiej im. L. Wyczółkowskiego, Radzyn Chełmiński . . . 032283
Muzeum Regionalne, Ośrodek Edukacji Plastycznej i Historycznej, Myślibórz . . . 032157
Muzeum Regionalne Dom Grecki, Myślenice . . . 032156
Muzeum Regionalne im. Adama Fastnachta, Brzozów . . . 031854
Muzeum Regionalne im. Albina Nowickiego, Ryn . . . 032297
Muzeum Regionalne im. Andrzeja Kaube, Wolin . . . 032510
Muzeum Regionalne im. Antoniego Minkiewicza, Olkusz . . . 032190
Muzeum Regionalne im. Dzieci Wrzesińskich, Września . . . 032536
Muzeum Regionalne im. Janusza Petera, Tomaszów Lubelski . . . 032388
Muzeum Regionalne im. Marcina Rożka, Wolsztyn . . . 032512
Muzeum Regionalne im. Seweryna Udzieli, Stary Sącz . . . 032340
Muzeum Regionalne im. Władysława Kowalskiego, Dobczyce . . . 031894
Muzeum Regionalne im Wojciechy Dutkiewicz, Rogozińskie Centrum Kultury, Rogoźno . . . 032292
Muzeum Regionalne Polskiego Towarzystwa Turystyczno-Krajoznawczego, Grodzisk Mazowiecki . . . 031950
Muzeum Regionalne PTTK, Golub-Dobrzyń . . . 031943
Muzeum Regionalne PTTK, Kępno . 031994
Muzeum Regionalne PTTK, Muszyna . . . 032155
Muzeum Regionalne PTTK, Puławy . 032273
Muzeum Regionalne PTTK, Starachowice . . . 032337
Muzeum Regionalne PTTK i Urzędu Gminy, Iwanowice . . . 031959
Muzeum Regionalne PTTK im. Hieronima Ławinczaka, Krotoszyn . . . 032079
Muzeum Regionalne PTTK im. J. Łukasiewicza, Gorlice . . . 031946
Muzeum Regionalne PTTK w Zagórzu Śląskim Zamek Grodno, Zagórze Śląskie . . . 032544
Muzeum Regionalne Siemiatycki Ośrodek Kultury, Siemiatycze . . . 032313
Muzeum Regionalne w Stęszewie, Stęszew . . . 032342
Muzeum Regionalne w Świebodzinie, Świebodzin . . . 032356
Muzeum Regionalne w Zagórzu Śląskim, Zamek Grodno, Jugowice . . . 031974
Muzeum Regionalne Ziemi Limanowskiej, Limanowa . . . 032103
Muzeum Regionalne Ziemi Sadowieńskiej, Sadowne . . . 032302
Muzeum Regionalne Ziemi Zbąszyńskiej PTTK, Zbąszyń . . . 032556
Muzeum Regionu Valšsko ve Vsetině - Zámek Vsetín, Vsetín . . . 008766
Muzeum Rekordů a Kuriozit, Pelhřimov . . . 008563
Muzeum Rolnictwa im. Ks. Krzysztofa Kluka, Ciechanowiec . . . 031879
Muzeum Romantyzmu, Opinogóra . 032195
Muzeum Ruchu Rewolucyjnego, Oddział Muzeum Okręgowego w Białymstoku, Białystok . . . 031828
Muzeum Rumburk, Rumburk . . . 008678
Muzeum Rybackie, Jastarnia . . . 031965
Muzeum Rybołówstwa, Centralne Muzeum Morskie w Gdańsku, Hel . . . 031955
Muzeum Rybołówstwa Morskiego, Świnoujście . . . 032360
Muzeum Rzemiosł Artystycznych i Precyzyjnych, Warszawa . . . 032464
Muzeum Rzemiosł Ludowych w Biłgoraju, Biłgoraj . . . 031839
Muzeum Rzemiosła, Krosno . . . 032078
Muzeum Rzemiosła Tkackiego, Turek . . . 032401
Muzeum Rzeźby im. Xawerego Dunikowskiego Królikarnia, Muzeum Narodowe w Warszawie, Warszawa . . . 032465
Muzeum s Historickou Expozicí, Hostinné . . . 008386
Múzeum Samuela Jurkoviča Sobotište-Nyaryiovský kaštiel', Sobotište . . 034427
Muzeum Sejmu, Warszawa . . . 032466
Muzeum Skansen, Pszczyna . . . 032267
Muzeum Skansen Kolejnictwa, Kościerzyna . . . 032017
Muzeum Skla, Harrachov v Krkonoších . . . 008364
Muzeum Skla a Bižuterie, Jablonec nad Nisou . . . 008399
Muzeum J.V. Sládka, Zbiroh . . . 008777
Muzeum Śląska Cieszyńskiego w Cieszynie, Cieszyn . . . 031881
Muzeum Śląska Opolskiego, Opole . 032199
Muzeum Śląskie, Katowice . . . 031989
Muzeum Ślężańskie im. Stanisława Dunajewskiego, Sobótka . . . 032325
Múzeum Slovenského Červeného Kríža, Martin . . . 034387
Muzeum Slovenského Narodného Povstania, Banská Bystrica . . . 034302
Múzeum Slovenskej Dediny, Martin 034388
Múzeum Slovenských Národných Rád, Slovenské Národné Múzeum, Myjava . . . 034395
Muzeum Sopotu, Sopot . . . 032329
Múzeum Špecialneho Školstva, Levoča . . . 034372
Múzeum Spiša, Spišská Nová Ves . 034432
Muzeum Społeczne, Strzyżów . . . 032344
Muzeum Sportu i Turystyki, Łódź . . 032117
Muzeum Sportu i Turystyki, Warszawa . . . 032467
Muzeum Sportu i Turystyki Regionu Karkonoszy, Karpacz . . . 031981
Muzeum Sportu i Turystyki Ziemi Gdańskiej, Muzeum Historii Miasta Gdańsk, Gdańsk . . . 031916
Muzeum Správy Krnap, Vrchlabí . . . 008762
Muzeum Sprzętu Gospodarstwa Domowego, Ziębice . . . 032560
Muzeum Śremskie, Śrem . . . 032333
Muzeum Środowiska Przyrodniczego i Łowiectwa, Muzeum Narodowe Rolnictwa i Przemysłu Rolno-Spożywczego w Szreniawie, Uzarzewo . . . 032406
Muzeum Stanisława Staszica, Piła . 032221
Muzeum Stanisława Wyspiańskiego, Muzeum Narodowe w Krakowie, Kraków . . . 032060
Muzeum Starożytnego Hutnictwa Mazowieckiego, Pruszków . . . 032259
Muzeum Starożytnego Hutnictwa Świętokrzyskiego im. prof. M. Radwana, Muzeum Techniki w Warszawie, Nowa Słupia . . . 032168
Muzeum Stefana Żeromskiego, Bolesława . . . 031847
Muzeum Stefana Żeromskiego, Nałęczów . . . 032161
Muzeum Středního Pootaví, Strakonice . . . 008695
Muzeum Strojíren Poldi, Kladno . . . 008433
Muzeum Šumavy, Kašperské Hory . 008431
Muzeum Šumavy, Sušice . . . 008701
Muzeum Svitidel a Chladičů, Nový Jičín . . . 008537
Muzeum Sztuk Użytkowych, Muzeum Narodowe w Poznaniu, Poznań . . 032252
Muzeum Sztuki Cmentarnej, Muzeum Miejskie Wrocławia, Wrocław . . . 032526
Muzeum Sztuki Dziecka, Warszawa 032468
Muzeum Sztuki Książki, Muzeum Narodowe, Wrocław . . . 032527
Muzeum Sztuki Medalierskiej, Muzeum Miejskie Wrocławia, Wrocław . . . 032528
Muzeum Sztuki Mieszczańskiej, Muzeum Miejskie Wrocławia, Wrocław . . . 032529
Muzeum Sztuki Nowoczesnem, Niepołomice . . . 032164
Muzeum Sztuki Sakralnej, Bardo . . 031818
Muzeum Sztuki w Łodzi, Łódź . . . 032118

Muzeum Sztuki Współczesnej, Muzeum im. Jacka Malczewskiego w Radomiu, Radom 032280
Muzeum Sztuki Współczesnej, Muzeum Narodowe, Wrocław 032530
Muzeum Sztuki Złotniczej, Kazimierz Dolny 031992
Múzeum Tatranského Národného Parku, Tatranská Lomnica 034441
Muzeum Tatrzańskie im. Tytusa Chałubińskiego, Zakopane 032550
Muzeum Teatralne, Warszawa 032469
Muzeum Teatralne, Muzeum Historycznego m. Krakowa, Kraków 032061
Muzeum Technik Ceramicznych, Koło 032009
Muzeum Techniki w Warzawie, Warszawa 032470
Muzeum Techniki Włókienniczej, Muzeum Okręgowego w Bielsku-Białej, Bielsko-Biała 031836
Muzeum Telč, Telč 008708
Múzeum Telesnej Kultúry VSR, Bratislava 034333
Muzeum Tělovýchovy a Sportu, Historické Muzeum, Praha 008629
Muzeum Těšínska, Český Těšín 008325
Muzeum Těšínska, Havířov 008366
Muzeum T.G. Masaryka, Rakovník 008665
Muzeum T.G. Masaryk's House, Čejkovice 008310
Muzeum Tkactwa Dolnośląskiego, Kamienna Góra 031978
Muzeum Tradycji i Perspektyw Huty im. B. Bieruta, Częstochowa 031888
Muzeum Tradycji Niepodległościowych, Łódź 032119
Muzeum Třešť, Třešť 008723
Muzeum Třineckých Železáren, Třinec 008724
Muzeum Twierdza Wisłoujście, Muzeum Historyczne Miasta Gdańska, Gdańsk 031917
Muzeum Týn nad Vltavou, Týn nad Vltavou 008730
Muzeum Tynecké Keramiky, Týnec nad Sázavou 008731
Muzeum Ubezpieczeń, Kraków 032062
Múzeum Ukrajinsko-Rusínskej Kultúry, Slovenské Národné Múzeum, Svidník 034439
Múzeum Umeleckých Remesiel, Mestské Múzeum v Bratislave, Bratislava 034334
Muzeum Umění, Benešov 008265
Muzeum Umění Olomouc, Olomouc 008542
Muzeum Uniwersytetu Jagiellońskiego - Collegium Maius, Kraków 032063
Muzeum Uniwersytetu Warszawskiego, Warszawa 032471
Muzeum Uniwersytetu Wrocławskiego, Wrocław 032531
Muzeum Úsov, Úsov 008736
Muzeum Uzbrojenia - Cytadela Poznańska, Wielkopolskie Muzeum Walk Niepodległościowych w Poznaniu, Poznań 032253
Muzeum v Bruntále, Bruntál 008301
Múzeum v Kežmarku a Mestský Hrad, Kežmarok 034362
Muzeum ve Štramberku, Štramberk 008696
Muzeum Velké Meziříčí, Velké Meziříčí 008748
Múzeum Vín, Prešov 034415
Múzeum vo Svätý Antone, Svätý Anton 034436
Múzeum Vojtecha Löfflera, Košice 034365
Muzeum Voskových Figurín České Historie, Praha 008630
Muzeum Voskových Figurín České Historie, Praha 008631
Muzeum Východních Čech v Hradci Králové, Oddělení Archeologické, Historické, Přírodovědecké, Hradec Králové 008389
Muzeum Vyškovska, Vyškov 008767
Muzeum Vysočiny Jihlava, Jihlava 008412
Muzeum w Bielsku Podlaskim, Muzeum Podlaskie w Białymstoku, Bielsk Podlaski 031833
Muzeum w Biskupinie, Państwowy Muzeum Archeologicznego w Warszawie, Głsawa 031938
Muzeum w Bochni im. Prof. Stanisława Fischera, Bochnia 031842
Muzeum w Chorzowie, Chorzów 031875
Muzeum w Chrzanowie, Chrzanów 031877
Muzeum w Darłowie, Zamek Książąt Pomorskich, Darłowo 031891
Muzeum w Elblągu, Elbląg 031901
Muzeum w Gliwicach, Gliwice 031934
Muzeum w Gorzowie Wielkopolskim, Gorzów Wielkopolski 031947
Muzeum w Gostyniu, Gostyń 031948
Muzeum w Grudziądzu, Grudziądz 031952
Muzeum w Grudziądzu w Klasztorna, Grudziądz 031953
Muzeum w Kętach, Kęty 031997
Muzeum w Kwidzynie, Muzeum Zamkowego w Malborku, Kwidzyn 032087
Muzeum w Lęborku, Lębork 032090
Muzeum w Łęczycy, Łęczyca 032092
Muzeum w Łowiczu, Łowicz 032123
Muzeum w Lubaczowie, Lubaczów 032124
Muzeum w Międzyrzeczu, Międzyrzecz 032143
Muzeum w Nysie, Nysa 032180
Muzeum w Oporowie, Oporów 032201
Muzeum w Przeworsku, Zespół Pałacowo-Parkowy, Przeworsk 032264
Muzeum w Raciborzu, Racibórz 032278
Muzeum w Rybniku, Rybnik 032296
Muzeum w Sosnowcu, Sosnowiec 032332
Muzeum w Stargardzie, Stargard 032338
Muzeum w Szklarskiej Porębie Hoffmanna, Szklarska Poręba 032376
Muzeum w Tarnowskich Górach, Tarnowskie Góry 032386
Muzeum w Tomaszowie Mazowieckim, Tomaszów Mazowiecki 032389
Muzeum w Tykocinie, Muzeum Okręgowego w Białymstoku, Tykocin 032402
Muzeum w Wałbrzychu, Wałbrzych 032414
Muzeum w Wodzisławiu Śląskim, Wodzisław Śląski 032508
Muzeum w Żywcu, Żywiec 032569
Muzeum Walewskich w Tubądzinie, Muzeum Okręgowe w Sieradzu, Wróblew 032513
Muzeum Walk o Wał Pomorski przy Miejsko-Gminnym Ośrodku Kultury, Mirosławiec 032149
Muzeum Walki i Męczeństwa w Treblince, Muzeum Regionalne w Siedlcach, Kosów Lacki 032018
Muzeum Warmii i Mazur, Olsztyn 032192
Muzeum Warmińskie, Muzeum Warmii i Mazur w Olsztynie, Lidzbark Warmiński 032102
Muzeum Westerplatte Sucharskiego, Muzeum Historyczne Miasta Gdańska, Gdańsk 031918
Muzeum Weterynarii, Muzeum Rolnictwa im. Rev. K. Kluka w Ciechanowcu, Ciechanowiec 031880
Muzeum Wiedzy o Środowisku, Poznań 032254
Muzeum Więzienia Pawiak, Muzeum Niepodległości, Warszawa 032472
Muzeum Wikliniarstwa i Chmielarstwa, Muzeum Narodowe Rolnictwa i Przemysłu Rolno-Spożywczego w Szreniawie, Nowy Tomyśl 032178
Muzeum Wikliny, Olkusz 032191
Muzeum Wisły, Centralny Muzeum Morskiego w Gdańsku, Tczew 032387
Muzeum Władysława Broniewskiego, Muzeum Literatury im. Adama Mieckiewicza w Warszawie, Warszawa 032473
Muzeum Wnętrz Dworskich, Muzeum Ziemi Wieluńskiej, Ożarów 032212
Muzeum Wnetrz Dworskich w Tubadzinie, Muzeum Okręgowe w Sieradzu, Wróblew 032513
Muzeum Wnętrz Pałacowych w Choroszczy, Muzeum Podlaskie w Białymstoku, Choroszcz 031873
Muzeum Wnętrz Zabytkowych, Muzeum Okręgowego w Tarnowie, Dębno 031893
Muzeum Wojsk Inżynieryjnych, Wyższej Szkoły Oficerskiej Wojsk Inżynieryjnych, Wrocław 032532
Muzeum Wojska, Białystok 031829
Muzeum Wojska Polskiego, Warszawa 032474
Muzeum Wojska Polskiego Galeria Sztuki, Warszawa 032475
Muzeum Woli, Muzeum Historycznego Miasta Starego Warszawy, Warszawa 032476
Muzeum Wsi Kieleckiej, Kielce 032001
Muzeum Wsi Lubelskiej, Lublin 032135
Muzeum Wsi Mazowieckiej, Sierpc 032316
Muzeum Wsi Opolskiej, Opole 032200
Muzeum Wsi Radomskiej, Radom 032281
Muzeum Wsi Słowińskiej w Klukach, Muzeum Pomorza Środkowego w Słupsku, Kluki 032007
Muzeum X Pawilonu Cytadeli Warszawskiej, Muzeum Niepodległości, Warszawa 032477
Muzeum Zabawek ze Zbiorow Henryka Tomaszewskiego, Karpacz 031982
Muzeum Zabawkarstwa, Kielce 032002
Muzeum Zachodnio-Kaszubskie, Bytów 031861
Muzeum Zagłębia, Będzin 031821
Muzeum Zaglebia Siarkowego, Zamek w Baranowie Sandomierskim, Baranów Sandomierski 031816
Muzeum Zagłębia Staropolskiego w Sielpi, Muzeum Techniki w Warszawie, Sielpia 032312
Muzeum Zakładowe im. St. Staszica Kieleckiej Fabryki Pomp Białogon, Kielce 032003
Muzeum Zamek, Zamek w Baranowie Sandomierskim, Baranów Sandomierski 031816
Muzeum-Zamek Górków, Państwowa Instytucja Kultury, Szamotuły 032361
Muzeum-Zamek w Bolkowie, Muzeum Okręgowego w Jeleniej Górze, Bolków 031850
Muzeum-Zamek w Gołuchowie, Gołuchów 031944
Muzeum Zamek w Łańcucie, Łańcut 032089
Muzeum Zamkowe, Pszczyna 032268
Muzeum Zamkowe w Malborku, Malbork 032139
Muzeum Zamku w Niedzicy, Niedzica 032163
Muzeum Zamoyskich w Kozłówce, Kamionka 031979
Muzeum Zbiorów Geologicznych, Kielce 032004
Muzeum-Zbiory Ludoznawcze im. Stefana i Tadeusza Szymańskich, Zakopane 032551
Muzeum Zbrojownia, Liw 032105
Múzeum Ždiarsky dom Ždiar, Ždiar 034450
Muzeum Zegarów Wieżowych, Muzeum Historyczne Miasta Gdańska, Gdańsk 031919
Múzeum Židovskej Kultúry, Slovenské Národné Múzeum, Bratislava 034335
Muzeum Ziemi Augustowskiej, Augustów 031814
Muzeum Ziemi Dobrzyńskiej, Rypin 032298
Muzeum Ziemi Kępińskiej, Kępno 031995
Muzeum Ziemi Kłodzkiej, Kłodzko 032005
Muzeum Ziemi Kociewskiej, Starogard Gdański 032339
Muzeum Ziemi Krajeńskiej, Nakło nad Notecią 032159
Muzeum Ziemi Krotoszyńskiej, Krotoszyn 032080
Muzeum Ziemi Krzeszowickiej, Krzeszowice 032084
Muzeum Ziemi Kujawskiej i Dobrzyńskiej, Włocławek 032504
Muzeum Ziemi Lubawskiej, Nowe Miasto Lubawskie 032170
Muzeum Ziemi Lubuskiej, Zielona Góra 032561
Muzeum Ziemi Mrągowskiej, Muzeum Warmii i Mazur w Olsztynie, Mrągowo 032153
Muzeum Ziemi Otwockiej, Otwock 032211
Muzeum Ziemi Pałuckiej, Żnin 032565
Muzeum Ziemi Piskiej, Oddział Muzem Okręgowego w Suwałkach, Pisz 032224
Muzeum Ziemi Polskiej Akademii Nauk, Warszawa 032478
Muzeum Ziemi Prudnickiej, Prudnik 032258
Muzeum Ziemi Puckiej, Puck 032270
Muzeum Ziemi Rawickiej, Rawicz 032286
Muzeum Ziemi Rawskiej, Rawa Mazowiecka 032285
Muzeum Ziemi Sochaczewskiej, Sochaczew 032328
Muzeum Ziemi Średzkiej Dwór w Koszutach, Koszuty 032020
Muzeum Ziemi Sulmierzyckiej im. S.F. Klonowica, Sulmierzyce 032347
Muzeum Ziemi Wałeckiej, Wałcz 032415
Muzeum Ziemi Wieluńskiej, Wieluń 032495
Muzeum Ziemi Wschowskiej, Wschowa 032537
Muzeum Ziemi Zaborskiej i Galeria Sztuki Ludowej, Wiele 032493
Muzeum Ziemi Zawkrzańskiej, Mława 032150
Muzeum Ziemi Złotowskiej, Złotów 032563
Muzeum Zoologiczne Instytutu Zoologii Uniwersytetu Jagiellońskiego, Kraków 032064
Muzeum Żup Krakowskich, Wieliczka 032494
Muzeum Żuraw, Centralne Muzeum Morskie, Gdańsk 031920
Muzeum Żydowskiego Instytutu Historycznego w Polsce, Warszawa 032479
Muzično-memorialnyj Muzej Solomiï Krušel'nic'koï, Lviv 038354
Muziekinformatie- en documentatiecentrum Ton Stolk, Vlaardingen 030274
Muziekinstrumenten-Museum, Peer 003702
Muziekinstrumentenmakersmuseum, Tilburg 030207
Muzikologické Pracoviště, Slezské Zemské Muzeum, Opava 008546
Muzium Alor Gajah, Melaka 027996
Muzium Angkatan Tentera, Malaysian Armed Force Museum, Kuala Lumpur 027971
Muzium Arkeologi, Merbok 028005
Muzium Brunei, Bandar Seri Begawan 004613
Muzium dan Galeri Seni, Universiti Sains Malaysia, Minden 028006
Muzium Darul Ridzwan, Ipoh 027950
Muzium Diraja Abu Bakar, Johor Bahru 027952
Muzium Jasin, Melaka 027997
Muzium Kecantikan, Melaka 027998
Muzium Layang Layang, Melaka 027999
Muzium Negara, Kuala Lumpur 027972
Muzium Negeri Kedah, Alor Setar 027946
Muzium Negeri Kelantan, Kota Bharu 027958
Muzium Negeri Perlis, Kangar 027953
Muzium Negeri Sarawak, Kuching 027986
Muzium Negeri Selangor, Shah Alam 028015
Muzium Negeri Sembilan, Seremban 028012
Muzium Negeri Trengganu, Kuala Terengganu 027984
Muzium Numismatik Maybank, Kuala Lumpur 027973
Muzium Perak, Taiping 028017
Muzium Polis Diraja Malaysia, Kuala Lumpur 027974
Muzium Rakyat, Melaka 028000
Muzium Sastera, Melaka 028001
Muzium Sejarah National, Kuala Lumpur 027975
Muzium Seni Asia, Kuala Lumpur 027976
Muzium Teknologi Melayu, Bandar Seri Begawan 004614

Muzium Tentera Laut Diraja Malaysia, Melaka 028002
Muzium Tuan Yang Terutama Melaka, Melaka 028003
Muzj Istorii Rossijskich Voennych Učilišč, Voenno-istoričeskij Muzej Artillerii, Inženernych Vojsk i Vojsk Svjazi, Sankt-Peterburg 033820
Muzyka i Vremja - Častnyj Muzej Džona Mostoslavskogo, Jaroslavl 033199
Muzzioli, Mario, Roma 076581
Muzzleloaders Etcetra, Minneapolis 090382
Muzzy, San Francisco 092850
M.V, Saint-Pierre-du-Val 067957
M.V.M., Bucureşti 109439
M.V.T, Greenford 113157
My Antique Trading Post, Tucson . . 093253
M.Y. Art Prospects, New York 118222
My Art Studio, Washington 120328
My Asian Gifts, San Francisco 119748
My Back Yard Nursery Art, San Diego 119527
My Collection, Verona 106799
My Daughter's Place, Oklahoma City 091521
My House Antiques, Los Angeles . . 089849
My Old Kentucky Home, Bardstown 042020
My Second Home, Nashville 090470
My Secret Garden, Memphis 090096
My Sisters Closet, Saint Paul 092379
My Sisters Stuff, Portland 091979
My Store, Moree 056255
My-Tho, Mons 058342
My Thuat, Ho Chi Minh City 136689
My Turn, Saint Paul 092380
M.Y. Williams Planet Earth Museum, Vancouver 006704
Mycènes, Champeix 062119, 124182
Myers, Charlotte 115301
Myers, Myrna, Paris 066317
Myers & Son, R.N., Gargrave 084454
Myers Museum, Eton 039460
Myerscough, Sarah, London 113784
Myfair Carpet Gallery, London 085550
Mykolaïvs'kyj Oblasnyj Chudožnij Muzej im. Vereščagina, Mykolaïv 038363
Mykolaïvs'kyj Oblasnyj Krajeznavčyj Muzej, Mykolaïv 038364
Mykonos Folklore Museum, Mykonos 021388
Myles, Eve, Houston 116376
Myles Hall, Toronto 059245
Mylin, Westerland 074369
Mylin, J., List 072285
Mylin, J., Sylt-Ost 074037
Mylin, Jens, Wyk auf Föhr 074550
Myllarheimen, Rauland 031131
Myllykolu, F.E. Sillanpään Syntymäkoti, Hämeenkyrö 009486
Myllymuseo, Juuka 009631
Myllynpuoti, Turku 137997
Myllysaaren Museo, Valkeakoski . . 010214
Myndlistaskólinn Akureyri, Akureyri 050287
Myndlistaskólinn i Reykjavík, Reykjavík 050289
Myntkabinett, Universitetets Kulturhistoriske Museer, Oslo 031088
Myntsafn Sedlabanka og Thjódminjasafns, Reykjavík 021968
Myôhôin Homotsukan, Kyoto 026753
Myohyang-san Museum, Hyangsan 027436
Myong Ji University Museum, Seoul 027587
Myopic, Providence 142818
Myra Powell Art Gallery and Gallery at the Station, Ogden 046630
Myra's Antiques, Cape Town 080685
Myra's Antiques, Columbus 088427
Myrbergsgården, Vörå 010251
Myrése, Maastricht 078615
Myreton Motor Museum, Aberlady . 038458
Myriad, Salisbury 086494, 131450
Myriad Antiques, London 085551
Myriade, Paris 066318
Les Myriades, Bruxelles 137454
Le Myricae, Roma 076582
Myrskylän Kotiseutumuseo, Myrskylä 009893
Myrtleville House Museum, Brantford 005147
Mysore Silk Museum, Bangalore . . 022016
Mystère de Chine, Saint-Denis 080129
Mysteria, Regina 097180
Mysteria Products, Fort Worth 088871
Mysterious Bookshop, New York . . . 142678
Mysterium, Las Vegas 116637
Mystery Cat, Honolulu 088968
Mystery One Bookshop, Milwaukee 142569
Mystic Ancient Art Gallery, Singapore 080532
Mystic Art Association, Mystic 054897
Mystic Art Association Museum, Mystic 046115
Mystic Coins, San Diego 092661
Mystic Island Books, Seattle 143002
Mystic Seaport, Mystic 046116
Mystique Designs, San Francisco . . 092851
Mystique Salon, Indianapolis 116481
Mystiques Antiques and Collectable, Mentone 056211
The Mystrey of the Egyptian History, Dallas 088576
Mythes et Légendes, Paris 066319
Mythos Art, Merimbula 094836
Mytton Antiques, Atcham 083347
Myung, Seoul 107274
Mzelaynius, San Antonio 092550
Mzuvele Art School, Kwamashu . . . 050704
Mzuzu Regional Museum, Mzuzu . . 027941
N 10 Antiquités, Châteaudun 062195
N & A Service, New York 132502
N Galereja, Tbilisi 101498
N. Hadjikyriakos-Ghikas Gallery, Benaki Museum, Athinai 021202
N & L Enterprises, Vancouver 097502
Na Bolšom, Sankt-Peterburg 109637
Na Dvorku, Hradec Králové 060021
Na Francouzské, Praha 060145
Na Kazimierzu, Kraków 140744
Na Královce, Praha 060146
Na Kramarskiej, Poznań 109058
Na Litejnom, Sankt-Peterburg 080313, 140936
Na Ochozu, Karlovy Vary 098372
Na Odwachu, Wrocław 109227
Na Piętęrku, Kraków 108965
Na Piętęrku, Warszawa 109163
Na Piętrze, Poznań 109059
Na Podhoří, Zlín 060202
Na Rynku, Hradec Králové 137784
Na Staronevskom, Sankt-Peterburg 080314
Na Staronevskom, Sankt-Peterburg 140937
Naaimachine Museum, Dordrecht . 029505
Naaimachinemuseum, Nieuweschans 029950
Naaji, Milwaukee 117209
Naantalin Museo, Naantali 009895
NAB Gallery, Chicago 042866
Nabaa, Elie, Beirut 077406
Naber, Groningen 108041
Nabis, Tokyo 107083
Nabrink, Gé, Amsterdam 140323
Nábytek jako umění a řemeslo, Uměleckoprůmyslové muzeum Praha, Duchcov 008356
Nábytek - Obrazy - Technické Starožitnosti, Příbram 060185
Nábytkové Múzeum, Markušovce . . 034381
Naccari, Elvira, Venezia 076960
Nachbar, Richard, Buffalo 087899
Nachman, Teresa, Buenos Aires . . . 094083
Nacht, Ernst, Zweisimmen 083048
Nachtgalerie, München 104275
Nachttopf-Museum, Zentrum für Außergewöhnliche Museen, Kreuth 018408
Nacionalen Archeologičeski Rezervat Kabile, Jambol 004696
Nacionalen Cărkoven Istoriko-archeologičeski Muzej, Sofia 004861
Nacionalen Etnografski Muzej, Bălgarska Akademija na Naukite, Sofia 004862
Nacionalen Istoričeski Muzej, Sofia 004863
Nacionalen Istoriko-archeologičeski Rezervat i Muzej Veliki Preslav, Veliki Preslav 004926
Nacionalen Istoriko-archeologičeski Rezervat Pliska, Pliska 004788
Nacionalen Literaturen Muzej, Sofia 004864
Nacionalen Muzej Bojanska Crkva, Sofia 004865
Nacionalen Muzej Georgi Dimitrov, Sofia 004866
Nacionalen Muzej na Bălgarskata Architektura, Veliko Tărnovo 004937
Nacionalen Muzej na Fizičeskata Kultura i Sport, Sofia 004867
Nacionalen Muzej na Obrazovanieto, Gabrovo 004685
Nacionalen Muzej na Transporta i Săobščenijata, Ruse 004822
Nacionalen Muzej Parachod Radecki, Kozloduj 004737
Nacionalen Muzej Rilski Manastir, Rilski Manastir 004816
Nacionalen Muzej Roženski Manastir, Rožen 004817
Nacionalen Muzej Zemjata i Chorata, Sofia 004868
Nacionalen Park-muzej Samuilova krepost, Istoričeski Muzej Petrič, Petrič . . . 004777
Nacionalen Park-muzej Šipka-Buzludža, Kazanlăk 004717
Nacionalen Politechničeski Muzej, Sofia 004869
Nacionalen Prirodonaučen Muzej, Sofia 004870
Nacionalen Selskostopanski Muzej, Sofia 004871
Nacionalen Voenno-morski Muzej, Varna 004922
Nacionalen Voennoistoričeski Muzej, Sofia 004872
Nacionalna Chudožestvena Galerija, Sofia 004873
Nacionalna Galerija za Čuždestranno Izkustvo, Sofia 004874
Nacionalna Galerija za Dekorativni Izkustva, Sofia 004875
Nacionalna Izložba na Narodnite Chudožestveni Zanajati i Priložni Izkustva, Orešak 004762
Nacionalnaja Galereja Respubliki Komi, Syktyvkar 033926
Nacionalnij Muzej u Lvovi, Lviv 038355
Nacionalnij Muzej u Lvovi - Viddil Narodnogo Mystectva, Lviv 038356
Nacionalnij Muzej u Lvovi - Viddil Starodrukiv ta Rukopysiv, Lviv . . . 038357
Nacionalnij Muzej u Lvovi - Viddil Sučasnogo Mystectva, Lviv 038358
Nacionalnyj Chudožestvennyj Muzej Respubliki Belarus, Minsk 003138
Nacionalnyj Chudožestvennyj Muzej Respubliki Sacha (Jakutija), Jakutsk 033189
Nacional'nyj Chudožnij Muzej Ukraïny, Kyïv 038317
Nacional'nyj Kyjevo-Pečerskyj Istoryko-kul'turnyj Zapovidnyk, Kyïv 038318
Nacional'nyj Muzej Čornobyl', Kyïv . 038319
Nacional'nyj Muzej Istorii Ukraïny, Kyïv 038320
Nacional'nyj Muzej Istorii Velykoï Vitčyznjanoï Vijny 1941-1945 Rokiv, Kyïv 038321
Nacionalnyj Muzej Kabardino-Balkarskoj Respubliki, Nalčik 033543
Nacional'nyj Muzej Literatury Ukraïny, Kyïv 038322
Nacional'nyj Muzej Medycyny Ukraïny, Kyïv 038323
Nacionalnyj Muzej Respubliki Baškortostan, Ufa 033995
Nacionalnyj Muzej Respubliki Komi, Syktyvkar 033927
Nacionalnyj Muzej Respubliki Marij Èl im. T. Evseeva, Joškar-Ola 033205
Nacionalnyj Muzej Respubliki Tatarstan, Kazan 033251
Nacional'nyj Muzej Tarasa Ševčenka, Kyïv 038324
Nacionalnyj Muzej Udmurtskoj Respubliki im. K. Gerda, Iževsk 033180
Nacional'nyj Muzej Zbrojnych Syl Ukraïny, Kyïv 038325
Nacional'nyj Zapovidnyk Chersones Tavrijs'kyj, Sevastopol 038389
Nacional'nyj Zapovidnyk Chorticja, Zaporižžja 038417
Nacional'nyj Zapovidnyk T.G. Ševčenka, Kaniv 038278
Nack, Saitama 106977
Nacke, Dieter, Bartenshagen 101740
Al-Nada, Katr, Cairo 098653
NADA Art Fair Miami, Miami Beach 094010
Nadaï, Michel de, Toulouse 124990
Nadalini, Gianpaolo, Paris 100717
Nádasdi Ferenc Múzeum, Sárvár . . 021838
Na.de., Roma 076583
Nadelmann, Berlin 138827
Nader, Port-au-Prince 105482
Nader, Gary, Miami 117115
Nader Mausoleum, Mashad 022583
Nadiani, Antonio, Roma . . 076584, 128130
Nadia's Antiques, Toronto 059246
Nadine, Warszawa 079772, 109164
Nadir, Annecy 098843
Nadir, Lyon 064167
Nadkarni, R.P., Mumbai 127087
Nadlerhaus, Hundshübel 018032
Nadrag, Nikolaus, Bielefeld 069833
NAEA News, Reston 136567
Naegele, Amyas, New York 118223, 132503
Nähmaschinen-Museum, Steckborn 037602
Nähmaschinen-Museum Gebr. Mey, Albstadt 015470
Näkövammaismuseo, Jiris 009620
Näpflin, Rosemarie, Hünenberg . . . 111563
Närpes Hembygdsmuseum, Närpes 009897
Næs Jernverksmuseum, Tvedestrand 031296
Naesa, Singapore 109842
Nässjö Auktionshall, Malmbäck . . . 122205
Næstved Museum, Næstved 009025
Näther, Gisela, Leipzig 103896
Naffouj, Landstuhl 103829
Nafplion Folklore Museum, Nafplion 021402
Naftalina, Montevideo 087334
Naftalina, Porto Alegre . . . 058514, 123696
Naga, New York 091105
Naga, Singapore 080533
Nagai, Tokyo 107084
Nagano-ken Shinano Bijutsukan, Higashiyama Kaiikan, Nagano . . . 026844
Nagaoka Cog Museum, Nagaoka . . 026847
Nagaoka Municipal Science Museum, Nagaoka 026848
Nagaoka-shiritsu Hakabutsukan, Nagaoka 026849
Nagaoka-shiritsu Kogyo Hakurankai, Nagaoka 026850
Nagasaki Atomic Bomb Museum, Nagasaki 026866
Nagasaki City Museum of History and Folklore, Nagasaki 026867
Nagasaki-kenritsu Bijutsu Hakubutsukan, Nagasaki 026868
Nagasaki-kenritsu Hakubutsukan, Nagasaki 026869
Nagasaki Kite Museum, Nagasaki . 026870
Nagasaki Science Museum, Nagasaki 026871
Nagasaki-shiritsu Hakabutsukan, Nagasaki 026872
Nagasaki-shiritsu Nyokodo Nagai Kinenkan, Nagasaki 026873
Nagasaki-shiritsu Ukiyo-e Bijutsukan, Nagasaki 026874
Nagashima Museum, Kagoshima . . 026605
Nagatoro Kyukokan, Chichibu 026441
Nagel, Leipzig 121496
Nagel, Neustadt an der Weinstraße 104434
Nagel, Phoenix 091757

Nagel, Reinheim 104707
Nagel, Santiago de Chile 059544
Nagel, Stuttgart 121606
Nagel, Verona 121741
Nagel, Ana Celina Freifrau von, München 072797, 104276
Nagel, B., West Hollywood 093489
Nagel, Christian, Köln 103684
Nagel, D., Dassendorf 070193
Nagel, Frauke, Heimsheim 103342
Nagel, Dr. Fritz, Bruxelles 120738
Nagel, Dr. Fritz, Haifa 121672
Nagel, Dr. Fritz, Tokyo 121746
Nagel, Dr. Fritz, Wien 120688
Nagel, Katharina, Hamburg 071298
Nagelschmiede, Sulz, Aargau 037615
Naghi, New Orleans 090593
Naghi, New Orleans 090594
Nagi Museum, Cairo 009315
Nagl, Helga, München 072798
Nagler & Eberle, Wien 120689
Nagon, Los Angeles 089850
Nagora, Martina, Cottbus 125436
Nagornaja Galereja, Moskva 109571
Nagoya-Boston Museum of Fine Arts, Nagoya 026881
Nagoya Castle Treasure House, Nagoya 026882
Nagoya City Hideyoshi and Kiyomasa Memorial Museum, Nagoya 026883
Nagoya Gallery, Nagoya 106927
Nagoya Geijutsu Daigaku, Nishiharu 050468
Nagoya-shi Bijutsukan, Nagoya . . . 026884
Nagoya-shi Hakubutsukan, Nagoya 026885
Nagoya-shi Kagakukan, Nagoya . . . 026886
Nagoya Zokei Geijyutsu Daigaku, Komaki 050457
Nagswood, El Paso 116115
Nagtegaal, Hans Peter, Apeldoorn . 128565
Nagtegaal, Roos, Bruntinge 128613
Nagu hembyggdsmuseum/Nauvon Kotiseutumuseo, Local Heritage Museum of Nagu/Nauvo, Nauvo 009901
Nagy, Michael, Woollahra 095429
Nagy, Tibor de, New York 118224
Nagy István Képtár, Baja 021618
Nagyházi, Budapest 105534, 121642
Nagytétényi Kastélymúzeum, Iparművészeti Múzeum, Budapest 021677
Naharro, Madrid 129650
Naharro, José-Luis, Lausanne 082557
Naharro Reyes, Luis, Zaragoza 081746
Nahas, Sharjah 083219
Nahkl Fort Museum, Nahkl 031351
Nahmad, Helly, London 113785
Nahmani, Daniel, Mont-de-Marsan . 064611
Nahnella, São Paulo 058728
Nahon, Pierre, Paris 100718
Nahsholim Museum, Hof Dor 022934
Nahum, Peter, London . . . 085552, 113786, 135239
Nahum Gutman's Museum, Tel Aviv 023088
Naicam Museum, Naicam 005974
Naïfs du Monde Entier, Paris 100719
Naigai, Tokyo 140195
Nail, Kathy, Seattle 119966
Naim, Anne-Maria, Paris 066320
Naim, Pascal, Paris 100720
Naimeh, Yousef, Damascus 083068
Naimski, Michael, London 113787
Naini Art Studio, Cockayne Hatley . 112883
Nairn Fishertown Museum, Nairn . . 040508
Nairn Museum, Nairn 040509
Naismith Memorial Basketball Hall of Fame, Springfield 048295
Naito Kinen Kusuri Hakubutsukan, Kawashima, Gifu 026648
Naiv Antikvarnaja Galereja, Sankt-Peterburg 080315
Najana, Warszawa 109165
Nakagawa Photo Gallery, Kyoto . . . 026754
Nakambale Museum, Ondangwa . . 029092
Nakamiya Gallery, Osaka 106969
Nakamiya Gallery-Midosuji Art, Osaka 106970
Nakamoura Kenichi Museum of Art, Koganei 026680
Nakamura, Kobijutsu, Hiroshima . . 077063
Nakamura Kogei, Kyoto 077119
Nakano Historical Museum, Tokyo . 027212
Nakao Shosen-do, Osaka 140172
Nakao Shoten, Osaka 140173
Nakaoka, Kyoto 077120
Nakashian-O'Neil, Saint Paul 092381
Nakayama Archaeological Museum, Matsumoto 026793
Nake, Erich, Wehrheim 105171
Naked Art, Birmingham 115119
Nakkilan Kotiseutumuseo, Juustomeijerimuseo, Nakkila 009899
Naklada Naprijed, Zagreb 133406
Nakota Curios, Hastings 084618
Nakusp Museum, Nakusp 005977
Nalbandian & Son, Loutfic, Beirut . . 077407
Nalbandian, Serge & Gaby, Beirut . . 077408
Nall, George, Louisville 116957
Nam, Kyeong, Seoul 107275
Nam, Son, Ha Noi 120475
Nam & Co., Thye, Singapore 080534
Nam, Y., Freiburg im Breisgau 139114
Nam Nao, Petchabun 037917
Namarook Antiques, Windsor, Victoria 056832
Namaste, Fort Worth 088872
Nambara Arts & Crafts, Nhulunbuy . 056346
Nambrok Antiques, Sale 056566
Namık Kemal Zindanı ve Müzesi, Gazimağusa 008238
Namikawa Banri Bukkyo Bijutsu Shashin Gallery, Hiroshima 026537
Namiraz, Monaco 077618
Namjin Art Museum, Imhoe 027509
Namsdalsmuseet, Namsos 031043
Namsskogan Bygdatun, Namsskogan 031045
N.A.M.T.A. News & Views, Huntersville 136568
Namy-Caulier, Martine, Paris 100721, 133656
Namyslok, Aschersleben 101606
Nan Bo's Southern Women Museum, Ho Chi Minh City 049539
Nan Leith's Brocanterbury, Canterbury 083864
Nan Yue Wang Palace Museum, Guangzhou 007091
Nanaimo Art Gallery and Exhibition Centre, Nanaimo 005980
Nanaimo District Museum, Nanaimo 005981
Nana's Imported Arts, Milwaukee . . 117210
Nana's Treasures and Antiques, El Paso 088809
Nanban Bunkakan, Osaka 026973
Nanbando, Tokyo 077285
Nanbooks, Settle 086538
Nance Museum, Lone Jack 045376
Nancéide, Nancy 138232
Nanchang City Museum, Nanchang 007194
Nancy Antiquités, Montréal 058980
Nancy Island Historic Site, Wasaga Beach 006765
Nancy's Christmas Collectibles, Denver 088717
Nandan Museum-Vichittra and Art Gallery, Santiniketan 022326
Nandewar Historical Museum, Barraba 000770
Nanfa, Antonio, Firenze 127379
Nanfria, Leonardo, Genova 127475
Nanhai Museum, Foshan 007070
Nanich Castañe, Maria Teresa, Barcelona 080891
Naninck & Lengaigne, Saint-Omer . 067692
Naniwa-no Umino Jikukan, Osaka . 026974
Nanji Guan, Qingdao 007222
Nanjing Academy of Fine Arts, Nanjing 049854
Nanjing Calligraphy and Painting Gallery, Nanjing 097875
Nanjing Children's Painting and Calligraphy Association, Nanjing 052800
Nanjing Folklorish Museum, Nanjing 007203
Nanjing International Culture and Arts Exchange Center, Nanjing 007204
Nanjing Museum, Nanjing 007205
Nanjingdi Zhen Science Museum, Nanjing 007206
Nanjingdi Zhi Museum, Nanjing . . . 007207
Nankai Broadcasting Sun Park Museum of Art, Matsuyama 026802
Nankang County Museum, Ganzhou 007078
The Nanking Porcelain &Co., London 085553
Nanni, Milano 075781
Nanni, Paolo, Bologna 105972
Nanning City Museum, Nanning . . . 007212
Nanny's Web, Bentleigh East 136801
Nanortallip Katersugaasivia, Nanortalik 021542
Nan's Hands, Indianapolis 089325
Nanshan Painting Gallery, Shenzhen 097988
Nansong Guanyao Museum, Hangzhou 007105
Nansong Qian Currency Museum, Hangzhou 007106
Nansouty, Bordeaux 061638
Nantais, Darryl, Linton 113402
Nante, Eggenfelden 070513
Nantenshi, Tokyo 107085
Nantgarw China Works Museum, Nantgarw 040510
Nanto, Nara 077162
Nanton Lancaster Air Museum, Nanton 005982
Nantong Museum, Nantong 007214
Nantucket Historical Association Museum, Nantucket 046126
Nantwich Antiques, Nantwich 086037
Nantwich Museum, Nantwich 040511
Nanwani & Co., London 085554
Nanyang Academy of Fine Arts, Middle Campus, Singapore 050687
Nanyang Academy of Fine Arts, Selegie Campus, Singapore 050688
Nanyang Academy of Fine Arts, Wilkie Campus, Singapore 050689
Nanyang Hanhua Guan, Nanyang . . 007215
Nanzig, M., Bonn 069935
Naomi Wood Collection at Woodford Mansion, Philadelphia 046966
Naomi's Antiques, San Francisco . . 092852
Naos, Barcelona 110225
Nap, Gödöllő 139935
Napa Valley Museum, Yountville . . . 049362
Naper Settlement Museum, Naperville 046128
Naphtaline, Bayeux 061228
Naphtaline, Saint-Amand-les-Eaux . 067346
Naphtaline, Valenciennes 068694
Napier Antique Centre, Napier 079167
Napier House, Sudbury, Suffolk . . . 086785
Napiórkowska, Katarzyna, Warszawa 109166
Napiórkowska, Katarzyna, Warszawa 109167
Naples Antiques Show, Naples 094011
Naples Museum of Art, Naples 046130
Napoléon Antiques, Montréal 058981
Napoleon- und Heimatmuseum, Deutsch Wagram 001776
Napoleonic Society of America, Clearwater 042971
Napoleonmuseum, Salenstein 037483
Napoli, Tommaso, Milano 075782
Napoli Capitale, Napoli 076015
Napoli Nobolissima, Roma 135927
Napotnikova Galerija, Šoštanj 034526
Naprawa Szkla Antycznego, Warszawa 129103
Náprstek Museum of Asian, African and American Cultures, Liběchov 008473
Náprstkovo Muzeum Asijských, Afrických a Amerických Kultur, Národní muzeum, Praha 008632
Nara City Museum of Photography, Nara 026895
Nara-kenritsu Bijutsukan, Nara . . . 026896
Nara-kenritsu Kashihara Kokogaku Kenkyujo Fuzoku Hakubutsukan, Kashihara 026634
Nara-kenritsu Minzoku Hakubutsukan, Yamato-koriyama 027326
Nara Koeki, Nara 077163
Nara Kokuritsu Hakubutsukan, Nara 026897
Naracoorte Art Gallery, Naracoorte . 001309
Naracoorte Museum, Naracoorte . . 001310
Naramata Museum, Naramata 005985
Naranjo, Albuquerque 114808
Naranjo, Albuquerque 114809
Naranjo Fernandez, Adolfo Leon, Medellín 098280
Il Narciso, Roma 106600
Narcisos, Los Angeles 132270
Narcissa Prentiss House, Prattsburgh 047224
Narcisse, Surry Hills 056655
Nardi, Francesco Neri, Venezia 076961
Nardin, Damascus 083069
Nardini, Jacques, Lyon 124370
Narducci, Largs 084905
Narducci, Saltcoats 086500
Narek, Queanbeyan 095108
Narek, Tanja 095318
Narembeen Historical Museum, Narembeen 001311
Naritasan History Museum, Narita . 026903
Narlıkuyu Mozaik Müzesi, Silifke . . 038172
Naroden Muzej, Ohrid 027914
Naroden Muzej, Veles 027927
Naroden Muzej Dr. Nikola Nezlobinski, Struga 027923
Narodna Galerija, Ljubljana 034487
Národní Dům na Smíchově, Praha . 008633
Národní galerie v Praze - Palác Kinských, Praha 008634
Národní Kulturní Památka Vyšehrad, Praha 008635
Národní Kulturní Památník - Valy, Mikulčice 008501
Narodni Muzej, Bački Petrovac 034141
Narodni Muzej, Beograd 034167
Narodni Muzej, Kragujevac 034206
Narodni Muzej, Leskovac 034212
Narodni Muzej, Pančevo 034233
Narodni Muzej, Požarevac 034246
Narodni Muzej, Smederevska Palanka 034261
Narodni Muzej, Štip 027922
Narodni Muzej, Užice 034278
Narodni Muzej, Vranje 034280
Narodni Muzej, Zadar 007825
Narodni Muzej, Zaječar 034283
Narodni Muzej, Zrenjanin 034285
Narodni Muzej Čačak, Čačak 034180
Narodni Muzej Crne Gore, Cetinje . . 034186
Narodni Muzej Kikinda, Kikinda . . . 034198
Narodni Muzej Kraljevo, Kraljevo . . 034208
Narodni Muzej Kruševac, Kruševac . 034210
Narodni Muzej Labin, Labin 007753
Narodni Muzej Niš, Niš 034218
Narodni Muzej Sabac, Sabac 034255
Narodni Muzej Slovenije, Ljubljana . 034488
Narodni Muzej Toplice, Prokuplje . . 034252
Narodni Muzej Valjevo, Valjevo 034279
Národní Muzeum, Praha 008636
Národní Technické Muzeum, Praha . 008637
Národní Zemědělské Muzeum, Praha 008638
Národní Zemědělské Muzeum Praha, Muzeum Českého Venkova, Kačina 008418
Národní Zemědělské Muzeum, Úsek Valtice, Valtice 008742
Narodnyj Geologičeskij Muzej Volgageologija, Nižnij Novgorod . . 033567

Narodnyj Istoriko-kraevedčeskij Muzej Tatarska, Novosibirskij oblastnoj kraevedčeskij muzej, Tatarsk . . . 033944
Národopisná Expozícia SARM Bardejovské Kúpele, Bardejovské Kúpele 034311
Národopisné Múzeum, Smižany . . . 034426
Národopisné Múzeum Liptova, Liptovský Hrádok 034374
Národopisné Muzeum Plzeňska, Západočeské Muzeum, Plzeň . . . 008571
Národopisné Muzeum Třebíz, Třebíz 008721
Národopisné Oddělení, Historické Muzeum, Národní Muzeum v Praze, Praha . 008639
Narok Museum, Narok 027431
Narooma Lighthouse Museum, Narooma 001312
Narosny, Anne, Cleveland 088346
Narovčatskij Rajonnyj Kraevedčeskij Muzej, Penzenskij gosudarstvennyj obedinennyj kraevedčeskij muzej, Narovčat . . 033547
Narrabri Antiques and Art, Narrabri . 056318
Narrabri Old Gaol Heritage Centre, Narrabri 001313
Narragansett Historical Society Museum, Templeton 048525
Das Narrenschiff, Amsterdam 140324
Narrenschopf, Fasnachtsmuseum, Bad Dürrheim 015687
Dat Narrenschyp, Vinkeveen 140562
Narrogin Gallery, Narrogin 001316
Narrogin Old Courthouse Museum, Narrogin 001317
Narrow Gauge Railway Museum, Tywyn 041255
Narryna Heritage Museum, Battery Point 000777
Narsaq Museum, Narsaq 021543
Nart, Paris 100722
Le Narthex, Paris 066321
Narukawa Bijutsukan, Hakone 026493
Narumi, San Francisco 092853
Naruyama, Tokyo 107086
Narva Muuseum, Narva 009381
Narwhal Inuit Art Gallery, London . . 040239
Narwhal Inuit Art Gallery, London . . 113788
Naš Realizm, Moskva 109572
NASA Lewis Research Center's Visitor Center, Cleveland 042995
Nasan, Seoul 077369
Nasca, New York 123004
Nascimento, Júlio Matos, Porto . . . 080099
Nascimento, Marcia, Belo Horizonte 096475
Do Nascimento, Toninho José, Brasília 058464
Nasenberg, Beate, Sprockhövel . . . 104939
Nasere, Reza, Los Angeles 116853
Nash, E. William, Jacksonville 089438, 132188
Nash, Garry, Auckland 108349
Nash, John, Ledbury 084922, 130868
Nash, Paul, Tetbury 086860
Nashan, Manama 057640
Al-Nashef, Mohammed Said, Damascus 083070
Nash's House and New Place, Shakespeare Birthplace Trust, Stratford-upon-Avon 041141
Nashua Center for Arts, Nashua . . . 046136
Nashville Gold Market, Nashville . . 090471
Nasionale Afrikaanse Letterkundige Museum en Navorsingsentrum, Bloemfontein 034561
Nasiotis Sotiris, G., Athinai 139898
Al-Nasir Sons, Abdullatif S., Al-Khobar 109673
Nasiri, A., Los Angeles . . . 089851, 132271
Nasiriya Museum, Nasiriya 022670
Nasjonalgalleriet, Nasjonalmuseet for Kunst, Oslo 031089
Nasledie, Kazan 080211
Naso, R.C., Cleveland 115731
Naß, Andreas, Waldems 074250
Nass, Frank-Dietmar, Gersfeld 070978
Naß, Dr. Markus, Berlin 069708
Al-Nassar, Al-Khobar 080353
Nassau, Lillian, New York . 091106, 118225
Nassau County Museum of Art, Roslyn 047547
Nassau Public Library and Museum, Nassau 003091
Nassauer, Armin, Siegen 139728
Nassauischer Kunstverein e.V., Wiesbaden 053516
Nasser, Awao, Wien 057507, 123520
Nasser, Marhoon, Al-Khobar 121970
Nassler, Neuburg an der Donau . . . 104404
Nassler, Neuburg an der Donau . . . 104405
Nast, Hartmund, Elmlohe 125585
Nast à Paris, Paris 100723
Nasta, Helsinki 060560
Nastolan Kotiseutumuseo, Nastola . 009900
Nastran, O., Kempfeld 071786
Nata-dera Homotsukan, Komatsu . . 026686
Natacha, Saint-Denis 080130
Natal Museum, Pietermaritzburg . . 034700
Natal Society of Arts, Durban 054067
Natale, Antonietta, Napoli 076016
Natale, Sonia, Roma 140112
Natale Labia Museum, Muizenberg 034684
Natali Restauri, Roma . . . 076585, 128131
Natalie and James Thompson Gallery, San Jose State University, San Jose . . 047899
Natalie Antiques, Chicago 088133
Nat'Antic, Menton 064494
Natascha, Gattikon 082386
Natchez Trace Parkway Study Collection, Tupelo 048658
Nategh, Basel 082160, 129929
Natesan, Bangalore 074777
Nathan, Ann, Chicago 115508
Nathan, Dr. Johannes, Zürich 112153
Nathan, John, Exeter 084361, 130695
Nathan Arts d'Asie, Saint-Ouen . . . 067856
Nathan Denison House, Forty Fort . 044015
Nathan Manilow Sculpture Park, University Park 048700
Nathanaelle, Neffe, Honfleur 099354
Nathaniel, Byron, Dallas 088577
Nathaniel W. Faison Home and Museum, La Grange 045066
Nation Museum, Beijing 006999
Nationaal Ambulance- en Eerste Hulpmuseum, Winschoten 030337
Nationaal Archief, Den Haag 029446
Het Nationaal Autominiaturen Museum, Asperen 029276
Nationaal Baggermuseum, Sliedrecht 030158
Nationaal Beiaardmuseum, Asten . . 029283
Nationaal Bevrijdingsmuseum 1944-1945, Groesbeek 029634
Nationaal Borstelmuseum, Izegem . 003539
Nationaal Brandweermuseum, Hellevoetsluis 029720
Nationaal Brilmuseum Amsterdam, Amsterdam 029212
Nationaal Centrum voor de Plastische Kunsten van de 16de en de 17 de Eeuw, Antwerpen 003155
Nationaal Coöperatie Museum, Schiedam 030132
Nationaal Fietsmuseum Velorama, Nijmegen 029963
Nationaal Glasmuseum, Leerdam . . 029835
Nationaal Historisch Orgelmuseum Elburg, Elburg 029553
Nationaal houtambachtenmuseum De Wimpe, Herenthout 003510
Nationaal Hunebedden Infocentrum, Borger 029333
Nationaal Jenevermuseum, Hasselt 003500
Nationaal Landschapskundig Museum, Dordrecht 029506
Nationaal Likeur- en Frisdrankenmuseum Isidorus Jonkers, Hilvarenbeek . . 029747
Nationaal Luchtvaart Museum Aviodome, Schiphol 030137
Nationaal Modelspoor Museum, Sneek 030168
Nationaal Monument Kamp Vught, Vught 030299
Nationaal Museum en Archief van Douane en Accijnzen, Antwerpen 003177
Nationaal Museum Historisch Landbouwtechniek, Wageningen . 030304
Nationaal Museum van de Speelkaart, Turnhout 003818
Nationaal Museum van Speelklok tot Pierement, Utrecht 030233
Nationaal Museum Verpleging en Verzorging, Zetten 030382
Nationaal Natuurhistorisch Museum Naturalis, Leiden 029851
Nationaal Oorlogs- en Verzetsmuseum, Overloon 030036
Nationaal Reddingmuseum Dorus Rijkers, Den Helder 029465
Nationaal Rijtuigmuseum, Leek . . . 029831
Nationaal Ruimtevaart Museum, Lelystad 029860
Nationaal Schaakmuseum, Den Haag 029447
Nationaal Scheephistorisch Centrum, Leylstad 029867
Nationaal Scheepvaartmuseum, Antwerpen 003178
Nationaal Schoeiselmuseum, Izegem 003540
Nationaal Schoolmuseum, Rotterdam 030094
Nationaal Scoutsmuseum, Leuven . 003580
Nationaal Sleepvaartmuseum, Maassluis 029892
Nationaal Smalspoormuseum - Stoomtrein Valkenburgse Meer, Valkenburg, Zuid-Holland 030250
Nationaal Spaarpottenmuseum, Amsterdam 029213
Nationaal Tinnen Figuren Museum, Ommen 029990
Nationaal Vakbondsmuseum De Burcht, Amsterdam 029214
Nationaal Visserijmuseum van Oostduinkerke, Oostduinkerke . . . 003683
Nationaal Vlas-, Kant- en Linnenmuseum, Kortrijk 003559
Nationaal Vlechtmuseum, Noordwolde 029976
Nationaal Volkssportmuseum voor de Vinkensport, Hulste 003527
Nationaal Wielermuseum, Roeselare 003720
National 1798 Visitor Centre, Enniscorthy 022785
National Aboriginal Cultural Centre, Harbour 055953
National Academy of Arts, Seoul . . 050513
National Academy of Design, School of Fine Arts, New York 051826
National Academy of Design Museum, New York 046380
National Afro-American Museum and Cultural Center, Wilberforce 049171
The National Agricultural Center and Hall of Fame, Bonner Springs 042298
National Air and Space Museum, Smithsonian Institution, Washington 048922
National Aivazovsky Picture Gallery, Feodosija 038264
National Alliance for Media Arts & Culture, San Francisco 054898
National and University Library, Zagreb 133407
National Antique Centre, Mornington 056258
National Apple Museum, Biglerville 042204
National Archives of Zambia, Lusaka 049572
National Army Museum, London . . . 040240
National Army Museum, Sandhurst Outstation, Camberley 038951
National Army Museum Sandhurst Departments, Sandhurst, Berkshire 040954
National Art & Antique Dealers Association, New York 054899
National Art Association of Denver, Denver 054900
National Art Connection, Minneapolis 117286
National Art Education Association, Reston 054901
National Art Gallery, Colombo 036133
National Art Gallery, Dhaka 003109
National Art Gallery, Islamabad . . . 031369
National Art Gallery, Minsk 003139
National Art Gallery of Armenia, Erevan 000686
National Art Gallery of Namibia, Windhoek 029106
National Art League, Douglaston . . 054902
National Art Materials Trade Association, Huntersville 054903
National Art Museum of Sport, Indianapolis 044752
National Art School, Darlinghurst . . 049611
National Artists Equity Association, Pacific Grove 054904
National Arts, Al-Ain 112443
National Arts Club, New York 046381
National Arts Coalition, Newtown . . 054068
National Arts Education Archive, Wakefield 041273
National Arts Stabilization, Washington 054905
National Assembly of State Arts Agencies, Washington 054906
National Association for the Visual Arts, Woolloomooloo 052480
National Association of Artists Organizations - NAAO, Birmingham 054907
National Association of Dealers in Antiques. Bulletin, Barrington 136569
National Association of Decorative and Fine Arts Societies, London 054442
National Association of Schools of Art and Design, Reston 054908
National Association of Women Artists, New York 054909, 136570
National Atomic Museum, Albuquerque 041620
National Automobile Museum, Harrah Collection, Reno 047371
National Automobile Museum of Tasmania, Launceston 001177
National Automotive and Truck Museum of the United States, Auburn 041886
National Aviation Museum, Ottawa . 006089
National Baseball Hall of Fame and Museum, Cooperstown 043139
National Birendra Art Gallery, Kathmandu 029115
National Border Patrol Museum and Memorial Library, El Paso 043643
National Bronze Art Museum, Lalitpur 029120
National Building Museum, Washington 048923
National Campaign for the Arts, London 054443
National Canal Museum, Easton . . . 043590
National Capital Trolley Museum, Silver Spring 048180
National Cartoonists Society, New York 054910
National Center for American Western Art, Kerrville 044977
National Center for the American Revolution, Valley Forge 048737
National Children's Museum, Delhi . 022086
National Civil Rights Museum, Memphis 045768
National Coal Mining Museum for England, Wakefield 041274
National Coin and Stamp Company, Omaha 091579
National College of Art and Design, Dublin 050345
National College of Arts, Lahore . . . 050586
National Commission for Museums and Monuments, Abuja 053937
National Conference of Artists, Detroit 054911
National Coracle Centre, Cenarth . . 039026
National Corvette Museum, Bowling Green 042367

National Council of Science Museums, Kolkata 053703
National Council on Education for the Ceramic Arts, Bandon 054912
National Cowboy and Western Heritage Museum, Oklahoma City 046647
National Cowgirl Museum and Hall of Fame, Fort Worth 044013
National Cryptologic Museum, Fort Meade 043949
National Cultural History Museum, Northern Flagship Institute, Pretoria 034722
National Cycle Collection, Llandrindod Wells 040048
National Czech and Slovak Museum, Cedar Rapids 042678
National D-Day Museum, New Orleans 046260
National Dairy Museum, Ashurst, Hampshire 038544
National Dinosaur Museum, Gungahlin 001087
National Doukhobour Heritage Village, Verigin 006725
National Dragonfly Biomuseum, Ashton, Oundle 038540
National Endowment for the Arts, Washington 054913
National English Literary Museum, Grahamstown 034623
National Exhibits by Blind Artists, Philadelphia 046967
National Fairground Museum, Northampton 040595
National Farm Toy Museum, Dyersville 043551
National Fine Arts and Antiques Fair, Birmingham 093939
National Firearms Museum, Fairfax 043783
National Fishing Heritage Centre, Grimsby 039642
National Folk Museum, Seoul 027588
National Folk Museum of Lesbos, Mytilini 021396
National Football Museum, Canton . 042608
National Football Museum, Preston 040780
National Fresh Water Fishing Hall of Fame, Hayward 044495
National Frontier Trails Center, Independence 044727
National Galleries of Scotland, Publications Department, Edinburgh 135144
National Gallery, Bangkok 037884
National Gallery, London 040241
National Gallery Bulawayo, Bulawayo 049578
National Gallery Company, London . 135240
National Gallery, London, Technical Bulletin, London 136255
National Gallery of Art, Washington 048924
National Gallery of Art, Publications Department, Washington 135522
National Gallery of Australia, Canberra 000888
National Gallery of Canada, Ottawa 006104
National Gallery of Corfu, Skripero . 021471
National Gallery of Ireland, Gailearaí Náisiúnta na hÉireann, Dublin . . . 022763
National Gallery of Ireland Publications, Dublin 134528
National Gallery of Jamaica, Kingston 026391
National Gallery of Modern Art, Delhi 022087
National Gallery of Modern Art, Mumbai 022266
National Gallery of Scotland, Edinburgh 039406
National Gallery of Victoria, Melbourne 001246
National Gallery of Zimbabwe, Harare 049583
National Gallery Shop, London 135241, 141852
National Gandhi Museum and Library, Delhi 022088
The National Gas Museum, Leicester 039975
National Geological Museum of China, Beijing 006985
National Glass Centre, Sunderland . 041158
National Hall of Fame for Famous American Indians, Anadarko 041706
National Handicrafts, Kampala 083170
National Hearing Aid Museum, London 040242
National Heisey Glass Museum, Newark 046429
National Heritage Museum, Van Gorden-Williams Library and Archives, Lexington 045270
National Heritage: The Museums Action Movement, London 054444
National Historic Oregon Trail Interpretive Center, Baker City 041952
National Historical Museum, Athinai 021203
National Historical Museum, Tiranë 000036
National Horseracing Museum, Newmarket 040562
National Infantry Museum, Fort Benning 043888
National Institute of Art and Disabilities, Richmond 047396
National Inventors Hall of Fame, Akron 041587
National Legal Posters, San Francisco 119749
National Liberty Museum, Philadelphia 046968
National Library, Valletta 028031
National Literary and Memorial Museum-Complex of Sabit Mukanov and Gabit Musrepov, Almaty 027392
National McKinley Birthplace Memorial, Niles 046488
National Magazine Company, London 135242
National Maritime Museum, Alexandria 009282
National Maritime Museum, Galle . . 036138
National Maritime Museum, London 040243
National Maritime Museum, Mokpo 027532
National Maritime Museum, Affiliated to Haifa Museum, Haifa 022926
National Maritime Museum Cornwell, Falmouth 039481
National Maritime Museum of Ireland, Dun Laoghaire 022779
National Memorabilia, Miami 090216
National Mining Museum, Kwekwe . 049586
National Model Aviation Museum, Academie of Model Aeronautics, Muncie . . . 046086
National Motor Museum, Birdwood . 000807
National Motor Museum, Brockenhurst 038879
National Motor Racing Museum, Bathurst 000776
National Motorcycle Museum, Bickenhill 038698
National Motorcycle Museum, Mitchell 001270
National Museum, Aden 049558
National Museum, Bangkok 037885
National Museum, Luang Prabang . 027645
National Museum, Malé 028018
National Museum, Monrovia 027826
National Museum, Nagara Pathama 037909
National Museum, Oshogbo 030702
National Museum, Ras-Al-Khaimah 038427
National Museum, Riyadh 034125
National Museum, Sanaa 049562
National Museum, Teheran 022636
National Museum, Victoria 034287
National Museum, Abuja, Abuja . . . 030672
National Museum and Art Gallery of Trinidad and Tobago, Port-of-Spain 037945
National Museum and Gallery, Cardiff 038990
National Museum at Ruwi, Ruwi . . . 031355
National Museum Bauchi, Bauchi . . 030676
National Museum Benin, Benin City 030677
National Museum Bloemfontein, Bloemfontein 034562
National Museum Directors' Conference, London 054445
National Museum Esie, Esie 030681
National Museum for Civilization, Cairo 009316
National Museum for Trading, Riyadh 034126
National Museum Ibadan, Ibadan . . 030683
National Museum Ile-Ife, Ife 030685
National Museum Kaduna, Kaduna . 030691
National Museum, Lagos, Onikan . . 030698
National Museum Makurdi, Makurdi 030695
National Museum Minna, Minna . . . 030696
National Museum Nairobi, Nairobi . 027430
National Museum of African Art, Smithsonian Institution, Washington 048925
National Museum of American Art, Washington 048926
National Museum of American History, Smithsonian Institution, Washington 048927
National Museum of American Illustration, Newport 046461
National Museum of American Jewish History, Philadelphia 046969
National Museum of American Jewish Military History, Washington 048928
National Museum of Archaeology, Tiranë 000037
National Museum of Archaeology, Valletta 028032
National Museum of Art and History, Yangon 029077
National Museum of Australia, Canberra 000889
National Museum of Australian Pottery, Wodonga 001625
National Museum of Baking, Blindley Heath 038769
National Museum of Bhutan, Paro . 003907
National Museum of Calabar, Calabar 030678
National Museum of Catholic Art and History, New York 046382
National Museum of Ceramic Art and Glass, Baltimore 042001
National Museum of Cham Sculpture, Da Nang 049519
National Museum of Chinese History, Beijing 007000
National Museum of Civil War Medicine, Frederick 044051
National Museum of Colonial History, Aba 030669
The National Museum of Communications, Irving 044780
National Museum of Contemporary Art, Athinai 021204
National Museum of Contemporary Art, Gwacheon 027500
National Museum of Damascus, Damascus 037828
National Museum of Dance, Saratoga Springs 048006
National Museum of Enugu, Enugu . 030679
National Museum of Ethiopia, Addis Ababa 009441
National Museum of Fine Arts, Valletta 028033
National Museum of Funeral History, Houston 044651
National Museum of Gardening, Helston 039723
National Museum of Health and Medicine, Armed Forces Institute of Pathology, Washington 048929
National Museum of History, Taipei . 007371
National Museum of Ilorin, Ilorin . . . 030687
National Museum of India, Delhi . . . 022089
National Museum of Kashan, Kashan 022566
National Museum of Korea, Seoul . . 027589
National Museum of Labour History, Manchester 040411
National Museum of Man, Bhopal . . 022035
National Museum of Mandalay, Mandalay 029059
National Museum of Medieval Art, Korçë 000027
National Museum of Modern Chinese Literature, Beijing 007001
National Museum of Mongolian History, Ulaanbaatar 029009
National Museum of Music, Beijing 007002
National Museum of Namibia, Windhoek 029107
National Museum of Natural History, Colombo 036134
National Museum of Natural History, Delhi 022090
National Museum of Natural History, Mdina 028026
National Museum of Natural History, Washington 048930
National Museum of Naval Aviation, Pensacola 046874
National Museum of Nepal, Kathmandu 029116
National Museum of Pakistan, Karachi 031373
National Museum of Photography, Film and Television, Bradford 038808
National Museum of Polo and Hall of Fame, Lake Worth 045119
National Museum of Racing and Hall of Fame, Saratoga Springs 048007
National Museum of Roller Skating, Lincoln 045308
National Museum of Science and Technology, Lahore 031384
National Museum of Science, Planning and Technology, Haifa 022927
National Museum of the American Indian, Washington 048931
National Museum of the American Indian, Smithsonian Institution, New York 046383
National Museum of the Imo State, Owerri 030703
National Museum of the Morgan Horse, Shelburne 048139
National Museum of the Ogun State, Abeokuta 030670
National Museum of the Ondo State, Akure 030673
National Museum of Turkmenistan, Ašgabat 038203
National Museum of Wildlife Art, Jackson 044809
National Museum of Women in the Arts, Washington 048932
National Museum of Woodcarving, Custer 043253
National Museum Oron, Oron 030699
National Museum Resources Exhibition, Birmingham 093940
National Museum Uyo, Uyo 030708
National Museums and Galleries of Northern Ireland, Belfast 054446
National Museums and Monuments of Zimbabwe, Harare 055128
National Museums of Scotland, Edinburgh 039407
National Music Museum, Bloemfontein 034563
National New York Central Railroad Museum, Elkhart 043662
National Oil and Acrylic Painters Society, Osage Beach 054914
National Ornamental Metal Museum, Memphis 045769
National Packard Museum, Warren . 048860
National Palace Museum, Taipei . . . 007372
The National Palace Museum Bulletin, Taipei 135657
The National Palace Museum Monthly of Chinese Art, Taipei 135658
The National Palace Museum Newsletter & Gallery Guide, Taipei 135659
The National Palace Museum Research Quarterly, Taipei 135660
National Philatelic Museum, Delhi . 022091
National Pioneer Women's Hall of Fame, Alice Springs 000737
National Police Museum and Ancient Police Museum, Qasr al-Gawharah, Cairo 009317
National Portrait Gallery, London . . 040244

National Portrait Gallery, Montacute 040491
National Portrait Gallery, Washington . . . 048933
National Postal Museum, Smithsonian Institution, Washington . . . 048934
National Print Museum, Dublin . . . 022764
National Rail Museum, Delhi . . . 022092
National Railroad Museum, Green Bay . . . 044310
National Railroad Museum and Hall of Fame, Hamlet . . . 044404
National Railway Museum, Port Adelaide . . . 001387
National Railway Museum, The National Museum of Science and Industry, York . . . 041480
National Railways of Zimbabwe Museum, Raylton . . . 049590
National Road/Zane Grey Museum, Norwich . . . 046570
National Route 66 Museum and Old Town Museum, Elk City . . . 043656
National Science Centre, Delhi . . . 022093
National Science Museum of Korea, Daejeon . . . 027483
National Scout Museum of New Zealand, Kaiapoi . . . 030526
National Scouting Museum, Irving . 044781
National Sculpture Society, New York . . . 054915
National Soaring Museum, Elmira . . 043692
The National Soccer Hall of Fame, Oneonta . . . 046690
National Society for Education in Art and Design, Corsham . . . 054447
National Society of Mural Painters, New York . . . 054916
National Society of Mural Painters. Newsletter, New York . . . 136571
National Society of Painters in Casein & Acrylic, Whitehall . . . 054917
National Society of Painters, Sculptors and Printmakers, London . . . 054448
National Society of the Children of the American Revolution Museum, Washington . . . 048935
National Society of Tole and Decorative Painters, Wichita . . . 054918
National Softball Hall of Fame and Museum Complex, Oklahoma City . . . 046648
National Space Centre, Leicester . . 039976
National Sportsmuseum, Patiala . . . 022292
National Sprint Car Hall of Fame and Museum, Knoxville . . . 045031
National Steinbeck Center, Salinas . 047759
National Taiwan Art Gallery, Taipei . 007373
National Taiwan College of Arts, Taipei . . . 049860
National Taiwan Science Education Center, Taipei . . . 007374
National Theatre Museum, Bloemfontein . . . 034564
The National Time Museum, Chicago . . . 042867
National Tobacco Museum, Wervik . 003851
The National Toy Train Museum, Strasburg . . . 048393
National Tramway Museum, Matlock . . . 040434
National Transport Museum, Dublin 022765
National Trust for Historic Preservation, Washington . . . 048936
National Trust Museum, Balaklava . 000759
National Trust Museum, Streaky Bay . . . 001495
National Union of Artists of Ukraine, Kyïv . . . 054262
National Vietnam Veterans Art Museum, Chicago . . . 042868
National Vintage, Los Angeles . . . 089852
National Vintage Wireless and Television Museum, Harwich . . . 039689
National Wall Art Gallery, Tampa . . . 120060
National Wallace Monument, Stirling . . . 041105
National War Museum of Scotland, National Museums of Scotland, Edinburgh . 039408
National War Museum of Umauhia, Umauhia . . . 030707
National Warplane Museum, Horseheads . . . 044624
National Watch and Clock Museum, Columbia . . . 043074
National Watercolor Society, Downey . . . 054919
National Waterways Museum, Gloucester . . . 039592
National Wireless Museum, Seaview . . . 040975
National Women's Hall of Fame, Seneca Falls . . . 048113
National Wood Working Museum, Bhaktapur . . . 029112
National Wool Museum, Geelong . . 001051
National Wrestling Hall of Fame, Stillwater . . . 048361
National Yiddish Book Center, Amherst . . . 041694
Nationale Antiekdagen, Genk . . . 093611
Det Nationale Fotomuseum, København . . . 008980
La Nationale Galerie d'Art Alyssa, Bardo . . . 037947
Nationalgalerie Friedrichswerdersche Kirche -Schinkelmuseum, Staatliche Museen zu Berlin - Stiftung Preußischer Kulturbesitz, Berlin . . . 016148
Det Nationalhistoriske Museum på Frederiksborg, Hillerød . . . 008909
Nationalmuseet, København . . . 008981
Nationalmuseum, Stockholm . . . 036648
Nationalpark-Haus, Museum Butjadingen, Butjadingen . . . 016527
Nationalparkhaus, Berchtesgaden . 015957
Nationalparkhaus, Zernez . . . 037749
Nationalparkmuseum, Mittersill . . . 002322
Nations Art, New York . . . 118226
Nations Art Gallery, Pittsburgh . . . 118943
Native American Art, Tulsa . . . 120201
Native American Exhibit, National Kateri Shrine, Fonda . . . 043883
Native American Heritage Museum at Highland Mission, Highland . . . 044536
Native American Images, Austin . . . 114997
Native American Museum, Terre Haute . . . 048531
Native American Resource Center, Pembroke . . . 046865
Native American Trading, Denver . . 116030
Native Art Exports, Calgary . . . 096830
Native Art of Australia, Alice Springs . . . 094142
Native Arts & Crafts, Rochedale . . . 056539
Native Books and Beautiful Things, Honolulu . . . 088969, 142418
Native Indian-Inuit Photographer's Association, Hamilton . . 052759, 096922
Native Investment, Vancouver . . . 097503
Native Nations Art, Oklahoma City . 118671
Nativelle, Françoise, Caen . . . 061879
Nativelle, Françoise, Paris . . . 066322
Nativi, Berto, Firenze . . . 075374
Natividad Arnaiz Martinez, Burgos . 129464
Natperfume, Brach . . . 061742
Natris, Wim de, Nijmegen . . . 108156
Natsagdorj Museum, Ulaanbaatar . . 029010
Natsara, Paris . . . 066323
Natsume, Saitama . . . 106978
Náttúrufrædaistofnun Islands, Akureyrarsetur, Akureyri . . . 021932
Natturufrædistofa Kopavogs, Kópavogur . . . 021954
Náttúrufræðlistofnun Íslands, Reykjavík . . . 021969
Náttúrugripasafnid i Neskaupstad, Neskaupstadur . . . 021955
Natur-Museum Luzern, Luzern . . . 037301
Natur-Museum mit Bauerngarten, Goldberg, Mecklenburg . . . 017476
Natur- und Heimatmuseum Vellberg, Vellberg . . . 020572
Natural Art Gallery, Los Angeles . . . 116854
Natural Elements Craft Gallery, Inveraray . . . 113294
Natural History and Antiquarian Museum; Penzance and District Museum, Penzance . . . 040693
Natural History Department, Hitchin 039758
Natural History Museum, Bhawalpur . . . 031358
Natural History Museum, Bangor, Gwynedd . . . 038591
Natural History Museum, Belfast . . 038663
Natural History Museum, Colchester . . . 039122
Natural History Museum, Gorgan . . 022556
Natural History Museum, Ife . . . 030686
Natural History Museum, Ilam . . . 022559
Natural History Museum, Karachi . . 031374
Natural History Museum, Kathmandu . . . 029117
Natural History Museum, Kingston . 026392
Natural History Museum, Lahore . . 031385
Natural History Museum, Las Cuevas . . . 003884
Natural History Museum, London . . 040245
Natural History Museum, Medani . . 036154
Natural History Museum, Nottingham . . . 040623
Natural History Museum, Port Louis 028072
Natural History Museum, Port Sudan . . . 036157
Natural History Museum, Portsmouth . . . 040768
Natural History Museum, Teheran . . 022637
Natural History Museum, Tring . . . 041240
Natural History Museum, Ulaanbaatar . . . 029011
Natural History Museum, Urmieh . . 022649
Natural History Museum, Yangon . . 029078
Natural History Museum, Bu-Ali University, Hamedan . . . 022558
Natural History Museum, Department of Antiquities, Tripoli . . . 027835
Natural History Museum, Eastern New Mexico University, Portales . . . 047153
Natural History Museum, Iranshahr High School, Yazd . . . 022652
Natural History Museum, Khorram-Abaad University, Khorram-Abaad . . . 022574
Natural History Museum, University of Kansas, Lawrence . . . 045205
Natural History Museum, University of Oslo, Oslo . . . 031090
Natural History Museum of Amarousio, Amarousio . . . 021127
Natural History Museum of Bombay Natural History Society, Mumbai . . . 022267
Natural History Museum of Cephalonia and Ithaca, Argostolion . . . 021146
Natural History Museum of Elassona, Elassona . . . 021253
Natural History Museum of Liberia, Monrovia . . . 027827
Natural History Museum of Los Angeles County, Los Angeles . . . 045455
Natural History Museum of Oeta, Ipati . . . 021283
Natural History Museum of the Aegean, Samos . . . 021459
Natural History Museum of the University of Basrah, Basrah . . . 022666
Natural History Museum of Tilos, Tilos . . . 021506
Natural History Museum of Zimbabwe, Bulawayo . . . 049579
Natural History Society and Folk Museum, Bacup . . . 038562
Natural Science Center of Greensboro, Greensboro . . . 044337
Natural Science Collections Alliance, Washington . . . 054920
Natural Science Museum, Marawi . 031743
Natural Science Museum, Victoria . 028042
Natural Sciences Collections Association, Scunthorpe . . . 054449
Natural Sciences Museum, Hulata . 022939
Natural Wood Framing, Tetbury . . . 131582
Naturama Aargau, Aarau . . . 036810
Nature by Design, Milwaukee . . . 117211
Nature en Provence, Riez . . . 014046
Nature in Art, Gloucester . . . 039593
Nature Museum, Charlotte . . . 042762
Nature Museum at Grafton, Grafton 044257
The Nature Museum of the Chicago Academy of Sciences, Chicago . . 042829
Nature Roots, Houston . . . 116377
Nature-Study and Folk Art Museum of Loutra Almopias, Loutraki . . . 021366
Naturens Hus, Stockholm . . . 036649
Natures Image Photography, Montville . . . 094872
Nature's Reflection, Houston . . . 089163
Natureum Niederelbe, Balje . . . 015865
Naturhistorisches Museum, Admont 001661
Naturhistorisches Museum, Heiden 037184
Naturhistorisches Museum, Nürnberg . . . 019368
Naturhistorisches Museum, Wien . . 002967
Naturhistorisches Museum, Landessammlung für Naturkunde Rheinland-Pfalz, Mainz . . . 018793
Naturhistorisches Museum, Städtische Museen Heilbronn, Heilbronn . . . 017850
Naturhistorisches Museum Basel, Basel . . . 036899
Naturhistorisches Museum der Burgergemeinde Bern, Bern . . . 036933
Naturhistorisches Museum Schloss Bertholdsburg, Schleusingen . . . 020044
Naturhistorisk Museum, Århus . . . 008808
Naturhistoriska Museet, Malmö Museer, Malmö . . . 036461
Naturhistoriska Museet i Göteborg, Natural History Museum of Göteborg, Göteborg . . . 036300
Naturhistoriska Riksmuseet, Stockholm . . . 036650
Naturhistoriske Samlinger, Bergen Museum, Bergen . . . 030769
Naturkunde-Museum, Bielefeld . . . 016240
Naturkunde-Museum, Coburg . . . 016577
Naturkunde-Museum Bamberg, Bamberg . . . 015877
Naturkunde-Museum K.-W. Donsbach, Herborn, Hessen . . . 017877
Naturkunde- und Feuerwehrmuseum, Dobersberg . . . 001782
Naturkundemuseum, Altdorf, Uri . . 036833
Naturkundemuseum, Kassel . . . 018197
Naturkundemuseum, Reutlingen . . 019810
Naturkundemuseum Erfurt, Erfurt . . 017020
Naturkundemuseum Freiberg, Freiberg, Sachsen . . . 017222
Naturkundemuseum Haus der Natur, Salzburg . . . 002561
Naturkundemuseum im Marstall, Paderborn . . . 019554
Naturkundemuseum im Tierpark, Hamm, Westfalen . . . 017732
Naturkundemuseum Leipzig, Leipzig . . . 018586
Naturkundemuseum Ludwigslust, Ludwigslust . . . 018710
Naturkundemuseum Niebüll, Niebüll 019306
Naturkundemuseum Ostbayern, Regensburg . . . 019756
Naturkundliche Sammlung, Altusried . . . 015526
Naturkundliche Sammlung, Königsbrunn . . . 018347
Naturkundliches Bildungszentrum, Ulm . . . 020532
Naturkundliches Museum, Wiesenfelden . . . 020881
Naturkundliches Museum in der Harmonie, Städtische Sammlungen Schweinfurt, Schweinfurt . . . 020143
Naturkundliches Museum und Schulungsstätte Alte Schmiede, Handeloh . . . 017746
Naturmuseum, Sankt Gallen . . . 037497
Naturmuseum, Sammlung Schliefsteiner, Neuberg an der Mürz . . . 002356
Naturmuseum, Städtische Kunstsammlungen, Augsburg . . . 015616
Naturmuseum Lüneburg, Lüneburg 018745
Naturmuseum Olten, Olten . . . 037401
Naturmuseum Solothurn, Solothurn 037578

Naturmuseum und Forschungsinstitut Senckenberg, Frankfurt am Main . 017193
Naturparkhaus Stechlin, Menz 018910
Naturschutzausstellung der Naturschutzstation, Neschwitz ... 019204
Naturum Stendörren, Nyköping ... 036510
Naturwissenschaftliche Sammlung, Stans 037596
Naturwissenschaftliche Sammlungen, Stiftung Stadtmuseum Berlin, Berlin 016149
Naturwissenschaftliche Sammlungen, Tiroler Landesmuseum Ferdinandeum, Innsbruck 002091
Naturwissenschaftliche Sammlungen der Stadt Winterthur, Winterthur 037728
Naturwissenschaftliche Sammlungen des Kantons Glarus, Engi 037068
Naturwissenschaftliches Museum, Aschaffenburg 015579
Naturwissenschaftliches Museum der Stadt Flensburg, Flensburg 017131
Naturwissenschaftliches Museum Duisburg, Duisburg 016859
Naturzentrum Nordfriesland, Bredstedt 016398
Natuur Historisch Museum en Heemkunde Centrum, Meerssen 029915
Natuurdiorama Holterberg, Holten . 029762
Natuurhistorisch en Volkenkundig Museum, Oudenbosch 030026
Natuurhistorisch Museum, Antwerpen 003179
Natuurhistorisch Museum Boekenbergpark, Deurne 003399
Natuurhistorisch Museum de Peel, Asten 029284
Natuurhistorisch Museum het Diorama, Nunspeet 029979
Natuurhistorisch Museum Maastricht, Maastricht 029898
Natuurmuseum Ameland, Nes 029940
Natuurmuseum Brabant, Tilburg ... 030208
Natuurmuseum de Wielewaal, Lopik 029876
Natuurmuseum Dokkum, Dokkum . 029492
Natuurmuseum E. Heimans, Zaandam 030365
Natuurmuseum Enschede, Enschede 029567
Natuurmuseum Groningen, Groningen 029642
Natuurmuseum het Drents-Friese Woud, Wateren 030313
Natuurmuseum Mar en Klif, Oudemirdum 030025
Natuurmuseum Nijmegen, Nijmegen 029964
Natuurmuseum Rotterdam, Rotterdam 030095
Natuurpunt Museum, Turnhout 003819
Natuurwetenschappelijk Museum, Antwerpen 003180
Nau 55, Porto 080100
Naucelle-Lepeltier, Caen 061880
Nauck & Co, Albert, Köln 134116
Naučno-issledovatelskij Institut i Muzej Antropologii im. D.N. Anučina, Moskovskij Gosudarstvennyj Universitet, Moskva 033507
Naučno-memorialnyj Muzej N.E. Žukovskogo, Moskva 033508
Naučnyj Morskoj Muzej, Atlantičeskij naučno-issledovatelskij institut morskogo rybnogo chozjajstva i okeanografii, Kaliningrad 033218
Naud, Daniel, Saint-Maixent-l'Ecole 067601
Naudet, Marguerite, Rilhac-Xaintrie 067146
Naudet, Michel, Limoges 063892
Naudin, Abbeville 060653, 098766
Naudin, Michel, Beaune 061288
Nauert, Christoph Dirk, Wien 057508, 120690
Naughton, Dun Laoghaire 139972
Naujieji Skliautai, Vilnius 107369
Nauka i Izkustvo, Sofia 133311
Naumann, Dr. Berthold, Stuttgart .. 105002
Naumann, Jens, Bad Heilbrunn ... 125097
Naumann, Ulrich, Cape Town 140973
Naumann-Museum, Köthen, Anhalt 018364
Naumburg, Barbara, Frankfurt am Main 125658
Naumkeag House, Stockbridge ... 048366
Nauportus, Vrhnika 080670
Nausicaa, Centre National de la Mer, Boulogne-sur-Mer 010913
Nautelankosken Museo, Lieto 009824
Nautic Hamburg, Hamburg 071299
Nautical Antique Centre, Weymouth 087117
Nautical Antiques, Norfolk 091393
Nautical Living, Kansas City 089512
Nautical Museum, Manx National Heritage, Castletown 039017
Nautical Museum of Crete, Chania . 021229
Nautical Museum of Galaxidi, Galaxidi 021271
Nautical Museum of Oinousses, Oinoussai 021412
Nauticals Limited, Dallas 088578
Nauticus, Hampton Roads Naval Museum, Norfolk 046502
Nautikon Mouseiontis Ellados, Piraeus 021434
Nautilus, Milwaukee 117212
Nautilus, Warszawa 079773
Nautilus Salon Antykwaryczny, Kraków 079646, 134856, 140745
Nauvoo Historical Society Museum, Nauvoo 046167
Nava-Hopi, Tucson 120152
Navajo Nation Museum, Window Rock 049235
Navajo National Monument, Tonalea 048575
Naval Academy Museum, Jinhae .. 027521
Naval and Maritime Museum, Ballina 000766
Naval Museum of Alberta, Calgary . 005195
Naval Undersea Museum, Keyport . 044993
Naval War College Museum, Newport 046462
Navan Centre, Armagh 038528
Navarra, Enrico, New York 118227
Navarra, Enrico, Paris 100724
Navarra, Enrico, Paris 100725
Navarra, Enrico, Paris 100726
Navarra, Enrico, Paris 133657
Navarra, G., Napoli 076017
Navarre-Duplantier, Hasparren 063133
Navarrete Alvárez, I.saac, Jerez de la Frontera 129541
Navarro, Megève 064467
Navarro, Nantes 099813
Navarro, Paris 066324
Navarro, Paris 124759
Navarro, Toronto 059247
Navarro, Ana, Barcelona 141000
Navarro, Ceferino, Granada 110380
Navarro, Françoise, Attin 061020
Navarro, Leandro, Madrid 081351, 110583
Navarro County Historical Society Museum, Corsicana 043168
Navarro Santa Cruz, Amparo, Murcia 081444
Navarro Zavaleta, Julio, Bogotá ... 123906
Navas, Enrique, Bogotá 098176
Navas & Navas, Bogotá 098177
La Nave, Valencia 110837
La Nave, Vigo 081707
Nave Museum, Victoria 048783
Navel, B., Berlin 101987
Naveri, Marius, Beaumont-Monteux 061261
La Navicella, Milano 106271
Il Navicello, Pisa 106469
Navier, Thierry, Azay-sur-Cher 061152
Navigator Contemporary Arts, Saint Just 114380
Naviglio, Milano 075783
Naviglio Piú, Milano 075784
Naviglio Piú, Milano 075785
Navikula Arts, Sankt-Peterburg 109638
Naviliat, Oscar Luis, Buenos Aires . 136742
Naville, Claude, Genève 122324
Naville & Christin, Genève 122325
Navire, Brest 099029
Naviscope Alsace, Strasbourg 014882
Navona Antiquariato, Roma 076586, 128132
Navoni, Roberto, Brescia . 075180, 127226
Navrátil, Miroslav, Praha 098475
The Navy Museum, Washington ... 048937
Naw, Osaka 106971
Al-Nawras, Sharjah 112469
Naxos, Wellington 108632
Nayarit, San Salvador 060479
Naylor, Timothy, Chertsey 130550
Nayong Pilipino Museum, Pasay ... 031758
Nayuma Museum, Limulunga 049567
Nazar, Fortaleza 137561
Nazarchuk, Regina 123812
Nazarri, Laura, Milano 075786
Naze, Michel, Doudeville 062730
Nazia Sultana, Brierfield 112710
Nazraeli, Tucson 135517
NB Style, Toowoomba 056723
NBS-Múzeum Minci a Medailí, Kremnica 034369
NCA Art Gallery, Lahore 108780
N.D., Austin 136572
nd-galerie, Bad Pyrmont 101687
NE Galerie, Rotterdam 108200
Néa Moni Collection, Chios 021234
Neal, New Orleans 122981
Neal, David, Oxted 141989
Neal Sons & Fletcher, Woodbridge . 122759
Neale, Joseph, Erina Heights 094511
Neales, Nottingham 122643
Neal's Gallery, Kansas City 116584
Nealway, Houston 089164
Neanderthal Museum, Mettmann .. 018928
Neary, C.F., Auckland 128909
Neary, Geoff, Huddersfield 084749, 130815
Nease, Joseph, Kansas City 116585
Neat Things, Toronto 059248
Neate, Gary C., Sudbury, Suffolk .. 086786
Neath Museum, Neath 040517
Nebbett, Andrew, London 085555
Nebehay, Christian M., Wien 057509, 137353
Nebehay, Dr. Stefan, Wien 057510
Nebel Verlag, Utting 134442
Nebelsieck, Gunther & Astrid, Berlin 069709
Nebelspalter-Verlag, Horn 135026
Nebengaus, Berlin 125264
Nebraska Conference United Methodist Historical Center, Lincoln 045309
Nebraska Museums Association, Aurora 054921
Nebraska Prairie Museum, Phelps County Historical Society, Holdrege 044570
Neby Eiendom, Grue Finnskog 121852
Nečekal, František, Cheb 137777
Necessary Angel, Keswick 113318
Neckarschiffahrts-Museum und Weinbau, Stadt- und Industriegeschichte, Städtische Museen Heilbronn, Heilbronn 017851
Nécropole de Louis Cauvin, Gareoult 011921
The Ned Shed Museum, Meldrum Bay 005854
Nedelcu, Stelian, Bucureşti 080166, 129222
Neder, Cornelia, Hammelburg 071365
Nederlands Architektuurinstituut, Rotterdam 030096
Nederlands Artillerie Museum, 't Harde 029668
Nederlands Bakkerijmuseum Het Warme Land, Hattem 029681
Nederlands Baksteen en Dakpanmuseum de Panoven, Zevenaar 030384
Nederlands Biermuseum de Boom, Alkmaar 029132
Nederlands Centrum voor Handwerken, Breda 029352
Nederlands Drogisterij Museum, Dutch Drugstore Museum, Maarssen ... 029887
Nederlands Economisch Penningkabinet, Rotterdam 030097
Nederlands Foto Instituut, Rotterdam 030098
Nederlands Goud-, Zilver- en Klokkenmuseum, Schoonhoven .. 030141
Nederlands Graanmuseum/Olie- en Korenmolen Woldzigt, Roderwolde 030071
Nederlands Instituut voor Mediakunst - Montevideo, Amsterdam 029215
Nederlands Kachelmuseum, Alkmaar 029133
Nederlands Kansspelmuseum, Den Haag 029448
Nederlands Leder- en Schoenenmuseum, Waalwijk 030302
Nederlands Militair Kustverdedigingsmuseum, Fort aan den Hoek van Holland, Hoek van Holland 029756
Het Nederlands Muntmuseum, Utrecht 030234
Nederlands Museum van Knipkunst, Schoonhoven 030142
Nederlands Museum voor Glas en Glastechniek, Hoogeveen 029767
Nederlands Openluchtmuseum, Arnhem 029271
Nederlands Parfumflessenmuseum, Winkel 030335
Nederlands Politie Museum, Apeldoorn 029255
Nederlands Scheepvaartmuseum, Amsterdam 029216
Nederlands Spoorwegmuseum, Utrecht 030235
Het Nederlands Sportmuseum Olympion, Lelystad 029861
Nederlands Steendrukmuseum, Valkenswaard 030253
Nederlands Stoommachinemuseum, Medemblik 029912
Nederlands Strijkijzer-Museum, Noordbroek 029972
Nederlands Tegelmuseum, Otterlo . 030017
Nederlands Textielmuseum, Tilburg 030209
Nederlands Uitvaartmuseum, Apeldorn 029257
Het Nederlands Vestingmuseum, Naarden 029935
Nederlands Waterleidingmuseum, Utrecht 030236
Nederlands Wijnmuseum, Arnhem . 029272
Nederlands Zouavenmuseum, Oudenbosch 030027
Nederlandsche Vereeniging Van Antiquaren, Den Haag 053898
De Nederlandse Museumvereniging, Amsterdam 053899
Nedervetil Hembygdsgård, Nedervetil 009902
Nedobeck, Milwaukee 117213
Nedomansky Brüder, Wien 057511
Née, Jean-Luc, Pierrecourt 066824
Née, Stéphane, Rozay-en-Brie 067316
Neeb, Hildegard, Westerburg, Westerwald 074360
Need to Read, Omaha 142730
Needful Things, Ulm 074149
Needful Treasures, Oklahoma City . 091522
Needles, Elva, Kansas City 089513
Neef, Helga, Köln 103685
Neel, Birmingham 131837
Neel, Saint-Paul-de-Vence 101215
Néel, Albert, Chazelles-sur-Lyon .. 099127
Neeltje Twiss, Den Haag 078223
Nees, Bartley, Wellington 108633
Nees Morfes, Athinai 105406
Neeses Farm Museum, Neeses ... 046173
Neesh, Mumbai 105789
Neess, Paris 100727, 124760
NEF, Kyïv 112420
La Nef des Fous, Paris 138509
Nef des Jouets, Soultz-Haut-Rhin .. 014844
Nefedov, D.V., Sankt-Peterburg ...080316, 140938
Nefertiti, Medellín 098281
Neff, Beat, Stäfa 082831
Neff, Charles, Mulhouse .. 064838, 138228
Neff, M., Frankfurt am Main 102804
Neff, Paul, Rastatt 134354

Neffe-Degandt, London 113789
Nefzger, Franz, Saaldorf-Surheim . . 126755
Negelein, Jörg C.G. von, Kiel 071840
Negev Museum, Be'ersheva 022897
Negrel, Austin 087598
Negrel, Austin 087599
Negri, Alberto, Roma 128133
Negri, Donatella, Villach 057342
Negri, Gabriella, Roma 128134
Negri, Vittorio, Milano 127639
Negrini, Maria Cristina, Bologna . . . 075095
Negrini, Maurizio, Verona 077014
The Negros Museum, Bacolod 031623
Negulescu, Sabina & Jean, Bucureşti 109440
Neher, Essen 102700
Nehmann, Wilhelm, München 072799
Nehring, S., Berlin 069710
Nehru Centre Art Gallery, Mumbai . 105790
Nehru Children's Museum, Kolkata . 022223
Nehru Memorial Museum and Library, Delhi 022094
Nehru Science Centre, Mumbai . . . 022268
Neidhardt, Fritz, Böblingen 138887
Neidhardt, S., Wiesbaden 127015
Neidhart Fresken, Wien Museum, Wien 002968
Les Neiges d'Antan, Paris 066325
Neighborhoood Gallery, New Orleans 117480
Neighbor's Antiques, Cleveland . . . 088347
Neil, Jacksonville 132189
Neil Armstrong Air and Space Museum, Wapakoneta 048851
Neill-Cochran Museum House, Austin 041933
Neill Museum, Fort Davis 043907
Neilmarie, Albuquerque 114810
Neils, E., Heidenheim an der Brenz . 103329
Neilson, T. & J.W., Edinburgh 084305
Neiraku Museum, Nara 026898
Neisser Haus - Heimathaus und Archiv, Hildesheim 017923
Neizvestniy, Ernst, New York 118228
Nej, Beograd 080400
Nejjoum, Ahmed Barghach, Casablanca 077666
Nejjoum, Larbi, Casablanca 077667
Nejman, Laure, Paris 066326
Neka Museum and Gallery, Gianyar 022418
Nel Corso del Tempo, Firenze 075375
Nela Alberca, Madrid 110584
Nelholt, Dennis, København 060358
Neligh Mills, Neligh 046175
Nelimarkka Museo . Etelä-Pohjanmaan Aluetaidemuseo ja Nelimarkka-resedenssi, Alajärvi 009454
Nelis, Jack, Den Haag 078224
Nelis, Jean, Bruxelles 096237
Nelis, Thom & Lenny, Amsterdam . . 077920
Nelis, Vincent, Amsterdam 077921
Nelis, Thom & Lenny, Haarlem 078473
Nell-Buch, Fürth, Bayern 125689
Nella Longari, Venezia 076962
Nellemann & Thomsen, Odense . . . 120875
Nellessen, S., Simmerath 073823
Nell'Incanto, Napoli 106383
Nello, Quiberon 101054
Nels Berggran Museum, Imperial . . 005635
Nelson, Antwerpen 057719
Nelson, Jacksonville 132190
Nelson, New York 091107
Nelson, Paris 100728
Nelson, John J., West Hollywood . . 093490
The Nelson-Atkins Museum of Art, Kansas City 044924
Nelson-Atkins Museum of Art. Calendar of Event, Kansas City 136573
Nelson Mandela Metropolitan Art Museum, Port Elizabeth 034705
Nelson Mandela Museum, Umtata . 034767
Nelson Monument, Edinburgh 039409
Nelson Museum, Nelson 005990
Nelson Museum and Local History Centre, Monmouth 040490
Nelson & Nelson, New York 091108
Nelson Pioneer Farm and Museum, Oskaloosa 046739
Nelson Provincial Museum, Nelson . 030548
Nelson & Tavares, Lisboa 129162
Nelson Tower, Forres 039518
Nelson's Antiques, Preston 086311
Nemany, Gerhard & Dorit, Dachau . 070169
Nemati Parviz, New York 091109
Nemec, Vaclav, Ingolstadt 103432
Nemes, Tamás, Budapest 127077
Német Nemzetiségi Muzeum, Ungarndeutsches Museum, Tata . 021905
I Nemici del Tarlo, Roma . 076587, 128135
Nemiranda, Angono 108814
Nemitz, Gröbenzell 103007
NEMLAC Annual Report, Newcastle-upon-Tyne 136256
NEMO, Amsterdam 029217
Nemo, San Antonio 092551
NEMO - Kunst in Nordeuropa, Eckernförde 102597, 133903
Nemorina, Helsinki 060561
Nemours Mansion and Gardens, Wilmington 049207
Nemzeti Történeti Emlékpark, Opusztaszer 021804
N'en Faites Pas un Roman, Liège . . 137521
Nenagh District Heritage Centre, Nenagh 022844
Nencioni, Daniele, Firenze 127380
Nene Antigüedades, Rosario 055296
Nene Valley Railway, Stibbington . . 041099
Neneckij Okružnoj Kraevedčeskij Muzej, Narjan-Mar 033544
Nénert, Didier-Jean, La Baule-Escoublac 063292
Nenert, Didier-Jean, Paris 066327
Nennmann, Wiesentheid 105288
Nenova, S.-R., Sofia 058765
Nentai Gallery, Bucureşti 109441
Nenthead Mines Heritage Centre, Nenthead 040520
Neo Galerie, Lagny-sur-Marne 099414, 124288
Neo Galleri, Stavanger 108758
Neon, Lyon 099608
Neon Graphics, Las Vegas 116638
Neon Lady, Saint Louis 092284
Neon Works & Nostalgia World, San Diego 092662
Neot Kedumim, The Biblical Landscape Reserve in Israel, Lod 023025
Nepal Antiques, Bhaktapur 077702
Nepal Crystal Works & Curio House, Kathmandu 077705
Nepcosons, Mumbai 074825
Nepean Historical Museum, Sorrento 001471
Nepean Museum, Nepean 005993
Népmüvészeti Tájház, Balatonszentgyörgy 021624
Nepomuk, Johann, Krefeld 072076
Néprajzi Gyűjtemény, Soproni Múzeum, Sopron 021846
Néprajzi Kiállítás, Janus Pannonius Múzeum, Pécs 021823
Néprajzi Múzeum, Budapest 021678
Néprajzi Múzeum, Nagyvázsony . . . 021800
Neptune, Nonancourt 065227
Neptune Art Marine, Biarritz 061470
Neptune Fine Art, New York 118229
Neptune Gallery, Dublin 074936
Neptune Gallery, Saint Blazey Par . . 114352
Neptune Township Historical Museum, Neptune 046179
Neptunus, Anjum 140351
Ner Hole Museum, Åndalsnes 030727
Néré, Henri, Saint-Malo (Ille-et-Vilaine) 067616
Nérel, Georges, Perpignan 066753
Neret-Minet, Paris 121177
Nergal Gate Museum, Mosul 022669
Neri, Alberto, Perugia 127881
Neri, Anna Maria, Firenze 075376
Neri, G., Cagliari 075217
Neri, Giuseppe, Cagliari 075218
Neri & Chas, Philadelphia 091671
Nerilee, Jamberoo 056019
Nerima Bijutsukan, Tokyo 027213
Nerima Home Town Museum, Tokyo 027214
Nering & Stern, Berlin 101988
Nerlich, Manfred, Neuwied 139592
Nerman, Winnipeg 059467, 137742
Nermesan, Elixhausen 056971
Nero, Bianco, Stokesley 114496
The Neroche Decorative and Fine Arts Society, Taunton 054450
Nero's Antiques, Norfolk 091394
Nes Lensemuseum, Skiptvet 031192
Nesbit & Co, D.M., Portsmouth 122661
Nesburg, Fort Worth 088873
Nesch-Museet, Ål 030716
Nesha, Jakarta 105839
Nesher, Barcelona 110226
Nesher, Barcelona 110227
Neskoromny, Andrzej, Łódź 079670
Nesle, New York 091110
Nesna Bygdemuseum, Nesna 031051
Nesplak, Karl, Wallhausen, Württemberg 074266
Ness Historical Society Museum, Port-of-Ness 040744
Nessim, Gabriel & Isabelle, Genève 082450
Nesstofusafn, Seltjarnarnes 021979
The Nest, Fresno 088913
Nest, Leicester 113374
Nest, San Francisco 092854
Nest, San Francisco 092855
Nester, Martin & Brigitte, Rottweil . 073608
Nestler, Reiner, Eisenach 070535
Nestor, Houston 132133
Net Loft Gallery, Porthleven 114278
Netaji Museum, Kolkata 022224
Netherland Inn House Museum, Kingsport 045011
Nettelbeck, Remscheid 104715
Nettels, Th., Münster 104372
Nettesheim, Gisela, Essen 070640
Nettis, Le Touquet-Paris-Plage 099463
Netuschil, Claus, Darmstadt 102347, 133857
Netuschil, Nicole, Wermelskirchen .074340, 105212
Netwerk Galerij, Aalst 096050
Network, Kunstverein Baden-Baden e.V., Gernsbach 053517
Network of European Museum Organisations, Helsinki 052876
Neu, A., Fröndenberg 070904
Neubacher, Toronto 097335
Neubacher, H.-D, Berlin 125265
Neubart, Yves-Marthus, Villeurbanne 068974
Neubarth, Michael, Hamburg 071300
Neubauer, Günter, Frankfurt/Oder . . 102843
Neubauer, Günther, Rödental 126726
Neubauer, Helmut, Hauneck 071435
Neubauer, Reiner, Bad Endorf 125092
Neuberger Museum of Art, Purchase College, State University of New York, Purchase 047285
Neuberin-Museum, Reichenbach, Vogtland 019776
Neubistritzer Heimatstube, Reingers 002519
Die Neue Aktionsgalerie, Berlin . . . 101989
Neue BildArt, Hünstetten 071588
Neue Galerie, Dachau 016620
Neue Galerie, Erlangen 102654
Neue Galerie, Landesmuseum Joanneum, Graz 001943
Neue Galerie der Stadt Linz, Wolfgang-Gurlitt-Museum, Linz 002250
Neue Galerie im Höhmann-Haus, Städtische Kunstsammlungen, Augsburg . . . 015617
Neue Galerie New York, New York . 046384
Neue Galerie New York, New York . 118230
Neue Galerie Oberschöneweide der Karl-Hofer-Gesellschaft, Berlin 016150
Neue Galerie, Staatliche und Städtische Kunstsammlungen, Staatliche Museen Kassel, Kassel 018198
Neue Gesellschaft für bildende Kunst e.V., Berlin 016151, 053518
Neue Holländerei, Meldorf 104056
Neue Kunstakakademie Rhein/Ruhr, Essen 050079
Neue Kunstschule, Basel 050757
Neue Kunstschule Zürich, Zürich . . 050781
Neue Münchener Künstlergenossenschaft, München 053519
Neue Nationalgalerie, Staatliche Museen zu Berlin - Stiftung Preußischer Kulturbesitz, Berlin 016152
Neue Pinakothek, Bayerische Staatsgemäldesammlungen, München 019095
Neue Plakat Kunst, Bad Münster . .101672, 133734
Neue Residenz, Bamberg 015878
Neue Sächsische Galerie, Chemnitz 016562
Neue Sammlung, Passau 019572
Die Neue Sammlung, Staatliches Museum für angewandte Kunst, München . 019096
Neuenschwander-Asuncion, Gockhausen 111520
Neuer Aachener Kunstverein e.V., Aachen 053520
Neuer Berliner Kunstverein, Berlin .016153, 053521
Neuer Jerxheimer Kunstverein, Jerxheim 053522
Neuer Kunstverein Aschaffenburg e.V., Aschaffenburg 053523
Neuer Kunstverein Gießen e.V., Gießen 053524
Neuer Leipziger Künstlerverein - soziale Vereinigung Kunst, Leipzig 053525
Neuer Leipziger Kunstverein e.V., Leipzig 053526
Neuer Sächsischer Kunstverein, Dresden 016808, 053527
Neues Glas/New Glass, Frechen . . . 135808
Neues Kunsthaus Ahrenshoop, Ostseebad Ahrenshoop 019517
Neues Kunstquartier, Berlin 053528, 135809
Neues Kunstquartier Berlin, Berlin . 016154
Neues Museum, Hollabrunn 002060
Neues Museum, Wien 135572
Neues Museum, Staatliches Museum für Kunst und Design in Nürnberg, Nürnberg 019369
Neues Museum Schwechat, Schwechat 002667
Neues Museum Weimar, Stiftung Weimarer Klassik und Kunstsammlungen, Weimar, Thüringen 020748
Neues Museum Weserburg Bremen, Bremen 016421
Neues Rheinland, Pulheim 135810
Neues Schloß Bayreuth, Bayreuth . 015922
Neues Schloß Herrenchiemsee, Herrenchiemsee 017898
Neues Schloß Meersburg, Meersburg 018874
Neues Schloß Schleißheim, Oberschleißheim 019417
Neues Schloß, Schloßmuseum, Tettnang 020427
Neues Schloß und Instrumentenmuseum, Kißlegg 018275
Neues Schloss Wallerstein, Wallerstein 020658
Neues Stadtmuseum Landsberg am Lech, Landsberg am Lech 018479
Les Neuf Muses, Paris 138510
Neufeld, Au, Sankt Gallen 134976
Neuffer, Gaston, Lausanne 082558, 130075
Neuffer, Simone, Lausanne 082559
Neugablonzer Industrie- und Schmuckmuseum im Isergebirgs-Museum, Kaufbeuren 018213
Neugebauer, München 126424
Neugebauer, Anita, Basel 111214
Neugebauer, Michael, Gossau (Zürich) 135024
Neugebauer, Michael, Salzburg . . . 133144

Neugebauer, W., Linz 137222
Neugebauer, Wolfgang, Satteins . . . 137257
Neugerriemschneider, Berlin 101990
Neuhäuser, Roland G., Mainz 072400
Neuhäuser, Ulrike, Mainz 126263
Neuhart, Denver 088718
Neuhaus, Albrecht, Würzburg 074505
Neuhaus, Beat, Fribourg 082379
Neuhaus, Beat, Fribourg . . 082380, 130025
Neuhaus, Lindy, Houston 089165
Neuhaus & Zigrahn, Moers 072583
Neuhausen, Angelika, Krefeld 126146
Neuheisel, Gernot, Saarbrücken . . . 073642
Neuhofer, Krems 057129
Neuhoff, New York 118231
Neuhoff, G., Waldbronn 105147
Neujack, Bernd, Krauchenwies 126143
Neukirch, C., Neckarbischofsheim . 072949
Neukomm, Doris, Zollikon 112020
Neuland-Bund und Verlag, München 134264
Neumann, Berlin 069711
Neumann, Duisburg 070484
Neumann, Krefeld 103782
Neumann, Neuruppin 073011
Neumann, Peine 104596
Neumann, San Francisco 132903
Neumann, Stuttgart 073997
Neumann, Doris, Hofheim, Unterfranken 125953
Neumann, Ernst, Günzburg 071140
Neumann, F., Saterland 073675
Neumann, Gerhard, Mühlenbeck . . 072604
Neumann, Jan, Praha 137840
Neumann, Käthe, Hesel 103369
Neumann, Karsten, Molsdorf 126331
Neumann, M., Gutach, Schwarzwaldbahn 139157
Neumann, Manfred, Schafflund . . . 073677
Neumann, Nicolas, Gmund 071016
Neumann, S., Grünwald 071137
Neumann, S. & K., Leipzig 103897
Das Neumann Haus Museum, Laidley 001167
Neumeister & Co., Hamburg 121433
Neumeister, München 121538
Neumeister, Wien 120691
Neunlist, André & Yannick, Battenheim 061219
Neunlist, Nathalie, Horbourg Wihr . . 063173
Neunte Kunst, Osnabrück 134336
Neuparth, Heike-Gabriele & Reimar, Pößneck 073349
Neupert, Herold, München 072800
Neurauter, Arthur, Chur 082316
Neuse, Bremen 070037
Neuser, Hermann, Siegen 104899
Neusser, Wien 095904
Neusser Auktionshaus, Neuss 121560
Neustadt Museum of Tiffany Art, New York 046385
Neustädter Rathaus, Hanau 017745
Neut Gallery, Wellington 108634
Neutral Art, Singapore 109843
Neutral Ground, Regina 097181
Neuville, Jean, Boyer 061739
Neuville Franck, Vaux-sous-Aubigny 068740
Neuwerk, Oldenburg, Oldenburg . . . 104543
Neuwerk, Rendsburg 104720
Neuwerk Kunsthalle, Konstanz 018378
Neuwirth, C., Bockenem 069897
Neuwirth, Dimitrij, Brno 123953
Neuwirth, Edith, Langenargen 103831
Neuwirth, Dr. Waltraud, Wien 133221
Neva-Ant, Sankt-Peterburg 080317
Nevada Art, Las Vegas 116639
Nevada County Historical Society Museum, Nevada City 046183
Nevada Historical Society Museum, Vevada Department Museums and Library, Reno 047372
Nevada Museum of Art, Reno 047373
Nevada Pastel Society, Las Vegas . 054922
Nevada State Fire Museum and Comstock Firemen's Museum, Virginia City . 048801
Nevada State Museum, Carson City 042635
Nevada State Museum, Las Vegas . 045191
Nevada State Museum. Carson City. Popular Series, Carson City 136574
Nevada State Museum Newsletter, Carson City 136575
Nevada State Railroad Museum, Carson City 042636
Nevado Cortes, Eva Maria, Pamplona 081525
Nevartos, Zürich 112154
Neve, Gunnar, Leck 072177
Never Ending Books, North Shore . . 140647
Never Too Old, Penola 056449
Neversink Valley Area Museum, Cuddebackville 043236
Neves, Ana, Lisboa 079975
Neves, Guilherme Gameiro, Lisboa . 109338
Nevill, Canterbury 112802, 130506
Nevill, Fred M., Houston 089166
Neville, Howard, Tunbridge Wells . . 086944
Neville Blakey Museum of Locks, Keys and Safes, Brierfield 038841
Neville Budhais Gallery, Montego Bay 106826
Neville Public Museum of Brown County, Green Bay 044311
Nevin, Skalko, Los Angeles 089853
Nevograf, Sankt-Peterburg 109639
Nevra Antik Galeri, İstanbul 083148
Nevşehir Devlet Güzel Sanatlar Galerisi, Nevşehir 038157
Nevşehir Müzesi, Nevşehir 038158
Nevska, Irina, San Francisco 119750
Nevyantik, Mladá Boleslav 060053, 137797
New Academy Gallery, London 113790
New Age Expressions, Buffalo 115261
New American Paintings, Boston . . 136576
New Ark, Moskva 109573
New Art, Hamburg 103199
New Art Centre, East Winterslow . . 039359
New Art Dealers Alliance, New York 054923
New Art Examiner, Chicago 136577
The New Art Gallery Walsall, Walsall 041286
New Art on Newbury, Boston 115211
New Art Portfolio, Stroud 114515
New Artform, Singapore 134892
New Arts Gallery, Toulon (Var) 101323
New Arts Program, Kutztown 054924
New Ashgate Gallery, Farnham 113057
New Asia Art Shop, Dallas 132019
New Avenue Fine Art, Miami 117116
New Bedford Whaling Museum, New Bedford 046190
New Beginning, Jacksonville 132191
The New Berlin Historical Society Museum, New Berlin 046192
New Bern Firemen's Museum, New Bern 046194
New Braunfels Conservation Society Museum, New Braunfels 046197
New Bridge Gallery, Truro 114605
New Brighton Art Gallery, Christchurch 108405
New Britain Museum of American Art, New Britain 046202
New Britain Youth Museum, New Britain 046203
New Britain Youth Museum at Hungerford Park, Kensington 044962
New British Artists, Bedford 112600
New Brunswick College of Craft and Design, Fredericton 049787
New Brunswick College of Craft and Design Gallery, Fredericton 005483
New Brunswick Healthcare Museum, Fredericton 005484
New Brunswick Mining and Mineral Interpretation Centre, Petit-Rocher 006144
New Brunswick Museum, Saint John 006354
New Brunswick Sports Hall of Fame, Fredericton 005485
New Bytes and Old Bits, Tucson . . . 093254
New Canaan Historical Society Museum, New Canaan 046208
New Canaan Nature Center, New Canaan 046209
New Castle Historical Society Museum, New Castle 046211
New Century, London 085556, 131118
New Century Antiquarian Books, Kew 136963
New Century Art, Cleveland 115732
New Century Artists, New York 118232
New Century Collector, Salt Lake City 092451
New Circle, Miami 117117
New Craftsman, Saint Ives, Cornwall 114366
New Creations, Dallas 088579
New Curiosity Shop, Tonbridge 086894, 131597
New Denmark Memorial Museum, New Denmark 005994
New Echota, Calhoun 042550
New Eltham Galleries, London 113791
New England Air Museum of the Connecticut Aeronautical Historical Association, Windsor Locks 049240
New England Antique Emporium, Uralla 056774
New England Antiques Journal, Ware 136578
New England Appraisers Association, Ludlow 054925
New England Brass and Iron Lace Foundry Museum, Uralla 001581
New England Carousel Museum, Bristol 042418
New England College Gallery, Henniker 044515
New England Fire and History Museum, Brewster 042400
New England House Antiques, Tring 086921, 131610
New England Maple Museum, Pittsford 047071
New England Maple Museum, Rutland 047580
New England Museum Association, Boston 054926
New England Quilt Museum, Lowell 045509
New England Regional Art Museum, Armidale 000752
New England School of Art and Design, Boston 051014
New England Science Center, Worcester 049305
New England Ski Museum, Franconia 044026
New England Watercolor Society, Boston 054927
New England Wireless and Steam Museum, East Greenwich 043562
New English Art Club, London 054451, 113792, 136257
New Farm Antique Centre, New Farm 056325
New Farm Art, New Farm 094934
New Forest Fine Art Gallery, Ashurst, Hampshire 112530
New Forest Museum and Visitor Centre, Lyndhurst 040367
The New Gallery, Birmingham 112654
The New Gallery, Calgary 096831
New Gallery, Ha Noi 120476
New Gallery, Houston 116378
New Gallery, Portscatho 114281
The New Gallery, Woolacombe 114733
New Gleanings, Albany 136579
New Grafton Gallery, London 085557
New Grafton Gallery, London 113793
New Grafton Gallery, London 131119
New Grounds Print Shop, Albuquerque 114811
New Hall, Dymchurch 039339
New Hall Women's Art Collection, Cambridge 038968
New Hampshire Antiquarian Society Museum, Hopkinton 044620
New Hampshire Antiques Monthly, Farmington 136580
New Hampshire Art Association, Boscawen 054928
New Hampshire Arts, Concord 136581
New Hampshire Farm Museum, Milton 045881
New Hampshire Institute of Art, Manchester 045621
New Hampshire Institute of Art, Manchester 051669
New Harmony Gallery of Contemporary Art, University of Southern Indiana, New Harmony 046221
New Harmony State Historic Site, New Harmony 046222
New Haven Colony Historical Society Museum, New Haven 046225
New Horizons, Ho Chi Minh City . . . 120519
New Iceland Heritage Museum, Gimli 005508
New Ideal Art, Singapore 109844
New Image Art, Los Angeles 045456
New Image Art, Philadelphia 118810
New Image Art, Philadelphia 118811
New Image Art, Philadelphia 118812
New Image Art, West Hollywood . . . 120403
New Image Gallery, Calgary 096832
New International Cultural Center, Antwerpen 003181
New Jade Gallery, Hong Kong 097816
New Jersey Association of Museums, Newark 054929
New Jersey Center for Visual Arts, Summit 048424
New Jersey Children's Museum, Paramus 046812
New Jersey Historical Society Museum, Newark 046424
New Jersey Museum of Agriculture, North Brunswick 046518
New Jersey Naval Museum, Hackensack 044377
New Jersey State House, Trenton . . 048604
New Jersey State Museum, Trenton 048605
New Jersey Watercolor Society, Parsippany 054930
The New Kelvin Gallery, East Kilbride 112976
New Lanark World Heritage Village, New Lanark 040524
New Land Gallery, Port Adelaide . . . 095079
New Langton Arts, San Francisco . . 047878
New Life, San Francisco 092856
New Life, Tucson 132988
New Life Art, Birmingham 115120
New Lisbon Antiques, Indianapolis . 089326
New Literature and Fine Arts Publishing House, Changchun 133342
New London County Historical Society Museum, New London 046239
New London Historical Society Museum, New London 046241
New London Public Museum, New London 046242
New Look, Minneapolis 132386
New Market Battlefield State Historical Park, New Market 046244
New Metropolis, Amsterdam 029217
New Mexico Art League, Albuquerque 054931
New Mexico Association of Museums, Albuquerque 054932
New Mexico Bureau of Mines Mineral Museum, Socorro 048210
New Mexico Farm and Ranch Heritage Museum, Las Cruces 045179
New Mexico Museum of Natural History and Science, Albuquerque 041621
New Mexico Museum of Space History, Alamogordo 041591
New Mexico State University Art Gallery, Las Cruces 045180

New Mexico State University Museum, Las Cruces 045181
New Mexico Wing-Commemorative Air Force, Hobbs 044563
New Milford Historical Society Museum, New Milford 046245
New Millennium Gallery, Saint Ives, Cornwall 114367
New Mills Heritage and Information Centre, New Mills 040525
New Museum Members' Bulletin, New York 136582
New Museum of Contemporary Art, New York 046386
New Museum of European and Eastern Art, Athinai 021205
New Nautilus, Parma 076217, 140090
New Nepal Art Palace, Lalitpuru . . . 107610
New Norcia Museum and Art Gallery, New Norcia 001323
New & Old Shop, San Antonio 092552
New Orleans Academy of Fine Arts, New Orleans 051803, 117481
New Orleans Artworks Gallery, New Orleans 046261
New Orleans Association of Conservators, New Orleans 054933
New Orleans Auction Galleries, New Orleans 122982
New Orleans Auction Saint Charles Gallery, New Orleans 090595, 122983
New Orleans Fire Department Museum, New Orleans 046262
New Orleans Glassworks and Printmaking Studio, New Orleans 117482
New Orleans Images, New Orleans . 117483
New Orleans Museum of Art, New Orleans 046263
New Orleans Pharmacy Museum, New Orleans 046264
New Otani Art Museum, Tokyo 027215
New Place, Kitchener 123777
The New Press, New York 135444
New Purva Elegance at Home, Hyderabad 074812
New Quay Gallery, Docklands 094479
The New Rembrandt Gallery, Newport, Isle of Wight 114137
New Satguru Art 'n' Frames 105592
New Selection, Knokke-Heist 096347
New Shakya Art, Kathmandu 107593
New South Wales Lancers Memorial Museum, Parramatta 001370
New Space Art Gallery, Hue 120547
New Space Art Gallery II, Hue 120548
New Stanley Hotel Gallery, Nairobi . 107163
New Street Antique Centre, Plymouth 086276
New Street Books, Penzance 141995
New Street Gallery, Plymouth 114260
New Sweden Farmstead Museum, Bridgeton 042410
New Sweden Historical Museum, New Sweden 046275
New Tingeling, Amsterdam 107775
New to You, Kuranda 056069
New Treasure Art Gallery, Yangon . .077701, 107568
New Trend Gallery, Frankfurt am Main 102805
New Tribal Arts, Toledo 120086
New Visions Gallery, Marshfield . . . 045708
New Visions Gallery, Salt Lake City . 119357
New Windsor Cantonment State Historic Site and National Purple Heart Hall of Honor, Vails Gate 048726
New World Antique, Detroit 088769, 132056
New World Antique Gallery, Detroit . 088770
New World Art Center, New York . . . 046412
New World Art Center, New York . . . 118233
New World Photo, New York 118234
New World School of the Arts, Miami 051701
New York Antiquarian Book Fair, New York 094012
New York Antique Almanac, New York 136583
New York Antique Center, New York 091111
New York Armory Antiques Show, New York 094013
New York Artists Equity Association, New York 054934
New York Arts of Pacific Asia Show, New York 094014
New York Bound Bookshop, New York 142679
New York Ceramics Fair, New York . 094015
New York City Fire Museum, New York 046387
New York City Police Museum, New York 046388
New York City's Antiques News, New York 136584
New York Doll Hospital, New York . . 132504
New York Galleries Antiques, New York 091112
New York Graphics, New York 118235
New York Hall of Science, Flushing . 043877
The New York Historical Society Museum, New York 046389
New York Institute of Photography, New York 051827
New York Institute of Technology, NYIT Finearts, Old Westbury 051881
New York International Arts and Antiques Show, New York 094016
New York Museum of Transportation, West Henrietta 049081
New-York New-York, Genève 082451, 111488
New York Print Fair, New York 094017
New York Public Library for the Performing Arts, New York 046390
New York Restoration Center, New York 132505
New York School of Interior Design, New York 051828
New York Society of Etchers, New York 118236, 135445
New York State College of Ceramics, Alfred University, Alfred 050884
New York State Museum, Albany . . 041599
New York Studio School of Drawing, Painting and Sculpture, New York 051829
New York Studio School of Drawing, Painting and Sculpture Gallery, New York 046391
New York Transit Museum, Brooklyn 042465
New York Tribal and Textile Arts Show, New York 094018
New Zealand Academy of Fine Arts, Wellington 050576
New Zealand Academy of Fine Arts Gallery, Wellington 030642
The New Zealand Antique Dealers' Association, Christchurch 053923
New Zealand Centre for Photography, Portrait Gallery, Wellington 030643
New Zealand Cricket Museum, Wellington 030644
New Zealand Fighter Pilots Museum, Wanaka 030624
New Zealand Fleet Air Arm Museum, Auckland 030446
New Zealand Journal of Photography, Wellington 136011
New Zealand Marine Studies Centre, Dunedin 030486
New Zealand Museums Journal, Wellington 136012
New Zealand National Maritime Museum, Auckland 030447
New Zealand Numismatic Journal, Auckland 136013
New Zealand Olympic and Commonwealth Games Association Museum, Wellington 030647
New Zealand On Art, Christchurch .079042, 108406
New Zealand Police Museum, Porirua 030578
New Zealand Portrait Gallery, Wellington 030645
New Zealand Society of Sculptors, Painters and Associates Inc., Auckland . . . 053924
New Zealands Rugby Museum, Palmerston North 030568
New Zone Virtual Gallery, Eugene . . 043747
Newark Air Museum, Newark-on-Trent 040533
Newark Antiques Centre, Newark-on-Trent 086054
Newark Antiques Warehouse, Newark-on-Trent 086055, 131301
Newark International Antiques and Collectors Fair, Newark-on-Trent . 093941
The Newark Museum, Newark 046425
Newark Museum, Newark-on-Trent 040534
Newark Museum Association, Newark 054935
Newark School of Fine and Industrial Art, Newark 051839
Newark Town Treasures and Art Gallery, Newark-on-Trent 040535
Newark Valley Depot Museum, Newark Valley 046434
Newarke Houses Museum, Leicester 039977
Newaygo County Museum, Newaygo 046435
Newberry Art, Dunsborough 094498
Newbridge House, Donabate 022727
Newburgh Antiques, Newburgh . . . 086059
Newburn Hall Motor Museum, Newburn 040540
Newbury Fine Arts, Boston 115212
Newby Hall, Ripon 040839
Newcastle Antique Centre, Hamilton, New South Wales 055937
Newcastle Antique Centre, Newcastle-upon-Tyne 086069, 131306
Newcastle Antiques & Collectables, Hamilton, New South Wales 055938
Newcastle Art Gallery, Newcastle, Co. Down 114117
Newcastle Art Space, Newcastle . . 094941
Newcastle Region Art Gallery, Newcastle 001326
Newcastle Region Maritime Museum, Newcastle 001327
Newcastle Regional Museum, Newcastle 001328
Newcomb Art Gallery, New Orleans 046265
Newcomb-Macklin, Chicago 115509
Newcomen Engine House, Dartmouth 039212
Newel, New York 091113
Newell Museum, Newell 046448
Newgate Gallery, Barnard Castle . . 112559
Newham, Richmond, Victoria 123297
Newham Grange Leisure Farm Museum, Middlesbrough 040462
Newham Heritage Centre, London . 040246
Newhampton Road Antiques, Wolverhampton 087211
Newhart, London 113794, 131120
Newhaven Fort, Newhaven 040558
Newhaven Heritage Museum, Edinburgh 039410
Newhouse, New York 118237
Newington Antiques, Newington . . .086071, 131308
Newland, Chris, London . . 085558, 131121
Newland & Son, L., London 131122
Newlove, B.M. & E., Surbiton 086793
Newlyfe Antiques, Boscastle 083578
Newlyn Antiques, Newlyn 056333
Newlyn Art Gallery, Penzance 040692
Newman, New York 091114
Newman, Toronto 097336
Newman, Addie, West Hollywood . . 093491
Newman, Nicholas J., West Ewell . . 131664
Newman & Co., W., Kolkata 134518
Newman, Walter Andrews, Philadelphia 118813
Newman & Co., W., Kolkata 139949
Newman House, Dublin 022766
Newmarket Antiques and Collectors Fair, Newmarket 093942
Newport Art Museum, Newport . . . 046463
Newport Art Museum School, Newport 051842
Newport Avenue Antique Center, San Diego 092663
Newport Avenue Antiques, San Diego 092664
Newport Beach Gallery, Newport . . 094946
Newport Gallery, Newport, Essex . . 086075
Newport Mansions, Newport 046464
Newport Pagnell Historical Society Museum, Newport Pagnell 040570
Newport Restoration, Newport, Gwent 131313
Newport Roman Villa, Newport, Isle of Wight 040568
Newport School of Art, Media and Design, University of Wales College, Newport, Newport, Gwent 050849
Newport State Park, Ellison Bay . . . 043682
Newport Temple Antiques, Newport 056334
Newquay Galleries, Newquay 114141
Newry and Mourne Arts Centre and Museum, Newry 040573
Newry Museum, Newry 040574
Newsbank Review of the Arts: Fine Arts and Architecture, New Canaan 136585
The Newseum, Arlington 041780
Newsletter, Russian Museums Association, Tula 136060
Newsletter East Asian Art & Archaeology, Ann Arbor 136586
Newsletter of the Southern African Museums Association, Grahamstown 136065
Newsletter on Contemporary Japanese Prints, Los Angeles 136587
Newsmall & Sterling, Vancouver . . . 097504
Newsome House Museum, Newport News 046471
Newspace, Los Angeles 116855
Newspace, Rozelle 095163
Newsstand Museum, Hirano Hakabutsukan, Osaka 026975
Newstead Abbey, Ravenshead 040802
Newstudio Gallery, Sacramento . . . 119155
Newton, Tokyo 077286
Newton, Barry, Goolwa 094595
Newton, Barry, Unley 095357
Newton Abbot Town and Great Western Railway Museum, Newton Abbot . 040575
Newton Andrews, Auckland 078966, 140601
Newton Andrews, North Shore 079196, 140648
Newton City Museum, Newton 046477
Newton Museum, Newton 046475
Newtons, Bury, Lancashire 083819, 130488
Newtown Historic Museum, Newtown 046482
Newtown Textile Museum, Newtown, Powys 040581
Newzones Gallery of Contemporary Art, Calgary 096833
Nexø Museum, Nexø 009026
Nexos, Wellington 108635
Next, Roma 135928
Next Graphics, Bucureşti 109442
Next Monet, San Francisco 119751
Next to New Shop, Austin 087600
Next to Nix Antiques, Fitzroy 055823
Nexus, Philadelphia 118814
Nexus Antiques, Wellington 079336
Nexus Books, Canterbury 141484
Nexus Contemporary Art Center, Atlanta 041845
Nexus Foundatoin for Today's Art, Philadelphia 046970
Nexus Gallery, Adelaide 094120
Nexus Gallery, New York 118238
Nexus Native Art, Vancouver 097505
Neyer, Durdica-Julie, Bludenz 095481
Neylon, Richard, Ultimo 137119
Neyrand, Bruno, Sarry 068135
Neyrand, Bruno, Villeurbanne 068975
Nez Perce County Museum, Lewiston 045247

Nez Perce National Historical Park, Spalding 048260
Nezu Bijutsukan, Tokyo 027216
NFA Space, Chicago 115510
Ng Viet Gallery, Ho Chi Minh City . . 120520
Ngai Leng, Hong Kong 059676
Ngarak, Swifts Creek 137099
Ngatea Antiques, Ngatea 079185
Ngaumatau Fine Art, Dunedin 108443
Nghe-Tinh Museum, Vinh 049555
Ngo, An, Ho Chi Minh City 120521
Ng's Art School, Hong Kong 049853, 097817, 133364
Ngurdoto Gate Museum, Arusha . . . 037847
Nguyen, Kim, Tulsa 120202
Nguyen, Serge, Paris 124761
Nguyen, Than, Ho Chi Minh City . . . 120522
Nguyên, T.P., Genève 082452
Nhabe Museum, Nhabe 003954
Nhat, Le, Ho Chi Minh City 120523
NHK Hoso Hakubutsukan, Tokyo . . . 027217
NHK Publishing, Tokyo 134728
Ni Tan Usados, Medellín 059933
Niagara, Lünen 103984
Niagara Apothecary, Niagara-on-the-Lake 006021
Niagara art and more, Düsseldorf . . 070419
Niagara County Historical Center, Lockport 045362
Niagara Falls Art Gallery - Kurlek Collection, Niagara Falls 006015
Niagara Fire Museum, Niagara-on-the-Lake 006022
Niagara Galleries, Richmond, Victoria 095140, 133054
Niagara Gorge Discovery Center, Niagara Falls 046483
Niagara Historical Museum, Niagara-on-the-Lake 006023
Niagara Power Project Visitors' Center, Lewiston 045250
Niagara Upholstery, Las Vegas 132217
Niakan, Los Angeles 089854
Niakan, West Hollywood 093492
Niavaran Palace, Teheran 022638
Niblett, A.G., Palma de Mallorca . . . 122079
Nic Nic, Amsterdam 077922
Nicaise, Pascal, Ons-en-Bray 065271
Nice Old Stuff, Wallacia 056796
Niceties, Los Angeles 089855
La Niche Art Gallery, West Burleigh 095390
La Nichée, Saint-Vit 068040
Nichido, Paris 100729
Nichido, Tokyo 107087
Nichido Bijutsukan, Kasama 026632
Nichol, Gerry, New York 091115
Nichol, Gordon, Dublin 074937
Nichol, J., Regina 123813
Nichola, Simon, Damascus 083071
Nicholas, London 135243
Nicholas, New York 091116
Nicholas, Antonio, Las Vegas 089594
Nicholas, Thaete, Philadelphia 132628
Nicholas Roerich Museum, New York 046392
Nicholls, John, Leigh, Staffordshire 084962
Nicholls, Paul, Milano 106272
Nicholls, Rene, Malmesbury 085902
Nichols, Indianapolis 089327
Nichols, Monroe 122972
Nichols, Arthur J., New York 118239
Nichols, Scott, San Francisco 119752
Nichols Antique Centre, Sheffield . .086561, 131475
Nichols House Museum, Boston . . . 042337
Nicholson, Bruxelles 058041
Nicholson, Cincinnati 088264
Nicholson, Launceston 136970
Nicholson, Richard A., Chester 141510
Nicholson Museum, Sydney 001521
Nici Self Museum, Centennial 042683
Nick, H. & D., Aubais 098870
Nick, Heinrich, Boppard 069952
Christiane Nick & Lis Butz, Düsseldorf 125541
Nick Nacks andre, Saint Louis 092285
Nickel, Heinz, Zweibrücken 134479, 139893
Nickels-Sortwell House, Wiscasset . 049271
Nicklaus & Bouvard, Berlin 069712, 125266
The Nickle Arts Museum, Calgary . . 005196
Nickleby, Kyneton 056074
Nicko, Nicole, Blois 061527
Nick's Art Gallery, Phoenix 118879
Nick's Baseball Cards, Dallas 088580
Nick's Upholstery, Chicago 131910
Nicky's Antiques, Brighton, Victoria 055552
Niclas-Paulhe, France, Paris 066328
NicNac Shop, Saint Louis 092286
Nico Gallery 619 Western Av, Seattle 119967
Nicod, Gérard, L'Isle-sur-la-Sorgue 063948
Nicod, Xavier & Gérard, L'Isle-sur-la-Sorgue 063949
Niçoise, Nice 138258
Nicol, Jacques-Henri, Montmorency 064720
Nicola Restauri, Torino 128339
Nicola Valley Museum, Merrit 005862
Nicolaï, Geneviève, Ménerbes 099703
Nicolai & Amend, Bühlerzell 125411
Nicolai Verlag, Berlin 133799
Nicolas, Michéle, Aizac 060731
Nicolas Antiquités, Aubenas 061033
Nicolas Denys Museum, Saint Peters 006391
Nicolas Galeria de Artă, Bucureşti . 109443
Nicolas & Osvaldo, Las Vegas 089595
Nicolau, Christophe, Nice 065119
Nicolau Relotgeria, Jose Maria, Barcelona 080892, 129373
Nicolaus August Otto Museum, Holzhausen 017993
Nicolaus-Schmidt-Künzel-Gedenkstätte, Tanna bei Schleiz 020402
Nicolay, Raymond de, Paris 121178
Nicolaysen Art Museum, Casper . . . 042647
Nicole Gallery, Chicago 115511
Nicole's Art Gallery, Tea Gardens . . 095321
Nicolet, Chantal, Uzès 125004
Nicolet, Claude, Paris 066329
Nicoletti, Roberto, Roma 076588
Nicolier, Josette, Limoges 063893
Nicolini, Mauro, Brescia 127227
Nicolle, Gerard, Nice 065120
Nicollet Book Store, Minneapolis . . 142586
Nicollier, Mainz 072401
Nicolo Fine Arts, New York 132506
Nicolosi, M., Köln 103686
Nicols, Düsseldorf 102531
Nicosia Municipal Arts Centre, Lefkosia 008224
Nidderdale Museum, Harrogate . . . 039678
Nidwaldner Museum, Stans 037597
Niece & Kimton, Tucson 120153
Niecke, Thomas, Stuttgart 105003
Nieder, B., Kerpen, Rheinland 071805
Nieder, Marcus, Winterberg 105308
Nieder-Eichholz, Dieter, Bochum . . 069890
Niederbayerisches Feuerwehrmuseum, Eggenfelden 016891
Niederbayerisches Landwirtschaftsmuseum, Regen 019743
Niederbayerisches Vorgeschichtsmuseum, Archäologische Staatssammlung München, Landau an der Isar . . . 018474
Niederberger, Kurt, Horw 130049
Niederbergisches Museum Wülfrath, Wülfrath 020991
Niederdeutsche Beiträge zur Kunstgeschichte, München 135811
Niederdorfer & Franc, Landskron . . 095640
Niederebersdorfer Heimat- und Archivstuben, Tutzing 020512
Niederecker, Ursula, München 072801
Niederer, Boris, Genève . . 082453, 111489
Niederer, Götz, Stuttgart 073998
Niederhauser, Catherine, Lausanne 111627
Niederhauser, Hans, Kreuzlingen . . 111594
Niederhauser, Th., Auslikon 082101
Niederhoffer, Annecy 060896
Niederkorn, Philadelphia 091672
Niederlausitz-Museum und Karl-Liebknecht-Gedenkstätte, Luckau, Niederlausitz 018689
Niederlausitzer Apothekenmuseum, Cottbus 016597
Niederlausitzer Heidemuseum, Regionale Forschungs- und Bildungsstätte für Geschichte, Volks- und Landschaftskunde, Spremberg 020269
Niederlintner, Frankfurt am Main . . 070770
Niedermaier, Erika, Barcelona 080893
Niedermann, Urs, Sankt Gallen 130164
Niedermayr, Josef, Antiquitätentischlerei, Punzing 137241
Niedermeyr, Rita Ellen, Bad Aibling . 069256
Niederoest, Urs S., Hamburg 071301
Niederöst-Brigger, Michael, Aarburg 082071
Niederösterreich-Gesellschaft für Kunst und Kultur, Wien 052580
Niederösterreichisches Dokumentationszentrum für Moderne Kunst, Sankt Pölten 002618
Niederösterreichisches Dokumentationszentrum für Moderne Kunst, Landesverband der Niederösterreichischen Kunstvereine, Sankt Pölten 052581
Niederösterreichisches Feuerwehrmuseum, Tulln 002760
Niederösterreichisches Freilichtmuseum, Haag, Niederösterreich 001999
Niederösterreichisches Landesjagdmuseum und Afrikamuseum, Marchegg . . . 002279
Niederösterreichisches Landesmuseum, Sankt Pölten 002619
Niederösterreichisches Landesmuseum, Verlagsabteilung, Sankt Pölten . . 133158
Niederösterreichisches Museum für Volkskultur, Groß Schweinbarth . . 001964
Niederösterreichisches Pressehaus, Sankt Pölten 133159
Niederösterreichisches Schulmuseum, Asparn an der Zaya 001703
Niederrheinischer Kunstverein e.V., Wesel 053529
Niederrheinisches Freilichtmuseum, Grefrath 017517
Niederrheinisches Motorradmuseum, Moers 018983
Niederrheinisches Museum für Volkskunde und Kulturgeschichte, Kevelaer . . 018240
Niedersächsisches Bergbaumuseum, Langelsheim 018493
Niedersächsisches Deichmuseum, Dorum 016773
Niedersächsisches Kleinbahn-Museum Bruchhausen-Vilsen, Bruchhausen-Vilsen 016452
Niedersächsisches Kutschenmuseum, Lilienthal 018644
Niedersächsisches Landesmuseum Hannover, Hannover 017765
Niedersächsisches Münzkabinett der Deutschen Bank, Hannover 017766
Niedersächsisches Museum für Kali- und Salzbergbau, Ronnenberg 019880
Niedersätz, Olaf, Berlin 138828
Niedheidt, Klaus, Düsseldorf 121386
Niedorf, Peter, Schwerin 073774
Niedworok, Rainer, Neukirchen-Vluyn 104409
Niehaus, Hans, Claremont 080690
Niehoff-Keussen & Keussen, Ohlsbach 073195
Niehusen, Klaus, Pronstorf 073378
Nielsen, Boston 115213
Nielsen, Charlottenlund 060219
Nielsen, Las Vegas 089596
Nielsen, Minneapolis 090383, 132387
Nielsen, Anne Julie, Læsø 098593
Nielsen, John, København 060359
Nielsen, Morten, Frederiksberg . . . 137872
Nielsen Slovakia, Bratislava 109913
Nielstrup Museum, Hadsten 008887
Niemann, Bärbel, Jever 103454
Niemann, Bodo, Berlin 101991
Niemann, Detlev, Hamburg 071302
Niemann, Heidrun & Thomas, München 072802
Niemann, Hermann, Hamburg 103200
Niemann, Rudolf, Seefeld, Oberbayern 126791
Niemann-Kröger, Karin, Husum, Nordsee 071600
Niemeijer, H., Zwolle 078892
Niemer, Korschenbroich 072060
Niemeyer, Bingen am Rhein 102138
Niemeyer, Anna Maria, Rio de Janeiro 096630
Niemeyer, C.W., Hameln 134028
Niemeyer, Jan Hendrik, Padingbüttel 104577, 139647
Niemeyer Tabaksmuseum, Groningen 029643
Niemiec, Jerzy, Landau in der Pfalz 072132
Niemirski, Marek, Warszawa 079774
Niemjetz, Karl, Hiddenhausen 071510
Nienaber, Christiane, New York . . . 118240
Niendorff, Austin 114998
Niepce, Christine, Grenoble 063070
Niepel, Düsseldorf 102532
Nierat, Bertrand, Sucy-en-Brie 068339
Nierendorf, Berlin 101992, 133800
Nierengarten-Smith, B.J., Saint Louis 119229
Niermeier, Johann, Landshut 072145
Nies, Jürgen, Pohlheim 073352
Nies, Marcel, Antwerpen 096083
Niese, de, Den Haag 078225
Niesen, Hubert, Rodgau 139693
Niespor, Franz, Zell, Mosel 127058
Niessen, A. & M., Kevelaer 071814
Niessen, Markus, Kevelaer 126037
Nieswandt, P., Rostock 104772
Nieszawer, Nadine, Paris 100730
Niethammer, Prof. Dr. Reiner, Mötzingen 072587
Nietsch, Sigurd, München 072803
Nietzsche-Archiv, Weimar, Thüringen 020749
Nietzsche-Haus, Naumburg, Saale . 019186
Nietzsche-Haus, Sils in Engadin . . . 037561
Nieuw Land Poldermuseum, Lelystad 029862
Nieuw Schoten, Haarlem 108060
De Nieuwe Linie, Bodegraven 078076, 128592
Nieuwe Republiek Museums - Vryheid, Vryheid 034773
De Nieuwe Toren, Kampen 029802
Nieuwenhuizen Segaar, G.J., Den Haag 078226
Nieuwlaat, Peter, Roosendaal 078688
Nievergelt, Felix, Zürich 112155
Niewerth, S., Reken 073482
NIFCA - Nordic Institute for Contemporary Art, Helsinki 009557
Niğde Müzesi, Niğde 038159
Nigel, West Winterslow 131668
Nigel, Milne, London 085559
Nigg, Franz, Balzers 077442
Nigoh, Köln 103687
Nigro, Gérald, Cormeilles-en-Vexin . 062479
Nigro, Horacio F., Montevideo 131731
Niguliste Muuseum, Eesti Kunstimuuseum, Tallinn 009408
Nihon Bijutsu Kyokai, Tokyo 053791
Nihon Bijutsu Nenkan, Tokyo 135982
Nihon Bijutsuin, Tokyo 053792
Nihon Bijutsuka Renmei, Tokyo . . . 053793
Nihon Camera Hakubutsukan, Tokyo 027218
Nihon Chokokukai, Tokyo 053794
Nihon Chosoka Kurabu, Tokyo 053795
Nihon Ga-In, Tokyo 053796
Nihon Gangu Shiryokan, Tokyo 027219
Nihon Geijutsu Gakuen, Tokyo 050490
Nihon Ginko Kin'yu Kenkyujo Kahei Hakubutsukan, Tokyo 027220
Nihon Hakubutsukan Kyokai, Tokyo 053797
Nihon Hanga Kyoukai, Sagamihara . 053798

Nihon Kindai Bungakukan, Tokyo . . 027221
Nihon Kinzoku Gakkai Fuzoku Kinzoku Hakubutsukan, Sendai 027049
Nihon Kogeikan, Tokyo National Museum, Tokyo 027222
Nihon Mangaka Kyokai, Tokyo 053799
Nihon Mingeikan, Tokyo 027223
Nihon Minka Shuraku Hakubutsukan, Osaka-fu Hakubutsukan Kyokai, Toyonaka 027291
Nihon Monki Senta Hakubutsukan, Inuyama 026568
Nihon Shodo Bijutsukan, Tokyo . . . 027224
Nihon Stained Glass Art Gallery, Tokyo 107088
Nihon Ukiyo-e Hakubutsukan, Matsumoto 026794
Nihotte, Pascal, Charleville-Mézières 062160
Nihoul, Pierre, Lille 063860
Niigata City Folk Museum, Niigata . 026908
Niigata-kenritsu Kindai Bijutsukan, Nagaoka 026851
Niigata-kenritsu Rekishi Hakubutsukan, Nagaoka 026852
Niigata Science Museum, Niigata . . 026909
Niigata-shiritsu Aizu Yaichi Kinenkan, Niigata 026910
Niigata-shiritsu Bijutsukan, Niigata 026911
Niimi Museum of Art, Niimi 026917
Niimi Sankodo, Tokyo 077287
Niitsu House, Niigata 026912
Nijenhuis, Hollandscheveld 128724
Nijhof & Lee, Amsterdam 140325
Nijinskas of Winnipeg, Winnipeg . . . 097596
Nijlunsing, Den Andel 128622
Nijmeegs Volkenkundig Museum, Nijmegen 029965
Nika, Chimki 109466
Nika, Moskva 140913
Nika, Sankt Silvester 111885
Nikau Gallery, Motueka 108503
Nikau Gallery, Whangarei 108663
Nikel, Edith & Dr. Johannes, Bad Homburg v.d.Höhe 101656
Nikh, Tilburg 108233
Nikitiny, Sankt-Peterburg 129246
Nikko Futarasan Jinja Hakubutsukan, Nikko 026918
Nikko Toshogu Treasure Museum, Nikko 026919
Nikman, Varna 058775
Nikoh, Yamanashi 134736
Nikolaos Perantinos Museum of Sculpture, Athinai 021206
Nikolaou, Lola, Thessaloniki 105451
Nikolaus Matz Bibliothek (Kirchenbibliothek), Michelstadt . . 018934
Nikolov, G., Sofia 096742
Nikolov, V., Halle, Saale 103074
Nikolov-Asja, Maksim, Sofia 058766
Nikon Gallery, Hiroshima 026538
Nikon Image House, Küsnacht 111600
Nikopolis ad Istrum-Antičen grad, Nikjup 004758
Nikos Nikolaides Theatrical Archives, Lemesos 008231
Nikou, Hamburg 103201
Nikou Collection, Mytilini 021397
Nikšićki Muzej, Nikšić 034216
Nilantik, İstanbul 083149
Nile, San Francisco 119753
Nile Art Gallary, Baltimore 115073
Nili Antiques, Miami 090217
Nilius, Joachim, Köln 103688
Nilma Collectables Emporium, Nilma 056348
Nils Aas Kunstverksted, Inderøy . . . 030920
Nilsen, Arendal 079369
Nilsiän Kotiseutumuseo, Nilsiä 009905
Nilsson, Bernt, Sunne 122273
Nilsson & Chiglien, Paris 066330
Svante Nilsson & Helene Hanes, Stockholm 129870
Nilu, Wiesbaden 105273
Nimba Art, Barcelona 110228
Nimberlee, Wyndham 095434
Nimbin Museum, Nimbin 001332
Nimbus Antiques, Whaley Bridge . . 087120, 131677
NIMBUS Kunst und Bücher, Wädenswil 141308
Nimmo & Spooner, London 085560
Nimoth, Torsten, Dresden 125504
N'Importe Quoi, Gent 058197
Nina Buceti, Messina 075567
Ninaber, Paulus, Granada 081146
Ninart Centro de Cultura, México . . 028541
Nina's Books, San Diego 142907
Nina's Galerie, Alpen 101561
Nine, Amsterdam 107776
Nine Arts Gallery, Antwerpen 096084
Nine-Teen Town, Shanghai 059759
Nineteenth Century Antiques, Norfolk 091395
Nineteenth Century Imprints, Portland 142805
Ninety, Charenton-le-Pont 135719
Ninety-Six National Historic Site, Ninety-Six 046489
Nineveh, Arundel 083313
Ninfea, Venezia 076963
Ningbo Baoguo Si Display Center, Ningbo 007216
Ningbo Museum, Ningbo 007217
Ningbo Painting Gallery, Ningbo . . . 097881
Ningyo no Ie, Kyoto 026755
Ninna-ji Temple Treasure House, Kyoto 026756
Ninni Esposito, Bari 105932
El Niño Seise, Sevilla 081598
Ninth Avenue Book Store, San Francisco 142959
Ninth Inning, Saint Paul 092382
Ninth Street Gallery, Saint Louis . . . 119230
Ninth Street Market Books, Philadelphia 142748
Nipawin and District Living Forestry Museum, Nipawin 006026
Nipigon Museum, Nipigon 006027
Nipissing Township Museum, Nipissing 006028
Nippon Art College, Tokyo 050491
Nippon Design Special Training College, Tokyo 050492
Nippon International Contemporary Art Festival, Tokyo 093801
Nippon Kokeshi Museum, Naruko . . 026904
Nippon Kokogakkai, Tokyo 053800
Nippon Shuppan Hanbai, Tokyo . . . 134729
Nippondo, Double Bay 094486
Niquelor, Badalona 129309
Nirmitee, Mumbai 105791
Nirmitee Interiors, Pune 074834
Nirvana Art Gallery, Kathmandu . . . 107594
Nisart, Launceston 094728
Nisha Art, Pune 105829
Nishida, Nara 077164
Nishida, Nara 106942
Nishiharu, Kyoto 077121
Nishijin Textile Center, Kyoto 026757
Nishimura, Kyoto 077122
Nishimura, Niigata 134716
Nishimura Museum, Iwakuni 026589
Nishio, Washington 133028
Nishna Heritage Museum, Oakland . 046602
Nisi, Salvatore, Milano 127640
Nisista, Haarlem 078474
Nisple, Agathe, Appenzell 111128
Niss Art, Nice 065121, 124519
Nissan, Genève 082454
Nissen, Sylvie, Cannes . . . 061950, 099075
Nissl, S., Eschen 107331
Nissou, Michel, Sarlat-la-Canéda . . 101257
Nisters, Josef, Speyer 104936
Nistri-Lischi, Pisa 134658
Nitrianska Galéria, Nitra 034398
Nitsch, Brigitte, Berlin 125267
Nitsch, Carolina, New York 135446
Nitsche, Wiesenbach, Baden 074430
Nitsche, Dr. Peter, Lübeck 103968
Nitsche, Tanja, Seefeld, Oberbayern 126792
Nittel, Dietmar, Graz 123365
Nitten - Japan Fine Arts Exhibition, Tokyo 027225, 053801
Nitzschmann, Regina, Nienburg, Weser 126550
Niu Art Museum, Northern Illinois University, DeKalb 043375
Niva Art, Wrocław 079801
Nivågårds Malerisamling, Nivå 009027
Nivalan Museo Katvala, Nivala 009907
Nivarlet, Mons 058343
Nivelle, Antoine, Bordeaux 124136
Niven, Janet, Woollahra 056873
Niveuwenhoven, Marie-Noelle, Cervières 062059
Niwa, Vancouver 097506
Nixdorf, Wolfgang, Völklingen 074227
Nizam, Samer, Damascus 083072
Nizami Ganjavi, Azerbaijan National Academy of Sciences, Baku 003084
The Nizam's Museum, Hyderabad . 022160
Nižegorodskaja Starina, Nižnij Novgorod 080282
Nižegorodskij Chudožestvennyj Muzej, Nižnij Novgorod 033568
Nižegorodskij Gosudarstvennyj Architekturno-stroitelnyj Universitet, Nižnij Novgorod 050650
Nižegorodskij Gosudarstvennyj Istoriko-architekturnyj Muzej-zapovednik, Nižnij Novgorod 033569
Nižegorodskij Kreml s Archangelskim Soborom, Nižnij Novgorod 033570
Nizhoni, Albuquerque 114812
Nižnetagilskij Municipalnyj Muzej Izobrazitelnych Iskusstv, Nižnij Tagil 033573
Nižnetagilskij Muzej-Zapovednik Gornozavodskogo Dela Srednego Urala, Nižnij Tagil 033574
Nizza, Giulio, Torino 076846
Njærheim Antik, Nærbø 079403
Njegošev Muzej, Cetinje 034187
Njudungs Hembygdsmuseum, Vetlanda 036786
NKD Enterprise, Miami 142559
NKKM-nytt, Oslo 136016
N.K.L. Artisanat, Québec 097154
NM Gallery, Yangon 107569
NMI-Museum IJkwezen, Delft 029415
NN-fabrik, Oslip 095700, 133124
N'Namdi, Chicago 115512
N'Namdi, George R., Detroit 116093
No. 1 Castlegate Antiques, Newark-on-Trent 086056
No 9 Antiques, Wolverhampton . . . 087212
No 90, Moskva 140914
No Kaiga Art Museum, Kyoto 026758
No Man's Land Historical Museum, Goodwell 044247
No Meio do Caminho, Rio de Janeiro 096631
No Name Exhibitions, Minneapolis . 117287
No Name Exhibitions @ Soap Factory, Minneapolis 045919
No News, 2x Provinz, Kassel 135812
Noa, Tokyo 077288
Noa Gallery, Washington 120329
Noack, Hollingstedt 071565
Noack, Hermann, Berlin 101993
Noack, Hermann, Berlin 101994
Noack, Joachim, Dresden 070326
Noack, Klaus, Mönchengladbach . . 104100
Noah Webster House - Museum of West Hartford History, West Hartford . . 049078
Noahs Ark Fine Art, Los Angeles . . . 116856
Noah's Art, San Antonio 119435
Noank Historical Society Museum, Noank 046490
Nob Hill Gallery, Albuquerque 114813
Nobel Museum, Stockholm 036651
Nobele, F. de, Paris 133658, 138511
De Nobele Baas, 's-Hertogenbosch 128715
Nobelmuseet och Bofors Industrimuseum, Karlskoga 036380
Nobi, Cairo 098654
Nobile, Angelo, Roubaix 067232
Nobile, Christopher, New York 132507
Nobile, Maurizio, Bologna 075096
Nobili, Mara S.F., Rio de Janeiro . . . 058624
Nobili, Noris, Firenze 075377
Noble Art, Bega 094231
Noble Collectibles, Albuquerque . . . 087413
Noble Maritime Collection, Staten Island 048332
Noble Upholstery, Hamilton 123772
NobleArt, Cambridge 112790
Nobleboro Historical Society Museum, Nobleboro 046491
Noblecourt, Marie, Paris 124762
Nobles County Art Center Gallery, Worthington 049314
Nobles County Historical Society Museum, Worthington 049315
Noblewoods, Woollahra . . 056874, 123330
Nobre, José M. Rosário, Lisboa . . . 129163
Nobrega, São Paulo 058729, 096682
Nobynäs Säteri, Aneby 036184
Nocchi, Jean-François, La Ferté-Bernard 063368
Il Noce, Napoli 076018
Nocera, Sergio, Napoli 127784
Noceti, Alejandro, Buenos Aires . . . 055229
Noceti, Angela, Genova 075487
Nocturnus Antiquarios, Rio de Janeiro 058625
Noczinski, Anke, Leipzig 126194
Noda, Nagoya 106928
Noddy, Port Noarlunga 056479
Nodrum, Charles, Richmond, Victoria 095141
Noeau, Hale O., Honolulu 116228
Der Nöck, Waiblingen 139823
Noehles, Martina, Mühlheim am Main 126338
Noel, Charlotte 115302
Noël, Daniel, Bruxelles 123601
Noël, Marcel, Bourges 061729
Noël, Robert, Vitry-le-François 069014
Noelanders Horizon, Knokke-Heist . 096348
Noelani, Honolulu 116229
Nöll, Nina, Hannover 071406
Nölle, Ute, Soest 104913
Noëlle & Gérard Antiquaires, Couhe 062502
Nöth, Doris, Kirchheim unter Teck . 103556
Noetzel, Florian, Wilhelmshaven . . . 134460
El Nogal, Bogotá 059848
Nogal, Oviedo 110663
Nogarotto, Danilo, Padova 076101
Nogata-shi Sekitan Kinenkan, Nogata 026925
Nogatsch, Zürich 083002
Nógrádi Megyei Múzeum, Salgótarján 021833
Nógrádi Történeti Múzeum, Salgótarján 021834
Nogurot, Eleonora, Trieste 076901
Nohea, Honolulu 116230
Nohea, Honolulu 116231
Nohea, Honolulu 116232
Nohl, Peter, Bremgarten bei Bern . . 129986
Nohle, Wolfram, Berlin 138829
Nohn, Markus, Frankfurt am Main . 102806
Nohrden, Jörg, Neumünster 073006
Nohrudi, Anne-Lise, Basel 082161
Noir, Alain, La Verpillière 063468
Noir d'Ivoire, Paris 100731
Noir d'Ivoire, Paris 100732
Noir Ebène, Paris 066331, 100733
Le Noir Forge, Arichat 005026
Noir sur Blanc, Bruxelles 137455
Noirmont, Jérôme de, Paris 100734
Noirmont Command Bunker, Saint Brelade 040903
Noirmont Prospect, Paris 100735
Nokian Kotiseutumuseo, Nokia 009908
Nokomis and District Museum, Nokomis 006029

Nolan, E.C., London 141853
Nolan, John, Southport 086658
Nolan & Eckman, New York 118241
Nolan Gallery, Tharwa 001546
Nolan-Rankin, Houston 116379
Nolan & Reid, Calgary 096834
Nolasco & Maia, Lisboa 079976
Nold, Berlin 069713
Nold, Dr. Meike, Varel 105102
Nold, R., Muggensturm 139578
Nolde-Museum, Stiftung Seebüll Ada und Emil Nolde, Neukirchen bei Niebüll 019245
Nolden-Daniels, Köln 103689
Noles-Davis, Dallas 132020
Nolhaga Slotts Konsthall, Alingsås . 036174
Nolhin Torppa, Laitila 009796
Noll, Ingrid & Günter, Bad Ems 069278
Nollan, Christophe, Chantilly 062142
Noller, Bertram, London 131123
Noller, Bertram, Reigate . . 086347, 131411
Noller, Reinhold, Heilbronn 071474
Nollet, Jean-Pierre, Gallardon 062956
Nollinger, Marie-Christine, Versailles 125019
Nolte, Bielefeld 069834
Nolte, Edelgard, Warburg 105158
Nolte, Klaus, Lippetal 072281
Nolte, Michael, Münster 072921
Nolte-Schmidt, U. & W., Düsseldorf 125542
Noltekuhlmann & Mayr, Berlin 069714
Nolting, Horst Joachim von, Bad Soden am Taunus 138705
Nolton Antiques, Bridgend 083666
Nolton Art Gallery, Bridgend Mid . . . 112699
Nomad Gallery, Cairo 098655
Nomad Gallery, Saint Paul 119302
Nomadenschätze, Zürich 083003
Nomadic Rug Traders, Pyrmont . . .056509, 123294
Le Nombre d'Or, Rontalon 067215
Nomel, Sofia 058767
Nomicos, Timişoara 080197
Nomikos Collection, Pyrgos 021445
Nominé, Fabienne, Reims 067074
Nomis Arts France, Paris 066332
The Nomma Art Gallery, Kampala . . 112375
Nommensen, Margret, Bad Segeberg 069382
Nomura Art Museum, Kyoto 026759
Non Solo Antico, Torino 076847
Nonnahûs, Akureyri 021933
Nonnenberg, Kerstin, Freiburg im Breisgau 125671
Nonnenbruch, Barbara, Bielefeld . .069835, 102126
Nonnenmacher, T., Freiburg im Breisgau 139115
Nonomura, Washington . . 093429, 133029
Nonsolotarli di Mulas, Cagliari 075219
Nonthaburi Natural History Museum, Nonthaburi 037916
Nonvaleurs, Zürich 141352
Nooit Gedacht, Amersfoort 077749
Nook, Sylvan, Dun Laoghaire 074965
Nooks & Crannies, Phoenix 091758
Nooks & Crannies, Ryde 086420
Noor Arts, Monaco 107539
Noord-Hollands Motoren Museum, Nieuwe Niedorp 029946
Noordbrabants Museum, 's-Hertogenbosch 029736
Noordelijk Busmuseum, Winschoten 030338
Noordelijk Scheepvaartmuseum, Groningen 029644
Het Noorderhuis, Zaandam 030366
Noordermeer, Birmingham 087775
De Noordwester, Vlieland 030282
Noortman, Maastricht . . . 078616, 108129
Noosa Regional Art Gallery, Tewantin 001543
Noosa Shire Museum, Pomona 001386
Noott, John, Broadway 083761
Noott, John, Broadway 083762
Noott, John, Broadway 112736
Noott, John, Broadway 112737
Noott, John, Broadway 130468
Nor West Bend Museum, Morgan . . 001283
Nor' Wester and Loyalist Museum, Williamstown 006825
Nora Auktionskammare, Nora 122218
Nora Barnacle House Museum, Galway 022792
Nora Dora, Saint Louis 092287
Nora Eccles Harrison Museum of Art, Logan 045365
Nora Museum, Gyttorp 036317
Noran, Lüdinghausen 103976
Noran, Panker 104581
Nora's Porch, San Francisco 092857
Norba: Arte, Cáceres 136097
Norbert, Houston 089167
Norbert G Collections, Paris 066333
Norchard Railway Centre, Dean Forest Railway Museum, Lydney 040363
Nord-Antique, Hamburg 093745
Nord Antique, Lille 063861
Nord Antique, Seclin 068181
Nord-Jarlsbergmuseene, Holmestrand 030898
Nord Ouest Antiquités, Bondues . . . 061554
Nord-Troms Museum, Sørkjosen . . 031210
Nord-Trøndelag Fylkesgalleri, Namsos 031044
Nordamerika Native Museum, Zürich 037791
Nordanstigs Konstförening, Bergsjö 054147
Nord'Antic, Liessies 063817
Nordantik, San Antonio 092553
NordArt, Bredstedt 069998
Norddal Museum, Valldal 031314
Norddeutsches Antiquariat, Rostock 139698
Norddeutsches Auto- und Motorrad-Museum, Bad Oeynhausen 015767
Norddeutsches Handwerkermuseum, Ovelgönne 019546
Norddeutsches Spielzeugmuseum, Soltau 020246
Norddeutsches Vogelmuseum, Sammlung Dr. Baumeister, Osterholz-Scharmbeck 019510
Norden, D., Antwerpen 057720
Norden, Jacob, Antwerpen 057721, 120707
Nordén, Johan, Stockholm 122257
Norden, Peter, Tetbury 086861
Nordenfjeldske Kunstindustrimuseum, Trondheim 031283
Nordenhake, Berlin 101995
Nordenhake, Stockholm 111065
Nordens Ark, Hunnebostrand 036352
Nordens Museer, Bergen 136017
Nordera, Bruno, Beaune 061289
Norderneyer Fischerhausmuseum, Norderney 019329
Nordfjord Folkemuseum, Sandane . 031164
Nordfriesische Kunstwerkstätten, Westerland 105227
Nordfriesisches Museum Ludwig-Nissen-Haus, Zweckverband Museumsverbund Nordfriesland, Husum, Nordsee . . 018035
Nordfyns Museum, Bogense 008823
Nordhagen, Jan, Oslo 121871
Nordhallands Hembygdsförening, Kungsbacka 036407
Nordhannoversches Bauernhaus-Museum, Wöhler-Dusche-Hof, Isernhagen . 018091
Nordhausen, H., Bruchhausen-Vilsen 102269
Nordia Art, Turku 120888
Nordic Art Promotion, Singapore . . 109845
The Nordic Art Review, Stockholm . 136115
Nordic Art School, Kokkola 049929
Nordic Heritage Museum, Seattle . . 048087
Nordica Homestead Museum, Farmington 043820
Nordico - Museum der Stadt Linz, Linz 002252
Nordico, Verlagsabteilung, Linz . . . 133114
Nordin, Cheptainville 062274
Nordische Botschaften Gemeinschaftshaus, Berlin 016155
Nordisk Galleri, Paris 066334
Nordisk Konservatorforbund, Den Danske Afdeling, Kongens Lyngby 052861
Nordiska Akvarellmuseet, Skärhamn 036575
Nordiska Auktionsbyrån, Stockholm 122258
Nordiska Konservatorförbundet, Svensk Sektion, Stockholm 054148
Nordiska Museet, Stockholm 036652
Nordiska Travmuseet i Årjäng, Årjäng 036192
Nordiskt Institut för Samtidskonst, Helsinki 009557
Nordjyllands Kunstmuseum, Aalborg 008799
Nordkappmuseet, Honningsvåg . . . 030905
Nordland Røde Kors Krigsminnemuseum, Narvik 031047
Nordlandsmuseet, Bodø 030784
Nordli Bygdemuseum, Nordli 031054
Nordlings Antikbod, Stockholm 081995
Nordmann, Lothar, Bissendorf 069858
Nordmarken, San Diego 119528
Nordmøre Museum, Kristiansund . . 030961
Nordnorsk Fartøyvernsenter og Båtmuseum, Gratangen 030861
Nordnorsk Kunstmuseum, Tromsø . 031276
Nordpfälzer Heimatmuseum, Rockenhausen 019855
Nordre Husan, Alvdal 030724
Nordseemuseum, Wissenschaftliche Sammlung des Alfred-Wegener-Instituts für Polar- und Meeresforschung, Bremerhaven 016433
Nordsjaellandsk Folkemuseum, Hillerød 008910
Nordsjøfartmuseet, Tælavåg 031258
Nordsømuseet, Hirtshals 008912
Nordstrand Visual Arts Gallery, Wayne State College, Wayne 049028
Nordström, Halmstad 141112
Nordun, Birgit & Olav, Hvidovre . . .060260, 124025
Nordvärmlands Jakt och Fiskemuseum, Sysslebäck 036701
Nordwestdeutsches Schulmuseum Friesland, Zetel 021057
Nordys, Birmingham 115121
Nore og Uvdal Bygdetun, Uvdal i Numedal 031308
Nores, Tampa 132958
Norfolk and Suffolk Aviation Museum, East Anglia's Aviation Heritage Centre, Flixton 039506
Norfolk Antique Company, Norfolk . 091396
Norfolk Contemporary Art Society, Norwich 054452
Norfolk Galleries, King's Lynn 084850
Norfolk Historical Museum, Norfolk 046495
Norfolk Historical Society Museum, Norfolk 046503
Norfolk House Galleries, Dorking . . 084200
Norfolk Island Museum, Kingston . . 030710
Norfolk Polyphon Centre, Bawdeswell 083455
Norfolk Rural Life Museum and Union Farm, Gressenhall 039641
Norfolk State University Art Department, Norfolk 051850
Norges Birøkterlags Museet, Billingstad 030774
Norges Fiskerimuseet, Bergen 030770
Norges Hjemmefrontmuseum, Oslo 031091
Norges Kunst- og Antikvitetshandlers, Oslo 053947
Norges Museumsforbund, Oslo 053948
Norges Olympiske Museum, Lillehammer 030985
Norgesauksjoner, Tønsberg 121879
Norgrove, P.W., Haslingden 084614
Nørholm, Homborsund 030900
Noria, Binic 061491
Norick Art Center, Oklahoma City University, Oklahoma City 051878
Noriega, Alejandro, Buenos Aires . .055230, 120554
Norilskaja Chudožestvennaja Galereja, Norilsk 033576
Noritz, Norbert, Hamburg 139202
Norlin, Kirk, Denver 116031
Normal's Book and Records, Baltimore 142229
Norman, Glenn, Woolloomooloo . . . 095432
Norman, Jennifer & Raymond, Needham 086041
Norman, Jeremy, San Francisco . . . 142960
Norman, Michael, Brighton 083706
Norman, Peter, Burwell . . 083818, 130487
Norman Cleveland County Historical Museum, Norman 046508
Norman No. 1 Oil Well Museum, Neodesha 046177
Norman R. Eppink Art Gallery, Emporia State University, Emporia 043705
Norman Rockwell Museum at Stockbridge, Stockbridge 048367
Norman Wells Historical Centre, Norman Wells 006031
Normanby Hall, Scunthorpe 040970
Normanby Park Farming Museum, Scunthorpe 040971
Normandie Antiquités, Montréal . . . 058982
Normandie Détection, Le Havre . . . 063639
Normanns, Rælingen 134850
Normanton Church Museum, Oakham 040632
Norminton, David, München 072804
Normisist Folk Inventions Museum, Northern Mindanao State Institute of Science and Technology (NORMISIST), Butuan 031641
Noronha, José Maria Pachero, Lisboa 079977
Noronha, José Maria Pacheco, Lisboa 079978
Noronha, Pedro Mendia, Lisboa . . . 079979
Noronha, Pedro José, Lisboa 079980
Norori, Luis, San Francisco 132904
Norr-Bygdens Auktionsbyrå, Skelleftehamn 122238
Norræna Húsid, Reykjavík 021970
Norrbottens Järnvägsmuseum, Luleå 036437
Norrbottens Museum, Luleå 036438
Norrbyskärs Museum, Hörnefors . . 036344
Norre Lorraine, Veneux-les-Sablons 068762
Norris & Co, Ben, Newbury 131304
Norris, B.J., Harrietsham 122534
Norris Museum, Saint Ives, Cambridgeshire 040917
Norrköpings Konstmuseum, Norrköping 036503
Norrköpings Stadsmuseum, Norrköping 036504
Norrmalm, Stockholm 081996
Norrtälje Auktionskammare, Norrtälje 122219
Norrtälje Konsthall, Norrtälje 036506
Norseman Historical and Geological Collection, Norseman 001334
Norsewood Pioneer Cottage Museum, Norsewood 030555
Norsk Antikvarbokhandlerforening, Oslo 053949
Norsk Barnemuseum, Stavanger . . 031226
Norsk Bergverksmuseum, Kongsberg 030948
Norsk Bremuseum, Fjærland 030835
Norsk Emballasje Museum, Oslo . . 031092
Norsk Farmasihistorisk Museum, Oslo 031093
Norsk Fiskeindustrimuseum, Melbu 031013
Norsk Fiskerværsmuseet, Sørvågen 031213
Norsk Fjellmuseum, Lom 030994
Norsk Folkemuseum, Norwegian Museum of Cultural History, Oslo 031094
Norsk Grafisk Museum, Stavanger . 031227
Norsk Hagebruks Museum, Grimstad 030864
Norsk Hermetikkmuseum, Stavanger 031228
Norsk Husflidsmuseum, Moen 031024
Norsk ICOM, Oslo 053950

Norsk Industriarbeidermuseet, Rjukan . . . 031139
Norsk Jernbanemuseum, Hamar . . 030874
Norsk Kartmuseum, Hønefoss 030903
Norsk Kjøretøyhistorisk Museum, Lillehammer . . . 030986
Norsk Klippfiskmuseum, Nordmøre Museum, Kristiansund . . . 030962
Norsk Landbruksmuseum, Ås 030741
Norsk Luftfartsmuseum, Bodø 030785
Norsk Megling & Auksjon, Bodø . . . 121847
Norsk Museum for Fotografi - Preus Fotomuseum, Horten . . . 030909
Norsk Oljemuseum, Stavanger 031229
Norsk Reiselivsmuseum, Balestrand 030753
Norsk Seminmuseum, Stange 031220
Norsk Sjøfartsmuseum, Oslo 031095
Norsk Skogbruksmuseum, Elverum 030822
Norsk Speidermuseum, Oslo 031096
Norsk Teknisk Museum, Oslo 031097
Norsk Telemuseum - Kristiansand, Kristiansand . . . 030957
Norsk Telemuseum - Lødingen, Lødingen . . . 030989
Norsk Telemuseum - Sørvågen, Norwegian Telecommunication Museum, Sørvågen . . . 031214
Norsk Telemuseum - Stavanger, Stavanger . . . 031230
Norsk Telemuseum - Trondheim, Trondheim . . . 031284
Norsk Tindemuseum, Åndalsnes . . 030728
Norsk Tollmuseum, Oslo 031098
Norsk Trikotasjemuseum, Salhus . . 031161
Norsk Utvandrermuseum, Ottestad . 031117
Norsk Vasskraft- og Industristadmuseum, Tyssedal . . . 031302
Norsk Vegmuseum, Fåberg 030827
Norsk Veterinærmedisinsk Museum, Oslo . . . 031099
Norske Billedkunstnere, Oslo 053951
Norske Grafikere, Oslo 053952
Norske Grenselosers Museum, Bjørkelangen . . . 030779
Norske Kunst- og Kulturhistoriske Museer, Oslo . . . 053953
Norske Museumspedagogiske, Forening, Bodø . . . 053954
Norske Naturhistoriske Museers, Landsforbund NNML, Bergen 053955
Norske Tekstilkunstnere, Oslo 053956
Nortan, Sharjah . . . 083220
Nortgate Auction Rooms, Newark-on-Trent . . . 122625
North, Desmond & Amanda, East Peckham . . . 084254, 130665
North Adelaide School of Art Gallery, Adelaide . . . 000708
North American Black Historical Museum, Amherstburg . . . 005008
North Andover Historical Museum, North Andover . . . 046512
North Anna Nuclear Information Center, Mineral . . . 045905
North Atlantic Aviation Museum, Gander . . . 005494
North Ayrshire Museum, Saltcoats . 040951
North Battleford Art Centre, North Battleford . . . 006033
North Bay and Area Museum, North Bay . . . 006037
North Beach Gallery, San Francisco 119754
North Bengal Science Centre, Siliguri . . . 022342
North Berwick Museum, North Berwick . . . 040590
North Carolina Central University Art Museum, Durham . . . 043546
North Carolina Maritime Museum, Beaufort . . . 042075
North Carolina Museum of Art, Raleigh . . . 047313
North Carolina Museum of Forestry, Whiteville . . . 049146
North Carolina Museum of History, Raleigh . . . 047314
North Carolina Museum of Life and Science, Durham . . . 043547
North Carolina Museum of Natural Sciences, Raleigh . . . 047315
North Carolina Museums Council, Raleigh . . . 054936
North Carolina Nature Artists Association, Cary . . . 054937
North Carolina Pottery Center, Seagrove . . . 048072
North Carolina State University Gallery of Art and Design, Raleigh . . . 047316
North Carolina Transportation Museum, Spencer . . . 048269
North Caroline Museum of Art. Bulletin, Raleigh . . . 136588
North Carr Lightship, Dundee 039310
North Castle Historical Society Museum, Armonk . . . 041783
North Coast Rare Books, Brunswick Heads . . . 136828
North Cornwall Museum and Gallery, Camelford . . . 038975
North Country Museum of Arts, Park Rapids . . . 046822
North Country Notes, Plattsburgh . . 136589
North Dakota Museum of Art, Grand Forks . . . 044262
North Devon Antiques Centre, Barnstaple . . . 083397
The North Devon Decorative and Fine Arts Society, Barnstaple . . . 054453
North Devon Maritime Museum, Appledore, Devon . . . 038516
North Down Heritage Centre, Bangor, County Down . . . 038589
North East Aircraft Museum, Sunderland . . . 041159
North East Museums, Libraries & Archives Council, Newcastle-upon-Tyne . . 054454
North Florida Community College Art Gallery, Madison . . . 045576
North Fremantle Antiques, North Fremantle . . . 056363
North Gallery, Saint Louis . . . 119231
North Hastings Heritage Museum, Bancroft . . . 005060
North Haven Historical Society Museum, North Haven . . . 046528
North Hertfordshire Museums, Letchworth . . . 039991
North Highland Community Museum, Dingwall . . . 005351
North Hills Museum, Granville Ferry 005543
North House Gallery, Manningtree . 114052
North House Museum, Lewisburg . . 045246
North Huron District Museum, Wingham . . . 006835
North Kerry Museum, Ballyduff 022686
North Lakes Antiquités, Saint-Martin-de-Ré . . . 067635
North Lanark Regional Museum, Almonte . . . 005000
North Lee County Historic Center and Santa Fe Depot Museum Complex, Fort Madison . . . 043947
North Leverton Windmill, North Leverton . . . 040591
North Light, Cincinnati . . . 136590
North Light Gallery, Huddersfield . . 113279
North Lincolnshire Museum, Scunthorpe . . . 040972
North London Clock Shop, London .085561, 131124
North Mountain Books, Phoenix . . . 142767
The North Museum of Natural History and Science, Lancaster . . . 045150
North Norfolk Railway Museum, Sheringham . . . 041009
North Oak Gallery, Columbus 115791
North of England Museums Libraries and Archives Council, Newcastle-upon-Tyne . . . 054455
North Otago Museum, Oamaru 030557
North Pacific Cannery Village Museum, Port Edward . . . 006181
North Paddock, Laura . . . 056091
North Park Collection, Chicago 088134
North Perth Antique Centre, North Perth . . . 056370
North Plainfield Exempt Firemen's Museum, North Plainfield . . . 046532
North Platte Valley Museum, Gering 044178
North Point Gallery, San Francisco . 119755
North Saint Mary's Brewing &Co., San Antonio . . . 132820
North Shore Art League, Winnetka .054938, 123139
The North Shore Arts Association, Gloucester . . . 044224
North Shore Arts Association, Gloucester . . . 054939
North Shropshire Reclamation, Burlton . . . 083800
North Somerset Museum, Weston-super-Mare . . . 041349
North Star Galleries, New York 091117, 118242
North Star Mining Museum, Grass Valley . . . 044295
North Star Scouting Memorabilia, West Saint Paul . . . 049097
North Stradbroke Island Historical Museum, Dunwich . . . 000998
North Thompson Museum, Barriere 005070
North Vancouver Museum, North Vancouver . . . 006045
North View Gallery, Portland 047173
North Wales Antiques, Colwyn Bay . 084068
North Weald Airfield Museum and Memorial, Epping . . . 039451
North West Arts Board, Manchester 054456
North West Books, Liverpool 141739
North West Federation of Museums and Art Galleries, Ellesmere Port 054457
North West Film Archive, Manchester . . . 040412
North West Sound Archive, Clitheroe . . . 039100
North West Style, Seattle 119968
North Western Agricultural Museum, Warracknabeal . . . 001596
North Wind Undersea Institute, Bronx . . . 042442
North Woolwich Old Station Museum, London . . . 040247
North Yorkshire and South Durham Decorative and Fine Arts Society, Darlington . . . 054458
North Yorkshire Moors Railway, Pickering . . . 040714
Northampton and Lamport Railway, Chapel Brampton . . . 039030
Northampton County Historical and Genealogical Society Museum, Easton . . . 043591
Northampton Museum and Art Gallery, Northampton . . . 040596
Northart Community Arts Centre, Auckland . . . 030448
Northborough Historical Museum, Northborough . . . 046547
Northcliffe Pioneer Museum, Northcliffe . . . 001341
Northcote, Robine, Saint-Quay-Portrieux . . . 067969
Northcote Gallery, London 113795
Northcote Gallery, London 113796
Northcote Pottery, Thornbury 001550
Northcote Road Antiques Market, London . . . 085562
Northcutt Steele Gallery, Montana State University Billings, Billings 042206
Northeast Classic Car Museum, Norwich . . . 046569
Northeast - Journal of Antiques & Art, Hudson . . . 136591
Northeast Louisiana Delta African American Heritage Museum, Monroe 045970
Northeast Martyrs Memorial Hall, Harbin . . . 007110
Northeast Mississippi Museum, Corinth . . . 043153
Northeast Mississippi Museums Association, Corinth . . . 054940
Northeast Oakland Historical Museum, Oxford . . . 046768
Northeastern Illinois University Art Gallery, Chicago . . . 042869
Northeastern Institute of Fine Arts, Shenyang . . . 049857
Northeastern Montana Threshers and Antique Association Museum, Culbertson . . . 043239
Northeastern Nevada Museum, Elko 043667
Northern Antiques Company, Norton, North Yorkshire . . . 086105
Northern Antiques Fair, Harewood . 093943
Northern Arizona University Art Museum and Galleries, Flagstaff . . . 043852
Northern Arts Board, Newcastle-upon-Tyne . . . 054459
Northern California Association of Museums, Chico . . . 054941
Northern California Coin Exchange, Oakland . . . 091430
Northern Clocks, Worsley . 087261, 131716
Northern Country Arts, Ottawa 097113
Northern Culture Museum, Yokogoshi . . . 027329
Northern Eye Gallery, Ceres 112829
Northern Galleries, Northern State University, Aberdeen . . . 041560
Northern Gallery, Saint Paul 119303
Northern Gallery for Contemporary Art, Sunderland . . . 041160
Northern Gateway Museum, Denare Beach . . . 005344
Northern Illinois University Art Gallery in Chicago, Chicago . . . 042870
Northern Illinois University Art Museum, DeKalb . . . 043376
Northern Image, Chicago 115513
Northern Image, Milwaukee 117214
Northern Image, Minneapolis 117288
Northern Image Studio of Fine Art, Ardersier . . . 112517
Northern Images, Edmonton 096891
Northern Images, Winnipeg 097597
Northern Indiana Arts Association, Munster . . . 046090
Northern Indiana Center for History, South Bend . . . 048227
Northern Ireland Museums Council, Belfast . . . 054460
Northern Kentucky University Art Galleries, Highland Heights . . . 044538
Northern Life Museum and National Exhibition Centre, Fort Smith . . . 005472
Northern Light Gallery, Brønshøj . . . 060215
Northern Lights Art Gallery, Mayville 045732
Northern Lights Gallery, Keswick . . 113319
Northern Lights Military Museum, Goose Bay . . . 005521
Northern Lights Studies in Creativity, Presque Isle . . . 136592
Northern Michigan University Art Museum, Marquette . . . 045696
Northern Traders, West Melbourne . 056815
Northern Virginia Fine Arts Association, Alexandria . . . 054942
The Northern Voyageur Trading Company, Winnipeg . . . 097598
Northfield Arts Guild, Northfield . . . 054943
Northfield Farm Museum, New Pitsligo . . . 040527
Northfield Historical Society Museum, Northfield . . . 046551
Northfleet Hill Antiques, Northfleet . 086100
Northgate, Chattanooga 122839
Northlake Coin and Stamp, Atlanta . 087506
Northland Books, Saskatoon 137685
Northland Exposure Artists Gallery, Kansas City . . . 116586
Northland Historical Society Museum, Lake Tomahawk . . . 045115
Northland Poster Collective, Minneapolis . . . 117289
Northland Upholstery, Columbus . . . 131986
Northland Viking Centre, Auckengill 038548
Northport Historical Society Museum, Northport . . . 046557

Northside Antiques, Clayfield 055687
Northside Antiques, Glenorchy 055890
Northside Restoration, Atlanta 131784
Northumberland Antique Restorations, Terrigal 123316
The Northumberland County Historical Society Museum, Sunbury 048429
Northumberland Fisheries Museum, Pictou 006150
Northumbria Pine, Whitley Bay 087137
Northwest Antiques, San Antonio .. 092554
Northwest Architectural Salvage, Saint Paul 092383
Northwest Art Center, Minot State University, Minot 045925
Northwest Camera, Portland 091980
Northwest Collectibles and Antique Paper, Portland 091981
Northwest Gallery and Sinclair Gallery, Northwest College, Powell 047217
Northwest Museum of Arts and Culture, Spokane 048275
Northwest Pastel Society, Gig Harbor 054944
Northwest Print Council, Portland .. 054945
Northwest Railway Museum, Snoqualmie 048207
Northwest Tribal Art, Seattle 119969
Northwest Watercolor Society, Sammamish 054946
Northwestern National Exhibition Centre, Hazelton 005611
Northwestern Oklahoma State University Museum, Alva 041676
Northwestern Ontario Sports Hall of Fame, Thunder Bay 006565
Northwich Antiques Center, Northwich 086104
Northwood, Edmonton 096892
Northwood Fine Art, Bournemouth . 112682
Norton, Pauline, Bridgnorth 112702
Norton, Richard, Chicago 115514
Norton & Co., W.W., London 135244
Norton Antiques, Twyford, Norfolk . 086971
Norton Conyers, Near Ripon 040515
Norton Museum of Art, West Palm Beach 049091
Norton Priory Museum, Runcorn ... 040871
Norton & Roberts, London 141854
Norton Simon Museum, Pasadena . 046833
Nortonbury, London 085563
Norton's Fine Art Studios, Saint Louis 119232
Norway Art, Minneapolis 117290
Norwegian-American Historical Museum, Northfield 046552
Norwegian Federation of Friends of Museums, Oslo 053957
Norwich and District Museum, Norwich 006055
Norwich Collectors Toyshop, Norwich 086121
The Norwich Decorative and Fine Arts Society, Bungay 054461
Norwich Gallery, Norwich 040609
Norwich Historical Society Museum, Norwich 046572
Norwich School of Art and Design, Norwich 050850
Norwich University Museum, Northfield 046555
Norwood, John, New York 091118
Norwood Cottage Antiques, Johannesburg 080711
Norwood Historical Association Museum, Norwood 046573
Norwood Museum, Holm 039761
Norwood Park Artists Guild, Chicago 054947, 115515
Nosbüsch, Manfred, Bonn 138905
Nose Creek Valley Museum, Airdrie 004989
Nosei, Annina, New York 118243
Nosorog, Beograd 080401
Nosorog, Beograd 109714
Nossereau-Hauff, Christine, L'Isle-sur-la-Sorgue 063950
Nossi College of Art, Goodlettsville . 051395
Noßmann, Andreas, Ennepetal 102628
Nosta, Bruxelles 058042
Nostalga Kunst- und Antiquitätentage mit Antiquariaten, Oldenburg, Oldenburg 093746
Nostalgia, Aix-en-Provence 060714
Nostalgia, Annecy 060897
Nostalgia, Arundel 083314
Nostalgia, Blackpool 083554
Nostalgia, Budapest 074697
Nostalgia, Cairo 098656
Nostalgia, Christchurch 079043
Nostalgia, Clevedon 084033
Nostalgia, Dubai 083196
Nostalgia, Köln 071987
Nostalgia, Los Angeles 089856
Nostalgia, Nelson 114113
Nostalgia, Nijmegen 078659
Nostalgia, Pforzheim 104604
Nostalgia, Solna 081897
Nostalgia, Stockport 086725
Nostalgia Antiques, Moonee Ponds . 056250
Nostalgia Antiques, Porthcawl 086293, 131390
Nostalgia Factory, Kangaroo Valley . 056033
Nostalgia Factory, Kangaroo Valley . 136955
Nostalgia Factory, Manly 056152
Nostalgia Gallery, Teddington 114559
Nostalgia on 19th Street, Houston . 089168
Nostalgia Shop, Saint Louis 092288
Nostalgia Shoppe, Toledo 093180
Nostalgia Traders, Mittagong 056238
Nostalgia World, Memphis 090097
Nostalgiaville, Miami 090218
Nostalgie, Pont-a-Marcq 066906
Nostalgie, Tilburg 078775
Nostalgie auf Rädern - Fahrzeugmuseum, Großklein 001973
Nostalgie & Cottage, Sprötze 073885
Nostalgie Museum, Brandenburg an der Havel 016374
Nostalgie-Museum, Wörth an der Donau 020947
Nostalgie-Stube, Marktredwitz 072464
Nostalgiebahnen in Kärnten, Museum für Technik und Verkehr, Ebental, Kärnten 001799
Nostalgiehaus, Rheda-Wiedenbrück 073510
Nostalgieladen, Zürich 083004
Nostalgipalatset, Stockholm 081997
Nostalgisches Musikparadies, Oberhasli 037388
Nostalgoteket, København 060360
Nostell Priory, Wakefield 041275
Nøstetangen Museum, Hokksund .. 030894
Nostitz, Charles von, New York 132508
Nostradamus Antiques, Weybridge . 087111
Nostradamus II, East Molesey 084252
Nostro Tempo, Torino 135929
Nostromo Books, Auckland 140602
Nosztalgia, Budapest 139923
Not Just Antiques, Tetbury 086862
Not Just Dolls, Dallas 088581
Not Just Silver, Weybridge 087112
Nota, La Paz 096444
Nota Bene, Düsseldorf 070420
Notable Accents, Dallas 088582
Notaphilie Dresden, Dresden 070327
Notari, Otello, Roma 128136
Het Notarishuis Arnhem, Arnhem .. 121783
Notebaart, P.C., Bussum 140377
De Notelaer, Hingene 029752
Notgeld-Sammlung 1918/20, Bad Wimsbach-Neydharting 001741
Noth, Elisabeth, Oberursel 126582
Nothe Fort Museum of Coastal Defence, Weymouth 041357
Nothelfer, Georg, Berlin 101996
Nothelfer, Georg, Berlin 101997
Nothing Definite, Saint Louis 092289
Nothing Trivial, Calgary 058796
Notions Antique Centre, Grantham .084497, 130741
Notiziario d'Arte, Roma 135930
Notiziario Vinciano, Brescia 135931
Notizie da Palazzo Albani, Urbino .. 135932
Notizie degli Scavi di Antichità, Roma 135933
Notodden Auksjonsforretning, Notodden 121860
Notojima Glass Art Museum, Notojima 026926
Notranjski Muzej Postojna, Postojna 034512
Notre Dame of Jolo College Museum, Sulu Culture Museum, Jolo 031675
Nottbohm, Göttingen 102980
Nottingham Antiques, Atlanta 087507
Nottingham Castle, Nottingham ... 040624
Nottingham Transport Heritage Centre, Ruddington 040862
Nottingham Trent School of Art and Design, Nottingham Trend University, Nottingham 050852
Nottingham University Museum, Nottingham 040625
Notus, New York 091119
Notus, New York 091120
Notz-Erkens, Nettetal 072964
Nou Cents, Barcelona 080894
Nouchka, La Bastide-des-Jourdans 063283
Nougues, Henri, Pontorson 066945, 124852
Nouh, Damascus 083073
Noujaim, Juliette, Paris 066335
Nouna R, Bruxelles 058043
Nour, Zürich 083005
Nourbakhsch, Giti, Berlin 101998
Nourisson, Philippe, Vern-sur-Seiche 125015
Nourry-Joannès, Claudine, Verneuil-sur-Avre 068782
Noury, Jacques, Tours 101382
Noüs-Verlag, Tübingen ... 134434, 139799
Nousbaum, Marie-France, Campagne 061927
Nousiaisten Kotiseutumuseo, Nousiainen 009910
Nouveaux Brocanteurs, La Chapelle-en-Serval 063314
Nouvelle Arche de Noé, Paris 133659
Nouvelle Art, Oslo 108737
Nouvelle Galerie, Grenoble 099308
Nouvelle Saison, Grenoble 138102
Nouvelle Tendance, Paris 124763
Nouvelles de l'Estampe, Paris 135720
Nouvelles Galeries de Paris, Bruxelles 120739
Nouvelles Hybrides, Courbevoie ... 062511
Nouvelles Images, Den Haag 107943
Nouvelles Images, Paris .. 100736, 133660
Nouvelles Images, Villemandeur ...101472, 133707
Nouvellet, Olivier, Paris 100737
Nova Conservação, Lisboa 129164
A Nova Eclética, Lisboa 140847
Nova Foresta, Southampton 142080
Nova Gallery, Calgary 096835
Nova Istoria na Veliko Tărnovo, Veliko Tărnovo 004938
Nova Kodl, Praha 098476
Nova Rúa, Lugo 110417
Nova Scotia Centre for Craft and Design, Halifax 005578
Nova Scotia College of Art and Design, Halifax 049790
Nova Scotia Museum, Halifax 005579
Nova Scotia Museum of Natural History, Halifax 005580
Nova Scotia Printmakers Association, RR 3 Centreville NS 052760
Nova Terra Antiek, Apeldoorn 078039
Nova Venezia, San Francisco 119756
Nova & Vetera, Bonn 138906
Novagraphics, Tucson 120154
Novaja Galereja, Ufa 109663
Novaja Kollekcija, Moskva 109574
Novak, Ljubljana 080657, 109979
Novak, C. & B., Gomaringen 071060
Novak, Johnathan, Los Angeles ... 116857
Novák, Karel, Kralupy nad Vltavou . 137788
Novak, Małgorzata, Kraków 108966
Novak-Spurny, Irma, Salzweg 104808
Nováková, L., Praha 137841
Novalis, Freiburg im Breisgau 102870, 139116
Novalis-Literaturgedenkstätte, Weißenfels 020783
Novalis-Museum, Wiederstedt 020855
Novanta Nove, Amsterdam 107777
Novara, Stockholm 081998
Novarese, Domenico, Torino 076848
Novarino, Enrico, Torino 076849
Novarino, Enrico Andrea, Torino ... 076850
Novartsib, Cassis 099092
Novato History Museum, Novato ... 046576
Novecento, Barcelona 080895
Novecento, Firenze 075378
Novecento, Modena 127738
Novecento, Padova 076102
Novecento & Dintorni, Roma 076589
Novecento Editrice, Palermo 134651
Novel Art, Männedorf 111713
Novellan, Hondarribia 110387
Novello, Michele, Venezia 106771
Novelty Art, Mumbai 074826
Noves, Laure de, La Ciotat 063333
Novgorod, Kouvola 137974
Novgorod-Siverskyj Istoriko-kulturnyj Muzej-zapovidnyk Slovo o Polku Igorevim, Novgorod-Sivers'kyj 038365
Novgorodskij Gosudarstvennyj Muzej-zapovednik, Velikij Novgorod 034028
Novi Vinodolski Regional Museum, Novi Vinodolski 007765
Novis, Arnsberg 069183
Novita' Bibliografiche, Roma 135934
Novo Século, Lisboa 109339
Novočerkasskij Muzej Istorii Donskich Kazakov, Novočerkassk 033579
Novodevičij Monastyr, Gosudarstvennyj istoričeskij muzej, Moskva 033509
Novoe Prostranstvo, Odesa 112433
Novohradská Galéria, Lučenec 034378
Novohradské Múzeum, Lučenec ... 034379
Novohradsky, Wolfgang, Freigericht 070870
Novokuzneckij Chudožestvennyj Muzej, Novokuzneck 033582
Novokuzneckij Kraevedeskij Muzej, Novokuzneck 033583
Novorossijskij Gosudarstvennyj Istoričeskij Muzej Zapovednik, Novorossijsk . 033584
Novosibirskaja Architekturno-chudožestvennaja Akademija, Novosibirsk 050652
Novosibirskaja Kartinnaja Galereja, Novosibirsk 033587
Novosibirskij Muzej Prirody, Novosibirsk 033588
Novosibirskij Oblastnoj Kraevedčeskij Muzej, Novosibirsk 033589
Novotroickij Istoriko-kraevedčeskij Muzej, Orenburgskij oblastnoj kraevedčeskij muzej, Novotroick 033592
Novum Forum, Neumarkt in Steiermark 002368
Nový Antik Bazar, Praha 060147
Nový Zamok Banská Štiavnica, Banská Štiavnica 034307
Novyj Ermitaž, Moskva 080255
Now & Again, Auckland 078967
Now & Again, Baltimore 087697
Now-Again, Los Angeles 089857
Now & Again at 57th Street, Sacramento 092172
Now and Again, Atlanta 087508
Now and Again, Tampa 093145
Now and Then, Edinburgh 084306
Now and Then, Saint Louis 092290
Now & Forever Images, Christchurch 108407
Now Gallery, Vichy 101465
Now & Then, Pittsburgh 091847
Now & Then, Vancouver 059391
Now & Then Collectibles, Miami ... 090219
Now & Then Shop, Indianapolis ... 089328
Nowack, W., Bredstedt 121357

Nowack & Roger, Düsseldorf 125543
Nowacki, Edwin, Poznań 079694
Nowacki, Peter, Iserlohn 071634
Nowak, Berlin 125268
Nowak, Gera 125718
Nowak, Hohen Neuendorf 125955
Nowak, Andreas, Petershagen, Weser 126621
Nowak, Britt, Altdorf bei Nürnberg . 125060
Nowak, Hiltraut, Dresden 102453
Nowak, Norbert, Dortmund 070291
Nowata County Historical Society Museum, Nowata 046577
Nowes, Howard, New York 118244
Nowhere Land, Bruxelles 096238
Nowicki, Andrzej Marek, Warszawa 129104
Nowicki, Piotr Tadeusz, Warszawa . 109168
Nowra Museum, Nowra 001347
Nowsky, Gerd, Oer-Erkenschwick . . 126585
Noyes, Michael, El Paso 132066
Noyes and Read Gallery and Herndon Gallery, Antioch College, Yellow Springs 049337
Noyes Art Gallery, Lincoln 045310
The Noyes Museum of Art, Oceanville 046621
Noyrigat, Jacques, Millau 064559
NRW-Forum Kultur und Wirtschaft, Düsseldorf 016842
NRW-Kunstkreis, Vettweiß 053530
NSE Medal, Nottingham 086142
NTT InterCommunication Center, Tokyo 027226
Nu Black Art Gallery, Charlotte 115303
Nuages, Milano 106273
Nuances, Issy-les-Moulineaux 135721
Nuantta Sunakkutaangit Musuem, Iqaluit 005646
Nubien Museum, Aswan 009287
Nucleo de Informatica e Cultura Itau Galeria, Belo Horizonte 096476
Núcleo Museológico do Santuário do Senhor Jesus da Pedra, Óbidos 032666
Núcleo Técnico Artístico, São Paulo 058730
Nudgee Road Antiques and Arts Centre, Hendra 055976
Nuding, Angelika, Sinsheim 073834
Nuding, Ursula, Pulheim 073384
Nüans Sanat Galerisi, İstanbul 112341
Nüchter, Albrecht, Schlitz 073702
Nüdling, Charlotte, Fulda . 070918, 102909
Nünlist, Octavè, Amriswil . 082089, 129897
Nürnberger, Dieter, Nürnberg 104485
Nürnberger Gobelin-Manufaktur, Nürnberg 126569
Nüssel, Erich F., München 126425
Nütt, Sybille, Dresden 102454
Nueva Era Arte y Diseño, Bogotá . . 098178
Nueva Roma, Buenos Aires 136743
Nueva Street Gallery, San Antonio . 119436
Nufer, Christoph, Aarwangen 082073, 129890
Nugget, Hong Kong 059677
Nugut, Tugun 056742
Nuijamaan Museo, Lappeenranta . . 009804
La Nuit de Varennes, Marseille 064379
Nukarin Koulumuseo, Nukari 009912
Nukke- ja Lelumuseo, Helsinki 009579
Nukke- ja Pukumuseo - Hatanpäa Mansion, Tampere 010124
Nukkemuseo Suruton, Savonlinna . 010066
Nukumuuseum, Tallinna Linnamuuseum, Tallinn 009409
Nullkommanix, Hamburg 103202
NUMA, Luxembourg 135987
NUMA-Revue internationale de numismatique, Luxembourg 134753
Numaga, Colombier 111365, 135006
Numark, Cheryl, Washington 120330
Number 1 Royal Crescent Museum, Bath 038629
Number 12, London 085564
Number 24 of Frinton, Frinton-on-Sea 084442
Number 28 Antiques, London 085565
Number 8, Auckland 108350
Number Nine the Gallery, Birmingham 112655
Numis, Praha 060148
Numis 21, Dijon 062670
Numis-Post & HMZ, Bad Ragaz . . . 136128
Numis'Aisne, Soissons 068250
Numisami, Nice 065122
Numiscarte, Saintes 068087
Numisma, Madrid 081352
Numismaatikko, Helsinki 060562
Numismatic Museum, Kathmandu . 029118
Numismatic Museum, Athens, Athinai 021207
Numismatic News, Iola 136593
Numismatic Review, New York 091121, 123005
Numismatic Society of India, Varanasi 053704
Numismatica, Brescia 135935
Numismatica, Madrid 081353
Numismatica Ajuriaguerra, Bilbao . 080985
Numismatica Ars Classica, Zürich . 083006
Numismatica Associacão de Artes e Antiguidades, Rio de Janeiro 058626
Numismatica Dracma, Logroño . . . 081184
Numismatica Metró, Milano 075787
Numismática, Monedas e Notas Antigas, Belo Horizonte 058439
Numismatics & Ancient Art Gallery, Zürich 083007
Numismatique du Port, Toulon (Var) 068466
Numismatique et Monnaie, Paris . . 066336
Numismatische Gesellschaft Speyer e.V., Speyer 053531
Numismatische Gesellschaft zu Berlin e.V., Berlin 053532
Numismatische Kommission der Länder in der Bundesrepublik Deutschland, Hannover 053533
Numismatische Studien, Hamburg . 135813
Numismatische Zeitschrift, Wien . . 135573
Numismatischer Verein, Bern 054203
Numismatisches Nachrichtenblatt, Speyer 135814
Numisporto, Porto 080101
Numiversal, Pirmasens 073332
Nummen Kotiseutumuseo, Nummi . 009913
Nummus et Ars, Venezia . 076964, 121740
Numthong, Bangkok 112235
Nun, Ghislaine, Elne 062773
Nunatta Katersugaasivia Allagaateqarfialu, Nuuk 021544
Nundah and Districts Historical Museum, Nundah 001348
Nundah Antiques, Nundah 056395
Nunes, Lisboa 140848
Nunes, Malakoff 064232
Nunes, Affonso, Rio de Janeiro . . . 058627
Nunes, Haroldo, Rio de Janeiro . . . 123707
Nunes, Joaquim Pereira, Lisboa . . . 079981
Nunes, Marilene B., Rio de Janeiro . 058628
Núñez, Elena, Montevideo 122786
Nuñez Narbona, Jose Maria, Toledo 081631
Nuni, Los Angeles 116858
Nunziati, Gianna, Firenze 127381
Nunzio, Salamone, Catania 075255, 127273
Nuova Abes Editrice, Bologna 134550
Nuova Arcadia, Padova 076103
Nuova Bianchi d'Espinosa, Napoli . . 106384
Nuova Conservazione, Roma 128137
Nuova Era, Bari 105933
Nuova Fauro, Roma 076590
Nuova Galleria Campo dei Fiori, Roma 106601
Nuova Gissi, Torino 106688
Nuova Gissi, Torino 106689
Nuova-Icona, Associazione Culturale per le Arti, Venezia 026261
Nuova Icona, Associazione Culturale per le Arti, Venezia 053763
Nuova Italia, Casellina-Scandicci . . 134562
Nuova Museologia, Brescia 135936
Nuova Rassegna, Cosenza 135937
Nuovo Accademia di Belle Arti, Milano 050393
Nuovo Fondaco, Genova 075488
Nuovo Istituto Italiano d'Arti Grafiche, Bergamo 134545
Nuovo Museo Provinciale Sannitico, Campobasso 023620
Nuovo Orizzonte, Genova 106100
Nurihiko, Tokyo 107089
Nurkkaus, Ranskalainen, Helsinki . 060563
Nurmeksen Museo, Nurmes 009915
Nurmi, J.A., Turku 098763
Nurmon Museo, Nurmo 009917
NUS Museum, Singapore 034295
Nusraty, New York 091122
Nussbaum, Louisville 116958
Nussbaum, Zeist 108274
Nussbaum, Scott F., Louisville 090014, 142533
Nussbaumer, Friedrich, Tobelbad . . 123476
Nusser, Ursula, München 121539
Nusser & Baumgart, München 072805, 104277, 134265
Nussknackermuseum, Neuhausen, Sachsen 019243
Nussle, Sarah, Paris 066337
Nussli, Stefan, Ittigen 130050
The Nut Point Gallery, Christchurch 108408
Nutcote Museum, Neutral Bay 001322
Nuti Loredana, Roma 076591
Nutimik Lake Museum, Seven Sisters Falls 006443
Nutley Antiques, Nutley 086146
Nuttall, Pennant Hills 056448
Nutzfahrzeugmuseum, Hartmannsdorf 017783
Nuuk Kunsttskolen, Eqqumiitsuliornermik Ilinniarfik, Nuuk 050274
Nuwaubian, London 141855
NVA-Museum, Ostseebad Binz 019527
Ny Ålesund By- og Gruvemuseum, Ny-Ålesund 031058
Ny Carlsberg Glyptotek, København 008982
Ny-Ram, Helsingborg 110944
Nya och Gamla Ting i Lövånger, Lövånger 122197
Nyabinghi, New York 118245
Nyahokwe Ruins Site Museum, Inyanga 049585
Nyborg, Oslo 079463
Nyborg og Omegns Museer, Nyborg 009033
Nydegg, Bern 111269
Nyerges, Suzanne, Los Angeles . . . 116859
NYFA Quarterly, New York 136594
Nyffeler & Co., Max, Langenthal . . .082524, 130061
Nyhuis, Emlichheim 070555
Nykarleby Museum, Uusikaarlepyy . 010193
Nylander Museum, Caribou 042620
Nýlistasafnið, Reykjavík 021971
Nymphenburger Porzellan-Sammlung Bäuml, München 019097
Nymphenburger Verlagshandlung, München 134266
Nynäs Slott, Västerljung 036768
Nynäshamns Järnvägsmuseum, Nynäshamn 036513
Nynorsk Antikvariat, Oslo 140704
Nyoirin-ji Treasure House, Yoshino . 027350
Nyons Antic, Nyons 065252
Nyozezo Private Museum, Nagaoka 026853
Nysà, Paris 066338
Nyslotts Landskapsmuseum, Nyslott 009919
Nystavka Iskusstva, Krasnojarsk . . 093852
Nyströmska Gården, Köpings Museum, Köping 036395
Nyt & Gammelt, København 060361
Nyt Nordisk Forlag, København . . . 133426
Nyugat, Budapest 139924
N.Z, Inglewood 079121
NZ Art Online, Christchurch 108409
NZ Arts, Auckland 108351
NZH Vervoers Museum, Haarlem . . 029657
LaO Antiquités, Sallanches 068098
O Art Museum, Tokyo 027227
O. Henry Home and Museum, Austin 041934
O Museu do Marajó, Cachoeira do Arari 004031
O N, Napoli 135938
O & O, Amsterdam 077923
O-Won, Daejeon 107195
Oadby Antiques, Foxton 079097
Oak Creek Pioneer Village, Oak Creek 046581
Oak Hall, Niagara Falls 006016
Oak House Museum, West Bromwich 041336
Oak & Kauri, Kumeu 079137
Oak Ridge Art Center, Oak Ridge . . 046587
Oakdale Museum, Oakdale 046588
Oakenshawe, Baltimore 087698
Oakes & Son, G., Bolton 083572
Oakham, London 085566, 113797
Oakham Castle, Rutland County Museum, Oakham 040633
Oakland Antiques, Belfast 083481
Oakland Coin and Jewelry, Oakland 091431
Oakland Museum of California, Oakland 046598
Oaklander, Irving, New York 142680
Oaklands Historic House Museum, Murfreesboro 046096
Oakleaf Antiques, Taupo 079256
Oakleigh and District Museum, Oakleigh 001352
Oakleigh House, Historic Mobile Preservation, Mobile 045951
Oakley Antique Mall, Cincinnati . . . 088265
Oakley Limited Upholstery, Chicago 131911
Oakley Pioneer Museum, Oakley . . 046604
Oakridge, El Paso 088810
Oakridge, Louisville 090015
Oaks House Museum, Jackson 044803
Oaktree Antiques, Lubenham 085859
Oakville Galleries, Centennial, Oakville 006058
Oakville Galleries, Gairloch, Oakville 006059
Oakville Museum at Erchless Estate, Oakville 006060
Oakwell Hall Country Park, Birstall . 038744
Oakwood Antiques, Hinuera 079116
Oakwood Gallery, Edwinstowe 113013
Oakwood Gallery, Leeds . . 084929, 130872
Oakwood House Gallery, Maldon . . 114033
Het Oale Meestershuus, Slagharen . 030157
Oale Smederie, Hellendoorn 029717
OAN-Oceanie Afrique Noire Books, New York 142681
Oasen, Valby 137910
Oasi, Mario Attilio, Roma 076592
Oasis, Manawatu 108491
Oasis, Seattle 093039
Oasis Antique, Sharjah 083221
Oasis Antiques, Brighton . 083707, 130447
Oasis-Centre, Genève 111490
The Oasis Company, Colombo 081761
Oasis Gallery, Portland . . . 091982, 123065
Oasis Superette, Tauranga 140660
Oates Memorial Museum and Gilbert White Museum, Selborne 040977
Oatlands Plantation, Leesburg 045232
Ob-Art, Barcelona 110229
Ob Luang, Chiang Mai 037896
Obach, Dieter, Velbert . . . 074186, 105112
Obadia, Nathalie, Paris 100738
Obalne Galerije - Galerija Loža, Koper 034469
Obalne Galerije - Mestna Galerija, Piran 034510
Oban Antiques, Oban 086152
Obecní Dům, Praha 008640
Obelar, Montevideo 087335
Obelisk Antiques, Warminster 087030
Obelisk Museum, Al-Matariyya 009270
Obelisque, Oslo 079464
Obéniche, Honfleur 099355
Oberacker, Rolf, Wiesbaden 074416

Oberbaumverlag, Berlin 133801
Oberbergischer Kunstverein Gummersbach e.V., Reichshof 053534
Oberburg Giebichenstein, Halle, Saale 017669
Oberdiek, H., Melle 072510
Oberdiek, Harald, Melle 072511
Oberfränkisches Bauernhofmuseum, Zell, Oberfranken 021052
Oberfränkisches Textilmuseum, Helmbrechts 017863
Oberharzer Bergwerksmuseum, Museum für Technik-und Kulturgeschichte, Clausthal-Zellerfeld 016569
Oberhausmuseum Passau, Passau . 019573
Oberkärntner Brauchtums- und Maskenmuseum, Oberdrauburg . . 002382
Oberkalkofen, Helga, Siegen 104900
Oberländer, Heike, Berlin 069715
Oberländer, Konrad, Augsburg 101618
Oberlander, Eberhard, Wurmannsquick 127054
Oberlausitzer Kunstverein e.V., Zittau 053535
Oberlausitzer Sechsstädtebund- und Handwerksmuseum Löbau, Löbau 018668
Oberle, Aline, Steuerberg 123473
Oberle, Frieder, Bad Schussenried . 069378
Oberlé, Gérard, Montigny-sur-Canne 138213
Oberlin College Gallery, Cleveland . 042996
Oberlin Historical and Improvement Organization Museum, Oberlin . . . 046608
Obermaier, R., Altötting 069157
Obermair, Rudolf, Wels . . . 057353, 123486
Obermann, Pierre, Genève 082455
Obermeier, Rosemarie, Neufarn . . . 072989
Obermeier, Rosemarie & Johann, Poing 073353
Obermeier, Rudolf, Regensburg . . . 126696
Obermeier, Siegfried, Berg bei Neumark, Oberpfalz 125152
Obermeyer & Reschke, Bonn 069936
Obermühle Hochburg-Ach, Ach . . . 001658
Obermühlviertler Denkmalhof Unterkagerer, Auberg 001706
Oberösterreichische Fotogalerie, Linz 002253
Oberösterreichischer Künstlerbund, Linz 052582
Oberösterreichischer Kunstverein, Linz 052583, 095669
Oberösterreichischer Musealverein, Gesellschaft für Landeskunde von Oberösterreich, Linz 052584
Oberösterreichischer Steingarten, Vorchdorf 002791
Oberösterreichisches Freilichtmuseum Sumerauerhof, Sankt Florian 002577
Oberösterreichisches Jagdmuseum, Schloß Hohenbrunn, Sankt Florian 002578
Oberösterreichisches Landesmuseum - Außenstelle Linz-Haag, Linz 002254
Oberösterreichisches Schiffahrtsmuseum, Grein an der Donau 001954
Oberpfälzer Fischereimuseum, Tirschenreuth 020442
Oberpfälzer Flußspat-Besucherbergwerk Reichhart-Schacht, Stulln 020341
Oberpfälzer Freilandmuseum Neusath-Perschen, Nabburg 019175
Oberpfälzer Handwerksmuseum, Rötz 019873
Oberpfälzer Künstlerhaus-Kebbel-Villa, Schwandorf 020123
Oberpfälzer Volkskundemuseum, Burglengenfeld 016520
Oberrheinische Narrenschau, Kenzingen 018238
Oberrheinisches Bäder- und Heimatmuseum Bad Bellingen, Bad Bellingen 015652
Oberrheinisches Tabakmuseum, Mahlberg 018779
Oberschlesisches Landesmuseum, Ratingen 019722
Oberschwäbische Barock-Galerie, Ochsenhausen 073169
Oberschwäbische Galerie Kloster Heiligkreuztal, Altheim bei Riedlingen 015508
Oberschwäbisches Museumsdorf Kreisfreilichtmuseum Kürnbach, Bad Schussenried 015794
Obersimmentaler Heimatmuseum, Zweisimmen 037823
Oberst, Carmen, Hamburg 103203
Oberto, Martino, Genova 127476
Oberweger, Innsbruck 095591
Oberweger, Werner, Schruns 095754
Oberweger, Werner & Philipp, Innsbruck 095592
Oberweißbacher Bergbahn, Mellenbach-Glasbach 018898
Oberwelt, Stuttgart 105004
Oberwemmer, Günter, Hamburg . . . 125832
Obieg, Warszawa 136030
Obir-Tropfsteinhöhlen, Bad Eisenkappel 001712
Object, Amsterdam 077924
Objectif Lune, Paris 066339
Objects and Posters, Staufenberg, Hessen 134403
Objects of Bright Pride, Seattle 119970
Objects of Desire, Louisville 116959
Objects of Vertu, Huddersfield 084750
Objedinenie Fotocentr Sojuza Žurnalistov, Moskva 033510
Objektief, Enschede 108022
L'Objet, Paris 066340
L'Objet Curieux, Genève 082456
Objet Trouvé, Stuttgart 073999
Objetos Diretos Multiplos Artes, Rio de Janeiro 096632
Objets D'art, East Grinstead 112975
Objets d'Art, Paris 066341
Objets d'Art, Paris 066342
Objets d'Arts, Paris 066343
Objets d'Hier, Casablanca 077668
Objets Inanimés, Perpignan 066754
Objets Plus, New York 091123
Objets Trou Ve', New Orleans 117484
Objets Trouvés, Paris 066344
Objex Studio & Gallery, Wellington . 108636
Oblasnyj Istoryčnyj Muzej im. V. Tarnovs'kogo, Černigiv 038232
Oblasnyj Krajeznavčyj Muzej, Žytomyr 038421
Oblasnyj Krajeznavčyj Muzej, Cherson 038249
Oblasten Istoričeski Muzej, Jambol 004697
Oblastnaja Kartinnaja Galereja Obraz, Kaluga 033226
Oblastní Galerie, Liberec 008474
Oblastní Galerie Vysočiny v Jihlavě, Jihlava 008413
Oblastní Muzeum, Chomutov 008335
Oblastní Muzeum, Most 008516
Oblastnoj Chudožestvennyj Muzej, Petropavlovsk-Kamčatskij 033657
Oblastnoj Kraevedčeskij Muzej, Ekaterinburg 033125
Oblastnoj Kraevedčeskij Muzej im A.A. Kuznecova, Čita 033095
Oblastnoj Muzejnyj Centr, Sankt-Peterburg 033821
Obligato, Francesco, Torino 076851
Oboro, Montréal 097059
Oboronna Bašta Malachova Kurgana, Muzei geroïčnoï oborony i vyzvolennja Sevastopolja, Sevastopol 038390
Obra de Arte, São Paulo 049768
Obra y Arte, Bucaramanga 098223
Obradović, Petar, Beograd 109715
Obrazárna Pražského Hradu, Praha 008641
O'Brien, F.M., Portland 142788
O'Brien, Liz, New York 091124
O'Brien, Michael & Ivan, Dublin . . . 134529
O'Brien and Son, R.J., Manchester . 085918
O'Brien, Stephen B., Boston 115214
O'Brien's, Masterton 108502
Øbro, København 060362
Obrock, Helmut, Rödinghausen . . . 073557
Obščinski Istoričeski Muzej, Etropole 004679
Obscura - Zeszyty fotograficzne PFFiAST, DSAFiTA, Dolnośląskie Stowarzyszenie Artystów Fotografików i Twórców Audiowizualnych, Wrocław 136031
Observatoire Galerie, Bruxelles . . . 096239
Observatoriemuseet, Stockholm . . . 036653
Observatory Museum, Grahamstown 034624
Obsession, Holt, Norfolk 135159
Obsession Antiques, Montréal 058983
Obsession Art Gallery, Kolkata 105743
The Obsession of Art, Bergen, Noord-Holland 107866
Obsidian, London 113798
Obsidian Gallery, Tucson 120155
Obsis, Gennevilliers 099287
Obsoleto, Alicante 080764
Obstbaumuseum, Werder, Havel . . . 020804
Obstmuseum, Sörup 020229
Obu, Tartu 098706
Óbuda, Budapest 139925
Obudai Helytörténeti Gyűjtemény, Budapest 021679
Óbudai Pincegaléria, Budapest 021680
Óbudai Társaskör Galéria, Budapest 021681
Obuvnické Muzeum, Zlín 008788
OCAD Gallery, Toronto 006619
Ocampo, Luis Alberto, Medellín . . . 059934
Ocara Antiquités, Lyon 064168
La Ocasion, Gijón 081125
Occasion, Helsinki 060564
Occasion 240, Paris 066345
O.C.C.M.P, Bordeaux 061639
Occultique, Northampton 141960
Occupation Tapestry Gallery and Maritime Museum, Saint Helier 040916
Occurence, Montréal 097060
Ocean Art, Indianapolis 116482
Ocean Art Gallery, Virginia Beach . . 120229
Ocean Beach Antique Mall, San Diego 092665
Ocean Beach Books, San Diego . . . 142908
Ocean City Art Center, Ocean City . . 046615
Ocean City Historical Museum, Ocean City 046616
Ocean Contemporary, Falmouth . . . 113052
Ocean County Historical Museum, Toms River 048574
Ocean Drive Space and Gallery, Miami 117118
Ocean Point, Atlanta 087509
Oceania Design, Wellington 030646
Oceanic Arts, Paddington, New South Wales 056420
Oceanographic Museum, Institute of Oceanography, Nhatrang 049549
Océanopolis, Brest 010987
Océarium du Croisic, Le Croisic . . . 012490
Ochanomizu Bijutsu Gakuin, Tokyo . 050493
Ochiai, Ichikawa 106861
Ochsenfarth, Lübeck 126243
Ochsenfarth, Paderborn 126610
Ocmulgee National Monument, Macon 045568
O'Connell, Adelaide 136774
O'Connor, Toronto 097337
O'Connor Bros., Windsor . 087182, 131698
O'Connor & Co., Cynthia, Swords . . 105902
O'Connor & Assoc., Tom, San Francisco 119757
Oconto County Historical Society Museum, Oconto 046622
Ocotillo, Houston 116380
Ocre, Lisboa 079982, 129165
Les Ocres du Sud, Carpentras 062001
Oct, Hiratsuka 106852
The Octagon, Washington 048938
Octagon Books, New York 142682
The Octagon Center for the Arts, Ames 041687
The Octagon House, Hudson 044664
Octagon House, Watertown 048998
Octave Chanute Aerospace Museum, Rantoul 047331
Octavia, Saint-Michel-Loubejou . . . 067678
Octavia Antiques, Petworth 086253
Octavia's Haze Gallery, San Francisco 119758
Octavo, Firenze 134586
Octo Studio, Philadelphia 091673
October, Cambridge 136595
October Gallery, London 113799
October Gallery, Philadelphia 118815
Oda Kolleksiyon, İstanbul 083150
Odalstunet Gårdsmuseum, Skarnes 031185
Odalys, Prados del Este . . 093553, 123144, 135529, 143057
Odapark, Venray 030270
OD'Art, Delft 107891
Odawara, Tokyo 140196
Odawara Castle Museum, Odawara 026931
Odawara Crustacea Museum, Tokyo 027228
Odd Book Shop, Kent Town 136962
The Odd Lot, Aberdeen . . 083239, 130280
Oddeleni Oblastni Muzeum Jihovýchodni Moravy, Napajedla 008520
Oddělení Oblastního Muzea Jihovychodní Moravy, Zlín, Luhačovice 008493
Oddentunet, Os Museum, Os i Østerdalen 031065
Odder Museum, Odder 009042
Oddi Baglioni, Emanuela, Roma . . . 106602
Oddlie Limited, Chicago . . 088135, 131912
Odds & Ends, Jacksonville 089439
Odds & Ends, Nairobi 077355
Oddvar Olsen, Drammen 121849
Oddział Literacki im. Marii Dąbrowskiej w Russowie, Muzeum Okręgowe Ziemi Kaliskiej w Kaliszu, Russów 032295
Oddział Sztuki Współczesnej, Muzeum Narodowe w Gdańsku, Gdańsk . . 031921
Oddział Zbiorów Graficznych i Kartograficznych, Biblioteka Jagiellońska, Kraków 032065
Odělene Likovne i Musičke Umetnosti, Srpske Akademije Nauka i Umetnosti, Beograd 050675
O'Dell Inn, Annapolis Royal 005017
Oden, Stockholm 111066
Odendahl & Kretschmer, Engelskirchen 070570, 125588
Odenwälder Freilandmuseum, Walldürn 020656
Odenwald- & Spielzeugmuseum, Michelstadt 018935
Odeon, Dublin 074938
Odeon Antiques, Leek . . . 084942, 130877
Oderlandmuseum, Bad Freienwalde 015701
Odermatt, Franz, Hergiswil, Nidwalden 082493
Odermatt, Peter & Beate, Schifferstadt 104823
Odermatt & Spatz, Neustadt an der Weinstraße 104435
Odermatt & Spatz, Schifferstadt . . . 134381
Odermatt-Vedovi, Paris 100739
Odes'kyj Chudožnij Muzej, Odesa . . 038370
Odes'kyj Istoriko-krajeznavčyj Muzej, Odesa 038371
Odes'kyj Literaturno-memorial'nyj Muzej K. Paustovskogo, Odes'kyj literaturnyj muzej, Odesa 038372
Odes'kyj Literaturnyj Muzej, Odesa 038373
Odes'kyj Muzej Zachidnogo ta Schidnogo Mystectva, Odesa 038374
Odessa Archaeological Museum, Odesa 038375
Odesser, Roman, München 072806
Odigia Ikonen-Museum, Den Haag . 029449
Odiham Gallery, Odiham 086154
Odile, Céret 099099
Odin Antiques, Brighton 083708
Odinani Museum, Awka 030675
Odinsborg, Uppsala 111093
Odisseus i Stockholm, Nacka 081886
Odlin Gallery, Wellington 108637
Odom, Fort Worth 142414
Odon Antik, Budapest 074698

O'Donnell, Chris & Lin, Wallingford . 087006
O'Donoghue Books, London 141856
Odontological Museum, London . . . 040248
Odsherreds Kulturhistoriske Museum, Højby 008918
Odsherreds Kunstmuseum, Asnæs . 008812
Odsherreds Museum, Asnæs 008813
Odsherreds Museum, Nykøbing Sjælland 009040
Oduon, Cairo 098657
Ody's Antiques, Miami 090220
Odyssée, Cannes 099076
Odyssée, Chur 111360
L'Odyssée, Lyon 138181
L'Odyssée, Paris 138512
Odyssée, Saint-Étienne 138599
Odyssey Books, Montréal 137666
Odyssey Fine Arts, London 085567
Oebel, Hildegard, Detmold 070229
Oechsle, Karl-Heinz, Lübeck 072334
Ödenburger Heimatmuseum, Bad Wimpfen 015833
Oedipus Rex Gallery, Auckland 108352
Ödmann, Gudrun, Stockholm 081999
Öffentliche Bibliothek der Universität Basel, Basel 036900
Oehl, Bruno, Wernersberg 126996
Öhman, Styrbjörn, Göteborg 141105
Oehmen-Krieger, Angelika, Neuss . 073016
Oehmig, Sven, Wasserburg am Inn . 126972
Öhrström, Göteborg 110926
L'Oeil de Poisson, Québec 097155
L'Oeil Soleil, Cliousclat 099156
Öjskogsparkens Museiområde, Närpes 009898
Ölands Auktionskammare, Borgholm 122110
Ölands Forngård, Borgholm 036227
Öle-Museum, Münsingen 037357
Oelert, Ober-Ramstadt 073134
Oelgart, D., Krefeld 126147
Oellermann, Eike, Heroldsberg 125919
Oelmann, Heinz, Herne 071492
Ölmühle Michelau, Rudersberg . . . 019935
Önningebymuseet, Mariehamn 009860
Öntödei Múzeum, Budapest 021682
von Oepen & Werner, Essen 070641
Örebro Konsthallen, Örebro 036521
Örebro Läns Museum, Örebro 036522
Oerka Irene Verbeek Museum, Raard 030052
Örnsköldsviks Museum, Örnsköldsvik 036527
Oertel, Ruth, Hannover 103292
Örterkomorek, Bettina, Rothenburg ob der Tauber 073591
Oerters, R., Gütersloh 103035
Oertijdmuseum De Groene Poort, Boxtel 029344
Öslénytani Telep, Rudabánya 021831
Oeß, Michael, Konstanz 126132
Östereichisches Brückenbaumuseum, Edelsbach bei Feldbach 001803
Östergötlands Auktions & Handelscenter, Linköping 122194
Östergötlands Länsmuseum, Linköping 036426
Österlens Museum, Simrishamn . . . 036572
Oesterling, Wardenburg 105159
Österlunds Auktioner, Kalmar 122174
Östermalm, Stockholm 082000
Österreichische Galerie Belvedere, Halbturn 002006
Österreichische Galerie Belvedere, Oberes Belvedere, Wien 002969
Österreichische Galerie Belvedere, Unteres Belvedere, Museum Mittelalterlicher Kunst, Barockmuseum, Wien 002970
Österreichische Gesellschaft für Christliche Kunst, Wien 052585
Österreichische Gesellschaft für Photographie, Wien 052586
Österreichische Kunsttopographie, Wien 135574
Das Österreichische Motorradmuseum, Eggenburg 001810
Österreichische Nationalbibliothek, Wien 002971
Österreichische Numismatische Gesellschaft, Wien 052587
Österreichische Zeitschrift für Kunst und Denkmalpflege, Horn 135575
Österreichischer Kunst- und Kulturverlag, Wien 133222
Österreichischer Kunstsenat, Wien . 052588
Österreichischer Museumsbund, Wien 052589, 133223
Österreichischer Restauratorenverband, Wien 052590
Österreichisches Circus- und Clown-Museum, Sammlung Unterhaltungskunst, Wien 002972
Österreichisches Donau- und Fischereimuseum, Orth an der Donau 002402
Österreichisches Felsbildermuseum, Spital am Pyhrn 002684
Österreichisches Filmmuseum, Verlagsabteilung, Wien 133224
Österreichisches Filmmuseum Wien, Wien 002973
Österreichisches Forstmuseum Silvanum, Großreifling 001978
Österreichisches Freilichtmuseum Stübing, Stübing bei Graz 002723
Österreichisches Freimaurermuseum, Rosenau Schloß 002540
Österreichisches Gartenbaumuseum, Wien 002974
Österreichisches Gesellschafts- und Wirtschaftsmuseum, Wien 002975
Österreichisches Getreidemuseum, Stadtmuseum Wels-Burg, Wels . . 002829
Österreichisches Ikonenmuseum, Potzneusiedl 002453
Österreichisches Institut für Photographie und Medienkunst, Wien 052591
Österreichisches Jüdisches Museum, Eisenstadt 001827
Österreichisches Kriminalmuseum, Scharnstein 002644
Österreichisches Kulturzentrum, Wien 052592
Österreichisches Luftfahrtmuseum, Feldkirchen bei Graz 001850
Österreichisches Museum für Volkskunde, Wien 002976
Österreichisches Olympia- und Sportmuseum, Wien 002977
Österreichisches Pfahlbaummuseum und Museum Mondseeland, Mondsee 002336
Österreichisches Schloß und Schlüsselmuseum, Graz 001944
Österreichisches Spiele Museum, Leopoldsdorf im Marchfelde 002232
Österreichisches Sprachinselmuseum, Wien 002978
Österreichisches Straßenbahn- und Lokalbahnbetriebsmuseum, Museumstramway Mariazell-Erlaufsee, Mariazell 002290
Österreichisches Theatermuseum, Wien 002979
Österreichisches Tonbandmuseum, Wien 002980
Österreichisches Wandermuseum, Alpl 001674
Österreichisches Werbemuseum, Wien 002981
Österreichisches Zuckermuseum, Tulln 002761
Östersunds Auktionsverk, Oviken . . 122226
Östgöta Auktionshall, Ljungsbro . . . 122195
Östra Södermanlands Museijärnväg, Mariefred 036469
Oestreich, M., Bruchsal 102272
Oestreicher, Marguerite, New Orleans 117485
Oeteldonks Gemintemuzejum, 's-Hertogenbosch 029737
Ötztaler Freilichtmuseum, Längenfeld 002191
A l'Œuvre, Montpellier 099761
Oeuvre Gravée, Bern 134995
Över Järva Antik, Solna 081898
Oevermann, Dr. Kristine, Frankfurt am Main 102807
Övermark Hembygdsmuseum, Övermark 009921
Övertorneå Hembygdsmuseum, Övertorneå 036534
Oexmann, München 072807
Özden Sanat Galerisi, İstanbul 112342
Özel, Ulusoy, Ankara 112264
Of All Things, Toronto 059249
Ofakim Art Gallery, Tel Aviv 105922
O'Fallon Historical Museum, Baker . 041950
Ofedo, Paris 066346
Ofedo, Paris 066347
Ofen- und Keramikmuseum Velten, Velten 020574
Ofenplattensammlung der Schwäbische Hüttenwerke, Aalen 015431
Oferta, Buenos Aires 136744
Off Beat Antiques, Pittsburgh 091848
Off Broadway Antique Dealers, Oakland 091432
Off Broadway Antiques, Saskatoon . 059101
Off Campus Book Store, Providence 142819
Off-Centre Gallery, Bristol 112727
Off Ramp Antiques, Los Angeles . . . 089858
Off the Beaten Way, New Orleans . . 117486
Off The Rails Collectables, Watsons Bay 056809
Off The Shelf Creations, Katherine . 056034
Off the Wall, Austin 087601
Off the Wall, Ayr 112535
Off the Wall, Denver 088719
Off the Wall, Hemel Hempstead . . . 084650
Off the Wall, Lanark 113347
Off the Wall, Los Angeles 089859
Off the Wall, Minneapolis 117291
Off the Wall, San Francisco 119759
Off the Wall Antiques, Saskatoon . . 059102
Off the Wall Gallery, Houston 116381
Off the Wall Hangings, Salt Lake City 119358
Offa, Knokke-Heist 096349
Offa's Dyke Antique Centre, Knighton 084886
Offay, Anthony d', London 113800
Offbeat Gallery, Wellington 108638
Offelder, Wolfgang, Neuss 073017
Offenbacher Kunstverein e.V, Dreieich 053536
Offeney, Burkhard, München 072808
Offer, Waterman & Co., London . . .085568, 113801, 131125
Offermann, Jens, Hamburg 103204
Offermanns, N., Mannheim 072428
Office Art, Boston 115215
Office Images, London 113802
Office Wide, Tokyo 107090
L'Officina, Roma 128138
Officina '96, Pomáz 134509
Officina del Restauro, Bologna 127170
L'Officina del Restauro, Firenze . . . 127382
Officina del Tempo, Roma 076593
Officinaarte, Magliaso 111714
Officinarte Conservazione e Restauro, Bologna 127171
Offizin Zürich Verlag, Zürich 135094
Oficina dos Anjos, Belo Horizonte . . 096477
Oficina Museu da Universidade Estácio de Sá, Rio de Janeiro 004414
Oficina Paulista Arte, São Paulo . . . 096683
Ofir, Kraków 108967
Ofoten Museum, Narvik 031048
Oftring, Reinhard, Hainburg, Hessen 103057
O'Gallerie, Portland 119023, 123066
O'Gara & Wilson, Chicago 142291
Ogarako Folk Museum, Misawa . . . 026810
Ogawa, Yamato 107137
Ogden, Harrogate 084583
Ogden, Richard, London 085569
Ogden Historical Society Museum, Spencerport 048270
Ogden House, Fairfield 043786
Ogden Union Station Museums, Ogden 046631
Oger & Dumont, Paris 121179
Oggetti del Passato, Modena 075925
L'Oggetto Ritrovato, Milano 075788, 106274, 127641
Oggiano, Paolo, Cagliari 127251
Ogham Gallery, Belfast 112617
Ogier, Jacques, Lyon 064169
Ogle, Portland 119024
Oglethorpe University Museum of Art, Atlanta 041868
O.G.N, Paris 066348
Ogni Moskvy - Muzej Istorii Gorodskogo Osveščenija, Moskva 033511
Ognibeni, Günter, Braunschweig . . . 125379
Ogniwo Polish Museum, Winnipeg . 006855
Ogólnopolskie Targi Antykwaryczne i Sztuki Współczesnej, Krakow 093840
O'Gorman, Lance, North Shore 108526
Ogres Vēstures un Mākslas Muzejs, Ogre 027718
Ogrodowicz, Piotr, Gdynia 129018
Ogunquit Museum of American Art, Ogunquit 046635
Ogura, Tokyo 077289
Ogurek, Lohmar 103935
Ogurek, Ferdinande, Lohmar 072298
O'Hara, Chicago 088136
O'Hara, Arthur P., Chicago 115516
Ohara Bijutsukan, Kurashiki 026701
Ohbayashi, Sendai 107002
Ohgiya, Nagoya 077153
Ohio Book Store, Cincinnati 142322
Ohio Ceramic Center, Roseville 047546
Ohio Estates Coins-Jewelry, Cleveland 088348
Ohio Historical Center, Columbus . . 043109
Ohio Historical Society Museum, Columbus 043109
Ohio Murals, Columbus 115792
Ohio Museums Association, Columbus 054948
Ohio Railway Museum, Worthington 049316
Ohio River Museum, Marietta 045673
Ohio University Art Gallery, Saint Clairsville 047622
Ohio University Department of Arts, Saint Clairsville 052069
Ohk, Manfred, Kaiserslautern 071683
Ohl, L., Schefflenz 073680
Ohl, Leo, Buchholz in der Nordheide 125408
Ohlbrock, Christoph, Gütersloh 071142
Ohlert, Rose Bay 056549
Ohletz, E., Brüggen, Niederrhein . . . 070071
Ohlídal, Vladimír, Luhačovice 098384
Ohme, Peter, München 139533
O.H.M.M. Impex, Bucureşti 080167
Ohno, Bryan, Seattle 119971
The Ohr-O'Keefe Museum of Art, Biloxi 042213
Ohsabanan museijärnväg, Växjö . . . 036771
Ohse, Rolf, Bremen 102254
The Ohsha'joh Museum of Art, Hiroshima 026539
OH+T Gallery, Boston 115216
Ohya-Shobo, Tokyo 077290, 140197
Oi Ling, Hong Kong 059678
Oiffer, Laurent, Paris 066349
Oijens, Marianne, Göteborg 110927
Oikos Antikon Gkeka, Athinai 074602
Oil and Gas Exhibition Centre, Qurm 031353
Oil Capital Rare Coins, Tulsa 093325
Oil Museum of Canada, Oil Springs 006065
Oil On Canvas, Athelstone 055414
Oil Painters of America, Crystal Lake 054949
Oil Painting Picture Gallery, Canning Vale 094366
Oil Pastel Association, Stockholm . . 054950
Oil Pastel Association International, New York 054951
Oil Pastel Society of Maine, Ocean Park 054952
Oil Patch Museum, Russell 047574
Oil Sands Discovery Centre, Fort McMurray 005466

Oinoussian Maritime Museum, Oinoussai 021412
Oise, Nagoya 106929
Oise Collections, Lamorlaye 063503
Oiseau d'Or, Montmirail 064715
L'Oiseau Livre, Paris 138513
Oishi, Fukuoka 106846
Oisin Gallery, Dublin 105881, 134530
Õisu Tehnikumi Muuseum, Halliste 009361
Oita-kenritsu Geijutsu Kaikan, Oita 026938
OJ Art Gallery, New York 118246
OJ Art Gallery, New York 118247
OJ Art Gallery, Philadelphia 118816
Ojai Art Center, Ojai 046638
Ojai Valley Museum, Ojai 046639
Ojala, Los Angeles 116860
Ojāra Vācieša Memoriālais Muzejs, Rīga 027760
Ojeblikket, København 008983
Ojeda, Manuel, La Palmas de Gran Canaria 110712
Ojitos, Miami 090221
Ojo al Arte Galería, Bogotá 098179
O.K Centrum für Gegenwartskunst, Linz 002255, 133115
Oka, Tokyo 107091
Okains Bay Maori and Colonial Museum, Okains Bay 030558
Okaiwa, Barcelona 129374
Okamoto, Kitakyushu 077073
Okanoyama Museum of Art, Nishiwaki 026924
O'Karma Jones, Atlanta 114908
Okaukuejo Museum, Okaukuejo 029089
Okawa, Osaka 077181, 128448
Okawa Bijutsukan, Kiryu 026652
Okaya Sericultural, Equipment and Literature and Silk Museum, Okaya 026939
Okayama-Kenritsu Bijutsukan, Okayama 026942
Okayama-kenritsu Hakubutsukan, Okayama 026943
Okayama-kenritsu Kibiji Local Museum, Soja 027087
Okayama-shiritsu Oriento Bijutsukan, Okayama 026944
Okayama Tenmon Hakubutsukan, Kamogata 026619
OKaz, Rouen 067286
Okazja, Warszawa 109169, 121908
Okefenokee Heritage Center, Waycross 049024
Okeresztény Mauzóleum, Pécs 021824
Okinawa-kenritsu Geijutsu Daigaku, Naha 050467
Okinawa-kenritsu Hakubutsukan, Naha 026888
Okkupasjonsmuseet, Eidsvoll Museum, Eidsvoll 030817
Oklahoma City Museum of Art, Oklahoma City 046649
Oklahoma Firefighters Museum, Oklahoma City 046650
Oklahoma Forest Heritage Center Forestry Museum, Broken Bow 042429
Oklahoma Heritage Book Center, Oklahoma City 142728
Oklahoma Indian Art Gallery, Oklahoma City 118672
Oklahoma Museum of African American Art, Oklahoma City 046651
Oklahoma Museum of Higher Education, Stillwater 048362
Oklahoma Museum of History, Oklahoma City 046652
Oklahoma Museums Association, Oklahoma City 054953
Oklahoma Route 66 Museum, Clinton 043019
Oklahoma Territorial Museum, Guthrie 044374
Okražen Istoričeski Muzej, Chaskovo 004656
Okražen Istoričeski Muzej, Montana 004756
Okražen Istoričeski Muzej, Pernik 004774
Okražen Istoričeski Muzej, Plovdiv 004795
Okražen Istoričeski Muzej, Sliven 004841
Okražen Istoričeski Muzej, Smoljan 004843
Okražen Istoričeski Muzej, Veliko Tărnovo 004939
Okražen Istoričeski Muzej, Vidin 004947
Okražen Istoričeski Muzej, Vraca 004949
Okražen Muzej na Văzraždaneto i Nacionalno-osvoboditelnite Borbi, Plovdiv 004796
Okražna Chudožestvena Galerija, Kardžali 004702
Okražna Chudožestvena Galerija, Stara Zagora 004884
Okražna Chudožestvena Galerija, Vraca 004950
Okražna Chudožestvena Galerija Dimităr Dobrovič, Sliven 004842
Okražna Chudožestvena Galerija Vladimir Dimitrov-Majstora, Kjustendil 004724
Okręgowe Muzeum Techniki Drogowej i Mostowej Okręgu Lubelskiego przy Zarządzie Dróg w Zamościu, Zamość 032554
Okresné Vlastivedné Múzeum, Humenné 034357
Okresní Muzeum, Chrudim 008342
Okresní Muzeum, Blovice 008271
Okresní Muzeum, Děčín 008347
Okresní Muzeum, Hořovice 008383
Okresní Muzeum, Ivančice 008397
Okresni Muzeum, Litoměřice 008480
Okresní Muzeum, Louny 008492
Okresní Muzeum, Pelhřimov 008564
Okresní Muzeum, Tachov 008706
Okresní Muzeum, Vlašim 008757
Okresní Muzeum Praha-východ, Brandýs nad Labem 008274
Okresní Muzeum v Kutné Hoře - Hradek, Kutná Hora 008463
Okresni Vlastivedné Muzeum, Svitavy 008703
Okresni Vlastivědné Muzeum, Nový Jičín 008538
Okresní Vlastivědné Muzeum, Šumperk 008700
Okresní Vlastivědné Muzeum Nový Jičín, Městské Muzeum, Příbor 008656
Okroy, Peter, Hilden 071520
Øksendal, Kristiansand 108697
Øksnes Bygdemuseum, Alsvåg 030721
Oktagon, Köln 134117
Oktibbeha County Heritage Museum, Starkville 048324
Oku Kokokan, Oku 026947
Okukiyotsu Electric Power Museum, Yuzawa 027353
Okupatsioonimuuseum, Kistler-Ritso Fond, Tallinn 009410
Okura, Tokyo 077291
Okura Shukokan Museum, Tokyo 027229
Okutama Kyodo Shiryokan, Okutama 026948
Okvir, Ivanč-Grad 123944
Okvir, Zagreb 123947
Okyo and Rosetsu Art Museum, Kushimoto 026706
Olabarri, Begoña, Bilbao 129441
Olaf-Gulbransson-Museum, Bayerische Staatsgemäldesammlungen, Tegernsee 020414
Olana State Historic Site, Hudson 044662
Olander, Ann, Falun 129837
Olav Bjaaland Museum, Morgedal 031033
Olav Holmegaards Samlinger, Mandal 031008
Olavinlinna Castle, Olavinlinna 009923
Olawa-Olawiński, Bogumił, Łódź 129052
Olbrich, Renate, Krefeld 103783
Olcese, Francesca, Genova 127477
Olck, Erich, Andernach 101582
Olczak, Dorota Ewa, Berlin 125269
Old, John, London 113803
The Old Aberdeen Book Shop, Aberdeen 141379
Old Aircraft Museum, Arnemuiden 029261
Old America, Milano 075789
Old and Curios Booksellers, Auckland 140603
Old and New Antiques, Highbury 055979
Old Armory, Cleveland 088349
Old Art, Roeselare 123669
Old & Art, Warszawa 079775, 109170
Old Arthur, Stockholm 082001
Old Arts Gallery, Pretoria 034723
Old & Asnew Book Traders, South Auckland 140653
Old Atwood House Museum, Chatham 042773
The Old Bakehouse, Chichester 112862
Old Bakehouse Antiques, Broughton Astley 083771
Old Bakehouse Antiques, Parramatta 056441, 123285
The Old Bakehouse Galleries, Edinburgh 113002
The Old Bakery, Woolhampton 087246
Old Bakery Antiques, Brasted 083653
Old Bakery Antiques, Cundletown 055735
The Old Bakery Antiques, Wheathampstead 087124
Old Bakery Antiques, Wymondham 087275
Old Bakery Cottage Book Shop, Warradyte 137129
Old Bakery Gallery, Lane Cove 094725
Old Ball Park, Oklahoma City 091523
Old Bank Antiques, Dungog 055768
Old Bank Antiques, Goomeri 055899
Old Bank Antiques Centre, Bath 083439
Old Bank Artel, McLaren Vale 094753
Old Bank Corner Collectables, Holbrook 056003
The Old Bank Craft Studio, Bewdley 112632
Old Bank Gallery, Pambula 095052
Old Bank House Antiques, Petworth 086254
Old Bank of New Brunswick Museum, Riverside-Albert 006296
Old Barn Antiques, Sutton Bridge 086798
Old Barn Antiques Warehouse, Sutton Bridge 086799
Old Barracks Heritage Centre, Cahersiveen 022699
Old Barracks Museum, Trenton 048606
Old & Beautiful, Genova 075489
The Old Beehive Bookshop, Mansfield 141941
Old Bell Museum, Montgomery 040492
Old Bell's Antiques, Kurrajong 056072
Old Bethpage Village Restoration, Old Bethpage 046660
The Old Blacksmith's Gallery, Dulverton 112961
Old Blue House Antiques, Houston 089169
Old Blythewood, Pinjarra 001380
Old Bogan Central Firefighters Museum, Baton Rouge 042050
Old Bohemia Historical Museum, Warwick 048868
Old Book Shop, Jacksonville 142468
Old Bookshop, Langport 141705
The Old Bookshop, Lisburn 141735
The Old Bookshop, Wolverhampton 142164
Old Borroloola Police Station Museum, Borroloola 000818
Old Bridge 2, Milano 075790
Old Bridge House Museum, Dumfries 039298
Old Brigade, Kingsthorpe 084856
Old Brooklyn Antiques, Cleveland 088350
Old Brown's Mill School, Chambersburg 042702
Old Brush Gallery, Brunkerville 094318
Old Brutus Historical Society Museum, Weedsport 049042
Old Butter Factory Art Gallery, Denmark 094475
Old Button Shop, Lytchett Minster 085888
Old Buttons, New York 091125
The Old Byre Heritage Centre, Dervaig 039233
Old Cable Station Museum, Apollo Bay 000743
Old Cairo, Cairo 060456
Old Canberra Tram Company Museum, Dickson 000984
Old Capitol Museum of Mississippi History, Jackson 044804
Old Carleton County Court House, Woodstock 006883
Old Castle Museum, Baker University, Baldwin City 041958
Old Cathedral Museum, Saint Louis 047675
Old Central School Art Centre, Auckland 108353
Old Channel, Delhi 074806
Old Chapel Antique Centre, Tutbury 086959
Old Chapel Antique Mall, Salt Lake City 092452
Old Charm Antiques, Knokke-Heist 058249
Old Charms, Genk 058163
The Old Children's Book, Edinburgh 141583
Old Children's Books, New Orleans 142621
The Old Church Bookshop, Carlingford 136849
Old Church Galleries, London 085570, 113804, 141857
The Old Cinema Antique Department Store, London 085571
Old City Arts Association, Philadelphia 054954
Old City Park - The Historical Village of Dallas, Dallas 043274
Old Classics, North Perth 056371
Old Clock Museum, Pharr 046916
Old Clock Shop, West Malling 087089
Old Coach House Gallery, Gillingham 113095
Old Codgers Antiques, Ulmarra 056759
Old Colonial, Tunbridge Wells 086945
Old Colonial Bank of Antiques, Mirboo North 056233
Old Colony Historical Museum, Taunton 048507
Old Constitution House, Windsor 049239
Old Conway Homestead Museum and Mary Meeker Cramer Museum, Camden 042575
The Old Cop Shop, Torquay 086901
The Old Corn Store, Stalbridge 114477
Old Corner House, Wittersham 087196
Old Cornstore Antiques, Arundel 083315
The Old Cottage, Hilversum 078538
Old Council Chambers Museum, Cleve 000928
Old Council Chambers Museum, Norton Summit 001343
Old Country, Manawatu 079142
Old Court House Museum, Durban 034602
Old Court House Museum, Guysborough 005559
Old Court House Museum-Eva Whitaker Davis Memorial, Vicksburg 048778
Old Courthouse Gallery, Ipswich 094662
Old Courthouse Heritage Museum, Inverness 044762
Old Courthouse Museum, Santa Ana 047946
Old Courtyard Museum, Kibbutz Ein Shemer 023002
Old Cowtown Museum, Wichita 049160
Old Craft, Warszawa 079776
Old Crofton School Museum, Crofton 005310
Old Crown Court and Shire Hall, Dorchester 039259
Old Cuba Collection, Miami 090222
Old Curiosity Shop, Chennai 074795
The Old Curiosity Shop, Dalkey 074884
Old Curiosity Shop, King's Lynn 084851
Old Curiosity Shop, Málaga 081428
Old Curiosity Shop, Rotterdam 078737
The Old Curiosity Shop, Sidmouth 086617
Old Curiosity Shop, Stockport 086726, 131542
Old Curiosity Shop & Art Galleries, Southampton 114458
Old & Curious, South Auckland 140654
Old Custom House, Penzance 086214
The Old Day's, Dordrecht 078312

Old Days, Kauniainen 060602
Old Depot Museum, Ottawa 046751
Old Dominion Railway Museum, Richmond 047422
Old Dominion University Gallery, Norfolk 046504
Old Door Store, San Antonio 092555
Old Dorchester State Historic Site, Summerville 048423
Old Dubbo Gaol, Dubbo 000995
Old Dutch Antique Shop, Johannesburg 080712
Old Dutch Parsonage, Somerville . . 048219
Old Economy Village Museum, Ambridge 041682
Old Editions Book Shop, Buffalo . . . 142264
Old England, Hilden 071521
Old England Gallery, Torino 076852
Old English Oak, Sandgate 086512
Old English Pine, Sandgate 086513
Old Erie Street Bookstore, Cleveland 142339
Old Exchange and Provost Dungeon, Charleston 042742
Old Falls Village, Menomonee Falls 045776
Old Fashioned Restoration, Toronto 059250, 123836
Old Fashioned Things, Houston . . . 089170
Old Father Antiques, B'Kara 077507
Old Father Time Clock Centre, London 085572
Old Fire Engine House Gallery, Ely . 113017
Old Fire House and Police Museum, Superior 048438
Old Fire Station Gallery, Caboolture 094340
Old Firehouse Museum, Greenville . 044343
Old Flames, Easingwold 084241
Old Flour Mill Gallery, Euroa 094518
The Old Forge Antiques, Stretton-under-Fosse 086781
Old Forge Studio, Pembridge 114221
Old Fort Bissell, Phillipsburg 047001
Old Fort Erie, Niagara Falls 006017
Old Fort Garland, Fort Garland 043916
Old Fort Harrod Museum, Harrodsburg 044452
Old Fort Harrod State Park Mansion Museum, Harrodsburg 044453
Old Fort House Museum, Fort Edward 043914
Old Fort Jackson, Savannah 048027
Old Fort Johnson, Fort Johnson . . . 043926
Old Fort Lauderdale Museum of History, Fort Lauderdale 043935
Old Fort Meade Museum, Fort Meade 043950
Old Fort Niagara, Youngstown 049358
Old Fort Number 4 Associates, Charlestown 042751
Old Fort Western, Augusta 041906
Old Fort William Historical Park, Thunder Bay 006566
Old Fox Antiques, Casino 055642
The Old French Mirror Company, Henley-on-Thames 084664
Old Fresno Auction, Fresno 122898
Old Friends, Portland 091983, 142806
Old Friends Antiques, Seattle 093040
Old Fuel Store Gallery, Wilcannia . . 095396
Old Furniture House, Claremont . . . 055676
Old Gala House, Galashiels 039533
Old Gaol and Courthouse, York 001649
Old Gaol Museum, Albany 000723
Old Gaol Museum, Buckingham . . . 038895
Old Gaol Museum, York 049343
Old George's Authentic Collectibles, Whitewood 006816
Old Gladstone Post Office Antiques, Gladstone 055879
Old Glow Company, Cincinnati 088266
Old & Gold, Durham 084236, 130659
Old Gold Antiques, Croydon 055730
Old Government House, Belair 000790
Old Government House, Fredericton 005486
The Old Governor's Mansion, Frankfort 044035
Old Graine Store, East Rudham . . . 084256
Old Grammar School, Manx National Heritage, Castletown 039018
Old Grammar School Museum, Kingston-upon-Hull 039886
Old Granary Antiques, King's Lynn . 084852
Old Green Cupboard, Jacksonville . 089440
Old Greer County Museum and Hall of Fame, Mangum 045625
The Old Guard Museum, Fort Myer . 043955
Old Guildhall Museum, Looe 040337
Old Haa, Yell 041466
Old Hall Antiques, Burton Salmon . . 083813
Old Hall Bookshop, Brackley 141430
Old Hall Farm, Long Clawson 085825, 131227
Old Harbour Masters Gallery, Porthleven 114279
Old Harbour Museum, Hermanus . . 034634
Old Hastings Bookshop, Hastings . . 141646
Old Hastings Mill Store Museum, Vancouver 006705
Old Hat Antiques, Thornbury 056709
Old Highercombe Museum, Tea Tree Gully 001539
Old Hill Antiques and Auction Rooms, Cradley Heath 122480
Old Home Supply House, Fort Worth 088874
Old House, Hereford 039736
The Old House, Saarburg 073649
Old House, Seaford 086528, 131462
Old House Antique Centre, Adversane 083256
Old House Gallery, Cairo 098658
Old House Gallery, Oakham 086147, 131339, 141977
Old House in Hog Hollow, Saint Louis 092291
Old House Museum, Bakewell 038568
Old House Museum, Durban 034603
Old House of Keys, Manx National Heritage, Castletown 039019
The Old House Revival Company, Winnipeg 059468
Old Hoxie House, Sandwich 047933
Old Imperial, Tampere 060631
Old Inn Gallery, Port Wakefield 095097
Old Iron County Courthouse Museum, Wisconsin State Historical Society, Hurley 044697
The Old Ironmongers Antiques Centre, Lechlade 084920
Old is Beautiful, Calgary 058797
Old Jaffa Gallery, Tel Aviv 105923
The Old Jail Art Center, Albany 041605
Old Jail House & Old Court House, Croydon 000960
Old Jail Museum, Albion 041609
The Old Jail Museum, Crawfordsville 043210
The Old Jail Museum, Warrenton . . 048866
The Old Jameson Distillery, Dublin . 022767
Old Japan, New York 091126
Old Jefferson Town, Oskaloosa . . . 046740
Old-Joy, Helsinki 060565
Old Khan, Cairo 060457
Old Kings Courthouse Museum, Kentville 005681
Old Lancaster Antiques, Fort Worth 088875
Old Library Gallery, Burgh-le-Marsh 112758
Old Lifeboat Museum, Poole 040739
Old Lighthouse Museum, Michigan City 045829
Old Lighthouse Museum, Stonington 048376
Old Lincoln County Courthouse Museum, Lincoln 045316
The Old Lincoln County Jail and Museum, Wiscasset 049267
Old Log Jail and Chapel Museums, Greenfield 044324
Old London, Milano 075791
Old Los Angeles Antiques, Los Angeles 089860
Old Mackinac Pointlightstation, Mackinac Island 045552
Old Magazines, Milwaukee 142570
Old Maitland Mill Antique Centre, Metford 056217
The Old Malthouse, Hungerford . . . 084762
Old Maltings Antique Centre, Louth 085855, 131240
The Old Manor, Heesch 128709
The Old Manse, Concord 043119
Old Map Gallery, Denver 142394
Old Maps and Prints, London 141858
Old Maps & Atlases, Murs 138229
Old Market House, Galena 044116
Old Master Gallery, Toronto 097338
Old Masters Art Shop, Portland 091984
Old Mearns Gallery, Glasgow 113124
Old Meeting House Museum, Barrington 005072
Old Melbourne Gaol and Penal Museum, Melbourne 001247
Old Memories, Toronto 059251
Old Memory, Roma 076594
Old Merchant's House and Row 111 Houses, Great Yarmouth 039635
Old Mike, Düren 070350
Old Mill Antique Centre, Bridgnorth 083671, 130438
Old Mill Museum, Cimarron 042914
Old Mill Museum, El Molino Viejo Museo, San Marino 047913
The Old Mint House, Pevensey 086267
Old Mission Antiques, Albuquerque 087414
Old Mission Santa Ines, Solvang . . . 048213
Old Money Antiques, Sacramento . . 092173
Old Monterey Jail, Monterey 045986
Old Mornington Post Office Museum, Mornington 001286
Old Mother Hubbard's, Biggleswade 083511
Old Museum Arts Centre, Belfast . . 038664
Old Music Shop, Chicago 088137
Old New York Book Shop, Atlanta . . 142207
Old Newcastle Gaol Museum, Toodyay 001554
Old Oak Tree, Minneapolis 090384
Old Oak Tree Antique Mall, Albuquerque 087415, 131747
Old Operating Theatre, Museum and Herb Garret, London's Museums of Health and Medicine, London 040249
Old Ordinary Museum, Hingham . . . 044556
Old Palace Antiques, Lostwithiel . . . 085853
Old Parliament House, Canberra . . . 000890
Old Pine House, Leamington Spa . . 084915
Old Police Station Museum Brookton, Brookton 000852
Old Pontville Shop, Pontville 056469
Old Post House, Axbridge 083355
Old Post Office Antiques, Fitzroy North 055829
Old Post Office Museum, Turriff . . . 041247
Old Post Office Seymour, Seymour . 095190
The Old Post Office Traders, Warkworth 079307
Old Print Gallery, Broadway 112738
Old Print Gallery, Washington 093430, 133030, 143048
Old Print Shop, New York . 091127, 142683
The Old Prison, Victoria 028043
Old Prison Museum, Deer Lodge . . 043366
Old Pueblo Gallery, Tucson 120156
The Old Queenslander Antiques Center, Cairns 055599
Old Railway Station Museum, Northam 001339
Old Reading Room, Kelling 113313
Old Rectory Museum, Loughborough 040343
Old Saint Edward's Anglican Church, Clementsport 005276
Old Saint Ferdinand's Shrine, Florissant 043872
Old Salem, Winston-Salem 049255
Old Sau's Antique Shop, Chicago . . 088138
Old School, London 085573
Old School Antiques, Penryn 086206
Old School Arts Workshop, Middleham 114080
The Old School Gallery, Muker 114099
Old School House, York 049344
Old School House Arts Centre, Qualicum Beach 006213
Old School House Gallery, Cleveland 094405
Old School Museum, Streaky Bay . . 001495
Old School Museum, Merimbula . . . 001256
Old Schoolhouse Museum, Ballintubber 022684
Old Schoolsrooms Antiques, Wincanton 087164, 131692
Old Schwamb Mill, Arlington 041772
Old Science Renovation, Minneapolis 132388
Old Scotland, Roma 076595
Old Seattle Paperworks, Seattle . . . 093041
Old Shanghai, Saint-Étienne 067461
Old Shawnee Town, Shawnee 048134
Old Shoe Box, Leominster 084975
The Old Shop, Dun Laoghaire 074966
Old Smithy, Feniscowles . 084398, 130708
The Old Smithy, West Burton 087083
The Old Smithy Studio, Bethlehem . 112625
Old South Antiques, Saint Louis . . . 092292
Old South Books, Nashville 142602
Old South Meeting House, Boston . 042338
Old South Restoration, San Antonio 132821
Old Spanish Fort and Museum, Pascagoula 046837
Old Speech Room Gallery, London . 040250
Old Springsure Hospital Museum, Springsure 001486
Old State Bank, Vincennes 048790
Old State Capitol, Springfield 048287
Old State House, Boston 042339
Old State House, Hartford 044462
The Old State House Museum, Little Rock 045345
The Old Station, London 085574
The Old Steam Bakery, Redruth . . .086344, 131407
Old Steamer, Turku 060643
Old Steeple, Dundee 039311
Old Stone Fort Museum Complex, Schoharie 048045
The Old Stone House, Washington . 048939
The Old Stone House Museum, Brownington 042479
Old Stone House Museum, Windsor 049236
The Old Stone Jail Museum, Palmyra 046803
Old Stuff, San Francisco 092858
Old Stuff Two, Vancouver 059392
Old Sturbridge Village, Sturbridge . . 048406
Old Style, Milanówek 079679
Old Style, Napoli 076019
The Old Surgery, Clun 112880
Old Tampa Book Company, Tampa . 143025
The Old Tavern Museum, Tuscaloosa 048664
Old Teazle House, Nailsworth 114104
Old Technology Shop, Seattle 093042
Old Templemore, Nannup 056312
Old Ten Chain Sawmill Company, Benaraby 094238
Old Things Shop, Roma 056548
Old Time, Austin 087602
The Old Time, 's-Hertogenbosch . . 078526
Old Time, San Marino 080348
Old-Time New England, Boston . . . 136596
Old Time Wooden Nickel, San Antonio 092556
Old Timer Antique Shop, Hong Kong 059679
Old Timers, Swinford 086817
Old Timers Antiques, Harrisville . . .055955, 123236
Old Timers Traeger Museum, Alice Springs 000738
Old Times, Helsinki 060566
Old Times Antiguidades, Brasília . . 058465
Old Times Antiques, Montréal 058984
The Old Tin Toy Shop, Auckland . . . 078968
Old Tobacco Sheds, Bright 055543
The Old Town, Cairo 060458

Old Town Antique Market, Portland . 091985
Old Town Antiques Centre, Eastbourne 084265
Old Town Bookshop, Edinburgh . . . 141584
Old Town Hall, Hemel Hempstead . . 039725
Old Town Hall Antique Centre, Midhurst 085987
Old Town Hall Antique Centre, Needham Market 086043, 131294
Old Town Hall Antiques, Falmouth . 084378
Old Town Hall Museum, Fifield 043841
Old Town Hall Museum, Margate . . 040424
Old Town Museum, Old Town 046666
Old Town San Diego, San Diego . . . 047828
Old Town Studio Gallery, San Diego 119529
Old Towne Antiques, Memphis 090098
Old Toy Shop, Ringwood 086368
Old Toy Show, Lincoln 040011
Old Toy Soldier, Pittsburgh 136597
Old Trail Museum, Choteau 042909
Old Troon Sporting Antiques, Troon . 086922
The Old Trouts Treasures, Bulls . . . 079001
Old Tythe Barn, Blackheath 055512
Old Valve Radios, South Auckland . 128957
Old Versailles, New York 091128
Old Versailles, New York 091129
Old Victoria Post Office Gallery, Mount Victoria 094915
Old Village Hall Museum, Lindenhurst 045324
Old Ware House Gallery, Maryborough, Queensland 001225
The Old Warehouse Antiques, Chester 083963
The Old Warehouse Gallery, Dorchester 112951
Old Wares, Burra 055589
Old Wares Curiosity Connection, Amphitheatre 055344
Old Washington Museum, Washington 048877
Old West Museum, Sunset 048434
Old West Publishing, Denver 135357
Old West Wax Museum, Thermopolis 048542
Old Westbury Gardens, Old Westbury 046667
Old Westend Antiques, Toledo 093181
Old Westend Antiques, Toledo 093182
Old Westend Antiques, Toledo 132973
Old Westend Antiques, Toledo 132974
Old Wood, Roma 076596, 128139
Old Wooden Pew, Tyabb 056752
Old Woodworks, Edmonton 123764
Old Wool and Grain Store Museum, Beachport 000779
The Old Works, Bramley 083637
Old World, Columbus 131987
Old World Accents, Richmond 092095
Old World Antiques, Minneapolis . . 090385
Old World Antiques, Salt Lake City . 092453
Old World Antiques, Stepney 056633
Old World Auctions, Sedona 123118
Old World Charm, Moe 056241
Old World do Brasil, Belo Horizonte 058440
Old World History, Miami 090223
Old World Mail Auction, Bethesda . . 122814
Old World Market, Detroit 088771
Old World Market Place, Birmingham 087776
Old World Prints, New Orleans 090596
Old World Refinishing, Farmington . 132069
Old World Restoration, Saint Paul . . 132771
Old World Restorations, Cincinnati . 131940
Old World Trading, London 085575
Old World Upholstery, Chicago 131913
Old World Warehouse, Philadelphia 091674
Old World Wisconsin, Eagle 043552
Old Wyche Gallery, Nantwich 114108
Old York Historical Museum, York . . 049345
Old Zhi Display Center, Xing Si Army, Nanchang 007195
Oldani, Hans-Rudolf, Mägenwil . . . 082645
d'Olde Bakkerieje, Deventer 078278
Olde Book Shop, Richmond 142828
Olde Books, Gulgong 136923
Olde Bostonian, Boston . . 087837, 131850
Olde Chicago Antiques, Chicago . . . 088139
Olde Colonial Courthouse, Barnstable 042026
Olde Favorites, Portland 091986
Olde Gallery, Jacksonville 089441
Olde Good Things, New York 091130
Olde Good Things, New York 091131
Olde Music and Cokery Books, Hobart 136945
'T Olde Ras, Doesburg 029489
The Olde Red Lion, Bedingfield . . .083473, 130364
Olde Shanghai Antiques, Singapore 080535
The Olde Shoppe, Windsor, Ontario 059442
Olde Stuff, Carrara 055639
Olde Stuff Antiques, Ashmore 055413
Olde Tyme Antiques, Calgary 058798
Olde Tyme Clock Shoppe, Toronto . 059252
Olde Tyme Clocks, Cincinnati 088267, 131941
Olde World Charm II, Houston 089171
Olden Asia, Beirut 077409
Olden Days, Dobwalls . . . 084171, 130637
Olden Days, Waikato 079294, 121838
Oldenbourg, Christoph W., Bristol . . 130458
Oldenbourg, R., München 134267
Oldenburg, Ulf, Berlin 069716
Oldenburg, Wilfried, Wiesbaden . . . 074417
Oldenburg-Museum, Unna 020538
Oldenburger Antiquariat, Oldenburg, Oldenburg 139631
Oldenburger Fahrradmuseum, Oldenburg, Oldenburg 019472
Oldenburger Kunstverein e.V., Oldenburg, Oldenburg 053537
Oldentime Furniture, Hawkes Bay . 128938
The Oldest House Museum, Key West 044990
Oldest House Museum Complex, Saint Augustine 047609
Oldest Stone House Museum, Lakewood 045131
Oldfield, Portsmouth 086300, 131395
Oldham, Elinor, Albuquerque 114814
Oldham, Thomas A., Sacramento . . 119156
Oldham County History Center, La Grange 045064
Oldies, Norwood 056390
Oldies, Goldies & Moldies, New York 091132
Oldies & Goodies, Pittsburgh 091849
OldieWeb, Ortenberg, Baden 139635
Olding, Manfred, Osnabrück 073245
Oldman River Cultural Centre, Brocket 005157
Oldswinford Gallery, Oldswinford . . 114186
Oldtimer-Galerie, Toffen . . 082857, 122353
Oldtimer-Museum, Arbon 036851
Oldtimer Museum, Groß Raden 017558
Oldtimer Museum, Rheinfelden . . . 037446
Oldtimercentrum Select, Joure 029796
Oldtimermuseum, Ardagger 001695
Oldtimermuseum De Rijke, Oostvoorne 030003
Oldtimermuseum De Ronkel, Kloosterburen 029814
Oldtimermuseum im Schloß, Blindenmarkt 001757
Oldwoods, Bristol 083745, 130459
Dat ole Hus, Aukrug 015627
Ole Moon and Other Tales, Dallas . . 115915
Ole Rømer Museet, Taastrup 009128
Olefanten, København 060363
Olejak, Bernhard, Neufahrn 126533
Olejárová, Mária, Poprad 109921
Oleos, Sara, Getxo 110355
Oleos and More, Miami 117119
Olevimäe Antiik, Tallinn 060485
Ølgod Museum, Ølgod 009057
Oliemolen de Zoeker, Zaandam . . . 030367
Oliemolen Het Pink, Koog aan de Zaan 029819
Oliewenhuis Art Museum, Bloemfontein 034565
Olim, La Varenne-Saint-Hilaire 063467
Olin Art Gallery, Gambier 044137
Olin Fine Arts Center, Washington and Jefferson College, Washington . . 048968
Oliva, Parma 076218
Oliva, Gilda, Paris 066350
Olivares Carayol, Norberto, Barcelona 080896
Olive Abella, Cristina, Barcelona . . . 129375
Olive Avenue Antiques, Fresno 088914
Olive DeLuce Art Gallery, Northwest Missouri State University, Maryville 045718
Olive Hyde Art Gallery, Fremont . . . 044075
Olive Schreiner House, National English Literary Museum, Cradock 034594
Oliveira, Braga 079812
Oliveira, Emídio Moreira, Porto 129195
Oliveira, João Esteves, Lisboa 109340
Oliveira, Joaquim Pereira, Porto . . . 129196
Oliveira, Pedro, Porto 109392
Oliveira, Rui Quintela, Lisboa 079983
Oliveira, Rui, Lisboa 079984
Oliver Bros., Boston 115217
Oliver, Claire, New York 118248
Oliver, Gerald, Haverfordwest 084626
Oliver, J., Minneapolis 090386
Oliver, Lyon, Oaksey 086151
Oliver, Patrick, Cheltenham 083925
Oliver Contemporary, London 113805
Oliver Cromwell's House, Ely 039442
Oliver House Museum, Penn Yan . . 046871
Oliver House Museum, Saint Martinville 047686
Oliver Kelley Farm, Elk River 043659
Oliver-Maneu, Joan, Palma de Mallorca 110695
Oliver Tucker Historic Museum, Beverly 042189
Oliveria, Lizabeth, Oakland 118639
Oliveria, Lizabeth, Oakland 118640
Olivers, Sudbury, Suffolk 122716
Olivers Antique, Kerava 060604
Olivers Bookshop, Whitley Bay 142154
Oliver's Collections, Auckland 078969
Olive's Oddments, Hamilton 058860
Olivier, Pierre, Annot 060908
Les Oliviers, Saint-Vincent-de-Tyrosse 068037
Oliwska, Gdańsk 108893
Olkijoen Rauhanpirtti, Pattijoki 009956
Olla Podrida, Minneapolis 090387
Olle Möbel, Duisburg 070485
Olle Olsson-Huset, Solna 036602
Ollier, Jacques, Paris 100740
Ollivary-Gauthier, Paris 066351
Olmes, Cincinnati 115647
Olmos, Gaspar, Murcia 081445
Olms, Georg, Hildesheim 134061
Olmstead Place State Park, Ellensburg 043672
Olmsted County Historical Society Museum, Rochester 047474
Olofsfors Bruksmuseum, Nordmaling 036497
Olofsson, Claes, Uppsala 141188
Oloneckaja Kartinnaja Galereja, Muzej izobrazitelnych iskusstv Respubliki Karelija, Olonec 033596
Oloneckij Nacionalnyj Muzej Karelov-Livvikov im. N.T.Prilukin, Olonec . 033597
Olorgesailie Prehistoric Site Museum, Olorgesailie 027432
O'Loughlin, Timaru 079272
Olschki, Leo S., Firenze 134587
Olsen, Bundaberg 055583
Olsen, Lucie, Montréal 058985
Olsen, Tim, Paddington 095037
Olson, Minneapolis 132389
Olsson, G.N., Kuwongbah 123251
Olsson, Gunnar, Stockholm 111067
Olsson & Uddenberg, Göteborg 110928
Olthuysen, Henk, Huijbergen 128730
Oltmanns, Teo, Unkel 105097, 134438
Oltre il Giardino, Milano 075792
Oltre L'Immagine, Milano 127642
Oltremare, Genova 106101
Oltznauer, Jan, München 126426
Olustee Battlefield, Olustee 046669
Olustvere Muuseum, Olustvere 009382
Oly-Galerie, Gelnhausen 102925
Olympia, Kraków 108968
Olympia Fine Art and Antiques Spring Fair, London 093944
Olympia Fine Art and Antiques Summer Fair, London 093945
Olympia Fine Art and Antiques Winter Fair, London 093946
Olympic Antique, Los Angeles 089861
Olympic Gallery, Southampton 086651
Olympic Hall of Fame and Museum, Calgary 005197
Olympic Museum, Wellington 030647
Olympic Upholsterers, Vancouver . . 123854
Olympus Cove Antiques, Salt Lake City 092454
Om Art Gallery, Ahmedabad 105598
Om El Hana, Cairo 060459
Om El Saad, Cairo 060460
Om igen - 1900-tal, Stockholm 082002
Oma-Freese-Huus, Dornum 016756
Omachi Alpine Museum, Omachi . . 026949
Omaha Antique Company, Omaha .091580, 132596
Omaha Auction Center, Omaha 123036
Omaha Center for Contemporary Art, Omaha 046682
Omaha Children's Museum, Omaha 046683
Omaha Clay Works, Omaha 118717
Omaha Furniture Clinic, Omaha . . . 132597
Omaha Gallery, Omaha 108531
O'Mahony, Diana, Cork 074880
O'Malley, C.H., Baltimore 087699
Oman, James & Angela, Dublin . . . 074939
Oman Museum, Muscat 031348
Oman Natural History Museum, Muscat 031349
Omani-French Museum Bait Fransa, Muscat 031350
Omani Heritage Gallery, Al-Qurum . 079512
Omar, Cairo 098659
Omar, Knaresborough . . . 084883, 130857
Omaruru Museum, Omaruru 029090
Oma's Schatzkästchen, Bamberg . . 069461
Oma's Schatzkammer, Bad Homburg v.d.Höhe 069296
Oma's Vitrine, Mödling 057186
Ombalantu Baobab Tree, Ombalantu 029091
Ombersley Gallery, Ombersley 114190
A L'Ombre du Clocher, La Colle-sur-Loup 063343
Ombre & Lumière, Toulon (Var) 101324
Ombres & Lumières, Paris 066352
Ombretta, Gardella, Genova 075490
Ome-shiritsu Bijutsukan, Ome 026951
Ome-shiritsu Hakubutsukan, Ome . 026952
Omega, Newport, Essex . . 086076, 131310
Omega, Warszawa 140794
Omega Art Expo, New York 118249
Omell, Ascot 083320, 130310
Omell 5060 N.R., London 113806
Omell Galleries, Ascot 112522
O'Melveny, Don, West Hollywood . . 120404
Omi Natural History Museum, Omi . 026953
Omi Shrine Clock Museum, Otsu . . 026998
Het Ommelander Antiquariaat, Appingedam 140354
Omni Art, Dallas 115916
Omni Chinatown, Singapore 080536
Omni Gallery, Portland 119025
Omni-Trading, Apeldoorn 078040
Omni View, Chicago 115517
Omnia, Sappemeer 078759, 121804
Omniart, Aham 133715
Omniguard Art Guarantee, New York 118250
Omniphil Prints, Chesham 083942, 141508

Omnisphere and Science Center, Wichita . . . 049161
Omodei, Mariella, Brescia . . . 127228
Omoide Museum, Kyoto . . . 026760
Omroepmuseum en Smalfilmmuseum, Hilversum . . . 029749
Omskij Gosudarstvennyj Istoriko-kraevedčeskij Muzej, Omsk . . . 033600
Omskij Gosudarstvennyj Literaturnyj Muzej im. F.M. Dostoevskogo, Omsk . . . 033601
Omskij Oblastnoj Muzej Izobrazitelnych Iskusstv im. M.A. Vrubelja, Omsk . 033602
Omuletz, Wilma, Eisenstadt . . . 056970
On a Shoestring, Birmingham . . . 087777
On Aura Tout Vu, Paris . . . 100741
On Canvass, Sydney . . . 095300
On Deck, Oklahoma City . . . 091524
On-Line Gallery, Southampton . . . 114459
On Paper, Providence . . . 119083
On Porpoise, San Diego . . . 119530
On Sight, Toronto . . . 097339
On the Air, Hawarden . . . 084627, 130775
On the Avenue, Buffalo . . . 087900
On the Avenue, Buffalo . . . 087901
On the Hill Cultural Arts Center, Yorktown . . . 049352
On the Nile, Chicago . . . 115518
On the Plaza Gallery, San Antonio . . 119437
On the Shelf, Wagga Wagga . . . 137127
On the Wild Side, Minneapolis . . . 117292
On Yedinci Yüzyıl Osmalı Evi, Bursa 038036
Onas, Bolzano . . . 075131
Once Again, Wellington . . . 079337
Once Read Books, Long Beach . . . 142484
Once Upon A Child, Canal Winchester . . . 142269
Once Upon A Crime, Minneapolis . . 142587
Once Upon a Time, Auckland . . . 078970
Once upon a Time, Miami . . . 090224
Once upon a Time, New York . . . 091133
Onckelinx, H., Bruxelles . . . 137456
Onda, Portland . . . 119026
Ondar-Bide, Donostia-San Sebastián . . . 081089
Onde, Danielle, L'Isle-sur-la-Sorgue 063951
Onder de Sint Maarten, Zaltbommel 140575
Ondergronds Museum, Kanne . . . 003549
't Onderhuys, Nieuw Beijerland . . . 128782
Onderska, Bogumiła, Poznań . . . 079695
Onderstepoort Veterinary History Museum, Onderstepoort . . . 034688
Onderwijskundig, Hilversum . . . 140462
Onderwijsmuseum Educatorium, Ootmarsum . . . 030006
One Bell, Lavenham . . . 084910
The One Below Gallery, London . . . 113807
One Club for Art and Copy, New York . . . 054955
One Eye Gallery, Wellington . . . 079338
One-Forty-Eight Shop, Hamilton . . . 058861
One Home, Denver . . . 088720
One of a Kind Antiuqes, San Diego . 092666
One Price Store, Singapore . . . 080537
One Step Back, Bungay . . . 083782
One Stop Antiques, Clayfield . . . 055688
One Stroke, San Jose . . . 119859
One To Z, Rotterdam . . . 108201
One Tree Two Bears Tradeing Post, Long Beach . . . 089645
One Twenty Eight, New York . . . 118251
One West Art Center, Fort Collins . . 043905
One18, Edinburgh . . . 113003
Oneida Community Mansion House, Oneida . . . 046688
Oneida County Historical Society Museum, Utica . . . 048720
Oneida Nation Museum, De Pere . . 043335
O'Neil, R.A., Toronto . . . 059253
O'Neill, Tam, Denver . . . 088721
Onesti, Olivia, Reims . . . 067075
Oneten, Houston . . . 116382
Oneto, Roberto, Genova . . . 127478
Ongakudori, Yokohama . . . 107149
Ongaonga Old School Museum, Ongaonga . . . 030559
Ongerup and Needilup District Museum, Ongerup . . . 001355
Onggi Folk Museum and Institute, Seoul . . . 027590
ONI Gallery, Boston . . . 115218
Onice, Madrid . . . 110585
Onichimiuk, Halina, Amiens . . . 060824, 124070
Oniris, Rennes (Ille-et-Vilaine) . . . 101086
Oniśko, Jan, Warszawa . . . 109171
Onken, Peter, Hiddenhausen . . . 121454
Onkodo, Tokyo . . . 077292
Online Exhibits, Earl Shilton . . . 112974
Only Collectables, Saint Paul . . . 092384
The Only Place for Pictures, London 113808
Onnen, Ewald, Bamberg . . . 125133
Ono, Nagoya . . . 106930
Ono, Tokyo . . . 107092
Ono Deco, Wien . . . 057512
Onomato Kunstverein, Düsseldorf . . 053538, 133894
Onomichi Shiritsu Bijutsukan, Onomichi . . . 026957
Onondaga Historical Association Museum, Syracuse . . . 048459
Oñoro Ortiz, Madrid . . . 129651
Oñoro-Ortiz 1890, Madrid . . . 129652
Onrust, Amsterdam . . . 107778
Ons Museum, Giessenburg . . . 029606
Ons Museum, Wintelre . . . 030340
Ons Winkeltje, Hilversum . . . 078539
Onset Contemporary Art, Chester . . 112852
Onslow, Stourpaine . . . 122712
Onslow Antiques, Shenton Park . . . 056587
Onslow County Museum, Richlands 047395
Onslow Goods Shed Museum, Onslow . . . 001356
Ontario Agricultural Museum, Milton . . . 005874
Ontario Association of Art Galleries, Toronto . . . 052761
Ontario College of Art & Design, Toronto . . . 049820
Ontario County Historical Society Museum, Canandaigua . . . 042594
Ontario Craft, Toronto . . . 135641
Ontario Museum Association, Toronto . . . 052762
Ontario Police College Museum, Aylmer . . . 005050
Ontario Science Centre, Toronto . . . 006620
Ontario Workers Arts and Heritage Centre, Hamilton . . . 005597
De Ontdekhoek Kindermuseum, Rotterdam . . . 030099
Ontem & Hoje, Rio de Janeiro . . . 058629
Ontmoetingscentrum de Veldkei, Expositie, Havelte . . . 029683
Ontonagon County Historical Society Museum, Ontonagon . . . 046698
Onufri Iconographic Museum, Bérat 000013
Onview, New York . . . 118252
Onyang Minsok Pakmulgwan, Asan 027450
Onyx Images, Indianapolis . . . 116483
Le Onze, Paris . . . 066353
Oola Boola Antiques, London . . . 085576
Oomes, P., Hilversum . . . 128720
Oonagh Black, Stow-on-the-Wold . 086756
Oorlogs- en Verzetsmuseum Johannes Post, Ridderkerk . . . 030059
Oorlogsmuseum, Bloemfontein . . . 034566
Oorlogsmuseum Bezinning 1940-1945, Borculo . . . 029329
Oorlogsverzetsmuseum Rotterdam, Rotterdam . . . 030100
Oost-Indisch Huis, Amsterdam . . . 029218
Oost Leeshal, Amsterdam . . . 140326
Oostends Historisch Museum De Plate, Oostende . . . 003688
Oosterkade Kunstonderneming, Groningen . . . 108042
Oosterlaar, Johan, Luttenberg . . . 128757
De Oosterport, Siegerswoude . . . 140530
Het Oosters Antiquarium, Leiden . . 140481
De Oostindische Compagnie, Gent . 058198
Oostplein Antiek, Rotterdam . . . 078738
Op de Beeck, J., Mechelen . . . 096388
Op de Muuren, Schalkhaar . . . 053900
Op den Berghe, Deventer . . . 078279
OPA Graphics, New Orleans . . . 117487
Opal and Gem Museum, Ballina . . . 000767
Opalescences, Saint-Ouen . . . 067857
L'Opaline, Perros-Guirec . . . 066769
Opaline, Tarbes . . . 068364
Opaline Rose, Teheran . . . 074845
Opatska Riznica Sv. Marka, Korčula 007742
Opbouw, Amsterdam . . . 140327
Opbouw, Rotterdam . . . 140523
Općinski Muzej, Mali Lošinj . . . 007757
OPD Restauro, Rivista dell'Opificio delle Pietre Dure e Laboratori di Restauro di Firenze, Firenze . . . 135939
Opelousas Museum, Opelousas . . . 046699
Opelousas Museum of Art, Opelousas . . . 046700
Open, Piazza del Galdo . . . 135940
Open-Air Water-Power Museum, Dimitsana . . . 021248
Open-Art-Gallery, München . . . 104278
Open Art Gallery, Zürich . . . 112156
Open Atelier, Leiden . . . 078576
Open Atelier, Zürich . . . 112157
The Open Book, Wellington . . . 140678
Open Books, Seattle . . . 143003
Open Door Studio, Los Angeles . . . 089862
The Open Eye Gallery, Edinburgh . . 084307
The Open Eye Gallery, Edinburgh . . 113004
The Open Eye Gallery, Edinburgh . . 130680
Open Eye Photography Gallery, Liverpool . . . 040036
Open Haven Museum, Amsterdam . 029219
Open Hunt, New York . . . 091134
Open Museum, Migdal-Tefen . . . 023032
Open Museum, Omer . . . 023041
Open Press, Denver . . . 135358
Open Space Gallery, Victoria . . . 006747
Open Studio, Toronto . . . 097340
Openbaar Vervoer Museum, Borculo 029330
Openbaar Vervoer Museum, Rotterdam . . . 030101
Opening Night Gallery, Minneapolis 117293
Maritiem Buitenmuseum; Openlucht Binnenvaartmuseum, Rotterdam . 030079
Openlucht Laagveenderij Museum Damshûs, Nij Beets . . . 029956
Openluchtmuseum De Duinhuisjes, Rockanje . . . 030067
Openluchtmuseum Ellert en Brammert, Schoonoord . . . 030144
Openluchtmuseum Erve Kots, Lievelde . . . 029870
Openluchtmuseum Het Hoogeland, Warffum . . . 030306
Openluchtmuseum Nieuw Amsterdam, Nieuw Amsterdam . . . 036159
Openluchtmuseum Ootmarsum, Ootmarsum . . . 030007
Openluchtmuseum voor Beeldhouwkunst Middelheim, Antwerpen . . . 003182
Opera Galeria, Warszawa . . . 109172
Opera Gallery, Ha Noi . . . 120477
Opera Gallery, New York . . . 118253
Opéra Gallery, Paris . . . 100742
Opera Gallery, Singapore . . . 109846
Operadora Claveles, Cancún . . . 128499
Opferkuch, Rolf, Stuttgart . . . 074000
Ophelia's Art Gallery, Birmingham . 115122
Ophey, Norbert, Geldern . . . 070950
Opie's Museum of Memories, Wigan . . . 041385
Opifex et Artifex, Milano . . . 127643
Opificio delle Arti Tessili, Milano . . . 075793
Opitz, Greiz . . . 071091
Opitz, J., Greiz . . . 071092
Opitz & Geschw., Manfred, Greiz . . 071093
Opitz, Rudolf, Gars am Kamp . . . 056987
Opium, Ajaccio . . . 060740
Opium, Warszawa . . . 079777
Oplenova Hiša, Gorenjski Muzej Kranj, Srednja Vas v Bohinju . . . 034527
Het Oplettende Lezertje, Bredevoort 140372
De Oplichterij, Rotterdam . . . 108202
O'Plus, Anglet . . . 060872
Opolski Rocznik Muzealny, Opole . . 136032
Opotiki Museum, Opotiki . . . 030560
Oppdal Bygdemuseum, Oppdal . . . 031059
Oppenberg, Bärbel, Dinslaken . . . 102378
Oppenheimer, Kenyon, Chicago . . . 088140, 131914, 135348, 142292
Oppenheimers Konsthall, Eldsberga 036248
Opper, Uwe, Kronberg im Taunus . . 103796
Oppitz, Karin Eleonore, Wels . . . 095781
Opposite, Paris . . . 066354
Opravy Starožitnosti, Svitavy . . . 060194, 124007
Oprecht, Dr., Zürich . . . 141353
Oprechte Veiling Haarlem, Haarlem 121792
Oprescu, Ion, Timişoara . . . 129233
Opsmuk, Amsterdam . . . 077925
De Opsteker, Amsterdam . . . 107779
Opštinski Muzej, Sremska Mitrovica 034267
Opti Art Galerie, Boppard . . . 102200
Optica, Montréal . . . 097061
Optima Gestion, Madrid . . . 129653
Optimum Fine Arts, Hornchurch . . . 113275
Option Art, Oostende . . . 058363
Options Gallery, New York . . . 118254
Optisches Museum, Carl Zeiss Ausstellungszentrum, Oberkochen 019394
Optisches Museum der Ernst-Abbe-Stiftung Jena, Jena . . . 018110
Opulent Era Gallery IV, Miami . . . 090225
Opus, Lefkosia . . . 098303
Opus, Wrocław . . . 109228
Opus 21, Paris . . . 066355
Opus 39 Gallery, Lemesos . . . 098317
Opus 391, Amsterdam . . . 140328
Opus 40 and the Quarryman's Museum, Saugerties . . . 048011
Opus 57, Charlottenlund . . . 060220
Opus Gallery, Ashbourne . . . 112525
Opus II, Kitchener . . . 096934
Opus One Gallery, Atlanta . . . 114909
Opus Restauri, Parma . . . 127859
Opus Zwei, Sankt Gallen . . . 082785
Opuscula Pompeiana, Roma . . . 135941
Oquendo, Madrid . . . 081354
D'Or Antiquitäten, Hamburg . . . 071303
Or & Bleu, Rouen . . . 067287, 124882
L'Or du Temps, Amiens . . . 138012
L'Or du Temps, Paris . . . 066356
L'Or du Temps, Paris . . . 066357
L'Or en Décor, Paris . . . 124764
Or et Change, Bayonne . . . 061236
Or et Change Comptoir des Minerais Précieux, Tarbes . . . 068365
Or et Monnaies Bordeaux, Bordeaux 061640
L'Or Limousin, Limoges . . . 063894
L'Or Verre, Paris . . . 066358
Oracle Junction, Buffalo . . . 142265
Orage, Barbizon . . . 098923
Al-Oraifi, Manama . . . 057641, 096020
Oran, Dresden . . . 102455
Orana Googars CDEP, Dubbo . . . 055763
Orandajin, 's-Hertogenbosch . . . 078527
Orang Asli Museum, Melaka . . . 028004
Orange, Los Angeles . . . 089863
Orange Collectable Auctions, Hamilton, Queensland . . . 120589
Orange County Historical Museum, Hillsborough . . . 044550
Orange County Museum of Art, Newport Beach . . . 046468
Orange County Regional History Center, Orlando . . . 046718
Orange Empire Railway Museum, Perris . . . 046884
Orange Group, New York . . . 091135
Orange Regional Gallery, Orange . . 001358
Orange Street Gallery, Uppingham . 114629
Orange Tree Antiques, Jacksonville 089442
Orangedale Railway Museum, Orangedale . . . 006073
De Orangerie, Delft . . . 078147
Orangerie, 's-Hertogenbosch . . . 029738

Orangerie, Kunstsammlung Gera, Gera 017373
Orangerie Benrath, Düsseldorf 016843
Orangerie Draenert, Immenstaad . . 103426
Orangerie im Englischen Garten, München 019098
Orangerie-Reinz, Köln 103690
Orangerie und Schloßpark Belvedere, Stiftung Weimarer Klassik und Kunstsammlungen, Weimar, Thüringen 020750
Orangeriet Antik Trädgårdskonst, Lund 081856
Orangetown Historical Museum, Pearl River 046854
Oranien-Nassau-Museum Oranienstein, Diez 016709
Oranje Museum, Baarn 029289
Oranmore Antiques, Dallas 088583
Orasis, Paphos 098322
Oravská Galéria, Dolný Kubín 034349
Oravská Galéria, Námestovo 034396
Oravské Múzeum Pavla Országha Hviezdoslava, Dolný Kubín 034350
Orawski Park Etnograficzny, Zubrzyca Górna 032566
Orbel Art, Sofia 096743
Orbetello, Los Angeles 116861
Orbicon, Cáceres 129472
Orbital Arts, Toronto 097341
Orblin, Ivan, Reims 067076
Orbost Gallery, Dunvegan 112972
Orcas Island Historical Museum, Eastsound 043592
Orcel, Jean-Paul, Vouvray 069034
Orchard Gallery, Londonderry 040329
Orchard Gallery, Singapore 109847
Orchard House - Home of the Alcotts, Concord 043120
Orchard Park Historical Society Museum, Orchard Park 046709
Orchid Art Gallery, Dallas 115917
Orchid Pavilion Art Gallery, Singapore 109848
Orci, Bucaramanga 098224
Ordemann, D., Schwalmstadt 104858
Orden und Militaria, Hamburg 071304
Ordenmuseum, Neuffen 019236
Ordensmuseum Abtei Kamp, Kamp-Lintfort 018147
Die Ordenssammlung - Historia Antiquariat, Berlin 138830
Order of Saint John Museum, Christchurch 030466
Ordinariat für Kunstgeschichte, Akademie der bildenden Künste, Wien 049665
Ordronneau, Yolande, Allouis 060783
Ordrupgaard, Charlottenlund 008829
Ordsall Hall Museum, Salford 040943
Ordu Devlet Güzel Sanatlar Galerisi, Ordu 038160
Ore-Petrographic Museum, Institute of Geology of Ore Deposits, Petrography, Mineralogy and Geochemistry of RAS, Moskva 033512
Les Oréades, Bagnères-de-Luchon 098907
Les Oréades, Bagnères-de-Luchon 098908
Les Oréades, Moskva 109575
Les Oréades, Paris 100743
Orebić Maritime Museum, Orebić . . 007768
Øregaard-Museum, Hellerup 008894
O'Regan, Donal, Cork 074881
O'Regan's, Cork 121658
Oregon Air and Space Museum, Eugene 043748
Oregon Coast History Center, Newport 046454
Oregon College of Arts and Crafts, Portland 051979
Oregon Electric Railway Historical Society Museum, Lake Oswego 045112
Oregon Gallery, Portland 119027
Oregon History Center, Portland . . . 047174
Oregon-Jerusalem Historical Museum, Oregon 046710
Oregon Military Museum, Clackamas 042935
Oregon Museum of Science and Industry, Portland 047175
Oregon Museums Association, Portland 054956
Oregon Scenics, Portland 119028
Oregon Sports Hall of Fame and Museum, Portland 047176
Oregon Trail Museum, Gering 044179
Oregon Trail Museum Association, Gering 054957
Oregon Trail Regional Museum, Baker City 041953
O'Reilly, Dublin 121666
O'Reilly & Son, Dublin 127099
O'Reilly & Co., William, New York . . 118255
Orel, Michael, Koblenz 103572
Orell Füssli, Zürich 141354
Orelya, Paris 066359
Orenburgskij Oblastnoj Kraevedčeskij Muzej, Orenburg 033615
Orenburgskij Oblastnoj Muzej Izobrazitelnych Iskusstv, Orenburg 033616
Orense Esculturas, Rio de Janeiro . 123708
Orep, Roma 128140
Orez, Den Haag 107944, 134806
Orfèo, Luxembourg 107408
Orfèvrerie, Evellin, Rennes (Ille-et-Vilaine) 124875
Organ Historical Trust of Australia, Camberwell 000879
Organisation Internationale des Experts, Paris 052964
Organizacion Bienal de Arte Contemporaneo, Sevilla 054120
Organization of Independent Artists, New York 054958
Organization of Military Museums of Canada, Gloucester 052763
Organization of Museums, Monuments and Sites of Africa OMMSA, Accra . . . 053660
Orgel-Art-Museum Rhein-Nahe, Windesheim 020909
Orgelbaumuseum, Ostheim vor der Rhön 019514
Orgelmuseet i Fläckebo, Salbohed . 036558
Orgelmuseum Altes Schloß, Valley . 020557
Orgelmuseum Borgentreich, Borgentreich 016343
Orgelmuseum Kelheim, Kelheim . . . 018222
Oriamu Museum, Izumiotsu 026594
Oriande, Bruxelles 058044
Oricchio, Fausto, Roma 076597
Oricha, Los Angeles 116862
Oriel, Dublin 105882
Oriel, Trefin 114598
Oriel Davies Gallery, Newtown, Powys 040582
Oriel Gallery, Ascot 094178
Oriel Gallery, Mold 040485
Oriel Gallery, Picton 108543
Oriel Glanymor Gallery, Fishguard . . 113067
Oriel Mostyn Gallery, Llandudno . . . 040052
Oriel Newydd, Llanerchymedd 113416
Oriel Plas, Llanbedrog 113412
Oriel Ynys Môn, Llangefni 040060
Orient Antique, Paris 066360
Orient Antiques, Bruxelles 058045
D'Orient et d'Ailleurs, Paris 100744
Orient Express, Cairo 060461
Orient Express, Cairo 098660
The Orient Express, Richmond, Victoria 056528
Orient Expressed Imports, New Orleans 090597
Orient House, Glebe 055882
Orient Lights, Holm-Seppensen . . . 071568
Orient Longman, Hyderabad 134516
Orient-Occident, Paris 066361
Orient-Teppich, Sankt-Peterburg . . 080318
Oriental Antique, Dallas 088584
Oriental Antique Gallery, Armadale, Victoria 055389
Oriental Antique House, Singapore . 080538
Oriental Antique Restorers, New York 132509
Oriental Antiques, Abu Dhabi 083176
Oriental Antiques Center, Dubai . . . 083197
Oriental Art, Amsterdam 077926
Oriental Art, Cairo 098661
Oriental Art Collections, New York . 118256
Oriental Art Gallery, San Francisco . 119760
Oriental Arts, Chennai 074796
Oriental Arts, Saint Louis 119233
Oriental Arts Gallery, Hong Kong . . . 059680
Oriental Artworks, Southend-on-Sea 114461
Oriental Bazaar, Tokyo 077293
Oriental Bronzes, Paris 066362
Oriental Cabinet, Hong Kong 059681
Oriental Ceramic Society, London . . 054462
The Oriental Collection, Ottawa . . . 059047
Oriental Danny, Dallas 088585
Oriental Danny, Dallas 088586
Oriental Decorations, New York . . . 091136
Oriental Furniture and Arts, London 085577, 131126
Oriental Furniture Repair, San Diego 132853
Oriental Gallery, Moreton-in-Marsh 086020
Oriental Gallery, Vancouver 059393
Oriental Handicrafts Exhibition, Manama 057642
The Oriental Haveli, Bangalore 074778
Oriental Heritage, Los Angeles 089864
Oriental House, Riyadh 080379
Oriental Imports, Oklahoma City . . . 091525
Oriental Institute Museum, University of Chicago, Chicago 042871
Oriental Interiors, Vancouver 059394
Oriental Museum, Durham 039337
Oriental Museum for Carpets, Riyadh 034127
Oriental Rug Gallery, Eton 084346
Oriental Rug Gallery, Guildford 084541
Oriental Rug Gallery, Oxford 086183
Oriental Rug Gallery, Sacramento . . 092174
Oriental Rug Gallery, Saint Albans . 086441
Oriental Rug House and Custom Furniture Center, Jacksonville . . . 089443, 132192
Oriental Rug Shop, Sheffield 086562
Oriental Rug Treasures, Long Beach 089646
Oriental Shop, Nashville 090472
Oriental Treasure Box, San Diego . . 092667
Oriental Treasures, Dallas 088587
Oriental Treasures, Singapore 080539
Orientalia Christiana Antiquariat, Bochum 138885
The Orientalia Journal, Little Neck . 136598
Orientalisches Münzkabinett Jena, Institut für Sprachen und Kulturen des Vorderen Orients, Friedrich-Schiller-Universität Jena, Jena 018111
Orientalist, London 085578
Orientalist, London 085579
Orientalist, London 131127
Orientalist, London 131128
l'Orientaliste, Marrakech 077685
L'Orientaliste, Thônex 082849
Orientalna, Warszawa 109173
Orientation, London 085580
Orientations, Hong Kong 135652
Orientations, San Francisco 092859
Orientique, Hong Kong 059682
Orientteppich-Museum, Hannover . 017767
Origami, Paris 100745
Origen, Budapest 074699
Origena, Milano 106275
Origin, Dublin 105883
The Original Aboriginal Art Company, Narangba 056314
Original Architectural Salvage, Dublin 074940
Original Art, Indianapolis 116484
Original Art Galleries, Subiaco 095234
The Original Art Report, Rockford . . 136599
The Original Art Shop, Colchester . . 112890
The Original Art Shop, Manchester . 114048
Original Art Shop, Stoke-on-Trent . . 114493
The Original Art Shop, Truro 114606
The Original Art Shop, Truro 131613
Original & Authentic Aboriginal Art, Melbourne 056197
Original & Authentic Aboriginal Art, Sydney 056686
Original Baltimore Antique Arms Show, Timonium 094019
Original Design, Colmar 062415
Original-Dorfschmiede Ehlen, Habichtswald 017613
The Original Dreamtime Art Gallery, Alice Springs 094143
The Original Dreamtime Art Gallery, Cairns 055600
Original Gallery, Hong Kong 097818
Original Gallery, Nice 099851
Original Garo, Sapporo 077199
Original Miami Beach Antique Show, Miami Beach 094020
Original Oz Art Gallery, Mount Martha 094909
Original Print Gallery, Dublin 105884
Original- und Abgußsammlung der Universität Trier, Trier 020482
The Original Wall Art, Langley 113351
Originality, Totnes 114592
Originals, Bridgnorth 112703
Original's in Glass, Tampa 132959
Origine, Beauvais 061313
Origine - Het Veilingtijdschrift, Haarlem 136005
Origines, Houdon 063178, 138107
Origins, Oostende 058364
Orillia Museum of Art and History, Orillia 006074
Orima, Stockholm 082003
Orimattilan Kotiseutumuseo, Orimattila 009926
Orimattilan Taidemuseo, Orimattila . 009927
Orinasukan, Kyoto 026761
Oriol, Barcelona 080897, 110230
Orion, Miami 090226
Orion Antique, Dallas 088588
Orion Antique, Oklahoma City 091526
Orion Art Gallery, Bruxelles 096240
Orion Book Store, Toronto 137714
Orion Editions, New York 135447
Orion Press, Tokyo 134730, 140198
The Orion Publishing Group, London 135245
Oriot, Jean-Marcel, Bagnoles-de-l'Orne 061169
Oripään Museo, Oripää 009929
Oriskany Battlefield, Oriskany 046714
Orissa, Milano 075794
Orissa State Museum, Bhubaneshwar 022039
Orit Art Gallery, Tel Aviv 105924
Oriti Niosi, Paolo Franco, Cagliari . . 075220
Oriveden Paltanmäen Museo, Orivesi 009930
Orkdal Bygdemuseum, Svorkmo . . 031256
Orkdal Bygdetun, Fannrem 030831
Orkney Farm and Folk Museum, Birsay 038743
Orkney Farm and Folk Museum, Harray 039674
Orkney Gallery, Kirkwall 113337
Orkney Museum, Kirkwall 039905
Orkney Wireless Museum, Kirkwall 039906
Orland Historical Museum, Orland . 046715
Orlandi, Franco, Roma 076598
Orlandini, Mauro, Torino 128340
Orlando, Zürich 112158
Orlando, John Baptist, Tarxien 128483
Orlando & Almeida, Lisboa 079985
Orlando Brown House, Liberty Hall Museum, Frankfort 044036
d'Orlando Griffe, Paris 066363
Orlando Museum of Art, Orlando . . 046719
Orlando Science Center, Orlando . . 046720
Orlaque, Paris 124765
Orleans, Toronto 059254
Orleans House Gallery, Twickenham 041254
Orlické Muzeum, Choceň 008333
Orlogsmuseet, København 008984

Orlovskij Gosudarstvennyj Institut Iskusstv i Kultury, Orël 050655
Orlovskij Oblastnoj Kraevedčeskij Muzej, Orël 033612
Orlovskij Oblastnoj Muzej Izobrazitelnych Iskusstv, Orël 033613
Orly, O.M. Wille, Basel 111215
Ormeau Baths Gallery, Belfast 038665
Ormond Memorial Art Museum, Ormond Beach 046724
Ornabi, São Paulo 137590
Ornament, San Marcos 136600
Ornament and Crime, Los Angeles . 089865
Ornamet Connection, Austin 087603
Ornatto, Porto Alegre 058515
Ornatto, Porto Alegre 058516
Ornatto, Porto Alegre 058517
Ornis Jagt- & Naturbøger, Skjern . . 137906
Ornithology and Entomology Museum, Cairo 009318
Ornunga Museum, Vårgårda 036781
Orny, Ludwig & Helga, München . . . 104279
Oro de Monte Alban, San Antonio . . 092557
Oro e Colore, Firenze 106067, 127383
ORO Fine Art Gallery, Albuquerque . 114815
Oro Gema, Valencia 081668, 122089
Oro Incenso e Mirra, Milano 075795
Oro y Plata, Sevilla 081599
Orobs, Toledo 120087
Orologio, Antwerpen 057722
Oroville Chinese Temple, Oroville . . 046729
Orphan Blues Magazine, Detroit . . . 116094
Orphée, Paris 066364
Orpiment, Paris 066365
Orr, San Diego 092668
Orr, C., Minneapolis 142588
Orr, Michael, Columbus 115793
Orrill, J., Los Angeles 122946
Orrú, Salvatore, Lippstadt 103930
Orsa Auktionsbyrå, Orsa 122224
Orsi, Carlo, Milano 075796
Orsini, Alessandro, Roma 076599
Orsini, Roberto, Milano 140058
Orskij Istoriko-kraevedčeskij Muzej, Orsk 033617
Orssich, Paul, London 141859
Országos Aluminiumipari Múzeum, Székesfehérvár 021869
Országos Geológia Múzeum, Budapest 021683
Országos Műszaki Múzeum, Budapest 021684
Országos Pedagógiai Könyvtár és Múzeum, Budapest 021685
Országos Színháztörténeti Múzeum és Intézet, Budapest 021686
Országos Zsidó Vallási és Történeti Gyüjtemény, Budapest 021687
Orta Oyunlari Sanat Gösteri Yan, İstanbul 112343
Ortega, Jacksonville 089444
Ortega, Santander 081557
Ortega, Sevilla 081600
Ortega, Alfonso, Alicante 110088
Ortega, Gilbert, Phoenix 118880
Ortega, Lola, Sevilla 081601
Ortega, Marie-Cristina, Versailles . . 068815
Ortega, Morales, Sevilla 081602
Ortega Machuca, Jose Ramon, Madrid 110586
Ortega Motilla, L., Denia 110329
Ortega Ortega, Enrique, Córdoba . . 129484
Ortega Ruiz, Manuel, Barcelona . . . 080898
Orteu, Jacques, Saint-Girons 067507
Orth, Seattle 119972
Orth, C., Lohmar 072299
Orth, Peter J., Bonn 102190
Orth-Blau, Sophie, Wien 057513
Ortillés-Fourcat, Paris 100746
Ortiz, Pierre, Calvisson 061914
Ortiz, Rafael, Sevilla 110773
Ortiz Aragon, Alicia, Granada 110381
Ortiz & Bello, Miami 090227
Ortiz Comas, Adriano Santiago, Madrid 110587
Ortiz & Dagenbela, San Antonio . . . 119438
Ortiz un Mundo Diferente, León . . . 110399
Ortmann, Jan-Stefan, Paris 124766
Ortner, Judith, Wien 137354
Orto Botanico, Palermo 025095
Orto Botanico Hanbury, Genova . . . 024326
Ortodoks Antik, Moskva 080256
Ortodoksinen Kirkkomuseo, Kuopio 009763
Ortolan, Giuseppe, Padova 076104
Orton, Stephen, Wantage . 087018, 131645
Orton, Stephen, Watlington 087057
Orton Geological Museum, Ohio State University, Columbus 043110
Orts Vidal, Alfredo, Alicante 080765
Orts, Gérard, Paris 066366
Orts, Gérard, Pau 066711
Orts- und Weinbaumuseum, Neftenbach 037369
Orts- und Wohnmuseum, Marthalen 037309
Ortsgeschichtliche Sammlung, Bovenden 016353
Ortsgeschichtliche Sammlung, Oberrieden 037392
Ortsgeschichtliche Sammlung Rebstein, Rebstein 037437
Ortsgeschichtliches Museum, Siegenburg 020203
Ortskundliches Museum Jois, Jois . 002106
Ortsmuseum, Amriswil 036841
Ortsmuseum, Andwil 036843
Ortsmuseum, Bergün 036922
Ortsmuseum, Binningen 036955
Ortsmuseum, Brachwitz 016356
Ortsmuseum, Bülach 036984
Ortsmuseum, Bütschwil 036987
Ortsmuseum, Häggenschwil 037174
Ortsmuseum, Jona 037206
Ortsmuseum, Kaltbrunn 037207
Ortsmuseum, Laax 037228
Ortsmuseum, Liesberg 037262
Ortsmuseum, Meilen 037320
Ortsmuseum, Merenschwand 037326
Ortsmuseum, Nürensdorf 037383
Ortsmuseum, Oftringen 037398
Ortsmuseum, Rafz 037431
Ortsmuseum, Roggwil 037458
Ortsmuseum, Rüti, Zürich 037468
Ortsmuseum, Sankt Stephan 037507
Ortsmuseum, Schänis 037521
Ortsmuseum, Thalwil 037626
Ortsmuseum, Unterengstringen . . . 037651
Ortsmuseum, Untersiggenthal 037656
Ortsmuseum, Vaz 037672
Ortsmuseum, Vnà 037685
Ortsmuseum, Wängi 037688
Ortsmuseum, Walenstadt 037691
Ortsmuseum, Weikertschlag 002814
Ortsmuseum, Zwentendorf 003073
Ortsmuseum Albisrieden, Zürich . . . 037792
Ortsmuseum Altes Rathaus, Balgach 036875
Ortsmuseum Altstetten, Altstetten . 036837
Ortsmuseum Beringen, Beringen . . 036923
Ortsmuseum Bern, Wangen an der Aare 037695
Ortsmuseum Brittnau, Brittnau 036975
Ortsmuseum Diessenhofen, Diessenhofen 037045
Ortsmuseum Dietikon, Dietikon . . . 037046
Ortsmuseum Eglisau, Eglisau 037057
Ortsmuseum Erlenbach, Erlenbach (Zürich) 037071
Ortsmuseum Eschlikon, Eschlikon . 037076
Ortsmuseum Flawil, Flawil 037086
Ortsmuseum Frenkendorf, Frenkendorf 037095
Ortsmuseum für Heimatkunde, Schlieren 037530
Ortsmuseum Gaiserwald, Altes Pfarrhaus, Sankt Josefen 037501
Ortsmuseum Hinwil, Hinwil 037189
Ortsmuseum Höngg, Zürich 037793
Ortsmuseum Kefiturm, Belp 036920
Ortsmuseum Kilchberg, Kilchberg, Zürich 037210
Ortsmuseum Küsnacht, Küsnacht . . 037225
Ortsmuseum Linthal, Linthal 037270
Ortsmuseum mit Karl-Jauslin-Sammlung, Muttenz 037367
Ortsmuseum Mollis, Mollis 037330
Ortsmuseum Mühle, Museen Maur, Maur 037319
Ortsmuseum Neunkirch, Neunkirch 037379
Ortsmuseum Oberes Bad, Marbach (Sankt Gallen) 037308
Ortsmuseum Oberuzwil, Oberuzwil . 037394
Ortsmuseum Oetwil, Oetwil am See 037396
Ortsmuseum Rüschlikon, Rüschlikon 037467
Ortsmuseum Sankt Veit, Sankt Veit im Mühlkreis 002633
Ortsmuseum Schleitheim, Schleitheim 037528
Ortsmuseum Schmitten, Schmitten (Albula) 037532
Ortsmuseum Spreitenbach, Spreitenbach 037589
Ortsmuseum Steinmaur, Sünikon . . 037613
Ortsmuseum Sust, Horgen 037194
Ortsmuseum Trotte, Arlesheim 036852
Ortsmuseum Urdorf, Urdorf 037659
Ortsmuseum Ursulastift, Gerstetten 017390
Ortsmuseum Vaz, Lenzerheide 037258
Ortsmuseum Vechigen, Boll 036962
Ortsmuseum Wallisellen, Wallisellen 037692
Ortsmuseum Weiach, Weiach 037699
Ortsmuseum Wetzikon, Wetzikon . . 037704
Ortsmuseum Wiesendangen, Wiesendangen 037708
Ortsmuseum Wila, Wila 037711
Ortsmuseum Wilchingen, Wilchingen 037712
Ortsmuseum Wilderswil, Wilderswil 037714
Ortsmuseum Wollishofen, Zürich . . 037794
Ortsmuseum Zollikon, Haus zum Felsengrund, Zollikon 037757
Ortsmuseum zur Farb, Stäfa 037592
Ortsmuseum zur Hohlen Eich, Wädenswil 037687
Ortssammlung Wettelsheim, Treuchtlingen 020470
Ortsstube, Bolligen 036963
Ortstein, Bremerhaven 070053
Ortstein, K., Bremerhaven 070054
Ortus, Montpellier 099762
Oružejnaja Palata, Gosudarstvennyj muzej-zapovednik Moskovskij Kreml, Moskva 033513
Orval Berry Museum, Frankford . . . 005475
Orvieto, Paolo, Milano 075797
Orville-Fasid, C., San Antonio 092558
Orwell Corner Historic Village, Prince Edward Island Museum and Heritage Foundation, Orwell 006078
Orwell Furniture, Ipswich . 084804, 130830
Orzcy, Budapest 074700
Osage County Historical Society, Lyndon 045532
Osage County Historical Society Museum, Pawhuska 046845
Osage Village Historic Site, Lamar . 045133
Osaka Antique Fair, Osaka 093802
Osaka Castle Museum, Osaka 026976
Osaka City Museum, Osaka 026982
Osaka-furitsu Gendai Bijutsu Center, Osaka 026977
Osaka-furitsu Senboku Koko Shiryokan, Sakai 027013
Osaka Geijutsu Daigaku, Kanan . . . 050453
Osaka Human Rights Museum, Osaka 026978
Osaka International Peace Center, Osaka 026979
Osaka-kenritsu Chikatsuasuka Hakubutsukan, Kanan 026621
Osaka-kenritsu Chu Hakabutsukan, Mino 026806
Osaka-kenritsu Sayamaike Hakubutsukan, Osaka-Sayama 026993
Osaka-kenritsu Waha Kamigata Bungeikan, Osaka 026980
Osaka Lottery Dream Museum, Osaka 026981
Osaka Museum of History, Osaka . . 026982
Osaka Museum of Natural History, Osaka 026983
Osaka Nippon Mingeikan, Suita . . . 027090
Osaka Prefectural Museum of Yayoi Culture, Izumi 026593
Osaka Science Museum, Osaka . . . 026984
Osaka-shiritsu Bijutsukan, Osaka . . 026985
Osaka-shiritsu Kindai Bijutsukan Kensetsu Jumbishitsu, Osaka 026986
Osaka-shiritsu Toyo Toji Bijutsukan, Osaka 026987
Osaka Zohkei Center, Osaka 050470
Osare, Camberwell 094360
Osbane Museet, Fana 030830
Osborn, Richard, London 113809
Osborn-Jackson House, East Hampton 043570
Osborne, Kirkcudbright 084877
Osborne, London 113810
Osborne & Allen, London 113811
Osborne Gallery, Nowra 094998
Osborne House, East Cowes 039347
Oscar, B., Miami 132352
Oscar Anderson House Museum, Anchorage 041715
Oscar Antyki, Łódź 079671
Oscar Getz Museum of Whiskey History, Bardstown 042021
Oscar Howe Art Center, Mitchell . . . 045943
Oscar Publications, Delhi 139948
Oscar Restauri, Venezia 128400
Oscars, Haslingden 113197
Oscar's Polishing and Plating, Indianapolis 132159
Oscarsborg Festningsmuseum, Forsvarsmuseet, Oscarsborg 031066
Oscarshall Slott, Oslo 031100
Osceola, San Francisco 119761
Osé, Hasselt 058230
Osebro, Porsgrunn 079484
Osen Bygdemuseum, Osen 031068
Osen Bygdetun, Steinsdalen 031239
Osenat, Jean-Pierre, Fontainebleau 121005
Osenat, Jean-Pierre, Paris 066367, 121180
Oseredok Ukrainian Art Gallery and Museum, Winnipeg 006856
Osgoode Township Museum, Vernon, Ontario 006729
Oshawa Sydenham Museum, Oshawa 006080
O'Shea, London 085581, 141860
Oshkosh Public Museum, Oshkosh . 046737
Osiak, Elizabeth, Portland 132699
Osinskij Kraevedčeskij Muzej, Osa . 033618
Osiris, Bruxelles 096241
Osiris, Helsinki 060567
Osiris Antiques, Southport 086659
Oskam-Neeven, Amstelveen 140274
Oskar Kokoschka Geburtshaus, Pöchlarn 002437
Oskar Luts Majamuuseum, Tartu . . 009422
Oskar Schlemmer Archiv, Staatsgalerie Stuttgart, Stuttgart 020361
Oskar Schlemmer Theatre Estate and Collection, Oggebbio 024990
Oskara Kalpaka Muzejs Airīšu Piemiņas Vietā, Zirņi 027805
Osler Historical Museum, Osler . . . 006082
Oslo Bymuseum, Oslo 031101
Oslo Kunstforening, Oslo 053958
Oslo Mynthandel, Oslo 079465
Osma, Guillermo de, Madrid 110588
Osmanbey Art Galeri, İstanbul 112344
Osmani Museum, Sylhet 003119
OsmoZ, Bulle 111320
Osmundo Antique Gallery, Makati . . 079561
Osona, Carlos, Buenos Aires 055231
Osona, Roberto, Cincinnati 115648
Osoyoos Art Gallery, Osoyoos 006083
Osoyoos Museum, Osoyoos 006084
Osper, Knut, Köln 103691
Osper, Rita, Köln 103692

Ośrodek Biograficzny Komisji Turystyki Górskiej, Gabinet prof. Kazimierza Sosnowskiego, Kraków 032066
Ośrodek Budownictwa Ludowego w Szymbarku z filia w Bartnem, Muzeum Budownictwa Ludowego w Szymbarku, Sękowa 032309
Ośrodek Historii Dęblińskiego Węzła Kolejowego, Dęblin 031892
Ośrodek Muzealno-Dydaktyczny Wielkopolskiego Parku Narodowego, Mosina 032152
Ośrodek Plenerowy w Kamionnej, Kąty Wrocławskie 108921
De Ossekop, Leiden 078577
Ossenpohl, Berlin 101999
Ossenpohl, Bonn 102191
Ossining Historical Society Museum, Ossining 046743
Osškij Objedinennyj Istoriko-Kulturnyj Muzej-Zapovednik, Oš 027639
Ossowski, London 085582
Ossowski, London 085583
Ossowski, London 131129
Ossowski, London 131130
Osswald, Harald, Meersburg 139470
Ost-West, Timişoara 080198
Ostapczuk, Barbara, Jülich 103458
Ostarrichi-Kulturhof, Neuhofen an der Ybbs 002358
Ostasiatika-Sammlung Ehrich, Museum Bochum, Hattingen 017797
Ostasiatische Zeitschrift, Neue Serie, Berlin 135815
Østasiatiska Museet, Stockholm . . 036654
Ostdeutsche Heimatstube, Bad Zwischenahn 015846
Ostdeutsche Heimatstube, Fellbach 017108
Ostdeutsche Heimatstube, Schwäbisch Hall 020118
Ostdeutsche Kultur- und Heimatstuben mit Schönbacher Stube, Heppenheim 017875
Osten, Andrea von der, Hilpoltstein . 139268
Ostendorf-Pfeiffer, Diepholz 102365
Ostendorff, Münster 104373, 139571
Ostendorff, Wiesbaden 105274
Ostendorff, Birthe, Heidelberg 103325
Oster, K., Haan 103040
Oster, Ralf, Kleve 126054
Østerbro Antik, København 060364
Osterburger Antiquariat, Osterburg . 139643
Osterburgsammlung, Bischofsheim an der Rhön 016251
Ostereimuseum, Sonnenbühl 020250
Osterley Park House, Isleworth 039828
Ostermann, Wuppertal 105358
Osterøy Museum, Lonevåg 030996
Osterson, Vancouver 097507
Ostertag, Freddy, Oberaach 082709
Osterville Historical Museum, Osterville 046744
Osterwalder, Hamburg 103205
Osterzgebirgsmuseum, Lauenstein . 018525
Das Ostfriesische Teemuseum und Norder Heimatmuseum, Norden 019326
Ostfriesisches Landesmuseum und Emder Rüstkammer, Emden 016961
Ostfriesisches Landwirtschaftsmuseum, Krummhörn 018428
Ostfriesisches Schulmuseum Folmhusen, Westoverledingen 020833
Ostharz-Antiquitäten, Aschersleben 069208
Osthofentor-Museum, Wehrkundlisches Museum zur Stadtgeschichte, Soest 020231
Osthoff, Daniel, Würzburg 139874
Ostholstein-Museum, Eutin 017095
Ostholstein-Museum Neustadt, Neustadt in Holstein 019294
Ostholt, K., Ahaus 101541
Ostia, New York 091137
Ostindiefararen Götheborg, Göteborg 036301
Ostindiska Kompaniet, Stockholm . 082004
Ostindiska Kompaniet, Stockholm . 082005
Ostler, Mittenwald 104081, 126321
Ostler, München 072809
Ostner, Schwabmünchen 073736
Osto- ja Myyntikeskus, Kotka 137972
Osto- ja Myyntiliike Kellari, Oulu . . 060618
Ostowar, Berlin 102000
Ostoya, Kraków 079647, 121891
Ostoya, Warszawa 121909
Ostoya, Warszawa 121910
Ostpreußisches Landesmuseum, Lüneburg 018746
Ostravská Antikva, Ostrava 060067
Ostravské Muzeum, Ostrava 008554
Ostrin, Joyce, New York 091138
Ostrobothnia Australis, Biological Museum, Vaasa 010202
Ostrogožskij Rajonnyj Istoriko-chudožestvennyj Muzej im. I.N. Kramskogo, I.N. Kramskoy Art Museum of Ostrogoshsk, Ostrogožsk 033621
Ostrov Sokrovišč, Moskva 080257
Østsamisk Museum, De Samiske Samlinger, Neiden 031049
Ostsee-Antik-Baabe, Ostseebad Baabe 073263
Ostsee-Antik-Zingst, Ostseebad Zingst 073266
Ostsee Galerie, Grömitz 103010
Østsjællands Museum, Stevns Museum, Store Heddinge 009118
Osuji, Wangen im Allgäu 074275
O'Sullivan, Dublin 074941
O'Sullivan, New York 091139
O'Sullivan, A.J., Darlton . . 084136, 130625
Osuna, Ramon, Washington 120331
Osusannah, Vancouver 097508
Osuuspankkimuseo, Helsinki 009558
Osvald, Oliver von, Sankt Gallen . . .130165, 141295
Oswald, Austin 114999
Oswald, Alfred, Göggenhofen 125734
Oswald, K., Lörrach 072293
Oswald & Kalb, Wien 057514
Oswego Historical Museum, Oswego 046745
Oswestry Transport Museum, Oswestry 040649
OSZK-Soros, Budapest 127078
Ota, Tokyo 107093
Ōta Kinen Bijutsukan, Tokyo 027230
Otago Art Society Gallery, Dunedin . 108444
Otago Military Museum, Dunedin . . 030487
Otago Museum, Dunedin 030488
Otago Settlers Museum, Dunedin . . 030489
Otago Studios, Glasgow 113125
Otago Vintage Machinery Club Museum, Dunedin 030490
Otakou Marae Museum, Dunedin . . 030491
Otani Memorial Art Museum Nishinomiya City, Nishinomiya 026922
Otar Memlekettik Archeologicalik Korik Muzej, Čimkent 027397
Otaru-shi Hakubutsukan, Otaru . . . 026995
Otaru-shi Seishonen Kagakugijutsukan, Otaru 026996
Otautau and District Local History Museum, Otautau 030561
Otello Kalesi, Gazimağusa 008239
Otemar, Jacques d', La Tour-d'Aigues 063453
Otende, Jocelyne, Avignon 061139
Otende, Jocelyne, Le Crès 063610
Oterelo, Claude, Paris 138514
Otéro, Saint-Paul-de-Vence 101216
Otford Antiques Centre, Otford 086172, 131350
Othegraven, Renée-Maria von, Wien 123521
Other Mark, Almere 107633
Other Shop II, San Francisco 092860
Other Side, Portland 091987
The Other Side, Tampa . . . 093146, 132960
The Other Side of the Mirror, Cholsey 112867
Other Times Antiques, Portsoy 086301
Other Times Books, Los Angeles . . 142516
Othmar Jaindl-Museum, Villach . . . 002775
Otis College of Art and Design, Los Angeles 051638
Otis Gallery, Otis College of Art and Design, Los Angeles 045457
Otley Antique Centre, Otley 086174
Otley Museum, Otley 040650
Otmezguine, Jane, Nice 099852
Otoe County Museum of Memories, Syracuse 048452
Otoko, Los Angeles 089866
O'Toole, Limerick 074989
O'Toole, Kay, Houston 089172
Otori, Nara 077165
Otranto, Barcelona 080899
Otrar State Archaeological Park Museum, Shymkent 027414
Otraženie - Muzej Voskovych Figur, Moskva 033514
Otsuka Textile Design Institute, Tokyo 050494
Ott, Egbert, Den Haag 078227
Ott, Herbert, Isen 103437
Ott, J.B.A.M., Zutphen 078879
Ott, Josef & Katharina, Schongau . . 104839
Ott, Joseph, Colmar 062416
Ott, Wilhelm, Düsseldorf . 102533, 133895
Ott-Berger, Christiane, Fuchstal . . . 125685
Ottavi, Marc, Paris 066368
Ottaviani, Pier Giuseppe, Roma . . . 076600
Ottawa Antique Market, Ottawa . . . 059048
Ottawa Conservation Studio, Ottawa 123799
Ottawa County Historical Museum, Port Clinton 047128
Ottawa Scouting Museum, Ottawa . 046750
Otte, Walter, Soest 128835
Otten, Rainer & Beate, Erwitte 070607
Ottenby Naturum, Degerhamn 036235
Ottenhausen, Irene, Piesport 134348
Otter, Amsterdam 140329
Otter, Groningen 078431
Otter, P. & B., Wallingford . 087007, 131643
Otter Antiques, Honiton 084728
Otter & Bear, Albuquerque 114816
Otter Tail County Historical Museum, Fergus Falls 043835
Otterbeck, Gertrud, Stuttgart 126870
Otterstetter, Claus, Bensheim 138726
Otterton Mill Centre and Working Museum, Budleigh Salterton 038899
Otterup Museum, Otterup 009059
Ottesen, Susanne, København 098579
Ottevanger & Weiman, Den Haag . . 078228
Ottin, Michel, Paris 066369
Ottlik, D., Meißen 072506
Ottmar-Mergenthaler-Museum, Bad Mergentheim 015751
Otto, Berlin 069717
Otto, Bologna 105973
Otto, Wien 095905
Otto, Wien 095906
Otto, Wien 095907
Otto, Wien 095908
Otto, Wien 095909
Otto, Wien 095910
Otto, Wien 095911
Otto, Wien 095912
Otto, Wien 095913
Otto, C. Claus, Bremen 138946
Otto, Jörg, Halle, Saale 125790
Otto, Jutta & Günter, Gevelsberg . . 070986
Otto, Kurt, Bad Sassendorf 069372
Otto, Manfred, Berlin 069718
Otto, R., Regensburg 126697
Otto, R.&B., Regensburg 073468
Otto, Renate, Friesenheim, Baden . 102890
Otto, Rositta, Bretten 125397
Otto, Rudolf, München 104280
Otto, Rudolf, Wien 095914
Otto, Ulrich, Roßdorf bei Darmstadt 126740
Otto-Dill Museum, Neustadt an der Weinstraße 019286
Otto-Dix-Haus, Kunstsammlung Gera, Gera 017374
Otto-Dix-Haus Hemmenhofen, Gaienhofen 017315
Otto Dix Stiftung, Vaduz 053840
Otto-Flath-Kunsthalle, Bad Segeberg 015799
Otto-Galerie, München 072810
Otto-Galerie, München 104281
Dat Otto Huus, Emden 016962
Otto & Jost, Davos Platz 111377
Otto-König von Griechenland-Museum, Ottobrunn 019544
Otto-Lilienthal-Museum, Anklam . . 015547
Otto Modersohn Museum, Ottersberg 019541
Otto-Nagel-Galerie, Berlin 102001
Otto Pankok Museum, Hünxe 018026
Otto-Schwabe-Museum, Hochheim am Main 017938
Otto & Trebeljahr, Hannover 071407
Otto-Ubbelohde-Haus, Lahntal 018462
Otto von Bylandt-Gesellschaft, Mönchengladbach 053539
Otto-von-Guericke-Museum in der Lukasklause, Magdeburg 018774
Otto Wagner Hofpavillion Hietzing, Wien Museum, Wien 002982
Otto Wagner Pavillion Karlsplatz, Wien Museum, Wien 002983
dell'Ottocento, Livorno 106127
Ottocento, Messina 075568
Ottocento, Roma 128141
Ottocento e Novecento, Milano 075798
Ottolina Antik, Billinge 081773
Ottomane, Lübeck 072335
Ottorino Nonfarmale, Venezia 128401
Ottrey, Mike, Wallingford 087008
Otumpa, London 113812
Otwarta, Wrocław 109229
Otway, Anglesea 094154
Ouaiss, Paris 066370
Ouaiss, Hady, Paris 066371
Ouaiss, Jacques, Beirut 077410
Ouaknine, Nantes 064937
Oud Amelisweerd Museum, Bunnik 029365
Oud Cortrijcke, Kortrijk 058267
Oud en Nieuw, Breda 078110
Oud Holland, Den Haag 136006
Oud Holland, Utrecht 078812
Ouddorps Raad- en Polderhuis, Ouddorp 030023
De Oude Aarde, Giethoorn 029611
Oude Ambachten en Speelgoedmuseum, Terschuur 030198
Oude Bakkerij, Medemblik 029913
De Oude Borze, Antwerpen 137402
De Oude Deel, Zutphen 078880
De Oude Doos, Eindhoven 078345
De Oude Doos, Utrecht 078813
De Oude Drostdy, Tulbagh 034762
d'Oude Fortuyne, Antwerpen 057723
Oude Fortuyne, Antwerpen 123550
Het Oude Glashuis, Nijmegen 078660
Het Oude Huis, Bergen op Zoom . . . 078074
Oude Kerk Volksmuseum, Tulbagh . 034763
De Oude Lantaerne, Leeuwarden . . 078554
De Oude Markt, Naarden 140499
Oude Pijpelade, Utrecht 078814
d'Oude Postkaart, Lier 137525
De Oude Prent, Hapert 140449
Oude Prenten, Rotterdam 078739
't Oude Raadhuis, Beek en Donk . . 029296
Het Oude Raadhuis, Leerdam 029836
Het Oude Raadhuis, Oud-Beijerland 030018
Het Oude Raadhuis, Urk 030221
Het Oude Slot Heemstede, Heemstede 029686
Oude Smederij, Enschede 078376
Het Oude Stadhuis, Hasselt 029679
De Oude Stal, Amsterdam 077927
Oude Vlaamse Galerij, Sint-Amands 096410, 123670
De Oude Wand, Zutphen 078881
Den Ouden Huis, 's-Hertogenbosch 078528
Oudhede & Geskenkwinkel, Pretoria 080740

Oudheidkamer, Vught 030300
Oudheidkamer, Bruinisse 029361
Oudheidkamer, Den Burg 029418
Oudheidkamer, Koudekerk 029821
Oudheidkamer, Steenwijk 030181
Oudheidkamer, Wijngaarden 030333
Oudheidkamer Beilen, Beilen 029300
Oudheidkamer Bleiswijk, Bleiswijk . 029316
Oudheidkamer Boerderij Strunk, Raalte 030050
Oudheidkamer Brederwiede, Vollenhove 030288
Oudheidkamer Buisjan Enter, Enter . 029573
Oudheidkamer Dantumadeel, Zwaagwesteinde 030406
Oudheidkamer de Oude Pastory, Heiloo 029707
Oudheidkamer Doorn, Doorn 029497
Oudheidkamer Eemnes, Eemnes . . 029528
Oudheidkamer Geervliet, Geervliet . 029595
Oudheidkamer Heerde, Heerde . . . 029688
Oudheidkamer Hellevoetsluis, Hellevoetsluis 029721
Oudheidkamer Hoolt'n, Holten 029763
Oudheidkamer Horst, Horst 029778
Oudheidkamer Ijsselstreek, Wijhe . 030331
Oudheidkamer in het Stadhuis, Bolsward 029324
Oudheidkamer Leiderdorp, Leiderdorp 029857
Oudheidkamer Lemster Fiifgea, Lemmer 029865
Oudheidkamer Leshuis, Dedemsvaart 029402
Oudheidkamer Lunteren, Lunteren . 029881
Oudheidkamer/ Museum Mr. Andreae, Kollum 029817
Oudheidkamer Nederlandse Kaap-Hoornvaarders, Hoorn 029773
Oudheidkamer Nunspeet, Nunspeet 029980
Oudheidkamer Renswoude, Renswoude 030056
Oudheidkamer Ridderkerk, Ridderkerk 030060
Oudheidkamer Rozenburg, Rozenburg 030111
Die Oudheidkamer tot Medenblick, Medemblik 029914
Oudheidkamer Vreeswijk, Nieuwegein 029949
Oudheidkamer Wassenaar, Wassenaar 030312
Oudheidkamer Weststellingwerf, Wolvega 030347
Oudheidkamer Wieringerwaard het Polderhuis, Wieringerwaard 030329
Oudheidkamer Willem Van Strijen, Zevenbergen 030386
Oudheidkundeige Verzameling, Schinveld 030135
Oudheidkundig Museum, Sint Michielsgestel 030150
Oudheidkundig Museum Arnemuiden, Arnemuiden 029262
Oudheidkundig Museum Sint-Janshospitaal, Damme 003385
Oudheidkundig Museum van de Bijloke, Gent 003451
Oudheidkundig Museum van het Begijnhof, Turnhout 003820
Oudheidkundige Verzameling, Sluis 030165
Oudin, Gilles, Paris 066372, 100747
Oudot & Fils, Fougerolles (Haute-Saône) 124243
Ouellette, Pierre-François, Montréal 097062
Ouestampille, Saint-Martin-de-Mailloc 067628
Oulaisten Kotiseutumuseo, Oulainen 009931
Oulan Bator, Orléans 099892
Ould Chibani, Casablanca 077669
Ouley, Eric, Izon 124266
d'Oultremont, Bruxelles 058046
Oulun Automuseo, Oulu 009933
Oulun Kirja-Antikvariaatti, Oulu . . . 137981
Oulun Taidemuseo, Oulu 009934
Oulun Yliopiston Eläinmuseo, Oulu . 009935
Oulun Yliopiston Geologinen Museo, Oulu 009936
Oulun Yliopiston Kasvimuseo, Oulu . 009937
Oulunsalon Kotiseutumuseo, Oulunsalo 009941
Oumow, Aude, Saint-Germain-en-Laye 101155
Oundle Museum, Oundle 040651
Our Dream Gallery, Portland 119029
Our Gallery, Sedbergh 114401
Our Heritage Museum, Adelaide . . . 034542
Our House, Honolulu 088970
Our House State Memorial, Gallipolis 044127
Our India Project Museum, Narendrapur 022282
Our Lady of Mercy Museum, Port-au-Port 006172
Our Talented Friends, Albuquerque . 087416
OurnaC, Eric, Clamart 062317
Ouro Brunido, Lisboa 129166
Ouroboros, Tucson 120157
A l'Ours d'Argent, Saint-André-de-Sangonis 067356
Ouse Valley Books, Sharnbrook . . . 142057
Oushabti, Toulouse 068531
Out of Africa, Philadelphia 118817
Out of Africa Gallery, Thetford 114568
Out of Asia, Los Angeles 089867
Out of Bounds, Seattle 119973
Out of Print, Caulfield South 136855
Out of Print Books, Cleveland 142340
Out-Of-Print Bookstore, Houston . . 142444
Out of the Blue Gallery, Marazion . . 114056
Out of the Blue Interiors, Townsville 056731
Out of the Closet, New Orleans 090598
Out of the Closet, New York 091140, 142684
Out of the East, Singapore 080540
Out of the Past, Austin 087604
Outagamie Museum and Houdini Historical Center, Appleton 041754
Outback Aboriginal Art, Hawthorn East 055958
Outback Art, Mayfield 056171
Outback Art, Mayfield 094797
Outback Colours Galleries, Quorn . . 095113
Outback Galleries, Silverton 095193
Outcast Book's, Hereford 141664
The Outcrop Gallery, Alice Springs . 094144
Outeniqua Railway Museum, Transnet Heritage Foundation, George 034617
Outerlimits, Mount Hawthorn 137013
Outfitters Gallery, Margate 114057
Outhwaite & Litherland, Liverpool . . 122575
Outjo Museum, Outjo 029094
Outlines Posters, London 113813
Outlook and District Heritage Museum and Gallery, Outlook 006106
Outokummun Kaivosmuseo, Outokumpu 009942
Outra Era, Lisboa 079986
Outrageous Art, Edinburgh 113005
Outre Antiques, Long Beach 089647
Outre Gallery, Melbourne 094822
Outre Jewel, Chicago 115519
Outre-Mer, Genève 082457
Outre Monde, Caen 099047
Outreach Collection, West Malling . 041340
Outred, Anthony, London 085584
Outremer, Morlaine, La Baule-Escoublac 099381
Outros Tempos, Porto 080102
Outside the Lines, Nashville 117363
Outsider Art Fair, New York 094021
Outters, Christophe, Reims 067077
Outward Bound Museum, Aberdovey 038454
Ouvrage de la Ligne Maginot, Leutenheim 012650
Ouvrage Décoration, Paris 066373
Ouyen Local History Resource Centre, Ouyen 001360
Ovalle Urbina, Mario, Santiago de Chile 059545
Ovarantigo Antiguidades, Ovar 080060
Ovens Museum, Riverport 006295
Over the Moon, Saint Agnes 114340
Over The Moon Antiques, Adelaide . 055318
Over Tijd, Eindhoven 078346
Overbeck, Hanstedt 103303
Overbeck-Gesellschaft, Verein von Kunstfreunden e.V., Lübeck 053540
Overbeck's Museum, Salcombe . . . 040940
Overfield Tavern Museum, Troy . . . 048621
Overhoff, Jürgen, Freiburg im Breisgau 070851
Overhoff, Jürgen, Freiburg im Breisgau 125672
Overholser Mansion, Oklahoma City 046653
Overland Trail Museum, Sterling . . . 048350
Overlook Press, New York 135448
Overlord, Saint Louis 092293
Overmans, R.M., Heusden 128717
Overmantels, London 085585, 131131
Overton, John, Atlanta 087510
Overwien, Köln 103693
Overy Gallery, Wells-next-the-Sea . 114658
Ovidi, Mario, Roma 128142
Owatonna Arts Center, Owatonna . . 046756
Owela Display Centre, National Museum of Namibia, Windhoek 029108
Owen, New York 118257
Owen, Debra, San Diego 119531
Owen, Faye W., Bonny Hills 094266
Owen, George, Dallas 142372
Owen, Patrick, Philadelphia 118818
Owen, Peter, London 135246
Owen & Ramsey, Richmond 142829
Owen Sound Marine and Rail Museum, Owen Sound 006109
Owens, Wellington 079339
Owens Art Gallery, Sackville 006318
Owens-Thomas House, Savannah . 048028
Owensboro Area Museum of Science and History, Owensboro 046760
Owensboro Museum of Fine Art, Owensboro 046761
Owlets, Hythe, Kent 084781
Owls Head Transportation Museum, Owls Head 046762
Owl's Rook Books, Calgary 137625
Owl's Roost Antiques, Miami 090228
Owo Museum, Owo 030704
O'Wyatt, Dion, New York 118258
Owyhee County Historical Museum, Murphy 046098
Oxbridge, Amsterdam 140330
Oxenfurter Antiquitätenhandel, Ochsenfurt 073168
Oxenstierna, Tamara, Stockholm . . 129871
Oxfam, Birmingham 141417
Oxfam, Newcastle-upon-Tyne 141953
Oxfam Book Shop, Edinburgh 141585
Oxfam Books, Colchester 141531
Oxfam Books, Lancaster 141704
Oxfam Bookshop, Chester 141511
Oxfam Bookshop, Chichester 141519
Oxfam Bookshop, Glasgow 141624
Oxfam Bookshop, London 141861
Oxfam Bookshop, London 141862
Oxfam Bookshop, Manchester 141938
Oxford Antique Restorers, New York 132510
Oxford Antiques, Unley . . . 056769, 123326
Oxford Architectural Antiques, Faringdon 084383
Oxford Area Arts Council, Oxford . . 054463
Oxford Art Journal, Oxford 136258
Oxford Bus Museum Trust, Long Hanborough 040334
Oxford County Museum School, Burgessville 005163
Oxford Court Antique Centre, Waikato 079295
Oxford Gallery, Arcachon 060952
Oxford Gallery, Mount Hawthorn . . . 094906
Oxford Library Museum, Oxford . . . 046767
Oxford Museum, Oxford 030564
Oxford Museum, Oxford 046766
The Oxford Story, Oxford 040662
Oxford Street Antique Centre, Leicester 084950
Oxford University Museum of Natural History, Oxford 040663
Oxford University Press, New York . 135449
Oxford University Press, Oxford . . . 135293
Oxford University Press Museum, Oxford 040664
The Oxfordshire Museum, Woodstock 041439
Oxl, Lysaker 121856
Oxley, Laurence, Alresford 083277, 130292, 141385
Oxley, Marc, Uppingham 086985
Oxley, Marc, Uppingham 114630
Oxley, Marc, Uppingham 131630
Oxley, P.A., Cherhill 083938
Oxmoor Circle Used Furniture, Birmingham 087778
Oxon Cove Park Museum, Oxon Hill 046777
Oxoxo Gallery, Baltimore 115074
Oyamazumi-jinja Kokuhokan, Omishima 026954
Øyfjell Bygdemuseum, Vinje 031340
The Oyster and Maritime Museum of Chincoteague, Chincoteague 042902
Oyster Bay Historical Society Museum, Oyster Bay 046779
Oyster Gallery, Torquay 114585
Oz Images Gallery, Cairns 094352, 123201
OZ Sculptures, Louisville 116960
Ozanne-Marcellin, Sophie, Paris . . . 066374
Ozark Folk Center, Mountain View . 046076
Ozark Pastel Society, Rogers 054959
Ozaukee Art Center, Cedarburg . . . 042680
Ozaukee County Historical Society Pioneer Village, Saukville 048014
Ozgul, Paris 138515
Oziol, Denis, Marvejols 064418
Ozone Art and Craft Gallery, Renmark 095128
P. and Al. Canellopoulos Museum, Athinai 021208
P-Art, Gent 096295
P Art Culture Antiques, İstanbul . . . 136140
P & L Furniture, Austin 131806
P-P-O-W Gallery, New York 118259
P & R Antiques, Fresno . . 088915, 132085
P & R Antiques, Halesworth 084555
P. Ramlee Memorial, Kuala Lumpur 027977
P Sanat Kültür Antika, İstanbul 136141
P Street Pictures, Washington 120332
P. Terlemezian State College of Arts, Erevan 049606
P.21 Arte, Roma 106603
Pa-Lin Arts School, Singapore 050690
Pa Objetos de Artes, Rio de Janeiro 096633
Paal, München 104282
Paalman, F., Bruxelles 123602
Paamiune Katersugausivik, Paamiut Museum, Paamiut 021545
Paape, Lewis, Hutt City . . 108474, 128939
Paarl Antiques, Paarl 080726
Paarl Museum, Paarl 034694
Paas, Kurt, Lüchow, Wendland 072344
Paattisten Kotiseutumuseo, Paattinen 009943
Paauwe, B.A., Utrecht 128858
Paavolan Kotiseutumuseo, Paavola 009944
Pabel, Reinhold, Hamburg 139203
Pabel-Moewig, Rastatt 134355
Pabetland Sanat Galerisi, İstanbul . 112345
Pabian, Stéphane, Paris 138516
Pabst, Eichenau 070519
Pabst, Neustadt an der Aisch 073025
Pabst, Josef, Puchheim 073381
Pabst, Michael, München 104283
Pabst, Michael, München 104284
PAC - Padiglione d'Arte Contemporanea, Milano 024731
PAC - Poste d'Arte Contemporain, Fribourg 037104
Pacaud, C., Audierne 098873
Pacault, Philippe, Vezinnes 068837
Pacchera, Dario, Roma 076601

Pacci, Raimondo, Firenze 127384
Pace, New York 118260
Pace, Saint Louis 119234
Pace, Edwin, Mqabba 128478
Pace Charles E., Houston 132134
Pace Prints, New York 135450
Pace & Wildenstein, New York 118261
Pace & Wildenstein, New York 118262
Pacem in Terris, Warwick 048869
Paces Bend Gallery, Atlanta 114910
Pacheco Art Gallery, Mandaluyong . 108838
Pachinger, M., München . . 072811, 126427
Pachmann, Roderich, München . . . 072812
Pachner, Siegfried, Steyr 123474
Pacht, Andreas, Kiel 071841
Pacht & Kiene, Gelsenkirchen 070958
Pacific Access California, Los Angeles 089868
Pacific American Gallery, Honolulu . 116233
Pacific Art, North Shore 079197
Pacific Arts Association, Sherman Oaks 054960
Pacific Arts Association, Europe, Genève 054204
The Pacific Arts Association Newsletter, New York 136601
Pacific Arts Center, Seattle 048088
Pacific Asia Museum, Pasadena . . . 046834
Pacific Book House, Antiques and Collectibles, Honolulu . . 088971, 142419
Pacific Bookshop, Christchurch . . . 140618
Pacific Coin, Tucson 093255
Pacific Collection, Baltimore 087700
Pacific County Historical Museum, South Bend 048231
Pacific Galleries, Seattle 123114
Pacific Galleries II, Seattle 093043, 123115
Pacific Gallery, Honolulu 116234
Pacific Gallery, Saskatoon 097196
Pacific Glass Auction, Sacramento . 123080
Pacific Great Eastern Station, North Vancouver 006046
Pacific Grove Art Center, Pacific Grove 046783
Pacific Grove Museum of Natural History, Pacific Grove 046784
Pacific Heights Antiques and Art, San Francisco 092861
Pacific House Publishing, Tucson . . 135518
Pacific Interiors, Chicago 088141
Pacific Islands Museums Association, Suva 052872
Pacific Lumber Company Museum, Scotia 048051
Pacific Museum, Yongin 027629
Pacific Northwest College of Art, Portland 051980
Pacific Northwest Truck Museum, Brooks 042473
Pacific Orient Traders, Honolulu . . . 088972
Pacific Orient Traders, Portland . . . 091988
Pacific Orient Traders, Vancouver . . 059395
Pacific Rim Focus, Pyrmont 056510
Pacific Science Center, Seattle 048089
Pacific University Museum, Forest Grove 043884
Pacific Woodblock Prints, Vancouver 059396, 097509
Pacitti, André, Paris 066375
Pacitti, Carla Adriana, Torino 076853
Packer, Aron, Chicago 115520
The Packhouse, Runfold 086416
Packmor, Marianne, Gronau, Westfalen 071108
Packnut, Indianapolis 089329
Packrat, Denver 088722
Packwood House, Lapworth 039932
Packwood House Museum, Lewisburg 045242
Paco Alonso, Sevilla 129739
Paço dos Duques de Bragança, Guimarães 032621
Paço Imperial, Rio de Janeiro 004415
Paco Imperial Antiguidades, Rio de Janeiro 058630
PACT, Rixensart 133296, 135606
Padasjoen Kotiseutumuseo, Nyystölä 009920
Padasjoen Kotiseutumuseo, Padasjoki 009945
Padasjoen Kotiseutumuseo, Torittu . 010154
Paddington Antique Centre, Paddington, Queensland 056432
Paddock, Woodhouse Eaves 087232
Paddy's Emporium, Panmure 056437
Padgett, Paul, Cincinnati 088268
Padovani, Luri 064036
Padovani, Penny, London 141863
Padovani, Walter, Milano 075799
Padovano, Roberto, New York 118263
Padre Burgos National Museum, Vigan 031807
Padrutt, Marlies, Chur 082317
Padstow Museum, Padstow 040669
Padua, Maria Lucia, Rio de Janeiro 123709
Padua Art Gallery, Padova 106405
Päämajamuseo, Mikkeli 009875
Paekakariki Arts, Paekakariki 079208
Paekakariki Railway Museum, Wellington 030648
Pängelanton-Eisenbahnmuseum, Münster 019151
Päpke & Janowitz, Düsseldorf 070421
Pärnu Muuseum, Pärnu 009384
Paeroa and District Historical Society Museum, Paeroa 030565
Paeroa Antiques, Paeroa 079209
Paes de Barros, Lya, São Paulo . . . 049769
Pätärin Talomuseo, Ylijärvi 010257
Paetzold, Ariane, Oberursel 126583
Pätzold, Kurt, Grabs 130040
Pätzold, Rainer, Aachen 069097
PAF Museum, Karachi 031375
Paffrath, G., Düsseldorf 102534
Pagan, Vigo 081708, 129793
Paganella, Armando, Torino 128341
Paganelli & C., G., Genova 106102
Paganini, Stéphane, Dunkerque . . . 062752
Pagazaurtundia, Paz Gimeno, Zaragoza 081747, 129820
Page, A. & H., London . . . 085586, 131132
Page, André E., Fribourg 130026
Page, Brian, Brighton 083709
Page, Colin, Brighton 141439
Page, Kevin, London 085587
Page, Roger, Yallambie 137146
Page 17, Charleville-Mézières 138071
Page Antiques, Armadale, Victoria . 055390
Page Antiques, Leek 084943
Page Conservation, Washington . . . 133031
Page Two, Fitzroy 136902
Pageafterpage, Box Hill 136815
Pageant, New York 142685
Pageau, Colette, Tours 068599
Pagenwood, Portland 091989, 132700
Pages, Frank, Baden-Baden 101725
Pagès, Gilbert, Badaroux 061158
Pagés, Jean, Bordeaux 138049
Pagès, Robert, Lunel 064028
Pages Art, North Shore . . . 079198, 128949
Pages d'Histoire, Paris 138517
Pages of Yesteryear, Sacramento . . 142846
Pages & Prints, Cincinnati 115649
Paggi, Claudia, Milano 127644
Paginas Antigas Livros, Belo Horizonte 137548
La Paglia, Modena 075926
Pagliarini, Enrico, Parma 106455
Pagliuca, Stefano, Napoli 076020
Pagnamenta & Co., Nicola Nik, Lugano 082604, 130094
Pagnier, Jean, Bonnefontaine 124108
Pagoa Restauración, Bilbao 129442
Pagoda Antiques, Seoul 077370
La Pagoda International, Padova . . 076105
Pagoda Red Antiques, Chicago 088142
Pagode de Chanteloup, Amboise . . 010361
Pagodenburg Rastatt, Rastatt 019714
Pagter, de, Middelburg 078641
Pahiatua and District Museum, Pahiatua 030566
Pahl Museum, Mainhardt 018783
Paier College of Art, Hamden 051431
Paige, New York 118264
Paignton and Dartmouth Steam Railway, Paignton 040672
Paikkarin Torppa, Sammatti 010062
Pailet, David E., New Orleans 117488
Pailhas, Roger, Marseille 099678
Paillard, Alain, Morez 064791
Pailler, Stéphane, Tours 068600
Paillette, Gisèle, Vimoutiers 068991
Pailleux, Daniel, Abbeville 060654
Paillous, Jacques, Villefranche-de-Rouergue 068896
Paimion Kotiseutumuseo, Paimio . . 009946
Paine, D., Gorseinon 084484
Paine Art Center, Oshkosh 046738
Paine Muñoz, Armando Germán, Punta Arenas 059481
Painen, Berlin 102002
Paini, Carlo, Brescia 106003
Paint & Sons, N.S. John, Saint Peter Port 086474, 131444
Paint 'n' Palette Club, Anamosa . . . 054961
Paint Pot Gallery, Yeppoon 095454
Paint Rag, Honolulu 136602
Paintbox Gallery, New York 118265
Paintbox Gallery 2, New York 118266
Painted Bride Art Center Gallery, Philadelphia 046971
Painted City Gallery, Toronto 097342
Painted Lady's Christmas Plums, Long Beach 089648
Painted Planet, Memphis 116999
Painted With Oil, Phoenix 118881
Painters's Hall, London 040251
Painting and Sculpture, Tel Aviv . . . 135856
Painting Conservation of Philadelphia, Philadelphia 132629
Painting Mart, San Jose 119860
Paintings Direct, Boston 115219
Paintings Galore, Victoria Point 056782
Paintings of the World, Tampa 120061
Paintings Plus, Phoenix 118882
Paintings Plus, Phoenix 118883
Paintingsandphotos Art Gallery, Washington 120333
Painvin, Olivier, Savigny-le-Temple . 068167
Paio, João Algarvio, Lisboa 079987
Paipoonge Historical Museum, Thunder Bay 006567
Pairel, Daniel, Angers 060861
Pairone, Mario, Nantes-en-Ratier . . 064957
Pairone Mario, La Mure-d'Isère . . . 063398
Pairs Antiques, London . . 085588, 131133
Paisley, Pretoria 080741
Paisley, Toronto 059255
Paisley Fine Books, Paisley 141991
Paisley Museum and Art Gallery, Paisley 040673
Paisnel, London 085589, 113814
Paiva, Maria Helena de Campos, São Paulo 058731
Pajar Museo, Ojacastro 035549
Pajaro Valley Historical Museum, Watsonville 049008
Pajdowska, E., Warszawa 109174
Pajulan Koulumuseo, Somero 010088
Pakan, Phoenix 132653
't Pakhuis, Den Haag 078229
Pakistan Air Force Museum Peshawar, Peshawar 031394
Pakistan Army Museum, Rawalpindi 031400
Pakistan Museum of Natural History, Islamabad 031370
Pakistani American Arts Council, Los Angeles 054962, 116863
Pákozdi Csata Emlékmüve, Pákozd 021807
Pakruojis Manor House, Šiauliai Aušros Museum, Pakruojis 027851
Pakzad, Freydoun, Hannover 071408
Pál & Társa, Budapest 074701
Pal de Rosa, Lleida 081177
Pałac Radziwiłłów w Nieborowie, Muzeum Narodowe w Warszawie, Nieborów 032162
Pałac Sztuki w Krakowie, Kraków . . 032067
Pałac w Dobrzycy, Muzeum Narodowe w Poznaniu, Dobrzyca 031897
Pałac w Rogalinie, Świątniki 032353
Palace, Den Haag 121787
Palace, Toronto 097343
Palace and Museum of Antiquities, Padmanabhapuram 022287
Palace Antiques, Bucureşti 080168
Palace Armoury, Valletta 028034
Palace Art, Karama 083207
Palace Editions, Bad Breisig 133729
Palace Galleries, New York 091141, 118267
Palace Huis Ten Bosch Museum, Sasebo 027040
The Palace Museum, Beijing 007003
Palace Museum, Ulaanbaatar 029012
Palace Museum, Zanzibar 037862
Palace of Holyroodhouse, Royal Collection, Edinburgh 039411
Palace of Royal Jewelleries, Zizinia 009351
Palace of the Governors, Museum of New Mexico, Santa Fe 047975
Palace of the Grand Masters, Rhodos 021454
Palace of Westminster, London . . . 040252
Palacerigg House, Palacerigg 040674
Palacete del Embarcadero, Santander 035814
Palacin, Jean-Pierre, Bordeaux . . . 124137
Palacio Arzobispal, Cusco 031506
Palácio Conde dos Arcos, Goiás . . . 004133
Palacio Condesa de Lebrija, Sevilla 035871
Palácio das Laranjeiras, Rio de Janeiro 004416
Palacio de Exposiciones Kiosko Alfonso, A Coruña 110323
Palacio de la Granja, Orihuela 035571
Palacio de Montemuzo, Ayuntamiento de Zaragoza, Zaragoza 036113
Palacio de Pedralbes, Barcelona . . 034959
Palacio de Viana, Córdoba 035118
Palacio del Mar, Donostia-San Sebastián 035154
Palacio del Mate, Posadas 000484
Palácio do Correio Velho, Lisboa . . 121939
Palácio dos Leilões, Belo Horizonte 096478
Palácio Guanabara, Rio de Janeiro . 004417
Palácio Gustavo Capanema, Rio de Janeiro 004418
Palácio Nacional da Pena, Sintra . . 032693
Palácio Nacional de Mafra, Mafra . . 032661
Palacio Nacional de Queluz, Queluz 032682
Palacio Real, Patrimonio Nacional, Madrid 035439
Palacio Real de Aranjuez, Aranjuez . 034846
Palacio Real de El Pardo, El Pardo . 035636
Palacio Real de Madrid, Museo de Carrozas y Real Armería, Madrid 035440
Palacio Real de Riofrío, Museo de la Caza, Riofrío 035705
Palacio Real y Museos de Tapices, San Ildefonso 035757
Palacio Taranco, Museo de Artes Decorativas, Montevideo 041545
Pałacyk, Warszawa 109175
Paladino, Langenhagen 103836
Palaeobotanisch Museum, Utrecht . 030237
Paläontologisches Museum, Offenhausen 002399
Paläontologisches Museum der Universität Zürich, Zürich 037795
Paläontologisches Museum München, München 019099
Paläontologisches Museum Nierstein, Nierstein 019316
Palaepaphos Museum, Kouklia 008206
Palæsamlingerne, Roskilde 009079
Palagraziussi, Giuliano, Venezia . . . 106772
Palaiopoleio o Sakis, Thessaloniki . 074640
Palaios, Milano 075800
Palais Bénédictine, Fécamp 011792
Palais de Glace, Buenos Aires 000250

Palais de la Découverte, Paris 013733
Palais de la Miniature, Lyon 012833
Palais de la Miniature, Saint-Pourçain-sur-Sioule 014495
Le Palais de l'Art Traditionnel, Constantine 000059
Palais de l'Ile, Centre d'Interprétation Urbain, Annecy 010413
Palais de Tokyo, Site de Création Contemporaine, Paris 013734
Le Palais des Arts, Trouville-sur-Mer 068639
Palais des Beaux-Arts, Bruxelles .. 003355
Le Palais des Beaux-Arts, Bruxelles 135607
Palais des Beaux-Arts, Charleroi .. 003371
Palais des Expositions Chinagora, Alfortville 010334
Palais des Papes et Musée du Vieil Avignon, Avignon 010598
Le Palais du Chocolat, La Côte-Saint-André 012244
Palais du Roure, Bibliothèque et Collections, Avignon 010599
Palais du Tau, Centre des Monuments Nationaux, Reims 014013
Le Palais Francais, Cairo 060462
Palais für aktuelle Kunst, Glückstadt 017435
Palais Grand Ducal, Luxembourg .. 027896
Palais Jacques Coeur, Bourges 010941
Palais Liechtenstein, Feldkirch 001847
Palais Minéral, Composition avec des Minéraux, Granville 011994
Palais Oriental, Paris 066376
Palais Palffy, Wien 002984
Palais Papius, Wetzlar 020846
Palais Princier, Monaco 028998
Palais Rihour, Lille 012686
Palais Surreal, Salvador Dalí im Palais Pallavicini, Wien 002985
Palamas Museum, Athinai 021209
Palamka, Lyon 099609
Palamuse O. Lutsu Kihelkonnakoolimuuseum, Palamuse 009386
Il Palanchino, Milano 075801, 127645
Paland, Karin, Weißbach, Gem. Kreuth 105199
Palanga, Pierina, Taranto 076751
Palanquin, Roscoff 067224
Palas, Varna 096776
Palata na Fizikata, Nacionalen Politechničeski Muzej Sofia, Kazanlăk 004718
Palatina, Buenos Aires 094084
Palatino, Roma 076602
Palatino, San Francisco .. 119762, 135493
Palau, Barcelona 080900
Palau de Caramany, Girona 110370
Palau Ducal dels Borja, Gandía 035213
Palau Reial de l'Almudaina, Palma de Mallorca 035618
Palawan Museum, Puerto Princesa . 031766
Palawan National Museum, Quezon 031768
Palawan State University Museum, Puerto Princesa 031767
Palazzina Marfisa, Ferrara 024115
Palazzo, Paolo, Palermo 127836
Palazzo Apostolico ed Archivio Storico della Santa Casa, Loreto 024533
Palazzo Armeria, Zurrieq 028051
Palazzo Attems-Petzenstein, Musei Provinciali di Gorizia, Gorizia 024353
Palazzo Barolo, Torino 026079
Palazzo Belgiojoso, Musei Civici, Lecco 024489
Palazzo Borromeo, Stresa 025959
Palazzo Bricherasio, Torino 026080
Palazzo Castelmur, Stampa 037595
Palazzo Castiglioni, Cingoli 023883
Palazzo del Principe, Genova 024327
Palazzo del Senato, Pinerolo 025250
Palazzo della Ragione, Padova 025067
Palazzo della Triennale, Milano ... 024732
Palazzo delle Esposizioni, Roma ... 025580
Palazzo Ducale, Genova 024328
Palazzo Ducale, Venezia 026262
Palazzo Fieschi, Genova 075491
Palazzo Grassi, Venezia 026263
Palazzo Litta, Milano 075802
Palazzo Medici Riccardi, Firenze .. 024199
Palazzo Orlandi, Busseto 023552
Palazzo Pfanner e Giardino, Lucca . 024549
Palazzo Pubblico, Opera di Francesco Azzurri 1884-1894, San Marino .. 034119
Palazzo Reale, Torino 026081
Palazzo Reale-Reggia di Caserta, Caserta 023691
Palazzo Taffini, Savigliano 025817
Palazzo Tozzoni, Collezioni d'Arte Comunali, Imola 024408
Palazzo Vertemate Franchi, Piuro .. 025283
Palazzo Vescovile, Reggio Emilia .. 025417
Palbert, Torino 076854, 106690
Pale Ink Antiquities, Phoenix 091759
't Paleis, Knokke-Heist 058250
Paleis Het Loo - Nationaal Museum, Apeldoorn 029256
Paleologo di Lemnos, Messina 127505
Paleontological and Geological Museum of the University of Athens, Athinai . 021210
Paleontologičen Muzej, Asenovgrad 004620
Paleontologičeskij Muzej im. Ju.A. Orlova, Paleontologičeskij institut RAN, Moskva 033515
Paleontologisk Museum, Universitets Naturhistoriske Museer, Oslo 031078
Paleontologiska Utställingar, Uppsala Universitet, Uppsala 036737
Paleontologo-stratigrafičeskij Muzej pri Kafedre Istorii Geologii, Sankt-Peterburgskogo Gosudarstvennogo Universiteta, Sankt-Peterburg ... 033822
Paleorama - Museo Itinerante, Don Torcuato 000331
Palermo, Rocco, Rio de Janeiro ... 058631
Palestinian Archaeological Museum, Birzeit 031411
Palestinian Artist House, Al-Khalil .. 108781
Palet en Tekenstift, Alkmaar 136007
Paleta, Lisboa 109341
Paletta, Athinai 105407
La Palette, Amiens 098822
Palette, Cairo 098662
Palette, Innsbruck 135576
Palette, Lorient 099522
Palette, North Shore 108527
Palette, Philadelphia 118819
Palette, Saint-Étienne 067462
Palette, Toulon (Var) 101325
Palette, Wardenburg 105160
Palette, Messine, Metz 099716
The Palette and Chisel Academy, Chicago 042872
Palette Bleue, Saint-Junien 067566
La Palette d'Or, Paris 100748, 124767
La Palette d'Or, Strasbourg 101300
Palette du Boucher, Brest 061777
Die Palette - Frankfurt am Main e.V., Frankfurt am Main 053541
Paletten, Göteborg 136116
Paletti, Parma 076219
Paley, Barbara K., New York 118268
The Paley Design Center of Philadelphia University, Philadelphia 046934
La Palferine, Paris 066377
Palimpsiston, Lemesos 059962
Palimpsiston, Lemesos 059963
Pálio Objetos de Arte, Rio de Janeiro 096634
Palisander, New York 091142
Palissandre, Bersillies ... 061374, 124098
Palissandre, Bruxelles 058047
Palissandres, Paris 124768
Palitra, Charkiv 112381
Palitra, Sankt-Peterburg 109640
Palitra, Sankt-Peterburg 109641
Palix, Yvonamor, México 107505
Palix, Yvonamor, Paris 100749
Paljas, Den Haag 078230
Paljas, Den Haag 078231
Pałka, Kazimierz, Kraków 129045
Pall, William, New York 118269
Pall Mall Antiques, Leigh-on-Sea .. 084957
Palladio, Memphis 090099
Palladio, M., Memphis 090100
Palladion, Basel 111216
Palladion, Toulouse 101367
Pallamar, Friederike, Wien 057515
Pallamar, Friederike, Wien 057516
Pallant House Gallery, Chichester .. 039073
Pallas, Breda 078111
Pallas, Praha 098477
Pallas Gallery, Turramurra 095354
Pallas & Janos, Den Haag 140398
Pallas-Palacio, Bruno, Bordeaux ... 124138
Palleau, Jean-Pierre, Paris 066378
Pallen, F., Brugge 057784
Pallesi, A., Roma 076603
Pallocca, Franco, Roma 076604
Palloni, A., Firenze 075379
Palloni Picchi, Loise, Firenze 075380
Pallotta, Giuseppe, Roma 128143
Palm, Werner, Bonn 069937
Palm Beach 3 - Contemporary-Photography-SOFA Design, West Palm Beach 094022
Palm Beach! America's International Fine Art and Antiques Fair, West Palm Beach 094023
Palm Beach Institute of Contemporary Art, Lake Worth 045120
Palm Springs Desert Museum, Palm Springs 046798
Palm Street Gallery, Westport 108656
Palma Ceia, Tampa 093147
Palma Rosa Museum, Hamilton, Brisbane 001094
Palmaverde, Bologna 139993
Palmdale Gallery, Motukarara 108504
Palme, K., Erftstadt 102642
Palme, Karin, Arnstorf 069186
Palmeblads Förlag, Göteborg 134958
Palmer, Birmingham 115123
Palmer, Richmond, Surrey 086360
Palmer, B., London 131134
Palmer, David, Ely 113018
Palmer, Dermot & Jill, Brighton ... 083710
Palmer, Herbert, West Hollywood .. 120405
Palmer, John, Houston 116383
Palmer, Mary, Stradbroke 086771
Palmer, Meredith, New York 118270
Palmer Auction Service, Lucas 122954
Palmer Galleries, Richmond, Surrey 114310
Palmer/Gullickson Octagon Home, West Salem 049099
Palmer House, Northfield 046554
Palmer Museum, Jewell 044862
Palmer Museum of Art, The Pennsylvania State University, University Park . 048703
Palmer Wirfs & Assoc., Portland ... 091990
Palmers Green Antiques Centre, London 085590
Palmerston North Community Arts Council, Palmerston North 108535
Palmieri, Saint-Ouen 067858
Palmieri, Vezio, Napoli 076021
Palmieri Sauveur, Nice 065123
Palmirotta, Ottavio, Torino 106691
Palmrose, David, Portland 091991
Palmu, Juhani, Helsinki 098741
Palmyra, Ygrande 069064
Palmyre, Bruxelles 058048, 123603
Palo Alto Art Center, Palo Alto 046804
Palo Alto Junior Museum, Palo Alto 046805
Palóc Múzeum, Nógrádi Megyei Múzeum, Balassagyarmat 021620
Paloma Art, Tucson 120158
Paloma Art at El Cortijo, Tucson ... 120159
Palombi, Roma 134681
Palomuseo, Helsinki 009559
Palomuseo, Kuusankoski 009772
Palomuseo, Lahti 009786
Palonta, Patrizia, Catania 127274
Palookaville, Portland 091992
Palos Verdes Art Center, Rancho Palos Verdes 047325
Palosanto Antiguedades, Almeria .. 080771
Palotavárosi Skanzen, Székesfehérvár 021870
Palpura, Lisboa 109342
Pålsjö Kvarn, Helsingborg 036338
Paltamon Kotiseutumuseo, Paltamo 009948
Paltani, Germinal, Nyon 082706
Paltenghi, Guerino, Château-d'Oex . 111342
Palthey, Jean-Christophe, Paris ... 066379
Paltinger, Walter, Wien 057517
Palu, Seattle 093044
Palucka Izba Muzealna, Muzeum Okręgowego im. Leona Wyczółkowskiego w Bydgoszczy, Kcynia 031993
Paludan-Bøger, København 137900
Palumbo, Buenos Aires 136745
Palumbo, New York 091143
Palumbo, Christina, Buenos Aires .. 136746
Palumbus, Antwerpen 096085
Palz, M., Beckingen 069501
Palzer, Michael, Ingolstadt 103433
Pama, Oslo 108738, 140705
Památky a Umění, Znojmo 060207
Památník, Dolní Domaslavice 008352
Památník Adolfa Kaspara, Loštice . 008489
Památník Antonína Dvořáka, Nelahozeves 008522
Památník Antonína Dvořáka, Vysoká u Příbrami 008768
Památník Antonína Dvořáka, Zlonice 008789
Památník Bedřicha Smetany, Jabkenice 008398
Památník Bedřicha Václavka, Čáslavice 008308
Památník Bible Kralické, Moravské Zemské Museum Brno, Kralice nad Oslavou 008451
Památník Bitvy 1813, Chlumec u Ústi nad Labem 008331
Památník Bitvy 1866 na Chlumu, Muzeum Východních Čech v Hradci Králové, Všestary 008765
Památník Bohuslava Martinů, Městské muzeum a galerie, Polička 008585
Památník Boženy Němcové, Červený Kostelec 008312
Památník Bratří Křičků, Kelč 008432
Památník Bratří Mrštíků, Diváky ... 008348
Památník Dr. Emila Axmana, Chropyně 008340
Památník Dr. Emila Holuba, Holice v Čechách 008378
Památník Dr. Františka Křižíka, Plánice 008568
Památník Františka Palackého, Hodslavice 008376
Památník Jana Ámoše Komenského, Bílá Třemešná 008267
Památník Jana Ámoše Komenského, Horní Branná 008381
Památník Jana Ámoše Komenského, Vlastivědné Mmuzeum Nový Jičín, Fulnek 008363
Památník Jiráskova Pokladu, Muzeum Orlických Hor, Rychnov nad Kněžnou, Potštejn 008588
Památník Jiřího Melantricha z Aventýna, Polabské muzeum Poděbrady, Roždalovice 008672
Památník Josefa Hybeše, Dašice .. 008346
Památník Josefa Ladislava Piče, Mšeno u Mělníka 008517
Památník Josefa Mánesa, Čechy pod Košířem 008309
Památník Josefa Suka, Křečovice .. 008456
Památník Karla Čapka, Stará Huť u Dobříše 008692
Památník Karla Havlíčka Borovského, Muzeum Vysočiny Havlíčkův Brod, Havlíčkův Brod 008369
Památník Karla Hynka Máchy, Doksy 008351
Památník Karla Jaromira Erbena, Miletin 008503

Památník Karla Václava Raise, Lázně Bělohrad 008468
Památník Krále Jiřího z Poděbrad a Lapidarium, Oblastni Muzeum, Poděbrady 008579
Památník Leoše Janáčka, Hukvaldy 008394
Památník Leoše Janáčka, Moravské Zemské Museum, Brno 008294
Památník Lidice, Lidice 008477
Památník Města, Police nad Metuji . 008581
Památník Mikoláše Alše, Mirotice . . 008505
Památník Mistra Jana Husa, Husinec 008396
Památník Mohyla míru, Prace u Brna 008589
Památník Národní Svobody, Hrabyně 008387
Památník Národního Písemnictví (Muzeum České Literatury), Praha 008642
Památník Otakara Štáfla, Muzeum Vysočiny Havlíčkův Brod, Havlíčkův Brod . . 008370
Památník Petra Bezruče, Muzeum Prostějovska, Kostelec na Hané . . 008446
Památník Petra Bezruče, Slezské zemské muzeum, Opava 008547
Památník Prokopa Diviše, Jihomoravské Muzeum ve Znojme, Znojmo 008793
Památník Románu Aloise Jiráska Skály, Teplice nad Metují 008711
Památník Selského Povstání, Městske Muzeum, Rtyně v Podkrkonoší . . . 008676
Památník Svatopluka Čecha, Obřiství 008540
Památník Svatopluka Čecha, Ostředek 008556
Památník Terezín, Terezín 008713
Památník Terezy Novákové, Proseč u Skutče 008660
Památník Václava Beneše Třebízského, Třebíz 008722
Památník Václava Beneše Třebízského a Svatopluka Čecha, Liten 008478
Památník Venkovského Lidu, Žumberk 008795
Památník W.A. Mozarta a Manželů Duškových, Bertramka, Praha . . . 008643
Památník Zdeňka Fibicha, Všeborice 008764
Památník Životické Tragedie, Muzeum Těšínska, Havířov 008367
Pambasang Museo ng Pilipinas, Manila 031733
Pambianco, Alberto, Milano 127646
Pamětní Síň Jana Ámoše Komenského, Brandýs nad Orlicí 008276
Pametnik na Kulturata Zemenski Manastir, Zemen 004951
Pami Antichità, Roma 076605
Pammer, Evelyn, Wien 057518
Pamminger, Reinhilde, Hamburg . . 071305
Pampa Centro de Artes y Diseño, Buenos Aires 055232
Pampaloni, Paolo, Firenze 140025
Pampaloni, Roberto, Firenze 127385
Pampaloni, Romeo, Roma 128144
Pampeana, Buenos Aires 136747
Pampille, Bernay 061368
Pamplin Park Civil War Site, Petersburg 046905
Pamukbank Fotoğraf Galerisi, İstanbul 112346
Pamyr, Paris 066380
Pan African Art Gallery, Long Beach 116677
Pan American Gallery, Dallas 115918
Pan-Art, Hong Kong 097819
Pan-Dan, Moskva 109576
PAN Kunstforum Niederrhein, Emmerich 016972
Pan-o-Rama, Bremen 138947
Panache, Los Angeles 089869
Panache, Tetbury 086863
Panache, West Hollywood 093493
Panache Antiques, Vancouver 059397
Panachrantos Monastery, Falika . . . 021260
Panaddaman-Cagayan State University Museum, Tuguegarao 031803
Panalba International, Marseille . . . 099679
Panamin Museum, Pasay 031759
Pananti, Piero, Milano 106276
Panarcadic Archeological Museum of Tripolis, Tripoli 021514
Panarelli, Andrea, Bari 127116
Panasia Galerie, Zürich 083008
Panay, Gérard, Bormes-les-Mimosas 061665
Panayi, Nicolas, Lefkosia 098304
La Pancarte, Nort-sur-Erdre 065230
Panchavati, Bangalore 074779
La Panchetta, Bari 105934
Pancho Lepina, Vigo 081709
Pancrazi, Jean-François, Toulon (Var) 124967
Panda, Smederevo 109747
Pandanus Palace, Noosaville 056353
Pander & Scholtens, Amsterdam . . 077928
Pandiris, André, Paris 066381
't Pandje, Utrecht 108258
Pandolfini Casa d'Aste, Firenze . . . 121687
Pandolfino, Daniele, Roma 128145
Pandora, Antwerpen 133251
Pandora Decor, Firenze 075381
Pandora Fine Art, Grantham 113146
Pandora Galéria, Budapest 105535
Pandora Old Masters, New York . . . 091144
Pandora's Box, Totnes 086907
Pandoras Gallery, Calgary 096836
Pánek, Bohumil, Říčany u Prahy . . . 124005
Panevėžio, Panevėžys 107355
Panhandle-Plains Historical Museum, Canyon 042609
Panhard, Gilles, Paris 124769
Panhellenic Union of Antiquities and Art Object Restorers, Athinai 053667
De Panhoeve, Berlicum 128585
Panicali, Carla, Roma 106604
Panico, Friederike, Amstetten 056918
Panico, Rocco, Kemmelbach 057094
Panier, Francine, Marseille 064380
Panini, Franco Cosimo, Modena . . . 134640
Panizza, Enrico Enzo, Milano 075803
Panje Tala, Teheran 074846
Panke Museum, Berlin 016156
Pankhurst Centre, Manchester 040413
Panlong Art Cooperative, Shanghai . 097934
Panlong Art Cooperative, Shanghai . 097935
Pannemann, K. & H., Westerstede . 105234
Panneterie, Saint-Ouen 067859
Pannetier, Gérard, Malemort-sur-Corrèze 064237
Pannhuis, Harald, Gummersbach . . 071148
Pannon Antik, Budapest 074702
Pannonhalmi Főapátság Gyűjteménye, Pannonhalma 021808
Pannonisches Heimatmuseum, Neusiedl am See 002372
Christiane von Pannwitz & Carolin Zuber, Berlin 125270
Panoptikum, Gelsenkirchen 070959
Panorama, Exeter 113039
Panorama, Wien 095915, 133225
Panorama Antiquariat, Lüneburg . . 139435
Panorama Antiques, Saint Louis . . . 092294
Panorama Art Gallery, Warszawa . . 121911
Panorama de la Bataille de Waterloo, Braine-l'Alleud 003253
Panorama Galleries, New York 091145
Panorama Großantiquariat, Wiesbaden 139853
Panorama Kreuzigung Christi, Einsiedeln 037060
Panorama Mesdag, Den Haag 029450
Panorama Museum, Bad Frankenhausen 015700
Panorama Numismatique, Paris . . . 066382
Panorama Oborona Sevastopolja 1854-1855 rr., Muzei geroïčnoï oborony i vyzvolennja Sevastopolja, Sevastopol 038391
Panorama Plevenska Epopeja 1877, Pleven 004783
Panorama Racławicka, Muzeum Narodowe, Wrocław 032533
Panorama, Salisbury University, Salisbury 136603
Panorama Šturm Sapun-gori 7 Travnja 1944 r., Muzei geroïčnoï oborony i vyzvolennja Sevastopolja, Sevastopol 038392
Panos Aravantinos Theatrical Museum of Painting and Stage Design, Piraeus 021435
Pansarmuséet, Axvall 036210
Pansi, Heinrich u Anita, Schwanberg 095755
Panssarimuseo, Parola 009955
Państwowa, Sopot 109075
Państwowe Muzeum Archeologiczne, Warszawa 032480
Państwowe Muzeum Etnograficzne, Warszawa 032481
Państwowe Muzeum Gross-Rosen w Rogoźnicy, Rogoźnica 032291
Państwowe Muzeum im. Przypkowskich, Jędrzejów 031969
Państwowe Muzeum na Majdanku, Lublin 032136
Państwowe Muzeum Stutthof, Sztutowo 032377
Państwowe Muzeum Stutthof w Sztutowie, Sopot 032330
Państwowe Muzeum w Białymstoku, Białystok 031830
Państwowe Muzeum w Oświęcimiu-Brzezince, Oświęcim 032208
Państwowe Zbiory Sztuki, Zamek Królewski na Wawelu, Sułoszowa 032348
Panta Rei Antiek, Leeuwarden 078555
Panta Rhei, Madrid 110589
Pantaleo, Fari, Zürich 130256
Pantaleón Rodríguez, Isabel, Salamanca 129715
Pantano, Grazia, Modena 127739
Pantazi, Agni & Georgiou, Piraeus . 074628
Panteão da Pátria Tancredo Neves, Brasília 004025
Pantechnicon Art Gallery, Daylesford 094466
Pantelejmonovskij, Sankt-Peterburg 080319, 140939
Panter, Richard, Bischheim 124101
Panter & Hall, London 113815
Pantera Roz, Bucureşti 109444
Panthéon, Paris 013735
Pantheon Arte, Roma 106605
Pantheon Books, New York 135451
Panther Decor, Vancouver 059398
Pantiles Antiques, Tunbridge Wells . 086946
Pantiles Spa Antiques, Tunbridge Wells 086947, 131621
Pantin, Ciprián A., Buenos Aires . . . 055233
Pantoja, Eliseo, Santiago de Chile . 097632
Pantokrátor, Budapest 074703
Panton, Milano 075804, 134625
Panton, Praha 133417
Panukrainskaja II, Dnipropetrovs'k . 112386
Panzano, Gian Carlo, Genova 075492
Panzano, Guido, Genova 075493
Panzano, Mario, Genova 075494
Pao Galleries at Hong Kong Art Centre, Hong Kong 007129
Pao & Moltke, Toronto . . . 059256, 097344
Paola Shop, Lima 079555
Paolella, Fabio, Napoli . . . 076022, 127785
Paoletti, Paolo, Firenze 075382
Paoli, de, Windsor, Ontario 097563
Paoli, Anna Loretta, Prato 076258
Paoli, Enrico, Prato 106477
Paolo, Cincinnati 115650
Pap, Mária, Budapest 127079
Papa Re, Roma 128146
Papadam, Nikos, Thessaloniki 105452
Papadato, Roma 076606
Papadopol's Art, Constanţa 080181
Papadopoulos, Charis, Thessaloniki 074641
Papadopoulos, Georgios, Thessaloniki 105453
Papadopoulos, Kleanthis, Thessaloniki 105454
Papadopoulos, Pavlos Georgios, Bologna 075097
Papadopoulos, Stephan, Kornwestheim 126139
Papadopoulos Picture Gallery, Evangelistria Holy Foundation, Tinos 021510
Papagena, Le Vésinet 099464
Papageno, Oviedo 081460
Papakura and District Historical Society Museum, Papakura 030571
Papakura Art Gallery, Auckland . . . 108354
Papaleo, Raffaele, Roma 128147
Papamoa Art Gallery, Tauranga 108577
Papasideris, Antwerpen 123551
Papaya, Hellerup 060254
Papazian, Paris 066383
Pape, Barbara, Rinteln 073542
Pape, Hans-Werner, Berlin 125271
Papelaria Moderna, Lisboa 140849
Papeler, Heinz, Krefeld 072077
Paper Antiquities, San Diego 092669, 142909
The Paper Bag Princess, West Hollywood 093494
Paper Chain, Mackay 136984
The Paper Conservator, Upton-upon-Severn 136259
Paper Heart Gallery, Phoenix 118884
Paper Moon, Portland 142807
Paper Peddlers Out-Of-Print Book, Cleveland 142341
Paper-Rock-Scissors, Baltimore . . . 115075
Paper Sculpture, San Francisco . . . 119763
Paper-Weight, Łódź 079672
Paperback Trading Post, Buffalo . . . 142266
Paperbark Gallery, Evans Head 094519
Papergraphica, Christchurch 079044
Paperimuseo, Espoo 009477
Papers d'Art, Girona 136098
Paperworks Gallery, Vancouver . . . 097510
Papezik, Ernst, Wien 057519
Paphos District Archaeological Museum, Paphos 008234
De Papieren Korf, Gent . . . 058199, 137500
Papierfabrik Hohenofen, Hohenofen 017974
Papiergeschichtliche Sammlung, Stiftung Zanders, Bergisch Gladbach 015969
Papiermachermuseum, Steyrermühl 002710
Papiermolen de Schoolmeester, Westzaan 030327
Papiermühle Weddersleben, Weddersleben 020693
Papiermuseum, Düren 016824
Papiers d'Antan, Bruxelles 058049, 137457
Papilio Antiques, Praha 060149
Papilio Starozitnosti, Brno 059981
Papiliorama-Nocturama Foundation, Kerzers 037208
Papillon, Bern 111270
Papillon, Joël & Paulette, Le Fidelaire 063619
Papillon Gallery, Los Angeles 089870
Papiri, Lugano 082605
Papiri, Adriana, Lugano 082606
Papiri, Adriana, Lugano 111667
Papiri, Adriana, Lugano 111668
Papiri, Adriana, Lugano 111669
Papírna Muzeum, Velké Losiny 008747
Papiro, Palermo 127837
Papiros, Denia 129494
Papita, Dubai 112456
Papon, Jean, Vevey 082884
Papp, Florian, New York 091146
Papp, Dr. Magdalene, Wien 095916, 123522
Papp, Th., Niddatal 104437
Pappabello, Cleveland 088351
Pappalardo, Valentina, Catania 106024
Pappe, Bernd, Bern 129969
Papplewick Pumping Station, Ravenshead 040803
Pappot, Peter, Amsterdam 077929
Pappy, Richmond 092096
Paprika Múzeum, Népművészeti Tájház, Kalocsa 021747
Paprikamúzeum, Szeged 021863

Paprsek, Kutná Hora 098377
Papua New Guinea Display Centre, Crafers 000954
Papua New Guinea National Museum and Art Gallery, Boroko 031435
Papunya Tula Artists, Alice Springs . 094145
Papworth, Barry, Lymington 085879, 131245
Papworth, Chris L., Kelvedon 084822
Papyri, Berlin 069719
Papyrud Secret, Cairo 060463
Papyrus, Brugge 057785
Le Papyrus, Bruxelles 137458
Papyrus, Voorburg 140564
Papyrus Antique Shop, San Diego . . 092670
Papyrus Books, New York 142686
Papyrus Salus, Tilburg 128844
Papyrusmuseum und Papyrussammlung, Wien 002986
Le Paquebot, La Flotte 063380
Paquebot, Saint-Ouen 067860
Paquebot Lacoste, Paris 066384
Para-Börse, Basel 082162
Para/Site Art Space, Hong Kong . . . 007130
Paracelso, New York 091147
Parachute, Montréal 135642
La Parada del Restaurador, Barcelona 080901
La Parada del Restaurador, Barcelona 080902, 129376
The Parade, Edmonton 058838
Parade, Toulouse 068532
Parade Antiques Market, Plymouth . 086277
Parade Galerie, Amsterdam 107780
Parade of Presidents Wax Museum, Keystone 044997
Paradigma, Moskva 109577
Le Paradis de l'Occasion, Nice 065124
Paradisboden, Bandhagen 081772
Paradise Antique Arts, Honolulu . . . 088973
Paradise Books, Surfers Paradise . . 137095
Paradise Found, Winnipeg 097599
Paradise Galleries, San Diego 119532
Paradise Gallery, Westcourt 095395
Paradise Mill Silk Industry Museum, Macclesfield 040378
Paradise Road, Colombo 081762
Paradise Road, Colombo 081763
Paradise Road Studio, Colombo . . . 081764
Paradise Road - The Gallery Shop, Colombo 081765
Paradise So Nice Interprizes, Los Angeles 116864
Paradise Valley Antiques, Phoenix . 091760
Paradiso, Baltimore 087701
Paradox, Edam 134808
Paradox, Harderwijk 140450
Parafia Ewangelicko - Augsburska Wang, Karpacz 031983
Parafialne Muzeum Regionalne, Krasnobród 032073
Parafita, Isabel Mota, Porto 080103
Paragon, Auckland 128910
Paragon Antiques, Birmingham . . . 087779
Paragon Antiques and Collectors Market, Bath 083440
Paragon Book Gallery, Chicago 135349, 142293
Paragon Furniture, London 131135
Paragon Press, London 135247
Paragona, Massimo, Napoli 076023
Paragona, Massimo, Napoli 076024
Paragone Gallery, West Hollywood . 120406
Parainen District Museum, Parainen 009949
Parainen Industrial Museum, Parainen 009950
Paraíso, C., Cruz Quebrada-Dafundo 121920
Paraíso, C., Lisboa 121940
Paralax Gallery, London 113816
Parallels Gallery, Philadelphia 118820
Paralos, London 141864
Parametro, Faenza 135942
Paramount Antiques, New York . . . 091148
Paramount Book Exchange, Manchester 141939
Paramount Décor, Montréal 123791
Paramythioti, Dominique, Paris . . . 100750
Parant, Marie, Paris 124770
Paraphernalia, Harrogate 084584
Paraphernalia, Sheffield 086563
Paraphernalia, Stockton-on-Tees . .086729, 131545
Paraplu, Nijmegen 108157
Parasaar, Hamme 120762
Parasite Museum, Faculty of Medicine, Mahidol University, Bangkok 037886
Paraskevova, Dr. Jaroslava, Frankfurt am Main 102808
Parasol Press, New York 135452
Parasol Unit, London 113817
Paratiritis, Thessaloniki 105455
Paratiritis, Thessaloniki 105456
Paravent, London 085591
Parazaar, Antwerpen 057724
Le Parc, München 072813
Parc, Vichy 101466
Parc Archéologique, Antoing 003151
Parc Archéologique de la Pointe-du-Buisson, Melocheville 005857
Parc Archéologique de Larina, Hières-sur-Amby 012103
Parc Archéologique Européen de Bliesbruck-Reinheim, Bliesbruck . 010840
Parc Ardèche Miniature, Soyons . . . 014847
Parc & Château de Valencay, Valençay 015093
Parc de la Préhistoire, Tarascon-sur-Ariège 014907
Parc de l'Artillerie, Québec 006230
Parc de Préhistoire de Bretagne, Malansac 012863
Parc de Reconstitution Archéologique, Villeneuve-d'Ascq 015269
Parc Howard Museum and Art Gallery, Llanelli 040056
Parc Miniature Alsace-Lorraine, Saint-Ame 014179
Parc Monceau, Atlanta 087511
Parc National de la Culture des Ethnies, Vientiane 027649
Parc Préhistorique Animalier Dino-Zoo, Charbonnières-les-Sapins 011244
Parc Préhistorique des Grottes de Fontirou, Castella 011137
Parc Préhistorique Imaginaire, Écomusée, Chamoux 011220
Parc Zoologique Arche de Noé et Amazonia, Saint-Clément-des-Baleines 014233
Parchemine, Lyon 138182
Parchman & Stremmel, San Antonio 119439
Parco, Nagoya 106931
Parco Monumentale di Pinocchio, Collodi 023933
Parco Museo Minerario, Abbadia San Salvatore 023109
Parco Nazionale delle Incisioni Rupestri, Capo di Ponte 023644
Parco Scherrer, Morcote 037339
Pardaf, Antwerpen 057725
Pardee Home Museum, Oakland . . 046599
Pardo, Lugo 081192
Pardo, Paris 100751
Pardo Gallery, Milano 106277
Pardo Sanchez, Jorge Antonio, Barcelona 080903
Pardo Sheenan, New York 118271
Pardoes, Amsterdam 077930
Pardon-Galerie und Verlag, Bad Homburg v.d.Höhe 101657, 133731
Parduhn, Ute, Düsseldorf 102535
La Pared Galería, Bogotá 098180
Paredis, T., Antwerpen 057726
Parent, Michelle, Montréal 058986
Parent, Xavier, Marseille 124430
Parente, Madrid 081355
Parenthou, Jacques, Lille 063862
Parenthou, Pierre & Jacques, Lille . 063863
Parenthou, Richard, Lille 063864
Parenza, G. & C., Roma 076607
Parenza, Marco, Roma . . . 076608, 128148
Paret Michel, Vermenton 068774
La Parete, Toronto 097345
Parfait, Yvon, Hudimesil 063181
Parfum-Flacon-Museum, München 019100
Parfummuseum, Hochfelden 037191
Pargon, D. & H., Nancy 064876
Parham Elizabethan House & Gardens, Pulborough 040785
Pari Nadimi, Toronto 097346
Pariente, Emé, Biarritz 061471
Parienté, Nathalie, Paris 100752
Parigi, Daniela, Torino 076855
Parikian, D., London 141865
Parikkalan Kotiseutumuseo, Parikkala 009952
Parin, Marie-Madeleine, Paris 124771
Paris, Nicole, Agon-Coutainville . . . 060674
Paris, Nicole, Rouen 067288
Paris Américan Art, Paris . 100753, 124772
Paris Antique Restoration, Los Angeles 132272
Paris Antiques, Ampthill . . 083298, 130302
Paris Antiques, New York 091149
Paris Antiques Gallery, Los Angeles 089871
Paris Book Store, Denver 142395
Paris Gibson Square Museum of Art, Great Falls 044301
Paris Images, New York 118272
Paris Manaus, Paris 066385
Paris-Musées, Paris 133661
Paris, Isabel & Carmen Pajares, Lleida 110408
Paris Photo, Paris 093669
Paris to Province, New York 091150
Parish, Norman, Washington 120334
von Parish-Kostümbibliothek, Münchner Stadtmuseum, München 019101
Parishville Museum, Parishville . . . 046818
Parisi, Franco, Roma 128149
Parisi, Giuseppe, Roma 128150
Parisi, Salvatore, Napoli 076025
Parisian Galerie, Singapore 109849
Parisot, René, Briançon 061790
Parizot, Alain, La Chapelle-Rablais . 063319
Park, New York 118273
Park Antique Restoration, Sherwood Park 059108, 123821
Park Antiques, Detroit . . . 088772, 132057
Park Antiques, Menston 085976
Park Avenue Antiques, Minneapolis 090388
Park Avenue Antiques Show, New York 094024
Park Avenue Gallery, Saint Louis . . 119235
Park Boulevard Art Works, San Diego 119533
Park Boulevard Gallery, San Diego . 092671
Park City Antiques Mall, Dallas 088589
Park City Museum, Park City 046820
Park Coin, Minneapolis 090389
Park Farm Museum, Milton Abbas . 040472
Park Gallery, Falkirk 039477
Park Gallery, Glasgow 113126
Park Gallery, Lalitpur 107602
Park Gallery, London 113818
The Park Gallery, Mosman Park . . . 094899
Park Gallery and Bookshop, Wellingborough 142145
Park Hill Cooperative Book Store, Denver 142396
Park House Antiques, Bladon 083555
Park House Museum, Amherstburg 005009
Park Lane Antiques Centre, Armadale, Victoria 055391
The Park-McCullough House, North Bennington 046516
Park-muzej General V.Z. Lavrov, Gorni Dabnik 004692
Park-muzej im. A.K. Tolstogo, Brjansk 033054
Park-Muzej Vladislav Varnenčik, Varna 004923
Park Ryu Sook Gallery, Seoul 107276
Park South Gallery, New York 118274
Park Street Antiques, Jacksonville . 089445
Park & Tilford, Vancouver 097511
Park View Antiques, Wadhurst 086997, 131637
Park-Villa Rieter, Museum Rietberg Zürich, Zürich 037796
Parkanon Kotiseutumuseo, Parkano 009953
Parkanon Metsämuseo, Parkano . . 009954
Parkdale-Maplewood Community Museum, Barss Corner 005074
Parke, Coventry 130610
Parke-West, San Diego 092672
Parker, Herzogenaurach 103365
Parker, Hunters Hill 056005
Parker, London . . 085592, 113819, 131136
Parker, Nashville 117364
Parker, Jack, Saint Louis . 092295, 119236
Parker, Kevin, Hendra 055977
Parker, William W., Washington . . .120335, 133032
Parker Middleton, London 113820
Parker-O'Malley Air Museum, Ghent 044187
Parker Tavern Museum, Reading . . 047342
Parker's Books, Sarasota 142973
Parkerson, Houston 116384
Parkett, Zürich 136129
Parkett Publishers, New York 135453
Parkett Verlag, Zürich 135095
Parkfields Gallery, Ross-on-Wye . . . 114326
Parkham Place Gallery, Surry Hills . 056656
Parkhouse, Mark, Barnstaple 083398
Parkhouse Antiques, Dallas 088590
Parkin, Michael, London 085593
Parkins, Cheam 122454
Parkinson, Anthony, Southport 142085
Parkland College Art Gallery, Champaign 042705
Parks Canada Visitor Reception Centre, Churchill 005271
Parks Johnson, Toronto 120820
Parkside Antiques, Melton Mowbray 085971
Parkside Cottage Museum, Narrandera 001314
Parkstone Press, Düren 133883
Parktown, Cannes 061951
Parkville Gallery, Flemington 094547
Parkway Galleries, Kansas City . . . 116587
Parkzicht, Ermelo 029581
Parlamentsausstellung des Deutschen Bundestages Wege, Irrwege, Umwege, Deutscher Dom, Berlin 016157
Parlatore, Prof. Maricetta, Bologna . 127172
Parliament House Art Collection, Canberra 000891
Parliamentary Memorial Museum, Tokyo 027231
Parlor, San Francisco 119764
Parlour Farm Antiques, Cirencester 084019
Parlour Gallery, Wolumla 095407
Parma, Luigi, Milano 127647
Parmakkapı İş Sanat Galerisi, İstanbul 112347
Parmantica, Parma 076220
Parme, Biarritz 061472
Parmegiani, Elisabetta, Milano 075805
Parmentier, Daniel, Egry 062765
Parmer, J., San Diego 142910
Parmiggiani, Marina, Modena 127740
Parnas, Katowice 108920
Parnas, Kraków 108969
Parnass, Wien 135577
Parnass Verlag, Wien 133226
Parnassos, Wassenaar 140570
Parnasszus, Budapest 139926
Parnell Gallery, Auckland 108355
Parnell Museum, Rathdrum 022849
Parnham House, Beaminster 038644
Parnitzke, G., Bessenbach 069810
Parochialkirche, Berlin 016158
Paroles, Avignon 138021
Parolini, Jean-Jacques, Lausanne . 082560
Parolini, Marietta & Jean-Jacques, Grandvaux 082483
La Parpaïolle, Marseille 064381
Parparov, Iva-I., Sofia 058768

Parpin, Parviz, Senden, Westfalen . 126795
Parque Arqueológico Cueva Pintada, Gáldar 035209
Parque Arqueológico El Caño, Natá 031420
Parque Etnográfico do Río Arnoia, Allariz 034823
Parque Museo el Catillo, Los Realejos 035693
Parque-Museo La Venta, Villahermosa 028939
Parque Regional de la Cuenca Alta del Manzanares, Manzanares el Real 035467
Parr, Stuart, New York 091151
Parra, Carlos Gil de la, Zaragoza . . 081748
Parra, Suzanne & Thierry, Montpellier 064752
Parrado, Arévalo 129306
Parramatta Antique Centre, Parramatta 056442
Parramón, Barcelona 134922
Parrasch, Franklin, New York 118275
Parreira, Candida de Azevedo, Brasília 096500
Parren, J., Thorn 128841
Parreño Navarro, Jose Joaquin, Madrid 129654
Parrin & Co., Kansas City 089514
Parris Island Museum, Parris Island 046827
Parrish, Susan, New York 091152
Parrish Art Museum, Southampton . 048254
Parrish & Reinish, New York 118276
Parriss, Sheringham 086590, 131490
Parroquia de Santa María, Oliva . . . 035553
Parruzot, William, Gap . . . 062964, 124245
Parry, H., Edinburgh 084308
Parry, H. & R.L., Sutton Coldfield . . 086802
Parry Mansion Museum, New Hope 046234
Pars, El Paso 088811
Pars, Miami 090229
Pars Museum, Shiraz 022598
Parsa, Saint-Ouen 067861
Parsa, Tucson 093256
Parschau, Günther, Frankfurt am Main 139094
Parshall, Margaret, Louisville 090016
Parson, Washington 133033
Parson Fisher House, Jonathan Fisher Memorial, Blue Hill 042273
Parsons, Atlanta 087512
Parsons Historical Society Museum, Parsons 046830
Parsons School of Design, New York 051830
Parsonsfield-Porter History House, Porter 047155
Parsy, Thierry, Paris 066386
La Part des Anges, L'Isle-sur-la-Sorgue 099514
Parter Galeria, Łódź 109015
Parthas Verlag, Berlin 133802
The Parthenon, Nashville 046150
Le Parthénon, Paris 100754
Parthenon, Sant Andreu de Llavaneres 134953
Particular, London 113821
Particular Art Gallery, Ho Chi Minh City 120524
Partikel, Luzern 111699
Partners and Crime, New York 142687
Partners in Pine, Coggeshall 084052
Partners in Time, Portland 091993
Partners in Time, Seattle 093045
Partnership, Dallas 088591
Partnership, Dallas 088592
Partridge, London 113822
Partridge, Loren, Oakland 118641
Partridge, Scott, Richmond 142830
Partridge, Timothy, Eastbourne 084266
Partridge Antique Shop, Glenelg . . . 055889
Partridge Island Museum, Saint John 006355
Parts, Toronto 097347
Parts and Pieces, Terborg 128839
Partyka, Kraków 108970
Parvulescu, Dan Adrian, București . 129223
Parys Museum, Parys 034695
Pasadena City College Art Gallery, Pasadena 046835
Pasadena Historical Museum, Pasadena 046836
Pasaż, Kraków 079648
Pascack Historical Society Museum, Park Ridge 046824
Pascal, Fukuoka 140157
Pascal, Anne-Mieke, Marseille 064382
Pascal, Jean-Claude, Le Soler 063707
Pascal, Jean-Pierre, Chambéry . . . 062106
Pascal, Patrick, Fontvieille 062914
Pascale, Michèle, Joigny (Yonne) . . 063246
Pascaline, Rueil-Malmaison 067322
Pascalis, Alexandre, Sainte-Olive . . 068074
Pascaud, Jean-Claude, Bordeaux . . 061641
Paschal, Nicole, Estang 062808
Pasche, Wuppertal 074534
Paschos, Grimaud 099316
Pasco & Co., Miami 090230
Pascual Ansotegui, Marisa, Pamplona 081526
Pascual Armengol, Jose, Barcelona 080904
Pascucci, Mario & Figli, Ferente, Roma 076609
El Paseante, Madrid 136099
Pasek, Mark, New York 118277
Pasek, Piotr, Köln 071988
Paseka, Litomyšl 137794
Paseka, Praha 098478, 133418
Pash & Sons, Arnold, London 085594
Pasha Antiques, West Hollywood . . 093495
Pashova Kăshta, Melnik 004750
Pasinger Fabrik - Ausstellungen, Kultur und Bürgerzentrum der Landeshauptstadt München, München 019102
Pasino, Debora, Roma 076610
Paslack, Armin, Friedrichshafen . . . 070895
Pasmans Huus, Ruinen 030113
Pasquer, Priska, Köln 103694
Pasquesi, Umberto, Kerken 071800
Pasquier, Yvette, Besançon 061394
Pasquier, Yvonne, Saint-Pierre-les-Nemours 067960
Pass, Jules L., Saint Louis 092296
Pass Collection, New York 091153
Pass of Killiecrankie Visitor Centre, Killiecrankie 039866
Passado Composto, São Paulo 058732
Le Passage, Paris 066387
De Passage, Zaandam 078852
Passage 125 Blaes, Bruxelles 058050
Passage Antiques, London 085595, 131137
Passage de Retz, Paris 100755
Passage du XXè Siècle, L'Isle-sur-la-Sorgue 063952
Passage-Kunstheft, Berlin 135816
Passage Saint-Michel, Bordeaux . . 061642
Passage-Verlag, Leipzig 134154
Passagen Verlag, Wien 133227
Passages Antique Gallery, New Orleans 090599
Passages Centre d'Art Contemporain, Troyes 015056
Passageway Gallery, Omaha 118718
Passaic County Community College Galleries, Paterson 046840
Passaic County Historical Society Museum, Paterson 046841
Passard, Gérard, Nevers 065012
Passardi, Gabriele, Viganello 130205
Passato Prossimo, Parma 076221
Passato Prossimo, Roma 076611
Passauer Glasmuseum, Passau . . . 019574
Le Passé Antérieur, Bordeaux 061643
La Passe Antiques, Dallas 088593
Passé au Présent, Iwuy 063228
Le Passé au Présent, Pau 066712
Passe Compose, Biarritz 061473
Passé Composé, Biarritz 061474
Passé Composé, Billy-sur-Ourcq . . 061486
Passé Composé, Craponne (Rhône) 062548
Passé-Composé, Montréal 058987
Le Passé Composé, Paris 138518
Passé Composé, Tournai 058387
Le Passé d'Aujourd'hui, Paris 066388
Le Passé de la Montagne, Les Houches 063767
Le Passé du Canton, Orgon 013508
Le Passé Intérieur, Bruxelles 058051
Passé Intérieur, Nice 065125
Passé Passion, Bruxelles 058052
Le Passé Présent, Lausanne 082561
Passé-Présent, Montréal 058988
Le Passé Présent, Nîmes 065184
Passé Présent, Paris 066389
Passé Présent, Paris 066390
Au Passé Présent, Toulon (Var) 068467
Passé Recomposé, Bordeaux 124139
Passé Recomposé, Bordeaux 124140
Le Passé Recomposé, Lyon 124371
Le Passé Retrouvé, Herblay 063145
Le Passé Retrouvé, Mortagne-au-Perche 064800
Passé Simple, Blérancourt 061514
Passé Simple, Boulogne-Billancourt 061688
Le Passé Simple, Bruxelles 058053
Passé Simple, Came 061924
Le Passé Simple, Cannes 061952
Passé Simple, Coignières 062391
Passé Simple, Eaubonne . 062759, 124229
Le Passé Simple, Grenoble 063071
Passé Simple, Guesnain 063102
Le Passé Simple, Kevelaer 071815
Le Passé Simple, La Cadière-d'Azur 063299
Passé Simple, Metz 064535
Le Passé Simple, Montluçon 064712
Passé Simple, Orléans 065306
Passebon, Pierre, Paris 066391
Passebon, Pierre, Paris 100756
Passelard, François, Riom 101092
Das Passepartout, Stuttgart 126871
Passer Marchen, København 060365
La Passerelle, Auxerre . . . 061104, 098884
Passerin, Maurice, Nice 065126
Passerose, Châteauneuf-sur-Charente 062208
Passers Buy, Llangollen 085040
Le Passeur de Lumière, Valbonne . . 101404
Passiflora, Brewood 083663
Passiflora, Saint-Ouen 067862
The Passing Show Antiques, Tawa Wellington 079268
Passion, Brugge 057786
La Passion d'Abord, La Chaux-de-Fonds 082303
Passion d'Antan, Chargey-les-Gray 062152
Passion des Meubles, Dijon 062671
Passion du Passé, Montréal 058989
Passion et Collection, Limoges 063895
Passion for the Past, Toronto 059257
Passion Maison, Toulon (Var) 068468
Passion Sanat Galerisi, İstanbul . . . 112348
Passions Past & Present, Palmerston North 079216
Passman, Bernard K., New Orleans 117489
Passman, Bernard K., New Orleans 117490
Past and Present, Bromley 083768
Past and Present, Clitheroe 084037
Past and Present, Hingham 084692
Past and Present, Honolulu 088974
Past and Present, Philadelphia 091675
Past and Present Furniture, Las Vegas 089597
Past and Presents, Haarlem 078475
Past Caring, Holt, Norfolk 084707
Past Centuries Pieces, Los Angeles 089872
Past Connection Antiques, Houston 089173
Past Connections, Mosman 056267
Past Era Antique Jewelry, Houston . 089174
Past Perfect, San Francisco 092862
Past & Present, Amsterdam 077931
Past & Present, Belfast 083482
Past & Present, Kortrijk 058268
Past & Present, Perranporth 086217
Past & Present, Saskatoon 059103
Past Present Future, Minneapolis . . 090390
Past & Present Shop, Long Beach . 089649
Past & Presents, Polperro 086283
Past Times, Albuquerque 087417
Past Times, Blindley Heath 038769
Past Times, Cincinnati 088269
Past Times, Dunedin 079088
Past Times, Long Beach 089650
Past Times, Singapore 080541
Past Times Antiques, Ormond 056410
Past Times Antiques, San Gwann . . 077527
Past Times Jewellery Workshop, Perth 056459
Pasteger, Yvan, Mulhouse 064839
Pastel Artists Canada, Flesherton . . 052764
Pastel Artists of New Zealand, Blenheim 053925
Pastel Painters of Maine, Springvale 054963
Pastel Painters Society of Cape Cod, Barnstable 054964
Pastel Society, London 054464
Pastel Society of America, New York 054965
Pastel Society of Australia, Moorooka 052481
Pastel Society of Canada, Ottawa . . 052765
Pastel Society of Colorado, Grand Junction 054966
Pastel Society of Eastern Canada, Montréal 052766
Pastel Society of El Paso, El Paso . . 054967
Pastel Society of New Mexico, Albuquerque 054968
The Pastel Society of North Carolina, Chapel Hill 054969
Pastel Society of North Florida, Fort Walton Beach 054970
Pastel Society of Oregon, Roseburg 054971
Pastel Society of San Diego, San Diego 054972
Pastel Society of Southeast Texas, Houston 054973
Pastel Society of the Northern Rockies, Idaho Falls 054974
Pastel Society of the Southwest, Dallas 054975
Pastel Society of the West Coast, Sacramento 054976
Pastel Society of Utah, West Valley . 054977
Pastel Society of Victoria, Canterbury 052483, 094369
Pastel Society of Victoria, Doncaster Heights 052482
Il Pastello, Roma 106606
Pasti, Irene & Bencini, Duccio, Firenze 075383
Pastiche Antiques, Los Angeles . . . 089873
Pastimes, Bristol 083746
Pastimes Antiques, South Auckland 079242
Pastimes Vintage Toys, Glasgow . . 084467
Pastl, Dr. Ute, Linz 057161, 120669
Pastor, Monique, Blois 061528
Pastor-Lloret, André, Nice 065127
Pastoral Gallery, Queanbeyan 095109
Pastorale, La Colle-sur-Loup 063344
Pastorale, Paris 066392
Pastorale, Quimper 067021
Pastorale Antiques, Lewes 084984
Pastorius, Den Haag 078232
Pastrana Greno, Pablo, Buenos Aires 055234
Pastre, Pierre, Béziers 098960
Pastrello, Francesco, Venezia 128402
Pásztói Múzeum, Nógrádi Megyei Múzeum, Pászto 021813
Pásztormúzeum, Bugac 021704
Patachine, Paris 066393
Pataka, Porirua 030579
Pataky Körgaléria, Budapest 105536
Patan, Lalitpur 107603
Patan Museum, Kathmandu 029119
Patch Magic, Singapore 080542
Patches Gallery, Lower Beechmont 094746
Patchings Farm Art Centre, Calverton 112782
Pate Museum of Transportation, Cresson 043214

Patee House Museum, Saint Joseph 047648
Patek Philippe Museum, Genève . . 037138
Pateley Bridge Antiques, Pateley Bridge 086194
Patella, Palermo 076167
Patelli, Nicola, Milano 127648
Pateniemen Sahamuseo, Pohjois-Pohjanmaan Museo, Oulu 009938
Patenschaftsmuseum Goldap in Ostpreußen, Stade 020278
Patent Model Museum, Fort Smith . 043981
Pater Peter Singer-Museum, Salzburg 002562
Paterae, New York 091154
Paterlini, Paola, Bologna 075098
Paternina, Alvaro de, Madrid 081356
Paternuosto, Luciano, Roma 128151
Paterson, Glasgow 122518
Paterson, A. & M., Paddington, Queensland 056433
Paterson, M., Ballarat 055436
Paterson, Patrick G., Bremen 070038
Paterson, Simon, Chichester 130564
Paterson Court House, Adamstown . 000700
Paterson Museum, Paterson 046842
Path, Aalst 096051
Pathe, Kobe 077083
Pathein Museum, Pathein 029067
Pathological Museum, London 040253
Pathologisch-anatomisches Bundesmuseum, Wien 002987
Pathology and Bacteriology Museum, Lucknow 022244
Pathology Museum, Kabul 000005
Pathology Museum, Pretoria 034724
Pathology Museum, Department of Pathology, Mumbai 022269
Pathway Antiques, Vancouver 059399
Pati, Giampaolo, Roma 128152
Patikamúzeum, Győr 021732
Patikamúzeum, Kőszeg 021776
Patina, Bern 082231
Patina, Budapest 074704
Patina, Madrid 129655
Patina, New York 091155
Patina, Szeged 074755
Patina Antik, Veszprém 074758
Patina Antikvitás, Budapest 074705
Patina Antiquitäten, Netphen 072958, 126523
Patina Art, Helsinki 060568
Patina Atelier, San Francisco 092863
Patina Consignment, Tucson 093257
Patinations, Gilmore 123228
Patine, Coimbra 079821
Patine, Maastricht 078617
Patine Antiquites, Chindrieux 062290
Patine du Temps, Bordeaux 061644
La Patine du Temps, Paris 066394
La Patine du Temps, Sainte-Geneviève-des-Bois 068064
Patine et Vieilles Dentelles, Lucciana 064023
Le Patio, Antibes-Juan-les-Pins . . . 060926
Al-Patio, Cairo 098663
El Patio, Sevilla 081603
Patio-Antiques, Hamburg 071306
Patio Art, Monaco 107540
El Patio de Pilar, Pilar 055290
Patio-Verlag, Dreieich 133875
Patna Museum, Patna 022294
Paton, Saint Albans 142030
Patou, Alain, Saint-Christoly-de-Blaye 067399
Patrascu, Manole, Galaţi 129231
Patrassi, Anna, Milano 075806
Patres, Eerbeek 128657
Patriarsheska Tsarkva na Tsarevets, Veliko Tărnovo 052709
Patrice, Brno 059982
Patrice-Alexis, Thonon-les-Bains . . 101313
Patrich, Simon, Vancouver 097512
Patrician Design, Albuquerque 087418
Patricia's Antiques, Buffalo 087902
Patricie, Brno 059983
Patrick, Hong Kong 133365
Patrick, Cidnee, Dallas 115919
Patrick, Jolly, Denver 116032
Patrick, Joseph, Toronto . . 059258, 137715
Patrick, Pierre, Cassis 099093
The Patrick and Beatrice Haggerty Museum of Art, Milwaukee 045898
Patrick Collection Motor Museum, Birmingham 038735
Patrick Taylor Cottage Museum, Albany 000724
Patrijaršie Palaty, Gosudarstvennyj muzej-zapovednik Moskovskij Kreml, Moskva 033516
Patrikiadis, George N., Athinai 074603
Patrimoine Historique et Études du Repassage, Sebourg 014738
Patrimonio Atelier de Conservacao e Restauracao, Belo Horizonte 123691
Patriots Point Naval and Maritime Museum, Mount Pleasant 046068
Patris, Françoise, Brest 061778
Patris, Gilles, Gouesnou 063020
Patron, Denver 116033
Patron, Prof. Riccardo, Bologna . . . 134551
Patronaggio, Michel, Lausanne . . . 111628
Patrone, Luigi, Roma 106607
Pat's Antiques, Cleveland 088352
Patscher, Stephan, Bodenheim 125343
Patsfall, Mark, Cincinnati 115651
Patten, Keith & Nancy, Saint Louis . 142860
Patten Lumberman's Museum, Patten 046843
Pattern Coins, Santa Monica 092941
Patterson, Anthony, Zürich 083009
Patterson, Isla Jean, Hawker, Australian Capital Territory 094618
Patterson, N., Tübingen 074114
Patterson, Nick, Tübingen 074115
Patterson, W.H., London . . 085596, 113823
Patterson Heritage Museum and Family History Centre, Birchington 038711
Patterson Homestead, Dayton 043323
Patterson Liddle, Bath 141398
Patterson's Spade Mill, Templepatrick 041195
Pattijoen Kotiseutumuseo Ojala, Pattijoki 009957
Pattinson, Betty, Yarram 095451
Pattison, Tony, Chorleywood 084004, 130577
Patton, Sainte-Savine 068082
Patton, Frank, Saint Louis 092297
Patton Museum of Cavalry and Armor, Fort Knox 043928
Patty's, Paddington, Queensland . . 137040
Patz, Robert, Magdeburg . 103992, 139440
Patzelt, Lambert, Ofterschwang . . . 126590
Patzelt, Michael, Wölfersheim 105315
Patzelt, W., Baddeckenstedt 069405
Patzer, Paul & Lilian, Nidau 111777, 141284
Patzer & Trenkle, Konstanz 139363
Patzschke, Claus, Vetschau 074200
Patzwall, Klaus D., Norderstedt . . . 134315
Pau-Santoantiguidades, Lisboa . . . 079988
Pauer, A., Leipzig 072213
Pauget, André, Cormoz 062481
Pauken, E., Bad Breisig 121302
Paul, Saint Kilda, Victoria 095174
Paul, Singapore 080543, 129264
Paul, Angela, Düsseldorf 102536
Paul, Anne-Marie le, Quimper 067022
Paul, Christoph & Brigitte, Stuttgart 074001
Paul, Diana, Calgary 096837
Paul, Frédéric, Larroque-sur-l'Osse 063543
Paul, Henri S., Bad Soden am Taunus 101701
Paul, Jon, Saint Louis 092298
Paul, Manuel Santiago, Valladolid . .081695, 110856
Paul, Maurizio, Berlin 125272
Paul, R.K., Dunedin 128935
Paul, W., Wegberg 074292
Paul, Wolfgang, München 072814
Paul Anton Keller-Museum, Lockenhaus 002262
Paul-Art Antique, Roye 067315
Paul Bunyan Logging Camp, Eau Claire 043597
Paul Dresser Memorial Birthplace, Terre Haute 048532
Paul Ernst-Gedenkstätte, Sankt Georgen an der Stiefing 002581
Paul-Galerie, Bremerhaven 102264
Paul Gugelmann-Museum, Schönenwerd 037534
Paul H. Karshner Memorial Museum, Puyallup 047290
Paul Jönska Gården, Viken 036791
Paul Laurence Dunbar State Memorial, Dayton 043324
The Paul Mellon Centre for Studies in British Art, London 050838, 135248
Paul Revere House, Boston 042340
Paul-Röder-Museum, Marktoberdorf 018847
Paul W. Bryant Museum, Tuscaloosa 048665
Paul Whitney Larson Gallery, University of Minnesota, Saint Paul 047708
Paula Modersohn-Becker-Stiftung, Bremen 016422
Paula Stradiņa Medicīnas Vēstures Muzejs, Rīga 027761
Paulan Taidemyynti, Tammela 060622
Pauler-Budde, Remscheid 073490
Paulette's Antiques, Cleveland 088353
Pauletti, Seattle 093046
Pauli, Alice, Lausanne 111629
Pauli, Monique, Marseille 064383
Pauli, Stefan, Bern 082232
Paulina Arts Center, Chicago 115521
Pauline E. Glidden Toy Museum, Ashland 041807
Pauline's Art, Las Vegas 116640
Paulise de Bush Costume Collection, Broadclyst 038872
Pauls, Rudi, Lübeck 072336
Paul's Antiques, Croydon 055731
Paul's Art Gallery, Houston 116385
Paul's Auction Mart, Southport 120639
Paul's Clock Repair, Pittsburgh 132671
Paulsen, Essen 139058
Paulsen, Barbara, Sinzig, Rhein . . . 126807
Paulsen, Harm, Schleswig 126769
Paulus, Antwerpen 096086
Paulus, A., Liège 058320
Paulus, Marcel, Toulouse 068533
Paulusgalerie, Albstadt 101555
Paupa, Donostia-San Sebastián . . . 110343
Pause Rétro, Montréal 058990
Pauselijk Zouavenmuseum, Roeselare 003721
Pautot, Alain, Clermont-Ferrand . . . 062353
Pauw, H. de, Gent 058200
Pauw, M., London 085597
Pauw-Müller, de, Gent 058201
Pauwels, Kortrijk 058269
De Pauweveer, Middelburg 108144
Pavanati, Cinzia, Padova 106406
Pavani, Marina, Genova 075495
Le Pavé dans la Mare, Besançon . . 061395
Pavesi, Arnaldo, Milano 075807
Pavia, Baden-Baden 069423
Paviglianiti, Patrizio, Firenze 106068
Paviglianiti, Patrizio, Firenze 106069
Pavignano, Claudia, Milano 075808
The Pavilion, Abu Dhabi 112439
Pavilion, Leeds 039958
Pavilion Antiques, Chicago 088143
Pavilion des Antiquaires et des Beaux-Arts, Paris 093670
Paviljon Katalnoj Gorki, Muzej-zapovednik Oranienbaum, Lomonosov 033336
Pavillon Audrey Hepburn, Tolochenaz 037637
Pavillon Chinois et Tour Japonaise, Bruxelles 003356
Pavillon de la Brocante, Sainte-Adresse 068046
Pavillon de l'Arsenal, Paris 013736
Pavillon de Vendôme, Aix-en-Provence 010298
Pavillon des Arts, Les Musées de la Ville de Paris, Paris 013737
Pavillon Flaubert, Canteleu 011100
Pavillon Saint-Arnaud, Trois-Rivières 006667
Pavilon Anthropos, Moravské Zemské Muzeum, Brno 008295
Pāvilostas Novadpētniecības Muzejs, Pāvilosta 027719
Paviot, Alain & Françoise, Paris . . . 100757
Paviot, Eric, Pont-de-l'Arche 066920
Pavito, Lagos 079839
Pavlik, Großschönau, Sachsen 071126
Pavlodarskij Istoriko-Kraevedčeskij Muzej, Pavlodar 027407
Pavlos Vrellis Museum of Greek History, Ioannina 021281
Pavlova, M., Miami 117120
Pavlovskij Istoričskij Muzej, Pavlovo 033629
Pavo Real Gallery, Boston 115220
Pavo Sanat Galerisi, İstanbul 112349
Pawdora Galéria, Budapest 105537
Pawelzik, Martin, Basel 129930
Pawilon, Kraków 136033
Pawilon Wystawowy, Muzeum Miasta Gdyni, Gdynia 031930
Pawlak, Caen 061881
Pawley, Jody, Drummoyne 094489
Pawlick, Lippstadt 103931
Pawlik, Nürnberg 073112, 126570
Pawlik, Witold J., Wien 057520
Pawnee City Historical Society Museum, Pawnee City 046848
Pawnee Indian Village, Republic . . . 047381
Pawsey & Payne, London 085598
Pawson, T.W., Somersham 086636, 131510
Pax, Knokke-Heist 096350
Pax, Kirsten, Berlin 069720
Paxson Gallery, University of Montana, Missoula 045935
Paxton, Loyd, Dallas 088594
Paxton House, Berwick-upon-Tweed 038686
Payer, Fritz, Zürich 083010
Payer, Josef, Wiener Neustadt 057597
Payer, Ursula, Leoben 095645
Paykel, Al, Sacramento 119157
Payne & Son, Oxford 086184, 131355
Payne & Sons, Tunbridge Wells . . .086948, 131622
Payne, Aaron, New York 118278
Payne, Clive, Chipping Norton 130572
Payne & Son, Geo. A., Bournemouth 083602, 130416
Payne Gallery, Bethlehem 042186
Paynes Creek Historic State Park, Bowling Green 042365
Payonne, Philippe, Rieux 067142
Payot, Genève 141252
Payot, Lausanne 135034
Payot, Lausanne 141264
Payrissat, Annie, Toulouse 068534
Paysan, Moritz, Stuttgart 126872
La Paz, Taranaki 079252
Paz, Fernando, Belo Horizonte 096479
Paz Feliz, Madrid 110590
Pazanis, Lyon 099610
Pazienza Fratelli, Milano 127649
Paznauner Bauernmuseum, Mathon 002294
Pazyryk, Aix-en-Provence 098791
Pazyryk, Saint Paul 092385
PB Gallery, New York 091156
P.Broc, Saint-Vigor-le-Grand 068035
PCOG Gallery, New York 118279
PDX Gallery, Portland 119030
AO Pe da Letra, São Paulo 137591
Pe de Boi Galeria de Arte Popular Brasileira, Rio de Janeiro 096635
Pé Palito & Cia, Porto Alegre 058518
Pea Configuracion Creativa, Madrid 110591
Pea Ridge National Military Park, Garfield 044147

Peabody Essex Museum, Salem . . . 047741
Peabody Museum of Archaeology and Ethnology, Cambridge 042567
Peabody Museum of Natural History, Yale University, New Haven 046226
Peabody Place Museum, Memphis . 045770
Peace Memorial Museum, Zanzibar 037863
Peace Museum, Bradford 038809
The Peace Museum, Chicago 042873
Peace River Centennial Museum, Peace River 006122
Peach Blossom Furniture, San Diego 092673
Peach Gallery, Stafford 114475
Peachgrove Antiques, Hamilton . . . 079107
Peachland Museum, Peachland . . . 006123
Peachtree Hill Gallery, Atlanta 114911
Peacock, Aberdeen 038450
Peacock, South Auckland 121831
Peacock, Deborah, Austin 115000
Peacock, Henry, London 113824
Peacock, Jay, San Francisco 092864
Peacock, Pristine, San Antonio 092559
Peacock, W. & H., Bedford 122405
Peacock, W. & H., Saint Neots 122681
Peacock Cottage Gallery, Linton . . . 094739
Peacock Heritage Centre, Chesterfield 039065
Peacock Visual Arts, Aberdeen 112479
Peak District Mining Museum, Matlock 040435
Peak Gallery, Toronto 097348
Peak Rail Museum, Matlock 040436
Peake, Barbara, Torquay 095347
Pear, Portland 119031
Pear Tree Gallery, Wahroonga 095368
Pearce, C., Hobart 136946
Pearce, Sara, London 113825
Pearce Institute, Glasgow 039567
Pearl, Hannover 125878
Pearl, Vebron 068742
Pearl Cross, London 085599, 131138
Pearl Gallery, Baltimore 115076
Pearl Gallery, Honolulu 116235
Pearl Publishing, Portland 119032, 135480
Pearl S. Buck Birthplace, Hillsboro . 044547
Pearl S. Buck House, Perkasie 046883
Pearle Dorrace, Dallas 088595
Pearlers Row Gallery, Broome 094316
Pearn's Steam World, Westbury . . . 001611
Péaron, Monique, Orgeval 065287
Pearsall, Louisville 090017
Pearse Lukies, Aylsham 083359
Pearse Museum, Dublin 022768
Pearson, Phoenix 091761
Pearson, Duncan, Dartford 112933
Pearson, Jim, Albuquerque 114817
Pearson, John A., Horton 084742
Pearson, Michael, Canterbury 083865, 130507
Pearson, Sebastian, Cambridge . . . 083848
Pearson, Sue, Brighton . . . 083711, 130448
Pearson Air Museum, Vancouver . . 048750
The Pearson Museum, Springfield . 048288
The Peary-MacMillan Arctic Museum, Bowdoin College, Brunswick 042488
Peasantries, Vancouver 059400
Pease-Cobb, Fort Worth 088876
Peasenhall Art and Antiques Gallery, Peasenhall 086196, 131364
Pebble Hill Plantation, Thomasville . 048549
Pebbles Yard Gallery, Saint David's . 114354
Peca, Severino, Lausanne 082562
Pecanins, México 107506
Peças Soltas, Faro 109252
Pecci, Laura, Milano 106278
Peccolo, Roberto, Livorno 106128
Péchaud, Camille, Crézancy-en-Sancerre 062568
Pecher, Marcus, Aschau am Inn . . . 069203
Pechermuseum, Hernstein 002039
Pêcheur d'Images, Pont-Aven 101035
Pecheur D'Images, Roscoff 101102
Peck, Joan, New York 118280
Peck & Hill, Birmingham 087780
Pecka, Praha 098479
Peckover House, Wisbech 041420
Peco, Hampton 084564, 130757
Pecorella, Napoli 076026
Pecorella, Luigi, Napoli 076027
Pecos Park, Pecos 046855
Pèda, Vilnius 107370
Pedagogické Muzeum Jana Ámoše Komenského, Praha 008644
Pedagoški Muzej, Beograd 034168
Peddler's Daughter, Milwaukee . . . 090318
Peddler's Daughter, Saint Louis . . . 092299
Peddlers Rack, Los Angeles 089874
Peddler's Village, Columbus 088428
Peddler's Wagon, San Antonio 092560, 123096
Peden, Ludij, Yungaburra 095460
Pedersen, Porto Alegre 096573
Pedersen, Gerd & Regine, Neckarsteinach 072952
Pedersen, Leif, Rungsted Kyst 120876
Pedersen, Tine Plantener, Holte . . . 124023
Pedestrian Gallery, Jacksonville . . . 116535
Pedlar, Maylands, South Australia . 056173
Pedlar's Pack Books, Totnes 142119
Pednault, Montréal 058991
Pedrazzi Cané, Angela, Bologna . . . 075099
Pedrero, Rafael Jimenez, Sevilla . . 081604
Pedretti, Felice, Roma 128153
Pedretti, Jean-Jacques, Porrentruy 082729
Pedro & Castro, Lisboa 079989
Pedrocchi, Sabrina, Losone 130089
Pedroni, Carlo, Muralto . . 082679, 141280
Pedrosa Garcia, Concha, Sevilla . . . 110774
Peebles, Tulsa 133000
Peege, Frank, Freiburg im Breisgau 121413
Peek, Ton, Utrecht 108259, 140553
Peek in the Attic, Dallas 088596
Peekskill Museum, Peekskill 046858
Peel Castle, Manx National Heritage, Peel 040680
Peel Heritage Complex, Brampton . 005134
Peeler, Alan, Memphis 117000
Peelmuseum, Ospel 030012
Peensalu, Stockholm 082006
Peep, Laine, Tartu 137920
't Peerd, Oostende 058365
Peerless, Calgary 123748
Peerlings, J., Kampen . . . 103482, 134075
Peerlings, Josef, Krefeld . 103784, 134132
Peet, Jan, Bussum 140378
Peeters, Leuven 133291, 137511
Peetsold, L.W., Hoofddorp 128725
Peetz, Sebastian, Hannover 103293
The Peg General Store, Vancouver . 059401
Pegaso, Roma 076612
Pegaso, West Hollywood 093496
Pegasus, Bari 075024
Pegasus, Bucureşti 129224
Pegasus, Dordrecht 107982
Pegasus Antiques, Geelong 055869
Pegasus Book Exchange, Seattle . . 143004
Pegasus Books, Wellington 140679
Pegasus Gallery, New York 118281
Pegasus Verlag, Wetzlar 134456
Pegasys-Körner, Wiernsheim 074391
Pegaz, Warszawa 109176
Pegaz, Zagreb 133408
Pegeot, Arlette, Besançon 061396
Peggottys, Teynham 086878
Peggy Guggenheim Collection, Venezia 026264
Peggy's Antiques, Indianapolis 089330
Peghaire, Michel, Magny-en-Vexin . 064215
Pegoud, Henri, Saint-Martin-de-Vaulserre 067639
Pehböck, Naarn im Machlande 095691
Pehböck, Erwin, Perg 095703
Pehrs, Magdalena, Münster 072922
Peichert, Uwe, Mülheim an der Ruhr 072614, 126340
Peiffer, Düsseldorf 070422
Peiffer, Ratingen 073429
Peiffer, Jacques, Herserange 124258
Peignet, Philippe, Nantes 064938
Peinelt, Scheibenberg 073681
Peintre, Christian, Paris 066395
Les Peintres Québecois, Québec . . 097156
Peintres sans Frontières, Paris 100758
Peinture Fraîche, Paris 100759
Peirce-Nichols House, Peabody Essex Museum, Salem 047742
Peironcely, Madrid 110592
Peithner-Lichtenfels, Praha 098480
Peithner-Lichtenfels, Wien 095917
Peitzmeier, Klaus, München 126428
Pejaten, Jakarta 105840
Pejepscot Historical Society Museum, Brunswick 042489
Peka Verlagsgesellschaft, Weßling . 134454
Pekel, Barbara, Köln 139351
Peking Arts and Antiques, San Francisco 092865
Peking Man in Zhoukoudian, Beijing 007004
Pékmúzeum, Soproni Múzeum, Sopron 021847
Pelagalli, Leonida, Roma 128154
Pelastusarmeijan Museo, Helsinki . 009560
Pelatan, Benoît, Suresnes 068343
Pelati, B. & C., Parma 076222
Pelati, Romano, Milano 106279
Pelavin, Cheryl, New York 118282
Pelayo, Seattle 093047
Pêle-Mêle, Bruxelles 137459
Pêle Mêle, Montmorot 064722
Pelée, Guy, Trélivan 068623
Pele's Dream, Honolulu 116236
Pelfini Vega, Gabriel, Cancún 128500
Pelgoron, Milano 075809
Pelgrom, J., Haarlem 078476
Pelgrom Museum Poorterswoning, Antwerpen 003183
Pelham Art Center, Pelham 046859
Pelham Galleries, London 085600
Pelias, Marilyn, New Orleans 090600
Pelican Art Gallery, Saint Michael . . 096041
Pelican Gallery, Forster 094555
Pelican Publishing, Gretna 135362
Peligro, New Orleans 117491
Peliti Associati, Roma 106608
Pelkosenniemen Kotiseutumuseo, Pelkosenniemi 009958
Pella Historical Village, Pella 046860
Pellas, Aldo, Paris 066396
Pellas & Blaise, Paris 124773
Pellat de Villedon, Jean-Yves, Versailles 068816
Pellé, Francis, Bordeaux 124141
Pellegrin, Chamonix-Mont-Blanc . . 062111
Pellegrin, Jacques, Paris 066397
Pellegrini, Alberto, Roma 128155
Pellegrini, Mario, Mendrisio 082657
Pellegrino, Bartolomeo, Torino 076856
Pellegrino, Marianna, Taranto 076752, 106652
Pellengahr, Dr. Ingo, Frankfurt am Main 070771
Pellerin, Claude & Stéphane, Longueville-en-Barrois 063989
Pellet, Patrice, Paris 124774
Pelletier, Annick, Vence 068753
Pelletier, Claude, Quiers-sur-Bezonde 067009
Pelletier, Pauline, Québec 097157
Pelligra Arredamenti, Catania 075256
Pellisier House Museum, Bethulie . 034553
Pellitteri, Frank, New York 132511
Pellitteri, Salvatore, Palermo 076168
Pellmont, Felix, Binningen 129980
Pellon Kotiseutumuseo, Pello 009959
Pellonpään Talonpoikaistalo, Pertteli 009963
Pelludat, Inga, München 126429
Pelly, William, Lyme Regis 114012
Pelmama Academy, Dobsonville . . . 050696
Pelorus Antiques, Havelock 079108
Pelosi, Annette, Aschaffenburg 101603
Pels-Leusden, Berlin 102003
Pels-Leusden, Zürich 112159
Pelster, Martin, Köln 071989
Peltier, Patrice, Le Mans 063662
Peltier-Quatrefages Bérangère, Sarzeau 068139
Peltolan Mäkitupalaismuseo, Tammijärvi 010115
Peltotyökalumuseo, Somero 010089
Peltriaux, Bernard, Reims 101070
Peltz, Milwaukee 117215
Pelz, Wunstorf 074518, 127046
Pelz, E., Hausmoning 071437
Pelzer, Alice Hélène & Gérard, Bougival 061674, 124151
Pelzer, Gérard, Bougival 061675
Pelzer, N. & N., Raesfeld 073406
Pelzerhaus, Emden 016963
Pema Arts Gallery, Kathmandu 107595
Pemba Museum, Chake Chake 037850
Pember Museum of Natural History, Granville 044289
Pemberton Museum, Pemberton . . 006125
Pembery, Michael, Bakewell 083366
Pembina Hills Regional Art Gallery, Morden 005960
Pembina Lobstick Historical Museum, Evansburg 005440
Pembina State Museum, Pembina . 046863
Pembina Threshermen's Museum, Winkler 006836
Pembleton, S., Nottingham 086143
Pembroke, Nashville 090473
Pembroke Antique Centre, Pembroke 086197
Pembroke Historical Museum, Pembroke 046864
Pemoht, J.F., Veghel 128864
De Pen, Peer 137535
Pen and Brush Museum, New York . 046393
Pen & Pencil Grafix, Portland 119033
Pena, Carvalho, Belo Horizonte . . . 058441
Pena, Rio de Janeiro 058632
Peña, J., Madrid 081357
Peña Leon, Juan, Madrid 081358
Pena-Peck House, Saint Augustine . 047610
Peñalosa Camargo, Consuelo, Bogotá 059849
Penang Forestry Museum, Pulau Pinang 028010
Peñas Ruiz, Enrique, Barcelona . . . 080905
Pencarrow House, Bodmin 038776
Pence, John, San Francisco 119765
Pence Gallery, Davis 043312
Penchée, Mondeville 064597
Penco, Sara, Roma 128156
Pendaries, Claude, Malemort-sur-Corrèze 064238
Pendariès, Virginie, Brive-la-Gaillarde 061816
Pendarvis, Mineral Point 045906
Pendeen Lighthouse, Pendeen 040684
Pendennis Castle, Falmouth 039482
Pender, Virginia 056785
Pendle Antiques Centre, Sabden . . . 086429
Pendle Heritage Centre, Barrowford 038606
Pendlebury Antiques, Dunedin 079089
Pendleton District Agricultural Museum, Pendleton 046868
Pendon Museum, Long Wittenham . 040336
Pendragon-Verlag, Bielefeld 133824
Pendulantic, Saint-Blaise 130155
La Pendule, Dortmund . . . 070292, 125481
La Pendule, Stolberg, Rheinland . . . 073928
La Pendulerie de Lyon, Lyon 064170, 124372
Pendulo, Lugo 081193
Pendulum, Fort Worth . . . 088877, 132072
Pendulum, Hamburg 071307
Pendulum Gallery, Sydney 095301
Pendulum of Mayfair, London 085601
Penello, R., Carouge 082293
Peneloux, Jocelyne, Bains-sur-Oust 061176
Penetanguishene Centennial Museum, Penetanguishene 006128

Penfold, Brisbane 055561
Peng Seng, Hong Kong 059683
Pengelly, Mike, Mitcham 137001
Penglai Art Cooperative, Shanghai . 097936
Pengsjö Nybyggarmuseum, Vännäs 036758
Penguin, Penguin Putman, New York 135454
Penguin Books, London 135249
Penha, Belo Horizonte 096480
Peninsula, Eindhoven 108005, 134809
Peninsula and Saint Edmunds Township Museum, Tobermory 006573
Peninsula Fine Arts Center, Newport News 046472
Peninsula Painting Restoration, Karingal 123248
Penkert, Rainer, München 072815
Penkill Castle, Girvan 039544
Penland School of Crafts, Penland . 051926
Penlee House Gallery and Museum, Penzance 040693
Penman, Spalding 086675, 131521
Penn, Saskatoon 059104
Penn Barn, Penn 141993
Penn Village Antique Centre, Penn . 086200
Penna, Carvalho, Belo Horizonte . . . 058442
Penna, Sandra, Belo Horizonte 058443
Pennard House Antiques, East Pennard 084255
Pennarz, Rainer, Pfaffenhofen an der Ilm 104602, 139653
Pennehaven Antik, Rungsted Kyst . 060399
Pennello, Cleveland 115733
Pennellotto Restauro, Firenze 127386
Penneshaw Maritime and Folk Museum, Penneshaw 001373
Penney, David, Bishop's Stortford . . 083544
Pennica, Gino, Modena 127741
Pennies, Topsham 086899
Pennies from Heaven, Göteborg . . . 141106
Pennings, Eindhoven 108006
Pennings, Willy, Delft 107892
Pennsbury Manor, Morrisville 046042
Pennsylvania Academy of the Fine Arts, Philadelphia 051945
Pennsylvania Academy of the Fine Arts Gallery, Philadelphia 046972
Pennsylvania Anthracite Heritage Museum, Scranton 048066
Pennsylvania Arts Alliance, Harrisburg 054978
Pennsylvania Dutch Folk Culture Society Museum, Lenhartsville 045235
Pennsylvania Federation of Museums and Historical Organizations, Harrisburg 054979
Pennsylvania German Cultural Heritage Center, Kutztown 045050
Pennsylvania Lumber Museum, Galeton 044123
Pennsylvania Military Museum and 28th Division Shrine, Boalsburg 042280
Pennsylvania Pine, Ashburton 083338, 130313
Pennsylvania School of Art and Design, Lancaster 051583
Pennsylvania State University Press, University Park 135519
Pennsylvania Trolley Museum, Washington 048969
Penny Farthing, North Berwick 141957
Penny Farthing Antiques, North Cave 086090
Penny Farthings Antiques Arcade, Swindon 086814
Penny Lane, Frederiksberg 137873
Penny Lane Antiques, Los Angeles . 089875
Penny Lane Antiques, Los Angeles .089876, 132273
Penny Lane Vintage Store, Los Angeles 089877, 132274
Penny Post Antiques, Buxton 083830
Pennyarts, New York 091157
Pennyfarthing Antiques, Boston . . . 083580
Pennypacker Mills, Schwenksville . 048047
Pennyroyal Area Museum, Hopkinsville 044619
Penny's Antiques, Northampton . . . 086098
Penny's Collectibles, Saint Louis . . 092300
Penobscot Marine Museum, Searsport 048073
Penrhos Cottage, Llanycefn 040068
Penrhyn Castle, Bangor, Gwynedd . 038592
Penrith Coin and Stamp Centre, Penrith 086204, 131366
Penrith Farmers & Kidds, Penrith . . 122650
Penrith Museum, Penrith 040688
Penrith Regional Gallery and The Lewers Bequest, Emu Plains 001022
Penryn Fine Art, Penryn 135295
Pensacola Historical Museum, Pensacola 046875
Pensacola Museum of Art, Pensacola 046876
Penselmuseet i Bankeryd, Bankeryd 036211
Pensez au Passé pour vos Présents, Casablanca 077670
Penshurst Place and Toy Museum, Penshurst 040690
Pensieri nel Tempo, Milano 075810
Pensler, Washington 120336
Pentagon Gallery, Cleveland 115734
Pentecoste, Daniel, Villeurbanne . . 068976
Pentes, Charlotte 115304
Penthouse Furniture, Denver 132042
Pentiment, Internationale Sommerakademie für Kunst und Gestaltung, Hamburg 050117
Pentimenti, Philadelphia 118821
Penwith Galleries, Saint Ives, Cornwall 040919
Natural History and Antiquarian Museum; Penzance and District Museum, Penzance 040693
Penzance Bookshop, Penzance . . . 141996
Penzenskaja Kartinnaja Galerija im. K.A. Savickogo, Penza 033638
Penzenskij Gosudarstvennyj Obedinennyj Kraevedčeskij Muzej, Penza 033639
Penzenskij Muzej Odnoj Kartiny, Penza 033640
Penzils, Saint Heliers 108558
Peola, Alberto, Torino 106692
Peony Antiques, Norwood 056391
People of Passion Galerie POP, Wien 095918
Peoples Art Hall, Dublin 105885
People's Fine Arts Publishing House, Beijing 133338
People's Gallery, El Paso 043644
The People's Gallery, Stalybridge . . 114478
The Peoples Gallery, Stowmarket . . 114509
People's History Museum, Manchester 040414
The People's Museum, Belfast 038666
People's Palace Museum, Glasgow 039568
People's Story Museum, Edinburgh 039412
Peoria Art Guild, Peoria 054980
Peoria Historical Society, Peoria . . . 046881
Pep & No Name, Basel . . . 111217, 141211
Pepe Merino, Lugo 081194, 129545
De Peperbusse, Oostende 096400
Pepés Antik, København . . 060366, 098580
Pepe's Special, Vantaa 138005
Pepin, Bruno, Paris 066398
Pépin, Guy, Amboise 060799
Pepin Press, Amsterdam 134787
Pepino, Timişoara 080199
Pepper Gallery, Boston 115221
Pepper Street Gallery, Magill 094758
Pepperall, Noel & Eva-Louise, Arundel 130306
Peppercorn Collectibles, Hall 055932
Peppergreen Trading, Berrima 055489
Pepperprojects, Berlin 102004
Peppers Art Gallery, Redlands 047361
Peppers Creek Antiques, Pokolbin . 056466
Peppin Brown Art Gallery, Whittlesford 041379
Peppitt, Judith, Snargate 086632
Pepys Antiques, Beckenham 083469
Pequeña Inglaterra, Málaga 081429
Pera Sanat Galerisi, İstanbul 112350
Perachora Museum, Perachora 021427
Perak Royal Museum, Kuala Kangsar 027964
Perard, André, Arles 060974
Perault, Sophie, Toulouse 124991
Perazzoli, Milano 140059
Perazzone-Brun, Paris 066399
Perbadanan Muzium Melaka, Melaka 053856
Perc-Peretz, M., Saarbrücken 121593
Perc Tucker Regional Gallery, Townsville 001564
Perce-Oreilles Productions, Fontenay-le-Comte 052965
Perchinelli, Felice, Genova 127479
Perchtold, Norbert, Wallern an der Trattnach 057345
Percival, R. & S.M., Ruthin 086419
Percival David Foundation of Chinese Art, School of Oriental and African Studies, University of London, London . . . 040254
Perco, Mario, Wien 057521
Percossi, Luisa, Milano 106280
Percy, Kevin, Hawkes Bay 108470
Percy House Gallery, Cockermouth . 112885
Percy Pilcher Museum, Lutterworth 040359
Perdijk, Tilburg 078776
Perdikakis, Gus, Cincinnati 088270
Père, Christophe, Semur-en-Auxois 068205, 124932
Peregrine Galleries, Montecito 090409
Pereira, Ângelo Augusto, Lisboa . . . 129167
Pereira, António Ferreira, Lisboa . . 079990
Pereira, Atta, Rio de Janeiro 058633
Pereira, Christina Cantinho, Lagos . 079840
Pereira, Mariana Costa, Lisboa 109343
Pereira, Mónica, Porto 109393
Peremiansky, Alberto, Buenos Aires 136748
Peres, Cornelia M., Roma 128157
Pères Blancs - Saint Anne, Jerusalem 022972
Pereslavl-Zalesskij Gosudarstvennyj Istoriko- architekturnyj i Chudožestvennyj Muzej-zapovednik, Pereslavl-Zalesskij 033644
Peretz, Jean-Claude, Villeneuve-sur-Lot 068922
Peretz & Ball, Saarbrücken 073643
Perey, Wollongong 137141
Perez, London 085602
Perez, London 085603
Perez, London 131139
Perez, London 131140
Perez, San Antonio 132822
Pérez, Andrés, Sevilla 081605
Perez, Ildefonso Lorite, Almeria . . . 110095
Pérez, Luis, Bogotá 098181
Perez, Michael, New York 118283
Perez, Mickael, Les Ulmes 063793
Pérez, Roberto, Medellín 059935
Pérez, Roberto, Medellín 123937
Pérez, Trinidad de, Bogotá 059850
Perez Arrans, Jose Antonio, Sevilla 081606
Pérez Barón, Elias, Bogotá 059851
Perez-Calahorra, Jordi Cirera, Barcelona 110231
Perez Carrasco, Tomas, Madrid . . . 081359
Perez de Albeniz, Moises, Pamplona 110721
Perez Gonzalez, Rafael, Valladolid . 110857
Perez-Hita Cugat, Pedro, Barcelona 080906
Perez Paya, Valencia 081669
Pérez-Paya, Valencia 141082
Perez Perez, Guillermo, Zaragoza . . 129821
Perez & Pires, Porto Alegre 096574
Pérez Sanleón, Antonio, Valencia . . 081670
Perfect Restorations, New York . . . 132512
Perfect Touch, Philadelphia 118822
Perfecto Da Lama, Saint-Pey-d'Armens 067951
Perfekta, Kraków 079649
Performance Space, Redfern 001425
Performing and Creative Arts Department, College of Staten Island, Staten Island 052213
Performing and Visual Arts Department, Marian College, Indianapolis 051500
Performing and Visual Arts Department, Wagner College, New York 051831
Performing Arts Collection of South Australia, Adelaide 000712
Performing Arts Museum, Victorian Arts Centre, Melbourne 001248
Perfume Museum, Niagara-on-the-Lake 006024
Pergamentum, Granada 129530
Pergamino, Madrid 081360
Pergamon, Bredevoort 140373
Pergamon Antique, Spišská Nová Ves 080640
Perhirin, Jacques, Le Relecq-Kerhuon 063705
Perhon Kotiseutumuseo, Perho 009961
Peribo, Mount Kuring-Gai 133051
Pericoi, Nathalie, Saint-Ouen 067863
Perides, Maria, Newstead 094951
Perier, Antoine de, Nantes 138245
Périer, Charles, Le Chesnay 063601
Périès, Jean-Claude, Montauban . . 064636
Périès, Jean-Claude, Montauban . . 064637
Perimeter Gallery, Chicago 115522
Perimeter Gallery, New York 118284
Perin, Attilio, Milano 127650
Perine, Paris 066400
Perini, Verona 140152
Period Antiques & Clocks, Seoul . . . 077371
Period Classics, Singapore 080544
Period Collections, Houston 116386
Period Features, Leek 084944
Period Fireplaces, Bristol . 083747, 130460
Period Furniture, York 131728
Period Furniture Showrooms, Beaconsfield 083462, 130357
Period Gallery, Omaha 118719
Period Picture Company, Washington 120337
Period Style Lighting, Enfield 084337
Perkins, Bryan, Wellingborough . . .087066, 131657
Perkins, James, Hitchin 113246
Perkins, R.G., Toronto 059259
Perkins, Steve, Whangarei 128985
Perkins Bull Collection, Peterborough 006141
Perkins Center for the Arts, Moorestown 046014
Perkins County Historical Society Museum, Grant 044285
Perkinson Gallery, Decatur 043353
La Perle des Puces, Cagnes-sur-Mer 061893
Perler, Herrmann & Co., Kehrsatz . .082512, 130053
Perlerin, Alain, Saint-Valéry-sur-Somme 068031
Perlés, Christophe, Paris 066401
Perlia, Ingrid, Kampen 071698
Perlin, Amy, New York 091158
Perlinger, Magarethe, München . . . 104285
Perlman, Trelleborg 082053
Perlmuttdrechslerei, Riegersburg, Niederösterreich 002529
Perlo, Jean-Louis, Reims 067078
Perlow Rich, Katharina, New York . . 118285
Permanent Exhibition of Votive Pictures Sanctuary of our Lady of Trsat, Rijeka 007781
De Permanente Kunsthuis, Groningen 108043
Permanenten Vestlandske Kunstindustrimuseum, Bergen . . . 030771
Permskaja Gosudarstvennaja Chudožestvennaja Galereja, Perm 033652
Permskij Gosudarstvennyj Institut Iskusstv i Kultury, Perm 050656
Permskij Oblastnoj Kraevedčeskij Muzej, Perm 033653
Pernáth, Praha 098481

Perner, Udo, Hof, Saale 139272
Perner, Udo, Hof, Saale 139273
Pernes, Civray 062308
Pernès, Michel, Beaune 098940
Pernička, Vojtěch, Brno 123954
Perniön Museo, Perniö 009962
Pernkopf, Dr. Johannes, Berlin 102005
Pernod, Jean-Pierre, Saint-Martin-du-Fresne 067643
Pernot, Alain, Vic-sur-Seille 068850
Pero, Beograd 109716
Péroline, L'Hospitalet 063811
Peron, Los Angeles 089878
Peron-François, Melun 121070
Peron - Galerie Českého Umění, Praha 098482
Perotti, Giacomo, Torino 128342
Perotto, Milano 134626
Perpetual, Hong Kong 059684
Perpetuum Art, Kostroma 109473
Perpignan Numismatique, Perpignan 066755
Perpitch, Antoine, Paris 066402
Perplies, Aachen 101521
Perquier, Jacques, Pont-Audemer . . 066912
Perra, Andrea, Catania 075257
Perramond, Alain, Tain-l'Hermitage 068349
Perranzabuloe Folk Museum, Perranporth 040695
Perras, Bernard, Paris 066403
Perrault, Gilles, Paris 066404
Perrault's Museum, Val Marie 006680
Perreau, Patrick, Châteauroux 124193
Perret, Francoise, Sergeac 124934
Perret, Gustave, Saint-Ouen 067864
Perret, Paul, Saint-Just-Saint-Rambert 067570
La Perricholi, Buenos Aires 055235
Perrier, Jean-Claude, Laval (Mayenne) 063554
Perrier, Michel, La Boisse 063295
Perrier, Suzanne, Régny 067049
Perrin, Montbéliard 099736, 138212
Perrin, Paris 100760
Perrin, Jacqueline, Nice . . 065128, 099853
Perrin, Jacques, Paris 066405
Perrin, Josiane, Aix-les-Bains 060725
Perrin, Marie-Jo, Lyon 064171
Perrin, Michelle, Tournus 068571
Perrin, Noël, Jasseron 063236
Perrin, Patrick, Paris 066406, 100761
Perrin, Royère, Lajeunesse, Vergez & Honta, Versailles 121282
Perrins Art Gallery, London 113826
Perritaz, Christian, Fribourg 082381
Perritaz, Christian, Fribourg 130027
Perrolle, Fabian, Biel 082260
Perron, Fabien, Besançon 061397
Perron, Ralph, Saint-Jeoire 067551, 124908
Perrone, Antonio, Biel . . . 082261, 129979
Perrot, Bernard, Châteauneuf-en-Thymerais 062205
Perrotin, Emmanuel, Paris 100762
Perrusson, Christian, Sennecey-le-Grand 068211
Perry, Charlotte 087970
Perry, Jacksonville 116536
Perry, George, Tauranga 108578
Perry County Lutheran Historical Society Museum, Altenburg 041670
Perry & Nicole, Memphis 117001
Perry & Phillips, Bridgnorth 122433
Perryman, Ian & Belinda, Woollahra 056875, 123331
Perry's Cider Mills, Ilminster 039796
Perry's Mart Masterton, Masterton . 079150
Perry's Victory and International Peace Memorial, Put-in-Bay 047286
Perryville Battlefield Museum, Perryville 046889
Persano, Giorgio, Torino 106693
Persaú, Ralf, München 126430
Persault, Michel, Albertville 060744
Il Perseo, Palermo 076169
Persepolis, Isfahan 074837
Persépolis, Palma de Mallorca 081490, 129709
Persian and Oriental Rug Gallery, Pittsburgh 091850
Persian Antiques Exhibition, Abu Dhabi 083177
Persian Arts & Crafts, Vancouver . . 059402
Persian Carpet Gallery of Petworth, Petworth 086255
Persian Carpet Museum, Raas 027633
The Persian Carpet Studio, Long Melford 085839
Persian Carpets and Antiques, Abu Dhabi 083178
Persian Gallery, Boston 087838
Persian Market, London 131141
La Persiana, Palermo 106437
Persico, Didier, La Valette-du-Var . . 063460
Persico, Didier, Pignans 066832
Persico Rosalba, Milano 075811
Persische Kunsthandelsgesellschaft, München 072816
Persmuseum, Amsterdam 029220
Person, Catherine, Seattle 119974
Personal Museum, Paris 100763
Personal Touch, Toledo 120088
Personé, Maria Adele, Bari 075025
Persone, Maria Adele, Bari 127117
Perspective, Vaduz 107342, 134743
Perspective Art, Ottawa 097114
Perspective Gallery, Blacksburg . . . 042246
Perspectives, Pont-Aven 101036
Persson, Malmö 141130
Persson, Åke, Piteå 122228
Persson, Lennart, Falun 129838
Perstorps Auktionsverk, Perstorp . . 122227
Perth Antiques, Perth 056460
Perth Antiques, Perth 086226
Perth Bookshop, Perth 141999
Perth Galleries, Subiaco 095235
Perth Institute of Contemporary Art, Perth 001376
Perth Museum, Perth 006134
Perth Museum and Art Gallery, Perth 040697
Perth Regiment Museum, Stratford . 006520
Perthuis, Serge, Saint-Arnoult-des-Bois 067362
Perticaro, Gaetano, Genova 127480
Perttelin Kotiseutumuseo, Pertteli . . 009964
Peruggi, Andrea, Padova 106407
Pesbar, Barbate 121991
Pesca, Nashville 090474
Pescali, Daniele, Milano 106281
Pesce, Sabrina, Bari 075026
Pesce Maurizio, Genova 075496
Pescetta, Verona 077015, 128432
Pescetta, Alessandro, Verona 077016
Pescetto, Rosa, Genova 075497
Peschar, Hannah, Ockley 114183
Pescheteau-Badin, Paris 121181
Peschke, J., Paderborn 073287
Pesciaioli, Luciano, Roma 076613
Pesenti, Bruno, Rochefort (Charente-Maritime) 067179
Peshawar Museum, Peshawar 031395
Peshtigo Fire Museum, Peshtigo . . 046896
Peshwa Satishchandra, Paris 066407
Pešková, Jitka, Český Krumlov 060004
Pesnel, Francette, Montgeron 064686
Pessah, Daniel, Fuengirola 081107
Pessin, Marc, Saint-Laurent-du-Pont 101167
Peštera Rabiša Muzej, Belogradčik . 004633
Pesterzsébeti Múzeum, Budapest . . 021688
Petalax Hembygdsmuseum, Petalax 009966
Petaluma Adobe State Historic Park, Petaluma 046897
Petaluma Wildlife and Natural Science Museum, Petaluma 046898
Petasecca Donati, Stefano, Roma . . 128158
Petchburi Gallery, Bangkok 112236
Pete and Susan Barrett Art Gallery, Santa Monica 047987
Peter, Buchholz in der Nordheide . . 102281
Peter, Buxtehude 070117
Peter, Margrit, Basel 082163
Peter, Michael, Halle, Saale 125791
Peter, Pia, Zürich 112160
Peter, Rosemarie, Korneuburg 095629
Peter Anich-Museum, Oberperfuss . 002389
Peter Anson Gallery, Buckie 038893
Peter Benoitmuseum, Harelbeke . . 003493
Peter Conser House, Heavener 044499
Peter et Martine, Beaumettes 061259
Peter Handke-Ausstellung, Griffen . 001959
Peter J. McGovern Little League Baseball Museum, South Williamsport 048253
Peter & Martine, L'Isle-sur-la-Sorgue 063953
Peter Pan's Bazaar, Gosport 084490
Peter Rice Homestead, Marlboro . . 045690
Peter Rosegger-Museum, Krieglach 002180
Peter Roseggers Geburtshaus, Alpl . 001675
Peter Scott Gallery, Lancaster 039924
Peter Stuyvesant Collection, Amsterdam 029221
Peter Stuyvesant Stichting, Zevenaar 030385
Peter Van den Braken Centrum, Sterksel 030185
Peter Wentz Farmstead, Worcester . 049312
Peter Whitmer Sr. Home and Visitors Center, Waterloo 048989
Peter-Wiepert-Museum, Burg auf Fehmarn 016502
Peter Yegen Jr. Yellowstone County Museum, Billings 042207
Pētera Barisona Muzejs, Staburags 027780
Pētera Upīša Pieminas Muzejs, Dobele 027676
Peterborough Arthouse, Peterborough 114244
Peterborough Centennial Museum and Archives, Peterborough 006142
Peterborough Historical Society Museum, Peterborough 046899
Peterborough Museum and Art Gallery, Peterborough 040700
Peterborough Sculpture Trust, Peakirk 054465
Peterburg, Sankt-Peterburg 080320
Peterburgskaja Restavracionnaja Kompanija, Sankt-Peterburg 129247
Peterhof, Paris 066408
Peterman, Kenneth O., Baltimore . . 087702
Peterpol', Sankt-Peterburg 134887
Peters, Calgary 096838
Peters, Calgary 096839
Peters, Düsseldorf 070423
Peters, München 072817
Peters, Axel, Wien 057522, 095919
Peters, Bodo, Bad Breisig 069271
Peters, Christian, Hamburg 125833
Peters, Christopher, Warwick 087042
Peters, C.M., Cape Town 080686
Peters, G., Husum, Nordsee 071601
Peters, Georg & Pascale, Ense 102631
Peters, Gerald, Dallas 115920
Peters, Gerald, New York 118286
Peters, Nina P, Hamburg 125834
Peters, Paul, Eerbeek 128658
Peters, Paul M., Harrogate 084585
Peters, P.L., Den Haag 078233
Peters, T., Rees 073448
Peters, Tijmen, Oosterbeek 128797
Peters Antik Aurorahuset, Göteborg 081818
Peter's Auction Sales, Winnipeg . . . 120830
Peters-Barenbrock, Ostseebad Ahrenshoop 104554
Peter's Barn Gallery, South Ambersham 114450
Peters Bookshop, Sheringham 142069
Peter's Gallery, Lemesos 098318
Peters & Isham, Fort Worth 142415
Peter's Oldies but Goodies, Saint Paul 092386
Petersburg Area Art League, Petersburg 046906
The Petersburg Museums, Petersburg 046907
Petersburg National Battlefield, Petersburg 046908
Petersen & Partner, Berlin 102006
Petersen, Salt Lake City 119359
Petersen, Ardén, Frederiksberg . . . 060242
Petersen, Christiane, Neuburg-Steinhausen 072978
Petersen, Dag-Ernst, Wolfenbüttel . 127032
Petersen, Eckart, Steinfeld 073905
Petersen, Hans-Christian, Esens . . . 102664
Petersen, J., Miami 132353
Petersens, Omeo 095007
Petersfield Antiques Fair, Petersfield 093947
Petersfield Bookshop, Petersfield . .131375, 142000
Petersfield Museum, Petersfield . . . 040706
Petersham Historical Museum, Petersham 046912
Petersohn, Jürgen, Waldbronn 126959
Peterson, Houdan 063176
Peterson, Toronto 097349
Peterson, Giles, South Auckland . . . 108561
Petersson, Kenneth, Hillerstorp . . . 081835
Pete's Furniture, Bangalore 074780
Pete's Furniture Refinishing, Fresno 132086
Petes Museigård, Havdhem 036331
Pete's Upholstery Shop, Fort Worth 132073
Petetin, Nicole, Saint-Claude 067401
Peth, Carl, Lübeck 072337
Petherick, Auburn 055416
Pethő, Budapest 074706, 105538
La Petit, Konstanz 103763
Petit, André François, Paris 100764
Petit, Francis, Brévonnes 061787
Petit, Marcel, Biécourt 061481
Petit, Pierre, Saint-Malo (Ille-et-Vilaine) 101174
Petit Antiquites, Paris 066409
Petit Broc, Senaud 068207
Petit Dénicheur, Carcassonne 061978
Petit Écomusée de Cinve, Pandrignes 013541
Le Petit Fouillis, Hayange 063138
Petit Galerie, Amsterdam 107781
Le Petit Jaunais, Nantes 099814
Petit Musée, Clair 005273
Petit Musée, Montréal 058992
Petit Musée Ambulant de la Musique Mécanique, Une Journée au Cirque, Villeneuve-la-Garenne 015274
Petit Musée d'Art Camerounais, Yaoundé 004983
Petit Musée d'Automat et du Vin de Pauillac, Pauillac 013756
Petit Musée de France, Albaret-Sainte-Marie 010311
Le Petit Musée de la Bicyclette, La Batie-Montgascon 012203
Petit Musée de la Chartreuse Saint-Hugon, Arvillard 010498
Petit Musée de la Poupée, Dijon . . . 011613
Petit Musée de la Table, Paris 013738
Petit Musée de l'Argenterie, Ateliers du Cuivre et de l'Argent, Paris 013739
Petit-Musée de Vin au Cave de la Dive Bouteille, Bourgueil 010946
Petit Musée des Chailloux, Chevagny-les-Chevrieres 011356
Petit Musée des Silos de Jouques, Jouques 012173
Petit Musée du Feu, Schoeneck . . . 014735
Petit Musée Fantastique de Guignol, Lyon 012834
Le Petit Musée Maison de Mariette, Saint-Laurent-du-Pont 014382
Petit Musée Minéraux et Faune de l'Alpe, Bourg-Saint-Maurice 010930
Petit Musée Rural, Varaire 015131
Petit Palais, Musée d'Art Moderne de Renoir à Picasso, Genève 037139
Petit-Palais, Musée des Beaux Arts de la Ville de Paris, Paris 013740
Le Petit Saint-Ouen, Montréal 058993

Le Petit Soldier Shop, New Orleans 090601
Petit Thomas, Paris 066410
Petitcollot, Bruno, Paris 066411
La Petite, Paris 100765
La Petite, Peine 104597
Petite Anglicane, Forestville 005453
Petite Brocante, Mer 064498
La Petite Brocante, Rochefort (Charente-Maritime) 067180
Petite Brocante, Saint-Malo (Ille-et-Vilaine) 067617
La Petite Curieuse, L'Isle-sur-la-Sorgue 063954
La Petite Galerie, Bruxelles 096242
La Petite Galerie, Paris 100766
La Petite Galerie, Quimper 101063
Petite Galerie, Reims 101071
La Petite Gallery, Los Angeles 116865
Petite Hirondelle, Chartres 062172
Petite Maison, Antibes-Juan-les-Pins 060927
Petite Maison de Le Corbusier, Corseaux 037035
La Petite Provence du Paradou, Le Paradou 012540
Petite Souris, Den Haag 128635
Les Petites Ecuries, Maisons-Laffitte 064227
Les Petites Folies, Tournai 058388
Petites Puces, Boulogne-sur-Mer . . 061699
Petitjean, Roland A., Basel 082164
Petitnicolas, Robert, Nice 065129
Petiton, Jean-Jacques, Eulmont . . . 062821
Petkov, Stan, Stockholm 129872
Petkov, Vasil, Šumen 137610
Petković, Beograd 080402, 109717
Petley, London 113827
Petley-Jones, Vancouver . 097513, 123855
P.e.t.ő., Budapest 074707
Petoëfi Irodalmi Múzeum, Budapest 021689
Petőfi Emlékmúzeum, Kiskoërös . . 021767
Petőfi Múzeum, Aszód 021617
Petone Settlers Museum, Te Whare Whakaarao o Pito-one, Wellington 030649
Petra Fine Art, Baltimore 115077
Petra Museum, Petra 027383
Petraglia, Antonella, Roma 076614
Petran Museum, Haltdalen 030871
Petrangeli, Valter, Roma 076615
Petrasek Landwehr 6000 OranienStr 171, Berlin 125273
Petrecca, Riccardo, Torino 106694
Petrefaktensammlung, Hanns-Seidel-Stiftung, Bad Staffelstein, Oberfranken 015808
Petrej, Peter, Zürich 141355
Petrequin, Daniel, Paris 138519
Petri, Karlheinz, Frankfurt am Main 070772
Petri Veijalainen, Verhoomo, Helsinki 124048
Petrich, Anja, Kiel 103542
Petrich, Tjark, Hemmoor 125913
Pétrides, Gilbert & Paul, Paris 100767
N. Petridis & Ch. Petridou, Thessaloniki 074642
Petrie Museum of Egyptian Archaeology, University College London, London 040255
Petrified Creatures Museum of Natural History, Richfield Springs 047391
Petrified Forest of the Black Hills, Piedmont 047017
Anna Petrik & Peter Rinnenburger, Frankfurt am Main 070773
Petrikat, P., Lüdenscheid 072347
Petrikat, P., Lüdenscheid 072348
Petrini, Giovanna, Firenze 075384
Petro, Paul, Toronto 097350
Pétroff-Rançon, Dinan 062683
Petroff-Rançon, Louis, Rennes (Ille-et-Vilaine) 101087, 124876
The Petroleum Museum, Midland . . . 045855
Petrolia Discovery, Petrolia 006145
Petropavlovskaja Krepost - Istoriko-kulturnyj Zapovednik, Sankt-Peterburg 033823
Petropol, Sankt-Peterburg 109642
Petrosemolo, Alberto, Roma 128159
Petrouchka, Paris 066412
Petroz, Jules & Aicha, Genève 082458
Petroz, Jules & Aicha, Saint-Julien-en-Genevois 067561
Petrů, M., Praha 137842
Petruni, Pietro, Milano 127651
Petryńska, Ewa, Wrocław 129129
Petschmann, Neckargemünd 104393, 134302
Pettaquamscutt Museum, Kingston 045017
Petteplace, Hamilton 123773, 137642
Petter, Eva-Maria, Nußbach 057194
Petter, Rainer, Berlin 069721
Petter Dass-Museet på Alstahaug, Sandnessjøen 031171
Petterson Museum of Intercultural Art, Claremont 042937
Pettersson, Inge, Sigtuna 110989
Petticoat, Lane, Ostfildern 073259
Petticoat Lane, Subiaco 056648
Pettigrew & Mail, Glasgow 113127
Pettigrews, Southport 114465
Pettinelli, Alberto, Milano 127652
Pettini, Antonio, Roma 140113
Pettis County Historical Society Museum, Sedalia 048102
Pettit, Anthony, Flatts 058392, 137542
Pettler & Lieberman, Los Angeles . . 142517
Petworth Affordable Fine Art Fair, Ducton 093948
Petworth Antique Market, Petworth 086256
Petworth Antiques and Fine Art Fair, Ducton 093949
The Petworth Cottage Museum, Petworth 040709
Petworth House and Park, Petworth 040710
Petzel, Friedrich, New York 118287
Petzold & Radermacher, Berlin 069722
Petzuch, Johannes, München 126431
Peuchet, Daniel, Pleyber-Christ . . . 066859
Peuples du Monde, Paris 133662
Peuran Museo, Rautalampi 010029
Peus Nachf., Dr. Busso, Frankfurt am Main 070774, 121408
Peute, P., Dordrecht 078313
Peveling, D., Köln 103695
Pew Corner, Guildford 084542
Pewabic Pottery Museum, Detroit . . 043455
Pewsey Heritage Centre, Pewsey . . 040712
Pewter Society, Monmouth 054466
Peyer, Zürich 112161
Peyer, Erwin, Horw 111562
Peyman, Los Angeles 116866
Peyralade, Marie-Thérèse, Paris . . . 066413
Peyre, Jean-Gabriel, Paris 066414
Peyre-Cornu, Elyette, Béziers 061443
Peyrecave, Anglet 060873, 124076
Peyrègne, Patrick, Saverdun 068164
Peyrolliers, Genève 082459
Peyron, Béatrix, Souppes-sur-Loing 068275
Peyronnet, Michel, Lanobre 063533
Peyronny, Jacqueline-Paule, Courtenay 062524
Peyrot, Ada, Torino 140140
Peyrou, Eric, Argentat 060960
Peyroulet & Cie., Gilles, Paris 100768
Peyton-Smith, Houston 122911
Pezellier, Jérôme, Tourcoing 068559
Pezon, Fabrice, Saussignac 068156
Pfadenhauer, A., Hof, Saale 071548
Pfadenhauer, Karl, München 072818
Pfaffenweiler Presse, Pfaffenweiler 134346
Pfahlbaumuseum Unteruhldingen, Uhldingen-Mühlhofen 020529
Pfahlbausammlung Dr. h.c. Carl Irlet, Twann 037646
Pfahlbautenmuseum, Pfyn 037414
Pfaller, Wien 057523
Pfalzgalerie Kaiserslautern, Kaiserslautern 018135
Pfalzmuseum, Forchheim, Oberfranken 017138
Pfalzmuseum für Naturkunde (POLLICHIA-Museum), Bad Dürkheim 015685
Pfannkuche, Preußisch Oldendorf . . 073372
Pfannstiel, Axel, Baden-Baden 125126
Pfanzelt, Kurt, Villach 137275
Pfarr, Peter, Bad Münder 125113
Pfarrmuseum, Dießen am Ammersee 016703
Pfarrmuseum, Flintsbach 017132
Pfau, Sabine, Darmstadt 070188
Pfau, Tamara, Basel 082165
Pfeffer, Eschau 139050
Pfefferkorn, Anne, Berlin 125274
Pfefferle, Karl, München 104286
Pfefferle, Karl, München 126432
Pfefferle, Karl, München 134268
Pfefferminzmuseum, Eichenau 016903
Pfeifer, Edgar, Schleiz 073695
Pfeifer, Erwin, Hamburg 139204
Pfeifer, Hildegard, Mühlacker 072603
Pfeifer, Robert A., Karlsruhe 103500
Pfeifer, Sven, Berlin 125275
Dagmar Pfeifer & Ursula Meiners, Düsseldorf 102537
Pfeiffenberger, Werner, Abtenau . . . 137148
Pfeiffer, Lörrach 139419
Pfeiffer, Philadelphia 118823
Pfeiffer, Sankt Wendel 104817
Pfeiffer, Wasserburg am Inn 074285
Pfeiffer, A., Kipfenberg 071850
Pfeiffer, C., Bruxelles 058054
Pfeiffer, Claus Jürgen, Berlin 133803
Pfeiffer, H., Dietersheim 070246
Pfeiffer, K.H., Schwäbisch Hall 073745
Pfeiffer, Martina, Wasserburg am Inn 074286
Pfeiffer, Olivier, Colmar 062417
Pfeiffer, Renate, Zeuthen 127064
Pfeifhofer, Helmut, Gmünd, Kärnten 056991
Pfeil, Heilbronn 071475
Pfeil, Klaus von, Karlsruhe 126004
Pfeil, Klaus von, Karlsruhe 126005
Pfeil, Wolf Graf von, Recklinghausen . 073446, 121583, 126684
Pfennig, Ingeborg, München 072819
Pferde-Eisenbahn Museum, Rainbach im Mühlkreis 002493
Pferde- und Kutschenmuseum, Chieming 016566
Pferdekuranstalt, Bern 036934
Pfeuffer, Georg, Landshut 072146
Pfiffaretti, Pascal, Littau 130083
Pfiffner, Sandra, Riedt bei Erlen . . . 082742
Pfingstritt-Museum Kötzting, Kötzting 018365
Pfingsttag, Böblingen 102168
Pfinzgaumuseum, Karlsruhe 018167
Pfirsch, Bernard, Strasbourg 068328
Pfister, Amstelveen 128525
Pfister, A.-M., Basel 141212
Pfister, Jackie, Zürich . . . 083011, 141356
Pfister, Michael, Weiterstadt 074330
Pfister, Oswald, Eibelstadt 125574
Pfister, Peter, Untrasried 126936
Pfister, Walter, Goldau 082479
PFL, Padova 076106
Pflaster, Lola, Dallas 088597
Pfleger, Lothar, Mannheim 126282
Pflüger, Bernd, Schwaigern 073748
Pflüger, Fernando, Kassel 071759
von Pflugh, Johnny, London 085604
Pflumm, Gerd A., Radolfzell 104653
Pflumm, Gerd A., Schramberg 104845
Pfo, Busan 107174
Pfortune, Indianapolis 116485
Pforzheimer Kunst-und Auktionshaus, Pforzheim 121574
Pfrang, Walter, Würzburg 074506
PFT Trading, Christchurch 079045
Pfundt, Sabine, Berlin 102007
Pfutsch, Susanne, Melk 057179
PG Antiques, Los Angeles . 089879, 132275
PG ART, İstanbul 112351
PGM Art World, Garching bei München 102916, 133970
PGM Art World, München 104287
P.H. Sullivan Museum and Genealogy Library, Zionsville 049378
PHA Gallery, New York 118288
Phänomen-Art, Pécs 105575
Phaidon Press, London 135250
Phal, Christine, Paris 100769
Phalippou, Marc, Rouen 067289
Phalsbourg d'Autrefois, Phalsbourg 066818
Phantique, Exeter 084362
Phantom of the Attic, Pittsburgh . . . 091851
Pharaoh's Finds, Buffalo 087903
Pharaoh's Gallery, Eau Claire Av NW, Calgary 096840
Pharaoh's Tomb & Burra Antique Centre, Burra 055590
Pharaonic Museum, Cairo 009319
Pharmaceutical and Medical Museum of Bohuslav Lavička, Ljubljana 034489
Pharmaceutical Society Late Victorian Pharmacy, Edinburgh 039413
Pharmacie-Musée de l'Hôtel Dieu le Comte, Troyes 015047
La Pharmacopée Antiquités, Lyon . . 064172
Pharmazie-Historisches Museum der Universität Basel, Apothekenmuseum, Basel 036901
Pharoahs Antiques Centre, Eastbourne 084267
Phase, Bologna 127173
Phase II Gallery, Chicago 115523
Phathai Cave, Lampang 037904
The Phatory, New York 118289
Phe, Rayong 037925
Pheasant Valley Gallery, Katikati . . . 079132
Pheljna, Pavone 134654
Phelps, Twickenham 086967, 131624
Phelps, T.L., Harrogate 130764
Phelps County Museum, Phelps County Historical Society, Holdrege 044570
Phelps House, Burlington 042515
Phelps Store Museum, Palmyra . . . 046802
Phenix 1880-1990, Antwerpen 057727
Phenotype Books, Penrith 141994
Phi Editions, Herborn 134748
Phi Kappa Psi Fraternity-Heritage Hall, Indianapolis 044753
Phidias, México 107507
Phiebig, Albert J., White Plains 143054
Philabaum, Tucson 120160
Philadelphia Antique Exchange, Philadelphia 091676
Philadelphia Art Alliance, Philadelphia 046973
Philadelphia Estate Antiques, Philadelphia 091677, 123047
Philadelphia Mummers Museum, Philadelphia 046974
Philadelphia Museum of Art, Philadelphia 046975
Philadelphia Museum of Judaica-Congregation Rodeph Shalom, Philadelphia 046976
Philadelphia Print Shop, Philadelphia 132630, 142749
Philadelphia Sketch Club, Philadelphia 054981
Philadelphia Trading Post, Philadelphia 091678, 123048
Philadelphia Upholstery, Philadelphia 132631
Philamarkt, Iserlohn 071635
Philatélie Lavalloise, Laval (Mayenne) 063555
Philatelistisches Museum der Vereinten Nationen, Genève 037140
Philbrook Museum of Art, Tulsa . . . 048656
Philicia Antiques, Kings Park 056055
Philim, Limoges 063896
Philip & Sons, Trevor, London 085605, 113828, 131142
Philip and Muriel Berman Museum of Art, Ursinus College, Collegeville 043047

Philip L. Wright Zoological Museum, University of Montana, Div. of Biological Sciences, Missoula 045936
Philipp, Absam 056909
Philipp, G., Quakenbrück 104647
Philipp-Matthäus-Hahn-Museum, Albstadt 015471
Philipp-Reis-Gedächtnisstätte, Museum für Post und Kommunikation Frankfurt am Main, Friedrichsdorf, Taunus 017268
Philipp-Reis-Haus Friedrichsdorf, Friedrichsdorf, Taunus 017269
Philipp Schäfer II Museum, Heimatmuseum Erfelden, Riedstadt 019839
Le Philippard, Narbonne 064965
Philippe, Antibes-Juan-les-Pins . . . 120902
Philippe, Croix 062573
Philippe, Auguste, Châteauneuf . . . 062201
Philippe, Catherine, Sancerre 068115, 101253
Philippe, Eric, Paris 066415
Philippe, Monique, Paris 066416
Philippe's French Antiques, Auckland 078971
Philippi, Julia, Dossenheim 102417
Philippi, Markus, Scheidegg 126765
Philippine Air Force Aerospace Museum, Pasay 031760
Philippine Army Museum, Makati . . 031699
Philippine House Museum, Shepparton 001465
Philippine Museum of Ethnology, Nayong Pilipino, Pasay 031761
Philippine Navy Museum, Cavite . . 031649
Philippine Presidential Museum, Malacañang 031702
Philippine Radiation Science Museum, Manila 031734
Philippine Science Centrum, Manila 031735
Philips, Malvern, Victoria 120606
Philips, Manchester 114049
Het Philips Gloeilampenfabriekje anno 1891, Eindhoven 029546
Philipse Manor Hall, Yonkers 049339
Philipsen, Piet, Tilburg 078777
Philler, Gudrun, Jena 103450
Phillip, Allen, Eastwood 055784
Phillip Antiques, Phillip 056464
Phillip Island Community Art and Craft Gallery, Cowes 000952
Phillips, Fort Worth 116158
Phillips, Mosman 094896
Phillips, Mumbai 074827, 139951
Phillips, New York 091159, 123006
Phillips, Roleystone 095155
Phillips, Saint Louis 092301
Phillips, Salt Lake City 119360
Phillips, Tulsa 093326
Phillips, Brian, Christchurch 140619
Phillips, Elaine, Harrogate 084586
Phillips, Marguerite, New York 118290
Phillips, Neil, London 085606
Phillips, Peter, San Diego 119534
Phillips, Ronald, London 085607
Phillips, S.J., London 085608, 131143
The Phillips Collection, Washington 048940
Phillips Countryside Museum, Brokerswood 038882
Phillips County Museum, Helena . . 044501
Phillips County Museum, Holyoke . . 044583
Phillips, de Pury & Co., Berlin 121338
Phillips, de Pury & Co., Genève . . . 122326
Phillips, de Pury & Co., London . . . 122596
Phillips, de Pury & Co., München . . 121540
Phillips, de Pury & Co., New York . . 123007
Phillips, de Pury & Co., Paris 121182
Phillips Historical Society Museum, Phillips 047000
Phillips Son & Neale, Paris 121183
Phillips of Hitchin, Hitchin 084694, 141669
Philly Coins, Philadelphia 091679
The Philmont Museum, Seton Memorial Library and Kit Carson Museum, Cimarron 042915
Philobiblion, Firenze 127387
Philothée, Annecy 060898
Philp, Richard, London 085609
Phils Arts and Antiques, Quezon City 079570
Phil'z, Toronto 059260
Phil'z, Toronto 059261
Phimasone, Tarbes 068366
Phipitapan Haeng Chart Phra Pathom Chedi, Nakhon Pathom 037910
Phipitapan Laeng Chart, Suphan Buri 037935
Phipitapan Laeng chart Chantharakasem, Ayutthaya 037865
Phipitapan Laeng chart Chao Sam Phraya, Ayutthaya 037866
Phipitapan Laeng Chart Ram Khamhaeng, Sukhothai 037933
Phipitapantasatan Haeng Chart Nakhon Si Thammarat, Nakhon Si Thammarat 037913
Phipittapan Tasatan Haengchart, Khon Kaen 037902
Phippen, Guy, Bois-Guillaume 061539
Phippen, Hubert, Malaunay 064234
Phippen Museum, Prescott 047225
Phipps & Pritchard, Bewdley 122409
Phipps & Pritchard, Cleobury Mortimer 122471
Phipps & Pritchard, Kidderminster . 122552
Phipps & Pritchard, Stourport-on-Severn 122713
Phititapan Haeng Chart, Chiang Mai 037897
Pho, Co, Ha Noi 120478
Pho, Hoa, Ho Chi Minh City 120525
Pho, Ngan, Ha Noi 120479
Phocéa, Marseille 099680
Phoebe Apperson Hearst Museum of Anthropology, University of California, Berkeley 042165
Phoebus, Rotterdam 108203
Phoebus (Tempe), Tempe 136604
Phoénix, Fort-de-France . 077553, 128489
Phoenix, Levin 079138
Phoenix, Paris 066417
Phoenix 369, Edinburgh 113006
Phoenix Antik, København 060367
Phoenix Antiques, Fordham 084421
Phoenix Antiques, Sherborne 086580
Phoenix Antiques, Tunbridge Wells . 086949
Phoenix Art Conservation, San Antonio 132823
Phoenix Art Gallery, Lavenham 113357
Phoenix Art Group, Phoenix 118885, 135476
Phoenix Art Museum, Phoenix 047011
Phoenix Auction, Dartford 122486
Phoenix Books and Records, San Francisco 142961
Phoenix Cabinet &Co., Phoenix 132654
Phoenix Egyptian Imports, Phoenix . 091762
Phoenix Fine Arts, Richmond, North Yorkshire 114306
Phoenix Gallery, New York 118291
Phoenix Museum of History, Phoenix 047012
Phoenix Potteries, Saint Louis 119237
Phoenix Rising Gallery, Seattle 119975
Phoenix Stamp and Coin, Phoenix . 091763
Phoenix Trading, Frinton-on-Sea . . 084443
Phonomuseum, Sankt Georgen im Schwarzwald 019986
Phorkys, Athinai 134489
Photage, Fort Worth 116159
Photantiques, Bowral 055531
Photantiques, Mittagong 056239
Photo Antiquities, Museum of Photographic History, Pittsburgh 047057
Photo Art Studio, Dubai 112457
Photo Factory Gallery, San Diego . . 119535
Photo Forum, Pittsburgh 118944
Photo Gallery On Line, Miami 117121
Photo-London, London 093950
Photo Planet, Stuttgart 126873
Photo Planet, Tokyo 135983
Photo Posters, Cincinnati 115652
Photo Suisse - Association Suisse pour la Photographie, Schweizerischer Verband für die Fotografie, Lausanne 054205
Photocollect, New York 118292
PhotoFolio, Saltaire 114392
Photoglob, Zürich 135096
Photograph Scotland, Callander . . . 112780
Le Photographe, Paris 135722
Photographers Gallery, Denver 116034
Photographers' Gallery, London . . . 040256
Photographers Gallery, Saskatoon . 006423
Photographers Gallery, Saskatoon . 097197
Photographers' Gallery, South Yarra 095212
Photographic Art Gallery, Marino . . 094790
Photographic Center Northwest 900 12th Av, Seattle 119976
Photographic Gallery, Dallas 115921
Photographic Image Gallery, Portland 119034
Photographic Investments Gallery, Atlanta 041869
Photographic Recollections, Broken Hill 094307
Photographic Resource Center, Boston 042341
Photographic Works of Art, Chicago 115524
Des Photographies, Paris . 100770, 138520
Photographisch-optisches Museum, Biedenkopf 016232
Photographische Gesellschaft, Wien 052593
Photographs Do Not Bend, Dallas . . 115922
Photography Gallery, Indianapolis . . 116486
Photography Gallery and Studio, Indianapolis 116487
Photography Monika Mohr Galerie, Hamburg 103206
Photography Museum, Stockholm . 036645
Photography Museum, Šiauliai Aušros Museum, Šiauliai 027855
Photology, Milano 106282
Photomuseum, Zarautz 036115
Photomuseum des Landes Oberösterreich, Bad Ischl 001727
Photonet, Wiesbaden 105275
Phot'Optic, Marseille 064384
Photoscapes, Urangan 095361
Photospace, Wellington 108639
Photoworld, Houston 116387
Phoung, Dong, Ho Chi Minh City . . . 120526
Phra Borommathat National Museum, Nakhon Si Thammarat 037914
Phra Chetuponwimonmangkhalaram National Museum, Bangkok 037887
Phra Phuttachinnarat National Museum, Phitsanulok 037922
Phu Khanh Museum, Phu Khanh . . . 049550
Phukradung, Loei 037907
Phulsanda Religious Arts Museum, Phulsanda 022296
Phuong, Ha Noi 120480
Phuong, Kim, Ho Chi Minh City 120527
Phuong, Nam, Ho Chi Minh City . . . 120528
Phuong, Nam, Ho Chi Minh City . . . 120529
Phupan, Sakon Nakhon 037926
Phuthadikobo Museum, Mochudi . . . 003953
Phyletisches Museum, Friedrich-Schiller-Universität, Jena 018112
Phyl's Memory Lane, Jacksonville . 089446
Physics Museum, Brisbane 000840
Pi y Margall, Madrid 110593
Pi Yandong Xue Yi Zhi Display Center, Guilin 007096
Pia, Francesca, Bern 111271
Piacenti, Daniele, Prato 127894
Piage & Pieta, Atlanta 114912
La Piana, Massimo, Palermo 106438
Pianet' Arte di Toninelli, Massagno . 082651
El Pianillo, Sevilla 081607
Piano Ciro, Roma 128160
Piano Museum Collection, Hereford 039737
Piano Nobile, Genève 111491
Piano Nobile, Kraków 108971
Piano Nobile Fine Paintings, London 085610, 113829, 131144
Piano Shop, Leeds 084930, 130873
Pianoforte-Museum, Meißen 018891
Pianola Museum, Amsterdam 029222
Pianos, Saint-Ouen 067865
Pianos Galore, Little Horsted 085013, 130901
Piano's Unlimited, Las Vegas 132218
Pia's Antique Gallery, Nashville . . . 090475
PIASA, Paris 121184
Piasecki, Piotr, Kórnik 129025
Piat, Bernard, Périgueux 066724
Piat, Bernard, Périgueux 066725
Piatt Castles, West Liberty 049086
Piatt County Museum, Monticello . . 046001
Piattelli, Lawrence, Firenze 127388
Piatti, Luca, Milano 075812
Piatti Nene, Milano 075813
Piave Antichitá, Milano 075814
Piazza on the Boulevard, Surfers Paradise 095244
Piazza Vecchia Moveis e Decoracoes, Rio de Janeiro 058634
Piazza Verdi, Roma 076616
Piazzini, Roma 076617, 128161
Piazzola, Alain, Ajaccio 138010
Pic Aepli Priska, Steinach 111936
Pic du Midi, La Mongie 012287
Le Pic Verre, Bruxelles 058055
Pica, Alvaro, Roma 128162
Pica Pica, Sundbyberg 141180
Picalle, Oostende 096401
Picaper, Axel, Berlin 069723
Picard, Ravensburg 104674
Picard, A. & J., Paris 133663, 138521
Picard, C., Ecouis 062760
Picard, Henri & Fils, Paris 138522
Picard, Jean-Louis, Paris 121185
Picard, Patrice, Rouen 067290
Picasso, Skopje 107426
Picasso, Carlo, Genova 127481
Picasso Art Gallery, Lefkosia 098305
Picasso Art Gallery and Art Coaching Centre, Hyderabad 105709
Picasso Gallery, Washington 120338
Picasso Graphic Station, Hiroshima 106856
Picasso-Museum, Donation Rosengart, Luzern 037302
Picasso Web, New York 118293
Piccadaci, Lilo, Montigny-lès-Metz . 064697
Piccadilly, Narbonne 064966
Piccadilly Antiques, Batheaston . . .083453, 130356
Piccadilly Arts, Houston 116388
Piccadilly Gallery, London 085611, 113830
Piccadilly Jewellers, Birmingham . . 083537
Piccapane, Raymond, Nice 124520
Piccardi, Monica, Firenze 127389
Picciati Armi, Roma 076618
Piccini Faneschi, Mirella, Firenze . . 127390
Fratelli Piccinini, Bologna . 075100, 127174
Piccirilli, Francesco, Roma 076619
Picco, P. de, Hameln 103240
Piccola Galleria d'Arte, Zürich 112162
Piccolezze, Bologna 075101
Piccoli Emmer, Nicoletta, Venezia . . 076965
Piccolo Antiquarium, Ex Palazzo Comunale, Fossato di Vico 024243
Piccolo Mondo Antico, Milano 075815
Piccolo Mondo Antico, Verona 077017
Piccolo Mondo Antico-Cattedrale, Lugano 082607
Piccolo Museo dei Popoli, Lodi 024522
Piccolo Museo della Moneta, Vicenza 026312
Piccolo Museo di San Paolo, Reggio Calabria 025410
Piccolo Museo Navale, Laives 024446
Piccolo Museo Parrocchiale, Torgnon 026044
Piccolo Museo Parrocchiale, Valsavarenche 026201
Al Piccolo Naviglio, Milano 075816
Picconi, Jean-Maxime, Lausanne . . 082563
Piccot, François, Yvoire 069070
Pich, Peter, München 104288

Pichard, Julien, Neuville-de-Poitou . 064998
Pichat, Marcel, Charmes-sur-l'Herbasse 062165
Pichlbauer, Rudolf, Mödling 057187, 120670
Pichlbauer, Rudolf, Salzburg 057271, 120674
Pichler, Eva M., Wien 057524
Pichler & Söhne, Gabriel, Wien 057525, 095920
Pichler, Manfred, Wien 057526
Pichot, Patrice, Trets 125002
Piciucchi, Massimiliano, Roma 076620
Pick & Poke, Clarence Park 055679
Pickard, Oklahoma City 118673
Pickens County Museum of Art History, Pickens 047015
Picker, Otto, Wassenaar 140571
Picker Art Gallery, Hamilton 044401
Pickering Antique Centre, Pickering 086269, 131380
Pickering & Chatto, London 141866
Pickering Museum Village, Pickering 006146
Picket Fence Antiques, Sacramento 092175
Pickett, Graham, Stamford 086686
Pickett & Watts, Jacksonville 116537
Pickford, Paul, Hayfield 084635
Pickford's House Museum, Derby . . 039227
Pickles, Parramatta 056443
Pickles Auctions, Fyshwick 120587
Pickles Auctions, Salisbury Plain . . 120635
Pickroth, Neckarsulm 104394
Pickup, David, Burford 083791
Pickwick, Katoomba 136957
Pickwick Antiques, Boscastle 083579
Pickwick Antiques, Preston 056502, 123291
Pickwick's Choice, Toronto 059262
Picma, Verona 106800
Picma, Verona 106801
Picoche, La Bresse 063298
Picpus, Montreux 111747
Picta, Firenze 127391
Picton Community Museum, Picton 030575
Picton Street Traders, South Auckland 079243
Pictor, Carcassonne 099083
Pictor Galerie, Mainz 104004
Pictorials, Shrewsbury 114432
Pictorica Galega, Vigo 110867
Pictou County Historical Museum, New Glasgow 005999
Pictura, Dordrecht 107983
Pictura, Gent 058202, 120759
Pictura, Groningen 108044
Pictura, Praha . . .060150, 098483, 120859
Pictura, Singapore 109850
Pictura, Witten 105311
Pictura Graphica, Bammental 101734
Pictural, Monaco 107541
The Picture Business, Bristol 112728
Picture Conservation and Restoration Studios, Buckingham 130473
Picture-Esq, Pocklington 114267
The Picture Factory, Heidelberg West 094632
Picture Frames, Eschwege 102660
Picture Gallery, Bhaktapur 029113
The Picture House, Crewe 112919
Picture House, Iklin 107445
The Picture House, Loughton 113998
The Picture House, Penryn 114228
The Picture House, Saint Ives, Cornwall 114368
The Picture House, Saint Mawes . . 114381
Picture House Gallery, Bury Saint Edmunds 112773
Picture House Gallery, Charlotte . . . 115305
Picture House Gallery, Padstow . . . 114212
Picture It, Albuquerque 114818
Picture Land, Austin 115001
Picture Map Company, Honolulu . . . 116237
Picture Nook Gallery, Prebbleton . . . 108547
Picture Options Gallery, Winnipeg . . 097600
Picture Palace, Wien 095921
Picture Parade, Sheffield 114420
Picture Paradise, Miami 117122
Picture Parlor, Mildura 056225
The Picture Parlour, Boscastle 112674
Picture Parts, Virginia Beach 120230
Picture Perfect, Berlin . . . 102008, 138831
Picture Perfect, Indianapolis 116488
Picture Perfect, Milwaukee 117216
Picture Perfect, Phoenix 118886
Picture Perfect, Phoenix 118887
Picture Perfect, Saint Paul 119304
Picture Perfect Art, Miami 117123
Picture Perfect Gallery, Charlotte . . 115306
Picture Perfect Gallery, Ilford 113286
Picture Perfect Gallery, London . . . 113831
Picture & Pottery, Cape Town 110029
Picture Restoration Studio, San Francisco 132905
Picture Restoration Studios, Arundel 130307
Picture Restoration Studios, Oxford 131356
The Picture Shop, Chorley 112868
Picture Shop, Wellington 108640
Picture Source Northwest, Seattle . 119977
Picture This, Borehamwood 112672
Picture This, Hong Kong . . 059685, 137749
Picture This, Indianapolis 116489
Picture This, Providence . . 119084, 142820
Picture This, Sandown 114394
Picture This, Wimborne 114701
Picture This, Windsor, Ontario 097564
Picture Us, Buddina 094321
Picturecraft Gallery, Holt, Norfolk . . 113260
Pictures, Bönningstedt 102171
Pictures, Bordeaux 138050
Pictures Are Beautiful, Houston . . . 116389
Pictures Etc, Winnipeg 097601
Pictures & Frames, Camberley 112783
Pictures & Frames, Craigavon 112911
Pictures & Frames, Crowthorne . . . 112926
Pictures & Frames, Farnham 113058
Pictures & Frames, Fleet 113069
Pictures & Frames, Guildford 113170
Pictures & Frames, Maidenhead . . . 114029
Pictures & Frames, Wokingham . . . 114720
Pictures Perfect - Downtown, Seattle 119978
Pictures Perfect - North, Seattle . . . 119979
Pictures Plus, Honolulu 116238
Pictures-Point, Paderborn 104573
Pictures & Things, Auckland 108356
Pictures To Delight, Newport, Essex 114133
Pictures to Go, Minneapolis 117294
Picturesque, Billericay 112640
Picturesque Photography, Pittsburgh 118945
Pictus Verlag, Schobüll 134383
Piddig Museum, Piddig 031763
Piderit, Kurt, Zürich 130257
Pidoux, Basel 082166
Pie Riera, Eugenio, Barcelona 080907
Piece Hall Art Gallery, Halifax 039663
Piece Hall Fine Art, Halifax 113179
Pièce Unique, Paris 100771
Pièce Unique, Paris 100772
Pieces of Olde Antiques, Louisville . 090018
Piechowiak, Krystyna, Poznań 079696, 129065
Piechura, Jan W., Warszawa 109177
Piécourt, Marie, Rueil-Malmaison . . 067323
Piedmont, Charlotte 131873
Piedmont Arts Museum, Martinsville 045714
Piedmont Lane Gallery, Oakland . . . 118642
Piedra Lumbre Visitors Center, Ghost Ranch Living Museum, Abiquiu 041572
Piedrahita, Felipe, Bogotá 059852
Pief, Köln 071990
Piehet, Ray J., New Orleans 090602
Pieksämäen Museo, Pieksämäki . . 009967
Piel, Michel, Cabourg 099042
Pielachtaler Heimatmuseum, Rabenstein an der Pielach 002487
Pielaveden Kotiseutumuseo, Pielavesi 009970
Pielisen Museo, Lieksa 009823
Pien, Amersfoort 077750
Pienmäen Talomuseo, Niemisjärvi . 009903
Pieper, Maria, Ulm 074150
Piepo, Wolfgang, Ronnenberg 126734
Pier Arts Centre, Stromness 041150
Pier One Imports, Houston 089175
Pier Pander Museum, Leeuwarden . 029842
Pierce Art Center, Minneapolis 117295
Pierce Manse, Concord 043125
Pierce's, Houston 089176, 122912
't Pierement, Leiden 078578
't Pierement, Middelburg 078642
Pierhuff, Indianapolis 089331
Pierides Museum, Laiki Cultural Centre, Larnaka 008210
Pierides Museum of Ancient Cypriot Art, Athinai 021211
Pierides Sculpture Garden, Larnaka 008211
Pierina Luti, Buenos Aires 055236
Pieringer, Anna, Tiefgraben 095769
Pierini, Alberto, Firenze 075385
Pierini, Filippo, Firenze 127392
Pierini, Robert, Biot 098972
Pierlot, Armelle, Lyon 064173
Piero, Yokohama 107150
Pierot, D., Bruxelles 123604
Pieroth, Heinz, Frankfurt am Main . 070775
Pierpont Morgan Library, New York . 046394
Pierre, 's-Hertogenbosch 108077
Pierre, Alain, Paris 124775
Pierre, Alain, Paris 124776
Pierre, Isabelle, Monaco 077619
Pierre Antiques, New York 091160
Pierre aux Loups, Cheval de Bois, Conflans-Sainte-Honorine 062458
Pierre d'Agate, Reims 067079
Pierre Gildesgame Maccabi Sports Museum, Ramat Gan 023052
Pierre-Hervouet, Dominique, Nantes 064939
Pierre Menard Home - State Historic Site, Ellis Grove 043681
Pierre Michel D., Paris 100773
Pierre & Nicolas, Cannes 099077
The Pierrepoint Gallery, Bridport . . . 112708
Pierrepont, Oxford 114202
Pierrepont Museum, Canton 042602
Pierres et Vestiges, Suresnes 068344
Pierres Passion, Vic-le-Comte 068846
Pierres Précieuses, Strasbourg 068329
Pierron, Laurent, Saint-Georges-du-Bois 067492
Pierrot, Warszawa 109178
Piers Pisani Antiques, Sherborne . .086581, 131485
Pierson, Marie-Françoise, Villers-la-Chèvre 068930
Pierson, Pat, Sainte-Foy-la-Grande 068057
Piert-Borgers, Barbara, Köln 126109
Pietarin Radan Museo, Lahti 009787
Pieter Claesen Wyckoff House Museum, Brooklyn 042466
Pieter Vermeulen Museum, Ijmuiden 029787
Pieternel, Deventer 078280
Pieters, Herzogenrath 071500
Pieters, Guy, Knokke-Heist 096351
Pieters, Guy, Saint-Paul-de-Vence . 101217
Pieters, Luc, Knokke-Heist 096352
Pietershuis, Haarlem 108061
La Pietra d'Agata, Milano 075817
Pietroforte, Manlio, Roma 128163
Piet's, Northampton 114154
Pifaçanes, Barcelona 129377
Piffl, Markus, Graz 057019, 123366
Pi.Ga., Roma 076621
Pigeon & Co, Lomas, Chelmsford . . 130529
Pigeon Island, Castries 034103
Pigeon Valley Steam Museum, Wakefield 030623
Piggelmee, Zwolle 078893
Pighouse Collection, Cornafean . . . 022723
Pigmalion, Postojna 110000
Pignatelli, Domenic R., North Providence 132564
Pignede, Yves, Maisons-Laffitte . . . 064228
Pignolo, Armando, Milano 127653
Pignolo, Giuliana, Milano 127654
Pigot, Jean-Michel, Sens 068218
Pig's Wings Bookshop of Dragon Hill, Coolangatta 136865
Pihan, Jenny, Frankston 094566
Pihay, Georgette, Québec 097158
Pihlajaveden Kotiseutumuseo, Pihlajavesi 009971
Pihtiputaan Kotiseutumuseo, Pihtipudas 009972
Pijpenkabinet & Smokiana, Amsterdam 029223
Pikaflor, Honfleur 063167
Pikari, Helsinki 060569
Pike County Museum, Milford 045869
Pikes Peak Pastel Society, Colorado Springs 054982
Pikinasso, Roanne 101096
Pikora, Cezary, Serock 079705
Piktúra Galéria, Budapest 105539
Pila Museum, Pila 031764
Pilar Martí, Barcelona 080908
Pilares Sanchez, J.L., Sevilla 110775
Pilat, Bianca, Chicago 115525
Pilat, Bianca, Milano 106283
Pilchard Works, Newlyn 040560
Pilchuck Glass School, Seattle 052167
Pile, Ronald, Ely 113019
Pilegaard, J., Aalborg 060209, 137860
Pilgrim Antiques, Ampthill 083299
Pilgrim Antiques, Honiton 084729
Pilgrim Books, Calgary 137626
Pilgrim Books, Dublin 139966
Pilgrim Gallery, London 113832
Pilgrim Hall Museum, Plymouth . . . 047097
Pilgrim Monument and Provincetown Museum, Provincetown 047267
Pilgrims Antique Centre, Dorking . . 084201
Pilgrims Antiques Centre, Gainsborough 084449
Pilgrim's Rest Museum, Pilgrim's Rest 034703
Pili, Lina, Berlin 069724
Pili, Rosetta, Cagliari 075221
Pilkington, Yelvertoft 135317
Pillantás, Budapest 105540
Pillars, Lyneham 085885
Pillars & Pomegranates, Fresno . . . 088916
Pille, T., Rostock 073581
Piller & Assoc., Stanley M., Oakland 091433
Piller, Yves, Corminboeuf 082326
Pillet, Lyons-la-Forêt 064198
Pilling, Detmold 070230, 121370
Pillon, Calais 120959
Pillon, Trieste 076902
Pilloni, Nunzia & C., Cagliari 075222
Pilloni, Rosaria, Cagliari 127252
Pillsbury, Michel, Houston 089177
The Pillsbury Art Collection, Minneapolis 045920
Pillu, François, Paris 100774
Pilney, Saint Paul 092387
Pilonova Galerija, Ajdovščina 034456
Pilorgé, Jean, Carnac 061992
Pilot Mound Cenntenial Museum, Pilot Mound 006152
Pilotgalerie, Luzern 111700
Pilots Cottage Museum, Kiama 001152
Pils, Erich, Krems 057130
Pils, John, Saint Louis 119238
Pilsen, Chicago 088144
Pilsen, Chicago 088145
Pilsen, Chicago 131915
Pilton Art Gallery, Barnstaple 112561
Piltzer, Gérald, Macherin 099623
Piluso, Karina, Aix-en-Provence . . . 098792
Pilz, Evelyn, Münster 072923
Pilz, Roman J., Mainburg 126254
Pilz-Lehrschau, Villach 002776

Pilzmuseum Taura, Schildau, Gneisenaustadt 020021
Pilzner, Fred, Hannover 103294
Pim, Heerlen 078502
Pima Air and Space Museum, Tucson 048640
Pimeria Alta Historical Society Museum, Nogales 046493
Pimlico, Chicago 088146
Pimlico Books, London 141867
Pimmingsdorfer, Angelika & Erich, Peuerbach 095704
Pin, Chen Tang, Hong Kong 059686
Pin, Xuan Ge, Singapore 109851
Le Pin Bleu, Beaune 061290
Le Pin Perdu, Carcassonne 061979
Pina, C., Charleroi 058151
La Pinacoteca, Barcelona 110232
La Pinacoteca, Bogotá 098182
Pinacoteca, Córdoba 000312
La Pinacoteca, Napoli 076028
Pinacoteca, Ploaghe 025288
Pinacoteca, Teramo 026004
Pinacoteca, Chiesa di Santa Verdiana, Castelfiorentino 023713
Pinacoteca, Palazzo dei Musei, Varallo Sesia 026208
Pinacoteca Ambrosiana, Milano . . . 024733
Pinacoteca Andrea Alfano, Castrovillari 023759
Pinacoteca Barão de Santo Angelo, Porto Alegre 004304
Pinacoteca Benedicto Calixto, Santos 004471
Pinacoteca Cantonale Giovanni Züst, Rancate 037432
Pinacoteca Capitolina, Roma 025581
Pinacoteca Carmelita del Convento del Carmen, Trujillo 031610
Pinacoteca Chiesa di San Giovanni, Pieve Torina 025241
Pinacoteca Chiesa di San Tomaso Becket, Padova 025068
Pinacoteca Civica, Abano Terme . . . 023107
Pinacoteca Civica, Ascoli Piceno . . 023271
Pinacoteca Civica, Asti 023291
Pinacoteca Civica, Baiardo 023325
Pinacoteca Civica, Cento 023790
Pinacoteca Civica, Cepagatti 023792
Pinacoteca Civica, Crotone 024008
Pinacoteca Civica, Iesi 024397
Pinacoteca Civica, Imola 024409
Pinacoteca Civica, Imperia 024413
Pinacoteca Civica, Montelupone . . . 024852
Pinacoteca Civica, Monza 024877
Pinacoteca Civica, Pieve di Cento . . 025238
Pinacoteca Civica, San Gimignano . 025684
Pinacoteca Civica, Santarcangelo di Romagna 025775
Pinacoteca Civica, Savona 025829
Pinacoteca Civica, Palazzo Canonici, Spello 025932
Pinacoteca Civica, Palazzo Priori, Fermo 024098
Pinacoteca Civica, Villa Grappallo, Vado Ligure 026182
Pinacoteca Civica A. Modigliani, Follonica 024218
Pinacoteca Civica A. Ricci, Monte San Martino 024817
Pinacoteca Civica Bruno Molajoli, Fabriano 024064
Pinacoteca Civica Carlo Servolini, Collesalvetti 023931
Pinacoteca Civica d'Arte Moderna, Latina 024477
Pinacoteca Civica e Gipsoteca U. Gera, Palazzo Bonomi, Ripatransone . . . 025445
Pinacoteca Civica F. Duranti, Palazzo Leopardi, Montefortino 024843
Pinacoteca Civica Francesco Podesti e Galleria Comunale d'Arte Moderna, Ancona 023201
Pinacoteca Civica G. Cattabriga, Bondeno 023476
Pinacoteca Civica Melozzo degli Ambrogi, Forlì 024233
Pinacoteca Civica Tosio Martinengo, Brescia 023525
Pinacoteca Comunale, Bosa 023498
Pinacoteca Comunale, Castiglion Fiorentino 023746
Pinacoteca Comunale, Cesena 023823
Pinacoteca Comunale, Città di Castello 023897
Pinacoteca Comunale, Deruta 024026
Pinacoteca Comunale, Locarno . . . 037273
Pinacoteca Comunale, Manciano . . 024593
Pinacoteca Comunale, Matelica . . . 024650
Pinacoteca Comunale, Narni 024927
Pinacoteca Comunale, Ostra 025036
Pinacoteca Comunale, Quistello . . . 025378
Pinacoteca Comunale, Ripe San Ginesio 025446
Pinacoteca Comunale, San Benedetto del Tronto 025653
Pinacoteca Comunale, Sarnano . . . 025791
Pinacoteca Comunale, Spoleto 025942
Pinacoteca Comunale, Verucchio . . 026296
Pinacoteca Comunale, Museo Civico, Mondavio 024789
Pinacoteca Comunale, Museo d'Arte della Città, Ravenna 025401
Pinacoteca Comunale, Palazzo Comunale, Massa Fermana 024633
Pinacoteca Comunale, Palazzo del Podestà, Massa Marittima 024644
Pinacoteca Comunale, Palazzo Tacchi Venturi, San Severino Marche . . . 025731
Pinacoteca Comunale, Palazzo Vallemani, Assisi 023285
Pinacoteca Comunale A. Moroni, Porto Recanati 025331
Pinacoteca Comunale Alberto Martini, Palazzo Foscolo, Oderzo 024983
Pinacoteca Comunale D. Stefanucci, Cingoli 023884
Pinacoteca Comunale d'Arte Antica e Moderna, Faenza 024073
Pinacoteca Comunale E. Giannelli, Parabita 025108
Pinacoteca Comunale e Museo A. De Felice, Terni 026012
Pinacoteca Comunale F. Galante Civera, Margherita di Savoia 024615
Pinacoteca Comunale Foresiana, Portoferraio 025339
Pinacoteca Comunale Francesco Cozza, Stilo 025952
Pinacoteca Comunale V. Bindi, Giulianova 024348
Pinacoteca D. Inzaghi, Budrio 023542
Pinacoteca Dantesca F. Bellonzi, Torre de Passeri 026086
Pinacoteca d'Arte Antica, Gemona del Friuli 024288
Pinacoteca d'Arte Contemporanea, Smerillo 025909
Pinacoteca d'Arte Francescana, Lecce 024485
Pinacoteca d'Arte Moderna, Avezzano 023310
Pinacoteca d'Arte Sacra, Alcamo . . 023161
Pinacoteca Davide Bergh', Calice al Cornovoglio 023583
Pinacoteca de la Escuela Provincial de Bellas Artes Dr. Figueroa Alcorta, Córdoba 000313
Pinacoteca de la Facultad de Bellas Artes, Manizales 007531
Pinacoteca de la Universidad de Concepción, Concepción 006914
Pinacoteca de Nuevo León, Monterrey 028572
Pinacoteca dei Cappuccini, Voltaggio 026366
Pinacoteca del Ateneo, Universidad Autónoma de Coahuila, Saltillo . . 028702
Pinacoteca del Centro de la Profesa, México 028542
Pinacoteca del Duomo, Cittadella . . 023900
Pinacoteca del Estado Juan Gamboa Guzmán, Mérida 028417
Pinacoteca del Pio Monte della Misericordia, Napoli 024921
Pinacoteca del Templo de La Compañía, Guanajuato 028309
Pinacoteca della Cassa di Risparmio, Cesena 023824
Pinacoteca della Certosa, Firenze . . 024200
Pinacoteca della Chiesa di San Francesco, Mercatello sul Metauro 024676
Pinacoteca della Rocca Ubaldinesca, Sassocorvaro 025808
Pinacoteca dell'Abbazia di Novacello, Varna 026217
Pinacoteca dell'Accademia Carrara, Bergamo 023381
Pinacoteca dell'Accademia dei Concordi e del Seminario, Rovigo 025615
Pinacoteca dell'Accademia di Belle Arti, Carrara 023675
Pinacoteca di Brera, Milano 024734
Pinacoteca di Corinaldo, Corinaldo . 023970
Pinacoteca di San Silvestro, Montecompatri 024832
Pinacoteca Diego Rivera, Xalapa . . 028944
Pinacoteca Diocesana di Arte Sacra, Senigallia 025854
Pinacoteca do Estado de São Paulo, São Paulo 004560
Pinacoteca d'Vinci, Medellín 098282
Pinacoteca e Biblioteca Rambaldi, Sanremo 025742
Pinacoteca e Musei Civici, Jesi . . . 024433
Pinacoteca e Musei Comunali, Macerata 024568
Pinacoteca e Museo Civici, Camerino 023607
Pinacoteca e Museo Civico, Palazzetto del Podestà 3, Bettona 023387
Pinacoteca e Museo Civico, Palazzo Minucci-Solaini, Volterra 026369
Pinacoteca e Museo de Napoli, Terlizzi 026005
Pinacoteca Eduardo Ramírez Castro, Aranzazu 007390
Pinacoteca G. A. Levis, Racconigi . . 025380
Pinacoteca Giovanni e Marella Agnelli, Palazzo Grassi, Torino 026082
Pinacoteca Giovanni Morscio, Dolceacqua 024033
Pinacoteca Giuseppe Stuard, Parma 025129
Pinacoteca in Palazzo Volpi, Como . 023947
Pinacoteca Internazionale dell'Età Evolutiva A. Cibaldi, Rezzato 025424
Pinacoteca Larraín, Santiago de Chile 123882
Pinacoteca M. Cascella, Museo Civico d'Arte Contemporanea, Ortona . . 025018
Pinacoteca Malaspina, Pavia 025146
Pinacoteca Manfrediana, Venezia . . 026265
Pinacoteca Municipal de Guadalupe, Guadalupe 028296
Pinacoteca Municipal de la Provincia de Corongo, Corongo 031495
Pinacoteca Municipal Ignacio Merino, Lima 031572
Pinacoteca Municipal Leoncio Lugo, Paucartambo 031580
Pinacoteca Municipal Miguel Ângelo Pucci, Franca 004121
Pinacoteca-Museo Beato Sante, Santuario Beato Sante, Mombaroccio 024781
Pinacoteca, Museo delle Ceramiche, Pesaro 025178
Pinacoteca Nazionale, Bologna 023461
Pinacoteca Nazionale, Cosenza . . . 023984
Pinacoteca Nazionale, Siena 025894
Pinacoteca Nazionale, Cittadella dei Musei, Cagliari 023571
Pinacoteca Nazionale, Palazzo Diamanti, Ferrara 024116
Pinacoteca Parrocchiale, Buonconvento 023546
Pinacoteca Parrocchiale, Castroreale 023756
Pinacoteca Parrocchiale, Corridonia 023974
Pinacoteca Provinciale Corrado Giaquinto, Bari 023345
Pinacoteca Repossi, Chiari 023844
Pinacoteca Rossetti Valentini, Santa Maria Maggiore 025755
Pinacoteca Todo Arte, Santiago de Chile 059546
Pinacoteca Universitaria, Colima . . 028172
Pinacoteca Vaticana, Musei Vaticani, Città del Vaticano 049435
Pinacoteca Virreinal de San Diego, México 028543
Pinacoteca Zelantea, Acireale 023114
Pinacotheca, Paderborn 104574
Pinakothek der Moderne, München 019103
Pinakotheke, Rio de Janeiro 096636
Pinakothiki Kouvoutsaki, Kifissia . . 021326
Piñanes Tena, Manuel, Sevilla 081608
Piñanes Tena, Manuel, Sevilla 081609
Pinard Etellin, Colette, Clermont-Ferrand 062354
Pin'Art Antiques, Bruxelles 058056
Pin.Arte, Torino 106695
Pinault, Jacques-Henri, Paris 124777
Pincacoteca E. Notte, Ceglie Messapica 023784
Pincas, Nathalie, Paris 124778
Pinceladas de Málaga, Málaga 110641
Pinchbeck Marsh Engine and Land Drainage Museum, Spalding 041075
Pincher Creek Museum, Pincher Creek 006153
Pinckaers, M., Limal 120776
Pindar Press, London 135251
Pine and Decorative Items, Ashbourne 083330
Pine and Design Imports, Chicago . 088147
Pine and Period Furniture, Grampound 084492
Pine Antiques, Olney 086163
Pine Antiques Workshop, Doveridge 084215
Pine-Apple Antiques, Kingston-upon-Hull 084863
The Pine Barn, Crawley 084105
Pine Cellars, Winchester 087175
The Pine Collection, Saint Peter Port 086475
Pine Collection and Ranelagh Antiques, Dublin 074942
The Pine Cottage, Jacksonville 089447
Pine County Historical Society Museum, Askov 041818
Pine Creek Museum, Pine Creek . . 001379
Pine Designs, London 131145
The Pine Emporium, Hemel Hempstead 084651
The Pine Emporium, Hursley 084774
Pine Finds, Bishop Monkton 130399
Pine Forest Art Centre, Dublin 050346
Pine Grove Historic Museum, Pontiac 047121
Pine House, Breda 078112
Pine Islet Lighthouse, Mackay 001201
The Pine Mine, London 085612
Pine Mine, Los Angeles 089880
Pine Parlour, Ampthill 083300
Pine Ridge Car Museum, Main Ridge 001205
The Pine Shop, Fremantle 055845
Pine Street Revolution Pantechnicon, Los Angeles 089881
Pine Stripping, Keighley 130838
Pine Stripping, London 131146
Pine Stripping Specialists, London . 131147
Pine Studio, Sankt-Peterburg 080321
Pine & Things, Shipston-on-Stour . . 086593
Pine Woodworks, Denver . 088723, 132043
Pineapple House Antiques, Alresford 083278
Pineau, Michel, Nantes 064940
Pineau, William, La Crèche 063360
Pineau, William, Saint-Maixent-l'Ecole 067602
Pinecrest Historical Village, Manitowoc 045637
Pineda, Bogotá 059853
Pinel & Partner, Bruxelles 058057
Pinel, Saskatoon 097198
Pines, Sylvia, New York 091161
Pinetum, Canterbury 083866, 130508

Pinetz, Walter, Wien 057527, 123523
Pinewood, Justin, Burton-upon-Trent 083816
Pinewood Furniture Studio, Halesowen 130756
Pinewood Museum, Wasagaming . . 006766
Ping Fan, Tianjin 098015
Ping Jin Zhan Yi, Old Zhi Display Center, Yangliuqing 007335
Pingdu City Museum, Pingdu 007219
Pingeon, Christian, Bézannes-lès-Reims 061425
Pinggu Shangzhai Cultural Display Center, Beijing 007005
Pinguin, Mainz 072402
Pingvin, Maffra 136986
Pinies, Patrick, Pointis-Inard 066884
Pink & Sons, Malvern, Victoria 056149
Pink Flamingos Antique Mall, Phoenix 091764
Pink Gallery, Helensburgh 113218
Pink Giraffe, San Antonio 092561
Pink Porch Antiques, Tucson 093258
Pink Summer, Genova 106103
Pinkerton, Heerlen 078503
Pinkhart, Gertraud, Wien 057528
Pinkney, Herbert, Memphis 117002
Pinn & Sons, W.A., Sible Hedingham 086613
Pinn Road Book Exchange, San Antonio 142892
Pinna, Henri, Plomodiern 066863
Pinnacles Gallery, Thuringowa Central 095335
Pinnacles National Monument, Paicines 046792
Pinnaroo Heritage Museum, Pinnaroo 001382
Pinnaroo Printing Museum, Pinnaroo 001383
Pinnau Antik, København 060368
Pinner, Stefan, Chemnitz 070140
Pinneys, Montréal 120807
Pino Pascual, S., Málaga 110642
Les Pins Maison des Arts, Cologny . 111364
Pinson, Françoise, Avranches 061147
Pinson, Joël, Saint-Quentin-sur-le-Homme 067979
Pinson, Yvon, Conques 062464
Pinson Mounds State Archaeological Area, Pinson 047031
Pint, Carlo, Napoli 076029
Pintar, Maria, Salzburg 057272
Pintassilgo & Almeida, Lisboa 079991
Pintér, Budapest 074708
Pintner, Hofheim am Taunus 103392
Pinto, António Reis, Lisboa 129168
Pinto, António Reis, Odivelas 129184
Pinto e Bourdain, Lisboa 121941
Pinto Torrijos, Francisco, Madrid . . 081361
Pinto Torrijos, Valentín, Madrid 081362
Pintuformas, Medellín 059936
Pintura Contemporánea, Lima 108811
Pinturas e Artes Especiais Ateliarte, São Paulo 049770
Pinturas Pueblo, Alicante 129303
Pinus, Leuven 058278, 123643
Pinx, Bochum 102159
Pinx, Helsinki 098742
Pinxit, Nashville 117365
Pinxit, Torino 106696
Pinzgauer Heimatmuseum, Saalfelden am Steinernen Meer 002546
Pio Cabello, Cristobal, Barcelona . . 080909
Pioneer Antiques, Phillip 056465
Pioneer Antiques, Tanunda 056697
Pioneer Arizona Living History Museum, Phoenix 047013
Pioneer Auto Museum, Murdo 046091
Pioneer Books, Seacombe Gardens 137084
Pioneer Corner Museum, New Holstein 046232
Pioneer Cottage Antiques, North Geelong 056367
Pioneer Farm Museum and Ohop Indian Village, Eatonville 043594
Pioneer Florida Museum, Dade City 043256
Pioneer Heritage Center, Cavalier . . 042660
Pioneer Heritage Center, LSU Shreveport, Shreveport 048161
Pioneer Historical Connors Museum, Connors 005292
Pioneer-Krier Museum, Ashland . . . 041799
Pioneer-Krier Museum, Ashland . . . 041800
Pioneer Log Cabin, Manhattan 045631
Pioneer Museum, Fabius 043778
Pioneer Museum, Fairmont 043794
Pioneer Museum, Silverton 034747
Pioneer Museum, Watford City 049002
Pioneer Museum, Wild Rose 049172
Pioneer Museum and Vereins Kirche, Gillespie County Historical Society, Fredericksburg 044054
Pioneer Museum of Alabama, Troy . 048615
Pioneer Rum Museum, Beenleigh . . 000788
Pioneer Settlement Museum, Swan Hill 001501
Pioneer Square Antique Mall, Seattle 093048
Pioneer Stripping and Refinish, Milwaukee 132370
Pioneer Tower Antiques, Kitchener . 058873
Pioneer Town, Wimberley 049227
Pioneer Tracks of Queensland Gallery, Nebo 094930
Pioneer Village, Farmington 043824
Pioneer Village, Silverdale 030594
Pioneer Village Museum, Beauséjour 005086
Pioneer Village Museum, Burnie . . . 000865
Pioneer Woman Statue and Museum, Ponca City 047118
Pioneerimuseo, Koria 009731
Pioneers of Aviation Museum, McGregor Museum, Kimberley 034664
Pioneers, Trail and Texas Rangers Memorial Museum, San Antonio 047799
Piontkowitz, S., Haan 071157
Piopio and District Museum, Piopio 030576
Pio's Antiques, Victoria 077545
Piot, Bad Kleinkirchen 095469
Piotrowski, Ryszard, Warszawa . . . 109179
Pip Antiques, Virginia 056786
Pipat & Morier, Blaye 061511
Pipat & Morier, Blaye 061512
Pipat & Morier, Bordeaux 061645
La Pipe, Oostende 058366
La Pipe Eric, Bruxelles 058058
Piper, Ulrike Margarete, Stuttgart . . 126874
Piper Antiques, Auckland 078972
Piper Aviation Museum, Lock Haven 045359
Piper Barn, Kyneton 056075
Piperaud, Pascale, Saint-Ouen 067866
Pipestone County Historical Museum, Pipestone 047032
Pipestone National Monument, Pipestone 047033
Pipik, Anna, Lambach 137208
Pipino, Vincenzo, Napoli 127786
Pippa, Luigi, Roma 128164
Pippa's Art Gallery, Whangarei 108664
Pippi, Firenze 075386
Pippi, Leonardo, Firenze 127393
Pippin, Clayfield 055689
Pippin, Kenneth, Baltimore 087703
Piqua Historical Area State Memorial, Piqua 047034
Pique-Puces, Bruxelles 137460
Piquet, Coudekerque-Branche 062499
Piqueux, Pierre, La Rochette 063442
Piraino, Pietro, Palermo 076170
Piramal Gallery, Mumbai 105792
Pirâmide, Lisboa 109344
La Piramide, Milano 075818
Piramidon, Barcelona 110233
Piras, Maria Giovanna, Torino 106697
Pirate, Denver 116035
Pirate Contemporary Art Oasis, Denver 043415
Pirate's Alley, Oklahoma City 118674
Pirmoradi, Hamburg 071308
Pirner, Gerhard, Edelsfeld 102599
Pirngruber, Alfred, Linz 137223
Piro, Hélène, Martel 064411
Piro, M., Buchholz in der Nordheide 102282
Pirontidi, Ernesto, Barcelona 080910
Pirotska Antikvariat, Sofia 137606
La Pirouette, Hyères 063197
Pirovano, Fabio, Pura 082735
Pirra, Stefano, Torino 106698
Pirri, Angela, Roma 076622
Pirzkall, Isabella, Worpswede 127036
Pisa, Den Haag 078234
Pisanelli, Tiziana, Roma 076623
Pisarski, Odenthal 073172
Pischetola, Giuseppe, Torino 076857
Piscopo, Nicola, Bari 127118
Piskarevskoe Memorialnoe Kladbišče - Muzej, Sankt-Peterburg 033824
Pismo, Denver 116036
Pisonero Ortega, Eduard, Barcelona 129378
Pistil, Seattle 143005
Pistiner, Albert, Paris 066418
Piston, Hyman E., New York 091162
Pisu, Giovanni, Cagliari . . 075223, 127253
Pit 21, Milano 106284
Pitäjämuseo ja Nymann Talo ja Apteekkimuseo, Tohmajärvi 010151
Pitäjäntupa-Museo, Joutseno 009628
Pitcairn, Scott 2207 Second Av, Seattle 119980
Pitchal, Virginie, Paris 066419
Pitcher, Nicholas S., London 085613
Piteå Museum, Piteå 036540
Pitfield, David, Sunninghill Ascot . . 114522
Piti Arte Ibiza, Eivissa 110348
Pitkänpellon Talomuseo, Kangasniemi 009661
Pitlochry Festival Theatre Art Gallery, Pitlochry 040717
Il Pitocchetto Tarquinio, Brescia . . . 106004
Piton, Saint-Raphaël 067986
Piton, J.P., Saint-Raphaël 067987
Pitot House Museum, New Orleans . 046266
Pitow, Bruck an der Mur 095490
Pitre, Honolulu 116239
Pitrelli, Vincenzo, Milano 127655
Pitstone Green Farm Museum, Pitstone 040718
Pitt, Helen, Vancouver 097514
Pitt Meadows Museum, Pitt Meadows 006154
Pitt Rivers Museum, Oxford 040665
Pitta-Settelmeyer, Rose-Maria, Konstanz 126133
Pittencrieff House Museum, Dunfermline 039318
Pittera, Jean, Marseille 124431
Pitti, Monaco 077620
Pittini, Matteo, Bari 127119
Pittock Mansion, Portland 047177
Pitton, Fabrizio, Torino 076858
Pittsburg State University Natural History Museum, Pittsburg 047038
Pittsburgh Antique Mall, Pittsburgh . 091852
Pittsburgh Center for the Arts, Pittsburgh 047058
Pittsburgh Children's Museum, Pittsburgh 047059
Pittsburgh Pastel Artists League, Pittsburgh 054983
Pittsburgh Plating and Lamp Service, Pittsburgh 132672
Pittsburgh Print Group, Pittsburgh . 054984
Pittsburgh Society of Illustrators, Monroeville 054985
Pittsford Historical Society Museum, Pittsford 047072
Pittsworth and District Historical Museum, Pittsworth 001384
Pitz, Ludwig, Stolberg, Rheinland . .073929, 104955
Pitzen, Christoph, Esslingen 125623
Pitzhanger Manor-House and Gallery, London 040257
Piulimatsivik - Nain Museum, Nain . 005975
Piva, Milano 075819
Piva, Milano 075820
Piva, Francesco, Milano 075821
Pivano, Pietro, Torino 128343
Pivot, Bernard, Basel 129931
Pivotal Galleries, Richmond, Victoria 095142
Pivovarské Muzeum, Plzeň 008572
Pivovarski Muzej, Ljubljana 034490
Pixel Gallery, Frankfurt am Main . . . 102809
Pixel Grain, Berlin 102009
Pixel Place, Hamilton 096923
Pixi & Cie., Paris 100775
Pixian Juan Calligraphy and Painting Gallery, Chengdu 097700
Pixian Museum, Pixian 007220
Pixtory, Marseille . 064385, 099681, 133495
Pizorno Azuara, Laura, Ourense . . . 081453
Pizzi, Amilcare, Cinisello Balsamo . 134570
Pizzi, Gabrielle, Melbourne 094823
Pizzigoni, Marco, Milano 121710
Pizzinelli, Gianfranco, Roma 128165
Pjatigorskij Kraevedčeskij Muzej, Pjatigorsk 033667
Pjazza Antiques, San Gwann 077528
P.J.K. Gallery, Skipton 114439
Pjóðminjasafn Islands, Reykjavík . . 021972
Pjot, Værløse 120877
Pjotr, Tilburg 108234
P.L. Déco, Saint-Médard-en-Jalles . 101182
Pla, Alfons, Barcelona 129379
PLA Naval Museum, Qingdao 007223
Plaar, Jonas, Zürich 083012, 130258
Plaaswinkel, Pretoria 080742
Plac-Art, Bremen 070039
Plac Zamkowy, Warszawa 109180
Placard Galerie, Mannheim 104027
The Place, Toulouse 101368
The Place Antiques, Golden Square 055894
Place Concore Antiquario, Rio de Janeiro 058635
Place des Arts, Paris 100776
Place des Vosges, New York 118294
La Place du Soleil, San Francisco . . 092866
Place Neuve Galerie, Vers-Pont-du-Gard 101451
Place Royale, Montréal 097063
Placemaker, Miami 117124
Placentia Area Museum, Placentia . 006156
Places and Spaces, London 085614
Plach, Johann, Gaweinstal 137174
Plachot, Christian, Ypreville-Biville .069065, 125040
Placier, Paris 100777
Plada, Maribor 080663
Pladeck, F., Bielefeld 069836
Plain Farm Workshop, Alton 130295
Plaine des Dinosaures, Mèze 013054
Plains Art Museum, Fargo 043815
Plains Indians and Pioneers Museum, Woodward 049301
Plains Vintage Railway and Historical Museum, Ashburton 030428
Plainsman Museum, Aurora 041916
Plaisio, Lagkadikia 105433
Plaisir d'Antan, La Roche-Guyon . . 063409
Plaisir des Yeux, Sierre 111903
Plaisirs d'Intérieur, Saint-Jean-de-Luz 067539
Plakart, Lauchringen 103839
Plakart am Dreiecksplatz, Kiel 103543
Plakat am Markt, Seligenstadt 104885
Plakatmuseum am Niederrhein, Emmerich 016972
Plakatsammlung, Museum für Gestaltung Zürich, Zürich 037797
Plakity, Michael, Dresden 138997
Plambeck, Rosamunde, Kiel 126042
Plamondon and District Museum, Plamondon 006157
Plan 2 B, Portland 137052
Plan-Art, Rheda-Wiedenbrück 104742
Plan-Weseritzer Heimatstuben mit Archiv, Tirschenreuth 020443

Plana, Ricard, Terrassa 110788
Planage, Binoist, Rouen 067291
Planaterra, Chur 111361
La Plancha, Heerlen 078504
Plane Space, New York 118295
Plane Tree, Christchurch 079046
Planet 22, Genève 111492
Planet Anime, Houston 089178
Planet Art, Cape Town 110030
Planet Art, Miami 117125
Planet Corroborce, Byron Bay 055594
Planet Earth Museum, Newhaven 040559
Planet Publishing, New Orleans 117492
Planet Rugs, Houston 089179
Planetron - Aards Paradijs, Dwingeloo 029515
Plank, Wien 095922
Plank, Alexander, Mauerbach 133118
Planque, Claudine, Lausanne 111630
Planšarski Muzej, Gorenjski Muzej Kranj, Bohinjsko Jezero 034460
Plantahaus - Chesa Planta, Samedan 037486
Plantard, Guer 063093
Plantard, Jean-Claude, Paris 066420
Plantation Agriculture Museum, Scott 048055
Plantation Antiques, Toronto 059263
Plantation Furniture & Antiques, Calgary 058799
Plantation Historical Museum, Plantation 047079
Plantation of Ulster Visitor Centre, Draperstown 039283
Plantation Shop, Atlanta 087513
Planteau du Maroussem, Eric, Aix-en-Provence 098793
Plantener Pedersen, Tine, Holte 060257
Planter, Singapore 080545
Plantier, Le Cheylard 063602
Plantier, Le Cheylard 063603
Plantijn, Den Haag 140399
Plantijn, C., Delft 140383
Plantiques, San Antonio 092562
Plantureux, Serge, Paris 138523
Plas Mawr, Conwy 039136
Plas Newydd, Llanfairpwll 040059
Plas Newydd, Llangollen 040065
Plasma, Prahran 056499
Plassard, Yves, Paris 066421
Plassart, Ch., Poitiers 121225
Plasse, Agnès, Boulogne-Billancourt 061689
Plassenburg, Kulmbach 018443
Plast-Art, Černigiv 112377
Plaster Rock Museum, Plaster Rock 006158
Plastic Club, Philadelphia 046977, 054986
Plastics Historical Society, Sidcup 054467
Plastique Kinetic Worms, Singapore 109852
Plastyka, Kraków 108972
Plastyka, Warszawa 109181
Plat, Hardegarijp 128701
Plat, Jean-Louis, Tours 068601
Plat Art, Buenos Aires 123156
El Plata, Sevilla 081610
De Plataan, Heerlen 078505
Plâté, Colombo 081766
Plâté, Colombo 081767
Plâté, Colombo 110895
Plâté, Colombo 110896
Plateaux Gallery, London 113833
Platenhäuschen, Erlangen 017035
Platero, Buenos Aires 136749
Platform 1 Heritage Farm Railway, Littlehampton 001189
Platform Artists Group, Melbourne 094824
Platform Gallery, Clitheroe 112878
Plati Galeria, Wrocław 109230
Platini, Sylvie, Portland 119035
Platini, Sylvie, Veyrier-du-Lac 101461
Platinum Collectibles, Las Vegas 089598
Platou, Bærums Verk 121844
Platt, Paris 066422
Platt, Kevin, Padstow 114213
Platt, Susan, Seattle 119981
Platt, Trevor, Wynnum 095437
Platt R. Spencer Special Collections and Archival Room, Geneva 044166
Platte, E. & H., Preußisch Oldendorf 104638
Platten, Frank, Suderburg 126891
Plattner, Rosina, Schladming 095749
Plattner Bienenhof Museum, Soprabolzano 025921
Plattsburgh Art Museum, State University of New York, Plattsburgh 047085
Platz, Danielle, Baden-Baden 125127
Platzer, G., Straßwalchen 095768
Platzer, Peter, Kornwestheim 072057
Plauener Spitzenmuseum, Plauen 019633
Play House Gallery, Baltimore 115078
Players Press, Studio City 135510
Plaza, Salamanca 081542
Plaza, Francisco, Madrid 081363
Plaza, Marina, Madrid 081364
Plaza Antigua, Deventer 078281
Plaza Antiques, Minneapolis 090391
Plaza de La Raza, Los Angeles 045458
Plaza & Janés, Barcelona 134923
Plazanet, Nicole, Malicorne-sur-Sarthe 064239
Plazanet, Yvonne, Le Chambon-sur-Lignon 063596
Plazzotta, London 113834
P.L.C, Tallard 068352
Pleasant Place Antiques, Wellington 079340
Pleasant Point Railway and Historical Society Museum, Pleasant Point 030577
Please Touch Museum, Philadelphia 046978
Pleasures of Past Times, London 141868
Plechaty, Zdenek, Bayreuth 069492
Pledger, Robert E., Houston 116390
Pleïade, Dunkerque 099244
Pléiade, Grenoble 099309
Pleiades Gallery, New York 118296
Le Pleiadi, Milano 106285
Le Pleiadi, Roma 076624
Plein Air Painters of America, Santa Fe 054987
Plein Air Scene, Vallejo 052304, 054988
Plein Gaz, Paris 066423
Plein Sud, Vaison-la-Romaine 068676
Plejada Galeria, Gdynia 108914
Pleša, Zlatko, Frankfurt am Main 070776
Plescoff, Nicolas, Paris 100778
Pleser, Cornelius, München 104289
Plesse, Bovenden 138914
Plessis, Nantes 099815
Plessis, du, Richmond, South Australia 120630
Plesskij Gosudarstvennyj Istoriko-Architekturnyj i Chudožestvennyj Muzej-Zapovednik, Ples 033670
Plester, Randy, London 058888, 123778
Plestor Barn Antiques, Liss 085009
Plett, Zeist 108275
Pleus, Gerd, Oldenburg, Oldenburg 073207
Plewnia, Michael, Weimar, Thüringen 074309
Plexihouse, Miami 090231
PLI Gallery, New York 091163
Plickert, Berlin 102010
Plietzsch, Freiburg im Breisgau 139117
Plimsoll Gallery, Hobart 001111
Plinth, Leeds 113365
Plischek, Hermann, Lanzenkirchen 137212
Plischke, Dr. Georg, Unterwössen 134441
Plitt, Rostock 073582
Ploch, Florentina, San Antonio 092563
Płóciennik & Sobczak, Łódź 140755
Plöchl, Bernhard, Freistadt, Oberösterreich 133069
Plöger, T., Bremen 138948
De Ploegh, Amersfoort 107642
Het Ploeghuis, Groningen 108045
Ploenes, Sabine, Wrohm 105336
Plötz, Maike, Wyk auf Föhr 105363
Plötz-Peters, Hannelore, Berlin 069725
Plof, Denver 116037
Plott, H.-G., Leipzig 139400
Plough House Interiors, Chepstow 083937, 130548
Ploutis, Loizou, Egkomi 059949
Plouviez, Martine, Montmorillon 064721
Plowden & Smith, London 131148
Plückbaum & Dr. Plückbaum-Burgardt, Bonn 121349
Plüm, H.-Günter, Delmsen 070215
Plümacher, H., Burgwald 070106
Plug In, Basel 036902
Pluimvee Museum, Barneveld 029293
Plum, Peter, Marbach am Neckar 126286
Plum Blossoms, Hong Kong 097820
Plum Blossoms, New York 118297
Plum Blossoms, Singapore 109853
Plum Blossoms, Singapore 109854
Plum Coulee and District Museum, Plum Coulee 006160
Plum Grove Historic Home, Iowa City 044766
Plumas County Museum, Quincy 047294
Plumb, Albert, Chichester 130565
Plumb Farm Museum, Greeley 044305
Plumbly, Trevor, Dunedin 079090, 121824
Plume Antiques, Campbell Town 055613
La Plume d'Oie, Liège 137522
La Plume Marinoise, Le Marin 140249
Plumershuuske, Diepenheim 029480
Plumettaz, Fernand, Payerne 082722
Plummer, Warren, Arncliffe 094175
Plums, Fresno 116181
Plunder Inn Antiques, Sacramento 092176
Plunder-Kabinett, Winterthur 082916
Plunket Museum of Irish Education, Dublin 022769
Plunkett, Thomas, Saint Albans 114345
Pluntke, Erdmut, Berlin 069726
Pluntke, Leslie, Mainz-Kostheim 126269
Pluperfect, Melton 056208
Plurabelle Books, Cambridge 141475
Pluraebello, Milano 106286
Pluriel, Narbonne 064967, 099821
Plus Art, Monaco 077621
Plus Books, London 141869
Plus Fours Gallery, Hyderabad 105710
Plus Galleries, Antwerpen 096087
Plus Loin, Paris 066424
Plus One Plus Two Galleries, London 113835
Pluskwa, David, Marseille 099682
Plymouth Plantation Museum, Plymouth 047098
Plymouth Antiquarian Society Museum, Plymouth 047099
Plymouth Arts Centre, Plymouth 040723
Plymouth Historical Museum, Plymouth 047101
P.M. Gallery, Columbus 115794
Pm Tung Arts, New York 091164
PMP Art, Timişoara 080200
PNT Prom, Zagreb 098290
Po, Kwai, Hong Kong 133366
Po, Kwai, Paris 133664
Po, Wing, Hong Kong 059687
PO Gallery, Providence 119085
Po Nu Fa, Liptovský Mikuláš 080628
Poble Espanyol, Barcelona 110234
Poble Espanyol, Palma de Mallorca 035619
Poblet Antiguitats, Tarragona 081625
Pocahontas County Iowa Historical Society Museum, Laurens 045200
Pocahontas County Museum, Marlinton 045694
Poch, A., Bielefeld 069837
Pochopova, Lidmila, Praha 060151
Pochyla, Iwona, Augsburg 125078
Pociao, Bonn 133830
Pocker & Son, J., New York 118298
Pocket Bookshop, Paignton 141990
O Poço Velho, Lisboa 079992
Počta, Josef, Praha 137843
Pod Kasztanami, Konstancin-Jeziorna 079611
Pod Kasztanami, Warszawa 109182
Pod Kinskou, Praha 060152
Pod Schodami, Łódź 109016
Pod Svícnem, Frýdek-Místek 137782
Pod trzema Gracjami, Gdańsk 079585, 108894
Pod Vintage, Toronto 059264
Pod Złotym Lewkiem, Kraków 079650, 108973
Podany, Pittsburgh 132673
Podbrzezie, Kraków 108974
Podhofer, Horst M., Düsseldorf 070424
Podhorácké Muzeum, Tišnov 008715
Podium Galerie, Kaufbeuren 103524
Podium Kunst, Schramberg 020096
Podium Kunst e.V., Schramberg 053542
Podjavorinské Múzeum, Nové Mesto nad Váhom 034402
Podještědské Muzeum Karoliny Světlé, Český Dub 008321
Podlipanské Museum, Regionální Kolín, Český Brod 008320
Podpolianske Múzeum Detva, Detva 034347
Podpolnaja Tipografija CK RSDRP, Moskva 033517
Podravka Museum, Koprivnica 007738
Podřipské Museum, Roudnice nad Labem 008671
Podska, Hawkes Bay 108471
Podszus, E.M., Düsseldorf 102538
Podtatranské Muzeum, Kežmarok 034362
Podtatranské Múzeum, Poprad 034411
Podunajské Múzeum, Komárno 034363
Podvin, Roselyne, Hazebrouck 063141
Podwysocka, Krystyna, Warszawa 129105
Poe, Steven, San Francisco 119766
Poe, Timothy, Birmingham 115124
Poech, Dieter & Erika, Trostberg 105070
Pöljän Kotiseutumuseo, Pöljä 009976
Pöll, Gerhard, Kufstein 057138
Poelman, Hengelo, Overijssel 128712
Pörtom Hembygdsmuseum, Pörtom 009977
Poestgens, Horst, Übach-Palenberg 121614
Poet Jovaras House, Šiauliai Aušros Museum, Šiauliai 027856
Pöter, A., Sulzheim 074031
Poetry Renaissance, Dallas 115923
Poets, Brigitte, Salzgitter 126760
Poets Gallery, Boston 115222
Pötter, Geert, Rosdorf 139695
Pötters, Ulrike, Dormagen 102388
Pöttinger, Martina, Linz 095670
Poetzsch-Meinhardt, Katarina, Buckenhof 125409
Pöytyän Kotiseutumuseo, Pöytyä 009978
Poggendorf, Renate, München 126433
Poggi, Eliane, Grenoble 099310
Poggi, Laura, Genova 075498
Poggi, Sandro, Roma 076625
Pogliano, Tommaso, Torino 128344
Poguy'Art, Toulouse 101369
Pohjanmaan Antikvariaatti, Vaasa 138002
Pohjanmaan Museo, Vaasa 010203
Pohjois-Karjalan Museo, Joensuu 009622
Pohjois-Pohjanmaan Museo, Oulu 009939
Pohjoismainen Konservaattoriliitto - Suomen Osasto, Helsinki 052877
Pohl, Joachim, Berlin 102011
Pohl, Max, Hamburg 071309
Pohl, U., Aldenhoven 069129
Pohle, Werner, Berlin 102012
Pohlkötter, Münster 104374
Pohlmann, Käthe, Hofheim am Taunus 071553
Pohronské Múzeum v Novej Bani, Nová Baňa 034401
Poiger, Oberndorf am Neckar 104505
Poignant, Jean-Marc, Nyons 065253, 124529
Poignant, Jean-Marc, Valréas 068702
Poilblan, Michel, Coucy-le-Château-Auffrique 062497
Le Poilu, Paris 066425
Poindessault, Bernard, Paris 066426
Poinot, Anne, Agon-Coutainville 060675

Poinsignon, Strasbourg 068330
Point, J., Paris 066427
Point Amour Lighthouse, Saint John's 006367
Point Cardinal, Paris 100779, 133665
Le Point d'Accroche, Paris 124779
Point-de-Vue, Saint-Paul-de-Vence 101218
Point du Jour, Douarnenez 099240
Point Ellice House, Victoria 006748
Point in Time, Vancouver 097515
Point Light, Surry Hills 095257
Point Loma Books, San Diego 142911
Point of Art, Hanau 103255
Point of Art Gallery, Calgary 096841
Point of Art Society, Calgary 052767
Point of Honor, Lynchburg 045529
Point Pelee Natural History Museum, Leamington 005760
Point Pleasant Battle Monument State Park, Point Pleasant 047112
Point Presse, Brignoles 138057
Pointe-à-Callière - Musée d'Archéologie et d'Histoire de Montréal, Montréal . 005947
Pointe Coupee Museum, New Roads 046273
Pointe-Noire - Parc Marin du Saguenay, Baie-Sainte-Catherine 005056
Poirier, Nicole, La Saulsotte 063444
Poirier, Sylviane, Montréal 097064
Poisa, Giuseppe, Brescia 127229
Poisat, Daniel, Paris 124780
Poissant Gallery, Houston 116391
Poisson, Anne-Marie, Crépon 062559
Poisson, Jean-François, Saint-Laurent-des-Bois 067577
Poisson, M.H., Fontenay-sour-Bois . 124242
Le Poisson à Plumes, Theoule-sur-Mer 101309
Poitou Tout'Occas, Châtillon-sur-Thouet 062238
Pojani Museum, Pojani 000030
Pokolbin Gallery, Pokolbin 095076
Pokrajac, Daniel, Chicago 088148
Pokrajinski Muzej, Kočevje 034468
Pokrajinski Muzej, Maribor 034500
Pokrajinski Muzej, Murska Sobota . 034507
Pokrajinski Muzej, Strumica 027924
Pokrajinski Muzej Celje, Celje 034463
Pokrajinski Muzej Koper, Koper . . . 034470
Pokrajinski Muzej Ptuj, Ptuj 034514
Pokrajinski Zavod za Zaštitu Prirode, Petrovaradin 050679
Pokrovskij Sobor-chram Vasilija Blažennogo, Gosudarstvennyj istoričeskij muzej, Moskva 033518
Pokstaavi, Helsinki 137954
Pokstaavi, Helsinki 137955
Pol, H.J., Borne 128597
Pol, Simon, Reims 067080
Pol-Art, Warszawa 109183
Polabské Muzeum, Poděbrady 008580
Polack, Bérengère, Paris 124781
Polajnarjeva Galerija, Bohinjska Bistrica 109932
Polak, Paris 138524
Polak, J., Amsterdam 077932
Polak, R., Den Haag 107945
Polanco, San Francisco 119767
Polar, Pascal, Bruxelles 096243
Polar Arts of Asia, Singapore 080546
Polaris, Paris 100780
Polarmuseet, Andenes 030731
Polarmuseet i Tromsø, Tromsø 031277
Polarolo & Sons, E., New York 132513
Polcraft, Chelmsford 112843
Poldark Mine and Heritage Complex, Helston 039724
Polder, J.A., Borne 107873, 128598
Poldermuseum, Antwerpen 003184
Poldermuseum, Puttershoek 030048
Poldermuseum de Hooge Boezem Achter Haastrecht, Haastrecht 029664
Poldermuseum Den Huijgen Dijck, Heerhugowaard 029694
Poldermuseum Het Grootslag - Nationaal Saet en Cruytmuseum, Andijk . . . 029248
Poldowrian Museum of Prehistory, Coverack 039156
Polemiko Mouseio, Athinai 021212
Polenmuseum Rapperswil, Rapperswil, Sankt Gallen 037435
Polenz, Dr. H., Senden, Westfalen . . 126796
Polenz-Museum, Cunewalde 016612
Poleschi Arte, Milano 106287
Polesden Lacey, Dorking 039264
Polesden Lacey, Great Bookham . . 039630
Poleski Ośrodek Sztuki, Łódź 109017
Poletti, Carlos, Milano 127656
Poley, Dennis, Alreswas 083280
Polgár, Budapest . 074709, 105541, 121643
Poli, Eugenio, Firenze 127394
Poli, Paolo, Firenze 127395
Poli Museo della Grappa, Bassano del Grappa 023356
Poliarts 2000, Milano 075822
Polibinskij Memoralnyj Muzej-usadba S.V. Kovalevskoj, Polibino 033672
Police and Pioneer Museum, Shoal Lake 006466
The Police Museum, Belfast 038667
Police Museum, Hong Kong 007131
Police Museum, Imphal 022172
Police Station and Courthouse, Auburn 000755
Police Station Museum, Mount Barker 001289
Polidori, Alberto, Perugia 127882
Poliedro, Roma 135943
Polifilo, Milano 134627
Il Polifilo, Milano 140060
Polifroni, Felice, Torino 128345
Polígrafa, Barcelona 134924
Polimento e Restauraçoes São Domingos, São Paulo 123720
Polish American Museum, Port Washington 047145
Polish Art Gallery, New York 118299
Polish Association of Members of the Museum Professions, Kraków . . . 053981
Polish Cultural Institution Gallery, London 040258
Polish Museum of America, Chicago 042874
Polisher, Tulsa 133001
Polishistoriska Museet, Stockholm . 036655
Polistekniska Museet, Solna 036603
Politeama Gallery, Roma 106609
Politechničskij Muzej, Moskva 033519
Politi, Giancarlo, Milano . . 134628, 140061
Political Life Museum, Amman 027377
Political Memorbilia Marketplace, Las Vegas 089599
Politie-Petten Museum, Slochteren . 030163
Politiemuseum, Wommelgem 003862
Politiemuseum Oudaan, Antwerpen 003185
Politikens Galleri, København 098581
Politimuseet i Oslo, Oslo 031102
Polizeihistorische Sammlung Berlin, Berlin 016159
Polizeimuseum, Aarau 036811
Polk County Heritage Gallery, Des Moines 043426
Polk County Historical Museum, Cedartown 042681
Polk County Historical Museum, Crookston 043224
Polk County Historical Museum, Osceola 046733
Polk County Historical Society, Des Moines 043427
Polk County Memorial Museum, Livingston 045355
Polk County Museum, Balsam Lake 041961
Polk Museum of Art, Lakeland 045124
Polk Place Antiques, Nashville 090476
Polkadot Gallery, Exeter 113040
Poll, Eva, Berlin 102013
Pollak, Tel Aviv 139980
Pollak, Patrick, South Brent 142075
Pollandt, Thomas, Berlin 069727
Pollard, Indianapolis 089332
Pollentier-Marechal, G. & M., Brugge 137418
Poller, Frankfurt am Main . 070777, 102810, 125659, 133951
Poller, Leah, New York 118300
Pollermann, Christel, Balingen 069438, 101726
Pollet & Desrumeaux, Lille 063865
Pollet Thiollier, Guy, La Clusaz 063338
Pollismolen, Bos-en Pijpenmuseum, Bree 003260
Pollmächer, Dr. Stefan, Bad Zwesten 101717
Pollmann, Herten 103364
Pollmer, Alexander, München 072820
Pollock, Los Angeles 089882
Pollock, Charles, West Hollywood . . 093497
Pollock's Toy Museum, London . . . 040259
Pollok House, Glasgow 039569
Polly, Venlo 108267
Polly Woodside Melbourne Maritime Museum, Southbank 001480
Polman, Emmerich 070563
Polnecq, Catherine, Paris 124782
Polnische Buchhandlung - Ksiegarnia Polska, Wien 137355
Polnischer Kultursalon e.V, Wiesbaden 105276
Polo-Lodge Antiques, Tulsa 093327
Polokwane Art Museum, Polokwane 034704
Polos, Brunswick Heads 055575
Polplakat, Warszawa 109184
Polska Federacja Fotograficznych i Audiowizualnych Stowarzyszeń Twórczych, Wrocław 053982
Polska Izba Artystów Konserwatorów Dzieł Sztuki, Warszawa 053983
Polskie Foto, Wrocław 136034
Polskie Towarzystwo Archeologiczne i Numizmatyczne Zarzad Główny, Warszawa 053984
Polson Park and Museum, Hoquiam 044621
Polstjernan, Stockholm 082007
Poltavs'kyj Chudožnij Muzej, Poltava 038377
Poltavs'kyj Krajeznavčyj Muzej, Poltava 038378
Poltavs'kyj Literaturno-memorial'nyj Muzej I.P. Kotljarevskogo, Poltava 038379
Poltavs'kyj Literaturno-memorial'nyj Muzej Panasa Myrnogo, Poltava 038380
Poltavs'kyj Literaturno-memorial'nyj Muzej V.G. Korolenka, Poltava 038381
Poltavs'kyj Muzej Aviacii ta Kosmonavtiki, Poltava 038382
Poltera, Jan-Reto, Lugano 111670
Põltsamaa Muuseum, Põltsamaa . . 009387
Poluschkin, S., Much 104125
Põlva Talurahvamuuseum, Karilatsi 009369
Polvere di Stelle, Padova 106408
Polvo Art Studio, Chicago 042875
Polvo Magazine, Chicago 136605
Poly, M.D., Floirac 099265
Poly, P., Assebroek 123564
Poly, P., Brugge 123568
Polyedre, Antwerpen 057728
Polyester, México 135991
Polygnotos Vagis Museum, Thassos 021484
Polygraphicum, Eberbach, Baden . .070492, 102590, 125562, 139029
Polylustre, Fortaleza 058477
Polymath Press, New York 135455
Polynesian Cultural Center, Laie . . . 045097
Polyphon, Heemstede 140453
Polytechnique, Bruxelles 137461
Polyteekkarimuseo, Espoo 009478
Polzin, Elisabeth, Wickede 127003
Polzin, Saskia Gesa, Paderborn . . . 126611
Pom Pom, Los Angeles 089883
Pom Pom, Los Angeles 089884
Poma, Paolo, Morcote 111749
Pomander, New York 142688
Pomar, María, Palma de Mallorca . . 110696
O Pomar dos Artistas, Lisboa 129169
Pomares Esparza, J., Pamplona . . . 110722
Pomarkun Kotiseutumuseo, Pomarkku 009984
Pomázer Heimatstube, Sinsheim . . 020223
Pomegranate Europe, Warwick 135311
Pomes Penyeach, Newcastle-under-Lyme 141952
Pomez, Olivier, Paris 066428
Pomfret Gallery, Pontefract 114268
Pomier, Lyon 064174
Pomiès, Yveline, Toulouse 124992
Pomme d'Ambre, Nancy 064877
Pomme de Pin, Bergerac 061363
La Pomme d'Or, Genève 082460
Pommerat, Gérard, Toulouse 068535
Pommersches Bettenmuseum, Flugplatzmuseum Peenemünde, Peenemünde 019578
Pommersches Landesmuseum, Greifswald 017524
Pommier, Gérard, Ferney-Voltaire . .062855, 099260
Pommois, Isabelle, Paris 066429
Pomona College Museum of Art, Claremont 042938
Pomone, Lutry 111675
Pomorski i Povijesni Muzej Hrvatskog Primorja, Rijeka 007782
Pomorski Muzej, Zadar 007826
Pomorski Muzej, Dubrovački Muzeji, Dubrovnik 007719
Pomorski Muzej Crne Gore, Kotor . . 034201
Pomorski Muzej Sergej Mašera, Piran 034511
Pomorskie Muzeum Wojskowe, Bydgoszcz 031857
Pomp, Thomas, Bottrop 133833
Pompallier House, Russell 030592
Pompejanum, Aschaffenburg 015580
Pompey Museum of Slavery and Emancipation, Nassau 003092
Pompili, Adele, Bologna 127175
Pompous Peasant, Tampa 093148
Pomsel, M., Brand-Erbisdorf 069975
Pomskizillious Museum of Toys, Xaghra 028047
Ponca City Art Association, Ponca City 054989
Ponce, Raquel, Madrid 110594
Ponce DeLeon Inlet Lighthouse, Ponce Inlet 047119
Ponce-Gallone, Marlène, Bogis-Bossey 082268
Ponceblanc, Jouannin, Saint-Rambert-en-Bugey 067981
Poncelet, David, Cambrai 061921
Poncet, Thierry, Chazelles-sur-Lyon 062263
Pond, Lily, Geelong 055870
Pond Cottage Antiques, Stillington . 086706
Pond Galleries, London 113836
Ponder, Richard, Wellington 108641
Pondicherry Museum, Pondicherry . 022299
Pongauer Heimatmuseum im Schloß Goldegg, Goldegg 001919
Pongratz, Alois, Bodenmais 069901
Pongratz, Alois, Kötzting 072044
Pongratz, Alois, Zwiesel 074582
Poniatowski, Marie-Sofia, Paris . . . 124783
Poniger Clocks and Watches, Armadale, Victoria 055392
Ponitrianske Múzeum, Nitra 034399
Pons, Chantal & Patrick, Lyon 064175, 124373
Ponse, Charenton-le-Pont 062150
Ponsford, A.J. & R.L., Barnwood . . .083402, 130342
Ponshu-kan-Echigo Sake Museum, Yuzawa 027354
Pont, Michel, Biarritz 061475
Pont, Philippe, Saint-Loubès 067589
De Pont, Stichting voor Hedendaagse Kunst, Tilburg 030210
Pont-Dépôt Ventes, Pont-Saint-Esprit 066932
Le Pont des Arts, Avignon 098901
Le Pont du Diable, Céret 062056

Pont & Plas, Gent 096296
Le Pont Traversé, Paris 138525
Pontaillac, Bordeaux 099009
Ponte, Beograd 080403
Il Ponte, Roma 106610
Il Ponte Casa d'Aste, Milano 075823, 106288, 121711
Il Ponte Contemporanea, Roma . . .106611, 134682
A Ponte - Galeria de Arte, São Paulo 096684
Pontecorboli, Firenze 134588
Ponteduro, Carlo, Bologna 075102
Pontefract Castle Museum, Pontefract 040729
Pontefract Museum, Pontefract . . . 040730
Ponterio & Assoc., San Diego 092674
Pontgirard, Monceaux 099729
Ponti, Alessio, Roma 106612
Ponti, Enea, Losone 082586, 130090
Ponticq, Michèle, Duras 062754
Ponticq, Michèle, Monpazier 064607
Pontifical Biblical Institute Museum, Jerusalem 022973
Pontiki Thalia, Lefkosia 098306
Ponting, Ben, Brighton 083712
Pontis'Antic, Valbonne 068680
Ponto de Antiguidades, Porto Alegre 123697
Pontremoli, Milano 075824
Pontremoli, Milano 075825
Pontual, Mauricio, Rio de Janeiro . . 096637
Pontypool and Blaenavon Railway, Blaenavon 038760
Pontypool Museums, Pontypool . . . 040733
Pontypridd Museum, Pontypridd . . . 040735
Pony Express Museum, Saint Joseph 047649
Ponziani, Firenze 127396
Pooker, Nils, Kiel 126043
Pool Dickynson, Madrid 129656
Pool Dickynson, Madrid 129657
Pool Dickynson, Madrid 129658
Poole, Douglas, Toronto 059265
Poor Man's Gallery, Virginia Beach . 120231
Poor Richard's Books, Felixstowe . . 141612
Poorhosaini, Seeheim-Jugenheim .073786, 121598
Poorter, Johanna de, Antwerpen . . . 096088
Poortere, J.-L. de, Bruxelles 058059
Pop, Zeno, Frankfurt am Main 070778
Pop Antik, Helsinki 060570
Pop-Art, Čačak 109730
Pop Art, Madrid 110595
Pop Art UK, Sheffield 114421
Pop Culture Classics, Phoenix 091765
Pop Indiana, Indianapolis 116490
Pope, Charlotte 115307
Pope, Philippe, Nice 065130
Pope, Philippe, Nice 065131
Pope County Historical Museum, Glenwood 044219
Popera, Chicago 115526
Pope's Tavern Museum, Florence . . 043866
Popescu, Victor, Düsseldorf 070425
Pophal, Veit, Dresden 125505
Poplar Antiques, Memphis 090101
Poplar Grove Historic Plantation, Wilmington 049215
Popmount, Richmond 119117
Popoff & Cie., Paris 100781
Popolini, Massimo, Roma 128166
Popp, Elisa, Heidelberg 134051
Popp, Evamaria, Blaustein 125337
Popp, Ludwig, München 104290
Popp, Margit & Matthias, Zell, Oberfranken 074560
Poppa, Austin 115002
Poppe, H. D., Nordstemmen 073088
Poppen, A., Esens 070615
Poppen en Poppenhuis Museum 't Duvelke, Breda 029353
Poppen- en Speelgoedmuseum, Tilburg 030211
Poppenhuis Carmen, Utrecht 030238
Poppenhuismuseum, Heesch 029700
Poppenmuseum, Ter Apel 029251
Poppenmuseum, Maastricht 029899
Poppenmuseum Christus Koning, Wetteren 003854
Poppenspe(e)lmuseum, Vorchten . . 030292
Poppin, Merry, Pretoria 080743
Poppo, Okutama 106949
Popppenhuismuseum Alida's Kleine Wereldje, Veendam 030254
Poptaslot Heringa-State, Marssum . 029910
Popular Art Centre, Al-Bireh 031406
Popular Arts Museum, San Juan . . . 032749
Popular Choice Antiques, Birmingham 130395
Popular Culture, Denver 088724
Popular Literature and Art Publishing House, Beijing 133339
Popular Traditions Museum Qasrelazem, Damascus 037829
Populart, Hong Kong 097821
Populart, Sevilla 081611
Populart, Weiden, Oberpfalz 105172
Porada, U., Schwalmstadt 104859
Poradowska-Werszler, Ewa, Wrocław 109231
Porcelain Repairs, Stockport 131543
Porcelain Room, New York 091165
Porcelánmúzeum, Hollóháza 021740
Porceleynboom, de, Breda 078113
Porcella, Antonio, Roma 106613
Porcelli, Micaela, Berlin 069728
Porch, Oakland 091434
Porch Cellar, Philadelphia 091680
Porch House Antiques, Tetbury 086864
Porcha, Detroit 088773
Porcher, Marseille 064386
Porcher, Dominique, Vern-sur-Seiche 068775
Porchester Antiques, Bristol 083748
Porchet, Carmen, Lausanne 082564
Porchet, Pierre, Lausanne 082565
The Porcine Gallery, Whangarei . . . 108665
Porcini, Vincenzo, Napoli 076030
Porcu, Lucia, Cagliari 075224
Porcupine Plain and District Museum, Porcupine Plain 006167
Porcupines, Bideford 141413
Pordes, Henry, London 141870
Porfirul Antichitati, Cluj-Napoca . . . 080179
Porfyrmuseet, Älvdalen 036168
Porin Taide ja Kehys, Pori 060621
Porin Taidemuseo, Pori 009986
Porirua Hospital Museum, Porirua . 030580
Porirua Museum of Arts and Cultures, Porirua 030579
Porky's Bits & Pieces, Ohingaiti . . . 079204
Porlammin Kotiseutumuseo, Porlammi 009990
Porro, Dijon 062672
Porro, Amedeo, Milano 106289
Porro, Francis, Dijon 062673, 124223
Porrua Hnos. y Cia., México 140257
Porrua, Manuel, México 140258
Porsanger Museum, Lakselv 030968
Porsch, Manfred, Gelnhausen 070953
Porsche Automuseum Helmut Pfeifhofer, Gmünd, Kärnten 001906
Porsche Museum, Stuttgart 020362
Porsche Traktorenmuseum, Altreiteregg 001685
Porselein Dierenpark, Wildervank . . 030334
De Porselijne Lampetkan, Delft . . . 078148
Porsgrunn Bymuseum, Porsgrunn . . 031123
Porslinsdoktorn Dimitar, Malmö . . . 129852
Porslinslagarna i Arvika, Arvika . . . 129835
Porst, Angelika, Gröbenzell 125756
Port Albert Maritime Museum, Port Albert 001391
Port Angeles Fine Arts Center, Port Angeles 047125
Port Antiques, Napier 079168
Port Arthur Historic Site, Port Arthur 001392
Port-au-Choix Site, Port-au-Choix . 006171
Port-aux-Basques Railway Heritage Centre, Port-aux-Basques 006174
Port Carling Pioneer Museum, Port Carling 006176
Port Chalmers Museum, Port Chalmers 030581
Port Clements Museum, Port Clements 006177
Port Colborne Historical and Marine Museum, Port Colborne 006178
Port Columbus National Civil War Naval Center, Columbus 043095
Port Community Art Centre, Port Adelaide 001388
Port Discovery - Children's Museum in Baltimore, Baltimore 042002
Port Dock Station Railway Museum, Port Adelaide 001387
Port Douglas Gallery of Fine Art, Port Douglas 095088
Port Douglas Oceanic Art Studio, Port Douglas 095089
Port Dover Harbour Museum, Port Dover 006180
Port Elizabeth Museum, Port Elizabeth 034706
Port Fairy Historic Lifeboat Station, Port Fairy 001395
Port Fairy History Centre, Port Fairy 001396
Port Gamble Historic Museum, Port Gamble 047129
Port Hardy Museum, Port Hardy . . . 006182
Port Hastings Museum, Port Hastings 006183
Port Huron Museum, Port Huron . . . 047133
Port Jackson Press, Fitzroy 094537
Port-la-Joye-Fort Amherst, Charlottetown 005249
Port MacDonnell and District Maritime Museum, Port MacDonnell 001399
Port Macquarie Antique Centre, Port Macquarie 056477
Port Macquarie Historic Museum, Port Macquarie 001400
Port Moody Art Association, Port Moody 052768
Port Moody Station Museum, Port Moody 006187
Le Port-Musée, Douarnenez 011642
Le Port-Musée, Douarnenez 011643
Port Natal Maritime Museum, Durban 034604
Port of Morgan Historic Museum, Morgan 001284
Port Phillip City Collection, Saint Kilda, Victoria 001450
Port Pirie National Trust Museum, Port Pirie 001401
Port Pirie Regional Art Gallery, Port Pirie 001402
Port Royal National Historic Site, Parks Canada, Annapolis Royal 005018
Port Royal Store, Los Angeles 089885
Port-Said Museum, Port Said 009343
Port Stephens Shell Museum, Corlette 000948
Port Sunlight Heritage Centre, Port Sunlight 040748
Port Townsend Marine Science Center, Port Townsend 047142
Port Union Museum, Port Union . . . 006190
Port Victor Gallery, Victor Harbor . . 001583
Port Victoria National Trust Museum, Port Victoria 001404
Porta Fratelli, Milano 127657
Porta, Luce, Knokke-Heist 096353
La Porta Antica, Milano 075826
Porta Borsari, Firenze 075387
Porta Cristina, Cagliari 075225
La Porta Michele, Catania 075258
Porta Romana, Firenze 075388
Porta-Verlag, München . . 104291, 134269
Portabella Córdoba, Barcelona 080911
Portage and District Arts Council, Portage-la-Prairie 006193, 052769
Portage County Historical Society Museum, Ravenna 047338
Portage County Museum, Stevens Point 048355
Portakal, Raffi, İstanbul . . 083151, 122381
Portal, Gdańsk . . . 079586, 108895, 129012
Portal, Catherine & Frédéric, Saint-Jean-de-Luz 101164
Portal Artes Galeria, Brasília 096501
Le Portal Artour, Québec 097159
Portal Galeria de Arte, São Paulo . . 096685
Portal Gallery, London . . . 085615, 113837
Portalibros, Ajijic 140254
Portals, Chicago 088149, 115527
Portanje's Vespa Scooter en Nostalgie Collectie, Bunnik 029366
La Portantina, Milano 075827
Portas, Danielle, Nîmes 065185
Portas do Sol, Lisboa 079993
Portchester Castle, Portchester . . . 040751
Portculli, Craven Arms 084104
Porte, Jacques, Paris 066430
La Porte Antique, Cairo 060464
La Porte County Historical Society Museum, La Porte 045075
Porte d'Amont, Meung-sur-Loire . . 064541
Porte de Hal, Musées Royaux d'Art et d'Histoire, Bruxelles 003357
Porte de la Monnaie, Bordeaux 061646
Porte des Gaultiers, Mirmande 099726
Porte Heureuse, Roussillon (Vaucluse) 101126
Porte Jacques, Paris 066431
Porte Rouge, Chicago 088150
Portéka-Antique, Budapest 074710
Portelli, Simon, Nadur 077519
Porteous, David, Newton Abbot . . . 135287
Porter, Coffs Harbour 055703
Porter & Son, A.W., Hartley Wintney 084603, 130770
Porter, David, Claremont 080691
Porter, James, Sandwich 086518
Porter, Les, Newcastle 094942
Porter, Liz, Ruthin 131432
Porter, R.E., Bournemouth 083603
Porter Almoneda, Madrid 081365
The Porter Bookshop, Sheffield . . . 142062
Porter County Old Jail Museum, Valparaiso 048742
Porter Davis, Seattle 093049
Porter-Phelps-Huntington Foundation, Hadley 044382
Porter Thermometer Museum, Onset 046693
La Porteria de Jorge Juan, Madrid . 110596
Porterville Historical Museum, Porterville 047156
Les Portes du Sud, Lyon 064176
Portfolio, Auckland 108357
Portfolio, London 113838, 131149
Portfolio, Saarlouis 139708
Portfolio Fine Art and Antiques, Braemar 055534
Portfolio Gallery, Edinburgh 039414
Portfolio Gallery, Saint Louis 119239
Portfolio Gallery, Saint Louis 119240
Portfolio Gallery, Vancouver 097516
Porthcawl and District Art Society, Porthcawl 054468
Porthcawl Museum, Porthcawl 040752
Porthcurno Telegraph Museum, Porthcurno 040753
Porthilly Crafts, Wadebridge 114637
Porthmadog Maritime Museum, Porthmadog 040754
Porthminster Gallery, Saint Ives, Cornwall 114369
Porthole Gallery, Falmouth 113053
Portholes Into the Past, Medina . . . 045748
Portia Gallery, Chicago 115528
Il Portico, Cagliari 106014
Portico, New York 142689
Portico Fine Art, New York 118301
Portico Gallery, Helensburgh 039717
Portico Gallery, Rotorua 108554
Portico Library and Gallery, Manchester 040415
Portier, Serret, Paris 066432
Portier, Thierry, Paris 066433

Portikus, Frankfurt am Main 017191
Portique, Bournemouth . . 083604, 130417
Portis, Will, Fresno 116182
Portland Antique Company, Portland 091994
Portland Antiques and Curios, West Bridgford 087081
Portland Art Museum, Portland 047178
Portland Art Museum Newsletter, Portland 136606
Portland Basin Museum, Ashton-under-Lyne 038543
Portland Castle, Portland 040756
Portland CEMA Arts Centre, Portland 001406
Portland Children's Museum Second Generation, Portland 047179
Portland Gallery, London . 085616, 113839
Portland House Antiques, Market Deeping 085933
Portland Maritime Discovery Centre, Portland 001407
Portland Museum, Louisville 045496
Portland Museum, Portland 040757
Portland Museum of Art, Portland . . 047162
Portland State University Galleries, Portland 047180
Portlandia Productions, Portland . . . 119036
Portmann, Alfred, Ebikon 082347
Portmoneum - Muzeum Josefa Váchala, Litomyšl 008484
Porto Bello, Buenos Aires 055237
Porto Bello, Den Haag 078235
Porto Bello, Den Haag 078236
Porto Belo, Porto 080104
Porto Coroa, Porto 080105
Porto Franco, Livorno 075536
Porto Novo, Nijmegen 108158
Porto Restauro, Porto 129197
Porto Velho Arte e Decoracao, Rio de Janeiro 058636
Portobello, Catania 075259
Portobello, Lemesos 059964
Portobello, Madrid 081366
Portobello, Paris 066434
Portobello, Paris 066435
Portobello, Philadelphia 091681
Portobello Antique, London 085617
Portobello Antique Dealers Association, London 054469
Portobello Antique Store, London . . 085618
Portobello Antiques, Auckland 078973
Portobello Antiques, Christchurch . . 079047
Portobello Antiques, Vancouver . . . 059403
Portobello Bookshop, London 141871
Portobello Gallery, Pittsburgh 118946
Portobello Gallery, Saint James . . . 003122
Portobello Road, Montevideo 087336
Portobello Road and Camel Antiques, Kansas City 089515
Portobello Road Antiques, Hamilton 058862
Portobello Row Antique & Collector's Centre, Boston 083581
Los Portones, Fuenlabrada 081108
Portrait Brokers of America, Birmingham 115125
Portrait Galery, Dordrecht 107984
Portrait Gallery, Blakesley 112665
Portrait Source, Fort Worth 116160
Portraits, Höhr-Grenzhausen 135817
Portraits, New York 118302
Portraits and Paintings, New York . . 118303
Portraiture, Atlanta 114913
Portret na Życzenie, Warszawa 109185
Portretgalerie, Den Haag 107946
Portrush Antiques, Nelson 079178
Portsmouth Athenaeum, Portsmouth 047189
Portsmouth Museum, Portsmouth . . 047195
Portsmouth Museum of Military History, Portsmouth 047201
Portsmouth Naval Shipyard Museum, Portsmouth Museums, Portsmouth 047202
Portsteffen, Hans, Köln 126110
The Portstewart Galleries, Portstewart 114284
The Portstewart Galleries, Portstewart 114285
Portuondo, Ramon, Madrid 081367
Portuondo Wakonigg, Jorge, Bilbao 080986
Portuondo Wakonigg, Ramón, Madrid 081368
Portus Antik, København 060369
Porvoon Museo, Porvoo 009996
Porzellan Klinik Leipzig, Leipzig . . . 126195
Porzellan-Werkstatt, Köln 126111
Porzellanklinik Karlsruhe, Karlsruhe 126006
Porzellanmuseum, Rödental 019863
Porzellanmuseum Reichmannsdorf, Reichmannsdorf 019778
Porzellansammlung, Staatliche Kunstsammlungen Dresden, Dresden 016809
Porzellanwerkstatt, Freiburg im Breisgau 125673
Pos-Art, Montréal 097065
Posada Alvarez, María Teresa, Medellín 098283
Posada Art Books, Bruxelles 137462
Posadovský, Bedřich, Praha 123994
Posalski, Nancy 064878
Posarnig, Erwin, Graz 133080
Posavski Muzej Brežice, Brežice . . 034461
Posch, Franz, Birkfeld 056947
Posch, Renate, Ternitz 137270
Poscharnig, Brigitta, Langenlois . . . 137210
Posion Kotiseutumuseo, Posio 010000
Posipal, Veit, Dresden 125506
Positive, Dijon 062674
Positive Images Art, Austin 115003
POSK Gallery, London 040260
Pospieszczyk, Jürgen, Regensburg . 073469
Pospíšil, Josef, Kutná Hora 123961
Pospísilova, Dr. Marie, Praha 098484, 123995
Poß, Ingo, Hetzerath 071504
Poßegger, Günter Walter, Sankt Gallen, Steiermark 057288
Posselt, M. I., Bonn 102192
Posset, 's-Hertogenbosch 108078
Possibilities, Jacksonville 089448
Possibilities, New Orleans 090603
Possum Art Gallery, Beenleigh 094229
Possum Brush Gallery, Taree 095320
Post, Enschede 078377
Post, Los Angeles 116867
Post, J.G., Breda 128607
Post, L.A., Benningbroek 128582
Post, Wilfried, Freiburg im Breisgau 102871
Post 10 Antiques, Oklahoma City . . 091527
Post Art, Amsterdam 077933
Post Card Shop, Saint Louis 142861
Post Gallery, Houston 116392
Post Horn Books, Settle 142054
Post House Antiques, Bletchingley . 083563
Post Rock Museum, Rush Co Historical Society, La Crosse 045055
Post & Salamon, Brunssum 107883, 134802
Post-Scriptum, Belfaux 111236
Post & Tele Museum, København . . 008985
Postal and Philatelic Museum, Tel Aviv 023089
Postal Museum, Amman 027378
Postal Museum, Cairo 009320
Postal Museum, Seoul 027591
Postal Museum, Stockholm 036656
Postal Museum, Taipei 007375
Postal Museum and Philatelic Library, Manila 031736
Postal Museum Botswana, Gaborone 003951
Postamúzeum, Balatonszemes 021623
Postamúzeum, Budapest 021690
Postamúzeum, Hollókö 021742
Postamúzeum, Nagyvázsony 021801
Postcard Art-Postcard Fiction, Brooklyn 136607
Postcard Museum, Holmfirth 039762
La Poste d'Antan, Paris 066436
La Poste d'Autrefois, Paris 138526
Poste de Traite Chauvin, Tadoussac 006553
Poste du Village, Rennes (Ille-et-Vilaine) 138582
Poster Art, Buffalo 115262
Poster Art, San Diego 119536
Poster Art Gallery, Genève 111493
Poster Art Place, San Antonio 119440
Poster Arts, Los Angeles 116868
Poster Dizajn, Moskva 109578
Poster-Galerie, Hamburg 103207
Poster-Galerie, Nürnberg 104486
Poster Galerie, Wettingen 111988
Poster- Galerie im Dez, Innsbruck . 095593
Poster Galerie Wien, Wien 095923
Poster Gallery, Albuquerque 114819
Poster Gallery, Kansas City 116588
Poster Planet, Sacramento 119158
Poster Plus, Chicago 115529
Poster Restoration Studio, Los Angeles 132276
The Poster Shack, Norfolk 118616
Poster Shoppe Gallery, Columbus . . 115795
Poster Source, San Francisco 119768
Poster Store, San Diego 119537
Poster World, Phoenix 118888
Postergalerie, Dortmund 102412
Postergalerie Flensburg, Flensburg 102732
Posteritati, New York 118304
Posterity Graphics, Toronto 097351
Posterman, Louisville 116961
Posteroptics, Windsor, Ontario 097565
Posterplanet, Portland 119037
Posters, Abu Dhabi 112440
Posters, San Antonio 119441
Posters and Frames, San Diego . . . 119538
Posters Etc, Toronto 097352
Posters Please, New York 091166
Posters Posters, Atlanta 114914
Posterworld, Saint Louis 119241
Posthoorn, Rotterdam 078740
Postimuseo, Helsinki 009561
Postma, G., Groningen 121790
Postmark Gallery, Kansas City 116589
Postmasters Gallery, New York 118305
Póstminjasafn Íslands, Hafnarfjörður 021947
Postmuseet, Oslo 031103
Postmuseum des Fürstentums Liechtenstein, Vaduz 027844
Postmuseum Mettingen, Mettingen 018924
Postmuseum Rheinhausen, Oberhausen-Rheinhausen 019389
Il Posto delle Briciole, Milano 075828
Postojannaja Požarno-techničeskaja Vystavka, Sankt-Peterburg 033825
Postons, Neil, Leominster 130887
Poštovní Muzeum, Praha 008645
Poštovní Muzeum, Poštovní Muzeum Praha, Vyšší Brod 008771
Postrotemuseet, Storby 010099
Postville Courthouse Museum, Lincoln 045294
Le Potager, Jacksonville 089449
Potala Art Gallery, Kathmandu 107596
Potamianos, Johann, München . . . 072821
Potapov, Andrej, Augsburg 069239
Potard, Simone, Dierre 062627
Potashnik, David, Coulsdon 084087, 130609
Potboard Antiques, Tenby 086842
Potbury & Sons, Sidmouth 122700
Potchefstroom Museum, Potchefstroom 034708
Le Poteau Rose, Lambersart 099418
Potemska, Maria, Łódź 129053
Potennec, Olivier, Verdun (Meuse) . 068770
Pothmann, Willi, Siegen 073812
't Pothuis, Haarlem 078477
't Pothuis, Zutphen 078882, 128888
Potiron, Marc, Saint-Sébastien-sur-Loire 068006
Potland Museum, Basildon 038609
Potluck, Nashville 090477
Potluck Art Show, San Francisco . . 094025
Potoroo, South Melbourne 095206
Potpourri, Lörrach 072294
Potpourri, Pittsburgh 118947
Potratz, Friedberg, Hessen 133963
Potrony, Miami 117126
Potsch, Otto, Wolkersdorf im Weinviertel 095978
Potsdam-Museum, Natur-Geschichte-Kunst, Potsdam 019657
Potsdam Public Museum, Potsdam . 047206
Potsdamer Kunstsalon, Potsdam . .073364, 121579
Potstada, Heike, Kiel 071842
Pottekarie, Dranouter 003411
Pottenbakkerij De Brinksteen, Dwingeloo 029516
Pottenbakkerij Het Ovenhuis, Ruinerwold 030116
Pottenbakkerij Museum, Kattendijke 029805
Potter, Houston 089180
Potter, Lewes 084985, 130892
Potter, Merredin 123265
Potter, Vancouver 059404
Potter, Barry, Stockton-on-Tees . . . 122708
Potter, Jonathan, London . 131150, 141872
Potter, Nick, London 113840
Potter & Son, W.G., Axminster 083356, 130318
The Potter Clarke Gallery, Saint Ives, Cornwall 114370
Potter County Historical Society Museum, Coudersport 043189
Potteries Antique Centre, Stoke-on-Trent 086733
The Potteries Museum and Art Gallery, Stoke-on-Trent 041121
Potteries Specialist Auctions, Stoke-on-Trent 122710
Potteries Specialist Auctions, Whitchurch, Shropshire 122746
Potters, Gladstone 094585
Potters, Chelsea, Auckland 108358
Potter's Antiques and Coins, Bristol 083749
Potters Bar Museum, Potters Bar . . 040774
Potters Cottage Gallery, Warrandyte 095371
Potter's Guild of San Diego, San Diego 054990
Potter's Museum of Curiosity and Smugglers's Museum, Bolventor . 038782
Potters Shop, Wellington 108642
Potterton, New York 142690
Potterton, Thirsk 142114
Pottery Art Cooperative, Wuxi 098042
The Pottery Buying Centre, Stocke-on-Trent 086717
Pottery Northwest Seattle Center, 305 Harrison St, Seattle 119982
Pottery Studio, Seattle 119983
Pottery Workshop, Hong Kong 097822
Pottier, Jean-Roger, Vitteaux 069018
The Potting Shed, Holkham 084698
Potton, Craig, Nelson 134846
Potts, Ludovic, Ely 130684
Potts Inn Museum, Pottsville 047209
Pottsgrove Manor, Pottstown 047208
Potuguesa, Tostedt 105051
Pou, Aura & S., Barcelona 129380
Poubeau, Anne, Sancerre 068116
Pouce Coupe Museum, Pouce Coupe 006194
Pouch, M., Český Krumlov 137775
Pouch Cove Museum, Pouch Cove . 006195
Pouffier, Elisabeth, Dijon 062675
Pouffier, Elisabeth, Dijon 062676
Pouillier, Michel, Saint-Maixme-Hauterive 067603
Pouillon, Bernard, Saarbrücken . . . 126758
Pouillon, Jacques, Versailles 068817
Poulain, Emile, Baud 061223
Poulain, Pierre, Paris 066437
Poulain & Le Fur, Paris 121186
Le Poulbot, Porto-Vecchio 066961
Poulet, Hervé, Paris 121187
Poulet, Isabelle, Paris 066438

Poulideto, Saint-Tropez 068021
Pouliquen, Jean-Christophe, Paris . 066439
Poulmarch, Armelle, Brest 099030
Poulter & Son, H.W., London 085619, 131151
Pound Gallery 1216 10th Av, Seattle 119984
Pound Ridge Museum, Pound Ridge 047216
Pound Sreat Gallery, Carshalton . . . 112821
Pounder, Los Angeles 116869
Pounder, Nicholas, Double Bay 136882
Pounders & Lewis, Birmingham . . . 131838
Pounds, Linda, Houston 089181
Poupard, Marguerite, Sers 068231
Poupée Merveilleuse, Marcy 064279
Poupée Passion, Longueil 124331
Poupées Retrouvées, Paris 066440, 124784
Pour Sourire, Paris 100782
Pourny, Christian, Fayence 062849
Pourrier, Nathalie, Arras 060989
Poursin, Paris 138527
Pousse-Cornet, Marie-Edith, Blois . 120932
Poussier, Charles, Nanterre 064887
La Poussière du Temps, Paris 138528
Poussières, Bruxelles 058060
Poussières d'Empires, Paris 066441
Poutrain, Pascal, Douai 062726
Poutsma, J., Kampen 140467
Pouyet, Gérard, Cluses 062371
Považská Galéria Umenia, Žilina . . . 034451
Považské Múzeum, Žilina 034452
Povčenno-agronomičeskij Muzej im. V.R. Viljamsa, Moskva 033520
Povi, Hvidovre 124026
Povijesno Društvo Istre, Pula 052823
Povijesno Društvo Zadar, Zadar . . . 052824
Powder Magazine, Beechworth . . . 000785
Powder Magazine, Charleston 042743
Powderham Castle, Kenton 039848
Powderhouse Antiques, New York . 091167
Powell, Chicago 142294
Powell, Chicago 142295
Powell, Chicago 142296
Powell, Columbus 088429
Powell, Columbus 088430
Powell, Columbus 115796
Powell Bros. & Sons, Salt Lake City 092455, 132791
Powell, Brian, Auckland . . 078974, 121813
Powell, James, Austin 087605
Powell, M., Portland 142808
Powell-Cotton Museum, Quex House and Gardens, Birchington 038712
Powell County Museum, Deer Lodge 043367
Powell River Historical Museum, Powell River 006196
Powell Street Gallery, San Francisco 119769
Power, Robyn, Kaleen 094671
Power Art, Rio de Janeiro 096638
Power Group, Vancouver 097517
Power House Gallery, New York . . . 118306
Power Plant Contemporary Art Gallery, Toronto 006621
Powerhouse Arts Centre, Casula . . 094384
Powerhouse Gallery, Montréal . . . 097066
Powerhouse House and Car Museum, Portland 001408
Powerhouse Museum, Science and Design, Ultimo 001575
Powerhouse Museum Yanco, Yanco 001641
Powers, Pamela, Seattle 119985
Powers Museum, Carthage 042643
Powis Castle, Welshpool 041330
Pownalborough Court House, Dresden 043508
Powysland Museum and Montgomery Canal Centre, Welshpool 041331
Pozłotnictwo - Pracownia Rzemiosła Artystycznego, Poznań . 053985, 109060
Pozza, Dario, Trieste 076903
Pozza, Neri, Vicenza 134710
Pozzi, Aldo, Riehen 130152
Pozzolini, Simonetta, Roma 128167
PP Gallery, Stafford 114476
PR Mønter, Århus 060210
PRA Antikvariat, Stockholm 141169
Pra Site Museum, Bogor 022407
Prabang Antiques, Los Angeles . . . 089886
Prabhas Patan Museum, Prabhas Patan 022300
Praça das Artes, Rio de Janeiro . . . 096639
Praca Paris Obras de Arte, Rio de Janeiro 058637
Prachatické Muzeum, Prachatice . . 008591
Prácheňské Muzeum, Písek 008567
Pracher, Peter Rudolf & Britta, Würzburg 127040
Prachner im MQ, Wien 137356
Pracownia Konserwacji Rzeźby, Warszawa 129106
Pracownia - Muzeum Józefa Ignacego Kraszewskiego, Biblioteka Raczyńskich, Poznań 032255
Practikal, Genève 111494
Practiqon Antik, Djursholm 081777
Pradarshak, Mumbai 105793
Pradelle, Hugues, Toulouse 124993
Pradilla, Fernando, Madrid 110597
Prado, Brugge 096118
Del Prado, Madrid 141057
El Prado, Montevideo 087337
Prado, Vasco, Porto Alegre 096575
Prado Antiguedades, Madrid 081369
El Prado Antiquarium, Rio de Janeiro 058638
Praedicantenbibliothek der Nikolaikirche, Isny 018096
Prähistorische Privatsammlung, Mühlen 002341
Prähistorische Siedlung Pestenacker, Weil am Lech 020714
Prähistorische Staatssammlung München, Museum für Vor- und Frühgeschichte, München 019033
Prähistorisches Heimatmuseum, Veringenstadt 020577
Prähistorisches Museum, Hallstatt . 002016
Prämonstratenser-Chorherrenstift mit Stiftssammlungen, Geras 001890
Präsenz, Mössingen 104111
Präsenz Galerie der Jesus Brüderschaft, Hünfelden 103410
Prag, Ken, San Francisco 092867
Praga, Moskva 080258
Prager Kunstsalon, Nürnberg 104487
Pragnell, George, Stratford-upon-Avon 086776
Prahart, Sale 114387
Prahse, Erlangen 070602
Le Praillot, Bonnay 098981
Prairie Avenue Bookshop, Chicago . 142297
Prairie Avenue Gallery, Chicago . . . 115530
Prairie County Museum, Des Arc . . 043423
Prairie du Chien Museum at Fort Crawford, Prairie du Chien 047219
Prairie Gallery, Weyburn 006802
Prairie Gallery, Grande Prairie 005540
Prairie Homestead, Philip 046998
The Prairie Museum of Art and History, Colby 043036
Prairie Panorama Museum, Czar . . 005320
Prairie Pioneer Museum, Craik 005305
Prairie River Museum, Prairie River 006197
Prairie Trails Museum of Wayne County, Corydon 043179
Prairie Village, Madison 045586
Prairie West Historical Centre, Eston 005436
Prairie Wind, Basel 111218
Prakrit Art Gallery, Chennai 074797, 105635
De Praktijk, Amsterdam 107782
Prandi, Marco, Brescia 127230
Pranee, Dallas 088598
Prangenberg, Thomas, Köln 071991
Pranger, J., Groningen 128680
Pranke, Ralph, Vellberg 105113
Prano Gudyno, Vilnius 128461
Prarin, Lavaur 063558
Prasad & Co, Giriraj, Jaipur, Rajasthan 105726
Praska, Warszawa 109186
Praske, Dieter, München 072822
Praske, Peter, Rheda-Wiedenbrück . 073511
Prassler, Cornelia Caroline, Bologna 127176
Prastiati, Doetinchem 078292
Prat, Alfred, Linz 095671
Prata, Mario da, São Paulo 123721
Sri Pratap Singh Museum, Srinagar 022344
Pratella & Sepe, Livorno 075537
Prater & Rouse, Norfolk 118617
Pratermuseum, Wien Museum, Wien 002988
Praters Mill, Varnell 048753
Prates, António, Lisboa 109345
Prates, António, Lisboa 109346
Pratesi, Giovanni, Firenze 075389
Prati, Franca, Palermo 106439
Pratley, Bathurst 055454
Prats, Joan, Barcelona 110235
Pratt, San Diego 119539
Pratt, Sevenoaks 114406, 135303
Pratt & Son, Leo, South Walsham . . 086646
Pratt Contemporary Art, Ightham . . 113285
Pratt County Historical Society Museum, Pratt 047223
Pratt Institute, Brooklyn 051042
Pratt Manhattan Gallery, New York . 046395
Pratt Museum, Homer 044587
The Pratt Museum of Natural History, Amherst 041695
Pratter, Josef, Erfurt 125599
Pratzon, Jill, New York 132514
Praud, Dominique, Pornichet 066953
Prause's Erben, Fritz, Klagenfurt . . 057110
Prause's Erben, Fritz, Pörtschach am Wörther See 057211
Prause's Erben, Fritz, Pörtschach am Wörther See 057212
Prause, Werner Friedrich, Wien . . . 057529
Pravato, Bonn 102193
Prawdzic, Gdynia 079598
Praxenthaler, Engelbert, Penzing . . 126618
Praxis Arte Internacional, Buenos Aires 094085
Praxis Arte Internacional, México . . 107508
Praxis Gallery, Toronto 097353
Praxis Gallery Cafe, Bideford 112637
Praxis International Art, New York . . 118307
Praz-Delavallade, Paris 100783
Pražské Starožitnosti, Praha 060153
PRD Antiques, Houston 089182
Pré, Jean-Marc, Limonest 063901
Pré aux Sources, Bruxelles 096244
Pre-Industrial Museum, Halifax . . . 039664
Pre Loved Books, Torquay 137113
Pre to Post Modern, Nashville 090478
Préard, Yannick, Nantes . . 064941, 124487
Precania, Stefana, Palermo 076171
Prechtl, Peter, Rottach-Egern 073602
Precious, Roy, Hartley Wintney 084604
Precious Little Things, Las Vegas . . 089600
Precious Metal and Stone Unlimited, Philadelphia 091682
Precious Metals of Arizona, Tucson 093259
Precious Moments, Honolulu 088975
Precuious Arts, Lalitpur 107604
Predela, Granada 129531
Predjamski Grad, Postojna 034513
Preetzer Kunstboutique, Preetz, Holstein 073369
Prefectural Assambly Memorial Hall, Niigata 026913
Préférences, Saint-Ouen 067867
The Preferred Perch, Winnipeg 097602
Pregão e Leilão, Lisboa 121942
Pregliasco, Torino 140141
Préhisto-Parc, Tursac 015068
Préhisto-Parc et Grottes, Réclère . . 037438
Le Préhistorama, Musée des Orgines de l'Homme, Rousson 014143
Prehistory Museum, Department of Antiquities, Tripoli 027836
Preilu Vēstures un Lietišķās Mākslas Muzejs, Preiļi 027724
Preiner, Graz 095538
Preis & Preis, Cham 125427
Preis & Preis, Parsberg 126613
Preis & Preis, Regensburg 126698
Preisegger, Saarbrücken 073644
Preisgalerie, Gladbeck 102960
Preiss, Landsberg am Lech 103823
Preiss, Los Angeles 116870
Preiss, Wolfgang, Overath 073276
Preißing, Ute, Flensburg 070707
Preißing, Ute, Handewitt 071372
Preißinger, Eva, Deggendorf 070199
Preißinger, Martin, Roding 126725
Préjean, Jean-Jérôme, Paris 066442
Prell, Lohne, Oldenburg 103936
Preller, M.C., München . . . 072823, 126434
Prem, Kurt, Salzburg 095732
Premier Antikvitás, Budapest 074711
Premier Art, Nashville 117366
Premier Artworks, San Antonio 119442
Premier Auction Gallery, Kansas City 122934
Premier Auctions, Las Vegas 122939
Premier Gallery, Minneapolis 117296
Premier Gallery of Art, Salt Lake City 119361
Premier Prints, Milton Keynes 114084
Premium Quality Coin, Minneapolis 090392
Premoli-Lorandi, Milano 075829
Prempeh II Jubilee Museum, Kumasi 021107
Premsela, Robert, Amsterdam 140331
Premsela & Hamburger, Amsterdam 077934
Premselaar, Amsterdam 077935
La Prendería, Zaragoza . . 081749, 122092
Prensa Cicuta, Cuevas del Almanzora 134930
't Prentarium, Leiden 078579
't Prentenkabinet, Ridderkerk 140514
Prentenkabinet Universiteit Leiden, Leiden 029852
De Prentenwinkel, Zwolle 140582
Prentwerk, Groningen 140435
Prenzel, Dieter & Daniel, Sülzhayn . 074024
Prenzlow, A., Leverkusen 103908
Le Presbytère, Aujac 061063
Presbyterian Historical Society Museum, Montreat 046009
Presbyterian Historical Society Museum, Philadelphia 046979
Prescot Museum, Prescot 040776
Prescott Fine Arts Association, Prescott 054991
Prescott House Museum, Port Williams 006191
Presekan, Reutlingen 073501
Présence du Passé, Marseille 064387
Presenhuber, Eva, Zürich 112163
Present, České Budějovice 098343
Present Moment Books, Minneapolis 142589
Presentatieruimte de Overslag, Eindhoven 029547
Presentation House Gallery, North Vancouver 006047
Presentation House Gallery, Vancouver 097518
Presentazione Scenografica Gioacchino Murat, Pizzo 025287
Presente Passado com Antiguidades, São Paulo 058733
Les Présents du Passé, Montfermeil 064683
Prešernov Spominski Muzej, Kranj . 034474
Preservation Hall Antiques, Portland 091995
Preservation Press, New York 135456
Preservation Services, Perth 123286
Preservation Solutions, London . . . 131152
Preservation Station, Nashville 090479, 132402
Preservation Tips, Columbia 136608
Présház, Tokaji 021909
President Andrew Johnson Museum, Greeneville 044322

President Benjamin Harrison Home, Indianapolis 044754
President Chester A. Arthur Historic Site, Fairfield 043792
President Pretorius Museum, Potchefstroom 034709
The Presidential Museum, Odessa . 046625
President's Cottage Museum, White Sulphur Springs 049145
Presidio La Bahia, Goliad 044243
Presnja Istoriko-memorialnyj Muzej, Moskva 033521
Presque Isle County Historical Museum, Rogers City 047525
Presqu'ile Provincial Park Museum, Brighton 005153
Press, Richard L., Sacramento 142847
The Press Gallery, Chippendale . . . 094395
Presses Universitaires de France, Paris 133666
Preßler, Bernd, Kassel 139309
Pressler, Guido, Hürtgenwald 134068
Pressler, Dr. Karl H., München 139534
Preßlmayer, Gertraud, Wien 057530, 123524
Pressmar, Johanna, München 072824, 104292
Presswood, Joe, Houston 122913
Prest, Nathalie, Mougon 124465
Prestel, München 134270
Prestel, F.A.C., Frankfurt am Main . 102811
Prestel International, New York 135457
Prestes, Luiz Cesar da Silva, Porto Alegre 096576
Prestes, Luiz Cesar da Silva, Porto Alegre 096577
Prestige, Barcelona 080912, 122011
Prestige, İstanbul 083152
Prestige, John, Brixham 083754
Prestige Art, New York 118308
Prestige Art Gallery, Nashville 117367
Prestige Art Gallery Amsterdam, Amsterdam 107783
Prestige Arts, Dallas 115924
Prestige de l'Art, Grignon 063079
Prestige du Passé, Paris 124785
Prestige Framing Gallery, Tauranga 108579
Prestige Gallery, College Park 094416
Prestige Gallery, Salt Lake City 119362
Prestige Pictures, Craigavon 112912
Prestige Rental, Fort Worth 116161
Prestileo, Giuseppe, Köln 071992
Prestinoni, Piero, Milano 127658
Prestl, P., Bruxelles 058061
Preston, Antony, Stow-on-the-Wold 086757
Preston Antique Centre, Preston . . . 086312
Preston Art Center, Dallas 115925
Preston Auctions, Preston 120629
Preston Book, Preston 142009
Preston Hall Museum, Stockton-on-Tees 041112
Preston Manor, Brighton 038850
Preston Mill and Phantassie Doocot, East Linton 039354
Prestongrange Museum, Prestongrange 040782
Prestwould Foundation, Clarksville . 042957
Presutti, Mario, Parma 127860
Prète, Antoine, Lyon 064177
Pretérito Mais Que Perfeito, Lisboa 079994
Preti, Bruno, Milano 075830
Pretoria Art Museum, Pretoria 034725
Pretti, Solange, Belo Horizonte 096481
Pretty Art Center, Taipei 098080
Pretty Bizarre, Deal 084144
Pretty Home, Helsinki 060571
Pretzsch, Göttingen 071051
Preußen-Museum Nordrhein-Westfalen, Museum für Preußische Geschichte im Rheinland, Wesel 020823
Preußen-Museum Nordrhein-Westfalen, Museum für Preußische Geschichte in Westfalen, Minden, Wetsfalen . . . 018954
Preuve par Trois, Angoulême 060878
Preux, Marie-José, Saint-Ouen . . . 067868
Preveli Monastery, Myrthios 021391
Previous Parrot Press, Witney 135314
Prévost, Paris 066443
Prévot, Buzancais 061842
Prevot, Philippe, Ruoms 067331
Preyß, Dorothea, München 126435
Prežihov Spominski Muzej, Ravne na Koroškem 034518
Preziophil, Genova 075499
Prialnic, Pierrette, Fontenay-sur-Loing 062909
Pribila, Paul, Turramurra 123322
Price, Andrew, Carnegie . . 055637, 123205
Price, A.R., Coventry 141543
Price, Graham, Polegate . . 086279, 131381
Price Guide (Dubuque), Dubuque . . 136609
Price Tower Arts Center, Bartlesville 042032
Prichard, Winchcombe 087170
Prichard, Pat, San Antonio 092564
Prichett, Frances, San Diego 132854
Pricketts Fort, Fairmont 043795
Prickwillow Drainage Engine Museum, Prickwillow 040783
Priddy, Denver 122885
Priddy, W.D., Chichester 083976
Pride, Eric, Cheltenham . . 083926, 130540
Pride and Joy Antiques, Houston . . 089183
Prides of London, London 085620
Priebe, E., Alken 101559
Prien, Jürgen, Goslar 071067
Priental-Museum, Aschau im Chiemgau 015587
Prieré d'Airaines, Airaines 010286
Priest House, West Hoathly 041338
Priest Popple Books, Hexham 141666
Priester, Jürgen, Bonn 069938
Priester, Pierre de, Rennes (Ille-et-Vilaine) 067119
Priester, Pierre de, Saint-Quentin (Aisne) 067976
Priesterhäuser, Städtische Museen Zwickau, Zwickau 021087
Priestley & Ferraro, London 113841
Priest's House, Easton-on-the-Hill . 039371
Priest's House Museum, Wimborne Minster 041393
Prieuré du Vieux Logis, Nice 013412
Le Prieuré Nantais, Nantes 064942
Prigent, Alain, Hardricourt 063129
Prignitz-Museum Havelberg, Havelberg 017811
Prili, David, Roma 076626, 128168
Prili, Franco, Roma 076627
Prili, Luciano, Roma 076628
Prili, Marcello, Roma 076629
Prili, Mario, Roma 076630
Prili, Walter, Roma 076631
Prima Art, Bratislava 140959
Prima Galleri, Örebro 081889
Prima Vista, Maastricht 078618
Primarily Portraits, Philadelphia . . . 118824
Primart Gallery, Claremont 110037
Primarte, Torino 106699
Primarte, Valencia 110838
Primary Source, Los Angeles 116871
Primavera, Cambridge 112791
Primavera Gallery, New York 091168
Prime Art 2000, Perth 095067
Prime Canvas, Hayfield 113212
Prime Gallery, Toronto 097354
Primer Museo de las Abejas en México, Colonia Condesa 028174
Primer Museo Permanente del Boxeo Argentino, Buenos Aires 000251
Primitive Art Works, Chicago 088151
Primitive Kitchen, Cincinnati 088271
Primitivismes, Paris 100784
Primona Art Gallery, Mumbai 105794
Primorskaja Kraevaja Kartinnaja Galereja, Vladivostok 034056
Primorskij Gosudarstvennyj Muzej im. V.K. Arseneva, Vladivostok 034057
Primrose Antiques, Enniskerry 074972
Primrose Antiques, Jacksonville . . . 089450
Primrose Hill Books, London 141873
Primrose Hill Press, Bicester 135120
Primstaven, Nesttun 079404, 108699
Primus Verlag, Darmstadt 133858
Princ, Sabine, München 126436
Le Prince, Cairo 098664
Prince, Ghislain, Caudry 062037
Prince Albert Historical Museum, Prince Albert 006204
Prince Albert National Park Nature Centre, Waskesiu Lake 006768
Prince Arthur Fine Arts, Toronto . . . 097355
Prince d'Orange, Bruxelles 058062
Prince Edward Island Heritage Foundation, Charlottetown 052770
Prince Edward Island Museum, Charlottetown 005250
Prince Edward Island Potato Museum, O'Leary 006070
The Prince Edward Island Regiment Museum, Charlottetown 005251
Le Prince Noir, Aubagne 061026
Prince of Serendip, Toronto 059266
Prince of Wales Fort, Churchill 005272
Prince of Wales Martello Tower, Halifax 005581
Prince of Wales Museum of Western India, Mumbai 022270
Prince of Wales Northern Heritage Centre, Yellowknife 006890
Prince & Pauper, San Diego 142912
Prince & Prince, Mannheim 072429
Prince Rupert, Trieste 140148
Prince Rupert Fire Museum, Prince Rupert 006210
Prince Street Gallery, New York . . . 118309
Princess Antique Centre, Shrewsbury 086606
Princess Gracie's Dowery, Jacksonville 089451
Princess of Wales's Royal Regiment and Queen's Regiment Museum, Dover 039277
Princess Patricia's Canadian Light Infantry Museum, Calgary 005198
Princessehof Leeuwarden, Nationaal Keramiekmuseum, Leeuwarden . 029843
Princeton and District Museum, Princeton 006212
Princeton Museum, Princeton 047239
Princeton University Art Museum, Princeton 047240
Princeton University Museum of Natural History, Princeton 047241
Princeton University Press, Princeton 135481
Principal Antiques, Mount Gambier . 056284
Principal Sombrerers, Barcelona . . 110236
Principe de Vergara, Madrid 081370
Principia Fine Art, Hungerford 084763
El Princito, Burgos 141011
Pringle, Andrew, Edinburgh 141586
Pringle Antiques, Fochabers 084417
Pringle Cottage Museum, Warwick . 001601
Pringle Gallery, Philadelphia 118825
Prins Eugens Waldemarsudde, Stockholm 036657
Prins Hendrik de Zeevaarder Museum, Egmond aan Zee 029534
Prinsheerlijk Antiek, Amsterdam . . 077936
Print and Drawing Council of Canada, Edmonton 052771
Print and Picture Collection, Philadelphia 046980
The Print Bin, Glen Osmond 094587
The Print Bin, Glenelg 094593
The Print Center, Philadelphia 046981
Print Club of Cleveland, Cleveland . 054992
Print Consortium, Kansas City 044925
Print Council of America, Cambridge 054993
Print Quarterly, London 136260
Print Studio, Gumpoldskirchen 095552
The Print Works, Haslingden 113198
Printed Image Photographic Bookshop, Prahran 137062
Printed Page, Louisville 142534
Printed Words, Frankston 136905
Printers Inc. Press, London 135252
Printfolio Gallery, Sydney 056687
Printing House Museum, Cockermouth 039113
The Printing Museum, Carson 042632
Printique Gallery, Woollahra 095430
Printmaker, Honolulu 116240, 132092
Printmaker Gallery, Fitzroy 094538
Printmakers Council, Clerkenwell Workshop, London 054470
Printmakers Council of Prince Edward Island, Prince Edward Island 052772
Printmakers Gallery, Saint Ives, Cornwall 114371
Printmakers of Cape Cod, South Orleans 054994
Printmaking Council of New Jersey, Somerville 054995
Printmaking Today, Witney 136261
Prints and Perspectives, Saint Paul . 119305
Prints Charming, Calgary 096842
Prints Charming, El Paso 116116
Prints Charming Gallery, Saint Louis 119242
Prints etc., Paris 133667
Prints Old and Rare, Pacifica 142731
Prints Plus, Albuquerque 114820
Prints Plus, Austin 115004
Prints Plus, Baltimore 115079
Prints Plus, Buffalo 115263
Prints Plus, Cincinnati 115653
Prints Plus, Cincinnati 115654
Prints Plus, Dallas 115926
Prints Plus, Fresno 116183
Prints Plus, Las Vegas 116641
Prints Plus, Memphis 117003
Prints Plus, Miami 117127
Prints Plus, Minneapolis 117297
Prints Plus, Portland 119038
Prints Plus, Portland 119039
Prints Plus, Saint Louis 119243
Prints Plus, Salt Lake City 119363
Prints Plus, San Diego 119540
Prints Plus, San Jose 119861
Prints Plus, Tampa 120062
Prints San Francisco, San Francisco 094026
Prints Unlimited, Chicago 115531
Prints Unlimited, Chicago 115532
Prints World, Belo Horizonte 058444
Printsonweb, Milano 106290
Printworks, Chicago 115533
Printworks Fine Art Gallery, Dallas . 115927
Printziples Fine Art, Toronto 097356
Prinz, Josef, Salzburg . . . 057273, 123453
Prinz, Leopoldine, Wien 057531
Prinz, Wolfgang, Düsseldorf 070426
Prinz-Dunst, Karin, Berlin . 069729, 121339
Prinzen, Freiamt 070814
Priollaud & Lavoissiere, La Rochelle 121025
Prior, Margret, Bochum 069891
Prior, Walter, Kassel 071760
Prior Restorations, Saint Paul 132772
Priors Reclamation Unit, Ditton Priors 084170
Priory Antiques, Bridlington 083674
Priory Antiques, Godalming 084481
Priory Bookshop, Great Malvern . . . 141634
Priory Collectables, Preston 086313, 131397
Priory Gallery, Bishop's Cleeve 083543
Priory Gallery, Broadway 112739
Priou, Paul, Civray 062309
Prioul, La Mézière 124279
Prirodnjački Muzej, Beograd 034169
Prirodnjački Muzej Crne Gore, Podgorica 034243
Prirodnyčyj Muzej, Oblasnyj krajeznavčnyj muzej, Cherson 038250
Prirodonaučen Muzej, Burgas 004651
Prirodonaučen Muzej, Černi Osăm . 004653
Prirodonaučen Muzej, Kotel 004735
Prirodonaučen Muzej, Plovdiv 004797
Prirodonaučen Muzej, Varna 004924

Prirodonaučen Muzej, Istoričeski Muzej, Belogradčik 004634
Prirodonaučen Muzej na Makedonija, Skopje 027920
Prirodoslovni Muzej, Rijeka 007783
Prirodoslovni Muzej, Split 007804
Prirodoslovni Muzej Slovenije, Ljubljana 034491
Prirodovedčeskij Muzej, Smolenskij Muzej-Zapovednik, Smolensk 033881
Přírodovědecké Muzeum, Národní muzeum, Praha 008646
Přírodovědecké Oddělení, Slezské zemské muzeum, Opava 008548
Prírodovedné Múzeum, Slovenské Národné Múzeum, Bratislava 034336
Priscilla, Paris 124786
Il Prisma, Milano 106291
El prisma, Sevilla 129740
Prison Arts Program, Saint Louis . . 119244
Prisoner's of Taste, Nashville 090480
Pristine Pieces, Edmonton 096893
Prithvi Art Gallery, Mumbai 105795
Pritt, Columbus 088431
Prittlewell Priory Museum, Southend-on-Sea 041065
Priuli & Verlucca, Pavone 134655
Privat, Paris 066444
Privat, B. & D., Paris 138529
Private Art Dealers's Association, New York 054996
Private Collection, Knokke-Heist . . 058251
Private Collection, Manama 057643, 096021
Private Collection-Antiques, Austin . 087606
Private Collections, Osprey 123037
Private Collector, San Diego 092675
Private Connection, New Orleans . . 117493
Private Connection, New Orleans . . 117494
Private Lebzelt- und Buttermodelabdrucksammlung, Pressbaum 002469
Private Sammlung Mechanischer Musikinstrumente, Wohlhausen . . 020948
Private Screening, Seattle 093050
Private View, Paris 100785
Private View, Paris 100786
Privatmuseum Hans Klein, Prichsenstadt 019672
Privatmuseum Im Blauen Haus, Appenzell 036848
Privatmuseum Sammlung Holzinger, Kunst der Autodidakten, München 019104
Privatsammlung A.F. Fleischer, Wien 002989
Privatsammlung Burg Runkel, Runkel 019955
Privatsammlung Franz Pinteritsch, Pichling 002429
Privatsammlung Hermine Brandstetter, Ostermiething 002404
Privatsammlung Leo Gesell, Triefenstein 020476
Privatsammlung Piaty, Waidhofen an der Ybbs 002802
Privatsammlung Silvester Berner, Lengenfeld bei Krems 002221
Prix, Barbara, Wien 057532
Priz, Sofia 096744
Prize, San Francisco 092868
Pro-Art, Bottrop 102209
Pro-Art, Gelsenkirchen 102930
Pro-Art, Lage, Lippe 103815
Pro Art, Verden 105114
Pro Art e.V., Göttingen 053543
Pro-Art Studio, Hong Kong 097823
Pro Arte, Bucureşti 136049
Pro Arte Christiana, Vaalbeek 052686
Pro-Arte-Edition, Hamburg 134020
Pro Arte Medii Aevi - Freunde des Museum Schnütgen e.V., Köln 053544
Pro Arts Gallery, Oakland 046600
Le Pro des Particuliers, Montagnole 064617
Pro Domo, Graz 057020
Pro Hart Gallery, Broken Hill 094308
Pro-Jex Gallery, Austin 115005
Pro Lab Imaging, Norwood 123281
Pro Litteris, Schweizerische Urheberrechtsgesellschaft für Literatur und bildende Kunst, Zürich 054206
Pro Marco, Roma 128169
Pro Rodeo Hall of Fame and Museum of the American Cowboy, Colorado Springs 043060
Pro Urba, Mosaiques Romaines, Orbe 037405
Pró Velho, Lisboa 079995
Pró Velho, Queluz 080120
Probst, Chicago 088152
Probst, Andrea, Gotha 071068
Probst, Hedi, Nonnenhorn 104458
Probst, Rochus von, Graz . 057021, 095539
Probst, Walter, Chambésy 082297
Probstei-Museum, Schönberg, Holstein 020071
Probsteier Heimatmuseum, Schönberg, Holstein 020071
Probsthain, Arthur, London 141874
El Procante, Donostia-San Sebastián 081090
Process Posters, Atlanta 114915
Procháska, Antonín, Brno 098336
Prochaska, Patrick, Blanco 122821
Procházková, Radka, Berlin 125276
Prochnow & Georg-Prochnow, Simmern, Hunsrück 104905
Prock, C., Bad Buchau 069274
Proconsult Kunstforlag, Snekkersten 133432
Procopius, Leuven 137512
Proctor, C.D. & H.M., Puddletown . . 142010
Proctor, Ralph, Pittsburgh 118948
Proctor House Museum, Brighton . . 005154
Prodejní Výstava Starožitností a Umění, Praha 093637
Productive Living, Saint Louis 119245
Produktionsmuseum Klostermühle, Boitzenburg 016307
Produzentengalerie, Düsseldorf . . . 102539
Produzentengalerie B27, Offenau . . 104527
Produzentengalerie e.V., München .053545, 104293
Produzentengalerie Falkenberg, Hannover 103295
Produzentengalerie Hamburg, Hamburg 103208
Produzentengalerie - OHa Kunst im Wasserturm, Eutin 017096
Produzentengalerie Passau, Passau 104590
Proed, Santiago de Chile 006940
ProexbA Coruña, A Coruña 141016
Prof. Aleksandra Biezina Muzejs, Madona 027712
Prof. Eidenberger-Museum, Niederwaldkirchen 002378
Prof.-Fritz-Behn-Museum, Bad Dürrheim 015688
Prof. Gerstmayr-Museum, Mauthausen 002305
Profanierte Marienkapelle, Ludwigsstadt 018713
Professional Art Dealers Association of Canada, Association des Marchands d'Art du Canada, Toronto 052724
Professional Arte Moderno, Miami . 117128
Professional Auction Galleries, Portland 123067
Professional Fine Arts, Washington . 120339
Professional Fine Arts Services, New York 118310
Professional Photography and Commercial Art, Graphic Design, Antonelli Institute, Erdenheim 051304
Professuren für Kunstgeschichte, Justus-Liebig-Universität Gießen, Gießen 050091
Proffitt, San Antonio 119443
Profil, Skopje 107427
Profil Scène, Perreuil 100997
Profila, Budapest 121644
Profilkolor, Biarritz 061476
Profiri, Maria-Létizia, Paris 124787
Profolio, Denise, Camperdown 055618
Profumo, Maria, Genova 127482
Profumo d'Antico, Napoli 076031
Progetto Restauro, Padova 135944
Progetto Venezia, Venezia 106773
Program for Art on Film, Brooklyn . 054997
Programa de Museo y Parques, San Juan 032750
Programme for Museum Development in Africa, Mombasa 053815
Programs in the Visual Arts, University of Wisconsin Superior, Superior 052230
Progres Torgovyj Dom, Moskva . . . 140915
Progressive Editions, Toronto 097357
Progressive Editions, Toronto 133328
Progressive Painters Association, Chennai 053705
Progresso & Sviluppo, Napoli 106385
Project Art, London 113842
Project Art-University of Iowa and Clinics, Iowa City 044767
Project Arts Center, Dublin 022770
Project Contemporary Artspace, Wollongong 095406
Project Gallery, Los Angeles 116872
Projection, Bruxelles 096245
Projects in Architecture, Los Angeles 116873
Projects United, Tägerwilen 111941, 135070
Projek, Amsterdam 077937
Projektgalerie Elsterpark, Leipzig . . 103898
Prokop & Th.Gartmann, D., Stallikon 082832
Proll, K., Morsum 072599
Prome Museum, Prome 029068
Promenade Antiques, Great Malvern 084516, 141635
Promif, New York 091169
Promoart, Roma 106614
Promoarte, México 107509
Promoção Arte, Lisboa 109347
Promocoupes, Caen 061882
Promont House Museum, Milford . . 045868
Promotora Internacional de Arte Grafico, Madrid 110598
Promotrice Belle Arti, Torino 053764
Promyk, Gdańsk 108896
Pron, Alessandro, Torino . 076859, 106700
Proniewski, Serge, Labarde 124285
Pronkkamer Uden-Museum Hedendaagse Kunst, Uden 030214
Proofs, London 113843
Prop Art, Chicago 115534
Prop-It, Toronto 059267
The Propeller Centre for the Visual Arts, Toronto 097358
Properly Staged Interiors, Albuquerque 087419
Property Antiques, Roseneath 056553
Propos d'Art, Montréal 097067
The Proposition, New York 118311
Propst, Innsbruck 095594
Propst House and Marple Grove, Hickory 044527
Propyläen Verlag, Berlin 133804
Prora-Museum, Ostseebad Binz . . . 019528
Prošek, Dr. Václav, Praha . 120860, 137844
Proserpine Historical Museum, Proserpine 001410
Proshine, Columbus 131988
Proske-Van Heerdt, Drs. Dorine, Amsterdam 140332
Prosotowitz, Hans, Schwegenheim . 073763
Prospect Antique Centre, Prospect . 056506
Prospect Books and Prints, Llanrwst 141742
Prospect Gallery, Nailsworth 094924
Prospect Hill Museum, Meadows . . 001229
Prospect House Books, Donaghadee 139958
Prospectus Art Gallery, Chicago . . . 115535
Prosper Decoracoes, Rio de Janeiro 058639
Prospero, Kansas City 142476
Prospero, Santa Fé 055304
Prospero, Gianantonio, Verona 128433
Prospettiva, Rivista di Storia dell'Arte Antica e Moderna, Firenze 135945
Prospettive d'Arte, Milano 106292, 134629
Prosser, Ronnie L., Oakland 118643
Prost, Alain, Chalon-sur-Saône 062091
Prost, Jean-Pierre, Bron 061818
Prosveta, Beograd 134888
Prot, Didier, Tours 068602
Protain, Frédéric, Jaux 063240
Protectart, Paris 066445
Protée, Paris 100787
Protetch, Max, New York 118312
Protze, Sabine, Berlin 125277
The Proud American, Washington . . 093431
Proud Camden Moss, London 113844
Proud Galleries, London 113845
Proudfoot, Peter & Penny, Berkeley 083492, 130372
Proulx & Synnett, Montréal 058994
Prouse, Oscar, Hawthorn, Victoria . . 055965
Prouse, Oscar, Hawthorn, Victoria . . 055966
Prouse, Oscar, Hawthorn, Victoria . . 120594
Prouté, Paul, Paris 100788, 138530
Prouty-Chew Museum, Geneva . . . 044164
Prouvot, Boulogne-sur-Mer 120948
Prova d'Artista, Venezia 106774
Provan Hall House, Glasgow 039570
Provand's Lordship, Glasgow 039571
Provan's Mechanical Museum, Colac 000938
Provasek, Frank, Fort Worth 088878
Provenance Fine Art, San Diego . . . 119541
Provenance Trade, Atlanta 087514
Provence et Fils, Gigean 062997
Provence Antique, Montauroux 064645
Provence Portes Anciennes, Roaix . 067161
Provence Retrouvée, L'Isle-sur-la-Sorgue 063955
Proviant-Eisen Museum, Gresten . . 001956
Providence, Atlanta 087515
Providence, Paris 066446
Providence Art Club, Providence . . . 054998
Providence Art Club, Providence . . . 119086
Providence Athenaeum, Providence 047260
Providence Children's Museum, Providence 047261
Province House, Charlottetown 005252
Provinces de France Antiques, San Antonio 092565
Provincetown Art Association, Provincetown 054999
Provincetown Art Museum, Provincetown 047268
Provincetown Arts, Provincetown . . 136610
Provincetown Heritage Museum, Provincetown 047269
Provinciaal Archeologisch Museum, Velzeke-Ruddershove 003823
Provinciaal Archeologisch Museum-Ename, Oudenaarde 003694
Provinciaal Archeologisch Museum van Zuid-Oost-Vlaanderen, Zottegem . 003874
Provinciaal Domein Rivierenhof Galerij, Deurne 003400
Provinciaal Molenmuseum, Wachtebeke 003839
Provinciaal Museum Bulskampveld, Beernem 003221
Provinciaal Museum Sterckshof - Zilvercentrum, Antwerpen 003196
Provinciaal Museum Stijn Streuvels, Ingooigem 003536
Provinciaal Museum van Drenthel, Assen 029279
Provinciaal Openluchtmuseum Bokrijk, Genk 003449
Provinciaal Textiel- en Kostuummuseum Vrieselhof, Antwerpen 003166
Provinciaal Utrechts Genootschap van Kunsten en Wetenschappen, Utrecht 053901
Provinciaal Veiligheidsinstituut, Antwerpen 003186
Provincial Antiques, Albert Park . . . 055323
Provincial Antiques, Milton 079155

Provincial Booksellers Fairs Association, Royston 054471
Provincial Museum of Alberta, Edmonton 005404
Provincial Museum of Newfoundland and Labrador, Saint John's 006368
Provincial Natuurhistorisch Museum Natura Docet, Denekamp 029469
Provinzialrömische Sammlung und Antikenkabinett, Landesmuseum Joanneum, Graz 001945
Provinzmuseum der Franziskaner, Wien 002990
Provost, Elizabeth, Salt Lake City . . 132792
Provost, Michel, Paris . . . 066447, 124788
Provost Skene's House, Aberdeen . 038451
Provot-Liénard, Laons 063535
Proyecta Arte, Bogotá 098183
Proyecta Arte, Bogotá 098184
Prøysenhuset, Rudshøgda 031155
Prucha, Th., Berlin 121340
Prudence Crandall Museum, Canterbury 042599
Prüss & Ochs, Berlin 102014
Prütz, Bad Pyrmont 069354
Prunier, Louviers 121040
Prunkräume in der Residenz, Residenz Kempten, Kempten 018236
Pruskin, London 085621
Pruvost, Michel, Crécy-la-Chapelle . 062554
Prvá Žilinská Aukčná, Žilina 080644, 121977
První České Muzeum Velocipédu, Chotěboř 008337
Pryor & Son, E., Liverpool 085026
Prywatne Muzeum Etnograficzne, Góra Kalwaria 031945
Prywatne Muzeum Etnograficzno-Historyczne, Bielsk Podlaski 031834
Pryzmat, Kraków 108975
Przhevalsk Regional Museum, Prževalsk 027641
Przy Piwnej, Warszawa 109187
PS, Amsterdam 107784
P.S. 1 Contemporary Art Center, Museum of Modern Art, Long Island City 045390
PS 122 Gallery, New York 118313
P.S. Art Studios and Gallery, Fremantle 094570
P.S. Arts Factory, Tokyo 077294
PS Galerie, Hamburg 103209, 125835
P.S. Galleries, Dallas 115928
P.S. Industry Museum, Renmark . . . 001428
Psaculia, Vassiliki, Milano 075831
Psarrou, Zoe, Chalandri 105417
Pšenský, Dr. Petr, Praha 060154
Psiman, Oklahoma City 118675
Psimar, Bruxelles 058063
Pskovskij Gosudarstvennyj Istoričesko-architekturnyj i Chudožestnennyj Muzej-zapovednik, Pskov 033677
Pskovskij Memorialnyj Muzej V.I. Lenina, Pskov 033678
Psotka, Walter, Toronto 123837
PST, Majenfelde 126270
Psyché, Budapest 139927
Psyche, Sapporo 077200
Psyché Antiquité, Quesnoy-sur-Deule 067005
Psychiatrie-Museum, Bern 036935
Psychiatrie-Museum, Emmendingen 016968
Psychiatrie Museum im Philippshospital, Riedstadt 019840
Psychiatriemuseum Haina, Haina, Kloster 017638
Psykiatrihistoriska Museet, Uppsala 036742
Psykiatrihistoriska Museet, Växjö . . 036772
Pszczulny, Ewa, Düsseldorf 125544
P.T. Boat Museum, Germantown . . . 044181
P.T. Color, Firenze 127397
Ptolemais Museum, Department of Antiquities, Tolmeitha 027830
PTT Muzej Zajednice Jugoslovenskih Pošta, Telegrafa i Telefona, Beograd . . . 034170
Pu 1 Xuan Art Gallery, Shanghai . . . 097937
Pu Le Temple, Chengde 007039
Public Art Fund, New York 136611
Public Art Gallery, Imst 095575
Public Art Review, Saint Paul 136612
Public Corporation for the Arts, Long Beach 055000
Public Hangings, Southampton 114460
Public Illumination Magazine, Long Island City 136613
Public Library and Museum, Herne Bay 039741
Public Library Gallery, Llanelli 040057
Public Museum of Grand Rapids, Grand Rapids 044278
Public Service Memorial, Kuala Lumpur 027978
Publicaciones de Estética y Pensamiento, Madrid 134948
Publicaciones Prensantigua, Medellín 059937
Publications d'Histoire de l'Art et d'Archéologie de l'Université Catholique de Louvain, Louvain-la-Neuve . . . 135608
Publick, Philadelphia 091683
Publiekscentrum voor Beeldende Kunst, Enschede 029568
Publix Books, Cleveland 142342
Pucci, A., Bruxelles 058064
Pucci, Bruno, Napoli 140080
Puccio, Salvatore, Palermo 076172
Puce a l'Oreille, Beirut 077411
Puce à l'Oreille, La Madeleine 063397
La Puce a l'Oreille, Lille 063866
La Puce Antiques, Linz 057162
La Puce d'Argent, Saint-Ouen 067869
O Puces, Beirut 077412
Puces, Bouville 061737
Puces, Villejuif 068905
Puces de Cherbourg, Équeurdreville-Hainneville 062794
Puces de la Côte, Grasse 063040
Puces d'Oc, Toulouse 068536
Les Puces Lascaris, Nice 065132
Les Puces Laurentaises, Saint-Laurent-en-Gâtines 067579
Les Puces Montluçonnaises, Montluçon 064713
Pucher, Dr. Christina, Graz 057022, 123367
Puchert, Sonja, Gröditz 103008
Puchol, Valencia 110839
Puck, Amsterdam 077938
Pucker, Boston 115223
Pucuk Rebung Royal Gallery Museum, Kuala Lumpur 027979
Pudasjärven Kotiseutumuseo, Pudasjarvi 010001
Pudelko, Bonn 102194
Pudong Duo Yun Xuan, Shanghai . . 097938
Pueblo County Historical Society Museum, Pueblo 047277
El Pueblo de Los Angeles Historical Monument, Los Angeles 045459
Pueblo Grande Museum, Phoenix . . 047014
Pueblo Viejo, San Miguel de Tucumán 055302
Puente, Carlos de la, New York 091170
Puente, Carlos de la, New York 091171
Puente, Jose, Madrid 110599
La Puente Valley Historical Society Museum, La Puente 045078
Puerta, Jesus, Granada 110382
Puerta de Alcalá, Belo Horizonte . . 058445
Puerta de Isabel II Gallery, Manila . 031737
Puerta Real, Granada 081147
La Puerta Verde de Españoleto, Madrid 129659
Las Puertas, Hong Kong 097824
Puertas Herrero, Sevilla 129741
Puerto Galera National Museum, Puerto Galera 031765
Puerto Rican Work Shop, New York 118314
Puerto Rican Work Shop, New York 118315
Püschner, Karsten, Hartmannsdorf . 125885
Püttner, Hans-Jürgen, Hof, Saale . . 125950
Pütz, Berthold & Paul, Berg, Kreis Ahrweiler 069528
Pütz, G., Freiburg im Breisgau 070852
Pütz, Gottfried, Müllheim, Baden . . 072620
Pueva, Düsseldorf 102540
Pueyo, Sevilla 110776
Puffing Billy Steam Museum, Menzies Creek 001255
Puga, George, Portland 119040
Puget, Sabine, Paris 100789
Puget Sound Coast Artillery Museum at Fort Worden, Port Townsend 047143
Pugh, Jan K., Pershore 141997
Pugh, Rosemary, Salisbury 142044
Pugh's Farm Antiques, Monkton . . . 086000
Pugin, Christine, Seewen 130176
Pugin, Max & Olivier, Genève 082461
Puhoi Historical Society Museum, Puhoi 030582
Puhr, Franz, Lannach 057143, 123405
Puhze, Günter, Freiburg im Breisgau 070853
Pui Kee, Hong Kong 059688
Puig Balaguer, Maria del Carmen, Castello de la Plana 110307
Puig Vidal, Manuel, Barcelona 080913
Pujol, Etienne, Perpignan 121223
Pujol, Joan, Castelnou 062018
Pujol & Martin, Toulouse 068537
Puke Ariki, New Plymouth 030553
Pukeberg, Stockholm 111068
Pukkilan Kartanomuseo, Piikkiö . . . 009973
Pukkilan Kotiseutumuseo, Pukkila . 010002
Pulandian City Museum, Dalian . . . 007060
La Pulce d'Acqua, Bari 075027
Pulci, Paolo, Firenze 075390, 140026
Pulgarín, Jorge, Medellín 123938
El Pulguero, Cali 059884
El Pulguero, Madrid 129660
Pulkauer Gewerbemuseum, Pulkau 002477
Pulkautaler Weinbaumuseum, Hadres 002002
Pulkkilan Kotiseutumuseo, Pulkkila 010003
Pulliam Deffenbaugh, Portland 119041
Pullman, London 085622
Pullman Museum, Historic Pullman Foundation, Chicago 042876
Pulp Fiction, Brisbane 136821
La Pulperie de Chicoutimi, Chicoutimi 005267
Puls, Bruxelles 096246
Pulszky Society - Hungarian Museums Association, Budapest 053678
Pulver Zajfman Collection, Toronto . 059268
Pulylac, Castellón de la Plana 129480
Pulzzart, Castres 099098
Pummer, Erich, Rossatz 123436
Pump House Center for the Arts, Chillicothe 042899
Pump House Gallery, London 040261
Pump House of Regional Arts, La Crosse 045057
Pump House Steam Museum, Kingston 005706
Pumphouse Educational Museum, London 040262
Punavuoren, Helsinki 060572
Punavuoren, Puu, Helsinki 124049
Punavuori, Helsinki 137956
Punch Gallery, Balmain 094205
Punchinello, Paris 066448
Mr Punch's Antique Market, Shaftesbury 086545, 131469
Punct Muzeal, Moroeni 032895
Punct Muzeal Gospodăria Tărănească, Enisala 032860
Pundole, Mumbai 105796
Pundole, Neville, Canterbury 112803
Punjab Archives Museum, Lahore . 031386
Punkaharjun Kotiseutumuseo, Punkaharju 010005
Punkt Etnograficzny w Rogierówku, Muzeum Pierwszych Piastów na Lednicy w Lednogórze, Rogierówko 032289
Punkt Galeria, Łódź 109018
Punkt Muzealny w Supraśli, Muzeum Okregowego w Białymstoku, Supraśl 032349
Punt de Llom, Palma de Mallorca . . 110697
Punti, A., Terrassa 081628
Puntland, Minneapolis 117298
Il Punto, Genova 106104
Punto Arte, Modena 106354
El Punto de las Artes, Madrid 136100
Puolakan Talomuseo, Kouvola 009745
Pupilles et Papilles, Valbonne 101405
Puppen-, Bären- und Spielzeugmuseum, Bad Wimpfen 015834
Puppen & Spielzeug, Duisburg 135818
Puppen- und Spielzeugmuseum, Davos Platz 037040
Puppen- und Spielzeugmuseum, Holzminden 017997
Puppen- und Spielzeugmuseum, Lichtenstein, Sachsen 018634
Puppen und Spielzeugmuseum, Mödling 002328
Puppen- und Spielzeugmuseum, Solothurn 037579
Puppen- und Spielzeugmuseum, Wien 002991
Puppen- und Spielzeugmuseum Sammlung Katharina Engels, Rothenburg ob der Tauber 019916
Puppenausstellung des Steinauer Marionetten-Theaters, Steinau an der Straße 020300
Das Puppenhaus, Nürnberg 073113
Puppenhausmuseum, Basel 036903
Puppenmuseum, Einöde 001817
Puppenmuseum, Oberlienz 002385
Puppenmuseum Falkenstein, Sammlung Elke Dröscher, Hamburg 017718
Puppenmuseum im Kunsthof, Herten 017905
Puppenmuseum in Villach, Villach . 002777
Puppenmuseum Jeannine, Kreuzlingen 037222
Puppenmuseum Kärntner Eisenwurzen, Hüttenberg 002067
Puppenmuseum Sasha Morgenthaler, Museum Bärengasse, Zürich 037798
Puppentheatermuseum, Kaufbeuren 018214
Puppentheatermuseum, Mistelbach an der Zaya 002317
Puppentheatermuseum mit Abteilung Schaustellerei, Münchner Stadtmuseum, München 019105
Puppentheatersammlung, Staatliche Kunstsammlungen Dresden, Dresden 016810
Puppet Centre, Toronto 006622
The Puppet Forge, Minneapolis . . . 117299
Puppich, Stefan, Hildesheim 125936
Puratatva Sangrahalaya, Rahul Sankratayan Sansthan, Gorakhpur 022126
Purcell, Francis J., Philadelphia . . . 091684
Purdon, Richard, Burford . 083792, 130478
Purdue University Calumet Library Gallery, Hammond 044406
Purdue University Galleries, West Lafayette 049085
Purdy's Furniture, Briar Hill 055540
Pure Design, Bangkok 083100
Pure Design Classics, Brighton 083713
Pure Galerie Art et Design, Caen . . 099048
Pure Nostalgia, Waihi 079279
Puri, Kassel 103516
Puri Gamelan Suar Agung, Denpasar 022414
La Purisima Mission, Lompoc 045372
Purist Gallery, Yallingup 095440
Puritan Values at the Dome, Southwold 086670
Purmerends Museum, Purmerend . 030046
Purnell, Baltimore 115080
Purple, Paris 135723
The Purple Cactus, Avalon 136787
Purple Cow, Saint Louis 092302
Purple Parrot, Jacksonville 116538
Purple Picture Gallery, Reading . . . 114300
Purple Picture Gallery, Windsor . . . 114710
Purschwitz, Manfred, Dossenheim . 070300
Purshottam & Sons, Sharjah 083222

Purtee, Indianapolis 132160
Purton Museum, Swindon 041176
Purutan Restorations, Delhi 074807, 127085
Purvattatva Sangrahalaya Madhya Pradesh Shasan, Damoh 022066
Pusaka, West Hollywood 093498
Pusat Latihan Kesenian & Pertukangan Tangan Brunei, Bandar Seri Begawan 004615
Puschner, Kerstin, Altenburg, Thüringen 101565
Pushman, New York 118316
Puškinskaja Observatorija - Galereja 103, Sankt-Peterburg 109643
Pusset, Jean-Jacques, Beaune . . . 061291
Pussinen, Kristiina, Helsinki 124050
Pustak, Hans-Jürgen, Wien 095924
Pustet, Anton, Salzburg 133145
Pustet, Friedrich, Regensburg 134361
Pustozerskij Kompleksnyj Istoriko-prirodnyj Muzej, Narjan-Mar 033545
Pusulan Museo, Pusula 010007
Pusz, Janina, Wrocław 140808
Putcuyns, Constant, Antwerpen . . . 123552
Putiikki, Helsinki 137957
Putinki, Helsinki 060573
Putkinotko, Savonlinna 010067
Putkiradiomuseo, Kouvola 009746
Putman, Catherine, Paris 133668
Putman, Robert, Amsterdam 140333
Putnam Cottage, Greenwich 044352
Putnam County Historical Society and Foundry School Museum, Cold Spring 043037
Putnam County Historical Society Museum, Kalida 044902
Putnam Museum of History and Natural Science, Davenport 043305
Putney Historical Society Museum, Putney 047287
Putot, Jacques, Le Perreux-sur-Marne 063681
Putte, René van de, Reims 124866
Putti, Toronto 059269
Putti, Albion, Groningen 108046
Puttnam, Annette, Petworth 086257
Il Putto, Amsterdam 077939
Il Putto, Amsterdam 077940
Putz, Gerhard & Beate, Eschwege . 070612
Puuhkalan Talomuseo, Ylivieska . . . 010260
Puukohola Heiau National Historic Site, Kawaihae 044939
Puupaja, Helsinki 060574
Puupaja, Helsinki 124051
Puur, Rotterdam 108204
Puy, Patrick, Bessieres 061407
Puyo, Antonia, Zaragoza 110888
Puyol, Marcelle, Auch 120910
Puzin, Georges, Versailles 138655
Puzo, Christian, Bayonne 061237
Puzone, Jean-Pierre, Genève 082462
Půžová, Marie, Jihlava 098367
P.W. Vorster Museum, Middelburg Cape 034680
Pybus, M., Whitby 114681
Pydar Gallery, Truro 114607
Pygmalion and Galatea, Toronto . . . 097359
Pyhäjärven Kotiseutumuseo, Pyhäjärvi 010009
Pyhäjoen Kotiseutumuseo, Pyhäjoki 010010
Pyhältö, Ipi & Pekka, Tampere 098761
Pyhämaan Kotiseutumuseo, Pyhämaa 010011
Pyhännän Kotiseutumuseo, Pyhäntä 010012
Pyhtään Kotiseutumuseo, Pyhtää . . 010013
Pyka, Henryk, Łódź 079673
Pykäri Nuutajärven Lasimuseo, Designor Oy Ab, Nuutajärvi 009918
Pyke, Beverley J., Alderney 083263
Pyl Vekov, Moskva 080259
Pyms Gallery, London . . . 085623, 113846, 131153
Pyo, Seoul 107277
Pyongyang Institut of Fine Arts, Pyongyang 050508
Pyramid Gallery, York 114755
Pyramid Hill and District Historical Museum, Pyramid Hill 001412
Pyramid Hill Sculpture Park and Museum, Hamilton 044403
Pyramida, Praha 098485
La Pyramide, Saint-Sauveur (Drôme) 068002
Les Pyramidions, Paris 066449
Pyro Gallery, Louisville 116962
Pyromania, Tauranga 108580
Pyttel, Peter, Bad Oeynhausen 069347
Pyynikinlinna, Tampere 010125
Q 14, Traunreut 105056
Q Antiques, Dun Laoghaire 074967
Q Antiques, Willingham . . 087151, 131687
Q Art Trading, New York 118317
Q Books, Nelson 140643
Q & C Militaria, Cheltenham 083927, 130541
Q Street Fine Crafts, Salt Lake City . 119364
Qalipakkanik Katersugaasivik, Ilulissat 021540
QANTAS Founders Outback Museum, Longreach 001194
Qaqortup Katersugaasivia, Qaqortoq Museum, Qaqortoq 021547
Qasigiannguit Katersugaasiviat, Christianshåb Lokalmuseum, Qasigiannguit 021548
Qasr Al-Gawharah, Cairo 009321
Qasr Al-Ibrahim, Cairo 009322
Qasr Ali Ibrahim, Zamalek 009349
Qassim, Yousif, Manama 096022
Qatar National Museum, Doha 032759
QCA Gallery, Brisbane 000841
QCC Art Gallery, Bayside 042066
Qdos, Lorne 056116
Qedem Museum, Kedumim 022990
Qeqertarsuaq Museum, Qeqertasuaq 021549
Qi Guo Gucheng Yi Zhi Museum, Zibo 007359
Qian Long Antiques Art Australia, Surry Hills 056657
Qianling Museum, Qian Xian 007221
Qijiang Stone Engraving Museum, Gunan 007098
Qilu, Jinan 097860
Qilu, Jinan 097861
Qin Dai Zhan Guan, Xian 007316
Qin Shi Huan Bingmayong Museum, Xian 007317
Qing Mi Ge Art Galley, Beijing 097673
Qing Ming Antikk, Oslo 079466
Qing Qi Shi, Qingdao 097889
Qingan Art Cooperative, Ningbo . . . 097882
Qingdao Art Galley, Qingdao 097890
Qingdao Art Galley, Qingdao 097891
Qingdao City Folklorish Museum, Qingdao 007224
Qingdao Municipal Museum, Qingdao 007225
Qingdao Oil Painting Factory, Qingdao 097892
Qingdao Oil Painting Institute, Qingdao 097893
Qingdao Painting Gallery, Qingdao . 007226
Qingpu Museum, Shanghai 007239
Qingpu Painting Gallery, Shanghai . 097939
Qingsong Art Service Center, Beijing 097674
Qinhuai Art Cooperative, Nanjing . . 097876
Qom Museum, Qom 022590
Qozhaya Museum, Qozhaya 027819
Q.'s Books, Hamilton, New South Wales 136928
Quaco Museum and Archives, Saint Martins 006386
Quadart, Christchurch 108410
Quaderni di Storia dell'Arte, Parma . 135946
Quadraat, Amsterdam 077941
Quadrat Bottrop, Josef-Albers-Museum, Moderne Galerie, Studio Galerie, Museum für Ur-und Ortsgeschichte, Bottrop 016352
Quadrata, Medellín 098284
Il Quadrato, Milano 134630
Quadreria Cesarini, Fossombrone . . 024245
Quadreria Comunale, Offida 024989
Quadreria Comunale, Prato 025366
Quadreria Comunale, San Constanzo 025669
Quadreria dei Girolamini, Napoli . . . 024922
Quadreria dell'800, Milano 106293
Quadreria della Cassa Depositi e Prestiti, Roma 025582
Quadreria della Società Economica, Chiavari 023850
Quadreria e Pinacoteca Civica, San Giovanni in Persiceto 025691
Quadrerie, Nice 065133
Quadreto, Pinner 114250
Quadri, Bruxelles 096247
Il Quadrifoglio, Livorno 075538
Il Quadrifoglio, Milano 075832
Quadrige, Nice 099854
Quadrille, London 085624
Quadrivium, Sydney 095302
Quadro, Zürich 112164, 130259
Quadrum Galeria de Arte, Belo Horizonte 096482
Quagga Art, Cape Town 110031
Quagliotti, Vittorio, Torino 128346
Quai de la Gare, L'Isle-sur-la-Sorgue 063956
Quaid-i-Azam Birthplace and Museum, Karachi 031376
Quaink, Thomas, Köln 126112
Quaint Notions, Jacksonville 089452, 122929, 132193
Quaker Museum, Ballytore 022690
Quaker Yearly Meeting House, Mount Pleasant 046067
Qualantoni, Salvatore, Milano 075833
Qualitas Antiquitas, Budapest 074712
Quality Antiques, Chicago 088153
Quality Coins, El Paso 088812
Quality Collectibles, Miami 090232
Quality Fine Arts, London 113847
Quality Frames and Art, Austin 115006
Quality Furniture Refinishing, Philadelphia 132632
Quality Furniture Repair Service, Tulsa 133002
Quality Upholstery, Cleveland 131969
Quan Hua Yuan, Wuxi 098043
Quandt-Verein Dittersbach zur Förderung der Künste e.V., Dittersbach 053546, 133868
Quantum Commercial, Wellington . 079341
Quantum Contemporary Art, London 113848
Quantum Gestion, Madrid 110600
Quanz, Herfried, Altenstadt, Hessen 101567
Quanzhou Maritime Museum, Quanzhou 007227
Quanzhou Painting Gallery, Quanzhou 007228
Quaranta, Renata, Roma 076632
Quaritch, Bernard, London 141875
Quarr Gallery, Swanage 114531
Quarry Bank Mill, Styal 041153
Quart Verlag, Luzern 135046
Quartair, Den Haag 107947
Quartana, Luca, Milano 127659
Quartel de Santa Cruz, Rio de Janeiro 004419
Quarterjack Antiques, Fontmell Magna 084420
Quartermaine, Paul, Morley 056256
Quartet Books, London 135253
Quartier Ephémère, Montréal 097068
Quartilho, Jorge Luiz Fernandes, Rio de Janeiro 096640
Quarto Bookshop, Saint Andrews . . 142035
Quarzsandbergwerk-Museum, Buchs, Zürich 036983
Quasar Antichitati, București 080169
Quaschinski, Brunhild, Limburg an der Lahn 072260
Quast, Anett, München 126437
Quast, F., Wernigerode 074345
Quaternary Period Qlacier Traces Exhibition Hall, Beijing 007006
Quatrain, West Hollywood 093499
Quatre A, Nice 065134
Quatrefoil, Fordingbridge 084423
Quatro Montras, Lisboa 129170
Quattrini, Anna, Roma 076633
Quattrocchi, Isabella, Roma 128170
Quattrocento, Madrid 129661
Quattrocento, Vannes (Morbihan) . . 068720
Quattroemme, Ponte San Giovanni . 134660
Quay Gallery, Sydney 095303
Quay Gallery Antiques Emporium, Exeter 084363
Quay Lombrail, Paris 121188
Quayside Antique Centre, Shrewsbury 086607, 131498
Quayside Antiques, Wanganui 079305
Quayside Art, Singapore 109855
Que Gallery, Ha Noi 120481
Que Milagro, Houston 116393
Que Van, Knokke-Heist 096354
Queanbeyan and District Historical Museum, Queanbeyan 001414
Quebec Art, Québec 097160
Quebec Art, Québec 097161
Quebec House, National Trust Chartwell, Westerham 041346
Quedar, Strasbourg 101301
Quedenbaum, Klein Kreutz 071869
Queen, New York 135458
Queen Anne Antiques, Lefkosia . . . 059957
Queen Anne Antiques & Raven's Nest Treasure, Seattle 093051
Queen Anne House, Chesham 083943
Queen Antiques, Toronto 059270
Queen Charlotte's Cottage, Richmond, Surrey 040833
Queen City Architectural Salvage, Denver 088725
Queen Elizabeth II Army Memorial Museum, Waiouru 030614
Queen Elizabeth National Park Museum, Lake Katwe 038221
Queen Elizabeth's Hunting Lodge, London 040263
Queen Emma Gallery, Honolulu . . . 044606
Queen Emma Summer Palace, Honolulu 044607
Queen Mary Museum, Long Beach . 045382
Queen of Hearts, Miami 117129
Queen of the South, Genk 058164
Queen Street Fine Arts, Blenheim . . 108375
Queen Street Mill Textile Museum, Burnley 038908
Queen Victoria Antiques Centre, Melbourne 056198
Queen Victoria Museum, Harare . . . 049584
Queen Victoria Museum and Art Gallery, Launceston 001178
Queen Victoria Rifles Museum - Hill 60, Zillebeke 003868
Queen West, Toronto 059271
Queens County Farm Museum, Floral Park 043864
Queens County Museum, Liverpool 005779
Queens County Museum, Tilley House and Court House, Gagetown 005492
Queen's Gallery, Charlotte 115308
Queens Gallery, Queenscliff 056513
The Queen's Gallery, Royal Collection, Edinburgh 039415
The Queen's Gallery, Royal Collection, London 040264
Queens Garden, Atlanta 087516
Queens Historical Museum, Flushing 043878
Queen's House, Teignmouth 086836
Queen's Key, Toronto 059272, 097360
Queen's Lancashire Regiment Museum, Preston 040781
Queens Library Gallery, Jamaica . . . 044826
Queen's Market, Lisboa . . 079996, 109348
Queens Museum of Art, Flushing . . 043879

Queen's Own Cameron Highlanders of Canada Regimental Museum, Winnipeg . . . 006857
Queen's Own Hussars Museum, Warwick . . . 041305
Queen's Own Rifles of Canada Regimental Museum, Toronto . . . 006623
Queen's Own Royal West Kent Regimental Museum, Maidstone . . . 040390
Queens Parade Antiques, Stow-on-the-Wold . . . 086758
Queens Park Conservation Studios, Manchester . . . 131257
Queen's Regiment Museum, Dover . 039277
Queens Road Gallery, Aberdeen . . . 112480
Queen's Royal Irish Hussars Museum, Eastbourne . . . 039363
The Queen's Royal Lancers Regimental Museum, Grantham . . . 039621
Queen's Royal Surrey Regiment Museum, Guildford . . . 039650
Queen's Royal Surrey Regiment Museum, West Clandon . . . 041337
Queen's York Rangers Regimental Museum, Toronto . . . 006624
Queenscliff Antiques, Queenscliff . . 056514
Queenscliffe Historical Museum, Queenscliff . . . 001416
Queenscliffe Maritime Museum, Queenscliff . . . 001417
Queensferry Museum, South Queensferry . . . 041048
Queensland Aboriginal Creations, Brisbane . . . 055562
Queensland Aboriginal Creations, South Brisbane . . . 056606
The Queensland Aborigine, Cairns . 055601
Queensland Air Museum, Caloundra 000877
Queensland Art Gallery, South Brisbane . . . 001474
Queensland Maritime Museum, South Brisbane . . . 001475
Queensland Military Memorial Museum, Fortitude Valley . . . 001037
Queensland Museum, South Bank . 001473
Queensland Pioneer Steam Railway, Blackstone . . . 000810
Queensland Police Museum, Brisbane . . . 000842
Queensland University of Technology Art Collection, Kelvin Grove . . . 001148
Queenstown and Frontier Museum, Queenstown . . . 034737
Queenstown Gallery, Dunedin . . . 108445
The Queenstown Story, Cobh . . . 022717
Quéhen, Catherine, Equihen-Plage . 062795
Queirós, Isabel, Porto . . . 080106
Quel Che Manca, Venezia . . . 076966
Quelle Belle Journée, Paris . . . 066450
Quelque part, Limoges . . . 099510
Quentin, Berlin . . . 069730, 121341
Quentin, Paris . . . 066451
Quentin, Yannick, Saint-Florentin . . 067477
Quentin-Molènes, Genève . . . 141253
Querch, Judith, Graz . . . 095540
Quercus, Debenham . . . 084151, 130629
Quercus, Noordlaren . . . 128792
Quereix, Bernard, Bordeaux . . . 061647
Quesnel, Pierre, Genouillac . . . 062985
Quesnel and District Museum, Quesnel . . . 006236
Quest, New Orleans . . . 090604
Quest, New York . . . 118318
Quest - Center for Earth Science And Discovery, Makati . . . 031700
Questa, Enrico, Torino . . . 076860
Questacon The National Science and Technology Centre, Canberra . . . 000892
Questel, Bruno, Rouen . . . 067292
Questel, Bruno, Rouen . . . 067293
Questel, Bruno, Rouen . . . 067294
Questron, Los Angeles . . . 135385
Quetico Provincial Park Heritage Pavilion, Atikokan . . . 005038
Quetsche, Verlag für Buchkunst, Witzwort . . . 134464
Quetzal, Knokke-Heist . . . 096355
Quetzalli, Denver . . . 116038
Quevedo, Lima . . . 079556
Queyrel, Luc, Paris . . . 100790
Quezel Mouchet, Andrée, Villeneuve-lès-Avignon . . . 068914
Quezonia Museum, Manila . . . 031738
Quibus, José, Toronto . . . 123838
Quick Strip, Cincinnati . . . 131942
Quicksilver, Berlin . . . 102015
Quicksilver, San Diego . . . 092676
Quidam de Revel, Paris . . . 066452
Quidi Vidi Battery, Saint John's . . . 006369
Quiet Street Antiques, Bath . . . 083441
Quiet Valley Living Historical Farm, Stroudsburg . . . 048402
The Quiet Woman Antiques Centre, Chipping Norton . . . 083993
Quigley, Harry & Judith, Adelaide . . 055319
Quigley, Michael A., San Antonio . . 092566
Quik, L., Den Haag . . . 078237
Quilichini, Ludovic, La Crau . . . 063359
Quilis-Semper, Brigitte, Grenoble . . 063072
Quill, Albuquerque . . . 131748
Quill Antiques, Deal . . . 084145
Quill Pen Antiques, Louisville . . . 090019
Quillet, Loix-en-Ré . . . 124330
Quillon, Tetsworth . . . 086872
Quilpie Museum, Quilpie . . . 001419
Quilt Garden, Kobe . . . 106883
Quilt Patch, Long Beach . . . 089651
Quilted Cat, Birmingham . . . 087781
Quilted Teddy, Denver . . . 088726
Quilter, John, Wellington . . . 140680
Quilter, Michael & Jackie, Amersham . . . 083291
Quilters Hall of Fame, Marion . . . 045679
Quimera Taller de Arte, Panamá City . . . 108794
La Quincaillerie, Veules-les-Roses . 101460
Quincy and Adams County Museum, Quincy . . . 047298
Quincy Art Center, Quincy . . . 047299
Quincy Historical Museum, Quincy . 047303
The Quincy Museum, Quincy . . . 047300
Quincy Society of Fine Arts, Quincy 055001
Quinéville Military Collectable, Quineville . . . 067027
Quiniou, Jessica, Quimper . . . 067023
Quinn, Camperdown . . . 055619
Quinn, Falls Church . . . 122895
Quinns, Taranaki . . . 121832
El Quinque Antiguedades, Zaragoza 081750
Quinque-Wessels, Heidrun, Berlin . 102016
Quinquis, Jean-Jacques, Ile-Tudy . . 099366
La Quinta, Madrid . . . 035441
Quinta das Cruzadas, Centro de Exposições, Arte e Multimédia, Sintra . . . 032694
Quinta Galería, Bogotá . . . 098185
Quintana, Portland . . . 119042
Quintana, Fernando, Bogotá . . . 098186
Quintana Diaz, Francisco Angel, Vitoria-Gasteiz . . . 081720
Quintana Loscos, Francisco, Barcelona . . . 129381
Quintanilla, Alonso de, Gordes . . . 063019
Quintavalla, Lorenzo, Milano . . . 127660
Le Quinte di Via dell'Orso, Milano . . 075834
Quinte Educational Museum, Ameliasburgh . . . 005005
Quintero, Sofia, Toledo . . . 120089
Quintessens, Utrecht . . . 108260
Quintessential Antiques, Saint Louis 092303
Quinto Bookshop, London . . . 141876
Quinto Bookshop, London . . . 141877
Quintrec, Yvon le, Lesneven . . . 063795
Le Quinze, Saint-Ouen . . . 067870
Quirindi and District Historical Cottage and Museum, Quirindi . . . 001420
Quiros Galdon, Marta Maria, Madrid 129662
Quisqualis Art, Paddington, Queensland . . . 095047
Quist, Rotterdam . . . 140524
Quitard, Pierre, Bazainville . . . 061242
Quittenbaum, Askan, Hamburg . . . 071310
Quittenbaum, Askan, München . . . 121541
Quivrin, Olivier, Etaples . . . 062814
Quixotics Gallery, Omaha . . . 118720
Qun-Yi, Singapore . . . 109856
Quorn Mill Museum, Quorn . . . 001421
Quorn Pine, Quorn . . . 086321, 131401
Quorum, Madrid . . . 110601
Quorum Art Gallery, Bogotá . . . 098187
Qurieus, Almelo . . . 077731
Qurm Museum, Qurm . . . 031354
Qurum Design, Seeb . . . 079522
Qusaibati, Mohammed Adib, Damascus . . . 083074
QUT Art Museum and Old Government House, Brisbane . . . 000843
Qutb Shahi Museum, Hyderabad . . 022161
Qvartinge Antik, Mariefred . . . 081882
R-Art, Praha . . . 060155
R E W Antiguidades, Rio de Janeiro 058640
R & F Antiques, Houston . . . 089184
R. Galerie, Český Krumlov . . . 098349
R & K Woodworks, Virginia Beach . 133012
R & Kim's Art Gallery, San Jose . . . 119862
R M Studio Gallery, Toronto . . . 097361
R & R Antiques, Fresno . . . 088917
R & R Antiques, Jolimont . . . 056024
R & R Auction, Cincinnati . . . 122860
R & R Coins, San Jose . . . 092932
R & R Galerie, Berlin . . . 102017
R & R Restoration, New York . . . 132515
R & S of Jacksonville, Jacksonville . 116539
R & T International, New York . . . 132516
Ra, Amsterdam . . . 107785
Ra del Rey, Madrid . . . 110602
RA Magazine, London . . . 136262
Råå Museum för Fiske och Sjöfart, Råå . . . 036541
Raab, Berlin . . . 102018
Raab, Helene, Fulda . . . 070919, 102910
Raab, I., Neustadt an der Weinstraße . . . 073032
Raab, Josef, München . . . 072825, 126438
Raab, Dr. M., München . . . 139535
Raabe-Haus, Braunschweig . . . 016391
Raabjerg, Folmer, København . . . 060370
Raad, Jan de, 's-Hertogenbosch . . 078529
Raadts & Godecke, Wesel . . . 074355
Raahen Museo, Raahe . . . 010014
Raaijmakers, Marijke, Nijmegen . . . 078661
Raasay Heritage Museum, Kyle . . . 039915
Raasch, D., Landsberg am Lech . . . 103824
Raasi, Chennai . . . 105636
Rabah, A., Gießen . . . 125730
Rabah, Salma, Damascus . . . 083075
Rábaközi Múzeum, Kapuvár . . . 021754
Rabasova, Rakovník . . . 098499
Rabasová, Kateřina, Praha . . . 098486
Rabb, Murphy, Chicago . . . 115536
Rabe, Barsbüttel . . . 101739
Der Rabe, Frankfurt am Main . . . 139095
Der Rabe, Hamburg . . . 139205
Rabe, Norderstedt . . . 126555
Rabe Verlag Zürich, Zürich . . . 135097
Rabeez, Riyadh . . . 140945
Rabekk Museum, Moss . . . 031036
Rabel, Monaco . . . 077622
Rabelaise, Nice . . . 138259
Rabenou, Yris, New York . . . 091172
Rabenschwarz, Braunschweig . . . 138931
Rabi, London . . . 085625
Rabier, Bruxelles . . . 058065
Rabigal, Nürnberg . . . 104488
Rabindra Bharati Museum, Kolkata 022225
Rabindra Bhavan Art Gallery, Delhi . 022095
Rabindra Bhavana, Santiniketan . . . 022327
Rabisch, Helmut Otto, Dresden . . . 125507
Rabourdin & Choppin de Janvry, Paris . . . 121189
Rabrooha, Ottawa . . . 059049
Rabu, Rémi-Claude, Paris . . . 124789
Rabun & Claiborne, New York . . . 091173
Rabus, Katrin, Bremen . . . 102255
Raby, John H., Bradford . . . 122429
Raby Castle, Darlington . . . 039207
Raccolata Comunale G.C. Corsi, Cantiano . . . 023634
Raccolta Alberto della Ragione e Collezioni del Novecento, Firenze . . . 024201
Raccolta Archeologica, Narni . . . 024928
Raccolta Archeologica, Scheggia . . 025839
Raccolta Archeologica, Terni . . . 026013
Raccolta Archeologica, Tolentino . . 026039
Raccolta Archeologica Alberto Pisani Dossi, Corbetta . . . 023961
Raccolta Archeologica e Paleontologica, Corciano . . . 023964
Raccolta Archeological, Bevagna . . 023390
Raccolta Civica, Città di Castello . . 023898
Raccolta Civica d'Arte Contemporanea, Molfetta . . . 024777
Raccolta Civiche di Storia, Albino . . 023154
Raccolta Comunale, Acquasparta . . 023117
Raccolta Comunale, Celenza Valfortore . . . 023787
Raccolta Comunale, Palazzo del Comune, Sigillo . . . 025896
Raccolta Comunale d'Arte, Frontone 024254
Raccolta d'Arte, Cattedrale, Città della Pieve . . . 023891
Raccolta d'Arte, Oratorio Santissima Crocifisso, Roccalbegna . . . 025457
Raccolta d'Arte C. Lamberti, Codogno . . . 023921
Raccolta d'Arte Contemporanea R. Pastori, Calice Ligure . . . 023584
Raccolta d'Arte della Provincia, Modena . . . 024767
Raccolta d'Arte e Archeologia, Piazza Armerina . . . 025218
Raccolta d'Arte Pagliara, Napoli . . . 024923
Raccolta d'Arte Sacra, Figline Valdarno . . . 024127
Raccolta d'Arte Sacra, Scarperia . . 025838
Raccolta d'Arte Ubaldiana, Piandimeleto . . . 025214
Raccolta d'Arte Votiva, Cesena . . . 023819
Raccolta dei Padri Passionisti, Paliano . . . 025098
Raccolta della Chiesa di Santa Maria Maggiore, Alatri . . . 023144
Raccolta dell'Avifauna delle Marche, Montefortino . . . 024844
Raccolta dell'Avifauna Lombarda, Arosio . . . 023254
Raccolta delle Piastrelle di Ceramica, Sassuolo . . . 025814
Raccolta dell'Opera del Duomo, Oristano . . . 025010
Raccolta di Cose Montesine, Montese . . . 024865
Raccolta di Fisarmoniche d'Epoca, Camerano . . . 023597
Raccolta di Fossili Francesco Angellotti, Ostra . . . 025037
Raccolta di Ingegneria Navale, Università di Genova, Genova . . . 024329
Raccolta di Opere d'Arte, Palazoo Comunale, Solarolo . . . 025910
Raccolta di Sant'Urbano, Apiro . . . 023221
Raccolta di Scienze Naturali, Vicenza . . . 026313
Raccolta di Vasi da Farmacia, Roccavaldina . . . 025460
Raccolta E Guatelli, Collecchio . . . 023928
Raccolta Etnografica, Cerreto di Spoleto . . . 023799
Raccolta Etnografica, Roseto Capo Spulico . . . 025598
Raccolta Etnografica, Vallo di Nera . 026199
Raccolta Etnografica del Centro Studi Pugliesi, Manfredonia . . . 024598
Raccolta Etnografica della Civiltà Contadina, San Giorgio Piacentino . . . 025686
Raccolta Guatelli, Ozzano Taro . . . 025043
Raccolta Judica, Palazzolo Acreide . 025077
Raccolta Kalefati, Oria . . . 025006
Raccolta Lapidaria Capitolina, Roma . . . 025583
Raccolta Memoria e Tradizioni Religiose, Serramanna . . . 025863

Raccolta Naturalistica, Tagliolo Monferrato 025983
Raccolta Ornitologica F. Stazza, Tempio Pausania 026000
Raccolta Osservatorio di Apicoltura Giacomo Angeleri, Pragelato 025350
Raccolta Paleontologica e Preistorica, ex Chiesa di San Domenico, Narni . . 024929
Raccolta Parocchiale, Valpelline . . . 026200
Raccolta Permanente sulla Lavorazione della Canapa, Buonconvento 023547
Raccolta Privata Toraldo di Francia, Tropea 026157
Raccolta Russo-Ortodossa, Merano 024672
Raccolta Storica della Vita Materiale dell'Antico, Altopascio 023182
Raccolta Temporanea, Cosenza . . . 023985
Raccolte d'Arte dell'Ospedale Maggiore di Milano, Milano 024735
Raccolte del Dipartimento di Scienze Radiologiche, Roma 025584
Raccolte dell'Istituto di Clinica delle Malattie Tropicali e Subtropicali, Roma 025585
Raccolte dell'Istituto di Clinica Otorinolaringoiatrica, Roma 025586
Raccolte dell'Istituto di Clinica Urologica, Roma 025587
Raccolte di Palazzo Tursi, Genova . 024330
Raccolte Frugone Villa Grimaldi-Fassio, Genova 024331
Race Fan Depot, Austin 087607
Racemotormuseum Lexmond, Lexmond 029866
Racers, Ricky, Fresno 088918
Rachana Open Air Museum, Rachana 027820
Rachel, Matthias, Heildelberg 071477
Rachel Carson Homestead, Springdale 048281
Rachel Kay Shuttleworth Textile Collections, Padiham 040668
Rachela, Kraków 079651
Rachel's, Houston 089185
Rachinger, Paul, Dießen am Ammersee 102366
Racht, Judiith, Chicago 115537
Rachtian, Shahla, Venezia 076967
Racim, Mohamed, Alger 094046
Racine, Bruxelles 133276
Racine, José, Lonrai 063993
Racine Heritage Museum, Racine . . 047306
Racines Architecturales, Casablanca 077671
Les Racines du Ciel, Rouen 101121
Racines et l'Oeil, Bruxelles 096248
Racional Moveis e Decoracoes, Rio de Janeiro 058641
Rack, Anne & Jürgen, Bad Orb 069352
Rackam, Paris 138531
Rackey, Joachim, Bad Honnef 101661
Rackstadmuseet, Arvika 036200
Racó del Colleccionista, Barcelona . 141001
Racourt, de, Bruxelles 058066
Raczeck, Peter, New York 118319
Rada Galerii České Republiky, Praha 052839
Radar-Sei, Bari 135947
Radbrook Culinary Museum, Shrewsbury 041021
Radcliffe, J., Hastings 084619
Radda, Dr. B., Klagenfurt . 057111, 123400
Råde Bygdetun, Råde 031127
Radecke, Inge von, Waldshut-Tiengen 074262
Radek-Rynkiewicz, Ewa, Łódź 109019
Rademacher, Bad Nauheim 101677
Rademacher, Hans-Werner, Olpe . . 126594
Rademacher, Jörg, Leer 072180
Rademachersmedjorna, Eskilstuna . 036254
Radermacher, Katrin, Laudenbach, Bergstraße 126176
Radermacher, Mara M., Rheinbach . 104746
Radermacher, Wolfgang, Kleve 071877
Radermacher, Wolfgang, Kleve 071878
Radetzky & Co., Wien 057533
Radetzky-Gedenkstätte Heldenberg, Kleinwetzdorf 002151
Radford University Art Museum, Radford 047307
Radgowska, Jolanta, Michałowice . 129056
Radial Access, Cincinnati 088272
Radice, Anna, Milano 075835
Radicke, Jutta, Sankt Augustin 104810
Radico, Cairo 060465
Radin, Bairnsdale 094190
Radinger, Rud & Fritz, Scheibbs . . . 137259
Radio Amateur Museum, Reusel . . . 030057
Radio and Television Museum, Šiauliai Aušros Museum, Šiauliai 027857
Radio- en Speelgoed Museum, Onstwedde 029993
Rádió és Televízió Múzeum, Diósd . 021713
Radio- ja TV-Museo, Lahti 009788
Radio Matterhorn Museum, Zermatt 037748
Radio- og Motorcykel Museet, Stubbekøbing 009120
Radio Ranch, Austin 087608
Radio-Television Museum, Bowie . . 042364
Radiomuseet i Göteborg, Göteborg . 036302
Radiomuseet i Jönköping, Jönköping 036362
Radiomuseum, Bad Bentheim 015655
Radiomuseum, Berneck 036942
Radiomuseum, Borculo 029331
Radiomuseum, Grödig 017546
Radiomuseum, Rottenburg an der Laaber 019929
Radiomuseum, Waldbronn 020631
Radionica Duše, Beograd 109718
Radius Gallery, Saint Paul 119306
Radix Gallery, Phoenix 118889
Radley, Boo, Los Angeles 089887
Radloff, Horst, Wismar 074451
Radman, Barbara, Witney 142161
Radmuseum anno dazumal, Altmünster 001684
Radnor House, Grampound 084493
Radnorshire Museum, Llandrindod Wells 040049
Radstädter Museumsverein, Radstadt 002491
Radtke, Dagmar, Berlin 125278
Radua Miralles, Maria Rosa, Palma de Mallorca 110698
Raduga, Moskva 140916
Radulescu, Paul, Paris 124790
Raduno Invernale di Antiquariato e Modernariato, Baganzola 093788
Radwan, Poznań 109061
Radwin, Jackie, San Antonio 092567
Radzuweit, H. & M., Westerland . . .074370, 105228
Rae, Dennis, San Francisco 119770
Rae, Dorian, Vancouver 097519
Rae, Jan, San Diego 132855
Rae, Jan, Virginia Beach 133013
Rae, Peter, Dunedin 108446
Rae, Peter, Dunedin 108447
Rae-Smith, London 085626, 113849
Rääkkylän Kotiseutumuseo, Rääkkylä 010015
Raeantiik, Tallinn 060486, 137919
Raeber, Luzern 135047
Räber, Alexander E., Zürich 112165
Räber, Alexander E., Zürich 112166, 135098
Räch, Judith, Gönnheim 071025
Raecke, Renate, Pinneberg 134349
Räderscheidt, Gisèle, Köln 103696
Raejuveel, Tallinn 060487
Rælingen Bygdetun, Fjerdingby . . . 030836
Raemaekers, C.J.M., Maastricht . . 128762
Ränkimäen Ulkomuseo, Lapua 009810
Rätisches Museum, Archäologische, historische und volkskundliche Sammlungen Graubündens, Chur . 037021
Raetsch, Barbara & Karl, Potsdam . 104630
Rättviks Konstmuseum och Naturmuseum, Rättvik 036542
Rätzel, Georg, Gießen . . . 070991, 102953
Raevangla Fotomuuseum, Tallinna Linnamuuseum, Tallinn 009411
Rafael, New York 091174
Rafael, Teheran 074847
Rafanelli, Fabio, Genova 106105
Rafanelli, Luca, Firenze 127398
Rafelman, Marcia, Toronto 097362
Rafer, Aline, Saint-Étienne 067463
Raff, Erwin, Denkendorf 125452
Raffael-Verlag, Ittigen 135027
Raffaelli, Giordano, Milano 106294
Raffaello, Providence 119087
Raffan & Kelaher, Leichardt 120602
Raffenel, Jean-Pierre, Domagné . . . 062701
Raffety & Walwyn, London 085627
Raffin, Jean-François, Paris 066453
Raffles, Singapore 109857, 121974
Raft Artspace, Parap 095055
Rag and Bone Books, Minneapolis . 142590
Ragailong Museum, Imphal 022173
Råger's Antik, Malmö 081878
Rageth, Jürg, Riehen 111842
Ragged School Museum, London . . 040265
Raggedy, Anne, Oklahoma City 091528
Ragici, Dr. Luigi, Milano 075836
Ragini Art Village, Lalitpur 107605
Ragione e Sentimento, Roma 076634
Raglan and District Museum, Raglan 030585
Raglan Dealers, Raglan 079225
Raglan Gallery, Cooma 094429
Raglan Gallery, Manly 094782
Raglan's Right Up My Alley, Raglan 079226
Ragley Hall, Alcester 038470
La Ragnatela, Milano 075837
La Ragnatela, Roma 076635, 128171
Ragona, Gioacchino, Palermo 076173
Ragot, Jones, Paris 066454
Ragtime, Bari 075028
Ragusa, Valerio, Padova 076107
Raguseo, Edward, New York 091175
Rah-Coco, Providence 092046
Raha- ja Mitalikokoelma, Helsinki . 009562
Rahäuser, H., Breisach am Rhein . . 070001
Rahardt, Mike, Leipzig 126196
Rahbarnia, Ahmad, San Marino . . . 129255
Rahic, A., Unlingen 074158
Al-Rahiq, Damascus 083076
Rahm-Nebling, Monika, Kaiserslautern 071684
Rahmanan, New York 091176
Rahmen und Bilder, Schwaz 095756
RahmenArt, Hamburg 103210
Rahn, C., Berlin 069731
Rahr West Art Museum, Manitowoc 045638
Raible, Stuttgart 074002, 105005
Raible, Aloys, Ellwangen . 070543, 102614
Raicri, Preto, Belo Horizonte 096483
Raicri, Preto, Belo Horizonte 096484
Raigné, Raymond, Fourcès 062931
Raike, Tucson 093260
Rail Transport Museum, Bassendean 000772
Railco Museum, Ravenshoe 001422
Railings Gallery, London 113850
Railroad and Heritage Museum, Temple 048523
Railroad House Historical Museum, Sanford 047942
Railroad Memories, Denver 088727
Railroad Museum of Long Island, Riverhead 047453
Railroad Museum of Pennsylvania, Strasburg 048394
Railroad Sales Agent, Milwaukee . . 090319
Railroad St Antiques, Louisville . . . 132303
Railroader's Memorial Museum, Altoona 041672
Rail's End Gallery, Haliburton 005564
Railway Age, Crewe 039175
Railway and Forestry Museum, Prince George 006207
Railway Bizarre, Ringwood 056532
The Railway Exposition, Covington . 043199
Railway Heritage Network, Linden . 045323
Railway Museum, Livingstone 049569
Railway Museum, Ravenglass 040799
Railway Preservation Society of Ireland, Whitehead 041372
Railway Square Antique Centre, Toowoomba 056724
Railway Station Gallery, Pomona . . 095078
Railway Station Museum, Castlegar 005235
Railway Station Museum, Uitenhage 034766
Railway Station Museum, Wonthaggi 001630
Railway Village Museum, Swindon . 041177
Railways to Yesterday, Rockhill Trolley Museum, Rockhill Furnace 047503
Railworld, Peterborough 040701
Raimbourg, Thierry, Barentin 061205
Raimo, Antonio, Atlanta . . 087517, 114916, 142208
Raimondi, Vincenzo, Roma 128172
Raimondi di Pettinaroli, Milano 106295
Raimondo, Guglielmo, Palermo . . . 106440
Raimund-Gedenkstätte, Gutenstein 001994
Raimundo Requixa, Maria Concepcion, Alicante 080766
Rain Dog Books, Chicago 142298
Raiņa Literatūras un Mākslas Vēstures Muzejs, Rīga 027762
Raiņa Memorālais Muzejs Jasmuiža, Aizkalne 027654
Raiņa Muzejs Tadenava, Tadaine . . 027781
Raiņa un Aspazijas Memoriālā Vasarnīca, Jūrmala 027699
Rainbird Art Gallery, Montville 094873
Rainbow Art, Shanghai 097940
Rainbow Art, Tampa 120063
Rainbow Art Expo, New York 118320
Rainbow Arts Gallery, Singapore . . . 109858
Rainbow Books, Brighton 141440
Rainbow Books, Wellington 140681
Rainbow Fine Art, New York 118321
Rainbow Gallery, Utting 105099
Raindre, Guy, Paris 066455
Raine, Harry, Consett 084076
Paul Rainer & Sabine Hetz, Prien . . 139666
Rainermuseum Salzburg, Salzburg . 002563
Rainforest Arts, Atherton 094180
Rainforest Gallery, Canungra 094371
Rainham Hall, Rainham 040790
Rainhof-Presse, Buchenbach 102279
Rainis and Aspazija Cottage, Majori Jūrmala 027713
Rainis and Aspazija House, Rīga . . . 027763
Rainis Museum, Preiļi 027725
Rainis Museum Tadenava, Jēkabpils 027690
Raintree Aboriginal Art Gallery, Darwin 094461
Raintree Abporiginal Art Gallery, Darwin 055739
Rainy Day Books, Kansas City 142473
Rainy Day Gallery, Penzance 114234
Rainy Hills Historical Society Pioneer Exhibits, Iddesleigh 005631
Rainy River District Women's Institute Museum, Emo 005427
Rais, Carlos J., Buenos Aires 055238
Rais Ali Delvary Museum, Bushehr . 022551
Rait Village Antiques Centre, Rait . . 086323
Raitioliikennemuseo, Helsingin Kaupunginmuseo, Helsinki 009563
Raitz von Frentz, Jürgen Freiherr, Wiesbaden 105277
Raizman, Adolphe, Draguignan 062737, 138084
Raj, Gent 058203
Raj, Gent 058204
Raj, New York 091177
Raja Dinkar Kelkar Museum, Pune . 022310
Rajaju, South Fremantle 095201
Rajalahden Talomuseo, Virrat 010247
Rajamäen Tehtaiden Museo, Nurmijärvi 009916
Rajamuseo, Imatra 009607

Rajcevic, Marinko, Neuwied 073047
Rajesk Chitrakar, Lalitpur 107606
Rajic, Hélène, Genève 082463
Rajkiya Sangrahalaya, Udaipur 022361
Rajoloteca Salvador Miquel, Vallromanes 036014
Rajpol, Warszawa 079778
Rajputana Museum, Ajmer 021997
Rajskij Sad, Moskva 109579
Rakennuskulttuuritalo Toivo ja Korsmanin talo, Pori 009987
Rakhine State Museum, Sitture . . . 029069
Rakhtshuy-Khaneh Museum, Zanjan 022655
Rakiura Museum, Stewart Island . . 030595
Rakkestad Bygdetun, Rakkestad . . 031128
Rákóczi Múzeum, Magyar Nemzeti Múzeum, Sárospatak 021835
Rakow, Johanna, Oberstaufen 104507
Raku, Singapore 109859
Raku Museum, Kyoto 026762
Rakushikan, Museum of Kyoto, Kyoto 026763
Rakvere Linnakodaniku Muuseum, Rakvere 009388
Rakvere Linnus-Muuseum, Rakvere 009389
Rakvere Näitustemaja-Muuseum, Rakvere 009390
Raleigh City Museum, Raleigh 047317
Raleigh Hill's Upholstery, Portland . 132701
Ralf's Antiques, West Hollywood . . 093500
Sri Rallabandi Subbarao Government Museum, Rajahmundry 022317
Rallarmuseet, Moskosel 036487
Ralli Museum, Caesarea 022900
Ralls, Marsha, Washington 120340
Ralls Historical Museum, Ralls 047319
Ralph Allen Memorial Museum, Oxbow 006111
Ralph Foster Museum, College of the Ozarks, Point Lookout 047109
Ralph Milliken Museum, Los Banos 045475
Ralph Waldo Emerson House, Concord 043121
Ram, Rotterdam 108205
Ram, Valencia 081671, 129781
Ram Art, Niš 109734
Ram Mala Museum, Comilla 003098
Ram-mannens Konstgalleri, Malmö 110978
Rama, Bangalore 074781
Rama Antiques, Bangkok 083101
Ramadier, Ludovic, Avignon 061140
Ramage, Christiane, Longpré-Corps-Saints 063985
Ramakers, Den Haag 107948
Ramalhete, Lisboa 121943
Raman Science Centre, Nagpur . . . 022280
Ramani, Utrecht 078815
Ramania Art Emporium, Kathmandu 107597
Rambaud, Gérard, Paris 100791
Rambert, Paris 100792
Rambert, Michel, Lyon 121054
Rambling Rose Antiques, Fort Worth 088879
Rambo Antigüedades, Buenos Aires 055239
Rambourg, Eric, Bordeaux 124142
Le Rameau d'Or, Lyon 138183
Ramee, Washington 120341
Rameix, Christophe, La Celle-Dunoise 063304, 099388
Ramer, Andreas, München 072826
Ramer, Andreas, Schnaitsee 073709
Ramer, Andreas, Seefeld, Oberbayern 073784
Ramex Galerie, Kassel 103517
Ramez, Cairo 060466
Ramge, B., Vaihingen 074179
Rami, Marinella, Bologna 075103
Ramirez, Angel, Miami 117130
Ramirez, Gabriel, Bogotá 123907
Ramirez, M., Phoenix 142768
Ramirez, Mario, Los Angeles 089888, 132277
Ramirez Perez-Lucas, Tomas, Madrid 110603
Ramiro, Madrid 081371
Ramiro, Madrid 081372
Ramiro, Madrid 122066, 141058
Ramiro & Leitão, Lisboa 079997
Ramitscheder-Mühle, Edlbach 001804
Ramkema, Dik, Overveen 140512
Ramla Museum, Ramla 023055
Ramlingappa Lamture Museum, Osmanabad 022286
Rammal, Damascus 083077
Rammelmüller, R., Wels . . 057354, 095782
Rammerscales, Lockerbie 040072
Ramón i Cabrera, Castello de la Plana 081039
Ramón Magsaysay Memorabilia Museum, Manila 031739
Ramona's Antiques, Atlanta 087518
Ramondon, Guéthary 099320
Ramoneda Soler, Maria Rosa, Barcelona 129382
Ramoni, Roberto, Roma 076636
Ramon's Antique Store, Los Angeles 089889
Ramon's Antique Store, West Hollywood 093501
Ramos, Dário, Porto 109394
Ramos, Noémio Santos, Faro 109253
Ramos Iznata, Jose Luis, Málaga . . 081430
Ramose, Maastricht 078619
Rampa, Ivano, Pratval 130142
Rampazzo, Luciana, Roma 128173
Rampoldt, Hartmut, Berlin 102019
Rampouch, Jaroslav, Olomouc 060063
Ramrath, Aachen 069098, 101522
Ramsauer, Angela, Geiselhöring . . . 125704
Ramsauer Getreidemühle, Ramsau am Dachstein 002498
Ramsay, John, Vancouver 097520
Ramsay, Roger, Chicago 115538
Ramsay Antiques, London 085628
Ramsay House, Alexandria 041647
Ramsay Museum, Honolulu 044608
Ramsdell, Nowa Nowa 094996
Ramsden Morrison, San Diego 119542
Ramseier, Ernst, Bern 082233
Ramses, Montevideo 087338
Ramsey, Saint Paul 119307
Ramsey, Alan, Darlington 084135
Ramsey, Jeremy, Singapore 109860
Ramsey Center for Arts, Shoreview 048157
Ramsey Garland, Philadelphia 091685
Ramsey House Museum Plantation, Knoxville 045043
Ramsey Rural Museum, Ramsey, Cambridgeshire 040791
Ramseyer, Stéphane, Sion 130178
Ramseyer & Kaelin, Bern 111272
Ramsgate Museum, Ramsgate 040795
Ramunni, Francesco, Bari 075029
Ramzi, Albuquerque 087420
Ramzia, Riyadh 080380
Ran, New York 118322
Ran, Mary, Cincinnati 115655
Ran In-Ting Gallery, Taipei 098081
Ran-In-Ting Museum, Taipei 007376
Rana Museum, Cultural History Department, Mo i Rana 031017
Rana Museum, Natural History Department, Mo i Rana 031018
Ranacher, Maria, Wien 123525
Ranaldi Freschi, Viviane, Lyon 099611
Ranasim Art Gallery, Hyderabad . . . 105711
Ranby Hall, Retford 086350
Ranchetti, Guido, Roma 128174
El Ranchito, Oklahoma City 091529
Rancho Los Alamitos, Long Beach . 045383
Rancho Los Cerritos, Long Beach . . 045384
Ranchu, Michèle & Serge, Manosque 064250
Randaberg Bygdemuseum, Randaberg 031130
Randall, Las Vegas 116642
Randall, San Diego 132856
Randall, Penelope, Woollahra 056876
Randall House Museum, Wolfville . . 006878
Randall Library Museum, Stow 048388
Randall Museum, San Francisco . . 047879
Randee & Co., Salt Lake City 092456
Randel, New York 118323
Randell, Colin, Newcastle 137029
Randelzhofer, Kurt, Ingolstadt 125970
Randers Kunstmuseum, Randers . . 009064
Randier, Henri, Paris 066456
Randolff, Düsseldorf 102541
Randolph, Suzanne, New York 118324
Randolph County Historical Museum, Winchester 049229
Randolph County Museum, Beverly 042191
Randolph Gallery, Edinburgh 113007
Randolph Gallery, Edinburgh 113008
Randolph Historical Society Museum, Randolph 047329
Random House Publishing, London . 135254
Randy's Antiques, Columbus 088432
Randy's Antiques, Saint Paul 092388
Randy's Auction Gallery, Norfolk . . . 123025
Ranfurly Antiques, Auckland 078975
Rangau-Handwerkermuseum, Markt Erlbach 018840
Rangau-Heimathaus, Cadolzburg . . 016533
Range Antiques, Toowoomba 056725
Rangiora Museum, Rangiora 030586
Rangpur Archaeological Museum, Rangpur 003117
Rani Laxmi Bai Palace Sculpture Collection, Jhansi 022189
Ranieri & Tenti, Milano 127661
Rank, Piotr, Bremen 125392
Rankin, George, London 085629
Rankin, Piers, London 085630
Daphne Rankin & Ian Conn, London 085631
Rankin House Museum, Miramichi . 005882
Rankin House State Memorial, Ripley 047442
Rankin Museum, Ellerbe 043675
Rankin Museum, Rankin 047330
Rannacher, Gertrude, Wien 137357
Rannarootsi Muuseum, Haapsalu . . 009359
Rannikkotykistömuseo, Helsinki . . . 009564
Rano, Cairo 060467
Ransberger, Fort Worth . . 088880, 122897
Ransdell, Alan C., Jacksonville 089453
Ransom, Mark, London 085632
Ransom, Mark, London 085633
Ransom County Historical Society Museum, Fort Ransom 043968
Rantasalmen Museo, Rantasalmi . . 010018
Rantsilan Kotiseutumuseo, Rantsila 010019
Ranuan Pappila- ja Pitäjämuseo, Ranua 010020
Ranz, Hans-Jörg, München 126439
Raoli, Milena, Roma 076637
Raos, Peter, North Shore 108528
Raphael, Birmingham 115126
Raphael, Napier 079169
Raphael, New York 091178
Raphael, New York 091179
Raphael, New York 132517
Raphael et Co, Saint-Ouen 067871
Raphaël's Auctions, Sion 122352
Raphaely, Miami 117131
Rapid City Museum, Rapid City . . . 006237
Rapid Eye Books, Battery Point . . . 136794
Rapin, Philippe, Paris 066457
Rapin, Renée, Corcelles-près-Payerne 111369
Rapinett, Alfred, Siggiewi 128481
Rapisarda, Giovanni, Livorno 075539
Rapisardi, Mario, Nice 124521
Rapp, Gisela & Hermann, Weilrod . . 134450
Rapp, Marianne, Wil 111994
Rapp, Yvonne, Louisville 116963
Rappaport, C.E., Roma 140114
Rappard, Bielefeld 102127
Rappenegger jun., Rudolf, Pentling . 126616
Rappo, Georges, Schaffhausen 082799
Rapsodija, Sankt-Peterburg 080322
Rapuano, Antonio, Napoli 076032
Rapuano, Pasquale, Napoli 076033
Raque Montagut, Barcelona 080914, 110237
Rara-Avis, Portland 091996
Rare and Racy, Sheffield . 131476, 142063
Rare Art, New York 118325
Rare Books, Leeds 141713
Rare Coin Buyers of Virginia, Richmond 092097
Rare Coin Company of America, Chicago 088154
Rare Coin Galleries of Seattle, Seattle 093052
Rare Collection, Hong Kong 059689
Rare Find Country Antiques, Metford 056218
Rare Finds, Memphis 090102
Rare Finds, New Orleans 090605
Rare Old Times, Brighton, South Australia 055544
Rare Oriental Book Company, Aptos 142193
Rare Posters, New York . . 118326, 123008
Rare Posters at DBA Art Wise, Brooklyn 135338
Rare Prints, Austin 087609
Rare Rabbit, Cincinnati 088273
Rare Reads, Atlanta 142209
Rare & Unusual, Long Beach 089652
Rarebit Galeria de Artes, São Paulo 096686
Rarebooks Dotcom, Brisbane 136822
Rarekiek, Amsterdam 077942
Raridade, Lisboa 079998
Raritäten-Kabinett, Cottbus 138969
Raritätensammlung Bruno Gebhardt, Zwönitz 021095
Rariteiten- en Ambachtenmuseum 't Krekelhof, Koksijde 003553
Raritet, Moskva 080260
Raritet, Murmansk 080279
Raritet Antikvarno-juvelirnyj Salon, Samara 080287
Raritet Rosvuzdizajn, Sankt-Peterburg 109644
Rarities Bazar, Praha 060156
Ras-al-Tin Palace Museum, Ras-al-Tin 009344
Rasan, Toronto 059273
Rasch, Bramsche 133835
Rasch, G., Wuppertal 105359
Rasch, Mario, Altenburg, Thüringen 069150
Rasch, Roger, Bergfelde 125154
Rasche, Stefan, Münster 104375
Raschella, Vincent, Montréal 058995
Raschoffer, Jacques, Cannes 061953
Rase, Lothar, Saarbrücken 073645
Rasen, Kunitachi 106888
Rasha, Damascus 083078
Rashi, Amsterdam 140334
Rashid, Manama 057644
Rashid Al-Oraifi Museum, Manama 003095
Rasht Museum, Rasht 022591
Rashtriya Lalit Kala Kendra, Kolkata 105744
Rasmus, København 098582
Rasmus, Alain, Besse-et-Saint-Anastaise 061402
Rasmussen, Erik, Ballerup 060212
Rasmussen, Erik, Smørum 060403
Rasmussen, Inge, København 060371
Rasmussen, Kent, København 060372
Rasmussen Art Gallery, Pacific Union College, Angwin 041726
Rasmusson, Claes Göran, Stockholm 122259
Rasoylis, San Francisco 119771
Rasoylis, San Francisco 119772
Raspail, Richard, Saint-Ouen 067872
Raspante, Marcello, Palermo 076174
Rassan Arabzadeh Carpet Museum, Teheran 022639
Raßbach, Christa, Loxstedt 072303
Rassbach, H., Bremerhaven 070055
Rassegna Attrezzi e Oggetti del Passato, Belluno 023364
Rassegna d'Arte, Napoli 135948
Rast, Bielefeld 069838
Rastrell, Valencia 081672

El Rastrillo, Bilbao 080987
El Rastro, Logroño 081185
El Rastro, Medellín 059938
El Rastro, Montevideo 087339
Il Rastro, Padova 076108
El Rastro, Palermo 076175
Rastro Crystty's, Valencia 081673
El Rastro Sur, Málaga 081431
Rasulo, Clodomira, Napoli 076034
Rat für Formgebung - German Design Council, Frankfurt am Main 053547
Le Rat Mort, Oostende 096402
Ratcliff, G.T., Kelvedon 084823
Ratel, Michèle, Poses 066962, 101046
Rath, Robert, Salzburg 057274
Rath, Sonja, Hamburg 071311
Ráth György Museum, Iparművészeti Múzeum, Budapest 021691
Elke Rath-Otto & Sebastian Ickrath, Marsberg 104038
Rath-Stephan, G., Hünfelden 071587
Rathaus Galerie, Euskirchen 102719
Rathaus-Galerie, Liestal 111646
Rathaus-Galerie, Kunstamt Reinickendorf, Berlin 016160
Rathausgalerie, Aalen 101535
Rathausgalerie, Bad Harzburg 015713
Rathausgalerie, Castrop-Rauxel 016544
Rathausgalerie, Sankt Veit an der Glan 002629
Rathausgalerie, Waidhofen an der Ybbs 002803
Rathausgalerie der Stadt Brühl, Brühl, Rheinland 016469
Rathausgalerie München, München 019106
Rathausgalerie Munster, Munster 019166
Rathausgalerie Vellmar, Vellmar 020573
Rathausmuseum, Sempach Stadt 037553
Rathausmuseum Nieder-Ohmen, Mücke 019004
Rathauspassage Antiquariat, Hamburg 103211
Rathaussammlung, Stein am Rhein 037608
Rathbone Law, Chichester 083977
Rathgeber, Karl-Heinz, Waltershausen 126965
Rathgeber, R., Ludwigshafen am Rhein 072316
Rathgen-Forschungslabor, Staatliche Museen zu Berlin - Stiftung Preußischer Kulturbesitz, Berlin 053548
Rathgory Transport Museum, Dunleer 022782
Rathjen, A., Lägerdorf 072112
Rathke, Dr. Ewald, Frankfurt am Main 102812
Ratier Frères, Olemps 065262
Ratliff, Las Vegas 089601
Ratnapura National Museum, Ratnapura 036143
Raton Museum, Raton 047337
Ratsch, Patrick, Potsdam 126653
Ratsuväkimuseo, Etelä-Karjalan Museo, Lappeenranta 009805
Rattlesnake Museum, Albuquerque 041622
Ratton Hourdé, Philippe, Paris 066458
Ratton & Ladrière, Paris 066459
Ratton & Ladrière, Paris 066460
Ratvolden, Røros 031149
Ratz, J. & B., Grafenau, Württemberg 139151
Ratzki, Mario, Boston 087839
Rau, Hans-Gerd, Rottenburg am Neckar 126747
Rau, Klaus-J., Münster bei Dieburg 126514
Rau, Peter, Staig 126823
Rau, Regina, München 126440
Rau, Walter, Düsseldorf 133896
Raub, Brest 099031
Raubach, Sankt Gallen 082786, 111874, 130166
Rauber, Ludwig, Vechta 105108
Raubiet, Philippe, Lille 124323
Raucci, Oreste, Roma 076638, 140115
Rauch, Hans Dieter, Wien 057534
Rauchfangkehrermuseum, RFK-Innung, Wien 002992
Rauchstubenhaus, Gündorf 001983
Rauchstubenhaus, Sankt Johann im Saggautal 002591
Raud, Christian, Paris 066461
Raudonat-Arndt, Ute, Mörfelden-Walldorf 126328
Raueiser, H., Saarbrücken 139707
Rauguth, Johann, Nürnberg 073114
Rauh, Helmut, Straubing 073940
Rauhaniemen Kotiseutumuseo, Sulkava 010100
Raule, Rolf, Deidesheim 070203
Raum 1, Hofheim am Taunus 103393
Raum Aktueller Kunst, Wien 095925, 133228
Raum für Aktuelle Kunst, Luzern 111701
Raum für Kunst, Altstätten 111119
Raum für Kunst und Kultur, Gummersbach 071149
Raum und Kunst, Kassel 103518
Rauman Antikvaarinen Kirjakauppa, Lappi 137977
Rauman Kirjasieppo, Rauma 137984
Rauman Museo, Rauma 010025
Rauman Taidemuseo, Rauma 010026
Raumkunst, Goch 102965
Raumschüssel, Heinz, Coburg 070148
RaumTraum, Bayreuth 101748
Raunet, Jean-Louis, Moncley 064593
Rauoff, Bin Abdul, Riyadh 080381
Raup, Günter, Bremen 070040
Rauriser Talmuseum, Rauris 002507
Rausch, Eva, Mödling 137234
Rausch, Uwe, Frankfurt am Main 102813, 139096
Rauscher, Norbert, Reutlingen 073502
Rautalammin Museo, Rautalampi 010030
Rautatieläiskotimuseo, Kouvola 009747
Rautenstrauch-Joest-Museum, Museum für Völkerkunde, Köln 018337
Rauter, Barcelona 134925
Rauter, Dorli, Bad Kleinkirchheim 137154
Raution Kotiseutumuseo, Rautio 010031
Raux Brothers, Colombo 081768
Rauzada, Alain, Saint-Ouen 067873
Rava & Co, Torino 128347
Ravá, Tobia, Venezia 106775
Ravaioli, Carlo, Bologna 127177
Raval Arte y Diseño, Zaragoza 110889
Ravalli County Museum, Hamilton 044396
Ravan, Atlanta 087519
Ravanel, Nathalie, Firenze 127399
Ravelingien, T., Gent 058205
Ravelli, Luigi, Brescia 127231
Ravelo e Hijos, Catalina de, Bogotá 059854
Raven, Minneapolis 117300
Raven, Portland 091997
Raven, San Francisco 119773
Raven Press Gallery, Dunvegan 112973
Raven & the Bear, Vancouver 097521
Ravenel, Saint Pierre 109667
Ravenna, Seattle 143006
Raven's Den Native Art Gallery, Vancouver 097522
Raven's Nest Antiques, Wellington 079342
Ravenswood, Chicago 142299
Raverty's Motor Museum, Echuca 001007
Ravestijn, Amsterdam 077943
Ravet, Marc, Boiscommun 061541
Raveyre, Antoine, Saint-Étienne 067464
Ravier, Joëlle & Daniel, Corps-Nuds 062485
Ravindra Art Palace, Delhi 105678
Ravintolamuseo, Lahti 009789
Ravizza, Norbert, Stuttgart 074003
Ravmuseet, Varde Museum, Oksbøl 009055
Ravon, Ph., Saintes 068088, 138610
Ravon, Xavier & Philippe, Dax 062607
Raw Art UK, Chester 112853
Raw Deluxe, Bristol 083750
Raw Vision, Radlett 136263
Rawhide Old West Museum, Scottsdale 048059
Rawls Museum Arts, Courtland 043196
Al-Rawwas, Mohammed Mwafaq, Damascus 083079
Ray, Tokyo 107094
Ray & Co, Harry, Welshpool 122742
Ray, Janette, York 142179
Ray, Simon, London 113851
Ray E. Powell Museum, Grandview 044283
Ray & Scott, Saint Sampson 086478, 131445
Raya, Singapore 109861
Raydon, New York 118327
Rayment, Derek & Tina, Barton, Cheshire 083407, 130344
Raymond, Cincinnati 115656
Raymond, Laurence, Persac 066774
Raymond Avenue Gallery, Saint Paul 119308
Raymond Chow Art Gallery, Vancouver 006706
Raymond M. Alf Museum of Paleontology, Claremont 042939
Raymond's Design Studio, New York 132518
Raymore Pioneer Museum, Raymore 006238
Raymundo's Art Gallery, Long Beach 116678
Raynalds Mansion, Much Wenlock 086030
Raynaud, Jean, La Roche-sur-Yon 121024
Raynaud, Jean-Louis, Aix-en-Provence 060715
Rayner, Port Macquarie 095095
Rayner, Michael, Cheltenham 141504
Raynham Hall Museum, Oyster Bay 046780
Raynor, Tom, New Orleans 090606
Rayo Rojo, Buenos Aires 136750
Rayon Vert, Nantes 099816
Rayons Verts, Niort 099874
Ray's Antiques, Callington 055603
Ray's Antiques, Chicago 088155
Ray's Hub, Long Beach 089653
Rayuela, Madrid 110604
Rayvec, Dallas 115929
Rayxart, Madrid 110605
Razstavna Galerija, Ljubljana 109980
Razstavna Galerija, Škofja Loka 110005
Razstavni Salon Rotovž, Maribor 034501
Razzano, Mario, Napoli 076035
Razzle Dazzle, Tucson 093261
R.B. Ferguson Museum of Mineralogy, Winnipeg 006858
R.B. Instruments, Mount Eliza 123274
RBM Fine Art Designs, Cincinnati 115657
RB's Settlers Antiques, Ulmarra 056760
R.C., Torino 076861, 128348
RC Arts, Poole 114271
R.C. Associates, Cullompton 084132
RCMP Centennial Celebration Museum, Fairview 005441
RCR Antique and Arts, New York 091180
RCS Libri, Milano 134631
RDS Diffusion, Paris 066462
RE, Praha 123996
Re, Francesco, Napoli 076036
RE-AL Kunstverlag, Nürnberg 134319
Re-Art, Moskva 109580
Re Artú, Padova 076109
Re Find, Cleveland 088354
Re & Mi, Paris 066463
Re Nova, Warszawa 129107
R.E. Olds Transportation Museum, Lansing 045165
Re-Soul, Seattle 093053
R.E. Stevenson Museum, Colenso 034590
Re-Vu, Lille 063867
Rea, Marcia, Freeman's Reach 094567
Rea Museum, Murfreesboro 046094
Read, Alan, Horncastle 084738
Read, John, Martlesham 085958, 131270
Read, Mike, Saint Ives, Cornwall 086458, 131441
Read Heeler, Echuca 136888
Read it Again Sam, Los Angeles 142518
Reader's Book Shop, Regina 137683
Readers Den, Windsor, New South Wales 137139
Reader's Digest Art Gallery, Pleasantville 047092
Readers Realm, Castle Hill 136854
Readers Rendezvous, Kingston 136966
Readers Rest, Lincoln 141734
Readers Teahouse, Kenmore 136959
Reader's Town, Mar del Plata 136762
Readers World, Birmingham 141418
Reading Abbay Gateway, Reading 040809
Reading Historical Society Museum, Reading 047343
Reading Historical Society Museum, Reading 047348
Reading Matters, Collingwood 136863
Reading Public Museum and Art Gallery, Reading 047347
Read's, Johannesburg 080713
Read's Rare Book Shop, Brisbane 136823
Readsboro Historical Society Museum, Readsboro 047350
Reaktion Books, London 135255
Real, A.M., London 131154
Real-73, Almeria 080772
Real Academia de Bellas Artes de la Purísima Concepción, Valladolid 050738
Real Academia de Bellas Artes de San Carlos, Valencia 050737
Real Academia de Bellas Artes de San Fernando, Museo de la Real Academia de Bellas Artes, Madrid 050726
Real Academia de Bellas Artes de San Telmo, Málaga 050728
Real Academia de Bellas Artes de Santa Isabel de Hungría, Sevilla 050734
Real Academia de Córdoba de Ciencias, Bellas Letras y Nobles Artes, Córdoba 050716
Real Academia de Nobles y Bellas Artes de San Luis, Zaragoza 050740
The Real Art Gallery, Shrewsbury 114433
Real Cartuja, Valldemosa 036010
Real Cartuja de Miraflores, Burgos 035010
Real Casa del Labrador, Aranjuez 034847
Real Fábrica de Tapices, Madrid 035442
Real Monasterio de San Jerónimo, Granada 035260
Real Monasterio de San Juan de la Peña, San Juan de la Peña 035759
Real Monasterio de Santa María de El Puig, El Puig de Santa María 035685
Real Mother Goose, Portland 119043
Real Mother Goose, Portland 119044
Real Museo Mineralogico, Napoli 024924
Real Pinacoteca, Tres Casas 035954
Real Pottery, Tring 136264
Real Reviews, Fort Worth 088881
Real TART Community Gallery, New Plymouth 030554
Real World Computer Museum, Boothwyn 042309
Reale, Francesco, Catania 127275
Reali Arte Contemporanea, Brescia 106005
Realidade Galeria de Arte, Rio de Janeiro 096641
Die Realismusgalerie, Fuldatal 102911
Realities Gallery, Toorak 095342
Realizations, New York 118328
Really Cool Stuff, Portland 091998
Really Good Stuff, Portland 091999
Rearasa, Zamora 081727, 129795
Reart, Banská Bystrica 129268
Reart, Bratislava 080610, 129272
Reart, Poprad 129281
ReArte, Zürich 112167
Réaux, Yves, Paris 100793
Rebassa Guardiola, Gabriel, Palma de Mallorca 081491
Rebbaumuseum am Bielersee, Ligerz 037268
Rebecca Gallery, Toronto 097363
Rebecca Nurse Homestead, Danvers 043294
Rebel, Marco, Luzern 130106
Rebel, Walter, Hamburg 139206

Rebelo, Antonio Silva, Lisboa 079999
Rebelo, Nuno A. Costa, Braga 079813
Rebensburg, Kirsten & Marcus, Bad Kreuznach 125105
Rebillot, Jean-Louis, Nohant-Vic . . 065215
Reblandmuseum, Baden-Baden . . . 015852
Rebok, T.H., Observatory 129295
Rebolledo Cuerno, Maria Antonia, Getxo 081118
Rebollini, Agnese, Genova 075500
Rebollo, Pepe, Zaragoza 110890
Reborn Antiques, Port Adelaide . . . 056471
Reborn Antiques, West Hollywood . 093502
Reboucas, Heriberto C., Fortaleza . 058478
Reboul, Jean-Michel, Paris 066464
Reboul, Patrice, Paris 066465
Rebound, Dunedin 140625
Rebound, Pittsburgh 091853
Rebourg, Claude, Neufchâteau 064981
Rebours, Johann, Sainte-Croix-sur-Aizier 068053
Rebuffel, San Francisco 092869
Rebuffel, Jean-Marie, Nice 065135
Rebus, Hamburg 103212
Rebuttini, Sergio, Modena 127742
Le Recamier, Bruxelles 058067
Récamier, Nice 065136
Recasens Art, Barcelona 110238
Recchi, Nicoló, Roma 076639
Recchia, Giuseppe, Torino 128349
Rech, Almine, Paris 100794
Rech, Manfred, Haan 071158, 103041
Rechberger, Rainer, Altmünster . . . 137149
Rechem, Flandre van, Lille 124324
Recherche du Passé, Sarzeau 138614
Rechnermuseum der Gesellschaft für wissenschaftliche Datenverarbeitung, Göttingen 017471
Rechnitzer, Berlin 125279
Rechsteiner, Franz, Appenzell 082093
Recht-Ullrich, Wilhelm, Hamburg . . 139207
Rechtshistorisches Museum, Karlsruhe 018168
Recidro, Manny, San Diego 142913
Recinto Casa Benito Juárez, Saltillo 028703
Reciprocity, Dallas 115930
Reck, Roswitha von der, München . 072827
Recke, Hilmar, Magdeburg 072375, 126251
Recker, H., Warendorf 074278
Recker, Michael, Mainz 126264
Reckermann, Winfried & Heidi, Köln 103697
Reckhaus, Rheda-Wiedenbrück . . . 104743
Recknagel, Weiden, Oberpfalz 105173
Recktenwald, L., Eppelborn 070574
Reckturm, Stadtmuseum Wiener Neustadt, Wiener Neustadt 003036
Reclaimed, Seattle 093054
Reclam jun., Philipp, Ditzingen 133869
Le Recoin, Voiron 069028
Recollect Dolls Hospital, Burgess Hill 083799, 130482
Recollection-Antiques, Los Angeles 089890
Recollections, Bournemouth 083605
Recollections, Brighton . . 083714, 130449
Recollections, Los Angeles 089891
Recollections, Omaha 091581
Recollections, Poynton 086307
Recollections, Saint Paul 092389
Recollections, Springston . 079245, 128959
Recollections Antiquea, London . . . 085634
Recollections Antiques, Indianapolis 089333
Recon, Dallas 088599
Record Detector, London 085635
Record of the Princeton University Art Museum, Princeton 136614
Record Office for Leicestershire, Leicester and Rutland, Leicester 039978
Recto-Verso, Strasbourg 068331
Rector, Tulsa 120203
Rectory Bungalow Workshop, Bingham 130384
Recuerdos de Bacolod Arts and Antiques, Manila 079566
Recuerdos Gallery, Zamboanga . . . 108860
O' Recuncho, A Coruña 081063
Recupero e Conservazione, Milano . 135949
Les Recyclables, Genève 141254
Red Art Gallery, Nelson . . 108517, 128946
Red Barn Antique Market, Indianapolis 089334
The Red Barn Antiques, Warkworth 079308
Red Barn Auction, Phoenix 123054
Red Barn Mall, Louisville 090020
Red Barn Museum, Morristown . . . 046039
Red Baron Antiques, Atlanta 087520
Red Bay Historic Site, Red Bay 006239
Red Brick Arts Centre and Museum, Edson 005418
Red Bridge Antiques, Providence . . 092047
Red Bridge Books, Kansas City 142477
The Red Bull Gallery, Longnor, Derbyshire 113992
Red Car Gallery, Milwaukee 117217
Red Cedar Gallery, Montréal 097069
Red Centre Art, Coolbinia 055713
Red Chair Antiques, Long Beach . . 089654
Red Cheery Art Gallery, Singapore . 109862
Red Clay State Historical Park, Cleveland 043005
Red Cloud's Auction Barn, Chicago .088156, 122845
Red Corner, Vancouver 059405
Red Deer and District Museum, Red Deer 006242
Red Desert Gallery, Eumundi 094516
Red Door Antiques, Oklahoma City . 091530
Red Door Bookshop, Warragul 137130
Red Door Gallery, Edinburgh 113009
Red Door on Charles Gallery, Launceston 094729
Red Dot, New York 118329
Red Dot Design Museum im Design Zentrum Nordrhein-Westfalen, Essen 017077
Red Dot Gallery, Cowbridge 112907
Red Eagle Gallery, Portland 119045
Red Eye, Chicago 088157
Red Gallery, Fitzroy North 094545
The Red Gallery, Marlow 114063
Red Gallery, Rosebank 110076
The Red Gallery, Thame 114566
Red Gate, Beijing 097675
Red Gate, West Hollywood 093503
Red Geranium, Albuquerque 087421
Red Geranium Shop, Louisville 090021
Red Hat Gallery, Johannesburg 110059
The Red Head Gallery, Toronto 097364
Red Hill Gallery, Red Hill 095118
Red Hill Gallery 141, Red Hill South 095123
Red Hill-Patrick Henry National Memorial, Brookneal 042472
Red Hill Studio Gallery, Telegraph Point 095322
Red House, Singapore 129265
Red House Antiques, Yoxford 087299
The Red House Antiques Centre, York 087294
Red House Books, San Francisco . . 142962
Red House Gallery, Adelong 094122
Red House Glass Cone Museum, Stourbridge 041128
Red House Museum, Gomersal . . . 039601
Red House Museum and Art Gallery, Christchurch 039087
Red Indian Art Deco, Toronto 059274
Red Kiln Connection, Salt Lake City 119365
Red Lake Museum, Red Lake 006243
Red Lantern, San Francisco 092870
Red Latern Antiques, Sacramento . 092177
The Red Lion Antiques, London . . . 085636
Red Lion Antiques, Petworth 086258
Red Lodge, Bristol 038867
Red Lodge Antiques, Screveton . . . 086525
Red Mansion, London 113852
Red Mill Museum Village, Clinton . . 043017
Red Mountain Museum, Birmingham 042224
Red Oak Gallery, Winnipeg 097603
The Red Pale, Eton 113034
The Red Peach, Singapore 080547
Red Peach Gallery, Hawkes Bay . . . 108472
Red Quill Antiques, Virginia Beach . 093364
Red Rag Gallery, Stow-on-the-Wold 114506
Red Ramia, Myrtleford 056309
Red River and Northern Plains Regional Museum, West Fargo 049073
Red River Art Gallery, Ha Noi 120482
Red River Book Shop, Winnipeg . . . 137743
Red River Gallery, Ha Noi 120483
Red River Historical Society Museum, Clay City 042959
Red River Valley Museum, Vernon . 048767
Red Rock Art, Kununurra 094711
Red Rock Museum, Church Rock . . 042913
Red Room, Lyon 099612
Red Room Antiques, Kansas City . . 089516
Red Rooster Antique Mall, Las Vegas 089602
Red Rooster Antique Mall, Las Vegas 089603
Red Rose Antique, Saint-Ouen 067874
Red Rose Antiques, Vancouver 059406
Red Rose Vintage Clothing, Indianapolis 089335
Red Sand Art Gallery, Alice Springs 094146
Red Sand Art Gallery, Ti Tree 095336
Red Sea Maritime Museum, Eilat . . 022905
Red Shop, Wolverhampton 087213
Red Sofa, Pittsburgh 091854
Red Star, Waikato 079296
Red Star International, Prahran . . . 137063
Red Tulip Art and Glass, Ottawa . . . 097115
Red Wagon Antiques, Nashville . . . 090481
Reda, Alexandria 060422
Redakcja Ośrodka Dokumentacji Zabytków, Warszawa 134863
Redaud, Anne, Nery 064978
Redback Art Gallery, Gordon Park . . 094599
Redbud, Houston 116394
Redcliff Museum, Redcliff 006244
Redcliffe Historical Museum, Redcliffe 001424
Redcoat Soldier Antiques, Sale 056567
Redd, San Diego 119543
Reddel, C., Melle 104057
Redding, Richard, Zürich 083013
Redding Museum of Art and History, Redding 047357
Reddingshuisje, Vliehors-Vlieland . . 030281
Reddingsmuseum Abraham Fock, Hollum 029761
Redecorate, Norwood 056392
Redel, Gordon, Düsseldorf 070427
Redfern, London 113853, 135256
Redford, Robert, Altrincham 083286
Redhill Museum, Redhill 001426
Redin, Uppsala 141189
Reding 41, Málaga 081432
Redington Museum, Waterville 049000
Rediscovered Treasures, San Antonio 092568
Redjala, Mohand, Paris 066466
Redland Museum, Cleveland 000929
Redlands Art Association, Redlands 055002
Redleaf Gallery, Tunbridge Wells . .086950, 114612
Redlitz, E., Konstanz 103764
Redmann Gönne, Berlin 069732
Redmonds, Melbourne 056199
Redningsselskapets Museum, Horten 030910
Redoña Residence Museum, Tacloban 031795
Redondo House, Long Beach 089655
Redpath Museum, Montréal 005948
Redpath Sugar Museum, Toronto . . 006625
Redpaths' Antiques, Newtown, Victoria 056343
Redpoint, Port Kembla 123287
Redrock Gallery, Southbank 095214
Red's Antique Galleries, Denver . . . 088728
Reðsafn Íslands, Reykjavík 021973
Redsky, Charlotte 115309
Reduta, Bratislava 080611
Redwater and District Museum, Redwater 006245
Redwitz, K. Freiin von, Rennertshofen 126714
Redwood County Museum, Redwood Falls 047365
Redwood Library and Athenaeum, Newport 046465
Ree, H., Amsterdam 077944
Reece, New York 118330
Reece, Gordon, London 085637
Reece, James, Salt Lake City 092457
Reed, Allansford 123175
Reed, Alan, Ponteland 114269
Reed, Jim, Birmingham 142240
Reed, Michael, Seattle 093055
Reed Arts, Columbus 115797
Reed Gold Mine, Midland 045849
Reed Gold Mine State Historic Site, Stanfield 048318
Reed & Reed, Atlanta 087521
Reedus, Dave, Detroit . . . 088774, 132058
Reedville Fishermen's Museum, Reedville 047366
Reef Gallery, Cairns 094353
Reeh, H. & K., Oberbillig 104495
Reek, O. & M., Ihlow 071610
Reeman & Son, Dansie & Howe, Colchester 122475
Rees, Margot Edwina, Armidale . . . 055399
Rees & O'Neill, London 141878
Reese, Philadelphia 091686
Reese, Margaret K., Houston 089186
Reese Bullen Gallery, Arcata 041761
Reeve, James, Warwick 087043
Reeves, Houston 089187
Reeves, New York 118331
Reeves, Alexander, Richmond 119118
Reeves, Paul, London 085638
The Reeves Center, Lexington 045281
Refectory of the Hosios Loukas Monastery, Boeotia 021221
Referat Volkskunde, Landesmuseum Joanneum, Graz 001946
Reference Works, Swanage 142102
Referência Galeria de Arte, Brasília 096502
Referência Galeria de Arte, Brasília 096503
Reffert, G., Mannheim 072430
Refinishing Shop, San Antonio 132824
Refinishing Shoppe, Austin 131807
Reflections, London 096955
Reflections, Lymm 085881
Reflections Antiques, Surry Hills . . . 056658
Reflections on Maling, Canterbury . 094370
Reflet d'Antan, Dormans-en-Champagne 062720
Le Reflet des Temps, Portet-sur-Garonne 066959
Reflet du Passé, Issoudun 063224
Reflet du Temps, Brassac 061751
Reflets d'Antan, Bordeaux 061648
Reflets d'Antan, Compiègne 062440
Reflets d'Autrefois, Aix-les-Bains . . 060726
Reflets d'Epoques, Paris 066467
Reflets du Temps, Biarritz 061477
Reflets du Temps, La Rochefoucauld 063421
Les Reflets du Temps, Paris 100795
Reflex, Breda 078114
Reflex, Mercin-et-Vaux . . 064499, 124443
Reflex Blue Communication, Clermont-Ferrand 099152
Reflex Magazine, Seattle 136615
Reflex Miniatuur Museum voor Hedendaagse Kunst, Amsterdam . 029224
Reflex Modern Art Gallery, Amsterdam 107786, 134788
Reform, Los Angeles 089892
Reform Vintage Modern, Philadelphia 091687
Reforma, Lisboa 080000
Reformas y Obras, Madrid 129663
Református Kollégiumi és Egyházművészeti Múzeum, Debrecen 021711
De Refter, Tilburg 078778, 140536

Le Refuge de Grasla, Les Brouzils . 012613
Refuge Fortifié Muséalisé, Dossenheim-sur-Zinsel . 011638
Refugio County Museum, Refugio . 047367
Regal, San Francisco . 119774
Regal Antiques, Westerham . 087100
Regal Art Gallery, Hamilton . 096425
Regal Art Gallery, Las Vegas . 116643
Regalia Antiques and Militaria, South Plympton . 056611
Regaliza, Palencia . 081462
Regalo Antiques, Atlanta . 087522
Regalos Atlas, Málaga . 081433
Regan, David M, Southport . 086660
Regard, Belo Horizonte . 096485
Regard, Genève . 111495
Regard, Nice . 065137
Regard, Paris . 100796
Regard 76, Bruxelles . 096249
Regard Antiquités, Carcassonne . 061980
Regard Contemporain, Aix-en-Provence . 098794
Regard sur le Passé, Troyes . 068653
Regards, Lorient . 064007
Regards, Metz . 099717
Reg'Art, Lys-lez-Lannoy . 099622
Regart, Paris . 100797
Regatta, Richmond, Surrey . 114311
Regatta Museum, Saint John's . 006371
Regele, Stuttgart . 121607
Regen, West Hollywood . 120407
Regenbogenstadl, Polling, Kreis Weilheim . 104620
Regence Comércio de Artes, Belo Horizonte . 058446
Regency, Barcelona . 080915
Regency, Miami . 132354
Regency Antique, Stourbridge . 086736
Regency Antique Restoration, Oakland . 132573
Regency Antiques, Baltimore . 087704
Regency Antiques, Boston . 087840
Regency Art and Antiques Gallery, West Hollywood . 093504
Regency Auction Gallery, New York 123009
Regency Fine Art, Harrogate . 130765
Regency Gallery, Cambridge . 112792
Regency Gallery, New York . 091181
Regency House, Genève . 082464
Regency House, Napoli . 076037
Regency House Antiques, Antwerpen . 057729
Regency House Antiques, New Orleans . 090607
Regency House Publishing, Broxbourne . 135126
Regency Paperbacks, Auckland . 140604
Regency Restoration, Calgary . 123749
Regency Wood Refinishing, Calgary 123750
Regeneration Furniture, New York . 091182
Régent, Paris . 066468
Regent Antiques, London . 085639, 131155
Regent Art Studio, Christchurch . 079048
Regent Auction, Winnipeg . 120831
Regent Galleries, Worcester . 114738
Regent House Gallery, London . 085640, 113854
Reger, Johannes Maximilian, Wiener Neustadt . 057598
Reggiani, Andrea, Milano . 075838
Reggiardo, T., San Francisco . 092871
Reggio, Gabriele, Torino . 128350
Reghion, Roma . 076640
Reghizzi, Enzo, Modena . 127743
Reghthuys, Giessenburg . 029607
Regia Art, New York . 118332
El Regillero Valiente, Madrid . 129664
Regiment, Bruxelles . 058068
Regimental Museum of 1st The Queen's Dragoon Guards, Cardiff . 038991
Regimental Museum of the 13th/18th Royal Hussars and Kent Dragoons, Cannon Hall Museum, Cawthorne . 039024
Regimental Museum of the 9th/12th Royal Lancers, Derby . 039228
Regimental Museum of the Black Watch, Perth . 040698
Regimental Museum of the Oxfordshire and Buckinghamshire Light Infantry, Oxford . 040666
Regimental Museum of the Royal Dragoon Guards and the Prince of Wales's Own Regiment of Yorkshire, York . 041481
Regimental Museum of the Royal Scots Dragoon Guards, Edinburgh . 039416
Regimental Museum of the Sherwood Foresters, Nottingham . 040626
Regimental Museum The Highlanders, The Queen's Own Highlanders Collection, Inverness . 039809
Regimentals Antiques, Victor Harbor . 056776
Régimódi bolt, Budapest . 074713
Régimódi Lakberendezések boltja, Budapest . 074714
Le Regina, Liège . 058321
Regina Antiguidades, Rio de Janeiro . 058642
Regina Firefighters Museum, Regina . 006259
Regina Plains Museum, Regina . 006260
Reginalde, Serrière-de-Briord . 068229
Reginalds Tower, Waterford . 022871
Regina's Gallery, Norfolk . 091397
Régine Décors, Benfeld . 061347
Regio Galerie, Basel . 111219
Regio Gallerie, Grenzach-Wyhlen . 103000
Regionaal Museum 1940-1945 Schagen en Omstreken, Schagen . 030125
Regionaal Natuurmuseum Westflinge, Sint Pancras . 030155
Regional Arts and Culture Council, Portland . 055003
Regional Galleries Association of Queensland, Fortitude Valley . 052484
Regional Museum, Xinhui . 007331
Regional Museum of Natural History, Bhopal . 022036
Regional Museum of Spartanburg County, Spartanburg . 048263
Regional Science and Discovery Center, Horseheads . 044625
Regional Science Centre, Bhopal . 022037
Regional Science Centre, Guwahati 022140
Regional Science Centre, Lucknow 022245
Regional Science Centre, Tirupati . 022355
Regional Science Centre and Planetarium, Kozhikode . 022231
Regional Science Centre Bhubaneswar, Bhubaneshwar . 022040
Regional- und Telegrafenmuseum, Stegersbach . 002692
Regionale Heemmusea Bachten de Kupe, Openluchtmuseum, Izenberge . 003542
Regionalen Istoričeski Muzej, Kardžali . 004703
Regionalen Istoričeski Muzej, Kjustendil . 004725
Regionalen Istoričeski Muzej, Pazardžik . 004772
Regionalen Istoričeski Muzej, Pleven . 004784
Regionalen Istoričeski Muzej, Ruse 004823
Regionalen Istoričeski Muzej, Stara Zagora . 004885
Regionalen Istoričeski Muzej, Šumen . 004893
Regionalen Istoričeski Muzej Varna, Varna . 004925
Regionales Eisenbahnmuseum der Museumseisenbahn Hamm im Maximilianpark, Hamm, Westfalen . 017733
Regionales Heimatmuseum für das Renchtal, Oppenau . 019474
Regionalgeschichtliche Sammlung mit Musikinstrumentensammlung Hans und Hede Grumbt Wasserburg Haus Kemnade, Hattingen . 017796
Regionalgeschichtliches Museum, Lutherstadt Eisleben . 018758
Regionali Muzej, Djakovica . 034189
Regionalmuseum, Harkerode . 017778
Regionalmuseum, Stockstadt am Rhein . 020321
Regionalmuseum Alsfeld, Alsfeld . 015486
Regionalmuseum Alte Schule, Kaufungen, Hessen . 018216
Regionalmuseum Binn, Binn . 036953
Regionalmuseum der Stadt Lobenstein, Lobenstein . 018667
Regionalmuseum des Amtes Malliß, Kaliß . 018139
Regionalmuseum Fritzlar, Fritzlar . 017277
Regionalmuseum Neubrandenburg, Neubrandenburg . 019219
Regionalmuseum Reichelsheim Odenwald, Reichelsheim, Odenwald . 019770
Regionalmuseum Schwarzwasser, Schwarzenburg . 037540
Regionalmuseum Wolfhagen, Neues Museum im Alten Renthof und in der Zehntscheune, Wolfhagen . 020958
Regionalmuseum Xanten, Xanten . 021034
Regionalna Izba Muzealna, Poddębice . 032228
Regionalne Muzeum Młodej Polski - Rydlówka, Kraków . 032068
Regionalne Muzeum Prasy i Drukarstwa Śląskiego, Pszczyna . 032269
Regionalni Muzej, Bihać . 003928
Regionální Muzeum, Český Krumlov 008323
Regionální Muzeum, Mělník . 008499
Regionální Muzeum, Mikulov na Moravě . 008502
Regionální Muzeum, Náchod . 008519
Regionální Muzeum, Žďár nad Sázavou . 008780
Regionální Muzeum a Galerie, Jičín 008409
Regionální Muzeum K.A. Polánka, Žatec . 008774
Regionální Muzeum v Chrudimi, Chrudim . 008342
Regionální Muzeum v Jílovém u Prahy, Jílové u Prahy . 008415
Regionální Muzeum v Kolíně, Kolín . 008441
Regionální Muzeum v Teplicích, Teplice . 008710
Regionální Muzeum ve Vysokém Mýtě, Vysoké Mýto . 008769
Regionalnyj Muzej Severnogo Priladožja, Sortavala . 033895
Regionmuseet Kristianstad, Kristianstad . 036402
Regionmuseum Västra Götaland, Vänersborg . 036756
Régipénz-Régiség Bolt, Pécs . 074749
Régiposta Antiquitás, Budapest . 074715
Régis, Gilbert, Nice . 065138
Regis-Saunier, Laurence, Paris . 066469
Régis & Thiollet, Argenteuil . 120904
Régiség & Használtcikk Kereskedés, Budapest . 074716
Régiség & Mûtárgy Kereskedés, Győr . 074738
Régiségbolt, Eger . 074734
Régiségbolt, Mosonmagyaróvár . 074743
Regler, Thomas, München . 126441
Regner, Johann, Graz . 137180
Regni, Daniela, Parma . 127861
Régnier, Jean-Claude, Saint-Ouen . 067875
Regoli, Silvia & Giorno, Giancarlo, Brescia . 075181
El Regreso del Sibarita, Salamanca 081543
Regresso Moveis Antigos, São Paulo . 058734
Het Regthuijs, Abbekerk . 029127
Regthuis Oudkarspel, Oudkarspel . 030032
Regthuis t'Schou, Schipluiden . 030139
Reguera Libreria, Sevilla . 141072
Řeháček, Ivan, Hradec Králové . 123957
Rehbein, Thomas, Köln . 103698
Rehberg, Annita, Hamburg . 125836
Rehberg, Dagmar, Mainz . 072403
Rehberg, Dagmar, Mainz . 104005
Rehberg, Dagmar, Mainz . 104006
Rehberger, R., Heidelberg . 139254
Reheis, Erich, Rosenheim . 126739
Rehm, Georg, Augsburg . 121300
Rehm, P., Ochsenhausen . 104518
Rehn, Stockholm . 082008
Rehnström, Mats, Stockholm . 141170
Rehoboth Art League, Rehoboth Beach . 047369, 055004
Rehoboth Museum, Rehoboth . 029095
Rehpenning, Bremervörde . 102266
Rehs, New York . 118333
Rei Desentupidora, Porto Alegre . 058519
Reial Academia Catalana Belles Arts Sant Jordi, Barcelona . 034960
Reial Acadèmia Catalana de Belles Arts de Sant Jordi, Barcelona . 050714, 134926
Reiartis Gestion, Valladolid . 110858
Reiat-Museum, Thayngen . 037627
Reibetanz, Herbert, Siegen . 139729
Reich, Curt, Baden-Baden . 133740
Reich, Dieter Bernd, Schärding . 057301
Reich, Waltraud, Bochum . 102160
Reichard, Hermann, Wiesbaden . 105278
Reichardt, Lothar, Hilders . 103377
Reichardt, Roland, Markkleeberg . 126292
Reichel, Robert, Nürnberg 073115, 126571
Reichelt, Braunschweig . 069991
Reichelt, E., Wietzen . 074434
Reichelt, Eberhard & Karin, Gundelsheim, Oberfranken . 125776
Reichenauer, Ingrid, Wien . 057535
Reichenbach, Jürgen, Freiburg im Breisgau . 070854
Reichenberger, Theo, Kassel . 134081
Reichenberger Heimatstube und Archiv, Augsburg . 015618
Reichenhaller Akademie, Bad Reichenhall . 050009
Reicher, Arthur, Düsseldorf . 070428
Reichert, Bad Staffelstein, Oberfranken . 069388
Reichert, A., Freiburg im Breisgau . 070855
Reichert, Chr., Burghausen, Salzach 070100
Reichert, Heinz, München . 072828
Reichert, Dr. Ludwig, Wiesbaden . 134459
Reichert, Siegmut, Kupferzell . 103808
Reichert, Ulrike, Köln . 126113
Reichert-Pinzl, Barbara, Königsdorf, Oberbayern . 126126
Reichl, Erich, Salzburg . 123454
Reichlin, Ernst & Urs, Küssnacht am Rigi . 082520, 111602, 130059
Reichmann, Alois, Wien . 137358
Reichmann, Bruno, Friesenheim, Baden . 070900
Reichold, Gabriele, Haimhausen . 103056, 121423
Reichold, Herman, Paderborn . 104575
Reichrath, Henning, Hildesheim . 125937
Reichsdorf-Museum Gochsheim, Gochsheim . 017440
Reichskammergerichtsmuseum, Wetzlar . 020847
Reichspräsident-Friedrich-Ebert-Gedenkstätte, Heidelberg . 017833
Reichsstadtmuseum, Rothenburg ob der Tauber . 019917
Reichsstadtmuseum im Ochsenhof, Bad Windsheim . 015839
Reichsstadtmuseum Weißenburg, Weißenburg in Bayern . 020775
Reichsstädtisches Archiv, Rathaushalle und Ratsstube, Mühlhausen, Thüringen . 019015
Reichstädtisches Museum, Bad Wimpfen . 015835
Reichstagsmuseum, Museen der Stadt Regensburg, Regensburg . 019757
Reichwald, Helmut F., Stuttgart . 126875
Reid, Douglas, Kingston . 106820
Reid & Reid, Edinburgh . 141587
Reidy, James, Houston . 132135
Reif, Erkrath . 070595
Reiff, Günther, Bad Urach . 125118
Reiff, Tove & Erik, Regstrup . 098600
Reiffenstein, Wien . 095926
Reigate Galleries, Reigate . 142015
Reigate Priory Museum, Reigate . 040820
Reijinsha, Osaka . 134717

Reijnboek, Apeldoorn 140352
Reik, Karl, Göppingen 071032
Reile, M., München 104294
Reilly, Frances, Eumundi 094517
Reilly, Jenny, Rockhampton 056545
Reim, Susanne, Altenburg, Thüringen 125062
Reimann, Detlef, Kirchzarten 126050
Reimann-Wehr, Cornelia, Werl 074339
Réimecher, Remich 077487
Reimer, Dietrich, Berlin 133805
Reimer, W., Wolfsburg 074480
Reimers, Dresden 138998
Reimert, Irma, Groningen 108047
Reimex, Mülheim an der Ruhr 072615
Reims Décor, Reims 124867
Reimus, Dagmar, Essen 102701
Rein, Jacques, Paris 066470
Rein, Michel, Paris 100798
Reinart, Oss 108161
Reinbeker Galerie, Reinbek 104704
Reinberger Galleries, Cleveland Institute of Art, Cleveland 042997
Reinbold, Friederike, Berchtesgaden 125151
Reincarnation, Cleveland 088355
Reindeer Antiques, London 085641
Reindeer Antiques, Potterspury . . . 086303
Reinders, J., Würselen 074489
Reindl, Hubert, Innsbruck 057085
Reindollar, Sheryl G., Charlotte 087971
A la Reine Victoria, Ruille-La Gravelle 067326
Reinegger, Peter, Fürstenfeldbruck . 070907
Reineke-Fuchs-Museum, Linden, Hessen 018657
Reinelt, Elisabeth & Wolfgang, Buxheim bei Memmingen 102297
Reiner, Hermann, Babenhausen, Schwaben 133728
Reiner, Thomas, Rottenburg am Neckar 126748
Reinessanceschloss Rosenburg, Rosenburg am Kamp 002541
Reinfeld, Bremen 070041
Reinfelder & Neumann, Nürnberg . . 073116
Reinhardt, Leipzig 072214
Reinhardt, Friedrich, Basel 134985
Reinhardt, Harry, Korbach 072056
Reinhardt, J., Halle, Westfalen 139163
Reinhardt, S., Rinteln 073543
Reinhardt, T., Extertal 070674
Reinhardt, Wilhelm, Bruchhausen-Vilsen 125400
Gebr. Reinher, Fußach . . . 056986, 123354
Reinhold, Emden 139038
Reinhold, Stockholm 129873
Reinhold, Zwickau 127068
Reinicke, Gudrun, Hamburg 125837
Reinicke & Biester, Hannover 071409
Reining, N., Borken, Westfalen 069957
Reining, Norbert, Borken, Westfalen 069958
Reinisch, Sabine, Wien 123526
Reinke, Hamm, Westfalen 071363
Reinke, S., Enger 102627
Reinkober, T., Winnigstedt 074448
Reinold Fils, Paris 124791
Reinprecht, Karl, Frohnleiten 123353
Reinshagen, Bad Oeynhausen 069348
Reinsma, Gabrielle, La Garenne-Colombes 063393
Reinwald, Joachim, Schwaigern . . . 073749
Reipin Museo, Pirkkala 009975
Reis, Hohenems 057066
Reis, Roland, Nürnberg 073117
Reis, Vítor Mendes, Lisboa 080001
Reisch, Elmar, Friedrichshafen 070896
Reisch, Sonja, Wien 057536
Reisch, Sonja, Wien 057537
Reisch, Sonja, Wien 133229
Reischl, Alfred, Amstetten 056919
Reischl, Friederike, Wieselburg an der Erlauf 137386
Reischl-Kaun, Ulrike, Sankt Florian 057287, 123463
Reisen, Brigitte, Erfurt . . . 102646, 125600
Reiser, K.-H., Spaichingen 073868
Reisjärven Kotiseutumuseo, Reisjärvi 010032
Reisler, Jo Ann, Vienna 143034
Reiss & Sohn, Königstein im Taunus 121481, 139359
Reiß, Florian, Steinweiler 126834
Reiss, Kurt, Enns 123349
Reiss-Engelhorn-Museen, Museum für Archäologie, Völkerkunde und Naturkunde, D5; Museum für Kunst-, Stadt-, Theater- und Musikgeschichte, C5, Mannheim 018809
Reiß & Latour, Lippstadt 072283
Reisser, M. & D., Wien . . . 095927, 133230
Reißmann, M., Mannheim 072431, 126283
Reisz, Gilles, Vitry-sur-Seine 138665
Reitbauer, Henrike, Freistadt, Oberösterreich 137167
Reith, Ingolstadt 103434
Reither, Colmar 062418
Reitinger, Hedwig, Grödig 057039
Reito, San Jose 119863
Reitschuster, Elisabeth, Burgau, Schwaben 070096
Reitz, Amsterdam 077945
Reitz, Monika, Frankfurt am Main . . 102814
Reitz Home Museum, Evansville . . . 043767
Reitzel, Ann, Hørsholm 060259
Reitzel, Daniel, Saint Paul 092390, 123092
Reitzin Säätiön Kokoelmat, Helsinki 009565
Reix, Chantal, La Rochelle 063439, 124283
Reixach Campanya Restauració, Barcelona 129383
Reizan, Kyoto 106903
Reizentolo, Pontevedra 110725
Rejans, İstanbul 083153
Rejuvenations, Port Pirie 056480
Rękawka, Kraków 108976
Rekeszus, Heiner, Wiesbaden 139854
Rekord-galerie, Berlin 102020
Rekow, Lydie, Crest 099188, 138080
Rekus, Irene, Heusenstamm 103371
Le Relais d'Alésia, Le Vaudioux . . . 063728
Relais de l'Antiquité, Saint-Jean-de-Gonville 067530
Le Relais des Arts, Puycelsi 067001, 101051
Relais des Arts, Sassenage 101261
Relais Des Epoques, Montréal 097070
Les Relais du Passé, Paris 066471
Relais Rétro, Paris 066472
Relart, Firenze 127400
Relf, Ian, Tunbridge Wells 086951
Relic Antiques, London 085642
Relic Antiques Trade, London 085643
Relicário Antiguidades, Belo Horizonte 058447
O Relicario Antiguidades, Rio de Janeiro 058643
O Relicário Antiguidades e Decorações, Brasília 058466
Relicario San Laureano, Bucaramanga 059869
Relics, Ilfracombe 084785
Relics, New Orleans 090608
Relics Antique Shop, Kingston 077032
Relics Antiques, North Fremantle . .056364, 123280
Relics Antiques, Wellington 079343
Relics - Pine Furniture, Bristol 083751
Relics Rescued, Strathalbyn 056638
Relief Bild, Bad Soden-Salmünster . 101703
Relier, Bertrand, Vemars 068748
Religieus Museum Kijk-je Kerk-Kunst, Gennep 029605
Religionskundliche Sammlung der Philipps-Universität, Marburg 018828
Religious and Church Art, Eindhoven 078347
Relin, Jean-Luc, Langres 063526
Le Reliquaire, Casablanca 077672
Reliquaire, Latrobe 056085
Reliure D'Art laTranchefile, Montréal 097071
Rella, Prof. Luigi, Bolzano 127196
Relojería Losada, Madrid . 081373, 129665
Relojeria Renovación, Cali 059885
Relojes Antiguos, Santiago de Chile 059547
El Relox de Arena, México 077581
Rem-Art, Kraków 129046
REM Gallery, San Antonio 119444
Remains Architectural Antiques, New York 091183
Remains Collectables, Fitzroy 055824
Remains To Be Seen, West Hollywood 093505
Remanguille, Madrid 129666
Remarkable Refinishing, Sacramento 132738
El Remate, Madrid 122067
Remates, Medellín 059939
Remates 488, Montevideo 122787
Remba, West Hollywood 120408
Rembar, Armadale, Victoria 094171
Rember Iberica, Madrid 129667
Rembert & Sons, Washington 133034
Rembrandt, Eindhoven . . . 078348, 140415
Rembrandt, Kraków 129047
Rembrandt, Salamanca 110736
Rembrandt, Santiago de Chile 059548
Rembrandt Antiek Galerie, Dallas . . 088600
Rembrandt Art Corp, Panamá City . 108795
Rembrandt Galéria, Budapest 074717
Rembrandt Galeria de Arte, Belo Horizonte 096486
REME Museum of Technology, Arborfield 038518
Remedia, Sopot 109076
Los Remedios, Málaga 081434
Remember That, Hobart 055998
Remember That, Richmond 092098
Remember the Alibi, San Antonio . . 142893
Remember This?, Balwyn North . . . 055446
Remember When, Gosford 055904
Remember When, Los Angeles 089893
Remember When, Saint Louis 092304
Remember When, San Antonio 092569
Remember When Antiques, Tampa . 093149
Remember When Shop, Dallas 088601, 115931
Remenber, Triel-sur-Seine 068630
Remer, Helmut, Mörfelden-Walldorf 104105
Remick Country Doctor Museum and Farm, Tamworth 048495
Remigius Antiquariat, Betzdorf 138870
Remille, Andrèe, Amponville 060829
Remillet, Guy, Beaune 061292
Remington, Cincinnati 088274
Remington, Reg & Philip, London . . 141879
Remington Carriage Museum, Cardston 005226
Remington Firearms Museum and Country Store, Ilion 044715
Reminiscence, Vancouver 059407
Reminiscence Antiques, Miami . . . 090233
Remise, Rheinbach 073517
Remise, Trigance 068631
Remmele, H., Gießen 102954
Remmert & Barth, Düsseldorf 102542
Remmet, Wiebelsheim 074385
Remmet, K.-Heinz, Bingen am Rhein 069849
Remmler, Trude, Moers 139484
Remnants of the Past, Toronto 059275
Remnisce Antique, Saint Paul 092391
Remolina & Assoc., Miami 117132
Remond, Jean-Louis, Le Havre . . . 063640
Rempex, Kraków 121892
Rempex, Warszawa 121912
Rempex Galeria, Warszawa 079779, 109188
Remuera, Auckland 078976
Remus, Gdańsk 129013
Rémy, Albert, Nancy 138233
Remzi, İstanbul 112352
Ren, Nagoya 106932
REN Antiques, West Hollywood 093506
Rena, Nara 106943
Renacentrum, Praha 123997
Renacimiento, Buenos Aires 055240
El Renacimiento, Madrid . 081374, 141059
Renacimiento, Santiago de Chile . . 059549
Renaissance, Dunedin 108448
La Renaissance, Granges-Paccot . .082484, 130042
La Renaissance, Randan 067040
Renaissance, Solihull 086633, 131507
Renaissance Antique Prints and Maps, Brighton, Victoria 136818
Renaissance Antiques, Cowbridge . 084094
Renaissance Art and Design Gallery, Boston 115224
Renaissance Book Shop, Milwaukee 142571
Renaissance Collection, Dallas 088602
Renaissance des Automates Éma, Lyon 012835
La Renaissance du Passé, Thaon-les-Vosges 068380
The Renaissance Furniture Store, Glasgow 084468
Renaissance Gallery, Bangalore . . . 105610
Renaissance Gallery, New York . . . 091184
Renaissance ou l'Amour de l'Art, Blacé 061503
Renaissance Relics, Jacksonville . . 089454
Renaissance Schloss Greillenstein, Röhrenbach 002533
Renaissance Shop, New Orleans . .090609, 132423
The Renaissance Society at the University of Chicago, Chicago 042877
Renaissance Square, Himeji 106851
Renaissance van het Boek, Gent . . 137501
Renaissances, Versailles 068818
Renaissanceschloss Nöthnitz, Bannewitz 015886
Renaissence, Dublin 074943
Renan, Rio de Janeiro . . . 058644, 123710
Renard, Mons 096391
Renard, Alexis, Paris 066473
Renard, Gaston, Ivanhoe 136953
Renard, Jean-Claude, Gien 121008
Renard, Jean-Claude, Paris 121190
Renard, Joël, Montmorot 124454
Renard, Olivier, Beaulieu-sur-Mer . . 061258
Des Renards, Bruxelles 137463
Renassia, Jacques, Saint-Flour . . . 067478
Renata, Kazan 080212
Renaud, Catherine, Saint-Denis-de-l'Hôtel 124892
Renaud, Christophe, Paris 066474
Renaud, Gilbert, Guyonnière 124255
Renaud, Paul, Paris 121191
Renaud, Sophie, Saint-Junien 067567
Renaudier, Serge, Mougins 099779
Renaudot, Les Sables-d'Olonne . . . 063786
Renault, Claude, Chatellerault 062220
Renault, Frédéric, Dinard 062689
Renault, Jack, Beaulieu-sur-Dordogne 061254
Rendell, Kenneth W., New York 091185
Rendells, Ashburton 122391
Rendells, Newton Abbot 122632
Rendelsmann, Heijo, Wiesbaden . . 074418
Rendez Vous, Angers 060862
Rendez-vous, Strasbourg 101302
Rendez-Vous du Collectionneur, Québec 059076
Rendezvous Art Gallery, Vancouver . 097523
Rendezvous Gallery, Aberdeen 083240
Rendon, San Antonio 119445
Rendtorff, Barbara, Kiel 126044
René, Denise, Paris 100799
René, Denise, Paris 100800, 133669
Renel, Milano 075839
Renes International, Winnipeg 059469
Renesans, Wolsztyn 129123
Renessans, Kazan 080213, 109471
Renessans, Sankt-Peterburg 080323
Renessans, Sankt-Peterburg 080324

Reneszánsz Kőtár, Pécs 021825
Renford Studio, Bridport 112709
Renfrew Museum, Waynesboro 049034
Rengebu-ji Temple, Kondo, Kotsudo and Kobodo Halls, Ogi 026934
Renggli, Carla, Zug 112221
Renishaw Antiques, Sheffield 086564
Renishaw Hall Museum and Art Gallery, Renishaw 040821
Renkert, Gaston, Montbertrand 064653
Renko, Warszawa 129108
Renmin Kang Ri Zhan Zhen Memorial Hall, Beijing 007007
Renn, Paris 100801
Renndorf, Manfred, Braunschweig 069992, 125380
Rennebu Bygdemuseum, Rennebu 031133
Renner, François, Velars-sur-Ouche 068744
Renner, Gerhard, Albstadt 138677
Renner, Kurt, Langenlois 057141
Renner, W., Heidelberg 071460
Rennesøy Bygdemuseum, Rennesøy 031134
Renney, Hexham 084679
Rennhofer, Udo, Zürich 083014
Rennies, Abergavenny 122383
Rennies, London 085644
Rennies, Monmouth 122620
Renninger's Antique Guide, Lafayette Hill 136616
Rennotte, Paris 124792
Reno, Montpellier 099763
Reno County Museum, Hutchinson 044704
Reno-Styl, Warszawa 079780
Reno-Styl, Warszawa 129109
Reno-Styl, Warszawa 129110
Renoir, Porto Alegre 096578
Renoir, Skopje 107428
Renoir Fine Art, Vancouver 097524
Renon, Violette, Saint-Ouen 067876
Renoncourt, Jean, Paris 066475
Renou & Poyet, Paris 100802
Renoud-Grappin, Jean-Paul, Besançon 120928
Renouf, Maria-Rosario, Montamy 064619
Renoux, Yves, Saint-Genis-de-Saintonge 067486, 124902
Renovace Stylového Nábytku, Praha 123998
Renov'Cuir, Fort-de-France 128490
Renowacja i Naprawa Przedmiotów Artystycznych i Zabytkowych, Warszawa 129111
Renowacja Mebli Pozłotnictwo, Poznań 129066
Renowacja Mebli Stylowych, Warszawa 129112
Renowacja Zegarów Antycznych, Warszawa 129113
Rens Lipsius, New York 118334
Rensselaer County Historical Society Museum, Troy 048619
Rensselaer Russell House Museum, Waterloo 048984
Rent-A-Center, Cleveland 115735
Rentoileur, Andréone, Reims 124868
Renton Museum, Renton 047379
Rentz, Richmond 119119
Renu, Sunisa, New York 091186
Renu-Grain, Los Angeles 132278
Renuar, Buenos Aires 094086
Renville County Historical Society Museum, Mohall 045957
Renwick Gallery of the Smithsonian American Art Museum, Smithsonian Institution, Washington 048941
Renwick Museum, Renwick 030587
Renz, Stuttgart 126876
Renz, Wilhelmsburg an der Traisen 057602
Renz, Josef, Sankt Pölten 057297, 123465
Repair Plus, Tampa 132961
Repartee Gallery, Salt Lake City 119366
Repeat Antiques, Charlotte 087972
Repeat Consignment, Houston 089188
Repeat Performance, Los Angeles 089894
Repères, Paris 135724
Repetto, Angelo, Genova 127483
Repetto, Francesca, Milano 106296
Replicas El Antaño, Medellín 059940
Replikate der Welt-Kunst im Schloss, Miltach 018941
Replot Hembygdsmuseum, Replot 010034
Reporcel, Cali 123919
Repphun, Konstanz 103765, 126134
Reppuniemen Ulkomuseo, Pöytyä 009979
Reprise, Amsterdam 077946
Repro Art Workshop, Singapore 109863
Reproduction Prints, Preston 114288
Repslagarmuseet, Älvängen 036166
Repton Clocks, Repton 131412
Republic County Historical Society Museum, Belleville 042108
Republican College of Arts, Academy of Arts of Uzbekistan, Taškent 052418
Republički Zavod za Zaštitu Spomenika Kulture, Beograd 050676
Republički Zavod za Zaštitu Spomenika Kulture-Cetinje, Cetinje 050678
Republika Antico, Warszawa 079781, 121913
République Numismatique, Paris 066476
Requena Lozano, Jesus, Madrid 129668
Rerat, Alexis, Montbéliard 064649
Res Allestimenti, Roma 076641
RES Antiqua, Wien 057538
Res Artis, Bucureşti 129225
Resa Termiño, Vitoria-Gasteiz 081721
Resch, Hans, Ruhstorf 126754
Resch & Resch-Schachten, Oberdolling 073139
Rescher, Werner, München 126442
Reschke, Torsten, Willich 074443
Rescon, Madrid 129669
Research Centre for Islamic History, Art and Culture, İstanbul 054253
Research Institute of Art Criticism, Academy of Arts of Uzbekistan, Taškent 052419
Resena Revista de Critica Cultural, Madrid 136101
Resenberg, Karl-Moritz, Hamburg 103213
Resenhof, Bernau, Baden 016201
Reserva Pessoal, São Paulo 058735
Reservation, San Antonio 119446
La Reserve, Knokke-Heist 096356
La Réserve, Paris 100803
La Reserve de Peau d'Ange, Paris 066477
Réserve Géologique de Haute-Provence, Digne-les-Bains 011595
Réserve Naturelle Géologique, Sisteron 014806
Réserves de l'Antiquaire, Florensac 062882
Réserves Nationales des Arts et Traditions Populaires Picardie, Saint-Riquier 014527
Reserviupseerikoulun Museo, Hamina 009501
Réservoir d'Images, Paris 100804
Resetarits, Wien 137359
Resettlers Market Place, Charlotte 087973
Reshaw Exhibit, Evansville 043768
Resi, Guglielmo, Milano 075840
La Résidence, Den Haag 078238
Résidence d'Artistes, Dompierre-sur-Besbre 011631
Residency Museum, York 001650
Residenz Ansbach, Ansbach 015557
Residenz Ellingen, Ellingen, Bayern 016938
Residenz und Hofgarten Würzburg, Würzburg 021004
Residenz Verlag, Salzburg 133146
Residenzgalerie Salzburg, Salzburger Landessammlungen, Salzburg 002564
Residenzmuseum, München 019107
Residenzschloß Oettingen, Oettingen 019451
Résillot, Michel, Vesoul 068829
Resim ve Heykel Müzesi, İstanbul 038095
Resin, Singapore 080548
Resin Wood, Bromma 081776
Resistance Museum, Akko 022885
Resma, Moskva 129238
Resnick, Ira, New York 118335
Resonans, Gent 096297
Resource for Art, San Francisco 119775
Respect Yourself, Chicago 115539
La Respelido, Saint-Rémy-de-Provence 067991
Respublikanskij Istoriko-Kraevedčeskij i Chudožestvennyj Muzej, Dušanbe 037839
Respublikanskij Istoriko-Kraevedčeskij Muzej im. Rudaki Abuabdullo, Pendžikent 037843
Respublikanskij Literaturnyij Memorialnyj Muzej Abaja, Semey 027410
Respublikanskij Vystavočnyj Zal, Muzej izobrazitelnych iskusstv, Joškar-Ola 033206
Resserre, Le Mans 063663
Ressmann, Köln 071993
Ressmann 6000 Breite Str 161, Anton, Köln 071994, 121476
Ressmann & Stieglmeier, München 072829
Rešt-Art, Bratislava 080612, 129273
Restall, Brown & Clennell, London 085645
Restart, Beograd 080404
Restart, Milano 127662
Restau-Moder, Barcelona 129384
Restaudecor, Alicante 129304
Restaur Arte-1997, Zaragoza 129822
Restaura, Getxo 081119, 129519
Restaura Cartagena, Cartagena 129475
Restauració de Llums, Barcelona 129385
Restauració de Paper, Barcelona 129386
Restauración D G, Donostia-San Sebastián 129514
Restauracion de Muebles Elizasu, Donostia-San Sebastián 129515
Restauracion de Tomo y Lomo, Madrid 129670
Restauracion Integral del Mueble, Buenos Aires 123157
Restauracion Santo Domingo 22, Madrid 129671
Restauración y Arte, Bogotá 059855, 123908
Restauración y Venta de Muebles Antigos, Medellín 059941, 123939
Restauraciones, Barcelona 129387
Restauraciones Albarium, Zaragoza 129823
Restauraciones Artísticas, Medellín 123940
Restauraciones Bilbao, Bilbao 129443
Restauraciones Carmelo, Santander 081558, 129722
Restauraciones Emilio, Madrid 129672
Restauraciones Fotograficas Vihuli, Cali 123920
Restauraciones la Dársena, A Coruña 081064, 129490
Restauraciones Larrea, Buenos Aires 055241, 123158
Restauraciones Narciso, Zaragoza 129824
Restauraciones Plumiers, Madrid 129673
Restauraciones Redó, Barcelona 129388
Restauraciones Religiosas de Imágenes, Medellín 123941
Restauraciones Siglo XXI, Bilbao 129444
Restauracja Mebli Antycznych, Wrocław 129130
El Restaurador de Antigüedades, Marbella 129707
La Restauradora, Barcelona 080916, 129389
Restauradora Arte Antiga, São Paulo 123722
Restaurare, Verona 128434
Restaur'Art, Lyon 124374
Restaurart, Porto Alegre 123698
Restaurarte, Roma 128175
Restaurarts, São Paulo 123723
Restaurateur M.C.E., Ees 128659
Restauratie Antiek, Gouderak 128677
De Restauration, Nantes 124488
Restauration de vos Meubles, Essey-lès-Nancy 124235
Restaurator, München 135819
Restauratore Mobili Iusco, Bari 127120
Arbeitsgemeinschaft der Restauratoren-Museen-Denkmalpflege-Grabungstechnik; Berufsverband staatlich geprüfter RestauratorInnen; Bundesverband Deutscher Diplom-RestauratorInnen; Deutscher Restauratoren Verband; Deutscher Verband Freiberuflicher Restauratoren; Restauratoren Fachverband; Restauratorenverband Sachsen, Bonn 053589
Restauratoren Team Bonn, Bonn 125358
Arbeitsgemeinschaft der Restauratoren-Museen-Denkmalpflege-Grabungstechnik; Berufsverband staatlich geprüfter RestauratorInnen; Bundesverband Deutscher Diplom-RestauratorInnen; Deutscher Restauratoren Verband; Deutscher Verband Freiberuflicher Restauratoren; Restauratoren Fachverband; Restauratorenverband Sachsen, Bonn 053589
Restauri Artistici Monumentali, Firenze 127401
Restauri del Sole di Buongiorno, Bari 127121
Restauri Formica, Milano 127663
Restauri Formica, Milano 127664
Restaurierung am Oberbaum, Berlin 125280
Restaurierungs Werkstätten Berlin, Berlin 125281
Restauro, Berlin 125282
Restauro, München 126443, 135820
Restauro, Verona 128435
Restauro, Warszawa 129114
Restauro Antigo, Porto 129198
Restauro Archeologico Ed Architettonico, Milano 127665
Restauro Art, Bologna 127178
Restauro Conservativo, Firenze 127402
Restauro Conservativo di Opere Su Carta, Firenze 127403
Restauro d'Arte, Roma 076642, 128176
Restauro di Mosaici e Materiali Lapidei, Firenze 127404
Restauro Due, Barcelona 129390
Restauro e Antiquariato, Verona 077018, 128436
Restauro e Arte, Torino 128351
Restauro e Idee, Milano 127666
Restauro Farnese, Roma 128177
Restauro Farnese al Vaticano, Roma 128178
Restauro Opere d'Arte, Verona 128437
Restauro San Giorgio, Roma 128179
Restauro van Dyck, Madrid 129674
Restauros, Porto 129199
Restaurum, Lengerich, Westfalen 126207
Restavracija 02, Sofia 123734
Restavracija EAD, Burgas 123726
Restavracija EAD, Sliven 123730
Restavracija EAD, Varna 123735
Restavracija EAD, Veliko Tărnovo 123736
Restavracija i Konservacija, Gabrovo 123727
Restavrator Anfilada, Sankt-Peterburg 129248
Restavrator-Peterburg, Sankt-Peterburg 129249
Reste-Langelier, Micheline, Rennes (Ille-et-Vilaine) 067120
Restelli, Filippo, Roma 076643
Restelo, Madrid 081375
Restigouche Gallery, Campbellton 005210
Restigouche Regional Museum, Dalhousie 005321
Resto Meubles, Saint-Denis 129209
Reston and District Historical Museum, Reston 006272
Restor Bois, Saméon 068105, 124923
Restorart, Toronto 123839
Restoration, New York 132519
Restoration and Design, Toledo 132975
Restoration and Design Studio, New York 132520
Restoration Antiques, New York 132521
Restoration Arts, Miami 132355

Restoration & Conservation of Art, Auckland . . . 128911
Restoration House, Mantorville . . . 045651
Restoration Shop, Austin . . . 131808
Restoration Studio, London . . . 131156
Restorations, Waikato . . . 128968
Restore, Madrid . . . 129675
Restore It, San Francisco . . . 132906
Restored Radios and Antiques, Deepdene . . . 055745
The Restorer, Santa-Venera . . . 128480
Restorers Barn, Castlemaine . . . 055647
Restorers Barn, Castlemaine . . . 123207
Restoring Australia, Yarck . . . 056896
Restoux, Elisabeth, Paris . . . 066478
Resurgam, Baltimore . . . 115081
Resurrected Furniture Gallery, San Diego . . . 092677
Resurrection Bay Historical Society Museum, Seward . . . 048119
Rét Galéria - Gazdagréti Kösségi Ház, Budapest . . . 105542
El Retablo, Bogotá . . . 098188
Retablo Arte, Pamplona . . . 110723
El Retaule, Terrassa . . . 081629
Retch, Cairo . . . 060468
Retelet, Pascal, Saint-Paul-de-Vence . . . 067943
Reti, Thomas, Saint-Ouen . . . 067877
El Retiro Art Gallery, Fyshwick . . . 094575
Rétközi Múzeum, Kisvárda . . . 021773
Reto a la Esperanza, Bilbao . . . 080988
Reto a la Esperanza, Santander . . . 081559
Retoc Restauracio, Barcelona . . . 129391
Retoque Rustilo, Lisboa . . . 129171
Retort, Amsterdam . . . 107787
Retriever Books, Dee Why . . . 136879
Retro, Gdynia . . . 079599
Retro, Rio de Janeiro . . . 058645
Retro, Stourbridge . . . 086737
Rétro Actif, Thémines . . . 068381
Rétro Activ, Paris . . . 066479
Retro-Active, Northcote . . . 056379
Retro Antiques, Lye . . . 085875
Retro-Art, Warszawa . . . 109189, 134864
Rétro Broc, La Gaude . . . 063394
Retro Collectibles, Norfolk . . . 091398
Rétro Désign, Rouen . . . 067295
Retro Fun, New Orleans . . . 090610
Retro Gallery, Hasselt . . . 058231
Retro Gallery, Houston . . . 116395
Retro Gallery, Los Angeles . . . 089895
Retro Home, London . . . 141880
Retro Inferno, Kansas City . . . 089517
Rétro Lumières Antiquités, Durtal . . 062757
Retro Modern, New York . . . 091187
Retro Modern Studio, New York . . . 091188
Retro Photo, Rognonas . . . 067198
Retro Rose, Salt Lake City . . . 092458
Retro Shop Bun Bun Do, Atlanta . . . 142210
Retro-Styl, Sopot . . . 079711, 140768
Retro Verso, Bayonne . . . 061238
Rétro Verso, Toulouse . . . 068538
Retro Ville, Calgary . . . 058800
Rétro Ville, Montréal . . . 058996
Retroactive, New Orleans . . . 090611
Retromania, Toronto . . . 059276
Retrospect, San Francisco 092872, 132907
Retrospection, Portland . . . 092000
Rétrospective, Paris . . . 066480
Retrospective, Wellington . . . 079344
Retrospective Antiques and Toys, Singapore . . . 080549
Retrostyl, Gdynia . . . 079600
Retrouvailles, Saint-Étienne . . . 067465
Les Retrouvailles, Saint-Sylvestre-sur-Lot . . . 068011
Retrouvailles, Stadtbredimus . . . 077492
Les Retrouvailles, Toulon (Var) . . . 068469
Retsas, Dimitris, Athinai . . . 139899
Rettel, Andreas, Kriftel . . . 126152
Retter, Frankfurt am Main . . . 102815
Retterath, Pia, Boos, Eifel . . . 069951
Retucci, Bolzano . . . 105989
Retureau, Alain, Châteauneuf . . . 062202
Returmakeriet, Huddinge . . . 081838
Returned Services League War Museum, Stawell Sub-Branch, Stawell . . . 001490
Réty, Michel, Flavigny-sur-Ozerain . 062867
Retzer Erlebniskeller, Retz . . . 002523
Reubacher Heimatmuseum, Rot . . . 019905
Reuben and Edith Hecht Museum, Haifa . . . 022928
Reuben H. Fleet Science Center, San Diego . . . 047829
Reubens Gallery, Leeds . . . 113366
Reuel B. Pritchett Museum, Bridgewater . . . 042412
Gebr. Reuer, Gladbeck . . . 071002
Reul & Hepp, Waldsolms . . . 074263
Reulens, Berlin . . . 069733
Réunion des Musées Nationaux, Nice . . . 013413
Réunion des Musées Nationaux, Paris . . . 052966, 133670
Reunion Gallery, Felixstowe . . . 113063
Reure, Dominique, Sainte-Foy-les-Lyon . . . 068058
Reure, Dominique, Villeurbanne . . . 068977
Reus, G. de, Amsterdam . . . 128551
Reuß, Bernhard, Gießen . . . 070992
Reußner, Reinhard, Essen . . . 070642
Reutelet, P., Bruxelles . . . 096250
Reuten, Amsterdam . . . 107788
Reuter, Jochen & Susan, Horn-Bad Meinberg . . . 125963
Reuter, Jutta, Bergheim, Erft . . . 069537
Reuter, Marianne, Salzburg . . . 057275
Reuter, Michel, Saint-Tropez . . . 068022
Reuter, R. & G., Essen . . . 070643
Reuter, Walter, Düsseldorf . . . 125545
Reuterhaus mit Richard-Wagner-Sammlung, Thüringer Museum Eisenach, Eisenach . . . 016923
Reuther, Christel, München . . . 072830
Reuther, Irmgard, Sankt Katharinen 126763
Reuther, R., Fürth, Bayern . . . 070911
Reutlinger Kunstkabinett, Reutlingen . . . 073503, 104734
Reutovskaja Gorodskaja Kartinnaja Galereja, Reutov . . . 033693
Reutter, S., Kempten . . . 071793
Revak & Co., M., Tucson . 120161, 143031
Reval Antiik, Tallinn . . . 060488
Révalle, Bronkhorst . . . 140374
Revalor, La Montagne . . . 124281
Revans & Waite, Greytown . . . 079106
Revantic, Paris . . . 066481
Rêve et Plaisirs, Mazières-de-Touraine . . . 064452
Au Réveil du Temps, Remiremont . .067091, 124870
Réveillaud, Richard, Chef-Boutonne 062267
Revel, Sylvain, Lyon . . . 138184
Revel Gallery, New York . . . 118336
Revelation Studios, San Francisco . 119776
Revell, Sheila, Hartley Wintney . . . 084605
Revellin, Logroño . . . 081186
Revelstoke Court House, Revelstoke . . . 006273
Revelstoke Museum, Revelstoke . . 006274
Revelstoke Railway Museum, Revelstoke . . . 006275
Revelution Graphics, New York . . . 118337
Re.Ve.Ma., Torino . . . 128352
Reventlow-Museet Pederstrup, Horslunde . . . 008937
Rêverie, Cannes . . . 061954
Revers, Berlin . . . 138832
Rêves d'Autrefois, Richelieu . . . 067136
Rêves de Poupées, Cormatin . . . 062476
Rêves d'Enfants, Nice . . . 065139
Reviejo Antigüedades, Bahía Blanca . . . 055142, 123146
Review, London . . . 136265
Revillon d'Apreval, Paris . . . 066482
Revillon Frères Museum, Moosonee 005958
Revista Arte Cubano, La Habana . . 135665
Revista de Estética, Buenos Aires . . 135533
Revista de Museólogia, Madrid . . . 136102
Revista muzeelor, Bucureşti . . . 136050
Revival, Abridge . . . 083252, 130285
Revival, Boston . . . 087841
Revival, Milano . . . 106297
Revival, Milton . . . 056229
Revivals on Adams, San Diego . . . 092678
Revive Art Gallery, Auckland . . . 108359
Reviver, Porto . . . 080107
Revol & Hermonville, Bolbec . . . 120933
Revol & Hermonville, Le Havre . . . 121031
Revolution Books, Detroit . . . 142403
Revolution House, Chesterfield . . . 039066
Revolution Studios, Chicago . . . 115540
Revolutionary History Museum, Guangzhou . . . 007092
Revolutionary Museum Ho Chi Minh City, Ho Chi Minh City . . . 049540
Revolutionary Museum of the Jinggang Mountains, Jinggang Mountains . 007160
Revolver Revue, Praha . . . 135668
Revolving Museum, Boston . . . 042342
Revue Belge de Numismatique et de Sigillographie, Bruxelles . . . 135609
La Revue de la Céramique et du Verre, Vendin-le-Vieil . . . 135725
Revue de l'Art, Paris . . . 135726
Revue du Louvre et des Musées de France, Noisiel . . . 135727
Revue la Part de l'Oeil, Bruxelles . .133277, 135610
Revue Noire, Paris . . . 135728
Revue Refinishing Studio, Oakland . 132574
Revue Roumaine d'Histoire de l'Art-Série Beaux-Arts, Bucureşti . . . 136051
Rewa Verlag, Ingolstadt . . . 134071
Rewa's Village, Kerikeri . . . 030532
Rewcastle, Geraldinge, Chesham . . 130552
Rewohl, A., Halle, Saale . . . 103075
Rex, Bratislava . . . 080613
Rex, Komárno . . . 080615
Rex, Oelsnitz, Vogtland . . . 073182
Rex, Verena, Markneukirchen . . . 072459
Rex Antiques, Chagford . . . 083902
Rey, Cahors . . . 120958
Rey, Clermont-Ferrand . . . 062355
Rey, Espoey . . . 062804
Rey, Firenze . . . 075391
Rey, Jacques, Châtillon-sur-Chalaronne . . . 062232
Rey & Cie., Jean, Lyon . . . 064178
Rey, Jean, Lyon . . . 064179
Rey, Jean, Lyon . . . 064180
Rey & Cie., Jean, Paris . . . 066483
Rey, Michel, Montpellier . . . 064753
Rey, Michel, Paris . . . 066484
Rey, Patrice, Capdenac-le-Haut . . . 061965
Rey, Patrice, Figeac . . . 062862
Rey Bello, Emilio, A Coruña . . . 129491
Rey Camara, Jose Maria del, Madrid . . . 081376
Rey Don Pedro, Burgos . . . 129465
Rey Valon, Denis, Saint-Cannat . . . 067391
Reyburn House Art Gallery, Whangarei . . . 108666
Reyer, Harry, Grieskirchen 057037, 123371
Reyes, Gonzalo, Granada . . . 081148
Reyes Espinola, Cecilio, Granada . . 129532
Reye's Shell, Chicago . . . 115541
Reyes Vargas, Eduardo, Santiago de Chile . . . 059550
Reyes Villalba, Daniel, Cali . . . 123921
Reygers, Hubertus, München . . . 104295
Reyghere, de, Brugge . . . 137419
Reymer-Jourdan, New York . . . 091189
Reymond, Charly, Censeau . . . 062050
Reymond, Charly, Nozeroy . . . 065246
Reymond, Jacques, Carouge . . . 129994
Reymond, Loic, Saint-Étienne . . . 067466
Reymondin, Genève . . . 111496
Reynaert, François, Remaugies . . . 067086
Reynal & Hervouet, Paris . . . 066485
Reynaud, Marie-Claire, Cabrieres-d'Avignon . . . 061852
Reynaud, Robert, Boulieu-les-Annonay . . . 061683
Reyne, Cincinnati . . . 088275
Reynold Rapp Museum, Spalding . . 006499
Reynolda House, Museum of American Art, Winston-Salem . . . 049256
Reynolds, Nashville . . . 090482, 132403
Reynolds, Richmond . . . 119120
Reynolds, Anthony, London . . . 113855
Reynolds, B.A.S., Easingwold . . . 084242
Reynolds, C., Oakham . . . 086148
Reynolds, C.H., Pickering . . . 086270
Reynolds, Douglas, Vancouver . . . 097525
Reynolds, Thomas R., San Francisco . . . 119777
Reynolds Homestead, Critz . . . 043221
Reynolds Museum, Wetaskiwin . . . 006799
Reyntens, Carl, Bruxelles . . . 058069
Reyre, Robert, Aix-en-Provence . . . 060716
Reza Abbasi Museum, Teheran . . . 022640
Reza Shah Museum, Johannesburg 034654
Rezag, Mohamed, Oran . . . 055138
Rezai, A., London . . . 085646
Reza's Antiques, Dallas . . . 088603
Řezbářství a Restaurátorské Práce, Hradec Králové . . . 123958
Rezek, Thomas, München . . . 139536
Rezerwat Archeologiczny-Gród Piastowski w Gieczu, Oddział Muzeum Pierwszych Piastów na Lednicy, Dominowo . . 031898
Rezerwat Archeologiczny i Muzeum w Krzemionkach k. Ostrowca, Muzeum Historyczno-Archeologicznego w Ostrowcu, Krzemionki koło Ostrowca . . . 032083
Rezerwat Archeologiczny na Zawodziu, Muzeum Okręgowego Ziemi Kaliskiej w Kaliszu, Kalisz . . . 031977
Rezydencja Księży Młyn, Muzeum Sztuki w Łodzi, Łódź . . . 032120
R.G. Antiques, Dunham-on-Trent . . 084232
RG Interiors, Birmingham . . . 087782
Rhayader and District Museum, Rhayader . . . 040823
Rhéa, Zürich . . . 083015
Rhea Gallery, Leominster . . . 113383
Rhein-Museum Koblenz, Koblenz . . 018297
Rheinberger, Singen, Hohentwiel . . 073830
Rheiner Auktionshaus, Rheine . . . 121587
Rheingauer Kunstauktionshaus, Eltville . . . 070549, 121392
Rheingauer Weinmuseum Brömserburg, Rüdesheim am Rhein . . . 019943
Rheinisch-Bergischer Künstlerkreis, Köln . . . 053549
Rheinische Münzfreunde, Bergisch Gladbach . . . 053550, 069542
Rheinischer Kunsthändler-Verband (RKV) e.V., Köln . . . 053551
Rheinisches Bildarchiv, Museen der Stadt Köln, Köln . . . 018338
Rheinisches Eisenkunstguss Museum, Bendorf, Rhein . . . 015943
Rheinisches Freilichtmuseum und Landesmuseum für Volkskunde Kommern, Mechernich . . . 018866
Rheinisches Industriemuseum, Außenstelle Engelskirchen, Engelskirchen . . . 016985
Rheinisches Industriemuseum, Außenstelle Ratingen, Ratingen . . . 019723
Rheinisches Industriemuseum, Schauplatz Solingen, Solingen . . . 020238
Rheinisches Industriemuseum, Zentrale, Oberhausen, Rheinland . . . 019391
Rheinisches Industriemuseum Bergisch Gladbach, Bergisch Gladbach . . . 015970
Rheinisches Industriemuseum Euskirchen, Tuchfabrik Müller, Euskirchen . . . 017093
Rheinisches Landes Museum Bonn, Landschaftsverband Rheinland, Bonn . . . 016333
Rheinisches Landesmuseum Trier, Trier . . . 020483
Rheinländer, Norbert, Magdeburg . . 126252
Rheinland-Pfälzisches Freilichtmuseum Bad Sobernheim, Bad Sobernheim . . . 015800
Rheinmuseum, Emmerich . . . 016973

Rheinstädtler, M., Mannheim 072432
Rhinebeck Aerodrome Museum, Rhinebeck 047386
Rhinelander Logging Museum, Rhinelander 047387
Rhinestone, Dublin 074944
Rhinestone, Rosie, Seattle 093056
Rhino, New Orleans 117495
Rhino, New Orleans 117496
Rhino Books, Nashville 142603
Rhinopolis, Gannat 011916
Rho, Seoul 107278
Rhode Island Black Heritage Society Museum, Providence 047262
Rhode Island Foundation Art Gallery, Providence 047263
Rhode Island Historical Society Exhibition, Providence 047264
Rhode Island Museum Network, Pawtucket 055005
Rhode Island School of Design, Providence 051995
Rhode Island Watercolor Society, Pawtucket 055006
Rhodes, Charles, South Auckland . . 128958
Rhodes, Isobel, Woodbridge 087224
Rhodes, Peter, Southampton 142081
Rhodes, Philip, Palmerston North . . 079217
Rhodes Cottage Museum, Muizenberg 034685
Rhodes & Mann, London 113856
Rhodes Memorial Museum and Commonwealth Centre, Bishop's Stortford 038749
Rhodes Museum of Classical Antiquities, Grahamstown 034625
Rhodes University School of Fine Art, Grahamstown 050700
Rhön-Museum, Fladungen 017128
Rhöner Naturmuseum, Tann, Rhön . 020401
Rhok - Academie voor Beeldende Kunsten Brussel, Bruxelles 049691
Rhomberg, Clemens, Innsbruck . . . 095595
Rhondda Heritage Park, Trehafod . . 041238
Rhondda Museum, Llwynypia 040070
Rhos Books, Colwyn Bay 141538
Rhuddlan Castle, Rhuddlan 040824
Rhudle Mill, Kilmichael Glassary . .084846, 130845
Rhyl Library, Museum and Arts Centre, Rhyl 040825
Riabitare, Perugia 127883
Rialto, Seattle 093057
Rialto Museum, Rialto 047388
Riarté, Venezia 106776
Riash, Cairo 098665
Riba-Mobley, South Glastonbury . . . 123123
RIBA Publications, London 135257
Ribaldi, Giuliana, Modena 127744
Ribalta, Budapest 074718
Ribarsko-Biološka Zbirka, Novi Dojran 034219
Ribaute, Roger, Pamiers 121105
Ribaux, Sankt Gallen 141296
Ribbentrop, Christiane von, Aschau im Chiemgau 069205
Ribbhagen, Kurt, Stockholm 082009
Ribblefort, Warton 114650
Ribbons, Delhi 074808, 105679
Ribchester Roman Museum, Ribchester 040826
Ribe Kunstmuseum, Ribe 009067
Ribe Raadhussamling, Ribe 009068
Ribeiro, Ana Maria Carmo, Lisboa .080002, 140850
Ribeiro, Cecilia, Rio de Janeiro 096642
Ribeiro, Manuel Santos, Porto 080108
Ribeiro de Sousa, Porto . . 080109, 121955
Ribeli, Stefan, Gräslikon 130041
La Ribera, Murcia 110653
Ribera Corona, Barcelona 129392
Ribes, Jean-Charles, Paris 066486
Ribes Garin, Salvador, Valencia . . . 081674
Ribes Garin, Salvador, Valencia . . . 081675
Ribière & Tuloup, Marseille 121065
Ribniški Muzej, Ribnica na Dolenjskem 034519
Ribolzi, Adriano, Monaco . 077623, 107542
Ribot, Michel, Anglès 060866
Rica Basagoiti, Bilbao 080989
Rica Basagoiti, Madrid 081377
Rica Basagoiti, Juan, Bilbao 080990
Ricard, Paul, Paris 100805
Ricart, Anna, Barcelona . . 080917, 110239
Ricaut, Guy, Pessac 066781
Riccadag Antiquities, Calgary 058801
Riccadonna, Monaco 107543
Riccardi, Angelo, Roma 076644
Riccardi, Maresca, Roma 140116
Riccardi, Pietro, Napoli 076038
Riccardo, Giuseppe, Napoli 127787
Ricci, Anna, Roma 076645
Ricci, Jacques-André, Chapareillan 062143
Ricci, Jean, Soisy-sur-Ecole 068257
Ricci, Sara, Firenze 127405
Ricci Arte, Livorno 106129
Ricciardi, Lucienne, Grenoble 063073
Ricciotti, Alain, Nice 065140
Ricco & Maresca, New York 118338
Rice, Denver 116039
Rice, Hamilton, New South Wales . . 136929
Rice, Houston 089189
Rice, Harold B., Buffalo 087904
Rice, Robin, New York 118339
Rice County Museum of History, Faribault 043816
The Rice Museum, Crowley 043232
The Rice Museum, Georgetown 044177
Rice University Art Gallery, Houston 044652
Ricerca d'Arte, Roma 106615
Ricerche Sul '600 Napoletano, Milano 135950
Ricewolrd Museum, Los Baños . . . 031690
Rich, Den Haag 078239
Rich, David, Denmark 094476
Rich, Ernsting, Indianapolis 116491
Rich, Michael & Steven, London . . . 113857
Rich, Steven & Michael, London . . . 085647
Rich Man Poor Man, Sacramento . . 092178
Richard, Appledore, Kent 083307
Richard, Bevaix 082253
Richard, Houston 089190
Richard, Long Jetty 136980
Richard, Rio de Janeiro 058646
Richard, Anne, Bethancourt-en-Vaux 061410
Richard, C. & M., Neuchâtel 111774
Richard, Ellen, Küsnacht 111601
Richard, F., Gent 096298
Richard, François, Saint-Ouen 067878
Richard, Jean-Luc & Takako, Paris . 100806
Richard, Laurent, Neuchâtel 082695
Richard, M., Cottenchy 062493
Richard, Marcel, Amiens 060825
Richard, Marie-Line, Saint-Pierre-Lafeuille 067959
Richard, Michel, Mainz . . . 072404, 126265
Richard, Michel R., Montréal 058997, 123792
Richard, R. & F., Bruxelles 058070
Richard Billinger-Gedenkraum, Sankt Marienkirchen bei Schärding 002600
Richard-Brandt-Heimatmuseum Bissendorf, Wedemark 020697
Richard F. Brush Art Gallery and Permanent Collection, Canton 042603
Richard Gallery and Almond Tea Gallery, Cuyahoga Falls 043254
Richard H. Schmidt Museum of Natural History, Emporia State University, Emporia 043706
Richard-Haizmann-Museum, Niebüll 019307
Richard Jefferies Museum, Swindon 041178
Richard L. Nelson Gallery and the Fine Arts Collection, Davis 043313
Richard Salter Storrs House, Longmeadow 045396
Richard-Simoncic-Museum, Volkskundemuseum, Rabensburg 002486
Richard Sparrow House, Plymouth . 047100
Richard Teschner-Gedenkraum, Theatersammlung der österreichischen Nationalbibliothek, Wien 002993
Richard-Wagner-Museum, Haus Wahnfried, Bayreuth 015923
Richard Wagner-Museum, Städtische Sammlung historischer Musikinstrumente Tribschen, Luzern 037303
Richard-Wagner-Museum Graupa, Pirna 019626
Richards, Sheffield 131477
Richards, D., Pittsburgh 142777
Richards & Sons, David, London . . .085648, 131157
Richards, Glenn, Seattle 093058
Richards, J., Charlotte 115310
Richards, Margo, Sydney 056688
Richards, Richard, Hong Kong 097825
Richards Antiques, Vancouver 059408
Richards-Dar House, Mobile 045952
Richard's Oriental Rug Gallery, Pittsburgh 091855
Richardson, Greys Green 113163
Richardson, Nantwich . . . 086038, 131291
Richardson, Rotherfield Greys 114327
Richardson, Nanette, San Antonio . 119447
Richardson, Nanette, San Antonio . 119448
Richardson-Bates House Museum, Oswego 046747
Richardson-Clarke, Boston 115225
Richardson & Kailas, London 085649
Richardson & Smith, Whitby 122745
Richardsons, Bourne 122422
Richarme & Polett, Paris 066487
Richborough Castle - Roman Fort, Sandwich 040959
Richco, San Diego 119544
Riche, Cairo 098666
Richel, Philippe, Pessac 066782
Richelieu, Constanţa 080182
Richelieu, Gijón 081126, 122026
Richelieu Numismatique, Paris 066488
Richens, Andrew, Toronto 059277
Riches, Cottonend 130608
Richet, Maurice, Tigy 068420
Richey Historical Museum, Richey . 047389
Richey Historical Society, Richey . . 047390
Richfield, New York 091190
Richfield, New York 091191
Richfield, New York 132522
Richibucto River Museum, Richibucto 006278
Richini, Mario Massimo, Genova . . 106106
Richland, Nashville 117368
Richland County Historical Museum, Wahpeton 048823
Richland County Museum, Lexington 045275
Richmond, London 113858
Richmond, Virginia Beach 120232
Richmond, David, Hyde Park 056009, 123243
Richmond, David, Unley 056770
Richmond and Surrey Auctions, Richmond, Surrey 122667
Richmond Antiques, Bowdon 083616
Richmond Antiques, Nelson 079179
Richmond Antiques, Richmond, Tasmania 056524
Richmond Art Center, Richmond . . . 047397
Richmond Art Gallery, Richmond . . 006283
Richmond Art Museum, Richmond . 047400
Richmond Barbers, Richmond, Surrey 114312
Richmond Book Shop, Richmond . . 142831
Richmond County Historical Society Museum, Melbourne 005852
Richmond Desk Leathers, Richmond 132721
Richmond Gaol Museum, Richmond, Tasmania 001429
Richmond Hill Gallery, Richmond, Surrey 114313
Richmond Main Mining Museum, Pelaw Main 001371
Richmond Museum, Richmond 006284
Richmond Museum, Richmond 034739
Richmond Museum of History, Richmond 047398
Richmond National Battlefield Park, Richmond 047423
Richmond Relics, Richmond, Victoria 056529
Richmond River Historical Museum, Lismore 001187
Richmond Vale Railway Museum, Pelaw Main 001372
Richmondshire Museum, Richmond, North Yorkshire 040829
Richomme, New York 132523
Richon, Christian, Balma 061182
Rich's Antiques, Columbus 088433
Rich's Oldies and Goodies, Chicago 088158
Richter, Berlin 102021
Richter, Düsseldorf 133897
Richter, Lübeck 072338
Richter, Nashville 090483
Richter, Varel 105103
Richter, Arndt, München 072831
Richter, B. & J., Baden-Baden 138710
Richter, E. & H., Lüdenscheid 103974
Richter, Günter A., Rottach-Egern . . 134374
Richter, H., Braunshorn 069997
Richter, Harald, Regensburg 126699
Richter, Helmuth, Weißenburg in Bayern 126987
Richter, Horace, Jaffa 105905
Richter, Klaus, Teltow 074053
Richter, L., Lörrach 072295
Richter, M., Leverkusen 103909
Richter, Marianne, Hamburg 071312
Richter, Markus, Berlin 102022
Richter, Reiner, Nordhorn 073084
Richter, U., Neustadt am Rübenberge 073022
Richter & Kavitz, Coburg 121368
Richter & Knoth, Leipzig 103899
Richter-Levsen, Martha, Wyk auf Föhr 074551
Richter & Masset, München 072832, 139537
Richters, E., Hilden 071522
Richters, Elfie, Düsseldorf 102543
Richy, Pierre-Maurice, Chalon-sur-Saône 062092
Richy, Pierre-Maurice, Montbellet . 064651
Rick, R., Frechen 070810
Rickard, Fred, Toledo 093183, 132976
Ricke, Rolf, Köln 103699
Ricke, Walter, Kottgeisering 139367
Ricker Pewter, Micheal, New Orleans 117497
Rickert, Hans, Stenten 104953
Rickett & Co., Shepperton 086572, 131481
Ricketty Rix, Traralgon 056734
Rick's Furniture Refinishing, San Antonio 132825
Ricky, Hong Kong 059690
Ricky's Galleria, Seattle 093059
Rico, Sainte-Foy-d'Aigrefeuille 124921
Ricochet, Toronto 059278
Ricoletto, Bogotá 098189
Riconti, Bernard, Paris 066489
Riconti, Bernard, Paris 066490
Ricordi, Milano 134632
Ricordi Rubati, Milano 127667
Il Ricordino, Napoli 076039
Ricordo, Porto Alegre 058520
Ricotta, Sergio, Roma . . . 076646, 128180
Ricour-Dumas, Christian, Paris 066491
Ricqlès, François de, Paris 121192
Ricros, Jean-Luc, Aurillac 061081
Ric's Art Boat, Bruxelles 003358
Al-Ridaa Museum, Damascus 037830
Ridard, Claudine, Jossigny 063253
Ridard, Claudine, Saint-Mandé 067621
Riddarholmskyrkan, Stockholm . . . 036658
Riddarhuset, Stockholm 036659

Riddell, Dallas . . . 142373
Ridder, Thierry de, Saint-Ouen . . . 067879
Ridder, Willem de, Antwerpen . . . 123553
Ridderhof Martin Gallery, Mary Washington College, Fredericksburg . . . 044062
Ridderhofstad Gunterstein, Breukelen . . . 029356
Riddett, Bournemouth . . . 122426
Riddiford Corner, Wellington . . . 079345
Riddoch Art Gallery, Mount Gambier 001290
Rideau District Museum, Westport . 006796
Ridente, Nicola, Bari . . . 127122
Rider University Art Gallery, Lawrenceville . . . 045212
Ridge House Museum, Ridgetown . 006287
Ridgeway Antiques, Westcliff-on-Sea . . . 087094
Ridgeway Battlefield Museum, Ridgeway . . . 006289
Ridglea, Fort Worth . . . 088882
Ridi & Madon, Roma . . . 128181
Ridna Chata, Kyïv . . . 112421
Ridnik, Versailles . . . 068819
Ridžina, Moskva . . . 109581
Rieber, Bernd, Stuttgart . . . 121608
Rieck-Haus / Vierländer Freilichtmuseum, Hamburg . . . 017719
Rieckhof, P.M., Kaarst . . . 071677
Riedel, Ratingen . . . 104664
Riedel, Christa, Frankenthal, Pfalz . 102738
Riedel, Friedrich, Marktl, Inn . . . 126295
Riedel, Gerhard, Mühlhausen, Thüringen . . . 072606
Riedel, Thomas, Beeskow . . . 125145
Riedenburger Bauernhofmuseum, Riedenburg . . . 019832
Rieder, München . . . 104296
Rieder, Jean-Paul, Bern . . 082234, 129970
Rieder, Lise-Marie, Chêne-Bougeries . . . 082306
Riedi, Ursula, Zürich . . . 083016
Riedl, Dr. Helmut Philipp, München 104297
Riedl, Lothar Joachim, Niederaichbach . . . 126546
Riedl-Seletzky, Wilhelm von, Wien . 057539
Riedmuseum, Stadtmuseum Rastatt, Rastatt . . . 019715
Riefel, Joseph, Maria Enzersdorf am Gebirge . . . 095676
Rieffel, Paris . . . 138532
Riegel, Nürnberg . . . 073118
Riegelhaus-Galerie, Heimberg . . . 111549
Riegner, Miami . . . 117133
Riegraf, P., Stuttgart . . . 074004
Riehl, Franck, Guidel . . . 063104
Riehle, Brigitte, Esslingen . . . 125624
Rieke, Barbara Maria, Kerpen, Rheinland . . . 071806
Rieker, Manfred, Heilbronn . . . 103334
Riel House, Winnipeg . . . 006859
Riemer, Christoph, Gelnhausen . . . 102926
De Riemkap, Heemstede . . . 128707
Riemland Museum, Heilbronn . . . 034633
Rien de Neuf, Montréal . . . 058998
Rien Poortvlietmuseum, Middelharnis . . . 029925
Rienzo, New York . . . 118340
Riepe, Gerhard, Herford . . . 071490
Riera, Daniel, Barcelona . . 080918, 141002
Riera Borrell, Manel, Barcelona . . . 141003
Ries, H., Heerlen . . . 078506
Ries, Judith, Zürich . . . 130260
Ries, K., Garbsen . . . 070930
Ries, K., Köln . . . 071995
Ries, Kurt, Waibstadt . . . 074245
Ries, Sandi, Charlotte . . . 087974
Ries, Wolfgang, Waibstadt 074246, 105144
Riese, Hannover . . . 071410
Riese, Horst, Bremen . . . 070042
Riesengebirgsmuseum, Marktoberdorf . . . 018848
Riesengebirgsstube, Würzburg . . . 021005
Riesenrundgemälde Schlacht am Bergisel, Innsbruck . . . 002092
Rieser, Mayen . . . 072477
Rieser, Franz, Ferlach . . . 095505
Rieser, Dr. Michael, Ravensburg . . . 073439
Rieser Bauernmuseum, Maihingen . . 018780
Rieskrater-Museum, Nördlingen . . . 019321
Riesner, Paris . . . 066492
Rießbeck, A., Hof, Saale . . . 071549
Riestra, Florencia, México . . . 107510
Rietdorf, Fredi, Zossen . . . 074574
Rietgaverstede, Streekmuseum van het Land van Nevele, Nevele . . . 003673
De Rietgors, Museum voor Moderne Kunst, Papendrecht . . . 030040
Rietjetoe, Den Haag . . . 078240
Rietpen, Bergen op Zoom . . . 107871
Rietschel, Weimar, Thüringen . . . 126979
Rietschel & Ruß, München 104298, 121542, 139538
Rietveld, Leiden . . . 078580
Rietveld, Leiden . . . 078581
Rietveld Schröderhuis, Centraal Museum Utrecht, Utrecht . . . 030239
Rieubon, Jean-Marc, Singapore . . . 080550
Rieunier, Bailly & Pommery, Paris . . 121193
't Rieuw, Nuis . . . 029978
Rievaulx Abbay, Rievaulx . . . 040836
Rieve, Haarlem . . . 078478
Riex, Milano . . . 140062
Rifai, Osman Shehadeh, Beirut . . . 077413
Rifaldi, Richard, Nice . . . 065141, 124522
Rıfat Ilgaz Kültür Merkezi, Kastamonu . . . 038121
Rifaut, Gilbis, Cambrai . . . 061922
Rifle Creek Museum, Rifle . . . 047438
Rig-Veda, Cluj-Napoca . . . 140887
Rigal, Jean, Paris . . . 066493
Rigaldo & Fils, Allaman . . 082082, 129895
Rigaldo & Fils, Lausanne . . . 082566
Rigaldo & Fils, Prilly . . . 130144
Rigamonti, Franco, Roma . . . 128182
Rigamonti, Margaret, Zürich . . . 083017
Rigamonti, Paolo, Milano . . . 127668
Riganti, Massimo, Chiasso . . . 082312
Rigaronne, Toulouse . . . 101370
Rīgas Doma Baznīca, Rīga . . . 027764
Rīgas Galerija, Rīga . . . 107320
Rīgas Kino Muzejs, Rīga . . . 027765
Rīgas Motormuzejs, Rīga . . . 027766
Rīgas Tehniskās Universitātes Muzejs, Rīga . . . 027767
Rīgas Ūdensapgādes Muzejs, Ādaži 027652
Rīgas Vēstures un Kugniecības muzejs, Rīga . . . 027768
Rīgas Vīni, Rīga . . . 107321
Rigassi, Raphael, Bern . . . 111273
Il Rigattiere, Bolzano . . . 075132
Rigaud, Alexis, Lembras . . . 063740
Rigault, Patrice, Lattes . . . 063547
Rigaut, Fabien, Reims . . . 124869
Riggauer, Konrad, München . . . 072833, 126444
Righi, Daniele, Firenze . . . 127406
Right Angle, Brackley . . . 083624, 130424
Right Brain Art Gallery, Atlanta . . . 114917
Rightlines Art Gallery, Bangalore . . 105611
Rigilio, Giovanni, Vezia . . . 082886, 130204
Rigoleto Curioso, Buenos Aires . . . 136751
Rigo's Antiques, San Antonio . . . 092570
Riihimäen Kaupunginmuseo, Riihimäki . . . 010035
Riihimäen Taidemuseo, Riihimäki . . 010036
Riihimuseo, Peräseinäjoki . . . 009960
Riihipiha Museo, Vuolijoki . . . 010253
Riise-Birger, Anita, Göteborg . . . 129841
Rijbroeck, Amsterdam . . . 107789
Rijdend Electrisch Tram Museum, Amsterdam . . . 029225
Rijk, de, Den Haag . . . 107949
Rijk, Walt de, Amsterdam . . . 107790
Het Rijk van Kralingen, Rotterdam . 108206
Rijkeboer, W., Enschede . . . 078378
Rijken, Tonnie, Geulle . . . 128672
Rijks, Amstelveen . . . 128526
Rijksakademie van Beeldende Kunsten, Amsterdam . . . 050553
Rijksarchief, Brugge . . . 003281
Rijksbureau voor Kunsthistorische Documentatie, Den Haag . . . 050556
Rijksmuseum, Amsterdam . . . 029226
Rijksmuseum Hendrik Willem Mesdag, Den Haag . . . 029451
Rijksmuseum Twenthe, Enschede . 029569
Rijksmuseum van Oudheden, Leiden . . . 029853
Rijksmuseum voor Volkenkunde, Leiden . . . 029854
Rijksprentenkabinet, Rijksmuseum, Amsterdam . . . 029227
Rijnders & Zoon, B.A.H., Arnhem . . 078058
Rijnders, B.H., Arnhem . . . 078059
Rijsdijk, Dordrecht . . . 078314
Rijsdijk, Saskia, Haarlem . . . 128694
Rijssens Museum, Rijssen . . . 030063
Rijtuigenmuseum, Bree . . . 003261
Rijwiel- en Bromfietsmuseum, Zoutkamp . . . 030395
De Rijzende Zon, Tilburg . . . 140537
Rik, Leiden . . . 078582
Rika Gallery, Waikato . . . 108594
Rike, K., Dallas . . . 115932
Rikey, Ingim, Reykjavík . . . 105590
Rikosmuseo, Vantaa . . . 010223
Riksantikvaren, Directorate for Cultural Heritage, Oslo . . . 031104
Riksföreningen Sverigekontakt, Göteborg . . . 054149
Riksutstallningar, Stockholm . . . 036660
Riley, Peter, Cambridge . . . 141476
Riley, Thomas R., Cleveland . . . 115736
Riley, Thomas R., Columbus . . . 115798
Riley County Historical Museum, Manhattan . . . 045632
Riley House Museum of African American History and Culture, Tallahassee . 048484
Riley Orrin, H., New York . . . 132524
Riley-Smith, Crispian, London . . . 085650
Riley-Smith, Crispian, London . . . 113859
Rillmann, G., Karlsruhe . . . 103501
Rilton, Stockholm . . . 082010
Římal, Pavel, Praha . . . 060157
Rimanque, Oostende . . . 058367
Rimari India, Mumbai . . . 105797
Rimbaud, Jean-Jacques, Paris . . . 066494
Rimbaud Verlag, Aachen . . . 133713
Rimbault, Jean Yves, Toucy . . . 068433
Rimbault-Joffard, Robert, Charly-sur-Marne . . . 062163
Rimfaxe, Esben, Farum . . 098524, 133421
Rimfaxe, Esben, København . . . 060373
Rimmele-Marzullo, Angela, Ulm . . . 074151
Rimrocker Historical Museum of West Montrose County, Naturita . . . 046165
Rimska Grobnitsa Silistra, Silistra . . 004832
Rimu Street Gallery, Wellington . . . 030650
Rinaldi, Alessandro, Roma . . . 128183
Rinaldi, Barbara, Napoli . . . 076040
Rinaldi, Luisa, Genova . . . 075501
Rinard, Guthrie, New Orleans . . . 117498
Rinaudo, Nicola, Milano . . . 075841
Rinck, Heiko, Fitzen . . . 070693
El Rincón, Montevideo . . . 087340
Rincón Artístico, Buenos Aires . . . 094087
Rincón de Historia, Salto . . . 000545
El Rincón de María Castaña, Caracas . . . 093541
Rincón del Antcuario, Buenos Aires 136752
Rincón Mexicano, Medellín . . . 098285
Rindal Bygdemuseum, Rindal . . . 031135
Rindlisbacher, Fritz, Zürich . . . 083018
Rinella, Diodato, Prato . . . 127895
Le Ring, Nantes . . . 052967, 099817
Ring bildender Künstler, Wuppertal . 053552
Ring of Fire, Milwaukee . . . 117218
Ringe Museum, Ringe . . . 009069
Ringel, Michael, Düsseldorf . . . 070429
Ringelnatz-Museum, Wurzen . . . 021025
Ringerikes Museum, Hønefoss . . . 030904
Ringius, Falköping . . . 122129
Ringkamp, Bernhard, Delbrück . . . 070208
Ringkøbing Antikmesse, Ringkøbing 093644
Ringkøbing Museum, Ringkøbing . . 009070
Ringles Cross Antiques, Uckfield . . 086977
Ringling School of Art and Design, Sarasota . . . 052146
Rings, Wellington . . . 079346
Ringsaker Vekter- og Brannhistoriske Museum, Moelv . . . 031021
Ringstead Gallery, Ringstead . . . 114314
Ringstead Village Antique Centre, Ringstead . . . 086364
Ringsted Museum, Ringsted . . . 009071
Ringström, Örebro . . . 122221
Ringve Museum, Trondheim . . . 031285
Ringwood Antique Market, Ringwood . . . 056533
Ringwood Miners Cottage, Ringwood . . . 001431
Rinn, Ch., Wetzlar . . . 074383
Rinn-Art Finland, Helsinki . . . 060575
Rinnelt, C., Wiesbaden . . . 074419, 139855
Rinno-ji Jokodo Treasure House, Nikko . . . 026920
Rinsche, Christian, Münster . . . 126506
Rinsen, Kyoto . . . 134713, 140163
Rio Grande Valley Museum, Harlingen . . . 044433
Rio Hondo College Art Gallery, Whittier . . . 049150
Rio Macanaz, Pedro del, Cádiz . . . 081029
Riocreux Michèle, Saint-Étienne . . . 067467
Riolo, Vincenzo, Palermo . . . 127838
Riondet, Bogdan, Lyon . . . 064181
Riordan Mansion, Flagstaff . . . 043853
Rios, Guatemala . . . 105481
Rios, Eli, New York . . . 132525
Rios Avelino, Genève . . . 082465
Riot, Paris . . . 124793
Ripa Antica, Milano . . . 075842
Ripert Grac, Isabelle, Marseille . . . 064388
Ripley, Dan, Indianapolis . 089336, 122923
Ripley Castle, Ripley, North Yorkshire . . . 040838
Ripley County Historical Society Museum, Versailles . . . 048773
Ripley's Believe it or not!, Key West 044991
Ripley's Believe It or Not Museum, Niagara Falls . . . 006018
Ripoll, Palma de Mallorca . . . 141067
Ripon College Art Gallery, Ripon . . . 047444
Ripon Historical Society Museum, Ripon . . . 047445
Ripon Prison and Police Museum, Ripon . . . 040840
Ripon Workhouse Museum, Ripon . 040841
Ripp, Ellen, Chicago . . . 115542
Rippa, Egidio, Napoli . . . 127788
Rippa, Salvatore, Napoli . . . 127789
Rippel, Arthur, Berlin . . . 069734
Rippert, Houston . . . 089191
Ripping Yarns, Caloundra . . . 136840
Ripping Yarns, London . . . 141881
Rippl-Rónai Emlékház, Kaposvár . . 021752
Rippon, Boswell & Co, London . . . 122597
Rippon, Boswell & Co, Wiesbaden . 121626
Rippon, Boswell & Co, Zürich . . . 122370
Rippon Lea Estate, Melbourne . . . 001249
Rippon Lea House Museum, Elsternwick . . . 001017
Rippstein, Pierre, Basel . . . 082167
Riquet, Sylvie, Soissons . . . 068251
Riquet'Broc, Toulouse . . . 068539
Risager, Jørgen, Odense . . . 060397
Risborough Art Gallery, Princes Risborough . . . 114290
The Risby Barn, Risby . . . 086382
Risby Cove, Strahan . . . 095226
Risch, Verena, Schaffhausen . . . 111891
Rischkopf, Günter, Starnberg . . . 073895
Riserva Naturale Speciale del Sacro Monte di Varalio, Varallo Sesia . . . 026209
Rishon Le-Zion Museum, Rishon Le-Zion . . . 023058
Rising Sun Tavern, Fredericksburg . 044063
Risley, David, London . . . 113860

Risør Museum, Festningsanlegget Urheia, Risør . . . 031136
Rispa-Hernández, Pilar, Flonheim . . 125645
Rispal, Antonin, Paris . . . 066495
Rispal, Antonin, Paris . . . 066496
Risque Art, Solihull . . . 114446
Riss, Samedan . . . 111862
Rissa Bygdemuseum, Rissa . . . 031138
Risse, Ildikó, Weßling . . . 105222
Risse, Martine, Bayonville-sur-Mad 061240
Risse, Martine, Nancy . . . 064879
Rissoan, Alain, Romans-sur-Isère . . 067203
Rissone, Gatti, Viganello . . . 111972
Ristea, Inge, København . . . 060374
Risten-Lakviks Järnväg, Åtvidaberg 036208
Risteski, Riste, Neustadt bei Coburg 073036
Ristolainen, M., Turku . . . 060644
Ristović, Beograd . . . 080405
Ristovski, Fulda . . . 070920
Rita's Antic Boutique, Luzern . . . 082633
Rita's Antique Cafe, New York . . . 091192
Rita's Antiques, San Francisco . . . 092873
Rita's Relics, Atlanta . . . 087523
Ritax, Lahti . . . 060610
Ritchie, A. & R., Saint Helier . . . 086451
Ritchie & Co, Colin, Toronto . . . 059279
Ritchie's, Toronto . . . 120821
Rite-Way, Tampa . . . 132962
Ritorna Moveis, São Paulo . . . 058736
Ritorno, Casablanca . . . 077673
Ritorno Bis, Bologna . . . 075104
Ritorto, Domenico, Roma . . . 076647
Ritorto, Ivan, Roma . . . 076648
Ritsch-Fisch, Jean-Pierre, Strasbourg . . . 101303
Ritschard, M. & U., Bern . . . 082235
Ritscher-Sandmeier, Helga, Berlin . 125283
Helga Ritscher-Sandmeier & Alexander Sandmeier, Berlin . . . 069735
Rittenhouse, Philadelphia . . . 118826
Ritter, Düsseldorf . . . 070430
Ritter, Klagenfurt . . . 095619
Ritter, Klagenfurt . . . 133102
Ritter, New York . . . 091193
Ritter, C., Bruxelles . . . 058071
Ritter, G., Rinteln . . . 073544
Ritter, Hans-Dieter, Jork . . . 103456
Ritter, Herbert M., München . . . 072834
Ritter, Luc, Bruxelles . . . 058072
Ritter, Marion, Hamburg . . . 071313
Ritter, Michael, Frankfurt am Main . 070779
Ritter, Michael, Gottmadingen . . . 071069
Ritter, P., Marienheide . . . 072458
Ritter, Patrice, Zürich . . . 083019
Ritterbach, Frechen . . . 133957
Rittergut Haus Laer, Bochum . . . 016282
Ritterhaus Bubikon, Bubikon . . . 036980
Rittersaalmuseum, Kirchbichl . . . 002127
Rittman Historical Society Museum, Rittman . . . 047446
Ritu Creations, Mumbai . . . 105798
Ritual Art Gallery, Kathmandu . . . 107598
Ritz, Reinhard, Naters . . . 111764
Ritzenhoff, Chicago . . . 088159
Ritzenthaler, Gassin . . . 062971
Ritzy Bits, Auckland . . . 078977
Rius Garrich, Claudio, Barcelona . . 080919
Riuttalan Talonpoikaismuseo, Karttula . . . 009672
Riva, New York . . . 118341
Riva, Adriano, Padova . . . 076110
Rivals Renaud, Villenouvelle . . . 068924
Rivas Martin, Juan, Madrid 081378, 129676
Rivchun, Heide, Cleveland 088356, 131970
Rive, H., Düsseldorf . . . 070431
Rive de Sorgues, L'Isle-sur-la-Sorgue . . . 063957
Rive Gauche, Auxerre . . . 061105
Rive Gauche, Den Haag . . . 078241
Rive Gauche Galerie d'Art Contemporain, Namur . . . 096393
Riveneuve, Marseille . . . 138198
River, Pittsburgh . . . 135478
River and Rowing Museum, Henley-on-Thames . . . 039728
River Art Group, San Antonio . . . 055007, 119449
River Arts Center, Clinton . . . 043011
River Brink, The Samuel E. Weir Collection, Queenston . . . 006235
River City Antiques, Saint Paul . . . 092392
River City Art and Antique Centre, Bangkok . . . 083102, 112237, 122377, 141371
River Emporium, Woodburn . . . 056844
River Gallery, Saint Paul . . . 119309
River Hills Park Museum, Chesterfield . . . 042806
River House Antiques, Pittsburgh . . 091856
River House Antiques, Washington . 093432
River Legacy Living Science Center, Arlington . . . 041776
River Market Antique Mall, Kansas City . . . 089518
River Museum, Wellsville . . . 049053
River Read, Noosaville . . . 137033
River Square Antiques, San Antonio 092571
River Valley School Museum, Virden 006755
River View Ethnographic Museum, Bear River . . . 005084
Riverbank, Petworth . . . 086259
Riverbank Antiques, Warrandyte . . . 056802
Riverbank Studios, Portsmouth . . . 114283
Riverchase Antique Gallery, Birmingham . . . 087783
Riverchase Gallery, Birmingham . . . 115127
Riverdale Mansion, Riverdale Park . 047451
Rivère-Pagnon, Nicole, Saint-Lizier 067587
Rivergum Art Gallery, Warrandyte . . 095372
Riverhouse, Steamboat Springs . . . 135509
Riverhouse Gallery, Saskatoon . . . 097199
Rivero Lake, Rodrigo, México . . . 077582
Rivers Gallery, Nailsworth . . . 114105
Riverside Antiques, Sawbridgeworth . . . 086521
Riverside Architectural Antiques, Saint Louis . . . 092305
Riverside Art Museum, Riverside . . 047459
Riverside Book Company, New York 135459
The Riverside Gallery, Golant . . . 113141
The Riverside Gallery, Inverness . . . 113299
Riverside Gallery, Looe . . . 113995
Riverside Gallery, Toronto . . . 097365
Riverside Gallery, Uppermill . . . 114626
Riverside Municipal Museum, Riverside . . . 047460
Riverside Museum, La Crosse . . . 045058
Riverside Museum at Blake's Lock, Reading . . . 040810
Riverstone, New Orleans . . . 117499
Riverton Museum, Riverton . . . 047463
Rivertown Galleries, London . . . 096956
Rivertown Gallery, Memphis . . . 117004
Riverview Antique Market, Milwaukee . . . 090320
Riverview at Hobson Grove, Bowling Green . . . 042368
Riverwest Artists Association, Milwaukee . . . 055008
Riverwest Arts Center, Milwaukee . 117219
Rivet, Gabriele, Köln . . . 103700
Rivett, Sue, Fakenham . . . 084375
Riviera Books, Harleston . . . 141642
Rivière, Christophe, Tournai . . . 058389, 123673
Rivière, Colette, Maisons-Laffitte . . 064229
Rivière, Guy, Charmoy . . . 062167
Riviere, Jean-Claude, Peujard . . . 066784
Rivière, Michel, Toulon (Var) . . . 068470
Riviere, Roger, Peujard . . . 066785
Rivière & Desnoe, Saint-Leu . . . 129210
Rivilla Calvo, T., Segovia . . . 110757
Rivilla Calvo, T., Segovia . . . 110758
Rivington Gallery, London . . . 113861
Rivista degli Studi Orientali, Roma . 135951
Rivista di Psicologia dell'Arte, Roma 135952
Rivista di Storia della Miniatura, Firenze . . . 135953
Rivista Ingauna e Intemelia, Bordighera . . . 135954
Rivkind, Robert, Toronto . . . 059280
Rivnens'kyj Krajeznavčyj Muzej, Rivne . . . 038383
Rivoli, Gladesville . . . 055878
Rivoli, Howard, Neutral Bay . . . 056323
Rivollier Alain, Vienne . . . 068866
Rivolta, Genève . . . 111497
Rivon, Alexandre, Parent . . . 065339
Riyahi Gallery, London . . . 085651
Riza, Sergiev Posad . . . 033868
Rizal Technological and Polytechnic Institute Museum, Morong . . . 031745
Rize Devlet Güzel Sanatlar Galerisi, Rize . . . 038163
Rizeanu, Dardu, Craiova . . . 129230
Riznica Franjevačkog Samostana Split, Poljud, Split . . . 007805
Riznica Katedrala, Dubrovnik . . . 007720
Riznica Katedrala, Split . . . 007806
Riznica Katedrala, Trogir . . . 007814
Riznica Manastira Studenica, Raška 034253
Riznica Samostana Svetog Frane, Zadar . . . 007827
Riznica Srpske Pravoslavne Crkve u Kotoru, Kotor . . . 034202
Riznica Zagrebačke Katedrala, Zagreb . . . 007855
Riznica Župne Crkve, Nin . . . 007763
Rizo, Bernard, Nîmes . . . 065186
Rizza, Roberto, Brescia . . . 127232
Rizzardi, Milano . . . 134633
Rizzato, Bruno, Venezia . . . 128403
Rizzi, Arcangelo, Milano . . . 127669
Rizzi, James, Tokyo . . . 107095
Rizzi, Renzo, Milano . . . 140063
Rizzitiello, Pasquale, Milano . . . 127670
Rizzo, Giovanni, Venezia . . . 076968
Rizzo Antiquari, Palermo . . . 076176
Rizzo Antiquari, Palermo . . . 076177
Rizzo Antiquari, Palermo . . . 076178
Rizzoli, Milano . . . 134634
R.J. Antiques, Bendigo . . . 055481
RJ Collectibles, Chicago . . . 088160
R.J. Galleries, Ballarat . . . 055437
Rjazanskij Gosudarstvennyj Istoriko-architekturnyj Muzej-zapovednik, Rjazan . . . 033697
Rjazanskij Oblastnoj Chudožestvennyj Muzej im. I.P. Požalostina, Rjazan . . . 033698
Rjazanskij Zaočnyj Institut Moskovskogo Gosudarstvennogo Universiteta Kultury i Iskusstv, Rjazan . . . 050657
RLB-Kunstbrücke, Innsbruck . . . 002093
R.L.S. Silverado Museum, Saint Helena . . . 047632
RM Antiquités, Pontoise . . 066944, 124851
R.M. Bohart Museum of Entomology, University of California, Davis . . . 043314
RM Fine Art, London . . . 113862
Ármaga, León . . . 110400
RMIT Gallery, Melbourne . . . 001250
RMN Italia, Roma . . . 106616
R.N. Atkinson Museum, Penticton . . 006130
Ro Gallery, Long Island City . . . 116688
Ro Gallery, New York . . . 118342
ROA Estudio, Madrid . . . 129677
Roach Tackle Folk Art, Toronto . . . 097366
Road, Sendai . . . 077218
Road of Odd Stones and Antiques, Shanghai . . . 059760
Roadhouse Relics, Austin . . . 115007
Roadshow Antique Jewellery, Nobby Beach . . . 056349
Roadshow Antiques, Southport . . . 056617
Roadside Antiques, Greystoke . . . 084534
Roald Amundsens Hjem Uranienborg, Svartskog . . . 031253
Roald Amundsens Minne, Borge Sarpsborg . . . 030787
Roan, Bob, Cogan Station . . . 122868
Roan Bygdetun, Roan . . . 031141
Roanoke Island Festival Park, Homeport of the Elizabeth II, Manteo . . . 045649
Roar Gallery, Wellington . . . 108643
Roaring Twenties Antique Car Museum, Hood . . . 044613
Roatzsch, Siegfried, Meinhard . . . 126300
Rob Piercy Gallery, Porthmadog . . . 114280
Rob Roy and Trossachs Victor Centre, Callander . . . 038947
Robache, Gérard, Vieille-Eglise . . . 068865
Robarick, Dorit, Lübbenau . . . 103958
Robb Street Gallery, Bairnsdale . . . 094191
Robben, Cincinnati . . . 131943
Robben Island Museum, Robben Island . . . 034741
Robbins, Martha, New Orleans . . . 117500
Robbins Hunter Museum, Avery-Downer House, Granville . . . 044293
Robbins Museum of Archaeology, Middleborough . . . 045831
Robbinsville, Miami . . . 090234
Roberson Museum and Science Center, Binghamton . . . 042217
Robert, Swansea . . . 142105
Robert, Brian, San Francisco . . . 092874
Robert, Claude, Paris . . . 121194
Robert, Claude, Paris . . . 121195
Robert, Daniel, Montréal . . . 123793
Robert, Didier, Saint-Étienne . . . 124899
Robert, Jacqueline, Villeurbanne . . 068978
Robert, J.C., Honfleur . . . 099356
Robert, Marie-Françoise, Paris . . . 121196
Robert, Maurice, Pézenas . . . 066810
Robert, Olivier, Capbreton . . . 061963
Robert, Olivier, Paris . . . 124794
Robert, Roland, Paris . . . 100807
Robert, Y., Agde . . . 060662
Robert A. Bogan Fire Museum, Baton Rouge . . . 042050
Robert A. Peck Gallery, Central Wyoming College, Riverton . . . 047464
Robert A. Vines Environmental Science Center, Houston . . . 044653
Robert and Mary Montgomery Armory Art Center, West Palm Beach . . . 049092
Robert Brady Museum, Cuernavaca 028209
Robert Burns Centre, Dumfries . . . 039299
Robert Burns House, Dumfries . . . 039300
Robert C. Williams American Museum of Papermaking, Atlanta . . . 041870
Robert E. Lee Memorial Association, Stratford . . . 048398
Robert Edward Hart Memorial Museum, Souillac . . . 028073
Robert Fulton Birthplace, Quarryville . . . 047292
Robert Gordon University Museum, Aberdeen . . . 038452
Robert Hamerling - Museum, Kirchberg am Walde . . . 002125
Robert Hull Fleming Museum, Burlington . . . 042526
Robert Hytha-Museum, Internationales Sonder-Museum Wildtiere der Welt, Oberwölbling . . . 002394
Robert-Koch-Museum, Berlin . . . 016161
Robert Langen Gallery, Waterloo . . 006776
Robert & Li, Tainan . . . 098058
Robert Louis Stevenson Memorial Cottage, Saranac Lake . . . 047996
Robert Louis Stevenson Museum, Vailima . . . 034109
Robert McLaughlin Gallery, Oshawa 006081
Robert McDougall Art Gallery, Christchurch . . . 030462
Robert Mills Historic House and Park, Columbia . . . 043084
Robert Musil-Literatur-Museum, Klagenfurt . . . 002147
Robert Newell House, DAR Museum, Saint Paul . . . 047711
Robert Opie Collection, Wigan . . . 041385
Robert Owen Memorial Museum, Newtown, Powys . . . 040583
Robert R. McCormick Museum at Cantigny, Wheaton . . . 049137
Robert S. Kerr Museum, Poteau . . . 047205
Robert S. Peabody Museum of Archaeology, Andover . . . 041723

Robert-Schumann-Haus Zwickau, Zwickau 021088
Robert Sheane's Agricultural Museum, Glenealy 022795
Robert-Sterl-Haus, Struppen 020339
Robert Stolz Museum Graz, Graz . . 001947
Robert Tait McKenzie Memorial Museum and Mill of Kintail, Almonte 005001
Robert Toombs House, Washington 048962
Robert V. Fullerton Art Museum, California State University, San Bernardino . 047812
Robert W. Ryerss Museum, Philadelphia 046982
Roberta e Basta, Milano 075843
Robertinum, Archäologisches Museum der Martin-Luther-Universität, Halle, Saale 017670
Roberto, Basilío Augusto, Lisboa . . 109349
Roberto's & Juliette's Antiques, Merbein 056215
Roberts, Lachlan 120598
Roberts, Nicholls 094965
Roberts, Tampa 120064
Roberts, Andrew, Gilles Plains 055876
Roberts, Bryan H., Columbus 115799
Roberts, Catherine, Washington . . . 093433
Roberts, Derek, Tonbridge 086895
Roberts, Elizabeth, Washington . . . 120342
Roberts, Jay, Chicago 088161
Roberts, John, Dallas 115933
Roberts, Mark, Welbeck 131656
Roberts, Peter, New York 091194
Roberts, R., Jacksonville 116540
Roberts, T.J., Uppingham 086986
Robert's Antiques, Saint Helier 086452
Robert's Antiques, Tulsa 093328
Roberts Auktioner, Kungsör 122187
Roberts County Museum, Miami . . . 045822
Roberts Emporium, Cardiff 083875, 130514
Roberts Gallery, Toronto 097367
Roberts & Little, Blackrock 074864
Robert's Quality Upholstering, Hamilton 123774
Roberts & Tilton, Los Angeles 116874
Robertson, Glenrothes 113135
Robertson, Melbourne 056200
Robertson, New York 118343
Robertson, Raymond, Dorchester . . 130643
Robertson Museum and Aquarium, Millport 040469
Robertson Recollections, Robertson 056537
Robespierre, Charleroi 058152
Robic, Albert, Vezins 068838
Robichon, François, Saint-Tropez . . 068023
Robillard, Clamart 062318, 124200
Robin, Eloi, Liège 058322
Robin, Jeanne & Roland, Cérilly . . . 099100
Didier Robin & James Fattori, Granville 121009
Robin Hood Antiques, Canterbury . . 055630
Robin Hood's Bay and Fylingdale Museum, Robin Hood's Bay 040843
Robinbois, Valencia 081676
Robins Antik, Stockholm 082011
Robin's Gallery, Nashville 117369
Robin's Nest, Miami 090235
Robin's Nest, Mount Tamborine . . . 094913
Robin's Nest, Richmond 092099
Robinson, New Orleans 090612
Robinson, Carol, New Orleans 117501
Robinson, Chris, Plymouth 114261
Robinson, E.N., Indianapolis 089337
Robinson, Georgia, Pittsburgh 142778
Robinson, James, New York 091195
Robinson, John, Wigan 087149
Robinson, Mariah, Richmond 092100
Robinson, Peter, Heacham 084639
Robinson, Peter, Wragby 114740
Robinson, Robert, Pittsburgh 118949
Robinson, Thomas, Will & Pascal, Houston 116396
Robinson Blaxill, Neill, Sevenoaks . 086542
Robinson & Reeves, Miami 117134
Robinson Visitors Center, Hartsville 044469
Robinsons, Knokke-Heist 096357
Robischon, Denver 116040
Robison, Holmfirth 113254
El Roble, Zaragoza 129825
Roble Center, Montevideo 087341
Robledo, Madrid 081379
Robson, Barnard Castle . . 083391, 130337
Robson, Northleach 086103
Robson Gallery, Halliwells House Museum, Selkirk 040982
Robuck, Jennifer, Austin 087610
Robundo, Tokyo 134731
Robur House Antiques, Perth, Tasmania 056463
Roby, Saint Paul 132773
Robyr, Annie, Montana-Vermala . . . 111740
Roca, Bucureşti 080170, 140881
Rocamora Brocante, La Bisbal d'Emporda 081008
Rocanville and District Museum, Rocanville 006300
Rocca, Venezia 076969
Rocca, Antoine, L'Haye-les-Roses . 063810
Rocca, Laura, Torino 076862, 128353
Rocca Borromeo, Museo dell'Abbigliamento Infantile, Angera 023206
Rocca Sanvitale, Fontanellato 024221
Rocchi, Sylvie, Blan 061506
Rocchini, Franca, Firenze 075392
Roccioletti, William, Frankfurt am Main 070780
Rocco, Rosaria, Napoli 076041
Rocco, Vincent, New York 091196
Roccolta d'Arte Sacra, Convento Francescano di Bosco, San Piero a Sieve 025723
Rocfort, Tony, La Baule-Escoublac . 099382
Rocfort, Tony, Rennes (Ille-et-Vilaine) 101088
Rocha, Barbizon 061204
Rocha, Paris 100808
Rocha, José Manuel M., Porto 129200
Da Rocha, Roselaine Bertoletti, Porto Alegre 058521
Rochan, Jeddah 080364
Rochas, Sylvain, Versailles 068820
Rochdale Art and Heritage Centre, Rochdale 040844
Rochdale Book Company, Rochdale 142020
Rochdale Pioneers Museum, Rochdale 040845
Roche, Bremen 070043
Roche, Tokyo 107096
Roche, Joseph, Marseille 064389
Roche, Lysiane, L'Isle-sur-la-Sorgue 063958
Roche, Michel, Paris 100809
Roche, Michel, Saint-Vincent-le-Paluel 068038
Roche, Philippe, La Ferté-sous-Jouarre 063376
Roche, Stéphane, Bordeaux 061649, 138051
Roche-Laclau, Francine, Laroin . . . 063538
Rochebonne, Paris 100810
Rochefort, London 131158
Rochelle & Co, Toronto 059281
Rocher, Alain, Paris 124795
Rocher Saint-Léon, Dabo 011558
Rochester Antiques, Rochester 056540
Rochester Art Center, Rochester . . . 047475
Rochester Hills Museum at Van Hoosen Farm, Rochester 047473
Rochester Historical and Pioneer Museum, Rochester 001434
Rochester Historical Society Museum, Rochester 047482
Rochester Museum, Rochester 047483
Rochet, Christophe, Bourg-en-Bresse 061709
Rochford, Minneapolis 132390
Rock, Rudolf, Zürich 083020
The Rock and Roll Hall of Fame and Museum, Cleveland 042998
The Rock Antiques, The Rock 056541
Rock County Historical Society Museum, Janesville 044839
Rock Creek Gallery, Washington . . . 120343
Rock Creek Station State Historic Park, Fairbury 043781
Rock House Museum, Wytheville . . 049323
Rock Island Arsenal Museum, Rock Island 047494
Rock Island County Historical Museum, Moline 045959
Rock 'n Roll Collectibles, New Orleans 090613
Rock 'n Roll Museum Arum, Arum . 029274
Rock 'n' Rustic, Maylands, South Australia 056174
Rock Pool Fine Art, Sidmouth 114435
Rock Springs Historical Museum, Rock Springs 047496
Rockarchive Gallery, London 113863
Rockart International, Montville . . . 094874
Rockart International, Noosa Heads 094967
Rockbourne Roman Villa, Fordingbridge 039511
Rockbridge Historical Society Museum, Lexington 045282
Rockcavern, Beechworth 000786
Rockefeller Archeological Museum, Israel Museum, Jerusalem, Jerusalem . 022974
Rockefeller Museum, Jerusalem . . 022975
Rockefeller's Antiques, Jacksonville 089455
Rocket Gallery, London 113864
Rocket to Mars, Providence 092048
Rocketart Gallery, Newcastle 094943
Rockford Art Museum, Rockford . . . 047500
Rockford College Art Gallery/Clark Arts Center, Rockford 047501
Rockhampton and District Historical Museum, Rockhampton 001435
Rockhampton Art Gallery, Rockhampton 001436
Rockhill Centre for Contemporary Arts, Glasgow 113128
Rockhill Trolley Museum, Rockhill Furnace 047504
Rockhurst Review, Kansas City . . . 136617
Rocking Chair Antiques, Warrington 087033
Rocking Horse, Oklahoma City 132583
Rocking Horse Antiques, Goomeri . 055900
Rockingham, Princeton 047242
Rockingham Art Gallery, Rockingham 095152
Rockingham Castle, Market Harborough 040428
Rockingham Free Museum, Bellows Falls 042123
Rockingham Road Antiques, Kettering 130841
Rockland Center for the Arts, West Nyack 052357
Rockland County Museum, New City 046215
Rockoxhuis, Antwerpen 003187
Rockport Art Association, Rockport 055009
Rockport Art Association Museum, Rockport 047508
Rockport Publishers, Gloucester . . . 135361
Rockridge Antiques, Oakland 091435
Rocks Centre Art Gallery, Sydney . . 095304
Rockston, Lusaka 120550
Rockwell, Ottawa 123800
Rockwell Museum of Western Art, Corning 043156
Rockwood Museum, Wilmington . . . 049208
Rocky Ford Historical Museum, Rocky Ford 047517
Rocky Lane School Museum, Fort Vermilion 005474
Rocky Mount Arts Center, Rocky Mount 047519
Rocky Mount Children's Museum, Rocky Mount 047520
Rocky Mount Museum, Piney Flats . 047029
Rocky Mountain Art, Denver 116041
Rocky Mountain Coin, Denver 088729
Rocky Mountain College of Art and Design, Denver 051252
Rocky Mountain College of Art and Design Galleries, Denver 043416
Rocky Mountain Conservation Center, University of Denver, Denver 043417
Rocky Mountain Doll Fantasy, Denver 088730
Rocky Mountain National Park Museum, Estes Park 043738
Rocky Mountain Quilt Museum, Golden 044235
Rocky Mountain Rangers Museum, Kamloops 005660
Rocky Reach Dam, Wenatchee 049057
Rocky Valley Gallery, Tintagel 114578
Rocky's Antiques and Books, San Diego 092679, 142914
Rococo Antiques, Weedon 087060
The Rocque, Hamilton 058863
Rocznik, Günter, Pfarrweisach 073314
Rocznik Muzeum Narodowego w Kielcach, Kielce 136035
Roczniki Sztuki Śląskiej, Wrocław . 136036
Rød Bygdetunet, Uskedalen 031305
Rod-Pol, Kraków 079652
Rode, Bordeaux 061650
Rode, Joëlle, Cadaujac 061855
Rode, Volker, Gelnhausen 125711
De Rode Cirkel, Leiden 108105
De Rode Deur, Dordrecht 078315
Rodecka, A., Gdynia 108915
Rodenberg, Geschw., Borken, Westfalen 069959
Rodenberg, Minden, Westfalen 072549
Rodenburg & Keus, Dordrecht 078316
Rodenkirch, Bertram, Oberschan . . 111792
Roderick, London 085652, 131159
Rodetoren4, Zutphen 108278
Rodgers, Paul, New York 118344
Rodgers & Nash, Malvern East 056137
Rodgers Tavern, Perryville 046890
Rodhain, Bruno, Paris 138533
Rodin, Seoul 107279
Rodin Museum, Philadelphia Museum of Art, Philadelphia 046983
Rodman Hall Arts Centre, Saint Catharines 006330
Rodney, Kreuztal 103789
Rodney, Arthur, Shoreham-by-Sea .086596, 131494
Rodney Fox Shark Museum, Glenelg 001065
Rodný Dom L'udovíta Štúra a Alexandra Dubčeka, Uhrovec 034449
Rodný Domek Adalberta Stiftera, Okresní muzeum Český Krumlov, Horní Planá 008382
Rodný Domek Aloise Jiráska, Hronov 008393
Rodný Domek Otokara Březiny, Městské muzeum, Počátky 008578
Rodon, Gent 058206
Rodrigue, New Orleans 117502
Rodrigue, Michel, Paris 066497
Rodrigues, Alberto Dias, Lisboa . . . 109350
Rodrigues, Arnaldo, Rio de Janeiro . 096643
Rodrigues, José Ribeiro, Lisboa . . . 080003
Rodrigues, José Esteves, Lisboa . . 129172
Rodrigues, José Manuel, Lisboa . . . 140851
Rodrigues, Luizandro A.G., Rio de Janeiro 058647
Rodrigues, Marco Antonio Silva, São Paulo 058737
Rodrigues, Maria Clara, Porto 080110
Rodrigues, Oscar Pereira, Lisboa . . 140852
Rodrigues & Lopes, Lisboa 080004
Rodriguez, Madrid 081380
Rodriguez, Albert, Saint-Ouen 067880
Rodríguez, Alvaro, Montevideo 087342
Rodríguez, Carlos Fernando, Bogotá 123909
Rodriguez, F. Javier, Zürich 130261
Rodriguez, José, Zürich 083021
Rodriguez, Lilian, Montréal 097072
Rodriguez, Roxane, Paris 100811
Rodríguez, Wolf, Montevideo 122788
Rodriguez Alvarez, Sevilla 129742

Rodriguez Carballo, Avelina, Valencia . . . 081677
Rodriguez Juarez, Ruben, Guadalajara . . . 077567
Rodriguez Martinez, Vicenta, Valencia . . . 081678
Rodriguez Perez, José, Sevilla . . . 129743
Rodriquez, Nancy, San Antonio . . . 092572
Rodts, M., Maldegem . . . 123661
Roduner, Bruno, Wetzikon . . . 082904
Roduner, Bruno, Wetzikon . . . 082905
Roe, Dallas . . . 115934
Roe, John, Islip . . . 084807
Roe & Moore, London . . . 141882
Röbbig, Gerhard, München . . . 072835
Röben, Wilhelmshaven . . . 074442
Roebling, New York . . . 118345
Roebourne Old Goal Museum, Roebourne . . . 001437
de Roeck-Van Dijck, Antwerpen . . . 057730
Röcker, Pascale, Pähl . . . 104578
Roedde House Museum, Vancouver 006707
Rödel, J., Rottach-Egern . . . 104778
Röder, Hermann, Rodershausen . . . 073550
Roeder, Margarete, Köln . . . 071996
Roeder, Matthias 6000 Schlüterstr 14, Berlin . . . 069736
Roeder, Roland, Uhldingen-Mühlhofen . . . 121616
Röder, Walter, Kaiserslautern . . . 103470
Rödner, Helmut, Haarlem . . . 140444
Röhnert, Werdau, Sachsen 105203, 126994
Roehr, Mirosław, Poznań . . . 129067
Röhsska Museet, Göteborg . . . 036303
Roelants, H., Genk . . . 058165
Röling, Amsterdam . . . 077947
Röll, Dr. Josef, Dettelbach . . . 133862
Rölli, Rudolf, Eschenz . . . 111400
Roelofs, Jan, Amsterdam . . . 077948
Roelofsz, Charles, Amsterdam . . . 077949
Roels, R., Gent . . . 123626
Römer, Heidi, Zürich . . . 083022, 112168
Römer Galerie, Weißenburg in Bayern . . . 105200
Römer und Bajuwaren Museum Burg Kipfenberg, Kipfenberg . . . 018257
Roemer- und Pelizaeus-Museum, Hildesheim . . . 017924
Römerbad, Schwangau . . . 020126
Römerbadmuseum, Hüfingen . . . 018017
Römerhalle, Bad Kreuznach . . . 015738
Römerhaus Walheim, Walheim . . . 020652
Römerkastell Saalburg, Bad Homburg v.d.Höhe . . . 015722
Römermuseum, Mainhardt . . . 018784
Römermuseum, Mautern, Niederösterreich . . . 002300
Römermuseum, Obernburg . . . 019396
Römermuseum, Zweigmuseum des Badischen Landesmuseums Karlsruhe, Osterburken . . . 019506
Römermuseum Augst, Augusta Raurica, Augst . . . 036863
Römermuseum Bedaium, Heimat-und Geschichtsverein Bedaium in Seebruck e.V, Seebruck . . . 020165
Römermuseum in der Grundschule Rißtissen, Ehingen, Donau . . . 016897
Römermuseum Kastell Boiotro, Archäologische Staatssammlung - Museum für Vor- und Frühgeschichte, Passau . . . 019575
Römermuseum Multerer, Grabenstätt . . . 017497
Römermuseum Stettfeld, Ubstadt-Weiher . . . 020513
Römermuseum Teurnia, Lendorf . . . 002220
Römermuseum Wallsee-Sindelburg, Wallsee . . . 002807
Römermuseum Weißenburg, Archäologische Staatssammlung München, Weißenburg in Bayern . . . 020776
Römerzeitliches Museum, Ratschendorf . . . 002503
Römisch-Germanisches Museum, Museen der Stadt Köln, Köln . . . 018339
Römisch-Germanisches Zentralmuseum, Forschungsinstitut für Vor- und Frühgeschichte, Mainz . . . 018794
Römische Baureste Am Hof, Wien Museum, Wien . . . 002994
Römische Ruinen unter dem Hohen Markt, Wien Museum, Wien . . . 002995
Römische Thermenanlage, Weißenburg in Bayern . . . 020777
Römische Villa Rustica Möckenlohe, Adelschlag . . . 015442
Römischer Weinkeller Oberriexingen, Zweigmuseum des Württembergischen Landesmuseums Stuttgart, Oberriexingen . . . 019409
Römisches Freilichtmuseum, Hechingen . . . 017818
Römisches Haus - Goethe-Nationalmuseum, Stiftung Weimarer Klassik und Kunstsammlungen, Weimar, Thüringen . . . 020751
Römisches Museum, Städtische Kunstsammlungen, Augsburg . . . 015619
Römisches Museum für Kur- und Badewesen, Neustadt an der Donau . . . 019280
Römisches Museum Remagen, Remagen . . . 019792
Römisches Museum und Naturkunde-Museum, Zumsteinhaus, Kempten 018237
Römisches Parkmuseum, Aalen . . . 015432
Römmeler, Jürgen, Rheine . . . 073524
Rönesans Sanat Galerisi, İstanbul . 112353
Rönne, V., Westerland . . . 074371
Rönnell, Stockholm . . . 141171
Rönnquist & Rönnquist, Malmö . . . 110979
Röntgen-Gedächtnisstätte, Würzburg . . . 021006
Röpke, Stefan, Köln . . . 103701
Roepzaal Ternesse, Wommelgem . . 120791
Roer, Münster . . . 104376
Rörbäcksnäs Hembygdsgård, Lima 036421
Het Roerkopje, Ede . . . 140413
Roerstreekmuseum, Sint Odiliënberg . . . 030151
Roesch, Jane, Pittsburgh . . . 091857
Roesch, Sonja, Houston . . . 116397
Rösch, Thomas, Reutlingen . . . 104735
Röseler, Jutta, Wehningen . . . 074293
Roesinger, Christa E., Köln . . . 103702
Röske, Horst, Alfdorf . . . 125054
Röske, Rainer, Berlin . . . 102023
Roesler, Nara, São Paulo . . . 096687
Rösli, Flaach . . . 082368
Roess, Michel, Munster . . 064842, 124466
Rössler, München . . . 104299
Rössler, Berthold, Ravensburg . . . 104675
Rössler, Verena, Rapperswil, Sankt Gallen . . . 082736
Rössler & Oswald, Wädenswil . . . 082896
Rössli, Balsthal . . . 111159
Rössli, Klosters . . . 082514
Rösti, Andreas, Gümligen . 082490, 130043
Rötger, Niels, Wuppertal . . . 074535
Röthel, M., Großpösna . . . 125767
Ria Röthinger & Michaela von Welck, Köln . . . 126114
Röttgen, Gladenbach . . . 071004
Röttges, Pforzheim . . . 073320
Rötzel & Co., Frankfurt am Main . . . 070781
Rötzer, Franz & Elke, Schwarzenbruck . . . 073761
Rövekamp, Ursula, Zürich . . . 112169
Röver, Ralf E., Donaueschingen . . . 070270
Röver, Sabine, Nürnberg . . . 104489
Roferber, Montevideo . . . 087343
Rogaland Bilmuseum, Vigrestad . . . 031335
Rogaland Fiskerimuseum, Åkrehamn . . . 030714
Rogaland Krigshistorisk Museum, Sola . . . 031206
Rogaland Kunstmuseum, Stavanger 031231
Rogaland Kunstnersenter, Stavanger . . . 108759
Rogalla, F. & K., Heide, Holstein . . . 071441
Rogalsky, Heinz, Hamburg 071314, 125838
Rogé, Emmanuel, Pertuis . . . 101001
Rogendorfer-Ausstellung, Sonderausstellung des Museumsvereins, Pöggstall . . . 002443
Rogeon, Pierre-Marie, Paris . . . 121197
Roger, Den Haag . . . 078242
Roger, Utrecht . . . 108261
Roger, Arthur, New Orleans . . . 117503
Roger, Arthur, New Orleans . . . 117504
Roger, Claude-Henri, Dreuil-les-Amiens . . . 062740
Roger, Hans-Peter, Neuss . . . 126539
Roger, Hassan, Paris . . . 066498
Roger 25, Barcelona . . . 129393
Roger Guffey Gallery, Kansas City . . 044926
Roger Raveelmuseum, Machelen . . 003621
Roger Tory Peterson Institute of Natural History Museum, Jamestown . . . 044831
Roger Williams National Memorial, Providence . . . 047265
Rogers & Co, London . . . 085653
Rogers, Alla, Washington . . . 120344
Rogers, Anthony, Ebikon . . . 111388
Rogers, Charles P., New York . . . 091197
Rogers, Clive, Staines . . . 086681
Rogers, Jolly, Hamilton . . . 058864
Rogers, Robert D., Omaha . . . 118721
Rogers, Rogers, London . . . 141883
Rogers, Wendy, Perth . . . 056461
Rogers Antikvariat, Malmö . . . 141131
Roger's Antiques Gallery, London . . 085654
Rogers Daisy Airgun Museum, Rogers . . . 047522
Rogers de Rin, London . . . 085655
Rogers Historical Museum, Rogers . 047523
Rogers House Museum and Gallery, Ellsworth . . . 043684
Roger's Upholstering, Pittsburgh . . 132674
Rogg & Trachsler, Basel . . . 082168
Rogge, Berlin . . . 125284
Rogge, B., Berlin . . . 125285
Roggenbuck, Dr. Stefan, Gelsenkirchen . . . 102931
Rogier & Rogier, London . . 085656, 131160
Rogin, Frank, New York . . . 091198
Rogner & Bernhard, Hamburg . . . 134021
Rogue Art Space, San Francisco . . . 119778
Rogue Buddha Gallery, Minneapolis 117301
Rogue Gallery and Art Center, Medford . . . 045742
Rogue Valley Art Association, Medford . . . 055010
Rogues, Hong Kong . . . 097826
Rogues, Phoenix . . . 091766
Rohain, Oostende . . . 058368
Rohan, Landerneau . . . 138113
Rohaut, Françoise, Honfleur . . . 063168
Rohaut Delassus, Françoise, Blonville-sur-Mer . . . 061532
Rohde, E., Potsdam . . . 073365
Rohde, Eberhard, Westerland . . . 105229
Rohen, Karen, Hagen, Westfalen . . 125781
Rohleder, Ilona, Berlin . . . 069737
Rohlfing, K.-H., Preußisch Oldendorf . . . 126661
Rohlmann, Heinz, Lebrade . . . 139384
Rohloff-Haluzàn, V., Nürnberg . . . 139613
Rohnstädter Heimatstube, Weilmünster . . . 020732
Rohr, F., Bern . . . 129971
Rohr, Hans, Bern . . . 141230
Rohr, Susan, Luzern . . . 111702
Rohrbach, Katharina, Obernburg . . 104504
Rohrer, A., Grenzach-Wyhlen . . . 071095
Rohrer, Ingrid, Konstanz . . . 103766
Rohrer, Karin, Höchstädt, Oberfranken . . . 071539
Rohs, L., Düren . . . 102463
Rohse, Otto, Hamburg . . . 134022
Le Roi David, Montauban . . . 064638
Le Roi Fou, Paris . . . 066499
Roider, Beatrix, München . . . 126445
Roig, Barcelona . . . 080920
Roig-Sabater, J., Mannheim . . . 072433
Roijen, J., Banholt . . . 128577
Roinet, Jacques, Plouguenast . . . 066873
Roiter, Marcio, Rio de Janeiro . . . 058648
Roja, Warszawa . . . 109190
Rojas, Miami . . . 132356
Rojas, Manolo, Madrid . . . 110606
Rojas Jūras un Zvejniecības Muzejs, Roja . . . 027772
Rojas Rodriguez, N., Granada . . . 129533
Rojaus Kalnas, Vilnius . . . 107371
Rojo Pinturas Española, Madrid . . . 081381
Rojstna Hiša Pesnika Otona Župančiča, Vinica . . . 034536
Rojstna Hiša Simona Gregorčiča, Vrsno . . . 034538
La Roka, Merano . . . 075549
Roka, Henriette, Røyken . . . 079487
Rokeby Museum, Rowland Evans Robinson Memorial Association, Ferrisburgh 043838
Rokko Heart, Kobe . . . 106884
Rokoko, Moskva . . . 080261
Rokoko, Warszawa . . . 129115
Rokokomuseum Schloß Belvedere, Stiftung Weimarer Klassik und Kunstsammlungen, Weimar, Thüringen . . . 020752
Rokuharamitsu-ji Treasure House, Kyoto . . . 026764
Rokuonji, Kyoto . . . 026765
Rokuzan Bijutsukan, Hotaka . . . 026548
Rol, Alain, Beaune . . . 061293
Rolan, Riyadh . . . 080382
Roland, Bremen . . . 121361
Roland, Köln . . . 071997
Roland, New York . . . 091199
Roland, C., Mons . . . 058344
Roland, Guy, Mons . . . 058345
Roland, Victor, Bruxelles . . . 058073
Roland, William, New York . . . 091200
Roland Gallery, Bath . . . 083442
Roland Gibson Gallery, Potsdam . . . 047207
Røldal Bygdemuseum, Røldal . . . 031144
Roldan Galeria, Sevilla . . . 110777
Roldan Marin, F., Sevilla . . . 110778
Roldo, Agostino, Modena . . . 075927
Rolevink, Bert, Armadale, Victoria . 055393
Rolf Bergendorffs Radio Museum, Lessebo . . . 036415
Rolfe, Susan, New York . . . 118346
Rolies, Antwerpen . . . 057731
Rolin, Gérard, Mazerulles . . . 064450
Rolla, Gian, Genova . . . 127484
Rolla Minerals Museum, University of Missouri, Rolla . . . 047530
Rollag Bygdetun, Rollag . . . 031145
Rollan & Reche, Madrid . . . 129678
Rolland, Emile, Courbevoie . . . 062512
Rolland, Jean-François, Sologny . . 068260
Rolland, Pierre, La Coquille . . . 063346
Rolland, René, Evron . . . 062830
Rolland, Roger, Saint-Ouen . . . 067881
Rolle, Madrid . . . 081382
Rolleston, Brian, London . . . 085657
Rollettmuseum, Baden bei Wien . . . 001746
Rollf's Gallery, Fresno . . . 116184
Rolli, Bernard, Bern . . . 082236, 129972
Rollin, Philippe, Limoges . . . 121037
Rollin, Pierre, Rouen . . . 101122, 124883
Rollin Art Centre, Port Alberni . . . 006170
Rolling Stone Press, Atlanta . . . 114918, 135323
Rollo Jamison Museum, Platteville . 047082
Rolls-Royce Museum, Dornbirn . . . 001788
Rolly, Pierre, Coulonges-les-Sablons . . . 062506
Rolly-Michaux, Boston . . . 115226
Rol'nícky Dom Vlkolínec, Liptovské Múzeum, Ružomberok . . . 034421
Rolnik, Robert, Pfaffenhofen an der Ilm . . . 126624
Rolo & Majoli, Roma . . . 128184
Roloff, Ostseebad Prerow . . . 126604
Roloff Pfeiffer, Marion, Santiago de Chile . . . 059551
Rom-Art-Galerie, Braunschweig . . . 102224
Roma, Don Torcuato . . . 123166
Roma Antiqua, Roma . . . 076649

Roma Color, Roma 076650, 128185
R.O.M.A. Consorzio, Roma 128186
Roma Roma Roma, Roma 106617
Romagne, Raymond, Fontclaireau . 062901
Romagnoli, Federica, Parma 127862
Romagny, Paris 100812
Romahn, Annemarie, Brüggen, Niederrhein 102274
Római Katolikus Egyházi Gyűjtemény, Sárospatak 021836
Római Katonai Fürdő, Budapest . . . 021692
Római Kötár, Szentendre 021885
Romain & Sons, A.J., Wilton, Salisbury 087160
Romain Rea, Paris 066500
Roman, Herbert, New York 118347
Román, Oscar, México 107511
Roman Army Museum, Greenhead . 039639
Roman Bath House, Lancaster 039925
Roman Baths Museum, Bath 038630
Roman Gil, Fernando, Barcelona . . 129394
Román Kori Kőtár, Pécs 021826
Roman Legionary Museum, Caerleon 038939
Roman Painted House, Dover 039278
Roman Theatre of Verulamium, Saint Albans 040888
Roman Villa, Brading 038815
Roman Villa Museum at Bignor, Pulborough 040786
Romana Antichitá, Roma 076651
Romana Antichitá, Roma 076652
Romanazzi, Luca, Bari . . . 075030, 127123
Romanengo, Laura, Genova 127485
Romanet, Paris 100813
Romanet, Jeannine, Montrichard . . 064773
Romang, Delio, Gstaad 111542
Romaní, Zamora 081728, 129796
Romani, Alberto, Roma 128187
Romanian Ethnic Art Museum, Cleveland 042999
Romann, Henri, München . 072836, 126446
Romano, Adliya 057614, 095985
Romano, Buenos Aires 136753
Romano, Alessandro, Firenze 075393
Romano, Filomena, Roma 076653
Romano, Giuseppe, Milano 127671
Romano, Laura, Palermo 106441
Romano, Paolo, Firenze 075394
Romano, Rosaria, Napoli 076042
Romano, Simone, Firenze 075395
Romano, Venerando, Rorschach . . . 082754
Romano, Vittorio, Firenze 075396
Romanos, Casablanca 077674
Romanov, Vancouver 097526
Romanovskie Palaty v Zarjade, Gosudarstvennyj istoričeskij muzej, Moskva 033522
The Romantic Agony Book and Print Auctions, Bruxelles 120740, 137464
Romantic Notions, Las Vegas 089604
Romantica Aina's, Jørpeland 079394
Romantica Antiek, Antwerpen 057732
Romanticismo e Dintorni, Napoli . . 135955
Romantika '96, Budapest 074719
Romantikerhaus, Jena 018113
Romantique, Auckland 078978
Romantique, Oslo 079467
La Romantique, Saint Paul 092393
Romantiques, Brookvale 055568
Romantiques, Manawatu 079143
Romantiques, Mona Vale 056243
Romantiques, Trevor 086917, 131607
Romany Folklore Museum and Workshop, Selborne 040978
Romark, Letchworth 130888
Romart, Amsterdam 107791
Rombach, Freiburg im Breisgau . . . 139118
Rombaut, Alexander, Gent 137502
Romberger, S., Landshut 072147
Rombourg, Franck, Isernhagen 071639
Rombouts & Zoon, H., Casteren . . . 128617
Romé, Auxerre 061106
Rome, de, Bradford 122430
Rome Antique-Antiquités, Romorantin-Lanthenay 067209
Rome Art and Community Center, Rome 047535
Rome Historical Society Museum, Rome 047536
Romeira, José, Sion 082814
Romela, Toronto 059282
Romeleit, M. L., Köln 071998
Romeny, Regi, Amsterdam 128552
Romeo, Fresno 088919
Romeo, Grazia, Catania 127276
Roméro, Bayonne 061239
Romero, Barbara, Caen 061883
Romero Zazueta, Enrique, México . 107512
Rometti, Olivier, Nice 138260
Romfeia, Plovdiv 096707
Romiley Antiques, Romiley 086396
Romiti, Rio de Janeiro 058649
Romito, Alfredo & Norberto, Rosario 055297
Romney Toy and Model Museum, Romney Hythe and Dymchurch Railway, New Romney 040528
Romsdalsmuseet, Molde 031030
Romsley Picture Gallery, Romsley . 114324
Ron Morel Memorial Museum, Kapuskasing 005664
Rona Gallery, London 113865
Rona Gallery, Wellington 108644
Ronacher, Josef, Wals . . . 057346, 123484
Ronald Reagan Boyhood Home, Dixon 043474
Ronald V. Jensen Living Historical Farm, Wellsville 049054
Ronan Gallery, Perth 114239
Ronbourg, J., Burgwedel 070110
Ronconi, Maurizio, Parma 127863
Ronda, Jean, Tours 068603
Ronda-Brou, Tours 068604
La Ronde des Bois, Auberives-sur-Varèze 061036
Ronde des Objets, Seilhac 068198
Rondeau Provincial Park Visitor Centre, Morpeth 005962
Rondet Sylvain, Aix-en-Provence . . 098795
Rondom 1920, Den Haag 078243
Rondula, Dölsach 056958, 095493, 123345, 133065
Ronen, Amsterdam 077950
Rong Xin, Zhai, Singapore 080551
Rongier, Maurice, Vic-sur-Cère 068849
Rongione, Sandro, Milano 127672
Rongyu Guan, Jiangyin 007146
Rønholt Iversen, Erik, Brønshøj 137863
Roniger Memorial Museum, Cottonwood Falls 043185
Ronin, New York 091201, 118348
Ronny Auto Dealer, Zebbug 077550
Ron's Attic, Baltimore 087705
Ron's Big Book, Southport 137089
Ron's Book Shop, Macquarie 136985
Ronsard, Paris 124796
Ronssin, Jean-Loup, Meung-sur-Loire 064542
Rontonton, Utrecht 078816
Ronvaux, J., Bruxelles 058074
Roodepoort Museum, Florida Park . 034612
Roohnikan, Renate, Bottrop 102210
Rooijen, H. den, Dordrecht 078317
Rook & Co., Curaçao 078897
Rookie, Jacksonville 089456
Rooksmoor, Bath 112582
Roola, Nagoya 106933
Room, Megève 064468
Room 125, Boston 087842
Room 403, Melbourne 094825
Room Service Vintage, Austin 087611
Room4, Ryde 114332
Rooma, Delhi 105680
Rooms and Gardens, New York 091202
Rooms and Gardens, San Antonio . . 092573
Rooms That Bloom, Kansas City . . . 089519
Roopa-Lekha, Delhi 135848
De Roos, Antwerpen 096089
Roos, Den Haag 078244
Roos, Eckhard, Tuttlingen 105080
Roos, M. & D., Frankfurt am Main . 070782
De Roos van Tudor, Leeuwarden . . . 108096
Roosens, Bruxelles 058075
Rooseum, Center for Contemporary Art, Malmö 036462
Roosevelt Campobello, Lubec 045515
Roosevelt Campobello International Park, Welshpool 006788
Roosevelt County Museum, Eastern New Mexico University, Portales 047154
Roosevelt Island Visual Arts, New York 118349
Rooster, Saint Louis 119246
Root, Sidney, Bruxelles 058076
Root House Museum, Marietta 045668
Root Seller, Phoenix 091767
Rooted in Wood, Baltimore 087706, 131827
Rootenberg, Robert, West Hollywood 120409
Roots of Norfolk at Gressenhall, Gressenhall 039641
Roots & Relics, Honolulu 088976
Rop, G. De, Aachen 101523
Ropac, Thaddaeus, Paris 100814
Ropac, Thaddaeus, Salzburg 095733, 133147
Ropars, Philippe, Rennes (Ille-et-Vilaine) 124877
Roparshaugsamlinga, Isdalstø 030923
Rope, Ted, Dargaville 108423
Ropers Hill Antiques, Staunton Harold 086698
Ropert, Claude, Lyon 064182
Roppongi Antique Fair, Tokyo 093803
Rops, Namur 096394
Rops, Saint-Servais 120787
Roq la Rue Gallery, Seattle 119986
Roque, Mario, Lisboa 080005
Roque Roque, Josefa, Barcelona . . 129395
Roques, Nice 065142
Roques, Fabienne, Sens 124933
Roques, Pierre-Edmond, Pau 066713
Roques, Teddy, Mondonville 064598
Roquette, Luísa, Lisboa 080006
Roquigny, Bruno, Ourville-en-Caux . 121104
Roquigny, Bruno, Saint-Valery-en-Caux 121253
Rori, Roma 076654
Rori, Parioli, Roma 076655
Rori, Priscilla, Roma 076656
Rørosmuseet, Røros 031150
Ros, Teia 134954
De Ros, Valencia 081679
Ro's Oriental Rugs, Nashville 090484
Rosa, Jacksonville 089457
Rosa, José, Carcavelos 121918
Rosa, José, Lisboa 121944
Rosa, Michael-Manuel de la, Berlin 138833
Rosa, Pietro, Roma 128188
Rosa, Roberto de la, Los Angeles . . 089896
Rosa, Umberto, Roma 128189
Rosa Studio, Indianapolis 132161
Rosado, Manuel, Nantes 064943
Rosales, Madrid 081383
Rosalie House, Eureka Springs 043756
Rosalie House Museum, Natchez . . 046161
Rosalie Shire Historical Museum, Goombungee 001070
Rosalie Whyel Museum of Doll Art, Bellevue 042116
Rosalux Gallery, Minneapolis 117302
Rosart, Québec 097162
Rosarta, Rotterdam 108207
Rosat, Aloïs, Les Moulins 082676
Rosatelli, Francesco, Roma 076657
Rosati, Renata, Firenze 075397
Roschewitz, B., Jersbek 071656
Roscoe Village Foundation, Coshocton 043181
Roscommon County Museum, Roscommon 022851
Roscrea Heritage Centre, Roscrea . 022852
Rose, Krefeld 072078, 126148
Rose, Tampa 132963
Rose, Anthony, Yass 095453
Rose, Charles, Melbourne 056201
Rose, Christine, New York 118350
Rose, Dianne, Fort Worth 088883
Rose, Dirk, Hamburg 103214
Rose, Giovanni, Bayreuth 069493
Rose, Giovanni, Bayreuth . 069494, 125141
Rose, Ludwig, Hamburg 071315
Rose, Marjorie, Pittsburgh 118950
Rose, Marjorie, San Francisco 092875
Rose, Michael, London 085658
Rose, Michael, London 085659
Rose, Michael, London 085660
Rose, Michael, London 085661
Rose, Monika, Detmold 070231
Rose, Peter, New York 118351
Rose, R.E., London 085662, 131161
Rose, R.L., Edinburgh 084309
Rose, R.L., Glasgow 084469
Rose, Dr. Ulrich, Greifswald 139152
Rose and Crown Antiques, West Malling 087090, 131667
Rose Antiques, Ashbourne 083331
Rose Antiques, Cleveland 088357
Rose Antiques, Toronto 059283
Rose Art, Vernantois 068776
Rose Art Museum, Brandeis University, Waltham 048847
Rose Center Museum, Morristown . 046041
Rose Cottage, Denver 116042
Rose Cottage Antiques, Birdwood . . 055504
Rose Cottage Antiques, Fyshwick . . 055856
La Rose des Vents, Le Cannet 063584
Rose Fine Art and Antiques, Stillington 086707, 131535
Rose Galleries, Saint Paul 092394, 123093
Rose Gallery, Northampton 114155
The Rose Garden, Baltimore 087707
Rose Hill Mansion, Geneva 044165
Rose Hill Museum, Bay Village 042065
Rose Hill Plantation State Historic Site, Union 048695
Rose House Museum, Picton 006148
Rose Lawn Museum, Cartersville . . 042640
Rose Museum at Carnegie Hall, New York 046396
La Rose noire, Peißenberg 073303
Rose Passé, Troyes 068654
Rose Rose, São Paulo 058738
Rose Seidler House, Wahroonga . . . 001589
Rose Street Gallery, Armadale, Victoria 094172
Rose Valley and District Heritage Museum, Rose Valley 006302
De Rose Winkel, Deventer 078282
Roseau County Historical Museum, Roseau 047540
Roseberry, Calgary 058802
Rosebery's, London 122598
Rosebud, El Paso 088813
Rosebud Centennial Museum, Rosebud 006303
Rosebud County Pioneer Museum, Forsyth 043886
Rosebud Studios, Surf Beach 095237
Rosebud's, Tampa 093150
Rosedale, Albany 108291
Rosedale Street Gallery, Dulwich Hill 094494
Rosefeld, Libbesdorf 072244
Rosehr, Kiel 071843, 126045
Roseland Antiques, Toronto 059284
Rosemann, Pegnitz 073298
Rosemann 413685, Susanna & Frank, Vilseck 105126
Rosemary and Time, Thame 086879, 131589
Rosemont Art Gallery, Regina 097182
Rosemont Plantation, Woodville . . . 049297
Rosemount Art Gallery, Regina 006261
Rosemount Gallery, Aberdeen 112481
Rosemount Lodge Art Gallery, Richmond, New South Wales 095131
Rosemount Museum, Pueblo 047278

Rosén, Götene 122145
Rosen, Andrea, New York 118352
Rosen Kavalier, Houston 089192
Rosenbach, Detlev, Hannover 103296
Rosenbach, Louis, Dallas 088604
Rosenbach Museum, Philadelphia 046984
Rosenbad, Stockholm 141172
Rosenbaum, Dallas 115935
Rosenbaum, Houston 116398
Rosenberg, Milano 106298
Rosenberg, A., Bremerhaven 070056
Rosenberg, Alex J., New York 118353
Rosenberg, C., Heswall 084675
Rosenberg & Co., Paul, New York 118354
Rosenberg, René, Holte 060258
Rosenberg Gallery, Goucher College, Baltimore 042003
Rosenberg & Kaufman, New York 118355
Rosenblatt, Minna, New York 091203
Rosenblom, Göteborg 110929
Rosenborg Slot, Danske Kongers Kronologiske Samling, København 008986
Rosendahler, Rosendahl 073569
Den Rosendahlske Bibelsamling, Esbjerg 008845
Rosendal, Durbanville 110040
Rosendals Slott, Stockholm 036661
Roseneath Gallery, Armidale 055400
Rosenfeld, Philadelphia 118827
Rosenfeld, Tel Aviv 105925
Rosenfeld, Michael, New York 118356
Rosenfeld, Michelle, New York 118357
Rosenfeld, Samuel, New York 118358
Rosenhagen, Johann, Öhringen 073178
Rosenhauer, Göttingen 102981
Rosenheimer Verlagshaus, Rosenheim 134371
Rosenholm Slot, Hornslet 008929
Rosenkranz, Chemnitz 102313
Rosenkranz, Magdeburg 072376
Rosenkranz, Christiane, Hamburg 125839
Rosenkranz, Conner, New York 118359
Rosenkranz, Ernst, Wien 137360
Rosenlew-museo, Pori 009988
Rosenlöfs Tryckerimuseum, Kungsgården 036408
Rosenmuseum Steinfurth, Bad Nauheim 015756
Rosenrod, Hovås 081837
Rosenstock, Denver 116043
Rosenstock, Denver 116044
Rosenstock, Denver 142397
Rosenthal, Berlin 102024
Rosenthal, Minneapolis 117303
Rosenthal, New Orleans 090614
Rosenthal, Ludwig, Leidschendam 140486
Rosenthal, Marcia, Pittsburgh 118951
Rosenthal, Marie-Eve, Saint-Ouen 067882
Rosenthal, Stan, Hastings 113201
Rosenthal Gallery of Art, Caldwell 042545
Rosenwald-Wolf Gallery, University of the Arts, Philadelphia 046985
Rosenzweig, M. & D., Bonn 102195
Rosequist, Tucson 120162
Rosersbergs Slott, Rosersberg 036546
Rose's Bookshop, Hay-on-Wye 141653
Il Roseto, Genova 075502
Rosetown Museum and Art Center, Rosetown 006305
Rosetzky, Marion, Red Hill 095119
Rosewall Memorial Shell Museum, Port Lincoln 001398
Rosewe, Klara, Pforzheim 073321
Rosewood, Bologna 075105
Rosewood, Oakland 091436
Rosewood Antiques, Traralgon 056735, 123320
Rosewood Furniture, Melbourne 056202
Rosewood Scrub Historical Museum, Marburg 001218
Roseworthy Agricultural Museum, Roseworthy 001439
Rosgartenmuseum, Konstanz 018379
Rosh, West Hollywood 093507
Rosicrucian Egyptian Museum, San Jose 047900
Rosies från Gammalt till Nytt, Spånga 081901
Rosin, Douglas, Chicago 088162
Rosin, Reinhard, Rottach-Egern 073603
Rosina's, Falmouth 084379, 130702
Rosing, H. & M, Bocholt 069878
Roskam, F.H., Broek in Waterland 128612
Roskamp, Hyma, Hamburg 125840
Roskamp, W., Kleve 071879
Roskell, Plymouth 114262
Roskilde Domkirkemuseum, Roskilde 009080
Roskilde Museum, Roskilde 009081
Roskilde Museums Købmandsgård, Roskilde 009082
Roslagens Sjöfartsmuseum, Väddö 036754
Roslagsmuseet, Norrtälje 036507
Roslavlskij Istoriko-chudožstvennyj Muzej, Roslavl 033699
Roslyn Oxley9 Gallery, Paddington 095038
Rosoff, Charles, New York 118360
Rosot, Jean, Pont-Aven 066915
Rosrestavracija, Moskva 129239
Ross, Dublin 127100
Ross, Goulburn 055909
Ross, Washington 133035
Ross, B., San Jose 132924
Roß, Betina, Berlin 125286
Roß, Betina, Ellerau 125583
Ross, Douglas, Woburn 122754
Ross, Hardie, Chipping Campden 083984
Ross, Jane, Carlton South 055633
Ross & Co., John, Belfast 122407
Ross, John, Tucson 093262
Ross, Luise, New York 118361
Ross, Marcus, London 085663
Ross, Morgan, Seattle 093060
Ross, Nancy, Chicago 088163
Ross, Simon, New York 091204, 132526
Ross Abbey Gallery, Sassafras 095185
Ross Antiques, Ross 056554
The Ross C. Purdy Museum of Ceramics, Westerville 049109
Ross Castle, Killarney 022810
Ross County Historical Society Museum, Chillicothe 042900
Ross Farm Museum, New Ross 006001
The Ross Gallery, Belfast 112618
Ross House Museum, Winnipeg 006860
Ross Memorial Museum, Saint Andrews 006323
Ross Old Book and Print Shop, Ross-on-Wye 142022
Ross-on-Wye Antiques Gallery, Ross-on-Wye 086404
Ross Thomson House Museum, Shelburne 006455
Ross Thomson Museum, Halifax 005582
Rossacher, Kurt & Simone, Steyr 133164
Rossaert, Antwerpen 137403
Roßberg, Markkleeberg 126293
Rossberg, Werner, Davos Platz 082338
Rossburn Museum, Rossburn 006306
Rossel, Paul Adam, Maastricht 128763
Rosselet, André, Auvernier 134977
Rosselli, John, New York 091205
Rosselli & Assoc. John, Washington 093434
Rossendale Footware Heritage Museum, Rawtenstall 040804
Rossendale Museum, Rawtenstall 040805
Rosseto, Volmir Luiz, Porto Alegre 096579
Rossetto, Roland, Chaumont (Haute-Marne) 062250
Rossi, San Francisco 092876, 132908
Rossi, Sankt-Peterburg 109645
Rossi, Toulon (Var) 068471
Rossi, André, Basel 082169
Rossi, Anna, Bologna 075106
Rossi, D., Bad Honnef 069303
Rossi, Flora, Roma 076658
Rossi, Dr. Giovanni, Milano 127673
Rossi, Jean-Pierre, Saint-Michel-l'Observatoire 067677
Rossi, Julcir, São Paulo 058739
Rossi, Laura, Roma 128190
Rossi, Leopoldo, Milano 075844
Rossi, Massimiliano, Roma 076659, 128191
Rossi, Paolo, Milano 127674
Rossi & Rossi, London 085664
Rossier, Pittsburgh 118952
Rossier, Claude, Fribourg 130028
Rossier, David & Colette, Rougemont 082756
Rossignol & Fils, Céret 124175
Rossignol, Daniel, Les Arcs 138118
Rossignol, Gabriel, Paris 138534
Rossignol, Gérard, Paris 100815
Rossignol, Henri, Cannes 138066
Rossignoli Picotti, Giuseppina, Verona 128438
Rossijskij Antikvarnyj Salon, Moskva 093853
Rossijskij Ėtnografičeskij muzej, Sankt-Peterburg 033826
Rossijskij Komitet Meždunarodnogo Soveta Muzeev (IKOM Rossii), Moskva 054023
Rossini, Paris 121198
Rossini, Aldo, Milano 075845
Rossini, Gianfranco, Lugano 082608
Rossiters, Crescent Head 094441
Rossland Historical Museum, Rossland 006307
Rosslyn, Dunedin 079091, 108449, 128936
Rosslyn Chapel, Roslin 040854
Rosso, Fulvio, Trieste 076904
Rosso, Mano, Oakland 091437
Rosso, Sonia, Torino 106701
Rosso, Yolande, Nice 065143
Rosso Bianco-Auto Museum, Aschaffenburg 015581
Rossolacca, Milano 075846
Rossum, E., Emmerich 070564
Rost, Rudolf & August, Wien 057540
Rost, Sebastian, Berlin 125287
Rosta-Buchladen, Münster 139572
Rostand, Michel, Paris 121199
Rosteck, Lemgo 072226, 103902
Rostenne, J., Bruxelles 137465
Rosthal, Meerbusch 121512
Rostovskij Filial Sankt-Peterburgskogo Gosudarstvennogo Universiteta Kultury i Iskusstv, Rostov-na-Donu 050658
Rostovskij Kreml - Gosudarstvennyj Muzej-zapovednik, Rostov (Jaroslavskaja obl.) 033701
Rostovskij Oblastnoj Muzej Kraevedenija, Rostov-na-Donu 033704
The Rostra Gallery, Bath 112583
Rostrum, South Petherton 086644, 131515
Rostrup Gaute, Sandnes 108751
Rostworowski, Dominik, Kraków 108977
Rosvall, C.W., Denver 122886
Roswell Museum and Art Center, Roswell 047554
Roszkov, Budapest 105543
Rot-Kreuz-Museum, Regenstauf 019762
Rota, Emmelshausen 070557
Rota, Nurieux-Volognat 065249
Rota, Bertram, London 141884
Rotary Museum of Police and Corrections, Prince Albert 006205
Rotas de Arte, Lisboa 109351
Rotation, Los Angeles 089897
Rotberg, H. W. Freiherr von, Heidelberg 125901
Rotch-Jones-Duff House and Garden Museum, New Bedford 046191
Rotenburg, Judi, Boston 115227
Roter Haubarg, Witzwort 020942
Rotermundt, Amsterdam 077951
Rotes Antiquariat, Berlin 138834
Roth, Leipzig 072215
Roth, Minneapolis 117304
Roth, München 126447
Roth, Reinach (Basel-Land) 082738
Roth, Valparaíso 059565, 123886
Roth, Artur, Mainhardt 072383
Roth, Eberhard, Schwaigern 126784
Roth, Gertrud & Ernst, Esselbach 102665, 125608
Roth, H., Magdeburg 072377
Roth, Heidy, Basel 082170
Roth, Hermann, München 072837
Roth, Hildegard, Gelsenkirchen 070960
Roth, Joachim, Theres 105046
Roth, Manfred, Gifhorn 070997
Roth, Michael, Kitchener 096935
Roth, Monika, Linz 123413
Roth, Rolf, Brugg 082274
Roth Horowitz, New York 118362
Roth Horowitz, West Hollywood 120410
Rothäuser, Michael, Essen 102702
Rothamel, Dr. Jörk, Erfurt 102647
Rothamel, Ursula, Darmstadt 125444
Rothas Art Gallery, Islamabad 108770
Rothballer, Markus, Weiden, Oberpfalz 074298
Rothballer, Peter, Pressath 073371
Rothe, Erfurt 070589
Rothe, Maria, Frankfurt am Main 102816, 133952
Rothe House Museum, Kilkenny 022805
Rothen, Zernsdorf 127059
Rothenbach, D. & R., Bad Kreuznach 069318
Rothenbücher, P., Bayreuth 121316
Rothenburger Künstlerbund e.V., Rothenburg ob der Tauber 053553
Rothenhäusler, Ulrike, Tiefenbronn 126902
Rother, Harald, Wien 057541, 123527
Rotherfold Antiques, Totnes 086908
Rotherham Art Gallery, Rotherham 040857
Rothfischer, Karin, Seeon 073788
Rothfuss-Stein, Elwine, Karlstein am Main 126011
Rothko Chapel, Houston 044654
Rothmühler Heimatmuseum und Archiv, Oestrich-Winkel 019446
Rothschild, Montréal 058999
Rothschild, New Orleans 090615
Rothschild, New Orleans 090616
Rothschild, Saint Louis 092306
Rothschild, Sigmund, New York 123010
Rothschild House, Port Townsend 047144
Rothwell & Dunworth, Dulverton 141561
Rotini, Eleonora, Livorno 106130
Rotkreuz-Museum, Nürnberg 019370
Rotkreuz-Museum Berlin, Berlin 016162
Rotkreuzmuseum, Hofheim, Unterfranken 017965
Rotor - Association for Contemporary Art, Graz 052594
Rotorua Museum of Art and History, Te Whare Taonga o te Arawa, Rotorua 030589
Rotovnik, Hanne, Klampenborg 137876
Rotstab, Liestal 111647
Rottar, Martina, Berlin 138835
Rottauer Museum für Fahrzeuge, Wehrtechnik und Zeitgeschichte bis 1948, Pocking 019645
Rotten Verlag, Visp 135073
Rotterdams Radio Museum, Rotterdam 030102
Rotterdamse Antiekhallen, Rotterdam 078741
Rottingdean Grange Art Gallery and National Toy Museum, Brighton 038851
Rottinghaus, Cincinnati 115658
Rottler, D., Riegel 073532
Rottloff, Karlsruhe 103502, 134078
Rottmann, Steinfurt 073906
Rottmann, Andreas, Wülfershausen 127037
Rottmann, Frank, Blomberg, Lippe 069870
Rottneros Park, Rottneros 036547
Rottnest Island Museum, Rottnest Island 001441
The Rotunda, Charlottesville 042767
Rotunda, Vilnius 107372
Rotunda Gallery, Brooklyn 042467
Rotunda Museum of Archaeology and Local History, Scarborough 040967
Rotušės, Alytus 107343

Rouayroux, Jean-Pierre, Montpellier 064754
Roubaud, Sylvia, München 104300
Roubin, Marc, Saint-Affrique 067342
Rouch, Yves, Carcassonne 061981
Rouchaléou, Montpellier 138223
Roucka, München 104301
Roudaut, Landerneau 063512, 124289
Rouden, André, La Seyne-sur-Mer . 063448
Roudillon, Jean, Paris 066501
Roudillon, Michel, Paris 066502
Roue Libre, Grignan 138104
Rouen Détection Numismatique, Rouen 067296
Rouenson, Marie-Josèphe, Coye-la-Forêt 062542
Rouffet-Goudier, Ascain 061006
de Rouffignac, Colin, Wigan 087150
Rouflay, Bernard, Perpignan 066756
Rouflay, Pierrette, Nîmes 065187
Rouge, Pierre, Mâcon 064207
Rouge 91, Brunoy 099039
Rouge-Pullon, Paris 124797
Rougeau, Richard, Bracieux 061744
Rougeaux Bayle, Martine, Pau 066714
Rouges, Jean-Marie, Montauban . . 064639
Rouget de Lisle Antiquités, Courlans 062514
Rough and Tumble Engineers Museum, Kinzers 045021
Rough Rustique, Kyneton 056076
Roughshed, Petworth 086260
Roughton, Dallas 115936
Rougier, Laurent, Bordeaux 124143, 138052
Rouhani, Saint Louis 092307
Rouif, Paris 100816
Rouillac, Philippe, Paris 121200
Rouillac, Philippe, Vendôme 121276
Rouilly, Orléans 065307
Rouje, Québec 097163
Rouleau and District Museum, Rouleau 006310
Roullet, Dominique, Rouen 067297
Roulmann, F., Paris 138535
Roulston Museum, Carstairs 005232
Roumet, Paris 066503
Roumieu, Claude, Cavaillon 062044
Round Corner Antiques, Dural 055772
The Round House, Penzance 114235
Round Top Antiques Fair, Round Top 094027
Round Top Center for the Arts - Arts Gallery, Damariscotta 043287
Roundabout Antiques, Wondai 056842
Roundabout Antiques Centre, Haywards Heath 084638
Roundell, James, London 113866
Rounds, Al, Salt Lake City 119367
Roura Comas, Juan Arturo, Barcelona 080921
Rourke, Peter, Vancouver 123856
Rouse Hill Estate, Rouse Hill 001442
Roussard, André, Paris 100817
Rousseau, Marcq-en-Barœul 064278
Rousseau, Florent, Paris 124798
Rousseau, Nadine, Bourges 138055
Rousseaux, Dominique, Paris 066504
Rousseaux, Dominique, Saint-Ouen 067883
Roussel, Toronto 059285
Roussel, Thérèse, Perpignan 066757, 100994
Roussel-Demaretz, Michèle, Nampont-Saint-Martin 064851
Rousselle, Henrianne, Ris-Orangis . 067154
Rousselot, Bouxières-aux-Dames . . 061738
Roussil, Montréal 097073
Roussillot, Yves & Marie-Claude, Drevant 062742
Roussos, Nikolaos, Athinai 074604
Roussou, Marilena, Athinai 074605, 127070
Route 66 Antique Connection, Albuquerque 087422
La Route D'Alexandre, Paris 066505
Route de la Soie et ses Merveilles, Paris 100818
Routledge, London 135258
Rouveloux, Christophe, Limoges . . . 063897
Rouvière, Gérard, Le Cailar 063582
Roux, Claude, Gannat 062960
Roux, Gilles, Mouriès 064818
Roux, Michel, Limay 063875
Roux, Philippe, Beaune 061294
Le Roux, Yves-Marie, Paris 121201
Roux & Troostwijk, Paris 121202
Rouyer, Michel, Liverdun 063969
Rouzaud, Jean-Marie, Le Cheylard . 063604
Rovana, Deisenhofen 070205
Rovani, Genova 106107
Rovaniemen Kotiseutumuseo, Rovaniemi 010045
Rovaniemen Taidemuseo, Rovaniemi 010046
Rovegno & C., Andrea, Genova 075503
Rovers, Haarlem 078479
Roversi, Giorgio, Bologna 075107
Rovi, Lugo 081195
Rovira, Barcelona 080922, 110240
Rovira, Jacques, Pia 066820
Rovira, Monique, Saint-Féliu-d'Avall 067473
Row, Charlotte 087975
Rowan, H., Bournemouth 141426
Rowan Gallery, Drymen 112959
Rowan Museum, Salisbury 047764
Rowe, Martyn, Chacewater 122453
Rowe, Phil, Chicago 088164
Rowland, Michael, Stow-on-the-Wold 086759
Rowland, Michelle, San Francisco . 119779
Rowland, Simon H., Chelmsford . . . 122456
Rowland Evans Robinson Memorial Association, Ferrisburgh 055011
Rowles & Co., Calgary 096843
Rowles & Co., Edmonton 096894
Rowles, Welshpool 087074, 114659
Rowletts of Lincoln, Lincoln 085000
Rowley, Ely 084328, 122502
Rowley, London 113867
Rowley, London 131162
Rowley Gallery, Holybourne 113261
Rowley Historical Museum, Rowley 047559
Rowley's House Museum, Shrewsbury 041023
Rowntree Antiques, Montréal 059000
Roxane's, Caen 061884
Roxborough, Newport Beach 056337
Roxburgh, U., Manawatu 128942
Roxbury, Houston 089193
Roxbury Historical Museum, Roxbury 047561
Roxy, Dallas 088605
Roxy Antik, Frederiksberg 060243
Roxy Klassik, Frederiksberg 060244
Roy, Elke, Bad Mergentheim 069327
Roy, Joël, Montamise 064618
Roy, Joël-Denis, Royan 067314
Roy, Martine, Paris 124799
Roy, Patrick, Lausanne 111631
Roy, Paule, Bourg-la-Reine 061712
Roy Boyd Gallery, Roy, Chicago . . . 042878
Le Roy Patrick, La Neuville-Roy . . . 063400
Roy Rogers-Dale Evans Museum, Branson 042388
The Roy Rogers-Dale Evans Museum, Victorville 048784
Roy Whalen Regional Heritage Centre, Deer Lake 005337
Royal Academy of Arts, London . . . 050839
Royal Academy of Arts Gallery, London 040266
Royal Academy Schools, Postgraduate Diploma in Fine Arts, London 050840
Royal Academy Shop, London 135259, 141885
Royal Air Force Air Defence Radar Museum, Norwich 040610
Royal Air Force Museum, London . . 040267
Royal Air Force Museum, Shifnal . . 041011
Royal Air Force Museum 201 Squadron, Saint Peter Port 040938
Royal Air Force Museum Reserve Collection, Stafford 041082
Royal Albert Memorial Museum and Art Gallery, Exeter 039465
Royal Anglian Regiment Museum, Imperial War Museum, Duxford 039338
Royal Antikvitás, Budapest 074720
Royal Antiques, New Orleans 090617
Royal Antiques, New York 091206
Royal Antiques, Panamá City 079529
The Royal Arcade Watch Shop, London 085665
Royal Architectural Institute of Canada, Ottawa 052773
Royal Armouries, London 040268
Royal Armouries at Fort Nelson, Fareham 039483
Royal Armouries Museum, Leeds . . 039959
Royal Army Dental Corps Historical Museum, Aldershot 038478
Royal Army Educational Corps Museum, Beaconsfield 038642
Royal Army Veterinary Corps Museum, Aldershot 038479
Royal Art, Aalst 057663
Royal Art, Brasília 096504
Royal Art, Frankfurt am Main 102817
Royal-Art, Genève 082466
Royal Art Galleries, Sliema 107452
Royal Art Gallery, Hamilton 096924
Royal Art Gallery, New Orleans 117505
Royal Art Museum, Berlin 016163
Royal Art Society of New South Wales, North Sydney 052485
Royal Arts Foundation, Newport . . . 046466
Royal Asiatic Society of Sri Lanka, Colombo 054127
Royal Athena Galleries, New York . . 091207
Royal Atlantic Wax Museum, Hunter River 005629
Royal Australian Air Force Museum, Point Cook 001385
Royal Australian Corps of Transport Museum, Puckapunyal 001411
Royal Australian Infantry Corps Museum, Singleton 001468
Royal Bank of Scotland Art Collection, London 040269
Royal Barges National Museum, Bangkok 037888
Royal Berkshire Yeomanry Cavalry Museum, Windsor 041416
Royal Birmingham Society of Artists, Birmingham 054472
Royal Birmingham Society of Artists, Birmingham 112656
Royal Borough Collection, Maidenhead 040386
Royal Borough Museum Collection, Windsor 041417
Royal Brierley Crystal Museum, Dudley 039291
Royal British Columbia Museum, Victoria 006749
Royal British Society of Sculptors, London 040270, 054473
Royal Brunei Armed Forces Museum, Bandar Seri Begawan 004616
Royal Cambrian Academy of Art, Conwy 039137
Royal Cameo Glass, New Orleans . . 117506
Royal Canadian Air Force Memorial Museum, Astra 005036
Royal Canadian Artillery Museum, Shilo 006465
Royal Canadian Military Institute Museum, Toronto 006626
Royal Canadian Mint, Winnipeg . . . 006861
Royal Canadian Mounted Police Museum, Regina 006262
Royal Canadian Ordnance Corps Museum, Montréal 005949
The Royal Canadian Regiment Museum, London 005793
Royal Carriage Museum, Bulaq-el-Dakrur 009288
Royal Ceremonial Dress Collection, London 040271
Royal Coin and Jewelry, Houston . . 089194
Royal Collectibles, Honolulu 088977
Royal Collectibles, San Francisco . . 092877
Royal College of Art, London 040272
Royal College of Art, London 050841
Royal College of Art Society, London 054474
Royal College of Obstetricians and Gynaecologists Collection, London 040273
Royal College of Surgeons in Ireland Museum, Dublin 022771
Royal Cornwall Museum, Truro 041243
Royal Crafts and Collectibles, Columbus 088434
Royal Crescent Antiques, New Orleans 090618
Royal Crown Derby Museum, Derby 039229
Royal de Paris, New York 091208
Royal Doulton Specialty Shop, Buderim 055579
Royal Electrical and Mechanical Engineers Museum, Arborfield 038518
Royal Engineers Museum, Chatham 039041
Royal Engineers Museum, Gillingham, Kent 039542
Royal Exchange Art Gallery, London 085666, 113868
Royal Exchange Art Gallery, London 113869
Royal Fine Art, Tunbridge Wells . . . 114613
Royal Fine Art Commission, London 054475
Royal Fine Art Commission for Scotland, Edinburgh 054476
Royal Flying Doctor Service Visitors Centre, Edge Hill 001010
Royal Furniture Refinishing, Edmonton 123765
Royal Fusiliers Regimental Museum, London 040274
Royal Gallery, Montréal 097074
Royal Gallery, San Francisco 119780
Royal Glasgow Institute of the Fine Arts, Glasgow 039572
Royal Gloucestershire, Berkshire and Wiltshire Regiment Museum, Salisbury 040948
The Royal Governor's Mansion, Perth Amboy 046892
Royal Green Jackets Museum, Winchester 041405
Royal Ground Art Gallery, Oakland . 118644
Royal Gunpowder Mills, Waltham Abbey 041291
Royal Hamilton Light Infantry Heritage Museum, Hamilton 005595
Royal Hampshire Regiment Museum, Winchester 041406
Royal Highland Fusiliers Regimental Museum, Glasgow 039573
Royal Holloway College Picture Gallery, Egham 039431
Royal Hospital Chelsea Museum, London 040275
Royal Incorporation of Architects in Scotland Gallery, Edinburgh 039417
Royal Inniskilling Fusiliers Regimental Museum, Enniskillen 039449
Royal Institute of Oil Painters, London 054477
Royal Institute of Painters in Watercolours, London 054478
Royal Irish Fusiliers Museum, Armagh 038529
Royal Irish Regiment Museum, Ballymena 038579
Royal Jewellery Studio, Auckland . . 108360
Royal Jewelry Museum, Alexandria 009283
Royal Lincolnshire Regiment Museum, Lincoln 040012
Royal Logistic Corps Museum, Deepcut 039221
Royal London Hospital Archives and Museum, London 040276
Royal London Wax Museum, Victoria 006750
Royal Malaysian Air Force Museum, Kuala Lumpur 027980
Royal Malaysian Navy Museum, Lumut 027987

Royal Marines Museum, Portsmouth 040769
The Royal Mews, Royal Collection, London 040277
Royal Mile Curios, Edinburgh 084310
Royal Military Academy Sandhurst Collection, Camberley 038952
Royal Military College of Canada Museum, Kingston 005707
Royal Military Police Museum, Chichester 039074
Royal Mill Gallery, Edinburgh 084311
Royal Mint Sovereign Gallery, London 040278
Royal Museum, Seoul 027592
Royal Museum, National Museums of Scotland, Edinburgh 039418
Royal Museum and Art Gallery, Canterbury 038982
Royal Museum Sri Menanti, Muzium Negeri Sembilan, Seremban 028013
Royal National Lifeboat Institution Headquarters Museum, Poole . . . 040740
Royal Naval Museum Portsmouth, Portsmouth 040770
Royal Naval Patrol Service Association Museum, Lowestoft 040352
Royal Navy Submarine Museum, Gosport 039611
Royal New Zealand Army Medical Corps Museum, Christchurch 030467
Royal New Zealand Navy Museum, Devonport 030478
Royal Newfoundland Constabulary Museum, Saint John's 006370
Royal Norfolk Regimental Museum, Norwich 040611
Royal Numismatic Society, London . 054479
Royal Numismatic Society of New Zealand, Wellington 053926
Royal Oak Traders, Auckland 078979
Royal Observatory Greenwich, National Maritime Museum, London 040279
Royal Observer Corps Museum, Eastleigh 039369
Royal Ontario Museum, Toronto . . . 006627
Royal Over-Seas League, London . . 054480
Royal Pavilion, Brighton 038852
Royal Photographic Society, Bath . . 054481
The Royal Photographic Society Octagon Galleries, Bath 038631
Royal Pump Room Museum, Harrogate 039679
Royal Queensland Art Society, Brisbane 052486
Royal Queensland Art Society, Broadbeach 052487
Royal Regiment of Fusiliers Museum, Warwick 041306
Royal Research Ship Discovery, Dundee 039312
Royal Saint John's Regatta Museum, Saint John's 006371
Royal Saskatchewan Museum, Regina 006263
Royal Scots Regimental Museum, Edinburgh 039419
Royal Scottish Academy, Edinburgh 050813
Royal Scottish Academy Collections, Edinburgh 039420
Royal Shakespeare Company Collection, Stratford-upon-Avon 041142
Royal Signals Museum, Blandford Forum 038766
Royal Society for the Encouragement of Arts, Manufactures and Commerce, London 054482
Royal Society of Antiquaries of Ireland, Dublin 053717
Royal Society of Arts and Sciences of Mauritius, Réduit 053862
Royal Society of British Artists, London 054483
Royal Society of British Artists. Publication, London 136266
Royal Society of Marine Artists, London 054484
The Royal Society of Miniature Painters, Sculptors and Gravers, Gillingham, Dorset 054485
Royal Society of Painter-Printmakers, London 054486
Royal Society of Portrait Painters, London 054487
Royal South Australia Society of Arts, Adelaide 052488
Royal South Australian Art Society, Adelaide 052489
Royal Sporting Antiques, Woodlands 056846
Royal Standard Antiques, Cowes . .084096, 130613
Royal Street Gallery, Paris 100819
Royal Sussex Regiment Museum, Eastbourne 039364
Royal Thai Navy Museum, Samut Prakan 037928
Royal Tyrrell Museum of Palaeontology, Drumheller 005362
The Royal Ulster Constabulary Museum, Belfast 038667
Royal Ulster Rifles Regimental Museum, The Royal Irish Rangers, Belfast . 038668
Royal Vending, Saint Louis 119247
Royal Watercolour Society, London . 054488
Royal Welch Fusiliers Regimental Museum, Caernarfon 038942
Royal West of England Academy, Bristol 050805
Royal Western Australian Historical Museum, Nedlands 001321
Royal Wiltshire Yeomanry Museum, Swindon 041179
Royal Winnipeg Rifles Museum, Winnipeg 006862
Royal York Auction Gallery, Pittsburgh 123058
Royale Silver Company, Los Angeles 089898
Royall, E. & C., Medbourne 131272
Royall House, Medford 045738
Royalton Historical Society Museum, Royalton 047564
Royalty Coins and Jewelry, San Antonio 092574
Royalty Fine Arts, Atlanta 114919
Le Royaume des Puces, Bruxelles . 058077
Le Royaume du Dahomey, Venezia . 076970
Royce Myers, Tulsa 120204
Roycroft Antiquarian Booksellers, Kew East 136964
Royden Prior Gallery, Eton 113035
Royer, Alain, Paris 066506
Royer, Elisabeth, Paris 100820
Royer, Elizabeth, Paris 100821
Royer, Jean-Pierre, Paris 124800
Royet, Auguste, Saint-Just-Saint-Rambert 067571
Royet, Auguste, Saint-Just-Saint-Rambert 067572
Royet, Georges, Panissieres 065334
Royo, Jésus, Espoey 062805
Røyrvik Bygdatun, Limingen 030988
Roy's Antiques, Clifton Hill 055695
Roy's Refinishing, Buffalo 131861
Roy's Upholstery, Ottawa 123801
Royston and District Museum, Royston 040860
Roz, Maria, Quintin 067031
Roza Azora, Moskva 109582
Różańska, Ewa, Gdynia 079601
Roždecetvenskaja Jarmarka Antikvariata, Moskva 093854
De Roze Patio, Sint-Niklaas 058376
Rozelle House Galleries, Ayr 038561
Rozenburg, Delft 078149
Rozendaal, N.E.J., Laren, Noord-Holland 140470
Rozet, Frédéric, Opoul- Perillos . . . 065274
Rozmarin, D., Olching 104534
Rožmberský Dům, Husitske Muzeum v Táboře, Soběslav 008689
Rózsa Naiv Art Galéria, Budapest . . 105544
R.P. Strathearn Historical Park, Simi 048183
RPA, Zagreb 123948
R.R., Madrid 081384
RR & H Specialty and Collectables, Cleveland 088358
R.R.1919, Genova 106108
R.S. Barnwell Memorial Garden and Art Center, Shreveport 048162
RS Fine Art, Tulsa 120205
RSA Journal, London 136267
RSA Library, London 040280
RSM Art Conservation, Fortitude Valley 123226
RSM Art Conservation, Mapleton . . 123262
R.S.V., Logroño 081187
RT Biz, Faversham 113061
RT Modern and Contemporary, Hong Kong 097827
Rubaiyat, Calgary 096844
Les Rubans Bleus, Vincennes 068999
Rubbers, Buenos Aires 094088
Rubbish, Los Angeles 089899
Rube, Eberhard, Koblenz 103573
Rubelle and Norman Schafler Gallery, Brooklyn 042468
Ruben, Los Angeles 132279
Ruben Goudsmid, H.J., Veendam . . 128863
Rubenianum, Antwerpen 003188
Rubens Maskinhistoriska Samlingar, Götene 036308
Rubens Schilderijen, Enschede 108023
Rubenshuis, Antwerpen 003189
Rubenstein, Paula, New York 091209
Ruberl, Richard, Wien . . . 057542, 095928
Rubi, Girona 081136
Rubicon Gallery, Dublin 105886
Rubin, Chuck, Louisville 090022
Rubin, Kaj, København 060375
Rubin, Lawrence, Milano 106299
Rubin, Lawrence, Zürich 112170
Rubin Museum, Tel Aviv 023090
Rubinacci, Genova 075504, 121691
Rubini, Fabrizio, Roma . . . 076660, 128192
Rubio, Mar del Plata 136763
Rubio, Pepe, Palma de Mallorca . . . 081492
Rubio Herrera, Jose, Palma de Mallorca 081493
Rubio Parra, M.J., Barcelona 080923
Ruby, J., Donaueschingen 070271
Ruby Antiques, Penryn 086207
Ruby Green Contemporary Arts Foundations, Nashville 046151
Ruby's Book Sale, New York 142691
Rucellai, Roma 106618
Rucellai, Roma 106619
Ruch, René, Paris 124801
Ruchi's Collection, Hyderabad 105712
Ruck, M., Gengenbach 070965
Rucker, Charles, San Diego 119545
Ruckers Hill Antiques, Northcote . . 056380
Ruckli, Andrea, Engelberg 111394
Ruckstuhl, Josef, Ruswil 082759
Rudd, Winnie, Jacksonville 089458
Rudd House Museum, Kimberley . . 034665
Ruddell Gallery, Black Hills State University, Spearfish 048268
Ruddick's Folly, Suffolk 048414
Ruddington Framework Knitters' Museum, Ruddington 040863
Ruddington Village Museum, Ruddington 040864
Ruddy Antiques, Petworth 086261
Rudenel, Rio de Janeiro 058650
Rudic, Apaculco 107463
Rudigier, Gertrud, München 072838
Rudloff, Claudia & Thomas, Scheinfeld 104820
Rudolf, Keitum 103525
Rudolf, Annegret, Oldenburg, Oldenburg 073208
Rudolf, Hans-Jürgen, Mannheim . .072434, 126284
Rudolf, Johann, Kassel 071761
Rudolf Steiner Archiv, Dornach 037050
Rudolf Steiner Archiv, Dornach 135008
Rudolf Weinwurm-Museum, Göpfritz 001915
Rūdolfa Blaumaņa Memoriālais Muzejs Braki, Ērgļi 027682
Rudolff, Britta, Köln 126115
Rudolf's, Fürstenfeldbruck 102897
Rudolfv, Amsterdam 107792
Rudolph, Jette, Berlin 102025
Rudolph, Nicole, Zwickau 074580
Rudolph, Werner, Neuburg-Steinhausen 072979
Rudolph E. Lee Gallery, Clemson . . 042977
Rudolph Tegners Museum, Dronningmølle 008836
Rudomino - Bibliografičeskaja Knižnaja Lavka, Moskva 140917
Rü-Bu Antik, Kirchhain 071857
Rue dans l'Art, Beauvais 098943
Rue de Rosa, Oss 078672
Rue de Siam, Donville-les-Bains . . 062715
Rue Jadis Antiguidades, Rio de Janeiro 058651
Rue Pouchkine, Strasbourg 101304
Rueb, Amsterdam 077952
Rübeländer Tropfsteinhöhlenmuseum, Rübeland 019938
Rübener, Inge, Sonsbeck 073864
Rübesams Da Capo Oldtimermuseum, Leipzig 018587
Rueckemann, Ilona, Wuppertal 139887
Rückert-Christ, G., Grünwald 103025
La Ruée Vers l'Art, Perthes 066776
Rüesch, Marianne, Zürich 130262
Ruef, Gabriele, München 072839
Ruef, Hugo, München 121543
Rüfenacht, Rudolf, Bern 082237
Rügen-Museum, Ostseebad Binz . . 019529
Rüger, Wolfgang, Frankfurt am Main 139097
Ruehl, Adrian, New York 091210
Rühl, Armin, Bad Homburg v.d.Höhe 069297
Rühmling, M., Kampen 071699
Ruellan, Jack-Philippe, Vannes (Morbihan) 121275
Ruelle, Jean-Luc, Creil 062556
Rue's Antiques, Austin 087612
Rüsch, Andreas, Hamburg 071316, 125841
Ruesch, Jeffrey, New York 118363
Ruesch, Jeffrey, New York 118364
Rüsch, Katja, Bad Endorf 125093
Rüsch, Max, Hamburg . . . 071317, 125842
Rüschitz-Cziglar, Helga Maria, Bad Radkersburg 095470
Rüstkammer, Staatliche Kunstsammlungen Dresden, Dresden 016811
Rüter, Franz-Jürgen, Oberhausen, Rheinland 073147
Rüter, Volker, Hannover 071411
Rüthemann, Roland, Hinwil 082497
Ruetten, Erlangen 121397
Rüttenauer, Ingrid, Tegernsee 074049
Rüttger, Goldbach, Unterfranken . . . 125742
Ruetz, Barbara, Augsburg 101619
Ruetz, Barbara, München 104302
Ruetz, Dr. Karl, Basel 141213
Ruf, Freiburg im Breisgau 070856
Ruf, München . . . 072840, 104303, 134271
Ruf, Theo, Zürich 135099
Rufener, Caroline, Winterthur 141314
Rufer, San Antonio 092575
Ruff, Oskar, Stuttgart 074005
Ruff and Ready, Washington 093435
Ruffier, Jean-Alain, Le Mont-sur-Lausanne 082663
Ruffier, Jean-Alain, Le Mont-sur-Lausanne 111738
Ruffing, Frank, Neunkirchen, Saar . 104417
Ruffini, Romedio, Fällanden 082364
Ruffini-Macherel, Joseph, Fribourg 082382
Rufford Old Hall, Rufford 040865
Rufin, Sylvie, Versailles 101456
Rufini, Perugia 076235
Rug Expo, Houston 089195
Rug Gallery, Cincinnati 088276
Rug Gallery, Leicester 084951

Rug Gallery, Tucson 093263, 132989
Ruga, A., Padova 127810
Rugby Art Gallery and Museum, Rugby 040868
Rugby Decorative and Fine Arts Society, Daventry 054489
Rugby Museum, Newlands 034686
Rugby School Museum, Rugby 040869
Rugeley Antique Centre, Brereton .. 083662
Ruggeri, Alessandro, Genova 075505
Ruggles House, Columbia Falls ... 043091
Rugol, Milano 075847
Rugs and Art, Los Angeles 089900
Rugs as Art, New York 091211
Rugs of the World, Tampa 093151
Ruh, B., Baden-Baden 069424
Ruh, Bernhard, Baden-Baden 069425
Ruhl, Helmut, Neustadt, Hessen ... 073038
Ruhlaer Tabakpfeifenmuseum und Museum für Stadtgeschichte, Ruhla 019946
Ruhlaer Uhrenmuseum, Ruhla 019947
Ruhmeshalle und Bavaria, München 019108
Ruhnu Muuseum, Ruhnu 009391
Ruhr, Dr. K., Fürth, Bayern 070912
Ruhr-Rhein-Antiquariat, Mülheim an der Ruhr 072616, 139491
Ruhrlandmuseum Essen, Essen ... 017078
Ruhrtalmuseum, Schwerte 020154
Ruichengzhai Biao Hua Jin Xia Cooperative, Beijing 097676
Ruifer, Madrid 129679
Ruimte Morguen, Antwerpen 096090, 133252
Ruine der Künste Berlin, Berlin 102026, 138836
Ruïne van Brederode, Santpoort ... 030119
Ruis, Michel, Saint-Ouen 067884
Ruiskumestarin Talo, Helsingin Kaupunginmuseo, Helsinki 009566
Ruitenberg, Jan, Zwolle 078894
Ruiz, Anna, Barcelona 110241
Ruiz, Dominique, Saint-Ouen 067885
Ruiz, J., Madrid 081385
Ruiz-Clavijo Fernandez, Palmira, Barcelona 129396
Ruiz Linares, Granada 081149
Ruiz Linares, Carmen, Granada ... 081150
Ruiz Linares, C.B., Granada 081151
Ruiz Linares, Hijos de, Granada ... 081152
Ruiz Manfredi, Lazaro, Sevilla 081612
Ruiz Sanchez, Joaquin Alberto, Madrid 110607
Ruiz-Vernaca Restauradores, Madrid 129680
Rūjienas Izstāžu Zāle, Rūjiena 027774
Rukaj, Nikola, Toronto 097368
Ruks, Helmut, Potsdam 126654
Ruländer, Worpswede 105333
Rule, Denver 116045
Rule & Cale, Windsor 087183
Rullier, Guillaume, Liguge 063824
Rullier, Michel, Paris 066507
Rullier, Michel, Poitiers 066894
Rullon, Jean-Michel, Tours 068605
Rulon-Miller, R., Saint Paul 142869
Rumale, Bangalore 105612
Rumble, Simon & Penny, Chittering 083999
Rumbler, Helmut H., Frankfurt am Main 139098
Rumbullion, Kamakura 106869
Rumelihisarı Müzesi, İstanbul Hisarlar Müzeleri, İstanbul 038096
Rumer, B., Los Angeles 089901
Rumford Historical Museum, North Woburn 046542
Rumitz, Johann F., Weilheim, Oberbayern 126977
Rumiz, Bardwell Park 094215
Rumma, Lia, Napoli 106386
Rummet, Röda, Uppsala 141190
Rumners Wobble, Kitchener 058874
Rumours, Nashville 117370
Rumpelkammer, Schwarzenberg, Erzgebirge 073760
Rumpff, Tanya, Haarlem 108062
Runako, Louisville 116964
Rund um Kunst, Kiel 103544
Rundāles Pils Muzejs, Pilsrundāle . 027721
Rundetaarn, København 008987
Rundfunkmuseum der Stadt Fürth, Fürth, Bayern 017289
Rundfunkmuseum Schloß Brunn, Emskirchen 016982
Rundgang Urchigs Terbil, Törbel ... 037636
Rundlet-May House, Portsmouth .. 047190
Rundlingmuseum Wendlandhof-Lübeln, Küsten 018436
Runebergin Antikvariaatti, Helsinki . 137958
Runebergs stugan, Jakobstad 009616
Runestone Museum, Alexandria ... 041633
Runge, Eferding 056969
Runge, Kiel 103545
Runge, Linz 057163
Runge, Wertheim 074348
Rungehaus, Wolgast 020971
Runkewitz, Carmen, Berlin 125288
't Runnertje, Amsterdam 077953
Runnquist, New York 091212
Runnquist & Runnquist, Toronto ... 059286
Runogalleria, Helsinki 137959
Runstuck, M., Neunkirchen-Seelscheid 073008
Runte, Carl, Wuppertal ... 074536, 127051, 139888
Ruocco, Gabriele, Napoli 076043
Ruokolahden Kotiseutumuseo, Ruokolahti 010047
Ruoveden Kotiseutumuseo, Ruovesi 010050
Rup Silver, Mumbai 074828
Rupert Cacendish Antiques, London 085667
Rupert Museum, Stellenbosch 034754
Rupertinum, Museum der Moderne Salzburg, Salzburg 002565
Rupertinum, Verlagsabteilung, Salzburg 133148
Rupf, Christof, Dobis 125470
Rupp, Lydia, Paris 066508
Ruppert, Bochum 102161
Ruppert, Engelbert, Eltville 070550
Ruppert, Tilo, Landau in der Pfalz .. 103820
Rupprecht, Neumünster 073007
The Rural Collection, New York 091213
Rural Life Centre, Farnham 039492
Rural Life Museum and Windrush Gardens, Baton Rouge 042051
Rus-Sov Antique, Helsinki 060576
Rus-Teak, Toronto 059287
Rusant, Sankt-Peterburg 080325
Rusca, Carola, Genova 127486
Rusch, Brunsbüttel 102278
Rusch, Günter, Hamburg 071318
Rusche, Egon, Oelde 073180
Ruschman, Indianapolis 116492
Rusconi, Donatella, Milano 075848
Rusconi, M., Milano 075849
Rush, New York 118365
Rush, John, Hamilton 137643
Rush County Historical Society Museum, Rushville 047569
Rush & Wicker, Cane, Virginia Beach 133014
Rushcutters Bay Gallery, Rushcutters Bay 095165
Rushen Abbey, Manx National Heritage, Ballasalla 038572
Rushton, Malcolm, London 085668
Rushworth Museum, Rushworth ... 001443
Rusk County Historical Society Museum, Ladysmith 045085
Ruskin, Stow-on-the-Wold 086760
Ruskin Gallery, Sheffield 040999
Ruskin Library, Lancaster 039926
Ruskin Museum, Coniston 039134
Ruskin School of Drawing and Fine Art, University of Oxford, Oxford 050853
The Ruskin Society of London, Oxford 054490
Ruskon Kotiseutumuseo ja Rindellin Mäkitupalaismuseo, Rusko 010051
Russ, Bissee 069855
Ruß, Sibylle, Bamberg 125134
Russakoff, J., Philadelphia 142750
Russeck, New York 118366
Russeck, San Francisco 119781
Russell, Austin 115008
Russell, Dr., Highgate, Western Australia 055984
Russell, Inglewood 056013
Russell, London 113870
Russell, London 141886
Russell, New Orleans 132424
Russell, Beverly, Montréal 059001
Russell, Davis, Queenscliff 095110
Russell, Jack, Chipping Sodbury .. 112865
Russell, Jean, New York 091214
Russell, M. & J., Yazor 087281
Russell, Sarah, Bath 083443
Russell, Sarah, Bath 141399
Russell, Sigi, New Orleans 090619
Russell, Brightwalls, Leominster .. 122564
Russell Cave Museum, Bridgeport . 042404
Russell-Clarke, Peter, Drysdale ... 094491
Russell Collection of Early Keyboard Instruments, University of Edinburgh, Edinburgh 039421
Russell-Cotes Art Gallery and Museum, Bournemouth 038795
Russell Court Studios, Salcombe .. 114385
Russell Gallery of Fine Art, Peterborough 006143
Russell Hill Rogers Galleries, Southwest School of Art and Craft, San Antonio 047800
Russell Museum, Russell 030593
Russell Rare Prints, Bath 112584
Russian Academy of Arts, Rossijskaja Akademija Chudožestv, Moskva .. 050647
Russian American Art Gallery, Chicago 115543
Russian Art Gallery, Portland 119046
Russian Art Gallery, Portland 119047
Russian Creations, Chicago 115544
Russian Hill Antiques, San Francisco 092878
Russian Hill Bookstore, San Francisco 142963
Russian Painting Collectors Club, Sankt-Peterburg 054024
The Russian Place, Chicago 115545
Russian World, New York 118367
Russkaja Emal', Moskva 080262
Russkaja Galereja na Vozdviženke, Moskva 109583
Russkaja Gallereja, Milano 075850
Russkaja Ikona, Moskva 080263
Russkaja Restavracija, Sankt-Peterburg 129250
Russkaja Starina, Sankt-Peterburg . 080326
Russkaja Usadba, Moskva 080264
Rußkamp, M., Bielefeld 069839
Russkie Galerei Sovremennoj Živopisi, Moskva 109584
Russkie Kraski, Sankt-Peterburg .. 109646
Russkij Gosudarstvennyj Muzej Arktiki i Antarktiki, Sankt-Peterburg 033827
Russkij Modern, Sankt-Peterburg .. 129251
Russkij Muzej Fotografii, Nižnij Novgorod 033571
Russkoe Iskusstvo, Sankt-Peterburg 109647
Russkoe Pole, Moskva 109585
Russo, La Coucourde 063355
Russo, New York 091215
Russo, Aldo, Milano 127675
Russo, Donatella, Torino 128354
Russo, F., Roma 106620
Russo, Felice, Milano 127676
Russo, Gianni, Milano 075851
Russo, John, Los Angeles 116875
Russo, Laura, Portland 119048
Russo, R., Ostseebad Binz 073265
Russo, Roberto, Roma 140117
Russo, Rosa, Prora 104640
Russow, Roland, Berlin 069738
Rust, Andreas, Frankfurt am Main . 070783
Rust, Iris, Köln 071999
Rust, R.S., Ipswich 130831
Rust, Yvonne, Whangarei 108667
Rust en Vreugd Museum, Cape Town 034582
Rust 'n Dust, Atlanta 087524
Rusterholtz, Basel 111220, 122306
Rustic, Dunedin 079092
Rustic and Industrial Antiques Warehouse, Newtown, New South Wales 056339
Rustic Good Looks, Lockhart 056110
Rustic Rose Antiques, Loch 056109
Rustic Steel Creations, Tampa 120065
Rustica Antiques, Calgary 058803
Rustica Antiques, Los Angeles 089902
Rusticas del Noroeste, Salamanca . 081544
Rusticas y Antigüedades El Roble, Bogotá 059856
Rustico, Zaragoza 081751, 129826
Rustington Heritage Exhibition Centre, Rustington 040872
Rustinoff, Vladimir, Saint-Paul-de-Vence 101219
Rustler, Adolf, Düsseldorf 125546
Rusty Relics Museum, Carlyle 005229
Rusų Meno, Vilnius 107373
Rutberg, Jack, Los Angeles 116876
Ruth, Peter, Bad Schönborn 125115
Ruth & Earl's Antiques, Baltimore .. 087708
Ruth Eckerd Hall, Clearwater 042972
Ruth Hall Museum of Paleontology, Abiquiu 041573
Ruth Youth Wing, The Israel Museum, Jerusalem 022976
Ruthenberg von Klein, Corinna, Berlin 125289
Rutherford, Melbourne 056203
Rutherford, Nelson 079180, 108518
Rutherford, Marlene, Chesterfield .. 083968
Rutherford B. Hayes Presidential Center, Fremont 044078
Rutherford House, Edmonton 005405
Rutherglen and District Artists Society, Rutherglen 052490
Ruthie, Miami 090236
Ruthin Craft Centre, Ruthin 040873
Ruthmere House Museum, Elkhart . 043663
Ruth's, San Diego 092680
Ruths, Walter, Usingen 074171
Ruthsatz, Bückeburg 070079
Rutishauser, Hans E., Kreuzlingen . 082517
Rutland Antiques Centre, Uppingham 086987
Rutland Area Art Association, Rutland 055012
Rutland Cottage, Christchurch 079049
Rutland County Museum, Oakham . 040634
Rutland Railway Museum, Cottesmore 039147
Rutten, Paul, Amsterdam 077954
Rutter-Tuchler, Claudia, Düsseldorf 102544
Ruttleigh, Philip A., Crudwell 084125
Ruttmann, Friedrich, Frankfurt am Main 070784
Rutz, Maria, Düsseldorf 070432
Ruununmylly, Hämeenlinna 009494
Ruurd Wiersma Hûs, Burdaard 029369
Ruys, T., Almere 077742
Ruyter, Pieter de, Delft 128621
Růžička, Jindřich, Praha 123999
Ruzza, Aureana, Padova 076111
RV/MH Heritage Foundation, Elkhart 043664
RW, Gouda 128675
RW Fine Arts Collection, Winterthur 112001
The R.W. Norton Art Gallery, Shreveport 048163
Ry, Jessica de, Paris 066509
Ryan, Las Vegas 116644
Ryan, London 113871
Ryan, Glenroy & Violet H., Tucson .. 093264
Ryan, Karlene K., Fresno 116185
Ryan, Mary, New York 118368
Ryan, Mary Ann, Portland 142809
Ryan, Peter K., Windsor, Ontario ... 059443
Ryan, William Henry, Tulsa 120206

Ryan Fine Arts Center, Abilene 041568
Ryan-Wood, Liverpool . . . 085027, 130904
Ryan's All Glass, Cincinnati 088277, 131944
Rybár, Antonín, Karlovy Vary 060033
Rybazaar, Chicago 088165
Rybinskij Gosudarstvennyj Istoriko-architekturnyj i Chudožestvennyj Muzej-zapovednik, Rybinsk 033708
Rychner, Rose-Marie, Studen 111939
Ryckeboer, Danièle, Wimereux 069053
Rycklösa, Linghem 122191
Rydal Mount, Ambleside 038506
Rydals Museum, Rydal 036549
Ryde Bookshop, Ryde 142024
The Ryde Gallery, Ryde 114333
Ryder, Georgina, Frampton 084437, 130719
Rye Art Gallery, Rye 040875
Rye Castle Museum, Rye 040876
Rye Heritage Centre Town Model, Rye 040877
Rye Historical Society Museum, Rye 047581
Ryecliff Antiques, Clayfield 055690
Ryedale Folk Museum, Hutton-le-Hole 039789
Ryerson, Tampa 120066
Ryerson, Toronto 097369
Ryesgades Möntgalleri, Århus 060211
Ryfylkemuseet, Sand 031163
Rygg, Kari, Bergen 079379
Rygge Museum, Larkollen 030971
Rygnestadtunet, Rysstad 031157
Ryhope Engines Museum, Sunderland 041161
Ryks, Hamburg 139208
Rymättylän Kotiseutumuseo, Rymättylä 010052
Rynek Sztuki, Łódź 109020
Ryö, Stockholm 141173
Ryosan Museum of History, Kyoto . 026766
Ryotsu Folk Museum, Ryotsu 027003
Ryrie Street Art Gallery, Geelong . . 094581
Ryton Galeria, Sopot 109077
Ryu, Tokyo 107097
Ryuga-Do Cave Museun, Tosayamada 027280
Ryukodo, Yokohama 077341
Ryusaido, Kyoto 106904
Ryushi Memorial Hall, Tokyo 027232
Ryuzen, Delhi 105681
Ryuzendo, Kyoto 077123
Ryvarden Galleri, Sveio 108760
S-D Coins, Oakland 091438
S-L-1, Milano 106300
S Quartilho, Rio de Janeiro 058652
S. Ray Miller Auto Museum, Elkhart 043665
S & S Antique, Kümmersbruck 072104
S & S Firearms, Fort Worth 088884
Sa, Hangang, Seoul 077372
Sa, Kogung, Busan 077359
Sa, Myungbo, Seoul 077373
SA Breweries World of Beer, Johannesburg 034655
Sa Costa, Palma de Mallorca 081494
Sá Costa, António, Lisboa 129173
Sa Nostra, Ciutadella de Menorca . 110311
Sa Nostra, Eivissa 110349
S.A. Otkrytka, Moskva 033523
Ibn Al-Saad, Dubai 083198
Saad, Ahmad, Beirut 077414
Saad Zaghlul Museum, Munira 009342
SAAF Museum Swartkop, Pretoria . 034726
SAAF Museum Ysterplaat, South African Air Force, Ysterplaat 034779
Saal, Klaus, Ludwigshafen am Rhein 103951, 134167
Saalburgmuseum, Bad Homburg v.d.Höhe 015722
Saalburgmuseum, Bad Homburg v.d.Höhe 015723
Saale-Galerie, Saalfeld, Saale 104786
Saalfelder Feengrotten, Saalfeld, Saale 019956
Saalig, Heinrich, Frankfurt am Main 102818, 125660, 133953
Saamelaismuseo Siida, Inari 009610
Saanich Historical Artifacts Society, Saanichton 006315
Saanich Pioneer Log Cabin Museum, Saanichton 006316
Saar, Martin, Zusmarshausen 127066
Saaremaa Muuseum, Kuressaare . . 009376
Saarijärven Museo, Saarijärvi 010054
Saarländischer Museumsverband e.V., Ottweiler 053554
Saarländisches Bergbaumuseum, Bexbach 016218
Saarländisches Künstlerhaus e.V., Saarbrücken 019962
Saarland Museum, Stiftung Saarländischer Kulturbesitz, Saarbrücken 019963
Saaser Museum, Saas Fee 037470
Saatchi Gallery, London 040281
Saatkamp, M., Lengerich, Westfalen 072230
Saavcedra Díaz, Juan Ramón, Santiago de Chile 059552
Saavedra, Ruben de, New York 091216
Saavedra, Víctor, Barcelona 110242
Saba, Worben 112009
Saba, Joël, Lille 124325
Sabae CCI Art Museum, Sabae 027005
Sabah Art Gallery, Kota Kinabalu . . 027960
Sabama, Eivissa 081096
Sabancı Kültür Sitesi, İmit 038077
Sabarsky, Serge, New York 118369
Sabartes, Pedro, Barcelona 080924
Sabas, Montevideo 122789
Sabā's House, Teheran 022641
Sabatelli, Franco, Milano . 075852, 127677
Sabathier-Habrial, Anne-Armelie, Bergnicourt 061364
Sabatier, Concarneau 099166
Sabatier, Annie, Lille 138121
Sabatier, Eduard, Verden . 074195, 105115
Sabatier, Jean-Frédéric, Apt 060943
Sabatier, Nadine, Saint-Ouen 067886
Al-Sabbar, Dubai 083199
Sabbatique, New York 118370
Sabelli, Fabrizio, Bolzano 127197
Sabera Trading Company, London . 085669
Sabet, Berlin 069739
Sabet, Los Angeles 089903
Sabiac, Pierre, Les Halles 063766
Sabin, Frank T., London 085670
Sabin, Frank T., London 113872
Sabina Antiquitäten, Essen 070644
Sabina's Gallery, Singapore 080552
Sabine, C.E., Stock 086709, 131538
Sable, Los Angeles 089904
Sable, V., New Orleans 117507
Sable-Castelli, Toronto 097370
Sable et Bruyère, Saint-Benoit-sur-Loire 067376, 101132
Le Sablier, Bruxelles 058078
Sablier, Montréal 059002
Sablone, Fabrizio, Roma 128193
Sablonier, Jacqueline, Schaan 077449
Saborit, Eugenia, Málaga 081435
Sabot, Henri, Bordeaux 061651
Sabot, Henri, Podensac 066881
Sabots de Bois, La Bourdiniere-Saint-Loup 063296
Saboudjian, Lucie, Paris 066510
Sabourin, Châtellerault 120973
Sabunati, Javad, Mülheim an der Ruhr 072617
Saby, Lazi, Stuttgart 105006
Saçaklı Ev - Kültür ve Sanat Merkezi, Lefkoşa 008258
Sacao Artes Utilidades, Fortaleza . . 096535
Sacchetti, Giuseppe, Roma 076661
Sacchetti, Jensen Giovanna, Ascona 111140
Sacchetti, Jensen Giovanna, Ascona 111141
Sacchi, Mariangela, Milano 127678
Sacchi, Paolo, Firenze 140027
Saccomani, Antonio, Verona 077019
Sacerdoti, Daniela, Milano 106301
Sacha, Ménerbes 064480
Sacha Gallery, Surry Hills 095258
Sacharow, Renate, Bad Neuenahr-Ahrweiler 069342
Sachem Historical Society Museum, Holbrook 044568
Sachs, Astrid, Minden, Westfalen . . 072550
Sachs, Karin, München 104304
Sachs Harbour Museum, Sachs Harbour 006317
Sachse, Freiberg, Sachsen 070815
Sachse, Ruth, Hamburg 103215
Sachse, Ruth, Hamburg 103216
Sachse & Heinzelmann, Hannover . 139243
Sacilotto, Sergio, Prato 076259
Sacilotto, Sergio, Prato 076260
Sack, Israel, New York 091217
Sackets Harbor Battlefield State Historic Site, Sackets Harbor 047583
Sackolah, Cincinnati 115659
Sacks, Beverly, New York 118371
Sacks, Kim, Johannesburg 110060
Sacks, Leslie, Los Angeles 116877
Saco, Miguel, New York . . 091218, 132527
Saco Museum, York Institute Museum, Saco 047584
Sacramento Mountains Historical Museum, Cloudcroft 043023
Sacramento Surplus Book Room, Sacramento 142848
Sacred Circle Gallery of American Indian Art, United Indians of All Tribes Foundation, Seattle 048090
Sacred Earth Arts, Kansas City 116590
Sacrewell Farm and Country Centre, Thornhaugh 041214
Sacro Convento Castillo de Calatrava la Nueva, Aldea del Rey 034815
Sa'dabad Museums, Teheran 022642
Al-Sadawi, Faisal Abdul Hamid, Riyadh 080383
Sadberk Hanım Müzesi, Vehbi Koç Vakfı, İstanbul 038097
Sadde, Philippe, Dijon 120989
The Saddle Room Antiques, Cookstown 084082
Saddlers Court Gallery, Richmond, Tasmania 095134
Saddleworth Museum and Art Gallery, Uppermill 041265
Sądecki Park Etnograficzny, Muzeum Okręgowego w Nowym Sączu, Nowy Sącz 032176
Sadega-Wafa, Gisela, Kerpen, Rheinland 071807
Sadelmakare Öbergs Hus, Solna . . 036604
Saden, Al-Khuwair 079510
Sadigh, New York 091219
Sadika, Marsa 112254
Sadikaj, Bashkim, Bologna 127179
Sadler, Stanley J., Houston 089196
Sadler Street Gallery, Wells 087070, 114657
Sado Hakabutsukan, Sawata 027043
Sado Kokokan, Ogi 026935
Sado-koku Ogi Folk Museum, Ogi . 026936
Sado Nohgaku-no-sato, Ryotsu . . . 027004
Sadowski & Farchmin, Lindenberg bei Berlin 072271
Sadri, Oklahoma City 091531, 132584
Sadriddin Aini Memorial Museum, Samarkand 049404
Sadza, A., Neunkirchen-Seelscheid 073009
Sääksmäen Kotiseutumuseo, Sääksmäki 010055
Säätyläiskotiseutumuseo, Kolkanlahti 009727
Sæby Museum and Sæbygaard Manor Museum, Sæby 009089
Sächsische Kunstwerk, Leipzig . . . 072216
Sächsischer Künstlerbund, Dresden 053555
Sächsischer Museumsbund e.V., Dresden 053556
Sächsisches Apothekenmuseum Leipzig, Leipzig 018588
Sächsisches Auktionshaus und Antiquariat, Leipzig 121497, 139401
Sächsisches Buch- und Graphikkabinett, Radebeul 139672
Sächsisches Eisenbahnmuseum, Chemnitz 016563
Sächsisches Industriemuseum Chemnitz, Chemnitz 016564
Sächsisches Lehr- & Besucherbergwerk-Himmelfahrt-Fundgrube, TU Bergakademie Freiberg, Freiberg, Sachsen 017223
Sächsisches Psychiatriemuseum, Leipzig 018589
Sächsisches Schmalspurbahn-Museum Rittersgrün, Rittersgrün 019852
Sächsisches Strafvollzugsmuseum, Waldheim 020642
Säffle Marinmotor Museum, Säffle . 036550
Säfsnäs Arbetarmuseum och Hembygdsgård, Fredriksberg 036277
Sägemühle, Thallwitz 020430
Säger, Jürgen, Grünstadt 125772
Sägereimuseum, Richterswil 037448
Sägmühlmuseum Marhördt, Oberrot 019410
Saegusa, Tokyo 107098
Säimenen Mylly, Rökönvaara 010041
Säkylän Kotiseutumuseo, Säkylä . . 010057
Sällskapet Länkarna, Grums 122147
Sällskapet Maneten, Göteborg 110930
Sämann, Wolfgang & Ursula, Frankfurt am Main 139099
Saendig, Vaduz 134744, 140225
Sändig, Elmar, Wiesbaden 139856
Sängermuseum, Feuchtwangen . . . 017117
Säntis, Gossau (Sankt Gallen) 111527
Saenz, Arana & Bernhard, Schaffhausen 082800
Saenz, Benjamin E., San Antonio . . 092576
Saenz de Maturana Aguirreurreta, Maria Carmen, Vitoria-Gasteiz 081722
Säräisniemen Kotiseutumuseo, Vaala 010198
Särestad Lantbruksmuseum, Grästorp 036312
Säreströniemi-Museo, Kaukonen . . . 009682
Särö Konst och Ram, Särö 110986
Säters Hembygdsmuseum, Säter . . 036553
Sætersgårds Samlinger Dølmotunet, Tolga 031268
Saetta, Maria Letizia, Roma 076662
Sättler, Harald, Erbach, Odenwald . 125593
Sättler, Harald, Michelstadt 072543, 126315
Saevars, Karls, Reykjavík 105591
Säyneisten Kotiseutumuseo, Säyneinen 010058
Saez Angulo, Rosa, Santander 081560
Saez Concha, Carlos A., Santiago de Chile 059553
Al-Safa, Cairo 060469
Safani, New York 118372
Safar, Khan, Cairo 098667
Ramsey Safar & Osama Ismail Abudawood, Jeddah 080365
Safari Imports, Houston 116399
Al-Safavi, Dubai 083200
Safe Haven, Oswego 046748
Safety Harbor Museum of Regional History, Safety Harbor 047598
Saffa-Janssen, Bruxelles 123605
Saffell, Michael & Jo, Bath 083444
Saffron, Mumbai 105799
Saffron Gallery, Saint Agnes 114341
Saffron Walden Antiques Centre, Saffron Walden 086434
Saffron Walden Auctions, Saffron Walden 122675
Saffron Walden Decorative and Fine Arts Society, Saffron Walden 054491
Saffron Walden Museum, Saffron Walden 040880
Saffroy, Gaston, Paris 138536
Safi, Carcassonne 061982
Safier Heimatmuseum, Safien 037473
Safita, Dubai 083201
Safn Rafmagnsveitu Reykjavíkur, Reykjavík 021974
Safn Ásgrims Jónssonar, Reykjavík 021975
Safnahús, Borgarfjardar, Borgarnes 105582
Safnahús, Skagfirdinga, Borgarnes . 105583

Safnahusid Húsavík, Húsavík 021951
Safnastofnun Austurlands, Egilsstadir 105584
Safont Molinero, Maria Luisa, Zaragoza 110891
Safor Galerie, Katzelsdorf, Leitha . . 095604
Safrai, Jerusalem 105913
Sag Harbor Whaling and Historical Museum, Sag Harbor 047601
Saga, Boulogne-Billancourt 061690
Saga-kenritsu Bijutsukan, Saga . . . 027006
Saga-kenritsu Hakubutsukan, Saga 027007
Saga-kenritsu Kyushu Toji Bunkakan, Arita 026419
Sagae, Seoul 107280
Sagalunds Museum, Kimito 009710
Sagamore Hill National Historic Site, Oyster Bay 046781
Sagan, Irene, Essen 102703
Sagar Mahal Art Gallery, Mumbai . . 105800
Sagarana, Belo Horizonte 137549
Sagasco Historical Group Museum, Brompton 000849
Sagasser, Dr. Jürgen, Amorbach . . . 069166
Sagasta, Logroño 081188
Sage, Ripley, Surrey 086374, 131416
S.A.G.E.M., Angoulême 060879
Sagemonoya, Tokyo 077295
Sagep, Genova 134594
Sager Studios, Fort Worth 051353
Sage's Quest, Buffalo 087905
Saget, Eric, Paris 066511
Saggi e Memorie di Storia dell'Arte, Firenze 135956
Il Saggiatore, Roma 106621
Al-Saghah, Sheikh Usamah, Damascus 083080
Saginaw Art Museum, Saginaw . . . 047603
Les Sagittaires, Paris 066512
Sagmeister, Ulrich, Pitten 057208
Sagot, Frédéric, Paris 100822
Sagot-Le Garrec, S., Paris 066513, 100823
Sagrera, Miguel, Palma de Mallorca 081495
Sagstua Skolemuseum, Sigurd Hoels Hjem, Sagstua 031159
Saguache County Museum, Saguache 047604
Såguddens Museum, Arvika 036201
Saguer, Vigneux-sur-Seine 068873
Sahan Museo, Puumala 010008
Sahara Imports, Long Beach 116679
Sahara Shoten, Yokohama 140214
Sahitya Parishad Museum, Midnapore 022258
Sahlender, Michael-Heinz, Stegaurach 126827
Sahlman, Peter Scott S., New York . 118373
Sahuc, Louis, New Orleans 117508
Sahuquet, Gerard, Bordeaux 120946
Sahuquet, Philippe, Millau 064560
SAI, Legionowo 108997
Sai Artefacts, Singapore 080553
SAI Oriental Art Corporation, Las Vegas 116645
Sai Swiss Auction International, Berikon 122310
Said, Emami, Bonn 125359
Said, G., Hamrun 128474
Said, Mohamed, Bamberg 125135
Said, Nasser Bin Mohamed Bin, Muttrah 079518
S.A.I.E. Editrice, Torino 134698
Saigon Art, Winchester 114706
Saigon Art Gallery, Ho Chi Minh City 120530
Saigon d'Art, Ho Chi Minh City 120531
Saigon Fine Arts, Den Haag 078245
Saijo Municipal Local Museum, Saijo 027008
Saikyo-ji Treasure Hall, Hirado 026517
Sailer, Innsbruck 057086, 095596
Sailor's Memorial Museum, Islesboro 044787
Sails Art, Plymouth 114263
Saimaan Kanavan Museo, Lappeenranta 009806
Sainsbury, John, Carlton, Victoria . . 136852
Sainsbury, R.P., Wallington 131644
Sainsbury Centre for Visual Arts, Norwich 040612
Sainsbury & Mason, London 085671
Sainsbury's, Camberwell 136842
Sainsburys of Bournemouth, Bournemouth 083606
Sainsere, Jacqueline, Saint-Ouen . . 067887
Saint, Philippe, Bruxelles 096251
Saint Albans Gallery, Saint Albans . 095166
Saint Albans Historical Museum, Saint Albans 047605
Saint Albans Organ Museum, Saint Albans 040889
Saint-André Antiquités, Saint-André-lez-Lille 067357
Saint Andrews Cathedral Museum, Saint Andrews 040895
Saint Andrews College Museum, Christchurch 030468
Saint Andrews Fine Art, Saint Andrews 086444
Saint Andrews Fine Art, Saint Andrews 114348
Saint Andrews Gallery, Hamilton . . . 108459
Saint Andrews Museum, Saint Andrews 040896
Saint Andrews Preservation Museum, Saint Andrews 040897
Saint Andrews University Museum Collections, University of Saint Andrews, Saint Andrews 040898
Saint Andrews Workshop, Saint Andrews 095167
Saint Angela's Museum, Prelate . . . 006198
Saint Anne's Chapel and Old Grammar School Museum, Barnstaple 038603
Saint Asaph Cathedral Treasury, Saint Asaph 040900
Saint Augustine, Porto Alegre 058522
Saint Augustine Historical Society Museum, Saint Augustine 047611
Saint Augustine Lighthouse and Museum, Saint Augustine 047612
Saint Augustine's Abbey, Canterbury 038983
Saint Barbe Museum and Art Gallery, Lymington 040366
Saint Barnabas Icon and Archaeological Museum, Gazimağusa 008240
Saint Bartholomew's Hospital Museum, London 040282
Saint Basile Chapel Museum, Saint-Basile 006326
Saint Benedicts Studio, Wallington . 114641
Saint Bernadette Institute of Sacred Art, Albuquerque 114821
Saint Bernard's Hospital Museum and Chapel, Southall 041053
Saint Bonaventure Art Collection, Saint Bonaventure 047616
Saint Brannocks Gallery, Mundesley 114103
Saint Breock Gallery, Wadebridge . .086995, 131635
Saint Bride's Crypt Museum, London 040283
Saint Catharines Museum, Saint Catharines 006331
Saint Catherine's National School Museum, Aughrim 022680
Saint Charles County Museum, Saint Charles 047621
Saint Charles Heritage Center, Saint Charles 047617
Saint Chrispin Antique Centre, Beverley 083501
Saint-Christophe, Soissons 068252
Saint-Clair Antiques, Toronto 059288
Saint Clair County Historical Museum, Belleville 042107
Saint-Clar Galerie, Sarlat-la-Canéda 101258
Saint Claude Museum, Saint Claude 006332
Saint Clements Antiques, Oxford . . 086185
Saint Clements Island-Potomac River Museum, Colton Point 043065
Saint-Cornély Antiquités, Carnac . . 061993
Saint-Cricq Antic, Auch 061054
Saint David's Hall, Cardiff 038992
Saint-Dizier, Montréal 097075
Saint Dominic Church Museum, Macau 007190
Saint Elie Pioneer Church Museum, Inglis 005638
Saint Francis Enterprise, Singapore 080554
Saint Gaudens National Historic Site, Cornish 043157
Saint George Epanosifis Monastery, Iráklion 021288
Saint George Gallery, Boston 115228
Saint George's, Stamford 086687
Le Saint-Georges, Toulouse 068540
Saint Georges Antiques, Battery Point 055456
Saint-Georges Antiquités Brocante, Lyon 064183
Saint George's Historical Society Museum, Saint George's 003904
Saint Georges Regional Museum, Hurstville 001123
Saint George's United Methodist Church Museum, Philadelphia 046986
Saint-Germain Antiquités, Ménerbes 064481
Saint-Germain Antiquités, Saint-Germain-en-Laye 067501
Saint Graal Gallery, Kraków 108978
Saint Helens, Swansea 131568
Saint Helens History Room, Saint Helens 001445
Saint Helens Transport Museum, Saint Helens 040909
Le Saint-Hubert, Nancy 064880
Saint Ives Collection, New York . . . 091220
Saint Ives Fine Arts, Saint Ives, Cornwall 114372
Saint Ives Gallery, Saint Ives, Cornwall 114373
Saint Ives Museum, Saint Ives, Cornwall 040920
Saint Ives Society of Artists, Saint Ives, Cornwall 054492
Saint Ives Society of Artists Members Gallery (Norway Gallery) and Mariners Gallery, Saint Ives, Cornwall 040921
Saint-Jacques, Pierre, Montréal . . . 059003
Saint James Antiques, Little Malvern 085014
Saint James Cavalier, Valletta 028035
Saint James' Gallery, Uitikon Waldegg 111952
Saint James' House, Fredericksburg 044064
Saint James House Antiques, Boroughbridge 083576, 130411
Saint James Museum and Library, Jerusalem 022977
Saint James's Art Books, London . . 141887
Saint James's Gallery, Bath 112585
Saint James's Gallery, Saint Peter Port 086476
Saint-Jean, Chalon-sur-Saône 099102
Saint-Job Auctions, Uccle 120789
Saint John, Stella, Christ Church . . 096037
Saint John and Coningsby Medieval Museum, Hereford 039738
Saint John Antiques, York 087295
Saint John Jewish Historical Museum, Saint John 006356
Saint John Sports Hall of Fame, Saint John 006357
Saint John Street Gallery, Ashbourne 112526
Saint John's Art and Heritage Centre, Listowel 022826
Saint John's Church and Parish Museum, Hampton 044416
Saint John's Co-Cathedral and Museum, Valletta 028036
Saint John's House, Warwick 041307
Saint John's Museum of Art, Wilmington 049216
Saint John's Northwestern Military Academy Museum, Delafield 043379
Saint John's Schoolhouse Museum, Reid 001427
Saint John's Theatre and Arts Centre, Listowel 022826
Saint Johnsbury Athenaeum, Saint Johnsbury 047639
Saint Joseph and the Angels Emporium, Edmonton 137635
Saint Joseph College Art Gallery, West Hartford 049079
Saint Joseph Island Museum Village, Richards Landing 006277
Saint Joseph Museum, Saint Joseph 047650
Saint Joseph's College Museum, Tiruchirappalli 022353
Saint Joseph's University Gallery, Philadelphia 046987
Saint Kilda Auction Rooms, Saint Kilda, Victoria 120634
Saint Lambert, Paris 138537
Saint-Laurent Art Museum, Montréal 005950
Saint-Laurent + Hill, Ottawa 097116
Saint Lawrence College Art Gallery, Kingston 005708
Saint Lawrence Memorial Miner's Museum, Saint Lawrence 006382
Saint Leonards Antique and Craft, Newton Abbot 086081, 131317
Saint Lifer Art Exchange, New York .118374, 123011
Saint-Louis, Lorient 099523
Saint-Louis, Nantes 064944
Saint Louis Architectural Art, Saint Louis 092308
Saint Louis Art Museum, Saint Louis 047676
Saint Louis Art Museum. Bulletin, Saint Louis 136618
Saint Louis Art Prints, Saint Louis . . 119248
Saint Louis Artists' Guild, Saint Louis 055013
Saint Louis Artists' Guild Museum, Saint Louis 047677
Saint Louis Car Museum, Saint Louis 047678
Saint Louis County Historical Museum, Duluth 043523
Saint Louis Irish Arts, Saint Louis . . 119249
Saint-Louis Posters, Paris 100824
Saint Louis Science Center Museum, Saint Louis 047679
Saint Louis University Museum of Arts and Culture, Baguio 031628
Saint-Loup, Namur 120782
Saint-Loup, Saint-Honore-les-Bains 067526
Saint Lucie County Historical Museum, Fort Pierce 043963
Saint Luke's Gallery, Washington . . 120345
Saint Luke's Gallery, Anna Maria College, Paxton 046851
Saint Mamas Manastırı İkon Müzesi, Güzelyurt 008248
Saint Margaret's Museum, Saint Margaret's Bay 040925
Saint-Martin, Montréal 133320
Saint-Martin, Paris 066514
Saint-Martin, Arnaud de, Paris 066515
Saint Martins Antiques Centre, Stamford 086688, 131527, 142088
Saint Martins Books, Bournemouth 141427
Saint Martin's Press, New York 135460
Saint Mary Magdalene Treasury, Newark-on-Trent 040536
Saint Marys and Benzinger Township Museum, Saint Marys 047688
Saint Mary's Chapel Antiques, Devizes 084163
Saint Marys Community Arts Centre, Saint Marys 001451
Saint Mary's Galeria, Orchard Lake 046708
Saint Marys Museum, Saint Marys . 006387
Saint Mary's Museum of Maxstone, Assiniboia 005035
Saint Mary's River Marine Centre, Museum Ship Norgoma, Sault Sainte Marie 006432

Saint Mary's University Art Center, San Antonio 047801
Saint Mary's University Art Gallery, Halifax 005583
Saint Mawes Castle, Truro 041244
Saint-Max Antiquités, Saint-Maximin-la-Sainte-Baume 067669
Saint Mel's Diocesan Museum, Longford 022828
Saint Michael's Historical Museum, Chatham, New Brunswick 005256
Saint Michael's Loft Museum, Christchurch 039088
Saint Michel, Toulouse 068541
Saint Mullins Heritage Centre, Saint Mullins 022855
Saint Mungo Museum of Religious Life and Art, Glasgow 039574
Saint Neots Museum, Saint Neots . 040928
Saint Nicholas Galleries, Carlisle . . 083879
Saint Nicholas Markets, Bristol 083752
Saint Nicholas Priory, Exeter 039466
Saint-Nicolas, Châteaubriand 062190
Saint Norbert Arts Centre, Winnipeg 097604
Saint Norbert Provincial Heritage Park, Winnipeg 006863
Saint Ouen, Puckeridge . . 086316, 131399
Saint Pancras Antiques, Chichester 083978, 130566
Saint Patrick's Museum, Cape Breton Centre for Heritage and Science, Sydney 006548
Saint Patrick's Trian, Armagh 038530
Saint-Paul, Saint-Félix-Lauragais . . 067475
Saint-Paul, Eric, Toulouse 068542
Saint Paul Apostolat des Editions, Lyon 133489
Saint Paul Gallery, Saint Paul 119310
Saint Paul Museum, Randleman . . . 047326
Saint Pauls Gallery, Birmingham . . . 112657
Saint-Père, Paris 100825
Saint Peter Hungate Church Museum, Norwich 040613
Saint Peter's Bunker, German Occupation Museum, Saint Peter 040933
Saint Peter's Church, Sunderland . . 041162
Saint Peter's Church Museum, Kanturk 022800
Saint Peter's College Art Gallery, Jersey City 044861
Saint Petersbourg Antiquités, Paris .066516, 138538
Saint Petersburg Gallery, Melbourne 056204
Saint Petersburg Museum of History, Saint Petersburg 047718
Saint Philips Books, Oxford 141987
Saint Photios Greek Orthodox National Shrine, Saint Augustine 047613
Saint-Remacle, Liège 058323, 120774
Saint-Remy, New York 091221
Saint Robert's Cave, Knaresborough 039909
Saint Seine, Isabelle de, Paris 066517
Saint Sharbel Museum, Annaya . . . 027806
Saint-Simond, Aix-les-Bains 060727
Saint Simons Island Lighthouse Museum, Saint Simons Island 047725
Saint Sophia of Kiev, Kyïv 038326
Saint Tammany Art Association, Covington 055014
Saint Tammany Art Gallery, Covington 043200
Saint Theresa's College Folklife Museum, Cebu 031658
Saint Thomas-Elgin Public Art Centre, Saint Thomas 006396
Saint Thomas More Art Gallery, Saskatoon 006424
Saint Thomas' Old Garrison Church Museum, Saint John's 006372
Saint Tropez Gallery, Surfers Paradise 095245
Saint-Viance Antiquités, Saint-Viance 068032
Saint Vigeans Museum, Arbroath . . 038522
Saint-Vincent, Châtillon-sur-Chalaronne 062233
Saint-Vincent Antiquités, Chalon-sur-Saône 062093
Saint Vincent Church Museum, Isandlwana 034637
Saint Volodymyr Museum, Ukrainian Catholic Archeparchy of Winnipeg, Winnipeg 006864
Saint Walburg and District Historical Museum, Saint Walburg 006400
Sainte-Anne, Armentières 060975, 124079
Sainte-Anne Antiquités, Peymeinade 066788
La Sainte-Aubaine, Saint-Aubin-sur-Mer 067364
Sainte Genevieve Museum, Sainte Genevieve 047728
Sainte-Hélène, Six-Fours-les-Plages 068247
Sainte Maison de la Flocellière, La Flocellière 012262
Sainte Marie among the Iroquois, Liverpool 045350
Sainte-Rita, Namur 120783
Sainteff, Denis, Strasbourg 068332
Saintfield Antiques & Fine Books, Saintfield 086485, 142042
Saints and Martyrs, Albuquerque . . 087423
Saints Gallery, Sans Souci 095182
Sainty Antique, Monetay-sur-Allier . 064599
Sainz López, Carlos, Zaragoza 129827
Sairaalamuseo, Lahti 009790
Saison, Raymond, Antibes-Juan-les-Pins 060928
La Saison des Pluies, Liège 058324
De Saisset Museum, Santa Clara . . 047953
Sait Faik Müzesi, Burgaz Adası . . . 038031
Saitama-kenritsu Hakubutsukan, Omiya 026955
Saitama-kenritsu Kindai Bijutsukan, Saitama 027009
Saitama-kenritsu Rekishi Shiryokan, Ranzan 027001
Saitama-kenritsu Sakitama Shiryokan, Gyoda 026476
Saitama-kenritsu Shizenshi Hakubutsukan, Nagatoro 026877
Saito, Chicago 088166
Saito, Nagoya 106934
Saito, Yokohama 140215
Saito Ho-on Kai Shizenshi Hakubutsukan, Sendai 027050
Saizowa, Jörg, Frankfurt/Oder 070807
Saja, Jeddah 080366
Sajam Umjetnosti i Umjetničke Opreme, Sarajevo 093615
Sajanskaja Kartinnaja Galereja, Sajansk 033709
Sajot, Thérèse, Touques 068555
SAK Galerie, Amsterdam 107793
Sakae, Hayama 077046
Sakai, Tokyo 077296
Sakai, Yokohama 107151
Sakai Antique Fair, Sakai 093804
Sakai Greenery Museum Harvest Hill, Sakai 027014
Sakai House, Hirano Hakabutsukan, Osaka 026988
Sakai Kokodo, Yokohama 077342
Sakai-shiritsu Hakubutsukan, Sakai 027015
Sakai-shiritsu Hamono Hakubutsukan, Sakai 027016
Sakaide Civic Art Museum, Sakaide 027018
Sakaimachi Art Gallery, Kyoto 106905
Sakakini, Hamburg 071319
Sakař, Jan, Pardubice 137807
Sakata, B. Garo, Sacramento 119159
Sake, Richmond 119121
Saker & Ting, Vaxholm 082064
Sakia, New York 118375
Sakr, Charles, Paris 066518
Sakrale Kunst in der Sankt-Anna-Kapelle, Cham 016552
Sakraler Austellungsraum, Groß Siegharts 001966
Sakralna Baština Muzej, Senj 007788
Saks, Denver 116046
Saks, Pune 105830
Sakshi, Bangalore 105613
Sakshi, Mumbai 105801
Saksische en Museumboerderij Erve Brooks Niehof, Gelselaar 029599
Sakura Bank Exhibition Room, Kyoto 026767
Sakura City Museum of Art, Sakura 027023
Sakuraya, Tokyo 077297
Sala, Xavier, La Seyne-sur-Mer . . . 063449
Sala 1 - Centro Culturale, Roma . . . 106622
Sala A. De Carolis, Montefiore dell'Aso 024841
Sala Antik & Auktionshall, Sala 081893, 122234
Sala Arte de Porto Alegre, Porto Alegre 096580
Sala Auktionskammare, Sala 122235
Sala Braulio, Castello de la Plana . . 110308
Sala Cadafe, Caracas 049478
Sala Cister, Málaga 110643
Sala Cristina, Milano 106302
Sala Dalmau, Barcelona 110243
Sala d'Arqueologia i Gabinet Numismàtic, Fundació Pública Institut d'Estudis Ilerdencs, Lleida 035352
Sala de Arqueología del Municipio de Mújica, Múgica 028587
Sala de Arte Carlos F. Sáez, Montevideo 041546
Sala de Arte Cuchilleros, Madrid . . 110608
Sala de Arte Jabalcuz, Jaén 110389
Sala de Arte Murillo, Oviedo 110664
Sala de Arte Prehispánico, Santo Domingo 009166
Sala de Arte Zeus, Zaragoza 081752, 110892
Sala de Cultura Carlos III, Pamplona 110724
Sala de Espera, Bogotá 098190
Sala de Exhibitiones Temporales del Banco Central, Museos del Banco Central de Costa Rica, San José 007682
Sala de Exposiciones, Barakaldo . . 034898
Sala de Exposiciones Conde Duque, Madrid 110609
Sala de Exposiciones Edificio Historico, Universidad de Oviedo, Oviedo . . 035587
Sala de Exposiciones El Pasaje, Alcázar de San Juan 034806
Sala de Exposiciones Rekalde, Bilbao 034989
Sala de los Bomberos, La Habana . 008021
Sala de Memorias Culturales, Mogotes 007547
Sala de Memórias de Chapada dos Guimarães, Chapada dos Guimarães 004065
Sala de Recuerdos de la Escuela Militar de Montaña, Jaca 035300
Sala de Trofeos del Duque de Arión, Plasencia 035658
Sala del Centro Cultural Provincial, Málaga 035457
Sala del Costume e delle Tradizioni Popolari, Chiesa di San Nicola, Corinaldo . . 023971
Sala Derenzi, Castello de la Plana . 110309
Sala d'Exposiciones de la Fundació la Caixa, Madrid 035443
Sala Fratelli, Milano 075853
Sala Gabernia, Valencia 110840
Sala Gestalguinos, Valencia 110841
Sala Girona de la Fundació la Caixa, Girona 035237
Sala Goya, Alicante 080767, 110089
Sala Guadalaviar, Valencia 122090
Sala Histórica de la Facultad de Medicina, Universidad Autónoma de Nuevo León, Mitras 028553
Sala Histórica del Regimiento de Infantería Mecanizado 24, Río Gallegos 000517
Sala Historica General Savio, Buenos Aires 000252
Sala Homenaje a Juárez, Guelatao de Juárez 028311
Sala Ipostel, Museo de Arte Contemporáneo de Caracas Sofía Imber, Caracas . 049479
Sala Josefa Rodriguez del Fresno, Santa Fé 000609
Sala La Fotografía, Caracas 120435
Sala Llotja del Peix, Alicante 110090
Sala Maior, Porto 109395
Sala Melchor Ocampo, Universidad Michoacana, Morelia 028585
Sala Mendoza, Caracas 049480
Sala Montcada de la Fundació la Caixa, Barcelona 034961
Sala Montseny, Mario, Barcelona . . 141004
Sala Moyua, Bilbao 080991, 122018
Sala Muncunill, Terrassa 035908
Sala Museo Literario, Archivo Histórico del Instituto Caro y Cuervo, Bogotá . . 007455
Sala Museo Pablo Sarasate, Pamplona 035633
Sala Parés, Barcelona . . . 080925, 110244
Sala Pelaires, Palma de Mallorca . . 110699
Sala Piano Museum, Cebu 031659
Sala Retiro, Madrid 122068
Sala Reus, Reus 035698
Sala Sergio Larrain, Santiago de Chile 006941
Sala Traktormuseum, Sala 036556
Salachas, Gilbert, Paris 133671
Saladin, Erich & Gaby, Blauen 082267
Saladino, Leonardo, Roma 076663
Salagoudi, S., Aachen 101524
Salah, Jacky, Appoigny 060940
Salah, Mohammad, Saint-Étienne . 067468
Salama, Cairo 098668
Salamah, Talebzen M.H., Madina . . 080369
Salamanca Arts Centre, Hobart . . . 001112
Salamanca Collection, Hobart 055999
The Salamanca Collection, Hobart . 094644
Salamanca Rail Museum, Salamanca 047730
De Salamander, Almere 140271
Salamander, Christchurch 079050, 108411
Salamandra, Zaragoza . . . 081753, 129828
Salamon, Milano . 075854, 106303, 127679
Salamon, Torino 106702
Salamon, Silverio, Torino . 076863, 140142
Salamone, Nunzio, Catania 075260, 127277
Salander & O'Reilly, New York 118376
Salangen Bygdetun, Sjøvegan 031183
Salant, Gerry, Paris 133672
Salão, Rio de Janeiro 096644
Salão Nacional de Antiguidades e Arte Sacra, Braga 093845
Salar Gallery, Hatherleigh 113202
Salar Jung Museum, Hyderabad . . . 022162
Salas Llibreteria, Barcelona 080926
Salas Municipales de Arte Sanz-Enea, Zarautz 036116
Salatino, Eugenia Correia, São Paulo 058740
Salaün, Anna, Caen 061885
Salaun, André, Brest 061779
Salaz, Medellín 059942
Salazar, Belo Horizonte 058448
Salazar, San Francisco 092879
Salbitani, Gabriella, Roma 076664
Salchow, Hamburg 139209
Salcido, San Diego 132857
Salcombe Maritime Museum, Salcombe 040940
Saldarriaga, Manolo, Medellín 059943
Saldus Vēstures un Mākslas Muzejs, Saldus 027777
Sale Historical Museum, Sale 001453
Saleh, Terry, Kurwongbah 056073
Saleh Kaki, Mustafa Yousuf, Jeddah 080367
Salehurst Auctioneers, Battle 122402
Salem 1630 Pioneer Village, Salem 047743
Salem Art Association, Salem 055015
Salem County Historical Society Museum, Salem 047747
Salem Historical Society Museum, Salem 047748
Salem Maritime National Historic Site, Salem 047744
Salem Museum, Salem 047754
Salem Witch Museum, Salem 047745

Salerno, Michael, Los Angeles 116878
Salerno, Paolo, Milano 075855
Sales, Alejandro, Barcelona 110245
Sales by Sylvia, Cincinnati 088278
Salese, Frank, Philadelphia 132633
Salet, Patrice, Saint-Ouen 067888
La Saletta, Milano 075856
Saleya, Nice 065144
Salford Museum and Art Gallery, Salford 040944
Salgado Fuentes, Juan Carlos, Santiago de Chile 059554
Salgo Trust for Education, Port Washington 047146
Salibello, John, New York 091222
Salida Museum, Salida 047755
Salies Antiquités, Salies-de-Béarn . 068092
Salina Art Center, Salina 047756
Salinas, M. Joaquín, Santiago de Chile 059555
Salinas Pueblo Missions National Monument, Mountainair 046077
Saline County Historical Society Museum, Dorchester 043480
Saline- und Heimatmuseum, Bad Sulza 015813
Salinenmuseum Unteres Bohrhaus, Rottweil 019933
Saling, Paris 066519
Salinpuoli, Helsinki 060577
Salis, Anif 095466
Salis, Christiane, Condom 062455
Salis, Michel, Nérac 064974
Salis & Vertes, Salzburg 095734
Salisbury and South Wiltshire Museum, Salisbury 040949
Salisbury Antiques Market, Salisbury 086495, 142045
Salisbury Antiques Warehouse, Salisbury 086496, 131451
Salisbury Folk Museum, Salisbury . 001454
Salisbury Historical Society Museum, Salisbury 047762
Salisbury House, Des Moines 043428
Salisbury Mansion, Worcester 049308
Salisbury State University Galleries, Salisbury 047760
Salisci, Francesco, Cagliari 075226, 127254
Salit, Jean-Norbert, Paris 066520
Salix, Banff 112555
Sallan Kotiseutumuseo, Salla 010059
Sallands Landbouwmuseum de Laarman, Luttenberg 029883
Sallaz, Michel, Paris 066521
La Salle à Manger, Bruxelles 058079
Salle Alfred Pellan, Laval 005756
Salle de Traditions de la Garde Républicaine, Paris 013741
Salle de Vente des Carmes, Marche-en-Famenne 120778
Salle de Vente Elisabeth, Namur ... 120784
Salle de Vente Regina, Liège 120775
Salle de Vente Saint-Jean, Bordères-sur-l'Echez 061663
Salle de Vente Sainte-Claire, Ensival 120753
Salle de Ventes du Béguinage, Bruxelles 120741
Salle de Ventes Européenne, Charleroi 120751
Salle de Ventes Nivelloise, Nivelles 120785
La Salle des Étiquettes, Musée de la Cave des Champagnes de Castellane, Épernay 011711
Salle des Illustres, Auch 010532
Salle des Souvenirs, Lisieux 012705
Salle des Ursulines, Vesoul 101459
Salle des Ventes, Aubervilliers 120909
Salle des Ventes, Coutras 062539
Salle des Ventes, Menton 121073
Salle des Ventes, Pau 066715
Salle des Ventes, Péronne 121222
Salle des Ventes Alésia, Paris 121203
Salle des Ventes de Nation, Paris .. 121204
Salle des Ventes des Particuliers, Chambéry 120968
Salle des Ventes des Particuliers, Joigny (Yonne) 063247
Salle des Ventes des Particuliers, Montmorot 064723
Salle des Ventes des Particuliers, Paris 121205
Salle des Ventes des Particuliers, Paris 121206
Salle des Ventes des Particuliers, Tinqueux 068423
Salle des Ventes du Particulier, Paris 121207
Salle des Ventes du Particulier, Paris 121208
Salle des Ventes du Particulier de l'Ariège, Mirepoix 064565
Salle des Ventes Guérandaise, Guérande 121013
Salle des Ventes Saint-Honoré, Paris 121209
Salle d'Exposition, Lure 099531
Salle d'Exposition Espace Lumière, Hénin-Beaumont 099328
Salle d'Exposition Haras du Pin, Le Pin-au-Haras 012543
Salle d'Honneur du 516e Régiment du Train, Toul 014971
Salle Exposition, Ile-d'Ouessant ... 099364
Salle Gallo-Romaine, Florange 011829
Salle Panoramique de Notre-Dame-de-Monts, Notre-Dame-de-Monts ... 013452
La Salle Raspail, Paris 066522
Salle Ventes Enchères Publiques, Etampes 121002
Salles, Pierre, Ambleville 060795
Salles de Vente de l'Ain, Replonges 067122
Les Salles du Palais, Genève 111498
Salles du Tresor, Prades 013940
Sallmann, Berlin 125290
Sallou, Hervé, Perros-Guirec 066770
Sallou, Hervé, Trégastel 068620
Sally, Cairo 060470
Sally, Dan-Cuthbert, Rose Bay 095158
Sally, Marie, Saint Paul 119311
Sally Lunn's Refreshment House and Kitchen Museum, Bath 038632
Sally's Collectables, Sacramento .. 092179
Salmagundi Museum of American Art, New York 046397
Salmagundi West, Vancouver 059409
Salmen, Thomas, Hemer 139261
Salmo Museum, Salmo 006406
Salmon, Richard, London 113873
Salmon Arm Museum, Salmon Arm 006407
Salmon Brook Historical Society Museum, Granby 044258
Salmon Galleries, McMahons Point 094756
Saló d'Antiquaris i Art Modern a Barcelona, Barcelona 093876
Saló d'Antiquaris i Brocanters a Lleida, Lleida 093877
Saloga Restauracion, Barcelona ... 129397
Saloisten Kotiseutumuseo, Arkkukari 009458
Salome, Nils, Bruxelles 058080
Salomon, Amstelveen 077762
Salomon, Wolfgang, Regensburg .. 126700
Salomon Lilian, Dr., Amsterdam ... 077955
Salomon Lilian, New York 091223
Salomon Stodel, Amsterdam 077956
Salomons Memento Rooms, Southborough 041062
Salon 5, Honolulu 116241
Salon Antičnega Pohištva, Maribor . 080664
Salon Antykwaryczny i Sztuki Współczesnej, Kielce 093841
Salon Artisanat d'Art, Albi-le-Séquestre 093671
Le Salon d'Art, Bruxelles 096252
Salon d'Automne - Antiquité et Brocante, Nancy 093672
Salon de Arte del Casino Nervion, Bilbao 110286
Salón de Artes Plásticas Antonia F. Rizzuto, Villa Carlos Paz 000661
Salón de la Fama del Beisbol Profesional de México, Monterrey 028573
Salon de la Société Nationale des Beaux-Arts, Paris 093673
Le Salon de l'Art et de la Décoration, Beirut 093811
Salon de l'Automobile Miniature, Ally 010341
El Salon de los Anticuarios, Cali ... 059886
Salon de Peinture Permanent, Montbard 013137
Salon de Thorigny, Paris 100826
Salón del Cuadro y sus Componentes, Madrid 093878
Salon des Antiquaires, Angers 093674
Salon des Antiquaires, Besançon .. 093675
Salon des Antiquaires, Bordeaux .. 093676
Salon des Antiquaires, Colmar 093677
Salon des Antiquaires, Lausanne .. 082567
Salon des Antiquaires, Lille 093678
Salon des Antiquaires, Metz 093679
Salon des Antiquaires, Nancy 093680
Salon des Antiquaires, Reims 093681
Salon des Antiquaires, Toulouse ... 093682
Salon des Antiquaires de Biarritz, Biarritz 093683
Salon des Antiquaires de Bourges, Bourges 093684
Salon des Antiquaires, de la Brocante et de l'Art Contemporain, Luxemburg .. 093813
Salon des Antiquaires de Lausanne, Lausanne 093893
Salon des Antiquaires et de la Belle Brocante, Tournai 093612
Salon des Antiquaires et de la Brocante, Dijon 093685
Salon des Antiquités, Orléans 093686
Salon des Antiquités et de la Brocante, Mouscron 093613
Salon des Antiquités et de la Brocante, Quimper 093687
Salon des Antiquités et de la Brocante, Troyes 093688
Salon des Artisans d'Art de Toulouse, Toulouse 093689
Salon du Collectionneur Paris, Salon International des Antiquaires Spécialisés, Paris 093690
Salon du Dessin, Paris 093691
Salon du Nord, Saint Paul 119312
Salon Dzieł Sztuki, Kraków 079653
Salon Dzieł Sztuki, Kraków 079654
Salon Dzieł Sztuki, Kraków 079655
Salon Dzieł Sztuki i Antykow Paga, Kielce 079609
Salon Dziel Udanych-Hall of Succesful Works, Wrocław 109232
Salón Electo Brizuela, Biblioteca Popular El Porvenir, Concepción del Uruguay 000285
Salon Europeen des Antiquaires, Grenoble 093692
Salon (Fort Collins), Fort Collins ... 136619
Salon-Galereja Éstetika, Saratov .. 109656
Salon Genevois de la Brocante et de l'Antiquité, Genève 093894
Salón Internacional de Grabado y Ediciones de Arte Contemporáneo, Madrid . 093879
Salon Libr'Art, Libramont 093614
Salon Muzyczny im. Fryderyka Chopina, Centrum Kultury i Sztuki w Kaliszu, Antonin 031813
Salón Nacional de Antigüedades, Sevilla 093880
Salon Natasha, Ha Noi 120484
Salon National des Antiquaires, Bourg-en-Bresse 093693
Salon Oven-Venera, Sankt-Peterburg 080327
Salon Printemps des Antiquités et de la Brocante, Troyes 093694
Le Salon Rouge, Amsterdam 107794
Salon s'Art, Ha Noi 120485
Salon Sprzedaży Antýkow, Warszawa 079782
Salon Sztuki Antyki i Sztuka Współczesna, Puck 079703
Salon Sztuki Współczesnej, Poznań 079697
Salon Sztuki Współczesnej-Antyki, Białystok 079571
Salon Sztuki Współczesnej - Antyki, Częstochowa 079574
Salon Utrechtse Kunstenaars, Utrecht 093835
Salon Verlag, Köln 134118
Salon Voltaire, Ferney-Voltaire 099261
Salon XX-XXI, Sankt-Peterburg 080328
Salone Aste, Cornici, Accessori, Grafica e Tecnologie, Bologna 093789
Salone della Numismatica, Medaglistica e Cartamoneta, Vicenza 093790
Salone dell'Antiquariato e del Libro Antico, Vicenza 093791
Salone Internazionale d'Arte Contemporanea, Bari 093792
Salone Italiano d'Antichità, Bari ... 093793
Salone Villa Romana, Firenze 024202
Salonik Chopinów, Muzeum Fryderyka Chopina, Warszawa 032482
Les Salons Démodés, Québec 059077
Salons voor Schone Kunsten, Sint-Niklaas 003760
Salotto, Arnhem 107857
Il Salotto, Milano 106304
Salpalinja-Museo, Miehikkälä 009868
Salpalinjan Bukkerialue, Ala-Philaja 009453
Salsi, Pier Antonio, Parma 127864
Salt, D.W., Cincinnati 131945
Salt, N.P. & A., Sheffield 086565
Salt, Steven, Crows Nest, Queensland 055729
Salt Archaeological Museum, Salt . 027384
Salt Box Collection, Portland 092001
Salt Folklore Museum, Salt 027385
Salt House Gallery, Saint Ives, Cornwall 114374
Salt Lake Antiques, Salt Lake City . 092459
Salt Lake Art Center, Salt Lake City 047775
Salt Lake Art Center, Salt Lake City 119368
Salt Museum, Liverpool 045351
Salt Museum, Northwich 040600
Salt Spring Island Museum, Ganges 005495
Salt Water Gallery, Burnham Market 112763
Saltar i Parar, La Bisbal d'Empordá . 081009
Saltash Heritage Centre, Saltash .. 040950
Saltburn Artists Projects, Saltburn-by-the-Sea 114393
Saltdal Museum, Rognan 031143
Salter, F.D., Clare 084027, 130587
Salter, Nicholas, London .. 085672, 141888
Salter Museum, Argonia 041768
Saltgate Antiques, Beccles 083467
Saltgrass Gallery, Lymington 114017
Salti, Lorenzo, Nice 124523
Saltiel, Le Castellet 063589
Saltire Society, Edinburgh 054493
Saltram House, Plymouth 040724
Saltrødbukta kunstformidling, Saltrød 079488
Saltstraumen Museum, Saltstraumen 031162
Saltworks Gallery, Atlanta 114920
Saltzaroen Aretoa, Bilbao 093881
Salud Segundino Antiguedades, Sevilla 081613
Saluden, Quimper 101064
Saluhallen, Sundsvall 122270
Salusbury, Tom, Hitchin .. 084695, 130796
Salva, Christian, Toulouse 124994
Salvador, Buenos Aires 136754
Salvador, Zaragoza 081754
Salvador Dali Museum, Saint Petersburg 047719
Salvadori, Roberto, Genova 075506
Salvadori, Sergio, Firenze 127407
Salvage Fisherman's Museum, Salvage 006408
Salvage Heaven, Milwaukee 090321
The Salvage Shop, Toronto 059289
Salvan, Christian, Le Dorat 063615
Salvan, Christian, Le Dorat 063616
Salvat, Barcelona 134927
Salvat, J., Miami 135392, 142560
Salvat, María, Barcelona 110246
Salvat Montserrat, Maria, Barcelona 110247

Salvation Army George Scott Railton Museum, Toronto 006628
Salvation Army International Heritage Centre, London 040284
Salvation Army Southern Historical Museum, Atlanta 041871
The Salvation Army Territorial Archives and Museum, Wellington 030651
Di Salvatore, Puyricard 067004
Salvatore, Bruno, Firenze 075398
Salvatori, Armando, Roma 128194
Salvatori, Maurizio, Roma 128195
Salvatorianerkloster, Dom zu Gurk, Gurk 001990
Salve 97, Sofia 096745
Salverda, Kiel-Windeweer 134818
Salveymühle, Geesow 017333
Salvi Garcia, Ruben, Oviedo 110665
Salvò, Rino, Padova 127811
SALVO, Scottish Arts Lobby, Edinburgh 054494
Salwender, H., Eppelheim 070576
Salzano, Giancarlo, Torino 106703
Salzbergwerk Berchtesgaden, Berchtesgaden 015958
Salzbergwerksmuseum und Schaustollen, Hallein 002014
Salzburger Barockmuseum, Sammlung Rossacher, Salzburg 002566
Salzburger Barockmuseum, Verlagsabteilung, Salzburg 133149
Salzburger Freilichtmuseum, Großgmain 001969
Salzburger Kunstverein, Salzburg . .052595, 095735, 133150
Salzburger Landes-Skimuseum, Werfenweng 002838
Salzburger Museum Carolino Augusteum, Salzburg 002567
Salzburger Museumsverein, Salzburg 052596
Salzer, Frank, Zwönitz 127069
Salzin, Namur 096395
Salzkammer, Pratteln 037424
Salzkammergut-Lokalbahn-Museum, Mondsee 002337
Salzmagazin, Nidwaldner Museum, Stans 037598
Salzmann, Dornbirn 123347
Salzmuseum, Bad Nauheim 015757
Salzmuseum, Bad Sooden-Allendorf 015806
Salzmuseum, Bad Sülze 015811
Salzwelten Altaussee, Altaussee . . 001677
Salzwelten Salzburg-Bad Dürrnberg, Hallein 002014
Sam Bell Maxey House, Paris 046817
Sam Brown Memorial Park, Browns Valley 042480
Sam Houston Historical Schoolhouse, Maryville 045720
Sam Houston Memorial Museum, Huntsville 044695
Sam Noble Oklahoma Museum of Natural History, Norman 046509
The Sam Rayburn Museum, Bonham 042297
Sam Roi Yod, Phachuab Khiri Khan . 037919
Sam the Chandelier Man, Toronto . . 059290
Sam Tung Uk Museum, Hong Kong . 007132
Sam Waller Museum, The Pas 006118
SAMAB, Southern African Museums Association, Grahamstown 136066
Samagra, Paris 100827
Samagundi Club, New York 055016
Saman, Teheran 074848
Samancıoğlu S. Resim Galerisi, İstanbul 112354
Samaniego Caballero, Pedro Antonio, Burgos 081019
Samans, Dr. Rainer, Eschweiler . . . 070613
SAMANTIX, Durban 136067
Samara, Amiens 060826
Samarcanda, Brasília 137554
Samarcanda, Perugia 076236
Samarkand Galleries, Edinburgh . . . 084312
Samarkand Galleries, Stow-on-the-Wold 086761, 131551
Samarkanda Otros Mundos, Girona 081137
Samarra Museum, Samarra 022673
Samarskaja Chudožestvennaja Galereja Marija, Samara 033721
Samarskaja Gosudarstvennaja Akademija Iskusstv i Kultury, Samara 050659
Samarskij Eparchialnyj Cerkovno-istoričeskij Muzej, Samara 033722
Samarskij Oblastnoj Chudožestvennyj Muzej, Samara 033723
Samarskij Oblastnoj Istoriko-kraevedčeskij Muzej im. P.V. Alabina, Samara . . 033724
Samarskij Zoologičeskij Muzej, Samara 033725
Samawat, Christa, Berlin 069740
Samb, Abdoulaye, Caen 061886
Sambataro, Placida, Catania 127278
Sambeau, Saint Louis 092309
Sambourne House Antiques, Swindon 086815
Sambulski & Körner-Sambulski, Haselau 071425
Samdan, İstanbul 083154
Samegården med Museum, Tärnaby 036703
Samford and District Historical Museum, Samford 001456
Sami, Austin 087613
Saminger, Erich, Linz 057164
Saminger, Erich, Salzburg 057276
Saminger, Erich, Wels . . . 057355, 123487
Saminger, Ferdinand, Linz 123414
Saminger, Ferdinand, Salzburg 057277, 123455
De Samiske Samlinger, Karasjok . . 030933
Samkyung, Seoul 107281
Samlarbutiken, Göteborg 081819
Samlarkällan, Upplands Väsby 082055
Samlarshopen, Göteborg 081820
Samler og Antikk Messen, Lillestrøm 093839
The Samlesbury Decorative and Fine Arts Society, Poulton-le-Fylde 054495
Samlesbury Hall, Samlesbury 086501
Sammann, Jesteburg 071660
Sammanns, Jesteburg 103453
Sammarino Selezione d'Arte Antica, San Marino 080349
Sammeck & Sammeck, München . . 104305
Sammel Surium, Nürnberg 073119
Sammelpunkt, Bünde 070084
Sammelpunkt, Zürich 141357
SammensIutningen af Grønlandske Lokalmuseer, Sisimiut 053668
Sammer Sidi, London 113874
Sammet, Detlef, Waldsassen 074258
Sammlung Antiker Kleinkunst, Institut für Altertumswissenschaften der Friedrich-Schiller-Universität Jena, Jena . . 018114
Sammlung Berger, Amorbach 015537
Sammlung Bodingbauer, Steyr 002704
Sammlung Buchheim - Museum der Phantasie, Bernried, Starnberger See 016209
Sammlung der Universität für angewandte Kunst Wien mit Oskar-Kokoschka-Zentrum, Wien 002996
Sammlung des Ägyptologischen Instituts, Universität Heidelberg, Heidelberg 017834
Sammlung Domnick, Nürtingen . . . 019378
Sammlung Dr. Berkowitz, Münzkabinett der Stadt Hannover, Hannover 017768
Sammlung Dr. Irmgard von Lemmers-Danforth, Europäische Wohnkultur aus Renaissance und Barock, Wetzlar 020848
Sammlung Ernst Schneider, Hetjens Museum, Düsseldorf 016844
Sammlung Essl - Kunst der Gegenwart, Klosterneuburg 002157
Sammlung Flörl, Hall in Tirol 002010
Sammlung Fossilien des Jura, Lichtenfels, Bayern 018632
Sammlung Franz Belting, Lehrte . . 018546
Sammlung Friedhof Hörnli, Riehen . 037453
Sammlung Friedrichshof, Zurndorf . 003072
Sammlung für Papier- und Druckgeschichte, Frankenberg, Sachsen 017148
Sammlung Gauselmann, Deutsches Automatenmuseum, Espelkamp . 017057
Sammlung Geyer-zu-Lauf, Emmendingen 016969
Sammlung Goetz, München 019109
Sammlung handgeschriebener Choralbücher, Kiedrich 018241
Sammlung Hauser und Wirth, Sankt Gallen 037498
Sammlung Heinrich Brechbühl, Steffisburg 037604
Sammlung Herzoglicher Kunstbesitz, Stiftung der Herzog von Sachsen-Coburg und Gotha'schen Familie, Coburg 016578
Sammlung historischer Maschinen und Geräte, Calau 016535
Sammlung historischer Mikroskope von Ernst Leitz, Wetzlar 020849
Sammlung historischer Prägestempel, Wien 002997
Sammlung historischer Tasteninstrumente Neumeyer-Junghanns-Tracey, Bad Krozingen 015741
Sammlung Hoffmann, Berlin 016164
Sammlung im Obersteg, Oberhofen am Thunersee 037390
Sammlung industrielle Gestaltung, Deutsches Historisches Museum, Berlin 016165
Sammlung Irmgard Friedl, Bad Griesbach im Rottal 015709
Sammlung Jagdkunde, Landesmuseum Joanneum, Graz 001948
Sammlung landwirtschaftlicher Geräte, Unterpleichfeld 020543
Sammlung Ludwig in Bamberg, Museen der Stadt Bamberg, Bamberg 015879
Sammlung Meinrad Burch-Korrodi, Sarnen 037515
Sammlung Mittelalterliche Kunst in Thüringen, Thüringer Museum Eisenach, Eisenach 016924
Sammlung Oskar Kokoschka, Wien 002996
Sammlung Oskar Reinhart 'Am Römerholz', Winterthur 037729
Sammlung Patt, Musik-Instrumente von gestern und heute, Willisau 037716
Sammlung Prinzhorn, Psychiatrische Universitätsklinik Heidelberg, Heidelberg 017835
Sammlung Religiöser Volkskunst, Wien 002998
Sammlung Rosengart Luzern, Luzern 037304
Sammlung Schloß Aichberg, Rohrbach an der Lafnitz 002537
Sammlung Warburg im Planetarium, Hamburg 017720
Sammlungen Burg Bernstein, Bernstein, Burgenland 001752
Sammlungen der Benediktiner-Abtei Braunau, Rohr, Niederbayern 019875
Sammlungen der Burg Hochosterwitz, Launsdorf 002208
Sammlungen der Schule für Gestaltung Basel, Basel 036904
Sammlungen der Stadt Amstetten auf Schloß Ulmerfeld, Ulmerfeld-Hausmening 002765
Sammlungen der Technischen Universität Dresden, Dresden 016812
Sammlungen des Archäologischen Instituts der Universität, Göttingen 017472
Sammlungen des Augustiner Chorherrenstiftes, Sankt Florian . 002579
Sammlungen des Instituts für Hochschulkunde der Deutschen Gesellschaft für Hochschulkunde, Würzburg 021007
Sammlungen des Kunstvereins, Ibbenbüren 018040
Sammlungen des Marktamtes, Wien 002999
Sammlungen des Stiftes Sankt Lambrecht, Volkskundemuseum, Galerie und Vogelsammlung, Sankt Lambrecht 002595
Sammlungen des Zisterzienserstiftes Rein, Rein 002518
Sammlungen im Adelmannschloß, Landshut 018485
Sammlungen Schloß Moosham, Mauterndorf 002302
Sammons, Timothy, London 113875
Sammy Marks Museum, Pretoria . . 034727
Sammy Miller Motorcycle Museum, New Milton 040526
Samobor Museum, Samobor 007786
Samocvet, Kiriši 109472
Samocvety, Moskva 033524
Samoticha, Mario, Bochum 069892
Samotracía, Buenos Aires 123159
Samovar Antiques, Hythe, Kent . . . 084782
Samoy Art Museum, Bacoor 031624
Sampl, Wolfgang, Baden . 082108, 111154, 129905
Sampler Antiques, Oklahoma City . 091532
Sampson, Alistair, London 085673
Sampson, Anthony, Dulverton 084227
Samrhea, Genolier 111512
Sams, Bad Ischl 095467
Sam's Antique Rugs, Dallas 088606, 132021
Sam's Cottage, Houston 089197
Sam's Refinishing, Houston 132136
Samson, Boston 115229
Samson, Paris 066523, 124802
Samson, Jean-François, Amboise . 060800
Samson-Haus, Leer 018541
Samson V Maritime Museum, New Westminster 006006
Samsun Atatürk Müzesi, Samsun . . 038166
Samsun Devlet Güzel Sanatlar Galerisi, Samsun 038167
Samsung Children's Museum, Seoul 027593
Samsung Foundation of Culture, Seoul 027594
Samsung Museum of Publishing, Seoul 027595
Samtleben, Ute, Potsdam 104631
Samtuh, Gangsang 107197
Samtuh, Seoul 107282
Samuel, Claude, Paris 100828
Samuel, Philippe, Paris 100829
Samuel Cupples House, Saint Louis 047680
Samuel Dorsky Museum of Art, New Paltz 046269
Samuel F.B. Morse Historic Site, Poughkeepsie 047214
Samuel Johnson Birthplace Museum, Lichfield 040001
Samuel K. Fox Museum, Dillingham 043469
Samuel P. Harn Museum of Art, Gainesville 044106
Samuel Palmer School of Fine Art, Shoreham 050857
Samuel S. Fleisher Art Memorial, Philadelphia Museum of Art, Philadelphia 046988
Samuel-Weis, Thierry, Marseille . . . 121066
Samuelis, Bielefeld 102128
Samuel's Gallery, Oakland 118645
Samvirkemuseet, Gjettum 030856
San Agustin Museum Intramuros, Manila 031740
San Angel Folk Art, San Antonio . . . 119450
San Angelo Art Club, San Angelo . . 055017
San Angelo Museum of Fine Arts, San Angelo 047785
San Antonio Abad, Madrid 035444
San Antonio Art League, San Antonio 055018
San Antonio Children's Museum, San Antonio 047802
San Antonio Cultural Arts, San Antonio 119451
San Antonio Missions Museum, Jolon 044877
San Antonio Missions Visitor Center, San Antonio 047803
San Antonio Museum of Art, San Antonio 047804

San Antonio Rare Coins and Jewelry, San Antonio . . . 092577
San Antonio Upholstering Company, San Antonio . . . 132826
San Antonio's Center for Antiques, San Antonio . . . 092578
San Barandan, Córdoba . . . 081051
San Barnaba, Milano . . . 106305
San Bernardino Art Association, San Bernardino . . . 055019
San Bernardino County Museum, Redlands . . . 047362
San Buenaventura Mission Museum, Ventura . . . 048758
San Carlos Cathedral Museum, Monterey . . . 045987
San Caterina, Brescia . . . 075182
San Diego Aerospace Museum, San Diego . . . 047830
San Diego Antique Tour, San Diego . 092681
San Diego Art Institute, San Diego . 052117
San Diego Automotive Museum, San Diego . . . 047831
San Diego Coin and Bullion, San Diego . . . 092682
San Diego Coin and Gold Exchange, San Diego . . . 092683
San Diego Hall of Champions Sports Museum, San Diego . . . 047832
San Diego Historical Society Museum, San Diego . . . 047833
San Diego Maritime Museum, San Diego . . . 047834
San Diego Mesa College Art Gallery and African Art Collection, San Diego . 047835
San Diego Model Railroad Museum, San Diego . . . 047836
San Diego Museum of African Art, San Diego . . . 047837
San Diego Museum of Art, San Diego . . . 047838
San Diego Museum of Man, San Diego . . . 047839
San Diego Natural History Museum, San Diego . . . 047840
San Diego Poster Distributor, San Diego . . . 119546
San Diego Sculptors Guild, San Diego . . . 055020, 119547
San Diego Shipping Antiguidades, São Paulo . . . 058741
San Diego W&S, San Diego . . . 142915
San Diego Watercolor Society, San Diego . . . 055021, 119548
San Dieguito Heritage Museum, Encinitas . . . 043708
San Domenico Stringed Instruments, Cardiff . . . 083876, 130515
San-Ee, Singapore . . . 109864
San el-Haggar Museum, Sharqiya . 009345
San Federico, Torino . . . 076864
San Fernando Historical Museum, Mission Hills . . . 045928
San Francisco African American Historical and Cultural Society Museum, San Francisco . . . 047880
San Francisco Antique and Design Mall, San Francisco . . . 092880
San Francisco Art Dealers, San Francisco . . . 119782
San Francisco Art Institute, San Francisco . . . 052124
San Francisco Arts of Pacific Asia Show, San Francisco . . . 094028
San Francisco Camerawork, San Francisco . . . 047881
San Francisco Craft and Folk Art Museum, San Francisco . . . 047875
San Francisco Fire Department Museum, San Francisco . . . 047882
San Francisco International Art Exposition, San Francisco . . . 094029
San Francisco Maritime National Historical Park, San Francisco . . . 047883
San Francisco Museum of Contemporary Hispanic Art, San Francisco . . . 047884
San Francisco Museum of Modern Art, San Francisco . . . 047885
San Francisco Rock Posters, San Francisco . . . 119783
San Francisco Tribal, Folk and Textile Arts Show, San Francisco . . . 094030
San Francisco Women Artists, San Francisco . . . 055022
San Gabriel Antigüedades, Lima . . . 079557
San Gabriel Mission Museum, San Gabriel . . . 047893
San Jacinto Museum, San Jacinto . 047894
San Jacinto Museum of History, La Porte . . . 045077
San Jaime, Palma de Mallorca . . . 081496
San Joaquin County Historical Museum, Lodi . . . 045363
San Joaquin Delta College, Fine Arts Division, Stockton . . . 052222
San Jose Antique Mall, Jacksonville 089459
San Jose Art League, San Jose . . . 055023
San Jose Coin Shop, San Jose . . . 092933
San Jose Collectibles, San Jose . . . 092934
San José de Flores, Buenos Aires . . 055242
San Jose Institute of Contemporary Art, San Jose . . . 047901
San Jose Museum of Art, San Jose 047902
San Jose Museum of Quilts and Textiles, San Jose . . . 047903
San Jose State University Art Galleries, San Jose State University, San Jose . . 047899
San Juan, Madrid . . . 129681
San Juan Bautista State Historic Park, San Juan Bautista . . . 047905
San Juan County Historical Museum, Silverton . . . 048182
San Juan County Museum, Bloomfield . . . 042252
San Juan Garcia, Federico, Valencia 129782
San Juan Historical Society Museum, Friday Harbor . . . 044083
San Juan Island National Historical Park, Friday Harbor . . . 044084
San Juan National Historic Site, San Juan . . . 032751
San Lorenzo Restoration, New York 132528
San Luis Obispo Art Center, San Luis Obispo . . . 047908
San Luis Obispo County Historical Museum, San Luis Obispo . . . 047909
San Marco Book Store, Jacksonville 142469
San Marco Gallery, Dominican University of California, San Rafael . . . 047922
San Marcos de Apalache Historic State Park, Saint Marks . . . 047684
San Martin, Carlos, Bordeaux . . . 124144
The San Mateo County Arts Council, Belmont . . . 042125, 055024
San Mateo County Historical Museum, Redwood City . . . 047364
San Miguel Mission Church, Santa Fe . . . 047976
San Pedro Market Antiques, San Antonio . . . 092579
San Pedro Museo de Arte, Puebla . . 028675
San Reus, Palma de Mallorca . . . 110700
San Román, Logroño . . . 129544
San Salvatore, Modena . . . 106355
San Tan Antiques, Phoenix 091768, 123053
San Telmo, Madrid . . . 081386
San Telmo, Madrid . . . 081387
San Vittore Comptoir, Marseille . . . 099683
Sana Hastakala, Lalitpur . . . 107607
Sanaa Exhibition, Sharjah . . . 083223
Sanace, Venezia . . . 076971
Sanada Ikkanart, New York . . . 118377
Al-Sanam, Manama . . . 096023
Sanandaj Museum, Sanandaj . . . 022593
Sanart, Frankfurt am Main . . . 070785
Sanat Dünyamız, İstanbul . . . 136142
Sanati Museum, Kerman . . . 022569
Al-Sanaya, Manama . . . 096024
Sanbrano, New York . . . 091224
Sancarlos, Lisboa . . . 080007
Sancerne, Pascal, Paris . . . 066524
Sanchez, Barcelona . . . 129398
Sanchez, Miami . . . 117135
Sanchez, Dana, Austin . . . 115009
Sanchez, Maika, Valencia . . . 110842
Sanchez, Pedro, Madrid . . . 081388
Sanchez Adobe Historic Site, Pacifica . . . 046786
Sanchez & Hijos, Juan, Barcelona . 080927
Sanchez Palma, Carmen, Granada . 110383
Sanchez Pinazo, Málaga . . . 110644
Sánchez & Priebe, Paloma, Valencia 129783
Sanchez Rigal y Otra, Murcia . . . 110654
Sanchez & Seydoux, Paris . . . 100830
Sanchez Suarez, L., Gijón . . . 110360
Sanchez Tapiz, Santiago, Donostia-San Sebastián . . . 110344
Sanchez Vazquez, Mercedes, Barcelona . . . 110248
Sanchez y Reyes, Madrid . . . 110610
Sancho Pallisa, Francisco, Barcelona . . . 080928
Sancta, Vilnius . . . 077456, 140234
Sancta Birgitta Klostermuseum, Vadstena . . . 036751
Sanctuary Cove Antique Gallery, Sanctuary Cove . . . 056569
Sanctuary Wood Museum - Hill 62, Zillebeke . . . 003869
Sand, Gérard, Bruxelles . . . 058081
Sand, Jean-Marie, Aubevoye . . . 061039
Sand Bakkens Medisinske Museum, Flekkefjord . . . 030840
Sand Castle Gallery, Sorrento . . . 095198
Sand Point Antiques, Seattle . . . 093061
Sand Springs Cultural and Historical Museum, Sand Springs . . . 047924
Sand Tchou Mengès, Paris . . . 133673
Sandaga Market, Dallas . . . 088607
Sandal Castle, Sandal . . . 040952
Sandal Magna Senteret, Sand . . . 108746
Sandaraca, Madrid . . . 129682
Sandauer Heimatstube, Arzberg, Oberfranken . . . 015570
Sandberg, Patrick, London . . . 085674
Sandblom, Victor, Seattle . . . 119987
Sande Historielags Bygdesamlinger, Sande . . . 031165
Sandefjord Bymuseum, Sandefjord . 031167
Sandefjord Sjøfartsmuseum, Sandefjord . . . 031168
Sandefjordmuseene, Sandefjord . . . 031169
Sandellmuseet, Ramkvilla . . . 036543
Sandels, Napoli . . . 076044
Sandelsches Museum, Kirchberg an der Jagst . . . 018259
Sander, Bad Soden am Taunus . . . 101702
Sander, Gunnar, Lund . . . 141124
Sander, H.A., Müllheim, Baden . . . 072621
Sander, Hans-Joachim, Berlin . . . 102027
Sander, Hans-Joachim, Darmstadt . 102348
Sander, Henning, Lehrte . . . 072188
Sander, R., Edemissen . . . 102600
Sander, Siegfried, Kassel . 103519, 134082
Sander, Stig, Frederiksberg 060245, 098528
Sanders, Capelle aan den IJssel . . . 128615
Sanders, Nashville . . . 090485, 132404
Sanders, Tucson . . . 120163
Sanders, Jack, Mönchengladbach . 072575
Sanders, Ken, Salt Lake City . . . 142875
Sanders, R.J., Auckland . . . 128912
Sanders & Sons, Robin, Woodstock 087242
Sanders, Tony, Penzance . . . 086215
Sanders, Yvonne, Auckland . . . 078980
Sanders of Oxford, Oxford . . . 086186
Sanderson, George & Peach, Holmfirth . . . 113255
Sanderus, Gent . . . 137503
Sandford, Dublin . . . 105887
Sandgate, Ayr . . . 122395
Sandgate and District Historical Museum, Sandgate . . . 001458
Sandgate Antiques, Penrith . . . 086205
Sandi, Gabriella, Venezia . . . 128404
Sandjon, J.P., Düren . . . 070351
Sandler, Hudson, Atlanta . . . 114921
Sandleson, Robert, London . . . 113876
Sandmann, Berlin . . . 102028
Sandmann, Dr. Marina, Pretzetze . . 104636
Sandmore, Calgary . . . 058804
Sandnes Kunstforening, Sandnes . . 079493
Sandnesmuseet, Sandnes . . . 031170
Sando, Sendai . . . 077219
Sandon Museum, New Denver . . . 005995
The Sandor Teszler Gallery, Wofford College, Spartanburg . . . 048264
Sandorfi, Maria, Paris . . . 066525
Sandoval, Phoenix . . . 118890
Sandoval, Vda de O., Barcelona . . . 080929
Sandown Historical Museum, Sandown . . . 047927
Sandpiper Gallery, Mousehole . . . 114096
Sandpoint Lighthouse, Delta County Historical Society, Escanaba . . . 043727
Sandra and Mary's Doll Shop, San Diego . . . 092684
Sandra & Márcio Objetos de Arte, Belo Horizonte . . . 058449
Sandras, Langenbernsdorf . . . 139380
Sandra's Sensations, Miami . . . 090237
Sandraz, Didier, Villeurbanne . . . 068979
Sandrelle, Lyon . . . 099613
Sandringham Antiques, Kingston-upon-Hull . . . 084864
Sandringham House Museum, Sandringham . . . 040957
Sandroni & Rey, Los Angeles . . . 116879
Sands & Co., New York . . . 118378
Sands-Willets House, Port Washington . . . 047147
Sandstein, Michael, Dresden . . . 133879
Sandsteinmuseum Kloster Cornberg, Cornberg . . . 016589
Sandtoft Transport Centre, Doncaster . . . 039252
Sandtorg Bygdetun, Sørvik . . . 031215
Sanduo Tang Museum, Taigu . . . 007277
Sandved, Kjell B., Washington . . . 120346
Sandvikens Konsthall, Sandviken . . 036563
Sandvoss, Dieter-Christian, Hannover . . . 071412
Sandwich, Chicago . . . 088167
Sandwich Auction House, Sandwich 123107
Sandwich Fine Books, Sandwich . . 142048
Sandwich Fine Books, Sandwich . . 142049
Sandwich Glass Museum, Sandwich . . . 047934
Sandwich Historical Society Museum, Center Sandwich . . . 042685
Sandwich Historical Society Museum, Sandwich . . . 047931
Sandy Bay Historical Museums, Rockport . . . 047509
Sandy K.'s Art Sales, Minneapolis . 117305
Sandy Spring Museum, Sandy Spring . . . 047938
Sandycove Fine Arts, Dublin . . . 074945
Sandy's Antiques, Bournemouth . . . 083607
Sandy's Gallery, Jacksonville . . . 089460
Sandz Gallery, Hamilton . . . 108460
Sanfeliu Gimeno, Maria Luz, Valencia . . . 129784
Sanfilippo, Giuseppa, Genova . . . 075507
Sanford Museum, Cherokee . . . 042791
Sanford Museum, Sanford . . . 047940
Sangat, Ufa . . . 109664
Sangeet Natak, Delhi . . . 135849
Sangenis, Albert, Barcelona . . . 080930, 129399
Sangerberger Heimatstube, Regenstauf . . . 019763
Sangji Vocational College Museum, Andong . . . 027448
Sangli State Museum, Sangli . . . 022325
Sangmoondang, Seoul . . . 107283
Sango, Leuven . . . 096373
Sangre de Cristo Arts Center and Buell Children's Museum, Pueblo . . . 047279
Sanguineti, Tito, Genova . . . 075508
Sanguinetti, Martínez . . . 055284
Sanguino, Toledo . . . 081632
Sani, Antonio, Firenze . . . 075399
Sani, Gladys, Paris . . . 066526, 100831
Sanilac County Historical Museum, Port Sanilac . . . 047139

Sanin Arenas, Ricardo, Cali 123922
Sanin Historical Collection, Yonago . 027347
Sanitärmuseum, Wien 003000
Sanitätsmuseum, Großpösna 017577
Sanjay Sharma Museum, Jaipur, Rajasthan 022180
Sanjaya, Singapore 080555
Sanjo, Paris 100832
Sanjo Gion Garo, Kyoto 106906
Sanjusangendo, Kyoto 026768
Sankara, Sylvie, Combs-la-Ville . . . 062433
Sankei-en Garden, Yokohama 027335
Sankofa, Cleveland 115737
Sankt-Annen-Museum und Kunsthalle Sankt-Annen, Museen für Kunst und Kulturgeschichte der Hansestadt Lübeck, Lübeck 018726
Sankt Eriks Antik, Stockholm 082012
Sankt Galler Brocante, Messe für Antiquitäten, Kuriositäten und Raritäten, Sankt Gallen 093895
Sankt Georgs Presse, Sankt Georgen an der Gusen 133156
Sankt Gertrude Antiquariat, Elmenhorst 139037
Sankt Gertrude Verlag, Hamburg . . 134023
Sankt Hans Gades Antik, København 060376
Sankt Jürgen, Flensburg 070708
Sankt Marien, Müntzergedenkstätte, Mühlhäuser Museen, Mühlhausen, Thüringen 019016
Sankt Matthäus-Kirche im Kulturforum, Berlin 016166
Sankt Patrokli-Dom-Museum Soest, Soest 020232
Sankt-Peterburg Club of Art Historians, Sankt-Peterburg 054025
Sankt-Peterburgskij Gosudarstvennyj Universitet Kultury i Iskusstv, Sankt-Peterburg 050661
Sankt-Peterburgskij Gosudarstvennyj Universitet Technologii i Dizajna, Sankt-Peterburg 050662
Sankt-Peterburgskij Muzej Chleba, Sankt-Peterburg 033828
Sankt-Peterburgskij Muzej Teatralnogo i Musykalnogo Iskusstva, Sankt-Peterburg 033829
Sankt-Peterburgskij Muzej V.V. Nabokova, Sankt-Peterburg 033830
Sankt-Peterburgskij Pastelnyj Sojuz, Sankt-Peterburg 054026
Sankt-Peterburgskij Sojuz Dizajnerov, Sankt-Peterburg 054027
Sankt Pöltner Künstlerbund, Sankt Pölten 052597
Sankta Karins Kyrkoruin, Visby 036800
Şanlıurfa Devlet Güzel Sanatlar Galerisi, Şanlıurfa 038168
Sanmei, Nagoya 106935
Sanming City Art Cooperative, Sanming 097901
Sanming City Calligraphy and Painting Gallery, Sanming 097902
Sanna, Gianfranco, Cagliari 075227
Sannergata, Oslo 079468
Sannidal Bygdetun, Sannidal 031172
Sannomiya Local Museum, Isehara 026572
Sano Art Museum, Mishima 026812
Sano Studio, New York 132529
Sanquhar Tolbooth Museum, Sanquhar 040961
Sans Ennui, San Francisco 119784
Sans Frontiers, Lefkosia 098307
Sans Tache, Mumbai 105802
Sanseido, Tokyo 140199
Sanselmo, Ciro, Napoli . . . 076045, 127790
La Sanseverina, Parma 106456
Šanšieva, Karina, Moskva 109586
Sanskar Cendra Musiam, Ahmedabad 105599
Sanske, Mary Anne, Zürich 112171
Sanskriti, Kolkata 105745
Sansom & Co., Bristol 135125
Sanson, Jacqueline, Nice 065145
Sanson, Xavier, Le Mans 121032
Sansone, Giovanni, Verona 077020
Sansoni, Milano 134635
Sansovini, Luigi, Roma 128196
Sansum, James, New York 091225
Sant-Yago, Madrid 081389
Santa, Banská Bystrica 129269
Santa Agueda, Zaragoza 129829
Santa Ana College Art Gallery, Santa Ana 047947
Santa Barbara Contemporary Arts Forum, Klausner Gallery and Norton Gallery, Santa Barbara 047948
Santa Barbara Historical Museum, Santa Barbara 047949
Santa Barbara Museum of Art, Santa Barbara 047950
Santa Barbara Museum of Natural History, Santa Barbara 047951
Santa Cruz Art League Museum, Santa Cruz 047959
Santa Cruz Museum of Natural History, Santa Cruz 047960
Santa Cruz Valley Art Association, Tuvac 055025
Santa Fe Children's Museum, Santa Fe 047977
Santa Fe Colonial, Miami 090238
Santa Fe Community Museum, Santa Fe 031785
Santa Fe Connections, San Antonio 119452
Santa Fe Gallery, Santa Fe Community College, Gainesville 044107
Santa Fe Trail Museum, Larned . . . 045176
Santa Fe Trail Museum, Trinidad History Museum, Trinidad 048613
Santa Fe Trail Museums of Gray County, Ingalls 044756
Santa Giulia - Museo della Città, Brescia 023526
Santa Lucia Antichitá, Firenze 075400
Santa Maria Museum of Flight, Santa Maria 047982
Santa Maria Valley Historical Society Museum, Santa Maria 047983
Santa Monica Museum of Art, Santa Monica 047988
Santa Paula Union Oil Museum, Santa Paula 047989
Santa Rosa Junior College Art Gallery, Santa Rosa 047993
Santacruz, Carlos, Bogotá 098191
Santagostini, Giorgio, Milano 127680
Santágueda, Madrid 129683
Santala, Ari, Joensuu 137967
Santamaria, Carlo, Napoli 106387
Santamaria, Claudia, Genova 127487
Santamaria, Nicolas Nicolaevich, Santander 129723
Santamaria, Paola, Padova 076112
Santamarías, Bogotá 059857
Santamarina Albertos, Elena, Burgos 129466
Santambrogio, Anna, Milano 075857
Santangelo, Massimiliano, Napoli . . 076046
Santarella Museum and Gardens, Tyringham 048682
Santarelli, William Maria, Torino . . . 128355
Santa'S, Barcelona 080931
Sante, Tania, Miami 090239
Santel, Bogotá 059858
Santi, Jakarta 105841
Santi, Giuffrida, Roma 128197
Santiago, Lisboa 140853
Santiago, Antoine, Descartes 062615
Santiago, Ray, Louisville 132304
Santiago Contreras, Jerez de la Frontera 081166
Santiago Cuadrado Rodriguez, Madrid 129684
Santiago do Cacém Museu Municipal, Santiago do Cacém 032684
Santiaoshi History Museum, Tianjin 007283
Santik Möbler, Stockholm 082013
Santillan, Julio, Buenos Aires 123160
Santo Calcagno, Catania 106025
Santo Niño Shrine and Heritage Museum, Tacloban 031796
Santo Rossi, Catania 075261
Santolin, Giustiniano, Milano 075858
Santolini, Antonio, Roma 128198
Santolini, Gérard, Paris 066527
Santom, William, Pittsburgh 132675
Santopietro, Montevideo 087344
Santos Júnior & Filhos, Lisboa 129174
Santos, Miami 117136
Santos, Augusto, Lisboa 080008
Santos, A.V., London 085675
Santos, Carlos Janeiro, Lisboa 080009
Santos, Carlos Janeiro, Lisboa 080010
Santos, Fernando Ferreira, Braga . . 140810
Santos, Fernando, Porto 109396
Santos, Florindo Ferreira, Lisboa . . 080011
Santos, J.F.J., Braga 079814
Santos, L., Madrid 110611
Santos, Maria Geraldo, Belo Horizonte 058450
Santos, Maria Isabel Ribeiro, Coimbra 079822
Santos, Silvia Lima, Fortaleza 096536
Santos, Virgínia, Coimbra 109247
Santos Gonzalez, Carlos, Barcelona 129400
Santos & Marcos, Lisboa 080012
Gonçalves Santos & Silveira, Lisboa 140854
Santos Vega, Rogelio, Madrid 129685
Santosh Art Gallary, Jaipur, Rajasthan 105727
Santostefano, Roberto, Buenos Aires 055243
Santuario Casa Santa Caterina, Siena 025895
Santuario de Nuestra Senora de Guadalupe, Santa Fe 047978
Santuario della Beata Vergine della Salute, Solarolo 025911
Santuario Eucaristico, Basilica di Santa Cristina, Bolsena 023465
Sanuki Folk Art Museum, Takamatsu 027105
Sanvido, Danilo, Milano 127681
Sanxia, Baoding 097639
Sanying Pagoda and Museum of Dinosaur, Shaoguan 007251
Sanyuan Gallery, Qingdao 097894
Sanz, Madrid 141060
Sanz, Daniel, Nogent-le-Rotrou . . . 065210
Sanz, Gonzalo, Barcelona . 080932, 129401
Sao, Paris 100833
São Gabriel, Lisboa 080013
São Marcos Restauracao Artistica em Prata, São Paulo 123724
Saona, Miami 117137
Saône Antiquités, Saint-Laurent-sur-Saône 067581
SAP Galeria - Spółdzielni Artystów Plastyków, Łódź 109021
Sapajou, B.D., Boulogne-Billancourt 138053
Sapet, Mirmande 099727
Sapet, Valence (Drôme) 101412
Sapet, Christian, Saint-Ouen 067889
Saphir, Paris 100834, 138539
Sapho, New York 091226
Sapin, de, Beek en Donk 128580
Sapino, Patrick, Briançon 061791
Sapiro, Paris 100835
Sapjo, Monaco 077624
Sapone, Antonio, Nice 099855
Sapori, Paolo, Milano 075859
Sappey, Huguette, Puget-Ville 066994
Sappey, Jacques, Puget-Ville 066995
Sappho, Glebe 136920
Sapporo Geijutsu no Mori Bijutsukan, Sapporo 027033
Sapporo International Print Biennale, Sapporo 093805
Sapporo Science Center, Sapporo . . 027034
Sapporo Sculpture Museum, Sapporo 027035
Sapporo Waterworks Memorial Museum, Sapporo 027036
Sapporo Winter Sports Museum, Sapporo 027037
Sapulpa Historical Museum, Sapulpa 047995
Sapumal Foundation Gallery, Colombo 036135
S.A.R. Restauro, Firenze 127408
Sara, Sendai 077220
Sara, Veneziano, Roma 076665
Sara Frances Antiques, Alderley Edge 083261, 130288
Sara Galleries, Houston 116400
Sara Hildénin Taidemuseo, Tampere 010126
Saracen's Lantern, Canterbury 083867
Sarafkina Kašta Gradski Bit, Veliko Tărnovo 004940
Sarah, Middelburg 078643
Sarah Campbell Blaffer Foundation, Houston 044655
Sarah Campbell Blaffer Gallery, Art Museum of the University of Houston, Houston 044656
Sarah Joan Antiques, North Rockhampton 056373
Sarah Moody Gallery of Art, University of Alabama, Tuscaloosa 048666
Sarah Orne Jewett House, South Berwick 048233
Sarah Spurgeon Gallery, Ellensburg 043673
Sarah Vaughan Museum, Sioux Lookout 006478
Sarajo, New York 118379
Sarakatsani Folklore Museum, Serres 021462
Saramito, Marie-Dominique, Cannes 061955
Sarang Art Gallery, Nairobi 107164
Sarasota Classic Car Museum, Sarasota 048000
Saraswaty, Kolkata 134519
Sarat Smriti Granthagar, Panitras . . 022290
Saratoga Museum, Saratoga 048004
Saratoga National Historical Park, Stillwater 048359
Saratoga Springs Museum, Saratoga Springs 048008
Saratovskij Ėtnografičeskij Muzej, Saratovskij oblastnoj muzej kraevedenija, Saratov 033857
Saratovskij Gosudarstvennyj Muzej Boevoj Slavy, Saratov 033858
Saratovskij Kraevedčeskij Muzej, Saratov 033859
Saravia, San Salvador 098689
Saray, Manama 057645
Saray, Manama 057646
Sarazin, L'Isle-sur-la-Sorgue 063959
Sarcander, Arthur, Gummersbach . . 071150
Sarcee People's Museum, Calgary . 005199
Sarda Ukil School of Arts, Delhi . . . 050301
Sardana's Art Centre, Delhi 105682
Sardar Patel University Museum, Vallabhvidyanagar 022369
Sardar Vallabhbhai Patel Museum, Surat 022346
Sardine, Noirmoutier-en-l'Ile 065221
Sareban, Verona 077021
Sarehole Mill, Birmingham 038736
Sarenhes, Québec 097164
Sargadelos, Madrid 110612
Sargadelos, Sevilla 110779
Sargant, Prof. Emil, Bregenz 095487
Sargeant, Alex, Seattle 119988
Sargeant, D. & A., Sevenoaks 086543, 131467
Sargent, Los Angeles 116880
Sargent, Peter M., Portland 092002
Sargent House Museum, Gloucester 044225
Sarget, Denis, Issoudun 121017
Sarginson, K.J., York 131729
Sarguinetti Century House Museum, Yuma 049371
Šarišská Galéria, Prešov 034416
Šarišské Múzeum, Bardejov 034310
Sarjeant Gallery - Te Whare o Rehua, Wanganui 030626

Şark Sigorta Sanat Galerisi, İstanbul 112355
Sarkander, H., München 072841
Sarkis, Saint-Ouen 067890
Sarkis, Khalil Jean, Beirut 077415
Sarkisian, Denver 088731
Sarkissian, Serge, Bordeaux 099010
Sárközi Népmüvészeti Tájház, Decs 021712
Sarkoezy, Helene, München 072842
Sarm-Sart, Montana-Vermala 082665
Sarnelli, Antonio, Napoli 127791
Sarnia Public Library and Art Gallery, Sarnia 006412
Sarno, Palermo 076179, 121714
Sarno, Allen, Seattle 143007
Saroj, Jaipur 074815
Saron, Porto Alegre 096581
Sárospataki Református Kollégium Tudományos Gyüjteményei Múzeum, Sárospatak 021837
Sarpy County Historical Museum, Bellevue 042111
Sarrance, Bernard, Pau 066716
Sarrat Museum, Sarrat 031788
Sarraute, Dominique, Carcassonne . 061983
Sarrazin, François, Orléans 065308
S.Art, Moskva 109587
Sarti, Enrico, Firenze 127409
Sarti, Giovanni, Paris 066528, 100836
Sarti, Marco, Bologna 127180
Sartoni & Cerveau, Paris 100837
Sartori, Rossana, Padova 076113
Sartori, Werner, Viernheim 074209
Sartun Sociedade de Artes Unidas, Rio de Janeiro 096645
Sarue Tatuagem, Fortaleza 058479
Saruyama, Tokyo 077298
Sarver, Paris 100838
Sasebo-shi Bunka Kagakukan, Sasebo 027041
Sasfra, Belo Horizonte 058451
Sash, Maastricht 078620
SASH Book and Papercare Restauratie, Maastricht 128764
Saskatchewan Arts Board Collection, Regina 006264
Saskatchewan Baseball Hall of Fame and Museum, Battleford 005082
Saskatchewan Craft Gallery, Saskatoon 006425
Saskatchewan Military Museum, Regina 006265
Saskatchewan Pharmacy Museum, Regina 006266
Saskatchewan River Valley Museum, Hague 005560
Saskatchewan Science Centre, Regina 006267
Saskatchewan Sports Hall of Fame and Museum, Regina 006268
Saskatchewan Western Development Museum, Yorkton 006893
Saskatchewan Wildlife Federation Museum, North Battleford 006035
Saskatoon Antique, Saskatoon 059105
Saslow, Judy A., Chicago 115546
Sasón E, Buenos Aires 055244
Saß, Linde & Karl Heinz, Lübeck . . . 126244
Sassen, Edith, Planegg 104612
Sassen, Luzia, Hennef . . . 103352, 134058
Sassénus, Paris 124803
Sassho, Sapporo 106988
Sassi, Enrico, Parma 127865
Sassi-Milici, Vallauris 101422, 133704
Sassin, Bernard, L'Isle-sur-la-Sorgue 063960
Il Sasso, Don Torcuato 055267
Sassolini, Alvaro, Firenze 127410
Sasson, Caracas 120436
Sasson, David, Mandelieu-La Napoule 064245
Sassone, Francesca, Milano 075860
Satakunnan Museo, Pori 009989
Satani, Kazuhiko, Tokyo 107099
Satellite Space Studio, Fortitude Valley 094561
The Satguru Art 'n' Frames, Jaipur, Rajasthan 105728
Satguru's, Mumbai 105803
The Satirical World Art Museum, Waco 048816
Satiricum, Staatliche Bücher und Kupferstichsammlung Greiz, Greiz 017527
Satkatar, Pune 074835
Sato Art Museum Toyama, Toyama . 027285
Sato Institute of Typography, Yokohama 050506
Sato-Stone, Tokyo 077299
Satoru, Honolulu 116242
Satrosphere, Aberdeen 038453
Satterlee Clark House, Horicon 044622
Sattler, Manfred, Schwangau 126788
Sattmann, Helmut, Bremen 070044
Satwa Art Gallery, Pune 105831
Satya Art Gallery, Mumbai 105804
Saubot, Roger, Bordeaux 061652
Saubot, Roger, Saint-Jean-de-Luz . 067540
Sauc, Surry Hills 095259
Sauda Museum, Sauda 031176
Saudan, Cédric, Veytaux 082885
Saudemont, Dominique, Arques (Pas-de-Calais) 060984
Saudou, Jean-Paul, Eysines 062832
Sauer, Karl-Ludwig, Berlin 133806
Sauer, Klaus-Kürgen, Remscheid . . 073491
Sauer, Peter, Wien 057543
Sauerbrei, K.-H., Einbeck 070531
Sauerland-Museum, Arnsberg 015566
Sauermann, Gottfried, Radebeul . . . 139673
Sauff, Weilheim, Oberbayern 074306
Saugus Iron Works, Saugus 048012
Sauk County Historical Museum, Baraboo 042019
Sauk Prairie Area Historical Society Museum, Prairie du Sac 047222
Saukkojärven Kotiseutu- ja Koulumuseo, Ranua 010021
Saul, Julie, New York 118380
Sauli, Joseph, Châtillon (Hauts-de-Seine) 062231
Saulneron, Patrick, Montréjeau . . . 064764
Sault de Sainte Marie Historical Sites, Sault Sainte Marie 048015
Sault Sainte Marie Museum, Sault Sainte Marie 006433
Saundarya Lahari, Amsterdam 134789
Saunders, Scullin 056579, 137083
Saunders, Charles, London 085676
Saunders, Lorrie M., Norfolk 091399
Saunders County Historical Museum, Wahoo 048822
Saunders Memorial Museum, Berryville 042173
Saunderson, Elaine, Dorking 084202, 130649
Saunier, Maryvonne, Paris 124804
Saunier, Maryvonne, Saint-Jean-de-Braye 124906
Saunier, Pierre, Paris 138540
Saunier, Raymond, Yvetot 069069
Saunier, Sylvain, Issoudun 063225
Saupe, Andre, Potsdam 073366
Saur, K.G., Leipzig 134155
Saur, K.G., München 134272
Saura Lluch, Vicenta, Barcelona . . . 129402
Saura Miret, Gabriel, Ciutadella de Menorca 081044
Sauri Pardo De Atin, Barcelona 129403
Saurier-Museum, Frick 037106
Sauriermuseum Aathal, Aathal-Seegräben 036814
Saurierpark, Traismauer 002749
Sauriol, H., Montréal 059004
Sauser, M.-J., Peseux 082723
Sauser, Pierre, Peseux . . . 082724, 130139
Saussez, Patrick, Tocane-Saint-Apre 068426
Sausverd, Patrick, Joigny (Yonne) . . 121018
Sautee-Nacoochee Museum, Sautee 048021
Sauter, Adolf Val., Langenenslingen 126169
Sauter, Friedericke, München 104306
Sauthier, Michel, Sion 082815
Sautter & Lackmann, Hamburg . . . 139210
Sauvage, Yannick, Andouillé 060835
Sauvageot, Daniel, Longjumeau . . . 063981
Sauvageot, Jean-Claude, Couches . 062495
Sauvant, Segonzac 068192
Sauveboeuf, Emmanuel de, Uzès . . 068671
Sauveur Bismuth, Paris 100839
Sauvon Kotiseutumuseo, Sauvo . . . 010065
Sauwald-Heimathaus, Sankt Roman 002622
Sauzéa Rambert, David de, Nice . . 065146
Savacou, New York 118381
Savage, Agoura Hills 136620
Savage, Portland 119049
Savage Carter, Nancy, Fort Worth . . 116162
Savage Fine Art, Harlestone 113183
Savageau, Denver 116047
Savannah College of Art and Design Galleries, Savannah 048029
Savannah Gallery, Atlanta 114922
Savannah House, Baltimore 087709
Savant, Vancouver 059410
Savant, Vancouver 059411
Savard, Jean-Christophe, Castelnau d'Estrétefonds 062013, 124172
Savardi & Rossi, Meilen 111727
Savaria Múzeum, Szombathely . . . 021898
Save On South, Edmonton 058839
Savelli, Roma 106623
Savenvalajamuseo, Somero 010090
Savery Antiques, Brighton 083715
Savery Books, Brighton 141441
Savez Muzejskih Društva Hrvatske, Zagreb 052825
Savez Udruženja Likovnih Umetnika, Beograd 054040
Savill, H.E., Scarborough 131460
Savill Galleries, Paddington 095039
Savina, Seoul 107284
Saving Grace, Fort Worth 088885
Savings Banks Museum, Ruthwell . 040874
Savings World Auction, Al-Wadi Al-Kabir 121883
Savino, Esposito, Firenze 075401
Savio, Gars am Kamp 095511
Savio, Costantino, Torino 128356
Savio-museet, Kirkenes 030937
Savoi, Bolzano 075133
Savoia & Fromm, South Cairo 123120
Savoir de Marie, Haguenau 063115
Savon Museo ja Taidemuseo, Varkaus 010229
Savon Radan Museo, Pieksämäki . . 009968
Savonlinnan Maakuntamuseo, Savonlinna 010068
Savonlinnan Taidemuseo, Savonlinna 010069
La Savonnerie, Bruxelles 058082
Savoy, William, Richmond 132722
Savremena Galerija Umetničke Kolonije Ečka, Zrenjanin 034286
Savreux, Marine, Biot 061493
Savupirttimuseo, Kuopio 009764
Savvas Thrasyvoulos, Michael, Montevideo 087345
Savvy Chic, Detroit 088775
Savvy Collector, Phoenix 118891
SAW Gallery, Ottawa 006105
SAW Gallery, Ottawa 097117
Sawa, Nagoya 106936
Sawanworanayok National Museum, Sukhothai 037934
Sawcc, New York 118382
Sawers, Robert G., London 085677, 141889
Sawhill Gallery, Duke Hall, James Madison University, Harrisonburg 044450
Sawhney, Dr. Jagdev S., Bonn 138907
Sawin Memorial Building, Dover . . . 043492
Sawtooth Center for Visual Design, Winston-Salem 052399
Sawyer's Sandhills Museum, Valentine 048733
Saxida, Paolo, Trieste 076905
Saxon, Dallas 088608
Le Saxon, Tours 068606
Saxon, Daniel, West Hollywood . . . 120411
Saxon Cross Antiques Emporium, Sandbach 086502
Saxonia, München 072843, 104307, 139539
Saxony Imports, Cincinnati 088279, 115660
Saxtead Green Post Mill, Saxtead . . 040964
Saxxon, Lichtenstein, Sachsen 103910
Al-Sayed, Hosam Abdul Majeed, Al-Khobar 080354
Al-Sayed Al-Khatat, Hanafi, Cairo . . 060471
Sayell, Graham, Vancouver 097527
Sayer, David A., Banstead 130330
Sayer, M. & R., New York 118383
Sayger, Indianapolis 089338
Sayk, Frederiksberg 060246
Saylor Byrd, Louisville 090023
Sayme-Arte, La Palmas de Gran Canaria 129710
Sayn-Wittgenstein, New York 118384
Sayner Gießhalle, Bendorf, Rhein . . 015944
Sayville Historical Society Museum, Sayville 048036
Sayward-Wheeler House, York Harbor 049350
SB, Paris 100840
SB Antik, Göteborg 081821
SB Antiquariat, Eurasburg 139063
SBA, Le Epouville 124294
Sbaffi, Hedy, Neunkirch 082698
SBS Antiques, Denver 088732
Scacchi, Bruno Roberto, Madonna del Piano 082644
Scaccianoce, Giuseppe, Palermo . . 106442
Scadding Cabin, Toronto 006629
Scaglia, Giulio, Brescia 075183
Scagliola, Henri, Genève 122327
Scagliola, Madeleine, Paris 124805
SCAI-The Bathhouse Gallery, Tokyo 107100
Scala, London 135260
Scala, Paris 133674
Scala, Giovanni, Napoli 076047
Scala Arte, Verona 106802
La Scala Gallery, San Diego 119549
Scala Group, Antella 134540
Scalamandre Archives, Long Island City 045391
Scaletta di Vetro, Milano 106306
Scalia, Carminella, Messina 127506
Scalloway Museum, Scalloway . . . 040965
Scalo Galerie, Zürich 112172
Scalo Verlag, Zürich 135100
Scalzotto, Claudio, Roma 076666
Scammell, Norwood 120621
Scan Art, Flensburg 070709
Scanabissi, Matteo, Bologna 075108
Scanderbeg Museum, Kruja 000028
Scandice, Tullamarine 123321
Scandinavia House, New York 046398
Scandinavian Antiques, Denver . . . 088733
Scandinavian Auction Systems, Oslo 121872
Scandinavian House, København . . 060377
Scandinavian Museum Association, Icelandic Section, Reykjavík 053684
Scaneg Verlag, München 134273
Scantic Academy Museum, East Windsor 043585
Scapa Flow Museum, Hoy 039779
Scaplen's Court Museum, Poole . . . 040741
Scarab Oracel, Miami 090240
Le Scarabée d'Or, Le Mans 063664
Scarabellin, Andrea, Roma 076667
Lo Scarabeo, Livorno 075540
Lo Scarabeo, Livorno 075541
Fratelli Scarano, Milano 127682
Scaravilli, Cleveland 115738
Scarborough Art Gallery, Scarborough 040968
Scarborough Fair Art Gallery, Scarborough 095187
Scarborough Historical Museum, Scarborough 006434

Scarborough Historical Museum, Scarborough 048037
Scarborough Perry Fine Art, Hove . . 122548
Scarfó, Rosina, Torino 076865
Scarfó Assunta, Palermo 076180
Scarfone and Hartley Galleries, University of Tampa, Tampa 048491
Scaringella, Silvia, Torino . 076866, 128357
Scaringi, Napoli 076048
Scarisbrick & Bate, London 085678, 131163
Scarlatella, Giacomo, Milano 127683
Scarlett, Paris 066529
Scarlett, Rouen 067298
Scarlett, Warszawa 109191
Scarpa, Paolo, Venezia 128405
Scarpa, Pietro, Venezia 076972
Scarpelli, Stefano, Firenze 127411
Scarpignato, Aldo, Roma . 076668, 140118
Scarpitti, Paolo, Roma 128199
Scarscelli, Dante, Nice 065147
Scarsdale Historical Society Museum, Scarsdale 048038
Scartazzini, Alex, Jegenstorf 082509, 130051
Scarthin Books, Cromford 141549
Scarthingwell Auction Centre, Scarthingwell 122689
Scatizzi, Mauro, Trieste 076906
Scatola Sfreddo, Anna Maria, Trieste 128377
Scauri, Elisabeth, Parma 076223
Scavengers, New York 091227
Scavi Archeologici di Velia, Ascea . 023261
Scavi di Ercolano, Ercolano 024053
Scavi di Oplontis, Villa di Poppea, Torre Annunziata 026085
Scavi di Ostia, Ostia Antica 025033
Scavi di Pompei, Pompei 025304
Scavi di Stabiae, Castellammare di Stabia 023718
Scavi e Museo Archeologico di S. Restituta, Napoli 024925
SCC & M Anticariat, Arad 140871
The Scein-Joseph International Museum of Ceramic Art, Alfred 041651
Scellier, Michel, Andainville 124071
Scène Antique, Paris 066530
Scene Gallery, New York 118385
Scène Plus, Longvic 099519
Scenetec, Vénissieux 101446
Scerra, Paolo, Firenze 075402
Scevù, Roma 140119
Schaab, Franz, Zwickau 105375
Schaab, Franz, Zwickau 105376
Schaad, Dieter, Therwil 082846
Schaaf, Dr. Hildegard, Köln 103703
Schaár Erzsébet Gyüjtemény, Székesfehérvár 021871
Schabel, Manfred, Berlin 069741
Schach, Horst, Karlsruhe 071728
Schachen-Galerie, Oensingen 111797
Schacherbauer, Erika, Aschau im Chiemgau 101605
Schachinger, Rudolf, Baden bei Wien 056941
Schachmuseum Ströbeck, Ströbeck 020337
Schack-Galerie, Bayerische Staatsgemäldesammlungen, München 019110
Schade, Meyhen 072540
Schade, Bernd, Karlsruhe 071729
Schade, Iris, Altenburg, Thüringen . 069151
Schade, Ralf, Naumburg, Saale . . . 072947
Schaden, Peter, Wien 095929
Schadow, Norbert, Berlin 069742
De Schaduw, Tilburg 140538
Schäbel, Gerlinde, Fischach 070688
Schäbel, R., Fischach 070689
Schädler, Karl, Oberstdorf 073157
Schaefer, Wiesbaden 105279
Schaefer, Wiesbaden 105280
Schaefer, Wiesbaden 127016
Schäfer, Anja, Groß-Gerau 125757
Schäfer, Beatrix, Stuttgart 126877
Schäfer, Bernhard, Bad Karlshafen . 138695
Schäfer, Christian, Wesendahl 074358
Schäfer, Claudia & Eduard, Utting . . 074176
Schäfer, Erika A., Seeheim-Jugenheim 126793
Schäfer, G., Kelberg 071778
Schäfer, Hermann, Roth-Eckersmühlen 073586
Schaefer, Iris, Köln 126116
Schäfer, J., Hürth 071594
Schäfer, Karl Günther, Gießen 102955, 133974
Schäfer, M., Sankt Augustin 073664
Schäfer, Michel, Wien 123528
Schäfer, Petra, Ochtendung 073170
Schäfer, Th., Hannover 134041
Schäfer, Torsten, Lich 072245
Schaefer Franck, La Frette-sur-Seine 063384
Schäferling, Dillingen an der Donau 070252
Schäferling, A., Bissingen, Schwaben 069860
Schäferling, M., Bissingen, Schwaben 069861
Schäfertanz-Kabinett, Rothenburg ob der Tauber 019918
Schäffer, Ralf, Falkensee 125629
Schaeffer House Museum, Grafton . 001079
Schäffler, Franz J., Ravensburg . . . 126681
Schäffner, Helmut, München 072844, 126448
Schaer & Wildbolz, Solothurn 111923
Schärer, Trudi & René, Sankt Gallen 082787
Schärz & Frey, Aarau 082069, 129888
Schäuffelhut, Stephanie, München . 126449
Schaffarzyk, G., Uplengen 074165
Schaffer, A., Halle, Saale 071179
Schaffer, Corky, Denver 088734
Schaffer, Ingrid, Wien 123529
Schafferer, Hermann, Innsbruck . . . 095597
Schaffernicht, C., Schwäbisch Gmünd 139720
Schaffhauser Weinbaumuseum, Hallau 037176
Schaffrath-Larché, Susanne, Pforzheim 073322
Schaffrin, Ruth, Konstanz 126135
Schafschetzy, Graz 057023, 095541
Schafschetzy, Günther, Graz 057024, 095542
Schaft, Hannie, Emmeloord 128665
Schaible, Hilde, Stuttgart 074006
Schaible, Volker, Herrenschwanden 130046
Schain, Cincinnati 115661
Schake, Mönchengladbach 072576
Schakenraad, Jos, Schijndel 128827
Schaks, H., Ahrensburg 101549
Schalk, Gerhard, München 072845
Schall, Alzey 069159
Schaller, Alfons, Neuhausen auf den Fildern 126534
Schaller, E. & N., Würzburg 074507
Schallmeiner, Karl, Ried im Innkreis 057224, 123433
Schamretta, Frankfurt am Main . . . 102819
Schamser Talmuseum, Tgea da Schons, Zillis 037752
Schana, B, Paris 100841
Schanbacher, Freudenstadt 070882
Schandog, Michael, Cottbus 070158
Schantl, Gerlinde, Wartberg im Mürztal 057347
Schantl, Peter, Linz 057165
Schaper, Dietrich, Hamburg 139211
Schaper, Eckehardt, Alsfeld 125058
Schaper, M. & H., Alfeld, Leine 133717
Schaper, Maya, New York 091228
Scharbach, V., Kempten 071794
Scharegg, Karl, Chur 082318
Scharf, Wolfsberg, Kärnten 057607
Scharfenbaum, Katrin, Konstanz . . . 126136
Scharfenberger, Hartmut, Meiningen 072503
Scharff, A., Kerpen, Rheinland 071808
Scharinger, Franz jun., Magdalenaberg 123416
Scharold, H. Karl, Houston 089198
Scharold, H. Karl, Houston 089199, 132137
Scharwath, Dr. Helga, Saarlouis . . . 104803
Schatkamer Sint Lambertuskerk, Horst 029779
Schatkamer Sint Walburgis Basiliek, Arnhem 029273
Schatkamer van de Basiliek van Onze Lieve Vrouwe, Maastricht 029900
Schatkamer van de Kathedrale Basiliek Sint-Bavo, Haarlem 029658
Schatkamer van de Sint-Salvatorskathedraal, Brugge 003282
Schatkamer van de Sint-Servaasbasiliek, Maastricht 029901
De Schatkammer van de Ouze-Lieve-Vrouwekerk, Sint-Truiden 003769
Schatt, Heidi & Bruno, Einsiedeln . . 082352
De Schatten van de Tsaar, Zaandam 078853
Schattenburg Feldkirch, Feldkirch . 001848
Schattleitenmühle, Garsten 001886
Schatz, Holger, Fürth, Bayern 125690
Schatz, Peggy, Chicago 115547
Schatz-Truhe, Saarburg 073650
Schatz von Sankt Johann, Osnabrück 019499
Schatzhaus in der Lausitz, Göda . . . 017441
Schatzkästchen Bischberg, Bischberg 069852
Schatzkammer, Altötting 015516
Schatzkammer, Frauenkirchen 001864
Schatzkammer, Volkach 074229
Schatzkammer der Basilika Sankt Ludgerus, Essen 017079
Schatzkammer der Evangelisch-Lutherischen Sankt Andreaskirche, Weißenburg in Bayern 020778
Schatzkammer der Kath. Pfarrkirche Sankt Servatius, Siegburg 020195
Schatzkammer der Residenz München, München 019111
Schatzkammer der Wallfahrtskirche, Hohenpeißenberg 017975
Schatzkammer der Wallfahrtskirche Maria Dreieichen, Stockern 002715
Schatzkammer der Wallfahrtskirche Maria Schutz, Maria Schutz am Semmering 002286
Schatzkammer des Münsters, Reichenau, Baden 019773
Schatzkammer Grafenrheinfeld, Grafenrheinfeld 017505
Schatzkammer Kloster Sankt Marienstern, Panschwitz-Kuckau 019558
Schatzkammer - Turmmuseum der Pfarrkirche, Sankt Wolfgang im Salzkammergut 002637
Die Schatzkiste, Ratingen 073430
Schatzl, Wolfgang, Salzburg 057278
Schatztruhe, Berlin 069743
Schatztruhe, Frankfurt am Main . . . 070786
Die Schatztruhe, Hamburg 071320
Schatzturm zu Schwyz, Schwyz . . . 037544
Schaub, Gun, Sickenhofen 073802
Schaubergwerk Barbarastollen, Leogang 002228
Schaubergwerk Büchenberg, Elbingerode, Harz 016936
Schaubergwerk Grillenberg, Payerbach 002409
Schaubergwerk Hochfeld, Neukirchen am Großvenediger 002359
Schaubergwerk Kupferplatte, Jochberg 002105
Schaubergwerk Seegrotte, Hinterbrühl 002044
Schaubergwerk Teufelsgrund, Münstertal 019160
Schaubergwerk und Heimatmuseum der Gemeinde Arzberg, Passail 002407
Schaubergwerk Zum Tiefen Molchner Stolln, Pobershau 019643
Schaudenkmal Gaszentrale, Unterwellenborn 020544
Schaudt, Gabriele, Burscheid, Rheinland 125419
Schauer, Franz, Krems 057131
Schauer, Markus, Frankfurt am Main 070787
Schauer, Markus, Sulzbach am Main 074027
Schaufler, Karin, Wien 133231
Schauglashütte, Uetendorf 037648
Schaulager, Laurenz-Stiftung, Münchenstein 037356
Schauland, H., Neuhausen, Enzkreis 072996
Schaum, Günter, Bad Schwalbach . 069379
Schaumberger, Elisabeth, Geras . . . 095513
Schaumburg, Stade 139739
Schaumburgisches Heimatmuseum Eulenberg, Historisches Museum Rinteln, Rinteln 019851
Schaumuseum Alte Huf-und Wagenschmiede, Gmünd, Niederösterreich 001908
Schaupp, Reinhard, Untergruppenbach 074162
Schauräume im Glockenturm, Graz 001949
Schauraum, Eggenfelden 016892
Schauraum für angewandte Kunst, Wien 095930
Schauraum über Geschichte und Brauchtum, Weitensfelder Kranzelreiten, Weitensfeld im Gurktal 002821
Schauß, Ulrike, Frankfurt am Main . 102820
Schauwerkstatt Historische Handweberei, Oederan 019438
Schawarz, Valentin, Ebental, Kärnten 056968
Scheck, Michael, Berlin 125291
Scheck, Peter, Wien 123530
Scheck, Wolfgang, Göppingen 071033
Scheding, Berry, Northwood 056381
Schedler, Amanda, Birmingham . . . 115128
Schedler, Patrik, Zürich 112173
Schedler - Edition und Galerie, Warth 111985, 135075
Scheel, Norbert, Tübingen 074116
Scheel & Melkonian, Amsterdam . . 077957
Scheel von Rodenberg, Jan, München 126450
von Scheele, Malmö 122210
Scheelen, Wolfgang, Düsseldorf . . . 070433
Scheepens & Vink, Amsterdam . . . 077958
Scheepers, H.P.M., Maastricht 078621
Scheepswerf De Delft, Rotterdam . . 030103
Scheepvaartmuseum, Baasrode . . . 003210
Scheepvaartmuseum, Bornem 003246
Scheepvaartmuseum, Gasselternijveen 029593
Scheer, Erich, Berlin 133807
Scheer, Sandra, Roost 077489
Scheers, P., Kortrijk 058270
Scheffel, Bad Homburg v.d.Höhe . . 101658
Scheffel, Walter, Bad Homburg v.d.Höhe 069298
Scheffers, Saskatoon 123820
Schefflenztal-Sammlungen, Schefflenz 020009
Schehezerade, Abu Dhabi 112441
Scheib, Georg & Helmut, Duisburg . 070486
Scheib, Volker, Biblis 125327
Scheibel, Dieter, Ober-Mörlen 134323
Scheibeler, Hein-Olof, Neubrandenburg 072973, 139586
Scheibler, A., Köln 103704
Scheibner, Sabine, Herrsching 125920
Scheich, Heinrich, Flieden 125642
Scheicher, Alois, Dirnbach 056957
Scheid, Karl M., Neubrunn 126529
Scheideck, Andreas, Konstanz 126137
Scheidegger, Affoltern am Albis . . . 141193
Scheidegger, Richterswil 111833
Scheidegger & Spiess, Zürich 135101
Scheidemann, Stephan, Friedrichroda 125681
Scheider, H., Bitburg 069863
Scheidl, Roman, Wien 095931
Scheidwimmer, Xaver, München . . . 072846
Scheikl, Gerhard Walter, Lieboch . . 057149
Scheil, Peter, Hamburg 121434
Scheinast, Andreas, Wien 095932, 123531

Scheiner, John, Ingolstadt 071626
Scheithauer, U., Neuffen 072992
Schelbergen, Geldern 070951
Scheldemuseum de Notelaer, Bornem 003247
Schell, Tecklenburg 074047
Schell, Christine, London . 085679, 131164
Schellbach, Doris, Grasbrunn 071087
Scheller, Oliver, Wörthsee 127029
Schellmann, München ... 104308, 134274
Schellmann, New York ... 118386, 135461
Schellnack, Iserlohn 103439
Schelma, Bruxelles 058083, 123606
Schelmenturm, Monheim am Rhein 018992
Schelpen Museum, Zaamslag 030359
Schemel, K., Schorndorf, Württemberg 104841
Schèmes Galerie, Lille 099495
Schemm, Constance, Schweickershausen 073764
Schempp, Kornwestheim 126140
Schendl, Dr. A., Wien 137361
Schenectady County Historical Society Museum, Schenectady 048043
Schenectady Museum, Schenectady 048044
Schenk, Edmonton 123766
Schenk, Haßfurt 103306
Schenk, B., Köln 103705
Schenk, Evamaria, Zofingen 082930
Schenk, Klaus, Calw 070122
Schenk, M. W., Engelskirchen 070571
Schenk, Dr. Rolf, Zürich 112174
Schenk zu Schweinsberg, Ekkehard, Marburg 139462
Schenker, Reussbühl 111828
Schenker, Zürich 112175
Schenker - Kunstraum, Luzern 111703
Schepenzaal Stadhuis, Zwolle 030413
Schepers, Dr. K. & R., Münster 072924
Schepke, Marek, Poznań . 079698, 140764
Schepp, N.J.R., Rotterdam 128823
Scheppe, K., Hügelsheim 071586
Scheppler & Müller, Neubiberg 139585
Scherb, Wolfgang, Freiburg im Breisgau 070857
Scherer & Fils, Saint-Maurice-sur-Huisne 067667
Schérer, Hélène-Elisabeth, Gironde-sur-Dropt 063003
Scherer Sohn, J. Otto, Bern 082238, 129973
Scherer, Paulo Frederico, Rio de Janeiro 058653
Scherer, Pedro Jose, Rio de Janeiro 058654
Scherer, Wolfgang, Miltenberg 104074
Scherer & Vandenburg, Hilversum . 078540
Schering Kunstverein, Berlin 053557
Scheringer, Georg, Konstanz 139364
Scherini, L., Balzers 077443
Scherjon's Klompenmakerij en Museum, Noardburgum 029968
Scherler, Hans & Antje, Berlin 069744
Schernig, Ursula, Fürth, Bayern ... 102904
Scherrer, Heinz, Minfeld 072552
Schermann, Peter, Kreßberg 072084
Scherz, Wolfgang, München 126451
Scherzer, Egon, Wien 095933
Schettino, Umberto, Roma 076669
Scheuch, Andreas, München 126452
Scheuch, Jochen, Köln 072000
Scheuer, Rosenheim 134372
Scheuermann, Hermann, Duisburg . 139028
Scheumüller, Walter, Ried im Innkreis 057225
Scheuring-Rojewski, Georg, Würzburg 074508
Scheuringer, Linz 137224
Scheuringer, Werner, Wien 057544
Scheuvens, Bernd, Bonn 125360
Schiaffino, Michela, Genova 075509
Schiaparelli, Giampaolo, Roma 076670
Schiavon, Vittorino, Padova 127812
Schiavone, Torino 076867
Schibig, Josef & Ursula, Steinen ... 130188
Schibli, Robert, Riehen ... 082744, 141291
Schibli-Doppler, Birsfelden 141234
Schicchi, Eva, Bologna 127181
Schicht, Renate, Düsseldorf 102545
Schichtwechsel, Triesen 107339
Schick, Johann B., Koblenz 126059
Schick, Silke, Metzingen 126313
Schick Art Gallery, Saratoga Springs 048009
Schickler, Howard, Brooklyn 115245, 142260
Schied, Jürgen, Kornwestheim 072058
Schiedams Prentenkabinet, Schiedam 140528
Schiefer- und Ziegelmuseum Dörfles-Esbach, Dörfles-Esbach 016733
Schiefermuseum, Ludwigsstadt ... 018714
Schiefke, Reinhard, Husum, Nordsee 103415
Schiel, Sankt Peter-Ording 104814
Schiele Museum of Natural History, Gastonia 044154
Schier, Hans-Georg, Bad Emstal ...101640, 125089
Schierding, Patrick, Delmenhorst .. 125450
Schierenberg, Dieter, Amsterdam .. 140335
Schierk, V., Bonn 138908
Schierl, Ludwig, München 072847
Schierstaedt, Eckehard von, Münster 126507
Schieske, Lothar, Herten 071496
Schiess, Patricia, Basel 141214
Schiffahrts- und Schiffbaumuseum, Wörth am Main 020946
Schiffahrtsmuseum, Spitz 002687
Schiffahrtsmuseum auf dem Traditionsschiff, Abteilung Schiffbaugeschichte des Schiffahrtsmuseum Rostock, Rostock 019903
Schiffahrtsmuseum der Oldenburgischen Weserhäfen, Brake, Unterweser . 016359
Schiffahrtsmuseum mit Nordseeaquarium Nordseeheilbad Langeoog, Langeoog 018513
Schiffahrtsmuseum Nordfriesland, Husum, Nordsee 018036
Schiffbau und Schifffartsausstellung Roßlau, Roßlau, Anhalt 019890
Schiffer, Atglen 135321
Schiffer, New York 118387
Schifferings, Poggenhagen 104618
Schiffermuseum, Zehdenick 021042
Schiffers, P.M., Warszawa 129116
Schifferstadt Architectural Museum, Frederick 044052
Schifffahrt Museum, Stadtmuseum Düsseldorf, Düsseldorf 016845
Schifffahrtsmuseum Haren (Ems), Haren 017777
Schifffahrtsmuseum Rostock, Rostock 019904
Schiffleutmuseum, Stadl-Paura ... 002688
Schiffmacher, Amsterdam 077959
Schiffmacher, Amsterdam 077960
Schiffmann, Reinhard, Forchheim, Oberfranken 133931
Schiffmühle Höfgen, Grimma 017539
Schiffner, Christine, Freiberg, Sachsen 102852
Schiffs- und Marinemuseum, Senden, Westfalen 020188
Schiffsmuseum Seitenradschleppdampfer Württemberg, Magdeburg 018775
Schikowski, Richard, Berlin 138837
Schild, Ursi, Rheinfelden 130146
Schild-Verlag, München 134275
Schilder- en Bakkerijmuseum 't Steenhuis, Niebert 029941
De Schildercamer, Oosterbeek 128798
De Schilderijenschuur, Zeist 108276
Schilderijenzaal Prins Willem V, Den Haag 029452
Schildgen, R., Bonn 069939
Schildger, Peter, Frankfurt am Main 125661
Schildt, Burghard, Kiel 103546
Schilgen, Eva Maria von, Großgmain 057045
Schilke, Richard, Pfungstadt 126630
Schillay, New York 118388
Schiller, Marbach am Neckar 139456
Schiller, L., Freiburg im Breisgau .. 139119
Schiller, Rosemarie, Nachrodt-Wiblingwerde 072940
Schiller & Bodo, New York 118389
Schiller-Museum, Stiftung Weimarer Klassik und Kunstsammlungen, Bauerbach 015895
Schiller-Nationalmuseum und Deutsches Literaturarchiv, Marbach am Neckar 018813
Schillerhäuschen, Stadtmuseum Dresden, Dresden 016813
Schillerhaus, Ludwigshafen am Rhein 018704
Schillerhaus, Stadtgeschichtliches Museum Leipzig, Leipzig 018590
Schillerhaus, Goethe-Nationalmuseum, Stiftung Weimarer Klassik und Kunstsammlungen, Weimar, Thüringen 020753
Schillers Gartenhaus der Friedrich-Schiller-Universität, Jena 018115
Schillers Geburtshaus, Marbach am Neckar 018814
Schilling, Agnes, Schorndorf, Württemberg 104842
Schilling, Hannemarie, Klagenfurt . 057112
Schilling, Helmut, Stuttgart 074007
Schilling, Helmut, Stuttgart 074008
Schilling, Helmut, Stuttgart 074009
Schilling, Lilo, Bonn 125361
Schillinger, Arnold, Breisach am Rhein 070002
Schilp, Ines, Iserlohn 071636
Schilp, Thomas, Hottenbach 125965
Schiltaere, Maastricht 078622
Schimmer, Dominique, Paris 100842
Schimmer, Reinhard, Nürnberg 073120
Schimper, K.F., Schwetzingen 134393
Schimpfle, Jörg-Dietr., Haimhausen 125785
Schimpl, Christa, Hamburg 071321
Schimschak, Franz, Köln 126117
Schimtz, Nathalie, Paris 066531
Schinart, Taranto 106653
Schindel, Wolfgang, Freiburg im Breisgau 070858
Schindelhauer, Manfred, München . 126453
Schindler, Bernhard, Bern 111274, 134996
Schindler, Bettina, Firenze 075403, 127412
Schindler, Christine, Bayreuth 069495
Schindler, Daniel, Bremgarten bei Bern 129987
Schindler, Eric, Richmond 119122
Schindler, Karin, Bamberg 069462
Schindler, L., Regensburg 073470
Schindler, Dr. O.H., Frankenthal, Pfalz 133933
Schindler, Reimar, Berlin 069745
Schingoethe Center for Native American Cultures, Aurora University, Aurora 041913
Schinko, Gerd, Wien 057545
Schinko, Gerd, Wien 057546
Schinn, Wolf, Lensahn 072233
Schinner, Mattersburg 095677
Schino, Michele, Bari 075031
Schipper, Stephanie, Mölln 126324
Schipper & Krome, Berlin 102029
't Schippertje, Leiden 078583
Schirhagl, Christian, Steyr 057325
Schirmer, Friedemann, Winterbach bei Schondorf 105307
Schirmer-Mosel, München 104309
Schirmer-Mosel, München 134276
Schirn Kunsthalle Frankfurt, Frankfurt am Main 017192
Schirow, Gerd, Overath 073277
Schirra, Saarlouis 073651, 121594
Schitke, Wofgang, Weimar, Thüringen 126980
Schitter, Jacqueline, Plouharnel ... 066875
Schitter, René, Dossenheim-sur-Zinsel 062721
Schkolnyk, Laurent, Nantes 099818
Schlächter, P., Münster 072925
Schläppi, J.R., Basel 111221
Schlaf, A., Giesen 070989
Schlafke, Gaby, Braunfels 125372
Schlag & Cie., Frank, Essen 102704
Schlager, Melbourne 056205
Schlapka, München 072848
Schlapp, H. L., Darmstadt 138975
Schlatter Navarro, Ángel Luis, Sevilla 129744
Schlebusch, Stefan, Berlin 069746
Schlechte, Monika, Meißen 072507
Schlee, Martina, Rothenburg ob der Tauber 073592
Schlee, Ute Friederike, Karlsruhe .. 126007
Schleede, Jens, Berlin 125292
Schlegel, Holger, Dresden 125508
Schlegel, Marika, Rolle 111844
Schlegel, Pascal, Nancy 064881
Schlegel, Volker, Mengen 126307
Schlegel, Walter, Kaufbeuren 071770
Schlégl, Nicole, Zürich ... 112176, 135102, 141358
Schleich, Dieter, Wiesloch 074432
Schleicher, T., Würzburg 139875
Schleichers Buchhandlung, Berlin . 138838
Schleifer, Ronald, Wien 137362
Gebr. Schleiffenbaum, Krefeld 072079, 126149
Schleifmühle Schwerin, Stadtgeschichts- und Museumsverein Schwerin e.V., Schwerin 020149
Schleimuseum, Kappeln 018151
Schleiper, Bruxelles 123607
Schleisner-Borgsmidt, Klampenborg 060261
Schlemer & Schatz, Hallstadt 125797
Schlemme, H., Erfurt 070590
Schlemmer, Dr., Deggendorf 070200
Schlensog, Ute, Crimmitschau 138970
Schlepper-, Auto- und Gerätemuseum Hesse, Aidhausen 015460
Der Schlern, Bolzano 135957
Schlesch, Arne, New York 091229
Schleser, Weimar, Thüringen 074310
Schlesinger, New York 118390
Schlesisch-Oberlausitzer Dorfmuseum, Markersdorf bei Görlitz 018833
Schlesisches Museum zu Görlitz, Görlitz 017455
Schless, Antwerpen 057733
Schleswig-Holsteinischer Kunstverein e.V., Kiel 053558
Schleswig-Holsteinisches Freilichtmuseum, Molfsee 018989
Schleswig-Holsteinisches Landwirtschaftsmuseum und Dithmarscher Bauernhaus, Meldorf 018895
Schleweis, W., Gelsenkirchen 070961
Schlicht, Bayreuth 138723
Schlicht & Geister, Berlin 138839
Schlichte Bergen, Amsterdam 077961
Schlichtenmaier, Grafenau, Württemberg ...071080, 102988, 133985
Schlichtenmaier, Stuttgart 105007, 134421
Schlichting, Dietfried, Göttingen ...071052, 125740
Schlichting, Horst, Göttingen 071053
Schlickeisen, Dortmund 070293
Schlidt, Köln 072001
Schlidt, Köln 072002
Schliekau-Museum, Bad Bevensen 015669
Schlienger, Valérie, Le Puy-Sainte-Reparade 063702
Schlieper, Michael, Hagen, Westfalen 103050, 133995
Schliephake, Jörg & Katharina, Königslutter 103747
Schlipf, Thomas, Rottweil 126752
Schlissinger, Michèle, Paris 124806
Schlitt, Reinhold, Wuppertal 074537
Schlobach, Marga, Bad Camberg .. 101633

Schlöbcke, Christian, Diez 125464
Schlöder-Kassner, Neustadt am Rübenberge 126542
Schlögl, Johannes Stephan, Innsbruck 123394
Schlögl, Josef, Gundertshausen ... 123376
Schlörer, Gerrit, Ulm 126931
Schlösschen Borghees, Emmerich . 016974
Schlößchen Vorder Bleichenberg Biberist, Biberist 036948
Schlötzer, Forchheim, Oberfranken . 070717
Der Schlondes, Aachen 069099
Schloß, Jegenstorf 037204
Schloss Achberg, Achberg 015439
Schloss Agathenburg, Agathenburg 015449
Schloß Ambras, Kunsthistorisches Museum Wien, Innsbruck 002094
Schloß Arolsen, Stiftung des Fürstlichen Hauses Waldeck und Pyrmont, Bad Arolsen 015647
Schloß Augustusburg, Brühl, Rheinland 016470
Schloß Baldern, Bopfingen 016341
Schloß Berleburg, Bad Berleburg .. 015665
Schloß Brake - Das Weserrenaissance-Museum, Lemgo 018607
Schloss Braunfels, Braunfels 016376
Schloß Bruchsal, Bruchsal 016459
Schloß Bürgeln, Schliengen 020045
Schloß Burgau, Burgau 001773
Schloss Cappenberg, Selm 020186
Schloss Dottenwil, Wittenbach 037737
Schloss Drachenburg, Königswinter 018357
Schloß Egg, Bernried, Niederbayern 016208
Schloß Eggenberg, Landesmuseum Joanneum, Graz 001950
Schloss Ehrenburg, Schloss- und Gartenverwaltung Coburg, Coburg 016579
Schloß Ettersburg, Ettersburg 017089
Schloß Faber-Castell, Stein, Mittelfranken 020297
Schloß Falkenlust, Brühl, Rheinland 016471
Schloß Farrach, Zeltweg 003069
Schloß Favorite, Staatliche Schlösser und Gärten Baden-Württemberg, Rastatt 019716
Schloss Freudenberg, Wiesbaden .. 020878
Schloß Friedberg, Volders 002786
Schloss Friedrichstein, Staatliche Museen Kassel, Bad Wildungen 015827
Schloss Galerie, Zürich .. 083023, 130263
Schloss Glienicke, Stiftung Preussische Schlösser und Gärten Berlin-Brandenburg, Berlin 016167
Schloß Groß Leuthen, Groß Leuthen 017555
Schloss Großkühnau - Verwaltung, Kulturstiftung DessauWörlitz, Dessau, Anhalt 016682
Schloss Güstrow, Staatliches Museum Schwerin, Güstrow 017601
Schloß Hämelschenburg, Emmerthal 016976
Schloß Hallwyl, Seengen 037549
Schloss Harburg, Harburg 017773
Schloss Hegi, Winterthur 037730
Schloß Heidelberg, Heidelberg 017836
Schloß Heiligenberg, Heiligenberg, Baden 017854
Schloß Heubach, Heubach, Württemberg 017913
Schloß Höchstädt, Höchstädt an der Donau 017944
Schloss Hof und Schloss Niederweiden, Engelhartstetten 001832
Schloß Hohenschwangau, Schwangau 020127
Schloss Homburg, Bad Homburg v.d. Höhe 015719
Schloss Hundisburg-Sammlung Apel, Hundisburg 018029
Schloss Johannisburg mit Schlossgarten und Pompejanum, Bayerische Staatsgemäldesammlungen, Aschaffenburg 015582
Schloß Kochberg mit Liebhabertheater, Stiftung Weimarer Klassik und Kunstsammlungen, Großkochberg 017573
Schloß Leitzkau, Stiftung Schlösser, Burgen und Gärten des Landes Sachsen-Anhalt, Leitzkau 018603
Schloß Lichtenstein, Lichtenstein, Württemberg 018635
Schloß Liebieg, Kobern-Gondorf ... 071887
Schloß Linderhof, Ettal 017088
Schloß Loosdorf mit Prunkräumen und Zinnfigurensammlung, Loosdorf, Bez. Mistelbach 002268
Schloss Ludwigsburg, Ludwigsburg, Württemberg 018697
Schloss Ludwigslust, Ludwigslust . 018711
Schloß Lustheim, Oberschleißheim . 019418
Schloß Mannheim, Mannheim 018810
Schloß Marienburg, Pattensen 019576
Schloß Miltach, Miltach 018942
Schloß Mörsburg, Stadel (Winterthur) 037591
Schloß Moosham, Tamsweg 002727
Schloss Mosigkau, Kulturstiftung DessauWörlitz, Dessau, Anhalt .. 016683
Schloß-Museum Welfenschloß Herzberg, Herzberg am Harz 017906
Schloß Naudersberg, Nauders 002353
Schloss Neuburg, Neuburg an der Donau 019224
Schloss Neuhardenberg, Neuhardenberg 019237
Schloß Neunhof, Germanisches Nationalmuseum, Nürnberg 019371
Schloß Neuschwanstein, Schwangau 020128
Schloss Oranienbaum, Kulturstiftung DessauWörlitz, Oranienbaum 019477
Schloß Peigarten, Dobersberg 001783
Schloß Pfaueninsel, Stiftung Preussische Schlösser und Gärten Berlin-Brandenburg, Berlin 016168
Schloß Plüschow, Plüschow 104616
Schloss Pöllau, Pöllau 002446
Schloß Reinbek, Reinbek 019781
Schloß Rheinsberg, Stiftung Preussische Schlösser und Gärten Berlin-Brandenburg, Rheinsberg 019825
Schloß Rosenau, Schloss- und Gartenverwaltung Coburg, Rödental 019864
Schloss Sachsenburg, Frankenberg, Sachsen 017149
Schloss Salem, Salem, Baden 019969
Schloß Sargans, Sargans 037511
Schloß Schallaburg, Loosdorf, Bez. Melk 002266
Schloß Schönbrunn, Wien 003001
Schloß Schwetzingen, Schwetzingen 020156
Schloß Seehof, Memmelsdorf 018903
Schloß Solitude, Stuttgart 020363
Schloß Spiez, Spiez 037585
Schloß Strünkede, Emschertal-Museum, Herne 017892
Schloß Tarasp, Tarasp 037621
Schloß Thunstetten, Thunstetten .. 037634
Schloß Trachselwald, Trachselwald 037639
Schloß Tratzberg mit Sammlungen, Jenbach 002102
Schloss Trebsen, Trebsen 020464
Schloß- und Goldbergbaumuseum, Großkirchheim 001970
Schloß und Gurschner Museum, Pram 002461
Schloss und Hofgarten Dachau, Schloss- und Gartenverwaltung Schleißheim, Dachau 016621
Schloss- und Kirche Sankt Bartholomä, Berchtesgaden 015959
Schloß und Park Schönbusch, Aschaffenburg 015583
Schloß und Schloßpark Bad Homburg, Bad Homburg v.d.Höhe 015724
Schloss und Schlosspark Charlottenburg mit Schinkelpavillon, Belvedere und Mausoleum, Stiftung Preussische Schlösser und Gärten Berlin-Brandenburg, Berlin 016169
Schloß und Schloßpark Wilhelmsthal, Calden 016538
Schloß- und Spielkartenmuseum, Altenburg, Thüringen 015503
Schloß Unteraufseß, Aufseß 015601
Schloß Urbach, Urbach 020545
Schloß Veitshöchheim, Veitshöchheim 020566
Schloß Vianden, Burgmuseum, Vianden 027907
Schloß Villa Ludwigshöhe mit Max-Slevogt-Galerie, Edenkoben 016884
Schloß vor Husum, Zweckverband Museumsverbund Nordfriesland, Husum, Nordsee 018037
Schloß Weikersheim, Weikersheim . 020712
Schloss Weilburg, Weilburg 020727
Schloß Weissenstein, Pommersfelden 019648
Schloß Werdenberg, Werdenberg .. 037701
Schloß Wernigerode, Zentrum für Kunst- und Kulturgeschichte des 19. Jahrhunderts, Wernigerode 020816
Schloß Wetzdorf-Fichtl, Kleinwetzdorf 002152
Schloß Weyer, Gmunden 001913
Schloss Wiederau, Pegau 019580
Schloß Wildegg, Wildegg 037713
Schloß Wilflingen, Langenenslingen 018507
Schloss Wilhelmshöhe/Weißensteinflügel, Kassel 018199
Schloß Wiligrad, Lübstorf 018730
Schloss Wörlitz und Englisches Landhaus, Kulturstiftung DessauWörlitz, Wörlitz 020945
Schloß Wolfstein mit Jagd- und Fischereimuseum und Galerie Wolfstein, Freyung 017257
Schloss Wolkenburg, Wolkenburg-Kaufungen 020972
Schloßausstellung, Staatliche Kunstsammlungen Dresden, Dresden 016814
Schlossberg-Cohen, Baltimore 115082
Das Schlossberg-Lädchen, Neustadt an der Weinstraße 073033
Schlossberger, Barbara, Germering 125723
Schloßbergmuseum, Chemnitz 016565
Schlosser, Augsburg 101620
Schloßgalerie, Brixlegg 095488
Schloßgalerie, Neuburg an der Donau 104406
Schloßgalerie Kastenscheuer, Eberdingen 016865
Schloßgalerie Mondseeland, Mondsee 002338
Schloßmuseum, Arnstadt 015568
Schloßmuseum, Bad Bentheim 015656
Schlossmuseum, Bad Iburg 015727
Schlossmuseum, Burgdorf 036993
Schloßmuseum, Ellwangen 016946
Schloßmuseum, Erbach, Donau ... 016999
Schloßmuseum, Gotha 017495
Schloßmuseum, Haitzendorf 002005
Schloßmuseum, Herberstein 002037
Schloßmuseum, Höchstädt, Oberfranken 017945
Schloßmuseum, Kirchberg an der Jagst 018260
Schlossmuseum, Kirchentellinsfurt . 018263
Schloßmuseum, Kronburg 018420
Schloßmuseum, Krummennaab ... 018425
Schlossmuseum, Langenburg 018506
Schloßmuseum, Oberhofen am Thunersee 037391
Schloßmuseum, Ortenburg 019486
Schloßmuseum, Schrozberg 020104
Schloßmuseum, Sigharting 002678
Schloßmuseum, Texing 002740
Schlossmuseum, Oberösterreichisches Landesmuseum, Linz 002256
Schlossmuseum, Staatliches Museum Schwerin, Schwerin 020150
Schloßmuseum, Städtische Museen Quedlinburg, Quedlinburg 019689
Schloßmuseum, Stiftung Weimarer Klassik und Kunstsammlungen, Weimar, Thüringen 020754
Schloßmuseum Amerang, Amerang 015534
Schloßmuseum Aulendorf-Kunst des Klassizismus-Altes Spielzeug, Zweigmuseum des Württembergischen Landesmuseums Stuttgart, Aulendorf 015628
Schlossmuseum Darmstadt, Darmstadt 016645
Schloßmuseum der Stadt Aschaffenburg, Aschaffenburg 015584
Schloßmuseum Heidegg, Gelfingen 037108
Schloßmuseum Hohenlohe-Schillingsfürst, Schillingsfürst 020024
Schloßmuseum Hubertusburg, Wermsdorf 020809
Schloßmuseum Ismaning, Ismaning 018093
Schloßmuseum Jagsthausen, Jagsthausen 018101
Schlossmuseum Jever, Jever 018122
Schloßmuseum Landeck, Landeck . 002195
Schloßmuseum Mespelbrunn, Mespelbrunn 018919
Schlossmuseum mit Bauernkriegsmuseum, Oberösterreichischer Landeskrippe und Georg-von-Peuerbach-Ausstellung, Peuerbach 002426
Schloßmuseum mit Brüder-Grimm-Gedenkstätte, Steinau an der Straße 020301
Schloßmuseum Murnau, Murnau .. 019168
Schloßmuseum Neuburg, Neuburg an der Donau 019224
Schloßmuseum Niederleis, Niederleis 002375
Schlossmuseum Oranienburg, Stiftung Preußische Schlösser und Gärten Berlin-Brandenburg, Oranienburg 019480
Schlossmuseum Reckahn, Reckahn 019738
Schloßmuseum Rimpar, Rimpar ... 019848
Schlossmuseum Sondershausen, Sondershausen 020248
Schloßmuseum Thun, Thun 037630
Schlossmuseum und Königliches Schloss, Berchtesgaden 015960
Schloßmuseum Warthausen, Warthausen 020683
Schlossmuseum Weitra, Weitra ... 002823
Schloßpark Tiefurt, Stiftung Weimarer Klassik und Kunstsammlungen, Weimar, Thüringen 020755
Schloßparkmuseum, Bad Kreuznach 015739
Schlottau, Wolfgang, Hamburg 103217
Schlotterbeck, Ursula, Horb 071580, 103406
Schlünsen, H., Heiligenhafen 071478
Schlürmann & Sönnichsen-Schlürmann, Sollerup 104919
Schlüsselberger, Richard Franz, Braunau am Inn 095483
Schlüter, Carl F., Hamburg 071322, 121435
Schlüter, Horst, Delbrück 070209
Schlüter, J., Buchenberg bei Kempten 070077
Schlüter, Marita, Everswinkel 125625
Schlüter & Fessmann, Heilbronn .. 071476
Schlütter, J., Köln 103706
Schlumberger Wein- und Sektkellerei, Wien 003002
Schlummer, Karin, Münster 072926
Schmahl, Karl-Heinz, Halberstadt .. 071172
Schmalfuß, Eberhard, Plauen 139661
Schmalfuß, Michael W., Marburg .. 104033
Schmallery, Portland 119050
Schmalspurbahn-Museum, Frojach 001874
Schmalstieg, Burgwedel 125417
Schmalstieg, Uwe, Hattorf 103311
Schmalz, Bad Gandersheim 069284
Schmautz, Dieter, Ludwigsburg, Württemberg 126232
Schmeja, Irmgard, Lippstadt 072284
Schmela, Düsseldorf 102546
Schmelenhaus Museum, Windhoek 029109
Schmelter, Eckhard, Münster 126508
Schmelter, Heine, Kevelaer 071816
Schmelter, Hubert, Münster 126509
Schmelz, Marktheidenfeld 072461

Schmelz, Bruno, Roden, Unterfranken . . . 073548
Schmerbach, Matthias, Falkensee . 125630
Schmetz, Aachen . . . 138670
Schmi-Dau, Dortmund . . . 070294, 125482
Schmid, Dettingen unter Teck . . . 070239
Schmid, Alfred, Augsburg . . . 138686
Schmid, Anna-Marie & Hans, Bützberg . . . 111319
Schmid, Beate, Neustadt an der Weinstraße . . . 134312
Schmid, E., Neuenhof . . . 082696
Schmid, Georg, Baden bei Wien . . . 056942
Schmid, H., Görnitz . . . 071039
Schmid, H., Illingen . . . 071613
Schmid, Helmut, Obertraubling . . . 104509
Schmid, Jürg, Chur . . . 130000
Schmid, Kathrin, Bad Wörishofen . . 069399, 101716
Schmid, Konrad, Chur . . . 082319
Schmid, Martin, Potsdam . . . 126655
Schmid, Rudolf-Ernst, München . . . 126454
Schmid & Rothhaar, Arnstein . . . 069185
Schmid & Rothhaar, Würzburg . . . 074509
Schmid-Schurig, Leonberg, Oberpfalz . . . 072234
Schmider, Andreas, Einhausen . . . 102608
Schmidgall, Markus, Bad Mergentheim . . . 125109
Schmidlin, Hans, Basel . . . 082171
Schmidt, Pretzfeld . . . 104637
Schmidt, Reichenbach, Vogtland . . 073475
Schmidt, Reith im Alpbachtal . . . 057219, 095709
Schmidt, Adriana, Stuttgart . . . 105008
Schmidt, Anton J, Sent . . . 082807
Schmidt, C., Ilsenburg . . . 071615
Schmidt, Ch., Zittau . . . 074571
Schmidt, Christel, Wadgassen . . . 105138
Schmidt, Daniel, Bern . . . 082239
Schmidt, Detlef, Wuppertal . . . 074538
Schmidt, E., Berlin . . . 102030, 125293
Schmidt, Elizabeth, Porto Alegre . . . 058523
Schmidt, Ernst, Düsseldorf . . . 070434
Schmidt, Friedrich Otto, Wien . . . 057547, 123532
Schmidt, George, New Orleans . . . 117509
Schmidt, Gérald, Rouen . . . 067299
Schmidt, H., Dußlingen . . . 070489
Schmidt, H., Köln . . . 139352
Schmidt, Hannes, Leipzig . . . 126197
Schmidt, Hans-Christian, Dresden . 070328
Schmidt, Hans & Edda, Bisingen . . 138879
Schmidt, Hans-Joachim, Kressbronn am Bodensee . . . 072085
Schmidt, Hans-Jürgen, Freiberg, Sachsen . . . 070816
Schmidt, Hartmut, Gießen . . . 070993
Schmidt, Heinrich, Burgwald . . . 070107
Schmidt, Heinrich, Grenzach-Wyhlen . . . 103001
Schmidt, Hermann, Mainz . . . 134182
Schmidt, Inga, Seevetal . . . 073792
Schmidt, Jean-Paul, Strasbourg . . . 068333
Schmidt, Johann, Wien . . . 057548
Schmidt, Joseph-Dieter, Klipphausen . . . 126055
Schmidt, Karin, Glaubitz . . . 071007
Schmidt, Lilo, Schneverdingen . . . 104833
Schmidt, M., Leißling . . . 072219
Schmidt, M., Weißenfels . . . 074328
Schmidt, M. & H., Tamins . . . 082842
Schmidt, Marion, Bad Essen . . . 125094
Schmidt, Martin, Satteldorf . . . 126764
Schmidt, Martin-Christian, Rostock 126742
Schmidt, Monika, München . . . 139540
Schmidt, Monika, München . . . 139541
Schmidt, Natalie, Bad Honnef . . . 125104
Schmidt, O., Nahrendorf . . . 121556
Schmidt, P., Frankenberg, Eder . . . 070721
Schmidt, P., Grande . . . 071084
Schmidt, P. & A., Bad Oeynhausen . 069349
Schmidt, Rainer, Frankfurt/Oder . . . 102844
Schmidt, Dr. Rainer, Tübingen . . . 074117
Schmidt, Raymond, Metz . . . 099718
Schmidt, Roland, Dessau, Anhalt . . 070223
Schmidt, Ruth, Berlin . . . 069747
Schmidt, Ruth, Witzenhausen . . . 139861
Schmidt, Sabine, Köln . . . 103707
Schmidt, Sebastian, Panker . . . 104582
Schmidt, Stefan, Regensburg . . . 121585
Schmidt, Sylvia, New Orleans . . . 117510
Schmidt, Thomas, Dresden . . . 138999
Schmidt, Thomas, Leisnig . . . 126204
Schmidt, Udo, Lüdenscheid . . . 103975
Schmidt, Valérie, Paris . . . 100843
Schmidt Bingham, New York . . . 118391
Schmidt & Dean, Philadelphia . . . 118828
Schmidt-Esters, Gudrun, Köln . . . 103708
Schmidt-Fleischmann, Gabriele, Schnaittach . . . 104831
Schmidt & Green, Wuppertal . . . 074539, 105360, 139889
Schmidt & Günther, Kelkheim . . . 139313
Schmidt House Museum, Grants Pass . . . 044287
Schmidt-Kühl, Sophia-Therese, Dresden . . . 102456, 125509
Schmidt & Pirec, Ahaus . . 069115, 101542
Schmidt-Rottluff, Chemnitz . . . 102314
Schmidtchen, Arno, Gastrose-Kerkwitz . . . 125699
Schmidtgen, H., Stuttgart . . . 139770
Schmidtová, Beata, Banská Bystrica . . . 140953
Schmidt's, Ypsilanti . . . 123141
Die Schmiede, Amsterdam . . . 140336
Schmiede Burg Schlitz, Burg Schlitz 016505
Schmiede im Hammergraben, Helfenberg . . . 002034
Schmiedemuseum, Fulpmes . . . 001877
Schmiedemuseum, Hatten, Oldenburg . . . 017793
Schmiedemuseum, Hohen Demzin . 017968
Schmiedemuseum, Lölling . . . 002264
Schmiedemuseum Arfeld, Bad Berleburg . . . 015666
Schmiedemuseum Bremecker Hammer, Lüdenscheid . . . 018734
Schmiedemuseum Kirchlauter, Kirchlauter . . . 018271
Schmierer, Harald, Schärding . . . 057302
Schmill, D., Neubrandenburg . . . 072974, 126527
Schminck Memorial Museum, Lakeview . . . 045127
Schmit, Robert & Manuel, Paris . . . 100844, 133675
Schmitt, Gerhard, Ingelheim am Rhein . . . 071621
Schmitt, Ingrid & Volker, Immenstadt . . . 071619
Schmitt, Jean-Pierre, Haguenau . . . 063116
Schmitt, Klaus, Schwäbisch Hall . . 104855
Schmitt, Marlen, Karlstadt . . . 103506
Schmitt, Michel, Paris . . . 066532, 100845
Schmitt, Norbert, Lahnstein . . . 126160
Schmitt, Sibylle, Köln . . . 126118
Schmitt, Winfried, Sundern . . . 105026
Schmitt-Jüssen, Bonn . . . 069940
Schmitt-Leibinger, Margit, Erlangen 102655
Schmitt & Mortimer, Hamburg . . . 071323
Schmitter, Th., Bornhöved . . . 069963
Schmittling, Gérard, Ceyrat . . . 062065
Schmitz, Hilpoltstein . . . 071527
Schmitz, Ratingen . . . 139675
Schmitz, Ratingen . . . 139676
Schmitz, Hans-Martin, Wuppertal . . 074540, 139890
Schmitz, Lieselotte, Moers . . . 072584
Schmitz, Maria, Bottrop . . . 069965
Schmitz, MarKos, Köln . . . 103709
Schmitz, Martin, Berlin . . . 102031, 133808
Schmitz, Susanne, Berlin . . . 125294
Schmitz, Uwe, Moers . . . 104109
Schmitz-Avila, Regina, Wiesbaden . 074420
Schmitz-Avila, Dr. Thomas, Bad Breisig . . . 069272
Schmitz-Call, Simmerath . . . 104904
Schmitz-Schneider, Renate, Remscheid . . . 073492
Schmitz & Steinfeld, Neuss . . . 073018
Schmitzer, Werner, Offenbach am Main . . . 126589
Schmock Broc, Paris . . . 066533
Die Schmökerkiste, Berlin . . . 138840
Schmölz, Cornelia, Dinkelscherben 125469
Schmölz, Helmut, Pirmasens . . . 073333
Schmoller, Dr. Bernd, Hamburg . . . 071324
Schmolling, Gabriele, Wedemark . . 105168
Schmolling, W., Hatzfeld . . . 103313
Schmolt, Axel, Krefeld . . . 121487
Schmuck Bros., New York . . . 091230
Schmuckgalerie im Palais, Linz . . . 057166
Schmuckli, Wädenswil . . . 130211
Schmuckmuseum Gablonzer Industrie, Enns . . . 001836
Schmuckmuseum Pforzheim im Reuchlinhaus, Pforzheim . . . 019608
Schmücker, Anita, Stuhr . . . 104960
Schmücking, Rolf, Archsum . . . 101592
Schmücking, Rolf, Sylt-Ost 105028, 134427
Schmutzler, H., Berlin . . . 069748
Schnabel, R., Großschwabhausen . 125771
Schnabl, Bernhard, Abensberg . . . 069107
Schnappauf, Ralf, Ransbach-Baumbach . . . 073415
Schnapsmuseum, Kötzting . . . 018366
Schnarch-Museum Alfeld, Alfeld, Leine . . . 015478
Schnauferlstall, Ruhpolding . . . 019954
Schneck, Johann, Möckmühl . . . 072557
Schneckenburger, M., Karlsruhe . . . 139299
Schneeberger, Carl, Traunstein . . . 074079
Schneeberger, Christian, Goldach . . 111521, 135023
Schneeberger, R., Straubing . . . 073941
Schneeberger, W. & J., Osnabrück . 073246
Schneemann, H., Detern . . . 070224
Schneeweiss, Elke, Geboltskirchen 056988
Schnegg, Emile, La Chaux-de-Fonds . . . 082304
Schneider, Berlin . . . 102032
Schneider, Chicago . . . 115548
Schneider, Netphen . . . 072959
Schneider, Carl, Frankfurt am Main 070788
Schneider, E.D., Meerbusch . . . 072489
Schneider, Eduard, Basel . . . 082172
Schneider, F., Düsseldorf . 070435, 102547
Schneider, G., Waldbröl . . . 105146
Schneider, Gerhard, Köln . . . 126119
Schneider, Dr. Gerhard, Olpe . . . 139634
Schneider, Dr. Hans, Tutzing . . . 074126, 139803
Schneider, Heidi, Horgen . . . 111559
Schneider, Joseph, Kitchener . . . 096936
Schneider jr., J.P., Frankfurt am Main . . . 102821
Schneider, Jutta, Niederbrombach . 073052
Schneider, Jutta, Weißenburg in Bayern . . . 126988
Schneider, Karin, Bayreuth . . . 069496
Schneider, Karl, Volkach . . . 126953
Schneider, Lothar, Vaduz . . . 077453
Schneider, Marc, Essen . . . 070645
Schneider, Michael, Bonn . . . 102196
Schneider, R., Potsdam . . . 104632
Schneider, Thomas, Augsburg . . . 138687
Schneider, Thomas, Dortmund . . . 070295
Schneider, Thomas, München . . . 072849, 104310
Schneider, Dr. Thomas Franz, Basel 141215
Schneider, Thomas M., London . . . 131165
Schneider, Ullrich, München . . . 072850
Schneider, W., Lauchringen . . . 072161
Schneider, Wilfried, Aachen . . . 101525
Schneider, Dr. Wolfgang, München . 126455
Schneider-Henn, Dietrich, München . . . 121544, 139542
Schneider Museum of Art, Southern Oregon University, Ashland . . . 041810
Schneider-Sato, Hardy, Karlsruhe . . 103503
Schneider-Steidle, Spiegelberg . . . 139738
Schneider-Wagener, F., Bonn . . . 069941
Schneiter, Dolores, Bern . . . 111275
Schnell, N. & M., Ellwangen . . . 070544
Schnell & Steiner, Regensburg . . . 134362
Schnell-Stöger, Irmgard, Oberammergau . . . 126574
Schnellbächer, Hans-Peter, Mainz . 126266
Schneph, Thomas E., Louisville . . . 116965
Schniedermeier, Essen . . . 070646
Schnieders, Wolfgang, Lingen . . . 072279
Schnitt, Köln . . . 103710
Schnitzer, Axel, Ummendorf . . . 126932
Schnitzler, Heinrich, Rheinbach . . . 126718
Schnitzschule Elbigenalp, Elbigenalp . . . 049620
Schnitzschule Oberammergau, Oberammergau . . . 050211
Schnoebelen, Gérard, Cornol . . . 082328
Schnopfhagen-Stüberl, Oberneukirchen . . . 002388
Schnupftabakmuseum, Grafenau, Niederbayern . . . 017500
Schobner, Hans-Günter, Geisenheim 070948
Schoch, Bad Bocklet . . . 069268
Schocken Institute of Jewish Research, Jerusalem . . . 022978
Schoder, Albrecht, Rheda-Wiedenbrück . . . 126717
Schöchlin, Margareta, Luzern . . . 130107
Schöchlin, Klaentschi & Micky, Sarmenstorf . . . 130171
Schöckel, Bredstedt . . . 102227
Schödel, Ottfried, Kernen . . . 071801
Schöfegger, Rupert, Wien . . . 137363
Schöfer, Peter, Haßloch . . . 071428
Schöffer Museum, Kalocsa . . . 021748
Schoefflen, Paris . . . 066534
Schoefflen, Guy, Crecy-en-Ponthieu 062552
Schoega & Schoeg, Rüthen . . . 073620
Schoeler, Clemens von, München . . 126456
Schoeller, Düsseldorf . . . 102548
Schoeller, Thomas, München . . . 126457
Schoellkopf Geological Museum, Niagara Falls . . . 046484
Schoemaker, R.J., Den Haag . . . 140400
Schoemansdal Museum, Louis Trichardt . . . 034674
Schömer, Anita & Johann, Hinzert-Pölert . . . 071531
Schömig-Biedermann, R., Laichingen . . . 072119
Schön, Bonn . . . 102197
Schön, Brigitte, Bodenheim . . . 125344
Schön, Elli, Bad Neuenahr-Ahrweiler . . . 069343
Schoen, Jason, Miami . . . 117138
Schoen & Nalepa, Berlin . 102033, 133809
Schoenauer, Arosa . . . 111131
Schönauer, Dieter, Balingen . . . 069439
Schönbeck, Heinz-D., Minden, Westfalen . . . 072551
Schönberg-Haus in Mödling, Mödling . . . 002329
Schönborn, R. von, Triberg . . . 074089
Schoenbrunn Village State Memorial, New Philadelphia . . . 046270
Schönbuch Museum, Dettenhausen 016694
Schöndorf, Manfred, Ottweiler . . . 126607
Schöne, Peter, Halle, Saale . . . 125792
Schöne, Thomas, Penzberg . . . 073305
Schöne Alte Möbel, Berlin . . . 069749
Schöne-Mühlen, Kristina, Westendorf . . . 127000
Schöneborn, K, Würzburg . . . 139876
Schöneich, M., Seligenstadt . . . 073799
Schönemann, Kempen . . . 071785
Schönemann, Wolfgang, Schwerin . 139724
Schoenen, Marcel & Karl, Aachen . 101526, 125042
Schönenberger, Brigitte, Kirchberg (Sankt Gallen) . . . 111584
Schönenberger, Daniela, Kirchberg (Sankt Gallen) . . . 111585
Schönenberger-Kyrimis, Maria, Zürich . . . 112177
Schönewald, Xanten . . . 105366
Schönfelder, Lindau, Bodensee . . . 072267

Schönfelder, Treibach-Althofen 095772
Schönhof, Jade 103445
Schönhuber, H., Dietfurt 070249
Schoeni, Hong Kong 097828
Schöni, Denis, Biel 082262
Schoeni, Markus, Zürich 130264
Schöni, Peter, Bern 082240
Schöning, Schwarzenbek 073759
Schöning, Philipp von, Eutin 070672
Schoening, Rita, Piding 073328
Schoening, Rudolf, Rödermark 073556
Schöninger & Co., München 121545
Schöninger, H., München 104311
Schöningh, Barbara, Hamburg 139212
Schöningh, F., Münster 139573
Schönlau, Rolf, Dörentrup 070266
Schönleiter, Albersdorf 069126
Schönleiter, Tino, Tellingstedt 074052, 121612
Schönleiter, W., Bunsoh 070090
Schönleiter, Wolfgang, Albersdorf . .069127, 121295
Schoenmakers, Borstel 069964
Schönmüller, München 104312
Schönpflug, Ingo, Innsbruck 057087
Schönpflug, Ingo, Innsbruck 057088
Schönpflug, Ingo, Innsbruck 120666
Schoentgen, Marie-José, L'Epine . . 063746
Schöpf, Uwe, Eppingen 070578
Schöpp, B., Ludwigsburg, Württemberg 103945
Schöppl, Gerhard, Salzburg 057279
Schöss, Kronach 072090
Schösser, Franz, Leuchtenberg 072237
Schötschel, Stephan, Biesenthal bei Bernau 125331
Schöttle, Rüdiger, München 104313
Schöttler, Zingst 105370
Schofield, Anne, Woollahra 056877
Schoharie Colonial Heritage Association Museum, Schoharie 048046
Schoharie County Arts Council, Cobleskill 055026
Schoharie Crossing, Fort Hunter ... 043922
Schokoland Alprose, Caslano 037000
SchokoMuseum in SchokoLand, Peine 019582
Schola San Zaccaria, Venezia 106777
Scholar's Books, Chicago 142300
Scholes Gallery, Rotorua 079231
Scholl, Sonnfriede, München 126458
Scholl, W., Wunstorf 139879
Scholl, Winfried, Wunstorf 139880
Schollaert, Aalst 057664
Scholler, Lotte von, Starnberg 073896
Des Schollum, Wellington 140682
Scholte House Museum, Pella 046861
Scholten & Sohn, H., Nordhorn 073085
Scholtes, Joël, Nice 065148
Scholtes, Joël, Nice 099856
Scholtissek, Reinhard, Bissendorf . 069859
Scholtz, H.-G., Berlin 069750, 138841
Scholz, Baden-Baden 069426
Scholz, A. von, Berlin 102034
Scholz, Artur, Heilbronn 125909
Scholz, Camille von, Haut-de-Cagnes 133474
Scholz, Heinrich, Reichenbach, Vogtland 073476
Scholz, Jens, Köln 121477
Scholz, Sylvia, Bad Dürkheim 069276, 125088
Scholz-Breznay, Livia, Gomaringen 125744
Scholz Park Museum, Riverton 001432
Scholzen, Werner, Hilden . 071523, 121456
Schomaker, Magdalena, Nordhorn .104467, 134316
Jürgen Schomaker & Michael Lehr, Berlin 138842
Schomann, Brigitta, Berlin 069751
Schomburg, Marl 104036
Schomburg Center for Research in Black Culture, New York 046399
Schommer, Rolf, Beckingen 069502
Schon, Kurt E., New Orleans 090620
Schon Kurt E., New Orleans 090621
De Schone Kunsten, Haarlem 108063
Schonfeld & Co., R.D., New York . . 118392
School Arts, Worcester 136621
School Books Museum, Salt 027386
School for Arts in Learning, WVSA Arts Connection, Washington 052334
School for the Contemporary Arts, Simon Fraser University, Burnaby 049776
School House Antiques, Chipping Campden 083985, 130568
School House Gallery, Bethany 094250
School House Gallery, Wighton 114695
School of Animation, Arts and Design, Sheridan Institute of Technology and Advanced Learning, Oakville 049807
School of Architecture, McGill University, Montréal 049804
School of Architecture, Montana State University, Bozeman 051020
School of Architecture, Ohio State University, Columbus 051196
School of Architecture, Pratt Institute, Brooklyn 051043
School of Architecture, Princeton University, Princeton 051991
School of Architecture, Rensselaer Polytechnic Institute, Troy 052276
School of Architecture, Southern University A & M College, Baton Rouge 050954
School of Architecture, Syracuse University, Syracuse 052237
School of Architecture, Tulane University, New Orleans 051804
School of Architecture, University of British Columbia, Vancouver 049829
School of Architecture, University of Detroit Mercy, Detroit 051259
School of Architecture, University of Texas, Austin 050937
School of Architecture, Yale University, New Haven 051793
School of Architecture and Planning, Massachusetts Institute of Technology, Cambridge 051065
School of Art, Gauhati 050302
School of Art, Tequesta 052255
School of Art, Arizona State University, Tempe 052252
School of Art, Bowling Green State University, Bowling Green 051019
School of Art, Chautauqua Institution, Chautauqua 051103
School of Art, Curtin University of Technology, Bentley 049609
School of Art, East Carolina University, Greenville 051420
School of Art, Illinois State University, Normal 051852
School of Art, Illinois Wesleyan University, Bloomington 050995
School of Art, Kent State University, Kent 051548
School of Art, Kent State University - Stark Campus, Canton 051073
School of Art, Louisiana State University, Baton Rouge 050955
School of Art, Louisiana Tech, Ruston 052062
School of Art, Montana State University, Bozeman 051021
School of Art, Munson-Williams-Proctor Institute, Utica 052299
School of Art, Northern Illinois University, DeKalb 051242
School of Art, Ohio University, Athens 050917
School of Art, Rhodes University, Grahamstown 050701
School of Art, University of Akron, Akron 050872
School of Art, University of Cincinnati, Cincinnati 051141
School of Art, University of Manitoba, Winnipeg 049834
School of Art, University of Oklahoma, Norman 051853
School of Art, University of Tennessee, Knoxville 051557
School of Art, University of Wales, Aberystwyth, Aberystwyth 050800
School of Art, University of Washington, Seattle 052168
School of Art, Victorian College of the Arts, Southbank 049618
School of Art, Washington University, Saint Louis 052080
School of Art, Yale University, New Haven 051794
School of Art and Art History, James Madison University, Harrisonburg 051445
School of Art and Art History, University of Denver, Denver 051253
School of Art and Art History, University of Florida, Gainesville 051370
School of Art and Art History, University of Iowa, Iowa City 051505
School of Art and Art History, University of South Florida, College of Visual and Performing Arts, Tampa 052249
School of Art and Art History Gallery, Denver 043418
School of Art and Cultures, Fine Art, University, Newcastle-upon-Tyne . 050848
School of Art and Design, Salford . . 050856
School of Art and Design, Georgia State University, Atlanta 050924
School of Art and Design, Mount Vernon College, Washington 052335
School of Art and Design, Northern Arizona University, Flagstaff 051336
School of Art and Design, Pratt Institute, Brooklyn 051044
School of Art and Design, Rochester Institute of Technology, Rochester 052045
School of Art and Design, San Jose State University, San Jose 052126
School of Art and Design, Southern Illinois University, Carbondale 051076
School of Art and Design, Suffolk College of Higher and Further Education, Ipswich 050819
School of Art and Design, Syracuse University, Syracuse 052238
School of Art and Design, University of Illinois at Urbana-Champaign, Champaign 051091
School of Art and Design, University of Michigan Ann Arbor, Ann Arbor . . 050903
School of Art and Design, University of Ulster, Belfast 050801
School of Art and Design, University of Wolverhampton, Wolverhampton . 050858
School of Art and Science, University of Richmond, Richmond 052023
School of Art, Design and Art History, San Diego State University,, San Diego 052118
School of Art Gallery, Baton Rouge . 042052
School of Art - Gallery, Montana State University, Bozeman 042376
School of Art Gallery and Museum, University of Wales, Aberystwyth . 038465
School of Art History and Archaeology, University of Manchester, Manchester 050846
School of Art, Media and Design, University of Gloucestershire, Cheltenham . . 050808
School of Arts, Gwalior 050304
School of Arts, McMaster University, Hamilton 049791
School of Arts, Manhattan College, Bronx 051035
School of Arts, Marymount University of Virginia, Arlington 050911
School of Arts, University of California Irvine, Irvine 051508
School of Arts, Virginia Commonwealth University, Richmond 052024
School of Arts and Humanities, Charles Stewart Mott Community College, Flint 051337
School of Arts and Sciences, Clark-Atlanta University, Atlanta 050925
School of Arts and Sciences, Eastern Oregon State College, La Grande . 051562
School of Arts and Sciences, Triton College, River Grove 052028
School of Contemporary Arts, Ramapo College of New Jersey, Mahwah . 051664
School of Design, North Carolina State University, Raleigh 052010
School of Earth Sciences Museum, Townsville 001565
School of Fine Art, De Montfort University, Leicester 050821
School of Fine Art, Indiana University Bloomington, Bloomington 050996
School of Fine Art, History of Art and Cultural Studies, University of Leeds, Leeds 050820
School of Fine Arts, Bob Jones University, Greenville 051424
School of Fine Arts, Fairmont State College, Fairmont 051322
School of Fine Arts, Memorial University of Newfoundland, Corner Brook 049781
School of Fine Arts, National Academy of Design, New York 051832
School of Fine Arts, San Jose City College, San Jose 052127
School of Fine Arts, University of Canterbury, Christchurch 050574
School of Fine Arts, University of Kansas, Lawrence 051594
School of Fine Arts, University of Mary Hardin-Baylor, Belton 050966
School of Fine Arts, University of Southern California, Los Angeles 051639
School of Fine Arts and Music, University of Guelph, Guelph 049788
School of Fine Arts, Classical Studies and Archaeology, University of Melbourne, Melbourne 049615
School of Fine Arts Gallery, Indiana University Bloomington, Bloomington 042265
School of Graphic Communications, George Brown College of Applied Arts and Technology, Toronto 049821
School of Interior Design and School of Art, Education Direct, Scranton 052158
School of Media Studies, Humber College of Applied Arts and Technology, Etobicoke 049786
School of Nations Museum, Elsah . 043693
School of Political and Social Inquiry Museum, Clayton 000926
School of Printing, Rochester Institute of Technology, Rochester 052046
School of the Art Institute of Chicago, Chicago 051130
School of the Art Institute of Chicago Gallery, Chicago 042879
School of the Arts, College of Charleston, Charleston 051095
School of the Arts, University of Wisconsin Milwaukee, Milwaukee 051721
School of the Museum of Fine Arts, Boston 051015
School of Visual and Performing Arts, Hillsborough Community College, Tampa 052250
School of Visual and Performing Arts, Long Island University, Brookville 051046
School of Visual and Performing Arts, University of Texas at Tyler, Tyler . 052288
School of Visual Arts, New York ... 051833
School of Visual Arts, University of Louisiana at Monroe, Division of Art, Monroe 051737
School of Visual Arts, University of North Texas, Denton 051247
School oft Art & Design, College Purchase, State University of New York, Purchase 052000
Schoolhouse Gallery, Rosny Park . . 095161
Schoolhouse Museum, Ridgewood . 047437
Schoolmuseum Michel Thiery, Gent 003466
Schooltijd Schoolmuseum, Terneuzen 030195
Schoon, Lier 137526
Schooneman, Oss 108162
Schoonens, A., Den Haag 078246

Schoonewelle, Centrum Natuur en Ambacht, Zwartsluis 030408
Schoonheim, Utrecht 078817, 128859
Schoonhovens Edelambachtshuys, Schoonhoven 030143
Schoormans, Lucas, New York 118393
Schoots, Willy, Eindhoven . 108007, 134810
Schopferer, Alfred, Waldkirch 074256
Schopmann, Hamburg . . . 071325, 121436
Schoppe, Angelika, Coesfeld 102323
Schoppe, E., Northeim 073089
Schoppmann & Weigt, Kevelaer . . .071817, 126038
Schorer, Fabian, Stuttgart 126878
Schorer, R., Rottweil 073609
Schorer, R., Villingen-Schwenningen 074217
Schorer, Walter, Neuburg an der Donau 121558
Schork, G., Karlsruhe 071730, 103504
Schorlemer, Werner von, Bergheim, Erft 125155
PetitSchorp, Stéphanie, Saint-Martin-de-Nigelles 067629
Schorr, Michael, Klosterfelde 126056
Schortgen, Esch-sur-Alzette 107386
Schortgen, Luxembourg 107409
Schots, Frédéric, Bruxelles 096253
De Schotse Huizen, Veere 030261
Schott, Wuppertal 074541
Schott, Alexander, München 139543
Schott, Matthias, München 139544
Schott, Pierre & Maria, Mainz 072405
Schott GlasMuseum, Schott Villa, Jena 018116
Schotte, T., Southwold 086671
Schotten, Manfred, Burford 083793, 130479
Schotten, R., Oberau 073137
Schotten, Robert, Farchant 070679
Schottenfeld & Partner, Wien 137364
Schouenberg, M.T.H., Maastricht . . 078623
Schouten, Kees, Amsterdam 077962
Schouten, R., Vriescheloo 128876
Schouteten, C., Capelle aan den IJssel 128616
De Schouw, Rotterdam 078742
Schouwey, Christian, Nods 130131
Schowalter, Albersweiler 125053
Schrade, Dorothea, Illereichen-Altenstadt 103423
Schrader, Nordkampen 073086
Schrader, Walsrode 074269
Schrag, Heinrich, Nürnberg 104490
Schrager, A., Milwaukee 122968
Schramek, Robert, Legau 072182
Schramkó, Pál, Solymár 127083
Schramm, Frankfurt am Main 102822
Schramm, Kiel 121465
Schramm, Kiel 139322
Schramm, Kiel 139323
Schramm, H., Greven 071096
Schramm, Jürgen, Pöcking 126639
Schrammel, Hermann, Wien 095934
Schrank, Herbert, Steyr 057326
Schraps, R., Dürrenuhlsdorf 070352
Schraube Museum, Halberstadt . . . 017648
Schraven, Justus, Göllheim 071024
Schredds, London 085680
Schreiber, Brescia 106006
Schreiber, Torino 076868
Schreiber, Elke & Werner, Mannheim 072435
Schreiber, F., Braunschweig 069993
Schreiber, J., Mannheim 104028
Schreiber, Klaus-Peter, Oldendorf . . 073216
Schreiber, L., Würzburg 074510
Schreiber, M., Marbach am Neckar 104031
Schreiber, Silke, München 134277
Schreiber, U., Köthen, Anhalt 072043
Schreiber & Leser, München 134278
Schreibmaschinen-Museum, Pfäffikon (Zürich) 037413
Schreibmaschinenmuseum Baggenstos, Wallisellen 037693
Schreilechner, Lorenz, Salzburg . . .057280, 123456
Schreindorfer, Fritz, Inning am Ammersee 125973
Schreiner, Steffen-Heinz, Meuselwitz 072539, 126314
Schreinereimuseum, Ibach 037197
Schreinermuseum, Altishofen 036835
Schreinermuseum, Ettiswil 037082
Schreiter, N., Frankfurt am Main . . . 070789
Schrem, Wilfried, Neu-Ulm 072970, 126526
Schrems, Dr. Verena, Salzburg 057281
Schreuder, Robert, Amsterdam 077963
Schreuders, J., Amsterdam 077964
Schreurs, M.H., Breda . . . 078115, 128608
Schreyer, Augsburg 138688
Schreyer, Chr., Berlin 121342
Schreyer, Hanno, Bonn 138909
Schriber, Martin, Winterthur 082917, 130224
Schriever, R., Köln 103711
Schrift-Art.ch, Rheineck 111829
Schrift- und Heimatmuseum Bartlhaus, Pettenbach 002425
Schriftmuseum J.A. Dortmond, Amsterdam 029228
De Schrijnwerker, Harlingen 128706
Schrinner, E., Bochum 125341
Schroder, Hokitika 108473
Schröck-Schmidt, Wolfgang, Neckargemünd 072951
Schröder, Den Haag 107950
Schroeder, von, Dunalley 094495
Schröder, Greven 071097
Schröder, Lüchow, Wendland 103970
Schröder, Schkeuditz 073691
Schröder, A., Lübeck 072339
Schröder, A., Mölschow 104089
Schröder, Alexander, Dresden 102457
Schroeder, B., Backnang 101623
Schroeder, B., Wachtberg 105133
Schröder, Detlef, Solingen 073856
Schröder, Hannelore, Essen 102705
Schröder, Helga, Düsseldorf 070436
Schröder, Ilse, Rottach-Egern 073604
Schröder, Janka, Sankt Augustin . . . 126762
Schröder, Joachim A., Berlin 069752
Schröder, Jörg, Lienen 072249
Schröder, Klaus, Oldenburg, Oldenburg 139632
Schröder, L., Hopsten 071579
Schröder, Madlen, Berlin 102035
Schröder, Ove, Julita 122171
Schröder, Renate & Rupert, Köln . .072003, 103712, 134119
Schröder & Dörr, Bergisch Gladbach 101767
Schröder & Salzbrenner, Baunatal . 069484
Alexander Schröder & Thilo Wermke, Berlin 102036
Schröer, Rolf, Gießen 070994
Schröer, Ursula, Hoyerswerda 103408
Schrörlücke, Gerlinde, Recklinghausen 073447
Schroer, Amsterdam 107795
Schröter, Hans, Wiesbaden 074421
Schroeter, K. & Ch., Sendenhorst . . 104886
Schroll, Anton, Wien 133232
Schrottmeyer, Michael, Berlin 138843
Schryver, Michael, Dorking 130650
Schryvers, Hochstadt, Pfalz 071536
Schubert, Goslar 102983
Schubert, Main Beach 094763
Schubert, Röbel 073555
Schubert, Andrea, Milano 106307
Schubert, B., Leipzig 139402
Schubert, Dieter, Lehrte 103847
Schubert, Erhard, Bürstadt 138955
Schubert, M., Neuss 073019
Schubert, Oscar, Münster 072927
Schubert, Rudolf, Salzburg 057282
Schubert, Walburga, Mannheim . . .072436, 139455
Schubert, Werner, Würzburg 074511, 105340, 127041
Schubert Geburtshaus und Adalbert Stifter-Gedenkräume, Wien Museum, Wien 003003
Schubert Sterbewohnung, Wien Museum, Wien 003004
Schublade, Braunschweig 069994
Schuch, Dieter, Linz am Rhein 126223
Schübbe, Christa, Düsseldorf 102549
Schuegraf, Josef, Stein, Mittelfranken 073902, 126829
Schüle & Co., Andreas, Ulm 074152
Schüler, Erich, Berlin 069753
Schüll, Michael G., Obertrubach . . . 104510
Schüller, E., Affalterbach 069113
Schüller, E., Remseck 073493
Schüller, Norbert, Wels 057356
Schüller, Wolfgang, München 104314
Schünemann, Carl Ed., Bremen . . . 133846
Schüpbach, Langenthal 082525
Schüppenhauer, Chris, Köln 103713, 134120
Schürenberg, Achim, Aachen 069100
Schürer, Rosmarie, Regensberg . . . 111824
Schürholz-Schäfer, Reichshof 126709
Schürmann, Heinz, Hagen, Westfalen 071164
Schürmann, Petra, Kamp-Lintfort . . 103477
Schürmann, R., Düsseldorf 070437
Schüßler, Alex, Ansbach 069175
Schüßler, Bernhard, München 139545
Schüßler, Frank, Sulzbach am Main 074028
Schuessler, Michael, Denver 116048
Schütte, B., Essen 102706
Schütte, Peter, Hamburg 071326
Schütte, Peter, Hamburg 103218
Schüttesägemuseum, Schiltach . . . 020027
Schüttler, Hans Ernst, Bonn 125362
Schütz, Frankfurt am Main 102823
Schütz, Linz 057167, 133116
Schütz, Wolfgang, Augsburg 125079
Schützdeller, P., Ratingen 073431
Schützenhaus Glaucha, Stadtmuseum Halle, Halle, Saale 017671
Schützenmuseum der Königlich privilegierten Feuerschützengesellschaft Weilheim, Weilheim, Oberbayern . 020730
Schützenscheibenmuseum, Scheibbs 002646
Schützenscheibensammlung, Mainbernheim 018781
Schuhmacher, Amsterdam 140337
Schuhmacher, Jörg, Frankfurt am Main 070790
Schuhmann, Norbert, Allershausen . 101560
Schul- und Heimatmuseum, Schönermark bei Angermünde 020079
Schule für künstlerische Photographie Wien, Wien 049666
Schuler, F., Chur 141238
Schuler, Horst, Düsseldorf 102550
Schuler, Philippe, Zürich 122371
Schuler School of Fine Arts, Baltimore 050950
Schulgeschichtliche Sammlung, Kulturhistorisches Museum, Magdeburg 018776
Schulgeschichtliche Sammlung Bremen, Bremen 016423
Schulgeschichtliche Sammlung im Main-Taunus-Kreis, Kriftel 018412
Schulhausmuseum, Hollingstedt bei Schleswig 017991
Schulheimatmuseum, Asbach-Bäumenheim 015572
Schulhistorische Sammlung Cruismannschule, Bochum 016283
Schullandheim Sassen, Heimatkundliche Einrichtung, Sassen, Vorpommern 019998
Schuller, Wolfgang, Wertheim 074349
Schulman, Helsinki 060578
Schulman, Laurens, Bussum 078136, 121785
Schulmuseum, Frankfurt/Oder 017205
Schulmuseum, Hundisburg 018030
Schulmuseum, Neumark 019250
Schulmuseum, Museen Schloss Aschach, Bad Kissingen 015732
Schulmuseum Bergisch Gladbach, Bergisch Gladbach 015971
Schulmuseum des Bezirkes Urfahr-Umgebung, Bad Leonfelden 001731
Schulmuseum des Bezirks Unterfranken, Schloß Aschach, Bad Bocklet . . . 015671
Schulmuseum Friedrichshafen am Bodensee, Friedrichshafen 017271
Schulmuseum Fronau, Roding 019860
Schulmuseum Lilienthal, Lilienthal . 018645
Schulmuseum Mozartschule Rheingönheim, Ludwigshafen am Rhein 018705
Schulmuseum Nordwürttemberg in Kornwestheim, Kornwestheim . . . 018385
Schulmuseum Nürnberg im Museum Industriekultur, Museen der Stadt Nürnberg, Nürnberg 019372
Schulmuseum Steinhorst, Museen des Landkreises Gifhorn, Steinhorst, Niedersachsen 020309
Schulmuseum und Hallenhaus, Mönchguter Museen, Middelhagen, Rügen . . . 018937
Schulmuseum Vechelde, Vechelde . 020562
Schulmuseum - Werkstatt für Schulgeschichte Leipzig, Leipzig . 018591
Schulmuseum Wildenhain, Wildenhain bei Großenhain, Sachsen 020889
Schulok, Iserlohn 103440
Schulstub'n-Glockenhäusl, Sankt Peter am Wimberg 002614
Schult, Köln 103714
Schulte, Düsseldorf 070438
Schulte, Christian, München 126459
Schulte, Jürgen, Kassel 071762
Schulte, Sigrid, Arnsberg 101596
Schulte, Thomas, Berlin 102037
Schulte, W., Bad Salzuflen 069366
Schulte, W., Bad Salzuflen 069367
Schulte-Hobein, Stefan, Lambsheim 072122
Schultehuis, Diever 029484
Schulten, Peter N., Siegburg 073808
Schulten, Ton, Ootmarsum 108160, 134827
Schultes, Rosemarie, Bad Hersfeld . 101649
Schultheiss, G.B., München 072851
Schultheiß, Wolfgang, Wien 057549
Schultz, Cleveland 131971
Schultz, Malmö 141132
Schultz, Wernigerode 105218
Schultz, Bruno, Stühlingen 073946
Schultz, Frederick, New York 091231
Schultz, Günter, Benzingerode 125148
Schultz, Julia, Moringen 126335
Schultz, Michael, Berlin . . 102038, 133810
Schultz, Pam, Babinda 094187
Schultz, Swaantje, Hamburg 071327
Schultze, Norbert, Düsseldorf 070439
Schultze-Ortloff, Baya-Renate, Meersburg 104051, 139471
Schulwitz, Giesbert & Irmgard, Plößberg 073347
Schulz, Meschede 104066
Schulz, Zutphen 078883
Schulz, Bernd, Kamp-Lintfort 071693
Schulz, Birgit, Mils 095681
Schulz, E., Offenburg 073190
Schulz, Edith, Wien 095935
Schulz, G., Oberstaufen 073153
Schulz, Gabriele, Hameln 125856
Schulz, Günter, Bad Soden am Taunus 069386
Schulz, Hans-Joachim, Leipzig 072217
Schulz, Henryk, Berlin 069754
Schulz, Johannes, Bremen 070045, 102256, 121362
Schulz, Karl-Friedrich, Mannheim . . 072437
Schulz, Martina, Hamburg 071328, 125843
Schulz, Michael, Berlin 125295
Schulz, Richard, Travemünde 074083
Schulz, Stefan, Poznań 129068
Schulz, Th., Esens 070616
Schulz, U., Hünxe 071592
Schulz-Aßmann, Ilona, Oegeln 073176

Schulz & Dahms, Hamburg 071329
Schulz-Falster, Susanne, London . . 141890
Schulz Marty, Annette, Gockhausen 130037
Schulze, Berlin 069755
Schulze, Hannover 103297
Schulze, Erika, Groß Grönau 139156
Schulze, H., Ergolding 070592
Schulze, Martin, Berlin 069756
Schulze, Monika, Großebersdorf . . . 125761
Schulze, N., Hessisch Lichtenau . . . 071501
Schulze, Norbert, Bremen 138949
Schulze, Thomas, Berlin 069757
Schulze-Delitzsch-Haus, Außenstelle des Museums Schloß Delitzsch, Delitzsch 016662
Schulze-Głazik, Grażyna, Kraków . . 129048
Schumacher, Badenweiler 069432
Schumacher, Berlin 069758
Schumacher, Müllheim, Baden 104132
Schumacher, G., Köln 072004
Schumacher, Heike, Überlingen . . . 105087
Schumacher, Michael J., New York . 118394
Schumacher, R., Düsseldorf 102551, 133898
Schumacher, Robert L.R., Seattle . . 119989
Schumacher & Conca, Zurzach 083047
Schumacher Gallery, Columbus . . . 043111
Schumacker, Liège 058325
Schumann, Louisville 090024, 132305
Schumann, Günter, Wiesbaden 074422
Schumann, Hellmut, Zürich 141359
Schumann & Co., Reinhold, Kassel . 071763
Schumann, Therese, Bad Salzuflen 069368
Schumann, Ursula, Freiburg im Breisgau 070859
Schumann-Haus, Leipzig 018592
Schumitz, Friederike, Hamm, Westfalen 125858
Schumm, Bernd, Hannover 071413
Schumshof, Tönisvorst 074068
Schunder, R., Guxhagen 071156
Schunkelhaus, Obercunnersdorf . . . 019384
Schunn, Heinz, Lechbruck am See . 072174
Schupp, Kai, Hamburg 125844
Schurig, Gunter, Lausitz 103844
Schurr, Dr. Ursula, Stuttgart 105009
Schuschu, Düsseldorf 102552
Schuster, Buffalo 131862
Schuster, Dresden 070329
Schuster, Frankfurt am Main 102824
Schuster, Torquay 142116
Schuster, Alex, Stuttgart 074010
Schuster, Karl F., Köngen 126125
Schuster, W., Stuttgart 126879
Schuster & Scheuermann, Berlin . . 102039
Schut, H.J., Laag-Keppel 128738
't Schuttershofke, Antwerpen 057734
Schutterskamer, Sneek 030169
Schutzverband Bildender Künstler, Nürnberg 053559
Schuwey, Luzern 111704
Schuwirth & Van Noorden, Maastricht 108130
Schuyler County Historical Society Museum, Montour Falls 046003
Schuyler-Hamilton House, Morristown 046038
Schuyler Jail Museum, Rushville . . 047568
Schuyler Mansion, Albany 041600
Schwaab, Gabriele, Köln 126120
Schwab, Eckhart, Miesbach 072545, 126317
Schwab, Gerhard, Bad Nauheim . . . 138700
Schwab, K., Phoenix 142769
Schwabach Galerie, Meilen 111728
Schwabacher Künstlerbund, Schwabach 053560
Schwabe & Co., Basel 134986
Schwabe, Angelika, Berlin 102040
Schwabenthal, Hans-Peter, Potsdam 126656
Schwabenverlag, Ostfildern 134339
Schwabinger Bilderbogen, SB Antiquariat, Eurasburg 139064
Schwabinger Münzstube, München 072852
Schwäbisches Bauern- und Technikmuseum, Eschach 017045
Schwäbisches Bauernhofmuseum Illerbeuren, Kronburg 018421
Schwäbisches Handwerkermuseum, Augsburg 015620
Schwäbisches Krippenmuseum im Jesuitenkolleg, Mindelheim 018946
Schwäbisches Schnapsmuseum, Bönnigheim 016300
Schwäbisches Schützenmuseum, Kronburg 018422
Schwäbisches Turmuhrenmuseum, Mindelheim 018947
Schwäbisches Volkskundemuseum und Bauernhofmuseum Staudenhaus, Gessertshausen 017399
Schwämmi's Gallery, Campo (Blenio) 111328
Schwärter, H., Bakum 069435
Schwagerle, Peter, Viktring 057340
Schwaighofer, Christian, Söchtenau 073841
Schwaighofer, Günther, Salzburg . . 057283
Schwald, Dagmar, München 104315
Schwald, G., Sinsheim . . . 073835, 104910
Schwalm & Menzel, Gerlingen 070975
Schwan, Fürth, Bayern 070913
Schwandt, Jörg, Berlin 069759
Schwaneberg, H., Haan 071159
Schwanke, Hamburg 121437
Schwartz, Rio de Janeiro 096646
Schwartz, Andrea, San Francisco . . 119785
Schwartz, Anna, Melbourne 094826
Schwartz, Carol, Philadelphia 118829
Schwartz, Gabriele, Berlin 125296
Schwartz, Nancy, New York 091232, 118395
Schwartz Collection of Skiing Heritage, Tiburon 048552
Schwartz Heritage House, Altona . . 005003
Schwartz Judaica, San Diego 142916
Schwartzsche Villa, Berlin 016170
Schwarz, Barßel 069477
Schwarz, Detmold 125458
Schwarz, Greifswald 102996
Schwarz, Heilbronn 103335
Schwarz, Philadelphia . . . 091688, 118830
Schwarz, Anton, Trun 082864, 130198
Schwarz, Barbara, Schorndorf, Württemberg 104843
Schwarz, Beat, Murten 082682
Schwarz, Hans, Springe 126820
Schwarz, Heinz, Kriens 130056
Schwarz, Hildegard, Keitum 103526
Schwarz, Hubert, Graz 123368
Schwarz, Karl & Barbara, Aarau . . . 082070
Schwarz, Karl-Heinz, Tübingen 074118
Schwarz, Leonhard, Georgensgmünd 125715
Schwarz, Linda, Cincinnati 115662
Schwarz, Max, Ingolstadt 071627
Schwarz, Monika, Volkach 074230
Schwarz, Peter, Berlin 138844
Schwarz, Rudolf, Pfronten 073325
Schwarz, Sigurd, Hamburg 139213
Schwarz, Ulrich, Korntal-Münchingen 139365
Schwarz, W., Altenkunstadt 069153
Schwarz-Afrika-Museum, Vilshofen 020602
Schwarz-Wrobel, Monika, Bochum . 069893
Schwarzacher, Gerhard, Sankt Anton am Arlberg 057285
Schwarzachtaler Heimatmuseum, Neunburg vorm Wald 019255
Schwarzbach, Peter, Nürnberg 073121
Schwarzbrot, Ahrensburg 101550
Schwarze, Dr. Wolfgang, Wuppertal 134474
Schwarze Kunst-Verlag, Bochum . . 133826
Schwarzenberger Skulpturenpark, Schwarzenberg am Böhmerwald . 002660
Schwarzer, Berlin 102041
Schwarzer, Düsseldorf 102553
Schwarzer, Klaus, Düsseldorf 070440
Schwarzer Elefant, Köln 072005
Schwarzfischer, Rosenheim 139696
Schwarzmann, Peter, Starnberg . . . 104943
Schwarzmeier, Jürgen, Arnsdorf . . .069184, 125065
Schwarzwälder, Manfred, Bad Tölz . 069389
Schwarzwälder Freilichtmuseum Vogtsbauernhof, Gutach, Schwarzwaldbahn 017610
Schwarzwälder Mineralienmuseum, Neubulach 019222
Schwarzwälder Mühlenmuseum, Grafenhausen 017504
Schwarzwälder Trachtenmuseum, Haslach 017787
Schwarzwald-Museum, Triberg . . . 020473
Schwazer Silberbergwerk, Schwaz . 002666
Schweden, Oliver, München 104316
Schwedenspeicher-Museum, Kulturgeschichtliches Museum im Elbe-Weser-Raum, Stade 020279
Schwedhelm, G., Duderstadt 070341
Schwedler, Holzgerlingen 071569
Schween, Bochum 102162
Schweig, Neil, Saint Louis 119250
Schweighofer, Bernd, Marktoberdorf 126296
Schweighofer, Johann, Hartberg . . . 123379
Schweihofen, J., Bielefeld 138876
Schweine-Museum, Bad Wimpfen . 015836
Schweinfurth Memorial Art Center, Auburn 041889
Schweins, Otto, Köln 103715
Schweinsteiger, Ilse, München 072853
Schweißhelm, H., Hannover 125879
Schweitzer, Lucien, Luxembourg . . 107410
Schweitzer, Lucien, Mondorf-les-Bains 107416
Schweitzer, Paul, Bonn 069942
Schweitzer, Rolf, Rothenburg ob der Tauber 073593
Schweizer, Bad Homburg v.d.Höhe .069299, 101659
Schweizer, Christof, Urnäsch 082868
Schweizer, Daniel, Genève 082467
Schweizer, Eglantine, Villars-le-Terroir 111973
Schweizer, Klaus, Konstanz 072050, 103767
Schweizer, Dr. René, Lampertheim .072124, 126161
Schweizer Filmmuseum, Basel 036905
Schweizer Grafiker Verband, Zürich 054178
Schweizer Jazzmuseum, Uster 037661
Schweizer Kamm-Museum, Mümliswil 037352
Schweizer Kindermuseum, Baden . 036873
Schweizer Kunst, Berufsverband visuelle Kunst, Zürich 054207
Schweizer Museum für Wild und Jagd, Utzenstorf 037663
Schweizerische Gesellschaft Bildender Künstlerinnen, Bern 054208
Schweizerische Gesellschaft der Freunde von Kunstauktionen, Zürich 054209
Schweizerische Interessengemeinschaft zur Erhaltung von Grafik und Schriftgut, Bern 054210
Schweizerische Landesbibliothek, Bern 036936
Schweizerische Theatersammlung, Bern 036937
Schweizerischer Ex Libris Club, Baden 054211
Schweizerischer Fachverband für Glasmalerei, Romont 054212
Schweizerischer Kunstverein, Zürich 054213
Schweizerischer Verband der Graveure, Stansstad 054214
Schweizerischer Verband für Konservierung und Restaurierung, Bern 054215
Schweizerischer Verband Graphisches Gewerbe, Basel 054216
Schweizerischer Werkbund, Zürich . 054217
Schweizerisches Alpines Museum, Bern 036938
Schweizerisches Dampfmaschinenmuseum Vaporama, Thun 037631
Schweizerisches Feuerwehrmuseum, Basel 036906
Schweizerisches Freilichtmuseum für ländliche Kultur, Brienz, Bern 036973
Schweizerisches Gastronomie-Museum, Thun 037632
Schweizerisches Institut für Kunstwissenschaft, Zürich 050782
Schweizerisches Meteoriten-und Mineralienmuseum, Schönenwerd 037535
Schweizerisches Museum für Landwirtschaft und Agrartechnik Burgrain, Alberswil 036827
Schweizerisches Schützenmuseum, Bern 036939
Schweizerisches Sportmuseum, Basel 036907
Schweizerisches Zentrum für Volkskultur, Burgdorf 036994
Schwemmgut-Museum, Finsing . . . 017121
Schwender, Jürgen, Münster 072928
Schwenk-Anger, Else, Alpirsbach . . 133719
Schwenkenbecher, Matthias, Nördlingen 126554
Schwenkfelder Library and Heritage Center, Pennsburg 046872
Schwenkkros, A., Osten 073253
Schwennesen, Heiko, Hamburg . . . 071330
Schwerd, Armin, Brühl, Rheinland . 138952
Schwerfeldreich, Stuttgart 105010
Schwerkolt Cottage Museum, Mitcham 001269
Schwetz, Claude, Saint-Ouen 067891
Schwicker - Tosi, Firenze 106070
Schwickerath, Udo, Langenfeld . . . 072155
Schwieder, Birgit, Morbach 126334
Schwilden, Bruxelles 137466
Schwind, Karlheinz, Frankfurt am Main 102825
Schwindel, Rudolf, Augsburg 125080
Schwingruber, Markus, Luzern 082634
Schwitter, Allschwil 134975
Schwörer & Sohn, March 072454
Schwörer, Udo, Engelsbrand 139039
Schwohn, D., Hörstel 071543
Schwules Museum, Berlin 016171
Schwurgerichtssaal 600, Museen der Stadt Nürnberg, Nürnberg 019373
Sci-Port Discovery Center, Shreveport 048164
Sci-Tech Center of Northern New York, Watertown 048995
Sciacca, Luigi, Messina 106140
Sciacchitano, Gaetano, Torino 128358
Sciacchitano, Giulio, Torino 128359
Scialom, Jean-Pierre, Zürich 141360
Scianca, Luciano, Roma 076671
Sciarra, Raniero, Roma 076672
Sciascia, Salvatore, Caltanissetta . . 134561
Sciberras, B'Kara 077508
Scibilia, Gabriela, Catania 127279
Sciboz-Cordier, Danielle, Nîmes . . . 065188
Scicali, Renata, Palermo 106443
Science Activity Centre, Sirsa 022343
Science Activity Corner, Gwalior . . . 022144
Science and Industry Collections Group, London 054496
Science and Technology Museum of Atlanta, Atlanta 041872
Science Center of Connecticut, West Hartford 049080
Science Center of Iowa, Des Moines 043429
Science Center of Pinellas County, Saint Petersburg 047720
Science Center of Thessaloniki and Technology Museum, Thessaloniki 021502
Science Center of West Virginia, Bluefield 042276
Science Centre for Education, Bangkok 037889
Science City Museum, Kolkata 022226
Science Discovery Center of Oneonta, Oneonta 046691
Science et Technologie de la Conservation et de la Restoration des Œuvres d'Art et du Patrimoine, Puteaux 135729

The Science Factory, Eugene 043749
Science Imaginarium, Waterloo ... 048985
The Science Museum, Cebu 031660
Science Museum, Dhaka 003110
Science Museum, Giza 009334
Science Museum, Kabul 000006
Science Museum, Upton 048711
Science Museum, Bibliotheca Alexandria, Alexandria 009284
Science Museum, The National Museum of Science & Industry, London 040285
Science Museum of Long Island, Manhasset 045626
Science Museum of Minnesota, Saint Paul 047709
Science Museum of Virginia, Richmond 047424
Science Museum of Western Virginia, Roanoke 047468
Science Museum Wroughton, The National Museum of Science & Industry, Wroughton 041459
Science North, Sudbury 006532
Science Spectrum, Lubbock 045514
Science Station Museum, Cedar Rapids 042679
Science Treasures, Oklahoma City . 091533
Science Works!, Marikina 031744
Sciencenter, Ithaca 044793
Scienceworks, Museum of Victoria, Spotswood 001483
Scienceworks Museum, Melbourne 001251
Scientific Researches Museum, Cairo 009323
Scipilliti, Liliana, Messina 106141
Scippa, Raffaele, Napoli 076049
Scisco, Vincent, Longwy 063992
Scitech, Aurora 041914
Scituate Historical Museum, Scituate 048048
Scituate Maritime and Irish Mossing Museum, Scituate 048049
Sciworks, Winston-Salem 049257
Sclanders, Andrew, London 141891
Scoazec, Jean-Louis, Pont-Aven .. 101037
Scognamiglio, Mimmo, Napoli 106388
Scognamiglio, Rodolfo, Milano 075861
Scohy, Serge, Antwerpen 096091
Scola Galleria, Oakland 118646
Scolar Fine Art, London 113877
Scoles, Saskatoon 097200
Scolton Manor Museum, Haverfordwest 039699
Scone and Upper Hunter Historical Museum, Scone 001460
Scone Palace, Perth 040699
Scope Antiques, London .. 085681, 131166
Scope London, London 093951
Scope Los Angeles, Los Angeles .. 094031
Scope Miami, Miami Beach 094032
Scope New York, New York 094033
Score, Stephen, Boston 087843
Le Scorpion, Les Baux-de-Provence 099469
Scorrano, Carlo, Roma 076673
Scorza, Angela M., Rio de Janeiro . 096647
Scorza, Daniela Menezes, São Paulo 096688
Scot, Paris 100846
Scotch Mist Gallery, Tucson 120164
Scotch Whisky Heritage Centre, Edinburgh 039422
Scotchtown, Beaverdam 042092
Scotia-Glenville Children's Museum, Scotia 048053
Scotland Art, Glasgow 113129
Scotland Heritage Chapel and Museum, Scotland 048054
Scotland Street School Museum, Glasgow 039575
Scotland Yard Antiques, Marburg .. 056158
Scotland's Secret Bunker, Saint Andrews 040899
Scotsman, Saint Louis 092310
Scott, Atlanta 087525
Scott, Edmonton 096895
Scott & Co., H., Norfolk 123026
Scott, James, Edinburgh 084313
Scott, Lee, Atlanta 087526
Scott, Marion, Vancouver 097528
Scott, Mike, Salisbury 131452
Scott, Richard, Holt, Norfolk 084708
Scott-Cooper, Cheltenham 083928, 130542
The Scott Gallery, Hawick Museum, Hawick 039704
Scott Monument, Edinburgh 039423
Scott Polar Research Institute Museum, Cambridge 038969
Scotti, Emidio, Roma 128200
Scottie's Guns and Militaria, Denver 088735
Scottish Antique, Doune 084214
Scottish Antique and Arts Centre, Abernyte 083248, 130282
Scottish Art Gallery, Dunoon 112968
Scottish Arts Council, Edinburgh ... 054497
Scottish Fine Art Group, Norwich .. 114167
Scottish Fisheries Museum, Anstruther 038513
Scottish Football Museum, Glasgow 039576
The Scottish Gallery, Edinburgh ... 113010
Scottish Industrial Railway Centre, Dalmellington 039203
Scottish Infantry Divisional Museum, Penicuik 040686
Scottish Jewish Museum, Glasgow 039577
Scottish Maritime Museum, Irvine . 039820
Scottish Mining Museum, Newtongrange 040578
Scottish Museum of Woollen Textiles, Walkerburn 041279
Scottish Museums Council, Edinburgh 054498
Scottish Museums Federation, Hamilton 054499
Scottish National Gallery of Modern Art Gallery, Edinburgh 039424
Scottish National Portrait Gallery, Edinburgh 039425
Scottish Pottery Historical Review, Edinburgh 136268
Scottish Rugby Union Museum, Edinburgh 039426
Scottish Society for Art History, Edinburgh 054500
Scottish Society for Conservation and Restoration, Edinburgh 054501
Scotts' Antiques of Battery Point, Hobart 056000
Scotts Bluff National Monument, Gering 044180
Scotts of Dorking, Dorking 084203, 130651
Scottsdale Artists' League, Scottsdale 055027
Scottsdale Artists' School, Scottsdale 052154
Scottsdale Museum of Contemporary Art, Scottsdale 048060
Scottsdale Village Antiques, Albuquerque 087424
Scotty's Trading Post, Southport ... 056618
Scout Gallery, London 113878
Scouting Museum de Ducdalf, Rotterdam 030104
Scouting Museum Haagse Randstad, Den Haag 029453
Scranton, Oklahoma City 091534
Screen Porch Arts, Houston 116401
Scremini, Clara, Paris 100847
Scribaen, de, Haarlem 128695
Scribes Books, Dunedin 140626
Scrimshaw, Glen, Saskatoon 097201
Scriporama, Spijkenisse 140533
Scripta Manent, Reggio Calabria .. 127899
Scriptum Art Books, Schiedam 134832, 140529
Lo Scrittoio, Roma 076674
Scriver Museum of Montana Wildlife and Hall of Bronze, Browning 042478
Scrocco, Roberto, Livorno 075542
Scroungers Antiques, Bridgetown .. 055541
Scrudato, Robert, Menton 064495, 138205
Scryption, Museum voor Schriftelijke Communicatie, Tilburg 030212
Scuderi, Carmelo, New York 091233
Scuderi, Daniel, New York 091234, 132530
Scuderi, Marisa, Palermo 106444
Scugog Shores Historical Museum, Port Perry 006188
Scuiller, Samy, Audierne 098874
Sculptastic, London 113879
Sculptors Guild of America, New York 055028
Sculptor's Society of Canada, Toronto 052774
Sculptors' Society of Ireland, Dublin 053718
Sculpture, Hamilton 136622
Sculpture Art Research Institute, Capital Normal University, Beijing 049845
Sculpture Center, Long Island City . 045392
Sculpture Center Gallery, New York 118396
Sculpture Gallery, San Francisco .. 119786
Sculpture Gallery, Sevenoaks 114407
Sculpture Internationale, Miami ... 094034
Sculptures, New York 118397
Scuola Dalmata dei Santi Giorgio e Trifone, Venezia 026266
Scuola di Specializzazione in Archeologia, Napoli 050399
Scuola Grande Arciconfraternita di San Rocco, Venezia 026267
Scuola Grande di San Giovanni Evangelista, Venezia 026268
Scuola Statale d'Arte, Priverno 050410
Scuola Superiore d'Arte Applicata del Castello Sforzesco, Milano 050394
Scuola Superiore d'Arte Cristiana Beato Angelico, Milano 050395
Scuoppo Musso, Marseille 064390, 124432
Scurr, Stuart, Mount Lawley 056290
Scurry County Museum, Western Texas College, Snyder 048209
Ščusev Museum, Chişinău 028988
SCW Reprographics, San Diego ... 119550
SD Galeria Mokotówa, Warszawa .. 109192
SD Galeria Panorama, Warszawa .. 109193
S.D. Galerie, Paris 066535
S.D.A.C., Paris 133676
SDV Saarbrücker Druckerei und Verlag, Saarbrücken 134376
SE Art and Design, New York 118398
Sea and See, Paris 100848
Sea Antiques, Helsinki 060579
Sea Country, Barcelona 080933
Sea & Country, Barcelona 080934
Sea & Country, Barcelona 080935
Sea Pictures, McCrae 094750
Sea View Antiques, Caernarfon ... 083834
Sea-Witch Antiques, Port Adelaide . 056472
Sea World, South African Association for Marine Biological Research, Durban 034605
Seabreeze Art Gallery, Southport .. 114466
Seabrook Antiques, Long Melford ..085840, 131231
Seabrook Village, Midway 045859
Seaby, London 085682
The SeaChange Gallery, Great Yarmouth 113154
Seaford Historical Museum, Seaford 048070
Seaford House Antiques, Moreton-in-Marsh 086021
Seaford Museum of Local History, Seaford 040973
Seaford's Barn Collectors Market, Seaford 086529, 142052
Seaforth Highlanders of Canada Regimental Museum, Vancouver 006708
Seagar, R.C., London 131167
Seagate Art Gallery, Toledo 120090
Seager, Arthur, Stow-on-the-Wold . 086762
Seagull, Singapore 109865
Seahaven Galleries, Providence ... 119088
Seal Island Light Museum, Barrington 005073
Seale, Jeremy, London 085683
Sealed Art, Hamilton 096925
Sealife Scheveningen, Den Haag .. 029454
Seanic Antiques, Newport 056335
Seans, Sankt-Peterburg 136061
Seaocean Book, Seattle 143008
Seaport Antique, Newport 056336
Seaport Antique Village, Delaware . 088632
SEARCH-Centre, Gosport 039612
Search Press, Tunbridge Wells 135309
Searcy County Museum, Marshall . 045697
Searle & Co., London 085684, 131168
Sears Canada, Calgary 096845
Sears-Peyton, New York 118399
Seashore Trolley Museum, Kennebunkport 044956
Seaside Art Gallery, Hong Kong ... 097829
Seasons Art, Singapore 080556
Seasons Art Gallery, Omaha 118722
Seasons Galleries, Den Haag 107951
Seasons in Time, Birmingham 087784
Seaton Delaval Hall, Seaton 040974
Seatons, Christchurch ... 079051, 128927
Seattle Antiquarian Book Fair and Book Arts Show, Seattle 094035
Seattle Antique Market, Seattle ... 093062
Seattle Art Museum, Seattle 048091
Seattle Arts, Seattle 136623
Seattle Asian Art Museum, Seattle . 048092
Seattle Auction Service, Seattle ... 123116
Seattle Book Center, Seattle 143009
Seattle Coin Shop, Seattle 093063
Seattle Intertribal Alliance, Seattle .055029, 119990
Seattle Mystery Bookshop, Seattle . 143010
Seattle Print Arts, Seattle 055030
Seauve, Philippe, Livron-sur-Drôme 063971
Seaver College, Pepperdine University, Malibu 051665
Seaview Antiques, Horncastle 084739
Seaview Artists Gallery, Moffat Beach 094864
Seaview Gallery, Queenscliff 056515, 095111
Seaway Gallery, Paignton 114214
Seaweed Art, Cape Town 110032
Seawinds, Columbus 088435
Sebag, Félix, Paris 066536
Sebão Livros Usados, Brasília 137555
Sebastian-Kneipp-Museum, Bad Wörishofen 015840
Sebastiano, Timo, Altendorf 082086
Sèbe, Alain, Vidauban 133705
Sebestyén, Georg, Waldenbuch ..074251, 105148
Sebestyen, M., Aachen 101527
Sebežskij Muzej Prirody, Sebež ... 033862
Sebley, Oswald, Norwich . 086122, 131333
Sebnitzer Kunstblumen- und Heimatmuseum Prof. Alfred Meiche, Sebnitz 020159
Sebo do Messias Livros Usados, São Paulo 137592
Sebo São João, São Paulo 137593
Sebök, Johann, Bamberg 121312
Seboga, Seoul 107285
Sebourne, Jose, Philadelphia 118831
Sebovero, São Paulo 137594
Sebra Galerii, Tartu 098707
Secesja, Kraków 079656
Secesja, Skawina 129071
Secesja, Warszawa 079783, 140795
Secker & Warburg, Martin, London . 135261
Secluded Alley Works, Seattle 119991
Seco, Virgilio Rodrigues, Lisboa ... 080014
Secol - Art, Torino 076869
Second Avenue Art Expo, New York 118400
Second Chance, Auckland 078981
Second Chance Antiques, Omaha .. 091582
Second City Resale, Cleveland 088359
Second Creek Antiques, Charlotte . 087976
Second Edition, Edinburgh 141588
Second Edition, Oakland 142710
Second Edition, Regina .. 059092, 123814
Second Edition-Books, Pambula ... 137043
Second Floor Antiques, Sacramento 092180
Second Glance Books, Portland ... 142810
Second Hand Design, Amsterdam . 077965

Second Hand Store and Antiques, Long Beach 089656
Second Juda, Banská Bystrica 140954
Second Life, Charlestown 131867
Second Look Book Store, San Antonio 142894
Second Notions Antiques, Kirkcaldy 084875
Second Sight Fine Art, Bath 112586
Second Story Books, Rockville 142835
Second Story Books, Washington . . 143049
Second Street Gallery, Charlottesville 042768
Second Thoughts Bookstore, Ottawa 137677
Second Time, Los Angeles 089905
Second Time Around, Hemswell Cliff 084655, 130782
Second Time Around, Providence . . 092049
Second Time Around, Vancouver . . 059412
Second Time Around Antiques, Buffalo 087906
Second Time Around Antiques, Richmond 092101, 132723
Second Time Around Books, Toronto 137716
Second World War Experience Centre, Leeds 039960
Seconde Modernité, Paris 100849
Secondo Mano, Gouda 078390
Secord, William, New York 118401
Secret d'Alcove, Bruxelles 058084
Secret Garden Gallery, North Tamborine 094984
Secrets, Port Isaac 114275
Secrets of Asia, Deventer 078283
Section d'Histoire de l'Art, Université de Lausanne, Lausanne 050769
Section d'Histoire de l'Art et d'Archéologie, Faculté de Philosophie et Lettres, Université Libre de Bruxelles, Bruxelles 049692
Section d'Histoire des Arts & d' Archeologie, Université de Bourgogne, Dijon . . 049948
Section Française de l'Institut International de Conservation des Œuvres d'Art. Core, Champs-sur-Marne 124183
Section Histoire de l'Art et Archéologie, Université de Toulouse, Toulouse . 049993
Section Sciences Humaines, Lettres et Arts, Université de Lille III, Villeneuve-d'Ascq 049997
Sécula, Alain-Nicolas, Beaune 061295
Sécula, Anthony, Beaune 061296
Sécula, Eric, Beaune 061297
Sécula, François, Beaune 061298
Sécula, Jacky, Beaune 061299
Sécula, Jean-Marc, Luzy 064044
Secula, Jean-Pierre, Saint-Ouen . . 067892
Sécula, Laurent, Beaune 061300
Sécula, Raymond, Beaune 061301
Sécula, Rodolphe, Beaune 061302
Sécula, Rodolphe, Paris 066537
Seculo XX Copacabana, Rio de Janeiro 058655
Séculos Passados, Porto 080111
Secundo, Liège 058326
Secundus, Terhole 140534
Secwepemc Museum and Heritage Park, Kamloops 005661
Sed Gallery, University of Georgia, Athens 041835
Sedan Numismatique, Sedan 068185
Sedarca, Oleyres 130136
Seddig, Ralph-André, Wedel 126974
Sederholmin Talo, Helsingin Kaupunginmuseo, Helsinki 009567
Seders, Francine, Seattle 119992
Sedgeberrow, Pershore 141998
Sedgewick Museum and Gallery, Sedgewick 006437
Sedgwick-Brooklin Historical Museum, Sedgwick 048104
Sedgwick Museum of Geology, Cambridge 038970
Sediwa, Hamburg 103219
Sedlák, František, Praha 060158
Sedlak, Karl, Offenhausen 057201
Sedman, Bridlington 083675
Sedona Arts Center, Sedona 048105
See Gallery, Toronto 097371
See Restoration, Atlanta 131785
Seebach, Jochen, Emkendorf 125587
Seedamm Kulturzentrum, Stiftung Charles und Agnes Vögele, Pfäffikon (Schwyz) 037411
Seedorn Verlag, Seuzach 135067
Seegartengalerie, Garding 102917, 133971
Seeger, Brigitte, Göppingen 071034
Seeger, Burgel, Fellbach 070683
Seegers, Marie-Louise, Blies-Ebersing 061516
Seekers Books, Toronto 137717
Seelackenmuseum, Sankt Veit im Pongau 002634
Seeland Galerie, Jens 111573
Seelhöfer, Hagen, Westfalen 071165
Seelhof, Ulrich, Dillenburg 125465
Seelhoff, Westerburg, Westerwald . 074361
Seemann, E.A., Leipzig 134156
Seemann, Helfried, Wien 137365
Seemeyer, Adolf, Hannover 071414, 125880, 139244
Seemuseum in der Kornschütte, Kreuzlingen 037223
Seeshells Antiques, Las Vegas 089605
Seethaphone, Bangalore 074782
Seeverlag, Höchst 133087
Seevogel-Museum Neusiedlersee, Rust, Burgenland 002543
Sefel Collection, Volos 021524
Ségal, Marie-Eva & Dr. Georges B., Basel 082173, 122307
Segal, Thomas, Baltimore 115083
Ségala, Badaroux 061159
Ségalat, Roger J., Lausanne 141265
Ségalen, Saint-Malo (Ille-et-Vilaine) 101175
Segalen, Roselyne, Paris 100850
Segalini, Italo, Brescia 106007
Segantini-Museum, Sankt Moritz . . 037506
Segarra, Maria Fernandez, Lisboa . 080015
Segas, Gilbert, Paris 066538
Sege, Geldrop 128670
Segedunum Roman Fort, Baths and Museum, Wallsend 041282
Seggern, J. von, Bremen 070046
Seghaier, Suzanne, Wien 095936
Seghers, P. & L., Oostende 096403
Il Segno del Tempo, Milano 075862
Il Segno del Tempo, Milano 075863
Sego Gallery, Salt Lake City 119369
Segonds, Jean-Claude, Limoges . . 063898
Segontium Roman Museum, Caernarfon 038943
Segonzac, Dunoyer de, Paris 066539
Segoura, Maurice, Paris . . 066540, 100851
Segovia Argudo, Marita, Madrid . . . 081390
Segrelles del Pilar, Valencia 110843
Seguin, Villeurbanne 125035
Seguin, Alain, Beaune 098941
Seguin, Patrick, Paris 100852
Seguin, Patrick, Paris 100853
Séguin Poirier, Bernard, Montréal . . 097076
Seguine House, Staten Island 048333
Séguineau, Eric, La Baule-Escoublac 121022, 138109
Seguinet, Arnaud, Duclair 120995
Ségur, Anne, Nice 138261
Seguso Viro, Venezia 106778
Segwun Heritage Centre, Gravenhurst 005546
Sehgalerie, Bordesholm 102202
Şehir Müzesi, Beşiktaş 038023
S.E.I. 1983, Roma 128201
Seï-un-do Galerie, Zürich 112178
Seian Zokei Daigaku, Otsu 050471
Seibert-Philippen, Gisela, Berlin . . . 102042
Seibido, Nara 077166
Seibold, Eleanor, New York 118402
Seibu, Tokyo 107101
Seidel & Sohn, Berlin 069760
Seidel & Sohn, Berlin 069761
Seidel, A., Bad Lauterberg 069321
Seidel, H., Neustadt in Holstein . . . 073040
Seidel, Konrad, Witten 127027
Seidel, Volker, Bochum 069894
Seidel & Richter, Kerstin, Berlin . . . 138845
Seidenath, Otto, Bamberg 125136
Seidenath, Thomas, Bamberg 125137
Seidenberg, David, New York 091235
Seidenfaden, Max, København 098583
Seidenstraßen Galerie, Gießen 102956
Seidl, Johannes, Gasteil 095512
Seidl, Josef, München 072854
Seidl, Josef, München . . . 072855, 121546
Seidl, Markus, Tiefenbach, Kreis Passau 074058
Seidler, Wilhelm, Linz 057168, 095672
Seifert, Edmund, Coburg 070149
Seifert, H., Köln 072006
Seifert, R., Schwabmünchen 073737
Seifert, Rolf, Dresden 139000
Seiffert, Albert, Nürnberg 073122
Seifudo, Kubo, Hiroshima 077064
Seigando, Jintsu, Tokyo 077300
Seigfred Gallery, Ohio University, Athens 041839
Seigne, Eric, Boisset Saint-Priest . . 124105
Seigneur, Jacques le, Ronchin 124881
Seiho, Tokyo 107102
Seiji, Honolulu 116243
Seiji Togo Memorial Sompo Japan Museum of Art, Tokyo 027233
Seikado Library and Art Museum, Tokyo 027234
Seiko, Sendai 107003
Seikosha, Osaka 077182
Seiler, Röslau 073560
Seiler, Andreas, Wöschnau 082920
Seiler, Anton, Bonstetten 111303
Seiler, Thomas, Heilbronn 103336
Seiler, Werner, Basel 129932
Seiler-Liepe, Ute, Berlin 125297
Seillé, Carcès 061984
Seillon, Jean-Marie, Saint-Martin-sur-Oust 067652
Seim, Bjørn, Oslo 079469
Seima, Tourriers 068574
Seimetz, Sankt Leon-Rot 073672
S.E.I.N.A., Milano 127684
Seinäjoen Lehti- ja Kirjapörssi, Seinäjoki 137987
Seinäjoen Luonto-Museo, Seinäjoki 010071
Seinerzeit, Bünde 070085
Seinerzeit, Leoben 057147
Seippel, Dr. R.-P., Köln 103716
Seiryu-do, Fukuoka 077045
De Seis a Ocho, Gijón 081127
De Seismograaf, København 060378
Seisonkaku, Kanazawa 026628
Seisser, Gudrun, Kronberg im Taunus 103797
Seissian & Fils, Hagop, Beirut 128454
Seith, H., Kempten 071795
Seitou, Hiroshima 106857
Seitre, Simone, Saint-Martin 105471
Seitz & Co., Saint Paul 092395
Seitz, K. & H., Rheinfelden 073526
Seitz, Werner, München 072856
Seitz & Partner, Berlin 102043
Seiwald, Dr. Emmerich, Sankt Oswald bei Freistadt 057294
Seiyo Inn, Sapporo 077201
Seiyun in Wadi Hadhramaut Museum, Seiyun 049563
Seize, Quimper 101065
Seize, Louis, Cairo 098669
Sejac, Poligny 124848
Sejallet, Jean, Saint-Rambert-d'Albon 067980
Sejarah Mesjid Banten Museum, Banten 022396
Sejong, Seoul 107286
Sejong College Museum, Seoul . . . 027596
Sejong Cultural Center Art Gallery, Seoul 107287
Sęk Galeria Korzenioplastyka, Halinów 108917
Sekaido, Sagamihara 077189
Sekaido, Tachikawa 077224
Sekaido, Tama 077226
Sekaido, Tokyo 077301
Sekaido, Tokyo 077302
Sekaido, Tokyo 077303
Sekcija na izobrazitelno izkustvo BAM, Sofia 052710
Sekelskifte Antikt & Annat, Stockholm 082014
Sekhmet, Vitoria-Gasteiz 141087
Sekiguchi Ko Museum Yuzawa, Yuzawa 027355
Sekitan Kinenkan, Ube 027300
Sekkeh Museum, Kerman 022570
Sekkeh Museum, Teheran 022643
Sekken Museum, Sekken 031177
Sekula, Sacramento 092181
Sekunda, Sankt-Peterburg 080329
Sel Inart, Firenze 075404
Selano, Benedetto, Genève 111499
Selbert, Rolf, Kassel 139310
Selbstständige Design-Studios e.V., Braunschweig 053561
Selbu Bygdemuseum, Selbu 031178
Selbu Strikkemuseum, Selbu Bygdemuseum, Selbu 031179
Selby Gallery, Ringling School of Art and Design, Sarasota 048001
Selch, Horst, Wörth am Main 105317
Selchow, Kerstin, Friedrichshafen . 102886
Selçuk Müzesi, Konya Museums, Konya 038137
Selden Emre, İstanbul 083155
Seldom Seen Designs, Cheltenham 112846
Select, Rotterdam 078743, 128824
Select Art, Dallas 115937
Select Art, Utrecht 078818, 140554
Select Art Galleries, London 096957
Select Stamp and Coin Studio, Buffalo 087907
Selected Antiques & Collectables, Barnstaple 083399, 130338
Selected Works, Chicago 142301
Selection Art, Torino 106704
Selections, Haarlem 078480
Selective Eye Gallery, Saint Helier .086453, 114356, 131440, 142037
Selective Prints, Willaston 114696
Selective Prints, Winsford 114712
Selenati, Ornella, Milano 106308
Self Help Graphics Gallery, Los Angeles 045460
Seliger, Gisela, Bremen 125393
Seligmann, M. & D., London 085685
Selims Antiques, Winnipeg 059470
Seling, Dr. H.W., München 072857
Selinheimo, Kari, Turku 137998
Seljuk, San Francisco 132909
Selkirk, Kambah 056027, 123246
Selkirk, Winnipeg 137744
Selkirk College Mansbridge Kootenay Collection, Castlegar 005236
Sell, Forchheim, Oberfranken 070718
Sell Antiques, Salt Lake City 092460
Sellack, Berlin 125298
Sellares, Alain, Montjoie-en-Couserans 064701
Sellarione, Dario, Roma 076675
Selle, Bjärred 110899
Sellem, Lund 134962
Sellem, Roger, Paris 066541
Sellerio, Palermo 134652
Sellers, Basil, Moruya 094890
Selli, Daniel, Gassin 062972
Selli, Daniel, Saint-Tropez 068024
Sellier, Eric, Neuilly-sur-Seine 064993
Sellier, Jean-Christian, Arras 060990
Selliez, Domnique, Hardifort 063127
Sellner Glashütte, Lohberg 018674
Sellos, Oscar B., Rio de Janeiro . . . 058656

Sellution Vintage Furniture, Vancouver 059413
Sellution Vintage Furniture, Vancouver 059414
Sellwood Antique Collective, Portland 092003
Sellwood Antique Mall, Portland . . . 092004
Sellwood Coins, Portland 092005
Selly Manor Museum, Birmingham . 038737
Selmersheim, Paris 100854
Selons, R. & B., Cuckfield 130620
Sels, Antwerpen 120708
Sels, Clara Maria, Düsseldorf 102554
Selsey Lifeboat Museum, Selsey . . 040984
Selsor Gallery of Art, Safari Museum, Chanute 042712
Šeltozerskij Vepsskij Ėtnografičeskij Muzej, Karelskij gosudarstvennyj kraevedčeskij muzej, Šeltozero 033863
Seltzer Lejeune, Paris 100855
Selvi, Carlo, Roma 076676
Selwoods, Taunton 086829
Selz, Beat, Perrefitte 111806, 135055
Selz, Dr. Gudrun, Freiburg im Breisgau 070860
Semaphore Antique Centre, Semaphore 056585
Semar, Rotterdam 108208
Sembritzki, Elisabeth, Oldenburg, Oldenburg 073209, 126592
Semenovskij Gosudarstvennyj Kraevedčeskij Istoriko-chudožestvennyj Muzej, Semenov 033864
Semenzato, Patrizia, Venezia 076973
Semerád, Petr, Klatovy 137787
Semerano, Dante, Roma 128202
Semet, Wolfgang, Speyer 126819
Semina Rerum, Zürich 112179
Seminar für Kunst und Kirche, Philosophisch-Theologische Hochschule Sankt Georgen, Frankfurt am Main 050085
Seminar für Kunstgeschichte, Heinrich-Heine-Universität, Düsseldorf . . . 050071
Seminar für Orientalische Kunstgeschichte, Rheinische Friedrich-Wilhelms-Universität Bonn, Bonn 050039
Seminario, Tampa 120067
Seminario de Arte Aragones, Zaragoza 136103
Seminario de Estudios de Arte y Arqueologia, Universidad, Valladolid 050739
Seminole Canyon State Historical Park, Comstock 043115
Seminole Nation Museum, Wewoka 049130
Seminyak, Coffs Harbour 094414
Semipalatinskij Istoriko-Kraevedčeskij Muzej, Semey 027411
Semler, Stefan & Rudolf, Fulda 070921
Semley Auctioneers, Shaftesbury . . 122694
Semmelweis Orvostörténeti Múzeum, Budapest 021693
Semmler, Lengdorf 103903
Semmler, Margitta, Wernigerode . . 074346
Semper, Franz, Laa an der Thaya . . 137206
Sempf, E., Nettetal 072965, 126524
Semsey Andor Múzeum, Balmazujváros 021625
Sen, San Francisco 092881
Sen-Garou, Tokyo 107103
Sen Trop, Beograd 080406
Fernandes Sena, Brasília 058467
Senac, Anna, Paris 124807
Senado Antiguidades, Rio de Janeiro 058657
Senagoo, Ahmad, Houston 089200
Senamiesčio, Vilnius 077457
Senasis Kuparas, Vilnius . 077458, 140235
Senate House, Kingston 045014
Senator George Norris State Historic Site, McCook 045544
Senator John Heinz Pittsburgh Regional History Center, Historical Society of Western Pennsylvania, Pittsburgh 047060
Senćanski Muzej, Senta 034256
Senckenberg-Forschungsinstitut und Naturmuseum, Frankfurt am Main 017193
Senda, Barcelona 080936, 110249
Senda-Espai 292, Barcelona 110250
Sendai Music Box Museum, Sendai 027051
Sendai-shi Hakubutsukan, Sendai . 027052
Sender, Rosalia, Valencia 110844
Sendergalerie Dobl, Dobl 001784
Seneca County Museum, Tiffin 048554
Seneca Falls Historical Society Museum, Seneca Falls 048114
Seneca-Iroquois National Museum, Salamanca 047731
Senemaud, Monique, Paris 066542
Senge, Raymond, München 126460
Senger, Bamberg 069463
Senger, Heinz & Matthias, Berlin . .069762, 121343
Senger, Karl Heinrich, Buxtehude . . 125422
Senhouse Roman Museum, Maryport 040431
Senior, E.E., Taringa 056700
Senior & Shopmaker, New York . . . 118403
Senj Municipal Museum, Senj 007789
Senjehesten Kystforsvarsmuseum, Midt-Troms Museum, Moen 031025
Senko-ji Treasure House, Ono 026956
Senn, Georg F., Binningen 129981
Senn, Martin, Sankt Gallen 082788, 130167
Sennacheribbo, Ida, Barcelona 110251
Sennerei-Museum und Heimatmuseum, Unterwasser 037658
Senninger, Eugène, Louverne 064015
Seno, Paolo, Milano 106309
Sen'oku Hakukokan Museum, Kyoto 026769
Senouhi, Cairo 060472
Sensburg, München 072858
Sensen-Schmiede-Museum/ Klangwelten, Micheldorf 002309
Sensen- und Heimatmuseum, Achern 015440
Sensi, Francesco, Roma 076677
Sensibly Chic, Salt Lake City 092461
Sensler Museum, Tafers 037620
Sensor K, Berlin 102044
Sensua, Atlanta 114923
Senterrammer, Oslo 079470
Sentimental Journey Antiques, Tampa 093152
Sentimento, Maylands, Western Australia 056177
Sentimento, New York 091236
Sentou, Paris 100856
Senza Zucchero, Milano 106310
Senzala Antiguidades, Belo Horizonte 123692
Senzatempo, Miami 090241
Seo, Dong, Masan 107201
Seoane, Roald, Montevideo 087346
Seojong, Seoul 107288
Seorim, Seoul 107289
Seoul Art Museum, Seoul 027597
Seoul Arts Data Center, Seoul 053828
Seoul Design Museum, Seoul 027598
Seoul Education Museum, Seoul . . 027599
Seoul Furniture and Antique Company, Seoul 077374
Seoul Metropolitan Museum of Art, Seoul 027600
Seoul National Science Museum, Seoul 027601
Seoul National University Museum, Seoul 027602
Seoul Olympic Museum, Seoul 027603
Seoul Station Hall, Railroad Museum, Seoul 027604
Seowha, Seoul 107290
S.E.P.A., Rennes (Ille-et-Vilaine) . . . 101089
Sepänmäen Käsityömuseo, Mäntsälä 009851
Sepant, Bucureşti 140882
Sepheriades, E., Athinai 074606
Sépia Galerie d'Art, Paris 100857
Sepia-The Alkazi Collection, New York 118404
Sepio, Claudio, Milano 075864
Sepon Penni, Helsinki . . . 060580, 137960
Seppmann, Dr. Werner, Haltern . . . 071184
Septem Maria Museum, Adria 023125
Septentrion Galerie Peinture, Marcq-en-Barœul 099637
Sepulchre, Bruno, Paris 138541
Sepúlveda, Maria Luísa, Lisboa . . . 080016
Sequeira, Mário, Braga 109240
Sequoïa, Le Havre 124301
Sequoyah, Dallas 142374
Sequoyah Cabin, Sallisaw 047766
Ser, Yong, Singapore 129266
Serafijn, Antwerpen 057735
Serafin, Wien 095937
Serafino, Paola, Genova 075510
Serai, Cairo 098670
Serai, Zivar, Teheran 074849
Seraphico, Oscar, Rio de Janeiro . . 096648
Seraphin, Philadelphia 118832
Serapi, Dallas 088609
Serbal, Madrid 129686
Serbian Heritage Museum of Windsor, Windsor, Ontario 006831
Serbischer Kultur- und Kunstverein, Stuttgart 053562
Serbski muzej - Sorbisches Museum, Bautzen 015900
Serbski muzej/ Wendisches Museum, Stadtgeschichtliche Sammlungen Cottbus, Cottbus 016598
Serck, Ph., Gent 096299
Serdar, Nikolas, Paris 100858
Serebrjanyj Rjad, Moskva 080265
Serebrjanyj Vek, Sankt-Peterburg . . 080330
Serebrjanyj Vek, Sankt-Peterburg . . 109648
Šeremetevskij Dvorec - Fontannyj Dom, Sankt-Peterburgskij Muzej Teatralnogo i Musykalnogo Iskusstva, Sankt-Peterburg 033831
Seren, Bridgend 135123
The Serendib Gallery, Colombo 081769, 110897
Serendipity, Deal 084146, 130628
Serendipity, Den Haag 078247
Serendipity, Edmonton 096896
Serendipity, Ledbury 084923, 130869
Serendipity, Preston 056503
Serendipity, Richmond 092102
Serendipity, Wolsingham 114722
Serendipity Antique Shows, Fresno 088920
Serendipity Antiques, Haslemere . .084608, 130772
Serendipity Antiques, Newcastle . . 056332
Serendipity Books, Leederville 136972
Serendipity Collectibles, Las Vegas 089606
Serendipity Gallery, Katoomba 094684
Serendipity Gallery, Las Vegas 089607
Serendipity on Magnolia, Los Angeles 089906
Serengeti Museum, Arusha 037848
Sereni, Renato, Brescia 075184
Serenity Designs, Congleton 112899
Serero, Caroline, Marseille 099684
Sergačskij Kraevedčeskij Muzej, Sergač 033866
Sergei Parajanov Museum, Erevan . 000687
Sergej Borodin Muzej, Taškent 049411
Serger, Helen, New York 118405
Sergievo-Posadskij Gosudarstvennyj Istoriko- chudožestvennyj Muzej Zapovednik, Sergiev Posad 033869
Seri Art Center, Bangkok 112238
Serie och Skivhandel, Stockholm . . 141174
Serieboden, Stockholm 141175
Seriehörnan, Göteborg 141107
Serieknodden, Göteborg 141108
Seriemuseet Comicland, Ullared . . . 036727
Seriesalarna, Malmö 141133
Serieuze Zaken, Amsterdam 077966
Sérignan, Avignon 061141
Sérignan, Jean-Jacques, Avignon . 098902
Sérignan, Philippe, Avignon 138022
Seriko, Helsinki 060581
Serindia Publications, London 135262
Serini, Marcello, Madrid 129687
Serio, Salvatore, Napoli 106389
Seriously Riches Collectables, Christchurch 079052
La Serlas, Sankt Moritz 082792
Serlick, Howard, Philadelphia 132634
Sermon, E., Bruxelles 058085
Sermoneta, Emma, Bologna 139994
Serna, Paris 100859
Sernissi, Massimiliano, Firenze . . . 127413
S.E.R.O.D., Paris 124808
Seromenho, J., Paris 066543
Seron, Sylvain, Paris 066544
Seronera, Paris 100860
Serot, Quiberon 101055
Serota, Jodi, New York 118406
Seroussi, Natalie, Paris 100861
Serpa, Luis, Lisboa 109352
Serpent Mound Museum, Peebles . 046857
Serpenta, Gert & Juliane, Immenstaad 103427
Serpente, Porto 109397
Serpentine Gallery, Aix-en-Provence 098796
Serpentine Gallery, London 040286
Serpentine Vintage Tractors and Machinery Museum, Serpentine 001462
Serpentinsteinmuseum Zöblitz, Zöblitz 021075
Serpuchovskij Istoriko-chudožestvennyj Muzej, Serpuchov 033870
Serra, Christian, Figeac . . 062863, 138088
Serra, Valeria, Torino 128360
Serra, Yvette & Marie-Françoise, Perpignan 124839
Serra d Arquet, Barcelona 129404
Serra Museum, San Diego 047841
Serraire, Patrick, Paris 066545
Serrano, Madrid 081391
Serrano, Juan, Gijón 081128, 129521
Serrano Pombo, Jenaro, Madrid . . . 081392
Serrant, Pierre, Saint-André-de-l'Epine 067352
Serrao, Napoli 076050
Serrao, Napoli 076051
Serrão, Filipe Silva, Arcozelo 121917
Serrão, Filipe, Porto 121956
Serrão, Filipe Silva, Porto 121957
De Serre, Arnhem 107858
Serrell, Philip, Great Malvern 122528
Serrenho, Pedro, Lisboa 109353
Serres, Paris 066546
Serres, Michel & Noël, Lunel-Viel . . 064030
Serres, Robert, Toulouse 068543
Serret, Fabiani, Neuilly-sur-Seine . . 099823
Serret & Portier, Paris 066547
Serrurier, Jean-Luc, Sens 068219
Serrurier, Jean-Luc, Sens 068220
Serrurier, Pierre, Sens 068221
Tavares Seruca, Lisboa 080017
Servarts, Salle de Ventes au Palais des Beaux-Arts, Bruxelles 120742
Servarts Thémis, Bruxelles 120743
Servas, François, Darvault 124217
Serventi, André, Grenade 099298
Servera, Francisco, Palma de Mallorca 081497
Servet, Colette, Murat (Cantal) 064845
Servet, Colette, Murat (Cantal) 064846
Service Historique de la Police, Historische Dienst van der Politie, Bruxelles . 003359
Servicemaster, Wiesbaden 127017
Serviceton Historic Railway Station, Serviceton 001463
Servicio de Publicaciones, Murcia . 134951
Servientis, Rosine, Pauillac 066717
Servinantes, Nantes 064945
Il Servo di Scena, Milano 075865
Servoir, Le Puy-en-Velay . 063700, 124308
Sésame, Lyon 064184
Sesame Art, London 113880

Sesanne Taideliike, Helsinki 060582, 098743
Sese, Marie, Tilburg 078779
Sesma Garcia, Julian, Bilbao 129445
Sesquicentennial Museum, Toronto 006630
Sessantasei, Napoli 076052
Session Cottage Museum, Turriff . . 041248
Sestieri, Andrea e Lorenzo, Roma . . 076678
Šestka, Třebíč 098505
Set Alkol, Manama 096025
Setagaya-kuritsu Bijutsukan, Tokyo 027235
Setareh & Söhne, Essen 070647
Setareh, Los Angeles 089907
Setesdalsbanen Stiftelsen, Vennesla 031329
Setesdalsmuseet, Rysstad 031158
Seti Arte, Milano 106311
Setiawan, Singapore 080557
Seto Inland Sea Folk History Museum, Takamatsu 027106
Seto-shi Rekishi Minzoku Shiryokan, Seto 027056
Seton Centre, Carberry 005221
Seton Hall University Museum, South Orange 048247
Setor de Malacologia, Juiz de Fora . 004176
Setsuryosha Bijitsukan, Niigata . . . 026914
Settlers Hardware, Houston 089201
Settlers Museum, Brewarrina 000832
Settlers Museum, Himeville 034635
Settlers' Museum, Mahone Bay . . . 005819
Settlers Store Antiques, Mudgee . . 056300
Settlers West Galleries, Tucson . . . 120165
Settlers West Gallery, Tucson 120166, 143032
Setton, Michele, Saxonwold 110079
Settore Cultura e Spettacolo. Rassegna di Studi e di Notizie, Milano 135958
Setzer, Ortrud, München 104317
Seufert, Matthias, Bad Kissingen . . 069308
Seurasaaren Ulkomuseo, Helsinki . 009568
Sevan, Chicago 115549
Sevan Art Gallery Limited, Toronto . 097372
Sevas, Bucureşti 080171
Seven Art, Helsinki 098744
Seven Colors, New York 118407
Seven Hills Books, Cincinnati 135351
Seven Oaks House Museum, Winnipeg 006865
Seven Sanat Galerisi, İstanbul 112356
Seven Sisters Antiques, Lanceston South 056078
Sévene, Suresnes 068345
Sevenheck, Fiona, Kiel 103547
Sevenoaks Museum and Gallery, Sevenoaks 040987
Seventeen O Eight, Richmond 119123
Seventh Heaven, Chirk 083996
Seventh Inning, Buffalo 087908
Severance, Detroit 116095
Severin, Gisela & Peter, Friedberg, Hessen 070887
Séverine, Oriot, Honfleur 063169
Severn Valley Railway, Bewdley . . . 038694
Severo-Kavkazskij Gosudarstvennyj Institut Iskusstv, Nalčik 050649
Severo-osetinskij Gosudarstvennyj Obedinennyj Muzej Istorii, Architektury i Literatury, Vladikavkaz 034038
Severo-osetinskij Literaturnyj Muzej im. K.L. Četagurova, Vladikavkaz 034039
Severočeská Galerie Výtvarného Umění v Litoměřice, Litoměřice 008481
Severočeské Muzeum v Liberci, Liberec 008475
Sevestre, Pascal, Cabourg 061850
Sévigné, Cesson-Sévigné 062061
Sévigné, Saint-Jean-sur-Vilaine . . . 067550
Sevilla, Victor, Paris 100862
Sevilla Decoracion, Sevilla 081614
Seville Great House and Heritage Park, Ocho Rios 026396
Sevimce Sanat Galerisi, İstanbul . . 112357
Sevin, Edouard de, Paris 066548
Sevret, René, Charenton-du-Cher . . 062145
Sewall-Belmont House, Washington 048942
Seward County Historical Society Museum, Goehner 044228
Seward House, Auburn 041890
Seward Museum, Seward 048119
Sewer, Ernest, Susten 082840
Sewerby Hall Art Gallery and Museum, Museum of East Yorkshire, Bridlington 038837
Sexmuseum Amsterdam Venustempel, Amsterdam 029229
Sextius, Aix-en-Provence 098797
Sexton, Esther, Dublin 074946
Sexton, Robert, San Francisco 119787
Sexton's Cottage Museum, Crows Nest, New South Wales 000958
Seyed-Ghaemi, Shamsadin, Landshut 103828
Seyfarth, Caputh 070123, 125424
Seyfert, Gudrun, Stuttgart 105011
Seyfert, Gudrun, Stuttgart 105012
Seyfert, Karsten, Berlin 125299
Seyhoun, Nader, Teheran 105844
Seyitgazi Müzesi, Seyitgazi 038170
Seymour, Rutherglen 056560
Seymour, Vancouver 097529
Seymour, Jane, Morrinsville 079157
Seymour and District Historical Museum, Seymour 001464
Seymour Art Gallery, North Vancouver 006048
Seymour Community Museum, Seymour 048122
Seywald, Dr. Thomas, Salzburg . . .095736, 133151
Sezam, Beograd 109719, 140949
Sezione Arte, Dipartimento di Scienza della Letteratura e dell'Arte Medioevale e Moderna, Pavia 050406
Sezione di Archeologia del Dipartimento di Scienze dell' Antichità, Università di Padova, Padova 050401
Sezione di Etruscologia e Antichità Italiche, Roma 050432
Sezione di Storia dell'Arte, Università Genova, Genova 050378
Sezon Museum of Modern Art, Karuizawa 026630
Sezoni, Sofia 096746
SFA Galleries, Nacogdoches 046117
S.F.E, Saint-Lunaire 067596
De Sfeer van Weleer, Rekken 030054
Sfeervol Wonen, Breda 078116
Sfeir-Semler, Dr. Andrée, Hamburg . 103220
Sfez, Victor, Paris 100863
Sforzini, Roma 140120
SGA Antiquités, Fontenay-sous-Bois 062908
S'Galeriele, Göppingen 102971
Sgambati, Antonio, Modena 127745
Sgambato, Angelique, Kaufbeuren . 126022
Sganga, Giuseppina, Roma 076679
Sgarban, Giovanni, Milano 140064
Sgouros, Ioannis, Thessaloniki 105457
Sgroi, Massimo, Palermo 076181
S.H. Ervin Gallery, Sydney 001522
Shaanxi Chinese Painting Gallery, Xian 007318
Shaanxi History Museum, Xian 007319
Shaanxi People's Fine Arts Publishing House, Xian 133390
Shab, Toronto 059291
Shaban, Yousef, Alexandria 060423
Shabben, Los Angeles 116881
Shabby, Hattie, Tucson 093265
Shabtai, Bahar, New York 132531
Shackerstone Railway Museum, Shackerstone 040988
Shackleton, Anthony, David & Ann, Snainton 086630, 131505
Shadeland Antique Mall, Indianapolis 089339
Shades International, Milano 106312, 127685
Shades of Africa, Miami 117139
Shades of Afrika, Long Beach 116680
Shades of Age, Clayfield 055691
Shades of Color, Portland 119051
Shades of Midnight, Peterborough . 137047
Shades of the Past, Carbonear 005223
Shades of the Past, Philadelphia . . 091689
Shadi, Damascus 083081
Shadi Abdel Salam Museum, Bibliotheca Alexandria, Alexandria 009285
Shadowland, Richmond 142832
The Shadows-on-the-Teche, New Iberia 046236
Shaffer, Portland 119052
Shafrazi, Tony, New York 118408
Shaftesbury Abbey and Museum, Shaftesbury 040989
Shaftesbury Town Museum, Shaftesbury 040990
Shaftsbury Historical Society Museum, Shaftsbury 048124
Shah Alam Art Gallery, Shah Alam . 028016
Shah Charu, Dallas 115938
Shaheed-e-Azam Bhagat Singh Museum, Khatkar Kalan 022204
Al-Shahid, Dubai 112458
Shahinian, Zare, Damascus 083082
Shahnama, Mumbai 105805
Shahrastan Bros., Damascus 083083
Shahrood Museum, Semnan 022595
Shahryar Museum, Tabriz 022603
Shah's Arts Collection, Brighton, Victoria 055553
Shaik & Son, London 085686
Shaiké I am Art Snir, Caulfield South 055657
Shain, Charlotte 115311
Shainman, Jack, New York 118409
Shaka, Saint Louis 119251
Shakan, Lausanne 111632
Shake Rattle and Read Book Box, Chicago 142302
Shaker Art, Milwaukee 117220
Shaker Heritage Society Museum, Albany 041601
Shaker Historical Society Museum, Shaker Heights 048125
Shaker Museum, New Gloucester . . 046218
Shaker Museum, Old Chatham 046662
Shaker Museum, South Union 048252
Shaker Square Antiques, Cleveland 088360
Shaker Village of Pleasant Hill, Harrodsburg 044454
Shakespeare & Co., München 139546
Shakespeare Birthplace Trust, Stratford-upon-Avon 041143
Shakespeare's Globe Exhibition and Tour, London 040287
Shakey, Philadelphia 091690, 132635
Shakir Ali Museum, Lahore 031387
Shaklee, Calgary 058805, 123751
Al Shakma, Cairo 098671
Shakowi Cultural Center, Oneida . . 046689
Shakris, San Francisco 092882
Shakti Art Gallery, Mumbai 105806
Shalimar Palace, Dubai 038424
Shalom, Miami 132357
Shalom Aleichem Museum, Tel Aviv 023091
Shalom Construction &Co., Pittsburgh 132676
Shalovelo, Regina 123815
Shamal, Villeurbanne 068980
Shambala, Hong Kong 059691
Shambhala, Boston 135335
Shambhalla Librairie, Lyon 138185
The Shambles, Ashburton 083339
The Shambles, Hillsborough 113244
Shambles Antiques, Kendal 084828
Shambles Museum, Newent 040556
Shamburger, Richmond 092103
Shambyu Museum, Shambyu 029096
Shamian Gallery, Guangzhou 097726
Shammah, Suzy, Milano 106313
Shamrock and Cotehele Quay Museum, National Maritime Museum Outstation, Saint Dominick, Cornwall 040905
Shamrock Antiques, Wellington . . . 079347
Shamrock Museum, Shamrock 006446
Shamwari, Oakland 118647
Shan, Fenglin, Guangzhou 097727
Shan, Riyue, Shanghai 097941
Shan Bao Zhai Art Gallery, Shanghai 097942
Shan Rong Cultural Display Center, Beijing 007008
Shan State Museum, Taunggyi 029071
Shan Xi, Shanghai 059761
Shanahan, Kilkenny 074982
Shand Galleries, Toronto 059292
Shand House Museum, Windsor, Nova Scotia 006829
Shandong Fine Arts Publishing House, Jinan 133368
Shandong Literature and Art Publishing House, Jinan 133369
Shandong Painting Gallery, Jinan . . 007154
Shandong Provincial Museum, Jinan 007155
Shandong Stone Engraving Art Museum, Jinan 007156
Shands Antiques, Christchurch 079053
Shandy Hall, Coxwold 039161
Shandy Hall, Geneva 044167
Shaner, Mark, Denver 116049
Shanez, Monaco 107544
Shang, Singapore 129267
Shangai, Bogotá 059859
Shanghai Antiques and Curios Store, Shanghai 059762
Shanghai Art Fair, Shanghai 093633
Shanghai Arts and Crafts, Shanghai 097943
Shanghai Arts & Crafts, Singapore . 080558
Shanghai Calligraphy and Painting Publishing House, Shanghai 133378
Shanghai Corner, Los Angeles 089908
Shanghai Curio, Shanghai 059763
Shanghai Fine Arts Gallery, Singapore 109866
Shanghai Friendship Store, Shanghai 059764
Shanghai Friendship Store, Shanghai 059765
Shanghai History Museum, Shanghai 007240
Shanghai Literature and Art Publishing House, Shanghai 133379
Shanghai Luxun House, Shanghai . 007241
Shanghai Museum, Shanghai 007242
Shanghai Natural History Museum, Shanghai Science & Technology Museum, Shanghai 007243
Shanghai Oil Painting Sculptural Institute, Shanghai 097944
Shanghai People's Fine Arts Publishing House, Shanghai 133380
Shanghai Science & Technology Museum, Shanghai 007244
Shanghai West, Los Angeles 089909
Shanghai'd, Philadelphia 091691
Shanghaied, Richmond, Victoria . . . 056530
Shango, Dallas 115939
Shangrila Art, Lalitpur 107608
Shank, Baltimore 115084
Shankar, Jaipur, Rajasthan 105729
Shankar's International Dolls Museum, Delhi 022096
Shanklin Auction Rooms, Shanklin . 122695
Shanklin Gallery, Shanklin 114409, 131472, 142056
Shannon's Gallery, Apollo Bay 094156
Shans, New York 091237
Shantala, Paris 066549
Shantou Archaeology Museum, Shantou 007249
Shantytown, West-Coast-Living Heritage, Greymouth 030507
Shanxi, Villeurbanne 068981
Shanxi Painting Gallery, Taiyuan . . . 007279
Shanxi Photographic Press, Xian . . 133391
Shaper, Zammie, Parramatta 056444
Shapero, London . 085687, 113881, 131169
Shapero, Bernard J., London 141892
Shapes Collection, West Hollywood 093508
Shapiro, Johannesburg 080714
Shapiro, San Francisco 119788

Shapiro, Estela, México 107513
Shapiro, Richard, West Hollywood . 093509
Shapiro Auctioneers, Armadale, Victoria 120561
Shapolsky, Anita, New York 118410
Sharadin Art Gallery, Kutztown 045051
Sharalan, Calgary 058806, 123752
Shardlow Antiques Warehouse, Shardlow 086549
Sharia Museum, Cairo 009324
Sharif, Manama 096026
Sharikat Kamsis Commercial Enterprise, Penang 077504
Sharjah Antiques, Sharjah 083224
Sharjah Archaeology Museum, Sharjah 038430
Sharjah Art Centre, Sharjah 050798
Sharjah Art Museum, Sharjah 038431
Sharjah Art Production, Sharjah . . . 112470
Sharjah Heritage Museum, Sharjah 038432
Sharjah International Art Biennial, Sharjah 093902
Sharjah Islamic Museum, Sharjah . 038433
Sharjah Natural History Museum, Sharjah 038434
Sharjah Science Museum, Sharjah . 038435
Al-Shark, Cairo 060473
Sharland & Lewis, Tetbury 086865
Sharlot Hall Museum, Prescott 047226
Sharon Arts Center, Sharon 048127
Sharon Museum, Emek Hefer 022908
Sharon Museum Emek Hefer, Midreshet Ruppin 023031
Sharon Temple Historic Site, Sharon 006447
Sharonville Coin, Cincinnati 088280
Sharp, Ian, Tynemouth 086974
Sharp Artists, Glasgow 113130
Sharp Artists, Uddington 114622
Sharp Edge, Paris 100864
Sharp Gallery, New York 118411
Sharp Shooter Studios, West Hollywood 120412
Sharp Street Glass, Philadelphia . . . 118833
Sharpe, Bellevue Hill 055469
Sharpe Selections, Saint Louis 092311
Sharpsteen Museum, Calistoga . . . 042551
Al-Sharq, Damascus 083084
Sharrington Antiques, Sharrington . 086550
Sharry, Buffalo 087909, 131863
Shasmoukine, Pierre, Sarlat-la-Canéda 101259
Shasta College Museum, Redding . 047358
Shaston Antiques, Shaftesbury 086546, 131470
Shaughnessy, Minneapolis 132391
Shaughnessy Antique, Vancouver . . 059415
Shaukat, Dubai 112459
Shaw, Goulburn 055910
Shaw &Co., Jack, Ilkley 084788
Shaw, Lawrence, Horncastle 084740
Shaw, Nicholas, Billingshurst 083516
Shaw, Nicholas, Petworth 086262
Shaw, Trish, Christchurch 108412
Shaw, Walter F., Phoenix 132655
Shaw a Park III, Albuquerque 087425, 131749
Shaw Island Historical Society Museum, Shaw Island 048131
Shaw & Zok, Bonn 102198
Shawano County Museum, Shawanao 048132
Shawbrook, Benalla 055474
Shawn Dulaney, New York 118412
Shawneetown Historic Site, Old Shawneetown 046665
Shawnigan Lake Historical Museum, Shawnigan Lake 006451
Shawqi Museum, Cairo 009325
Shaw's Corner, Ayot-Saint-Lawrence 038557
Shay, Robert, Saint Louis . 092312, 132753
Shazar, Maité, Lausanne 130076
Sha'Zeez, Las Vegas 116646
Shearburn, William, Saint Louis . . . 119252
Shearwater Aviation Museum, Shearwater 006452
Sheather, Willy, Wagga Wagga 095367
Sheba, Cairo 098672
Sheba, New York 091238, 132532
Sheboygan County Historical Museum, Sheboygan 048137
The Shed, Coatesville 079075
Shed im Eisenwerk, Ausstellungsraum für zeitgenössische Kunst, Frauenfeld 037093
Shedhalle-Rote Fabrik, Zürich 037799
Shedhalle Sankt Pölten, Sankt Pölten 002620
Shee Alms House, Kilkenny 022806
Sheeba, Sharjah 083225
Sheehan, Portland 132702
Sheehan, Kevin, Tetbury 131583
Sheehan, Steve, Bunbury 094325
Sheehan, Susan, New York 118413
Sheehan Gallery at Whitman College, Walla Walla 048835
Sheen, New York 118414
Sheen, Max, Hong Kong 059692
Sheen Gallery, London 113882
Sheffield, E., Genève 082468
Sheffield Antiques Emporium, Sheffield 086566, 131478, 142064
Sheffield Bus Museum, Sheffield . . 041000
Sheffield City Museum and Mappin Art Gallery, Sheffield 041001
Shefton Museum of Greek Art and Archaeology, Newcastle-upon-Tyne 040553
Shehady, Pittsburgh 091858
Shehail, Abdullah Ali, Sharjah 083226
Sheikan Museum, Sudan National Museum, El-Obeid 036145
Sheikh Saeed's House, Dubai 038425
Sheila's Gallery, Singapore 080559
Sheker, Gus, Denver 132044
Shekhtman, Irene, New York 132533
Shelburne County Museum, Shelburne 006456
Shelburne Museum, Shelburne 048140
Shelby, Portland 092006
The Sheldon Art Museum, Middlebury 045833
Sheldon Fish Fine Arts, New York . .118415, 123012
Sheldon Jackson Museum, Sitka . . 048197
Sheldon Jaffery, Cleveland 142343
Sheldon Memorial Art Gallery and Sculpture Garden, Lincoln 045311
Sheldon Museum, Haines 044389
Sheldon Peck Museum, Lombard . . 045369
Shell House Gallery, Ledbury 113361
Shell Lake Museum, Shell Lake . . . 006457
Shelley, Yass 056904
Shelley, Julian, Aberystwyth 141382
Shellin Antiques and Irish Lace Museum, Enniskillen 039450
Shelter House, Emmaus 043701
Shelter Island Historical Society Museum, Shelter Island 048146
Shem-Tov Shani, Barcelona 110252
Shen, Chen, Singapore 080560
Shenandoah Valley Folk Art and Heritage Center, Dayton 043327
Shenchang, Hangzhou 059583
Sheng Kun, Shanghai 059766
Shengjing Hua Yuan, Shenyang . . . 097968
Shenlong, Wuxi 098044
Shenn, Singapore 109867
Shenshu-Bunko Museum, Tokyo . . . 027236
Shenton, Rita, Twickenham 086968, 142131
Shenton Park Antiques, Shenton Park 056588
Shenyang Art Society- Hua Yuan, Shenyang 052801, 097969
Shenyang Palace Museum, Shenyang 007257
Shenzhen Art Gallery, Shenzhen . . . 007262
Shenzhen Museum, Shenzhen 007263
Shenzhen Painting Gallery, Shenzhen 007264
Shepard, Joel, Seattle 132943
Shepard, Paul S., Tucson 093266
Sheperd & Derom, New York 118416
Shephela Museum, Kibbutz Kfar Menahem 023009
Shepherd, New York 132534
Shepherd, Peter, Hurst . . . 084775, 141684
Shepherd Wheel, Sheffield 041002
Shepherdson, Andrew, Sorell 056601
Sheppard Fine Arts Gallery, University of Nevada, Reno, Reno 047374
Sheppard & Son, C.B., Sutton-in-Ashfield 122717
Sheppard Street Antiques, Richmond 092104
Shepparton Art Gallery, Shepparton 001466
Sheppee, William, Salisbury 086497
Sheppy's Farm and Cider Museum, Bradford-on-Tone 038811
Shepton, Denver 088736
Shepton Mallet Antiques and Collectors Fair, Shepton Mallet 093952
Shepton Mallet Museum, Shepton Mallet 041005
Sher, Miami 117140
Sheraton House, Torquay 086902
Sherborne Castle, Sherborne 041006
Sherborne Museum, Sherborne . . . 041007
Sherborne World of Antiques, Sherborne 086582, 131486
Sherbrooke Art Society, Belgrave . .052491, 094234
Sherbrooke Village, Sherbrooke, Nova Scotia 006458
Sherburne County Historical Museum, Becker 042093
Shere Antiques Centre, Shere 086588
Sheridan, Ian, Hampton 141641
Sheridan, Keith, New York 091239
Sheridan Brown, Hawthorn, Victoria 055967
Sheringham Museum, Sheringham . 041010
Sherlock Holmes Museum, London 040288
Sherlock Holmes-Museum, Meiringen 037322
Sherm, Sacramento 132739
Sherman, Los Angeles 132280
Sherman, Barry, Prahran 056500
Sherman Galleries, Paddington . . . 095040
Sherman Galleries, Paddington . . . 095041
Sherman House, Lancaster 045142
Sherrier Resources Centre, Lutterworth 040360
Sherry, Houston 089202
Sherry, Kelly, Houston 089203
Sherry's Antiques, Salt Lake City . . 092462
Sherwood, Houston 116402
Sherwood, Anthony, Ashgrove 055412
Sherwood, D.W., Rushden 086418
Sherwood-Davidson House, Newark 046430
Sherwood Forest Plantation, Charles City 042719
Shetland Croft House Museum, Dunrossnes 039325
Shetland Museum, Lerwick 039988
Shettler, Gavin, Portland 119053
Sheung Yiu Folk Museum, Hong Kong 007133
Shevlin, Toronto 097373
Shewen Art Cooperative, Shanghai . 097945
Sheyenne Valley Arts & Crafts Association, Fort Ransom 055031
Shfela Museum, Kibbutz Kfar Menahem 023010
Shi Liao Display Center, Nanjing . . . 007208
Shibayama, Tokyo 107104
Shibayama Haniwa Hakubutsukan, Shibayama 027058
Shibden Hall Museum, West Yorkshire Folk Museum, Halifax 039665
Shibunkaku, Kyoto 077124
Shibunkaku, Kyoto 140164
Shibunkaku Bijutsu, Tokyo 077304, 140200
Shibunkaku Museum of Art, Kyoto . 026770
Shicheng County Museum, Ganzhou 007079
Shickman, H., New York 118417
Shido-dera Treasure House, Shido . 027060
Shido-ji Homotsukan, Shido 027061
Shield, Richmond 092105
Shield, Robin, Swinstead 086818
Shieling, Harrogate 084587
Shiell, Miriam, Toronto 097374
Shifara Kunsti-ja Antiigigalerii, Tallinn 060489
Shifflett, Los Angeles 116882
Shifrin, Judy, Cleveland 115739
Shiga-kenritsu Kindai Bijutsukan, Otsu 026999
Shiga-kenritsu Omi Fudoki-No-Oka Shiryokan, Azuchi 026432
Shigaraki-yaki Pottery Museum, Koga 026678
Shige, San Francisco 092883
Shigeki Komori Atelier, Gifu 106850
Shigihara-Goede, S., Bonn 069943
Shihezi Junken Museum, Shihezi . . 007266
Shijiazhuang City Museum, Shijiazhuang 007268
Shiki, Kobe 106885
Shiki, Tokyo 107105
Shikoku Minka Hakubutsukan, Takamatsu 027107
Shiling Art, Guangzhou 097728
Shilla, Daegu 107191
Shillong Tribal Research Institute, Shillong 022334
Shiloh Museum of Ozark History, Springdale 048280
Shiloh National Military Park and Cemetery, Shiloh 048153
Shilpi Kendra, Mumbai 105807
Shima Marineland, Ago 026402
Shimamoto, Tokyo 077305
Shimane Daigaku Hobungakubu Kokogaku Kenkyushitsu-nai, Matsue 026786
Shimane-kenritsu Hakubutsukan, Matsue 026787
Shimane Prefectural Yakumodatsu Fudoki No Oka History Hall, Matsue 026788
Shimazu Foundation Memorial Hall, Kyoto 026771
Shimeru, Bairnsdale 094192
Shimizu, Tokyo 077306
Shimizu, Yokohama 107152
Shimoda Marine Biological Station, Kamo, Izu 026618
Shimonoseki City Art Museum, Shimonoseki 027068
Shimosuwa Museum, Shimosuwa . 027070
Shin-Yokohama Ramen Hakubutsukan, Yokohama 027336
Shinagawa Historical Museum, Tokyo 027237
Shinano Drawing Museum, Ueda . . 027301
Shinanobashi Gallery, Osaka 106972
Shinchon Museum, Shinchon 027442
Shindler, Hutt City 121827
Shine, Nelson 108519
Shine Gallery, London 113883
Shiners, Snobs Knobs, Jesmond . . 084815
Shing, Singapore 080561
Shing, Singapore 109868
Shingen-Ko Treasure House, Enzan 026452
Shinko, Kobe 077084
Shinn, Catherine, Cheltenham 083929, 130543
Shinobazu, Tokyo 107106
Shinsegae Gana Art, Seoul 107291
Shinseidoo-Hatanaka, Tokyo 107107
Shinseisha, Osaka 077183
Shinshu-shinmachi Art Museum, Shinshiyuushin 027071
Shinuiju Historical Museum, Shinuiju 027443
Shinwa, Tokyo 121747
Shiny Things Collectables, Oxenford 056414
Shinyanga Mazingira Museum, Shinyanga 037858
Shinyoung Cinema Museum, Namwon 027535
Shio-no-michi Hakabutsukan, Itoigawa 026583

Shiogama Shrine Museum, Shiogami 027072
Shiota, T.Z., San Francisco 092884, 119789
Shiozawa Tsumugi Commemorative Museum, Shiozawa 027075
Ship Model Gallery of New York, New York 091240
Ship to Shore, Vancouver 059416
Shipahoy, Killarney 056051
Shipley, London 141893
Shipley Art Gallery, Gateshead 039537
Shipley Gallery, Blackheath 094257
Shippensburg Historical Society Museum, Shippensburg 048156
Ships of the Sea Maritime Museum, Savannah 048030
Shipshapes Maritime Prints, Thornton Hough 114573
The Shipwreck, Brightlingsea 083680
Shipwreck Heritage Centre, Hastings 039694
Shipwreck Museum, Bredasdorp . . 034568
Shipwreck Museum, Cairns 000875
Shirahata Shiro World Mountains Photograph Collection, Yuzawa . . 027356
Shirakawadai Shoten, Kobe 140160
Shirane Memorial Museum, Tokyo . 027238
Shiraz, Tampa 093153
Shiraz Persian Rug Gallery, Goodwood 055896, 123231
Shire, Alnwick 112497
Shire, Princes Risborough 135298
Shire, Andrew, Los Angeles 116883
Shire Hall Gallery, Stafford 041083
Shire of Landsborough Historical Society, Landsborough 001171
Shire of Wondai Museum, Wondai . 001628
Shirehall Museum, Little Walsingham 040023
Shiretoko Museum, Shari 027057
Shirley-Eustis House, Boston 042343
Shirley Plantation, Charles City 042720
Shirley's Antiquitäten, Neuenstadt . 072986
Shiromatsu, Sendai 107004
Shirota, Tokyo 107108
Shiseido, Tokyo 107109
Shiseido Art House, Kakegawa 026607
Shisha Art, Wiesbaden 105281
Shishi Kaikan, Takayama 027126
Shishu, Chengdu 097701
Shishu, Guangzhou 097729
Shitamachi Museum, Tokyo 027239
Shizuoka City Toro Museum, Shizuoka 027081
Shizuoka-kenritsu Bijutsukan, Shizuoka 027082
Shkodër Museum, Shkodër 000032
SHM Smith Hodgkinson, Chorley . . 122466
Sho, Tokyo 107110
Sho Art, Tokyo 107111
Shoal Creek Gallery, Austin 115010
Shoal Creek Living History Museum, Kansas City 044927
Shoalhaven Art Gallery, Old Erowal Bay 095003
Shobhana, Bangalore 074783
Shodo Hakubutsukan, Tokyo 027240
Shoe Museum, Street 041148
Shofi-Hollowell, Sylvia, Tampa 120068
Shogun's Gallery, Portland 092007
Shohada Museum, Ghazvin 022553
Shohten, Inami, Tokyo 077307
Shoji Ueda Museum of Photography, Kishimoto 026655
Shojudo, Tokyo 077308
Shoko Shuseikan Historical Museum, Kagoshima 026606
Shokokan Museum, Mito 026820
Shokokuji Jotenkaku Museum, Kyoto 026772
Sholem Asch House, Bat Yam 022895
Al Shomou Art Gallery, Cairo 098673
The Shooting Gallery, San Francisco 119790
Shooting Star Art Gallery, New Orleans 117511
Shop Front Antiques and Restoration, Chicago 088168, 131916
Le Shoppe, Oklahoma City 091535
Shore Galleries, Chicago 122846
Shore Line Trolley Museum, East Haven 043571
Shore Road Pumping Station, Birkenhead 038715
Shore Village Museum, Rockland . . 047505
Shoreham Aircraft Museum, Shoreham 041014
Shoreham Airport Historical Exhibition, Shoreham-by-Sea 041016
Shoreline Historical Museum, Seattle 048093
Shoreline Studio, Aberdour 112482
Shoreman, Taipei 098082
Shoren-in Treasure House, Kyoto . . 026773
Shores, Ken, Portland 092008
Shores Space, Amsterdam 107796
Shorewood Coins, Milwaukee 090322
Shorey & Co., Kevin, Cairns 055602
Short, C., Great Torrington 084524
Short North Gallery, Columbus 115800
The Short Poppy, Wellington 079348
Shorter Mansion Museum, Eufaula . 043740
Shortmead Antiques, Biggleswade . 083512
Shoshone Tribal Cultural Center, Fort Washakie 043990
Shosoin Treasure Repository, Nara . 026899
The Shoto Museum of Art, Tokyo . . 027241
Shotton, J., Durham 141562
Shotts Heritage Centre, Shotts 041017
Shoun, Nara 106944
Shout!, Singapore 080562
Show Gallery, Toronto 006631
Show of Hands, Denver 116050
Show Off New Zealand, Raglan . . . 108549
Showcase, Las Vegas 089608
Showcase, Richmond 092106
Showcase Antiques, Randwick 056519
Showcase Antiques Art, Dubai 083202
Showplace Gallery, Houston 089204
Showroom, Chicago 115550
Showroom, Montréal 059005
SHP Special Historical Products, Düsseldorf 070441
Shreemanthi Bai Memorial Government Museum, Mangalore 022254
Shreve, Crump & Low, Boston 087844
Shreves, New York 123013
Shrewsbury Antique Centre, Shrewsbury 086608
Shrewsbury Antique Market, Shrewsbury 086609
Shrewsbury Castle, Shrewsbury . . . 041022
Shrewsbury Museum and Art Gallery, Shrewsbury 041023
Shrewsbury Windle House, Madison 045581
Shri Chhatrapati Shivaji Maharaj Museum, Satara 022329
Shri Girdharbhai Sangrahalaya, Amreli 022008
Shrikrishna Science Centre, Patna . 022295
Shrine of the Book, Israel Museum, Jerusalem 022979
Shrishti, Delhi 105683
Shrishti, Hyderabad 105713
Shrishti Art Gallery, Lucknow 105748
Shropshire Regimental Museum, Shrewsbury 041024
Shrubsole, S.J., New York 091241
Shtekelis Prehistory Museum, Haifa 022929
Shua Quan, Beijing 097677
The Shudehill Book Center, Manchester 141940
Shufunotomo, Tokyo 134732
Shugborough Estate Museum, Milford, Staffordshire 040466
Shugoarts, Tokyo 107112
Shugu, Shanghai 059767
Shumpudo, Tokyo 107113
Shumway, George, York 135526
Shun Da, Qingdao 097895
Shungeng, Jinan 097862
Shunyam, Amsterdam 107797
Shutter Door Antiques, Virginia Beach 093365
Shuttleworth Collection, Old Warden 040639
Shuttleworths, Scarborough 086523
Shwan, Saint-Malo (Ille-et-Vilaine) . 101176
Shyam Art, Kathmandu 107599
Si, Bao Zhai, Singapore 109869
Si-Am Trading, Hong Kong 097830
Si-Art, Windsor 114711
Si Como No, San Antonio 119453
Si Salon, Wellington 030652
S.I.Ag., Firenze 106071
Siag, Mona, Cairo 060474
Siagne, Saint-Cezaire-sur-Siagne . . 067396
The Siam Gallery, Plymouth 114264
Siam Gems Center, Paris 066550
SIAM- Société Internationale Art Moderne, Paris 100865
The Siam Society under Royal Patronage, Bangkok 054243, 112239
Siano, Philadelphia 118834
Siatista Botanical Museum, Siatista 021464
Šiauliai Aušros Museum, Šiauliai . . 027858
Siaulio, Alfonso, Vilnius 128462
Sibbel, Knut, Paris 066551, 100866
Sibbesgården, Sipoo 010080
Sibbo Jordbruksmuseum, Sipoo . . . 010081
Sibeliuksen Syntymäkoti, Hämeenlinna 009495
Sibelius Museum, Turku 010169
Sibenaler, Jean-Claude, Bondy 061556
Sibenaler, Jean-Claude, Noisy-le-Sec 065224
Sibley, Landshut 072148
Sibley, Rosenheim 073575
Sibley County Historical Museum, Henderson 044508
Sibley Historic Site, Mendota 045774
Sibman Gallery, Paris 100867
Siboney, Santander 110752
Siboni, Mabille & Vankemmel, Sceaux 121257
Sibony, Ariel, Paris 100868
Sibrium, Milano 140065
Sibsagar College Museum, Hiranya Probha Memorial Library and Museum, Sibsagar 022339
Sicamous and District Museum, Sicamous 006467
Sicard, Christian, Saint-Julien-de-Peyrolas 067556
Sicardi, Houston 116403
Sicare, Auxonne 098885
Sichert, Georg, Laufen, Salzach . . . 139383
Sichuan Fine Arts Institute, Chongqing 049847
Sichuan Fine Arts Publishing House, Chengdu 133345
Sichuan Museum, Chengdu 007044
Sichuan University Museum, Chengdu 007045
Sicolo, Luigi, Milano 127686
Sicot, Jacky, Salon-de-Provence . . 068103
Siculan, Mike, Saint Louis 092313
Sicurani, Ajaccio 060741, 124063
Sid Richardson Collection of Western Art, Fort Worth 044014
Sidac, Leiden 108106
Side Door Antiques, Tulsa 093329, 133003
Side Door Antiques, Winnipeg 059471
Side Müzesi, Side 038171
Side Roads Publications, Miami . . . 117141
Side Roads Publications, Miami . . . 135393
Side Street Projects, Los Angeles . . 045461
Sidelines Gallery, Watchet 114652
Sidenstein, Anna Marianne, Düshorn 102467
Sidenväveri Museum, Stockholm . . 036662
Sidewalk Gallery, Battery Point 094221
Sidmouth Antiques Centre, Sidmouth 086618, 142071
Sidmouth Museum, Sidmouth 041027
Sidney and Gertrude Zack Gallery, Vancouver 006709
Sidney Historical Association Museum, Sidney 048173
Sidney Historical Museum, Society of Saanich Peninsula Museums, Sidney 006469
Sidney Lanier Cottage, Middle Georgia Historical Society, Macon 045569
Sidney Marine Museum, Society of Saanich Peninsula Museums, Sidney 006470
Sidney Mishkin Gallery of Baruch College, New York 046400
Sidoti, Salvatore, Palermo 106445
Sidra, Manama 096027
Sidvik Collections, Bangalore 105614
Sié, Henri, Saint-Tropez 101234
Siebel, Kurt, Siegen 104901
Sieben-Keltern-Museum, Metzingen 018929
Sieben-Schwaben-Museum, Türkheim 020505
Siebenberg House, Jerusalem 022980
Siebenberg-Verlag, Waldeck, Hessen 134447
Siebenbürgisches Museum Gundelsheim, Gundelsheim, Württemberg 017605
Siebengebirge & Zeuthen, Wünsdorf 139866
Siebengebirgsbuchhandlung, Bonn . 138910
Siebengebirgsmuseum, Königswinter 018358
Das Siebente Zimmer, Hamburg . . . 071331
Siebenthal, Anna, Crans-sur-Sierre 082335, 111375
Sieber, Bruno, Luzern 111705, 130108
Siebers, Yves, Stuttgart 121609
Siebert, Fritz, Frankfurt am Main . .070791, 102826, 125662
Siebert, Petra, Ratingen 073432
Siebert, Ulrich, Wettenberg 074378
Siebert-Singh, Bad Sooden-Allendorf 101705
Siebler, Mike, Püttlingen 104641
Sieblos-Museum Poppenhausen, Paläontologisch-geologisches Museum, Poppenhausen, Wasserkuppe . . . 019649
Siebold Memorial Museum, Nagasaki 026875
Siebold-Museum, Würzburg 021008
Siebolts, Maria, Oberhaching 073141
Siebrecht, A., Westerstede 074375
Siedler, Georg-Wilhelm, Wien 057550
Siedow, Fred, Portland 132703
Siedow, Fred, Portland 132704
Siefert, Ronald, Buskirk 122832
Sieff, Simon, Tetbury 086866
Siegburger Kunst- und Auktionshaus, Siegburg 073809, 121599
Siege Museum, Petersburg 046909
Siegel, Allan, Pittsburgh 132677
Siegel, Eliot, London 113884
Siegel, Evelyn, Fort Worth 116163
Siegel, Robert, New York 123014
Siegelmuseum Schloß Waldenburg, Waldenburg, Württemberg 020639
Siegemund, Reichartshausen 073473
Siegerlandmuseum mit Ausstellungsforum Haus Oranienstraße, Siegen 020201
Siegert, Hans-Jürgen, Basel 134987
Siegert, O.W., München 126461
Siegfried Charoux-Museum, Langenzersdorf 002203
Siegfried H. Horn Archaeological Museum, Berrien Springs 042172
Siegle, Franz, Mühlhausen, Kraichgau 139490
Siegler, Joseph, Pézenas 066811
Siegmayer, H., Seeheim-Jugenheim 073787
Siegmayer, Thomas, Bad Windsheim 069398
Siekerman, R.P., Amsterdam 128553
Siekkötter, Marie, Bad Mergentheim 069328
Sieler, Andreas, Gera 125719
Sielhafenmuseum der niedersächsischen Nordseeküste, Wittmund 020932

Sielmuseum der Hamburger Stadtentwässerung, Hamburg . . . 017721
Siemandel-Feldmann, Herbert, Essen . . . 102707
Siemens-Forum in Berlin, Berlin . . . 016172
SiemensForum, München . . . 019112
Siemer, Bischofszell . . . 111297
Siemer, Bischofszell . . . 111298
Siemer, Bischofszell . . . 135001
Siemers, Rüde . . . 073616
Siemers, Petra, Bad Fallingbostel . . 069282
Siemon, K.& M., Homberg, Efze . . . 071575
Siempre Viva Art, Denver . . . 116051
Sień Biała Galeria Sztuki, Gdańsk . . 108897
Sień Mała Galeria, Gdańsk . . . 108898
Siena, Salamanca . . . 081545, 129716
Siena, Zaragoza . . . 129830
Sienna, Pamela, Boston . . . 115230
Siennes, Paris . . . 124809
Siepmann, Markus, Essen . . . 070648
Siepmann, Markus, Essen . . . 070649
Siera, B.M., Sleeuwijk . . . 128833
Sieracki, Baltimore . . . 087710
Sierantuur, Rotterdam . . . 078744
Sierra, Amparo, Bogotá . . . 098192
Sierra, Dolores de, Madrid . . . 110613
Sierra Arts Foundation, Reno . . . 047375
Sierra Colina, Fernando de la, Barcelona . . . 129405
Sierra Colours, Nashville . . . 117371
Sierra Leone National Museum, Freetown . . . 034288
Sierra Pastel Society, Placerville . . 055032
Sierro Sánchez, Alvaro, Santiago de Chile . . . 123883
Sies & Höke, Düsseldorf . . . 102555
Sieso, Laurent, Hindisheim 063157, 124261
Siete Revueltas, Sevilla . . . 081615
Sieur, Pierre, Paris . . . 138542
Sievert, Hans-Jörg, Gmund . . . 071017
Sievi, Brigitte, Berlin . . . 102045
Sievin Kotiseutumuseo, Sievi . . . 010075
Siewert, Uta, Bad Bevensen . . . 069267
Sifang Buyun Xuan, Qingdao . . . 097896
Sigalas, Olaf, Hildrizhausen . . . 121457
La Sigalière, Civray . . . 062310
De Sigarenfabriek, Delft . . . 107893
Sigaroudinia, Parvis, Lisburn . . . 085008
Sigdal og Eggedal Museum, Prestfoss . . . 031126
Siggebohyttans Bergmansgård, Nora . . . 036495
Sigi's Antiquitäten, Staad . 082828, 130184
Sigle, New Orleans . . . 090622
Siglhaus, Sankt Georgen bei Salzburg . . . 002583
El Siglo XX, Barcelona . . . 141005
Sigma, Zutphen . . . 140580
Sigma Antiques and Fine Art, Ripon 086380, 131419
Sigmund Freud-Museum, Wien . . . 003005
Sign, Groningen . . . 108048
Sign of the Times, Wellington . . . 079349
Sign Today, New Orleans . . . 117512
Signal 66, Washington . . . 120347
Signal Art Centre, Bray . . . 105850
Signal Gallery, Auckland . . . 108361
Signal Hill Gallery, Weyburn . . . 006802
Signal Hill National Historic Site, Saint John's . . . 006373
Signatur, Aachen . . . 069101
Signatur, Remagen . . . 135821
Signature Arts, Saint Louis . . . 119253
Signature Gallery, Atlanta . . . 114924
Signature Gallery, Boston . . . 115231
Signature Gallery, Saint Paul . . . 119313
The Signature Gallery, Swansea . . . 114536
Signatures Gallery, London . . . 113885
Signed Sealed Delivered, Houston . 142445
Signet, Praha . . . 137845
Significant Books, Cincinnati . . . 142323
Signman, Indianapolis . . . 116493
Signorello, Salvatore, Havixbeck . . 125891
Signorini, Alberto, Milano . . . 075866
Signorini, Erminio, Verona . . . 128439
Signorini, Mariarita Anna, Firenze . . 127414
Signs by George, El Paso . . . 116117
Signs Now, Miami . . . 117142
Signs Now, Omaha . . . 118723
Signs of Significance, Toronto . . . 097375
Signstore, Sacramento . . . 119160, 142849
Signum Antiquariat, Margit, Königstein im Taunus . . . 139360
Sigogne & Ko, Paris . . . 066552
Sigoloff, San Antonio . . . 119454
Sigrid, Paris . . . 066553
Sigtuna Museer, Sigtuna . . . 036566
Sigtuna Rådhus, Sigtuna . . . 036567
Sigui, Angers . . . 098831
Sigurhaedir - Hús Skáldsins Museum, Literary Museum, Akureyri . . . 021934
Sigwart, Klaus, Hüfingen . . . 125966
Sigynn, Bertram, Lüneburg . . . 103982
Siikaisten Kotiseutumuseo, Siikainen . . . 010076
Siivari, T., Siilinjärvi . . . 137988
Sijben, Bert, Amsterdam . . . 107798
Sika, Los Angeles . . . 116884
Sika Galerie, Liberec . . . 060044
Sikander, Torino . . . 076870
Sikar Museum, Sikar . . . 022340
Sikes, Bobby, Atlanta . . . 114925
Sikinos Archeological Collection, Sikinos . . . 021467
Sikkema, Brent, New York . . . 118418
Sikkens Schildersmuseum, Sassenheim . . . 030122
Sikoronja, Marija, Rosegg . . . 095711
Sikorska, Jadwiga, Warszawa . . . 140796
Sikorski, Gdańsk . . . 108899
Siksika Nation Museum, Siksika . . 006472
Silas Wright Jr. Historic House, Canton . . . 042604
Silax, Havlíčkův Brod . . . 060017
Silbag, Littau . . . 130084
Silber, Jakub, Hradec Králové . . . 123959
Silberberg, Dr. Helmut K., Tulbagh .080750, 110081
Silberberg, Nathan, New York . . . 118419
Silberbergwerk, Ramingstein . . . 002495
Silbereisenbergwerk Gleißinger Fels, Fichtelberg . . . 017118
Silberfund, Hildesheim . . . 071525
Silberman, Fred, New York . . . 091242
Silberman, Jane W., Dallas . . . 088610
Silbernagl, Volker Erwin, Milano . . . 106314
Silbernberg, Drs. Ph.M., Amsterdam 077967
Silbersack, Wolfgang, Würzburg . . . 127042
Silberstein, Claude, Paris . . . 066554
Silberstollen Geising, Geising . . . 017343
Silberwaren- und Bijouteriemuseum, Ott-Pausersche Fabrik, Schwäbisch Gmünd . . . 020112
Silcher-Museum Schnait, Weinstadt 020768
Síldarminjasafnid a Siglufirdi, Siglufjörður . . . 021980
Silex Ediciones, Madrid . . . 134949
Silgjerd, Stavanger . . . 121878
Silhouette Antiques, New York . . . 091243
Silhouette Antiques, Seattle . . . 093064
Siliato, Pasquale, Roma . . . 128203
Silicon Pulp Gallery, Stanmore . . . 095220
Silicon Valley Clock Repair, San Jose . . . 132925
Silifke Müzesi, Silifke . . . 038173
Siliman University Anthropology Museum, Dumaguete . . . 031670
Silio, Fernando, Santander . . . 110753
Silipo, Assunta, Reggio Calabria . . . 127900
Silis, Fuenlabrada . . . 081109
Siljansfors Skogsmuseum, Mora . . 036484
Siljustøl Museum, Edvard Grieg Museum, Paradis . . . 031121
Silk Hakubutsukan, Yokohama . . . 027337
Silk Museum, Gangnae . . . 027485
Silk Museum, Soufli . . . 021472
Silk 'n Crafts, Manama . . . 057647
Silk Road, Nashville . . . 090486
The Silk Road, Roma . . . 076680
Silk Road Collection, New Orleans . 090623
Silk Road Textiles, Kathmandu . . . 077706
Silk Top Hat Gallery, Ludlow . . . 114006
Silk Winds, Honolulu . . . 088978
Silkeborg Kulturhistoriske Museum, Silkeborg . . . 009090
Silkeborg Kunstmuseum, Silkeborg 009091
Silken Tent, Braidwood . . . 094277
The Silky Oak Shop, Woolloongabba 056887
Silla University Museum, Busan . . . 027462
Sillack, Manto & Angelika, Dresden 102458
Sillage, Lyon . . . 064185
Siller, Klaus, Ludwigshafen am Rhein . . . 126236
Silly Galah Gallery, Meadows . . . 094800
Silly Renaud, Josnes . . . 063251
Silme, Roma . . . 076681
Siloam Springs Museum, Siloam Springs . . . 048174
Siloé, Laval (Moselle) . . . 133477
Silom Art Space, Bangkok . . . 112240
Silom Galleria, Bangkok . . . 083103
Silomuseum, Waidhofen an der Thaya . . . 002800
Silpakorn University Art Centre, Bangkok . . . 037890
Silsh Way, Killiney . . . 074983
Silva, Nilton, Fortaleza . . . 096537
Silva, Lisboa . . . 121945
Silva, Geraldes da, Porto . . . 109398
Da Silva, Toronto . . . 123840
Silva, Antonio J. Caldeira, Lisboa . . 080018
Silva, Armando, Coimbra . . . 129142
Silva, Claudionor B., Fortaleza . . . 137562
Silva, Edmundo, Lisboa . . . 129175
Silva, Edmundo, Lisboa . . . 129176
Silva, Eduardo Carvalho, Lisboa . . . 080019
Silva, Ezequiel Faria, Torres Vedras 080125
Silva, Fabio, New York . . . 091244
Silva, Francisco Marques, Lisboa . . 080020
Silva, Henrique, Lisboa . . . 129177
Silva, Joani P., Fortaleza . . . 096538
Silva, Júlio Gomes, Lisboa . . . 080021
Silva, Mamede Cerqueira, Braga . . 109241
Silva, Manoel Bezerra, Rio de Janeiro . . . 058658
Silva, Maria Dulce, Lisboa . . . 080022
Silva, Maria Idalina, Lisboa . . . 080023
Silva, Pedro, Lisboa . . . 080024
Silva, Rodolfo da, Paris . . . 124810
Silva, Victor, Bogotá . . . 098193
Silva Bastos, Lisboa . . . 080025
Silva Carvalho Gomes Mendes, Lisboa . . . 080026
Silva & Martinho, Lisboa . . . 080027
Silva P., Pedro, Santiago de Chile . . 123884
Silva Rafael Lopes, Lisboa . . . 129178
Silva-Rerum, Łódź . . . 140756
Silvana, Zurrieq . . . 077552
Silvano, Raymond, Marseille . . . 138199
Silvanum Skogsmuseet, Ockelbo . . 036514
Silveira, Yara Vianna, São Paulo . . . 096689
Silver, Jay, Houston . . . 089205
Silver, Tom, Bondi Beach . . . 055519
Silver Art, Norderstedt . . . 073076
Silver Blue Traders, Vancouver . . . 097530
Silver City Art Centre, Broken Hill . . 094309
Silver City Museum, Silver City . . . 048176
Silver Cliff Museum, Silver Cliff . . . 048178
Silver Cloud Galleries, Chicago . . . 115551
Silver Corner, Dubai . . . 083203
Silver-Craft Company, Atlanta . . . 131786
Silver Dollar Gallery Auctions, Baltimore . . . 122811
Silver Eagle and Gold Coins, Cleveland . . . 088361
Silver Eye-Center for Photography, Pittsburgh . . . 047061
Silver Fish Books, Taupo . . . 140658
Silver for Sale, Seattle . . . 093065
Silver Fox Gallery, London . . . 085688
The Silver Fund, London . . . 113886
Silver Gallery, San Francisco . . . 092885
Silver Horse Antiques, Las Vegas . . 089609
Silver K, Upper Mount Gravatt . . . 095359
Silver K Gallery, Armadale, Victoria . 055394
Silver K Gallery, Chadstone . . . 055660
Silver Ledge Hotel Museum, Ainsworth Hot Springs . . . 004988
Silver Line, Warszawa . . . 109194
Silver Line and More, Atlanta . . . 087527
Silver Magazine, Rancho Santa Fe . 136624
Silver Moon Trading Company, Vancouver . . . 059417
The Silver Mouse Trap, London . . .085689, 131170
Silver Museum, Al-Khobar . . . 034122
Silver Owl, Albuquerque . . . 131750
Silver River Museum, Ocala . . . 046613
Silver Sands Art, Jacksonville . . . 116541
Silver Screen, Saint Louis . . . 119254
Silver Sensations, Atlanta . . . 087528
Silver Services, Wellington . . . 128977
Silver Set, El Paso . . . 088814
Silver Shadow Picture & Prints, Swansea . . . 114537
Silver Shears, Seattle . . . 093066
Silver Shop, Dublin . . . 074947
The Silver Shop, Vancouver . . . 059418
Silver Society, London . . . 054502
Silver Society of Australia, Sydney South . . . 052492
Silver Star, Salt Lake City . . . 092463
Silver Stream Railway Museum, Hutt City . . . 030520
Silver Street Antiques & Things, Cirencester . . . 084020
Silver Street Gallery, Ilminster . . . 113292
Silver Thimble, Kendal . . . 084829
Silver Thistle, Houston . . . 089206
Silver Treasures, Dubai . . . 083204
Silveragent, Nashville . . . 090487
Silverbell, Tucson . . . 120167
Silverbox, Köln . . . 072007
Silvercreek Museum, Freeport . . . 044072
Silvercrest and More, Toledo . . . 093184
Silverenberg, Max, Eindhoven . . . 140416
The Silverhalide Gallery, Whitstable 114688
Silverleaf Antiques, San Jose . . . 092935
Silverman, Jackie & Manny, West Hollywood . . . 120413
Silverman, Michael, London . . . 141894
Silverman Heritage Museum, Toronto . . . 006632
Silvermine Guild Arts Center, New Canaan . . . 046210
Silvermine School of Art, Silvermine Guild Arts Center, New Canaan . . . 051788
Silvermist Studio Gallery, Healesville . . . 094629
Silvermuseet, Arjeplog . . . 036193
Silversmith, New Orleans . . . 090624
Silversmiths, Werner, Milwaukee . . 132371
Silverstein, New York . . . 118420
Silverstone, Franklin, Montréal . . . 097077
Silverstream Gallery, Timaru . . . 108583
Silvertime, Brecon . . . 083659
Silverton Gaol Museum, Silverton . . 001467
Silvery Slocan Museum, New Denver . . . 005996
Silvesters, Wingham . . . 087186
Silvestre, Jean-Pierre, Marseille . . . 099685
Silvestri, Claudio, Milano . . . 075867
Silvestri, Claudio, Milano . . . 075868
Silvestri, Luca, Napoli . . . 076053
Silvi's Antiques, Houston . 089207, 132138
Silvy, Jean-François, Cannes . . . 061956
Silz, Ursula, Budenheim . . . 138954
Sim, Michael, Chislehurst 083998, 130575
Sim, Roy, Blairgowrie . . . 083558
Simader, Herberg, Sankt Johann am Wimberg . . . 123464
Símaminjasafnið, Reykjavík . . . 021976
Simancas, Santander . . . 110754
Simão, José Vasconcelos, Lisboa . . 080028
Simcoe County Museum, Minesing . 005877
Simeon, Minneapolis . . . 132392
Simeon Perkins House, Queens County Museum, Liverpool . . . 005780

Simerneq, Nuuk 053669
Simeza, Bucureşti 109445
Simferopolskij Chudožestvennyj Muzej, Simferopol 038395
Simfonia Lemnului, Bucureşti 129226
Simil Art Gallery, Paris 100869
Simingshan Revolutionary Martyr Memory, Yuyao 007343
Simiolus, Utrecht 136008
Simmering, Calgary 123753
Simmerl, Gmund 071018
Simmerling, J., Chicago 088169
Simmermacher, René, Staufen 073900, 139741
Simmi, Stefano, Roma 106624
Simmond's & Sons, S.F., Catonsville 131866
Simmonite, Peter, Sheffield 114422
Simmons & Sons, Henley-on-Thames 122542
Simmons, Hong Kong 097831
Simmons, London 085690
Simmons, San Francisco 119791
Simmons, Wednesbury 142144
Simmons & Son, J.C., Saltburn-by-the-Sea 122686
Simmons, S.L., Brighton 083716
Simmons & Simmons, Albuquerque 087426, 142191
Simmor, Los Angeles 089910
Simms, Henry S., San Antonio 092580
Simoens, Andre, Knokke-Heist 096358
Simões & Irmãos, Carlos Domingues, Lisboa 080029
Simolan Taide ja Kehys, Lahti 060611, 098756
Simon, Charleroi 058153
Simon, Filderstadt 102728
Simon, Fürth, Bayern 125691
Simon, Hannover 071415
Simon, Madrid 129688
Simon, New Orleans 090625
Simon, Schrecksbach 073732
Simon, Seoul 107292
Simon, Wien 057551
Simon, Wiesbaden 074423
Simon, Brigitte & Karl-Heinz, Oldenburg, Oldenburg 073210
Simon, Dany, Uzès 068672
Simon, Didier, Héry 063152
Simon, Gilles, Nonancourt 065228
Simon, Helene, Köln 072008
Simon, Johann, Kassel 071764
Simon, Julian, London 085691
Simon, Marie-Josée, Perpignan . . . 066758
Simon, R. & M., Herzogenrath 103368
Simon, Dr. Ulrich, Frankfurt am Main 102827
Simon & Belmann, Telgte 105040
Simon Fraser Gallery, Burnaby 005171
Simon Gfeller-Gedenkstube, Heimisbach 037185
Simon i Patiño, La Paz 096445
Simon Kotiseutumuseo, Simo 010079
Simon Michael School of Fine Arts, Rockport 052054
Simon Paneak Memorial Museum, Anaktuvuk Pass 041709
Simon van Gijn Museum aan Huis, Dordrechts Museum, Dordrecht . . 029507
Simon Wiesenthal Center, Los Angeles 045462
Simon Wiesenthal Center - Museum of Tolerance, Los Angeles 045463
Simonato, Lorenzo, Padova 127813
Simoncini, Luxembourg 107411
Simone, Francesco, Torino 076871, 128361
Simone, Neil, Whixley 114692
Simone, Sonia, Chicago 088170
Simonet, Serge, Saint-Ouen 067893
Simonetti, Torino 076872
Simonetti, Maria-Pina, Islikon 111571
Simoni, Dino, Bologna 127182
Simonian, N. & Dr. S., Hamburg . . . 071332
Simonida, Niš 109735
Simonini, Michèle, Bédarieux 120922
Simonis, Düsseldorf 102556
Simonis, Paris 100870
Simonis & Buunk, Ede . . . 107991, 128656
Simonnæs, Bergen 079380
Simonot-Amigues, Versailles 068821
Simons, Bendorf, Rhein 069520
Simons, Herwig, Antwerpen 057736
Simon's Town Museum, Simon's Town 034748
Simonson, Bruxelles 120744
Simonson, Carol & James, Minneapolis 117306
Simotti, Rocchi Marcello, Roma . . . 076682
Simper, Murray & Ann, Warrnambool 137132
Simple Treasures, Manly 056153
Simpli, Sue, Toledo 120091
Simplicism, New York 118421
Simply Antiques, Moreton-in-Marsh 086022
Simply Gorgeous, Wellsford 079360
Simply Oak, Biggleswade . 083513, 130383
Simply Unique, Los Angeles 089911
Simpson, Buenos Aires . . 055245, 123161
Simpson, Hemel Hempstead 113223
Simpson, Stanmore 056628
Simpson, Wylam 114741
Simpson, Andrew, Woollahra 056878
Simpson, Catherine, London 096958
Simpson & Assoc., G., New Orleans 090626
Simpson & Sons, H.C., Oldham . . .086159, 131343
Simpson, Marianne, Fochabers . . . 141615
Simpson, R.J., Houston 132139
Simpson, Russell, Los Angeles 089912
Simpson, William, Houston 089208, 122914, 142446
Simpsons, Brentwood 083661
Sims, Michael, Lowestoft 141926
Sims, Paul, Richmond 092107
Sims Reed, London 085692, 141895
Sims Reed Gallery, London 113887
Simsbury Historical Society Museum, Simsbury 048184
Le Simserhof, Musée National de la Fortification Maginot, Siersthal . . 014798
Sin, Hua, Singapore 109870
Sin Ken, Ken, Bagnères-de-Bigorre 061163
Sin-Mi, Daegu 107192
Sinai, London 085693
Sincheonji Art Museum, Aeweol . . . 027445
Sinclair, Melbourne 094827
Sinclair, John, Stamford 086689
Sinclair-Barclay, Waikato 108595
Sinclair-Haus, Bad Homburg v.d.Höhe 015725
Sinclair Lewis Museum, Sauk Centre 048013
Sinclairs, Ardross 055352
Sind Provincial Museum, Hyderabad 031365
Sindaco-Domas, Claudia, Paris . . . 124811
Sindbad Antiques, Sharjah 083227
Sindbad Books, Carnegie 136853
Sindel, Heinz, München 126462
Sindelfinger Kabinett, Sindelfingen . 139730
Sindens, R.J., Calgary . . . 058807, 096846
Sindler, Richard, Baltimore 087711
Sindringer Heimatmuseum - Stadtmühle, Forchtenberg 017140
Sinebrychoffin Taidemuseo, Valtion Taidemuseo, Helsinki 009569
Sineo, Marina, Roma 076683
Sinesy Aboriginal Art & Design, Ballina 055442
Sineux, Précey 066979
Sinfield, Brian, Burford . . . 083794, 112756
Sing, Hong Kong 059693
Sing Kai Hong, West Hollywood . . . 093510
Singapore Art Museum, Singapore . 034296
Singapore Art Society, Singapore . . 054050
Singapore History Museum, National Museums of Singapore, Singapore 034297
Singapore History Museum at Riverside Point, National Museums of Singapore, Singapore 034298
Singapore National Corporation, Singapore 109871
Singapore Science Centre, Singapore 034299
Singe, Violet, Leiden 128744
Le Singe Blanc, Paris 066555, 100871
Au Singe Bleu, Bordeaux 061653
Singel 91 Antiquiteiten, Amsterdam 077968
Singer, Seattle 093067
Singer, Dorothy, Wien 137366
Singer Museum, Laren, Noord-Holland 029828
Singida Museum, Singida 037859
Singidunum, Beograd 109720
Single Tree Antiques, Richmond . . . 092108
Singleton Antiques, Skenfrith 086621
Singleton Historical Museum, Singleton 001469
Singsås Museum, Singsås 031181
Singshop, Bad Segeberg 101699
Siniawski, Janus, Kassel . 071765, 126018
Sining Makiling Gallery, University of the Philippines Los Baños, Los Baños 031691
Siniscalco, Maurizio, Napoli 076054
Sinjuku Art Gallery, Tokyo 107114
Sink, Mark, Denver 116052
Sinka, Laszlo, New York 132535
Sinkel, Jürgen, Griesstätt 071104
Sino Arts, Singapore 109872
Sino-Japanese Museum, Corfu . . . 021242
Sinop Devlet Güzel Sanatlar Galerisi, Sinop 038174
Sinop Kültür Merkezi, Sinop 038175
Sinop Müzesi, Sinop 038176
La Sinopia, Roma 076684
Sinopis, Roma 076685, 128204
Sinquin, René, Quiberon 101056
Sint-Baafskathedraal Gent, Gent . . 003467
Sint Catharinadal, Oosterhout 140509
Sint-Dimpna en Gasthuismuseum, Geel 003444
Sint-Godelievemuseum, Gistel 003478
Sint-Janshuismolen en Koeleweimolen, Stedelijke Musea Brugge, Brugge 003283
Sint Jansmuseum De Bouwloods, 's-Hertogenbosch 029739
Sint Joseph Galerie, Leeuwarden . . 108097
Sint-Lucas Beeldende Kunst, Hogeschool voor Wetenschap en Kunst, Gent . 049701
Sint Lucas Society, Leiden 078584, 108107, 140482
Sint-Pieters Museum op de Lichtenberg, Maastricht 029902
Sint-Plechelmusbasiliek met Schatkamer, Oldenzaal 029988
Sinte, Kathrien, Eindhoven 078349, 128662
Sintesi, Bologna 134552
Sintitulo, Mougins 099780
Sintot, Arbois 060944
Sintot, Santans 068121
Sintra Galleri & Butik, Göteborg . . . 110931
Sinu-Galerie, München 104318
Sion Hill Hall, Thirsk 041210
Sioux City Art Center, Sioux City . . . 048185
Sioux City Public Museum, Sioux City 048186
Sioux Empire Medical Museum, Sioux Falls 048192
Sioux Indian Museum, Rapid City . . 047336
Sioux Lookout Museum, Sioux Lookout 006479
Siouxland Heritage Museums, Sioux Falls 048193
Sipahi Ay. Trias Bazilikası ve Kantara Kalesi, Kantara 008250
Sipalaseequtt Museum, Pangnirtung 006113
Il Sipario, Parma 106457
Sipek, Harald, Mainz 139449
Siping City Museum, Siping 007270
Sipiora, Leonard P., El Paso 088815
Sipiweske Museum, Wawanesa . . . 006779
Sipma, Zwolle 078895
Sippel, Detlef, Pforzheim 126628
Sippolan Kotiseutumuseo, Sippola . 010082
Siqueira, Aelcio A., Belo Horizonte . 137550
Sir Alexander Galt Museum, Lethbridge 005767
Sir Alfred Munnings Art Museum, Dedham 039220
Sir Choturam Memorial Museum, Sangaria 022324
Sir Edgeworth David Memorial Museum, Kurri Kurri 001162
Sir Francis Cook Gallery, Augrès . . . 038549
Sir Frank Hutson Sugar Museum, Saint James 003123
Sir Henry Doulton Gallery, Stoke-on-Trent 041122
Sir Henry Jones Museum, Llangernyw 040061
Sir Henry Royce Memorial Foundation, Paulerspury 040676
Sir Hermann Black Gallery, Sydney . 001523
Sir Isaac and Lady Edith Wolfson Museum, Hechal Shlomo, Jerusalem 022981
Sir J.J. Institut of Applied Arts, Mumbai 050317
Sir John Soane's Museum, London 040289
Sir Max Aitken Museum, Cowes . . . 039159
Sir Seewoosagar Ramgoolam Memorial Centre, Plaine Verte 028069
Sir Walter Scott's Courtroom, Selkirk 040983
Sir Wilfred Grenfell College Art Gallery, Corner Brook 005294
Sir William, Paris 066556
S.I.R.A., Roma 128205
Sirapian, Agkop, Athinai 074607
Sirba Sirba, Fernando, Sevilla 081616
Sırçalı Medrese Müzesi, Konya 038138
Sirén, Helsinki 098745, 124052
La Sirena, Miami 090242
La Sirene, Liège 137523
Sireyzol, Serge, Belmont-Bretenoux 061340
Siri Drawing and Oil Painting Institute, Hyderabad 105714
Sirius, Basel 111222
Sirius-Alfa, Moskva 109588
Sirrs, J., Cottingham 130607
Sisi Museum zum Andenken an Kaiserin Elisabeth, München 019113
Sisimiut Katersugaasiviat, Sisimiut . 021550
Šiškin, Leonid, Moskva 109589
Siskin Museum of Religious and Ceremonial Art, Chattanooga 042782
Siskiyou County Museum, Yreka . . 049366
Siskos, Konst., Athinai 074608
Sisley, Bruxelles 133278, 137467
Sisman, Mathieu, Paris 066557
Sismanoglou, Thessaloniki 105458
Siso Difusiones, Lleida 081178
Sissoko, New York 118422
Sissoko, Philadelphia 118835
Sissons, William, Helmsley 113221
Sister Dragonfly Gallery, Louisville . 116966
Sister Studios, Saint Louis 119255
Sisters Antiques, Saint Paul 092396
Sistig, Manfred, Köln 072009
Sistu, Gianna, Paris 100872
Sit'Art, Magny-en-Vexin 099625
Sitch & Co., W., London . . 085694, 131171
Sitcoske, Marcel, San Francisco . . . 119792
Site Archéologique, Village Mediéval, Alba-la-Romaine 010310
Site Archéologique de Saint-Blaise, Saint-Mitre-les-Remparts 014446
Site Archéologique La Cave Peinte, Brain-sur-Allonnes 010960
Site-Chantier de Fouilles Archéologiques, Charavines 011243
Site Fortifié des Bois de Cattenom, Sentzich, Cattenom 011153
Site Gallery, Winnipeg 006866
Site Gallery, Winnipeg 097605
Site Gallo-Romain de Grand, Grand 011982
Site-Historique du Banc-de-Paspébiac, Paspébiac 006119
Site Odéon 5, Paris 100873

Site Préhistorique de Castel Merle, Sergeac . . . 014766
Site Santa Fe, Santa Fe . . . 047979
Siteau, Michel, Mazières-sur-Béronne . . . 064453
Sitges Subastas, Sitges . . . 122085
El Sitial, Zaragoza . . . 129831
Sitio Arqueológico de Cumbemayo, Cumbemayo . . . 031496
Sítio Roberto Burle Marx, Rio de Janeiro . . . 004420
Sitjas Antiquaris, Barcelona . . . 080937
Sitka National Historical Park, Sitka 048198
Sitorai Mochi-Khosa, Buchara . . . 049386
Sitting Pretty, Great Glen . 084507, 130745
Sitting Pretty Antiques, Sudbury, Suffolk . . . 086787, 131558
Sitting Room, Houston . . . 089209
Sittingbourne and Kemsley Light Railway, Sittingbourne . . . 041034
Sittingbourne Heritage Museum, Sittingbourne . . . 041035
Situ, Y., San Francisco . . . 132910
Situation Kunst, Bochum . . . 016284
Sity South Dealers, Christchurch . . 079054
Sitzenfrei, Axel, Wien . . . 057552, 123533
Siuntion Kotiseutumuseo, Siuntio . . 010083
Siuta, Albert, Ottersberg . . . 104560
Sivas Devlet Güzel Sanatlar Galerisi, Sivas . . . 038180
Siwik, Olaf, Berlin . . . 069763
Six, Luc, Bousbecque . . . 124159
Six Chapel Row Contemporary Arts, Bath . . . 112587
Six Eight Three Haight Street, San Francisco . . . 119793
Six Nations Indian Museum, Onchiota . . . 046686
Six Principles, Vancouver . . . 059419
Sixbid, Waibling . . . 121619
Sixel, Herbert, Viersen . . . 074213
Sixspace, Los Angeles . . . 116885
Sixth Avenue Antiques, San Francisco . . . 092886
Sixth Chamber Used Books, Saint Paul . . . 142870
Sixth Floor Museum at Dealey Plaza, Dallas . . . 043275
Sixtos, San Antonio . . . 132827
Sixty West Antique Mall, Richmond 092109
Sixways Antique Centre, Cheltenham . . . 083930, 130544
Sizad, Abdelziz, Paris . . . 124812
Sizdah Aban Museum, Teheran . . . 022644
Sizemore, Mary, Oklahoma City . . . 091536
Sizergh Castle, Kendal . . . 039847
Sjöberg, Inga Lill, Göteborg . . . 081822
Sjöfartmuseet, Oskarshamn . . . 036537
Sjöfartsmuseet, Göteborg . . . 036304
Sjöfartsmuseet, Kristiinankaupunki 009751
Sjöhistoriska Institutet vid Åbo Akademi, Turku . . . 010170
Sjöhistoriska Museet, Stockholm . . 036663
Sjösten, Johan, Göteborg . . . 081823
Sjöström, Hans Göran, Stockholm .082015, 111069
Sjøfartsmuseet i Porsgrunn, Porsgrunn . . . 031124
Sjølingstad Uldvarefabrik, Mandal . 031009
Sjóminja- og Vélsmiðjusafn, Reykjavík . . . 021977
Sjóminjasafn Austurlands, Eskifjörður . . . 021941
Sjóminjasafn Islands, Hafnarfjörður 021948
Sjóminjasafnid á Eyrarbakka, Eyrarbakki . . . 021943
Sjukehusmuseet i Molde, Molde . . . 031031
Sjukehusmuseet i Skien, Skien . . . 031190
SK Upholstery, San Diego . . . 132858
Ska-Nah-Doht Iroquoian Village and Museum, Mount Brydges . . . 005967
Skaalurensamlinga - Skipsbyggingsmuseet i Rosendal, Rosendal . . . 031154
Skácelík, Olomouc . . . 098392
Skådan, Uppsala . . . 082060
Skade Service Gruppen, Herlev . . . 124021
Skärgårdens Sågverksmuseum, Holmsund . . . 036346
Skärgårdsmuseet, Lappoby-Åland . 009809
Skärgårdsmuseet, Stavsnäs . . . 036610
Skagen By- og Egnsmuseum, Skagen . . . 009095
Skagens Museum, Skagen . . . 009096
Skaggs, Glen C., San Antonio . . . 092581
Skagit County Historical Museum, La Conner . . . 045053
Skagway City Museum, Skagway . . 048199
Skaj, Curt, Stockholm . . . 082016
Skali, N., Bonn . . . 138911
Skambraks, Klaus Udo, Frankfurt am Main . . . 125663
Skambraks, Klaus Udo, Frankfurt am Main . . . 125664
Skanderborg Museum, Skanderborg 009097
Skandinavisk Museumförbund - Skandinaavinen Museoliitto, Finnish Section, Helsinki . . . 052878
Skandinavisk Museumsforbund, Danske Afdeling, København . . . 052862
Skandinavisk Museumsforbund, Norwegian Section, Tønsberg . . . 053959
Skandinavisk Museumsforbund, Swedish Section, Stockholm . . . 054150
Skånes Konstförening, Malmö 054151, 110980
Skånland Museum, Evenskjer . . . 030825
Skansen Archeologiczny w Mrówkach, Muzeum Okręgowego w Koninie, Mrówki . . . 032154
Skansen Górniczy Królowa Luiza, Muzeum Górnictwa Węglowego w Zabrzu, Zabrze . . . 032542
Skansen i Muzeum Pszczelarstwa im prof. Ryszarda Kosteckiego, Muzeum Narodowe Rolnictwa i Przemysłu Rolno-Spożywczego w Szreniawie, Swarzędz . . . 032352
Skansen Kultury Ludowej Pogórza Sudeckiego, Kudowa Zdrój . . . 032085
Skansen Kurpiowski im. Adama Chętnika, Muzeum Regionalne, Nowogród . 032172
Skansenowska Zagroda Sitarska, Biłgoraj . . . 031840
Skånska Lasses Hus, Mjölby . . . 036478
Skanzen - Múzeum L'udovej Architektúry, Bardejovské Kúpele . . . 034312
Skara Järnvägsmuseum, Skara . . . 036576
Skarabäus, Köln . . . 072010
Skarabé Mynt & Föremål från Antiken, Göteborg . . . 081824
Skarbiec, Kraków . . . 108979
Skarics, Gerhard, Baden bei Wien . 056943
Skattkammaren, Stockholm . . . 036664
Skattkammaren - Uppsala Domkyrkas Museum, Uppsala . . . 036743
Skaun Bygdamuseum, Børsa . . . 030789
Skazka, Moskva . . . 080266
Skeaping, Lydford . . . 114009
Skeaping Gallery, Lydford . . . 085873
Skeen, Joseph, Greenbank . . . 055913
Skellefteå Museum, Skellefteå . . . 036580
Skellgate Curios, Ripon . . . 086381
Skelsey, K.L., Beverly Hills . . . 055501
Skepparn, Göteborg . . . 081825
Skeppsvarvet sjöfartsutställning, Sagalund Museum, Västanfjärd . . . 010211
Skepsi on Swanston, Carlton, Victoria . . . 094378
Skerryvore Museum, Hynish . . . 039790
Ski- und Heimatmuseum, Kurort Oberwiesenthal . . . 018446
Ski- und Heimatmuseum, Sankt Anton am Arlberg . . . 002574
Ski- und Heimatmuseum Upfingen, Sankt Johann, Württemberg . . . 019989
Skiba, Hans-Peter, Berlin . . . 069764
Skibinski, Josef, Ibbenbüren . . . 071603
Skibinski, Marc, Montmirail . . . 064716
Skibsted, Ove, Struer . . . 060404
Skidans Hus, Boden . . . 036219
Skidby Windmill and Museum of East Riding Rural Life, Skidby . . . 041037
Skien Antikk, Skien . . . 140708
Skiles, David, Louisville . . . 090025
Skillbeck, Charlotte . . . 115312
Skillen, Peter, Cockermouth . . . 112886
Skilton, Charles, London . . . 135263
Skimo Arte, Madrid . . . 110614
Skimuseet, Oslo . . . 031105
Skimuseum, Oberreute . . . 019407
Skimuseum, Vaduz . . . 027845
Skinner, Boston . . . 087845, 122826
Skinner, Helen, Stockholm . . . 129874
Skinner Museum of Mount Holyoke College, South Hadley . . . 048241
Skinner Wallace, John, Cleveland . . 142344
Skippergata Antikviteter, Kristiansand . . . 079398
Skipton Antiques Centre, Skipton . . 086626
Skiptvet Bygdemuseum, Skiptvet . . 031193
Skira, Milano . . . 134636
Skirball Cultural Center, Hebrew Union College, Los Angeles . . . 045464
Skirball Museum of Biblical Archaeology, Jerusalem . . . 022982
Skiri, Angela, München . . . 072859
Skironio Centrum Kifissa, Skironio Museum Polychronopoulos, Néa Kifissia . . 021408
Skironio Museum Polychronopoulos, Mégara . . . 021373
Skissernas Museum, Lund . . . 036447
Skive Kunstmuseum, Skive . . . 009098
Skive Museum, Skive . . . 009099
Skivesset, Malmö . . . 141134
Skjalm, H., København . . . 060379
Skjern-Egvad Museum, Skjern . . . 009103
Skjern Vindmølle, Skjern . . . 009104
Skjoldborgs Barndomshjem, Vesløs 009144
Sklářské Muzeum, Kamenický Šenov . . . 008423
Sklářské Muzeum Moser, Karlovy Vary . . . 008426
Sklářské Muzeum Nový Bor, Nový Bor . . . 008534
Skleder, Frank W., Pittsburgh . . . 142779
Sklenka Muzeum v Železném Brodě, Železný Brod . . . 008784
Sklep z Antykami, Warszawa . . . 079784
Sklerijenn, Saint-Malo (Ille-et-Vilaine) . . . 101177
Sklo en Zo, Rotterdam . . . 108209
Sklorz, M., Ludwigsburg, Württemberg . . . 072310
Skobelev Park-muzej, Pleven . . . 004785
Škoda Auto Museum, Mladá Boleslav . . . 008507
Skövde Konsthall och Konstmuseum, Skövde . . . 036581
Skövde Stadsmuseum, Skövde . . . 036582
Skogs- och Motorsågsmuseum, Sunne . . . 036694
Skogsmuseet i Lycksele, Lycksele . 036449
Skogsmuséet på Römmen, Mörsil . 036482
Skogsmuseum, Åsele . . . 036203
Skoindustrimuseet, Kumla . . . 036406
Skokloster Motormuseum, Skokloster . . . 036583
Skoklosters Slott, Skokloster . . . 036584
Skol, Montréal . . . 097078
Skolen for Mediekunst, Kongelige Danske Kunstakademi, København . . . 049907
Skolen for Mur og Rum, Kongelige Danske Kunstakademi, København . . . 049908
Skolmuseet, Östra Ljungby . . . 036533
Skolmuseum Bunge, Farösund . . . 036268
Školoto Muzej, Trjavna . . . 004906
Školska knjiga, Zagreb . . . 133409
Školska Zbirka Odžaci, Odžaci . . . 034231
Skoob, Bath . . . 141400
Skoob Russell Square, London . . . 141896
Skoogs Antik, Malmö . . . 081879
Skopia, Genève . . . 111500
Skorianetz, Dr. Werner, Genève . . . 141255
Skoto, New York . . . 118423
Skottvångs Gruva, Värdshus och Museum, Mariefred . . . 036470
Skovbrugsmagasinet på Corselitze, Nykøbing Falster . . . 009035
Skovgaard Museet i Viborg, Viborg . 009149
Skovle & Skovle, København . . . 137901
Skowhegan History House, Skowhegan . . . 048200
Skowhegan School of Painting and Sculpture, New York . . . 051834
Skowronek, Heinz, Kirchdorf auf Poel . . . 103551
Skowronska, Berlin . . . 138846
SKP Licht + Kunst, Wolfenbüttel . . . 105320
Skrajewski, A., Dessau, Anhalt . . . 102357
Skrebowski, Justin F., London 085695, 141897
Skrętowicz & Spółka, Kraków . . . 129049
Skrifter & Tal, Stockholm . . . 141176
Skrindo, Olav, Oslo . . . 079471
Skrobanek, E., Bruchköbel . . . 070063
Skrobek, B., Gaildorf . . . 070924
Skrodzki, Hattstedt . . . 103312
Skrolsvik Fiskebruksmuseum, Moen . . . 031026
Skrypt, Kraków . . . 140746
Skrypzak, Georg, Berne . . . 125323
Skufca, Dorothy, San Francisco . . . 132911
Skulpturen-Kabinett, Freiburg im Breisgau . . . 102872
Skulpturen-Museum, Städtische Museen Heilbronn, Heilbronn . . . 017852
Skulpturengarten am Schwarzen Haus, Bielefeld . . . 102129
Skulpturenhain vor Marleben, Trebel . . . 020463
Skulpturenmuseum Glaskasten Marl, Marl, Westfalen . . . 018852
Skulpturenmuseum im Hofberg, Stiftung Koenig, Landshut . . . 018486
Skulpturenpark, Bad Nauheim . . . 015758
Skulpturenpark Kramsach, Kramsach . . . 002169
Skulpturenpark Motzen, Motzen . . . 104124
Skulpturens Hus, Stockholm . . . 036665
Skulpturensammlung, Staatliche Kunstsammlungen Dresden, Dresden . . . 016815
Skulpturensammlung und Museum für Byzantinische Kunst, Staatliche Museen zu Berlin - Stiftung Preußischer Kulturbesitz, Berlin . . . 016173
Skulpturenweg, Emmendingen . . . 016970
Skulpturhalle Basel, Abguss-Sammlung des Antikenmuseums, Basel . . . 036908
Skultura Galeria de Arte, São Paulo 096690
Skupin, Rudolf, Bremen . . . 138950
Skupnost Muzejev Slovenije, Ljubljana . . . 054058
Skye and Lochalsh Area Museums, Portree . . . 040758
Skyhawk Rugs, Albuquerque . . . 087427
Skylark 2, London . . . 113888
Skylark Gallery, London . . . 113889
Skylark Studio, Cockermouth . . . 112887
Skylark Studios, Tydd Gote . . . 114620
Skylight Galleries, Cape Town . . . 110033
Skylight Gallery, Chicago . . . 115552
Skyline Books and Records, New York . . . 142692
Skyscraper, New York . . . 091245
Skyscraper Museum, New York . . . 046401
Skysun, Hong Kong . . . 097832
Skyttalan Museo, Parainen . . . 009951
Skywalk, Cincinnati . . . 142324
SL Galerie, Bielefeld . . . 102130
Slaait'n Hoes, Onstwedde . . . 029994
Slabsides, West Park . . . 049094
Slaby, Dietmar, Ried im Innkreis . . . 057226
Slaby, Gerhard, Sankt Martin im Innkreis . . . 057293
Slack & Warren, Sanderstead . . . 142047
Slade, John, Saint-Christophe . . . 067400
Slade, Michael, London . . 085696, 131172
The Slade Centre, Gillingham . . . 113096
Slade School of Fine Art, University College London, London . . . 050842
Sládečkovo Vlastivědné Muzeum v Kladně, Kladno . . . 008434
Sladmore Gallery, London . . . 113890

The Sladmore Gallery of Sculpture, London 040290
Slag van de Somme Museum, Schagen 030126
Slagelse Museum for Handel, Håndværk og Industri, Slagelse 009109
Slager, Mandy, Amsterdam 128554
Slagterbutikken anno 1920, Roskilde 009083
Sláma, Plzeň 060082
Slama, Hans, Klagenfurt 057113, 095620
Slama, Michael A., Portland 092009
Śląski Salon Sztuki, Wrocław 079802
Slate Run Living Historical Farm, Ashville 041817
Slate Valley Museum, Granville 044290
Slater, Indianapolis 089340
Slater, Sacramento 092182
Slater, Sacramento 123081
Slater, Gloria, New Orleans 090627
Slater, Kathy, New Orleans 090628
Slater, Phillip, Barnt Green 130341
Slater Memorial Museum, Norwich 046567
Slater Mill Historic Site, Pawtucket 046849
Slatkine, Genève 135021, 141256
Slaughter House Gallery, Pittsburgh 118953
Slaughter Ranch Museum, Douglas 043483
Slavejkov Antikvariat, Sofia 137607
Slaviero, Josilane, São Paulo 058742
Slavik, Renate, Wien 095938
Slavjanskij Dom, Moskva 109590
Slavonic Benevolent Order of the State of Texas Museum, Temple 048524
Slawenburg Raddusch, Raddusch 019694
Sledmere House, Sledmere 041041
Sleeping Beauty Antique Beds, Brighton 083717, 130450
Sleepy Poet Antique Mall, Charlotte 087977
Sleepy Poet Stuff on Park, Charlotte 087978
Slegers, P.T., Venlo 078846
Sleghem, Jacques & Sylvie, Lille 063868
De Slegte, Antwerpen 137404
Slegte de, Antwerpen 137405
De Slegte, Bruxelles 137468
De Slegte, Gent 137504
Slegte, J. de, Amersfoort 140273
Slegte, J. de, Arnhem 140356
Slegte, J. de, Breda 140366
Slegte, J. de, Den Haag 140401
Slegte, J. de, Eindhoven 140417
Slegte, J. de, Enschede 140420
Slegte, J. de, Groningen 140436
Slegte, J. de, Haarlem 140445
Slegte, J. de, Leiden 140483
Slegte, J. de, Maastricht 140495
Slegte, J. de, Rotterdam 140525
Slegte, J. de, Tilburg 140539
Slegte, J. de, Utrecht 140555
Slegte, J. de, Zwolle 140583
Slegte, Roel de, Amsterdam 077969
Sleigh Beds, Harriet Ann, Rolvenden 086394
Slein, Philip, Saint Louis 119256
Sleire Skulemuseum, Hosteland 030911
Slesvigske Vognsamling, Haderslev 008886
Sleuth, Toronto 137718
Slevarenske Muzeum Komarov, Komárov 008442
Slevogthof Neukastel, Sitz des Malers Prof. Max Slevogt mit Gemäldegalerie, Leinsweiler 018554
Slewe, Amsterdam 107799
Slezáček, České Budějovice 060001
Slezské Zemské Muzeum, Opava 008549
Slidell Art Center, Slidell 048201
Sliedrechts Museum, Sliedrecht 030159
Slifer House, Lewisburg 045243
Slim, R.T., Halesowen 141639
Slinger, Adrian, Noosa Heads 094968
Slingue, Michel, Angoulême 060880
Šlisselburgskaja Krepost Orešek, Šlisselburg 033874
Slitine, Chakib, Paris 066558
Slo Mak, Skopje 107429
Sloan, Buffalo 087910
Sloan Museum, Flint 043862
Sloane, Denver 116053
Sloane, Houston 116404
Sloane-Stanley Museum and Kent Furnace, Kent 044964
Sloans & Kenyon, Bethesda 122815
Slöinge Lanthandelsmuseum, Slöinge 036588
Slöjdmuseet, Ånge 036187
Slongo, Timothy P., Indianapolis 142458
Slootmans, Westervoort 128881
Slope, Eric D., Southampton 058394
Sloss Furnaces National Historic Landmark, Birmingham 042225
Slot Loevestein, Poederoijen 030043
Slot Zeist, Zeist 030379
Slot Zuylen, Oud-Zuilen 030021
Slough Museum, Slough 041042
Slovácké Muzeum, Uherské Hradiště 008732
Slovart Publishing, Bratislava 134893
Slovenská Národná Galéria, Bratislava 034337
Slovenská Národná Galéria - Galéria Insitného Umenia - Schaubmar Mill, Pezinok 034407
Slovenská Národná Galéria - Kaštiel' Strážky, Spišská Béla 034430
Slovenská Národná Galéria - L'udovit Fulla Galéria, Ružomberok 034422
Slovenská Národná Galéria - Zvolenský Zámok, Zvolen 034455
Slovenská Výtvarná Únia, Bratislava 054053
Slovenské Banské Múzeum, Banská Štiavnica 034308
Slovenské Múzeum A.S. Puškina, Matica Slovenská, Brodzany 034342
Slovenské Múzeum Ochrany Prírody a Jaskyniarstva, Liptovský Mikuláš 034377
Slovenské Národné Literárne Múzeum, Slovenská Narodná Knižnica, Martin 034389
Slovenské Národné Múzeum, Bratislava 034338
Slovenské Národné Múzeum - Muzeologický kabinet, Bratislava 054054
Slovenské Národné Múzeum - Múzeum Betliar, Betliar 034313
Slovenské Národné Múzeum - Múzeum Bojnice, Bojnice 034315
Slovenské Polnohospodárske Múzeum, Nitra 034400
Slovenské Technické Múzeum, Košice 034366
Slovenski Etnografski Muzej, Ljubljana 034492
Slovenski Gasilski Muzej, Metlika 034504
Slovenski Gledališki Muzej, Ljubljana 034493
Slovenski Šolski Muzej, Ljubljana 034494
Slovensko Arheološko Društvo, Ljubljana 054059
Slovensko Konservatorsko Društvo, Ljubljana 054060
Slovensko Muzejsko Društvo, Ljubljana 054061
Slovo, Moskva 134879
Slugfest, Austin 115011
Sluijters, R., Hilversum 128721
't Sluisje, Amersfoort 077751
Sluisman, P., Gouda 078391
Sluk, Eduard, Ubstadt-Weiher 074130
Slunkaríkí, Isafjörður 105585
Slusariuc, Freiburg im Breisgau 070861
Sluys, Cl., Bruxelles 058086
S.M. Fine Art UK, London 131173
SM Restauri, Roma 128206
Små Kära Ting, Göteborg 081826
Smågårde Auktioner Tofta, Visby 122299
Smagghe, Véronique, Paris 100874
Smajgl, Andreas, Salzkotten 073658
Smålands Bil, Musik och Leksaksmuseum, Rydaholm 036548
Smålands Konstarkiv, Värnamo 036760
Smålands Militärhistoriska Museum, Eksjö 036247
Smålands Museum, Sveriges Glasmuseum, Växjö 036773
Small Comforts Antiques, Vancouver 059420, 123857
Small Furniture Store, New York 091246, 132536
Small Mansions Arts Centre, London 040291
Small Museums Association, Clinton 055033
The Small Plaice Art Gallery, Upper Stowe 114624
Small Pleasures, Boston 087846
Small Pleasures, New York 091247
Small Pleasures Perfect Timing, Boston 087847
Small Space, Ha Noi 120486
Small & Whitfield, Parkside 056440
Small & Whitfield, Parkside 120625
Small Wonder Gallery, Murrumbeena 094923
Small World, San Antonio 092582
Small World Antiques, Saint Louis 092314
Smallwood, Memphis 090103
Smallwood's Retreat, Marbury 045660
Smallworks Gallery, Las Vegas 116647
Smal'ta, Charkiv 112382
Smart, Jonathan, Christchurch 108413
The Smart Gallery, Batley 112590
Smart t'Art Gallery, Cleveland 115740
Smashed Pipi, Mangawhai 108493
Smatolánová, Zdenka, Vrchlabí 060201, 137858
Smeaton's Tower, Plymouth 040725
Smedemuseet, Øster-Assels 009058
Smederij Museum Wijlen dhr Verkley, Nieuwkoop 029952
Smedley, Durwyn, Indianapolis 089341
Smeets, Weil am Rhein 074301
Smelik & Stokking, Amsterdam 107800
Smelik & Stokking, Den Haag 107952
Smelik & Stokking, Rotterdam 078745
Smellie & Son, L.S., Hamilton 122533
Smend, Rudolf, Köln 103717
Smeraldo, Verona 077022
Smetanamuseet, Göteborg 036305
SMG Sales and Originals, Montréal 097079
SMH-Art, Basel 111223
Smibert, Tony, Deloraine 094473
Smid, Großenkneten 071119
Smid, Klaus J., Oldenburg, Oldenburg 073211
Smidt Múzeum, Szombathely 021899
Śmigiel, Józef, Wrocław 079803, 129131
Smink, Hoofddorp 128726
Smiraglia, Rocco, Roma 128207
Smiske Museum, Rijmenam 003715
Smit, Emmen 078365
Smit, Louise, Amsterdam 107801
Smit, N., Amsterdam 140338
Smit & Bos, Harlingen 140451
Smital, Adolf, Schorndorf, Württemberg 073725
Smiterlöwsche Sammlung, Franzburg 017207
Smith, Campbells Creek 055614
Smith, Christchurch 108414, 140620
Smith, Cincinnati 088281
Smith, Cork 074882
Smith, New York 091248
Smith, Norfolk 132561
Smith, Sacramento 119161
Smith, Teddington 114560
Smith, Toledo 132977
Smith, Wellington 140683
Smith, Wellington 140684
Smith, A.H., Miami 132358
Smith & Co., A.J., Seattle 093068
Smith, Allan, Swindon 086816
Smith, Alun Courtney, London 131174
Smith, Alvin G ., San Antonio 092583
Smith, Anne, Baltimore 087712
Smith, Betty A., Dallas 115940
Smith, Chad, Salt Lake City 132793
Smith, C.W., Minneapolis 090393
Smith, Daren, Norwich 141967
Smith, David, Manton 085925
Smith, Dick, London 113891
Smith, D.J., Pamber Heath 131361
Smith, D.J., Silchester 131501
Smith, E.F., Houston 132140
Smith, Elliot, New York 118424
Smith, Elliot, Saint Louis 119257
Smith, Elsie, San Francisco 092887
Smith, Eric, Darwen 130626
Smith, Frank, Newcastle-upon-Tyne 141954
Smith, Graham, Jesmond 048816
Smith, Granny, Saint Paul 092397
Smith, J., York 087296
Smith, Jack, Albuquerque 131751
Smith, James, Richmond, Surrey 142017
Smith, Jannene, Rozelle 137078
Smith, Jennie, Tampa 093154
Smith, Keith, Ledbury 141710
Smith, Ken, Enderby 084335
Smith, L. Royden, Lichfield 084992, 141731
Smith, Lana, Louisville 090026
Smith, Larry, West Hollywood 120414
Smith, Lesley, Nottingham 141976
Smith, Leslie, Den Haag 107953
Smith, Louise, Kew 056048
Smith, Louise, Toronto 097376
Smith, Neal R., Denver 116054
Smith, Niall, New York 091249
Smith, Peter, Sunderland 086788, 131559
Smith, Peter Bain, Cartmel 141496
Smith, Robert Dale, Omaha 091583, 132598
Smith, Roger, New York 118425
Smith, T., Chalfont Saint Giles 083906, 130522
Smith & Son, W.H., Bruxelles 137469
Smith Art Gallery, Brighouse 038843
Smith & Burstert, Kansas City 089520
Smith College Museum of Art, Northampton 046545
Smith County Historical Society Museum, Tyler 048680
Smith & Ferguson, Birmingham 131839
The Smith Gallery, Colchester 112891
Smith-Hill, Indianapolis 089342
Smith-Hill, Indianapolis 132162
Smith & Kramer, Kansas City 116591
Smith-McDowell House Museum, Asheville 041796
Smith Robertson Museum, Jackson 044805
Colin Smith & Gerald Robinson, London 085697
Smith & Roelants, Auckland 078982
Smith Street Galleries, Honolulu 116244
Smith & Ward, Wellington 079350
Smith & Wong, Vancouver 059421
Smith-Zimmermann Museum, Madison 045587
Smithen, Calgary 058808
Smithers Furniture, Austin 131809
Smithers Public Art Gallery, Smithers 006483
Smithills Hall Museum, Bolton 038781
Smiths, Christchurch 121819
Smith's, Harrogate 084588
Smith's Cove Historical Museum, Smith's Cove 006484
Smiths Falls Railway Museum of Eastern Ontario, Smiths Falls 006487
Smith's Fort Plantation, Surry 048443
Smithsonian American Art Museum, Washington 048943
Smithsonian Institution, Washington 048944
Smithtown Historical Society Museum, Smithtown 048204
Smitz, J., Knokke-Heist 058252
Smocked Frock, Houston 089210
Smoglian, Guido, Fairfield 055813
Smoki Museum, Prescott 047227
Smoky Hill Museum, Salina 047757
Smøla Museum, Smøla 031200
Smolarczyk-Stepniak, Krystyna, Gdańsk 079587, 108900

Smolenskaja Chudožestvennaja Galerja, Smolensk 033882
Smolenskaja Regionalnaja Organizacija Sojuza Chudožnikov Rossii, Smolensk 054028
Smolenskij Gosudarstvennyj Institut Iskusstv, Smolensk 050663
Smolenskij Istoričeskij Muzej, Smolenskij Muzej-Zapovednik, Smolensk . . . 033883
Smolenskij Muzej-Zapovednik, Smolensk 033884
Smolenskij Sobor, Novodevičij muzej, Smolensk 033885
Smolka, Wilhelm, Wien . . 057553, 095939, 123534
Smollett Antique, Albury 120560
Smollett Antique Furniture, Albury . 055332
Smoorenburg, A., Raalte 140513
Smrček, Znojmo 060208
Smrčkův Dům, Husitske Muzeum v Táboře, Soběslav 008690
Šmrnc, Bratislava 129274
Smrsch, Helmut, Rodgau 073554
Smruti Mirani, Mumbai 105808
Smyrnios Gallery, Prahran 095106
Smyth, J., Dun Laoghaire 074968
Smyth, Peta, London 085698
Smyth, Spencer, San Francisco . . . 119794
Smyth County Museum, Marion . . . 045687
Smythe & Co., New York . 091250, 123015, 142693
Smythe & Co., R.M., Washington . . 093436
Smythe, Son & Walker, Cleveleys . . 122473
S.N.A.B., Paris 133677
Snäckan, Stockholm 082017
Snake River Heritage Center, Weiser 049044
Snap Dragon, South Molton 086642, 131514
Snap Galleries, Canons Ashby 112798
Snapdragon, Ottawa 097118
Snape Antiques, Snape 086631
Snappertunan Talomuseo, Snappertuna 010084
Snåsa Bygdamuseum, Snåsa 031201
S.N.C de Corbez, Saint-Germain-les-Corbeil 052968
S.N.E.C., Annonay 060907
Snel, Loděnice 060050
Snell, Tim, Bath 083445
Śniadewicz, Grażyna, Milanówek . . 129057
Snibston Discovery Park, Coalville . 039108
Snidaro, Mario Luis, Reus 129711
Snider, Desiree, Milano 127687
Snider Plaza Antique Shops, Dallas 088611
Sniders, Jeremy, Glasgow 084470, 130730
Snijders, Jos, Roermond 078680
The Snite Museum of Art, University of Notre Dame, Notre Dame 046574
Snitzer, Fredric, Miami 117143
Snivling Sibbling, Los Angeles 089913
Snob, Bari 075032
Snook, Wadebridge 114638
Snook, Jason, Caulfield East 123208
Snoop Antiques, Malvern, South Australia 056139
Snooty Wombat Antiques, Mount Pleasant 056294
Snooz'ease Furniture, Denver 088737
Snoqualmie Valley Historical Museum, North Bend 046515
Snoriguzzi, Michel, Courgenay 082332
Snow, Tulsa 093330
Snow, Catherine, Nashville 090488
Snow Country Tree Museum, Shiozawa 027076
Snow Goose Associates, Seattle . . . 119993
Snow Goose Canadian Arts, Ottawa 097119
Snowbird Gallery, Edmonton 096897
Snowden, Ruby, Yarm 087279
Snowden House, Waterloo 048986
Snowdonia Antiques, Llanrwst 085043, 130911
Snowline Collectibles, Las Vegas . . 089610
Snowshill Manor, Broadway 038877
Snowy Mountains Galleria de Art, Jindabyne 094668
Snuffel, Hasselt 137507
Snug Harbor Cultural Center, Staten Island 048334
De Snuifdoos, Rotterdam 078746
Snyder, Columbus 131989
Snyder, Alice R., Pittsburgh 118954
Snyder, Gary, New York 118426
Snyder, J.R., San Diego 132859
Snyder, Susan, San Diego 119551
The Snyder County Historical Society Museum, Middleburg 045832
Snyder Museum and Creative Arts Center, Bastrop 042036
Snyderman, Philadelphia 118836
Snyers, Alain & Caroline, Paris 124813
So, Hyun, New York 118427
SO:AK Galerie, Wien 095940
So Art, Norwich 114168
So Be It, Portland 119054
So Bell Antiques, San Francisco . . . 092888
So-Bigraphics, Omaha 118724
So Gallery, Kamakura 106870
So Much More, Columbus 088436
Soames County Auctions, Witney . . 122753
Soapbox Gallery, Fortitude Valley . . 094562
Soardi, Nice 099857
Soares, António Pinto, Porto 109399
Soares, Vítor Fernandes, Coimbra . 109248
Soares, Vítor Fernandes, Lagos . . . 109256
Soares & Mendonça, Lisboa 080030, 121946
Soaring Eagle, Saint Paul 092398
Soaring Eagle Gallery, Albuquerque 114822
Sober, Michael, New York 142694
Sobo, Columbus 088437
Sobocinska, Elzbieta, Bonn 125363
Sobol, Leszek, Kraków . . . 079657, 140747
Sobottka, Aachen 069102
Sobottka-Braun, Ute, Pulheim 126666
El Sobrao de la Abuela, Salamanca 081546, 129717
Sobunkan, Tokyo 140201
Søby Brunkulslejer og Brunkulsmuseet, Herning 008906
Søbygård, Søby Ærø 009111
Socabep, Saint-Just-en-Chevalet . . 067569
Soccodato, Ferdinando, Roma 128208
Soccorsi, Raffaela, Roma 128209
Sochaři, Olomouc 123965
Sochi, Saint Paul 092399
Social History Collections, Iziko Museums of Cape Town, Cape Town 034583
Social History Curators Group, Newcastle-upon-Tyne 054503
Socialmuseet Det Gamle Syge-Plejehjem, Hinnerup 008911
Sociedad Argentina de Artistas Plásticos, Buenos Aires 052447
La Sociedad de Arte Moderno, México 053865
Sociedad de Exposiciones San Vicente Paul, Madrid 054121
Sociedad Estatal para el Desarrollo del Diseño y la Innovación, Madrid . . 054122
Sociedad Iberoamericana de Estudios Numismáticos, Madrid 054123
Sociedad Mayagüezana Pro Bellas Artes, Mayagüez 054010
Sociedade Nacional de Belas Artes, Lisboa 054006, 109354
Sociedade Nacional de Leilões, Porto 054007
Sociedade Portuguesa de Leilões a Pregoeira, Lisboa 054008
Societá di Belle Arti, Milano 053765
Societá Editrice Antiquariato Bologna, Bologna 075109, 139995
Società Editrice Internazionale, Torino 134699
Società Editrice Napoletana, Napoli 134645
Società Nazionale di Scienze, Lettere ed Arti, Napoli 053766
Società Numismatica Italiana, Milano 053767
Società per le Belle Arti, Milano . . . 053768
Società per le Belle Arti ed Esposizione Permanente, Milano 024736
Società Promotrice delle Belle Arti, Torino 053769
Società Tiburtina di Storia e d'Arte, Tivoli 053770
Societätsverlag, Frankfurt am Main 133954
Societas Museologia, Český Těšín . 052840
Societatea Colecţionarilor de Artă din România, Bucureşti 054014
Societatea Profesorilor de Muzica şi Desen dîn România, Bucureşti 054015
Société Biblique, Les Abymes 139907
Société de l'Historie de l'Art Français, Paris 052969
Societé d'Ébénisterie et de Menuiserie de style et décoration, Rabat 077697, 128514
Société des Amis du Louvre, Paris . 052970
Société des Amis du Musée National d'Art Moderne Centre Pompidou, Paris . 052971
Société des Artistes Décorateurs, Paris 052972
Société des Artistes Indépendants, Paris 052973
Société des Arts, Paris 100875
Société des Auteurs dans les Arts Graphiques et Plastiques (ADAGP), Paris 052974
Société des Expositions du Palais des Beaux-Arts, Bruxelles 052655
Société des Musées Québécois, Montréal 052775
Société des Peintres-Graveurs Français, Paris 052975
Société des Peintres, Sculpteurs et Architectes Suisses, Lausanne . . 054238
Société d'Investissement et de Restauration (S.I.R.), Lacave 099413, 124287
Société du Dessin, Paris 052976
Société E.D.P.A, Sté Européenne de Diffusion de Peintures Artistiques, Brainville-sur-Meuse 052977
Société Française d'Art Contemporain, Paris 052978
Société Mâconnaise Cheminées Anciennes, Mâcon 064208
Société Mutuelle Artistique, Carouge 054218
Société Nationale des Beaux-Arts, Paris 052979
Société Neubourgeoise d'Antiquité et de Brocantes, Le Neubourg 052980, 063674
Société Normande d'Art et d'Antiquités, Honfleur 052981, 063170
Societé Pastel de Lyon, Carponne . 052982
Society for Art Publications of the Americas, San Francisco 055034
Society for Arts, Chicago . 055035, 115553
Society for Contemporary Craft Museum, Pittsburgh 047062
Society for Contemporary Photography, Kansas City 044928, 055036
Society for Japanese Arts, Bergeijk 053902, 134799
Society for Renewal of Christian Art, New York 055037
Society of American Graphic Artists, New York 055038
Society of American Historical Artists, Osysterbay 055039
Society of Antiquaries of London, London 054504
Society of Antiquaries of Scotland, Edinburgh 054505
Society of Architectural Historians of Great Britain, London 054506
Society of Arts and Crafts, Boston . 055040
Society of Arts and Crafts Exhibition Gallery, Boston 042344
The Society of Arts, Literature and Welfare, Chittagong 052634
The Society of Botanical Artists, Gillingham, Dorset 054507
Society of Contemporary Artists, Kolkata 053706
Society of County Museum Officers, Taunton 054508
Society of Decorative Art Curators, Liverpool 054509
Society of Fine Art Auctioneers and Valuers, Woking 054510
Society of Illustrators, New York . . . 055041
Society of Illustrators Museum of American Illustration, New York 046402
Society of Jewellery Historians, London 054511
Society of London Art Dealers, London 054512
Society of Miniaturists, Ilkley 054513
Society of Museum Archaeologists, London 054514
Society of Photographers & Artists Representatives, New York 055042
The Society of Scottish Artists, Edinburgh 054515
Society of the Cincinnati Museum, Washington 048945
The Society of the Four Arts Gallery, Palm Beach 046796
Society of Wildlife Artists, London . 054516
The Society of Women Artists, Gillingham, Dorset 054517
Society of Wood Engravers, Northamptonshire 054518
Sočinskij Chudožestvennyj Muzej, Soči 033890
Soco, Austin 115012
Socorro, de, New York 091251
Socotom, Paris 066559
Socotti, Brugge 096119
Socrates Sculpture Park, Long Island City 045393
Sod House Museum, Aline 041653
Sod House Museum, Arctic Bay . . . 005025
Sod House Museum, Gothenburg . . 044253
Sodal, Nancy 099798
Sodankylän Kotiseutumuseo, Sodankylä 010085
Sodbury Antiques, Chipping Sodbury 083995
Sodbuster Archives Museum, Strome 006524
Sodosha, Tokyo 107115
Sodus Bay Historical Society Museum, Sodus Point 048211
Soe Moe, Yangon 107570
Söderbärke Hembygdsgård, Ekomuseum Bergslagen, Söderbärke 036591
Söderhamns Auktionshall, Sandarne 122236
Söderhamns Stadsmuseum, Söderhamn 036592
Söderklenoden, Stockholm 082018
Söderlångvikin Museo, Dragsfjärd . 009464
Soeders, Manfred, Göteborg 129842
Söderström, Leif, Stockholm 082019
Söderström, Werner, Helsinki 133443
Södertälje Konsthall, Södertälje . . . 036594
Södertälje Konsthandel och Galleri, Södertälje 110991
Södra Dalarnas Auktioner, Hedemora 122154
Södra Galleriet, Stockholm 111070
Södra Skattkammaren, Stockholm . 082020
Söhn, Fritz-Dieter, Marburg 139463
Söhn, Gerhart, Düsseldorf 102557
Söhn-Veigl, Barbara, Düsseldorf . . . 125547
Soelberg, Christina E, Oslo 128994
Soelberg, Jytte, København 060380
Sölje Bygdegård, Glava 036286
Söllner, Gabriele, Braunschweig . . . 069995
Sölvesborgs Museum, Sölvesborg . 036598
Sörgel, Karlheinz, Pommelsbrunn . . 126641
Sörmlands Museum, Nyköping 036511
Sörmlandsgården, Eskilstuna 036255
Sörries, Gerhard, Eckental 125566
Soester Münzcabinett, Soest 073847
Soeten, M., Gronau, Westfalen 103012
Sofa, Enschede 078379
Sofa, İstanbul 083156
Søfarts og Fiskerimuseet, Læsø . . . 009007

Søfartssamlingerne i Troense, Svendborg 009124
Sofec, Saint-Brieuc 138593
Sofer, Paris 066560
La Soffitta, Venezia 076974
La Soffitta della Nonna, Palermo . . 076182
Sofia, Cleveland 115741
Sofia Arte, Roma 076686
Sofia Kamburova, Sofia 096747
Sofiero Slott, Helsingborg 036339
Sofijska Gradska Chudožestvena Galerija, Sofia 004876
Sofijski Istoričeski Muzej, Sofia . . . 004877
Sofistic, Buenos Aires 055246
Sofranor, Paris 066561
Soft, Paris 066562
Software Museum, Hünfeld 018022
S.O.G.A.C., Marseille 064391
SO.GE.FI, Nice 065149
Sogetsu Bijutsukan, Tokyo 027242
Søgne Bygdemuseum, Søgne 031203
Sogo Museum of Art, Yokohama . . . 027338
Soh, Tokyo 107116
Soheili, München 072860
Soho, Seoul 107293
Soho 20, New York 118428
El Soho Antique, Bogotá 059860
Soho Art Gallery, Vancouver 097531
Soho Arte Millenium, Bogotá 098194
Soho Fine Art Gallery, Las Vegas . . 116648
Soho Fort Worth Art Gallery, Fort Worth 116164
Soho Galería, Bogotá 098195
Soho Galleries, Sydney 095305
Soho Gallery, San Francisco 119795
Soho House, Birmingham 038738
Soho Mid-Century Gallery, Memphis 090104
Soho Myriad, Atlanta 114926
Soho Photo Gallery, New York 046403
Soil Artist Cooperative, Seattle 119994
Soin, München 072861, 104319
Soin, Margarete, München 072862
Soinin Museo, Soini 010087
Soissons Antiquités, Soissons 068253
Soizic, La Ciotat 063334
Sojo, Amsterdam 107802
Sojun Art Museum, Siheung 027618
Sojus Chudožnikov Kitovras, Moskva 054029
Sojus Chudožnikov Moskvy, Moskva 054030, 109591
Sojuz Chudožnikov Rossii, Moskva . 054031
Sojuz Chudožnikov Sankt Peterburga, Sankt-Peterburg 054032
Soka, Taipei 098083
Sokang University Museum, Seoul . 027605
Sokei Bijutsu Gakko, Kunitachi 050458
Sokendo, Tokyo 077309
Soker, Don, San Francisco 119796
Sokličev Muzej, Slovenj Gradec . . . 034524
Soknedal Bygdemuseum, Soknedal 031204
Soko African Stone Art, Newtownabbey 114144
Sokoloff, San Francisco 119797
Sokolowski, Harry, Los Angeles . . . 132281
Sokolowski, Heinz, Sömmerda 073844
Sokolowski, Heinz, Weimar, Thüringen 074311
Sokrovišča Peterburga, Sankt-Peterburg 080331
Sol, Niš 109736
Sol del Rio Art Gallery, San Antonio 119455
Sol Floris Antiques, Seattle 093069
Sola, Guido, Roma 076687
Sola kulturhus, Sola 108753
Solagro, Venezia 076975
Solajian, Kivork, Damascus 083085
La Solana Antigüedades, Caracas . 093542
Solander, Yarralumla 095449
Solanet, Lucien, Paris 121210
Solange, Fresney 062945
Solange, Montevideo 087347
Solano, C., Vitoria-Gasteiz 110873
Solar, Lisboa 080031
Solar Boats Museum, Giza 009335
Solar de Dom João VI, Rio de Janeiro 004421
Solar Grandjean de Montigny, Rio de Janeiro 004422
Solari, Elisabetta, Genova 127488
Solari Arte, Milano 106315
Solarte, Roma 076688
Solatès, Montreux 082670
Solazoque, Oviedo 110666
Solazzi, Francesco, Milano 127688
Solberg, Esaias, Oslo 079472
Sold, Richmond 092110
Soldan, Romina, Roma 106625
Le Soldat Artiste, Nouvron-Vingre . . 013453
Soldattorpet i Ytterjeppo, Uusikaarlepyy 010194
Solder, Michael, Münster 139574
Soldi, Daniele, Firenze 075405
Soldier and Scholar, Fitzroy North . . 136904
Soldiers' Memorial Military Museum, Saint Louis 047681
Soldiers National Museum, Gettysburg 044186
Soldiers of Gloucestershire Museum, Gloucester 039594
Il Sole, Perugia 106461
Solé, Marie-José, Paris 124814
Sole Art, Philadelphia 118837
Il Sole Cornici, Roma 106626, 121725
Soleado Stichting, Utrecht 078819
Soledad Arroyo Gil, Toledo 081633, 110792
Soledad Lorenzo, Madrid 110615
Soledad Lorenzo, Madrid 110616
Soledad Lorenzo, Madrid 110617
Soleil, Le Noirmont 082702
Soleil Bleu, Caracas 120437
Le Soleil Bleu, Versailles 101457
Soleil d'Art, Arcachon 098856
Soleil d'Art, Sanguinet . . . 068118, 101254
Soleil Ethnic, Vincennes 101485
Soleil Rouge, Villeurbanne 068982
Le Soleil sur la Place, Lyon 099614
Soleiman & Haroun, Teheran 074850
Soleimani, Rosa, New York 091252
Soleleitungsmuseum Brunnhaus Klaushäusl, Grassau, Chiemgau 017513
Soler, Silvia, Barcelona 080938
Soler & Llach, Barcelona 122012
Solers, Sofia 096748
Soletti, Bruna, Milano 106316
Soli Archaeological Site, Lefke 008251
Solidair, Rotterdam 108210
Solidor, Cagnes-sur-Mer 099050
Soligo, Aldo, Roma 076689
Solihull Art Gallery, Solihull 114447
Solikamskij Gorodskoj Kraevedčeskij Muzej, Solikamsk 033891
Soliman, Riad, Cairo 098674
Solin, Stockholm 082021, 111071
Solinas, Salvatore, Weißenburg in Bayern 126989
Solinger Auktionshaus, Solingen . . 121602
Solinger Fotoforum, Solingen 020239
Soliño, Donostia-San Sebastián . . . 129516
Solitaire Galerie, Berlin 102046
Sollefteå Museum, Sollefteå 036599
Søllerød Museum, Holte 008928
Sollertis, Toulouse 101371
de Solliès, Paris 100876
Solna Auktionsbyrå, Vingåker 122295
Solna Hembygdsmuseum, Solna . . 036605
Solniční, Brno 059984
Solo, Lyon 099615
Solo, Joseph, New York . . 091253, 132537
Solo Books, Ottawa 137678
Soloman & Co., New York 118429
Soloman Island National Museum and Cultural Centre, Honiara 034540
Soloman & Soloman, Chicago 115554
Solomon, Dublin 105888
Solomon, Indianapolis 132163
Solomon, London 085699, 131175
Solomon, New York 118430
Solomon, Seattle 119995
Solomon, Jerry, Los Angeles 116886
Solomon, Nancy, Atlanta 114927
Solomon, Richard, New York 118431
Solomon Dubnick, Sacramento . . . 119162
Solomon Malvina, New York 091254
Solomon R. Guggenheim Museum, New York 046404
Solomon & Whitehead, Lichfield . . . 135169
Solomons, John, Armidale 055401
Solomos Museum, Corfu 021244
Solonoy, Cairo 060475
Solopark, Cambridge 083849
Soloveckij Gosudarstvennyj Istoriko-Architekturnyj i Prirodnyj Muzej-Zapovednik, Soloveckij 033894
Solstice, Los Angeles 116887
Solstices, Lille 138122
Soltani, Kiu, Köln 072011
Solvay Centrum Sztuki, Kraków . . . 108980
Sølvfunn, Oslo 079473
Solvis, Minsk 057655
Sølvkælderen, København 060381, 124029
Solway, Carl, Cincinnati 115663
Solway Aviation Museum, Crosby-on-Eden 039185
Soma Gyofu Kinenkan, Itoigawa History and Folk Museum, Itoigawa 026584
Somali National Museum, Mogadishu 034541
Sombra Township Museum, Sombra 006489
Somdet Phra Narai National Museum, Lopburi 037908
Somenzi, Roméo, Lausanne 082568
Someron Museo, Somero 010091
Someron Torppamuseo, Somero . . . 010092
Somers, Axel, Liège 058327
Somers, Elaine, Belfast 112619
Frans Somers & Katrin Coaching, Ernst 102657
Somers Historical Society Museum, Somers 048214
Somers Mansion, Somers Point . . . 048216
Somerset, B.V.M., Tonbridge 086896, 131598
Somerset and Dorset Railway Trust Museum, Washford 041312
Somerset Brick and Tile Museum, Bridgwater 038833
Somerset County Museum, Taunton 041190
Somerset Cricket Museum, Taunton 041191
Somerset East Museum, Somerset East 034751
Somerset Historical Center, Somerset 048217
Somerset Military Museum, Taunton 041192
Somerset Place, Creswell 043219
Somerset Rural Life Museum, Glastonbury 039581
Somerton Antiques, Somerton 086638, 131511
Somervale Antiques, Midsomer Norton 085988
Somervell County Museum, Glen Rose 044205
Somerville, Plymouth 114265
Somerville, Stephen, London 085700, 113892
Somerville Museum, Somerville . . . 048218
Somesville Museum, Mount Desert 046055
Somethin' Special, Windsor, Ontario 097566
Something Different, Cleveland . . . 115742
Something Different Antiques, Brighton, Victoria 055554
Something Else, New York 091255
Something Fishy, Cleveland 115743
Something for Everyone, Cleveland 088362
Something Old Something New, Bowness-on-Windermere 083618
Something Old Something New, Brampton, Cumbria 083640
Something Special Antiques, Fort Worth 088886
Something Special Gallery, Invercargill 108477
Something Unique, Virginia Beach .093366, 133015
Sometime Ago Antiques, Wellington 079351
Somewhere in Time, Denver 088738
Somewhere in Time, Minneapolis . . 090394
Somix, Bucureşti 080172
Somlo, London 085701, 131176
Somma, Salvatore, Napoli 076055
Sommazzi, Paolo, Firenze 127415
Somme Heritage Centre, Newtownards 040587
Sommer, Saarbrücken 073646
Sommer, Sankt Blasien 073666
Sommer, A., München . . . 126463, 133547
Sommer, Bruno, Frankfurt am Main 070792
Sommer, Erhard, Bamberg 101732
Sommer, Gerhard, Graz . . 057025, 095543
Sommer, Gerhard, Innsbruck 123395
Sommer, Gertraud, München 104320
Sommer, Karin, Bad Salzdetfurth . . 101691
Sommer-Blum, Bernadette, Willisau 130217
Sommer-Fuchs, Christine, Königsberg in Bayern 072031
Sommerer, Hannes & Sonja, Feuchtwangen 070686
Sommerfeld, Doris, Bottrop 069966
Sommerfeld, Ursula, Greiz 071094
Sommerhoff, Daniel, Mehlbek 072495
Sommerhuber-Kachelofenmuseum, Steyr 002705
Sommerset Art Konzeption, München 104321
Sommerset House Books, Blackheath 136805
Sommerville, Vancouver 059422
Sømna Bygdetun, Sømna 031207
Somnis, Girona 081138
Somogy Editions d'Art, Paris 133678
Somogyi Megyei Múzeumok Igazgatósága, Kaposvár 021753
Somoza & Sims, Houston 116405
Somuchso, Berlin 102047
Son-Et-Lumiere, Mumbai 105809
Šon Gallery, Moskva 080267
Sona, Bayreuth 101749
Sonargaon Folk Art and Craft Museum, Sonargaon 003118
Sonath, Paris 100877
Sonawala, Madhavi, Mumbai 105810
Soncin, Rinaldo, Torino 128362
Sonda, Den Haag 107954
Sondaar, P.Y., Utrecht 128860
SonderBa, Nienburg, Weser 104454
Sonderegger, R. & M., Bäretswil . . . 082110
Sønderjyllands Kunstmuseum, Tønder 009131
Søndhordland Motormuseum, Valevåg 031313
Sondre Nordheimstova, Morgedal . . 031034
Sonetec Sud Ouest, Saint-Morillon . 101183
Song, København 060382
Song, Sam, New York 091256
Song Qingling Former Residence, Shanghai 007245
Song Qingling Tongzhi Former Residence, Beijing 007009
Songam Art Museum, Incheon 027512
Songcheng, Hangzhou 097739
Songha, Busan 107175
Songha, Changwon 107178
Songjiang County Museum, Shanghai 007246
Songline, Amsterdam 107803
Songsin Teachers College Museum, Seoul 027606
Songyun Zhai Art Galley, Tianjin . . . 098016
Songyun Zhai Art Galley, Tianjin . . . 098017
Soni, Crawford 110039
Sonia, Singapore 080563
Sonic Arts Gallery, San Diego 119552
Sonkajärven Kotiseutumuseo, Sonkajärvi 010095
Sonnabend, New York 118432

Sonne + Mond Galerie, Heinsberg 103348
Sonnen-Galerie, Beilstein, Württemberg 101752
Sonntag, Stefan, Stuttgart 074011
Sonoma County Museum, Santa Rosa 047994
Sonoma State Historic Park, Sonoma 048223
Sonoran, Phoenix 091769
Sonrier, Jean-Pierre, Colmar 062419
Sonrisa, Los Angeles 116888
Sons of the American Revolution, Roselle 047544
Sons of the American Revolution Museum, Louisville 045497
Sonsbeek, Arnhem 107859
Sontg Hippolytus, Veulden 037674
Sontheim, Ernst, Kempten 126029
Sony Gallery, Cairo 098675
Sony Wonder Technology Lab, New York 046405
Sonya's Treasures, Indianapolis 089343
Sonzogni, Luisa, Milano 075869
Soo, Seoul 107294
Soo Line Historical Museum, Weyburn 006803
Soo San, London 085702, 131177
Soo Tze Oriental Antiques, Prahran 056501
Soo Visual Arts Center, Minneapolis 045921
Soobin, Singapore 109873
Sood Sangvichien Prehistoric Museum, Bangkok 037891
Sooke Region Museum, Art Gallery and Historic Moss Cottage, Sooke 006490
Sookmyung Women's University Museum, Seoul 027607
Sooner Collectibles, Oklahoma City 091537
Sooner Ga Museum, Dhaka 003111
Sopel, Lyle, Vancouver 097532
Sopel, Lyle, Vancouver 097533
Sopena, Ramón, Barcelona 134928
Sophia Antiquités, Saint-Ouen 067894
Sophie & Joe's Emporium, Saint Paul 092400
Sophie & Van Twist, Breda 078117
Sophienburg Museum, New Braunfels 046198
Sophie's Books, Moss Vale 137011
Sophisticated Traveller, Zeist 078870
Sophonisbe, Carthage 112245
Sopocki Dom Aukcyjny, Gdańsk 079588, 121886
Sopocki Dom Aukcyjny, Gdynia 079602, 121889
Sopocki Dom Aukcyjny, Kraków 079658
Sopocki Dom Aukcyjny, Kraków 079659
Sopocki Dom Aukcyjny, Kraków 121893
Sopocki Dom Aukcyjny, Kraków 121894
Sopocki Dom Aukcyjny, Sopot 079712, 121898
Sopot-Art, Sopot 109078
Soppe, Anne, Essen 070650
Sopwell Nunnery, Saint Albans 040890
Sør-Senja Museum, Midt-Troms Museum, Stonglandseidet 031243
Sorai, Kyoto 077125
Soranthe, Eindhoven 078350
Sorbische Bauernstube, Heinersbrück 017858
Sorbische Heimatstube Rohne, Schleife-Rohne 020034
Sordes, Christian, Grenoble 063074
Sordini, Marseille 099686
Sordo Rue, Pedro Sergio, Barcelona 080939
Sordoni Art Gallery, Wilkes-Barre 049175
Sorecomodata, Porto 080112, 129201
Sorel, Portland 092010
Sorell Antique Centre, Sorell 056602
Sorell Station Antiques, Sorell 056603
Soren, Christensen, New Orleans 117513
Sørensen, Oslo 079474
Soret, Hervé, Saint-Ouen 067895
Soret, Philippe, Saint-Ouen 067896
Sorge, Klaus, Milano 127689
Sorgenfrei, Gisela, Bad Schwartau 069380
Sorgenicht, Margarete, Berlin 069765
Sørlandets Kunstmuseum, Kristiansand 030958
Sørlandsutstillingen, Saltrød 108745
Sørli Museum, Sørli 031211
Sorma, Sharjah 083228
Sormani, Milano 140066
Soro, Los Angeles 089914
Sorø Amts Museum, Sydvestsjællands Museum, Sorø 009114
Sorokko, Serge, San Francisco 119798
Sorokko, Serge, San Francisco 119799
Sorolla Galeria, Sevilla 110780
Soroptimist Book Shop, Port Pirie 137051
Soroptimist International, Kansas City 116592
Soroush, Teheran 134524
Sørsamiske Samlinger, Snåsa 031202
Sós, Budapest 139928
SOS Art, Bologna 127183
Sos Moveis, São Paulo 058743
Sosa, Lourdes, México 107514
Sósaiati, Coimbra 079823
Soshoku Design, Tokyo 135984
Sosin & Sosin, Minneapolis 117307
Soskine, Michel, New York 118433
Sosnitza, Michael, Göttingen 125741
Sosnovoborskij Chudožestvennyj Muzei Sovremennogo Iskusstva, Sosnovyj Bor 033897
Sossdorf, Hans Georg, Lübeck 072340
Sóstói Múzeumfalu, Sóstógyógyfürdő 021851
Søsveen Antikk, Sola 079495
Sota Zorraquin, Pedro de la, Bilbao 110287
Sotamuseo, Helsinki 009570
El Sótano, Montevideo 087348
Sotavallan Tuulimylly, Lempäälä 009817
Soteau, Christian, Souvigny 068280
Sotheby's, Amsterdam 121779
Sotheby's, Atlanta 122802
Sotheby's, Bangkok 122378
Sotheby's, Beverly Hills 122818
Sotheby's, Billingshurst 122414
Sotheby's, Bofferdange 121755
Sotheby's, Boston 122827
Sotheby's, Bruxelles 120745
Sotheby's, Buenos Aires 120555
Sotheby's, Caracas 123142
Sotheby's, Cheltenham 122460
Sotheby's, Chester 122463
Sotheby's, Chicago 122847
Sotheby's, Clyde 122867
Sotheby's, Constantia 121982
Sotheby's, Dallas 122876
Sotheby's, Dublin 121667
Sotheby's, Edinburgh 122500
Sotheby's, Frankfurt am Main 121409
Sotheby's, Genève 122328
Sotheby's, Glasgow 122519
Sotheby's, Hamburg 121438
Sotheby's, Harrogate 122537
Sotheby's, Haverford 122900
Sotheby's, Helsinki 120887
Sotheby's, Hong Kong 120840
Sotheby's, Honolulu 122903
Sotheby's, Houston 122915
Sotheby's, Jakarta 121653
Sotheby's, Johannesburg 121986
Sotheby's, København 120873
Sotheby's, Köln 121478
Sotheby's, Kuala Lumpur 121760
Sotheby's, Lehre 121491
Sotheby's, London 122599
Sotheby's, London 122600
Sotheby's, Lugano 122336
Sotheby's, Lyon 121055
Sotheby's, Madrid 122069
Sotheby's, Melbourne 120610
Sotheby's, México 121768
Sotheby's, Miami 122963
Sotheby's, Milano 121712
Sotheby's, Minneapolis 122970
Sotheby's, Monaco 121775
Sotheby's, Montchanin 122973
Sotheby's, Monterrey 121769
Sotheby's, München 121547
Sotheby's, New York 123016
Sotheby's, Newcastle-upon-Tyne 122630
Sotheby's, Newmarket 122631
Sotheby's, Newtownards 122634
Sotheby's, Oslo 121873
Sotheby's, Palm Beach 123040
Sotheby's, Paris 121211
Sotheby's, Praha 120861
Sotheby's, Riderwood 123077
Sotheby's, Rio de Janeiro 120796
Sotheby's, Roma 121726
Sotheby's, Särö 122233
Sotheby's, Salisbury 122684
Sotheby's, San Francisco 123106
Sotheby's, Sankt Moritz 122349
Sotheby's, Santa Barbara 123109
Sotheby's, Santiago de Chile 120836
Sotheby's, São Paulo 120798
Sotheby's, Seattle 123117
Sotheby's, Shanghai 120843
Sotheby's, Singapore 121975
Sotheby's, Skurup 122240
Sotheby's, Stockholm 122260
Sotheby's, Stocksfield 122707
Sotheby's, Sydney 120644
Sotheby's, Taipei 120845
Sotheby's, Tel Aviv 121676
Sotheby's, Tiverton 122727
Sotheby's, Tokyo 121748
Sotheby's, Torino 121735
Sotheby's, Toronto 120822
Sotheby's, Warwick 120793
Sotheby's, Wien 120692
Sotheby's, Zürich 122372
Sotheby's Art at Auction, London 136269
Sotheby's Newsletter, New York 136625
Sotheby's Restoration, New York 132538
Sotheran, Henry, London 131178, 141898
Sotheran, Henry, London 141899
Sotilaslääketieteen Museo, Lahti 009791
Sotiropoulos, Athinai 105408
Sotis, Mitzy, Roma 128210
Sotkamon Kotiseutumuseo, Sotkamo 010096
Soto, Boston 115232
Soto, Blanca, Madrid 110618
Soto de Collins, Lucía, Bogotá 059861
Soto Valle, Luís Miguel, Bilbao 080992
Sotscheck, Helmut, Potsdam 126657
Sotterley Plantation Museum, Hollywood 044580
Sottocorno 9, Milano 106317
Sou, Sendai 107005
Soubizantik, Saint-Ouen 067897
Soubrier, Paris 066563
Souček, Vladislav, Plzeň 060083
Soucheby, Nelson 079181, 108520
Souchet, Albert, Rennes (Ille-et-Vilaine) 124878
Souchet, Fabien, Paris 124815
Souchko, Vladimir, Rouen 067300, 124884
Souchon, Michel, Paris 066564
Souchot, Patrice, Cepoy 062051
Souchot, Patrice, Cepoy 062052
Soudan Corners, Toronto 059293
Souders, Fort Worth 116165
Soudry-Tharaud, Annie, Carnac 061994
Soufer, New York 118434
Souffle du Passé, Kfarhabab 077437, 140221
Soufir, Hélène, Maulette 064433
Souflard, Jean-Pierre, Ampuis 060830
Sougyo, Aoitori, Tokyo 077310
Souillac, Michel, Paris 066565
Souk, Sam, New York 118435
Souka, Sapporo 077202
Soukaïna, Casablanca 077675
Soul 42, Bern 082241
Soul Mates Adventures, Amsterdam 107804
Soul of Africa, Vancouver 097534
Soulard, Saint Louis 119258
Soulard, Claude, Saint-Georges-de-Montaigu 067489
Soulard, Jacqueline & Christian, Flayosc 062868, 138089
Soulard, Marie-Hélène, Nantes 124489
Soulas, Didier, La Roche-sur-Yon 063418
Soulé-Roig, Béatrice, Perpignan 100995, 124840
Soulié, Béatrice, Paris 100878
Soulié, Jacqueline, Finhan 062864
Soulie, José, Bourganeuf 061717
Soulier, Marc, Montpellier 064755
Soulières, Roger, Montréal 097080
Soun Museum, Ashikaga 026425
Sound School House Museum, Mount Desert 046056
Sound Visitor Centre, Manx National Heritage, Port Saint Mary 040746
Soundarte-Galería, Medellín 098286
Soundiata, Seattle 119996
Sounds of Yesteryear, Winnipeg 006867
Sour, Patrick, Niort 065198
Sourbié, Didier, Sigean 068241
Source, Bath 083446
Source, Buffalo 087911
Source Antiques, Dubbo 055764
Source aux Trouvailles, Nanterre 064888
Source Enterprises, Vancouver 059423
Source Fine Arts, Kansas City 116593
Source Graphics and Arts, Abu Dhabi 112442
Source: Notes in the History of Art, New York 136626
Sources, London 136270
Sourgnes, Michel, Ascot 094179
Sourice, Daniel, Vitry-sur-Seine 069016
Sourillan International, Toulouse 068544, 101372
La Souris Verte, Paris 066566
Sourzat, Jean-Louis, Saint-Céré 067395
Sous le Ciel Tibétain, Perpignan 066759
Sous-les-Toits-de-Paris, Paris 066567
Sousa &Filhos, Lisboa 080032
Sousa & Roquette, Lisboa 080033
Soussana, Jacques, Jerusalem 105914, 134537
Soustre, François, Saint-Hilaire-Luc 067521
Souter Johnnie's House, Kirkoswald 039904
Souterroscope des Ardoisières, Caumont-l'Eventé 011160
South Africa National Association for the Visual Arts, Pretoria 054069
South African Antique Dealers' Association, Fontainebleau 054070
South African Cultural History Museum, Iziko Museums of Cape Town, Cape Town 034583
South African Jewish Museum, Cape Town 034584
South African Maritime Museum, Cape Town 034585
South African Mint Museum-Coin World, Centurion 034589
South African Museum, Iziko Museums of Cape Town, Cape Town 034586
South African National Gallery, Iziko Museums of Cape Town, Cape Town 034587
South African National Museum of Military History, Saxonwold 034746
South African National Railway Museum, Auckland Park 034546
South African Police Service Museum, Pretoria 034728
South Arkansas Arts Center, El Dorado 043627
South Australian Aviation Museum, Port Adelaide 001389
South Australian Maritime Museum, Port Adelaide 001390
South Australian Museum, Adelaide 000713
South Australian Police Museum, Thebarton 001548
South Bank Galleries, Pittsburgh 091859, 118955

South Bank Printmakers, London . . 113893
South Bannock County Historical Center, Lava Hot Springs 045203
South Bay Auctions, Long Island City 122941
South Bend Regional Museum of Art, South Bend 048228
South Boston-Halifax County Museum of Fine Arts and History, South Boston 048234
South Bronx Art Workshop, Baltimore 115085
South Canterbury Museum, Timaru 030605
South Cariboo Historical Museum, Clinton 005278
South Carolina Artisans Center, Walterboro 048844
South Carolina Confederate Relic Room and Museum, Columbia 043085
South Carolina Cotton Museum, Bishopville 042235
South Carolina Federation of Museums, Columbia 055043
South Carolina Historical Society Museum, Charleston 042744
South Carolina Law Enforcement Officers Hall of Fame, Columbia 043086
South Carolina Military Museum, Columbia 043087
South Carolina National Guard Museum, Sumter 048425
South Carolina State Museum, Columbia 043088
South Carolina Tennis Hall of Fame, Belton 042134
South Charles Street Gallery, Baltimore 115086
South Charleston Museum, South Charleston 048235
South Coast Auction, Santa Ana . . . 123108
South Coast Railroad Museum at Goleta Depot, Goleta 044240
South Coast Wood Works Gallery, Youngs Siding 095458
South County Antique Mall, Saint Louis 092315
South County Art Association, Kingston 055044
South County Museum, Narragansett 046133
South Dakota Amateur Baseball Hall of Fame, Lake Norden 045111
South Dakota Art Museum, Brookings 042449
South Dakota Discovery Center, Pierre 047019
South Dakota Hall of Fame, Chamberlain 042700
South Devon Railway, Buckfastleigh 038889
South-East Armed Force Museum, Ho Chi Minh City 049541
South East Art Society, Mount Gambier 052493
South East European Contemporary Art Network, Skopje 053853
South Eastern Federation of Museums and Art Galleries, Bromley 054519
South Fitzroy Antiques and Interiors, Fitzroy 055825, 123224
South Florida Art Institute, Dania . . 051225
South Florida Museum, Bradenton . 042380
South Florida Museum of Natural History, Dania Beach 043292
South Florida Science Museum, West Palm Beach 049093
South Front Antique Market, Memphis 090105
South Gate Gallery, Exeter 113041
South Gippsland Auctions, Korumburra 120597
South Gippsland Shire Museum, Foster 001038
South Grey Museum and Historical Library, Flesherton 005447
South Hero Bicentennial Museum, South Hero 048243
South Hill Park Arts Centre, Bracknell 038802
South Hills Antique Center, Pittsburgh 091860
South Hills Antique Gallery, Cleveland 088363
South Hills Art Center, Pittsburgh . . 118956
South Holland Historical Museum, South Holland 048244
South Indian Society of Painters, Chennai 053707
South London Antique and Bookcentre, London 141900
South London Gallery, London 040292
South Louisville Antique Mall, Louisville 090027
South Midlands Museums Federation, Saffron Walden 054520
South Milwaukee Historical Society Museum, South Milwaukee 048245
South Molton and District Museum, South Molton 041045
South Nottinghamshire Hussars Museum, Bulwell 038900
South of Market, Atlanta 087529
South Otago Historical Museum, Balclutha 030452
South Park City Museum, Fairplay . 043796
South Pass City State Historic Site, South Pass City 048248
South Peace Centennial Museum, Beaverlodge 005088
South Perth Antiques, South Perth . 056610
South Perth Heritage House, South Perth 001477
South Rawdon Museum, South Rawdon 006495
South Ribble Museum and Exhibition Centre, Leyland 039997
South River Meeting House, Lynchburg 045530
South Shields Museum and Art Gallery, South Shields 041050
South Shore Gallery, Milwaukee . . . 117221
South Simcoe Pioneer Museum, Alliston 004998
South Similkameen Museum, Keremeos 005683
South Street Seaport Museum, New York 046406
South Sutton Old Store Museum, South Sutton 048251
South Taranaki District Museum, Patea 030574
South Texas Museum, Alice 041652
South Tipperary County Museum, Clonmel 022715
South Tynedale Railway Preservation Society, Alston 038497
South Wales Borderers and Monmouthshire Regimental Museum of the Royal Regiment of Wales, Brecon 038827
South Wales Miner's Museum, Port Talbot 040750
South Wales Police Museum, Bridgend 038828
South West Academy of Fine & Applied Arts, Exeter 050815
South West Museums Council, Bathpool 054521
South Western Federation of Museums and Art Galleries, Bournemouth 054522
South Wood County Historical Museum, Wisconsin Rapids 049272
Southam, Salt Lake City 119370
Southampton Art Gallery, Southampton 006497
Southampton Art School, Southampton 049815
Southampton City Art Gallery, Southampton 041058
Southampton Hall of Aviation, Southampton 041059
Southampton Historical Museum, Southampton 048255
Southampton Maritime Museum, Southampton 041060
Southam's, Thrapston 122726
Southchurch Hall Museum, Southend-on-Sea 041066
Southdown Antiques, Lewes 084986
Southdown House Antique Galleries, Brasted 083654, 130432
Southeast Arts Center, Atlanta 041873
Southeast Asia Art, Singapore 109874
Southeast Coin, Portland 092011
Southeast Missouri State University Museum, Cape Girardeau 042613
Southeast Museum, Brewster 042401
Southeast Museum of Photography, Daytona Beach Community College, Daytona Beach 043331
Southeastern Center for Contemporary Art, Winston-Salem 049258
Southeastern College Art Conference, Chapel Hill 055045
Southeastern Front, Cleveland 136627
Southeastern Museums Conference, Baton Rouge 055046
Southeastern Pastel Society, Dawsonville 055047
Southeastern Railway Museum, Duluth 043517
Southend Central Museum, Southend-on-Sea 041067
Southend Limited, Charlotte 087979
Southend Pier Museum, Southend-on-Sea 041068
Southerbee, Oklahoma City 091538
Southern African Development Community Association of Museums and Monuments, Harare 055129
Southern Alberta Art Gallery, Lethbridge 005768
Southern Alleghenies Museum of Art, Loretto 045404
Southern Alleghenies Museum of Art at Johnstown, Johnstown 044874
Southern Antique Centre, Kogarah . 056060
Southern Antique Centre, Kogarah . 056061
Southern Arizona Watercolor Guild, Tucson 055048
Southern Artist Union, Jacksonville 055049
Southern Arts Federation, Atlanta . . 055050
Southern California Chapter Railway and Locomotive Museum, Los Angeles 045465
Southern Cross Relics, Koroit 056067
Southern Crossing Antique Mall, Jacksonville 089461
Southern Exposure Gallery, San Francisco 047886
Southern Exposure Gallery, San Francisco 119800
Southern Expressions, New Orleans 117514
Southern Firearms, Clovelly Park . . 055697
Southern Forest World Museum, Waycross 049025
Southern Graphics Council, Athens . 055051
Southern Highland Craft Guild at the Folk Art Center, Asheville 041797
Southern Historical Showcase, Nashville 090489
Southern Museum of Flight, Birmingham 042226
Southern Newfoundland Seamen's Museum, Grand Bank 005528
Southern Ohio Museum and Cultural Center, Portsmouth 047194
Southern Oregon Historical Society Museum, Medford 045743
Southern Oregon University Museum of Vertebrate Natural History, Ashland 041811
Southern Plains Indian Museum, Anadarko 041707
Southern Settings, Birmingham . . . 115129
Southern & Southeast Arts, Winchester 054523
Southern Splendor, Nashville 090490
Southern Ute Indian Cultural Center, Ignacio 044714
Southern Vermont Art Center, Manchester 045624
Southern Vermont College Art Gallery, Bennington 042147
Southern Vermont Natural History Museum, Marlboro 045693
Southey and District Museum, Southey 006498
Southgate Auction Rooms, London . 122601
Southgate Bookshop, London 141901
The Southland Art Collection, Dallas 043276
Southland Art Society, Invercargill .053927, 108478
Southland Fire Service Museum, Invercargill 030523
Southland Museum and Art Gallery, Invercargill 030524
Southold Historical Society Museum, Southold 048257
Southold Indian Museum, Southold 048258
Southport Antique Mall, Indianapolis 089344
Southport Antiques, Chicago 088171
Southport Antiques Centre, Southport 086661
Southport Art, Chicago 115555
Southport-Westport Antiques Show, Greens Farms 094036
Southsea Castle, Portsmouth 040771
Southside Antiques, Saint Louis . . . 092316
Southside Antiques Centre, Annerley 055349
Southside Auction, Tulsa 123130
Southside Furniture Stripper, Jacksonville 132194
Southside House, London 040293
Southward Museum, Paraparaumu . 030573
Southwest Antiques, Houston 089211
Southwest Art, Invercargill 108479
Southwest Art League Seminars, Santa Fe 052143
Southwest Coin, Oklahoma City . . . 091539
Southwest Cornerhouse, Albuquerque 114823
Southwest Florida Pastel Society, Naples 055052
Southwest Gallery, Dallas 115941
Southwest Mercado Gallery, Albuquerque 114824
Southwest Museum, Los Angeles . . 045466
Southwest Museum of Science and Technology, Dallas 043277
Southwest Numismatic Corporation, Dallas 088612
Southwest School of Art and Craft, San Antonio 052111
Southwest Studios, El Paso 116118
Southwest Virginia Museum, Big Stone Gap 042201
Southwestern Art, Denver 116055
Southwestern Artists Association, San Diego 055053
Southwestern College Art Gallery, Chula Vista 042912
Southwestern Michigan College Museum, Dowagiac 043499
Southwestern Ontario Heritage Village, Kingsville 005710
Southwestern Saskatchewan Oldtimer's Museum, Maple Creek 005831
Southwestern University Museum, Cebu 031661
Southwestern Utah Art Gallery, Saint George 047631
Southwick, David L.H., Kingswear . 084868
Southwick Hall, Peterborough 040702
Southwold Museum, Southwold . . . 041073
Souto, Rui, Porto 080113
Souvenance, Bourges . . . 061730, 124157
Souvenances, Montreuil-sur-Mer . . 064771
Souvenir, Singapore 080564
Souvenir Antiques, Carlisle 083880
Souvenir Press, London 135264
Souverain, Michel, Nueil-sur-Layon 065247
Souvré, Christian, Courmelles 062517
Souyris, Christian, Salles-Curan . . . 068100
Souza, Toninho de, Brasília 096505
Souzy, Pierre de, Paris 100879
Sov Art, Moskva 109592
Sovenirs de Provence, Cassis 099094
Sovereign Antiques, Gateshead . . . 084455
Sovereign Antiques, Middle Park . . 056221

Sovereign Antiques, Seacliff Park . . 056580
Sovereign City Auctions, Sebastopol 120636
Sovereign Collection, Portland 119055
Sovereign Furniture Gallery, Chesham 083944, 130553
Sovereign Hill, Ballarat 000765
Soviart, Kyïv 112422
Soviet Carpet and Art Galleries, London 085703
Sovremennaja Galereja-muzej Nikor, Sobranie N.I. Kornilova, Moskva . 033525
Sovremennoe Iskusstvo, Sankt-Peterburg 109649
Sowade, Reimund, Dresden 070330
Soweto Art, Johannesburg 110061
Sowinski, Christiane, Noailles 065204
Sozzani, Carla, Milano 106318
Sozzi, Romeo, Milano 106319
Sozzi, Romeo, Milano 106320
S.P. Engelbrecht Museum of the Nederduitsch Hervormde Kerk van Afrika, Pretoria 034729
S.P. Fine Arts, Dallas 115942
Spa & Assoc., Los Angeles 089915
Spa 64, New York 091257
Spaans Galjoen, Amsterdam 077970
Spaarnestad Fotoarchief, Haarlem . 029659
Space 101 Gallery, Brew House Association, Pittsburgh 047063
Space 1026, Philadelphia 118838
Space 237, Toledo 120092
The Space Center, Alamogordo . . . 041591
Space Center, Houston 116406
Space Center Houston, Houston . . . 044657
Space d'Arte, New York 118436
Space Expo, Noordwijk, Zuid-Holland 029975
Space Farms Zoological Park and Museum, Sussex 048444
Space & Form, Montréal 059006
Space & Form, Montréal 059007
Space Gallery, Denver 116056
Space Gallery, Kraków 108981
Space Gallery, New Orleans 117515
Space Invaders, Long Beach 089657
Space of Art, Baabdet El-Metn 077378
Space of Art, Beirut 077416
Space One Eleven, Birmingham . . . 042227
Space One Eleven, Birmingham . . . 115130
Space Station, Denver 088739
Space Time Dreamworld, Marseille 099687
Space Untitled, New York 118437
Spaces, Cleveland 043000
Spaces, Cleveland 115744
Spacial Anomaly Gallery, Philadelphia 118839
Spadafora, Giuseppe, Torino 106705
Spadari, Fréjus 062939
Spaddeline, München 072863
Spadina Museum, Toronto 006633
Spagl, Hutthurm 134069
Spagna, Anna Maria, Milano 127690
Spagnoletto, Pacifico, Roma 076690
Spagnoli, Sebastiano, Napoli 076056
Spagnolo, Mario, Roma 128211
Spagnolo, Rosaria, Foggia 127430
Spahn, R., Flieden 070710
Spaite, Monique, Ternuay-Melay-Saint-Hilaire 068372
Spak, Stockholm 082022
Spakenburgs Museum 't Vurhuus, Bunschoten Spakenburg 029368
Spalding Antiques, Spalding 056620
Spalding Antiques, Spalding 086676
Spalding Gentlemen's Society Museum, Spalding 041076
Spalk, Dieter, München 072864
The Spam Museum, Austin 041918
Span Art Gallery, Tokyo 107117
Span Galleries, Melbourne 094828
Spang, Cincinnati 088282
Spanierman, New York 091258
Spanish Cross Home Furnishings, Tucson 093267
Spanish Governor's Palace, San Antonio 047805
Spanish Institute, New York 046407
The Spanish Quarter Museum, Saint Augustine 047614
Spannagel, H., Seebad Heringsdorf 073782
Spanos, Konst., Athinai 139900
Spantidaki, Athinai 074609
Spare Room, Edithburgh 055790
Sparebankmuseet, Oslo 031106
Sparekassemuseet, Korsør 009003
Sparenberg, Friedrich, Göttingen . . 071054
Spargelmuseum, Schlunkendorf . . . 020052
Spark, Denver 116057
Spark Gallery, Denver 043419
Sparkassen-Museum, Greding 017516
Sparkassen-Museum der Erste Bank, Wien 003006
Sparnaay, Tjalf, Amsterdam 107805
Sparresholm Vognsamling, Holme-Olstrup 008922
Spart, Michel, Corcelles . . 082325, 130004
Spartanburg County Art School, Spartanburg 052199
Spartanburg County Museum of Art, Spartanburg 048265
Spartanburg Science Center, Spartanburg 048266
Sparts - Art in Sports, Amsterdam .107806, 134790
Spårvägsmuseet, Stockholm 036666
Spas, Sankt-Peterburg 109650
Spathareion Museum of the Shadow Theatre, Maroussi 021368
Spazierer, Schrems 137261
Spazio, Erasmus, Milano 106321
Spazio Arte, Milano 106322
Spazio Arte, Perugia 106462
Spazio Idea Arredamenti, Roma . . . 076691
Spazzio, Porto Alegre 058524
SPC Pioneer Museum, San Francisco 047887
SPCK Bookshops, Winchester 142159
Speakeasy Antiques, San Antonio . 092584
Speakeasy Antiques, San Antonio . 092585
Speakeasy Antiques, San Antonio . 132828
Spears, Indianapolis 116494
De Specht, Zetten 128886
Special Pieces, Paddington, New South Wales 056421
Special T Gallery, Edmonton 096898
Specialcolour, Nottingham 114178
The Specialist, Shorncliffe 123304
Specialty Finishes Unlimited, Columbus 131990
The Speckled Hen, Townsville 056732
Spectator Bookstore, Oakland 142711
Spector, Warren, Houston 089212
Spector Gallery, Philadelphia 118840
Spectra, Wörgl 095974
Spectrum, East Grinstead 130661
Spectrum, Euskirchen 102720
Spectrum (Amherst), Amherst 136628
Spectrum Arts, New York 118438
Spectrum Books, Warrnambool . . . 137133
Spectrum-Friends of Fine Art, Toledo 055054, 120093
Spectrum Gallery, Balwyn 094208
Spectrum Gallery, Fresno 116186
Spectrum Gallery, Machynlleth 114025
Spectrum Gallery, Toronto 097377, 123841
Spectrum Gallery, Washington 120348
Spectrum Photos, Leicester 113375
Spectrum plus, Liebefeld 082577
Spectrum Sotos, Zaragoza 110893
Speculum Orbis, Bad Neustadt an der Saale 135822
Speeckaert, E., Bruxelles 137470
Speed, J. & J., Cobham 130592
Speed Art Museum, Louisville 045498
Speedway, Judy, Houston 116407
Speedway Antique Mall, Tucson . . . 093268
Speedway Bookshop, Christchurch . 140621
Speedway Coins, Indianapolis 089345
Speelgoedmuseum De Brug, Eerbeek 029530
Speelgoedmuseum De Kijkdoos, Hoorn 029774
Speelgoedmuseum Deventer, Deventer 029475
Speelgoedmuseum Mechelen, Mechelen 003634
Speelgoedmuseum Op Stelten, Oosterhout 030000
Speelman, A. & J., London 085704
Speelman, Edward, London 113894
Speer, Zürich 135103
Speer, Torsten, Uetersen 074137
Speezey, Los Angeles 116889
Speicher im Stegengraben, Rendsburg 104721
Speicherstadtmuseum, Hamburg . . 017722
Speight, Elisabeth, Philadelphia . . . 132636
Speight 5060 Martin, Storrington . . 114499
Speijer, J., Hilversum 078541
Speke Hall, Liverpool 040037
Spektar, Veliko Tărnovo 096781
Spektrum, Jilemnice 098368
Spektrum, Internationale Vierteljahresschrift für Dichtung und Originalgrafik Zürich, Regensberg 136130
Spelbos, Utrecht 128861
Spelbos, R.H., Utrecht 078820
Speldjesmuseum, Klaaswaal 029810
Speller, Annie, Clermont-Ferrand . . 062356
Spellman Museum of Stamps and Postal History, Weston 049123
Spelman, Ken, York 142180
Spelman College Museum of Fine Art, Atlanta 041874
Spelthorne Museum, Staines 041085
Spence, Larry, Austin 087614
Spenceola Antiques Center, Bel Air . 087726
Spencer, Boston 142256
Spencer, Bridlington 122435
Spencer, Houston 116408
Spencer, Des, Main Beach 094764
Spencer, Don, Warwick 087044
Spencer, Jolly, Chicago 088172
Spencer, R., Portland 092012
Spencer and Gillen Gallery, Alice Springs 000735
Spencer Entomological Museum, Vancouver 006710
Spencer House, London 040294
Spencer Museum of Art, University of Kansas, Lawrence 045206
Spencer Museum of Art. Register, Lawrence 136629
Spencer-Peirce-Little Farm, Newbury 046440
Spencer Street Gallery, West Melbourne 095392
Spencer's Treasures, Phoenix 091770
Spendiarians Museum, Erevan 000688
Spengler-Museum, Sangerhausen . 019980
Spenner, H., Waltrop 139825
Spennick, Jacques, Lens 063742
Spenster, Ole, København 060383
Spéos - Formation et Stages de Photographie, Paris 049980
La Speranza, Luigi, Wien 095941
Sperberg, Michael J., Richmond . . .092111, 132724
Sperka, Peter, Paunzhausen 073297
Sperl, Potsdam 104633
Sperlhofer, Michael, Bad Ischl 056932, 095468
Sperling, Linthe 072280, 121500
Sperling, Reinhard, Dresden 125510
Spermann, Klaus, Berlin 102048
Spero, Simon, London 085705
Sperone, Gian Enzo, New York 118439
Sperone, Gianenzo, Roma 106627
Sperone, Gianenzo, Roma 106628
Sperone & Westwater, New York . . 118440
Sperrgebiet Museum, Oranjemund . 029093
Sperrin Heritage Centre, Plumridge 040720
Sperrle, Volker, Schwäbisch Gmünd 073740
Spertus Museum, Chicago 042880
Spessartmuseum, Lohr am Main . . 018680
Speth, D., Lalling 072120
Spetses Museum, Spetses 021478
Spettel, Alain, Bruguières 061825
Speybrouck, Bruno, Kortrijk 058271
Speyer, Darthea, Paris 100880
SPG Gallery, Richmond, Victoria . . . 095143
Sphinx, Groningen 140437
Sphinx, Milano 127691
Sphinx, Toronto 059294
Sphinx-Antiques, Zürich 083024
Spica, Martina-Erica, Lugano 082609
Spice, Hastings 084620
Spice's Gewürzmuseum, Hamburg . 017723
Spicilège, Paris 100881
Spider Web Painting Australia, Buxton 094334
spiegel, München 019114
De Spiegel, Zaltbommel 078858
Spiegel, Reinhard, Wiesbaden 105282
Spiegel, Robert, Windisch Minihof . 057604
Spiegel, Theodor, Würzburg 127043
Spiegel Fine Framing, New York . . . 132539
Spiegelbeeld, Breda 128609
Spiegelbeeld, Emmen 108015
Spiegeling Art, Amsterdam 107807
Spiegelman, K., West Hollywood . . 093511
't Spieghel, Leiden 078585
't Spieghelhuis, Almelo 107626
Spieker, Werner, Gelnhausen 070954
Spiel Kultur, München 019115
SpielArt-Galerie, Frankfurt am Main 102828
Spielberger, Karl, Freistadt, Oberösterreich 137168
Spielkartensammlung Piatnik, Wien 003007
Spielvogel, Gudrun, München 104322, 134279
Spielzeug anno dazumal - Museum Beilngries, Beilngries 015939
Spielzeug-Museum Bad Herrenalb, Bad Herrenalb 015714
Spielzeug- und Kinderwelt Museum, Steinhude 020311
Spielzeugeisenbahn- und Zweiradmuseum, Affoltern am Albis 036818
Spielzeugmuseum, Bad Lauterberg 015747
Spielzeugmuseum, Davos Platz . . . 037040
Spielzeugmuseum, Görlitz 017456
Spielzeugmuseum, Hemau 017869
Spielzeugmuseum, Loosdorf, Bez. Melk 002267
Spielzeugmuseum, Michelstadt . . . 018936
Spielzeugmuseum, Schkeuditz 020031
Spielzeugmuseum, Trier 020484
Spielzeugmuseum, Zwiesel 021090
Spielzeugmuseum, Museen der Stadt Nürnberg, Nürnberg 019374
Spielzeugmuseum, Salzburger Museum Carolino Augusteum, Salzburg . . . 002568
Spielzeugmuseum, Stadtmuseum Ingolstadt, Ingolstadt 018075
Spielzeugmuseum Alsfeld, Alsfeld . 015487
Spielzeugmuseum, Dorf- und Rebbaumuseum, Riehen 037454
Spielzeugmuseum im Alten Rathausturm, München 019116
Spielzeugmuseum im Alten Schloß, Jan und Manuela Kube, Sugenheim 020379
Spielzeugmuseum/Kellerkunstmuseum im Auktionshaus Boltz, Bayreuth . . . 015924
Spielzeugmuseum - Sammlung Depuoz, Zürich 037800
Spielzeugmuseum Solz, Bebra 015928
Spiers Gallery, Brevard College, Brevard 042398
Spies, H., Merzenich 072528
Spies, Margit, Stuttgart 126880
Spieß, Karin, Hamburg 071333
Spiess, Michel, Aarburg . . 082072, 129889
Spiess, Sibylle, Kirkel 103560
Spiess & Walther, Heidelberg 071461
Spijker, F., Eindhoven 078351
Spik, Leo, Berlin 069766, 121344
Spike Gallery, New York 118441

Spike Hughes Rare Books, Innerleithen 141688
Spiliotopoulos, Andreas, Thessaloniki 105459
Spillemands-Jagt og Skovbrugsmuseet i Rebild, Skørping 009105
Spiller, Jacksonville 116542
Spiller, Jacksonville 116543
Spiller, Axel, Gronau, Westfalen . . . 103013
Spiller, Vincenty, Jacksonville 116544
Spillmann, Bea, Zürich . . . 112180, 135104
Lo Spillo, Firenze 075406
Spin Gallery, Toronto 097378
La Spina, Pisa 106470
Spinabroc, Épinal 062789
De Spinde, Amersfoort 077752
De Spindelaar, Amersfoort 077753
Spindler, Klaus, München 072865
Spindler, Thomas, Marseille 124433
Spindletop and Gladys City Boomtown Museum, Beaumont 042088
Spine, Phoenix 091771
Spinelli, Andrea, Milano 075870
Spink & Son, London 085706
Spink, John, London 085707
Spinning Wheel, Southport 086662
Spinoza, Amsterdam 140339
Het Spinozahuis, Rijnsburg 030062
Spinrath, Düsseldorf 070442
Spira, Max, Paris 066568
Spira, Thierry, Paris 100882
Spiral Art Gallery, Auckland 108362
Spiral Gallery, Bega 094232
The Spiral Gallery, Settle 114404
Spiral Studios, Perth 095068
La Spirale 2000, Milano 106323
Spirale Arte, Milano 106324
Spirali/Vel, Milano 134637
Spires Art, Omagh 114189
Spires Gallery, Olney 114188
Spirig, Kurt, Lugano 082610, 141269
Spirig & Schnellmann, Rheineck . . . 082739
Spirit, Amsterdam 107808
Spirit Echoes Gallery, Austin 115013
Spirit Gallery, Vancouver 097535
Spirit of '76 Museum, Elyria 043699
Spirit of '76 Museum, Wellington . . 049051
The Spirit Wrestler, Vancouver 097536
Spiritual Art Gallery, Louisville 090028
Spiro Mounds Archaeological Center, Spiro 048272
Spironello, J., Bruxelles 123608
Spirres, Hannelore, Bottrop 102211
Spirta, Paris 100883
Spisanie Karikatura, Sofia 135617
Spisanie Kartinna Galeriia, Sofia . . 135618
Spisanie Panorama, Sofia 135619
Spišské Múzeum, Slovenské Národné Múzeum, Levoča 034373
Spitäle, Würzburg 105341
Spital Hengersberg, Hengersberg . . 017871
Spitalieri, Palermo 127839
Spitalmuseum, Aub 015594
Spitfire and Hurricane Memorial Museum, Ramsgate 040796
Spittka, Martin, Freiburg im Breisgau 139120
Spittler, Florianne, Kaiserslautern . . 103471
Spitz, Jean-Marie, Charleville-Mézières 099119
Spitzer, Bernd, Hamburg 071334
Spivack, Wellesly 093446, 133040
Spivey, Kansas City 142478
Spivey, Oklahoma City 091540
Spleiss, Margrit, Zürich 112181
SPLIA Gallery, Cold Spring Harbor . 043039
Spliethoff, G. & T., Billerbeck 102137
Splinter, Christine, Berlin 102049
Splinter, Juffrouw, Amsterdam 077971
Splinters Antiques, Forster 055835
Splinters Antiques, Myaree 056307
Split Rock Lighthouse Historic Site, Two Harbors 048677
Spode, David, Darlinghurst 136875
Spode Museum, Stoke-on-Trent . . . 041123
Spøk og spenning, Oslo 140706
Spoke Wheel Car Museum, Charlottetown 005253
Społeczne Muzeum Konstantego Laszczki, Dobre 031896
Spolidoro, Gilberto, Porto Alegre . . . 058525
Spomen Galerija Ivana Meštrovića, Vrpolje 007822
Spomen Kuća Bitke na Sutjesci, Tjentište 034273
Spomen-Kuća Vladimira Gortana, Beran 007698
Spomen-Muzej Prosvetitelja i Pisca Kirila Pejčinovića, Lesak kod Tetova . . . 034211
Spomen Muzej Prvog Zasjedania ZAVNOBiH-a, Mrkonjić Grad 034214
Spomen Muzej Prvog Zasjedanja ZAVNOBiH-a, Mrkonjić Grad 003935
Spomen Muzej Stojana Araliče, Otočac 007770
Spomen-Park Kragujevački Oktobar, Kragujevac 034207
Spomen Park-Kumrovec, Kumrovec 007750
Spomen-Zbirka Pavla Beljanskog, Novi Sad 034226
Spominska Zbirka Pisatelja Ivana Cankarja, Vrhnika 034537
Spong, Lindfield 085004
Spontanart, Laupen, Bern 111607
Spooner & Son, Michael, Ottawa . .059050, 120810
Spoor, Fred, Den Haag 078248
Spoor- en Tramweg Verzameling, Loppersum 029877
Spoorwegmuseum van Miniatuurmodellen, Heist-op-den-Berg 003507
Sport Images, Edmonton 096899
Sporting Antiques, Tunbridge Wells 086952
Sporting Art Gallery, Toronto 097379
The Sporting Gallery, Tetbury 086867
Sportis, Fréderic, Paris 066569
Sportmuseum Berlin, Stiftung Stadtmuseum Berlin, Berlin 016174
Sportmuseum Leipzig, Stadtgeschichtliches Museum Leipzig, Leipzig 018593
Sportmuseum Vlaanderen, Hofstade 003517
Sports Car Museum of Japan, Gotemba 026475
Sports Hall of Memories, Trail 006649
Sports Images, Columbus 088438
Sports Legacy Art Gallery, Pittsburgh 118957
Sports Legends, El Paso 088816
Sports Legends, El Paso 088817
The Sports Museum of New England, Boston 042345
Sports World Specialties, Pittsburgh 091861
Le Sportsman, Paris 138543
Sportsman's Edge Gallery, Houston 116409
Sportsman's Gallery, Atlanta 114928
Sportsman's Gallery, West Horndon 114667
Sporveismuseet Vognhall 5, Oslo . . 031107
Sporvejsmuseet Skjoldenæsholm, Jystrup Midtsj 008946
Spot Antiques, Saint Louis 092317
Spotsylvania Historical Museum, Spotsylvania 048276
Spoutnik, Montréal 059008
Spoutz, Eric I., Detroit 116096
Sprafka & O'Neill, Saint Paul 092401
Spratley, David, Paris 066570
Spratt, Frederick, San Jose 119864
Spratt, Jack, Newark-on-Trent 086057
Spread Eagle, London 085708
Spread Eagle, London 085709
Spread Eagle, London 131179
Spread Eagle, London 131180
Spread Eagle, London 141902
Sprebitz, Peter, Torgau 074072
Spreen, Heinrich, Preußisch Oldendorf 073373
De Spreeuwenpot, Den Haag 078249
Spreewald-Museum Lübbenau/Lehde, Lübbenau 018716
Sprengel Museum Hannover, Hannover 017769
Sprenger, G., Velburg 074187
Sprenger, G., Velburg 074188
Spriggs, J., New York 142695
Spring Creek Gallery, Beechworth . 094228
Spring Fair Birmingham-Gallery, Birmingham 093953
Spring Gallery, New York 118442
Spring Garden Book Supply, Philadelphia 142751
Spring Gate Galleries, Tampa 120069
Spring Gate Galleries, Tampa 120070
Spring Gate Galleries, Tampa 120071
Spring London Park Lane Arms Fair, London 093954
Spring Mill State Park Pioneer Village and Grissom Memorial, Mitchell 045939
Spring Mountain Art Gallery, Las Vegas 116649
Spring Mountain Art Gallery, Las Vegas 116650
Spring Street Historical Museum, Shreveport 048165
Spring Sunshine Art Gallery, Sydney 095306
Springbank Visual Arts Centre, Mississauga 005893
Springdale Coin and Antique Shop, Cincinnati 088283
Springer & Winckler, Berlin 102050
Springerin - Hefte für Gegenwartskunst, Wien 135578
Springfield, Amsterdam 077972
Springfield, Jacksonville 116545
Springfield Armory Museum, Springfield 048296
Springfield Art and Historical Society, Springfield 055055
Springfield Art Association, Springfield 055056
Springfield Art Gallery, Springfield . 048289
Springfield Art League, Springfield . 055057
Springfield Art Museum, Springfield 048301
Springfield Historical Society Museum, Springfield 048302
Springfield Library & Museums Association, Springfield 055058
Springfield Museum, Springfield . . . 048305
Springfield Museum of Art, Springfield 048304
Springfield Museum of Old Domestic Life, High Point 044535
Springfield Science Museum, Springfield 048297
Springfields Art, Mellieha 107446
Springhill Costume Museum, Moneymore 040486
Springhill House, Magherafelt 040384
Springhill Miner's Museum, Springhill 006502
Springmann, Josef, Freiburg im Breisgau 070862
Springs Museum, Springs 048308
Springtide Gallery, Bath 112588
Springvale and District Historical Museum, Springvale 001487
Springville Museum of Art, Springville 048310
Het Sprinozahuis, Rijnsburg 053903
Sprinz, Claudia, Feldafing 133927
Sprookjes, Antwerpen 057737
Sprossa, Else, Lillesand 128992
Sprott, W., Memphis 090106
Sprovieri Gallery, London 113895
Spruce Row Museum, Waterford . . 006769
Spruck, Gisela, Glauburg 125731
Sprüth, Monika, Köln 103718
Monika Sprüth & Philomene Magers, München 104323
Sprugnoli, Marie-Christine, Nice . . .065150, 099858
Sprugnoli, Michel, Nice . . 065151, 099859
Spruill, Atlanta 114929
Spruill Gallery, Atlanta 041875
Spruit, Sjaak, Maastricht 128765
Sprung, H., Zetel 127060
Sprung, Ralf-Peter, Berlin 069767
Spruth, Magers & Lee, London 113896
Claire Spry & Hermann Luther, Burg auf Fehmarn 125413
Spude, Christoph, Kassel 126019
't Spulleke, Bergen op Zoom 078075
Spunk, Minneapolis 117308
Spurlock Museum, University of Illinois at Urbana-Champaign, Urbana 048713
Spurn Lightship, Kingston-upon-Hull 039890
Spurrier-Smith, I., Ashbourne 083332
Spydeberg Bygdetun, Spydeberg . . 031217
Squam Lakes Natural Science Center, Holderness 044569
Squamish Valley Museum, Garibaldi Heights 005496
The Square Gallery, Saint Mawes . . 114382
Squatriti, Mario, Roma 128212
Squatters Antiques, Murray Bridge .056304, 123276
Squeri, Robert, San Francisco 119801
Squerryes Court, Westerham 041347
Squibbs, London 131181
Squillace, Armando, Roma 128213
Squires Antiques, Altrincham 083287
Squires Antiques, Faversham 084395
Squire's Pantry Antiques, Cowfold . 084097
Squirrel, Seattle 093070
Squirrel Collectors Centre, Basingstoke 083408
Squirrel Hill Jewelry, Pittsburgh . . .091862, 132678
Squirrels, Brockenhurst 083764
S.R. Furnishing and Antiques, Halesowen 084553
Sragow, Ellen, New York 118443
Średzki Ośrodek Kultury Galeria, Środa Śląska 032335
Sridharani Gallerie, Delhi 105684
Srinakharinwirot Art Exhibition Hall, Bangkok 037892
Srna, Manfred, Graz-Gösting 057036, 095549, 120664
Srna-Modlitby, Martha, Wien 057554
Srna-Modlitby, Martha, Wien 095942
SS Great Britain Museum, Bristol . . 038868
S.S. Meteor Maritime Museum, Barkers Island 042022
S.S. Moyie National Historic Site, Kaslo 005667
Ssangin, Gwangju 107198
SSCR Journal, Bathgate Hills 136271
ST Antik, Gävle 081787
St Paul's Street, Stamford 142089
Staas, B., Wassenberg 074282
Staatliche Akademie der Bildenden Künste Karlsruhe, Karlsruhe 050145
Staatliche Akademie der Bildenden Künste Stuttgart, Stuttgart 050250
Staatliche Antikensammlungen und Glyptothek, München 019117
Staatliche Bücher- und Kupferstichsammlung Greiz, Stiftung der Älteren Linie des Hauses Reuß, Greiz 017528
Staatliche Fachschule für Keramik, Höhr-Grenzhausen 050133
Staatliche Fachschule für Keramik Landshut, Landshut 050163
Staatliche Fachschule für Porzellan, Johann-Friedrich-Böttger-Institut, Selb 050236
Staatliche Galerie Moritzburg Halle, Kunstmuseum des Landes Sachsen-Anhalt, Halle, Saale 017672
Staatliche Graphische Sammlung München, München 019118
Staatliche Hochschule für Bildende Künste, Städelschule, Frankfurt am Main . 050086
Staatliche Hochschule für Gestaltung Karlsruhe, Karlsruhe 050146
Staatliche Kunsthalle Baden-Baden, Baden-Baden 015853
Staatliche Kunsthalle Karlsruhe, Karlsruhe 018169

Staatliche Kunstsammlungen Dresden, Generaldirektion, Dresden 016816
Staatliche Münzsammlung, München 019119
Staatliche Museen Kassel, Direktion und Verwaltung, Kassel 018200
Staatliche Museen zu Berlin - Preußischer Kulturbesitz, Generaldirektion, Berlin 016175
Staatliche Museumsberatung für Nordhessen, Staatliche Museen Kassel, Kassel 018201
Staatliche Porzellan Manufaktur Meissen, Restaurierwerkstatt, Meißen 126301
Staatliche Sammlungen in der Residenz, München 019120
Staatliche Zeichenakademie Hanau, Hanau 050118
Staatlicher Schloßbetrieb Schloß Nossen / Kloster Altzella, Nossen 019341
Staatliches Museum Ägyptischer Kunst, München 019121
Staatliches Museum für Ägyptische Kunst, Seefeld, Oberbayern 020166
Staatliches Museum für Naturkunde, Karlsruhe 018170
Staatliches Museum für Naturkunde Görlitz, Görlitz 017457
Staatliches Museum für Naturkunde Stuttgart, Museum am Löwentor und Museum Schloss Rosenstein, Stuttgart 020364
Staatliches Museum für Naturkunde und Vorgeschichte, Oldenburg, Oldenburg 019471
Staatliches Museum für Völkerkunde Dresden, Dresden 016817
Staatliches Museum für Völkerkunde München, München 019122
Staatliches Naturhistorisches Museum, Braunschweig 016392
Staats- und Stadtbibliothek, Augsburg 015621
Staats- und Universitätsbibliothek Hamburg Carl von Ossietzky, Hamburg 017724
Staatsarchiv Bamberg, Bamberg . . 015880
Staatsbibliothek Bamberg, Bamberg 015881
Staatsbibliothek zu Berlin, Preußischer Kulturbesitz, Berlin 016176
Staatsbibliothek zu Berlin, Preußischer Kulturbesitz, Berlin 016177
Staatsburgh State Historic Museum, Staatsburg 048312
Staatsgalerie am Schaezler-Palais, Bayerische Staatsgemäldesammlungen, Augsburg 015622
Staatsgalerie im Hohen Schloß, Bayerische Staatsgemäldesammlungen, Füssen 017292
Staatsgalerie im Leeren Beutel, Bayerische Staatsgemäldesammlungen, Regensburg 019758
Staatsgalerie im Neuen Schloß, Bayerische Staatsgemäldesammlungen, Oberschleißheim 019419
Staatsgalerie in der Benediktiner-Abtei, Bayerische Staatsgemäldesammlungen, Ottobeuren 019543
Staatsgalerie in der Burg, Bayerische Staatsgemäldesammlungen, Burghausen, Salzach 016516
Staatsgalerie in der Kunsthalle, Bayerische Staatsgemäldesammlungen, Augsburg 015623
Staatsgalerie in der Neuen Residenz, Bayerische Staatsgemäldesammlungen, Bamberg 015882
Staatsgalerie in der Residenz, Bayerische Staatsgemäldesammlungen, Ansbach 015558
Staatsgalerie in der Residenz Würzburg, Bayerische Staatsgemäldesammlungen, Würzburg 021009
Staatsgalerie moderner Kunst in der Pinakothek der Moderne, Bayerische Staatsgemäldesammlungen, München 019123
Staatsgalerie Stuttgart, Stuttgart . . 020365
Stabbursnes Naturhus og Museum, Indre Billefjord 030921
Staberock, Heinz, Potsdam 126658
Stabile, Ivana, Brescia 075185
The Stable, Salt Lake City 119371
Stable Antiques, Lindfield 085005
Stable Antiques, Sedbergh 086533
Stable Antiques, Storrington 086735
Stable Antiques, Thornton Dale . . . 086884
Stable Antiques at Houghton, Houghton 084743
Stable Art, Twickenham 114618
Stable Gallery, Inveraray 113295
Stablegate Antiques, Barham 083379
Stabler, Monty, Birmingham 115131
Stabler-Leadbeater Apothecary Museum, Alexandria 041648
Stables, Grasmere 084501
Stables Antique Centre, Hatton 084623
Stables Art Gallery of Taos Art Association, Taos 048499
Stables Gallery, Ballymoney 112546
S.T.A.C., Montesson 064680
Staccioli, Ugo, Roma 128214
Stacey, Alan & Kathy, Yeovil 131724
Stacey & Son, John, Leigh-on-Sea .084958, 122562
Stachowiak, Poznań 109062
Stachowiak, W., Blomberg, Lippe . . 069871
Stack, New York 091259, 123017
Stackstreet Books, Auckland 140605
Stacpoole, George, Adare 074855
Stacy-Marks, Helmsley 113222
Stacy-Marks, E., Helmsley 084644
Stacy-Marks, E., Polegate 086280
Stacy-Marks, Nigel, Auchterarder . . 083351
Stacy-Marks, Nigel, Perth 086227
Stacy-Marks, Nigel, Perth 114240
Stacy-Marks, Nigel, Perth 131372
Stacy's Tavern Museum and Glen Ellyn Historical Society, Glen Ellyn 044202
Stadelmann, Burkhard, Langen in Hessen 139378
Stader, Johann Joseph, Neuss 126540
Stadhuis, Gent 003468
Stadhuis van Antwerpen, Antwerpen 003190
Stadhuismuseum, Zierikzee 030390
Stadion, Trieste 076907, 121736
Stadium, Dieulefit 062628
Stadium, Hyères 063198
Stadium, Nantes 064946
Stadler, Konstanz 134130
Stadler, Gertraud, München 072866, 126464
Stadler, Jonny W., Wilhelmsfeld . . . 127020
Stadsboerderij Het Wevershuisje, Almelo 029138
Stadsgalerie Engels Tuin, Ootmarsum 030008
Stadsgalerie Gouda, Gouda 029627
Stadsgalerij Heerlen, Heerlen 029697
Stadshil, København 060384
Stadsmuseet i Gråbrödraklostret, Ystad 036805
Stadsmuseet och Ahlbergshallen, Östersund 036531
Stadsmuseum Doetinchem, Doetinchem 029491
Stadsmuseum Groenlo, Groenlo . . . 029632
Stadsmuseum Ijsselstein, Ijsselstein 029791
Stadsmuseum Woerden, Woerden . 030344
Stadsmuseum Zoetermeer, Zoetermeer 030392
Stadt-Galerie, Maisach 104014
Stadt-, Glas- und Steinmuseum, Gmünd, Niederösterreich 001909
Stadt-Museum, Weil der Stadt 020721
Stadt- und Bädermuseum, Bad Salzuflen 015787
Stadt- und Bädermuseum Bad Doberan, Bad Doberan 015680
Stadt-und Bergbaumuseum der Stadt Staßfurt, Staßfurt 020292
Stadt- und Bergbaumuseum Freiberg, Freiberg, Sachsen 017224
Stadt- und Brauereimuseum, Pritzwalk 019676
Stadt- und Burgmuseum, Eppstein . 016997
Stadt- und Dampfmaschinenmuseum, Werdau, Sachsen 020803
Stadt- und Fachwerkmuseum Alte Universität, Eppingen 016995
Stadt- und Festungsmuseum im Ludwigstor, Germersheim 017381
Stadt- und Heimatmuseum, Heidenreichstein 002029
Stadt- und Heimatmuseum, Kusel . 018450
Stadt- und Heimatmuseum, Malchow, Mecklenburg 018800
Stadt- und Heimatmuseum, Marienberg 018830
Stadt- und Heimatmuseum der Stadt Marl, Marl, Westfalen 018853
Stadt- und Heimatmuseum mit Galerie, Haus des Gastes, Burg Waischenfeld, Waischenfeld 020627
Stadt- und Hochstiftmuseum, Dillingen an der Donau 016714
Stadt- und Industriemuseum-Lottehaus, Wetzlar 020850
Stadt- und Kreisgeschichtliches Museum, Hünfeld 018023
Stadt- und Kulturgeschichtliches Museum, Torgau 020453
Stadt- und Landesbibliothek Dortmund, Artothek, Dortmund 016769
Stadt- und Manfred-Kyber-Museum, Löwenstein 018673
Stadt- und Parkmuseum, Bad Muskau 015755
Stadt- und Regionalmuseum Landshut, Museen der Stadt Landshut, Landshut 018487
Stadt- und Steirisches Eisenmuseum, Eisenerz 001819
Stadt- und Turmmuseum, Bad Camberg 015678
Stadt- und Universitätsbibliothek, Frankfurt am Main 017194
Stadt-und Wagenmuseum Oschatz, Oschatz 019488
Stadt- und Wallfahrtsmuseum, Walldürn 020657
Stadtarchiv mit städtischen Sammlungen, Lauf an der Pegnitz 018527
Stadtarchiv und Stadtbibliothek, Lindau, Bodensee 018653
Stadtbibliothek Reutlingen, Reutlingen 019811
Stadtbibliothek Trier - Schatzkammer und Ausstellung, Trier 020485
Stadtgalerie, Osnabrück 019500
Stadtgalerie Alte Post, Westerland . 020830
Stadtgalerie Altena, Altena 015495
Stadtgalerie Altötting, Altötting 015517
Stadtgalerie am Minoritenplatz, Wolfsberg, Kärnten 003059
Stadtgalerie Bamberg - Villa Dessauer, Museen der Stadt Bamberg, Bamberg 015883
Stadtgalerie Bern, Bern 036940
Stadtgalerie im alten Herrenhaus, Ternitz 002738
Stadtgalerie im Elbeforum, Brunsbüttel 016475
Stadtgalerie in Bruneck, Brunico . . 023536
Stadtgalerie Kiel, Heinrich-Ehmsen-Stiftung, Kiel 018251
Stadtgalerie Klagenfurt, Klagenfurt . 002148
Stadtgalerie Lünen, Lünen 018748
Stadtgalerie Saarbrücken, Saarbrücken 019964
Stadtgeschichtliche Sammlung, Norderstedt 019331
Stadtgeschichtliche Sammlung, Velbert 020569
Stadtgeschichtliches Museum, Hilpoltstein 017926
Stadtgeschichtliches Museum, Pfullingen 019613
Stadtgeschichtliches Museum, Tangermünde 020399
Stadtgeschichtliches Museum im Landrichterhaus, Karlstadt 018176
Stadtgeschichtliches Museum Jülich, Jülich 018131
Stadtgeschichtliches Museum Leipzig - Altes Rathaus, Leipzig 018594
Stadtgeschichtliches Museum Leipzig - Neubau, Leipzig 018595
Stadtgeschichtliches Museum Schabbellhaus, Wismar 020921
Stadtgeschichtliches Museum Spandau, Berlin 016178
Stadtgeschichtliches Museum Weißensee, Berlin 016179
Stadtgeschichtliches Zentrum, Städtische Sammlungen, Lutherstadt Wittenberg 018764
Stadtgeschichts- und Schradenmuseum, Ortrand 019487
Stadtgeschichtsmuseum Arnstadt Haus zum Palmbaum mit Bachgedenkstätte und Literatenkabinett, Arnstadt 015567
Stadtgeschichtsmuseum Schwerin, Museen der Landeshauptstadt Schwerin, Schwerin 020151
Das Stadthäuschen, Düsseldorf . . . 070443
Stadthaus am Dom, Wetzlar 020851
Stadthaus-Galerie, Luzern 111706
Stadthaus-Galerie, Münster 019152
Stadthaus Olten, Olten 037402
Stadthaus Ulm, Ulm 020533
Stadthistorisches Museum, S+K-Bergbaumuseum, Bad Salzdetfurth 015785
Stadtmauermuseum Nördlingen, Nördlingen 019322
Stadtmuseum, Apolda 015563
Stadtmuseum, Baunatal 015898
Stadtmuseum, Freilassing 017241
Stadtmuseum, Melk 002306
Stadtmuseum, Penzberg 019588
Stadtmuseum, Rothenburg, Oberlausitz 019922
Stadtmuseum, Wusterhausen 021027
Stadtmuseum Aarau, Aarau 036812
Stadtmuseum Alte Burg Wittenberge, Wittenberge 020928
Stadtmuseum Alte Post, Ebersbach an der Fils 016871
Stadtmuseum Amberg, Amberg, Oberpfalz 015529
Stadtmuseum Amtsturm, Lübz 018731
Stadtmuseum Andernach, Andernach 015539
Stadtmuseum Arelape-Bechelaren, Pöchlarn 002438
Stadtmuseum Bad Bergzabern, Bad Bergzabern 015658
Stadtmuseum Bad Berneck, Bad Berneck 015667
Stadtmuseum Bad Cannstatt, Stuttgart 020366
Stadtmuseum Bad Soden, Bad Soden am Taunus 015803
Stadtmuseum Bad Wildungen, Bad Wildungen 015828
Stadtmuseum Baden-Baden, Baden-Baden 015854
Stadtmuseum Baden-Baden, Zweigstelle im Neuen Schloss, Baden-Baden . . . 015855
Stadtmuseum Battenberg, Battenberg, Eder 015894
Stadtmuseum Bautzen, Regionalmuseum der sächsischen Oberlausitz, Bautzen 015901
Stadtmuseum Beckum, Beckum . . 015932
Stadtmuseum Bendorf im Schloss Sayn, Bendorf, Rhein 015943
Stadtmuseum Bergkamen, Bergkamen 015973
Stadtmuseum Bocholt, Bocholt . . . 016273
Stadtmuseum Bonn, Bonn 016334
Stadtmuseum Borken, Westfalen, Borken, Westfalen 016345
Stadtmuseum Brakel, Brakel 016360
Stadtmuseum Bretten, Bretten 016447

Stadtmuseum Breuberg-Neustadt, Breuberg 016449
Stadtmuseum Bruck an der Leitha, Bruck an der Leitha 001769
Stadtmuseum Burgdorf, Burgdorf, Kreis Hannover 016509
Stadtmuseum Burgstädt, Burgstädt 016524
Stadtmuseum Coesfeld und Städtische Turmgalerie, Coesfeld 016584
Stadtmuseum Colditz, Museum der Stadt Colditz, Colditz 016587
Stadtmuseum Cottbus, Cottbus . . . 016599
Stadtmuseum Cuxhaven, Cuxhaven 016613
Stadtmuseum Damme, Damme, Dümmer 016629
Stadtmuseum Deggendorf, Deggendorf 016657
Stadtmuseum Delmenhorst, Delmenhorst 016666
Stadtmuseum der Landeshauptstadt Düsseldorf, Düsseldorf 016846
Stadtmuseum Ditzingen, Ditzingen . 016729
Stadtmuseum Döbeln/Kleine Galerie, Döbeln 016731
Stadtmuseum Dornbirn, Dornbirn . . 001789
Stadtmuseum Dresden, Dresden . . 016818
Stadtmuseum Eilenburg, Eilenburg . 016916
Stadtmuseum Eisenberg, Eisenberg, Thüringen 016928
Stadtmuseum Erlangen, Erlangen . . 017036
Stadtmuseum Esslingen, Esslingen 017086
Stadtmuseum Eupen, Eupen 003430
Stadtmuseum Euskirchen, Euskirchen 017094
Stadtmuseum Fellbach, Fellbach . . 017109
Stadtmuseum Fembohaus mit Noricama, Museen der Stadt Nürnberg, Nürnberg 019375
Stadtmuseum Friesach, Friesach . . 001872
Stadtmuseum Fürstenfeldbruck, Fürstenfeldbruck 017284
Stadtmuseum Fürth, Fürth, Bayern . 017290
Stadtmuseum Gardelegen, Gardelegen 017323
Stadtmuseum Gehrden, Gehrden, Hannover 017336
Stadtmuseum Geithain, Geithain . . 017346
Stadtmuseum Gera, Gera 017375
Stadtmuseum Gerlingen - Gerlinger Heimatmuseum - Museum der Deutschen aus Ungarn, Gerlingen 017379
Stadtmuseum Giengen, Giengen an der Brenz 017404
Stadtmuseum Göhre, Städtische Museen Jena, Jena 018117
Stadtmuseum Grafenau, Grafenau, Niederbayern 017501
Stadtmuseum Groß-Gerau, Groß-Gerau 017553
Stadtmuseum Gütersloh, Gütersloh 017603
Stadtmuseum Gunzenhausen, Gunzenhausen 017608
Stadtmuseum Hadamar, Hadamar . 017617
Stadtmuseum Hagen, Hagen, Westfalen 017627
Stadtmuseum Hall in Tirol, Hall in Tirol 002011
Stadtmuseum Hartberg, Hartberg . . 002019
Stadtmuseum Hattingen, Hattingen 017798
Stadtmuseum Haus Kupferhammer, Warstein 020682
Stadtmuseum Herrenmühle, Hammelburg 017734
Stadtmuseum Herzogenaurach, Herzogenaurach 017908
Stadtmuseum Hildburghausen, Hildburghausen 017917
Stadtmuseum Hofgeismar, Hofgeismar 017962
Stadtmuseum Hofheim am Taunus, Hofheim am Taunus 017963
Stadtmuseum Holzminden, Holzminden 017998
Stadtmuseum Horb, Horb 018006
Stadtmuseum Hornmoldhaus, Bietigheim-Bissingen 016241
Stadtmuseum Hüfingen, Hüfingen . 018018
Stadtmuseum im Alten Forstamt, Stockach 020319
Stadtmuseum im Augustinerkloster, Bad Langensalza 015744
Stadtmuseum im Knochenhauer-Amtshaus, Hildesheim 017925
Stadtmuseum im Prinz-Max-Palais, Karlsruhe 018171
Stadtmuseum im Spital, Crailsheim 016600
Stadtmuseum im Weveldhaus, Neuburg an der Donau 019225
Stadtmuseum Ingolstadt im Kavalier Hepp, Ingolstadt 018076
Stadtmuseum Iserlohn, Iserlohn . . . 018087
Stadtmuseum Judenburg, Judenburg 002107
Stadtmuseum Kassel, Kassel 018202
Stadtmuseum Kaufbeuren, Kaufbeuren 018215
Stadtmuseum Kelsterbach, Kelsterbach 018226
Stadtmuseum Killingerhaus, Idstein 018047
Stadtmuseum Klostermühle, Bad Urach 015817
Stadtmuseum Klosterneuburg, Klosterneuburg 002158
Stadtmuseum Leimen - Sankt Ilgen, Leimen, Baden 018549
Stadtmuseum Leonberg, Leonberg, Württemberg 018619
Stadtmuseum Leun, Leun 018621
Stadtmuseum Lichtenfels, Lichtenfels, Bayern 018633
Stadtmuseum Lindau, Lindau, Bodensee 018654
Stadtmuseum Ludwigshafen, Ludwigshafen am Rhein 018706
Stadtmuseum Lüdenscheid, Museen der Stadt Lüdenscheid, Lüdenscheid . 018735
Stadtmuseum Meersburg, Meersburg 018875
Stadtmuseum Meißen, Meißen 018892
Stadtmuseum Meppen, Meppen . . . 018911
Stadtmuseum mit Weinmuseum, Bad Vöslau 001738
Stadtmuseum Mosbach, Mosbach, Baden 019002
Stadtmuseum Mühlberg, Elbe, Mühlberg, Elbe 019008
Stadtmuseum Mühlheim, Mühlheim am Main 019017
Stadtmuseum Münster, Münster . . . 019153
Stadtmuseum Mutzschen, Mutzschen 019171
Stadtmuseum Naumburg, Haus zur Hohen Lilie, Naumburg, Saale 019187
Stadtmuseum Neumarkt, Neumarkt, Oberpfalz 019253
Stadtmuseum Neuötting, Neuötting 019262
Stadtmuseum Neustadt an der Waldnaab, Neustadt an der Waldnaab 019281
Stadtmuseum Nittenau, Nittenau . . 019319
Stadtmuseum Nördlingen, Nördlingen 019323
Stadtmuseum Norderstedt, Norderstedt 019331
Stadtmuseum Nürtingen, Nürtingen 019379
Stadtmuseum Obermühle, Braunfels 016377
Stadtmuseum Oberwölz und Österreichisches Blasmusikmuseum, Oberwölz 002395
Stadtmuseum Offenbach am Main, Offenbach am Main 019454
Stadtmuseum Oldenburg, Oldenburg, Oldenburg 019473
Stadtmuseum Oschatz, Oschatz . . . 019488
Stadtmuseum Pforzheim, Pforzheim 019609
Stadtmuseum Pinkafeld, Garnisions-Feuerwehr- und Kirchenmuseum, Pinkafeld 002431
Stadtmuseum Pinneberg, Pinneberg 019619
Stadtmuseum Pirna, Pirna 019627
Stadtmuseum Povelturm, Nordhorn 019337
Stadtmuseum Pulsnitz, Pulsnitz . . . 019678
Stadtmuseum Quakenbrück, Quakenbrück 019681
Stadtmuseum Radolfzell, Radolfzell 019700
Stadtmuseum Rastatt, Rastatt 019717
Stadtmuseum Rottweil, Rottweil . . . 019934
Stadtmuseum Saalfeld im Franziskanerkloster, Saalfeld, Saale 019957
Stadtmuseum Sachsenheim, Sachsenheim 019966
Stadtmuseum Sankt Pölten, Sankt Pölten 002621
Stadtmuseum Sankt Veit, Sankt Veit an der Glan 002630
Stadtmuseum Schelklingen, Schelklingen 020012
Stadtmuseum Schladming, Schladming 002648
Stadtmuseum Schleswig, Schleswig 020041
Stadtmuseum Schloß Hoyerswerda, Hoyerswerda 018013
Stadtmuseum Schloss Wolfsburg, Wolfsburg 020966
Stadtmuseum Schlüsselfeld, Schlüsselfeld 020051
Stadtmuseum Schongau, Schongau 020090
Stadtmuseum Schorndorf, Schorndorf, Württemberg 020093
Stadtmuseum Schramberg, Schramberg 020097
Stadtmuseum Schwabach, Schwabach 020106
Stadtmuseum Schwandorf mit Falkenauer Heimatstube, Schwandorf 020124
Stadtmuseum Schwedt, Städtische Museen Schwedt/Oder, Schwedt 020137
Stadtmuseum Siegburg, Siegburg . 020196
Stadtmuseum Sindelfingen, Sindelfingen 020217
Stadtmuseum Stadtoldendorf, Stadtoldendorf 020287
Stadtmuseum Steinfurt, Steinfurt . . 020304
Stadtmuseum Stolpen, Stolpen . . . 020327
Stadtmuseum Stubenhaus, Staufen 020294
Stadtmuseum Sulzbach-Rosenberg, Sulzbach-Rosenberg 020385
Stadtmuseum Teterow, Teterow . . . 020423
Stadtmuseum Teterow, Teterow . . . 020424
Stadtmuseum Tharandt, Tharandt . 020434
Stadtmuseum Traiskirchen, Möllersdorf 002331
Stadtmuseum Traiskirchen, Traiskirchen 002746
Stadtmuseum Trostberg, Trostberg . 020490
Stadtmuseum Tübingen, Tübingen . 020500
Stadtmuseum und Fürstlich Starhembergisches Familienmuseum, Eferding 001805
Stadtmuseum und Riesengebirgsmuseum, Marktoberdorf 018848
Stadtmuseum Waldkraiburg, Waldkraiburg 020646
Stadtmuseum Weilheim, Weilheim, Oberbayern 020731
Stadtmuseum Weimar, Weimar, Thüringen 020756
Stadtmuseum Wels, Wels 002830
Stadtmuseum Wels-Burg - Agrargeschichtliche Sammlung, Wels 002831
Stadtmuseum Wiener Neustadt, Wiener Neustadt 003037
Stadtmuseum Wienertor Hainburg, Hainburg an der Donau 002004
Stadtmuseum Wil, Wil 037710
Stadtmuseum Zistersdorf, Zistersdorf 003071
Stadtmuseum Zweibrücken, Zweibrücken 021083
Stadtmuseum Zwettl, Zwettl, Niederösterreich 003077
Stadtraum Vilshofen, Vilshofen 020603
Stadtresidenz Landshut, Landshut . 018488
Stadtteilmuseum Nowaweser, Potsdam 019658
Stadttormuseum, Wehrheim 020703
Stadtturmgalerie, Innsbruck 095598
Stäbler, Erwin, Zürich 083025
Staeck, Prof. Klaus, Heidelberg . . .103326, 134052
Stäcker, Peter, Bischofszell 111299
Das Städel, Städelsches Kunstinstitut und Städtische Galerie, Frankfurt am Main 017195
Städelscher Museums-Verein e.V., Frankfurt am Main 053563
Städtische Ausstellungshalle Am Hawerkamp, Münster 019139
Städtische Dauerausstellung zur Geschichte der Aschaffenburger Juden, Aschaffenburg 015585
Städtische Galerie; Fürstbischöfliches Museum, Meersburg 018874
Städtische Galerie, Würzburg 021003
Städtische Galerie, Bietigheim-Bissingen 016242
Städtische Galerie, Dreieich 016779
Städtische Galerie, Eisenhüttenstadt 016930
Städtische Galerie, Lienz 002236
Städtische Galerie, Ravensburg . . . 019734
Städtische Galerie, Traunstein 020459
Städtische Galerie, Museum alter lippischer Maler, Schieder-Schwalenberg . . 020016
Städtische Galerie, Museum der Stadt Ettlingen, Ettlingen 017092
Städtische Galerie, Sammlung des 20. Jahrhunderts, Paderborn 019555
Städtische Galerie ada Meiningen, Meiningen 018885
Städtische Galerie am Markt Wurzen, Wurzen 021026
Städtische Galerie Böblingen, Böblingen 016296
Städtische Galerie Brückenturm, Mainz 018795
Städtische Galerie Delmenhorst, Haus Coburg Sammlung Stuckenberg, Delmenhorst 016667
Städtische Galerie Die Fähre, Bad Saulgau 015789
Städtische Galerie Eichenmüllerhaus, Lemgo 018608
Städtische Galerie Erlangen, Erlangen 017037
Städtische Galerie Fauler Pelz, Überlingen 020516
Städtische Galerie Filderhalle, Leinfelden-Echterdingen 018552
Städtische Galerie Filderstadt, Filderstadt 017120
Städtische Galerie Fruchthalle Rastatt, Rastatt 019718
Städtische Galerie Grimma, Grimma 017540
Städtische Galerie Haus Seel, Siegen 020202
Städtische Galerie im Alten Rathaus, Fürstenwalde, Spree 017285
Städtische Galerie im Amtshimmel, Baden 036871
Städtische Galerie im Buntentor, Bremen 016424
Städtische Galerie im Cordonhaus, Cham 016553
Städtische Galerie im Königin-Christinen-Haus, Zeven 021064
Städtische Galerie im Kornhaus, Kirchheim unter Teck 018269
Städtische Galerie im Kulturforum, Offenburg 019457
Städtische Galerie im Lenbachhaus und Kunstbau, München 019124
Städtische Galerie im Park, Viersen 020589
Städtische Galerie im Rathaus, Balingen 015864
Städtische Galerie im Rathauspark, Gladbeck 017421
Städtische Galerie im Schloßpark Strünkede, Emschertal-Museum, Herne 017893
Städtische Galerie im Theater Ingolstadt, Museum für konkrete Kunst, Ingolstadt 018077
Städtische Galerie in der Alten Schule, Sigmaringen 020209
Städtische Galerie In der Badstube, Wangen im Allgäu 020672
Städtische Galerie in der Reithalle, Paderborn 019556

Städtische Galerie Iserlohn, Iserlohn 018088
Städtische Galerie Jesuitenkirche, Aschaffenburg 015578
Städtische Galerie Kaarst, Kaarst . . 018134
Städtische Galerie Karlsruhe, Karlsruhe 018172
Städtische Galerie Leerer Beutel, Museen der Stadt Regensburg, Regensburg 019759
Städtische Galerie Lehrte, Lehrte . . 018546
Städtische Galerie Liebieghaus, Museum Alter Plastik, Frankfurt am Main . 017196
Städtische Galerie Lovis-Kabinett, Villingen-Schwenningen 020596
Städtische Galerie Lüdenscheid, Museen der Stadt Lüdenscheid, Lüdenscheid 018736
Städtische Galerie Mennonitenkirche, Neuwied 019300
Städtische Galerie Nordhorn - Kunstwegen, Nordhorn 019338
Städtische Galerie Ostfildern, Ostfildern 019513
Städtische Galerie Peschkenhaus, Moers 018984
Städtische Galerie Peter Breuer, Zwickau 021089
Städtische Galerie Reutlingen, Reutlingen 019812
Städtische Galerie Rosenheim, Rosenheim 019887
Städtische Galerie Schwarzes Kloster, Freiburg im Breisgau 017237
Städtische Galerie sohle 1, Stadtmuseum Bergkamen, Bergkamen 015974
Städtische Galerie Stapflehus, Weil am Rhein 020718
Städtische Galerie Villa Streccius, Landau in der Pfalz 018475
Städtische Galerie Villa Zanders, Bergisch Gladbach 015972
Städtische Galerie Waldkraiburg, Waldkraiburg 020647
Städtische Galerie Wesseling, Wesseling 020827
Städtische Galerie Wolfsburg, Wolfsburg 020967
Städtische Gemäldegalerie, Füssen 017293
Städtische Kunstgalerie im Deutschordenshaus, Donauwörth 016745
Städtische Kunstgalerie Torhaus Rombergpark, Dortmund 016770
Städtische Kunsthalle, Museen der Stadt Recklinghausen, Recklinghausen . 019740
Städtische Kunsthalle Mannheim, Mannheim 018806
Städtische Kunstsammlung, Murrhardt 019170
Städtische Kunstsammlung, Kulturzentrum Talbahnhof, Eschweiler 017052
Städtische Kunstsammlung Schloß Salder, Salzgitter 019971
Städtische Kunstsammlungen, Ausstellungsgebäude, Institut Mathildenhöhe, Darmstadt 016646
Städtische Münzsammlung im Archiv der Hansestadt Lübeck, Lübeck 018727
Städtische Museen Heilbronn, Heilbronn 017853
Städtische Museen Junge Kunst und Viadrina, Frankfurt/Oder 017206
Städtische Museen Wangen im Allgäu, Wangen im Allgäu 020673
Städtische Sammlungen, Amstetten 001687
Städtische Sammlungen, Bauländer Heimatmuseum, Adelsheim 015446
Städtische Sammlungen Freital, Freital 017248
Städtische Wessenberg-Galerie, Konstanz 018380
Städtisches Feuerwehr-Museum, Eisenhüttenstadt 016931
Städtisches Heimatmuseum, Osterode am Harz 019511
Städtisches Heimatmuseum, Ballenstedt 015866
Städtisches Heimatmuseum, Höchstadt an der Aisch 017942
Städtisches Heimatmuseum, Landau in der Pfalz 018476
Städtisches Heimatmuseum, Lippstadt 018665
Städtisches Heimatmuseum, Mengen 018907
Städtisches Heimatmuseum, Meßkirch 018921
Städtisches Heimatmuseum, Naila . 019178
Städtisches Heimatmuseum, Reinfeld, Holstein 019782
Städtisches Heimatmuseum, Taucha bei Leipzig 020406
Städtisches Heimatmuseum Erding, Erding 017004
Städtisches Heimatmuseum im Waldemarturm, Dannenberg, Elbe 016631
Städtisches Hellweg-Museum, Geseke 017398
Städtisches Hutmuseum, Lindenberg im Allgäu 018658
Städtisches Kießling-Museum, Drosendorf an der Thaya 001792
Städtisches Kramer-Museum, Kempen 018230
Städtisches Kunstmuseum Singen, Singen, Hohentwiel 020219
Städtisches Kunstmuseum Spendhaus Reutlingen, Reutlingen 019813
Städtisches Lapidarium, Stuttgart . 020367
Städtisches Museum, Hechingen . . 017817
Städtisches Museum, Schleswig . . 020041
Städtisches Museum, Aschersleben 015589
Städtisches Museum, Bad Reichenhall 015775
Städtisches Museum, Bruchsal . . . 016460
Städtisches Museum, Eisenhüttenstadt 016932
Städtisches Museum, Halberstadt . 017649
Städtisches Museum, Herborn, Hessen 017878
Städtisches Museum, Iserlohn 018089
Städtisches Museum, Kalkar 018141
Städtisches Museum, Kitzingen . . . 018277
Städtisches Museum, Korbach 018383
Städtisches Museum, Menden 018906
Städtisches Museum, Mülheim an der Ruhr 019024
Städtisches Museum, Pfungstadt . . 019615
Städtisches Museum, Schärding . . 002639
Städtisches Museum, Überlingen . . 020517
Städtisches Museum, Welzheim . . . 020791
Städtisches Museum, Werl 020808
Städtisches Museum, Wiesloch . . . 020884
Städtisches Museum, Zeulenroda . . 021060
Städtisches Museum Abteiberg, Mönchengladbach 018978
Städtisches Museum Abtshof, Regionalmuseum des Niederen Flämings, Jüterbog 018132
Städtisches Museum Braunschweig, Braunschweig 016393
Städtisches Museum/ Daniel-Pöppelmann-Haus, Herford 017883
Städtisches Museum Einbeck, Einbeck 016919
Städtisches Museum Engen + galerie, Engen 016986
Städtisches Museum Fürstenwalde, Fürstenwalde, Spree 017286
Städtisches Museum Gelsenkirchen, Gelsenkirchen 017357
Städtisches Museum Göppingen im Storchen, Göppingen 017451
Städtisches Museum Göttingen, Göttingen 017473
Städtisches Museum Grevesmühlen, Grevesmühlen 017534
Städtisches Museum Hann. Münden, Hann Münden 017749
Städtisches Museum im ehemaligen Heiliggeistspital, Munderkingen . . 019163
Städtisches Museum im Hospital, Nidderau 019304
Städtisches Museum im Kornhaus Bad Waldsee, Bad Waldsee 015820
Städtisches Museum Kamen, Kamen 018143
Städtisches Museum Ludwigsburg, Ludwigsburg, Württemberg 018698
Städtisches Museum Peterskirche, Vaihingen 020555
Städtisches Museum Rosenheim, Rosenheim 019888
Städtisches Museum Schloß Rheydt, Mönchengladbach 018979
Städtisches Museum Seesen, Seesen 020174
Städtisches Museum Simeonstift, Trier 020486
Städtisches Museum Sprucker Mühle, Guben 017593
Städtisches Museum Tuttlinger Haus, Museen der Stadt Tuttlingen, Tuttlingen 020510
Städtisches Museum Vogthaus, Ravensburg 019735
Städtisches Museum Wesel, Wesel 020824
Städtisches Museum Wesel, Schill-Kasematte und Festungsgeschichtliche Abteilung, Wesel 020825
Städtisches Museum Zirndorf, Zirndorf 021070
Städtisches Naturkundliches Museum, Göppingen 017452
Städtisches Ortsmuseum Schwamendingen, Zürich 037801
Städtisches Propsteimuseum mit Römerthermen, Zülpich 021080
Städtisches Schulmuseum, Lohr am Main 018681
Städtisches Zentrum für Geschichte und Kunst, Riesa 019842
Städtligalerie, Wangen an der Aare 111984
Stähle, Prof. Walter, Meersburg . . . 072492
Stähli, M. & M., Oberdiessbach . . . 111788
Stähli, Marc, Auvernier 129902
Stähli, Pablo, Köln 072012
Stähli, Pablo, Zürich 112182
Stähli, Simon, Urdorf 141307
Stählin, Betli, Altendorf 082087
Stämpfli Verlag, Bern 134997
Ständerhaus, Buus 036996
Staetshuijs, Amsterdam 077973
Staetshuijs, Amsterdam 077974
Stäubli, Ernst Adolf, Neuenhof 111775
Stäudter, Anita, Neustadt an der Aisch 073026
Staf, Antwerpen 057738
Staff College Museum, Camberley . 038953
Staffanstorps Konsthall, Staffanstorp 036608
Staffelbach, Elisabeth, Aarau 111104
Staffin Museum, Isle-of-Skye 039826
Staffin Museum, Staffin 041080
Stafford, Barcelona 080940
Stafford, Ulla, Binfield 083518
Stafford Castle and Visitor Centre, Stafford 041084
Staffords, London 113897
Staffordshire House Antiques, Oakland 091439
Staffordshire Pride, London 085710
Staffordshire Regiment Museum, Lichfield 040002
Stafforte, Andrea, Bern 082242
Stafsjö Bruksmuseum, Falkenberg . 036261
Stage, Sapporo 077203
Stage 21 Gallery, Tokyo 107118
Stage Door Prints, London 085711, 141903
Stage Nine, Sacramento . 092183, 119163
Stage & Screen, London 141904
Stagecoach Inn Museum Complex, Newbury Park 046441
Stages Gallery, Machynlleth 114026
Stagnani, Andrea, Milano 127692
Ståhl, Lund 141125
Stahl, Oersberg 121570
Stahl, Detlef, Speichersdorf 073874
Stahl, Hans, Hamburg . . . 071335, 121439
Stahl, Jochem, Hirrlingen 125941
Stahl, Wilfried, Memmingen 072514
Stahlberger, Weil am Rhein 105176
Stahler, Arno, Haßloch 121447
Stahlmach, Adelbert, Berlin 069768
Stahmer, D. & H., Meinersen 072497
Stained Glass, Raytown 136630
Stained Glass Attractions, Metford . 056219
Stained Glass Museum, Ely 039443
Stainless, Frank, Schauenstein . . . 073678
Stainsby, Graham, Walsdorf 074267
Stair & Co, London 085712, 131182
Stair & Co., New York 091260
Staithe Antiques, Brancaster Staithe 083641
Staithe Lodge Gallery, Swafield . . .086807, 131565
Stal, Dominique, Paris 100884
Stal, Kevin, Aiguèze 098778
Stała Ekspozycja Muzealna Ziemi Sierakowickiej, Sierakowice 032315
Stalder, Hanspeter, Sursee 130191
Staley & Son, Sandy Bay 095181
Staley, Carolyn, Seattle . . 093071, 119997
Staley, Earl V. & Suzanne C., Houston 116410
Staley & Wise, New York 118444
Stalham Antique Gallery, Stalham .086682, 131524
Stalheim Folkemuseum, Stalheim . 031219
Stalke, København 098584
Stalker, Varna 096777
Stalker, Ruth, Montréal 059009
Stall-Lädeli, Dübendorf 082345
De Stalling, Zaltbommel 108272
Stallings, Steve, Las Vegas 116651
La Stalluccia Antichitá, Firenze . . . 075407
Stalmann, Dietrich, München 126465
Stalna Izložba Stilskog Namještaja 18.-19. St., Čelarevo 034183
Stalzer, Andreas, Wien . . . 095943, 133233
Stam, H., Haarlem 078481
Stamataris, Nikos, Chalandri 074618
Stamati, Paul, New York 091261
Stambak, Jean-Marc, Toulouse . . . 124995
Stambolov, Todor, Amsterdam 128555
Stamford, New York 123018
Stamford Artists Galleries, Stamford 114480
Stamford Brewery Museum, Stamford 041088
Stamford Historical Society Museum, Stamford 048314
Stamford Museum, Stamford 041089
Stamford Museum and Nature Center, Stamford 048315
Stamkunsten, København 098585
Stamm, Hamburg 071336
Stamm, Wiesbaden 074424
Stamm, Ronald, Friedeburg, Ostfriesland 125680
Stammegna, Marc, Marseille 064392, 099688
Stammegnia, Paris 066571
Stammerjohann, Jürgen, Hamburg . 139214
Stammersdorfer Kleinkunst, Wien . 057555
Stamnes, Morten, Oslo 079475
Stamp & Sons, J., Market Harborough 085940, 131263
Stamp and Coin Shop, Seattle 093072
Stampa, Basel 111224, 141216
Stampa, Chur 082320, 111362
Stamparte, Bologna 105974, 134553, 139996
Stampbach, Gunten 111543
Stamperia Artistica Nazionale, Torino 134700
Stampfl, W., Bayrischzell 069498
Stampwise Info Square, Pretoria . . 034730
Stan, Saint Louis 092318
Stan Hywet Hall and Gardens, Akron 041588
Stanbet, Moskva 109593
Stanczyk, Kraków 108982
Standard 1437 N Bosworth Av, Chicago 115556
Standard Bank Gallery, Johannesburg 034656
Standi, Geza, Fürstenfeld 056983
Standing Bear Antiques, Omaha . . . 091584

Standing Conference on Archives and Museums, York 054524
Stanford, Nashville 117372
Stanford Hall Motorcycle Museum, Lutterworth 040361
Stanfords, Colchester 122476
Stange, Egmont, Waltersdorf bei Königs Wusterhausen 074270
Stanger, Estelle, New York 091262
Stanglmeier, Udo, Sinzig 139731
Staniland, Stamford 142090
Stanislas, Nancy 064882
Stanislas, Nancy 064883
Stanislaus, Neufeld 072990
Stanjohn, Chicago 088173, 131917
Stanka, Heinz & Lilian, Rehau 073471
Stanko, Wrocław 109233
Stanko, Bernie, Johannesburg 080715
Stankus, M., Oakland 118648
Stankus Conway, San Francisco . . . 119802
Stanley, Chicago 088174
Stanley, Chicago 088175
Stanley & Co., Denver 122887
Stanley, Hyderabad 105715
Stanley, Rockdale 095151
Stanley, Barbara, London 113898
Stanley, Dalia, Sydney 120645
Stanley, Julian, Bourton-on-the-Water 083614, 130421
Stanley Gallery, Hong Kong 097833
Stanley Gallery, Hong Kong 097834
Stanley Gallery, Hong Kong 097835
Stanley Museum, Kingfield 045005
The Stanley Picker Gallery, Kingston-upon-Thames 039894
Stanley Spencer Gallery, Cookham . 039138
Stanley Street Buy and Sell, East Brisbane 055781
Stanley-Whitman House, Farmington 043819
Stanly County Historic Museum, Albemarle 041607
Stanmer Rural Museum, Brighton . . 038853
Stanmore, Victor Harbor 056777
Stanmore Galleries, Stanmore 095221
Stanovsky, Dallas 088613, 132022
Stanowski, Warszawa 079785
Stanowski, Warszawa 129117
Stanowski, Warszawa 129118
Stan's Antiques, Los Angeles 089916
Stansbury Museum, Stansbury 001488
Stansted Mountfitchet Windmill, Stansted Mountfitchet 041092
Stanthorpe Regional Art Gallery, Stanthorpe 001489
Stanton, G., Dallas 115943
Stanton, Louis, Mere 085977
Stanton, Louis, Mere 085978
Stanton County Museum, Pilger . . . 047020
Stantondale, El Paso 132067
Stantschev, Matey, Oostende 123668
Stanworth, P., Market Bosworth . . . 085931
La Stanzina, Milano 106325
Stanzione Ciro, Roma 076692
Lo Stanzone, Trieste 076908
Stapel, R., Burg auf Fehmarn 070092
Stapel, R., Stralsund 073934
Stapelfeldt, Günter, Reinbek 104705
Stapf, Helmut, Gernsheim 070977
Staplehurst Antiques, Staplehurst . .086697, 131530
Staples, Richmond 119124
Stapleton, Unley 056771
Stapleton, Serena, London 131183
Stapper, Venlo 140561
Star Antiques, San Francisco 092889
Star Books, Adelaide 136775
Star Bookshop, Southsea 142087
Star City Heritage Museum, Star City 006507
Star Furniture, El Paso 088818
Star Gallery, Godalming 113140
Star Gazers, Windsor, Ontario 097567
Star Mound School Museum, Snowflake 006488
Star of the Republic Museum, Blinn College, Washington 048973
Star Peddler, Houston 089213
Star-Spangled Banner Flag House and 1812 Museum, Baltimore 042004
Star Troc, Epinay-sur-Seine 062791
Stara Galeria, Warszawa 109195
Stara Galeria BWA, Lublin 109028
Stará Huť v Josefovském Údolí, Adamov 008260
Stará Plzeň, Plzeň 060084
Stara Praga, Warszawa . . 079786, 129119
Stará Škola, Police nad Metují 008582
Stara Synagoga, Muzeum Historyczne Miasta Krakowa, Kraków 032040
Staraja Kniga, Sankt-Peterburg . . . 140940
Staraja Kniga, Sankt-Peterburg . . . 140941
Staraja Kniga, Sankt-Peterburg . . . 140942
Staraja Moneta, Sankt-Peterburg . . 080332
Starbase 21, Tulsa 093331
Starchild, Columbus 088439
Starcik, Bärbel, Frankfurt am Main . 070793
Starck, Rüdiger, Pforzheim 073323
Starczewski, Hans Joachim, Höhr-Grenzhausen 134062
Stardust, New York 091263
Stardust Antik, Stockholm 082023
Starfish Gallery, Whangarei 108668
Starfish Gallery, Woody Point 095413
Stargardt, J.A., Berlin 121345, 138847
Stargate, Richmond 119125
Stari Majstori, Sofia 058769
Starina, Moskva 080268, 129240
Starinarnica Marajna, Ljubljana . . . 080658
Starinárstvo Jukas, Ružomberok . . 080637
Starinnaja Mebel', Moskva 080269
Starinnye Časy, Sankt-Peterburg . . 080333
Starinnyj Interjer, Moskva 080270
Starinnyj Interjer, Sankt-Peterburg . 080334
Stark, Christian, Waldalgesheim . . . 074248
Stark, Martina, Magdeburg 103993
Stark Museum of Art, Orange 046703
Starkey, Milton 056230
Starkey, James H., Beverley 083502, 130377
Starkey James H., Beverley 112630
Starkie, Simon, Cartmel 083890
Starlight, Wansford 087016
Starlight Room, Long Beach 089658
Starling, New Orleans 142622
Starmach, Teresa, Kraków 108983
Staro Selo Kumrovec, Kumrovec . . 007751
Staročerkasskij Istoriko-architekturnyj Muzej-zapovednik, Staročerkassk 033904
Starocie w Sopocie, Sopot 079713
Staroladožskij Istoriko-Architekturnyj i Archeologičeskij Muzej-Zapovednik, Staraja Ladoga 033901
Staromiejski, Ratusz, Gdańsk 121887
Starooskolskij Kraevedčeskij Muzej, Staryj Oskol 033907
Starorusskij Kraevedčeskij Muzej, Staraja Russa 033903
Staroświecki Styl, Kraków 140748
Staroświecki Syl, Kraków 079660
Staroveteśnictví a Kramářství Antik, Děčín 060009
Starožitnictví, České Budějovice . . . 060002
Starožitnictvi, Kolín 060037
Starožitnictví, Praha 060159
Starožitnictví MK, Praha 060160
Starožitnictví u Zlaté uličky, Praha . 060161
Starožitnosti, Bělá pod Bezdězem . 059968
Starožitnosti, Benešov 059969
Starožitnosti, Brno 059985
Starožitnosti, Brno 059986
Starožitnosti, Brno 059987
Starožitnosti, Jablonec nad Nisou . . 060026
Starožitnosti, Levice 080625
Starožitnosti, Nové Zámky 080631
Starožitnosti, Praha 060162
Starožitnosti, Praha 060163
Starožitnosti, Praha 060164
Starožitnosti, Praha 060165
Starožitnosti - Antik, Ostrava 060068
Starožitnosti Antiqua, Jihlava 060029
Starožitnosti Baru, Brno 059988
Starožitnosti CS, Brno 059989
Starožitnosti Déco, Prostějov 060186
Starožitnosti Golem, Prostějov 060187
Starožitnosti - Kabinet, Brno 059990
Starožitnosti Matouš, Jilemnice . . . 060031
Starožitnosti - Militaria, Litomyšl . . 060049
Starožitnosti Ninive, Domažlice . . . 060013
Starožitnosti Pola, Ostrava 060069
Starožitnosti Přikryl, Prostějov 060188
Starožitnosti R & T, Frýdek-Místek . 060016
Starožitnosti Royal, Prešov 080634
Starožitnosti Sandra, Týn nad Vltavou 060197
Starozitný Nábytek, Praha 060166
Starr, Denver 088740
Starr, Belle, Saint Louis 123089
Starr, Jana, New York 091264
Starr, Steve, Chicago 088176
Stars, Portland 092013
Stars and Splendid, Portland 092014
StArt, London 113899
Start, New York 118445
St'Art Up, L'attrape-Coulems, Lyon 099616
Startgallery, Wellington 108645
Starting Line Antiques, Indianapolis 089346
Starved Rock State Park, Utica 048717
Stary Dom, Kraków 079661
Starý Královsky Palác, Praha 008647
Stary Sklep, Kraków 108984
Starý Zámek, Moravské zemské museum Brno, Jevišovice 008408
Starý Zamok Banská Štiavnica, Banská Štiavnica 034309
Starye Gody, Moskva 080271
Starye Gody, Sankt-Peterburg 080335
Starye Kartiny, Sankt-Peterburg . . . 080336
Staschen, Wolfgang, Berlin 138848
Staschull, Bernd, Niederndodeleben 126547
Statarmuseum Mejeriet, Örebro . . . 036523
State Agricultural Heritage Museum, Brookings 042450
State Apartments of the Royal Palace, Stockholm 036667
State Archaeological Museum, Kolkata 022227
State Archives of West Bengal, Kolkata 022228
State Art Gallery, Ahmedabad 021993
State Art Museum R. Mustafaev, Baku 003085
State Authority of Museums, Rīga . 053836
State Ayurvedic College Museum, Hardwar 022149
State Capital Publishing Museum, Guthrie 044375
State Coal Mine Museum, Wonthaggi 001631
State Folk Art Museum of Armenia, Erevan 000689
State Fretwork Museum, Erevan . . . 000690
State Gallery of Contemporary Cypriot Art, Lefkosia 008225
State Health Institute Museum, Lucknow 022246
State Historical and Architectural Museum-reserve Shirvan Shahs' Palace, Baku 003086
State Historical Museum of Kyrgyzstan, Biškek 027636
State Historical Museum of Wisconsin, Madison 045595
State Historical Society of Iowa Museum, Des Moines 043430
State Historical Society of Missouri Museum, Columbia 043073
State Historical Society of North Dakota Museum, Bismarck 042239
State History Museum of Armenia, Erevan 000691
The State House-Museum of I.V. Stalin, Gori 015402
State Kala Akademi Museum, Imphal 022174
State Library and Museum, Kyaukpyu 029058
State Library and Museum, Mawlamyine 029063
State Literature Museum of Georgia, Tbilisi 015412
State Museum, Hyderabad 022163
State Museum, Kohima 022209
State Museum, Mandalay 029060
State Museum, Trichur 022358
State Museum, Edward Museum, Bhopal 022038
State Museum of Abkhasia, Suchumi 015404
State Museum of Adjar, Batumi . . . 015400
State Museum of Azerbaijan Carpets and Applied Art Letif Kerimov, Baku . . 003087
State Museum of Ethnography, Arts and Crafts, Lviv 038359
State Museum of Georgia, Tbilisi . . 015413
State Museum of History, Oklahoma City 046652
State Museum of Natural History of NAS of Ukraine, National Academy of Sciences of Ukraine, Lviv 038360
State Museum of Pennsylvania, Harrisburg 044444
State Museum of the South-Ossetian Autonomous District, Chinvali . . . 015401
State of the Art, Kansas City 116594
State of the Arts, Darlinghurst 133048
State Theatrical Museum, Tbilisi . . 015414
State Tribal Museum, Chhindwada . 022061
Statek-Muzeum Dar Pomorza, Centralne Muzeum Morskie, Gdańsk 031922
Statek-Muzeum Dar Pomorza, Centralne Muzeum Morskie w Gdańsku, Gdynia 031931
Statek-Muzeum Sołdek, Centralne Muzeum Morskie, Gdańsk 031923
Statements Gallery, Napier 108506
Staten Island Children's Museum, Staten Island 048335
Staten Island Ferry Collection, Staten Island 048336
Staten Island Historical Society Museum, Staten Island 048337
Staten Island Institute of Arts and Sciences, Staten Island 048338
Statens Håndverks- og Kunstindustriskole, Oslo 050582
Statens Historiska Museum, Stockholm 036668
Statens Kunstakademi, Kunsthøgskolen i Oslo, Oslo 050583
Statens Museum for Kunst, København 008988
Statens Världskulturmuseet, Göteborg 036306
Stathopoulos, Stelios, Pagkrati 139902
Static Line, Sainte-Mère-Eglise . . . 068073
The Station Gallery, Whitby 006806
Station House, Culcairn 000962
Station Master's Cottage, Toronto . 095346
Station Mill Antiques, Chipping Norton 083994, 130573
Station Nord, Berlin 102051
Station Peinture, Avignon 061142
Station Road Picture Framing and Art Studio, Margaret River 123263
Station Square Gallery, Pittsburgh . 118958
The Stationery Office, London 135265
Stationhouse Gallery, Williams Lake 006823
Štátna Galéria, Banská Bystrica . . . 034303
Státní Galerie Výtvarného Umění, Cheb 008329
Státní Hrad a Zámek, Frýdlant v Čechách 008362
Státní hrad Bouzov, Bouzov 008273
STATT-Museum, Herbstein 017882
Statthaus Böcklerpark, Berlin 016180
Statue Museum Balai Arca, Nganjuk 022479
Statue of Liberty National Monument and Ellis Island Immigration Museum, New York 046408

Staub g*fzk!, Zürich 112183
Stauber, Traudl, Freinberg 095508
Stauch, Karin, Falkenstein, Vogtland 070678
Staudermann, Maria & Werner, Bexbach 069814
Staudinger, Elfriede, Bad Vöslau . . . 137155
Staufer, Münsingen 121553
Staufergedächtnisstätte und Museum Wäscherschloß, Wäschenbeuren . 020615
Stauffenberg-Schloß und Stauffenberggedächtniszimmer, Albstadt 015472
Stauffer, Frédéric, Monaco 077625
Stauffer, Pierre, Jussy 082510
Staufferhaus - Sammlung Alt Unterentfelden, Unterentfelden . . 037652
Staukewitz, Gisela & Herbert, Hannover 071416
Stauner, Markus, Monzingen 072593
Staunton Augusta Art Center, Staunton 048345
Staunton Fine Arts Association, Staunton 055059
Staurothek, Domschatz und Diözesanmuseum Limburg, Limburg an der Lahn 018651
Stauss, Ursula, Stuttgart 126881
Stauth Memorial Museum, Montezuma 045992
Stavanger Brannmuseum, Stavanger 031232
Stavanger Faste Galleri, Stavanger . 031231
Stavanger Kunstforening, Stavanger 053960
Stavanger Maritime Museum, Stavanger Museum, Stavanger 031233
Stavanger Museum, Stavanger 031234
Staveley Antiques, Staveley 086699, 131532
Stavropolskij Kraevedčeskij Muzej im. G.N. Prozriteleva i G.K. Prave, Stavropol 033911
Stavropolskij Muzej Izobrazitelnych Iskusstv, Stavropol 033912
Stawe, Jörn, Seestermühe 073790
Stawell Antiques, Stawell 056630
Stawell Historical Museum, Stawell 001491
Stawski Gallery, Kraków 108985
Sté Anciens ets Bacqueville, Argenteuil 060964
Steach, Los Angeles 116890
Stead, Geoffrey, Todenham 086890
The Steading Gallery, Borgue 112673
Steadman, Saint Louis 119259
Steals & Deals, Atlanta 087530
Steam Engine Museum, Mabel 045538
Steam Gallery, Beer 112604
Steam Museum, Penrith 040689
The Steam Museum, Kew Bridge Steam Museum, Straffan 022860
STEAM Museum of the Great Western Railway, Swindon 041180
Steamboat Arabia Museum, Kansas City 044929
Steamboat Bertrand Museum, Missouri Valley 045937
Steamboat Dock Museum, Keyport . 044992
Steamboat Museum, Bowness-on-Windermere 038800
Steammodels.uk.com, Alfreton . . .083267, 130289
Steamship Collection, University of Baltimore, Baltimore 042005
Steamship Keewatin, Douglas 043484
Steamship William G. Mather Museum, Cleveland 043001
Steamtown National Historic Site, Scranton 048067
Steamtown Railway Museum, Carnforth 039004
Stearns, David, Memphis 090107
Stearns Collection of Musical Instruments, University of Michigan, School of Music, Ann Arbor 041735
Stearns History Museum, Saint Cloud 047626
Stebel, Sühlen 074023
Stebesmehl, Stolberg, Rheinland . . 073930
Stebler, Heinz, Dornach 130006
Stecher, Thomas, Stephanskirchen, Simssee 073916
Stechow, Barbara von, Frankfurt am Main 102829
Steckdaub, Andreas, Stuttgart 126882
Steckelberg, Uwe, Ochsenfurt 104517
Steckenpferd, Lauf an der Pegnitz . 072170
Stecker, Eva, Paderborn 073288
Stedelijk Archeologisch Museum, Oudenburg 003697
Stedelijk Brouwerijmuseum, Leuven 003581
Stedelijk Museum, Alkmaar 029134
Stedelijk Museum, Damme 003386
Stedelijk Museum, Oudenaarde . . . 003695
Stedelijk Museum Aalst, Aalst 003142
Stedelijk Museum Alfons Blomme, Roeselare 003722
Stedelijk Museum Amsterdam, Amsterdam 029230
Stedelijk Museum Brusselpoort, Mechelen 003635
Stedelijk Museum Bureau Amsterdam, Amsterdam 029231
Stedelijk Museum De Lakenhal, Leiden 029855
Stedelijk Museum Diest, Diest 003403
Stedelijk Museum Diksmuide, Diksmuide 003406
Stedelijk Museum Het Domein, Sittard 030156
Stedelijk Museum Het Toreke, Tienen 003795
Stedelijk Museum-Hoevemuseum, Sint-Truiden 003770
Stedelijk Museum Hof van Busleyden, Mechelen 003636
Stedelijk Museum Hoogstraten, Hoogstraten 003519
Stedelijk Museum Huize Ernest Claes, Scherpenheuvel 003745
Stedelijk Museum Ieper, Ieper 003534
Stedelijk Museum Kampen, Kampen 029803
Stedelijk Museum Lokeren, Lokeren 003611
Stedelijk Museum Roermond, Roermond 030072
Stedelijk Museum Schepenhuis, Mechelen 003637
Stedelijk Museum Schiedam, Schiedam 030133
Stedelijk Museum Van der Kelen-Mertens, Leuven 003582
Stedelijk Museum Vianen, Vianen . . 030271
Stedelijk Museum Vlissingen, Vlissingen 030284
Stedelijk Museum voor Actuele Kunst, Gent 003469
Stedelijk Museum voor Folklore en Regionale Geschiedenis, Ronse . . 003729
Stedelijk Museum voor Heemkunde en Folklore, Aarschot 003143
Stedelijk Museum voor Pijp en Tabak, Harelbeke 003494
Stedelijk Museum Zutphen, Zutphen 030405
Stedelijk Museum Zwolle, Zwolle . . 030414
Stedelijk Onderwijsmuseum Ieper, Ieper 003535
Stedelijk Prentenkabinet, Antwerpen 003191
Stedelijk Textielmuseum, Ronse . . . 003730
Stedelijk Waagmuseum, Enkhuizen 029562
Stedelijke Academie voor Beeldende Kunst, Ieper 049709
Stedelijke Academie voor Beeldende Kunst, Menen 049720
Stedelijke Academie voor Beeldende Kunst-Filiaal Wervik, Wervik 049739
Stedelijke Academie voor beeldende Kunsten, Geluwe 049697
Stedelijke Academie voor beeldende Kunsten, Herentals 049706
Stedelijke Academie voor beeldende Kunsten, Lauwe 049712
Stedelijke Academie voor Plastische Kunsten, Genk 049698
Stedelijke Academie voor Schone Kunsten, Deinze 049694
Stedelijke Academie voor Schone Kunsten, Eeklo 049696
Stedelijke Academie voor Schone Kunsten, Hasselt 049705
Stedelijke Academie voor Schone Kunsten, Roeselare 003723, 049728
Stedelijke Academie voor Schone Kunsten, Sint-Niklaas 049729
Stedelijke Akademie voor Beeldende Vorming, Harelbeke 049703
Stedelijke Kunstacademie, Tielt, West-Vlaanderen 049734
Stedelijke Musea, Sint-Niklaas 003761
Stedelijke Musea, Torhout 003804
Stedelijke Musea Kortrijk, Kortrijk . 003560
Stedelijke Oudheidkamer, Genemuiden 029601
Stedelijke Oudheidkamer De Roos, Geertruidenberg 029594
Stedman Art Gallery, Camden 042577
Steeb, Dr. Christian, Graz 057026
Steed, Dallas 115944
Steedehuys Antiek, Haarlem 078482
Steedman, Robert D., Newcastle-upon-Tyne 141955
Steeg, Baar 069249
Steeg, Kurt, Steinmaur 111937
Steel, Danielle, San Francisco 119803
Steele, Rick, Porsgrunn 128995
Steele, Robert, New York 118446
Steele County Museum, Hope 044616
Steelelife Gallery, Chicago 115557
Steeler Antiquariat, Essen 139059
Steen, I., Almelo 077732
Steenbakkerijmuseum Rupelklei te Terhagen, Terhagen 003788
Steenbakkerijmuseum 't Gelleg te Rumst, Rumst 003733
Steendrukkerij Amsterdam, Amsterdam 107809
Steenis, Oss 078673
Steenkolenmijn Daalhemergroeve, Valkenburg, Limburg 030248
Steenmuseum, Gent 003470
Steensland Art Museum, Saint Olaf College, Northfield 046553
Steensma & Van der Plas, Amsterdam 077975
Steenuil, 's-Hertogenbosch 108079
Steep and Brew Gallery, Madison . . 045593
Steephill Studio, Maleny 094771
Steeple Antiques, Ceres 083897
Steeple Antiques, Falkirk 084377
Stefan Fadinger-Museum, Sankt Agatha 002573
Stefan-George-Museum im Stefan-George-Haus, Bingen am Rhein 016246
Stefanelli, Annamaria, Perugia 106463
Stefanelli, Luigi, Genève 111501
Stefanelli Naderi, Seyed Ebrahim, Firenze 075408
Stefani, Liverpool 085028, 130905
Stefani, Paolo, Firenze 075409
Stefani, Roberta, Bologna 075110
Stefanini, Aurelio, Firenze 106072
Stefano, Betty de, Bruxelles 058087
Stefano, Natali, Roma . . . 076693, 128215
Stefanov, V., Veliko Tărnovo 137613
Stefanović, Dusan, Beograd 109721
Stefanovic, Josip, Stuttgart 139771
Stefanovich, Bruxelles 058088
Stefanovska, Maja, Skopje 107430
Steff, Tuntange 077494
Steffani, Pärnu 098691
Steffarli, Bardon 055449
Steffek, Michael, Brunn am Gebirge 056954
Steffek, Michael, Wien 057556
Steffen, Luxembourg 107412
Steffny, Christa & Ernst, Merzkirchen 126309
Steffny, Thomas, München 126466
Stegehuis, Henk, Almelo 077733
Stegentritt, Dr. Erwin, Saarbrücken . 134377
Steger, H., Auerbach, Oberpfalz . . . 069213
Steger, Hans, Zeulenroda 105369
Stegmaier, Ludwig & Marianne, München 104324
Stegner, Heinz, Mainz 139450
Stehle, Jörg-Uwe, Bensheim 101757
Stehmann, Ira, München 104325
Stehr, Volker J., Bielefeld 069840
Steib, Cochem 102321
Steib, R., Lappersdorf 072159
Steibo, Stadtlohn 073891
Steidl Bernd, Dresden 070331
Steidle & Douglas, Rottenburg am Neckar 126749
Steiermärkischer Kunstverein Werkbund, Graz 052598
Steiff, Düsseldorf 102558
Steiff, Hamburg 103221
Steiger, Erwin, Luzern 082635
Steiger, Thilo, Bad Schwartau 069381
Steiglitz Court House, Steiglitz 001492
Steigrad, Lawrence, New York 091265
Steilacoom Historical Museum, Steilacoom 048348
Stein, Bad Oeynhausen 101685
Stein, Alois, Inzell 125974
Stein, Angela, Wuppertal 074542
Stein, Axel, Bonn 069944
Stein, Benjamin J., Amsterdam . . . 077976
Stein, Carolyn von, Cincinnati 131946
Stein, Christian, Milano 106326
Stein, Daniel, San Francisco 092890
Stein & Co., David, Sydney 123314
Stein, Fabien, Seichamps 068197
Stein, Gertrude, New York 118447
Stein, Horst-Detlev von, München . 072867
Stein, Irmgard & Heinz, Gelsenkirchen 102932
Stein, Margitta, Siegen 073813
Stein, Martin, Karlstein am Main . . 126012
Stein, Robert, Saint Louis 119260
Stein, Vernice, Buffalo 115264
Stein-Reich, Berlin 102052
Stein- und Bauernmuseum Großdöllnerhof, Rechberg 002508
Stein- und Beinmuseum, Weiterstadt 020788
Stein- und Fossiliensammlung Albert, Sulzdorf 020388
Steinacker, U., Koblenz 103574
Steinbach, Krefeld 072080
Steinbach, Michael, München 139548
Steinbach, Wendelin, Krefeld 103785
Steinbauer, Franz, Opfenbach 073221, 126596
Steinbaum, Bernice, Miami 117144
Steinbeck, Renate, Aachen 069103
Steinbeck, Romy, Richterswil 082741
Steinbeißer, W., Ingolstadt 139284
Steinberg, Nettetal 104398
Steinberg, Barry, Los Angeles 116891
Steinberg, Peter, Linz 137225
Steinberger, Ludwig, Ulm 074153
Steinbrich-Fricke, I., Dachau 070170
Steinbrink, H., Osnabrück 073247
Steinburg, Mollhagen 072588
Steinegger, Iris Claudia, Rüdlingen . 111852
Steinek, H.S., Wien 095944
Steinek, H.S., Wien 095945
Steinemann & Co., Luzern 111707
Steiner, San Francisco 119804
Steiner, Sydney 056689
Steiner, A., Bamberg 069464
Steiner, Alain, Homburg 071577
Steiner, Emil, Stadel (Winterthur) . . 082829
Steiner, Franz, Stuttgart 134422
Steiner, Gerhard, Graz 057027
Steiner, Dr. Günther, Graz 057028
Steiner, Max, Zürich 083026, 130265
Steiner, Nelly, Bern 082243
Steiner, Nordfrid, Basel 082174
Steiner, Nordfrid, Basel 129933

Steiner, René, Bussigny-près-Lausanne . . . 082284
Steiner, René, Erlach . . . 111396, 135010
Steiner, Silvia, Biel . . . 111291
Steiner, Urs, Zürich . . . 141361
Steiner, Victor, Graz . . . 123369
Steiner, Walo, Densbüren . . . 111380
Steinert & Kühn, Burgstädt . . . 070102
Steinfeld, Gent . . . 058207
Steinfeld, A., Westerland . . . 105230
Steinhauermuseum, Randersacker . 019709
Steinhauermuseum Mühlbach, Eppingen . . . 016996
Steinhausen-Museum, Frankfurt am Main . . . 017197
Steinhauser, Freiburg im Breisgau . 070863
Steinhauser, Werner, Graz . . . 057029
Steinhauser, Werner, Judendorf-Straßengel . . . 057093
Steinhauzer, Leo, Eindhoven . . . 108008
Steinhöfel, Adendorf . . . 138671
Der Steinhof, Berlin . . . 125300
Steinhoff, Almere . . . 077743
Steinhuder Spielzeugnuseum, Steinhude . . . 020311
Steiniger, Siegburg . . . 104892
Steinigeweg, W., Tecklenburg . . . 074048
Steininger, Hans-Rudolf, Staad . . . 111929
Steininger, Ric J., Cairns . . . 094354
Steinitz, Bernard, Paris . . 066572, 100885
Steinitz-Baruch, Bernard, Saint-Ouen . . . 067898
Steinkohlen-Besucherbergwerk Rabensteiner Stollen, Ilfeld . . . 018049
Steinkopf, J.F., Stuttgart . . . 139772
Steinle, M., Neustadt am Rübenberge . . . 073023
Steinmag, Gümligen . . . 130044
Steinmayr, B., Bergisch Gladbach . . 069543
Steinmeier, Udo, Nussdorf, Chiemgau . . . 073132
Steinmetz, Jon, Ahrensburg . . . 069122
Steinmeyer, Ulli, Ottobrunn . . . 073271
Steinmuseum, Solothurn . . . 037580
Steinrötter, Münster . . . 104377
Steinsburg-Museum, Römhild . . . 019869
Steinscher Hof Kirberg, Freiherr-vom-Stein-Gedenkstätte, Hünfelden . . . 018025
Steinsiek, Tulsa . . . 093332, 133004
Steinsland Klyngetun, Trondarnes Distriktsmuseum, Harstad . . . 030878
Steinsträsser, Manfred, Köln . . . 072013
Steintor-Verlag, Lübeck . . . 134172
Steintor-Verlag, Möhnesee 104085, 134206
Steinzeitdorf Kussow, Kussow bei Grevesmühlen . . . 018451
Steinzeitmuseum, Thunstetten . . . 037635
Steinzeitmuseum, Sammlung Reinhard, Korb . . . 018382
Steirische Antiquitäten- und Sammlermesse, Unterpremstätten 093586
Steirisches Feuerwehrmuseum, Gross Sankt Florian Kunst und Kulturzentrum, Groß Sankt Florian . . . 001963
Steirisches Glaskunstzentrum und Glasmuseum Bärnbach, Bärnbach 001748
Steirisches Holzmuseum, Sankt Ruprecht . . . 002623
Steirisches Obstbaumuseum, Puch bei Weiz . . . 002473
Steirisches Uhren-, Musikalien- und Volkskundemuseum, Arnfels . . . 001696
Stelio, Davia, Trieste . . . 076909
Stelio, J., Fortaleza . . . 096539
Stella, Breda . . . 107881
Stella, Giorgia, Verona . . . 128440
Stella, L., Paris . . . 100886
Stella, Pierangelo, Padova . . . 140085
Stella A., Berlin . . 102053, 133811, 138849
Stella Books, Chepstow . . . 141507
Stellan, Holm, New York . . . 118448
Stellenbosch Museum, Stellenbosch . . . 034755
Steller, Jacksonville . . . 116546
Stelling Projecten, Leiden 108108, 128745
Stelten, Worpswede . . . 074487
Stelten, A., Grasberg . . . 071085
Steltman, Amsterdam . . . 077977, 107810, 134791
Stelzer, Hannelore, Lörrach . . . 072296
Stelzer, Hubert, Bielefeld . . . 069841
Dr. Stelzer & Zaglmaier, Halle, Saale . . . 103076
Stema, Brescia . . . 127233
Stemmer, Ismaning . . . 125977
Stemmer, Owing Mills . . . 135474
Stemp, Alfred, Eichenau . . . 125576
Stencil, Barcelona . . . 080941
Stendahl, Los Angeles . . . 116892
Stenderhoff, T., Münster . . . 139575
Stenderhoff, Theresia, Münster . . 072929, 139576
De Stenen Uil, Eindhoven . . . 108009
Stenenexpositie de Molen - Museum Batjuchin, Borculo . . . 029332
Stenersenmuseet, Oslo . . . 031108
Stengel-True Museum, Marion . . . 045686
Stenhuset, Stockamöllan . . . 081903
Stenlund, Barbro, Stockholm . . . 111072
Stenneset Bygdetun, Rana Museum, Mo i Rana . . . 031019
Steno Museet, Århus . . . 008809
Stense, Stockholm . . . 082024
Stenstrøm, Frederiksberg . 060247, 124018
Stenstrup Museum, Højby . . . 008918
Stenton Gallery, Stenton . . . 114484
Stenvert-Mittrowsky, Antonia, Köln .103719, 134121
Stenzel, Thomas, Northeim . . . 126558
Step Back Antiques, Hawthorn, Victoria . . . 055968
Step Back in Time, Columbus . . . 088440
Stepenik - Kcb, Beograd . . . 109722
Stephan, Bad Zwischenahn . . . 069403
Stephan, Grödig . . . 057040
Stéphan, Nantes . . . 064947
Stephan, Bernd, Pirmasens . . . 073334
Stephan, Christian, Beaune . . . 061303
Stephan, Dr. Georges, Hamburg . . . 071337
Stephan, Henri, Juvigny . . . 063269
Stéphan, Jean-Marc, Beaune . . . 061304
Stephan, Josef, Heubach, Württemberg . . . 071506
Stephan, Kai, Jena . . . 071655
Stéphan, Monique, Saint-Pol-de-Léon . . . 067964
Stéphan, Robert, Paris . . . 066573
Stéphan, Roger, Varennes-Vauzelles 068728
Stephan, Sébastien, Beaune . . . 061305
Stéphan, Yannick, Coatréven . . . 062373
Stéphan, Yannick, Perros-Guirec . . 066771
Stephanie Ann Roger Gallery, Frostburg . . . 044091
Stephanie's Antique, New York . . . 091266
Stephanie's Antiques, New York . . . 091267
Stephansson House, Edmonton . . . 005406
Stephen, Saint Paul . . . 119314
Stephen, Jean, Minneapolis . . . 117309
Stephen A. Douglas Tomb, Chicago 042881
Stephen C. Foster State Park, Fargo 043811
Stephen Foster Folk Culture Center, White Springs . . . 049143
Stephen G. Beaumont Museum, Wakefield . . . 041276
The Stephen Girard Collection, Girard College, Philadelphia . . . 046989
Stephen Leacock Museum, Orillia . 006075
The Stephen Phillips Memorial House, Salem . . . 047746
Stephens, Chris, Charlotte . . . 087980
Stephens, Francis, Corringham . . . 084084
Stephens, John, Auckland . . . 078983
Stephens African-American Museum, Shreveport . . . 048166
Stephens Collection, London . . . 040295
Stephens County Historical Society Museum, Duncan . . . 043529
Stephen's Gallery, Houston . . . 116411
Stephens Museum, Fayette . . . 043829
Stephenson, Glenna, Kansas City . . 089521
Stephenson, Joseph, Cincinnati . . . 088284
Stephenson, Robert, London . . . 085713
Stephenson County Historical Society Museum, Freeport . . . 044073
Stephenson Railway Museum, North Shields . . . 040592
Stephensons, York . . . 122767
Stephenville Museum, Stephenville 048349
Steppan, Robert, Augsburg . . . 069240
Steppé, Bruxelles . . . 058089
Steppes Hill Farm Antiques, Stockbury . . . 086716
Steppingstone Museum, Havre de Grace . . . 044485
Steps, Delhi . . . 105685
Steps Gallery, Carlton, Victoria . . . 094379
Sterbehaus Ferdinand Raimunds, Gedenk- und Informationsstätte, Pottenstein . . . 002452
Sterenberg, M., Groningen . . . 078432
Sterenfeld, Xavier, Perpignan . . . 066760, 100996
Sterkau, Ralf, Bochum . . . 069895
Sterkstroom Museum, Sterkstroom 034760
Sterkwerk Galerie, Tilburg . . . 108235
Sterl, Thomas Georg, Homburg . . . 071578, 125959
Sterling, Charlotte . . . 087981
Sterling, Eden, Cincinnati . . . 088285
Sterling and Francine Clark Art Institute, Williamstown . . . 049187
Sterling Books, Weston-super-Mare 142147
Sterling Coins and Medals, Bournemouth . . . 083608
Sterling Hill Mining Museum, Ogdensburg . . . 046633
Sterling Historical Society Museum, Sterling . . . 048352
Sterling Hundley, Richmond . . . 119126
Sterling Publishing Company, New York . . . 135462
Sterling-Rock Falls Historical Society Museum, Sterling . . . 048351
Sterling Studios, London . 113900, 131184
Stern, New York . . . 091268
Stern, Tel Aviv . . . 105926, 127105
Stern, Anita, New York . . . 091269
Stern, Anita, New York . . . 091270
Stern, Barry, Paddington . . . 095042
Stern, Franz, Wien . . . 137367
Stern & Co., Harvey M., Philadelphia . . . 132637
Stern, Lynne, London . . . 113901
Stern Pissaro Gallery, London . . . 085714, 113902, 131185
Stern und Hungler, Wien . . . 095946
Stern-Verlag Janssen & Co., Düsseldorf . . . 133899, 139020
Sternat, Dr. Reinhold, Wien . . . 057557
Sternberg, Frank, Zürich . 083027, 122373
Sternberg, Heinz, Hamburg . . . 071338
Sternberg, Maurice, Chicago . . . 115558
Sternberg, Maurice, Chicago . . . 115559
Sternberg Museum of Natural History, Hays . . . 044490
Šternberský Palác, Národní Galerie v Praže, Praha . . . 008648
Sterne-Hoya Museum, Nacogdoches . . . 046118
Sternisa, Manfred, Linz . . . 057169
Sternitzky, Hugues, Wasserbourg . . 069047
Sternmann, M., Crailsheim . . . 070160
Šternová, Viera, Trenčín . . . 109923
Sterr, Franz Xaver, Starnberg . . . 073897
Sterr, F.X., Starnberg . . . 126826
Sterrenburg, Marius, Amsterdam . . 077978
Sterry, John Henry, Louisville . . . 090029
Sterz, P. & I., Wolfsburg . . . 105325
Sterzenbach, Heinz, Berlin . . . 102054
Sterzenbach, Mathias, Longeville-lès-Metz . . . 063980
Stetten, Isabelle Anne, Paris . . . 124816
Stettler Town and Country Museum, Stettler . . . 006510
Steuben House Museum, River Edge . . . 047448
Steuder, La Chaux-de-Fonds . . . 082305
Steuer, Helmut, Worms . . . 074483
Steurer, A., Bietigheim, Baden . . . 069844
Steven H. Oliver Art Center, California College of Arts and Crafts, Oakland . . . 046592
Stevenage Museum, Stevenage . . . 041095
Stevens, Houston . . . 089214, 132141
Stevens & Son, Lubenham 085860, 131241
Stevens, Elliot, New York . . . 118449
Stevens, J.G., Maastricht . . . 128766
Stevens, John, Nashville . . . 132405
Stevens, Larry, Baltimore . . . 115087
Steven's Art, Buffalo . . . 115265
Stevens-Coolidge Place, North Andover . . . 046513
Stevens County Gas and Historical Museum, Hugoton . . . 044667
Stevens County Historical Society Museum, Morris . . . 046031
Stevens Museum, Salem . . . 047732
Stevenson, Hamilton . . . 058865
Stevenson, Mandrake, Ibstock . . . 084783, 130822
Stevenson, R.B., San Diego . . . 119553
Stevenson Academy of Traditional Painting, Sea Cliff . . . 052159
Stevenson Galleries, Tunbridge Wells . . . 114614
Stevenson-Hamilton Memorial Information Centre, Skukuza . . . 034749
Steves Homestead Museum, San Antonio . . . 047806
Steveston Museum, Richmond . . . 006285
Stevington Windmill, Stevington . . . 041096
StewArt, Battle . . . 112591
Stewart, Bexhill-on-Sea . . 112634, 130381
Stewart, Eastbourne . . . 084268, 130671
Stewart, Glenorie . . . 055891
Stewart, Jacksonville . . . 132195
Stewart, Charles, Atlanta . . . 087531
Stewart, Cynthia, Tulsa . . . 120207
Stewart, Dennis E., San Antonio . . . 119456
Stewart, Edward, New York . . . 091271
Stewart, Inessa, Dallas . . . 088614
Stewart, Lauri, London . . . 085715
Stewart Antiques, Los Angeles . . . 089917
Stewart Collection, Pocklington . . . 040726
Stewart Historical Museum, Stewart . . . 006511
Stewart Indian Cultural Center, Carson City . . . 042637
Stewart M. Lord Memorial Museum, Burlington . . . 042517
Stewart, Tabori & Chang, New York 135463
Stewarton and District Museum, Stewarton . . . 041097
The Stewartry Museum, Kirkcudbright . . . 039901
Stewner, Lübeck . . . 103969
Stey, Villemomble . . . 068907
Steyaert, C., Bruxelles . . . 058090
Steyaert, Claire, Minneapolis . . . 090395
Steyning Museum, Steyning . . . 041098
Østfold Auksjonsforretning, Mysen . 121858
Sticht, Uwe, Gevelsberg . . . 139136
Stichting Archipel, Apeldoorn . . . 107844
Stichting Atlas Van Stolk, Rotterdam . . . 030105
Stichting de Appel, Amsterdam . . . 029232
Stichting De Brakke Grond, Amsterdam . . . 029233
Stichting Huis Bergh, 's-Heerenberg 029690
Stichting Joden Savanna, Paramaribo . . . 036160
Stichting Niggendijker, Groningen . . 108049
Stichting Noorderlicht, Groningen . . 108050, 134811
Stichting Oosterkerk, Amsterdam . . 029234
Stichting Outline, Amsterdam . . . 107811
Stichting Santjes en Kantjes, Maastricht . . . 029903
Stichting Veranneman, Kruishoutem 003562
Stichting Werkplaats tot Herstel van Antiek Textiel, Haarlem . . . 128696
Stichting Zeeland 1939-1945, 's-Heer Abtskerke . . . 029687

Stichting Zeeuwse Schaapkudde, Heinkenszand . . . 029710
Stickan, Marion, Köln . . . 072014
Stickereimuseum Eibenstock, Eibenstock . . . 016902
Stickmaskinsmuseum, Glemminebro . . . 036287
Sticks and Stones, Christchurch . . . 079055
Sticks And Stones, Christchurch . . . 079056
Sticks and Stones House, Corner Brook . . . 005295
Sticks & Stones, Montrose . . . 086004
Sticks & Stones, Toronto . . . 059295
Stiebeling, Klaus, Wuppertal . . . 074543
Stieber, Anni, Würzburg . . . 074512
Stiebner, München . . . 134280
Stiefelhagen, Klaus, Lindlar . . . 072275
Stiefelhagen, Kunibert, Siegburg . . 073810
Stiefelmachermuseum, Rechnitz . . 002510
Stiefler, G., Pottenstein . . . 139665
Stiegemann-Schöpper, I., Rheine . . 073525
Stieglitz, Martha, Stuttgart . . . 105013
Stieler, Rittersgrün . . . 073547
Stien, Daniel, San Francisco . . . 092891
Stieren, San Antonio . . . 119457
Stierhübelteichhaus, Trift- und Holzfällermuseum, Karlstift . . . 002115
Stierle, Heinz, Salzburg . . . 137248
Sties, Paul, Kronberg im Taunus . . . 103798
Stiffkey, Norwich . . . 086123
Stiffkey Antiques, Stiffkey . . . 086704
Stiffkey Lamp Shop, Stiffkey . . . 086705
't Stift, Schatkamer en Bezoekerscentrum, Susteren . . . 030190
Stift Dürnstein, Dürnstein, Niederösterreich . . . 001793
Stift Fischbeck, Hessisch Oldendorf 017910
Stift Melk, Stiftsmuseum, Melk . . . 002307
Stift Obernkirchen, Obernkirchen . . 019402
Stiftelsen, Stockholm . . . 111073
Stiftelsen Musikkulturens Främjande, Stockholm . . . 036669
Stiftlandmuseum, Waldsassen . . . 020649
Stiftsbibliothek, Einsiedeln . . . 037061
Stiftsgalerie Sankt Georgen, Sankt Georgen am Längsee . . . 095741
Stiftsgården, Trondheim . . . 031286
Stiftskirchenmuseum, Himmelkron . 017929
Stiftsmuseum, Bad Buchau . . . 015677
Stiftsmuseum, Garsten . . . 001887
Stiftsmuseum, Mattsee . . . 002298
Stiftsmuseum, Millstatt . . . 002314
Stiftsmuseum, Vomp . . . 002787
Stiftsmuseum, Zwettl, Niederösterreich . . . 003078
Stiftsmuseum der Stadt Aschaffenburg, Aschaffenburg . . . 015586
Stiftsmuseum Praemonstratenser-Chorherren Stift Schlägl, Aigen-Schlägl . . . 001669
Stiftsmuseum Schatzhaus Kärntens, Sankt Paul . . . 002613
Stiftsmuseum Steyr-Gleink, Steyr-Gleink . . . 002707
Stiftsmuseum und Domschatzkammer, Xanten . . . 021035
Stiftssammlungen des Zisterzienserstiftes Rein, Gratwein . . . 001924
Stiftssammlungen Lambach, Lambach . . . 002193
Stiftssammlungen Wilten, Innsbruck . . . 002095
Stiftung Aratym, Gutenstein . . . 001995
Stiftung Aschenbrenner, Garmisch-Partenkirchen . . . 017327
Stiftung AutoMuseum Volkswagen, Wolfsburg . . . 020968
Stiftung Bauhaus Dessau, Dessau, Anhalt . . . 016684
Stiftung B.C. Koekkoek-Haus, Kleve 018281
Stiftung Brandenburgische Gedenkstätten, Oranienburg . . . 019481
Stiftung Bundeskanzler-Adenauer-Haus, Bad Honnef . . . 015726
Stiftung DKM, Duisburg . . . 016860
Stiftung Dr. Edmund Müller, Beromünster . . . 036945
Stiftung Ernst Schneider, Hetjens Museum, Düsseldorf . . . 016844
Stiftung Fritz und Hermine Overbeck, Bremen . . . 016425
Stiftung für Eisenplastik, Sammlung Dr. Hans Koenig, Zollikon . . . 037758
Stiftung für Konkrete Kunst, Reutlingen . . . 019814
Stiftung für Konkrete Kunst Roland Phleps, Freiburg im Breisgau . . . 017238
Stiftung Hans Arp und Sophie Taeuber-Arp, Remagen . . . 019793
Stiftung Haus der Geschichte der Bundesrepublik Deutschland, Bonn . . . 016335
Stiftung Haus der Geschichte der Bundesrepublik Deutschland, Zeitgeschichtliches Forum Leipzig, Leipzig . . . 018596
Stiftung Käthe-Kollwitz-Gedenkstätte, Moritzburg . . . 018998
Stiftung Keramion, Zentrum für morderne und historische Keramik, Frechen 017215
Stiftung Kloster Michaelstein/Museum, Blankenburg, Harz . . . 016261
Stiftung Kohl'sche Einhorn-Apotheke, Weißenburg in Bayern . . . 020779
Stiftung Künstlerhaus Boswil, Boswil . . . 036965
Stiftung Mecklenburg, Ratzeburg . . 019728
Stiftung Moritzburg, Kunstmuseum des Landes Sachsen-Anhalt, Halle, Saale . . . 017672
Stiftung Preußische Schlösser und Gärten Berlin-Brandenburg, Park Sanssouci (Schloß Sanssouci, Neue Kammern, Chinesisches Haus, Neues Palais, Schloß Charlottenhof, Römische Bäder, Normannischer Turm, Orangerieschloß, Historische Mühle), Neuer Garten (Schloß Cecilienhof mit Historischer Stätte der Potsdamer Konferenz, Marmorpalais, Gotische Bibliothek), Park Babelsberg (Schloß Babelsberg, Flatowturm), Moschee (Dampfmaschinenhaus), Belvedere Pfingstberg, Pomonatempel, Jagdschloß Stern, Schloß und Park Caputh, Schloß und Park Rheinsberg, Schloß und Park Sacrow, Schloß und Park Königs Wusterhausen, Schloß und Park Paretz, Schloß Oranienburg, Park Charlottenburg (Schloß Charlottenburg, Neuer Pavillon, Mausoleum, Belvedere), Park Glienicke (Schloß Glienicke, Casino), Jagdschloß Grunewald, Potsdam . 019659
Stiftung Rebhaus Wingreis, Twann . 037647
Stiftung Römermuseum Homburg-Schwarzenacker, Homburg . . . 018003
Stiftung Sammlung E.G. Bührle, Zürich . . . 037802
Stiftung Scheibler-Museum Rotes Haus, Monschau . . . 018993
Stiftung Schloß Ahrensburg, Ahrensburg . . . 015456
Stiftung Schloß Eutin, Eutin . . . 017097
Stiftung Schloß Glücksburg, Glücksburg, Ostsee . . . 017433
Stiftung Schloss und Park Benrath, Museum für Europäische Gartenkunst, Museum Corps de Logis (Hauptschloß), Museum für Naturkunde, Orangerie, Park, Düsseldorf . . . 016847
Stiftung Sculpture at Schoenthal, Langenbruck . . . 037230
Stiftung Springhornhof, Neuenkirchen, Lüneburger Heide . . . 104407
Stiftung Stadtmuseum Berlin, Landesmuseum für Kultur und Geschichte Berlins, Generaldirektion und Verwaltung, Berlin . . . 016181
Stiftung Stadtmuseum Sursee, Sursee . . . 037619
Stiftung Starke, Berlin . . . 016182
Stiftung Stift Neuzelle, Neuzelle . . . 019301
Stiftung Weimarer Klassik und Kunstsammlungen, Weimar, Thüringen . . . 020757
Stiftung Wilhelm Lehmann, Niederhelfenschwil . . . 037381
Stiftung Wilhelm Lehmbruck Museum, Zentrum Internationaler Skulptur, Duisburg . . . 016861
De Stijl, Dordrecht . . . 078318
Stiklestad Nasjonal Kultursenter, Verdal . . . 031331
Stiko Karoliukai, Vilnius . . . 107374
Stil, Beograd . . . 080407
Stilbruch, Berlin . . . 069769
Stilke, Magdeburg . . . 072378
Stilkunst, Starnberg . . . 073898
Still Life, Edinburgh . . . 084314
Still National Osteopathic Museum, Kirksville . . . 045023
Stilla Nova, Maastricht . . . 078624
Stille, Maastricht . . . 140496
Stille Nacht-Museum, Hallein . . . 002015
Stille-Nacht- und Heimatmuseum Bruckmannhaus, Oberndorf bei Salzburg . . . 002387
Stiller, Hans-Dirk, Düsseldorf . . . 139021
Stillman, Georgie, San Diego . . . 092685
Stills, Nijmegen . . . 108159
Still's Corner, Timaru . . . 108584
Stills Gallery, Edinburgh . . . 039427
Stills Gallery, Paddington . . . 095043
Stillwater, Seattle . . . 119998
STIM, Nesle-Hodeng . . . 064979
Stima, Breda . . . 107882
Stima, Bruxelles . . . 096254
Stingl, Renate, Frankfurt am Main . 070794
Stingray, Columbus . . . 115801
Stinson, New Orleans . . . 117516
Stinzenmuseum, Tsjerke en Uniastate Beers, Beers . . . 029297
Stirk Cottage, Kalamunda . . . 001139
Stirling Antiques, Abinger Hammer . 083251
Stirling Old Town Jail, Stirling . . . 041106
Stirling Smith Art Gallery and Museum, Stirling . . . 041107
Stirnemann, M.V., Zürich . . . 141362
Stirt, James, Vevey . . . 122355
Stith, Norfolk . . . 132562
Stivanin-Bouquet, Céline, Castanet-Tolosan . . . 124171
Stix, Karlsruhe . . . 071731
Stix, W., Baden-Baden . . . 069427
Stjepan Gruber Museum, Županja . 007863
Stjernsunds Slott, Askersund . . . 036205
Stjørdal Museum KF, Stjørdal . . . 031240
Stoani Haus der Musik, Gasen . . . 001889
Stobi, Skopje . . . 107431
Stock, Toronto . . . 123842
Stock, Colin, Rainford . . . 086322
Stock, D., Wienhausen . . . 074390
Stock, Karl-Heinz, Kamen . . . 071691
Stock, Martin, Hohenems . 095570, 133088
Stock, Michaela, Wien . . . 057558
Stock, Ray, Denver . . . 116058
Stock Exchange Consignment Shop, Saint Louis . . . 092319
Le Stock Room, Montréal . . . 059010
Stock Solution, Salt Lake City . . . 119372
Stockbridge Library Historical Room, Stockbridge . . . 048368
Stocké, Rainer, Frankenthal, Pfalz . 133934
Stocker, Andreas, Gletzow . . . 071008
Stocker, Jos., Zürich . . . 141363
Stocker, Leopold, Graz . . . 133081
Stocker-Schmid, Dietikon . . . 135007
Stockermann, W., Düsseldorf . . . 070444
Stockhammer, Hall in Tirol . . . 133086
Stockholm Art Fair, Sollentuna . . . 093885
Stockholm Historical Society Museum, Stockholm . . . 048369
Stockholms Auktionsverk, Degeberga . . . 122116
Stockholms Auktionsverk, Göteborg 122144
Stockholms Auktionsverk, Malmö . 122211
Stockholms Auktionsverk, Stockholm . . . 122261
Stockholms Auktionsverk, Strängnäs . . . 122264
Stockholms Internationella Antikmässan, Stockholm . . . 093886
Stockholms Länsmuseum, Stockholm . . . 036670
Stockholms Medeltidsmuseum, Stockholm . . . 036671
Stockholms Skolmuseum, Stockholms Stadsmuseum, Stockholm . . . 036672
Stockholms Stadsmuseum, Stockholm . . . 036673
Stockholms Universitet Konstsamlingar, Stockholm . . . 036674
Stocking, Sarah, San Francisco . . . 119805
Stocklassa, Stockholm . . . 129875
Stockman, Bakers Swamp . . . 094194
Stockmans, Jos, Haarlem . . . 078483
Stockport Art Gallery, Stockport . . . 041109
Stockport Museum, Stockport . . . 041110
Stocks and Chairs, Poole . 086289, 131388
Stockspring, London . . . 085716
Stockton-on-Tees Museums and Heritage Service, Stockton-on-Tees . . . 041113
Stockwood Craft Museum and Mossman Gallery, Luton . . . 040358
Stockyard Galleries, Foster . . . 094564
Stockyard Gallery, Mataranka . . . 094795
Stockyards Station Gallery, Fort Worth . . . 116166
Stoddard, James A., Washington . . 133036
Stoddard, Richard, New York . . . 142696
Stodel, Inez, Amsterdam . . . 077979
Stodel, Jacob, London . . . 085717
Stodola, Václav, Praha . . . 060167
Stöberdiele, Büsum . . . 070088
Stöberkiste, Grambin . . . 071083
Stöberlein, Günter, München . . . 134281
Stöberstube Siebengebirge, Wünsdorf . . . 139867
Stöckli, Stans . . . 130187
Stoedtner, Dr. F., Meerbusch . . . 134197
Stöger, Martin & Monika, Piding . . . 126631
Stöhr, Wien . . . 137368
Stöhr, Beate, Meerbusch . . . 072490
Stöhr, Edith, Wien . . . 057559
Stöhr, Dr. H. & W., Wuppertal . . . 105361
Stöhr, Helmut, Bayreuth . . . 125142
Stör, Hans, Frankfurt am Main . . . 070795
Stöver, L., Hamminkeln . . . 134031
Stoff, Graz . . . 057030
Stoffels, Joh., Trier . . . 074098
Stoffer, Nicole, Gelsenkirchen . . . 102933
Stofnun Arna Magnússonar, Reykjavík . . . 021978
Stoilov, Valletta . . . 107455
Stokes, Val, Waikato . . . 108596
Stokes, William H., Cirencester . . . 084021
Stokes Books, Dublin . . . 139967
Stokke Bygdetun og Galleri Bokeskogen, Stokke . . . 031241
Stolarski, M., Lesznowola . . . 079665
Stoldt, Helgo, Krempel . . . 072083
Stolen Buick Studio, Chicago . . . 115560
Stolica, Moskva . . . 140918
Stolica, Moskva . . . 140919
Stolk, F., Amsterdam . . . 077980
Stolk, Henk Martin, Linz . . . 123415
Stolker, Maud, Breda . . . 078118
Stoll, R., Sinsheim . . . 073836
Stolla-Holten, Gisela, Neustadt an der Weinstraße . . . 073034
Stolle, Wolf-Rüdiger, Berlin 069770, 125301
Stoller, Silvia, Horgen . . . 111560
Stollhoff, Joachim, Weil am Rhein . 074302
Stollman, Steve, New York . . . 091272
Stoltefuß, Thomas, Hamm, Westfalen . . . 071364
Stoltenburg, Limburg an der Lahn . 072261
Stoltz, Virginia C., Columbus . . . 088441
Stoltze-Turm und Stoltze-Museum der Frankfurter Sparkasse, Frankfurt am Main . . . 017198
Stolz, Gerhard, Starnberg . . . 073899
Stolz, Dr. Ruprecht, Berlin . . . 102055
Stondon Museum, Lower Stondon . 040349
Stone, Allan, New York . . . 118450
Stone, Frank, Minneapolis . . . 117310
Stone, Jeremy, San Francisco . . . 119806

Stone, June & Tony, London 085718
Stone, Keith, Bessacarr 083496
Stone, M. Lee, San Jose 119865
Stone Age Antiques, Miami 090243
Stone and Press Galleries, New Orleans 117517
Stone Art, Bakewell 112538
Stone Arts, South Auckland 079244
The Stone Barn Glass Gallery, Newcastle-upon-Tyne 114127
Stone by Stone Gallery, Dallas 115945
Stone Cottage Antiques, Fort Worth 088887
Stone Cottage Antiques, Toronto . . 059296
Stone Engraving Art Museum, Beijing 007010
Stone Engraving Museum, Fu 007071
Stone Fort Museum, Stephen F. Austin State University, Nacogdoches 046119
The Stone Gallery, Burford 083795
Stone House Gallery, Fredonia 044065
The Stone House Museum, Belchertown 042102
Stone Legacy Gallery, Genève 111502
Stone Mountain Art, Atlanta 114930
Stone Museum, Monroe Township . 045974
Stone Shop Museum, Grimsby 005553
Stone-Tolan House, Rochester 047484
Stone Trough Books, York 142181
Stonecrop Fine Art Galleries, Violet Town 095365
Stonefield Historic Site, Cassville . . 042650
Stonehouse Gallery, Warrandyte . . . 095373
Stonehouse Museum, Vale 048731
Stoner, Ben, Chippendale . 055670, 123213
Stones River National Battlefield, Murfreesboro 046097
Stone's Tavern Museum, Ligonier . . 045289
Stoneware Gallery, Winnipeg 097606
Stoneway Gallery, Bridgnorth 112704
Stoneycroft Farm, Betchworth 083497
Stonington, Seattle 119999
Stonington Stables Museum of Art, Deakin University, Malvern, Victoria 001210
Stonnington Local History Collection - Malvern, Malvern, Victoria 001211
Stonnington Local History Collection - Prahran, Prahran 001409
Stonor Park, Henley-on-Thames . . . 039729
Stony Plain and District Pioneer Museum, Stony Plain 006515
Stony Point Battlefield State Historic Site, Stony Point 048380
Stoob, Urban, Sankt Gallen 135063
Tin Stoodley & Celia Jennings, Dinah, Brasted 083655
De Stoof, Deventer 107971
De Stoof, Enschede 078380
Stoomgemaal Halfweg, Halfweg . . . 029666
Stoomgemaal Hertog Reijnout en Bezoekerscentrum Arkemheen, Nijkerk 029957
Stoomgemaal Mastenbroek, Genemuiden 029602
Stoomhoutzagerij, Groenlo 029633
Stoomtrein Goes-Borsele, Goes . . . 029616
Stoottroepen Museum, Assen 029281
Stop Monnaie, Pointe-à-Pitre 074646
Stopalo, Jean & Carsten, Stockholm 082025
Stopin, Camille, Lille 124326
Stoppenbach & Delestre, London . .085719, 113903
Stor-Elvdal Museum, Koppang 030950
Stora Nyckelvikens Gård, Nacka . . . 036492
Storai, Luciano, Prato 127896
Storbecher, Daniel, Millau 064561
Storch, Erich, Krefeld 072081, 139368
Storchenturm-Museum, Zell am Harmersbach 021050
Storck, Wolframs-Eschenbach 074476
Stordel, Peter, Neuenbrook 072980, 126531
De Store, Zaltbommel 078859
The Store Antiques, Great Shelford . 084522
The Store Antiques, Toronto 059297
Store II, Portland 092015
Store Mæla Gård Merdin, Skien . . . 121877
The Store Upstairs, New York 118451
Storefront for Art and Architecture, New York 118452
Storehouse 22, Buffalo 115266
The Stores, Great Waltham 084525
Storey, London 085720, 141905
Storia della Miniatura. Studi e Documenti, Firenze 135959
Storia dell'Arte, Scandicci 135960
Stories, Richmond 142833
Storkower Bogen, Berlin 102056
Storm, Bagsværd 133419
Storm, Great Shelford . . . 084523, 113152
Storm Fine Arts, Cambridge 112793
Storm King Art Center, Mountainville 046079
Storm P.-Museet, Frederiksberg . . . 008863
Stormarnsches Dorfmuseum, Altes Bauernhaus am Thie, Hoisdorf . . . 017986
Stormbroek, Eindhoven 078352
Stormcloud Trading, Saint Paul 119315
Storme, Frédéric, Lille 099496
Storme, Jacqueline, Lille 099497
Storms, Berlin 102057
Storms, Düsseldorf 102559
Storms, Walter, München 104326
De Stormvogel, Siegerswoude 140531
Storno Collection, Soproni Múzeum, Sopron 021848
Storo, Oslo 079476
Storoževoj Korabl' 'Krasnyj Vympel' 1911 g., Voenno-istoričeskij Muzej Tichookeanskogo Flota, Vladivostok 034058
Storrer, Erich, Zürich 112184
Storrowton Village Museum, West Springfield 049101
Storstrøms Kunstmuseum, Maribo . 009020
Storti, Daniela, Roma 128216
Story House Historical Museum, Yamba 001639
Story of Castle Cornet, Saint Peter Port 040939
Story of People, Western Development Museum, Yorkton 006894
Stoßberg, R., Wermelskirchen 074341
Stossel, Willy, Thiais 124954
Stothert Old Books, Chester 141512
Stott Park Bobbin Mill, Ulverston . . 041262
Stoughton and District Museum, Stoughton 006516
Stoughton Historical Museum, Stoughton 048386
Stoup, John, San Diego 119554
Stourhead House, Stourton 041129
Stout, William, San Francisco 142964
Stouvenel, Marie-Rose, Niort 065199
Stoves, Mantels & More, Oklahoma City 091541
Stovner Rammer, Oslo 079477
Stow Antiques, Stow-on-the-Wold . 086763
Stow Gallery, Penn 114224
Stow House, Museum of Goleta Valley History, Goleta 044241
Stow West 1825 School Museum, Stow 048389
Stowarzyszenie do Pielegnacij Kultury i Sztuki Slaskiej, Łomnica Dolna . . 053986
Stowarzyszenie Miłośników Dawnej Broni i Barwy, Kraków 053987
Stowarzyszenie Muzeów na Wolnym Powietrzu, Toruń 053988
Stowarzyszenie Polskich Artystów Karykatury, Warszawa 053989
Stowarzyszenie Polskich Artystów Kowali, Gdańsk 053990
Stowarzyszenie Robotnicze Twórców Kultury, Wrocław 053991
Stowarzyszenie Zwiazek Muzeów Polskich, Kraków 053992
The Stoy Museum of the Lebanon County Historical Society, Lebanon 045225
Straat Antiquaren, Amsterdam 140340
Strabally Steam Museum, Stradbally 022859
Strachan, Glasgow 084471
Strachey, Julie, Connor Downs 084075
Strachur Smiddy Museum, Strachur 041133
Stracke, Dr. Gottfried, Köln 103720, 126121
Stradbroke Gallery, Stradbroke 114510
Stradlings, New York 091273
Strängnäs Museum, Strängnäs 036684
Strafvollzugsmuseum, Ludwigsburg, Württemberg 018699
Stragapede-Didra, Konstanz 103768
Strahan Woodworks, Strahan 095227
Strahovská Obrazárna, Praha 008649
Strais Auktionshall, Ystad 122300
Straits, Harvest, Singapore 080565
Straits Antiques, Singapore 080566
Straits Literature and Art Publishing House, Fuzhou 133347
Straka, Erich, Bad Wimsbach-Neydharting 056938, 123340
Strakeljahn, M., Hiddenhausen 071511
Strakova, Bad Salzuflen 069369
Strakova, B., Bad Salzuflen 138704
Stramitz, Leonhard, Wien 123535
Stramowska, Teresa, Piaseczno . . . 129059
Stranahan House, Fort Lauderdale . 043936
Strand Antiques, London 085721
Strand Antiques, Port Elliot 056473
The Strand Antiques, Taranaki 079253
Strand Art Conservation, Lne Cove . 123255
The Strand Art Gallery, Brixham . . . 112729
Strand Book Annex, New York 142697
Strand Book Store, New York 142698
Strand Coins, Sydney 056690
Strand Gallery, Aldeburgh 112490
The Strand Gallery, Bideford 112638
Strand Gallery, Southend-on-Sea . . 114462
Strand Objetos de Arte, Rio de Janeiro 096649
Stranda Hembygdsförening, Mönsterås 036481
Strandberg, Stockholm . . 082026, 122262
Strandgaarden Museum, Ringkøbing Museum, Ulfborg 009133
Strandgalerie, Zürich 112185
Strandgalleriet, Södertälje 110992
Strandhalle Ahrenshoop, Ostseebad Ahrenshoop 019518
Strandingsmuseum St. George, Ringkøbing Museum, Ulfborg 009134
Strandt, Johan, Bad Schwartau . . . 101698
Strang, Hanspeter, Tobel . 082855, 130195
Strang, Jan, Helsinki 137961
Strang Print Room, University College London, London 040296
Strange Days, Indianapolis 089347
Strange Days, Indianapolis 089348
Strange Frames On Whyte, Edmonton 096900
Le Strange Old Barns Antiques, Hunstanton 084768
Strangers Hall Museum of Domestic Life, Norwich 040614
Stranieri, Paolo, Milano 075871
Straniquario, Firenze 075410
Stranraer Museum, Stranraer 041135
Stranski, Edith, Wien 123536
Stransky, Michael, München 126467
Strasbourg and District Museum, Strasbourg 006517
Strasburg Museum, Strasburg 048396
Strašifták, Peter, Pezinok 129280
Strass, Wien 137369
Straßenbau - einst und jetzt, Waldbüttelbrunn 020633
Strassenbaumuseum, Sayda 020003
Straßer, A., Wörthsee 139862
Strasser, Johann, Schlößl 123468
Strasser, Wolfgang, Ravensburg . . . 073440
Strassner, Schärding 057303
Strategic Air Command Museum, Ashland 041805
Strategic Air & Space Museum, Ashland 041805
Strategic Corporate Partnership, London 113904
Stratemann, Kurt-R., Göttingen . . . 071055
Strater Hotel, Durango 043536
Stratfield Saye House and Wellington Exhibition, Basingstoke 038612
Stratfield Saye House and Wellington Exhibition, Stratfield Saye 041136
Stratford, Columbus 115802
Stratford and District Museum, Stratford 001493
Stratford Antique Centre, Stratford-upon-Avon 086777
Stratford Antiques & Interiors Centre, Stratford-upon-Avon 086778
Stratford Bookshop, Stratford-upon-Avon 142094
Stratford Hills Antique Market, Richmond 092112
The Stratford Historical Society and Catherine B. Mitchell Museum, Stratford 048397
Strathalbyn Antique Market, Strathalbyn 056639
Strathalbyn National Trust Museum, Strathalbyn 001494
Strathclair Museum, Strathclair . . . 006521
Strathcona, Edmonton 137636
Strathcona Archaeological Centre, Edmonton 005407
Strathcona County Heritage Foundation Museum, Sherwood Park 006464
The Strathearn Gallery, Crieff 112923
Strathearn Gallery & Studio, Castle Douglas 112826
Strathmore, Montréal 059011
Strathnairn Homestead Gallery, Holt 094652
Strathnaver Museum, Thurso 041221
Strathpeffer Spa Pumping Room Exhibition, Strathpeffer 041147
Strathroy Middlesex Museum, Strathroy 006523
Strathspey Railway, Aviemore 038552
Strathwork Galerie, Ladbergen 103811
Straub, Schwäbisch Gmünd 073741
Straub, Angelika, Lechbruck am See 103846
Straub, Hermann, Stockdorf 126836
Straub & Lambert, Ruderting 073611
Straubhaar, Daniel, Thun 082853
Straubinger, F., Amberg, Oberpfalz . 069161
Strauch, Düsseldorf 125548
Strauhof Zürich, Literaturausstellungen, Zürich 037803
Straumsnes Bygdemuseum, Kanestraum 030931
Strauß, Saarbrücken 073647
Strauß, Heidemarie, Berlin 069771
Strauß, Johann, Schnega 104832
Strauß Gedenkstätte, Wien Museum, Wien 003008
Stravridis, Stravros E., Athinai 139901
Straw and Grass Handicraft Museum, Seoul 027608
Strawbale Gallery, Woodend 095411
Strawberry Hill Antiques, Johannesburg 080716
Strawbery Banke, Portsmouth 047191
Mr. Straw's House, Worksop 041449
The Stray Show, Chicago 094037
Streamer, J., Leigh-on-Sea 084959
Streamer, J., Leigh-on-Sea 084960
Streamline Antiques, Boston 087848
Strebel, Wiesbaden 074425
Streck, Ernst, München 126468
Streck, H. P., Bonn 069945
Strecker Museum Complex, Waco . 048817
Středočeské Muzeum, Roztoky u Prahy 008675
Stredoslovenské Múzeum, Banská Bystrica 034304
Streekheemmuseum den Aanwas, Ossendrecht 030014
Streekhistorisch Centrum, Stadskanaal 030178
Streeklandbouwmuseum Agrimuda, Sluis 030166
Streeklandbowmuseum Agrimunda, Sint Anna ter Muiden 030147
Streekmuseum, Oudenaarde 003696

Streekmuseum Alphen, Alphen, Noord-Brabant 029142
Streekmuseum De Groote Sociëteit, Tiel 030204
Streekmuseum de Meesthof, Sint Annaland 030148
Streekmuseum de Moennik, Helden 029712
Streekmuseum De Oude Wolden, Bellingwolde 029303
Streekmuseum de Tolbrug, Bakel . . 029290
Streekmuseum De Vier Ambachten, Hulst 029786
Streekmuseum Goeree en Overflakkee, Sommelsdijk 030174
Streekmuseum Het Admiraliteitshuis, Dokkum 029493
Streekmuseum Het Dorp van Bartje, Rolde 030073
Streekmuseum Het Land van Axel, Axel 029285
Streekmuseum Het Rondeel, Rhenen 030058
Streekmuseum Hoeksche Waard, Heinenoord 029708
Streekmuseum Jan Anderson, Vlaardingen 030275
Streekmuseum Land van Valkenburg, Valkenburg, Limburg 030249
Streekmuseum Leudal, Haelen 029665
Streekmuseum Ommen, Ommen . . 029991
Streekmuseum Opsterland, Gorredijk 029621
Streekmuseum Oudheidkamer Reeuwijk, Reeuwijk 030053
Streekmuseum Schippersbeurs, Elsloo 029556
Streekmuseum Stevensweert/ Ohé en Laak, Stevensweert 030186
Streekmuseum Tholen en Sint-Philipsland, Sint Annaland 030148
Streekmuseum van Klein-Brabant De Zilverreiger, Weert 003848
Streekmuseum Volkssterrenwacht, Burgum 029376
Streekmuseum voor de Krimpenerwaard Crimpenerhof, Krimpen aan den Ijssel 029823
Streekmuseum West Zeeuws-Vlaanderen, Ijzendijke 029792
Street Gallery, Street 114513
Street Level, Glasgow 113131
Street Scene Gallery, New Orleans . 117518
Street Scene Gallery, New Orleans . 117519
Street Scene Studios, New Orleans 117520
Street Store Angeles, Long Beach . 089659
Streetcar and Electric Railway Museum, Milton 005875
Streetlife Museum, Hull Museum of Transport, Kingston-upon-Hull . . . 039891
Streffer, Walter, Stuttgart 139773
Strehl, G., Weiden, Oberpfalz 074299
Streicher, Hana, Berlin 125302
Streichinstrumentensammlung, Einsiedeln 037062
Streiff, Barbara, Glarus 111517
Strein, Theodor, Villach 137276
Streit, Gottfried, Basel 129934
Streitenfeld, Dirk, Oberursel 104513
Streiter, Franz, Soest 073848
Streithoff, Wolfgang, Gebesee 125701
Strelow, Hans, Düsseldorf 102560
Streminski, Köln 072015
Stremitzer, Sabine, Wasendorf 133169
Strempel, C.-P., Hamburg 139215
Streppel, J.A.J., Amsterdam 140341
Střeštíková, Jiřina, Brno 098337
Stretham Old Engine, Stretham . . . 041149
dello Stretto, Messina 106142
Stretton Antiques Market, Church Stretton 084011
Stretton Water Mill, Farndon 039487
Streubel, Paul, Recklinghausen . . . 139680
Strey-Froom & Strey, Berlin 069772
Strey-Froom & Strey, Kloster Zinna . 071884
Strey-Froom & Strey, Ließen 072251
Striatus, Kiel 103548
Strick, Agnes, Köln 072016
Stricker, Aachen 101528
Stricker, Karl-Heinz, Nettetal 104399
Stricker, Sybill, Bad Sauerbrunn . . . 095471
Strickhausen, Helmut, Teisendorf . . 126896
Strickland, Hobart 094645
Strickland & Daughters, Jane, Honiton 084730
Stricklin, D., Washington 093437
Stricoff, New York 118453
Strictly Limited Editions, San Francisco 119807, 135494
Stride, Calgary 096847
Stride & Son, Chichester 122465
Strides Gallery, Driffield 112958
Striebeck, Bernd & Helga, Hagen, Westfalen 071166, 103051
Striegel, W., Dietersheim 070247
Strienz, Cornelia, Uhingen 126929
Striffler, Andreas, Gerlingen 125721
Strigazzi, Dr. Giancarlo, Haan 125778
Strigel-Museum und Antoniter-Museum, Memmingen 018905
Strijk, H.J., Groningen 078433
Strik, J.W., Deventer 078284
Strike Me Lucky, Aldgate 136780
Strike One, London 085722, 131186
Strike Zone, Houston 089215
Strina, Luisa, São Paulo 096691
Strindberg-Museum Saxen, Saxen . 002638
Strindbergsmuseet Blå Tornet, Stockholm 036675
Stringer, Brian, Houston 089216
Strip-Ease Refinishing, Louisville . . 132306
Strip-It, Omaha 132599
Strip Joint, Norfolk 132563
Strip Shop, Charlotte 131874
Strip Shop, San Diego 132860
Striped House Museum of Art, Tokyo 027243
Strippel, Grete, Sittenbach 073839
Stripper, Salt Lake City 132794
Strippers Furniture Restoration, Saint Paul 132774
Stripping Workshop, Albuquerque . . 131752
Stripping Workshop, Washington . . 133037
Stripwinkel, Beo, Antwerpen 137406
STRM, Saint-Ouen 067899
Strømstad Auktionsservice, Strømstad 122265
Strømstads Museum, Strømstad . . 036687
Strobel, Berlin 069773
Strobel, Buffalo 087912
Strobel, Labrador 056077
Strobel, Christian, Stöttwang-Thalhofen 139743
Strobel, Siefried, Hagenbach 103053
Strobele, Prof. Dr. Charlotte, Wien . 095947
Strobelt, H., Muggensturm 072935
Strobl, Ingrid, München 126469
Ströhlein, R., Bamberg 069465
Strömforsin Teollisuusmuseo, Ruotsinpyhtää 010048
Strömsholms Slott, Kolbäck 036397
Strömsunds Auktionstjänst, Strömsund 122267
Ströter, Michael, Bielefeld 138877
Strötzbacher Mühle, Mömbris 018973
Stroganovskaja Roždestvenskaja Cerkov, Niżegorodskij Istoričesko-architekturnyj Muzej- zapovednik, Nižnij Novgorod 033572
Stroganovskij Dvorec, Gosudarstvennyj Russkij Muzej, Sankt-Peterburg . . 033832
Strøgets Guld & Sølv, København . .060385, 124030
Strogguou, Alexandra, Athinai 074610
Strohhaus, Muhen 037361
Strohhaus und Dorfmuseum, Kölliken 037215
Strohmenger, A., Weilerswist 074304
Strohschneider, Zürich 112186
Strømann, Marianne, Charlottenlund 060221, 124012
Stromberg, C. von, Neumarkt, Oberpfalz 073005
Strømberg, Steen, København 060386, 124031
Stromboni, Dominique, Paris 066574
Stromer, Mia, Frensdorf 070877
Stromingen, Den Haag 078250
Stromness Museum, Stromness . . . 041151
Strong Museum, Rochester 047485
Strood Library Gallery, Rochester . . 040849
Stroom - Haags Centrum voor Visueel Kunst, Den Haag 029455
Štros, Martin, Praha 124000
Strossmayerova Galerija Starih Majstora, Zagreb 007856
Strothotte, B., Gütersloh . . 071143, 121421
Stroud House Gallery, Stroud 114516
Stroud Mansion, Stroudsburg 048403
Stroud Museum, Stroud 041152
Strouds, Southwell 086666
Strouk, Laurent, Paris 100887
Strover, Lynne, Cambridge 112794
Strub & Co., Zürich 083028
Strube, Henning, München 126470
Struchen, H., Tagelswangen 141304
Struck, Nicolaus, Berlin 138850
Struck, Nikolaus, Koblenz 139330
Struck, Vera, Atlanta 114931
Structure 17, Perpignan 124841
The Structurist, Saskatoon 135643
Strübhaus-Haus der Malkunst, Veringenstadt 020578
Strümann, Heilbronn 103337
Strümann, Mosbach, Baden 104123
Strümper, Hans, Erwitte 070608
Struer Museum og Johs. Buchholtz Hus, Struer 009119
Strugalla, Johannes, Mainz 134183
Struggletown Fine Arts Complex, Narellan 094927
Struktur, Hamburg 071339, 125845
Struś, Jan, Poznań 079699
Struś, Jan, Poznań 079700
Struts Gallery, Sackville 006319
Struwwelpeter-Museum, Sammlung der Originale Dr. Heinrich Hoffmanns (Nachlaß), Frankfurt am Main . . . 017199
Strydom, George 110042
Strzelczyk, Warszawa 079787
Strzelczyk, Tadeusz, Warszawa 129120
Strzelecki, Krzysztof, Wrocław 129132
Stuart, Barrington 083404
Stuart, D.M., Bulli 055581
Stuart, Herbert, Newport, Gwent . . 131314
Stuart-Buchanan, Denver 088741
Stuart Collection, University of California, San Diego, La Jolla 045069
Stuart House Antiques, Chipping Campden 083986, 130569
Stuart House City Museum, Mackinac Island 045553
Stuart Livraria e Galeria, Lisboa . . .109355, 140855
Stuart Street Gallery, Dunedin 108450
Stuart Town Gaol Museum, Alice Springs 000739
Stubbs, Kristy, Dallas 115946
Stubengesellschaft Engen, Engen . . 053564
Stubenrauch, Holde, Langgöns 103837
Stubnitz Gallery, Adrian College, Adrian 041581
Stucco, Madrid 081393
Stuchley, A.F. & J., Port Macquarie . 056478
Stuckert, Düsseldorf 070445
Stuckert, Herbert, Düsseldorf 070446
Stuckert, M., Düsseldorf 070447
Stuckhardt, W., Karlsruhe 139300
Stuckhaus Cöpenick, Berlin 125303
Stucky, Bruno, Mörel 082661
Stud Farm Gallery, Bakewell 112539, 130323, 135116
Studebaker National Museum, South Bend 048229
Student Art League, Washington . . 055060
Student Center Gallery, Asbury College, Wilmore 049218
Studer, Schwanau 134390
Studer, Beate, Luzern 082636
Studer, Elisabeth, Hagenbuch 082491, 130045
Studer, Susanne, Mörschwil 111736
Studi di Storia dell'Arte, Todi 135961
Studi e Testi di Storia e Critica dell'Arte, Napoli 135962
Studi Sul Settecento Romano, Roma 135963
Studia Muzealne, Poznań 136037
Studiecentrum Perk, Eindhoven . . . 029548
Studien zu Denkmalschutz und Denkmalpflege, Wien 135579
Studien zur Österreichischen Kunstgeschichte, Wien 135580
Studiengalerie Fach Kunst an der Pädagogischen Hochschule Ludwigsburg, Ludwigsburg, Württemberg 103946, 134166
Studiengang Architektur Holzminden, Hochschule für angewandte Wissenschaft und Kunst, Holzminden 050134
Studiengang Bildende Kunst, Hochschule für Gestaltung und Kunst Luzern, Luzern 050770
Studiengang Kunsttechnologie, Konservierung und Restaurierung von Kunst- und Kulturgut, Hochschule für Bildende Künste Dresden, Dresden 050066
Studiengang Kunstwissenschaft/-pädagogik, Universität Bremen, Fachbereich Kulturwissenschaften, Bremen 050046
Studiengang Restaurierung, Fachbereich Kommunikationsgestaltung, FH Hildesheim/ Holzminden, Hildesheim 050132
Studiengang Restaurierung/ Grabungstechnik, Fachhochschule für Technik und Wirtschaft, Berlin . . . 050030
Studiengemeinschaft Darmstadt, Darmstadt 050054
Studienrichtung Bildhauerei, Burg Giebichenstein-Hochschule für Kunst und Design Halle, Halle, Saale 050100
Studienrichtung Glas, Burg Giebichenstein-Hochschule für Kunst und Design Halle, Halle, Saale 050101
Studienrichtung Grafik, Burg Giebichenstein-Hochschule für Kunst und Design Halle, Halle, Saale 050102
Studienrichtung Keramik, Burg Giebichenstein-Hochschule für Kunst und Design Halle, Halle, Saale 050103
Studienrichtung Konzeptkunst Buch, Burg Giebichenstein-Hochschule für Kunst und Design Halle, Halle, Saale 050104
Studienrichtung Kunsterziehung/ Diplomkunstpädagogik, Burg Giebichenstein-Hochschule für Kunst und Design Halle, Halle, Saale 050105
Studienrichtung Malerei, Burg Giebichenstein-Hochschule für Kunst und Design Halle, Halle, Saale 050106
Studienrichtung Schmuck, Burg Giebichenstein-Hochschule für Kunst und Design Halle, Halle, Saale 050107
Studienrichtung Textil, Burg Giebichenstein-Hochschule für Kunst und Design Halle, Halle, Saale 050108
Studiensammlung der Lübecker Bodenfunde, Lübeck 018728
Studiensammlung der Universität Leipzig, Kustodie der Universität Leipzig, Leipzig 018597
Studiensammlung historischer Ziegel, Irdning 002099
Studies in Art Education, Reston . . . 136631
Studies in Conservation, London . . 136272
Studies in Iconography, Tempe 136632
Studies in Modern Art, New York . . 136633
Studies in the Decorative Arts, New York 136634
Studies in the History of Art, Landover 136635
The Studio, Gateshead 113089

The Studio, Gomshall 084483
The Studio, Hamilton 096926
The Studio, Hyderabad 105716
Studio, Madrid 110619
The Studio, Otford 114194
Studio, Tel Aviv 135857
Studio 101, Eton 084347
Studio 107, Austin 115014
Studio 107, Norfolk 118618
Studio-13, Moskva 109594
Studio 18 Gallery, New York 118454
Stúdió 1900, Budapest . . . 074721, 105545
Studio 2, Appledore, Devon 112515
Studio 2, Hong Kong 097836
Studio 2 Gallery, Austin 115015
Studio 2 Gallery, Chermside 094389
Studio 2000, Brampton, Cumbria . . 112694
Studio 21, Maryborough, Queensland 056166
Studio 215, Auckland 108363
Studio 220, Tucson 120168
Studio 23, Cincinnati 115664
Studio 236, Hope Island 094653
Studio 24, San Francisco 119808
Studio 2507, Portland 119056
Studio 261, Montréal 097081
Studio 28, Stockholm 111074
Studio 3, Roma 128217
Studio 33, Portland 119057
Studio 34, Houston 116412
Studio 34, Ourense 110657
Studio 4, Firenze 127416
Studio 4, Lamlash 113344
Studio 407, San Diego 119555
Studio 48, New Lambton 094936
Studio 52, Sharjah 112471
Studio 55, Delhi 105686
Studio 67, Akaroa 128892
Studio 7, Starnberg 104944
Studio 71, Palermo 106446
Studio 728, Vancouver 097537
Studio 8 Graphics, Toronto 097380
Studio 84 West, Long Beach 116681
Studio 86, Wanganui 108604
Studio A Otterndorf, Museum gegenstandsfreier Kunst Landkreis Cuxhaven, Otterndorf 019538
Studio Aesthetic, Mumbai 105811
Studio AF, Roma 128218
Studio Agram, Budapest 074722
Studio Ah Lala, Mile End 094847
Studio am Burgplatz, Düsseldorf . . 070448
Studio Amaranto, Verona 106803
Stúdió Antikvárium, Budapest 139929
Studio Antiques, Oklahoma City . . . 091542
Studio Ardiglione, Firenze 127417
Studio Arga, Venezia 106779
Studio Art, Karachi 108776
Studio Art and Frame, Minneapolis . 117311
Studio Art Department, Manhattanville College, Purchase 052001
Studio Art Gallery, Bridgetown 096036
Studio Art II, Washington 120349
Studio Artis, Ettelbruck 107387
Studio Arts, Norfolk 118619
Studio Arts Department, Transylvania University, Lexington 051603
Studio Arts Gallery, Lancaster 113348
Studio ASH, Columbus 115803
Studio Associates, Philadelphia . . . 118841
Studio Associato Restauro Opere d'Arte, Brescia 127234
Studio B, Columbus 115804
Studio B2, Genova 106109
Studio Bibliografico Vecchi Libri, Firenze 140028
Studio Bookshop, Brighton 141442
Studio Capricornus, Eckernförde . . 102598
Studio Cavalieri, Bologna 105975
Studio Celtia, London 096959
Studio d'Arte Firenze, Firenze 075411
Studio d'Arte F.Russo, Roma 106629
Studio d'Arte Grafica, Milano 106327
Studio d'Arte Spazia, Bologna 105976
Studio d'Arte Verbano, Locarno . . . 111654
Studio de l'Image, Paris 100888
Studio Della, Ostrava 098404
Studio dell'Arte, Montréal . 059012, 123794
Studio di Val Cervo, Roma 106630
Studio Editions, London 135266
Studio Fine Art, San Diego 119556
Studio Forni, Milano 106328
Studio Fusion, London 113905
Studio Fyra Årstider, Stockholm . . . 111075
Studio G 7, Bologna 105977
Studio-Galerie, Berlin 102058
Studio-Galerie, Berlin 102059
Studio Galerie, Linz 095673
Studio-Galerie, Regensburg 104701
Studio Gallerie, Klausdorf 103562
The Studio Gallery, Datchet 084141, 130627
Studio Gallery, Denver 116059
The Studio Gallery, Fresno 116187
Studio Gallery, Manly 094783
Studio Gallery, New York 118455
Studio Gallery, Oklahoma City 118676
The Studio Gallery, Slough 114442
Studio Gallery, Washington 048946
Studio Gallery, Washington 120350
Studio Gallery 106, Toronto 097381
Studio Ghiglione, Genova . 075511, 121692
Studio Gi, Gagliano del Capo 134591
Studio Glass Gallery, London 040297
Studio Graphics & Fine Arts, Calgary 096848
Studio G.S., Roma 121727
Studio Guastalla, Milano 106329
Studio Hermitage, New York 118456
Studio III Gallery, Austin 115016
Studio im Hochhaus, Berlin 016183
Studio im Zumikon, Nürnberg 019376
Studio Johannes, Helsinki 098746
Studio La Città, Verona 106804
Studio La Duchesse, Montréal 059013
Studio M, Bamberg 101733
Studio M, Warszawa 109196
Studio Maastricht, Maastricht 108131
Studio Moderne, Nantes 064948
Studio-Museo di Giuseppe Pellizza, Istituto Giuseppe Pellizza, Volpedo 026365
Studio Museum in Harlem, New York 046409
Studio of Artists, Newtown, New South Wales 094959
Studio of Contemporary Art, Auckland 108364
Studio on J, Sacramento 119164
Studio on the Quay, Yarmouth 114744
Studio One, Cleveland 115745
Studio One, Honolulu 116245
Studio One Gallery, Mount Gambier 094904
Studio Philatélique de Provence, Avignon 061143
Studio Plus, Geelong 094582
Le Studio PM, Montréal 097082
Studio Potter, Goffstown 136636
Studio Quadro, Radlett 114293
Studio Restauro Antichità, Brescia . 127235
Studio Restauro Santa Trinita, Firenze 127418
Studio Ripetta, Roma 076694
Studio Roze Antiques, Rio de Janeiro 123711
Studio S, Pune 105832
Studio S Arte, Roma 106631
Studio Saint-Sulpice, Paris 066575
Studio San Damiano, Milwaukee . . 117222
Studio San Giuseppe Art Gallery, Cincinnati 042928
Studio Santa Trinita, Firenze 127419
Studio Six Art, Oklahoma City 118677
Studio Sixteen Seventeen, Los Angeles 116893
Studio Sixty, Glasgow 113132
Studio Soligo, Roma 106632
Studio Soligo, Roma 106633
Studio Solstone, Seattle 120000
Studio Suardo, Milano 127693
Studio Swiss, Tucson 132990
Studio Ten, Saint Paul 119316
Studio Tommaseo, Trieste 106719
Studio Vizio, Budapest 134508
Studio Wildflower Paintings, Denmark 094477
Studio Windsor, Mumbai 105812
Studio Works Gallery, Nailsworth . . 114106
Studio X, Images de Presse, Limours 133484
Studio za Umetničku Keramiku, Arandjelovac 109679
Studiogalerie Kaditzsch, Denkmalschmiede Höfgen, Grimma 017541
Lo Studiolo, Firenze 127420
Studios of Jack Richard Creative School of Design, Cuyahoga Falls 051217
Studios on High, Columbus 115805
Studo San Domenico, Milwaukee . . 117223
The Study Gallery, Poole 114272
Stüber, Olaf, Berlin 102060
Stübiger, A., Grevenbroich 071099
Stübler, Michael, Hannover 103298, 134042
Stückler, Helga, Spielberg 095762
Stühler, Berlin 102061
Stühlinger Gewerbehof e.V., Freiburg im Breisgau 053565, 070864
von Stülpnagel, Neumünster 104416
Stülpnagel, Karl-Heinrich von, Leipzig 126198
Stuempfig, Anthony, Philadelphia . . 091692
Stümpges, V., Heidelberg 071462
Stützer, Carla, Köln 103721
Stützer, Thomas, Heiligenstadt 125910
Stützle, Wolfram, Waldkirch 126961
Stuff 2 Gold, Phoenix 091772
Stuff Antiques, Phoenix . . 091773, 132656
Stuff & Nonsense, Chesham 083945
Stuff & Such, Houston 089217
Stugans, Röda, Torslanda 082051
Stuhlbau- und Heimatmuseum, Rabenau, Sachsen 019693
Stuhlgalerie, Bad Arolsen 069259
Stuhlmann, Wedel 105167
Stuhlmuseum Burg Beverungen, Beverungen 016216
Stuhr Museum of the Prairie Pioneer, Grand Island 044265
Stuker, Zürich 112187
Stuker, Jürg, Bern 111276, 122314
Stumbaum, Regina, Herrsching . . . 125921
Stumm, Gert, Düsseldorf 070449
Stummer, Jörg, Zürich 112188
Stumpf, Hong Kong 097837
Stumpf, Hermann, Neckarsteinach . 072953
Stumpf-Behrens, Karin, Kronberg im Taunus 072094
Stumpy Gully Antiques, Tyabb 056753
Stumvoll, Herbert, Hirschegg, Kleinwalsertal 057061
Stundner, Salzburg 123457
Stupack, Winnipeg 120832
Sturdivant Hall, Selma 048110
Sturgeon River House, Sturgeon Falls 006525
Sturges Fine Arts Center, San Bernardino 047813
Sturgis Station House Museum, Sturgis 006526
Sturies, Dr. Andreas, Düsseldorf . . .070450, 121387
Sturm, von, Hamburg 103222, 125846
Sturm, Matthias, Ehrenfriedersdorf . 070516
Sturm, Michael, Stuttgart 105014
Sturm-Larondelle, Berlin 125304
Sturman, Hawes 084629
Sturman Institute Museum of Regional Science, Afula 022882
Sturmio, Sevilla 129745
Sturni, Daniela, Roma 128219
Sturt, Mittagong 094863
Sturt House, Grange 001080
Sturt Street Antiques and Art, Ballarat 055438
Sturzenegger, Markus, Zürich 083029, 130266
Stuteville, Seattle 093073, 132944
Stutsman County Memorial Museum, Jamestown 044833
Stuttfeld, Köln 103722
Stuttgart Agricultural Museum, Stuttgart 048412
Stuttgarter Feuerwehrmuseum, Feuerwehrverein Stuttgart e.V, Stuttgart 020368
Stuttgarter Gesellschaft für Kunst und Denkmalpflege, Stuttgart 053566
Stuttgarter Gesellschaft für Kunst und Denkmalpflege, Studiensammlung Möbel, Stuttgart 020369
Stuttgarter Künstlerbund, Stuttgart .053567, 105015
Stuttgarter Kunstverein, Stuttgart . .020370, 053568
Stuttgarter Porzellan Werkstatt, Stuttgart 126883
Stutzhäuser Brauereimuseum, Luisenthal 018752
Stux, Stefan, New York 118457
Stuyck Miguel, Madrid 129689
Styl, Pruszków 129070
Styl Antikvitás, Pécs 074750
Style, Le Chambon-sur-Lignon 063597
Style, Denis, Bucureşti 109446
Style 1900, Lambertville 136637
Style 25, Lausanne 082569
Style Art Publishing, Phoenix 135477
Style D'Art, Rio de Janeiro 058659
Style Deco, München 072868
Style et Décor, Saint-Tropez 068025
Style French Antiques, Los Angeles 089918
Style French Antiques, West Hollywood 093512
Style Gallery, London 085723
Style Junkies, Nelson 079182
Styles of Stow, Stow-on-the-Wold . 086764
Styles Silver, Hungerford . 084764, 130818
Stylo, Robert, Mendoza 055287
Styl'Vieil, Brignoles 061800, 124162
Stypmann, David, New York 091274
Styria, Judenburg 137200
Suan Pakkad Palace, Bangkok 037893
Suarez, Graciela, Miami 090244
Suarez, Pascal, Saint-Jean-de-la Ruelle 067531
Suarez Doradores, Valencia 129785
Suarsana, Putu & Nicole, Bad Mergentheim 069329
Suau, Robert, Saint-Paulet-de-Caisson 067946
Suaudeau, Marie-Pierre, Montpellier 064756
Suay y Serra, Valencia 129786
Subak, Chicago 088177
Subak Museum, Banjar Senggulan . 022394
Subal, Anton, Wien 057560, 095948
Subarna, Barcelona 080942, 122013
Subarunoki, Sapporo 106989
Subastas, Madrid 136104
Subastas Alicante, Alicante 121988
Subastas de Barcelona, Barcelona . 122014
Subastas la Villa Vieja, Alicante . . . 080768
Subastas La Villa Vieja, Alicante . . . 121989
Subastas San Gervasi, Barcelona . . 122015
Subastas Segre, Madrid 122070
Subastas y Exposiciones, Marbella .081437, 122073
Subastas y Galeria de Arte, Valencia 081680, 110845
Suberg, J., Olsberg 104546
Subert, Alberto, Milano 075872
Subex, Barcelona 110253
Subgang, Alfons, Gronau, Westfalen 071109
Subiaco, Alpirsbach 101562
Subiaco Museum, Subiaco 001497
Subjektiv, Sankt-Peterburg 136062
Sublett, R.D., Louisville . . 090030, 132307
Submarine Force Museum and Historic Ship Nautilus, Groton 044364

Subra, Catherine, Toulouse 068545
Subra, Eric, Paris 066576
Subun-so, Tokyo 140202
Suburb Jinying Graphics Art Gallery, Wuxi 098045
Suburban 312 Gallery, Brighton, Victoria 094283
Succès, La Chevrolière 063331
Successories, Cincinnati 115665
Succotash, Saint Paul 092402
Sucesores de Giganto, Madrid 129690
Sucharduv Dům, Městské Muzeum, Nová Paka 008528
Suchecki, Waclaw, Düsseldorf 070451, 125549
Suchna Kendra Gallery, Lucknow . . 105749
Suchomsky, Gerd, Köln 072017
Suchow & Seigel, New York 091275
Suciu, Emilia, Ettlingen 102714
Suckau, Irmgard, Berlin 125305
Suckau-Pirow, K., Westerland 074372
Sucksdorff, Jürgen, Berlin 069774
Sucret, Lionel, Rodez 067196
Sud 70, Cannes 061957
Sud Antik, Montauban 064640
Sud Loire, Pont-Saint-Martin 066934
Sud Textiles, Bobigny 098977
Sudan National Museum, Khartoum 036152
Sudan Natural History Museum, University of Khartoum, Khartoum 036153
Suddaby, Blairgowrie 136807
Sude Nachf., L. & J., Hamburg 071340
Sudeley Castle, Winchcombe 041395
Sudetendeutsches Archiv, München 019125
Sudhaus Sorgendorf, Bleiburg 001755
Sudley House, Liverpool 040038
Sudmann, Brigitte, Stuttgart 105016
Sue Ellen Gallery, Main Beach 056125
Sue Ryder Museum, Cavendish . . . 039022
Suecia Antik Affär, Tumba 082054
Sueck, Ursula, Coesfeld 070152
Sueclaytables, Unley 056772
Süd West Galerie, Hüttlingen 071596
Süddeutsche Verlagsgesellschaft Ulm, Ulm 134437
Südharzer Eisenhüttenmuseum, Bad Lauterberg 015748
Südhessisches Handwerksmuseum, Roßdorf bei Darmstadt 019889
Südmährer Heimatmuseum, Laa an der Thaya 002190
Südmährisches Landschaftsmuseum, Geislingen an der Steige 017345
Südostbayerisches Naturkunde- und Mammut-Museum, Siegsdorf . . . 020204
Südpfälzische Kunstgilde e.V., Bad Bergzabern 053569
Südsauerlandmuseum, Attendorn . . 015593
Südschwäbisches Archäologiemuseum im Jesuitenkolleg, Mindelheim 018948
Südschwäbisches Vorgeschichtsmuseum im Jesuitenkolleg, Mindelheim 018948
Südtiroler Gesellschaft für Photographie, Bolzano 053771
Südtiroler Landesmuseum für Volkskunde, Brunico 023537
Süess, Robert, Dierikon 111383
Sülchgau-Museum, Rottenburg am Neckar 019927
Suermondt-Ludwig-Museum, Aachen 015425
Süßmeier, Peter, Manching 072409
Sütel, Hans-Richard, Preetz, Holstein 073370
Suezumi, Kobe 077085
Suffolk City Council Libraries and Heritage, Ipswich Library, Ipswich 039815
Suffolk County Historical Society Museum, Riverhead 047454
Suffolk County Vanderbilt Museum, Centerport 042686
Suffolk House Antiques, Yoxford . . . 087300
Suffolk Museum, Suffolk 048415
Suffolk Punch Heavy Horse Museum, Woodbridge 041433
Suffolk Rare Books, Sudbury, Suffolk 142100
Suffolk Regiment Museum, Bury Saint Edmunds 038926
Suffolk Resolves House, Milton . . . 045880
The Suffolk Table Company, Debenham 084152, 130630
Suffren, Saint-Tropez 068026, 101235
Suga, Tokyo 107119
Sugan, Dublin 074948
Sugar, Houston 089218
Sugar Antiques, London . . 085724, 131187
Sugar Barrel Antiques, Vancouver . 059424
Sugar Bear Antiques Mall, Jacksonville 089462
The Sugar Refinery, Vancouver 097538
Sugarhill Arts Center, New York . . . 118458
Sugarhouse, Salt Lake City 092464
Sugarhouse, Salt Lake City 092465
Sugarhouse, Salt Lake City 119373
Sugarhouse, Salt Lake City 132795
Sugarman, Budd, Toronto 059298
Sugarplums, Las Vegas 089611
Suger, Paris 066577
Sugères, Bruno, Clermont-Ferrand . 062357
Sugesa, Madrid 081394
Sugihara, Tokyo 140203
Sugimoto Bijutsukan, Mihama 026803
Sugino Gakuen Isho Hakubutsukan, Tokyo 027244
Sugiura, Kyoto 106907
Suhm, Walter, Thal 082844
Suhrkamp, Frankfurt am Main 133955
Suhube, Riyadh 109675
Sui Tangyao Zhi Display Center, Chengdu 007046
Suider-Afrikaanse Museum-Assosiasie, Grahamstown 054071
Suidobata Fine Arts Academy, Tokyo 050495
Suifu Meitokukai Foundation Tokugawa Museum, Mito 026821
Suijkerbuijk, C., Antwerpen 057739
Suipacha, Buenos Aires 094089
Suissa, Alice, Versailles 068822
Suite 106, New York 118459
Suite Lorain Antiques, Cleveland . . 088364
Suk Joo-sun Memorial Museum of Korean Folk Arts, Seoul 027609
Suka Academy, Busan 050509
Suka Art Space, Busan 027463
Sukagawa-shiritsu Hakubutsukan, Sukagawa 027092
Sukanen Ship Pioneer Village and Museum of Saskatchewan, Moose Jaw . . . 005955
Sukellusvene Vesikko, Helsinki . . . 009571
Sukhotai Antiques, Bangkok 083104
Sukiennice. Galeria Związku Polskich Artystów Plastyków, Kraków 032069
Suksimuseo, Vimpeli 010242
Sukuma Museum - Bujora, Mwanza 037857
Sulabh International Museum of Toilets, Delhi 022097
Sułek, Kazimierz, Kraków 129050
Suleyman, Duisburg 070487
Sulgrave Manor, Sulgrave 041156
Sulitjelma Gruvemuseum, Sulitjelma 031249
Sulivan, Teheran 105845
Sulivan Gallery, Teheran 074851
Sulk, U., Greifswald 102997
Sullivan, Sacramento 092184
Sullivan, Michael T., Indianapolis . . 116495
Sullivan, Terence Paul, Ryde 114334
Sullivan County Historical Society Museum, Hurleyville 044698
Šulo, Jozef, Prievidza 129282
Sulphide Street Station Railway and Historical Museum, Broken Hill . . 000848
Sulphur Creek Nature Center, Hayward 044493
Sultan, Fawzi H., Safat 077377
Sultan Abdul Aziz Royal Gallery, Kelang 027954
Sultan Abu Bakar Museum Pahang, Pekan 028007
Sultan Ali Dianr Museum, Sudan National Museum, El-Fasher 036144
Sultan Mahmud Badaruddin II Museum, Palembang 022486
Sultana Center, Cairo 060476
Sultane, Zeina, Beirut 077417
Sultan's Armed Forces Museum, Ruwi 031356
Sulu National Museum, Jolo 031676
Sum Gallery, London 113906
Suma Aqualife Museum, Kobe 026669
Sumelocenna - Römisches Stadtmuseum, Rottenburg am Neckar 019928
Sumer, Los Angeles 089919
Sumisho Art Gallery, Tokyo 077311
Sumiti, Maurizio, Venezia 128406
Sumiyoshi-jinja Treasure House, Shimonoseki 027069
Summa, New York 118460
Summer, Polegate 086281
Summer, Celeste, Tucson 120169
Summerfield & Co., T.R., Albury . . . 055333
Summerland Antiques, Ballina 055443
Summerland Museum, Summerland 006533
Summerleaze Gallery, East Knoyle . 112977
Summerlee Heritage Park, Coatbridge 039109
Summerley Auction Rooms, Bognor Regis 122420
Summerlin, Las Vegas 089612
Summers, Margarita, Madrid 110620
Summers, Martin, London 113907
Summers, Ralph & Sheila, Woodford Green 135316
Summers, Richard, Richmond 092113
Summers, Sharon, Charlotte 087982
Summers Art, Dorking 112955
Summers Art, West Clandon 114665
Summers Davis, Wallingford 087009
Summersgill, York 122768
Summerson, Ed, Hong Kong 133367
Summersons, Warwick 087045
Summit Arts, Los Angeles 116894
Summit Auction Rooms, Summit . . 123124
Summit County Historical Society Museum, Akron 041589
Sumner, David, Toorak Gardens . . . 095343
Sumner Art Gallery, Christchurch . . 108415
Sumner & Dene, San Diego 119557
Sumner/Redcliffs Historical Museum, Christchurch 030469
Sumo Hakubutsukan, Nihon Sumo Kyokai, Tokyo 027245
Sumpter, Edward, New York 091276
Sumpu Museum, Shizuoka 027083
Sums'kyj Chudožnij Muzej im. N. Onac'kogo, Sumy 038399
Sums'kyj Oblasnyj Krajeznavčyj Muzej, Sumy 038400
The Sumter County Museum, Sumter 048426
Sumter Gallery of Art, Sumter 048427
Sun, Nagoya 077154
Sun, Chong Hong, New York 091277
Sun, Gaju, Los Angeles 116895
Sun Antics, Magagnosc 064212
Sun Art Gallery, Los Angeles 116896
Sun Craft, Singapore 109875
Sun Gallery, Minneapolis 090396
Sun Gallery, Paris 100889
Sun Gallery, Seoul 107295
Sun Gallery, Hayward Area Forum of the Arts, Hayward 044494
Sun Prairie Historical Museum, Sun Prairie 048428
Sūna, Agija, Rīga 107322
Sunam, Busan 107176
SunAmerica Collection, Los Angeles 045467
Sunart, Sofia 096749
Sunbury Great House, Saint Phillip . 003126
Sunbury Shores Arts and Nature Centre, Saint Andrews 006324
Sunce, Beograd 109723
Sund Bygdemuseum, Skogsvåg . . . 031195
Sund Fiskerimuseum, Ramberg . . . 031129
Sunda, Fabrizio, Cagliari . 075228, 127255
Sundag, Günter, Schüttorf 073735
Sundance Art, Phoenix 118892
Sundblad, Emily, New York 118461
Sundby Samling Bryggergården, Nørresundby 009031
Sundby Samling Raschgården, Nørresundby 009032
Sundbybergs Museum, Sundbyberg 036689
Sunderland Museum, Sunderland . . 041163
Sundermann, Rüdiger, Würzburg . . 105342
Sundheimer, Florian, München 104327
Sundheimer, Florian, München 139549
Sundial Antiques, Amersham 083292
Sundomin Kotiseutumuseo, Sundom 010104
Sundquist, Poni, San Diego 132861
Sundridge Gallery, Sundridge 086789
Sundridge Gallery, Sundridge 114520
Sundridge Gallery, Sundridge 131560
Sundsbergs Gård Museum och Konsthall, Sunne 036695
Sundsvalls Auktionsverk, Sundsvall 122271
Sundsvalls Museum, Sundsvall . . . 036692
Sundvik, Annika, New York 118462
Sunflower Cottage, Louisville 090031
Sunflower Gallery, Calgary 096849
Sung, San Francisco 092892
Sung-Am Archives of Classical Literature, Seoul 027610
Sung Kyun Kwan University Museum, Seoul 027611
Sungem, Southport 056619
Sungjon University Museum, Seoul . 027612
Sungkok Art Museum, Seoul 027613
Sunjin, Singapore 109876
Sunland Art Gallery, El Paso 116119
Sunnansjö Herrgård Galleri, Sunnansjö 036693
Sunndal Bygdemuseum, Sunndalsøra 031251
Sunnfjord Museum, Førde 030846
Sunnhordland Folkemuseum og Sogelag, Stord 031244
Sunnmøre Museum, Ålesund 030719
Sunny Sky, Saint Paul 092403
Sunny Systems, Chennai 105637
Sunnyhurst Wood Visitor Centre, Darwen 039213
Sunnyside Historical Museum, Sunnyside 048431
Sunnyside Museum, Hillside 039752
Sunnyvale Historical Museum, Sunnyvale 048433
Sunporch, Baltimore 087713
Sunrise Art and Sculpture Gallery, Las Vegas 116652
Sunrise Museum, Charleston 042748
Sunrise Southwest, Denver 116060
Sunrise Stained Glass, Tucson 120170
Sunrise Trail Museum, Tatamagouche 006555
Sunset Antiques, Miami 090245
Sunset Bazaar, Los Angeles 089920
Sunset Gallery, Miami 117145
Sunset Gallery, Milton 094859
Sunset Orange, Los Angeles 089921
Sunset Studio Gallery, Cobram 094409
Sunshine, Roger, Miami 090246
Sunshine Art Gallery, Boreen Point . 094268
Sunshine Artist, Orlando 136638
Sunshine Coast Auctions, Maroochydore 120607
Sunshine Coast Museum, Gibsons . 005505
Suntory Bijutsukan, Tokyo 027246
Suntory Museum, Osaka 026989
Sunwatch Indian Village - Archaeological Park, Dayton 043325
Suojeluskuntamuseo, Seinäjoki . . . 010072
Suolahden Museo, Suolahti 010107
Suomalainen Kirjakauppa, Helsinki . 137962
Suomen Antikvariaattiyhdistys, Helsinki 052879

Suomen Finnish Honeybee Museum, Juva . . . 009633
Suomen Ilmailumuseo, Vantaa . . . 010224
Suomen Jääkiekko-Museo, Tampere . . . 010127
Suomen Järvikalastusmuseo ja Kerimäen Ulkomuseoalue, Kerimäki . . . 009699
Suomen Jalkapallomuseo, Valkeakoski . . . 010215
Suomen Joutsen, Turku . . . 010171
Suomen Käsityön Museo, Jyväskylä 009645
Suomen Kansallismuseo, Helsinki . 009572
Suomen Kansansoitinmuseo, Kaustinen . . . 009684
Suomen Kellomuseo, Espoo . . . 009479
Suomen Koulumuseo, temporary closed, Tampere . . . 010128
Suomen Lasimuseo, Riihimäki . . . 010037
Suomen Matkailumuseo, Imatra . . . 009608
Suomen Merimuseo, National Board of Antiquities, Helsinki . . . 009573
Suomen Metsästysmuseo, Riihimäki . . . 010038
Suomen Muinaismuistoyhdistys, Helsinki . . . 052880
Suomen Museoliitto, Helsinki . . . 052881
Suomen Nyrkkeilymuseo, Tampere . 010129
Suomen Partiomuseo, Turku . . . 010172
Suomen Rakennustaiteen Museo, Helsinki . . . 009574
Suomen Rautatiemuseo, Hyvinkää . 009597
Suomen Taiteilijaseura, Helsinki . . . 052882
Suomen Tietojenkäsittelymuseo, Jyväskylä . . . 009646
Suomen Urheilumuseo, Helsinki . . . 009575
Suomen Värimuseo, Kemi . . . 009693
Suomen Valimomuseo ja Högforsin Masuuni, Karkkila . . . 009669
Suomen Valokuvataiteen Museo, Helsinki . . . 009576
Suomenlinna-Museo, Helsinki . . . 009577
Suomenlinna-Sveaborg, Helsinki . . 009578
Suomenlinnan Lelumuseo, Helsinki 009579
Suomi Galleri, Stockholm . . . 111076
Suomi International College of Art and Design, Hancock . . . 051438
Suomusjärven Kotiseutumuseo, Suomusjärvi . . . 010108
Suonenjoen Kotiseutumuseo, Suonenjoki . . . 010109
Supa-Ngwao Museum Centre, Francistown . . . 003949
Super Paintings, Glasgow . . . 113133
Super Poster, Panamá City . . . 108796
Superior Antique Mall, Toledo . . . 093185
Superior Art Corporation, New York 118463
Superior Galleries, Beverly Hills . . . 122819
Superlatives, Kansas City . . . 089522
Super's Design, Miami . . . 090247
Superstar Collectibles, Nashville . . 090491
Supico & Sousa, Lisboa . . . 140856
Suppan, Martin, Wien . . . 057561
Suppan, Martin, Wien . . . 095949
Suppan, Martin, Wien . . . 120693
Suppan, Martin, Wien . . . 120694
Suppan, Martin, Wien . . . 133234
Supper, Pforzheim . . . 104605
Suppes, Alexander, Ober-Ramstadt 073135
Suppes, Bernd, Wiesbaden . . . 139857
The Supreme Court of the United States Museum, Washington . . . 048947
Suquamish Museum, Poulsbo . . . 047215
Suquamish Museum, Suquamish . . 048439
Sur, Rottenburg am Neckar . . . 073607
Sur la Route du Chineur, Sens . . . 068222
Sur les Ailes du Temps, Paris . . . 066578
Sur Meuse, Maastricht . . . 108132
Surahammars Bruksmuseum, Surahammar . . . 036698
Surapon, Bangkok . . . 112241
Surbhi Arts and Crafts, Jaipur, Rajasthan . . . 105730
Surchondarë Vilojati Archeologija Muzeji, Termiz . . . 049414
Surcontre, Napoli . . . 076057
Surek-Becker, Marie-Luise, Berlin . 138851
Surer, Théodore D., Allaman . . . 082083
Surface Design Association, Sebastopol . . . 055061
Surface Design Journal, Sebastopol 136639
Surface Gallery, Nottingham . . . 114179
Surinaams Museum, Paramaribo . . 036161
Surnadal Bygdemuseum, Surnadal . 031252
Surprise! Surprise!, New York . . . 091278
Surprises, Houston . . . 116413
Surratt House Museum, Clinton . . . 043012
Surrey, Cincinnati . . . 088286
Surrey Antiques, Horley . . . 084733
Surrey Antiques Fair, Guildford . . . 093955
Surrey Art Gallery, Surrey . . . 006539
Surrey Clock Centre, Haslemere . . .084609, 130773
Surrey Crescent Traders, Auckland . 078984
Surrey Heath Museum, Camberley . 038954
Surrey Hills Art Gallery, Surry Hills . 095260
The Surrey Institute of Art & Design, Farnham . . . 050816
Surrey Museum, Surrey . . . 006540
Surroundings, Indianapolis . . . 089349
Survey Museum, Roorkee . . . 022322
Survivors, Kerikeri . . . 079136
Surya, Michelfeld . . . 139476
Surya Gallery, Hyderabad . . . 105717
Susan B. Anthony House, Rochester 047486
Susan Gallery, Kraków . . . 108986
Susane, R., Miami . . . 090248
Susannah, Bath . . . 083447
Susannah Place Museum, Sydney . 001524
Susan's Antiques, Hamilton . . . 058866
Susan's Antiques, Toronto . . . 059299
Susan's Selections, Richmond . . . 092114
Susen, Bernard, Chailly-en-Bière . . 062070
Sushart, Pune . . . 105833
Sushi Performance and Visual Art Museum, San Diego . . . 047842
Susini, Aix-en-Provence . . . 098798
Susini, Bruno, Bachant . . . 061156
Susini, Pierre, Montpellier . . . 124462
Suslow, Larissa, Fürstenfeldbruck . 070908
Suso, Palmira, Lisboa . . . 109356
Susquehanna, Washington . . . 093438
Susquehanna Art Museum, Harrisburg . . . 044445
Susquehanna County Historical Society, Montrose . . . 046012
Susquehanna Museum of Havre de Grace, Havre de Grace . . . 044486
Sussex Combined Services Museum, Eastbourne . . . 039365
Sussex County Historical Society Museum, Newton . . . 046478
Sussex Farm Museum, Heathfield . 039711
Sussex Galleries, Edmonton . . . 096901
Sussi, Rīga . . . 107323
Sussman, Arthur, Albuquerque . . . 114825
Suszyńska, Leonarda, Poznań . . . 109063
Sutcliffe, Malcolm, Penryn . . . 114229
Sutcliffe, Tony & Anne, Southport . . 086663
Sutcliffe Galleries, Harrogate 084589, 130766
Sutcliffe Gallery, Whitby . . . 041366
Sutcliffe Gallery Publication, Whitby 135313
Suter, Owen, Richmond . . . 092115
The Suter, Te Aratoi o Whakatu, Nelson . . . 030549
Suthburgh Antiques, Long Melford .085841, 131232, 141924
Sutherland, New York . . . 118464
Sutherland Art Gallery, Sutherland . 095261
Sutherland Steam Mill, Denmark . . 005346
Suti Galerie und Edition, Bern 111277, 134998
Sutter, Cleveland . . . 088365
Sutter's Fort, Sacramento . . . 047594
Sutton, Fitzroy . . . 094539
Sutton, New Orleans . . . 117521
Sutton, Jack, New Orleans . . . 090629
Sutton, Lea, Tulsa . . . 093333
Sutton-Ditz House Museum, Clarion 042945
Sutton Gallery, Melbourne . . . 094829
Sutton-Grenée, Martine, Paris . . . 066579
Sutton Lane, London . . . 113908
Sutton Park, Sutton-on-the-Forest . 041165
Sutton Valence Antiques, Maidstone 085896
Sutton Valence Antiques, Sutton Valence . . . 086805
Sutton Windmill and Broads Museum, Sutton, Norwich . . . 041164
Suur - Helsingin Vaihtopörssi, Helsinki . . . 060583
Suur-Miehikkälän Kylämuseo, Miehikkälä . . . 009869
Suur-Savon Museo, Mikkeli . . . 009876
Suwa-shi Bitjutsukan, Suwa . . . 027094
Suworow-Museum, Glarus . . . 037150
Suze, Jean-Michel, Périgueux . . . 121221
Suzhou, Suzhou . . . 059789
Suzhou Art Gallery, Suzhou . . . 007271
Suzhou City Art Base, Suzhou . . . 097998
Suzhou Engraved Stone Museum, Suzhou . . . 007272
Suzhou Museum, Suzhou . . . 007273
Suzhou National Treasure Numismatics Museum, Suzhou . . . 007274
Suzhou Silk Museum, Suzhou . . . 007275
Suzuki Bokushi Kinenkan, Shiozawa . . . 027077
Svalbard-Museum, Longyearbyen . 030998
Svaneholms Slott, Skurup . . . 036586
Svato Verlag, Hamburg . . . 134024
Svatopluk Čech, Louny . . . 060051
Svaz Antikváru CR, Praha . . . 052841
Svedinos Bil- och Flygmuseum, Slöinge . . . 036589
Sveindal Museum, Kollungtveit . . . 030943
Svelvik Museum, Svelvik . . . 031254
Svendborg og Omegns Museum, Svendborg . . . 009125
Svendsen, Annalena, New York . . . 091279
Svensk Konsthandel, Uppsala . . . 082061
Svenska Antikvariatföreningen, Stockholm . . . 054152
Svenska Galleriförbundet, Stockholm . . . 054153
Svenska Julkort, Henån . . . 134960
Svenska Konstgalleriet, Malmö . . . 110981
Svenska Konstkritikersamfundet, Stockholm . . . 054154
Svenska Konstnärernas Förening, Stockholm . . . 054155
Svenska Mobler, Los Angeles . . . 089922
Svenska Museer, Stockholm . . . 136117
Svenska Museiföreningen, Stockholm . . . 054156
Svenska Rum Antikt, Stockholm . . . 082027
Svenska Statens Porträttsamling, Mariefred . . . 036471
Svenska Transportmuseet, Huskvarna . . . 036354
Svensson, Kurt, Stockholm . . . 111077
Sverdlovskaja Kartinnaja Galereja, Ekaterinburg . . . 033109
Sveriges Allmänna Konstförening, Stockholm . . . 054157
Sveriges Järnvägsmuseum, Gävle . 036284
Sveriges Konst och Antikhandlarförening, Stockholm . . . 054158
Sveriges Konstföreningars Riksförbund, Malmö . . . 054159
Sveriges Konsthantverkare och Industriformgivare, Stockholm . . . 054160
Sveriges Museimannaförbund, Nacka . . . 054161
Sveriges Riksidrottsmuseum, Farsta 036269
Sveriges Rundradiomuseum, Motala . . . 036490
Sveriges Sjömanshusmuseum, Uddevalla . . . 036726
Sveriges Teatermuseum, Nacka . . . 036493
Sveriges VVS-Museum, Katrineholm 036389
Sverko, Mario, Toulouse . . . 124996
Švestka, Jiří, Praha . . . 098487
Svet-L, Kyïv . . . 112423
Svettini, Adele, Milano . . . 075873
Švihov Hrad, Švihov . . . 008702
Svijažskij Architekturno-chudožestvennyj Muzej, Gosudarstvennyj Muzej izobrazitelnych iskusstv Respubliki Tatarstan, Svijažsk . . . 033918
Svindersvik, Nacka . . . 036494
Svjato-Troickij Sobor, Sankt-Peterburg . . . 033833
Svjatogorskij Monastyr, Puškinskie Gory . . . 033690
Svoboda, J., Bad Wimpfen . . . 101714
Svojanov Hrad, Polička . . . 008586
Svolis, Giannis, Zografou . . . 105465
S.W. Antiques, Pershore . . . 086221
Swaen, Paulus, Paris . . . 121212, 138544
Swaffer, Spencer, Arundel . . . 083316
Swaffham Museum, Swaffham . . . 041166
Swahnberg, Henric, Kristinehamn . 122183
Swain, Marilyn, Grantham . . . 122524
Swainbanks, Liverpool . . . 085029
Swakopmund Military Museum, Swakopmund . . . 029098
Swakopmund Museum, Swakopmund . . . 029099
Swalcliffe Barn, Swalcliffe . . . 041167
Swaledale Folk Museum, Reeth . . . 040817
Swallow Tail, San Francisco . . . 092893
Swan, London . . . 085725
Swan, Moonah . . . 137002
The Swan, Tetsworth . . . 086873, 131585
Swan, Michael, Dockyard . . . 096417
Swan, Michael, Hamilton . . . 096426
Swan Antiques, Bawtry . . . 083456
Swan Antiques, Baythorne End . . . 083457
Swan Antiques, Cranbrook . . . 084102
Swan Books, Billericay . . . 141414
Swan Coach House Gallery, Atlanta 041876
Swan Fine Art, London . . . 113909
Swan Gallery, Burford . . . 083796, 130480
Swan Gallery, Sherborne . 086583, 114428, 131487
Swan Hill Regional Art Gallery, Swan Hill . . . 001502
Swan Street Antique Mall, Louisville 090032
Swan Valley Historical Museum, Swan River . . . 006543
Swanage Railway, Swanage . . . 041168
Swanberg, Sacramento . . . 092185
Swangrove, New York . . . 091280
Swann, New York . . . 091281, 123019
Swann, Nice . . . 138262
Swann, Paris . . . 066580
Swans Antique Centre, Oakham . . .086149, 131340
Swansea Antiques Centre, Swansea 086813
Swansea Museum, Swansea . . . 041174
Swanson, Minneapolis . . . 117312
Swanson, Trevor V., Phoenix . . . 118893
Swanson Cralle, Louisville . . . 116967
Swanson Cralle, Louisville . . . 116968
Swanton Mill, Ashford . . . 038538
Swarovski, Saint Louis . . . 092320
Swarovski Kristallwelten, Wattens . 002812
Swart, J.A., Hercules . . . 129293
De Swarte Leeuw, Middelburg . . . 078644
Swarthout Memorial Museum, La Crosse . . . 045059
Swastika, Delhi . . . 105687
Swatosch, Wiesbaden . . . 074426
Swayambunath Museum, Swayambunath . . . 029121
Swaziland National Museum, Lobamba . . . 036163
Sweden Antique, Helsingborg . . . 081834
Swedenborg, Boston . . . 115233, 142257
Swedenborgs Antik, Stockholm . . . 082028
Swedish American Museum Association of Chicago, Chicago . . . 055062
Swedish American Museum Association of Chicago Museum, Chicago . . . 042882
Swedish Federation of Friends of Museums, Stockholm . . . 054162
Sweeney Art Gallery, Riverside . . . 047461
Sweerts de Landas, Ripley, Surrey .086375, 131417

Sweet Briar College Art Gallery, Sweet Briar . . . 048448
Sweet Briar Museum, Sweet Briar . 048449
Sweet Home, Hamburg . . . 071341
Sweet Memories, Tampa . . . 093155
Sweet Repeats, Charlotte . . . 087983
Sweet Slumber Antiques, Kempsey 056040
Sweetbriar Gallery, Helsby . . . 084647
Sweetings, Belper . . . 083485, 130369
Sweetow, Patricia, San Francisco . . 119809
Sweetwater County Historical Museum, Green River . . . 044313
Swensbylijda, Svensbyn . . . 036700
Swenson, Austin . . . 122806
Swenson Memorial Museum of Stephens County, Breckenridge . . . 042394
Swertz, André, Utrecht . . . 140556
Swetec, Franz, Düsseldorf . . . 102561
Swetec, Franz, Griesheim . . . 103005
Swets & Zeitlinger, Lisse . . . 140490
Swift, K.W., Ludlow . . . 141927
Swift County Historical Museum, Benson . . . 042148
Swigart Museum, Huntingdon . . . 044674
Swindler's Ridge Museum, Benton . 042149
Swindon, Hong Kong . . . 137750
Swindon Museum and Art Gallery, Swindon . . . 041181
Swinford Museum, Filkins . . . 039500
Swinkels, Berry, Eindhoven . . . 078353
Swiridoff Verlag, Künzelsau . . . 134135
Swisher County Museum, Tulia . . . 048651
Swiss Historical Village, New Glarus 046217
Swiss Institute - Contemporary Art, New York . . . 046410
Swiss Time, Atlanta . . . 087532, 131787
Swiss Village, Saint Louis . . . 142862
Swissminiatur, Melide . . . 037323
Świtalscy, Dariusz & Irena, Gdańsk . 079589
Switzerland County Historical Society Museum, Vevay . . . 048775
Swoboda, Bockenheim . . . 069898
Swoboda, Peter, Köln . . . 103723
Swoboda, R., Vogtsburg . . . 105128
Swope, Albuquerque . . . 114826
Swope Art Museum, Terre Haute . . 048533
Sworder & Sons, Hertford . . . 122543
Sworder & Sons, Stansted Mountfitchet . . . 122706
Swords and Ploughshares Museum, Manotick . . . 005827
Swords Into Plowshares Peace Center and Gallery, Detroit . . . 043456
Swuste, Bosch en Duin . . . 128599
Syarikat, Abdul, Melaka . . . 077500
Syber, Saint Kilda, Victoria . . . 137081
Syber, Windsor, Victoria . . . 137140
Sycomore, Lyon . . . 064186
Syddansk Universitetsforlag, Odense . . . 133430
Sydenham Antiques Centre, London . . . 085726, 131188
Sydhimmerlands Museum, Nørager 009028
Sydney Affordable Art Show, Moore Park . . . 093574
Sydney and Louisburg Railway Museum, Louisbourg . . . 005803
Sydney Antique Centre, Surry Hills . 056659
Sydney Art on Paper-International Art Fair, Castlecrag . . . 093575
Sydney Children's Museum, Merrylands . . . 001260
Sydney Coins and Jewellery, Parramatta . . . 056445
Sydney Galleries, Sydney . . . 095307
Sydney Galleries, Sydney . . . 095308
Sydney Heritage Fleet, Pyrmont . . . 001413
Sydney Jewish Museum, Darlinghurst . . . 000971
Sydney Observatory, Museum of Applied Arts and Sciences, Sydney . . . 001525
Sydney Road Old Things, Balgowlah 055425
Sydney Tramway Museum, Loftus . 001190
Sydsjællands Museum, Vordingborg 009153
Sydslesvigs Danske Kunstforening, Flensburg . . . 053570
Sydys, J. G., Sankt Pölten . . . 137253
Sygun Copper Mine, Beddgelert . . . 038652
Sykepleiemuseum, Oslo . . . 031109
Sykes, Christopher, Woburn . . . 087200
Sykkylven Naturhistorisk Museum, Sykkylven . . . 031257
Syl'Antic, Le Peage-de-Roussillon . 063677
Syllavethy Gallery, Alford . . . 112495
Syllectiki, Athinai . . . 093751
Syllogy Art Gallery, Toronto . . . 097382
Sylter Gemälde Cabinett, Westerland . . . 105231
Sylter Heimatmuseum, Sylt-Ost . . . 020392
Sylter Kunstfreunde e.V., Westerland . . . 053571
Sylvain, Jacqueline, Gonfreville-l'Orcher . . . 063015
Sylvan, Kolkata . . . 074817
Sylvan Mall Antiques, Toledo . . . 093186
Sylvania Galleries, Sylvania . . . 095310
Sylvester, Günter, Hatten, Oldenburg . . . 071430
Sylvester & Sons, H.W., Kalk Bay . . 080723
Sylvia Art Antic, Gracay . . . 063027
Sylvia Plotkin Judaica Museum, Scottsdale . . . 048061
Sylvia's Attic, New Orleans . . . 090630
Symboles de l'Art, Saint-Palais . . . 067933
Symes, Robin, London . . . 085727, 113910
Symphonie des Arts, La Baule-Escoublac . . . 099383
Synagóga - Centrum Súčasného Umenia, Galéria Jána Koniarka v Trnave, Trnava . . . 034446
Synagoge, Bourtange . . . 029339
Synagoge und Jüdisches Museum Ermreuth, Neunkirchen am Brand 019258
Synagogen-Museum, Urspringen . . 020548
Syndicat Belge de la Librairie Ancienne et Moderne, Liège . . . 052687
Syndicat de la Librairie Ancienne et du Commerce de l'Estampe en Suisse, Vereinigung der Buchantiquare und Kupferstichhändler in der Schweiz, Saint-Prex . . . 054219
Syndicat des Antiquaires, Brocanteurs et Galeries d'Art de Marseille et la Région, Marseille . . . 052983
Syndicat des Antiquaires et Brocanteurs Audois, Carcassonne . . . 052984
Syndicat des Antiquaires et Brocanteurs des Vosges, Bains-les-Bains . . . 052986
Syndicat des Antiquaires et Brocanteurs des Vosges, Saint-Dié-des-Vosges . . . 052985
Syndicat Français des Experts Professionnels en Oeuvres d'Art et Objets de Collection, Paris . . . 052987
Syndicat Lorrain Professionnel de l'Antiquité, Rosières-aux-Salines . 052988
Syndicat Mixte de Brouage, Corps de Garde, Hiers-Brouage . . . 012104
Syndicat Nacional des Artistes Auteurs, Paris . . . 052989
Syndicat Nacional des Artistes Plasticiens, Paris . . . 052990
Syndicat Nacional des Artistes Professionnels, Paris . . . 052991
Syndicat Nacional des Créateurs en Arts Graphiques, L'Haye-les-Roses . . . 052992
Syndicat Nacional des Graphistes, Paris . . . 052993
Syndicat Nacional des Sculpteurs et Plasticiens, Paris . . . 052994
Syndicat National de la Librairie Ancienne et Moderne, Paris . . . 052995
Syndicat National de l'Arquebuserie et du Commerce de l'Arme Historique et de Coll, Avallon . . . 052996
Syndicat National des Antiquaires, Paris . . . 052997
Syndicat National du Commerce de l'Antiquité et de l'Occasion, Paris 052998
Syndicat Romand des Antiquaires, Paudex . . . 054220
Syndikat, Leipzig . . . 139403
Synopsis m, Lausanne . . . 111633
Syntax Medienproduktion + Verlag, Mannheim . . . 134190
Synthese, Bruxelles . . . 096255
Synthèse, Paris . . . 100890
Synthese GmbH für Restaurierung, Budapest . . . 127080
Syon House, London . . . 040298
Sýpka, Brno . . . 098338
Syplacz, Arnold, Hagen, Westfalen .071167, 103052
Syracuse University Art Collection, Syracuse . . . 048460
Syracuse University Press, Syracuse . . . 135512
Syrlin-Kunstverein e.V., Stuttgart . . 053572
Syropoulou, Dimitra, Kalamaria . . . 105426
Sysmäen Kotiseutumuseo, Sysmä . 010110
Syvert, Mandal . . . 079400
Syvertsen, Kristiansand . . . 079399
Syzranskij Gorodskoj Kraevedčeskij Muzej, Syzran . . . 033929
Szaal, Wien . . . 057562
Szaal, Horst & Wolfgang, Wien . . . 095950
Szabadtéri Néprajzi Gyűjtemény, Szenna . . . 021877
Szabadtéri Néprajzi Múzeum, Szalafő . . . 021854
Szabadtéri Néprajzi Múzeum, Szentendre . . . 021886
Szabadtéri Vizügyi Múzeum, Szolnok . . . 021897
Szadadtéri Erdei Múzeum, Szilvásvárad . . . 021895
Szafrańska, Stanisława, Łódź . . . 079674
Szaivert, Dr. Eva, Wien . . . 057563
Szalay-Gyûjtemény - Petróház, Miskolci Galéria, Miskolc . . . 021791
Szalinski, I., Osnabrück . . . 073248
Szalom, Kraków . . . 108987
Szántó Kovács Múzeum, Orosháza . 021805
Szarka, David, Luzern . . . 130109
Szatmári Múzeum, Mátészalka . . . 021781
Szczepanski, G., Meppen . . . 072518
Szczypka-Kozłowska, Grażyna, Łomianki . . . 129055
Széchenyi Emlékmúzeum, Nagycenk . . . 021796
Széchenyi Irodalmi és Művészeti Akadémia, Budapest . . . 050285
Szedlarik, W., Bad Hofgastein . . . 137153
Szelag, Saint Louis . . . 132754
Szélmalom, Szeged . . . 021864
Szent Imre Antikvárium, Budapest .121645, 139930
Szent István Király Múzeum, Székesfehérvár . . . 021872
Szentendrei Képtár, Szentendre . . . 021887
Szepanski, Peter, Stuttgart . . . 074012
Szepe, Helena, Chicago . . . 142303
Szépművészeti Múzeum, Budapest 021694
Szerb Egyházy Múzeum, Szentendre . . . 021888
Szezląg, Warszawa . . . 109197
Sziget, Budapest . . . 074723
Sziget Galéria, Budapest . . . 105546
Szigetszentmiklós-Honismereti Gyûjtemény, Szigetszentmiklós . . . 021892
Szín-Tér Galéria, Győr . . . 105560
Szindlowski, Kuno, Allensbach . . . 069135
Színháztörténeti és Színészmúzeum, Miskolci Galéria, Miskolc . . . 021792
Szkatułka, Warszawa . . . 109198
Szkolne Muzeum Morskie, Bolesławiec . . . 031849
Szlos, Lisette, Paris . . . 066581
Szlovák Tájház, Békéscsaba . . . 021630
Szoborpark, Budapest . . . 021695
Szőnyi István Emlék Múzeum, Zebegény . . . 021927
Szövöház, Hollókö . . . 021743
Szoke, John, New York . . . 135464
Szokoly, Veszprém . . . 139944
Szombathelyi Képtár, Szombathely . 021900
Szőnyi, Budapest . . . 139931
Szopinski, Neustadt an der Weinstraße . . . 073035
Szórakaténusz Játékmúzeum, Kecskemét . . . 021763
Szpitalki, Muzeum Ziemi Puckiej, Puck . . . 032271
Sztuka, Kraków . . . 121895
Sztuka, Warszawa . . . 136038
Sztuka Dalekiego Wschodu, Muzeum Okręgowe w Toruniu, Toruń . . . 032396
Sztuka Dawna, Sopot . . . 079714
Sztuka Dawna, Starogard Gdański . 079715
Sztuka i Antyki, Bielsko-Biała 079572, 108862
Sztuka - Stowarzyszenie Artystyczne, Warszawa . . . 053993
Szuhay, Peter, London . . . 113911
Szukits, Szeged . . . 139942
Szwajcer, Micheline, Antwerpen . . . 096092
Szy, Dénes, Düsseldorf . . . 070452
Szymański, Sławomir, Gdynia . . . 140727
Szymkowicz, Paris . . . 100891
T E S Art, Mosta . . . 107447
T. & G. Art Gallery, Hoi An . . . 120543
T K H, Bad Königshofen . . . 069310
T Rue A, Paris . . . 100892
T Studio, Los Angeles . . . 116897
T20, Murcia . . . 110655
Ta' Hagrat Copper Age Temples, Mgarr . . . 028027
Ta' Kola Windmill, Xaghra . . . 028048
Ta Matete Living Gallery, Roma . . . 106634
Taalintehtaan Ruukinmuseo, Dalsbruk . . . 009463
Taarup, Dorthe, Hellerup . . . 060255
Taba, Murcia . . . 129708
Tabak-Museum der Stadt Hockenheim, Hockenheim . . . 017940
Tabak- und Zigarrenmuseum, Reinach (Aargau) . . . 037442
Tabakhistorische Sammlung Reemtsma, Hamburg . . . 017725
Tabakmuseum, Lorsch . . . 018687
Tabakmuseum, Oberzeiring . . . 002397
Tabako to Shio no Hakubutsukan, Tokyo . . . 027247
Tabakspeicher, Museum für Nordhäuser Handwerks- und Industriegeschichte, Nordhausen . . . 019335
La Tabard, Booterstown . . . 105849
Tabasso, Maddalena, Milano . . . 075874
Tabbernee, D., Rotterdam . . . 078747
Taber, Sacramento . . . 092186
Taber and District Museum, Taber . 006550
Taberna Livraria, Fortaleza . . . 137563
Tabiah, Mohammed Samir, Damascus . . . 083086
Tabla y Lienzo, Madrid . . . 081395
Table Rock Historical Society Museum, Table Rock . . . 048461
Tabler, Joseph, San Diego . . . 142917
Tabley House Collection, Knutsford . 039913
Taboada, Austin . . . 115017
Tabor Opera House Museum, Leadville . . . 045221
Tábua Rasa, Lisboa . . . 129179
Tabula, Zamora . . . 081729, 129797
Tabula Buch & Kunst, Tübingen . . . 139800
Tabula Rasa, Paris . . . 124817
Tabusintac Centennial Museum, Tabusintac . . . 006551
Hervé Tabutin & Gérard de Dianous, Marseille . . . 121067
Taby, Paul, Sens . . . 068223
Tačauz Muzej, Tačauz . . . 038210
Tacconi, Dina, Modena . . . 127746
Tache, Carles, Barcelona . . . 110254
Tache d'Argent, Mons . . . 096392
Taché-Levy, Bruxelles . . . 096256
Tachibana, Kyoto . . . 077126
Tachmes, Leonard, Miami . . . 117146
Tacit, Thornbury . . . 095332
Tacken, Bloemendaal . . . 128591
Tacoma Art Museum, Tacoma . . . 048469
Tacticos, Timişoara . . . 080201
Tactual Museum, Greek Lighthouse for the Blind, Athinai . . . 021213

Tactual Museum, Greek Lighthouse for the Blind, Kallithea 021300
Tacussel, Paul, Marseille 133496
Tadema, London 085728, 113912
Tadman, Shelley, Winnipeg 097607
Tadmor, Dubai 083205
Tadre Mølle, Hvalsø 008941
Tadu, Bangkok 112242
Tadzio, Kyïv 112424
Tändsticksmuseet, Jönköping 036363
Täuber, Claudia, Wien 057564
Täuber, Hans-Joachim, Bad Salzuflen 069370
Taff, James F., Sacramento 092187
Taft Museum of Art, Cincinnati 042929
TAG Art Gallery, Nashville 117373
Tag Diamond Jewelry, Buffalo 087913
Taganrogskaja Kartinnaja Galereja, Taganrog 033933
Taganrogskij Gosudarstvennyj Literaturnyj i Istoriko-architekturnyj Muzej-zapovednik, Taganrog 033934
Taganrogskij Kraevedčeskij Muzej, Taganrogskij gosudarstvennyj literaturnyj i istoriko-architekturnyj muzej-zapovednik, Taganrog 033935
Taganrogskij Muzej im. A.P. Čechova, Taganrog 033936
Tagawa Bijutsukan, Tagawa 027098
Tage, E ., Philadelphia 091693
Tages, Lidingö 081846
Taggart, Hollis, Chicago 115561
Taggart, Hollis, New York 118465
Taglialatella, Dominic J ., New York 118466
Tagliapietra, Ivano, Torino 128363
Tagliapietra, Lino, Seattle 120001
Tagliapietra, Maurizio, Verona 128441
Tagliareni, Salvatore J., Philadelphia 118842, 132638
Taha Hussien Museum, Haram 009338
Tahiti Imports, Honolulu 088979
Tahydromiko Moyseio, Athinai 021214
Tai, Hong Kong 059694
Tai & Co., J.T., New York 091282
Tai Hao Ling Museum, Zhoukou . . . 007354
Tai Sing, Hong Kong 059695
Tai Wo & Co., Hong Kong 059696
Taichang City Museum, Taichang . . 007276
Taide, Helsinki 135679
Taide Fox, Tampere 060632
Taide ja Kehys Pekkala, Oulu 098758
Taidehistorian Seura, Föreningen för Konsthistoria, Helsinki 052883
Taidekeidas, Turku 060645
Taidekeskus Mältinranta, Tampere . 010130
Taidekoti Kirpilä, Helsinki 009580
Taidelainaamo Tampereen Taideyhdistys, Tampere 060633
Taidemaalariliiton Galleria, Helsinki 098747
Taidemuseo, K.H. Renlund Museum, Kokkola 009726
Taidesalonki, Helsinki . . . 060584, 098748
Taidesalonki Piirto, Helsinki 098749
Taideteollisuusmuseo, Helsinki 009518
Taieri Historical Museum, Outram . . 030562
Taifa Llibres, Barcelona 141006
Taiga, Tobetsu 077228
Taihape and District Museum, Taihape 030596
Taiheiyo Bijutsukai, Tokyo 053802
Taikomosios dailės, Vilnius 107375
Taikoo Books, York 142182
Tain and District Museum, Tain . . . 041183
The Taipa Houses Museum, Macau 007191
Taipei Fine Arts Museum, Taipei . . . 007377
Taipei National University of the Arts, Taipei 049861
Taiping Museum, Nanjing 007209
Tairawhiti Museum, Gisborne 030501
The Taise Gallery, Ballycastle 112542
Taish-Machi Kominkan Fuzoku Taisha Kokokan, Taishiya 027101
Taiteiden Tutkimuksen Laitos, Helsingin Yliopisto, Helsinki 049926
Taivalkosken Kotiseutumuseo, Taivalkoski 010112
Taivassalon Museo, Taivassalo 010113
Taiwan Antique Dealers' Association, Taipei 052807
Taiwan Craft Center, Taipei 007378
Taiwan Folk Arts Museum, Taipei . . 007379
Taiwan Museum, Taipei 007380
Taiwan Museum of Art, Taichung . . 007363
Taiyi, Shanghai 097946
Taiyuan Painting Gallery, Taiyuan . . 007280
Taizz Museum, Taizz 049564
Le Taj, Cairo 060477
Tajan, Lausanne 122331
Tajan, Paris 121213
Tájház, Buzsák 021705
Tájház, Mezőkövesd 021783
Tajiri Hyoguten, Tokyo 077312
Tajmyrskij Okružnoj Kraevedčeskij Muzej, Dudinka 033105
TAK - Tiroler Autor/inn/en Kooperative, Innsbruck 133093
Takács, Dezső, Győr 074739
Takada, San Francisco 119810
Takahashi, Kyoto 077127
Takahashi, Imono Kojo, Kyoto 077128
Takako, Tsuji, New York 118467
Takamatsu City Museum of Art, Takamatsu 027108
Takamatsuzuka Wall Painting Museum, Asuka 026429
Takamiya, Osaka 106973
Takamura Art Museum, Minami-tsuru 026804
Takaoka Bijutsukan, Takaoka 027110
Takaoka Shiritsu Hakubutsukan, Takaoka 027111
Takara, Hiroshima 106858
Takarada, T. & M., Yokohama 077343
Takarazuka Daigaku Hakabutsukan, Takaraduka 027112
Takarazuka Zokei Geijutsu Daigaku, Takaraduka 050475
Takasaki-shi Bijutsukan, Takasaki . 027116
Takasawa Folk Craft Museum, Niigata 026915
Takashimaya, Singapore 109877
Takayama Jinya, Takayama 027127
Takayama-shiritsu Hakubutsukan, Takayama 027128
Take Another Look-Books, Seattle . 143011
Take it for Granted, Johannesburg . 080717
Takehisa Yumeji Ikaho Memorial Hall, Ikaho 026554
Takenaka, Kyoto 077129
Takenouchi Kaido Rekishi Hakubutsukan, Taishi 027100
Takeuchi, Tokyo 140204
Takht-e-Jamshid, Marvdashd 022580
Takht-e-Jamshid, Shiraz 022599
Takhté-Djamchid, Teheran 105846
Taki, Ayse, İstanbul 112358
Takii, Osaka 106974
Takkenberg, M., Zaandam 078854
Tako no Hakubutsukan, Tokyo 027248
Taksu, Singapore 109878
Takumi, Tokyo 077313
Tal, Bordeaux 061654
Tal 20, München 104328
Tal-Museum, Engelberg 037067
Talabardon & Gautier, Paris 100893
Talacea, Vigo 081710
Talana Museum and Heritage Park, Dundee 034595
Talaos, Auray 061070
Talas, New York 132540
Talavan Moraleda, Felipe, Madrid . . 129691
Talaverano, Manuela, Sevilla 110781
Talboom, Antwerpen 137407
Talbot Arts and Historical Museum, Talbot 001530
Talbot & Co, Edwin, Carlisle 112816
Talbot Court Galleries, Stow-on-the-Wold 086765, 114507, 131552
Talbot House, Poperinge 003705
Talbot Rice Gallery, Edinburgh 039428
Talbot Walk Antique Centre, Ripley, Surrey 086376
Talebloo, New Orleans 090631
Talec, Agnès, Paris 138545
Talen, K., Staphorst 128838
Talens, Leeuwarden 078556
Talent Arts Gallery, Singapore 109879
Talents, Manama 096028
Talents Fine Arts, Malton . 085904, 131250
Talents Fine Arts, Malton North . . . 114034
Tales of the Old Gaol House, King's Lynn 039879
The Talish Gallery, Edinburgh 084315
Talisman, Gillingham, Dorset 084458
Talisman, Washington 120351
Talisman Antiques, Oakland 091440
Talisman Fine Art, Looe 113996
Talisman Gallery, Little Hartley 094742
Talisman Gallery, Portland 119058
Talk of the Town, Dallas . . 088615, 132023
Talk of the Town, Houston 089219
Talkeetna Historical Society Museum, Talkeetna 048477
Talking Machine, London 085729
Talking Point Antiques, Sowerby Bridge 086673
Tall Ships Bookshop, Manawuta . . . 140638
Tall Stories, San Francisco 142965
Tallahassee Museum of History and Natural Science, Tallahassee 048485
Tallbo, Järbo 036358
Tallec, Bordeaux 061655
El Taller, Bogotá 123910
Taller, Miró, Santiago de Chile 059556
El Taller Antigüedades y Restauración, Medellín 059944, 123942
Taller Cuatro, Madrid 129692
El Taller de Angelo, Lugo 129546
Taller de Arte y Galería Universal, Medellín 098287
Taller de Arte y Restauración El Moral, Bogotá 059862, 123911
Taller de Artes, San Antonio 119458
Taller de Artes Ecuador, Bogotá . . . 059863
Taller de Ceramica Nerea, Cali 123923
Taller de Esculturas Pátinas y Bronces, Medellín 123943
El Taller de Marcos, Castellón de la Plana 129481
Taller de Marcos Goya, Concepción 059479
Taller de Restauración, Cali 123924
Taller de Restauracion, León 081173, 129543
Taller de Restauración del Patrimonio, Madrid 129693
Taller del Artista, Granada 129534
Taller el Trastam, Valencia 129787
Taller Escuela de Grabado Tres en Raya, Madrid 050727
Taller Escuelas Arte Fuego, Caracas 120438
Taller Galería de Robles, Madrid . . . 129694
Taller Galeria Fort in Cadaqués, Barcelona 110255, 134929
El Taller Gallery, Austin 115018
Taller Malaca, Madrid 129695
Taller Puertorriqueno, Philadelphia . 046990
Taller Puertorriqueno, Philadelphia . 118843
Taller Restauracion Antiguedades, Zaragoza 129832
Taller Textil, Madrid 129696
Taller y Almacén de Artes Aplicadas el Arcano, Cali 123925
Talleres Creativos Reojo, Madrid . . 129697
Talleres de Restauración Arti, Bogotá 123912
Talleres Exposiciones Libres, Lima . 108812
Tallgauer, G., Stuhr 073949
Tallgauer, Udo, Bassum 069482
Tallieu & Tallieu, Gent 096300
Tallinna Linnamuuseum, Tallinn . . . 009412
Tallkrogens Gammalt & Nytt, Enskede 081782
Tally Antique Auctions, Tallygaroopna 120646
Talma Mill Art Gallery, Christ Church 096038
Talmuseum, San Nicolò Ultimo 025719
Talmuseum Andreas Hofer, San Leonardo in Passiria 025698
Talmuseum Chasa Jaura, Valchava 037666
Talmuseum Kaunertal, Feichten . . . 001841
Talmuseum Lachitzhof, Klein Sankt Paul 002150
Talmuseum Samnaun, Chasa Retica, Samnaun Compatsch 037487
Talmuseum Ursern, Andermatt 036842
Talomuseo, Kuortane 009766
Taloni, Cristiano, Roma 076695
Taloni, Piero, Roma 076696
Talonpoikaismuseo Yli-Kirra, Punkalaidum 010006
Talonpojanmuseo, Kälviä 009649
Talsu Novadpētniecības un Mākslas Muzejs, Talsi 027783
Talton, J.W., Long Sutton, Lincolnshire 085847, 131236
Talvisen Työläismökki, Humppila . . 009595
Talvisotanäyttely, Kuhmo 009754
Talwar, New York 118468
Tam, Hong Kong 097838
Tam, Hong Kong 097839
Tam, Hong Kong 097840
Tam O'Shanter Experience, Alloway 038490
Tama Bijutsu Daigaku, Tokyo 050496
Tama County Historical Museum, Toledo 048565
Tama Seiseki Kinenkan, Tama 027132
Tamagawa Modern Art Museum, Tamagawa 027133
Tamagnini, Massimo, San Marino . .080350, 129256
Taman Warisan Merimbun, Tutong . 004618
Tamar, New York 118469
Tamara, Tel Aviv 121677
Tamara's Antiques, Minneapolis . . .090397, 122971
Tamarillo, Wellington 108646
Tamarind Institute, University of New Mexico, Albuquerque 050881
Tambaran, New York 118470
Tambasco, Montevideo 122790
Tamblyn, Alnwick 083274
Tambo Gallery, London 113913
Tamborine Mountain Heritage Centre, Eagle Heights 000999
Tambovskaja Oblastnaja Kartinnaja Galereja, Tambov 033938
Tambovskij Gosudarstvennyj Universitet, Tambov 050664
Tambovskij Oblastnoj Kraevedčeskij Muzej, Tambov 033939
Tamburelli, Claudio, Roma 076697
Tamburini, Joseph, Uzer 068665
Tamburrini, Roland, Paris 066582
Tamenaga, Paris 100894
Tamia, Atlanta 087533
Tamin, Paris 066583
Tamlyn & Son, Bridgwater 122434
Tammaro, Luciano, Napoli 127792
Tammen, R. & U., Oldenburg, Oldenburg 073212
Tammen & Busch, Berlin 102062
Tammiharjun Sairaalamuseo, Ekenäs 009468
Tammio Museo, Tammio 010116
Tampa Antiquarian Book Company, Tampa 143026
Tampa Bay History Center, Tampa . 048492
Tampa Museum of Art, Tampa 048493
Tampa Realistic Artists, Tampa 055063
Tampereen Kaupunginmuseo, Tampere 010131
Tampereen Kirja- ja Lehtiantikva, Tampere 137993
Tampereen Luonnontieteelinen Museo, Tampere 010132
Tampereen Nykytaiteen Museo, Tampere 010133
Tampereen Taidemuseo - Pirkanmaan Aluetaidemuseo, Tampere 010134

Tampereen Taidemuseon Muumilaakso, Tampere . . . 010135
Tampereen Teknillinen Museo, Tampere . . . 010136
Tampico, San Francisco . . . 092894
Tamralipta Museum and Research Center, Tamluk . . . 022347
Tamsen Munger, Fresno . . . 116188
Tamura, Tokyo . . . 140205
Tamworth Castle Museum, Tamworth . . . 041184
Tamworth City Gallery, Tamworth . . 001532
Tamyang Bamboo Museum, Tamyang . . . 027620
Tamy's Antiques, New York . . . 091283
Tan, Ah Han, Singapore . . . 080567
Tan, C. K., Singapore . . . 080568
Tan, Sim, Kuala Lumpur . . . 107438
Tan Oe Pang Art Studio, Singapore . 034300
Tana Museum, Tana . . . 031259
Tanabe Museum of Art, Matsue . . . 026789
Tanagra, Montceau-les-Mines . . . 064666
Tanagra, Strasbourg . . . 068334
Tanah Art Museum, San Antonio . . . 003885
Tanaka, Nagasaki . . . 077144
Tanaka, Nagoya . . . 077155
Tanaka, Nara . . . 077167
Tanaka, Tokyo . . . 107120
Tanakami Mineral Museum, Otsu . . 027000
Tanakaya, Paris . . . 066584, 100895
Tanawha Antiques, Tanawha . . . 056694
Tanazawa, Tokyo . . . 140206
Tanca, Giuseppe, Roma . . . 076698
Tanca, Milena, Roma . . . 076699
Tandanya, National Aboriginal Cultural Institute, Adelaide . . . 000714
Tandart, Bois-Colombes . . . 061537
Tandem Press, Madison . . . 135388
Tandläkarmuseum, Sunne . . . 036696
Tandy, Robert, Bristol . . . 130461
Tandy, Robert, Clevedon . . . 130589
Tanfer, Madrid . . . 129698
Tang, Dapiao, Shanghai . . . 097947
Tang, Dapiao, Shanghai . . . 097948
Tang, Dapiao, Shanghai . . . 097949
Tang, Donghai, Shanghai . . . 097950
Tang, G.E., Shanghai . . . 059768
Tang, G.E., Shanghai . . . 059769
Tang, Sarina, New York . . . 118471
Tang, Sarina, New York . . . 118472
Tang Dai Art Museum, Xian . . . 007320
T'ang Horse, Singapore . . . 080569
Tang Teaching Museum and Art Gallery, Saratoga Springs . . . 048010
Tange, Valenciennes . . . 068695
Tångeberg, Elkea & Peter, Tystberga . . . 129885
Tangente, Eschen . . . 107332
Tanger, Albert, Fort-de-France . . . 128491
Tangerding-Dörner, Bocholt . . . 069879
Tanglewood, Vancouver . . . 137732
Tanglin Antique Gallery, Singapore . 080570
Tango, Montréal . . . 059014
Tango Art Deco, Warwick . . . 087046
Tango Photographie, Montréal . . . 097083
Tangram, Cannes . . . 099078
Tanguy, Jean-Pierre, Crézancy-en-Sancerre . . . 062569
Tania's Gallery, Atlanta . . . 114932
Tanimura Bijutsukan, Itoigawa . . . 026585
Tanis, Paris . . . 066585
Tanis, Jean-Louis, Le Castera . . . 063592
Tanit, München . . . 104329
Tanja, Beograd . . . 080408
Tanjore Collection, Chennai . . . 105638
Tank Museum, Bovington . . . 038798
Tankerton Antiques, Whitstable . . . 087141
Tankosha, Kyoto . . . 134714
Tankosha, Tokyo . . . 134733
Tanks Art Centre, Edge Hill . . . 094504
The Tanks of Aden, Aden . . . 049559
Tann, Iris von der, Berlin . . . 102063
Tanneberger, Rüdiger, Zwickau . . . 074581
Tanner, Bern . . . 134999
Tanner, Daniel, Basel . . . 111225
Tanner, Robert, Zürich . . . 083030, 130267
Tanner Chaney, Albuquerque . . . 114827
Tannhäuser, Braunschweig . . . 102225
Tans Place, Blenheim . . . 140608
Tansu, Montréal . . . 097084
Tansu Design, San Francisco . . . 092895
Tanta Museum, Tanta . . . 009347
Tantalus Antiques, Troon . . . 086923
Tantaquidgeon Indian Museum, Uncasville . . . 048687
Tante Blanche Museum, Madawaska . . . 045573
Tante Pose ANS, Bergen . . . 079381
Tantekin Antik, İstanbul . . . 083157
Tanti, Paul, Sliema . . . 077531, 128482
Tantius, Hans-Gerd, Lübbecke . . . 103954, 134169
Tanuki la Galerie, Lyon . . . 099617
Tanums Hällristningsmuseum, Tanumshede . . . 036704
Tanybryn Gallery, Tanybryn . . . 095319
Tanzer, Dianne, Fitzroy . . . 094540
Tanzer, Jack, New York . . . 118473
Tanzilli, Roland, Meximieux . . . 064544
Tanzillo, Gaetano, Napoli . . . 127793
Tanzimat Müzesi, İstanbul . . . 038098
Tanzini, Armando, Malindi . . . 077346
Tao, Mumbai . . . 105813
Tao, Paris . . . 066586
Taos Art Association, Taos . . . 055064
Taos Historic Museums, Taos . . . 048500
Taos/Western Fine Arts Publishing Company, Taos . . . 135514
Taowu Yiyuan, Suzhou . . . 097999
TAP Gallery, Darlinghurst . . . 094455
TapaFa, Wellington . . . 108647
Tapestry, Cheltenham . . . 083931, 130545
Tapestry Antiques, Hertford . . . 084674
Tápies, Toni, Barcelona . . . 110256
Het Tapijtmuseum, Genemuiden . . . 029603
Tapinquiri, La Paz . . . 096446
Tapiola-Antikvariaatti, Espoo . . . 137922
Tapiolan Taide ja Kehys, Espoo . . . 098710
Tapis, Seattle . . . 093074
Tapisseries Jean Lurçat, Rocamadour . . . 014069
Tapissier, Michel, Reims . . . 067081
Tapissier, Michel, Tinqueux . . . 068424
Tappantown Historical Society Museum, Tappan . . . 048501
Tappenden, London . . . 113914
Tapper-Popermajer, Malmö . . . 110982
Tapsell, Beechworth . . . 136795
Tapsell, Rutherglen . . . 137079
Tapsell, C., London . . . 085730
Tapsell, Gillian, Rye . . . 114336
Tapulimuseo, Lempäälä . . . 009818
Tar Tunnel, Coalport . . . 039107
Tara and District Pioneer Memorial Museum, Tara . . . 001535
Tara Antiques, Atlanta . . . 087534
Tara Antiques, London . . . 085731
Tara & Kys, Ho Chi Minh City . . . 120532
Tara & Kys, Siem Reap . . . 096782
Tara Verde, Lugano . . . 111671
Taragna, Giulio, Il Leggio, Torino . . . 140143
Taraj, Fatmir, Saint-Ouen . . . 067900
Taralga Historical Museum, Taralga 001536
Taranaki Arts Centre, Taranaki . . . 108571
Tarangau Caravan Park, Broome . . 094317
Taranna, Barcelona . . . 110257
Tarantino, Nicola, Bari . . . 127124
Tarantino, Nunzio, Napoli . . . 127794
Tarantino, Vincenzo, Milano . . . 127694
Tarantola, Lucia, Milano . . . 127695
Taraporevala, D.B., Mumbai . . . 134521
Tara's Hall, Hadleigh . . . 084548
Tarasiève, Suzanne, Barbizon . . . 098924
Tarasiève, Suzanne, Paris . . . 100896
Tarazi, Michel Emile, Broumana . . . 077424
Tarble Arts Center, Eastern Illinois University, Charleston . . . 042722
Tarbouriech, Guy & Martine, Bagnols-sur-Cèze . . . 061171
Tardieu, Loic, Bordeaux . . . 124145
Tardif, François, Jouars-Pontchartrain . . . 063256, 124270
Tardino, Claudio, Milano . . . 127696
The Tardis, Christchurch . . . 079057
Tardy, Dany, Fontaine-le-Dun . . . 062892
The Tareq Rajab Museum, Hawelli . 027630
Targa, Stefano, Torino . . . 076873
Target, Moskva . . . 129241
Target Gallery, London . . . 113915
Targhetta, Andrea, Venezia . . . 128407
Tarık Zafer Tunaya Kültür Merkezi, İstanbul . . . 112359
Tarka Books, Barnstaple . . . 141391
Tarkasis Pantelis, Eptalofos . . . 105421
Tarkiainen, Helsinki . . . 060585
Tarkis, Madrid . . . 081396, 122071
Tarlee Antiques, Tarlee . . . 056701
Tarli e Dintorni, Civitanova Marche . 093794
Il Tarlo, Catania . . . 075262
Il Tarlo, Padova . . . 076114
Il Tarlo, Torino . . . 076874
Tarlo d'Oro, Palermo . . . 127840
Tarnished Treasures, Phoenix . . . 091774
Tarpon Springs Cultural Center, Tarpon Springs . . . 048503
Tarporley Antique Centre, Tarporley 086823
The Tarporley Gallery, Tarporley . . . 114550
Tarquini, Nathalie, Marseille . . . 099689
Tarquinio, Lille . . . 063869
Tarr, Mike, Taunton . . . 114556
Tarrade, Arnault, Saumur . . . 068153
Tarrade, Arnault, Villebernier . . . 068887
Tarrago, Nicole, Montady . . . 064615
Tarrant, Lorraine, Ringwood . . . 086369
Tarrazi, Jean-Pierre, Marseille . . . 064393
Tarrytowns Museum, Tarrytown . . . 048506
Tarskij Istoriko-kraevedčeskij Muzej, Tara . . . 033940
Tarsus Müzesi, Tarsus . . . 038181
Tarsus Müzesi, Tarsus . . . 038182
Tarszys, José, Buenos Aires . . . 136755
Tartaglia, Riccardo, Roma . . . 106635
Tartari, Roberto, Modena . 075928, 127747
Tartarotti, Clara, Milano . . . 127697
Le Tartarughe, Roma . . . 076700
Tarter, Thannhausen . . . 139781
Tartière, Jean, Chabris . . . 062067
Tartous Museum, Tartous . . . 037836
Tartt, Washington . . . 120352
Tartu Kunstimaja, Tartu . . . 009423
Tartu Kunstimuuseum, Tartu . . . 009424
Tartu Linnamuuseum, Tartu . . . 009425
Tartu Mänguasjamuuseum, Tartu . . 009426
Tartu Ülikooli Ajaloomuuseum, Tartu 009427
Tartu Ülikooli Geoloogiamuuseum, Tartu . . . 009428
Tartu Ülikooli Kunstimuuseum, Tartu 009429
Tartu Ülikooli Zooloogiamuuseum, Tartu . . . 009430
Tartumaa Muuseum, Elva . . . 009356
Tarusskaja Kartinnaja Galereja, Kalužskij oblastnoj chudožestvennyj muzej, Tarusa . . . 033941
Tarusskij Kraevedčeskij Muzej, Tarusa . . . 033942
Tarusskij Muzej Semji Cvetaevych, Kalužskij oblastnoj kraevedčeskij muzej, Tarusa . . . 033943
Tarvasjoen Kotiseutumuseo, Tarvasjoki . . . 010142
Tarvastu Kihelkonnamuuseum, Tarvastu . . . 009431
Tarzan, Köln . . . 072018
Taş Eserler Müzesi - Lapidari, Lefkoşa . . . 008259
Tasb, Las Vegas . . . 089613
Tasbach, Elvira, Berlin . . . 138852
Tasca, Stella, Roma . . . 106636
Taschen, Köln . . . 134122
Taschen, London . . . 135267
Taschen, Paris . . . 133679
Tasende, West Hollywood . . . 120415
Tashkent Historical Museum of the People of Uzbekistan, Taškent . . . 049412
Tasiilap Katersugaasivia, Ammassalik Museum, Tasiilaq . . . 021551
Tåsinge Skipperhjem og Folkemindesamling, Svendborg . . 009126
Tasmania Distillery Museum, Hobart . . . 001113
Tasmania Gallery, Hobart . . . 094646
Tasmanian Copper and Metal Art Gallery, Carrick . . . 094380
Tasmanian Museum and Art Gallery, Hobart . . . 001114
Tasmanian School of Art, University of Tasmania, Hobart . . . 049612
Tasmanian Wool Centre, Ross . . . 001440
Tasmania's Antique Directory, Battery Point . . . 055457
Tasneem Arts Gallery, Peshawar . . 031396
Tassart, Mireille, Verdun (Meuse) . . 068771
Tassenmuseum Hendrikje, Amstelveen . . . 029161
Tassotti, Bassano del Grappa . . . 134543
Tassy, Jean, Alès . . . 060774
Tassy, Philippe, Barjac . . . 061210
Taste of San Antonio, San Antonio . 092586
Tastet, André, Amiens . . . 060827
Tat, Tong, Singapore . . . 109880
Tatabánya Múzeum, Tatabánya . . . 021906
Tatafiore, Mario & Bruno, Napoli . . . 127795
Tatar, Alexander, Toronto . . . 097383
Tatarskij Gosudarstvennyj Muzej Izobrazitelnych Iskusstv, Kazan . . 033252
Tatarskoe Gorodišče - Archeologičeskij i prirodnyj Muzej-zapovednik, Stavropol . . . 033913
Tate, New York . . . 118474
Tate and Antique Shop, Houston . . . 089220
Tate Britain, London . . . 040299
Tate Gallery, Austin . . . 115019
Tate Gallery of British Art, London . 040299
Tate Gallery Publishing, London . . . 135268
Tate Geological Museum, Casper . . 042648
Tate House, Portland . . . 047163
Tate Liverpool, Liverpool . . . 040039
Tate Members, London . . . 054525
Tate Modern, London . . . 040300
Tate Saint Ives, Saint Ives, Cornwall 040922
Tate Shop, London . . . 141906
Tate: The Art Magazine, London . . . 136273
Tatham Art Gallery, Pietermaritzburg . . . 034701
Tatham-Losh, Julian, Andoversford 083303
Tatham-Losh, Julian, Cheltenham . 083932
Tatiana, Singapore . . . 109881
Tatintsian, Gary, New York . . . 118475
Tatistcheff, New York . . . 118476
Tator, Roger, Lyon . . . 099618
Tatort Galerie, Frankfurt am Main . . 102830
Tátrai Galéria, Piliscsaba . . . 105576
Tatranská Galéria, Poprad . . . 034412
Tatsumiya, Sendai . . . 077221
Tatsuno Bijutsukan, Tatsuno . . . 027136
Tatsuuma Archaeological Museum, Nishinomiya . . . 026923
Tatsuya, Higashi-Osaka . . . 077047
Tatsuya, Higashi-Osaka . . . 077048
A Tattered Page, Fort Worth . . . 142416
Tattersall's, Uppingham . . 086988, 131631
Tattershall Station Gallery, Tattershall . . . 114551
Tatti, Steven, New York . . . 118477
Tatton Park, Knutsford . . . 039914
Tattoo Art Museum, San Francisco . 047888
Tattoo Museum, Amsterdam . . . 029235
Tatty Old Bits, Carrum . . . 055640
Tatura Irrigation and Wartime Camps Museum, Tatura . . . 001538
Tatyana Gallery, New York . . . 118478
Tatyana Gallery, Praha . . . 098488
Tatze & Peter Müller, Richard Sylvia, Zofingen . . . 112018
Taub, New York . . . 118479
Tauber, Elisabeth & Kurt, Pegnitz . . 073299, 104593

Tauber, Laurence, Surbiton 086794
Tauberfränkisches Landschaftsmuseum, Tauberbischofsheim 020405
Tauberländer Dorfmuseum, Weikersheim 020713
Tauberová, Zdeňka, České Budějovice 137774
Taubert, Thomas, Düsseldorf 102562
Taubitz, Laatzen 134136
Tauchmann, Alfred, Söchau 057316
Tauchnitz, A., Leipzig 139404
Tauer, Markkleeberg 134195
Tauernstraßen-Museum, Eben im Pongau 001794
Taugeron, Anthony, Nantes 124490
Taunton Antiques Market, Taunton . 086830
Taunton Press, Newton 135469
Taunton Studio Gallery, Taunton . . . 114557
Taunusladchen, Idstein 071609
Taupe, Ingrid, Villach 133167
Taupiri Antiques, Waikato 079297
Taupo District Museum of Art and History, Taupo 030597
Tauranga Museum, Tauranga 030599
Taureilles, Annecy 060899
Taurino José Puente, Madrid 110621
Taurisano, Rio de Janeiro 096650
Tauriska-Galerie, Leopold Kohr Akademie, Neukirchen am Großvenediger . . . 002360
Tauriska Galerie Verlag, Neukirchen am Großvenediger 133123
Taurus Gallery, Oxford 114203
Taurus-Kunstkarten, Brackenheim . 133834
Taurus Verlag Leipzig, Leipzig 134157
Tausch, Stade 073888
Tausch, Dieter, Innsbruck . 095599, 137198
Tauscher, Günther, Salzburg 123458
Tauzy, Georges, Saint-Ouen 067901
Tavanarasi, İstanbul 083158
Tavard, Freddy, Niort 065200
Tavares, Maria Gouveia, Lisboa . . . 080034
Tavastilan Kotiseutumuseo, Mietoinen 009870
Tavecchio, Giorgio, Milano 127698
Tavener Colin, Timsbury 114577
Tavernier, Bruxelles 120746
Tavistock Antiques, Saint Neots . . . 086469
Tawaraya, Nagoya 077156
Tawhiti Museum, Hawera 030515
Tawi-Tawi Ethnological Museum, Mindanao State University, Bongao 031634
Taxameter-Museum, Hamburg 017726
Taxandriamuseum, Turnhout 003821
Taxi Mauve, Auxerre 061107
Taxi Photo, Lima 136018
Taxinge Slott, Nykvarn 036512
Tayler & Fletcher, Bourton-on-the-Water 122427
Taylor, Belfast 112620
Taylor, Dublin 105889
Taylor, London 085732, 113916
Taylor, Montrose 122622
Taylor, Tarragindi 056702
Taylor, B. R., Kelling 084819
Taylor, Brenda, New York 118480
Taylor, Christopher, Auckland 108365
Taylor, David Martin, London 085733
Taylor, Duncan, Bellevue Hill 055470
Taylor, Erin, Minneapolis . 117313, 135397
Taylor, Frederieke, New York 118481
Taylor, Henry, Johannesburg 110062
Taylor, Jardine, London 113917
Taylor, Jenny, Busselton 094333
Taylor, John, Georgensgmünd 125716
Taylor, Jude, Middle Swan 094843
Taylor, Karen, Twickenham 114619
Taylor, Louis, Stoke-on-Trent 122711
Taylor, Martin, Wolverhampton 087214
Taylor, Max, Balgowlah 094197
Taylor, M.C., Bournemouth 083609, 130418
Taylor & Son, Peter, Watford 142143
Taylor, Rankine, Cirencester 084022
Taylor, Robin, Wakefield 086999
Taylor, Véra, Ligueil 063823
Taylor Brown and Sarah Dorsey House, Midland 045856
Taylor & Francis, Stockholm 134971
Taylor-Grady House, Athens 041836
Taylor-Jensen, Palmerston North . . 079218
Taylor & Parry, Cobham 130593
Taylor-Pick, Beverley 112631
Taylor-Smith, Westerham 087101
Taylor-Smith, Westerham 142146
Taylors, Castlebaldwin 105851
Taylor's Coins, Toronto 059300
Taymori Hall, Isfahan 022563
Tayrac, Régine de, Paris 124818
Tayru's, Villa Ballester 055307
Al-Tayyeb, Dubai 112460
Tazl, Wolfgang, Weiz 057349
T.B. Ferguson Home, Watonga 049005
TBA Exhibition Space, Chicago 042883
Tbilisi State Museum of Anthropology and Ethnography, Tbilisi 015415
T.C. Steele State Historic Site, Nashville 046139
TD Art Collection, Dallas 115947
Te, Jie, Beijing 097678
Te Acordás, Hermano, Buenos Aires 136756
Te Amorangi Trust Museum, Rotorua 030590
Te Awamutu Books & Stamps, Waikato 140666
Te Awamutu Museum, Te Awamutu 030600
Te Kauri Lodge Museum, Hamilton . 030510
Te Koop Gevraagd, Alkmaar 077718
Te Kowhai Print Trust, Whangarei . .053928, 108669
Te Kuiti and District Historical Society Museum, Te Kuiti 030601
Te Manawa Art, Palmerston North . 030569
Te Manawa Life Mind, Te Whare Pupuri Taonga o Manawatu, Palmerston North 030570
Te Mei Si Art Gallery, Guangzhou . . 097730
te Neues, Tonbridge 135307
te Neues Book Division, Kempen . . 139314
te Neues Verlag, Kempen 134086
Te Papa, Museum of New Zealand Te Papa Tongarewa, Wellington 030653
Te Toi Mana Maori Gallery, Christchurch 108416
te tuhi - the mark, Auckland 030449
Te Wa The Space Gallery, Wanganui 108605
Te Whare Taonga O Akaroa, Akaroa 030420
Te Whare Whakaaro o Pito-one, Hutt City 030521
Tea and Tattered Pages, Paris 138546
Tea & Antiques, Felixstowe 084397
Tea Museum, Bois-Cheri 028064
Teaberry Press, San Francisco 135495
Teackle Mansion, Princess Anne . . 047231
Teak Sentiments, Singapore 080571
Team of Art, Berlin 102064
Teaparty, J.J., Boston 087849
Teapot World, Conwy 084078
Teardo, Carlo, Milano 075875
Teardo, Carlo, Milano 075876
Teardo, Carlo, Milano 075877
Teardo, Carlo, Milano 140067
Teatermuseet i Hofteatret, København 008989
Teatermuseet i Oslo, Oslo 031110
Teatralnaja galereja, Moskva 109595
Teatralnyj Muzej, Kazanskij akademičeskij Bolšoj dramatičeskij teatr im V.I. Kačalova, Kazan 033253
Teatre-Museu Dalí, Figueres 035194
Teatterimuseo, Helsinki 009581
Teb, Paris 066587
Tebo, Brian, Jacksonville . 089463, 122930
Teboul, Jacqueline, Paris 066588
La Teca, Padova 076115
Tecck an Phiarsaigh, Rosmuck 022853
Tech, Malte, Eutin 102722
Techne, La Science au Service de l'Histoire de l'Art et des Civilisations, Paris . 135730
Techne Galeria, Poznań 109064
Techni-Macedonian Artistic Association Kilkis, Kilkis 021328
Technical Art-Electronic Paint, Dietzenbach 133866
Technichsche Sammlung der Bergakademie Freiberg, TU Bergakademie Freiberg, Freiberg, Sachsen 017225
Technické Muzeum, Muzeum Těšínska, Petřvald u Karviné 008565
Technické Muzeum Tatra, Kopřivnice 008445
Technické Muzeum v Brně, Brno . . 008296
Techniek Museum Delft, Delft 029416
Techniekmuseum Heim, Hengelo, Overijssel 029728
Technik anno dazumal - Museum Kratzmühle, Kinding 018255
Technik Museum Speyer, Speyer . . 020265
Technik- und Verkehrsmuseum, Stade 020280
Technikmuseum Hugo Junkers, Dessau, Anhalt 016685
Technikmuseum Magdeburg, Magdeburg 018777
Technikmuseum U-Boot Wilhelm Bauer, Bremerhaven 016434
Technikon Natal Gallery, Durban . . . 034606
Techniquest, Cardiff 038993
Technische Museum Alte Ziegelei, Ermsleben 017043
Technische Sammlungen der Stadt Dresden, Dresden 016819
Technisches Denkmal Gaswerk, Neustadt, Dosse 019291
Technisches Denkmal Kupferhammer, Thießen bei Dessau 020437
Technisches Denkmal Museumkalkwerk Lengefeld, Zweckverband Sächsisches Industriemuseum, Lengefeld, Erzgebirge 018609
Technisches Denkmal Neue Hütte, Schmalkalden 020054
Technisches Denkmal Neumannmühle, Ottendorf bei Sebnitz 019535
Technisches Denkmal Tobiashammer, Ohrdruf 019461
Technisches Denkmal Turmwindmühle, Ermsleben 017044
Technisches Denkmal Ziegelei Hundisburg, Hundisburg 018031
Technisches Halloren- und Salinenmuseum, Halle, Saale 017673
Technisches Landesmuseum, Schwerin 020152
Technisches Museum, Großröhrsdorf, Oberlausitz 017579
Technisches Museum Alte Wasserkunst, Bautzen 015902
Technisches Museum der Pforzheimer Schmuck- und Uhrenindustrie, Pforzheim 019610
Technisches Museum Frohnauer Hammer, Annaberg-Buchholz 015551
Technisches Museum Holzschleiferei Weigel, Rittersgrün 019853
Technisches Museum Ölmühle, Pockau 019644
Technisches Museum Papiermühle, Zwönitz 021096
Technisches Museum Silberwäsche Antonsthal, Breitenbrunn, Erzgebirge 016405
Technisches Museum Wien, Wien . . 003009
Technisches Schaudenkmal Gießerei Heinrichshütte, Wurzbach 021023
Technology & Conservation, Somerville 136640
Technology Museum of Thessaloniki, Thessaloniki 021502
Technopolis, Mechelen 003638
Technorama, Winterthur 037731
Técnica, Asunción 108802
Tecnireco, Roma 128220
Tecno, Pisa 076245
Tecno-Art-Center, Sankt-Peterburg . 109651
Tecno Art Società Cooperativa, Catania 127280
Tecolote Tiles and Gallery, Albuquerque 114828
Ted, Genova 075512
T.E.D., Le Puy-en-Velay 063701
Tedden, Peter, Düsseldorf 102563
Teddy Bear, Avranches 061148
Teddy Bear Museum, Seogwipo . . . 027541
The Teddy Bear Museum, Stratford-upon-Avon 041144
Teddy Bear Museum of Naples, Naples 046131
Teddy Bear Shop and Museum, Ironbridge 039818
Teddy Bear Trail, San Diego 092686
Teddy Museum Berlin in Hof/Bayern, Hof, Saale 017958
Teddybären Guide Österreich, Wien 135581
Teddyland, Rothenburg ob der Tauber 073594
Teddymuseum, Klingenberg am Main 018282
Teddy's Antiques, Jacksonville 089464
Teddy's Galerie, Luzern . . 111708, 130110
Tedesco, Enrica, Firenze 075412
Ted's Refinishing, Fresno 132087
Tee & Son, R.H.V., Vancouver 059425
Teekengenootschap Pictura, Dordrecht 053904
Tees Archaeology, Hartlepool 039686
Teeterville Pioneer Museum, Delhi . 005340
Teeterville Pioneer Museum, Teeterville 006556
Teetzmann, Peter, Hamburg 071342
Teezer, Cincinnati 088287
Teger, London 085734, 131189
Tegethoff, Ruth, Senden, Westfalen 126797
Tegfryn Art Gallery, Menai Bridge . . 114076
Teglgårdsstrædes Kunsthandel, København 060387, 098586
Teglia, Marco & Luca, Firenze 075413
Tegliucci, Franca Maria, Roma 128221
TEH Gallery, Berlin 102065
Tehkummah Township Museum, Tehkummah 006557
Tehnička knjiga i antikvarijat, Zagreb 137766
Tehnički Muzej, Zagreb 007857
Tehniški Muzej Slovenije, Ljubljana 034495
Tei, Wing, Hong Kong 059697
Teichmühle, Steinwiesen 020313
Teifi Valley Railway, Llandysul 040054
Teignmouth & Son, Pamela, London 085735
Teignmouth and Shaldon Museum, Teignmouth 041194
Teijink, Antwerpen 057740
Teijink, Den Haag 078251
Teine Memorial Museum, Sapporo . 027038
Teishin Sogo Hakubutsukan, Tokyo . 027249
Teiskon Kotiseutumuseo, Tampere . 010137
Teissèdre, Paris 100897
Teissedre, Tucson 120171
Teissèdre, F., Paris 138547
Teissèdre, F., Paris 138548
Teissèdre, Lionel, Murat (Cantal) . . 064847
Teissedre, René François, Paris . . . 100898
Teixeira, Armando Gonçalves, Porto 109400
Teixido, Carlos, Barcelona 110258
Teixido, Carlos, Madrid 110622
Tekakwitha Fine Arts Center, Sisseton 048195
Tekel Sanat Galerisi, İstanbul 112360
Tekiho Memorial Museum of Art, Ogose 026937
Tekirdağ Devlet Güzel Sanatlar Galerisi, Tekirdağ 038183
Tekirdağ Müzesi, Tekirdağ 038184
Tekisui Art Museum, Ashiya 026427
Tekniikan Museo, Helsinki 009582
Teknikens Hus, Luleå 036439
Teknikens och Sjöfartens Hus, Malmö Museer, Malmö 036463
Teknillinen Korkeakoulu, Helsinki . . 049927
Tekniska Kvarnen, Örebro 036524
Tekniska Museet, Stockholm 036676

Tekovské Muzeum v Leviciach, Levice 034371
Tel, Guglielmo, Roma 106637
Tel Aviv Museum of Art, Tel Aviv . . . 023092
Tel Hai Museum, Tel Hai 023096
Tela, Lisboa 129180
La Telaccia, Torino 106706
Telar Artesanía Textil, Bilbao 129446
Telart, Cali 123926
Teleborgs Slott, Växjö Universitet, Växjö 036774
Telechea, Domingo Isaac, São Paulo 123725
Telefonmuseet, Hellerup 008895
Telefonmuseum Hittfelder Bahnhof, Seevetal 020176
Telefonmuseum im Greuterhof, Islikon 037202
Telefoonmuseum, Drouwen 029513
Telegalleria, Sonera 010093
Telemark Kunstnersenter, Porsgrunn 031125
Telemark og Grenland Museum, Skien 031191
Telemuseum, Stockholm 036677
Telephone Historical Collection, Halifax 005584
Telephone Pioneer Communications Museum, San Francisco 047887
Telephone Pioneer Museum, Saint John 006358
Telephone Pioneer Museum of New Mexico, Albuquerque 041623
Teles Atelier de Arte, Antonieta, São Paulo 049771
Telfair Museum of Art, Savannah . . 048031
Teline, Concarneau 062444
Telkamp, Karoline, München 072869
Telkmann, Annette, Lienen 072250
Telkwa Museum, Telkwa 006558
Tell-Museum, Bürglen 036986
Tell Qasile Archaeological Site, Eretz-Israel Museum, Tel Aviv 023093
Teller, Susan, New York 118482
Telles, Claudio Franco Netto, Brasília 096506
Telles, Richard, Los Angeles 116898
Tello, Damascus 083087
Tellogleion Foundation, Thessaloniki 021503
De Telloor, Alkmaar 107620
Telohe, Karin, Bad Honnef 069304
Telorama, Regina 006269
Telstra Museum Brisbane, Clayfield 000924
Tem Sanat Galerisi, İstanbul 112361
Tema Celeste, Milano 135964
Tema Galería de Arte, Buenos Aires 094090
Temecula Valley Museum, Temecula 048515
Temel Sanat Kolleksiyon, İstanbul . 038099
Téméraire, Colombey-les-Deux-Eglises 062430
Temiskaming Art Gallery, Haileybury 005562
Temlett House, Grahamstown 034626
Temme, Karin, Düsseldorf 125550
Temmeksen Kotiseutumuseo, Temmes 010144
Temmes, Mia, Würzburg 105343
Témoin, 0142221620, Paris 100899
Tempantigo Antiguidades, Lisboa . . 080035
Tempe Arts Center, Tempe 048521
Tempe Historical Museum, Tempe . 048522
Tempel Kroonluchterreparaties, Amsterdam 128556
Tempelhoff von, Karlsruhe 103505
Tempelmuseum Frauenberg, Leibnitz 002217
A Tempera, Bordeaux 124146
Tempera, Bruxelles 096257
Tempéra, Cusset 099193
A Tempera, Paris 100900
Tempera, Ville-d'Avray 068884
Tempérance, Bruxelles 058091
Temperance Tavern, Newcomerstown 046446
Temperley, David, Birmingham 130396, 141419
Temperli, Alfred & Sonja, Lachen, Schwyz 111603
Tempesta, Marly, Saint-Ouen 067902
Tempestini, Daniele, Prato 127897
Tempi Antichi, Bologna 075111
Tempietto Rossiniano della Fondazione Rossini, Pesaro 025179
Il Tempio Ritrovato, Napoli 127796
Tempio Voltiano, Como 023948
Temple, Jeanne, Milton Keynes . . . 085993
Temple, Katherine, Denver 132045
Temple, Steven, Toronto 137719
Temple Auctions, Lisburn 122573
Temple Bar Gallery and Studios, Dublin 105890, 134531
Temple de Diane, Aix-les-Bains . . . 060728
Temple des Mille Bouddhas, La Boulaye 012206
Temple Gallery, Birmingham 112658
Temple Gallery, Dunedin 079093
Temple Gallery, London 085736
Temple Gallery, London 113918
Temple Gallery, London 131190
Temple Gallery, Tyler School of Art, Temple University, Philadelphia 046991
Temple Museum of Religious Art, Beachwood 042067
Temple Museum of Religious Art, Cleveland 043002
Temple Newsam House, Leeds Museums and Galleries, Leeds 039961
Temple of Aphrodite, Kouklia 008207
Temple Réformé Mulhouse, Mulhouse 013299
Templecrest Art, Cape Town 110034
Templecrest Art, Oxford 114204
Templeman, Loughton 113999
Templerhaus, Amorbach 015538
Templin Historical Village, Boonah . 000814
Templo Románico de San Martín, Fromista 035201
Templon, Daniel, Paris 100901
Templon, Jean-Claude, Chanteloup 062137
Il Tempo, Verona 077023
O Tempo Antiguidades, Porto Alegre 058526
Tempo Interiores, Porto 080114
Il Tempo Ritrovato, Brescia 075186
Il Tempo Ritrovato, Cagliari 075229
Temporäre Galerie Schloß Neersen, Willich 020899
Temporale, Lugano 136131
Temporary Contemporary, Kraków . 108988
Temporis Matériaux Anciens, Trezioux 068628
Tempos Antigos, Porto . . . 080115, 129202
Les Temps Anciensdas, Châteauneuf-du-Rhône 062204
Temps d'Alice, Nantes 064949
Temps de Choses, Bougival 061676
Le Temps de Vivre, Dijon 062677
Le Temps des Cérises, Charleville-Mézières 138072
Le Temps des Cerises, Honfleur . . . 063171
Le Temps du Livre, Le Marin 140250
Le Temps Jadis, Soisy-sous-Montmorency 068256
Les Temps Mêlés, Albi 060761
Temps Passé, Villefranche-sur-Saône 068903
Le Temps Perdu, Genova 075513
Temps qui Passe, Genolier 082474, 111513
Le Temps Retrouvé, Brest 061780
Le Temps Retrouvé, Champlost . . . 062126
Temps Retrouvé, Isles-sur-Suippe . 063218
Temps Retrouvé, Sceaux 068175
Temptations, Ashtead 083343
Téms Swíya Museum, Sechelt 006436
Temuka Courthouse Museum, Temuka 030602
Ten Boom, Den Haag 078252
Ten Broeck Mansion, Albany 041602
Ten Duinen 1138, Koksijde 003554
Ten in One Gallery, New York 118483
Ténat, René, Mirande 064562
Tenbury and District Museum, Tenbury Wells 041196
Tenby Museum and Art Gallery, Tenby 041197
Tenchi Shobo, Osaka 140174
Tenchini, Giacomo, Brescia 075187
Il Tendaggista, Genova 075514
Tendance Temps Danse, Paris 066589
Tendances, Paris 100902
Tendances-Mikado, Luxembourg . . 107413
Tender Buttons, New York 091284
Tendille, Patrick, Bonson 124109
Tenement House, Glasgow 039578
Tenenbaum, Henri, Saint-Ouen 067903
Tengalerie.ch, Adligenswil 111108
Tengyu, Suita 140180
Tenholan Kotiseutumuseo, Tenala . . 010145
Teniers, Oostende 096404
Tenino Depot Museum, Tenino 048527
Tenmon Museum of Art, Hirakata . . 026522
Tennants, Harrogate 122538
Tennants, Leyburn 122569
Tennengauer Kunstkreis e.V, Hallein 052599
Tennent Art Foundation Gallery, Honolulu 044609
Tennessee Antique Mall, Nashville . 090492
Tennessee Art League, Nashville . . 055065
Tennessee Art League Gallery, Nashville 117374
Tennessee Arts Report, Nashville . . 136641
Tennessee Association of Museums, Piney Flats 055066
Tennessee Central Railway Museum, Nashville 046152
Tennessee Historical Society Museum, Nashville 046153
Tennessee State Museum, Nashville 046154
Tennessee Valley Art Association, Tuscumbia 048670
Tennessee Valley Art Association, Tuscumbia 055067
Tennessee Valley Railroad Museum, Chattanooga 042783
Tennismuseum Gasber, Oberhausen, Rheinland 019392
Tennyson's Bookshop, Hawkes Bay 140631
Tennyson's Bookshop, Hawkes Bay 140632
Tenpyo, Nara 106945
Tenpyodo, Kyoto 077130
Tenri Gallery, Tokyo 027250
Tenri University Sankokan Museum, Tenri 027138
Tenschert, Heribert, Rotthalmünster 139700
Tenschert, Klaus, Hirschaid 125942
Tenshodo, Aki, Hiroshima 077065
Tent-Centrum Beeldende Kunst, Rotterdam 108211
La Tentation du Mandarin, Paris . . . 066590
Tentei, Tokyo 107121
Tenterden and District Museum, Tenterden 041201
Tenterden Antiques and Silver Vaults, Tenterden 086845
Tenterfield Centenary Cottage, Tenterfield 001540
Tentoonstellingsruimte 't Oute Hus, Burgh-Haamstede 029375
Tentoonstellingzaal Hessenhuis, Antwerpen 003192
Teo Leo, Paris 066591
Teo Otto-Gedenkraum, Wien 003010
Teodoro P. Resurreccion Memorial Museum, Ilocos Museum of Music and Fine Arts, Luna 031692
Teodra Art Gallery, Toronto 097384
Teollisuustyöväen Asuntomuseo, Imatra 009609
Tepco Denryokukan, Tokyo 027251
Tepes, Zoran, Beograd 109724
Tepia, Kikai Sangyo Kinenkan, Tokyo 027252
Teplahis, Atlanta 114933
Teplitz-Schönauer Heimatmuseum, Frankfurt am Main 017200
Tepper, New York 091285, 123020
Tepper, Burkhardt, Hamburg 071343, 139216
Tepper & Takayama, Boston 115234
Teppich und Heimatmuseum, Museum Schloß Voigtsberg, Oelsnitz, Erzgebirge 019442
Tequila Bookworm, Toronto 137720
Ter, Daniel, Etoile-sur-Rhône 062818
Tér Galéria, Budapest 105547
Teranga, Kraków 108989
Terbrüggen, Wehr 074294
Tercelin de Joigny, Benoît, Mons . . 058346
Tercera Gallery, San Francisco 119811
Tere Pastoriza, Miami 117147
Terebeck, Coesfeld 102324
Terenzi, Luciana, Roma 076701
Teresa Antiques, Madrid 081397
Teresia ja Rafael Lönnströmin kotimuseo, Rauma 010027
Tereza Antiguidades, Belo Horizonte 058452
Teriade Museum, Mytilini 021398
Teri's Authentic Restoration, Los Angeles 132282
Terjärvs Hembygdsgård, Teerijärvi . 010143
Terlinden, Dendermonde . 058155, 120752
Terme, Jean-Louis, Montpellier . . . 064757
Terme Saint-Eloi, Montauroux 064646
Természettudományi Múzeum, Aggetelek 021616
Terminal 2, Værløse 060407
Ternopil's'kyj Oblasnyj Chudožij Muzej, Ternopil' 038402
Ternopil's'kyj Oblasnyj Krajeznavčyj Muzej, Ternopil' 038403
TerpenTijn, Dordrecht 107985
Terpstra, Joanna, Brushgrove 094320
Terra, Arnhem 107860
Terra, Delft 107894
Terra, Donec'k 112387
Terra, Winterthur 112002
Terra À Vista, Lagos 109257
Terra Art Gallery, Drummoyne 094490
Terra Cotta, Las Vegas 089614
Terra Cotta, Saint-Ouen 067904
Terra dei Volsci Annali, Roma 135965
Terra Incognita, Praha 137846
Terra Incognita Antique Maps, Calgary 137627
Terra Museum of American Art, Chicago 042884
Terra Mystica, Bad Bleiberg 001710
Terra Nova Gallery, Kuranda 094718
Terra Promessa, Bergen op Zoom . . 107872
Terra Publishing House, Moskva . . . 134880
Terra Sancta Museum, Nazareth . . . 023038
Terra-Vinea, Portel-des-Corbières . 013925
Terrace Antiques, Belfast . 083483, 130368
Terrace Antiques, London 085737
Terrace Antiques, South Fremantle . 056607
Terrace Book Shop, Paddington, Queensland 137041
Terrace Gallery, Harewood 039670
The Terrace Gallery, Loxton 094747
Terrace Gallery, Orlando 046721
Terrace Glory Box, Kiama 056050
Terrace Hill Historic Site and Governor's Mansion, Des Moines 043431
Terrace House Factory, Ultimo 056761
Terracota, Madrid 129699
Terracotta Warriors Museum, Dorchester 039260
Terrada, Ada, Cazilhac 062046
Terrades, Gabriel, Paris 100903
Terrahe, Peter, München 139550
Terrail, Paris 133680
Terrain Gallery, New York 046411
Terrain Gallery, New York 118484
Terralong Gallery, Kiama 094698
Terrapin, New York 118485
Terrasi, Jolanda, Palermo 127841
Terravechia Antigüedades, Don Torcuato 123167
Terre d'Arte, Catania 075263
Terre de Chine, Paris 100904

Terre de Sienne, Beirut .. 077418, 128455
Terre de Sienne, Paris 124819
Terre del Fuoco, Bologna 135966
Terre des Arts, Paris 100905, 133681
Terre d'Ivoire, Tours 068607
Terre et Feu, Paris 066592
Terre et Toiles, Alès 098816
Terre Rare, Bologna 105978
Terrebonne Museum, Houma 044633
Terreiro, Ana Paula, Lisboa 080036
Terreiro, Ana Paula, Lisboa 080037
Terrel, Calgary 123754
Terres, La Ciotat 099391
Terres Anciennes Antiquités, Montpellier 099764
Terres Contemporaines, Moret-sur-Loing 099771
Terres d'Ailleurs, Les Rosiers-sur-Loire 063780
Terres d'Ailleurs, Paris 066593
Terres d'Ailleurs, Toulouse 124997
Terres d'Autrefois, Beire-le-Châtel . 061323
Terres Sauvages, Chalons-en-Champagne 062097
Terret, Stéphane, Bordeaux 124147
Terrier, Christian, Grenoble 063075
Terrill, Suzanna, Cincinnati 115666
Territoires du Jazz, Marciac 012892
Territorial Capital-Lane Museum, Lecompton 045227
Territorial Statehouse State Museum, Fillmore 043843
Territory Colours, Darwin 094462
Territory Town USA, Old West Museum, Okemah 046640
Terry's Antiques, Manila 079567
Tersløsegaard, Dianalund 008830
Tertia, Sankt-Peterburg 080337
Teruz, Rogerio A., Rio de Janeiro .. 096651
Tervajärven Talomuseo, Sotkamo .. 010097
Tervakanava, Kajaani 009653
Terwagne, Liège 058328
Terwagne, Liège 123657
Terwen, Dr. Pier A., Leiden 128746
Terwilliger Museum, Waterloo 048990
Terzo Millennio, Milano 106330
Terzo Occhio, Bologna 135967
Teschner, Volker, Kromsdorf 126153
Tesi, Pierre, Saint-Ouen 101190
Tesio Gallery, Milano 106331
Teske, U., Echternacherbrück 070500
Teson, Singapore 080572
Tesori dal Tempo, Verona 093795
Tesoro del Duomo, Enna 024050
Tesoro del Duomo, Messina 024683
Tesoro del Duomo, Milano 024737
Tesoro del Duomo, Monreale 024797
Tesoro del Duomo, Vigevano 026324
Tesoro della Cattedrale, Palermo .. 025096
Tesoro della Cattedrale, Rimini 025436
Tesoro della Chiesa di San Pietro, Calascibetta 023574
Tesoro della Santa Maria della Scala, Chieri 023857
Tesoro di Santa Maria La Stella, Militello in Val di Catania 024743
Tesoros Trading, Austin 115020
Tesouro-Museu da Sé de Braga, Braga 032585
Tess, Pruszków 109067
Tessa, Kościerzyna 079612
Tessai Museum, Takaraduka 027113
Tessaido, Kyoto 077131
Tessaido, Kyoto 077132
Tessandra, Den Haag 107955
Tessedik Sámuel Múzeum, Szarvas 021855
Tesser, London 113919
Tessier, Marc, Saint-Ouen 067905
Tessiers, London 085738, 131191
Tessin, Heinz, Quickborn 139670
Tesson, Robert, Paris 066594
Tesson, Serge, Parthenay 121219
Test, Warszawa 109199
Testa, Stefano, Torino 128364
Testard-Letêtu, Aigues-Mortes 098776
Testard-Letêtu, Nîmes 099870
Testnevelési és Sportmúzeum, Budapest 021696
Testoni, Piero, Verona 106805
Testsmart, Birmingham 142241
Teşvikiye Sanat Galerisi, İstanbul .. 112362
Tetbury Antique Dealers Association, Tetbury 054526
Tetbury Gallery, Tetbury .. 086868, 114564
Tetbury Old Books, Tetbury 142112
Tetbury Police Museum, Tetbury ... 041202
Tételin, Max, Rouen 067301, 124885
Tetley's Brewery Wharf, Leeds 039962
Tettamanti, Massimo, Firenze 075414
Il Tetto 87, Roma 106638
Teubner, Dr. Manfred, Nordhausen . 139598
Teubner, Ole, Otterwisch 126605
Teuchler, M., Leipzig 126199
Teulère, Michel, Annecy 120900
Teulings, Den Haag 078253
Teulon and District Museum, Teulon 006561
Teumer, Dortmund 138984
Teumer, I., Miltenberg 072546
Teumer, Michael, Dortmund 070296
Teunissen, Eindhoven 078354
Teunissen, H.A.J., Nijmegen 128788
Teutloff, Lutz, Bielefeld 102131
Teutloff, Lutz, Bielefeld 102132
Teutoburger Münzauktion, Borgholzhausen 121352
Teutopolis Monastery Museum, Teutopolis 048537
Teutschbein, G., Frankfurt am Main 070796
Teuvan Museo, Teuva 010146
Tevel, Montréal 097085
Teviot District Museum, Roxburgh . 030591
Tew, Timothy, Atlanta 114934
Tewari-Bergert, Marianne, Zürich .. 112189
Tewkesbury Antique Centre, Tewkesbury 086876, 142113
Tewkesbury Museum, Tewkesbury . 041205
Texacola Collectables, San Antonio 092587
Texan, Joe, Houston 089221
Texan Art Schools, Auckland 050571, 108366
Texana Museum, Edna 043616
Texarkana Museums System, Texarkana 048539
Texas Air Museum, Rio Hondo 047441
Texas Art Galleries, Dallas 115948
Texas Association of Museums, Austin 055068
Texas Auction Academy, Frisco ... 051363
Texas Baptist Historical Center Museum, Brenham 042397
Texas Choice, San Antonio 119459
Texas City Museum, Texas City ... 048540
Texas Energy Museum, Beaumont . 042089
Texas Forestry Museum, Lufkin ... 045520
Texas Furniture, San Antonio 132829
Texas Gallery, Houston 116414
Texas Gas Collectables, Fort Worth . 088888
Texas Governor's Mansion, Austin . 041935
Texas Heritage Museum, Hillsboro . 044546
Texas Historical Museum, Texas ... 001544
Texas International Fine Art Fair, Houston 094038
Texas Junk Company, Houston 089222
Texas Maritime Museum, Rockport 047511
Texas Memorial Museum of Science and History, Austin 041936
Texas Military Forces Museum, Austin 041937
Texas Music Museum, Austin 041938
Texas Pharmacy Museum, Amarillo 041681
Texas Ranger Hall of Fame and Museum, Waco 048818
Texas Seaport Museum, Galveston . 044136
Texas Sports Hall of Fame, Waco .. 048819
Texas Woman's University Art Galleries, Denton 043395
Texograph, Southport 114467
Text Traders, Brisbane 136824
Text und Töne, Hamburg 139217
Text und Töne, Hamburg 139218
Texte zur Kunst, Berlin 135823
Textil-Forum-Service, Hannover ... 134043
Textil- und Heimatmuseum, Stiftung Paul Aebi-Gaissmaier, Sennwald 037554
Textil- und Rennsportmuseum, Hohenstein-Ernstthal 017980
Textilarkivet Västernorrland, Sollefteå 036600
Textildruckmuseum Mittelweiherburg, Hard, Vorarlberg 002017
Textile Conservancy Company, Tenterden 131580
Textile Conservation, Banwell 130331
Textile Conservation Centre, East Molesey 054527
Textile Conservation Centre, University of Southampton, Winchester 041407
Textile Conservation Workshop, Harbury 050818
Textile Museum, Kuala Lumpur ... 027981
The Textile Museum, Washington .. 048948
Textile Restoration, Chicago 131918
Textile Restoration Studio, Altrincham 130298
Textilforum, Hannover 135824
Textilforum, Herning 008907
Textilkonservering, Stockholm 129876
Textilkunst, Alfeld, Leine 135825
Textilmaschinenmuseum Neuthal, Bäretswil 036874
Textilmuseet, Borås 036226
Textilmuseet Högbo, Sandviken ... 036564
Textilmuseum, Hauptwil 037179
Textilmuseum, Neumünster 019254
Textilmuseum, Sankt Gallen 037499
Textilmuseum Die Scheune, Spinnen/Weben + Kunst, Nettetal 019207
Textilmuseum Firma Franz Pischl, Telfs 002736
Textilmuseum im Jesuitenkolleg, Mindelheim 018949
Textilmuseum Max Berk im Kurpfälzischen Museum der Stadt Heidelberg, Heidelberg 017837
Textilmúzeum, Budapest 021697
Textilní Muzeum TIBA, Česká Skalice 008315
Texture Antiques, Austin 087615
Textures Design, Québec 097165
Teylers Museum, Haarlem 029660
Teysen's Woodland Indian Museum, Mackinaw City 045557
Teyssandier, Auxerre 061108
Teyssen, Jürgen, Bremerhaven ... 102265
Teyssendier de la Serve Luc, Fleurance 138090
T.F. Chen Cultural Center, New York 046412
TG Art, Wokingham 114721
Tgeasa Rustica, Lantsch 082526
Thabuis, Jean-Paul, La Roche-sur-Foron 063411
Thackeray Gallery, London 113920
Thackray Museum, Leeds 039963
Thad, Chicago 115562
Thaddeus, Portland 142811
Thakeham, Pulborough .. 086318, 131400
Thalassa - Aghia Napa Municipal Museum, Pierides Foundation, Aghia Napa . 008203
Thaler, Schlüchtern 073704
Thaler, Claudia, Salzburg 123459
Thaler, Friedrich, Hart 123378
Thaler, Friedrich, Salzburg 123460
Thaler, Werner, Basel 111226, 129935
Thaler Keramikmuseum und Maria-Felchin-Sammlung, Matzendorf 037317
Thames Art Gallery, Chatham, Ontario 005261
Thames Auction House, Waikato .. 121839
Thames & Hudson, London 135269
Thames & Hudson, New York 135465
Thames Museum, Newport 046467
Thames Oriental Rug Company, Henley-on-Thames 084665, 130787
Thames Police Museum, London .. 040301
Thames School of Mines and Mineralogical Museum, Thames 030603
Thames Valley Antiques, Atlanta ... 087535
Thames Valley Art Dealers' Association, Dorchester-on-Thames 054528
Thames Valley Museum School, Burgessville 005163
Thameside Aviation Museum, East Tilbury 039358
Thamesware, London 113921
Thamshavnbanen, Orkla Industrimuseum, Løkken Verk 030992
Than, Mai, Ha Noi 120487
Thanet Antiques, Ramsgate 086328
Thang, Long, Ha Noi 120488
Thanhardt-Burger, Chicago 115563
Thanjavur Art Gallery, Thanjavur ... 022348
Thanka, Frankfurt am Main 102831
Thanks for the Memories, West Hollywood 093513
Thar Art Gallery, Bangalore 074784, 105615
That About Covers it, San Francisco 132912
That and This, Victoria Park 056780
That Antique Place, Houston 089223, 132142
That Gypsy Woman, Daylesford ... 055743
Thavibu Gallery, Bangkok 112243
Thaw & Co., E.V., New York 118486
The Collection, Estepona 081102
The Dalles Art Association, The Dalles 055069
Thea G. Korver Visual Art Center, Northwestern College, Orange City 046706
Theale Fireplaces, Theale 131590
Theater Museum, Amsterdam 029236
Theatergalerie, Wien 057565
Theatergeschichtliche Sammlung und Hebbel-Sammlung, Kiel 018252
Theatermuseum der Landeshauptstadt, Dumont-Lindemann-Archiv, Düsseldorf 016848
Theatermuseum Hannover, Hannover 017770
Theatermuseum in der Reithalle, Meininger Museen, Meiningen 018886
Theaterstübli, Basel 082175
Theaterwissenschaftliche Sammlung, Universität zu Köln, Köln 018340
Theatre and Fine Arts Department, Pace University, New York 051835
Theatre Antiques, Minneapolis 090398
The Theatre Antiques Center, Framlingham 084436, 130718
Théâtre d'Automates-Le Village Enchanté, Bellefontaine (Manche) 010740
Theatre Museum, Victoria and Albert Museum, London 040302
Thébaud, Concarneau 062445
Thébaud, Nantes 064950
Théberge, Claude, Montréal 097086
Thee Metropolitan Gallery, Detroit . 088776
De Theefabriek, Houwerzijl 029780
Theel, T., Berlin 125306
Theelen, Edda, Bad Kreuznach 069319
Theeuwes, J.C.A.M., Oisterwijk ... 128794
Theile, Johanna M., Santiago de Chile 123885
Theilmann, Klaus, Pfaffenhofen an der Ilm 073312
Theimer, François, Toucy 133702
Thein, F., Preußisch Oldendorf 073374
Theis, Heinz-Joachim, Berlin 102066
Theise, Sascha, Koblenz 071896
Theisen, Ursula, Köln 103724
Theiss, Saint Louis 132755
Theiss, Hartmut, Darmstadt 070189
Theiss, Kellie Rae, Minneapolis ... 117314
Theiss, Konrad, Stuttgart 134423
Theißen, E., Aachen 101529
Theißen, Helga Maria, Aachen 101530
Theleman, Ludwig, Weimar, Thüringen 139836
Thelen, Bonn 069946
Thelen, Gertrud, Baden-Baden 138711
Thelen, Ingrid, Bonn 069947

Thellier, Paris 100906, 124820
Thelma Miles Museum, Matheson . 005843
Thélot, Fontenay-le-Comte 121006
Thelow, Jörg, Wedemark 126975
Themapark Openluchtmuseum De Spitkeet, Harkema 029673
Themes and Variations, London . . . 085739
Themes Antiquaire, Saint-Ouen . . . 067906
Themes & Variations, London 113922
Then Again, Gosford 055905
Then & Now, Manawatu 079144
Theng, Petra, Memmingen 072515
Theo-Steinbrenner-Turm-Museum, Sommerach 020247
Theo Swagemakers Museum, Haarlem 029661
Theo Thijssen Museum, Amsterdam 029237
Theodor-Mommsen-Gedächtnisstätte, Garding 017324
Theodor-Storm-Haus, Husum, Nordsee 018038
Theodor-Zink-Museum und Wadgasserhof, Kaiserslautern 018136
Théodore, Biarritz 061478
Theodore Roosevelt Birthplace, New York 046413
Theodore Roosevelt Inaugural National Historic Site, Buffalo 042506
Theodosiou, Theod., Thessaloniki . . 105460
Theomaria Gallery, Lemesos 098319
Theomin Gallery, Olveston Dunedin's Historic Home, Dunedin 030492
Theophilos Kairis Museum, Andros . 021135
Theotokopoulos, Madrid 081398
Ther, Anne-Gabriele, Vierhöfen 074207, 126949
Thereses Kunstsalong, Oslo 108739
Theresienthaler Glasmuseum, Zwiesel 021091
Theriault, Annapolis 122795
Therien & Co., San Francisco 092896
Therien & Co., West Hollywood . . . 093514
Therisso Museum of Eleftherios Venizelos, Chania 021230
Thermen-Museum Juliomagus, Schleitheim 037529
Thermenmuseum, Heerlen 029698
Thermostat Gallery, Manawatu 108492
Théron, Didier, Nogent-sur-Marne .065212, 124527
Thérond, Jean-Pierre, Montpellier . 064758
Théry, Christophe, Le Mee-sur-Seine 063666
Thery, Jocelyne, Cleguer 062322
Thesauros, Messina 075569
Thesaurus, Saint Helier 142038
Thesing, M., Borken, Westfalen . . . 069960
Thesing, Michael, Raesfeld 073407
Thesmar, François, Paris 066595
Thessaloniki Museum for the Macedonian Struggle, Thessaloniki 021504
Theßeling, Ochtrup 104519
Theta-Museet, Bergen 030772
Thetford Historical Society Museum, Thetford 048545
Theuermann, Georg, Wien 057566
Theuermann, Valentin, Wien 057567
Theunissen, L., Heerlen 078507
Theunissen, O., Bruxelles 058092
Thévenaz, Willy, Le Locle 082584
Thévenod, Léon, La Tour 063452
Thézan, Nice 065152
Thiam, Metz 099719
Thian Hwa, Ang, Singapore 109882
Thibaudière Brocante, Lyon 064187
Thibault, G., Tours 068608
Thibault de la Châtre, Paris 066596
Thibaut, Mons 058347
Thiboumery, Jean-Yves, Rennes (Ille-et-Vilaine) 067121
Thiebaud, Paul, San Francisco 119812
Thiébaut, Bertrand, Paris 066597
Thieblemont, Gabriel, Chaumont (Haute-Marne) 062251
Thiede, Berlin 102067
Thiel, J., Knokke-Heist 058253
Thiel, Karl, Wiener Neustadt 137384
Thiel, L., Schleiden 073694
Thiele, Markus, Linz 095674
Thiele, Ulrich, Bad Lippspringe 069324
Thiele & Schwarz, Kassel 134083
Thielen, H., Sankt Ingbert 073669
Thielens, Luc, Gent 058208
Thielitz, A., Rantum 073416
Thielmann, Siegfried, Wuppertal . . 127052
Thielsch, Gottfried, Görlitz 125737
Thielsch, Gottfried, Markersdorf bei Görlitz 126291
Thielsen, London 096960
Thielska Galleriet, Stockholm 036678
Thieme, Axel, Darmstadt 102349
Thieme, Nicoline, Leipzig 139405
Thiénot, Jacqueline, Saint-Tropez . 068027
Thieroff, Annett, Dresden 070332
Thierry, B., Paris 066598
Thierry, Elisabeth, Domfront 062704
Thierry, Elisabeth, Domfront 062705
Thierry, Laurent, Paris 066599
Thierry-Lannon et Associés, Brest . 120952
Thierry Winsall, Paris 066600
Thiersch, Brigitte, Weimar, Thüringen 074312
Thierstein, Daniel, Bern 141231
Thierstein, Daniel, Biel 141233
Thiery, Elisabeth Maria, Wien 057568
Thies, Andreas, Nürtingen 121568
Thiesse, Jean-Pierre, Les Forges . . 063764
Thiessen, Elke, Kandern 125992
Thiessen, N., Düren 102464
Thijs, André, Beveren 123565
Thil, Stéphane, Épernay 062784
Thimbleby & Shorland, Reading . . . 122664
Thimblena's Thimbles, Dallas 088616
Thingbaek Kalkminer Bundgaards Museum, Skørping 009106
Things-Antiques, Los Angeles 089923
Things From the Past, San Antonio . 092588
Things II, Denver 088742
Things Jamaican, Montego Bay . . . 106827
Things Japanese, New York 091286
Things To Do, Manama 057648
Think Modern, Oakland 091441
Th'ink Tank, Denver 116061
Thinkers Bookshop, Tweed Heads South 137118
Thinktank, The Museum of Science and Discovery, Birmingham 038739
Thiollière, Philippe, Saint-Étienne . . 124900
Thion, François, Evreux 121003
Third Avenue Antiques, Mount Lawley 056291
Third Avenue Gallery, Vancouver . . 097539
Third Canyon Gallery, Denver 116062
Third Cavalry Museum, Fort Carson 043899
Third Eye, San Diego 119558
Third Floor Antiques, San Diego . . . 092687
Third Street Gallery, Philadelphia . . 118844
Third Street Gallery, Seattle 120002
Third Text, Third World Perspectives on Contemporary Art and Culture, London 136274
Third World Ethnic Books, Los Angeles 142519
Thiriassa, Los Angeles 116899
Thirion, D., Bruxelles 058093
Thirion, Jean-Luc, Bordeaux 124148
Thiriot, Alain, Saint-Ouen 067907
Thirkill Antiques, Leyburn 084987
Thirlestane Castle, Lauder 039936
Thirroul Antique Centre, Thirroul . . . 056707
Thirsk Museum, Thirsk 041211
Thirst Shop, Larnaka 059951
Thirteen Hundred, Cleveland 115746
Thirteenth Floor Gallery, Chicago . . 115564
Thirty 60, Dallas 088617
Thirty Victoria Street, Potts Point . .056485, 095103
This and That, Abu Dhabi 083179
This and That, Hermanville-sur-Mer 063150
This and That, Providence 092050
This Century Art Gallery, Williamsburg 049184
This is Art, Nottingham 114180
This is the Place Heritage Park, Salt Lake City 047776
This Old House Antiques, Albuquerque 087428
This Old Warehouse, Jacksonville . 089465
This, That and the Other, New York . 091287
Thistle Antique, Houston 089224
Thistle Antiques, Aberdeen 083241
Thistle Antiques, Hamilton 058393
Thistle Books, Glasgow 141625
Thistlethwaite, E., Settle 086539
Tho, Seoul 107296
Thoemmes, Bristol 141458
Thöni, Franz, Chur 111363
Thörnblom, Christina, Stockholm . . 129877
Tholozé, Paris 100907
Thoma, Pähl 104579
Thoma, Hans, Karlsruhe 134079
Thoma, Peter, Köln 103725
Thoman, Elisabeth & Klaus, Innsbruck 095600
Thomas, Bruxelles 137471
Thomas, Milwaukee 132372
Thomas, New York 118487
Thomas, Paris 066601
Thomas, Waikato 108597
Thomas, Andrew, Boston 115235
Thomas, Andrew, Stamford 086690
Thomas, Barry, Auckland 078985
Thomas, Barry, Minneapolis 117315
Thomas, C., Gent 058209
Thomas, C.E., Stockholm 141177
Thomas, Dale, Artarmon 094176
Thomas, Dominique, Pont-à-Mousson 066910
Thomas, Frédérique, Saubrigues . . 124927
Thomas, Hartmut, Zittau 074572
Thomas, Hugh A., New York 118488
Thomas, I.S., Paris 100908
Thomas, Jeffrey, San Francisco . . . 142966
Thomas, Marie-Josée & Claude, Perpignan 066761
Thomas, Olaf, Hamburg 071344
Thomas, Patrick, Dorking . 084204, 130652
Thomas, Raimund, München 104330
Thomas, Richard, San Francisco . . 119813
Thomas, Richard C ., New Orleans . 117522
Thomas, Simone, Paris 138549
Thomas, Tamara B., Los Angeles . . 116900
Thomas & Alexander, Paddington, Queensland 056434
Thomas Bewick's Birthplace, Mickley 040455
Thomas-Bourgneuf, Jean-Paul, Cesson-Sévigné 062062
Thomas Carlyle's Birthplace, Ecclefechan 039374
Thomas Center Galleries, Gainesville 044108
Peter Thomas & Gaby Churchill, Ottawa 123802
Thomas Clarke House-Princeton Battlefield, Princeton 047243
Thomas-Dubarry, Arcachon 098857
Thomas E. McMillan Museum, Brewton 042402
Thomas Edison Birthplace Museum, Milan 045861
Thomas Edison House, Louisville . . 045499
Thomas-Foreman Home, Muskogee 046111
Thomas Foster Memorial Temple, Uxbridge 006676
Thomas Handforth Gallery, Tacoma 048470
Thomas Haney House, Maple Ridge 005834
Thomas Hart Benton Home and Studio, Kansas City 044930
Thomas-Hines, Richmond 092116
Thomas & Hirsch, New York 118489
Thomas J. Boyd Museum, Wytheville 049324
Thomas J. Walsh Art Gallery and Regina A. Quick Center for the Arts, Fairfield University, Fairfield 043787
Thomas Jefferson House Monticello, Charlottesville 042769
Thomas K. Lang Gallery, Webster University, Wien 003011
Thomas L. Kane Memorial Chapel, Kane 044907
Thomas-Mann-Archiv, Zürich 037804
Thomas McCulloch Museum, Dalhousie University, Halifax 005585
Thomas-Müntzer-Gedenkstätte, Heldrungen 017862
Thomas Muir Museum, Bishopbriggs 038746
Thomas Newcomen Museum, Exton 043777
Thomas P. Adams, Blackrock 121657
Thomas P. Kennard House, Lincoln . 045312
Thomas Price House, Woodruff . . . 049287
Thomas Sappington House Museum, Crestwood 043218
Thomas-Scheler, Paris 138550
Thomas T. Taber Museum, Williamsport 049185
Thomas Warne Historical Museum, Old Bridge Township 046661
Thomas Wolfe Memorial, Asheville . 041798
Thomassen, Göteborg 110932
Thomasset, Jean-Pierre, L'Isle-sur-la-Sorgue 063961
Thomasson, Gérard, Grenoble 124254
Thomaston Historical Museum, Thomaston 048547
Thomasville Cultural Center, Thomasville 048550
Thome, New York 091288
Thome, New York 132541
Thome, H., Königsfeld im Schwarzwald 072034
Thomi, Albert, Basel 141217
Thomine Demazures Alban, Neuilly-sur-Seine 064994
Thomire, Paris 066602
Thompson, Aldeburgh 130287
Thompson, Atlanta 114935
Thompson, Atlanta 114936
Thompson, Charlotte 087984, 122837
Thompson, Fort Worth 142417
Thompson, Ipswich 084805
Thompson, Louisville 090033
Thompson, Windsor, New South Wales 056827
Thompson, Anthony, London 113923
Thompson, Bob & Pam, Charlotte . . 122838
Thompson, Brad, New Orleans 117523
Thompson, Carole, Memphis 117005
Thompson, Damian, Yamanto 095442
Thompson, Gary, Salt Lake City . . . 092466
Thompson, James, Kirkby Lonsdale 122557
Thompson, John, Knaresborough . . 084884
Thompson, John, Tunbridge Wells . 086953
Thompson, John W., Sydney 123315
Thompson, Michael, Los Angeles . . 142520
Thompson, O.O. & Jane, Charlotte . 087985
Thompson's, London 113924
Thompson's Gallery, Aldeburgh . . . 112491
Thomrom, Paris 066603
Thomsen, Erik, Bensheim 069525
Thomsen, Inge, Siegen 104902
Thomsen, Jim & James, Oakland . . 132575
Thomsen, Leif, København 124032
Thomson, Hannover 125881
Thomson, C., New York 118490
Thomson, Graeme, Auckland 078986
Thomson, Percy, Taranaki 108572
Thomson Bagley, Whangarei 121843
Thomson & Burrows, Salt Lake City 092467
Thomson, Roddick & Laurie, Annan 122389
Thomson, Roddick & Medcalf, Carlisle 122450
Thomson, Roddick & Medcalf, Dumfries 122493
Thomson, Roddick & Medcalf, Edinburgh 122501

Thomson's, Saint Helier 086454
Thomüller, Josef, Wuppertal 074544
Thon, Matthias, Ahlen . . . 121293, 138672
Thonet & Karolinsky, Wien 057569
Thonet-Museum, Friedberg 001870
Thong Nhat Palace, Ho Chi Minh City 049542
Thor, Long Beach 089660
Thoral, Pierre, Lyon 064188
Thorburn Gallery, Dobwalls 039245
The Thoreau Institute at Walden Woods, Lincoln 045300
Le Thorel, Jocelyne, Ploisy 066861
Thorens, Daniel Blaise, Basel 111227
Thorma János Múzeum, Kiskunhalas 021771
Thorn, David J., Budleigh Salterton 083778
Thornbury and District Museum, Thornbury, Gloucestershire 041212
Thornbury Antiques, Thornbury, Gloucestershire 086883
Thornby Cottage Antiques, Exton . . 055812
Thorndon Antiques, Wellington 079352
Thorne-Sagendorph Art Gallery, Keene State College, Keene 044947
Thorney Heritage Centre, Thorney . 041213
Thornhill, London 085740, 131192
Thornhill Gallery, Avila College, Kansas City 044931
Thornhill Historic Site and 19th Century Village, Chesterfield 042807
Thornquest Gallery, Southport 095216
Thornthwaite Galleries, Thornthwaite 114571
Thornton, Auckland 121814
Thornton, Hamilton 108461
Thornton, Andy, Halifax 084560
Thornton, Diane, York 114756
Thornton, John, London 141907
Thornton, Joseph, Windermere . . . 087179
Thornton, J.W., Bowness-on-Windermere 083619
Thornton, Lynne, Paris 066604
Thornton Tomasetti, Philadelphia . . 118845
Thornton W. Burgess Museum, Sandwich 047935
Thorntons, Harrogate 084590
Thornwood, Houston 116415
Thornwood Auctions, Epping 122503
Thorp &Bros., New York 132542
Thorp, Edward, New York 118491
Thorp, P.A. Lee, Cape Town 080687
Thorp, Thomas, Guildford 141638
Thorp, Thomas, Saint Albans 142031
Thorpe Water Mill, Bothwell 000819
Thorpold, Frank R., Johannesburg . 080718
Thorsens, Grimstad 140693
Thorsheim, M.J., Minneapolis 117316
Thorvaldsens Museum, København 008990
Thorvaldsens Samlingen på Nysø, Præstø 009062
Those were the Days, Cambridge . . 083850
Those Were the Days, Uddingston . 114621
Thosh, Cluj-Napoca 109452
Thost, Hans-Joachim, Lemgrabe . . 126206
Thoth, Bussum 134804
Thoumyre, François, Conches-en-Ouche 062447, 099169
Thoumyre, Perrine, Oppède 124530
Thousand Islands Craft School, Clayton 051151
Thousand Islands Museum of Clayton, Clayton 042964
Thouvenot, Robert, Haroué 063130
Thrai Kao, Battani 037894
Thrasher, Angela R., Baltimore 087714
Thrasher Carriage Museum, Frostburg 044092
Three Art Clubs of Chicago, Chicago 115565
Three Buckets Full, Hutt City 079119
Three Centuries Shop, Vancouver . . 059426
Three Dee Art, Soldiers Point 095195
Three East Third Street Corporation, New York 118492
Three Fishes, Toronto 097385
Three Friends Studio, Chicago 088178
Three Georges' Imperial Art Academy, Beijing 049846
Three Lions Antiques, Jacksonville . 089466
Three-O-Five-Shop, New Orleans . . 090632
Three Pagodas, Minneapolis 090399
Three Rivers Auction, Pittsburgh . . 123059
Three Rivers Gallery, Pittsburgh . . . 118959
Three Rivers Museum, Muskogee . 046112
Three Rivers Museum and Local History, Rickmansworth 040835
Three Rooms, Minneapolis 117317
Three Treasures Fine Arts Centre, Singapore 080573
Three Village Historical Society Museum, Setauket 048117
Three Women and an Armoire, Sacramento 092188
Threepenny Books, Pittsburgh 142780
Threlkeld Quarry and Mining Museum, Threlkeld 041218
Threshing Museum, Mullinahone . . 022840
The Thrie Estaits, Edinburgh 084316
Thrifty Joe's, San Diego 142918
Thrifty Upholstery, Albuquerque . . . 131753
Throckmorton, New York . 091289, 118493
Throll, Berlin 138853
Thronateeska Heritage Foundation, Albany 041596
Through the Lens, Arundel 083317, 130308
Through the Looking Glass, Dun Laoghaire 074969
Through the Looking Glass, London 085741
Through the Quay Hole, Salcombe . 114386
Thua Thien Hue Museum, Thua Thien Hue 049554
Thünen-Museum-Tellow, Warnkenhagen 020681
Thüring, Lydia, Basel 082176
Thüringer Freilichtmuseum Hohenfelden, Hohenfelden 017970
Thüringer Landesmuseum Heidecksburg, Rudolstadt 019936
Thüringer Museum Eisenach, Eisenach 016925
Thüringer Universitäts- und Landesbibliothek Jena, Jena 018118
Thürmer, Lutz, Potsdam 126659
Thuillier, Paris 100909
Thuillier, Alain, Herblay 063146
Thuillier, Serge, Noirmoutier-en-l'Ile 065222
Thuillier, William, London 085742
Thulin & Ohlson, Göteborg 141109
Thull, K., Bonn 069948
Thulla, Howth 105896
Thum, D., Meersburg 072493
Jacques Thum & Stefan Hörler, Jacques, Sankt Gallen 111875
Thumm, Barbara, Berlin 102068
Thun-Hohenstein, Praha 060168
Thun-Hohenstein, Sven, Klagenfurt 095621
Thunder Bay, New York 091290
Thunder Bay Art Gallery, Thunder Bay 006568
Thunder Bay Historical Museum Society, Thunder Bay 006569
Thunder Bay Military Museum, Thunder Bay 006570
Thunderbird Museum, Merrillan . . . 045790
Thunér, Lars, Stockholm 082029
Thunnissen, Claudia, Leiderdorp . . 128748
Thuns, Michael, Bonn 125364
Thurgauische Kunstgesellschaft, Kreuzlingen 054221
Thurles Famine Museum, Thurles . . 022863
Thurn und Taxis Museum, Bayerisches Nationalmuseum, Regensburg . . . 019760
Thurner, Martin, Breitenfeld an der Rittschein 056952
Thurner & Sagmeister, Marion u Ulrich, Seebenstein 057311
Thurow, Gerhard, Berlin 125307
Thurrock Museum, Grays 039626
Thursch, Detlef, Düsseldorf 139022
Thursch & Frank, Düsseldorf 139023
Thursford Collection, Fakenham . . . 039475
Thurso Heritage Museum, Thurso . . 041222
Thury György Múzeum, Nagykanizsa 021797
Thwaite Mills Watermill, Leeds 039964
Thwaites, Watford 087055, 131655
Thyade, Rotterdam 108212
Tiafit, Emmetten 082353
Tiagarra Aboriginal Culture Centre and Museum, Devonport 000982
Tian Chan Xuan Art Galley, Beijing . 097679
Tiandu, Singapore 109883
Tianjin Art Museum, Tianjin 007284
Tianjin Drama Museum, Tianjin . . . 007285
Tianjin History Museum, Tianjin . . . 007286
Tianjin Museum of Natural History, Tianjin 007287
Tianjin Painting Gallery, Tianjin 007288
Tianjin People's Fine Arts Publishing House, Tianjin 133386
Tianjin People's Science Hall, Tianjin 007289
Tianlong, Shanghai 059770
Tianyi Ge Museum, Ningbo 007218
Tiara, Singapore 080574
Tib Lane Gallery, Manchester 114050
Tibaudo, François, Lyon 124375
Tiber Bookshop, Baltimore 142230
Tibet, Lille 063870
Tibet House Museum, Delhi 022098
Tibet Songtsen House, Zürich 037805
Tibet Treasure, New York 091291
The Tibetan Gallery, Hong Kong . . . 059698
Tibetan Traditional Thangka Arts, Kathmandu 107600
Tibetan Village Store, New York . . . 091292
Tibooburra Local Aboriginal Land Council Keeping Place, Tibooburra 001552
Tibro Museum, Tibro 036706
Tic Toc Clock Shop, Dallas 132024
Tichadou, Philippe, Richebourg . . . 067134
Tichenor, Scott, Louisville 090034
Tichmann, Andreas, Wuppertal 074545
Ticho House, Jerusalem 022983
Tichý, O., Praha 137847
Ticktock Media 4D, Tunbridge Wells 135310
Tidaholms Konstförening, Tidaholm 054163
Tidaholms Konsthall, Tidaholm 036707
Tidaholms Museum, Tidaholm 036708
Tidal Access Gallery, Nelson 108521
Tidal Wave Gallery, Hereford 113238
Tiderne Skifter, København 133427
Tidevarvet Bokmagasinet, Stockholm 141178
Tie Pen Jinshi, Shanghai 097951
Tiedong Qian Hua Art Cooperative, Anshan 097637
Tiedt, Gudrun, Goslar 102984, 133979
Tiedt, J., Feldberg, Mecklenburg . . 102724
Tiefenauer, Charly, Rüti, Zürich 082758
Tiegs, R.-Peter, Spremberg 073884
Tieling City Museum, Tieling 007292
Tielker, Jürgen, Bochum 069896
Tiemeyer, Ria, Berlin 125308
Tiempo's Antiques Curiosidades, Valencia 093555
De Tiempos de Antaño, Bilbao 080993
Tiempos Modernos, Madrid 081399
Tiemuseo, Helsinki 009583
Tien, Kee, Singapore 080575
Tienda Guadalupe, San Antonio . . . 119460
La Tienda Latina, Bruxelles 137472
Tiendschuur, Tilburg 128845
Tienne, Modena 075929
Tienti, D., Genova 075515
Tientong, Los Angeles 089924
Tiepolo, Singapore 080576
Tieppo, Oscar Luigi, Roma 076702
Tier- und Jagdmuseum, Bad Dürrheim 015689
Tiercin, Christian, Dijon 099219
Tierens, Hugo, Londerzeel 123659
Tiermuseum, Burgau, Schwaben . . 016508
Tiermuseum, Lenggries 018615
Tierra, Dornbirn 056966
Tiers, Serge, Marseille 124434
Tierwelt-Panorama, Ebikon 037053
Tieste, Reinhard, Bremen . 070047, 133847
Tieteelliset Kokoelmat, Forssa 009484
Tietjen & Co., Dagmar & Detlef, Hamburg 071345, 121440, 139219
Tietze, Meudt 134201
Tifani, Beograd 109725
Tiffany, Bologna 075112
Tiffany, Chicago 088179, 131919
Tiffany, Enschede 078381
Tiffany, Luzern 082637
Tiffany, West Hollywood 093515
Tiffany Antiques, Shrewsbury 086610
Tiffany Glass Gallery, Calgary 096850
Tiffany Inn, Kansas City 089523
Tiffany Touch Studio, Virginia Beach 133016
Tiffany Ursta, Wrocław 109234
Tiffany's Antiques, Chennai 074798
Tiffany's Decor, Edmonton 058840
Tiffany's Decor On Whyte, Edmonton 058841
Tiffins Antiques, Emsworth 084334
Tiflološki Muzej, Zagreb 007858
Tiftickjian & Sons, David, Buffalo . . 087914
Tiftickjian jr., David, Buffalo 087915
Tifus, Clermont-Ferrand 099153
Tiger Paws, Minneapolis 090400
Tighes Hill Gallery, Tighes Hill 095337
Tighnabruaich Gallery, Tighnabruaich 114576
Tignish Cultural Centre Museum, Tighish 006571
Tigressblue Gallery, Kirkhill 113336
Tijani, Dortmund 102413
De Tijd, Doetinchem 078293
Tijdloos, Den Haag 107956
Tijdloos, Leiden 078586
De Tijdspiegel, Den Haag 078254
De Tijdspiegel, Middelburg 078645
Tijssen, Venlo 078847
Tik Tak Antiikki, Turku 060646
Tikanojan Taidekoti, Vaasa 010204
Tikotin Museum of Japanese Art, Haifa Museums, Haifa 022930
Tilba Woodturning Gallery, Central Tilba 094386
Tilbury, Draguignan 062738, 124227
Tilbury, Genova 075516
Tilbury Fort, Tilbury 041223
Tilbury West Agricultural Museum, Comber 005288
Tilché, Jean-Marc, Carcassonne . . 099084
Tilden-Foley, New Orleans 117524
Tilden-Thurber, Providence 092051
Tiles and Architectural Ceramics Society, Leeds 054529
Tilia, Giuseppe, Roma 128222
Tilings Antiques, Brasted 083656
Tilk, Helina, Tallinn 098703
Till-Eulenspiegel-Museum, Schöppenstedt 020089
Tillamook County Pioneer Museum, Tillamook 048556
Tillamook Naval Air Station Museum, Tillamook 048557
De Tille, Leeuwarden 140473
Tiller, Amsterdam 107812
Tiller, Wien 095951
Tiller & Ernst, Wien 095952
Tilley, Sheffield 086567, 142065
Tilleys, Solihull 086634, 131508
Tillier, Vincent, Paris 066605
Tillie's Collectibles, San Antonio . . . 092589
Tillman, Potterspury 086304
Tillou, Dana, Buffalo 087916, 115267
Tillou, Peter, New York 118494
Till's Bookshop, Edinburgh 141589
Tillybs, Heinz, Quarrendorf 073392
Tilly's Antiques, Leigh-on-Sea 084961, 130881
Tilman, Powhatan 123068
Tilmant d'Auxy, Bruno, Château-Chervix 062179, 124190

Tilsam, Paris 066606
Tilt, Ferntree Gully 094524
Tilton, Jack, New York 118495
Tim & Avi's Salvage Store, Indianapolis 089350
Timar Italia, Parma 076224
Timber Creek Police Station Museum, Timber Creek 001553
Timber Museum of New Zealand, Putaruru 030584
Timber Village Museum, Blind River 005105
The Timbers Antique Centre, Lavenham 084911
Timbert, Odette, Espaubourg 062802
Timbertown Museum, Wauchope . . 001603
Timbery, Laddie, Huskisson 056007
Timbres et Monnaies, Paris 066607
Timbres et Monnaies, Tours 068609
Timbuctoo II, Amsterdam 140342
Timbuktu, Amsterdam 077981
Timbuktu to Kathmandu, Noosaville 094969
Time and Again, Pittsburgh 091863, 132679
Time and Motion, Beverley 083503, 130378
Time and Tide Antiques, Portaferry .086290, 131389
Time Bandit, Baltimore 087715
Time Booksellers, Frankston 136906
Time Bygdemuseum, Undheim 031304
Time Capsule, El Paso 088819
Time Frame, Edmonton 096902
Time Gallery, New York 091293
Time Gallery, Paris 066608
Time in Hand, Shipston-on-Stour . .086594, 131493
Time Keeper, Chicago 115566
Time Less, Amsterdam . . 077982, 128557
Time Machine, Merimbula 136999
The Time Machine, Virginia Beach .093367, 133017
Time Machine, Weston-super-Mare 041350
The Time Museum, Chicago 042867
The Time Museum, Newark-on-Trent 040537
Time Museum, Teheran 022645
Time 'n' Again, Thirroul 056708
Time Shop, Milwaukee . . . 090323, 132373
Time Tested Books, Sacramento . . 142850
Time & Tide, Christchurch 079058
Time Traders, Boston 087850
Time Traveler Book Store, Milwaukee 142572
Time Traveller, Paeroa 079210
Time Treasures Antiques, Chicago . 088180
Time Treasures Antiques, Chicago . 088181
Time Tunnel, San Jose 092936
Time Tunnel, Zürich 083031
Time Well, Chicago 088182
Time Will Tell, New York 091294
Time Wonderland, Kawagoe 077072
Timeball Tower, Deal 039219
Timecraft Clocks, Sherborne 086584
Timeless, Bruxelles 058094
Timeless, Hibiscus Coast 079115
Timeless, Tauranga 128966
Timeless Antiques, Basel 082177
Timeless Antiques, Chicago 088183
Timeless Art Gallery, Singapore . . . 109884
Timeless Beds, Malvern 085907
Timeless Books, Angaston 136782
Timeless Books, Angaston 136783
Timeless Collectable, San Diego . . 092688
Timeless Gallery, Zürich 083032
Timeless Pieces, Silverton 056595
Timeless Stitches, Everson 088823
Timeless Treasures, Kansas City . . 089524
Timeless Treasures, San Francisco . 092897
Timelines, Saint Paul 092404
Timely Treasures, Houston 089225
Timepeice Repairs, Lincoln 085001, 130898
Timepiece, Dublin 074949, 127101
Timepiece, Teignmouth 086837
Timepiece City, New York 091295
Times and Chimes, Houston 089226
Times Books, London 135270
Times Gone By, Jacksonville 132196
Time's Lost Toys, Saskatoon 059106
Times Oriental Rugs, Houston 089227
Times Past Antiques, Auchterarder .083352, 130316
Times Past Antiques, Eton 084348, 130693
Times Past Antiques, Potter Heigham 086302
Timespan Museum and Art Gallery, Helmsdale 039718
Timgems, Norwich 086124
Timios Stavros Monastery, Mavradzei 021370
Timken Museum of Art, San Diego . 047843
Timm, A., Elsdorf 070548
Timm, Carl V., Salt Lake City 132796
Timm, Gesa, Schleswig 126770
Timme, Hannover 139245
Timmen, H., Borculo 128596
Timmermann, Heinz, Cottbus 070159
Timmermans, Juanita, Bad Salzuflen 069371
Timmermans-Opsomerhuis, Lier . . 003604
Timmins Museum, National Exhibition Centre, South Porcupine 006494
Timms, S. & S., Shefford 086569
Timoléonthos, François, Nevers . . .065013, 124494
Timoteo, Burgos 129467
Timothy, Slijk Ewijk 121805
Timothy Hackworth Victorian Railway Museum, Shildon 041012
Het Timpaan, Apeldoorn 078041
Tim's Book Exchange, Winnipeg . . . 137745
Tin Angel Antiques, Baltimore 087716
Tin Drum Books, Leicester 141719
Tin Horse Antiques, Louisville 090035
Tin Man, Miami 090249
Tin Museum - Gedung Raja Abdullah, Kelang 027955
Tin Sheds Gallery, Chippendale . . . 094396
Tinakori Antiques, Wellington 079353
Tinakori Gallery, Wellington 079354
Tinakori Gallery, Wellington 128978
Tinakori Gallery, Wellington 128979, 140685
Tinarelli, Evelina, Bologna 075113
Tina's Antiques, Codford 084047
Tincan Alley, Tulsa 120208
Tincu, Timişoara 080202
Tindell, Nashville 132406
Tindley & Chapman, London 141908
El Tinell, Barcelona 080943
Tinelmuseum, Sinaai-Waas 003750
Tineriba Fine Art, Adelaide 055320
Tineriba Fine Art, Adelaide 094121
Tineriba Tribal Gallery and Museum, Hahndorf 001092
Ting, Amstelveen 077763
Ting Qin Antiques, Shanghai 059771
Tinguely, Peter, Tafers 082841
Tingvoll Museum, Tingvoll 031265
Tingwall Agricultural Museum, Gott 039613
Tinhorn Press Gallery, San Francisco 119814
Tinius, Ursula, Wustrow, Niedersachsen 127055
Tinkelbel, Maastricht 108133
Tinker, Richmond 132725
Tinker Swiss Cottage Museum, Rockford 047502
Tinley Park Historical Society Museum, Tinley Park 048558
Tinn Museum, Rjukan 031140
Tinney, Martin, Cardiff 112814
Tino, Norberto, La Paz 096447
Tino's Treasures, Omaha . 091585, 132600
Tinslay, Peter, Crows Nest, New South Wales 055727, 136870
TinT, Thessaloniki 105461
Tinter, Gerhard, Wien 137370
Tintern Abbey, Chepstow 039056
Tintern Antiques, Tintern 086886
Tinti, Olivier, Rouen 067302
Tinti, Polo, Bologna 127184
Tinti, Rosanna, Bologna 075114
Tintic Mining Museum, Eureka 043755
The Tiny Clock Shop, Windsor, Ontario 059444
Tiny Factory-Comeprima, Toulouse 101373
Tinzl, Christoph, Salzburg 123461
Tioda, Gijón 110361
Tioga County Historical Society Museum, Owego 046757
Tioga Point Museum, Athens 041840
Tippecanoe Battlefield, Battle Ground 042057
Tippecanoe County Historical Museum, Lafayette 045089
Tippl, Gerd, Bamberg 125138
Tipton, Steve, Louisville 090036
Tipton County Museum, Covington . 043201
Tipton-Haynes Museum, Johnson City 044868
Tiptree Museum, Tiptree 041224
Tipu Sahib Museum, Srirangapatna 022345
Tiqueibles of Irvington, Indianapolis 089351
Tiramisu, Sundbyberg 082046
Tirau Antique Centre, Waikato 079298
Tirdad, Wädenswil 111979
Tire la Chevillette, Dinard 062690
Tire Müzesi, Tire 038185
Tirenna, Palermo 076183
Tires, Terry, Jacksonville 089467
Tiroche, Micky, London 113925
Tirol Edition, Innsbruck 133094
Tiroler Bauernhausmuseum, Kitzbühel 002134
Tiroler Bergbau- und Hüttenmuseum, Brixlegg 001767
Tiroler Kaiserjägermuseum Obergricht, Serfaus 002675
Tiroler Künstlerschaft, Innsbruck . . 052600
Tiroler Kunst- und Antiquitätenmesse, Innsbruck 093587
Tiroler Kunstpavillon Kleiner Hofgarten, Innsbruck 002096
Tiroler Landesmuseum Ferdinandeum, Innsbruck 002097
Tiroler Volkskunstmuseum, Innsbruck 002098
Tirotta, Ilario, Genova 106110
Tirpitz-Stillingen, Varde Museum, Blåvand 008822
Tisato, Massimo, Verona 128442
Tisch Beere Gallery, Cardiff 112815
Tischbein & Partner, Mühlhausen, Thüringen 072607
Tish, Anya, Houston 116416
Tison, Claude, Piacé 066821
Tison, Jacky, Mareschè 064283
Tissen, Ralf, Überlingen 105088
Tisserant, Paris 066609
Tiszeker, Krisztina, Roma 076703
Titan Missile Museum, Green Valley 044314
Titanicmuseum, Bad Wildungen . . . 015829
Titbits, Milano 075878
Titchener, Mary, South Yarra 056615
Titcher & Sons, John, Littleton, Cheshire 085018
Titchiner, Mark, Halesworth 113175
Titgemeyer-Heck, Lucia, München . 072870
Tithe Barn Museum and Art Centre, Swanage 041169
Titi, Gianna, Roma 076704
Titian, Rodrigo, London 131193
Titian, Salvatore, London 131194
Titian Gallery, Stow-on-the-Wold . . 086766
Titiana, Chaskovo 096700
Title Wave, Portland 142812
Titles Book Gallery, Howick 140633
Titlewave Books, Seattle 143012
Tito Arte, Torino 106707
Titon, San Francisco 092898, 132913
Titre Ni Signature, Coustellet 099183
Titren, Beaune 098942
Tittelbach, Elke, Cismar 102317
Tittiskåpet, Sollentuna 081895
Titus Brandsma Museum, Bolsward 029325
Tiverton Museum of Mid Devon Life, Tiverton 041225
Tivoli Gallery, Salt Lake City 119374
Tiwi Art Network, Darwin 055740
TJ Furniture Land, Houston 089228
TJK Antiques, San Francisco 092899
Tjolöholms Slott, Fjärås 036274
T.J.'s Gallery on Evans, Mackay . . . 094751
Tjumenskaja Kartinnaja Galereja, Tjumen 033957
Tjumenskij Gosudarstvennyj Institut Iskusstv i Kultury, Tjumen 050665
Tjumenskij Oblastnoj Kraevedčeskij Muzej im. I.Ja. Slovcova, Tjumen 033958
Tjumenskij Oblastnoj Muzej Izobrazitelnych Iskusstv, Tjumen 033959
Tjust Auktion & Antikt, Hjorted 081836, 122162
TK Projects, New York 118496
Tkalec, Helmut, Oberalm . 057197, 123424
Tlaqueparte Monterrey, Monterrey . 093819
TLC Exchange, Tucson 093269
TLC Gallery, Houston 116417
TLC Gallery, Houston 116418
Tlon Books, London 141909
TM Gallery, Crestview 043217
To, Seoul 107297
To-ji Homotsukan, Kyoto 026774
To Life, Chicago 115567
TOAAC, Lutry 111676
Toad Hole Cottage Museum, Ludham 040353
Toale, Bernard, Boston 115236
Toast Gallery, Paris 100910
Tobacciana Report, Houston 136642
Tobacco Farm Life Museum, Kenly . 044953
Tobacco Museum, Texas 001545
Tobačni Muzej, City Museum of Ljubljana and Tobachna Ljubljana, Ljubljana 034496
Tobajas, Antoni, Barcelona 080944
Tobaks- och Tändstickmuseum, Stockholm 036679
Tobey, New York 118497
Tobias and The Angel, London 085743
Tobias Community Historical Society Museum, Tobias 048563
Tobias-Mayer-Museum, Marbach am Neckar 018815
Tobias Smollett Museum, Alexandria 038480
Tobiassen, Alf Georg, Stavanger . . . 079507
Tobien, Husum, Nordsee 103416
Tobilane Designs, Penrith 131367
Tobin-Hewett, Louisville 116969
Tobis Editions, Preding 133128
Tobogan, Paris 066610
Tobogan, Saint-Ouen 067908
Toboggan Centre Culturel, Decines-Charpieu 099202
Tobolskaja Kartinnaja Galereja, Tobolsk 033960
Tobolskij Gosudarstvennyj Istoriko-architekturnyj Muzej-zapovednik, Tobolsk 033961
Tobwabba Art, Forster 055836
The Toby Jug, Johannesburg 080719
Toby's Antiques, Portland 092016
Toby's Antiques, Torquay 086903
Toccaceli, Monica, Roma 076705
Tocchetti, Lugano 111672, 122337
Tochigi-kenritsu Bijutsukan, Utsunomiya 027311
Tochigi-kenritsu Hakubutsukan, Utsunomiya 027312
Todai-ji Treasure Hall, Nara 026900
Today's Memories, Singapore 080577
Todd, Don, Portland 132705
Todd, Sue, Dunedin 079094
Todd & Austin, Winchester 087176
Todd Madigan Gallery, California State University Bakersfield, Bakersfield 041956
Todd's, Launceston 084908
Tode, Berlin 138854
Todescat, Liliana, Santiago de Chile 059557
Todeschini, Attilia, Verona 128443
Todi, Tiziana, Roma 106639
Todisco, Carl, Boston 087851

Todmorden Antiques Centre, Todmorden . . . 086892
Todmorden Fine Arts, Todmorden . . 114581
Todmorden Mills Heritage Museum and Arts Centre, Toronto . . . 006634
Todorov, T., Loveč . . . 137597
Toebosch, Amsterdam . . . 077983
Tölke, Christoph, Krefeld . . . 126150
Tölke, Dr. Dirk, Aachen . . . 125043
Töllinmäen Museo, Hämeenkyrö . . 009487
Töllstorps Industrimuseum, Gnosjö Industrimuseum, Gnosjö . . . 036291
Toennissen, Monika, Köln . . . 103726
Toepfer, Dr. Eva, Contern . . . 077463
Toepfer, Kelly, Northwood . . . 056382
Töpferei und Museum im Kannenofen, Höhr-Grenzhausen . . . 017950
Töpfereimuseum, Langerwehe . . . 018514
Töpfereimuseum Raeren, Raeren . . 003708
Töpfermuseum, Duingen . . . 016849
Töpfermuseum, Kohren-Sahlis . . . 018371
Töpfermuseum, Rödermark . . . 019865
Töpfermuseum, Stoob . . . 002717
Töpfermuseum Im alten Kannenofen, Ransbach-Baumbach . . . 019711
Töpfermuseum Thurnau, Thurnau . . 020438
Töpferstube mit Keramikmuseum, Bad Wiessee . . . 015821
Törk, Darmstadt . . . 070190
Törngrens Krukmakeri, Falkenberg . 036262
Török, Ferenc, Sankt Gallen . . . 111876, 130168
Töysän Museo, Töysä . . . 010149
Toffoletto Colombo, Laura, Milano . 127699
Tofield Historical Museum, Tofield . 006574
Toftum, Lars, Valby . . . 124034
Togei Bijutsu Kenkyujo, Kawasaki . 050455
Togen, Hiroshima . . . 077066
Toggenburger Museum, Lichtensteig . . . 037261
Toggenburger Schmiede- und Handwerksmuseum, Bazenheid . . 036911
Togni, Marco, Roma . . . 128223
Tognola, Chantal, Bellinzona . . . 082190
Tognolini, Carola, Verona . . . 128444
Tognon, Caterina, Venezia . . . 106780
Tognon, Olivia, Bari . . . 075033
Togonon, Julina E., San Francisco . 119815
Toguna, Amersfoort . . . 077754
Toguna, Luxembourg . . . 107414
Toguna, Toulouse . . . 068546
Toh, Seoul . . . 107298
Toh, Foong, Singapore . . . 080578
Toho, Kyoto . . . 077133
Toho, Kyoto . . . 140165
Tohoku Daigaku, Kokoshiryoshitsu, Sendai . . . 027053
Tohoku Geijutsu Koka Daigaku, Yamagata . . . 050504
Tohoku Rekishi Shiryokan, Tagajou 027097
Toifl, Brigitta, Wien . . . 057570
Toiles, E., Quimper . . . 101066
Toiles et Feuilles, Sanary-sur-Mer . 101252
Toison, Madrid . . . 110623
Tøjhusmuseet, København . . . 008991
Tokai Daigaku Kaiyo Kagaku Hakubutsukan, Shizuoka . . . 027084
Tokaji Múzeum, Tokaji . . . 021910
Tokat Müzesi ve Örenyerleri, Tokat . 038186
Token Hakubutsukan, Tokyo . . . 027253
Token-Team, Oldenburg, Oldenburg 073213
Toki-no Sato History Hall, Mano . . . 026780
Toki-no Wasuremono, Tokyo . . . 107122
Tokmachi, Nemat, Albuquerque . . . 087429
Toko, San Diego . . . 092689
Toko, San Francisco . . . 119816
Tokodo Shoten, Tokyo . . . 140207
Tokomairiro Historical Society Museum, Milton . . . 030541
Tokomaru Steam Engine Museum, Tokomaru . . . 030607
Tokoname Togei Kenkyujyo, Tokoame Institute of Ceramic Art, Tokoname . . . 027140
Toku, Tokyo . . . 077314
Tokugawa, Phoenix . . . 118894
Tokugawa Art Sword Exhibition Fair, Nagoya, Aichi . . . 093806
Tokugawa Bijutsukan, Nagoya . . . 026887
Tokusa, Honolulu . . . 088980
Tokushima-kenritsu Hakubutsukan, Tokushima . . . 027141
Tokushima-kenritsu Kindai Bijutsukan, Tokushima . . . 027142
Tokushima-kenritsu Torii Kinen Hakubutsukan, Naruto . . . 026906
Tokushima Prefectural Local Culture Hall, Tokushima . . . 027143
Tokyo Art Auction, Tokyo . . . 121749
Tokyo Art Creation, Tokyo . . . 077315
Tokyo Bienial, Tokyo . . . 053803
Tokyo Bijutsu, Tokyo . . . 134734
Tokyo Bijutsu Club, Tokyo . . . 053804
Tokyo Central Bijutsukan, Tokyo . . . 027254
Tokyo Design Academy, Tokyo . . . 050497
Tokyo Designer Gakuin, Tokyo . . . 050498
Tokyo Fuji Art Museum, Hachioji . . 026482
Tokyo Gallery, Tokyo . . . 107123
Tokyo Geijutsu Daigaku, Tokyo . . . 050499
Tokyo Honten Art Gallery, Tokyo . . . 107124
Tokyo Kaikan Gallery, Tokyo . . . 107125
Tokyo Kikaku, Musashino . . . 077142
Tokyo Kokuritsu Hakubutsukan, Tokyo . . . 027255
Tokyo Kokuritsu Kindai Bijutsukan, Tokyo . . . 027256
Tokyo Kokuritsu Kindai Bijutsukan, Film Center, Tokyo . . . 027257
Tokyo Kokuritsu Kindai Bijutsukan Kogeikan, Crafts Gallery, Tokyo . . . 027258
Tokyo Kokusai Bijutsukyoukai, Tokyo . . . 027259
Tokyo Lease, Tokyo . . . 077316
Tokyo Metropolitan Geijutsu High School Museum, Tokyo . . . 027260
Tokyo Modern Art Gallery, Tokyo . . 107126
Tokyo Noko Daigaku Kogakubu Fuzoku Sen'i Hakubutsukan, Koganei . . . 026681
Tokyo Senshoku Bijutsu Gakuin, Tokyo . . . 050500
Tokyo Station Gallery, Tokyo . . . 027261
Tokyo-to Bijutsukan, Tokyo . . . 027262
Tokyo-to Gendai Bijutsukan, Tokyo . 027263
Tokyo-to Shashin Bijutsukan, Tokyo 027264
Tokyo-to Teien Bijutsukan, Tokyo . . 027265
Tokyo University Archaeological Collection, Tokyo . . . 027266
Tokyo Zokei Daigaku, Hachiouji . . . 050452
Tol, Jaap, Bergen, Noord-Holland . . 107867
Tolarno, Melbourne . . . 094830
Tolbooth Art Centre, Kirkcudbright . 039902
Tolbooth Museum, Stonehaven . . . 041125
Tolch, Andrew, Saint Louis . . . 092321
Toldedo Antique Gallery, Miami . . . 090250
Tole World, Concord . . . 136643
Toledano, Jean-Daniel & Anne, Arcachon . . . 120903
Toledano, Jean-Daniel & Anne, Bordeaux . . . 120947
Toledo Artists' Club, Toledo . . . 055070
Toledo Museum of Art, Toledo . . . 048569
Toledo Museum of Science, Toledo . 048568
Tolga Eti Sanatevi, İstanbul . . . 112363
Tolga Woodworks Gallery, Tolga . . . 095339
Tolgus Tin Mill and Streamworks, Redruth . . . 040816
Tolhouse Museum and Brass Rubbing Centre, Great Yarmouth . . . 039636
Tolis, Gerasimos, Thessaloniki . . . 105462
Tolksdorf, Hattingen . . . 071432
Tolksdorf, Wilma, Frankfurt am Main . . . 102832
Toll Gallery, Thurso . . . 114574
Toll House Bookshop, Holmfirth . . . 141672
Tolland County Jail and Warden's Home Museum, Tolland . . . 048571
Tollemans, Bruxelles . . . 058095
Tollmann, Grevenbroich . . . 071100
Tollrian, Ulrich, Worms . . . 074484
Tolmach, James, Atlanta . . . 131788
Tolman, Miami . . . 117148
Tolman Collection, Tokyo . . . 027267
Tolminski Muzej, Tolmin . . . 034528
Tolotti, Luigi, Venezia . . . 076976
Tolpuddle Martyrs Museum, Tolpuddle . . . 041228
Tolsey Museum, Burford . . . 038903
Tolson, Tom, Fort Worth . . . 132074
Tolson Memorial Museum, Huddersfield . . . 039782
Toltec Mounds Archeological State Park, Scott . . . 048056
Toluian, Palermo . . . 106447
Tolvmansgården, Kruunupyy . . . 009752
Tolvskillingen, Kungsbacka . . . 081843
Tom, Warszawa . . . 079788, 140797
Tom Antique, Auckland . . . 128913
Tom Brown School Museum, Uffington . . . 041259
Tom Collins House, Swanbourne . . 001503
Tom Mix Museum, Dewey . . . 043462
Tom Thomson Memorial Art Gallery, Owen Sound . . . 006110
Tom Tits Experiment, Södertälje . . . 036595
Toma, San Antonio . . . 132830
Toma, Nick, Heerlen . . . 078508
Toma, Sheila, New York . . . 091296
Tomada, Andreina, Roma . . . 076706
Tomakomai-shi Seishonen, Tomakomai . . . 027279
Tomanek, Herbert, Wien . . . 137371
Tomaro, Antonio, Roma . . . 128224
Tomaru, Tokyo . . . 140208
Tomasella, Albert, Grenoble . . . 063076
Tomaselli, Kristina, Stuttgart . . . 105017
Tomasi, Carla, Roma . . . 128225
Tomasi, Carla, Roma . . . 128226
Tomassetti, Maria Cristina, Roma . . 128227
Tomatis, Francis, Lézignan-Corbières . . . 063807
Tombak, İstanbul . . . 083159
Tombak, İstanbul . . . 136143
Tomball Community Museum Center, Tomball . . . 048572
Tombe Reali di Casa Savoia, Torino 026083
Tombeur, Josette, Saint-Paul-de-Vence . . . 101220
Tombland Antiques Centre, Norwich . . . 086125, 131334
Tombland Bookshop, Norwich . . . 141968
Tombland Jewellers and Silversmiths, Norwich . . . 086126
Tome Parish Museum, Tome . . . 048573
Tome Pires, Los Angeles . . . 089925
Tomedi, Irene, Bolzano . . . 127198
Tomelilla Auktionshall, Tomelilla . . . 122277
Tomelilla Konsthall, Tomelilla . . . 036709
Tomeo, Cleveland . . . 115747
Tomescheit, Stefan, Ingelheim am Rhein . . . 071622
Tomicek, Jürgen, Werl . . . 105208
Tomiello, Luigi, Lugano . . 082611, 130095
Tomimoto Kenkichi Memorial Museum, Ando . . . 026414
Tomini, Alessio, Mendrisio 082658, 141278
Tomintoul Gallery, Ballindalloch . . . 112541
Tomintoul Museum, Tomintoul . . . 041229
Tomioka Museum, Tokyo . . . 027268
Tomita, Fukuyama . . . 106848
Tomita, Hiroshima . . . 106859
Tomita, Washington . . . 120353
Tomlin, Dallas . . . 088618
Tomlin, Gerald, Dallas . . . 088619
Tomlinson, Tockwith . . . 086889
Tomm, Meyhen . . . 072541
Tommasone, Lucio, Firenze . . . 127421
Tommy Q, Los Angeles . . . 089926
Tommys Allservice & Antik, Stockholm . . . 082030
Tommy's Furniture, Albuquerque . . 131754
Tomorrow's Antique, Helsinki . . . 060586
Tomorrow's Treasures Today, Los Angeles . . . 089927
Tomos, Tokyo . . . 107127
Tomos, Vigo . . . 129794
Tompkins & Robandt, Chicago . . . 088184
Toms Curio's, Dublin . . . 074950
Tom's Furniture and Collectables, Tucson . . . 093270
Tom's Furniture and Collectables, Tucson . . . 093271
Tom's Terrific Antiques Shop, Omaha . . . 091586
Tom's Trains & Miniatures, Fresno . 088921
Tomsich, Saint Louis . . . 119261
Tomskij Muzej Derevjannogo Zodčestva, Tomsk . . . 033963
Tomskij Oblastnoj Chudožestvennyij Muzej, Tomsk . . . 033964
Tomskij Oblastnoj Kraevedčeskij Muzej, Tomsk . . . 033965
Tomtom, London . . . 085744
Ton Duc Thang Museum, Ho Chi Minh City . . . 049543
Ton Sak Yai, Uttaradit . . . 037939
Ton Smits Huis, Eindhoven . . . 029549
Ton Trai, Phuket . . . 037924
Tonawandas Museum, Tonawanda . 048576
Tønder Museum, Tønder . . . 009132
Tondinelli, Floriana, Roma . . . 106640
Tondorf, Düsseldorf . . . 102564
Tone, Saitama . . . 106979
Tone Art, Belfast . . . 112621
Tonella, Danielle, Lugano . . . 082612
Tonelli, Chicago . . . 115568
Tonelli, Milano . . . 106332
Tonello, Alfio & Emilio, Milano . . . 127700
Tonen, Erik, Antwerpen . . . 137408
Tonen, Erik, Antwerpen . . . 137409
Tong, Singapore . . . 080579
Tong, Mern Sern, Singapore . . . 080580
Tong-Jin Irrigation Folk Museum, Kimje . . . 027524
Tongan County Museum, Xiamen . . 007312
Tongarra Museum, Albion Park . . . 000727
Tongass Historical Museum, Ketchikan . . . 044979
Tongdosa Museum, Yangsan . . . 027624
Tongerlohuis Heyderadey, Roosendaal . . . 108170
Tongin, Seoul . . . 077375
Tongue, Dr., Portland . . . 092017
Tongxian Museum, Beijing . . . 007011
Tongzhou District Museum, Beijing . 007012
Toni-Merz-Museum, Sasbach bei Achern, Baden . . . 019997
Tonic General, Calgary . . . 058809
Tonkin, Ha Noi . . . 120489
Tonkin, Ha Noi . . . 120490
Tonkonow, Leslie, New York . . . 118498
Tonner, Jean-Marie, Saint-Mihiel . . 067680
Tonner, Joseph, Pons . . . 066905
Tonnerre, Joseph, Groix . . . 063085
Tonning, Magnus, Vellinge . . . 111097
Tonnoirs, Townsville . . . 137114
Tonon, Paolo & Josy, Genève . . . 082469
Tonon, Paolo & Josy, Genève . . . 082470
Tonon, Paolo & Josy, Genève . . . 111503
Tonon, Paolo & Josy, Genève . . . 111504
Tonson Gallery, Bangkok . . . 112244
Tonto National Monument, Roosevelt . . . 047538
Tony, Madrid . . . 129700
Tony Galeria de Arte e Antiguidades, São Paulo . . . 058744, 096692
Tony's Antiques, Portland . . . 092018
Tony's Furniture Refinishing, Cleveland . . . 131972
The Tool Shop, Needham Market . . 086044
Tooley, M.V., Chesham . . . 083946, 130554
Tooley, Adams & Co., Wallingford . . 142139
Tools Galerie, Paris . . . 100911
Toomey & Tourell, San Francisco . . 119817
Toon Art, Cincinnati . . . 115667
Toon-in Gallery, Melbourne . . . 094831
De Toonkamer, Amersfoort . . . 077755
Toons On, Philadelphia . . . 118846
Toop, Bill, Broadmayne . . . 112730
Tooraj, Los Angeles . . . 089928
Toorak Auctions, Caulfield South . . 120577

Tooronga Hall Antiques, Armadale, Victoria 055395, 123184
Tooronga Hall Antiques, Caulfield East 055650, 123209
De Toorts, Haarlem 134813
Toos Museum, Mashad 022584
Toowoomba Antiques Gallery, Toowoomba 056726
Toowoomba Art Society, Toowoomba 052494
Toowoomba Historical Museum, Toowoomba 001558
Toowoomba Regional Art Gallery, Toowoomba 001559
Toowoon Bay Gallery, Toowoon Bay 095345
Top, T.T., Kloosterburen 128737
Top Art, Hiroshima 077067
Top Art, Jeddah 080368
Top Art, Kiel 071844
Top Art, San Diego 119559
Top Artist, Chicago 115569
Top Banana Antiques Mall, Tetbury . 086869
Top Coins & Fine Art, Mall Darwin . 056134
Top Drawer Antiques, San Diego . . 092690
Top Drawer Auction, New Orleans .090633, 122984
Top Fresh Arts Gallery, Singapore . . 109885
Top Hat Antiques, Nottingham 086144
Top of Oklahoma Historical Museum, Blackwell 042247
Top of the Hill, Stoke-on-Trent 086734
Top of the Ninth, Columbus 088442
Top Pictures, Hull 113281
Top Rockz Gallery, Kununurra 094712
Topalian, Malcolm F., New York . . . 091297
TopArt Expositie Dagen, Rotterdam . 093836
Topkapi, Maubeuge 064425
Topkapı Sarayı Müzesi, İstanbul . . . 038100
Topografika Antikvariat, Oslo 140707
Topographie des Terrors, Berlin . . . 016184
Topoisten Ulkomuseoalue, Nousiainen 009911
Topp, Derek, Rowsley 114329
Topp, Hans-Jürgen, Limburg an der Lahn 072262, 103917, 139415
Topp & Bußkamp, Münster 126510
Toppenish Museum, Toppenish 048584
Topper, Victor & Renee, Toronto . . . 059301
Toppings, Thomas, Montréal 097087
Toppler-Schlößchen, Rothenburg ob der Tauber 019919
Topsfield Historical Museum, Topsfield 048585
Topsham Museum, Topsham 041230
Topsham Quay Antique Centre, Topsham 086900
Tor 1, Georgsmarienhütte 070966
Tor Sanguigna, Roma 076707
Tora, Guido, Roma 128228
Torajiro Kojima Memorial Hall, Ohara Bijutsukan, Kurashiki 026702
Torba Sanat Evi, Muğla 112373
Torbandena, Trieste 106720
Torbati, F., Hamburg 103223
Torbay Museum, Torbay 006577
Torbey, M., Mansourih El-Metn 077438
Torbogenmuseum, Königsbronn . . . 018344
Torch, Amsterdam 107813
Il Torchio, Roma 134683
Il Torchio Artistico e Letterario, Bassano Romano 135968
Il Torchio di Porta Romana, Milano . 106333
Torcular, Milano 134638
Torekällbergets Museum, Södertälje 036596
Torekovs Sjöfartsmuseum, Torekov 036710
De Toren Antiekcentrum, Breda . . . 078119
Torenmuseum, Goedereede 029614
Torenmuseum, Mol 003647
Torenverplaatsingsmuseum, Bocholt 003237
Toretti, Danièle, Aix-en-Provence . . 060717
Torfaen Museum, Pontypool 040734
Torfmuseum, Neustadt am Rübenberge 019278
Torfs, Leonardo, Antwerpen 096093
Torfschiffwerftmuseum, Worpswede 020989
Torhalle, Frauenchiemsee 017210
Torhalle Frauenchiemsee und Vikarhaus, Chiemsee 016567
Torhaus Atelier, Alsfeld 101564
Torhaus Dölitz, Leipzig 018598
Torhaus-Galerie, Berufsverband Bildender Künstlerinnen und Künstler Braunschweig e.V., Braunschweig 102226
Torhaus Markkleeberg, Museum der Völkerschlacht 1813, Markkleeberg 018835
Torhaus-Museum, Siegburg 020197
Torhaus Otterndorf, Sammlung Labiau/ Ostpreußen, Otterndorf 019539
Torhof-Galerie, Köln 103727
Tori Tori, Tokyo 077317
Torindo, Tokyo 107128
Torkild, Malfait, Bruxelles . 058096, 123609, 133279
Torlet, Paris 124821
Tornabuoni Arte, Firenze 106073
Tornabuoni Arte, Milano 106334
Tornar, Elena, Pisa 076246
Tornare, Genève 111505
Tornaritis Pierides Municipal Museum of Paloentology, Larnaka 008212
Tornberg, Lund 110956
Tornionlaakson Maakuntamuseo, Tornio 010157
Tornow, Löwenberg 072297
Tornyai János Múzeum, Hódmezővásárhely 021739
Toro Mera, Margarita Rosa, Cali . . . 123927
Toronski, W., Bruxelles 058097
Toronto Aeropspace Museum, Toronto 006635
Toronto Antique Centre, Toronto . . . 059302
Toronto Art Therapy Institute, Toronto 049822
Toronto Center for Contemporary Art, Toronto 006636
Toronto Dominion Gallery of Inuit Art, Toronto 006637
Toronto International Art Fair, Toronto 093628
Toronto Outdoor Art Exhibition, Toronto 006638
Toronto Outdoor Art Exhibition, Toronto 097386
Toronto Photographers Workshop, Toronto 097387
Toronto School of Art, Toronto 049823
Toronto Scottish Regimental Museum, Fort York Armoury, Toronto 006639
Toronto Sculpture Garden, Toronto . 006640
Toronto Vintage Paper Show-Canada Antiquarian Book Fair, Toronto . . . 093629
Toronto's First Post Office, Toronto . 006641
Toronto's Waterfront Museum, Toronto 006642
Torossian, Armand & Gérard, Grenoble 121012
Torpedo Factory Art Center, Alexandria 041649
Torquay Museum, Torquay 041231
Torquay Pottery Collectors Society, Saint Albans 142032, 142032, 086442, 086442
Torquay Pottery Collectors Society Magazine, Saint Albans 136243
The Torrance Gallery, Edinburgh . . . 113011
De la Torre, Madrid 081400
Torre, de la, Santiago de Chile 059558
La Torre, Verona 077024
Torre Abbey Historic House and Gallery, Torquay 041232
La Torre de Lulio, Oaxaca 140259
Torre del Conde, San Sebastián de La Gomera 035773
Torre dels Enagistes, Manacor 035461
La Torre di Corba Colombo, Milano . 106335
La Torre di Giada, Trieste 076910
Torre Enrica, Genova 075517
I Torre Guaita, San Marino 034120
Torrebianca, Trieste 076911
Torredimare, Pasquale, Milano 075879
Torrens, Jean, Paris 066611, 124822
Torrent, David, Vic-le-Comte 068847
Torreón Fortea, Ayuntamiento de Zaragoza, Zaragoza 036114
Torres, Madrid 081401
Los Torres, San Salvador 098690
Torres, Albert, Barcelona 129406
Torres, Bárbara, Porto . . . 080116, 109401
Torres, Eugénio, Porto 109402
Torres, Miguel Alberto, Bucaramanga 098225
Torres, Veronica, Asunción 079532
Torres Gonzalo, Pedro, Logroño . . . 110411
Torres Muñiz, Jesus, Granada 110384
Torres Strait Museum, Thursday Island 001551
Torresan, Marina, Milano 127701
Torresdale Station Antiques, Philadelphia 091694
Torretta, Locarno 082583, 130088
La Torretta, Roma 076708
Torri, Angelo, Brescia 075188
Torrington Historical Society Museum, Torrington 048588
Torrington Museum, Torrington 041234
Torris Barrois, Marc-André, Sainte-Cathérine-lès-Arras 068050
Torrisi, Alfio, Catania 127281
Torrisi, Massimo Teodoro, Catania . 127282
Torsby Finnkulturcentrum, Torsby . . 036711
Torsby Fordonsmuseum, Torsby . . . 036712
Torsegno, Francesco, Genova 127489
Torshälla Auktionsbyrå, Torshälla . . 122278
Tort, Andrée, Mirepoix 064566
Torta, Giulio, Palermo 076184
Torterat, Joël, Saulxures-lès-Nancy 101262
Tortoise Shell, Columbus 088443
Tortora, Bari 105935
Tortora, Antonio, Roma 128229
Tortora, Julien, Nice 124524
Tortori, Alfredo, Roma 076709
La Tortue Eléctrique, Paris 066612
Torukumen, Yokohama 077344
Torus, Antwerpen 057741
Tørvikbygd Bygdemuseum, Tørvikbygd 031271
Tosaka, Paris 100912
Toscado, David, Guadalajara 077568
Toscana, Murcia 081446
Toserco Gallery, Ha Noi 120491
Toshiba Kagakukan, Kawasaki 026647
Toshin, Hiroshima 077068
Toshodai-ji Treasure House, Nara . . 026901
Tot Antic, Barcelona 080945, 129407
Total Antiques, Sharjah 083229
Total Art Resources, Singapore 109886
Total Open-Air Museum, Yangju . . . 027623
Totally Essential, London 113926
Totara Peak Gallery, Omarama 108532
Totem Gallery, Johannesburg 110063
Totem Gallery, Rosebank 110077
Totem Gallery, Venezia 106781
Totem Gallery, Venezia 106782
Toten Økomuseum, Bøverbru 030791
Toten Økomuseum, Kapp 030932
Tóth, Amsterdam 077984
Tóth, Róbert, Budapest 074724
Totius House Museum, Potchefstroom 034710
Totnes Costume Museum, Totnes . . 041236
Totnes Elizabethan Museum, Totnes 041237
Toto, Bari 127125
Totonchian, Houston 089229
Totteridge Gallery, London 085745, 113927, 131195
Totters of Knightsbridge, Vancouver 059427
Tottori Folk Art Museum, Tottori . . . 027281
Tottori-kenritsu Hakubutsukan, Tottori 027282
Touati, Le Raincy 063704
Touba, Providence 119089
Toubas & C., Alain, Milano 106336
Toucan, London 131196
Toucan Art, Cheadle 112838
Touch of Antique, Toronto 059303
Touch of Art, Albuquerque 114829
Touch of Art, Mumbai 074829
Touch of Design, Saint Paul 119317
Touch of Difference, Toronto 059304
Touch Wood, B'Kara 077509
Touché, Hilversum 078542
Touche Contemporary Art, Stroud . . 114517
Le Touche of Class, Long Beach . . . 089661
Touchons du Bois, Angoulême 098834
Touchstone Center for Crafts, Farmington 043823
Touchstone Center for Crafts, Farmington 051328
Touchstone Gallery, Washington . . . 120354
Touchwood, Ottawa 123803
Tougaloo College Art Collection, Tougaloo 048589
Touhfa, Casablanca 077676
Touijar, Bruxelles 096258
Toujouse, Vaux-sur-Mer . . 068741, 125009
Toulemont, Martin, Sauxillanges . . . 068160
Toulouse, Paris 124823
Toulouse Antique Gallery, West Hollywood 093516
Toulza, Daniel, Foix 062885
Touma, Michael, Leipzig . 103900, 134158
Tounkara, Rotterdam 108213
Tounta, Ileana, Athinai 105409
La Tour Camoufle, Metz 064536
La Tour Camoufle, Paris 066613
La Tour Camouflé, Paris 066614
Tour de Constance, Monument D'Aigues-Mortes, Aigues-Mortes 010279
Tour de la Brocante et de l'Antiquité, Manom 064248
Tour de la Motte-Forte, Arnay-le-Duc 010478
Tour de Moricq, Angles 010400
La Tour des Cardinaux, Marseille . . 099690
Tour des Voleurs, Riquewihr 014060
Tour d'Oriol, Marseille . . . 064394, 138200
De la Tour Fine Art, Amsterdam . . . 077985
La Tour Fine Arts, New York 118499
Tour-Musée de Velaux, Le Donjon, Velaux 015153
La Tour Royale, Toulon (Var) 014980
Tourdot, Jean-Claude, Châtenois . . 062226
La Tourelle, Chaumont-sur-Tharonne 062254
Tourelle, Lamotte-Beuvron 063505
La Tourelle Castle Gallery, Tanawha 095317
Les Tourelles, Arnay-le-Duc 060980
Tourenne, Robin, Paris 124824
Touring Exhibitions Group, London . 054530
Touristik-Museum, Unterseen 037654
Tourmondeur, Menton 064496
Tournebize, Guy, Sainte-Maxime . . 068070
Tournebize, Jean-François, Vichy . . 068862
Tourneboeuf, Alice, Saint-Ouen . . . 067909
Tournelle, Marie, Paris 066615
Tournesol, Maastricht 078625
Les Tournesols, Saint-Étienne 101151
Tournevire, Tarascon (Bouches-du-Rhône) 068360
Tournié, Françoise, Paris 100913
Tournigand, Yvette, Saint-Ouen . . . 067910
Tourny's, Bordeaux 061656
Tourraton, Patrick, Rouen 067303
Toussaint, Daniel, Paris 066616
Toussaint, Denis, Aydoilles 061150
Toussaint, Françis, Paris 066617
Toussaint, Georges, Le Havre 063641
Toussaint, Jean-Pierre, La Ferrière-sur-Risle 063366
Toussaint Antiekhandel, Den Haag . 078255
Toussaint Forge, Givet 011958
Tout le Monde, New York 091298
Tout pour le Plaisir, Dourdan 062733
Tout Style Antiquités, Ponte Capriasca 082728
Tout un Art, Saint-Cyr-au-Mont-d'Or 101139
Tout un Peu, Saint-Martin-Lalande . 067650
Toutain, Gilles, Vire 121287

Toutantroc, Aïcirits-Camou-Suhast . 060676
Toutencadre, Saint-Privat-des-Vieux 067966
Toutoccas', Noidans-lès-Vesoul . . . 065216
Tovar, Dallas 132025
Tovar, Leon, New York 118500
Tovar, Luis, Sheffield 131479
Toveks Auktioner, Åtran 122094
Tovey, Brian, Henley-in-Arden 113228
Tovi, Jacques, Paris 066618
Towada Natural History Museum, Towadako 027284
Towarzystwo Przyjaciół Sztuk Pięknych, Kraków 053994
Towe Auto Museum, Sacramento . . 047595
Tower Antiques, Cranborne 084099
Tower Arts, Fresno 116189
Tower Books, Taranaki 140657
Tower Bridge Antiques, London . . . 085746
Tower Bridge Exhibition, London . . 040303
Tower Fine Arts Gallery, Brockport . 042425
Tower Grove Antiques, Saint Louis . 092322
Tower Grove East Studios, Saint Louis 119262
Tower Museum, Londonderry 040330
Tower Museum of Prosphorion, Ouranoupoli 021413
Tower of David, Museum of the History of Jerusalem, Jerusalem 022984
Towers, Robert, Dublin 139968
Town and Country Antiques, Houston 089230
Town and Country Antiques, Saintfield 086486, 131448
Town and Country Antiques, San Antonio 092590
Town and Country Auctioneers, Dublin 121668
Town and Country Decorative, Richmond, Surrey 086361
Town and Country Gallery, Yarragon 095447
Town and Country Shop, Milwaukee 090324
Town and Crown Exhibition, Windsor 041418
Town and Village Art, New York . . . 118501
Town & Country Antiques, West Hollywood 093517
Town & Country Antiques and Collectables, Caulfield South 055658
Town Creek Indian Mound Historic Site, Mount Gilead 046058
The Town Gallery, Ballymoney 112547
Town Gallery, Kansas City 089525
Town Gallery, Toledo 120094
Town Gallery and Japan Room, Brisbane 094298
Town Hall Art & Antiques, Woburn . 087201
Town House, Culross 039192
Town House Antiques, Marple Bridge 085956
Town House Galleries, Morecambe . 114089
Town House Gallery, Kirkby Lonsdale 113332
Town House Gallery, Lancaster 113349
Town House Museum of Lynn Life, King's Lynn 039880
Town Museum, East Grinstead 039349
Town Museum, Gödöllő 021727
Town of Clarence Museum, Clarence 042943
Town of Manlius Museum, Manlius . 045644
Town of North Hempstead Museum, Westbury 049104
Town of Ontario Historical and Landmark Preservation Society Museum Complex, Ontario 046696
Town of Warwick Museum, Warwick 048870
Town of York Antiques, Toronto . . . 059305
Towne, Louisville 090037, 132308
Towne Center Gallery, Long Beach . 116682
Towneley Hall Art Gallery and Museums, Burnley 038909
Towner Art Gallery and Local Museum, Eastbourne 039366
Towngate Gallery & Art Centre, Poole 114273, 135297
Townhead Antiques, Newby Bridge . 086060
Townhouse, Dublin 134532
The Townhouse Gallery, Belfast . . . 112622
Townhouse Gallery of Contemporary Art, Cairo 098676
Townlife Art, Toronto 097388
Townsend, Pittsburgh 142781
Townsend, John P., Cheltenham . . . 083933
Townsend & Bateson, Tetbury 086870
Townsend Gallery, Burnley 112768
Townsend Gallery, Los Angeles . . . 116901
Townsends, London 085747
Townsends, London 085748
Townsford Mill Antiques Centre, Halstead 084562
Townshend, James, Bath 083448
Township Museum, Migrant Labour Museum and Arts and Crafts Centre, Lwandle 034675
Townsville Museum, Townsville . . . 001566
Towteck, Singapore 109887
Toxana Basement Gallery, Richmond, New South Wales 095132
Toy and Miniature Museum, Stellenbosch 034756
Toy and Miniature Museum of Kansas City, Kansas City 044932
Toy and Teddy Bear Museum, Lytham Saint Anne's 040374
Toy Crazy, Louisville 090038
The Toy Museum, Stow-on-the-Wold 041130
Toy Museum, Valletta 028037
Toy Nostalgia, Auckland 078987
Toy Shop, Vancouver 059428
Toy Shoppe, Fort Worth 088889
Toy Soldier Shoppe, Milwaukee . . . 090325
Toy-Toy Museum, Rotterdam 030106
Toy Train Depot, Oakland 091442
Toyama Kenminkaikan Bijutsukan, Toyama 027286
Toyama-kenritsu Kindai Bijutsukan, Toyama 027287
Toyama Kinenkan, Hiki 026507
Toyama Kinenkan Fuzoku Bijutsukan, Kawashima, Saitama 026649
Toyama Municipal Folkcraft Village, Toyama 027288
Toyama Museum, Toyama 027289
Toyko Art Projects, New York 118502
Toynbee-Clarke, London 085749
Toyo, Tokyo 077318
Toyo Bijutsu Gakko, Tokyo 050501
Toyo Calligraphy Art Association, Hachioji 053805
Toyohashi-shiritsu Bijutsukan, Toyohashi 027290
Toyota Automobile Museum, Nagakute 026841
Toyota Municipal Museum of Art, Toyota, Aichi 027292
Toys of Yesteryear, Las Vegas 089615
Tozzi, Franco, Firenze 127422
T.R.A., Paris 100914
Trabarro, Brasília 096507
Trabzon Devlet Güzel Sanatlar Galerisi, Trabzon 038188
Trabzon Müzesi, Trabzon 038189
Tracé, Maastricht 108134
Trace, Newport, Isle of Wight 136275
Trace Ecart, Bulle 111321
Tracery Book Searcher, Dallas 142375
Traces, Journal of the International Stone Sculpture Community, Blacksburg 136644
Tracey's Antiques, Drummoyne . . . 055760
Trachten- und Heimatmuseum, Weiltingen 020734
Trachten- und Volkskunstmuseum, Seebach, Baden 020162
Trachtenhaus Jatzwauk, Hoyerswerda 018014
Trachtenmuseum, Ochsenfurt 019433
Trackside Antiques, Detroit 088777
Tracy, Columbus 115806
Tracy Maund Historical Collection, Carlton South 000900
Trada, Chipping Norton 141522
Tradart Genève, Genève 082471
Trade Antiques, Alford, Lincolnshire 083265
Trade Antiques, Napoli . . . 076058, 106390, 127797, 140081
Trade Art, Madrid 081402
Trade Picture Services, London . . . 131197
Trade Wind, Rottingdean 086410
Trader, Sam, San Francisco 092900
Trader Windmill, Sibsey 041026
Traders of the Lost Art, Calgary . . . 058810
Tradestone Gallery, Baltimore 115088
Tradewind East, Honolulu 116246
Tradewind Fine Art, Tintagel 114579
Tradice, Praha 060169, 124001
Tradíció, Győr 074740
Tradición Revista, Albuquerque . . . 136645
Trading Arts & Crafts Aboriginal Corporation, Mount Isa 056286
Trading Post, Mountain Ash 086026
Trading Post, Saskatoon 097202
Trading Post Antiques, Tauranga . . . 079266
Tradisjonsbygg AS, Kviteseid 128991
Traditiekamer Regiment Stoottroepen, Assen 029282
Traditiekamer Typhoon, Volkel 030287
Traditiekamer Vliegbasis Twenthe, Enschede 029570
Traditio Antiguidades e Decoracoes, Rio de Janeiro 058660
Tradition Faïence, Montereau-Fault-Yonne 124450
Traditional Art Gallery, New York . . . 118503
Traditional Heritage Museum, Sheffield 041003
Traditions, Baltimore 087717
Traditions and Treasures, San Antonio 092591
Traditions East Gallery, Makati 108829
Traditions Fine Furniture, Tulsa 093334
Træe, Bryne 030798
Träg, Elfriede & Klaus, Nürnberg . . . 073123
Traen, J., Brugge 057787, 123569
Tränkle, M., Ettenheim 070666
Tränkle, Michael, Mahlberg 072379
Trafalgar Antiques Centre, Woodlesford 087233
Trafalgar Art, Valletta 107456
Trafalgar Bookshop, Brighton 141443
Trafalgar Devenport, Devenport . . . 079077
Trafalgar Galleries, London 085750
Trafalgar Galleries, London 113928
Trafalgar Square Collectors Centre, London 085751
Trafalgars Antiques, Auckland 078988
Trafalgars Antiques, North Shore . . 079199
Trafelet, V., Dettighofen bei Lanzenneuform 082340
Traffey, Moirans 064576
Trafico de Arte, León 110401
Trafo - Galerie 5020 in Print, Salzburg 135582
Trag-Art, Bern 111278
Tragor Ignác Múzeum, Vác 021913
Trail End State Historic Museum, Colorado-Wyoming Association of Museums, Sheridan 048149
Trail Museum, Trail 006650
Trailer Gallery, Saint-Martin 105472
Traill County Historical Society Museum, Hillsboro 044543
Trailside Nature and Science Center, Mountainside 046078
Trailside Nature Center and Museum, Cincinnati 042930
Trailside Nature Museum, Cross River 043229
Traiman, Louis, Philadelphia 123049
Train Historique du Lac de Rillé, Rillé 014049
Traineau, Versailles 138656
The Training Center, Sanaa 120549
Trainland U.S.A., Colfax 043040
Les Trains de Saint-Eutrope, Musée Vivant, Evry 011764
Trains Limited, Saint Louis 092323
Trains & Toys, Omaha 091587
Traisentaler Antiquitäten- und Sammlermesse, Traismauer 093588
Traits Singuliers, Dijon 062678
Trakai Historical Museum, Trakai . . 027861
Trakijska Grobnica, Kazanlăk 004719
Traktoren-Museum Kempen, Horn-Bad Meinberg 018007
Traktorenmuseum, Vordernberg . . . 002794
Traktorenmuseum, Westerkappeln . 020829
Traktorveteranensammlung Dorf an der Pram, Wendling 002833
Trallero, Barcelona 080946
Tram Museum Rotterdam, Rotterdam 030107
Tram Museum Zürich, Zürich 037806
Trama, Barcelona 080947, 110259
Trama, Madrid 110624
Trambahn-Museum, München 019126
Tramer, Irma, Bünde 070086
Trammell and Margaret Crow Collection of Asian Art, Dallas 043278
Trammuseum, Schepdaal 003744
Tramway Museum, Bendigo 000796
Tramway-Museum Graz, Graz 001951
Tran, Hau Tuan, Ho Chi Minh City . . 120533
Tranby House, Maylands, Western Australia 001228
Tranchina, Pietro, Modena 127748
Traner, Valencia 081681
Trang, An, Ha Noi 120492
Tranmeçon, Armel, Les Sables-d'Olonne 063787
Trannod, Concarneau 099167
Tranquilino Sandalio de Noda Museo de Ciencias Naturales, Pinar del Río . 008097
Trans, New York 136646
Trans-Art Gallery, San Antonio 119461
Trans Wien, Wien 052601
Transamerican Antiques, Virginia Beach 093368
TransArt, Köln 103728
Transatlantic Antiques & Fine Art, Ampthill 083301
Transatlantique, Bruxelles 137473
Transcona Historical Museum, Winnipeg 006868
Transdeco, Espoo 098711
Transee Antik, Altmünster 056916, 123335
Transenantic, Nice 065153
Transference, Flinders 055832
Transference, Hampton 055952
Transformation Treasures, Pittsburgh 091864
Transgariep Museum, Philippolis . . 034697
Transição, Lisboa 080038
Transition Books, San Francisco . . . 142967
TransNamib Museum, Windhoek . . 029110
Transnet Heritage Foundation Library, Johannesburg 034657
Transoceanea, Chicago 115570
Transparence, Biot 098973
Transparence, Paris 100915
Transportation Exhibits, Nevada City 046184
Transportation Museum, Cairo 009326
Transvaal Museum, Northern Flagship Institution, Pretoria 034731
Transylvania Museum, Lexington . . 045265
Tranviaser, Zaragoza 129833
Trap, København 098587
Trapenat, Châteaudun 120971
Trapezium House, The Petersburg Museums, Petersburg 046910
Trapholt, Museum of Modern Danish Art, Applied Art and Furniture Design, Kolding 008998
Trapp & Aumüller, Backnang 069253
Trappin, Raffaelle, Bolzano 127199
Traquair House, Innerleithen 039799
Traralgon and District Arts Society, Traralgon 052495, 095352
Traralgon Antiques, Traralgon 056736

Trasa-Urban Arts Collective, Salt Lake City 055071
Trash From the Past, Honolulu 088981
Trash 'n' Treasure, Alsager 083281
Trash n'Treasure, Ottawa 059051
Trash or Treasure 2000, Baltimore . 087718
Trash Palace Epilogue, Auckland . . 078989
Trash to Treasures, Indianapolis . . . 089352
Trash & Treasures, Manawatu 140636
Trash & Treasures Too, Manawatu . 140637
Traslucido, Firenze 075415
Trastad Samlinger, Borkenes 030788
El Trastero, Logroño 081189
La Trastienda, Burgos 081020
La Trastienda, Cali 059887
La Trastienda, León 081174
La Trastienda de Felcar, Gijón 081129
La Trastienda de Felcar, Gijón 081130
Tratteggio, Santander 081561, 129724
Traub, Johann, Eichstätt 070521
Traub, Johann & Anneliese, Eichstätt 070522
Traube, D., Bruxelles 058098
Traube & von Hardenberg, Nörten-Hardenberg 073064
Traudisch, I., Wiehl 105238
Traumpfade, Worpswede 105334
Trauner, Chlothilde, Mauthausen . . 137231
Trauque, Betty, Lézignan-Corbières 063808
Trautmann, Stéphanie-C., Lausanne 082570, 130077
Trautmann & Meeßen, Aachen 101531
Trautner, Elfriede, Innsbruck 057089, 095601
Trauzettel, Stolberg, Rheinland 139744
Trave, Reinfeld, Holstein 073479
Trave Antik, Travemünde . 074084, 139785
Travel Art Galéria, Szeged 105578
Travel Thru Time, Phoenix 091775
Travel Town Museum, Los Angeles . 045468
Traveler's Rest State Historic Site, Toccoa 048564
Traveling Exhibition Information Service Newsletter, Largo 136647
Traveller Antiques, Edmonton 058842
Travellers Rest Historic House Museum, Nashville 046155
Traveller's Trading Post, Enmore . . 055801
Traver, William, Seattle 120003
Traver, William, Seattle 120004
Travers, Scott, New York 091299
Traverse County Historical Society Museum, Wheaton 049139
Traversothèque, Musée du Chemin de Fer, Mulhouse 013300
Travis, Atlanta 087536
Travis, Matthew, Houston 116419
Travis & Emery, London 141910
Trawler Pictures, Cleethorpes 112876
Trax In Time, Tauranga 079267
Trayecto, Vitoria-Gasteiz 110874
Trazit, Lionel, Trizac 068632
Trazos, Bogotá 098196
Trazos, Cali 098241
Trazos Tres, Santander 110755
Treadgolds Museum, Portsmouth . . 040772
Treadway Gallery, Cincinnati 115668
Tréanton, Morlaix 064793
Trearte, Burgdorf 111325
Treasure Aisles, Saint Louis 092324
The Treasure Box, Hickling 113240
Treasure Chest, Berwick-upon-Tweed 083494, 130373
Treasure Chest, Blackrock 074865
Treasure Chest, Felixstowe 141613
Treasure Chest, North Scituate 136648
Treasure Chest, Weymouth 087118, 142151
Treasure Chest, Whitley Bay 087138
Treasure Chest Antiques, Vancouver 059429
Treasure Chest by BM, Cincinnati . . 088288
Treasure Chest of Indy, Indianapolis 089353
Treasure Earth, Brunswick 055574
Treasure Gallery, Fremantle 094571
Treasure House, Charlotte 087986
Treasure House of Books, Fitzroy . . 136903
Treasure House of Flowers & Art, Kingston 106821
Treasure House of the Eiheiji Temple, Eiheiji 026451
Treasure Hunt, Houston 089231
Treasure Hunt, Jacksonville 142470
Treasure Hunt, Pittsburgh 091865
Treasure Ireland, Dublin 074951
Treasure Island, Fort Worth 088890
Treasure Island, Louisville 090039
Treasure Mart, Omaha 091588
Treasure of the Sierra Madre, Fresno 088922
Treasure Shop, Tucson 093272
Treasure Trove, Beirut 077419
Treasure Trove, San Diego 092691, 123100
Treasure Trove Antiques, Columbus 088444
Treasure Trove Shipwreck Museum, Port Douglas 001394
Treasured Restorations, San Antonio 132831
Treasured Scarab, Denver 088743
Treasurehouse, Washington 120355
Treasurer's House, York 041482
Treasures, Den Haag 078256
Treasures, Exmouth 084366
Treasures, Four Elms 084428
Treasures and Collectibles, Houston 089232
Treasures and Pleasures, New York 091300
Treasures and Trifles, New York . . . 091301
Treasures and Trifles, San Antonio . 092592
Treasures Antique Mall, Salt Lake City 092468
Treasures From The Past, Yarra Glen 056898
Treasures of Ballater, Ballater 083374
Treasures of Ours, Saint Louis 092325
Treasures of the Earth, Corpach . . . 039144
Treasures of the Sea Exhibit, Delaware Technical and Community College, Georgetown 044172
Treasures of Time, Toronto 059306
Treasures of Yarraville, Yarraville . . 056903
Treasures of Yesterday, Coorparoo . 055716
Treasures Recycled, Charlotte 087987, 131875
Treasures & Trifles, Denver 088744
Treasures Unlimited, Charlotte 087988
Treats & Treasures, Coolamon 055710
Treaty House, Waitangi National Trust, Waitangi, Auckland 030619
Treaty Site History Center, Saint Peter 047713
Třebechovické Muzeum Betlémů, Třebĕchovice pod Orebem 008717
Trebellar, A Coruña 110324
Trebosc & Van Lelyveld, Amsterdam 077986
Trébuquet, Raymond, Toulon (Var) . 124968
Trecastle Antiques Centre, Trecastle 086913
Treco e Breguetes Comercio de Antiguidades, Rio de Janeiro 058661
Tredant, J.R., South Molton 086643
Tredegar House and Park, Newport, Gwent 040564
Tree, Chicago 088185
Tree Frog Gallery, Maleny 094772
Treeck, Gustav van, München 126471
Treedale Antiques, Little Dalby 085011, 130899
Treedale Antiques, Oakham 086150, 131341
Treefrogs, West Hollywood 093518
Treen Antiques, Manchester 131258
Trees of Stone, Salt Lake City 119375
Treff, Baabe 069248
Treff, Chemnitz 070141
Treff, H., Zingst 074569
Treffeisen, Ruth, Wiggensbach 105293
Treffer, Hans, Klagenfurt . 057114, 095622
Treffpunkt Kunst, Ottobrunn 053573, 104562
Treffpunktgalerie, Stuttgart 105018
Trefpunt, Deurne 137490
Tregaskis, Raymond & Victoria, Paddington, New South Wales 056422
Treger, Richard, Paris 100916
Treglown, Roger J., Macclesfield . . 141931
Tregoning Antiques, Bournemouth .083610, 130419
Tregony Antiques, Tregony 086914
Tregony Gallery, Tregony 114599
Treherne Museum, Treherne 006651
Treibholz, Düsseldorf 070453
Treichel, Gerhard, Kippenheim 134090
Treillage, New York 091302
Treille Marine, Saint-Martin-de-Ré . 067636
Le Treize, Bruxelles 058099
De Trekbel, Haarlem 078484
Het Trekkermuseum, Nisse 029967
Trelleborgs Museum, Trelleborg . . . 036716
Treloar, Michael, Adelaide 136776
Trelyon Gallery, Saint Ives, Cornwall 114375
Trema, Lisboa 109357
Trémaud, Catherine, Nieulle-sur-Seudre 065163
Trémaud, Jean-Pierre, Doizieux . . . 062693
Tremayne, Saint Ives, Cornwall . . . 086459
Trembath Welch, Great Dunmow . . 122525
Tremblay, Pierre, Toronto 059307
Trembley, London 058889
Trembowla Cross of Freedom Museum, Dauphin 005330
Tréméac, Jean-Marie, Pontrieux . . . 066947
Tremeaux, Claude, Beaune 061306
Tremmel, Manfred, Waldsee 126962
Trémont, Gérard Sérgio M., Porto . . 140869
Tremont Gallery, Boston 042346
Trench Puzzles, Stowmarket 086770
Trenčianske Múzeum, Trenčín 034443
Trenck, Stefan von der, Lensahn . . . 126212
TrenDepot, Buffalo 115268
Trender, Robert, London 131198
Trengarin Gallery, Narrogin 094929
Trengove, Warlingham 087024
Trent, West Hollywood 093519
Trentham Agricultural and Railway Museum, Trentham 001568
Trentham Treasures, Wellington . . . 079355
Fratelli Trenti, Brescia 127236
Trenton City Museum, Trenton 048607
Trenton Historical Museum, Trenton 048599
Trepanier Baer Gallery, Calgary . . . 096851
Trepassey Area Museum, Trepassey 006652
Trèpetie, Maastricht 078626
Treppengalerie und Edition Treppen, Oldenburg, Oldenburg . . 104544, 134335
Treppenhauer, U., Berlin 069775
Treptau, Axel, München 126472
Trepte, Dresden 070333
Trerice, Newquay 040572
Tres Petite Shoppe, Saint Louis . . . 092326
Tres Serveis Culturals, Palma de Mallorca 110701
Três Xelins, Lisboa 080039
Tresfjord Museum, Tresfjord 031273
Tresillian Antiques, Tresillian 086916, 131606
Tresoar, Frysk Histoarysk en Letterkundich Sintrum, Leeuwarden 029844
Le Trésor, Monthey 082666
Tresor am Römer, Frankfurt am Main 070797, 139100
Trésor de Grand-Mère, Rodez 067197
Trésor de la Basilique Saint-Materne, Walcourt 003841
Tresor de la Catedral, Girona 035238
Trésor de la Cathédrale de Troyes, Troyes 015057
Trésor de la Cathédrale Notre-Dame, Moulins (Allier) 013272
Trésor de la Cathédrale Notre-Dame, Tournai 003812
Trésor de la Cathédrale Notre-Dame-du-Glarier, Sion 037568
Trésor de la Cathédrale Saint-Nicolas, Chapitre Cathédral de Saint-Nicolas, Fribourg 037105
Trésor de la Collégiale, Huy 003530
Trésor de la Collegiale Sainte-Waudru, Mons 003654
Trésor de l'Eglise Primaire Saint-Sebastien, Stavelot 003784
Trésor de Paris, Paris 066619
Trésor de Saint Foy, Conques 011469
Trésor d'Église, Art Sacré, Marseille 012954
Trésor d'Église, Cathédrale Saint-Just-et-Saint-Pasteur, Narbonne 013355
Trésor des Nomades, Marrakech . . 077686
Trésor du Frère Hugo d'Oignies, Namur 003669
Trésor du Passé, Jounieh 077434
Trésor et Musée de la Collegiale Sainte-Begge, Andenne 003147
Trésor Public, Blois 061529
Trésor Saint-Gervais, Avranches . . . 010606
Tresorama, La Ferté-Macé 012252
Trésorerie Générale, Moulins (Allier) 064816
Trésorerie Générale de la Gironde, Bordeaux 061657
Trésorient, Paris 066620
Trésoriers de France, Montpellier . . 064759
Aux Trésors d'Antan, Alès 060775
Trésors d'Antan, Dômevre-en-Haye 062702
Trésors d'Asie, Paris 066621
Trésors de l'Afrique et de l'Orient, Zürich 083033
Trésors des Siècles, La Ferté-sous-Jouarre 063377
Trésors du Monde, Arzon 061005
Les Trésors du Passé, Montréal . . . 059015
Tress, Horst, Köln 103729
Tressage & Rempaillage, Québec . . 123808
Tresure Room Gallery of the Interchurch Center, New York 046414
Tretene, Massimiliano, Bologna . . . 075115
Tret'ja Galereja, Moskva 109596
Treubmann, Rolf, Lehe 072184
Treussier, Ronan, Nantes 064951
Treussier, Ronan, Nantes 064952
Treuter, Siegi, Bodman-Ludwigshafen 102166
Trev Deeley Motorcycle Museum, Richmond 006286
Trevi Flash Art Museum, Trevi 026116
Trévise Antiquités, Paris 066622
Trevithick Cottage, Camborne 038957
Trevizanutto, Sylvio, Montréal 059016
Trevor, Allan, Toronto 097389
Tri-Art, Los Angeles 116902
Tri-Cities Museum, Grand Haven . . 044264
Tri-County Historical Society and Museum, Herington 044518
Tri-State Mineral Museum, Joplin . . 044883
Tria Phylla, Athinai 134490
Triad, New York 118504
Triada, Gdańsk 108901
Triada, Sopot 109079
Triade, Barbizon 098925
Triadis, Sofia 096750
Triangelns Prylbod, Malmö 081880
Triangle Art Gallery, San Francisco . 119818
Le Triangle Blanc, Le Croisic 099433
Triangle de Verre, Poligny 101017
Triangle Editions, New York 118505, 135466
Triangle Gallery, Calgary 096852
Trianglens Antikvariat, København . 137902
El Trianon, Málaga 081436
Trianon, Marseille 064395
Trianon, Monaco 107545
Trianon Museum and Art Gallery, Denver 043420
TriArt Gallery, Louisville 116970
Trias Art Gallery, Toronto 097390
Trias-Museum, Ochsenfurt 019434
Tribal, Bordeaux 099011
Tribal Art, Donaghadee 112949
Tribal Art, 's-Hertogenbosch 108080
Tribal Art Gallery, Melbourne 094832
Tribal Arts, Bruxelles 058100
Tribal Design, Amsterdam 077987
Tribal Eye, Toronto 097391
Tribal Gallery, Gosford 055906

Tribal Gathering London, London . . 113929
Tribal Hut, Houston 116420
Tribal Museum, Ahmedabad 021994
Tribal & Oriental Arts & Antiques, Lesmurdie 056096
Tribal - The Magazine of Tribal Art, San Francisco 136649
Tribbia, Edgar, Champ-sur-Drac . . . 062113
Tribbia, Edgar, Laffrey 063481
Tribble, J., Atlanta 087537
Tribe & Son, Tom, Sturminster Newton 086782, 131556
Tribeca, New York 118506
Tribes Gallery, New York 118507
Tribuzio, Paolo, Roma 128230
Tricard, Maurice, Arras 060991
Tricia's Treasures, Birmingham . . . 087785
Tricia's Treasures, Gosnells 055907
Tricromia, Roma 106641
Tridaya Eka Dharma Museum, Bukittinggi 022409
Le Trident, Nice 065154
Trident, Regency Park . . . 056523, 137069
Trident Antiques, Long Melford 085842, 131233
Trident Booksellers, Boston 142258
Trident Galleries, Leicester 113376
Il Tridente, Verona 077025
Triebel, M., Bad Sachsa 069362
Triebold, Alexandra, Riehen 111843
Trier, Dieter, Leipzig 139406
Trierer Münzfreunde e.V., Trier 053574
Triestingtaler Heimatmuseum, Weissenbach an der Triesting 002816
Triff-Daumas, Henri, Paris 100917
Trift- und Holzfällermuseum, Bad Großpertholz 001720
Trigano, Patrice, Paris . . . 066623, 100918
Trigg Ison, Los Angeles 116903
Triglavska Muzejska Zbirka, Mojstrana 034505
Trigon Gallery, Plzeň 098409
Trillarium, Waffensammlung und Heimatmuseum, Cleebronn 016570
Triller, Ina-Amélie, München 126473
Trilles, Marti, Castello de la Plana . 081040
Trilogy, New Farm 094935
Triluz, Bilbao 080994, 129447
Trim, Nagoya 077157
Trimarchi, Bologna 105979
Trimboli, Pietro, Bologna 127185
Trimbridge Galleries, Bath 083449
Trimbridge Galleries, Bath 112589
Trinca, Vittorio, Roma 076710
Trindade, Porto 109403
Trindade, António, Lisboa 080040
Trindade, João Campos Pereira, Lisboa 080041
Trindade, Luís Miguel, Lisboa 129181
Trindade, Tereza, Belo Horizonte . . 058453
Trinder, Neil, Sheffield 131480
Trinder, P.D. & R., Sudbury, Suffolk . 142101
Trinders' Fine Tools, Clare 084028
Tring Market, Tring 122728
Trinidad Antigüedades, Buenos Aires 055247
Trinité Art'Gallery, Troyes 101393
Trinity Antiques, Perth 056462
Trinity Antiques Centre, Colchester .084058, 141532
Trinity Arcade Bookshop, Perth 137046
Trinity Arts Guild, Fort Worth 055072, 116167
Trinity Books, Randburg 140975
Trinity Curious, Edinburgh 084317, 130681
Trinity Fine Art, Milano 075880
Trinity Gallery, Atlanta 114937
Trinity Heights - Saint Joseph Center-Museum, Sioux City 048187
Trinity House, Newcastle-upon-Tyne 040554
Trinity House National Lighthouse Centre, Penzance 040694
Trinity Interpretation Centre, Trinity . 006655
Trinity Museum, Trinity 006656
Trinity Museum of the Parish of Trinity Church, New York 046415
Trintignan, Hélène, Montpellier 099765
Triny, C F, Piazzogna 111809
Trio-Antiek, Antwerpen 123554
Trio Antik, København 060388
Trio Silversmiths, Philadelphia 132639
Triod, Dobrič 058753, 137596
Triolo, Pietrina, Messina 127507
Triomphe Arte e Antiguidades, Rio de Janeiro 058662
Triomphe Arte e Antiguidades, Rio de Janeiro 058663
Trionfante, Palermo 076185
Trionfante, Palermo 076186
Trionfante, Palermo 076187
Trionfante, Palermo 127842
La Trionfante di Precania, Stefana, Palermo 076188, 106448, 121715
Tripet, Raoul, Vaulion 082872
Tripier, Antoinette, Paris 121214
Triple Candie, New York 118508
Trippel, V., Braunschweig 069996
Triptiek, Breda 078120
Triptychon Verlag, Essen 133919
Triptyque, Paris 066624, 124825
Triquart, B., Ober-Hilbersheim 073133
Trish, Cleveland 088366
Trish's Dungeon, North Fremantle . 056365
Triskelion, Toronto 137721
Trist, William, Edinburgh 130682
Tristan's, Wadebridge 114639
Triton Collection, New York 118509
Triton Galleries, Exeter 113042
Triton Gallery, Cheltenham 083934
Triton Gallery, New York 118510
Triton Gallery, Paignton 114215
Triton Gallery, Torquay 114586
Triton Museum of Art, Santa Clara . 047954
Triton Verlag, Wien 133235
Tritonia 2, Hamburg 103224
Tritonus, Krummhörn 103799
Trnka, Jozef, Lausanne 130078
Troadec, Pierre, Perros-Guirec 066772
Troadkasten, Freinberg 001866
Troadkasten, Sauerlach 020000
Troadkasten, Schardenberg 002641
Troadkasten Fornach, Fornach 001860
La Trobe, Newtown, Victoria 056344
Le Troc 2, Roma 076711
Troc 34, Le Crès 063611
Troc 40, Herm 063148, 138106
TROC 79, Niort 065201
Troc 89, Avallon 061119
Troc 89, Avallon 061120
Troc Ambiance, Angers 060863
Troc-Antic, La Rochelle 063440
Troc Antik, Metz 064537
Troc Broc 49, Saumur 068154
Troc Broc Antiquités, Beaune 061307
Le Troc de la Gloire, Toulouse 068547
Troc de l'Ile, Chavelot 062259
Troc-de-l'Ile, Orgeval 065288
Troc de l'Ile, Troyes 068655
Troc-de-l'Ile Floride, Saint-Maur . . 067655
Troc de l'Ile Occase, Bourg-en-Bresse 061710
Troc de l'Ile Verfer, Narbonne 064968
Troc en Ville, Marseille 064396
Troc et Chine, Mougins 064807
Troc Pérignon, Toulouse 068548
Troc & Puces, Châteauroux 062211
Troc Salonais, Salon-de-Provence . 068104
Troc-Vente 89, Auxerre 061109
La Trocade du Sablon, Bruxelles . . . 058101
Trocadero Antiguidades, Lisboa . . . 080042
Trocadore, Isle 063217
Trocante, Béziers 061444
Trocante, Moulin-Neuf 064810
La Trocante, Nice 065155
La Trocante, Nîmes 065189
Trocante, Rotterdam 078748
La Trocante, Saint-Avold 067368
Le Troc'Antic, Vizille 069021
Trocaz, Michel, Beaune 061308
Trocfouille, Les Mages 063769
Trochu and District Museum, Trochu 006657
Trocmeubles, Cannes 061958
Trocmez, Bertrand, Clermont-Ferrand 099154
Troc'n'Roll, Bruxelles 058102
Trocque, Chantal & Michel, Brionne 061805
Troc'Tout, Cherveix-Cubas 062279
Troc'Truc, Montauban 064641
Trödelstübchen, Hagen, Westfalen . 071168
Trödler & Sammler Journal, Reichertshausen 135826
Tröger, K., Lörrach 139420
Trösch, Armin, Zürich 141364
Tröster, Herbert, Schmallenberg . . . 073706
Trog, Denver 088745
Troge, Birgit, Hamburg 071346
Trøgstad Bygdemuseum, Trøgstad . 031274
Trohay, Jean-Claude, Fréjus 062940
Troickij Sobor, Serpuchovskij istoriko-chudožestvennyj muzej, Serpuchov 033871
Trois, Vittorio, Venezia 076977
Trois Fois Passera, Montréal 059017
Troise, Nicola, Napoli 127798
La Troisème Veille, Paris 138551
Le Troisième Oeil, Bordeaux 099012
Trojahn, Martina & Michael, Berlin . 102069
Trojner, Audrey, Buffalo 087917
Troll, Halle, Saale 125793
Trollenäs Slott, Eslöv 036258
Trolley Museum of New York, Kingston 045015
Trolley Square Gallery, Salt Lake City 119376
Trollhättans Museum och Saab Museum, Trollhättan 036720
Tromayer, Erich, Wien . . . 095953, 133236
Trombacco, Dr. Federica, Bologna . 127186
Trommsdorf-Galerie, Erfurt 102648
Trompat, Yvette, Orléans 065309
Trompetenmuseum, Bad Säckingen 015782
Trompka, Gerd, Köln 072019
Het Tromp's Huys, Vlieland 030283
Troms Forsvarsmuseum, Bardu . . . 030755
Tromsø Folkemuseum, Tromsø 031278
Tromsø Universitets Museum, Tromsø 031279
Tron, Lesznowola 079666
Troncin, Sabine, Nancy 124471
Troncone, Gabriele, Napoli 076059
Troncone, Giovanni, Napoli 076060
Troncone, Maria, Napoli 076061
Troncone & Laezza, Napoli 076062
Trondarnes Distriktmuseum, Harstad 030879
Trøndelag Folkemuseum, Trondheim 031287
Trondheim Kunstmuseum, Trøndelag Kunstgalleri, Trondheim 031288
Trondheim Politimuseum, Trondheim 031289
Troner Art, Düsseldorf 070454
Troops of Time, Jacksonville 089468
Troost, Marja, Amstelveen 077764
Tropea, Mario, Basel 129936
Tropea, Sebastiano, Catania 075264
Trophäensaal, Altenfelden 001679
Trophée 89, Auxerre 061110
Tropical Decorators and Upholsters, Jacksonville 132197
Tropical Giclees, Honolulu 116247
Tropical Trading, Paris 100919
Tropico del Cancro, Bari 105936
Tropico del Cancro 2, Bari 075034
Tropique Bouquinerie, Saint-Étienne 138600
Trosiner, Hamburg 071347
Trost, Lippstadt 103932
Trost, André, Juigné-sur-Loire 063265
Trost, Heiner, München 072871
Trostbach, Gisela, München 126474
Trosterud Skolemuseum, Rømskog 031147
Troszkiewicz, Warszawa 140798
Trotman, Ken, Cambridge 141477
Trotot, Emmanuel, Bougival 061677
Trottenmuseum, Schliengen 020046
Trotters, Masterton 079151
Trottmann, Dr. Helene, München . . 139551
Troubadour, Paris 066625
Troubetzkoy, New York 118511
Troubetzkoy, Paris 100920
Troussier, Rémy, Thury-Harcourt . . 068418
Troussillé, Guy, Toulouse 068549
Trout Farm, San Francisco 092901
Trout Gallery, Carlisle 042622
Troutmark Books, Cardiff 141489
Trouvaille, Bern 082244
La Trouvaille, Bruxelles 137474
Trouvaille, Cannes 061959
La Trouvaille, Marseille 064397
La Trouvaille, Milano 075881
Trouvaille, Roosendaal 108171
Trouvaille, Toulouse 068550
La Trouvaille, Trouville-sur-Mer . . . 068640
Trouvailles, Boulogne-sur-Mer 061700
Trouvailles, Cambrai 061923
Trouvailles, Epagny 062779
Trouvailles, Lezignan-La Cebe 063809
Trouvailles, Lyon 124376
Trouvailles, Nantes 064953
Les Trouvailles, Paris 066626
Trouvailles, Paris 135731
Les Trouvailles, Saint-Ouen 067911
Trouvailles Antiquités, Lyon 064189
Les Trouvailles de Léonard, Québec 059078
Trouvailles et Envies, Missillac 064570
Trouvé Lorelay, Pisa 076247
Les Trouvères, Bruxelles 058103
Les Trouveres, Bruxelles 123610
Trova Foundation, Saint Louis 047682
Trovato, Ben, Brugge 096120
Il Trovatore, Cagliari 075230
Trowbridge, Atlanta 114938
Trowbridge, Chicago 115571
Trowbridge, London 113930, 131199
Trowbridge, Martin, New York 118512
Trowbridge Gallery, Claremont 055677, 136860
Trowbridge Gallery, Crowborough . . 112925
Trowbridge Museum, Trowbridge . . 041242
Troxell-Steckel House and Farm Museum, Egypt 043623
Troy Museum and Historic Village, Troy 048616
Troyanski Manastir, Orešak 004763
Troyer, Washington 120356
Trub, Dieter, Gundelsheim, Württemberg 071152
Trubarjev, Ljubljana 140969
Truchelut, Daniel, Houilles 063180
TRUCK Centre, Calgary 005200
True Blue Antiques, Mangerton 056150
True Blue Fine Art Gallery, Hobart . . 094647
True Devotion Design, Oakland 091443
True Frame and Art, Cobram 094410
True Reflections, Hamilton 096427
True to Form, Jacksonville 116547
Trübendörfer, S. & I., Weinsberg . . . 105196
True's Yard Fishing Heritage Centre, King's Lynn 039881
Trützschler's Milch- und Reklamemuseum, Hildburghausen 017918
Truffi, Rinalda, Venezia 106783
Trulla, Joël, Fontenay-le-Comte . . . 062904
Trulli, Massimo, Roma 106642
Truman Corners Antique Mall, Kansas City 089526
Trummer, August, Graz 095544
Trump, Manfred, Öhringen 104522
The Trumpet (New York), New York . 136650
Trumpington, Guildford 113171
Trumpington Fine Art, Cambridge . . 112795
Trumpington Gallery, Cambridge . . . 112796
Trunke, Friedrich, Memmingen 072516
Trunz, Hartwig, Spiez 130183
Trunz, M., Eschbach 102659

Truong, Hélène, Paris 066627
Truppe, Matthäus, Graz 137181
Truppe, Peter, Wien 137372
Truppenmuseum, Straß in Steiermark 002719
Truro Center for the Arts at Castle Hill, Truro 052277
Truscott, Christina, London 085752
Trussart, Daniel, Rouen 101123
Truva Müzesi Örenyeri, Çanakkale . 038040
Try Museum, Dronninglund 008834
Tryart Gallery, Louisville Visual Art Association, Louisville 045500
Tryon, London 085753, 113931
Tryon Palace, New Bern 046195
Trysil Bygdemuseum, Trysil 031292
Trzcina, Gdańsk 079590
Trzebiatowski, Krzysztof, Hamburg . 071348
Tržiška Galerija, Tržič 034532
Tržiški Muzej, Tržič 034533
TS-Auto- & Viestintämuseo, Turku . 010173
Tsa Mo Ga Memorial Museum, Plains 047075
Tsangarakis, Kallitheathinas 105427
Tsannis, Paylos, Athinai 074611
Tsantilas, Margit, Velden 057339
Tsantilis, Athinai 074612
Tsarinas, Sydney 056691
Tschanun, Eugen, Bregenz 056951
Tschanz, Jean-Roch, Bern 082245
Tschauder, B., Hameln 103241
Tschechisches Zentrum-CzechPoint, Berlin 016185
Tschernitz, Herbert, Wien 057571
Tscheschlog, H.-G., Schwelm 073770
Tschetschorke, Rolf, Kirchhundem . 103559
Tschierske, Monika, Berlin 125309
Tschinkl, Andreas, Marktleuthen . . 072462
Tschirren, René, Basel 141218
Tschirschky, Isabelle, Überlingen . . 074134
Tschöpe, Reinhild, Kaarst . 071678, 121460
Tschofen, Helmut, Sankt Gallenkirch 057290
Tschoppe, Manfred & Uschi, Hattstedt 071433
Tschudi, Glarus 111518, 135022
Tschudi, Zuoz 112222
Tse, C.Y., Hong Kong 059699
Tsé Wan, Lyon 064190
Tsé Wan, Lyon 064191
Tsekouras, Andreas, Athinai 074613
Tsenka, Paris 100921
Tsepelidis, Grigorios, Thessaloniki . 074643
Tshuapa, Bruxelles 058104
Tsilalis, Athinai 105410
Tsimpiskaki, Tzeni, Thessaloniki . . 105463
Tsiridis, Georgios, Thessaloniki . . . 105464
Tsochantaridis, R., Heidelberg 071463
Tsuchida Bakusen Bijutsukan, Sawata 027044
Tsui Museum of Art, Hong Kong . . . 007134
Tsukamoto, Tokyo 077319
Tsukuba Bijutsukan, Ibaraki-ken Kindai Bijutsukan, Tsukuba 027296
Tsukushi, Yokohama 107153
Tsumeb Cultural Village, Tsumeb . . 029101
Tsumeb Museum, Tsumeb 029102
Tsumugi, Grace, London 113932
Tsurui Bijutsukan, Niigata 026916
Tsuruki & Co., Y., Kyoto 077134
Tsurumoto, Hiroshima 077069
Tsuwano Gendai Photo Gallery, Tsuwano 027299
Ttaka Bazar, Donostia-San Sebastián 081091
TTD Museum, Tirupati 022356
Tu Do, Ho Chi Minh City 120534
Tu Do, Ho Chi Minh City 120535
Tu Do, Houston 116421
TU-Endie-Wei State Park, Point Pleasant 047112
Tuam Mill Museum, Tuam 022866
Tuapsinskij Kraevedčeskij Muzej im. N.G. Poletaeva, Tuapse 033970
Tuatapere Bushmans Museum, Tuatapere 030608
Tub King, Jacksonville 089469
Tubac Center of the Arts, Tubac . . . 048624
Tube, Düsseldorf 139024
Tube Gallery, Bedlington 112601
Tuberculosemuseum Beatrixoord, Appelscha 029259
Tubman African-American Museum, Macon 045570
Tubman Centre of African Culture, Cape Mount 027824
Tuchel, Piet, Grafschaft 071082
Tucher, Bernhard von, Kaisheim . . . 125987
Tucherschloss mit Hirsvogelsaal, Museen der Stadt Nürnberg, Nürnberg . . . 019377
Tuchlauben Galerie, Wien . 057572, 095954
Tuchmacher-Museum Bramsche, Bramsche 016361
Tuchmuseum Lennep der Anna-Hardt-Stiftung, Remscheid 019798
Tuck Museum, Hampton 044411
Tucker, Alan & Joan, Stroud 142098
Tucker, E., Pittsburgh 142782
Tucker, Phyllis, Houston 089233
Tucker, Jonathan & Antonia Tozer, London 113933
Tucker House Museum, Saint George's 003905
Tucker Station Antiques, Louisville . 090040
Tucker Tower Nature Center Park Museum, Ardmore 041767
Tuckerbox Antiques, Gundagai 055925
Tucson Auction Service, Tucson . . . 123127
Tucson Children's Museum, Tucson 048641
Tucson Coin, Tucson 093273
Tucson Museum of Art and Historic Block, Tucson 048642
Tucson Plein-Air Painters Society, Tucson 055073
Tucumcari Historical Research Institute Museum, Tucumcari 048648
Tuddal Bygdetun, Tuddal 031293
Tudisco, Pascal, Borgo . . . 061664, 124150
Tudo Usado, Lisboa 080043, 129182
Tudor, Alresford 083279, 130293
Tudor, Richard, London 113934
Tudor, Tony, Brugge 057788
Tudor Antiques, Long Melford 085843, 131234
Tudor Antiques, Napier 079170
Tudor Books, Weston-super-Mare . 142148
Tudor Galleries, Norwich 114169
Tudor House, Barnstaple . 083400, 130339
Tudor House, Stow-on-the-Wold . . 086767
Tudor House, Hosking Memorial Museum, Margate 040425
Tudor House, Weymouth Civic Soc, Weymouth 041358
Tudor House Antiques, Christchurch 084008
Tudor House Antiques, Halesowen . 084554
Tudor House Antiques, Henley-on-Thames 084666
Tudor House Antiques, Ironbridge . . 084806
Tudor House Fine Arts and Antiques, Darwin 055741
Tudor House Galleries, Charlotte . . 115313
Tudor House Museum, Southampton 041061
Tudor Manor, New York 091303
Tudor Manor, New York 091304
Tudor Place Museum, Washington . 048949
Tudor Rose Antiques, Faulconbridge 055815
Tudor Rose Antiques, Faulconbridge 055816
Tudor Rose Antiques, New York . . .091305, 132543
Tudor Rose Antiques, Petworth 086263
tuduv Verlag, München 134282
Tübinger Kunstverein e.V., Tübingen 053575
Tückmantel, Guido, Düsseldorf 070455
Tüm Sanat Galerileri Derneği, Ankara 054254
Tuena, Filippo Maria, Roma 076712
Tüötten-Museum, Mettingen 018925
Türk Nümismatik Derneği, İstanbul . 054255
Türk Vakıf Hat Sanatları Müzesi, İstanbul 038101
Türk ve İslâm Eserleri Müzesi, Edirne 038055
Türk ve Islam Eserleri Müzesi, İstanbul 038102
Türke, Erhard, Bad Salzuflen 101695
Türkiye Ekonomık ve Toplumsal Tarih Vakfı, İstanbul 054256
Türkiyede Sanat, İstanbul 136144
Türr István Múzeum, Baja 021619
Tüshaus-Mühle, Dorsten 016760
Tüzoltó Múzeum, Budapest 021698
Tufariello, Giuseppe, Milano 075882
Tuffier, Thierry, Les Andelys 099466, 124311
Tufts University Art Gallery, Medford 045739
Tugnet Ice House, Spey Bay 041079
Tugu Nasional Museum, Jakarta . . 022455
Tuileries Images, Paris 100922
Les Tuilleries, Lys-lez-Lannoy 064199
Tuition, Entertainment, News, Views, Oxford 136276
Tuits, Dallas 088620
Tukano, Fortaleza 096540
Tukuma Audēju Darbnīcas, Tukums 027788
Tukuma Muzejs, Tukums 027789
Tula, Richard, Atlanta 114939
Tula & Niles, Nelson 079183, 108522
Tulane University Art Collection, Tulane University, New Orleans 046267
Tulare County Museum, Visalia 048803
Tularosa Basin Historical Society Museum, Alamogordo 041592
Tulbagh Antiques, Tulbagh 080751
Tule Antik, Stockholm 082031
Tulhoff & Volk, Berlin 102070
Tulip Antiques, Silvan 056594
Tulip Tree Antiques, Indianapolis . . 089354
La Tulipe Noire, San Francisco 092902, 132914
Tulkens, Fl., Bruxelles 137475
Tulklana Kumbi Aboriginal Galleries, Dareton 094448
Tull, Gottfried, Wadgassen 126956
Tullgarns Slott, Vagnhärad 036777
Tullie House - City Museum and Art Gallery, Carlisle 038999
Tullio, Emilio, Milano 075883
Tullis-Toledano Manor, Biloxi 042214
Tullmuseum, Stockholm 036680
Tullner Museen im Minoritenkloster, Tulln 002762
Tulloch, Launceston 120601
Tullow Museum, Tullow 022867
Tully, Denver 088746
Tulsa, Chennai 074799
Tulsa Antique Mall, Tulsa 093335
Tulsa Artists Coalition, Tulsa 055074, 120209
Tulsa Card, Tulsa 093336
Tulsa Coin and Stamp, Tulsa 093337
Tulsa Watch and Clock Repair, Tulsa 133005
Tulsi Sangrahalaya Ramvan, Satna . 022330
Tulskij Filial Moskovskogo Gosudarstvennogo Universiteta Kultury i Iskusstv, Tula 050666
Tul'skij Gosudarstvennyj Muzej Oružija, Tula 033979
Tulskij Muzej Izobrazitelnych Iskusstv, Tula 033980
Tulskij Oblastnoj Kraevedčeskij Muzej, Tula 033981
Tulum, Yunüs, Gießen 070995
Tuma, Alexander, Wien 137373
Tumanyans Museum, Erevan 000692
Tumbergs Skol- och Hembygdsmuseum, Vårgårda 036782
Tumbling Tumbleweed, Tucson 093274
Tumlaren, Teckomatorp 082050
Tummers & Tummers, Den Haag . . 078257
Tumulka 6000 Prinzregentenstr 97a, München 104331
Tumut and District Historical Museum, Tumut 001572
Tun Abdul Razak Memorial, Kuala Lumpur 027982
Tunabygdens Gammelgård, Borlänge 036229
Tunbridge Wells Antique Centre, Tunbridge Wells 086954
Tunbridge Wells Museum and Art Gallery, Tunbridge Wells 041245
Tunc, Neset, Friedrichshafen 070897
Tuncurry Museum, Tuncurry 001573
Tune Bygdemuseum, Sarpsborg . . . 031175
Túnel do Tempo, Porto Alegre 058527
Tung Jing, Modena 075930
Tung Salaeng Luang, Phitsanulok . . 037923
Tunger, Flensburg 102733
Tungsten, New Orleans 117525
Tunica-Biloxi Native American Museum, Marksville 045689
Tunicia, Madrid 081403
Tunick, David, New York 118513
Tunkl, David, Los Angeles 116904
Tunkl, David, West Hollywood 120416
Tunku Abdul Rahman Memorial, Kuala Lumpur 027983
Le Tunnel, Véretz 101449
Tuns Press, Dalhousie University, Halifax 133314
Tunsons, Denver 116063
Tuomarinkylän Museo, Helsingin Kaupunginmuseo, Helsinki 009584
Tupa, Helsinki 060587, 124053
Tupelo Artist Guild Gallery, Tupelo . 048659
Tupou College Museum, Nuku'alofa 037944
Tupperville School Museum, Bridgetown 005149
Turabo University Museum, Gurabo 032716
Turaidas Muzejrezervāts, Sigulda . . 027778
Turak, Philadelphia 118847
Turakina Antiques, Turakina 079275
Al-Turath, Dubai 083206
Turati, Milano 106337
Turati Arte, Firenze 106074
Turbulence, New York 091306
Turchetti, Manuela, Milano 075884, 106338, 127702
Turchetto, Rita, Venezia 076978
Turchi, G., Firenze 075416
Turchi, Valerio, Roma 076713
Turčianska Galéria, Martin 034390
Turetsky, Rosa, Genève 111506
De Turfschuur, Kolhorn 029816
Turiaf, Bernard, Montfort-l'Amaury . 064684
Turianelli, Massimo, Roma 128231
Turin Gallery, Torino 106708
Turion, Patrick, Saint-Ouen 101191
Turk, W.F., London 085754, 131200
Turkaly, Cleveland 115748
Turkana, Los Angeles 116905
Turkana, New York 091307
Turkana, New York 091308
Turkansaaren Ulkomuseo, Pohjois-Pohjanmaan Museo, Oulu 009940
Turkeyenhof, Bredene 003257
Turki Gharli, Mazen, Damascus . . . 083088
Turkish Sports Museum, Şişli 038178
Turkmen Carpet Museum Gurbansoltan Eje, Așgabat 038204
Turks Head Antiques, Eton 084349
Turkuvaz Sanat Galerisi, Ankara . . . 038013
Turlej, Kraków 134857
Turlough Park House, Castlebar . . . 022706
Turlure, Emilienne, Le Havre 099443
Der Turm, Trausdorf an der Wulka . 095771
Turm 9 - Stadtmuseum Leonding, Leonding 002230
Turm-Galerie-Bonn, Wachtberg . . . 105134
Turmbund, Innsbruck 052602, 133095
Turmgalerie 333, Helmstedt 103349
Turmmuseum, Breitenbrunn, Neusiedlersee 001766
Turmmuseum, Pillichsdorf 002430
Turmmuseum Sankt Magnus, Esens 017056
Turmmuseum Schloß Mengerskirchen, Mengerskirchen 018908

Turmmuseum Stadt Blankenberg, Hennef 017873
Turmuhren- und Heimatmuseum Bockenem, Bockenem 016287
Turmuhrenmuseum, Naunhof 019188
Turn o' the Century, Sherwood 056591
Turn of the Century, New York 091309
Turn of the Century Antiques, Austin 087616
Turn of the Century Hardware, Indianapolis 132164
Turn of the Century Lighting, Toronto 059308
Turn On Lighting, London 085755
Turn the Fox Century, Barcelona 080948
Turnage Place Antiques, Atlanta 087538
Turnbull Bros., Milton 056231
Turnburrys, Jesmond 084817, 130836
Turner, Birmingham 112659
Turner, Exeter 113043
Turner, London 096961
Turner, New York 091310
Turner, A.F.J., East Molesey 084253
Turner, Annmarie, Marlborough 085952
Turner, Dennise, Pontefract 086286
Turner, Helen, New York 118514
Turner, Malcolm, Norwich 086127
Turner, Peter, Gmunden 056995
Turner, Peter, Gmunden 123356
Turner, R. & M., Jedburgh 084811
Turner, S. & E.M., Beeston 083476
Turner, Sally, Wendover 087076
Turner Clayton, Fresno 116190
Turner Curling Museum, Weyburn 006804
Turner Helton, Seattle 093075
Turner House Gallery, Penarth 040682
Turner House Museum, Hattiesburg 044477
Turner, Hugh & Curtis jr., Richmond 119127
The Turner Museum, Sarasota 048002
Turner Society, London 054531
Turner Valley Gas Plant, Turner Valley 006670
Turning Page, Milwaukee 090326
Turning Point Gallery, Washington 120357
Turnip Truck Antiques, San Diego 092692
Turnor, Philip, Rotherham 086409
Turnover Shop, Baltimore 087719
Turnover Shop, Baltimore 087720
Turnowsky, W., Tel Aviv 134539
Turnpike Gallery, Leigh, Lancashire 039980
The Turnstone Gallery, Sandsend 114395
Turpault, René, Tours 068610
Turpin, Alain, Guéret 121014
Turpin, M., London 085756, 131201
Turpins Antiques, Hungerford 084765
Turquat, Paul, Montpellier 064760
Turquin, Eric, Paris 121215
Turquoise, Honfleur 099357
Turquoise Museum, Albuquerque 041624
Turquoise Trading Post, Austin 115021
Turrero Lucia, Manuel, Madrid 081404
Turret House, Wymondham, Norfolk 087277, 142175
Turri, Gobbi & Mirta, Ascona 111142
Turszynski, Uwe, München 139552
Turtle Creek Antiques, Chicago 088186
Turtle Dove, Clayfield 055692
Turtle Fine Art, Rye 114337
Turtle Mountain Chippewa Heritage Center, Belcourt 042103
Turtolan Kylämuseo, Turtola 010181
Turton Tower, Turton Bottoms 041249
Turudda, Lüneburg 072361
Turun Antiikki ja Taide, Turku 060647
Turun Biologinen Museo, Turku 010174
Turun Kaupungin Historiallinen Museo, Turun Linna, Turku 010175
Turun Maakuntamuseo, Turku 010176
Turun Taidemuseo, Turku 010177
Turun Taideyhdistys / Konstföreningen i ÅBO, Turku 052884
Turun Terveydenhuoltomuseo, Turku 010178
Turun Tuomiokirkkomuseo, Turku 010179
Turys Antiquitäten, Oberschan 082712
Tuš i Pero, Sofia 096751
Tuscany, Manchester 114051
Tuscany Fine Arts, Letchworth 113384
Tuscany Galleries, Healesville 094630
Tusculum, Putbus 104646
Tushinsky-Merlette, Ella, Paris 124826
Tushita, Duisburg 133900
Tuskegee Institute National Historic Site, Tuskegee Institute 048672
Tuskulum, Schaffhausen 111892
Tusmore Antiques, Tusmore 056748
Tut-Uncommon Antiques, Memphis 090108
Tutankhamun Exhibition, Dorchester 039261
Tutbury Mill Antiques Centre, Tutbury 086960
Tute-Natura, Bennekom 029306
Tutino, Dominique, Paris 066628
Tutt, J.C., Petworth 086264
TuttAntico, Genova 093796
Tuttantico, Roma 076714
Tuttle, Charles E., Tokyo 134735
Tutto Diverso, Hasselt 058232
Tutzek, Merseburg 072523
Tutzer Pattis, Helga, Bolzano 075134
Tuupalan Museo, Kuhmo 009755
Tuur Galerie, Venlo 108268
Tuusniemen Kotiseutumuseo, Tuusniemi 010184
Tuvikese Shop, Tartu 098708
Tuvinskij Filial Moskovskogo Gosudarstvennogo Universiteta Kultury i Iskusstv, Kyzyl 050642
Tuvinskij Respublikanskij Kraevedčeskij Muzej im. Aldan Maadyr, Kyzyl 033324
TV-Galereja, Moskva 109597
TV Toys Dieren, Dieren 029481
Två Sekel, Uppsala 082062
TVDART, Berlin 016186
Tvedestrand Museum, Tvedestrand 031297
Tveit Bygdemuseum, Tveit 031298
Tveitens Samlinger, Eggedal 030813
Tverskaja Oblastnaja Kartinnaja Galereja, Tver 033986
Tverskoj Gosudarstvennyj Obedinennyj Muzej, Tver 033987
Tvorčeskij Centr i Vystavočnyj Zal Fëdor, Sankt-Peterburg 033834
Tvorčestvo Rodiny, Moskva 080272, 109598
T.W. Wood Gallery and Arts Center, Montpelier 046005
De Twee Pauwen, Den Haag 107957
De Twee Wapens, Den Haag 078258
Tweed and Area Heritage Centre, Tweed 006671
Tweed Museum of Art, University of Minnesota, Duluth 043524
Tweed River Regional Art Gallery, Murwillumbah 001303
Tweeddale Museum, Peebles 040678
Het Tweede Leven, Rotterdam 078749
Tweede Lezer, Brasschaat 137413
Tweewielermuseum Tankstop, Workum 030351
Twentieth Century, London 085757
Twentieth Century Antiques, Coolangatta 055712
Twentieth Century Collectables & Antiques, Hutt City 079120
Twentieth Century Design, Mornington 056259
The Twentieth Century Gallery, Williamsburg 049184
Twentieth Century Gallery, London 113935, 131202
Twentieth Century Limited Goods, Boston 087852
Twenty First Century Gallery, Denver 116064
Twenty Twenty Applied Arts, Much Wenlock 114097
Twenty Two Gallery, Philadelphia 118848
Twerenbold, Luzern 111709, 130111
Twice Around, Orange 056407
Twice Loved, Pittsburgh 091866
Twice Loved Tales, Jacksonville 142471
Twice Sold Tales, Seattle 143013
Twice Sold Tales, Seattle 143014
Twice Sold Tales, Seattle 143015
Twice Told Tales, Houston 142447
Twice Told Tales, Providence 142821
Twice Treasured, Pittsburgh 091867
Twice Upon A Time, Albion 055327
Twickenham Antique Warehouse, Twickenham 086969, 131625
Twickenham Homestead, Katikati 079133
Twig, New York 118515
Twiga, San Francisco 119819
Twigger's Bookshop, London 141911
Twiggs & Moore, Salt Lake City 119377
Twigs, New Orleans 090634
Twillingate Museum, Twillingate 006672
Twin Cities Galleries, Minneapolis 117318
Twin Falls County Museum, Twin Falls 048674
Twin Falls Museum, Mullens 046081
Twinhouse Gallery, Atlanta 114940
Twinkle Art Gallery, Delhi 105688
Twinsburg Historical Society Museum, Twinsburg 048675
Twiss, Rodney, Eastwood 055785
Twist Art & Design, London 113936
Two 07 Art, New York 118516
TWO 10 Gallery, London 040304
Two 12 Pottery, Minneapolis 117319
Two Angels, Seattle 093076
Two Boys and a Girl, El Paso 116120
Two Cans Antiques, Seaford 056582
Two Coats, Tucson 120172
Two Columbia Road, London 113937
Two Divas, Toronto 059309
Two Dollar Rare Bookstore, Cleveland 142345
Two Dragons, Llanerchymedd 085037
Two Four Seven, Petone Wellington 079221
Two Hills and District Museum, Two Hills 006673
Two Leaves Design, Clitheroe 112879
Two Lions, Washington 093439
Two Ninty Two, Dallas 132026
Two Sisters, Charlotte 087989
Two Swans, Wodonga 056839
Two Turtle Iroquois Fine Art Gallery, Ohsweken 006064
Two Way Books, Brighton 141444
Two Zero, London 113938
Twój Magzyn Fotograficzny, Warszawa 136039
Tworczosc, Warszawa 136040
La Txatarreria, Donostia-San Sebastián 081092
Txindoki, Madrid 129701
Txoko'S 96, Bilbao 080995
Ty Aven, Pont-Aven 101038
Ty Gwyn and Ty Crwn, Barmouth 038595
Ty Korn, Brest 138056
Ty Mawr Wybrnant, Dolwyddelan 039247
Tyabb Antique Centre, Tyabb 056754
Tyabb Grain Store Antiques, Tyabb 056755
Tyabb Packing House Antiques, Tyabb 056756
Tybee Museum and Tybee Island Light Station, Tybee Island 048678
Tydal Museum, Tydal 031299
Tyholmen, Arendal 079370
Tykarpsgrottan Kalkmuseum, Hässleholm 036320
Tyldesleys, Vancouver 059430, 120826
Tylecek, Jiri, Paris 100923
Tyler, Charlotte 087990
Tyler, Mount Kisco 135400
Tyler, Philadelphia 091695
Tyler, Singapore 109888
Tyler Art Gallery, Oswego 046749
Tyler Museum of Art, Tyler 048681
Tyler School of Art, Temple University, Elkins 051294
Tyllack, Norbert, Berlin 125310
Tylldalen Bygdetun, Tylldalen 031300
Tymiński, Jakub, Warszawa 079789
Tymperleys Clock Museum, Colchester 039123
Tyndalemuseum, Vilvoorde 003832
Tynemouth Architectural Salvage, Tynemouth 086975
Tyneside Decorative and Fine Arts Society, Ponteland 054532
Tynset Bygdemuseum, Tynset 031301
Työväen Keskusmuseo, Tampere 010138
Työväenasuntomuseo, Kuusankoski 009773
Työväenasuntomuseo, Helsingin Kaupunginmuseo, Helsinki 009585
Typhaine, Courbevoie 062513
Typhoon, Pittsburgh 091868
Typical Trading, Cairo 060478
Typos-Verlag, Herten 134059
Tyresö Slott, Tyresö 036723
Tyringe Auktionskammare, Tyringe 122282
Tyrnävän Kotiseutumuseo, Tyrnävä 010188
Tyrolia, Innsbruck 137199
Tyrolia Verlag, Innsbruck 133096
Tyrrell, Portland 092019
Tyrvään Seudun Museo, Vammala 010218
Tyrwhitt-Drake Museum of Carriages, Maidstone 040391
Tyson, Morecambe 086006
Tytell, New York 091311
Tyto Alba, Vilnius 134745
Tytyrin Kalkkikaivosmuseo, Lohja 009835
Tzen, Singapore 080581
TZR Galerie, Bochum 102163
Tzschentke, Bernd, Cottbus 125437
Tzwern, Maurice, Bruxelles 096259
U Ambrože, Hradec Králové 060022
U Červeného Beránka, Praha 098489
U Draka, Znojmo 098519
U Dvou Čápů, Karlovy Vary 098373
U Floriána, Ostrava 060070
U Harleya, Banská Bystrica 140955
U Ignáce, Praha 060170
U Jakoba, Opava 098397
U Jakuba, Frýdek-Místek 098357
U Jakubské Věže, Brno 137769
U Kamenného Stolu, Praha 060171
U Keplera, Praha 060172
U Konvice, Hradec Králové 060023
U Kostela, Písek 060078
U Kováře, Brno 098339
U Král'a Mateja, Poprad 080632
U Madony, Brno 059991
U Maxima, Minsk 096043
U Michala, Telč 098502
U Mloka, Olomouc 098393
U Nádraží, Hradec Králové 060024
U Nádraží, Šumperk 060192
The U. Nahon Museum of Italian Jewish Art, Jerusalem 022985
U Parnasa, Sankt-Peterburg 140943
U Pražkeho Jezulátka, Praha 098490, 137848
U R My Sunshine, Philadelphia 091696
U Radnice, Čelákovice 098341
U Rotundy, Týnec nad Sázavou 098506
U Sediaceho Anjela, Kežmarok 109915
U Slona, Písek 137809
U Sveti Jošta, Český Krumlov 098350
U Synagogy, Liberec 060045
U. T. E. T., Torino 134701
U-Turn E-Zine, Oak Park 136651
U Uhelného Trhu, Praha 060173
U Vinohradského Pavilonu, Praha 060174
U Vlašského Dvora, Kutná Hora 098378
U Zlaté Číše, Praha 137849
U Zlaté Korony, Telč 098503
U Zlaté Koruny, Muzeum města Brna, Brno 008297
U Zlatého Lva, Praha 060175
U.A.B. Visual Arts Gallery. Selections from the Permanent Selection, Birmingham 136652
U.A.P., Constanţa 109455
Ubach, Madrid 081405
Ubach, Maria, Barcelona 080949
Ubaldi, Sandro, Frankfurt am Main 070798

UBC Fish Museum, Vancouver 006711
Ubeda, Yolande, Valros 068705
UBMB, Thise 068397
U.B.R Galerie-Raum für aktuelle Kunst, Salzburg 095737
Ubu, New York 118517
Učebno-chudožestvennyj Muzej im. I.V. Cvetaeva, Moskva 033526
Ucher, A., Köln 103730
Uchida, Kyoto 077135
Uchida, Tokyo 077320
Uckermärkische Heimatstuben, Fürstenwerder 017287
Uckermärkisches Volkskundemuseum Templin, Templin 020420
Udell, Douglas, Edmonton 096903
Udell, Douglas, Vancouver 097540
Udivitelnoe v Kamne - Muzej Mineralov, Rud, Samocvetov, Teberda 033946
Udmurtskij Respublikanskij Muzej Izobrazitelnych Iskusstv, Iževsk . . 033181
Udruženje Likovnih i Umetnika Primenjenih Umetnosti i Dizajnera Vojvodine, UPIDIV, Novi Sad 054041
Udruženje Likovnih Umetnika Primenjenih Umetnosti i Dizajnera Srbije, Beograd 054042
Udruženje Likovnih Umetnika Srbije, Beograd 054043
Udruženje Likovnih Umjetnika Bosne i Hercegovine, Sarajevo 052699
Udruženje Likovnih Umjetnika Crne Gore, Podgorica 054044
Udruženje Likovnih Umjetnika Primjenjenih Umjetnosti Bosne i Hercegovine, Sarajevo 052700
Udruženje Likovnih Umjetnika Primjenjenih Umjetnosti Hrvatske, Zagreb 052826
UDT-SEAL Museum, Fort Pierce . . . 043964
Überall, J., Schwäbisch Gmünd . . . 073742
Überseemuseum Bremen, Bremen . 016426
Überwälder Heimatmuseum, Wald-Michelbach 020628
Ügora, Schwäbisch Hall 073746
Uelner, S., Königswinter 072040
Ueltzen, Doris, Sommerhausen . . . 104924
Uelze, Dresden 125511
Ündüz, Gülay, İstanbul 083160
Üniversite Devlet Konservatuvari, Ankara 050791
Ueno Royal Museum, Tokyo 027269
Ürgüp Müzesi, Ürgüp 038190
Uerpmann, Oerlinghausen 073184
Ürün Sanat Galerisi, İstanbul 112364
Uesugi Shrine Treasure House, Yonezawa 027349
Uffelmann, Björn, Hagen, Westfalen 071169
Uffenheimer Gollachgaumuseum, Uffenheim 020525
Ufimskaja Kartinnaja Galereja, Ufa . 033996
U.F.R d'Art et d'Archéologie, Université de Paris I - Panthéon-Sorbonne, Paris 049981
Ugalde, Pedro, Getxo 081120
Uganda Artists Association, Kampala 054260
Uganda Museum, Kampala 038220
Ugarte Bejega, Victor, Vitoria-Gasteiz 081723
Ugas, Renzo, Locarno 111655
Ugbrooke House, Chudleigh 039089
Ugglas Antikhandel, Stockholm . . . 082032
Ugglas Antikhandel, Stocksund . . . 082044
Ughetto, Henry, Villeurbanne 101483
Ugly Otter Trading Post, Albuquerque 087430
Ugly Stuff Antiques, Birregurra 055506
Ugolini, Daniele, Firenze 106075
Uğur, İstanbul 083161
Uhde, Margrit, Dassel 070192
Uhl, Dr. Alfons, Nördlingen 134314
Uhl, Peter, Freiburg im Breisgau . . . 139121
Uhlig & Polz, Dettingen unter Teck . 102363
Uhlmann, Jean-Pierre, Colmar 062420
Uhn, Hofheim am Taunus 103394
Uhren- und Musikgerätemuseum-Museum zu Putbus, Putbus 019680
Uhren- und Pfeifenmuseum, Ruhla . 019946
Uhrenindustriemuseum, Villingen-Schwenningen 020597
Uhrenmuseum, Bad Grund 015711
Uhrenmuseum, Bad Iburg 015728
Uhrenmuseum, Regensburg 019761
Uhrenmuseum, Wien Museum, Wien 003012
Uhrenmuseum Beyer, Zürich 037807
Uhrenmuseum Glashütte, Glashütte, Sachsen 017424
Uhrenmuseum Matthäus, Obernzenn 019405
Uhrensammlung Kellenberger, Gewerbemuseum, Winterthur . . . 037732
Uhrentechnische Lehrschau Hennig, Kurort Hartha 018444
Uhrig, Weingarten, Baden 074314
Uhrig, Gustav, Gedern 070941
Uhrig, Iris, Alsheim 125059
Uhrig, James W., Indianapolis 116496
Uhrlau, Brigitte, Hamburg 125847
Uibel, Birgit, Cottbus 102326
Uilenspiegel Museum, Damme 003387
Uiryeong Museum, Uiryeong 027621
Uit de Kunst, Utrecht 078821
Uit Steppe en Oase, Gent 058210
Uitamonkosken Myllymuseo, Multia 009882
Het Uitgelezen Boek, Zoelen 140578
Uitgeverij 010 Publishers, Rotterdam 134831
Uitgeverij Sun, Amsterdam 134792
Uivel, Amsterdam 077988
Ujlaky, Richard, Palis 065333
UK Arts 'N' Crafts, Lowestoft 114003
Ukiyo-e, New York 091312
Ukiyo-e and Pottery Museum, Hirano Hakabutsukan, Osaka 026990
Ukiyo-e Dealers Association of Japan, Tokyo 053806
Ukiyo-e Society of America, New York 055075
Ukraina Museum, Saskatoon 006426
Ukraine National Gallery, Kyïv 038327
Ukrainian-American Archives and Museum, Hamtramck 044418
Ukrainian-American Museum, Warren 048857
Ukrainian Art Center, Los Angeles . . 045469
Ukrainian Canadian Archives and Museum of Alberta, Edmonton 005408
Ukrainian Catholic Women's League Museum, Edmonton 005409
Ukrainian Cultural Heritage Museum, Sandy Lake 006409
Ukrainian Cultural Heritage Village, Edmonton 005410
Ukrainian Museum, Cleveland 043003
Ukrainian Museum, New York 046416
Ukrainian Museum, Torrens Park . . 001561
Ukrainian Museum of Canada, Saskatoon 006427
Ukrainian Museum of Canada, Vancouver 006712
Ukrainian Museum of Canada - Alberta Branch, Edmonton 005411
Ukrainian Museum of Canada - Manitoba Branch, Winnipeg 006869
Ukrainian Museum of Canada - Ontario Branch, Toronto 006643
Ukrainian National Museum, Chicago 042885
Ukrainian Peoples Home of Ivan Franco, Angusville 005015
Ukraińska Galeria Sztuki, Kraków . . 108990
Ulaanbaatar City Museum, Ulaanbaatar 029013
Ulargiu, Raffaele, Roma 128232
Ulaszewski, Alexius, Dolgenbrodt . . 102382
Ulbricht, Dr. Michael, Machern 121506, 139438
Ulenspiegel Art Gallery, Oostende . . 096405
Uleybury School Museum, One Tree Hill 001354
Ulferts, G., Stolberg, Rheinland . . . 073931
Ulibarri Junior, Mario Peres, Porto Alegre 058528
Ulises Libros, Madrid 141061
Ulisse, Perugia 140092
Ulivi, V., Prato 106478
Uljanovskij Oblastnoj Chudožestvennyj Muzej, Uljanovsk 034016
Uljanovskij Oblastnoj Kraevedčskij Muzej im. I.A. Gončarova, Uljanovsk . . . 034017
Ullapool Museum, Ullapool 041260
Ullenius, Stockholm 129878
Ullensaker Bygdemuseum, Jessheim 030925
Ullevål Sykehus Museum, Oslo 031111
Ullman, Sylvia, Cleveland 115749
Ullmann, A.R., London . . . 085758, 131203
Ullmann, Robert, Schaffhausen . . . 082801
Ullrich, Angelika C., Düsseldorf . . . 070456
Ullrich, Beppo, Düsseldorf 125551
Ullrich, Ewald, Hamburg 103225
Ullrich, Markus, Reichertshausen . . 126708
Ullwer, Werner, Obergünzburg 073140
Ulmann, Angélo, Amberieux-en-Dombes 060789
Ulmer, Detlef, Norderstedt 073077
Ulmer, Maria, Meersburg 072494
Ulmer Museum, Ulm 020534
Ulmer Verein e.V., Bochum 053576
Ulricehamns Museum, Ulricehamn . 036728
Ulrich, Elizabeth, Honolulu 116248
Ulrich, Herbert P., Berlin 069776
Ulrich, Hugo, Buchrain 129991
Ulrich, Sarah, Saint Louis 092327
Ulrichs, Prof. Timm, Hannover 103299, 134044
Ulrika museum, Ulrika 036729
Ulriksdals Slott, Solna 036606
Ulster-American Folk Park, Museums and Galleries of Nothern Irland, Omagh 040643
Ulster County Historical Society Museum, Marbletown 045659
Ulster Folk and Transport Museum, Holywood 039766
Ulster History Park, Omagh 040644
Ulster Museum, Museums and Galleries of Northern Ireland, Belfast 038669
Ulsyn Töw Muzei, Ulaanbaatar 029014
Ultiart, Sofia 096752
Ultima Thule, Warszawa 140799
Ultimate Editions, London 135271
Ultime Atome, Gent 096301
Ultramarine, Ventnor 086994
Ultrapiktura, Moskva 109599
Ultraviolet, Southsea 114469
Ultreya, Milano 134639
Ulucam, Lüdenscheid 072349
Ulug-Beg Memorial Museum, Samarkand 049405
Ulukaya, İstanbul 083162
Uluslararası Plastik Sanatlar Derneği, İstanbul 054257, 112365
Ulva Konst & Kuriosa, Uppsala 141191
Ulverstone Local History Museum, Ulverstone 001576
Ulysses, Wien 095955
Ulysses Aukciók, Budapest 121646
Ulysses Bookshop, London 141912
Um Gallery, Seoul 107299
Umanome, Nara 106946
Umatilla County Historical Society Museum, Pendleton 046866
Umbrella, Santa Monica 136653
Umbrella Studio, Townsville 095351
Umbria, Amsterdam 077989
Umeå Energicentrum, Umeå 036731
Umekoji Steam Locomotive Museum, Kyoto 026775
Umělecké Předměty a Galerie, Poděbrady 098410
Uměleckoprůmyslové Muzeum v Praze, Praha 008650
Umělecký Bazar, Brno 059992
Umění, Praha 135669
Umetnička Galerija Nadežda Petrović, Čačak 034181
Umetnička Zbirka Flögel, Beograd . 034171
Umetnostna Galerija Maribor, Maribor 034502
Umetnostna Galerija Maribor, Maribor 109992
Umetnostni Paviljon, Slovenj Gradec 034522
Umezawa Memorial Gallery, Tokyo . 027270
Umhey, Roland, Lampertheim 072125
Umi-no Hakubutsukan, Toba 027139
U'Mista Cultural Centre, Kwakwaka'wakw museum, Alert Bay 004993
Umjetnička Galerija, Dubrovnik . . . 007721
Umjetnička Galerija, Mostar 003934
Umjetnička Galerija, Skopje 027921
Umjetnička galerija Bosne i Hercegovine, Sarajevo 003940
Umjetnička Galerija Josip-Bepo Benkovic, Herceg-Novi 034193
Umjetnička Galerija Rizah Stetić, Brčko 003931
Umjetnička Galerija Velimir A. Leković, Bar 003927
Umjetnički Paviljon u Zagrebu, Zagreb 007859
Umla, Helmut & Silvia, Völklingen . . 139822
Umlauf, Felicitas Susanne, Düsseldorf 102565
Umlauf, Osswald, Bad Vilbel 069390, 125119
Umlauf Sculpture Garden and Museum, Austin 041939
Umm Qais Archaeological Museum, Umm Qais 027387
Ummels, C.E., Nieuwegein 128784
Umoja Art Village, Chicago 115572
Umoona Opal Mine and Museum, Coober Pedy 000943
Umstädter Museum Gruberhof, Groß-Umstadt 017562
Un Autre Regard, Paris 100924
Un Coin du Passé, Aix-les-Bains . . . 060729
Un Francais á Londres, London . . . 085759
Un Jour a Paris, Warszawa 109200
Un Meuble Une Histoire, Le Havre . 124302
Un Regard Moderne, Paris 138552
Un Souffle d'Antan, La Daguenière . 063363
Un Sourire de Toi, Paris 100925
Un Tuffo nel Passato, Bari 075035, 127126
Un Village se Raconte, Ecomusée de la Vallee d'Aspe, Lourdios-Ichère . . 012781
Unamuno Sobrino, Consuelo, Burgos 081021, 129468
Uncle Davey's Americana, Jacksonville 089470, 132198
Uncle Edgar's Mystery Bookstore, Minneapolis 142591
Uncle Hugo's Science Fiction, Minneapolis 142592
Uncle Remus Museum, Eatonton . . 043593
Uncle Richard's Antiques, San Diego 092693
Uncle Tom's Cabin Historic Site, Dresden 005359
Uncle Vick's, Norfolk 091400
Uncommon Objects, Austin 087617
Underground, Alice, New York 091313
Underground Gallery, Seattle 120005
Underground Passages, Exeter 039467
Underground Prisoners Museum, 1918-1948, Jerusalem 022986
Underhill Museum, Idaho Springs . . 044713
Underwood Gallery, Milwaukee . . . 117224
Underwoodhall Antiques, Woodhall Spa 087230
Une Autre Epoque, Brie-Comte-Robert 061795
Une Maison, Saint-Ouen 067912
Une Page d'Histoire, Caylus 062045
Une Si Belle Journée, La Colle-sur-Loup 063345
UNESCO Publishing, Paris 133682
Unexpected Joy, New York 091314
Unexpected Treasures, Richmond . . 092117
Unfer, Leutenheim 063798

Ungar, Eduard, Ybbs 137387
Ungarie Museum, Ungarie 001577
Ungarische Botschaft, Berlin 016187
Ungarn-deutsche Heimatstuben, Langenau, Württemberg 018502
Ungarndeutsches Heimatmuseum Backnang, Backnang 015640
Unge Kunstneres Samfund, Oslo . . 053961
Ungefroren, Gerhard, Halle, Saale . 071180
Ungelenk, Rainer, Wandersleben . . 074272
Unger, Siegmar, Bad Königshofen . . 069311
Unger, Urs von, Basel 082178
Unger, Urs von, Saanen 082762
Ungern-Sternberg, Dr. Wolfgang von, Regensburg 139685
Ungheretti, Piero, Livorno 127496
Ungurmuiža, Raiskums 027726
Unhyang Art Museum, Bugil 027452
Uni-Antiquariat, Graz 137182
Uni Mat, Chaskovo 058752, 137595
Uniacke Estate Museum, Mount Uniacke 005969
UniBuch, Darmstadt 138976
Unicat, Oranienburg 104547
Unicon Art, Košice 109917
Unicorn, Miami 090251
Unicorn Antiques, Edinburgh 084318
Unicorn Antiques, Kingswinford . . .084869, 130853
Unicorn Gallery, Chippendale 094397
Unicorn Gallery, Wilmslow 114699
Unicorn Studio, Baltimore 115089
Unicorn Unique, Camberwell 055609
Unicum, Krefeld 072082
Unidad Museológica Municipal de La Banda, La Banda 000372
Unie Výtvarných Umělců, Plzeň . . . 008573
Unie Výtvarných Umělců Plzeňské Oblasti, Plzeň 052842
Uniepers, Abcoude 134763
UNIKA, Innermanzing 057071
Unikart, Essen 070651, 125617
Unikat, Kraków 079662
Unikat, Remagen 073485
Unimex International, San Antonio . 119462
Union, London 113939
Union Art Gallery, Baton Rouge 042053
Union-Art Gallery, University of Wisconsin-Milwaukee, Milwaukee 045899
Union Avenue Antique Mall, Memphis 090109
Union Bay Antiques, Seattle 093077
Union County Heritage Museum, New Albany 046188
Union County Historical Complex, Creston 043216
Union County Historical Foundation Museum, Union 048696
Union County Historical Society Museum, Blairsville 042248
Union County Historical Society Museum, Marysville 045717
Union County Museum, Lewisburg . 045244
Union County Museum, Union 048694
Union County Public Library Union Room, Monroe 045973
Union de Arte, Barcelona 110260
Unión de Asociaciones de Artistas Visuales, Barcelona 054124
Union des Photographes Créateur, Paris 052999
Union Française des Experts, Paris . 053000
Union Freischaffender Künstler und Kunstfreunde, Stuttgart 053577
Union Gallery, Adelaide 000715
Union Méditerranéenne d'Art Contemporain, Megève 099701
Union Méditerranéenne d'Art Contemporain, Saint-Paul-de-Vence 053001
Union Mills Homestead and Grist Mill, Westminster 049117
Unión Nacional de Escritores y Artistas de Cuba, La Habana 052831
Union Nacionale des Peintres Illustrateurs, Paris 053002
Union Nationale des Artistes Professionnels des Arts Plastiques et Graphiques, Bruxelles 052688
Union Nationale des Arts Culturels, Alger 052437
Union of Artists of the Kyrgyz Republic, Biškek 053830
Union of Belarusian Artists, Minsk .052639, 096044
Union of Bulgarian Artists, Sofia . . . 052711
Union Square Ceramic Center, New York 118518
Union Syndicale des Artisans des Métiers d'Art, Grenoble 053003
Union Trading, Chinese Antique Objects, Hong Kong 059700
Unione Sindacale Artisti Italiani Belle Arti, Roma 053772
Unique, Den Haag 078259
L'Unique, Montréal 097088
Unique Antique, Tucson 093275
Unique Antiques, New York 091315
Unique Antiques, Pittsburgh 091869
Unique Antiques, San Diego 092694
Unique Antiques, Singapore 080582
Unique Design, Ulset 079509
Unique Finds, New York 091316
Unique Finds, Seattle 093078
Unique Fine Art, Shenstone 114423
Unique Pieces, Calgary 058811
Unique Place, Singapore 080583
Unique Resale, Houston 089234
Unique Stuff, Kansas City 089527
Unique Treasure & Antiques, Regina 059093
Unique Treasures, Columbus 088445
Uniques, Cincinnati 088289
Uniques, Vancouver 059431
Uniquities Architectural Antiques, Calgary 058812
UNISA Art Gallery, Pretoria 034732
Unité Musée Numismatique, Banque de République d'Haïti, Port-au-Prince 021606
Unitechas, Vilnius 140236
United Art Gallery, Hong Kong 097841
United Caribbean Art Gallery, Jacksonville 116548
United Counties Museum, Cornwall 005298
United Empire Loyalist Museum, Bloomfield 005106
United Grand Lodge of England Library and Museum, London 040225
United Independent Art Community, San Francisco 055076, 119820
United Kingdom Institute for Conversation of Historic and Artistic Works, London 054533
United Oil Painting, Virginia Beach . 120233
United Oil Paintings, Norfolk 118620
United Planets - Space Art Galerie, München 072872, 104332
United Society of Artists, London . . 054534
United States Air Force Academy Museum, El Paso 043631
United States Air Force Museum, Wright-Patterson Air Force Base 049319
United States Army Air Defense Artillery Museum, Fort Bliss 043892
United States Army Aviation Museum, Fort Rucker 043972
United States Army Center of Military History, Fort McNair 043946
United States Army Chaplain Museum, Fort Jackson 043924
United States Army Communications-Electronics Museum, Fort Monmouth 043952
United States Army Engineer Museum, Fort Leonard Wood 043942
United States Army Finance Corps Museum, Fort Jackson 043925
United States Army Heritage and Education Center, Carlisle 042623
United States Army Medical Department Museum, Fort Sam Houston 043974
United States Army Military History Institute Museum, Carlisle 042623
United States Army Museum of Hawaii, Fort DeRussy 043908
United States Army Ordnance Museum, Aberdeen Proving Ground 041561
The United States Army Quartermaster Museum, Fort Lee 043940
United States Army Signal Corps and Fort Gordon Museum, Fort Gordon . . . 043918
United States Army Transportation Museum, Fort Eustis 043915
United States Army Women's Museum, Fort Lee 043941
United States Brig Niagara, Homeport Erie Maritime Museum, Erie 043724
United States Capitol Visitor Center, Washington 048950
United States Cavalry Museum, Fort Riley 043971
United States Coast Guard Museum, New London 046240
United States Coin and Currency Shop, Philadelphia 091697
United States Commission of Fine Arts, Washington 055077
United States Department of the Interior Museum, Washington 048951
United States Federation of Friends of Museums, Baltimore 055078
United States Figure Skating Association, Colorado Springs 055079
United States Grant Ancestral Homestead, Dungannon 039321
United States Grant's Home, Galena 044117
United States Hockey Hall of Fame, Eveleth 043769
United States Holocaust Memorial Museum, Washington 048952
United States-International Council on Monuments and Sites, Washington 055080
United States Marine Corps Air-Ground Museum, Quantico 047291
United States Marine Corps Museum, Washington 048953
United States Mint-Philadelphia, Philadelphia 046992
United States National Ski Hall of Fame and Museum, Ishpeming 044782
United States Naval Academy Museum, Annapolis 041744
United States Navy Art Gallery, Washington 048954
United States Navy Supply Corps Museum, Athens 041837
United States Porcelain, Albuquerque 131755
United States Senate Commission on Art, Washington 055081
United States Senate Commission on Art Collection, Washington 048955
United States Space and Rocket Center, Huntsville 044694
Unites States National Committee of the ICOM, Washington 055082
Unity and District Heritage Museum, Unity 006675
Uniunea Artiştilor Plastici din România, Bucureşti 054016
l'Univers, Lausanne 141266
L'Univers du Bronze, Paris 100926, 138553
Univers du Livre, Paris 124827
Univers Maurice Rocket Richard, Montréal 005951
Universal Art, Silverton 080747
Universal Arts Galerie Studio, München 104333
Universal Arts Gallery, Memphis . . . 117006
Universal Books and Old Wares, Taralga 056698, 137107
Universal Comics, Baltimore 142231
Universal Prints Verlag, Hamburg . . 134025
Universal - Sociedade de Leilões, Porto 054009
Univers'Art, Le Mans 099449
Universe Antiques, New York 091317
Universe Publishing, New York 135467
Universeum, Göteborg 036307
Universidad de Granada. Cuadernos de Arte, Granada 136105
Universidad de Sevilla. Serie: Bellas Artes, Sevilla 136106
Universita degli Studi di Parma. Istituto di Storia dell'Arte. Cataloghi, Parma 135969
Universita degli Studi di Roma. Seminario di Archeologia e Storia dell'Arte Greca e Romana. Studi Miscellanei, Roma 135970
Università Internazionale dell'Arte, Firenze 050370
Universität der Künste Berlin, Berlin 016188
Universität der Künste Berlin, Berlin 050031
Universität für angewandte Kunst Wien, Wien 049667
Universität für künstlerische ind industrielle Gestaltung, Linz 049640
Universitäts- und Landesbibliothek Bonn, Bonn 016336
Universitäts- und Landesbibliothek Münster, Münster 019154
Universitätsbibliothek, München . . . 019127
Universitätsbibliothek der Humboldt-Universität zu Berlin, Berlin 016189
Universitätsbibliothek der Universität Leipzig, Leipzig 018599
Universitätsbibliothek Salzburg, Salzburg 002569
Universitätsbibliothek Wien, Wien . . 003013
Universitätsbuchhandlung, Bochum 138886
Universitätsmuseum Hohenheim, Stuttgart 020360
Universitätssammlung antiker und nachantiker Münzen und Medaillen, Tübingen 020501
Universitätssammlungen Kunst+Technik, Technische Universität Dresden, Dresden 016820
Université du Vin, Suze-la-Rousse . 014892
Universiteitsbiliotheek Gent, Gent . . 003471
Universiteitsmuseum, Groningen . . 029645
Universiteitsmuseum De Agnietenkapel, Amsterdam 029238
Universiteitsmuseum Utrecht, Utrecht 030240
Universitetets Oldsaksamling, Universitetets Kulturhistoriske Museer, Oslo . . . 031112
University Additions, Memphis 117007
University Archaeology Museum, Birmingham 038740
University Art, Sacramento 119165
University Art Association of Canada, North York 052776
University Art Galleries, Murray State University, Murray 046100
University Art Galleries, University of South Dakota, Vermillion 048764
University Art Gallery, Bridgeport . . 042409
University Art Gallery, Carson 042633
University Art Gallery, Chico 042893
University Art Gallery, Jacksonville . 044820
University Art Gallery, Mount Pleasant 046065
University Art Gallery, North Dartmouth 046524
University Art Gallery, Pittsburgh . . 047064
University Art Gallery, Potchefstroom 034711
University Art Gallery, Rohnert Park 047527
University Art Gallery, Stony Brook . 048379
University Art Gallery, Turlock 048660
University Art Gallery, Claire Trevor School of the Arts, Irvine 044778
University Art Gallery, Indiana State University, Terre Haute 048534
University Art Gallery, San Diego State University, San Diego 047844
University Art Gallery, Union University, Jackson 044807
University Art Gallery, University of California, San Diego, La Jolla . . . 045070
University Art Museum, Albany 041603
University Art Museum, Binghamton 042218
University Art Museum, Santa Barbara 047952
University Art Museum, University of Louisiana at Lafayette, Lafayette . 045092

University Art Museum, University of New Mexico, Albuquerque 041625
University at Buffalo Art Galleries, Buffalo 042507
University College Dublin Classical Museum, Dublin 022772
University College of Cape Breton Art Gallery, Sydney 006549
University College Zoological Museum, Cork 022722
University Fine Art Collection, Hobart 001115
University Galleries, Akron 041590
University Galleries, Art Dept., University of Texas Pan American, Edinburg . . . 043610
University Galleries, Clarion University of Pennsylvania, Clarion 042946
University Gallery, Alexandria 041632
University Gallery, Boca Raton 042286
University Gallery, Gainesville 044109
The University Gallery, Newcastle-upon-Tyne 040555
University Gallery, Oxford 046769
University Gallery, Fort Hays State University, Hays 044491
University Gallery, Texas A & M University, Commerce 043114
University Gallery, University of Delaware, Newark 046421
University Gallery, University of Massachusetts at Amherst, Amherst 041696
University Gallery Leeds, Leeds . . . 039965
The University Gallery of the University of the South, Sewanee 048118
University Historical Museum, Musuan 031747
University Medical Museum, Medical University of South Carolina, Charleston 042745
University Museum, Dundee 039313
The University Museum, Edwardsville 043619
University Museum, Martin 045711
University Museum, Port Harcourt . 030706
The University Museum, Tokyo 027271
University Museum, Vallabhvidyanagar 022370
The University Museum, Indiana University of Pennsylvania, Indiana 044733
University Museum, Southern Illinois University, Carbondale 042619
The University Museum, University of Arkansas, Fayetteville 043830
University Museum and Art Gallery, Hong Kong 007135
University Museum of Anthropology, University of the Philippines, Quezon City 031779
University Museum of Archaeology and Anthropology, Cambridge 038971
University Museum of Science and Culture, Aligarh 021999
University Museum of Zoology, Cambridge 038972
University Museum - Sasol Art Museum, Stellenbosch 034757
University Museums, Oxford 046770
University Museums Group, Liverpool 054535
University of Alaska Museum, Fairbanks 043780
University of Alberta Museums, Edmonton 005412
University of Architecture, Ho Chi Minh City 052432
University of Arizona Mineral Museum, Tucson 048643
University of Arizona Museum of Art, Tucson 048644
University of Arizona Union Galleries, Tucson 048645
University of Arkansas at Little Rock Art Galleries, Little Rock 045346
University of Art and Design Helsinki, Helsinki 049928
University of Brighton Gallery, Brighton 038854
University of Bristol Theatre Collection, Bristol 038869
University of Calgary Museum of Zoology, Calgary 005201
University of California Berkeley Art Museum, Berkeley 042166
University of California Press, Berkeley 135327
University of Chicago Press, Chicago 135350
University of Colorado Museum, Boulder 042354
University of Dundee Exhibitions Department, Dundee 039314
University of Essex Exhibition Gallery, Colchester 039124
University of Exeter Press, Exeter . . 135146
University of Fort Hare Museum, Alice 034543
University of Hawaii Art Gallery, Honolulu 044610
University of Hawaii Press, Honolulu 135365
University of Illinois at Urbana-Champaign. School of Art and Design. Newsletter, Champaign 136654
University of Iowa Museum of Art, Iowa City 044768
University of Iowa Museum of Natural History, Iowa City 044769
University of Kansas Ryther Printing Museum, Lawrence 045207
University of Kentucky Art Museum, Lexington 045266
University of Lethbridge Art Gallery, Lethbridge 005769
University of Liverpool Art Gallery, Liverpool 040040
University of Mandalay Collections, Bawdigon Archaeological Museum, Mandalay 029061
University of Michigan Museum of Art, Ann Arbor 041736
University of Michigan Press, Ann Arbor 135318
University of Nebraska Art Gallery at Omaha, Omaha 046684
University of Nebraska Press, Lincoln 135376
University of Nebraska State Museum, Lincoln 045313
University of New Brunswick Art Centre, Fredericton 005487
University of New Mexico Art Museum. Bulletin, Albuquerque 136655
University of North Dakota Zoology Museum, Grand Forks 044263
University of North Texas Art Gallery, Denton 043396
University of Northern Iowa Museum Museums & Collections, Cedar Falls 042668
University of Northern Philippines Museum, Vigan 031808
University of Nueva Caceres Museum, Naga 031750
University of Oregon Museum of Art, Eugene 043742
University of Pennsylvania Museum of Archaeology and Anthropology, Philadelphia 046993
University of Pretoria Art Collection, Pretoria 034733
University of Queensland Art Museum, Brisbane 000844
University of Rhode Island Fine Arts Center Galleries, University of Rhode Island, Kingston 045018
University of Richmond Museums, Richmond 047425
University of Rochester Memorial Art Gallery, Rochester 047487
University of San Carlos Anthropology Museum, Cebu 031662
University of San Carlos Biological Museum, Cebu 031663
University of Santo Tomas Museum of Arts and Sciences, Manila 031741
University of South Australia Art Museum, Adelaide 000716
University of South Carolina at Spartanburg Art Gallery, Spartanburg 048267
University of South Carolina Beaufort Art Gallery, Beaufort 042077
University of Southern Philippines Museum, Cebu 031664
University of Southern Queensland Art Collection, Toowoomba 001560
University of Stellenbosch Art Gallery, Stellenbosch 034758
University of Swaziland Library Museums Collection, Kwaluseni 036162
University of Sydney Art Collection, Sydney 001526
University of Toronto Art Centre, Toronto 006644
University of Toronto Press, Toronto 133329
University of Virginia Art Museum, Charlottesville 042770
University of Wales Press, Cardiff . . 135134
University of Washington Press, Seattle 135505
University of Waterloo Art Gallery, Waterloo 006777
University of West Florida Art Gallery, Pensacola 046877
University of Wisconsin Zoological Museum, Madison 045594
University of Wyoming Anthropology Museum, Laramie 045169
University of Wyoming Art Museum, Laramie 045170
University of Zambia Library Museums Collection, Lusaka 049573
University Place Art Center, Lincoln 045314
University Press of New England, Hanover 135363
University Used and Rare Books, Seattle 143016
Universum, Moskva 080273
Universum, Wien 057573
Universum, Museo de las Ciencias de la UNAM, México 028544
Universum Science Center Bremen, Bremen 016427
Univerzitet Umetnosti u Beogradu, Beograd 050677
Univerzsitatea Naţională de Airte din Bucureşti, Bucureşti 050621
Unlimited Corporate Art, Chicago . . 115573
UNLV Barrick Museum, Las Vegas . 045192
Unna, Chicago 115574
Uno A, Bogotá 098197
Unrau, Sabine, Kiel 071845
Uns lütt Schiffsmuseum, Cuxhaven 016614
Unser kleines Museum, Gries im Pinzgau 001957
Unsodo, Kyoto 077136, 134715
Unsodo, Tokyo 077321
UNSW Art Collection, Sydney 001527
Unsworth, Robin, Olney 086164
Unsworths, London 141913
Unsworths, Oxford 141988
Untamalan Kotiseutumuseo, Laitila 009797
Untch, Karl, Bad Rappenau 101688
Unterberg, A., Göttingen 071056
Unterberger, Franz, Feldkirch 137166
Unterfränkisches Grenzmuseum, Bad Königshofen 015734
Unterfränkisches Verkehrsmuseum, Gemünden am Main 017360
Unterlöhner, Erwin, Kuchen 072100
Unterrabnitzer Malergruppe, Unterrabnitz 052603
Untersbergmuseum Fürstenbrunn, Grödig 001961
Unterwarter Heimathaus, Unterwart 002770
Untitled, London 136277
Untitled Fine Arts Service, Albuquerque 114830
Untitled Gallery, Oklahoma City . . . 118678
Untitled Mixed Media, Amsterdam . 077990
Untitled Press, Captiva Island 135342
Untucht, Bernd, Magdeburg 126253
Untzi Museoa - Museo Naval, Donostia-San Sebastián 035155
Unverzagt, S., Köln 139353
Uodu Buried Forest Museum, Uodo . 027308
Uodu History and Folklore Museum, Uodo 027309
Up & Co., New York 118519
Up Against the Wall, Denver 116065
Up Country, Tunbridge Wells 086955
Up East Associates, New York 118520
Up Six, Saint Paul 092405
Up the Creek Antiques, Buffalo 087918
Upchurch, Kenneth, Ashbourne . . . 083333
Updike, John, Edinburgh 141590
Upernavik Museum, Upernavik 021552
Upham Mansion, Marshfield 045709
Uphill Galleries, New Orleans 117526
Upholstery by Design, Portland 132706
Upholstery of the Stars, Miami 132359
Upholstery Restored, Heidelberg Heights 123241
Upholstery Shop, Calgary 123755
Upholstery Shoppe, Kansas City . . . 132212
Upholstery Special, Saint Paul 132775
Upholstery Unlimited, New Orleans . 132425
Upholstery Workroom, San Jose . . . 132926
UPIDIV Galerija, Novi Sad 034227
Upminster Mill, Upminster 041263
Upminster Tithe Barn Museum, Agricultural and Folk Museum, Upminster . . . 041264
Upp, Albin, Oslo 108740
Uppark Exhibition, Petersfield 040707
Upper Bay Gallery, Houston 116422
Upper Canada Village, Morrisburg . 005964
Upper Canadian Antique Mart, Ottawa 059052
Upper Court Manor Antiques, Dublin 074952
Upper Court Manor Antiques, Freshford 074974
Upper East Antiques, Portland 092020
Upper East Region Museum, Bolgatanga 021100
Upper Level Antique Mall, Seattle . . 093079
Upper Midwest Conservation Association, Minneapolis 055083
Upper Musselshell Historical Society Museum, Harlowtown 044434
Upper Paxton Township Museum, Millersburg 045873
Upper Room Chapel Museum, Nashville 046156
Upper Rust Antiques, New York . . . 091318
Upper Snake River Valley Historical Museum, Rexburg 047385
Upper Waitaki Pioneer Museum and Art Gallery, Kurow 030533
Upper Wharfdale Folk Museum, Grassington 039624
Upper Yarra Valley Museum, Yarra Junction 001644
Upperbridge Antiques, Holmfirth . . . 084700
Upperlands Eco-Museum, Derry . . . 039232
Uppertown Firefighters Museum, Astoria 041826
Upplands Auktioner, Uppsala 122285
Upplandsmuseet, Uppsala 036744
Uppsala Auktionskammare, Uppsala 122286
Uppsala Konst- & Ramaffär, Uppsala 111094
Uppsala Konstmuseum, Uppsala . . 036745
Uppsala Medicinhistoriska Museum, Uppsala 036746
Uppsala Universitet Myntkabinett, Uppsala 036747
Uprka, J., Praha 098491
Upside-Down Turtle, Charlotte 087991
Upstairs Antiques, Auckland 078990
Upstairs Art, Christchurch 108417
Upstairs Books, Engadine 136891
Upstairs Downstairs, Curaçao 108287
Upstairs, Downstairs, Devizes 084164, 130633
Upstairs, Downstairs, Honiton 084731
Upstairs Downstairs, Nairne 056311
Upstairs Downstairs, Oamaru 079202
Upstairs Downstairs Antiques, Boston 087853
Upstairs Downtown Antiques, New York 091319

Upstairs Gallery, Lismore 094741
Upstairs Gallery, Winnipeg 006870
Upstairs Gallery, Winnipeg 059472, 097608
Upstairs Gallery Of Fine Arts, Waikato 108598
Upsters Gallery, Eastleigh 112978
Upton House, Banbury 038585
Uptown Archeology, Cleveland 088367
Uptown Center Hull House Association, Chicago 055084
Uptown Gallery, Fresno 116191
Uptown Gallery, Las Vegas 116653
Uptown Gallery, New York 118521
Uptown Gallery, Richmond 119128
Uptown Images, Saint Paul 119318
Uptown Restoration, New Orleans . 132426
Uptowner Antiques, New Orleans . . 090635
Uptowner Antiques, New Orleans . . 090636
Ur-Donautal-Museum, Torbogenhaus, Wellheim 020790
Ur- und Frühgeschichtliche Ausstellung, Sömmerda 020228
Ur- und frühgeschichtliche Eisenindustrie im Bezirk Oberpullendorf - Schauraum, Oberpullendorf 002390
Ur- und Frühgeschichtliche Sammlung, Friedrich-Alexander-Universität Erlangen-Nürnberg, Erlangen 017038
Ur-und frühgeschichtliche Sammlungen, Landesmuseum Joanneum, Graz . 001952
Ur-Wolpertinger-Museum, Zentrum für Außergewöhnliche Museen, Kreuth 018409
Urahoro-cho Kyodo Hakubutsukan, Urahoro 027310
Urajärven Kartanomuseo, Urajärvi . 010189
Uralla Gallery, Uralla 095360
Uralla Trading Post, Uralla 056775
Uralskaja Gosudarstvennaja Architekturno-chudožestvennaja Akademija, Ekaterinburg 050632
Uralskij Geologičeskij Muzej V.V. Vachrušev, Ekaterinburg 033126
Uralskij Istoriko-Kraevedčeskij Muzej, Uralsk 027416
Uran Sanat Galerisi, İstanbul 112366
Uranga, Cástor, Donostia-San Sebastián 081093, 141018
Urània, Budapest 139932
Urania-Fotogalerie am Eisernen Tor, Graz 095545
Urania-Galerie im Palais Trauttmansdorff, Graz 095546
Urart Sanat Galerisi, İstanbul 112367
Urban, Auckland 108367
Urban, Baltimore 115090
Urban, Chicago 115575
Urban, New York 091320
Urban, New York 091321
Urban, New York 118522
Urban, Washington 120358
Urban, Georg, München 072873
Urban, Klaus-Peter, Fellbach 125634
Urban, Patrick, Illkirch-Graffenstaden 063206
Urban, Peter, Grafing bei München . 102989
Urban, Zdeněk, Olomouc . 060064, 098394
Urban Archaeology, Eastwood 055786
Urban Art, Los Angeles 116906
Urban Art Retreat, Chicago 115576
Urban Artifacts, Chicago 088187
Urban Artifacts, Philadelphia 091698
Urban Artifacts, Richmond 092118
Urban Artifacts Gallery, Houston . . . 116423
Urban Chateau, San Francisco 092903
Urban Cottage, Houston 089235
Urban Desires, New York 136656
Urban Gallery, Miami 117149
Urban Institute for Contemporary Arts, Grand Rapids 044279
The Urban Jungle, Singapore 080584
The Urban Settler, Vancouver 059432
Urban Shaman, Winnipeg 097609
Urban Treasures, Austin 087618
Urbana, Barcelona 080950
Urbana, Barcelona 080951
Urbanarts, Boston 042347
Urbaneck, Wolfgang, Porta Westfalica 126642
Urbanek, Dieter, Paderborn 073289
Urbanek, Regina, Brühl, Rheinland . 125405
Urbani, Claude, Antibes-Juan-les-Pins 098852
Urbaniak, Piotr, Poznań 079701
Urbano, Ourense 081454
Urbano Plaza, Buenos Aires 123162
Urbauer, Hans Joachim, Siegsdorf . 073815
Urbauer, Hans Joachim, Vachendorf 074178
Urben, Thomas, Urnäsch 111956
Urbes, Gräfelfing 133983
Urbieta 66, Donostia-San Sebastián 081094
Urbina, Vitoria-Gasteiz 081724
Urbs et Orbis, Rheinbach 139692
Urdang, Bertha, Jerusalem 105915
Urdang, Beth, Boston 115237
Urdangarin Unzueta, Aitor, Vitoria-Gasteiz 110875
Ure Museum of Greek Archaeology, Reading 040811
Urfa Müzesi, Urfa 038191
Urgeschichtliche Sammlung, Engerwitzdorf 001834
Urgeschichtliches Freilichtmuseum Keltendorf Mitterkirchen, Mitterkirchen 002319
Urgeschichtliches Museum und Galerie Vierzigtausend Jahre Kunst, Blaubeuren 016266
Urgeschichtssammlung und Heimtmuseum, Jedenspeigen 002100
Urho Kekkonen Museo Tamminiemi, Helsinki 009586
Uri and Rami Nechushtan, Kibbutz Ashdot Yaakov 022995
Uribe, Daniel, Valenciennes 068696
Urios College Museum, Butuan . . . 031642
Urioste, Marta N. de, La Paz 058399
Urjalan Museo, Urjala 010190
Urlass, Rüdiger, Frankfurt am Main 070799, 102833
Urli-Vernenghi, Paris 066629
Urmensch-Museum, Steinheim an der Murr 020308
Uroomieh Museum, Uroomieh 022650
Urquhart Castle, Drumnadrochit 039287
Urquijo, Guillermo, Bilbao 080996
Urras Eachdraibh Sgire Bhearnaraidh, Bernera 038680
Urrutia Cutiño, Marta, Badalona . . . 110099
Ursini, Ennio, Trieste 076912
Ursino, Carnely, Fortaleza 096541
Urskog-Hølandsbanen, Sørumsand . 031212
Urso, Josiane, Paris 066630
Ursula Blickle Stiftung, Kraichtal . . 018391
Ursuline Hallway Gallery, Southwest School of Art and Craft, San Antonio 047807
Ursus, New York 142699
Ursus, Penzance 086216, 131370
Urubamba, Paris 100927, 138554
Urumchi City Museum, Urumchi . . . 007295
Urwelt-Museum Hauff, Holzmaden . 017995
Urwelt-Museum Oberfranken, Bayreuth 015925
Urweltmuseum, Pirna 019628
Urweltmuseum Aalen, Aalen 015433
Urwyler, Hansueli, Interlaken 111570
Urzeitmuseum Nußdorf ob der Traisen, Traismauer 002750
US Army Military Police Corps Museum, Fort Leonard Wood 043943
US CoinNection, Jacksonville 089471
US Coins and Jewelry, Houston . . . 089236
US Patent and Trademark Office - Museum, Arlington 041781
US Rare Coin, Austin 087619
US Toy Collector Magazine, Helena 136657
US1 Antiques, Chicago 088188
USA 916, Sacramento 119166
Usadba Izmajlovo, Moskva 033527
Usage, Bruxelles 096260
Uşak Arkeoloji Müzesi, Uşak 038192
L'Usato della Contrada, Brescia . . . 075189
USed, New York 091322
Used Stuff, Los Angeles 089929
Uselding, S., Bruxelles 058105
Usenko, H., Delmenhorst 125451
Usha Mirchandani, Mumbai 105814
Usher, Barcelona 080952, 141007
Usher & Son, James, Lincoln 085002
Usher, John, Boston 142259
Usher, Richard, Cuckfield . 084127, 130621
Usher Gallery, Lincoln 040013
l'Usine, Charleroi 058154
Usk Rural Life Museum, Usk 041266
USM Art Gallery, Gorham 044250
Usman Jusupov Memorial Museum, Jalta 038274
Uspenskij Sobor, Gosudarstvennyj muzej-zapovednik Moskovskij Kreml, Moskva 033528
Uss, Zdzisław, Gdańsk 129014
USS Alabama Battleship Memorial Park, Mobile 045953
USS Arizona Memorial, Honolulu . . 044611
USS Bowfin Submarine Museum, Honolulu 044612
USS Constitution Museum, Boston . 042348
USS Lexington Museum on the Bay, Corpus Christi 043165
USS North Carolina Battleship Memorial, Wilmington 049209
USS Radford National Naval Museum, Newcomerstown 046447
USS Silversides and Maritime Museum, Muskegon 046104
Ussishkin House, Kibbutz Dan 022998
Ust'-Ilimskaja Kartinnaja Galereja, Ust'-Ilimsk 034019
Ustav dějin umění AV ČR, Praha . . . 049893
Ústecká Bus Historické Muzeum, Chlumec u Ústi nad Labem 008332
Usual and Unusual Antiques, Milwaukee 090327
Usus, Offenbach am Main 134329
Uta, Kraków 079663, 140749
Uta, Warszawa 109201
Utah Artist Hands, Salt Lake City . . 119378
Utah Artists, Salt Lake City 055085
Utah Book and Magazine, Salt Lake City 142876
Utah Field House of Natural History State Park, Vernal 048766
Utah Museum of Fine Arts, University of Utah, Salt Lake City 047777
Utah Museum of Natural History, Salt Lake City 047778
Utah Museums Association, Salt Lake City 055086
Utah Potters, Salt Lake City 119379
Utah State Historical Society Museum, Salt Lake City 047779
Ute Indian Museum, Montrose 046011
Uter, Peter, Rüdersdorf bei Berlin . . 126753
Utermann, Wilfried, Dortmund 102414
Utica Museum, Hobson 044564
L'Utile e il Dilettevole, Milano 075885
Utilidades Raclima, Lisboa 080044
Utke, A., Sankt Augustin 073665
Utopia, Gent 137505
Utopia, Haarlem 078485
Utopia Antiques, Low Newton 085856
Utopia Art Sydney, Waterloo 056808
Utopia Art Sydney, Waterloo 095379
Utopia Fine Art Gallery, Alice Springs 094147
Utrecht, Pittsburgh 118960
Utropet, Falköping 122130
Utsi, Nils Olaf, Oslo 079478
Utställningar & Konsthandel, Jönköping 110947
Utställningssalongen, Stockholm . . 111078
Utstein Kloster, Mosterøy 031037
Utsukushigahara Kogen Bijutsukan, Takeshi 027130
Uttar Pradesh State Museum, Lucknow 022247
Uttenrodt, Michael, Ludwigsburg, Württemberg 126233
Uttoxeter Heritage Centre, Uttoxeter 041267
UTU Artworks, Singapore 109889
Utvandrarnas Hus, Växjö 036775
Utz, Brigitte, Dresden 102459
Utzt, Inge, Stuttgart 139774
Uudenkaupungin Kultuurihistoriallinen Museo, Uusikaupunki 010197
Uummannap Katersugaasivia, Uummannaq 021553
Uus't Olde Maat, Giethoorn 029612
UVAN Historical Museum, Winnipeg 006871
Uwajima-shiritsu Date Hakubutsukan, Uwajima 027313
Uxbridge - Howick's Creative Centre, Auckland 030450
Uxbridge-Scott Museum, Uxbridge . 006677
Uyttenhove, L., Oostende 058369
Uzal, M. & N., Bruxelles 058106
Uzbekistan Art Academy, Taškent . . 049413
Uzbekistan Art Academy, Taškent . . 052420
Uzunov, Dečko, Sofia 096753
Užupio Galerija, Vilnius 107376
Uzzell, Phillip, Richmond 132726
V Dinastia, Madrid 081406
V I Prints, Selkirk 114402
V. K. Janyno, Druskininkai 107344
V + K Publishing, Blaricum 134801
V Podloubí, Mladá Boleslav 098387
V & R Fine Art, Tampa 120072
V & R Unipress, Göttingen 133977
V. & V., 's-Hertogenbosch 078530
V2 Galerie, Rotterdam 108214
Vaagsvold, Alfred, Borhaug 108686
Vaajakosken Työläiskotimuseo, Jyväskylä 009647
Vaal Teknorama Cultural Museum, Vereeniging 034769
Vaas, Vence 101443
Vaas, Alois, Ellwangen 070545
Vaasan Auto- ja Moottorimuseo, Vaasa 010205
Vaasan Merimuseo, Vaasa 010206
Vaasen, R., Jülich 103459
Vacaro Venuto, Valros 068706
Vacaville Museum, Vacaville 048722
Vaccaretti, Laurent, Castellane 062010
Vaccari, A. & L., Bologna 075116
Vaccari, Paolo, Firenze 127423
Vaccher, Dr. Daniela, Roma 128233
Vache, Josian, Boisseron 061544
Vachel Lindsay Home, Springfield . 048290
Vachtanov, Moskva 109600
Vacquet-Journiac, Charlette, Angers 060864
Vadala & Busch, Frankfurt am Main 102834
Vadertje Tijd, Leiden 078587
Vadhera, Delhi 105689
Vadillo Vadillo, Blas Jose, Sevilla . . 129746
Vadrot, Jean-Louis, Pont-Authou . . 066913
Vadsbo Museum, Mariestad 036474
Vadsø Museum - Ruija Kvenmuseum, Vadsø 031310
Vadstena Slott, Vadstena 036752
Vadstena Stadsmuseum, Vadstena . 036753
Vääksyn Vesimylly- ja piensähkölaitosmuseo, Vääksy . . 010208
Väderstad Auktionshall, Mjölby 122215
Vähänkyrön Museo, Vähäkyrö 010209
Väike-Männiku Talumuuseum, Kõpu 009374
Väinontalo - Järviseudun Museo, Vasikka-Aho 010231
Välkesalmi, Kimmo, Helsinki 137963
Vämöparken, Karlskrona 036385
Vänermuseet, Lidköping 036419
Vänersborgs Museum, Vänersborg . 036757
Værløse Museum, Værløse 009136
Värmdö Auktionsverk, Djurhamn . . 122117
Värmlands Museum, Karlstad 036387
Värtsilän Myllymuseo, Värtsilä 010210
Väsby Kungsgård, Sala 036557
Västby Auktionskammare, Helgum . 122156

Västerås Flygande Museum, Västerås . . . 036762
Västerås Flygmuseum, Västerås . . . 036763
Västerås Konstmuseum, Västerås . . 036764
Västerås Skolmuseum, Västerås . . 036765
Västerbottens Museum, Umeå 036732
Västergötlands Museum, Skara . . . 036577
Västerviks Auktionsbyrå, Västervik . 122288
Västerviks Museum, Västervik 036770
Västkustauktioner, Hunnebostrand . 122165
Västmanlands Läns Museum, Västerås . . . 036766
Västra Auktionsverket, Jönköping . . 122169
Västra Göinge Hembygdsmuseum, Hässleholm . . . 036321
Vättehult - Pälle Nävers Diktarstuga, Vetlanda . . . 036787
Vätterbygdens Auktionskammare, Jönköping . . . 122170
Växjö Auktionskammare, Växjö 122289
Vafiadis, Theo, Pirmasens 073335
Vafias, Nineta, Kifissia 105432
Vaga Publishers, Vilnius 134746
Våga Se, Stockholm 111079
Vagabond Books, Los Angeles 142521
Vaganay, Luc, Lyon 124377
Il Vaglio, Bari 105937
Vagnmuseet, Malmö Museer, Malmö . . . 036464
Vagnshistoriska Museet, Fristad . . . 036278
Vagonářské Muzeum, Studénka . . . 008699
Vagt, Ingeborg, Berlin 102071
Vagues à l'Ame, Sucy-en-Brie 068340
Vai, Denver 088747
Vaiani, Viviano, Livorno 075543
Vaidoto Žuko, Vilnius 107377
Vaijnorský L'udovy Dom - Etnografická Expozícia, Mestské Múzeum v Bratislave, Bratislava . . . 034339
Vail Galleries, Solihull 114448
Vail Valley Arts Council, Avon 055087
Vaila Fine Art, Shetland 114429
Vaile Mansion - Dewitt Museum, Independence . . . 044728
Vaillant, Gérard, Le Breuil 063578
Vaillant, Michel, Avignon 098903
Vaisy, Patricia, Messery 064514
Vaitai, Vilnius 107378
Vajda Lajos Emlékmúzeum, Ferenczy Múzeum, Szentendre . . . 021889
Vajra, Paris 066631
Vakanas, Lucien, Sault (Vaucluse) . 068145
Vakgroep Kunst-, Muziek- en Theaterwetenschappen, Universiteit Gent, Fakulteit Letteren en Wijsbegeerte, Gent . . . 049702
Vakıf Halı Müzesi, İstanbul 038103
Vakıf Inşaat ve Sanat Eserleri Müzesi, İstanbul . . . 038104
Vakıf Kilim ve Düz Dokuma Yaygılar Müzesi, İstanbul . . . 038105
Vakil & Sons, Mumbai 134522
Vakko Sanat Galerisi, İstanbul 112368
Vakko Sanat Galerisi, İstanbul 112369
Vakoilumuseo, Tampere 010139
Val-d'Oise Documents & Collections, Deuil-la-Barre . . . 062619
Val House, Bucureşti 109447
Val I 30, Valencia 110846
Valaamskij Naučno-issledovatelskij Cerkovno- archeologičeskij i Prirodnyj Muzej-zapovednik, Sortavala 033896
Valabrega, Vittorio, Torino 076875
Valade, François, Gençay 062980
Valade, François, Lussac-les-Châteaux . . . 064037
Valadier, Roma 076715
Valahia, Bucureşti 080173
Valansi, Claudio, Rio de Janeiro . . . 096652
Valantin, Hugues, Dordives 062718
Valaria, Detroit 116097
Valašské Muzeum v Přírodě, Rožnov pod Radhoštěm . . . 008674
Valat, Eric, Erquy 062798
Valberg, Ottawa 097120
Valbusa, Verona 077026
Valdajskij Kraevedčeskij Muzej, Valdaj . . . 034021
Valdemārpils Mežu Muzejs, Valdemārpils . . . 027790
Valderrama, Mia, New York 132544
Valdés Costales, José Manuel, Oviedo . . . 141065
The Valdez Museum, Valdez 048728
Valdivia Museo, Valdivia 009267
Valdo, Paris 100928
Valdosta State University Fine Arts Gallery, Valdosta . . . 048730
Valdres Folkemusum, Fagernes . . . 030828
Vale and Downland Museum, Wantage . . . 041295
Vale Antiques, Easingwold 084243
Vale Antiques, London 085760
Vale do Paraiba Antiguidades, São Paulo . . . 058745
Vale Stamps and Antiques, London . 085761
Valeda, Felix Hector, Cancún 128501
Valemount and Area Museum, Valemount . . . 006682
Valence House Museum and Art Gallery, Dagenham . . . 039199
Valenne, Luxembourg 077480
Valens Log Cabin, Ancaster 005013
Valensi, Gilbert, Belgentier 061330
Valensija, Sankt-Peterburg 109652
Valent, Modena 075931
Valentia Island Heritage Centre, Knightstown . . . 022818
Valentien, Dr. Freerk, Stuttgart 105019
Valentijn, Den Haag 078260
Valentijn, Antonius, Berlin 069777, 125311
Valentin, Carqueiranne 062003
Valentin, Etienne, Cluny 062368
Valentin, Françoise, Serverette 068232
Valentin, Gilbert, Vallauris 101423
Valentin, Jean-Pierre, Montréal . . . 097089
Valentin, Martin, Geldern 070952
Valentin Antiguedades, Madrid 081407
Valentin-Karlstadt Musäum, München . . . 019128
Valentina, Manama 096029
Valentina, Winterthur 082918
Valentine & Co., Owen F., Richmond 123076
Valentine Antiquités, Toulouse 068551
Valentine Richmond History Center, Richmond . . . 047426
Valentine's Antique Gallery, Bendigo 055482
Valentin's, Paris 100929
Valentis, Bordeaux 124149
Valentown Museum, Victor 048781
Valenzuela & Klenner, Bogotá 098198
Våler Torvdriftsmuseum, Våler i Solør . . . 031312
Valéra, Tarbes 101308
Valeri, Diego, Padova 076116, 140086
Valeria Bella, Milano 140068
Valeria Belvedere, Milano 106339
Valette, Paris 138555
Valeur Collection Télécartes, Nice . 065156
Valga Muuseum, Valga 009433
Valhalla Museum, Tresco 041239
Vali, London 113940
The Valiant Soldier, Buckfastleigh . . 038890
La Valigia del Viaggiatore, Brescia . 075190
Valík, Jozef, Košice 080624
Valiño, Alicia & Jorge, Montevideo . 142188
Valiño Fernández, Jorge, Montevideo . . . 087349
Valis, Apostolos, Ludwigsburg, Württemberg . . . 126234
Valjanov, Osnabrück 073249
Valkama, Jorma-Tapio, Jämsä 098750
Valkas Novadpētniecības Muzejs, Valka . . . 027791
Valks, Jan, Haarlem 078486
Vall-Alemany, R., Lleida 122028
Vallaci, Cannes 061960
Valladares Rascon, Jose Ignacio, Salamanca . . . 081547
Vallade, Robert, Cachan 061854
Vallance Cottage, Alexandra 030422
Vallanzasca, Maria Antonietta, Padova . . . 106409
Vallard House Fine Art Gallery, Mount Tamborine . . . 094914
Vallby Friluftsmuseum, Västerås . . . 036767
Valldeperas Ulloa, Alfonso, San Salvador . . . 124037
Vallé, Chrstiane, Clermont-Ferrand . 099155
Del Valle Anticuarios, Toledo 081634
Valle de los Caídos, Valle de Cuelgamuros . . . 036011
Vallebona, Silvano, Genova 106111
Valledor Aguerri, Javier, Zaragoza . 081755
Vallée, Florence, Guingamp 063109
Vallee, Yvonne, Martel 064412
Vallée Verte, Grandchamp 099294
Vallejo Naval and Historical Museum, Vallejo . . . 048734
Valleriaux, François, Paris 138556
Vallerini, Andrea, Pisa 140093
Vallette-Jaquenoud, Paula, Marseille . . . 064398
Valley Antiques, Paeroa . . 079211, 128950
Valley Antiques, Wrentham 087269
Valley Art Center, Clarkston 042953
Valley Auctions, Folkestone 122512
Valley Coin, Minneapolis 090401
Valley Coin, Gold and Silver Exchange, San Jose . . . 092937
Valley Community Historical Society Museum, Valley . . . 048735
Valley County Pioneer Museum, Glasgow . . . 044197
The Valley Forge Museum, Valley Forge . . . 048737
Valley Forge National Historical Park, Valley Forge . . . 048738
Valley House Gallery, Dallas 115949
Valley Museum, McBride 005813
Valley of the Kings, Los Angeles . . . 116907
Valley Oriental, Las Vegas 116654
Valley Originals Art, Bega 094233
Valley Trophies, Phoenix 091776
Valley Upholstering, Louisville 132309
Valli, Tuula, Tampere 060634
Vallier, Valencia 141083
Valligiano, Roma 076716
Vallois, Paris 100930
Vallois, Georges-Philippe & Nathalie, Paris . . . 100931
Vallois, Robert, Paris 100932
Vallotton, Philippe, Lausanne 082571
Valls, Rafael, London 085762
Valls, Rafael, London 085763
Valls, Rafael, London 113941
Valls, Rafael, London 113942
Valluet, Christine, Paris 100933
Valmar, Miami 117150
Valmar, Stansted Mountfitchet 086695
Valmay, Hamilton 108462
Valmieras Novadpētniecības Muzejs, Valmiera . . . 027793
Valmont, Buenos Aires 094091
Valoir, Orléans 121103
Valokuva, Helsinki 135680
Valparadiso, Palermo 076189
Valsts Elektrotehniskās Fabrikas Vēstures Muzejs, Rīga . . . 027769
Valsts Mākslas Muzejs Izstazu Zale Arsenāls, Rīga . . . 027770
Valsts Mākslas Muzeju, Rīga 027771
Valsyra, Saint-Ouen 067913
Valta, Bernhard, Vasoldsberg 123482
Valtakunnallinen Työväentalomuseo, Riihimäki . . . 010039
Valu Oria Galeria de Artes, São Paulo . . . 096693
Value, Christian, Christchurch 140622
Value Plus, Columbus 088446
Valued History, Cambridge 083851
Valverde, Décio, São Paulo 058746
Valverde Lacambra, Fernando, Zaragoza . . . 081756, 129834
V.A.M.P, Pierrefitte-sur-Seine 066826
Vampulan Museo, Vampula 010219
Ván, Ha Noi 120493
Ván, Ho Chi Minh City 120536
Van, M., Paris 100934
Van Aacken, Rudolf, Oberhausen, Rheinland . . . 073148, 126575
Van Aalst, A., Breda 078121, 128610
Het Van Abbemuseum, Bonheiden . 003240
Van Abbemuseum, Eindhoven 029550
Van Acker, Akko, Paris 066632
Van Ackeren, Kleve 071880
Van Allemeersch, Knokke-Heist . . . 058254
Van Almsick, Georg, Gronau, Westfalen . . . 071110, 103014
Van Alsenoy, Antwerpen 120709
Van Art Antiguidades, Rio de Janeiro . . . 058664
Van Assche, S., Gent 058211
Van Baalen, J.M., Goes 128673
Van Baars, M., Lochem 128756
Van Balberghe, Emile, Bruxelles . . . 137476
Van Banning, Herman, Amsterdam . 077991
Van Basten Batenburg, Nazie, Maastricht . . . 078627
Van Beek, G., Aalsmeer 128515
Van Beers, Jan, London 085764
Van Bekhoven, Anton W., Naarden .134824, 140500
Van Benthem-Doppegieter, A.M.E., Bodegraven . . . 128593
Van Berchem, J.-S., Bruxelles 137477
Van Beuzekom, Cees, Gouda 128676
Van Borkulo, Loes, Amsterdam . . . 077992
Van Buren County Historical Society Museum, Keosauqua . . . 044973
Van Bussel, M ., Amsterdam 077993
Van Camp-Magermans, Jenny, Antwerpen . . . 096094
Van Campen & Rochtus, Antwerpen 096095
Van Canneyt, Ignace, Kortrijk 058272
Van Catwijck, Leiden 078588
Van Cleemput & Schietekat, Sint-Niklaas . . . 058377
Van Coevorden, Doornspijk 140409
Van Cortlandt House Museum, Bronx . . . 042443
Van Daele, R., Antwerpen 057742
Van Dalen, Jan, Rotterdam 078750
Van Dam, Adriaan, Utrecht 128862
Van Dam, Drs. Michiel, Amsterdam 077994
Van Damme, James, Bruxelles 096261
Van de Beuque, Antoine, Paris 100935
Van de Laar, Maurits, Den Haag . . . 107958
Van de Laar, Michel, 's-Hertogenbosch . . . 128716
Van de Loo, München 104334
Van de Loo, Marie-José, München .104335, 134283
Van de Loo, P., Eindhoven 128663
Van de Loo, Peter, Eindhoven 078355
Van de Moosdijk, Eindhoven 078356
Van de Nieuwe Dingen, Tilburg 108236
Van de Plas Ets, Bruxelles 137478
Van de Pol, Arnhem 078060
Van de Poll-Stichting, Zeist 030380
Van de Raadt, S., Rotterdam 108215
Van de Velde, Denise, Aalst 096052
Van de Velde, L., Antwerpen 057743
Van de Velde, Ronny, Berchem 096109, 133253
Van de Ven, Alexander, Den Haag . . 078261
Van de Vijver, Bruxelles 058107
Van de Water, Eindhoven 108010
Van de Weghe, Christophe, New York . . . 118523
Van de Wiele, G., Knokke-Heist . . . 058255
Van de Wiele, M., Brugge 137420
Van Dekken, B., Rötgesbüttel 073564
Van Delden & Cie., Dr., Osnabrück . 073250
Van Delft, George, Tilburg 078780
Van den Berg, Leeuwarden 108098
Van den Berg, E., Breda 128611
Van den Berg, Jos, Den Haag 107959
Van den Besselaar, Anny, Maastricht . . . 108135

Van den Bogaerde, D., Bruxelles . . 058108
Van den Bogart, J., Roosendaal . . . 078689
Van den Bos, M.W., Haarlem 128697
Van den Bosch, L., Bruxelles 058109
Van den Bout & Zoon, H.A.C., Langerak 128739
Van den Brulle, Kristine, Antwerpen 123555
Van den Bulcke, R., Brugge 057789
Van den Burg, Henk, Rotterdam . . . 140526
Van Den Bussche, Dominique, Martigues 064416
Van den Eijnde, Bruxelles 058110
Van den Elshout, J.A.P., Den Haag . 078262
Van den Ende, M., Den Haag 128636
Van den Gaag, J.A., Den Haag 128637
Van den Ham & Tijdink, Bilthoven . . 128589
Van den Minkelis, T., Hardinxveld Giessendam 128704
Van den Putte, G., Gent 123627
Van den Sommen, F., Eindhoven . . . 078357
Van den Tillaar, Uden 128850
Van der Aa, T., Sliedrecht 128834
Van der Aa & de Boer, Maastricht . . 078628
Van der Beek, P.J., Stadskanaal . . . 128837
Van der Ben, Hans, Geldrop 140425
Van der Does, Dorle, Carouge 082294
Van der Donk, Ineke, Zaltbommel . . 078860
Van der Donk, Jan, New York 142700
Van der Donk, Pimm, Amsterdam . . 107814
Van der Donk, Pimm, Hamburg . . . 103226
Van der Eems, Bolsward 128594
Van der Eerden, B.L., Rotterdam . . 078751
Van der Eerden, L., Rotterdam 078752
Van der Elst, Bruxelles 137479
Van der Graaf, Tom, Ottoland 128803
Van der Gucht, A., Bruxelles 058111
Van der Gulik, A.K.J., Haarlem 078487
Van der Heijden, Arno, Amsterdam .077995, 128558
Van der Heyde, Paopaoe 101491
Van der Horst, Frank, Weesp 128879
Van der Kamp, H.J.G.E., Zwolle . . . 078896
Van der Klift, Hans, Den Burg 140385
Van der Koelen, Dr. Dorothea, Mainz 104007
Van der Linden, Amersfoort 077756, 128524
Van der Loo, Hans & Ulrike, Hettenleidelheim 071503
Van der Marel, A., Heemstede 140454
Van der Meer, Datchet 135137
Van der Meer, A., Amsterdam 077996
Van der Mel, Amsterdam 107815
Van der Most, Jürgen & Andrea, Leutershausen 126217
Van der Neut, R.A.G., Haarlem 078488
Van der Peet, C.P.J., Amsterdam . . 140343
Van der Perre, Francine, Bruxelles . 137480
Van der Perre, Micheline, Bruxelles 058112, 096262, 137481
Van der Planken, Antwerpen 096096
Van der Schoot, Ad, Tilburg 128846
Van Der Schueren, Jean-Luc, Bruxelles 058113
Van der Stappen, W.C.M., Tilburg . . 078781
Van der Steur, A.G., Haarlem 140446
Van der Straeten, Amsterdam 107816
Van der Teen, Dordrecht 078319
Van der Veen, Geert, Toronto 097392
Van der Ven, 's-Hertogenbosch . . .078531, 140461
Van der Vlist, Frederiek & Ingrid, Leiden 108109
Van der Voort, Eivissa 110350
Van der Weide, H.J., Zwolle 128891
Van der Werff, Auke, Amsterdam . . 077997
Van-der-Werf's Wedgwoodmuseum, Zuidwolde, Groningen 030401
Van der Wis, J.C., Groningen 078434
Van der Woude, J.M., Amsterdam . 128559
Van Deudekom, Johannes, Monaco 128509
Van Devlet Güzel Sanatlar Galerisi, Van 038193
Van Dexter-Grover, New York 091323
Van Dieten-d'Eendt, Ferdinand, Amsterdam 107817
Van Dijk, Kampen 140468
Van Dijk, Jaap, Sint Michielsgestel . 128831
Van Dijk & Van Schaik, Naarden . . . 128781
Van Dijken, H.C., Haarlem 078489
Van Dishoeck, Eduard, Amsterdam . 140344
Van Doorn, Franeker 140422
Van Dorssen, Irene, Yandina 095445
Van Dreven, Amsterdam 077998
Van Driel, Rotterdam 078753
Van Durme, O. & F., Gent 058212
Van Duyvendijk Brouwer, Amsterdam 077999
Van Dyck, Gijón 110362
Van Dyck, Gijón 110363
Van Dyke Coins, Detroit 088778
Van Eck, Frank P., Triesen 134740
Van Ee, Richmond, Victoria 095144
Van Eeghen-de Laaf, H.A.C., Haarlem 128698
Van Eick, Manfred, Düsseldorf 125552
Van Eijck, Maastricht 078629
Van Eijck, Rotterdam 108216
Van Elst, E., Amsterdam 078000
Van Erp-Broekhans, Tilburg 078782
Van Eyck, Buenos Aires 094092
Van Frankfoort & P. Beudel, Hamburg 071349
Van Galen, San Francisco 132915
Van Ganzenwinkel, G.T.J., Eindhoven 128664
Van Ganzenwinkel, M.F.G., Someren 128836
Van Geel, Jan, Apeldoorn 128566
Van Geenen, Delft 078150
Van Gelder, Amsterdam . . 107818, 134793
Van Gendt, Amsterdam 121780
Van Gennep, Amsterdam 134794
Van Gogh, Amsterdam 128560
Van Gogh, Bitola 107419
Van Gogh Documentatiecentrum, Nuenen 029977
Van Gogh Museum, Amsterdam . . . 029239
Van Gold, Alicante 121990
Van Gouygem, Jean-Pierre, Saint-Ouen 067914
Van Gremberghe, Kathy, Vallauris . . 101424
Van Grover, J.J., New York 091324
Van Gybland-Oosterhoff Collection, Pretoria 034734
Van Haeften, Johnny, London 085765, 113943, 131204
Van Ham, Köln . . . 072020, 103731, 121479
Van Ham, P., Antwerpen 057744
Van-Hay, Geoffrey, Merstham 085980
Van Heekern, Peter, Essen 125618
Van Heemst-Pallay, Middelharnis . . 128776
Van Hefflin, Kirton-in-Lindsey 084879
Van Heijningen, Den Haag 107960
Van Heijningen, Den Haag 107961
Van Heijst, Bergen op Zoom 128583
Van Helden, Wellington 108648
Van Herck, Antwerpen 123556
Van Herck, Jan, Antwerpen 057745, 123557
Van Hier tot Tokyo, Amsterdam . . . 078001
Van Hoeter, F., Bruxelles 137482
Van Hoevelaak & Zoon, Zeist 078871
Van Hoof, Eindhoven 078358
Van Hoof, Jan, 's-Hertogenbosch . . 108081
Van Hoorebeke, Guy, Brugge 057790
Van Hoorn, Nijmegen 140507
Van Hoorn, H., Lettele 128750
Van Horn & Hayward, Houston 089237
Van Houtte, Charenton-le-Pont 062151
Van Houtte, Jean-Louis, Maisons-Alfort 064224
Van Hove, Bruxelles 058114
Van Hove, Monique, Quimper 067024
Van Iperen, G.H.A., Oss 078674
Van Kaam, R.G., Ijmuiden 128733
Van Kammen, A., Leeuwarden 078557
Van Kampen, Doesburg 128647
Van Keulen, Matty, Uden 128851
Van Kio, Nara 077168
Van Kleef, Oakland 118649
Van Kranendonk, Den Haag 107962
Van Kuik, Paul, Voorschoten 140565
Van Laarhoven, A., Dordrecht 078320
Van Laer, Frank, Antwerpen 123558
Van Laere, Antwerpen 096097
Van Langenhove, Gent . . . 058213, 096302, 120760
Van Leest, Utrecht 078822
Van Leeuwen, Amsterdam 140345
Van Leeuwen, Woerden 128885
Van Leeuwen, Remco, Eindhoven . . 078359
Van Leeuwen, S., Den Haag 078263
Van Leeuwenhoek, Anthonie, Delft . 140384
Van Lieshout, J.C., Oss 128801
Van Liew, Marcia, Seattle 093080
Van Lijf-Van Leeuwen, N ., Enschede 078382
Van Lindenberg, G.J., Zutphen 078884
Van Lines, Detroit 088779
Van Loock, Albert, Bruxelles 137483
Van Loock, Claude, Bruxelles 133280, 137484
Van Loon, J.M., Tilburg . . 078783, 128847
Van Meeuwen, J.W.T., Den Haag . . 140402
Van Megchelen, Cock, Eindhoven . . 078360
Van Menen, L. & J., Brugge 057791
Van Meter State Park, Miami 045821
Van Middelem, Luc, Oostende 096406
Van Mourik, Culemborg 128618
Van Müzesi, Van 038194
Van Mullem, Jan, Brugge . 057792, 123570
Van Nie, Amsterdam 078002
Van Nieuwenhuyse, H., Gent 123628
Van Noppen, Providence 119090
Van Nostrand-Starkins House, Roslyn 047548
Van Oorschot, Nico, Amsterdam . . . 078003
Van Opdorp, Hoogerheide 128728
Van Orsouw, Oss 078675
Van Orsouw, Bob, Zürich 112190
Van Os, Ignas, Arnhem 128572
Van Os, Margot, Hilversum 128722
Van Os, Peter, Arnhem . . . 078061, 140357
Van Otterloo, Doorn 140408
Van Overstraeten, J., Bruxelles 058115
Van Paddenburgh, L., Leiden 140484
Van Paridon, Eloy, Sassafras 056577
Van Peborgh, Raymonde, Sarlat-la-Canéda 068127
Van Poelgeest, W., Amsterdam 107819, 128561, 140346
Van Raalte, Drs. G., Amsterdam . . . 078004
Van Reekum Museum; Historisch Museum Apeldoorn, Apeldoorn 029252
Van Remmen, Solingen 073857
Van Riel, Buenos Aires 094093
Van Rijn, Paris 100936
Van Rijn, Utrecht 078823
Van Rijn, Rob, Maastricht 078630
Van Rijswijck Galerie, Antwerpen . . 096098
Van Rijt, F.J.K., Apeldoorn 140353
Van Riper-Hopper House, Wayne . . 049031
Van Rompaey, Robert, Antwerpen . . 096099
Van Roon, Haarlem 078490
Van Rossem, Adriaan, Nijmegen . . . 128789
Van Rossum, T.N.R., Middenbeemster 128777
Van Roy, R., Antwerpen 123559
Van Ruiten & Zoon, Leiden 078589
Van Rycke, Bordeaux 061658
Van Sabben, Oostwoud 140510
Van Sabben, Piet, Hoorn 121794
Van Schaik, Oss 078676
Van Schaik, Pretoria 140974
Van Schalkwyk, Kathryn, Pretoria . . 080744
Van Schouten, Ruud, Amsterdam . . 128562
Van Spijk, Pascal, Venlo 134837
Van Staden, Gerrit, Delmenhorst . . 102355
Van Stekelenburg, Hein & Marion, Amsterdam 140347
Van Stijn & Van Stijn, Arnhem 107861
Van Stockum, Den Haag 121788
Van Strub, Kurt, Genève 111507
Van 't Hof, A., Haarlem 078491
Van 't Hof, Jeroen, Heemstede 128708
Van 't Hul, L., Kampen 128735
Van 't Hull, Karin, Detmold 125459
Van 't Lindenhoutmuseum, Nijmegen 029966
Van Tendeloo, L., Antwerpen 137410
Van Thienen, C., Bruxelles 123611
Van Tilburg Collection, Pretoria . . . 034735
Van Turnhout, Breda 140367
Van Uffelen, Palmerston North 108536
Van Valkengoed, Nijkerk 128787
Van Veen, Meppel 140497
Van Veen, Claudia, Freising 070874
Van Vliet, F., Hilversum 078543
Van Vliet, H.C., Amsterdam 078005
Van Vugt, J., Eindhoven 078361
Van Vyve, E., Bruxelles 123612
Van Wal, Milwaukee 117225
Van Waning, Rotterdam 108217
Van Wassenaar, J.C., Rotterdam . . . 078754
Van Weerde, Amsterdam 078006
Van Welsenes, Bernard, Bergen, Noord-Holland 107868
Van Wersch, A.F., Heerlen 078509
Van Weydevelt, Philippe, Corné . . . 062483
Van Weyenbergh, Los Angeles 116908
Van Wijland, P., Dordrecht 078321
Van Wijngaarden, Amsterdam 107820
Van Wingerden, Groot Ammers 128683
Van Wisselingh & Co., E.J., Haarlem 078492
Van Witteloostuijn, Delft 078151
Van Wüllen, Legden 072183
Van Wyck Homestead Museum, Fishkill 043847
Van Zoetendaal, Amsterdam 107821
Vanajan Kotiseutumuseo, Hämeenlinna 009496
Vanavara, Tallinn 060490
Vanbeselaere, René, Oudon 065314
Vanbienne, Mons 058348
Vanbraekel, A., Mouscron 133294
Vanbrugh House Antiques, Stow-on-the-Wold 086768, 142091
Vanbrunt, New York 118524
Vance Kirkland Museum, Denver . . 043421
Vancoppenolle, Gent 058214
Vancouver Antique Centre, Vancouver 059433
Vancouver Art Gallery, Vancouver . . 006713
Vancouver Arts Centre, Albany 000725
Vancouver Arts Centre, Albany 094126
Vancouver Chinese Art Gallery, Vancouver 097541
Vancouver Holocaust Education Centre, Vancouver 006714
Vancouver Life Drawing Society, Vancouver 052777
Vancouver Maritime Museum, Vancouver 006715
Vancouver Museum, Vancouver . . . 006716
Vancouver Naval Museum, West Vancouver 006794
Vancouver Police Centennial Museum, Vancouver 006717
Vancso, Olga, Lustenau 137229
Vanczak, François, Nancy 064884
Vandalia State House, Vandalia . . . 048752
Vandelanoitte, Lille 124327
Vandeleur Antiquarian Books, Epsom 141600
Vandelft, Mornington 123272
Vandenberghe, Philippe, Crozon . . . 099192
Vandenhaute, Rouen 067304
Vander, Jenny, Dublin 074953
Vander-Chine, Bruxelles 133281
Vanderbilt Mansion National Museum, Hyde Park 044709
Vanderbilt University Fine Arts Gallery, Nashville 046157
Vanderbor, Barcelona 080953, 110261
Vanderhoof Community Museum, Vanderhoof 006719
Vanderkindere, Bruxelles 120747
Vanderleelie, Edmonton 096904
Vanderslyen, Bruxelles 058116

Vanderstelt, Voorburg 121808
Vandevoorde, Paris 100937
Vandewater, Seattle 143017
Vandilli, Antonio, Roma 128234
Vandiver-Williams, Atlanta 087539
Vane, London 085766
Vaned Art Gallery, Miami 117151
Vanessa Vintage Treasures, Baltimore 087721
Vang Olsen, Mimi, New York 091325
Vangelisti, Bruno, Lucca 121693
Vangelli dé Cresci, Francesco, Roma 106643
Vangeon, Guy, Luisant 064024
Vanghendt, E., Bruxelles 058117
Vanghi, Lucia, Bologna 127187
Vanguard, Long Beach 089662
Vanguard, San Francisco 119821
Vanguard Centennial Museum, Vanguard 006720
Vanguardia, Bilbao 110288
Vanha Kerttu, Sysmä 137989
Vanha-Rantalan Talomuseo, Pertunmaa 009965
Vanhaa & Kaunista, Helsinki 060588
Vanhaecke, D., Bruxelles 058118
Vanhaisäntä, Igor, Helsinki 060589
Vanhalst, R., De Haan 123616
Vanhat Neidit, Helsinki 060590
Vanhoecke, Pascal, Cachan 099043
Vanhoegaerde, Samuel, Knokke-Heist 096359
Vanholme, Philippe, Lille 124328
Vanhoogstraat, William R., Saint Louis 119263
Vanhove, Leuven 137513
Vania, Jakarta 105842
Vanic, Wien 095956
Vanier, Tucson 120173
Vanini, Oakland 091444
Vanishing Point Gallery Of Arts, Benowa 094243
Vankilamuseo, Hämeenlinnan Kaupungin Historiallinen Museo, Hämeenlinna 009497
Vanleeuwen, Nieuwerkerk aan den IJssel 128785
Vann, Bill, Saint Louis 119264
Vann House, Chatsworth 042774
Vannacci, Pier Augusto, Firenze . . . 127424
Vannier, Jean-Paul, Gradignan 063028
Vannini, Brescia 106008
Vanonkelen, L., Bruxelles 058119
Vanot, Michel, Marseille 124435
Vanrell, Palma de Mallorca 110702
Vans, Lord, New York 118525
Vansalon, Indianapolis 116497
Vanseer, C. & Y., Liège 058329
Vanstone, Peter, Los Angeles 089930
Vantaan Kaupunginmuseo, Vantaa . 010225
Vantaan Kaupunginmuseo - Kuvataideasiat, Vantaa 010226
Vantaggio, Uno, Roma 076717
Vantan Design Kenkyujo, Tokyo . . . 050502
Vantul de Rasarit, Bucureşti 140883
Vanuatu Cultural Centre and National Museum, Port Vila 049416
Vanuxem, Paris 100938
Vanuxem, Roland, La Crèche 099393
Vanzo, Saint-Laurent-des-Vignes . . 067578
Vaos Collection, Athinai 021215
Vapentekniska Museet, Eskilstuna . 036256
Vaquer Neri, Maria Carmela, Cagliari 075231
Vara del Rey, Sevilla 081617
Varadero, Porto 140870
Varalan Liikuntamuseo, Tampere . . 010140
Varando, Silvio, Firenze 075417
Varanger Museum Sør, Grenselandmuseet, Kirkenes 030938
La Varangue, Paris 066633
Varart, Firenze 106076
Varas, Teodoro Anton, Barcelona . . 080954
Varas, Teodoro Anton, Barcelona . . 080955
Varaždinske Toplice Muzej, Varaždinske Toplice 007817
Varbanova, V. Ju., Sofia 058770
Varbanova, V. Ju., Sofia 058771
Varde Artillerimuseum, Varde Museum, Varde 009140
Varden Redningsmuseum, Jahrmuseet, Narbø 031046
Vardømuseene, Vardø 031318
Varekamp, Amsterdam 078007
Varela, Martínez 055285
Varela, Martínez 055286
Varendra Research Museum, Rajshahi 003116
Varenne, Alexandre, Paris 100939
Varenne, Daniel, Genève 111508
Varese, Maria Rosa, Torino 076876
Varet, Cyrille, Paris 100940
Várfok Galéria, Budapest 105548
Varga Imre Kiallitas, Budapest 021699
Vargas, Sevilla 081618
Vargas Museum and Art Gallery, Mandaluyong 031710
Vargha & Bettega, Montevideo 122791
Varia, Liège 137524
Variété, Nice 065157
Variety, Chicago 088189, 142304
Variety Box, Tunbridge Wells 086956
Variety Trading, Timaru 121835
Varine-Gincourt, Paris 100941
Varini, Arnaldo, Brescia 127237
Varissuon Antikvariaatti, Turku 137999
Varistaipaleen Kanavamuseo, Karvion Kanava 009674
Varjjat Sámi Musea, Varanger Samiske Museum, Varangerbotn 031317
Varkauden Museo, Varkaus 010228
Varkauden Taidemuseo, Varkaus . . 010229
Varlet, Claude, Paris 066634
Varma, Ravi, Chennai 074800, 105639
Varma Arts Gallery, Hyderabad 074813
Varmegalleriet, København 098588
Varmès-Hinaekian, Peggy, Genève . 111509
Vármúzeum, Dunaföldvár 021714
Vármúzeum, Kisvárda 021774
Vármúzeum, Siklós 021840
Vármúzeum, Simontornya 021841
Vármúzeum, Sümeg 021853
Vármúzeum, Veszprém 021920
Vármúzeum, Magyar Nemzeti Múzeum, Esztergom 021725
Varner-Hogg Plantation, West Columbia 049071
Varnier, Paris 100942
Varnum Memorial Armory and Military Museum, East Greenwich 043563
Városi Képtár, Orosháza 021806
Városi Képtár, Székesfehérvár 021873
Városi Múzeum, Kőszeg 021777
Városi Tömegközlekedési Múzeum, Budapesti Közlekedési Részvénytársaság, Budapest 021700
Városmajor, Budapest 074725
Városmajor Antikvárium, Budapest . 139933
Városmajor Galéria, Budapest 105549
Várostörténeti Kiállitás, Soproni Múzeum, Sopron 021849
Várostörténeti Múzeum, Pécs 021827
Várostörténeti Múzeum, Uj Magyar Képtár, Székesfehérvár 021874
Varpaisjärven Kotiseutumuseo, Varpaisjärvi 010230
Várrom és Népi Müemlék, Kisnána . 021772
Varšavka, Moskva 109601
Varsinais-Suomen Kehys ja Taide, Turku 060648
Varszinhaz Galeria, Budapest 105550
Varteig Bygdemuseum, Varteig 031321
Vartigian, Harry, Milwaukee 142573
Vartroc a'Plus, La Valette-du-Var . . 063461
Varusschlacht im Osnabrücker Land, Museum und Park Kalkriese, Bramsche 016362
Vasa, Bad Mergentheim 069330
Vasa Konst, Uppsala 111095
Vasa Lutheran Church Museum, Vasa 048754
Vasalopps Museet Mora, Mora 036485
Vasalopps Museet Sälen, Transtrand 036714
Vasamuseet, Statens Sjöhistoriska Museer, Stockholm 036681
Vasarely Múzeum, Janus Pannonius Múzeum, Pécs 021828
Vasarely Múzeum, Szépmüvészeti Múzeum, Budapest 021701
Vasastadens Antikvariat, Göteborg . 141110
Vasco, João, Lisboa 080045
Vaseaux Lake Galleries, Oliver 006072
Vashon Maury Island Heritage Museum, Vashon 048755
Vasi Múzeumfalu, Savaria Múzeum, Szombathely 021901
Vasica, Diane, San Francisco 119822
Vasilevskij Ostrov, Sankt-Peterburg 109653
Vasistas, Montpellier 099766
Vaskikari, Ruben A., Turku 138000
Vasneto, Lisboa 080046
Vasoli, Vincenzo Luigi, Milano 075886
Vasquez, Giuseppa, Padova 076117
Vasquez Ramon, Patricia, Nîmes . . 065190
Vassallo, J., Sliema 077532
Vassallo, J., Sliema 121763
Vassallo, Thomas, Valletta 077541
Vassallo Paléologo, Renato, Paris . . 124828
Vassdragsmuseet Labro, Lågdalsmuseet, Skollenborg 031196
Vasse, Pierre, Lille 099498
Vassilev, Assen, Sofia 096754
Vassiliou Collection, Thessaloniki . . 021505
Vassivière en Limousin, Centre National d'Art et du Paysage, Beaumont-du-Lac 010710
Vassy & Jalenques, Clermont-Ferrand 120978
Vaste Choix de Curiosités, Draguignan 062739
Vastra Kosh, Mumbai 105815
Vat Sisaket, Vientiane 027650
Vat Xiengkhouane, Vientiane 027651
Vatika, Chennai 105640
Vattani, Rita, Roma 076718
Vaubourgeix, Serge, Maroilles 064298
Vauclair, Barbara, Morges 082675
Vaucluse House, Vaucluse 001582
Vaudoyer, Dominique, Paris 100943
Vaughan, Christchurch 079059
Vaughan, Christchurch 079060
Vaughan, Christchurch 128928
Vaughan, London 085767
Vaughan, Stamford 086691
Vaughan, Robert, Stratford-upon-Avon 142095
Vaugrante, Jean-Pierre, Granville . . 063035
Vault Gallery, Murchison 108505
Vaupel, H., Bad Bramstedt 101632
Vaupel, P. & R., Issum 071644
Vaut d'Age, Marie, Paris 138557
Vauth, Datteln 102350
Vautrin & Audouy, Paris 066635
Vauvre, Jean Yves de la, Cusset . . . 062586
Vavasour Godkin, Auckland 108368
Vaxholms Fästnings Museum, Vaxholm 036784
Vay Adám Múzeum, Vaja 021914
Vayhinger, Helena & Werner, Radolfzell 104654
Vazquez Pousa, Alberto, Sevilla . . . 081619
VB Gallery, Saint Louis 119265
VBKD Stichting, Dordrecht 107986
VC Gallery, El Paso 116121
Východoslovenská Galéria, Košice . 034367
V.D.A., Paris 066636
VDA Antiquités, Flayosc 062869
VdB Galerie, Zwolle 108285
Veaux, Thierry, Labastide-Rouairoux 063473
Veaux, Thierry, L'Isle-sur-la-Sorgue 063962
Vebr, Dr. Jan, Praha 060176
Vecchi, M.C. de, Villeneuve-sur-Lot 068923
Vecchia Europa, Philadelphia 091699, 132640
Vecchio, Cannes 099079
Vecchio, Lotto, Firenze 075418
Il Vecchio Melo, Torino 140144
Il Vecchio Mobile, Torino 128365
Vecchioli, La Plata 055276
Vecciarelli, Leopoldo, Roma 128235
Vechelde, Wendeburg 074332
Vecht, A., Amsterdam 078008
Vectis, Bembridge 130370
Vector Verve, Madrid 110625
Vedanta Gallery, Chicago 115577
Vedder, Ratingen 073433
Vedovi, Bruxelles 096263
Vee & Cranston, Melrose 085969
Veeda, Washington 093440
Veen, Haarlem 078493
Veen Park, Barger Compascuum . . 029292
Veenendaal de la Haye, Amsterdam 078009
Het Veenkoloniaal Museum, Veendam 030255
Veenmuseum het Vriezenveense Veld, Vriezenveen 030296
Veensma, Ute, Bremen 070048
Veenstra, S., Groningen 078435
Vefsn Museum, Mosjøen 031035
De la Vega, León 081175
Vega, Virgen de la, Valencia 081682
Vega Bygdemuseum, Vega 031325
Végállomás, Budapest 105551
Vegårshei Bygdetun, Vegårshei . . . 031326
Veghs, Danny, Cleveland 088368
Vegmuseet - Rogaland, Stavanger . 031235
Vegreville Regional Museum, Vegreville 006723
Vegueta, La Palmas de Gran Canaria 110713
Vehbi Koç Vakfı, İstanbul 054258
Vehmaan Kivityömuseo ja Huolilan Kotiseutumuseo, Vehmaa 010232
Vehrs, Jens, Schlotfeld 073703
Veiga, João Carlos, Lisboa 080047
Veiga, Maria Conceição, Lisboa . . . 140857
Veiga, Sancho, Madrid 081408
Veil of Years, Morpeth 056262
La Veille Cassine, Maignelay-Montigny 064218
Veillerette, Francis, Châteauvillain . 062212
Veillon, Cédric, Honfleur 063172
Veillon, Margo, Cairo 098677
Veirhanen, København 060389
Veith, B., Berlin 069778
Veith, Ingrid, Ludwigsburg, Württemberg 103947
Vejeces, Alex, Cali 059888
Vejen Kunstmuseum, Vejen 009141
Vejle Kunstmuseum, Vejle 009142
Vejle Museum, Vejle 009143
Vekkilän Kotiseutumuseo, Tammela 010114
Veksølund, Veksø Sjælland 060414
Vektermuseet i Valbergtårnet, Stavanger 031236
Vela Galleri, Frederiksberg 098529
Velan, Torino 106709
Velasco, José María, México 107515
Velasquez, Deventer 078285
Veldhorst, W.A., Rotterdam 078755
Velera, Madrid 110626
Veletržní Palác, Národní galerie v Praze, Praha 008651
Velez, Jesus Santos, Lisboa 080048
Velfjord Bygdemuseum, Hommelstø 030901
Velge & Noirhomme, Bruxelles 096264
Velha Lapa Antiguidades, Rio de Janeiro 058665
Velhage, U., Forst, Baden 070719
Velharias, Imelda, Lisboa 080049
Velharias Alfarrabista, Lisboa 080050
Velharias Pompeia, Lisboa 080051
Velho Armazém, Porto Alegre 058529
Velhos Tempos, Coimbra 079824
Velhos Tempos, Coimbra 079825
Velhustro, Coimbra 079826

Velikolukskij Kraevedčeskij Muzej, Velikie Luki . . . 034024
Velikoustjugskij Gosudarstvennyj Istoriko-Architekturnyj i Chudožestvennyj Muzej-Zapovednik, Velikij Ustjug . . . 034029
Velin, Minneapolis . . . 117320
Velin, Rumen, Varna . . . 096778
Veliz, J. & A., Barcelona . . . 129408
Velká Synagoga, Plzeň . . . 008574
Vella Canonja, Girona . . . 081139
Vellantiques, Richmond, Surrey . . . 086362
Velliet, Alexis, Paris . . . 121216
Vellinga, G.J., Rotterdam . . . 078756
Vello, G., Aachen . . . 101532
Velmerig, Hans-Günter, Düsseldorf . 070457
Velona, Firenze . . . 075419
Velryba, Praha . . . 098492
Velten, Elke, Trier . . . 074099
Veltia, Rio de Janeiro . . . 096653
Veluws Klederdrachtenmuseum, Epe . . . 029576
Veluws Museum Nairac, Barneveld . 029294
Veluws Museum van Oudheden - Stadsmuseum, Harderwijk . . . 029671
Velvet, Torino . . . 076877
Velvet Cabbage, Miami . . . 090252
Velvet Da Vinci, San Francisco . . . 119823
Velvet Swing Antiques, Pittsburgh . 091870
Velykosoročynskyj literaturno-memorialnyj Muzej Gogolja, Velyki Soročynci . 038410
Vemedetudo, Porto Alegre . . . 058530
Venango Museum of Art, Science and Industry, Oil City . . . 046637
Venant, Robert, Luzancy . . . 064042
Venard, Jean-Paul, Pérouges . . . 066731
Venator & Hanstein, Köln . 121480, 139354
Venbroek, Deventer . . . 078286
Venbroek, Deventer . . . 128644
Venclauskiu House, Šiauliai Aušros Museum, Šiauliai . . . 027859
Vendôme, Montréal . . . 059018
Vendôme, Paris . . . 066637, 100944
Vendsyssel Historiske Museum, Hjørring . . . 008913
Vendsyssel Kunstmuseum, Hjørring 008914
Vendu Notarishuis, Rotterdam . . . 121803
Venduehuis Dickhaut, Maastricht . . 121798
Venegas García, Alvaro, Bogotá . . . 059864
Venerosi Pesciolini, Lisa, Firenze . . 127425
Venetia's Antiques, Crows Nest, New South Wales . . . 055728
Veneto Gallery, San Francisco . . . 092904
Venetoulis, Genève . . . 082472
Venetsanos Museum of Modern Art, Piraeus . . . 021436
Veneziano, Giuseppe, Firenze . . . 075420
Venice Design, Venezia . . . 106784
Venice Design, Venezia . . . 106785
Venice to Paris, New York . . . 091326
Venis-Art & Antik, Zürich . . . 083034
Venkatappa Art Gallery, Bangalore . 105616
Sri Venkateswara Sculpture Centre, Tirupati . . . 050329
Venn, Edward, Williton . . . 087153, 131688
Vennel Gallery, Irvine . . . 039821
Vennesla Bygdemuseum, Museene i Vennesla, Vennesla . . . 031330
Vennini, Casablanca . . . 077677
Venon-Clays, Claude, Troo . . . 068634
Venot & Chavent, Bernard, Bordeaux . . . 061659
Vent de Chine, Ibos . . . 063200
Le Vent des Cimes, Grenoble . . . 099311
Vent d'Images, Caen . . . 061887
Vent Haven Museum, Fort Mitchell . 043951
Ventana, Sacramento . . . 119167
Ventana Gallery, San Antonio . . . 119463
El Ventanal, Buenos Aires . . . 136757
Ventanals, L'Hospitalet de Llobregat 110388
Ventanas y Puertas Antiguas, Medellín . . . 059945
Les Ventes Jacques, Bruxelles . . . 120748
Ventnor Heritage Museum, Ventnor 041269
Ventnor Rare Books, Ventnor . . . 142136
Vento, Berlin . . . 125312
Ventosa, Grégorio, Arlanc-en-Livradois . . . 060967
Vents d'Ouest, Issy-les-Moulineaux 133476
Ventspils Jūras Zvejniecības Brīvdabas Muzejs, Ventspils . . . 027798
Ventspils Muzejs, Ventspils . . . 027799
Ventura, Rio de Janeiro . . . 135612
Ventura, Muriel, Torino . . . 076878
Ventura College Art Galleries, Ventura . . . 048759
Ventura County Maritime Museum, Oxnard . . . 046776
Ventura County Museum of History and Art, Ventura . . . 048760
Venture, Tucson . . . 120174
Venturini, Assad Cavalieri, Rio de Janeiro . . . 058666
Venturoli, Walter, Bologna . . . 127188
Vénuat, Olivier, Limoges . . . 063899
Venus, Haarlem . . . 078494
Venus, Palma de Mallorca . . . 110703
Venz, H.-J., Dresden . . . 070334
Venz, Hans-Joachim, Ottendorf-Okrilla . . . 073268
Venzke, Günter, Berlin . . . 069779
Venzlaff, Peter, Nürnberg . . . 073124
Ver-Art, Milano . . . 075887
Le Ver-Vert, Nevers . . . 138247
Le Ver-Vert, Paris . . . 100945, 138558
Vera, de, New York . . . 118526
Véra, Jean-Pierre, Noirétable . . . 065218
Veran, Antwerpen . . . 096100
La Véranda, Châtenay-Malabry . . . 062221
Veranda, Manama . . . 096030
Veranda, Oakland . . . 091445
La Verandah, Monaco . . . 077626
Verandah, Oxford . . . 114205
Verandah Gallery, Mareeba . . . 094786
Vérand'Artistes, Bougival . . . 099014
Verarte, Roma . . . 106644
Verband Süddeutscher Kunsthändler e.V.; Verband Bayerischer Kunst- und Antiquitätenhändler e.V., Berlin . . 053129
Verband Bildender Künstler, Bezirksverband Magdeburg, Magdeburg . . . 053578
Verband Bildender Künstler Sachsen-Anhalt, Halle, Saale . . . 053579
Verband Bildender Künstler Thüringen e.V., Erfurt . . . 053580
Verband bildender Künstler und Künstlerinnen Württemberg e.V., Stuttgart . . . 053581
Verband Bildender Künstler und Künstlerinnen Württemberg e.V., Region Rems-Murr, Remshalden . . . 053582
Verband der Antiquare Österreichs, Wien . . . 052604
Verband der Berliner Kunst- und Antiquitätenhändler e.V., Berlin . . 053583
Verband der deutschen Münzhändler, Hamburg . . . 053584
Verband der freiberuflichen Restauratoren in Norddeutschland e. V., Emkendorf 053585
Verband der Grafik-Designer e.V., Berlin . . . 053586
Verband der Grafik-Designer Österreichs, Wien . . . 052605
Verband der Händler für Historische Wertpapiere, Wiesbaden . . . 053587
Verband der Münzhändler im APHV, Köln . . . 053588
Verband der Museen der Schweiz, Association des Musées Suisses, Zürich . . . 054222
Verband der Restauratoren e.V., Bonn . . . 053589
Verband der Restauratoren, Ländergruppe Baden-Württemberg, Stuttgart . . . 053590
Verband der Restauratoren, Ländergruppe Brandenburg, Berlin . . . 053591
Verband der Restauratoren, Ländergruppe Bremen, Bremen . . . 053592
Verband der Restauratoren, Ländergruppe Hamburg, Hamburg . . . 053593
Verband der Restauratoren, Ländergruppe Hessen, Neu-Anspach . . . 053594
Verband der Restauratoren, Ländergruppe Mecklenburg-Vorpommern, Rostock . . . 053595
Verband der Restauratoren, Ländergruppe Niedersachsen, Hannover . . . 053596
Verband der Restauratoren, Ländergruppe Sachsen, Dresden . . . 053597
Verband der Restauratoren, Ländergruppe Sachsen-Anhalt, Magdeburg . . . 053598
Verband der Restauratoren, Ländergruppe Schleswig-Holstein, Kiel . . . 053599
Verband der Restauratoren, Ländergruppe Thüringen, Friedrichroda . . . 053600
Verband der Sächsischen Kunst- und Antiquitätenhändler e.V., Dresden 053601
Verband des Hessischen Antiquitäten- und Kunsthandels e.V., Wiesbaden . . . 053602
Verband Deutscher Antiquare e.V., Elbingen . . . 053603
Verband Deutscher Kunst- und Antiquitätenhändler e.V., Borken, Hessen . . . 053604
Verband Deutscher Kunsthistoriker e.V., München . . . 053605
Verband Norddeutscher Kunsthändler e.V., Hamburg . . . 053606
Verband Oberösterreichischer Freilichtmuseen, Linz . . . 052606
Verband Österreichischer Galerien moderner Kunst, Wien . . . 052607
Verband Österreichischer Privatmuseen, Bad Wimsbach-Neydharting . . . 052608
Verband Rheinischer Museen, Solingen . . . 053607
Verband Saarländischer Kunst- und Antiquitätenhändler e.V., Saarbrücken . . . 053608
Verband Schweizer Galerien, Basel 054223
Verband schweizerischer Antiquare und Kunsthändler, Zürich . . . 054224
Verband Schweizerischer Auktionatoren von Kunst und Kulturgut, Bern . . . 054225
Verband Schweizerischer Bildhauer- und Steinmetzmeister, Association suisse des maîtres sculpteurs sur pierre et maîtres marbriers, Bern . . . 054226
Verband Schweizerischer Holzbildhauer, Sankt Gallen . . . 054227
Verband Schweizerischer Münzenhändler, Zürich . . . 054228
Verband Süddeutscher Kunsthändler e.V.; Verband Bayerischer Kunst- und Antiquitätenhändler e.V., Berlin . . 053129
Verbaus, Vilnius . . . 128463
Verbeeck, Paul, Antwerpen . . . 057746
Verbeek-Schuttelaar, Margriet, Gouda . . . 078392
Verbeelding, Amsterdam . . . 134795
De Verbeelding Kunst Landschap Natuur, Zeewolde . . . 030378
Verbeke, Bart, Gent . . . 123629
Verbièse, P., Cluses . . . 062372, 124205
Verbiest, Y., Bruxelles . . . 058120
Verbizier, Solange de, Paris . . . 124829
Verbo, Lisboa . . . 134872
De Verborgen Tuin, 's-Hertogenbosch . . . 108082
Das Verborgene Museum, Dokumentation der Kunst von Frauen e.V., Berlin . 016190
Vercauteren, Antwerpen . . 057747, 123560
Vercauteren, H., Gent . . . 058215
Vercel, Félix, Paris . . . 100946
Vercelli, Christophe, Antibes-Juan-les-Pins . . . 060929
Verchi, Marialieta, Trieste . . . 076913
Verd House, Barcelona . . . 080956
A Verdadeira Antiquária, Lisboa . . . 080052
Verdala, Naxxar . . . 077521
Verdant Works, Dundee . . . 039315
Verde, Roma . . . 076719
Verdenet, Alain, Vuillafans . . . 069037
Verdes Soto Arten Colombia, Cali . . 098242
ver.di, FG Bildende Kunst, Berlin . . . 053609
Verdier, Nérac . . . 064975
Verdier, Paris . . . 066638
The Verdier House, Beaufort . . . 042078
Verdière, René, Ménilles . . . 064485
Verdière Christophe, Alençon . . . 060767
Verdini, C., Roma . . . 076720
Verdini, Costantino, Roma . . . 076721
Verdmont Historic House Museum, Smith's Parish . . . 003906
Verdonck & Zoon, Gent . . . 123630
Verdonk, J., Amsterdam . . . 078010
Verdreau Dufresne, Paris . . . 066639
Verdugo, Manuel, Sevilla . . . 129747
Vereeniging van Handelaren in oude Kunst in Nederland, Amsterdam . . . 053905
Verein Atelier 8-80, Chemnitz . . . 053610
Verein August Macke Haus e.V., Bonn . . . 053611
Verein Beethoven-Haus, Bonn . . . 053612
Verein Berliner Künstler, Berlin . . . 053613
Verein Berner Galerien, Bern . . . 054229
Verein Bildender Künstler Schaffhausen, Forum Vebikus, Schaffhausen . . . 054230
Verein der Freunde des Kupferstich-Kabinetts Dresden e.V, Dresden . . 053614
Verein der Freunde und Förderer des Clemens-Sels-Museum, Neuss . . 053615
Verein der Freunde von Schloss Prangins, Association des Amis du Château de Prangins, Prangins . . . 054231
Verein der Hobbykünstler, Bruck an der Leitha . . . 052609
Verein der Kunstfreunde e.V, Bad Zwischenahn . . . 053616
Verein der Kunstfreunde für Wilhelmshaven e.V., Wilhelmshaven . . . 053617
Verein der Münzfreunde für Westfalen und Nachbargebiete, Münster . . . 053618
Verein der Museumsfreunde in Wien, Wien . . . 052610
Verein Dorf-eigen-Art, Zierenberg . . 053619
Verein Freunde zeitgenössischer Kunst, Kramsach . . . 052611
Verein für aktuelle Kunst, Oberhausen, Rheinland . . . 053620
Verein für bildende Kunst-Atelier Yin Yang, Graz . . . 052612, 095547
Verein für Christliche Kunst im Erzbistum Köln und Bistum Aachen, Köln . . . 053621
Verein für Christliche Kunst in der Evangelisch-Lutherischen Kirche in Bayern e.V., Neuendettelsau . . . 053622
Verein für Geschichte und Kunst des Mittelrheins, Koblenz . . . 053623
Verein für Kunst und Altertum in Ulm und Oberschwaben, Ulm . . . 053624
Verein für Kunst und Kultur, Eichgraben, Niederösterreich . . . 052613
Verein für Original Radierung München, München . . . 053625, 104336
Verein für Originalgraphik, Zürich . .054232, 135105
Verein für visuelle Kommunikation, Hannover . . . 053626
Verein Haus Salmegg, Rheinfelden . 053627
Verein KulturAXE, Wien . . . 052614
Verein Kunst im Museumsquartier, Wien . . . 052615
Verein Kunstsammlung Unterseen, Unterseen . . . 037655, 054233
Verein Kunst.Werk, Graz . . . 052616
Verein Schichtwechsel, Vaduz . . . 053841
Verein zur Bert Hubl Kunst-Förderung e.V., Angelburg . . . 053628
Verein zur Förderung bildender Künstler Köln-Porz e.V., Köln . . . 053629
Verein zur Förderung der Künstlerischen Tätigkeiten, Trier . . . 053630
Verein zur Förderung der Kunst - Kassel e.V, Kassel, Kassel . . . 053631
Verein zur Förderung der Kunst und der 'Art Innsbruck', Innsbruck . . . 052617
Verein zur Förderung der Ostkirchlichen Kunst, Herten . . . 053632
Verein zur Förderung des Kunsthistorischen Instituts in Florenz, München . . . 053633
Verein zur Förderung künstlerischer Fotografie und artverwandter Künste, Wien . . . 052618
Verein zur Förderung moderner Kunst e.V., Goslar . . . 053634, 133980

Verein zur Förderung von Grafik und Buchkunst e.V., Leipzig 053635
Verein zur Förderung zeitgenössischer Kunst, Linz 052619
Vereinigung Bildender Künstler Steiermarks, Graz 052620
Vereinigung Bildender Künstlerinnen Österreichs, Wien 052621
Vereinigung der Freunde antiker Kunst, Basel 054234
Vereinigung der Freunde von Kunst und Kultur im Bergbau e.V., Bochum . 053636
Vereinigung der Kunsthistorikerinnen und Kunsthistoriker in der Schweiz, Zürich 054235
Vereinigung der Mund- und Fussmalenden Künstler in aller Welt e.V., Schaan 027838
Vereinigung der Mund- und Fussmalenden Künstler in aller Welt e.V., Schaan 053842
Vereinigung Deutscher Restauratorenverbände, Köln 053637
Vereinigung Freunde des Klingspor-Museums e.V., Offenbach am Main 053638
Vereinigung Malerstübchen Willingshausen e.V., Alsfeld 053639, 133721
Vereinigung Pfälzer Kunstfreunde, Kaiserslautern 053640
Vereinigung Steirischer Kunsthändler, Graz 052622
Vereinigung Westfälischer Museen, Münster 053641
Vereniging Sint Lucas, Amsterdam . 053906
Vereniging van beeldende Kunstenaars De Brug, Duivendrecht 053907
Vereniging van Rijksgesubsidieerde Musea, Amsterdam 053908
Vereniging van Vrienden der Aziatische Kunst, Soest 053909
Vereniging voor het Museum von Hedendaagse Kunst, Gent 052689
Vereniging voor Penningkunst, Gorinchem 053910
Véret, Patrick, Arras 098865
Verfaille, G., Tournai 058390
Verfmolen de Kat, Zaandam 030368
Vergain, Philippe, Paris 124830
Vērgales Pagasta Muzejs, Vērgale . 027800
Vergani, Orio, Milano 106340
Verge, Linda, Québec 097166
Vergitsis Tsortsis, Pagkrati 105437
Vergnais, Colette, Vourles 069033
Vergon, Vincent, Cosges 124210
Vergougnou, André, Nantes 064954
Verhaeghe, M., Gent 058216
Verhaeren, Bruxelles 096265
Verhaest, M., Oostende 096407
Verhage, Middelburg 121799
Verheijen, Albert, Goirle 128674
Verhoeven, Bussum 140379
Verhoeven, Barbara, Duisburg 102586
Verhulst, Middelburg 078646
Verhulst, Middelburg 078647
Veria Byzantine Museum, Veria . . . 021519
Vérité & Mensonge, Québec 097167
Verjura & Corondel, Bilbao 129448
Verkehrsdrehscheibe Schweiz, Basel 036909
Verkehrshaus der Schweiz, Schweizerisches Museum für Verkehr und Kommunikation, Luzern 037305
Verkehrsmuseum, Frankfurt am Main 017201
Verkehrsmuseum Dresden, Dresden 016821
Verkehrsmuseum Karlsruhe, Karlsruhe 018173
Verkehrsmuseum Sankt Veit an der Glan, Sankt Veit an der Glan 002631
Verkerke, Bogotá 098199
Verkerke, Satwa 112463
Verkerke, Veenendaal 134836
Verkeste, J., Serooskerke Walcheren 128829
Verkoopzaal Erik, Brugge 120715
Verkoopzaal van de Kust Romain, Oostende 120786
Verkoopzalen D.V.C., Gent 120761
Verksted, Godvik 128989
Verlag Atelier im Bauernhaus, Ottersberg 134340
Verlag Der Apfel, Wien 133237
Verlag der Kunst, Dresden 133880
Verlag der Kunsthalle zu Kiel, Kiel . 134088
Verlag des Germanischen Nationalmuseums, Nürnberg 134320
Verlag des Kunstgeschichtlichen Instituts der J.-W.-Goethe-Universität, Frankfurt am Main 133956
Verlag des Kunstvereins Coburg, Coburg 133851
Verlag für moderne Kunst Nürnberg, Nürnberg 134321
Verlag für Photographische Literatur, Wien 133238
Verlag für Sammler, Graz 133082
Verlag für zeitgenössische Kunst, Berlin 133812
Verlag Galerie B.O.A., München . . . 134284
Verlag & Galerie Steyrdorf, Steyr . .095766, 133165, 137268
Verlag Haus am Checkpoint Charlie, Berlin 133813
Verlag im Atelierhaus, Mainhardt . . 134177
Verlag Kunst und Design, München 134285
Verlag Passauer Glasmuseum, Tittling 134428
Verlag Pfälzer Kunst, Landau in der Pfalz 134138
Verlag Sammlerfreund, Hamburg . . 134026
Verlag Urachhaus, Stuttgart 134424
Verlagshaus Würzburg, Würzburg . . 134471
Verlagsmuseum der Unternehmensgruppe Ravensburger, Ravensburg 019736
Verlaine Antiquités, Saint-Ouen . . . 067915
Verlan Tehdasmuseo, Verla 010233
Verlat Gallery, Antwerpen 096101
Verleyen, Michel & Alexandra, Seine-Port 068200
Verloop, J., Noordwijk, Zuid-Holland 140508
Vermar, Caracas 093543
Vermaten, Fons, Baarn 128575
Vermeer, Buenos Aires 094094
Vermeersch, P., Antwerpen 057748
Vermeille, Montréal 097090
Vermesova Vila, Slovenská Národná Galéria, Dunajská Streda 034351
Vermessungskundliche Sammlung, Linz 002257
Vermeulen, Gent 123631
Vermeulen & Zoon, G., Dordrecht . . 078322
Vermeulen & Zoon, G., Dordrecht . . 078323
Vermilion, Atlanta 114941
Vermilion, San Francisco 119824
Vermilion County Museum, Danville 043296
Vermillion, Chicago 088190
Vermillion County Museum Society, Danville 055088
Vermom Artes em Decor, São Paulo 058747
Vermont Folklife Center, Middlebury 045835
Vermont Historical Society Museum, Montpelier 046006
Vermont Marble Museum, Proctor . 047245
Vermont Museum and Gallery Alliance, Woodstock 055089
Vermont Pastel Society, Saint George 055090
Vermont State Craft Center at Frog Hollow, Middlebury 045836
The Vermont State House, Montpelier 046007
Vermorel, Bernard, Lyon 138186
Vermote, Jacky, Marignier 064285
Vern Carver & Beard, Minneapolis . 117321
Verna, Annemarie, Zürich 112191
Vernacular Art 'n' Craft, Nagpur . . . 105822
Vernay-Chantrel, Bernard, Lyon . . . 064192
Vernay-Chantrel, Bernard, Lyon . . . 064193
Vernay-Chantrel, Bernard, Lyon . . . 124378
Verne, Cleveland 115750
Verner Amell, London 113944
Verneuil, Paris 100947
Vernex, Andrée, Paris 066640
Verney-Caron, Georges, Villeurbanne 101484
Verney-Carron, Georges, Lyon 099619
Vernhes, Guillaume, Sainte-Christie 068051
La Vernice, Bari 105938
Vernisaž Art Podvalčik, Chabarovsk 033083
Vernisaž Pljus, Charkiv 112383
Vernissage, Heidelberg . . 134053, 135827
Vernissage, Hochstadt am Main . . . 103384
Vernissage, Lima 079558
Vernon, Peter, Toronto 059310
Vernon, Tony, Topsham 131600
Vernon County Museum, Viroqua . . 048802
Vernon Dath Galleries, Newstead . . 094952
Vernon Diab, G., Louisville 090041, 122953
Vernon Historical Museum and Pond Road Chapel, Vernon 048768
Vernon Public Art Gallery, Vernon, British Colombia 006728
Vernonia Historical Museum, Vernonia 048770
Vernoze Antiquités, Champeix 062120
Veron, Paul, Greifswald 102998
Verona Arts, New York 118527
Veronese, Guatemala 074651
Véronèse, Nantes 099819
Veronese, F., Bologna 139997
Verongalli, Plinio, Roma 128236
Veronica's Treasures, Swan Hill . . . 056661
Verp'Hier, La Verpillière 063469
Verpleeghuis Cornelia, Zierikzee . . . 030391
Verpleegkundig Historisch Bezit, Amersfoort 029155
Verran Museum, Malm 031004
De Verrassing, Utrecht 108262
Verrechia, Chris, Le Pré-Saint-Gervais 063694
Verrechia, Chris, Saint-Ouen 067916
Verreglass, Paris 066641
Les Verres de nos Grand Mères, Saint-Ouen 067917
Verrier, Jean, Saint-Jean-de-Luz . . 067541
Verrier, Jean, Saint-Jean-de-Luz . . 067542
Verrière, Meyrin 111732
Verrimst, Concarneau 099168
Verrina, Maria Giovanna, Bologna . . 075117
Verroios-Stergakis, Nikos, Patrai . . 074627
Le Vers à Bois, Montréal 059019
Vers les Arts, Calignac 133456
Versailles, B'Kara 128473
Versailles Antiques, Saint-Ouen . . . 067918
Versailles Artes e Antiguidades, Belo Horizonte 058454
Versailles Elegance, Toronto 059311
Versailles Galeria de Artes, Rio de Janeiro 096654
Versailles Lighting, New York 132545
Versalles, Bilbao 080997
Versalles, Bilbao 080998
Versantic, Vichy 068863
De Verschijning, Tilburg 108237
Verschoor, Olga, Thoiré-sur-Dinan . 068398
Verschueren & Co., Mechelen 123665
Verschueren, J.L., Amsterdam 078011
Versmolder Kunstkreis e.V., Versmold 053642, 105116
Verso Arts et Lettres, Paris 133683, 135732
Verstegen, Rosel & Willy, Herxheim bei Landau, Pfalz 071498
Versteigerer-Verband Baden-Württemberg e.V., Tübingen 053643
Versteigererverband Baden-Württemberg e.V., Stuttgart 053644
Vert Galant, Antibes-Juan-les-Pins . 060930
Vértes Múzeum, Csákvár 021707
Vértesszőllősi Bemutatóhely, Magyar Nemzeti Múzeum, Vértesszőllős . 021917
Vértice, Oviedo 110667
De Vertico, Rhenen 128811
Vertige, Pontevès 066940
Vertigo Galleries, London 113945
Vertigo Gallery, London 113946
Vertigo Studios, Memphis 117008
Vertiko, Brietlingen 070060
Das Vertiko, Herten 071497
Vertu, Cincinnati 115669
Verulamium Museum, Saint Albans 040891
Vervarcke, J., Knokke-Heist 058256
Vervat, Muriel, Firenze 127426
Verve Gallery, Los Angeles 116909
Verveer, Arnold, Nieuwpoort 128786
Verveer, C.B., Waal 128877
Het Vervolg, Utrecht 140557
Vervondel, H., Gent 058217
Verwertungsgesellschaft Bild-Kunst, Bonn 053645
Verwertungsgesellschaft Bildender Künstler, Wien 052623
Verwood Community Museum, Verwood 006731
Very Affordable Art, Rye 114338
The Very Idea, New York 118528
The Very Nice Group, Paddington, New South Wales 056423
Very Small Shop, Den Haag 078264
Very Special Arts Gallery, Albuquerque 041626
Very Special Arts Gallery, Albuquerque 114831
Very Special Arts Singapore, Singapore 054051
Veryan Galleries, Veryan Green . . . 114633
De Verzamelaar, Roosendaal 078690
De Verzamelaar, Tilburg 078784
Verzamelaars Beurs, Eindhoven . . . 093837
Verzameld Werk, Gent 096303
Verzameling Steenbakker Ten Bokkel Huinink, Neede 029938
Verzamelmuseum, Veendam 030256
Verzeletti, Serge, Saint-Étienne . . . 067469
Verzetsmuseum Amsterdam, Amsterdam 029240
Verzetsmuseum Friesland, Leeuwarden 029845
Verzetz Museum Zuid-Holland, Gouda 029628
Vescovi, Luigino, Morecambe 086007
Vesko, Gertrude, Bad Aussee 056926
Vespa, Roland, Nice 065158
Vesse, Didier, Pézenas 101008
Vessel, Los Angeles 116910
Vest-Agder Fylkesmuseum, Kristiansand 030959
Vest-Lindsey House, Frankfort 044037
Vest-Telemark Museum, Dalen i Telemark 030803
Vestal Museum, Vestal 048774
Vestegnens Antikvariat, København 137903
Vesterålsmuseet, Melbu 031014
Vesterheim Norwegian-American Museum, Decorah 043358
Vesterheim Rosemaling Letter, Decorah 136658
Vestfold Fylkesmuseum, Tønsberg . 031270
Vestfyns Hjemstavnsgård, Glamsbjerg 008875
Vesthimmerlands Museum, Års . . . 008810
Vestiges, Portland 092021
Vesting Bourtange, Bourtange 029340
Vestingmuseum, Nieuweschans . . . 029951
Vestingmuseum Oudeschans, Oudeschans 030029
Vestisches Museum, Recklinghausen 019741
Vestlandske Brukshandel, Voss . . . 121882
Vestlandske Skolemuseum, Stavanger 031237
Vestnik Asociace Muzei a Galerii České Republiky, Praha 135670
Vestry House Museum, London . . . 040305
Vestsjællands Kunstmuseum, Sorø . 009115
Vesttry Antiques, Cranbrook 084103
Vestvågøy Museum, Leknes 030978
Vetelin Museo, Veteli 010234
Veterans Federation of the Philippines Museum, Taguig 031798
Veterans'Memorial Military Museum, Kensington 005679
Veterinärhistoriska Museet, Skara . 036578

Veterinärmedizinhistorisches Museum der Tierärztlichen Hochschule Hannover, Hannover 017771
Veterinærmuseet, Oslo 031099
Veterinary Museum, London 040306
Vetlanda Museum, Vetlanda 036788
Vetlanda Skolmuseum, Vetlanda . . 036789
Vetlužskij Kraevedčeskij Muzej, Vetluga 034033
Vetmas, Buenos Aires . . . 055248, 094095
Vetri, Seattle 120006
La Vetrina del Tempo, Pordenone . . 093797
Větrný Mlýn, Rudice 008677
Vetter, Düren 102465, 133884, 139002
Vetter, Günter, München 126475
Vetter, Jörg H., Osnabrück 073251
Vettori & Figli, Paolo, Firenze 127427
Vêtu, Patrice, Canteleu 061961
Veturimuseo, Locomotive Museum, Toijala 010153
Vetus, Firenze 075421
Vetusta Libros, Santiago de Compostela 141070
Il Vetusto, Milano 075888
Veurink, J.P., Middelburg 108145
Vevelstad Bygdetun, Vevelstad 031334
Vexer, Sankt Gallen 135064
Veyrac, Henri, Nantes 121090
Veyrat, Thérèse, Bourgoin-Jallieu . . 099024
Veyret, Renaud & Bruno, Thônes . . 068402
Veysset, Jacques, Moutier-Rozeille 064821, 138225
Veyssière, Jean-Paul, Saint-Cyr-sur-Loire 138594
Vezzali, Emilio, Modena 127749
Vezzoli Cabrioli, Maria, Brescia . . . 075191
Vezzosi, Massimo, Firenze 075422
VF Fine Arts, Houston 116424
VHS-Photogalerie, Stuttgart 105020
VI Antiques & Fine Art, Montréal . . . 059020
Via Antica, Manila 079568
Via Antica, Paris 066642
Via Antigüedades, Caracas 093544
Via Appia, Timişoara 080203
Via Artis, Bad Aussee 001709
Via Galleria, Helsinki 060591
Via Giulia 187, Roma 076722
Via Kunst, Rotterdam 108218
Via Sollertia Jewel Art, Christchurch 108418
Via Varenne, Paris 066643
Vía Veneto Antiguedades, Don Torcuato 055268
Via Venezia, Tilburg 078785
Viafrika, Indianapolis 116498
Vial, Henri, Dourdan 133467
Vial, Marie-Thérèse, Marseille 124436
Viala, Joël, La Capelle-Balaguier . . 063303
Vianden, von, Waren 105161
Vianello, Ponzano 134661
Vianello, Bruno, Venezia 128408
Viani, Nadia, Venezia 106786
Vianna, Ivanir G., Brasília 096508
Viant, André, Épinal 062790, 124233
Viar, Antwerpen 057749
Viarius, Frauenfeld 141241
Viart, London 113947
Viart, New York 118529
Viart, Sofia 096755
Viborg Stiftsmuseum, Viborg 009150
Vibrant Art, Stow-on-the-Wold 114508
Vibrant Fine Art, Los Angeles 116911
Vibroc, Bordeaux 061660
Vic Antic, Vic-en-Bigorre 068840
Vicar Antiques, Pittsburgh 091871
Vicar Lane Antique Centre, Beverley 083504
Vice, New York 136659
Vicens Piera, Barcelona 110262
Vicens Piera, Barcelona 110263
Vicent, Peter, Berlin 069780
Vicente, José Ferreira, Lisboa 140858
Vicente, José Ferreira, Paço de Arcos 140860
Vicente Manansala Museum, Binangonan 031632
Vicentini, Aristide, Verona 128445
Vichitchai Antiques Co. Ltd., Bangkok 083105
Vichot, Philippe, Paris 066644
Vichot Corboz, Montmorot 064724
Vicino, Paul, Baltimore 131828
Vick, New York 118530
Vickers, S., Cambridge 141478
Vickery's, Martock 122615
Vickie's Collectibles, Long Beach . . 089663
Vicko, Hong Kong 097842
Vicksburg National Military Park-Cairo Museum, Vicksburg 048779
Vicky's Art and Crafts Gallery, Mumbai 105816
Vicky's Jewellery, Toronto 059312
Vico, Jesús, Madrid 081409, 122072
Il Vicolo, Genova 106112
Il Vicolo, Genova 106113
Il Vicolo, Milano 127703
Vicor Restauraciones, Barcelona . . 129409
Vicor Restauraciones, Barcelona . . 129410
Vic's Coin Shop, San Jose 092938
Vic's Upholstery, Edmonton 123767
Victis Auctions, Stockton-on-Tees . 122709
Victoire, Boulogne-Billancourt 061691
Victor Harbor Antique Centre, Victor Harbor 056778
Victor Harbor Gallery, Victor Harbor 095364
Victor i Fills, Barcelona 080957
Victor i Fills, Madrid 081410
Victor Jara, Salamanca 081548
Victor-Schultze-Institut für christliche Archäologie und Geschichte der kirchlichen Kunst, Greifswald . . . 017525
Victor Trading Post, Victor Harbor . . 056779
Victor Valley Museum and Art Gallery, Apple Valley 041751
Victoria, Caen 061888
Victoria, Praha 060177
Victoria, Claudette, San Antonio . . . 132832
Victoria and Albert Museum, London 040307
Victoria and Albert Museum, Mumbai 022271
Victoria and Albert Museum Bookshop, London 141914
Victoria and Albert Museum Publications, London 135272
Victoria and Edward Antiques Centre, Dorking 084205
Victoria Antique, Hörden 071541
Victoria Antiques, Alderney 083264
Victoria Antiques, Glasgow 084472
Victoria Antiques, London . 085768, 131205
Victoria Antiques, Praha 060178
Victoria Antiques, Ryde 086421
Victoria Antiques, Wadebridge 086996, 131636
Victoria Antiques, Wallasey 087002, 131638
Victoria Art Gallery, Bath 038633
Victoria Art Gallery, Regina 097183
Victoria Book, Wanganui 140667
Victoria Bookshop, Swindon 142108
The Victoria Centre, Saltaire 086499
Victoria County Historical Society Museum, Lindsay 005776
Victoria County Museum, Baddeck . 005053
Victoria Dreams, Headley . 084641, 130779
Victoria Falls Field Museum, Livingstone 049570
Victoria Falls Information Centre, Livingstone 049570
Victoria Gallery, Camborne 083839
Victoria Gallery, Widnes 114694
Victoria Gallery II, Caerleon 112777
Victoria Hydro Station Museum, Carbonear 005224
Victoria Imports, Stockport 086727
Victoria Jubilee Museum, Cawthorne 039025
Victoria Jubilee Museum, Vijayawada 022376
Victoria Mansion, Portland 047164
Victoria Memorial Hall, Kolkata 022229
Victoria Prints, Ludlow 114007
Victoria Road Antique Centre, Rozelle 056558
Victoria School Museum, Carleton Place 005228
Victoria School Museum and Archives, Edmonton 005413
Victoria Tower, Huddersfield 039783
Victoria Trophées, Saint-Apollinaire 067360
Victoria West Regional Museum, Victoria West 034771
Victorian Antique Dealer's Guild, Ascot Vale 052496
Victorian Art Society, Melbourne . . . 052497
Victorian Artists Society, Melbourne 052498
Victorian Brass Bedstead Company, Cocking 084046
Victorian Chairman, Bournemouth .083611, 130420
Victorian College of the Arts Gallery, Southbank 001481
Victorian Fireplace, Canterbury . . .083868, 130509
Victorian Gallery, Dallas 115950
Victorian Gallery, Shrewsbury 114434
Victorian Gilt, Auckland 078991
The Victorian Ironmonger, Brinklow 083723
Victorian Memories, Minneapolis . . 090402
Victorian Railway Workshops Art and Antiques, Oakleigh 056397
Victorian Railway Workshops Art and Antiques, Windsor, Victoria 056833
The Victorian Shop, Saint Annes-on-Sea 086445
Victorian Sitting Room, Omaha 091589
Victorian Society, London 054536
Victorian Society of Ireland, Dublin . 053719
Victorian Tapestry Workshop, South Melbourne 095207
The Victorian Village Antiques, Glasgow 084473
Victoriana, Parma 076225
Victoriana, Parma 076226
Victoriana Antiques, Naxxar 077522, 107448
Victoriana Dolls, London 085769
Victorias, Cork 074883
Victoria's Antique, Christchurch . . . 079061
Victoria's Design, Birmingham 087786
Victoria's First Hardware Museum, Sorrento 001472
Victoria's Home, Toledo 093187
Victoria's Tramway Museum, Bylands 000870
Victoria's Treasure's, Wanganui . . . 079306
Victorine, Den Haag 078265
Victors Konst & Ram i Slottsstaden, Malmö 110983
Victors Konsthandel & Ramateljé, Stockholm 111080
Victory, Alkmaar 140269
Victory Antiques, Christchurch 079062
Victory Gardens, New York 091327
Victory Lane Enterprise, Cleveland . 088369
Victory Theatre Antique Centre, Blackheath 055513
Vida, České Budějovice 098344
Vida, Dordrecht 107987
Vidal, Aix-les-Bains 098801
Vidal, New York 091328
Vidal, Nîmes 065191
Vidal, Aline, Paris 100948
Vidal, Dominique, Idron 063201
Vidal, Emmanuelle, Toulouse 068552
Vidal, Marie, Campagnan 061926
Vidal, Marie, Pézenas 066812
Vidal, Michel, Paris 100949
Vidal, Patricia, Ham 063119
Vidal Saint-Phalle, Paris 100950
Vidart, Chicago 115578
Le Vide Grenier, Chasseneuil-sur-Bonnieure 062176
Le Vide Grenier, Orchies 065283
Video Museum and Theater, Grass Valley 044296
Videomixmedia, Genève 054236
Vido, Isabella, Padova 076118
La Vie au Château, Paris 066645
Vie au Vert, Gouda 078393
La Vie d'Antan, La Roche-sur-Foron 063412
La Vie de Château, Brest 061781
La Vie de Château, Paris 066646
Vie-en-B, Dommartin (Rhône) 062710
La Vie en Rose, Paris 066647
Viebahn, Worpswede 074488
Viecenz, Anne, Halle, Saale 103077, 125794
Viehrig, Thilo, Kaulsdorf 126023
Le Vieil Orfèvre, Paris 124831
La Vieille Epoque, Reuland 077488
La Vieille Epoque, Saint-Ouen 067919
La Vieille Fontaine, Lausanne 082572, 130079
Vieille Fontaine, Obernai 065258
La Vieille Forge, Vulaines 069039
Vieille Garde, Mulhouse 064840
Vieille Garde, Mulhouse 064841
Vieille Maison des Jésuites, Québec 006231
Vieille Poste, Saint-Ouen-de-Thouberville 067931
Vieille Saintonge, Tesson 068376
Vieilles Choses, Nice 065159
Vieilleurop, Paris 066648
Vieira, Lisboa 109358
Vieira, Graciano, Porto 129203
Vieira, João Sarmento, Lisboa 129183
Vieira, Marcus, Belo Horizonte 096487
Vieira, Pedro Sousa, Lisboa 080053
Vieira & Irmão, Funchal 079838
La Vieja Esquina, Tandil 055306
La Vieja Mecedora, Madrid 129702
Viejo París, Montevideo 087350
Viejo Patio - San Telmo, Buenos Aires 055249
Vieleers, Amsterdam 107822
Vielhauer, A., Coesfeld 070153
Vielhescaze, Renaud, Gennevilliers 062983
Viellieber, Stuttgart 074013
Vielmann, Los Angeles . . . 089931, 132283
Vielmetter, Susanne, Los Angeles . . 116912
Vielstedter Bauernhaus, Heimatmuseum der Delmenhorster Geest, Vielstedt . . 020584
Vien Bao Tang Lich Sa Viet Nam, Ha Noi 049530
Viennaartguide, Wien 135583
Vienne Collection, Vienne 068867
Viennot, Franck, Saint-Pierre-de-Boeuf 124916
Viento y Agua Gallery, Long Beach . 116683
De Vier Gemeten, Middelburg 108146
De Vier Winden, Katwijk aan Zee . . 128736
Vierinzwanzig, Hatten, Oldenburg . . 103308
Vierny, Dina, Paris 100951
Vierschaar Museum, Veere 030262
Viersener Auktionshaus, Viersen . . 121617
Vierth, Hans-Heinrich, Düsseldorf . .070458, 125553
Vies Privées, Paris 066649
Viestikeskus Lokki, Mikkeli 009877
Viestimuseo, Riihimäki 010040
Viet Fine Arts Gallery, Ha Noi 120494
Viet Nam College of Fine Arts, Ha Noi 052429
Viet Nam Conservatory of Culture and Art, Ha Noi 052430
Viet Nam Fine Arts Association, Ha Noi 055123
Viet Nam History Museum Ho Chi Minh City, Ho Chi Minh City 049544
Viet Nam National Fine Arts Museum, Ha Noi 049531
Viet Nam Oil Painting, Ho Chi Minh City 120537
Viet Nam Revolution Museum, Ha Noi 049532
Viet Nam Women's Museum, Ha Noi 049533
Vietnam Art Design, New York 118531
Vietnam Era Educational Center, Holmdel 044582
Vietnam Veterans Museum, San Remo 001457

Le Vieux Charme, Bruxelles 058121
Au Vieux Chéroy, Chéroy 062278
Vieux Grand Port Archaeological Site, Old Grand Port 028068
Le Vieux Logis, Musées Chanoine Puissant, Mons 003655
Vieux Lutry, Lutry 082615
Le Vieux Manoir, L'Isle-sur-la-Sorgue 063963
Le Vieux Manoir, L'Isle-sur-la-Sorgue 063964
Le Vieux Manoir, Paris 066650
Le Vieux Matos, Blois 061530
Vieux Meubles de Cluny, Cluny 062369
Vieux Moulin de Palette, Aix-en-Provence 060718
Vieux Ordinaires, Toulon (Var) 138630
Vieux Porche, Ranspach 067041
Vieux Presbytère de Batiscan, Batiscan 005078
Les Vieux Salons, Romans-sur-Isère 067204
View Design International, Salammbô 083107
View Point, Bern 111279
View Street Bazaar, Bendigo 055483
View Two Gallery, Liverpool 113411
Vieweger, Thomas, Blaslay 124102
Viewpoint Gallery, New York 118532
Vigado Galeria, Budapest 021702
Vigan House Museum, Vigan 031809
Vigatunet, Ryfylkemuseet, Hjelmeland 030893
Vigeland, Gustav, Sør-Audnedal . . . 031209
Vigeland-Museet, Oslo 031113
Vigelius, Egon, Köln 072021
Viggiani, Rosastella, Roma 076723
La Vigie, Nîmes 099871
Vigie, Bruno, Marseille 064399
Vigier, Roquefort 067219
Viglia, Maurizio, Roma 076724
Vigliero, Cristina, Genova 075518
Viglietti, Giuseppe, Roma 128237
Vigna, Françoise, Nice 099860
Vigna, Paolo, São Paulo 058748
Vignal, Claude, Plailly 066837
Vignal, Hélène, Saules 124928
Vignale, Maria Cristina, Bologna . . . 127189
Vignali, Pretoria 110072
Vignati & Pirruccio, Milano 127704
Vigne, Jean-Bruno, Paris 066651
Vigneras, Jacques & Régis, Limoges 063900
Vigneron, Etienne, Levallois-Perret . 063803
Vigneron, Françoise & Marc, Cholet 062301
Vignes, Henri, Paris 138559
Vignettes, San Diego 092695
Vigneux, Le Blanc 063571
Vigo Carpet Gallery, London 085770
Vigo County Historical Museum, Terre Haute 048535
Vigo-Sternberg, New York 091329
Vigoiz, Vigo 081711
Vigoiz, Vigo 110868
Vigoureux, Antoine, Varennes-le-Grand 068727
Vigoureux, Philippe, Verberie 068764, 101448
Vigreux, Jean-Jacques, Rouen 124886, 138592
Vigué, Jean-Luc, Béziers 061445
Viguié, Pierre, Paris 066652
Vihannin Kotiseutumuseo, Vihanti . . 010236
Vihavuoden Myllymuseo, Sappee . . 010063
Vihdin Museo, Vihti 010237
Viirilän Kotiseutumuseo, Ruotsinpyhtää 010049
Viiskulman, Helsinki 060592
Viitainahon Kotiseutumuseo, Piippola 009974
Viitasaaren Metsätyömuseo, Viitasaari 010240
De Vijf Eijken, Arnhem 107862
De Vijf Vergulde Fleschjes, Delft . . . 078152
Vijs'kovo-istoryčnyj Muzej, Oblasnyj istoryčnyj muzej im. V. Tarnovs'kogo, Černigiv 038233
Vika Antikk, Oslo 079479
Vikedal Bygdemuseum, Vikedal . . . 031338
Vikens Sjöfartsmuseum, Viken 036792
Viking Antikhandel, Täby 082049
Viking City of Jorvik, York 041478
Viking Historical Museum, Viking . . 006752
Viking Union Gallery, Western Washington University, Bellingham 042119
Vikingbergs Konstmuseum, Helsingborgs Museer, Helsingborg 036332
Vikingemuseet Moesgård, Højbjerg 008917
Vikingeskibsmuseet, Roskilde 009084
Vikingmuseet på Borg, Bøstad 030790
Vikingsholm, Tahoma 048476
Vikingskiphuset, Universitetets Kulturhistoriske Museer, Oslo . . . 031114
Vikram Kirti Mandir Museum, Ujjain 022363
Viks Auksjonsforretning, Brevik . . . 121848
Viktor Rydbergsmuseet, Jönköping . 036364
Viktoria, Bern 082246, 129974
Viktoria, Püttlingen 104642
Viktoria Antik, Stockholm 082033
Viktoria ir Darius, Vilnius . 077459, 140237
Viktorija, Nesebăr 123728
Vila, Xavier, Barcelona 080958
Vila A, Ljubljana 109981
Vila Art, Barcelona 110264
Vila de Arte, Fortaleza 058480
Vila Plūdoņa Memoriālā Māja Muzejs, Ceraukste 027668
Vila Rabella, Marta, Barcelona 129411
Vila Tugendhat, Muzeum města Brna, Brno 008298
Vilain, M., Deurne 137491
Vilardo, Pietro, Roma 106645
Vilars, Claude, Vire 069003
Vilarte, Madrid 129703
Vilas Fine Art, Letchworth 113385
Vilatte Fabre, Agnès, Grasse 121010
Vilbert Diffusion, Cholet 062302
Vildy, Lydie, Gièvres 062995
Vilela, José Manuel, Lisboa 140859
Vilhena, Gaspar L. Manuel, Braga . . 129141
Vilho, Helsinki 137964
Viljamakasiinimuseo, Vihti 010238
Viljandi Muuseum, Viljandi 009436
Viljandimaa Gümnaasiumi Muuseum, Viljandi 009437
The Villa, Hamilton 058867
Villa, Giuseppina, Milano 127705
Villa, Dr. Paola, Milano 127706
Villa, Peter L., New York 118533
Villa Adriana, Paris 066653
Villa Adriana, Valencia 081683
Villa Aichele, Städtische Galerie der Stadt Lörrach, Lörrach 018671
Villa am Aabach, Städtische Galerie für zeitgenössische Kunst und Gestaltung, Uster 037662
Villa Amadeus Galerias, Monterrey . 077592
Villa Antica, Paris 066654
Villa Antique Mall, Oklahoma City . . 091543
Villa Antiques, Christchurch 079063
Villa Arson, Centre National d'Art Contemporain, Nice 013414
Villa Arson, Département d'Edition, Nice 133504
Villa Arte, Hamm, Westfalen 134030
Villa Bagatelle, Sillery 006474
Villa Bergzicht/Brouwerijmuseum Raaf, Heumen 029742
Villa Blau, Sommerhausen 104925
Villa Bougainvillea, Miami 090253
Villa Carlo Taidetalo, Turku 098764
Villa Cicogna Mozzoni, Bisuschio . . 023405
Villa de Bank, Enschede . . 108024, 140421
Villa de Bondt, Gent 096304
Villa dell'Arte, Porto Alegre 096582
Villa d'Este, Tivoli 026028
Villa du Jardin, Meyrin 111733
Villa du Parc Centre d'Art Contemporain, Annemasse 098845
Villa et Jardins Ephrussi de Rothschild, Saint-Jean-Cap-Ferrat 014338
Villa Farnesina, Roma 025588
Villa Flath, Bad Segeberg 101700
Villa Flora Winterthur, Sammlung Hahnloser, Winterthur 037733
Villa Foscari La Malcontenta, Mira . 024747
Villa Gallo-Romaine de Saint-Ulrich, Haut-Clocher 012077
Villa Gallo-Romaine de Séviac, Montréal-du-Gers 013216
Villa Godi Malinverni, Lugo di Vicenza 024557
Villa Grècque Kérylos, Beaulieu-sur-Mer 010707
Villa Grisebach Auctions, New York . 123021
Villa Grisebach Auktionen, Berlin . . 121346
Villa Grisebach Auktionen, Caracas 123143
Villa Grisebach Auktionen, Hamburg 121441
Villa Grisebach Auktionen, Leopoldshöhe 121498
Villa Grisebach Auktionen, London . 122602
Villa Grisebach Auktionen, Morcote 122343
Villa Grisebach Auktionen, Mülheim an der Ruhr 121517
Villa Grisebach Auktionen, München 121548
Villa Grisebach Auktionen, Paris . . . 121217
Villa Grisebach Auktionen, Ramat Hasharon 121674
Villa Grisebach Auktionen, Wien . . . 120695
Villa Grisebach Auktionen, Zürich . . 122374
Villa Grisebach Gallery, Berlin 102072
Villa Gyllenberg, Helsinki 009587
Villa Imperiale, Pesaro 025180
Villa Kruger, Clarens 037023
Zur Villa Kunterbunt, Plochingen . . . 073345
Villa Lattes, Istrana 024426
Villa Louis Historic Site, Prairie du Chien 047220
Villa Majorelle, Nancy 013329
Villa Manin, Codroipo 023922
Villa Mansi, Capannori 023640
Villa Marie-José, Lamothe-Montravel 063504
Villa Médicis, Bonnieux 061566
Villa Médicis, Saint-Rémy-de-Provence 067992
Villa Melrose, Los Angeles 089932
Villa Menafoglio Litta Panza, Varese 026214
Villa Merkel, Galerien der Stadt Esslingen, Esslingen 017087
Villa Mirabello, Musei Civici, Varese 026215
Villa Mobili, Milano 075889
Villa Montezuma Museum, San Diego 047845
Villa Museo Puccini, Viareggio 026302
Villa Obermeier, München 072874
Villa Oppenheim, Forum für Kunst, Kultur und Medien, Berlin 016191
Villa Pelsser, Henri-Chapelle 003508
Villa Pisani, Strà 025955
Villa Roman Ateljeet, Turku 098765
Villa Romana, Piazza Armerina 025219
Villa Romana a Mosaici, Desenzano del Garda 024029
Villa Safron, Rajagiraya 081770
Villa San Michele, Anacapri 023194
Villa Serra, Bologna 075118, 121679, 134554
Villa Strassburger, Deauville 011567
Villa Stuck Museum, München 019093
Villa 't Eksternest, Roeselare 003724
Villa Terrace Decorative Arts Museum, Milwaukee 045900
Villa Torrigiani, Camigliano 023609
Villa Vauban, Galerie d'Art de la Ville de Luxembourg, Luxembourg 027897
Villa Verdi, Villanova sull'Arda 026335
Villa Wessel, Iserlohn 018090
Villacher Fahrzeugmuseum, Villach 002778
Villag, Manama 096031
Village Aldest, Genève 082473
Village Antique Mall, Denver 088748
Village Antique Market, Weedon . . . 087061
Village Antiques, Albuquerque 087431
Village Antiques, Berrima 055490
Village Antiques, Buffalo 087919
Village Antiques, Cheam 083914
Village Antiques, Cobham . 084042, 130594
Village Antiques, Geelong 055871
Village Antiques, Manchester 085919
Village Antiques, Omaha 091590
Village Antiques, Saint Louis 092328
Village Antiques, Tampa . . 093156, 132964
Village Antiques, Weybridge 087113, 131676
Village Art and Crafts Association, Mitcham 052499, 094862
Village Bazaar, Milwaukee 090328
Village Book Shop, Columbus 142356
Village Book-Tique, Hornsby 136948
Village Books, East Dereham 141563
Village Boutique, Memphis 117009
Village Bygones Antiques, Christchurch 079064
Village Clocks, Coltishall . 084067, 130605
Village Clocks, Long Melford 085844, 131235
Village Coin, Tampa 093157
Village Coin Shop, Austin 087620
Village Collectibles, Indianapolis . . 089355
Village Créole, Les-Trois-Ilets 107461
Village Crudère, Marseille 064400
Village Custom, Edmonton 096905
Le Village de Passy, Paris 066655
Village des Antiquaires, Beaune . . . 061309
Village des Antiquaires, Besançon . 061398
Le Village des Pêcheurs, Canet-en-Roussillon 011094
Village Galeria de Arte, Rio de Janeiro 096655
The Village Gallery, Ballymoney . . . 112548
The Village Gallery, Delhi 105690
The Village Gallery, Heswall 113239
The Village Gallery, Hook 113270
Village Gallery, Palm Cove 095050
Village Gallery, San Antonio 119464
Village Gallery, Washington 120359
Village Gallery of Arts, Portland . . . 119059
Village Historical Society Museum, Harrison 044448
Village Historique Acadien, Caraquet 005219
Village Marketplace, Nashville 090493
Village Miniature, Marchesieux 012888
Village Miniature avec Jardins et Plan d'Eau in Situ, Saint-Martin-de-Villenglose 014421
Village Minier de Bourlamaque, La Cité de l'Or, Val d'Or 006679
Village-Musée, Fos-sur-Mer 011870
Village Museum, Kfar Tavor 022993
Village Museum, Stellenbosch 034759
Village Museum, National Museums of Tanzania, Dar-es-Salaam 037852
Village Museum of Local History, Chihaya-Akasa 026442
Village Notre-Dame, Bordeaux 061661
Village of Elsah Museum, Elsah . . . 043694
Village Painters, Birmingham 115132
Village Peddler, Houston 089238
Village Périgord Antiquité, Trélissac 068622
Village Pump Antiques, Exeter 055811
Village Québecois d'Antan, Drummondville 005365
Village Smithy, San Antonio 132833
Village Treasures, Long Beach 089664
Village Treasures II, Oklahoma City . 091544
Village Upholstery, Seattle 132945
Village Vault Antiques, Long Beach . 089665
Villageois, Gaston, Ducos 128487
Villages Antiques, Houston 089239, 132143
Villain, Jean-Paul, Paris 100952
Villalba i Badia, Maria, Barcelona . . 110265
Villani, Fabio, Forres 130714
Villani, Fabio & Luigi Maria, Forres . 130715
Villani & C., Marco, Firenze 106077
Villaniza, Caracas 093545
Villanova University Art Gallery, Villanova 048785

Villanueva 23, Madrid 129704
Villanueva Riu, Pedro, Burgos 129469
Villar Jambrina, Vicente, Barcelona 129412
Villard Lalande, Paris 100953
Villaret, Claire de, Paris 100954
Villarino, Jose y Otro, Bilbao 080999, 129449
Villars, Bruxelles 058122
Villars, Paris 100955
Villás Galéria és Aukciós Ház, Debrecen 074730, 121647
Ville delle Rose, Galleria d'Arte Moderna, Bologna 023462
Villegas-Inagaki, San Francisco . . . 119825
Villemin, Catherine, Pompey 066900
Villeneuve, Arnaud de, Asnières-sur-Seine 124080
Villeneuve, Sabrice de, Atlanta 114942
Villepoix, Anne de, Paris 100956
Villermet, Rolande, Paris 124832
Villermin, Daniel, Besançon 061399
Villers, T. de, Bruxelles 123613
Villiers, Paris 100957
Villiers, Paris 100958
Villiers, Cherie de, Rosebank 110078
Villinger-Schmeller, Radegundis, Veitshöchheim 105109
Villino, Rasdorf 073418
Villoresi, Simonetta, Bologna 075119
Villoresi, Simonetta, Bologna 075120
Vilmorin, Antoine de, Paris 066656
Vilniaus Paveikslu Galerija, Lietuvos Dailes Muziejus, Vilnius 027866
Vilniaus Praeitis, Vilnius . . 077460, 140238
Vilniaus Restauratorius, Vilnius 128464
Vilnius Academy of Fine Arts, Vilnius 050523
Vilo Distribution, Paris 133684
Vilppulan Museo, Vilppula 010241
Vilstaler Bauernmuseum, Eichendorf 016905
Vimal, Emmanuel, Vic-le-Comte . . . 068848
Vimm Trans, Bucureşti . . . 109448, 129227
Vimonisha, Chennai 105641
Vimont, Jacques, Bollène 061550
Vin Acco Time Repair, Cincinnati . . 131947
Vin- och Sprithistoriska Museet, Stockholm 036682
Vina Cooke Museum of Dolls and Bygone Childhood, Newark-on-Trent 040538
The Vinalhaven Historical Society Museum, Vinalhaven 048786
Vinarium, Weinbaumuseum und Weinbaufreilichtmuseum, Cleebronn 016571
Viñas, Alfredo, Málaga 110645
Vina's Gallery, Sacramento 119168
Vinc-Alex Galerie, Lyon 099620
Vince &Son., Pittsburgh 132680
Vince-Or, Vincennes 069000
Vincent & Sons, Jacksonville 132199
Vincent, New Orleans 117527
Vincent, Saint-Pierre 109412
Vincent, Bernard, Juvisy-sur-Orge .063271, 124273
Vincent, Garth, Allington 083269
Vincent, Gil, Gent 123632
Vincent, Julien, Lyon 124379
Vincent Art Gallery, Townsville 001567
Vincent Mit L'Ane, L'Isle-sur-la-Sorgue 063965
Vincent Price Art Gallery, Monterey Park 045990
Vincent Viry René, La Bresse 099387, 124275
Vincentz, Colmar 062421
Vinciguerra, Vincenzo, Palermo . . . 106449
Vinck, E., Aalst 057665
Vincy, Lara, Paris 100959
Vindelådalens Antik & Auktionshall, Vindeln 082066, 122294
Vindonissa-Museum, Aargauische Kantonsarchäologie, Brugg 036978
The Vinery, Dorking 084206, 130653
Vingåkers Auktionstjänst, Vingåker . 122296
Vingedal, Stockholm 129879
Vingelen Kirke- og Skolemuseum, Vingelen 031339
Vingerhoedmuseum, Veenendaal . . 030258
Vingt Neuf Rue Grande, Moret-sur-Loing 064790
Vingtième Siècle, Saint-Ouen 067920
Vinh, Loi, Ho Chi Minh City 120538
Vinh, Xuan, Ho Chi Minh City 120539
Vinha d'Arte, Lisboa 109359
Vinhas, António, Porto 080117
Vinhático, Porto 080118
Vinhatti, Porto Alegre 058531
Vinings, Atlanta 087540
Vinizky, Irina, München 104337
Vinjestoga, Vinje 031341
Vink, Kleve 071881
Vink, R., Groningen 078436
Vinke, Thomas, Herford 139264
Vinnyc'kyj Literaturno-memorial'nyj Muzej M.M. Kocjubyns'koho, Vinnycja . . 038412
Vinnyc'kyj Nacional'nyj Muzej-sadiba im. Pirogova, Vinnycja 038413
Vinnyc'kyj Oblasnyj Chudožnij Muzej, Vinnycja 038414
Vinnyc'kyj Oblasnyj Krajeznavčyj Muzej, Vinnycja 038415
Vinorama - Musée du Vin, Bordeaux 010896
Vint - Trenta, Barcelona . . 080959, 129413
Vintage, Los Angeles 089933
Vintage 429, New Orleans 142623
Vintage Acco Time, Cincinnati 088290
Vintage Acco Time, Cincinnati 088291
Vintage Aircraft Museum, Masterton 030538
Vintage and More, Albuquerque . . . 087432
Vintage Antique Centre, Warwick . . 087047
Vintage Antiques, Charlotte 087992
Vintage Antiques, Edmonton 058843
Vintage Antiques, El Paso 088820
Vintage Art Gallery, Singapore 109890
Vintage Art Prints, Honolulu 116249
Vintage Cameras, London 085771
Vintage Car and Carriage Museum, Inishowen 022798
Vintage Clobber, Bournemouth 083612
Vintage Clothing, Philadelphia 091700
Vintage Country Antiques, Willunga 056825
Vintage Decor, Cincinnati 088292
Vintage Designs, New York 091330
Vintage Furniture, Indianapolis 132165
Vintage Interiors, Phoenix 091777
Vintage Isle, Honolulu 088982
Vintage Loft, New York 091331
Vintage Mania, Memphis 090110
Vintage Modern, San Francisco . . . 092905
Vintage Motor Cycle Museum, Laxey 039941
Vintage Museum of Photography, London 040308
Vintage Nest, Houston 089240
Vintage on College Avenue, Oakland 091446
Vintage Pine, Chicago 088191
Vintage Pine, Long Melford 085845
Vintage Poster Art, San Francisco . . 119826
Vintage Poster Bank, Cincinnati . . . 115670
Vintage Posters International, Chicago 115579
Vintage Prints and Paper, Buffalo . .087920, 142267
Vintage Radio & Gramaphone, Toronto 059313
Vintage Restoration, New York 132546
Vintage Revival, Charlotte 087993
Vintage Revivals, Jacksonville 089472
Vintage Revivals at Regency Mall, Jacksonville 089473
Vintage Rose, Ballarat 055439
The Vintage Shop, Bangalore 074785
Vintage Sounds, Houston 089241
Vintage Stock, Tulsa 093338
Vintage to Vogue, Bath 083450
Vintage Toy and Train Museum, Sidmouth 041028
Vintage Toy and Train Museum, Sidmouth 086619
Vintage Universe, Houston 089242
Vintage Vantage, Chicago 115580
Vintage Veruca, Winnipeg 059473
Vintage Watch Company, Tunbridge Wells 086957
Vintage Wireless Museum, London . 040309
Vintage Wireless Shop, Nottingham 086145
Vintler, Bolzano 075135
Vinton Street Antiques, Omaha 091591
Vintrlík, Petr, Brno 137770
Vintti, Jussin, Helsinki 060593
Vinttikamari, Helsinki 060594
Viñuela Fernandez, Antonio, Barcelona 129414
Vinyasa, Chennai 105642
Vinzentz, Düsseldorf 102566
Vinzenz, Rolf, München 126476
Viola, Aldo, Roma 128238
Viola, André, Metz 064538, 138207
Viola, Carlo, Bologna 075121
Viola, Rodolfo, Milano 106341
Violaris Eitle, Lefkosia 059958
Violeau, Jean-Claude, Pezou 066816
Violet, Gent 058218
Violet Town Antiques, Violet Town . 056783
La Violetera, Paris 066657
Violin Shop, Hexham 084680
Vion, Jean-Paul, Pézenas 066813
VIP Antik, İstanbul 083163
VIP Antiques, Washington 093441
Vip's International, Rotterdam 108219
Viragem, Lisboa 080054
Virago Arte, Fitzroy North 094546
Virago Arte, Torino 106710
Viranşehir Kültür Merkezi, Viranşehir 038195
Virden Pioneer Home Museum, Virden 006756
Virgil I. Grissom State Memorial, Mitchell 045940
Virgilio, Carlo, Roma 106646
Virgilkapelle, Wien Museum, Wien . 003014
Virgil's Antiques, Railway Estate . . . 056516
Virgin Gallery, Villeurbanne 068983
Virginia, London 085772
Virginia, Carmen, Barcelona 110266
Virginia Air and Space Center, Hampton 044417
Virginia Association of Museums, Richmond 055091
Virginia Aviation Museum, Richmond International Airport 047432
Virginia Baptist Historical Society Museum, Richmond 047427
Virginia Beach Antique Mall, Virginia Beach 093369
Virginia Beach Art Gallery, Virginia Beach 120234
Virginia Beach Maritime Museum, Virginia Beach 048798
Virginia City Madison County Historical Museum, Virginia City 048800
The Virginia Discovery Museum, Charlottesville 042771
Virginia Fine Art Gallery, Bendigo . . 094242
Virginia Groot A. Foundation, Chicago 042886
Virginia Historical Society Museum, Richmond 047428
Virginia Institute of Marine Science, Fish Collection, Cloucester Point 043022
Virginia Living Museum, Newport News 046473
Virginia M. McCune Community Arts Center, Petoskey 046915
Virginia Marine Science Museum, Virginia Beach 048799
Virginia Military Institute Museum, Lexington 045283
Virginia Museum of Fine Arts, Richmond 047429
Virginia Museum of Fine Arts (Calender), Richmond 136660
Virginia Museum of Fine Arts Publishing Department, Richmond 135483
Virginia Museum of Natural History, Martinsville 045715
Virginia Museum of Transportation, Roanoke 047469
Virginia Sports Hall of Fame and Museum, Portsmouth 047203
The Virginia War Museum, Newport News 046474
Virginia Wright Fund, Seattle 048094
Virginia's, Los Angeles 089934
Virgo Labour Museum, Oravais 009925
Viridian Artists, New York 118534
Virje Local History Museum and Fine Arts Gallery, Virje 007819
Virkki-käsityömuseo, Helsinki 009588
Viroconium Museum, Wroxeter Roman City, Wroxeter 041460
Virolahden Kotiseutumuseo, Virolahti 010243
El Virrey, Córdoba 055255
Virtain Perinnekylä, Virrat 010248
Virtanen, Armadale, Victoria 055396
Virtanen, J. K., Highett 055980
Virtanen, Kent & Sharen, Mosman Park 056271
Virtasalmen Kotiseutumuseo, Virtasalmi 010249
Virtual Art Gallery, Las Vegas 116655
Virtual Art Gallery, Milwaukee 117226
VirtuArtNet Galéria, Budapest 105552
Virtudes 20, Madrid 129705
Les Virtuoses de la Réclame, Paris . 100960
Virtuti Militari, Paris 066658
Virus Arts, Toronto 097393
Vis, Delft 107895
Vis à Vis, Chalon-sur-Saône 099103
Vis-á-Vis, Karlsruhe 071732
Vis à Vis, Marseille 053004, 099691, 133497, 135733
Visafslag Elburg, Elburg 029554
Visage Galerie, Berlin 102073
Visarte Berufsverband Visuelle Kunst Schweiz, Sociéte des Artistes Visuels Suisse, Zürich 054237
Visarte Vaud, Lausanne 054238
Visca, Umberto, Roma 076725
Visceglia Art Gallery, Caldwell College, Caldwell 042547
Visceglie, Giuseppe, Bari 075036
Vischer, Erwin, Mönchengladbach . 072577
Vischetti, Flavia, Roma 128239
Vischpoort en Kazematten, Elburg . 029555
Visconti, Paris 100961
Visconti Berger, Firenze 075423
De Vishal, Haarlem 108064
Vishwakarma, Hyderabad 105718
Vision 21 Art School, Los Angeles . 051640
Vision Graphics, Philadelphia 118849
Vision Quest Trading Company, Winnipeg 097610
Visions, Croydon 112929
Visions in Black, Dallas 115951
Visions of Gold, Houston 089243
Visiting Arts, London 054537
Viski Károly Múzeum, Kalocsa 021749
Vismara, Luigi, Milano 127707
Visol, Ourense 110658
Visser, Dick, Antwerpen . . 057750, 123561
Visser, Peter, Cape Town 080688
Visserij- en Cultuurhistorisch Museum, Woudrichem 030354
Visserijmuseum, Breskens 029355
Visserijmuseum, Bruinisse 029362
Visserijmuseum, Vlaardingen 030276
Visserijmuseum Zoutkamp, Zoutkamp 030396
Visseron, Bernadette, Poursac 066972
Vista Fine Arts, Dallas 115952
Vista Fine Arts, West Hollywood . . . 120417
Vista Point, Köln 134123
Visual, Madrid 136107
Visual and Performing Arts, Aims Community College, Greeley 051409

Visual and Performing Arts Department, Fairfield University, Fairfield 051321
Visual and Performing Arts Department, Finger Lakes Community College, Canandaigua 051068
Visual and Performing Arts Division, Cabrillo College, Aptos 050907
Visual and Performing Arts Division, Glendale Community College, Glendale 051387
Visual and Performing Arts Division, Marygrove College, Detroit 051260
Visual and Performing Arts Division, Yavapai College, Prescott 051987
Visual Art, Edgware 112980
Visual Art Department, Dean Junior College, Franklin 051356
Visual Art Department, Golden West College, Huntington Beach 051488
Visual Art Department, Mitchell Community College, Statesville 052215
Visual Art Galleries, Singapore 109891
Visual Art School of Trenton, Trenton 052271
Visual Art Studio, Richmond 119129
Visual Artists and Galleries Association, New York 055092
Visual Arts, Minneapolis 117322
Visual Arts, University of Windsor, Windsor, Ontario 049832
Visual Arts Alliance of Nashville, Nashville 055093
Visual Arts and Galleries Association, Ely 054538
Visual Arts and Media Studies, Pasadena City College, Pasadena 051918
Visual Arts Annex Gallery, Guadalupe Cultural Arts Center, San Antonio . 047808
Visual Arts Center, Mount Hood Community College, Gresham 051427
Visual Arts Center, Tidewater Community College, Portsmouth 047204
Visual Arts Center of Northwest Florida, Panama City 046810
Visual Arts Department, Antioch College, Yellow Springs 052410
Visual Arts Department, Bemidji State University, Bemidji 050967
Visual Arts Department, Bergen Community College, Paramus 051913
Visual Arts Department, Brewton-Parker College, Mount Vernon 051761
Visual Arts Department, Colby Community College, Colby 051170
Visual Arts Department, Flagler College, Saint Augustine 052067
Visual Arts Department, Florida International University, Miami 051702
Visual Arts Department, Goldsmith's College, London 050843
Visual Arts Department, Hutchinson Community Junior College, Hutchinson 051494
Visual Arts Department, Kilgore College, Kilgore 051551
Visual Arts Department, Miami-Dade Community College, Miami 051703
Visual Arts Department, Middlesex County College, Edison 051286
Visual Arts Department, New College of Florida, Sarasota 052147
Visual Arts Department, Pine Manor College, Chestnut Hill 051107
Visual Arts Department, Rio Hondo College, Whittier 052369
Visual Arts Department, School of Fine Arts, Willoughby 052384
Visual Arts Department, Seward County Community College, Liberal 051605
Visual Arts Department, Southwestern Oregon Community College, Coos Bay 051201
Visual Arts Department, State University of New York College at Old Westbury, Old Westbury 051882
Visual Arts Department, University of California San Diego, La Jolla 051564
Visual Arts Department, University of Maryland, Baltimore County, Baltimore 050951
Visual Arts Division, Bennington College, Bennington 050969
Visual Arts Gallery, Birmingham 042228
Visual Arts Gallery, New York 118535
Visual Arts Gallery, Pensacola 046878
Visual Arts Museum, New York 046417
Visual Arts Program, Johnson County Community College, Overland Park 051905
Visual Arts Program, University of Illinois at Springfield, Springfield 052206
Visual Arts Publishing, London 135273
Visual Communications Class, Atlanta Area Technical School, Atlanta 050926
Visual Galeria Artes, Brasília 096509
Visual History Gallery, Cincinnati .. 088293
Visual Jazz Art Gallery, New Orleans 117528
Visual, Performing and Applied Arts Division, Harford Community College, Bel Air 050960
Visual Resources, Chicago 115581
Visual Resources Association Bulletin, Ann Arbor 136661
Visual Spaces, Montréal 097091
Visualize, San Francisco 119827
Visuart Galéria, Nyíregyháza 105568
Visvesvaraya Industrial and Technological Museum, Bangalore 022017
Vita Valvet, Stockholm 082034
Vitale, Alessandrina, Venezia 076979
Vitale Family Galleries, San Diego . 119560
Vitali, Stefano, Milano 075890
Vitenskapsmuseet, Trondheim 031290
Vites, Armando, Rosario 136764
Vitiello, Christophe, Marseille 124437
Vitlycke Museum, Tanumshede 036705
Vito, Chicago 131920
Vitold, Mary, Seattle 120007
Vitosha, Sofia 096756
Vitoux, Pierre-Marie, Paris 100962
Vitovec, Basel 141219
Vitra, Varna 096779
Vitra Design Museum, Weil am Rhein 020719
Vitra Design Museum Berlin, Berlin 016192
Vitralls Hernandez, Barcelona 080960
Vitreous, Salt Lake City 092469
Vitrine, Bern 082247
Vitrine, Klagenfurt 057115
Die Vitrine, Limburg an der Lahn .. 072263
Vitrine, Maria Enzersdorf am Gebirge 057175
Die Vitrine, Ostfildern 073260
Vitrine 144, Mülheim an der Ruhr .. 072618
Vitrine Antiguidades, Belo Horizonte 058455
La Vitrine des Antiquaires, Nevers . 065014
Vitrine Présentée à la Médiathèque, Rougiers 014138
Vitro, Skopje 107432
Vitrotto, Clotilde, Torino 076879
Vitry, Antoine, Marnes-la-Coquette . 064297
Vitt, Walter, Köln 134124
Vittet, Claude, Paris 066659
Vittori, Claudia, Venezia 128409
Vittoria Art Gallery, Manly 094784
Vitvar, Jaroslav, Zürich 083035
Viva, Zlín 098516
Viva-Artis, Sopot 109080
Viva Galerie, Montréal 059021
Vivace, Jounieh 077435
Vivaldi, Paris 066660
Vivant, Seattle 093081
Vivanti, David, Roma 076726
Viv'Antique im Holländischen Viertel, Potsdam 073367
Vivarium, Musée de la Nature, Lautenbach-Zell 012440
Vivarium, Museo de Historia Natural, Quito 009257
Vivaropets Auktionsbyrå, Hammerdal 122152
Vivement Jeudi, Paris 066661
Vivendi, Paris 100963
Vives-Atsara, Jose, San Antonio 119465
Vivian, Marseille 064401
Viviani, Pisa 106471
Vivianna, Leura 094738
Vivid, Rotterdam 108220
Vivier, Luxeuil-les-Bains 064040
Vivier & Christophe, Michel, Saint-Sauveur 068001
Vivier d'Oie, Bruxelles 058123
Vivioli, Genova 075519, 127490
Vivliofilia-Myriovivlos, Athinai 121633
Vivre, Nijmegen 078662
Vivre l'Art, Bruxelles 096266
Vixseboxse, Cleveland 115751
Vizcaya Museum, Miami 045818
Vizija, Beograd 109726
Vízivárosi, Budapest 105553
Vizmathy, Cecil Béla, Budapest 074726
Vizzavona, Paris 066662
Vizzotto, Mattia, Milano 127708
VJ 22, Delft 107896
Vjatskaja Kunstkamera, Kirovskij oblastnoj kraevedčeskij muzej, Kirov 033268
V.K. Krishna Menon Museum and Art Gallery, Kozhikode 022232
Vlaams Mijnmuseum, Beringen 003228
Vlaams Tram- en Autobusmuseum, Berchem 003227
Vlaamse Museumvereniging, Antwerpen 052690
Vlaamse Vereniging van Experten voor Kunst en Antiquiteiten, Knokke .. 052691
Vlaamse Zaal, Antwerpen 096102
Vlachos Collection, Mytilini 021399
Vlada, Moskva 109602
Vladimir's Antiques, New York 091332
Vladimirskij, Sankt-Peterburg 080338
Vladislava Loča Latgaliešu Rakstniecības Muzejs, Pilcene 027720
Vladivostokskaja Krepost' - Voenno istoričeskij Fortifikacionnyj Muzej, Vladivostok 034059
Het Vlaemsche Erfgoed, Groede 029631
Vlam, Michiel de, Den Haag 078266, 128638
Vlasbewerkingsmuseum It Braakhok, Ee 029524
Vlasblom, Arnhem 107863
Vlastivedné a Literárne Múzeum, Svätý Jur 034437
Vlastivědné Muzeum, Bělá pod Bezdězem 008263
Vlastivědné Muzeum, Horšovský Týn 008384
Vlastivědné Muzeum, Kamenice nad Lipou 008422
Vlastivědné Muzeum, Kyjov 008465
Vlastivědné Múzeum, Nové Zámky . 034404
Vlastivědné Muzeum, Nymburk 008539
Vlastivedné Múzeum, Považská Bystrica 034413
Vlastivědné Muzeum, Slany 008685
Vlastivědné Muzeum, Žirovnice 008785
Vlastivědné Muzeum, Muzeum Broumovska, Broumov 008299
Vlastivědné Muzeum a Galerie, Česká Lípa 008313
Vlastivědné Muzeum Dr. Hostaše v Klatovech, Klatovy 008436
Vlastivědné Muzeum Jesenicka, Jeseník 008407
Vlastivědné Muzeum pro Vysoké nad Jizerou a Okolí, Vysoké nad Jizerou 008770
Vlastivedné Múzeum v Galante, Galanta 034354
Vlastivedné Múzeum v Hlohovci, Hlohovec 034355
Vlastivědné Muzeum v Olomouci, Olomouc 008543
Vlatten, M., Heidelberg 071464
Vlcek, Maria, Landshut 072149
Vleeshal, Middelburg 029923
Vleeshuis, Antwerpen 003193
Vleeshuismuseum, Dendermonde . 003394
Vliegend Museum Lelystad, Lelystad 029863
Vliegend Museum Seppe, Bosschenhoofd 029337
Vliegenthart, Amsterdam 128563
Vloedbeld, Almelo 077734
Vloemans, John A., Den Haag 140403
Vlok, A., Utrecht 078824
VN Art, Ho Chi Minh City 120540
Voas Museum, Minburn 045902
Voborník, Ústí nad Labem 124009
Vobruba, Milan, Munster 104381
V.O.C. Antiques, Woodhall Spa 087231
Vock, Carl, Zürich 083036, 130268
Vodné Kasárne, Slovenská Národná Galéria, Bratislava 034340
Vodnikova Domačija, Ljubljana 109982
Vöbam, Stockholm 082035, 141179
Vögeli-Buchwalder, Ronny & Jus, Luzern 082638
Vögtli, Benno, Hochwald 082498
Völcker, Dr. Wolfram, Berlin 102074
Völkel, Gisela, Berkatal 069546
Völkel, Steffen, Beratzhausen 138727
Völkerkundemuseum der Archiv- und Museumsstiftung Wuppertal, Wuppertal 021020
Völkerkundemuseum der Universität Zürich, Zürich 037808
Völkerkundemuseum der von Portheim-Stiftung, Heidelberg 017838
Völkerkundemuseum Herrnhut, Außenstelle des Staatlichen Museums für Völkerkunde Dresden, Herrnhut 017902
Völkerkundemuseum Sankt Gallen, Stiftung Sankt Galler Museen, Sankt Gallen 037500
Völkerkundesammlung, Museen für Kunst und Kulturgeschichte der Hansestadt Lübeck, Lübeck 018729
Völkerkundliche Sammlung, Winterthur 037734
Völkerkundliche Sammlung der Philipps-Universität, Marburg 018829
Völkerkundliche Sammlung der Universität, Institut für Ethnologie, Göttingen . 017474
Völkerkundliches exotisches, zoologisches und heimatkundliches Missionsmuseum, Bad Driburg 015683
Völkerschlachtdenkmal und Forum 1813, Museum zur Geschichte der Völkerschlacht, Stadtgeschichtliches Museum Leipzig, Leipzig 018600
Völkl, Ingo, Straubing 139746
Voellmy & Co., Basel 129937
Völz, Rainer, Essen 070652
Vömel, Dorothee, Düsseldorf 102567, 139025
Voenno-istoričeski Muzej, Gorna Studena 004691
Voenno-istoričeski Muzej, Pleven .. 004786
Voenno-istoričeski Muzej Osvoboditelna Vojna 1877-1878, Bjala 004638
Voenno-istoričeskij Muzej Artillerii, Inženernych Vojsk i Vojsk Svjazi, Sankt-Peterburg 033835
Voenno-istoričeskij Muzej Tichookeanskogo Flota, Vladivostok 034060
Voenno-medicinskij Muzej, Sankt-Peterburg 033836
Voenno-morskoj Muzej Severnogo Flota, Murmansk 033537
Voergård Slot, Dronninglund 008835
Voerman Museum Hattem, Hattem . 029682
Vörösmarty Mihály Emlékmúzeum, Kapolnásnyék 021750
Voerster, J., Stuttgart 139775
De Voetboog, Amsterdam 107823
Vötter's Oldtimermuseum, Kaprun . 002114
Vöyrin Kotiseutumuseo, Vörå 010252
Vog Art, Toulouse 068553
Vogdt, Stefan A., München 104338
Vogel, Barenthin 125139
Vogel, Hannover 071417
Vogel, Heilbronn 103338
Vogel, Mannheim 104029

Vogel, Potsdam 104634
Vogel, Albert, Würzburg 074513
Vogel, Donald S., Dallas 115953
Vogel, E., Den Haag 140404
Vogel, Fritz, Schlatt bei Winterthur .082803, 130174
Vogel, Hans-Detlev, Königstein im Taunus 072035
Vogel, Hans-Joachim, Kaiserslautern 125986
Vogel, Horst, Heidelberg 071465
Vogel, Jürgen, Jestetten 071662
Vogel, Roland, Rain am Lech 126676
Vogel, Rudolf & Freia, Schlüsselfeld 126773
Vogel & Vogel, Garbsen 070931
Vogelmuseum, Waging 020620
Vogelmuseum-Die Vogelwelt des Böhmerwaldes, Aigen im Mühlkreis 001667
Vogels, Aard, Veldhoven 128866
Vogels, Leon, Helmond 128710
Vogelsberger Heimatmuseum, Schotten 020094
Vogelsperger, Basel 111228, 134988
Voges & Partner, Frankfurt am Main 102835
Gebr. Vogl, Augsburg 069241
Vogl, Franz A., München 126477
Vogl, Monika, Mönchengladbach . . 104101
Vogler, Philippe, Basel . . . 082179, 122308
Voglhofer, Stefan, Schwertberg . . .057310, 095758, 123469
La Voglia del Passato, Verona 077027
Voglmair, Manfred, Gmunden 056996
Vogt, A., Köln 103732
Vogt, Armin, Basel 111229
Vogt, Barbara, Hamburg 103227
Vogt, Bernardete Nadal de, Porto Alegre 123699
Vogt, Bettina, Hannover 125882
Vogt, George, Houston 089244
Vogt, Inge, Hilzingen 139269
Vogt, M., Alling 069136
Vogt, Peter, München 072875, 121549
Vogteimuseum mit Blumenauer Heimatstube, Aurach 015630
Vogtländisches Dorfmuseum, Erlbach 017039
Vogtländisches Freilichtmuseum, Erlbach 017040
Vogtländisches Freilichtmuseum Landwüst, Landwüst 018489
Vogtlandmuseum Plauen, Plauen . . 019634
La Vogue Antiques and Collectables, Johannesburg 080720
Vogue Antiquités, Tournai 058391
Vogue Art and Crafts Gallery, Mumbai 105817
Vohr, Erika, Reutlingen . . . 073504, 126716
Void, New York 118536
Voigt, Nürnberg 104491
Voigt, Gerard, Stuttgart 126884
Voigt, Markus, Wildenberg 105294
Voigtländer, Hartmannsdorf 071423
Voilà, Dordrecht 107988
Voimalamuseo, Helsingin Kaupunginmuseo, Helsinki 009589
Voipaalas Taidekeskus, Sääksmäki 010056
Voissier, Roselyne, Clermont-Ferrand 062358
Voit, Gisela, Rottach-Egern 073605
Voit, Robert, Warmensteinach 126968
Voithenberghammer, Hammerschmiede von 1823, Furth im Wald 017306
La Voiture Ancienne d'Alsace, Zehnacker 069072
't Voiturke, Antwerpen 057751
Vojenské Múzeum Trenčín, Trenčín . 034444
Vojenské Starožitnosti, Praha 060179
Vojenské Technické Muzeum, Krhanice 008457
Vojni Muzej Beograd, Beograd 034172
Vojvodjanski Muzej, Novi Sad 034228
Vokaer, Michel, Bruxelles . 096267, 133282
Vol du Papillon, Lausanne 111634
Volcano Art Center, Hawaii National Park 044487
Volda Bygdetun, Volda 031343
Voldemāra Jākobsona Memoriālā Māja Muzejs, Bebri 027664
Voldère, Bernadette de, Paris 066663
Voldère, Florence de, Paris 066664
Volek, Roman, Praha 060180, 124002
Volendam Windmill Museum, Milford 045867
Volendams Museum, Volendam . . . 030286
Volets Bleus, Angresse 060881
Volgogradskij Gosudarstvennyj Institut Iskusstv i Kultury, Volgograd 050671
Volgogradskij Memorialno-istoričeskij Muzej, Gosudarstvennyj muzej-panorama Stalingradskaja Bitva, Volgograd . 034065
Volgogradskij Muzej Izobrazitelnych Iskusstv, Volgograd 034066
Volgogradskij Oblastnoj Kraevedčeskij Muzej, Volgograd 034067
Volk, Bruno, Lülsfeld 072352
Volk, Konrad, Würzburg . . 074514, 105344
Volkening Heritage Farm at Spring Valley, Schaumburg 048042
Volkenkundig Museum Gerardus van der Leeuw, Groningen 029646
Volker, Monika, Hildesheim 071526
Volkers, Neu-Isenburg 072967
Volkert, Traunstein 139784
Volkert, Andreas, Münster 072930, 126511
Volkmer, Peter & Renate, Aichhalden 125051
Volkoff & von Hohenlohe, Solvang . 143018
Volksbuurtmuseum, Den Haag 029456
Volksbuurtmuseum Wijk, Utrecht . . 030241
Volkskunde-Museum, Thüringer Bauernhäuser, Rudolstadt 019937
Volkskunde Museum Hesterberg, Stiftung Schleswig-Holsteinische Landesmuseen Schloß Gottorf, Schleswig 020042
Volkskunde Sammlung, Staatliche Museen Kassel, Kassel 018203
Volkskunde- und Freilichtmuseum, Konz 018381
Volkskunde- und Mühlenmuseum, Waltersdorf bei Zittau 020663
Volkskundemuseum, Antwerpen . . 003194
Volkskundemuseum, Mödling 002330
Volkskundemuseum, Reitzengeschwenda 019786
Volkskundemuseum, Schönberg, Mecklenburg 020073
Volkskundemuseum, Salzburger Museum Carolino Augusteum, Salzburg . . . 002570
Volkskundemuseum des Bezirks Unterfranken, Museen Schloss Aschach, Bad Bocklet 015672
Volkskundemuseum Deurne, Deurne 003401
Volkskundemuseum Spiralschmiede, Lasberg 002207
Volkskundemuseum Treuchtlingen, Treuchtlingen 020471
Volkskundemuseum Wyhra, Wyhratal 021030
Volkskundig Educatie Museum, Susteren 030191
Volkskundlich-Landwirtschaftliche Sammlung, Landesmuseum Joanneum, Stainz 002690
Volkskundliche Sammlung, Mömbris 018974
Volkskundliche Sammlung, Naturwissenschaftliches Museum Osnabrück, Osnabrück 019501
Volkskundliche Sammlung alter bäuerlicher Geräte, Ludesch 002270
Volkskundliche Sammlung des Fichtelgebirgsvereins, Weidenberg 020709
Volkskundliche Sammlungen, Stiftung Schleswig-Holsteinische Landesmuseen Schloß Gottorf, Schleswig 020042
Volkskundliche Sammlungen, Erlebnispark Ziegenhagen, Witzenhausen 020941
Volkskundliche und kirchliche Sammlungen, Straßburg 002720
Volkskundliches Berufe- und Handwerker-Museum, Aspang 001701
Volkskundliches Freilichtmuseum im Stadtpark Speckenbüttel, Bremerhaven 016435
Volkskundliches Gerätemuseum, Arzberg, Oberfranken 015571
Volkskundliches Museum, Deutschlandsberg 001780
Volkskundliches Museum Alois Alphons, Hirschwang 002047
Volksmuseum Deurne, Antwerpen . 003195
Volksschulmuseum, Maria Taferl . . 002287
Voll, Karlheinz, Frankfurt am Main .070800, 102836
Volland, Andrea, Düsseldorf 070459
Volle, Bernard, Saint-Ambroix 067350
Le Volle Blaes, Bruxelles 058124
Vollert, Peter, Üchtelhausen 126927
Vollmer, Karin, Karlsruhe 126008
Vollstedt, Andreas, Rendsburg 073498
Volmant, Linda, Cabrieres-d'Avignon 061853
Volo Antique Auto Museum and Village, Volo 048806
Volodymyr-Volyns'kij Istoryčnyj Muzej, Volodymyr-Volyns'kij 038416
Vologodskaja Oblastnaja Kartinnaja Galereja, Vologda 034071
Vologodskij Gosudarstvennyj Istoriko-Architekturnyj i Chudožestvennyj Muzej-Zapovednik, Vologda 034072
Volos, Roma 106647
Voloviec, Claude, Les Alleuds 063751
Volpe, New York 118537
Volpin, Stefano, Padova 127814
Volpin Foscarini, Maristella, Padova 127815
Volta Regional Museum, Ho 021103
Le Voltaire, Lillebonne 063874
Voltaire Fine Art, Paris 100964
Voltaire & Rousseau, Glasgow 141626
Volterra, Firenze 075424
Volubilis, Casablanca 077678
The Volume Framer, Amersham . . . 136278
Volumina, Milano . 075891, 127709, 140069
Volumnia, Perugia 134656
Volunteer Committees of Art Museum, New Orleans 055094
Volunteer Firemen's Mall and Museum of Kingston, Kingston 045016
Volyns'kyj Krajeznavčyj Muzej, Luc'k 038330
Volz, Kandern 103485, 125993
Vom Kloster zum Dorf, Creglingen . 016603
Vomáčka, František, Praha 060181
Von der Heydt-Museum, Wuppertal 021021
The von Liiebig Art Center, Naples . 046132
Vonbank, Christl, Bürs 095491
Vonderau Museum, Fulda 017302
Vonderbank, J., Bad Reichenhall . . 069357
Vonderbank, Roland, Frankfurt am Main 125665
Vondst, de, Utrecht 078825
Vonesch, Roland, Ensisheim 099249
Vonholdt, Birgit, Burrweiler 102296
Vonrüti, Regi, Wetzikon 111989
Vonta, Katerina, Athinai 074614
Vonthron, William, Paris 066665
Vontobel, Feldmeilen 135011
Voor de Oude Jan, Delft 078153
Voorhistorisch Museum, Zonhoven . 003871
Voorhuis, Arnhem 078062
Voorhuis, Doetinchem 078294
Voormalig Stoombierbrouwerij De Keijzer N.A. Bosch, Maastricht 029904
Voortrekker Monument Heritage Site, Pretoria 034736
Voortrekker Museum, Pietermaritzburg 034702
Voorvelt, F., Amsterdam 078012
Vopravilova, Ludmila, Porta Westfalica 126643
Vor- und Frühgeschichtliche Sammlung, Staatliche Museen Kassel, Kassel 018204
Vor- und Frühgeschichtliches Museum, Thalmässing 020431
Vorarlberger Kunst- und Antiquitätenmesse Art Design, Feldkirch 093589
Vorarlberger Kunstverein, Bregenz . 052624
Vorarlberger Landesmuseum, Bregenz 001763
Vorarlberger Militärmuseum, Bregenz 001764
Vorarlberger Naturschau, Dornbirn . 001786
Vorarlberger Verlagsanstalt, Dornbirn 133067, 137162
Vorauer, Karl, Großwilfersdorf 057048
Vorbach, Gangelt 102913
Vorbasse Museum, Vorbasse 009152
Vorderasiatisches Museum, Staatliche Museen zu Berlin - Stiftung Preußischer Kulturbesitz, Berlin 016193
Vorgeschichtliche Sammlung, Nabburg 019176
Vorgeschichtsmuseum der Oberpfalz, Archäologische Staatssammlung München, Amberg, Oberpfalz . . . 015530
Vorgeschichtsmuseum im Grabfeldgau, Archäologische Staatssammlung München, Bad Königshofen 015735
Vorkink-Heeneman, Den Haag 140405
Vorkutinskij Mežrajonnyj Kraevedčeskij Muzej, Vorkuta 034076
Vormayr, Christian, Riedau 123434
Voronežskij Chudožestvennyj Muzej im. I.N. Kramskogo, Voronež 034083
Voronežskij Oblastnoj Kraevedčeskij Muzej, Voronež 034084
Vorpal, New York 118538
Vorpal, San Francisco 119828
Vorselaars, Berlin 069781
Vorspohl, K., Senden, Westfalen . . . 073800
Vortex, London 141915
Võrumaa Muuseum, Võru 009438
Vorwerk, Jürgen, Marburg 072450
Vos, Anita, Amsterdam 107824
Vos, C. de, Aalst 096053
Vos, C.J.M. de, Amsterdam 140348
Vos, Ingrid, Amsterdam 078013
Vos, Jacques de, Paris . . . 066666, 100965
Vos, J.H., Groningen 078437
Vos, M . de, Knokke-Heist 096360
Vos, P.F., Haarlem 128699
Vose, Boston 087854, 115238
Vosges Antiquités, Paris 066667
Voskuil, Babs, Delft 107897
Voß, Angelika, Trittau 105067
Voss, Anne, Dortmund 102415
Voss, Claudia, Hamburg 071350
Voss, D., Isernhagen 071640
Voss, Gisela, Gütersloh 071144
Voss, Kurt, San Antonio 132834
Voss, P., Merzen 072526
Voss, Rüdiger, Düsseldorf 102568
Voß, U. & B., Wesselburen 139842
Voss, Viktor, Luzern 082639
Voss Folkemuseum, Skulestadmo . 031198
Voß-Heitbrink, R., Stemwede 073913
Vosse, M.C., Liège 058330
Voßkuhl, Emsdetten 070568
Vostell, Madrid 110627
Vostell, Rafael, Berlin 102075
Vostell, Rafael, Berlin 102076
Vostočnaja Galereja, Moskva 109603
Vostočno Kazachstanskij Ėtnografičeskij Muzej, Ust-Kamenogorsk 027418
Vostočno-Sibirskaja Gosudarstvennaja Akademija Kultury i Iskusstva, Ulan-Udė 050667
Vostok Galereja, Ufa 109665
Vostry, Erfurt 102649
Le Votaire, Beirut 077420
Votat, Pierre, Paris 066668, 124833
Votava, Petr, Liberec 060046
Votivsammlung der Wallfahrtskirche Maria Kirchental, Sankt Martin bei Lofer 002603
Votivschatz der Wallfahrtskirche, Sankt Jakob-Breitenau 002588
Votre Galeria de Arte, Rio de Janeiro 096656
Vouga, Elizabeth & Claude, Kirchdorf (Aargau) 082513

La Vouivre, Paris 138560
Vouros Eftaxias Museum, Athinai . . 021216
Vous Etes Ici, Amsterdam 107825
Vous Etes Ici, Amsterdam 134796
Vouvalis Mansion, Kalymnos 021303
Vox Centre, Montréal 097092
Vox Populi Gallery, Philadelphia . . . 046994
Voxxx Galerie, Chemnitz 102315
Voyage Intérieur Nice, Nice 099861
Voyager Toys, Houston 089245
Voyages, Paris 066669
Voyageur Heritage Centre, Mattawa 005845
Voyageurs National Park Museum, International Falls 044761
Voyer, Michel, Poitiers 066895
Voyer, Roland, Lugo 081196
Voz Alta, San Diego 119561
Vozroždenie, Moskva 109604
Vrain, Jean Claude, Paris 138561
De Vranse Gans, Amstelveen 077765
Vrbický, Petr, Hradec Králové 137785
Vredenbregt-Timmer, Rotterdam . . 078757
Vredes Museum, Amsterdam 029208
Vredespaleis, Den Haag 029457
Vredespijp, Amsterdam 078014
Vredevoogd, Amsterdam 078015
Vree, J.F.M. de, Oss 078677
Vree, Mathilde de, Rotterdam 108221
Vree, Paul, Hildesheim 139267
Vreeze, Nanky de, Amsterdam 107826
De Vregille & Bizouard, Dijon 120990
Vrienden van de Stedelijke Musea Oostende, Oostende 052692
Vries, de, Haarlem 140447
Vries, de, Leeuwarden 078558
Vries, B. de, Amsterdam 078016
Vries, Croibien de, Bruxelles 058125
Vries, Fenna de, Rotterdam 108222
Vries, Rob de, Haarlem 108065
Vries, Rob de, Haarlem 108066
Vrin, Paris 138562
Vrin, Paris 138563
Vrindavan Research Institute Museum, Mathura 022256
Vring, Cornelia, München 126478
Vrolijk, Rotterdam 078758
Vrolijk, Maurice, Dordrecht 107989
Vromans, Amsterdam 107827
Vrouwen in Druk, Amsterdam 140349
Het Vrouwenhuis, Zwolle 030415
Vrublevskaja, Elena, Moskva 109605
Vryburg Museum, Vryburg 034772
VSA Arts, Salt Lake City 119380
VSE Elektro-Museum, Illingen 018054
Vserossijskij Istoriko-ėtnografičeskij Muzej, Toržok 033968
Vserossijskij Memorialnyj Muzej-zapovednik V.M. Šukšina, Srostki 033899
Vserossijskij Muzej Dekorativno-Prikladnogo i Narodnogo Iskusstva, Moskva . . 033529
Vserossijskij Muzej Puškina, Sankt-Peterburg 033837
Vserossiskij Chudožestvennyj Naučno-restavracënnyj Centr im. Akademika Igorja Grabarja, Moskva 129242
Vsevoložskij Gosudarstvennyj Istoriko-kraevedčeskij Muzej, Vsevoložsk . 034088
VTO Gallery, London 113948
VU Centre de Diffusion et de Production de la Photographie, Québec 006232
Vu Sous 7 Anglès, Lourmarin 099527
Vuaille, Jean-Paul, Lyon 124380
Vucci, Pasquale, Bari 075037, 139982
Vue de l'Abbaye, Brantome 061750
Vughts Historisch Museum, Vught . 030300
Vuille, Louis, Yverdon-les-Bains . . .082924, 112012, 141315
Vuillemo, Jean-Marc, Besançon . . .061400, 098955
Vuitton, Anne, Paris 124834
Vukov i Dositejev Muzej, Beograd . . 034173
Vulcan International, Osaka 077184
Vulliod, François, Lyon 064194
Vuni Sarayi, Lefke 008252
Vuyk, Wout, Amsterdam 140350
de Vuyst, Lokeren 058332, 096381, 120777
De Vuyst, Sankt Johann im Pongau 095742
V.V.95, Sevilla 081620
VW-Käfermuseum, Ingering 002072
Vyborgskij Kraevedčeskij Muzej, Vyborg 034090
Vychino, Moskva 109606
Východočeská Galerie, Pardubice . . 008560
Východočeské Muzeum, Pardubice . 008561
Východoslovenské Múzeum, Košice 034368
Vylym-Hütte, Userin 020550
The Vyne, Basingstoke 038613
Vysoká Škola Uměleckoprůmyslová v Praze, Praha 049894
Vysoká Škola Výtvarných Umení v Bratislave, Bratislava 050692
Vystavka Izjaščnych Iskusstv, Novosibirsk 093855
Výstavní Sín Mánes, Praha 098493
Výstavní Síň Muzea, Ústí nad Orlicí . 008739
Výstavní Síň Muzea Těšínska, Orlová 008550
Výstavní síň Muzea Těšínska, Muzeum Těšínska, Český Těšín 008326
Výstavní síň Muzeum Těšínska, Muzeum Těšínska, Jablunkov 008402
Vystavočnye Zaly v Dome Aksakovych, Moskva 033530
Vystavočnyj Zal, Čerepovec 033077
Vystavočnyj Zal, Krasnoturinsk 033307
Vystavočnyj Zal, Ekaterinburgskij Tvorčeskij Sojus Dejatelej Kultury, Ekaterinburg 033127
Vystavočnyj Zal, Kirovskij Oblastnoj Chudožestvennyj Muzej im. Viktora i Apollinarija Vasnecovych, Kirov . . 033269
Vystavočnyj Zal, Kirovskij oblastnoj kraevedčeskij muzej, Kirov 033270
Vystavočnyj Zal, Tulskij muzej izobrazitelnych iskusstv, Tula 033982
Vystavočnyj Zal, Volgogradskij muzej izobrazitelnych iskusstv, Volgograd 034068
Vystavocnyj Zal, Vologodskij Gosudarstvennyj Istoriko-Architekturnyj i Chudožestvennyj Muzej-Zapovednik, Vologda 034073
Vystavočnyj Zal Biblioteki im. A.A. Bloka, Sankt-Peterburg 033838
Vystavocnyj Zal Doma Učenych, Sibirskoe otdelenie Rossijskoj akademii nauk, Novosibirsk 033590
Vystavočnyj Zal g. Smolenska, Smolenskij Muzej-Zapovednik, Smolensk . . . 033886
Vystavočnyj Zal Karelskoj Gosudarstvennoj Filarmonii, Petrozavodsk 033665
Vystavočnyj Zal Moskovskogo Sojuza Chudožnikov, Moskva 033531
Vystavočnyj Zal Permskogo Oblastnogo Kraevedčeskogo Muzeja, Perm . . 033654
Vystavočnyj Zal Raduga, Čeboksary 033066
Vystavočnyj Zal - Russkie Chudožniki v Samarskoj Gubernii, Žigulevsk . . 034097
Vystavočnyj Zal Sojuza Chudožnikov Rossii, Sankt-Peterburg 033839
Vystavočnyj Zal Spasskaja Cerkov, Irkutsk 033165
Vystavočnyj Zal Tverskoj Oblastnoj Kartinnoj Galerei, Tver 033988
Vystavočnyj Zentr -Galereja, Muzejno-vystavočnyj kompleks M.T. Kalašnikova, Iževsk 033182
Vystavočnyj Zentr Sankt-Peterburgskogo Otdelenija Sojuza Chudožnikov Rossii, Sankt-Peterburg 033840
Vytautas The Great War Museum, Kaunas 027850
Výtvarná Řemesla, Praha 124003
Výtvarná Škola Václava Hollara, Praha 049895
Výtvarné Centrum Chagall, Ostrava 008555
Výtvarný Život, Bratislava 136064
Vzgljad, Sankt-Peterburg 109654
W 139, Amsterdam 107828
W. Henry Duvall Tool Museum, Upper Marlboro 048707
W. Hourston Smithy Museum, Saint Margaret's Hope 040926
W & L Antiquitäten, Eicklingen 070525
W & W Antiqua, Basel 082180
W & W Antiques, Norfolk 091401
W125 Galerie, Tilburg 108238
W.13 Antiques, London 085773
Wa, Kwan Kai, Hong Kong 059701
Wa, Kwan Wing, Hong Kong 059702
Wa-Ni, Göteborg 110933
W.A. Scout Museum, West Perth . . 001609
WAAC Newsletter, Los Angeles 136662
De Waag, Alkmaar 077719
De Waag, Hilversum 078544
De Waagschaal, Delft 078154
Het Waaierkabinet, Amsterdam . . . 029241
Waal, Hans de, Lith 128752
Het Waalres Museum, Waalre 030301
Waanders, Zwolle 134842
Waba Cottage Museum, White Lake 006808
Wabash Frisco and Pacific Association Museum, Glencoe 044206
Wabasha County Museum, Reads Landing 047349
Wabasso Historical Society Museum, Wabasso 048808
Wabaunsee County Historical Museum, Alma 041666
Wabberi, Columbus 115807
Waber, G., München 126479
Wable, Annie, Boulogne-sur-Mer . . 099021
Wable, Annie, Lille 099499
Wabowden Historical Museum, Wabowden 006757
Wace, Rupert, London . . . 085774, 113949
Wachauer Antiquitäten- und Sammlermesse, Spitz 093590
Wachaumuseum, Weißenkirchen in der Wachau 002819
Wachholtz, Neumünster 134306
Wachiraprasat Museum, Phetchaburi 037920
Wachner, Lydia, Göppingen 071035
Wachniak & Sons, J., Winnipeg . . . 120833
Wachs, Gottfried, Dresden 125512
Wachsstöcklkabinett - Wachzieher- und Lebzelter-Museum, Viechtach . . . 020583
Wachtelaer, Bruxelles 058126
Wachter, Winston, Seattle 120008
Wachter Mayer, Winston, New York 118539
Wachters, Sabine, Knokke-Heist . . 096361
Wack, Kaiserslautern 103472
Wackenhut, Houston 089246
Wacker, Bernd, Bad Rodach 069359
Wacker, Hans, Hannover 071418
Wacker, M., Heidelberg 071466
Wacker & Rohm, Stuttgart 105021
Wackernah, Gösta, Karlsruhe 071733
Wada, Steve, New York 118540
Wada Takashi, New York 118541
Waddesdon Manor, The Rothschild Collection, Waddesdon 041270
Waddington, Trevor, Bradford-on-Avon 083633, 130426
Waddington Galleries, London 113950
Waddington's, Toronto 120823
Wade, Birmingham 131840
Wade, Colin, Balmain 055445
Wade, Ray, Poulton-le-Fylde 086305
Wade, Sara, Korora 094709
Wade House and Wesley Jung Carriage Museum, Greenbush 044316
Wade Maxx, New York 118542
Wadena and District Museum and Gallery, Wadena 006758
Wadeye Arts & Crafts, Darwin 055742
Wadge, Chris, Salisbury 086498
Wadham, Peter, Exeter . . . 084364, 130696
Wadsworth Atheneum, Hartford . . . 044463
Wadsworth-Longfellow House, Portland 047165
Wäger, Hans, Bielefeld 138878
Wäger, Hans, Herford 139265
Wähning, Andrea, Karlsruhe 126009
Währungsreform von 1948 und Konklave in Rothwesten, Fuldatal 017303
Wäinö Aaltosen Museo, Turku 010180
Wälchli, Peter, Solothurn 082823
Wälde, Christiane, Marburg 072451
Wälderbähnle, Bezau 001754
Wäller, Westerburg 105224
Wälti, Thérèse H., Bern 082248
Waentig, Friederike, Köln 126122
Wäschepflegemuseum, Rainbach im Mühlkreis 002494
Wäscherei-Museum Omas Waschküche, Berlin 016194
Wafangdian City Museum, Wafangdian 007298
Waffenkammer im Munot-Turm, Schaffhausen 037525
Waffenmuseum, Oberndorf am Neckar 019399
Waffenmuseum Suhl, Suhl 020381
Waffensammlung Willibald Folger, Bruck an der Mur 001770
Wage, Philadelphia 091701
Wagenbach, Klaus, Berlin 133814
Wagenburg im Schloß Schönbrunn, Kunsthistorisches Museum, Wien 003015
Wagener, Heino, Leer 072181
Wagenknecht, Rainer E., Berlin . . . 069782
Wagenmakersmuseum, Leiden . . . 029856
Wagga Antique Centre, Wagga Wagga 056790
Wagga Wagga Art Gallery, Wagga Wagga 001587
Wagin Historical Village Museum, Wagin 001588
Wagman & Son, Stanley, Toronto . .059314, 097394
Wagnalls Memorial, Lithopolis 045336
Wagner, Gemmerich 070962
Wagner, Paddington 095044
Wagner, Wallisellen 111982
Wagner, Armand, Luxembourg 077481
Wagner, Barbara, Grafing bei München 125751
Wagner, Claus, Baden 082109
Wagner, Corinne, Saint-Tropez 068028
Wagner, F., Wesselburen 139843
Wagner, Gabriele, Dresden 125513
Wagner, H., Stegersbach 137264
Wagner, H.-J., Regensburg 139686
Wagner, Hajo, Wuppertal 074546
Wagner, Horst, Innsbruck 057090
Wagner, Howard B., Louisville 090042
Wagner, Karl Dieter, Hamburg 139220
Wagner, M., Ditzingen 070261
Wagner, Marie-Claude, Paris 066670
Wagner, Matthias, Berlin 138855
Wagner, N., Wolfenbüttel 074474
Wagner, Odon, Toronto . . . 097395, 123843
Wagner, P., Garching bei München . 070932
Wagner, Richard, Den Haag 078267
Wagner, Rolf, Büdingen 125410
Wagner, Shirley, Palm Beach 056436
Wagner, Siegfried, Münsingen 126492
Wagner, Thomas E., Kindsbach, Pfalz 103550
Wagner, Dr. Wolfgang, Kassel 121462
Wagner Bazarin, São Paulo 096694
Wagner Chavanis, Lyon 124381
Wagner Free Institute of Science, Philadelphia 046995
Wagner P.A. Museum, Rondebosch . 034743
Wágnerova, Pruhonice 098498
Wagon Wheel Antiques, Louisville .090043, 132310
Wagon Wheel Regional Museum, Alix 004995
Wags Curios, Semaphore 056586
Wagstädter Heimatstube, Bad Neustadt an der Saale 015764
Wagstaff, Oxted 086187, 131357
Wah, Chun Kwok, Hong Kong 059703
Wah, Leong Shin, Singapore 109892
Wah, Tsui Shem, San Francisco . . . 119829
Wah, Tung, Hong Kong 059704

Wahab, Manama 096032
Wahkiakum County Historical Museum, Cathlamet 042657
Wahl, Heilbronn 139259
Wahl, Neuhäusel 072994
Wahl, Alicja & Bożena, Warszawa . . 109202
Wahl, Annelie, Koblenz 071897
Wahl & Søn, Ib, Frederiksberg 060248, 124019
Wahl, Dr. J., Bernburg 138869
Wahl, Markus, Erwitte 070609
Wahl, O. & R., Moonah 137003
Wahlandt, Edith, Stuttgart 105022
Wahle, Exeter 113044
Wahlrab, Nürnberg 073125
Wahlström, B. & L., Stockholm 082036
Wahrenberger, Daniel, Zürich 112192
Wahrenbrock, San Diego 142919
Wahres Deutsch- Historisches Lügenmuseum und Kunsthaus, Gantikow 017318
Wai, Poon Chin, Hong Kong 059705
Wai & Teng, Singapore 109893
Waibel, Wolfgang, Schramberg . . . 073730
Waidelich, Christina, Heiden 111548
Waiheke Community Art Gallery, Auckland 030451
Waiheke Island Historical Society Museum, Waiheke Island 030610
Waihi Arts Centre and Museum Association, Waihi 030611
Waikato Museum of Art and History, Hamilton 030511
Waikato School Of Arts, Waikato . . 050575
Waikawa District Museum, Tokanui 030606
Waikiki Beach Gallery, Honolulu . . . 116250
Waikouaiti Museum, Waikouaiti . . . 030612
Waimate Historical Museum, Waimate 030613
Waimer, Jettingen-Scheppach 071665
Waimer, S., Reutlingen 073505
Waimer, Walfriede, Günzburg 103030
Wain, Peter, Menai Bridge 085973
Wainscot, Vancouver 059434, 123858
Waintraub, Henri, Paris 066671
Wainwright Museum, Wainwright . . 006759
Waipara County Historical Society Museum, Hawarden 030514
Waipu Art Gallery, Whangarei 108670
Waipu Heritage Centre, Waipu 030616
Waipukurau Museum, Waipukurau . 030617
Wairarapa Arts Foundation and Print Council of New Zealand, Masterton 053929
Wairoa Museum Koputuntanga, Toanga o Te Wairoa, Wairoa 030618
Waitoki Antiques, Auckland 078992
Waitomo Museum of Caves, Waitomo Caves 030621
Waiuku Museum, Waiuku 030622
Waka Huia Art & Craft Gallery, Picton 108544
Wakaw Heritage Museum, Wakaw . 006761
Wakayama-kenritsu Hakubutsukan, Wakayama 027315
Wakayama-kenritsu Kindai Bijutsukan, Wakayama 027316
Wake Forest University Fine Arts Gallery, Winston-Salem 049259
Wakefield, Anthony, Dorking 084207
Wakefield, Colin, Wellington 128980
Wakefield & Co., Robert, Houston . . 089247
Wakefield Antiques, Masterton 079152
Wakefield Art Gallery, Wakefield . . . 041277
Wakefield Historical Museum, Wakefield 048828
Wakefield House Museum, Blue Earth 042272
Wakefield Museum, Wakefield 041278
Wakefield Museum, Wakefield 048827
Wakelin & Linfield, Billingshurst . . . 083517
Wakeman & Sons, A.E., Tedburn Saint Mary 086834
Wakeman, Frances, Carlton 141491
Wakim, Brunswick 123199
De Wakkere Jongens, Amsterdam . 078017
Wako Hakubutsukan, Yasugi 027328
Waksberg, Daniel, Neuilly-sur-Seine 064995
Walbrecht, Julius, Wuppertal 074547
Walbröl, Ursula, Düsseldorf 102569
Walch, René, Lichtenberg 099480
Walcha, Hans-Martin, Dresden 125514
Walcot Reclamation, Bath 083451, 130355
Walczuk, Eugeniusz, Jabłonna 079604, 129020
Walczyński, Andrzej, Warszawa . . .079790, 129121
Wald- und Lönsmuseum, Heinade . 017857
Wald- und Moormuseum Berumerfehn, Großheide 017572
Waldbauernmuseum, Gutenstein . . 001996
Waldburg-Zeil, Franz-Clemens, Hohenems 123386
Waldeck, Dr. Hans, Gau-Algesheim 070939
Walden, Amsterdam 107829
Walden, London 141916
Walden, New York 118543
Walden Pond, Oakland 142712
Walderdorff, Emmanuel, Köln 103733
Waldgeschichtliches Museum Sankt Oswald, Sankt Oswald, Niederbayern 019992
Waldhauer, A., Mannebach 104018
Waldherr, Kirchheimbolanden 103558, 134091
Waldhorn & Adler, New Orleans . . . 090637
Waldhufen-Heimatmuseum Salmbach, Engelsbrand 016984
Waldinger, Andreas, Ravensburg . . 073441
Waldmann & Busch, Bad Segeberg 069383
Waldmühle, Dettenheim 070232
Waldmuseum, Burg, Dithmarschen 016504
Waldmuseum, Furth im Wald 017307
Waldmuseum, Mehlmeisel 018879
Waldmuseum, Münstertal 019161
Waldmuseum, Surwold 020389
Waldmuseum, Zwiesel 021092
Waldmuseum Dr. Kanngiesser, Braunfels 016378
Waldmuseum Göhrde, Göhrde 017442
Waldmuseum im Wildpark Neuhaus, Holzminden 017999
Waldmuseum Stendenitz, Stendenitz 020317
Waldmuseum Wassermühle, Wingst 020911
Waldmuseum Watterbacher Haus, Kirchzell 018272
Waldnaabtal-Museum in der Burg Neuhaus, Windischeschenbach 020910
Waldner, Erich R., Ludwigsburg, Württemberg 121502
Waldner-Millesi, Sigrid, Basel 129938
Waldo Antique Center, Kansas City . 089528
Waldo Antiques, Kansas City 089529
Waldock, Blackrock 105848
Waldon, Minneapolis 090403
Waldrich, Christiane, München 104339
Waldrich, Joachim, München 134286
Waldron, Patrick, Cirencester 084023, 130584
Waldschmidt-Ausstellung, Eschlkam 017049
Waldschmidthaus Waldfrieden, Kötzting 018367
Waldviertler Atelier Werkstätte, Hoheneich 095568
Waldviertler Bauernhaus-Museum, Weitra 002824
Waldviertler Bauernhof-Museum, Gföhl 001894
Waldviertler Eisenbahnmuseum, Sigmundsherberg 002679
Waldviertler Puppenmuseum, Waldkirchen 002806
Walenda, Günther, Wiesloch 074433
Walendowski, Michał, Łódź 079675
Walentowski, Dresden 102460
Walentowski, Werl 105209
Walentowski, H. & C., Seebad Ahlbeck 104875
Walford, Leslie, Double Bay 055757
Walhalla, Donaustauf 016739
Walhalla Old Wares, Walhalla 056795
Walinska, Ewa, Arnhem 107864
Walison, Marieke, Epen 128668
Walk a Crooked Mile Books, Philadelphia 142752
Walk Gallery, London 113951
Walkabout Gallery, Leichhardt 094732
Walkatjara Art Centre, Yulara 056907
Walkaway Station Museum, Walkaway 001590
Walker, Austin 087621
Walker, Denver 116066
Walker, Denver 116067
Walker, Harrogate 084591
Walker, Harrogate 113194
Walker, Harrogate 130767
Walker, Indianapolis 089356
The Walker, Liverpool 040041
Walker, Nepean 059024, 120808
Walker, Toronto 059315
Walker, Alan, Halfway 084556
Walker, Alfred J., Boston 115239
Walker, Charles, Seattle 093082
Walker, John, Dorchester 084180
Walker, John, New York 091333
Walker, Judith, Hermagor 095564
Walker, Judith, Klagenfurt 095623
Walker, Melissa Inez, San Diego . . . 119562
Walker Art Center, Minneapolis . . . 045922
Walker Art Center Publications, Minneapolis 135398
Walker Art Collection of the Garnett Public Library, Garnett 044150
Walker Art Gallery, Liverpool 040041
Walker Art Gallery Shop, Liverpool . 141740
Walker, Barnett & Hill, Cosford 122479
Walker Galleries, Honiton 113268
Walker & Hall, Wellington 079356
Walker Hill Art Center, Seoul 027614
Walker Street Gallery, Dandenong . 000970
Walker Wildlife and Indian Artifacts Museum, Walker 048832
Walkers, Beechworth 055464
Walker's Point Artists Association, Milwaukee 055095
Walker's Point Center for the Arts, Milwaukee 045901
Walking Stick Shop, Arundel 083318
Walkner, M., Salzburg 137249
Walkter & Hall, Auckland 078993
The Wall, Ely 113020
Wall, E. F., Woodbridge . . 087225, 131710
Wall, Kandy, Columbus 115808
Wall, Thomas, Djursholm 129836
Wall Impressions, Jacksonville 116549
Wall-Museum, Museumshof, Oldenburg in Holstein 019466
Wall Roman Site and Museum - Letocetum, Lichfield 040003
Wall Street Exchange, Richmond, Victoria 095145
Wall Street Gallery, Calgary 096853
Wallace, Auckland 108369
Wallace, Brookfield 055567
Wallace, Calgary 096854
Wallace, Fort Worth 088891
Wallace, Memphis 132332
Wallace, Portland 142813
Wallace, Barbara, Philadelphia 118850
Wallace, Robert, Armadale, Victoria 055397
Wallace, Robert, Paddington, New South Wales 056424
Wallace Area Museum, Wallace Bridge 006762
The Wallace Collection, London . . . 040310
Wallace District Mining Museum, Wallace 048836
Wallace Early Settlers Museum, Riverton 030588
Wallace House, Somerville 048220
The Wallace Museum Foundation, Montgomery 045996
Wallack, Ottawa 097121
Wallaroo Heritage and Nautical Museum, Wallaroo 001591
Wallbrecht, Dr. R.E., Hannover 125883
Wallenfang, Heidi, Rösrath 073562
Wallenfels'sches Haus, Abteilung Vor- und Frühgeschichte, Archäologie und Völkerkunde, Oberhessisches Museum und Gail'sche Sammlungen, Gießen 017413
Waller, Amsterdam 107830
Waller, Blaise, Paris 066672
Waller, Christoph, Gottenheim 125747
Wallet Fouque, Amiens 098823
Wallett, Shirley, Griffith 055921
Wallfahrts- und Heimatmuseum, Altötting 015518
Wallfahrtsbasilika Mariazell, Schatzkammern, Galerien, Reliquienkammer und Krippenkammer, Mariazell 002291
Wallfahrtsmuseum, Legau 018542
Wallfahrtsmuseum, Maria Enzersdorf am Gebirge 002280
Wallfahrtsmuseum, Maria Taferl . . . 002288
Wallfahrtsmuseum, Neukirchen beim Heiligen Blut 019246
Wallfahrtsmuseum, Steingaden . . . 020305
Wallfahrtsmuseum, Katholische Kirchenstiftung Weihenlinden-Högling, Bruckmühl 016462
Wallfahrtsmuseum Inchenhofen, Inchenhofen 018062
Wallflower Gallery, Miami 117152
Wallin, Ingemar, Stockholm 082037
Wallin, Johan, Stockholm 111081
Wallin, Ralph, Seattle 132946
Wallin, Sture, Märsta 122204
Walling, Julia, Saint Albans 114346
Wallingford Gallery, Wallingford . . . 114640
Wallingford Historical Society Museum, Wallingford 048837
Wallingford Museum, Wallingford . . 041280
Wallington Hall, Cambo 038955
Wallis Museum at Connors State College, Warner 048854
Wallis & Wallis, Lewes 122568
Walliser, Hans, Herrliberg 082495
Walliser, Hans, Meilen 082653
Walliser Reb- und Weinmuseum, Salgesch 037484
Wallmark, Jan, Stockholm 111082
Wallner, Chicago 088192
Wallner, Doris, Mank 137230
Wallpaper History Society, London . 054539
Wallraf, Köln 103734
Wallraf-Richartz-Museum - Fondation Corboud, Museen der Stadt Köln, Köln 018341
Wallrock, Woolloongabba 056888
Walls, Amsterdam 107831
Walls Art, Nashville 117375
Walls of Art, Los Angeles 116913
Wallscapes, Las Vegas 116656
Wallsend Heritage Centre, Wallsend 041282
Wallspace, New York 118544
Wallstraßen-Galerie, Mönchengladbach 104102
Wallwitz, Angela Gräfin von, München 072876
Wally's Antiques, Milwaukee 090329
Wally's Antiques, Milwaukee 090330, 132374
Walmer Castle, Walmer 041283
Walmstedtska Gårdens Museivåning, Uppsala 036748
Walnut Canyon National Monument, Flagstaff 043854
Walnut Grove Plantation, Roebuck . 047521
Walonia, Utrecht 078826
Walpole, London 085775, 113952
Walpole, Monaco 077627
Walpole, Graham, London 085776
Walpurgishalle Thale, Thale 020429
Walpurgius, Theodor, Nassau, Lahn 139580
Walrus Gallery, Wellington 108649
Walry, Gent 096305

Walsall Leather Museum, Walsall . . 041287
Walsall Local History Centre, Walsall 041288
Walsall Museum, Walsall 041289
Walsall Museum and Art Gallery, Walsall 041286
Walschot, Roermond 078681
Walsemann, D.G.C., Utrecht 078827
The Walsenburg Mining Museum and Fort Francisco Museum of La Veta, Walsenburg 048842
Walser, Philippe, Mazerulles 124440
Walser, Rupert, München 104340
Walser Heimatmuseum, Triesenberg 027840
Walserhaus Gurin, Bosco/Gurin . . . 036964
Walsermuseum, Alagna Valsesia . . 023141
Walsermuseum, Riezlern 002532
Walsermuseum Lech-Tannberg, Lech 002215
Walsh, Chicago 115582
Walsh, Chris, Seattle 120009
Walsh, Frank O., Atlanta . . 087541, 142211
Walsh & Co, John, Wakefield 122734
Walt Whitman Birthplace State Historic Site, Huntington Station 044689
Walt Whitman House, Camden 042578
Walter, A., Freiburg im Breisgau . . . 070865
Walter & Son, A., Hamilton 123775
Walter, Alfredo, Lugano . . 082613, 130096
Walter, Alwin, Bad Zwesten 069402
Walter, David, Claremont 055678
Walter, Erika, Wien 057574
Walter, Fabian & Claude, Basel 111230
Walter, Fabian & Claude, Zürich . . . 112193
Walter, François, Colombier 130003
Walter, Hans-Willi, Leonberg, Württemberg 134159
Walter, Irénée, Ballersdorf 061181
Walter, Lutz J., Stuttgart 126885
Walter, Lutz Joseph, Wernigerode . 126997
Walter, M., Pforzheim 073324
Walter, Manfred, Freigericht 070871
Walter, Manfred, Kleinschmalkalden 126053
Walter, Peter, Krems 095634
Walter, P.J., Lindau, Bodensee 072268
Walter, Roland, Wien 057575
Walter, W., Edingen-Neckarhausen . 121390
Walter-Adams, San Francisco 119830
Walter and McBean Galleries, San Francisco Art Institute, San Francisco 047889
Walter Anderson Museum of Art, Ocean Springs 046618
Walter Elwood Museum, Amsterdam 041701
Walter-Honig-Heimatmuseum, Hitzacker 017934
Walter P. Chrysler Boyhood Home and Museum, Ellis 043680
Walter P. Chrysler Museum, Auburn Hills 041893
Walter Phillips Gallery, Banff 005064
Walter Rothschild Zoological Museum, Tring 041241
Walter Runebergin Veistoskokoelma, Porvoo 009997
Walter Wright Pioneer Village, Dawson Creek 005335
Walter W.S. Cook Alumni Lecture, Locust Valley 136663
Walters, Eileen, New York 118545
Walters, J.D. & R.M., Rolvenden . . .086395, 131424
Walters Art Museum, Baltimore . . . 042006
Walters Art Museum. Journal, Baltimore 136664
Walter's Sweet Antiques, Minneapolis 090404
Walterwoods Antiques, Masterton . 079153
Waltham Historical Society Museum, Waltham 048848
The Waltham Museum, Waltham . . 048849
Walther, Ratingen 104665, 134356
Walther, Caroline, Stuttgart 126886
Walther, Konrad, Prösen 073377
Waltl, Helga & Karl, Wies, Steiermark 137385
Waltner, Angela, Schneeberg, Erzgebirge 126775
Walton, Michael, Dublin 074954
Walton, Stephen, Bradfield Saint George 112687
Walton Galleries, Guisborough 113172
Walton Gallery, London 113953
Walton Hall Heritage Centre, Warrington 041302
Walton Hall Museum, Linford 040014
Walton House Museum, Centerville 042688
Walton Maritime Museum, Walton-on-the-Naze 041292
Waltscher Heimatstube, Neckargemünd 019194
Waltzer, Stewart, New York 118546
Waltzer, Stewart, New York 118547
Waltzing Matilda Centre and Qantilda Museum, Winton 001623
Walvis Bay Museum, Walvis Bay . . 029103
Walz, Bobenheim-Roxheim 069873
Walz, Winden 074445
Walz, Ed., Feldafing 139069
Walz, Michael F., Potsdam 073368, 139664
Walz, Wolfgang & Marianne, Großwallstadt 071128
Walzinger, A. & A., Saarlouis 104804
Wamco, Oakland 091447
Wameling Richon, Cäcilia, Baden . . 111155
Wan-Bo, Shanghai 059772
Wan Qing Art Cooperative, Shanghai 097952
Wan Qing Tang Art Cooperative, Wuxi 098046
Wan Zhou District Museum, Chongqing 007053
Wanapum Dam Heritage Center, Beverly 042190
Wandel, Düsseldorf 070460, 125554
Wandle, London 085777
Wandle Industrial Museum, Mitcham 040481
Wandsworth Museum, London 040311
Wanecq, Jean, Paris 066673
Wang, Oslo 079480
Wang, Oslo 108741
Wang, San Jose 119866
Wang, Chen, Singapore 080585
Wang, Chen, Singapore 080586
Wang, Elizabeth, New York 118548
Wang, Kwong, Hong Kong 059706
Wang, Lucy, San Diego 119563
Wang, Maggy, Thezac 068385
Wang, Marcel, Wien 057576
Wangal Aboriginal Arts & Crafts, Kuranda 056070
Wangaratta Exhibitions Gallery, Wangaratta 001593
Wangaratta Museum, Wangaratta . 001594
Wangmiao Display Center, Dujiangyan 007066
Wangsmo, Trondheim 140710
Wanha-Aika, Helsinki 060595
Wanhan Puoti, Fiskars 137923
Wanke, Tilman A., München 126480
Wannemacher, W., Langen in Hessen 072151
Wannenes, Milano 075892
Wannenes & C., Genova 075520
Wannenmacher-Museum, Emsdetten 016980
Wanner, Anita, Zürich 130269
Wanner, Anne-Marie, La Cadière-d'Azur 063300
Wanner, Gerda, Kloten 082515
Wansink, Roermond 108167
Wanuskewin Heritage Park, Saskatoon 006428
Wanzke, Dr. Wolfgang, Augsburg . . 138689
Wao, Fukuoka 106847
Waow Gallery, Bruxelles 058127
Wapello County Historical Museum, Ottumwa 046753
Wapler, Gerd, Regensburg 126701
Wapler, Vincent, Paris 121218
Waquet, Patrick, Fismes 062865
War and Peace Exhibition, Oban . . . 040636
War in the Pacific National Historical Park, Asan 021567
War in the Pacific National Historical Park, Piti 021569
War Memorial, Dublin 022773
War Memorial Carillon Tower and Military Museum, Loughborough 040344
War Memorial Gallery of Fine Arts, Sydney 001528
War Museum, Addis Ababa 009442
War Museum, Valletta 028038
War Museum, Yangon 029079
War Remnants Museum, Ho Chi Minh City 049545
War Room and Motor House Collection, Harrogate 039680
War Shop, Tampa 093158
War Souvenirs, Auckland 078994
Wara, Lewis, Seattle 120010
Waragil, Blackheath 094258
Waratah Rural Auctions, Wickham . 120654
Warba Mirdawaji Aboriginal Art, Roebourne 095153
Warbinek, Siefersheim 104888
Warburg Institute Publications, London 135274
Ward, London 085778
Ward, Saint Paul 132776
Ward, Sidcup 086615
Ward, Tampa 132965
Ward, Howard E., Southport 086664
Ward, Keith, Tulsa 133006
Ward & Son, L.L., Brandsby 083642
Ward, Mark, North Geelong 056368
Ward, Michael, New York 091334
Ward, Michael, New York 091335
Ward, Paul, Sheffield 086568
Ward, Peter, Cheltenham . 083935, 130546
Ward & Chowen, Tavistock 122722
Ward County Historical Society Museum, Minot 045926
Ward Hall, Georgetown 044174
The Ward Museum of Wildfowl Art, Salisbury University, Salisbury . . . 047761
Ward-Nasse, New York 118549
Ward O'Hara Agricultural Museum of Cayuga County, Auburn 041891
Ward Thomas, Christian, Balsham .083375, 130326
Ward-Thompson, Willoughby 095399
Ward & Ward, Kansas City 116595
Warden's House Museum, Stillwater 048358
Wardil, Marco A., Belo Horizonte . . 058456
Wardrobe, Brighton 083718
Ware, Kamakura 077071
Ware Museum, Ware 041296
Wareham Town Museum, Wareham 041297
The Warehouse, Amsterdam 078018
Warehouse Artworks, Winnipeg . . . 097611
The Warehouse Gallery, Henley-on-Thames 113234
Warehouse Gallery, Houston 116425
Warehouse Gallery, Lee 045228
Wares for Art, New York 118550
Warger, Doris, Frauenfeld 130015
Warhol Family Museum of Modern Art, Medzilaborce 034391
Waringarri Arts Aboriginal, Kununurra 094713
Warings of Hereford, Hereford 084670
Warisan, Los Angeles 089935
Waritsch, Marie-Luise, Innsbruck . . 057091
Warkums Erfskip, Workum 030352
Warkworth and District Museum, Warkworth 030631
Warlenius, Agneta, Stockholm 129880
Warley Antique Centre, Birmingham 083538
Warminster Antiques Centre, Warminster 087031
Warmun Art Centre, Warmun 095369
Warndorff, Ton, Haarlem 108067
Warnecke-Tamaschke & Prof.Dr. Tamaschke, Ravenstein 104677
Warner & Son, Robert, Worthing . . . 087266
Warner, W.W., Brasted 083657
Warner Archive, Milton Keynes 040475
Warner Museum, Springville 048309
Warning, Brigitte, Hamm, Westfalen 103246
Warnke, Uwe, Berlin 133815
Warooka and District Museum, Warooka 001595
Waroschitz, L., Berlin 069783
Warracknabeal Historical Centre, Warracknabeal 001597
Warragul and District Historical Museum, Warragul 001598
Warrandyte Historical Museum, Warrandyte 001599
Warren, New York 132547
Warren, San Francisco 132916
Warren, Fizzy, Stockbridge 086714
Warren, F.J., Paris 133685
Warren, Jimmy, Littlebourne 085015, 130902
Warren, Joan, San Diego 119564
Warren, John F., Philadelphia 142753
Warren County Historical Society Museum, Lebanon 045224
Warren County Museum, Warren . . 048862
Warren Historical Museum, Warren 048856
Warren ICBM and Heritage Museum, Frances E. Warren Air Force Base 044025
Warren Rifles Confederate Museum, Front Royal 044090
Warren & Wignall, Leyland 122570
Warrender & Co, S., Sutton 086795, 131562
Warrens, Leiston 084966, 130883
Warrick County Museum, Boonville 042306
Warringah, Brookvale 094313
Warrington Museum and Art Gallery, Warrington 041303
Warrnambool Art Gallery, Warrnambool 001600
Warrumbungles, Coonabarabran . . 094430
Warsaw Historical Museum, Warsaw 048867
Warshaw, Karen, New York 091336
Warshaw, Karen, New York 091337
Warson Woods Antique Gallery, Saint Louis 092329
Warszawskie Centrum Numismatyczne, Warszawa 079791, 121914
Wartburg, Eisenach 016926
Wartel, Jean-Paul, Couterne 062536
Wartenberg, Bad Bellingen 101626
Warth, Willy von der, Krefeld 121488
Warther Museum, Dover 043495
Wartmann, Maya, Windisch 130218
Wartski, London 085779, 131206
Warumpi Arts, Alice Springs 055339
Warwick Antique Centre, Warwick .087048, 142141
Warwick Art Gallery, Warwick 095375
Warwick Castle, Warwick 041308
Warwick Doll Museum, Warwick . . 041309
Warwick Gallery, Beaconsfield 112592
Warwick Henderson, Auckland 108370
Warwick Leadlay, London 113954, 141917
Warwick Museum of Art, Warwick . 048872
Warwick Oakman, Newtown, Tasmania 056340
Warwick Regional Art Gallery, Warwick 001602
Warwick & Warwick, Warwick 122738
Warwickshire Museum, Warwick . . 041310
Warwickshire Museum of Rural Life, Moreton Morrell 040498
Warwickshire Yeomanry Museum, Warwick 041311
Waś, Andrzej, Kraków 129051
Was Designs, Tucson 120175
Wasa Antik, Stockholm 082038
Wasa Ramar, Göteborg 110934
Wasch-en Strijkmuseum, Boxtel . . . 029345
Waschhaus Potsdam, Potsdam 104635
Waschkau, R., Wolgast 074481

Waschkowitz, Christiane, Aschaffenburg 069201
De Wascht en Strekt, Gilze 029613
Wasco County Historical Museum, The Dalles 043282
Wascoe's Siding Antiques, Glenbrook 055886
Het Wase Pijprokerssalon, Sint-Niklaas 003756
Waseca County Historical Society Museum, Waseca 048874
Waseda Daigaku Tsubouchi Hakushi Kinen Engeki Hakubutsukan, Tokyo 027272
Washakie Museum, Worland 049313
Washburn, New York 118551
Washburn County Historical Society Museum, Shell Lake 048145
Washburn Historical Museum, Washburn 048876
Washington, Sherry, Detroit 116098
Washington Antiques Show, Washington 094039
Washington Area Lawyers Committee for the Arts, Washington 055096
Washington Art Association, Washington Depot 055097
Washington Art Dealers Association, Washington 055098
Washington Center for Photography, Washington 048956
Washington County Historical Association Museum, Fort Calhoun 043897
Washington County Historical Society Museum, Portland 047181
Washington County Historical Society Museum, Washington 048964
Washington County Historical Society Museum, Washington 048970
Washington County Historical Society Museum, West Bend 049063
Washington County Museum, Akron 041585
Washington County Museum, Sandersville 047926
Washington County Museum of Fine Arts, Hagerstown 044386
Washington Crossing Historic Park, Washington Crossing 048975
Washington Dolls House and Toy Museum, Washington 048957
Washington Framing and Art, Washington 120360
Washington Gallery, Penarth 114223
Washington Green, Newcastle-upon-Tyne 135285
Washington Green Fine Art Publishing, Birmingham 135122
Washington Historical Museum, Washington 048963
Washington International Arts Letter, Washington 136665
Washington Irving, New York 118552
Washington Museum, Washington . 048965
Washington Museum Association, Bellevue 055099
Washington National Cathedral, Cathedral Church of Saint Peter and Saint Paul, Washington 048958
Washington Old Hall, Washington . . 041314
Washington Pavillion of Arts and Science, Sioux Falls 048194
Washington Printmakers, Washington 055100
Washington Printmakers Gallery, Washington 120361
Washington Square Gallery, Philadelphia 091702
Washington Square Outdoor Art Exhibit, New York 118553
Washington State Capital Museum, Olympia 046673
Washington State Historical Society Museum, Tacoma 048471
Washington Studio School, Chevy Chase 051108
Washington University Gallery of Art, Saint Louis 047683
Washington Very Special Arts, Washington 055115
Washington's Headquarters, Newburgh 046438
Washington's Lands Museum and Sayre Log House, Ravenswood 047339
Wasilewski, Margarete, Bad Berleburg 069263
Waskada Museum, Waskada 006767
Wasmuth, Berlin 138856
Wasmuth, Ernst, Tübingen 134435
Wassenberg, Maria Helena, Chur . .082321, 130001
Wassenberg Art Center, Van Wert . . 048746
Wasser- und Fischkundemuseum, Wendorf bei Sternberg 020798
Wasserburg Haus Kemnade, Museum Bochum, Hattingen 017799
Wasserkraftmuseum, Vattenfall Europe Generation (VE-G), Ziegenrück . . . 021065
Wasserkraftmuseum Leitzachwerk, Feldkirchen-Westerham 017106
Wasserkunst von 1535, Bad Arolsen 015648
Wasserleitungsmuseum, Reichenau an der Rax 002511
Wasserleitungsmuseum, Wildalpen 003043
Wassermann, Gudrun, Schönkirchen 104837
Waßermann, Wolfgang, Feldkirchen-Westerham 102725
Waßermann, Wolfgang, München . . 104341
Wassermühle Höfgen, Grimma 017542
Wassermühle Kuchelmiß, Kuchelmiß 018429
Wasserschloß Mitwitz, Mitwitz 018964
Wassertor-Museum, Städt. Museen Isny, Isny 018097
Wasserwelt Erlebnismuseum, Ostseebad Binz 019530
Wassmuth, Agathe, Hann Münden . 103256
Wastlbauernhof, Siegsdorf 020205
Wastlmühle, Lainbach 002192
WaSu Galleries, Tucson 120176
Wasyl Negrych Pioneer Homestead, Gilbert Plains 005506
Waszkowiak, Christiane, Berlin . . . 102077
Wat Ko Museum, Phetchaburi 037921
Wat Phra Thart Lampang Luang Museum, Lampang 037905
Watabe, Sapporo 077204
Watanabe, Brooklyn 135339
Watanabe, S., Tokyo 107129
Watari-Um, Tokyo 027273
Watatu Gallery, Nairobi 107165
The Watch Doctor, Los Angeles . . .089936, 132284
Watch Out, Portland 092022
Watch This Space, Alice Springs . . 094148
Watchet Market House Museum, Watchet 041315
Watelet, Paris 066674
Water and Colors Gallery, Miami . . 117153
Water Gallery, Angono 108815
Water Gallery, Bourton-on-the-Water 112683
Water Meadow Barn Gallery, Isles-of-Scilly 113309
Water Mill Museum, Water Mill . . . 048978
Water Ski Hall of Fame, American Water Ski Educational Foundation, Polk City 047114
Water Supply Museum, Weymouth . 041359
Water Tower, Louisville 116971
Water Tower Museum, Gunnedah . . 001088
Waterbolk, Niek, Utrecht 140558
Waterbridge Gallery, Bacup 112536
Watercolor, New York 136666
Watercolor Art Society Houston, Houston 055101
Watercolor Gallery, Tucson 120177
Watercolor Magic, Cincinnati 136667
Watercolor Society of Alabama, Birmingham 055102
Watercolors Gallery, Pittsburgh . . . 118961
Watercolour Society of Queensland, West End 052500
Watercolour Society of Wales, Raglan 054540
The Watercolours & Drawings Fair, London 093956
Waterfall Antiques, Ross-on-Wye . . 086405
Waterfall's, Buffalo 131864
Waterford Gallery, Altrincham 112504
Waterford Historical Museum, Waterford 048981
Waterford Treasures at the Granary, Waterford 022872
Waterfront Antiques Market, Falmouth 084380
Waterfront Galerie, Gent 096306
Waterfront Gallery, Honolulu 116251
Waterfront Gallery, Westport 022873
Waterfront Museum, Poole 040742
Waterfront Museum and Showboat Barge, Brooklyn 042469
Watergate Antiques, Chester 083964
Watergate Gallery, Washington 120362
The Watergate Street Gallery, Chester 112854
Waterhouse & Dodd, London 085780, 113955, 131207
Waterhouse Gallery, Barton-under-Needwood 112563
Wateridge, Barry J., Hindhead 130795
Waterland Neeltje Jans, Vrouwenpolder 030297
Waterlane & Dorset, Salisbury 142046
Waterloo Area Farm Museum, Grass Lake 044294
Waterloo Center of the Arts, Waterloo 048987
The Waterloo Trading Company, London 085781
Waterman, Amsterdam 078019
Waterman, London 085782, 113956
Watermark, Cockermouth 112888
The Watermark, Preston 114289
Watermark Studio, Penrith 114226
Watermen's Museum, Yorktown 049353
Waters, Geoffrey, London 085783
Waters, W.W., Vancouver 097542
Waterside Antiques Centre, Ely 084329
Waterside Arts, Edinburgh 113012
Waterside Gallery, Bideford 112639
Waterside Gallery, Saint Mawes Truro 114383
Waterstone, Portland 119060
Watertown Historical Society Museum, Watertown 048991
The Watervliet Arsenal Museum, Watervliet 049001
Waterway Gallery, Armadale, Western Australia 094174
Waterways Museum, Goole 039604
Waterways Visitor Centre, Dublin . . 022774
Waterwheel Museum, Salisbury . . . 001455
Waterworks Museum - Hereford, Hereford 039739
Waterworks Visual Arts Center, Salisbury 047765
Wates, E. & A., London 131208
Watford Museum, Watford 041317
Watkins Bros., Denver 116068
Watkins, London 141918
Watkins, Chuck, Fort Worth 132075
Watkins, Islwyn, Knighton 084887
Watkins Community Museum of History, Lawrence 045208
Watkins Gallery, American University, Washington 048959
Watkins Institute Art Gallery, Nashville 046158
Watkins Museum, Taylorsville 048510
Watkins Woolen Mill, Lawson 045213
Watling, Bruce, Newstead 094953, 123278
Watling Antiques, Crayford 084106
Watling Street Galleries, Towcester 114596
Watson, Hamburg 071351
Watson, B., Johannesburg 110064
Watson, Barry, Christchurch 121820
Watson, G. & J., Turramurra 056746
Watson, G. & J., Williamstown 056822
Watson, Gordon, London 085784
Watson, Peter, Armadale, Victoria . . 055398
Watson and Son, Thomas, Darlington 122485
Watson Arts Centre, Watson 095381
Watson Crossley Community Museum, Grandview 005542
Watson-Curtze Mansion, Erie 043725
Watson Farm, Jamestown 044835
Watson Gallery, Norton 046561
Watson-Guptill, New York 135468
Watson Museum, Rajkot 022318
Watson & Vincent, Nelson 128947
Watsons Bay Art Gallery, Watsons Bay 095382
Watson's Creek Antiques, Kangaroo Ground 056031
Watson's Mill, Manotick 005828
Watt Space Gallery, Newcastle 094944
The Watteau Society, London 054541
The Watteau Society Bulletin, London 136279
Wattebled, Xavier, Lille 121036
Watten Cane Furniture, Singapore . 080587
Wattenbach, Philippsthal, Werra . . . 104607
Watterott, Gilbert, Leinefelde 126180
Watters, Frank, Sydney 095309
Watters Smith, Lost Creek 045478
Wattis, Hong Kong 097843
Wattlebark, Mogo 094867
Watts Gallery, Compton, Surrey . . . 039130
Watts Towers Arts Center, Los Angeles 045470
Watzke, Barbara, Aschaffenburg . . 069202
Watzl, Ludwigsburg, Württemberg . 072311
Watzlawik, S., Regensburg 104702
Wauchope District Historical Museum, Wauchope 001604
Wauconda Township Museum, Wauconda 049010
Waude, Ignaz, Korschenbroich 072061
Waukesha County Museum, Waukesha 049012
Wauman, Knokke-Heist 096362
Wave Gallery, Philadelphia 118851
Waveland Museum, Lexington 045267
Wavelength Gallery, Falmouth 113054
Waverley Antiques, Upper Largo . . . 086982
Waverley City Gallery, Wheelers Hill 001613
Waverly, Bethesda 122816, 142232
Waves, New York 091338
Wavriensia, Wavre 135611
Wavrin, Ludovic de, Paris 100966
Wawana, Maastricht 108136
Wawel Art, Kraków 108991
Wawota and District Museum, Wawota 006780
Wax Museum, Byblos 027817
Wax Museum, Dublin 022775
Wax Museum Český Krumlov, Muzeum Voskových Figurín České Historie, Český Krumlov 008324
Wax Museum Karlštejn, Muzeum Voskových Figurín České Historie, Karlštejn . 008429
Waxin, Marie-Thérèse, Roubaix . . . 067233
Way, R.E. & G.B., Newmarket 141956
Way, Richard, Henley-on-Thames . . 141660
Way We Wore, Houston 089248
Wayfarer, Launceston 141707
Wayfarer Books, Old Hall Bookshop, Looe 141925
Wayland, Washington 120363
Wayland Historical Museum, Wayland 049026
Wayne, Arthur, Winnipeg 097612
Wayne, Neil, Belper 083486
Wayne Art Center, Wayne 049033
Wayne Center for the Arts, Wooster 049303
Wayne County Historical Museum, Richmond 047401
Wayne County Historical Society Museum, Lyons 045536
Wayne County Historical Society Museum, Wooster 049304
Wayne County Museum, Honesdale 044590
Wayne State University Museum of Anthropology, Detroit 043457

Wayne State University Museum of Natural History, Detroit 043458
Wayne's World, Timaru 108585
Ways, Ryde 122673
Wayser, Saint-Ouen 101192
Wayside Antiques, Duffield 084224
Wayside Antiques, Tattershall 086826
Wayside Folk Museum, Zennor 041489
Wayside Shop, Oklahoma City 091545
Wayside Treasures, Philadelphia . . 091703
Wayville Latvian Museum, Brooklyn Park 000850
Waywood, Byron Bay 094339
Waywood Furniture, Wellington . . . 128981
Wazee Deco, Denver 088749
Wazzau, Iris, Davos Platz 111378
W.C. Handy Home Museum, Florence 043867
WCK Galleries, Taman Melawati . . . 107441
W.D.O. Gallery, Charlotte 115314
Weald and Downland Open Air Museum, Singleton 041031
Wear It Again Sam, San Diego 092696
Weardale Museum, Weardale 041319
Weasel Pop Studio, Saint Paul 119319
Weather Dicovery Center, North Conway 046523
Weatherell, Harrogate 084592
Weatherford, David, Seattle 093083
Weatherhill, Trumbull 135515
Weathersby, Virginia Beach 093370, 133018
Weatherspoon Art Museum, University of North Carolina at Greensboro, Greensboro 044338
Weaver, Blackheath 094259
Weaver, Tucson 132991
Weaver, Bernard, Cirencester 084024
Weaver, Trude, London 085785
Weaver Gallery, Chester 112855
Weaver Gallery, Nantwich 114109
Weaver Gallery, Northwich 114157
Weaver Neave & Daughter, London . 131209
Weaver's Cottage, Kilbarchan 039863
Weavers' Triangle Visitor Centre, Burnley 038910
Weaverville Joss House, Weaverville 049039
Web Fine Art, Basingstoke 112566
Webantik, Strasbourg 068335
Webb, Buffalo 087921
Webb, Winchester 087177
Webb, Winchester 114707
Webb, Winchester 131697
Webb, Dan F., Oakland 142713
Webb, Michael, Llangristiolus 085041
Webb, Roy, Wickham Market 087146
The Webb-Deane-Stevens Museum, Wethersfield 049128
Webb House Museum, Newark 046431
Webb's, Auckland 078995, 121815, 128914
Webbs Road Fine Art, London 113957
Weber, Baltimore 087722
Weber, Chicago 131921
Weber, Firenze 127428
Weber, Fort Worth 088892
Weber, Köln 072022
Weber, Saint Louis 092330
Weber, Viechtach 105117
Weber, Andrea, Dresden 070335
Weber, Carola, Wiesbaden 105283
Weber, Christian, Meißen 104055
Weber, Detlef, Merzig 072530
Weber, Dieter, Hamburg 071352
Weber, Edith, New York 091339
Weber, Eugen, Stuttgart 074014
Weber, Frank, Saarbrücken 073648
Weber, Friedhelm, Dortmund 070297
Weber, Günter, Bad Homburg v.d.Höhe 125102
Weber, Günter, Niedernhausen 126548
Weber, H., Lambrecht 072121
Weber, Hans, Holzkirchen, Oberbayern 125958
Weber, Helga Maria, Hamburg 125848
Weber, Jakob, Bad Tölz 101709
Weber, Jamileh, Zürich 112194
Weber, Jean, Wiltz 107418
Weber, Joachim, Stockdorf 073922
Weber, Josef, Mainz 104008, 134184
Weber, Karin, Hong Kong 097844
Weber, L., Badem 069407
Weber, L.& M., Erkerode 070594
Weber, M., Frei-Laubersheim 070812
Weber, Malavé von, Caracas 093546
Weber, Maria, München 134287
Weber, Michael, Friedrichshafen . . 102887
Weber, Michael, Guldental 071145
Weber, Michael, Poole 114274
Weber, Milada, Wimmelbach bei Forchheim 105305
Weber, Monika, Trier 126916
Weber, Peter, Köln 139355
Weber, Peter, Offenburg . . 073191, 104533
Weber, Peter, Trier 074100
Weber, Peter, Unterpleichfeld 126935
Weber, Thomas, Niederzissen 073055
Weber, W., Kaufungen, Hessen 071771
Weber, W. & E., Mannheim 072438
Weber, Wolfgang, Starnberg 104945
Weber-Kiffe, Fritz, Kleve 071882
Weber-Kiffe, Fritz, Wesel 074356
Weber-Schwenk, Petra, Castrop-Rauxel 102302
Weber State University Art Gallery, Ogden 046632
Weber & Weidemeyer, Kassel 134084
Weberei- und Heimatmuseum, Laichingen 018467
Weberei- und Heimatmuseum Ruedertal, Schmiedrued 037531
Webereimuseum, Breitenberg, Niederbayern 016403
Webereimuseum, Haslach 002024
Weberhaus Marlesreuth, Naila 019179
Weberhausmuseum, Schauenstein . 020007
Webermuseum, Heidenreichstein . . 002030
Weberstube Jonsdorf, Kurort Jonsdorf 018445
Webster, Fresno 088923
Webster, Leatherhead 113360
Webster, E.T., Blythburgh 083566
Webster & Co., G., Wellington 108650
Webster, Janice, Bacchus Marsh . . 094188
Webster, Sande, Philadelphia 118852
Webster County Historical Museum, Red Cloud 047353
Webster House Museum, Elkhorn . . 043666
Webtiques, Louisville 090044
Wechsler, Ruedi, Buochs 082282
Weckmans, G. & C., Bruxelles 058128
Weckström, Björn, Espoo 098712
Wed Galerie, Utrecht 108263
Wedde, Peter, Wellington 079357
Wedding, Jane, Råholt 079485
Wedding and Custom Museum, Kuah 027963
Wedel, Martina von, Hamburg 125849
Wedel, Martina von, Hamburg 125850
Weder, Johannes, Bayreuth 069497
Wedgewood Studio, Phoenix 132657
Wedgwood Museum, Stoke-on-Trent 041124
Wedler, J., Ganderkesee 070925
Wednesbury Museum and Art Gallery, Wednesbury 041320
Wee Jumble Shop, Sacramento . . . 092189
Weecke, B., Horn-Bad Meinberg . . 139280
Weedon, Mike, London 085786
Weedon Antiques, Weedon 087062
Weegmuseum de Oude Waag, Someren 030173
De Weegschaal, Bussum 078137
Weeks Air Museum, Miami 045819
The Weem, Pittenweem 114253
Weemaels, P. & M., Bruxelles 058129
Weems, Albuquerque 114832
Weems, Albuquerque 114833
Weems, Michael, Baltimore 115091
Weems-Botts Museum, Dumfries . . 043527
Frankie G. Weems Gallery & Rotunda Gallery, Meredith College, Raleigh 047318
Weenen Museum, Weenen 034774
Weeping Water Valley Historical Society Museum, Weeping Water 049043
Weerd, H. de, Ruinen 128825
Weerenbeck, Maastricht 078631
Weerheijm, H., Zaandam 078855
Weerts & Van Gijsel, Roermond . . . 078682
Weetslade Fine Art, Dudley 130657
Weg des Friedens, Purgstall an der Erlauf 002480
Wegendt, Ingrid, Bad Kleinkirchheim 056935
Wegener, Gitana, Burgdorf, Kreis Hannover 138957
Wegener, Lydia, Recklinghausen . . 104686
Weger, Ute & Klaus, Mühltal 104128
Wegiel, Michel, Villeurbanne 068984
Wegmachermuseum, Wasserburg am Inn 020688
Wegmann, L., Baden-Baden 069428
Wegner, Alfons, Rosenheim 104764
Wegner, Carl, Berlin 138857
Wegner, Josef, Köln 103735
Wegner, U., Schweinfurt 104863
Wehlburg, Quakenbrück 073391
Wehling & Fülscher, Hamburg 071353
Wehmeyer, Martina, Düsseldorf . . . 102570
Wehner, Gordon, Storkow, Mark . . . 073933
Wehr, K., Frechen 102849
Wehr, K., Pulheim 104644
Wehr, Rainer, Stuttgart 105023
Wehrens, Horst, Düsseldorf 070461
Wehrgeschichtliches Museum Rastatt, Rastatt 019719
Wehrlin-Bieli, Michaela, Liestal . . . 082579
Wehse, R., Münster 072931
Wei, Bruxelles 058130
Weichelt, Klaus, Großhartmannsdorf 071120
Weicheltmühle, Reichenau bei Dippoldiswalde 019774
Weichhart, Felicitas, Wien 057577
Weick, Werner, Düsseldorf 102571
Weick, Wilhelm, Berlin 069784
Weidenfeld & Nicolson, London . . . 135275
Weidenholzer, Erna, Andorf 095465
Weider, Auray 098878
Weider, Auray 098879
Weidle, Bonn 133831
Weidler, Herbert, Nürnberg 121567
Weidman, West Hollywood 120418
Weidmann Cottage Heritage Centre, Muswellbrook 001305
Weidner, Lisl, Kitzbühel . . 057100, 095608
Weies, Martin, Fröndenberg 125684
Weig, M., Kehl am Rhein 071776
Weigand, Heinz-Martin, Ettlingen . . 102715
Weigelt, Jörg, Hannover 121446
Weigl, Erwin, Nürnberg 104492
Weigl, Gitta, Maxhütte-Haidhof 104041
Weigt, Paul, Lübeck 072341
Weihermüller, C., Leverkusen 139411
Weihermüller-Curylo, C., Leverkusen 139412
Weihnachts-Sammlerbörse Zürich, Zürich 093896
Weihoek, de, Roosendaal 078691
Weijand, Karel, Farnham . 084391, 130706
Weijburg, H.A., Hilversum 078545
Weil, Alain, Paris 066675
Weil, Christiane, Mirepoix 064567
Weil, Claudia, Friedberg, Bayern . . . 102881
Weil, Pascal, Fegersheim 062851
Weil Antiquités, Montréal 059022
Weil Art Gallery, Corpus Christi 043166
Weiland, Dieter, Magdala 126250
Weiland, Gustav, Lübeck 139429
Weiland, Klaus, Limburg an der Lahn 072264
Weilandt, Dieter, Göttern 125738
Weilenmann & Co., Felix, Zürich . . . 083037
Weiler, Neukirchen-Vluyn 104410
Weiler, Prof. Dr. Dieter ter, Tegernsee 105037
Weilinger, Dr. Arthur, Salzburg 095738
Weill, Etienne, Bogny-sur-Meuse . . 061534
Lucie Weill & Seligmann - Charles Zoller, Paris 133686, 138564
Weiller, Paris 100967
Weiller, Patrick, Paris 100968
Weimann, Alexander, Weimar, Thüringen 126981
Weimer, Josef, Elz 125586
Wein, Eva, Berlin 125313
Wein- und Heimatmuseum, Durbach 016862
Weinbau-Museum, Chur 037022
Weinbau Museum, Neckermarkt . . 002354
Weinbau- und Heimatmuseum, Klingenberg am Main 018283
Weinbau- und Landwirtschaftsmuseum, Hadersdorf 002001
Weinbaumuseum, Flörsheim-Dalsheim 017134
Weinbaumuseum, Oetwil am See . . 037397
Weinbaumuseum, Reidling 002517
Weinbaumuseum Alte Kelter, Erlenbach, Kreis Heilbronn 017041
Weinbaumuseum am Zürichsee, Au, Zürich 036859
Weinbaumuseum der Winzergenossenschaft, Ortenberg, Baden 019483
Weinbaumuseum im Herrenhof, Neustadt an der Weinstraße 019287
Weinbaumuseum Jenins, Jenins . . 037205
Weinbaumuseum Meersburg, Meersburg 018876
Weinbaumuseum Stuttgart-Uhlbach, Stuttgart 020371
Weinbeer, K., Diebach 070243
Weinberg, Daniel, Los Angeles 116914
Weinberg, Dieter, Köln 072023
Weinberg, Lin, New York 091340
Weinberg Nature Center, Scarsdale 048039
Weinberger, København 098589
Weinbrenner, Ulrike, Stuttgart 126887
Weinek, Linz 137226
Weinek, Salzburg 137250
Weinel, Christel, Dormagen 121373
Weiner, Josef, München . . 072877, 121550
Weiner, Patricia, Cincinnati 115671
Weingärtner, Bad Wörishofen 069400
Weingärtner, Speyer 104937
Weingärtner, Harald, Speyer 073883
Weingart Galleries, Los Angeles . . . 045471
Weingartner, Dominik, Luzern 082640
Weingreen Museum of Biblical Antiquities, Dublin 022776
Weingutmuseum Hoflößnitz, Radebeul 019697
Weinheimer, Corinna, Trondheim . . 128996
Weinheimer Auktionshaus, Weinheim, Bergstraße 121621
Weinlandgalerie im Land um Laa an der Thaya, Wulzeshofen 095979
Weinlandmuseum, Asparn an der Zaya 001704
Weinmann, H.-J., Berlin 125314
Weinmann, Liz, Köln 103736
Weinmuseum, Güssing 001986
Weinmuseum, Vaihingen 020556
Weinmuseum Kitzeck, Kitzeck im Sausal 002135
Weinmuseum Prellenkirchen, Prellenkirchen 002467
Weinmuseum Schlagkamp-Desoye Senheim, Senheim 020191
Weinreiter, Erfurt 121395
Weinstadtmuseum Krems, Dominikanerkirche, Krems 002175
Weinstein, Minneapolis 117323
Weinstein, San Francisco 119831
Weinstein, Harvey, New York 091341
Weintraub, Michael, New York 142701
Weinviertler Museumsdorf, Niedersulz 002377

Weinviertler Naturmuseum, Jetzelsdorf 002103
Weinviertler Oldtimermuseum Poysdorf, Poysdorf 002457
Weinzierl, Paul, Moosthenning 126333
Weir, Gerald, Ipswich 130832
Weir Farm, Wilton 049224
Weir Gallery, Mundarin 094920
Weird Sisters, Minneapolis 117324
Weird Stuff, Carnegie 055638
Weird Stuff Antique, Kansas City . . 089530
Weis & Eckert, Tauberbischofsheim 074042
Weisberg, Emanuel, New York 091342
Weise, Gitte, Paddington 095045
Weise, H.-D., Weinheim, Bergstraße 074319
Weise, Regine & Bernd, Chemnitz . 102316
Weise, Uwe, Elmshorn 070547
Weisenberger, Thomas, Dinkelsbühl 102373
Weiser-Wehner, Hochstetten-Dhaun 071538
Weisert, Sascha, Düsseldorf 125555
Weisflog, Ursula, München 126481
Weisgerber, Andreas, Billerbeck . . . 125333
Weishäupl, München 139553
Weiß, Altenstadt, Iller 101568
Weiss, London 085787, 113958
Weiss, London 113959
Weiss, Wien 137374
Weiß, Witten 074456
Weiß, Annerose, Rodewisch 073552
Weiß, B., Eschelbronn 070610
Weiss, Barbara, Berlin 102078
Weiß, Brigitte, Gefrees 070945
Weiß, Brigitte, Münchberg 072624
Weiss, Brigitte, Zürich 112195
Weiß, Fritz, Rothenburg ob der Tauber 073595
Weiss, H., Köln 072024
Weiss, H., Mödling 095686, 133121
Weiss, Helga, Graz 057031
Weiß, Isolde, München 104342
Weiß, Jörg-Peter, Schleiden 126767
Weiß, Katharina, Hilden . . 103376, 125926
Weiss, L., Dettighofen 070233
Weiss, Lothar, Jestetten 071663
Weiss, Mike, New York 118554
Weiß, Peter, Rothenburg ob der Tauber 073596
Weiss, Sharon, Columbus 088447
Weiss, Wilhelm, Spittal an der Drau 095764
Weiß, Wolfgang & Maritta, Römerberg 073559
Weiss & Klebel, Bregenz 123343
Weiss-Weingart, Ebbe, Salem, Baden 104806
Weißenhorner Heimatmuseum, Weißenhorn 020785
Weißenrieder, Wiesbaden 074427
Weissenstein-Museum, Weissenstein bei Solothurn 037700
Weissert, Friedrich, Paris 138565
Weissert, Nikolaus, Tübingen 139801
Weißgerbermuseum, Doberlug-Kirchhain 016730
Weissing, Alsfeld 069142
Weisův Dům, Husitské Muzeum v Táboře, Veselí nad Lužnicí 008751
Weisz, Spencer, Chicago 115583
Weithauer, Gert, Bayreuth 101750
Weitz, Harold B., Pittsburgh 091872
Weitz, Pascal, Clamart 062319
Weitz & Coleman, New York 142702
Weitze, Heinrich, Weimar, Thüringen 126982
Weitze, Helmut, Hamburg 071354, 139221
Weitze, Wolfgang, Jena 139288
Weitzel, Regina 097184
Weitzel, Saskatoon 097203
Weixin Antique Store, Shanghai . . . 059773
Weixler, Charles, Louisville 132311
Weiyuan, Quanzhou 097899
Weizmann Archives and House, Rehovot 023056
Weka, Frankfurt am Main 070801
Welbourne House, Mitcham 056234
Welbry, Lemesos 098320
Welch, Barney K., Dallas 088621
Welch, K. & A., Warminster 087032
Welch, M.G., Taunton 086831, 131576
The Welch Regiment Museum (41st/ 69th Foot) of the Rpyal Regiment of Wales, Cardiff 038994
Welco International, Chennai 105643
Welcome Home Antiques, New York 091343
Weldon, Southport 086665, 131519
Weldon, J.W., Dublin 074955
Weldon, J.W., Dublin 074956
Welholme Galleries, Grimsby 039643
Welker, Karl & Karin, Homburg 125960
Welker, Rudolf & Erika, Dannstadt-Schauernheim 138972
Frank Welker & Heike Pfaff-Welker, Oberthal, Saar 073159
Welkom Museum, Welkom 034775
Well Art, Warszawa 109203
Well Cottage Antiques Centre, Princes Risborough 086315
Well-Dressed Wall, Milwaukee 117227
Well Federal Artist, Philadelphia . . . 118853
Well House Antiques, Tilston 086885
Well Hung, London 113960
Well Read Book Shop, Wellington . . 140686
Wella Museum, Darmstadt 016647
Wellage & Schaff, Cincinnati 115672
Welland Historical Museum, Welland 006782
Wellandgalerie, Aalen 101536
Wellbrook Beetling Mill, Cookstown 039139
Wellby, H.S., Haddenham, Buckinghamshire 084545, 130751
Wellcome Library for the History and Understanding of Medicine, London 040312
Wellcome Museum of Anatomy and Pathology, London 040313
Wellcome Museum of Medical Science, London 040312
Weller, Markus, Düsseldorf 070462
Weller, Sam, Salt Lake City 142877
Weller & Cwalinski, Houston 116426
Weller & Dufty, Birmingham 122417
Weller-Plate, Peter, Ockenheim . . . 126584
Wellerdiek, Juliane, Berlin 102079
Wellesbourne Wartime Museum, Wellesbourne 041323
Wellesley, New York 118555
Wellesley College Friends of Art Newsletter, Wellesley 136668
Wellesley Historical Society, Wellesley Hills 049047
Wellfleet Historical Society Museum, Wellfleet 049049
Wellford, Memphis 090111
Wellhausen, Houston 116427
Welling & Co., Kansas City 089531
Welling, Anthony, Ripley, Surrey . . . 086377
Wellingborough Heritage Centre, Wellingborough 041325
Wellings Landsbymuseum, Lintrup . 009012
Wellington Arch, London 040314
Wellington Arts Centre, Wellington . 030654
Wellington Aviation Museum, Moreton-in-Marsh 040497
Wellington B. Gray Gallery, Greenville 044345
Wellington Coin Club, Wellington . . 053930
Wellington Community Historical Museum, Wellington, Ontario 006783
Wellington County Museum, Fergus 005443
Wellington Courthouse Museum, Wellington 001606
Wellington Gallery, Hobart 094648
Wellington Gallery, Kilmarnock 113323
Wellington Gallery, London 085788, 131210
Wellington Museum, London 040077
Wellington Salerooms, Wellington . 122740
Wellington Sculpture Trust, Wellington 053931, 108651
Wellm, Horst, Pattensen 139650
Wellmann, E., Derschen 070219
Wellmer, Elisabeth-Christiane & Dietrich, Himbergen 125939
Wellmer, Elisabeth-Christiane & Dietrich, Westensee 127001
Wellnitz, Rudolf, Darmstadt 138977
Wells, Los Angeles 089937
Wells Antique Centre, Wells-next-the-Sea 087072
Wells Auction Rooms, Wells 122741
Wells Auto Museum, Wells 049052
Wells County Historical Museum, Bluffton 042277
Wells County Museum, Fessenden . 043840
Wells Fargo History Museum, Los Angeles 045472
Wells Fargo History Museum, Minneapolis 045923
Wells Fargo History Museum, Sacramento 047596
Wells Fargo History Museum, San Diego 047846
Wells Fargo History Museum, San Francisco 047890
Wells Fargo History Museum Old Sacramento, Sacramento 047597
Wells Museum, Wells 006786
Wells Museum, Wells 041326
Wells Walsingham Light Railway, Wells-next-the-Sea 041328
Welsch, Trier 074101
Welser Antiquitäten-, Sammler- und Nostalgiemesse, Wels 093591
Welser Puppenweltmuseum, Wels . 002832
Welsh, Jorge, Lisboa 080055
Welsh, Jorge, London . . . 085789, 131211
Welsh Art, Tywyn 086976
Welsh Highland Railway Museum, Porthmadog 040755
Welsh Slate Museum, Llanberis . . . 040046
Welshpool and Llanfair Light Railway, Llanfair Caereinion 040058
Weltbild Bechtermünz, Augsburg . . 133727
Welter, Gert, Lauenförde 072166
Welters, Fons, Amsterdam 107832
Welti, Rolf, Zürich 112196
Weltkulturerbe Völklinger Hütte, Europäisches Zentrum für Kunst und Industriekultur, Völklingen 020604
Weltkunst, München 135828
Weltkunst Verlag, München 134288
Weltwoche-ABC-Verlag, Zürich . . . 135106
Welvaars, Holman, Antwerpen 057752
Welvaars, Odette, Amsterdam 078020
Welwert, Christine, Kitzbühel 057101
Welwyn Roman Baths Museum, Welwyn 041332
Welz, Salzburg . . . 095739, 133152, 137251
Welz, F., Heidelberg 139255
H. Welzer & S. Czichi, Hannover . . . 103300
Wemaere, Bertrand, Versailles 068823
Wemaere, Frederic, Verneuil-sur-Avre 068783
Wemken, Bad Zwischenahn 069404
Wen Bao Zhai Art Shop, Shanghai . 097953
Wen Baozhai, Xian 098053
Wen-Kai, Taipei 133396
Wen Tianxiang Temple, Beijing 007013
Wenatchee Valley Museum, North Central Washington Museum, Wenatchee 049058
Wenceslao Vinzons Historical Landmark Museum, Vinzons 031810
Wende, Düsseldorf 070463
Wendel, Georg, Frankfurt am Main . 070802
Wendelin-Briner, Basel 082181
Wendell Gilley Museum, Southwest Harbor 048259
Wenderoth, Georg, Kassel 134085
Wendezeit, Berndorf 095476
Wending, Amsterdam 078021
De Wending, Delft 078155
Wendl, Martin, Rudolstadt 073615
Wendl, Martin, Rudolstadt 121591
Wendland, Holger R., Dresden 102461, 133881
Wendler, Jörg, Merchweiler 072520
Wendouree, Ballarat 136791
Wendover Antique Centre, Wendover 087077, 131661
Wendrich, Ursula (04632) 7533, Steinbergkirche 104948
Wendt, Leipzig 072218
Wendt, G., Meine 072496
Wendt, J., Berlin 138858
Wendys Portraits, Hazel Grove 113217
Wengenroth, Ute, Montabaur 104119
Wenger, Brigitte, Steinenbronn 104949
Wenham Museum, Wenham 049059
Wening, P.B.J., Groningen 128681
Weninger, Erich, Wien 057578
Wenk, Neckargemünd 126519
Wenk, Heinz, Dortmund 102416
Wenke, Christfried, Tübingen 074119, 126921
Wenke, Wolfgang, Eisenach 125580
Wenling, Quanzhou 097900
Wenlock Fine Art, Much Wenlock . .114098, 131289
Wenmeizhai, Tianjin 098018
Wenmiao Museum, Tianjin 007290
Wennekes & Zoon, J., Den Haag . . 140406
Wenner, H.Th., Osnabrück 121572, 139641
Wenping, Qingdao 097897
Wenping, Qingdao 097898
Wenske & Jehmlich, Potsdam 126660
Wensley, Ramsbottom 114294
Wensleydale Galleries, Northallerton 114151
Wenten, Heinz, Xanten 074556
Wentholt, Leiden 078590
Wentscher, Jürgen, Meckenheim, Rheinland 126298
Wentworth, Atlanta 114943
Wentworth, Boston 115240
Wentworth, Charlotte 115315
Wentworth, Columbus 115809
Wentworth, Las Vegas 116657
Wentworth, Los Angeles 116915
Wentworth, Miami 117154
Wentworth, Miami 117155
Wentworth, Saint Louis 119266
Wentworth-Coolidge Mansion, Portsmouth 047192
Wentworth Galleries, Waterloo 095380
Wentworth Gardner and Tobias Lear Houses, Portsmouth 047193
Wenz, Ginsheim-Gustavsburg 071000, 121417
Wenz, Renate, Mainz 072406
Wenz, Wolfgang, Berlin 069785
Wenzel, München 072878, 126482
Wenzel, Zürich 083038, 130270
Wenzel, D., Eichholz 070520
Wenzel, Dorothea, Werther 105221
Wenzel, Frauke, Borken, Westfalen 125368
Wenzel, Gabriele, München 072879
Wenzel, Heinz, Niederaula 073051
Wenzel, M., Bamberg 069466
Wenzel, S., Usedom 074170
Wenzel Abu, Ulrike, Frankfurt am Main 125666
Wenzel-Hablik-Museum, Itzehoe . . 018100
Wenzel-Schütz, Ulrike, Nassau, Lahn 104389
Weoley Castle, Birmingham 038741
Wepf & Co., Basel 141220
Werbe Design Akademie, Innsbruck 049632
Werberger Stuben, Motten 019003
Werdenfelser Museum, Garmisch-Partenkirchen 017328
Werder, A., Zürich 112197
Wereld Bodem Museum, International Soil Reference and Information Centre, Wageningen 030305
Wereldgalerie, Maastricht 108137
Wereldmuseum Rotterdam, Rotterdam 030108
Werk Art-Galerie, Köln 103737
WerkART, Sankt Gallen 111877
Werkbund-Galerie und Art-Office, Graz 095548
Werkgalerie am Läuferplatz, Bern . 111280

Werkhof Bistrica, Sankt Michael . . . 002604
Werkladen, Aachen 125044
Werkladen, Singen, Hohentwiel . . . 073831
Werkmann, Olomouc 123966
Werksmuseum Achse, Rad und Wagen, Wiehl 020856
Werksmuseum der Amazonen-Werke, Gaste 017331
Werksmuseum der Firma Linke-Hofmann-Busch, Salzgitter 019972
Werksmuseum der MTU, München . 019129
Werksmuseum der Waechtersbacher Keramik, Brachttal 016355
Werksmuseum Koenig & Bauer AG, Würzburg 021010
Werkspoor Museum, Amsterdam . . 029242
Die Werkstatt, Essen 070653
Die Werkstatt, Rotenhahn 073585
Werkstatt 52, Karlsruhe 126010
Werkstatt Bleichhäuschen, Rheda-Wiedenbrück 104744
Werkstatt für Kunst, Bonn 069949
Werkstatt Kollerschlag, Kollerschlag 095628
Werkstattgalerie Uranus, Ellenberg . 102612
Werkstattpresse, Wien 133239
Werkzeugmuseum Zur Eisenbahn, Ermatingen 037072
Werle, Andreas, Eppelheim 070577
Wern Mill Gallery, Nannerch 114107
Werner, São Paulo 058749
Werner, Wiesbaden 074428
Werner, Wildhagen 074439
Werner, Helmut, Bergholz-Rehbrücke 125156
Werner, I., Weimar, Thüringen 139837
Werner, L., München 139554
Werner, L., München 139555
Werner, Michael, Köln 103738
Werner, Michael, New York 118556
Werner, P., Heide, Holstein 071442
Werner, Peder, Stockholm 129881
Werner, Pia Anna, Kalbach 125988
Werner, Ralf & Margit, Radolfzell . .073403, 126674
Werner, Th., Gladbeck 071003
Werner, Walter, Oberursel 073167
Werner, Wolfgang, Berlin . 069786, 102080
Werner, Wolfgang, Bremen 102257
Werner-Berg-Galerie der Stadt Bleiburg, Bleiburg 001756
Werner-Egk-Begegnungsstätte, Donauwörth 016746
Wernersche Verlagsgesellschaft, Worms 134465
Wernher Collection at Ranger's House, London 040315
Wernigeröder Kunst- und Kulturverein e.V., Wernigerode 053646, 105219
Wernz, U. & G., Tuttlingen 105081
Werra-Kalibergbau-Museum, Heringen, Werra 017886
Werribee and District Historical Museum, Werribee 001608
Wersching, J., Elchingen 070537
Werstener Kreuz, Düsseldorf 102572
Werth, Dr. Wolfgang, Düsseldorf . . . 102573
Wertheimers, New York 091344
Werthmüller, Lucius, Basel 141221
Wertpapier-Museum, Zürich 037809
Wertz Bros., Los Angeles 089938
Wertz Bros., Los Angeles 089939
De Wervel, Dordrecht 078324
Werwein, Erich, Neunkirchen am Brand 126536
Werz, Bernd, Ludwigshafen am Rhein 126237
Werz, J., Bolsward 128595
Weschler & Son, Adam A., Washington 093442, 123138
Wescott's Station Antiques, Saint Paul 092406
Wesemeyer, A., Köln 072025
Wesendonk, Marie-Rose von, München 126483
Weskamp, Stephan, Höxter 071544, 103389
Weslaco Bicultural Museum, Weslaco 049060
Wesley's House and Museum, London 040316
Wesner, Konstanz 072051, 103769
Wesner, Klaus, Berlin 102081
Weßel, C., Hamburg 125851
Weßel, Klaus, Hamburg 103228
Wesselhoefft, A., Burgdorf, Kreis Hannover 070098
Wesselstuerne, København 008992
Wessendorf, G., Kaarst 071679
Wessex, Wareham 114645
Wessex Antiques, Sherborne 086585, 131488
Wessling, Robert, Berlin 069787
Wessling, Robert, Berlin 125315
Weßolowski, Oberhausen, Rheinland 126576
West, Brian, Sandgate 086514
West, John T., Portland 092023
West, J.R., Vancouver 123859
West, Mark J., London 085790
West, Seb, Saint Ives, Cornwall . . . 114376
West 10 Frame, Vancouver 097543
West Allis Historical Society Museum, West Allis 049061
West Antic, Brest 061782
West Antique, Oslo 079481
West-Art, Clarence 135352
West Baton Rouge Museum, Port Allen 047123
West Bend Art Museum, West Bend 049064
West Bengal State Akademie of Dance, Drama, Music and Visual Arts, Rabindra Bharati University, Kolkata 050313
West Berkshire Museum, Newbury . 040542
West Blatchington Windmill, Hove . 039778
West Burton Antiques, Los Angeles 089940
West Chicago City Museum, West Chicago 049070
West Coast Antiques, Portland 092024
West Coast Gallery, Osborne Park . 095010
West Coast Historical Museum, Hokitika 030517
West Coast Maritime Museum, Tofino 006575
West Coast Museum of Flying, Sidney 006471
West Coast Peddler, Whittier 136669
West Coast Pioneer's Memorial Museum, Zeehan 001652
West Cork Model Railway Village, Clonakilty 022712
West Cork Regional Museum, Clonakilty 022713
West Country Pictures, South Molton 114452
West End Antiques, Elgin 084324
West End Antiques, Leicester 084952
West End Antiques, Saint Louis . . . 092331
West End Antiques Mall, Richmond 092119
West End Exchange, Edmonton . . . 058844
West End Galleries, Buxton 083831
West End Gallery, Edmonton 005414
West End Gallery, Edmonton 096906
West End Gallery, Miami 117156
West End Gallery, Milwaukee 117228
West End Gallery, Richmond 119130
West End Gallery, Wirksworth 114713
West End Trading, Lisboa 109360
West Essex Antiques, Matching Green 085961
West Expansion, Casablanca 107557
West Gallery, Quezon City 108858
West Gallery @ Art Center, Mandaluyong 108839
West Gate Towers, Canterbury 038984
West Highland Museum, Fort William 039520
West Hoe Auctions, Fareham 122509
West Kilbride Museum, West Kilbride 041339
West London Antiques and Fine Art Fair, London 093957
West Los Angeles Book Center, Los Angeles 142522
West Louisville Antiques, Louisville 090045
West Midlands Arts Board, Birmingham 054542
West Midlands Police Museum, Birmingham 038742
West Neuk Gallery, Forfar 113073
West of the Pecos Museum, Pecos . 046856
West Overton Museums, Scottdale . 048057
West Palm Beach Antique and Collectables Show, West Palm Beach 094040
West Park Museum and Art Gallery, Macclesfield 040379
West Parry Sound District Museum, Parry Sound 006117
West Pasco Historical Society Museum, New Port Richey 046271
West Point, Den Haag 078268
West Point Lighthouse Museum, O'Leary 006071
West Point Museum, West Point . . . 049096
West Port Books, Edinburgh 141591
West Portal Books, San Francisco . 142968
West River Museum, Philip 046999
West Rock Antiques, Warwick 087049, 131653
West Sea Company Nautical Antiques, San Diego 092697
West Sølv og Mynt, Oslo . 079482, 121874
West Somerset Railway, Minehead . 040476
West Somerset Rural Life Museum, Allerford 038485
West Southwest Gallery, Denver . . . 116069
West Stow Anglo-Saxon Centre, Bury Saint Edmunds 038927
West Street Antiques, Dorking 084208
West Street Gallery, Crewkerne . . . 112921
The West Suffolk Decorative and Fine Art Society, Bury Saint Edmunds 054543
West Surrey Decorative and Fine Arts Society, Godalming 054544
West Texas Connection, Austin 087622
West Torrens Railway, Signal Telegraph and Aviation Museum, Brooklyn Park . 000851
West Valley Art Museum, Sun Cities Museum of Art, Surprise 048440
West Vancouver Museum, West Vancouver 006795
West Virginia Independence Hall, Wheeling 049141
West Virginia Northern Community College Alumni Association Museum, Wheeling 049142
West Virginia State Farm Museum, Point Pleasant 047113
West Virginia State Museum, Charleston 042749
West Virginia University Mesaros Galleries, Morgantown 046028
West Wales Antiques, Murton 086031
West Wales Arts Centre, Fishguard . 039503
West Wycombe Motor Museum, West Wycombe 041343
West Wycombe Park House, West Wycombe 041344
Westallgäuer Heimatmuseum, Weiler-Simmerberg 020729
WestArt, Auburn 136670
Westbeth, New York 118557
Westbury Antiques, Melbourne 056206
Westbury Manor Museum, Fareham 039484
Westchester Art Workshop, White Plains 052365
Westchester Books, Miami 142561
Westcliff Picture Gallery, Westcliff-on-Sea 114673
Westcliffe Gallery, Sheringham 086591, 131491
Westcott, Montréal 137667
Westcott Gallery, Dorking . 084209, 112956
Westdale Bookworm, Hamilton 137644
Westdale Gallery On Augusta, Hamilton 096927
Westdeutsche Kunst Messe Köln, Köln 093747
Westdeutsche Kunst- und Antiquitätenausstellung, Dortmund 093748
Westdeutscher Künstlerbund, Bochum 053647
Westelynck, Serge, Flêtre 062874
Westenburger, Gisela, Wiesbaden . . 105284
Westend Antik, Stuttgart 074015
Westende Gemtime, Christchurch . 079065
Westendgalerie, Berlin 102082
Westendorp, C.J., Meppel 128772
Westenhoff, Klauspeter, Hamburg . . 103229
Westenholz, London 085791
Wester, Rathjensdorf 126679
Westerberg, Stockholm 082039
Westerham Antiques Warehouse, Westerham 087102
Westerham House Antiques, Westerham 087103
Westerhaus, Michael, Wuppertal . . 127053
Westerhof, J.B., Burgwerd 078123, 121784
Westermeier, Sebastian, Hausham . 125887
Western, C., Karlsruhe 139301
Western Aerospace Museum, Oakland 046601
Western Approaches, Liverpool . . . 040042
Western Archeological and Conservation Center, Tucson 048646
Western Art Association, Ellensburg 055103
Western Art Gallery and Museum, The University of Montana, Dillon 043471
Western Association for Art Conservation, Oakland 055104
Western Australian Maritime Museum, Fremantle 001043
Western Australian Medical Museum, Subiaco 001498
Western Australian Museum, Perth . 001377
Western Australian Museum Geraldton, Geraldton 001054
Western Canada Aviation Museum, Winnipeg 006872
Western Center for Conservation of Fine Arts, Denver 132046
Western Coin, San Diego 092698
Western Collectables, Killarney Vale 056052
Western Colorado Center for the Arts, Grand Junction 044268
Western Connecticut-Western Massachusetts, Rhinebeck 136671
Western Development Museum, Saskatoon 006429
Western Gallery, Western Washington University, Bellingham 042120
Western Hennepin County Pioneers Museum, Long Lake 045394
Western Heritage Center, Billings . . 042208
Western Heritage Gallery, Albuquerque 087433
Western Hotel Museum, Lancaster . 045137
Western Illinois University Art Gallery, Macomb 045564
Western Jewelry and Coin Exchange, Seattle 093084
Western Kentucky University Gallery, Bowling Green 042369
Western Life Gallery, San Francisco 119832
Western Museum, Abilene 041566
Western Museum of Mining and Industry, Colorado Springs 043061
Western Museums Association, Oakland 055105
Western New Mexico University Museum, Silver City 048177
Western New York Artists Group, Buffalo 055106, 115269
The Western Railway Museum, Suisun City 048418
Western Ranger, Bridgnorth 112705
Western Reserve Historical Society Museum, Cleveland 043004
Western Rhode Island Civic Museum, Coventry 043197
Western Springs Museum, Western Springs 049106
Western States Arts Federation, Denver 055107

Westerwolds Crashmuseum, Oude Pekela . . . 030024
Westfälisch-Niederländisches Imkereimuseum, Museen der Stadt Gescher, Gescher . . . 017396
Westfälische Münz- und Sammlerbörse, Dortmund . . . 093749
Westfälischer Künstlerbund Dortmund e.V., Herdecke . . . 053648
Westfälischer Kunstverein, Münster 019155, 053649
Westfälisches Feldbahnmuseum, Lengerich, Westfalen . . . 018613
Westfälisches Freilichtmuseum Detmold, Landesmuseum für Volkskunde, Detmold . . . 016691
Westfälisches Freilichtmuseum Hagen, Landesmuseum für Handwerk und Technik, Hagen, Westfalen . . . 017628
Westfälisches Glockenmuseum, Museen der Stadt Gescher, Gescher . . . 017397
Westfälisches Industriemuseum, Altes Schiffshebewerk Henrichenburg, Waltrop . . . 020666
Westfälisches Industriemuseum, Glashütte Gernheim, Petershagen, Weser . . 019594
Westfälisches Industriemuseum, Henrichshütte Hattingen, Hattingen . . . 017800
Westfälisches Industriemuseum, Landesmuseum für Industriekultur, Dortmund . . . 016771
Westfälisches Industriemuseum, Zeche Hannover, Bochum . . . 016285
Westfälisches Industriemuseum, Textilmuseum, Bocholt . . . 016274
Westfälisches Landesmuseum für Kunst und Kulturgeschichte Münster, Münster . . . 019156
Westfälisches Museum für Archäologie, Herne . . . 017894
Westfälisches Museum für Naturkunde, Landesmuseum und Planetarium, Münster . . . 019157
Westfälisches Römermuseum, Haltern . . . 017678
Westfälisches Schulmuseum, Dortmund . . . 016772
Westfalen Verlag, Bielefeld . . . 133825
Westfalia-Auto-Museum, Rheda-Wiedenbrück . . . 019818
Westfield Heritage Village, Rockton 006301
Westfries Museum, Hoorn . . . 029775
Westgate Books, Saskatoon . . . 137686
Westgate Gallery, North Berwick . . 114147
Westgate Museum, Winchester . . . 041408
Westhorpe Antiques, Southwell . . .086667, 131520
Westhues, W., Ahlen . . . 069117
Westin, Frösön . . . 122137
Westlake Gallery, Seattle . . . 120011
Westland & Co, London . . . 085792
Westlands Museum voor Streek- en Tuinbouwhistorie, Honselersdijk . 029764
WestLicht, Wien . . . 095957
Westman y Muñoz, Santiago de Chile . . . 059559
Westmansmors stugan, Jakobstad . 009617
Westmeyer, Angelika, Essen . . . 070654
Westminster Abbey Museum, London . . . 040317
Westminster College Art Gallery, New Wilmington . . . 046277
Westminster Dragoons Museum, London . . . 040318
Westminster Historical Society Museum, Westminster . . . 049118
Westminster Mint, Minneapolis . . . 090405
Westmoreland Museum of American Art, Greensburg . . . 044340
Westmoreland Sanctuary, Bedford Corners . . . 042101
Westmorland Clocks, Kendal . . . 084830
Weston, William, London . 085793, 113961
Weston Antiques, Weston . 087104, 131672
Weston Art Gallery, Cincinnati . . . 115673
Weston Park, Weston-under-Lizard 041351
Westonzoyland Pumping Station Museum, Bridgwater . . . 038834
Westover Antique Gallery, Saint Louis . . . 092332
Westover House, Charles City . . . 042721
Westpac Gallery, Victorian Arts Centre, Melbourne . . . 001237
Westpac Museum, Sydney . . . 001529
Westphal, Berlin . . . 102083
Westphal, Paderborn . . . 104576
Westphal, Herbert, Horn-Bad Meinberg . . . 125964
Westphal, M., Appenheim . . . 069178
Westphal, Martin, Ingelheim am Rhein . . . 071623
Westphal, Volker, Berlin . . 069788, 102084
Westphalsches Haus, Markkleeberg 018836
Westport Bookstore, Kansas City . . 142479
Westport Gallery, Dundee . 084230, 130658
Westport Historical Museum, Westport . . . 049126
Westport House, Westport . . . 022874
Westport Maritime Museum, Westport . . . 049127
Westpreussisches Landesmuseum, Münster . . . 019158
Westra, Irene, Groningen . . . 078438
Westrope, I., Birdbrook . . . 083522
Westsächsisches Textilmuseum Crimmitschau, Crimmitschau . . . 016607
Westside Antique Mall, El Paso . . . 088821
Westside Books, Denver . . . 142398
Westside Frames & Art Gallery, Clondalkin . . . 105852
Westside Moods, Los Angeles . . . 089941
Westville Historic Handicrafts Museum, Lumpkin . . . 045522
Westville House Antiques, Littleton, Somerset . . . 085019
Westwallmuseum Gerstfeldhöhe, Pirmasens . . . 019624
Westway Pine, Helmsley . . . 084645
Westwind Art Editions, Edmonton . . 096907
Westwind Art Editions, Edmonton . . 133313
Westwind (Los Angeles), Los Angeles . . . 136672
Westwood, New York . . . 118558
Westwood, A., Cincinnati . 088294, 122861
Westwood, Mark, Hay-on-Wye . . . 141654
Westwood House Antiques, Tetbury 086871
Westwords, Greenock . . . 141637
Westwords, Plymouth . . . 136280
Westzaanse Bodemvondsten Kok-Voogt, Westzaan . . . 030328
Weswal, Tamworth . . . 095316
Weta Design, Waikato . . . 108599
Wetaskiwin and District Museum, Wetaskiwin . . . 006800
Wetering, Amsterdam . . . 107833
Weth, R., Würzburg . . . 127044
Wethersfield Museum, Wethersfield 049129
Wetsfälisches Industriemuseum Zeche Nachtigall, Witten . . . 020926
Wetter, F., Wachtberg . . . 074233
Wetterau-Museum, Friedberg, Hessen . . . 017262
Wettergrens Bokhandel, Göteborg . 141111
Wetterling, Stockholm . . . 111083
Wetterling, Theo, Singapore . . . 109894
Wetterwald & Rannou-Cassegrain, Nice . . . 121096
Wettstein, Dierks, Düsseldorf . . . 070464
Wettstein, Karl-Heinz, Weingarten, Württemberg . . . 074315
Wetz Museum, Uffikon . . . 037649
Wetzel, Christian, Erfurt . . . 070591
Wetzel, Hannelore, Kassel . . . 071766
Weuffen, P., Vechta . . . 074184
Wever, Peter, Berlin . . . 133816
Wever Van Wijnen, Franeker . . . 140423
Weverijmuseum, Geldrop . . . 029598
Wewerka, M. J., Berlin . . . 102085, 133817
Wexford Arts Centre, Wexford . . . 022877
Wexford County Historical Museum, Cadillac . . . 042541
Wexford County Museum, Enniscorthy . . . 022786
Wexler, Philadelphia . . . 118854
Wexner Center for the Arts, Columbus . . . 043112
Wey & Co., Luzern . . . 082641
Weyers-Sampson Art Gallery, Greenville . . . 044347
Weygang-Museum, Öhringen . . . 019440
Weyhe, E., New York . . . 118559
Weymouth Museum, Timewalk and Brewery Museum, Weymouth . . . 041360
Weymouth Woods-Sandhills Nature Preserve Museum, Southern Pines . . . 048256
Weyrauch, I., Frei-Laubersheim . . . 070813
Weyrich, Albuquerque . . . 114834
Weyrich, A., Halle, Saale . . . 103078
Weyrich, J., Graal-Müritz . . . 071071
Weywoda, Manfred, Wien . 057579, 120696, 137375
WG Expozaal, Amsterdam . . . 107834
W.G.B. Antiquitäten, Witzhave . . . 074459
W.H. Over Museum, Vermillion . . . 048765
W.H. Smith Museum, Newtown, Powys . . . 040584
The W.H. Stark House, Orange . . . 046704
Whakatane District Museum and Gallery, Whakatane . . . 030656
Whale Bone Gallery, Port Fairy . . . 095091
Whale Museum, Friday Harbor . . . 044085
Whales Tale Antiques, Napier . . . 079171
Whalesong Digital Arts, Honolulu . . 116252
Whaleworld Museum, Albany . . . 000726
Whaley Thorns Heritage Centre and Museum, Whaley Thorns . . . 041361
Whanau Gallery, Wellington . . . 108652
Whanganui Arts Trust, Wanganui . . 053932
Whanganui Regional Museum, Wanganui . . . 030627
Whanganui Riverboat Centre Museum, Wanganui . . . 030628
Whangarei Art Museum, Te Wharetaonga o Whangarei, Whangarei . . . 030658
Whangarei Museum, Whangarei . . . 030659
Whangaroa County Museum, Kaeo . 030525
Whanki Museum, Seoul . . . 027615
Whariti Antiques, Woodville . . . 079366
Wharton, Charlotte . . . 115316
Wharton, Tim, Redbourn . . . 086339
Wharton County Historical Museum, Wharton . . . 049132
Wharton Esherick Museum, Malvern . . . 045609
What Cheer Antiques, Providence . . 092052
What Mama Had, San Diego . . . 092699
What Now Antiques, Buxton . . . 083832
Whatcom Museum of History and Art, Bellingham . . . 042121
Whately, Rollo, London . . . 085794, 131212
Whatnots, Strathblane . . . 086779
What's Art Gallery, Sendai . . . 107006
Whats in Store, Los Angeles . . . 089942
Whay, Kevin, Hoylake . . . 084746, 130811
Wheal Martyn Cornwall's Museum of the Clay, Saint Austell . . . 040902
Wheat Ridge Sod House Museum, Wheat Ridge . . . 049133
Wheatcroft & Son, Noel, Matlock . . 122616
Wheatleys, Great Yarmouth . . . 084530
Wheaton History Center, Wheaton . 049138
Wheatsheaf Antiques, Chester . . . 083965
Wheel a Deal, Regina . . . 059094
Wheeler, Providence . . . 119091
Wheeler, Genevieve E., New York . . 091345
Wheeler, Jack & Kate, Austin . . . 087623
Wheeler, Simon, Midhurst . . . 141945
Wheeler Gallery, Providence . . . 047266
Wheeler Historic Farm, Salt Lake City . . . 047780
Wheels, Parramatta . . . 137045
Wheels O' Time Museum, Peoria . . 046882
Wheelwright Museum of the American Indian, Santa Fe . . . 047980
Where Art Is At, Armadale, Victoria . 094173
Where On Earth Did You Get That, Calgary . . . 058813
Whetung Craft Centre and Art Gallery, Curve Lake . . . 005318
Whichcraft Jewellery, Writtle 087271, 131720
Whiddons Antiques and Tearooms, Chagford . . . 083903
Whillock, David, San Francisco . . . 132917
Whillock, F., Litton Cheney . . . 141736
Whim Antiques, Toronto . . . 059316
Whimsey Shoppe, Dallas . . . 088622
Whimsey Shoppe, Dallas . . . 088623
Whimsical Notions, Warrimoo . . . 056803
Whimsy Antiques, Toronto . . . 059317
Whipple House Museum, Ashland . . 041808
Whipple Museum of the History of Science, Cambridge . . . 038973
Whippoorwill, Atlanta . . . 087542, 131789
Whirligig, Chicago . . . 088193
Whisnant, New Orleans . . . 090638
Whisnant, New Orleans . . . 090639
Whisson, Kallangur . . . 094677
Whistle Stop Treasure Shop, Birmingham . . . 087787
Whistler, Barry, Dallas . . . 115954
Whistler House Museum of Art, Lowell Art Association, Lowell . . . 045510
Whitaker, Charles A., Philadelphia . 123050
Whitaker Center for Science and the Arts, Harrisburg . . . 044446
Whitbourne Museum, Whitbourne . . 006805
Whitburn Community Museum, Whitburn . . . 041363
Whitby Abbey Museum, Whitby . . . 041367
Whitby Museum, Whitby . . . 041368
Whitchurch Silk Mill, Whitchurch, Hampshire . . . 041369
Whitchurch-Stouffville Museum, Gormley . . . 005523
White, Albert, Toronto . . . 097396
White, Charlie, Portland . . . 119061
White, Christopher, Uttoxeter 086991, 131633
White, David N., Wellington 079358, 108653
White, E. & B., Brighton . . . 083719
White, Frank, Cincinnati . . . 115674
White, Gordon, Hyde Park . . . 056010
White, Harlan, San Diego . . . 092700
White, Joan & David, Barnard Castle . . . 083392
White, Joan & David, Manfield . . . 085920
White, M. & M., Reigate . . . 086348
White, Marcie, San Francisco . . . 119833
White, Wilford, Oklahoma City . . . 123032
White Cat Book Company, Saskatoon . . . 137687
White & Co, Madrid . . . 110628
White Cockade Publishing, Oxford . 135294
White Columns, New York . . . 118560
White County Historical Museums, Ratcliff Inn, L.Haas Store, Matsel Cabin, Robinson-Stewart House, Carmi . 042628
White County Historical Society Museum, Cleveland . . . 042980
White County Historical Society Museum, Monticello . . . 046002
White Crane Gallery, Omaha . . . 118725
White Cube, London . . . 113962
White Dacha, Minsk . . . 096045
White & Day, Houston . . . 089249
White Deer Land Museum, Pampa . 046806
White Dove Art Gallery, Albuquerque . . . 087434
White Dragon Collectibles, Jacksonville . . . 089474
White Elephant Antiques, Dallas . . . 088624
White Fox Museum, White Fox . . . 006807
White Gallery, Portland . . . 047182
The White Gallery, Wincanton . . . 114702
White Gloves Art, Clayfield . . . 094403
White Hall Historic Site, Richmond . 047403
White Harvest Fine Art, Holden Hill . 094650
White Hill Gallery, Red Hill . . . 095120
White Hills Antiques, White Hills . . . 056819

The White House, Washington 048960
The White House, Waverton 087058
White House, Westbury 001612
White House Antiques, Houston . . . 089250
White House Art Gallery, Washington 120364
White House Farm Antiques, Easingwold 084244
White House Gallery, Castle Hill . . . 094381
White House Gallery, Manama 057649
White House Gallery, Oklahoma City 118679
White House Museum of Buildings and Country Life, Aston Munslow 038546
White Light Edition, Mossautal 134210
White Line Gallery, Exeter 113045
White Lotus, Bangkok . . . 135109, 141372
White Memorial Conservation Center, Litchfield 045334
White Mill Rural Heritage Centre, Sandwich 040960
White Oak Gallery, Minneapolis . . . 117325
White Park Antiques, Malvern, South Australia 056140
White Patch Gallery, Bribie Island . . 094278
White Pillars Museum, De Pere . . . 043336
White Pine Public Museum, Ely . . . 043697
White Plains Antique Shows, White Plains 094041
White River Architectural Antiques, Indianapolis 089357
White River Museum, Meeker 045749
White River Valley Museum, Auburn 041892
White Rock Museum, White Rock . . 006810
White Roding Antiques, White Roding 087135
The White Room, Meltham 114074
White Room Gallery, West Hollywood 120419
White Rose, Mumbai 074830
White Space Contemporary Art, Totnes 114593
White Swan Antiques, Saint Louis . 092333
White Tiger, Nashville 117376
White Trash, New York 091346
White Wall Gallery, Chapel Allerton . 112835
White Walls, Chicago 136673
White Water Gallery, North Bay 006038
Whitechapel Art Gallery, London . . . 040319
Whitecliffe College of Arts and Design, Te whaare Takiura o Wikiriwhi, Auckland 050572, 108371
Whitecrow, San Diego 119565
Whitefield House Museum, Moravian Historical Society, Nazareth 046168
Whitefriars, Coventry 039155
Whitehall, Cheam 039043
Whitehaven Museum and Art Gallery, Whitehaven 041370
Whitehead House Antiques, Austin . 087624
Whitehead Memorial Museum, Del Rio 043377
Whitehern Historic House and Garden, Hamilton 005596
WhiteImage.com, Hillsborough 113245
Whitelaw & Sons, John, Auchterarder 083353
Whitemoor, Shenton 086571
Whitemouth Municipal Museum, Whitemouth 006815
Whiters of Leicester, Hoby 084696, 130797
Whiteshell Natural Historic Museum, Seven Sisters Falls 006444
Whitespace, Auckland 108372
Whitewater Canal Historic Site, Metamora 045798
Whitewater Historical Museum, Whitewater 049148
Whiteway & Waldron, London 085795
Whiteway-Wilkonson, G.A., Maidencombe 085893
Whitewood Historical Museum, Whitewood 006817
Whitfield, London 113963
Whitfield, James, New York 118561
Whitfield, Laurence, Cirencester . . . 130585
Whitfield, Robert, London 085796
Whitford, London 085797, 113964
Whitgift Centre Gallery, Croydon . . . 112930
Whitgift Galleries, Croydon 084124
Whitgift Galleries, Croydon 112931
Whitgift Galleries, Croydon 130619
Whithner, Baltimore 115092
Whithorn - Cradle of Christianity, Whithorn 041374
Whithorn Priory and Museum, Whithorn 041375
Whitingham Historical Museum, Whitingham 049149
Whitley, Miami 090254
Whitley County Historical Museum, Columbia City 043090
Whitmore, Great Malvern 084517
Whitmore, Vancouver 059435
Whitney, Minneapolis 090406, 142593
Whitney, Adam, Omaha 118726
Whitney, Susan, Regina 097185
Whitney Museum of American Art, New York 046418
Whitney Museum of American Art at Champion, Stamford 048316
Whitstable Fine Art, Whitstable 114689
Whitstable Museum and Gallery, Whitstable 041376
Whitstable Oyser and Fishery Exhibition, Whitstable 041377
Whitt Kraus, San Diego 119566
Whittaker & Biggs Auction Room, Congleton 122477
Whittier Fine Arts Gallery, Wichita . . 049162
Whittington, Henley-on-Thames . . . 113235
Whittlesey Museum, Whittlesey . . . 041378
Whittlesford Gallery, Whittlesford . . 114691
Whittmann, Lawrence, Vancouver . 097544
Whitton & Laing, Exeter 122506
The Whitworth Art Gallery, Manchester 040416
Whitworth Historical Society Museum, Whitworth 041380
Who New, Pittsburgh 091873
Whodunit, Philadelphia 142754
Wholesale Antique Center, Miami . . 090255
Wholesale Art, Minneapolis 117326
Wholesale Art, San Antonio 119466
Who's Who in Art, Calne 136281
Who's Who in International Art, Lausanne 135035
Who's Who International-Art Management, Lausanne 111635
Whowhatwherewhenwhy W5, Belfast 038670
Whyalla Maritime Museum, Whyalla 001614
Whyte, Dublin 121669
Whyte, Jill, Mullingar 105899
Whyte, John, Edinburgh 084319
Whyte Museum of the Canadian Rockies, Banff 005065
Whytock & Reid, Edinburgh 084320, 130683
Wibaux, Hugues, Lyon . . . 064195, 124382
Wiberg, Alex, Stockholm 111084
Neil Wibroe & Natasha MacIlwaine, London 085798
Wich, G. E., Fürth 102899
Wich, Joan, Houston 116428
Wicher, Helga, Wuppertal . 105362, 134475
Wichers, Den Haag 078269
Wichert, Georg, Gangelt 070927
Wichert, P., Wedemark 074290
Wichert-Pollmann, Dr. Ursula, Altenbeken 138679
Wichita Art Museum, Wichita 049163
Wichita Center for the Arts, Wichita 049164
Wichita Center for the Arts, Wichita 052372
Wichita Falls Museum and Art Center, Wichita Falls 049167
Wichita-Sedgwick County Historical Museum, Wichita 049165
Wichmann, Carl J., Bevern, Kreis Pinneberg 102102
Wichmann, Horst P., Seeham 057313
Wichmann, W., Aachen 069104
Wick, Eugen, Solingen 073858
Wick Antiques, Lymington 085880, 131246
Wick Heritage Centre, Wick 041382
Wickaninnish Gallery, Vancouver . . 006718
Wickaninnish Gallery, Vancouver . . 097545
Wicker, Seattle 093085
Wicker Gazebo, New Orleans 090640
Wicker Shop, Minneapolis 090407, 132393
Wicker Shop, Saint Paul . . 092407, 132777
Wicker Witch, Chicago 088194
Wickert, Bernhard, Spangenberg . . 139735
Wickert, H., Ulm 074154
Wickerwood Lamp Shop, Houston . 132144
Wicki, Tom, Malters 111716
Wickiser, Walter, New York 118562
Wickliff, Karen, Columbus 142357
Wickliffe Mounds, Museum of Native American Village, Wickliffe 049169
Wickman Maritime Collection, Zabbar 028049
Widdas, Roger, Moreton-in-Marsh .086023, 114093, 131287
Widder, Roland, Wien 057580
Wide Bay and Burnett Historical Museum, Maryborough, Queensland 001226
Wide Bay Gallery, Maryborough, Queensland 094792
Wide Bay Hospital Museum, Maryborough, Queensland 001227
Wide Horizons Gallery, Cooks Hill . . 094427
Wide House Antique, Middle Dural . 056220
Widener Gallery, Hartford 044464
Widener University Art Collection and Gallery, Chester 042802
Widenfels, Saint-Paul-de-Vence . . . 101221
Wider, Hermann, Fribourg 082383, 130029
Widmann, Rainer, Stuttgart 074016
Widmen, Las Vegas 116658, 135375
Widmer, Anton, Bern 082249, 129975
Widmer, Christoph, Sankt Gallen . .111878, 141297
Widmer, Hans, Sankt Gallen 082789, 111879, 122348
Widmerpool House Antiques, Maidenhead 085894
Widor, Paris 066676
Widrich, Salzburg 133153
Widrich, Mechtild, Wien 133240
Widukind-Museum, Enger 016987
Widurski, Maciej, Kraków 079664
Widzewska, Łódź 109022
Wiebe-Sahlender, P., Neustadt am Rübenberge 073024
Wiebold, Cincinnati 131948
Wiebold & Colby, Indianapolis 089358, 132166
Wiebus, Arndt, Oberhausen, Rheinland 139617
Wiechern, Gardy, Hamburg 103230
Wiechers Woon Oase, Dwingeloo . . 029517
Wiechmann, Bardowick 069470
Wiechmann, Deggenhausertal 133860
Wiechmann, K.-Heinz, Bad Bramstedt 069269
Wiechmann, Kai, Hamburg 071355
Wiechmann, Kai, München 072880
Wieck, Thomas, Stuttgart 126888
Wieckowski, Hartmut von, Nehlitz . 126521
Wieczorek, Peter K., Düsseldorf . . .070465, 125556
Wieczorek, Zbigniew, Warszawa . . 079792
Wiedebusch, Max, Hamburg 139222
Wiedemann, Frank, Düsseldorf 070466, 125557
Wiedenig, Renate Sofie, Rottenmann 057230
Wiedenkeller, Ursula, Zürich 112198
Wiedenroth, Alfred, Hannover 071419
Wieder, Bergheim 056945
Wiederhold, Imke, Berlin 138859
Wiedmann, Willy, Stuttgart 074017
Wiegand, Wolfgang, Wernarz 105213
The Wiegand Gallery, Notre Dame de Namur University, Belmont 042126
Wiegele, Edwin, Haimburg 095555
Wiegerling, Peter, Gaißach 125697
Wiegmann, D., Lübbecke 072318
Wiehager, Schieder-Schwalenberg . 073686
Wiehl, Blanka, Dormagen 070274
Wieland, Angelika, Berlin 102086
Wieland-Archiv, Biberach an der Riß 016220
Wieland-Gartenhaus, Biberach an der Riß 016221
Wieland-Gedenkzimmer, Achstetten 015441
Wieland-Schauraum, Biberach an der Riß 016222
Wielandgut Ossmannstedt mit Wieland-Gedenkstätte, Stiftung Weimarer Klassik und Kunstsammlungen, Ossmannstedt 019502
Wielkopolski Park Etnograficzny, Muzeum Pierwszych Piastów na Lednicy, Lednogóra 032094
Wielkopolskie Muzeum Pożarnictwa PTTK, Rakoniewice 032284
Wielkopolskie Muzeum Wojskowe, Muzeum Narodowe w Poznaniu, Poznań . . 032256
Wiemann, Rolf, Hamburg 071356
Wiemann, Dr. Wolfgang, Heidelberg 139256
Wien, Barbara, Berlin 133818, 138860
Wien, Leonardo, Wien 057581
Wien Museum Hermesvilla mit Schauräumen der Modesammlung, Wien 003016
Wien Museum Karlsplatz, Wien . . . 003017
Wienand, Köln 134125
Wienands, B., Köln 072026
Wiend Books & Collectables, Wigan 142156
Wieneman, Tom, Saint Louis 092334
Wiener, Nancy, New York 091347
Wiener Antiquariat, Wien 137376
Wiener Bestattungsmuseum, Wien . 003018
Wiener Dom-Verlag, Mistelbach an der Zaya 137233
Wiener Feuerwehrmuseum, Wien . . 003019
Wiener Glasmuseum, Sammlung Lobmeyr, Wien 003020
Wiener Interieur, Wien 057582
Wiener Kriminalmuseum, Museum der Bundespolizeidirektion Wien, Wien 003021
Wiener Kunst Auktionen im Kinsky, Wien 120697
Wiener Kunsthefte - Zeitschrift für Druckgraphik, Wien 135584
Wiener Kunstschule, Wien 049668
Wiener Messing Manufaktur, Wien . 057583
Wiener Münzensalon, Wien 057584
Wiener Neustädter Künstlervereinigung, Wiener Neustadt 052626
Wiener Neustädter Künstlervereinigung, Wiesen 052625
Wiener Porzellanmanufaktur Augarten, Wien 003022
Wiener Secession, Vereinigung bildender Künstler, Wien 052627, 133241
Wiener Secession, Vereinigung bildender Künstler und Küntlerinnen, Wien . 003023
Wiener Stadt- und Landesbibliothek, Wien 003024
Wiener Straßenbahnmuseum, Wien 003025
Wiener Teddybärenmuseum, Wien . 003026
Wiener Tramwaymuseum, Wien . . . 003027
Wiener Ziegelmuseum, Wien 003028
Wienerroither & Kohlbacher, Wien . 095958
't Wienkeltje van Wullempje, Hoedekenskerke 029755
Wieringer Boerderij, Den Oever . . . 029466
Wiese, Basel 134989
Wiese, B., Überlingen 139805
Wiese, O., Neubrandenburg 072975, 126528
Wiesenmeisterei, Neustadt-Glewe . 019293
Wieser, Franz Karl, Fürstenfeld 056984
Wieser, Helmuth & Bärbel, München 072881
Wiesinger, Eleonore, Wels 057357
Wiesinger, Hubert, Wels 057358
Wiesmann-Emmerling, Adelheid, Darmstadt 125445
Wiesmeier, Jasmin, Schlangenbad . 139712
Wiesner, Eduard, Wernstein am Inn 133172, 137281

Wiesner, V., Leipzig . . . 126200
Wießner, H., Regen . . . 073449
Wietschorke, Edeltrud, Sonsbeck . . 073865
Wieuw, de, Antwerpen . . . 096103, 123562
Wieża Więzienna i Katownia, Muzeum Historyczne Miasta Gdańska, Gdańsk . . . 031924
Wigan Pier, Wigan . . . 041386
Wigerdal, Stockholm . . . 082040
Wiggertaler Museum, Schötz . . . 037537
Wiggins & Sons, Arnold, London . . . 085799
Wiggins, Peter, Chipping Norton . . . 130574
Wight Light Gallery, Ventnor . . . 114632
Wightwick Manor, Wolverhampton . 041431
Wigington, Bryan, Hay-on-Wye . . . 130777
Wigmore, London . . . 113965
Wigmore, D., New York . . 091348, 118563
Wignacourt, B'Kara . . . 077510
Wignall Museum and Gallery, Chaffey College, Rancho Cucamonga . . . 047322
Wihlborg, Magnus, Lund . . . 129849
Wijk, Jacoba, Groningen . . . 108051
Wijnhoven, T., Brugge . . . 096121
Wijnklder Soniën, Overijse . . . 003700
Het Wijnkopersgildehuys, Amsterdam . . . 029243
Wijnmuseum Maastricht, Cadier en Keer . . . 029380
Wijsmuller, Lara, Amsterdam . . . 078022
Wikinger Museum Haithabu, Stiftung Schleswig-Holsteinische Landesmuseen Schloß Gottorf, Busdorf bei Schleswig . . . 016526
Wik's Mynt & Kuriosa, Kil . . . 081841
Wiktor, Tord, Stockholm . . . 129882
Wiktorsson, Jörgen, Basel . . . 129939
Wilber Czech Museum, Wilber . . . 049170
Wilberforce House, Kingston-upon-Hull . . . 039892
Wilbert, Bruxelles . . . 137485
Wilbert, Stanley, Calgary . . . 096855
Wilbrand, Dieter, Köln . . . 103739, 134126
Wilbur D. May Museum, Reno . . . 047376
Wilbur Wright Birthplace and Interpretive Center, Hagerstown . . . 044383
Wilbye, Jonathan, Kirkby Stephen . 130855
Wilce, Christine, Le Touquet-Paris-Plage . . . 063720
Wilce, Christine, Neuville-sous-Montreuil . . . 064999
Wilce Trading, Reims . . . 067082
Wilcockson, John, Marburg . . . 072452
The Wilcox Collection, London . . . 113966
Wild, Ulm . . . 074155, 105096
Wild, Adolf, Lahr, Schwarzwald . . . 103816
Wild, Alexander, Bern . . . 141232
Wild y Cia, Alfred, Bogotá . . . 098200
Wild, Eva Maria, Frankfurt am Main 102837
Wild, George, New York . . . 132548
Wild, Rose, Seattle . . . 093086
Wild, Wolfgang, Zürich . . . 130271
Wild About Music, Austin . . . 115022
Wild Art, Cape Town . . . 110035
Wild Earth Images, Salt Lake City . . 119381
Wild Goose Antiques, Modbury . . . 085999
Wild Honey, Guildford . . . 094609
Wild Oates Gallery, Doonan . . . 094482
Wild Orchid Antiques, Richmond . . . 092120
Wild Pitch, Portland . . . 092025
Wild Rose Antiques, Edinburgh . . . 084321
Wild Rose Antiques and Auctions, Virginia Beach . . . 093371, 123135
Wild Strawberry-Muddy Wheel Gallery, Albuquerque . . . 114835
Wild Things, Denver . . . 116070
Wild Walls Gallery, Bentleigh East . 094244
Wild Wings Gallery, Saint Paul . . . 119320
Wilde, Chris, Harrogate . . . 084593
Wilde, H-J., Hamburg . . . 103231
Wilde, Olaf, Braunschweig . . . 125381
Wilde, P.S., Toronto . . . 059318
Wilde, Yvan de, Périgueux . . . 066726
Wilde Art, Arrington . . . 112519
Wilde-Meyer, Tucson . . . 120178
Wildeboer, Groningen . . . 078439
Wildeboer, Toon, Hilversum . . . 108088
Wildenauer, Hans, Friedenfels . . . 070891
Wildenstein & Co., London 085800, 113967
Wildenstein & Co., New York . . . 118564
Wildenstein, Paris . . . 133687
Wildenstein, Tokyo . . . 107130
Wilder, Salzhemmendorf . . . 139709
Wilder Memorial Museum, Strawberry Point . . . 048399
Wilderer-Museum Sankt Pankraz, Sankt Pankraz . . . 002609
Wilderness Park Museum, El Paso . 043645
Wilderness Reflections Gallery, Kansas City . . . 116596
Wilderness Road Regional Museum, Newbern . . . 046436
Wildfellner, Georg, Grieskirchen . . .057038, 095550
Wildfowl Art Journal, Salisbury . . . 136674
Wilding, R., Wisbech . . . 087191, 131700
Wildlife Art, Burnsville . . . 136675
The Wildlife Art Gallery, Lavenham . 113358
Wildlife Education Centre, Entebbe . 038215
Wildlife Gallery, Toronto . . . 006645
Wildlife Gallery, Toronto . . . 097397
Wildlife Interpretive Gallery, Royal Oak . . . 047563
Wildlife Museum, Ulaanbaatar . . . 029015
Wildlife Wonderlands Giant Worm Museum, Bass . . . 000771
Wildman, Barbara, Nelson . . . 131296
Wildmeister, Würzburg . . . 074515
Wildner, L., Graz . . . 137183
Wildner, Wolfgang, Passau . . . 104591
Wildschut, Amsterdam . . . 078023
Wildwood, Bury Saint Edmunds . . . 112774
Wildwood, Edmonton . . . 096908
Wildwood, Fitzroy Falls . . . 094541
Wildwood Center, Nebraska City . . . 046170
Wile Carding Mill Museum, Bridgewater . . . 005151
Wiles, A. Allen, Woodridge . . . 056847
Wilfing, Josef, Salzburg . . . 123462
Wilford & Assoc., Cleveland . . . 088370
Wilford, Hong Kong . . . 059707
Wilford, H., Wellingborough . . . 122739
Wilfrid Israel Museum of Oriental Art and Studies, Kibbutz Hazorea . . . 023007
Wilhelm, Beckingen . . . 069503
Wilhelm, Eleonore, Ludwigshafen am Rhein . . . 103952, 134168
Wilhelm, Hohmann, Stuttgart . . . 139776
Wilhelm, M., Aldingen . . . 069130
Wilhelm, Otto, Frankfurt am Main . . 070803
Wilhelm-Busch-Geburtshaus, Wiedensahl . . . 020854
Wilhelm-Busch-Gedenkstätte, Wilhelm-Busch-Gesellschaft, Seesen . . . 020175
Wilhelm-Busch-Gesellschaft e.V., Hannover . . . 053650
Wilhelm-Busch-Mühle, Ebergötzen . 016867
Wilhelm-Busch-Museum Hannover, Deutsches Museum für Karikatur und kritische Grafik, Hannover . . . 017772
Wilhelm Fabry-Museum, Hilden . . . 017920
Wilhelm-Hack-Museum Ludwigshafen am Rhein, Ludwigshafen am Rhein . . 018707
Wilhelm Kienzl-Museum, Waizenkirchen . . . 002804
Wilhelm-Morgner-Haus, Soest . . . 020233
Wilhelm-Ostwald-Gedenkstätte, Großbothen . . . 017566
Wilhelmietenmuseum, Huijbergen . 029781
Wilhelmsturm Dillenburg Museum, Dillenburg . . . 016712
Wilimzig, Ewald, Worpswede . . . 105335
Wilk, Warszawa . . . 109204
Wilk, M., Brühl, Rheinland . . . 070074
Wilke, C., Lehrte . . . 103848
Wilke, Nikolaus, Sinsheim . . . 126805
Wilkens, Silvia, Mainz . . . 104009
Wilkerson, New Orleans . . . 090641
Wilkes, Minneapolis . . . 117327
Wilkes Art Gallery, North Wilkesboro . . . 046541
Wilkie, Saskatoon . . . 059107
Wilkie and District Museum, Wilkie 006821
Wilkin, Elizabeth, Paraparaumu . . . 079220
Wilkin County Historical Museum, Breckenridge . . . 042393
Wilkins, Brett, Lichfield . . . 084993
Wilkins, David J., London . 085801, 131213
Wilkins, Joan, Witney . . . 087194
Wilkins & Wilkins, London . . . 113968
Wilkinson, Doncaster . . . 122489
Wilkinson, London . . . 085802
Wilkinson, London . . . 085803
Wilkinson, London . . . 113969
Wilkinson, London . . . 131214
Wilkinson, London . . . 131215
Wilkinson, Marcus, Grantham 084498, 130742
Wilkinson, Marcus, Sleaford 086628, 131504
Wilkinson, Tony, Petworth . . . 086265
Wilkinson & Beighton Auctioneers, Rotherham . . . 122671
Wilkinson County Museum, Woodville . . . 049298
Wilkinson & Rhodes, San Antonio . . 092593
Wilkinsons, Brighton . . . 083720
Will, Astrid, Berlin . . . 125316
Will, H.-D., Kerpen, Rheinland . . . 071809
Will, Joël, La Chapelle-Bertrand . . . 063310
Will, John, Virginia Beach . . . 093372
Will Rogers Memorial Museums, Claremore . . . 042942
Will Rogers State Historic Park, Pacific Palisades . . . 046785
Willa Cather State Historic Site, Red Cloud . . . 047354
Willamette Science and Technology Center, Eugene . . . 043750
Willand, Detlef, Hirschegg, Kleinwalsertal . . . 095566
The Willard House, WCTU Museum, Evanston . . . 043764
Willard House and Clock Museum, Grafton . . . 044255
Willborg, J.P., Stockholm . 082041, 129883, 134972
Willburn Antiques, Christchurch . . . 079066
Willburn Antiques, Christchurch . . . 079067
Willburn Antiques, Christchurch . . . 128929
Willcox & Nightingale, Penryn . . . 086208
Wille, Irmgard, Füssen . . . 070916
Willeke, Angela, Werenzhain . . . 105204
Willem de Kooning Academie, Hogeschool Rotterdam, Rotterdam . . . 050567
Willem Prinsloo Museum, Rayton . . 034738
Willemoesgårdens Mindestuer, Assens . . . 008815
Willems, Düsseldorf . . . 121388
Willems, Gerard, Hobart . . 056001, 094649
Willems, M., Bruxelles . . . 123614
Willem's Winkel, Middelburg . . . 078648
Willemsen, H., Treuen . . . 074087
Willen, Luzern . . . 111710, 130112
Willenhall Lock Museum, Willenhall 041387
Willenhall Museum, Willenhall . . . 041388
Willer Brocante, Willer-sur-Thur . . . 069051
Willermann, F.-J., Steinfurt . . . 073907
Willi, H.-P., Tübingen . . . 139802
Willi Dickhut Museum, Gelsenkirchen . . . 017358
Willi the Clockman, Lesmurdie . . . 056097
William, Ascott-under-Wychwood . . 083321
William, Joseph, Portland . . . 119062
William, Robert, Vancouver . . . 059436
William A. Farnsworth Art Museum and Wyeth Center, Rockland . . . 047506
William A. Quayle Bible Collection, Baker University, Baldwin City . . . 041959
William B. Ide Adobe State Historic Park, Red Bluff . . . 047352
The William Benton Museum of Art, University of Connecticut, Storrs . 048384
William Blizard Gallery, Springfield . 048298
William Bonifas Fine Arts Center, Escanaba . . . 043728
William Booth Birthplace Museum, Nottingham . . . 040627
William Breman Jewish Heritage Museum, Atlanta . . . 041877
William Carey Museum, Leicester . 039979
William Clark Market House Museum, Paducah . . . 046788
William Cullen Bryant Homestead, Cummington . . . 043246
William D. Lawrence House, Nova Scotia Museum, Halifax . . . 005586
William Fehr Collection, Cape Town 034588
William Grant Still Art Center, Los Angeles . . . 045473
William H. Harrison Museum/ Grouseland, Vincennes . . . 048791
William H. Van Every jr. and Edward M. Smith Galleries, Davidson . . . 043308
William Hammond Mathers Museum, Bloomington . . . 042266
William Henry Steeves House, Hillsborough . . . 005617
The William Herschel Museum, Bath . . . 038634
William Holmes McGuffey Museum, Oxford . . . 046774
William Howard Taft National Historic Site, Cincinnati . . . 042931
William Humphreys Art Gallery, Kimberley . . . 034666
William & Joseph, New Orleans . . . 117529
William King Regional Arts Center, Abingdon . . . 041569
William Lamb Memorial Studio, Montrose . . . 040496
William M. Colmer Visitor Center, Ocean Springs . . . 046619
William Morris Gallery and Brangwyn Gift, London . . . 040320
The William Morris Society, London 040321
William Pryor Letchworth Museum, Castile . . . 042652
William Ray House, Dartmouth . . . 005326
William S. Hart Museum, National History Museum of Los Angeles County, Newhall . . . 046451
William S. Webb Museum of Anthropology, Lexington . . . 045268
William Scarbrough House, Ships of the Sea Museum, Savannah . . . 048032
William Street Gallery, South Yarra . 095213
William Trent House, Trenton . . . 048608
William Whitley House, Stanford . . . 048320
William Woods University Art Gallery, Fulton . . . 044098
William'S, Barcelona . . . 080961
Williams, Houston . . . 116429
Williams & Son, London . . . 085804, 113970
Williams, Mornington . . . 094886
Williams, Nashville . . . 117377
Williams, Nashville . . . 117378
Williams, Salt Lake City . . . 119382
Williams, Tulsa . . . 093339, 123131
Williams, Wellington . . . 079359, 108654
Williams, Adam, New York . . . 118565
Williams, Brian, Charlotte . . . 131876
Williams, Christopher, Parkstone . . 141992
Williams, David, London . . . 141919
Williams, E & B, Levallois-Perret . . 063804
Williams, Ehoodin, Cincinnati . . . 115675
Williams, George, Kells . . . 074980
Williams & Co., H., Toronto . . . 120824
Williams, Huw, Porthmadog . . . 086294
Williams, Jean, Seattle . . . 093087
Williams, Melvin D ., Pittsburgh . . . 091874
Williams, Nigel, London . . . 141920
Williams, Peter, Tetbury . . . 131584
Williams, Philip, New York . . . 118566
Williams, Philip, New York . . . 118567
Williams, Scott, Richmond . . . 092121
Williams, Steve, Jacksonville . . . 116550
Williams, Thayne A., Baltimore . . . 087723
Williams, Thomas, London 085805, 113971
Williams, Tom, Calgary . . . 137628
Williams, Tracy, New York . . . 118568
Williams, Trevor, Plymouth . . . 142005

Williams & Clark, Vancouver 097546, 137733
Williams & Co., Toronto 059319
Williams College Museum of Art, Williamstown 049188
Williams County Historical Museum, Montpelier 046004
Williams Lake Museum, Williams Lake 006824
Williamsburg Decorative Arts Series, Williamsburg 136676
Williamson, New Orleans 090642
Williamson, Connie, Dallas 088625
Williamson, P., Houston 089251
Williamson, Patrice, Nantes 124491
Williamson, William, Stoke-on-Trent 114494
Williamson Art Gallery and Museum, Birkenhead 038716
Williamson County Historical Society Museum, Marion 045677
Williamstown Historical Museum, Williamstown 001618
Willibaldsburg, Eichstätt 016913
Willicher Kunstverein e.V., Nettetal . 053651
Willie Monks Museum, Lusk 022830
Willinger Milchmuhmuseum, Willingen, Upland 020903
Willinghäuser Gemäldekabinett und Industrie @ Fine Art, Schwalmstadt 073751
Willingham Auctions, Willingham . . 122748
Willis, Memphis 117010
Willis, Henry, Sherborne . . 086586, 131489
Willis, James, San Francisco 119834
Willis Museum, Basingstoke 038614
Willisch, Susanne, München 104343, 126484
Willistead Manor, Windsor, Ontario . 006832
Willmitzer, H., Hilpoltstein 071528
Willoughby-Baylor House, Norfolk . 046505
Willoughby Historical Museum, Niagara Falls 006019
Willow, Denver 088750
Willow, Dumfries 112962
Willow, Dunedin 079095
Willow, Phoenix 118895
Willow, Sacramento 119169
Willow, Toronto 097398
Willow, Weybridge 114676
Willow, Glen, San Jose 092939
Willow Antiques, Nettlebed 086047, 131298
Willow Art Gallery, Long Beach 116684
Willow Auctions, Uckfield 122731
Willow Bunch Museum, Willow Bunch 006827
Willow Gallery, Weybridge 087114
Willow Place Antiques, Richmond . . 092122
Willow Pool, Lymm 085882
Willow Street Gallery, Washington . 120365
Willow Woodstock, New York 118569
Willowa, Warszawa 109205
Willowbank at Taggerty, Taggerty . . 095311
Willowbrook at Newfield, Newfield . 046449
Will's, London 113972
Wills Lane Gallery, Saint Ives, Cornwall 114377
Willunga Antiques, Willunga 056826
Willy's Coins, Omaha 091592
Willys Ram, Lund 110957
Wilma's Workshop, Tampa 132966
Wilmer Jenning, New York 118570
Wilmersdorf Archiv, Berlin 016195
Wilmette Historical Museum, Wilmette 049199
Wilmington Priory, Wilmington 041390
Wilmington Railroad Museum, Wilmington 049217
Wilmink, Louis, Velp 128867
Wilmsen, Münster 072932
Wilmslow Antiques, Wilmslow 087154
Wilner & Co., Eli, New York 132549
Wilnitsky, Boris, Wien 057585
Wilnitsky, Leonid, Wien 057586
Wilsmann, M., Oelde 139623
Wilson, Columbus 131991
Wilson, Oklahoma City 118680
Wilson, Robe 095149
Wilson, Windsor, Ontario 097568
Wilson, A&K, Harpenden 113186
Wilson, Amanda L., Phoenix 091778
Wilson, Frank, Worthing 087267
Wilson, Greg, Pokolbin 095077
Wilson, H.W., Bronx 135336
Wilson, Jerome, New York 091349
Wilson, John, Hawthorn, Victoria . . 055969
Wilson, Maralyn, Birmingham 115133
Wilson, O.F., London 085806
Wilson, Peter, Nantwich 122624
Wilson, Philip, London 135276
Wilson & Sons, R.S., Boroughbridge 083577
Wilson, Susan M., Kilmacolm 113322
Wilson, Virginia, Darlinghurst 055738
Wilson & Buttle, London 131216
Wilson Castle, Proctor 047246
Wilson County Historical Society Museum, Fredonia 044066
Wilson Historical Museum, Wilson . 049221
Wilson MacDonald Memorial School Museum, Selkirk 006441
Wilson Museum of Narberth, Narberth 040513
Wilsons', Haverfordwest 113206
Wilson's Creek National Battlefield, Republic 047383
Wilton, Agnes, London 085807
Wilton Historical Museums, Wilton . 049225
Wilton House, Wilton, Salisbury . . . 041392
Wilton House Museum, The National Society of the Colonial Dames of America in the Commonwealth of Virginia, Richmond 047430
Wilton Windmill, Wilton, Marlborough 041391
Wiltondale Pioneer Village, Bonne Bay 005116
Wiltshire, Helen, Mission Beach . . . 094860
Wiltshire, Helen, Port Douglas 095090
Wiltshire Fire Defence Collection, Potterne 040773
The Wiltshire Gallery, Salisbury . . . 114390
Wiltshire Heritage Museum and Gallery, Devizes 039235
Wiltshire Regiment Museum, Devizes 039236
Wilzek, A., Mühlbeck 139489
Wimberger, Ludwig, Linz 057170
Wimbledon Fine Art, London 113973, 131217
Wimbledon Lawn Tennis Museum, London 040322
Wimbledon School of Art, London . . 050844
Wimbledon Society Museum of Local History, London 040323
Wimbledon Windmill Museum, London 040324
Wimetz, Yves, Templeuve 068370
Wimmel, Eduard, Bad Sooden-Allendorf 101706
Wimmel, Werner, Stegen 126828
Wimmer, München 104344
Wimmer, Elga, New York 118571
Wimmer, Gerti, Frontenhausen 070905
Wimmer, Josef, Obermühl 057198
Wimmer, Kathrin, Miesbach 104070
Wimmer, Otto, München 126485
Wimmer, Volker, Wien 137377
Wimmera Mallee Pioneers Museum, Jeparit 001132
Wimpole Hall and Home Farm, Royston 040861
Wimtetz, Yves, Seclin 068182
Win Art Gallery, Roubaix . . 067234, 101104
Wincanton Antiques, Wincanton . . . 087165
Wincanton Museum, Wincanton . . . 041394
Winchbooks of Canberra, Fyshwick 136913
Winchcombe Folk and Police Museum, Winchcombe 041396
Winchcombe Railway Museum, Winchcombe 041397
Winchelsea and District Historical Records Centre, Winchelsea 001621
Winchelsea Museum, Winchelsea . 041398
Winchendon Historical Museum, Winchendon 049228
Winchester, Minneapolis 117328
Winchester Bookshop, Winchester . 142160
Winchester Cathedral Triforium Gallery, Winchester 041409
Winchester City Museum, Winchester 041410
Winchester College Treasury, Winchester 041411
Winchester-Frederick County Historical Society Museum, Winchester . . . 049232
Winchester Furniture, Winchester . . 087178
Winckelmann-Museum, Stendal . . . 020316
Wind, E.-W., Bremen 070049, 125394
Wind, Mary, La Rochelle . . 063441, 099408
Wind, Mary, Saint-Martin-de-Ré . . . 067637
Wind Horse Gallery, Denver 088751
Wind Margery Studio, Saint Louis . . 119267
Wind River Historical Center Dubois Museum, Dubois 043511
Wind & Water Gallery, Houston 089252
Windermere Fine Art, London 113974
Windermere Steamboat Museum, Windermere 041412
Windermere Valley Museum, Invermere 005642
Winders, S., Newcastle-under-Lyme 086063, 131305
Windfall Gallery, Palmerston North . 108537
Windham Textile and History Museum, Willimantic 049190
Windham Township Pioneer Museum, Delhi 005340
Windheuser, Höxter 139271
Windhill Antiquary, Bishop's Stortford 083545
Windhorse Gallery, Bangalow 094211
Windibank, P.F., Dorking 122491
The Winding Stair, Galway 074975
Winding Stair Bookshop, Dublin . . . 139969
Windjammer Gallery, Hamilton 096428
Windle, John, San Francisco 142969
Windmann, Bad Oeynhausen 069350
Windmann, B., Vlotho 074223
Windmill and Milling Museum, Polegate 040728
Windmill Antiques, Bembridge 083487
Windmill Antiques, Stafford 086679
Windmill Fine Art, High Wycombe . . 084683
Windmill Gallery, Birmingham 083539, 130397
Windmill Gallery, Kuranda 094719
Windmill Island Municipal Park Museum, Holland 044576
Windmill Wood Works, San Antonio 132835
Windmühle, Podersdorf 002434
Windmühle, Retz 002524
Windmühle Vahrel, Varel 020561
Windoows, Bruxelles 096268
Window on the Past, Seattle 093088
Window to the Past, Singapore 080588
Windows Gallery, Nashville 090494
Windows on Church Galleries, Richmond, Victoria 095146
Winds of Change, Winchcombe . . . 114703
Windsong, Omaha 118727
Windsor, Deauville 062611
Windsor, Alain, Luynes 064041
Windsor, Alain, Tours 068611
Windsor, David, Bangor, Gwynedd .083378, 130329
Windsor, Jean-Pierre, Saint-Denis-des-Monts 067419
Windsor Antique, New York 091350
Windsor Antique Centre, Windsor, New South Wales 056828
Windsor Antiques, Dublin 074957
Windsor Castle, Royal Collections, Windsor 041419
Windsor Collections, New Orleans . 090643
Windsor Cottage Antiques, Windsor, New South Wales 056829
Windsor Fine Art, New Orleans 117530
Windsor Gallery, Christchurch 079068, 108419
Windsor Gallery, Hythe 113284
Windsor Hall, Charlotte 087994
Windsor House, Hong Kong 059708
Windsor House, San Francisco 092906
Windsor House Antiques, London . . 085808
Windsor House Antiques Centre, Moreton-in-Marsh 086024
Windsor Kulturgintza, Bilbao 110289
Windsor Market, Tulsa 093340
Windsor Productions, Long Beach . 116685
Windsor's Community Museum, Windsor, Ontario 006833
Windwood, Charlotte 087995
Windwood, New York 118572
Wine, Louis, Toronto 059320
The Wine Museum, Kelowna 005674
Wine Museum of Greyton H. Taylor, Hammondsport 044408
Wine Street Gallery, Devizes 112947
Winedale Historical Center, University of Texas, Round Top 047556
Wing, Hong Kong 097845
Wing, Cheong, Hong Kong 059709
Wing, Cheong Hong, Hong Kong . . . 059710
Wing, Hing, Hong Kong 059711
Wing Luke Asian Museum, Seattle . 048095
Wingaba-Vision, Yangon 107571
Wingates Fine Art, Hatherleigh 113203
Winges, Köln 139356
Wings Metaphysical Books, Denver 142399
Wings of Freedom, Huntington 044677
Wings of History Air Museum, San Martin 047914
Wings of Love, Clinton 043013
Winiger, Barbara, Zürich 112199
Winistörfer, René, Herzogenbuchsee 082496
Wink, Bernhard, Gengenbach 125714
Wink, Gregor & Alexander, Neunkirchen-Seelscheid 073010
Winkel, Wolfgang, Bayrischzell 069499
Winkel, Wolfgang, Bielefeld 069842, 121347
Winkelbach, Jochen, Bielefeld 125330
't Winkelke, Roermond 078683
Winkelmann, Düsseldorf 102574
Winkelmann, A. & R., Gifhorn 070998
Winkelmann, Erika M., München . . 072882
Winkelmann, Gerda, Hallstatt 057054
Winkelmann, Ilse-H., Lemförde . . . 072220
Winkelmann, P., Kaiserslautern . . .071685, 103473, 139290
Winkelmann, Ulrich, Köln 126123
Winkelriedhaus, Nidwaldner Museum, Stans 037599
't Winkeltje, Nijmegen 078663
Winkens, Geilenkirchen 070947
Winkhardt, Jörg, Cuxhaven 125440
Winkler, Crimmitschau 125439
Winkler, Erfurt 125601
Winkler, Osnabrück 073252, 126600
Winkler, Papeete 069074
Winkler, Christoph, Gütersloh 125774
Winkler, Dr. Hildegard, Wien 137378
Winkler, Kerstin, Riesa 073534
Winkler, W., Würzburg 127045
Winklmeier, J., Straubing 073942
Winn & Devon, Seattle . . . 120012, 135506
Winnebago Area Museum, Winnebago 049245
Winnemöller, Birgit, Hamburg 103232
Winner Fraisse Demey, Nantes 064955
Winnetka Historical Museum, Winnetka 049246
Winnie Davis Museum of History, Gaffney 044102
Winnie's Antique Resale, Milwaukee 090331
Winnikes, K., Heidelberg 071467
Winning, Wener, München 072883
Winnipeg Art Gallery, Winnipeg 006873
Winnipeg Police Museum, Winnipeg 006874

Winnipegosis Museum, Winnipegosis 006876
Winn's Antik, Bergisch Gladbach . . 069544
Winns Historic Bakehouse Museum, Coromandel Valley 000949
Winn's Used Books, Salt Lake City . 142878
Winona County Historical Museum, Winona 049249
Winram's Bookshop, Aberdeen 141380
Win's Gallery, Ravenshoe 095115
Winser Museumshof, Winsen, Aller 020915
Winslow Antiques Centre, Winslow . 087187
Winslow Crocker House, Yarmouth Port 049333
Winslow Saleroom - Geo. Wigley & Sons, Winslow 122750
Winston, Amsterdam 078024
Winston, San Francisco 119835
Winston Churchill Memorial and Library in the United States, Westminster College, Fulton 044099
Winston Mac, Bury Saint Edmunds .083824, 130491
Winter, Gross Rohrheim 125759
Winter, New York 118573
de Winter, Paris 100969
Winter, Plainville 123060
Winter, Rottweil 073610
Winter, Wiesbaden 105285
Winter, A., Bad Waldsee 069392
Winter, Alfred, Salzburg 133154
Winter, Dieter, Nürnberg 073126
Winter, Douglas, Dallas 088626
Winter, Eveline, Rugeley 086414
Winter, Fritz, Dießen am Ammersee 102367
Winter, Heinrich, Düsseldorf 070467, 121389
Winter, Hubert, Wien 095959
Winter, Ursula, Ofterdingen 073193
Winter Antiques Show, New York . . 094042
C.-M.Winter & F.Königshoff, Dornum 070277
Winter & Winter, München 104345
Winterberg, Arno, Heidelberg 103327, 121452, 139257
Winterbranch, San Francisco 119836
Winterer & Klimscha, Wien 057587
Winterhager, M., Freiburg im Breisgau 070866
Winterhoff, Lissy, Köln 103740
Wintering, Rita, Hannover 071420
Winter's, Weston-super-Mare 087106
Winterset Art Center, Winterset . . . 049264
Wintersport-Museum, Davos Platz . 037041
Wintersteiger, Magnus, Enns 123350
Wintersteiger, Magnus, Kronstorf . . 123402
Winterstein, Charles, Chanos-Curson 062136
Winterthur Museum, Winterthur . . . 049265
Winterton, Lichfield 122571
Wintgens, Elizabeth, Marlow 114064
Winthrop University Galleries, Rock Hill 047489
Winton Hall Antiques, Ravenstonedale 086331
Winzer, Dr. Axel, Kronberg im Taunus 072095
Winzer Museum, Eggenburg 001811
Winzerhaus, Poppendorfberg 002450
Winzermuseum Rauenberg, Rauenberg 019729
Wippermann, Hans, Bruckmühl . . . 125402
Wir, Livorno 075544
Wired Art Gallery, London 096962
Wiregrass Gallery, Eltham 094506
Wiregrass Museum of Art, Dothan . 043482
Wireless Hill Telecommunications Museum, Applecross 000745
Wirker- und Strickermuseum, Apolda 015563
Wirkner, Harald, Kitzingen 071867
Wirkus, Ehlscheid 139031
Wirrabara Forestry Museum, Wirrabara 001624
Wirral Museum, Birkenhead 038717
Wirrimbah Aboriginal Art, Emerald Creek 055800
Wirth, Ranskill 114296
Wirth, Angelika, Wiesbaden 127018
Wirth, Marie-Louise, Hochfelden . . 111556
Wirth, Ralf, Leipzig 126201
Wirth, Renate, Kölleda 071899
Wirth, Sonia, La Chaux-de-Fonds . . 111347
Wirthmore, New Orleans 090644
Wirthmore, New Orleans 090645
Wirthner, Karolin, Münster 130122
Wirtschaftsgeschichtliches Museum Villa Grün, Dillenburg 016713
Wirtz, Miami 117157
Wirtz, Ilse, Essen 102708
Wirtz, Stephen, San Francisco 119837
Wirtz Gallery, First National Bank of South Miami, Miami 045820
Wisbech and Fenland Museum, Wisbech 041421
Wischer, Lars, Klettwitz 071874
Wischer, S., Altlandsberg 069155
Wischhausen, Rolf, Kiel 071846
Wisconsin Automotive Museum, Hartford 044465
Wisconsin Federation of Museums, Wausau 055108
Wisconsin Fine Arts Association, Cedarburg 055109
Wisconsin Historical Museum, Madison 045595
Wisconsin Maritime Museum, Manitowoc 045639
Wisconsin National Guard Memorial Library and Museum, Camp Douglas 042586
The Wisconsin Union Galleries, Madison 045596
Wisconsin Veterans Museum King, King 045004
Wisconsin Veterans Museum Madison, Madison 045597
Wisdom Books, Kolkata 139950
Wisdom Hut Book Store, Washington 143050
Wise, Mary, London 085809, 122603
Wise County Heritage Museum, Decatur 043356
Wiseman, London 113975
Wiseman, Ruth & Carl D., Dallas . . 115955
Wiseman, Sarah, Oxford 114206
Wiseman and Fire House Galleries, Grants Pass 044288
Wish Barn Antiques, Rye 086427
Wishes, New Orleans 090646
Wishful Things, Milwaukee 090332
Wishing Corner, Portland 092026
Wishing Well, Fort Worth 088893
Wishing Well Antiques, Ullapool . . .086979, 131626
Wishnow, Houston 089253, 132145
Wishtower Puppet Museum, Eastbourne 039367
Wisma, Trigg 056738
Wismes, Michel de, Nantes 064956
Wißdorf, Olaf, Köln 103741
Wissel-Eggimann, Simone, Basel . . 129940
Wisselink, L., Den Haag 107963
Wissenschaftliche Buchgesellschaft, Darmstadt 133859
Wissenschaftliches Kabinett, Wien . 057588
Wissing, Magitte, Bocholt 102146
Wistariahurst Museum, Holyoke . . . 044585
Wisteria, Dallas 088627
Wisteria, Dallas 088628
Wisteria Gallery, Wootton Bridge . . 114734
De Wit - Royal Manufacturers of Tapestries, Mechelen 003639
The Witch, Hasselt 058233
Witch Ball, Brighton 083721, 141445
The Witchball, London . . . 085810, 113976
Witchcliffe Art Gallery, Witchcliffe . . 095403
Witchhill, Sittard 078763
With Paint, Oakland 118650
With You in Mind, Washington 093443
With You in Mind, Washington 093444
Witham, Norman, Shirley 086595
Withcott Antiques, Withcott 056838
Witherells, Sacramento 092190
Withernsea Lighthouse Museum, Withernsea 041422
The Withindale Gallery, Long Melford 113990
Withington, Richard W., Hillsboro . . 122901
Without Pier Gallery, Sandringham . 095180
Witke, Herbert, Wien 057589
Witkowski, Heinz-Georg, Adendorf . 069110
Witmeur, J.-P., Bruxelles 058131
Witney and District Museum and Art Gallery, Witney 041425
Witney Antiques, Witney . . 087195, 131702
Wit's End, McKinnon 056120
Witt, Dordrecht 107990
Witt, Dortmund 125483
Witt, Oldenburg, Oldenburg 073214
Witt, Claude, Riquewihr 067152
Wittamer, M., Bruxelles 096269
Wittchen, Friedhelm, Naumburg, Saale 126517
Witte, C. de, Gent 058219
Witte, Donald de, Antwerpen 057753, 123563
Witte, F., Roosendaal 128816
Witte, Georges de, Gent 123633
Witte de With, Centrum voor Hedendaagse Kunst, Rotterdam 030109
De Witte Eenhoorn, Utrecht 078828
De Witte Lelie, Delft 107898
Witte Museum, San Antonio 047809
De Witte Rosieren, Roosendaal . . . 078692
De Witte Voet, Amsterdam 107835
Wittebol, Joseph, Helmond 128711
Wittels & Co., F., Caracas 093547
Wittelsbachermuseum Aichach, Archäologische Staatssammlung München, Aichach 015458
Wittenberger Freilichtmuseum, Tollhus up'n Wurnbarg, Edewecht 016886
Wittenborn, San Francisco 119838, 142970
Wittenborn-Czubaszek, Angelika, Berlin 069789
Wittenbrink, Bernhard & Hanna, München 104346
Wittenbrink, Bernhard & Hanna, München 104347
Wittenbrink, Bernhard & Hanna, München 134289
Wittenbrink, Bernhard & Hanna, München 134290
Witter, San Francisco 092907
Witter Gallery, Storm Lake 048381
Witte's Museum, Axel 029286
Witteveen, Amsterdam 107836
Wittgensteiner Kunst Gesellschaft '80 e.V., Bad Berleburg 053652
Witthoeft, Heinz, Stuttgart 105024
Wittig, Friedrich, Kiel 134089
Wittke, Bodo, Rosenheim 073576
Wittke, Hans-Joachim, Adliswil . . . 129893
Wittköpper, Markus, Münster 126512
Wittkowski, Evelyn, Berlin 125317
Wittmann, Dachau 070171, 138971
Wittmann, Rohrbach, Ilm 073566
Wittmann, D., Rohrbach, Kreis Pfaffenhofen 126729
Wittmann, Jutta, Wien 095960
Wittmann, Karin, Neubeuern 072971
Wittrock, Wolfgang, Berlin 069790
Wittrock, Wolfgang, Düsseldorf . . . 070468
Wittumsmuseum, Urbach 020546
Wittumspalais - Goethe-Nationalmuseum, Stiftung Weimarer Klassik und Kunstsammlungen, Weimar, Thüringen 020758
Wittwe, Elisabeth, Metz 099720
Witula, Alex, Bologna 075122
Witzel, Erhard, Wiesbaden 105286
Witzel, H., Stiege 073919
Witzenbacher, Berlin 138861
Wixhäuser Dorfmuseum, Darmstadt 016648
Wizani, Manfred, München 126486
Wizard of A-Z, Seattle 093089
Wizard of Was, Nashville 090495
Wizards Wood Works, Austin 087625, 131810
W.K.P. Kennedy Gallery, North Bay . 006039
Władyka, Zbigniew, Łódź 129054
W.M. Keck Museum, Reno 047377
Wobst, Bad Salzungen 101696
Wobst, Werner & Sigrid, Möhnesee 104086
Woburn Abbey, Woburn 041426
The Woburn Abbey Antiques Centre, Woburn 087202
Woburn Book Shop, London 141921
Woburn Fine Arts, Woburn 087203, 114716, 131704
Wocher-Panorama der Stadt Thun um 1810, Thun 037633
Wocoal Art Center, Spiral, Tokyo . . . 027274
Woefke, Mortsel 137533
Woehl, Gerald, Marburg 126288
Wöhlers, Bad Wimpfen 069396
Woehlert, Michael, Bad Bederkesa . 125085
Wöhlke, H., Jork 103457
Wöhrl, Erwin, Egweil 125573
Wölbert, Otto, Stuttgart 126889
Wölfle, Robert, München 139556
Woeller, Thomas, Frankfurt am Main 102838
Woellner jr., W.C., Cincinnati 088295
Woensampresse, Werkgemeinschaft Deutscher Graphiker, Essen 053653, 133920
Woerdehoff, Esther, Paris 100970
Wörfel, Peter & Christel, Schweinfurt 104864
Wörner, Reinhard & Petra, Nidderau 104438
Wöste, Bösel 102172
Woeste, Jörn-Uwe & Barbara, Augsburg 138690
Wofsy, Alan, San Francisco 119839, 142971
Wogrolly, Graz 123370
Wohl, Dietmar, Münster 126513
Wohl, Lorraine, New York 091351
Wohl, Lorraine, New York 091352
Wohl Archaeology Museum Herodian Mansions, Jerusalem 022987
Wohlers & Co., Dr. Robert, Hamburg 139223
Wohlfarth, Washington 120366
Wohlgemuth, Jürgen, München . . . 072884
Wohlgemuth, Luise, Zollikon 130226
Wohlgenannt, Egon, Neukirch 072997
Wohlgenannt-Zincke, Johannes, Groß Gerungs 057041
Wohlhüter, Werner, Leibertingen . . . 103849
Wohlhuter, Paris 066677
Wohlleb, Wien 123537
Wohlleben, Reinhold, Calw 102298
Wohlrab, A., Plauen 073339
Wohnmaschine, Berlin 102087
Wohnmuseum Egga, Visperterminen 037683
Wohnmuseum Schellenberg, Aussenstelle des Liechtensteinischen Landesmuseums, Schellenberg 027839
Wohnorama, Kloten 082516
Wohnwerk, Wuppertal 074548
Wojciechowski, Jerzy, Poznań 129069
Wojewódzkie Muzeum Pożarnictwa, Włocławek 032505
Wojtachnio, Elżbieta & Stanisław, Warszawa 079793
Wojtasiak, Adam, Milanówek 140758
Wojtok, Christa, Hannover 103301
Wójtowicz, Kraków 140750
WOKA, Wien 095961
Wokingham Antiques Centre, Wokingham 087206, 131706
Woksengs Samlinger, Rørvik 031152
Wolber, Kerben 071797, 126030
Wolber, Karl, Bonn 069950
Wolcott House Museum Complex, Maumee 045727
Wold Galleries, Bourton-on-the-Water 112684
Woldaschl, Michael, Wien 095962

Wolf, Berlin 138862
Wolf, Cincinnati 115676
Wolf, Cleveland 115752
Wolf, Coswig bei Dresden 125434
Wolf, Eichstetten 070523
Wolf, Meinerzhagen 072498
Wolf, Cäcilia, Bad Oeynhausen 121304
Wolf, Christin, Albuquerque 114836
Wolf, Daniel, New York 118574
Wolf, Doris, Wien 095963
Wolf, Elfriede, München 104348
Wolf, Ernst, Wien 057590
Wolf, Gregor, Grafenau, Niederbayern 071078
Wolf, Günter, Karlsruhe 071734
Wolf, Günter, Schmitten 073707
Wolf, Gustav, Östringen 104525
Wolf, Hagen, Bodenheim 069899
Wolf, Hans-Werner, Göttingen 071057
Wolf, Hermann, Crailsheim 070161
Wolf, James, Cincinnati 088296
Wolf, Joachim, Pforzheim 126629
Wolf, Lone, Fort Worth 116168
Wolf, Michael J., San Diego 119567
Wolf, Peter & Eva, Sulzbach am Main 074029
Wolf, U., Eichstetten 070524
Wolf, Ulrich, Gross-Zimmern 071117
Wolf & Eckert, Dresden . . 070336, 125515
Wolf House Museum, Manhattan . . 045633
Wolf-Kurz, Renate, Erbach, Odenwald 139040
Wolf Point Area Historical Society Museum, Wolf Point 049274
Wolf-Schirmer, Juliane, Kandern . . 125994
Der Wolf-Verlag, Sankt Michael, Lavanttal 133157
Wolf & Wolf, Liebenau 095648
Wolfaert-Masson, Knokke-Heist . . . 096363
Wolfe, Ernie, Los Angeles 116916
Wolfe & Wolfe, Stockholm 082042
Wolfeboro Historical Society Museum, Wolfeboro 049275
Wolfenbütteler Barock-Nachrichten, Wolfenbüttel 135829
Wolfenbütteler Renaissance Mitteilungen, Wolfenbüttel 135830
Wolff, Den Haag 078270
Wolff, München 139557
Wolff, Schwelm 104865
Wolff, B., Haguenau 099322
Wolff, Frank Freiherr von, Oldenburg, Oldenburg 126593
Wolff, Gérard, Liverdun 063970
Wolff, Gisela, Fulda 125696
Wolff, Jocelyn, Paris 100971
Wolff, Jürgen, Nürnberg 134322
Wolff, Klaus, Schweinfurt 073768
Wolff, Michael, Marburg 072453
Wolff, Reinhard, Berlin . . . 069791, 102088, 125318
Wolff, Tatjana, Kiel 126046
Wolff, Torsten, Bremen 102258
Wolffersdorff, Thomas von, Leipzig . 126202
Wolfgang Lettl-Verein zur Förderung surrealer Kunst e.V., Augsburg . . . 053654
Wolfhound Press, Dublin 134533
Wolfinger, Willy, Balzers 140222
Wolfram, Lohfelden 126227
Wolfrum, Wien 133242
Wolfrum, Hubert, Wien . . . 095964, 133243, 137379
Wolfs, Maastricht 108138
Wolfsberg Center, Ermatingen 111399
Wolfsberg-Verlag, Zürich 135107
Wolfsen, Aalborg 098520
Wolfson Museum, Heichal Shlomo, Jerusalem 022988
The Wolfsonian, Florida International University, Miami Beach 045826
Wolfsteiner Heimatmuseum im Schramlhaus, Freyung 017258
Woljeon Art Museum, Seoul 027616
Die Wolkenpumpe, Luzern 141276
Die Wolkenpumpe, Osnabrück 139642
Wolkoffin Talomuseo, Etelä-Karjalan Museo, Lappeenranta 009807
Wolkowitz, Bryce, New York 118575
Wollaston Heritage Museum, Wollaston 041428
Wollenweber, Andreas, Frankfurt am Main 102839
Woller, Helmut, Schwechat 137262
Wollner, Wilhelm, Bonn 138912
Wollny, Katharina, Wolfratshausen . 127034
Wollombi Barn Antiques, Wollombi . 056840
Wollondilly Heritage Centre, The Oaks 001353
Wollongong City Gallery, Wollongong East 001627
Wollwert, Birgel 069850
Wolm'Art, Souffelweyersheim 068269
Wolnik, Edward, Wrocław 129133
Wołosz, Bogdan, Kraków 140751
Wolseley, London 085811, 113977
Wolseley Community Museum, Wolseley 006879
Wolter, Freiburg im Breisgau 139122
Wolter, Raesfeld 073408
Wolter, Reinhard, Welt 074331
Wolter, U., Königswinter 072041
Wolters, Maastricht 078632, 128767
Wolters, A., Edemissen 070503
Wolters, Thomas, Berlin 125319
Wolthaus, Düsseldorf 070469
Wolvekamp, J., Utrecht 140559
Wolverhampton Antique Market, Wolverhampton 087215, 142165
Wolverhampton Art Gallery, Wolverhampton 041432
Wolverine Hobby and Historical Society Museum, Spy Hill 006505
Wolzik, Claudia, Essen 070655
Womack, Kathy, Austin 115023
Woman Made Gallery, Chicago 042887
Womankraft, Tucson 048647
Woman's Art, Laverock 136677
Women and Their Work, Austin . . . 041940
Women Art Jia Association, Suzhou 052802, 098000
Women in the Arts, Indianapolis . . . 116499
Women in the Arts, Washington . . . 136678
Women in the Arts Newsletter, New York 136679
Women & Their Work, Austin 115024
Women's Army Corps Museum, Fort Lee 043941
Women's Art Association of Canada, Toronto 052778
Women's Art Registry of Minnesota, Saint Paul 055110
Women's Art Registry of Minnesota Gallery, Saint Paul 047710
Women's Caucus for Art, Philadelphia 055111
Women's Caucus for Art. National Update, Philadelphia 136680
Women's Heritage Museum, San Francisco 047891
Women's History Museum, West Liberty 049087
Women's Museum, Dallas 043279
Won, Seoul 107300
Won, Dong, Daegu 107193
Won Kwang College Museum, Iri . . 027513
Wondai Shire Art Gallery, Wondai . . 095408
Wonder Graphics, Washington 120367
Wonder Graphics, Washington 120368
Wonder Works Children's Museum, The Dalles 043283
Wonderful Department Store, Singapore 109895
Wonderful World of Antiques, Detroit 088780
Wonderland, Gouda 108028
Wonderland, Tilburg 078786
Wonderland Multivintage, Chicago . 088195
Wonderword, Hamburg 139224
Wong & Partners, Ruwi 079521
Wong, Edmond, Hong Kong 059712
Wong, Kwong, Hong Kong 059713
Wong, T., Hong Kong 097846
Wong, Wylie, San Francisco 092908
Wong Man Chun, Hong Kong 059714
Wongan Ballidu and District Museum, Wongan Hills 001629
Wonnerup House and Old School, Busselton 000868
Wonsan Historical Museum, Wonsan 027444
Wonthaggi Auctions, Wonthaggi . . . 120657
Woo-Bong Art Museum, Daegu . . . 027477
Woo Sheung Tak, Hong Kong 059715
Woo Sheung Tak, Hong Kong 059716
Woocoo Museum, Brooweena 000855
Wood, Bruce, Chicago 115584
Wood, Christopher, London 113978
Wood, Colin, Aberdeen . . . 083242, 141381
Wood, J. & K., Barnsley, South Yorkshire 112560
Wood, Jeremy, Billingshurst 112642
Wood, Marcia, Atlanta 114944
Wood, Martin Frank, Dallas 115956
Wood, Michael, Plymouth 086278
Wood, Michael, Plymouth 114266
Wood, Pat & Brian, Lynton 085887
Wood, Peter, Cambridge 141479
Wood, P.N., Rugby 131431
Wood, Vanessa, Mosman 056268
Wood Artists, New York 132550
Wood Be Goods, London 131218
Wood County Historical Center, Bowling Green 042371
Wood Creations, Austin 115025
Wood Doctor, Albuquerque 131756
The Wood Doctor, Las Vegas 132219
Wood Doctor, Phoenix 132658
Wood End Museum, Scarborough . . 040969
Wood Gallery, Hazmieh 077426
Wood & Hogan, New York 091353
Wood Intentions, London 096963
Wood Jack, Cincinnati 115677
Wood Library-Museum of Anesthesiology, Park Ridge 046823
Wood Mountain Post, Regina 006270
Wood Mountain Ranch and Rodeo Museum, Wood Mountain 006880
Wood Pile Antiques, Portland 092027, 132707
Wood Shop Art Gallery, Chicago . . . 115585
Wood-Stock, Hasselt 058234
Wood Street Antiques, Myrtleford . . 056310
Wood Street Galleries, Pittsburgh . . 047065
Wood Street Gallery, Chicago 115586
Wood Stripping and Refinishing, Toledo 132978
Wood Tobe-Coburn School, New York 051836
Wood Works, London 131219
Woodall & Emery, Balcombe 083367
Woodard & Greenstein, New York . . 091354
Woodart, Marsa 128476
Woodart Picture Framers, Mowbray 080724
Woodbine, Spalding 114472
Woodbine, Whaplode Drove 114678
Woodbine International Fire Museum, Woodbine 049279
Woodbourne, Cincinnati 115678
Woodbridge Museum, Woodbridge . 041434
Woodbridge Pine & Collectables, Woodbridge 087226
Woodburn Plantation, Pendleton . . . 046869
Woodburn & Westcott, Indianapolis 116500
Woodbury Antiques, Woodbury 087227
Woodchester Villa, Bracebridge . . . 005128
Woodchurch Village Life Museum, Woodchurch 041435
Woodco, Jacksonville 132200
Woodcraft, Omaha 132601
Woodcraft and Decor, Singapore . . 080589
Woodcraft Gallery, Christchurch . . . 108420
Woodd, Anthony, Edinburgh 084322
Wooden Bird, Columbus 115810
The Wooden Bird, Minneapolis 117329
Wooden Bird, Saint Paul 119321
Wooden Box Antiques, Woodville . . 087243
Wooden Elephant Furniture, Saint Louis 132756
Wooden Gallery, Chicago 115587
The Wooden Goose, Drouin 055759
Wooden Horse, Minneapolis 090408
Wooden Horse Antique, Jacksonville 089475, 132201
Wooden Nickel, Tampa 093159
Wooden Nickel Antiques, Cincinnati 088297, 122862, 131949
Wooden Nickel Coins, Seattle 093090
Wooden Nickel Historical Museum, San Antonio 047810
Wooden Pew, Tyabb 056757
The Wooden Rose, Kaiapoi 079130
Wooden Spoon Antiques, Coffs Harbour 055704
Wooden Things II, Norfolk 091402
Wooden Ways and Olden Days, Omaha 091593
Woodend and District Local and Family History Resource Centre, Woodend 001632
Woodford, Louisville 090046
Woodha, Boston 115241
Woodhall Spa Cottage Museum, Woodhall Spa 041436
Woodhams, W.J., Shaldon 086548, 131471
Woodhead, Geoffrey M., Honiton . . 141677
Woodhorn Colliery Museum, Ashington 038539
Woodhouse, R.C., Hunstanton 084769, 130819
Woodland, Birmingham 130398
Woodland Art Gallery, Glasgow 113134
Woodland Heritage Museum, Westbury 041345
Woodlands Art Gallery, London 040325
Woodlands Auction Rooms, Ocean Grove 120622
Woodlands Gallery, Falkland 113049
Woodlands Gallery, Winnipeg 097613
Woodlands Pioneer Museum, Woodlands 006882
Woodlawn Museum, Ellsworth 043685
Woodlawn Plantation, Alexandria . . 041650
Woodley, A.R., Ascot 130311
Woodloes Homestead Folk Museum, Cannington 000893
Woodman's House Antiques, Uppingham 086989, 131632
Woodmere Art Museum, Philadelphia 046996
Woodnuts & Co., Chicago 088196
Woodpecker, Calgary 096856
Woodpecker, Roma 076727
The Woodpigeon, London . 085812, 131220
Woodrising Gallery, Isle-of-Skye . . . 113305
Woodrow Wilson Birthplace and Museum, Staunton 048346
Woodrow Wilson House, Washington 048961
Woodruff Museum of Indian Artifacts, Bridgeton 042411
Woods, Michael, Toledo 120095
Woods, Stuart, New Town 056328
Woods Hole Oceanographic Institution Exhibit Center, Woods Hole 049288
Wood's Refinishing and Restoration, Richmond 132727
Woods Street Gallery, Darwin 094463
Wood's Wharf Antiques Bazaar, Haslemere 084610
Woodshed Antiques, Ballarat 055440
Woodside & Braseth, Seattle 120013
Woodside Finishers, San Francisco . 132918
Woodside National Historic Site, Kitchener 005719
Woodside Reclamation, Berwick-upon-Tweed 083495
Woodside Store Historic Site, Woodside 049289
Woodson, Charlotte, Birmingham . . 087788
Woodson County Historical Museum, Yates Center 049334

Woodstock Art, Woodstock 114732
Woodstock Art Gallery, Woodstock . 006884
Woodstock Artists Association, Woodstock 055112
Woodstock Artists Gallery, Woodstock 049293
The Woodstock Bookshop, Woodstock 142171
Woodstock Historical Society Museum, Bryant Pond 042492
Woodstock Historical Society Museum, Woodstock 049291
Woodstock Historical Society Museum, Woodstock 049295
Woodstock Museum, Woodstock . . 006885
Woodstock Museum of Shenandoah County, Woodstock 049296
Woodstock School of Art, Woodstock 052403
Woodstrip International, Gent 058220, 123634
Woodtech, Windsor, Ontario 123863
Woodville Museum, Rogue River . . 047526
Woodville Pioneer Museum, Woodville 030661
Woodward, New York 118576
Woodward Antiques, Jacksonville . 089476
Woodware Art, Skipton 114440
Woodworking Wizard, Denver 132047
Woodworks, Dallas 132027
The Woodworks Gallery, Vancouver 097547
Woodworm Antiques, Fairy Meadow 055814, 123222
Wookey Hole Cave Diving and Archaeological Museum, Wookey Hole 041440
Woolaroc Museum, Bartlesville . . . 042033
Woolff, London 113979
Woolfsons of James Street, Stewarton 086701, 131533
Woolgoolga Art Gallery, Woolgoolga 095414
Woollahra Antiques Centre, Woollahra 056879
Woollahra Art Removals, North Melbourne 094977
Woollahra Decorative Arts Gallery, Bondi Junction 055520
Woollahra Times Art Gallery, Woollahra 095431
Woolley, Mark, Portland 119063
Woolley & Wallis, Salisbury 122685
Woolpit and District Museum, Woolpit 041441
Woolstaplers Hall Museum, Chipping Campden 039078
Wooltrak Store, Lismore 136978
Woomera Heritage Centre, Woomera 001635
Woonbootmuseum, Amsterdam . . . 029244
De Woonstee, Dordrecht 128652
Woori, Seoul 107301
Wooster Gallery, New York 091355
Wooster Gardens, New York 118577
Wooster Projects, New York 118578
Wooten, Dallas 088629
Wooth, Alexander Georg, Baden-Baden 069429, 125128
Wootton, Baltimore 087724, 131829
Worby, Russell, Colwyn Bay 084069
Worcester Antiques Centre, Worcester 087260, 131715
Worcester Art Museum, Worcester . 049309
Worcester Center for Crafts, Krikorian Gallery, Worcester 049310
Worcester City Museum and Art Gallery, Worcester 041446
Worcester Historical Museum, Worcester 049311
Worcester Museum, Worcester 034778
Worcester of Christchurch, Christchurch 079069
Worcestershire County Museum, Kidderminster 039861
Worcestershire Yeomanry Cavalry Museum, Worcester 041447
The Word Bookstore, Montréal 137668
Word & Image, London 136282
Wordelmann, Lutz, Berlin 069792
Words and Pictures Museum, Northampton 046546
Words Etcetera, Dorchester 141556
Words Worth Books, Calgary 137629
Wordsworth House, Cockermouth . 039114
Worgull, Wienhausen 105239
Work of Art, Houston 116430
Work of Artist, Phoenix 118896
The Work of Our Hands, Atlanta . . . 114945
Worker Gallery, Xining 098056
Workers Arts and Heritage Centre, Hamilton 005597
Worker's Home Museum, South Bend 048230
Workhouse Museum, Londonderry . 040331
Working Classroom, Albuquerque . . 114837
Working Wood, Cobargo 094408
Workman, Wally, Austin 115026
Workman and Temple Family Homestead Museum, City of Industry 042934
The Works, Ohio Center for History, Art and Technology, Newark 046432
The Works Antiques Centre, Llandeilo 085031, 130906
Works Galerie, Montfort-l'Amaury . 099745
Works of Art, Antwerpen 057754
Works of Art, Paisley 114218
Works of Art Collection, University of Cape Town, Rosebank 034745
Works on Paper, Los Angeles 116917
Works on Paper, New York 094043
Works on Paper, North Melbourne . 094978
Works on Paper, Philadelphia 118855
Works San Jose Gallery, San Jose . 119867
The Workshop, Roma 076728
Workshop and Stores, Grangemouth 039618
Workshop Arts Centre, Willoughby . 095400
Workshop Editions, Carlton North . . 133046
Workshop Glas und Keramik, Berlin 102089
Workshop Print Gallery, Chicago . . . 115588
Workshop Wales Gallery, Fishguard 113068
Worksop Museum, Worksop 041450
Workspace, Honolulu 116253
World 4 You, Wien 095965
World Accents, Portland 119064
World Africa, New York 118579
World Antique Dealers Association, Mansfield 055113
World Antique Fair, Osaka 093807
World Art, Denville 136681
World Art Center, New York 118580
World Art Gallery, Eindhoven 108011
World Art Gallery, Ho Chi Minh City . 120541
World Art Gallery, Seoul 107302
World Arts, Beijing 135653
World Class Collectibles, Jacksonville 089477
World Coin Company of America, Chicago 088197
World Coin News, Iola 136682
World Coins, Canterbury 083869
World Coins and Antiques, Chicago 088198
World Famous Portobello Market, London 085813, 131221
World Figure Skating Museum and Hall of Fame, Colorado Springs 043062
World Fine Art, Scottsdale 136683
World Fine Art Gallery, New York . . 118581
World Fine Art Gallery, New York . . 118582
World Forestry Center, Portland . . . 047183
World Golf Hall of Fame, Saint Augustine 047615
World in Wax Museum, Echuca . . . 001008
World Kite Museum and Hall of Fame, Long Beach 045385
World Line Arts, Dubai 112461
World Map Company, New Orleans . 142624
World Methodist Museum, Lake Junaluska 045109
World Money Fair, Basel 093897
World Museum of Mining, Butte . . . 042536
World Museum of Natural History, Riverside 047462
World O' Tools Museum, Waverly . . 049019
The World of Antiques & Art, Bondi Junction 135542
World of Art, Cairo 098678
World of Books, Belfast 141407
World of Centuries Art, Woollahra . . 056880
World of Country Life, Exmouth . . . 039469
World of Energy, Fremantle 001044
World of Energy at Keowee-Toxaway, Seneca 048112
World of Glass, Saint Helens 040910
The World of Toyism, Emmen 053911
World of Wings Pigeon Center Museum, Oklahoma City 046654
The World Organization of China Painters, Oklahoma City 046655, 055114
World Research Company, Washington 093445
World Sculpture News, Hong Kong . 135654
World Trade Art Gallery, New York . 118583
World Wide Art Products, Hong Kong 097847
World Wide Arts Resources, Columbus 115811
World Wide Gallery, Washington . . . 120369
Worldgallery.co.uk, London 113980
Worlds End Bookshop, London 141922
World's Money Exchange, Chicago . 088199
World's Treasures, Houston 089254
Worldtisic Art, Chicago 115589
Worldwide Butterflies and Lullingstone Silk Farm, Sherborne 041008
Worldwide Numismatic Galleries, Sacramento 092191
Wormsloe State Historic Site, Savannah 048033
Worpsweder Verlag, Lilienthal 134160
Worrell, Norman, Nashville 117379
Worsbrough Mill Museum, Barnsley, South Yorkshire 038601
Worsch, Otto, Klagenfurt 057116
Worsfold, Deborah, Vancouver 097548
Worshipful Company of Glaziers and Painters of Glass, London 054545
Worth & Co., Jacksonville 089478
Worthing Auction Galleries, Worthing 122764
Worthing Museum and Art Gallery, Worthing 041451
Worthington, Chicago 115590
Worthington, Chicago 115591
Worthington, Los Angeles 089943
Worthington, Mac, Columbus 115812
Worthington, Nancy, Houston 116431
Worthington Historical Society Museum, Worthington 049317
Worthy's Upholstering Company, Washington 133038
Wortley Top Forge, Thurgoland 041220
Worx of Art, Hitchin 113247
Wosimsky, Dietgard, Gießen 102957
Wosinsky Mór Megyei Múseum, Szekszárd 021876
Wosnitza, Franziska, Dresden 125516
Wotton Auction Rooms, Wotton-under-Edge 122765
Wotton Heritage Centre, Wotton-under-Edge 041452
Woudenberg, Den Haag 128639
Woulfe, Angela, Limerick 105898
Wouters, Louis, Haacht 123637
Woven Magic, Sevenoaks 086544
Wow, Denver 088752
Wow Art Gallery, Mumbai 105818
Wow & Zen, Chicago 088200
Wowan and District Museum, Wowan 001636
Woźniak, Magdalena, Poznań 109065
Woznik, Michael, Bonn 125365
Wrackmuseum, Cuxhaven 016615
Wrather West Kentucky Museum, Murray State University, Murray 046101
Wray Museum, Wray 049318
Wrede, Heinz, Bad Reichenhall 069358
Wrede, Stella, Heidelberg 125902
Wren, Burford 083797, 130481
Wren, Portland 092028
Wren, Christopher, Melton Mowbray 114075
Wren Gallery, Burford 112757
Wren House Antiques, Wrentham . . 087270
Wren's Nest House Museum, Atlanta 041878
Wrest Park, Silsoe 041030
Wrexham Arts Centre, Wrexham . . . 041457
Wrexham County Borough Museum, Wrexham 041458
Wrigglesworth, Linda, London 085814, 131222
Wright, Albuquerque 087435
Wright, Albuquerque 122794
Wright, Chicago 088201, 122848
Wright, Christchurch 079070
Wright, New York 118584
Wright, Andrew, Moonah 120614
Wright, B.J. & M.A., Burra 055591
Wright, Clifford, London 085815
Wright, Eli, Portarlington 056482
Wright, Gary, Moreton-in-Marsh . . .086025, 131288
Wright, Gordon, Edinburgh 141592
Wright, Mick & Fanny, Minchinhampton 085995
Wright, Peter, Great Missenden . . .084519, 130747
Wright, Tim, Glasgow 084474
Wright, Wayne, Christchurch 079071, 128930
Wright Brothers National Memorial, Kill Devil Hills 045000
Wright County Historical Museum, Buffalo 042497
Wright Manley, Tarporley 122719
Wright Museum, Wolfeboro 049277
Wright Museum of Art, Beloit 042133
Wright State University Art Galleries, Dayton 043326
Wright's Ferry Mansion, Columbia . 043075
Wrightway Studios, Auckland 128915
Wrigley-Cross, Portland 142814
Wriston Art Center Galleries, Appleton 041755
Writers Museum, Dublin 022777
The Writers' Museum, Edinburgh . . 039429
Wrobel, Claude, Paris 124835
Wroblewski, Richard, Hannover . . . 071421
W.R.S. Architectural Antiques, Low Newton 085857
WSA Gallery, Hamilton 108463
WTC Art Gallery, Rotterdam 108223
Wu, Lima 134854
Wucher, Francis, Storckensohn . . . 068283
Wucherer, Prof. Egon, Klagenfurt . . 095624
Wucherpfennig, O. & M., Taunusstein 074044
Wüest, Josef F., Ascona 111143
Wülker, Th., Lage, Lippe 072114
Wünnenberg, Eckhard, Essen 139060
Würstlein, Michelau 072542
Würth, Steffi, Haßloch 071429
Würthle & Sohn, Wien . . . 057591, 137380
Württembergische Landesbibliothek, Stuttgart 020372
Württembergischer Kunstverein Stuttgart, Stuttgart 020373
Württembergischer Kunstverein Stuttgart, Stuttgart 053655
Württembergisches Landesmuseum Stuttgart, Stuttgart 020374
Württembergisches Trachtenmuseum, Pfullingen 019614
Würzburger Kunstauktionshaus, Würzburg 121629
Wüst, Arno, Gossau (Sankt Gallen) . 082481
Wüst, Ursula, Berlin 125320
Wüstendörfer-Heid, Pedra, Eckental 125567
Wüstenhöfer, Armin, Leidersbach . . 072190
Wüthrich, Debora, Bern 082250
Wüthrich, Tony, Basel 111231
Wuhan City Museum, Wuhan 007302
Wuhou Museum, Chengdu 007047

Wuilliot Franck, L'Isle-sur-la-Sorgue . . . 063966
Wujiang Museum, Wujiang . . . 007305
WUK, Wien . . . 095966
Wulastook Museums, Fredericton . . 005488
Wulf, Dele, Konstanz . . . 103770
Wulfert, Fritz, Kevelaer . . . 071818
Wulff, C., Rostock . . . 139699
Wulff, N., Krummwisch . . . 072099
Wullschleger, John R., Zürich . . . 112200
Wunderbaldinger, Sankt Pölten . . . 137254
Wunderkammer, Carlton, Victoria . . 055636
Wunderlich, Dr. Chr.-H., Halle, Saale . . . 125795
Wunderlich & Co., Gerold, New York 118585
Wunderlich, Roland, Bad Mergentheim . . . 125110
Wunderlich, Wolfgang, München . . 072885
Wunderskirchner, Manfred, Böbing . 125345
Wunram, Emmerthal . . . 070565
Wunschel, Hervé, Villeurbanne . . . 068985
Wunschik, Hubertus, Mönchengladbach . . . 104103
Wupatki National Monument, Flagstaff . . . 043855
Wuppertaler Uhrenmuseum, Wuppertal . . . 021022
Wurlitzer Antiques, Miami . . . 090256
Wurm, Lippstadt . . . 103933
Wurm, Malen, Herne . . . 103360
Wurm, Thomas, Erfurt . . . 125602
Wurzel- und Heimatmuseum, Amel 003145
Wurzer, Gerhard, Houston . . . 116432
Wurzinger, Andrea, Freistadt, Oberösterreich . . . 137169
Wutzke, Koblenz . . . 103575
Wuxi City Calligraphy and Painting Gallery, Wuxi . . . 098047
Wuxi City Museum, Wuxi . . . 007307
Wuxi Engraved Stone Display Center, Wuxi . . . 007308
Wuxi Revolutionary Display Center, Wuxi . . . 007309
Wuzhong, Suzhou . . . 098001
Wuzhong, Suzhou . . . 098002
WVSA Arts Connection, Washington 055115
WWH Restoration, Washington . . . 133039
www.galleryonthe.net, Rotherham . 114328
Wyalkatchem C.B.H. Agricultural Museum, Wyalkatchem . . . 001637
Wyalong Park Private Museum, Maddington . . . 001202
Wyandot County Historical Society Museum, Upper Sandusky . . . 048710
Wyandotte County Museum, Bonner Springs . . . 042299
Wyandotte Museum, Wyandotte . . . 049320
Wyannie Malone Historical Museum, Hope Town . . . 003088
Wyards, Faversham . . . 113062
Wyatt, Buffalo . . . 115270, 131865
Wyatt Earp Birthplace, Monmouth . 045963
Wychwood, Taynton . . . 086833
Wyck Museum, Philadelphia . . . 046997
Wyckaert, Bruxelles . . . 058132, 123615
Wycombe Museum, High Wycombe 039749
Wydawnictwa Artystyczne i Filmowe, Warszawa . . . 134865
Wydawnictwo Artystyczne, Zdzisław, Wołomin . . . 109210
Wydler, Kurt, Bern . . . 129976
Wydra, Tereza E., Gdańsk . . . 108902
Wye College Museum of Agriculture, Dover . . . 039271
Wye Gallery, Hay-on-Wye . . . 113211
Wyeth, New York . . . 091356
Wykeham, Stockbridge . . . 086715
Wykeham, Stockbridge . . . 114487
Wykeham, Stockbridge . . . 131539
Wylam Railway Museum, Wylam . . 041461
Wyland, Honolulu . . . 116254
Wyland, Honolulu . . . 116255
Wyland, Honolulu . . . 116256
Wyland, Las Vegas . . . 116659
Wyland, Las Vegas . . . 116660
Wyland, San Diego . . . 119568
Wyland, San Francisco . . . 119840
Wyland, Seattle . . . 120014
Wylde, Trigg . . . 056739
Wylder, Jonathan, London . . . 113981
Wyler, S., New York . . . 091357
Wylie House Museum, Bloomington 042267
Wyllie, London . . . 085816, 113982
Wymondham Antique and Collectors Centre, Wymondham, Norfolk . . . 087278
Wymondham Heritage Museum, Wymondham . . . 041462
The Wynd Gallery, Melrose . . . 114073
Wyndham, Omaha . . . 091594
Wyndham Museum, Wyndham . . . 030662
Wyndham Shopping Arcade, Kingston . . . 106822
Wyndhams, Stow-on-the-Wold . . . 086769
Wyngaert, de, Bruxelles . . . 137486
Wynick-Tuck, Toronto . . . 097399
Wynn, Allen, Boston . . . 115242
Wynn Collection, Las Vegas . . . 045193
Wynter, New York . . . 118586
Wynyard and District Museum, Wynyard . . . 006886
Wyoming Arts Council Gallery, Cheyenne . . . 042816
Wyoming Dinosaur Center, Thermopolis . . . 048543
Wyoming Pioneer Home, Thermopolis . . . 048544
Wyoming Pioneer Memorial Museum, Douglas . . . 043486
Wyoming State Museum, Cheyenne 042817
Wyoming Territorial Park, Laramie . 045171
Wyrardisbury Antiques, Wraysbury .087268, 131719
Wyreena Gallery, Croydon . . . 094445
Wysing Arts, Bourn . . . 038793
Wysocki, André, Zürich . . 083039, 130272
Wyss & Partner, Zollikon . 112021, 122360
Wyss, Jaime, Dübendorf . 082346, 130007
Wyss, Markus, Zürich . . . 112201
Wyss-Chodat, Yvonne, Thônex . . . 130193
Wystan Hugh Auden-Dokumentationsräume, Kirchstetten . . . 002131
Wyters, Saint-Ouen . . . 067921
Wyters, Chantal, Paris . . . 066678
Wythenshawe Hall, Manchester City Art Gallery, Manchester . . . 040417
X-21 Modern, San Francisco . . . 119841
X 21 Modern Design, Sacramento . 092192
X-Art, Amsterdam . . . 107837
X-Art Studios für Computergrafik, Pinkafeld . . . 049643
X F Upholstery, San Jose . . . 132927
X-Pression, Indianapolis . . . 116501
XA Ytem Museum, Mission . . . 005886
Xabier Sabi i Lopez, Barcelona . . . 141008
Xairel, Lisboa . . . 080056
Xanadu, Maastricht . . . 078633
Xanadu, Sittard . . . 078764
Xanadu Gallery, San Francisco . . . 119842
Xandi, Ponta Delgada . . . 080061
Xanthippe Antichitá, Venezia . . . 076980
Xanthos, Glebe . . . 055883
Xantus János Múzeum, Győr . . . 021733
Xarrie, Barcelona . . . 080962
Xavante, Saint Kilda, Victoria . . . 095175
Xavier, Sliema . . . 077533, 107453
Xavier, Tereza, Rio de Janeiro . . . 096657
Xavier-Bender, Michèle, Paris . . . 066679
Xavier Square Antiques, Phoenix . . 091779
Xavier University Art Gallery, Cincinnati . . . 042932
Xavier University Museum (Museo de Oro), Cagayan de Oro City . . . 031644
Xavier's, Detroit . . . 088781
Xcape, Long Beach . . . 089666
Xcape, Long Beach . . . 089667
Xenos, Basel . . . 129941
Xenos, Hamburg . . . 134027
Xhenseval, A., Liège . . . 123658
Xhenseval, Philippe, Marseille . . . 124438
Xhibit Art Contemporary & Design, McMahons Point . . . 094757
Xi Bao Celadon Museum, Shenzhen 007265
Xi Xin Yuan, Shanghai . . . 059774
Xiamen Calligraphy and Painting Gallery, Xiamen . . . 098049
Xiamen City Art Cooperative, Xiamen . . . 098050
Xiamen City Museum, Xiamen . . . 007313
Xian Banpo Museum, Xian . . . 007321
Xian Beilin Museum, Xian . . . 007322
Xian Forest of Stone Tablets Museum, Xian . . . 007323
Xian Highway Display Center, Xian . 007324
Xian National Art Academy, Xian . . . 049859
Xiangshen, Shanghai . . . 059775
Xiangtan City Museum, Xiangtan . . 007326
Xiangyu, Indianapolis . . . 116502
Xianyang City Museum, Xianyang . . 007327
Xiao Xiao, Shanghai . . . 059776
Xiaoshan City Museum, Xiaoshan . . 007329
Xiaoshan Hua Institute, Hangzhou . 097740
Xiaoyanta Bag Guan Museum, Xian 007325
Xibit, Mumbai . . . 105819
Xicali, El Paso . . . 088822
Xiguan, Guangzhou . . . 059580
Xihu Calligraphy and Painting Gallery, Hangzhou . . . 097741
Xiling, Hangzhou . . . 097742
Xiling Shishu Painting Gallery, Chengdu . . . 097702
Xilobi, Barcelona . . . 129415
Ximena, Urioste, Ensdorf . . . 102630
Ximenes, Maria Pires, Setúbal . . . 129206
Xin, Yun, Singapore . . . 080590
Xin Hai Shouyi Mausoleum of Fallen Heroes, Wuhan . . . 007303
Xin-Shenzhou, Singapore . . . 109896
Xincheng District Museum, Nanning 007213
Xing, West Hollywood . . . 120420
Xinghua, Shanghai . . . 097954
Xingping Maoling Museum, Xianyang . . . 007328
Xingshansi Art Association, Xian . . .052803, 098054
Xinguang, Shanghai . . . 059777
Xinguang Art Gallery, Shenzhen . . . 097989
Xinjiang Museum, Urumchi . . . 007296
Xinjiang Painting Gallery, Urumchi . 007297
Xinjiang Photography and Fine Arts Publishing House, Urumchi . . . 133387
Xinle Yi Zhi Museum, Shenyang . . . 007258
Xiongfeng Tang Art Cooperative, Chengdu . . . 097703
Xippas, Renos, Paris . . . 100972
Xizhou Yandu Yi Zhi Museum, Shan Zhou Museum, Beijing . . . 007014
X.M.X. Art and Antique Centre, Lefkosia . . . 059959
Xoio, Porto . . . 080119
Xperiment Huset, Växjö . . . 036776
Xu, Huaiyu, Shanghai . . . 097955
Xu Bei-Hong Memorial Hall, Beijing 007015
Xuan Art Gallery, Ningbo . . . 097883
Xuanhua, Singapore . . . 109897
Xuchang, Shanghai . . . 059778
Xuchang City Museum, Xuchang . . 007332
Xue Lai Er, Shanghai . . . 097956
Xue Qin, Beijing . . . 097680
Xukou Gusu Art Cooperative, Suzhou . . . 098003
Xuzhou Gupeng, Xuzhou . . . 059791
Xuzhou Museum, Xuzhou . . . 007333
XX Multiple, Rotterdam . . . 108224
XXième Art, Paris . . . 066680
xxs Galerie im Studio, Celle . . . 102306
XXXX Antique Complex, Castlemaine . . . 055648
Xydis, Antonis, Athinai . . . 074615
XYLON Internationale Vereinigung der Holzschneider, Deutsche Sektion, Reutlingen . . . 053656
Xylon Museum, Schwetzingen . . . 020157
XYZ Antiques, New York . . . 091358
The Y, Hong Kong . . . 097848
Y & B Brocanteurs, Bruxelles . . . 058133
Y P Art Expo, Paris . . . 100973
Y & Z Oriental Furniture, Los Angeles . . . 089944
Ya, Akane, Kitakyushu . . . 077074
Ya, Roman, Sapporo . . . 077205
Ya Hui Art Gallery, Shenzhen . . . 097990
Ya Pian Zhan Zhen Museum, Dongguan . . . 007064
Ya Ya Gallery, New Orleans . . . 117531
Ya Yun Zhai, Tianjin . . . 098019
Yabane-Sagemonoya, Tokyo . . . 077322
Yachay Wasi, Training Center of Conservation and Restoration, Lima . . . 050593
Yacimiento-Museo Arqueologico, Ambrona . . . 034835
Yacimiento-Museo Arqueológico, Garray . . . 035214
Yacoubian, G.H., Lefkosia . . . 098308
Yad Labanim Museum and Memorial Center, Petah Tikva . . . 023044
Yad Lashiryon Museum, Latrun . . . 023024
Yad-Lebanim Memorial Center, Rehovot . . . 023057
Al-Yad Al-Mahira, Baghdad . . . 074852
Yad Vashem Art Museum, Museum of Holocaust Art, Jerusalem . . . 022989
Yad Yaari Museum of Jewish Youth Movement, Givat Haviva . . . 022910
Yaegaki-jinja Treasure Storehouse, Matsue . . . 026790
Yaelle, Toronto . . . 097400
Yaeyama Museum, Ishigaki . . . 026574
Yagai Hakubutsukan, Gashozukuri Minkaen, Shirakawa . . . 027078
The Yager Museum, Oneonta . . . 046692
Yagi, Kyoto . . . 077137
Yagi, Tokyo . . . 140209
Yağmur Kayabek, İstanbul . . . 083164
Yaguarundi Galería, Cali . . . 098243
Yague, Barcelona . . . 080963, 129416
Yahiko-jinja Treasure House, Yahiko 027318
Yakage Museum, Yakage . . . 027319
Yakima Valley Museum, Yakima . . . 049327
Yakushi-ji Treasure House, Nara . . . 026902
Yaky, Roma . . . 076729
Yaky, Roma . . . 076730
Yakyu Taiiku Hakubutsukan, Tokyo . 027275
Yaldhurst Museum of Transport and Science, Christchurch . . . 030470
Yale Center for British Art, New Haven . . . 046227
Yale Gallery, Vancouver . . . 097549
Yale Publications in the History of Art, New Haven . . . 136684
Yale University Art Gallery, New Haven . . . 046228
Yale University Art Gallery Bulletin, New Haven . . . 136685
Yale University Collection of Musical Instruments, New Haven . . . 046229
Yale University Press, London . . . 135277
Yale University Press, New Haven . . 135402
Yallingup Galleries, Yallingup . . . 095441
Yalvaç Müzesi, Yalvaç . . . 038196
Yalvaç Müzesi, Yalvaç . . . 038197
Yamada Shoten, Tokyo . . . 140210
Yamagata Bijutsukan, Yamagata . . . 027320
Yamagata-kenritsu Hakubutsukan, Yamagata . . . 027321
Yamaguchi, Osaka . . . 106975
Yamaguchi Hoshun Memorial Hall, Hayama . . . 026502
Yamaguchi-kenritsu Bijutsukan, Yamaguchi . . . 027322
Yamaguchi-kenritsu Hakubutsukan, Yamaguchi . . . 027323
Yamaguchi Tokenten, Tokyo . . . 077323
Yamaki Art Gallery, Osaka . . . 106976
Yamamoto, Hiroshima . . . 106860
Yamamoto Isoroku Kinenkan, Nagaoka . . . 026854
Yamamoto Kanae Memorial Museum, Ueda . . . 027302
Yamamoto Shoten, Tokyo . . . 140211

Yamana Artsalon, Tokyo 077324
Yamanashi-kenritsu Bijutsukan, Kofu 026677
Yamanashi-kenritsu Koko Hakubutsukan, Higashi-Yatsushiro 026506
Yamanouchi-jinja Treasure History Hall, Kochi 026674
Yamashita, Ito 077070
Yamaso, Kyoto 106908
Yamatane Bijutsukan, Tokyo 027276
Yamato, Lille 063871
Yamato, Paris 066681
Yamauchi Library, Yokohama 027339
Yamazaki Museum of Art, Kawagoe 026639
Yan, Hong Kong 097849
Yan Ku, Tong, Hong Kong 059717
Yanaga Hokkaido Museums, Sapporo 027039
Yanbian Autonomous Prefecture Museum, Yanji 007337
Yancey Richardson, New York 118587
Yancey's Antiques, Austin 087626
Yanchyshyn, Yuri, New York 132551
Yanda Aboriginal Art, Alice Springs . 055340
Yanda Aboriginal Arts Melbourne, Mentone 056212
Yande Meannjin Antiques, Narangba 056315
Yande Meannjin Antiques, Paddington, Queensland 056435
Yandina Trading Post, Yandina 056895
Yaneff International Art, Caledon East 005177
Yanes, Miami 090257
Yang, C., Tokyo 077325
Yangliu Gallery, Tianjin 098020
Yangliuqing Gallery, Tianjin 098021
Yangliuqing Museum, Tianjin 007291
Yangliuqing New Year Picture Cooperative, Tianjin 098022
Yangpyong Batangol Gallery, Gangha 107196
Yangtze River Antiques, Seattle . . . 093091
The Yangtze River Literature and Art Press, Wuhan 133389
Yangzhou Museum, Yangzhou 007336
Yanhuang, Jinan 097863
Yanhuang Art Center, Beijing 007016
Yanjing Art Cooperative, Beijing . . . 097681
Yanjing Art Cooperative-Biyun Si, Beijing 097682
Yanjing Art Cooperative Changcheng, Beijing 097683
Yanjing Art Cooperative Liulichang, Beijing 097684
Yanjing Art Cooperative-Qi Nian Hall, Beijing 097685
Yanjing Art Cooperative-Shisanling, Beijing 097686
Yanjing Art Cooperative-Wofosi, Beijing 097687
Yank Azman, Toronto 059321
Yankalilla District Historical Museum, Yankalilla 001642
Yankee Air Museum, Belleville 042110
Yankee Air Museum, Willow Run Airport 049196
Yankee Candle Car Museum, South Deerfield 048238
Yankee Peddler Antiques, Pittsburgh 091875
Yankee Trader, Denver 088753
Yankee Trader, Fresno 088924
Yannick, David, Bruxelles 058134
Yannis Tsarouchis Museum, Maroussi 021369
Al-Yanora, Sharjah 083230
Yant, Wrocław 129134
Yao Xian Museum, Yao Xian 007338
Yapı Kredi Kazım Taşkent Sanat Galerisi, İstanbul 112370
Yapı Kredi Vedat Nedim Tör Müzesi, İstanbul 038106
Yard Art, San Francisco 092909
Yard Dog Folk Art, Austin 087627
Yard Gallery, Nottingham 040628
Yarliyil Art Centre, Halls Creek 055933
Al-Yarmouk, Manama 096033
Yarmouth County Museum, Yarmouth 006889
Yarnton Antiques Centre, Yarnton . . 087280
Yarra Sculpture Gallery, Abbotsford 094112
Yarra Valley Antique Centre, Yarra Glen 056899
Yarralumla Gallery, Yarralumla 095450
Yarraman Heritage Centre, Yarraman 001645
Yarrawonga, Yarrawonga 120661
Y'Artecre Faso, Ouagadougou 052715
Yarton, Don, San Antonio 092594
Yashi Hua Yuan, Shenzhen 097991
Yasmeen, Sidi Bou Saïd 112259
Yass Railway Museum, Yass 001648
Yasuda, New York 118588
Yasui, Osaka 077185
Yasumi, Honolulu 088983, 132093
Yataro Noguchi Art Museum, Nagasaki 026876
Yates, David & Constance, New York 118589
Yates, Kenneth W., Shorncliffe 056592
Yato, San Diego 119569
Yatsuhashi-An & Shishu-Yakata, Kyoto 026776
Yau, Yick Hong, Hong Kong 059718
Yau Annie, New York 118590
Yawa, Washington 143051
Yaya, Tokyo 077326
Yayo Bajo, Pamplona 081527
Yayoi Gallery, Tokyo 107131
Yayoi Museum, Tokyo 027277
Yazdan, Manama 096034
Yazdi, Frank, Calgary 096857
Yazici, Kemal, Köngen 072029
Yazılıkaya Müzesi, Çifteler 038043
Yazoo Historical Museum, Yazoo City 049335
Ybor City State Museum, Tampa . . . 048494
Ydais, Annick, Biarritz 061479
Ydessa Hendeles Art Foundation, Toronto 006646
Ye Auld Curiosité Boutique, Montréal 059023
Ye Olde Antique Furniture House, Edmonton 058845
Ye Olde Bookshop, Kwinana 136968
Ye Olde Cupboard, Miami 090258
Ye Olde Village Clock Shop, Freshwater 084440, 130720
Year, Taipei 059797, 098084
Year Dot, Leeds 084931
Years Gone Buy, Chicago 088202
Yeasung, Seoul 107303
Yeats Tower - Thoor Ballylee, Gort . 022796
Yeemock, Seoul 107304
Yefief, Santa Fe 136686
Yeh, Seoul 107305
Yeiser Art Center, Paducah 046789
Yelde Hall Museum, Chippenham . . 039077
Yelen, Milano 075893
Yelens, Nowa Nowa 094997
Yeleswasam Pavilion, Hyderabad . . 022164
Yell Crafts, Shetland 114430
Yellow Aster, Los Angeles 089945
Yellow Lantern Antiques, Brighton . 083722
Yellow Medicine County Historical Museum, Granite Falls 044284
Yellow Moon Gallery, Holcombe . . . 113248
Yellowstone Art Museum, Billings . . 042209
Yellowstone Gateway Museum of Park County, Livingston 045353
Yelmo, Cartagena 081032
Yelmo, Cartagena 081033
Yelmo, Cartagena 122022
Yelmo, Cartagena 122023
Yelverton Paperweight Centre, Yelverton 041468
Yemac, Seoul 107306
Yemac, Seoul 107307
Yenar, Seoul 077376
Yeongil Folk Museum, Pohang 027538
Yepes, Los Angeles 116918
Yeppoon Collectables, Yeppoon . . . 056905
Yeraltı Müzesi, Kaymaklı 038122
Yeramian, J., Den Haag 107964
Yerba Buena Center for the Arts, San Francisco 047892
Yerebatan Sarnıcı, İstanbul 038107
Yeremiyew, Luc, Héry 124260
Yerevan Children's Picture Gallery, Erevan 000693
Yerewan State Humanitarian College, Erevan 049607
Yerevan State Institute of Fine Arts, Erevan 049608
Yes Books, Portland 142789
Yeshiva University Museum, New York 046419
Yesim, Hurlstone Park 094655
Yesong, Daegu 107194
Yester-Days, Haddington 084547
Yester-Year, Iver 084808, 130833
Yester-Year Artifacts Museum, Rowley 006313
Yester-Years Community Museum, Dinsmore 005352
Yesterday, Torino 076880
Yesterday and Today, Miami 090259
Yesterday and Today, Sutton-in-Ashfield 086803
Yesterday Antiquitäten, Wiesbaden . 074429
Yesterday Child, London . . 085817, 131223
Yesterday Once More, Miami 090260
Yesterday Once More, Wagga Wagga 056791
Yesterday Tackle and Books, Bournemouth 141428
Yesterday, Today and Tomorrow, Atlanta 087543
Yesterday, Today, Tomorrow, Dundee 084231
Yesterdays, Pörtschach am Wörther See 057213, 123429
Yesterdays, Wareham 087020
Yesterdays Antique & Curios, Singapore 080591
Yesterday's Antiques, Cleethorpes .084029, 130588
Yesterday's Antiques, Victoria Park . 056781
Yesterdays Books, Bournemouth . . 141429
Yesterday's Books, Wauchope 137134
Yesterday's Child, Denver 088754
Yesterday's Gems, Coffs Harbour . . 055705
Yesterdays Memories, Los Angeles . 116919
Yesterdays Memories, Miami 090261
Yesterday's Memories, Milwaukee . 142574
Yesterday's Memories and More, Pittsburgh 091876
Yesterday's News, Pittsburgh 091877
Yesterday's News, Tulsa 093341
Yesterday's Today, Perth 086228
Yesterdays Treasures, Ariah Park . . 055353
Yesterday's Treasures, Cleveland . . 088371
Yesterday's Treasures, Houston . . . 089255
Yesterdaze, Seattle 093092
Yesterdey's Art, Roma 076731
Yesteryear, Christchurch 079072
Yesteryear, Philadelphia 091704
Yesteryear, Princeton 136687
Yesteryear - A Step Back in Time, Los Angeles 089946
Yesteryear Antiques, Columbus . . . 088448
Yesteryear Antiques, Dublin 074958
Yesteryear Antiques, Phoenix 132659
Yesteryear Book Shop, Atlanta 142212
Yesteryear Costume Gallery, Orroroo 001359
Yesteryear House-Central Mine, Clarkston 042952
Yesteryear Mart, Las Vegas 089616
Yesteryear Museum, Captains Flat . 000894
Yesteryear Museum, Pamplin 046807
Yesteryears, Cincinnati 088298
Yesteryears Doll and Toy Museum, Sandwich 047936
Yeungnam University Museum, Kyongsan 027528
Les Yeux Fertiles, Paris 100974
Yew, Miaw, Singapore 080592
Yew Tree Antiques, Four Elms 084429
Yew Tree Antiques, Wiveliscombe . . 087199
Yewon, Seoul 107308
Yezerski, Howard, Boston 115243
Ygrego, Lisboa 109361
Y.H.F. Lardy, Toulon (Var) 068472
Yi, Seoul 107309
Yi, Hong, Seattle 120015
Yi, Xuan, Singapore 109898
Yi, Xuan Bao, Singapore 109899
Yi Jun Peace Museum, Den Haag . . 029458
Yi Zhi Shi Liao Guan, Shanghai 007247
Yiannoulis Halepas Museum and Museum of Tinian Artists, Panormos Tinou . . 021417
Yichang City Museum, Yichang 007339
Yigal Allon Center, Ginnosar 022909
Yiğit, İsmail, İstanbul 083165
Yih Feng, Taipei 059798
Yıldız Sarayi^BY Müzesi, İstanbul . . 038108
Yilpinji, Nice 099862
Yin & Co., I.T., Houston 116433
Yin Gui, Shanghai 059779
Ying, Kee Hong, Singapore 080593
Ying & Co., Ton, New York 118591
Yingkou City Museum, Yingkou . . . 007341
Yip Shu Lap, Hong Kong 097850
Yip's Rainbow, Hong Kong 097851
Yip's Rainbow, Hong Kong 097852
Yiti, Al-Qurum 108765
Yitti, Ruwi 108768
Yixing Porcelain Corporation Museum, Yixing 007342
Yiyuan, Shanghai 059780
Yiyuan, Shanghai 097957
Yksi, Eindhoven 108012
Ylä-Savon Kotiseutumuseo, Iisalmi . 009599
Ylämaan Jalokivimuseo, Ylämaa . . 010254
Yläneen Kotiseutumuseo, Yläne . . . 010255
Yli-Lauroselan Talomuseo, Ilmajoki 009603
Yli-Tolppa J & K, Turku 060649
Ylihärmän Kotiseutumuseo, Ylihärmä 010256
Ylikiimingin Kotiseututalo ja Museo, Ylikiiminki 010258
Ylistaron Kotiseutumuseo, Ylistaro . 010259
Yma, Tokyo 107132
Ymir Museum, Ymir 006891
Ynik, Amsterdam 078025
Yoder, Dean, Cleveland 131973
Yogen-In Homotsukan, Kyoto 026777
Yogi Berra Museum, Little Falls . . . 045339
Yojigen, Osaka 077186
Yokogaki Suikodo, Osaka 077187
Yokohama Bijutsu Club, Yokohama . 053807
Yokohama Bijutsukan, Yokohama . . 027340
Yokohama Doll Museum, Yokohama 027341
Yokohama Kaikou Shiryokan, Yokohama 027342
Yokohama Maritime Museum and Nippon-Maru Memorial Park, Yokohama . 027343
Yokohama Ogimura Shikko, Yokohama 077345
Yokosuka-shi Hakubutsukan, Yokosuka 027345
Yokota, Kyoto 077138
Yokoyama, Kyoto 077139
Yokoyama, Tokyo 077327
Yokoyama Taikan Memorial Hall, Tokyo 027278
Yolande's Gallery, Enniskillen 113026
Yoldosh Oxunboboev Memorial Muzeyi, Margelan 049396
Yolk, Los Angeles 116920
Yolo County Historical Museum, Woodland 049285
Yonaa Antiques, Los Angeles 089947, 132285
Yonago-shi Bijutsukan, Yonago 027348
Yonan, Serge F., Beirut 077421
Yong, Yuan Cheng, Singapore 109900
Yongfeng, Shenzhen 097992
Yongfeng County Museum, Enjiang . 007067
Yonghong, Shanghai 097958

Yonsei University Museum, Seoul . . 027617
Yook Yung, Seoul 107310
Yoon, Sebastian, Calgary 096858
Yorba-Slaughter Adobe Museum, Chino 042903
The Yorck Project, Gesellschaft für Bildachivierung, Berlin 133819
York, Roma 076732
York, San Antonio 092595
York, Sydney 056692
York, Caroline, Saint Petersburg . . . 119322
York, Graham, Honiton . . . 084732, 141678
York, Richard, New York 118592
York and Lancaster Regimental Museum, Rotherham 040858
York Antiques, Launceston 056090
York Antiques Centre, York 087297
York & Caning, New York 132552
York City Art Gallery, York 041483
York Cottage Antiques, Helmsley . . 084646
York County Museum, York 049349
York Decorative and Fine Arts Society, York 054546
York Gallery, London 085818
York Gallery, London 085819
York Gallery, Torquay 114587
York Minster Undercroft Treasury and Crypt, York 041484
York Quay Gallery at Harbourfront Centre, Toronto 006647
York Racing Museum, York 041485
York Story, York 041486
York Sunbury Historical Society Museum, Fredericton 005489
Yorke, Moonta 056252
Yorke, John H., Saint Leonards-on-Sea 086467
Yorks, Shona, New York 118593
Yorkshire, New York 118594
Yorkshire Air Museum, Elvington . . 039440
Yorkshire Air Museum, Canada Branch, Saint-Laurent 006381
Yorkshire and Humberside Federation of Museums and Art Galleries, Doncaster 054547
Yorkshire and Humberside Museums Council, Leeds 054548
Yorkshire Art, Swinton 114544
Yorkshire Arts, Dewsbury 054549
Yorkshire Artscene, Halifax 136283
Yorkshire Museum, York 041487
Yorkshire Museum of Carriages and Horse Drawn Vehicles, Wensleydale . . . 041333
Yorkshire Museum of Farming, York 041488
Yorkshire Museums Council, Leeds 054550
Yorkshire Pine, San Diego 092701
Yorkshire Sculpture Park, West Bretton 041334
The Yorkshire Watercolour Society, Brighouse 054551
Yorkton Arts Council, Yorkton 006895, 052779
Yorktow, Launceston 094730, 136971
Yorktown Historical Museum, Yorktown 049351
Yorktown Museum, Yorktown Heights 049356
Yorktown Visitor Center, Yorktown . 049354
Yorktown Visitor Center Museum, Colonial National Historical Park, Yorktown 049355
Yorkville, New York 118595
Yorkville House, Toronto 097401
Yorozu Tetsugoro Memorial Museum of Art, Towa 027283
Yoseido, Tokyo 107133, 128452
The Yosemite Museum, Yosemite National Park 049357
Yoshida, Portland 092029, 119065
Yoshii, New York 118596
Yoshii, Osaka 077188
Yoshii, Paris 100975
Yoshimizu-jinja Yoshinoyama, Yoshino 027351
Yoshimoto Bungeikan, Yoshimoto Comedians Museum, Osaka 026991
Yoshimura, Emile, Mitaka 128447
Yoshinogawa Sake Museum Hisago-tei, Nagaoka 026855
Yoshizawa Kinenkan, Joetsu 026601
Yoshizumi, Sapporo 077206
Yossi Milo, New York 118597
Yossi S. Masters Workshop, Jerusalem 075000
Yotvata Museum and Visitors Center, Yotvata 023102
Youll, Hungerford 084766
Young, Edinburgh 084323
Young, Hawthorn East 120593
Young & Son, London 085820, 131224
Young, Saint Louis 119268
Young, Salt Lake City 119383
Young, Donald, Chicago 115592
Young, Jackie, Pittsburgh 142783
Young & Son, John, Keswick 084833
Young, John, Toronto 059322
Young, K.C., Seattle 093093
Young, R.M., South Molton 142076
Young, Robert, London 085821
Young at Art Children's Museum, Davie 043309
Young Blood Galleries, Atlanta 114946
Young Classics, Reutlingen 104736
Young Originals Gallery of Fine Art, Paddington, Queensland 095048
Youngs, John & Rebecca, Christchurch 079073
Young's Brewery Museum, London . 040326
Younis, A., Ascona 111144
Your Art Gallery, Knokke-Heist 096364
Your Decor, Las Vegas 116661
Your Hearts Desire, Las Vegas 089617
Your Heritage House, Detroit 043450
Your Treasure Is Here, Tampa 093160
Yours Truly Antiques, Jacksonville . 089479
Youth Museum of Southern West Virginia, Beckley 042094
Youth Science Institute, San Jose . . 047904
Yoxall Antiques, Solihull . . 086635, 131509
Yoyogi Seminar, Tokyo 050503
Yozgat Devlet Güzel Sanatlar Galerisi, Yozgat 038198
Yozgat Kültür Merkezi, Yozgat 038199
Ypäjän Kotiseutumuseo, Ypäjä 010261
Ypey, Erik, Stockelsdorf 126838
Ypsilanti Historical Museum, Ypsilanti 049364
Yrjar Heimbygdslag, Opphaug 031061
Yrjö A. Jäntin Taidekokoelma, Porvoo 009998
Yrjö Liipolan Taidekokoelma, Koski . 009739
Yrjönkadun Antikvariaatti, Helsinki . 137965
Yrwing, Stockholm 111085
Y.S.F. Bookshop, Sheffield 142066
Ystads Konstmuseum, Ystad 036806
Ystwyth Books, Aberystwyth 141383
Ythurbide, Olivier d', Saint-Cloud . . 067404
d'Ythurbide, Olivier, Saint-Ouen . . . 067922
Yttilän Museokoulu, Yttilä 010262
Yturri-Edmunds Historic Site, San Antonio 047811
Yu, Ogaki 106947
Yu, Jing, San Francisco 119843
Yu-I Institut, Bruxelles 096270
Yu Yuen Antique Market, Shanghai . 059781
Yuan, Hong, Singapore 109901
Yuan Meng Art, Beijing 097688
Yuan You, Shanghai 059782
Yubi, Nagoya 106937
Yucaipa Adobe, Yucaipa 049369
Yucca Art Gallery, Albuquerque 114838
Yue, Chung Hin, Hong Kong 059719
Yue, Fung, Hong Kong 059720
Yue Gu, Zhai, Hong Kong 059721
Yue Po Chai, Hong Kong 059722
Yuen, Singapore 109902
Yugtarvik Regional Museum, Bethel 042177
Yuhang Painting Gallery, Hangzhou . 097743
Yukara Ori Folkcraft Museum, Asahikawa 026423
Yuki Bijutsukan, Osaka 026992
Yukon Beringia Interpretive Centre, Whitehorse 006813
Yukon Historical and Museums Association, Whitehorse 052780
Yukon Transportation Museum, Whitehorse 006814
Yuma Fine Arts Association, Yuma . 055116
Yuma Territorial Prison Museum, Yuma 049372
Yumak, Reutlingen 073506
Yumak, Ahmet, Dettingen unter Teck 070240
Yume, Mitaka 106911
Yume-Ya, Honolulu 088984
Yumeji Art Museum, Okayama 026945
Yumi, Kobe 106886
Yun Yu, Zhai, Beijing 059579
Yuna, Seoul 107311
Yung Lee, Hong, Hong Kong 059723
Yuni, Kobe 106887
Yunji Zhai Arts, Wuhan 098027
Yunlin, Wuxi 098048
Yunnan Fine Arts Publishing House, Kunming 133370
Yunnan Museum Provincial, Kunming 007167
Yunus Emre Müzesi, Yunus Emre . . 038200
Yurara Art Gallery, Thornlands 095334
Yurt, Engin & Türkan, Dettingen unter Teck 070241
Yurttaş Kitabevi, İstanbul 083166
Yushodo, Tokyo 140212
Yusuf, Ravensburg 104676
Yutaka, Kanazawa 106871
Yutoku Shrine Museum, Kashima, Saga 026636
Yuyuan Antique Market, Shanghai . 059783
Yuzawa History and Folk Museum, Yuzawa 027357
Yuzhang Bo Wu Yuan, Nanchang . . 007196
Yvana, Marseille 064402
Yvart, Yverdon-les-Bains 112013
Yveline, Paris 066682
Yvernault, Marie-Alexandrine, Saint-Ouen 067923
Yverneau, Christophe, Auch 061055
Yvert et Tellier, Amiens . . . 060828, 133446
Yvert & Tellier, Lille 063872
Yvert & Tellier, Paris 066683, 133688
Yvinec, Pierre Adrien, Paris 138566
Yvonne, Haarlem 078495
Yvonne Fine Art, Christchurch 079074, 108421
YYZ Artists' Outlet, Toronto 006648
YYZ Artists' Outlet, Toronto 097402
Z-Bau Galerie, Nürnberg 104493
Z-Galerie, Baar 111149
Z Galerie, Long Beach 116686
Z Gallerie, Denver 116071
Z Gallerie, Los Angeles 116921
Z Gallerie, Sacramento 119170
Z Gallerie, San Diego 119570
Z Gallerie, San Diego 119571
Z Gallerie, San Francisco 119844
Z Gallerie, Tucson 120179
Z33, Provinciaal Centrum voor Beeldende Kunsten-Begijnhof, Hasselt 003501
Z9A, Mainz 104010
Za Bramką, Poznań 109066, 140765
Zaaijer, Pieter, Den Haag 078271
De Zaal, Delft 107899
Zaal Anselmo, Borgerhout 120711
Zaane, Alma van, Blaricum 140363
Zaanlandse Oudheidkamer Honig Breet Huis, Zaandijk 030371
Zaans Museum, Zaandam 030369
De Zaanse Schans, Zaandam 030370
Zaar, New Gloucester 090496
Zabala Madina, Amaia, Irún 081159, 129540
Zabari, Avner, Miami 117158
Zabbar Sanctuary Museum, Zabbar 028050
Zabbeni, André, Vevey . . . 111968, 122356
Zaberfelder Kunstkabinett und Verlag, Zaberfeld 105367, 134476, 139892
Zabern, Philipp von, Mainz 134185
Zabert, Gilberto, Torino 076881
Zabert, Gilberto, Torino 076882
Zabert, Gilberto, Torino 106711
Zabert, Gilberto, Torino 106712
Zabol Museum, Zabol 022653
Zabriskie, New York 118598
Zabytkowa Cerkiew w Bartnem, Muzeum Budownictwa Ludowego w Szymbarku, Bartne 031820
Zabytkowa Huta Żelaza, Filia Muzeum Techniki w Warszawie, Chlewiska 031866
Zabytkowa Kuźnia Wodna, Muzeum Techniki w Warszawie, Gdańsk 031925
Zabytkowa Kuźnia Wodna w Starej Kuźnicy, Filia Muzeum Techniki w Warszawie, Stara Kuźnica 032336
Zabytkowa Zagroda Świętokrzyska, Bodzentyn 031843
Zaccaria, Paolo, Bologna . 075123, 127190
Zaccaro, Carmine, Napoli 076063
Zaccaro, Luigi, Napoli 076064
Žáček, Miroslav, Praha 060182
Zach, Gerald, Graz-Puntigam 137184
Zacharias, Kelheim 103527
Zacharias, Lemesos 098321
Zacharias, Karl, Feldkirchen bei Graz 056977
Zacharias, Karl, Graz 057032
Zachary, Gertrude, Albuquerque . . . 087436
Zachęta, Warszawa 109206
Zacheta Państwowa Galeria Sztuki, Warszawa 032483
Zack, Karlsruhe 071735
Zacke, Wien 095967, 120698
Zac's Attic, San Diego 092702
Zadah, London 085822
Zadelhoff, Hilversum 078546, 121793
Zadick, Lion B., Überlingen 121615
Zadick, Robert, München . 072886, 104349
Zado, Portland 119066
Zadruga na Majstorite na Narodnite Chudožestveni Zanajati, Sofia . . . 052712
Zaduzbina Kralja Petra I Karađorđevića, Topola 034274
Zählermuseum, München 019130
Zähringer, Gerhard, Zürich 112202, 141365
Zafira, Paris 100976
Zagar, Isaiah, Philadelphia 118856
Zaghloul, Kamal, Cairo 098679
Zagni, Jean, Lavardac 063556
Zaguan, Barcelona 129417
Zaguan, Valencia 110847
Zahedan Museum, Zahedan 022654
Zahn, Andrea, Mainz 104011
Zahn, Hans, Peiß 073301
Zahn, Hans, Stephanskirchen, Simssee 073917
Zahnärztliches Museum, Tübingen . 020502
Zahnhistorische Sammlung, Coburg 016580
Zahnradbahnschuppen, Puchberg . 002474
Záhorská Galéria Senica, Senica . . 034424
Záhorské Múzeum, Skalica 034425
Zahraa, Cairo 098680
Al-Zaim, Louai, Damascus 083089
Zaïnal, Françoise, Quiberon 101057
Zak, Sacramento 123082
Žák, Milan, Brno 059993
Zakarpats'kyj Chudožnij Muzej im. J. Bokšaja, Užgorod 038407
Zakarpats'kyj Kraeznavčyj Muzej, Užgorod 038408
Zakarpats'kyj Muzej Narodnoï Architektury ta Pobutu, Užgorod 038409
Zakian Bros., Philadelphia 091705
Het Zakkendragershuisje, Historisch Museum Rotterdam, Rotterdam . . 030110
Zakład Narodowy im. Ossolińskich, Wrocław 032534
Zaks, Sonia, Chicago 115593
Zakurozaka Gallery, Tokyo 107134
Zakynthos Byzantine Museum, Zakynthos 021532
Zakynthos Museum of the Natural Heritage, Zakynthos 021533

Zalacain, Jean-François, Sarlat-la-Canéda . . . 068128
Zaldivar Museum, Albuera . . . 031618
Zalipianki, Kraków . . . 108992
Žaliūkių Windmill, Šiauliai Aušros Museum, Šiauliai . . . 027860
Záložňa, Senica . . . 080638
Zaltbommels Stoom- en Energiemuseum, Zaltbommel . . . 030373
Zamaan, Beirut . . . 077422
Zamaan, Can, Cairo . . . 098681
Zaman, Zay, Cairo . . . 098682
Zamanda Sanat, İstanbul . . . 112371
Zambakejian, Jiwan, Saint-Ouen . . 067924
Zambakejian, Zohrab, Saint-Ouen . 067925
Zambaldo, Alessandra, Verona . . . 128446
Zambelli, Daniela & C., Brescia . . . 075192
Zambezi, Amsterdam . . . 078026, 107838
Zambezi, Valençay . . . 101406
Zambezi, Valençay . . . 101407
Zambezi Gallery, Lagos . . . 109258
Zambezi Imports, Canning Vale . . . 055623
Zamboanga National Museum, Zamboanga . . . 031811
Zamboni, Pierre, Congerville-Thionville . . . 062462
Zámecké Muzeum, Kravaře . . . 008455
Zámek, Hradec nad Moravicí . . . 008390
Zámek, Nové Město nad Metují . . . 008532
Zámek, Vrchotovy Janovice . . . 008763
Zámek, Okresní muzeum Chomutov, Jirkov . . . 008417
Zámek Brandýs, Brandýs nad Labem . . . 008275
Zámek Budišov, Moravské Zemské Museum Brno, Budišov u Třebíče . . . 008303
Zámek-Kinski, Chlumec nad Cidlinou . . . 008330
Zámek Kinských, Muzeum Regionu Valšsko ve Vsetině, Valašské Meziříčí . . . 008741
Zamek Królewski na Wawelu - Państwowe Zbiory Sztuki, Kraków . . . 032070
Zamek Królewski w Warszawie, Pomnik Historii i Kultury Narodowej, Warszawa . . . 032484
Zámek Lemberk, Jablonné v Podještědí . . . 008401
Zámek Libochovice, Libochovice . . 008476
Zámek Líčkov - Galerie O. Brázda, Žatec . . . 008775
Zámek Lysice, Lysice . . . 008495
Zámek Manětín, Muzeum a galerie severního Plzeňska, Manětín . . . 008497
Zámek Moravský Krumlov - Galerie Slovanská Epopej Alfonse Muchy, Galerie Hlavního Města Prahy, Moravský Krumlov . . . 008514
Zámek Nelahozeves, Nelahozeves . 008523
Zámek Sychrov, Sychrov . . . 008704
Zámek Troja, Galerie Hlavního Města Prahy, Praha . . . 008652
Zámek Velké Březno, Velké Březno . 008745
Zámek Veltrusy, Veltrusy . . . 008749
Zámek Vizovice, Vizovice . . . 008756
Zamek w Czersku, Czersk . . . 031884
Zamek w Gniewie, Gniew . . . 031940
Zammit, Mosta . . . 077518, 128477
Zamoskvorečje Galereja, Moskva . . 109607
Zampardi, Massimiliano, Palermo . 076190
Zanabazar Museum of Fine Arts, Ulaanbaatar . . . 029016
Zanardelli, Roma . . . 076733
Zanardi, Bruno, Parma . . . 127866
Zanardi, Bruno, Roma . . . 128240
Zanarini, Achille, Bologna . . . 105980
Zanasi, Carlotta, Bologna . . . 127191
Zanasi, Giuseppe, Bologna . . . 139998
Zanazanian, John, Philadelphia . . . 132641
Zanchiello, Cosimo, Nyon . . . 082707
Zancopé, Paolo Emanuele, Venezia 076981
Zandbergen, Dick, Maarssen . . . 140491
Zandenbos, Nunspeet . . . 029981
Zander, Erika, Graz . . . 057033
Zander, Erika, Graz . . . 057034
Zander, Ingo, Segeletz . . . 073793
Zander, Dr. R., Schönwölkau . . . 139715
Zander, S., Köln . . . 103742
Zander, T., Köln . . . 103743
Zander, Thomas, Köln . . . 103744
Zandi, Berlin . . . 102090
Zandlopermuseum Glanerbrug, Enschede . . . 029571
Zandner, Roland, Wildpoldsried . . . 074440
Zandoozi, Austin . . . 115027
Zandvoorts Museum, Zandvoort . . . 030374
Zane Grey Museum, Lackawaxen . . 045081
Zane Moss, New York . . . 091359
Zanella, Carlo, Torino . . . 128366
Zanella, F., Passau . . . 073296
Zanella, Léon, Vaison-la-Romaine . 101403
Zanella, Roberto, Torino . . . 128367
Zanelli, London . . . 131225
Zanesville Art Center, Zanesville . . . 049374
Zanetta, Franco, Nyon . . . 082708
Zanettini, Chiara, Padova . . . 076119
Zanfrognini, Sergio, Milano . . . 127710
Zangbieri, Basel . . . 111232
Zangrilli & Co, London . . . 113983
Zangs Atlandia, São Paulo . . . 058750
Zanichelli, Baroni Giliana, Modena . 140074
Zanikos, Anne, San Antonio . . . 119467, 132836
Zanin, Stefano, Venezia . . . 128410
Zanna, Alessandro, Roma 076734, 128241
Zannettacci-Stephanopoli, Sonia, Genève . . . 111510
Zannoni, Adelino, Genova . . . 127491
Zannoth, Wilhelm, München . . . 072887
Zannotti, Gennaro, Roma . . . 076735
Zanol, Alain, Montréal-la-Cluse . . . 064762
Zanoletti, Giulia, Brescia . . . 075193
Zanoli, Marco, Milano . . . 127711
Zanon, Mauro, Bolzano . . . 127200
Zanone, Pierre, Lussy-sur-Morges . 082614
Zanoni, Luigi, Milano . . . 127712
Zanoni, Peter, Eglisau . . . 082349, 130008
Zanotti, William, Modena . . . 127750
Zantout, Majida, Beirut . . . 077423
Zantt, Vanessa, Baltimore . . . 087725
Zanutto, Vincenzo, Venezia . . . 076982
Zanzibar, Memphis . . . 117011
Zanzibar, Napoli . . . 076065
Zanzibar National Archives and Museums Department, Zanzibar . . . 037864
Zaor, Québec . . . 059079, 097168
Západočeská Galerie v Plzni, Plzeň . 008575
Západočeské Muzeum, Plzeň . . . 008576
Západomoravské Muzeum v Třebíči, Třebíč . . . 008720
Západomoravské Muzeum v Třebíči - Muzeum Jemnice, Jemnice . . . 008405
Západoslovenské Múzeum v Trnave, Trnava . . . 034447
Zapata, Eduardo, Granada . . . 129535
Zapata, Rodrigo, Cali . . . 098244
Zapel, Mario, Berlin . . . 138863
Zapf, David, San Diego . . . 119572
Zapf, Matthias, Bad Berka . . . 069261
Zapffe, Carl, Seattle . . . 093094, 132947
Zaporiz'kyj Chudožnij Muzej, Zaporižžja . . . 038418
Zaporowski, Jakub, Gdańsk . . . 140722
Zaporožeskij Kraevedčeskij Muzej, Zaporože . . . 038419
Zapotec, Houston . . . 116434
Zapovidnyk-muzej Gogolja, Gogoleve . . . 038265
Zapp, Bad Kreuznach . . . 101668
Zapp Magazine, Amsterdam . . . 136009
Zappe, J., Eimen . . . 070528
Zappoli, Tina, Porto Alegre . . . 096583
Žar-Ptica, Belgorod . . . 109464
ZAR Works, Johannesburg . . . 080721
Zara Clark Folk Museum, Charters Towers . . . 000908
Zaralli, Alceste, Roma . . . 128242
Zarco, Lisboa . . . 080057
Zard, Ghassan, Jal-el-Dib 077428, 107329
Zardin, Luciano, Venezia . . . 076983
Zaremski, Marcin, Warszawa . . . 109207
Zargari, Gabriela, Walsrode . . . 105154
Zarit, Jeffrey S., Dallas . . . 088630
Zarposh, Houston . . . 089256
Zarre, Andre, New York . . . 118599
Zarrilli, Michele, Firenze . . . 075425
Zart, Zürich . . . 130273
Zatzka, Bucaramanga . . . 098226
Zauner, Andreas, Baden bei Wien . .056944, 123341
Zauner, Christa, Leonding . . . 095647
Zauner-Mayerhofer, Silvia, Wien . . . 123538
Zaunmüller, Karl-Heinz, Trier . . . 139791
Zausch, R., München . . . 072888
Zavelberg-Torrekens, Bruxelles . . . 058135
Zavelle, Philadelphia . . . 142755
Zavičajna Galerija, Novi Sad . . . 034229
Zavičajni Muzej, Bar . . . 034143
Zavičajni Muzej, Baška . . . 007696
Zavičajni Muzej, Bileća . . . 003929
Zavićajni Muzej, Bileća . . . 034176
Zavičajni Muzej, Biograd na Moru . . 007699
Zavičajni Muzej, Buzet . . . 007705
Zavičajni Muzej, Čazma . . . 007709
Zavičajni Muzej, Danilovgrad . . . 034188
Zavičajni Muzej, Doboj . . . 034190
Zavičajni Muzej, Herceg-Novi . . . 034194
Zavičajni Muzej, Jaša Tomić . . . 034196
Zavičajni Muzej, Nikšić . . . 034217
Zavičajni Muzej, Nova Gradiška . . . 007764
Zavičajni Muzej, Ogulin . . . 007766
Zavičajni Muzej, Otočac . . . 007771
Zavičajni Muzej, Pljevlja . . . 034238
Zavičajni Muzej, Prijedor . . . 003936
Zavičajni Muzej, Ruma . . . 034254
Zavičajni Muzej, Travnik . . . 003942
Zavičajni Muzej, Trebinje . . . 034275
Zavičajni Muzej, Ulcinj . . . 034277
Zavičajni Muzej, Visoko . . . 003947
Zavičajni Muzej Aleksinac, Aleksinac . . . 034139
Zavičajni Muzej Grada Rovinja, Rovinj . . . 007785
Zavičajni Muzej Našice, Našice . . . 007760
Zavičajni Muzej Ozlja, Ozalj . . . 007772
Zavičajni Muzej Poreštine, Poreč . . 007774
Zavičajni Muzej Trebinje, Trebinje . . 003943
Zavičajni Muzej u Jagodini, Jagodina . . . 034195
Zavičajni Muzej Zemuna, Zemun . . 034284
Zavod za Zaštita na Spomenicite na Kulturata na Grad Skopje, Skopje 050525
Zavod za Zaštita na Spomenicite na Kulturata, Prirodnite Retkosti i Muzej, Institute for Protection of Cultural Monuments, Natural Rarities and Museum, Strumica . . . 027925
Zavrtálek, Jan, Brno . . . 059994, 098340
Zazo, Madrid . . . 081411
Zazou, San Diego . . . 119573
Les Zazous, Annecy . . . 098844
Zazzaretta, Franco, Pfronten . . . 073326
Zbiory Historyczne Ziemi Wadowickiej, Wadowice . . . 032410
Zbiory Historyczno-Etnograficzne, Oświęcim . . . 032209
Zbiory Metrologiczne Głównego Urzędu Miar, Warszawa . . . 032485
Zbiory Sprzętu Ratownictwa Kolejowego, Poznań . . . 032257
Zbiory Sztuki, Muzeum Ziemi Kujawskiej i Dobrzyńskiej, Włocławek . . . 032506
Zbiory Sztuki na Jasnej Górze, Częstochowa . . . 031889
Zbirka Anke Gvozdanović, Museum of Arts and Crafts, Zagreb . . . 007860
Zbirka Bratovštine Gospe od Utjehe, Korčula . . . 007743
Zbirka Bratovštine Sv. Roka, Korčula . . . 007744
Zbirka Crkve Gospe od Skrpjela, Perast . . . 034235
Zbirka Crkve Sv. Nikole, Perast . . . 034236
Zbirka Crkvene Umjetnosti, Šibenik 007792
Zbirka Eparhije Banatski, Vršac . . . 034282
Zbirka Franjevačkog Samostana, Sinj . . . 007794
Zbirka Franjevačkog Samostana Visovac, Visovac . . . 007821
Zbirka Ikona Bratovštine Svih Svetih, Korčula . . . 007745
Zbirka Poduzeća Naftagas, Novi Sad . . . 034230
Zbirka Rudnika Majdanpek, Majdanpek . . . 034213
Zbirka Umjetnina Franjevačkog Samostana, Hvar . . . 007727
Zbirka Umjetnina Juraj Plančić, Stari Grad . . . 007809
Zbirka Umjetnina KAIROS, Benediktinski Samostan Sv. Nikole, Trogir . . . 007815
Zbirka Župne Crkve, Prčanj . . . 034247
Zborowska, Nina, Painswick 114216, 131359
Zdeb, Erich, Hörsching . . . 057065, 123382
Zdeb, Erich, Wien . . . 057592, 123539
Zderzak, Kraków . . . 108993
Zdrenka, Barabara, Warszawa 079794, 140800
ZeaYou, Waikato . . . 108600
Zeb, Parma . . . 076227
Zeberg, Antwerpen . . . 057755
Zebone, Indianapolis . . . 089359
Zebra Crafts, Nairobi . . . 077356
Zebra Gallery, Hahndorf . . . 094611
Zebra One, London . . . 113984
Zebra Street Project, Kensington . . 054072
Zebra Two, London . . . 113985
Zebrak, Monaco . . . 077628
Żebrowski, Krysztof, Warszawa . . . 129122
Zebulon B. Vance Birthplace, Weaverville . . . 049040
Zecchi, Firenze . . . 075426
Zecchini, Napoleone, Milano . . . 075894
Zecchino, Angelo, Torino . . . 128368
Zecchino, Ottavia, Torino . . . 076883
Zecconi, Auguste, Saint-Bonnet-en-Champsaur . . . 067379
Zech, Hans, Ingolstadt . . . 071628, 103435
Zechmeister, Michael, Lanzenkirchen . . . 123406
Zeck, Michael, Eberbach, Baden . . 070493
Zedd, San Francisco . . . 119845
Zedes, Bruxelles . . . 096271
Zedler, Dörte Maria, Naumburg, Saale . . . 126518
Zee, Hong Kong . . . 097853
Zee- en Havenmuseum de Visserijschool, IJmuiden . . . 029788
Zeemuseum, Den Haag . . . 029459
Zeeuws Biologisch Museum, Oostkapelle . . . 030002
Zeeuws Maritiem Muzeeum, Vlissingen . . . 030284
Zeeuws Museum, Middelburg . . . 029924
Zeeuws Poppen- en Klederdrachten Museum, Zoutelande . . . 030394
Zeezicht, Eindhoven . . . 078362
De Zegel, Utrecht . . . 078829
Zeh, Wolfgang, Berlin . . . 069793
Zehetbauer, Michaela, Winhöring . . 074447
Zehetner, Linz . . . 057171
Zehm, Bodo, Melle . . . 126302
Zehnder, Alfred, Bowil . . . 082270
Zehnder, Monika, Gallaria Caspar Badrutt, Sankt Moritz . . . 082793
Zehnthaus, Jockgrim . . . 018123
Zehntscheune, Kastellaun . . . 103520
Zehntscheune, Uting . . . 074172
Zehrfeld, Manfred, Dresden . . . 125517
Zeichenakademie Peter Grenacher, Zürich . . . 050783
Zeidel-Museum, Feucht . . . 017113
Zeidler, Freiberg, Sachsen . . . 102853
Zeidler, Gdańsk . 079591, 108903, 121888, 129015, 140723
Zeidler, Monika, Berlin . . . 069794
Zeidler, Ulrike, Ebern . . . 125563
Zeier, Edith, Aristau . . . 082094
Zeil-Antiquariat, Frankfurt am Main 139101
Zeile & Judish, Denver . . . 116072

Zeiler, Bernd Restaurator, Pfaffenhofen an der Ilm . . . 126625
Zeiler Foto- und Filmmuseum, Zeil am Main . . . 021043
Zeilopleidingsschip Mercator, Oostende . . . 003689
Žeimelis Žiemgalos Museum, Šiauliai Aušros Museum, Žeimelis . . . 027867
Zeimes, Nathalie, Liège . . . 058331
Zein, Evelyne, Berlin . . . 069795
Zeiner, Franz, Hamburg . . 103233, 125852
Zeiner, Helmut, Puchenau . . . 137240
Zeiringer, Franz, Ottendorf an der Rittschein . . . 057203
Zeise, Leobersdorf . . . 137216
Zeiselmairhaus, Schrobenhausen . . 020103
Zeisig, Kurt-Georg, Berlin . . . 138864
Zeisler, Anke, Berlin . . . 102091
Zeit-Foto Salon, Tokyo . . . 107135
Zeitbrücke-Museum, Gars am Kamp . . . 001885
Zeitgeist, Detroit . . . 116099
Zeitgeist, Timmendorfer Strand . . . 105048
Zeitgeist, Travemünde . . . 139786
Zeitgeist Gallery, Nashville . . . 117380
Zeitkunstgalerie, Halle, Saale . . . 103079
Zeitkunstgalerie, Kitzbühel . . . 095609
Zeitlos, Hamburg . . . 071357
Zeitlos, Schongau . . . 073718
Zeitoun, Angel, Paris . . . 066684
Zeitoun, Elie, Paris . . . 066685
Zeitraum, Mannheim . . . 072439
Zeitreise, Bamberg . . . 069467
Zeitreise - Renner Villa Gloggnitz, Gloggnitz . . . 001901
Zeitschrift für Kunstgeschichte, München . . . 135831
Zeitschrift für Kunsttechnologie und Konservierung, Worms . . . 135832
Zeitschrift für Literatur und Kunst, Wien . . . 135585
Zeitspurenmuseum Altheim, Altheim . . . 001682
Zeittunnel Wülfrath, Wülfrath . . . 020992
Zeitwandel, Bielefeld . . . 069843
Zeitwende, München . . . 072889
Zeitzeichen, Kleve . . . 139328
Zejda, Rodenbach . . . 104755
Zelano, Washington . . . 120370
Zelewski, Bodo von, Alfter . . . 125055
Zeleznički Muzej, Beograd . . . 034174
Zelienople Historical Museum, Zelienople . . . 049375
Zelinski, Christel, Berlin . . . 102092
Zelko, Emmanuel, Saint-Gervais . . 067504
Zelko, Emmanuel, Saint-Ouen . . . 067926
Zeller, Andreas & Erika, Trimstein . . 082862
Zeller, Christian, Bern . . . 111281
Zeller, Dr. Klaus Robert, Lindau, Bodensee . . . 139416
Zeller, Michael, Lindau, Bodensee . 121499
Zeller, Michèle, Bern . . . 082251
Zellermayer, Berlin . . . 102093
Zell's Curios, Durban . . . 080696
Zellweger, Harry, Basel . . . 111233
Zellweger, Harry, Carabietta . . . 111329
Zelman, Guy, Paris . . . 066686
Zem Goldrähmli, Pratteln . 111816, 130141
Zemaljski Muzej, Sarajevo . . . 003941
Zemanek-Münster, Würzburg . . . 074516, 121630, 139877
Zemědělská Sbírka na Zámku Kačina, Kutná Hora . . . 008464
Zemědělské Muzeum Ohrada, Ohrada . . . 008541
Zemljepišni Muzej Slovenije, Ljubljana . . . 034497
Zemmrich, Michael, Berlin . . . 069796
Zempléni Muzeum, Szerencs . . . 021891
Zemplínske Múzeum, Michalovce . . 034392
Zen, Miami . . . 090262
Zen, Miami . . . 090263
Zen Art, Hamburg . . . 071358
Zen Gallery, Bruxelles . . . 058136
Zenatti, Tiziano, Merano . . . 075550
Zendron, Manfred, Wien . . . 057593
Zenen Art, Wooburn Common . . . 114726
Zenetörténeti Múzeum, Budapest . . 021703
Zenetsis Vasilis, S., Athinai . . . 105411
Zengcheng City Museum, Zengcheng . . . 007345
Zengen, von, Bonn . . . 121350
Zengiaro, Aldo Carlo Vittorio, Firenze . . . 075427
Zenit Galleri, København . . . 098590
Zenith, Maastricht . . . 078634
Zenith Antiques, Pittsburgh . . . 091878
Zenith Gallery, Washington . . . 120371
Zenkel, Petra, Steinbach am Wald . 126830
Zenko-ji Tendai Sect Treasure House, Nagano . . . 026845
Zeno Arte, Roma . . . 106648
Zeno X Gallery, Antwerpen . . . 096104
Zenobi, Roma . . . 076736
Zenoficinas, Porto . . . 129204
Zentgrafen Antiquitäten, Kassel . . . 071767
Zentilin, Daniela, Venezia . . . 106787
Zentique, Los Angeles . . . 089948, 116922
Zentral-und Landesbibliothek Berlin, Gotisches Haus, Berlin . . . 016196
Zentralantiquariat, Leipzig . . . 139407
Zentralantiquariat Leipzig, Leipzig . 139408
Zentralarchiv, Staatliche Museen zu Berlin - Stiftung Preußischer Kulturbesitz, Berlin . . . 016197
Zentrales Verzeichnis Antiquarischer Bücher, Berlin . . . 138865
Zentralinstitut für Kunstgeschichte, München . . . 050198
Zentralschweizer Antiquitätentage und Antik-Börse, Luzern . . . 093898
Zentrum für Außergewöhnliche Museen, Kreuth . . . 018410
Zentrum für Außergewöhnliche Museen, München . . . 019131
Zentrum für Bucherhaltung, Leipzig 126203
Zentrum für Internationale Lichtkunst, Unna . . . 020539
Zentrum für phantastische Künste e.V., Remagen . . . 053657
Zentrum Höngg, Zürich . . . 112203
Zenz & Hillebrand, Pullach . . . 073386
Zepf, Manfred, Karlsruhe . . . 071736
Zephyr Gallery, Louisville . . . 116972
Zepp, Eugen, München . . . 126487
Zeppelin-Museum, Neu-Isenburg . . 019211
Zeppelin Museum Friedrichshafen, Friedrichshafen . . . 017272
Zeppelin-Museum Meersburg, Meersburg . . . 018877
Zepter, Beograd . . . 109727
Zerain Cultural Park, Zerain . . . 036118
Zerbisch, G., Wernigerode . . . 074347
Zerkalo, Sankt-Peterburg . . . 109655
Zerline, Saint-Ouen . . . 067927
Helmut Zernickel & Eva Sperner-Zernickel, München . . . 126488
Zero Karati, Padova . . . 106410
Zéro l'Infini, Etuz . . . 099253
Zero to Sixties, New York . . . 091360
Zerovnik, Annerl, Apolda . . . 069177
Zerrenner, Rolf, Reichenbach, Vogtland . . . 126707
Zerrer, Stuttgart . . . 126890
Zerrouki, Ch, Strasbourg . . . 138623
Zerrouki, Karim, Rueil-Malmaison . 067324
Zerunian, Ingrid, Wien . . . 057594
Zervudachi, Peter, Trelex . . . 082860
Zet-Zet Galeria, Łódź . . . 109023
Zeta, Piran . . . 080668
Zetel, Amsterdam . . . 107839
Zetera, Neuhausen auf den Fildern . 072995
Zetland Lifeboat Museum, Redcar . 040813
Zetlin Museum, Yechiel Nahari Museum of Far Eastern Art, Ramat Gan . . . 023053
Zettelmeier, Erika & Wilhelm, Wachtberg . . . 105135
Zetterquist, New York . . . 118600
Zettl, Brigitte, Mallersdorf-Pfaffenberg . . . 104017
Zettl Langer Gyüjtemény, Sopron . . 021850
Zettlmeissl-Satzinger, Thea, Gunzenhausen . . . 103038
Zettner, Andreas, Veitshöchheim . . 134444
Zeugs, Peißen . . . 073302
Zeus 120, Roma . . . 076737
De Zeven Pijlen, Gouda . . . 078394
De Zevende Hemel, Haarlem . . . 078496
Zezschwitz, von, München . . . 121551
Zezula, Brno . . . 120849
Zezula, Praha . . . 120862
Zg Gallery, Chicago . . . 115594
Zgodovinski Arhiv i Muzej Univerze v Ljubljani, Ljubljana . . . 034498
Zhabei Revolutionary Shi Liao Display Center, Shanghai . . . 007248
Zhan Tianyou Former Residence, Wuhan . . . 007304
Zhan Tianyou Memorial Hall, Beijing 007017
Zhangjiagang City Gallery, Zhangjiagang . . . 007346
Zhangqiu Arts and Crafts Guan, Jinan . . . 007157
Zhangqiu Chua Ren Art Shop, Jinan 097864
Zhangqiu Museum, Jinan . . . 007158
Zhao Hua Fine Arts Publishing House, Beijing . . . 133340
Zhaoling Museum, Liquan Xian . . . 007174
Zhe, Chen, Shenyang . . . 097970
Zhejiang Academy of Fine Arts Press, Hangzhou . . . 133351
Zhejiang Literature and Art Publishing House, Hangzhou . . . 133352
Zhejiang Museum, Hangzhou . . . 007107
Zhejiang Natural Museum, Hangzhou . . . 007108
Zhejiang Painting Gallery, Hangzhou 097744
Zhejiang People's Fine Arts Publishing House, Hangzhou . . . 133353
Zhejiang Photography Publishing House, Hangzhou . . . 133354
Zhen Gu, Shanghai . . . 059784
Zhengding County Display Center, Shijiazhuang . . . 007269
Zhenghe, Nanjing . . . 097877
Zhengpinzhai, Beijing . . . 097689
Zhengzhou Museum, Zhengzhou . . 007350
Zhenjiang Museum, Zhenjiang . . . 007351
Zhenjianhai, Shanghai . . . 059785
Zheong Zhong Jia Yuan, Shanghai . 059786
Zhi Li Victory Museum, Baoding . . . 006958
Zhiyin Ren Hai Art Gallery, Shanghai 097959
Zhon Art Corporation and Xiyuan Art Cooperative, Urumchi . . . 098025
Zhonghua Art, Beijing . . . 097690
Zhonghua Nation Museum, Beijing . 007018
Zhonghua Xin Road Antiques, Shanghai . . . 059787
Zhonglu, Jinan . . . 097865
Zhongshan, Jinan . . . 097866
Zhongshan Art Cooperative, Liaoyang . . . 097870
Zhongshan Museum, Zhongshan . . 007353
Zhou Hejing County Museum, Hejing . . . 007112
Zhou Man Xia, Verona . . . 077028
Zhouzhi County Farmer Art Association, Xian . . . 052804, 098055
Zhuhai Museum, Zhuhai . . . 007357
Zhumin, Shanghai . . . 059788
Zi Yuan Art Scheme, Shenzhen . . . 097993
Ziad, Chahin, Ingelheim am Rhein . 103431
Ziarsolo, Paul, Bilbao . . . 129450
Ziarsolo de Zuazua, Paul, Bilbao . . . 081000, 129451
Ziba, Honarhayeh, Isfahan . . . 074838
Žibel, Minsk . . . 096046
Zibelius, Sven, Hannover . 071422, 103302
Zibetti, Solduno . . . 082817, 130180
Zibo City Museum, Zibo . . . 007360
Zichy Galéria, Budapest . . . 105554
Zichy Mihály Emlékmúzeum, Zala . 021923
Zidarics, Norbert, Frankfurt am Main . . . 070804
Zidella, R., Oldenburg, Oldenburg . . 073215
Židovské Muzeum v Praze, Praha . . 008653
Ziebold, Santiago de Chile . . . 097633
Ziebold, Jörg, Emmedingen . . . 070556
Ziegel- und Kalkmuseum, Winzer . . 020918
Ziegelbauer, Dieter, Maulbronn . . . 072474
Ziegelei Benzin, Benzin . . . 015952
Ziegelei-Museum, Cham . . . 037007
Ziegeleimuseum, Jockgrim . . . 018124
Ziegeleipark Mildenberg, Mildenberg . . . 018940
Ziegler, Tulsa . . . 120210
Ziegler, Eva-Maria, Velden . . . 123483
Ziegler, Eva & Peter, Bad Endorf . . . 069279
Ziegler, Loredana & Arthur, Zürich . 083040
Ziegler, Renée, Zürich . . . 112204
Ziegler, Serge, Zürich . . . 112205
Ziegler Arteus Palace, Sankt Moritz 082794
Ziegler Arteus Palace, Zürich . . . 083041
Ziehm, Rolf, Zeulenroda . . . 074567
Ziehm, Rolf, Zeulenroda . . . 127061
Ziehm, Rolf, Zeulenroda . . . 127062
Ziehn & Dickmeis, Düren . . . 102466
Ziekenhuis- en Verpleegkundig Museum, Deventer . . . 029476
Zielhaus am Klausenpass, Spiringen . . . 037587
Zieliński, Jerzy, Warszawa . . . 140801
Zielke, Cornelia & Wolfgang, Kirtorf 071865
Ziemann, Bremen . . . 070050, 102259
Ziemann, Bremen . . . 102260
Ziemer, Maisach . . . 104015
Ziemer, L., Buchholz in der Nordheide . . . 121363
Ziems, Katrin-Andrea, Berlin . . . 125321
Ziern & Hanon Dorothy, Saint Louis 092335
Ziesler, Gustav, Groß-Umstadt . . . 071116
Zietz, Rainer, London . . . 085823, 113986
Zig Zag Antiques, Chicago . . . 088203
Zig Zag Collectables, Toronto . . . 059323
Zigafoos, Louisville . . . 090047
Zigan, Klaus, Kirchheim unter Teck 103557
Ziggurat, Warszawa . . . 134866
The Zigler Museum, Jennings . . . 044854
Zij van Hiernaast, Breda . . . 078122
Zijdemuseum, Meliskerke . . . 029917
Zijper Museum, Schagerbrug . . . 030127
Zika, Beograd . . . 080409
Žilinsko, J., Vilnius . . . 077461
Žilka, Janoš a Petr, Brno . . . 137771
Zilken, Elmer, Riedering . . . 126721
Zilla Samgrahasala, Purulia . . . 022313
Ziller, Agathon, Göttingen . . . 071058
Ziller, Helmut, Adnet . . . 123333
Zillertaler Goldschaubergwerk, Zell am Ziller . . . 003067
Zillich-Raudies, Isabell, München . . 126489
Zilverberg, M., Amsterdam . . . 078027
De Zilverdistel, Antwerpen . . . 137411
De Zilveren Passer, Gent . 058221, 123635
De Zilveren Toren, Antwerpen . . . 096105
Zilvermuseum Sterckshof Povincie Antwerpen, Antwerpen . . . 003196
Zimart Galleria, Los Angeles . . . 116923
Zimbabwe Military Museum, Gweru 049580
Zimmer, Bitburg . . . 102141
Zimmer, Neu-Isenburg . . . 072968
Zimmer, Reinheim . . . 073480
Zimmer, Elke & Werner, Düsseldorf 102575
Zimmer, Hansjörg, Oldenburg, Oldenburg . . . 139633
Zimmer, U., Traben-Trarbach . . . 105053
Zimmer, Xavier, Marseille . . . 138201
Zimmer Children's Museum, Los Angeles . . . 045474
Zimmerdahl, Lund . . . 081857
Zimmerdahl, Stockholm . . . 082043
Zimmerei-Museum, Feldkirch . . . 001849
Zimmergalerie, Schwetzingen . . . 104873
Zimmerman, Baltimore . . . 135325
Zimmermann, Köln . . . 103745
Zimmermann, Neu Isenburg . . . 104401
Zimmermann, Anneliese, Düsseldorf . . . 070470

Zimmermann, Franz-Josef, Trier . .074102, 126917
Zimmermann, Fritz, Filderstadt 070687
Zimmermann, Fritz, München 126490
Zimmermann, Gerd, Konstanz 126138
Zimmermann, Helmut, Frankfurt am Main 070805, 102840, 121410
Zimmermann, Horst, Neutraubling . 073043
Zimmermann, Ines, Köln 126124
Zimmermann, Jean, Paris 100977
Zimmermann, Jörg, Heusenstamm . 071509
Zimmermann, Jürgen, Raubling . . . 073436
Zimmermann, Karin, Freiburg im Breisgau 070867
Zimmermann, Kurt & Silvia, Flaach 082369, 130014
Zimmermann, N., Boppard 069953
Zimmermann, P., Mannheim 072440
Zimmermann, Peter, Mannheim . . . 104030
Zimmermann, U. & H., Sexau 073801
Zimmermann, W., Karlsruhe 071737
Zimmermann, W., Sachsenheim . . . 104805
Zimmermann, W. & R., Breisach am Rhein 070003
Zimmermann, Waltraud, Breisach am Rhein 102228
Zimmermann, Wilhelm, Wien 137381
Zimmermann & Franken, Mönchengladbach 104104, 134207
Zimmermannhaus, Brugg 111310
Zimmermannshaus Lackinger, Windhaag bei Freistadt 003055
Zimmertoren, Lier 003605
Zimolong, Gladbeck 102961
Zimports, Dallas 088631
Zinato, Maria Luisa, Venezia 076984
Zinelli, Roma 076738
Zingales, Emanuela, Roma 076739
Zingarelli, Raffaele, Torino 128369
Zingerle, Percha 127867
Zingg, Tokyo 077328
Zingmagazine, New York 136688
Zingrebe, Philipp, Essen 125619
Michael Zink & Andreas Gegner, München 104350
Zink & Jestedt, Erfurt 139046
Zinkwazi, Newcastle-upon-Tyne . . . 114128
Zinn, Heidi, Wegberg 105170
Zinnfiguren-Klause im Schwabentor, Museum für Geschichte in Dioramen mit Zinnfiguren, Freiburg im Breisgau 017239
Zinnfiguren-Museum, Bad Bergzabern 015659
Zinnfigurenmuseum, Gusow 017609
Zinnfigurenmuseum, Grüningen . . . 037168
Zinnfigurenmuseum, Herzberg am Harz 017907
Zinnfigurenmuseum, Zürich 037810
Zinnfigurensammlung, Linow 018664
Zinngießerhäusl, Mattighofen 002297
Zinngrube Ehrenfriedersdorf, Besucherbergwerk - Mineralogisches Museum, Ehrenfriedersdorf 016899
Zinnkann, Elfriede, Landau in der Pfalz 072133
Zinnkeller, Weidenberg 020710
Zinongo, South Fremantle 095202
Zins, Michel, Paris 066687
Zintl, Herbert, Altdorf bei Nürnberg . 069145
Zintl, Herbert, Nürnberg 073127
Zintl, Maria, Ludwigshafen am Rhein 072317
Zinzulusa, Roma 076740
Zion, Salt Lake City 132797
Zion Historical Museum, Zion 049376
Zion National Park Museum, Springdale 048282
Ziontalis, New York 091361
Zip 37, Denver 116073
Zipfel, Roland, Mannheim 072441
Zippel, Christina, Essen 070656
Zippel, Dietrich, Uetze 126928
Zipperer, Isolde, Darmstadt 125446
Zippo and Case Visitors Center Company Museum, Bradford 042381
Zipprich, D., München 139558
Zira, Montevideo 087351
Zirbenlandgalerie, Obdach 095699
Zirkelmuseum, Wilhelmsdorf, Mittelfranken 020892
Zirkus und Varieté Archivsammlung Reinhard Tetzlaff, Hamburg 017727
Zirngibl, Petra, Regensburg 126702
Zisa, New York 118601
Ziska Gallery, Bracebridge 005129
F. Zisska & R. Kistner, München . . .121552, 139559
Zisterzienserabtei Mehrerau, Bregenz 001765
Zisterzienserkloster Bebenhausen, Staatliche Schlösser und Gärten Baden-Württemberg, Tübingen 020503
Zisterziensermuseum Riddagshausen, Braunschweig 016394
Zisterzienserstift, Lilienfeld 002239
Zisterzienserstift und Stiftssammlungen, Stams 002691
Zita, K. & K., Sankt Wolfgang im Salzkammergut 057298
Žitnoostrovné Múzeum, Dunajská Streda 034352
Zitzewitz, Jutta von, Lübeck 072342
Zitzmann, Klaus, Sonneberg, Thüringen 073863
Zitzmann, Peter, Nürnberg 073128
Ziva Antiques, İstanbul 083167
Ziwna, Gerald, Wien 095968
Ziya Gökalp Müzesi, Diyarbakır . . . 038052
ZKM Medienmuseum, ZKM Zentrum für Kunst- und Medientechnologie Karlsruhe, Karlsruhe 018174
Zlámal, Michal, Praha 124004
Zlatá Reneta, České Budějovice . . . 098345
Zlatorog, Sofia 058772
Zlaty Klíč Muzeum, Karlovy Vary . . . 008427
Zlatý Kříž, České Budějovice 098346
Zlot & Assoc., Mary, San Francisco . 119846
Zlotowski, Paris 100978
Zmuda, Wien 137382
Zniva, Josef, Graz-Straßgang 137185
Znojemský Hrad, Jihomoravské Muzeum ve Znojmě, Znojmo 008794
Zoar State Memorial, Zoar 049379
Zobel, Bräunlingen 069972
Zobl, Angele, Salzburg 133155
Zoboli, Domolo, Modena 127751
Zodiac, Dunedin 079096
Zoe, Milwaukee 117229
Zöhrer, Schwaz 057308, 095757
Zöhrer-Vogt, Viktoria D., Graz 057035
Zoellick, Scott, Milwaukee 117230
Zöllner, Köln 072027
Zoetmulder, Burt, Salt Lake City . . .092470, 132798
Zöttl, Hermann, Ergoldsbach 125603
Zoffoli, Renato, Roma 076741
Zografia, Paiania 105438
Zograph, Oostende 096408
Zograph, Toronto 123844
Zohar, Haifa 074998
Zohar, Toronto 097403
Zohiko, Tokyo 077329
Zoja, Alberto, Milano 127713
Zokyudo, Kyoto 106909
Zolino, Jorio, Torino 106713
Zoll, S., Gemünden, Wohra 070963
Zoll- und Finanzgeschichtliche Sammlung, Oberösterreichisches Landesmuseum, Linz 002258
Zoll- und Heimatmuseum, Perwang 002422
Zolla & Lieberman, Chicago 115595
Zoller, Sankt Gallen 082790, 130169
Zoller, Tulsa 093342
Zollikofer, Olga, Zürich 130274
Zollinger &Co., Saint Louis 132757
Zollmuseum, Wegscheid 020701
Zollmuseum Friedrichs, Aachen . . . 015426
Zollverein Ausstellungen, Gesellschaft für zeitgenössische Kunst, Essen . . . 017080
Zolotaja Kniga, Moskva 140920
Zolotnik, Moskva 080274
Zolotoe Runo, Moskva 080275
Zolotoj Larec, Moskva 080276
Zoltán, Tamás, Budapest 074727
Zomerkoestal uut 't Wold, Ruinerwold 030117
Zompenmuseum, Enter 029574
De Zon, Gouda 078395
Zona Arte Gallery, San Francisco . . 119847
Zona D, São Paulo 058751
Zonal, San Francisco 092910
Zonal Anthropological Museum, Shillong 022335
Zonal Museum, Dehradun 022074
Zonca & Zonca, Milano 106342
Zonco, Carlo, Nice 065160
Zone France Edition d'Art, Paris . . . 133689
Zone Gallery, Adelaide 000717
Zône Vormgeving, Leiden 108110
Zonengrenz-Museum Helmstedt, Helmstedt 017868
Zong Lian Zhai Biao Gallery, Tianjin 098023
Zonguldak Devlet Güzel Sanatlar Galerisi, Zonguldak 038201
Zonin, Licia, Roma 128243
De Zonnebloem, Amstelveen 077766
De Zonnehof, Centrum voor Moderne Kunst, Amersfoort 029156
Het Zonnetje, Haarlem 078497
Zoo Antik, København . . . 060390, 124033
Zoo Galerie, Nantes 099820
Zoölogisch Museum Amsterdam, Amsterdam 029245
Zoological Museum, Addis Ababa . . 009443
Zoological Museum, Bukittinggi . . . 022410
Zoological Museum, Dublin 022778
Zoological Museum, Faizabad 022116
Zoological Museum, Gorakhpur . . . 022127
Zoological Museum, Hardwar 022150
Zoological Museum, Jaunpur 022185
Zoological Museum, Lahore 031388
Zoological Museum, Meerut 022257
Zoological Museum, Pematangsiantar 022494
Zoological Museum, Teheran 022646
Zoological Museum, Tel Aviv 023094
Zoological Museum, Zografou 021537
Zoological Museum at Agricultural College, Karaj 022565
Zoological Museum of the Institute of Zoology, Erevan 000694
Zoologičeskij Muzej, Dal'nevostočnyj gosudarstvennyj universitet, Vladivostok 034061
Zoologičeskij Muzej, Kazanskij gosudarstvennyj universitet, Kazan 033254
Zoologičeskij Muzej, Syktyvkarskij Gosudarstvennyj Universitet, Syktyvkar 033928
Zoologičeskij Muzej Kafedry Zoologii Pozvonočnych, Sankt-Peterburgskogo Gosudarstvennogo Universiteta, Sankt-Peterburg 033841
Zoologičeskij Muzej Moskovskogo Gosudarstvennogo Universiteta M.V. Lomonosova, Moskva 033532
Zoologičeskij Muzej Rossijskogo Gosudarstvennogo Pedagogičeskogo Universiteta im. A.I. Gercena, Sankt-Peterburg 033842
Zoologičeskij Muzej Rossijskoj Akademii Nauk, Sankt-Peterburg 033843
Zoologičeskij Muzej Tomskogo Gosudarstvennogo Universiteta, Tomsk 033966
Zoologische Sammlungen des Institutes für Zoologie, Martin-Luther-Universität Halle-Wittenberg, Halle, Saale 017674
Zoologische Schausammlung, Tübingen 020504
Zoologische Staatssammlung, München 019132
Zoologisches Forschungsinstitut und Museum Alexander Koenig, Bonn 016337
Zoologisches Museum der Universität, Institut für Zoologie und Anthropologie, Göttingen 017475
Zoologisches Museum der Universität Hamburg, Hamburg 017728
Zoologisches Museum der Universität Heidelberg, Heidelberg 017839
Zoologisches Museum der Universität Zürich, Zürich 037811
Zoologisches Museum zu Kiel, Christian-Albrechts-Universität, Kiel 018253
Zoologisches und Tiermedizinisches Museum der Universität Hohenheim, Stuttgart 020375
Zoologisk Museum, Grindsted 008881
Zoologisk Museum, København . . . 008993
Zoologisk Museum, Universitetets Naturhistoriske Museer, Oslo 031115
Zoologisk Museum Svendborg, Svendborg 009127
Zoologiska Museet, Lund 036448
Zoologiska Utställingar, Evolutionsmuseet Uppsala Universitet, Uppsala 036749
Zoology and Botany Museum, Ernakulam 022111
Zoology Museum, Annamalai Nagar 022010
Zoology Museum, Brisbane 000845
Zoology Museum, Ibadan 030684
Zoology Museum, Johannesburg . . 034658
Zoology Museum, Kanpur 022199
Zoology Museum, Kingston 026393
Zoology Museum, Legon 021111
Zoology Museum, Lucknow 022248
Zoology Museum, Muzaffarnagar . . 022274
Zoology Museum, Winnipeg 006875
Zoom Gallery, Bruxelles 096272
Zoonekynd, Ludwig, Calais 061906
Zopf, Rheinsberg 104750
Zoppi, Den Haag 128640
Zoppi, Giovanni, Torino 076884
Zordan, Pierre, Toulouse 068554
Zorn, Askolf W., München 072890
Zorn, Inge, Jesteburg 071661
Zorndt, Elke & Jost, Rantzau 073417
Zornsamlingarna, Mora 036486
Zorzycki, Regina, Dortmund 133874
Zoshukan, Hanamaki 026498
Zotos, Christos, Amsterdam 078028
Zott, Peter, Memmingen 072517
Zotti, Marco, Sankt Gallen 111880, 130170
Zouari Mardochee, Fabien, Paris . . 066688
Zouein, Paris 138567
Zouied, Hemiad Farag Ahmad, Yanbu 080384
Zouke & Cie., Paris 100979
Zoumboulakis, Athinai 074616
Zoumboulakis, Daphne, Athinai . . . 105412
Zoumpoulaki, Athinai 105413
Zoutmuseum Delden, Delden 029404
Zowe, James Helmut, Bonn 138913
Zrinyi Miklós Vármúzeum, Szigetvár 021893
Zscheyge, Theresia, München 072891
Zschiesche, Bernhard, Dresden . . . 125518
Zsidai, Péter, Budapest 074728
Zsolna Galéria, Budapest 105555
Zsolnay Kerámia Kiállítás, Janus Pannonius Múzeum, Pécs 021829
Zsolnay-Keramik-Porzellan-Museum, Potzneusiedl 002454
Ztichlá Klika, Praha 098494, 137850
Zubal, John T., Cleveland 142346
Zubelli, Sergio, Brescia 075194
Zubia, Eduardo, Montevideo 087352
Zubiller, L., Freiburg im Breisgau . . 139123
Zubrycki, Fontaine-de-Vaucluse . . . 099267
Zuccaro, Madrid 110629
Zucchetti, Serenella, Perugia 076237
Zucker-Museum, Berlin 016198
Zuckmantler Heimatstube, Bietigheim-Bissingen 016243
Züge, Stralsund 073935
Zühlsdorf, Karl Heinz, Köln 072028
Zühmendorf, A., Waldenburg, Württemberg 074253
Zülow-Gruppe, Linz 052628

Zürcher, Cornelia, Kirchberg (Bern) . 141261
Zürcher Abwassermuseum Kläranlage Werdhölzli, Zürich 037812
Zürcher Chronik, Winterthur 136132
Zürcher Kunstgesellschaft, Zürich . 054239
Zürcher Spielzeugmuseum, Zürich . 037813
Zürich Kosmos Galerie, Wien 095969
Zürichsee Auktionen, Erlenbach (Zürich) 082356, 122317
Zürichsee Zeitschriftenverlag, Stäfa 135069
Zuid-Limburgse Stoomtreinmaatschappij, Simpelveld 030146
Zuiderkerk, Amsterdam 029246
Zuiderzeemuseum, Enkhuizen 029563
Zuidwestbrabants Museum, Halle . . 003487
Zuigan-ji Hakabutsukan, Matsushima 026797
Żukowska, Likia, Kraków 108994
Žula, Peter, Maribor 109993
Zulauf, Dr. Günther, Freinsheim . . . 102874
Zulauf, Peter, Essen 102709
Žulebinskij, Moskva 080277
Zulu-African Art Shop, New Orleans 117532
Zululand Historical Museum, Eshowe 034610
Žulys, G., Klaipėda 077454
Zum Alten Laempli, Zürich 083042
Zum Arkantus, Binningen . 082264, 129982
Zum Basilisk, Basel 082182
Zum blauen Pfauen, Birrwil 082266, 111294, 129984
Zum Bühlhof, Iffwil 082505
Zum Gambiross, Basel 082183
Zum goldige Nüüteli, Aarau 111105
Zum Goldspiegel, Binningen 129983
Zum Grauen Wind, Zürich 112206
Zum Holzwurm, Bachenbülach 082104
Zum Holzwurm, Basel . . . 082184, 129942
Zum Kunos Thor, Basel . . 111234, 122309
Zum Louvre, Basel 082185
Zum Taubenschlag, Linz 057172
Zum Unteren Wildenstein, Basel . . . 082186
Zumklei, Martina, Wesel 074357
Zumkley, Beate, Wesel 126999
Zumkley, Norbert, Hamminkeln . . . 071368
Zumpicchiat, Frédéric, Origny-en-Thierache 065289
Zumsteinhaus mit Römischem Museum und Naturkunde-Museum, Zumsteinhaus, Kempten 018237
Zunfthaus zur Meisen Keramiksammlung, Musée Suisse-Schweizerisches Landesmuseum, Zürich 037814
Zungeninstrumenten-Sammlung Zwota, Sammlung historischer und neuzeitlicher Zungeninstrumente, Zwota 021097
Zunhamer, Martin, Altötting 125064
Zunino, Ada, Milano 106343
Zupan, Viktor, Radolfzell 073404
Zuppinger, R., Altwis 111120
Zuppinger, R., Hunzenschwil 111565
Zupski Muzej Lopud, Lopud 007754
Zupski Ured, Ston 007810
Zur Kaffeemühle, Winterthur 082919
Zur Sache..., Wien 135586
Zurcher, Paris 100980
Zurell, Manfred, Remchingen 126712
Zurholt, E., Altenberge 069148
Zurolo, Maria Rosaria, Brescia 075195
Zuzarte, José Azevedo, Lisboa 080058
Zuzarte, José Azevedo, Lisboa 080059
Zväz muzei na Slovensku, Liptovský Mikuláš 054055
Zvenigorodskij Istoriko-architekturnyj i Chudožestvennyj Muzej, Zvenigorod 034099
Zverevskij Centr Sovremennogo Iskusstva, Moskva 033533
Zveza Društev Slovenskih Likovnih Umetnikov-Galerija, Ljubljana . . . 054062
Zvezda, Moskva 080278
De Zwaan, Amsterdam 121781
Zwaanenburg, Peter, Dordrecht . . . 078325
Zwach, Käthe, Schörfling am Attersee 095751
De Zwaluw, Oosthuizen 134826
Zwanenbroedershuis, Illustre Lieve Vrouwe Broederschap, 's-Hertogenbosch . 029740
Het Zwanepand, Antwerpen 057756, 096106
Zwang, Christian, Berlin 102094
Zwang, Christian, Hamburg 103234, 125853
Zwangsarbeiter Gedenkstätte, Leipzig 018601
Het Zwart Huis, Knokke-Heist 096365
De Zwarte Panter, Antwerpen 096107
Zweckverband Deutsches Porzellanmuseum, Wunsiedel . . . 053658
Die Zwei, Düsseldorf 070471
Zwei-Burgen Antik, Weinheim, Bergstraße 074320
Zweiffel, B., Bad Münstereifel 069335
Zweig, Linda, New York 118602
Zweigmuseum des Staatlichen Museum für Völkerkunde, Residenzschloß Oettingen, Oettingen 019452
Zweiradmuseum Bühler, Wolfhausen 037740
Zweiradmuseum Havel-Auen-Werder, Werder, Havel 020805
Das Zweitbuch, Berlin 138866
Zweymüller, Baden bei Wien 137156
Związek Artystów Rzeźbiarzy, Gdańsk 053995
Związek Polskich Artystów Plastyków, Gdańsk 053997
Związek Polskich Artystów Plastyków, Łódź 053996
Związek Polskich Artystów Plastyków, Zarząd Główny, Warszawa 053998
Związek Polskich Artystów Plastyków Zarząd Okręgu Kraków, Kraków . . 053999
Związek Polskich Artystów Rzeźbiarzy zar, Wrocław 054000
Zwiebelzwerg Verlag, Willebadessen 134461
Zwierlein, Oswin, Bad Königshofen . 069312
Zwiers, Christina, Enschede 108025
Zwijvekemuseum, Dendermonde . . 003395
Zwinger, Jean, Espalion 062801
Zwinger Galerie, Berlin 102095
Zwingligeburtshaus, Wildhaus 037715
Zwirbels Trödelei, Nürnberg 073129
Zwirner, David, New York 118603
Zwirner, Dr. Dorothea, Berlin 102096
Zwirner & Wirth, New York 118604
Zwischen den Deichen, Büsum . . . 016500
Zwischenraum-Galerie, Münster . . 104378
Zwolf, Denver 116074
Zwolinska-Gasiorowska, Anna, Düsseldorf 125558
Zwosta, Alfons, Litzendorf 072286
Zyanya, Los Angeles 089949
Zygote, Cleveland 115753, 135354
Zymner, Ulla, Olfen 104545
Zynger, Rio de Janeiro 058667
Zynwala, Jacek, Wrocław 129135
Zypr Gallery, Toronto 097404